The Librarians Phone Book 1981

The Librarians Phone Book 1981

Edited by Jaques Cattell Press

R. R. Bowker Company
New York & London 1979

Copyright © 1980 by Xerox Corporation
Published by R. R. Bowker Company
1180 Avenue of the Americas, New York, N.Y. 10036

International Standard Book Number: 0-8352-1321-8
International Standard Serial Number: 0195-332X
All rights reserved. Reproduction of this book, in
whole or in part, without the written permission
of the publisher is prohibited.
Printed and bound in the United States of America.

All precautions have been made to avoid errors.
However, the publishers do not assume and hereby
disclaim any liability to any party for any loss or
damage caused by errors or omissions, whether such
errors or omissions result from negligence, accident
or any cause.

PREFACE

Complementing the *American Library Directory, The Librarians Phone Book 1981* is designed to aid further communication in the library and publishing world. In its second edition, the directory alphabetically lists over 55,000 librarians, heads of library networks and consortia, and faculty of library science programs throughout the United States and Canada.

Each listing begins with the person's name and title. This is followed by the library and/or institution with which the person is affiliated; branch and department libraries are identified in parentheses. Ending the entry is the city and state in which the library is located and its phone number.

When a librarian holds more than one position within an institution, the person is listed once for each assignment; thus, multiple entries occur.

The publishers do not assume and hereby disclaim any liability to any party for any loss or damage caused by errors or omissions in *The Librarians Phone Book 1981* whether such errors or omissions result from negligence, accident or any other cause.

We welcome your comments and suggestions along with notes of omissions and errors.

Linda Burns, *Editor*
Anne Rhodes, *Managing Editor*
Information Directories
Steve Nichols, *General Manager*
JAQUES CATTELL PRESS

September, 1980

The Librarians Phone Book 1981

A

Aagaard, James S, *Info Syst Dir,* Northwestern University Library, Evanston IL. 312-492-7658

Aagesen, Odile, *Librn,* Genesee District Library (Baker Park), Burton MI. 313-742-7860

Aaker, Ordelle, *Librn,* Aid Association for Lutherans, Founders Library, Appleton WI. 414-734-5721, Ext 2295

Aalto, Madeleine, *Chief Librn,* East York Public Library, Toronto ON. 416-423-6218

Aanonson, Dorothy, *Ch,* Estherville Public Library, Estherville IA. 712-362-3869

Aaron, Arthur, *Supvr,* New York Times (Photo Library), New York NY. 212-556-7220

Aaron, Betty, *Librn,* Pure Carbon Co Library, Saint Marys PA. 814-781-1573

Aaron, Jane H, *Acq,* Swarthmore College, McCabe Library, Swarthmore PA. 215-447-7477, 447-7480

Aaron, Shirley, *Assoc Prof,* Florida State University, School of Library Science, FL. 904-644-5775

Aas, E A, *Supvr,* Sandia Laboratories, Technical Library, Livermore CA. 415-455-2928

Aasen, M, *ILL,* Kelsey Institute of Applied Arts & Sciences, Learning Resources Center, Saskatoon SK. 306-664-6417

Aasen, Marjory, *Cat,* Sioux Falls Public Library, Sioux Falls SD. 605-339-7081

Abahamsen, Veva, *Dir,* Parchment Community Library, Parchment MI. 616-381-3566

Abaray, Anna J, *Ref & ILL,* Schenectady County Community College Library, Library Resources Center, Schenectady NY. 518-346-6211, Ext 240, 241

Abaray, Michael, *Acq,* Indiana University Northwest Library, Gary IN. 219-980-6580

Abbaticchio, Donna, *Librn,* New York Public Library (Job Opportunities Information Center - Learner's Advisory Service), New York NY. 790-6588 (Job Opportunities); 790-6589 (Learner's Advisory)

Abbe, Elizabeth, *Librn,* Connecticut Historical Society Library, Hartford CT. 203-236-5621

Abbett, Phillip, *Fiscal Officer,* South State Cooperative Library System, Los Angeles CA. 213-974-6501

Abbey, Anne, *Librn,* Harvard Public Library, Harvard MA. 617-456-3678

Abbey, Eugenia H, *Chief Librn,* Veterans Administration, Medical Center Library, Decatur GA. 404-321-6111, Ext 254

Abbey, Karen, *Cat,* University of Michigan-Dearborn Library, Dearborn MI. 313-593-5400

Abblitt, Dennis, *Asst Librn, Ref & Spec Coll,* University of New Brunswick, Saint John Campus, Ward Chipman Library, Saint John NB. 506-657-7310

Abbott, Ann, *Librn,* Lambton County Library (Lambton Mall), Sarnia ON. 519-542-2580

Abbott, Billye, *ILL,* Southeastern Oklahoma State University Library, Durant OK. 405-924-0121, Ext 245

Abbott, Bruce, *Libr Coordr,* Charity Hospital of Louisiana, School Of Nursing Media Center, New Orleans LA. 504-568-6431

Abbott, Carrie, *Acq,* Oconee County Library, Walhalla SC. 803-638-5837

Abbott, Donna, *Librn,* Willard Memorial Library (North Fairfield Branch), North Fairfield OH. 419-744-2285

Abbott, Edith, *Librn,* Our Lady of the Lake Medical Center Library, Baton Rouge LA. 504-769-3100, Ext 8140

Abbott, George, *Media & On-Line Servs,* Syracuse University Libraries, Ernest S Bird Library, Syracuse NY. 315-423-2575

Abbott, Joan, *Librn,* Andover Public Library, Andover CT. 203-742-7428

Abbott, John C, *Dir,* Southern Illinois University at Edwardsville, Elijah P Lovejoy Library, Edwardsville IL. 618-692-2711

Abbott, Laura P, *Librn,* Vermont Historical Society Library, Montpelier VT. 802-563-2320

Abbott, Marjorie, *Tech Serv,* Stillwater Public Library, City Library, Stillwater OK. 405-372-3633

Abbruzzese, Marie G, *Librn,* Mary's Help Hospital Library, Daly City CA. 415-992-4000

Abdo, Fatima, *Acq,* Mary H Weir Public Library, Weirton WV. 304-748-7070

Abdulhuq, A M, *Assoc Prof,* Saint John's University, Div of Library & Information Science, NY. 212-969-8000, Ext 200

Abdulia, Elizabeth, *ILL,* University of Florida Libraries, Gainesville FL. 904-392-0341

Abel, Gladys, *Librn,* Humphreys County Library System (Humphrey's County), Belzoni MS. 601-247-3606

Abel, Lorraine C, *Acq,* Lehigh University Libraries, Bethlehem PA. 861-3026 (Dir), 861-3050 (Ref), 861-3030 (Circ), 861-3055 (ILL)

Abel, Marguerite E, *Asst Dir & Ref,* West Virginia University (Medical Center Library), Morgantown WV. 304-293-2113

Abel, Marian, *ILL,* Washoe County Library, Reno NV. 702-785-4039

Abel, Mrs Dale, *Librn,* Broadwater Public Library, Broadwater NE. 308-489-5678

Abel, Mrs F, *Librn,* Scarborough Public Library (Agincourt Branch), Agincourt ON. 416-293-7811

Abel, Virginia, *Librn,* New York Public Library (Dance & Drama), New York NY. 212-790-6262

Abele, Jessie, *In Charge,* Nogales City-Santa Cruz County Library (Patagonia Public Library), Patagonia AZ. 602-287-3343, 287-6310

Abell, Elaine D, *Librn,* Montgomery Free Library, Montgomery Center VT. 802-326-4785

Abell, J Richard, *Hist & Lit,* Public Library of Cincinnati & Hamilton County, Cincinnati Public Library, Cincinnati OH. 513-369-6000

Abell, Millicent D, *Dir,* University of California, San Diego, University Libraries, La Jolla CA. 714-452-3336

Abella, Rose, *Latin Am,* University of Miami, Otto G Richter Library, Coral Gables FL. 305-284-3551

Abelow, Ruth M, *Librn,* Temple Emanu-El, Rosenhaus Library, Miami Beach FL. 305-538-2503, Ext 35

Abelson, Burton, *Librn,* New York Public Library (Bronx Reference Center), New York NY. 212-220-6575

Aber, Jeanne M, *Acting Curator Irish Coll,* Boston College Libraries (Bapst (Central Library)), Chestnut Hill MA. 617-969-0100, Ext 3205

Aberbach, Moses, *Curator,* Baltimore Hebrew College (Jewish Historical Society of Maryland Library), Baltimore MD. 301-466-4443

Aberman, Nancy, *Ref,* Saugus Public Library, Saugus MA. 617-233-0530

Abernathy, Bonnie, *AV,* Kinchafoonee Regional Library, Dawson GA. 912-995-2902

Abernathy, M R, *Librn,* Foote Mineral Co, Research & Engineering Department Library, Exton PA. 215-363-6500, Ext 264

Abernathy, William F, *Dir, Acq & Bibliog Instr,* Columbia Bible College, Columbia Graduate School of Bible & Missions, Learning Resources Center, Columbia SC. 803-754-4100, Ext 276 & 277

Abid, Ann B, *Librn,* Saint Louis Art Museum, Richardson Memorial Library, Saint Louis MO. 314-721-0067

Abner, Anna L, *Librn,* Lee County Public Library, Beattyville KY. 606-464-8014

Abner, Judith, *Librn,* Limestone College, A J Eastwood Library, Gaffney SC. 803-489-7151, Ext 179

Abney, Ella M, *Librn,* Academy of Medicine of Queens County Inc, Carl Boettiger Memorial Library, Forest Hills NY. 212-268-7300, Ext 6

Abney, Lucille, *Bkmobile Coordr,* Monroe County Public Library, William B Harland Memorial Library, Tompkinsville KY. 502-487-5301

Abney, Robert, *Mgr Commun Info Servs,* Public Library of the District of Columbia, Martin Luther King Memorial Library, Washington DC. 202-727-1101

Abplanalp, Eleanor, *Asst Librn,* Scott County Library, Scott City KS. 316-872-3855

Abraham, Deborah V H, *Librn,* Public Library of Brookline (Putterham), Brookline MA. 617-469-0750

Abraham, Elizabeth G, *Librn,* Second Presbyterian Church, Capen Memorial Library, Bloomington IL. 309-828-6297

Abraham, Lynn R, *Assoc Librn,* Simpson, Thacher & Bartlett, Law Library, New York NY. 212-483-9000, Ext 537

Abraham, Sandra, *Ref,* Mississippi Gulf Coast Junior College, Jackson County Campus Library, Gautier MS. 601-497-4313, Ext 226, Libr; 497-4313, Ext 255 Media Ctr

Abrahamson, Agnes, *Dir,* Falmouth Memorial Library, Falmouth ME. 207-781-2351

Abrahamson, Aina, *Dir,* California Lutheran College Library, Thousand Oaks CA. 805-492-2411, Ext 205

Abrahamson, Elaine, *Librn,* Atlantic County Historical Society Library, Somers Point NJ. 609-927-5218

Abrahamson, Patricia, *On-Line Servs & Bibliog Instr,* United States Army (Technical Library), White Sands Missile Range NM. 505-678-1317

Abram, Mary S, *Librn,* Veterans Administration, Hospital Library, West Roxbury MA. 617-323-7700, Ext 451

Abram, Persis, *Tech Serv & Cat,* Richmond Hill Public Library, Richmond Hill ON. 416-884-9288

Abram, Winifred, *Librn,* Hastings Public Library, Hastings PA. 814-247-8231

1

Abramo, Peggy, *Asst Dir & Acq,* Fairfield Public Library, Fairfield CT. 203-259-8303
Abramov, III, Peter, *Dir,* Sayville Library, Sayville NY. 516-589-4440
Abramovitz, Miriam, *Librn,* United States Army (Electronics R & D Command Technical Library), Fort Monmouth NJ. 201-532-9000
Abramowicz, Dina, *Librn,* Yivo Institute for Jewish Research Library & Archives, New York NY. 212-535-6700
Abrams, Carolyn, *Librn,* William Carey College (William Carey College on the Coast Library), Gulfport MS. 601-582-5051, Ext 245 & 246
Abrams, Douglas M, *Asst Librn,* University of Texas of the Permian Basin, Learning Resources Center, Odessa TX. 915-367-2114
Abrams, Faye, *Chief Librn,* Bank of Montreal, Head Office Library, Montreal PQ. 514-877-6890
Abrams, Faye, *Ref & Coll Develop,* University of Waterloo Library, Waterloo ON. 519-885-1211
Abrams, Joan, *Ref,* Marple Public Library, Broomall PA. 215-356-1510, 356-0550
Abrams, Leslie, *Ref,* College of Charleston, Robert Scott Small Library, Charleston SC. 803-792-5530
Abrams, Milton C, *Dir,* Utah State University, Merrill Library & Learning Resources Program, Logan UT. 801-750-2637
Abrams, Ruth, *Ad,* Hastings-On-Hudson Public Library, Hastings-on-Hudson NY. 914-478-3307
Abramson, Edna, *Librn,* Union Trust Co of Maryland Library, Baltimore MD. 301-332-5369
Abramson, Jenifer, *Cat,* Loyola Marymount University (Loyola Law School Library), Los Angeles CA. 213-642-2934
Abramson, Mark, *Senior Librn,* Kings Park Psychiatric Center, Dept of Libraries, Kings Park NY. 516-544-2671
Abruzzo, Judy, *Librn,* Preble County District Library (Eaton), Eaton OH. 513-456-4331
Absetz, Peg, *Asst Librn,* United States Army (Walson Army Hospital Medical Library), Fort Dix NJ. 609-562-5741, 562-2664
Absher, Helen L, *Librn,* Enumclaw Public Library, Enumclaw WA. 206-825-2938
Abshire, Charles, *Librn,* Mount Hood Community College Library, Gresham OR. 503-667-1561
Abshire, Eleanor, *Librn,* United States Bureau of Mines, Albany Metallurgy Research Center, Technical Library, Albany OR. 503-967-5864
Abugov, Leslie, *Media,* Bloomfield College Library, Bloomfield NJ. 201-748-9000, Ext 281
Abusch, Susan, *Librn,* American Science & Engineering, Inc, Research Library, Cambridge MA. 617-868-1600, Ext 326
Acanfora, Esther, *Librn,* Upper Darby Township & Sellers Free Public Library (Municipal Branch), Upper Darby PA. 215-789-4400
Accardi, Joseph, *Exten Serv,* Janesville Public Library, Janesville WI. 608-752-8934, Ext B
Accardi, Rosa, *In Charge,* Boces Cultural Arts Center Library, Syosset NY. 516-
Aceto, Vincent J, *Prof,* State University of New York at Albany, School of Library & Information Science, NY. 518-455-6288
Acevedo, Carlos A, *Dir & Media,* Quincy Junior College, Learning Resource Center, Quincy MA. 617-786-8777
Ach, William, *Microtext,* Wake Forest University, Z Smith Reynolds Library, Winston-Salem NC. 919-761-5480
Achee, Henri, *Pub Serv,* Louisiana State University, LeDoux Library, Eunice LA. 318-457-7311, Ext 38
Achee, Nicholas, *Asst Dir,* Tennessee Technological University, Jere Whitson Memorial Library, Cookeville TN. 615-528-3408
Acheff, Lawrence, *Asst Dir,* Gary Public Library, Gary IN. 219-886-2484
Achenbach, Erna, *Librn,* Krotona Institute of Theosophy Library, Ojai CA. 805-646-1139
Achleitner, Herbert, *Circ,* New Mexico Highlands University, Donnelly Library, Las Vegas NM. 505-425-7511, Ext 331
Achneepenesbum, Hannah, *Librn,* Northeastern Regional Library System (Martin Falls Bend), Ogoki Port ON. 705-567-7043
Acker, Jean R, *Librn,* New York State Department of Commerce Library, Albany NY. 518-474-5664

Acker, Joe D, *Dir Libr Serv,* Brewer State Junior College, Main Campus Library, Fayette AL. 205-922-3221, Ext 244
Acker, Thomas B, *Cat,* Nova Scotia Teachers College Library, Truro NS. 902-895-5347, Ext 30
Ackerman, Carolyn, *Coll Develop,* Hofstra University Library, Hempstead NY. 516-560-3475
Ackerman, Fannie C, *Librn,* Howard University Libraries (Chemistry Library), Washington DC. 202-636-6881
Ackerman, Heidi J, *Librn,* Temple Emanuel of Great Neck, Irving G Trattler Library, Great Neck NY. 516-482-5701
Ackerman, Joan B, *Commun Servs,* Westfield Athenaeum, Westfield MA. 413-568-7833
Ackerman, Marjorie, *Librn,* Mount Vernon Public Library (Dennis Memorial), Fredericktown OH. 614-694-2046
Ackerman, Mary, *Librn,* Guttenberg Public Library, Guttenberg IA. 319-252-3108
Ackerman, Mrs Richard, *Librn,* New Berlin Library, New Berlin NY. 607-847-8564
Ackerman, Pat, *Supvr,* McDonnell Douglas Corp, Douglas Aircraft Co Technical Library, Long Beach CA. 213-593-9541
Ackerman, Patricia, *Archivist,* New York University (New York University Archives), New York NY. 212-598-2484
Ackermann, Susan J, *Librn,* Coopers & Lybrand Library, Boston MA. 617-423-4200, Ext 308
Ackeroyd, Richard, *Pub Servs,* Denver Public Library, Denver CO. 303-573-5152, Ext 271
Ackerson, Dorothy, *Librn,* Grout Museum of History & Science Library, Waterloo IA. 319-234-6357
Ackerson, Eleanor, *Dir,* Tappan Library, Tappan NY. 914-359-3877
Ackerson, Margaret, *Librn,* Creare Engineering Research Library, Hanover NH. 603-643-3800
Ackles, Linda, *Librn,* Horry County Memorial Library (Surfside Branch), Surfside Beach SC. 803-238-0122
Ackley, Donald, *Film,* Orange Coast College Library, Costa Mesa CA. 714-556-5885
Ackley, Judith, *Media,* Golden West College Library, Huntington Beach CA. 714-892-7711, Ext 541
Ackroyd, Clare M, *Ad,* Public Library of the City of Somerville, Somerville MA. 617-623-5000
Ackterkirch, Margaret, *Storytelling & Puppetry,* Gaston-Lincoln Regional Library, Gastonia NC. 704-866-3756
Acosta, Lydia, *Librn,* University of Tampa, Merl Kelce Library, Tampa FL. 813-253-8861, Ext 385
Acosta, Lydia M, *Chmn,* Library Affairs Committee of the Associated Mid-Florida Colleges, FL. 813-253-8861, Ext 464
Acosta, Marty, *Librn,* Artec Associates Inc Library, Hayward CA. 415-785-8080
Acosta, Trini B, *Librn,* El Paso Herald-Post Library, El Paso TX. 915-747-6950
Acs, Imre, *Librn,* Cuyahoga County Commissioners Reference Library, Archives of Cuyahoga County, Cleveland OH. 216-623-7272
Acton, Lois M, *Librn,* Provost Municipal Library, Provost AB. 403-753-2801
Acuff, Barbara, *Tech Serv,* Central Bible College Library, Springfield MO. 417-833-2551, Ext 37
Adair, Garnet, *Asst Librn,* Jackson City Library, Jackson OH. 614-286-2609
Adalian, Paul, *Ref,* California Polytechnic State University Library, San Luis Obispo CA. 805-546-2345
Adam, Audrey, *Librn,* National School Boards Association Library, Washington DC. 202-337-7666
Adam, Beatrice M, *Commun Servs,* Maplewood Memorial Library, Maplewood NJ. 201-762-1622
Adamcewicz, Marjorie, *Acq,* Eastern Connecticut State College, J Eugene Smith Library, Willimantic CT. 203-456-2231, Ext 374, 422
Adamczyk, Judith, *Bkmobile Coordr,* Bay County Library System, Bay City MI. 517-894-2837
Adamedes, Artemis, *Per,* Newport Public Library, Newport RI. 401-847-8720
Adamowicz, Joanne, *ILL,* Kelley Library, Salem Public Library, Salem NH. 603-898-7064
Adams, Ann, *Head, Cat Dept,* Houston Public Library, Houston TX. 713-224-5441

Adams, Barbara S, *Chief Librn,* Veterans Administration, Center Library, Martinsburg WV. 304-263-0811, Ext 416
Adams, Barbara W, *Librn,* Silvermine Guild of Artists Library, New Canaan CT. 203-866-0411, Ext 25
Adams, Billye H, *Librn,* Wolfe County Library, Campton KY. 606-668-6571
Adams, C, *Doc,* University of Regina Library, Regina SK. 306-584-4132
Adams, Carolyn, *Bkmobile Coordr,* Calloway County Public Library, Murray KY. 502-753-2288
Adams, Charles, *Librn,* Broward County Division of Libraries (South County Regional), Hollywood FL. 305-987-9944
Adams, Connie, *Ch,* Callaway County Public Library, Fulton MO. 314-642-7261
Adams, Deborah L, *Librn,* Zieger Hospital Inc, Botsford General Hospital (Osteopathic) Medical Library, Farmington MI. 313-476-7600, Ext 341, 212
Adams, Dene, *Librn,* Pickens County Library (Village), Pickens SC. 803-878-4718
Adams, Donna, *Librn,* Celanese Fibers Co, Technical Library, Rock Hill SC. 803-366-4121
Adams, E M, *Librn,* East Texas Baptist College Library, Marshall TX. 214-938-0377
Adams, Edwarda, *Librn,* Langley Porter Psychiatric Institute Library, University of California at San Francisco, San Francisco CA. 415-681-8080, Ext 380
Adams, Eileen, *Librn,* Northumberland Union Public Library (Roseneath Branch), Roseneath ON. 416-352-2841
Adams, Elaine, *Media,* Texas Southern University Library, Houston TX. 713-527-7121
Adams, Eleanor, *Dir,* South Chicago Community Hospital (Nursing School Library), Chicago IL. 312-978-2000, Ext 5548
Adams, Florence N, *Librn,* Hartford Public Library (Goodwin), Hartford CT. 203-522-8496
Adams, Florence N, *Librn,* Hartford Public Library (Park), Hartford CT. 203-527-2387
Adams, Geraldine, *Bkmobile Coordr,* Marion County Public Library, Lebanon KY. 502-692-4698
Adams, Ida G, *Asst Dir,* Florida Agricultural & Mechanical University, Samuel H Coleman Memorial Library, Tallahassee FL. 904-599-3370
Adams, J Robert, *Dir,* Wesleyan University, Olin Memorial Library, Middletown CT. 203-347-9411, Ext 296
Adams, Jean, *ILL,* Wolfsohn Memorial Library, King of Prussia PA. 215-265-5151
Adams, Jeanne L, *Dir,* Woodside Receiving Hospital, Staff Resource Library & Patients' Library, Youngstown OH. 216-788-8712, Ext 267
Adams, John M, *Dir,* Moline Public Library, Moline IL. 309-762-6883
Adams, John P, *Dir,* Frederick E Parlin Memorial Library, Everett MA. 617-387-2550
Adams, Joyce, *Librn,* Akron-Summit County Public Library (North), Akron OH. 216-535-9423
Adams, June B, *Dir,* Somerset County Library, Somerville NJ. 201-725-4700, Ext 234
Adams, Karen, *Develop Servs,* Manitoba Department of Cultural Affairs & Historical Resources, Public Library Services Branch, Winnipeg MB. 204-453-7549
Adams, Kay, *Outreach,* Monroe County Library System, Rochester NY. 716-428-7345
Adams, Kay, *Cat,* Southeastern Louisiana University, Linus A Sims Memorial Library, Hammond LA. 504-549-2234
Adams, Kerstin, *Ad,* Longmont Public Library, Longmont CO. 303-776-2236
Adams, Libby, *Librn,* First Regional Library (Batesville Public), Batesville MS. 601-563-3545
Adams, Loretta, *Librn,* Sioux City Public Library (Riverside), Sioux City IA. 712-279-6179
Adams, Lorna, *Librn,* Lake Park Public Library, Lake Park FL. 305-848-6070
Adams, Louise, *ILL,* Chapman College, Thurmond Clarke Memorial Library, Orange CA. 714-997-6806
Adams, Lowell, *Dir,* Oklahoma Art Center Library, Oklahoma City OK. 405-946-4477
Adams, Marcia, *Librn,* Wayne Presbyterian Church (Library), Wayne PA. 215-688-8700

Adams, Marie, *Tech Serv & Acq,* Nova Scotia Technical College Library, Halifax NS. 902-429-8300, Ext 254
Adams, Marion, *Circ,* Texas Southern University Library, Houston TX. 713-527-7121
Adams, Mary, *Librn,* Metropolitan Council Library, Saint Paul MN. 612-291-6464
Adams, Mary L, *Librn,* La Crosse County Library, La Crosse WI. 608-785-9638
Adams, Medora, *Librn,* Piedmont Regional Library (Maysville Branch), Maysville GA. 404-867-2762
Adams, Mignon, *Bibliog Instr,* State University of New York, College of Arts & Science at Oswego, Penfield Library, Oswego NY. 315-341-4232
Adams, Muriel J, *Ch,* Forbes Library, Northampton MA. 413-584-8399
Adams, Nancy, *Regional Coordr,* San Diego County Library (Region F), San Diego CA. 714-565-5100
Adams, Paul, *Supvr,* Southern Ohio Correctional Facility Library (Law Library), Lucasville OH. 614-259-5544, Ext 51
Adams, Peggy, *Acq,* Herbert H Lehman College Library, Bronx NY. 212-960-8577, 960-8582
Adams, Raquel, *Cat,* Utah State Library, Salt Lake City UT. 801-533-5875
Adams, Reginald, *Supervisor,* Chicago Public Library (Woodlawn), Chicago IL. 312-752-3761
Adams, Robert M, *Dir,* Southern Union State Junior College, McClintock Library, Wadley AL. 205-395-2211, Ext 35
Adams, Rosalie, *Asst Librn,* Bliss Memorial Public Library, Bloomville OH. 419-983-4675
Adams, Ruth A, *Librn,* Woodbine Public Library, Woodbine IA. 712-647-2750
Adams, Ruth C, *Librn,* Francis M Harrison Memorial Library, Stamford CT. 203-327-3851
Adams, Sarah, *Asst Librn,* Lake Placid School of Art, Nettie Marie Jones Fine Arts Library, Association for Music, Drama & Art, Lake Placid NY. 518-523-2591, 523-2592, Ext 31
Adams, Shirley, *Librn,* Atchison County Library (Fairfax Branch), Fairfax MO. 816-744-5404
Adams, Susan, *Ch,* Ponca City Library, Ponca City OK. 405-762-6311
Adams, Thomas R, *Librn,* Brown University (John Carter Brown Library), Providence RI. 401-863-2725
Adams, Ursel, *Actg Librn,* Woodside United Methodist Church Library, Silver Spring MD. 301-587-1215
Adams, Virginia J, *Asst Dir,* Price Waterhouse Information Center, Boston MA. 617-423-7330, Ext 219
Adams, Virginia M, *Librn,* Old Dartmouth Historical Society Library, New Bedford MA. 617-997-0046
Adams, W K, *Asst Dir,* Dan River Inc, Research Library, Danville VA. 804-799-7100
Adams-Molloy, Carolyn, *Librn,* Hillsborough Community College Library (Dale Mabry Campus Library), Tampa FL. 813-879-7222, Ext 554
Adamshick, Robert, *Librn,* New York Institute of Technology, Metropolitan Center Library, New York NY. 212-399-8340, 399-8341
Adamson, Genny Wise, *Librn,* Metropolitan Library System (Edmond Branch), Edmond OK. 405-235-0571
Adamson, Joan, *Librn,* Lambton County Library (Port Lambton Branch), Port Lambton ON. 519-677-5217
Adamson, Kurt, *Ref,* University of New Mexico General Library (Law Library), Albuquerque NM. 505-277-6236
Adamson, Madeline, *Circ,* University of Calgary Library, Calgary AB. 403-284-5954
Adamson, Martha C, *Cat,* United States Air Force (Air Force Weapons Laboratory Technical Library), Kirtland AFB NM. 505-844-7449
Adamson, Mrs C M, *Librn,* Parker Memorial Baptist Church Library, Anniston AL. 205-236-5628
Adamson, Mrs Gordon F, *Librn,* Grand Saline Public Library, Grand Saline TX. 214-962-3122
Adamson, Paula, *Tech Serv,* Northwest Regional Library, Thief River Falls MN. 218-681-4325
Adamson, Tom M, *In Charge,* University of New Mexico, Gallup Branch, Learning Resources Center, Gallup NM. 505-863-9327

Adamy, Charlotte, *Librn,* Big Horn County Library (Greybull Branch), Greybull WY. 307-568-2388
Adcock, Mrs Briley, *Dir,* Rutherford County Library System, Linebaugh Public Library, Murfreesboro TN. 615-893-4131
Addams, Elizabeth, *Ref,* William Woods College, Dulany Memorial Library, Fulton MO. 314-642-3269
Addico, John, *Human Kinetics & Leisure Studies,* University of Waterloo Library, Waterloo ON. 519-885-1211
Addington, Leone, *Librn,* Harrison Public Library, Harrison ID. 208-689-3529
Addis, Albert, *Dir,* McCowan Memorial Library, Pitman Library, Pitman NJ. 609-589-1656
Addis, Beth, *Tech Serv,* Anderson County Library, Anderson SC. 803-225-1429
Addison, Anna M, *Librn,* Hartford Public Library (Dwight), Hartford CT. 203-236-2112
Addison, Anna M, *Librn,* Hartford Public Library (Mark Twain), Hartford CT. 203-522-0857
Addison, Mary Ellen, *Librn,* Public Library of Cincinnati & Hamilton County (Northern Hills), Cincinnati OH. 513-369-6036
Addison, Mrs Clifton, *Librn,* Southeast Alabama Cooperative Library System (Ashford), Dothan AL. 205-899-3121
Addison, Sarah M, *Librn,* Cambridge City Public Library, Cambridge City IN. 317-478-3335
Addison, Sunny, *Ad, ILL & Ref,* Public Library of Anniston & Calhoun County, Liles Memorial Library, Anniston AL. 205-237-8501, Ext 8503
Addleman, Louise, *Ch,* Germantown Public Library, Germantown OH. 513-855-4001
Addlesperger, Boyd, *Spec Coll,* Mansfield-Richland County Public Library, Mansfield OH. 419-524-1041
Addy, Mary, *Ser,* Dartmouth College, Baker Memorial Library, Hanover NH. 603-646-2235
Adelman, George, *Librn,* Massachusetts Institute of Technology, Neuroscience Research Program Library, Boston MA. 617-522-6700
Adelman, Irving, *On-Line Servs,* East Meadow Public Library, East Meadow NY. 516-794-2570
Adelman, Jean, *Librn,* University of Pennsylvania Libraries (Museum), Philadelphia PA. 215-243-7840
Adelson, Natalie, *Librn,* Scranton Public Library (Bookmobile Office), Scranton PA. 717-343-2661
Adelsperger, Robert J, *Rare Bks & Spec Coll,* University of Illinois at Chicago Circle Library, Chicago IL. 312-996-2716
Adeniran, Dixie D, *Dir,* Ventura County Library Services Agency, Ventura County Library, Ventura CA. 805-654-2627
Aderhold, Margaret, *Librn,* Automation Industries, Inc, Vitro Laboratories Division Library, Silver Spring MD. 301-871-7200
Adinolfi, Eleanor, *Librn,* Buffalo & Erie County Public Library System (Mead), Buffalo NY. 716-892-4525
Adkins, Ann, *Circ,* Baraboo Public Library, Baraboo WI. 608-356-6166
Adkins, Bette, *Librn,* Walla Walla Union-Bulletin Library, Walla Walla WA. 509-525-3300
Adkins, Julia, *Librn,* Union Carbide Corp (Engineering Department Library), South Charleston WV. 304-747-4608
Adkins, Marge, *Libr Clerk,* Holzer Medical Center, School of Nursing Library, Gallipolis OH. 614-446-5264
Adkins, Marjorie, *Chief,* Chicago Public Library (Fine Arts Div), Chicago IL. 312-269-2839
Adkins, Rebecca, *Administrator,* Northwest Regional Library, Winfield AL. 205-487-2330
Adkins, Rebecca, *Dir,* Northwest Regional Library (Winfield Branch), Winfield AL. 205-487-2484
Adkins, Russell, *Assoc Dir for Media Resources,* Wichita State University, Library & Media Resources Center, Wichita KS. 316-689-3586
Adler, Estelle C, *Chief Librn,* Canadian Department of External Affairs, Canadian Consulate General Library, New York NY. 212-586-2400
Adler, Lorna, *YA & Ref,* Larchmont Public Library, Larchmont NY. 914-834-1960
Adler, Marianne, *Librn,* Los Angeles Public Library System (Cahuenga), Los Angeles CA. 213-664-6418
Adler, Steve, *Dir,* Stauffer Chemical Co, Information Services, Dobbs Ferry NY. 914-693-1200

Adler, Valerie, *Cat,* Marshfield Free Library, Marshfield WI. 715-384-2929, 387-1302
Adley, Delores, *Librn,* San Carlos Public Library, San Carlos AZ. 602-475-2295
Adley, Sharon, *Circ,* Lake County Public Library (Talking Book Service), Merrillville IN. 219-769-3541, Ext 37
Adomeit, Katharine F, *Ch,* West Hartford Public Library, Noah Webster Memorial Library, West Hartford CT. 203-236-6286
Adorno, Miriam, *Librn,* New York Eye & Ear Infirmary Library, New York NY. 212-598-1431
Adreani, Earl, *Dir,* Boston University Libraries (School of Education), Boston MA. 617-353-3272
Adrian, Audrey, *Asst Librn,* Winnipeg Bible College & Theological Seminary Library, Otterburne MB. 204-284-2923, Ext 141
Adrian, Donna, *Lectr,* Concordia University, Library Studies Program, PQ. 514-482-0320, Ext 324
Adriance, Lois, *Pub Servs,* Northeast Kansas Library System, Shawnee Mission KS. 913-831-4993
Adrianopoli, Barbara, *Dir,* Schaumburg Township Public Library (Hoffman Estates), Hoffman Estates IL. 312-885-3511
Aducci, Patricia J, *Librn,* Colt Industries, Crucible Research Center Library, Pittsburgh PA. 412-923-2955, Ext 255
Aebischer, Joanne, *Tech Serv & Cat,* Salem Public Library, Salem OR. 503-588-6071
Aedy, Leonora, *Assoc Prof,* Lakehead University, School of Library Technology, ON. 807-345-2121, Ext 240
Aer, Elvi, *Acq,* University of Toronto Libraries (University Library), Toronto ON. 416-978-2294
Affleck, Betty, *Librn,* Prince Edward Island Provincial Library (Mount Stewart Branch), Mount Stewart PE. 902-892-3504, Ext 54
Affleck, D, *Educ,* University of Regina Library, Regina SK. 306-584-4132
Affleck, Del, *Dir & Acq,* Capilano College, Media Centre, North Vancouver BC. 604-986-1911, Ext 241
Afflerbach, Betty, *Librn,* Texas Medical Association, Memorial Library, Austin TX. 512-477-6704, Ext 191
Affolter, Ruth, *Librn,* Cedar Hills Alcoholism Treatment Center Library, Maple Valley WA. 206-228-5115
Africk, Lenore, *Librn,* Armak Co Library, McCook IL. 312-565-1846
Aga, Fuafanua P, *Librn,* American Samoa-Office of Library Services (Betty Lunnon), Faga'itua Village PI. 622-5704
Agar, Mrs W S, *Hist Librn,* Institute for Advanced Study Libraries, Princeton NJ. 609-924-4400
Agar, Peg, *Librn,* Carnegie Public Library, Browns Valley MN. 612-695-2318
Agard, Robert M, *Dir,* Bennington College, Crossett Library, Bennington VT. 802-442-5401, Ext 278, 279, 290
Agazarian, M V, *Chmn,* Westbrook College, Library Technology Program, ME. 207-797-7261, Ext 78
Agazarian, Marian V, *Dir,* Westbrook College Library, Portland ME. 207-797-7261, Ext 280
Agbim, Mrs Ngozi, *Librn,* Fiorello H LaGuardia Community College, Long Island City NY. 212-626-5518
Agee, Harold, *Cat,* Liberty Baptist College Library, Lynchburg VA. 804-528-0821
Agen, Jerry, *Dir Mgr Servs,* Seattle Public Library, Seattle WA. 206-625-2665
Ager, Susan, *Librn,* Oak Terrace Nursing Home, DPW Medical Library, Minnetonka MN. 612-934-4100, Ext 237
Agler, Raymond, *Humanities Coordr,* Boston Public Library, Eastern Massachusetts Library System, Boston MA. 617-536-5400
Agnella, Sister Mary, *Librn,* Our Lady of Peace Hospital, Medical Library, Louisville KY. 502-451-3330
Agner, Pamela, *Librn,* Veterans Administration (Patients Library), Miami FL. 305-324-4455, Ext 3622
Agnew, Beatrice W, *Dir,* Palisades Free Library, Palisades NY. 914-359-0136

Agnew, Brad, *Dir,* Northeastern Oklahoma State University, John Vaughan Library-Learning Resource Center, Tahlequah OK. 918-456-5511, Ext 385

Agnew, Ellen Y, *Librn,* Richmond Public Library (Ginter Park), Richmond VA. 804-780-6236

Agnew, Mrs Fred, *Cat,* Frankfort Community Public Library, Frankfort IN. 317-654-8746

Agnew, Nancy R, *Dir,* Wheeler Basin Regional Library, Decatur Public Library, Decatur AL. 205-353-2993

Agnoni, Leah, *Ref,* Rodman Public Library, Alliance OH. 216-821-1410

Agrawal, G P, *Dir, Libr Servs,* Robert Morris College Library, Coraopolis PA. 412-264-9300

Agrawal, G P, *Dir, Libr Servs,* Robert Morris College Library, Pittsburgh PA. 412-227-6839

Agricola, Grace, *Ch,* Coshocton Public Library, Coshocton OH. 614-622-0956

Agriesti, Paul A, *Deputy State Librn,* New Mexico State Library, Santa Fe NM. 505-827-2033

Aguilar, Juan F, *Dir,* Drake University (Drake Law Library), Des Moines IA. 515-271-2141

Aguilar, William, *Dir,* Pikeville College, O'Rear-Robinson Library, Pikeville KY. 606-432-9372

Aguirre, Anthony, *Assoc Dir,* University of Connecticut Health Center, Lyman Maynard Stowe Library, Farmington CT. 203-674-2739

Agus, Tamar, *Librn,* Milbank, Tweed, Hadley & McCloy Library, New York NY. 212-530-5200

Aharonion, Arsine, *Librn,* Shawmut Bank of Boston Library, Boston MA. 617-292-2296

Ahearn, Helen G, *Librn,* Derby Public Library, Derby CT. 203-734-4173

Ahearn, John, *Media,* Xavier University of Louisiana Library, New Orleans LA. 504-486-7411, Ext 317

Ahearn, Mrs John, *Acq,* Bedford Free Public Library, Bedford MA. 617-275-9440

Ahern, Camille, *Acq & Ref,* New Hampshire College, Shapiro Library, Manchester NH. 603-668-2211, Ext 211

Ahl, Ruth E, *Asst Dir, Resources & Ref,* Purdue University Libraries & Audio-Visual Center, West Lafayette IN. 317-749-2571

Ahlborn, Joy W, *Librn,* Greeley District Court Law Library, Greeley CO. 303-353-8050, Ext 359

Ahlf, Marguerite, *Dir,* Edson Municipal Library, Edson AB. 403-723-3117

Ahlgren, D, *Librn,* Dakota County Library System (Hastings Branch), Hastings MN. 612-437-5286

Ahlquist, Audrey, *Acq,* Tulsa City-County Library, Tulsa OK. 918-581-5221

Ahlquist, Bernice, *Dir,* Cherry Hill Free Public Library, Cherry Hill NJ. 609-667-0300

Ahlquist, Nancy, *Br Librn,* Wisconsin State Department of Natural Resources (Department Library), Madison WI. 608-266-2621

Ahmad, Carol, *Humanities,* Oklahoma State University Library, Stillwater OK. 405-624-6313

Ahmad, Riaz, *Oriental studies,* University of Arizona Library, Tucson AZ. 602-626-2101

Ahmad, Riaz, *Librn,* University of Arizona Library (Oriental Studies Collection), Tucson AZ. 602-626-3695

Ahmad, S A, *Tech Serv & Cat,* Florida Agricultural & Mechanical University, Samuel H Coleman Memorial Library, Tallahassee FL. 904-599-3370

Ahmed, Elizabeth, *Art & Archit,* New York Institute of Technology Library, Old Westbury NY. 516-686-7657, 686-7658

Ahmed, Khalil, *Ref,* J Sargeant Reynolds Community College (Downtown Campus-Learning Resources Center), Richmond VA. 804-786-6249

Ahouse, John, *Spec Coll,* California State University, Long Beach, University Library, Long Beach CA. 213-498-4047

Ahrens, Carol, *Ref & Spec Coll,* Hempstead Public Library, Hempstead NY. 516-481-6990

Ahrens, Fausta W, *Asst Librn,* Eagle Grove Public Library, Eagle Grove IA. 515-448-4115

Aichele, April, *On-Line Servs,* Muskingum Area Technical College, Herrold Hall Learning Resource Center, Zanesville OH. 614-454-2501, Ext 311, 312

Aichele, Jean, *Instr,* Saint Cloud State University, Center for Library & Audiovisual Education, MN. 612-255-2022

Aiches, Alan, *Dir,* Saint John's Art Gallery Library, Wilmington NC. 919-763-0281

Aide, Katherine S, *Libr Tech,* United States Army (Military Police School Library), Fort McClellan AL. 205-238-3737

Aiello, Hellen M, *Ser,* Wheaton College Library, Norton MA. 617-285-7722, Ext 518

Aiello, Joan, *Librn,* Carnegie Library of Pittsburgh (South Side), Pittsburgh PA. 412-622-3100

Aiken, Chris, *Ch,* Middle Georgia Regional Library, Macon GA. 912-745-5813

Aiken, Mary, *Ch,* Greenville County Library, Greenville SC. 803-242-5000

Aikens, Bonnie, *Ch,* Corry Public Library, Corry PA. 814-664-7611

Aikens, Jean, *Librn,* Bledsoe County Public Library, Pikeville TN. 615-447-2817

Aimore, Alan C, *Military Hist,* United States Military Academy Library, West Point NY. 914-938-2230

Ainer, Mary Ethel, *Librn,* Butte County Library (Chico Memorial Way), Chico CA. 343-4211 or 343-4216

Ainley, Gerrie, *Librn,* Wellington County Public Library (Centre Wellington), Fergus ON. 519-846-5761

Ainsworth, Mary Lynn, *In Charge,* Pitney Bowes, Technical Library, Stamford CT. 203-853-0727, Ext. 506, 507

Airel, Walter F, *Dir,* Livingston County Library System, Avon NY. 716-226-2770

Airhart, La Rue, *Acq,* Girard Free Public Library, Girard OH. 216-545-2508

Airoldi, Joan D, *Dir,* Legion Memorial Library, Mellen WI. 715-274-8331

Aitken, Leslie, *Librn,* Alberta Education Library (Special Education Services Materials Resource Center for Visually Impaired), Edmonton AB. 403-427-4681

Aitken, M I, *Chief Librn,* Canada Department of Finance & Treasury Board Library, Ottawa ON. 613-996-8211

Aitner, Helen, *ILL,* Connecticut College Library, New London CT. 203-442-1630

Aja, Loretta, *ILL,* Saint Joseph's University Libraries (Drexel Library), Philadelphia PA. 215-879-7559

Aja, Sandy, *Librn,* Vermont Department of Transportation Library, Vermont Department Of Highways, Montpelier VT. 802-828-2544

Akana, Sandra, *Librn,* Hawaii State Library System (Waimanalo Community-School), Waimanalo HI. 808-259-9925

Akehurst, M, *Librn,* Geological Survey of Canada, Information Services Library, Vancouver BC. 604-666-3812

Aken, Irene, *Cat,* College of Lake County, Learning Resource Center, Grayslake IL. 312-223-6601, Ext 392

Aker, Christopher, *Media,* Public Library of Johnston County & Smithfield, Smithfield NC. 919-934-8146

Aker, Patricia, *Librn,* Abilene Free Public Library, Abilene KS. 913-263-3082

Akers, Christina, *Asst Dir,* Northern Oklahoma College Library, Tonkawa OK. 405-628-2581, Ext 48

Akers, John E, *Librn,* Veterans Administration Center Library, Hot Springs SD. 605-745-4101, Ext 226

Akers, Mrs Ralph M, *Librn,* Free Public Library, West Liberty IA. 319-627-2084

Akerson, Amelia, *Librn,* Upton Town Library, Upton MA. 617-529-6272

Akey, Sharon, *Librn,* Patton State Hospital, Patients Library, Patton CA. 714-862-8121, Ext 487

Aki, Hareko, *Tech Serv,* Maui Community College, Learning Resource Center, Kahului HI. 808-242-5433, 242-5498

Akimoto, Takashi, *In Charge,* Hawaii State Library System (Centralized Processing Center), Honolulu HI. 808-537-6381

Akins, Harold, *Coordr, Video Production Ctr,* Oconee Regional Library, Laurens County Library, Dublin GA. 912-272-5710

Akiyama, Emi, *Asst Dir,* Cornell University Medical College, Samuel J Wood Library, New York NY. 212-472-5300

Akiyama, Wilfrid S, *Librn,* Fulton State Hospital (Medical Library), Fulton MO. 314-642-3311

Akonful, John, *Acting Head of Tech Servs,* North Carolina Agricultural & Technical State University, F D Bluford Library, Greensboro NC. 919-379-7782, 379-7783

Akos, Marian, *Librn,* Sigma Alpha Epsilon Fraternity, Levere Memorial Foundation Library, Evanston IL. 312-475-1856

Akram, Zakkiyya Y, *Librn,* Kaiser Permanente Medical Center, Health Sciences Library, Bellflower CA. 213-920-4247

Aksamit-Petzel, Mary, *Ref,* Harvey Public Library, Harvey IL. 312-331-0757

Aksler, Samuel M, *Librn,* Yeshiva University Libraries, New York NY. 212-960-5382

Al-Ashari, Theone, *Librn,* Ingham County Library (Waverly), Lansing MI. 517-676-9088

Al-Hussaini, Maida, *Branch Librns,* Hinds Junior College, George M McLendon Library, Raymond MS. 601-857-5261, Ext 253

Al-Hussaini, Maida, *Librn,* Hinds Junior College, Vicksburg-Warren County Branch Library, Vicksburg MS. 601-638-0600

Alajajian, Hilda, *Ch,* Anderson County Library, Anderson SC. 803-225-1429

Alala, Frances, *Librn,* Paterson Free Public Library (Southside), Paterson NJ. 201-881-3783

Alaniz, Miguel, *Young Adult & Outreach Librn,* San Bernardino County Library, San Bernardino CA. 714-383-1734

Alarie, Maurice, *Dir,* University of Ottawa Libraries (Vanier Library (Medicine, Science & Engineering)), Ottawa ON. 613-231-2324

Alayon, Gloria H Mendez, *Cat,* Inter-American University of Puerto Rico, School of Law Library, Santurce PR. 809-754-7215

Albanese, Bro Charles, *Librn,* Saint Benedict's Monastery Library, Snowmass CO. 303-927-3311

Albeck, Doris, *Ch,* Long Beach Public Library System, Long Beach CA. 213-436-9225

Albee, Jr, Lowell, *Dir,* Lutheran School of Theology at Chicago, Krauss Library, Chicago IL. 312-667-3500, Ext 226

Alber, Kathleen, *Acq,* Russell Sage College, James Wheelock Clark Library, Troy NY. 518-270-2249

Alberda, Stanley E, *Dean,* Imperial Valley College, Spencer Library Media Center, Imperial CA. 714-352-8320, Ext 270

Alberding, Margaret G, *Librn,* Kiowa Public Library, Kiowa KS. 316-825-4272

Alberico, Ralph, *Ref & Bibliog Instr,* Loyola University Library, Main Library, New Orleans LA. 504-865-3346

Alberigi, Terence, *Ref,* City College of San Francisco Library, San Francisco CA. 415-239-3404

Albert, Margaret, *Bkmobile Coordr,* Fond Du Lac City-County Library Service, Fond du Lac WI. 414-921-3670

Albert, Nancy, *Librn,* Swedesboro Free Public Library, Swedesboro NJ. 609-467-0111

Albert, Nancy, *Librn,* Timken Mercy Medical Center (Mercy School of Nursing Library), Canton OH. 216-489-1140

Albert, Ronald, *Cat,* Long Beach Community College Learning Resources Division (Liberal Arts Campus Library), Long Beach CA. 213-420-4231

Albert, Susan A, *Ref,* Pawtucket Public Library & Regional Library Center, Deborah Cook Sayles Memorial Library, Pawtucket RI. 401-725-3714

Albert, Warren, *Librn,* Illinois Central Community Hospital, Medical Library, Chicago IL. 312-643-9200, Ext 361

Alberti, Dino A, *Hist,* Louisiana Tech University, Prescott Memorial Library, Ruston LA. 318-257-2577

Alberts, Pearl, *Ref,* Boston College Libraries (School of Management Library), Chestnut Hill MA. 617-969-0100, Ext 3216

Albertsen, Arla, *Asst Librn,* Canton Public Library, Canton SD. 605-987-5831

Albertson, Christopher, *Dir,* Orange Public Library, Orange TX. 713-883-7323

Albina-Gazaille, Sister, *Chief Librn,* Rivier College, Regina Library, Nashua NH. 603-888-1311, Ext 42

Albrecht, Cheryl C, *Coordr,* Greater Cincinnati Library Consortium, OH. 513-475-6152

Albrecht, Doris B, *Librn,* Analytical Psychology Club of New York, Kristine Mann Library, New York NY. 212-697-7877

Albrecht, Jean, *Librn,* University of Minnesota (Forestry), Saint Paul MN. 612-373-1407

Albrecht, Lois, *Librn,* Bayfield Carnegie Library, Bayfield WI. 715-779-3953

Albrecht, Lois K, *Bur of Libr Develop, Actg Dir & Adv Servs,* State Library of Pennsylvania, Harrisburg PA. 717-787-2646
Albrecht, Patricia, *Librn,* Sanilac Township Library, Port Sanilac MI. 313-622-8623
Albrecht, Sterling J, *Dir,* Brigham Young University, Harold B Lee Library, Provo UT. 801-378-2905
Albrich, E, *Librn,* Queen's University at Kingston (Art), Kingston ON. 613-547-2633
Albrich, E, *Librn,* Queen's University at Kingston (Music), Kingston ON. 613-547-2873
Albright, Elaine, *Dir,* Lincoln Trail Libraries System, Champaign IL. 217-352-0047
Albright, Estalee, *Pub Servs,* Hartnell College, Learning Resources Center, Salinas CA. 408-758-8211, Ext 400
Albright, Frances L, *Asst Librn & Cat,* Kansas Wesleyan, Memorial Library, Salina KS. 913-827-5541, Ext 233
Albright, Jane, *Bibliog Instr,* Carson-Newman College Library, Jefferson City TN. 615-475-9061, Ext 247
Albright, Janet, *Ref,* North State Cooperative Library System, Willows CA. 916-934-2173
Albright, Julia C, *ILL,* Pottstown Public Library, Pottstown PA. 215-326-2532
Albright, Marilyn, *Reader Serv,* Carnegie-Mellon University, Hunt Library, Pittsburgh PA. 412-578-2446, 578-2447
Albright, Penny E, *Librn,* Kershaw County Library, Camden SC. 803-432-5183
Albright, Thomas E, *Asst Dir,* Michigan State University Library, East Lansing MI. 517-355-2344
Albright, Virginia, *Librn,* East Lansing Public Library, East Lansing MI. 517-351-2420
Albritton, Henry, *Per & Bibliog Instr,* Norfolk State University, Lyman Beecher Brooks Library, Norfolk VA. 804-623-8873
Albro, Elizabeth, *Librn,* Edison National Historic Site Library, West Orange NJ. 201-736-0550
Albsmeyer, Betty, *Ref,* Quincy Public Library, Quincy IL. 217-223-1309
Albury, Lenora, *In Charge,* Monroe County Public Library (Key Largo Branch), Key Largo FL. 305-451-2396
Albus, Betty, *Librn,* Bancroft Public Library, Bancroft NE. 402-648-3350
Alchuk, Daniel, *Instr,* Seneca College of Applied Arts & Technology, Library Techniques, ON. 416-491-5050
Alcorn, Chris, *Librn,* Grace Lutheran Church Library, La Grange IL. 312-352-0730
Alcorn, Cynthia, *Tech Serv,* Emerson College, Abbot Memorial Library, Boston MA. 617-262-2010, Ext 281
Alcorn, Florence, *Librn,* Oliver Springs Public Library, Oliver Springs TN. 615-435-7248
Alcorn, Marianne, *ILL & Circ,* University of Washington Libraries (Law Library), Seattle WA. 206-543-4089
Alcorn, Maxine, *Librn,* Houston Public Library (Looscan), Houston TX. 713-622-6525
Alcott, Colleen, *Bibliog Instr,* Beckman Instruments, Inc, Research Library, Fullerton CA. 714-871-4848, Ext 8958
Aldana, Willelma M, *Librn,* Cleveland Public Library (Treasure House), Cleveland OH. 216-795-4383
Alden, Janet M, *Dir,* Warwick Public Library, Orange MA. 617-544-2775
Alder, Marianne, *Bibliog Instr,* William Marsh Rice University, Fondren Library, Houston TX. 713-527-4022
Alderdice, Sally, *Librn,* Claverack Free Library, Claverack NY. 518-851-7120
Alderfert, William K, *State Historian,* Illinois State Historical Library, Springfield IL. 217-782-4836
Alderman, Mrs Dan, *In Charge,* Volusia County Public Libraries (Oak Hill Branch), Oak Hill FL. 904-252-8374
Alderman, Pamela, *Librn,* Mount Sinai Hospital of Cleveland, George H Hays Library, Cleveland OH. 216-795-6000, Ext 249
Aldous, Mary, *Librn,* United States Navy (Thompson Medical Library), San Diego CA. 714-225-6640
Aldous, Patricia, *Librn,* Douglas County Library System (Drain Public), Drain OR. 503-836-2648
Aldred, Richard, *Acq & Cat,* Hahnemann Medical College & Hospital of Philadelphia, Warren H Fake Library, Philadelphia PA. 215-448-7186

Aldredge, Shirley, *Pub Servs,* National Oceanic & Atmospheric Administration, Environmental Research Laboratories Library, Boulder CO. 303-499-1000, Ext 3271
Aldrich, Hazel, *Librn,* Homedale Public Library, Homedale ID. 208-337-4228
Aldrich, Mary M, *Librn,* Hawarden Public Library, Hawarden IA. 712-552-2244
Aldrich, Mrs Willie L, *Dir & Acq,* Livingstone College (Hood Theological Seminary), Salisbury NC. 704-633-7960, Ext 45, 41
Aldrich, Russell Edward, *Librn,* Connecticut Mental Health Center Library, New Haven CT. 203-789-7300
Aldrich, Sister Michele, *Tech Serv & Cat,* Thomas More College, Learning Resources Center, Fort Mitchell KY. 606-341-5800, Ext 61
Aldridge, Ruth, *Dir,* Holmes County Library, Durant MS. 601-653-3451
Aldridge, Ruth, *Librn,* Mid-Mississippi Regional Library System (Durant Public), Durant MS. 601-653-3451
Aldus, Judith, *Tech Serv,* University of New Brunswick, Harriet Irving Library, Fredericton NB. 506-453-4740
Aleccia, Janet, *Librn,* DuPage County Health Dept, John P Case Library, Wheaton IL. 312-682-7372
Aleshire, Joan, *Librn,* Shrewsbury Public Library, Cuttingsville VT. 802-492-3410
Alessi, Susan, *Dir,* Merrick Library, Merrick NY. 516-379-3476
Alex, Joni M, *Librn,* Saint Vincent Health Center, Health Sciences Library, Erie PA. 814-459-4000, Ext 523
Alexander, Andrew G, *Dir,* Rolla Free Public Library, Rolla MO. 314-364-2604
Alexander, April, *Per,* Simmons College, Beatley Library, Boston MA. 617-738-2241
Alexander, Becky, *Ch,* Hutchinson County Library, Borger TX. 806-274-6221
Alexander, C A, *Eng Librn,* General Dynamics Corp, Convair Div, Research Library, San Diego CA. 714-277-8900, Ext 1073
Alexander, Cam, *Librn,* South Carolina Historical Society Library, Charleston SC. 803-723-3225
Alexander, Carolyn, *Chief Librn,* United States Army (Combat Developments Experimentation Command, Technical Library), Fort Ord CA. 408-242-3618, 242-4706
Alexander, Catherine, *Librn,* Flint Public Library (North Flint Branch), Flint MI. 313-785-7879
Alexander, Catherine, *Librn,* Flint Public Library (Potter), Flint MI. 313-742-9300
Alexander, Colleen J, *On-Line Servs,* General Dynamics Corp, Convair Div, Research Library, San Diego CA. 714-277-8900, Ext 1073
Alexander, David, *Archivist,* Auraria Libraries, Denver CO. 303-629-2805
Alexander, Eleanore, *Librn,* Pike-Amite-Walthall Library System (Alpha Center), McComb MS. 601-684-8312
Alexander, Elinor M, *Librn,* Pillsbury, Madison & Sutro, Law Library, San Francisco CA. 415-983-1130
Alexander, Elizabeth, *Ch,* Shelby Township Library, Utica MI. 313-739-7414
Alexander, Evelyn, *Admin Asst,* San Bernardino Public Library, San Bernardino CA. 714-889-0264
Alexander, Gerard L, *Chief,* New York Public Library (Map), New York NY. 212-790-6286
Alexander, Ginger, *Librn,* Washington State Library (Department of Energy Library), Olympia WA. 206-754-1369
Alexander, Harriet, *ILL,* Flint Memorial Library, North Reading MA. 617-664-4942
Alexander, Janet, *Librn,* Southwest Regional Library, Rutland VT. 802-773-3088
Alexander, Janice, *Librn,* Nutter, Mcclennen & Fish, Law Library, Boston MA. 617-973-9700
Alexander, Julie, *Reader Serv,* University of Texas at Arlington Library, Arlington TX. 817-273-3391
Alexander, K M, *Librn,* Lakewood Memorial Library, Lakewood NY. 716-763-6234
Alexander, Laurel, *Librn,* New York Public Library (Stapleton), New York NY. 212-727-0427
Alexander, Lee, *Archivist,* Atlanta University, Trevor Arnett Library, Atlanta GA. 404-681-0251, Ext 225

Alexander, Marian, *Cat,* Western Washington University, Mabel Zoe Wilson Library, Bellingham WA. 206-676-3050
Alexander, Mary, *Cat,* Monroe County Public Library, Key West FL. 305-294-7100
Alexander, Mary Ann, *Dir,* Greene County Public Library, Greeneville TN. 615-638-5034
Alexander, Merle I, *Chief Librn,* Veterans Administration, Hospital Library, Marion IN. 317-674-3321
Alexander, Paula R, *ILL & Ref,* Northeastern Oklahoma A&m College, Learning Resources Center, Miami OK. 918-542-8441, Ext 220
Alexander, S O, *Ser,* Lakehead University Library, Thunder Bay ON. 807-345-2121
Alexander, Samuel O, *Lectr,* Lakehead University, School of Library Technology, ON. 807-345-2121, Ext 240
Alexander, Sheila, *Librn,* Portland Public Library (Munjoy Hill), Portland ME. 207-772-4581
Alexander, Susanna, *Asst Dir,* Missouri State Library, Jefferson City MO. 314-751-4214
Alexander, Thelma, *Librn,* Piedmont Regional Library (Commerce Branch), Commerce GA. 404-867-2762
Alexander, Thomas, *Librn,* University of California, Berkeley (Public Health), Berkeley CA. 415-642-2511
Alexander, Valerie, *Librn,* Atlantic City Medical Center, Medical Library, Atlantic City NJ. 609-344-4081
Alexander, Veronica C, *Librn,* Wayne County Public Library, Honesdale PA. 717-253-1220
Alexander, Wendy, *Dir,* Rosendale Library, Rosendale NY. 914-658-9013
Alexander, IV, William D, *Dir,* South Portland Public Library, South Portland ME. 207-799-2204
Alexis, Charlene, *Asst Dir Pub Servs,* Auraria Libraries, Denver CO. 303-629-2805
Alfin, Ellen L, *In Charge,* Ville Marie Social Service Centre, Centre City Division Library, Montreal PQ. 514-937-9581
Alfold, Mrs G, *Br Supvr,* Scarborough Public Library (Morningside), Scarborough ON. 416-282-3485
Alfonso, Lucinda, *ILL,* Miami Dade Community College (Niles Trammel Learning Resources), Miami FL. 305-596-1293
Alford, Anne, *Outreach,* Albany County Public Library, Laramie WY. 307-745-3365
Alford, Dorothy, *Librn,* Bossier Parish Public Library (Haughton Branch), Haughton LA. 318-949-0196
Alford, H Wendell, *Asst Dir & Tech Serv,* University of Northern Iowa Library, Cedar Falls IA. 319-273-2737
Alford, James, *Media,* Olympic College, Learning Resources Center, Bremerton WA. 206-478-4609
Alford, John, *Prof,* University of Wyoming, Library Media Program, WY. 307-766-2349
Alford, Marilyn, *Asst Librn,* Stephenville Public Library, Stephenville TX. 817-965-5665
Alford, Mary A, *Asst Dir & Ch,* Bellaire City Library, Bellaire TX. 713-664-4098
Alford, Ruth, *Tape Technician,* District of Columbia Library for the Blind & Physically Handicapped, Washington DC. 212-727-2142
Alford, Thomas, *Dir,* Library Cooperative of Macomb, Mount Clemens MI. 313-286-5750
Alford, Thomas, *Dir,* Macomb County Library, Mount Clemens MI. 313-469-5300
Alfveby, Wayne, *Dir,* Northwest Regional Library, Thief River Falls MN. 218-681-4325
Algaze, Selma, *Training Coordr,* Broward County Division of Libraries, Broward County Library, Pompano Beach FL. 305-972-1100
Alger, Margaret, *Librn,* Sutton Free Public Library (Manchaug), Sutton MA. 617-865-6939
Algermissin, Virginia, *Dir,* Texas A&m University Libraries (Medical Sciences), College Station TX. 713-845-7427, 845-7428
Algoo, Stanley, *Tech Serv,* Scarborough Public Library, Scarborough ON. 416-291-1991
Alig, Katherine, *Chief Librn, Acq & Ref,* Airco Inc, Information Center, Murray Hill NJ. 201-464-2400
Alkema, Margaret, *Ch,* Malden Public Library, Malden MA. 617-324-0218
Alkire, Leland, *Per,* Eastern Washington University, John F Kennedy Memorial Library, Cheney WA. 509-359-2261

Alkire, Leland, *Bibliog Instr,* Eastern Washington University, John F Kennedy Memorial Library, Cheney WA. 509-359-2261
Allaire, M Jane, *Dir,* Rhode Island Junior College, Knight Campus Library, Warwick RI. 401-825-2215
Allan, Ann, *Asst Prof,* Kent State University, School of Library Science, OH. 216-672-2782, 672-7988
Allan, Betsy, *Asst Librn,* J Herman Bosler Memorial Library, Bosler Free Library, Carlisle PA. 717-243-4642
Allan, David, *Media,* Mankato State University, Memorial Library, Mankato MN. 507-389-6201
Allan, Elizabeth, *Ref,* Stevens Memorial Library, North Andover MA. 617-682-6260
Allan, Erma, *Cat,* University of New Brunswick, Harriet Irving Library, Fredericton NB. 506-453-4740
Allan, Ferne C, *Dir,* Texaco, Inc, Jefferson Chemical Co, Inc Technical Literature Section Library, Austin TX. 512-465-6543
Allan, Margaret B, *Librn,* United States Air Force (Medical Library), Elmendorf AFB AK. 907-752-5328
Allan, Marie, *Ch,* Cedar Falls Public Library, Cedar Falls IA. 319-266-2629
Allan, Michael F, *Asst Librn,* Union Carbide Corp, Battery Products Div Technical Information Center, Cleveland OH. 216-631-3100, Ext 367
Allan, Viola, *Br Coordr,* Franklin Township Free Public Library, Malaga NJ. 609-694-2833
Allar, Dorraine, *Librn,* Marathon County Public Library (Unity Branch), Unity WI. 715-845-7214, Ext 21
Allard, Armand, *Dir,* Bibliotheque Municipale Des Trois-Rivieres, Trois-Rivieres PQ. 819-374-3521, Ext 71
Allard, C Gabriel, *Dir,* College De Maisonneuve Bibliotheque, Montreal PQ. 514-254-7131, 254-4035
Allard, Diane, *Librn,* Bibliotheque De La Ville De Montreal (Salaberry Children), Montreal PQ. 514-872-4048
Allard, Gail, *ILL,* Windsor Public Library, Windsor CT. 203-688-6433
Allard, Joan, *Ref,* Adams Library, Chelmsford MA. 617-256-5521
Allard, Kay, *Dir,* Lincoln First Bank, Library Services, Rochester NY. 716-262-2306, 262-2307
Allard, Mary Margaret, *Dir,* Beck Bookman Library, Holton KS. 913-364-3532
Allard, Micheline, *Librn,* Abbott Laboratories Limited Library, Montreal PQ. 514-341-6880
Allard, Serge, *Dir,* College Du Nord-Quest La Bibliotheque, Rouyn PQ. 819-762-0931, Ext 134
Allard, Serge, *Librn In Charge,* Universite Du Quebec: Centre d'etudes Universitaires Dans L'ouest Quebecois Bibliotheque, Rouyn PQ. 819-762-0971, Ext 350
Allbach, Ronald, *AV,* Haverhill Public Library, Haverhill MA. 617-373-1586
Allbaugh, Leni, *Librn,* Penn Area Library (Harrison City Reading Center), Harrison City PA. 412-744-4414
Allbert, Portia, *Librn,* Kansas State Historical Society Library, Topeka KS. 913-296-3251
Allbritton, Joy, *Asst Librn,* LaSalle Parish Library (Olla), Jena LA. 318-495-5570
Alldredge, Noreen G, *Asst Dir Coll Develop,* Texas A&m University Libraries, College Station TX. 713-845-6111
Allely, Mary, *Librn,* San Diego Public Library (Linda Vista), San Diego CA. 714-277-3637
Alleman, David, *Bibliog Instr & Ref,* Hillsdale College, Mossey Learning Resources Center, Hillsdale MI. 517-437-7341, Ext 225
Alleman, Virginia, *Tech Serv,* Golden West College Library, Huntington Beach CA. 714-892-7711, Ext 541
Allen, Adrian E, *Libr Supvr,* Argonne National Laboratory, Argonne-West Technical Library, Idaho Falls ID. 208-526-7237
Allen, Alice, *Head,* University of Minnesota Libraries-Twin Cities (Serials Acquisitions), Minneapolis MN. 612-373-3112
Allen, Angela A, *Librn,* Southern California College, O Cope Budge Library, Costa Mesa CA. 714-556-3610, Ext 264
Allen, Anita, *Librn,* San Antonio Public Library (Young Peoples Room), San Antonio TX. 512-299-7821

Allen, Anna Foster, *Librn,* Lehigh County Historical Society, Scott Andrew Trexler, II Memorial Library, Allentown PA. 215-435-1074
Allen, Anne, *Librn,* United States Navy (Correctional Center Library), Charleston SC. 803-743-6490
Allen, Anne, *Admin Librn,* United States Navy (Naval Station Base Library), Charleston SC. 803-743-5399
Allen, Arlene, *Ad & Ref,* Silver City Public Library, Silver City NM. 505-538-3672
Allen, Barbara, *Br Coordr & Bkmobile Coordr,* Kalamazoo Public Library, Kalamazoo MI. 616-342-9837
Allen, Barbara, *Media,* Robbins Library, Arlington MA. 617-643-0026
Allen, Barbara, *Cat,* University of Denver (Westminster Law Library), Denver CO. 303-753-3405
Allen, Beatrice S, *Librn,* Worcester County Library (Snow Hill), Snow Hill MD. 301-632-2600
Allen, Beth, *Librn,* McMinn Co, Edward Gauche Fisher Public Library, Athens TN. 615-745-7782
Allen, Betty, *Ch,* Library Association of Portland, Multnomah County Library, Portland OR. 503-223-7201, Ext 40
Allen, Beverly, *ILL,* Lake Ontario Regional Library System, Kingston ON. 613-546-9400
Allen, Beverly, *Cat,* Saint Norbert College, Todd Wehr Library, De Pere WI. 414-337-3280
Allen, Beverly E, *Dir,* Morehouse College School of Medicine, Multi-Media Center, Atlanta GA. 404-681-2800, Ext 202
Allen, Bill, *Am & English Lit,* Stanford University Libraries, Stanford CA. 415-497-2016
Allen, Bonnie E, *Dir,* Saint Charles District Library, Hartley Memorial Library, Saint Charles MI. 517-865-9451
Allen, Bonnie J, *Librn,* IRM United States of America, Inc, International Research & Marketing Library, New York NY. 212-751-3970
Allen, Cameron, *Law Librn,* Rutgers University, the State University of New Jersey (School of Law), Newark NJ. 201-648-5675
Allen, Carla, *Circ,* Calloway County Public Library, Murray KY. 502-753-2288
Allen, Charmaine, *Circ,* Indiana University at South Bend Library, South Bend IN. 219-237-4440
Allen, Debra, *Dir,* White River Regional Library, Batesville AR. 501-793-7347
Allen, Dick, *Br Coordr,* Osceola Public Library, Osceola NE. 402-747-4301
Allen, Dolores E, *Librn,* Chicopee Public Library, Chicopee MA. 413-594-6679
Allen, Doris, *Cat,* California State University, Hayward Library, Hayward CA. 415-881-3664
Allen, Dorothy, *Acq,* Houston Baptist University, Moody Memorial Library, Houston TX. 713-774-7661, Ext 303
Allen, Dorothy, *Librn,* Montreal Association for the Blind Library, Montreal PQ. 514-489-8201
Allen, Dorothy R, *Librn,* Litton Educational Publishing Inc, Editorial Library, New York NY. 212-265-8700, Ext 447
Allen, Drucilla, *Cat,* Catonsville Community College, Learning Resources Div, Baltimore MD. 301-455-4586
Allen, Edna, *Ref,* Warner-Lambert Canada Limited, Reference Library, Scarborough ON. 416-750-2360
Allen, Edwin, *Acq,* Wesleyan University, Olin Memorial Library, Middletown CT. 203-347-9411, Ext 296
Allen, Eleanor B, *Librn,* University of Pennsylvania Libraries (Lippincott-Wharton School), Philadelphia PA. 215-243-5921
Allen, Emily, *Librn,* Westminster Presbyterian Church, John H Holmes Library, Cincinnati OH. 513-921-1623
Allen, Eulalia, *Librn,* York Public Library, York AL. 205-392-4950
Allen, Eva, *Ch, YA & Acq,* Newmarket Public Library, Newmarket ON. 416-895-5196
Allen, Fern L, *Librn,* Kinderhook Memorial Library, Kinderhook NY. 518-758-6192
Allen, Gary, *ILL,* Carroll College Library, Helena MT. 406-442-3450, Ext 245, 247 & 442-1295
Allen, Gary R, *Dir, Acq & Cat,* Hazel Park Memorial Library, Hazel Park MI. 313-542-0940

Allen, Glenn, *Ser,* Carnegie Library, Rome GA. 404-291-7568
Allen, Gordon, *Librn,* United States Army (Computer Systems Command Technical Library), Fort Belvoir VA. 703-664-6071
Allen, Helen M, *Librn,* Bunker Hill Public Library, Bunker Hill IL. 618-585-4736
Allen, Imogene, *Librn,* Greenville County Library (Simpsonville), Simpsonville SC. 803-963-7870
Allen, Irene, *Per,* Seattle University, A A Lemieux Library, Seattle WA. 206-626-6859
Allen, Jacqueline, *Librn,* Rock Island Public Library (Martin Luther King), Rock Island IL. 309-794-9809
Allen, James A, *Dir,* University of Arkansas at Little Rock Library, Little Rock AR. 501-569-3120
Allen, Jane, *Librn,* Chatham-Effingham-Liberty Regional Library (Liberty County), Hinesville GA. 912-876-3574
Allen, Jeanette, *Cat,* Saint Joseph College, Pope Pius XII Library, West Hartford CT. 203-232-4571, Ext 208
Allen, Jeanne, *Librn,* Hale Center Public Library, Hale Center TX. 806-839-2055
Allen, Joan, *ILL,* Middlebury College, Egbert Starr Library, Middlebury VT. 802-388-7621
Allen, Joanne, *Circ,* Bayard Taylor Memorial Library, Kennett Square PA. 215-444-2702
Allen, John P, *Assoc Dean,* Illinois Valley Community College, Library Technical Assistant Program, IL. 815-224-2720
Allen, Joseph, *Relig,* Bob Jones University, J S Mack Library, Greenville SC. 803-242-5100, Ext 296
Allen, Joseph, *Asst Dir,* Bob Jones University, J S Mack Library, Greenville SC. 803-242-5100, Ext 296
Allen, Joyce S, *Librn,* Methodist Hospital of Indiana, Inc, Library Department, Indianapolis IN. 317-924-8021
Allen, Judy, *Librn,* Tulsa City-County Library (East Second), Tulsa OK. 918-592-0001
Allen, Judy, *Librn,* Tulsa City-County Library (Florence Park), Tulsa OK. 918-936-0730
Allen, Julia, *Dir,* Carnegie Free Library, Connellsville PA. 412-628-1380
Allen, June, *ILL & Acq,* Saint Mary's College of California, Saint Albert Hall Library, Moraga CA. 415-376-4411, Ext 229, 230
Allen, Kay, *Librn,* Cleveland Public Library (West Park), Cleveland OH. 216-941-3730
Allen, Kenneth S, *Assoc Dir & Spec Programs,* University of Washington Libraries, Seattle WA. 206-543-1760
Allen, Kenneth W, *Dean,* Waubonsee Community College, Learning Resources Center, Sugar Grove IL. 312-466-4811, Ext 303
Allen, Lawrence A, *Prof,* University of Kentucky, College of Library Science, KY. 606-258-8876
Allen, Linda G, *Tech Serv & Cat,* Louisville Free Public Library, Louisville KY. 502-584-4154
Allen, Lois L, *Librn,* Price Waterhouse & Co Library, Chicago IL. 312-565-1500
Allen, Marcia K, *Librn,* Catholic Medical Center, Health Science Library, Manchester NH. 603-668-3545
Allen, Margaret, *Spec Coll,* Grace A Dow Memorial Library, Midland Public Library, Midland MI. 517-835-7151
Allen, Margaret, *ILL & Cat,* Salem College, Benedum Learning Resources Center, Salem WV. 304-782-5238
Allen, Margaret, *Librn,* Victoria County Public Library (Fenelon Falls Branch), Fenelon Falls ON. 705-324-3104
Allen, Margaret A, *Librn,* Saint Joseph's Hospital, School of Nursing Learning Resource Center, Marshfield WI. 715-387-7374
Allen, Margaret B, *Dir,* Bennington Free Library, Bennington VT. 802-442-9051
Allen, Margaret B, *Supvr,* United States Air Force (Hospital Patient's Library), Elmendorf AFB AK. 907-752-5328
Allen, Margery, *Head Metro Libr,* Metropolitan Toronto Library Board, Metropolitan Toronto Library, Toronto ON. 416-928-5150
Allen, Marguerite M, *Librn,* Arms Library Association, Shelburne Falls MA. 413-625-2024
Allen, Marion, *Acq,* Colby-Sawyer College, Fernald Library, New London NH. 603-526-2010, Ext 245

Allen, Marsha, *Librn,* Detroit Public Library (Chaney), Detroit MI. 313-833-9757

Allen, Martha, *Tech Serv & Cat,* Keuka College, Lightner Library, Keuka Park NY. 315-536-4411, Ext 224, 248 & 338

Allen, Marti, *Tech Serv & On-Line Servs,* Bethany Nazarene College, R T Williams Memorial Library, Bethany OK. 405-789-6400, Ext 276

Allen, Mary Alice, *Librn,* Georgia Pacific Corp Library, Atlanta GA. 404-491-1244

Allen, Mary W, *Librn,* Washington Psychoanalytic Society, Hadley Memorial Library, Washington DC. 202-338-5453

Allen, Mrs Leland, *Librn,* Webster Parish Library (Springhill Branch), Springhill LA. 318-539-4117

Allen, Myrna, *Librn,* Dayton & Montgomery County Public Library (Burkhardt Avenue Branch), Dayton OH. 513-224-1651, Ext 240

Allen, Nan, *Librn,* Brooksville Free Public Library, Inc, Brooksville ME. 207-326-4518

Allen, Nancy, *Librn,* Birmingham Public & Jefferson County Free Library (East Lake), Birmingham AL. 205-254-2551

Allen, Nancy, *Librn,* University of Illinois Library at Urbana-Champaign (Communications), Urbana IL. 217-333-2216

Allen, Nancy S, *Librn,* Museum of Fine Arts, William Morris Hunt Memorial Library, Boston MA. 617-267-9300, Ext 388

Allen, Neta, *Librn,* Northeast Regional Library (Baldwyn Library), Baldwyn MS. 601-365-3305

Allen, Norma, *Sci & Indust,* Reuben McMillan Free Library Free Library Association, Public Library of Youngstown & Mahoning County, Youngstown OH. 216-744-8636

Allen, Pamela, *ILL,* Corpus Christi Public Libraries, La Retama Public Library, Corpus Christi TX. 512-882-1937

Allen, Pat, *Librn,* Sheridan County Fulmer Public Library (Story Community), Story WY. 307-683-2922

Allen, Patty, *Librn,* Olden County Center (Patients' Library), Anchorage KY. 502-241-0300

Allen, Pauline B, *Librn,* University of Nebraska Medical Center (Nebraska Psychiatric Institute Library), Omaha NE. 402-541-4624

Allen, Rebecca, *Asst Librn,* North Scituate Public Library, North Scituate RI. 401-647-5133

Allen, Richard, *Asst,* Evansville State Hospital, Medical Library, Evansville IN. 812-473-2261

Allen, Richard, *Northern Network Coordr,* Nebraska Library Commission, Lincoln NE. 402-471-2045

Allen, Rita, *Librn,* Lyons Falls Free Library, Lyons Falls NY. 315-348-8633

Allen, Robert L, *Librn,* United States Air Force (ESMC Technical Library), Patrick AFB FL. 305-494-6638

Allen, Rosanna P, *Humanities & Soc Sci,* Pennsylvania State University, Fred Lewis Pattee Library, University Park PA. 814-865-0401

Allen, Rose, *Librn,* Frontenac County Library (Kingston Township Centre 70), Kingston ON. 613-389-2616

Allen, Sandra, *Librn,* Stratton Free Library, Swanzey NH. 603-352-7169

Allen, Sarah, *In Charge,* Florida Agricultural & Mechanical University (Instructional Materials Center School of Pharmacy), Tallahassee FL. 904-599-3301

Allen, Sharon, *Dir,* Humboldt County Library, Winnemucca NV. 702-623-5081, Ext 315 & 316

Allen, Shirley A, *In Charge,* Indiana Baptist College Library, Indianapolis IN. 317-882-2327

Allen, Susan, *Tech Serv,* Laramie County Community College Library, Cheyenne WY. 307-634-5853

Allen, Susan, *Circ,* Logan Library, Logan UT. 801-752-2365

Allen, Susan M, *Dir,* Greenville Public Library, Carnegie Branch, Greenville OH. 513-548-3915

Allen, Tracy S, *Librn,* Kettleson Memorial Library, Sitka AK. 907-747-8708

Allen, Valentine, *ILL,* College of Medicine & Dentistry of New Jersey, George F Smith Library of the Health Sciences, Newark NJ. 201-456-4580

Allen, Viola, *Librn,* Franklin Township Free Public Library (Franklinville Library), Franklinville NJ. 609-694-1028

Allen, Virginia, *Doc,* Victoria College - University of Houston Victoria Campus Library, Victoria TX. 512-575-7436

Allen, Walter C, *Assoc Prof,* University of Illinois, Graduate School of Library Science, IL. 217-333-3280

Allen, William R, *Librn,* Devry Institute of Technology, Information Resource Center Library, Atlanta GA. 404-452-0288

Allen, Jr, Edwin H, *Asst Dir,* League of Iowa Municipalities Library, Des Moines IA. 515-265-9961

Allender, Robert K, *Regional Librn,* Lake Cumberland Regional Library, Columbia KY. 502-384-4211

Allensworth, James, *Ref,* North State Cooperative Library System, Willows CA. 916-934-2173

Allert, Dan, *Media,* Carl Sandburg College, Learning Resources Center, Galesburg IL. 309-344-2518, Ext 247 & 257

Alleva, Rose Marie, *Librn,* Applied Psychological Services, Inc Library, Wayne PA. 215-688-4874

Alley, Brian, *Asst Dir,* Miami University, Edgar W King Library, Oxford OH. 513-529-2944

Alley, Debra J, *Circ,* Eastern Nazarene College, Nease Library, Wollaston MA. 617-773-6350, Ext 251

Alley, Dorothy, *Librn,* Hercules Inc, Systems Division, Bacchus Plant Lab Library, Magna UT. 801-250-5911

Alley, Katherine, *Asst Librn,* University of Maine at Machias, Merrill Library, Machias ME. 207-255-3313, Ext 234

Allie, Jean Leon, *Acq,* Saint Paul University Library, Ottawa ON. 613-235-1421, Ext 54

Alligood, Elaine C, *Chief, Libr Servs,* Veterans Administration, Hospital Library Service, Baltimore MD. 301-467-9932, Ext 5464

Allis, Jeannette B, *Govt Publications,* Bureau of Libraries, Museums & Archaeological Services, Saint Thomas VI. 809-774-3407

Allison, Anne Marie, *Asst Dir,* Florida Atlantic University, S E Wimberly Library, Boca Raton FL. 305-395-5100, Ext 2448

Allison, Dee Ann, *Dir,* Hastings Regional Center, Medical Center Library, Hastings NE. 402-463-2471, Ext 342

Allison, Estaline, *Asst Librn,* Hobe Sound Bible College Library, Hobe Sound FL. 305-546-6166

Allison, Eugene S, *Pub Serv Coordr,* Volusia County Public Libraries, Daytona Beach FL. 904-252-8374

Allison, Evelyn, *Ref,* Bucks County Community College Library, Newtown PA. 215-968-5861, Ext 306, 307

Allison, Frederick E, *Dir,* Grove City Public Library, Grove City OH. 614-875-6716

Allison, George B, *Dep Dir,* United States Air Force, Air University Library, Maxwell AFB AL. 205-293-2888

Allison, James M, *Librn,* Bexar County Law Library, San Antonio TX. 512-227-8822

Allison, Jean A, *Chrmn,* Trinity United Church of Christ, Edith L Stock Memorial Library, Saint Louis MO. 314-352-6645

Allison, Jo-Anne, *Librn,* Northwest Library, Yellowknife NT. 403-873-7628

Allison, Monica, *Admin Asst,* Winnipeg Public Library, Winnipeg MB. 204-985-6450

Allison, Mrs M, *Librn,* Holmes County District Public Library (Killbuck Branch), Killbuck OH. 216-674-5972

Allison, Robert, *Librn,* East York Public Library (Dawes Road), Toronto ON. 416-757-8649

Allison, Theodore R, *Dir,* Bellevue Public Library, Bellevue OH. 419-483-4769

Allmand, Linda, *Chief, Branch Servs,* Dallas Public Library, Dallas TX. 214-748-9071

Allmandinger, Helen, *Cat,* Dwyer-Mercer County District Library, Celina OH. 419-586-2314

Allmon, Marialis, *Librn,* Cherokee Regional Library (Chickamauga Public), Chickamauga GA. 404-638-2992

Allred, Carol B, *Asst Librn Pub Servs,* Southern Methodist University Libraries (Underwood Law Library), Dallas TX. 214-692-3258, 692-3230

Allshouse, Jane W, *Librn,* Dow Corning Corp (Technical Information Service Library), Midland MI. 517-496-4957

Allshouse, John W, *Ad,* South Bend Public Library, South Bend IN. 219-288-4413

Allstrom, Barbara, *Librn,* American Cyanamid Co Library, Stamford CT. 203-348-7331, Ext 784

Allwardt, Donna, *Ad & Bkmobile Coordr,* Sutter County Free Library, Yuba City CA. 916-673-5773

Allwardt, Richard E, *Asst Dir,* Mansfield-Richland County Public Library, Mansfield OH. 419-524-1041

Alm, Mary E, *Librn,* Pine Plains Free Library, Pine Plains NY. 914-398-1927

Almack, Julie, *Asst Dir & Commun Servs,* Carlsbad City Library, Carlsbad CA. 714-438-5614

Almagro, Bertha, *Asst Librn for Processing Servs,* University of Arizona Library (Arizona Health Sciences Center Library), Tucson AZ. 602-626-6121

Almand, Jean, *Librn,* Western Kentucky University (Science Library), Bowling Green KY. 502-745-3958

Almeica, Pauline, *Librn,* United States Navy (Naval Air Station Library), Fallon NV. 702-423-5161, Ext 2599

Almeida, Carlos, *Dir,* Portuguese Union of the State of California, J A Freitas Library, San Leandro CA. 415-483-7676

Almeida, Ruth, *Librn,* Public Library of Annapolis & Anne Arundel County Inc (Kuethe), Glen Burnie MD. 301-766-8788

Almeida, Ruth, *Librn,* Public Library of Annapolis & Anne Arundel County Inc (North County Area), Harundale MD. 301-768-4320

Almes, June, *Coordr,* Lock Haven State College, PA. 717-748-5351, Ext 478

Almquist, Deborah T, *Chmn,* Boston Biomedical Library Consortium, MA. 617-782-7000, Ext 2177

Almquist, Helen, *Librn,* Essex Public Library, Essex IA. 712-379-3355

Aloisa, Francine, *Asst Dir,* Kent Memorial Library, Suffield CT. 203-668-2325

Alonso, Guillermo A, *Librn,* San Antonio Light Library, San Antonio TX. 512-226-4271

Alonzi, Mary, *Librn,* Toledo-Lucas County Public Library (Toledo Heights), Toledo OH. 419-255-7055

Alonzo, Kate, *Dir,* Henrietta Public Library, Rochester NY. 716-334-3401

Aloyse, Sister M John, *Cat,* Saint Charles Borromeo Seminary, Ryan Memorial Library, Philadelphia PA. 215-839-3760, Ext 275

Alper, Freda P, *ILL, Cat & Ref,* Gloucester City Library, Gloucester City NJ. 609-456-4181

Alper, Rhea, *Librn,* Free Public Library of Woodbridge (Port Reading Branch), Port Reading NJ. 201-541-5201

Alper, Rhea, *Librn,* Free Public Library of Woodbridge (Sewaren Branch), Sewaren NJ. 201-634-7571

Alpern, Florence L, *Dir,* West Long Branch Public Library, West Long Branch NJ. 201-222-5993

Alquist, Kay, *Media,* Rolling Meadows Library, Rolling Meadows IL. 312-259-6050

Alrutz, Tom, *Dir,* Newark Public Library, Newark NJ. 201-733-7800

Alsaker, L, *Ref,* Luther College, Preus Library, Decorah IA. 319-387-1163

Alsbach, George, *Cat,* Southwestern Oklahoma State University, Al Harris Library, Weatherford OK. 405-772-6611, Ext 5311

Alschlager, Barbara, *ILL & Ch,* Rock County Community Library, Luverne MN. 507-283-8569

Alsfeld, Jane, *Librn,* Wilton Public & Gregg Free Library, Wilton NH. 603-654-2581

Alsip, James B, *Dir,* George Washington University Library, Washington DC. 202-676-6455

Alsmeyer, Jr, Henry L, *Dir & Acq,* Hendrix College, Olin C Bailey Library, Conway AR. 501-329-9323

Alsop, Rosemary, *Asst Dir & Ch,* Working Men's Institute Library, New Harmony IN. 812-682-4806

Alston, Barbara, *Librn,* Wake County Department of the Public Library (South Raleigh Branch), Raleigh NC. 919-755-6106

Alston, Jane C, *Dir,* H Grady Bradshaw Chambers County Library and Cobb Memorial Archives, Shawmut AL. 205-768-3150

Alsum, Mariann, *ILL & Reader Serv,* Saint Mary's College, Fitzgerald Library, Winona MN. 507-452-4430, Ext 232

Alsworth, Frances, *Dept Chmn,* Central State University, Library Science Dept, OK. 405-341-2980, Ext 681

Alt, Diane, *Media,* Central College, Geisler Learning Resource Center, Pella IA. 515-628-4151, Ext 233

Altberg, Rose, *Ch,* Veterans Administration, Medical Center Library, Altoona PA. 814-943-8164

Altenburg, William, *Ref,* Santa Maria Public Library, Santa Maria CA. 805-925-0994, Ext 261

Alter, Forrest, *Art, Drama, Music,* Flint Public Library, Flint MI. 313-232-7111

Alterman, Sara Katsh, *Librn,* Association of Operating Room Nurses Library, Denver CO. 303-755-6300

Altfuldisch, Florian, *Ch,* Sudbury Public Library, La Bibliotheque Publique de Sudbury, Sudbury ON. 705-673-1155

Altgilbers, Cynthia, *Asst Librn,* Quincy College Library, Quincy IL. 217-222-8020, Ext 225

Altgilbers, Cynthia, *Instr,* Quincy College, Library Science Program, IL. 217-222-8020, Ext 225

Altherr, Janet W, *Librn,* Reading Public Library, Reading VT. 802-457-3737

Altis, E E, *Doc,* Southwest Missouri State University Library, Springfield MO. 417-836-5104

Altman, Ellen, *Dir,* University of Arizona, Graduate Library School, AZ. 602-626-3565

Altman, Philip L, *Dir,* Federation of American Societies for Experimental Biology Library, Bethesda MD. 301-530-7121

Altman, Shalom, *Dir,* Gratz College Library (Abner & Mary Schreiber Jewish Music Library), Philadelphia PA. 215-329-3372

Altner, Patricia, *On-Line Servs,* United States Army (Armament R & D Command, Scientific & Technical Information Div), Dover NJ. 201-328-2914

Altomar, Mary, *Librn,* Schwarz Services International, Ltd Library, Mount Vernon NY. 914-664-1100

Altomaro, Rita, *Ref & Spec Coll,* Free Public Library of the Borough of Fort Lee, Fort Lee NJ. 201-461-8020

Alton, Mary, *Librn,* Saint Jerome Hospital, Medical Library, Batavia NY. 716-343-3131

Altonn, Elva, *Ref & Per,* San Jose City College Library, San Jose CA. 408-298-2181, Ext 410

Aluffo, Pier, *Asst Librn,* Betz Laboratories, Inc Library, Trevose PA. 215-355-3300, Ext 507

Alvano, Erlinda F, *Librn,* Value Engineering Co, Technical Library, Alexandria VA. 703-960-4600

Alvarado, Eliam, *Circ,* University of Puerto Rico - Bayamon Regional College, Learning Resources Center, Bayamon PR. 809-786-5225

Alvarado, Migdalia, *Asst Librn,* Ponce Public Library, Ponce PR. 809-843-4820

Alvarez, Adoracion A, *Dir,* Oregon School for the Deaf Library, Salem OR. 503-378-6252

Alvarez, Grace, *Librn,* Avantek Inc, Corporate Library, Santa Clara CA. 408-249-0700

Alvarez, Ivette, *Librn,* Commonwealth of Puerto Rico (Department of State Library), San Juan PR. 809-724-6869

Alvarez, Octavio, *Librn,* National Institute on Aging, Gerontology Research Center Library, Baltimore MD. 301-396-9403

Alvarez, Ofelia, *Tech Serv,* Catholic University of Puerto Rico (Encarnacion Valdes Library), Ponce PR. 809-844-4150, Ext 119

Alvarez, Robert S, *Dir,* South San Francisco Public Library, South San Francisco CA. 415-877-8521

Alverson, Margaret H, *Librn,* Veterans Administration, Hospital Library, Minneapolis MN. 612-725-6767

Alves, Lillian, *Dir,* Benicia Public Library, Benicia CA. 707-745-2265

Alves, Jr, C Douglass, *Dir,* Wethersfield Historical Society, Old Academy Museum Library, Wethersfield CT. 203-529-7656

Alvey, Celine, *Librn,* Naval Medical Research Institute, Technical Reference Library, Bethesda MD. 301-295-0060, 295-0061

Alvy, C, *Librn,* Mudge, Rose, Guthrie & Alexander Library, New York NY. 212-422-6767

Alwady, Mrs S, *Reader Serv,* Southern University Library, Baton Rouge LA. 504-771-4990, 771-4991, 771-4992

Alward, Judy, *ILL,* University of Alaska, Arctic Environmental Information & Data Center Library, Anchorage AK. 907-279-4523

Amabile, Helen, *Head, Ref Branch,* International Communication Agency (Agency Library), Washington DC. 202-724-9214

Amadi, Adolphe O, *Instr,* Cambrian College of Applied Arts & Technology, Library Techniques Program-Programme en Bibliotechniques, ON. 705-566-8101

Aman, Mohammed, *Dean,* University of Wisconsin-Milwaukee, School of Library Science, WI. 414-963-4707

Amantia, A M, *Asst Librn,* National Wildlife Federation, Frazier Memorial Library, Washington DC. 202-797-6829

Amara, Margaret, *Librn,* Center for Advanced Study in the Behavioral Sciences Library, Stanford CA. 415-321-2052

Amaral, Anne, *Librn,* University of Nevada-Reno (Life & Health Science), Reno NV. 702-784-6616

Amaro, Margarita, *Bi-lingual Serv,* Dodge City Public Library, Dodge City KS. 316-225-0248

Amaya, Larue, *Asst Librn,* Ohio Valley Medical Center, Inc, Hupp Medical Library, Wheeling WV. 304-243-0123

Ambardeker, Raj, *Pub Serv,* Middle Georgia College, Roberts Memorial Library, Cochran GA. 912-934-6221, Ext 274

Ambelang, Audrey, *Dir,* Sparta Free Library, Sparta WI. 608-269-2010

Ambergay, Joyce, *Librn,* Letcher County Public Library (Lillian Webb Memorial), Neon KY. 606-855-7913

Ambrose, Ethel, *Ch,* Stockton-San Joaquin County Public Library, Stockton Public Libr, Stockton CA. 209-944-8415

Ambrose, Frances, *Librn,* Freedom Public Library, Freedom PA. 412-775-7160

Amburgey, Don, *Dir,* Kentucky River Regional Library District, Hazard KY. 606-439-1531

Amburn, Kathy, *Coodr,* Central Counties Center for Mental Health & Mental Retardation Services, Information Resource Center Library, Temple TX. 817-778-4841, Ext 76

Amdahl, Ruth, *Librn,* Saint Louis Park Medical Center, Arneson Library, Minneapolis MN. 612-927-3097

Amdor, Robert, *Librn,* National Park Service, Fort Vancouver National Historic Site Library, Vancouver WA. 206-696-4041

Amdursky, Saul J, *Admin,* Racine County Federated Library System, Racine WI. 414-637-1661

Ameduri, Jean, *Librn,* Saint Louis Public Library (Gravois), Saint Louis MO. 314-481-3125

Amee, Charlotte, *Asst Librn,* Rice Public Library, Kittery ME. 207-439-1553

Amee, Louise P, *Librn,* Arvin A Brown Public Library, Richford VT. 802-848-3313

Ameely, Lucille, *Dir,* Dartford Public Library, Green Lake WI. 414-294-3572

Amelang, Jean, *Reader Serv,* Elbert Ivey Memorial Library, Hickory NC. 704-322-2905

Ameling, Linda, *ILL,* Lake County Public Library, Merrillville IN. 219-769-3541

Ameling, Russ, *Maps,* Mankato State University, Memorial Library, Mankato MN. 507-389-6201

Amelung, Mary Alice, *Librn,* Johnson County Library (Oak Park), Overland Park KS. 913-831-1550

Amelung, Richard, *Cat,* Saint Louis University (Omer Poos Law Library), Saint Louis MO. 314-658-2755

Amen, Kathleen, *Doc, On-Line Servs & Bibliog Instr,* Saint Mary's University (Academic Library), San Antonio TX. 512-436-3441

Amend, Edna, *Librn,* Richmond Heights Memorial Library, Richmond Heights MO. 314-645-6202

Ament, Deborah, *Bkmobile Coordr,* Wheeler Basin Regional Library, Decatur Public Library, Decatur AL. 205-353-2993

Amer, Rosalie, *Tech Serv,* Cosumnes River College, Learning Resources Center, Sacramento CA. 916-421-1000, Ext 266

Amerski, Audrey, *Doc,* Old Dominion University Library, Norfolk VA. 804-440-4141

Ames, Audrey E, *Librn,* Defence Research Establishment, Suffield Library, Suffield AB. 403-455-3701

Ames, Barbara, *ILL,* Twin Falls Public Library, Twin Falls ID. 208-733-2965

Ames, Jan, *Dir,* Washington Regional Library for the Blind & Physically Handicapped, Seattle WA. 464-6930. SCAN 576-6930

Ames, Kathryn S, *Assoc Dir & Acq,* Athens Regional Library, Athens GA. 404-543-0134

Ames, Mark J, *Dir,* Loutit Library, Grand Haven MI. 616-842-5560

Ames, Roy P, *Dir,* John Marshall Law School, Sidney T Schell Memorial Library, Atlanta GA. 404-659-8121

Ames, Ruth, *Archivist Reporter Records,* Wake Forest University, Z Smith Reynolds Library, Winston-Salem NC. 919-761-5480

Amey, Lorne J, *Asst Prof,* Dalhousie University, School of Library Service, NS. 902-424-3656

Amicarella, Effie, *Librn,* Lafayette Public Library, Lafayette CO. 303-665-5200

Amick, Betty, *Librn,* Platte County Public Library (Glendo Branch), Glendo WY. 307-735-4480

Amidjaya, Mary, *Ref,* Rock Valley College Educational Resources Center, Rockford IL. 815-226-3762

Amies, D R, *Dir,* Moose Jaw Union Hospital, Medical Library, Moose Jaw SK. 306-692-1841, Ext 377, 378

Amiot, Carol, *Librn,* College de Rimouski (CEGEP) Bibliotheque, Rimouski PQ. 418-723-1880

Amirault, Cerina, *Libr Asst,* Western Counties Regional Library (Pubnico Branch), Pubnico NS. 902-762-2204

Amirault, Mary Louise, *Librn,* Nature Center for Environmental Activities Library, Westport CT. 203-227-7253

Amiryar, Quadir, *ILL,* George Washington University Library, Washington DC. 202-676-6455

Amis, Helen C, *Ad,* Richard H Thornton Library, Oxford NC. 919-693-1121

Amis, Joe, *Librn,* South Plains College Library, Levelland TX. 806-894-9611

Amis, Patricia, *Asst Dir,* Marysville Public Library, Marysville OH. 513-642-1876

Amis, Terence, *Asst Dir,* Albert-Westmorland-Kent Regional Library, Moncton NB. 506-389-2631

Ammer, William, *Librn,* Pickaway County Law Library Association Library, Circleville OH. 614-474-6026

Ammerman, Robert C, *Librn,* Germantown Public Library, Germantown OH. 513-855-4001

Ammirati, John, *Dir,* Cathedral College of the Immaculate Conception, Cathedral College Library, Douglaston NY. 212-631-4600, Ext 213

Ammon, F Elaine, *Librn,* Parkesburg Free Library, Parkesburg PA. 215-857-3345

Ammons, Betty, *Bibliog Instr,* United Methodist Historical Society, Lovely Lane Museum Library, Baltimore MD. 301-889-4458

Ammons, Shirley, *Librn,* Amarillo Public Library (Southwest), Amarillo TX. 806-378-3056, 378-3057

Amos, Billie, *Librn,* Mid-Continent Public Library (Camden Point Branch), Camden Point MO. 816-445-3384

Amos, Geraldine O, *Assoc Dir & Tech Serv,* Dillard University, Will W Alexander Library, New Orleans LA. 504-949-2123, Ext 256, 257

Amos, Margie, *Asst Librn,* Scott Sebastian Regional Library, Greenwood AR. 501-996-2856

Amos, Mary L, *Assoc Prof,* Bowling Green State University, Dept of Library & Educational Media, OH. 419-372-2461

Amos, Nancy, *Librn,* Louisville Free Public Library (Northeast), Louisville KY. 502-423-0908

Amos, Robert, *In Charge,* Art Gallery of Greater Victoria Reference Library, Victoria BC. 604-384-4101

Amoury, Gloria, *Librn,* Mystery Writers of America, Inc Library, New York NY. 212-473-8020

Amrhein, Ed, *Youth Facility,* Great Neck Library, Great Neck NY. 516-466-8055

Amrhein, John K, *Dir,* Kutztown State College, Rohrbach Library, Kutztown PA. 215-683-4480

Amrhein, Susan, *Media,* Loudoun County Public Library, Leesburg VA. 703-777-0368

Amrit, Paul, *Librn,* Steger-South Chicago Heights Public Library District, South Chicago Heights IL. 312-755-5040

Amsbary, Kristine, *ILL & Ser,* Mount Vernon Public Library, Mount Vernon IL. 618-242-6322

Amtzis, Selma, *Librn, On-Line Servs & Bibliog Instr,* Sea View Hospital & Home Medical Library, Staten Island NY. 212-390-8689
Amy, Jenny, *Ch,* Nepean Public Library, Ottawa ON. 613-224-4338
Amyoony, Adelia, *Circ,* Halifax City Regional Library, Halifax NS. 902-426-6980
Amyot-Rainville, Carole, *Librn,* Saint Vincent-De-Paul Hospital, Medical Library, Sherbrooke PQ. 819-563-2366, Ext 255
Amyotte, Cecile, *Librn,* National Capital Commission Library, Ottawa ON. 613-992-4231
An, Virginia, *AV,* Houston Baptist University, Moody Memorial Library, Houston TX. 713-774-7661, Ext 303
Anable, Richard, *Assoc Dir,* State University of New York at Binghamton Library, Binghamton NY. 607-798-2194
Anaclerio, C R, *Chief, Tech Libr Br,* United States Army (Technical Library), Aberdeen Proving Ground MD. 301-671-2934
Anama, Shirley, *Ch,* Free Public Library of the City of Trenton, Trenton NJ. 609-392-7188
Ananda, Peter, *Librn,* University of California, Berkeley (South-Southeast Asia Library Service), Berkeley CA. 415-642-3095
Anas, Roberta J, *Librn,* Symmers, Fish & Warner Library, New York NY. 212-751-6400
Anastasiou, Joan D, *Coordr,* Vancouver Community College at Langara Campus, Library Technician Program, BC. 604-324-5418
Anchors, Barbara, *Acq,* Chatham-Effingham-Liberty Regional Library, Savannah Public Library, Savannah GA. 912-234-5127
Ancilla, Sister M, *Dir,* Maria Regina College Library-Media Center, Syracuse NY. 315-474-4891, Ext 28
Ancilla, Sister M, *Asst Prof,* Mary Regina College, Library Service Program, NY. 315-474-4891
Anctil, Donna L, *Acq,* Nashua Public Library, Nashua NH. 603-883-4141, 883-4142
Anderberg, Debra, *Tech Serv & Cat,* Franklin Square Public Library, Franklin Square NY. 516-488-3444
Anderegg, Jeanne, *Acq,* Boston University Libraries (Mugar Memorial Library), Boston MA. 617-353-3710
Anderes, Wilma, *Librn,* Chapman Public Library, Chapman KS. 913-922-6548
Anderjaska, Marilyn, *Dir,* Hayes Center Public Library, Hayes Center NE. 308-286-3411
Anderl, Robert, *Tech Serv,* University of Nevada, Las Vegas, James R Dickinson Library, Las Vegas NV. 702-739-3286
Anderl, Susan, *Spec Coll,* University of Nevada, Las Vegas, James R Dickinson Library, Las Vegas NV. 702-739-3286
Anderle, Donald F, *Chief,* New York Public Library (Art & Architecture), New York NY. 212-790-6205
Anderman, Nancy E, *Ref,* Montgomery County Community College, Learning Resources Center, Blue Bell PA. 215-643-6000, Ext 340
Anders, Lorraine, *Librn,* Henry Wyles Cushman Library, Bernardston MA. 413-648-9595
Anders, Ora, *Ref,* City Colleges of Chicago, Kennedy-King College Library, Chicago IL. 312-962-3262
Andersen, Herbert, *Librn,* Judith Basin County Free Library (Raynesford Library Station), Raynesford MT. 406-738-4345
Andersen, Jeff, *Dir,* Lyme Historical Society Library, Old Lyme CT. 203-434-5542
Andersen, Joan, *Circ,* West Hartford Public Library, Noah Webster Memorial Library, West Hartford CT. 203-236-6286
Andersen, Linda, *Librn,* Linn County Library District Two, La Cygne KS. 913-757-2151
Andersen, Lois, *Librn,* Hennepin County Library (Medina), Hamel MN. 612-475-1201
Anderson, A Gerald, *Scandanavia,* University of Washington Libraries, Seattle WA. 206-543-1760
Anderson, A J, *Assoc Prof,* Simmons College, Graduate School of Library & Information Science, MA. 617-738-2225
Anderson, A Troy, *Dir,* College of Eastern Utah Library, Price UT. 801-637-9943
Anderson, Agnes, *Asst Librn,* Alberta RCMP Century Library, Beaverlodge AB. 403-354-2569
Anderson, Agnes, *Trade Spec,* United States Department of Commerce, Regional Office Library, Los Angeles CA. 213-824-7591

Anderson, Althea, *Ch,* Clearwater Public Library, Clearwater FL. 813-462-6800
Anderson, Amelia, *Librn,* Libbie A Cass Memorial Library, Springfield NH. 603-763-4381
Anderson, Angannetta, *Media,* Rowan Technical College, Learning Resource Center, Salisbury NC. 704-637-0760, Ext 69
Anderson, Ann M, *Asst Dir,* Winchester Public Library, Winchester MA. 617-729-3770
Anderson, Anna Mary, *In Charge,* Mariska Aldrich Memorial Foundation, Inc, Library of Music, Pearl City HI. 808-456-2201
Anderson, Annabelle L, *Librn,* Jacksonville College Library, Jacksonville TX. 214-586-2518, Ext 27
Anderson, Audrey, *Data Processing Ctr,* Saint Paul Public Library, Saint Paul MN. 612-292-6311
Anderson, Audry, *Librn,* Washoe County Library (Incline Branch), Incline Village NV. 702-785-4039
Anderson, B L, *Chief, Libr Doc Ctr,* National Library of Canada, Ottawa ON. 613-995-9481
Anderson, Barbara, *Librn,* Red Rock Public Library, Red Rock ON. 807-886-2558
Anderson, Barbara, *Librn,* San Bernardino County Library, San Bernardino CA. 714-383-1734
Anderson, Barbara, *Ch,* Warren County Library, Monmouth IL. 309-734-6412
Anderson, Barbara, *Librn,* West Virginia Forestry Camp, Davis Center Library, Davis WV. 304-259-5241
Anderson, Barbro, *Librn,* Erik A Lindgren & Associates, Inc Library, Chicago IL. 312-784-0710
Anderson, Bernece, *Librn,* Wake County Department of the Public Library (Chavis Heights Neighborhood), Raleigh NC. 919-755-6105
Anderson, Bertha, *Librn,* Elk Horn Public Library, Elk Horn IA. 712-764-5514, 764-5687
Anderson, Bette, *Librn,* Junction City Public Library, Junction City OR. 503-998-8942
Anderson, Betty, *Librn,* Atwater Public Library, Atwater MN. 612-974-8760
Anderson, Betty J, *Librn,* Fort Vancouver Regional Library (Battle Ground Community), Battle Ground WA. 206-687-2322
Anderson, Calvin, *Circ,* Los Angeles City College Library, Los Angeles CA. 213-663-9141, Ext 412
Anderson, Carol, *Ad,* Sudbury Public Library, La Bibliotheque Publique de Sudbury, Sudbury ON. 705-673-1155
Anderson, Carol L, *Acq,* University of Oklahoma MUniversity Libraries, Norman OK. 405-325-2611
Anderson, Carolyn, *Librn,* Mennonite Hospital & School of Nursing, Health Sciences Library, Bloomington IL. 309-827-4321, Ext 367
Anderson, Charlotte, *Librn,* Ocmulgee Regional Library (Wilcox County), Abbeville GA. 912-374-4711
Anderson, Charlotte, *Regional Librn,* Tulsa City-County Library, Tulsa OK. 918-581-5221
Anderson, Charlotte, *Regional Librn,* Tulsa City-County Library (North Regional Library & Social Services Center), Tulsa OK. 918-582-8654
Anderson, Charlotte, *Asst Dir,* University of New Hampshire, Ezekiel W Dimond Library, Durham NH. 603-862-1540
Anderson, Christine, *Acq,* Johnson County Community College Library, Overland Park KS. 913-888-8500, Ext 532
Anderson, D, *ILL & Circ,* Rockville Public Library, George Maxwell Memorial Library, Vernon CT. 203-875-5892
Anderson, Darlene, *Librn, On-Line Servs & Bibliog Instr,* Granite Falls Public Library, Granite Falls MN. 612-564-3738
Anderson, David, *Clinical Med Librns,* Wake Forest University (Bowman Gray School of Medicine Library), Winston-Salem NC. 919-727-4691
Anderson, David C, *Tech Serv,* University of California at Davis (Health Sciences Library), Davis CA. 916-752-1214
Anderson, Dawn, *ILL,* North Richland Hills Public Library, Fort Worth TX. 817-281-8416
Anderson, Debra, *Admin Asst,* Sussex County Department of Libraries, Georgetown DE. 302-856-7701, Ext 292
Anderson, Dorothy, *Dir,* Heginbotham Library, Holyoke CO. 303-854-2597

Anderson, Dorrine A, *Dir,* Gladstone Area School & Public Library, Gladstone MI. 906-428-4224
Anderson, Douglas M, *Assoc Dean,* Delta College, Learning Resources Center, University Center MI. 517-686-9000
Anderson, Earnesteen, *Librn,* Shreve Memorial Library (David Raines Branch), Shreveport LA. 318-222-0824
Anderson, Ed, *Dir,* Illinois Valley Community College, Jacobs Memorial Library, Oglesby IL. 815-224-2720
Anderson, Elaine, *Cat,* Sioux Falls Public Library, Sioux Falls SD. 605-339-7081
Anderson, Eleene, *Librn,* Central Florida Regional Library (Cedar Key), Ocala FL. 904-629-8551
Anderson, Elizabeth A, *Libr Tech,* Hazeltine Public Library, Busti NY. 716-487-1281
Anderson, Elizabeth M, *Librn,* Hempfield Public Library, Irwin PA. 412-864-1469
Anderson, Ellen, *Librn,* Joice Public Library, Joice IA. 515-588-3330
Anderson, Ellen, *Ref,* Northern Virginia Community College Libraries (Loudoun Campus), Sterling VA. 703-323-4657
Anderson, Elma, *Per,* Marywood College Library, Scranton PA. 717-343-6521, Ext 289
Anderson, Emma, *Librn,* Santa Maria Public Library (Orcutt Station), Orcutt CA. 805-937-6483
Anderson, Esther, *Librn,* Tillamook County Public Library (Manzanita Branch), Manzanita OR. 503-368-5137
Anderson, Frances, *Librn,* Delia Community Library, Delia AB. 403-364-3777
Anderson, Frances, *Branch Librn,* South Shore Regional Library, Bridgewater NS. 902-543-2548
Anderson, Frank J, *Dir, Rare Bks & Spec Coll,* Wofford College, Sandor Teszler Library, Spartanburg SC. 803-585-4821, Ext 396
Anderson, Fred, *Media,* Hartnell College, Learning Resources Center, Salinas CA. 408-758-8211, Ext 400
Anderson, G, *Fine Arts,* Calgary Public Library, Calgary AB. 403-268-2880
Anderson, G David, *On-Line Servs,* Columbus College, Simon Schwob Memorial Library, Columbus GA. 404-568-2042
Anderson, Genene, *AV,* Rockford Public Library, Rockford IL. 815-965-6731
Anderson, Glenda E, *Librn,* City of Savannah (Municipal Research Library), Savannah GA. 912-233-9321, Ext 240
Anderson, Grace, *Librn,* Sparks Hospital-University of Arkansas for Medical Sciences, Regional Health Sciences Library, Fort Smith AR. 501-661-5000
Anderson, Greg, *Librn,* University of North Dakota-Williston Center, North Dakota Masonic Memorial Library, Williston ND. 701-572-6736
Anderson, H Vince, *Chmn,* Western Council of State Libraries, Inc, NV. 702-885-5130
Anderson, Hazel, *Circ,* Association for Research & Enlightenment, Edgar Cayce Memorial Library, Virginia Beach VA. 804-428-3588, Ext 178
Anderson, Hazel, *Librn,* Wakefield Public Library, Wakefield MI. 906-229-5236
Anderson, Hermione, *Librn,* Saint Joseph Hospital Library, Tacoma WA. 206-627-4101, Ext 252
Anderson, Herschel V, *State Librn,* South Dakota State Library, Pierre SD. 605-773-3131
Anderson, Ida M, *Librn,* Cotuit Library, Cotuit MA. 617-428-8141
Anderson, Ingeborg, *Librn,* George Holmes Bixby Memorial Library, Francestown NH. 603-547-2730
Anderson, Irene, *Librn,* Polson City Library, Polson MT. 406-883-4003
Anderson, Irene, *Librn, Blind & Physically Handicapped,* Roanoke City Public Library System, Roanoke VA. 703-981-2475, Ext 2476
Anderson, Isabel, *Librn,* Virden Public Library, Virden IL. 217-965-3015
Anderson, Isabella, *Librn,* Argonne National Laboratory (Chemistry), Argonne IL. 312-972-3566
Anderson, J D, *Librn,* Canada Department of National Defense (Technical Library), Ottawa ON. 613-993-2105
Anderson, James C, *Curator,* University of Louisville Library (Photographic Archives), Louisville KY. 502-588-6752

Anderson, James D, *Assoc Prof,* Rutgers-The State University of New Jersey, Graduate School of Library & Information Studies, NJ. 201-932-7500

Anderson, James F, *Dir,* First Regional Library, DeSoto County Library, Hernando MS. 601-368-4439

Anderson, Jan, *Tech Serv,* Malone College, Everett L Cattell Library, Canton OH. 216-454-3011, Ext 311

Anderson, Jane, *Librn,* Chesterfield Public Library, Chesterfield NH. 603-363-4621

Anderson, Janet, *In Charge,* Lycoming College Library, Williamsport PA. 717-326-8153

Anderson, Janet, *Librn,* Tuolumne County Law Library, Sonora CA. 209-532-7752

Anderson, Janice, *Ser,* George Washington University Library, Washington DC. 202-676-6455

Anderson, Janice, *Interim Coordr,* Malone College, Everett L Cattell Library, Canton OH. 216-454-3011, Ext 311

Anderson, Jean R, *Librn,* University of South Florida, Fort Myers Campus Library, Fort Myers FL. 813-332-3365

Anderson, Jennifer, *Testing,* Moraine Valley Community College, Learning Resources Center, Palos Hills IL. 312-974-4300, Ext 222

Anderson, Jerry, *Media,* College of the Mainland, Learning Resources Center, Texas City TX. 713-938-1211, Ext 447

Anderson, Joan, *Br Coordr,* Middle Georgia Regional Library, Macon GA. 912-745-5813

Anderson, Joanne, *Librn,* San Diego Public Library (Valencia Park), San Diego CA. 714-264-8370

Anderson, JoDon, *Bkmobile Coordr,* Southwest Wisconsin Library System, Fennimore WI. 608-822-3393

Anderson, Jody, *Librn,* Saint Patrick Hospital Library, Missoula MT. 406-543-7271, Ext 382

Anderson, Joe, *Senior Librn,* Mercantile Library Association, New York NY. 212-755-6710

Anderson, John F, *Dir,* Tucson Public Library, Tucson AZ. 602-791-4391

Anderson, Jorita, *Librn,* Nicholas County Public Library, Carlisle KY. 606-289-5595

Anderson, Joseph J, *State Librn,* Nevada State Library, Carson City NV. 702-885-5130

Anderson, Josephine, *Ch,* Alamogordo Public Library, Alamogordo NM. 505-437-9058

Anderson, Joyce, *Dir,* Fullerton Public Library, Fullerton NE. 308-536-2382

Anderson, Judith P, *Asst Librn,* Fairfax County Public Central Library, Fairfax VA. 703-691-2741

Anderson, Julia Lee, *Librn,* Perry County District Library (Crooksville Branch), Crooksville OH. 614-982-4821

Anderson, Julie, *Librn,* Celesco Industries Inc, Technical Library, Costa Mesa CA. 714-546-8030

Anderson, Karen, *Cat,* California State University, Northridge, Delmar T Oviatt & South Libraries, Northridge CA. 213-885-2271

Anderson, Kathie P, *Corp Librn,* Reynolds Metals Co (Executive Office Library), Richmond VA. 804-281-2804

Anderson, Kathie P, *Librn,* Reynolds Metals Co (Law Library), Richmond VA. 804-281-2804

Anderson, Kathryn, *Tech Serv,* Warwick Public Library and Regional Center, Warwick RI. 401-739-5440

Anderson, Kathy, *Librn,* Atlantic County Library (Hammonton Branch), Hammonton NJ. 609-561-2264

Anderson, Kathy, *Tech Serv & Cat,* Lower Merion Library Association, Bryn Mawr PA. 215-527-3889

Anderson, Kathy, *Cat,* Ludington Public Library, Bryn Mawr PA. 215-527-1550, 525-1776

Anderson, Kathy, *Ch,* Tuolumne County Free Public Library, Sonora CA. 209-532-7842

Anderson, Kay, *Librn,* Kitsap Regional Library (Silverdale Station), Tracyton WA. 206-377-3571

Anderson, Keith, *Acq & Cat,* San Diego Mesa College Library, San Diego CA. 714-279-2300, Ext 385

Anderson, Kenneth N, *Librn,* Coffee Information Institute Library, New York NY. 212-687-6640

Anderson, L V, *Dir,* Western Texas College, Learning Resource Center, Snyder TX. 915-573-8511, Ext 265

Anderson, LaVern, *Circ,* Norfolk State University, Lyman Beecher Brooks Library, Norfolk VA. 804-623-8873

Anderson, Lawrence A, *Librn,* Cunningham & Walsh, Inc Library, New York NY. 212-683-4900, Ext 350

Anderson, LeMoyne W, *Dir,* Colorado State University, William E Morgan Library, Fort Collins CO. 303-491-5911

Anderson, Linda, *Ch & Commun Servs,* Brighton City Library, Brighton MI. 313-229-6571

Anderson, Linda, *Pub Servs & On-Line Servs,* Brock University Library, Saint Catharines ON. 416-684-7201

Anderson, Linda, *Acq,* Duluth Public Library, Duluth MN. 218-723-3800

Anderson, Linda, *Librn,* Kenosha Public Library (Washington), Kenosha WI. 414-656-6053

Anderson, Lynn, *Tech Serv & On-Line Servs,* Evangel College Library, Springfield MO. 417-865-2811, Ext 267

Anderson, Lynnette, *Actg Dir,* Casper College, Goodstein Foundation Library, Casper WY. 307-268-2269

Anderson, Marcia, *Tech Serv, On-Line Servs & Bibliog Instr,* Huron Valley Library System, Ann Arbor MI. 313-971-6056

Anderson, Marcia, *Extramural Coordr,* Ohio State University Libraries (Health Sciences Library), Columbus OH. 614-422-9810

Anderson, Marcia, *Tech Serv,* Washtenaw County Library, Ann Arbor MI. 313-971-6056

Anderson, Margaret, *Asst Librn,* Babbitt Public Library, Babbitt MN. 218-827-3345

Anderson, Margaret, *Instr,* Middle Tennessee State University, Department of Library Service, TN. 615-898-2740 & 898-5555

Anderson, Margaret, *Librn,* Muskegon County Library (Ravenna Branch), Ravenna MI. 616-853-6205

Anderson, Margaret J, *Dir,* Augsburg College, George Sverdrup Library, Minneapolis MN. 612-330-1014

Anderson, Margaret R, *Mgr,* R & D Associates Library, Technical Information Center, Marina Del Rey CA. 213-822-1715

Anderson, Maria P, *Tech Serv,* Newport News Public Library System, Newport News VA. 804-247-8506

Anderson, Marjorie, *Media,* Pacific Union College, W E Nelson Memorial Library, Angwin CA. 707-965-6241

Anderson, Marjorie E, *Dir,* East Hampton Public Library, East Hampton CT. 203-267-2635

Anderson, Marna, *Ad,* Monterey Public Library, Monterey CA. 408-646-3930

Anderson, Marquita W, *Circ,* Loyola University Library (School of Law), New Orleans LA. 504-865-3426, 865-3427, 865-3136

Anderson, Marvis, *Tech Serv,* Grambling State University, A C Lewis Memorial Library, Grambling LA. 318-247-6941, Ext 220

Anderson, Mary, *Cat,* Clark University, Robert Hutchings Goddard Library, Worcester MA. 617-793-7573

Anderson, Mary, *Asst Librn,* Hancock School Public Library, Hancock MI. 906-482-2750

Anderson, Mary B, *Assoc Dir,* Iowa Lutheran Hospital (School of Nursing Library), Des Moines IA. 515-283-5647

Anderson, Mary E, *Librn,* Emmetsburg Public Library, Emmetsburg IA. 712-852-4009

Anderson, Mary Ellen, *Librn,* Lambton County Library (Thedford Branch), Thedford ON. 519-296-4459

Anderson, Mary Jane, *Per,* Minot State College, Memorial Library, Minot ND. 701-857-3200

Anderson, Mary L, *Librn,* Springdale Free Public Library, Springdale PA. 412-274-9717

Anderson, Maxine, *Dir,* Louise Childress Library, Highland Park Public Library, Dallas TX. 214-521-4161

Anderson, Morry R, *Librn,* Starved Rock Library System (Subregional Library for the Blind & Physically Handicapped), Ottawa IL. 815-434-7537, Ext 9

Anderson, Mrs John, *In Charge,* Oxford County Library (Princeton Library), Princeton ON. 519-458-4430

Anderson, Mrs P, *ILL,* Algonquin Regional Library System, Parry Sound ON. 705-746-9161

Anderson, Mrs Robert V, *Curator of Photog,* Valentine Museum Library, Richmond VA. 804-649-0711

Anderson, Myrna, *Librn,* Kirkendall Public Library, Ankeny IA. 515-964-3165

Anderson, Nancy, *Librn,* Carbon County Public Library (Hanna Branch), Hanna WY. 307-325-9357

Anderson, Nancy, *Librn,* University of Illinois Library at Urbana-Champaign (Mathematics), Urbana IL. 217-333-0258

Anderson, Nancy S, *Tech Serv,* School of the Ozarks, Lyons Memorial Library, Point Lookout MO. 417-334-6411, Ext 460

Anderson, Nancy S, *Ch,* Utica Public Library, Utica NY. 315-735-2279

Anderson, Natalie, *Asst Dir & Ch,* Topsfield Town Library, Topsfield MA. 617-887-2914

Anderson, Noel, *Lit,* University of Texas at Arlington Library, Arlington TX. 817-273-3391

Anderson, Norma, *Ref & Bibliog Instr,* Gordon-Conwell Theological Seminary, Burton L Goddard Library, South Hamilton MA. 617-468-7111, Ext 255, 256

Anderson, Oriole P, *Librn,* Manulife, Business Library, Toronto ON. 416-928-4104

Anderson, Pamela, *Librn,* Nuclide Corp, State College PA. 814-238-0541

Anderson, Patricia, *Dir,* Englewood Library, Englewood NJ. 201-568-2215

Anderson, Paul, *Circ,* University of Cincinnati Libraries, Central Library, Cincinnati OH. 513-475-2218

Anderson, Paul, *Spec Coll,* Washington University Libraries (School of Medicine Library), Saint Louis MO. 314-454-3711

Anderson, Peter G, *Curric Mat,* California State University, Chico Library, Chico CA. 916-895-6212

Anderson, Phyllis, *Librn,* McKean County Law Library, Smethport PA. 814-887-5571

Anderson, Phyllis D, *Ch,* Ilion Free Public Library, Ilion NY. 315-894-2151

Anderson, Robert E, *Head Librn,* School of the Ozarks, Dept of Library Science, MO. 417-334-6411, Ext 460

Anderson, Robert E, *Dir,* School of the Ozarks, Lyons Memorial Library, Point Lookout MO. 417-334-6411, Ext 460

Anderson, Ronald E, *AV,* South Carolina State Library, Columbia SC. 803-758-3181

Anderson, Rose K, *Dir,* Sandhills Community College Library, Carthage NC. 919-692-6185, Ext 221, 223

Anderson, Rosemary, *Ch,* Lawton Public Library, Lawton OK. 405-248-6287

Anderson, S, *Mgr,* Ministry of Education Library, Toronto ON. 416-965-1451

Anderson, Sandra C, *Librn,* Union Carbide Corp, Linde Division Technical Library, Tonawanda NY. 716-877-1600, Ext 395 & 396

Anderson, Sharon, *Ref,* Dickinson School of Law, Sheely-Lee Law Library, Carlisle PA. 717-243-4611, Ext 9

Anderson, Sharon, *Doc,* University of California, San Diego, University Libraries, La Jolla CA. 714-452-3336

Anderson, Sheridan Cash, *Librn,* South Dakota Supreme Court Law Library, Pierre SD. 605-773-4898

Anderson, Sherrie, *Librn,* Gerber Products Co, Corporate Library, Fremont MI. 616-928-2631

Anderson, Sherry, *Tech Serv,* East Carolina University (Health Affairs Library), Greenville NC. 919-757-6961, Ext 261

Anderson, Sherry, *Asst Librn,* Polk City Community Library, Polk City IA. 515-984-6119

Anderson, Shirley, *Librn,* Jones Library, Inc (North Amherst), Amherst MA. 413-549-1565

Anderson, Sister Joseph Marie, *Dir,* University of Dallas, William A Blakley Library, Irving TX. 214-438-1123, Ext 328

Anderson, Sonia, *Ch,* Torrance Public Library, Torrance CA. 213-328-2251

Anderson, Steven W, *Dir,* Meeker Public Library, Meeker CO. 303-878-5911

Anderson, Stuart H, *Librn,* New Jersey Department of Labor & Industry Library, Trenton NJ. 609-292-2035

Anderson, Susan, *Dir,* Coshocton Public Library, Coshocton OH. 614-622-0956

Anderson, Susan, *L R C Supvrs,* Pasco-Hernando Community College Library, Dade City FL. 904-567-6701

Anderson, Susan, *Learning Res Supvr,* Pasco-Hernando Community College, North Campus Learning Resources Center, Brooksville FL. 904-796-6726

Anderson, T J B, *Chief Librn,* Ontario Ministry of Correctional Services Staff Library, Scarborough ON. 416-750-3481

Anderson, Teresa, *Actg Dir,* University of Wisconsin-Madison (Agricultural Library), Madison WI. 608-262-3521

Anderson, Verlyn D, *Dir,* Concordia College, Carl B Ylvisaker Library, Moorhead MN. 218-299-4641

Anderson, Vicki, *Instr,* Grossmont College, Library Technology Program, CA. 714-465-1700, Ext 319

Anderson, Victor, *Librn,* University of Puerto Rico Library (Graduate School of Public Administration), Rio Piedras PR. 809-764-0000, Ext 3290

Anderson, Virginia, *Librn,* California Institute of Technology (Aeronautics-Energy Research Library), Pasadena CA. 213-795-6811, Ext 1521

Anderson, William, *Gen Mgr,* EG&G, Inc Library, Los Alamos NM. 505-667-5061

Anderson, Wilma, *Ref,* Fort Valley State College, Henry Alexander Hunt Memorial Library, Fort Valley GA. 912-825-6342

Anderson, Wilma E, *Librn,* Cantril Public Library, Cantril IA. 319-397-2214

Anderson, Woody W, *Librn,* Luling Public Library, Luling TX. 512-875-2813

Anderson, III, Yeatman, *Curator,* Inland Rivers Library, Cincinnati OH. 513-369-6000

Anderson, III, Yeatman, *Rare Bks,* Public Library of Cincinnati & Hamilton County, Cincinnati Public Library, Cincinnati OH. 513-369-6000

Anderson, Jr, A G, *Dir,* Clark University, Robert Hutchings Goddard Library, Worcester MA. 617-793-7573

Anderson, Jr, A G, *Dir,* Worcester Polytechnic Institute, George C Gordon Library, Worcester MA. 617-753-1411, Ext 410

Anderson-Imbert, Margarita, *Bk Selection Specialists,* Harvard University Library (Harvard College Library (Headquarters in Harry Elkins Widener Memorial Library)), Cambridge MA. 617-495-2401

Anderson-Laid, Cheryl, *ILL,* Saint Paul Public Library, Saint Paul MN. 612-292-6311

Andersson, Meila, *Librn,* Shell Canada Resources Ltd, Technical Library, Calgary AB. 403-232-3512

Andow, Norrie, *Librn,* Alnor Instrument Co Library, Niles IL. 312-647-7866

Andrade, Alice, *Acq,* Alameda Free Library, Alameda CA. 415-522-5413, 522-3578

Andrade, Kathleen M, *Ad, YA & Acq,* Lodi Public Library, Lodi CA. 209-334-3973

Andre, John, *Libr Asst,* National Rural Electric Cooperative Association, Norris Memorial Library, Washington DC. 202-857-9788

Andre, Leslie, *Ser,* Eastern Illinois University, Booth Library, Charleston IL. 217-581-2210

Andre, Sister Lorayne, *Librn,* Saint Bede Priory Library, Eau Claire WI. 715-834-3176

Andreae, Jeannette, *Bkmobile Coordr,* Ames Public Library, Ames IA. 515-232-4404

Andreen, Elizabeth M, *Chief Librn,* United States Marine Corps (Pacific Logistic Supply Base Library), Barstow CA. 714-577-6211

Andresen, Tish, *Exten Serv,* Boise Public Library & Information Center, Boise ID. 208-384-4466

Andress, Loretta, *Cat,* Alaska Health Sciences Library, Anchorage AK. 907-263-1870

Andrew, Bruce, *Reader Serv,* State University College at Buffalo, Edward H Butler Library, Buffalo NY. 716-878-6302

Andrew, Gloria, *Adminr,* Control Data Corp, Corporate Library Information Center, Bloomington MN. 612-853-4229, 4375 & 5147

Andrew, Helen, *Curator,* Walt Whitman House State Historic Site, Research Library & Museum, Huntington Station NY. 516-427-5240

Andrews, Alice, *Lectr,* Atlanta University, School of Library & Information Studies, GA. 404-681-0251, Ext 312

Andrews, Alice, *ILL,* Marion Public Library, Marion OH. 614-387-0992

Andrews, Anne E, *Ext Asst Dir,* Central North Carolina Regional Library, Burlington NC. 919-227-2096

Andrews, Barbara P, *Dir,* Nantucket Atheneum, Nantucket MA. 617-228-1110

Andrews, Charles R, *Dean,* Hofstra University Library, Hempstead NY. 516-560-3475

Andrews, Clair, *ILL & Ref,* Kutztown State College, Rohrbach Library, Kutztown PA. 215-683-4480

Andrews, Constance H, *Per & Micro,* Providence Public Library, Providence RI. 401-521-7722

Andrews, Dean Timothy, *Dir & Bibliog Instr,* Hellenic College & Holy Cross Greek Orthodox School of Theology, Cotsidas-Tonna Library, Brookline MA. 617-731-3500, Ext 43, 44, 45

Andrews, Elizabeth, *Asst Librn,* New England College of Optometry Library, Boston MA. 617-261-3430, Ext 42, 43

Andrews, Elliott E, *State Librn,* Rhode Island State Library, Providence RI. 401-277-2473

Andrews, Gail P, *Circ,* Mississippi University for Women, John Clayton Fant Memorial Library, Columbus MS. 601-328-4808

Andrews, Gene, *Media,* Kellogg Community College, Emory W Morris Learning Resource Center, Battle Creek MI. 616-965-3931, Ext 333

Andrews, Helen, *Dir,* Cambridge Springs Public Library, Cambridge Springs PA. 814-398-2123

Andrews, J E, *Librn,* Andrew Jergens Co, Research Library, Cincinnati OH. 513-421-1400

Andrews, James C, *Dir,* Rensselaer Polytechnic Institute, Folsom Library, Troy NY. 518-270-6673

Andrews, Janet A C, *Circ,* Westminster College, McGill Library, New Wilmington PA. 412-946-8761, Ext 342

Andrews, Jean M, *Dir,* Waterford Township Public Library, Pontiac MI. 313-674-4831

Andrews, Judith B, *Librn,* Thomas Beaver Free Library, Danville PA. 717-275-4180

Andrews, Karen, *Librn,* University of California Los Angeles Library (Engineering & Mathematical Sciences), Los Angeles CA. 213-825-4951

Andrews, Kathy, *Cat,* Roxanne Whipple Memorial-Navajo County Library, Winslow City-Navajo County Library, Winslow AZ. 602-289-4982

Andrews, Loretta, *Cat,* Saint Mary's Seminary & University, School of Theology Library, Baltimore MD. 301-323-3200, Ext 70

Andrews, Lucy A, *Librn,* Wellfleet Public Library, Wellfleet MA. 617-349-6009

Andrews, Mae, *Sci-Tech,* Emporia State University, William Allen White Library, Emporia KS. 316-343-1200, Ext 205

Andrews, Mae, *On-Line Servs,* Emporia State University, William Allen White Library, Emporia KS. 316-343-1200, Ext 205

Andrews, Marcella, *Librn,* Madera County Law Library, Madera CA. 209-674-4641, Ext 210

Andrews, Mary, *Librn,* Alpine Club of Canada Library, Banff AB. 403-762-2291

Andrews, Mary, *Librn,* Peter & Catharine Whyte Foundation, Archives of the Canadian Rockies Library, Banff AB. 403-762-2291

Andrews, Mrs I, *Librn,* Milton Public Library, Milton IA. 515-656-4454

Andrews, Mrs Otome, *Librn,* United States Navy (Rodman Library), Vallejo CA. 707-646-3338

Andrews, Nancy, *Librn,* San Diego Museum of Art, Reference Library, San Diego CA. 714-232-7931

Andrews, Pamela, *Pub Servs,* Oklahoma State University, Oklahoma City Branch, Technical Institute Library, Oklahoma City OK. 405-947-4421, Ext 251

Andrews, Phyllis, *Bibliog Instr,* University of Rochester, Rush Rhees Library, Rochester NY. 716-275-4461

Andrews, Reid, *In Charge,* Pan American Society, Shattuck Library, Boston MA. 617-266-2248, 2249

Andrews, Robert, *Govt Docs,* Duluth Public Library, Duluth MN. 218-723-3800

Andrews, Roberta, *Librn,* United States Department of Health & Human Services, National Institute for Occupational Safety & Health Library, Cincinnati OH. 513-684-8321

Andrews, Sally, *Ref,* University of Vermont & State Agricultural College (Dana Medical), Burlington VT. 802-656-2200

Andrews, Susanne, *Ref,* Plymouth Public Library, Russell Memorial Library, Plymouth MA. 617-746-1927

Andrews, Theodora, *Librn,* Purdue University Libraries & Audio-Visual Center (Pharmacy), West Lafayette IN. 317-494-8517

Andrews, Virginia, *On-Line Servs,* Texas Tech University Library, Lubbock TX. 806-742-2261

Andrews, William M, *Dir,* University of Minnesota, Waseca, Learning Resource Center, Waseca MN. 507-835-1000

Androczi, Ferenc F, *Assoc Prof,* West Virginia Wesleyan College, Dept of Library Science, WV. 304-473-8059

Androczi, Ference F, *Ref,* West Virginia Wesleyan College, Annie Merner Pfeiffer Library, Buckhannon WV. 304-473-8059

Andrus, Elena, *Librn,* Kent County Library System (Alpine Branch), Comstock Park MI. 616-784-0206

Andrus, Mary, *ILL,* Princeton Public Library, Princeton NJ. 609-924-9529

Andrus, Roger D, *Librn,* Oregon Supreme Court, Law Library, Salem OR. 503-378-6030

Andry, Margaret, *ILL,* New Orleans Public Library, Simon Heinsheim & Fisk Libraries, New Orleans LA. 504-586-4905

Andrysiak, Vera, *Head, Bk mobile & Extension Servs,* Winnipeg Public Library (West End), Winnipeg MB. 204-775-7941

Anduha, Isabel T, *Librn,* United States District Court Library, Honolulu HI. 808-546-3163

Anesi, Elizabeth, *Librn,* Portland District Library, Portland MI. 517-647-6981

Ang, Wende, *Ref,* Salisbury State College, Blackwell Library, Salisbury MD. 301-546-3261, Ext 351

Ang, Wende, *Ser & Doc,* University of Maryland-Eastern Shore, Frederick Douglass Library, Princess Anne MD. 301-651-2200, Ext 229

Angel, Carrie L, *Librn,* Dayton Mental Health Center, Dayton OH. 513-258-0440

Angel, Michael, *Ref & On-Line Servs,* University of Manitoba Libraries, Winnipeg MB. 204-474-9881

Angeletti, Louise, *Tech Serv,* Scott Sebastian Regional Library, Greenwood AR. 501-996-2856

Angeline, Sister, *Librn,* Sainte Therese Hospital Medical Library, Waukegan IL. 312-688-5969

Angelini, Angella, *Cat,* East Stroudsburg State College, Kemp Library, East Stroudsburg PA. 717-424-3467

Angelini, Anna, *French, Portuguese, Spanish & German Languages,* Stockton-San Joaquin County Public Library, Stockton Public Libr, Stockton CA. 209-944-8415

Angell, John, *Acting Head,* Free Library of Philadelphia (Literature), Philadelphia PA. 215-686-5322

Angell, June, *Tech Serv,* Saugus Public Library, Saugus MA. 617-233-0530

Angell, Mary, *Managing Ed,* State Medical Society of Wisconsin Library, Madison WI. 608-257-6781

Angelo, Alice Marrie, *Dir & Bibliog Instr,* Saint Joseph College, Pope Pius XII Library, West Hartford CT. 203-232-4571, Ext 208

Angelo, Constance C, *Librn,* Evergreen Park Public Library, Evergreen Park IL. 312-422-8522

Angelotti, Marie E, *Dir,* Florida Atlantic University, College of Humanities, Library Science, FL. 305-395-5100, Ext 2431, 2448

Angenent, Tina, *Librn,* Rideau Lakes Union Library (Seeley's Bay Branch), Seeley's Bay ON. 613-359-5315

Angiolillo, Birgitta, *ILL,* Dickinson College, Boyd Lee Spahr Library, Carlisle PA. 717-245-1396

Anglaola, Juliana, *Ref,* Inter-American University of Puerto Rico, Metropolitan Campus Library, Hato Rey PR. 809-754-7215, Ext 246, 245, 256

Angle, Bruce, *Librn,* Controls for Environmental Pollution, Inc Library, Santa Fe NM. 505-982-9841

Angle, Nina K, *Librn,* Columbia Gas Transmission Corp, Law Library, Charleston WV. 304-346-0951, Ext 554

Angle, Sally, *Cat,* Pennsylvania State University, Capitol Campus Heindel Library, Middletown PA. 717-787-7771

Anglemeyer, Glenwyn, *Dir,* Wakarusa Public Library, Wakarusa IN. 219-862-2465

ANGLERO

Anglero, Sarah J, *Dir,* Harcum Junior College Library, Bryn Mawr PA. 215-525-4100, Ext 221

Anglim, Alice, *Librn,* San Diego Public Library (Beckwourth), San Diego CA. 714-264-1288

Anglim, Sister Eileen, *Ref,* Rockhurst College, Greenlease Library, Kansas City MO. 816-363-4010, Ext 253

Anglin, Barbara, *Tech Serv,* Lee-Itawamba Library System, Lee County Library, Tupelo MS. 601-844-2377

Anglin, Gary J, *Asst Prof,* University of Arkansas, Instructional Resources Education, AR. 501-575-5444

Anglin, Richard V, *Ad,* Ramapo Catskill Library System, Middletown NY. 914-343-1131, 352-4825, 565-3030

Angst, Elaine, *Librn,* Blair-Preston Public Library, Blair WI. 608-989-2502

Angstadt, Susan, *Asst Librn,* South Park Township Community Library, Library PA. 412-833-5585

Anguilano, Michel, *Music,* Miami-Dade Public Library System, Miami FL. 305-579-5001

Anguilano, Michel, *Media,* Miami-Dade Public Library System, Miami FL. 305-579-5001

Angus, Bill, *Media,* Mott Community College, C S Mott Library, Flint MI. 313-762-0400

Angus, Elizabeth, *Librn,* Crown Life Insurance Co, Home Office Library, Toronto ON. 416-928-4650

Angus, Henrietta, *Acq, Doc & Ser,* Robert Morris College Library, Coraopolis PA. 412-264-9300

Angus, Jacqueline A, *Libr Supervisor,* General Mills Inc (James Ford Bell Technical Information Services), Minneapolis MN. 612-540-3464

Anhalt, Lenore, *Art & Music,* Shelter Rock Public Library, Albertson NY. 516-248-7363

Anich, Myralyn, *Librn,* Mukwonago Public Library, Mukwonago WI. 414-363-4640

Ankenman, Beverly, *Dir,* Wilsonville Public Library, Wilsonville NE. 308-349-3465

Ankerson, Elizabeth, *Asst Dir,* Cathedral College of the Immaculate Conception, Cathedral College Library, Douglaston NY. 212-631-4600, Ext 213

Ankudowich, Mary, *Librn,* Smith College Library (Werner Josten Library), Northampton MA. 413-584-2700, Ext 457

Ann, Sister Mary, *Asst Librn,* Lourdes College, Mother Adelaide Hall & Duns Scotus Library, Sylvania OH. 882-2016 Ext 230

Anna, Sister Mary, *Tech Serv,* Notre Dame College, Clara Fritzsche Library, Cleveland OH. 216-381-1680, Ext 59

Annable, Dorothy, *ILL & Ref,* Santa Barbara City College Library, Santa Barbara CA. 805-965-0581, Ext 242

Annand, Stewart, *Librn,* McCutchen, Black, Verleger & Shea Law Library, Los Angeles CA. 213-381-3411

Anne, Sister M, *Dir,* Manor Junior College, Basileiad Library, Jenkintown PA. 215-885-2360, Ext 9

Annenberg, Lester, *Librn,* Time, Inc (Sports Library), New York NY. 212-841-3397

Annese, Lucius, *Librn,* Saint Francis Seraphic Seminary Library, Andover MA. 617-851-3391

Annett, Anne, *Supvr,* Middlesex County Library (Melbourne Branch), Melbourne ON. 519-438-8368

Annis, Betty S, *Bkmobile Coordr,* Eastern Shore Public Library, Accomac VA. 804-787-3400

Annis, L Arvilla, *Librn,* Didymus Thomas Library, Remsen NY. 315-831-8761

Annon, Ruth, *Chief Librn,* National Enquirer, Research Department Library, Lantana FL. 305-586-1111

Anolik, Ruth B, *Reader Serv,* Holy Family College Library, Philadelphia PA. 215-637-7700, Ext 51

Ansari, Mary, *Librn,* University of Nevada-Reno (Engineering), Reno NV. 702-784-6945

Ansari, Mary, *Librn,* University of Nevada-Reno (Mines), Reno NV. 702-784-6596

Ansel, Phyllis, *Doc,* New England School of Law Library, Boston MA. 617-267-9655, Ext 50

Ansell, Sherman, *In Charge,* Wisconsin Board of Vocational-Technical & Adult Education, Research Coordination Unit Library, Madison WI. 608-266-3705

Anske, Helen, *Librn,* Lacon Public Library, Lacon IL. 309-246-3855

Anske, Kay, *Dir,* Oblate College of the Southwest Library, San Antonio TX. 512-341-1366, Ext 35

Ansley, Celia, *Per,* Transylvania County Library, Inc, Brevard NC. 704-883-9880

Ansley, Celia, *Circ,* Transylvania County Library, Inc, Brevard NC. 704-883-9880

Anson, Brooke, *Pub Servs,* University of Wisconsin-Stout, Pierce Library, Menomonie WI. 715-232-1184

Anson, Marion, *Senior Citizens & Outreach Servs,* Millville Public Library, Millville NJ. 609-825-7087

Anspaugh, Judith, *Pub Servs,* Mississippi College (Law Library), Clinton MS. 601-924-5131, Ext 280

Anspaugh, Sheryl, *Dir,* Houston Community College, Library & Learning Resources Center, Houston TX. 713-524-3925, 524-2921

Anstine, Francesca, *On-Line Servs,* University of Illinois, Library of the Health Sciences, Urbana IL. 217-333-4893

Antes, E Jean, *Librn & On-Line Servs,* Robert Packer Hospital Library, Sayre PA. 717-888-6666, Ext 220

Anthofer, Bernadette, *Librn,* Granger Public Library, Granger IA. 515-999-2261

Anthony, Audree, *Libr Supvr,* Lorillard Research Center Library, Greensboro NC. 919-373-6895

Anthony, Bolton, *Ad,* Cumberland County Public Library, Anderson Street Library, Frances Brooks Stein Memorial Library, Fayetteville NC. 919-483-1580

Anthony, Carol, *Instr,* Auburn University, Dept of Educational Media, AL. 205-826-4529

Anthony, Donald C, *Dir,* Syracuse University Libraries, Ernest S Bird Library, Syracuse NY. 315-423-2575

Anthony, Dorothy, *Librn,* East Cleveland Public Library (Caledonia Branch), Cleveland Heights OH. 216-451-8017

Anthony, Emily H, *Dir,* Northeast Georgia Regional Library System, Clarkesville GA. 404-754-4413

Anthony, Eva, *Asst Librn,* Prospect Public Library, Prospect CT. 203-758-6625, 758-6626

Anthony, G Michael, *Media,* Davidson County Community College, Grady E Love Learning Resources Center, Lexington NC. 704-249-8186, Ext 270

Anthony, Helen, *Cat,* Middletown Free Library, Middletown RI. 846-1573 & 846-1584

Anthony, Karen, *Librn,* Amos Memorial Public Library (Fort Laramie Branch), Fort Laramie OH. 513-295-3155

Anthony, Kate, *Math,* Wilkes Community College, Learning Resources Library, Wilkesboro NC. 919-667-7136, Ext 26

Anthony, Kay, *ILL, Acq & Ref,* Coalinga District Library, Coalinga CA. 209-935-1676

Anthony, Kenneth H, *Dir,* Maine Maritime Academy, Nutting Memorial Library, Castine ME. 207-326-4311, Ext 328

Anthony, Marjorie, *Librn,* Raymond A Sapp Memorial Library, Wyanet IL. 815-699-2342

Anthony, Mary, *Librn,* Tulare County Law Library, Visalia CA. 209-733-6395, Ext 293

Anthony, Mary M, *Librn,* MacKenzie, Smith, Lewis, Mitchell & Hughes, Law Library, Syracuse NY. 315-474-7571

Anthony, Paul L, *Dir,* Cardinal Newman College Library, Saint Louis MO. 314-261-2600, Ext 27

Anthony, Peter, *Librn,* University of Manitoba Libraries (Architecture & Fine Arts), Winnipeg MB. 204-474-9216

Anthony, Peter, *In Charge,* University of Manitoba Libraries (Music Reading Room), Winnipeg MB. 204-474-9567

Anthony, Sister Rose Mary, *Ch,* Oak Creek Public Library, Oak Creek WI. 414-764-4400

Antioco, Jurate, *Librn,* Pennie & Edmonds Library, New York NY. 212-986-8686, Ext 295

Antipa, Susan, *Librn,* Nevada County Library (Truckee Branch), Truckee CA. 916-587-3062

Antipin, Rose, *Librn,* United Engineers & Constructors, Inc Library, Philadelphia PA. 215-422-3374

Antles, Margaret, *Actg Librn,* Jay County Public Library, Portland IN. 317-726-7890

Antoinette, Sister Mary, *Dir,* Trocaire College Library, Buffalo NY. 716-826-1200, Ext 239

Anton, Roberta T, *Librn,* Greentree Public Library, Pittsburgh PA. 412-921-9292

Antonietti, Reno, *Media,* Rochester Institute of Technology, Wallace Memorial Library, Rochester NY. 716-475-2566

Antony, Arthur, *On-Line Servs,* University of California, Santa Barbara Library, Santa Barbara CA. 805-961-2741

Antosiak, Dolores A, *Dir,* Hamtramck Public Library, Albert J Zak Memorial Library, Hamtramck MI. 313-365-7050

Antrim, Carol, *Librn,* Denver Public Library (Ross-University Hills), Denver CO. 303-573-5152, Ext 271

Anttila, Faith, *Per,* Fitchburg State College Library, Fitchburg MA. 617-345-2151, Ext 137

Antunes, Mary, *Librn,* Havre Public Library, Havre MT. 406-265-2123

Anzalone, Alfred M, *Librn & On-Line Servs,* United States Army (Dept of Defense, Plastics Technical Evaluation Center Library), Dover NJ. 201-328-2778

Anzul, Clement J, *Librn & On-Line Servs,* Fordham University Library at Lincoln Center, New York NY. 212-841-5130, 841-5133

Anzul, Margaret, *Adjunct Instr,* Kean College of New Jersey, Library-Media Program, NJ. 201-527-2626, 527-2071

Aoki, Janet, *Libr Tech,* Hawaii State Library System (Pahoa Community-School), Pahoa HI. 808-965-8574

Aoki, Toshiyuki, *Asst Librn,* Harvard University Library (Harvard-Yenching Library), Cambridge MA. 617-495-3327

Apel, H W, *Librn,* United States Army (Engineer Division, Ohio River Technical Library), Cincinnati OH. 513-684-3001

Api, Rose D, *Off Mgr,* Soap & Detergent Association Library, New York NY. 212-725-1262

Apley, Shirley, *Cat,* Minnehaha County Library, Hartford SD. 605-528-3532

Apling, Debby, *ILL,* Robbins Library, Arlington MA. 617-643-0026

Apmadoc, Virginia, *Ch,* Downey City Library, Downey CA. 213-923-3256

Aponte, Jose, *Librn,* Tucson Public Library (El Pueblo), Tucson AZ. 602-791-4733

Apostolos, Margaret, *Per,* Kutztown State College, Rohrbach Library, Kutztown PA. 215-683-4480

Appel, Anne M, *Dir,* Denville Free Public Library, Denville NJ. 201-627-6555

Appel, Gayle, *Librn,* Le Sueur-Waseca Regional Library (Waterville Public), Waterville MN. 507-362-8462

Appel, Marylou, *Ch,* Ontario Cooperative Library System, Newark NY. 315-331-2176

Appel, Marylou, *Ch,* Wayne County Library System, Newark NY. 315-331-2176

Appelbaum, Sara, *Bkmobile Coordr,* Tampa-Hillsborough County Public Library System, Tampa FL. 813-223-8947

Appelbaum, Sara, *Talking Bk Librn,* Tampa-Hillsborough County Public Library System (Subregional Library for the Blind & Physically Handicapped), Tampa FL. 813-223-8851

Appenzellar, Terry, *Chief Readers' Serv,* United States Department of Justice Library, Washington DC. 202-633-3775

Apple, Barbara, *Librn,* News-Sun Library, Waukegan IL. 312-689-7000, Ext 6969

Apple, Ethel, *Ref,* Elgin Community College, Renner Learning Resources Center, Elgin IL. 312-697-1000, Ext 258

Apple, Hope, *Ref,* Skokie Public Library, Skokie IL. 312-673-7774

Applebaum, Edmond L, *Assoc Librn Mgt,* Library of Congress, Washington DC. 202-287-5000

Appleby, Bertha, *Cat,* Mount Prospect Public Library, Mount Prospect IL. 312-253-5675

Applegate, Rachel, *Spec Coll,* Grant County Library, Ulysses KS. 316-356-1433

Appleton, Janet W, *Librn,* Gellman Research Associates Library, Jenkintown PA. 215-884-7500

Appleton, Joan C, *Bibliog Instr,* Lock Haven State College, George B Stevenson Library, Lock Haven PA. 717-893-2309

Aprill, Karen, *Br Coordr,* Jefferson-Madison Regional Library, McIntire Public Library, Charlottesville VA. 804-296-6157

Apschnikat, Kenneth, *Chief Park Interpreter,* National Park Service, Richmond National Battlefield Park Headquarters Library, Richmond VA. 804-226-1981

Aquan-Yuen, Margaret, *Geog & Planning,* University of Waterloo Library, Waterloo ON. 519-885-1211

Aquiar, Joan, *Librn,* New Bedford Free Public Library (Casa da Saudade), New Bedford MA. 617-999-3900
Aquire, Barbara, *Librn,* Southern West Virginia Community College, Logan Campus Library, Logan WV. 304-235-2800
Aragon, Lauren J, *Librn,* United States Air Force (Homestead Air Force Base Library), Homestead AFB FL. 305-257-8433
Aranda-Coddou, Patricia, *Asst Librn,* University of Nebraska-Lincoln (College of Law Library), Lincoln NE. 402-472-3547
Arant, Gayle, *ILL,* Colusa County Free Library, Colusa CA. 916-458-7671
Arbaugh, Linda, *Librn,* Burlington County Library (Bordentown Branch), Bordentown NJ. 609-298-9622
Arbogast, Laoma, *Librn,* Osawatomie Carnegie Library, Osawatomie KS. 913-755-2136
Arbogast, Mrs C J, *Librn,* Polymer Corp Library, Reading PA. 215-929-5858, Ext 248
Arbuckle, Marybeth, *Dir,* Deschutes County Library, Bend OR. 503-382-5191
Arbus, I, *ILL & On-Line Servs,* Medgar Evers College Library, Brooklyn NY. 212-735-1851
Arcacha, Ana, *Librn,* Austin Public Library (Southwood), Austin TX. 512-472-5433
Arcand, Fernande, *Bkmobile Coordr,* Ottawa Public Library, Ottawa ON. 613-236-0301
Arcand, Fernande, *Librn,* Ottawa Public Library (South/Mobile Library Services), Ottawa ON. 613-236-0301, Ext 270, 271, 277
Arcari, Ralph D, *Dir,* University of Connecticut Health Center, Lyman Maynard Stowe Library, Farmington CT. 203-674-2739
Arcega, Vicente L, *Librn,* Title Insurance & Trust Co, Law Library, Los Angeles CA. 213-852-6000
Arceneaux, Lucille, *Dir,* Lafayette Parish Public Library, Lafayette LA. 318-233-0587
Arch, Roberta, *Librn,* Qualla Boundary Public Library (Snowbird Community), Robbinsville NC. 704-479-3917
Archambault, Pauline, *Librn,* Bibliotheque Publique, Saint Hyacinthe PQ. 514-773-1830
Archer, Cheryl, *Librn,* Argonne National Laboratory (Environmental Science), Argonne IL. 312-972-3981
Archer, Cheryl, *Ref,* Cora J Belden Library, Rocky Hill CT. 203-529-2379
Archer, Colleen, *Librn,* Toledo-Lucas County Public Library (Washington), Toledo OH. 419-255-7055
Archer, Edgar A, *Dir,* Lincoln Memorial University Library, Harrogate TN. 615-869-3611, Ext 57
Archer, Florence, *ILL,* Danville Public Library, Danville VA. 804-799-5195
Archer, Jane, *Librn,* Memorial Public Library, Medfield MA. 617-359-4544
Archer, Jim, *Graphics,* Clark College Library, Vancouver WA. 206-699-0251
Archer, Lunelle, *Asst Dir, Ref & Commun Servs,* Ridgewood Public Library, Ridgewood NJ. 201-652-5200
Archer, Phyllis, *Librn,* Hancock Free Public Library, Hancock VT. 802-767-3378
Archer, Robert, *Dir TV Servs,* Southeastern Massachusetts University, Library Communications Center, North Dartmouth MA. 617-999-8662
Archibald, Genni, *Librn,* Nova Scotia Department of Recreation Library, Halifax NS. 902-424-7734
Archibald, Jean K, *Dir, Rare Bks & Spec Coll,* Macalester College, Weyerhaeuser Library, Saint Paul MN. 612-647-6346
Archibald, John D, *Dir,* Mishawaka-Penn Public Library, Mishawaka IN. 219-259-5277
Archie, Monie B, *Dir,* Waterloo Public Memorial Library, Waterloo WI. 414-478-3344
Archuleta, Alice, *Librn,* San Diego Public Library (Benjamin), San Diego CA. 714-583-2428
Arden, Sandra, *Asst Dir, Ad & Ref,* Troy Public Library, Troy MI. 313-689-5665
Arden, Sylvia, *Chief Librn,* San Diego Historical Society, Library & Manuscripts Collection, San Diego CA. 714-297-3258
Ardis, Bruce, *Dir,* South Chicago Community Hospital (Hospital Library), Chicago IL. 312-978-2000, Ext 205
Ardis, Susan, *Librn,* University of Texas Libraries (Engineering), Austin TX. 512-471-1610

Ardner, Larry, *Coordr,* Madisonville Community College Media Center, Madisonville KY. 502-821-2250, Ext 66
Ardoin, Evelyn, *Media,* De Anza College, Learning Center, Cupertino CA. 408-996-4761
Ardrey, Richard L, *Dir,* Indiana University at Kokomo, Learning Resource Center, Kokomo IN. 317-453-2000, Ext 237
Arellano, Rachel, *Cat,* University of Santa Clara (Heafey Law Library), Santa Clara CA. 408-984-4451
Arends, Paul E, *Dir, Bus Servs,* University of Cincinnati Libraries, Central Library, Cincinnati OH. 513-475-2218
Areoeste, Jean, *Ref,* Princeton University Library, Princeton NJ. 609-452-3180
Arey, Carol, *Acq,* Robbins Library, Arlington MA. 617-643-0026
Arfa, Sherry J, *Librn,* Presbyterian Hospital (Milbank Library), New York NY. 212-694-2760
Arfield, John, *Dir of Educ Media,* Harcum Junior College Library, Bryn Mawr PA. 215-525-4100, Ext 221
Argentati, Ronald, *Acq,* United States Navy (General Library Services), Pensacola FL. 904-452-1380
Argudin, Linda, *Tech Serv, Acq & Cat,* Irving Public Library System, Irving TX. 214-253-2639
Arguelles, Gil, *Media,* Merced College, Lesher Library, Merced CA. 209-723-4321, Ext 274
ArguellodeCardona, Elena, *Librn,* Inter-American University of Puerto Rico, Metropolitan Campus Library, Hato Rey PR. 809-754-7215, Ext 246, 245, 256
Arguin, Louise, *Prof,* College de Jonquiere, Techniques de la Documentation, PQ. 418-547-2191, Ext 270
Ariail, Julius F, *Circ,* Georgia Southern College Library, Statesboro GA. 912-681-5115
Ariano, Vicki, *Tech Serv,* Regis College, Dayton Memorial Library, Denver CO. 303-458-4030
Ariaratnam, Lakshmi, *Head, Central Libr,* Riverside City & County Public Library, Riverside CA. 714-787-7211
Arida, Robert, *Librn,* Saint Herman's Theological Seminary Library, Kodiak AK. 907-486-3524
Arie, Barbara, *Librn,* American Heart Association, Inc Library, Dallas TX. 214-750-5408
Ariel, Joan, *Librn,* Alameda County Library (Albany Branch), Albany CA. 415-526-3720
Aristoff, Eugene, *Info Specialist,* Atlantic Richfield Co, ARCO Chemical Co, Research & Engineering Library, Glenolden PA. 215-586-4700, Ext 345, 346
Arkin, Cynthia R, *Librn,* American Telephone & Telegraph Co (Law Library), New York NY. 212-393-3651
Arklie, Harriet A, *Actg Dir, Tech Serv & On-Line Servs,* North Central College Library, Naperville IL. 312-355-0597, 420-3425
Arlen, Philippe, *Librn,* College Ahuntsic Bibliotheque, Montreal PQ. 514-389-5921, Ext 246
Arleth, Hettie, *Librn,* Fort Worth Star-Telegram Reference Library, Fort Worth TX. 817-336-9271
Armand, Elizabeth, *ILL & Ref,* Salem Public Library, Salem MA. 617-744-0860
Armbruster, Mrs K, *Librn,* Brooks Municipal Library, Brooks AB. 403-362-2947
Armendt, Jean K, *Librn,* Harford County Library (Havre de Grace Branch), Havre de Grace MD. 301-939-3380
Armendt, Katherine E, *Librn,* Maryland Department of General Services, Maryland Hall of Records Commission Library, Annapolis MD. 301-269-3916
Armes, Patti, *Asst Dir Tech Servs,* University of Texas Health Science Center at Dallas Library, Dallas TX. 214-688-3368
Armington, Joyce E, *Dir & Ad,* Prospect Heights Public Library District, Prospect Heights IL. 312-259-3500
Armintor, Bob, *Self Learning Lab Media,* Pikes Peak Community College, Learning Materials Center, Colorado Springs CO. 303-576-7711, Ext 536
Armistead, Henry T, *Coll Develop,* Thomas Jefferson University (Scott Memorial Library), Philadelphia PA. 215-928-8848

Armistead, Myra A, *Doc,* Clemson University, Robert Muldrow Cooper Library, Clemson SC. 803-656-3026
Armitage, Andrew, *Dir,* Owen Sound Public Library, Owen Sound ON. 519-376-6623
Armitage, Katherine Y, *Dir,* Haywood County Public Library, Waynesville NC. 704-452-5169
Armitage, Regina, *Librn,* Chillicothe Township Free Public Library, Chillicothe IL. 309-274-2719
Armitage, Thomas, *Dir,* Fort Dodge Public Library, Fort Dodge IA. 515-573-8167
Armon, Margaret, *Patients' Librs,* Veterans Administration, Hospital Library, Perry Point MD. 301-642-2411
Armor, R D, *Assoc Librn,* Southwest Research Institute, Thomas Baker Slick Memorial Library, San Antonio TX. 512-684-5111, Ext 2125
Armour, Charles, *Lectr,* Dalhousie University, School of Library Service, NS. 902-424-3656
Armour, Geoffrey, *Acq, Rare Bks & Spec Coll,* Carlsbad City Library, Carlsbad CA. 714-438-5614
Armour, James, *Pub Serv,* Northern Arizona University Libraries, Flagstaff AZ. 602-523-9011
Armour, Jean, *Commun Servs,* Liverpool Public Library, Liverpool NY. 315-457-0310
Armour, M, *Acq,* Carleton University, Murdoch Maxwell MacOdrum Library, Ottawa ON. 613-231-4357
Armour, Mrs E, *Coordr,* Canadian Association for the Mentally Retarded, John Orr Foster Memorial Library, Downsview ON. 416-661-9611
Armour, Rayne, *Tech Serv,* College of Lake County, Learning Resource Center, Grayslake IL. 312-223-6601, Ext 392
Armoza, Ann S, *Dir,* Deer Park Public Library, Deer Park NY. 516-586-3000
Armstead, Bernice M, *Actg Dir & On-Line Servs,* Meharry Medical College Library, Kresge Learning Resource Center, Nashville TN. 615-327-6319
Armstrong, A, *Librn,* Ministry of Education, Science & Technology Library, Victoria BC. 604-387-6279
Armstrong, Addie, *Cat,* Lewisville Public Library, Lewisville TX. 214-436-1812
Armstrong, Alice, *Librn,* EMR Telemetry Systems, Technical Information Center Library, Sarasota FL. 813-371-0811
Armstrong, Betty, *Librn,* Reuben McMillan Free Library Free Library Association (South Branch), Youngstown OH. 612-747-6424
Armstrong, Carl H, *Dir,* Indiana State Museum Library, Indianapolis IN. 317-232-1637
Armstrong, Carole, *Acq,* Southwest State University Library, Marshall MN. 507-537-7021
Armstrong, Cesar J, *Librn,* Blackwell, Walker, Gray, Powers, Flick & Hoehl Library, Miami FL. 305-358-8880
Armstrong, Daniel, *Dir,* Plymouth Public Library, Plymouth IN. 219-936-2324
Armstrong, Donna, *Librn,* Victoria County Public Library (Downeyville), Lindsay ON. 705-324-3104
Armstrong, Dorothy, *Librn,* Hill County Rural Free Library, Havre MT. 406-265-5481, Ext 49
Armstrong, Dorothy, *Librn,* Hoeganaes Corp Library, Riverton NJ. 609-829-2220, Ext 261
Armstrong, Douglas, *Chief Librn,* Ontario Ministry of Labour (Staff Library), Toronto ON. 416-965-1641
Armstrong, Elizabeth, *Dir,* California Institute of the Arts Library, Valencia CA. 805-255-1050, Ext 227
Armstrong, Evelyn W, *Dir Libr Serv,* Merck Sharp & Dohme (Library Services), West Point PA. 215-699-5311, Ext 6026
Armstrong, Geneva M, *Librn,* Euless Public Library, Euless TX. 817-283-5151
Armstrong, Grace A, *Chief Librn,* Southern Alberta Institute of Technology, Learning Resources Centre, Calgary AB. 284-8647; 284-8648
Armstrong, Helen Jane, *Maps,* University of Florida Libraries, Gainesville FL. 904-392-0341
Armstrong, J, *Dir & Media,* Muskingum College Library, New Concord OH. 614-826-8152
Armstrong, Jane, *Librn,* Environmental Protection Agency, Motor Vehicle Emission Lab Library, Ann Arbor MI. 313-668-4311

ARMSTRONG

Armstrong, Jane, *Librn,* Rutgers University (Center for Alcohol Studies), New Brunswick NJ. 201-932-3510

Armstrong, Janet, *Librn,* Mississauga Public Library (Park Royal), Mississauga ON. 416-822-3476

Armstrong, Jeanne, *Librn,* Chicago Public Library (North Lake View), Chicago IL. 312-525-2870

Armstrong, Joan, *Supvr,* Sir Sandford Fleming College of Applied Arts & Technology Library (Peterborough), Peterborough ON. 705-743-5620, Ext 34

Armstrong, Joan L, *Dir,* James Blackstone Memorial Library, Branford CT. 203-488-1441

Armstrong, John W, *Selection,* United States Air Force (Air Force Geophysics Laboratory, Research Library), Hanscom AFB MA. 617-861-4895

Armstrong, Joy A, *Librn,* Abitibi-Price, Inc, Research Centre Library, Mississauga ON. 416-822-4770, Ext 69

Armstrong, Judith, *Dir,* Drury College, Walker Library, Springfield MO. 417-865-8731, Ext 282

Armstrong, Judy Beth, *Tech Serv, Acq & Cat,* Owen Sound Public Library, Owen Sound ON. 519-376-6623

Armstrong, Lena, *Dir,* Belton City Library, Belton TX. 817-939-1161

Armstrong, Lewis, *Libr Asst,* University of Kansas Libraries (Map), Lawrence KS. 913-864-4420

Armstrong, Linda S, *Ch,* Haysville Community Library, Haysville KS. 316-524-5242

Armstrong, Marty, *Ref,* Governors State University, University Library, Park Forest South IL. 312-534-5000, Ext 2231

Armstrong, Michael, *Librn,* Public Library of Cincinnati & Hamilton County (Glendale), Cincinnati OH. 513-771-6024

Armstrong, Michael, *Librn,* Public Library of Cincinnati & Hamilton County (Bonham), Wyoming OH. 513-369-6014

Armstrong, Nancy, *On-Line Servs,* Illinois Agricultural Association, IAA & Affiliated Companies Library, Bloomington IL. 309-557-2552

Armstrong, P A, *Librn,* Cranbrook Public Library, Cranbrook BC. 604-426-4063

Armstrong, Patricia, *Dir,* Saint Albans Correctional Facility Library, Saint Albans VT. 802-524-6771

Armstrong, Roberta, *Librn,* John McIntire Public Library Public Library (New Concord Branch), New Concord OH. 614-453-0391

Armstrong, Rodney, *Dir,* Boston Athenaeum, Boston MA. 617-227-0270

Armstrong, Sandra, *Librn,* Keewatin Community College Learning Resources Centre, The Pas MB. 204-623-3416, Ext 161

Armstrong, Vicki, *Ad,* Spokane County Library, Spokane WA. 509-924-4122

Arn, Lisa, *Cat,* Burton Public Library, Burton OH. 216-834-4258

Arn, Nancy, *Librn,* Barton Library, El Dorado AR. 501-863-5447

Arndal, R E, *Info Spec,* General Dynamics Corp, Convair Div, Research Library, San Diego CA. 714-277-8900, Ext 1073

Arndt, Alba B, *Librn,* Hailey Public Library, Hailey ID. 208-788-4221

Arndt, Arleen, *Cat,* Adrian College, Shipman Library, Adrian MI. 517-265-5161, Ext 220

Arndt, Eleanor, *Dir,* Meridian District Library, Meridian ID. 208-888-4451

Arndt, John, *ILL, Ref & Coll Develop,* Wilfrid Laurier University Library, Waterloo ON. 519-884-1970

Arner, Samuel Dewalt, *Dir,* Museum of Antiquities & Art Library, Cathedral City CA. 714-328-4532

Arnesen, Sandra L, *AV,* Creighton University (Health Sciences), Omaha NE. 402-449-2908

Arneson, Anne, *Music,* University of Colorado at Boulder (University Libraries), Boulder CO. 303-492-7511

Arneson, Dorothy, *Doc,* Kansas City Public Library, Kansas City MO. 816-221-2685

Arneson, Rosemary, *Librn,* Chestatee Regional Library (Talking Book Center), Gainesville GA. 404-534-2671

Arnett, Annamae, *Librn,* Rotan Public Library, Rotan TX. 915-735-3362

Arnett, Betty S, *Librn,* Choctawhatchee Regional Library (Headland Public), Headland AL. 205-693-2706

Arnett, Jane C, *Dept Head,* Lenoir Community College, Library Media Technical Assistant Program, NC. 919-527-6223, Ext 235

Arnett, Kathleen, *Learning Lab,* Dodge City Community College, Learning Resources Center, Dodge City KS. 316-225-1321, Ext 220

Arnett, Mary Ruth, *Cat,* Cumberland College, Norma Perkins Hagan Memorial Library, Williamsburg KY. 606-549-0558

Arnett, II, Stanley K, *Exten Servs,* Blue Water Library Federation, Port Huron MI. 313-987-7323

Arnett, II, Stanley K, *Librn,* Blue Water Library Federation (Subregional Library for the Blind & Physically Handicapped), Port Huron MI. 313-982-3600

Arnett, II, Stanley K, *Br Coordr,* Saint Clair County Library System, Port Huron MI. 313-987-7323

Arney, Freda, *Librn,* New Hanover County Public Library (Carolina Beach Branch), Carolina Beach NC. 919-458-5016

Arnn, Judith, *Librn,* United States Air Force (Wilford Hall Medical Center Library), Lackland AFB TX. 512-671-1110

Arnold, Arleen, *Librn,* Stamford's Public Library (Turn of the River), Stamford CT. 203-322-7628

Arnold, Arlene, *Br Librn,* Stamford's Public Library, Ferguson Library, Stamford CT. 203-325-4354

Arnold, Brenda, *Circ,* Saint Clair County Library System, Port Huron MI. 313-987-7323

Arnold, Brenda, *Librn,* Salvation Army Church Library, Las Vegas NV. 702-878-1004

Arnold, Carol W, *Librn,* University of Hawaii School of Public Health, Reference Library, Honolulu HI. 808-948-8666

Arnold, Clarence, *AV,* J Sargeant Reynolds Community College (Downtown Campus-Learning Resources Center), Richmond VA. 804-786-6249

Arnold, Cynthia, *ILL & Ref,* Maine State Library, Augusta ME. 207-289-3561

Arnold, Darlene M, *Ref & ILL,* Minnesota State Library Agency, Office of Public Libraries & Interlibrary Cooperation, Saint Paul MN. 612-296-2821

Arnold, Donna, *Circ,* Oceanside Public Library, Oceanside CA. 714-439-7330

Arnold, Doris, *Librn,* Kentucky Department of Commerce, Div of Research & Planning, Research Library, Frankfort KY. 502-564-4886

Arnold, Dorothy, *Ch,* Delphos Public Library, Delphos OH. 419-692-1339

Arnold, Elaine, *Dir,* Rushville Public Library, Rushville IN. 317-932-3496

Arnold, Elaine, *Librn,* University of Detroit Library (Architecture), Detroit MI. 313-927-1065

Arnold, Electa E, *Librn,* Melvin Public Library, Melvin IL. 217-388-2421

Arnold, George, *Head, Tech Servs,* American University (Acquisitions Department), Washington DC. 202-686-2328

Arnold, George D, *Tech Serv & Acq,* American University, Jack I & Dorothy G Bender Library & Learning Resources Center, Washington DC. 202-686-2323

Arnold, Glenda, *Acq,* University of Tennessee Center for the Health Sciences Library, Memphis TN. 901-528-5638

Arnold, Inedia, *Librn,* Blue Mound Community Library, Fort Worth TX. 817-232-0661

Arnold, Jacqueline, *YA,* Mamie Doud Eisenhower Public Library, Broomfield Public Library, Broomfield CO. 303-469-1821

Arnold, Jean, *Librn,* Sinking Spring Public Library, Sinking Spring PA. 215-678-4311

Arnold, Joan, *Cat,* School of Visual Arts Library, New York NY. 679-7350 Ext 67, 68

Arnold, Josephine, *Circ,* Bloomington Public Library, Bloomington IL. 309-828-6091

Arnold, Kathryn, *Dir,* Chattanooga-Hamilton County Bicentennial Library, Chattanooga TN. 615-757-5320

Arnold, Kathryn, *Rare Bks,* Ely Public Library, Ely IA. 319-848-9197

Arnold, Kathy, *Librn,* Reading Public Library (Southeast), Reading PA. 215-373-7006

Arnold, Kim, *Planetarium Dir,* Saint Charles Parish Library, Luling LA. 504-785-8471

Arnold, Linda, *Cat,* State University of New York, College at Oneonta, James M Milne Library, Oneonta NY. 607-431-2723

Arnold, Lois, *Librn,* Pershing County Library, Lovelock NV. 702-273-2216

Arnold, Lois, *Librn,* Washington County Library (Valley), Afton MN. 612-436-5882

Arnold, Margaret J, *Dir,* Wellesley Free Library, Subregional Headquarters for Eastern Massachusetts Regional Library System, Wellesley MA. 617-235-1610

Arnold, Marilyn, *Dir,* David City Public Library, David City NE. 402-367-3100

Arnold, Marilyn, *Ch,* River Grove Public Library, River Grove IL. 312-453-4484

Arnold, Marjorie, *Librn,* Fresno Bee Editorial Library, Fresno CA. 209-441-6111

Arnold, Mary J, *Librn,* Ohio State University Libraries (Engineering Library), Columbus OH. 614-422-2852

Arnold, Mary J, *Librn,* Ohio State University Libraries (Materials Engineering Library), Columbus OH. 614-422-9614

Arnold, Mrs M, *Librn,* Middle Georgia Regional Library (Jeffersonville Public), Jeffersonville GA. 912-945-3910

Arnold, Mrs P, *Supvr,* Edmonton Public Library (Capilano), Edmonton AB. 403-469-6488

Arnold, Peggy A, *Librn,* Laurel Public Library, Laurel MT. 406-628-4961

Arnold, Richard, *Br Admin Asst,* Maine State Library, Augusta ME. 207-289-3561

Arnold, Ruth, *Ref,* Jersey City State College, Forrest A Irwin Library, Jersey City NJ. 201-547-3026

Arnold, Sharon, *Librn,* United States Navy (Naval Station Library), Cecil Field FL. 904-778-5675

Arnold, Wilnora Barton, *Assoc Prof,* San Antonio College, Library Technology Program, TX. 512-734-7311, Ext 2482

Arnoldi, Ardell, *Librn,* Lamberton Public Library, Lamberton MN. 507-752-7859

Arnot, J, *Librn,* Lakehead University Library (Education), Thunder Bay ON. 807-345-2121, Ext 719

Arnott, Barbara A, *Librn,* United States Navy (Crew's Library), Oakland CA. 415-639-2220

Arnott, F Davidson, *Dir,* Centennial College of Applied Arts & Technology, Resource Centre, Scarborough ON. 416-439-7180

Arnsan, Daniel, *Ch & YA,* Carlsbad City Library, Carlsbad CA. 714-438-5614

Arnsmeier, Carol, *Tech Serv,* Dundee Township Library, Dundee IL. 312-428-3661

Arola, David J, *Asst Librn,* United States Army (Fort McPherson Library System), Fort McPherson GA. 404-752-2528, 752-3045

Aromaa, Karl, *ILL,* Goodnow Library, Sudbury MA. 617-443-9112

Aromaa, Karl, *Dir,* Hudson Public Library, Hudson MA. 617-562-7521, 7522

Aronoff, Carol A, *Dir,* Santa Monica Public Library, Santa Monica CA. 213-451-5751

Aronoff, Darwin, *Acq,* Los Angeles City College Library, Los Angeles CA. 213-663-9141, Ext 412

Aronovsky, Manne, *Librn,* Minnie Cobey Memorial Library, Columbus OH. 614-253-8523

Aronson, Marcia, *Librn,* Public Archives of Nova Scotia, Halifax NS. 902-423-9915

Aronson, Shirley, *Govt Doc,* Maryland State Law Library, Annapolis MD. 301-269-3395

Aronwits, Jacqueline, *Ref,* Warren Public Library, Warren MI. 313-264-8720

Arpoika, Sharon, *Librn,* Stanislaus County Free Library (Riverbank Branch), Riverbank CA. 209-869-1001

Arps, Joyce, *Tech Serv,* Texas College, D R Glass Library, Tyler TX. 214-593-8311, Ext 37

Arrasmith, Virginia, *Dir,* Guthrie Center Public Library, Guthrie Center IA. 515-747-8110

Arredondo, Liza, *Ch,* Nicholson Memorial Library, Garland TX. 214-494-7187

Arrigoni, Sylvia, *Phys Sci,* Chicago Public Library (Business, Science & Technology Div), Chicago IL. 312-269-2814, 269-2865

Arrington, Debrah, *Librn,* Fayette County Public Library (Fayetteville), Fayetteville WV. 304-574-0070

Arrington, Frances, *Chief Librn,* Lee College Library, Cleveland TN. 615-472-2111, Ext 329

Arris, Jean, *Ad,* Rice Public Library, Kittery ME. 207-439-1553

Arrondo, Ondina, *Librn,* Miami-Dade Public Library System (Hispanic), Miami FL. 305-579-5492

Arros, Jeno, *Librn,* Montreal Botanical Garden Library, Montreal PQ. 514-872-4543
Arrott, Diane, *Ch & YA,* Tom Green County Library System, San Angelo TX. 915-655-7321
Arrowood, Bruce, *Dir,* Parkersburg Community College, Learning Resources Center, Parkersburg WV. 304-424-8260
Arroyo, Wilfredo Alequin, *Media,* Antillian College Library, Mayaguez PR. 809-832-9595, Ext 209
Arroyo-Carrion, Ramon, *Dir,* Caribbean Regional Library, Rio Piedras PR. 809-764-0000
Arruti, Beth M, *Librn,* Bureau of Land Management Library, Winnemucca NV. 702-623-3676
Arsenault, Cori, *Librn,* Clifton-City-Greenlee County Library, Clifton AZ. 602-865-2461
Arsenault, Henri J, *Supvr,* Polysar Ltd, Polysar Information Center, Sarnia ON. 519-337-8251, Ext 711
Arsenault, Kathleen, *Cat,* Minneapolis College of Art & Design Library, Minneapolis MN. 612-870-3291
Arsenault, Lucia, *Librn,* Prince Edward Island Provincial Library (Abram Village Branch), Abram Village PE. 902-892-3504, Ext 54
Arsenault, Virginia, *Librn,* Prince Edward Island Provincial Library (Wellington Branch), Wellington PE. 902-892-3504, Ext 54
Arseneault, Mrs A, *Librn,* Smooth Rock Falls Public Library, Smooth Rock Falls ON. 705-338-2318
Arseneault, Therese, *ILL & Ref,* Albert-Westmorland-Kent Regional Library, Moncton NB. 506-389-2631
Arsh, Judy, *Librn,* Upper Darby Township & Sellers Free Public Library (South Branch), Primos PA. 215-789-4400
Arshem, James, *In Charge,* Denver Public Library (Conservation), Denver CO. 303-573-5152, Ext 271
Arshem, James, *In Charge,* Denver Public Library (Science & Engineering), Denver CO. 303-573-5152, Ext 271
Artandi, Susan A, *Prof,* Rutgers-The State University of New Jersey, Graduate School of Library & Information Studies, NJ. 201-932-7500
Arter, Judy, *Ch,* Okanagan Regional Library District, Kelowna BC. 604-860-4033
Arterbery, Vivian J, *Dir,* Rand Corp Library, Santa Monica CA. 213-393-0411, Ext 369
Arthur, Irene, *Media,* Chatham Public Library, Chatham ON. 519-354-2940
Arthur, Jacqulyn, *Librn,* Haleyville Public Library, Haleyville AL. 205-486-7450
Arthur, Mary Lynn, *Dir & Cat,* Riviera Beach Public Library, Riviera Beach FL. 305-845-4194, 845-4195, 845-4196
Artz, Theodora, *Acq,* University of Dayton Libraries (Law School Library), Dayton OH. 513-229-2314
Artzberger, John A, *Dir,* Oglebay Institute Mansion Museum Library, Wheeling WV. 304-242-7272
Arundell, Art, *Br Libr Asst,* Ventura County Library Services Agency (Fillmore Branch), Fillmore CA. 805-524-3355
Arves, Miriam, *Dir,* West Fargo Public Library, West Fargo ND. 701-282-0415
Arvin, Carolyn R, *Asst Librn,* Frances L Folks Memorial Library, Loogootee Public Library, Loogootee IN. 812-295-3713
Arvin, Charles, *Ref,* Genesee District Library, Flint MI. 313-732-0110
Arvin, Charles, *ILL & Media,* Mideastern Michigan Library Cooperative, Flint MI. 313-232-7119
Arwas, Clement, *Librn,* University of Montreal Libraries (Geology), Montreal PQ. 514-343-6831
Asare, Shirley, *Librn,* Aurora Public Library (North), Aurora CO. 303-364-9358
Asawa, Edward E, *Librn,* Los Angeles County Department of Mental Health Library, Mental Health Services Library, Los Angeles CA. 213-937-2380, Ext 270
Asay, Voleta, *Librn,* Saguache County Public Library (Center Branch), Center CO. 303-655-2551754-3156
Asbeck, Harriet, *Interlibr Loan,* Lake-Sumter Community College, Learning Resources Center, Leesburg FL. 904-787-3747, Ext 33

Asbell, Mary M, *Extension Serv,* University of Texas Medical Branch, Moody Medical Library, Galveston TX. 713-765-1971
Asbell, Mildred, *Librn,* Connecticut Valley Hospital, Hallock Medical Library, Middletown CT. 203-344-2304
Asbury, Katherine, *Ser,* Portland State University, Branford Price Millar Library, Portland OR. 503-229-4424
Ascher, Lionel, *Chief Librn,* Orange County Public Library (Westminster Branch), Westminster CA. 714-893-5057
Ascherman, Ruth, *Chief Librn,* Ohio County Public Library, Rising Sun IN. 812-438-2257
Ash, Joan, *Assoc Librn,* University of Oregon Health Sciences Center (Health Sciences Library), Portland OR. 503-225-8026
Ash, Joyce, *Librn,* Pinellas Park Public Library, Pinellas Park FL. 813-544-4868
Ash, Linda, *In Charge,* Saint Paul Public Library (Hamline), Saint Paul MN. 612-292-6632
Ash, Mary, *Chief Librn,* Canadian Forces College, Keith Hodson Memorial Library, Toronto ON. 416-224-4015
Ash-Jones, Mirian, *Media,* Gardner-Webb College, Dover Memorial Library, Boiling Springs NC. 704-434-2361
Ashbrook, Lorain, *Ad,* Amos Memorial Public Library, Sidney Public Library, Sidney OH. 513-492-8354
Ashby, Marilyn, *Librn,* Spanish Fork City Library, Spanish Fork UT. 801-798-6403
Ashby, Mattie Lou, *Librn,* Shreve Memorial Library (Blanchard Branch), Blanchard LA. 318-221-2614
Ashcraft, David L, *Librn & AV,* Woodward State Hospital-School (Resident-School Library), Woodward IA. 515-438-2600, Ext 248
Ashcroft, Edward, *Psychol,* Morton Grove Public Library, Morton Grove IL. 312-965-4220
Ashcroft, Edward, *Tech Serv & Cat,* Morton Grove Public Library, Morton Grove IL. 312-965-4220
Ashe, Kathleen, *Tech Serv,* University of Minnesota, Waseca, Learning Resource Center, Waseca MN. 507-835-1000
Ashe, Lyn, *Dir,* Rogers Memorial Library, Southampton NY. 516-283-0774
Ashe, Mary, *Art & Music,* San Francisco Public Library, San Francisco CA. 415-558-4235
Asheim, Lester, *Prof,* University of North Carolina at Chapel Hill, School of Library Science, NC. 919-933-8366
Asher, Doris H, *Librn,* Edward W Sparrow Hospital, Medical Library, Lansing MI. 517-487-2788
Asher, Judy, *Ch,* Bronxville Public Library, Bronxville NY. 914-337-7680
Asher, Mrs Gunvanti, *Tech Serv,* Holy Family College Library, Philadelphia PA. 215-637-7700, Ext 51
Ashford, Denise, *Mgr Tech Servs, Sr Librn,* Motorola Inc, Integrated Circuit Div Technical Library, Mesa AZ. 602-962-3417
Ashford, Denise, *Librn & On-Line Servs,* Motorola, Inc, Semiconductor Products Group Library, Phoenix AZ. 602-244-6065
Ashford, John C, *Dir,* South Seattle Community College, Instructional Resources Center, Seattle WA. 206-764-5395
Ashford, Mrs Freddye G, *Dir,* Lincoln University, Inman E Page Library, Jefferson City MO. 314-751-2325, Ext 326
Ashford, Richard, *Instr,* Simmons College, Graduate School of Library & Information Science, MA. 617-738-2225
Ashin, Elizabeth, *Librn,* Louisiana State University Medical Center Library (School of Dentistry), New Orleans LA. 504-568-6100
Ashley, Becky, *Bkmobile Coordr,* Polk County Public Library, Columbus NC. 704-894-8721
Ashley, Betty, *Cat,* Holliston Public Library, Holliston MA. 617-429-6070
Ashley, Carrie G, *Ad,* Aiken-Bamberg-Barnwell-Edgefield Regional Library, Aiken SC. 803-648-8961
Ashley, E M, *Dir,* Middlesex County College Library, Edison NJ. 201-548-6000, Ext 240
Ashley, Grover, *Dir,* University of Southern Mississippi, Cook Memorial Library, Hattiesburg MS. 601-266-7301
Ashley, Janet L, *On-Line Servs,* State University of New York, College at Oneonta, James M Milne Library, Oneonta NY. 607-431-2723

Ashley, Lillian W, *Ch,* Appomattox Regional Library, Maud Langhorne Nelson Library, Hopewell VA. 804-458-6329
Ashley, Martha, *Librn,* Prince George's County Memorial Library System (Fairmount Heights Branch), Fairmount Heights MD. 301-925-9700
Ashley, Patrick, *Monographic Acq,* Northwestern University Library, Evanston IL. 312-492-7658
Ashley, Ruby, *Ref,* Bacone College Library, Muskogee OK. 918-683-4581, Exts 214,227,246
Ashmore, Mary R, *Asst Dir,* Utica Public Library, Utica NY. 315-735-2279
Ashook, Kathleen, *Loan Librn,* United States Naval War College Library, Newport RI. 401-841-2641
Ashton, Elizabeth, *Librn,* Madawaska Public Library, Madawaska ME. 207-728-7749
Ashton, Lucy, *Librn,* Prescott Public-Yavapai County Library System (Black Canyon Public), Black Canyon City AZ. 206-374-9913
Ashton, Rick J, *Asst Dir,* Public Library of Fort Wayne & Allen County, Fort Wayne IN. 219-424-7241
Ashton, Jr, Ray E, *Dir,* North Carolina State Museum of Natural History, H H Brimley Memorial Library, Raleigh NC. 919-773-7451
Ashworth, Margaret W, *Librn,* Crane Packing Co, Technical Library, Morton IL. 309-967-3790
Askelson, Rod, *Acq,* Uncle Remus Regional Library, Madison GA. 404-342-1206, 342-2955
Askelson, Rodney, *Librn,* Washington State Library (Washington State Reformatory Library), Monroe WA. 206-794-8077
Askew, Elizabeth E, *Bus, Sci & Tech,* Richmond Public Library, Richmond VA. 804-780-4256
Asmundson, J Michael, *Loan,* University of California at Davis, General Library, Davis CA. 916-752-2110
Asmussen, Virginia, *ILL,* Sioux City Public Library, Sioux City IA. 712-279-6179
Asp, William G, *Dir,* Minnesota State Library Agency, Office of Public Libraries & Interlibrary Cooperation, Saint Paul MN. 612-296-2821
Aspelmeir, Charlene, *Librn,* Wapello Public Library, Keck Memorial Library, Wapello IA. 319-523-5261
Asper, Cheryl, *Asst Librn,* Quincy College Library, Quincy IL. 217-222-8020, Ext 225
Asper, Cheryl, *Dir,* Quincy College, Library Science Program, IL. 217-222-8020, Ext 225
Aspinall, Ellen A, *Ch,* Gladwyne Free Library, Gladwyne PA. 215-642-3957
Asplund, Colleen, *Ch,* Albany County Public Library, Laramie WY. 307-745-3365
Asquith, April, *ILL & AV,* Needham Free Public Library, Needham MA. 617-444-0087, 444-0090
Asquith, Joan L, *Dir,* King Memorial Library, Machias NY. 716-353-9915
Asquith, Natalie, *Librn,* Ingham County Library (Stockbridge Branch), Stockbridge MI. 517-676-9088
Asselstine, Beulah, *Librn,* Frontenac County Library (Mountain Grove Branch), Mountain Grove ON. 613-335-5360
Astell, Joan, *Librn,* Millers Falls Library, Millers Falls MA. 413-659-3801
Astheimer, Bernice, *Dir,* Dunlap & Associates, Inc Library, Darien CT. 203-655-3971
Aston, Charles, *Spec Coll,* University of Pittsburgh, Hillman Library, Pittsburgh PA. 412-624-4400
Aston, Marcia, *Asst Dir,* Northeastern Pennsylvania Bibliographic Center, PA. 717-824-9931
Astraquillo, Divinia J, *Librn,* Milwaukee County Law & Reference Library, Milwaukee WI. 414-278-4321
Astrinsky, Aviva, *Tech Serv,* Union Theological Seminary Library, New York NY. 212-662-7100, Ext 274
Aswald, Beth, *Asst Librn,* Brown County Regional Library, Aberdeen SD. 605-225-8580
Atanian, Alice T, *ILL,* Central Massachusetts Regional Library System, Worcester MA. 617-752-3751
Atay, D, *Librn,* Borough of York Public Library (Mount Dennis), Toronto ON. 416-762-1101
Atcher, Tagalie, *Dir,* Group Health Cooperative of Puget Sound, Medical Library, Seattle WA. 206-326-6093
Atcheson, Pearl, *Dir,* Washoe Medical Center Library, Reno NV. 702-785-5693

Atchison, Helen K, *Dir,* Cary Library, Houlton ME. 207-532-3967
Atchison, Mary, *Cat,* Bates College, George and Helen Ladd Library, Lewiston ME. 207-784-2949
Athanasiadis, Genevieve, *Librn,* Longview State Hospital, Patients' Library, Cincinnati OH. 513-948-3600
Atherton, Joy, *Acq,* Kitchener Public Library, Kitchener ON. 519-743-0271
Atherton, Karen, *Ch,* New Albany Floyd County Public Library, New Albany IN. 812-944-8464
Atherton, Pauline, *Prof,* Syracuse University, School of Information Studies, NY. 315-423-2911
Atherton, Valerie, *Ref,* Martinsburg-Berkeley County Public Library, Martinsburg Service Center, Martinsburg WV. 304-267-8933
Athey, Barbara, *Librn,* Saint Margaret Memorial Hospital (Paul Titus Memorial Library), Pittsburgh PA. 412-622-7120
Athy, Doris J, *Dir,* Thomas Jefferson Library, Jefferson City MO. 314-634-2464
Atisano'e, Olive, *Librn,* American Samoa-Office of Library Services (Feleti Pacific), Fagatogo Village PI. 633-4556
Atisano'e, Olive, *Rare Bks & Spec Coll,* American Samoa-Office of Library Services, Pago Pago, Samoa PI. 633-5869
Atkins, Abbie, *Chief, Info Syst Section,* Defense Intelligence Agency, Central Reference Div Library, Washington DC. 202-692-5311
Atkins, Ada-Marie, *Humanities,* University of Calgary Library, Calgary AB. 403-284-5954
Atkins, Anita, *Chief Librn,* United Lodge of Theosophists, Theosophy Hall Library, New York NY. 212-535-2230
Atkins, Ann, *Acctg Lab Tech,* State Technical Institute at Memphis, George E Freeman Library, Memphis TN. 901-377-4106
Atkins, Charles K, *Dir,* Santa Cruz Public Library, Santa Cruz CA. 408-429-3533
Atkins, Cynthia Fuller, *Asst Librn,* Hopkinsville Community College Library, Hopkinsville KY. 502-886-3921, Ext 39
Atkins, Donna A, *Librn,* Amax Extractive Research & Development, Inc, Technical Information Center, Golden CO. 303-279-7636, Ext 262
Atkins, Dorothy, *Bkmobile Coordr,* Carl Elliott Regional Library, Jasper AL. 205-221-2567
Atkins, Edith, *Librn,* Richmond Public Library, Richmond NH. 603-239-6076
Atkins, Edith W, *Librn,* Conant Public Library, Winchester NH. 603-239-4331
Atkins, Gene D, *Cat,* Abilene Public Library, Abilene TX. 915-677-2474
Atkins, Jane, *Media,* American Samoa Community College, Learning Resources Center, Pago Pago, Samoa PI. 688-9155, Ext 24
Atkins, Letha, *Librn,* Artesia Public Library, Artesia NM. 505-746-4252
Atkins, M A, *Tech Serv,* Fountaindale Public Library District, Bolingbrook IL. 312-759-2102
Atkins, Manon, *Archivist,* Oklahoma Historical Society (Division of Library Resources), Oklahoma City OK. 405-521-2491
Atkins, Nancy F, *Chief Librn,* Tennessee Valley Authority, Chattanooga Technical Library, Chattanooga TN. 755-2811
Atkins, Susan, *Librn,* Saint Anthony Hospital Library, Milwaukee WI. 414-271-1965
Atkinson, Anne, *Librn,* Buffalo & Erie County Public Library System (North Park), Hertel NY. 716-875-3748
Atkinson, Bonnie, *Acq,* Mid Michigan Community College, Charles A Amble Library, Harrison MI. 517-386-7792, Ext 258
Atkinson, Calberta O, *Librn,* Rust Engineering Co, Whellabrator-Frye Inc, Birmingham AL. 205-254-4000
Atkinson, D, *AV,* Barrie Public Library, Barrie ON. 705-728-1010
Atkinson, Donna, *Supvr,* Middlesex County Library (Lucan Branch), Lucan ON. 519-227-4682
Atkinson, Geraldine, *Dir,* Claymont School District Public Library, Uhrichsville OH. 614-922-3626
Atkinson, Hugh, *Univ Librn,* University of Illinois Library at Urbana-Champaign, Urbana IL. 217-333-0790

Atkinson, Jean, *Chief Librn,* Eisenhower Medical Center, Walter M Leuthold Medical Library, Rancho Mirage CA. 714-346-3911, Ext 1416, 1417
Atkinson, Joan, *Asst Prof,* University of Alabama, Graduate School of Library Service, AL. 205-348-4610
Atkinson, Judith, *Mgr,* Burroughs Corp, Technical Information Resource Center, Pasadena CA. 213-351-6551, Ext 2316
Atkinson, Rosalind, *Librn,* Valatie Free Library, Valatie NY. 518-758-9321
Atlas, Aime, *Sr Librn,* Pilgrim Hospital (Health Sciences Library), West Brentwood NY. 516-231-8000, Ext 583
Atlas, Aime, *Sr Librn,* Pilgrim Hospital (Harry J Worthington Memorial Library), West Brentwood NY. 516-231-8000, Ext 546
Atmore, Sam, *AV,* Colby College, Miller Library, Waterville ME. 207-873-1131, Ext 209
Atri, Bianca G D, *Acq,* United States Army (Natick Research & Development Command, Technical Library), Natick MA. 617-653-1000, Ext 2248
Attebery, Joyce A, *Librn,* National Park Service, Mesa Verde Museum Library, Mesa Verde National Park CO. 303-529-4475, Ext 4
Attinello, Salvatore, *Ref,* City Colleges of Chicago, Kennedy-King College Library, Chicago IL. 312-962-3262
Attridge, Evalyn, *Acq,* Huntington Beach Library, Information & Cultural Resource Center, Huntington Beach CA. 714-842-4481
Attuquayefio, Vernice, *Spec Coll,* Grambling State University, A C Lewis Memorial Library, Grambling LA. 318-247-6941, Ext 220
Attwood, Florence, *Circ,* Memorial University of Newfoundland Library, Saint John's NF. 709-753-1200
Attwood, Sally, *Dir,* Palmer Public Library, Palmer AK. 907-745-4690
Atwell, Wanda, *Librn,* Annapolis Valley Regional Library Headquarters (Wolfville Branch), Wolfville NS. 902-532-2260
Atwood, Donna, *Librn,* Jasper County Library, Newton IA. 515-792-8502
Atwood, Edna, *Dir,* Carnegie Public Library, Trinidad CO. 303-846-6841
Atwood, Janet, *Tech Serv,* Wilkes Community College, Learning Resources Library, Wilkesboro NC. 919-667-7136, Ext 26
Atwood, Margaret S, *Dir,* York College of Pennsylvania Library, York PA. 717-846-7788, Ext 353
Atwood, Olin D, *Librn,* Platte Valley Bible College Library, Scottsbluff NE. 308-632-6933
Atwood, Pamela C, *Librn,* Krause Milling Co Technical Library, Milwaukee WI. 414-272-6200, Ext 55
Atwood, Pearl, *Ch,* Pelham Public Library, Pelham NH. 603-635-7581
Atwood, Ruth C, *Res & Develop,* University of Louisville, Louisville KY. 502-588-6745
Atz, James W, *Curator,* American Museum of Natural History Library (Dean Memorial Library, Dept Of Ichthyology), New York NY. 212-873-1300, Ext 308
Au, Eleanor, *Head of Spec Coll,* University of Hawaii (University of Hawaii Library), Honolulu HI. 808-948-7205
Au, Marcia, *Ref,* Toledo-Lucas County Public Library, Toledo OH. 419-255-7055
Aubrey, Irene, *Chief, Children's Lit Serv,* National Library of Canada, Ottawa ON. 613-995-9481
Aubrey, John, *Actg Supvr Spec Coll,* Newberry Library, Chicago IL. 312-943-9090
Aubuchon, Ruth, *Pub Info,* Wyoming State Library, Cheyenne WY. 307-777-7281
Aubut, Roland, *Prof,* College de Jonquiere, Techniques de la Documentation, PQ. 418-547-2191, Ext 270
Auch, Eldora, *Librn,* Saint Clair County Library System (Memphis Public), Memphis MI. 313-392-2980
Auchstetter, Rosann, *Media,* Art Institute of Chicago (Ryerson & Burnham Libraries), Chicago IL. 312-443-6666
Aud, R A, *Dir,* Nicholson Area Library, Nicholson PA. 717-942-6295
Aud, Thomas F, *Dir,* Jackson-Madison County Library, Jackson TN. 901-423-0225
Audant, Colette, *Librn,* Hotel-Dieu De Levis, Bibliotheque Medicale, Levis PQ. 418-833-3710

Audet, Mrs J E, *Librn,* Kathleen B Potter Memorial Library, Matheson Public Library, Matheson ON. 705-273-2760
Audet, Roger, *Librn,* College De Levis Bibliotheque, Levis PQ. 418-837-7544
Audretsch, Robert W, *Dir,* Three Rivers Regional Library Service System, New Castle CO. 303-984-2887
Auer, Grace, *Librn,* Cook County Hospital, Tice Memorial Library, Chicago IL. 312-633-6725
Auer, Margaret, *Coordr Instructional Servs,* University of Detroit Library, Detroit MI. 313-927-1090
Auerbach, Rita, *Ch,* Connetquot Public Library, Bohemia NY. 516-567-5115
Aufdenkamp, Jo Ann, *Admin, Info Servs,* Lincoln National Life Insurance Co (Law Library), Fort Wayne IN. 219-424-5421, Ext 7492
Auffrey, Virginia, *Circ,* Rock Island Public Library, Rock Island IL. 309-788-7627
Augelli, John, *Dir,* Denison Public Library, Denison TX. 214-465-1797
Auger, Maurice, *Dir,* Universite Du Quebec A Trois-Rivieres Bibliotheque, Trois-Rivieres PQ. 819-376-5706
Auger, Roland, *Spec Coll,* Bibliotheque Nationale Du Quebec, Montreal PQ. 514-873-4553
Augsburger, Pauline, *Librn,* Chatsworth Township Library, Chatsworth IL. 815-635-3004
August, Sidney, *Dir,* Community College of Philadelphia, Division of Educational Resources, Philadelphia PA. 215-972-7250
Augusten, Dorothy, *ILL,* Baldwin Public Library, Birmingham MI. 313-647-1700
Augustine, Janis C, *Supvr,* Salem Public Library, Salem VA. 703-389-0247
Augustino, Diane, *Librn,* Research Institute on Alcoholism Library, Buffalo NY. 716-887-2511
Augustson, D, *Doc,* Barrie Public Library, Barrie ON. 705-728-1010
Augustus, Ethel, *Librn,* Acadia Parish Library (Bunche), Rayne LA. 318-788-1880
Augustus, Franke, *Librn,* Lee-Itawamba Library System (A M Strange Branch), Tupelo MS. 601-842-3354
Auh, John, *Chief Librn,* Wagner College, Horrmann Library, Staten Island NY. 212-390-3001
Auld, Lawrence, *Instr,* University of Illinois, Graduate School of Library Science, IL. 217-333-3280
Auld, Skip, *Hist,* Public Library of Charlotte & Mecklenburg County, Inc, Charlotte NC. 704-374-2725
Aulds, Lou, *Media,* Miami University, Edgar W King Library, Oxford OH. 513-529-2944
Aulik, Sister Humbeline, *Acq,* College of Saint Teresa, Mary A Molloy Library, Winona MN. 507-454-2930, Ext 210
Ault, Betty, *Asst Librn,* Deaconess Hospital, Drusch Professional Library, Saint Louis MO. 645-8510, Ext 2194
Ault, Linnie, *In Charge,* Eureka-Humboldt County Library (Fortuna), Fortuna CA. 707-725-3460
Ault, Sherry, *Ch,* Hubbard Public Library, Hubbard OH. 216-534-3512
Aultice, Mary, *ILL,* Lynchburg Public Library, Lynchburg VA. 804-847-1565
Aurenz, Margaret, *Cat,* Albert A Wells Memorial Library, Tippecanoe County Contractual Library, Lafayette IN. 317-423-2602
Auriene, P A, *Circ,* Fountaindale Public Library District, Bolingbrook IL. 312-759-2102
Ausman, Nancy, *ILL,* Indianhead Federated Library System, Eau Claire WI. 715-839-5082
Ausman, Nancy, *ILL,* L E Phillips Memorial Public Library, Eau Claire WI. 715-839-5002
Aussenberg, Lynda, *Video Coordr,* South Park Township Community Library, Library PA. 412-833-5585
Austen, Lillian M, *Librn,* Bethlehem Steel Corp (Charles H Herty, Jr Memorial Library), Bethlehem PA. 215-694-6441
Austin, A, *Librn,* Calgary Public Library (Bowness), Calgary AB. 403-288-5885
Austin, Betty, *Librn,* Cutler Memorial Library, Farmington ME. 207-778-4312
Austin, Bonney, *Librn,* Saint Mary's Hospital, Medical Library, Duluth MN. 218-727-4551
Austin, Colena, *Librn,* Partridge Public Library, Partridge KS. 316-567-2493

Austin, Dan, *Cent Serv,* Palm Beach County Public Library System, West Palm Beach FL. 305-686-0895

Austin, David, *Librn,* National Asthma Center Medical Library, Denver CO. 303-458-1999, Ext 259

Austin, Dennis D, *Dep Libr,* Wisconsin Supreme Court, Wisconsin State Law Library, Madison WI. 608-266-1424, 266-1600

Austin, Elizabeth, *Ch,* E C Scranton Memorial Library, Madison CT. 203-245-7365

Austin, Elizabeth R, *Per & Doc,* Maine Maritime Academy, Nutting Memorial Library, Castine ME. 207-326-4311, Ext 238

Austin, Gertrude, *Asst Librn,* White County Public Library, Sparta TN. 615-836-3613

Austin, Grace, *Librn,* Currituck County Public Library, Coinjock NC. 919-453-8345

Austin, JoAnn, *Librn,* Lamb County Library, Littlefield TX. 806-385-5223

Austin, Joanne, *Librn,* Osterhout Free Library (North), Wilkes-Barre PA. 717-822-4660

Austin, Joanne D, *Dir,* Morris Public Library, Morris CT. 203-567-0160

Austin, John, *Cat,* De Paul University Libraries (Law Library), Chicago IL. 312-321-7710

Austin, Judie, *Librn,* Forsyth County Public Library (Kernersville Branch), Kernersville NC. 919-993-8141

Austin, Judith, *Media,* Montgomery County-Norristown Public Library, Norristown PA. 215-277-3355

Austin, Kathy, *AV,* University of Southern Mississippi (Teaching-Learning Resources Center), Hattiesburg MS. 601-266-7307

Austin, Loretta E, *Librn,* Colorado River Board of California Library, Los Angeles CA. 213-620-4480

Austin, Mabel D, *Bkmobile Coordr,* Currituck County Public Library, Coinjock NC. 919-453-8345

Austin, Marilyn, *Librn,* York Regional Library (Chipman Public), Chipman NB. 506-339-5842

Austin, Marion, *Librn,* Victoria County Public Library (Kinmount Branch), Kinmount ON. 705-324-3104

Austin, Martha L, *Librn,* University of Washington Libraries (Physics), Seattle WA. 206-543-2988

Austin, Maurene, *Librn,* Andrews County Library, Andrews TX. 915-523-2680

Austin, Nancy, *Commun Servs,* Lima Public Library, Lima OH. 419-228-5113

Austin, Nava, *Librn,* Wright County Library, Hartville MO. 417-741-7595

Austin, Neal F, *Dir,* High Point Public Library, High Point NC. 919-885-8411

Austin, Norma, *ILL,* Stanislaus County Free Library, Modesto CA. 209-526-6821

Austin, Richard H, *Chief, Financial Mgt Off,* Library of Congress, Washington DC. 202-287-5000

Austin, Roxanna, *Dir,* Athens Regional Library, Athens GA. 404-543-0134

Austin, Susanna, *ILL & Ref,* Frederick E Parlin Memorial Library, Everett MA. 617-387-2550

Austin, William, *Circ,* Fordham University Library at Lincoln Center, New York NY. 212-841-5130, 841-5133

Austreih, Sylvia, *Librn,* Temple Beth Torah Library, Upper Nyack NY. 914-358-2248

Ausubel, Hillel, *Music,* New Rochelle Public Library, New Rochelle NY. 914-632-7878

Auten, John F, *In Charge,* Sonoco Products Co, Inc, Technical Information Center, Hartsville SC. 803-383-7510

Auth, Judith, *Ch & YA Coordr,* Riverside City & County Public Library, Riverside CA. 714-787-7211

Autio, Elizabeth, *Asst Librn,* Republic-Michigamme Public Library, Republic MI. 906-376-8401

Autis, John, *Inst Servs,* Starved Rock Library System, Ottawa IL. 815-434-7537

Autry, Brick, *Dir,* Rhoads Memorial Library, Dimmitt TX. 806-647-3532

Avant, Robert, *ILL, Ref & On-Line Servs,* Carl Elliott Regional Library, Jasper AL. 205-221-2567

Avdzej, Tamara, *Acq,* Kean College of New Jersey, Nancy Thompson Library, Union NJ. 201-527-2017

Avenick, Karen, *Ref,* Camden County Free Library, Voorhees NJ. 609-772-1636

Averdick, Michael, *Ad,* Kenton County Public Library, Covington KY. 606-292-2363

Averill, Dorothy, *Cat,* James Blackstone Memorial Library, Branford CT. 203-488-1441

Aversa, Mary E, *Mgr,* Doane Agricultural Service, Inc, Doane Information Center, Saint Louis MO. 314-968-1000, Ext 530, 531

Avery, Alice, *Librn,* Taber Municipal Library, Taber AB. 403-223-4343

Avery, Ann, *ILL,* Sampson-Clinton Public Library, Clinton NC. 919-592-4153

Avery, Ann, *Librn,* Sampson-Clinton Public Library (J C Holliday Memorial), Clinton NC. 919-592-4153

Avery, Bonny, *Ch & YA,* Troy Public Library, Troy MI. 313-689-5665

Avery, Cleorae, *Librn,* Grand Rapids Public Library (Creston), Grand Rapids MI. 616-456-4433

Avery, Connie S, *Librn,* Paw Paw Public Library, Paw Paw IL. 815-627-9396

Avery, Janet, *Media,* Angelina College Library, Lufkin TX. 713-639-1301

Avery, Joan C, *Librn,* Los Angeles Public Library System (Atwater), Los Angeles CA. 213-664-1353

Avery, Mary Ann, *Librn,* Newark Public Library (Branch Brook), Newark NJ. 201-733-7760

Avery, Mary F, *Dir,* Rowan Technical College, Learning Resource Center, Salisbury NC. 704-637-0760, Ext 69

Avery, Patsy J, *Librn,* Haskell County Public Library, Stigler OK. 918-967-4801

Avery, William, *Research Ed,* Fawcett Books, Research Library, New York NY. 212-975-4321

Aves, Cornelia, *Librn,* Baltimore County Public Library (Towson Area), Towson MD. 301-296-8500

Avietene, Madeleine, *Librn,* Sisters of the Immaculate Conception Convent Library, Putnam CT. 203-928-5828

Avila, Blanca A, *Librn,* Highway Users Federation Library, Washington DC. 202-857-1225

Avins, Wesley, *Bus & Tech,* Public Library of Fort Wayne & Allen County, Fort Wayne IN. 219-424-7241

Avison, L, *Librn,* University of Toronto Libraries (Audio Visual), Toronto ON. 416-978-6522

Avlon, Mary, *Librn,* Central Islip State Psychiatric Center (Health Science Library), Central Islip NY. 516-234-6262, Ext 2248

Avotte, Doris, *Librn,* Menominee County Library (Hermansville Branch), Hermansville MI. 906-498-2253

Avram, Henriette, *Dir, Network Develop Off,* Library of Congress, Washington DC. 202-287-5000

Awald, Ruth L, *Librn,* Hamlet Public Library, Hamlet IN. 219-867-6033

Awdy, Janet, *Ch & YA,* Macomb County Library, Mount Clemens MI. 313-469-5300

Awkard, J C, *Ref & On-Line Servs,* Florida Agricultural & Mechanical University, Samuel H Coleman Memorial Library, Tallahassee FL. 904-599-3370

Axeen, Marina E, *Chmn & Prof,* Ball State University, Dept of Library Science, IN. 317-285-7180, 285-7189

Axelrod, Velma, *Med Librn,* University of Pittsburgh (Howard Anderson Power Memorial Library), Pittsburgh PA. 412-647-4288

Axelson, Sally, *Per,* Anoka County Library, Blaine MN. 612-784-1100

Axford, H William, *Actg Dean,* Sangamon State University, Norris L Brookens Library, Springfield IL. 217-786-6597

Axman, Donald, *Tech Serv,* Four County Library System, Binghamton NY. 607-723-8236

Axon, Catherine, *ILL & Ref,* Suffolk University College Library, Boston MA. 617-723-4700, Ext 241

Axthelm, Jean, *Asst Dir & Ref,* Glen Ellyn Public Library, Glen Ellyn IL. 312-469-0879

Axthelm, Kenneth, *AV,* Brooklyn Public Library (Central Library), Brooklyn NY. 212-780-7712

Axtmann, Margaret Maes, *Librn,* National Center for State Courts Library, Williamsburg VA. 804-253-2000

Axton, Vivian, *Asst Librn,* Hancock County Library, Hawesville KY. 502-927-6760

Ayajanion, A H, *On-Line Servs,* IBM Corp, Data Systems Division Library, Hopewell Junction NY. 914-897-6219

Ayala, John, *Librn,* Long Beach Community College Learning Resources Division (Pacific Coast Campus Library), Long Beach CA. 213-420-4548

Ayama, Ma Deva, *Ad,* Fullerton City Library, Fullerton CA. 714-738-6333, Ext 301

Ayars, Virginia, *Acq,* Michigan City Public Library, Michigan City IN. 219-879-4561

Aycock, Bessie, *Asst Librn,* Bay Ridge Christian College Library, Kendleton TX. 713-532-3982

Aycock, Mrs B D, *ILL & Ref,* Union Theological Seminary in Virginia Library, Richmond VA. 804-355-0671, Ext 311

Aycock, Sue, *Lit,* Arlington Public Library, Arlington TX. 817-275-2763, 265-3311, Ext 347

Aye, Dorothy, *Asst Librn,* North Lyon County Library, Allen KS. 316-528-3451

Ayers, Eleanor Y, *Librn,* Moody's Investors Service Inc Library, New York NY. 212-553-0300

Ayers, Linda E, *Dir,* Sandpoint-East Bonner County Free Public Library District, Sandpoint ID. 208-263-6930

Ayers, Mary Lou, *Dir,* Bollinger County Library, Marble Hill MO. 314-238-2713

Ayers, Randy, *ILL,* Kentucky State University, Blazer Library, Frankfort KY. 502-564-5852

Aylward, James, *Librn,* United States Navy (Naval Education & Training Center), Newport RI. 401-841-3044, 841-4352

Ayoub, E A, *Librn,* Teledyne, Inc, Teledyne Engineering Services Library, Waltham MA. 617-890-3350

Ayoub, Eleanor, *Librn,* New York Public Library (New Dorp), New York NY. 212-351-2977

Ayoung, Rita, *Librn,* Imperial Tobacco (Research Library), Montreal PQ. 514-932-6161

Ayres, Felix, *Cat,* Glendale Public Library, Glendale CA. 213-956-2030

Ayres, Jean, *Librn,* Augusta Regional Library (Appleby), Augusta GA. 404-736-6244

Ayres, Lauribel, *Actg Librn,* Bryan-Bennett Library, Salem IL. 618-548-2822

Ayres, Madeline, *Dir,* Garwood Free Public Library, Garwood NJ. 201-789-1670

Azeltine, Mary R, *Dir,* Monticello Public Library, Monticello IA. 319-465-3354

Azukas, Lynda, *Acq,* West Haven Public Library, West Haven CT. 203-932-2221

Azukas, Mary Ann, *Tech Serv,* Chicago Ridge Public Library, Chicago Ridge IL. 312-423-7753

Azusenis, Helen, *ILL,* Cleveland Public Library, Cleveland OH. 216-623-2800

B

Baade, Harley D, *Librn,* General Electric Co, Apollo Systems, Reference Services Library, Houston TX. 713-332-4511

Baak, Odella, *Instr,* Morningside College, Library Science Dept, IA. 712-277-5125

Baar, Beverly, *Librn,* Pathfinder Community Library, Baldwin MI. 616-745-4010

Baar, Hazel, *Social & Educ,* Grand Rapids Public Library, Grand Rapids MI. 616-456-4400

Baarson, Elaine, *Doc,* Tucson Public Library, Tucson AZ. 602-791-4391

Baatz, Wilmer, *Asst Dir Coll Develop,* Indiana University at Bloomington, University Libraries, Bloomington IN. 812-337-3403

Baatz, Wilmer H, *Librn,* Indiana University at Bloomington (Education), Bloomington IN. 812-337-1798

Babb, Antonia, *Germanic,* University of California Los Angeles Library, Los Angeles CA. 213-825-1201

Babb, Dortha Fae, *Librn,* Craig-Moffat County Public Library, Craig CO. 303-824-5116

Babb, Jan, *Librn,* Austin Public Library (Le Roy Public), LeRoy MN. 507-324-5641

Babb, Julia, *Librn,* Greenville County Library (Wade Hampton-Taylors), Taylors SC. 803-268-5955

Babb, Mary E, *Dir,* Umatilla Public Library, Umatilla FL. 904-669-2911

Babb, Sandra, *Librn,* Burleson Public Library, Burleson TX. 817-295-6131

Babbitt, Dennis, *Br Coordr,* Elkhart Public Library, Elkhart IN. 219-294-5463

Babbitt, Dennis, *Librn,* Elkhart Public Library (Pierre Moran), Elkhart IN. 219-294-6418

Babcock, Elria M, *Librn,* Gilman Public Library, Gilman VT. 802-892-7783
Babcock, Lillian, *Librn,* Green Hills Public Library District, Palos Hills IL. 312-598-8446
Babcock, Maralyn, *Ch,* Collier County Free Public Library, Naples FL. 813-262-4130, 261-8208
Babcock, Mary Jane, *Circ,* San Diego State University Library, San Diego CA. 714-286-6014
Babcock, Rosa, *Ref,* El Centro College, Learning Resources Center, Dallas TX. 214-746-2292
Babcock, Sharon, *Librn,* University of Washington Libraries (K K Sherwood Library), Seattle WA. 206-223-3360
Babcock, Warren, *ILL, On-Line Servs & Bibliog Instr,* Washington State University Library, Pullman WA. 509-335-4557
Babel, Rayonia, *ILL & Ref,* Aurora College, Charles B Phillips Library, Aurora IL. 312-892-6431, Ext 61, 62
Babel, Therese, *YA,* Rock Springs Public Library, Rock Springs WY. 307-362-6212
Babicki, Joseph, *Tech Serv,* Decatur Public Library, Decatur IL. 217-428-6617, Ext 33
Babikow, Mary Beth, *Pub Servs,* Baltimore County Public Library, Towson MD. 301-296-8500
Babin, Joseph M, *Dir,* Saint Joseph Seminary College, Pere Rouquette Library, Saint Benedict LA. 504-892-9895
Babineair, Francine, *Librn,* J E Baker Co Library, York PA. 717-848-1501
Babits, Ann, *ILL,* New Brunswick Free Public Library, New Brunswick NJ. 201-745-5337
Baca, Dan, *Classified Report Libr,* Los Alamos Scientific Laboratory Libraries, Library Services Group, Los Alamos NM. 505-667-4448
Baca, Deloisa, *Librn,* Bureau of Land Management, Socorro District Office Library, Socorro NM. 505-835-0412
Bacak, Laverne, *Librn,* Wharton County Library (El Campo Branch), El Campo TX. 713-543-2362
Baccus, Donald, *Librn,* Sacramento Public Library (Elk Grove Branch), Elk Grove CA. 916-685-4798
Bach, Andrew W, *Assoc Prof,* Slippery Rock State College, Dept of Library Science, PA. 412-794-7321
Bach, Barbara, *Librn,* Beth El Synagogue, Max Shapiro Memorial Library, Saint Louis Park MN. 612-920-3512
Bachand, Michelle, *Librn,* University of Ottawa Libraries (Teacher Training Library), Ottawa ON. 613-231-5986
Bacharach, Martin M, *Supvr,* William Douglas McAdams Medical Library Medical Library, New York NY. 212-759-6300, Ext 276
Bachers, Herman B, *Librn,* Borough of Folcroft Public Library, Folcroft PA. 215-586-1690
Bachman, Tom, *Dir,* Brewer Public Library, Richland Center WI. 608-647-6444
Bachmann, George T, *Dir & Acq,* Western Maryland College, Hoover Library, Westminster MD. 301-848-7000, Ext 281
Bachrach, Joseph, *Asst Librn, Acq & Circ,* Hebrew Theological College, Saul Silber Memorial Library, Skokie IL. 312-267-9800
Bachus, Edward J, *Tech Serv,* Skidmore College, Lucy Scribner Library, Saratoga Springs NY. 518-584-5000, Ext 234
Bacino, Janice, *Pub Servs,* Lewis & Clark Library, Helena MT. 406-442-2380
Back, Carrie, *Per,* Morehead State University, Johnson Camden-Julian Carroll Library, Morehead KY. 606-783-2250
Backes, Elizabeth, *Per,* South Seattle Community College, Instructional Resources Center, Seattle WA. 206-764-5395
Backes, James C, *Asst Librn,* New York Law Institute, New York NY. 212-732-8720
Backes, John, *Ref,* Shoreline Community College, Library/Media Center, Seattle WA. 206-546-4663
Backes, John P, *Librn,* Honeywell Inc, Marine Systems Center Technical Library, Seattle WA. 206-789-2000, Ext 335
Backie, Faye, *ILL,* University of Southwestern Louisiana, Dupre Library, Lafayette LA. 318-264-6396
Backlund, Betty, *Tech Serv & Asst Dir,* Algonquin Area Public Library District, Algonquin IL. 312-658-4343

Backlund, Caroline, *Bibliog Instr,* National Gallery of Art Library, Washington DC. 202-737-4215
Backsen, Marcella, *Librn,* Immaculate Heart of Mary Parish Library, Los Alamos NM. 505-662-6193, 672-9061
Backus, Betty, *Ad,* Graham Public Library, Union Grove WI. 414-878-2910
Backus, Marjorie, *Dir,* Heuvelton Free Library, Heuvelton NY. 315-344-6550
Baclawski, Mary Ann, *Coll Develop & Tech Serv,* Troy Public Library, Troy NY. 518-274-7071
Bacon, Agnes K, *Librn,* Nordson Corp, Corporate Library, Amherst OH. 216-988-9411, Ext 433
Bacon, Aurora, *Dir,* Edison Free Public Library, Edison NJ. 201-287-2298
Bacon, Bryan L, *Librn,* Burnaby Municipal Library, Burnaby BC. 604-294-7234
Bacon, Constance M, *Librn,* Insurance Society of Philadelphia, Inc Library, Philadelphia PA. 215-627-5306
Bacon, Ethel, *Music,* University of Hartford, Mortensen Library, West Hartford CT. 203-243-4265
Bacon, Linda A, *Librn,* Chatfield College Library, Saint Martin OH. 513-875-4091
Bacon, Mary, *Librn,* Stinson Memorial Library, Anna IL. 618-833-2521
Bacon, Patricia, *Ref,* Franklin Township Free Public Library, Somerset NJ. 201-545-8032
Bacon, Reitha, *Librn,* Barry-Lawrence Regional Library (Mount Vernon Branch), Mount Vernon MO. 417-466-2921
Bacsany, Karen, *Ref,* Wayne State University Libraries (Kresge Library), Detroit MI. 313-577-4035
Bader, Hazel B, *Librn,* Rutan & Tucker Library, Santa Ana CA. 714-835-2200, Ext 230
Bader, Jaci, *Circ,* Central Wyoming College Library, Riverton WY. 307-856-9291, Ext 33
Bader, Kathleen D, *Dir,* Snow Library, Orleans MA. 617-255-3848
Bader, Rochelle, *Reader Serv,* George Washington University Library (Paul Himmelfarb Health Sciences Library), Washington DC. 202-676-2850
Badersnider, Jackie, *Dir,* Alvah N Belding Library, Belding MI. 616-794-1450
Badertscher, David G, *Dir,* Milbank, Tweed, Hadley & McCloy Library, New York NY. 212-530-5200
Badger, Barbara, *Media,* De Paul University Libraries (Lincoln Park Campus Library), Chicago IL. 312-321-7934
Badger, Betty, *Librn,* Landgrove Public Library, Landgrove VT. 802-824-6703
Badger, Hal, *Chief Librn,* Freedoms Foundation Library, Valley Forge PA. 215-933-8825
Badger, Joan A, *Ref,* University of Charleston, Andrew S Thomas Memorial Library, Charleston WV. 304-346-1400
Bading, Kathryn E, *Processing Supervisor,* Trinity University Library, San Antonio TX. 512-736-8121
Badion, N, *Ref,* Napa City - County Library, Napa CA. 707-253-4241
Badis, Sylvia, *Ch,* Mary H Weir Public Library, Weirton WV. 304-748-7070
Badome, Jacqueline, *Librn,* Brundage, Story & Rose, Investment Counsel Library, New York NY. 212-269-3050, Ext 78
Bae, Frank S, *Dir,* New England School of Law Library, Boston MA. 617-267-9655, Ext 50
Baechtold, Marguerite, *Assoc Prof,* Western Michigan University, School of Librarianship, MI. 616-383-1849
Baedler, Elfriede A, *ILL & Ref,* Eau Gallie Public Library, Melbourne FL. 305-254-1739
Baer, D Richard, *Dir,* Hollywood Film Archive Library, Los Angeles CA. 213-933-3345
Baer, E Alex, *Ref,* Virginia Polytechnic Institute & State University Library, Blacksburg VA. 703-961-5593
Baer, Ferdinand, *In Charge,* University of Maryland at College Park (Meteorology), College Park MD. 301-454-2708, 454-2709
Baer, Karl A, *Chief Librn,* National Association of Home Builders, National Housing Center Library, Washington DC. 202-452-0200
Baer, Mark H, *Dir,* Hewlett-Packard Co (Corporate Library), Palo Alto CA. 415-856-3091
Baer, N, *Ser,* University of Rhode Island Library, Kingston RI. 401-792-1000

Baer, Robert, *ILL, Ad & Ref,* Piscataway Township Free Public Library, John F Kennedy Memorial Library, Piscataway NJ. 201-463-1633
Baesler, Carol, *Librn,* Washington State Library (Olympic Center Staff Library), Bremerton WA. 206-478-4886
Baez, Lourdes, *Librn,* Persing & Company, Inc, Research Library, New York NY. 212-964-4300, Ext 379
Bagby, Felicia, *Librn,* Clark & Dietz-Engineers, Inc Library, Urbana IL. 217-384-1400
Bagby, Sterling, *Dir,* Halifax County-South Boston Regional Library, Halifax VA. 804-476-2327
Bagen, John J, *Dir,* Saint Mary's Seminary College, Saint Mary's of the Barrens Library, Perryville MO. 314-547-6300
Bagg, Deborah, *Acq,* Albion College, Stockwell Memorial Library, Albion MI. 517-629-5511, Ext 285
Baggett, Carolyn, *Asst Prof,* University of Mississippi, Graduate School of Library & Information Science, MS. 601-232-7440
Baggett, Marjorie D, *Govt Doc,* University of Alabama in Birmingham, Mervyn H Sterne Library, Birmingham AL. 205-934-6360
Baggett, Viola, *Librn,* Pinebluff Public Library, Pinebluff NC. 919-947-2931
Baggs, Jr, Robert N, *Dir,* Ocean City Free Public Library, Ocean City NJ. 609-399-2434
Baginski, Doris A, *Ref,* United States Naval War College Library, Newport RI. 401-841-2641
Bagley, Elizabeth, *Tech Serv & Cat,* Mercy College of Detroit Library, Detroit MI. 313-592-6000
Bagley, Josephine, *Tech Serv,* College of New Rochelle, Gill Library, New Rochelle NY. 914-632-5300, Ext 347
Bagley, Marcy, *Chief Librn,* Arizona Republic & Phoenix Gazette Library, Phoenix AZ. 602-271-8000, Ext 8555
Bagnerise, Charles L, *Asst Chief,* Veterans Administration, Medical Center Library, New Orleans LA. 504-589-5272
Bagoff, Robert, *Librn,* Nova University Libraries (Behavioral Sciences), Fort Lauderdale FL. 305-475-8300, Ext 264, 245
Bagordo, Constant, *Librn,* Bibliotheque Municipale, Granby PQ. 514-372-6678
Bagwell, Anne, *Librn,* Richland County Public Library (Devine Street), Columbia SC. 803-799-5873
Bagwell, L R, *Librn,* Southwest Texas Genealogical Association Library, Del Rio TX. 512-775-4507
Baham, Mrs Binnie, *ILL & Ref,* Southeastern Louisiana University, Linus A Sims Memorial Library, Hammond LA. 504-549-2234
Bahn, Gilbert S, *In Charge,* Schuyler Technical Library, Newport News VA. 804-877-5860
Bahr, Alice, *Ref,* Cedar Crest College, Cressman Library, Allentown PA. 215-437-4471, Ext 264
Bahr, Christine, *Librn,* United Hospital Fund of New York, Reference Library, New York NY. 212-754-1080, Ext 256
Bahre, Stephen A, *Dir,* Merrimack College, McQuade Library, North Andover MA. 617-683-7111, Ext 210
Bahu, Rebecca, *Ad,* South Bend Public Library, South Bend IN. 219-288-4413
Baie, Dorothy, *Asst Librn,* Clinton Township Public Library, Waterman IL. 815-264-3339
Baier, Linda, *Asst Librn,* Institute of Paper Chemistry Library, Appleton WI. 414-734-9251
Bailey, Alice R, *Asst Librn,* Marion Military Institute, Baer Memorial Library, Marion AL. 205-683-9593
Bailey, Ann, *Cat,* Borough of Etobicoke Public Library, Weston ON. 416-248-5681
Bailey, Barbara J, *ILL & Ref,* Welles-Turner Memorial Library, Glastonbury CT. 203-633-1300
Bailey, Beatrice, *Sci & Indust,* Saint Paul Public Library, Saint Paul MN. 612-292-6311
Bailey, Brenda, *Librn,* Antaeus Lineal Research Associates, Antaeus Institute Library, Fayetteville AR. 501-443-3050
Bailey, Camilla, *Media & Acq,* Elbert County Library, Elberton GA. 404-283-5375
Bailey, Carol B, *Librn,* Blue Ridge Summit Free Library, Blue Ridge Summit PA. 717-794-2240
Bailey, Carolyn, *Circ,* Valdez Public Library, Valdez AK. 907-835-4632
Bailey, Cheryl M, *Dir,* Mary College Library, Bismarck ND. 701-255-4681, Ext 502

Bailey, Chris H, *Mgt Dir,* American Clock & Watch Museum, Inc, Edward Ingraham Library, Bristol CT. 203-583-6070
Bailey, Darlene, *Ch & YA,* Umatilla County Library, Pendleton OR. 503-276-1881
Bailey, Darlene, *Librn,* Van Buren County Library (Gobles Branch), Gobles MI. 616-423-4771
Bailey, Dianne M, *Librn,* Public Library of Johnston County & Smithfield (Kenly Public), Kenly NC. 919-934-8146
Bailey, Donald, *Librn,* Lake Lanier Regional Library (Buford Public), Buford GA. 404-945-4196
Bailey, Donald K, *Librn,* Texas State Library, Division for the Blind & Physically Handicapped, Austin TX. 512-475-4758
Bailey, Ernie, *Circ,* Murray State University, Harry Lee Waterfield Library, Murray KY. 502-762-2291
Bailey, Evelyn, *Librn,* Cabell County Public Library (Douglass Public), Huntington WV. 203-523-7437
Bailey, Franceta, *Dir,* Iowa Western Community College-Clarinda Center, Edith Lisle Library, Clarinda IA. 712-542-5117, Ext 263
Bailey, George M, *Assoc Dir,* Claremont Colleges Libraries, Claremont CA. 714-621-8000, Ext 3721
Bailey, Jane, *Program Coordr,* Calloway County Public Library, Murray KY. 502-753-2288
Bailey, Jane J, *Bkmobile Coordr,* Dorchester County Library, Saint George SC. 803-563-9189
Bailey, Jean, *Librn,* Rhode Island Junior College, William F Flanagan Campus Library, Lincoln RI. 401-333-7053
Bailey, Jean M, *Librn,* P H Glatfelter Co, Research Library, Spring Grove PA. 717-225-4711, Ext 212
Bailey, Joan, *Circ,* Cherokee County Public Library, Gaffney SC. 803-489-4381
Bailey, Joe H, *Assoc Dir,* North Texas State University Library, Denton TX. 817-788-2411
Bailey, Joyce, *Asst Librn,* Tenney Memorial Library, Inc, Newbury VT. 802-866-5955
Bailey, Judith H, *Librn,* French American Metals Corp Library, Lakewood CO. 303-232-4966
Bailey, Kay, *Librn,* Texas Eastern Transmission Corporate Library, Houston TX. 713-759-3070
Bailey, Lisa, *Librn,* Carter County Library (Olive Hill Branch), Olive Hill KY. 606-286-2351
Bailey, Lois, *Librn,* Circleville Bible College Library, Circleville OH. 614-474-8896
Bailey, Lucille, *Bibliog Instr,* Hunter College of the City University of New York Library, New York NY. 212-570-5511
Bailey, Lugene, *Per,* Central State University, Hallie Q Brown Memorial Library, Wilberforce OH. 513-376-7212
Bailey, Madeleine, *Librn,* Alberta Federal & Intergovernmental Affairs Library, Edmonton AB. 403-427-2611
Bailey, Mamie, *Librn,* Public Library of Johnston County & Smithfield (Atkinson Memorial), Selma NC. 919-934-8146
Bailey, Margaret, *Ad & Ref,* Clark Public Library, Clark NJ. 201-388-5999
Bailey, Marlene, *Librn,* Journal & Courier Library, Lafayette IN. 317-423-5511
Bailey, Martha, *Librn,* Purdue University Libraries & Audio-Visual Center (Life Science), West Lafayette IN. 317-749-2284
Bailey, Mary Frances, *Chief Historian,* National Park Service, Colonial National Historical Park Library, Yorktown VA. 804-898-3400
Bailey, Mary Jane, *Dir,* Mamie Doud Eisenhower Public Library, Broomfield Public Library, Broomfield CO. 303-469-1821
Bailey, Mary W, *Ref,* Virginia State College, Johnston Memorial Library, Petersburg VA. 804-520-6171
Bailey, Mercedes M, *Librn,* Inter-American Defense College Library, Washington DC. 202-693-8154
Bailey, Patti, *External Librn,* Safford City-Graham County Library, Safford AZ. 602-428-1531
Bailey, Richard, *AV,* American River College Library, Sacramento CA. 916-484-8293
Bailey, Richard C, *Dir,* Kern County Museum Library, Bakersfield CA. 805-861-2132
Bailey, Robert J, *Librn,* Mississippi State Department of Archives & History, Jackson MS. 601-354-6218

Bailey, Rose Marie, *Librn,* San Antonio Public Library (San Pedro), San Antonio TX. 512-733-1454
Bailey, Ruth, *Librn,* Iosco-Arenac Regional Library (Whittemore Library), Whittemore MI. 517-362-2651
Bailey, Ruth, *Asst Librn & Reader Serv,* Nyack College Library, Nyack NY. 914-358-1710, Ext 270, 271
Bailey, Sheila M, *Tech Serv,* High Point College, Wrenn Memorial Library, High Point NC. 919-885-5101
Bailey, Theresa, *Commun Servs,* Jefferson County Public Library, Lakewood CO. 303-238-8411
Bailey, Virginia, *Librn,* Rensselaer Polytechnic Institute (Architecture), Troy NY. 518-270-6465
Bailey, Vivian L, *Ref,* Eisenhower Public Library District, Harwood Heights IL. 312-867-7828, 452-8989
Bailey, William M, *Librn,* Hillsborough County Law Library, Tampa FL. 813-272-5818
Bailey, III, James F, *Dir,* Indiana University (School of Law Library), Indianapolis IN. 317-264-4028
Bailin, Debra, *ILL,* Washington University Libraries (School of Dental Medicine Library), Saint Louis MO. 314-454-0385
Baillio, Dallas, *Dir,* Mobile Public Library, Mobile AL. 205-438-7073
Bailly, Cecilia F, *Librn,* Ramsdell Public Library, Housatonic MA. 413-274-3738
Bails, Barbara, *Dir,* Stanwood Public Library, Stanwood IA. 319-945-3531
Baily, Diette, *Librn,* Brooklyn College Library (Music), Brooklyn NY. 212-780-5289
Baily, Martha B, *ILL & Ref,* Abbeville-Greenwood Regional Library, Greenwood SC. 803-223-4515
Bain, Charles T, *Dir,* Northeastern Oklahoma A&m College, Learning Resources Center, Miami OK. 918-542-8441, Ext 220
Bain, Christine, *Assoc Librn,* New York State Library (Science, Health Science & Technology), Albany NY. 518-474-7041
Bain, Christine A, *Dir,* Albany Medical Center College of Union University (Capital District Psychiatric Center Library), Albany NY. 518-445-6609
Bain, Janice W, *Librn, On-Line Servs & Bibliog Instr,* National Academy of Sciences, Transportation Research Board Library, Washington DC. 202-389-6841
Bain, June, *Librn,* Hunter Public Library, Hunter NY. 518-263-4655
Bain, Marjorie, *Librn,* Tufts Library (Fogg), South Weymouth MA. 617-337-0410
Bain, Mrs I, *Libr Tech,* George Brown College of Applied Arts & Technology Library (Nightingale Campus), Toronto ON. 416-967-1212
Bain, Patrick F, *Librn,* Castor Community Library, Castor AB. 403-882-3451
Baines, Grace E, *Cat,* Buffalo & Erie County Public Library System, Buffalo NY. 716-856-7525
Bains, Susan F, *Librn,* Railroad Commission of Texas, Oil & Gas Library, Austin TX. 512-445-1100
Bair, Harold A, *In Charge,* Philadelphia Zoological Society Library, Philadelphia PA. 215-243-1100, Ext 218
Baird, Bobbie, *Cat,* Warren Wilson College Library, Swannanoa NC. 704-298-3325, Ext 45
Baird, Dennis W, *Soc Sci,* University of Idaho Library, Moscow ID. 208-885-6534
Baird, Dorothy S, *Actg Chmn,* East Tennessee State University, Library Service Division, TN. 615-929-4244
Baird, Lynn, *Ser,* University of Idaho Library, Moscow ID. 208-885-6534
Baird, M Lucille, *Coordr,* Eastern New Mexico University, Library Science, Dept of Instructional Resources, NM. 505-562-3111
Baird, Marcia, *Tech Serv,* Goldey Beacom College, J Wilbur Hirons Library, Wilmington DE. 302-998-8814, Ext 47
Bak, Elaine, *Asst Librn,* Long Island Historical Society Library, Brooklyn NY. 212-624-0890
Bake, A S J, *Humanities & Soc Sci,* Royal Military College of Canada, Massey Arts & Science-Engineering Library, Kingston ON. 613-545-7305
Bake, Blaine, *Rare Bks & Spec Coll,* Ricks College, David O McKay Learning Resources Center, Rexburg ID. 208-356-2351

Baker, A, *Librn,* University of Southern California (Seaver Science & Engineering), Los Angeles CA. 213-743-5614
Baker, Alberta, *Librn,* Cities Service Co (Law Library), Tulsa OK. 918-586-2272
Baker, Alzina, *Librn,* Coldwater District Library (Wilmore Branch), Wilmore KS. 316-738-4464
Baker, Antonie, *Assoc Dir,* Florida International University, North Miami Campus Library, North Miami FL. 305-940-5730
Baker, Aurelia S, *Librn,* Central State Hospital, Staff Library, Indianapolis IN. 317-633-7461
Baker, B, *Asst Librn,* Barrie Public Library, Barrie ON. 705-728-1010
Baker, B Gene, *Dir,* Florida State Legislature Joint Legislative Management Committee, Division of Legislative Library Services, Tallahassee FL. 904-488-2812
Baker, Barbara, *Instr Serv,* Gaston College, Learning Resources Center, Dallas NC. 704-922-3136, Ext 315
Baker, Barbara W, *Asst Librn,* Osterville Free Library, Osterville MA. 617-428-2565
Baker, Bruce S, *Dir,* Western Regional Public Library System, Springfield MA. 413-732-3115
Baker, Bryan, *Assoc Prof,* Sam Houston State University, Library Science Department, TX. 713-295-6211, Ext 1151
Baker, Carol, *Ch,* Newton Falls Public Library, Newton Falls OH. 216-872-1282
Baker, Carole, *On-Line Servs,* University of Cincinnati Medical Center Libraries (Media Resources Center), Cincinnati OH. 513-872-4173
Baker, Carolina, *Ser,* Florida International University, Tamiami Campus, Athenaeum, Miami FL. 305-552-2461
Baker, Caroline, *Cat,* Larchmont Public Library, Larchmont NY. 914-834-1960
Baker, Charles L, *Dir,* Maitland Art Center, Maitland FL. 305-645-2181
Baker, Cleona, *Librn,* Concord Public Library, Concord VT. 802-695-2236
Baker, Connie, *Chief Librn,* Veterans Administration Medical Center, Library Service, San Diego CA. 714-453-7500, Ext 3421
Baker, Deanna, *ILL,* Hutchinson County Library, Borger TX. 806-274-6221
Baker, Donald E, *Dir,* Willard Library of Evansville, Evansville IN. 812-425-4309
Baker, Donna, *Ch,* Palatine Public Library District, Palatine IL. 312-358-5881
Baker, Dorothy, *Cat,* Danbury Public Library, Danbury CT. 203-797-4505
Baker, Dorothy, *Librn,* Detroit Public Library (Gray), Detroit MI. 313-833-9155
Baker, Dot, *Librn,* Ocmulgee Regional Library (M E Roden Memorial), Hawkinsville GA. 912-892-3155
Baker, Douglas, *Dir,* Northwest Wisconsin Library System, Ashland WI. 715-682-8027
Baker, Elaine, *YA,* Southern Adirondack Library System, Saratoga Springs NY. 518-584-7300, 792-3343, 885-1073
Baker, Elizabeth, *Librn,* Eastern Kentucky University (Music), Richmond KY. 606-622-4944
Baker, Emily, *Ad,* Nyack Library, Nyack NY. 914-358-3370
Baker, Gayle, *Circ,* Vanderbilt University Medical Center Library, Nashville TN. 615-322-2292
Baker, Glena, *Librn,* Evansville Public Library & Vanderburgh County Public Library (Howell), Evansville IN. 812-425-2621
Baker, Gretchen, *Circ,* Leavenworth Public Library, Leavenworth KS. 913-682-5666
Baker, Harold, *Libr Systs,* Indiana State University, Cunningham Memorial Library, Terre Haute IN. 812-232-6311, Ext 2451
Baker, Helen C, *Librn,* Springfield United Methodist Church Library, Springfield VA. 703-451-2375
Baker, Ilene, *Ch,* Rockville Centre Public Library, Rockville Centre NY. 516-766-6258
Baker, Irene, *Tech Serv,* Missouri Baptist College Library, Saint Louis MO. 314-434-1115, Ext 73
Baker, J Wayne, *Dir,* Ohio Northern University, Heterick Memorial Library, Ada OH. 419-634-9921, Ext 370, 490
Baker, Jacqueline, *County Librn,* Clarion County Library System, Clarion PA. 814-226-7172
Baker, Jacqueline, *Head Librarian,* Clarion Free Library, Clarion PA. 814-226-7172

BAKER

Baker, James D, *Dir,* Broome Community College, Cecil C Tyrrell Learning Resources Center, Binghamton NY. 607-772-5020

Baker, James J, *Librn,* Minnesota State Prison Library, Stillwater MN. 612-439-1910, Ext 271

Baker, Janet R, *Dir,* Conant Free Public Library, Sterling MA. 617-422-6409

Baker, Jean S, *ILL, Ref & Bibliog Instr,* Siena Heights College Library, Adrian MI. 517-263-0731, Ext 242

Baker, John P, *Conservation Chief,* New York Public Library (Preparation Services), New York NY. 212-790-6262

Baker, Joseph, *Commun Servs,* Musser Public Library, Muscatine IA. 319-263-3065

Baker, Judith, *Assoc Dir,* Hahnemann Medical College & Hospital of Philadelphia, Warren H Fake Library, Philadelphia PA. 215-448-7186

Baker, Judy, *Cat,* Alameda County Library, Hayward CA. 415-881-6337

Baker, Judy, *Librn,* Putnam County District Library (Continental Branch), Continental OH. 419-523-3747

Baker, Karen, *Librn,* Austin Public Library (North Village), Austin TX. 512-472-5433

Baker, Karen, *YA,* Chappaqua Central School District Public Library, Chappaqua Library, Chappaqua NY. 914-238-4779

Baker, Kathryn F, *Librn,* Grant Park Public Library, Grant Park IL. 815-465-6531

Baker, Letha F, *Librn,* Nevada County Law Library, Nevada City CA. 916-265-2461, Ext 200

Baker, Linda, *Librn,* Sutherland, Asbill & Brennan, Law Library, Atlanta GA. 404-658-8907

Baker, Lisa L, *Librn,* Musick, Peeler & Garrett Library, Los Angeles CA. 213-629-3322

Baker, Lois, *Librn,* Trafford Community Public Library, Trafford PA. 412-372-5115

Baker, Loris, *Media,* Bethlehem Public Library, Bethlehem PA. 215-867-3761

Baker, Margaret, *ILL & Ref,* Fort Dodge Public Library, Fort Dodge IA. 515-573-8167

Baker, Margaret, *Ad,* Paris Public Library, Paris TX. 214-785-8531

Baker, Margaret M, *Info & ILL,* Westfield Athenaeum, Westfield MA. 413-568-7833

Baker, Marie, *Supvr,* Chicago Public Library (Rockwell Gardens Reading & Study Center), Chicago IL. 312-243-4534

Baker, Marion F, *Dir & Br Coordr,* Susquehanna County Historical Society & Free Library Association, Montrose PA. 717-278-1881

Baker, Martha A, *Librn,* Hobart Brothers Co Technical Center, John H Blankenbuehler Memorial Library, Troy OH. 513-339-6011, Ext 4603

Baker, Mary, *Exten Servs,* Eugene Public Library, Eugene OR. 503-687-5450

Baker, Mary, *ILL & Ref,* Franklin Pierce College Library, Rindge NH. 603-899-5111, Ext 215, 216

Baker, Mary E, *Dir,* Houston Antique Museum Library, Chattanooga TN. 615-267-7176

Baker, Mary E, *Librn,* 3M (The 235 Technical Library), Saint Paul MN. 612-733-2592

Baker, Mary Faith, *Bkmobile Coordr,* Public Library of the City of Somerville, Somerville MA. 617-623-5000

Baker, Mary L, *Chief Librn,* Coopersville District Library, Coopersville MI. 616-837-6809

Baker, Melva, *Ser,* University of Texas at Arlington Library, Arlington TX. 817-273-3391

Baker, Michael, *Systemwide Circ: Coordr,* Chicago Public Library, Chicago IL. 312-269-2900

Baker, N W, *Librn,* IBM Corp, Office Products Div Headquarters, Business Info Center, Franklin Lakes NJ. 201-848-2041

Baker, Nancy, *Librn,* Saugerties Public Library, Saugerties NY. 914-246-4317

Baker, Nancy, *Ref,* University of Kentucky, Margaret I King Library, Lexington KY. 606-257-3801

Baker, Naydean L, *Librn,* Ventura County Law Library, Ventura CA. 805-654-2695

Baker, Nettie, *Cat,* University of Dallas, William A Blakley Library, Irving TX. 214-438-1123, Ext 328

Baker, Norabel, *Librn,* Hope Welty Township Library, Cerro Gordo IL. 217-763-5001

Baker, Pearl, *Asst Dir,* Brooke County Public Library, Wellsburg WV. 304-737-1551

Baker, Phoebe, *Bd,* Longwood Gardens Inc Library, Kennett Square PA. 215-388-6741, Ext 510

Baker, Phyllis, *Actg Dir,* Washington County Public Library, Marietta OH. 614-373-1057

Baker, Robert, *Coordr of Instrnl Servs,* Spokane Community College, East Mission Campus Library, Spokane WA. 509-455-7699

Baker, Roberta, *Tech Serv,* New Martinsville Public Library, New Martinsville WV. 304-455-4545

Baker, Ronald, *Librn,* Lambton County Library, Wyoming ON. 519-845-3324

Baker, Rowena, *Circ,* Tennessee State University, Martha M Brown - Lois W Daniel Library, Nashville TN. 615-320-3682, 251-1417

Baker, Sara W, *Dir Libr Serv,* Huron Road Hospital Library & Audiovisual Center, Library & Audiovisual Center, Cleveland OH. 216-761-3300, Ext 3206

Baker, Sarah, *Librn,* Washington County Free Library (Sharpsburg Public), Sharpsburg MD. 301-432-8825

Baker, Sarah D, *Dir & Br Coordr,* Pulaski County Public Library, Winamac IN. 219-946-3432

Baker, Scott, *Ref,* Troy Public Library, Troy NY. 518-274-7071

Baker, Sharon, *In Charge,* Trinity Lutheran Church Library, Madison WI. 608-249-8527

Baker, Sharon D, *Acq,* University of California at Davis, General Library, Davis CA. 916-752-2110

Baker, Susan, *Librn,* Hardy County Public Library (East Hardy County Branch), Baker WV. 304-538-6560

Baker, Sylva, *Librn,* Academy of Natural Sciences Library, Philadelphia PA. 215-299-1041

Baker, Verna T, *ILL & Ref,* King's College Library, Briarcliff Manor NY. 914-941-7200, Ext 243

Baker, Virginia P, *Dir,* Maple Woods Community College Library, Kansas City MO. 816-436-6500, Ext 73, 74

Baker, William, *Librn,* Norfolk Public Library (Berkley), Norfolk VA. 804-441-2853

Baker, Wylene, *Asst Dir & ILL,* York College, Levitt Library, York NE. 402-362-4441, Ext 244

Baker, Jr, Samuel M, *Dir,* University of New Haven, Marvin K Peterson Library, West Haven CT. 203-934-6321

Bakes, Hiram, *Ref,* Aquinas College, Learning Resource Center, Grand Rapids MI. 616-459-8281, Ext 234

Bakewell, Dennis, *Rare Bks & Spec Coll,* California State University, Northridge, Delmar T Oviatt & South Libraries, Northridge CA. 213-885-2271

Bakies, Alice, *Circ,* Findlay-Hancock County Public Library, Findlay OH. 419-422-1712

Bakke, Dan, *Librn,* Public Library of Des Moines (Franklin), Des Moines IA. 515-283-4271

Bakken, Lavola J, *Res,* Douglas County Museum History Research Library, Roseburg OR. 503-672-5961

Bakos, Karen, *Librn,* Lake County Public Library (Lake Station Public), Lake Station IN. 219-962-2409

Bakunas, Pat, *Rare Bks & Maps,* Balzekas Museum of Lithuanian Culture, Library & Information Center, Chicago IL. 312-847-2441

Balassone, Bro Gabriel, *Dir,* Duns Scotus Library, Southfield MI. 313-357-3070

Balatti, Sheila, *Librn,* Bank of Canada Library, Ottawa ON. 613-563-8246

Balay, Robert E, *Head Librn Ref Dept,* Yale University Library (Sterling Memorial Library), New Haven CT. 203-436-8335

Balazs, Andrew, *Librn,* Alberta Attorney General Law Library, Edmonton AB. 403-427-5021, 5022

Balcer, Betty, *ILL,* Saint Mary's Seminary & University, School of Theology Library, Baltimore MD. 301-323-3200, Ext 70

Balcerzak, Judy A, *Librn,* Burlington Northern Energy & Minerals Library, Billings MT. 406-249-4521, Ext 398

Balch, Carole, *Preparation & Bd,* Dallas Public Library, Dallas TX. 214-748-9071

Balch, Gay M, *Circ,* Abilene Public Library, Abilene TX. 915-677-2474

Balcken, Fran, *Ch,* Wauwatosa Public Library, Wauwatosa WI. 414-258-5700

Balcom, Karen S, *President,* Council of Research & Academic Libraries (Marciue Users Group (MUG)), San Antonio TX. 512-734-7311, Ext 2489

Balcom, Ted, *Dir,* Villa Park Public Library, Villa Park IL. 312-834-1164

Balconi, William, *ILL,* John Carroll University, Grasselli Library, University Heights OH. 491-4233 & 491-4231

Bald, Margaret, *Acq,* Bob Jones University, J S Mack Library, Greenville SC. 803-242-5100, Ext 296

Baldaia, Mary Jane, *Per,* Fall River Public Library, Fall River MA. 617-676-8541

Baldasaro, Claire, *Librn,* Hamilton Memorial Library, Chester MA. 413-354-7808

Baldau, Gretchen, *Curric Laboratory,* State University College at Buffalo, Edward H Butler Library, Buffalo NY. 716-878-6302

Balderas, Lynn Pete, *Dir,* Cameron County Library System, Brownsville TX. 512-541-1241, Ext 356

Balderas, Lynn Pete, *Dir,* City-College Library, Brownsville TX. 512-541-1241, Ext 356, 541-1662, Ext 356

Balderston, Ann, *Asst Librn,* Newtown Library Co, Newtown PA. 717-968-9928

Baldi, Joyce P, *Ad,* Westwood Free Public Library, Westwood NJ. 201-664-0583

Baldinger, Esther, *Ref, On-Line Servs & Bibliog Instr,* Washington University Libraries (School of Medicine Library), Saint Louis MO. 314-454-3711

Baldini, Bernie, *Tech Serv,* University of Kentucky (Medical Center Library), Lexington KY. 606-233-5300

Baldino, Bernadette, *Media,* Bridgeport Public Library, Bridgeport CT. 203-576-7777

Baldino, Marilyn, *Ch,* Field Library, Peekskill Library, Peekskill NY. 914-737-0010

Baldock, Margaret, *Librn,* University of Saskatchewan Library (Education), Saskatoon SK. 306-343-3793

Baldonado, Charles, *Librn,* El Paso Public Library (Lower Valley), El Paso TX. 915-543-2954

Baldridge, Alan, *Librn,* Stanford University, Hopkins Marine Station Library, Pacific Grove CA. 408-373-0464

Baldridge, Alan, *Librn,* Stanford University Libraries (Hopkins Marine Station), Pacific Grove CA. 408-373-0464

Baldridge, Sheila, *Librn,* Moss Landing Marine Laboratories of the California State University Library, Moss Landing CA. 408-633-3304

Baldwin, Alberta, *Per,* Southern Connecticut State College, Hilton C Buley Library, New Haven CT. 203-397-4505

Baldwin, Betsy, *Tech Serv,* Plattsburgh Public Library, Plattsburgh NY. 518-563-0921

Baldwin, C M, *Librn,* Tetra Tech, Inc Library, Pasadena CA. 213-449-6400

Baldwin, Dee, *Asst Librn,* University of Florida Libraries (Latin American Collection), Gainesville FL. 904-392-0359, 392-0360

Baldwin, Elmer, *Spec Servs,* Oregon State Library, Salem OR. 503-378-4243

Baldwin, Evelyn, *Pres,* Atlantic County Historical Society Library, Somers Point NJ. 609-927-5218

Baldwin, Jean D, *Dir,* Guilford Free Library, Guilford CT. 203-453-6561

Baldwin, Jerome C, *Librn,* Minnesota Department of Transportation Library, Saint Paul MN. 612-296-2385

Baldwin, Julie, *Doc,* University of Toledo, William S Carlson Library, Toledo OH. 419-537-2324

Baldwin, Mae, *Tech Serv,* Peru Public Library, Peru IN. 317-473-3069

Baldwin, Marilyn, *Tech Serv,* Midwestern Regional Library System, Kitchener ON. 519-576-5061

Baldwin, Mark, *Librn,* Raytheon Co, Submarine Signal Div, Technical Information Center, Portsmouth RI. 401-847-8000

Baldwin, Mary S, *Mgr,* Saint Regis Paper Co, Roy K Ferguson Technical Center Library, West Nyack NY. 914-624-3523

Baldwin, Mike, *Bus Mgr,* Fort Worth Public Library, Fort Worth TX. 817-870-7700

Baldwin, Nadine, *Ser,* University of British Columbia Library, Vancouver BC. 604-228-3871

Baldwin, Paula, *Librn,* Fitzwilliam Town Library, Fitzwilliam NH. 603-585-6503

Bale, Mrs H, *Librn,* Bibliotheque Municipale, Temiscaming PQ. 819-627-3273

Bale, William R, *Librn,* Parkland Regional Library, Lacombe AB. 403-782-3850
Bales, Miriam, *Acq,* Dayton & Montgomery County Public Library, Dayton OH. 513-224-1651
Bales, Mrs D A, *Librn,* Inland Cement Industries Ltd Library, Edmonton AB. 403-452-8290
Bales, Sydney, *Coordr,* Community Hospital at Glen Cove, Medical Library, Glen Cove NY. 516-676-5000, Ext 609
Balester, Vivian S, *Librn,* Squire, Sanders & Dempsey, Law Library, Cleveland OH. 216-696-9200
Balgach, Nancy T, *ILL,* Virginia Polytechnic Institute & State University Library, Blacksburg VA. 703-961-5593
Balge, Elizabeth S, *Dir,* Broward County Historical Commission Library, Fort Lauderdale FL. 305-765-5872
Balikos, Jeanne O, *Supvr,* Hughes Aircraft Co (Information Research), Culver City CA. 213-391-0711, Ext 3474
Balk, Arnold, *Soc Sci,* University of Georgia Libraries, Athens GA. 404-542-2716
Balkan, Harriett C, *Librn,* Little Silver Public Library, Little Silver NJ. 201-747-9649
Balkema, John B, *Librn,* National Council on the Aging, Inc Library, Washington DC. 202-223-6250
Balkema, Laurel, *ILL,* Grand Valley State Colleges, Zumberge Library, Allendale MI. 313-895-6611, Ext 252
Balko, Pat, *Cat,* University of Pittsburgh, Johnstown Campus Library, Johnstown PA. 814-266-9661, Ext 314
Ball, Alice Dulany, *Exec Dir,* Universal Serials & Book Exchange, Inc, (USBE), DC. 202-529-2555
Ball, Ardella Patricia, *Dir Asst Prof,* Armstrong State College, Library Media, GA. 912-927-5332
Ball, Barbara, *AV & Media,* Oakland Community College, Highland Lakes Campus Library, Union Lake MI. 313-363-7191, Ext 335
Ball, Betty Jo, *Chief Librn,* Illinois Valley Community College, Jacobs Memorial Library, Oglesby IL. 815-224-2720
Ball, Darlene L, *Mgr,* Burlington Industries Inc, Information Services Library, Greensboro NC. 919-379-2613
Ball, Gladys E, *Co Chairman,* Lantana Community Library, Lantana FL. 305-586-4320
Ball, Helen, *Rare Bks & Spec Coll,* Miami University, Edgar W King Library, Oxford OH. 513-529-2944
Ball, Howard G, *Dean & Prof,* Alabama Agricultural & Mechanical University, School of Library Media, AL. 205-859-7216 or 859-7238
Ball, J, *Librn,* University of Toronto Libraries (Scarborough College), Toronto ON. 416-284-3245
Ball, Jean, *Librn,* Northumberland Memorial Library, Lottsburg VA. 804-529-7363
Ball, John L, *Assts To Chief Librarian,* University of Toronto Libraries (University Library), Toronto ON. 416-978-2294
Ball, Joyce, *Pub Servs,* University of Nevada-Reno, Noble H Getchell Library, Reno NV. 702-784-6533
Ball, Martha L, *Pub Servs,* College of Charleston, Robert Scott Small Library, Charleston SC. 803-792-5530
Ball, Martha L, *Pub Servs,* College of Charleston, Robert Scott Small Library, Charleston SC. 803-792-5530
Ball, Michael, *Sci Tech & Docs,* Grand Rapids Public Library, Grand Rapids MI. 616-456-4400
Ball, Robert, *ILL,* University of Nevada, Las Vegas, James R Dickinson Library, Las Vegas NV. 702-739-3286
Ball, Susan C, *Librn,* Puget Sound Power & Light Co Library, Bellevue WA. 206-454-6363
Ballantyne, Jean, *Librn,* Listowel Public Library, Listowel ON. 519-291-4621
Ballard, Candace, *Librn,* Chicago Public Library (Eckhart Park), Chicago IL. 312-226-6069
Ballard, Debbie, *Librn,* Southwire Co, Research & Development Library, Carrollton GA. 404-832-4242, Ext 5080
Ballard, Jan, *YA,* Orlando Public Library, Orlando FL. 305-425-4694
Ballard, Jeannette E, *Librn,* INA Corp Library, Philadelphia PA. 215-241-4677

Ballard, Kathie, *Librn,* Williamsburg Community Library, Williamsburg IA. 319-668-1195
Ballard, Martha G, *Tech Serv, Acq & Circ,* Marion Public Library, Marion IN. 317-664-7363
Ballard, Mary R, *Dir,* Waldorf College Library, Forest City IA. 515-582-2450, Ext 274
Ballard, Natalie C, *Librn,* Lawrence Law Library, Lawrence MA. 617-687-7754
Ballard, Patricia, *Librn,* Garrard County Public Library, Lancaster KY. 606-792-3424
Ballard, Robert M, *Assoc Prof,* North Carolina Central University, School of Library Science, NC. 919-683-6485
Ballard, Tom, *Librn,* Chicago Public Library (Logan Square), Chicago IL. 312-235-5295
Ballard, Jr, Lockett Ford, *Dir,* Litchfield Historical Society, Ingraham Memorial Library, Litchfield CT. 203-567-5862
Ballas, Kathleen, *Asst Dir,* Herkimer County Community College Library, Herkimer NY. 315-866-0300, Ext 55
Ballasch, Sandra S, *Librn,* University of Iowa Libraries (Library Science), Iowa City IA. 319-353-3946
Ballenger, Mable, *Tech Serv,* Daniel Boone Regional Library, Columbia MO. 314-443-3161
Ballentine, Rebecca, *Librn,* University of North Carolina at Chapel Hill (Institute of Government), Chapel Hill NC. 919-933-1304
Ballew, James D, *Dir,* Athens State College Library, Athens AL. 205-232-1802, Ext 291
Balliet, Roger, *Pub Info Officer,* Pierce County Rural Library District, Tacoma WA. 206-572-6760
Ballinger, Barbara, *Dir,* Oak Park Public Library, Scoville Institute, Oak Park IL. 312-383-8200
Balliot, Robert L, *Dir,* University of Pittsburgh at Bradford Library, Bradford PA. 814-362-3801, Ext 126
Ballou, Helen, *Tech Serv,* West Nyack Free Library, West Nyack NY. 914-358-6081
Ballou, Patricia, *Spec Coll,* Columbia University (Barnard College), New York NY. 212-280-3846
Balluffi, Gloria, *Librn,* Kentucky Correctional Institution for Women Library, Pewee Valley KY. 502-241-8454, Ext 37
Balmer, Mary, *Tech Serv,* University of Connecticut Library, Storrs CT. 203-486-2219
Balog, Betty, *Ch,* Harris County Public Library, Houston TX. 713-221-5350
Balog, Linda, *Librn,* Fairfax Public Library, Fairfax IA. 319-846-2994
Balog, Rita J, *Librn,* Harbor Public Library, Ashtabula Harbor OH. 216-964-9645
Balogh, Joyce H, *Dir,* Rolling Hills Consolidated Library, Saint Joseph MO. 816-232-5479
Balok, Becki, *ILL,* Herrick Public Library, Holland MI. 616-392-3114
Balon, Brett, *Ad,* Southeast Regional Library, Weyburn SK. 306-842-4402, 842-3432
Balon, Brett, *Br Coordr,* Southeast Regional Library, Weyburn SK. 306-842-4402, 842-3432
Balon, Yolanda, *Acq,* Cary Memorial Library, Lexington MA. 617-862-6288
Balonis, Christine K, *Circ & Ref,* College of Physicians of Philadelphia Library, Philadelphia PA. 215-561-6050
Balsam, Frances G, *Librn,* Hampton Bays Public Library, Hampton Bays NY. 516-728-6241
Balshone, Cathy S, *Dir,* Boston Conservatory of Music, Albert Alphin Music Library, Boston MA. 617-536-6340, Ext 281
Baltes, Jack, *Dir, Info Serv & Publications,* International Foundation of Employee Benefit Plans, Information Center, Brookfield WI. 414-786-6700
Balthasar, Luiza, *RML Coordr,* New York Medical College, Westchester Medical Center Library, Valhalla NY. 914-347-5237
Baltis, Nancy, *Manager,* Syntex USA, Inc, Corporate Library-Information Services, Palo Alto CA. 415-855-5814
Baltuska, Josephine D, *Librn,* Wyandotte County Law Library, Kansas City KS. 913-573-2899, 342-4225
Balz, Elizabeth L, *Asst Dir,* Trinity Lutheran Seminary Library, Columbus OH. 614-236-7116
Balzer, Grace, *Librn,* International Nickel Co, Inc (Law Library), New York NY. 212-742-4141

Bamattre, Robert, *Ref & ILL,* Biola College & Talbot Theological Seminary, Rosemead Graduate School of Professional Psychology, Rose Memorial Library, La Mirada CA. 213-944-0351, Ext 3255
Bamba, Elizabeth, *Librn,* Jourdanton Community Library, Jourdanton TX. 512-769-3087
Bamber, Mary, *Tech Serv,* Cherry Hill Free Public Library, Cherry Hill NJ. 609-667-0300
Bamberger, Bethia, *Ref,* Bloomfield Township Public Library, Bloomfield Hills MI. 313-642-5800
Bambino, Josephine, *Librn,* Siskiyou County Public Library (McCloud Branch), McCloud CA. 916-964-2169
Bambrick, Jane, *On-Line Servs,* William Paterson College of New Jersey, Sarah Byrd Askew Library, Wayne NJ. 201-595-2113
Bana, Joseph J, *Dir,* Euclid Public Library, Euclid OH. 216-261-5300
Banach, Ann, *Acq,* University of Miami, Rosentiel School of Marine & Atmospheric Sciences, Miami FL. 305-350-7207
Banasch, Barb, *Media,* Medicine Hat College, Learning Resource Center, Medicine Hat AB. 403-527-7141, Ext 245
Banash, Maxine W, *Librn,* Historical Society of Palm Beach County Library, Palm Beach FL. 305-655-1492
Banaticla, Moises, *Cat,* Lima State Hospital, Forensic Psychiatric Library, Lima OH. 419-227-4631, Ext 224
Bancroft, Ann M, *Librn,* Museum of New Mexico (Museum of International Folk Art Library), Santa Fe NM. 505-827-2544
Band, Richard A, *Librn,* Lancaster County Library, Lancaster SC. 803-285-1502
Bandemer, June, *Asst Dir,* University of Pittsburgh (Maurice & Laura Falk Library of the Health Sciences), Pittsburgh PA. 412-624-2521
Bander, Edward J, *Librn,* Suffolk University College Library (Law), Boston MA. 617-723-4700, Ext 176
Bandilli, Janet, *Librn,* Attleboro Public Library (South Attleboro), South Attleboro MA. 617-761-6232
Bandura, Barbara, *Ref,* New City Free Library, New City NY. 914-634-4997
Bandurraga, Peter, *Librn,* Ventura County Historical Museum & Ventura County Library Services Agency, Ventura County Historical Museum Library, Ventura CA. 805-653-0323
Bandy, Charles, *Dir,* University of Colorado Health Sciences Center (Denison Memorial Library), Denver CO. 303-394-5125
Bandy, Margaret, *Librn,* Saint Joseph Health Science Library, Denver CO. 303-837-7188
Banek, Barbara Minne, *Librn,* Inland Steel Co, Research Library, East Chicago IN. 219-392-5824
Banghart, Peggy May, *Librn,* First Presbyterian Church Library, Ann Arbor MI. 313-662-4466
Bangsberg, Nadine, *Librn,* United States Navy (Coronado Library), San Diego CA. 714-437-2473
Banker, Esther B, *Librn,* Greenwich Library (Byram Shubert), Greenwich CT. 203-622-7950
Banker, Sanford J, *Ch,* Veterans Administration, Medical Center Learning Resources Center, Saint Cloud MN. 252-1670 Ext 270
Banker, Sharon, *Librn,* Memphis State University Libraries (Chemistry), Memphis TN. 901-454-2625
Banko, Carole, *Acq & Spec Coll,* John Jay College of Criminal Justice Library, New York NY. 212-489-5169
Banks, Acklen, *Librn,* Metropolitan Library System (Ralph Ellison), Oklahoma City OK. 405-235-0571
Banks, Barbara, *Librn,* Comfort Public Library, Trenton NC. 919-324-5061
Banks, Brenda, *Librn,* Edmonton Art Gallery Library, Edmonton AB. 403-429-6781
Banks, Doris, *Pub Servs,* Whitworth College, Harriet Cheney Cowles Memorial Library, Spokane WA. 509-466-3260
Banks, George S, *Librn,* Naropa Institute Library, Boulder CO. 303-444-0202
Banks, Grace, *Commun Servs, Br Coordr & Bkmobile Coordr,* Louisville Free Public Library, Louisville KY. 502-584-4154
Banks, Janet J, *Librn,* Casey County Public Library, Liberty KY. 606-787-9381

BANKS

Banks, LaVerne, *Libr Asst,* Rusk County Memorial Library (McMillan Memorial), Overton TX. 214-657-8557

Banks, Margaret, *Libr,* University of Western Ontario (Law Library), London ON. 519-679-2857

Banks, Mary E, *Cat,* Stark County District Library, Canton OH. 216-452-0665, Ext 31

Banks, Mary Ellen, *Libr,* Schlumberger-Dall Research Center Library, Ridgefield CT. 203-438-2631, Ext 325, 342

Banks, Nicolena, *Tech Serv,* Baraboo Public Library, Baraboo WI. 608-356-6166

Banks, Paul N, *Conservator & Head Conservation Dept,* Newberry Library, Chicago IL. 312-943-9090

Banks, S Leone, *Libr,* Saint Boniface General Hospital, School of Nursing Library, Winnipeg MB. 403-237-2955

Banks, Shirley, *Libr,* Lambton County Library (Petrolia Branch), Petrolia ON. 519-882-0771

Banner, Charla, *Pharmacy,* Butler University, Irwin Library, Indianapolis IN. 317-283-9225

Banner, Charla, *Libr,* Butler University (Science Library, Holcomb Research Institute), Indianapolis IN. 317-283-9401

Bannigan, Bernice G, *Ref,* Utica Public Library, Utica NY. 315-735-2279

Bannigan, Margaret Mary, *Acq,* Saint Paul Seminary, John Ireland Memorial Library, Saint Paul MN. 612-690-4355

Bansal, Arlene, *Libr,* Arizona State Regional Library for the Blind & Physically Handicapped, Phoenix AZ. 602-255-5578

Banser, Elaine, *Libr,* A Herr Smith & E E Smith Library, Loda Township Library, Loda IL. 217-386-2783

Banta, John J, *Chief Libr,* White & Case, Law Library, New York NY. 212-732-1040, Ext 365

Banta, Vickie, *Libr,* Knight-Ridder Newspaper Corp, Lexington Herald-Leader Co Library, Lexington KY. 606-254-6666, Ext 260

Bantner, Deanna, *Libr,* Assumption Public Library, Assumption IL. 217-226-3915

Banwart, Emmy, *Libr,* West Bend Public Library, West Bend IA. 515-887-6411

Baptista, Stuart F, *Acq,* Salt Lake City Public Library, Salt Lake City UT. 801-363-5733

Baptiste, Mary, *Libr,* Gloucester Lyceum & Sawyer Free Library (McPherson Park), Gloucester MA. 617-281-1118

Baptiste, Renate, *Acq,* Digital Equipment Corp, Corporate Library, Maynard MA. 617-493-6231, 493-5821

Baptiste, Syria, *Br Dist Supvr,* Oakland Public Library, Oakland CA. 415-273-3281

Baquet, Sheila, *Libr,* Shelton State Community College, Junior College Division, Tuscaloosa AL. 205-759-1583

Bar-Tzur, Judy, *Dir,* Western States Chiropractic College, W A Budden Library, Portland OR. 503-256-3180

Barad, Morton, *Libr,* Reid & Priest Library, New York NY. 212-344-2233

Barager, Wendy A, *Chief Libr,* Sentinel Star Newspaper Library, Orlando FL. 305-420-5510

Barajas, Eduardo, *Libr,* United States Penitentiary Library, Steilacoom WA. 206-588-5281

Baran, Charlotte, *Manager,* Pfizer Inc, Pharmaceuticals Library, New York NY. 212-573-2323

Baran, Walter, *Libr,* River Rouge Public Library, River Rouge MI. 313-843-2040

Barata, Ellen, *Personnel & Pub Relations,* Stamford's Public Library, Ferguson Library, Stamford CT. 203-325-4354

Baratta, Rosemarie, *Dir,* Island Park Public Library, Island Park NY. 516-432-0122

Barbalas, Louis X, *Libr,* Motor Vehicle Manufacturers Association of the United States, Inc (Engineering), Detroit MI. 313-872-4311, Ext 373

Barbare, Tom, *Media,* Cerro Coso Community College, Learning Resources Center, Ridgecrest CA. 714-375-5001, Ext 47

Barbarick, Jean, *Libr,* Knoxville-Knox County Public Library (Millertown), Knoxville TN. 615-522-7627

Barbarin, Erskine, *Libr,* New Orleans Public Library (Broadmoor), New Orleans LA. 504-822-4520

Barbash, Mrs B, *Libr,* Miami Heart Institute, Medical Library, Miami Beach FL. 305-672-1111, Ext 4133

Barber, Alice, *Libr,* Chicago Technical College Library, Chicago IL. 312-225-8200

Barber, Barbara, *Ref & Commun Servs,* Topeka Public Library, Topeka KS. 913-233-2040

Barber, Betty A, *Libr,* Ohio Bell Telephone Co, Public Relations & Film Library, Cleveland OH. 216-822-2740

Barber, Beverly, *Dir,* Saint Clair County Library, Pell City AL. 205-884-1685

Barber, Catherine, *Libr,* Missouri Historical Society Library, Saint Louis MO. 314-361-1424

Barber, Cheryl, *Acq,* Kalamazoo Public Library, Kalamazoo MI. 616-342-9837

Barber, Donna, *Media & Circ,* Governors State University, University Library, Park Forest South IL. 312-534-5000, Ext 2231

Barber, Doris, *Dir,* Middlesex County Hospital, Medical Library, Waltham MA. 617-894-4600

Barber, Eleanor, *Libr,* Cedar Springs Public Library, Cedar Springs MI. 616-696-1910

Barber, Elinore, *Dir,* Baldwin-Wallace College (Riemenschneider Bach Institute), Berea OH. 216-826-2207

Barber, Frank T, *Patent Counsel,* Greyhound Corp, Patent Law Dept Library, Scottsdale AZ. 602-991-3000, Ext 365

Barber, Gary, *Ref & Bibliog Instr,* State University of New York College, Daniel A Reed Library, Fredonia NY. 716-673-3183

Barber, Geraldine E, *Libr,* Orangeville Public Library, Orangeville ON. 519-941-0610

Barber, Marion W, *Libr,* Davisville Free Library, North Kingstown RI. 401-884-5524

Barber, Mary S, *Extramural Libr & Bibliog Instr,* University of Louisville Library (Kornhauser Health Sciences), Louisville KY. 502-588-5771

Barber, Paula L, *Design & Exhibits,* Dallas Public Library, Dallas TX. 214-748-9071

Barber, Peggy A, *Libr,* State Services Organization Library, Washington DC. 202-624-5483

Barber, Raymond, *Asst Prof,* Drexel University, School of Library & Information Science, PA. 215-895-2474

Barber, Raymond R, *Libr,* Corning Glass Works, Technical Information Center, Corning NY. 607-974-3258

Barber, Vivian, *Libr,* Gibson County Memorial Library, Trenton TN. 901-855-1991

Barberi, Jean D, *Libr,* Enoch Pratt Free Library (Brooklyn), Baltimore MD. 301-396-5430, 396-5395

Barbezat, Gloria, *YA,* Gail Borden Public Library District, Elgin IL. 312-742-2411

Barbosa, Mary Lee, *Libr,* Dallas Public Library (Skyline), Dallas TX. 214-381-1149

Barbour, Donna, *Libr,* North Memorial Medical Center, Medical Library, Minneapolis MN. 612-588-0616, Ext 431

Barbour, Harriet, *Head, Govt Servs,* Oklahoma Department of Libraries, Oklahoma City OK. 405-521-2502

Barbour, Wendell A, *Reader Serv,* Georgia Southern College Library, Statesboro GA. 912-681-5115

Barbre, Betty, *Libr,* Union Carbide Corp Library, Paducah KY. 502-444-6311, Ext 438

Barclay, Betty, *Dir,* Takoma Park Maryland Library, Takoma Park MD. 301-270-1717

Barclay, Dot, *Ch & YA,* Palos Verdes Library District, Palos Verdes Peninsula CA. 213-541-2559, 2550

Barclay, Elizabeth, *Libr,* Forbes Health System, East Suburban Health Center Library, Monroeville PA. 412-273-2422

Barclay, Julius, *Rare Bks,* University of Virginia, Alderman Library, Charlottesville VA. 804-924-3026

Barclay, Mrs Powell, *Supvr,* Middlesex County Library (Mount Brydges Branch), Mount Brydges ON. 519-264-1061

Barclay, Susan, *Dir,* Durham College of Applied Arts & Technology Library, Oshawa ON. 416-576-0210, Ext 214

Bard, Harriet E, *Dir,* Wayne Township Library, Morrisson-Reeves Library, Richmond IN. 317-966-8291

Bard, Therese B, *Asst Prof,* University of Hawaii, Graduate School of Library Studies, HI. 808-948-7321

Bardolph, Anne D, *Cat & Spec Coll,* Florida State University (Law Library), Tallahassee FL. 904-644-1004

Bardot, Maja, *Ref,* Rhode Island School of Design Library, Providence RI. 401-331-3507, Ext 229

Bardsley, Sylvia, *Ch,* Oregon City Library, Oregon City OR. 503-655-8398, 655-8399

Bardwell, John D, *Media,* University of New Hampshire, Ezekiel W Dimond Library, Durham NH. 603-862-1540

Barefield, Margaret S, *Libr,* Gulf Coast Community College Library, Panama City FL. 904-769-1551, Ext 294

Barefoot, Gary Fenton, *Dir & Spec Coll,* Mount Olive College, Moye Library, Mount Olive NC. 919-658-2502, 658-2503, Ext 25, 26

Barefoot, Jan, *Outreach,* Sampson-Clinton Public Library, Clinton NC. 919-592-4153

Barela, Gloria, *Ref,* Colorado Mountain College-West Campus, Learning Center, Glenwood Springs CO. 303-945-7481, Ext 66

Bareno, Laura, *Outreach Coordr,* San Diego County Library, San Diego CA. 714-565-5100

Barensfeld, Thomas, *Head Libr,* Cleveland Press Editorial Library, Cleveland OH. 216-623-6741

Baretski, Charles, *Libr,* Newark Public Library (Van Buren), Newark NJ. 201-733-7750

Barette, Pierre, *Asst Prof,* Southern Illinois University at Carbondale, Educational Media Program, IL. 618-453-5764

Barfell, Louise, *Libr,* Columbia-Lafayette-Ouachita-Calhoun Regional Library (Calhoun County), Hampton AR. 501-234-1991

Barfield, Carolyn, *ILL,* Cumberland County Public Library, Anderson Street Library, Frances Brooks Stein Memorial Library, Fayetteville NC. 919-483-1580

Barfield, Harvey, *Media,* Arlington Heights Memorial Library, Arlington Heights IL. 312-392-0100

Barfield, Isaac R, *Dir,* Howard University Libraries (Allen Mercer Daniel Law Library), Washington DC. 202-686-6684

Barfield, Mrs J K, *Libr,* Fort Sumner Public Library, Fort Sumner NM. 505-355-2832

Barge, Silvey W, *In Charge,* Hanson Engineers, Inc, Technical Library, Springfield IL. 217-788-2450

Barham, Mary, *Asst Dir,* San Jacinto College, Lee Davis Library, Pasadena TX. 713-476-1850, 476-1501, Ext 241

Barhydt, Gordon, *Chief Libr,* North York Public Library, Willowdale ON. 416-494-6838

Barie, Dennis, *Dir,* Archives of American Art, Midwest Area Center, Detroit MI. 313-226-7544

Baril, Bonnie, *Dir,* Gunnison County Library, Gunnison CO. 303-641-3485

Baringer, Jeanine, *Dir,* Van Horn Public Library, Pine Island Public Library, Pine Island MN. 507-356-8558

Barkalow, Pat, *Syst Coordr,* University of Tennessee, Knoxville, James D Hoskins Library, Knoxville TN. 615-974-0111

Barkdull, Margery K, *Map Libr,* National Geographic Society Map Library, Gaithersburg MD. 202-857-7000, Ext 1401

Barker, Betsy, *Libr,* Gemological Institute of America, Research Library, Santa Monica CA. 213-829-2991

Barker, Dale L, *Assoc Dir,* University of Miami, Otto G Richter Library, Coral Gables FL. 305-284-3551

Barker, Diane, *Media,* West Texas Library System, Lubbock TX. 806-762-5442

Barker, Ernest C, *Internal Auditor,* Library of Congress, Washington DC. 202-287-5000

Barker, Fletcher, *Cat,* Woodbury University Library, Los Angeles CA. 482-8491, Ext 25

Barker, Grace, *Libr,* Bremer Pond Memorial Library, Pittsburg NH. 603-538-6653

Barker, Grace, *Libr,* Victoria County Public Library (Bobcaygeon Branch), Bobcaygeon ON. 705-738-2088

Barker, Judith, *Libr,* Arnprior Public Library, Arnprior ON. 613-623-2279

Barker, Lauren, *ILL,* University of South Florida (Medical Center Library), Tampa FL. 813-974-2399

Barker, Lillian, *Libr,* Prince George's County Memorial Library System (Laurel Branch), Laurel MD. 301-776-6790

Barker, Lytton T, *Tech Serv & Cat,* Guilford Technical Institute, Learning Resource Center, Jamestown NC. 919-292-1101, 454-1126

Barker, M, *Tech Serv,* Napa City - County Library, Napa CA. 707-253-4241

Barker, Marilyn, *Librn,* Knoxville-Knox County Public Library (West Haven), Knoxville TN. 615-522-1915

Barker, Marjorie, *Br Coordr & Bkmobile Coordr,* Okanagan Regional Library District, Kelowna BC. 604-860-4033

Barker, Mrs Dale, *Librn,* South Haven Township Library, South Haven KS. 316-892-5891

Barker, Mrs E T, *Librn,* Hemphill County Library, Canadian TX. 806-323-5282

Barker, Ray, *Librn,* Coastal Plain Regional Library (Tifton-Tift County Branch), Tifton GA. 912-382-2448

Barker, Ray S, *Asst Dir,* Coastal Plain Regional Library, Tifton GA. 912-386-3400

Barker, Richard T, *Librn,* Appalachian State University, Carol Grotnes Belk Library, Boone NC. 704-262-2186

Barker, Robin, *Consult Libr Develop,* Nevada State Library, Carson City NV. 702-885-5130

Barker, S E, *Librn,* Ministry of Forests Library, Victoria BC. 604-387-5985

Barker, III, John S, *Librn,* Farmville Public Library, Farmville NC. 919-753-3355

Barkey, Patrick T, *Dir,* Claremont Colleges Libraries, Claremont CA. 714-621-8000, Ext 3721

Barkholz, Gerald, *Asst Prof,* University of South Florida, Graduate Department of Library, Media & Information Studies, FL. 813-974-2557

Barkley, Bruce, *Aux Serv,* Champaign Public Library & Information Center, Champaign IL. 217-356-7243

Barkley, Marlene, *Librn,* Daniel, Mann, Johnson & Mendenhall Library, Los Angeles CA. 213-381-3663, Ext 126, 127

Barkley, William, *Tech Serv & Cat,* Kalamazoo Public Library, Kalamazoo MI. 616-342-9837

Barkman, Gladys, *Librn,* Steinbach Public Library, Steinbach MB. 204-326-6841

Barkman, John D, *Dir,* Blinn College, W L Moody Jr Library, Brenham TX. 713-836-6566

Barks, Margaret, *Children's Div,* Indianapolis-Marion County Public Library, Indianapolis IN. 317-635-5662

Barksdale, Eleanor, *Ch,* Simsbury Public Library, Simsbury CT. 203-658-5382

Barksdale, Kenneth, *Acq,* Eastern Kentucky University, John Grant Crabbe Library, Richmond KY. 606-622-3606

Barlas, Julie Sandall, *Librn,* Harvard University Library (Blue Hill Meteorological Observatory Library), Cambridge MA. 617-495-2836

Barlas, Julie Sandall, *Librn,* Harvard University Library (Gordon McKay Library), Cambridge MA. 617-495-2836

Barloga, Carolyn, *Asst Librn,* Saint Francis Hospital, Health Science Learning Center, Milwaukee WI. 414-647-5156

Barlow, B, *Doc,* University of Saskatchewan Library, Saskatoon SK. 306-343-4216

Barlow, E Garrett, *In Charge,* Genealogical Society, Church of Jesus Christ of Latter-Day Saints, Los Angeles Branch Genealogical Library, Los Angeles CA. 213-272-8726

Barlow, Edward V, *Librn,* Rhode Island State Law Library, Providence RI. 401-277-3275

Barlow, Jane, *Librn,* Wentworth Library (Mount Albion), Stoney Creek ON. 416-526-4126

Barlow, Jr, George W, *Chief Librn,* McGraw-Hill, Inc (Corporate Library), New York NY. 212-997-1221

Barlup, Judy E, *Circ,* University of Washington Libraries, Seattle WA. 206-543-1760

Barmann, Edgar, *In Charge,* Catholic Universe Bulletin Library, Cleveland OH. 216-696-6525

Barnabei, Betty, *Pre School Coord,* Mary H Weir Public Library, Weirton WV. 304-748-7070

Barnard, Cindy, *Ch,* Saint Charles City County Library, Saint Peters MO. 314-441-2300

Barnard, Delores, *Librn,* North Dakota Historical Society, Research & Reference Div Library, Bismarck ND. 701-224-2668

Barnard, Janie, *Ref,* Monterey Bay Area Cooperative Library System, Salinas CA. 408-758-9818

Barnard, Mellissa, *Bkmobile Coordr,* Lansing Public Library, Lansing MI. 517-374-4600

Barnard, Richard E, *Library Supv,* United States Department of Defense (Defense Mapping Agency Aerospace Center, Technical Library), Saint Louis MO. 314-263-4267

Barnard, Roy, *Ser,* Kearney State College, Calvin T Ryan Library, Kearney NE. 308-236-4218

Barnard, Ruth, *Librn,* Andrews Carnegie Library, Andrews NC. 704-321-5956

Barndt, Laura T, *Librn & Media,* Columbus Developmental Center, Grove School Library, Columbus OH. 614-272-0509

Barner, Barry, *Librn,* Canada Department of the Environment, Maritimes Forest Research Centre Library, Fredericton NB. 506-452-3541

Barnes, Brenda, *Librn,* Driscoll Foundation Children's Hospital Library, Corpus Christi TX. 512-854-5341

Barnes, Brooks M, *Asst Dir,* Eastern Shore Public Library, Accomac VA. 804-787-3400

Barnes, Bruce, *Spec Coll,* State Library of Massachusetts, Boston MA. 617-727-2590

Barnes, Carol G, *Asst Dir,* Granby Public Library, Granby CT. 203-653-2800

Barnes, Caroline, *Circ,* Black Hawk College, Learning Resource Center, Moline IL. 309-796-1311, Ext 344

Barnes, Christopher R, *Librn,* Keene State College, Wallace E Mason Library, Keene NH. 603-352-1909, Ext 266

Barnes, Dee Dee, *Dir,* Bud Werner Memorial Library, Steamboat Springs CO. 303-879-0240

Barnes, Doris, *Dir, Acq & Cat,* Arkansas State University, Beebe Branch, Abington Memorial Library, Beebe AR. 501-882-3393, Ext 33

Barnes, Edna, *Librn,* Stevens County Library, Hugoton KS. 316-544-2301

Barnes, Elizabeth, *Librn,* Saxtons River Public Library, Saxtons River VT. 802-869-2312

Barnes, Elizabeth Ann, *Librn,* Blanche K Werner Public Library, Trinity TX. 713-594-2087

Barnes, Eugene B, *Acq,* University of Oregon Library, Eugene OR. 503-686-3056

Barnes, Jean, *Ch,* Saint Albans Free Library, Saint Albans VT. 802-524-3804

Barnes, Jean, *Tech Serv & Cat,* South Charleston Public Library, South Charleston WV. 304-744-6561

Barnes, Katie, *Librn,* Wilson County Public Library (East), Wilson NC. 919-237-2627

Barnes, Kenneth S, *Dir,* Hicksville Public Library, Hicksville NY. 516-931-1417

Barnes, Laura Mae, *Librn,* Tulsa City-County Library (Page Memorial), Sand Springs OK. 918-245-4595

Barnes, Leonard, *Librn,* Florida State University (Nursing), Tallahassee FL. 904-644-1291

Barnes, Marjorie, *Librn,* Tipton Public Library, Tipton IA. 319-886-6266

Barnes, Martha, *Ch,* Westchester Library System, Hartsdale NY. 914-761-7620

Barnes, Mattie L, *Librn,* Acacia Mutual Life Insurance Co Library, Washington DC. 202-628-4506, Ext 536

Barnes, Muriel, *Ref,* Benton & Bowles Inc Library, New York NY. 212-758-6200, Ext 3156

Barnes, Myrna, *Librn,* Collier County Free Public Library (Immokalee Branch), Immokalee FL. 813-262-4130, 261-8208

Barnes, Nell, *Ref,* Norfolk State University, Lyman Beecher Brooks Library, Norfolk VA. 804-623-8873

Barnes, Pamela, *Librn,* West Linn Public Library, West Linn OR. 503-656-7853

Barnes, Robert, *Fine Arts,* Tampa-Hillsborough County Public Library System, Tampa FL. 813-223-8947

Barnes, Robert F, *Div Head,* Lehigh University, Div of Computing & Information Science, PA. 215-861-3000

Barnes, Ruth, *Technician,* Textron Inc, Dalmo Victor Co Technical Library, Belmont CA. 415-595-1414

Barnes, S Helen, *Teacher-Librn,* Wisconsin Department of Health & Social Services, Northern Wisconsin Center for the Developmentally Disabled, Chippewa Falls WI. 715-723-5542

Barnes, Shaleen, *Bibliog Instr,* Wheaton College Library, Norton MA. 617-285-7722, Ext 518

Barnes, Suzanne O, *Librn,* Hoechst Fibers Industry, Technical Information Center, Spartanburg SC. 803-579-5750

Barnes, Versie, *Librn,* Chicago Public Library (Wendell Smith), Chicago IL. 312-995-1700

Barnett, Ann, *Ch,* Chattahoochee Valley Regional Library, W C Bradley Memorial Library, Headquarters, Columbus GA. 404-327-0211

Barnett, Bernice, *Librn,* Assumption Seminary Library, San Antonio TX. 512-734-5137

Barnett, Doris, *Librn,* Ottawa Public Library (West), Ottawa ON. 613-236-0301, Ext 273

Barnett, Dorothy, *Librn,* Kansas State University (Architecture & Design), Manhattan KS. 913-532-5968

Barnett, Florence, *Humanities,* Warner Southern College, Learning Resource Center, Lake Wales FL. 813-638-1426, Ext 28

Barnett, Helen, *Dir,* Delaware Technical & Community College Library, Newark DE. 302-368-6985

Barnett, Helen K, *Librn,* Delaware Technical & Community College, Wilmington Campus Learning Resources Center, Wilmington DE. 302-571-2113

Barnett, Janie, *Librn,* Cass County Public Library (Peculiar Branch), Peculiar MO. 816-758-5412

Barnett, Juanita M, *Librn, On-Line Servs & Bibliog Instr,* Ouachita Baptist University, Riley Library, Arkadelphia AR. 501-246-4531, Ext 121

Barnett, Judith B, *Asst Librn,* University of Rhode Island, Graduate School of Oceanography, Pell Marine Science Library, Narragansett RI. 401-792-6161

Barnett, Marilyn, *ILL,* University of Kansas Medical Center, College of Health Sciences & Hospital, Clendening Library, Kansas City KS. 913-588-7166

Barnett, Mrs Douglas, *Dir,* Morganton-Burke Library, Inc, Morganton NC. 704-437-5638

Barnett, Nancy, *Acq,* Tom Green County Library System, San Angelo TX. 915-655-7321

Barnett, Noda, *In Charge,* Howard County Library (Wilde Lake), Ellicott City MD. 301-997-8000

Barnett, Noda, *In Charge,* Howard County Library (Wilde Lake), Savage MD. 301-997-8000

Barnett, Sally, *Ref,* Juniata College, L A Beeghly & O R Myers Science Library, Huntingdon PA. 814-643-4310, Ext 57

Barnett, Stanley, *Librn,* First Baptist Church Library, Booneville MS. 601-728-6272

Barnett, Virginia, *Asst Dir,* Scarsdale Public Library, Scarsdale NY. 914-723-2005

Barnett, Jr, William, *Librn,* Saint Petersburg Beach Public Library, Saint Petersburg Beach FL. 813-360-0438

Barnette, Susan, *Librn,* Mcdowell County Public Library (Old Fort Branch), Old Fort NC. 704-668-7111

Barney, Alan, *Admin Serv,* Center for Research Libraries, Chicago IL. 312-955-4545

Barney, Frances J, *Librn,* United States Forest Service, Rocky Mountain Forest & Range Experiment Station Library, Fort Collins CO. 303-221-4390

Barney, Janet, *Spec Coll,* Central Bible College Library, Springfield MO. 417-833-2551, Ext 37

Barnhard, Neil K, *Pub Servs,* University of Arkansas for Medical Sciences Library, Little Rock AR. 501-661-5980

Barnhill, Roy L, *Librn,* Cape Fear Technical Institute, Library Learning Resource Center, Wilmington NC. 919-343-0481, Ext 230

Barnhouse, M, *Librn,* Jean Bailey Memorial Library, Burnaby BC. 604-437-4511

Barnow, Erik, *Chief, Motion Picture Broadcasting & Recorded Sound Div,* Library of Congress, Washington DC. 202-287-5000

Barnstable, Mildred, *Librn,* Nokomis Public Library, Nokomis IL. 217-563-2734

Barnthouse, Dorothy, *Librn,* Baldwin City Library, Baldwin City KS. 913-594-3411

Barnum, Betty, *Asst Dir,* Largo Library, Largo FL. 813-584-8671, Ext 281, 282

Barnum, Sally J, *Librn,* United Way of Metropolitan Chicago Library, Chicago IL. 312-263-1756

Baron, Anita E, *Librn,* Westport Free Public Library, Westport MA. 617-636-4317

Baron, Emma, *Ch,* Pawtucket Public Library & Regional Library Center, Deborah Cook Sayles Memorial Library, Pawtucket RI. 401-725-3714

Baron, James, *Librn,* Brooklyn Public Library (Eastern Parkway), Brooklyn NY. 212-756-5150

Baron, Krystyna, *Librn,* Polish Institute of Arts & Sciences in America Library, New York NY. 212-988-4338

Baron, Lorraine, *Librn,* Ionics Inc Research Dept Library, Watertown MA. 617-926-2500

Baron, Thelma, *Tech Serv,* Long Beach Public Library, Long Beach NY. 516-432-7201

Barone, Jean, *Ch,* Hoyt Library, Kingston PA. 717-287-2013

Barone, Kristine M, *Dir,* Somerset County Library System, Princess Anne MD. 301-651-0852

Barone, Rita, *Dir,* Metropolitan Life Insurance Co (Law Library), New York NY. 212-578-3111

Baroni, L, *Br Coordr,* North Castle Public Library, Armonk NY. 914-273-3887

Baroski, Margaret, *Music,* Free Library of Springfield Township, Philadelphia PA. 215-836-5300

Baroski, Margaret A, *Dir,* Free Library of Springfield Township, Philadelphia PA. 215-836-5300

Barr, Daniel J, *ILL,* Buffalo & Erie County Public Library System, Buffalo NY. 716-856-7525

Barr, Larry T, *Asst Librn & Acq,* Blue Island Public Library, Blue Island IL. 312-388-1078

Barr, Marion, *Librn,* Tillamook County Public Library (Bay City Branch), Bay City OR. 503-377-2288

Barr, Mary, *Dir & Acq,* Butler County Community College Library, Butler PA. 412-287-8711, Ext 198

Barr, Mary, *Pub Servs,* University of California Library, San Francisco CA. 415-666-2334

Barr, Michael B, *Librn,* Bureau of Indian Affairs, Village of Gambell Library, Gambell AK. 907-746-8001

Barr, Pamela K, *Librn,* Suffolk Cooperative Library System (Reading for the Handicapped), Bellport NY. 516-286-1600

Barr, Robert S, *Dir,* Greater Philadelphia Chamber of Commerce Library, Philadelphia PA. 215-568-4040

Barr, Sarah, *ILL,* Miami University, Edgar W King Library, Oxford OH. 513-529-2944

Barr, William E, *Acq,* Eastern Washington University, John F Kennedy Memorial Library, Cheney WA. 509-359-2261

Barra, Carol H, *Librn,* Breed, Abbott & Morgan Library, New York NY. 212-888-0800

Barraclough, A, *Asst Librn,* Nesbitt Thomson & Co Ltd Library, Montreal PQ. 514-844-0131, Ext 375, 372

Barras, Marian T, *ILL,* Saint Martin Parish Library, Saint Martinville LA. 318-394-4086

Barratt, Mrs Toby, *Librn,* Pakenham Township Library, Pakenham ON. 613-624-5430

Barravecchia, Mary N, *Head Libr Section,* United States Navy, Newport RI. 401-841-4338

Barre, Andree, *Tech Serv,* Bibliotheque De La Ville De Montreal, Montreal PQ. 514-872-5923

Barrecchia, Joyce, *Librn,* Supreme Court, Third Judicial District Law Library, Kingston NY. 914-339-5680, Ext 210

Barresi, Patricia, *YA,* New Rochelle Public Library, New Rochelle NY. 914-632-7878

Barrett, Amy, *ILL,* La Grange Public Library, La Grange IL. 312-352-0576, Ext 6

Barrett, Arline R, *Librn,* Eastman Kodak Co (Photographic Technology Library), Rochester NY. 716-722-2341

Barrett, Barbara, *Librn,* Escanaba Carnegie Public Library, Escanaba MI. 906-786-4463

Barrett, Buckley, *Dir,* Marymount Palos Verdes College Library, Rancho Palos Verdes CA. 213-377-5501, Ext 29

Barrett, Carol A, *Librn,* Bell Helicopter Textron Technical Library, Fort Worth TX. 817-280-3608

Barrett, Donald J, *Asst Dir, Pub Serv,* United States Air Force Academy Library, United States Air Force Academy CO. 303-472-2590

Barrett, Donna, *Asst Dir,* Huntsville-Madison County Public Library, Huntsville AL. 205-536-0021

Barrett, Dorothy, *In Charge,* United Daughters of the Confederacy, Caroline Meriwether Goodlett Library, Richmond VA. 804-355-1636

Barrett, Elizabeth, *Librn,* TRW Equipment Library, Cleveland OH. 216-383-3417

Barrett, Elizabeth, *Spec Coll,* Whittier College School of Law Library, Los Angeles CA. 213-938-3621, Ext 24

Barrett, Eva, *Librn,* Sutton Public Library, Sutton WV. 304-765-7224

Barrett, Evelyn, *Librn,* Union County Public Library (College Corner Branch), College Corner IN. 317-458-5355

Barrett, Fawna, *Librn,* Randall City Library, Randall KS. 913-739-2380

Barrett, Gertrude, *Ch,* Saint John Regional Library, Saint John NB. 506-693-1191

Barrett, Jaia, *Doc,* Duke University, William R Perkins Library, Durham NC. 684-2034 (Main).

Barrett, Jane, *Librn,* Canadian Institute of International Affairs Library, Toronto ON. 416-979-1851

Barrett, John T, *Librn,* Boston Public Library (Charlestown Branch), Charlestown MA. 617-242-1248

Barrett, Judy, *Librn,* Sullivan County Public Library (Moody Memorial), Kingsport TN. 615-349-7651

Barrett, Laura, *Media,* College of Medicine & Dentistry of New Jersey, George F Smith Library of the Health Sciences, Newark NJ. 201-456-4580

Barrett, Lee, *Ref & Bibliog Instr,* Shelby State Community College Library, Memphis TN. 901-528-6743

Barrett, M Elva, *Librn,* Clearfield County Public Library Federation (Curwensville Branch), Curwensville PA. 814-236-0355

Barrett, Margaret, *Ch,* Free Public Library of Woodbridge, Woodbridge NJ. 201-634-4450

Barrett, Patsy, *Librn,* Stair Public Library, Morenci MI. 517-458-6510

Barreva, N, *Asst Librn,* Santa Rosa Medical Center, Health Science Library, San Antonio TX. 512-228-2284

Barrick, Susan O, *Librn,* Virginia Institute of Marine Science Library, Gloucester Point VA. 804-642-2111, Ext 119

Barrie, John, *Media,* Long Island University, Brooklyn Center Libraries, Brooklyn NY. 212-834-6060, 834-6064

Barrier, Catherine, *Ref,* Cypress College Library, Cypress CA. 714-826-2220, Ext 124, 125

Barringer, George, *Spec Coll,* Georgetown University, Joseph Mark Lauinger Library, Washington DC. 202-625-4095

Barringer, Judith, *Librn,* Lincoln Library (North), Springfield IL. 217-753-4970

Barringer, Judith, *Librn,* Lincoln Library (South), Springfield IL. 217-753-4980

Barrios, Richard, *Media,* Wharton County Junior College, J M Hodges Learning Center, Wharton TX. 713-532-4560, Ext 36

Barrioswahdan, Josephine, *County Librn,* San Benito County Free Library, Hollister CA. 408-637-2013

Barron, Barbara J, *Chief Librn,* Veterans Administration Medical Center, Medical Library, Salt Lake City UT. 801-582-1565

Barron, Edwina T, *Librn,* Preformed Line Products Co, Research & Engineering Library, Cleveland OH. 216-461-5200, Ext 345

Barron, Helen, *Arts,* Indianapolis-Marion County Public Library, Indianapolis IN. 317-635-5662

Barron, J L, *Librn,* Bowaters Newfoundland Limited, Technical Service Library, Corner Brook NF. 709-634-5151

Barron, Joan W, *Dir,* Harbridge House Library, Boston MA. 617-267-6410, Ext 447

Barron, Kay, *Media,* Eastern Ontario Library System, Ottawa ON. 613-238-8457

Barron, Margaret, *Librn,* Cuyahoga Community College (Metropolitan Campus Library), Cleveland OH. 216-241-5966, Ext 217

Barron, Robert E, *Assocs,* New York State Library, Albany NY. 518-474-5930

Barron, Shirley, *Asst Dir,* Kelley Library, Salem Public Library, Salem NH. 603-898-7064

Barron-Rios, Maria, *Ref,* Pinal County Library System, Florence AZ. 602-868-5801, Ext 456

Barroner, Marion A, *Librn,* Hollidaysburg Free Public Library, Hollidaysburg PA. 814-695-5961

Barrow, Cynthia, *Asst Dir,* Del Norte Public Library, Del Norte CO. 657-2633

Barrow, John, *Librn,* American Academy of Dramatic Arts Library, New York NY. 212-686-9244, Ext 39

Barrow, Mary, *Librn,* Petro-Tex Chemical Corp, Research Library, Houston TX. 713-477-9211

Barrow, Sarilou, *Librn,* Orange County Law Library, Orlando FL. 305-420-3240

Barrow, Scott, *Bkmobile Coordr,* Dartmouth Public Libraries, Southworth Library, South Dartmouth MA. 617-997-1252

Barrows, Eleanor, *Ref,* University of Washington Libraries (Law Library), Seattle WA. 206-543-4089

Barrows, Richards, *Librn,* United States Department of the Navy, Alexandria VA. 202-694-3299

Barrows, William, *Librn,* United States Court of Appeals, Ninth Circuit Library, Seattle WA. 206-442-4475

Barry, Carol, *Ref,* Central State University Library, Edmond OK. 405-341-2980, Ext 494, 495 & 496

Barry, Carol, *Ref,* On-Line Servs & Bibliog Instr, Elmhurst College, A C Buehler Library, Elmhurst IL. 312-279-4100, Ext 255

Barry, Carol, *Librn,* Scotland Public Library, Scotland CT. 203-423-0925

Barry, Colette, *Dir,* Bibliotheque Des Archives Nationales Du Quebec, Quebec PQ. 418-643-2167

Barry, Gloria, *Librn,* Hennepin County Library (Oxboro), Bloomington MN. 612-888-3369

Barry, Gloria, *Librn,* Hennepin County Library (Penn Lake), Bloomington MN. 612-884-3667

Barry, J Kevin, *Media & Acq,* York College Library, Jamaica NY. 212-969-4026

Barry, James P, *Dir,* Martha Kinney Cooper Ohioana Library Association, Columbus OH. 614-466-3831

Barry, Kevin, *Librn,* Princeton University Library (Industrial Relations), Princeton NJ. 609-452-3180

Barry, Leigh, *Br Coordr,* Douglas County Library System, Roseburg OR. 503-673-1111, Ext 310

Barry, Lois, *Ref,* Douglas County Library System, Roseburg OR. 503-673-1111, Ext 310

Barry, Louise C, *Librn,* United States Army (US Army Armor Center Library System), Fort Knox KY. 502-624-1232

Barry, Richard, *Librn,* Manhattan College (Engineering), Bronx NY. 212-548-1000, Ext 275

Barry, Richard, *Ref,* Manhattan College, Cardinal Hayes Library, Bronx NY. 212-548-1400, Ext 366 & 367

Barry, Roger, *Media,* Iowa Western Community College, Hoover Media Library, Council Bluffs IA. 712-325-3247

Barry, Rose, *Tech Serv,* Mundelein College, Learning Resource Center, Chicago IL. 312-262-8100, Ext 301, 302 & 303

Barsch, Terttu M, *Tech Serv & Cat,* Winter Park Public Library, Winter Park FL. 305-647-1638

Barsi, Carol, *Asst Librn,* San Diego Society of Natural History Library, San Diego CA. 714-232-3821

Barsnmyan, Silva, *Dir,* Union City Free Public Library, Union City NJ. 201-866-7500

Barson, Norman, *Supvr,* Celanese Research Co, Technical Information Center, Summit NJ. 201-273-6600, Ext 515

Bart, Hans, *Librn,* Arizona State Museum Library, Tucson AZ. 602-626-4695

Barta, Shirley, *Dir,* Antigo Public Library, Antigo WI. 715-623-3631

Bartel, Bernice, *Librn,* Kansas State University (Physics), Manhattan KS. 913-532-6827

Bartels, Eileen K, *Librn,* United States Fish & Wildlife Service, Northern Prairie Wildlife Research Center Library, Jamestown ND. 701-252-5363

Barten, Pauline, *Media,* Hammond Public Library, Hammond IN. 219-931-5100

Barth, Barbara, *Librn,* San Diego Public Library (Tierra Santa), San Diego CA. 714-268-3284

Barth, Joseph M, *Coll Dev,* United States Military Academy Library, West Point NY. 914-938-2230

Barth, Paul, *Dir Libr Serv,* Bellevue Hospital Center, Clarence E de la Chapelle Medical Library, New York NY. 212-561-6535, 561-6536

Barthe, Margaret, *Ref & On-Line Servs,* Florida Southern College, Roux Library, Lakeland FL. 813-683-5521, Ext 211

Barthelette, Carl A, *Cat,* Ontario Public Library, Ontario CA. 984-2758 Ext 38

Bartholomew, Gail, *Asst Dir,* Maui Community College, Learning Resource Center, Kahului HI. 808-242-5433, 242-5498

Bartholomew, Jean, *Librn,* Bement Public Library, Saint Johns MI. 517-224-4702

Bartko, Yvonne, *In Charge,* Hawaii State Library System (Materials Evaluation & Programming), Honolulu HI. 808-732-7769

Bartkovich, Jeff, *Dir,* New River Community College, Learning Resource Center, Dublin VA. 703-674-4121, Ext 303

Bartkowiak, Dale, *AV & YA,* McMillan Memorial Library, Wisconsin Rapids WI. 715-423-1040

Bartleson, Carol, *Cat & Circ,* Fanwood Memorial Library, Fanwood NJ. 201-322-6400

Bartlett, Alan, *Acq,* Allegheny College, Lawrence Lee Pelletier Library, Meadville PA. 814-724-3363

Bartlett, Choice, *Librn,* Brook-Iroquois Township Public Library, Brook IN. 219-275-2471

Bartlett, Danny, *Tech Serv & Cat,* Kingsport Public Library, J Fred Johnson Memorial Library, Kingsport TN. 615-245-3141

Bartlett, Debbie, *Librn,* Sweetwater County Library (Bairoil Branch), Bairoil WY. 307-875-3615

Bartlett, Dorma, *Tech Serv,* University of Wisconsin-Green Bay, Library Learning Center, Green Bay WI. 414-465-2382

Bartlett, E, *On-Line Servs & Bibliog Instr,* Bell Canada (Information Resource Centre), Montreal PQ. 514-870-8922

Bartlett, Eleanor A, *Hist, Travel & Geog,* Public Library of the District of Columbia, Martin Luther King Memorial Library, Washington DC. 202-727-1101

Bartlett, Eudora F, *Librn,* Public Library of Catasauqua, Catasauqua PA. 215-264-4151

Bartlett, Judith, *Curric Mats Ctr Librn,* York College Library, Jamaica NY. 212-969-4026

Bartlett, Kathleen, *Circ,* City-County Library of Missoula, Missoula MT. 406-728-5900

Bartlett, Lynda S, *Librn,* Missouri Research Laboratories, Southwest Library, Albuquerque NM. 505-243-6772

Bartlett, Nancy, *Per,* Montreat-Anderson College, L Nelson Bell Library, Montreat NC. 704-669-2382

Bartlett, Opal, *Librn,* Simon Schwob Medical Library, Columbus GA. 404-324-4711, Ext 6516-7

Bartlett, Phyllis, *Librn,* Bradley Beach Public Library, Bradley Beach NJ. 201-775-2175

Bartlett, Shirley, *Librn,* Saranac Public Library, Saranac MI. 616-642-9146

Bartley, Audra, *Librn,* Umatilla County Library (Stanfield Branch), Stanfield OR. 503-276-1881

Bartley, Barbara G, *Assoc Prof,* University of Wisconsin-Milwaukee, School of Library Science, WI. 414-963-4707

Bartley, David, *Tech Serv,* Lubbock City-County Library, Lubbock TX. 806-762-6411, Ext 2828

Bartley, Patricia, *In Charge,* Malcolm X College Library, Chicago IL. 312-942-3237

Bartlow, Anne, *ILL, On-Line Servs & Bibliog Instr,* Iowa Wesleyan College, Chadwick Library, Mount Pleasant IA. 319-385-8021, Ext 131

Bartman, Marie, *Librn,* Congregation Agudas Achim, Bernard Rubinstein Library, San Antonio TX. 512-736-4216

Bartolini, R Paul, *Dir,* Knoxville-Knox County Public Library, Lawson McGhee Library, Knoxville TN. 615-523-0781

Bartolo, Laura M, *Librn,* Phillips, Lytle, Hitchcock, Blaine & Huber Library, Buffalo NY. 716-847-7086

Barton, Barbara, *Librn,* Bank of California Library, San Francisco CA. 415-765-2116

Barton, Betty, *Librn,* Glidden Public Library, Glidden IA. 712-659-2781

Barton, Christine, *Librn,* Fentress County Public Library, Jamestown TN. 615-879-7512

Barton, David, *Exten,* Arrowhead Library System, Virginia MN. 218-741-3840

Barton, Edith G, *Librn,* Drayton Valley Public Library, Drayton Valley AB. 403-542-5327

Barton, Erigid S, *Dir,* De Saisset Art Gallery & Museum Library, Santa Clara CA. 408-984-4528

Barton, Gary, *Commun Servs,* Albany Dougherty Public Library, Albany GA. 912-435-2104

Barton, J A, *Ref,* British Columbia Government, Legislative Library, Victoria BC. 604-387-6500

Barton, Janet E, *Librn,* Miami Christian College Library, Miami FL. 305-685-7431

Barton, Kimberly, *Media,* Frederick County Public Library, Frederick MD. 301-694-1613

Barton, Mrs J Floyd, *Curator,* Kent Historical Society Library, Kent CT. 203-927-3761

Barton, Phillip K, *Dir,* Rowan Public Library, Salisbury NC. 704-633-5578

Barton, Richard, *Bus & Finance,* Detroit Public Library, Detroit Associated Libraries, Detroit MI. 313-833-1000

Barton, Richard, *Asst Dir,* North Dakota State University Library, Fargo ND. 701-237-8876

Barton, Virginia L, *Assoc Dir,* Timberland Regional Library, Olympia WA. 206-943-5001

Bartos, Mary, *AV,* Notre Dame College, Clara Fritzsche Library, Cleveland OH. 216-381-1680, Ext 59

Bartosh, Edith, *Dir,* River Falls Public Library, River Falls WI. 715-425-2180

Bartosh, Eloise, *Asst Librn,* Mercy Hospital, Medical Library, Scranton PA. 717-344-8571

Bartosh, John, *Lectr,* Marywood College, Dept of Librarianship, PA. 717-342-6521

Bartow, Barbara, *Cat,* University of Delaware, Hugh M Morris Library, Newark DE. 302-738-2231

Bartow, Berneice E, *Librn,* Ridley Park Public Library, Ridley Park PA. 215-583-7207

Bartsch, Robert, *Librn,* Louisville Free Public Library (Frost), Louisville KY. 502-933-3002

Bartshron, Bob, *Pub Servs,* Mesa Community College Library, Mesa AZ. 602-833-1261, Ext 291, 201

Bartucca, Peter J, *Librn,* Burke & Burke, Law Library, New York NY. 212-489-0400

Bartusiewicz, Pamela, *Asst Dir,* Glenwood-Lynwood Public Library District, Glenwood IL. 312-758-0090

Bartz, Pauline, *Librn,* Hardtner Public Library, Hardtner KS. 316-296-4677

Bartzis, Ethel, *Librn,* Pike Library Association, Haverhill NH. 603-989-5806

Barulich, Olivia, *Librn,* Kern County Library (Buttonwillow), Bakersfield CA. 805-861-2130

Barus, Sister M Celinette, *Asst Librn,* Villa Maria College of Buffalo Library, Buffalo NY. 716-896-0703

Barwick, Irene, *ILL,* New Berlin Public Library, New Berlin WI. 414-786-2990

Basar, Dorothy, *Librn,* Beaver County Times, Editorial Department Library, Beaver PA. 412-775-3200

Basarab, Violet, *Librn,* High Prairie Municipal Library, High Prairie AB. 403-523-3838

Basdekas, Sylvia, *Librn,* Suburban Hospital, Medical Library, Bethesda MD. 301-530-3100

Baselmagel, Dorothea, *Librn,* Garden Center of Rochester, Inc Library, Rochester NY. 716-473-5130

Basigkow, Mary L, *Dir,* Orion Township Public Library, Lake Orion MI. 313-603-1888

Basil, Evelyn, *Media,* North Baltimore Public Library, North Baltimore OH. 419-257-2196

Basile, Anne J, *Librn,* Epworth United Methodist Church Library, Toledo OH. 419-531-4236

Basile, Victor, *Tech Serv,* College of Medicine & Dentistry of New Jersey, George F Smith Library of the Health Sciences, Newark NJ. 201-456-4580

Basinger, Annie Belle, *Circ,* Charles A Cannon Memorial Library, Concord NC. 704-788-3167

Basiuk, Emil, *Dentistry,* Loyola University of Chicago Libraries (Medical Center), Maywood IL. 312-531-3192

Baskett, Adeline T, *Dir,* Cleveland State Community College Library, Cleveland TN. 615-472-7141, Ext 278

Baskett, Mrs G E, *Chief Librn,* Mary Cotton Public Library, Sabetha KS. 913-284-3160

Baskin, Bernard, *Librn,* International Harvester Co, Corporate Communications, Chicago IL. 312-836-2000

Baskin, Claribel, *ILL,* Miami Dade Community College (North Campus Library), Miami FL. 305-685-4436

Baskin, Jeff, *AV,* University of Arkansas for Medical Sciences Library, Little Rock AR. 501-661-5980

Baskin, Pat, *Librn,* Congregation B'nai Israel, Isidore Bloch Memorial Library, Albuquerque NM. 505-266-0155

Basler, Annette, *Admin Asst,* McMillan Memorial Library, Wisconsin Rapids WI. 715-423-1040

Basler, Beatrice K, *Coll Develop,* Medical College of Georgia Library, Augusta GA. 404-828-3441

Basler, Ellen, *Librn,* Athol Murray College of Notre Dame, Lane Hall Memorial Library, Wilcox SK. 306-732-2080, Ext 29

Basler, Thomas G, *Dir,* Medical College of Georgia Library, Augusta GA. 404-828-3441

Bass, Dave, *Bus Mgr,* Los Angeles Public Library System, Los Angeles CA. 213-626-7555

Bass, Donna R, *Dir,* John A Gupton College Memorial Library, Nashville TN. 615-327-3927

Bass, Geraldine, *Librn,* Johnson County Library (Spring Hill Branch), Spring Hill KS. 913-686-2304

Bass, Harold L, *Dept Head,* Union University, Library Certification Program, TN. 901-668-1818, Ext 269

Bass, Harold L, *Dir,* Union University, Emma Waters Summar Library, Jackson TN. 901-668-1818, Ext 269

Bass, Kathy, *Tech Serv,* Oklahoma Department of Libraries, Oklahoma City OK. 405-521-2502

Bass, Mary Ellen, *ILL Librn,* CTUW Project, CT. 203-436-1972

Bass, Mary Ellen, *ILL,* Yale University Library (Sterling Memorial Library), New Haven CT. 203-436-8335

Bass, Muriel, *Fine Arts,* Fairfield Public Library, Fairfield CT. 203-259-8303

Bass, Sarah, *Librn,* Baltimore City Department of Planning Library, Baltimore MD. 301-396-5920

Bass, III, David, *On-Line Servs,* Dauphin County Library System, Harrisburg PA. 234-4961

Bassange, Hector, *Dir,* McLean Hospital, Medical Library, Belmont MA. 617-855-2460

Bassen, Irmgard, *Chief, Pub Servs,* Orange County Public Library, Orange CA. 714-634-7645

Bassett, Annette, *Admin Asst,* Suffolk Cooperative Library System, Bellport NY. 516-286-1600

Bassett, Betty A, *Mgt,* Xerox Research Centre of Canada, Technical Information Centre, Mississauga ON. 416-828-6200, Ext 256

Bassett, Beverly, *Tech Serv,* Washington Bible College-Capital Bible Seminary, Oyer Memorial Library, Lanham MD. 301-552-1400, Ext 232

Bassett, Clancy, *Ser,* Santa Monica College Library, Santa Monica CA. 213-450-5150

Bassett, Irene, *Ch,* La Grange Public Library, La Grange IL. 312-352-0576, Ext 6

Bassett, Nell, *ILL,* Troy State University Library, Troy AL. 205-566-3000, Ext 263

Bassett, Pegeen, *Doc,* Suburban Library System, Burr Ridge IL. 312-325-6640

Bassett, Richard V, *Bkmobile Coordr,* Shiawassee County Library, Corunna MI. 517-743-3421, Ext 278

Bassett, Robert J, *Ref,* University of Tennessee, Knoxville, James D Hoskins Library, Knoxville TN. 615-974-0111

Bassett, Ruth, *Librn,* Brandywine Conservancy, Inc, Brandywine River Museum Library & Study Center, Chadds Ford PA. 215-388-7601, Ext 17

Bassett, Wayne R, *Dir,* Marathon County Public Library, Wausau WI. 715-845-7214, Ext 21

Bassett, Wayne R, *Dir,* Wisconsin Valley Library Service, System Headquarters, Wausau WI. 715-845-7214, Ext 35, 49, 50 & 51

Bassist, Norma, *Librn,* Bassist College Library, Portland OR. 503-228-6528

Bassnett, Peter J, *Dir,* Scarborough Public Library, Scarborough ON. 416-291-1991

Bast, Sarah Jeanne, *Dir,* Batavia Public Library District, Batavia IL. 312-879-1393

Bastedo, Nellie, *Biol & Optometry,* University of Waterloo Library, Waterloo ON. 519-885-1211

Bastedo, Russell, *Dir,* Long Island Historical Society Library, Brooklyn NY. 212-624-0890

Bastien, Carol, *Acq,* Southwestern Baptist Theological Seminary, Fleming Library, Fort Worth TX. 817-923-1921, Ext 277

Bastin, Pat J, *Librn,* Lexington Public Library (Eastland), Lexington KY. 606-254-0344

Bastow, E, *Cat,* Rockville Public Library, George Maxwell Memorial Library, Vernon CT. 203-875-5892

Batchelder, Bob, *Maps,* University of Calgary Library, Calgary AB. 403-284-5954

Batchelder, Virginia, *Librn,* Pembroke Town Library, Pembroke NH. 603-485-7851

Batchelor, Dianne S, *Librn,* McCormick County Library, McCormick SC. 803-465-2821

Batchelor, Lorraine, *Asst Librn,* Tri-County Community College Library, Murphy NC. 704-837-6810

Batchelor, Mrs R L, *Librn,* Thomas Public Library (Byron Public), Byron GA. 912-825-8540
Bate, Jane E, *Dir,* Blanchester Public Library, Blanchester OH. 513-783-3585
Bate, Mary, *Librn,* Victoria County Public Library (Cameron Branch), Cameron ON. 705-324-3104
Bateman, Audray, *Spec Coll,* Austin Public Library, Austin TX. 512-472-5433
Bateman, Brenda J, *Ref & ILL,* Lynchburg College, Knight Memorial & Capron Libraries, Lynchburg VA. 804-845-9071, Ext 271
Bateman, Mary Ruth, *Librn,* Union Carbide Corp, Corporate Research Laboratory Library, Tuxedo Park NY. 914-351-2131, Ext 213
Bateman, Mrs Douglas, *Dir,* Lowndes County Library System, Columbus Public Library, Columbus MS. 601-328-1056
Bateman, Patti, *Librn,* Aurora Public Library (Municipal Reference), Aurora CO. 303-755-4880
Bateman, S, *Librn,* Calgary Public Library (Alexander Calhoun), Calgary AB. 403-244-7686
Bater, Richard E, *Media,* Stockton State College Library, Pomona NJ. 609-652-1776, Ext 343
Bates, Agnes C, *Librn,* Gloucester Public Library, Gloucester VA. 804-693-2998
Bates, Alyce, *Ref,* Huron Public Library, Huron SD. 605-352-3778
Bates, Charles, *Coord Syst Servs,* Fond Du Lac City-County Library Service, Fond du Lac WI. 414-921-3670
Bates, Charles, *Syst Coordr,* Fond du Lac County, Mid-Wisconsin Federated Library System, Fond du Lac WI. 414-921-3670
Bates, Darlene, *Agr Doc,* West Hills Community College Library, Coalinga CA. 209-935-0801, Ext 47
Bates, David W, *Dir,* North Adams Public Library, North Adams MA. 413-662-2545, 663-3317
Bates, Evelyn, *Acq,* Cambria County Library System, Johnstown PA. 814-536-5131
Bates, Iain, *Asst Dir,* Acadia University, Harold Campbell Vaughan Memorial Library, Wolfville NS. 902-542-2201, Ext 215
Bates, Jim, *Librn,* Florida Junior College at Jacksonville (North Campus Learning Resources Center), Jacksonville FL. 904-757-6311
Bates, Jo, *Librn,* Union Public Library, Union IA. 515-486-5561
Bates, Karla, *ILL, Ch & On-Line Servs,* Muskegon County Library, Muskegon MI. 616-724-6248
Bates, Kathleen K, *ILL,* Baltimore County Public Library, Towson MD. 301-296-8500
Bates, Klair, *Dir,* Otsego District Public Library, Otsego MI. 616-694-9690
Bates, Lounsbury D, *Librn,* Harvard Club of New York City Library, New York NY. 212-682-4600
Bates, Mabell, *Spec Coll,* Bridgewater State College, Clement C Maxwell Library, Bridgewater MA. 617-697-8321, Ext 441, 442
Bates, Marcia, *Assoc Prof,* University of Washington, School of Librarianship, WA. 206-543-1794
Bates, Marilyn Dee, *Librn,* Mississippi State Board of Health (Health Science Library), Jackson MS. 601-354-6614
Bates, Mary, *Chief Librn,* Blue Mountain Community College Library, Pendleton OR. 503-276-1260, Ext 234
Bates, Muriel S, *Spec Coll,* San Antonio College Library, San Antonio TX. 512-734-7311, Ext 2480
Bates, Nancy E, *Dir Libr Operations,* Fairfax County Public Library, Administrative Offices, Springfield VA. 703-321-9810
Bates, Patricia, *Librn,* Alexandria Library (Talking Book Department), Alexandria VA. 703-750-6357
Bates, Peta, *Librn,* Law Society of Saskatchewan Libraries (Saskatoon), Regina SK. 306-569-8020
Bates, Tom, *ILL,* University of Houston (Clear Lake City), Houston TX. 713-488-9280
Bates, Jr, Henry E, *Dir,* Milwaukee County Federated Library System, Milwaukee WI. 414-278-3210
Bates, Jr, Henry E, *City Librn,* Milwaukee Public Library, Milwaukee WI. 414-278-3000
Bateson, Janet, *Ch,* Corona Public Library, Corona CA. 714-736-2381

Batey, Deborah, *Librn,* United States Navy (Medical Library), Camp Pendleton CA. 714-725-1322
Batey, Emily, *Actg Dir & Commun Servs,* West Florida Regional Library, Pensacola Public Library, Pensacola FL. 904-438-5479
Batey, Marion, *Librn,* Mason County Public Library (New Haven Public), New Haven WV. 304-675-2913
Batey, Mary E, *Librn,* Veterans Administration (Medical Center Patients' Library), Ann Arbor MI. 313-769-7100, Ext 620
Bathalon, Real, *In Charge,* Bibliotheque Interculturel Monchanin, Monchanin Cross-Cultural Library, Montreal PQ. 514-288-7229
Bathurst, Gary, *Bus Mgr,* Pierce County Rural Library District, Tacoma WA. 206-572-6760
Batjiaka, John, *Media,* City of Cerritos Public Library, Cerritos CA. 213-924-5775
Batlaglia, Terri, *Electronic Learning Dir,* Louisiana Tech University, Prescott Memorial Library, Ruston LA. 318-257-2577
Batliner, Doris J, *Chief Librn,* Courier-Journal & Louisville Times Co, Inc Library, Louisville KY. 502-582-4184
Batsel, John David, *Dir,* Graduate Theological Union Library, Berkeley CA. 415-841-9811
Batsel, John David, *Librn,* Graduate Theological Union Library (San Anselmo Branch), Berkeley CA. 415-841-9811
Batson, Darrel, *Librn,* Clark County Library District (Outreach Services), Las Vegas NV. 702-733-7810
Batson, Rebecca, *Circ,* Virginia Union University, William J Clarke Library, Richmond VA. 804-359-9331, Ext 256, 257
Batson, Sue, *Libr Tech Program,* Spokane Falls Community College, Library Media Services, Spokane WA. 509-456-2860
Batt, Fred, *On-Line Servs,* Mansfield State College Library, Mansfield PA. 717-662-4071
Batt, Richard, *Dean,* Washington University, School of Continuing Education, Librarianship Program, MO. 314-889-6700
Batten, Helen, *Librn,* Lambton County Library (Arkona Branch), Arkona ON. 519-828-3406
Batten, Marian, *Librn,* Webb Sadle Memorial Library, Pleasantville IA. 515-848-5617
Batten, Peggy Young, *Dir,* Martinsburg-Berkeley County Public Library, Martinsburg Service Center, Martinsburg WV. 304-267-8933
Batterman, Rene, *Librn,* Temple Emanuel Library, Cherry Hill NJ. 609-665-0669
Battillo, Kathryn, *Syst Coordr,* Plymouth Public Library, Russell Memorial Library, Plymouth MA. 617-746-1927
Battin, Patricia, *V-Pres & Univ Librn,* Columbia University (University Libraries), New York NY. 212-280-2241
Battipaglia, Nicholas S, *Math, Sci & Engineering,* United States Military Academy Library, West Point NY. 914-938-2230
Battis, Cynthia J, *ILL,* Public Library of Brookline, Brookline MA. 617-734-0100
Battison, Sara, *On-Line Servs,* Yale University Library (Medical Library), New Haven CT. 203-436-4784, 436-2961
Battisti, Josephine, *Librn,* University of Wyoming (Geology), Laramie WY. 307-766-3374
Battle, Bettie, *Ch,* Kershaw County Library, Camden SC. 803-432-5183
Battle, Constance G, *Dir,* Oak Ridge Public Library, Oak Ridge TN. 615-483-6386
Battle, Theresa, *Asst Librn, Tech Serv & Cat,* Utica Junior College, William H Holtzclaw Library, Utica MS. 601-885-6062, Ext 48
Battles, Elizabeth, *Bkmobile Coordr,* Westborough Public Library, Westborough MA. 617-366-2812
Battles, Helen, *Circ,* Caldwell College Library, Caldwell NJ. 201-228-4424, Ext 34
Battles, Janet, *Reader Serv,* James Blackstone Memorial Library, Branford CT. 203-488-1441
Batton, Delma H, *Dir,* Dover Public Library, Dover DE. 302-734-4419, 734-9711
Batton, Nancy S, *Librn,* Harriette Person Memorial Library, Port Gibson MS. 601-437-5202
Battram, John V, *Media,* University of Wisconsin-Whitewater, Library & Learning Resources, Whitewater WI. 414-472-1000
Batty, C David, *Lectr,* University of Maryland, College of Library & Information Services, MD. 301-454-5441

Batty, Carol, *Ch,* Champaign Public Library & Information Center, Champaign IL. 217-356-7243
Batty, Dolores, *Librn,* Oglesby Public Library, Oglesby IL. 815-883-3619
Baty, Roger M, *Dir,* University of Redlands, George & Verda Armacost Library, Redlands CA. 714-793-2121, Ext 472
Batz, Christeen, *Librn,* Adams County Public Library (Brighton), North Glenn CO. 303-659-2572
Baucom, Charles V, *Dir,* York College, Levitt Library, York NE. 402-362-4441, Ext 244
Baucom, Charles V, *Tech Serv,* York College, Levitt Library, York NE. 402-362-4441, Ext 244
Bauder, Ellen, *ILL,* Allentown College of Saint Francis De Sales Library, Center Valley PA. 215-282-1100, Ext 266
Bauder, Jean, *Tech Serv,* Allentown Public Library, Allentown PA. 215-820-2400
Bauer, Alice, *Cat,* University of Virginia, Alderman Library, Charlottesville VA. 804-924-3026
Bauer, Charles K, *Lectr,* Atlanta University, School of Library & Information Studies, GA. 404-681-0251, Ext 312
Bauer, Charles K, *Mgr,* Lockheed-Georgia Company, Technical Information Dept Library, Marietta GA. 404-424-2928
Bauer, David J, *Vice Pres for Admin & Finance,* New York Public Library, Astor, Lenox & Tilden Foundations Library, New York NY. 212-790-6262
Bauer, George R, *Pub Servs,* University of Wisconsin-Green Bay, Library Learning Center, Green Bay WI. 414-465-2382
Bauer, Helen T, *Librn,* Gillespie Public Library, Gillespie IL. 217-839-3614
Bauer, Jo Ann, *Ch,* Eureka-Humboldt County Library, Eureka CA. 707-445-7284, 445-7513
Bauer, Louise, *Dir,* Waunakee Public Library, Waunakee WI. 608-849-4217
Bauer, Margaret D, *Dir,* Juniata County Library, Mifflintown PA. 717-436-6378
Bauer, Marjorie, *In Charge,* Monticello Library, Monticello MN. 612-295-2322
Bauer, Marsha, *Interlibr Coop Consult,* Kaskaskia Library System, Smithton IL. 618-235-4220
Bauer, Nancy, *Librn,* Science Associates International, Inc Library, New York NY. 212-265-4995
Bauer, Patricia M, *Dir,* Patten College of the Bible Library, Oakland CA. 415-533-8300, Ext 21
Bauer, Peggy, *Ch,* Sioux Falls Public Library, Sioux Falls SD. 605-339-7081
Bauer, Roger, *Cat,* Capital Library Cooperative, Mason MI. 517-676-9511
Bauer, Roger, *Cat,* Ingham County Library, Library Service Center, Mason MI. 517-676-9088
Bauer, Rose Marie, *Clerk,* Mid-Columbia Regional Library (Connell Branch), Connell WA. 509-234-4971
Bauer, Virginia, *Acq,* University of Wisconsin Center, Washington County Library, West Bend WI. 414-338-8753, Ext 60
Bauer, Jr, Frederick E, *Assoc Librn,* American Antiquarian Society Library, Worcester MA. 617-755-5221
Bauerle, Evelyn C, *Dir,* Pottstown Public Library, Pottstown PA. 215-326-2532
Baugh, Joanne D, *Head Librn,* Pennsylvania State University, Fayette Campus Library, Uniontown PA. 412-437-2801
Baugh, Marguerite, *Librn,* Taylor County Public Library, Grafton WV. 304-265-5015
Baugh, Nita, *Program Coordr,* Calloway County Public Library, Murray KY. 502-753-2288
Baugh, Polly, *Librn,* Arlington Public Library (Southwest), Arlington TX. 817-277-5265
Baughan, III, Charles A, *Support Servs,* Johns Hopkins University Libraries (Milton S Eisenhower Library), Baltimore MD. 301-338-8325
Baugher, Philip, *Dir,* Westchester Public Library, Thomas Memorial Library, Chesterton IN. 219-926-7696, Ext 7697 & 7698
Baughman, James C, *Assoc Prof,* Simmons College, Graduate School of Library & Information Science, MA. 617-738-2225
Baughman, Kathryn L, *Bus Mgr,* Conococheague District Library System, Chambersburg PA. 717-263-1054

Baughman, Steve, *Tech Serv,* Middle Georgia College, Roberts Memorial Library, Cochran GA. 912-934-6221, Ext 274

Baughman, Susan, *Librn,* Boston University Libraries (Educational Resources Library), Boston MA. 617-353-3734

Baule, Edith, *Acq,* Schools of Theology in Dubuque Library, Dubuque IA. 319-589-3100, 556-8151

Baum, Audrey, *Librn,* Kirkwood Public Library, Kirkwood MO. 314-821-5770

Baum, Christina, *Librn,* Maysville Community College Library, Maysville KY. 606-759-7141, Ext 28

Baum, Ingeborg R, *Librn,* Scottish Rite Supreme Council Library, Washington DC. 202-232-3579, Ext 39

Baum, Joel, *Ad & Ref,* Ohio County Public Library, Wheeling WV. 304-232-0244

Baum, L, *Librn,* Oakland Public Library (Montclair), Oakland CA. 415-339-9505

Baum, Marsha, *Asst Librn,* Center for Governmental Research, Inc Library, Rochester NY. 716-325-6360, Ext 38

Baum, Mary, *Librn,* Cleveland Museum of Natural History, Harold T Clark Library, Cleveland OH. 216-231-4600, Ext 22

Bauman, Alice, *Tech Serv,* College of Great Falls Library, Great Falls MT. 406-761-8210, Ext 280

Bauman, Jean M, *Dir,* Glen Rock Public Library, Glen Rock PA. 717-235-1127

Bauman, Mabel M, *Librn,* Allison Public Library, Allison IA. 319-267-2562

Bauman, Robert, *Instructional Servs,* Hamline University, Bush Memorial Library, Saint Paul MN. 612-641-2373

Baumann, Anne, *Asst Dir,* Cote Saint-Luc Public Library, Cote Saint-Luc PQ. 514-481-5676

Baumann, Charles H, *Dir,* Eastern Washington University, John F Kennedy Memorial Library, Cheney WA. 509-359-2261

Baumann, Ellen, *Librn,* Memorial Library of Little Valley, Little Valley NY. 716-938-6301

Baumann, Jane, *Cat,* Hoyt Library, Kingston PA. 717-287-2013

Baumer, Mary, *Librn,* Mercy Hospital of Johnstown, Medical Library, Johnstown PA. 814-536-4461, Ext 394

Baumgardner, Cathie, *Acq,* Northern Illinois University, College Law Library, Glen Ellyn IL. 312-858-7200

Baumgardner, Margie, *Librn,* East Ridge City Library, East Ridge TN. 615-867-7717

Baumgardner, Sandra, *Tech Serv, Acq & Cat,* Stonewall Jackson Regional Library, Buckhannon WV. 304-472-5475, 472-5581

Baumgartner, Robert W, *Govt Publications,* Northwestern University Library, Evanston IL. 312-492-7658

Baumruk, Robert, *Chief,* Chicago Public Library (Social Sciences & History Div), Chicago IL. 312-269-2830

Baumwart, Kathleen E, *Dir, Acq & Cat,* New Mexico State University at Alamogordo Library, Learning Resource Center, Alamogordo NM. 505-437-6864

Bauner, Ruth, *Librn,* Southern Illinois University at Carbondale (Education-Psychology), Carbondale IL. 618-453-2274

Baur, Estar, *Dir,* Laney College Library-Learning Resources Center, Oakland CA. 415-763-4791

Baur, Joyce E, *Dir,* Jenkintown Library, Abington Library Society, Jenkintown PA. 215-884-0593

Baurer, Joan, *Librn,* American Hospital Supply Corporation, Dade Division, Miami FL. 305-633-6461, Ext 357

Baurgoin, Jeanette, *Librn,* Saint Boniface College Library Centre, Saint Boniface MB. 233-0210 & 237-6671

Bausch, Ronald L, *Dir,* Garfield County Public Library, New Castle CO. 303-984-2346

Bausom, Nancy R, *Ch,* Glenside Public Library District, Glendale Heights IL. 618-858-0840

Baussman, Patricia, *Tech Serv,* Meadville Library Art & Historical Association, Meadville PA. 814-336-1773

Baut, Maria, *Librn,* Fife Lake Public Library, Fife Lake MI. 616-879-4101

Bautista, Deborah, *Asst Librn,* New Mexico State University, Grants Branch Library, Grants NM. 505-287-7981, Ext 14

Bautz, Karen, *Librn,* Prince George's County Memorial Library System (Bowie Branch), Bowie MD. 301-262-7000

Bauyes, Roy, *Per,* University of Toledo, William S Carlson Library, Toledo OH. 419-537-2324

Baxter, Ann, *Dir,* College of Medicine & Dentistry of New Jersey, Spritzer Memorial Library, Green Brook NJ. 201-968-6000, Ext 240

Baxter, Anne, *Per,* Reformed Theological Seminary Library, Jackson MS. 601-922-4988, Ext 52

Baxter, Barbara, *Tech Serv,* San Bernardino Public Library, San Bernardino CA. 714-889-0264

Baxter, Charlene Adams, *Cat & Bibliog Instr,* La Grange College, William & Evelyn Banks Library, La Grange GA. 404-882-2911, Ext 34

Baxter, Deborah, *Librn,* Orono Public Library, Orono ME. 207-866-2226

Baxter, Ellen, *Librn,* University of Kentucky (Chemistry/Physics), Lexington KY. 606-258-5954

Baxter, Jill, *Tech Serv,* Clark County Library District, Las Vegas NV. 702-733-7810

Baxter, Kathleen, *Ch,* Anoka County Library, Blaine MN. 612-784-1100

Baxter, Mary, *Acq,* Ventura County Library Services Agency, Ventura County Library, Ventura CA. 805-654-2627

Baxter, Mary, *Chmn,* West Georgia College, Library Media Program, GA. 404-834-1325

Baxter, Nancy, *Librn,* Windwood Presbyterian Church Library, Cypress TX. 713-376-2017

Baxter, Pat, *Librn,* Alberta Hospital Association Library, Edmonton AB. 403-423-1776

Baxtresser, Betty, *Chief Librn,* Bureau of the Census Library, Suitland MD. 301-763-5040, 763-5042

Bay, Steven, *Sci,* University of Bridgeport, Magnus Wahlstrom Library, Bridgeport CT. 203-576-4740

Bayard, Mary Ivy, *Librn,* Temple University of the Commonwealth System of Higher Education (Tyler School of Fine Arts), Eklins Park PA. 215-224-7575, Ext 246

Bayel, R, *Librn,* Loyalist College, Anderson Resource Centre, Belleville ON. 613-962-9501, Ext 249

Bayer, Arlyne, *Asst Librn,* Soho Center for Visual Artists Library, New York NY. 212-226-1993

Bayer, Bernard, *In Charge,* Ohio State University Libraries (Mechanized Information Center), Columbus OH. 614-422-3480

Bayer, Bernard, *Mech Info Serv,* Ohio State University Libraries (William Oxley Thompson Memorial Library), Columbus OH. 614-422-6151

Bayer, Brunhilde, *Tech Serv,* College Misericordia Library, Dallas PA. 717-675-2181, Ext 225

Bayer, Sister Carolyn Ann, *Asst Dir,* Seward County Community College, Learning Resource Center, Liberal KS. 316-624-1951

Bayer, Susan, *Cat,* Prairie State College, Learning Center, Chicago Heights IL. 312-756-3110, Ext 113

Bayhi, Jo Ann, *Librn,* Livingston Parish Library (Denham Springs Branch), Denham Springs LA. 504-665-8118

Bayle, Stephen, *Asst Dir & Commun Servs,* Watertown Free Public Library, Watertown MA. 617-924-5390

Bayles, Alice H, *Dir,* Dover Free Library, East Dover VT. 802-348-7951

Bayles, Carmen L, *Dir,* Hutchinson Community Junior College, John F Kennedy Library & Learning Resources Center, Hutchinson KS. 316-663-5781, Ext 125

Bayles, Florence, *Ad,* Euclid Public Library, Euclid OH. 216-261-5300

Bayles, Mark, *ILL,* Fontana Regional Library, Bryson City NC. 704-488-2382

Bayles, Mark S, *Librn,* Marianna Black Library, Bryson City NC. 704-488-3030

Bayless, Donna, *Commun Servs,* South Bend Public Library, South Bend IN. 219-288-4413

Bayless, June E, *Dir,* Whittier Public Library, Whittier CA. 213-698-8949

Bayless, Lyn, *Asst Librn,* Columbia State Community College, John W Finney Memorial Library, Columbia TN. 615-388-0120, Ext 234

Bayliss, Mrs Leland, *Librn,* Warren County Library (Oxford Public Library), Oxford NJ. 201-475-5361, Ext 114

Bayne, Eva, *Librn,* Dell Publishing Co, Inc Library, New York NY. 212-832-7300, Ext 460, 461

Bayne, Pauline Shaw, *Librn,* University of Tennessee, Knoxville (Music), Knoxville TN. 615-974-3474

Bayorgeon, Mary M, *Librn & On-Line Servs,* Saint Elizabeth Hospital, Health Science Library, Appleton WI. 414-731-5261, Ext 375

Bayrak, Bettie, *Librn,* Grande Prairie Regional College Library, Grande Prairie AB. 403-532-8830, Ext 302

Bays, Diane, *Chief Librn,* Canadian Department of Regional Economic Expansion Library, Ottawa ON. 819-997-6074

Bayus, Lenore W, *Pub Rel Dir,* Carnegie Library of Pittsburgh, Pittsburgh PA. 412-622-3100

Baza, Rosalia, *Librn,* Guam Public Library (Barrigada), Agana, Guam PI. 472-8507

Bazie, Lorna, *Librn,* Brooklyn Public Library (Brower Park), Brooklyn NY. 212-778-6262

Bazillion, Mrs H, *Librn,* Sault Sainte Marie Public Library (East), Sault Sainte Marie ON. 705-949-8553

Bazillion, Mrs H, *Librn,* Sault Sainte Marie Public Library (Koram), Sault Sainte Marie ON. 705-949-2871

Bazillion, Mrs H, *Librn,* Sault Sainte Marie Public Library (Steelton), Sault Sainte Marie ON. 705-253-1501

Bazillion, Richard J, *Chief Librn,* Algoma University College Library, Sault Sainte Marie ON. 705-949-2301

Bazin, Carmen, *Tech Serv & Acq,* Bibliotheque Municipale Des Sources, Sources Public Library, Roxboro PQ. 514-684-8247, 684-8260

Bazinet, Pierre A, *Dir,* Bureau D'amenagement Et De Gestion Du Complexe Scientifique De Quebec, Service de Documentation et de Bibliotheque, Sainte Foy PQ. 418-657-2426

Bazydlo, Gretchen, *Dir,* Marstons Mills Public Library, Marstons Mills MA. 617-428-5175

Bazzell, Barbara, *Librn,* Louisiana Office of Commerce & Industry, Research & Planning Library, Baton Rouge LA. 504-342-5383

Beach, Babette, *Dir,* George Smith Public Library, Junction City KS. 913-238-4311

Beach, Carolyn, *ILL,* Richland Parish Library, Rayville LA. 318-728-4806

Beach, Cecil, *Dir,* Broward County Division of Libraries, Broward County Library, Pompano Beach FL. 305-972-1100

Beach, Earle, *Bus Mgr,* Temple University of the Commonwealth System of Higher Education, Samuel Paley Library, Philadelphia PA. 215-787-8231

Beach, Ellen, *Librn,* Reinbeck Public Library, Reinbeck IA. 319-345-2652

Beach, Linda M, *Librn,* Saint Luke's Hospital (Trexler Library), Bethlehem PA. 215-691-4355

Beach, Marv, *Ch,* Neptune Public Library, Neptune NJ. 201-775-8241

Beach, Mrs M, *Librn,* Coldwater Memorial Public Library, Coldwater ON. 705-686-3601

Beach, Rose Mary, *Dir,* Goldey Beacom College, J Wilbur Hirons Library, Wilmington DE. 302-998-8814, Ext 47

Beach, Sister Dorothy, *Dir,* Trinity College Library, Washington DC. 202-269-2252

Beach, Susan, *Ref,* Great River Library System, Quincy IL. 217-223-2560

Beachy, Dorothy, *Librn,* Pikes Peak Regional Library District (Monument Hill Branch), Monument CO. 303-481-2293

Beachy, Dorothy, *Librn,* Pikes Peak Regional Library District (Palmer Lake Community), Palmer Lake CO. 303-481-2587

Beacock, E Stanley, *Dir,* London Public Libraries & Museums, London ON. 519-432-7166

Beadle, Constance, *Librn,* Fallsington Free Library Co, Fallsington PA. 215-295-4449

Beadle, Elizabeth, *Bkmobile Coordr,* Somerset County Library, Somerville NJ. 201-725-4700, Ext 234

Beadle, June F, *Librn,* Lake Wales Public Library, Lake Wales FL. 813-676-4521

Beagle, Don, *Ad, Tech Serv & Cat,* Robeson County Public Library, Lumberton NC. 919-738-4859

Beaird, A Michael, *Librn,* University of Mississippi, Law Library, University MS. 601-232-7361

Beal, Jean, *YA,* Novi Public Library, Novi MI. 313-349-0720

Beal, LaTroy, *Librn,* Richwood Public Library, Richwood WV. 304-846-6222

Beal, Vernon L, *Librn,* Ohio Soldiers' & Sailors' Home Library, Sandusky OH. 419-625-2454
Beale, Joel, *Librn,* Gulf Oil Corporation (Gulf Oil Chemicals Co, Business Information Center), Houston TX. 713-750-2511
Beale, Wm G, *Ref,* College of Southern Idaho Library, Twin Falls ID. 208-733-9554, Ext 236
Beales, Carol, *Librn,* Copley Newspapers Inc, James S Copley Library, La Jolla CA. 714-454-0411
Beall, Babara A, *In Charge,* National Forest Products Association, Information Center, Washington DC. 202-797-5836
Beall, Mary, *Programming,* Englewood Library, Englewood NJ. 201-568-2215
Bealmer, Diana, *Librn,* Kern County Library (Rosamond Branch), Rosamond CA. 805-861-2130
Beals, Martha, *Govt Doc & Educ Curric Laboratory,* Campbell University, Carrie Rich Memorial Library, Buies Creek NC. 919-893-4111, Ext 238
Beam, Deborah, *On-Line Servs,* Southwestern Baptist Theological Seminary, Fleming Library, Fort Worth TX. 817-923-1921, Ext 277
Beam, Patricia, *Tech Serv,* Pittsburgh Theological Seminary, Clifford E Barbour Library, Pittsburgh PA. 412-362-5610, Ext 280
Beam, Shirley, *Librn,* Newark Public Library (Johnstown Branch), Johnstown OH. 614-967-2982
Beaman, Barbara, *Supvr Libr,* Hercules Inc (Fourteenth-T Library), Wilmington DE. 302-575-5401
Beaman, Patricia, *Librn,* San Antonio State Chest Hospital Library Services, San Antonio TX. 512-534-8857, Ext 242, 324
Beamer, K, *Soc Sci,* Mount San Antonio College, Learning Resources Center, Walnut CA. 714-594-5611, Ext 260
Bean, Arlen K, *Librn,* California Taxpayers Association Library, Sacramento CA. 916-441-0490
Bean, Catherine, *In Charge,* Depauw University (Music), Greencastle IN. 317-653-9721, Ext 2825
Bean, Christopher, *ILL & Ref,* Sweet Briar College Library, Sweet Briar VA. 804-381-5541
Bean, Christopher, *Bibliog Instr,* Sweet Briar College Library, Sweet Briar VA. 804-381-5541
Bean, Douglas J, *Dir,* Middletown Public Library, Middletown OH. 513-424-1251
Bean, Elaine, *Bibliog Instr,* Rivier College, Regina Library, Nashua NH. 603-888-1311, Ext 42
Bean, Elinore F, *Acq,* Dean Junior College, E Ross Anderson Library, Franklin MA. 617-528-9100, Ext 261
Bean, Estelle, *Asst Dir & Ref,* Lebanon Public Library, Lebanon OH. 513-932-4725
Bean, Gordon, *Prof,* Ryerson Polytechnical Institute, Library Arts Dept, ON. 416-595-5285
Bean, Janet, *Cultural Ctr,* Chicago Public Library, Chicago IL. 312-269-2900
Bean, Janet, *Dir,* Chicago Public Library (Cultural Center), Chicago IL. 312-269-2820
Bean, Nancy L, *YA,* Warren Library Association, Warren Library, Warren PA. 814-723-4650
Bean, Norma, *Ref,* Texas Southern University Library, Houston TX. 713-527-7121
Bean, Reita I, *Librn,* Reuben Hoar Library, Littleton MA. 617-486-4046
Bean, Reita I, *Librn,* Albert J Sargent Memorial Library, Boxborough MA. 617-263-4680
Bean, Ron, *Ref,* Frankfort Community Public Library, Frankfort IN. 317-654-8746
Beane, Joel N, *Dir & Bibliog Instr,* Kingwood Public Library, Kingwood WV. 304-329-1499
Bear, Iris, *Librn,* Shannon-Glow Inc, Shannon Luminous Materials Co Library, Los Angeles CA. 213-876-2660
Beard, Barbara A, *ILL,* Missouri Southern State College, George A Spiva Library, Joplin MO. 417-624-8100, Ext 251
Beard, Charles E, *Dir,* West Georgia College Library, Carrollton GA. 404-834-1370
Beard, Dora, *Govt Publication,* Northeast Louisiana University, Sandel Library, Monroe LA. 318-342-2195
Beard, John R, *Dir,* Dowling College Library, Oakdale NY. 516-589-6100, Ext 218 or 219
Bearden, Jacqueline, *Admin Librn,* Saint Augustine Historical Society Library, Saint Augustine FL. 904-829-5514

Bearden, Joan, *Pub Servs,* Florida Junior College at Jacksonville (Kent Campus Learning Resource Center), Jacksonville FL. 904-387-8222
Bearden, Joseph M, *Librn,* Dallas Public Library (Jefferson), Dallas TX. 214-946-8104
Bearden, William, *Acq,* Fordham University, Duane Library, Bronx NY. 212-933-2233, Ext 230, 259
Beardslee, Elaine, *ILL,* Northwestern Michigan College, Mark Osterlin Library, Traverse City MI. 616-946-5650, Ext 541
Beardslee, R, *Dir,* Bio-Science Laboratories Library, Van Nuys CA. 213-989-2520, Ext 271
Beardsley, Elizabeth W, *Dir,* Katonah Village Library, Katonah NY. 914-232-3508
Beardsley, Glenna, *ILL,* Ellensburg Public Library, Ellensburg WA. 509-962-9863, Ext 250
Beardsley, Jeanne, *Ch,* Maywood Public Library, Maywood NJ. 201-845-7755
Beardsley, S A, *Librn,* Westinghouse Nuclear Training Center Library, Zion IL. 312-872-4585
Bearer, Annabeth, *Librn & On-Line Servs,* Phillips Petroleum Co (Natural Resources Group Library), Bartlesville OK. 918-661-7515
Bears, H E, *Tech Serv,* Standard Oil Co (Indiana), Library-Information Center, Chicago IL. 312-856-5961
Bearss, Cathy, *Supvr,* Elgin County Public Library (Springfield Branch), Springfield ON. 519-633-0815
Beary, Eugene G, *Chief Librn,* United States Army (Natick Research & Development Command, Technical Library), Natick MA. 617-653-1000, Ext 2248
Beary, Marjorie, *On-Line Servs,* Florida International University, Tamiami Campus, Athenaeum, Miami FL. 305-552-2461
Beasecker, Robert, *Archivist,* Grand Valley State Colleges, Zumberge Library, Allendale MI. 313-895-6611, Ext 252
Beasley, Helen W, *Dir,* Dekalb Community College, Central Campus Library, Clarkston GA. 404-292-3994
Beasley, James F, *Dir,* Central Colorado Library System, Aurora CO. 303-344-1871
Beasley, Kaye, *Librn,* Westfield Public Library, Westfield IN. 317-896-5253
Beasley, Lorna Lee, *Librn,* American Insurance Association Law Library, New York NY. 212-433-4476
Beasley, Marion, *Librn,* Leslie County Library, Hyden KY. 606-672-2460
Beasley, Marion, *President,* Southeastern Kentucky Regional Library Cooperative, KY. 606-666-7521
Beasley, Mary, *Librn,* Chicago Public Library (Brainerd), Chicago IL. 312-445-5559
Beasley, Roger, *Tech Serv,* Kenyon College, Gordon Keith Chalmers Memorial Library, Gambier OH. 614-427-2244, Ext 2186
Beasley, Ruth, *Librn,* Big Spring State Hospital Library, Big Spring TX. 915-267-8216
Beasley, Vivian A, *Bibliog Instr,* State Law Library, Frankfort KY. 502-564-4848
Beasley, Jr, Clarence W, *Dir,* Saint John the Baptist Parish Library, LaPlace LA. 504-652-2144
Beatley, Beryl, *Ch,* Newton Free Library, Newton MA. 617-527-7700, Ext 24
Beatlee, Beryl, *Librn,* Newton Free Library (Junior Library), Newton MA. 617-527-7700, Ext 24
Beaton, Adele, *Librn,* Chicago Public Library (Walker), Chicago IL. 312-233-1920
Beaton, Maxine, *Librn,* Presbyterian Medical Center, H A Bradford Memorial Library, Denver CO. 303-839-6440
Beaton, Patricia, *Acq & Ref,* New Hampshire College, Shapiro Library, Manchester NH. 603-668-2211, Ext 211
Beattie, Brian, *Dir,* Bradford Memorial Library, El Dorado KS. 316-321-3363
Beattie, Lyn, *Ref,* Esso Resources Canada Ltd (Production Research-Technical Services), Calgary AB. 403-259-0671
Beattie, Mrs M, *Librn,* Cochrane Community Library, Cochrane AB. 403-932-3239
Beattie, Stella, *Supvr,* Huron County Public Library (Seaforth Branch), Seaforth ON. 519-527-1430
Beatty, Betty, *Asst Dir & Tech Serv,* Wittenberg University, Thomas Library, Springfield OH. 513-327-7016
Beatty, Dave, *Librn,* Montana State Prison Library, Deer Lodge MT. 406-846-2314

Beatty, Jean, *ILL,* Hingham Public Library, Hingham MA. 617-749-0907
Beatty, Madge, *Librn,* Catawba County Library (Sherrills Ford Branch), Sherrills Ford NC. 704-464-2421
Beatty, Mae, *Circ,* Cumberland County Public Library, Anderson Street Library, Frances Brooks Stein Memorial Library, Fayetteville NC. 919-483-1580
Beatty, Peg, *Librn,* Middletown Public Library (Union Township), West Chester OH. 513-777-3131
Beatty, Ruby, *Librn,* Keosauqua Public Library, Keosauqua IA. 319-293-3766
Beatty, Samuel B, *Dir,* American Society for Information Science Library, Washington DC. 202-659-3644
Beatty, Sister Mary Patricia, *Cat,* Barry College, Monsignor William Barry Memorial Library, Miami Shores FL. 305-758-3392, Ext 263
Beatty, Susan, *Librn,* Alberta Library Services To the Handicapped, Calgary AB. 403-268-5296
Beatty, Suzanne D, *Librn,* Chicago Bridge & Iron Technical Library, Oak Brook IL. 312-654-7279
Beatty, Suzanne H, *Dir,* Shellsburg Public Library, Shellsburg IA. 319-436-2112
Beaty, Mary, *Asst Librn, ILL & Ref,* Davidson College, E H Little Library, Davidson NC. 704-892-2000, Ext 331
Beaty, Patricia J, *Ch,* Moline Public Library, Moline IL. 309-762-6883
Beaubien, Bea, *Ch,* Adams Library, Chelmsford MA. 617-256-5521
Beauchamp, Jacques, *Dir,* Bibliotheque Municipale De Lachine, Lachine PQ. 514-637-2568
Beauchamp, Louise, *Ch,* Chateauguay Municipal Library, Chateauguay PQ. 514-691-1934
Beauchamp, Mary, *Librn,* M C River Valley Public Library District, Meredosia IL. 217-584-1571
Beauchamp, Norman, *Cat,* University of Missouri-Kansas City Libraries (Music), Kansas City MO. 816-363-4300
Beauchamp, Norman, *Cat,* University of Missouri-Kansas City Libraries (Medical Library), Kansas City MO. 816-474-4100, Ext 280
Beauchemin, Lisette, *Ch,* Bibliotheque Municipale Des Trois-Rivieres, Trois-Rivieres PQ. 819-374-3521, Ext 71
Beaucher, Ann, *Librn,* Timrod Library, Summerville SC. 803-871-4600
Beaudet, Francoise, *Librn,* University of Montreal Libraries (Theology-Philosophy), Montreal PQ. 514-343-6592
Beaudet, Normand, *Librn,* Institute Philippe Pinel De Montreal Bibliotheque, Montreal PQ. 514-648-8461, Ext 274
Beaudette, Gerard P, *Acq,* Bates College, George and Helen Ladd Library, Lewiston ME. 207-784-2949
Beaudette, Robert, *Per,* Skokie Public Library, Skokie IL. 312-673-7774
Beaudin, Marion M, *Librn,* Woodland Clinic Medical Group, Woolsey Medical Library, Woodland CA. 916-666-1631, Ext 289
Beaudoin, Kathleen, *Chief Librn,* Canadian Medical Association Library, Ottawa ON. 613-731-9331, Ext 72
Beaudoin, Michel, *Dir,* Universite De Sherbrooke Bibliotheque (Bibliotheque des Sciences), Sherbrooke PQ. 819-565-5475
Beaudoin, Yolande, *Librn,* University of Montreal Libraries (Psycho-Education), Montreal PQ. 514-382-2972
Beaudot, William, *In Charge,* Milwaukee Public Library (East), Milwaukee WI. 414-278-3058
Beaudrie, Kay, *Cat,* Rosary College, Rebecca Crown Library, River Forest IL. 312-366-2490, Ext 305
Beaudrie, Ronald, *Ref,* Dowling College Library, Oakdale NY. 516-589-6100, Ext 218 or 219
Beaudry, Claude, *Music,* Universite Laval Bibliotheque, Quebec PQ. 418-656-3344
Beaudry, Joanne, *ILL,* North Central Regional Library System, Sudbury ON. 705-675-6467
Beauford, Roland, *Acq,* Jefferson-Madison Regional Library, McIntire Public Library, Charlottesville VA. 804-296-6157
Beaufort, Suzanne, *Librn,* Augusta Regional Library (Maxwell), Augusta GA. 404-793-2020
Beaulac, Sister Lillian, *Dir & Acq,* Anna Maria College Library, Paxton MA. 617-757-4586, Ext 56

Beaumont, Esther, *Dir Programs & Commun Relations,* Fairfax County Public Library, Administrative Offices, Springfield VA. 703-321-9810

Beaumont, Rosemary, *ILL & Ad,* Riviera Beach Public Library, Riviera Beach FL. 305-845-4194, 845-4195, 845-4196

Beaumont, Virginia, *Librn,* Sequoia Hospital, Medical Staff Library, Redwood City CA. 415-369-5811, Ext 554

Beaupre, Linda, *Acting Asst Dir for Pub Servs,* University of Texas Libraries (General), Austin TX. 512-471-3811

Beauregard, John, *Dir,* Gordon College, Winn Library, Wenham MA. 617-927-2300, Ext 233

Beauregard, Louise, *Bibliog Instr & Ref,* College De Maisonneuve Bibliotheque, Montreal PQ. 514-254-7131, .254-4035

Beausoleil, Marion, *Librn,* Union Free Public Library, Stafford Springs CT. 203-684-4913

Beauvais, Rose Cordier, *Info Officer,* Sinte Gleska College Library, Mission SD. 605-856-4550

Beaver, Jane, *Ch,* Olathe Public Library, Olathe KS. 913-764-2259

Beaver, Lucile E, *Dir,* United States Department of Transportation, Library Services Div, Washington DC. 202-426-2565, 426-1792

Beavers, Carolyn, *YA,* Rockingham County Public Library, Eden NC. 919-627-1106

Beavers, Ila, *Librn,* Fayetteville-Lincoln County Public Library, Fayetteville TN. 615-433-3286

Beavers, James F, *Libr Dir,* Oscar Rose Junior College, Learning Resources Center, Midwest City OK. 405-733-7323, 733-7322

Beavin, Daniel S, *Librn,* Midstate Regional Library, Berlin VT. 802-828-2320

Beavon, Constance, *Art,* City University of New York, Library of Graduate School & University Center, New York NY. 212-790-4541

Beazizo, Phyllis, *Librn,* Whatcom County Public Library (Newhalem), Rockport WA. 206-397-4371

Bebout, Judith, *YA,* Sussex County Library System, Sussex County Area Reference Library, Newton NJ. 201-948-3660

Bebout, Lois, *Flm & Rec,* Louisiana State Library, Baton Rouge LA. 504-342-4922

Bebout, Susan M, *Librn,* Bracewell & Patterson, Law Library, Houston TX. 713-223-2900

Becham, Gerald, *Instr,* Georgia College, Education Library Media, GA. 912-453-4047 & 453-5573

Becham, Gerald C, *Asst Dir,* Georgia College, Ina Dillard Russell Library, Milledgeville GA. 912-453-4047, 453-5573

Bechanan, H Gordon, *Dir,* Virginia Polytechnic Institute & State University Library, Blacksburg VA. 703-961-5593

Bechard, C, *Asst Librn,* Port Leyden Community Library, Port Leyden NY. 315-348-6077

Becherer, Susan, *Librn,* Genesee District Library (Mount Morris Library), Mt Morris MI. 313-686-6120

Becherx, Mary Jo, *Dir,* Waupun Public Library, Waupun WI. 414-324-3931

Bechtel, Joan, *Cat,* Dickinson College, Boyd Lee Spahr Library, Carlisle PA. 717-245-1396

Bechtel, Nancy G, *Dir,* Connecticut State Department of Community Affairs, Resource Center Library, Hartford CT. 203-566-3559

Bechthold, Ruth, *ILL, Tech Serv & Cat,* Lodi Public Library, Lodi CA. 209-334-3973

Beck, Agnes, *Coordr of Ancillary Servs,* New York Association for the Blind, Lighthouse Library, New York NY. 212-355-2200, Ext 397

Beck, Alisa, *YA,* Jackson-George Regional Library System (Pascagoula City Branch), Pascagoula MS. 601-762-3406

Beck, Ann W, *Librn,* Lake Bluff Public Library, Lake Bluff IL. 312-234-2540

Beck, Beatrice M, *Librn,* Rancho Santa Ana Botanic Garden Library, Claremont CA. 714-626-3922

Beck, Clara, *Librn,* Elizabeth Township Library, Elizabeth IL. 815-858-2212

Beck, Doris, *Dir,* Midwestern Baptist College, B R Lakin Library, Pontiac MI. 313-334-0961

Beck, Dorothy, *Bkmobile Coordr,* Northeast Georgia Regional Library System, Clarkesville GA. 404-754-4413

Beck, Elizabeth F, *Librn,* FMC Corp, Chain Division, Technical Center Library, Indianapolis IN. 317-267-2200

Beck, Harold, *Libr Technician,* United States Army (US Disciplinary Div Library), Fort Leavenworth KS. 913-684-4021

Beck, Ina, *Librn,* Woodward Public Library, Woodward IA. 515-438-2636

Beck, James M, *Rec Mgt Supvr,* Ohio Power Co Library, Canton OH. 216-456-8173

Beck, Janice J, *Librn,* Southwest Regional Library Service System, Durango CO. 303-247-4782

Beck, Joyce, *Librn,* Southwest Arkansas Regional Library (Foreman Branch), Foreman AR. 501-777-4564

Beck, Lois, *Cat,* University of Minnesota, Saint Paul Campus Libraries, Saint Paul MN. 612-373-0904

Beck, Lucy, *Children's Servs & Outreach Servs,* Kenosha Public Library, Kenosha WI. 414-656-6034

Beck, Margaret, *Librn,* Flathead County Free Library (Olney Branch), Olney MT. 406-881-2412

Beck, Margie H, *Librn,* Canton Public Library, Canton MO. 314-288-5279

Beck, Marianne, *Spec Coll,* Wartburg College, Engelbrecht Library, Waverly IA. 319-352-1200, Ext 244

Beck, Miriam, *Asst Librn,* Thomas County Historical Library, Colby KS. 913-462-6972

Beck, Paul, *Archivist,* Dallas Public Library, Dallas TX. 214-748-9071

Beck, Richard J, *Assoc Dir & Pub Serv,* University of Idaho Library, Moscow ID. 208-885-6534

Beck, Shirley, *In Charge,* Tusculum College Library (Instructional Materials Center), Greeneville TN. 615-639-3751

Beck, Thomas, *Curator Photog,* University of Maryland Baltimore County Library, Baltimore MD. 301-455-2457

Beck, Wanda, *Librn,* Northeast Georgia Regional Library System (Clayton), Clarkesville GA. 404-754-4413

Beck, William L, *Dir,* California State College, Louis L Manderino Library, California PA. 412-938-4091

Beck, Zelma, *Librn,* Gallitzin Public Library, Gallitzin PA. 814-886-4041

Beckemeier, DeWayne, *Dir,* Poplar Bluff Public Library, Poplar Bluff MO. 314-785-8436

Becker, Agnes, *Librn,* Garfield County Library, Burwell NE. 308-346-4711

Becker, Alan, *Tech Servs Coordr,* Broward County Division of Libraries, Broward County Library, Pompano Beach FL. 305-972-1100

Becker, Barbara, *Asst Librn,* Hartington Public Library, Hartington NE. 402-254-6245

Becker, Barbara, *Librn,* Parke, Davis & Company Research Library, Ann Arbor MI. 313-994-3500

Becker, Barbara A, *Asst Dir, Commun Servs & Br Coordr,* New Britain Public Library, New Britain CT. 203-224-3155

Becker, Betty, *Circ,* Fulton County Public Library, Rochester IN. 219-223-2713

Becker, Beverly, *ILL,* Harford County Library, Bel Air MD. 301-838-7484

Becker, Bradley H, *Asst Dir,* Harrison Public Library, Harrison NY. 914-835-0324

Becker, Catherine, *ILL & Ref,* Westfield State College Library, Westfield MA. 413-568-3311

Becker, Cheryl, *Librn,* Detroit Lakes Public Library, Detroit Lakes MN. 218-847-8322

Becker, Deloras, *Tech Serv,* North Platte Public Library, Lincoln Keith Perkins Regional Library, North Platte NE. 308-532-6560

Becker, Dorothy, *Librn,* Minnesota Valley Regional Library (North Mankato), Mankato MN. 507-345-5120

Becker, Dorothy K, *Rd Servs,* Boston Public Library, Eastern Massachusetts Library System, Boston MA. 617-536-5400

Becker, Eileen, *In Charge,* Richmond Library, Richmond MN. 612-597-2075

Becker, Jacquelyn B, *Librn,* Helene Curtis Industries, Inc, Research & Development Library, Chicago IL. 312-292-2121

Becker, Jeanne, *Librn,* Cabrini Medical Center, Dr Massimo Bazzini Memorial Library, New York NY. 212-725-6631, 725-6632

Becker, Jeanne P, *Tech Serv & Cat,* Roanoke College Library, Salem VA. 703-389-2351, Ext 202

Becker, Jill, *Librn,* Sotheby Parke Bernet, Inc Library, New York NY. 212-472-3554

Becker, John, *Dir,* Otterbein College, Courtright Memorial Library, Westerville OH. 614-890-3000, Ext 164

Becker, Josephine M, *Dir,* Solano County Library, Fairfield-Suisun Community, Fairfield CA. 707-429-6601

Becker, Joyce, *Librn,* Colusa County Free Library, Colusa CA. 916-458-7671

Becker, Kate E, *Asst Librn,* University of Nebraska-Lincoln (College of Law Library), Lincoln NE. 402-472-3547

Becker, L K, *Librn,* Western Electric Co, Inc, Technical Library, Lee's Summit MO. 816-251-4000

Becker, Lawrence, *Asst Librn,* Porter Public Library, Westlake OH. 216-871-2600

Becker, Margaret, *Librn,* Celanese Plastics Co, Research & Development Library, Greer SC. 803-877-8471

Becker, Mary J, *Librn,* Cahill Gordon & Reindel Library, Washington DC. 202-659-3030

Becker, Mrs Herbert, *Dir,* Alexander Public Library, Alexander IA. 515-692-3228

Becker, Nancy, *Ser,* Central Missouri State University, Ward Edwards Library, Warrensburg MO. 816-429-4141

Becker, Nita, *Librn,* Jerome Public Library, Jerome ID. 208-324-5427

Becker, Roger, *Librn,* University of North Dakota (Olaf H Thormodsgard Law Library), Grand Forks ND. 701-777-2204

Becker, Solomon, *Chief Librn,* Municipal Reference & Research Center (Haven Emerson Public Health Library), New York NY. 212-566-5169

Becker, Solomon, *Librn,* New York City Municipal Reference & Research Center, Haven Emerson Public Health Library, New York NY. 212-566-5169

Becker, Stephen, *Interpretative Specialist,* Riverside County Historical Commission Library, Rubidoux CA. 714-787-2551

Beckerdite, L Ann, *Librn,* Chicago Public Library (Midwest), Chicago IL. 312-278-7788

Beckerman, Edwin P, *Dir,* Free Public Library of Woodbridge, Woodbridge NJ. 201-634-4450

Beckert, Doris, *Head Ref,* American River College Library, Sacramento CA. 916-484-8293

Beckham, Carol, *Dir,* Mercedes Memorial Library, Mercedes TX. 512-565-2371

Beckham, Helen, *Exten,* Bolivar County Library, Robinson-Carpenter Memorial Library, Cleveland MS. 601-843-2774

Beckles, Marjorie, *Manager,* Institute of International Education, Harkness Reading Room, New York NY. 212-883-8470

Beckley, Aleccea, *Br Supvr,* La Crosse County Library (Sias Branch), Onalaska WI. 608-783-1586

Beckley, Sarah, *Librn,* Vigo County Public Library (West Terre Haute Library), West Terre Haute IN. 812-533-2480

Beckman, Dennis D, *Librn,* Tosco Corp Information Center, Los Angeles CA. 213-552-7093

Beckman, Margaret, *Chief Librn,* University of Guelph Library, Guelph ON. 519-824-4120, Ext 3617

Beckman, Patricia, *Librn,* Boonslick Regional Library (Cole Camp Branch), Cole Camp MO. 816-668-3887

Beckman, Shirley, *Pub Info,* Ingham County Library, Library Service Center, Mason MI. 517-676-9088

Beckwith, Doris, *Librn,* San Joaquin Local Health District Library, Stockton CA. 209-466-6781, Ext 60

Beckwith, Herbert H, *Cat,* National Maritime Museum, J Porter Shaw Library, San Francisco CA. 415-556-8177

Beckwith, Jo, *On-Line Servs,* Waukegan Public Library, Waukegan IL. 312-623-2041

Beckwith, Patricia, *Librn,* Liquid Carbonic Corp, Houston Natural Gas R&D Library, Chicago IL. 312-855-2500

Beckwith, Terry Lee, *Asst Dir, Acq & Ref,* Vermont Law School Library, South Royalton VT. 802-763-8307

Becton, Marshall, *Circ,* Wayne County Public Library, Inc, Goldsboro NC. 919-735-1824

Bedard, Alice, *Dir,* Jolys Regional Library, Saint Pierre MB. 204-433-7729

Bedard, Jerel, *Librn,* Carnegie Public Library, Perry OK. 405-336-4721

Bedard, Mme Lucien, *Librn,* Bibliotheque Publique, Riviere-du-Loup PQ. 418-862-4252

Beddington, M Bower-Wolterman & M, *Info Specialists,* Engelhard Minerals & Chemicals Corp, Technical Information Center, Edison NJ. 201-321-5271

Beddoes, Thomas, *State & Local Hist,* State Library of Pennsylvania, Harrisburg PA. 717-787-2646

Beddoes, Thomas, *State & Local Hist,* State Library of Pennsylvania, Harrisburg PA. 717-787-2646

Bedell, Audry, *Bkmobile Coordr,* Ector County Library, Odessa TX. 915-332-0633

Bedell, Barbara, *Ref,* Pensacola Junior College, Learning Resource Center, Pensacola FL. 904-476-5410

Bedford, Janet, *Media,* Illinois Wesleyan University Library, Bloomington IL. 309-556-3172

Bedford, Joyce, *Librn,* Mississauga Public Library (Malton Branch), Malton ON. 416-677-5878

Bedigian, Deena Sivart, *Librn,* Roger Williams Park Museum of Natural History Library, Providence RI. 401-941-5640

Bedikian, Elizabeth, *Bus & Sci,* New Orleans Public Library, Simon Heinsheim & Fisk Libraries, New Orleans LA. 504-586-4905

Bedor, Donna, *ILL,* University of Colorado at Colorado Springs, Library, Colorado Springs CO. 303-593-3296

Bedore, Carol, *Acq,* Clinton-Essex-Franklin Library System, Plattsburgh NY. 518-563-5190

Bedrosky, Nanette, *Cat,* Creighton University (Health Sciences), Omaha NE. 402-449-2908

Bedwell, Moneta, *Librn,* Graham Hospital Association, Medical Staff Library, Canton IL. 309-647-5240, Ext 318

Bedworth, Steven, *Outreach,* Wilkinsburg Public Library, Pittsburgh PA. 412-244-2940

Beebe, Ann, *Librn,* Selah Public Library, Selah WA. 509-697-4373

Beebe, Emma, *Commun Servs,* Pawtucket Public Library & Regional Library Center, Deborah Cook Sayles Memorial Library, Pawtucket RI. 401-725-3714

Beebe, Emma D, *Dir,* Cumberland Public Library, Edward J Hayden Library, Cumberland RI. 401-333-2552

Beebe, Shirley J, *Librn,* Newaygo Carnegie Library, Newaygo MI. 616-652-6723

Beech, Beatrice, *Librn,* Western Michigan University (Institute of Cistercian Studies), Kalamazoo MI. 616-383-4985

Beecher, Andrew, *Coordr,* Madison Public Library (Municipal Video Service), Madison WI. 608-266-6501

Beecher, John W, *Librn,* University of Illinois Library at Urbana-Champaign (Agriculture), Urbana IL. 217-333-2416

Beecher, Raymond, *Librn,* Greene County Historical Society, Vedder Memorial Library, Coxsackie NY. 518-731-6822

Beekman, Ruth, *Librn,* Kentucky Christian College, Lusby Memorial Library, Grayson KY. 606-474-6613

Beel, Dorothy, *Librn,* Tampa-Hillsborough County Public Library System (Ybor City Public), Tampa FL. 813-223-8497

Beel, Dorothy, *Librn,* Tampa-Hillsborough County Public Library System (West Tampa Public), Tampa FL. 813-251-3678

Beeler, Carol, *Librn,* Snyder Research Laboratory Inc Library, Pico Rivera CA. 213-949-5471

Beeler, Cathy, *Asst Prof,* California State University, Chico, Dept of Education, Librarianship Program, CA. 916-895-6421

Beeler, M G, *Librn,* Florida Department of Health & Rehabilitative Services, Sunland Center at Miami Library, Opa Locka FL. 305-624-9671, Ext 237

Beeler, Richard J, *Bus & Econ,* Colorado State University, William E Morgan Library, Fort Collins CO. 303-491-5911

Beeley, Freda, *Librn,* Bluffs Public Library, Bluffs IL. 217-754-3032

Beem, Virginia, *Dir,* Fennville District Library, Fennville Area Public Library, Fennville MI. 616-561-5050

Beeman, Virginia, *Tech Serv,* Hackley Public Library, Muskegon MI. 616-722-7276

Beemer, Chris, *Dir,* Sharon Springs Public Library, Sharon Springs KS. 913-852-4527

Beemer, Judy, *Librn,* Sharon Springs Public Library, Sharon Springs KS. 913-852-4527

Beer, Richard L, *Dir,* Adams-Pratt Oakland County Law Library, Pontiac MI. 313-858-0011

Beerman, Mrs Tibor, *Librns,* Temple B'nai Israel, Lasker Memorial Library, Galveston TX. 713-765-5796

Beers, F Earl, *Librn,* Nurad Inc Library, Baltimore MD. 301-462-1700

Beers, George, *Media,* Community College of Philadelphia, Division of Educational Resources, Philadelphia PA. 215-972-7250

Beers-Schnock, Margaret, *ILL,* Cornell University Libraries (Law Library), Ithaca NY. 607-256-7236

Beery, Carl, *Librn,* Suburban Library System (Blind & Physically Handicapped Services), Burr Ridge IL. 312-325-6640

Beery, Lorita E, *Librn,* Summit United Methodist Church Library, Columbus OH. 614-291-3324

Beesley, Della, *Librn,* Public Library of Cincinnati & Hamilton County (Harrison Branch), Harrison OH. 513-367-4728

Beesley, Henrietta, *Librn,* Public Library of Cincinnati & Hamilton County (Overlook), Cincinnati OH. 513-921-6247

Beeson, John Richard, *Dir,* Orem Public Library, Orem UT. 801-224-7050

Beestrum, Edna, *Asst Dir,* University of Houston (Clear Lake City), Houston TX. 713-488-9280

Beetle, Marie, *Librn,* Saint Lucie County Library Systems (Port Saint Lucie Libr), Port Saint Lucie FL. 305-878-1467

Beeton, Elizabeth, *Tech Serv,* Borough of Etobicoke Public Library, Weston ON. 416-248-5681

Begg, Barbara A, *Librn,* University of California, San Diego (Science & Engineering), La Jolla CA. 714-452-3257

Begg, Robert, *Media,* Skyline College Library, San Bruno CA. 415-355-7000, Ext 311

Begg, Robert T, *Dir,* Ohio Northern University (Jay P Taggart Memorial Law Library), Ada OH. 419-634-9921, Ext 339

Beggerly, Maurine, *Librn,* Jackson Metropolitan Library (Richland Library), Jackson MS. 601-352-3677

Begin, Diane, *Bibliog Instr,* Ecole Des Hautes Etudes Commerciales De Montreal Bibliotheque, Montreal PQ. 514-343-4481

Begleiter, Ronni, *Ref,* Drake University (Drake Law Libr), Des Moines IA. 515-271-2141

Beglo, Jo, *Archit, Art & Relig,* University of Waterloo Library, Waterloo ON. 519-885-1211

Behan, Mary C, *Dir,* Township of Shaler North Hills Library, Glenshaw PA. 412-486-0211, 486-0212

Behar, Solomon, *Anglo-American,* University of California, Berkeley (University Library), Berkeley CA. 415-642-3773

Behers, Janice, *Librn,* United States Bureau of Mines, Reno Research Center Library, Reno NV. 702-784-5348

Behler, Patricia, *Ch & YA,* Missouri State Library, Jefferson City MO. 314-751-4214

Behles, Richard, *Ser,* Loyola-Notre Dame Library, Inc, Baltimore MD. 301-532-8787

Behimann, Sister Jane, *Media,* Fontbonne College Library, Saint Louis MO. 314-862-3456, Ext 352

Behm, Kathy, *Media,* Washington University Libraries (School of Dental Medicine Library), Saint Louis MO. 314-454-0385

Behn, Gail, *Librn,* Fosston Public Library, Fosston MN. 218-435-1320

Behr, Alice Shaver, *Librn,* Union Carbide Corp (Research & Development Department Building 770 Library), South Charleston WV. 304-747-5119

Behrends, Viola, *Librn,* Baldwin Memorial Library, Wells River VT. 802-757-2693

Behrendt, Elizabeth, *Actg Librn,* United States Geological Survey Library, Golden CO. 303-234-4133

Behrens, Elizabeth, *Librn,* Memorial University of Newfoundland Library (Sir Walter Grenfell College Library), Corner Brook NF. 709-639-8981

Behrens, Faith, *Tech Serv,* Santa Barbara Public Library, Santa Barbara CA. 805-962-7653

Behrens, Ferne, *Librn,* United States Navy (Naval Amphibious Base General Library), Norfolk VA. 804-464-7691

Behrens, Marge, *Slavic & Oriental,* Rand Corp Library, Santa Monica CA. 213-393-0411, Ext 369

Behrens, Patricia, *Dir,* Huntingdon Valley Library, Huntingdon Valley PA. 215-947-5138

Behringer, Mary, *Dir, Cat & Ref,* Blauvelt Free Library, Blauvelt NY. 914-359-2811

Behrman, June, *ILL,* William Jeanes Memorial Library, Lafayette Hill PA. 215-828-0441

Behsman, Brenda, *Librn Blind,* North Platte Public Library (Library for the Blind & Physically Handicapped), North Platte NE. 308-532-6560

Beidler, Susan, *Tech Serv,* Lycoming College Library, Williamsport PA. 717-326-8153

Beigel, Carol, *Librn,* Watkins-Johnson Co, CEI Division Engineering Library, Gaithersburg MD. 301-948-7550

Beilby, Mary, *Educ,* State University of New York College, Memorial Library, Cortland NY. 607-753-2525, 753-2221

Beilby, Mary, *Coll Develop,* State University of New York College, Memorial Library, Cortland NY. 607-753-2525, 753-2221

Beiler, Dorthea, *Librn,* First Presbyterian Church Library, De Land FL. 904-734-6212

Beiler, Eileen, *Librn,* American Institute for Research in the Behavioral Sciences, Research Library, Pittsburgh PA. 412-681-3000

Beilke, Jayne, *Dir,* Indiana Vocational Technical College, Learning Resources Center, Columbus IN. 812-372-9925

Beilke, Patricia F, *Assoc Prof,* Ball State University, Dept of Library Science, IN. 317-285-7180, 285-7189

Beimesch, Barbara, *Librn,* Procter & Gamble Co (Miami Valley Laboratories Technical Library), Cincinnati OH. 513-562-1100

Beinbrech, Pauline, *Librn,* Petrolite Corp, Research Library, Saint Louis MO. 961-3500 Ext 325

Beining, Ellen, *Asst Librn,* Berlin Public Library, Berlin WI. 414-361-2650

Beintema, William, *Librn,* Oklahoma City University (Law Library), Oklahoma City OK. 405-521-5271

Beiser, Karl A, *District Consult,* Northeastern Maine Library District, Bangor ME. 207-947-8336, 947-8337

Beiter, Elizabeth, *Librn,* Stillwater Free Library, Stillwater NY. 518-664-6255

Bejarano, Rose, *Librn,* Family Planning Resource Center of Planned Parenthood of San Antonio, Planned Parenthood-World Population South Central Region Library, San Antonio TX. 512-227-2227

Bejster, Barbara, *Ch,* Graves Public Library, Mendota Library, Mendota IL. 815-538-5142

Bekar, Carol, *Librn,* McGill University Libraries (Northern Studies), Montreal PQ. 514-392-8233

Bekassy, Eva, *Sci,* Saint John's University Library, Jamaica NY. 212-969-8000, Ext 201

Bekkedal, Tekla, *Assoc Prof,* University of Wisconsin-Eau Claire, Dept of Library Science & Media Education, WI. 715-836-2635

Belair, M Phyllis, *Chief Librn,* Willimantic Public Library, Willimantic CT. 203-423-6182

Beland, Andre, *Acq & Ref,* College Du Nord-Quest La Bibliotheque, Rouyn PQ. 819-762-0931, Ext 134

Beland, Andre, *Acq & Ref,* Universite Du Quebec: Centre d'etudes Universitaires Dans L'ouest Quebecois Bibliotheque, Rouyn PQ. 819-762-0971, Ext 350

Beland, Noel, *Dir,* Seminaire Saint-Augustin Bibliotheque, Cap-Rouge PQ. 418-872-0954

Belanger, Brien, *Circ,* Moody Bible Institute Library, Chicago IL. 312-329-4138

Belanger, R P Conrad, *Supvr,* Seminaire Saint-Sacrament Library, Terrebonne PQ. 514-471-6615

Belanger, Richard, *ILL,* Teachers College - Columbia University Library, New York NY. 212-678-3022, 678-3020

Belanger, Yvette, *Libr Tech,* Agriculture Canada (Ottawa Research Station Library), Ottawa ON. 613-995-9428

Belanger, Jr, Edward, *Admin Servs,* Catholic University of America, John K Mullen of Denver Memorial Library, Washington DC. 202-635-5055

Belch, C Jean, *Curric,* University of Washington Libraries, Seattle WA. 206-543-1760

Belch, David, *Pub Info,* San Francisco Public Library, San Francisco CA. 415-558-4235

Belcher, Dona, *Librn,* United States Navy (Naval Ammunition Disposal Library), Colts Neck NJ. 201-462-9500

Belcher, Faye, *Asst Dir,* Morehead State University, Johnson Camden-Julian Carroll Library, Morehead KY. 606-783-2250

Belcher, John R, *Librn,* Public Library of the District of Columbia (Southeast), Washington DC. 202-727-1377

Belden, Margaret, *Tech Serv,* Fanwood Memorial Library, Fanwood NJ. 201-322-6400

Belding, James, *Librn,* Detroit Public Library (Campbell), Detroit MI. 313-833-9178

Beldon, Marilyn, *Ch,* Hurst Public Library, Hurst TX. 817-485-5320

Beleutz, M, *ILL,* Saint Thomas Public Library, Saint Thomas ON. 519-631-6050

Belgum, Kathie, *Asst Dir,* University of Iowa Libraries (Law Library), Iowa City IA. 319-353-5968

Belh, Norman, *Librn,* Greenville County Library (Eastside Branch), Greenville SC. 803-292-1603

Belisle, Earl, *Ref,* College of Saint Thomas, O'Shaughnessy Library, Saint Paul MN. 612-647-5720

Belisle, Germain, *Dir & Acq,* Bishop's University & Champlain Regional College, John Bassett Memorial Library, Lennoxville PQ. 819-569-9551, Ext 341

Belk, Patricia H, *Asst Librn,* Lancaster County Library, Lancaster SC. 803-285-1502

Belknap, Elizabeth, *Librn,* Inman Public Library, Inman KS. 316-585-2474

Belknap, Gerda, *Br Coordr & Bkmobile Coordr,* Richland County Public Library, Columbia SC. 803-799-9084

Belknap-Jones, Marylou, *Asst Librn & Bks By Mail,* Washington County Cooperative Library Services, Portland OR. 503-645-5112

Bell, Francis, *Humanities,* Dallas Public Library, Dallas TX. 214-748-9071

Bell, Annie Lee, *Librn,* True Vine Baptist Church Library, Alexandria LA. 318-445-6730

Bell, Barbara, *Librn,* Satilla Regional Library (Willacoochee Public), Willacoochee GA. 912-534-5252

Bell, Beatrice, *Librn,* Sno-Isle Regional Library (Freeland Branch), Freeland WA. 206-321-4383

Bell, Bernice L, *Asst Librn,* Jackson State University, Henry Thomas Sampson Library, Jackson MS. 601-968-2123

Bell, Beverly, *Tech Serv,* Saint Charles Public Library District, Saint Charles IL. 312-584-0076

Bell, Carol A, *Librn,* Bechtel Power Corp Library, Gaithersburg MD. 301-948-2700

Bell, Charlotte M, *Dir of Media Servs,* First Baptist Church Library, Greensboro NC. 919-274-3286

Bell, Christina C, *Librn,* Littlefield Library, Tyngsboro MA. 617-649-7361

Bell, Christine L, *Bibliog Instr,* Boston University Libraries (Alumni Medical Library), Boston MA. 617-247-6187

Bell, D V, *Dir of Research,* Electric Furnace Co Library, Salem OH. 216-332-4661

Bell, Della, *ILL,* El Dorado County Library, Placerville CA. 916-626-2561

Bell, Doris, *Res Coord,* Barton-Aschman Associates, Inc Library, Evanston IL. 312-491-1000

Bell, Eleanor, *Librn,* Jerseyville Free Library, Jerseyville IL. 618-498-4511

Bell, Elisabeth, *Ref & On-Line Servs,* University of California Library, San Francisco CA. 415-666-2334

Bell, Elizabeth, *Librn,* Colquitt-Thomas Regional Library (Meigs Public Branch), Meigs GA. 912-985-6540

Bell, Ellen, *Librn,* Meigs Local School District Public Library, Pomeroy OH. 614-992-5813

Bell, Elsie, *Librn,* Metropolitan Library System (Main Libr), Oklahoma City OK. 405-235-0571

Bell, Gretchen, *Media,* Piedmont Technical College, Learning Resources Center, Roxboro NC. 919-599-1181, Ext 266

Bell, Gwen, *Ref,* Clayton Junior College Library, Morrow GA. 404-961-3520

Bell, Helen, *Ref & On-Line Servs,* University of Texas at El Paso Library, El Paso TX. 747-5683; 747-5684

Bell, Inez D, *Learning Laboratory,* Wilson County Technical Institute, Learning Resource Center, Wilson NC. 919-291-1195, Ext 235

Bell, Inglis F, *Assoc Librn,* University of British Columbia Library, Vancouver BC. 604-228-3871

Bell, James B, *Dir,* New England Historic Genealogical Society Library, Boston MA. 617-536-5740

Bell, James R, *Librn,* Tri-County Community College Library, Murphy NC. 704-837-6810

Bell, Jo Ann, *Dir,* East Carolina University (Health Affairs Library), Greenville NC. 919-757-6961, Ext 261

Bell, John, *Ref,* University of Tennessee at Martin, Paul Meek Library, Martin TN. 901-587-7060

Bell, Kathleen, *Cat,* Wentworth Institute of Technology Library, Boston MA. 617-442-9010, Ext 344

Bell, Katie R, *Coordr,* Alabama State University, Library Educational Media Program, AL. 205-832-6072, Ext 502

Bell, Louise, *Librn,* Randolph Public Library (Seagrove Branch), Seagrove NC. 919-873-7521

Bell, M, *Ref,* Ventura College, D R Henry Library, Ventura CA. 805-642-3211, Ext 201

Bell, Marion V, *Gen Info,* Enoch Pratt Free Library, Baltimore MD. 301-396-5430, 396-5395

Bell, Mary, *Asst Librn,* Oak Forest Hospital (Medical Library), Oak Forest IL. 312-928-4200

Bell, Mary J, *Tech Serv,* Knoxville-Knox County Public Library, Lawson McGhee Library, Knoxville TN. 615-523-0781

Bell, Matthew J, *Librn,* Rockland Memorial Library, Rockland MA. 617-878-1236

Bell, Mertys W, *Dir,* Guilford Technical Institute, Learning Resource Center, Jamestown NC. 919-292-1101, 454-1126

Bell, Miriam Lee, *Ch,* Edison Free Public Library, Edison NJ. 201-287-2298

Bell, Mrs D N, *Librn,* Ross Township Public Library, Forester's Falls ON. 613-646-2543

Bell, Mrs Glen, *Genealogy,* City of Nanticoke Library Board, Waterford Public Library, Waterford ON. 519-443-7682

Bell, Mrs Glenn, *Dir,* City of Nanticoke Library Board, Waterford Public Library, Waterford ON. 519-443-7682

Bell, Mrs Leon, *Librn,* Hamilton Public Library (Locke), Hamilton ON. 416-522-7154

Bell, Myra, *Librn,* George S Houston Memorial Library (Ashford Branch), Dothan AL. 205-899-3121

Bell, Nancy B, *Librn,* Shelburne Free Public Library, Shelburne Falls MA. 413-625-9728

Bell, Natalie, *Asst Librn,* Perrot Memorial Library, Old Greenwich CT. 203-637-1066

Bell, Phyllis J, *Dir,* Blue Island Public Library, Blue Island IL. 312-388-1078

Bell, Rebecca, *Tech Serv & Cat,* South Dakota State Library, Pierre SD. 605-773-3131

Bell, Richard, *ILL,* University of Wisconsin-Eau Claire, William D McIntyre Library, Eau Claire WI. 715-836-3715

Bell, Richard H, *Coordr,* Nova University Libraries (Media Center Library), Fort Lauderdale FL. 305-475-8300, Ext 264, 245

Bell, Robert E, *Ref & ILL,* University of California at Davis, General Library, Davis CA. 916-752-2110

Bell, Sarah, *Librn,* Midrasha College of Jewish Studies Library, Southfield MI. 313-354-3130

Bell, Shelah A, *Dir,* Irving Public Library System, Irving TX. 214-253-2639

Bell, Susanne, *Asst Librn,* Washington University Libraries (Gaylord Music), Saint Louis MO. 314-889-5560

Bell, Thomas, *Librn,* University of Wisconsin-Milwaukee School of Social Welfare, Region V Child Abuse & Neglect Resource Center, Milwaukee WI. 414-963-6010

Bell, Virginia, *Librn,* Fayette County Public Library (Herbert Jones Library), Oakhill WV. 304-469-9890

Bell, W Wayne, *Asst Dean,* Hofstra University Library, Hempstead NY. 516-560-3475

Bell, Wanda R, *Libr Asst II,* Pennsylvania Department of Environmental Resources (Technical Reference Library), Harrisburg PA. 717-787-9646

Bell, Winnie, *Dir & Acq,* Harding University, Beaumont Memorial Library, Searcy AR. 501-268-6161, Ext 354

Bell, Jr, Whitfield J, *Librn,* American Philosophical Society Library, Philadelphia PA. 215-627-0706

Bellamy, Judy, *Librn,* Contra Costa County Library (El Sobrente Branch), El Sobrante CA. 415-223-1491

Bellamy, Richard, *Bibliog Instr,* Sonoma State University, Ruben Salazar Library, Rohnert Park CA. 707-664-2397

Bellardo, Pamela, *Mgr,* Advanced Micro Devices, Inc, Technical Library, Sunnyvale CA. 408-732-2400, Ext 2260

Bellardo, Trudi, *Librn,* International House of Philadelphia Library, Philadelphia PA. 215-387-5125

Bellardo, Trudi, *On-Line Servs,* University of Kentucky, Margaret I King Library, Lexington KY. 606-257-3801

Bellati, Lynn Doddridge, *Librn,* Deloitte, Haskins & Sells, San Francisco CA. 415-393-4330

Bellavance, Pauline, *Librn,* Bibliotheque Publique Barbel, Gagnon PQ. 418-532-4471

Belleau, Micheline, *Tech Serv & Cat,* College De Maisonneuve Bibliotheque, Montreal PQ. 514-254-7131, 254-4035

Bellefeuille, Sister Julie, *Dir,* College of Notre Dame Library, Belmont CA. 415-593-1601, Ext 57

Bellefontaine, Edgar J, *Librn,* Social Law Library, Boston MA. 617-523-0018

Bellehumeur, Lynn, *ILL,* Milwaukee County Federated Library System, Milwaukee WI. 414-278-3210

Bellehumeur, Lynn, *ILL,* Milwaukee Public Library, Milwaukee WI. 414-278-3000

Beller, Betty, *YA,* Long Beach Public Library, Long Beach NY. 516-432-7201

Bellicha, Terry, *Dir,* National Clearinghouse for Alcohol Information Library, Rockville MD. 301-468-2600

Bellinger, Martha, *Ref,* Claflin College, H V Manning Library, Orangeburg SC. 803-534-2710, Ext 56

Bellinger, Patricia, *Asst Dir,* Erwin Library & Institute, Boonville NY. 315-942-4834

Bellinger, Randy, *Dir,* Mitchell Public Library, Hillsdale MI. 517-437-2581

Bellinger, Robert, *Librn,* Long Beach Public Library System (Bret Harte), Long Beach CA. 213-424-2345

Bellingham, Susan, *Spec Coll,* University of Waterloo Library, Waterloo ON. 519-885-1211

Bellis, Margaret, *Librn,* Johnson Memorial Library, Millersburg PA. 717-692-2658

Belliveau, Jr, Gerard J, *Librn,* Racquet & Tennis Club Library, New York NY. 212-753-9700

Bello, Raymond, *Auto Cat,* Louisiana State University (Troy H Middleton Library), Baton Rouge LA. 504-388-2217

Bellomy, Anne G, *Librn,* Bureau of Geology & Energy Resources Library, Jackson MS. 601-354-6228

Bellstrom, Regina, *Librn,* Townshend Public Library, Townshend VT. 802-365-4039

Belonger, Roland, *Archiviste,* Societe Historique du Saguenay, Chicoutimi PQ. 418-549-2805

Below, Joy, *Librn,* Hubbard Public Library, Hubbard IA. 515-864-2771

Belsito, Karen, *ILL,* University of Massachusetts Medical School, Medical Center Library, Worcester MA. 617-856-2511

Belsterling, Jean I, *Librn,* West Jersey Hospital, Eastern Division, Staff Medical Library, Voorhees NJ. 609-795-3000, Ext 387

Belt, Beth, *Dir,* Boonslick Regional Library, Sedalia MO. 816-826-6195

Belt, Jane, *Librn, On-Line Servs & Bibliog Instr,* Central Washington Hospital, Health Sciences Library, Wenatchee WA. 509-662-1511, Ext 328

Beltran, Ann, *Ref,* Indiana University at Bloomington, University Libraries, Bloomington IN. 812-337-3403

Beltran, Aurora, *Asst Librn,* El Mirage Public Library, El Mirage AZ. 602-933-8407

Beluschak, Robert J, *Dir,* Lee County Library System Administrative Office, Fort Myers FL. 813-334-3221

Belvedere, Dorothy, *Librn,* National Park Service, Ozark National Scenic Riverways Reference Library, Van Buren MO. 314-323-4236

Belvin, Robert J, *Dir,* Geneva Free Library, Geneva NY. 315-789-5303

Bemesderfer, Joy, *Librn,* Kanawha County Public Library (Glasgow Branch), Glasgow WV. 304-595-3131

Bemis, Dorothy, *Asst Dir & Acq,* Musser Public Library, Muscatine IA. 319-263-3065

Bemis, Michael F, *Librn,* Wisconsin Department of Justice, Law Library, Madison WI. 608-266-0325

Bemis, Zoe, *Ref,* Bryn Mawr College, Canaday Library, Bryn Mawr PA. 215-645-5279

Bemmert, Maryellen, *Asst Dir,* Robbins Library, Arlington MA. 617-643-0026

Ben-Chain, Rachel, *Per,* Spertus College of Judaica, Norman & Helen Asher Library, Chicago IL. 312-922-9012, Ext 50

Ben-Zvi, Hava, *Librn,* Jewish Federation Council of Greater Los Angeles, Jewish Community Library, Los Angeles CA. 213-852-1234, Ext 341

Benamati, Dennis, *Tech Serv,* University of Maine School of Law, Donald L Garbrecht Library, Portland ME. 207-780-4350

Benavides, Marilyn, *Librn,* Smithfield City Library, Smithfield UT. 801-563-3555

Benavidez, Sally, *ILL,* New Mexico Highlands University, Donnelly Library, Las Vegas NM. 505-425-7511, Ext 331

Benawa, Violet, *Librn,* BA Investment Management Corp Library, San Francisco CA. 415-622-6883

Benchik, Barbara, *Chief Librn,* Peoples Gas Light & Coke Co Library, Chicago IL. 312-431-4677

Bencivengo, G, *Spec Coll,* William Paterson College of New Jersey, Sarah Byrd Askew Library, Wayne NJ. 201-595-2113

Benda, Janice, *Ad,* Pittsford Community Library, Pittsford NY. 716-586-1251

Bendell, Beverley, *Librn,* Montreal Engineering Co Ltd, Monenco Library, Calgary AB. 403-263-1680, Ext 3710

Bender, Ann, *Librn,* Brooklyn Public Library (Walt Whitman), Brooklyn NY. 212-855-1508

Bender, Barbara, *Librn,* Dallas Public Library (Fretz Park), Dallas TX. 214-233-8262

Bender, Betty W, *Dir,* Spokane Public Library, Comstock Building Library, Spokane WA. 509-838-3361, Ext 65

Bender, Cheryl Geyer, *Librn,* Little Falls Public Library, Little Falls NY. 315-823-1542

Bender, John, *Dir,* Taylor Memorial Public Library, Cuyahoga Falls Public Library, Cuyahoga Falls OH. 216-928-2117

Bender, Kay, *Ad,* Atlantic County Library, Pleasantville NJ. 609-646-8699, 645-7121, 625-2776

Bender, Miriam, *Dir,* Davis Junior College of Business Library, Toledo OH. 419-255-0700

Bender, Jr, Thomas R, *Fisheries Biologist,* Pennsylvania Fish Commission, Benner Spring Fish Research Station Library, Bellefonte PA. 814-355-4837

Bendix, Linda A, *Librn & Bibliog Instr,* Lakeland College, Community Memorial Library, Sheboygan WI. 414-565-1238

Bendure, Bobbie, *Librn,* Chronicle-Telegram Library, Lorain County Printing & Publishing Co, Elyria OH. 216-323-3321

Benedetti, Joan M, *Coordr,* Craft & Folk Art Museum Library, Media Resource Center, Los Angeles CA. 213-939-4952, 937-5544

Benedict, Dixie, *Per,* Humboldt State University Library, Arcata CA. 707-826-3441

Benedict, Lorraine L, *Asst Prof,* San Antonio College, Library Technology Program, TX. 512-734-7311, Ext 2482

Benedict, Mary Jane, *Librn,* Louisville School of Art, Inc Library, Louisville KY. 502-245-8836

Benedict, Michael, *Coordr, Mat Selection,* Houston Public Library, Houston TX. 713-224-5441

Benedict, Richard F, *Syst Coordr,* United States Air Force, Air University Library, Maxwell AFB AL. 205-293-2888

Benefield, Marian, *Librn,* Daphne Public Library, Daphne AL. 205-626-3441

Benelisha, Eleanor, *Dir,* Saint Mary's Hospital & Medical Center, Medical Library, San Francisco CA. 415-668-1000

Benemann, William E, *Tech Serv,* Golden Gate University (School of Law Library), San Francisco CA. 415-442-7260

Benes, Ellen, *AV,* Loutit Library, Grand Haven MI. 616-842-5560

Benet, S, *Music,* University of Victoria, McPherson Library, Victoria BC. 604-477-6911, Ext 4466

Benetz, Stephen, *Pub Servs,* New Orleans Public Library, Simon Heinsheim & Fisk Libraries, New Orleans LA. 504-586-4905

Benford, Elizabeth S, *Librn,* University of Michigan (English Language Institute Library), Ann Arbor MI. 313-764-2417

Bengisser, Bartholomew, *Dir,* Franciscan Monastery Library, Washington DC. 202-526-6800

Benglas, Gitta, *Asst Librn,* Fritzsche, Dodge & Olcott, Inc Library, New York NY. 212-929-4100

Bengston, Lisa, *Acting Asst,* Ontario County Historical Society Library, Canandaigua NY. 716-394-4975

Bengtson, Betty, *Cat,* Georgetown University, Joseph Mark Lauinger Library, Washington DC. 202-625-4095

Benham, Blanche, *Librn,* Thompson-Brumm-Knepper Clinic Library, Saint Joseph MO. 816-233-9711

Benham, Virginia, *Librn,* Miracle Valley Regional Library (McMechen Public Branch), McMechen WV. 304-232-9720

Beninghave, Martha, *Asst Librn,* Howard County Library (Wilde Lake), Columbia MD. 301-465-8980

Benish, Carol J, *Dir,* Bloomsburg Public Library, Bloomsburg PA. 717-784-0883

Benitez-Sharpless, Mercedes, *Librn,* Lafayette College (Kirby Library of Government & Law), Easton PA. 215-253-6281, Ext 321

Benjamin, Bernadette, *In Charge,* Saint Michael's College (Serials), Colchester VT. 802-655-2000, Ext 2400

Benjamin, Doris, *Dir,* Itawamba Junior College, Learning Resource Center, Fulton MS. 601-862-3101, Ext 237

Benjamin, Doris, *Dir,* Itawamba Junior College Vocational-Technical Center, Itawamba Junior College-Tupelo Branch, Learning Resources Ctr, Tupelo MS. 601-842-5621, Ext 25

Benjamin, Elinor, *Librn,* Newfoundland Public Library Services (Western Region), Corner Brook NF. 709-634-7333

Benjamin, Mary, *Librn,* Hesperia District Library, Hesperia MI. 616-854-5125

Benjamin, Merla, *Librn,* Donnellson Community Library, Donnellson IA. 319-835-5545

Benjamin, Mrs M, *Librn,* Canadian Marconi Co Library, Montreal PQ. 514-341-7630

Benjamin, Virginia, *Sci Ref,* University of Georgia Libraries, Athens GA. 404-542-2716

Benkert, Alan, *Br Ad Serus,* Fairfield Public Library, Fairfield CT. 203-259-8303

Benn, Diane, *Librn,* Veterans Memorial Library (Gladys McArthur Memorial), Weidman MI. 517-664-3316

Benn, James R, *Regional Coordr,* Southeastern Connecticut Library Association, (SECLA), CT. 203-448-1554

Benne, Mae, *Prof,* University of Washington, School of Librarianship, WA. 206-543-1794

Bennen, Jr, Thomas J, *Dir,* Watonwan County Library, Saint James MN. 507-375-3791

Benner, Evangeline, *Librn,* Baltimore County Public Library (Dundalk Branch), Dundalk MD. 301-284-3660

Benner, Evangeline, *Librn,* Baltimore County Public Library (Edgemere Minilibrary), Towson MD. 301-477-1515

Benner, Evangeline, *Librn,* Baltimore County Public Library (North Point Area), Baltimore MD. 301-285-5000

Benner, Evangeline, *Librn,* Baltimore County Public Library (Turner's Station Branch), Turner's Station MD. 301-284-7570

Benner, Marie, *Ch,* Waterville Public Library, Waterville ME. 207-872-5433

Bennet, R, *Dir,* Souris Valley Extended Care Hospital Library, Weyburn SK. 306-842-7481

Bennett, Helen L, *Americana,* University of Missouri-Kansas City Libraries, Kansas City MO. 816-276-1531

Bennett, Agnes, *Cat,* California State College, Stanislaus Library, Turlock CA. 209-633-2232

Bennett, Ann, *Librn,* New Mexico School for the Deaf Library, Santa Fe NM. 505-983-3321, 982-1721

Bennett, Bernard, *Ref,* Blinn College, W L Moody Jr Library, Brenham TX. 713-836-6566

Bennett, Betsy, *Bkmobile Coordr,* Valparaiso-Porter County Public Library System & Administrative Headquarters, Valparaiso IN. 219-462-0524

Bennett, Betty, *Doc,* Stephen F Austin State University, Ralph W Steen Library, Nacogdoches TX. 713-569-4109

Bennett, Bill, *Dir,* F H Hayhurst Co Ltd, Research Library, Toronto ON. 416-487-4371

Bennett, Bill A, *Dir,* L'anse Township School & Public Library, L'Anse MI. 906-524-6213

Bennett, Bridget, *Ch,* Memorial Hall Library, (Subregional Headquarters for Eastern Massachusetts Regional System), Andover MA. 617-475-6960

Bennett, C, *Librn,* Newcastle Public Library (Newcastle Memorial), Newcastle ON. 416-987-4844

Bennett, Charlene W, *Media,* Abilene Public Library, Abilene TX. 915-677-2474

Bennett, Charles G, *Genealogical Librn,* Bennington Museum, Genealogical Library, Bennington VT. 802-442-2180

Bennett, Claire, *Rare Bks & Spec Coll,* Southern Connecticut State College, Hilton C Buley Library, New Haven CT. 203-397-4505

Bennett, Claudine, *Librn,* Jennings City Library, Jennings KS. 913-678-2306

Bennett, Cynthia, *Dir,* Lewisville Public Library, Lewisville TX. 214-436-1812

Bennett, Dave, *Media,* Durham College of Applied Arts & Technology Library, Oshawa ON. 416-576-0210, Ext 214

Bennett, Della, *Dir,* Stillwater Public Library, City Library, Stillwater OK. 405-372-3633

Bennett, Diane, *Dir,* Nancy Carol Roberts Memorial Library, Brenham TX. 713-836-2312

Bennett, Dorothea E, *Chief Libr Servs,* Veterans Administration, Hospital Medical Library, Martinez CA. 415-228-6800, Ext 298

Bennett, Emerson, *ILL,* Mott Community College, C S Mott Library, Flint MI. 313-762-0400

Bennett, Esther, *Tech Serv,* Sunflower County Library System, Indianola MS. 601-887-2153, 887-2298

Bennett, Florence, *Ch & YA,* Trumbull Library, Trumbull CT. 203-261-6421

Bennett, Floyd H, *Cat,* Louisiana State University at Alexandria Library, Alexandria LA. 318-445-3672, Ext 46

Bennett, Frank, *Ref,* Statesboro Regional Library, Statesboro GA. 912-764-7573

Bennett, Gladys, *In Charge,* Packwood Community Library, Packwood IA. 515-695-5131

Bennett, Gordon L, *Dir,* Park County Public Library, Bailey CO. 303-838-5539

Bennett, Helen, *Ref,* California State University, Northridge, Delmar T Oviatt & South Libraries, Northridge CA. 213-885-2271

Bennett, J, *Librn,* Okanagan Regional Library District (Westbank Branch), Westbank BC. 604-768-4369

Bennett, Jack, *Dir,* Clayton Junior College Library, Morrow GA. 404-961-3520

Bennett, Joanne, *Librn,* Beebe Hospital, Medical Library, Lewes DE. 302-645-3283

Bennett, Joanne, *Librn,* Beebe Hospital (Nursing School Library), Lewes DE. 302-645-3251

Bennett, Joyce, *Librn,* Fremont County Library (Hudson Branch), Hudson WY. 307-332-5194

Bennett, Joyce A, *Dir,* Bentley College, Solomon R Baker Library, Waltham MA. 617-891-2231

Bennett, Kenneth, *Coll Develop,* California State University Dominguez Hills, Educational Resources Center, Carson CA. 213-515-3700

Bennett, Klara, *Dir,* Dows Community Library, Dows IA. 515-852-4326

Bennett, Lisa, *Ch,* West Haven Public Library, West Haven CT. 203-932-2221

Bennett, Lynne, *Librn,* Kansas Community Memorial Library, Kansas IL. 217-948-5484

Bennett, M A, *Librn,* Atlanta Public Library (Greenbriar), Atlanta GA. 404-344-4052

Bennett, Madaleine G, *Librn,* Raytheon Co (Research Division Library), Waltham MA. 617-899-8400, Ext 2196

Bennett, Marcia, *Librn,* Long Beach Public Library System (Burnett), Long Beach CA. 213-591-8614

Bennett, Marcia, *Health Occupations,* Wake Technical College Library, Raleigh NC. 919-772-0551, Ext 236

Bennett, Margaret, *Tech Serv,* Saint Andrews Presbyterian College, DeTamble Library, Laurinburg NC. 919-276-3652, Ext 307, 289

Bennett, Marion, *Dir, Ad & Acq,* Marshall Public Library, Marshall MI. 616-781-7821

Bennett, Mary, *Genealogy,* Fort Bend County Library, Richmond TX. 713-342-4455

Bennett, Mary Ann, *ILL,* Eastfield College, Learning Resources Center, Mesquite TX. 214-746-3168

Bennett, Michael Wayne, *Librn,* Sacramento County Medical Society, Paul H Guttman Library, Sacramento CA. 916-452-2671, Ext 7

Bennett, Myrtle C, *Dir,* North Carolina Agricultural & Technical State University, F D Bluford Library, Greensboro NC. 919-379-7782, 379-7783

Bennett, Nancy, *ILL,* Pinal County Library System, Florence AZ. 602-868-5801, Ext 456

Bennett, Pauline, *ILL & Ref,* Qualla Boundary Public Library, Cherokee NC. 704-497-9023

Bennett, Peg, *Cat,* Southern Missionary College, McKee Library, Collegedale TN. 615-396-4290

Bennett, Peggy, *Asst Prof,* Southern Missionary College, Library Science Program, TN. 615-396-4291

Bennett, Peter, *Regional Reference Librn,* Northern Interrelated Library System, Pawtucket RI. 401-723-5350

Bennett, Phyllis, *Librn,* Baptist Medical Center of Oklahoma, Medical Library, Oklahoma City OK. 405-949-3766

Bennett, Richard, *Archives & Rare Bks,* University of Manitoba Libraries, Winnipeg MB. 204-474-9881

Bennett, Rolland L, *Librn, Rare Bks & Spec Coll,* Asbury College, Morrison-Kenyon Library, Wilmore KY. 606-858-3511

Bennett, Rowland, *Dir,* Maplewood Memorial Library, Maplewood NJ. 201-762-1622

Bennett, Ruth, *Ad & Ref,* Newmarket Public Library, Newmarket ON. 416-895-5196

Bennett, Sally H, *Cat,* Eastern College, Frank Warner Memorial Library, Saint Davids PA. 215-688-3300, Ext 210

Bennett, Sharon, *Librn,* Charleston Museum Library, Charleston SC. 803-722-2996, Ext 3

Bennett, Sherry, *ILL,* Robert J Kleberg Public Library, Kingsville TX. 512-592-6381

Bennett, Shirley, *Librn,* Keyport Free Public Library, Keyport NJ. 201-264-0543

Bennett, Sister Marie Cecile, *Ref,* Fontbonne College Library, Saint Louis MO. 314-862-3456, Ext 352

Bennett, Susan, *Ad & YA,* Carnegie Public Library District, Fortville IN. 317-485-5432

Bennett, Virginia, *Librn,* Alameda County Library (Dublin Branch), Dublin CA. 415-828-1315

Bennett, Y S, *Ref & Bibliog Instr,* Medgar Evers College Library, Brooklyn NY. 212-735-1851

Bennetts, M, *Librn,* Teck Centennial Library, Kirkland Lake ON. 705-567-7966

Benney, Sue, *ILL,* California State Polytechnic University Library, Pomona CA. 714-598-4671

Benninghoff, R N, *Educ,* Cleveland State University Libraries, Cleveland OH. 216-687-2486

Benninghoff, Robert N, *On-Line Servs,* Cleveland State University Libraries, Cleveland OH. 216-687-2486

Bennis, Patricia P, *Librn,* United Food & Commercial Workers International Union Library, Washington DC. 202-223-3111, Ext 212

Bennorth, Barbara, *Dir,* Kent Free Public Library, Carmel NY. 914-225-8585

Beno, Henry, *Dir,* Fox Valley Technical Institute, Educational Resource Center, Appleton WI. 414-735-5746

Benoit, Anthony H, *Dir,* Morehouse Parish Library, Bastrop LA. 318-281-3683

Benoit, Anthony H, *Librn,* Morehouse Parish Library (Bastrop Branch), Bastrop LA. 318-281-3683

Benoit, Francine, *Bibliog Instr,* Science Council of Canada Library, Ottawa ON. 613-996-1729

Benoit, Graham, *Dir,* Owatonna Free Public Library, Owatonna MN. 507-451-4660

Benolken, Marjorie, *Ch,* West Chicago Public Library, West Chicago IL. 312-231-1552

Bensmiller, Robert, *Media,* Iowa Wesleyan College, Chadwick Library, Mount Pleasant IA. 319-385-8021, Ext 131

Benson, Bobbie, *Cat,* Logan-Helm Woodford County Public Library, Versailles KY. 606-873-5191, 873-9703

Benson, Doreen, *Dir,* Laurel Springs Library, Laurel Springs NJ. 609-627-4888

Benson, Elfrida C, *Librn,* Richmond Public Library (East End), Richmond VA. 804-780-4474

Benson, Elizabeth, *Librn,* Topinabee Public Library, Topinabee MI. 616-238-7514

Benson, Esther, *Librn,* Citronelle Memorial Library, Citronelle AL. 205-866-7319

Benson, George R, *AV,* Centre College of Kentucky, Grace Doherty Library, Danville KY. 606-236-5211, Ext 237

Benson, Harold W, *Librn,* New York City Human Resources Administration Library, New York NY. 212-460-8555

Benson, Hazel B, *Asst Dir & Ref,* Ohio State University Libraries (Health Sciences Library), Columbus OH. 614-422-9810

Benson, Isabel, *Ref,* Stockton-San Joaquin County Public Library, Stockton Public Libr, Stockton CA. 209-944-8415

Benson, James, *Assoc Prof,* University of Alabama, Graduate School of Library Service, AL. 205-348-4610

Benson, Jane, *Librn,* Frank Hughes Memorial Library, Liberty MO. 816-781-3611

Benson, Jean M, *Dir,* Muscoda Public Library, Muscoda WI. 608-739-3182

Benson, Joseph, *Dir,* Chicago Transit Authority Library, Chicago IL. 312-664-7200, Ext 754

Benson, Karl A, *Librn,* Danville-Boyle County Public Library, Danville KY. 606-236-8466

Benson, Liz, *Cat,* College of Wooster, Andrews Library, Wooster OH. 216-264-1234, Ext 483

Benson, Margaret, *Circ,* Public Library of Nashville & Davidson County, Nashville TN. 615-244-4700

Benson, Marion, *Librn,* Argonne National Laboratory (Reactor Safety & Applied Physics), Argonne IL. 312-972-4825

Benson, Mary, *Librn,* Packaging Corporation of America, Research Library, Grand Rapids MI. 616-459-4581

Benson, Mary Margaret, *Cat,* School of Theology at Claremont, Theology Library, Claremont CA. 714-626-3521, Ext 263

Benson, Maxine, *Curator,* Colorado Historical Society, Documentary Resources Department, Denver CO. 303-839-2305

Benson, Mrs Arlo, *Librn,* Marathon Public Library, Marathon IA. 712-289-2261

Benson, Nancy D, *Ad,* Neill Public Library, Pullman Public Library, Pullman WA. 509-334-3595

Benson, Pat, *In Charge,* Cokato Library, Cokato MN. 612-286-5760

Benson, Ruth M, *ILL, YA & Ref,* Floral Park Public Library, Floral Park NY. 516-354-0666

Benson, Stanley H, *Dir, Acq & Bibliog Instr,* Oklahoma Baptist University, Mabee Learning Center, Shawnee OK. 405-275-2850, Ext 245

Benson, Virginia, *Librn,* North Brevard Public Library, Titusville FL. 305-269-7323

Bent, Geoffrey, *Asst Librn,* Sonnenschein, Carlin, Nath & Rosenthal, Law Library, Chicago IL. 312-876-7906

Bent, Ruth, *Pub Servs,* Antioch College, Olive Kettering Memorial Library, Yellow Springs OH. 513-767-7331, Ext 229

Bente, June E, *Manager,* Ortho Pharmaceutical Corp, Hartman Library, Raritan NJ. 201-524-2240

Bentley, Carol, *Mat Ctr,* Chicago State University, Paul & Emily Douglas Library, Chicago IL. 312-995-2254

Bentley, Carrie, *Librn,* Chattahoochee Valley Regional Library (Chattahoochee County Public), Cusseta GA. 404-327-0211

Bentley, Elizabeth, *On-Line Servs,* New York Public Library, Astor, Lenox & Tilden Foundations Library, New York NY. 212-790-6262

Bentley, Elizabeth, *Acting Chief,* New York Public Library (Cooperative Services Div), New York NY. 212-790-6262

Bentley, Jane, *Librn,* San Diego Museum of Man, Scientific Library, San Diego CA. 714-239-2001, Ext 23

Bentley, Janice Babb, *Librn,* Mayer, Brown & Platt Law Library, Chicago IL. 312-782-0600

Bentley, LeMerle, *Ref,* Morehead State University, Johnson Camden-Julian Carroll Library, Morehead KY. 606-783-2250

Bentley, Louise, *Librn,* Birmingham Public & Jefferson County Free Library (Avondale), Birmingham AL. 205-254-2551

Bentley, Margaret Ann, *Ad,* Owosso Public Library, Owosso MI. 517-725-5134

Bentley, Martha J, *Libr Chairman,* Monterey History & Art Association, Mayo Hayes O'Donnell Library, Monterey CA. 408-372-2608

Bentley, Sara A, *YA,* Field Library, Peekskill Library, Peekskill NY. 914-737-0010

Benton, Claudia, *Cat,* Kanawha County Public Library, Kanawha County Service Center, Charleston WV. 304-343-4646

Benton, Dena J, *Librn,* Granville Public Library, Granville MA. 413-357-8531

Benton, Evelyn F, *Dir,* Deer Park Public Library, Deer Park TX. 713-479-5276

Benton, Joanne, *Dir,* Good Samaritan Hospital Library, Vincennes IN. 812-885-3333

Benton, Marjorie, *Music & Art,* Public Library of Des Moines, Des Moines IA. 515-283-4152

Benton, Rita B, *Librn,* University of Iowa Libraries (Music), Iowa City IA. 319-353-3797

Benton, Susan, *Librn,* Irving Public Library System (Southwest), Irving TX. 214-253-2546

Bentz, Dale M, *Librn,* University of Iowa Libraries, Iowa City IA. 319-353-4450

Bentz, Marlene A, *Librn,* Sheldon Public Library, Sheldon IA. 712-324-2442

Bentzler, Georgiane, *Librn,* University of Wisconsin Center, Marshfield-Wood County Library, Marshfield WI. 715-387-1147

Benyo, John C, *Asst Librn,* Saint Vincent College & Archabbey Libraries, Latrobe PA. 412-539-9761, Ext 378

Benz, Allen, *Librn, On-Line Servs & Bibliog Instr,* Aerial Phenomena Research Organization, Inc, APRO Library-Information Services, Tucson AZ. 602-323-1825

Beran, Lois, *Librn,* Caldwell Carnegie Library, Caldwell KS. 316-845-6879

Beran, Mary Lou, *Cat,* Idaho State University Library, Pocatello ID. 208-236-3202

Berardi, Darlene, *Tech Serv,* Transylvania University, Frances Carrick Thomas Library, Lexington KY. 606-233-8225

Berberena, Felix, *Media,* Inter-American University-Fajardo Regional College, Centro de Recursos para el Aprendizaje, Fajardo PR. 809-863-2390

Berberich, Patricia L, *Admin Asst & Coordr Exten Servs,* Hartford Public Library, Hartford CT. 203-525-9121

Berch, Victor, *Spec Coll,* Brandeis University, Goldfarb Library, Waltham MA. 617-647-2514

Bercik, Ed, *Circ,* Edinboro State College, Baron-Forness Library, Edinboro PA. 814-732-2780

Bercik, Elaine, *Curric Mat,* Edinboro State College, Baron-Forness Library, Edinboro PA. 814-732-2780

Berdel, Mary Ellen, *Librn,* East Brunswick Public Library (Alice Appleby DeVoe Memorial), East Brunswick NJ. 201-257-8376

Berenbak, Margaret M, *Asst Dir,* Morris County Free Library, Whippany NJ. 201-285-6101

Berenson, Irwin R, *Ref,* Peninsula Public Library, Lawrence NY. 516-239-3262

Beresini, Katrina, *Librn,* San Benito County Law Library, Hollister CA. 408-637-3786

Berezin, Evelyn, *Librn,* Framingham Public Library (Saxonville), Framingham MA. 617-877-3636

Berg, Ann, *ILL & Ref,* Purdue University, North Central Campus Library, Westville IN. 219-785-2541

Berg, Ann, *Govt Ref,* Tucson Public Library, Tucson AZ. 602-791-4391

Berg, Ann, *Librn,* Tucson Public Library (Local Government Information Center), Tucson AZ. 602-791-4041

Berg, Barbara J, *Librn,* United States Army (Corps of Engineers, Alaska District Library), Anchorage AK. 907-752-4910

Berg, Betty, *Librn,* Redwood City Public Library (Schaberg), Redwood City CA. 415-368-8628

Berg, Carmen, *Ch,* Fergus Falls Public Library, Fergus Falls MN. 218-739-9387

Berg, Donna, *On-Line Servs,* University of Wyoming, William Robertson Coe Library, Laramie WY. 307-766-3279

Berg, Dorothy, *Ad,* Lorain Public Library, Lorain OH. 216-244-1192

Berg, Edith, *Coordr,* Saskatchewan Consumer Affairs Resource Center, Regina SK. 306-565-5549

Berg, Evelyn, *Secy,* Peoria Historical Society, Harry L Spooner Memorial Library, Peoria IL. 309-674-1921

Berg, Frances, *Librn,* General Electric Co (Branch Library), Philadelphia PA. 215-823-3405

Berg, Helen, *Circ,* Kutztown State College, Rohrbach Library, Kutztown PA. 215-683-4480

Berg, Janet, *Dir,* Marion Public Library, Marion OH. 614-387-0992

Berg, Janis D, *Dir,* Kilbourn Public Library, Wisconsin Dells WI. 608-254-2146

Berg, Joanne, *Librn,* Spring Valley Public Library, Spring Valley MN. 507-346-2100

Berg, Margaret, *ILL,* Delaware Technical & Community College Library, Newark DE. 302-368-6985

Berg, Richard R, *Media,* United Theological Seminary Library, Dayton OH. 513-278-5817

Berg, Valborg Hansing, *Librn,* Freeborn County Historical Society, Research Library, Albert Lea MN. 507-373-8003

Bergen, Daniel, *Prof,* University of Rhode Island, Graduate Library School, RI. 401-792-2878 or 792-2947

Bergen, Florence, *Tech Serv,* Wolcott Public Library, Wolcott CT. 203-879-3663

Bergeon, Ethel, *Librn,* Hall-Fowler Memorial Library, Ionia MI. 616-527-3680

Berger, Alvin C, *Circ,* East Stroudsburg State College, Kemp Library, East Stroudsburg PA. 717-424-3467

Berger, Bernice, *Br Coordr,* El Dorado County Library, Placerville CA. 916-626-2561

Berger, Betty, *Librn,* Tipton County Public Library (Windfall Branch), Windfall IN. 317-945-7655

Berger, Brenda, *AV,* East Brunswick Public Library, East Brunswick NJ. 201-254-1220

Berger, Carol A, *Mgr Libr & Info Servs,* Beatrice Foods Co, Research Center Library, Chicago IL. 312-791-8292

Berger, Claudia, *Librn,* Berkeley Public Library (South), Berkeley CA. 714-644-6860

Berger, David O, *Dir,* Concordia College, Rincker Library, Milwaukee WI. 414-344-3400, Ext 526

Berger, Jason S, *In Charge,* Sinai Temple Library, Springfield MA. 413-736-3619

Berger, Jeanne A, *Librn,* Henry C Adams Memorial Library, Prophetstown IL. 815-537-5462

Berger, Jeff, *Asst Dir & YA,* Franklin Public Library, Franklin NH. 603-934-2911

Berger, Leslie, *Ref,* East Stroudsburg State College, Kemp Library, East Stroudsburg PA. 717-424-3467

Berger, Leslie, *Ref, Rare Bks & Spec Coll,* Easton Area Public Library, Easton PA. 215-258-2917

Berger, Lewis W, *On-Line Servs & Bibliog Instr,* United States Steel Corp, Research Laboratory Technical Information Center, Monroeville PA. 412-372-1212, Ext 2344

Berger, Linda, *Bkmobile Coordr,* Hutchinson Public Library, Hutchinson KS. 316-663-5441

Berger, Mary, *Ad,* Norfolk Public Library, Lewis & Clark Regional Library, Norfolk NE. 402-371-4590

Berger, Morey, *Librn,* Monmouth County Library (Eastern), Shrewsbury NJ. 201-842-5995

Berger, Patricia W, *Dir Libr Serv,* National Bureau of Standards (Bureau of Standards Library), Washington DC. 301-921-3405

Berger, Sister Frances Loretta, *Circ & Educ Mat Ctr,* Mundelein College, Learning Resource Center, Chicago IL. 312-262-8100, Ext 301, 302 & 303

Bergeron, Cheri, *In Charge,* Montana Office of Public Instruction, Resource Center, Helena MT. 406-449-2082

Bergeron, Gilles, *Ref,* University du Quebec: Centre d'Etudes Universitaires Dans L'Ouest Quebecois, Centre de Hull Bibliotheque, Hull PQ. 819-776-8381

Bergeron, Rita E, *Librn,* Renegotiation Board Library, Washington DC. 202-254-8221

Bergeron, Sister Leon, *Assoc Prof,* Silver Lake College, School Librarianship Program, WI. 414-684-6691, Ext 34

Bergeron, William, *Librn,* Cranston Public Library (Oaklawn), Cranston RI. 401-942-1787

Bergeson, Alan, *Bibliog Instr,* College of DuPage, Learning Resources Center, Glen Ellyn IL. 312-858-2800, Ext 2351

Bergeson, Hal, *Media,* Pikes Peak Community College, Learning Materials Center, Colorado Springs CO. 303-576-7711, Ext 536

Berggren, Britta, *Librn,* Lindberg Corp Library, Chicago IL. 312-693-2021

Bergin, Dorothy O, *Librn,* Mobil Tyco Solar Energy Corp Library, Waltham MA. 617-890-0909, Ext 362

Bergin, Margaret, *Talking Bks,* Arlington County Department of Libraries, Arlington Public Library, Arlington VA. 703-527-4777

Bergles, Frances, *Fine & Performing Arts,* Saskatoon Public Library, Saskatoon SK. 306-664-9555

Berglin, Mary, *Commun Servs,* Vermillion Public Library, Vermillion SD. 605-624-2741

Berglund, Edean, *Librn,* Saint Luke's Hospital, Medical Library, Duluth MN. 218-727-6636, Ext 5320

Berglund, Faith, *Librn,* Marathon County Public Library (Joseph Dessert), Mosinee WI. 715-693-2144

Berglund, Nina, *Cat,* Mansfield State College Library, Mansfield PA. 717-662-4071

Bergman, Betty, *Pub Servs,* Waterloo Public Library, Waterloo IA. 319-291-4521

Bergman, Edward, *ILL & Media,* Leominster Public Library, Leominster MA. 617-537-0941

Bergman, Joyce, *Asst Librn,* Runnemede Public Library, Runnemede NJ. 609-939-4688

Bergman, Sherrie S, *Librn,* Wheaton College Library, Norton MA. 617-285-7722, Ext 518

Bergmann, Mary Jane M, *Dir,* Margaret R Grundy Memorial Library, Bristol PA. 215-788-7891

Bergmann, Randall W, *Circ, Ref & On-Line Servs,* United States Air Force (Air Force Geophysics Laboratory, Research Library), Hanscom AFB MA. 617-861-4895

Bergmark, Nancy, *Acq,* Georgia Department of Education (Div of Public Library Services), Atlanta GA. 404-656-2461

Bergner, Helen, *Dir,* Gillett Public Library, Gillett WI. 414-855-6224

Bergon, Helen, *Biog,* Public Library of the District of Columbia, Martin Luther King Memorial Library, Washington DC. 202-727-1101

Bergquist, Jeannette, *Librn,* Waterville Public Library, Waterville KS. 913-785-2769

Bergquist, Martha, *ILL,* Reed College, E V Hauser Memorial Library, Portland OR. 503-771-1112, Ext 260

Bergsing, Patricia M, *Librn,* Burlingame Public Library, Burlingame CA. 415-344-7107

Bergstad, K, *Asst Librn,* Inyo County Law Library, Independence CA. 714-878-2411, Ext 269

Beringer, H Joy, *Librn,* West Haven Public Library (Ora B Mason Branch), West Haven CT. 203-933-9381

Berk, Jack M, *Dir,* Bethlehem Public Library, Bethlehem PA. 215-867-3761

Berk, Janet B, *History of Med,* University of Rochester (Edward G Miner Library, School of Medicine & Dentistry), Rochester NY. 716-275-3364

Berk, Lawrence S, *Assoc Dir,* Hudson Valley Community College Learning Resources Center, Dwight Marvin Library, Troy NY. 518-283-1100, Ext 629

Berk, Robert A, *Assoc Prof,* University of Arizona, Graduate Library School, AZ. 602-626-3565

Berkan, Esther, *Librn,* Delta College, Learning Resources Center, University Center MI. 517-686-9000

Berkebile, Hazel, *Librn,* First Baptist Church Library, North Kansas City MO. 816-842-1175

Berkeley, Edmund, *Manuscripts,* University of Virginia, Alderman Library, Charlottesville VA. 804-924-3026

Berkeley, Rebecca, *Librn,* Enoch Pratt Free Library (Pennsylvania Ave), Baltimore MD. 301-396-5430, 396-5395

Berkeley, Rebecca, *In Charge,* Enoch Pratt Free Library (Reservoir Hill), Baltimore MD. 301-396-5430, 396-5395

Berkeley, Roberta, *Cat,* Antillian College Library, Mayaguez PR. 809-832-9595, Ext 209

Berkemeier, Sister Hildemar, *ILL & Ref,* Christ the King Seminary Library, East Aurora NY. 716-652-8959

Berkey, Trudy, *Public Serv,* West Virginia Northern Community College, New Martinsville Campus Library, New Martinsville WV. 304-233-5900

Berkhofer, G H, *Dir,* Clark County Historical Society Library, Springfield OH. 513-324-0657

Berkley, Audrey Kargus, *Librn,* Saint Louis Society for Medical & Scientific Education Library, Saint Louis MO. 314-371-5225

Berkley, Audrey L, *Librn,* Saint Louis Metropolitan Medical Society, Saint Louis Society for Medical & Scientific Education Library, Saint Louis MO. 314-371-5225

Berkley, Robert J, *Dir,* Nasson College, Anderson Learning Center Library, Springvale ME. 207-324-5340, Ext 26

Berkness, Chris, *Ch,* Loveland Public Library, Loveland CO. 303-667-4040

Berkowitz, Dorothy J, *Librn,* United States International Trade Commission Library, Washington DC. 202-523-0013

Berkowitz, Nancy, *Instr,* Lansing Community College, Library Media Technology Program, MI. 517-373-9978

Berlin, Charles, *Bibliogr in Judaica,* Harvard University Library (Harvard College Library (Headquarters in Harry Elkins Widener Memorial Library)), Cambridge MA. 617-495-2401

Berlin, Deborah, *Cat,* Kelley Library, Salem Public Library, Salem NH. 603-898-7064

Berlin, N, *Librn,* Borough of York Public Library (Mobil Library Service (Shut-in)), Toronto ON. 416-781-5208

Berliner, Donna, *Librn,* Temple Emanu El Library, Alex Weisberg Library, Dallas TX. 214-368-3613, Ext 411

Berling, John, *Dean,* Saint Cloud State University, Center for Library & Audiovisual Education, MN. 612-255-2022

Berling, John G, *Dean,* Saint Cloud State University, Centennial Hall Learning Resources Center, Saint Cloud MN. 612-255-2084

Berman, Arthur, *Dir,* East Arkansas Community College, Learning Resources Center, Forrest City AR. 501-633-4480, Ext 28

Berman, Estelle, *Dir,* Scarsdale Public Library, Scarsdale NY. 914-723-2005

Berman, Gertrude L, *Librn,* Congregation B'nai Israel Synagogue Library, Woonsocket RI. 401-762-3651

Berman, Jenny, *Librn,* Public Library of Charlotte & Mecklenburg County, Inc (Metrolina Library for the Blind & Physically Handicapped), Charlotte NC. 704-334-4358

Berman, Joan, *Cat,* Humboldt State University Library, Arcata CA. 707-826-3441

Berman, Leslie M, *Planning & Res,* Connecticut State Library, Hartford CT. 203-566-4301

Berman, Mary, *Librn,* New York Public Library (Sedgwick), New York NY. 212-294-1182

Berman, Sanford, *Cat,* Hennepin County Library, Edina MN. 612-830-4944

Berman, Susan, *Ad & Ref,* North Kingstown Free Library, North Kingstown RI. 401-294-2521

Bermann, Ruth L, *Dir,* New London Public Library, New London WI. 414-982-3521

Bermel, Margaret, *Librn,* Deschutes County Library (Sisters Public), Sisters OR. 503-549-2921

Bermingham, Margaret L, *Ad,* Mount Vernon Public Library, Mount Vernon NY. 914-668-1840

Bermudez, Edna, *Librn,* West Georgia Regional Library (Warren P Sewell Memorial Library of Bremen), Bremen GA. 404-832-1381

Bernadette, Sister Catherine, *Per,* Caldwell College Library, Caldwell NJ. 201-228-4424, Ext 34

Bernal, Emilia, *Prof,* University of Puerto Rico, Graduate School of Librarianship, PR. 809-764-0000, Ext 3522, 3526

Bernard, B A, *Librn,* Emery Industries Inc, Research Library, Cincinnati OH. 513-482-2157

Bernard, Bobbi, *Librn,* AMF Inc, Technical Information Center, Stamford CT. 203-325-2211, Ext 4510

Bernard, Hugh Y, *Dir & Acq,* George Washington University Library (Jacob Burns Law Library), Washington DC. 202-676-6646

Bernard, J David, *Dir,* Saint Joseph's Hospital, Medical Library, Stockton CA. 209-943-2000

Bernard, Janet, *Librn,* Spring Valley Public Library, Spring Valley IL. 815-663-4741

Bernard, Jeannette, *Librn,* Saint Louis County Library (Lewis & Clark), St Louis MO. 314-868-0331

Bernard, Lowell F, *Dir,* Cleveland Health Education Museum Library, Cleveland OH. 216-231-5010

Bernard, Mlle Gaby, *Librn,* Bibliotheque Municipale, Warwick PQ. 819-358-6187

Bernard, Mrs C, *Librn,* La Rocca Laboratories, Inc Library, Dumont NJ. 201-384-8509

Bernard, Richard, *Asst Prof,* University of British Columbia, School of Librarianship, BC. 604-228-2404

Bernard, Virginia B, *Dir,* Haverhill Public Library, Haverhill MA. 617-373-1586

Bernardi, Eunice, *Librn,* Weir Public Library, Weir KS. 316-396-8214

Bernardi, Toni, *Ch & YA,* Grove City Public Library, Grove City OH. 614-875-6716

Bernardin, Luce, *Dir,* Bibliotheque Municipale, Saint Bruno-de-Montarville PQ. 514-653-2474

Bernasek, Carol, *Cat, Music & Rec,* North Carolina School of the Arts, Semans Library, Winston-Salem NC. 919-784-7170, Ext 2566

Bernath, Mrs E, *Librn,* Bryan Public Library (Stryker Public), Stryker OH. 419-682-5081

Bernaudo, Richard P, *Dir,* Nutley Public Library, Nutley NJ. 201-667-0405

Berndt, Audrey, *ILL & Ref,* Winona State University, Maxwell Library, Winona MN. 507-457-2040

Berndt, Fred, *Dir,* Saint Paul Technical Vocational Library, Saint Paul MN. 612-221-1410

Berne, Beth, *Tech Serv,* Jefferson-Madison Regional Library, McIntire Public Library, Charlottesville VA. 804-296-6157

Berner, Richard C, *Archives,* University of Washington Libraries, Seattle WA. 206-543-1760

Berney, Bruce R, *Dir,* Astoria Public Library, Astoria OR. 503-325-6581

Bernhard, Pat, *Librn,* Greece Public Library (North Greece Branch), North Greece NY. 716-392-6620

Bernhardt, Debra, *Oral Historian,* New York University (Tamiment Library & Robert F Wagner Labor Archive), New York NY. 212-598-2484

Bernhardt, Homer, *Librn,* University of Pittsburgh (Engineering), Pittsburgh PA. 412-624-4484

Bernhardt, Homer, *Librn,* University of Pittsburgh (Mathematics), Pittsburgh PA. 412-624-4488

Bernhardt, Ruth, *ILL,* Northbrook Public Library, Northbrook IL. 312-272-6224

Bernhardt, Sister Virginia, *Tech Serv,* Mercyhurst College Learning Resource Center, Erie PA. 814-864-0681, Ext 228, 234

Bernholdt, Jocelyn A, *Librn,* Alexian Brothers Medical Center, Medical Library, Elk Grove Village IL. 312-437-5500, Ext 4756

Bernier, Gaston, *Asst Dir Dept of Political Docs & Res,* Assemblee Nationale, Bibliotheque de la Legislature, Quebec PQ. 418-643-2121

Berninghausen, David K, *Prof,* University of Minnesota, Library School, MN. 612-373-3100

Berns, Norma J, *Asst Dir,* Carroll Public Library, Carroll IA. 712-792-3432

Berns, Phyllis, *Librn,* Greene County District Library (Spring Valley Branch), Spring Valley OH. 513-862-4538

Bernstein, Bernice, *Assoc Librn,* Maryland State Law Library, Annapolis MD. 301-269-3395

Bernstein, Gloria, *Manager,* Thomas J Lipton Inc, Technical Research Library, Englewood Cliffs NJ. 201-567-8000

Bernstein, Jill P, *Corp Libr,* Sunkist Growers, Inc, Corporate Library, Sherman Oaks CA. 213-986-4800, Ext 516 & 445

Bernstein, Judith, *Librn,* University of New Mexico General Library (Anderson Schools of Management Memorial Library), Albuquerque NM. 505-277-5912

Bernstein, Lillian, *Librn,* Newark Beth Israel Medical Center, Dr V Parsonnet Memorial Library, Newark NJ. 201-926-7233, 926-7441

Bernstein, Merle, *Librn,* United States Bureau of Mines Library, Twin Cities MN. 612-725-4503

Bernstein, Neil, *Dir,* Point-Of-Purchase Advertising Institute, Inc, Industry Information Center, New York NY. 212-682-7041

Bernstein, Norbert, *Dir,* Scotch Plains Public Library, Scotch Plains NJ. 201-322-5007

Bernstein, Paul, *Librn,* Jewish Community Center of Metropolitan Detroit, Henry & Delia Meyers Memorial Library, West Bloomfield MI. 313-661-1000, Ext 163

Bernstein, Robin R, *ILL,* Bellevue College, F Hoyte Freeman Library, Bellevue NE. 291-8100 Ext 64

Bernsten, Pat, *ERIC,* University of North Dakota, Chester Fritz Library, Grand Forks ND. 701-777-2617

Berquam, David, *Sci,* University of Toledo, William S Carlson Library, Toledo OH. 419-537-2324

Berreman, Barbara, *ILL,* Spokane County Library, Spokane WA. 509-924-4122

Berrettini, Joellen, *Librn,* Pepper, Hamilton & Scheetze, Law Library, Philadelphia PA. 215-893-3080

Berring, Robert, *Lectr,* Simmons College, Graduate School of Library & Information Science, MA. 617-738-2225

Berring, Jr, Robert C, *Asst Dir,* Harvard University Library (Law School Library), Cambridge MA. 617-495-3170

Berrios, Angel M, *Acq,* University of Puerto Rico, Humacao University College Library, Humacao PR. 809-852-2525, Ext 200

Berrios, Angela, *Cat,* University of Puerto Rico, Cayey University College Library, Cayey PR. 809-738-2161, Ext 221, 738-5651

Berrios, Luis R, *Dean,* Puerto Rico Junior College (Cupey Campus Learning Resources Center), Rio Piedras PR. 809-765-1716

Berrios, Roman R, *Cat,* Florida, State University System, Extension Library, Saint Petersburg FL. 813-893-9120

Berrisford, Paul, *Dir,* University of Minnesota Libraries-Twin Cities (Central Technical Services), Minneapolis MN. 612-373-2883

Berrocal-Lopez, Ramon, *Dir,* University of Puerto Rico, Arecibo Regional College Library, Arecibo PR. 809-878-2830, Ext 332

Berry, Alma E, *Librn,* Saint Anthony Hospital, Medical Staff Library, Louisville KY. 502-587-1161, Ext 756

Berry, Anna, *Asst Dir,* College of Saint Joseph the Provider Library, Rutland VT. 802-775-0806

Berry, Diane, *Librn,* Library Co of Burlington, Burlington NJ. 609-386-1273

Berry, Dorothy, *Librn,* Camargo Township Public Library, Villa Grove IL. 217-832-5211

Berry, Edna, *Librn,* George Library, Swanquarter NC. 919-926-8841

Berry, Elizabeth L, *Cat,* Fitchburg Public Library, Fitchburg MA. 617-343-3096

Berry, Gayle C, *ILL,* Clarkson College of Technology, Harriet Call Burnap Memorial Library, Potsdam NY. 315-268-6645

Berry, Grace, *Asst Dir,* South Mississippi Regional Library, Columbia MS. 601-736-5516

Berry, Gracia, *Librn,* Frost Free Library, Marlborough NH. 603-876-4479

Berry, Gwendolyn B, *Dir,* Speedway Public Library, Speedway IN. 317-243-8959

Berry, James, *Res Coordr,* Housing Association of Delaware Valley Library, Philadelphia PA. 215-563-4050

Berry, John, *Ref, Spec Coll & Bibliog Instr,* Elmira College, Gannett-Tripp Learning Ctr, Elmira NY. 607-734-3911, Ext 287

Berry, Kathleen, *Br Librn,* Wissahickon Valley Public Library, Ambler PA. 215-646-1072

Berry, Leona, *Spec Coll,* Eastern Michigan University, Center of Educational Resources, Ypsilanti MI. 313-487-0020

Berry, Madeline, *Asst Librn,* Gorham Public Library, Gorham NH. 603-466-2525

Berry, Margaret, *Librn,* Bay County Public Library Association (Holmes County Branch), Bonifay FL. 904-547-3573

Berry, Marie, *Librn,* San Antonio Public Library (History, Social Science & General Reference), San Antonio TX. 512-299-7813, 299-7814

Berry, Marilyn, *Dir, On-Line Servs & Bibliog Instr,*Bad Axe Public Library, Bad Axe MI. 517-269-8538

Berry, Mary, *Librn,* Cherokee-City-County Public Library, Cherokee OK. 405-596-2366

Berry, Mary Jane, *Librn,* Porterville State Hospital (Professional Library), Porterville CA. 209-784-2000

Berry, Mary Jane, *Librn,* Porterville State Hospital (Residents' Library), Porterville CA. 209-784-2000

Berry, Mary Wallace, *Librn,* Carbarrus Memorial Hospital Library, Concord NC. 704-786-2111, Ext 367

Berry, Nancy, *Bibliog Instr,* Arthur D Little Inc, Research Library, Cambridge MA. 617-864-5770, Ext 3019

Berry, Nancy C, *Ch,* Lancaster County Library, Lancaster SC. 803-285-1502

Berry, Patrick, *Librn,* Ladish Co, Metallurgical Dept Library, Cudahy WI. 414-747-3011

Berry, R Edwin, *Assocs,* New York State Library, Albany NY. 518-474-5930

Berry, Rachel, *In Charge,* Pillsbury Company (Main Office Library), Minneapolis MN. 612-330-4047

Berry, Roger, *Spec Coll,* University of California Library, Irvine CA. 714-833-5212

Berry, Vernice W, *In Charge,* First Pennsylvania Bank, Marketing Information Center, Philadelphia PA. 215-786-8354

Berry, Jr, R H, *Librn,* General Electric Co (Technical Information Center), Erie PA. 814-455-5466

Berson, Bella Z, *Asst Librn for Personnel,* Yale University Library (University Library), New Haven CT. 203-436-8335

Bert, Rita, *Ch,* Oak Lawn Public Library, Oak Lawn IL. 312-422-4990

Bertalan, Frank J, *Prof,* Texas Woman's University, School of Library Science, TX. 817-387-2418 & 566-1455

Bertalmio, Lynne, *Dir,* Stillwater Public Library, Stillwater MN. 612-439-1692

Bertels, Henry J, *Dir,* Georgetown University (Woodstock Theological Center Library), Washington DC. 202-625-3120

Berthel, Martha M, *Dir & Spec Coll,* Bethune-Cookman College, Carl S Swisher Library, Daytona Beach FL. 904-255-1401, Ext 321

Berthelot, Benoit, *Tech Serv,* College Dominicain De Philosophie Et De Theologie, Bibliotheque du College Dominicain, Ottawa ON. 613-233-5696, 233-5697

Berthoff, R, *Poetry,* State University of New York at Buffalo, University Libraries, Buffalo NY. 716-636-2965

Bertholf, R, *Curator,* State University of New York at Buffalo (Poetry-Rare Books Collection), Buffalo NY. 716-636-2917

Bertholf, Robert, *Spec Coll,* State University of New York at Buffalo, University Libraries, Buffalo NY. 716-636-2965

Berthrong, Merrill G, *Dir,* Wake Forest University, Z Smith Reynolds Library, Winston-Salem NC. 919-761-5480

Bertini, Rosemarie, *Librn,* Madrid Public Library, Madrid IA. 515-795-3846

Bertolucci, Ysabel R, *Librn,* Kaiser Permanente Medical Center Library, South San Francisco CA. 415-876-0408

Berton, Alberta D, *Dir,* College of Physicians of Philadelphia Library (Medical Documentation Service), Philadelphia PA. 215-561-6050

Berton, Barbara, *Librn,* Stanislaus County Free Library (Valley Home Branch), Valley Home CA. 209-847-1120

Bertozzi, Patricia, *ILL, Tech Serv & Cat,* Vermont Law School Library, South Royalton VT. 802-763-8307

Bertram, Lucille, *Ref,* Teaneck Public Library, Teaneck NJ. 201-837-4171

Bertram, S, *Assoc Prof,* University of Alberta, Faculty of Library Science, AB. 403-432-4578

Bertrand, Helen, *Librn,* Mary I Blood Memorial Library, Brownsville VT. 802-484-7887

Bertrand, Jean, *Librn,* Essex County Public Library (Amherstburg Libr), Amherstburg ON. 519-776-5241

Bertrand, John, *Media & Ref,* Shasta College Library, Redding CA. 916-241-3523, Ext 377

Bertrand, Robert, *Ref,* Findlay-Hancock County Public Library, Findlay OH. 419-422-1712

Bertsch, Christine, *Ref,* University of Maine at Presque Isle Library, Presque Isle ME. 207-764-0311, Ext 223

Bertsch, Verna, *Bookkeeper & Asst,* Cambridge City Public Library, Cambridge City IN. 317-478-3335

Berwick, Bruce, *Cent Servs,* North Central Regional Library, Wenatchee WA. 509-663-1117

Besant, Larry X, *Pub Servs,* Ohio State University Libraries (William Oxley Thompson Memorial Library), Columbus OH. 614-422-6151

Besecker, Linda, *Librn,* Bluffton-Richland Public Library, Bluffton OH. 419-358-5016

Besemer, Susan, *Media,* State University College at Buffalo, Edward H Butler Library, Buffalo NY. 716-878-6302
Beshara, Jean, *Librn,* Nelsonville Public Library (Glouster Branch), Glouster OH. 614-767-3959
Beshears, Carol, *Librn,* Yuma City County Library, Somerton AZ. 602-627-2149
Beshears, Carroll, *Librn,* Yuma City-County Library (Somerton), Somerton AZ. 602-782-1871
Beskid, Stephan J, *Circ,* Saint Vladimir's Orthodox Theological Seminary Library, Father Georges Florovsky Library, Yonkers NY. 914-961-8313, Ext 10
Beson, Carolyn, *Librn,* Standard Oil Co (Indiana) (Amoco Production Co, Research Center), Tulsa OK. 918-625-3400
Besse, Jan, *Ch,* Seekonk Public Libraries, Seekonk MA. 617-761-6424
Besserman, Frances, *Ref & Bibliog Instr,* Kishwaukee College Library, Malta IL. 815-825-2086, Ext 225
Bessette, Irene, *Librn,* Queen's University at Kingston (Law), Kingston ON. 613-547-5934
Bessette, Madeleine, *Asst Dir & Acq,* Bibliotheque Municipale Des Trois-Rivieres, Trois-Rivieres PQ. 819-374-3521, Ext 71
Bessey, Win, *Cat,* Albany County Public Library, Laramie WY. 307-745-3365
Bessie, Doris, *Librn,* Strathmore Municipal Library, Strathmore AB. 403-934-5440
Bessler, Joanne, *Ref & Pub Servs,* University of Wyoming, William Robertson Coe Library, Laramie WY. 307-766-3279
Best, Dee, *Ref,* Lake Land College, Virgil H Judge Learning Resource Center, Mattoon IL. 217-235-3131, Ext 267
Best, Donald A, *Dir,* Cadillac-Wexford Public Library, Cadillac MI. 616-775-6541
Best, Donald A, *Dir,* Mid-Michigan Library League, Cadillac MI. 616-775-6541
Best, Donna Jo, *Bus Off,* Wyoming State Library, Cheyenne WY. 307-777-7281
Best, Laurel, *Librn,* Hall Memorial Library, Ellington CT. 203-875-6881
Best, Patricia, *Ad,* Flesh Public Library, Piqua OH. 513-773-6753
Best, Susan, *Librn,* Wilkinson County Library System (Kevin Poole Van Cleave Memorial), Centreville MS. 601-645-5771
Best, Jr, Edwin J, *On-Line Servs,* Tennessee Valley Authority, Chattanooga Technical Library, Chattanooga TN. 755-2811
Besterman, Elaine, *Mgr Libr Servs,* Richardson-Merrell Inc, Merrell Research Center Library, Cincinnati OH. 513-948-9111, Ext 2400
Betancourt, J A, *Dir,* Hostos Community College Library, Bronx NY. 212-960-1093
Betcher, William, *Pub Servs,* Ohio University, Vernon R Alden Library, Athens OH. 614-594-5228
Beth, Sandra, *ILL & Ad,* Winona Public Library, Winona MN. 507-452-4582
Bethany, Loraine, *Cat,* Jackson Metropolitan Library, Jackson MS. 601-352-3677
Bethke, Leonora, *Librn,* Moore Memorial Library, Moore MT. 406-374-2472
Bethune, Margaret, *Librn,* Annapolis Valley Regional Library Headquarters (Berwick Branch), Berwick NS. 902-538-9517
Bettencourt, Judy, *Cat,* Watsonville Public Library, Watsonville CA. 408-722-2408
Bettencourt, Nancy J, *Dir,* Pickens County Library, Easley SC. 803-859-9679
Bettendorf, James B, *Dir,* Flint Newman Center Library, Flint MI. 313-239-9391
Betterholm, Beverly, *Librn,* Pyromet Industries Library, San Carlos CA. 415-591-7161
Bettes, Frances M, *Librn,* Mercy Regional Medical Center Library, Vicksburg MS. 601-636-2131
Bettis, Gary, *Doc, Spec Coll & State Govt Servs,* Idaho State Library, Boise ID. 208-334-2150
Bettis, Kathleen, *ILL & Ref,* Idaho State Library, Boise ID. 208-334-2150
Betts, Eula, *Tech Serv,* Mississippi State University, Mitchell Memorial Library, Mississippi State MS. 601-325-4225
Betts, Jean, *Asst Librn,* Garnett Public Library, Garnett KS. 913-448-3388
Betts, Mrs Charles, *Librn,* Lowndes County Library System (Caledonia Public), Caledonia MS. 601-356-6384

Betts, Sue, *Tech Serv,* Tyler Junior College, Edgar H Vaughn Memorial Library, Tyler TX. 214-592-5993, 593-3342
Betts, Vicki, *On-Line Servs,* University of Texas at Tyler, Tyler TX. 214-566-1471
Betz, Pat, *Asst Dir,* Glenn A Jones Md Memorial Library, Johnstown Public Library, Johnstown CO. 303-587-2459
Betz, Peter, *Asst Librn,* Fulton-Montgomery Community College Library, Johnstown NY. 518-762-4651, Ext 396
Betzenderfer, Anne, *Librn,* W A Wahler & Associates Library, Palo Alto CA. 415-968-6250
Beuefeville, Louise De, *Librn,* La Laurentienne Compagnie Muturelle D'assurance Library, Quebec PQ. 418-688-3433
Beugin, Susan, *Librn,* Alberta Department of the Attorney General & Law Society of Alberta Library, Calgary AB. 403-261-7475
Beulick, Jacqueline, *TV,* Saint Louis Community College (Forest Park Campus), Saint Louis MO. 314-644-9209
Beuson, George R, *Dir,* Kentucky School for the Deaf Library, Danville KY. 606-236-5132
Beuttenmiller, Shirley, *Sci-Tech,* Metropolitan Toronto Library Board, Metropolitan Toronto Library, Toronto ON. 416-928-5150
Bevan, Barbara H, *Chief Librn,* York Hospital Library, York PA. 717-771-2495
Bevan, David, *Info Serv,* North Carolina Department of Cultural Resources, Division of State Library, North Carolina State Library, Raleigh NC. 919-733-2570
Bevan, John, *Circ,* University of Utah (Law Library), Salt Lake City UT. 801-581-6438
Bevan, Leah, *ILL,* Pittsburg State University Library, Pittsburg KS. 316-231-7000, Ext 431
Beverage, J W, *Librn,* Rolls-Royce (Canada) Ltd Library, Lachine PQ. 514-631-3541, Ext 349
Beverage, John, *Reader Serv,* Dallas Theological Seminary, Mosher Library, Dallas TX. 214-824-3094, Ext 285
Beveridge, Jean, *ILL & Bibliog Instr,* Acadia University, Harold Campbell Vaughan Memorial Library, Wolfville NS. 902-542-2201, Ext 215
Beverly, Frances, *Librn,* Owen County Public Library, Owenton KY. 502-484-3450
Beversdorf, Anne, *Suprv,* Indiana University Social Studies Development Center, Curriculum Resource Center, Bloomington IN. 812-337-3584
Bevilacqua, Ann F, *Doc,* Franklin & Marshall College Library, Lancaster PA. 717-291-4223
Beville, Mitchell, *Librn,* University of South Dakota (Governmental Research Bureau), Vermillion SD. 605-677-5242
Bevington, Audrey, *Librn,* Cold Spring Harbor Laboratory Library, Cold Spring Harbor NY. 516-692-6660, Ext 750
Bevoin, Luellen, *Circ,* Lethbridge Community College, Buchanan Resource Centre, Lethbridge AB. 403-327-2141, Ext 350
Bewley, Gladys P, *Dir,* Haddonfield Public Library, Haddonfield NJ. 609-429-1304
Bewley, Gladys P, *Librn,* Haledon Free Public Library, Haledon NJ. 201-790-3808
Bewley, Lois A, *Assoc Prof,* University of British Columbia, School of Librarianship, BC. 604-228-2404
Bey, Lois A, *Chief Librn,* Travenol Laboratories, Inc Library, Morton Grove IL. 312-965-4700
Beye, Sandra, *Ref,* Rowan Public Library, Salisbury NC. 704-633-5578
Beyea, Marion, *Prov Archivist,* New Brunswick Provincial Archives, Fredericton NB. 506-453-2637, 453-2122
Beyer, Robyn, *Librn,* Pepper, Hamilton & Scheetze, Law Library, Philadelphia PA. 215-893-3080
Beyersdorf, M, *Acq,* College of New Rochelle, Gill Library, New Rochelle NY. 914-632-5300, Ext 347
Beyett, Kathleen, *Librn,* National Marine Fisheries Service, W F Thompson Memorial Library, Kodiak AK. 907-487-4961, 487-4962
Beymer, Charles R, *Asst Dir,* California Polytechnic State University Library, San Luis Obispo CA. 805-546-2345
Beynon, S, *ILL & Ref,* Saint Catharines Public Library, Saint Catharines ON. 416-688-6103
Bez, Marianne, *Librn,* Hall of Flame, Richard S Fowler Memorial Library, Phoenix AZ. 602-275-3473

Bezich, Ronda R, *Librn,* Clearwater Sun Newspaper Library, Clearwater FL. 813-448-2127
Bezpaletz, Margaret J, *Acq,* South Dakota State Library, Pierre SD. 605-773-3131
Bezugloff, Natalia B, *In Charge,* Cleveland Public Library (Foreign Literature), Cleveland OH. 216-623-2895
Bhargava, Asha, *Ref,* Warren County Library, Belvidere NJ. 201-475-5361, Ext 114
Bhatnagar, Margaret, *Librn,* Alberta Agriculture Library, Edmonton AB. 403-427-2107
Bhullar, Goodie, *Bibliog Instr,* University of Missouri-Columbia, Elmer Ellis Library, Columbia MO. 314-882-4701
Biagini, Mary Kay, *Asst Prof,* Kent State University, School of Library Science, OH. 216-672-2782, 672-7988
Bial, Ray, *Acq,* Parkland College, Learning Resource Center, Champaign IL. 217-351-2241
Bialac, Verda, *Cat,* Omaha Public Library, W Dale Clark Library, Omaha NE. 402-444-4800
Bialecki, Anthony G, *Librn,* United States Air Force (Office of Scientific Research Library), Bolling AFB DC. 202-767-4910
Biamonte, Rose, *Tech Serv,* Center Moriches Free Public Library, Center Moriches NY. 516-878-0940
Bianchi, Rosemary, *Pub Rel,* Kenosha Public Library, Kenosha WI. 414-656-6034
Bianchini, Lucian, *Dir,* Mount Saint Vincent University Library, Halifax NS. 902-443-4450, Ext 120, 121, 125
Bias, Georgene I, *Dir,* Saint Philip's College Library, San Antonio TX. 512-532-4211, Ext 200
Biasiol, Virgilio, *Dir,* Santa Barbara Mission Archive Library, Santa Barbara CA. 805-682-4713
Bibby, Elizabeth A, *In Charge,* Canadian Consulate General Library, Chicago IL. 312-427-1031
Bibby, Julia E, *Cat,* Ansonia Library, Ansonia CT. 203-734-6275
Bibko, Neva A, *Librn,* Phoenix Public Library, Phoenix NY. 315-695-4355
Biblarz, Dora, *Acq & Spec Coll,* Arizona State University Library, Tempe AZ. 602-965-3417
Bible, Amanda, *Librn,* Whiteville Public Library, Columbus County Public Library, Whiteville NC. 919-642-3116
Bible, Amanda R, *Dir,* Columbus County Public Library, Whiteville NC. 919-642-3116
Bible, June, *Librn,* McCracken Public Library, McCracken KS. 913-394-2444
Bible, Lynne, *Asst Dir,* Alhambra Public Library, Alhambra CA. 213-570-5008
Biblo, Herbert, *Reader Serv,* John Crerar Library, Chicago IL. 312-225-2526
Biblo, Herbert, *Dir,* Illinois Institute of Technology, James S Kemper Library, Chicago IL. 312-567-3355
Biblo, Jean, *Librn,* Miami-Dade Public Library System (Northeast), Miami FL. 305-579-5001
Bick-Gregoire, Lorraine, *Mgr Tech Info Servs,* Raytheon Company, Missle Systems Div, Bedford Laboratories Technical Information Center Library, Bedford MA. 617-274-7100, Ext 2231
Bickel, Bernice, *Ch,* Evansville Public Library & Vanderburgh County Public Library, Evansville IN. 812-425-2621
Bickel, Jane, *Ch,* Chappaqua Central School District Public Library, Chappaqua Library, Chappaqua NY. 914-238-4779
Bickel, Lois A, *Librn,* Bismarck Hospital, School of Nursing Library, Bismarck ND. 701-223-4700, Ext 271
Bickel, M L, *Librn,* Bryan Public Library (Edgerton Public), Edgerton OH. 419-298-3230
Bickers, Mary, *Tech Serv & Acq,* Greensboro Public Library, Greensboro NC. 373-2474; 373-2471
Bickerton, Agnes, *Librn,* Virden-Elkhorn Regional Library (Elkhorn Branch), Elkhorn MB. 204-845-2292
Bickett, Brenda, *Arabic Mat,* Georgetown University, Joseph Mark Lauinger Library, Washington DC. 202-625-4095
Bickford, Christopher, *Asst Dir,* Connecticut Historical Society Library, Hartford CT. 203-236-5621
Bickford, Margaret, *Dir,* Blackwell Public Library, Blackwell OK. 405-363-1809

Bickford, Priscilla, *Librn,* Maine Department of Environmental Protection & Department of Conservation Library, Augusta ME. 207-289-2691

Bickler, Betty, *Librn,* Central Florida Regional Library (Belleview), Ocala FL. 904-245-5552

Bickman, Linda A, *Animal Sci,* University of California at Davis, General Library, Davis CA. 916-752-2110

Bickram, Mrs B, *Group Leader,* George Brown College of Applied Arts & Technology Library (Casa Loma Campus), Toronto ON. 416-967-1212

Bickston, Deverett D, *Librn,* Southern Methodist University Libraries (Science-Engineering), Dallas TX. 214-692-2271

Bickston, Deverett D, *Librn,* Southern Methodist University Libraries (Industrial Information Services), Dallas TX. 214-692-2272

Bicsak, Ilona, *Cat Maintenance,* Columbia University (University Libraries), New York NY. 212-280-2241

Biczak, Cathleen, *Spec Servs,* Ingham County Library, Library Service Center, Mason MI. 517-676-9088

Biddison, Donald, *Ref,* University of Wisconsin-Milwaukee, Golda Meir Library, Milwaukee WI. 414-963-4785

Biddle, Emily D, *Dir,* Knox County Public Library, Vincennes IN. 812-882-6007

Biddle, Ruby, *Acq,* University of Arkansas Libraries (Law), Fayetteville AR. 501-575-5604

Biddle, Stanton F, *Assoc Dir Lib Plan & Develop,* State University of New York at Buffalo, University Libraries, Buffalo NY. 716-636-2965

Biddle, Virginia, *Asst Librn,* South Dakota Supreme Court Law Library, Pierre SD. 605-773-4898

Bidlack, Russell E, *Dean,* University of Michigan, School of Library Science, MI. 313-764-9376

Bidwell, Robert G, *Asst Dir,* George Washington University Library (Jacob Burns Law Library), Washington DC. 202-676-6646

Biebel, Helen, *ILL,* University of Miami, Otto G Richter Library, Coral Gables FL. 305-284-3551

Bieber, Doris M, *Librn,* Vanderbilt University School of Law Library, Nashville TN. 615-322-2568

Bieber, Eliza D, *Dir,* Prairie Trails Public Library District, Burbank IL. 312-430-3688

Bieber, Judith, *Ref,* Oregon City Library, Oregon City OR. 503-655-8398, 655-8399

Biehl, Jane, *Ch Consult,* Mideastern Ohio Library Organization, (MOLO), OH. 216-875-4269

Biel, Sally, *Asst Librn,* AMP, Inc Library, Harrisburg PA. 717-780-8131

Bielawski, Sue, *Ref,* Corning Community College, Arthur A Houghton, Jr Library, Corning NY. 607-962-9251

Bielecki, C, *Asst Info Spec,* Air Products & Chemicals, Inc (Corporate Library), Allentown PA. 215-398-7288

Bielefield, Arlene F, *Dir Readers Servs,* Connecticut State Library, Hartford CT. 203-566-4301

Bielenberg, W Larry, *Dir,* Concordia Seminary Library, Ludwig E Fuerbringer Hall Library, Saint Louis MO. 314-721-5934, Ext 293

Bieler, Wallace H, *Comptroller,* Union National Bank & Trust Co Library, Souderton PA. 215-723-9841

Bielitz, Gerda, *Asst Librn,* Grosse Pointe Public Library, Grosse Pointe MI. 313-343-2074

Bielmeier, Sonia, *Dir,* Brookfield Public Library, Brookfield WI. 414-782-4140

Bien, Stanley, *Chief Librn,* Livonia Public Library, Livonia MI. 313-421-6600

Bienemann, Bruce, *Dir,* Sioux City Art Center, Art Center Association of Sioux City Library, Sioux City IA. 712-279-6272

Bienkowski, Alexander C, *AV,* University of Texas Medical Branch, Moody Medical Library, Galveston TX. 713-765-1971

Bienvenue, Yvette, *Cat,* Fall River Public Library, Fall River MA. 617-676-8541

Bierbaum, E Louise, *Librn,* Robertson Memorial Library, Higginsville MO. 816-584-2880

Bierbaum, Esther G, *Librn,* Pasadena Presbyterian Church Library, Saint Petersburg FL. 813-345-0148

Biere, Verlyn, *Dir,* Justice Public Library District, Justice IL. 312-496-1790

Bieri, Mary, *Librn Blind,* Hastings - Adams County Library, Hastings NE. 402-463-9855

Bierlein, John Francis, *Dir,* Democratic National Committee, Issues-Research Library, Washington DC. 202-797-5900, Ext 281

Bierly, Kristin S, *Asst Dir,* Maynard Public Library, Maynard MA. 617-897-8481

Bierman, Kenneth J, *Asst Dir Tech Serv,* Tucson Public Library, Tucson AZ. 602-791-4391

Bierman, Sandy, *Librn,* Bannock Memorial Hospital Library, Pocatello ID. 208-232-6150

Biersborn, Mary C, *Mgr,* Sperry Corp, Sperry UNIVAC Div, Information Service Center, Roseville MN. 612-631-5386

Bierschenk, Nancy, *Asst Librn,* Texas Medical Association, Memorial Library, Austin TX. 512-477-6704, Ext 191

Bievenour, Ruth, *Arts & Sciences,* Martin Memorial Library, York PA. 717-843-3978

Biewer, Alice, *Librn,* Lidgerwood Public Library, Lidgerwood ND. 701-538-4084

Bigbee, Elizabeth, *Dir,* Riverside City College, Martin Luther King Library, Riverside CA. 714-684-3240, Ext 328

Bigelow, Alice, *Cat,* Hyconeechee Regional Library, Yanceyville NC. 919-694-6241

Bigelow, Therese, *Ch & YA,* Charles H Taylor Memorial Library, Hampton Public Library, Hampton VA. 804-727-6234

Bigger, Mary Beth, *Humanities Res Ctr Cat,* University of Texas Libraries (General), Austin TX. 512-471-3811

Biggerstaff, Barbara, *Librn,* Vance Township Library, Fairmount IL. 217-758-2164

Biggerstaff, Judith, *Librn,* Dallas County Public Library (Coppell Branch), Coppell TX. 214-462-0312

Biggerstaff, Vicki, *Tech Serv,* North American Baptist Seminary, Kaiser-Ramaker Library, Sioux Falls SD. 605-336-6805, Ext 8

Biggio, Eugene, *Dir,* Kent Memorial Library, Suffield CT. 203-668-2325

Biggs, Catherine, *Librn,* Hewlett-Packard Cupertino Library, Cupertino CA. 408-257-7000, Ext 2465

Biggs, Donald W, *Librn,* New Jersey Neuro-Psychiatric Institute, Medical Library, Princeton NJ. 609-466-0400, Ext 420

Biggs, Kay, *Librn,* Corbin Public Library, Corbin KY. 606-528-6366

Bigler, Evelyn T, *Librn,* Payson Public Library, Payson UT. 801-465-3793

Bigler, Nancy, *Asst Librn,* University of Wisconsin Center, Washington County Library, West Bend WI. 414-338-8753, Ext 60

Bigman, Lorraine, *Acq,* Navajo Community College, Naaltsoos Ba'Hooghan Library, Tsaile AZ. 602-724-6132

Bignell, Carol, *Librn,* Detroit Public Library (Douglass), Detroit MI. 313-833-9714

Bigus, Sonia K, *Dir,* Baldwinsville Public Library, Baldwinsville NY. 315-635-5631

Bihon, Connie S, *Librn,* Pennzoil Company, Research Department Library, Shreveport LA. 318-861-4531

Bikowski, Leonard, *ILL & Circ,* United States Department of the Interior, Natural Resources Library, Washington DC. 202-343-5821

Bilbrey, Dale E, *Librn,* Upper Room Devotional Library, Nashville TN. 615-327-2700, Ext 444

Bilecki, Anthony, *Librn,* Ivan Franko Museum & Library Society, Inc Library, Winnipeg MB. 204-589-4397

Bilek, Kenneth L, *Ad,* Hennepin County Library, Edina MN. 612-830-4944

Bilicke, Thomas, *Media,* Northrop University, Alumni Library, Inglewood CA. 213-776-5466

Bilinski, Donald, *Dir,* Polish Museum of America Library, Chicago IL. 312-384-3352

Bilk, Marjorie, *Librn,* Moore College of Art Library, Philadelphia PA. 215-568-4515

Bill, Karen, *Librn,* Dunhill Business Research Library, Fort Lauderdale FL. 305-484-8300

Bill, Ruby, *Librn,* Lakeland Counseling Center Library, Elkhorn WI. 414-723-5400, Ext 253

Billert, Julia A, *Cat,* Tidewater Community College, Virginia Beach Campus Library, Virginia Beach VA. 804-427-3070, Ext 123, 126

Billesbach, Ann E, *Curator,* Willa Cather Historical Center Library, Red Cloud NE. 402-746-3285

Billey, Barbara, *Librn,* Navajo Community College, Shiprock Campus Library, Shiprock NM. 505-368-5291

Billick, Pam, *Dir Libr Serv,* Mercy Hospital, Edward L Burns Health Sciences Library, Toledo OH. 419-259-1327

Billings, Carol, *Ref,* Law Library of Louisiana, New Orleans LA. 504-568-5705

Billings, Harold W, *Chmn,* Amigos Bibliographic Council (Council of Academic Research Libraries), Austin TX. 214-750-6130

Billings, Harold W, *Dir,* University of Texas Libraries (General), Austin TX. 512-471-3811

Billingsley, Crystal, *Dir,* Yates Community Library, Lyndonville NY. 716-765-9041

Billingsley, Robert, *Libr Supvr & On-Line Search Coordr,* Hughes Aircraft Co, Santa Barbara Research Center Library, Goleta CA. 805-968-3511, Ext 2541, 2542

Billingsly, Sharon, *Librn,* Mound Valley Public Library, Mound Valley KS. 316-328-3341

Billips, Irene, *Librn,* Valparaiso-Porter County Public Library System & Administrative Headquarters (Kouts Public), Kouts IN. 219-766-2116

Billman, Bethany, *Librn,* Wyoming Seminary, Kirby Library, Kingston PA. 717-288-7541

Billmeyer, Doris S, *Librn,* Spring Lake Public Library, Spring Lake NJ. 201-449-6654

Bills, James F, *Asst Dir,* Case Western Reserve University Libraries, Cleveland OH. 216-368-3506

Bills, Seth, *Media,* Ricks College, David O McKay Learning Resources Center, Rexburg ID. 208-356-2351

Billy, Paul Louis, *Dir,* Deerfield Beach Public Library, Deerfield Beach FL. 305-427-3337

Billyou, L E, *Librn,* Technicon Instruments Corp, Technical Division Library, Tarrytown NY. 914-631-8000

Billyou, Ruth, *Coordr,* Greater Hartford Consortium for Higher Education, CT. 203-236-1203

Binder, Ann, *Spec Serv,* Kewanee Public Library, Kewanee IL. 309-852-4505

Binder, Michael, *Dir,* Fairleigh Dickinson University, Messler Library, Rutherford NJ. 201-933-5000, Ext 252

Binder, Mitzi, *YA,* Ridgewood Public Library, Ridgewood NJ. 201-652-5200

Binder, Richard, *Bibliog Instr,* Drexel University Library, Philadelphia PA. 215-895-2750

Binder, Richard, *Humanities & Soc Sci,* Drexel University Library, Philadelphia PA. 215-895-2750

Bindley, Ruby, *Dir,* Montezuma Township Library, Montezuma KS. 316-846-4183

Bindseil, Heather, *Acq,* Midwestern Regional Library System, Kitchener ON. 519-576-5061

Bingaman, Joseph, *Curator Latin Am Coll,* Hoover Institution on War, Revolution & Peace, Stanford CA. 415-497-2058

Bingaman, Priscilla, *Librn,* Missouri Bankers Association Library, Jefferson City MO. 314-636-8151

Bingert, Alice S, *Dir,* Washington Public Library, Washington NJ. 201-689-0201

Bingham, Beth, *Ad,* East Baton Rouge Parish Library, Baton Rouge LA. 504-389-3360

Bingham, Betty L, *Dir,* Jackson County Public Library, McKee KY. 606-287-8113

Bingham, Florence, *Dir,* Silsby Free Public Library, Charlestown NH. 603-826-7793

Bingham, Jim, *AV & Circ,* Houston Academy of Medicine, Texas Medical Center Library, Houston TX. 713-797-1230

Bingham, Keith, *Librn,* South Bend Public Library (LaSalle), South Bend IN. 219-234-2734

Bingham, Lois, *Librn,* Randolph Public Library (Archdale Branch), Archdale NC. 919-431-3811

Bingham, Marie, *Cat,* University of Alabama, Amelia Gayle Gorgas Library, University AL. 205-348-5298

Bingham, Sherrill, *ILL,* Weber County Library, Ogden UT. 801-399-8516

Bingleman, Gladys, *Librn,* Victoria County Public Library (Dunsford Branch), Dunsford ON. 705-324-3104

Bingman, Richard M, *Field Util Specialist,* Mid-Continent Regional Educational Laboratory Library, Kansas City MO. 816-361-7700

Binion, Francie G, *Ch,* Analytic Services Inc, ANSER Library, Arlington VA. 703-979-0700

Binkley, Andrea, *Media,* Metropolitan Technical Community College, Instructional Resource Center, Omaha NE. 402-457-5100

Binkley, Dorothy, *Chief Librn,* Wesley Medical Center, Medical & Nursing Library, Wichita KS. 316-685-2151

Binkley, Nancy A, *Bkmobile Coordr,* Tri-County Regional Library, Rome GA. 404-291-9360

Binkley, Yildiz, *Ser,* Tennessee State University, Martha M Brown - Lois W Daniel Library, Nashville TN. 615-320-3682, 251-1417

Binn, Lucy, *Ch,* Free Public Library of the Borough of Fort Lee, Fort Lee NJ. 201-461-8020

Binnington, J, *Dir & Ch,* Lakefield Public Library, Lakefield ON. 705-652-8623

Binnington, Joan, *Librn,* Lakefield Public Library (Library of Smith Township Ward), Bridgenorth ON. 705-292-5065

Binns, Mrs W G, *Librn,* Reveille United Methodist Church Library, Richmond VA. 804-359-6041

Binotti, Betty, *Ad,* Acorn Public Library District, Oak Forest IL. 312-687-3700

Binsted, Donna, *Librn,* Meaford Public Library, Meaford ON. 519-538-3500

Birch, Barbara, *Librn,* Readsboro Public Library, Readsboro VT. 802-423-8204

Birch, Doris, *Librn,* Genesee District Library (A J Phillips Library), Fenton MI. 313-629-7612

Birch, Grace M, *Librn,* Trumbull Library, Trumbull CT. 203-261-6421

Birch, Jane, *Ref,* County College of Morris, Sherman H Masten Learning Resource Center, Randolph Township NJ. 201-361-5000, Ext 470

Birchard, Jane M, *Dir,* Flint Hills Area Vocational-Technical School Library, Emporia KS. 316-342-6404

Birchmore, Patricia, *Librn,* SYVA Company Library, Palo Alto CA. 415-493-2200

Bird, Carol, *Librn,* La Salle Public Library, La Salle IL. 815-223-2341

Bird, F, *Librn,* Okanagan Regional Library District (Salmon Arm Branch), Salmon Arm BC. 604-832-6161

Bird, Janet, *Librn,* Victor Valley College Library, Victorville CA. 714-245-4271, Ext 262

Bird, Judith C, *Acq,* State University Agricultural & Technical College at Farmingdale, Thomas D Greenley Library, Farmingdale NY. 516-420-2011, 420-2012

Bird, Lillian L, *Librn,* Nassau County Department of Health, Central Research Library, Mineola NY. 516-535-3368, 69

Bird, Viola, *Librn,* Preston, Thorgrimson, Ellis & Holman Library, Seattle WA. 206-623-7580

Bird, Warren P, *Dir,* Duke University (Medical Center Library), Durham NC. 919-684-2092

Birdcell, Gail, *Adminr,* Northwest Indiana Area Library Services Authority, (NIALSA), IN. 219-926-1146

Birdsall, Douglas, *Humanities,* Idaho State University Library, Pocatello ID. 208-236-3202

Birdsall, Lucy, *In Charge,* United States Geological Survey, Public Inquiries Office Library, Los Angeles CA. 213-688-2850

Birdsall, W F, *Assoc Dir Pub Servs,* University of Manitoba Libraries, Winnipeg MB. 204-474-9881

Birdsey, Betty, *Music,* Ithaca College Library, Ithaca NY. 607-274-3182

Birdsong, Gail, *Librn,* Baltimore County Public Library (Reisterstown Branch), Reisterstown MD. 301-833-1550

Birdsong, Mrs Homer, *Librn,* La Porte County Library (Kingsford Heights Branch), Kingsford Heights IN. 219-393-3280

Birdwell, Effie N, *Chief Librn,* Monsanto Chemical Intermediates Co, Process Technology Dept Library, Texas City TX. 713-945-4431, Ext 2367

Biren, I B, *Computing Supvr,* Bell Telephone Laboratories (Bell Telephone Laboratories Technical Library), Murray Hill NJ. 582-4612 (Supvr); 582-3740 (Circ); 582-3604 (Info Alerting Servs); 582-3901 (Systs Design Program); 582-3453 (Computing Info Serv); 582-7330 (Computing)

Birge, Ilene A, *Ser,* Indiana University at South Bend Library, South Bend IN. 219-237-4440

Birkel, Paul, *Dir,* University of San Francisco, Richard A Gleeson Library, San Francisco CA. 415-666-6167

Birkemeier, Wendy, *Ch,* East Brunswick Public Library, East Brunswick NJ. 201-254-1220

Birkemeier, Naomi, *Dir,* Lincoln Park Public Library, Lincoln Park NJ. 201-694-8283

Birkey, Grace, *Librn,* Wabco, Construction & Mining Equipment Group, Engineering Technical Library, Peoria IL. 309-672-7223

Birkhead, Ruth, *Dir,* Appleton Public Library, Appleton WI. 414-734-7171

Birknes, Margaretha E H, *Librn,* New Bedford Bar Association Library, New Bedford MA. 617-992-8077

Birks, Grant, *Info Servs II,* Bell-Northern Research, Technical Information Center, Ottawa ON. 613-596-2469

Birladeanu, Ludmila, *Librn,* Harvard University Library (Chemistry Library), Cambridge MA. 617-495-4079

Birlem, Lynne, *Lectr,* Simmons College, Graduate School of Library & Information Science, MA. 617-738-2225

Birman, Bonnie, *Librn,* New York Public Library (Tremont), New York NY. 212-299-5177

Birmingham, Frank, *Dept Head,* Mankato State College, Library Media Education, MN. 507-389-1965

Birmingham, John T, *Librn,* Cuyahoga County Public Library (North Olmsted Branch), North Olmsted OH. 216-777-6211

Birmingham, Mary, *Librn,* Bethany Lutheran College & Seminary, Memorial Library, Mankato MN. 507-625-2977

Birnbaum, Denise, *Tech Serv,* Airesearch Manufacturing Co, Engineering Library, Phoenix AZ. 602-267-2062

Birnbaum, Henry, *Librn,* Pace University Library, New York NY. 212-285-3333

Birnbaum, Iza, *Media,* Jericho Public Library, Jericho NY. 516-935-6790

Birnbaum, Kerry G, *Tech Serv,* Aiken-Bamberg-Barnwell-Edgefield Regional Library, Aiken SC. 803-648-8961

Birney, Ann, *Librn,* Rolling Hills Consolidated Library (Belt), St Joseph MO. 816-232-5479

Biro, Julie, *Ch,* Mount Kisco Public Library, Mount Kisco NY. 914-666-8041

Biro, Ruth G, *Dir,* Duquesne University, School of Education, Library Science Program, PA. 412-434-6100

Birriolo, Esther, *Librn,* Blossburg Memorial Library, Blossburg PA. 717-638-2197

Birschel, Dee B, *Assoc Dir,* International Foundation of Employee Benefit Plans, Information Center, Brookfield WI. 414-786-6700

Birula, Kay, *Librn,* AMP, Inc Library, Harrisburg PA. 717-780-8131

Bisaillon, Blaise, *Dir,* Forbes Library, Northampton MA. 413-584-8399

Bisaillon, Edmond, *Dir,* Hastings Museum Library, Hastings NE. 402-463-7126

Bisbee, Betty, *Librn,* Fremont County Library (Riverton), Riverton WY. 307-856-3556

Bisbee, Helen, *Circ,* Millicent Library, Fairhaven MA. 617-992-5342

Bisch, Thelma, *Librn,* Kitchener-Waterloo Hospital, Health Sciences Library, Kitchener ON. 519-742-3611, Ext 2235

Bischel, Daniel, *ILL & Reader Serv,* University of Puget Sound, Collins Memorial Library, Tacoma WA. 206-756-3257

Bischoff, Frances, *Media,* William N Wishard Memorial Hospital, Library & Media Services, Indianapolis IN. 317-630-7028

Bischoff, Mary, *Acq & Tech Serv,* Christ Seminary-Seminex Library, Saint Louis MO. 314-534-7535

Bischoff, Mrs Arthur, *Librn,* Benson Public Library, Benson AZ. 602-586-9535

Bish, Dianne Lee, *Adminr,* Novi Public Library, Novi MI. 313-349-0720

Bishoff, Lizbeth J, *Dir,* Ela Area Public Library District, Lake Zurich IL. 312-438-3433

Bishoff, Paul, *Librn,* Geneva College (Placement Center), Beaver Falls PA. 412-846-5100, Ext 297

Bishop, Barbara, *Actg Dir,* Umatilla County Library, Pendleton OR. 503-276-1881

Bishop, David, *Dir,* University of California Library, San Francisco CA. 415-666-2334

Bishop, David F, *Dir,* University of Georgia Libraries, Athens GA. 404-542-2716

Bishop, Delbert A, *Dir,* National Archives & Records Service, Philadelphia Branch Library, Philadelphia PA. 215-951-5591

Bishop, Dolores, *Asst Librn,* Philo Township Public Library, Philo IL. 217-684-2896

Bishop, Dorothy J, *Librn,* Soldotna Public Library, Joyce Carver Memorial Library, Soldotna AK. 907-262-4227

Bishop, Emma, *ILL & Ad,* Beaufort County Library, Beaufort SC. 803-524-0762

Bishop, Erlene, *Ref,* Mount Vernon College Library, Washington DC. 202-331-3475

Bishop, Gwynneth, *Sci & Med,* University of Toronto Libraries (University Library), Toronto ON. 416-978-2294

Bishop, James P, *Dir,* Carthage College, John Mosheim Ruthrauff Library, Kenosha WI. 414-551-8500, Ext 530

Bishop, Janet, *Media,* Nichols Library, Naperville IL. 312-355-1540

Bishop, Jean, *Circ,* Montana College of Mineral Science and Technology Library, Butte MT. 406-792-8321, Ext 371

Bishop, Judy, *Librn,* Middle Georgia Regional Library (Rocky Creek), Macon GA. 912-745-5813

Bishop, Kenneth E, *Coordr,* Blue Ridge Community College Library, Weyers Cave VA. 703-234-9261, Ext 247

Bishop, Linda, *Ref & Per,* Saint Mary's University (School of Law Library), San Antonio TX. 512-436-3435

Bishop, Marcia, *Librn,* Bureau of Land Management, Las Vegas District Office Library, Las Vegas NV. 702-385-6403

Bishop, Marian, *Cat,* Albion College, Stockwell Memorial Library, Albion MI. 517-629-5511, Ext 285

Bishop, Marjory, *Ch,* Rathbun Free Memorial Library, East Haddam CT. 203-873-8210

Bishop, Mary C, *Librn,* Holland Public Library, Southbridge MA. 413-245-3607

Bishop, Mrs Chilson, *Dir,* Crawfordsville District Public Library, Crawfordsville IN. 317-362-2242

Bishop, Robert, *Present Dir,* Museum of American Folk Art, Research Library, New York NY. 212-581-2474

Bishop, W Sanders, *Dir,* Samford University (Learning Resources (Media) Center), Birmingham AL. 205-870-2893

Bishop, Walt, *Librn,* National Semiconductor Corp, Technical Library, Danbury CT. 203-744-0060

Bisignano, Anthony, *Media,* Jamestown Community College, Hultquist Library Learning Center, Jamestown NY. 716-665-5220, Ext 210

Bismuti, Gene, *Chief, Info Servs,* Washington State Library, Olympia WA. 206-753-5592

Bissell, Priscilla E, *Librn,* Jackson Public Library, Jackson NH. 603-383-9731

Bissett, John P, *Cat,* Mary Washington College, E Lee Trinkle Library, Fredericksburg VA. 703-899-4666

Bisson, Linda, *Asst Librn,* Rathbun Free Memorial Library, East Haddam CT. 203-873-8210

Bissonnette, Pauline, *Asst Librn,* Groton Public Library, Groton MA. 617-448-6761

Bistline, Marian, *Hosp Librn,* La Porte Public Library, La Porte IN. 219-362-6156

Bitman, Leslie, *Assoc Librn,* Squire, Sanders & Dempsey, Law Library, Cleveland OH. 216-696-9200

Bitner, Lucy McLaughlin, *Ch,* Annie Halenbake Ross Library, Lock Haven PA. 717-748-3321

Bittel, Ann B, *Dir,* Northeast Alabama State Junior College Library, Rainsville AL. 205-228-6001, Ext 26

Bitter, Jane, *Librn,* Mobil Research & Development Corp, Technical Information Service Library, Paulsboro NJ. 609-423-1040, Ext 2429

Bitting, Judith C, *Librn,* Smith Kline & French Laboratories (Research & Development Information Center Library), Philadelphia PA. 215-854-4000

Bittle, Kathryn, *Librn,* Norristown State Hospital (Noyes Memorial Library), Norristown PA. 215-631-2613

Bittner, Christina, *ILL,* Hibbing Public Library, Hibbing MN. 218-262-1038

Bittner, Doris L, *Librn,* Prairie du Chien Memorial Library, Prairie du Chien WI. 608-326-6211

Bivins, Hulen, *AV,* Alabama Public Library Service, Montgomery AL. 205-832-5743

Biwer, Terry, *Research Tech,* Waukesha County Museum Research Center Library, Waukesha WI. 414-544-8430

Bixby, Barbara, *Librn,* Bowie Public Library, Bowie TX. 817-872-2681

Bixby, Constance, *Librn,* Fletcher Memorial Library, Ludlow VT. 802-228-2681

Bixby, Gwen, *ILL,* New Orleans Baptist Theological Seminary Library, New Orleans LA. 504-282-4455, Ext 289

Bixel, Robert, *Librn,* Baptist University of America Library, Decatur GA. 404-288-4660, Ext 19

Bixler, Beverly, *Ch,* Tyler Public Library, Tyler TX. 214-595-4267

Bixon, Shirley, *Librn,* Duncan Public Library, Duncan AZ. 602-359-2094

Bjarnar, Vilhjalmur T, *Curator,* Cornell University Libraries (Icelandic Collection), Ithaca NY. 607-256-6462

Bjarnar, Vilhjalmur T, *Icelandic Coll,* Cornell University Libraries (University Libraries), Ithaca NY. 607-256-4144

Bjella, Arlene, *Librn,* Silver Bay Public Library, Silver Bay MN. 218-226-4331

Bjelland, Jeanette, *Asst Librn,* Lake Mills Public Library, Lake Mills IA. 515-592-2202

Bjerke, Cheryl A, *Dir,* Northwestern College of Chiropractic Library, Saint Paul MN. 612-690-1735, Ext 22

Bjerke, Robert A, *Dir,* University of Wisconsin Center-Manitowoc County Library, Manitowoc WI. 414-682-8251, Ext 27

Bjerken, Lisa, *Librn,* Fairview-Southdale Hospital, Mary Ann King Health Sciences Library, Edina MN. 612-920-4400, Ext 333

Bjoin, Cheryl, *Dir,* East Central Regional Library, Cambridge MN. 612-689-1901

Bjordahl, Hilda M, *Dir,* De Smet City Library, De Smet SD. 605-854-3842

Bjork, Carol, *Librn,* Museum of Fine Arts School Library, Boston MA. 617-267-9300, Ext 511

Bjork, Margaret, *Librn,* Harlowton Public Library, Harlowton MT. 406-632-5523

Bjork, Phillip B, *Dir,* South Dakota School of Mines & Technology (James Dye Bump Memorial Library), Rapid City SD. 605-394-2467

Bjorke, Wallace S, *Librn,* University of Michigan Libraries (Music), Ann Arbor MI. 313-764-2512

Bjorklund, Edith, *Asst Dir Coll Develop,* University of Wisconsin-Milwaukee, Golda Meir Library, Milwaukee WI. 414-963-4785

Bjorkman, Mildred, *Br Asst,* La Crosse County Library (Bangor), La Crosse WI. 608-486-4084

Bjormerantz, Leslie B, *Educ,* Northwestern University Library, Evanston IL. 312-492-7658

Bjornberg, Linda, *Librn,* Willmar State Hospital Library, Willmar MN. 612-235-3322

Bjorner, Susan, *Asst Dir, Ad & Ref,* Burlington Public Library, Burlington MA. 617-272-2520

Black, Betty, *Ad & West Br Coordr,* Ventura County Library Services Agency, Ventura County Library, Ventura CA. 805-654-2627

Black, Carolyn, *Tech Serv,* Texarkana Public Library, Texarkana TX. 214-794-2149

Black, Emma, *Acq,* Ligonier Valley Library Association, Inc, Ligonier PA. 412-238-6451

Black, Ferne, *Asst Librn,* Cuyahoga Community College (Metropolitan Campus Library), Cleveland OH. 216-241-5966, Ext 217

Black, Fran, *Cat,* Portsmouth Public Library, Portsmouth NH. 603-431-2000, Ext 252

Black, Frances, *Tech Serv, Acq & Br Coordr,* Grove City Public Library, Grove City OH. 614-875-6716

Black, George W, *On-Line Servs,* Southern Illinois University at Carbondale, Delyte W Morris Library, Carbondale IL. 618-453-2522

Black, Goldie, *Acq,* Grove City College, Henry Buhl Library, Grove City PA. 412-458-6600, Ext 270

Black, Harriette C, *Librn & Curator,* Newcomen Society in North America, Thomas Newcomen Library in Steam Technology & Industrial History, Downingtown PA. 215-363-6600

Black, Isabella, *Librn,* Queens Children's Psychiatric Center, The Lauretta Bender Child Psychiatry Library, Bellerose NY. 212-464-2900, Ext 1194

Black, J B, *Librn,* University of Toronto Libraries (University of Saint Michael's College), Toronto ON. 416-921-3151

Black, Jane, *Acq,* Richmond Public Library, Richmond VA. 804-780-4256

Black, Janet, *Librn,* Frontenac County Library (Cloyne Branch), Cloyne ON. 613-336-8744

Black, Junivee, *Ch,* Hutchinson Public Library, Hutchinson KS. 316-663-5441

Black, Kate, *Librn,* Estill County Public Library, Irvine KY. 606-723-3030

Black, Larry, *Dir,* Public Library of Columbus & Franklin County (Main Library-Hq), Columbus OH. 614-222-7151

Black, Lawrence, *Librn,* New York State Office of Mental Retardation & Developmental Disabilities, Institute for Basic Research in Mental Retardation Library, Staten Island NY. 212-698-1122, Ext 610

Black, Lillie, *Librn,* Kansas City Public Library (Prospect), Kansas City MO. 816-924-1184

Black, Lois, *ILL, Ref & Commun Servs,* North Bellmore Public Library, North Bellmore NY. 516-785-6260

Black, Margaret, *Acq,* Upsala College Library, East Orange NJ. 201-266-7295

Black, Ralph E, *Assoc Prof,* State University of New York, College of Arts & Science, School of Library & Information Science, NY. 716-245-5322

Black, Robert F, *Dir,* Lawrence County Public Library, Lawrenceburg TN. 615-762-4627

Black, Sandra, *Asst Dir,* Mohawk College of Applied Arts & Technology, Library Resource Centre, Hamilton ON. 416-389-5665

Black, Sophie K, *Assoc Univ Librn for Pub Servs,* Northeastern Illinois University Library, Chicago IL. 312-583-4050, Ext 469, 470, 471, 472

Black, Sylvia, *In Charge,* Norfolk Public Library (Park Place Branch), Norfolk VA. 804-627-8076, Ext 6441

Black, Thelma, *Librn,* Brooklyn Public Library (Park Slope), Brooklyn NY. 212-768-0593

Black, Valerie, *Assoc Librn,* Yellowstone Library & Museum Association, Yellowstone National Park WY. 307-344-7381

Black, William K, *Asst to Dean,* University of Louisville Library, Louisville KY. 502-588-6745

Black, Jr, George, *Librn,* Southern Illinois University at Carbondale (Science), Carbondale IL. 618-453-2700

Black, Jr, Hugh G, *Pub Servs,* Southwest Texas State University, Learning Resources Center, San Marcos TX. 512-245-2132

Blackaby, Sandra, *Chief Librn,* Treasure Valley Community College Library, Ontario OR. 503-889-6493, Ext 68

Blackbeard, Bill, *Dir,* San Francisco Academy of Comic Art Library, San Francisco CA. 415-681-1737

Blackburn, Alice K, *Dir,* Neill Public Library, Pullman Public Library, Pullman WA. 509-334-3595

Blackburn, Frank M, *Dir,* West Texas State University, Cornette Library, Canyon TX. 806-656-2761

Blackburn, Joy M, *Librn,* Washington National Insurance Co, Information Resources Center, Evanston IL. 312-866-3651

Blackburn, Linda, *Ref,* Georgetown University (John Vinton Dahlgren Memorial Library), Washington DC. 202-625-7577

Blackburn, Mary, *Asst Librn,* Mount Pulaski Township Library, Mount Pulaski IL. 217-792-5919

Blackburn, Rebecca, *Acq,* Otterbein College, Courtright Memorial Library, Westerville OH. 614-890-3000, Ext 164

Blackburn, Robert H, *Chief Librn,* University of Toronto Libraries (University Library), Toronto ON. 416-978-2294

Blackburn, Virginia, *Librn,* Corpus Christi Public Libraries (Flour Bluff), Corpus Christi TX. 512-937-5222

Blacker, Rhoda, *Librn,* Boston Public Library (North End), Boston MA. 617-227-8135

Blacker, Rhoda, *Librn,* Boston Public Library (West End), Boston MA. 617-523-3957

Blackledge, Theresa, *Dir,* Jones County Junior College Memorial Library & Media Center, Ellisville MS. 601-477-9311, Ext 298

Blackman, Annie F, *Librn,* Anderson College Library, Anderson SC. 803-226-6181, Ext 264

Blackman, Betty J, *Dir,* Loyola Marymount University, Charles Von Der Ahe Library, Los Angeles CA. 213-642-2788

Blackman, Libby, *Asst Librn,* Free Library of Philadelphia, Library for the Blind & Physically Handicapped, Philadelphia PA. 215-925-3213

Blackman, Stephen, *Librn,* Banks Community Library, Banks OR. 503-324-3111

Blackman, W Dee, *Dir,* Big Country Library System, Abilene TX. 915-673-2311

Blackmon, E Terrell, *Media,* Jackson Metropolitan Library, Jackson MS. 601-352-3677

Blackmon, W Dee, *Dir,* Abilene Public Library, Abilene TX. 915-677-2474

Blackmore, Cathy, *Librn,* Saint Joseph Township Library, Swearingen Memorial Library, Saint Joseph IL. 217-469-2159

Blackmore, Elodie E, *Dir, Acq & Cat,* East Smithfield Public Library, Esmond RI. 401-231-5150

Blackstock, Dicksie, *Librn,* Occidental Research Corp Library, Irvine CA. 714-957-7450

Blackston, Jeanette, *Librn,* Metropolitan Pittsburgh Broadcasting Corp, WQED Library, Pittsburgh PA. 412-622-1524

Blackstone, Hazel, *Librn,* Ellsworth City Library, Ellsworth ME. 207-667-2307

Blackstone, Mary Ann, *Asst Dir & ILL,* Scottsbluff Public Library, Scottsbluff NE. 308-632-4424

Blackwell, Anita, *Ch,* Tombigbee Regional Library, Bryan Public Library, West Point MS. 601-494-4872

Blackwell, Betty, *Library Asst,* Spartanburg County Public Library (Chesnee Branch), Chesnee SC. 803-461-2423

Blackwell, Carolyn, *Asst Librn,* Jackson-George Regional Library System (Pascagoula City Branch), Pascagoula MS. 601-762-3406

Blackwell, Doris B, *Librn,* North Carolina Central University (Academic Skills Center), Durham NC. 919-683-6368

Blackwell, Eunice, *Librn,* Mondamin Public Library, Mondamin IA. 712-646-2888

Blackwell, Kathy, *Tech Serv,* Pike-Amite-Walthall Library System, McComb Public Library (Headquaters), McComb MS. 601-684-7034

Blackwell, Juanita, *Librn,* Blountsville Public Library, Blountsville AL. 205-429-3156

Blackwood, Judy, *Librn,* Aspen Systems Corporation, Library & Information Center, Rockville MD. 301-428-0700

Blackwood, Julia, *Librn,* Somerville-Fayette County Library, Somerville TN. 901-465-2091

Blackwood, Philip T, *Librn,* First Presbyterian Church, William Faulds Memorial Library, Ardmore PA. 215-642-6650

Blades, Jane, *Dir,* Humboldt Public Library, Humboldt KS. 316-473-2243

Blaesing, Margaret, *ILL,* Quincy College Library, Quincy IL. 217-222-8020, Ext 225

Blaetz, Monika, *Tech Serv,* Canajoharie Library & Art Gallery, Canajoharie NY. 518-673-2314

Blagg, Pearl, *Acq,* Free Public Library of the City of Trenton, Trenton NJ. 609-392-7188

Blahnik, Mary Ann, *Asst Dir,* Hales Corners Library, Hales Corners WI. 414-425-8050

Blaine, Barry Richard, *Librn,* Uniontown Public Library, Uniontown PA. 412-437-1165

Blaine, Martha, *Chief Librn,* Oklahoma Historical Society (Division of Library Resources), Oklahoma City OK. 405-521-2491

Blaine, Nann, *Librn,* Pittsburg Public Library, Pittsburg KS. 316-231-8110

Blair, Anita, *Librn,* Saint Clair College of Applied Arts & Technology Library, Windsor ON. 519-966-1656

Blair, Barbara, *Librn,* Greene County District Library (Bellbrook-Winters), Bellbrook OH. 513-848-2751

Blair, C G, *Librn,* Chavis County District Court Library, Roswell NM. 505-623-8460

Blair, Carole, *Tech Serv,* Old Bridge Public Library, Old Bridge NJ. 201-679-5622

Blair, Helen E, *Librn,* Virginia Memorial Public Library, Virginia IL. 217-452-3846

Blair, Jean, *Cat,* Chillicothe & Ross County Public Library, Chillicothe OH. 614-773-4145

Blair, Jeanne, *Ref,* Kitsap Regional Library, Bremerton WA. 206-377-7601

Blair, John, *On-Line Servs & Bibliog Instr,* Texas A&m University Libraries (Medical Sciences), College Station TX. 713-845-7427, 845-7428

Blair, Lavonne, *Dir,* Horicon Free Public Library, Horicon WI. 414-485-2791

Blair, Lynne M, *Dir,* Southwestern at Memphis, Burrow Library, Memphis TN. 901-274-1800, Ext 365, 366

Blair, Margaret, *Acq,* University of Maryland at Baltimore (Health Sciences Library), Baltimore MD. 301-528-7545

Blair, Marva, *Asst Librn,* American Express Co, Card Division, Systems Library, Fort Lauderdale FL. 305-473-3750

Blair, Maxine G, *Librn,* Camden-Clark Memorial Hospital Library (Medical Library), Parkersburg WV. 304-424-2111, 424-2237

Blair, Maxine G, *Librn,* Camden-Clark Memorial Hospital Library (Nursing Library), Parkersburg WV. 304-424-2111, 424-2237

Blair, Maxine G, *Librn,* Camden-Clark Memorial Hospital Library (Pathology Library), Parkersburg WV. 304-424-2111, 424-2237

Blair, Patricia L, *Ch,* Jackson County Library System, Medford OR. 503-776-7281

Blair, Ruth, *Ms Cat,* Connecticut Historical Society Library, Hartford CT. 203-236-5621

Blair, Ruth, *Librn,* NASA, Michoud Assembly Facility Library, New Orleans LA. 504-255-3311

Blais, Gaston, *Librn,* Bibliotheque Municipale, Saint Jean PQ. 514-347-1305

Blais, P P, *In Charge,* Ministere Du Revenu Bibliotheque, Sainte-Foy PQ. 418-643-6255

Blaise, Sue Ann, *Librn,* University of California, San Diego (San Diego Medical Society, University Hospital), San Diego CA. 714-294-6520

Blake, Ernestine, *Librn,* Durham County Library (McDougald Terrace), Durham NC. 919-596-8332

Blake, Ethel, *Ch,* Chester C Corbin Public Library, Webster Public Library, Webster MA. 617-943-0131

Blake, Gregory, *Ref,* York Regional Library, Fredericton NB. 506-454-4481

Blake, Gregory, *Ref,* York Regional Library (Fredericton Public), Fredericton NB. 506-454-2431

Blake, Helen, *Dir,* Southwick Public Library, Southwick MA. 413-569-6612

Blake, James B, *Librn,* University of the Pacific, Pacific Marine Station Library, Dillon Beach CA. 707-878-2278

Blake, John, *Librn,* Durham County Library (Parkwood), Durham NC. 919-544-2171

Blake, Jon W, *Media,* University of Washington Libraries, Seattle WA. 206-543-1760

Blake, Jon W, *Librn,* University of Washington Libraries (Media Center), Seattle WA. 206-543-1760

Blake, Martha A, *Chief Librn,* United States Army (Construction Engineering Research Laboratory Library), Champaign IL. 217-352-6511, Ext 253

Blake, Mary K, *Tech Serv,* J Sargeant Reynolds Community College (Media Processing Center), Richmond VA. 804-257-0208

Blake, Ruth, *Tech Serv,* Tulsa City-County Library, Tulsa OK. 918-581-5221

Blakebrough, Arden, *Librn,* Orange County Sheriff-Coroner, Laboratory of Criminalistics Library, Santa Ana CA. 714-834-3073

Blakeley, Mary, *Map,* University of Arizona Library, Tucson AZ. 602-626-2101

Blakeley, Mary L, *Librn,* University of Arizona Library (Map Collection), Tucson AZ. 602-626-2596

Blakely, Florence, *Coll Develop,* Duke University, William R Perkins Library, Durham NC. 684-2034 (Main).

Blakely, Jan, *Head, Admin Office,* Oklahoma Department of Libraries, Oklahoma City OK. 405-521-2502

Blakeman, Mary James, *Ad,* Bolivar County Library, Robinson-Carpenter Memorial Library, Cleveland MS. 601-843-2774

Blakeman, Randolph, *Librn,* Humphreys County Library System, Belzoni MS. 601-247-3606

Blakes, Mary, *Librn,* East Baton Rouge Parish Library (Carver), Baton Rouge LA. 504-343-7810

Blakeslee, Anita, *YA,* Fairport Public Library, Fairport Harbor OH. 216-354-8191

Blakley, Alma E, *Per,* Lincoln University, Inman E Page Library, Jefferson City MO. 314-751-2325, Ext 326

Blakslee, Rika, *Librn,* Lennox & Addington County Public Library (Yarker Branch), Yarker ON. 613-354-2585

Blalock, Louise, *Librn,* Island Interrelated Library System, Barrington RI. 401-245-3875

Blalock, Patricia S, *Dir,* Public Library of Selma & Dallas County, Selma AL. 205-875-3535

Blanchard, Danielle, *Librn,* Bibliotheque Municipale De Sorel, Sorel PQ. 514-743-4013

Blanchard, Debra, *ILL & AV,* Athol Public Library, Athol MA. 617-249-9515

Blanchard, Joan, *Dir Ext & Libr Develop,* New Hampshire State Library, Concord NH. 603-271-2392

Blanchard, Julia, *Librn,* Dunbarton Public Library, Dunbarton NH. 603-774-3546

Blanchard, Laura, *Ch,* Charleston County Library, Charleston SC. 803-723-1645

Blanchard, Margaret, *Headquarters Asst Dir,* Central North Carolina Regional Library, Burlington NC. 919-227-2096

Blanchard, Mary Gene, *Librn,* CH2M Hill, Technical Library, Gainesville FL. 904-377-2442, Ext 224, 225, 363

Blanchard, Patricia, *Librn,* Jennie Edmundson Memorial Hospital Library, Council Bluffs IA. 712-328-6130

Blanchet, Johanne, *Asst Librn,* Bell Canada (Law Library), Montreal PQ. 514-870-2683

Blanco, Sue, *Librn,* Saint Mary Parish Library (Patterson Branch), Patterson LA. 318-395-2777

Bland, Catherine V, *Dir,* Virginia State College, Johnston Memorial Library, Petersburg VA. 804-520-6171

Bland, Janet, *Rare Bks & Spec Coll,* Arkansas State University, Dean B Ellis Library, Jonesboro AR. 501-972-3078, 972-3079

Bland, Robert, *Cat,* Western Carolina University, Hunter Memorial Library, Cullowhee NC. 704-293-7306

Bland, Robert L, *Coordr Law Libr & Legislative Ref Servs,* New Jersey State Library, Trenton NJ. 609-292-6200

Bland, Rodney L, *Youth Servs & Continuing Educ Coordr,* Nicolet Federated Library System, Green Bay WI. 414-497-3443

Blanda, Tom, *AV & YA,* Gates Public Library, Gates Robert Abbott Memorial Library, Rochester NY. 716-247-6446

Blander, Murray, *Ad,* North Bellmore Public Library, North Bellmore NY. 516-785-6260

Blanding, Cynthia, *ILL,* University of California, Riverside (Bioagricultural), Riverside CA. 714-787-3238

Blanding, Sylvia, *Develop Countries,* Kansas State University, Farrell Library, Manhattan KS. 913-532-6516

Blandy, Susan, *ILL & Ref,* Hudson Valley Community College Learning Resources Center, Dwight Marvin Library, Troy NY. 518-283-1100, Ext 629

Blank, Annette C, *Cent Ch,* Enoch Pratt Free Library, Baltimore MD. 301-396-5430, 396-5395

Blank, Charles S, *Librn,* Washington County Free Library, Hagerstown MD. 301-739-3250

Blank, Janet, *Librn,* Trane Co, Engineering Library, La Crosse WI. 608-787-3583

Blank, Marianne, *ILL,* Saint Clair County Library System, Port Huron MI. 313-987-7323

Blank, Ruth, *Librn,* Indian Center of San Jose, Inc Library, San Jose CA. 408-259-9722, Ext 23

Blankenship, Alma, *Librn,* Bristol Public Library (Avoca), Bristol VA. 615-968-9663

Blankenship, Beth, *Librn,* Sylvia Public Library, Sylvia KS. 316-486-2472

Blankenship, David, *Media,* Parkersburg & Wood County Public Library, Wood County Service Center, Parkersburg WV. 304-485-6564

Blankenship, Dorothy, *Librn,* Southeast Arkansas Regional Library (Gould Public), Gould AR. 501-367-3336

Blankenship, Penelope M, *Librn,* Florence-Lauderdale Public Library, Florence AL. 205-764-6563

Blankenship, Theresa C, *Dir,* Avery-Mitchell-Yancey Regional Library, Spruce Pine NC. 704-765-4866

Blanton, Howard, *Dept Head,* Wake Technical College, Library Technical Assistant Program, NC. 919-772-0551

Blanton, Michael M, *Chief Librn & On-Line Servs,* Veterans Administration, Medical Center Library, Durham NC. 919-286-0411, Ext 6344

Blaschak, M, *On-Line Servs & Bibliog Instr,* Bendix Corp, Engineering Development Center Library, Southfield MI. 313-827-5620

Blasciak, Jean F, *Dir,* Public Library of Northfield, Northfield NJ. 609-646-4476

Blase, Susan, *Librn,* United States Army (Recreation Services Library), Newburgh NY. 914-564-7000

Blaser, Kathleen, *Librn,* Saint Nicholas Hospital, Health Sciences Library, Sheboygan WI. 414-459-4713

Blasick, Hank, *Dir,* Montgomery County Library, Conroe TX. 713-756-4486

Blasick, Mary, *Tech Serv,* Jackson State Community College Library, Jackson TN. 901-424-3520, Ext 248

Blasingame, Ralph, *Prof,* Rutgers-The State University of New Jersey, Graduate School of Library & Information Studies, NJ. 201-932-7500

Blasjo, Richard, *Librn,* Dakota County Area Vo-Tech Institute Library, Instructional Materials Center, Rosemount MN. 612-423-2281

Blaske, Virginia, *Asst Prof,* Saint Cloud State University, Center for Library & Audiovisual Education, MN. 612-255-2022

Blasko, Teri L, *Ref,* Pennsylvania State University Altoona Campus, Robert E Eiche Library, Altoona PA. 814-946-4321

Blatchford, Ruth, *Librn,* Hampton Falls Free Public Library, Hampton Falls NH. 603-926-3682

Blatchley, Alice E, *Librn,* Maryland State Governor's Commission on Law Enforcement Library, Towson MD. 301-321-3875

Blatt, Anne, *Ref,* Greenburgh Public Library, Elmsford NY. 914-682-5265

Blatt, Warren, *Librn,* Knesseth Israel Synagogue Library, Gloversville NY. 518-725-0649

Blattner, Julie, *Librn,* Harvard University Library (Center for International Affairs Library), Cambridge MA. 617-495-2173

Blattner, Julie, *Librn,* Harvard University Library (International Development Institute), Cambridge MA. 617-495-3650

Blauet, Doris, *Librn,* Flint Osteopathic Hospital, Dr Eugene C Herzog Medical Library, Flint MI. 313-762-4587

Blaylock, James C, *Dir,* Baptist Missionary Association Theological Seminary, Kellar Library, Jacksonville TX. 214-586-2501, Ext 6

Blazek, Ronald, *Assoc Prof,* Florida State University, School of Library Science, FL. 904-644-5775

Blazer, Virginia, *Librn,* Ocmulgee Regional Library (Cochran-Bleckley Public), Cochran GA. 912-934-2904

Blazina, Vesna, *Librn,* University of Montreal Libraries (Biology), Montreal PQ. 514-343-6801

Bleakmore, R, *Dir,* Tucson General Hospital Library, Tucson AZ. 602-327-5431

Blean, Jr, Keith C, *Asst Dir Tech Processes,* University of California, Santa Barbara Library, Santa Barbara CA. 805-961-2741

Blechl, Sue, *Librn,* Brown County Library (De Pere Branch), De Pere WI. 414-336-9010

Bledsoe, Randolph, *Librn,* Washoe County Library (Sparks Branch), Sparks NV. 702-785-4170

Bleecker, Mary I, *Librn,* College of the Virgin Islands, Saint Croix Campus Library, Saint Croix VI. 809-778-1620

Bleecker, Ruth, *Music Cur,* Boston Public Library, Eastern Massachusetts Library System, Boston MA. 617-536-5400

Blei, Barbara, *Cat,* Stockton-San Joaquin County Public Library, Stockton Public Libr, Stockton CA. 209-944-8415

Bleich, Marlene, *Librn,* Los Angeles Institute of Contemporary Art Library, Los Angeles CA. 213-559-5033

Bleier, Ruth, *Acq,* Nassau Library System, Uniondale NY. 516-292-8920

Bleiweis, Maxine, *Dir,* Lucy Robbins Welles Library, Newington CT. 203-666-9350

Blenkhorn, Patricia, *Librn,* New Brunswick Telephone Company, Ltd, Education Library, Saint John NB. 506-693-6845

Blenkush, Sharon, *Cat,* Ohio Northern University, Heterick Memorial Library, Ada OH. 419-634-9921, Ext 370, 490

Blesse, Robert, *Spec Coll & Archivist,* California Polytechnic State University Library, San Luis Obispo CA. 805-546-2345

Blevins, Donald L, *Librn,* United States Department of Agriculture, Science & Education Administration, Northern Region Research Center Library, Peoria IL. 309-685-4011, Ext 235 or 337

Blevins, Elliott, *Asst Librn,* General Dynamics Corp, Public Affairs Library, Saint Louis MO. 314-862-2440

Blevins, Judy, *Bkmobile Coordr,* Public Library of Pine Bluff & Jefferson County, Pine Bluff AR. 501-534-4802, 534-4818

Blevins, Mary, *Librn,* Arkansas Enterprises for the Blind Library, Little Rock AR. 501-664-7100

Blevins, Susan, *Cat,* University of Baltimore, Langsdale Library, Baltimore MD. 301-727-6350, Ext 444

Blight, Judith, *Ser,* University of Lowell Libraries (O'Leary Library), Lowell MA. 617-452-5000 Ext 480

Blinn, J, *Librn,* Oakland Public Library (Elmhurst), Oakland CA. 415-632-1500

Bliske, Carol, *Librn,* Nekoosa Public Library, Nekoosa WI. 715-886-3109

Bliss, Anthony, *Rare Bks & Spec Coll,* Northern Illinois University, Founders Memorial Library, De Kalb IL. 815-753-1094

Bliss, Deborah, *Vision Sci,* University of Alabama in Birmingham (Lister Hill Library of the Health Sciences), Birmingham AL. 205-934-5460

Bliss, Dorothy, *Dir,* Morton-James Public Library, Nebraska City NE. 402-873-5609

Bliss, Ina, *Dir,* Planned Parenthood Association of Orange County, H E Chatfield Library, Orange CA. 714-973-1727

Bliss, June, *Librn,* Public Library of Charlotte & Mecklenburg County, Inc (Sharon), Charlotte NC. 704-374-2109

Bliss, Robin, *Libr Aide,* Watertown Township Library, Fostoria MI. 517-795-2127

Blissert, Frederic M, *Dir,* East Los Angeles College Library, Monterey Park CA. 213-265-8650

Blixrud, Julia, *OCLC Coordr,* Minnesota Interlibrary Telecommunications Exchange, (MINITEX), MN. 612-376-3925, 376-3926

Bloch, Majorie, *Librn,* Kemper-Newton Regional Library (DeKalb Branch), DeKalb MS. 601-743-5981

Blocher, Joan, *Asst Dir,* Chicago Theological Seminary, Hammond Library, Chicago IL. 312-752-5757, Ext 55 & 56

Block, Eleanor, *Librn,* Ohio State University Libraries (Journalism Library), Columbus OH. 614-422-8747

Block, Ellen, *Ch,* Public Library of the City of Somerville, Somerville MA. 617-623-5000

Block, Grace, *Librn,* Harrison Public Library (West Harrison), White Plains NY. 914-948-2092

Block, Joan, *Bkmobile Coordr,* Broward County Division of Libraries, Broward County Library, Pompano Beach FL. 305-972-1100

Block, Joann, *Bkmobile Coordr,* Broward County Division of Libraries (Bookmobiles), Pompano FL. 305-972-1107

Block, Marylaine, *Asst Dir, ILL & Ref,* Saint Ambrose College, Learning Resource Center, Davenport IA. 319-324-1681, Ext 241

Block, Milton P, *Dir,* Monmouth Museum Library, Lincroft NJ. 201-747-2266

Block, Robert M, *Dir,* Medicine Hat Public Library, Medicine Hat AB. 403-527-5551

Block, Sally, *Librn,* Edgewater Hospital, Medical Library, Chicago IL. 312-878-6000

Blocker, Martha, *Head Librn,* Indianapolis Museum of Art Reference Library, Indianapolis IN. 317-923-1331, Ext 46

Blodgett, Elizabeth, *Dir,* Ontario Cooperative Library System, Newark NY. 315-331-2176

Blodgett, Elizabeth, *Dir,* Wayne County Library System, Newark NY. 315-331-2176

Blodgett, Lucy C, *Librn,* Kensington Social & Public Library, Kensington NH. 603-772-5423

Blodgett, Phyllis, *Cat,* Lynn Public Library, Lynn MA. 617-595-0567

Bloesch, Ethel, *Lectr,* University of Iowa, School of Library Science, IA. 319-353-3644

Bloesch, Leda G, *Dir,* Phillips County Community College Library, Helena AR. 501-338-6474, Ext 246

Bloetkle, Pamela, *Asst Librn,* Medaille College, Scholastica Library, Buffalo NY. 716-884-3281, Ext 238

Blok, Marsha, *Classics,* University of Waterloo Library, Waterloo ON. 519-885-1211

Blom, Dorothy, *Ch,* Free Public Library of Hasbrouck Heights, Hasbrouck Heights NJ. 201-288-0488

Blomberg, Hildur E, *Dir,* Grantsburg Public Library, Grantsburg WI. 715-463-2244

Blomeke, Linda, *Librn,* Knoxville-Knox County Public Library (Norwood), Knoxville TN. 615-688-2454

Blomquist, Laura, *Librn,* Ohio State University Libraries (Education Library), Columbus OH. 614-422-6275

Blomstrann, Lois, *Asst Dir,* New Britain Museum of American Art Library, New Britain CT. 203-229-0257

Blomstrom, Nancy, *Circ & Ref,* Eureka College, Melick Library, Eureka IL. 309-467-3721, Ext 219-258

Blondeau, Gilbert, *Librn,* Bibliotheque Municipale De Sainte-Foy, Sainte Foy PQ. 418-657-4252

Blood, Helen L, *Dir,* Tiffin-Seneca Public Library, Tiffin OH. 419-447-3751

Blood, Richard, *Circ,* San Francisco State University, J Paul Leonard Library, San Francisco CA. 415-469-1681

Bloodworth, Ferne, *In Charge,* Texas Education Agency (Region IX), Witchita Falls TX. 817-322-6928

Bloodworth, Jean, *ILL,* Rollins College, Mills Memorial Library, Winter Park FL. 305-646-2000, Ext 2676

Bloom, Charles, *Ref,* Humboldt State University Library, Arcata CA. 707-826-3441

Bloom, Ellen, *Ad,* East Rockaway Public Library, East Rockaway NY. 516-599-1664

Bloom, Linda, *Tech Serv & Acq,* Our Lady of the Lake University Libraries, San Antonio TX. 512-434-6711, Ext 272

Bloom, Marie A, *Librn,* Edmeston Free Library, Edmeston NY. 607-965-8208

Bloom, Marvin K, *Exec Dir,* Tobacco Merchants Association of the United States, Howard S Cullman Library, New York NY. 212-239-4433

Bloom, Olive, *Cat & Ref,* Maywood Public Library, Maywood NJ. 201-845-7755

Bloom, Wendy, *YA & AV,* Harrison Public Library, Harrison NY. 914-835-0324

Bloomer, Jerry M, *Librn,* R W Norton Art Gallery, Reference & Research Library, Shreveport LA. 318-865-4201

Bloomer, Nona, *Hist,* Guilford Free Library, Guilford CT. 203-453-6561

Bloomfield, Masse, *Supvr,* Hughes Aircraft Co (Technical Library), Culver City CA. 213-391-0711, Ext 2615

Bloomfield, Rosemary, *YA,* Mount Vernon Public Library, Mount Vernon WA. 206-336-2418

Bloomingburg, Mary, *Cat & Rare Bks,* Freed-Hardeman College, Loden-Daniel Library, Henderson TN. 901-989-4611, Ext 133

Bloomquist, Jennie, *Asst Librn,* Greenwood Public Library, Greenwood NE. 402-789-2300

Bloomquist, Mary Jane, *Bkmobile Coordr,* Washington County Library System, William Alexander Percy Memorial Library, Greenville MS. 601-335-2331

Bloomquist, Pamela, *Chief Librn,* Sebring Public Library, Sebring FL. 813-385-6350

Bloomsburgh, Esther G, *Librn,* Temple University, Ambler Campus Library, Ambler PA. 215-643-1200, Ext 250

Bloomstein, Carole, *Librn,* Bureau of Jewish Education, Jewish Community Library, San Francisco CA. 415-751-6983, Ext 12

Bloos, Arnold, *Librn,* American Maize-Products Co, Corn Processing Division Research Department Library, Hammond IN. 219-659-2000

Blosser, Gaele G, *Ser & Doc,* College of Charleston, Robert Scott Small Library, Charleston SC. 803-792-5530

Blossom, Amy, *Ref,* Loveland Public Library, Loveland CO. 303-667-4040

Blostein, Fay, *Instr,* University of Toronto, Faculty of Education, ON. 416-978-3242

Blouin, A W O, *Librn,* Employment & Immigration Bibliotheque, Vanier ON. 613-993-9810

Blouin, Deborah, *Bibliog Instr,* Arizona State University Library, Tempe AZ. 602-965-3417

Blouin, Robert J, *Ad,* Berkshire Athenaeum, Pittsfield Public Library, Pittsfield MA. 413-442-1559

Blouke, Jessie S, *Librn,* Washington County Library, Chatom AL. 205-847-2097

Blount, Ada, *Librn,* Birmingham Public & Jefferson County Free Library (Georgia Road), Birmingham AL. 205-254-2551

Blount, Edward F, *Asst,* Holyoke Public Library, Holyoke MA. 413-534-3357

Blount, Nancy, *Cat,* Westmont College, Roger John Voskuyl Library, Santa Barbara CA. 805-969-5051, Ext 378

Blovin, Jr, Francis X, *Asst Prof,* University of Michigan, School of Library Science, MI. 313-764-9376

Blovine-Cliche, Odette, *Dir,* Quebec Ministere Des Communications, Bibliotheque Administrative, Quebec PQ. 418-643-1529

Blowers, Malcolm E, *Librn,* University of North Carolina at Asheville, D Hiden Ramsey Library, Asheville NC. 704-258-0200

Blue, Jo Anne, *Librn,* Dixie Regional Library (Vardaman Branch), Vardaman MS. 601-489-3522

Blue, Josephine, *Librn,* Mount Vernon Public Library (Danville Public), Danville OH. 614-599-6216

Blue, Margaret, *Tech Serv,* Chula Vista Public Library, Chula Vista CA. 714-427-1151

Bluemel, Edward, *Info Officer,* Lever Brothers Co, Research And Development Division Research Library, Edgewater NJ. 201-943-7100, Ext 341

Bluemel, Nancy, *Ch,* Sherman Public Library, Sherman TX. 214-892-4545, Ext 242

Bluestein, Patricia, *Librn,* American Banker, Editorial Library, New York NY. 212-563-1900

Blum, Frieda, *Actg Dir,* Hampton Public Library, Hampton IA. 515-456-4451

Blum, John P, *Dir,* New Mexico State Supreme Court Law Library, Santa Fe NM. 505-827-2515

Blum, Phyllis, *Librn,* National Naval Medical Center (Naval School of Health Sciences Library), Bethesda MD. 301-295-0393

Blumberg, Janet, *Chief Consult Serv,* Washington State Library, Olympia WA. 206-753-5592

Blume, Peter F, *Curator,* Allentown Art Museum Reference Library, Allentown PA. 215-432-4333

Blumenshine, Joyce, *Spec Servs,* Pekin Public Library, Pekin IL. 309-347-7111

Blumenstein, Joan, *Ch,* Orange Public Library, Orange CA. 714-532-0391

Blumenthal, Sandra, *Librn,* Denver Public Library (Smiley), Denver CO. 303-573-5152, Ext 271

Blumstein, Barbara, *Dir,* Eager Free Public Library, Evansville WI. 608-882-4230

Blundell, Janet, *Librn,* Monmouth County Library (Township Ocean), Oakhurst NJ. 201-531-5092

Blunt, Carol, *Ch,* Litchfield Public Library, Litchfield MN. 612-693-2483, 693-2484

Blush, Robert, *Admin Asst,* Iberville Parish Library, Plaquemine LA. 504-687-2520

Blust, Sandra, *Librn,* Pennsylvania Department of Environmental Resources (Bureau of Topographic & Geologic Survey Library), Harrisburg PA. 717-787-6029

Bly, Matthew, *Cat,* Gaston County Public Library, Gastonia NC. 704-866-3756

Blyth, Barbara, *Dir,* Southeast Regional Library, Weyburn SK. 306-842-4402, 842-3432

Board, Joyce, *Librn,* Wake County Department of the Public Library (Wake Forest Public), Wake Forest NC. 919-556-2276

Boardman, Charlotte K, *Librn,* EDO Corp, Engineering Library, College Point NY. 212-445-6000

Boardman, Doris, *Dir,* Crafton Hills College Library, Yucaipa CA. 714-794-2161, Ext 222

Boardman, Elizabeth G, *Plant Sci,* University of California at Davis, General Library, Davis CA. 916-752-2110

Boardman, June M, *Librn,* Rosewood Center, Miriam Lodge Medical & Professional Library, Owings Mills MD. 301-363-0300, Ext 342

Boardman, Marilyn G, *Asst Dir,* Saint Johnsbury Athenaeum Inc Library, Saint Johnsbury VT. 802-748-8291

Boardman, Terese, *In Charge,* W A Foote Memorial Hospital Library, Jackson MI. 517-788-4800

Boatman, Sandra, *Librn,* Kent County Library System (Grandville Branch), Grandville MI. 616-534-8536

Boatright, Mrs J V, *Librn,* Oconee Regional Library (Woodrow Wilson), Tennille GA. 912-854-7466

Boaz, Judy, *Librn,* Pennyrile Regional Library, Princeton KY. 502-365-6674

Bob, Murray L, *Dir,* Chautauqua-Cattaraugus Library System, Jamestown NY. 716-484-7135

Bob, Murray L, *Dir,* James Prendergast Library Association, Jamestown NY. 716-484-7135

Boback, Freda, *Librn,* Peace River Municipal Library, Peace River AB. 403-624-4076

Bobb, Frank W, *Librn & Curator,* Free & Accepted Masons of Pennsylvania, R W Grand Lodge Library & Museum, Philadelphia PA. 215-988-1933, 988-1934

Bobeen, Jeanette, *Ch & YA,* Dodge City Public Library, Dodge City KS. 316-225-0248

Boben, Marian, *Dir,* Tredyffrin Public Library, Strafford PA. 215-688-7092

Bobersky, Noreen, *Librn,* Bristol Public Library, Bristolville OH. 216-889-3651

Bobick, James, *Sci,* Temple University of the Commonwealth System of Higher Education, Samuel Paley Library, Philadelphia PA. 215-787-8231

Bobinski, George S, *Dean,* State University of New York at Buffalo, School of Information & Library Studies, NY. 716-636-2412

Bobinski, Mary F, *Dir,* Amherst Public Library, Williamsville NY. 716-688-4919

Boblin, Ingrid, *Ad,* Sangudo Junior Senior High School and Public Library, Sangudo AB. 403-785-2212

Bobo, Paul, *Librn,* University of Kansas Libraries (Art), Lawrence KS. 913-864-3020

Bobowski, Alan, *Instr,* Lansing Community College, Library Media Technology Program, MI. 517-373-9978

Bobrovich, Mildred, *ILL & Ref,* American Museum of Natural History Library, New York NY. 212-873-1300, Ext 494

Bobula, Patty, *Dir,* New Hampshire Vocational-Technical College Library, Laconia NH. 603-524-8084

Bobzien, Barbara, *Cat,* Janesville Public Library, Janesville WI. 608-752-8934, Ext B

Boccetti, Louis G, *Librn,* E I Du Pont De Nemours & Co, Inc, Dacron R & D Library, Kinston NC. 919-527-0111

Boccier, Kathyrn, *Librn,* Franklin General Hospital, Medical Library, Valley Stream NY. 516-825-8800

Boch, Kirby, *Librn,* University of Wisconsin-Whitewater (Music Listening Center & Art Slide Library), Whitewater WI. 414-472-1756

Bochanyin, Curtis, *Divinty & Philos,* University of Chicago, Joseph Regenstein Library, Chicago IL. 312-753-2977

Bock, D Joleen, *Instr,* Appalachian State University, Department of Educational Media: Librarianship & Instructional Technology, NC. 704-262-2243

Bockman, Elizabeth W, *Librn,* Elkins Park Free Library, Elkins Park PA. 215-635-5000

Bockman, Marilyn, *In Charge,* American Association of Advertising Agencies, Member Information Service, New York NY. 212-682-2500, Ext 214

Bocks, Phyllis, *Exhibits,* Herrick Public Library, Holland MI. 616-392-3114

Bocksenbaum, Howard, *Coordr,* Island Interrelated Library System, Barrington RI. 401-245-3875

Bodansky, Ruth, *Librn,* Ayerst Laboratories (Information Center on the Mature Woman), New York NY. 212-826-3300

Boddy, Michael P, *ILL,* Asbury Theological Seminary, B L Fisher Library, Wilmore KY. 606-858-3581, Ext 246

Bodenheimer, Rosy, *Ref,* Baltimore Hebrew College, Joseph M Meyerhoff Library, Baltimore MD. 301-466-7900, Ext 307

Boder, Viola, *Tech Serv,* Duluth Public Library, Duluth MN. 218-723-3800

Bodewin, Lana, *Tech Serv,* New Mexico Highlands University, Donnelly Library, Las Vegas NM. 505-425-7511, Ext 331

Bodge, Richard A, *Dir,* Amesbury Public Library, Amesbury MA. 617-388-0312

Bodi, Sonia, *Asst Librn,* Kendall College Library, Evanston IL. 312-869-5240, Ext 247, 248

Bodien, Carol, *Per & Doc,* Bemidji State University, A C Clark Library, Bemidji MN. 218-755-2955

Bodien, Carol, *Instr,* Bemidji State University, Library Science Program, MN. 218-755-2955

Bodine, Jean, *Deputy Chief Librn,* Time, Inc (Main Library), New York NY. 212-841-3745

Bodke-Roberts, Alice, *Biomed,* University of California, Riverside (Bioagricultural), Riverside CA. 714-787-3238

Bodley, Margaret J, *Dir,* National Council on Family Relations, Family Resource-Referral Center, Minneapolis MN. 612-331-2776

Bodnar, John F, *Librn,* Affiliated Colleges & Universities Inc, New York Ocean Science Laboratory Library, Montauk NY. 516-668-5800, Ext 10

Bodnar, Marta, *Librn,* Ortho Pharmaceutical Ltd Library, Don Mills ON. 416-444-4461

Bodoh, Lois C, *Librn,* U S Industrial Chemicals Co Division of National Distillers & Chemical Corp, Technical Information/Records Library, Tuscola IL. 217-253-3311, Ext 497

Bodsford, Janet, *Acq,* Piedmont Bible College, George M Pamuel Memorial Library, Winston-Salem NC. 919-725-8345, Ext 311

Bodwin, Kathryn A, *Librn,* Mackinac Island Public Library, Mackinac Island MI. 906-847-3421

Boeckel, Olga, *Librn,* Daily Register Library, Shrewsbury NJ. 201-542-4000, Ext 206

Boeder, Thelma, *In Charge,* United Methodist Church, Archives & Historical Library, Minneapolis MN. 612-870-3637

Boegen, Anne, *Ch & YA,* Miami-Dade Public Library System, Miami FL. 305-579-5001

Boegenold, Julie, *Public Services,* Providence Athenaeum, Providence RI. 401-421-6970

Boehler, Sister Anthony, *Librn,* Saint John's Hospital (School of Nursing Learning Resource Center), Springfield IL. 217-525-6655

Boehles, Mary, *Librn,* Union Carbide Corp (Linde Division Marketing Communications Library), New York NY. 212-551-4602

Boehm, Hildegarde, *Dir,* Lakewood Public Library, Lakewood OH. 216-226-8275

Boehm, Joanne, *Librn,* Reformed Bible College Library, Grand Rapids MI. 616-458-0404, Ext 11

Boehm, Roanne, *Ch,* Woodland Public Library, Woodland CA. 916-662-6616

Boehme, Richard, *Tech Serv & Cat,* Framingham State College, Henry Whittemore Library, Framingham MA. 617-620-1220, Ext 273

Boehner, Margaret, *Librn,* Onondaga County Public Library System (Soule), Syracuse NY. 315-473-6808

Boehnert, M, *Librn,* London Public Libraries & Museums (Byron Memorial), London ON. 519-471-4000

Boehning, Karen, *Tech Serv,* Oshkosh Public Library, Oshkosh WI. 414-424-0473

Boelke, Joanne H, *Librn,* Northwestern University Library (Undergraduate Services Dept), Evanston IL. 312-492-7682

Boen, Tom, *Training Spec,* Florida State Department of Criminal Law Enforcement (Division of Staff Services, Bureau of Staff Development Library), Tallahassee FL. 904-488-1340

Boender, Mrs L, *Dir,* Emily Carr College of Art Library, Vancouver BC. 604-681-9525, Ext 26

Boepple, Rolland E, *Dir,* Santa Ana College, Library Technology Program, CA. 714-835-3000, Ext 357

Boepple, Rolland E, *Dir,* Santa Ana College, Nealley Library, Santa Ana CA. 714-835-3000, Ext 357

Boer, Aileen C, *Librn,* Federal Reserve Bank of Philadelphia, Philadelphia PA. 215-574-6540

Boermeester, Eva, *Cat,* Ventress Memorial Library, Marshfield MA. 617-837-5035

Boes, Warren N, *Dir,* Michigan Technological University Library, Houghton MI. 906-487-2500

Boesch, Mrs William, *Librn,* Portsmouth Athenaeum, Inc Library, Portsmouth NH. 603-964-8284, 436-5723

Boese, Robert A, *Dir,* Western Plains Library System, Montevideo MN. 612-269-5644

Boesen, Mary, *In Charge,* Depauw University (Prevo Science & Mathematics Library), Greencastle IN. 317-653-9721, Ext 2660

Boettcher, Barry J, *Librn,* United States Air Force (Myrtle Beach Air Force Base Library), Myrtle Beach AFB SC. 803-238-7086

Boettcher, Elinor, *Librn,* Newman Grove Public Library, Newman Grove NE. 402-447-2331

Boettcher, Myron D, *Dir,* Concordia College, Scheele Memorial Library, Bronxville NY. 914-337-9300, Ext 138

Boettner, Dorothy, *Libr Tech,* Nevada County Library (Nevada City Branch), Nevada City CA. 916-265-4606

Boevingloh, Vicki, *Ref,* Syntex USA, Inc, Corporate Library-Information Services, Palo Alto CA. 415-855-5814

Boewe, Karl, *Media,* University of Kentucky (Medical Center Library), Lexington KY. 606-233-5300

Bogan, Jeannie, *Asst Librn,* Shelby County Library District, Shelbyville KY. 502-633-3803

Bogan, Mary E, *Spec Coll,* Emporia State University, William Allen White Library, Emporia KS. 316-343-1200, Ext 205

Bogart, Harold, *ILL & Tech Serv,* New Mexico State Library, Santa Fe NM. 505-827-2033

Bogart, Harold L, *Head,* New Mexico Information System, (NEMISYS), NM. 505-827-2033

Bogart, Kurt, *Ref,* Ithaca College Library, Ithaca NY. 607-274-3182

Bogart, Ron, *Genealogist,* United Methodist Church Central Illinois Conference, Peter Cartwright Memorial Library, Bloomington IL. 309-828-5092, Ext 38

Bogash, Marcella, *Circ,* Center Moriches Free Public Library, Center Moriches NY. 516-878-0940

Bogatz, June, *Asst Dir,* Meriden Public Library, Meriden CT. 203-238-2344

Bogdon, Edith M, *Records Mgt Spec,* Bureau of Land Management, Elko District Office Library, Elko NV. 702-738-4071

Bogdoyan, Helen, *On-Line Servs,* Georgetown University (John Vinton Dahlgren Memorial Library), Washington DC. 202-625-7577

Bogen, Betty, *Chief Librn,* Veterans Administration, Health Sciences Library, Dayton OH. 513-268-6511, Ext 335

Bogen, Mitchell A, *Librn,* Metropolitan Hospital Center (Draper Hall Library), New York NY. 212-360-6262

Boger, Karl, *Librn,* Ed Burnett Consultants, Inc, Research Library, New York NY. 212-679-0630

Bogey, Daniel P, *Librn,* Easton Public Library, Easton CT. 203-261-0134

Boggan, Kay, *Librn,* Mid-Mississippi Regional Library System (Goodman Public), Goodman MS. 601-472-2095

Boggess, Clarabelle, *Librn,* Potomac Public Library, Potomac IL. 217-987-6506

Boggs, Bonnie F, *Librn,* Pickerington Public Library, Pickerington OH. 614-837-4104

Boggs, Ida, *Br Coordr,* Shreve Memorial Library, Shreveport LA. 318-221-2614

Boggs, Parker, *Dir & Ref,* Southeast Community College, Learning Resources Center, Cumberland KY. 606-589-2145, Ext 25

Boghiu, Rodica, *Librn,* Saint Joseph's Preparatory Seminary Library, Princeton NJ. 609-452-2144

Bogie, Thomas M, *Hist & Soc Sci,* Dallas Public Library, Dallas TX. 214-748-9071

Bogis, Nana E, *Dir,* Free Public Library of Monroe Township, Williamstown NJ. 609-629-1212

Bogle, Carlene, *Cat,* Loma Linda University Library, Riverside CA. 714-785-2022

Bogle, Clara J, *Librn,* Wauconda Township Library, Wauconda IL. 312-526-6225

Bogle, Clara M, *Librn,* Richmond Public Library (Belmont), Richmond VA. 804-780-6139

Bogle, Janet, *Librn,* Atlanta Public Library (Hobgood-Palmer), Fairburn GA. 404-964-5525

Bogle, Jr, Robert G, *Asst Dir,* Schreiner College, W M Logan Library, Kerrville TX. 512-896-5411, Ext 64

Bognar, Dorothy, *Librn,* University of Connecticut Library (Music), Storrs CT. 203-486-2502

Bogner, Patricia, *Ch,* Waterford Township Public Library, Pontiac MI. 313-674-4831

Bogner, Susan, *Librn,* LaSalle Bank Building Law Library, Chicago IL. 312-558-3135

Bogue, Donald J, *Dir,* Andon College of Vocational Health Careers Library, San Jose CA. 408-244-8777

Bogue, James W, *Ref,* Phoenix College Library, Phoenix AZ. 602-264-2492, Ext 621

Bohachevsky, Roman S, *Dir,* Pasadena Public Library, Pasadena TX. 713-477-0276

Bohaning, Stella M, *Librn,* TRW Inc, Technical Library, Cape Canaveral FL. 305-783-0870

Bohen, Mary Lou, *Librn,* Mauston Public Library, Mauston WI. 608-847-4454

Bohi, Etha, *Librn,* Teton County Library (Alta Library), Driggs ID. 307-733-2164

Bohlen, Jeanne, *Field Rep,* Foundation Center-Cleveland, Kent H Smith Library, Cleveland OH. 216-861-1933

Bohley, Ronald, *Dir,* University of Missouri-Rolla Library, Rolla MO. 314-341-4227

Bohling, Kathleen, *Circ,* Marquette University Memorial Library, Milwaukee WI. 414-224-7214

Bohling, Raymond, *Librn,* University of Minnesota Libraries-Twin Cities (Engineering), Minneapolis MN. 612-373-2975

Bohn, Dorothy, *Head,* University of Minnesota Libraries-Twin Cities (Public Services), Minneapolis MN. 612-373-2565

Bohn, Mel, *Ref & Bibliog Instr,* University of Nebraska at Omaha, University Library, Omaha NE. 402-554-2361

Bohn, Sue, *Ch,* Satellite Beach Public Library, Satellite Beach FL. 305-773-9411

Bohne, J, *In Charge,* University of Toronto Libraries (Faculty of Forestry), Toronto ON. 416-978-6016

Bohnert, Lea, *Asst Prof,* University of Rhode Island, Graduate Library School, RI. 401-792-2878 or 792-2947

Bohrer, Jeanne, *Ch,* Middlesex Public Library, Middlesex NJ. 201-356-6602

Boilard, David W, *Assoc Dir & Prog Develop,* University of South Dakota, Christian P Lommen Health Sciences Library, Vermillion SD. 605-677-5347

Boily, Denis, *Prof,* CEGEP Francois-Xavier Garneau, Techniques de la documentation, PQ. 418-688-8310, Ext 290

Boinay, George, *Acq,* Columbia University (University Libraries), New York NY. 212-280-2241

Boisclair, Nicole Mathieu, *Bibliothecaire,* Centre De Documentation Du Conservatoire De Musique De Montreal, Montreal PQ. 514-873-4031, Ext 37

Boisse, Joseph A, *Dir,* Temple University of the Commonwealth System of Higher Education, Samuel Paley Library, Philadelphia PA. 215-787-8231

Boissevain, Ellen, *Ref, On-Line Servs & Bibliog Instr,* Agency for International Development, Development Information Center, Washington DC. 202-632-8571

Boissonnas, Christian, *Acq,* Cornell University Libraries (University Libraries), Ithaca NY. 607-256-4144

Boisvert, Donald J, *Librn,* State of Rhode Island Department of Community Affairs Library, Providence RI. 401-277-2857

Boisvert, Robert, *Cat,* Bibliotheque Municipale Des Trois-Rivieres, Trois-Rivieres PQ. 819-374-3521, Ext 71

Boitscha, Roberta, *Librn,* Hillsboro Public Library, Hillsboro IA. 319-253-3645

Boivin, Richard, *Asst Librn,* Universite Du Quebec A Trois-Rivieres Bibliotheque, Trois-Rivieres PQ. 819-376-5706

Boksenbaum, Howard, *Regional Coordr,* Island Interrelated Library System, RI. 401-245-3875

Bolan, Suzanne, *Dir,* Rosenbach Museum & Library, Philadelphia PA. 215-732-1600

Boland, Ann R, *Commun Servs,* Nashua Public Library, Nashua NH. 603-883-4141, 883-4142

Boland, Christine, *Ref,* Lawrence Public Library, Lawrence MA. 617-682-1727

Boland, Miriam, *Librn,* Georgia Department of Human Resources Library, Atlanta GA. 404-656-4969

Bolanso, Marie K, *Librn,* Saint John Hospital, Medical Library, Detroit MI. 313-343-3733

Bolce, Frederica, *Ref,* Case Western Reserve University & Cleveland Medical Library Association, Cleveland Health Sciences Library, Cleveland OH. 216-368-3426

Bolch, Leona, *Librn,* Atlanta Public Library (Alpharetta Branch), Alpharetta GA. 404-475-9506

Bolden, Barbara, *Tech Serv,* Rockingham County Public Library, Eden NC. 919-627-1106

Bolden, C E, *State Law Librn,* Washington State Law Library, Olympia WA. 206-753-6524

Bolden, Elizabeth C, *Librn,* United States Army (Madigan Army Medical Center Medical Library), Tacoma WA. 206-967-6837

Bolden, Joyce B, *Dir,* W R Holley Memorial Library, Atmore AL. 205-368-3052

Boldrick, Mary D, *Ad,* Lynchburg Public Library, Lynchburg VA. 804-847-1565

Boldrick, S J, *Florida,* Miami-Dade Public Library System, Miami FL. 305-579-5001

Boldt, John, *Librn,* Wisconsin State Reformatory Library, Green Bay WI. 414-432-4877, Ext 78

Boldt, Julia A, *Librn,* Wanatah Public Library, Cass Township Library, Wanatah IN. 733-2595

Boldt, M, *Librn,* First Mennonite Church Library, Reedley CA. 209-638-2917

Boldt, Stella, *Librn,* Dewey County Library (Isabel Branch), Isabel SD. 605-865-3541

Bolduc, Pauline, *Tech Serv & Commun Servs,* New Bedford Free Public Library, Subregional Headquarters for Eastern Massachusetts Regional Library System, New Bedford MA. 617-999-6291

Bolef, Doris, *Dir,* Rush-Presbyterian-Saint Luke's Medical Center (Library of Rush University), Chicago IL. 312-942-2271, 942-5950

Boleman, Richard, *ILL,* Brandeis University, Goldfarb Library, Waltham MA. 617-647-2514

Boles, Carolyn, *Librn,* Western Kentucky University (Educational Resources Center), Bowling Green KY. 502-745-2491

Boles, Louise, *Tech Serv,* Emporia State University, William Allen White Library, Emporia KS. 316-343-1200, Ext 205

Boles, Suzanne, *Commun Servs,* Tulsa City-County Library, Tulsa OK. 918-581-5221

Bolger, Dorothy, *Librn,* Prince Edward Island Provincial Library (Hunter River Branch), Hunter River PE. 902-892-3504, Ext 54

Bolgiano, Christina, *Tech Serv,* James Madison University, Madison Memorial Library, Harrisonburg VA. 703-433-6150

Bolher, Kathleen, *Acq,* International Nickel Co of Canada Ltd, Technical Library, Toronto ON. 416-361-7641

Bolin, Ann, *Library Asst,* Spartanburg County Public Library (Lyman Branch), Lyman SC. 803-439-4759

Bolin, Bonnie, *ILL,* Watonwan County Library, Saint James MN. 507-375-3791

Bolin, Carbilene G, *Dir,* Fulton Public Library, Fulton KY. 502-472-3439

Bolin, Jean, *Librn,* Johnson County Library (Cedar Roe), Roeland Park KS. 913-831-1550

Bolin, Nancy, *Dir,* Cambridge Mental Health & Mental Retardation Center, Staff & Resident Resource Center, Cambridge OH. 614-439-1371, Ext 320

Bolin, Ruth, *Ad,* Finkelstein Memorial Library, Spring Valley NY. 914-352-5700, Ext 230

Bolin, Vern, *Librn,* Bolin Laboratories, Inc Library, Phoenix AZ. 602-942-8220

Boling, Alice, *Br Asst,* Timberland Regional Library (Elma Branch), Elma WA. 206-482-3737

Bolinger, Barbara, *Dir,* Illinois Department of Mental Health & Development Disabilities (Residents Library), Decatur IL. 217-877-3410, Ext 323

Bolkcom, Aileen, *Clerk,* Long Beach Public Library (Point Lookout Branch), Point Lookout NY. 516-432-8951

Boll, Carolyn, *Info Assts,* Colgate-Palmolive Co, Technical Information Center Library, Piscataway NJ. 201-463-1212, Ext 277

Bolles, Charles, *Dir,* Emporia State University, School of Library Science, KS. 316-343-1200, Ext 203, 204

Bolles, Shirley, *Dir,* Rutgers University (Library of Science & Medicine), Piscataway NJ. 201-932-3850

Bollier, John A, *Ref & Bibliog Instr,* Yale University Library (Divinity School), New Haven CT. 203-436-8440

Bolling, Elizabeth, *Librn,* Cincinnati Milacron, Inc, Electronics Systems Div Technical Information Center, Lebanon OH. 513-494-1200

Bollinger, Barbara, *Cat,* Cedar Crest College, Cressman Library, Allentown PA. 215-437-4471, Ext 264

Bollinger, Barbara, *Cat,* Muhlenberg College, John A W Haas Library, Allentown PA. 215-433-3191, Ext 214

Bollinger, Faye, *Librn,* Grifton Public Library, Grifton NC. 919-524-5545

Bollinger, Joan, *Dir,* Roseland Free Public Library, Roseland NJ. 201-226-8636

Bollinger, Marian E, *Dir,* South Whitley-Cleveland Township Public Library, South Whitley IN. 219-723-5321

Bollinger, Sherry, *Librn,* Riverside Regional Library (Center 5), Morley MO. 314-262-3094

Bollinger, Thomas, *Media,* National College of Chiropractic, Sordoni-Burich Library, Lombard IL. 312-629-2000, Ext 50

Bollman, E H, *In Charge,* Saint John's Hospital (Patient Library), Saint Paul MN. 612-228-3600

Bollman, Mary A, *Ch,* Lake Forest Library, Lake Forest IL. 312-234-0636

Bolotine, David, *Cat,* State University of New York, Frank Melville Jr Memorial Library, Stony Brook NY. 516-246-5650

Bolstad, Bethel, *Librn,* Great Falls Clinic Medical Library, Great Falls MT. 406-454-2171, Ext 212

Bolstad, Robert, *Librn,* New York Public Library (Ottendorfer), New York NY. 212-647-0947

Bolt, Alvin, *Radio Sta,* Public Library of Nashville & Davidson County, Nashville TN. 615-244-4700

Bolt, Nancy, *Branch Chief, Pub Libr,* Maryland State Department of Education, Division of Library Development & Services, Baltimore MD. 301-796-8300, Ext 284

Bolt, Reba, *Librn,* McDowell Public Library (Coalwood Branch), Coalwood WV. 304-436-3070

Bolte, Becky, *Tech Serv,* Maitland Public Library, Maitland FL. 305-647-7700

Bolte, Bill, *Info Network (KENCLIP) & Pub Servs,* Kentucky Department of Library & Archives, Frankfort KY. 502-564-7910

Bolten, Doris C, *Acq,* Hughes Aircraft Co (Technical Library), Culver City CA. 213-391-0711, Ext 2615

Bolton, Barbara, *Librn,* Domtar Inc, Research Centre Library, Senneville PQ. 514-457-6810, Ext 236

Bolton, Emily, *Librn,* National Park Service, Midwest Regional Library, Omaha NE. 402-221-3472

Bolton, Lucile I, *Dir,* Greenfield Public Library, Greenfield MA. 413-772-0989, 772-6305

Bolton, Mae, *Ref,* Sacramento Public Library, Sacramento CA. 916-440-5926

Bolton, Patricia, *Dir,* Grangeville Centennial Library, Grangeville ID. 208-983-0951

Bolton, Patricia, *Ref,* Red Deer College, Learning Resources Center, Red Deer AB. 403-346-6450

Bolton, Phyllis L, *Dir,* GAF Corp, Technical Information Services Library, Wayne NJ. 201-628-3320

Bolton, Stephen B, *Librn,* Carthage Free Library, Carthage NY. 315-493-2620

Bolttcher, Joline, *Tech Serv,* Columbia College, Kirtley Library, Columbia MO. 314-449-0531, Ext 221

Bolvin, Boyd M, *In Charge,* Bellevue Community College, Library Media Center, Bellevue WA. 206-641-0111

Bombard, Marlene, *Bkmobile Coordr,* Saint Clair County Library System, Port Huron MI. 313-987-7323

Bomgardner, Barbara E, *Librn,* Veterans Administration, Medical & Patients' Libraries, Lebanon PA. 717-272-6621, Ext 268, 247

Bomgardner, Martha Ann, *Librn, On-Line Servs & Bibliog Instr,* United States Attorney's Office Library, Newark NJ. 201-645-2387

Bomstad, Evelyn, *Tech Serv,* Crow River Regional Library, Willmar MN. 612-235-3162

Bonander, Madeline C, *Librn,* Chicago-Read Mental Health Center, Professional Library, Chicago IL. 312-794-4000

Bonar, Dale, *Media,* Aims Community College Library, Greeley CO. 303-330-8008, Ext 326

Bonar, Honey Lou, *Ch,* Hastings - Adams County Library, Hastings NE. 402-463-9855

Bonar, Mrs Tom G, *Asst Librn,* Aguila Public Library, Aguila AZ. 602-685-2295

Bonath, Gail, *Cat,* Grinnell College, Burling Library, Grinnell IA. 515-236-6181, Ext 598
Bond, A, *Librn,* Algonquin College of Applied Arts & Technology (Parkdale Campus), Ottawa ON. 613-725-2195
Bond, Amy, *Librn,* Lonesome Pine Regional Library (Scott County Public), Gate City VA. 703-386-3302
Bond, Art, *Dir,* John C Calhoun State Community College (Developmental Learning Center), Decatur AL. 205-353-3102
Bond, Barbara, *Dir & Ref,* Dyer Library, Saco ME. 207-283-3861
Bond, Carolyn, *Ad,* Prince William Public Library, Manassas VA. 703-361-8211
Bond, Gwen, *ILL,* Mesa Public Library, Mesa AZ. 602-834-2207
Bond, Jo Ann, *Registration,* Valparaiso-Porter County Public Library System & Administrative Headquarters, Valparaiso IN. 219-462-0524
Bond, JoAnne L, *Asst Dir,* Willows Public Library, Willows CA. 916-934-5156
Bond, Monica, *Librn,* Roxbury Community College Library, Roxbury MA. 617-445-3040
Bond, Vivian, *Asst Librn,* University of Maine at Fort Kent, Blake Library, Fort Kent ME. 207-834-3165, Ext 215
Bond, William H, *Librn,* Harvard University Library (Houghton Library-Rare Books & Manuscripts), Cambridge MA. 617-495-2441
Bondarovich, Mary F, *Mgr Tech Info Ctr,* Bristol-Myers Products, Technical Information Center, Hillside NJ. 201-926-6691
Bondi, Mary, *Dir,* Berkeley Public Library, Berkeley IL. 312-544-6017
Bondow, Louise, *Tech Serv,* Western New Mexico University, Miller Library, Silver City NM. 505-538-6731
Bonds, Evan, *Librn,* Western Michigan University (Music), Kalamazoo MI. 616-383-1817
Bone, Janet, *ILL,* Morris County Free Library, Whippany NJ. 201-285-6101
Bone, Jean, *Dir,* Haskell Township Library, Sublette KS. 316-675-2771
Bone, Larry Earl, *Dir,* Mercy College Libraries, Dobbs Ferry NY. 914-693-4500, Ext 260
Bone, Maydene, *Asst Librn,* South Ryegate Public Library, Inc, South Ryegate VT. 802-584-3655
Bone, Peter W, *Dir Pub Relations,* Rothman's of Pall Mall Canada Ltd, Automotive Reference Library, Toronto ON. 416-789-3432
Bonebreak, Doris, *Ser,* Illinois Wesleyan University Library, Bloomington IL. 309-556-3172
Boner, Marian O, *Dir,* Texas State Law Library, Austin TX. 512-475-3807
Boner, Marion Christopher, *Dir,* Callaway Educational Association, Coleman Library, La Grange GA. 404-882-0946
Bonett, Susan, *Asst Dir & Br Coordr,* Trails Regional Library, Johnson County-Lafayette County Library, Warrensburg MO. 816-747-9177
Bongar, Audrey, *Pub Servs,* Annie Halenbake Ross Library, Lock Haven PA. 717-748-3321
Bonge, Barbara, *Ref,* Thomas M Cooley Law School Library, Lansing MI. 517-371-5140
Bongiorno, Mary E, *Librn,* Air Products & Chemicals, Inc, Houdry Laboratories Library, Linwood PA. 215-485-1135, Ext 223, 229
Bonhomme, M S, *Librn,* Cabot Corp, Stellite Div Library, Kokomo IN. 317-456-6140
Bonhomme, Mary, *Ref,* Indiana University at Kokomo, Learning Resource Center, Kokomo IN. 317-453-2000, Ext 237
Boniface, Priscilla, *Cat,* Monessen Public Library, Monessen PA. 412-684-4750
Bonilla, Maria G, *Librn,* United States Army (Fort Buchanan Post Library), Fort Buchanan PR. 809-783-2424
Bonin, Claude-Andre, *Chief Librn,* Hydro-Quebec Bibliotheque, Montreal PQ. 514-285-1711, Ext 1617
Bonin, Lionel, *Librn,* Laurentian University Library (School of Education), Sudbury ON. 705-675-1151, Ext 474
Bonin, Roger, *Dir,* Ecole Polytechnique De Montreal Bibliotheque, Montreal PQ. 514-344-4847
Bonis, Eva M, *Librn,* Dennison Manufacturing Co Research Library, Framingham MA. 617-879-0511, Ext 509
Bonjour, Barbe, *Ad,* Smithtown Library, Smithtown NY. 516-265-2072

Bonkemeyer, Patty, *Librn,* Gulf Shores Public Library, Gulf Shores AL. 205-968-7394
Bonn, Marie J, *Chief Librn,* Eastman Kodak Co (Kodak Apparatus Div Library), Rochester NY. 716-726-3418
Bonn, Thomas, *Media,* State University of New York College, Memorial Library, Cortland NY. 607-753-2525, 753-2221
Bonn, Thomas, *PE Recreation & Polit Sci,* State University of New York College, Memorial Library, Cortland NY. 607-753-2525, 753-2221
Bonnaffon, Anne, *Librn,* United States Army (Walson Army Hospital Medical Library), Fort Dix NJ. 609-562-5741, 562-2664
Bonnar, A J, *Dir Finance & Property Servs,* Toronto Public Library, Toronto ON. 416-484-8015
Bonnell, Pamela G, *Librn,* City of Dallas, Management Services Research Library, Dallas TX. 214-670-4248
Bonnelli, Ann, *Librn,* Detroit Public Library (Sherwood Forest), Detroit MI. 313-833-9810
Bonnelly, Claude, *Asst Dir,* Universite Laval Bibliotheque, Quebec PQ. 418-656-3344
Bonner, Craig, *Eng Servs Chief,* Hampshire College, Harold F Johnson Library Center, Amherst MA. 413-549-4600
Bonner, Dora, *Librn,* Fairfield Library Association, Inc, Fairfield TX. 214-389-3574
Bonner, Evelyn K, *Librn,* Sheldon Jackson College, Stratton Library, Sitka AK. 907-747-5235, 747-5259
Bonner, Gina, *Circ & Coll Develop,* Lewis & Clark College, Aubrey R Watzek Library, Portland OR. 503-244-6161, Ext 400
Bonner, Jean, *Cat,* Schoolcraft College, Eric J Bradner Library, Livonia MI. 313-591-6400, Ext 412
Bonner, Leona, *Librn,* Swaledale Public Library, Swaledale IA. 515-995-2352
Bonner, Robert J, *Dir,* Indiana University-Purdue University at Indianapolis, University Library, Indianapolis IN. 317-264-4101
Bonner, Sandra J, *Asst Librn & Ref,* Marymount Manhattan College, Thomas J Shanahan Library, New York NY. 212-472-3800, Ext 460, 461
Bonner-Johnson, Patricia, *Cat,* Gonzaga University (Law Library), Spokane WA. 509-328-4220, Ext 3781
Bonnet, Anna Belle B, *ILL,* Lafayette Parish Public Library, Lafayette LA. 318-233-0587
Bonnet, Paul, *Ref & On-Line Servs,* West Valley College, Learning Resource Center, Saratoga CA. 408-867-2200, Ext 284
Bonnette, Nancy R, *Librn,* Aiken-Bamberg-Barnwell-Edgefield Regional Library (Wagener Branch), Wagener SC. 803-648-8961
Bonnette, Paul, *Cat,* Saint Michael's College, Durick Library, Colchester VT. 802-655-2000, Ext 2400
Bonneville, Geraldine, *Librn,* Isle La Motte Free Library, Isle La Motte VT. 802-928-8293
Bonneville-McGhee, Janet, *Pub Info,* Tacoma Public Library, Tacoma WA. 206-572-2000
Bonney, Frances, *Librn,* Science Council of Canada Library, Ottawa ON. 613-996-1729
Bonney, Francis L, *ILL, Ref & Spec Coll,* Buena Park Library District, Buena Park CA. 714-826-4100
Bonney, Shirley, *Acq,* David Thompson University Centre, Nelson BC. 604-352-2241, Ext 29
Bonnifield, Patricia P, *Dir,* Saint Martin's College Library, Lacey WA. 206-491-4700
Bonning, Mrs John, *Librn,* Bremen Library Association, Medomak ME. 207-529-5572
Bonniuee, Judy, *Librn,* Dakota County Library System (Farmington Branch), Farmington MN. 612-463-7990
Bono, Bernadette, *Librn,* Frederick E Parlin Memorial Library (West Everett), Everett MA. 617-387-0830
Bonsall, Bonnie, *Librn,* Central Florida Regional Library (Crystal River), Ocala FL. 904-795-3716
Bonser, Patricia, *Cat,* Arlington County Department of Libraries, Arlington Public Library, Arlington VA. 703-527-4777
Bonsteel, Sue, *Dir,* Stratford Public Library, Stratford ON. 519-271-0220
Bonta, Bruce, *Gen Ref,* Pennsylvania State University, Fred Lewis Pattee Library, University Park PA. 814-865-0401

Bonville, Barbara, *Librn,* Russell Memorial Library, Acushnet Public Library, Acushnet MA. 617-995-5414
Bonynge, Jeanne R, *Librn,* United States Tax Court Library, Washington DC. 202-376-2707
Boock, Carol, *Cat,* Deschutes County Library, Bend OR. 503-382-5191
Booher, Harold H, *Dir,* Episcopal Theological Seminary of the Southwest Library, Austin TX. 512-472-4134
Booher, Patricia, *ILL,* Episcopal Theological Seminary of the Southwest Library, Austin TX. 512-472-4134
Book, Nancy, *Ref,* Emory University Libraries (General Libraries), Atlanta GA. 404-329-6861
Booker, Nell, *Librn,* Butler, Binion, Rice, Cook & Knapp, Law Library, Houston TX. 713-237-3111
Booker, Patricia, *Fine Art,* Austin Public Library, Austin TX. 512-472-5433
Booker, Patricia, *On-Line Servs,* Austin Public Library, Austin TX. 512-472-5433
Booker, Susan, *Tech Serv,* Midwestern Baptist Theological Seminary Library, Kansas City MO. 816-453-4600, Ext 248
Booker, Toula, *Librn,* Wichita Public Library (Boulevard), Wichita KS. 316-262-0611
Bookhout, Polly, *Librn,* New York Public Library (Columbus), New York NY. 212-586-5098
Bookmeyer, Jane, *On-Line Servs & Bibliog Instr,* PPG Industries Inc (Glass Research Center Library), Pittsburgh PA. 412-665-8566
Bookmyer, Jane, *Supvr,* PPG Industries Inc (Glass Research Center Library), Pittsburgh PA. 412-665-8566
Bookstein, Abraham, *Assoc Prof,* University of Chicago, Graduate Library School, IL. 312-753-3482
Boone, Arthur, *Instr,* University of the District of Columbia-Mount Vernon Square Campus, Dept of Library Science & Instructional Systems Technology, DC. 202-727-2756, 727-2757 & 727-2758
Boone, Beth A, *Librn,* University of North Carolina, Highway Safety Research Center Library, Chapel Hill NC. 919-933-2202
Boone, Blanche, *In Charge,* Schenectady County Public Library (Quaker Street Station), Quaker Street NY. 518-895-2719
Boone, Deborah C, *Librn,* Saint Elizabeth Hospital, Health Science Library, Beaumont TX. 713-892-7171, Ext 4732
Boone, Jon, *Acq,* Northern Illinois University, Founders Memorial Library, De Kalb IL. 815-753-1094
Boone, Lou Ann, *Dir,* Charlotte Public Library, Carnegie Library, Charlotte MI. 517-543-1300
Boone, Louise V, *Dir,* Albemarle Regional Library, Winton NC. 919-358-7631
Boone, Mary L, *Dir,* Chapel Hill Public Library, Chapel Hill NC. 919-942-5455
Boone, Morell D, *Dean,* University of Bridgeport, Magnus Wahlstrom Library, Bridgeport CT. 203-576-4740
Boone, Roberta J, *Librn,* Clinton Public Library, Clinton TN. 615-457-0519
Boone, Sam, *Newsp & Micro,* Duke University, William R Perkins Library, Durham NC. 684-2034
Boone, Samuel M, *ILL,* University of North Carolina at Chapel Hill, Louis Round Wilson Academic Affairs Library, Chapel Hill NC. 919-933-1301
Boone, Susan, *Cat,* Cedar Falls Public Library, Cedar Falls IA. 319-266-2629
Boone, Susan, *Curator,* Sophia Smith Collection, Women's History Archive, Smith College, Northampton MA. 413-584-2700, Ext 622
Boone, Jr, Edward J, *In Charge,* MacArthur Memorial Library & Archives, Norfolk VA. 804-441-2256
Boonstra, Harry, *Dir,* Hope College, Van Zoeren Library, Holland MI. 392-5111, Ext 2130
Boor, Elizabeth E, *Librn,* Free Public Library, Hannibal MO. 314-221-0222
Boorkman, Jo Anne, *Pub Servs,* University of North Carolina at Chapel Hill (Health Sciences Library), Chapel Hill NC. 919-966-2111
Boorstin, Daniel J, *Librn of Congress,* Library of Congress, Washington DC. 202-287-5000
Booth, Anna Jane, *Librn,* Oscoda County Library, Mio MI. 517-826-3613

Booth, Betsy, *Admin Asst & Ch*, Taylor Memorial Public Library, Cuyahoga Falls Public Library, Cuyahoga Falls OH. 216-928-2117

Booth, Bev, *Librn*, Santa Clara County Free Library (Campbell Public), Campbell CA. 408-378-8122

Booth, Brenda, *Acq*, Alabama Public Library Service, Montgomery AL. 205-832-5743

Booth, Dehlia, *Bkmobile Coordr*, Edmonson County Public Library, Brownsville KY. 502-597-2146

Booth, Elizabeth, *Librn*, University of Pittsburgh (Henry Clay Frick Fine Arts), Pittsburgh PA. 412-624-4124

Booth, Elizabeth Ann, *Librn*, Bartholomew County Library (Subregional Library for the Blind & Physically Handicapped), Columbus IN. 812-379-1277

Booth, Jackie, *Librn*, Sanborn Library of North Danville, Danville NH. 603-642-3351

Booth, Jane, *Ref*, Southeastern Massachusetts University, Library Communications Center, North Dartmouth MA. 617-999-8662

Booth, Janet, *Chief Librn*, Haldimand Public Library, Caledonia ON. 416-765-2634

Booth, Janet A, *Librn*, Creighton Public Library, Creighton NE. 402-358-5115

Booth, Lois M, *Librn*, United States Army (Martin Army Hospital Library), Fort Benning GA. 404-544-3343

Booth, Malcolm A, *Ser*, Orange County Community of Museums & Galleries Library, Goshen NY. 914-294-5657

Booth, Mrs Alex, *Librn*, Fruitland Baptist Bible Institute Library, Hendersonville NC. 704-685-8886

Booth, Mrs Willmynor E, *Librn*, Cuero Public Library, Cuero TX. 512-275-2864

Booth, Robert E, *Dir*, Wayne State University, Div of Library Science, MI. 313-577-1825

Booth, Shirley, *Acq*, Newark Free Library, Newark DE. 302-731-7550

Booth, Thomas, *Operations Mgr*, Digital Equipment Corp, Corporate Library, Maynard MA. 617-493-6231, 493-5821

Boots, Frederic, *Media*, Alexandria Library, Alexandria VA. 703-750-6351

Boots, Frederick C, *Librn*, Westgate Friends Meeting Library, Columbus OH. 614-274-5131

Boots, Saundra, *Librn*, Adel Public Library, Adel IA. 515-993-3512

Booz, Richard, *Mgt Consult*, Information Systems Consultants Inc Library, Bethesda MD. 617-522-0204, 301-299-6606

Boppert, Peter, *Asst Dir*, Southern Connecticut State College, Hilton C Buley Library, New Haven CT. 203-397-4505

Boram, Hilary, *Librn*, Asheville-Buncombe Library System (North Asheville), Asheville NC. 704-254-3028

Boram, Joan, *Librn*, Constructions Consultants, Inc Library, Detroit MI. 313-874-2770

Borave, Kathleen, *Tech Serv*, Verona Free Public Library, Verona NJ. 201-239-0050

Borbely, Jack, *Mgr*, American Telephone & Telegraph Company, Long Lines Information Research Center, Bedminster NJ. 201-234-3280

Borchert, Brenda, *Asst Librn & ILL*, Pennwalt Corp, Lucidol Div, Research Library, Buffalo NY. 716-877-1740, Ext 262, 276

Borchuck, Fred, *Dir & Media*, Shippensburg State College, Ezra Lehman Memorial Library, Shippensburg PA. 717-532-1463

Borda, Eva, *Ref*, University of Western Ontario (Health Sciences Library), London ON. 519-679-6175

Bordeaux, Carolyn, *Asst Dir*, Pender County Library, Burgaw NC. 919-259-4521

Borden, Faye, *On-Line Servs*, Science Council of Canada Library, Ottawa ON. 613-996-1729

Borden, Jeanne, *Dir & Acq*, Rhode Island School of Design Library, Providence RI. 401-331-3507, Ext 229

Borden, Sharon, *Acq*, Metropolitan Technical Community College, Instructional Resource Center, Omaha NE. 402-457-5100

Border, Nick, *Librn*, San Jose Public Library (Berryessa), San Jose CA. 408-272-3554

Borders, Delores, *Vice Pres & Info Dir*, Gardner Advertising Co, Inc, Library, Saint Louis MO. 314-444-2357

Borders, Evelyn, *Tech Serv*, Logan-Helm Woodford County Public Library, Versailles KY. 606-873-5191, 873-9703

Borders, Florence E, *Archivist*, Amistad Research Center Library, New Orleans LA. 504-944-0239

Borders, Jane, *YA*, Bloomington Public Library, Bloomington IL. 309-828-6091

Bordner, Ellen, *Media*, Long Branch Public Library, Long Branch NJ. 201-222-3900

Bordner, George, *Tech Serv*, State Library of Pennsylvania, Harrisburg PA. 717-787-2646

Bordonaro, Victoria, *Librn*, Sussex County Library System (Byran-Southern District), Stanhope NJ. 201-347-2535

Bordonaro, Victoria, *Librn*, Sussex County Library System (Hopatcong-Southern District), Hopatcong NJ. 201-398-6120

Borek, Mary, *Cat*, Nassau Library System, Uniondale NY. 516-292-8920

Boren, Lynne, *Librn*, Oakley Library District, Oakley ID. 208-862-3869

Boren, Phyllis, *Librn*, George Amos Memorial Library (Wright Branch), Wright WY. 307-682-3223

Boren, Sheila, *Tech Serv*, Findlay-Hancock County Public Library, Findlay OH. 419-422-1712

Borg, Anne, *Asst Dir*, Kent Memorial Library, Suffield CT. 203-668-2325

Borg, Joan, *Librn*, First Presbyterian Church, Thomas E Boswell Memorial Library, Evanston IL. 312-864-1472, Ext 27

Borgen, Wanda, *Dir*, Harrington Park Public Library, Harrington Park NJ. 201-768-5675

Borgendale, Marilyn, *ILL*, University of Baltimore, Langsdale Library, Baltimore MD. 301-727-6350, Ext 444

Borger, Beatrice C, *Librn*, American Trucking Associations General Library, Washington DC. 202-797-5291

Borges, Anne, *Librn*, Day Kimball Hospital, Lapalme Memorial Library, Putnam CT. 203-928-6541, Ext 327

Borgeson, Earl C, *Librn*, Southern Methodist University Libraries (Underwood Law Library), Dallas TX. 214-692-3258, 692-3230

Borgman, Betty, *Ref*, Wayne State University Libraries (Kresge Library), Detroit MI. 313-577-4035

Borgmeyer, Sister Raymond, *Librn*, Incarnate Word Hospital Library, Saint Louis MO. 314-664-6500

Borgo, Jessie, *Coordr*, Berkshire Athenaeum (West Side Community Public Library), Pittsfield MA. 413-442-8230

Boria, Marilyn, *Chief*, Chicago Public Library (General Information Service Div), Chicago IL. 312-269-2800

Boris, Christine, *Ch & AV*, Lindenhurst Memorial Library, Lindenhurst NY. 516-888-7575

Boris, M H, *Librn*, NL Baroid Library, Houston TX. 713-527-1282

Boris, Raymond, *Asst Prof*, Dalhousie University, School of Library Service, NS. 902-424-3656

Borja, Beata C, *Br Coordr*, Guam Public Library, Nieves M Flores Memorial Library, Agana, Guam PI. 472-6417

Bork, Harry J, *Dir*, Fox Lake District Library, Fox Lake IL. 312-587-0198

Borkowski, Shirley, *ILL*, Middletown Free Library, Middletown RI. 846-1573 & 846-1584

Borkum, Judith, *Tech Serv*, Syosset Public Library, Syosset NY. 516-921-7161

Borland, Dollie, *Bkmobile Coordr*, Saint Lucie County Library Systems, Fort Pierce FL. 305-461-5708

Borland, Jacqueline, *Librn*, Essex County Public Library (Kingsville Branch), Kingsville ON. 519-776-5241

Borman, John, *Asst Dir*, Stanly County Public Library, Albemarle NC. 704-982-0115

Borman, Lois, *Librn*, Torrance Public Library (Isabel Henderson Branch), Torrance CA. 213-371-2075

Borman, Sister Clara, *Cat*, Mundelein College, Learning Resource Center, Chicago IL. 312-262-8100, Ext 301, 302 & 303

Born, Jean, *Librn*, Akron-Summit County Public Library (Richfield Branch), Richfield OH. 216-659-4343

Born, Jean, *Tech Serv*, Mesa Community College Library, Mesa AZ. 602-833-1261, Ext 291, 201

Born, Jean, *Instr*, Mesa Community College, Library Technician Program, AZ. 602-833-1261

Borner, Albert P, *Librn*, Donovan Leisure Newton & Irvine Library, New York NY. 212-489-4293

Bornfleth, Marcus, *Head Info Ctr*, Swift & Co, Research & Development Information Center, Oak Brook IL. 312-325-9320, Ext 141

Bornt, Phyllis, *Br Coordr*, Schenectady County Public Library, Schenectady NY. 518-382-3500

Borntrager, Mary, *Libr Administrator*, Destin Library, Inc, Destin FL. 904-837-8572

Borock, Mrs Freddie, *Librn*, Brookhaven Memorial Hospital, Medical Library, Patchogue NY. 516-654-7074

Borodacz, W, *Polish*, State University of New York at Buffalo, University Libraries, Buffalo NY. 716-636-2965

Borom, Florence, *Librn*, Burke County Library, Waynesboro GA. 912-554-3277

Borovansky, Vladimir, *Sci*, Arizona State University Library, Tempe AZ. 602-965-3417

Borowski, Joseph, *Dir*, Oakton Community College, Learning Resource Center, Morton Grove IL. 312-967-5120, Ext 331

Borron, Carol, *Librn*, Park County Library (Powell Branch), Powell WY. 307-754-2481

Borroughs, Sister Louise, *Archivist*, Lutheran Deaconess Community Library, Gladwyne PA. 215-642-8838

Bors, Nancy, *Asst Dir*, A Holmes Johnson Memorial Library, Kodiak Public Library, Kodiak AK. 907-486-3312

Borschell, Betty, *Librn*, American Concrete Institute Library, Detroit MI. 313-532-2600

Bortell, Bonnie, *Media*, Jackson District Library, Jackson MI. 517-788-4087

Bortner, Alba, *Ch*, Montclair Free Public Library, Montclair NJ. 201-744-0500

Borton, Jeannine, *Br Coordr*, Troy-Miami County Public Library, Troy OH. 513-339-0502

Borton, Jeannine, *Librn*, Troy-Miami County Public Library (Oakes-Beitman Memorial), Pleasant Hill OH. 513-676-2731

Borum, Hill, *Librn*, Spring Hill Community Library, Spring Hill TN. 615-486-2932

Borus, Rita Halle, *Librn*, Jewish Community Centers Association, Tannie Lewin Judaica Library, Saint Louis MO. 314-432-5700

Borys, Orest, *Librn*, Colonial Penn Group, Marketing Research Library, Philadelphia PA. 215-988-7414

Borysko, Elizabeth, *Ch*, Mount Clemens Public Library, Mount Clemens MI. 313-465-1906

Bosa, Real, *Pub Servs & Bibliog Instr*, Bibliotheque Nationale Du Quebec, Montreal PQ. 514-873-4553

Bosca, David, *Chief*, Chicago Public Library (Literature & Philosophy Div), Chicago IL. 312-269-2800

Bosch, Allan, *Pub Servs*, Kenyon College, Gordon Keith Chalmers Memorial Library, Gambier OH. 614-427-2244, Ext 2186

Bosco, John, *Ref*, Garden City Public Library, Garden City NY. 516-742-8405

Bosco, Julius C, *Dir*, Philadelphia College of Bible, Scofield-Hill Memorial Library, Philadelphia PA. 215-561-8612

Bosco, Sister John, *Dir*, Saint Mary's College of O'fallon Library, O'Fallon MO. 314-272-3420, Ext 224

Bose, Anindya, *Instr*, University of Denver, Graduate School of Librarianship and Information Management, CO. 303-753-2557

Bosen, Shirley E, *Dir*, Fullerton College, William T Boyce Library, Fullerton CA. 714-871-8000

Bosen, Shirley E, *Assoc Dean Educ Resources Libr*, Fullerton College, Library Technician Program, CA. 714-871-8000, Ext 244

Boshears, Jr, Onva K, *Dean*, University of Southern Mississippi, School of Library Service, MS. 601-266-7168

Boski, Marina M, *Med Librn, On-Line Search Coordr & Bibliog Instr*, Montreal Neurological Institute & Montreal Neurological Hospital Library, Montreal PQ. 514-284-4651

Bosler, Deborah M, *Librn*, Metropolitan Edison Company System Library, Reading PA. 215-929-3601, Ext 589

Bosler, Gerald, *Ref*, Macomb County Community College-South Campus, Max Thompson Learning Media Center, Warren MI. 313-445-7401

Bosley, Jane M, *Librn*, Institute for Cancer Research Library, Talbot Research Library, Philadelphia PA. 215-728-2710, 728-2711

Bosma, Jan, *Ref & Ser,* Grand Rapids Baptist College & Seminary, Ketcham Library, Grand Rapids MI. 616-949-5300, Ext 228
Boss, Catherine M, *Dir,* Elizabeth General Hospital & Dispensary, Health Science Library, Elizabeth NJ. 201-289-8600, Ext 208
Bossard, Carolyn, *Ad,* Steele Memorial Library, Chemung-Southern Tier Library System, Elmira NY. 607-733-9173, 733-9174, 733-9175
Bosse, June, *Ch,* Lakeville Public Library, Lakeville MA. 617-947-9028
Bosse, Maurice H, *Dir,* Massachusetts Maritime Academy, Captain Charles H Hurley Library, Buzzards Bay MA. 617-759-5761, Ext 281
Bosse, Rita, *Libm,* Town of Ayden Public Library, Ayden NC. 919-746-3101
Bosseau, Don L, *Univ Libm,* University of Hawaii (University of Hawaii Library), Honolulu HI. 808-948-7205
Bossen, Michael, *Asst Libm,* Central Wyoming College Library, Riverton WY. 307-856-9291, Ext 33
Bosshardt, Margaret E, *Dir,* Marshall-Lyon County Library, Marshall MN. 532-2646; 532-2849
Bossler, Kathryn C, *Libm,* Columbia Gas System Service Corp, Law Library, Wilmington DE. 302-429-5320
Bostetter, Sandra, *Libm,* Arizona State School for the Deaf & Blind, Phoenix Day School for the Deaf Library Media Center, Phoenix AZ. 602-255-3448
Bostic, Linda, *Commun Servs,* Pasadena Public Library, Pasadena TX. 713-477-0276
Bostic, Mary, *Acq,* Long Island University, Brooklyn Center Libraries, Brooklyn NY. 212-834-6060, 834-6064
Bostic, Mary, *Elem Educ, Eng & Am Lit,* Long Island University, Brooklyn Center Libraries, Brooklyn NY. 212-834-6060, 834-6064
Bostick, Catherine B, *Libm,* Buckman Laboratories, Inc Library, Memphis TN. 901-278-0330
Bostick, Sharon, *Ref Hotline,* Oakland University, Kresge Library, Rochester MI. 313-377-2486, 377-2474
Bostick, Virginia, *Spec Coll,* Morris County Free Library, Whippany NJ. 201-285-6101
Boston, Marietta, *Libm,* El Dorado County Library (Pollock Pines Branch), Pollock Pines CA. 916-644-2498
Bostwick, Elizabeth A, *Libm,* Huntington Art Galleries Library, Huntington WV. 304-529-2701
Bostwick, Joan, *Servs to the Institutionalized Consult,* Massachusetts Board of Library Commissioners, Office for the Development of Library Services, Boston MA. 617-267-9400
Boswell, Judith A, *Libm,* Palmyra Public Library, Palmyra PA. 717-838-1347
Boswell, Pam Kiefer, *Asst Libm,* Mary Esther Public Library, Mary Esther FL. 904-243-5731
Boswell, Peggy, *Coordr Region One,* Denver Public Library, Denver CO. 303-573-5152, Ext 271
Botcun, Tania, *research,* Sutherland, Asbill & Brennan, Law Library, Atlanta GA. 404-658-8907
Botelho, Cynthia, *Libm,* Falmouth Public Library (East Falmouth), Falmouth MA. 617-548-6340
Botes, Doris, *Ad & Ref,* Algonquin Area Public Library District, Algonquin IL. 312-658-4343
Both, Stephanie, *Libm,* McGill University Libraries (Library Science), Montreal PQ. 514-392-5931
Botham, Barbara, *Ch,* Finkelstein Memorial Library, Spring Valley NY. 914-352-5700, Ext 230
Botham, Jane, *Consults,* New York State Library, Albany NY. 518-474-5930
Bothe, Jeane, *Curator,* Museum of the Great Plains, Research Center, Lawton OK. 405-353-5675
Bothmer, A James, *Libm & On-Line Servs,* McKennan Hospital, Medical Staff Library, Sioux Falls SD. 605-339-8000
Bothwell, Betty, *Asst Dir,* Crown Point-Center Public Library, Crown Point IN. 219-663-0270
Bothwell, Garcie, *Cat,* Elbert Ivey Memorial Library, Hickory NC. 704-322-2905
Bott, Audrey L, *Dir Libr Serv,* Business International Research Library, New York NY. 212-750-6383
Bott, Cynthia, *Coordr,* University of Kentucky (Law), Lexington KY. 606-258-8686
Bott, Lois A, *Circ,* C F Lawrence Memorial Library, Pepperell MA. 617-433-6933

Botta, Gail, *Acq,* Albany Medical Center College of Union University, Schaffer Library of Health Sciences, Albany NY. 518-445-5534
Botto, Denise, *Reserves,* Southern Connecticut State College, Hilton C Buley Library, New Haven CT. 203-397-4505
Bottomley, Anne, *Libm,* Contra Costa County Library (Kensington Branch), Kensington CA. 415-524-3043
Bottoms, Jane R, *Libm,* Children's Medical Center, Medical Library, Dayton OH. 513-461-4790
Bottoms, Rita, *Rare Bks & Spec Coll,* University of California, University Library, Santa Cruz CA. 408-429-2076
Botts, H M, *Libm,* Pullman Kellogg, Research & Engineering Development Library, Houston TX. 713-626-5600
Botts, Joy, *Coordr,* Tri-County Library Council, Inc, WI. 414-553-2617
Botts, Virginia, *Libm,* Foxburg Free Library, Foxburg PA. 412-659-3431
Botwinick, Marshall, *Dir,* Henry Waldinger Memorial Library, Valley Stream NY. 516-825-6422
Boubel, Margaret, *Ref & Pub Servs,* Chabot College, Learning Resource Center, Hayward CA. 415-786-6762
Boublitz, Harry H, *Libm,* Enoch Pratt Free Library (Hamilton), Baltimore MD. 301-396-5430, 396-5395
Bouchard, Andre R, *Media,* CEGEP de Chicoutimi, Centre De Documentation, Chicoutimi PQ. 418-549-9520, Ext 212, 312
Bouchard, James, *Libm,* Toledo-Lucas County Public Library (Oregon Branch), Oregon OH. 419-255-7055
Bouchard, Jeanette, *ILL,* South Portland Public Library, South Portland ME. 207-799-2204
Bouchard, Joyce, *Libm,* Butte-Silver Bow Free Public Library, Butte MT. 406-792-3410
Bouchard, Marcel, *Libm,* Bibliotheque Municipale, Mont-Laurier PQ. 819-623-1833
Bouchard, N, *Libm,* P S Ross & Partners Library, Montreal PQ. 514-861-7481, Ext 282
Bouchard, Patricia, *Cat,* Port Authority of New York & New Jersey Library, New York NY. 212-466-4067, 4068
Bouchard, Rita, *Ref,* Colby College, Miller Library, Waterville ME. 207-873-1131, Ext 209
Bouche, Anne Marie, *Rare Bks & Cat,* Mills College Library, Oakland CA. 415-632-2700, Ext 260, 261, 262
Boucher, Jean, *Libm,* Shannon & Wilson Inc, Technical Library, Seattle WA. 206-632-8020
Boucher, Micheline M, *In Charge,* Canadian Museums Association, Museum Documentation Centre Library, Ottawa ON. 613-233-5653
Boucher, R, *Dir,* Seminaire Saint-Alphonse Library, Peres Redemptoristes, Sainte Anne-de-Beaupre PQ. 418-827-2751
Boucher, Shirley, *Asst Libm,* Missouri State Chest Hospital, Medical Library, Mount Vernon MO. 417-466-3711
Boucher, Virginia, *ILL,* University of Colorado at Boulder (University Libraries), Boulder CO. 303-492-7511
Boucias, Karen I, *ILL,* Santa Fe Community College Library, Gainesville FL. 904-377-5161, Ext 315
Boudreau, Allan, *Libm & Curator,* Grand Lodge Free & Accepted Masons of the State of New York Library & Museum, New York NY. 212-741-4500
Boudreau, Berthe, *Libm,* Universite De Moncton (Centre de Ressources Pedagogiques), Moncton NB. 506-858-4356
Boudreau, Gerald, *Acq,* Ecole Des Hautes Etudes Commerciales De Montreal Bibliotheque, Montreal PQ. 514-343-4481
Boudreau, James A, *Dir,* Babson College, Sir Isaac Newton Library, Babson Park MA. 617-235-1200
Boudreau, Jocelyne, *Dir & Acq,* Bibliotheque Municipale, Sept-Iles PQ. 418-968-6722
Boudreau, Martha, *Bkmobile Coordr,* New Bedford Free Public Library, Subregional Headquarters for Eastern Massachusetts Regional Library System, New Bedford MA. 617-999-6291
Boudreau, Richard A, *Dir,* Thomas College, Marriner Library, Waterville ME. 207-873-0771, Ext 17

Boudreault, Mireille, *Libm,* Bibliotheque Municipale De Jonquiere, Jonquiere PQ. 418-548-7101, Ext 50
Bouey, Elaine, *Develop Servs,* University of Calgary Library, Calgary AB. 403-284-5954
Bougas, Stanley J, *Dir,* United States Department of Commerce Library, Washington DC. 202-377-5511
Boughner, Mary Jane, *On-Line Servs,* Michigan State Library, Lansing MI. 517-373-1580
Boughton, Nancy, *Support Serv,* Kokomo Public Library, Kokomo IN. 317-457-5558
Bouillet, Adriana, *Libm,* Evergreen Regional Library, Gimli Centennial Library, Gimli MB. 204-642-7912
Boulet, Marcel, *Libm,* College Universitaire De Saint-Boniface Bibliotheque, Winnipeg MB. 204-233-0210, Ext 130
Boulet, Paul E, *Dir,* Universite Du Quebec A Chicoutimi Bibliotheque, Chicoutimi PQ. 418-545-5642, 545-5011
Bouley, Mary Lou, *Tech Serv,* Richards Memorial Library, North Attleboro Public Library, North Attleboro MA. 617-695-6411
Boulter, Belinda, *Libm,* Ecotope Group, Energy Resource Center, Seattle WA. 206-322-3753
Boulton, Earl M, *Ref,* Creighton University (Health Sciences), Omaha NE. 402-449-2908
Boulton, James P, *Dir,* Hemet Public Library, Hemet CA. 714-658-7293
Bounds, Charlotte, *Dir,* Crowley's Ridge College Library, Paragould AR. 501-236-6901, Ext 31
Bouquet, Sarah, *Dir,* Cottonwood Public Library, Cottonwood AZ. 602-634-8601
Bouquet, Verna, *Libm,* Pointe Coupee Parish Library (New Roads Branch), New Roads LA. 504-638-7593
Bourassa, Lise, *AV,* Bibliotheque De La Ville De Montreal, Montreal PQ. 514-872-5923
Bourdages, Celine, *Libm,* Canadian General Electrical Co, Ltd, Dominion Engineering Works Ltd Library, Lachine PQ. 514-634-3411
Bourdo, E A, *Dir,* Michigan Technological University, Ford Forestry Center Library, L'Anse MI. 906-524-6181
Bourdon, Bonnie, *Libm,* Vermont Institute of Natural Science Library, Woodstock VT. 802-457-1207
Bourdon, Huguette, *Libm,* Saint Isidore De Prescott Public Library, Saint Isidore de Prescott ON. 613-524-2109
Bourduas, Claire, *Actg Libm,* Bibliotheque Municipale, Port-Cartier PQ. 418-766-2368
Bourelle, Connie, *AV,* Dwyer-Mercer County District Library, Celina OH. 419-586-2314
Bourgault, Kathleen, *Libm,* Alvan Bolster Ricker Memorial Library, Poland ME. 207-998-4390
Bourgeois, Annette E, *Libm,* Canada Department of Energy, Mines & Resources (Geological Survey of Canada Library), Ottawa ON. 613-995-4151
Bourgeois, Catherine, *Libm,* IBM Corp, Reference Library, Montreal PQ. 514-874-6271
Bourgeois, Jean Marc, *Libm,* Bibliotheque Centrale De Pret Du Saguenay-Lac-Saint-Jean, Alma PQ. 418-662-6427
Bourguin, David, *ILL & Bibliog Instr,* University of Redlands, George & Verda Armacost Library, Redlands CA. 714-793-2121, Ext 472
Bourke, Marion, *Libm,* California State Library, Books for the Blind & Physically Handicapped, Sacramento CA. 916-322-4090
Bourke, Robert, *Dir,* Seminaire Des Peres Maristes Bibliotheque, Sillery PQ. 418-651-4944
Bourland, Beth, *Media,* Midland College, Learning Resources Center, Midland TX. 915-684-7851, Ext 214
Bourne, Elizabeth, *ILL & Ref,* Cranston Public Library, William H Hall Free Library (Administrative & Reference Center), Cranston RI. 401-781-2450, 781-9580
Bourne, Lorene J, *Dir,* Brun Memorial Library, Humboldt Memorial Library, Humboldt NE. 402-862-2914
Bourneuf, Henri, *Ref,* Endicott College, Fitz Memorial Library, Beverly MA. 617-927-0585, Ext 280
Bournise, Eileen Collier, *Dir,* San Fernando Valley College of Law Library, Sepulveda CA. 213-894-5711
Bourque, Bro Sylvio, *Libm,* Alfred Public Library, Alfred ON. 613-679-4404

Bourque, Dora, *In Charge,* Albert-Westmorland-Kent Regional Library (Shediac Public), Shediac NB. 506-389-2631

Bourret, Mrs F, *Librn,* Elizabethtown Township Public Library, Addison ON. 613-924-9525

Boushe, Mary Sue, *Librn,* Memphis & Shelby Counties Bar Association Library, Memphis TN. 901-527-7041

Bouskill, Ann, *Librn,* Cheektowaga Public Library (North), Cheektowaga NY. 716-634-4424

Bousquet, Ann M, *Librn,* Fanny Allen Hospital Library, Winooski VT. 802-655-1234

Bousquet, Jean M, *Music & Arts,* Berkshire Athenaeum, Pittsfield Public Library, Pittsfield MA. 413-442-1559

Bousquet, Lucille, *Asst Librn,* Bridgewater Public Library, Bridgewater MA. 617-697-3331

Bousquet, Virginia, *Tech Serv,* Brevard Community College, Melbourne Campus Learning Resources Center, Melbourne FL. 305-254-0305, Ext 227, 228

Bouthillette, Jean, *Acq,* College De Sainte-Foy, Centre des Medias, Sainte Foy PQ 418-657-3624

Boutilier, Brian G, *YA,* Reading Public Library, Reading MA. 617-944-0840

Boutinon, Elizabeth R, *Librn,* Shearson Loeb Rhoades, Inc Library, New York NY. 212-577-5253

Bouton, Marla, *Central Network Coordr,* Nebraska Library Commission, Lincoln NE. 402-471-2045

Boutwell, Meda, *Librn,* Eastern New Mexico University, Clovis Campus Library, Clovis NM. 505-762-3823

Boutwell, Sheryl A, *Librn,* Clarke College, Sanders Memorial Library, Newton MS. 601-683-2061

Boux, Rene, *Fine Arts,* University of Bridgeport, Magnus Wahlstrom Library, Bridgeport CT. 203-576-4740

Bova, Patrick, *Librn,* National Opinion Research Center Library, Chicago IL. 312-753-1487

Bovarnick, Esther W, *Ch,* Hempstead Public Library, Hempstead NY. 516-481-6990

Bovee, Dena, *Instr,* Northern Michigan University, Dept of Library Science, MI. 906-227-2250

Bovee, Dena, *ILL,* Northern Michigan University, Lydia M Olson Library, Marquette MI. 906-227-2250

Bovee, Martha, *Tech Serv,* University of California, San Diego, University Libraries, La Jolla CA. 714-452-3336

Boverie, Edward, *Media,* City of Inglewood Public Library, Inglewood CA. 213-649-7380

Bovi, Carolynn Deli, *ILL & Circ,* Case Western Reserve University Libraries (School of Law Library), Cleveland OH. 216-368-2792

Bow, Clifford, *Librn,* Wayne County Public Library, Monticello KY. 606-348-8565

Bow, Joan Hagberg, *Librn,* Robert R Nathan Associates, Inc Library, Washington DC. 202-833-2200, Ext 78

Bow, Judith, *Librn,* Washtenaw County Library (Library for the Blind & Physically Handicapped), Ann Arbor MI. 313-971-6059

Bow, Judity, *Librn Blind,* Huron Valley Library System, Ann Arbor MI. 313-971-6056

Bowden, Ann, *Assoc Dir,* Austin Public Library, Austin TX. 512-472-5433

Bowden, Jay, *Librn,* Sherburne Library, Killington VT. 802-422-9765

Bowden, John M, *Librn,* West Hills Community College Library, Coalinga CA. 209-935-0801, Ext 47

Bowden, Virginia M, *Assoc Dir,* University of Texas Health Science Center at San Antonio Library, San Antonio TX. 512-691-6271

Bowden, William, *Librn,* Collier County Free Public Library (Marco Island Branch), Marco Island FL. 813-262-4130, 261-8208

Bowen, Ada M, *Commun Servs, On-Line Servs & Bibliog Instr,* University of South Florida (Medical Center Library), Tampa FL. 813-974-2399

Bowen, Albertine, *Pub Servs,* University of the District of Columbia, Learning Resources Division, Washington DC. 202-282-7536

Bowen, Christopher, *Fine Arts & Music,* Akron-Summit County Public Library, Akron OH. 216-762-7621

Bowen, Debbie, *Librn,* Tombigbee Regional Library (Mathiston Public), Mathiston MS. 601-263-4772

Bowen, Ellen, *Librn,* Perquimans County Library, Hertford NC. 919-426-5319

Bowen, Heini, *Librn,* Sudbury Public Library (Regency Mall), Sudbury ON. 705-673-1155, Ext 44

Bowen, Johanna, *Per & Ser,* State University of New York College, Memorial Library, Cortland NY. 607-753-2525, 753-2221

Bowen, Jomarjo, *Librn,* New York Public Library (Countee Cullen), New York NY. 212-281-0700

Bowen, Kay, *Librn,* United States Public Health Service Hospital Library, Nassau Bay TX. 713-333-5503, Ext 149

Bowen, Kay, *Ch,* Wayne County Public Library, Wooster OH. 216-262-0916

Bowen, Laurel, *Ms Curator,* Illinois State Historical Library, Springfield IL. 217-782-4836

Bowen, Marguerite E, *Librn,* Foster Advertising Ltd, Information Center, Toronto ON. 416-928-8166

Bowen, Sherrel, *Librn,* Tulare County Library System (Earlimart Branch), Earlimart CA. 805-849-2525

Bowen, Virginia, *Ad,* Lucius Beebe Memorial Library, Wakefield MA. 617-245-0790

Bower, Cynthia, *Doc,* University of Arizona Library, Tucson AZ. 602-626-2101

Bower, Cynthia, *Librn,* University of Arizona Library (Government Documents Dept), Tucson AZ. 602-626-4871

Bower, Donald E, *Dir,* National Writers Club Library, Aurora CO. 303-751-7844

Bower, Janice F, *Librn,* Massachusetts Institute of Technology, Lincoln Laboratory Library, Lexington MA. 617-862-5500, Ext 7195

Bower, JoAnne, *Librn,* Weston County Public Library, Newcastle WY. 307-746-2206

Bower, Lester, *Acq,* Borough of Manhattan Community College Library, Martin B Dworkis Library, New York NY. 212-262-3530

Bower, Wayne, *Tech Serv,* Albuquerque Public Library, Albuquerque NM. 505-766-7882

Bowers, Alyce, *Dir,* Rockaway Township Free Public Library, Rockaway Township NJ. 201-627-6871

Bowers, Betsy, *Ref,* East Central State University, Linscheid Library, Ada OK. 405-332-8000

Bowers, Donna, *Asst Librn,* Lower Arkansas Valley Regional Library, Las Animas CO. 303-456-1770

Bowers, Elizabeth A, *Dir,* Weld County Library, Greeley CO. 303-330-7691

Bowers, James R, *Supvr,* Allied Chemical Corp (Business Library), Morristown NJ. 201-455-6061

Bowers, Jean, *Cat & AMIGOS,* Public Library of Enid & Garfield County, Enid Public Library, Enid OK. 405-234-6313

Bowers, Jeri, *Ch,* J Herman Bosler Memorial Library, Bosler Free Library, Carlisle PA. 717-243-4642

Bowers, Laura J, *Dir,* University of Southern Mississippi-Natchez Library, Natchez MS. 601-442-7326

Bowers, Linda, *Tech Serv,* Cedar Crest College, Cressman Library, Allentown PA. 215-437-4471, Ext 264

Bowers, Linda, *Tech Serv,* Muhlenberg College, John A W Haas Library, Allentown PA. 215-433-3191, Ext 214

Bowers, Louise, *Librn,* Hamburg Public Library, Hamburg PA. 215-562-2843

Bowers, Lue A, *Asst Librn,* Ashland Public School District Library, Ashland OH. 419-289-8188

Bowers, Lutrell, *Ch,* Pottsville Free Public Library, Pottsville Library District Center, Pottsville PA. 622-8105; 622-8880

Bowers, Margaret, *Librn,* Louisville Free Public Library (Shawnee), Louisville KY. 502-774-5122

Bowers, Marjorie E, *Librn,* Skidompha Library, Damariscotta ME. 207-563-5513

Bowers, Miriam, *Ref,* Chaffey College Library, Alta Loma CA. 714-987-1737, Ext 303

Bowers, Pat, *Acq,* McCook Community College, Learning Resource Center, McCook NE. 308-345-6303

Bowers, Richard, *Librn,* Kreutz Creek Valley Library Center, Hellam PA. 717-252-4080

Bowers, Richard, *Librn,* York County Library System (Kreutz Creek Valley Branch), York PA. 717-846-0677

Bowersox, Twila, *Librn,* Belleville Public Library, Belleville KS. 913-527-5305

Bowery, Mrs J, *ILL,* Red Deer College, Learning Resources Center, Red Deer AB. 403-346-6450

Bowes, Winifred B, *Librn,* Alcan Aluminum Corp Library, Cleveland OH. 216-523-6860

Bowie, Claire, *Ref,* City University of New York, Library of Graduate School & University Center, New York NY. 212-790-4541

Bowlby, Phyllis E, *Librn,* Library Development Commission, North Central Branch, Prince George BC. 604-562-7226

Bowler, Richard, *Anglo-Am,* University of Chicago (Law Library), Chicago IL. 312-753-3425

Bowles, Barbara, *Librn,* Pamunkey Regional Library (Rockville Branch), Rockville VA. 804-749-3146

Bowles, David M, *Cat,* University of Virginia (Claude Moore Health Sciences Library), Charlottesville VA. 804-924-5444

Bowles, Gay, *Circ,* Central College, Geisler Learning Resource Center, Pella IA. 515-628-4151, Ext 233

Bowles, Nancy, *Chief Librn,* Dillon, Read & Co, Inc Library, New York NY. 212-285-5690

Bowles, Nancy A, *Librn,* United States Army (Fitzsimons Army Medical Center, Post Library), Aurora CO. 303-341-8104

Bowley, Jane, *Librn,* East Kingston Public Library, East Kingston NH. 603-642-8333

Bowlin, Lavinda, *Librn,* Hot Springs Public Library, Hot Springs SD. 605-745-3151

Bowling, Carol L, *Ref,* Aiken-Bamberg-Barnwell-Edgefield Regional Library, Aiken SC. 803-648-8961

Bowman, Bernard, *Asst Librn,* Hampshire County Public Library, Romney WV. 304-822-3185

Bowman, D Harold, *Dept Chmn,* University of Northern Colorado, Department of Educational Media, CO. 303-351-2807

Bowman, Dona, *Librn,* Madison General Hospital (Memorial Medical Library), Madison WI. 608-267-6202

Bowman, Frances, *On-Line Servs,* Atlantic Richfield Co (Headquarters Library), Los Angeles CA. 213-486-2400

Bowman, Jerry, *Ref,* Watertown Regional Library, Watertown SD. 605-886-8521, 886-8282

Bowman, John B, *Librn,* North Smithfield Public Library, Slatersville RI. 401-767-2780

Bowman, Lucille S, *Asst Librn,* Piedmont Bible College, George M Manuel Memorial Library, Winston-Salem NC. 919-725-8345, Ext 311

Bowman, Lyle, *Librn,* Tahlequah Carnegie Library, Tahlequah OK. 918-456-2581

Bowman, M, *Cat,* Leamington Public Library, Leamington ON. 519-326-3441

Bowman, Marsha, *Cat,* Greenville Public Library, Carnegie Library, Greenville OH. 513-548-3915

Bowman, Martha, *Assoc Librn,* George Washington University Library, Washington DC. 202-676-6455

Bowman, Mary, *ILL,* Louisiana State University in Shreveport Library, Shreveport LA. 318-797-7121, Ext 203

Bowman, Patricia, *Ref,* Kaubisch Memorial Public Library, Fostoria OH. 419-435-2813

Bowman, Patricia R, *Dir,* Blackfoot Public Library, Edna Gillespie Memorial Library, Blackfoot ID. 208-785-1251

Bowman, R J, *Coordr,* Niagara College of Applied Arts & Technology, Library Technicians Course, ON. 416-735-2211

Bowman, Rebecca, *Librn,* Cleveland Public Library, Cleveland TN. 615-476-8431

Bowne, Debra, *Circ,* Teaneck Public Library, Teaneck NJ. 201-837-4171

Bowring, Margaret, *Librn,* Agriculture Canada Library, Vineland Station ON. 416-562-4113, Ext 41

Bowser, Eileen, *Asst Dir,* Bell Memorial Public Library, Mentone IN. 219-353-7234

Bowser, Elizabeth S, *Dean of Special Servs,* Roanoke-Chowan Technical Institute, Learning Resource Center, Ahoskie NC. 919-332-5921

Bowser, Susan, *Librn,* Elizabethtown Public Library, Elizabethtown PA. 717-367-7467

Bowsfield, Hartwell, *Archives,* York University, Scott Library, Downsview ON. 416-667-2235

Bowshier, Mary Ann, *Librn,* Mechanicsburg Public Library, Mechanicsburg OH. 513-834-2004

Bowyer, Dorothy, *Librn,* Harris County Public Library (Jacinto City), Houston TX. 713-673-3237

Bowyer, Rose, *Librn,* Pocahontas County Free Library, Green Bank WV. 304-653-4936
Bowyer, Valerie, *In Charge,* Consulate-General of Japan in Edmonton Library, Edmonton AB. 403-422-3752, 429-3052
Box, Betty, *Librn,* Herman Brown Free Library (Bertram Branch), Bertram TX. 512-756-2328
Box, Betty, *Librn,* Herman Brown Free Library (Briggs Branch), Briggs TX. 512-756-2328
Box, Betty, *Librn,* Herman Brown Free Library (Oakalla Branch), Oakalla TX. 512-756-2328
Box, Thelma, *Asst Librn,* Crane County Library, Crane TX. 915-558-3142
Boyadjieff, Katherine, *Librn,* Calistoga Public Library, Calistoga CA. 707-942-4833
Boyarski, Jennie S, *Librn,* Paducah Community College Library, Paducah KY. 502-442-6131, Ext 17
Boyce, Barbara, *Asst Librn,* Tufts University (Edwin Ginn Library), Medford MA. 617-628-5000, Ext 235
Boyce, Bert, *Assoc Prof,* University of Missouri-Columbia, School of Library & Informational Science, MO. 314-882-4546
Boyce, Emily S, *Prof,* East Carolina University, Dept of Library Science, NC. 919-757-6621, 757-6627
Boyce, Harold W, *Dir,* Marion College Library, Marion IN. 317-674-6901, Ext 228
Boyce, Jan T, *Ref,* Boston College Libraries (Bapst (Central Library)), Chestnut Hill MA. 617-969-0100, Ext 3205
Boyce, Joan, *Pub Servs,* Flagstaff City-Coconino County Public Library System, Flagstaff AZ. 602-774-0603
Boyce, Joseph A, *Dir,* Coppin State College, Parlett Moore Library, Baltimore MD. 301-383-5926
Boyce, Linda Neal, *Ch,* Ridgefield Library & Historical Association, Ridgefield CT. 203-438-2282
Boychuk, Elaine, *Media,* University of Alberta (University Libraries), Edmonton AB. 403-432-3790
Boyd, A, *Librn,* Okanagan Regional Library District (Naramata Branch), Naramata BC. 604-496-5679
Boyd, Alberta, *Librn,* Public Library of Charlotte & Mecklenburg County, Inc (Pineville Branch), Pineville NC. 704-889-7121
Boyd, Alice, *Ref,* Hutchinson County Library, Borger TX. 806-274-6221
Boyd, Alice, *Asst Dir,* Phillipsburg City Library, Phillipsburg KS. 913-543-5325
Boyd, Barbara G, *County Librn,* Alameda County Library, Hayward CA. 415-881-6337
Boyd, Betty, *Acq,* Butler University, Irwin Library, Indianapolis IN. 317-283-9225
Boyd, Charles, *Evening Coordr,* Tulsa Junior College, Learning Resource Center, Tulsa OK. 918-587-6561, Ext 363
Boyd, Constance, *Librn,* Harrisville Public Library, Harrisville NH. 603-827-3431
Boyd, D Alex, *Asst Prof,* University of Alabama, Graduate School of Library Service, AL. 205-348-4610
Boyd, Dean, *Librn,* York County Library (Clover Public), Clover SC. 803-222-3474
Boyd, Doris, *Librn,* Tipton County Public Library, Covington TN. 901-476-8289
Boyd, Effie, *Doc,* ARO Inc, Arnold Engineering Development Center Technical Library, Arnold AFS TN. 615-455-2611, Ext 431
Boyd, Effie W, *Tech Librn & On-Line Searchers,* United States Air Force (Arnold Engineering Development Center Library), Arnold AFS TN. 615-455-2611
Boyd, Elizabeth, *Tech Serv,* Wilson College, John Stewart Memorial Library, Chambersburg PA. 717-264-4141, Ext 344
Boyd, Frances P, *Chmn Libr Cont,* Central Presbyterian Church Library, Terre Haute IN. 812-232-5049
Boyd, Harmon, *Exten Servs,* Vigo County Public Library, Terre Haute IN. 812-232-1113
Boyd, Jacqueline, *Librn,* Bud Werner Memorial Library (West Routt Library District), Hayden CO. 303-276-3343
Boyd, Julia G, *Dir,* Upper Cumberland Regional Library, Cookeville TN. 615-526-4016
Boyd, Kathleen, *Dir,* Saint Elizabeth's Hospital, School of Nursing Library, Brighton MA. 617-782-7000, Ext 2304

Boyd, Lynn, *Doc,* Alabama Supreme Court, Supreme Court & State Law Library, Montgomery AL. 205-832-6410
Boyd, Mary A, *Cat,* Rockbridge Regional Library, Lexington VA. 703-463-4324
Boyd, Mary Lou, *Ref,* Helen Matthes Library, Effingham IL. 217-342-2464
Boyd, Molly, *Librn,* El Paso Community College (Learning Resources Center), El Paso TX. 915-532-9971, Ext 211
Boyd, Mrs Eldon, *Librn,* Frederick Public Library, Frederick OK. 405-335-3601
Boyd, Mrs M, *Librn,* Borough of Etobicoke Public Library (Humber Bay), Toronto ON. 416-248-5681
Boyd, Pat, *Acq,* Wingate College, Ethel K Smith Library, Wingate NC. 704-233-4061, Ext 155
Boyd, Rena, *Asst Librn,* Bogle & Gates Library, Seattle WA. 206-682-5151
Boyd, Ron, *Media,* Columbia Basin College, Library Media Center, Pasco WA. 509-547-0511, Ext 287, 289, 290 & 294
Boyd, Sandra, *Ref & Bibliog Instr,* Episcopal Divinity School, Sherrill Hall Library, Cambridge MA. 617-868-3450, Ext 31
Boyd, Sandra, *Bibliog Instr,* Weston School of Theology Library, Cambridge MA. 617-868-3450, Ext 31
Boyd, Sandra H, *Libr Asst,* Tennessee Eastman Co (Business Library), Kingsport TN. 615-246-2111, Ext 2071
Boyd, Stanley E, *Ref & ILL,* United States Air Force (Academic Library), Wright-Patterson AFB OH. 513-255-5894
Boyd, Susan, *Librn,* Greenville County Library (Augusta), Greenville SC. 803-277-0161
Boyd, Susie, *Librn,* Suwannee River Regional Library, Seven-County Region (Trenton (Gilchrist County)), Live Oak FL. 904-463-2210
Boyd, Trenton, *Dir,* University of Missouri-Columbia (Veterinary Medical Library), Columbia MO. 314-882-2461
Boyd, Virginia, *Asst Dir, ILL & Ref,* Brunswick Junior College, Clara Wood Gould Memorial Library, Brunswick GA. 912-264-7270
Boyd, William B, *AV,* Saint Petersburg Junior College, Saint Petersburg Campus Library, Saint Petersburg FL. 813-546-0011, Ext 353
Boyden, Patrick, *Computer Assisted Instruction,* Kent State University Libraries, Kent OH. 216-672-2962
Boydston, Jo Ann, *John Dewey Ctr,* Southern Illinois University at Carbondale, Delyte W Morris Library, Carbondale IL. 618-453-2522
Boyea, Pat, *Librn,* Monmouth County Library (Manalapan), Englishtown NJ. 201-536-6026
Boyeff, Colette L, *Circ,* Minot State College, Memorial Library, Minot ND. 701-857-3200
Boyer, Anita, *Tech Serv & Cat,* Alsip-Merrionette Park Library, Alsip IL. 312-371-5666
Boyer, Betty, *Librn,* Meadow Grove Public Library, Meadow Grove NE. 402-634-2266
Boyer, Calvin, *Dir,* University of California Library, Irvine CA. 714-833-5212
Boyer, Calvin J, *Dir,* University of Mississippi Library, University MS. 601-232-7091
Boyer, Carol, *Librn,* Boulder Community Hospital, Boulder Valley Medical Library, Boulder CO. 303-442-8190, Ext 435
Boyer, Catherine, *Libr Inst,* Orange Coast College Library, Costa Mesa CA. 714-556-5885
Boyer, Denis, *Dir,* Bibliotheque Municipale de Hull, Hull PQ. 819-777-4341
Boyer, Doris G, *Dir,* Mississippi Delta Junior College, Stanny Sanders Library, Moorhead MS. 601-243-8672
Boyer, Eleanor, *Cat,* Warren Public Library, Warren OH. 216-399-8807
Boyer, Fay E, *Librn,* Georgia Baptist Medical Center (Medical Library), Atlanta GA. 404-659-4211, Ext 2481
Boyer, Francine, *Asst Dir,* Bibliotheque Municipale De Longueuil, Longueuil PQ. 514-670-1410
Boyer, Francine, *Librn,* Bibliotheque Municipale De Longueuil (Succursale Place Desormeaux), Longueuil PQ. 514-670-1410
Boyer, Harold, *Institutions,* Burlington County Library, Mount Holly NJ. 609-267-9660
Boyer, Jack K, *Dir,* Kit Carson Memorial Foundation, Inc Historical Research Library, Taos NM. 505-757-4741
Boyer, Jean, *Librn,* Robesonia Community Library, Robesonia PA. 215-693-3474

Boyer, Laura, *Ref,* University of the Pacific, Irving Martin Library, Stockton CA. 209-946-2431
Boyer, Marc, *ILL,* Ogdensburg Public Library, Ogdensburg NY. 315-393-4325
Boyer, Margaret Jane, *Dir,* Missouri Baptist College Library, Saint Louis MO. 314-434-1115, Ext 73
Boyer, Mary, *Librn,* Library Association of Portland (Home & Institutional Services), Portland OR. 503-223-7201, Ext 27
Boyer, Norma, *Dir,* Old Tappan Free Public Library, Old Tappan NJ. 201-664-3499
Boyer, Robert E, *Assoc Librn,* Arlington Public Library, Arlington TX. 817-275-2763, 265-3311, Ext 347
Boyer-Caya, G, *Librn,* Hopital Hotel-Dieu De Montreal, Medical Library, Montreal PQ. 514-844-0161, Ext 592
Boyes, Kathy, *Manager,* Bell-Northern Research, Technical Information Center, Ottawa ON. 613-596-2469
Boyesen, Persis, *Ref,* Ogdensburg Public Library, Ogdensburg NY. 315-393-4325
Boykin, Carol, *Librn,* McGladrey, Hendrickson & Co Library, Davenport IA. 319-326-5111, Ext 267
Boykin, Jr, Joseph F, *Dir,* University of North Carolina at Charlotte, J Murrey Atkins Library, Charlotte NC. 704-597-2221
Boylan, Merle N, *Dir,* University of Washington Libraries, Seattle WA. 206-543-1760
Boylan, Nancy G, *Librn,* Federal Aviation Administration (Aeronautical Center Library), Oklahoma City OK. 405-686-4709
Boylan, Pat, *Cat,* Charles M White Memorial Public Library, Stevens Point WI. 715-346-2841
Boylan, Patricia, *YA,* Smithtown Library, Smithtown NY. 516-265-2072
Boylan, Ray, *Asst Dir,* Center for Research Libraries, Chicago IL. 312-955-4545
Boyle, Aurelia, *Librn,* Hazleton Area Public Library (Freeland), Hazleton PA. 717-636-2125
Boyle, Joan, *ILL,* Phillips University (John Rogers Graduate Seminary Library), Enid OK. 405-237-4433, Ext 227
Boyle, Joanne, *Tech Serv,* Gogebic Community College, Alex D Chisholm Learning Resource Center, Ironwood MI. 906-932-4231, Ext 211
Boyle, John M, *Librn,* New York State Supreme Court (Law Library), New York NY. 212-374-8384
Boyle, Phylis, *Ad,* Corning Public Library, Corning NY. 607-936-3713
Boyle, Sister Mary David, *Librn,* Saint Agnes Hospital, Robert C Gavin Memorial Library, Fond du Lac WI. 414-921-2300, Ext 233
Boyle, Thomas, *Dir,* Midland Lutheran College Library, Fremont NE. 402-721-5482, Ext 4
Boyles, Emily, *Per,* San Francisco Public Library, San Francisco CA. 415-558-4235
Boyles, Linda K, *Ch,* Santa Fe Regional Library, Gainesville Public Library Headquarters, Gainesville FL. 904-374-2091
Boyles, Olga M, *Librn,* Henry County Library, Clinton MO. 816-885-2612
Boylls, Virginia, *Librn,* San Diego Public Library (Rancho Bernardo), San Diego CA. 714-236-5800
Boynton, Janet H, *Tech Serv,* University of Rochester (Edward G Miner Library, School of Medicine & Dentistry), Rochester NY. 716-275-3364
Boynton, Jean, *ILL,* Lake County Library, Lakeport Library, Lakeport CA. 707-263-2291
Boynton, Jean, *Librn,* Lake County Library (Upper Lake Branch), Upper Lake CA. 707-275-2049
Boynton, John, *Media,* Maine State Library, Augusta ME. 207-289-3561
Boynton, Yvonne, *Librn,* Galesburg Mental Health Center, Himwich Library of Neurosciences, Galesburg IL. 309-344-2141
Boysen, Jessica, *Librn,* Community-General Hospital of Greater Syracuse, Medical Library, Syracuse NY. 315-492-5500
Boytinck, Paul W, *Cat,* Bucknell University, Ellen Clarke Bertrand Library, Lewisburg PA. 717-524-3056
Bozak, Paul, *Librn,* Moose Jaw Law Society Library, Moose Jaw SK. 306-693-6105
Bozarth, Rebecca, *Librn,* Mid-Continent Public Library (Oak Grove Branch), Oak Grove MO. 816-625-3213

Bozone, Billie, *Dir,* Smith College Library, Northampton MA. 413-584-2700, Ext 501
Bozorgizard, Joy, *Pub Servs,* Paul Sawyier Public Library, Frankfort KY. 502-223-1658
Bozyk, Patricia K, *Dir,* Red River Community College, Learning Resources Center, Winnipeg MB. 204-632-2232
Braafladt, Mary E, *Per,* College of Saint Scholastica Library, Duluth MN. 218-723-6143
Braafladt, Mary Ellen, *Instr,* College of Saint Scholastica, Library Science Program, MN. 218-723-6143
Braam, Dora, *In Charge,* Albert-Westmorland-Kent Regional Library (Hillsborough Public), Hillsborough NB. 506-389-2631
Brabec, Georgine, *Tech Serv & Cat,* North Park College & Theological Seminary (Wallgren Library), Chicago IL. 312-583-2700
Brabham, J, *Libm,* Gates Rubber Co, Gates Learjet Corp Library, Wichita KS. 316-946-2000
Brace, Betty, *Circ,* University of Massachusetts at Amherst Library, Amherst MA. 413-545-0284
Bracewell, R G, *Libm,* University of Toronto Libraries (Emmanuel College Library), Toronto ON. 416-978-3864
Bracey, Ann, *Libm,* Fort Worth Public Library (Northeast Branch), Fort Worth TX. 817-838-6931
Bracey, Linde, *Ser,* Vanderbilt University Medical Center Library, Nashville TN. 615-322-2292
Brack, Lola, *Libm,* Otis Community Library, Otis KS. 913-387-2403
Bracken, Elva, *Ch,* Washington County Library, Saint George UT. 801-673-2562
Bracken, Leath Parker, *Acq,* Mary Riley Styles Public Library, Falls Church VA. 703-241-5030
Bracker, James K, *Ref, On-Line Servs & Bibliog Instr,* Knox College, Henry W Seymour Library, Galesburg IL. 309-343-0112, Ext 246
Brackett, Gwendolyn, *Asst Libm,* Loyal Public Library, Loyal WI. 715-255-8189
Brackett, Doris, *Ch,* Greenfield Public Library, Greenfield MA. 413-772-0989, 772-6305
Brackett, N Scott, *Libm,* Lear Siegler Inc Engineering Library, Grand Rapids MI. 616-241-7467
Brackett, Sarah, *Libm,* Washington State Library (Yakima Valley School Staff Library), Selah WA. 509-697-7272
Brackman, Selma, *In Charge,* Freelance Photographer's Guild Library, New York NY. 212-777-4210
Brackney, Virginia, *Br Coordr & Bkmobile Coordr,* Lima Public Library, Lima OH. 419-228-5113
Brackney, William H, *Dir,* American Baptist Historical Society, Samuel Colgate Baptist Memorial Library, Rochester NY. 716-473-1740
Brackstone, Deborah, *ILL,* Memphis State University Libraries, Memphis TN. 901-454-2201
Bracy, Pauletta, *Instr,* University of Iowa, School of Library Science, IA. 319-353-3644
Bradberry, Richard, *Dir,* Langston University, G Lamar Harrison Library, Langston OK. 405-466-2231, Ext 231
Bradbury, Daniel J, *Dir,* Janesville Public Library, Janesville WI. 608-752-8934, Ext B
Bradbury, Frances J, *Dir,* Northbrook Public Library, Northbrook IL. 312-272-6224
Braddock, Theda, *Ch,* Haddonfield Public Library, Haddonfield NJ. 609-429-1304
Braddock, Virginia, *Municipal Govt Ref Serv,* Boulder Public Library, Boulder CO. 303-441-3100
Braddy, John E, *Mgr,* Owens-Illinois, Inc (Technical Information Services), Toledo OH. 419-247-9323
Braden, Nancy, *Ch,* Weld County Library, Greeley CO. 303-330-7691
Braden, Robert C, *Project Mgr,* Belfour Stulen, Inc, Mechanical Properties Data Center, Traverse City MI. 616-947-4500
Bradford, David, *Instr,* United States Department of Agriculture Graduate School, Certificate Program for Library Technicians, DC. 202-447-5885
Bradford, Edwina, *Ad,* Liberal Memorial Library, Liberal KS. 316-624-0148
Bradford, Jane W, *Dir,* Westerville Public Library, Westerville OH. 614-882-7277
Bradford, Jeannette, *Dir,* Carmel Public Library, Carmel IN. 317-844-3361
Bradford, Mary, *ILL,* West Virginia Institute of Technology, Vining Library, Montgomery WV. 304-442-3141
Bradford, Rosalie, *Libr Suprv,* Woodland Public Library, Woodland CA. 916-662-6616
Bradley, A, *Bibliog Instr,* Mount Royal College Library, Calgary AB. 403-246-6111
Bradley, Albert P, *Ch,* NASA, Johnson Space Center, Technical Library Branch, Houston TX. 713-483-6461
Bradley, Alcyone B, *Libm,* National Park Service, Everglades National Park Reference Library, Homestead FL. 305-245-5266, Ext 23
Bradley, Annette, *Ser,* Laurentian University Library, Bibliotheque de l'Universite Laurentienne, Sudbury ON. 705-675-1151, Ext 251 & 252
Bradley, Audrey, *Libm,* Knoxville-Knox County Public Library (Carter), Knoxville TN. 615-933-5438
Bradley, Barbara, *Media,* Monroe County Library System, Monroe MI. 313-241-5277
Bradley, Barbara, *Media,* Southeast Michigan Regional Film Library, Monroe MI. 313-241-5277
Bradley, Bess, *Libm,* Val Verde County Library, Del Rio TX. 512-774-3611
Bradley, Catherine, *Libm,* Illinois Supreme Court Library, Springfield IL. 217-525-2424
Bradley, Diane, *Per & Doc,* Hardin-Simmons University, Richardson Library, Abilene TX. 915-677-7281, Ext 236
Bradley, Diane, *Libm,* Rayside-Balfour Public Library, Chelmsford ON. 705-855-9333
Bradley, Diane, *ILL,* South Georgia Regional Library, Valdosta-Lowndes County Public Library, Valdosta GA. 912-247-3405
Bradley, Emily H, *Asst Dir & Ref,* Carnegie Library, Rome GA. 404-291-7568
Bradley, Florene Jordan, *Libm,* Columbia-Lafayette-Ouachita-Calhoun Regional Library, Asa C Garrett Memorial Library, Magnolia AR. 501-234-1991
Bradley, Gail, *Br Coordr,* Sullivan County Public Library, Blountville TN. 615-323-5301
Bradley, Helen, *Cat,* La Porte County Library, La Porte IN. 219-362-6156
Bradley, Helen, *Cat,* La Porte Public Library, La Porte IN. 219-362-6156
Bradley, Hortense C, *Libm,* Pine Forest Regional Library (McHenry Public), McHenry MS. 601-788-6539
Bradley, James, *Acq,* Community College of Philadelphia, Division of Educational Resources, Philadelphia PA. 215-972-7250
Bradley, Jana, *Dir,* William N Wishard Memorial Hospital, Library & Media Services, Indianapolis IN. 317-630-7028
Bradley, John, *Dir,* Bucks County Community College Library, Newtown PA. 215-968-5861, Ext 306, 307
Bradley, John, *Dir,* Film Library Intercollege Cooperative of Pennsylvania, (FLIC), PA. 215-968-5861
Bradley, Judith, *ILL, Ref & Bibliog Instr,* Mercyhurst College Learning Resource Center, Erie PA. 814-864-0681, Ext 228, 234
Bradley, Larry C, *Dir,* Nevada Public Library, Nevada MO. 417-667-2831
Bradley, Lynne E, *Video Serv,* Public Library of the District of Columbia, Martin Luther King Memorial Library, Washington DC. 202-727-1101
Bradley, Murray L, *Reader Serv,* United States Naval War College Library, Newport RI. 401-841-2641
Bradley, Nancy, *Libm,* Atlanta Public Library (East Atlanta), Atlanta GA. 404-525-8802
Bradley, R T, *Dir,* Sarnia Public Library and Art Gallery, Sarnia ON. 519-337-3291
Bradley, Robena, *Asst Dir & Cat,* Shaw University, Learning Resources Center, Raleigh NC. 919-755-4930
Bradley, Ruth, *Ch,* Harvey Public Library, Harvey IL. 312-331-0757
Bradley, Susan, *ILL & Ref,* Musser Public Library, Muscatine IA. 319-263-3065
Bradley, Verdelle V, *Dir,* Virginia Union University, William J Clarke Library, Richmond VA. 804-359-9331, Ext 256, 257
Bradner, Peg, *Dir,* Mansfield Public Library, Mansfield MA. 617-339-8803
Brado, Marilyn, *Ch,* South Portland Public Library, South Portland ME. 207-799-2204
Bradow, Margaret, *Br Coordr,* Cedar Rapids Public Library, Cedar Rapids IA. 319-398-5123
Bradow, Margaret, *Libm,* Cedar Rapids Public Library (Kenwood), Cedar Rapids IA. 319-398-5123
Bradrick, Dolores, *Libm,* Butler County Law Library, Butler PA. 412-285-4731
Bradshaw, Emily, *Dir Info Serv,* Family Service Association of America Library, New York NY. 212-674-6100, Ext 49, 50
Bradshaw, Lillian M, *Dir,* Dallas Public Library, Dallas TX. 214-748-9071
Bradshaw, Lillian M, *Dir,* Northeast Texas Library System, Dallas TX. 214-651-9266
Bradshaw, Lucy Hyman, *Libm,* Winston-Salem State University, C G O'Kelly Library, Winston-Salem NC. 919-761-2128
Bradshaw, Marcia, *Dir,* Mitchell Community College Library, Statesville NC. 704-873-2201, Ext 220
Bradshaw, Margaret, *Libm,* Birchard Public Library of Sandusky County (Gibsonburg Branch), Gibsonburg OH. 419-332-1121
Bradsher, Elizabeth D, *Libm,* Saint Louis County Department of Community Health & Medical Care, Medical Staff Library, Clayton MO. 314-727-6300, Ext 386
Bradstreet, Lana, *Libm,* Wheeler Public Library, Wheeler TX. 806-826-5977
Bradt, Donna M Sontas, *Head Libr,* Economics Laboratory Inc, Information Center, Saint Paul MN. 612-451-5651
Bradt, Kathleen Ruth, *Pub Servs,* Baker University Library, Baldwin City KS. 913-594-6451, Ext 414
Brady, Ann, *Libm,* Indianapolis-Marion County Public Library (Spades Park), Indianapolis IN. 317-635-5662
Brady, Ann, *In Charge,* Newspaper Advertising Bureau, Inc, Information Center, New York NY. 212-557-1822, 557-1823
Brady, Ben, *Assoc State Libm for Libr Develop,* Louisiana State Library, Baton Rouge LA. 504-342-4922
Brady, Blanch, *Libm,* Hot Springs Public Library, Hot Springs MT. 406-741-3491
Brady, Brenda, *Bkmobile Coordr,* Prince Edward Island Provincial Library, Charlottetown PE. 902-892-3504, Ext 54
Brady, Dorothy L, *Libm,* Geological Survey of Alabama Library, University AL. 205-348-5095
Brady, Dorothy L, *Libm,* Georgia Power Co Library, Atlanta GA. 522-6060; Ext 2651
Brady, Edith, *Libm,* Richmond State Hospital Library, Richmond IN. 317-966-0511, Ext 208
Brady, Emma Jean, *Libm,* Walter Cecil Rawls Regional Library System (Benjamin P Chapman Memorial Library), Smithfield VA. 804-357-2264
Brady, James, *On-Line Servs,* University of Southern Maine, Gorham ME. 207-780-5340, 780-4273
Brady, James J, *In Charge,* General Electric Co, AEG Technical Information Center, Cincinnati OH. 513-243-4333
Brady, Jill, *District Libm,* Scarborough Public Library, Scarborough ON. 416-291-1991
Brady, Joan, *Libm,* University of Colorado Health Sciences Center (Rene A Spitz Psychiatric Library), Denver CO. 303-394-7039
Brady, Lila, *Dir,* Northern Illinois Library System, Rockford IL. 815-229-0330
Brady, Lois, *Ad,* Martinsburg-Berkeley County Public Library, Martinsburg Service Center, Martinsburg WV. 304-267-8933
Brady, M, *Tech Serv,* Northern Montana College Library, Havre MT. 406-265-7821, Ext 3306, 3307
Brady, M M, *Assoc Libm,* University of Saskatchewan Library, Saskatoon SK. 306-343-4216
Brady, Margaret, *ILL,* Salt Lake City Public Library, Salt Lake City UT. 801-363-5733
Brady, Mary, *Tel Ref Serv Libm,* New York Public Library (General Reference Service), New York NY. 790-6575; 790-6161 (Tel Ref); 790-6234 (Union Cat)
Brady, Mary Ann, *Libm,* Union Carbide Corp, Linde Division Library, Indianapolis IN. 317-241-2311, Ext 2520

Brady, Mary L, *Learning Resources & Curric,* California Polytechnic State University Library, San Luis Obispo CA. 805-546-2345

Brady, Mary T, *Interbranch Loan,* New York Public Library (The Branch Libraries), New York NY. 212-790-6262

Brady, Peggy M, *Ref,* North Olympic Library System, Port Angeles WA. 206-457-4464

Brady, Richard, *Media,* Moraine Valley Community College, Learning Resources Center, Palos Hills IL. 312-974-4300, Ext 222

Brady, Sara, *Ref,* Trail Blazer Library System, Monroe LA. 318-323-8494

Brady, Shirley M, *Ch & YA,* Saint Paul Public Library, Saint Paul MN. 612-292-6311

Brady, Sister Mary William, *Rare Bks,* College of Saint Catherine, Saint Catherine Library, Saint Paul MN. 612-690-6650

Brady, Verla, *Librn,* Brooke County Public Library (Hooverson Heights), Follansbee WV. 304-527-0860

Brady, Virginia, *Librn,* Wehran Engineering Library, Middletown NY. 914-343-0660

Braeuer, M, *Mat Sci,* State University of New York at Buffalo, University Libraries, Buffalo NY. 716-636-2965

Braford, Merle, *Librn,* Kent County Library System (Sand Lake Branch), Sand Lake MI. 616-774-3250

Brag, Terry A, *Spec Coll,* Clark University, Robert Hutchings Goddard Library, Worcester MA. 617-793-7573

Brager, Beverly, *Art & Music,* Madison Public Library, Madison WI. 608-266-6300

Bragg, Alethea, *Librn,* Memphis-Shelby County Public Library & Information Center (Arlington Branch), Arlington TN. 901-867-2561

Bragg, Martha, *Librn,* La Plata Public Library, La Plata MO. 816-332-7474

Bragg, Rosa, *Librn,* Chesterfield County Central Library (Ettrick-Matoaca Branch), Ettrick VA. 804-526-8087

Bragg, Terry A, *Actg Librn,* Clark University (Special Collections), Worcester MA. 617-793-7572

Brain, Virginia, *Librn,* Mid-Continent Public Library (Lee's Summit Branch), Lee's Summit MO. 816-524-0567

Brainard, Elsie, *Adjunct Instr,* Kean College of New Jersey, Library-Media Program, NJ. 201-527-2626, 527-2071

Brainin, Grace, *Commun Servs,* Royal Oak Public Library, Royal Oak MI. 313-541-1470

Brajsa, Bogdana, *Librn,* University of Western Ontario (Engineering), London ON. 519-679-6119

Brake, Beth, *Monographs,* University of Texas at Arlington Library, Arlington TX. 817-273-3391

Brakovec, J, *Ser,* Montana College of Mineral Science and Technology Library, Butte MT. 406-792-8321, Ext 371

Braley, Barbara M, *Librn,* Richards Memorial Library, Paxton MA. 617-754-0793

Bralow, Janet, *Librn,* Island Park Public Library, Island Park NY. 516-432-0122

Brambilla, Andrew P, *Dir,* Immaculate Conception College Library, Troy NY. 518-271-6000

Bramble, Laura, *Soc Sci,* Indianapolis-Marion County Public Library, Indianapolis IN. 317-635-5662

Bramlett, Loretta, *AV,* Sunland Center at Tallahassee Library, Tallahassee FL. 904-877-4161, Ext 231

Bramlett, Susan, *Bkmobile Coordr,* Oconee County Library, Walhalla SC. 803-638-5837

Bramley, Mary A, *Cat,* Woburn Public Library, Woburn MA. 617-933-0148

Brammer, Linda, *Asst Dir,* Cecil County Public Library, Elkton MD. 301-398-0914

Brammer, Mrs William, *Librn,* Narrows Public Library, Narrows VA. 703-726-2884

Bramson, Cynthia, *Dir,* Temple Resource Center Library, Sylvania OH. 419-885-3341

Bramwell, Jane, *Dir,* Reedsburg Public Library, Reedsburg WI. 608-524-3316

Branch, Brenda, *Program Develop,* Austin Public Library, Austin TX. 512-472-5433

Branch, Frederick W, *Media,* Bloomfield Public Library, Northwest Essex Area Library, Bloomfield NJ. 201-429-9292

Branch, Jean, *Head, Acq Dept,* Houston Public Library, Houston TX. 713-224-5441

Branch, Mary, *Librn,* Greenwood-Leflore Public Library System (Morgan City Branch), Morgan City MS. 601-254-7790

Branch, Olive H, *Coll Develop,* University of Tennessee, Knoxville, James D Hoskins Library, Knoxville TN. 615-974-0111

Branch, Sonya, *Ch,* Lafayette Parish Public Library, Lafayette LA. 318-233-0587

Branchcomb, Harriette, *Per,* Norfolk State University, Lyman Beecher Brooks Library, Norfolk VA. 804-623-8873

Brand, Alice, *Librn,* Menninger Foundation, Professional Library, Topeka KS. 913-234-9566, Ext 3601

Brand, Barbara, *Ref,* State University of New York, Frank Melville Jr Memorial Library, Stony Brook NY. 516-246-5650

Brand, Charles, *Dir,* University of Maryland at College Park (M Lucia James Curriculum Laboratory), College Park MD. 301-454-5466

Brand, Diana, *Librn,* Los Angeles Public Library System (Memorial), Los Angeles CA. 213-934-0855

Brand, Dorothy, *Librn,* Joplin Regional Center Materials Center, Joplin MO. 417-624-7004

Brand, Joanne, *Asst Librn,* Barryton Public Library, Barryton MI. 517-382-5288

Brand, Mary, *Librn,* Washington Parish Library System, Franklinton LA. 504-839-5336

Brand, Mina, *ILL,* Harvard University Library (Museum of Comparative Zoology Library), Cambridge MA. 617-495-2475

Brand, Rosalie, *Cat,* University of Southern Mississippi, Cook Memorial Library, Hattiesburg MS. 601-266-7301

Brandau, Christie, *Asst Librn,* Sage Public Library, Osage IA. 515-732-3323

Brandeal, Bea, *Circ,* North Haledon Free Public Library, North Haledon NJ. 201-427-6213

Brandeau, John, *AV,* Mercy College Libraries, Dobbs Ferry NY. 914-693-4500, Ext 260

Brandeis, R, *Librn,* University of Toronto Libraries (Victoria College), Toronto ON. 416-978-3821

Brandel, Jo, *Ref,* Detroit Bible College, Farmington Hills MI. 313-553-7200

Branden, Shirley, *Ref & On-Line Servs,* University of Tennessee Center for the Health Sciences Library, Memphis TN. 901-528-5638

Brandenburger, Laddie, *Librn,* Silver Creek Public Library, Silver Creek NE. 308-773-2594

Brandenbury, Ronnie E, *Bkmobile Coordr,* Lee County Public Library, Beattyville KY. 606-464-8014

Brandes, Linda, *Acq,* Malone College, Everett L Cattell Library, Canton OH. 216-454-3011, Ext 311

Brandewie, Dennis, *ILL & Ref,* Evansville Public Library & Vanderburgh County Public Library, Evansville IN. 812-425-2621

Brandhorst, W T, *Dir,* ERIC Processing & Reference Facility, MD. 301-656-9723

Brandi, Michael, *Computerized Searching,* College of Medicine & Dentistry of New Jersey, George F Smith Library of the Health Sciences, Newark NJ. 201-456-4580

Brandis, Rushton, *Consult to State Agencies,* Washington State Library, Olympia WA. 206-753-5592

Brandl, Leslie, *Librn,* Moore Public Library, Lexington MI. 313-359-8267

Brandolino, Richard, *Dean,* Joliet Junior College, Learning Resource Center, Joliet IL. 815-729-9020, Ext 282

Brandon, Dorothy, *Ch & AV,* Mohawk Valley Library Association, Schenectady NY. 518-355-2010

Brandon, Dorothy, *Librn,* Philbrick-James Library, Deerfield NH. 603-463-8329

Brandon, Freda, *Librn,* Antlers Public Library, Antlers OK. 405-298-3756

Brandon, Louise, *Ch,* Huntsville-Madison County Public Library, Huntsville AL. 205-536-0021

Brandreth, Sister Elizabeth Anne, *Librn,* Mercy Hospital, Medical Library, Scranton PA. 717-344-8571

Brandriff, Dorothy, *Librn,* Modale Public Library, Modale IA. 712-645-2267

Brandt, Evelyn K, *Librn,* Phillips County Public Library, Malta MT. 406-654-2407

Brandt, Faye, *Dir,* Peru State College Library, Peru NE. 402-872-3815, Ext 218

Brandt, Kandy, *Media,* Seattle Public Library, Seattle WA. 206-625-2665

Brandt, Patricia, *Lang-Lit,* Oregon State University, William Jasper Kerr Library, Corvallis OR. 503-754-3411

Brandwein, Larry, *Dep Dir,* Brooklyn Public Library, Brooklyn NY. 212-780-7712

Branin, Joseph, *Humanities,* University of Georgia Libraries, Athens GA. 404-542-2716

Brann, Andrew, *Acq,* University of Kansas Libraries (School of Law), Lawrence KS. 913-864-3025

Brannan, Nancy C, *Librn,* Talmudical Academy of Baltimore Library, Baltimore MD. 301-484-6600

Brannen, Catherine, *Librn,* Watertown Free Public Library (West Branch/Browne School), Watertown MA. 617-926-7716

Brannin, Thomas, *Librn,* Brooklyn Public Library (Flatlands), Brooklyn NY. 212-252-6115

Brannon, Charles E, *Dir,* Tumbling Waters Museum of Flags, National Center for the Study of Contemporary American Culture Library, Montgomery AL. 205-262-5335

Brannon, Luci, *Librn,* Ozark-Mahoning Co, Research Library, Tulsa OK. 918-585-2661

Brannon, Shannon, *Books-by-Mail,* Birmingham Public & Jefferson County Free Library, Birmingham AL. 205-254-2551

Branscombe, Thelma, *Librn,* Lincoln Public Library, Lincoln NH. 603-745-8159

Bransford, Eleanor, *Cat,* Greensboro Public Library, Greensboro NC. 373-2474; 373-2471

Branson, Margaret, *Interlibrary Coop,* Wisconsin Department of Public Instruction (Public & Cooperative Library Service), Madison WI. 608-266-7270

Brant, Leah, *Librn,* First Church of the Brethren Library, York PA. 717-755-0307

Brant, Lynne, *ILL & Circ,* Lutheran Theological Seminary, Krauth Memorial Library, Philadelphia PA. 215-248-4616

Brant, Marjorie, *Librn,* Columbia Gas Systems (Service Corp Research Libr), Columbus OH. 614-486-3681

Brantigan, Patsy, *Cat,* Xavier University of Louisiana Library, New Orleans LA. 504-486-7411, Ext 317

Brantley, Carol A, *Pub Servs,* High Point College, Wrenn Memorial Library, High Point NC. 919-885-5101

Brantley, Peggy, *Librn,* Wake County Department of the Public Library (Wendell Public), Wendell NC. 919-365-7646

Branton, Charles N, *Dir,* Richland Parish Library, Rayville LA. 318-728-4806

Branton, Elsie, *Cat,* Oscar Rose Junior College, Learning Resources Center, Midwest City OK. 405-733-7323, 733-7322

Brantz, Malcolm, *Media,* University of Connecticut Health Center, Lyman Maynard Stowe Library, Farmington CT. 203-674-2739

Brasche, Ann, *Librn,* United States Navy (Wilkins Biomedical Library), San Diego CA. 714-225-4474

Brasel, Nancy, *Librn,* Northeast Regional Library (Marietta Library), Marietta MS. 601-728-9320

Brasher, Rose Anne, *Dir,* Temple Junior College, Hubert M Dawson Library, Temple TX. 817-773-9961, Ext 42

Brasile, Caryl A, *Librn,* Matson Public Library, Princeton IL. 815-875-1331

Brasilton, Annette, *Librn,* Piedmont Regional Library (West Jackson Public), Braselton GA. 404-867-2762

Brassard, Georgette, *Librn,* Bibliotheque Municipale, La Tuque PQ. 819-523-3100

Brassard, Helen E, *Librn,* Foxboro Co, Research Center Library, Foxboro MA. 617-543-8750

Brassell, Daniel P, *Dir,* Carnegie-Ellsworth Public Library, Iowa Falls IA. 515-648-2872

Brassfield, Doris, *Librn,* International University Library, Kansas City MO. 816-931-6374

Brassil, Ellen, *Bibliog Instr,* University of North Carolina at Chapel Hill (Health Sciences Library), Chapel Hill NC. 919-966-2111

Brasslow, Trish, *Librn,* Brockton Public Library System (Montello), Brockton MA. 617-583-3968

Brast, Bernice, *Librn,* Austin County Library System (Robert M Knox Memorial (Hqs)), Wallis TX. 713-478-6813

Braswell, Laura, *ILL,* Columbia Bible College, Columbia Graduate School of Bible & Missions, Learning Resources Center, Columbia SC. 803-754-4100, Ext 276 & 277

Braswell, Margaret, *Librn,* Avery County Library, Newland NC. 704-733-9393
Braswell, Nell P, *Asst Prof,* Winthrop College, School Librarianship Program, SC. 803-323-2136
Braswell, Rita, *Dir,* Mansfield Library, Mansfield Center CT. 203-423-2501
Braton, Diane, *Ref,* Union City Free Public Library, Union City NJ. 201-866-7500
Brattland, Shirley, *Cat,* Moorhead State University, Livingston Lord Library, Moorhead MN. 218-236-2922
Bratton, Helen, *Librn,* Mifflin County Library (Rothrock), McVeytown PA. 717-899-6851
Bratton, Rose, *Ref,* National League of Cities, Muncipal Reference Service, Washington DC. 293-5878; Ref 293-2631; ILL 293-2356
Braude, Robert, *Dir,* Midcontinental Regional Medical Library Program, NE. 402-541-4646, 541-4006
Braude, Robert M, *Dir,* University of Nebraska Medical Center, Library of Medicine, Omaha NE. 402-541-4006
Brault, Jean-Remi, *Dir,* Bibliotheque Nationale Du Quebec, Montreal PQ. 514-873-4553
Brault, Laura K, *Tech Serv,* Coe College, Stewart Memorial Library, Cedar Rapids IA. 319-399-8585, 399-8586
Braun, Alice, *Librn,* Greenwood Public Library, Greenwood WI. 715-267-7103
Braun, Alison M, *Dir,* American College of Emergency Physicians, Emergency Medical Serv Info Center Library, Dallas TX. 214-659-0911
Braun, Bill, *Librn,* Delta City Library, Delta UT. 801-864-2759
Braun, Carl F, *Soc Sci,* Syracuse University Libraries, Ernest S Bird Library, Syracuse NY. 315-423-2575
Braun, Constance, *Librn,* Geneva College (Brooks Educational Curriculum Center), Beaver Falls PA. 412-846-5100, Ext 297
Braun, Henry, *Librn,* Congregation Beth Emeth, Judaica Library, Albany NY. 518-436-9761
Braun, Kathleen C, *Librn,* Stewartville Public Library, Stewartville MN. 507-533-4902
Braun, Marilyn, *Info Serv,* Bartholomew County Library, Cleo Rogers Memorial Library, Columbus IN. 812-379-1255
Braun, Sister Joan, *Instr,* College of Saint Scholastica, Library Science Program, MN. 218-723-6143
Braunagel, Judith, *Asst Prof,* State University of New York at Buffalo, School of Information & Library Studies, NY. 716-636-2412
Braunstein, Binnie Syril, *Coll Develop,* University of Maryland Baltimore County Library, Baltimore MD. 301-455-2457
Brautigam, David K, *Acq,* Westminster College, McGill Library, New Wilmington PA. 412-946-8761, Ext 342
Bravard, Robert S, *Dir,* Lock Haven State College, George B Stevenson Library, Lock Haven PA. 717-893-2309
Braver, Norma, *Ref,* University of Louisville Library (Kornhauser Health Sciences), Louisville KY. 502-588-5771
Braverman, Miriam, *Asst Prof,* Columbia University in the City of New York, School of Library Service, NY. 212-280-2292
Bravo, Joanne J, *In Charge,* Becton, Dickinson Co, Endevco Library, San Juan Capistrano CA. 714-493-8181, Ext 301
Bravy, Gary, *Media,* State University of New York, College of Arts & Science at Oswego, Penfield Library, Oswego NY. 315-341-4232
Brawner, Lee B, *Dir,* Metropolitan Library System, Oklahoma City OK. 405-235-0571
Braxton, Ann B, *Librn & On-Line Servs,* Ciba-Geigy Corp Library, Greensboro NC. 919-292-7100, Ext 2860
Braxton, Anne, *Art & Architecture,* Ohio University, Vernon R Alden Library, Athens OH. 614-594-5228
Braxton, Anne, *Librn,* Ohio University (Art), Athens OH. 614-594-5065
Bray, Mary, *Librn,* Lakeland Hospital, Medical Library, Elkhorn WI. 414-723-2960, Ext 2490
Bray, Mrs O, *Librn,* Sperry Rand Corp, Sperry Marine Systems Engineering Library, Charlottesville VA. 804-973-3371
Bray, Ruth, *Ch,* Albert-Westmorland-Kent Regional Library, Moncton NB. 506-389-2631
Bray, Sally, *Bkmobile Coordr,* Durham County Library, Durham NC. 919-683-2626
Bray, Velma, *Librn,* Middle Georgia Regional Library (Oglethorpe Public), Oglethorpe GA. 912-472-6485
Brayfield, Mary Jane, *Librn,* Bendix Corp, Energy Controls Divisions Library, South Bend IN. 219-237-2761
Braymer, Lois, *Librn,* Frank Phillips College, James W Dillard Library, Borger TX. 806-274-5311
Brayson, Sandra, *Chief Librn,* Veterans Administration, Medical Center Library, Portland OR. 503-222-9221, Ext 382
Brayton, Gretchen H, *Librn,* Sumner Public Library, Sumner IA. 515-224-3324
Brazelle, Eugenia H, *Librn,* Weldon Memorial Library, Weldon NC. 919-536-3837
Brazier, James, *Educ,* Jacksonville State University Library, Jacksonville AL. 205-435-9820, Ext 213, 214
Brazile, Orella, *Librn,* Southern University, Shreveport-Bossier City Campus Library, Shreveport LA. 318-424-6552, Ext 238
Brazin, Lillian R, *Dir,* Albert Einstein Medical Center (Daroff Division Medical Library), Philadelphia PA. 215-465-1100, Ext 386
Brazynetz, Helen, *Acq,* Case Western Reserve University Libraries (School of Law Library), Cleveland OH. 216-368-2792
Breaden, Richard P, *Dir,* Saint Joseph's Seminary, Corrigan Memorial Library, Yonkers NY. 914-969-0794
Brearley, N, *Reader Serv,* Carleton University, Murdoch Maxwell MacOdrum Library, Ottawa ON. 613-231-4357
Breault, Claude, *Librn,* Bibliotheque De La Ville De Montreal (Langelier), Montreal PQ. 255-2770 (Adult); 255-1811 (Children)
Breaux, Cheryl, *Librn,* Lafayette Charity Hospital, Health Science Library, Lafayette LA. 318-233-2525
Brech, Maria, *Librn,* Mercy College, Yorktown Heights Branch Campus, Yorktown Heights NY. 914-962-9486
Brecha, Elaine, *Dir,* Shoreham-Wading River Public Library, Shoreham NY. 516-929-4488
Brecher, Hazel C, *In Charge,* Joseph Schlitz Brewing Co, Consumer Research Library, Milwaukee WI. 414-224-5000
Brechka, Frank T, *Hist,* University of California, Berkeley (University Library), Berkeley CA. 415-642-3773
Brechner, Margaret, *Librn,* World Education Inc, Library, New York NY. 212-838-5255
Brecht, Albert, *Dir,* University of Southern California (Asa V Call Law Library), Los Angeles CA. 213-743-6487
Breckunitch, Jean, *Librn,* Buffalo Center Public Library, Buffalo Center IA. 515-562-2546
Bredehoft, Linda, *Librn,* Saint John's College Library, Winfield KS. 316-221-4000, Ext 68
Bredemeier, Virginia, *In Charge,* E I Du Pont De Nemours & Co, Inc (Stine Laboratory), Newark DE. 302-366-5353, 336-5354
Breeden, Lois, *Librn,* Jefferson-Madison Regional Library (Greene County), Stanardsville VA. 804-985-2370
Breeding, Noreen A, *Ref,* Idaho Falls Public Library, Idaho Falls ID. 208-529-1450
Breedlove, Elizabeth, *Tech Serv,* New Jersey State Library, Trenton NJ. 609-292-6200
Breedlove, James, *Latin Am,* Stanford University Libraries, Stanford CA. 415-497-2016
Breedlove, Stephen, *Govt Ref Suprv,* New Jersey State Library, Trenton NJ. 609-292-6200
Breedlove, William, *Dir,* Louis Bay Library, Hawthorne NJ. 201-427-5745
Breen, Jon, *Ref,* Rio Hondo Community College Library, Whittier CA. 213-692-0921, Ext 371
Breen, Richard, *Dir,* Willamette University Library (College of Law Library), Salem OR. 503-370-6387
Breese, John K, *Librn,* J J Keller & Associates, Inc, Library Research Center, Neenah WI. 414-722-2848, Ext 308
Bregaint, B J, *Dir,* Cambrian College of Applied Arts & Technology Library, Sudbury ON. 705-566-8101, Ext 320
Bregaint, C, *Chief Librn,* Secretary of State Department Library, Ottawa ON. 613-997-0028
Bregent, Ann, *Doc,* Washington State Library, Olympia WA. 206-753-5592
Bregman, Steven, *AV & Tech Serv,* Bryant Library, Roslyn NY. 516-621-2240
Bregoli, Marilyn, *Asst Dir,* Auburn Public Library, Auburn MA. 617-832-2081
Bregzis, Ritvars, *Assoc Librn,* University of Toronto Libraries (University Library), Toronto ON. 416-978-2294
Brehm, Jocelyn, *Head Librn & Dir,* Colby Public Library, Colby WI. 715-223-2000
Brehman, Maribelle, *Cat,* Mansfield-Richland County Public Library, Mansfield OH. 419-524-1041
Breidt, Cheryll, *Librn,* Pinehurst-Kingston Free Library District, Pinehurst ID. 208-682-3483
Breiholz, Grace, *Librn,* Pomeroy Public Library, Pomeroy IA. 712-468-2311
Breiner, Arlene K, *Tech Serv,* Albright College Library, Reading PA. 215-921-2381, Ext 224
Breinich, John A, *Dir,* Hawaii Medical Library, Inc, Honolulu HI. 808-536-9302
Breisach, Herma, *Ser,* Western Michigan University, Dwight B Waldo Library, Kalamazoo MI. 616-383-4961
Breit, Alice, *Librn,* Ashland City Library, Ashland KS. 316-635-2509
Breit, Marquita, *Cat & Circ,* Bellarmine College Library, Louisville KY. 502-452-8137
Breit, Pauline, *Ch,* Gates Public Library, Gates Robert Abbott Memorial Library, Rochester NY. 716-247-6446
Breitenback, Dorie, *Librn,* Pamunkey Regional Library (Goochland Branch), Goochland VA. 804-556-4774
Breitenfeld, Marilyn, *Asst Dir, ILL & Ref,* Upper Moreland Free Public Library, Willow Grove PA. 215-659-3638
Breitenfeldt, Jean, *Librn,* Spokane County Library (Cheney Branch), Cheney WA. 509-235-4164
Breitenfeldt, Miriam, *Librn,* Wibaux Public Library, Wibaux MT. 406-795-2452
Breitenstein, Bradley, *Dir,* Massapequa Public Library, Massapequa NY. 516-798-4607
Breitenstein, Paul R, *In Charge,* Harry C Trexler Masonic Library, Allentown PA. 215-434-2831
Breithaupt, Betty, *Librn,* Kaskaskia College Library, Centralia IL. 618-532-1981
Breivik, Patricia S, *Dir,* Auraria Libraries, Denver CO. 303-629-2805
Breland, Joyce, *Librn,* Pine Forest Regional Library (Beaumont Public), Beaumont MS. 601-788-6539
Breland, Marguerite, *Dir,* Noxubee County Library System, Macon MS. 601-726-5461
Breland, Zoe Lee, *Librn,* Pine Forest Regional Library (Leakesville Public), Leakesville MS. 601-788-6539
Brem, Verna, *Circ,* Mount Lebanon Public Library, Pittsburgh PA. 412-531-1912
Bremer, Alice, *Dir,* Brandon Public Library, Brandon WI. 414-356-5415
Bremer, Glenda, *Dir,* Rock County Community Library, Luverne MN. 507-283-8569
Bremer, Julius, *Librn,* Cleveland Public Library (East 79th Street), Cleveland OH. 216-881-7266
Bremer, Marian, *Librn,* Newton Free Library (Nonantum), Newton MA. 617-527-7700, Ext 24
Bremser, Estelle, *Ch & Ref,* Wharton County Library, Wharton TX. 713-532-4822
Brendel, Shirley, *Acq & Ser,* University of Arkansas Libraries, Fayetteville AR. 501-575-4101
Brender, Mary, *Asst Librn & Acq,* Dallas County Public Library, Dallas TX. 214-749-8566, 749-8886
Brendza, Robin, *Librn,* American Instrument Co Library, Silver Spring MD. 301-589-1727
Breneau, Donald, *Tech Serv,* Wayne State University Libraries, Detroit MI. 313-557-4020
Brenegan, Stella, *Cat,* Dawson College Library, Montreal PQ. 514-525-2501, Ext 297
Brengle, Laurie, *Ad,* Gaston-Lincoln Regional Library, Gastonia NC. 704-866-3756
Brening, Dorothy, *Tech Serv,* Nova University Libraries (Law Center Library), Fort Lauderdale FL. 522-2300 Ext 113
Brennan, Ann, *Ch,* Round Lake Area Public Library District, Round Lake IL. 312-546-7060
Brennan, Ann M, *Info Specialist,* World Data Center-A for Glaciology Library, Boulder CO. 303-492-5171
Brennan, Charlotte, *Dir,* Yavapi College Learning Resources Center, Prescott AZ. 602-445-7300, Ext 272

Brennan, David K, *Dir,* University of Alabama (School of Law Library), University AL. 205-348-5925

Brennan, Deborah B, *Dir & Acq,* North Kingstown Free Library, North Kingstown RI. 401-294-2521

Brennan, Ellen, *Librn,* Pennsylvania Economy League, Inc, Eastern Div Library, Philadelphia PA. 215-985-0510

Brennan, Francis C, *Rare Bks,* Xavier University, McDonald Memorial Library, Cincinnati OH. 513-745-3881

Brennan, Helen A, *Librn,* Boston Public Library (Roslindale Branch), Roslindale MA. 617-323-2343

Brennan, Joan, *Ad,* Worthington Public Library, Worthington OH. 614-885-3185

Brennan, Merrie, *Asst Dir, ILL & Br Coordr,* Manistee County Library, Manistee MI. 616-723-2519

Brennan, Mrs Exir, *Bibliog Instr,* University of Alabama, Amelia Gayle Gorgas Library, University AL. 205-348-5298

Brennan, Patricia, *Circ,* Lake Forest College, Donnelley Library, Lake Forest IL. 312-234-3100, Ext 405

Brennan, Patricia, *Circ,* Saint Charles Public Library District, Saint Charles IL. 312-584-0076

Brennan, Robert G, *Ref & Pub Servs,* California State University, Chico Library, Chico CA. 916-895-6212

Brennan, Terrance, *Dir,* Clinton Community College, Learning Resources Center, Clinton IA. 319-242-6841, Ext 27

Brenneise, Harvey, *On-Line Servs,* Andrews University, James White Library, Berrien Springs MI. 616-471-3264, 471-3275

Brenneman, Betsey, *Acq,* Worcester State College, Learning Resources Center, Worcester MA. 617-752-7700, Ext 132, 135

Brennen, Patrick W, *Dir,* University of South Dakota, Christian P Lommen Health Sciences Library, Vermillion SD. 605-677-5347

Brenner, Barbara J, *Dir,* Danville Public Library, Danville IL. 217-446-7420

Brenner, Carol, *Circ,* Park College Library, Parkville MO. 816-741-2000, Ext 254

Brenner, Elizabeth, *Librn,* Los Angeles Public Library System (Loyola Village), Los Angeles CA. 213-670-5436

Brenner, Ellen, *Analysts,* Cornell University Medical College, Samuel J Wood Library, New York NY. 212-472-5300

Brenner, Helen Ann, *Ch,* Wayne Township Library, Morrisson-Reeves Library, Richmond IN. 317-966-8291

Brenner, Helen Ann, *Librn,* Wayne Township Library (Scott Boys' Club of Richmond), Richmond IN. 317-966-8291

Brenner, Lawrence, *Librn,* Boston City Hospital (Department of Health & Hospitals), Boston MA. 617-424-4198

Brenner, M Diane, *Archivist,* Anchorage Historical & Fine Arts Museum Archives, Anchorage AK. 907-264-4326, 264-4327

Brenner, Marilyn, *Librn,* Temple Beth El, Prentis Memorial Library, Birmingham MI. 313-851-1100

Brenner, Nancy, *Dir,* Randolph Public Library, Asheboro NC. 919-629-3329

Brenner, Willis, *Asst Prof,* Augustana College, Library Science Program, SD. 605-336-4921

Brenner, Willis, *Ref,* Augustana College, Mikkelsen Library & Learning Resources Center, Sioux Falls SD. 605-336-4921

Brenny, Nancy, *Bibliog Instr,* Pillsbury Company (Main Office Library), Minneapolis MN. 612-330-4047

Brent, Sherry, *Tech Serv & Ref,* Great Bend Public Library, Great Bend KS. 316-792-2409

Brent, Stanford, *In Charge,* Explorers Club, James B Ford Library, New York NY. 212-628-8383, Ext 5

Brentlinger, Jane W, *Bkmobile Coordr,* Finger Lakes Library System, Ithaca NY. 607-273-4074

Breon, Norine D, *Librn,* Hedrick Memorial Library, Hedrick IA. 515-653-4912

Bresie, Mayellen, *Dir,* Laredo Junior College, Harold R Yeary Library, Laredo TX. 512-724-7544, 722-0521

Bresie, Mayellen, *Dir,* Laredo State University, Harold R Yeary Library, Laredo TX. 512-722-8001, Ext 42

Breslauer, Kathryn, *Dir,* Priest Lake Community Library, Priest River ID. 208-443-2454

Breslauer, Lester M, *Chief Librn,* Bell Aerospace Textron, Larry D Bell Memorial Library, Buffalo NY. 716-297-1000, Ext 7167

Breslin, D, *Ref,* Ventura College, D R Henry Library, Ventura CA. 805-642-3211, Ext 201

Bresnahan, Alice, *Librn,* 3M (The 209 Technical Library), Saint Paul MN. 612-733-6973

Bress, Susan C Pynchon, *Dir,* Little Falls Public Library, Little Falls NY. 315-823-1542

Bressler, Nancy, *Curator,* Princeton University Library (Seeley G Mudd Manuscript Library), Princeton NJ. 609-452-3180

Bressman, Ann, *Soc Sci,* Phoenix Public Library, Phoenix AZ. 602-262-6451

Breting, Elizabeth, *Ch & Commun Servs,* Kansas City Public Library, Kansas City MO. 816-221-2685

Breton, Francine, *In Charge,* Ministere Des Consommateurs, Cooperatives Et Institutions, Financieres Bibliotheque, Quebec PQ. 418-643-5236

Breton, Lise, *Librn,* Northeastern Regional Library System (Val Cote Public), Mattise ON. 705-567-7043

Breton, Pierre Le, *Asst Dir,* College De L'immaculee Conception, Bibliotheque de Theologie, Montreal PQ. 514-737-1465

Bretscher, Carolyn, *Librn,* Warwick, Welsh & Miller, Inc, New York NY. 212-751-4700

Brett, Beverly, *ILL,* Kingston Public Library, Kingston ON. 613-549-8888

Brett, Marianne E, *Librn,* North York General Hospital, W Keith Welsh Library, Willowdale ON. 416-492-4748

Brettschneider, Sharon, *Ref,* Manchester Community College Library, Manchester CT. 203-646-4900, Ext 295

Bretz, Carma, *Librn,* Lucas Public Library, Lucas KS. 913-525-6305

Bretz, Linda, *Dir,* Monroe County Library System, Rochester NY. 716-428-7345

Bretz, Linda M, *Admin Agent,* Pioneer Library System, Rochester NY. 716-428-7345

Bretz, Linda M, *Dir,* Rochester Public Library, Rochester NY. 716-428-7300

Bretz, Robert, *Librn,* Visual Studies Workshop Research Center, Rochester NY. 716-442-8676

Breu, Constance R, *Librn,* Rochester Public Library, Rochester VT. 802-767-3927

Breuer, Karin, *Curator,* Robert Gore Rifkind Foundation, Art Library & Graphics Collection, Beverly Hills CA. 213-278-0970, Ext 323

Brevard, E, *Librn,* Sports World Library, Pelham NY. 914-738-5505

Brewer, Annie, *Librn,* Gale Research Co Library, Detroit MI. 313-961-2242

Brewer, Calvin, *Phys Sci & Eng,* Oklahoma State University Library, Stillwater OK. 405-624-6313

Brewer, Charles, *Dir,* Saint Francis Xavier University, Angus L Macdonald Library, Antigonish NS. 902-867-2267

Brewer, Chris, *On-Line Servs,* Kern County Museum Library, Bakersfield CA. 805-861-2132

Brewer, Elizabeth, *Program Dir,* Southeast Missouri State University, Library Science Program, MO. 314-651-2235

Brewer, Elizabeth, *ILL,* Virginia Commonwealth University (James Branch Cabell Library), Richmond VA. 804-257-1105

Brewer, Fred, *Sci Tech,* Louisiana Tech University, Prescott Memorial Library, Ruston LA. 318-257-2577

Brewer, Jeaneice, *Lang & Lit,* University of Missouri-Columbia, Elmer Ellis Library, Columbia MO. 314-882-4701

Brewer, Joan P, *Librn,* Allendale-Hampton-Jasper Regional Library (Allendale), Allendale SC. 803-584-3513

Brewer, Joan Scherer, *On-Line Servs,* Institute for Sex Research, Research Collections & Information Services, Bloomington IN. 812-337-7686

Brewer, John, *Dir,* Bureau of Governmental Research Library, New Orleans LA. 504-525-4152

Brewer, Judy E, *Ch,* Sapulpa Public Library, Sapulpa OK. 918-224-5624

Brewer, Karen, *Librn,* Northeastern Ohio Universities College of Medicine, Basic Medical Sciences Library, Rootstown OH. 216-325-2511

Brewer, Margaret A, *Librn,* United States Army (Seneca Army Depot, Post Library), Romulus NY. 607-869-3061

Brewer, Marjorie, *ILL & Cat,* Monrovia Public Library, Monrovia CA. 213-358-0174

Brewer, Mrs Waymon, *Tech Serv,* White River Regional Library, Batesville AR. 501-793-7347

Brewer, Opal, *Citizens Info Serv,* Tulsa City-County Library, Tulsa OK. 918-581-5221

Brewer, Stanley E, *Chief Librn,* Gulf Oil Corporation (Gulf Refining & Market Co, Library & Information Center), Houston TX. 713-226-1632, 226-1811

Brewer, Sue, *Librn,* Cumberland County Public Library (Spring Lake Branch), Spring Lake NC. 919-497-3650

Brewers, Patricia A, *Adjunct Lectr,* Dalhousie University, School of Library Service, NS. 902-424-3656

Brewin, Charles K, *Soc Sci,* Tulane University of Louisiana, Howard-Tilton Memorial Library, New Orleans LA. 504-865-5131

Brewster, David J, *Acq & Cat,* Genesee Community College, Alfred C O'Connell Library, Batavia NY. 716-343-0055, Ext 350

Brewster, Doris H, *Dir,* Milton College, Shaw Memorial Library, Milton WI. 608-868-2912

Brewster, Evelyn, *Librn, Pub Librs,* Colorado State Library, Colorado Department of Education, Denver CO. 303-839-3695

Brewster, John, *Spec Coll,* North Texas State University Library, Denton TX. 817-788-2411

Brewster, John, *Librn,* North Texas State University Library (Special Collections), Denton TX. 817-788-2411

Brewster, Nancy, *Cat,* Wayne Township Library, Morrisson-Reeves Library, Richmond IN. 317-966-8291

Brewster, Olive N, *Cat,* United States Air Force (Strughold Aeromedical Library), Brooks AFB TX. 512-536-3321

Brey, Francis, *Ref,* Indiana University-Purdue University at Indianapolis, University Library, Indianapolis IN. 317-264-4101

Breyfogle, J Wm, *Librn,* Johnson County Law Library, Olathe KS. 913-782-5000, Ext 512

Breyley, Dorothy B, *Head Librn,* Sterling Drug Inc, Hilton-Davis Chemical Co Div Library, Cincinnati OH. 513-841-4074

Breymaier, Jacquelyn, *Librn,* House of the Good Samaritan Hospital Library, Watertown NY. 315-785-4000

Brezger, Jean, *Asst Librn,* Kaskaskia Library System (Subregional Library for the Blind & Physically Handicapped), Smithton IL. 618-235-4220

Brezinski, Mary Ann, *Admin Asst,* Charles M White Memorial Public Library, Stevens Point WI. 715-346-2841

Brian, Barbara, *Librn,* Mercy Medical Center, Medical Library, Coon Rapids MN. 612-427-2200

Brian, Ray, *Librn,* California Academy of Sciences, J W Mailliard, Jr Library, San Francisco CA. 415-221-4214, 221-5100, Ext 275

Brian, Rita, *Dir,* La Marque Public Library, La Marque TX. 713-935-5821

Brice, Carol, *Asst Head,* Chicago Public Library (Chicago Library Service for the Blind & Physically Handicapped (Subregional)), Chicago IL. 312-738-9200

Brice, Heather W, *Dir,* Laurel Highlands Health Sciences Library Consortium, PA. 814-266-9661, Ext 305

Brice, Ora, *Curator,* Sauk County Historical Society, Museum Library, Baraboo WI. 608-356-6016

Briceland, V Diane, *ILL,* Marshall University, James E Morrow Library, Huntington WV. 304-696-3120

Briceland, Virginia, *Acq,* Washington & Jefferson College Library, Washington PA. 412-222-4400, Ext 271

Brich, George M, *Dir,* Elkhart Public Library, Elkhart IN. 219-294-5463

Brichford, Maynard J, *Archivist,* University of Illinois Library at Urbana-Champaign (University Archives), Urbana IL. 217-333-0798

Brick, Kay, *Librn,* University of Mississippi Library (Chemistry), University MS. 601-232-7301

Bricker, George H, *Archivist,* Historical Council of the United Church of Christ Archives, Lancaster PA. 717-393-0654, Ext 46

Bricker, George H, *Dir & Acq,* Lancaster Theological Seminary, Philip Schaff Library, Lancaster PA. 606-252-0361

Bricker, Norma Jean, *Ch,* Grant County Library, Ulysses KS. 316-356-1433

Brickson, Marvin E, *President,* Madison Federation of Labor AFL-CIO Library, Madison WI. 608-256-5111

Bridegam, Willis, *Librn,* Amherst College, Robert Frost Library, Amherst MA. 413-542-2212

Bridewell, Juanita, *Ref & Bibliog Instr,* Louisiana State University at Alexandria Library, Alexandria LA. 318-445-3672, Ext 46

Bridge, Mary M, *Librn,* Saint Joseph's Hospital, Educational Resources Center, Parkersburg WV. 304-424-4111

Bridges, Dorothy, *Librn,* Flin Flon Public Library, Flin Flon MB. 204-687-3397

Bridges, Douglas W, *Dir,* Malaspina College, Learning Resources Center, Nanaimo BC. 604-753-3245

Bridges, Jacqueline, *Cat,* Winthrop College, Ida Jane Dacus Library, Rock Hill SC. 803-323-2131

Bridges, John, *Media & Commun Servs,* Asheville-Buncombe Library System, Asheville NC. 704-252-8701

Bridges, Kitty, *Info Analyst,* Exxon Co USA, Medical Department, Linden NJ. 201-474-2506

Bridges, L, *Acq,* Calgary Public Library, Calgary AB. 403-268-2880

Bridges, Marguerite, *Librn,* Eufaula Public Library, Eufaula OK. 918-689-2291

Bridges, Marian, *Acq,* Central Carolina Technical Institute, Learning Resource Center, Sanford NC. 919-775-5401, Ext 244

Bridges, Roger D, *Chief Librn,* Illinois State Historical Library, Springfield IL. 217-782-4836

Bridges, Sherwood, *Dir Instruc Resources,* Central Michigan University, Charles V Park Library, Mount Pleasant MI. 517-774-3500

Bridges, Shirley S, *Librn,* Northampton Area Public Library, Northampton PA. 215-262-7537

Bridges, Tammy, *Asst Librn,* Clara Lander Library, Winnipeg MB. 204-338-2028

Bridges, Virginia, *Acq,* South Georgia Regional Library, Valdosta-Lowndes County Public Library, Valdosta GA. 912-247-3405

Bridgewater, Hope, *Ch,* Halifax City Regional Library, Halifax NS. 902-426-6980

Bridgman, William G, *Dir,* Sandhill Regional Library System, Rockingham NC. 919-997-3388

Briedis, Liga L, *ILL, Ref & Bibliog Instr,* Drake University, Cowles Library, Des Moines IA. 515-271-3993

Briell, Robert, *Librn,* Tampa-Hillsborough County Public Library System (North Tampa Public), Tampa FL. 813-932-7594

Brien, I, *Exec Secy,* Institute of Occupational & Environmental Health Library, Montreal PQ. 514-844-4955

Brier, Edward J, *Cat,* Providence Public Library, Providence RI. 401-521-7722

Briese, Noma, *Librn,* Sioux City Public Library (Leeds), Sioux City IA. 712-279-6179

Brigach, Carmen E, *Librn,* New York State Supreme Court Library, Syracuse NY. 315-425-2063

Brigg, Mrs J, *Librn,* Evergreen Regional Library (Arborg Branch), Arborg MB. 204-376-2778

Briggs, Barbara, *Cat & Ref,* Barrington College Library, Barrington RI. 401-246-1200, Ext 291

Briggs, Carol, *Librn,* Hillsdale Library, Hillsdale NY. 518-325-4101

Briggs, Catherine, *Asst Librn,* Dayton Memorial Library, Dayton WA. 509-382-4131

Briggs, Evelyn, *Librn,* Kent County Library System (Lowell Branch), Lowell MI. 616-897-9596

Briggs, Frances M, *Librn,* General Electric Co, Carboloy Systems Department, Detroit MI. 313-536-9100, Ext 320

Briggs, G H, *Dir,* Carleton University, Murdoch Maxwell MacOdrum Library, Ottawa ON. 613-231-4357

Briggs, John, *Bkmobile Coordr,* Muskegon County Library, Muskegon MI. 616-724-6248

Briggs, Mary Kay, *Librn,* United States Air Force (Mather Air Force Base Library), Mather AFB CA. 916-364-2942

Briggs, Mrs Michael, *Cat,* West Los Angeles College Library, Culver City CA. 213-836-7110, Ext 301

Briggs, Nathalia, *Cat,* Narragansett Pier Free Library, Narragansett RI. 401-789-9507

Briggs, Nina Pearl, *Librn,* Saint Luke's United Methodist Church Library, Oklahoma City OK. 405-232-1371

Briggs, Ramona, *In Charge,* Computer Sciences Corp Technical Library, Falls Church VA. 703-533-8877, Ext 6260

Briggs, Ramona, *Manager,* Computer Sciences Corporation, Technical Library, Falls Church VA. 703-533-8877

Briggs, Richard L, *Tech Serv,* Harford Community College Learning Resources Center, Bel Air MD. 301-838-1000, Ext 268

Briggs, Ruth, *Cat,* Lithgow Public Library, Augusta ME. 207-622-6368

Briggs, Sonja, *Dir & Acq,* Iowa Western Community College, Hoover Media Library, Council Bluffs IA. 712-325-3247

Brigham, Bruce A, *Librn,* Division of Correction, Reception & Medical Center Library, Lake Butler FL. 904-496-2222

Brigham, Diane, *Ref,* Ormsby Public Library, Carson City NV. 702-882-5665

Brigham, Jeffrey L, *Asst Librn & Tech Serv,* Nyack College Library, Nyack NY. 914-358-1710, Ext 270, 271

Brigham, Sybil J, *Head, Ref Servs,* Vermont Resource Sharing Network, VT. 802-828-3261

Bright, Alice, *ILL,* Carnegie-Mellon University (Engineering & Science), Pittsburgh PA. 412-578-2426, 578-2427

Bright, Franklyn F, *Tech Serv,* University of Wisconsin-Madison, Memorial Library, Madison WI. 608-262-3521

Bright, Leta, *Librn,* Wagoner Carnegie Library, Wagoner OK. 918-485-2126

Bright, Martha, *Asst Librn,* Maharishi International University Library, Fairfield IA. 515-472-5031, Ext 152, 232

Bright, Renate, *Librn,* Spectra-Physics Inc, Autolab Division Library, Santa Clara CA. 805-249-5200

Bright, Velma, *Dir,* Akron Carnegie Public Library, Akron IN. 219-893-4113

Brightbill, George, *Doc,* Temple University of the Commonwealth System of Higher Education, Samuel Paley Library, Philadelphia PA. 215-787-8231

Brightenback, Carla, *Bibliog Instr,* Middlebury College, Egbert Starr Library, Middlebury VT. 802-388-7621

Brightwell, Juanita S, *Dir,* Lake Blackshear Regional Library, Americus GA. 912-924-8091

Brigiotta, Mary, *Ref,* Binghamton Public Library, Binghamton NY. 607-723-6457

Brigstock, Frances, *Per,* Richard Bland College Library, Petersburg VA. 804-732-0111, Ext 226

Bril, Patricia, *Ref & Bibliog Instr,* California State University Fullerton Library, Fullerton CA. 714-773-2714

Briles, Kathy, *Librn,* Nashville Public Library, Nashville IL. 618-327-3827

Briley, Anne, *Ser,* East Carolina University, J Y Joyner Library, Greenville NC. 919-757-6514

Briley, John B, *Mgr,* Ohio Historical Society, Campus Martius Museum Library, Marietta OH. 614-373-3750

Brilhart, Linda, *Librn,* Stanislaus County Free Library (Florence L Gondring Library), Ceres CA. 209-537-8938

Brill, Betty, *Librn,* Nipigon Township Public Library, Nipigon ON. 807-887-3142

Brill, Faye, *On-Line Servs,* Foote, Cone & Belding Advertising, Inc, Information Center, Chicago IL. 312-467-9200

Brill, Gloria, *Ad,* San Bernardino County Library, San Bernardino CA. 714-383-1734

Brill, Judith, *Librn,* New York Public Library (Sixty-Seventh Street), New York NY. 212-734-1717

Brill, Wesley A, *Libr Adminr,* Colt Industries, F M Engine Division Library, Beloit WI. 608-364-4411, Ext 2366

Brillault, Ruth, *Librn,* Long Beach Public Library System (Ruth Bach), Long Beach CA. 213-421-5411

Brilmyer, Betty, *Librn,* Grosse Pointe Public Library (Park), Grosse Pointe Park MI. 313-343-2071

Brindamour, Mary E, *Librn,* Dynamics Research Corp Library, Wilmington MA. 617-658-6100

Bringer, Charles O, *Drafting,* Indiana Vocational Technical College, Learning Resource Center, Gary IN. 219-981-1111, Ext 28

Bringer, Sharon, *Tech Serv & Cat,* Culver-Stockton College, Carl Johann Memorial Library, Canton MO. 314-288-5221, Ext 21

Bringham, Sybil, *Ref,* State of Vermont Department of Libraries, Montpelier VT. 802-828-3261

Bringman, Victoria, *In Charge,* Enoch Pratt Free Library (Hampden), Baltimore MD. 301-396-5430, 396-5395

Brink, Clarence, *Ref,* Vigo County Public Library, Terre Haute IN. 812-232-1113

Brinkley, Charles, *Circ,* California State University, John F Kennedy Memorial Library, Los Angeles CA. 213-224-2201

Brinkley, Helen L, *Librn,* United States Air Force (Medical Center Library), Wright-Patterson AFB OH. 513-257-4506

Brinkley, Margot, *Dir,* Foundation Center Library, Washington DC. 202-331-1400

Brinkley, Thelma, *Librn,* Northeast Missouri Library Service (Lewis County), LaGrange MO. 314-655-2288

Brinkman, Donna, *Spec Servs,* Amos Memorial Public Library, Sidney Public Library, Sidney OH. 513-492-8354

Brinkman, Katherine D, *Dir,* John Jermain Memorial Library, Sag Harbor NY. 516-725-0049

Brinkman, Mike, *Media,* Pacific University, Harvey W Scott Memorial Library, Forest Grove OR. 503-357-6151, Ext 301

Brinkman, Mrs B, *Asst Dir,* Lomira Public Library, Lomira WI. 414-269-4115

Brinkmier, Hermina, *Librn,* Monsanto Co Library, Monsanto Research Corp Mound Facility, Miamisburg OH. 513-865-3942

Brinks, Herbert, *Archives,* Calvin College & Seminary Library, Grand Rapids MI. 616-949-4000, Ext 297

Brinsfield, Gail E, *Librn,* Mary M Campbell Public Library, Marcus Hook Public Library, Marcus Hook PA. 215-485-6519

Brinsmead, Ann, *Librn,* HJK & A Library, Washington DC. 202-333-0700

Brinson, Elizabeth, *Actg Librn & Tech Serv,* Fort Valley State College, Henry Alexander Hunt Memorial Library, Fort Valley GA. 912-825-6342

Brinten, Yuki Takahaslie, *Librn,* Pendle Hill Library, Wallingford PA. 215-566-4507

Brinton, Harry, *Dir,* Jacksonville Public Library System, Haydon Burns Library, Jacksonville FL. 904-633-6870

Brisbane, Patty, *Librn,* Genesee District Library (Swartz Creek Area Library), Swartz Creek MI. 313-635-3900

Briscoe, Bessie, *Tech Serv,* Atlanta University, Trevor Arnett Library, Atlanta GA. 404-681-0251, Ext 225

Briscoe, Georgia, *ILL,* University of San Diego (Marvin Kratter Law Library), San Diego CA. 714-293-4541

Briscoe, Marianne, *Dir of Develop,* Newberry Library, Chicago IL. 312-943-9090

Briscoe, Peter, *Coll Develop,* University of California, Riverside, University Library, Riverside CA. 714-787-3221

Brislin, Jane F, *Dir,* Industrial Health Foundation, Inc Library, Pittsburgh PA. 412-687-2100

Brisman, Shimeon, *Jewish Studies,* University of California Los Angeles Library, Los Angeles CA. 213-825-1201

Brister, Janet, *Librn,* Fayette County Memorial Library, Fayette AL. 205-932-6625

Bristor, Patricia, *Acq,* Wayne State University Libraries (Vera P Shiffman Medical Library), Detroit MI. 313-577-1088

Bristow, Carol, *Acq, Cat & On-Line Servs,* Evergreen Valley College Library, San Jose CA. 408-274-7900, Ext 310

Bristow, Wauneta, *Librn,* Platte County Public Library (Guernsey Branch), Guernsey WY. 307-836-2816

Britain, Karla, *Librn,* Washington Adventist Hospital, Medical Library, Takoma Park MD. 301-891-7324, 891-7325

Brite, Agnes, *Librn,* New England Mutual Life Insurance Co, Business Library, Boston MA. 617-266-3700, Ext 2306

Britsch, Christine, *Tech Serv & Cat,* Weber County Library, Ogden UT. 801-399-8516

Britt, Caroline S, *Librn,* Dow Chemical Co, Dowell Div Research & Develop Library, Tulsa OK. 918-582-0101

Britt, Gladys L, *Dir,* Bienville Parish Library, Arcadia LA. 318-263-2930

Britt, Joyce, *Tech Serv,* Wesley College, Parker Library, Dover DE. 302-736-2413

Britt, Ruth C, *Librn,* Fort Gay Public Library, Fort Gay WV. 304-648-5338

Britt, Terry, *Assoc Dir,* Naval Postgraduate School, Dudley Knox Library, Monterey CA. 408-646-2341

Britt, Wayne, *AV,* Chadron State College Library, Chadron NE. 308-432-4451, Ext 271

Brittain, Barbara, *Ch,* Beaufort County Library, Beaufort SC. 803-524-0762

Britten, Doreen, *Ch,* T B Scott Free Library, Merrill Public Library, Merrill WI. 715-536-7191

Britter, Robert, *Libr Asst,* Bethany Medical Center, Medical Library, Kansas City KS. 913-281-8400

Britton, Anne, *Ref,* Scottsdale Community College Library, Scottsdale AZ. 602-941-0999

Britton, Barbara, *Librn,* Black Economic Research Center Reference Library, New York NY. 212-666-0345

Britton, Catherine, *Librn,* Palm Beach County Public Library System (Del Trail), Delray Beach FL. 305-498-3110

Britton, Constance, *Tech Serv,* College of Wooster, Andrews Library, Wooster OH. 216-264-1234, Ext 483

Britton, Gail, *Asst Dir,* Greene County Public Library, Greeneville TN. 615-638-5034

Britton, Helen, *Cat & Processing,* University of Houston (M D Anderson Memorial Library), Houston TX. 713-749-4241

Britton, Jerie J, *Librn,* Central Presbyterian Church Library, Houston TX. 713-621-2424

Britton, Marjorie, *Librn,* Le Sueur-Waseca Regional Library (Janesville Public), Janesville MN. 507-234-6605

Britton, Phyliss, *Librn,* New York State Craig Developmental Center, Health Science Library, Sonyea NY. 716-658-2221

Britton, R, *Librn,* University of Southern California (Social Work), Los Angeles CA. 213-743-7932

Britton, Robert P, *Librn,* Maine Regional Library for the Blind & Physically Handicapped, Augusta ME. 207-289-3959

Britton, Terry, *Learning Resources Ctr Dir,* Oscar Rose Junior College, Learning Resources Center, Midwest City OK. 405-733-7323, 733-7322

Britz, Daniel, *Africana,* Northwestern University Library, Evanston IL. 312-492-7658

Brivio, Carlo, *Librn,* Maryglade College Seminary Library, Detroit MI. 313-861-2866

Brizendine, Margaret S, *Dir,* Russell Public Library, Russell NY. 315-347-3210

Brkic, Beverly, *Cat,* North Dakota State University Library, Fargo ND. 701-237-8876

Broad, Julia, *Librn,* Harris-Stowe State College Library, Saint Louis MO. 314-533-3366, Ext 36

Broad, Patricia, *Librn,* Saint Petersburg Public Library (Mirror Lake), Saint Petersburg FL. 813-893-7268

Broadbent, III, H E, *Dir,* Ursinus College, Myrin Library, Collegeville PA. 215-489-4111, Ext 290

Broaddus, Billie, *Asst Dir,* University of Cincinnati Medical Center Libraries (Health Sciences Library), Cincinnati OH. 513-872-5627

Broadhead, Barbara Jo, *Chief Librn,* International Paper Co, Science & Technology-Information Services, Mobile AL. 205-457-8911, Ext 375

Broadhead, Sandra, *Acq,* Jones County Junior College Memorial Library & Media Center, Ellisville MS. 601-477-9311, Ext 298

Broadnax, Lavonda K, *Learning Resources Librn,* Saint Paul's College, Russell Memorial Library, Lawrenceville VA. 804-848-3111, Ext 221

Broadus, Laurie A, *Librn,* Saint Mary of Nazareth Hospital (School of Nursing Library), Chicago IL. 312-384-5360

Broadus, Robert, *Prof,* University of North Carolina at Chapel Hill, School of Library Science, NC. 919-933-8366

Broadwater, Deborah, *Cat,* University of Baltimore, Langsdale Library, Baltimore MD. 301-727-6350, Ext 444

Broadwater, Maxine, *Librn,* Ruth Enlow Library of Garrett County (Grantsville Br), Grantsville MD. 301-895-5298

Broadwell, Sara, *Branch Asst,* Abbeville-Greenwood Regional Library (Calhoun Falls Branch), Calhoun Falls SC. 803-447-8724

Broadwin, J, *Librn,* United States Army (Medical Research Library), Presidio of San Francisco CA. 415-561-2600, 561-4781

Broady, Jessie, *Tech Serv, Cat & Bibliog Instr,* Essex Community College, James A Newpher Library, Baltimore MD. 301-682-6000, Ext 320

Brock, Betty, *Ch,* Nyack Library, Nyack NY. 914-358-3370

Brock, Clifton, *Pub Servs,* University of North Carolina at Chapel Hill, Louis Round Wilson Academic Affairs Library, Chapel Hill NC. 919-933-1301

Brock, Edith, *Dir,* Ruth Enlow Library of Garrett County, Oakland MD. 301-334-3996

Brock, James P, *Dir,* Adriance Memorial Library, Poughkeepsie NY. 914-485-4790

Brock, Jeanne, *Asst Dir, Media & Tech Serv,* Butler Carnegie Library, Butler IN. 219-868-2351

Brock, Kenneth, *Media,* Pan American University, Learning Resource Center, Edinburg TX. 512-381-2751

Brock, L Alan, *Dir,* Cedarville College Library, Cedarville OH. 513-766-2211, Ext 207

Brock, Lois, *Librn,* General Tire & Rubber Co, Research Division Information Center, Akron OH. 216-798-3496

Brock, Mary Beth, *Acq,* Hinds Junior College, George M McLendon Library, Raymond MS. 601-857-5261, Ext 253

Brock, Ruth, *Bus,* University of Texas at Arlington Library, Arlington TX. 817-273-3391

Brock, Verna LS, *Dir,* Wakulla County Public Library, Crawfordville FL. 904-926-7415

Brock, William D, *Dir Member Serv,* United Way of America, Information Center Library, Alexandria VA. 703-836-7100, Ext 384

Brockamp, Nita J, *Librn,* Kitchell Memorial Library, Morrisonville IL. 217-526-4553

Brockgreitens, L H, *Librn,* ACF Industries, Inc, Amcar Div, Technical Center Library, Saint Charles MO. 314-723-9600

Brockland, M Dionysia, *Dir & Acq,* Cardinal Ritter Library, Saint Louis MO. 314-544-0455, Ext 56

Brockman, Pat, *Circ,* Orlando Public Library, Orlando FL. 305-425-4694

Brockman, Wanda, *Librn,* University Christian Church Library, Seattle WA. 206-522-0169

Brockman, William, *Doc,* Drew University, Rose Memorial Library, Madison NJ. 201-377-3000, Ext 469

Brockmann, Dorothy, *Circ,* East Carolina University, J Y Joyner Library, Greenville NC. 919-757-6514

Brockway, Duncan, *Dir,* Schools of Theology in Dubuque Library, Dubuque IA. 319-589-3100, 556-8151

Brockway, Paula R, *Librn,* United States Air Force Academy Library (Medical (SGAL)), United States Air Force Academy CO. 303-472-5107

Brodak, Elizabeth W, *Dir,* Western Colorado University Library, Grand Junction CO. 303-245-3950

Brodbeck, Jeanne, *Librn,* Palm Beach County Public Library System (Southwest County), Boca Raton FL. 305-482-4554

Broderick, Donald C, *Dir,* University of Maine at Augusta, Learning Resources Center, Augusta ME. 207-622-7131

Broderick, James T, *Cat,* Public Library of Fort Wayne & Allen County, Fort Wayne IN. 219-424-7241

Broderick, John C, *Asst Librn Res Servs,* Library of Congress, Washington DC. 202-287-5000

Brodersen, Margaret, *Librn,* Scott Community College, Palmer Campus Library, Davenport IA. 319-324-1611, Ext 272,242

Brodhead, Thomasene, *Librn,* Hawaii State Library System (Ewa Beach Community-School), Ewa Beach HI. 808-689-8391

Brodie, Debra, *Dir,* Hillsboro Public Library, Hillsboro OR. 503-648-6669

Brodie, P, *Librn,* Norland Associates Library, Janesville WI. 608-754-1451

Brodine, Leola M, *Librn,* Loup County Public Library, Taylor NE. 308-942-8545

Brodkin-Schneider, Lonnie J, *Librn,* William M Mercer Ltd, Library-Information Center, Montreal PQ. 514-285-1802

Brodman, Estelle, *Dir,* Washington University Libraries (School of Medicine Library), Saint Louis MO. 314-454-3711

Brodner, Larson, *Info Spec,* Esso Resources Canada Ltd (Technical Information Services), Calgary AB. 403-267-1494

Brodsky, Carol, *ILL,* Finkelstein Memorial Library, Spring Valley NY. 914-352-5700, Ext 230

Brodt, Janice, *ILL,* Dearborn Department of Libraries, Henry Ford Centennial Library, Dearborn MI. 313-271-1000

Brodt, Janice, *Ref,* Dearborn Department of Libraries, Henry Ford Centennial Library, Dearborn MI. 313-271-1000

Brody, Catherine T, *Dir,* New York City Community College, Namm Hall Library, Brooklyn NY. 212-643-5240

Brody, Catherine T, *Graphic Arts,* New York City Community College, Namm Hall Library, Brooklyn NY. 212-643-5240

Brody, Catherine T, *Researcher,* Typophiles Inc, Typographic Reference Library, Brooklyn NY. 212-462-2017

Brody, Julia J, *Chief,* New York Public Library (Mid-Manhattan), New York NY. 212-790-6566

Brody, Lynn, *Librn,* University of Texas Libraries (Undergraduate), Austin TX. 512-471-5222

Broeker, Mary Ann, *Dir,* Culver Public Library, Culver IN. 219-842-2941

Broeksmit, Jane M, *Librn,* Dwight Public Library, Dwight IL. 815-584-3061

Broering, Naomi, *Librn,* Georgetown University (John Vinton Dahlgren Memorial Library), Washington DC. 202-625-7577

Broersma, Nancy, *Librn,* Allendale Township Library, Allendale MI. 616-895-4178

Brofft, Dottie, *Ref,* Environmental Protection Agency, Environmental Research Center Library, Cincinnati OH. 513-684-7701

Brogan, Gerald E, *Dir,* College of the Redwoods Library, Eureka CA. 707-443-8411, Ext 249

Brogden, Thera, *Ref,* Andalusia Public Library, Andalusia AL. 205-222-6612

Brogdon, Crystal G, *Dir,* LaVista Public, LaVista NE. 402-331-9519

Broglie, Margaret L, *Librn,* Crafton Public Library, Crafton PA. 412-922-6877

Broidy, Ellen, *Assoc Librn,* Bancroft, Avery & McAlister Library, San Francisco CA. 415-788-8855, Ext 301

Brokalakis, Melissa C, *Asst Dir,* Wayland Free Public Library, Wayland MA. 617-358-2311, 358-2308

Bromberg, Nicolette, *Media,* Lower Columbia College, Learning Resource Center, Longview WA. 206-577-2310

Brome, Eleanor, *Dir,* Cranford Public Library, Cranford NJ. 201-276-1826

Bromer, Susan, *Curric Mat,* East Stroudsburg State College, Kemp Library, East Stroudsburg PA. 717-424-3467

Bromley, Carolyn, *Circ,* North Kingstown Free Library, North Kingstown RI. 401-294-2521

Bromley, Jo Ann, *Librn & Cat,* Lake View Public Library, Lake View IA. 712-657-2310

Bromley, Joan D, *Librn,* S L Griffith Memorial Library, Danby VT. 802-293-5106

Bromley, Patricia, *Librn,* Toledo-Lucas County Public Library (Point Place), Toledo OH. 419-255-7055

Bromwich, G, *Librn,* Reed Stenhouse Ltd, Research Department Library, Toronto ON. 416-868-5520

Brongers, Rein, *Sci,* University of British Columbia Library, Vancouver BC. 604-228-3871

Brongers, Rein, *On-Line Servs,* University of British Columbia Library, Vancouver BC. 604-228-3871

Bronner, Edwin B, *Dir & Spec Coll,* Haverford College, James P Magill Library, Haverford PA. 215-649-9600, Ext 281

Bronson, Diane, *Cat & Pub Relations,* Palm Beach County Public Library System, West Palm Beach FL. 305-686-0895

Bronson, Gwen, *Dir,* Beaumont District Library, Beaumont CA. 714-845-1357

Bronson, John O, *Librn,* Chesapeake College Library, Learning Resources Center, Wye Mills MD. 301-758-1537, 822-5400, Ext 56, 57

Bronson, Que, *Librn,* Public Library of Annapolis & Anne Arundel County Inc (Eastport-Annapolis Neck), Annapolis MD. 301-224-7655

Brontley, Dorothy, *Gen Libr Serv,* Worcester Public Library, Worcester MA. 617-752-3751

Brook, Barry S, *Co-Directors,* Research Center for Musical Iconography, New York NY. 212-790-4282

Brookbank, Frances A, *Librn,* Connersville Public Library, Fayette County Public Library, Connersville IN. 317-825-4681

Brooke, Anna, *Librn,* Smithsonian Institution Libraries (Hirshhorn Museum Library), Washington DC. 202-381-6702

Brooke, Lee, *Dir,* Chicago College of Osteopathic Medicine Library, Alumni Memorial Library, Chicago IL. 312-947-3000

Brooke, Lee, *Dir Libr Serv,* Olympia Fields Osteopathic Medical Center Library, Olympia Fields IL. 747-4000 Ext 1190

Brooke, Lou, *Dir,* Southwestern Regional Library, Silver City NM. 505-538-2871

Brooke, M, *Media,* Red River Community College, Learning Resources Center, Winnipeg MB. 204-632-2232

Brookens, Kenneth, *Assoc Prof,* Central Missouri State University, Dept of Library Science and Instructional Technology, MO. 816-429-4835

Brooker, Margaret, *Ch,* Franklin Sylvester Library, Medina OH. 216-725-0588

Brooker, Valerie, *Librn,* York Regional Library (Florenceville Public), Florenceville NB. 506-392-5294

Brooker, Virginia, *Librn,* Midlands Technical College, Beltline Campus Library, Columbia SC. 803-782-5471, Ext 265

Brookes, Betty, *AV,* Webster College, Eden Theological Seminary, Eden-Webster Libraries, Saint Louis MO. 314-968-0500, Ext 235

Brookhart, Ray F, *Bibliog Instr,* Carlsbad City Library, Carlsbad CA. 714-438-5614

Brooking, Ruth P, *Chief Librn,* Oshawa Public Library, Oshawa ON. 416-579-6111

Brookins, Charles, *Ref,* Langston University, G Lamar Harrison Library, Langston OK. 405-466-2231, Ext 231

Brookman, Janice, *Asst Dir,* Carnegie Public Library, East Liverpool OH. 216-385-2048

Brookman, Janice, *Film Librn,* Carnegie Public Library, East Liverpool OH. 216-385-2048

Brookman, Joyce, *Dir,* Sadie Pope Dowdell Library, South Amboy NJ. 201-721-6060

Brookreson, Frances, *Librn,* Hendrick Medical Center, Mary Meek School of Nursing Library, Abilene TX. 915-677-3551

Brooks, Allen, *Ad & Ref,* Blue Ridge Regional Library, Martinsville VA. 703-632-7125

Brooks, Anita, *Acq,* Gadsden-Etowah County Library, Gadsden Public Library, Gadsden AL. 205-547-1611

Brooks, Ann K V, *Librn,* Barrington Public Library, Barrington NH. 603-286-3967

Brooks, Beulah, *Librn,* Camas County Public Library, Fairfield ID. 208-764-2439

Brooks, Beverly, *Head,* Trident Technical College (North Campus Learning Resources Center), Charleston SC. 803-572-6094

Brooks, Boyden, *Mail Order Servs,* North Central Regional Library, Wenatchee WA. 509-663-1117

Brooks, Carolyn, *Ch,* Chippewa Library League, Mount Pleasant MI. 517-773-3242

Brooks, Carolyn, *Chief Librn,* Evangelical Covenant Church Library, Muskegon MI. 616-728-5385

Brooks, Carolyn, *Ch,* Veterans Memorial Library, Mount Pleasant MI. 517-773-3242

Brooks, Cassandra, *Librn,* Vigo County Public Library (Meadows Libr), Terre Haute IN. 812-232-6738

Brooks, Cathy, *Ch & YA,* Boynton Beach City Library, Boynton Beach FL. 732-2624 or 732-8111, Ext 223, 224 & 225

Brooks, Connie, *Librn,* Lovington Public Library, Lovington NM. 505-396-3144

Brooks, Darlene J, *Librn,* Palmer Public Library, Palmer TN. 615-779-5292

Brooks, Diane, *Librn,* Atlantic Institute of Education Library, Halifax NS. 902-425-5430

Brooks, Edith, *Librn,* Public Library of Nashville & Davidson County (Hadley Park), Nashville TN. 615-329-4774

Brooks, Elizabeth, *ILL,* Delaware County District Library, Delaware OH. 614-362-3861

Brooks, Elizabeth, *Med Libr,* Veterans Administration, Hospital Library, Perry Point MD. 301-642-2411

Brooks, Etta, *Librn,* Jacksonville Public Library System (Dallas Graham), Jacksonville FL. 904-633-5605

Brooks, Frances, *Asst Librn,* State Technical Institute at Memphis, George E Freeman Library, Memphis TN. 901-377-4106

Brooks, Grover, *Education,* Wright State University Library, Dayton OH. 513-873-2380

Brooks, Grover, *Bibliog Instr,* Wright State University Library, Dayton OH. 513-873-2380

Brooks, Jane, *Librn,* Torrance Public Library (North Torrance), Torrance CA. 213-323-7200

Brooks, Janet, *Chief Librn,* United States Department of Defense, Defense Communications Agency, Technical & Information Library Center, Arlington VA. 703-692-2468

Brooks, Jeanne, *Asst Librn,* Central Carolina Technical Institute, Learning Resource Center, Sanford NC. 919-775-5401, Ext 244

Brooks, Jerrold L, *Exec Dir,* Historical Foundation of the Presbyterian & Reformed Churches Library, Montreat NC. 704-669-7061

Brooks, Joseph, *Bus & Tech,* Lansing Public Library, Lansing MI. 517-374-4600

Brooks, Lois, *ILL,* Wilmette Public Library District, Wilmette IL. 312-256-5025

Brooks, Lorraine P, *Cat,* Orange Public Library, Orange CT. 203-795-0288

Brooks, Mary, *Librn,* Los Angeles Public Library System (Ascot), Los Angeles CA. 213-759-4817

Brooks, Maureen, *Acq,* Cerro Coso Community College, Learning Resources Center, Ridgecrest CA. 714-375-5001, Ext 47

Brooks, Phyllis, *Ref,* Lake Erie College, James F Lincoln Learning Resource Center, Painesville OH. 216-352-3361, Ext 280

Brooks, Phyllis, *Librn,* Lambton County Library (Wyoming Library), Wyoming ON. 519-845-0181

Brooks, Richard, *Asst Dir & Bkmobile Coordr,* Dakota County Library System, Burnsville MN. 612-435-8111

Brooks, Robert A, *Ref,* Yale University Library (Law Library), New Haven CT. 203-436-2215

Brooks, Robert M, *Acq,* Monmouth College, Guggenheim Library, West Long Branch NJ. 201-222-6600, Ext 264

Brooks, Roger D, *Librn,* Kansas Supreme Court Law Library, Topeka KS. 913-296-3257

Brooks, Ruth, *Librn,* Parsons State Hospital & Training Center Libraries (Patients Library), Parsons KS. 316-421-6550

Brooks, Ruth H, *Asst Librn,* Southwest Foundation for Research & Education, Preston G Northrup Memorial Library, San Antonio TX. 512-674-1410, Ext 226

Brooks, Sandra, *Ref,* Niagara College of Applied Arts & Technology, Tecumseh Resource Centre, Welland ON. 416-735-2211, Ext 297

Brooks, Shirley, *Librn,* Hay River Library, Hay River NT. 403-874-6531

Brooks, Terrill, *Ser,* University of Michigan-Flint Library, Flint MI. 313-762-3400

Brooks, Tom J, *Tech Serv,* Fresno County Free Library, Fresno CA. 209-488-3191

Brooks, IV, Harry F, *Chief Librn,* Veterans Administration, Medical Center Library, Montgomery AL. 205-272-4670, Ext 260, 261

Brookshier, Doris, *Educ,* Central Missouri State University, Ward Edwards Library, Warrensburg MO. 816-429-4141

Brookshire, Doris, *ILL,* Meridian Public Library, Meridian MS. 601-693-6771, 693-4913

Brookshire, Sherry, *Asst Librn,* United States Air Force (Hospital Patient's Library), Elmendorf AFB AK. 907-752-5328

Broom, Harriet, *Dir,* Mid State Technical Institute Library, Wisconsin Rapids WI. 715-423-5650

Broom, Harriet, *Dir,* Mid-State Technical Institute, Marshfield Campus Library, Marshfield WI. 715-387-2538

Broom, Harriet, *Dir,* Mid-State Technical Institute, Stevens Point Campus Library, Stevens Point WI. 715-344-3063

Broom, June E, *Librn,* Suwannee River Regional Library, Seven-County Region (Cross City (Dixie County)), Live Oak FL. 904-498-3949

Broom, Sandra R, *Exec Libr,* E C Scranton Memorial Library, Madison CT. 203-245-7365

Broom, Susan, *Asst Dir,* Saint Lucie County Library Systems, Fort Pierce FL. 305-461-5708

Broomall, Susan, *Librn,* Orlando Public Library (Northgate), Orlando FL. 305-295-3613

Broome, Bettye, *Gen Consult,* Mississippi Library Commission, Jackson MS. 601-354-6369

Broome, Debbie, *Librn,* Jackson Metropolitan Library (Terry Library), Terry MS. 601-352-3677

Broome, J Sue, *Exten Servs,* Chatham-Effingham-Liberty Regional Library, Savannah Public Library, Savannah GA. 912-234-5127

Brophy, Sister Annette, *Music,* College of Saint Benedict Library, Saint Joseph MN. 612-363-5011

Brose, Jean M, *Chief Librn,* Rochester Methodist Hospital, Methodist-Kahler Library, Rochester MN. 507-286-7425

Brosius, Karen, *ILL,* Susquehanna University, Roger M Blough Learning Ctr, Selinsgrove PA. 717-374-0101, Ext 329

Brosius, M E, *In Charge,* Organization for Economic Cooperation & Development, Publications & Information Center, Washington DC. 202-724-1857

Brosk, Carol A, *Librn,* McDermott, Will & Emery Library, Chicago IL. 312-372-2000, Ext 371

Broskoff, Alice, *Ch,* Albert Lea Public Library, Albert Lea MN. 507-373-8862

Brosky, Catherine, *Sci & Tech,* Carnegie Library of Pittsburgh, Pittsburgh PA. 412-622-3100

Brosman, Geraldine Y, *Librn,* United States Air Force (Minot Air Force Base Library), Minot AFB ND. 701-727-4761

Brostrom, David, *Extension Coordr,* Northwest Wisconsin Library System, Ashland WI. 715-682-8027

Broten, A, *Librn,* Balfour Technical School Library, Regina SK. 306-522-0672

Brothers, Joyce D, *Tech Serv & Cat,* Dean Junior College, E Ross Anderson Library, Franklin MA. 617-528-9100, Ext 261

Brotherton, Barbara, *Librn,* Orange Public Library (El Modena), Orange CA. 714-639-7181

Brotherton, Lise, *Prof,* College de Maisonneuve, Techniques de la Documentation, PQ. 514-254-7131

Broude, Jeffrey, *Acq,* California State University Dominguez Hills, Educational Resources Center, Carson CA. 213-515-3700

Brough, Lorna L, *Acq,* Del Mar College Library, Corpus Christi TX. 512-881-6308

Broughton, Ann, *Ref,* Jackson-George Regional Library System (Pascagoula City Branch), Pascagoula MS. 601-762-3406

Broughton, Pansy D, *Librn,* R J Reynolds Tobacco Company (Engineering Dept Library), Winston-Salem NC. 919-777-5000

Broughton, Rita, *Flm Libr Servs Suprv,* Saint Louis Public Library, Saint Louis MO. 314-241-2288

Broukes, Linda, *Librn,* Canadian Association for Mentally Retarded Library, Winnipeg MB. 204-783-7147

Broumley, Evlyn, *Genealogy & Local Hist,* Weatherford Public Library, Weatherford TX. 817-594-2767

Brounell, Mildred, *Asst Librn,* Cities Service Co (Law Library), Tulsa OK. 918-586-2272

Broussard, Harry C, *Syst & Develop,* University of New Mexico General Library, Albuquerque NM. 505-277-4241

Broussard, Mrs J W, *Librn,* Cameron Parish Library, Cameron LA. 318-775-5421

Broussard, Ruth E, *Librn,* Vermilion Parish Library (Kaplan Branch), Kaplan LA. 318-643-7209

Brouwer, Carol H, *Dir,* Whitinsville Social Library Inc, Whitinsville MA. 617-234-2151

Brovhard, H, *Librn,* Blanden Art Gallery Reading Library, Fort Dodge IA. 515-573-2316

Brow, Ellen, *Latin Am & Span Bibliog,* University of Kansas Libraries, Watson Memorial Library, Lawrence KS. 913-864-3601

Browand, Kenneth S, *Dir,* Lansing Public Library, Lansing MI. 517-374-4600

Brower, Dorothy, *Librn,* Blaine County Library (Harlem Public), Harlem MT. 406-357-2932

Brower, Dorothy, *Librn,* Harlem Public Library, Harlem MT. 406-353-2712

Brower, Kate, *Ref & Bibliog Instr,* Johnson Free Public Library, Hackensack NJ. 201-343-4169

Brower, Kate, *Govt docs, Bus & Law,* Johnson Free Public Library, Hackensack NJ. 201-343-4169
Brower, M Bertha, *Librn,* Spring City Free Public Library, Spring City PA. 215-948-4130
Brower, Milt, *Instr,* Highline Community College Library, Library Technician Program, WA. 206-878-3710, Ext 233
Brower, Nancy, *Ch & YA,* Butte County Library, Oroville CA. 916-534-4525
Brower, Viola, *Librn,* Kanawha Public Library, Kanawha IA. 515-762-3595
Brower, Wini, *Ch,* Kearney Public Library, Kearney NE. 308-237-5133
Brown, A T, *Librn,* Timken Co, Research Library, Canton OH. 216-453-4511, Ext R 373
Brown, Alice, *Doc,* University of Nevada, Las Vegas, James R Dickinson Library, Las Vegas NV. 702-739-3286
Brown, Alma, *In Charge,* Miami-Dade Public Library System (Dixie Park), Miami FL. 305-579-5322
Brown, Andrea P, *Chief Librn,* Saint Mary's College, Sarah Graham Kenan Library, Raleigh NC. 919-828-2521, Ext 313, 314
Brown, Ann, *Librn,* Mid-Continent Public Library (South Kansas City Branch), Kansas City MO. 816-523-1611
Brown, Anna Sue, *Cat & On-Line Servs,* Drury College, Walker Library, Springfield MO. 417-865-8731, Ext 282
Brown, Anne, *Librn,* Ontario Ministry of the Attorney General, Supreme Court of Ontario Judges Library, Toronto ON. 416-363-4101, Ext 259
Brown, Arthur, *Librn,* Maryknoll Seminary Library, Maryknoll NY. 914-941-7590, Ext 427
Brown, Audrey, *Dir & Acq,* Port Hope Public Library, Port Hope ON. 416-885-4712
Brown, Audrey, *Dir,* Southington Public Library, Southington CT. 203-628-0947
Brown, Barbara, *Librn,* Granby Public Library, Granby VT. 802-328-4494
Brown, Barbara, *Ch,* Louis T Graves Memorial Public Library, Kennebunkport ME. 207-967-2778
Brown, Barbara, *Librn,* New York Supreme Court Law Library, Auburn NY. 315-253-1279
Brown, Barbara, *ILL,* Park Forest Public Library, Park Forest IL. 312-748-3731
Brown, Barbara, *Asst Librn for Gen Reader Servs,* Princeton University Library, Princeton NJ. 609-452-3180
Brown, Barbara B, *Dir,* Terryville Public Library, Terryville CT. 203-582-3121
Brown, Bernice, *Br Coordr,* Raleigh County Public Library, Beckley WV. 304-255-0511
Brown, Bernice, *Librn,* Raleigh County Public Library (Marsh Fork), Stickney WV. 304-854-2677
Brown, Bernita, *Librn,* Sno-Isle Regional Library (Tulalip Libr), Marysville WA. 206-659-1512
Brown, Betsy, *Librn,* Kenosha Public Library (West and Bookmobile), Kenosha WI. 414-656-6038
Brown, Betty, *Mgr, Program Servs,* Dallas Public Library, Dallas TX. 214-748-9071
Brown, Betty, *Asst Librn,* Hoesch Memorial Public Library, Alma NE. 308-928-2600
Brown, Betty, *Doc,* Oklahoma Department of Libraries, Oklahoma City OK. 405-521-2502
Brown, Betty L, *Cat,* Wheaton College Library, Norton MA. 617-285-7722, Ext 518
Brown, Betty R, *Librn,* Coloma Township - Rock Falls Public Library, Rock Falls IL. 815-626-3958
Brown, Bettye A, *Librn,* State Community College of East Saint Louis, Learning Resource Center, East Saint Louis IL. 618-875-9100, Ext 238, 378
Brown, Beulah M, *Librn,* San Bernardino County Law Library, San Bernardino CA. 714-383-2701
Brown, Billie K, *Librn,* Athens Regional Library (Oconee County), Watkinsville GA. 404-769-6177
Brown, Bonnie, *ILL,* Chickasaw Library System, Ardmore OK. 405-223-3164
Brown, Bonnie, *Librn,* Louisiana State University (Chemistry), Baton Rouge LA. 504-388-2530
Brown, Bruce, *Librn Blind,* Corn Belt Library System, Normal IL. 309-452-4485
Brown, Bruce M, *Dir & Rare Bks,* Colgate University, Everett Needham Case Library, Hamilton NY. 315-824-1000
Brown, C, *Ref,* Patten Free Library, Bath ME. 207-443-5141
Brown, Caren, *Dir,* Free Public Library of the Township of Berkeley Heights, Berkeley Heights NJ. 201-464-9333
Brown, Carmen, *Ref,* Worcester Polytechnic Institute, George C Gordon Library, Worcester MA. 617-753-1411, Ext 410
Brown, Carol, *Librn,* Butte County Library (Chico Downtown), Chico CA. 916-343-6070
Brown, Carol, *Ch,* Concord Public Library, Concord NH. 603-225-2743
Brown, Carol, *Admin Asst,* West Georgia Regional Library, Neva Lomason Memorial Library, Carrollton GA. 404-832-1381
Brown, Carol, *Acq & Cat,* Western Wyoming Community College, Library Learning Resources Center, Rock Springs WY. 307-382-2121, Ext 154
Brown, Carol A, *Librn,* Consolidated Natural Gas Service Co, Inc Library, Cleveland OH. 216-421-6302
Brown, Carol N, *Archivist,* Curtis Publishing Co Library, Indianapolis IN. 317-634-1100
Brown, Carolyn, *Dir,* Executive Office of the President Information Management & Services Division, Washington DC. 202-395-4862, 395-3654
Brown, Cecil R, *Ad,* Spartanburg County Public Library, Spartanburg SC. 582-4123 & 585-2441
Brown, Charles A, *Librn,* Amarillo Hospital District, Health Science Library, Amarillo TX. 806-376-4431
Brown, Charles A, *Librn,* Memorial Medical Center Library, Corpus Christi TX. 512-881-4197
Brown, Christine B, *Librn,* United States Department of Commerce, Industry & Trade Administration Library, Atlanta GA. 404-881-4873
Brown, Claire L, *Librn,* United States Navy (Naval Air Test Center Library), Patuxent River MD. 301-863-3000
Brown, Clara Mae, *Asst Dir, Acq & Ref,* Chestatee Regional Library, Gainesville GA. 404-532-3311
Brown, Clayton, *Ref,* California State University, John F Kennedy Memorial Library, Los Angeles CA. 213-224-2201
Brown, Connis O, *Local & State Records,* Virginia State Library, Richmond VA. 804-786-8929
Brown, Consuella H, *Vault Librn,* United States Army (Morris Swett Library), Fort Sill OK. 405-351-4525, 351-4477
Brown, Craig, *Ser,* Boston University Libraries (Mugar Memorial Library), Boston MA. 617-353-3710
Brown, Daniel A, *In Charge,* National Park Service, Kennesaw Mountain National Battlefield Park Library, Marietta GA. 404-974-2689
Brown, Darmae, *Dir,* Northeast Colorado Regional Library, Wray CO. 303-332-4715
Brown, David, *Asst Dir,* Murray Public Library, Murray UT. 801-266-1137
Brown, David, *Librn,* Murray Public Library (Vine St), Murray UT. 801-266-1261
Brown, David C, *Librn,* United States Marine Corps (James Carson Breckinridge Library), Quantico VA. 703-640-2248
Brown, Deborah, *Asst Librn,* Bowling Green State University, Firelands College Library, Huron OH. 419-433-5560, Ext 252, 281 & 211
Brown, Diana M, *Dir,* Saint Charles Public Library District, Saint Charles IL. 312-584-0076
Brown, Donald R, *Mat Selection,* State Library of Pennsylvania, Harrisburg PA. 717-787-2646
Brown, Donna, *Br Coordr,* Stockton-San Joaquin County Public Library, Stockton Public Libr, Stockton CA. 209-944-8415
Brown, Donnie, *Ch,* Delray Beach Public Library Association, Inc, Delray Beach FL. 305-276-6482
Brown, Doris, *Ch & YA,* Atikokan Public Library, Atikokan ON. 807-597-4406, 597-4230
Brown, Doris, *In Charge,* Eureka-Humboldt County Library (McKinleyville Branch), McKinleyville CA. 707-839-1510
Brown, Dorothy, *Librn,* Fort Smith Public Library (Midland Blvd), Ft Smith AR. 501-782-2204
Brown, Dorothy, *Cat,* Letcher County Public Library, Whitesburg KY. 606-633-7547
Brown, Dorothy, *Librn,* University of Alabama (Business), University AL. 205-348-6096
Brown, Dorothy E, *Librn,* Emerson Hospital, Dr George E Titcomb Medical Library, Concord MA. 617-369-1400, Ext 249
Brown, Dorothy N, *Librn,* Eastern Wyoming College Library, Torrington WY. 307-532-7111
Brown, Dorothy S, *Dir,* Webster Memorial Library, Wentworth NH. 603-764-5818
Brown, Duncan, *Tech Serv,* Maharishi International University Library, Fairfield IA. 515-472-5031, Ext 152, 232
Brown, E, *Librn,* University of Toronto Libraries (Engineering), Toronto ON. 416-978-3101
Brown, Edna, *Cat,* Ames Public Library, Ames IA. 515-232-4404
Brown, Edna Earle, *Tech Serv & On-Line Servs,* Georgia Southern College Library, Statesboro GA. 912-681-5115
Brown, Edna H, *Librn,* Smyth Public Library, Manchester NH. 603-483-8245
Brown, Elaine A, *ILL, Sci,* Brown University (University Library), Providence RI. 401-863-2167
Brown, Eleanor, *Circ,* Amherst College, Robert Frost Library, Amherst MA. 413-542-2212
Brown, Eleanor, *Librn,* Amherst College (Merrill Science Library), Amherst MA. 413-542-2076
Brown, Elisabeth P, *Asst Librn,* American College, Vane B Lucas Memorial Library, Bryn Mawr PA. 215-896-4507, 896-4508
Brown, Elizabeth B, *Librn,* Montgomery Museum of Fine Arts Library, Montgomery AL. 205-834-3490
Brown, Ellen, *Tech Serv,* Commerce Public Library, Commerce CA. 213-722-6660
Brown, Elnor, *Librn,* Imperial Public Library, Imperial NE. 308-882-4754
Brown, Eloise P, *ILL & Ref,* Lebanon Valley College, George D Gossard Memorial Library, Annville PA. 717-867-4411, Ext 217
Brown, Elsie, *Librn,* Colusa County Free Library (Maxwell), Maxwell CA. 916-438-2250
Brown, Emma Lee, *Health,* West Chester State College, Francis Harvey Green Library, West Chester PA. 215-436-2643
Brown, Emma Lee, *Coll Develop,* West Chester State College, Francis Harvey Green Library, West Chester PA. 215-436-2643
Brown, Ethel, *Tech Serv,* Frederick Community College, Learning Resource Center, Frederick MD. 301-694-1242
Brown, Eva, *Coordr, Interlibr Coop,* Chicago Public Library (Central Library), Chicago IL. 312-269-2900
Brown, Florence L, *Librn,* Logan County Library, Stapleton NE. 308-636-2343
Brown, Florence S, *Dir,* Concord Pike Library, Wilmington DE. 302-478-7961
Brown, Forrest E, *Dir,* Saint Olaf College, Rolvaag Memorial Library, Northfield MN. 507-663-2222
Brown, Frances, *Librn,* Jackson County Library System (Gold Hill Branch), Gold Hill OR. 503-855-1994
Brown, Georgia W, *Dir,* Southern University Library, Baton Rouge LA. 504-771-4990, 771-4991, 771-4992
Brown, Gerald, *Asst Librn,* Pulitzer Publishing Co, Saint Louis Post Dispatch Reference Library, Saint Louis MO. 314-621-1111, Ext 535
Brown, Gerald A, *Dir,* Waupaca Free Public Library, Waupaca WI. 715-258-3393
Brown, Geraldine M, *Librn,* Xerox Corp, Law Library, Stamford CT. 203-329-8700, Ext 3415
Brown, Geri, *Librn,* Memphis-Shelby County Public Library & Information Center (Germantown Libr), Germantown TN. 901-754-3702
Brown, Gertrude S, *Dir,* Harborfields Public Library, Greenlawn NY. 516-757-4200
Brown, Gertude, *Librn,* Waterville Town Library, Waterville VT. 802-644-5039
Brown, Gloria H Terwilliger, *Dir,* Northern Virginia Community College Libraries (Alexandria Campus), Alexandria VA. 703-323-4231
Brown, Grace, *Circ,* Hofstra University Library, Hempstead NY. 516-560-3475
Brown, Grace, *Librn,* Houston Public Library (Kashmere Gardens), Houston TX. 713-674-8461
Brown, Harold, *Asst Librn,* Northrop University, Alumni Library, Inglewood CA. 213-776-5466

Brown, Harold, *Tech Serv & Media,* Northrop University, Alumni Library, Inglewood CA. 213-776-5466
Brown, Harriet, *Librn,* Brimfield Public Library, Brimfield MA. 413-245-3518
Brown, Hazel, *Librn,* Tinicum Memorial Public Library, Essington PA. 215-521-9344
Brown, Hazel, *Dir,* Yale Public Library, Yale OK. 918-387-2135
Brown, Helen, *Media,* Barrhead Elementary School Public Library, Barrhead AB. 403-674-2160
Brown, Helen J, *Mgr Info Systs & On-Line Search Coordr,* Kennecott Copper Corp, Information Center, Lexington MA. 617-862-8268, Ext 333, 334
Brown, Helen L, *Dir,* Hiram Halle Memorial Library, Pound Ridge NY. 914-764-5085
Brown, Helen-Ann, *Librn,* National Jewish Hospital & Research Center-National Asthma Center, Medical Library, Denver CO. 303-388-4461, Ext 473,474
Brown, Inez, *Librn,* Los Angeles Public Library System (Washington Irving), Los Angeles CA. 213-734-6303
Brown, Irene, *Dir,* Cassville Public Library, Cassville WI. 608-725-5180
Brown, Jack Perry, *Librn,* Cleveland Museum of Art Library, Cleveland OH. 216-421-7340
Brown, James A, *Media,* Amarillo College, Learning Resource Center, Amarillo TX. 806-376-5111, Ext 2420
Brown, James J, *Dir,* Waterloo Public Library, Waterloo ON. 519-886-1310
Brown, Jane, *Ch,* Novi Public Library, Novi MI. 313-349-0720
Brown, Jane Walsh, *Librn,* Westchester Public Library (Hageman Memorial), Porter IN. 219-926-7696
Brown, Janet, *Librn,* Carroll County Public Library (Taneytown), Westminster MD. 301-756-6316
Brown, Janet, *Fine Arts Coordr,* State University of New York at Binghamton Library (Fine Arts), Binghamton NY. 607-798-4927
Brown, Janet D, *Librn,* Dudley-Tucker Library, Raymond NH. 603-895-2633
Brown, Janette, *Tech Serv,* Moore Memorial Public Library, Texas City TX. 713-948-3111, Ext 160
Brown, Janice A, *Media,* Washburn University of Topeka (School of Law Library), Topeka KS. 913-295-6688
Brown, Jay M, *Librn,* Congregation Mishkan Israel Library, Hamden CT. 203-288-3877
Brown, Jean, *Cat & Rare Bks & Spec Coll,* Fulton County Public Library, Rochester IN. 219-223-2713
Brown, Jean, *Dir,* Tyringham Institute Library, Tyringham MA. 413-243-3216
Brown, Jeanine, *Chief, Libr Serv,* Veterans Administration, Medical Center Library Service, Muskogee OK. 918-683-6321, Ext 240
Brown, Jeanne, *Doc,* Urbana Free Library, Urbana IL. 217-367-4057
Brown, Jessica, *ILL,* University of Wisconsin-Milwaukee, Golda Meir Library, Milwaukee WI. 414-963-4785
Brown, Jo Nell, *Ch,* Canon City Public Library, Canon City CO. 303-275-3669
Brown, Joan, *Dir,* W J Niederkorn Public Library, Port Washington WI. 414-284-5031
Brown, Joanne, *Bkmobile Coordr,* Baker County Public Library, Baker OR. 503-523-6414, 523-6419
Brown, Johanna B, *Automated Retrieval & ILL,* California Polytechnic State University Library, San Luis Obispo CA. 805-546-2345
Brown, John R, *In Charge,* Florida Power Corporation Library, Saint Petersburg FL. 813-866-5458
Brown, Jonna, *Librn,* Seminole Junior College, David L Boren Library, Seminole OK. 405-382-9950, Ext 243
Brown, Jovana J, *Dean,* Evergreen State College, Daniel J Evans Library, Olympia WA. 206-866-6262
Brown, Joy, *Bkmobile Coordr,* Whitley County Library, Williamsburg KY. 606-549-0818
Brown, Judith, *Asst Dir & Ch,* Natrona County Public Library, Casper WY. 307-235-9272
Brown, Judith H, *Librn,* Wheeler Library, North Stonington CT. 203-535-0383
Brown, Julanne, *Librn,* Omaha Public Library (Willa Cather), Omaha NE. 402-444-4851

Brown, June E, *Univ Librn & Acq,* Alfred University (Herrick Memorial Library), Alfred NY. 607-871-2184
Brown, K, *Librn,* Dakota County Library System (West Saint Paul Branch), West St Paul MN. 612-457-8497
Brown, Karen, *Ch & YA,* Robeson County Public Library, Lumberton NC. 919-738-4859
Brown, Karla, *Librn,* Muskegon County Library (Fruitport), Muskegon MI. 616-865-3461
Brown, Katherine M, *Asst Librn,* Muncie-Center Township Public Library, Muncie IN. 317-288-9971
Brown, Kathleen, *Media,* Bates College, George and Helen Ladd Library, Lewiston ME. 207-784-2949
Brown, Kathleen, *US Doc,* Cambria County Library System, Johnstown PA. 814-536-5131
Brown, Kathryn, *Librn,* Newbury Public Library, Newbury MA. 617-465-0539
Brown, Kathryn E, *Librn,* Clear Lake City Library, Clear Lake SD. 605-874-2013
Brown, Kathy, *Media & Cat,* Centenary College of Louisiana, Magale Library, Shreveport LA. 318-869-5170
Brown, Keith G, *Asst Librn,* General Dynamics-Fort Worth Division, Technical Library, Fort Worth TX. 817-732-4811, Ext 4319, 4320
Brown, Kenneth, *Dir,* Asheville-Buncombe Library System, Asheville NC. 704-252-8701
Brown, Laura Ferris, *Librn,* American Arbitration Association, Eastman Arbitration Library, New York NY. 212-484-4127
Brown, Laure H, *Librn,* National Capital Planning Commission, Washington DC. 202-724-0174
Brown, Laurie, *Acq,* Millsaps College, Millsaps-Wilson Library, Jackson MS. 601-354-5201, Ext 324
Brown, Leah M, *Sci,* Slippery Rock State College Library, Slippery Rock PA. 412-794-2510
Brown, Leander T, *Librn,* Olwine, Connelly, Chase, O'donnell & Weyher Library, New York NY. 212-688-0400, Ext 212
Brown, Lee C, *Dir,* Widener College, Wolfgram Memorial Library, Chester PA. 215-876-5551, Ext 424
Brown, Lena, *Librn,* Centralia Community Library, Centralia KS. 913-857-3331
Brown, Leslie, *Librn,* Harwich Port Library Association, Harwich Port MA. 617-432-3320
Brown, Lillian, *Librn,* Wakefield Public Library, Wakefield NH. 603-522-3335
Brown, Lillian, *Tech Serv & Cat,* Willard Library, Battle Creek MI. 616-968-8166
Brown, Linda, *Librn,* Cumberland County Public Library (Hope Mills Branch), Hope Mills NC. 919-425-8455
Brown, Linda, *Media & Tech Serv,* Manistee County Library, Manistee MI. 616-723-2519
Brown, Linda, *In Charge,* Yale University Library (Observatory), New Haven CT. 203-436-3460
Brown, Linda S, *Dir,* Palisade Public Library, Palisade NE. 308-285-3320
Brown, Lisle G, *Rare Bks & Spec Coll,* Marshall University, James E Morrow Library, Huntington WV. 304-696-3120
Brown, Liz, *ILL,* Worcester County Library, Snow Hill MD. 301-632-2600
Brown, Lois, *Acq,* Drexel University Library, Philadelphia PA. 215-895-2750
Brown, Lola, *Librn,* Eugene Bible College Library, Eugene OR. 503-485-1780
Brown, Lorene B, *Assoc Prof,* Atlanta University, School of Library & Information Studies, GA. 404-681-0251, Ext 312
Brown, Lorna, *Librn,* Ontario Ministry of Revenue Library, Toronto ON. 416-965-3832
Brown, Louise, *Archivist,* H Grady Bradshaw Chambers County Library and Cobb Memorial Archives, Shawmut AL. 205-768-3150
Brown, Louise, *Librn,* Platte County Public Library (Chugwater Branch), Chugwater WY. 307-422-3366
Brown, Louise R, *Dir,* Wayland Free Public Library, Wayland MA. 617-358-2311, 358-2308
Brown, Lucille, *Bibliog Instr,* State University of New York, College at New Paltz, Sojourner Truth Library, New Paltz NY. 914-257-2204
Brown, Lynn, *Librn,* Milford Public Library (Devon), Devon CT. 203-874-3021
Brown, Lynne, *Actg Dir,* Chatham Public Library, Chatham ON. 519-354-2940

Brown, M, *Ch,* Barrie Public Library, Barrie ON. 705-728-1010
Brown, Mae, *Librn,* Piedmont Public Library, Piedmont AL. 205-447-8274
Brown, Mae A, *Adminr,* Southwest Missouri Library Service, Inc, MO. 417-326-4395
Brown, Margaret, *Regional Admin,* Central Massachusetts Regional Library System, Worcester MA. 617-752-3751
Brown, Margaret, *ILL & Ref,* Nichols Library, Naperville IL. 312-355-1540
Brown, Mariam E, *Dir,* Winterset Public Library, Winterset IA. 515-462-1731
Brown, Marie, *Ref,* Rogers Memorial Library, Southampton NY. 516-283-0774
Brown, Marie, *Librn,* Shoals Public Library, Shoals IN. 812-247-3591
Brown, Marina, *Acq,* Wells College, Louis Jefferson Long Library, Aurora NY. 315-364-3351
Brown, Martha, *Librn,* YWCA Library, Montreal PQ. 514-866-9941
Brown, Marva C, *Cat, Ref & Rare Bks,* Washington County Library, Saint George UT. 801-673-2562
Brown, Mary, *Bkmobile Coordr,* Washington County Free Library, Hagerstown MD. 301-739-3250
Brown, Mary A, *Dir,* Rye Free Reading Room, Rye NY. 914-967-0480
Brown, Mary Alice, *Librn,* Indianapolis-Marion County Public Library (Westlane), Indianapolis IN. 317-635-5662
Brown, Mary Ann, *Reader Serv,* Duke University (Medical Center Library), Durham NC. 919-684-2092
Brown, Mary Anna, *Dir,* Seward County Community College, Learning Resource Center, Liberal KS. 316-624-1951
Brown, Mary Grace Hawkins, *Librn,* Petersburg General Hospital, Medical Health Sciences Library, Petersburg VA. 804-732-7220, Ext 250, 251
Brown, Mary Ruth, *Assoc Dir,* University of Kentucky, Margaret I King Library, Lexington KY. 606-257-3801
Brown, Maxine, *Bus Mgr,* Aurora Public Library, Aurora CO. 303-750-5000, Ext 410
Brown, Melody, *Ch,* Rhode Island Department of State Library Services, Providence RI. 401-277-2726
Brown, Michael, *Assoc Librn & Acq,* Messiah College, Murray Learning Resources Center, Grantham PA. 717-766-2511, Ext 380
Brown, Mirneal C, *Acq,* University of Tennessee at Chattanooga Library, Chattanooga TN. 615-755-4701
Brown, Morton R, *Librn,* Smith Barney Harris Upham & Co, Inc Library, New York NY. 212-399-6294
Brown, Mrs Floyd S, *Librn,* Bethlehem Public Library, Bethlehem NH. 603-869-2409
Brown, Mrs G, *Asst Librn,* Sangudo Junior Senior High School and Public Library, Sangudo AB. 403-785-2212
Brown, Muriel, *Tech Serv,* Wascana Institute of Applied Arts & Sciences, Resource & Information Center, Regina SK. 306-565-4321
Brown, N A, *Librn,* University of Saskatchewan Library, Saskatoon SK. 306-343-4216
Brown, Nancy, *Librn,* Chenoa Free Public Library, Chenoa IL. 815-945-4253
Brown, Nancy, *Librn,* Essex County Public Library (McGregor Branch), McGregor ON. 519-776-5241
Brown, Nancy Jo, *Cat,* Turner Free Library, Randolph MA. 617-963-3000
Brown, Nancy W, *Librn,* Mildred Stevens Williams Memorial Library, Appleton ME. 207-785-3448
Brown, Norene, *Librn,* Tidioute Public Library, Tidioute PA. 814-484-3581
Brown, Pamala J, *Librn,* Harford County Library (Aberdeen Branch), Aberdeen MD. 301-272-0520
Brown, Pamela, *Tech Serv,* Oak Lawn Public Library, Oak Lawn IL. 312-422-4990
Brown, Pamela, *Dir,* Waushara-Green Lake Cooperative Library Service, Berlin WI. 414-361-1916
Brown, Patricia, *Health Network Librn,* Eastern Oregon State College, Walter M Pierce Library, La Grande OR. 503-963-2171, Ext 240

Brown, Patricia, *Ch,* Pittsford Community Library, Pittsford NY. 716-586-1251

Brown, Patricia B, *Dir, On-Line Servs & Bibliog Instr,* National College of Chiropractic, Sordoni-Burich Library, Lombard IL. 312-629-2000, Ext 50

Brown, Patricia F, *Librn,* Interchurch Center, Ecumenical Library, New York NY. 212-678-6081

Brown, Patricia I, *Asst Librn,* Suffolk University College Library (Law), Boston MA. 617-723-4700, Ext 176

Brown, Paula, *Ref & Supvr,* Batten, Barton, Durstine & Osborn, Inc, Information Retrieval Center, New York NY. 212-355-5800, Ext 101

Brown, Peter, *Humanities & Urban Studies,* Ryerson Polytechnical Institute, Donald Mordell Learning Resources Centre, Toronto ON. 416-595-5331

Brown, Philip, *Bibliog Instr,* South Dakota State University, Hilton M Briggs Library, Brookings SD. 605-688-5106

Brown, Pia, *Philos-Relig,* Oregon State University, William Jasper Kerr Library, Corvallis OR. 503-754-3411

Brown, Pollye, *Librn,* Houston Public Library (Johnson), Houston TX. 713-733-1983

Brown, R W, *Librn,* Sidney Public Library, Sidney NE. 308-254-3110

Brown, Ralphina, *Asst Librn,* Fiske Public Library, Wrentham MA. 617-384-2761

Brown, Raymond K, *Media,* Roanoke College Library, Salem VA. 703-389-2351, Ext 202

Brown, Rebecca, *Cat,* Assemblies of God Graduate School Library, Cordas C Burnett Library, Springfield MO. 417-862-2781, Ext 5505

Brown, Regina A, *Librn,* Ohio State University Libraries (Geology Library), Columbus OH. 614-422-2428

Brown, Rhunetta, *Bkmobile Coordr,* Bladen County Public Library, Elizabethtown NC. 919-862-8171

Brown, Richard, *Bkmobile Coordr,* Topeka Public Library, Topeka KS. 913-233-2040

Brown, Richard E, *Asst Dir,* Berkeley Public Library, Berkeley CA. 415-644-6095

Brown, Richard H, *Dir Res & Educ,* Newberry Library, Chicago IL. 312-943-9090

Brown, Richard L, *Librn,* Colorado Division of Planning, Planning Library, Denver CO. 303-839-2351

Brown, Richard L, *Asst Dir,* Florida State University (Law Library), Tallahassee FL. 904-644-1004

Brown, Ricki, *Ad,* Chattahoochee Valley Regional Library, W C Bradley Memorial Library, Headquarters, Columbus GA. 404-327-0211

Brown, Robert, *Dir,* Archives of American Art, New England Area Center, Boston MA. 617-223-0951

Brown, Robert, *Librn, ILL & Rare Bks,* Northeastern Christian Junior College, Anna Whitworth Library, Villanova PA. 215-525-6780

Brown, Robert M, *Adjunct Prof,* East Carolina University, Dept of Library Science, NC. 919-757-6621, 757-6627

Brown, Robin, *Librn,* Alberta Treasury Department Library, Edmonton AB. 403-427-7595

Brown, Ronda, *YA & Ref,* Jennings County Public Library, North Vernon IN. 812-346-2091

Brown, Ruth, *Acq,* Shreve Memorial Library, Shreveport LA. 318-221-2614

Brown, Ruth H, *Librn,* Mary E Bartlett Memorial Library, Brentwood NH. 603-642-3355

Brown, Ruth I, *Asst Dir & Ch,* Paramus Public Library, Paramus NJ. 201-265-1800

Brown, Ruth J, *Cat,* Methodist Theological School in Ohio Library, Delaware OH. 614-363-1146, Ext 242

Brown, Sallie, *Librn,* Jackson Public Library, Jackson AL. 205-246-4962

Brown, Sally, *Acq,* West Virginia University (Medical Center Library), Morgantown WV. 304-293-2113

Brown, Sandra, *Circ & Per,* Mount Marty College Library, Yankton SD. 605-668-1555

Brown, Sarah K, *Librn,* Southern Company, Birmingham AL. 205-870-6011

Brown, Sharon, *Librn,* Conoco, Inc, Minerals Department Library, Denver CO. 303-575-6025

Brown, Sharon, *Asst Librn,* New York Society Library, New York NY. 212-288-6900

Brown, Sheryl, *Librn,* Northwood Institute Library (Freedom Education Center), Cedar Hill TX. 214-291-7466

Brown, Shirley, *Librn,* Durham County Library (Stanford L Warren), Durham NC. 919-688-8027

Brown, Shirley, *Librn,* Leesburg Public Library (Branch Number 1), Leesburg FL. 904-787-6607

Brown, Shirley, *Librn,* Sherwin-Williams Co of Canada Ltd, Technical Library, Montreal PQ. 514-933-8611, Ext 206

Brown, Shirley G, *Librn,* First United Presbyterian Church Library, Norwalk OH. 419-668-1923

Brown, Sister Elizabeth, *Dir,* College of Mount Saint Joseph on the Ohio, Archbishop Alter Library, Mount Saint Joseph OH. 513-244-4216

Brown, Sonja I, *Librn,* Carnegie Library, Jefferson TX. 214-665-8911

Brown, Stanley W, *Pub Serv,* Dartmouth College, Baker Memorial Library, Hanover NH. 603-646-2235

Brown, Stephen, *Asst Dir,* Cedarville College Library, Cedarville OH. 513-766-2211, Ext 207

Brown, Stephen, *USDA,* University of Georgia Libraries, Athens GA. 404-542-2716

Brown, Sue, *Acq,* Louisiana State University in Shreveport Library, Shreveport LA. 318-797-7121, Ext 203

Brown, Susan, *Ch,* Boise Public Library & Information Center, Boise ID. 208-384-4466

Brown, Suzanne, *Librn,* Newport News Public Library System (Virgil I Grissom), Newport News VA. 804-877-0111

Brown, Tim, *Librn,* Washington State Library (Washington State Penitentiary Library), Walla Walla WA. 509-525-3610

Brown, Timothy A, *Librn,* Boise State University Library, Boise ID. 208-385-1234

Brown, Travis, *In Charge,* Texas Education Agency (Region XVII), Lubbock TX. 806-763-4127

Brown, Vada, *ILL,* Davidson County Public Library System, Lexington NC. 704-246-2520

Brown, Viola, *Reclass,* Saint Louis University (Omer Poos Law Library), Saint Louis MO. 314-658-2755

Brown, Walter, *Dept Head,* Georgia Southern College, Library - Media, GA. 912-681-5204

Brown, Wanda, *Ch,* Niobrara County Library, Lusk WY. 307-334-3490

Brown, Wendell, *Proc,* Public Library of the District of Columbia, Martin Luther King Memorial Library, Washington DC. 202-727-1101

Brown, Wendy, *Culture,* Lake Ontario Regional Library System, Kingston ON. 613-546-9400

Brown, Wendy, *Pub Servs,* Lake Ontario Regional Library System, Kingston ON. 613-546-9400

Brown, Wendy, *Librn,* Northumberland Union Public Library, Trenton ON. 613-392-1400

Brown, Wilda, *Acq,* University of Albuquerque, Center for Learning & Information Resources, Albuquerque NM. 505-831-1111, Ext 230

Brown, Wilma E, *Dir,* Malheur County Library, Ontario Public Library, Ontario OR. 503-889-6371

Brown, Winnie, *Librn,* San Saba County Library, Rylander Memorial Library, San Saba TX. 915-372-3079

Brown, Wm G, *Dir,* Fairbanks Museum & Planetarium Library, Saint Johnsbury VT. 802-748-2372

Brown, Yvonne C, *Librn,* Port of Portland Library, Portland OR. 503-233-5000

Brown, Jr, Bennie, *Librn,* Gunston Hall Plantation Library, Lorton VA. 703-550-9220

Brown, Jr, George, *Asst Dir & Ch,* Burlington County Library, Mount Holly NJ. 609-267-9660

Brown-Hicks, Joan, *Commun Servs,* Halifax City Regional Library, Halifax NS. 902-426-6980

Browne, Ann C, *Circ,* Sacred Heart College, McCarthy Library, Belmont NC. 704-825-5146

Browne, D A, *Coordr,* Hercules Inc, Technical Information Center, McGregor TX. 817-840-2811, Ext 1503

Browne, Emily, *Librn,* New York Public Library (Todt Hill-Westerleigh), New York NY. 212-442-8373

Browne, Joseph P, *Dir,* University of Portland, Wilson W Clark Memorial Library, Portland OR. 503-283-7111

Browne, Joseph P, *Libr Sci, Sci & Theol,* University of Portland, Wilson W Clark Memorial Library, Portland OR. 503-283-7111

Browne, Mamie G, *Archivist,* Alabama Agricultural & Mechanical University, Joseph F Drake Memorial Learning Resources Center, Normal AL. 205-859-7309

Browne, Russell A, *Dir,* Dalton Junior College, Library Resource Center, Dalton GA. 404-278-3113, Ext 237, 247

Browne, Walt, *Dir,* Northeast Regional Library, Corinth MS. 601-287-2441

Brownell, Diane C, *Librn,* Tunbridge Public Library, Tunbridge VT. 802-889-3341

Brownell, Richard, *Librn,* Solano County Library, Fairfield-Suisun Community, Fairfield CA. 707-429-6631

Brownfield, Tom, *Dir,* Canal Fulton Public Library, Canal Fulton OH. 216-854-4148

Browning, Donna, *Librn,* Deaconess Hospital, Medical Library, Buffalo NY. 716-886-4400

Browning, Eva, *Media Spec,* Pasco-Hernando Community College, North Campus Learning Resources Center, Brooksville FL. 904-796-6726

Browning, Grace F, *Librn,* Jackson County Library System (Phoenix Branch), Phoenix OR. 503-535-4102

Browning, James, *Librn,* The Citadel (Chemistry), Charleston SC. 803-792-7793

Browning, Mary, *Ch, Reader Serv & On-Line Servs,* United States Air Force (Academic Library), Wright-Patterson AFB OH. 513-255-5894

Browning, Paul D, *Dir,* Hubbard Memorial Library, Ludlow MA. 413-583-3408

Browning, Phyllis, *Librn,* Beckman Instruments, Inc, Spinco Div Technical Library, Palo Alto CA. 415-326-1970

Browning, Ruth, *Ref,* Upper Arlington Public Library, Upper Arlington OH. 614-486-9621

Browning, Ruth H, *Librn,* Christopher Public Library, Christopher IL. 618-724-7534

Browning, Sue, *Librn,* Miami-Dade Public Library System (Coconut Grove), Miami FL. 305-442-8695

Brownlee, Annette, *Instrnl Servs,* Barat College Library, Lake Forest IL. 312-234-3000, Ext 237

Brownlee, Brenda, *Interpretation Officer,* Parks Canada, Fort Malden National Historic Park Library, Amherstburg ON. 519-736-5416

Brownlee, Doris F, *Librn,* Saint Clair County Library (Springville), Springville AL. 205-884-1685

Brownlee, Jerry W, *Dir,* Palm Beach County Public Library System, West Palm Beach FL. 305-686-0895

Brownlee, Mrs D M, *Librn,* Stettler Municipal Library, Stettler AB. 403-742-2305

Brownlee, Richard S, *Dir,* State Historical Society of Missouri Library, Columbia MO. 314-443-3165

Brownlow, Jennifer, *Librn,* Nova Scotia Institute of Technology Library, Halifax NS. 902-424-4333

Brownlow, Judith, *Librn,* National Marine Fisheries Service, Northeast Fisheries Center Library, Woods Hole MA. 617-548-5123, Ext 60

Brownridge, Ina C, *Chmn,* Five Associated University Libraries, NY. 315-423-3021

Brownridge, Ina C, *Dir,* State University of New York at Binghamton Library, Binghamton NY. 607-798-2194

Brownson, Charles W, *Ref & Bibliog Instr,* Christopher Newport College, Captain John Smith Library, Newport News VA. 804-599-7130

Broxton, Rita, *Librn,* Central Florida Regional Library (Bronson), Ocala FL. 904-486-2354

Brozena, Susan, *Ch,* Township of Hamilton Free Public Library, Trenton NJ. 609-890-3460

Brubaker, Constance, *Instr,* Georgia Southern College, Library - Media, GA. 912-681-5204

Brubaker, Eva M, *Librn,* Nappanee Public Library, Nappanee IN. 219-773-4932

Brubaker, Jan, *Librn,* Warder Public Library (Houston Memorial), South Charleston OH. 513-462-8047

Brubaker, Maryellen, *Dir,* Cortez City Library, Cortez CO. 303-565-8117

Brubaker, Robert L, *Chief Librn,* Chicago Historical Society Library, Chicago IL. 312-642-4600

Brubeker, Marcia J, *Librn,* Jerome Public Library, Jerome AZ. 602-634-8992

Bruce, Ann Minnick, *Librn,* Florida State Hospital, Health Science Library, Chattahoochee FL. 904-663-7453

Bruce, Betty, *Spec Coll,* Monroe County Public Library, Key West FL. 305-294-7100
Bruce, Danny, *Librn,* Penniman & Browne Inc Library, Baltimore MD. 301-825-4131
Bruce, Dennis L, *Dir,* Spartanburg County Public Library, Spartanburg SC. 582-4123 & 585-2441
Bruce, Elizabeth, *Special Services,* Lewis & Clark College, Aubrey R Watzek Library, Portland OR. 503-244-6161, Ext 400
Bruce, Gerald, *Oral Hist,* Lancaster County Library, Lancaster PA. 717-394-2651
Bruce, Helen, *Librn,* British Columbia Ministry of Economic Development Library, Victoria BC. 604-387-3315
Bruce, Jane, *Ref,* Girard Free Public Library, Girard OH. 216-545-2508
Bruce, Lorne D, *Dir,* King Township Public Library, King City ON. 416-833-5101
Bruce, Marie, *Librn,* Ripley Free Library, Ripley NY. 716-736-3913
Bruce, Mary, *Librn,* Forsyth County Public Library (Thruway), Winston-Salem NC. 919-727-2337
Bruce, Nancy, *Librn,* Garnavillo Public Library, Garnavillo IA. 319-964-2119
Bruce, Pamela, *Librn,* National Film, Television & Sound Archives Library, Public Archives of Canada, Ottawa ON. 613-995-1311, Ext 23, 25
Bruce, Patricia, *Tech Serv,* John C Calhoun State Community College, Albert P Brewer Library, Decatur AL. 205-353-3102
Bruce, Robert, *Hist & Travel,* Minneapolis Public Library & Information Center, Minneapolis MN. 612-372-6500
Bruce, Ruth, *Ad,* Scottsbluff Public Library, Scottsbluff NE. 308-632-4424
Brucha, Beverly, *Dir,* Champlain Regional College, Saint Lambert Campus Resource Centre, Saint Lambert PQ. 514-672-7360, Ext 220, 221
Bruchey, Margaret, *Librn,* Frederick County Public Library (Thurmont), Frederick MD. 301-694-1613
Brucker, Linn, *AV,* Columbus College, Simon Schwob Memorial Library, Columbus GA. 404-568-2042
Brucker, Wonja K, *Librn,* Schenectady County Public Library (Duane), Schenectady NY. 518-382-3504
Bruckner, Sue, *Librn,* First Regional Library (Crenshaw Public), Crenshaw MS. 601-382-5272
Brude, Deborah, *Coordr,* Anoka Area Vocational Technical Institute, Media Center, Anoka MN. 612-427-1800, Ext 250
Bruder, Boris, *Ser,* University of Waterloo Library, Waterloo ON. 519-885-1211
Bruder, Catherine, *Asst Supvr,* Waterloo Regional Library (Bloomingdale), Bloomingdale ON. 519-745-3151
Bruder, Helen, *Librn,* Niagara Falls Public Library (Chippawa), Niagara Falls ON. 416-295-3541
Brudvig, Glenn, *Dir,* University of Minnesota Libraries-Twin Cities (Bio-Medical Library), Minneapolis MN. 612-373-5585
Brudvig, Karen, *Librn,* Baptist Hospital Fund, Midway School of Nursing Library, Saint Paul MN. 612-641-5500
Brudwick, Marlys, *Librn,* Ferndale Public Library, Ferndale WA. 206-384-1472
Brueck, Lora, *Spec Coll,* Worcester Polytechnic Institute, George C Gordon Library, Worcester MA. 617-753-1411, Ext 410
Bruegging, Carol, *Librn,* Nevada State Hospital, Patients Library, Nevada MO. 417-667-3355
Bruemmer, Alice, *Librn,* Allstate Insurance Law Library, Northbrook IL. 312-291-5407, 6014
Bruemmer, Bruce, *Archivist,* Northeast Minnesota Historical Center, Duluth MN. 218-726-8526
Bruening, Grace C, *Asst Dir & Ref,* Glen Rock Public Library, Glen Rock NJ. 201-445-4222, 445-4223
Bruening, Julian C, *Dir,* Illinois Library Materials Processing Center, IL. 815-398-2441
Bruenjes, Alice, *Librn,* Jewish Hospital of Saint Louis (School of Nursing), Saint Louis MO. 314-454-8474
Bruff, William, *Media,* Foothill College, Hubert H Semans Library, Los Altos Hills CA. 415-948-8590, Ext 390, 391
Brugger, Arden, *Ad,* Jacksonville Public Library System, Haydon Burns Library, Jacksonville FL. 904-633-6870
Brugger, Jane E, *Cat,* Marshall University, James E Morrow Library, Huntington WV. 304-696-3120

Bruguera, Jorge, *ILL & Ref,* Foothill College, Hubert H Semans Library, Los Altos Hills CA. 415-948-8590, Ext 390, 391
Bruhl, Ella May, *Dir,* Fox River Grove Public Library District, Fox River Grove IL. 312-639-2274
Bruhn, Mildred S, *Librn,* UOP, Inc (Patent Library), Des Plaines IL. 312-391-2008
Bruhn, Mrs V, *Ad & Tech Serv,* Vaughan Public Libraries, Maple ON. 416-832-1432
Bruhn, Pauline, *Asst Librn,* Antioch Township Library, Antioch IL. 312-395-0874
Bruington, Harry, *Ref,* Pacific Union College, W E Nelson Memorial Library, Angwin CA. 707-965-6241
Bruland, Magdalene, *Tech Serv & Cat,* Clatsop Community College Library, Astoria OR. 503-324-0910
Bruland, Osborne Y, *Dir,* Faith Evangelical Lutheran Seminary Library, Tacoma WA. 206-752-2020
Brule, Francoise, *Prof,* College Lionel-Groulx, Techniques de la Documentation, PQ. 514-430-3120, Ext 261
Brumback, Sister Una M, *Librn,* Avila College, Hooley-Bundschu Library, Kansas City MO. 816-942-8400, Ext 220
Brumbaugh, Dorothy, *Librn,* Lowell Observatory Library, Flagstaff AZ. 602-774-3358, Ext 29
Brumbaugh, Mary C, *Dir,* Putnam Public Library, Putnam CT. 203-928-6489
Brumfield, Cindy, *Librn,* Cumberland College of Tennessee, Mitchell Library, Lebanon TN. 615-444-2562
Brumfield, Linda, *Librn,* Cabell County Public Library (West Huntington Public), Huntington WV. 304-525-2181
Brumley, Sherry, *Asst Librn,* Sabine Parish Library (Converse Branch), Converse LA. 318-256-2212
Brun, Christian, *Rare Bks & Spec Coll,* University of California, Santa Barbara Library, Santa Barbara CA. 805-961-2741
Brundage, Louise, *Computerized Serv,* Hamden Library, Miller Memorial, Hamden CT. 203-248-7747
Brundin, R, *Assoc Prof,* University of Alberta, Faculty of Library Science, AB. 403-432-4578
Brune, Christopher, *Ad, Tech Serv & Auto Proj Dir,* Pequannock Township Public Library, Pompton Plains NJ. 201-835-7460
Bruneau, Andre, *Tech Serv,* Bibliotheque Municipale De Sherbrooke, Sherbrooke Municipal Library, Sherbrooke PQ. 819-565-5860, 565-5861 & 565-5862
Bruneau, Theresa, *Librn,* Conference Board in Canada, Information Div Library, Ottawa ON. 613-746-1261
Brunelle, Eugene A, *Adjunct Prof,* East Carolina University, Dept of Library Science, NC. 919-757-6621, 757-6627
Brunelle, Eugene A, *Dir,* East Carolina University, J Y Joyner Library, Greenville NC. 919-757-6514
Brunelle, Margaret, *ILL,* North Park College & Theological Seminary (Wallgren Library), Chicago IL. 312-583-2700
Bruner, Gilda, *Dir,* Greenwood Lake Public Library, Greenwood Lake NY. 914-477-8377
Bruner, M R, *Librn & Tech Serv,* R Stresau Laboratory, Inc Library, Spooner WI. 715-635-2777
Bruner, Mary Ann, *County Bookmobile Librn,* Hattiesburg Public Library System, Hattiesburg MS. 601-582-4461
Bruneske, Kathy J, *Dir,* Alexander Hamilton Free Memorial Library, Waynesboro Library, Waynesboro PA. 717-762-3335
Brunet, Fran, *Chief Librn,* Esherick Homsey Dodge & Davis Library, San Francisco CA. 415-285-9193
Brunet, Jocelyne, *Cat,* Chateauguay Municipal Library, Chateauguay PQ. 514-691-1934
Brunet, Lise, *Asst Prof,* University of Montreal, Ecole de Bibliotheconomie, PQ. 514-343-6044
Brungard, Freda, *Pub Servs,* Annie Halenbake Ross Library, Lock Haven PA. 717-748-3321
Brunjes, Elizabeth, *Ch,* Milford Public Library, Milford IN. 219-658-4312
Brunk, Erma H, *Acq,* Eastern Mennonite College & Seminary Library, Harrisonburg VA. 703-433-2771, Ext 171
Brunka, Veronica, *Librn,* Ontario Ministry of Health Library, Toronto ON. 416-965-7881

Brunner, Helen, *Coordr,* Visual Studies Workshop Research Center, Rochester NY. 716-442-8676
Brunner, Karen B, *Librn,* Morris County Law Library, Morristown NJ. 201-285-6497
Brunning, Diana, *Pub Servs & Bibliog Instr,* Lincoln Land Community College, Learning Resources Center, Springfield IL. 217-786-2354
Brunnschweyer, Tamara, *Latin Am,* Michigan State University Library, East Lansing MI. 517-355-2344
Bruno, Barbara, *Asst Dir, ILL & Ref,* Beverly Public Library, Beverly MA. 617-922-0310
Bruno, Florence, *Ch,* Oakfield Public Library, Haxton Memorial Library, Oakfield NY. 716-948-9900
Bruno, Frank P, *Chief Bk Delivery,* Boston Public Library, Eastern Massachusetts Library System, Boston MA. 617-536-5400
Bruno, Melba, *Librn,* National Agricultural Library (DC Branch), Washington DC. 301-344-4248
Bruns, Edna R, *Asst Dir,* South Whitley-Cleveland Township Public Library, South Whitley IN. 219-723-5321
Bruns, Joyce, *Media,* Radford University, John Preston McConnell Library, Radford VA. 703-731-5471, 5472
Bruns, Robert, *Instr,* University of Colorado, Educational Technology Program, CO. 303-492-5141 & 492-6715
Brunsman, Patricia, *Dir,* Nanuet Public Library, Nanuet NY. 914-623-4281
Brunson, Madelon, *Archivist,* Reorganized Church of Jesus Christ of Latter Day Saints, Independence MO. 816-833-1000, Ext 400
Brunson, Ruth, *Dir,* University of Arkansas at Little Rock Library (University of Arkansas at Little Rock School of Law & Pulaski County Law Library), Little Rock AR. 501-371-1071
Brunswick, Sheldon, *Judaica,* University of California, Berkeley (University Library), Berkeley CA. 415-642-3773
Bruntjen, Scott, *Exec Dir,* Pittsburgh Regional Library Center, (PRLC), PA. 412-441-6409, 661-8868
Brunton, Angela, *Librn,* California Division of Mines & Geology Library, San Francisco CA. 415-557-0308
Brunton, David W, *Asst Dir,* Englewood Public Library, Englewood CO. 303-761-4376
Brunton, Marilyn, *Ch,* Lake Agassiz Regional Library, Moorhead MN. 218-233-7594
Brunton, Shirley, *Librn,* Dakota City Public Library, Dakota City NE. 402-987-3778
Bruntsen, Scott, *Coordr,* Interlibrary Delivery Service of Pennsylvania, PA. 412-441-6409
Brusa, June, *Librn,* Santa Cruz Public Library (Boulder Creek Branch), Boulder Creek CA. 408-336-5639338-6340
Bruser, Barbara, *Librn,* Rosenberg Capital Management, Research Library, San Francisco CA. 415-777-5474
Brush, Carolyn, *Cat,* Muncie-Center Township Public Library, Muncie IN. 317-288-9971
Brush, Maryanne, *Asst Dir,* Jefferson County Public Library, Lakewood CO. 303-238-8411
Brustman, Mary Jane, *Ch,* Rice Public Library, Kittery ME. 207-439-1553
Bruun, Lila, *Librn,* Bemidji Public Library, Bemidji MN. 218-751-3963
Bruvelheide, Janis H, *Dir & Prof,* Montana State University, Library Science Dept, MT. 406-994-2851, 994-4752
Bryan, Arthur L, *Dir,* Jacob Edwards Library, Southbridge MA. 617-764-2544
Bryan, Barbara D, *Dir & Acq,* Fairfield University, Gustav & Dagmar Nyselius Library, Fairfield CT. 203-255-5411, Ext 2451
Bryan, Carla, *Dir,* Northwood Institute Library, Cedar Hill TX. 291-1541 Ext 28
Bryan, Deborah, *Ch,* Macomb City Public Library, Macomb IL. 309-833-2714
Bryan, Ed, *Dir,* Panhandle State University, Marvin E McKee Library, Goodwell OK. 405-349-2611
Bryan, Eleanor, *Acq,* University of Calgary Library (Faculty of Medicine Medical Library), Calgary AB. 403-284-6858
Bryan, Jane, *Ref,* University of Pennsylvania Libraries, Van Pelt Library, Philadelphia PA. 215-243-7091
Bryan, Jane C, *Dir,* Pike-Amite-Walthall Library System, McComb Public Library (Headquarters), McComb MS. 601-684-7034

Bryan, Linda, *Ref,* Johns-Manville Corporation (Research Information Center), Denver CO. 303-979-1000, Ext 4471, 4374

Bryan, Linda S, *Librn,* Dun & Bradstreet Business Library, New York NY. 212-285-7304

Bryan, Margaret, *Librn,* Guymon Public Library, Guymon OK. 405-338-7330

Bryan, Marie E, *Librn,* Willows Public Library, Willows CA. 916-934-5156

Bryan, Marquerite, *Librn,* Wellington County Public Library (Arthur Branch), Arthur ON. 519-848-3493

Bryan, Patricia, *Librn,* Elkin Public Library, Elkin NC. 919-835-5586

Bryan, Rebecca, *Ser,* Eastern Oregon State College, Walter M Pierce Library, La Grande OR. 503-963-2171, Ext 240

Bryan, Virgina, *Dir,* Bossier Parish Community College Library, Bossier City LA. 318-746-9851

Bryan, Vivian, *Law & Doc,* State of Vermont Department of Libraries, Montpelier VT. 802-828-3261

Bryan, Jr, Edwin H, *Dir,* Pacific Scientific Information Center, Honolulu HI. 808-847-3511

Bryant, Allison D, *Librn,* Edgecliff College, Brennan Memorial Library, Cincinnati OH. 513-961-3770

Bryant, Audrey, *Librn,* Sacramento Public Library (Fruitridge), Sacramento CA. 916-440-5926

Bryant, Barton, *Asst Librn,* Kinnelon Public Library, Kinnelon NJ. 201-838-1321

Bryant, Beverly, *Librn,* Brandon Township Public Library, Ortonville MI. 313-627-2804, Ext 44

Bryant, Brenda, *Dir,* Abilene Christian University at Dallas, Resources Center, Garland TX. 214-279-6511

Bryant, Catherine M, *ILL & AV,* Colquitt-Thomas Regional Library, Moultrie-Colquitt County Library, Moultrie GA. 912-985-6540

Bryant, Charles R, *Curator SE Asia Coll,* Yale University Library (Sterling Memorial Library), New Haven CT. 203-436-8335

Bryant, Dorothy, *Librn,* KLI, Inc, Medical Technology Internationale, Inc Library, Ivyland PA. 215-322-0210

Bryant, Ellen, *Librn,* Centre County Library & Historical Museum (Aaronsburg Branch), Aaronsburg PA. 814-349-5328

Bryant, Ellen K, *YA,* Glencoe Public Library, Glencoe IL. 312-835-5056

Bryant, Fred D, *Dir & Spec Coll,* University of South Florida (Medical Center Library), Tampa FL. 813-974-2399

Bryant, Hazel, *Asst Dir & Tech Serv,* Transylvania County Library, Inc, Brevard NC. 704-883-9880

Bryant, Jean, *Dir,* Industry Hills Exhibit Conference Center, Ralph W Miller Golf Library, City of Industry CA. 213-965-0861, Ext 221

Bryant, John, *Tech Serv,* University of Kentucky, Margaret I King Library, Lexington KY. 606-257-3801

Bryant, Juanita, *Librn,* Pike County Free Public Library, Waverly OH. 614-947-4921

Bryant, June, *Asst Dir & Cat,* Brooks Memorial Library, Brattleboro VT. 802-254-5290

Bryant, Karen, *Doc,* Florida International University, North Miami Campus Library, North Miami FL. 305-940-5730

Bryant, Kay, *Librn,* Cotton Free Public Library, Weybridge VT. 802-545-2166

Bryant, Kay, *Librn,* Manchester Public Library, Manchester IA. 319-927-3719

Bryant, L, *In Charge,* State of California Bay Area Quality Control District, Technical Library, San Francisco CA. 415-771-6000, Ext 266

Bryant, Ludmila, *Ad,* Barrington Public Library District, Barrington IL. 312-382-1300

Bryant, Marion, *Acq,* Shaw University, Learning Resources Center, Raleigh NC. 919-755-4930

Bryant, Marjory H, *Librn,* Wilton Free Public Library, Goodspeed Memorial Library, Wilton ME. 207-645-4831

Bryant, Mary, *Librn,* Pike-Amite-Walthall Library System (Martin Luther King Community Center), McComb MS. 601-684-9940

Bryant, Mary L, *Asst Dir & Tech Serv,* Northeastern Oklahoma A&m College, Learning Resources Center, Miami OK. 918-542-8441, Ext 220

Bryant, Maureen E., *Libr Tech,* United States International Trade Commission Library (Law Library), Washington DC. 202-523-0333

Bryant, Mrs James C, *Librn,* Whitewright Public Library, Whitewright TX. 214-364-2510

Bryant, Norah P, *Chief Librn,* Westmount Public Library, Westmount PQ. 514-937-2486

Bryant, Pat K, *ILL & Ref,* New College of the University of South Florida, Sarasota Campus Library, Sarasota FL. 813-355-7671, Ext 214

Bryant, Paul F, *Tech Librn,* Champion International (Champion Papers Technical Library), Hamilton OH. 513-868-4578

Bryant, Prudence W, *Pub Servs,* Alabama Agricultural & Mechanical University, Joseph F Drake Memorial Learning Resources Center, Normal AL. 205-859-7309

Bryant, Sister Nathalee, *Ref & On-Line Servs,* Xavier University of Louisiana Library, New Orleans LA. 504-486-7411, Ext 317

Bryant, Thelma, *Librn,* Dallas County Public Library (Sachse), Garland TX. 214-495-1212

Bryant, Tyrone, *Aid to the Disadvantaged Project Dir,* Broward County Division of Libraries, Broward County Library, Pompano Beach FL. 305-972-1100

Bryant, Tyrone, *Librn,* Broward County Division of Libraries (Collier City Branch), Collier City FL. 305-973-7115

Bryant, Willard, *Librn,* Flint River Regional Library (Peachtree City Branch), Peachtree City GA. 404-487-8557

Bryden, Cathy, *Librn,* Wentworth Library (Lynden Branch), Lynden ON. 416-526-4126

Bryden, Dawn, *Dir,* Dundas Public Library, Dundas ON. 416-627-3507

Brydges, Michael, *Chief Librn,* Red Deer College, Learning Resources Center, Red Deer AB. 403-346-6450

Brydges, Nancy, *Coordr,* Red River Community College, Library Technician Course, MB. 204-632-2150

Bryer, Bruce, *Dir,* Dixon Unified School District Public Library, Dixon Public Library, Dixon CA. 916-678-5447

Bryk, Christine, *Ch,* Your Home Public Library, Johnson City NY. 607-797-4816

Bryk, Donald, *Sci,* Queensborough Community College Library, Bayside NY. 212-631-6226

Bryne, Amanda, *Librn,* Louisville Free Public Library (Crescent Hill), Louisville KY. 502-896-1012

Brynildsen, Palmer, *Librn,* New York University (Tamiment Library & Robert F Wagner Labor Archive), New York NY. 212-598-2484

Brynolfson, Gaylord, *Lit,* Princeton University Library, Princeton NJ. 609-452-3180

Brynteson, Susan, *Dir,* University of Delaware, Hugh M Morris Library, Newark DE. 302-738-2231

Bryson, Emily M, *On-Line Servs,* Chicago State University, Paul & Emily Douglas Library, Chicago IL. 312-995-2254

Bryson, Juliette, *Dir,* Ashland Public Library, Ashland KY. 606-324-4195

Bryson, Kathleen, *Ref,* Transylvania University, Frances Carrick Thomas Library, Lexington KY. 606-233-8225

Bryson, Mary Lee, *Librn,* Shreve Memorial Library (Higginbotham Branch), Greenwood LA. 318-221-2614

Bryson, Natalia, *Librn,* Chatham-Effingham-Liberty Regional Library (Ola Wyeth), Savannah GA. 912-232-5488

Bryson, Rebecca C, *Tech Serv,* Abbeville-Greenwood Regional Library, Greenwood SC. 803-223-4515

Bryson, Ronald, *Chmn & Dir,* Spalding College, Dept of Library Science, KY. 502-585-9341

Bryson, Rozanne L, *Librn,* Systems, Science & Software Library, San Diego CA. 714-453-0060, Ext 384

Bryson, Verena, *Commun Servs,* Greenville County Library, Greenville SC. 803-242-5000

Buback, Joanne, *Librn,* First National City Bank, Advance Mortgage Corp Library, Southfield MI. 313-424-2200

Bublick, Raisa L, *Librn,* Richmond Memorial Library, Marlborough CT. 203-295-0712

Bubnick, Rita, *ILL,* Kewanee Public Library, Kewanee IL. 309-852-4505

Bucci, John, *Ref & Bibliog Instr,* Saint Mary's College of Maryland Library, Saint Mary's City MD. 301-994-1600, Ext 216

Buch, Hanne, *Librn,* Danish Consulate General Library, New York NY. 212-697-5107

Buch, Jane, *ILL,* Delaware Division of Libraries, Dept of Community Affairs & Economic Development, Dover DE. 302-678-4748

Buchan, Janet, *Tech Serv,* Mount Laurel Free Public Library, Mount Laurel NJ. 609-234-7319

Buchan, Phyllis, *Librn,* Fernie Centennial Library, Fernie BC. 604-423-7017

Buchanan, Barbara R, *Librn,* Dow Chemical of Canada, Ltd Library, Sarnia ON. 519-339-3131

Buchanan, Edna M, *Librn,* United States Forest Service, Forestry Sciences Laboratory Library, Princeton WV. 304-425-8106, Ext 263

Buchanan, Gale, *AV,* Schoolcraft College, Eric J Bradner Library, Livonia MI. 313-591-6400, Ext 412

Buchanan, Gerald, *Asst Dir,* Mississippi Library Commission, Jackson MS. 601-354-6369

Buchanan, Gerald, *Assoc Dir,* Mississippi Library Commission, Jackson MS. 601-354-6369

Buchanan, Holly S, *Dir,* Norton-Children's Hospitals, Medical Library, Louisville KY. 502-589-8171

Buchanan, Jack, *Librn & Acq,* Santa Maria Public Library, Santa Maria CA. 805-925-0994, Ext 261

Buchanan, Jack T, *Librn,* Eastman Kodak Co, Texas Eastman Co Research & Development Laboratory, Longview TX. 214-757-6611

Buchanan, Jill, *Ref,* San Diego Mesa College Library, San Diego CA. 714-279-2300, Ext 385

Buchanan, Jim, *Librn,* Housing Advocates, Inc, Law & Consumer Affairs Library, Cleveland OH. 216-579-0575

Buchanan, Karen E, *Librn,* American Stock Exchange, Inc, Martin J Keena Memorial Library, New York NY. 212-938-2280

Buchanan, Matylde M, *Librn,* Natchez College Library, Natchez MS. 601-445-9702

Buchanan, Nancy, *Circ,* Pima Community College, West Campus Learning Resource Center, Tucson AZ. 602-884-6821

Buchanan, Raymond F, *Dir,* Fairport Public Library, Fairport NY. 716-223-9091

Buchanan, William C, *Asst Prof,* East Carolina University, Dept of Library Science, NC. 919-757-6621, 757-6627

Buchen, David, *Media,* University of Wisconsin Center-Rock County Library, Janesville WI. 608-755-2831

Bucher, Mary, *ILL & Ref,* State University of New York Agricultural & Technical College at Canton, Southworth Library, Canton NY. 315-386-7229

Bucher, Ruth, *Ad,* Mount Pleasant Public Library, Pleasantville NY. 914-769-0548

Bucher, Victoria, *Bkmobile Coordr,* South Bend Public Library, South Bend IN. 219-288-4413

Buchheit, Doris, *Dir,* Plumb Memorial Library, Shelton CT. 203-734-3386

Buchheit, Mary, *Librn,* Kingsbrook Jewish Medical Center, Medical Library, Brooklyn NY. 212-756-9700

Buchholz, Chris, *Librn,* Tacoma Department of Public Utilities Library, Tacoma WA. 206-383-2471, Ext 168

Buchholz, Janis, *Ser,* Wayne State University Libraries (Science Library), Detroit MI. 313-577-4066

Buchkovich, Grace, *Librn,* Windber Public Library, Inc, Windber PA. 814-467-4950

Buchman, Kay, *Asst Libr Dir,* Oscar Rose Junior College, Learning Resources Center, Midwest City OK. 405-733-7323, 733-7322

Buchman, Sandra, *Registrar,* Chesapeake Bay Maritime Museum Library, Saint Micheals MD. 301-745-2916

Buchta, Tom, *Dir,* College of Lake County, Learning Resource Center, Grayslake IL. 312-223-6601, Ext 392

Buck, A M, *Libr Supvr,* Bell Telephone Laboratories (Western Electric Technical Library), Reading PA. 929-7493 (Supvr); 929-7250 (Ref)

Buck, Gene, *Librn,* Madison City-County Library, Richmond KY. 606-623-4098

Buck, Jeremy R, *Asst Dir & Ad,* Dayton & Montgomery County Public Library, Dayton OH. 513-224-1651

Buck, Jeremy R, *Asst Dir,* Erie County Library System, Erie PA. 814-452-2333

Buck, Jessie Fern, *Librn,* Dunklin County Library (Senath Branch), Senath MO. 314-738-2363

Buck, Lauretta, *Ser,* Auburn University, Ralph Brown Draughton Library, Auburn AL. 205-826-4500

Buck, Lucy, *Librn,* Riverside Regional Library (Center 4), Altenburg MO. 314-824-5267

Buck, Marjorie, *Asst Dir,* Clyde Public Library, Clyde OH. 419-547-7174

Buck, Marjorie L, *Librn,* First National Bank of Boston, Research Library, Boston MA. 434-2200

Buck, Mary Jane, *Librn,* Duluth Public Library (Woodland), Duluth MN. 218-724-1268

Buck, Michael D, *Dir,* TSTI Harlingen Library, Harlingen TX. 512-425-4922, Ext 50

Buck, Mrs Paul C, *Librn,* Deposit Free Library, Deposit NY. 607-467-2577

Buck, Pat, *Libr Technician,* San Diego County Library (Spring Valley Branch), Spring Valley CA. 714-463-3006

Buck, Patricia, *Asst Librn,* School District of Philadelphia, Pedagogical Library, Philadelphia PA. 215-299-7783

Buck, Phyllis, *Dir,* Livingston Manor Free Library, Livingston Manor NY. 914-439-5440

Buck, Sadie Mae, *Music Librn,* Rochester Public Library, Olmsted County Library System, Rochester MN. 507-285-8000

Buck, Sylvia G, *Librn,* Warren Public Library, Warren MA. 413-436-7690

Buck, William, *Cat,* Fargo Public Library, Fargo ND. 701-241-1490

Buckel, W L, *On-Line Servs,* Battelle Columbus Laboratories Library, Columbus OH. 614-424-6306

Bucker, Elliot D, *Librn,* Portsmouth Bar & Law Library, Portsmouth OH. 614-353-8319

Buckert, Joyce, *Librn,* Memorial Hospital Library, Medical Records Department, Carthage IL. 217-357-3131

Buckeye, Robert, *Rare Bks & Spec Coll,* Middlebury College, Egbert Starr Library, Middlebury VT. 802-388-7621

Buckholtz, Donald, *Librn,* Massachusetts Taxpayers Foundation Library, Boston MA. 617-357-8500

Buckingham, Barbara, *Media,* Macomb County Library, Mount Clemens MI. 313-469-5300

Buckingham, Mary Jo, *Librn,* Klamath County Library (Keno Branch), Keno OR. 503-882-8894

Buckingham, Rebecca M, *Ch,* Neill Public Library, Pullman Public Library, Pullman WA. 509-334-3595

Buckingham, Thomas, *Librn,* Erie County Law Library, Sandusky OH. 419-626-4823

Buckland, Lawrence F, *Pres,* Inforonics, Inc Library, Littleton MA. 617-486-8976

Buckland, Michael, *Dean,* University of California, Berkeley, School of Library & Information Studies, CA. 415-642-6000 & 642-1464

Buckland, Nancy, *Librn,* Jackson District Library (Parma Branch), Parma MI. 517-531-4785

Buckle, Judith, *Ch,* Saskatoon Public Library, Saskatoon SK. 306-664-9555

Buckley, Alice, *Librn,* Cardinal Spellman Philatelic Museum Library, Weston MA. 617-894-6735

Buckley, Barbara, *Librn,* Winchester Public Library, Winchester IL. 217-742-3150

Buckley, Charles, *Librn,* Great Neck Library (Parkville), New Hyde Park NY. 516-466-8055, Ext 234

Buckley, David M, *Journals,* University of Dayton Libraries, Roesch Library, Dayton OH. 513-229-4221

Buckley, Donald G, *Bkmobile Coordr,* Westfield Athenaeum, Westfield MA. 413-568-7833

Buckley, Hope T, *ILL,* Rider College, Franklin F Moore Library, Lawrenceville NJ. 609-896-5111

Buckley, James W, *Dir,* Torrance Public Library, Torrance CA. 213-328-2251

Buckley, Jeanne, *Media,* Saint Joseph's University Libraries (Drexel Library), Philadelphia PA. 215-879-7559

Buckley, John A, *Assoc Dir, Admin,* United States Public Health Service Hospital Library, Nassau Bay TX. 713-333-5503, Ext 149

Buckley, Marie, *Librn,* Rock Valley Community Library, Rock Valley IA. 712-476-5651

Buckley, Martha F, *Instr,* Emory University, Div of Librarianship, GA. 404-329-6840

Buckley, Peggy, *Librn,* Des Moines Art Center Library, Des Moines IA. 515-277-4405, Ext 24

Buckley, Steven, *Asst Dir Tech Servs,* State University of New York College at Brockport, Drake Memorial Library, Brockport NY. 716-395-2140

Buckley, Veronica, *AV,* Lawrence Public Library, Lawrence MA. 617-682-1727

Buckley, Jr, Jay S, *In Charge,* Pfizer, Inc, Medical Research Laboratories, Library, Groton CT. 203-445-5611, Ext 687

Bucklin, Susan, *Ch,* Oliver Wolcott Library, Litchfield Public Library, Litchfield CT. 203-567-8030

Buckmaster, Bruce, *Ref,* Long Branch Public Library, Long Branch NJ. 201-222-3900

Buckmaster, Bruce A, *Dir,* Fanwood Memorial Library, Fanwood NJ. 201-322-6400

Bucknall, Carolyn F, *Asst Dir for Coll Develop,* University of Texas Libraries (General), Austin TX. 512-471-3811

Buckner, Dessie, *Librn,* Tulsa City-County Library (Brookside), Tulsa OK. 918-749-1664

Buckner, Juanita, *Dir,* Paul Sullins Public Library, Crossett Public Library, Crossett AR. 501-364-2230

Buckner, Marion, *Cat,* San Diego Public Library, San Diego CA. 714-236-5800

Buckner, Mildred, *Dir,* Salem Public Library, Salem MO. 314-729-4331

Buckner, Mrs William, *Tech Serv,* Virginia Intermont College, J F Hicks Memorial Library, Bristol VA. 703-669-6101, Ext 26

Buckner, Rebecca, *Librn,* Talladega Public Library, Talladega AL. 205-362-4211, 362-4251

Bucks, Richard, *Asst Prof,* University of Wisconsin-Eau Claire, Dept of Library Science & Media Education, WI. 715-836-2635

Buckwalter, Margaret V, *Spec Coll,* Clarion State College, Rena M Carlson Library, Clarion PA. 814-226-2343

Bucove, David A, *Dir,* Anderson City-Anderson & Stony Creek Township Public Library, Anderson Public Library, Anderson IN. 317-644-0938

Bucy, Frances A, *ILL,* Denver Public Library, Denver CO. 303-573-5152, Ext 271

Bucy, Norma B, *In Charge,* Immanuel Lutheran Church Library, Terre Haute IN. 812-232-4972

Budahn, Karen, *In Charge,* Southeastern Wisconsin Health Systems Agency Library, Milwaukee WI. 414-271-9788

Buday, Magda, *Librn,* Washington University Libraries (Business), Saint Louis MO. 314-889-6334

Budd, Pamela, *Ch,* Avery-Mitchell-Yancey Regional Library, Spruce Pine NC. 704-765-4866

Budde, Jacqueline, *Librn & On-Line Servs,* University of Minnesota, Hormel Institute Library, Austin MN. 507-433-8804

Budet, Ramon, *Ref,* University of Puerto Rico, Humacao University College Library, Humacao PR. 809-852-2525, Ext 200

Budge, Edwin S, *Dir,* Josephine County Library System, Grants Pass Library, Grants Pass OR. 503-474-5480

Budge, Ronnie L, *Headquarters Libr & Ad,* Jackson County Library System, Medford OR. 503-776-7281

Budington, William S, *Dir,* John Crerar Library, Chicago IL. 312-225-2526

Budrevics, D, *Librn,* Gulf Canada Ltd, Calgary AB. 403-233-3804

Budrew, John, *Acq & Ser,* University of Texas Health Science Center at Dallas Library, Dallas TX. 214-688-3368

Budwick, James, *Ad,* Mamaroneck Free Library, Mamaroneck NY. 914-698-1250

Buechler, John, *Spec Coll,* University of Vermont & State Agricultural College, Bailey-Howe Memorial Library, Burlington VT. 802-656-2020

Buehler, Ann, *Librn,* Saint Louis County Library (Thornhill), St Louis MO. 314-878-7730

Buehler, Dale A, *Dir,* Wilkes College, Eugene Shedden Farley Library, Wilkes-Barre PA. 717-824-4651, Ext 331 & 332

Buehler, Margaret, *Librn,* Lincoln County Library, Kemmerer WY. 307-877-4886

Buell, Carol Dick, *Dir,* Metropolitan Technical Community College, Instructional Resource Center, Omaha NE. 402-457-5100

Buell, Linda, *Librn,* Flint Public Library (Civic Park), Flint MI. 313-234-2639

Buell, Martha, *Librn,* Saint Maries Public Library, Saint Maries ID. 208-245-3732

Bueno, Luis, *Librn,* Miami Herald Library, Reference Herald Plaza, Miami FL. 305-350-2419

Buerham, Gail, *Outreach,* Sampson-Clinton Public Library, Clinton NC. 919-592-4153

Buerkle, Marvine, *Ch & Cat,* Craighead County & Jonesboro Public Library, Jonesboro AR. 501-935-5133

Buescher, Barbara, *Librn,* Wake County Department of the Public Library (Cary Public), Cary NC. 919-467-8908

Bueschlen, Wava, *Chief Librn,* Fort Wayne Bible College, S A Lehman Memorial Library, Fort Wayne IN. 219-456-2111, Ext 223

Buesing, R G, *Dir,* Saint Paul's College Library, Concordia MO. 816-463-2238, Ext 27

Buettner, Vicki, *On-Line Servs & Bibliog Instr,* Western Plains Library System, Clinton OK. 405-323-0974

Bufano, Ralph A, *Dir,* Paine Art Center & Arboretum Library, Oshkosh WI. 414-235-4530

Buffaloe, Ann, *Cat,* Faulkner-Van Buren Regional Library, Conway AR. 501-327-7482

Buffett, Bryan C, *Dir,* Dryden Public Library, Dryden ON. 807-223-4314

Buffington, Josephine, *ILL & Circ,* David Lipscomb College, Crisman Memorial Library, Nashville TN. 615-385-3855, Ext 282, 283

Buffington, Karyl L, *Librn,* Coffeyville Public Library, Coffeyville KS. 316-251-1370

Buffington, Louise, *Librn,* West Florida Regional Library (Jay Branch), Jay FL. 904-675-6293

Buffington, Mina, *Librn,* Elizabethville Area Library, Elizabethville PA. 717-362-9825

Bugbee, Monica, *Asst Librn,* Lehigh County Historical Society, Scott Andrew Trexler, II Memorial Library, Allentown PA. 215-435-1074

Bugbee, Pearl, *Media,* Goddard College, William Shipman Library, Plainfield VT. 802-454-8311, Ext 232

Bugden, Gloria, *Asst Librn,* C F Lawrence Memorial Library, Pepperell MA. 617-433-6933

Buggs, Susie, *Librn,* Public Library of Fort Wayne & Allen County (Pontiac), Fort Wayne IN. 219-444-0403

Bugnitz, Patrice M, *Museum Tech,* Jefferson National Expansion Memorial Library, Saint Louis MO. 314-425-6023

Bugnone, Cheryl, *Librn,* Kinsman Free Public Library, Kinsman OH. 216-876-2461

Buhl, Betsy D, *Librn,* Bureau of Land Management Library, Winnemucca NV. 702-623-3676

Buhman, Lesley, *Circ & Ref,* Lewis & Clark College (Paul L Boley Law Library), Portland OR. 503-244-1181, Ext 685

Buhr, Helen B, *Librn,* Sallie Logan Public Library, Murphysboro IL. 618-684-3271

Buhr, Rosemary, *Librn,* Barnes Hospital, School of Nursing Library, Saint Louis MO. 314-454-2554

Buhrman, Charles B, *Per,* Saint Petersburg Junior College, Saint Petersburg Campus Library, Saint Petersburg FL. 813-546-0011, Ext 353

Buhrmann, June, *Ch,* Altadena Library District, Altadena CA. 213-798-0833

Buhse, Moira B, *Dir,* Westmont Public Library, Westmont IL. 312-969-5625

Bui, Dominic, *Ref,* Fayetteville Technical Institute, Paul H Thompson Library, Fayetteville NC. 919-323-1961

Buick, Margaret, *Acq,* Phoenix Public Library, Phoenix AZ. 602-262-6451

Buika, Gina, *Dir,* Bird S Coler Hospital, Medical Library, New York NY. 212-688-9400

Buikema, Nancy K, *Dir,* Schmaling Memorial Public Library District, Fulton IL. 815-589-2045

Buiter, MaryAnn, *Librn,* Perry Memorial Hospital Library, Princeton IL. 815-875-2811, Ext 477

Bulaong, Grace, *Cat,* Metropolitan Toronto Library Board, Metropolitan Toronto Library, Toronto ON. 416-928-5150

Bulch, Helen, *Librn,* Lennox & Addington County Public Library (Stella Public), Stella ON. 613-354-2585

Bulger, Janet, *Actg Librn,* American Electric Power Service Corp Library, New York NY. 212-422-4800, Ext 8476, 8477

Bulkeley, Mary, *Asst Librn,* John Mosser Public Library, Abingdon IL. 309-462-3129

Bulko, Pat, *Asst Librn,* Bullard-Sanford Memorial Library, Vassar MI. 517-823-2171

Bull, Ai-Lua, *Librn,* Western Missouri Mental Health Center Library, Kansas City MO. 816-471-3000, Ext 378
Bull, Mary, *ILL & Ref,* University of South Carolina, Coastal Carolina College Kimbel Library, Conway SC. 803-347-3161, Ext 242
Bull, Sharon, *Asst Librn,* Canadian Nazarene College, Winnipeg MB. 204-269-2120
Bull, Susie, *Asst Dir,* Ricks Memorial Library, Yazoo-Sharkey-Issaquena Library System, Yazoo City MS. 601-746-5557
Bullard, Anita, *Librn,* Katherine J Barclay Free Library, Brewerton NY. 315-676-7484
Bullard, Ann H, *Ref,* Scotland County Memorial Library, Laurinburg NC. 919-276-0563
Bullard, Ann H, *Librn,* Scotland County Memorial Library (Wagram Branch), Wagram NC. 919-276-2638369-2966
Bullard, Eleanor, *Ch,* Ellsworth City Library, Ellsworth ME. 207-667-2307
Bullard, Gregory N, *Asst Dir for Tech Servs,* Syracuse University Libraries, Ernest S Bird Library, Syracuse NY. 315-423-2575
Bullard, Janice, *Ad,* San Mateo Public Library, San Mateo CA. 415-574-6955
Bullard, Jean, *Circ,* Cullman County Public Library, Cullman AL. 205-734-2720
Bullard, Louise, *Librn,* Sacramento Public Library (North Sacramento), Sacramento CA. 916-927-0652
Bullard, Mary, *Info & Referral Coordr,* Monroe County Library System, Monroe MI. 313-241-5277
Bullard, Mary Nell, *Librn,* Scurry County Library, Snyder TX. 915-573-5572
Bullard, Sheilah, *Librn,* Southwestern College Library, Oklahoma City OK. 405-947-2331, Ext 214
Bullen, George, *Librn,* Pouce Coupe Public Library, Pouce Coupe BC. 604-786-5765
Bullen, Ida A, *Asst Dir & Admin Servs,* DuPage Library System, Geneva IL. 312-232-8457
Bullen, Robert W, *Admin Servs,* North Suburban Library System, Wheeling IL. 312-459-1300
Bullerman, Carol, *Librn,* Alta Vista Public Library, Alta Vista IA. 515-364-2975
Bulley, Joan S, *Librn,* Mary Washington Hospital Library, Fredericksburg VA. 703-373-4110, Ext 642
Bullman, Virginia, *Librn,* Waterford Public Library, Waterford PA. 814-796-4729
Bulloch, Lillian H, *Dir,* Cedar City Public Library, Cedar City UT. 801-586-6661
Bullock, Ednita W, *Tech Serv,* Bennett College, Thomas F Holgate Library, Greensboro NC. 919-273-4431, Ext 139
Bullock, Esther, *Acq,* Joliet Junior College, Learning Resource Center, Joliet IL. 815-729-9020, Ext 282
Bullock, Judy, *Gen Serv,* Jacksonville Public Library System, Haydon Burns Library, Jacksonville FL. 904-633-6870
Bullock, Penelope L, *Prof,* Atlanta University, School of Library & Information Studies, GA. 404-681-0251, Ext 312
Bullock, Robbie, *Stenog,* State Technical Institute at Memphis, George E Freeman Library, Memphis TN. 901-377-4106
Bullock, Susan, *President,* Southern Connecticut Library Council, CT. 203-387-3690
Bullock, Susan M, *Dir,* Cheshire Public Library, Cheshire CT. 203-272-2245
Bullock, Sybil H, *Dir,* United States Army (Aeromedical Research Laboratory Scientific Information Center), Fort Rucker AL. 205-255-6919
Bullock, Victoria, *Ch,* Oyster Bay-East Norwich Public Library, Oyster Bay NY. 516-922-1212
Bullock, Virginia G, *Adjunct Prof,* Case Western Reserve University, School of Library Science, OH. 216-368-3500
Bullock, W M, *Dir,* Mountain Empire Community College Library, Big Stone Gap VA. 703-523-2400, Ext 267
Bulman, Learned T, *Tech Serv,* County College of Morris, Sherman H Masten Learning Resource Center, Randolph Township NJ. 201-361-5000, Ext 470
Bulmer, Helen, *Librn,* Devon Public Library, Devon AB. 403-987-3720
Bulow, Dorothy, *Cat,* Cleveland Heights-University Heights Public Library, Cleveland Heights OH. 216-932-3600

Bulow, Jack, *Assoc Dir, Exten Servs,* Birmingham Public & Jefferson County Free Library, Birmingham AL. 205-254-2551
Bulson, Christine, *Ref,* State University of New York, College at Oneonta, James M Milne Library, Oneonta NY. 607-431-2723
Bulstrode, Roblyn L, *Librn,* Vortex Institute, Inc, Library of Esoteric Studies, Fairbanks AK. 907-479-4413
Bult, Conrad J, *Asst Dir(Col), ILL, & Ref,* Calvin College & Seminary Library, Grand Rapids MI. 616-949-4000, Ext 297
Bulter, Carol, *Dir,* Shell Lake Public Library, Shell Lake WI. 715-468-2074
Buma, Doris L, *Dir,* Ashland Public Library, Ashland MA. 617-881-2490
Bumgardner, Erlene, *Librn,* Mason County Public Library (Mason City Public), Mason WV. 304-773-5580
Bump, Priscilla, *Asst Librn,* Albany Public Library, Albany WI. 608-862-3491
Bumpass, Donald E, *Dept Head,* University of Arkansas, Instructional Resources Education, AR. 501-575-5444
Bumpus, Esta Sue, *Librn,* Wichita Public Library (Ford Rockwell), Wichita KS. 316-262-0611
Bumstead, Ann L, *Ch,* Willimantic Public Library, Willimantic CT. 203-423-6182
Bumstead, Ginny, *Ch,* Marshalltown Public Library, Marshalltown IA. 515-754-5738
Bunce, Jack D, *Pres,* Jackson Business University Library, Jackson MI. 517-789-6123
Bunce, William C, *Dir,* University of Wisconsin-Madison (Kohler Art Library), Madison WI. 608-263-2256
Bunch, Carol Ann, *Ch,* Orangeburg County Library, Orangeburg SC. 803-534-1429
Bunch, Cathye, *Dir,* Saint Louis Community College Administrative Center Instructional Resource Technical Services, MO. 314-644-9589
Bunch, Cathye, *Dir,* Saint Louis Community College (Administrative Center), Saint Louis MO. 314-644-9589
Bunch, Corrie, *Acq,* University of Southern Mississippi, Cook Memorial Library, Hattiesburg MS. 601-266-7301
Bunch, Robert L, *Librn,* Oklahoma State Reformatory Library, Granite OK. 405-535-2186
Bunch, Ruby, *Librn,* Thomas Jefferson Library (Miller County Service Center), Eldon MO. 314-392-6657
Bunco, Merle, *Micromedia,* Southern Connecticut State College, Hilton C Buley Library, New Haven CT. 203-397-4505
Bunco, Paulette, *Ref & On-Line Servs,* Trumbull Library, Trumbull CT. 203-261-6421
Bund, Jeannette, *ILL,* Bryant Library, Roslyn NY. 516-621-2240
Bundick, Mrs Boone, *Librn,* Stella Hart Memorial Public Library, Smiley TX. 512-587-2701
Bundy, Annalee, *Dir,* Providence Interrelated Library System, Providence RI. 401-521-7722
Bundy, Annalee M, *Dir,* Providence Public Library, Providence RI. 401-521-7722
Bundy, Marlene, *Librn,* Anaconda Copper Co Library, Denver CO. 303-575-4425
Bundy, Mary L, *Prof,* University of Maryland, College of Library & Information Services, MD. 301-454-5441
Bundy, William P, *Dir,* UOP Inc, Air Correction Division Library, Darien CT. 203-655-8711
Bung, Rosalie, *Librn,* Normandale Community College, Learning Resources Center, Bloomington MN. 612-830-9300
Bunge, Charles A, *Dir,* University of Wisconsin-Madison, Library School, WI. 608-263-2900
Bunger, Barbara, *Dir,* Jensen Memorial Library, Minden NE. 308-832-2648
Bunker, Dorothy, *Librn,* Oak Bluffs Public Library, Oak Bluffs MA. 617-693-9433
Bunker, Eugene G, *Dir,* Saint Norbert College, Todd Wehr Library, De Pere WI. 414-337-3280
Bunker, Nathaniel, *Bibliogr in Am Hist,* Harvard University Library (Harvard College Library (Headquarters in Harry Elkins Widener Memorial Library)), Cambridge MA. 617-495-2401
Bunker, Neil, *Bibliog Specialist,* University of Rochester (Sibley Music Library), Rochester NY. 716-275-3018

Bunker, Norman J, *Librn,* Michigan Department of Transportation Library, Lansing MI. 517-373-1545
Bunkley, Barbara, *Tech Serv,* Statesboro Regional Library, Statesboro GA. 912-764-7573
Bunn, Doris, *Librn,* Seneca East Local School District Library, Attica OH. 419-426-3825
Bunn, Dumont, *Asst Dir & ILL,* Mercer University, Stetson Memorial Library, Macon GA. 912-745-6811, Ext 284
Bunn, Margie Y, *Librn,* Baltimore City Public Schools, Professional Media Center, Baltimore MD. 301-396-6983
Bunnell, Chet, *Ref,* University of Mississippi, Law Library, University MS. 601-232-7361
Bunner, Mary, *Tech Serv,* Manatee County Public Library System, Bradenton FL. 813-748-5555
Buntin, Steven Leslie, *Bibliothecar,* KXE6S Verein Chess Society, Special Research Library Division, Durham NC. 919-489-9146
Bunting, Anne C, *Tech Serv & Spec Coll,* University of Tennessee Center for the Health Sciences Library, Memphis TN. 901-528-5638
Bunting, Christine, *Art,* University of California, University Library, Santa Cruz CA. 408-429-2076
Bunting, Larry, *Media,* Scottsdale Community College Library, Scottsdale AZ. 602-941-0999
Bunyan, Linda E, *Librn,* Saint Thomas Hospital, Medical Library, Akron OH. 216-379-1111, Ext 7505
Buocher, Patricia, *Librn,* City of Hope National Medical Center, Piness Medical & Scientific Library, Duarte CA. 213-359-8111
Burbridge, Florence, *Librn,* Second Congregational Church Library, Grand Rapids MI. 616-361-2629
Burch, Della, *ILL & Ref,* ARO Inc, Arnold Engineering Development Center Technical Library, Arnold AFS TN. 615-455-2611, Ext 431
Burch, Della C, *Tech Librn & On-Line Searchers,* United States Air Force (Arnold Engineering Development Center Library), Arnold AFS TN. 615-455-2611
Burch, Jeannette S, *Dir,* Cannon Falls Library, Cannon Falls MN. 507-263-2804
Burch, Leona E, *Librn,* Madill City Library, Madill OK. 405-795-2749
Burch, Marion J, *Librn,* Newton Public Library, Newton IA. 515-792-4108
Burch, Mary S, *Librn,* New York State Supreme Court Library, Troy NY. 518-270-5238
Burchard, Gertrude, *Acq,* Macomb County Library, Mount Clemens MI. 313-469-5300
Burchill, Mary D, *Cat,* University of Kansas Libraries (School of Law), Lawrence KS. 913-864-3025
Burckel, Nicholas, *Spec Coll & Archivist,* University of Wisconsin-Parkside Library, Kenosha WI. 414-553-2221
Burdash, David H, *Dir,* Wilmington Institute Library, Wilmington DE. 302-571-7400
Burden, Geri, *Dir,* Bernardsville Public Library, Bernardsville NJ. 201-766-0118
Burden, Karen, *Ref,* Kankakee Public Library, Kankakee IL. 815-939-4564
Burden, Mary C, *Librn,* Lima Public Library (Harrod Branch), Harrod OH. 419-228-5113
Burden, Peg, *Librn,* Onondaga County Public Library System (White), Syracuse NY. 315-473-6769
Burden, Ruth B, *Librn,* Sallie Harrell Jenkins Memorial Public Library, Aulander NC. 919-345-4461
Burdett, Ollie M, *Librn,* Phillips Petroleum Co (Gas & Gas Liquids Library), Bartlesville OK. 918-661-6600
Burdick, Elizabeth B, *Dir,* International Theatre Collection of the International Theatre Institute of the United States, Inc, New York NY. 212-245-3950
Burdick, Lois, *Circ,* Florida State University, Robert Manning Strozier Library, Tallahassee FL. 904-644-5211
Burdick, Mary, *Ad,* Maurice M Pine Free Public Library, Fair Lawn NJ. 201-796-3400
Burdick, Oscar C, *Librn,* Pacific School of Religion, Charles Holbrook Library, Berkeley CA. 415-848-0528
Burdick, Robert, *Librn,* Public Library of Cincinnati & Hamilton County (Cumminsville), Cincinnati OH. 513-541-0630

Burdine, Judy, *Librn,* Pulaski County Public Library, Somerset KY. 606-679-1734
Burdirk, Oscar, *Assoc Libr for Collection Mgt,* Graduate Theological Union Library, Berkeley CA. 415-841-9811
Burditt, Jean, *Librn,* Hildebrand Memorial Library, Boscobel WI. 608-375-5723
Burek, Ann, *Asst Librn,* Northland Pioneer College (District Learning Resources Center), Holbrook AZ. 602-524-6111, Ext 234 & 243
Burek, Ann, *Asst Librn,* Northland Pioneer College (Holbrook Center Library), Holbrook AZ. 602-524-6111, Ext 243 & 234
Burel, Mary G, *Acq,* Gettysburg College, Schmucker Memorial Library, Gettysburg PA. 717-334-3131, Ext 366
Bures, Loran T, *Dir,* Republican Associates of Southern California, Research Library, Glendale CA. 213-242-3146
Buresh, Vitus, *Spec Coll,* Illinois Benedictine College, Theodore Lownik Library, Lisle IL. 312-968-7270, Ext 286
Burfisher, Eloise, *Commun Servs,* Des Plaines Public Library, Des Plaines IL. 312-827-5551
Burford, James V, *Librn,* Mississippi Gulf Coast Junior College, Jefferson Davis Campus Learning Resource Center, Gulfport MS. 601-896-3355, Ext 46
Burford, Jennifer, *Librn,* Saint Francis Hospital Library, Beech Grove IN. 317-783-8106
Burford, Richard, *Dir,* Kent County Municipal Public Library, Chatham ON. 519-352-2520
Burford, Robert S, *Dir,* Marian J Mohr Memorial Library, Johnston RI. 401-231-4980
Burg, Corinne, *Rare Bks & Spec Coll,* University of the South, Jessie Ball duPont Library, Sewanee TN. 615-598-5931, Ext 265, 267
Burg, Jayson, *Asst Librn,* Union County Technical Institute, Scotch Plains NJ. 201-889-2000, Ext 280
Burg, Joan C, *Ch,* Brookfield Library, Brookfield Center CT. 203-775-6241
Burg, Nan C, *Librn,* Pennsylvania Department of Community Affairs Library, Harrisburg PA. 717-787-6904
Burg, Roger, *Librn,* Hennepin County Library (Augsburg Park), Richfield MN. 612-869-8863
Burgan, Christine D, *Dir & Acq,* Cynthiana Public Library, Harrison County Library District, Cynthiana KY. 606-234-4881
Burgan, John S, *Cent Librn,* Enoch Pratt Free Library, Baltimore MD. 301-396-5430, 396-5395
Burgarella, Mary, *Head Libr Develop Servs,* Massachusetts Board of Library Commissioners, Office for the Development of Library Services, Boston MA. 617-267-9400
Burger, Gary, *Dir,* Berkshire Museum, Art & Science Library, Pittsfield MA. 413-443-7171
Burgerhoff, Carol, *Tech Serv & Cat,* Spartanburg County Public Library, Spartanburg SC. 582-4123 & 585-2441
Burgess, A, *Librn,* University of Toronto Libraries (Knox College), Toronto ON. 416-923-7644
Burgess, Agnes, *Librn,* Russell & District Regional Library, Russell MB. 204-773-3127
Burgess, Barbara, *Asst Librn,* Hobe Sound Bible College Library, Hobe Sound FL. 305-546-6166
Burgess, Barbara, *Media,* Leonia Public Library, Leonia NJ. 201-944-1444
Burgess, Beverly C, *Librn,* Goliad County Library, Goliad TX. 512-645-2291
Burgess, Dean, *Dir,* Portsmouth Public Library, Portsmouth VA. 804-393-8501, 393-8502
Burgess, Edwin, *Ref & On-Line Servs,* United States Army (Combined Arms Research Library), Fort Leavenworth KS. 913-684-3282
Burgess, Frances, *Librn,* Athens Regional Library (Bogart Branch), Bogart GA. 404-543-0134
Burgess, James W, *Circ,* Public Library of the District of Columbia, Martin Luther King Memorial Library, Washington DC. 202-727-1101
Burgess, Larry E, *Rare Bks & Spec Coll,* A K Smiley Public Library, Redlands CA. 714-793-2201
Burgess, M R, *Per,* California State College, San Bernardino Library, San Bernardino CA. 714-887-7321
Burgess, Mrs J, *Librn,* Middle Georgia Regional Library (Jones County Public), Gray GA. 912-986-6626
Burgess, Nancy, *Archives,* Thomas Nelson Community College Library, Hampton VA. 804-825-2868, 825-2876
Burgess, Richard, *Librn,* Gary Public Library (John F Kennedy), Gary IN. 219-887-8112
Burgess, Robert S, *Prof,* State University of New York at Albany, School of Library & Information Science, NY. 518-455-6288
Burgess, William E, *Market Operations Mgr,* SDC Search Service, CA. 213-829-7511
Burgess, Winona, *Librn,* Mid-Continent Public Library (Grain Valley Branch), Grain Valley MO. 816-443-2316
Burghardt, James H, *Dir,* Library Association of Portland, Multnomah County Library, Portland OR. 503-223-7201, Ext 40
Burgher, Rosalie, *Librn,* Olive Free Library Association, West Shokan NY. 914-657-2482
Burgin, Joyce, *Librn,* Los Angeles Public Library System (Woodland Hills), Los Angeles CA. 213-887-0160
Burgin, Michelle, *Media,* North Central Regional Library System, Mason City IA. 515-423-6917
Burgin, Robert, *Asst Dir,* Forsyth County Public Library, Winston-Salem NC. 919-727-2556
Burgin, Robert, *Dir,* Wayne County Public Library, Inc, Goldsboro NC. 919-735-1824
Burgis, G C, *Librn,* Thunder Bay Public Library, Thunder Bay ON. 807-344-3585
Burgman, Sylvia, *ILL & Tech Serv,* Jericho Public Library, Jericho NY. 516-935-6790
Burgner, C, *Tech Serv,* Florida Institute of Technology, Jensen Beach Library, Jensen Beach FL. 305-334-4200, Ext 60, 61
Burgoyne, Gail, *Librn,* Pine River Library, Pine River MN. 218-587-2171
Burhans, Grace, *In Charge,* Delano Library, Delano MN. 612-972-3467
Buri, Gertrude, *Ref,* Wissahickon Valley Public Library, Ambler PA. 215-646-1072
Buri, Maura, *Per,* Villanova University (Pulling Law Library), Villanova PA. 215-527-2100, Ext 702, 703, 704
Burich, Nancy, *Librn,* University of Kansas Libraries (Regents Center), Overland Park KS. 913-841-2147
Burich, Nancy J, *Dir & Ref,* University of Kansas Regents Center Library, Overland Park KS. 913-341-4554
Burimaukas, Janet, *Acq,* Nazareth College of Rochester Library, Lorette Wilmot Library, Rochester NY. 716-586-2525, Ext 232
Burinski, Walter W, *ILL,* Michigan State University Library, East Lansing MI. 517-355-2344
Burk, Alan, *Librn,* University of Western Ontario (Business), London ON. 519-679-3255
Burk, Anne Petersen, *Librn,* Livonia Public Library, Livonia NY. 716-346-3450
Burk, Janet L, *Tech Serv & Cat,* Principia College, Marshall Brooks Library, Elsah IL. 618-374-2131, Ext 325
Burk, Leslie, *Ch,* Napa City - County Library, Napa CA. 707-253-4241
Burk, William, *Librn,* University of North Carolina at Chapel Hill (Botany), Chapel Hill NC. 919-933-3783
Burkart, Charles, *Librn,* Murray State University (Media), Murray KY. 502-762-2291
Burkart, Jeff, *AV,* Concordia College, Buenger Memorial Library, Saint Paul MN. 612-641-8240
Burke, Audrey, *Bus Mgr,* Saint Charles City County Library, Saint Peters MO. 314-441-2300
Burke, Barbara, *Librn,* Colorado State University (Engineering Sciences Library), Fort Collins CO. 303-491-8694
Burke, Bettie, *Pub Servs,* Mount San Jacinto College Library, San Jacinto CA. 714-654-7321, Ext 242
Burke, Billie Jean, *Dir,* Morrison-Talbott Library, Waterloo IL. 618-939-6232
Burke, Ella L, *Admin Asst,* Consortium of East Jersey, NJ. 201-527-2387
Burke, Ellen, *Circ,* State Historical Society of Wisconsin Library, Madison WI. 608-262-3421
Burke, Frank G, *Lectr,* University of Maryland, College of Library & Information Services, MD. 301-454-5441
Burke, Grace, *Librn,* La Grange Public Library, La Grange NC. 919-566-3722
Burke, J Lois, *Chief Librn,* Benton & Bowles Inc Library, New York NY. 212-758-6200, Ext 3156
Burke, Jeanette, *Librn,* Willard Memorial Library (Wakeman Branch), Wakeman OH. 216-839-2976
Burke, Joseph, *Librn,* United States Air Force Academy Library (Community Library), United States Air Force Academy CO. 303-472-4665
Burke, Judith, *Ref,* San Jacinto College, Lee Davis Library, Pasadena TX. 713-476-1850, 476-1501, Ext 241
Burke, Karl, *AV,* King's College, D Leonard Corgan Library, Wilkes-Barre PA. 717-824-9931, Ext 245
Burke, Lu, *Libr Tech,* Queen's University at Kingston (Psychology), Kingston ON. 613-547-3172
Burke, M Nancy, *ILL & Ref,* Gateway Technical Institute, Learning Resources Center, Kenosha WI. 414-656-6924, 656-6923
Burke, Marilyn, *Tech Serv & Cat,* Malden Public Library, Malden MA. 617-324-0218
Burke, Redmond, *Assoc Prof,* University of Wisconsin-Oshkosh, Dept of Library Science, WI. 414-424-2313
Burke, Richard, *Ad,* West Bloomfield Township Public Library, West Bloomfield MI. 313-682-2120
Burke, Roberta, *Ch,* Franklin Public Library, Franklin NH. 603-934-2911
Burke, Saretta, *ILL & Ref,* Rossford Public Library, Rossford OH. 419-666-0924
Burke, Sharon E, *Acq & Doc,* Loyola University of Chicago Libraries (Law School Library), Chicago IL. 312-670-2952
Burke, Susan, *Librn,* FMC Corp, OED Technical Library, San Jose CA. 408-289-2852
Burke, Tina, *Librn,* Prince George's County Memorial Library System (Magruder), Hyattsville MD. 301-277-3432
Burke, Vivienne C, *Asst Librn,* Rainier National Bank Library, Seattle WA. 206-621-4088
Burkert, Theresa J, *Asst Dean,* Western Piedmont Community College, Learning Resources Center, Morganton NC. 704-437-8688, Ext 234
Burkes, Ann, *Librn,* East Central Junior College, Burton Library, Decatur MS. 601-635-2111, Ext 219
Burkett, Phyllis, *Dir,* Craighead County & Jonesboro Public Library, Jonesboro AR. 501-935-5133
Burkett, Phyllis, *Dir,* Crowley Ridge Regional Library, Jonesboro AR. 501-935-5133
Burkett, Phyllis, *Librn,* White County Public Library, Searcy AR. 501-268-2449
Burkett, Tim, *Media,* West Hills Community College Library, Coalinga CA. 209-935-0801, Ext 47
Burkhardt, Lela G, *Librn,* Wabasha Public Library, Wabasha MN. 612-565-3927
Burkhardt, Lona, *Librn,* Harriman Public Library, Harriman TN. 615-882-3195
Burkhardt, Robert, *Tech Serv,* Athens State College Library, Athens AL. 205-232-1802, Ext 291
Burkhart, Gayle K, *Ref,* Grace A Dow Memorial Library, Midland Public Library, Midland MI. 517-835-7151
Burkhart, Hilda Sue, *Asst Prof,* Middle Tennessee State University, Department of Library Service, TN. 615-898-2740 & 898-5555
Burkhart, Rebecca, *Ch,* Verona Free Public Library, Verona NJ. 201-239-0050
Burkhart, Velda B, *Cat,* Virginia Polytechnic Institute & State University Library, Blacksburg VA. 703-961-5593
Burkhauser, Jude, *Commun Servs,* Mercer County Library, Trenton NJ. 609-989-6917
Burkheart, Sue, *Cat,* Middle Tennessee State University, Andrew L Todd Library, Murfreesboro TN. 615-898-2622
Burkholder, Barry, *Instructional Develop,* J Sargeant Reynolds Community College (Parham Campus Learning Resources Center), Richmond VA. 804-264-3220
Burkholder, Dorothea, *Asst Cat,* Cardinal Ritter Library, Saint Louis MO. 314-544-0455, Ext 56
Burkholder, Florence, *Dir,* Collinsville Memorial Public Library, Collinsville IL. 618-344-1112
Burkholder, Ruth, *Librn,* Peabody Township Library, Peabody KS. 316-983-2494
Burkholder, Sue, *Cat,* University of Missouri Saint Louis, Thomas Jefferson Library, Saint Louis MO. 314-453-5221

Burkland, Sharon W, *Res Dir*, Whitney Communications Corporation, Research Library, New York NY. 212-582-2300, Ext 48, 49
Burks, Wanda, *Librn*, Kansas City Life Insurance Co, General Library, Kansas City MO. 816-753-7000
Burleigh, Joan, *Librn*, Mendocino Art Center Library, Mendocino CA. 707-937-5818
Burley, Betty J, *Librn*, Miracle Valley Regional Library (Cameron Public Branch), Cameron WV. 304-686-2140
Burling, Alice, *Librn*, Aurora Public Library, Aurora NE. 402-694-2272
Burlingame, Dwight F, *Dean*, Bowling Green State University Library, Bowling Green OH. 419-372-2856
Burlingame, Margaret, *Librn*, El Paso Public Library (Westside), El Paso TX. 915-543-2164
Burlingham, Esther H, *Dir*, Oxford Public Library, Oxford PA. 215-932-9625
Burlingham, Merry, *South Asian Librn*, University of Texas Libraries (Asian), Austin TX. 512-471-3135
Burlunk, Penny, *Supr & Tech Servs*, Saint Lawrence College of Applied Arts & Technology Library Services, Kingston ON. 613-544-5400, Ext 163
Burman, Becky, *AV*, Coca-Cola Co (Business Information Services), Atlanta GA. 404-898-2124
Burmeister, Erwin, *Tech Serv & Cat*, University of the Pacific, Irving Martin Library, Stockton CA. 209-946-2431
Burmeister, Florence, *Ch*, Skokie Public Library, Skokie IL. 312-673-7774
Burmeister, Sally, *Librn*, Oak Harbor Public Library, Oak Harbor OH. 419-898-7001
Burn, Barbara, *Dir*, Grand View College Library, Des Moines IA. 515-266-2651
Burn, Harry T, *Librn*, Oak Ridge Associated Universities (MERT Division Library), Oak Ridge TN. 615-576-3408
Burna, George, *In Charge*, Scott Paper Co (Research Library & Technical Information Service), Philadelphia PA. 215-521-5000, Ext 2416
Burnam, Paul D, *Dir*, Orient Developmental Center, Resident Library, Orient OH. 614-877-4361, Ext 210
Burnap, Elizabeth, *Asst Dir*, Ritter Memorial Library, Lunenburg MA. 617-582-7817
Burndorfer, Hans, *Librn*, University of British Columbia Library (Music), Vancouver BC. 604-228-3589
Burnell, Rachel M, *Librn*, Spaulding Memorial Library, Sebago ME. 207-787-2730
Burnes, Richard P, *Cat*, Massachusetts Institute of Technology, Lincoln Laboratory Library, Lexington MA. 617-862-5500, Ext 7195
Burnett, Barbara J, *Librn*, Montgomery Ward, Corporate Library & Information Center, Chicago IL. 312-467-2333
Burnett, Betty, *Main Libr*, Los Alamos Scientific Laboratory Libraries, Library Services Group, Los Alamos NM. 505-667-4448
Burnett, Charles, *Popular Libr*, Public Library of the District of Columbia, Martin Luther King Memorial Library, Washington DC. 202-727-1101
Burnett, Donald E, *Librn*, Anna Mental Health & Development Center, Staff Library, Anna IL. 618-833-5161, Ext 213
Burnett, Mrs R E, *Dir*, Saint George's Episcopal Church, John A Howe Memorial Library, Schenectady NY. 518-374-3163
Burnett, Rosa S, *Dir*, Mississippi Industrial College Library, Holly Springs MS. 601-252-4754, 252-3411
Burnett, Rosa S, *Librn*, State Technical Institute at Memphis, George E Freeman Library, Memphis TN. 901-377-4106
Burnett, Ruth, *Acq*, State University of New York, College at Oneonta, James M Milne Library, Oneonta NY. 607-431-2723
Burnette, Frances, *Ref*, Lima Public Library, Lima OH. 419-228-5113
Burnette, Jeanne, *Cat*, Colby College, Miller Library, Waterville ME. 207-873-1131, Ext 209
Burnette, Louis, *Librn*, Warren County Community Center Library, Warrenton NC. 919-456-2147
Burney, Dorothee, *Librn*, Goethe Institute of Boston, German Cultural Center for New England Library, Boston MA. 617-262-6050
Burney, Sara, *Librn*, Tombigbee Regional Library (Choctaw County Public), Ackerman MS. 601-285-6348
Burnham, Anna C, *Dir*, Charles City Public Library, Charles City IA. 515-228-5532
Burnham, Elinor, *Dir*, Somers Public Library, Somers CT. 203-749-8845
Burnham, Helen A, *Dir*, Croton Free Library, Croton-on-Hudson NY. 914-271-4098
Burnham, John P, *Librn*, University of Maine at Farmington, Mantor Library, Farmington ME. 207-778-3501, Ext 225
Burnham, John P, *Curator Numismatics Coll*, Yale University Library (Sterling Memorial Library), New Haven CT. 203-436-8335
Burnham, Kay, *Ref*, South Windsor Public Library, South Windsor CT. 203-644-1541
Burnham-Kidwell, Deborah, *Asst Dir*, Mohave Community College, Resource Center, Kingman AZ. 602-757-4331, Ext 19
Burnie, Valerie, *ILL & Ref*, University of South Carolina at Spartanburg Library, Spartanburg SC. 803-578-1800, Exts 410, 411, 420 & 421
Burnley, Lilian W, *Librn*, East Cheltenham Free Library, Cheltenham PA. 215-379-2077
Burnley, Lillian, *Librn*, Holy Trinity Lutheran Church Library, Abington PA. 215-659-2642
Burns, Anna C, *Cat*, Louisiana State University at Alexandria Library, Alexandria LA. 318-445-3672, Ext 46
Burns, Arlene, *Cat*, Holdrege Public Library System, South Central Regional Library, Holdrege NE. 308-995-6556
Burns, Barbara, *Librn*, Proctor Free Library, Proctor VT. 802-459-3539
Burns, Barbara, *Bkmobile Coordr*, Wayne County Public Library, Wooster OH. 216-262-0916
Burns, Barbara A, *In Charge*, Anchor Corp, Research Library, Fair Lawn NJ. 201-423-4660
Burns, Barrie, *Acting Dir Cat Br*, National Library of Canada, Ottawa ON. 613-995-9481
Burns, Bernettie H, *Librn*, Fallon County Library, Baker MT. 406-778-2222
Burns, Bernita, *Librn*, Community Library of Allegheny Valley, Tarentum PA. 412-226-0770
Burns, Carol, *Cat*, Library Association of Portland, Multnomah County Library, Portland OR. 503-223-7201, Ext 40
Burns, Carol A, *Asst Librn Pub Servs*, Emory University Libraries (A W Calhoun Medical Library), Atlanta GA. 404-329-5810
Burns, Carol S, *Librn*, Princeton Public Library, Princeton IN. 812-385-4464
Burns, Catherine, *Br Coordr*, Morris County Free Library, Whippany NJ. 201-285-6101
Burns, Cynthia, *Ch*, Providence Athenaeum, Providence RI. 401-421-6970
Burns, Dean, *Chief Librn*, United States Army (Fort Myer Post Library), Fort Myer VA. 703-692-9574, 692-9650
Burns, Diane, *Ch*, Beech Grove Public Library, Beech Grove IN. 317-788-4203
Burns, Dorothy, *Per*, Loyola University of Chicago Libraries (Medical Center), Maywood IL. 312-531-3192
Burns, Dorothy, *Librn*, Orlando Public Library (Booker T Washington), Orlando FL. 305-425-7319
Burns, Elisabeth S, *ILL, Ser & Bibliog Instr*, Roger Williams College Library, Bristol RI. 401-255-2361
Burns, Freddye, *Cat*, Tuskegee Institute, Hollis Burke Frissell Library, Tuskegee Institute AL. 205-727-8894
Burns, Glenda L, *Librn*, Pacific Coast Banking School Library, Seattle WA. 206-624-7618
Burns, Grant, *Libr Publ*, University of Michigan-Flint Library, Flint MI. 313-762-3400
Burns, Helen N, *Librn*, Brookfield Carnegie Library, Brookfield MO. 816-258-7439
Burns, Janice, *Librn*, Nestle Enterprises, Inc, Technical Service Library, Fulton NY. 315-598-1234, Ext 348
Burns, Jerry, *Hist Projects*, Credit Union National Association, Inc, Information Resource Center, Madison WI. 608-231-4170
Burns, Jesse N, *Librn*, Stark County District Library (Madge Youtz), Canton OH. 216-452-2618
Burns, Joan P, *Asst Dir*, University of Baltimore, Langsdale Library, Baltimore MD. 301-727-6350, Ext 444
Burns, John A, *Dir*, Wayne Public Library, Wayne NJ. 201-694-4272
Burns, Jonathan, *Ref & Spec Coll*, Portland Public Library, Baxter Library, Portland ME. 207-773-4761
Burns, Judith V, *Librn*, Sheridan Public Library, Sheridan MT. 406-842-5431
Burns, Julie, *Asst Librn*, Wesley College, Parker Library, Dover DE. 302-736-2413
Burns, Jurate, *Librn*, Destin Library, Inc, Destin FL. 904-837-8572
Burns, Karen, *Mgr*, Direct Mail-Marketing Association, Inc, Information Central, New York NY. 212-689-4977
Burns, Karen, *ILL & Ref*, Walworth County Library Services, Lake Geneva WI. 414-248-8312
Burns, Karen M, *ILL & Ref*, Lake Geneva Public Library, Lake Geneva WI. 414-248-8311
Burns, Keith P, *Dept Chmn*, West Virginia Wesleyan College, Dept of Library Science, WV. 304-473-8059
Burns, Keith P, *Dir*, West Virginia Wesleyan College, Annie Merner Pfeiffer Library, Buckhannon WV. 304-473-8059
Burns, Lillias, *Commun Servs*, Public Library of Nashville & Davidson County, Nashville TN. 615-244-4700
Burns, Lora, *Acq*, Mercer University, Stetson Memorial Library, Macon GA. 912-745-6811, Ext 284
Burns, Marcia, *Cat*, Saint Mary's College, Alumnae Centennial Library, Notre Dame IN. 219-284-4242
Burns, Margaret, *Trustee*, Gilmanton Iron Works Public Library, Gilmanton NH. 603-364-7786
Burns, Marie T, *Librn*, United Charities of Chicago Library, Chicago IL. 312-939-5930, Ext 158
Burns, Mary, *Librn*, Indianapolis-Marion County Public Library (Wishard Hospital), Indianapolis IN. 317-635-5662
Burns, Mary Frances, *Ref*, Palatine Public Library District, Palatine IL. 312-358-5881
Burns, Mary M, *Curriculum & Children's Lit*, Framingham State College, Henry Whittemore Library, Framingham MA. 617-620-1220, Ext 273
Burns, Max L, *Dir*, Westark Community College, Holt Library, Fort Smith AR. 501-785-4241, Ext 308
Burns, Michael, *Dir*, Bay De Noc Community College, Learning Resources Center, Escanaba MI. 906-786-5802, Ext 31
Burns, Michael F, *Dir*, Cloverland Processing Center, MI. 906-786-5802, Ext 22
Burns, Norma, *Librn*, West Stewartstown Library, Stewartstown NH. 603-246-8813
Burns, Ross, *Librn*, Waco-McLennan County Library (South Waco), Waco TX. 817-754-0358
Burns, Ruth S, *Librn*, Franklin Mint Corp, Information Research Services, Franklin Center PA. 215-459-6374
Burns, Sheila, *Children's Rm*, Tampa-Hillsborough County Public Library System, Tampa FL. 813-223-8947
Burns, Simone, *Librn*, Wentworth Military Academy, Sellers-Coombs Library, Lexington MO. 816-259-4261
Burns, Sister Mary Claudia, *AV*, College of Mount Saint Joseph on the Ohio, Archbishop Alter Library, Mount Saint Joseph OH. 513-244-4216
Burns, Susan, *Librn*, Houston Public Library (Walter), Houston TX. 713-771-5797
Burns, Susan, *Br Mgr*, United States General Accounting Office Library System (Office of Information Systems & Services), Washington DC. 275-3691 (Br Mgr), 275-5180 (Audit Ref Servs), 275-2585 (Law), 275-2555 (Tech Servs)
Burns, Susan K, *ILL*, Palmer College of Chiropractic, Davenport IA. 319-324-1611, Ext 242
Burns, Suzanne, *Bkmobile Coordr*, Miami Beach Public Library, Miami Beach FL. 305-673-7535
Burns, Tom, *Circ*, Humboldt State University Library, Arcata CA. 707-826-3441
Burns, Virginia, *Librn*, Stockton-San Joaquin County Public Library (Tracy Branch), Tracy CA. 209-944-8415
Burns, William A, *Exec Dir*, Florence Museum, Evans Research Center Library, Florence SC. 803-662-3351

Burnweit, Richard, *Circ,* Westmont College, Roger John Voskuyl Library, Santa Barbara CA. 805-969-5051, Ext 378

Burr, Bessie, *Librn,* Saint Francis Public Library, Saint Francis KS. 913-332-3292

Burr, Charlotte A, *Circ,* Ripon College Library, Ripon WI. 414-748-8328

Burr, Joanne, *Ch,* Southern Adirondack Library System, Saratoga Springs NY. 518-584-7300, 792-3343, 885-1073

Burr, Josephine, *ILL, Ad & On-Line Servs,* West Haven Public Library, West Haven CT. 203-932-2221

Burr, June G, *Librn,* Gorham-MacBane Public Library, Springfield TN. 615-384-5123

Burr, Margaret R, *Dir,* Deming Public Library, Deming NM. 505-546-9202

Burr, Mary Louise, *Librn,* East Mississippi Regional Library (Enterprise Public), Enterprise MS. 601-659-9127

Burr, Myrtis, *Asst Librn,* Chesterfield County Library, Chesterfield SC. 803-623-7489

Burr, Ravilla, *Acq,* Southwestern Adventist College, Findley Memorial Library, Keene TX. 817-645-3921, Ext 242

Burr, Robert L, *Dir,* Gonzaga University, Crosby Library, Spokane WA. 509-328-4220, Ext 3132

Burrell, Brenda, *Pub Servs,* Novi Public Library, Novi MI. 313-349-0720

Burrell, Eugene, *ILL & Ref,* Elkhart Public Library, Elkhart IN. 219-294-5463

Burrier, Donald H, *Dir,* Elyria Public Library, Elyria OH. 216-323-5747

Burrill, Amy J, *Librn,* Monroe Public Library, Monroe NH. 603-638-2590

Burris, Jim, *Librn,* Salt Lake County Judges' Law Library, Salt Lake City UT. 801-535-7518

Burritt, Beverly, *Librn,* Superior Public Library, Superior AZ. 602-689-2327

Burroughs, Carol, *Ref,* Gonzaga University, Crosby Library, Spokane WA. 509-328-4220, Ext 3132

Burroughs, Phyllis E, *Librn,* Dailey Memorial Library, Derby VT. 802-766-5063

Burrow, Neva L, *Librn,* Ledyard Public Library, Ledyard IA. 515-888-3311

Burrow, Sue, *Ch,* Humboldt County Library, Winnemucca NV. 702-623-5081, Ext 315 & 316

Burrowes, Mark, *Asst Dir,* Cooke County College, Mary Josephine Cox Memorial Library, Gainesville TX. 817-668-7731, Ext 237

Burrows, Ann Lewis, *Exec Dir,* Mary Ball Washington Museum & Library Inc, Lancaster VA. 804-462-7280

Burrows, E, *Actg Librn,* Agbabian Associates Library, El Segundo CA. 213-640-0576

Burrows, Jean, *Librn,* Deaconess Hospital, Library Resource Center, Oklahoma City OK. 405-946-5581, Ext 308

Burruss, Marsha, *Ref,* Principia College, Marshall Brooks Library, Elsah IL. 618-374-2131, Ext 325

Bursik, Martina, *Librn,* Buckham Memorial Library, Faribault MN. 507-334-2089

Burson, Phyllis, *Dir,* South Texas Library System, Corpus Christi TX. 512-882-6502

Burson, Phyllis S, *Librn,* Corpus Christi Public Libraries, La Retama Public Library, Corpus Christi TX. 512-882-1937

Burstein, Rose Anne, *Dir,* Sarah Lawrence College, Esther Raushenbush Library, Bronxville NY. 914-337-0700, Ext 479

Burston, Madeline H, *Librn,* Nassau County Department of Health, Div of Laboratories & Research Medical Library, Hempstead NY. 516-483-9158

Burt, D L, *Dir,* Nova Scotia Teachers College Library, Truro NS. 902-895-5347, Ext 30

Burt, David L, *Lectr,* Dalhousie University, School of Library Service, NS. 902-424-3656

Burt, DeVere, *Dir,* Cincinnati Museum of Natural History Library, Cincinnati OH. 513-621-3889

Burt, Eleanor Jones, *Librn,* Tennessee State Planning Office Library, Nashville TN. 615-741-2363

Burt, Lesta N, *Dir,* Sam Houston State University, Library Science Department, TX. 713-295-6211, Ext 1151

Burt, Sandra, *Librn,* Canadian Forestry Service, Great Lakes Forest Research Centre Library, Sault Sainte Marie ON. 705-949-9461, Ext 205

Burtch, Solglad, *Cat,* Stoneham Public Library, Stoneham MA. 617-438-1324

Burtis, Farida, *Dir Pub Relations,* Queens Borough Public Library, Jamaica NY. 212-990-0700

Burtniak, John, *Tech Serv & Acq,* Brock University Library, Saint Catharines ON. 416-684-7201

Burton, Ann, *Cat,* Midlands Technical College, Beltline Campus Library, Columbia SC. 803-782-5471, Ext 265

Burton, Annie Laurie, *Ch & YA,* Twin Falls Public Library, Twin Falls ID. 208-733-2965

Burton, Arlynn R, *Librn,* Cuyahoga County Public Library (Maple Heights Regional), Maple Heights OH. 216-475-5000

Burton, Audrey, *Ref,* George Fox College, Shambaugh Library, Newberg OR. 503-538-8383, Ext 303

Burton, Bob, *AV,* Oakton Community College, Learning Resource Center, Morton Grove IL. 312-967-5120, Ext 331

Burton, Cathy P, *Ch,* Lake Alfred Public Library, Lake Alfred FL. 813-956-3434

Burton, D, *ILL,* University of Missouri-Rolla Library, Rolla MO. 314-341-4227

Burton, Debra, *Librn,* Huntsville Public Library, Huntsville ON. 705-789-5232

Burton, Doris, *Librn,* Uintah County Library, Vernal UT. 801-789-0091

Burton, E Christine, *Librn,* William Ross Public Library, Chaplin CT. 203-455-9424

Burton, Elisabeth, *Librn,* Lloyd Noland Hospital, David Knox McKamy Medical Library, Fairfield AL. 205-783-5121

Burton, Ella, *Librn,* Crowsnest Municipal Library (Bellevue Municipal Public Library), Bellevue AB. 403-564-4849

Burton, Evelyn, *Librn,* Stillwater County Library (Reedpoint Soldier Boy Memorial County), Reedpoint MT. 406-322-5337

Burton, Frances, *Acq,* Northport Public Library, Northport NY. 516-261-6930

Burton, Geneva, *Acq & ILL,* Cincinnati Bible Seminary Library, Cincinnati OH. 513-471-4800, Ext 49

Burton, Graydon, *Circ,* Ricks College, David O McKay Learning Resources Center, Rexburg ID. 208-356-2351

Burton, Jean, *Cat,* Tom Green County Library System, San Angelo TX. 915-655-7321

Burton, Johanna, *Cat,* Haltom City Public Library, Haltom City TX. 817-834-7341

Burton, John, *Dir,* Flathead County Free Library, Kalispell MT. 406-755-5300, Ext 357

Burton, Lois, *Librn,* Indiana Academy of Science, John Shepard Wright Memorial Library, Indianapolis IN. 317-633-6425

Burton, Mel, *Ch,* Natrona County Public Library, Casper WY. 307-235-9272

Burton, Mrs F H, *Mgr,* Church of England Institute Library, Saint John NB. 506-693-2295

Burton, Robert E, *Dir,* State University of New York College at Plattsburgh, Benjamin F Feinberg Library, Plattsburgh NY. 518-564-3180

Burton, Ruth D, *Asst Dir,* Newburgh-Ohio Township Public Library, Newburgh IN. 812-853-5468

Burtt, Mabel, *Librn,* Sacramento Public Library (Hagginwood), Sacramento CA. 916-922-8455

Burtt, Richard, *On-Line Servs,* Hope College, Van Zoeren Library, Holland MI. 392-5111, Ext 2130

Burwell, David, *Librn,* Lawrence County Bar & Law Library Association, Ironton OH. 614-532-0582

Burwell, Edward, *Librn,* Union Carnegie Library, Union SC. 803-427-7140

Burwell, Pat M, *Films & Media,* North Texas Library System, Fort Worth TX. 817-335-6073

Bury, Barbara, *Librn,* University of Texas Health Science Center at San Antonio Library (Robert B Green Educational Resources Center), San Antonio TX. 512-223-6361, Ext 234

Bury, Jack C, *Dir,* Saddle Brook Free Public Library, Saddle Brook NJ. 201-843-3287

Bury, Mary Ann, *In Charge,* Celanese Corp, Celanese Plastics Co Information Center, Chatham NJ. 201-635-2600, Ext 4244

Bury, Mrs Pat, *Bkmobile Coordr,* Rockbridge Regional Library, Lexington VA. 703-463-4324

Bury, Peter, *Dir,* Glenview Public Library, Glenview IL. 312-724-5200

Burylo, Michelle, *Librn,* Air Products & Chemicals, Inc (Business Library), Allentown PA. 215-398-7442

Busboso, Jean, *Librn,* Fairfax County Public Library (Centreville Branch), Springfield VA. 703-451-8055

Busby, Bob, *Librn,* Speech Center Organization Parent Education, Speech & Language Development Center, Buena Park CA. 714-821-3620

Busby, Ollie, *Media,* Northland Pioneer College (District Learning Resources Center), Holbrook AZ. 602-524-6111, Ext 234 & 243

Busch, Anita, *Librn,* Dixon Township Library, Argonia KS. 316-435-6632

Busch, B J, *Librn,* University of Alberta (H T Coutts (Education) Library), Edmonton AB. 403-432-5555

Busch, Betty, *Librn,* Dayton Law Library Association, Dayton OH. 513-225-4505

Busch, Celesta, *On-Line Servs,* General Dynamics, Pomona Division Library, Pomona CA. 714-629-5111, Ext 4151, 4161

Busch, Constance, *Tech Serv & Cat,* Fairfield Public Library, Fairfield CT. 203-259-8303

Busch, Joseph, *Tech Serv,* Hampshire College, Harold F Johnson Library Center, Amherst MA. 413-549-4600

Busch, Nancy, *Pan Handle Network Coordr,* Nebraska Library Commission, Lincoln NE. 402-471-2045

Busenbark, Beverly V, *Librn,* Bell & Howell Co, Research Laboratories Library, Pasadena CA. 213-796-9381, Ext 2222

Busenlehner, Mrs Joe, *Librn,* Carnegie Public Library, Ballinger TX. 915-365-3616

Busey, Madge, *Librn,* United States Army (Army Engineer Center & Fort Belvoir Van Noy Library), Fort Belvoir VA. 703-664-6255

Busey, Madge, *Dir,* United States Army (Engineer School Library & Learning Resources Center), Fort Belvoir VA. 703-664-1140

Bush, Alfred, *Mss,* Princeton University Library, Princeton NJ. 609-452-3180

Bush, Bernard, *Exec Dir,* New Jersey State Library (New Jersey Historical Commission), Trenton NJ. 609-292-6062

Bush, Diane E, *Librn,* Canadian Baptist Archives, Hamilton ON. 416-525-9140, 4401

Bush, Douglas K, *Asst Dir, Pub Servs,* Brigham Young University, Harold B Lee Library, Provo UT. 801-378-2905

Bush, Ernest W, *Media,* Dallas Baptist College, Vance Memorial Library, Dallas TX. 214-331-8311, Ext 213

Bush, Gail, *Librn,* Heidrick & Struggles Inc, Library Research Center, Chicago IL. 312-372-8811

Bush, Gail, *Dir,* National College of Education, Chicago Campus Library, Chicago IL. 312-621-9676

Bush, Geneva, *Hosp Librn,* University of South Alabama (Biomedical Library), Mobile AL. 205-460-7043

Bush, Geneva L, *Tech Serv & Cat,* Mobile College, J L Bedsole Library, Mobile AL. 205-675-5990

Bush, George A, *Supvr,* Michigan Department of Corrections, Marquette Branch Prison State House of Correction Library, Marquette MI. 906-226-6531, Ext 326

Bush, Janet E N, *Librn,* Children's Hospital, Inc, Medical Library, Baltimore MD. 301-462-6800, Ext 209

Bush, Jo Ann, *Librn,* United States Department of the Interior (Heritage Conservation and Recreation Service Library), Denver CO. 303-234-6462

Bush, Jo Ann, *Librn,* United States Department of the Interior, Heritage Conservation & Recreation Service, Mid-Continent Regional Office Library, Lakewood CO. 303-234-2634

Bush, Kathy, *Media,* Muscatine Community College Library, Muscatine IA. 319-263-8250, Ext 112

Bush, Lael Laning, *Librn,* Rooks, Pitts, Fullagar & Poust Library, Chicago IL. 312-372-5600

Bush, Lael Laning, *Librn,* Sonnenschein, Carlin, Nath & Rosenthal, Law Library, Chicago IL. 312-876-7906

Bush, Lois, *Ref,* Suffolk County Community College (Selden Campus Library), Selden NY. 516-233-5181

Bush, Mary, *Asst Dir,* Long Beach Public Library, Long Beach MS. 601-863-0711

Bush, Nancy W, *Assoc Prof,* Auburn University, Dept of Educational Media, AL. 205-826-4529

Bush, Patricia A, *Mgt*, Northwestern University Library, Evanston IL. 312-492-7658

Bush, Rebecca C, *Acq & Cat*, Dallas Baptist College, Vance Memorial Library, Dallas TX. 214-331-8311, Ext 213

Bush, Richard, *Librn*, Choteau County Free Library (Big Sandy Branch), Big Sandy MT. 406-622-5222

Bush, Thelma R, *Librn*, Coolidge Library, Coolidge KS. 316-372-8631

Bushell, Margaret, *Supvr*, Huron County Public Library (Goderich Branch), Goderich ON. 519-524-9261, 524-7734

Bushey, Kathleen, *Librn*, Modoc County Library (Canby), Canby CA. 916-233-2719

Bushey, Marge, *Asst Dir*, Agness Community Library, Agness OR. 503-247-6083

Bushman, James, *ILL*, Rockefeller University Library, New York NY. 212-360-1000

Bushnell, C Patricia, *Ch*, South Milwaukee Public Library, South Milwaukee WI. 414-762-8692

Bushnell, Judith A, *Librn*, State University of New York College at Geneseo (School of Library & Information Science), Geneseo NY. 716-245-5334

Bushnell, Marietta P, *Dir*, Pennsylvania Academy of Fine Arts, Philadelphia PA. 215-972-7611

Bushong, Sharon, *Librn*, Findlay-Hancock County Public Library (Arlington Branch), Arlington OH. 419-365-5755

Bushong, Sharon, *Librn*, Findlay-Hancock County Public Library (Mount Blanchard Branch), Mount Blanchard OH. 419-422-1712

Busick, Christopher, *On-Line Servs*, Wayne State University Libraries (G Flint Purdy Library), Detroit MI. 313-577-4032

Buske, Angela, *On-Line Servs*, Dow Chemical Co (Technical Information Services), Midland MI. 517-636-0972

Buskey, John L, *Dir*, Alabama State University, Library & Learning Resources, Montgomery AL. 205-832-6072

Busler, Mary Ann, *Commun Servs*, Muscle Shoals Regional Library System, Florence AL. 205-764-6563

Busman, Sheryl, *Asst Librn*, Allendale Township Library, Allendale MI. 616-895-4178

Buss, David, *Ref, On-Line Servs & Bibliog Instr*, Pima Community College, West Campus Learning Resource Center, Tucson AZ. 602-884-6821

Buss, Margaret, *Librn*, California Department of Transportation, District 4 Library, San Francisco CA. 415-577-3894

Busse, Lawrence R, *Asst Prof*, Saint Cloud State University, Center for Library & Audiovisual Education, MN. 612-255-2022

Busse, S, *Doc, On-Line Servs & Bibliog Instr*, Addiction Research Foundation Library, Toronto ON. 416-595-6144

Busselle, Patricia S, *Legis Ref & On-Line Serv*, New Hampshire State Library, Concord NH. 603-271-2392

Bussert, Elizabeth, *Librn*, Sheldon Township Public Library, Sheldon IL. 815-429-3521

Bussinger, Madelyn, *Librn*, Saint Charles City County Library (O'Fallon Branch), O'Fallon MO. 314-272-4999

Busta, Mrs Paul, *Asst Librn*, Granville Public Library, Granville OH. 614-587-0196

Bustamante, Pauline, *Br Libr Asst*, Ventura County Library Services Agency (El Rio Branch), El Rio CA. 805-485-4515

Bustamonte, Pauline, *Br Libr Asst*, Ventura County Library Services Agency (Avenue), Ventura CA. 805-643-6393

Bustetter, Stan, *Exten*, Forsyth County Public Library, Winston-Salem NC. 919-727-2256

Butchart, Glenn, *Dir*, Parkland Regional Library Service, Dauphin MB. 204-638-6410

Butchart, Lorraine, *Pub Servs*, Jackson District Library, Jackson MI. 517-788-4087

Butcher, Jeanne, *Ad*, Emporia Public Library, Emporia KS. 316-342-6524

Butcher, Jo Ellen, *Assoc Librn*, Borg-Warner Corp, Chemicals Library, Washington WV. 304-863-7335, Ext 335

Butcher, Theresa M, *Lectr*, Concordia University, Library Studies Program, PQ. 514-482-0320, Ext 324

Buten, David, *Dir*, Buten Museum of Wedgwood Library, Merion PA. 215-664-6601

Buterbaugh, James G, *Dept Chmn*, University of Utah, Dept of Educational Systems & Learning Resources, UT. 801-581-7123

Buth, Olga, *Music Librn*, University of Texas Libraries (Fine Arts), Austin TX. 512-471-4777

Buthod, Craig, *Bus & Tech*, Tulsa City-County Library, Tulsa OK. 918-581-5221

Buthod, Craig, *Librn*, Williams Brothers Engineering Co, Technical Information Center, Tulsa OK. 918-496-5020

Butkovich, Margaret, *Assoc Dir*, University of Colorado Health Sciences Center (Denison Memorial Library), Denver CO. 303-394-5125

Butler, Allene, *Librn*, Mechanicsville Public Library, Mechanicsville IA. 319-432-7135

Butler, Alycia Smith, *Librn*, Hubbardston Public Library, Hubbardston MA. 617-928-4775

Butler, Anne H, *Librn, On-Line Servs & Bibliog Instr*, Alston, Miller & Gaines, Law Library, Atlanta GA. 404-586-1500, Ext 1508, 1509

Butler, Anne J, *Lectr*, Emory University, Div of Librarianship, GA. 404-329-6840

Butler, Anthony M, *Dir*, Bridgeton Free Public Library, Bridgeton NJ. 609-451-2620

Butler, Antoinette, *Ref*, American Telephone & Telegraph, Business & Technical Resources Center, Piscataway NJ. 201-699-2169

Butler, Barbara, *Asst Librn*, Newbury Public Library, Newbury MA. 617-465-0539

Butler, Beverly E, *Librn*, Hunton & Williams Law Library, Richmond VA. 804-788-8245

Butler, David, *Instr*, University of Denver, Graduate School of Librarianship and Information Management, CO. 303-753-2557

Butler, Dean L, *Librn*, IBM Corp, Boulder Library, Boulder CO. 303-447-5064

Butler, Dottie, *Librn*, Forsyth County Public Library (East Winston Branch), Winston-Salem NC. 919-727-2202

Butler, Douglas, *Tech Serv, Cat & On-Line Servs*, Asbury College, Morrison-Kenyon Library, Wilmore KY. 606-858-3511

Butler, Eva K, *Librn*, Scott Paper Co (Marketing Library), Philadelphia PA. 215-521-5000, Ext 2262

Butler, Evelyn, *Librn*, University of Pennsylvania Libraries (Social Work), Philadelphia PA. 215-243-5509

Butler, Ilean, *Librn*, Philomath Public Library, Philomath OR. 503-929-3016

Butler, Iva, *Dir*, Charles Ralph Holland Memorial Library, Jackson County Public Library, Gainesboro TN. 615-268-9190

Butler, Janice, *Neighborhood Br Coordr*, New Orleans Public Library, Simon Heinsheim & Fisk Libraries, New Orleans LA. 504-586-4905

Butler, Janice, *Coll Develop*, University of Colorado Health Sciences Center (Denison Memorial Library), Denver CO. 303-394-5125

Butler, Joan, *Ch*, Peterborough Town Library, Peterborough NH. 603-924-6401

Butler, Joan, *Dir*, Public Library of New London, New London CT. 203-447-1411, 447-1412

Butler, Joyce, *Librn*, Rockingham Public Library (Page Public), Luray VA. 703-743-6867

Butler, Kenneth W, *Actg Dir*, Portland State University, Branford Price Millar Library, Portland OR. 503-229-4424

Butler, Lucy K, *Librn*, Veterans Administration, Hospital Library, Providence RI. 401-521-1700, Ext 537, 539

Butler, Lynne, *Dir*, Vernon Area Public Library, Prairie View IL. 312-634-3650

Butler, Margaret, *Librn*, New York Life Insurance Co (Law Library), New York NY. 212-576-6458

Butler, Marian, *Br Coordr*, Selby Public Library, Sarasota County Federated Library System, Sarasota FL. 814-366-7303

Butler, Marian, *Librn*, Selby Public Library (Betty W Service Branch), Sarasota FL. 814-921-5901

Butler, Mary Austin, *Librn*, Dewey County Library (Dakota Club), Eagle Butte SD. 605-964-7661

Butler, Meredith, *Asst Dir Pub Servs*, State University of New York College at Brockport, Drake Memorial Library, Brockport NY. 716-395-2140

Butler, Nancy, *Librn*, Greenville County Library (Fountain Inn), Fountain Inn SC. 803-862-2576

Butler, Naomi W, *Sch Libr Media Specialists*, Maryland State Department of Education, Division of Library Development & Services, Baltimore MD. 301-796-8300, Ext 284

Butler, Patricia, *Ref*, Wichita State University, Library & Media Resources Center, Wichita KS. 316-689-3586

Butler, Patrick, *Dir*, Schoolcraft College, Eric J Bradner Library, Livonia MI. 313-591-6400, Ext 412

Butler, Randall, *Assoc Dir*, California State University, John F Kennedy Memorial Library, Los Angeles CA. 213-224-2201

Butler, Ruth G, *Dir*, Houghton College-Buffalo Extension Campus, Ada M Kidder Memorial Library, West Seneca NY. 716-674-6363

Butler, Thelma, *Librn*, Lennox & Addington County Public Library (Newburgh Branch), Newburgh ON. 613-354-2585

Butler, Thomas, *Media*, Staley Library, Millikin University, Decatur IL. 217-424-6214

Butler, Jr, Joseph T, *Tech Serv*, Nicholls State University, Allen J Ellender Memorial Library, Thibodaux LA. 504-446-8111, Ext 401, 402

Butorac, Frank G, *Dir*, Mercer County Community College Library, Trenton NJ. 609-586-4800, Ext 358

Butorac, Frank G, *Dept Chmn*, Mercer County Community College, Library-Media Center Technical Assistant Program, NJ. 609-586-4800, Ext 360

Butson, Linda C, *Dir*, Mountain Area Health Education Center, Health Sciences Library, Asheville NC. 258-0881 Ext 210

Butt, Jean, *Ref & Spec Coll*, Tufts University, Nils Yngve Wessell Library, Medford MA. 617-628-5000, Ext 235

Butt, Karen, *Ch*, Dare County Library, Manteo NC. 919-473-2372

Butt, Minnie, *Librn*, Hards Memorial Library, Central City NE. 308-946-2512

Butt, Mrs M, *Supvr*, Edmonton Public Library (Strathcona), Edmonton AB. 403-439-6450

Buttars, Gerald, *Blind Servs*, Utah State Library, Salt Lake City UT. 801-533-5875

Buttars, Gerald A, *Librn*, Utah State Library Commission, Division for the Blind & Physically Handicapped, Salt Lake City UT. 801-533-5855

Butter, Karen, *ILL & Pub Servs*, University of Utah (Spencer S Eccles Health Sciences Library), Salt Lake City UT. 801-581-8771

Butter, Pat, *Librn*, Regional Memorial Hospital, Health Sciences Library, Brunswick ME. 207-729-0181, Ext 365

Butterbaugh, Pauline, *Asst Librn*, Kendallville Public Library, Kendallville IN. 219-347-3554

Butterfield, Eileen, *Ch*, Waterford Public Library, Waterford CT. 203-442-8551

Butterfield, Elaine A, *Librn*, Carbon County Public Library (Saratoga Branch), Saratoga WY. 307-326-8209

Butterfield, Margaret D, *Librn*, Caribou Public Library, Caribou ME. 207-496-5411

Butterfield, Rita, *Circ*, University of British Columbia Library, Vancouver BC. 604-228-3871

Butterwick, Ann, *Librn*, Wentworth Library (Millgrove Branch), Millgrove ON. 416-526-4126

Buttler, Charlotte, *Instr*, Northwestern College, Library Science Program, IA. 712-722-4821

Buttler, Margaret, *Librn*, Rutgers University (Physics), New Brunswick NJ. 201-932-2500

Buttner, Michael, *Recording Specialist*, New York Association for the Blind, Lighthouse Library, New York NY. 212-355-2200, Ext 397

Button, Evelyn, *Librn*, Huxley Public Library, Huxley IA. 515-597-2552

Button, Katherine, *Librn & On-Line Servs*, Massachusetts General Hospital (Treadwell Library), Boston MA. 617-726-8600

Button, Marge, *Tech Serv*, Southbury Public Library, Southbury CT. 203-264-0606, Ext 239

Button, Mary L, *Librn*, Clifton Springs Hospital & Clinic, Medical Library, Clifton Springs NY. 315-462-9561

Butts, Carol, *Tech Serv*, Lawrence University, Seeley G Mudd Library, Appleton WI. 414-739-3681, Ext 264

Butts, Dorothea, *Media*, Willard Library, Battle Creek MI. 616-968-8166

Butts, Gordon Keith, *Prof*, Southern Illinois University at Carbondale, Educational Media Program, IL. 618-453-5764

Butts, Joan, *Dir*, Lyons Public Library, Lyons KS. 316-257-2961

Butts, Kay, *Asst Librn*, Oneonta Public Library, Oneonta AL. 205-274-7641

Butts, Roberta, *Libr Technicians,* Veterans Administration, Hospital Library, Miles City MT. 406-232-3060, Ext 305

Butts, Rosie, *Librn,* Uncle Remus Regional Library (Hancock County), Sparta GA. 404-444-5389

Butts, III, H Daniel, *Dir,* Mansfield Art Library, Mansfield Fine Arts Guild, Inc, Mansfield OH. 419-756-1700

Butzer, Patricia, *Librn,* Meals for Millions Foundation Library, Santa Monica CA. 213-829-5337

Buurma, Clarence, *Dir,* Mescalero Community Library, Mescalero NM. 505-671-4494, Ext 205 & 206

Buurstra, Annette, *Educ,* Northeastern Illinois University Library, Chicago IL. 312-583-4050, Ext 469, 470, 471, 472

Buus, David, *Instr,* Pima Community College, Library Technology Program, AZ. 602-884-6821

Buvinger, Jan, *Dep Dir,* Charleston County Library, Charleston SC. 803-723-1645

Buxton, Anne, *Bkmobile Librns,* Athens Regional Library, Athens GA. 404-543-0134

Buxton, Helen L, *Librn,* Skowhegan Free Public Library, Skowhegan ME. 207-474-9072

Buxton, Kathy, *Ch,* George Amos Memorial Library, Campbell County Library, Gillette WY. 307-682-3223

Buxton, Reginald C, *Librn,* Ellinwood School Community Library, Ellinwood KS. 316-564-2306

Buxton, Suzanne, *Media,* Richmond Hill Public Library, Richmond Hill ON. 416-884-9288

Buzan, Norma, *Commun Servs,* Troy Public Library, Troy MI. 313-689-5665

Buzas, John P, *Librn,* United States Navy (Naval Air Station Library), Norfolk VA. 804-444-3583

Buzas, Mary, *Ad,* Butler Public Library, Butler PA. 412-287-5576

Buzzard, Deborah, *Circ,* Niles Community Library, Niles MI. 616-683-8545, 683-8546

Buzzard, Marion, *Acq,* University of California Library, Irvine CA. 714-833-5212

Buzzell, Marguerite, *Librn,* Maxfield Public Library, Loudon NH. 603-798-5153

Byam, Mildred, *Asst Dir, ILL & Acq,* Saint Bernard's Seminary Library, Rochester NY. 716-254-1020, Ext 25, 26, 27

Byan, Phyllis, *ILL,* Sarah Lawrence College, Esther Raushenbush Library, Bronxville NY. 914-337-0700, Ext 479

Byard, Anne, *Dir,* Blue Mound Memorial Public Library, Blue Mound IL. 217-692-2774

Bybell, Betsy, *Br Coordr,* Moscow-Latah County Library System, Moscow ID. 208-882-3925

Bye, John, *Archivist,* North Dakota State University Library, Fargo ND. 701-237-8876

Byer, Janice, *Asst Dir,* Mount Ida Junior College, Hallden Library, Newton Centre MA. 617-969-7000, Ext 152

Byergo, Fredrick H, *Dir,* Cook Memorial Public Library District, Libertyville IL. 312-362-2330

Byerly, Barbara, *Librn,* Jacksonville Public Library System (Murray Hill), Jacksonville FL. 904-633-3787

Byerly, Mary, *Asst Librn,* Cornell College, Russell D Cole Library, Mount Vernon IA. 319-895-8811, Ext 117

Byers, Barbara, *Ad, Commun Servs & Br Coordr,* Washington County Library, Lake Elmo MN. 612-777-8143

Byers, Bertina, *Doc,* United States Army (Combined Arms Research Library), Fort Leavenworth KS. 913-684-3282

Byers, Dorothy, *Head,* University of Cincinnati Libraries (Engineering), Cincinnati OH. 513-475-3761

Byers, Edward W, *Dir,* Laramie County Library System, Cheyenne WY. 307-634-3561

Byers, Laura, *Librn Ctr for Studies in Landscape Archit,* Harvard University Library (Dumbarton Oaks Research Library, Bliss Pre-Columbian Collection & Garden Library), Washington DC. 202-232-3101

Byers, Marie, *Ref & Bibliog Instr,* David Lipscomb College, Crisman Memorial Library, Nashville TN. 615-385-3855, Ext 282, 283

Byers, Mary Katherine, *Tech Serv, Cat & On-Line Servs,* Waco-McLennan County Library, Waco TX. 817-754-4694

Byers, Montez G, *Actg Librn,* Bennett College, Thomas F Holgate Library, Greensboro NC. 919-273-4431, Ext 139

Byers, Rosemarie, *Tech Serv,* Grace A Dow Memorial Library, Midland Public Library, Midland MI. 517-835-7151

Byers, Ruth, *Ref & ILL,* York County Library, Headquarters Rock Hill Public Library, Rock Hill SC. 803-328-8402

Byers, Sarah L, *Librn,* Frederick Eugene Lykes Jr Memorial County Library, Brooksville FL. 904-796-3480

Byfield, Mary, *Cat,* Pasadena Public Library, Pasadena TX. 713-477-0276

Byington, Edith, *Librn,* Alford Town Library, Alford MA. 413-528-4536

Byington, Sally A, *Librn,* Wonewoc Public Library, Wonewoc WI. 608-464-7625

Bykowski, James, *Production Servs Coordr,* McHenry County College, Learning Resource Center System, Crystal Lake IL. 815-455-3700, Ext 276

Bylkas, Helen V, *Cat,* Michigan Technological University Library, Houghton MI. 906-487-2500

Byman, Judith A, *ILL, On-Line Servs & Bibliog Instr,* Monroe Community College, LeRoy V Good Library, Rochester NY. 716-442-9950, Ext 2310

Bynagle, Hans E, *Dir,* Friends University, Edmund Stanley Library, Wichita KS. 316-263-9131, Ext 220

Bynes, Betty, *Librn,* Chatham-Effingham-Liberty Regional Library (Carnegie), Savannah GA. 912-232-1420

Bynkoski, Ruth, *Librn,* Rainy River Public Library, Rainy River ON. 807-852-3375

Bynon, George E, *Instrnl Media Ctr,* University of Oregon Library, Eugene OR. 503-686-3056

Bynum, Elizabeth, *Librn,* Wentworth Library (Greensville), Hamilton ON. 416-526-4126

Bynum, Helen, *Librn,* John Henderson Memorial Library, Westville OK. 918-723-5002

Byra, Susan, *Dir,* DeSoto Parish Library, Mansfield LA. 318-872-2441

Byra, Susan T, *Asst Dir,* East Mississippi Regional Library, Quitman MS. 601-776-2492

Bryant, Riette Susie, *Dir,* Walker College, Irma D Nicholson Library, Jasper AL. 205-387-0511, Ext 37

Byrd, Ada, *Dir,* Beaufort County Community College, Washington NC. 919-946-6194, Ext 244

Byrd, Anne, *Librn,* Northeast Regional Library (Iuka Library), Iuka MS. 601-423-6300

Byrd, Annette, *Librn,* Hartselle Public Library, Hartselle AL. 205-773-9880

Byrd, Coleen, *Chief Librn,* Gulfport-Harrison County Library, Gulfport MS. 601-863-6411

Byrd, Darlene F, *In Charge,* Presbyterian Hospital, School of Nursing Library, Charlotte NC. 704-371-4258

Byrd, Ethel G, *Acq,* Benedict College, Benjamin F Payton Learning Resources Ctr, Columbia SC. 803-256-4220

Byrd, Fay, *Dir,* Wilkes Community College, Learning Resources Library, Wilkesboro NC. 919-667-7136, Ext 26

Byrd, Gary, *Dir of Media Ctr,* Arkansas College, Mabee Learning Resources Center, Batesville AR. 501-793-9813

Byrd, Gary, *President,* Kansas City Library Network Inc, MO. 816-932-2333

Byrd, Gary D, *Librn,* University of Missouri-Kansas City Libraries (Medical Library), Kansas City MO. 816-474-4100, Ext 280

Byrd, Gladys H, *Dir,* Brewton Public Library, Brewton AL. 205-867-4626

Byrd, Julia, *Libr Technician,* Veterans Administration, Medical Center Library, Lake City FL. 904-752-1400, Ext 272

Byrd, Lorna, *Librn,* Pikes Peak Regional Library District (East), Colorado Springs CO. 303-591-0091

Byrd, Ron, *Cat,* Fresno City College, Learning Resources Center, Fresno CA. 209-442-8204

Byrd, Rose, *In Charge,* Miami-Dade Public Library System (Model City), Miami FL. 305-638-6978

Byrd, T, *Ref,* J Sargeant Reynolds Community College (Parham Campus Learning Resources Center), Richmond VA. 804-264-3220

Byrd, Theresa, *ILL & Bibliog Instr,* J Sargeant Reynolds Community College (Parham Campus Learning Resources Center), Richmond VA. 804-264-3220

Byrd-Watts, Doris, *Librn,* Buffalo & Erie County Public Library System (North Jefferson), Buffalo NY. 716-883-4418

Byrne, C C, *Librn,* Atomic Energy of Canada Ltd, Engineering Company Library, Mississauga ON. 416-823-9040, Ext 2247

Byrne, Dorothy, *Dir,* Seguin-Guadalupe County Public Library, Seguin TX. 512-379-1531

Byrne, Elizabeth, *Head Librn,* University of Cincinnati Libraries (Design, Architecture & Art), Cincinnati OH. 513-475-3238

Byrne, Frederick, *Librn,* Columbia University (Burgess-Carpenter Classics Library), New York NY. 212-280-2241

Byrne, Frederick, *Librn,* Columbia University (Columbia College Library), New York NY. 212-280-3534

Byrne, Frederick, *Bibliog Instr,* Columbia University (University Libraries), New York NY. 212-280-2241

Byrne, Janice Durack, *Librn,* Chicago Public Library (Garfield Ridge), Chicago IL. 312-582-6094

Byrne, Joan, *Asst Dir & Ref,* Dodge City Public Library, Dodge City KS. 316-225-0248

Byrne, Margaret A, *Librn,* United States Air Force (Offutt Air Force Base Library), Offutt AFB NE. 402-294-2533

Byrne, Mary, *ILL,* Winnetka Public Library District, Winnetka IL. 312-446-5085

Byrne, Mary Ann, *Ad & Commun Servs,* Altadena Library District, Altadena CA. 213-798-0833

Byrne, Mary M, *Dir,* Delaware Technical & Community College, Terry Campus Learning Resources Center, Dover DE. 302-678-5404

Byrne, Nadene, *Head Librn,* Art Institute of Chicago (Art School Library), Chicago IL. 312-443-3748

Byrne, Paula E, *Librn,* New Bedford Free Public Library (Howland-Green), New Bedford MA. 617-992-4595

Byrne, Sister Ann, *Dir & On-Line Servs,* Caldwell College Library, Caldwell NJ. 201-228-4424, Ext 34

Byrne, Sister Ann, *Chmn,* Caldwell College, Library Science Program, NJ. 201-228-4424

Byrne, Suzanne W, *Librn,* South Fulton Hospital, Health Sciences Library, East Point GA. 404-763-5174

Byrne, Tim, *Govt Doc,* Virginia Commonwealth University (James Branch Cabell Library), Richmond VA. 804-257-1105

Byrne, Tina, *Co-Director,* Regional Information & Communication Exchange, TX. 713-528-3553

Byrne, W, *In Charge,* Alberta Department of Culture (Archeological Survey of Alberta), Edmonton AB. 403-427-2355

Byrne, Jr, Frank P, *Chief Librn,* United States Marine Band Music Library, Washington DC. 202-433-4298

Byrnes, Letha, *Librn,* Illinois Prairie District Public Library (Roanoke Branch), Roanoke IL. 309-923-7686

Byrnes, Martha C, *Asst Dir,* Whittier College School of Law Library, Los Angeles CA. 213-938-3621, Ext 24

Byrns, James, *Librn,* Brooklyn Public Library (Midwood), Brooklyn NY. 212-377-7972

Byron, Sister Berenice, *Acq,* Thomas More College, Learning Resources Center, Fort Mitchell KY. 606-341-5800, Ext 61

Byrum, Lois, *On-Line Servs,* Minnesota Department of Education Professional Library, Saint Paul MN. 612-296-6104

Byrum, Jr, John D, *Chief, Descriptive Cat Div,* Library of Congress, Washington DC. 202-287-5000

Bysiewicz, Shirley R, *Librn,* University of Connecticut at Hartford (Law Library), West Hartford CT. 203-523-4841, Ext 347, 370

Bystrom, Esther B, *Dir,* Marquette County Historical Society, J M Longyear Research Library, Marquette MI. 906-226-6821

C

Caballero, Cesar, *Rare Bks & Spec Coll,* University of Texas at El Paso Library, El Paso TX. 747-5683; 747-5684

Caballero, Isabel S, *Hist of Medicine*, University of Miami (Louis Calder Memorial Library), Miami FL. 305-547-6441

Cabeceiras, James, *Prof*, San Jose State University, Division of Library Science, CA. 408-277-2292

Cabeen, Kirk, *Dir*, Engineering Societies Library, New York NY. 212-644-7611

Cabell, Leo, *Assoc Dir*, University of Colorado at Boulder (University Libraries), Boulder CO. 303-492-7511

Cabello, Roberto, *Librn*, Anaheim Public Library (Elva L Haskett), Anaheim CA. 714-821-0553

Cable, Carole, *Librn*, University of Texas Libraries (Architecture & Planning), Austin TX. 512-471-1844

Cable, Carole, *Architecture & Fine Arts Librn*, University of Texas Libraries (Fine Arts), Austin TX. 512-471-4777

Cabrera, Lupe, *In Charge*, Talley Industries, Dynamic Science, Inc Library, Phoenix AZ. 602-869-9331

Cace, Elga, *Librn*, New York Public Library (Fordham Library Center), Bronx NY. 212-220-6572

Cacharelis, Jane, *Ref*, Truman College, Learning Resources Center, Chicago IL. 312-878-1700, Ext 2230

Cackowski, Irene, *Dir*, South River Public Library, South River NJ. 201-254-2488

Caddell, Claude W, *Dir*, Frankfort Community Public Library, Frankfort IN. 317-654-8746

Caddell, Peggy, *AV*, Odessa College, Murry H Fly Learning Resources Center, Odessa TX. 915-337-5381, Ext 299

Caddy, James L, *Librn*, Saint Mary Seminary Graduate School of Theology, Mullen Library, Cleveland OH. 216-721-2100

Cade, Roberta G, *Asst Dir for Programs & Servs*, Mid-York Library System, Utica NY. 315-735-8328

Cadieu, Betsy R, *Bus Mgr*, Sandhill Regional Library System, Rockingham NC. 919-997-3388

Cadieu, Cheryl, *Dir*, Spies Public Library, Menominee MI. 906-836-3911

Cadieux, Jacques, *Librn*, Canada Department of National Defense, National Department Headquarters Library, Ottawa ON. 613-996-0831

Cadle, Dean, *Tech Serv*, University of North Carolina at Asheville, D Hiden Ramsey Library, Asheville NC. 704-258-0200

Cadman, Mrs Marion C, *Librn*, Gulf Canada Ltd, Head Office Library, Toronto ON. 416-924-4141, Ext 287, 297

Cadmus, Pamela, *Librn*, Montgomery-Floyd Regional Library (Floyd Branch), Floyd VA. 703-745-2947

Cadwell, Annette G, *Info Specialist*, National Restaurant Association, Information Resource Center, Chicago IL. 312-787-2525

Cady, Louise M, *Librn*, Canaan Town Library, Canaan NH. 603-523-4266

Cael, Zita, *Acq*, Florida Atlantic University, S E Wimberly Library, Boca Raton FL. 305-395-5100, Ext 2448

Caez, Ana, *Circ*, Bayard Taylor Memorial Library, Kennett Square PA. 215-444-2702

Caffarel, Sister Agnes, *Librn*, Hotel Dieu Hospital Library, New Orleans LA. 504-588-3470

Caffrey, Margaret, *Cat*, Johnson County Community College Library, Overland Park KS. 913-888-8500, Ext 532

Caffrey, Margaret M, *Librn*, Allentown State Hospital, Heim Memorial Library, Allentown PA. 215-821-6265

Cagan, W Daniel, *Librn*, Oral Roberts University, John D Messick Learning Resources Center, Tulsa OK. 918-492-6161

Cage, Alvin C, *Dir*, Stephen F Austin State University, Ralph W Steen Library, Nacogdoches TX. 713-569-4109

Cage, Lee, *Dir*, Nacogdoches Public Library, Nacogdoches TX. 713-569-8282

Caggiano, Alice C, *Librn*, Butterfield Library, Westminster VT. 802-722-4324

Cagle, Brantley, *Doc*, McNeese State University, Lether E Frazar Memorial Library, Lake Charles LA. 318-477-2520, Ext 271

Cagle, Marion, *Ch*, Lee-Itawamba Library System, Lee County Library, Tupelo MS. 601-844-2377

Cagle, Phyllis, *Acq*, Charles A Cannon Memorial Library, Concord NC. 704-788-3167

Cagle, William, *Librn*, Indiana University at Bloomington (Lilly Rare Books), Bloomington IN. 812-337-2452

Cagle, William, *Rare Bks*, Indiana University at Bloomington, University Libraries, Bloomington IN. 812-337-3403

Cahalan, Lee, *Librn*, Rollman Psychiatric Institute, Medical Library, Cincinnati OH. 513-559-3200

Cahalan, Thomas H, *Acq*, Northeastern University Libraries, Boston MA. 617-437-2350

Cahall, Marcia K, *Librn*, Procter & Gamble Co (Company Library), Cincinnati OH. 513-562-1100

Cahall, Mary, *Dir*, Sussex County Department of Libraries (Greenwood Public), Greenwood DE. 302-349-5309

Cahen, Stephanie, *Librn*, Wardsboro Free Public Library, Wardsboro VT. 802-869-2551

Cahill, Ann, *Syst Coordr*, Kansas City Public Library, Kansas City MO. 816-221-2685

Cahill, Anne, *Ref*, Skagit Valley College, Library Media Center, Mount Vernon WA. 206-424-1031, Ext 111

Cahill, Brian, *On-Line Servs & Bibliog Instr*, Larder Lake Public Library, Larder Lake ON. 705-643-2222

Cahill, Brian L, *Dir*, Northeastern Regional Library System, Kirkland Lake ON. 705-567-7043

Cahill, Fred, *Admin Asst*, New Jersey State Library, Trenton NJ. 609-292-6200

Cahill, L, *Librn*, Nesbitt Thomson & Co Ltd Library, Montreal PQ. 514-844-0131, Ext 375, 372

Cahill, Mary Clare, *Librn*, Smithsonian Institution Libraries, Radiation Biology Laboratory Library, Rockville MD. 301-443-2307

Cahill, Nan, *Acq*, Marianopolis College Library, Montreal PQ. 514-931-8792

Cahoon, Andrea R, *Dir*, Ringwood Public Library, Ringwood NJ. 201-962-6256

Cahoon, Nadine B, *Librn*, Ladies Library Association, East Burke VT. 802-626-9823

Cail, Nada, *Cat*, Villanova University (Pulling Law Library), Villanova PA. 215-527-2100, Ext 702, 703, 704

Cain, Elizabeth, *Librn*, Halstead Public Library, Halstead KS. 316-835-2170

Cain, Glenda, *Circ*, George S Houston Memorial Library, Dothan AL. 205-793-9767

Cain, H C, *Librn*, Lamont Memorial Free Library, McGraw NY. 607-836-6767

Cain, Jacquelyn S, *Librn*, Ketchum Macleod & Grove Inc, Library Services, Pittsburgh PA. 412-456-3600

Cain, Kaye, *Bkmobile Coordr*, Hayner Public Library District, Alton IL. 618-462-0651

Cain, Linda, *Hist & Geog*, Jacksonville State University Library, Jacksonville AL. 205-435-9820, Ext 213, 214

Cain, Marie, *Librn*, Albia Public Library, Albia IA. 515-932-2469

Cain, Mary E, *Asst Dir & Ch*, Whitewater Public Library, Whitewater WI. 414-473-3906

Cain, Melissa, *Actg Librn*, University of Illinois Library at Urbana-Champaign (English), Urbana IL. 217-333-2220

Cain, Robert E, *Asst Librn*, Fitchburg Public Library, Fitchburg MA. 617-343-3096

Cain, Tom, *Govt Docs*, Golden Gate University (School of Law Library), San Francisco CA. 415-442-7260

Cain-Seiler, Kathi, *Bibliog Instr*, Community College of Denver, North Campus Learning Materials Center, Westminster CO. 303-466-8811, Ext 500

Caine, B, *Acq*, Georgia Institute of Technology, Price Gilbert Memorial Library, Atlanta GA. 404-894-4510

Caine, Carol, *Librn*, Miami-Dade Public Library System (Lemon City), Miami FL. 305-638-6909

Caine, Cathy, *Librn*, Austin Public Library (Little Walnut Creek), Austin TX. 512-472-5433

Caine, Cathy, *Librn*, Austin Public Library (North Oaks Branch), Austin TX. 512-472-5433

Caine, Phyllis, *Acq & Ref*, Shasta College Library, Redding CA. 916-241-3523, Ext 377

Cainen, Barbara, *Librn*, Essex County Public Library (Malden Rd), Windsor ON. 519-776-5241

Caintic, Zenaida L, *Librn*, Catholic Newman Center Library, Lexington KY. 606-255-0467

Cairns, Alvene, *Librn*, Western Plains Library System (Appleton Branch), Appleton MN. 612-289-1681

Cairns, Eleanor C, *Ch*, Maine Medical Center, Health Science Library, Portland ME. 207-871-2201

Cairns, P, *Dir*, Braille Institute of America, Inc, Library, Los Angeles CA. 213-660-3880

Cairns, Patricia Newton, *Librn*, Ellwood City Area Public Library, Ellwood City PA. 412-758-6458

Cairns, Roberta A E, *Dir*, Barrington Public Library, Barrington RI. 401-245-3106

Cairns, Roberta A E, *Dir*, East Providence Public Library, Weaver Memorial Library, East Providence RI. 401-434-2453

Cairns, Sister Marie L, *Assoc Prof*, Louisiana State University, Graduate School of Library Science, LA. 504-388-3158

Cairo, Margaret, *Sr Librns*, New York State Library (Monographic Processing), Albany NY. 518-474-5948, 474-7866

Cakste, Anastasija, *Librn*, Northeastern University Libraries (Physics-Electrical Engineering Graduate Engineering), Boston MA. 617-437-2363

Calabrese, Alice, *Dir*, Geneva Public Library District, Geneva IL. 312-232-0780

Calabrese, Anthony, *Fishery Biologist*, National Marine Fisheries Service, Milford Laboratory Library, Milford CT. 203-878-2459

Calahan, Ellen, *Librn*, San Diego Public Library (Mira Mesa), San Diego CA. 714-271-8410

Calaway, Charlene, *Librn*, Wharton County Library (Louise Branch), Louise TX. 713-648-2363

Calbick, Ian M, *In Charge*, Wentworth Library, Hamilton ON. 416-526-4126

Calbreath, Leah, *Special Servs*, Dickinson Public Library, Dickinson ND. 701-225-2162

Calby, Anne, *Tech Serv & Cat*, Gallaudet College, Edward Miner Gallaudet Memorial Library, Washington DC. 202-651-5566

Calcagno, Philip, *Ser*, Southern Illinois University at Edwardsville, Elijah P Lovejoy Library, Edwardsville IL. 618-692-2711

Calcaterra, Lori, *On-Line Servs*, Washington University Libraries, Saint Louis MO. 314-889-5400

Calcese, Sarah, *Librn*, Wisconsin State Department of Local Affairs & Development Library, Madison WI. 608-266-2423

Calderelli, Leatrice, *Cat*, New Cumberland Public Library, New Cumberland PA. 717-774-0403

Caldiero, Dominick, *Media*, Manhattan College, Cardinal Hayes Library, Bronx NY. 212-548-1400, Ext 366 & 367

Caldwell, Alva R, *Librn*, Garrett-Evangelical Theological Seminary Library, Evanston IL. 312-866-3911

Caldwell, Beverly, *Ref*, Merritt Island Public Library, Merritt Island FL. 305-452-3834

Caldwell, Beverly, *Tech Serv*, Prince William Public Library, Manassas VA. 703-361-8211

Caldwell, Catherine L Pat, *Librn*, United States Army (Gaffey Hall Library), Fort Knox KY. 502-624-5449

Caldwell, Chris, *ILL*, California State University, John F Kennedy Memorial Library, Los Angeles CA. 213-224-2201

Caldwell, Dorothy J, *Librn*, Mount Carroll Township Public Library, Mount Carroll IL. 815-244-1751

Caldwell, Evelyn B, *Librn*, American Enterprise Institute for Public Policy Research Library, Washington DC. 202-862-5831, 862-5832

Caldwell, Jane, *Ch*, Catawba County Library, Newton NC. 704-464-2421

Caldwell, John, *Dir*, Augustana College, Denkman Memorial Library, Rock Island IL. 309-794-7266

Caldwell, Jon, *Librn*, Philadelphia College of Art Library (Slide Library), Philadelphia PA. 215-893-3117

Caldwell, Judy, *Ch & Tech Serv*, Jefferson County Library, Nederland TX. 713-727-2735, 727-2736

Caldwell, Justine M, *Librn*, Cooley Dickinson Hospital (Richard H Dolloff Medical Library), Northampton MA. 413-584-4090, Ext 2291

Caldwell, Linda M, *Librn*, Frederick Memorial Hospital, Walter F Prior Medical Library, Frederick MD. 301-662-5111, Ext 351

Caldwell, Lou, *Librn*, Houston Public Library (Humanities), Houston TX. 713-224-5441

Caldwell, Mary Louise, *Librn,* Madison County-Canton Public Library (Flora Public), Flora MS. 601-879-8686
Caldwell, Mrs A, *Librn,* Campbellford Public Library, Campbellford ON. 705-653-3611
Caldwell, Mrs A E, *Librn,* Viking Municipal Library, Viking AB. 403-336-3466
Caldwell, Patricia, *Librn,* California State Prison, San Quentin, Library Information Center, San Quentin CA. 415-454-1460
Caldwell, Ruby, *Asst Librn,* Amarillo Art Center Library, Amarillo TX. 806-372-8356
Caldwell, Sherry, *Ch,* Elbert County Library, Elberton GA. 404-283-5375
Caldwell, Violet L, *Asst Dir,* Parsons Public Library, Parsons KS. 316-421-5920
Caleen, Kathy, *Librn,* Florida Department of Environmental Regulation Library, Tallahassee FL. 904-488-0870
Calese, Robert, *Librn,* New York Public Library (Edenwald), New York NY. 212-798-3355
Caley, Diane, *Dir,* Ward County Public Library, Minot ND. 701-852-1045
Calfa, Joni, *Coordr,* Job Information Center (East), Riverhead NY. 516-727-3741
Calhoon, William, *Librn,* Wesleyan University (Science), Middletown CT. 203-347-9411, Ext 818
Calhoun, Catherine C, *Dir,* Torrington Historical Society Library, Torrington CT. 203-482-8260
Calhoun, Clayne, *Librn,* Roanoke Law Library, Roanoke VA. 703-981-2268
Calhoun, Dorothy E, *Librn,* United States Air Force (Maxwell Community Library), Maxwell AFB AL. 205-293-6484
Calhoun, Glovina, *Librn,* Marlow Public Library, Marlow OK. 405-658-5354
Calhoun, John, *Ser,* Louisiana Tech University, Prescott Memorial Library, Ruston LA. 318-257-2577
Calhoun, John, *ILL,* Sumter County Library, Sumter SC. 803-773-7273
Calhoun, Karen L, *Librn,* Kern Health Sciences Library, Bakersfield CA. 805-323-7651, Ext 257
Calhoun, Margie, *Ref,* Norfolk State University, Lyman Beecher Brooks Library, Norfolk VA. 804-623-8873
Calhoun, Suzanne S, *Dir,* Clearwater Memorial Public Library, Orofino Library, Orofino ID. 208-476-3411
Calhoun, Wanda J, *Dir,* Augusta Regional Library, Augusta-Richmond County Public Library, Augusta GA. 404-724-1871
Cali, Joseph, *Asst Dir & Ref,* Antioch College, Olive Kettering Memorial Library, Yellow Springs OH. 513-767-7331, Ext 229
Caliendo, Lorraine, *Librn,* American Marketing Association Information Center, Chicago IL. 312-648-0536
Caliguiri, Cathy A, *Librn,* West Rutland Free Library Corp, West Rutland VT. 802-438-2964
Calish, Esther H, *Dir,* Beverly Public Library, Beverly MA. 617-922-0310
Calisoff, Wilmadean, *Librn,* Forman Public Library, Manito IL. 309-968-6093
Calkins, Larry, *Ref,* Elko County Library, Elko NV. 702-738-3066
Call, Arlan, *Dir,* Magic Valley Library System, Twin Falls ID. 208-734-6857
Call, Arlan, *Dir,* Twin Falls Public Library, Twin Falls ID. 208-733-2965
Call, Isaac, *Media,* Broward Community College, Learning Resources Center, Fort Lauderdale FL. 305-475-6500
Call, Mary E, *Librn,* Stamford Community Library, Stamford VT. 802-694-1392
Call, Rona, *Tech Serv & Cat,* Greenfield Public Library, Greenfield MA. 413-772-0989, 772-6305
Callaghan, C, *Media,* University of Prince Edward Island, Robertson Library, Charlottetown PE. 902-892-1243
Callaghan, Patrice, *Media,* Public Library of Cincinnati & Hamilton County, Cincinnati Public Library, Cincinnati OH. 513-369-6000
Callah, Paul C, *Chief Librn,* Baltimore City Department of Housing & Community Development Library, Baltimore MD. 301-396-4100
Callaham, Betty E, *Dir,* South Carolina State Library, Columbia SC. 803-758-3181
Callahan, Anne W, *Librn,* Dalton Free Public Library, Dalton MA. 413-684-0049

Callahan, Doris A, *Librn,* Trinity County Library, Weaverville CA. 916-623-6182
Callahan, Ellen, *Bk Servs,* Time, Inc (Main Library), New York NY. 212-841-3745
Callahan, Frances, *Librn,* Berkshire Athenaeum (Morningside Community Public Library), Pittsfield MA. 413-442-5457
Callahan, Harriet, *Louisiana Dept,* Louisiana State Library, Baton Rouge LA. 504-342-4922
Callahan, John, *Librn,* Department of Public Libraries & Information (Great Neck), Virginia Beach VA. 804-481-6094
Callahan, Kathleen, *Libr Asst,* Michigan Department of Agriculture, East Lansing MI. 517-373-6410, Ext 49
Callahan, Norma C, *Librn,* Orange Public Library, Orange CT. 203-795-0288
Callahn, Virginia, *Media,* Leavenworth Public Library, Leavenworth KS. 913-682-5666
Callan, Ann, *Librn,* Fort Lauderdale Museum of the Arts, Art Reference Library, Fort Lauderdale FL. 305-463-5184
Callan, Henry T, *Librn,* Elizabeth Taber Library, Marion MA. 617-748-1252
Callanan, Mary, *Circ,* Johnson Free Public Library, Hackensack NJ. 201-343-4169
Callard, Joanne, *ILL,* University of Oklahoma Health Sciences Center Library, Oklahoma City OK. 405-271-2285
Callaway-Martin, Dorothy D, *Dir,* Saint Johns-Apache County Library, Saint Johns Public Library, Saint Johns AZ. 602-337-4405
Callen, Robert V, *Archivist,* Marquette University Memorial Library, Milwaukee WI. 414-224-7214
Callender, Rebecca, *Dir,* Logan County District Library, Bellefontaine OH. 513-599-4189
Callery, Bernadette G, *Librn,* Hunt Institute for Botanical Documentation, Hunt Botanical Library, Pittsburgh PA. 412-578-2437
Callinan, Mary L, *Librn,* Union Dime Savings Bank Library, New York NY. 212-221-2057
Callis, Mary Lou, *Ch,* Greentown & Eastern Howard School & Public Library, Greentown Library, Greentown IN. 317-628-3534
Callis, Peggy, *Asst Librn,* Owensville Public Library, Owensville IN. 812-724-3335
Callis, Virginia, *Librn,* Fort Branch Public Library, Fort Branch IN. 812-753-4212
Callison, Jan, *Librn,* Public Library of Annapolis & Anne Arundel County Inc (Crofton), Crofton MD. 301-721-7515, 7516
Calloway, Dave, *Asst Dir,* Montgomery County Library, Conroe TX. 713-756-4486
Calloway, Josephine, *Librn,* Metropolitan Life Western Head Office Library, San Francisco CA. 415-546-3000
Calloway, Linda K, *Librn,* Holme, Roberts & Owen, Law Library, Denver CO. 303-861-7000, Ext 260
Calman, John Douglas, *Librn,* Florida Department of Natural Resources, Division of Resource Management, Tallahassee FL. 904-488-5139
Calogero, Susan, *Librn,* Utica Public Library (East Utica), Utica NY. 315-733-6316
Calogero, Susan, *Librn,* Utica Public Library (North Utica), Utica NY. 315-735-9141
Calonne, Rachele, *Dir,* CEGEP de Saint-Laurent Bibliotheque, Montreal PQ. 514-747-6521
Calovich, Rose Mary, *Fine Arts,* Kansas City Kansas Public Library, Kansas City KS. 913-621-3073
Caltabiano, Marilyn, *Dir,* Memorial Library of Radnor Township, Wayne PA. 215-687-1124
Calvano, Mary, *Librn & On-Line Servs,* Lord Corp, Information Centers, Erie PA. 814-868-3611, 456-8511
Calvano, Michael, *Acting Chief,* New York Public Library (Photographic Services (Photostat, Photog, Microfilm, Quick-copy)), New York NY. 212-790-6262
Calve-Woodrough, Lise, *Prof,* College Lionel-Groulx, Techniques de la Documentation, PQ. 514-430-3120, Ext 261
Calvert, Ann, *Ref,* Wolfsohn Memorial Library, King of Prussia PA. 215-265-5151
Calvert, Gail A, *Ref & MEDLINE,* Medical College of Georgia Library, Augusta GA. 404-828-3441
Calvert, John, *Video Servs,* West Virginia Library Commission, Science & Cultural Center, Charleston WV. 304-348-2041

Calvert, Mrs Frankie, *Dir,* Rowan County Public Library, Morehead KY. 606-784-7137
Calvert, Myrl L, *Librn,* Wilkinson County Library System (Woodville Public), Woodville MS. 601-886-6712
Calvert, Raymond, *Tech Serv, On-Line Servs & Bibliog Instr,* Florida Regional Library for the Blind & Physically Handicapped, Daytona Beach FL. 904-252-4722
Calvin, Besty, *Librn,* New York Botanical Garden, Cary Arboretum Library, Millbrook NY. 914-677-5343, Exts 270 & 275
Calvin, Lynn M, *Librn,* Benjamin Franklin University Library, Washington DC. 202-737-2262, Ext 28
Calvins, Duane K, *Asst Librn,* Brooklyn Law School, Henry L Ughetta Law Library, Brooklyn NY. 212-625-2200, Ext 53 or 55
Cam, Y, *Librn,* Oakland Public Library (West Oakland), Oakland CA. 415-832-3519
Cama, Maryann, *ILL & Ref,* Kaye, Scholer, Fierman, Hays & Handler Law Library, New York NY. 212-759-8400, Ext 312
Camacho, Nancy, *Coordr,* Heart of Illinois Library Consortium, IL. 309-691-4702, Ext 3073
Camarigg, Elizabeth, *Spec Coll,* Mason City Public Library, Mason City IA. 515-423-7552
Cambier, Pearl, *Librn,* Alton Public Library, Alton IA. 712-756-4516
Camboa, Carlos, *Librn,* Pan American Documentation & Health Information Office, Washington DC. 202-861-3200, Ext 87, 88
Cambre, C J, *Coordr,* University of South Carolina, Thomas Cooper Library, Columbia SC. 803-777-3142
Cambron, Carol, *Acq,* Central Missouri State University, Ward Edwards Library, Warrensburg MO. 816-429-4141
Camerieri, Cheryl, *Media,* Camden County Free Library, Voorhees NJ. 609-772-1636
Camero, Olga, *Supvr Libr Servs,* Conoco Inc (International Exploration & Production Library), Houston TX. 713-965-2499
Cameron, A A, *Chief Librn,* Georgina Public Library Administration, Keswick ON. 416-476-7233
Cameron, Bruce, *Dir,* Wheatland Regional Library, Saskatoon SK. 306-652-5077
Cameron, Candace, *Ch,* Escondido Public Library, Escondido CA. 714-741-4683
Cameron, Connie, *ILL, Ref & Bibliog Instr,* Bryant College, Edith M Hodgson Memorial Library, Smithfield RI. 401-231-1200, Ext 300
Cameron, D, *Ch,* Patten Free Library, Bath ME. 207-443-5141
Cameron, Eleanor, *Nursing Libr,* Humber College, Learning Resource Centre, Rexdale ON. 416-675-3111, Ext 331
Cameron, Erma, *Inner City Branch Coordr,* Chatham-Effingham-Liberty Regional Library, Savannah Public Library, Savannah GA. 912-234-5127
Cameron, G, *Librn,* Saugeen Public Library, Chippewa Hill ON. 519-797-3089
Cameron, Jennie, *Librn,* Richards Library, Warrensburg NY. 518-623-5611
Cameron, Laura, *Cat,* Wheaton College Library, Wheaton IL. 312-682-5101
Cameron, Lorraine, *Asst Librn,* Rye Public Library, Rye NH. 603-964-8401
Cameron, Marcia, *ILL,* Superiorland Library Cooperative, Marquette MI. 906-228-7697
Cameron, Mary T, *Ch,* Chapel Hill Public Library, Chapel Hill NC. 919-942-5455
Cameron, Pat, *Librn,* Trinity Memorial Hospital Library, Cudahy WI. 414-769-9000, Ext 383 & 384
Cameron, Priscilla, *Asst Librn,* Eugene Bible College Library, Eugene OR. 503-485-1780
Cameron, Richard A, *Head Field Servs,* Minnesota Historical Society (Division of Archives & Manuscripts), Saint Paul MN. 612-296-6980
Cameron, Richard T, *In Charge,* Buchanan County Historical Society Library, Saint Joseph MO. 816-364-1485
Cameron, Sister M Francesca, *Dir,* Saint Catharine College, Media Center, Saint Catharine KY. 606-336-9303
Cameron, Ulysses, *Libr Servs, Assoc Dir,* University of the District of Columbia, Learning Resources Division, Washington DC. 202-282-7536

Cameron, Virginia, *Media,* State University of New York College at Brockport, Drake Memorial Library, Brockport NY. 716-395-2140

Cameron, William J, *Dean,* University of Western Ontario, School of Library & Information Science, ON. 519-679-3542

Cameron, Winnifred, *Bkmobile Coordr,* York Regional Library, Fredericton NB. 506-454-4481

Camlioglu, Ergun, *Chief, Canadian Bk Exchange Ctr,* National Library of Canada, Ottawa ON. 613-995-9481

Camp, Anne M, *Librn,* Muleshoe Area Public Library, Muleshoe TX. 806-272-4707

Camp, Beverly, *Librn,* Stevens Public Library, Ashburnham MA. 617-827-4404

Camp, Brian, *Assoc Librn,* Educational Film Library Association, New York NY. 212-246-4533

Camp, Emily, *Ref,* Central College, Geisler Learning Resource Center, Pella IA. 515-628-4151, Ext 233

Camp, P E, *Librn,* University of South Florida (Florida Historical Society Library), Tampa FL. 813-974-2731

Camp, Thomas E, *Librn,* University of the South (School of Theology), Sewanee TN. 615-698-5931, Ext 281

Camp, Thomas Edward, *Assoc Dir,* University of the South, Jessie Ball duPont Library, Sewanee TN. 615-598-5931, Ext 265, 267

Campa, Lina, *Librn,* Irwindale Public Library, Irwindale CA. 962-5255 or 962-3381, Ext 38

Campagna, Jane, *Ch,* River Bend Library System, Coal Valley IL. 309-799-3131

Campaigne, Laura E, *Librn,* Saint Peter's Hospital, Medical Staff Library, Albany NY. 518-471-1490

Campbell, A, *Librn,* Public Service Commission Library, Ottawa ON. 613-992-4808, 997-3606

Campbell, Alice P, *Acq,* Northeastern University Libraries (School of Law), Boston MA. 617-437-3338

Campbell, Alma B, *Supv,* Sperry UNIVAC Computer Systems, Information Center, Blue Bell PA. 215-542-2458

Campbell, Anne, *Ref,* Champlain Regional College, Saint Lambert Campus Resource Centre, Saint Lambert PQ. 514-672-7360, Ext 220, 221

Campbell, Anne, *Ref,* Chula Vista Public Library, Chula Vista CA. 714-427-1151

Campbell, B Heather, *ILL,* Jacksonville Public Library System, Haydon Burns Library, Jacksonville FL. 904-633-6870

Campbell, Barbara, *Ref,* Bryant Library, Roslyn NY. 516-621-2240

Campbell, Barbara J, *Dir,* Santa Clara County Free Library, San Jose CA. 408-293-2326

Campbell, Bertha, *Librn,* Atlanta Public Library (Paces Ferry), Atlanta GA. 404-262-1124

Campbell, Beverly, *Librn,* Montgomery County Library, Mount Ida AR. 501-867-3812

Campbell, Billy W. *Supvr,* Hughes Aircraft Co (Company Technical Document Center Library), Culver City CA. 213-391-0711, Ext 6187

Campbell, Carol L, *Librn,* Manhattan Community Library, Manhattan MT. 406-284-6644

Campbell, Catherine, *Ch,* Bartow Public Library, Bartow FL. 813-533-4985

Campbell, Cathrin, *Instr,* Concordia University, Library Studies Program, PQ. 514-482-0320, Ext 324

Campbell, Charles, *Librn,* Judith Basin County Free Library (Utica Library Station), Utica MT. 406-566-2389

Campbell, Charles E, *Asst Prof,* Saint Cloud State University, Center for Library & Audiovisual Education, MN. 612-255-2022

Campbell, Clara, *Librn,* Rosicrucian Order, AMORC, Research Library, San Jose CA. 408-287-9171, Ext 218

Campbell, Corinne A, *Tech Librs Mgr,* Boeing Co (Kent Technical Library), Seattle WA. 206-773-0590

Campbell, Corinne A, *Tech Librs Mgr,* Boeing Co (Renton Technical Library), Seattle WA. 206-237-8311

Campbell, Donna, *Soc Sci,* University of Calgary Library, Calgary AB. 403-284-5954

Campbell, Donna M, *Librn,* Agawam Public Library, Agawam MA. 413-789-1550

Campbell, Dorothy W, *Asst Prof,* North Carolina Central University, School of Library Science, NC. 919-683-6485

Campbell, Edward I, *Dir,* Frederick Community College, Learning Resource Center, Frederick MD. 301-694-1242

Campbell, Elizabeth, *Librn,* Municipal Library (Preville), Saint Lambert PQ. 514-671-2152

Campbell, Ellie, *On-Line Servs,* Glenview Public Library, Glenview IL. 312-724-5200

Campbell, Errol V, *Librn,* Florida State Prison Library, Starke FL. 904-964-8125, Ext 322

Campbell, Fern, *Ch,* Norfolk Public Library, Norfolk VA. 804-441-2887

Campbell, Frances D, *Librn,* Colorado Supreme Court Library, Denver CO. 303-861-1111, Ext 173

Campbell, Frank C, *Chief,* New York Public Library (Music Division), New York NY. 212-790-6262

Campbell, Gail, *ILL, Ad & Ref,* Mayne Williams Public Library, Johnson City TN. 615-928-3116

Campbell, Gene, *Librn,* Saint Cloud State University (Campus School Learning Resources Center), Saint Cloud MN. 612-255-3195

Campbell, Gillian, *Ref,* Coquitlam Public Library, Coquitlam BC. 604-931-2416

Campbell, Gladys, *Librn,* Voluntown Public Library, Voluntown CT. 203-376-0485

Campbell, Gloria, *Librn,* Public Library of Columbus & Franklin County (Driving Park), Columbus OH. 614-222-7612

Campbell, Gwen, *Asst Librn,* Dorion Public Library, Dorion ON. 807-857-2289

Campbell, Helen G, *Librn,* Mirror Lake-Tomlinson Adult Education Center, School Board of Pinellas County Library-Media Center, Saint Petersburg FL. 813-821-4593

Campbell, Helen W, *Dir,* Indiana University (School of Dentistry Library), Indianapolis IN. 317-264-7204

Campbell, Irene, *Asst Librn,* Lake City Public Library, Lake City IA. 712-464-3413

Campbell, James, *Librn,* United States Department of Defense, DISAM Library, Wright-Patterson AFB OH. 513-255-5567

Campbell, Jane, *Librn,* Northeast Regional Library (Chalybeate Library), Chalybeate MS. 601-223-6768

Campbell, Jeannette, *Librn,* Lafe Allen Memorial Library of North Miami Beach, North Miami Beach FL. 305-947-8100, Ext 169

Campbell, Jerry D, *Dir,* Iliff School of Theology, Ira J Taylor Library, Denver CO. 303-744-1287, Ext 30

Campbell, Joan, *Tech Serv,* Fairbanks North Star Borough Public Library & Regional Center, Fairbanks AK. 907-452-5177

Campbell, John, *Br Coordr & Bkmobile Coordr,* Great Falls Public Library, Pathfinder Federation of Libraries Headquarters, Great Falls MT. 406-453-0349

Campbell, John K, *Dir,* Bushnell-Sage Memorial Library, Sheffield Free Library, Sheffield MA. 413-229-7788

Campbell, Joyce, *Librn,* Dallas Public Library (Lancaster-Kiest), Dallas TX. 214-371-3446

Campbell, Joyce, *Ad,* Newburgh Free Library, Newburgh NY. 914-561-1836

Campbell, Joylene, *Librn,* Lakeland Library Region, North Battleford SK. 306-445-6108

Campbell, Juanita, *Librn,* Newbern City Library, Newbern TN. 901-627-3153

Campbell, Judith, *Acq,* Holyoke Community College Library, Holyoke MA. 413-538-7000, Ext 261

Campbell, Judith, *Ref,* Holyoke Community College Library, Holyoke MA. 413-538-7000, Ext 261

Campbell, Kathleen, *Librn,* Morrill Memorial & Harris Library, Strafford VT. 802-765-4037

Campbell, L, *Circ,* Barrie Public Library, Barrie ON. 705-728-1010

Campbell, Laurel, *Librn,* Warder Public Library (Park Branch), Springfield OH. 513-322-2651

Campbell, Lillian, *Librn,* East Palestine Memorial Public Library, East Palestine OH. 216-426-3778

Campbell, Linda N, *Librn,* Fort Meade Public Library, Fort Meade FL. 813-285-8287

Campbell, Louise, *Ref & Bibliog Instr,* Roberts Wesleyan College, Kenneth B Keating Library, Rochester NY. 716-594-9471, Ext 133

Campbell, Marc T, *ILL,* Fort Hays State University, Forsyth Library, Hays KS. 913-628-4431

Campbell, Margaret, *Librn,* Central Soya Company, Inc, Food Research Library, Fort Wayne IN. 219-489-1511, Ext 248

Campbell, Margaret, *Ad,* Normal Public Library, Normal IL. 309-452-1757

Campbell, Margaret E, *Librn,* Maritime Resource Management Service Library, Information Centre, Amherst NS. 902-667-7231

Campbell, Marge, *Librn,* Rome Historical Society, William E & Elaine Scripture Memorial Library, Rome NY. 315-336-5870

Campbell, Marie N, *Asst Librn,* New Mexico Junior College, Pannell Library & Instructional Resources Center, Hobbs NM. 505-392-6526, Ext 231 & 233

Campbell, Martha, *Librn,* Paton Public Library, Paton IA. 515-968-4559

Campbell, Mary, *Asst Librn,* Edson Municipal Library, Edson AB. 403-723-3117

Campbell, Mary Jane, *Librn,* Ferro Corp, Chemical Library, Bedford OH. 216-641-8580

Campbell, Mary K, *Dir,* First Baptist Church, Media Center Library, Abilene TX. 915-673-5031

Campbell, Mary Katherine, *Educ Serv,* Hardin-Simmons University, Richardson Library, Abilene TX. 915-677-7281, Ext 236

Campbell, Mary L, *Librn,* Robert W Ryerss Library & Museum, Philadelphia PA. 215-745-3061

Campbell, Mary Lou, *Ch & YA,* Roseville Public Library, Roseville CA. 916-783-7158

Campbell, Nancy, *Asst,* E I Du Pont De Nemours & Co, Inc (Stine Laboratory), Newark DE. 302-366-5353, 336-5354

Campbell, Nancy, *Acq,* Northern Kentucky University, W Frank Steely Library, Highland Heights KY. 606-292-5483

Campbell, Nancy, *Librn,* York Regional Library (Marysville Public), Fredericton NB. 506-472-4196

Campbell, Nina, *Librn,* Lane Public Library (Lindenwald), Hamilton OH. 513-893-4691

Campbell, Nina S, *Assoc Dir,* Indiana University (School of Medicine Library), Indianapolis IN. 317-264-7182

Campbell, Patty, *Instr,* Highline Community College Library, Library Technician Program, WA. 206-878-3710, Ext 233

Campbell, Paul, *Dir,* Rhode Island Historical Society Library, Providence RI. 401-331-0448

Campbell, Phyllis, *Cat,* Endicott College, Fitz Memorial Library, Beverly MA. 617-927-0585, Ext 280

Campbell, Ray, *Dir,* Carbondale Public Library, Carbondale IL. 618-457-0354

Campbell, Regina, *Dir,* Brighton Memorial Library, Rochester NY. 716-473-8805

Campbell, Richard J, *Ref Librn,* Wilbur Wright College, Library Technology Program, IL. 312-777-7900, Ext 82, 83

Campbell, Robertina, *Ref,* Bloomfield Public Library, Northwest Essex Area Library, Bloomfield NJ. 201-429-9292

Campbell, Rosalind C, *Librn,* Blue Ridge Technical College Library, Flat Rock NC. 704-692-3572

Campbell, Ruth, *Ch,* Hudson Public Library, Hudson MA. 617-562-7521, 7522

Campbell, Sally S, *Librn,* Bank of Hawaii, Information Center, Honolulu HI. 808-537-8375

Campbell, Sharon, *Librn,* Genoa Public Library, Genoa IL. 815-784-2627

Campbell, Stanley R, *Ref & ILL,* Centre College of Kentucky, Grace Doherty Library, Danville KY. 606-236-5211, Ext 237

Campbell, Stella Thurmond, *Field Librn,* Caney Fork Regional Library, Sparta TN. 615-836-3335

Campbell, Susan, *Sci,* Colgate University, Everett Needham Case Library, Hamilton NY. 315-824-1000

Campbell, Susan L, *In Charge,* Vanier Institute of the Family, Resource & Information Center, Ottawa ON. 613-232-7115

Campbell, Ted Thaxton, *Dir,* Ector County Library, Odessa TX. 915-332-0633

Campbell, Victoria, *Ch,* Great Falls Public Library, Pathfinder Federation of Libraries Headquarters, Great Falls MT. 406-453-0349

Campbell, Victoria J, *Librn,* Thayer Public Library, Braintree MA. 617-848-0405

Campbell, Virginia, *ILL & Circ,* Lynnfield Public Library, Lynnfield MA. 617-334-5411

Campbell, Vivian, *Acq,* Georgetown University (Fred O Dennis Law Library), Washington DC. 202-624-8260

Campbell, W Glenn, *Dir,* Hoover Institution on War, Revolution & Peace, Stanford CA. 415-497-2058

Campbell, Jr, Edward D C, *Dir,* Museum of the Confederacy Library, Richmond VA. 804-649-1861

Campbell, Jr, Francis D, *Librn,* American Numismatic Society Library, New York NY. 212-234-3130, Ext 20

Campbell, Jr, Wayne T, *Media,* Greenwich Library, Greenwich CT. 203-622-7900

Camper, Frances, *Acq,* Virginia Military Institute, J T L Preston Library, Lexington VA. 703-463-6228

Campese, Michael A, *Librn,* Saint Elizabeth's Hospital, Medical Library, Belleville IL. 618-234-2120, Ext 233

Campfield, Mary, *Dir,* Winnebago Mental Health Institute, Medical Library, Winnebago WI. 414-235-4910, Ext 327

Campfield, Mary E, *Asst Dir & Ref,* Essex Community College, James A Newpher Library, Baltimore MD. 301-682-6000, Ext 320

Campion, Carol Mae, *Librn,* Lackawanna Junior College, Seeley Memorial Library, Scranton PA. 717-961-7831

Campion, Serge G, *Chief Librn,* Transport Canada Library & Information Centre, Ottawa ON. 613-996-7121, 996-5861

Campo, June, *Librn,* Biloxi Public Library (West Biloxi), Biloxi MS. 601-388-5696

Campo, Palma, *Librn,* Dykema, Gossett, Goodnow, Spencer & Trigg, Dykema, Gossett Law Library, Detroit MI. 313-568-6715

Campoli, Lois, *Librn,* Welkind Neurological Hospital Library, Chester NJ. 201-584-8145

Campora, Barbara, *Br Coordr,* Calaveras County Library, San Andreas CA. 209-754-4266

Campton, Delores, *Tech Serv,* Alexander Mitchell Library, Aberdeen Public Library, Aberdeen SD. 605-225-4186

Canaan, Sibyl, *Ch,* North Country Libraries, Moolilauke Public Library, North Woodstock NH. 603-745-8752

Canada, Charlyn M C, *Dir,* Vail Public Library, Vail CO. 303-476-5613, Ext 215

Canada, Mary, *Ref,* Duke University, William R Perkins Library, Durham NC. 684-2034

Canady, Carole, *Bkmobile Coordr,* Granite City Public Library, Granite City IL. 618-876-0550

Canas, Yolanda, *Cat,* Baptist Sunday School Board of the Southern Baptist Convention, Dargan-Carver Library, Nashville TN. 615-251-2133

Canavan, June, *Media,* Danbury Public Library, Danbury CT. 203-797-4505

Candau, Eugenie, *Librn,* San Francisco Museum of Modern Art, Louise Sloss Ackerman Fine Arts Library, San Francisco CA. 415-863-8800

Candelmo, Emily, *Librn,* Tippetts-Abbett-McCarthy-Stratton, TAMS Library, New York NY. 212-867-1777, Ext 500

Candia, Sylvia, *Librn,* San Antonio Public Library (Las Palmas Library Center), San Antonio TX. 512-434-6394

Cane, Betsey, *Circ,* Digital Equipment Corp, Corporate Library, Maynard MA. 617-493-6231, 493-5821

Cane, Ena M, *Librn,* S White Dickinson Memorial Library, Whately MA. 413-665-2170

Canelas, Dale B, *Assoc Dir,* Stanford University Libraries, Stanford CA. 415-497-2016

Caneschi, Ceal, *ILL,* Meriden Public Library, Meriden CT. 203-238-2344

Canfield, Dee, *Librn,* River Bend Library System (Books for the Blind & Physically Handicapped), Coal Valley IL. 309-799-3131

Canfield, Dolores, *Librn Blind,* River Bend Library System, Coal Valley IL. 309-799-3131

Canfield, Earl, *Chief, Educ & Pub Welfare Dir,* Library of Congress, Washington DC. 202-287-5000

Canfield, Helen S, *Ch,* Hartford Public Library, Hartford CT. 203-525-9121

Canfield, Mary, *Librn,* Lyon Township Library, New Hudson MI. 313-437-8800

Canipe, Hubert, *ILL & OCLC,* United States Army (United States Army Institute for Military Assistance, Marquat Memorial Library), Fort Bragg NC. 919-396-9383

Cann, Cheryle J, *Librn,* Malcolm Bliss Mental Health Center, Robert J Brockman Memorial Library, Saint Louis MO. 314-241-7600, Ext 391

Cann, Sharon Lee, *Librn,* Northside Hospital, Woodruff Health Sciences Library, Atlanta GA. 404-256-8744

Cannaday, Deborah, *Librn,* Toledo Law Association Library, Toledo OH. 419-259-8951

Cannan, Jodie, *Dir,* Grand County Libraries, Granby CO. 303-887-2149

Cannan, Julia, *Librn,* Kent State University Libraries (Chemistry & Physics Library), Kent OH. 216-672-2532

Cannavan, Lea, *Rec Supvr,* San Jacinto College, Lee Davis Library, Pasadena TX. 713-476-1850, 476-1501, Ext 241

Cannetti, Margaret, *Librn,* Saint Mary's County Memorial Library (Lexington Park Branch), Lexington Park MD. 301-475-2846

Canning, Eileen, *Instr,* Highline Community College Library, Library Technician Program, WA. 206-878-3710, Ext 233

Canning, Karen, *Asst Librn,* Esther Washburn Public Library, Tremont IL. 309-925-5432

Canning, Nancy, *Ref,* Anoka Area Vocational Technical Institute, Media Center, Anoka MN. 612-427-1800, Ext 250

Cannon, Anne, *Librn,* York University (Government Documents-Administrative Studies), Downsview ON. 416-667-2545

Cannon, Barbara J, *ILL,* Greenfield Public Library, Greenfield MA. 413-772-0989, 772-6305

Cannon, Linda W, *Librn,* Mount Morris Library, Mount Morris NY. 716-658-4412

Cannon, Marion, *Media,* Nicholson Memorial Library, Garland TX. 214-494-7187

Cannon, Mary, *Librn,* Tucson Public Library (Nanini), Tucson AZ. 602-791-4626

Cannon, Perry G, *Asst Dir,* University of Alabama in Birmingham, Mervyn H Sterne Library, Birmingham AL. 205-934-6360

Cannon, Perry G, *Humanities,* University of Alabama in Birmingham, Mervyn H Sterne Library, Birmingham AL. 205-934-6360

Cannon, Robert E, *Dir,* Kern County Library, Bakersfield CA. 805-861-2130

Cannon, Ruth M Eggleston, *Librn,* Federal Reserve Bank of Richmond Research Library, Richmond VA. 804-643-1250, Ext 3131

Cannon, Theresa, *Ad,* Paramus Public Library (Midland Ave), Paramus NJ. 201-444-4911

Cannon, Jr, Carl F, *Librn,* Newport News Shipbuilding & Dry Dock Co, Library Services Department, Newport News VA. 804-380-2610

Cano, Margarita, *Art,* Miami-Dade Public Library System, Miami FL. 305-579-5001

Canon, Charles, *Tech Serv & Cat,* Roberts Wesleyan College, Kenneth B Keating Library, Rochester NY. 716-594-9471, Ext 133

Canose, J A, *Cat Coordr,* Bell Telephone Laboratories (Bell Telephone Laboratories Technical Library), Holmdel NJ. 949-3912 (Supvr); 949-5966 (Libr Network Support); 949-7986 (Cat); 229-7810 (W Long Branch Info)

Cant, Janet, *Librn,* Westminster Church Library, Detroit MI. 313-341-2697

Canter, Jo, *Librn,* Ashe County Public Library, West Jefferson NC. 919-246-2041

Canter, Louis, *Librn,* Mount San Jacinto College Library, San Jacinto CA. 714-654-7321, Ext 242

Cantone, Sister Pachal Marie, *Librn,* Saint Francis Medical Center, Medical Library, Trenton NJ. 609-396-7676, Ext 248

Cantone, Sister Paschal Marie, *Librn,* Saint Francis Hospital Library, Wilmington DE. 302-421-4123

Cantor, Beverly L, *Librn,* American Home Products Corp, Wyeth Laboratories Inc Library, West Chester PA. 215-696-3100, Ext 338

Cantor, Mel L, *Librn,* Coronado Public Library, Coronado CA. 714-435-4187

Cantrall, Sharon, *Asst Dir,* Mendocino County Library, Ukiah CA. 707-468-4491

Cantrell, Ann, *Librn,* Northwest Regional Library (Sulligen Branch), Sulligent AL. 205-698-8631

Cantrell, Durene, *Librn,* Douglas County Library System (Glendale Public), Glendale OR. 503-832-2360

Cantrell, Gary, *Music,* Adelphi University Library, Garden City NY. 516-294-8700

Cantwell, Barbara, *Librn & Doc,* Skagit County Historical Museum Library, La Conner WA. 206-466-3365

Cantwell, Judith H, *Librn,* Gulf South Research Institute Library, New Orleans LA. 504-283-4223

Cantwell, Mary, *AV,* Bexley Public Library, Columbus OH. 614-231-2784

Cantwell, Mrs John B, *Librn,* Hatfield Public Library, Hatfield MA. 413-247-9097

Canty, Donald, *Media,* Bronx Community College Library, Bronx NY. 212-367-7300, Ext 315

Canute, Sandy, *Tech Serv,* White Pine Library Cooperative, Saginaw MI. 517-792-0001

Canuti, Teresa D, *Dir,* Dansville Public Library, Shepard Memorial Library, Dansville NY. 716-335-6720

Canzoneri, Ellen, *Circ,* College Misericordia Library, Dallas PA. 717-675-2181, Ext 225

Capadona, Frank, *Librn,* California Men's Colony Library, San Luis Obispo CA. 805-543-2700

Caparoon, Darlene, *Librn,* Mellinger Memorial Public Library, Morning Sun IA. 319-868-7936

Capel, Gloria, *In Charge,* Crown Zellerbach Corp, Corporate Information Center, San Francisco CA. 415-823-5403

Capell, Joyce, *Media,* Mission College, Learning Resource Services, Santa Clara CA. 408-988-2200, Ext 1531

Capen, Margaret L, *Ch,* Brewer Public Library, Brewer ME. 207-989-7943

Capers, Loretta, *Librn,* College for Human Services Library, New York NY. 212-989-2002, Ext 28, 36

Capitolo, Giaconda, *Mormons, Western History & Utah,* Salt Lake City Public Library, Salt Lake City UT. 801-363-5733

Capitolo, Gioconda, *Rare Bks & Spec Coll,* Salt Lake City Public Library, Salt Lake City UT. 801-363-5733

Caplan, Frances J, *ILL, Ref & Bibliog Instr,* Robert Morris College Library, Pittsburgh PA. 412-227-6839

Caplan, Nora, *Librn,* Montgomery County Department of Public Libraries (Noyes Children's Branch), Kensington MD. 301-949-3780

Caplinger, Wanda, *Librn,* Lubbock City-County Library (Idalou Branch), Idalou TX. 806-762-6411, Ext 2828

Capobianco, Camille, *Ad, Ref & Commun Servs,* Glen Cove Public Library, Glen Cove NY. 516-676-2130

Capone, Theresa, *Cat,* John Jay College of Criminal Justice Library, New York NY. 212-489-5169

Caponigro, A, *Chief Librn,* Saint Agnes Medical Center, Health Science Library, Philadelphia PA. 215-339-4448

Caporicci, Mary, *Asst Dir,* Cote Saint-Luc Public Library, Cote Saint-Luc PQ. 514-481-5676

Caporicci, Mary, *English ILL, Cat & Ref,* Reginald J P Dawson Library, Bibliotheque de Ville Mont Royal, Mount Royal PQ. 514-342-1892

Capp, Sandy, *Asst Dir,* Comstock Township Library, Comstock MI. 616-345-0136

Cappannari, Suzzanne, *ILL,* Vanderbilt University Medical Center Library, Nashville TN. 615-322-2292

Cappell, Anita, *Dir,* Marlboro Free Library, Marlboro NY. 914-236-7272

Cappiello, Angela, *Media & Pub Servs,* New Hyde Park Public Library, New Hyde Park NY. 516-354-1413

Cappiello, Angela, *Asst Librn,* New York Historical Society Library, New York NY. 212-873-3400

Capps, Marie T, *Maps & Mss,* United States Military Academy Library, West Point NY. 914-938-2230

Capps, Paullean, *Tech Serv,* West Florida Regional Library, Pensacola Public Library, Pensacola FL. 904-438-5479

Capron, Louise, *ILL,* Drew University, Rose Memorial Library, Madison NJ. 201-377-3000, Ext 469

Capron, Mrs Orlando, *Librn,* Bridge Memorial Library (North Walpole Library), North Walpole NH. 603-756-9806

Capron, Shirley, *Dir,* School for International Training, Donald B Watt Library, Brattleboro VT. 802-257-7751, Ext 216

Capshaw, Mrs W R, *Librn,* Texarkana Public Library, Texarkana TX. 214-794-2149

Captain, Sue W, *Reader Serv,* Southwest Virginia Community College Library, Richlands VA. 703-964-2555

Capute, Virginia B, *Librn,* Columbus Law Library Association, Columbus OH. 614-221-4181

Caputo, Carmella, *Librn,* Claymont School District Public Library (Dennison Branch), Dennison OH. 614-922-5851

Caputo, Valentina, *ILL & Tech Serv,* Bayard Taylor Memorial Library, Kennett Square PA. 215-444-2702

Cara, James, *Librn,* Berkeley Public Library (Claremont), Berkeley CA. 714-644-6880

Caraher, Michael, *Tech Serv,* Eisenhower College of the Rochester Institute of Technology, Ellis Slater Library, Seneca Falls NY. 315-568-7171

Caravello, Gloria, *Circ,* Barrington Public Library District, Barrington IL. 312-382-1300

Caraway, Claudia, *Cat,* Angelo State University, Porter Henderson Library, San Angelo TX. 915-942-2222

Caraway, Lulane, *Asst Librn,* Texarkana Public Library, Texarkana TX. 214-794-2149

Caraway, Virginia, *Librn,* Lytle Public Library, Lytle TX. 512-772-9492

Carberry, Mrs Donald, *Asst Dir,* Bolton Free Library, Bolton Landing NY. 518-644-2233

Carbery, Mance, *Cat,* Ontario Legislative Library, Research & Information Services, Toronto ON. 416-965-4545

Carbo, Maryjane, *Ch,* Wayne County Public Library, Inc, Goldsboro NC. 919-735-1824

Carbone, Carmela, *Ref,* Engineering Societies Library, New York NY. 212-644-7611

Carbone, Jerry, *ILL & Ref,* Brooks Memorial Library, Brattleboro VT. 802-254-5290

Carbonell, Marilyn, *On-Line Servs,* University of Missouri-Kansas City Libraries, Kansas City MO. 816-276-1531

Carbonell, Marilyn, *Art, Pharmacy, Ethnic Studies,* University of Missouri-Kansas City Libraries, Kansas City MO. 816-276-1531

Card, Judy, *Librn,* Memphis-Shelby County Public Library & Information Center (Children's), Memphis TN. 901-528-2950

Card, June, *Librn,* Tower-Porter Community Library, Tower City PA. 717-647-4900

Card, Larry, *Librn,* Valparaiso Technical Institute Library, Valparaiso IN. 219-462-2191

Card, Laurel, *Cat,* Oceanside Public Library, Oceanside CA. 714-439-7330

Card, Mrs Everett, *Librn,* Guilford Smith Memorial Library, South Windham CT. 203-423-5159

Cardell, Betty, *Acq,* Center for Disease Control Library, Atlanta GA. 404-329-3396

Cardella, Mary Ann, *Asst Librn,* Bausch & Lomb Corporate Library, Rochester NY. 716-338-6053

Carden, Betty, *Librn,* Breckinridge County Public Library, Hardinsburg KY. 502-756-2323, Ext 1

Carden, Micki, *Commun Servs,* Miami-Dade Public Library System, Miami FL. 305-579-5001

Carden, Mrs William, *Asst Dir,* Winfield Public Library, Winfield IA. 319-257-3247

Carder, Shirley, *Librn,* Bonham Public Library, Bonham TX. 214-583-3128

Cardiff, Eleanor, *Br Coordr,* Northport Public Library, Northport NY. 516-261-6930

Cardillo, Wayne, *Doc,* University of Kansas Libraries (School of Law), Lawrence KS. 913-864-3025

Cardin, Celine, *ILL,* Bibliotheque Nationale Du Quebec, Montreal PQ. 514-873-4553

Cardona, Carmen, *Acq,* Antillian College Library, Mayaguez PR. 809-832-9595, Ext 209

Cardoza, Eleanor, *Librn,* Nova Scotia Commission on Drug Dependency Library, Halifax NS. 902-424-4270

Cardoza, Virginia, *Dir,* Hepburn Library of Madrid, Madrid NY. 315-322-5673

Cardozo, Carol L, *Ref,* Belmont Public Library, Belmont MA. 617-489-2000

Cardozo, Manuel, *Curator,* Catholic University of America (Oliveira Lima), Washington DC. 202-635-5059

Carducci, Frances, *Systs Analyst,* Monroe County Library System, Rochester NY. 716-428-7345

Cardwell, Beulah B, *Librn,* Johnston Public Library, Baxter Springs KS. 316-856-5591

Cardwell, Katherine E, *In Charge,* United States Forest Service, Institute of Northern Forestry, Science Laboratory Library, Fairbanks AK. 907-479-7443

Cardwell, Margaret, *Genealogy & Local Hist,* Kokomo Public Library, Kokomo IN. 317-457-5558

Care, John H C, *Librn,* Erving Public Library, Erving MA. 617-544-6339

Carey, Beverly, *Librn,* Wilder Clubhouse & Library, Wilder VT. 802-295-2169

Carey, Eleanor, *Librn,* Putney Public Library, Putney VT. 802-387-4407

Carey, Esther D, *Librn,* Torrington Library, Torrington CT. 203-489-6684

Carey, Kjestine, *ILL,* Montana State University, Roland R Renne Library, Bozeman MT. 406-994-3119

Carey, Lee, *Asst Dir,* Bergen Community College, Learning Resources Center Library, Paramus NJ. 201-447-1500, Ext 405

Carey, Lois, *Ref,* United States Army (Army Engineer Center & Fort Belvoir Van Noy Library), Fort Belvoir VA. 703-664-6255

Carey, Mary H, *Ch,* Finger Lakes Library System, Ithaca NY. 607-273-4074

Carey, Mrs E, *Librn,* Pensacola Junior College (Milton Center), Milton FL. 904-476-5410

Cargill, Jean, *Tech Serv, Acq & Cat,* Allan Hancock Joint Community College Library, Santa Maria CA. 805-922-6966, Ext 215, 242

Cargill, Jennifer, *Acq,* Miami University, Edgar W King Library, Oxford OH. 513-529-2944

Carhart, Jr, Forrest F, *Exec Dir,* New York Metropolitan Reference & Research Library Agency, (METRO), NY. 212-398-0290

Carini, Helen, *Tech Serv,* GAF Corp, Technical Information Services Library, Wayne NJ. 201-628-3320

Carlburg, David, *Librn,* California Department of Justice Library, Los Angeles CA. 213-736-2196

Carleton, Don E, *Librn,* University of Texas Libraries (Barker Texas History Center), Austin TX. 512-471-3811

Carlin, Elizabeth J, *Dir,* Oakmont Carnegie Library, Oakmont PA. 412-828-9532

Carlin, Lawrence, *Ad,* Rocky River Public Library, Rocky River OH. 216-333-7610

Carlisle, Betty, *Librn,* Shreve Memorial Library (Mooringsport Branch), Mooringsport LA. 318-221-2614

Carlisle, Carol, *Dir,* Mineola Memorial Library Inc, Mineola TX. 214-569-2767

Carlisle, Donna, *Ad,* Hays Public Library, Hays KS. 913-625-9014

Carlisle, Donna H, *Dir,* Jackson County Library, Kadoka SD. 605-837-2689

Carlisle, Donna H, *Dir,* Jackson County Library (Kadoka Library), Kadoka SD. 605-837-2689

Carlisle, Hilda, *Chief Librn,* First United Methodist Church, Gertrude Callihan Memorial Library, San Marcos TX. 512-392-3848

Carlley, Caroline, *Librn,* Fredonia Public Library, Fredonia AZ. 643-5395

Carlombe, Solange, *Acq,* Trois-Rivieres College Library, Trois-Rivieres PQ. 819-376-1721, Ext 286

Carlon, Marilyn, *Ref, Tech Serv & Cat,* Harford County Library, Bel Air MD. 301-838-7484

Carlon, Patsy, *Librn,* Lake County Library (Paisely Branch), Paisley OR. 503-943-3911

Carlsen, Harle S, *Librn,* South Dennis Free Public Library, South Dennis MA. 617-394-8954

Carlsen, Mildred, *Asst Dir,* North Iowa Area Community College Library, Mason City IA. 515-421-4232

Carlson, Allen B, *Dir,* Montgomery County Community College, Learning Resources Center, Blue Bell PA. 215-643-6000, Ext 340

Carlson, Carl A, *In Charge,* United States Naval Photographic Center (Motion Picture Film Depository Library), Washington DC. 202-545-6700

Carlson, David, *Bibliog Instr,* University of Evansville, Clifford Memorial Library & Learning Resources, Evansville IN. 812-479-2462

Carlson, Dorothy, *Ch,* Memorial Library of Radnor Township, Wayne PA. 215-687-1124

Carlson, Dudley, *Ch,* Princeton Public Library, Princeton NJ. 609-924-9529

Carlson, Edna N, *Librn,* Bayport Public Library, Bayport MN. 612-439-7454

Carlson, George, *Librn,* Choteau County Free Library (Geraldine Branch), Geraldine MT. 406-737-4326

Carlson, Gertrude A, *Educ,* Tarleton State University Library, Stephenville TX. 817-968-9246

Carlson, Gordon, *Librn,* United States Public Health Service, NIOSH Appalachian Laboratory for Occupational Safety & Health Library, Morgantown WV. 304-599-7416

Carlson, Jacquelynn, *Librn,* Saint Mary's Hospital, Staff Library, Minneapolis MN. 612-338-2229

Carlson, James F, *Asst Dean, Libr-Media,* American River College Library, Sacramento CA. 916-484-8293

Carlson, Jean S, *Bibliog Instr,* Mid-Michigan Library League, Cadillac MI. 616-775-6541

Carlson, Joan, *Librn,* Lindstrom Public Library, Lindstrom MN. 612-257-2817

Carlson, Joan, *Librn,* Rhode Island School for the Deaf Library, Providence RI. 401-277-3525

Carlson, John B, *Dir,* Montcalm Community College Library, Sidney MI. 517-328-2111, Ext 261

Carlson, Jolene, *Ref,* Trinity College Library, Deerfield IL. 312-945-6700, Ext 217

Carlson, Lillian V, *Asst Librn,* Dunwoody Industrial Institute Library, John A Butler Learning Center, Minneapolis MN. 612-374-5800

Carlson, Linda, *ILL & Ref,* Johns Hopkins University School of Advanced International Studies, Sydney R & Elsa W Mason Library, Washington DC. 202-785-6296

Carlson, Livija, *Librn,* University of Minnesota (Veterinary Med), Saint Paul MN. 612-373-1455

Carlson, Margaret, *Bibliog Instr & Maps,* Michigan Technological University Library, Houghton MI. 906-487-2500

Carlson, Marie, *ILL & Media,* Bethlehem Public Library, Delmar NY. 518-439-9314

Carlson, Marilyn, *Librn,* Northwest Hospital, Effie M Storey Learning Center, Seattle WA. 206-364-0500, Ext 686

Carlson, Mary, *Bus, Sci-Tech,* Phoenix Public Library, Phoenix AZ. 602-262-6451

Carlson, Melinda, *Media,* Eastern Shore Regional Library, Salisbury MD. 301-742-1537

Carlson, Melvin, *Info processing,* University of Massachusetts at Amherst Library, Amherst MA. 413-545-0284

Carlson, Mina, *Asst Dir,* Estherville Public Library, Estherville IA. 712-362-3869

Carlson, Mrs Roy, *Librn,* Lincoln Township Library, Wausa NE. 402-586-2454

Carlson, Nellie, *Asst Librn,* Lincoln County Library, Kemmerer WY. 307-877-4886

Carlson, Pat, *Dir,* Southern California College of Optometry, M B Ketchum Memorial Library, Fullerton CA. 714-870-7226, Ext 315

Carlson, Ralph, *Acq & Cat,* Norfolk Public Library, Norfolk VA. 804-441-2887

Carlson, Robyn L, *Dir,* Lewis County War Memorial & Lewis Bennet Public Library, Weston WV. 304-260-5151

Carlson, Ruth, *Dir,* Weix Memorial Library, Dorchester Public Library, Dorchester WI. 715-654-5402

Carlson, Sandy, *Ch,* Kitsap Regional Library, Bremerton WA. 206-377-7601

Carlson, Stan W, *Dir & Archivist,* Unity Hospital Medical Library, Fridley MN. 612-786-2200, Ext 378

Carlson, Vicki, *Librn,* Carpenter Memorial Library, Cle Elum WA. 509-674-2313

Carlsten, Marcia, *Ch,* Flint Public Library, Flint MI. 313-232-7111

Carlstrom, Elizabeth, *Ch,* Jefferson Public Library, Jefferson IA. 515-386-2836

Carlton, Bruce, *Ref,* Contra Costa College Library, San Pablo CA. 415-235-7800, Ext 213

Carlton, Carol, *Media,* Southeast Community College, Learning Resources Center, Cumberland KY. 606-589-2145, Ext 25

Carlton, Janet, *Librn,* Virginia Polytechnic Institute & State University Library (Reserve Collection, VPI & SU Northern Virginia Graduate Center), Washington DC. 703-961-5593

Carlton, Jeane, *Outreach Librn,* Forked Deer Regional Library Center, Trimble TN. 901-297-5810

Carlton, Peggy, *Ch,* Gulfport Public Library, Gulfport FL. 813-347-0218
Carlton, Roland G, *Dir,* Mineola Public Library, Mineola NY. 516-746-8488
Carlton, Winifred, *Librn,* Hancock Public Library, Hancock WI. 715-249-5496
Carlucci, Nancy D, *Librn,* Ministry of the Solicitor General, Office of the Fire Marshal Library, Toronto ON. 416-965-4855
Carmack, Bob, *Dean,* University of South Dakota, I D Weeks Library, Vermillion SD. 605-677-5371
Carmack, Mona S, *Dir,* Ames Public Library, Ames IA. 515-232-4404
Carmack, Norma J, *Social Science,* Trinity University Library, San Antonio TX. 512-736-8121
Carman, Stanley B, *Librn,* Milford Public Library, Milford CT. 203-878-7461
Carmel, Joel, *Cat,* Immaculate Heart College Library, Los Angeles CA. 213-462-1301, Ext 271
Carmichael, Cecily, *Educ, Psychol, Sociol,* West Chester State College, Francis Harvey Green Library, West Chester PA. 215-436-2643
Carmichael, Eleanor, *Cat & On-Line Servs,* Depauw University, Roy O West Library, Greencastle IN. 317-653-9721, Ext 250
Carmichael, H Dodson, *Dir,* Dallas Health & Science Museum Library, Dallas TX. 214-428-8351
Carmichael, James, *Instr,* Georgia College, Education Library Media, GA. 912-453-4047 & 453-5573
Carmichael, James V, *Ref,* Georgia College, Ina Dillard Russell Library, Milledgeville GA. 912-453-4047, 453-5573
Carmichael, M Fairlie, *Librn,* Waterbury Hospital, Health Center Library, Waterbury CT. 203-573-6148
Carmichael, Rosemary, *Librn,* Wake County Department of the Public Library (Garner Public), Garner NC. 919-772-5210
Carmona, Emily, *Cat,* Topeka Public Library, Topeka KS. 913-233-2040
Carmona, Rita, *On-Line Servs,* Florida Institute of Technology Library, Melbourne FL. 305-723-3701, Ext 270
Carnahan, David J, *Assoc Dean,* Evergreen State College, Daniel J Evans Library, Olympia WA. 206-866-6262
Carnahan, Joan A, *Librn,* Tenneco Chemicals, Inc Library, Piscataway NJ. 201-981-5252
Carnahan, Mabel, *Librn,* Jacksonville Public Library System (Regency Square), Jacksonville FL. 904-633-3020
Carnall, Kathleen, *Dir,* Porter Public Library, Westlake OH. 216-871-2600
Carnegie, Sandra, *Supvr,* Middlesex County Library (Newbury Branch), Newbury ON. 519-438-8368
Carnell, Helen J, *Librn,* United Co-operatives of Ontario, Harmon Library, Mississauga ON. 416-270-3560, Ext 245
Carnelli, Sandra, *Ad,* Warren-Newport Public Library District, Gurnee IL. 312-244-5150
Carnes, Kathleen, *Librn,* Choate Hospital Library, Woburn MA. 617-933-6700
Carney, Eileen, *Asst Librn,* Brundage, Story & Rose, Investment Counsel Library, New York NY. 212-269-3050, Ext 78
Carney, Karen, *Librn,* Simon's Rock Early College Library, Great Barrington MA. 413-528-0771, Ext 273
Carney, Lynn, *Tech Serv,* Georgetown University (Fred O Dennis Law Library), Washington DC. 202-624-8260
Carney, Patrick J, *Dir,* United States Navy (United States Marine Corps Base Library), Camp Pendleton CA. 714-725-5104
Carney, Thomas L, *Dir,* Cedar Rapids Public Library, Cedar Rapids IA. 319-398-5123
Carney, Tom, *Adjunct Asst Prof,* University of Iowa, School of Library Science, IA. 319-353-3644
Carnow, Annette, *ILL & Bibliog Instr,* Chicago Public Library (General Information Service Div), Chicago IL. 312-269-2800
Carnright, Jason J, *Dir,* Clinton Community College, LeRoy M Douglas Memorial Library, Plattsburgh NY. 518-561-6650, Ext 360
Caro, Eva K, *Librn,* California State Department of Transportation (Laboratory Technical Library), Sacramento CA. 916-444-4752

Caro, Juana, *Librn,* Donna Public Library, Donna TX. 512-464-4091
Carol, Marcel C, *Librn,* Baylor University in Dallas Library, Dallas TX. 214-820-2372
Carolan, Robert H, *Librn,* Rhode Island Association for the Blind Library, Providence RI. 401-941-5421
Carolin, Janice, *Asst Librn,* Manulife, Business Library, Toronto ON. 416-928-4104
Carollo, Michael Thomas, *Dir,* Page Public Library, Page AZ. 602-645-2231
Caron, Barbara A, *Dir,* Viking Library System, Fergus Falls MN. 218-739-2896
Caron, E Rose, *Librn,* Nashua Public Library (Chandler Memorial), Nashua NH. 603-882-4461
Caron, Gail, *Librn,* Aurora Public Library (Southwest), Aurora CO. 303-750-5000, Ext 410
Caron, Gisele, *ILL,* College Du Nord-Quest La Bibliotheque, Rouyn PQ. 819-762-0931, Ext 134
Caron, Gisele, *ILL,* Universite Du Quebec: Centre d'etudes Universitaires Dans L'ouest Quebecois Bibliotheque, Rouyn PQ. 819-762-0971, Ext 350
Caron, Mary L, *Instrl Mat Asst,* Illinois Benedictine College, Theodore Lownik Library, Lisle IL. 312-968-7270, Ext 286
Caron, Richard A, *Dir,* Cities Service Research & Development Co, Central Library, Cranbury NJ. 609-655-7140
Caron, Ted, *Cat,* Mayo Foundation (Medical Library), Rochester MN. 507-284-2061
Carothers, Evelyn, *Librn,* Tulare County Library System (Ducor Branch), Ducor CA. 209-534-2251
Carothers, Evelyn, *Librn,* Tulare County Library System (Terra Bella Branch), Terra Bella CA. 209-535-4621
Carpenter, Angelica, *Librn,* Springfield-Greene County Library (Green County Branch), Springfield MO. 417-865-5558
Carpenter, Barbara, *Per,* Harrisburg Area Community College, McCormick Library, Harrisburg PA. 717-236-9533, Ext 257
Carpenter, Becky, *Librn,* Goldfield Public Library, Goldfield NV. 702-485-3236
Carpenter, Betty M, *Librn,* Suffolk County Historical Society Library, Riverhead NY. 516-727-2881
Carpenter, Bruce, *Media,* Quinnipiac College Library, Hamden CT. 203-288-5251, Ext 271
Carpenter, Cecile L, *Asst Dir,* Library Association of Portland, Multnomah County Library, Portland OR. 503-223-7201, Ext 40
Carpenter, Doreen, *Dir,* Bibliocentre, Division of Centennial College of Applied Arts & Technology, ON. 416-694-5201
Carpenter, Dorothy, *Acq,* Reuben McMillan Free Library Free Library Association, Public Library of Youngstown & Mahoning County, Youngstown OH. 216-744-8636
Carpenter, E, *English, Theatre & Cinema,* State University of New York at Buffalo, University Libraries, Buffalo NY. 716-636-2965
Carpenter, Gai, *Dir,* Hampshire College, Harold F Johnson Library Center, Amherst MA. 413-549-4600
Carpenter, Harlow, *Dir,* Bundy Foundation, Inc, Bundy Art Gallery Library, Waitsfield VT. 802-496-3882
Carpenter, Janet, *Librn,* Oswego Public Library, Oswego KS. 316-795-4921
Carpenter, Janet S, *Librn,* Ashley County Library, Hamburg AR. 501-853-8781
Carpenter, Juanita, *Librn,* Oak Grove Luthern Church Library, Richfield MN. 612-869-4917
Carpenter, Kenneth, *Spec Coll,* University of Nevada-Reno, Noble H Getchell Library, Reno NV. 702-784-6533
Carpenter, Kenneth E, *Kress Libr Curator,* Harvard University Library (Baker Library), Boston MA. 617-495-3650
Carpenter, Lois, *Ref,* Manitoba Department of Education Library, Winnipeg MB. 204-786-0218
Carpenter, Marjorie L, *ILL,* Northwestern University Library, Evanston IL. 312-492-7658
Carpenter, Max H, *Dir,* Maritime Institute of Technology & Graduate Studies Library, Linthicum Heights MD. 301-636-5700
Carpenter, Maxine P, *Asst Librn,* Ashley County Library, Hamburg AR. 501-853-8781
Carpenter, Peggy, *Ch,* Burlington County Library, Mount Holly NJ. 609-267-9660

Carpenter, Peggy, *Librn,* Zeigler Public Library, Zeigler IL. 618-596-2041
Carpenter, Raymond, *Assoc Prof,* University of North Carolina at Chapel Hill, School of Library Science, NC. 919-933-8366
Carpenter, Thelma M, *Librn,* Oregon Township Public Library, Oregon IL. 815-732-2724
Carpenter, Violet, *Librn,* Martins Ferry Public Library (Powhatan Point Public), Powhatan Point OH. 614-633-0314
Carpenter, Jr, Robert E, *Librn,* Newport News Public Library System (West Avenue), Newport News VA. 804-247-8505
Carper, Ann M, *Dir,* Elizabethtown College, Zug Memorial Library, Elizabethtown PA. 717-367-1151, Ext 222
Carper, Carleta, *Librn,* Northeast Missouri Library Service (Lewis County), LaBelle MO. 816-462-3600
Carpino, Eileen, *Dir,* Wheeling College, Bishop Hodges Learning Center, Wheeling WV. 304-243-2226
Carpino, Linda, *Ch,* Toledo-Lucas County Public Library, Toledo OH. 419-255-7055
Carr, Ann A, *Acq,* Harvard University Library (Francis A Countway Library of Medicine), Boston MA. 617-732-2142
Carr, Barbara, *Head Off Servs,* Hughes Aircraft Co, Electron Dynamics Div Technical Library, Torrance CA. 213-534-2121, Ext 2143
Carr, Barbara, *ILL & Ref,* Saint Lawrence College of Applied Arts & Technology Library Services, Kingston ON. 613-544-5400, Ext 163
Carr, Charles, *Ad,* Burlington County Library, Mount Holly NJ. 609-267-9660
Carr, Charles, *Librn Blind,* Burlington County Library, Mount Holly NJ. 609-267-9660
Carr, Charles E, *Asst Prof,* University of North Alabama, Dept of Education & Library Science, AL. 205-766-4100, Ext 266
Carr, Deborah, *Asst Librn,* West Tisbury Free Public Library, West Tisbury MA. 617-693-3366
Carr, Edna, *ILL,* Pinellas Park Public Library, Pinellas Park FL. 813-544-4868
Carr, Elizabeth, *In Charge,* Florida Agricultural & Mechanical University (School of Business & Industry Library), Tallahassee FL. 904-599-3457
Carr, H Isabel, *Per,* Montgomery College-Takoma Park Campus Library, Takoma Park MD. 301-587-4090, Ext 242
Carr, Jeanette, *ILL,* Hammond Public Library, Hammond IN. 219-931-5100
Carr, Marion, *Librn,* Worcester Public Library (Greendale), Worcester MA. 617-853-0230
Carr, Marjorie, *Librn,* Enfield Free Public Library, Enfield NH. 603-632-7145
Carr, Mary, *Cat,* Gonzaga University, Crosby Library, Spokane WA. 509-328-4220, Ext 3132
Carr, Melba, *Librn,* Montgomery County Public Library (Mount Gilead Branch), Mt Gilead NC. 919-439-6651
Carr, Melissa, *Pub Servs,* Daniel Boone Regional Library, Columbia MO. 314-443-3161
Carr, Mildred L, *Circ,* University of North Carolina at Greensboro, Walter Clinton Jackson Library, Greensboro NC. 919-379-5880
Carr, Peggy, *Dir,* Feather River College, Quincy CA. 916-283-0202, Ext 36
Carr, Susan, *Per,* Doane College, Perkins Library, Crete NE. 402-826-2161, Ext 224, 287
Carr, Susan, *Ch,* Newark Public Library, Newark OH. 345-1750 & 345-8972
Carr-Harris, Ian, *Dir,* Ontario College of Art Library, Toronto ON. 416-977-5311, Ext 54 & 55
Carraccino, Joseph, *Bkmobile Coordr,* Chelsea Public Library, Chelsea MA. 617-884-2335
Carrell, Esther M, *Librn,* Plainview Public Library, Plainview NE. 402-582-4507
Carrer, Gloria, *Bibliog Instr,* East Longmeadow Public Library, East Longmeadow MA. 413-525-7813
Carreta, Anne, *On-Line Servs,* Westchester County Historical Society Library, Tuckahoe NY. 914-337-1753
Carriar, Nancy, *Ser,* University of Minnesota, Duluth (Health Science Library), Duluth MN. 218-726-8585
Carrick, Kathy, *Assoc Dir,* State University of New York at Buffalo (Charles B Sears Law Library), Buffalo NY. 716-636-2043

Carrico, Evea Lou, *Librn,* Athens Mental Health & Mental Retardation Center (Patients' Library), Athens OH. 614-592-3031, Ext 335
Carrico, Philip N, *Dir,* Northern Kentucky Regional Library System, Covington KY. 606-431-1043
Carrier, Barbara, *Tech Serv & Cat,* New College of the University of South Florida, Sarasota Campus Library, Sarasota FL. 813-355-7671, Ext 214
Carrier, Eileen, *Librn,* Bennington College (Music), Bennington VT. 802-442-5401, Ext 201
Carrier, Esther J, *ILL,* Lock Haven State College, George B Stevenson Library, Lock Haven PA. 717-893-2309
Carrier, Katherine, *Librn,* Prince Edward Island Provincial Library (Kensington Branch), Kensington PE. 902-892-3504, Ext 54
Carrier, Lois, *Soc Sci,* University of British Columbia Library, Vancouver BC. 604-228-3871
Carrier, Marjorie, *Librn,* North Stratford Public Library, Stratford NH. 603-922-3884
Carrier, Walter, *Librn,* Moody Bible Institute of Chicago, Moody Aviation Library, Elizabethton TN. 615-543-3534
Carriere, Jeanne, *Librn,* Winnipeg Public Library (Coronation Park), Winnipeg MB. 204-233-7766
Carrigan, Brenda, *Librn,* Oshawa Public Library (Jess Hann Branch), Oshawa ON. 416-728-2441
Carrigan, J Michael, *Exhibits Officer,* Library of Congress, Washington DC. 202-287-5000
Carrigan, Jean, *Chief Librn,* Equitable Life Assurance Society of the United States (General Library), New York NY. 212-554-2491
Carrigan, John L, *Librn,* City of Hope National Medical Center, Piness Medical & Scientific Library, Duarte CA. 213-359-8111
Carrigan, Sister Mary E, *Asst Dir & Ref,* Elizabeth Seton College Library, Yonkers NY. 914-969-4000, Ext 261
Carrigan, Theresa, *Librn,* Hamilton Township Library, Mays Landing NJ. 609-625-1572
Carrillo, Sherry J, *ILL,* Florida International University, Tamiami Campus, Athenaeum, Miami FL. 305-552-2461
Carrillo, Teri, *Librn,* Bureau of Land Management, Las Cruces District Office Library, Las Cruces NM. 505-523-5571
Carringer, Doris B, *Librn,* Murphy Public Library, Murphy NC. 704-837-2417
Carrington, Sandra, *Librn,* Austin Public Library (Manchaca Road), Austin TX. 512-472-5433
Carrington, Jr, Samuel M, *Librn,* William Marsh Rice University, Fondren Library, Houston TX. 713-527-4022
Carrison, Dale, *Dir,* Mankato State University, Memorial Library, Mankato MN. 507-389-6201
Carrison, Dale, *Chmn,* Southcentral Minnesota Inter-Library Exchange, (SMILE), MN. 507-389-6201
Carriveau, Kenneth, *Dean,* University of Guam, Library Science Program, GU. 734-2921
Carro, Jorge L, *Head Law Librn,* University of Cincinnati Libraries (Robert S Marx Law Library), Cincinnati OH. 513-475-3016
Carroad, Eva, *Librn,* University of California, Berkeley (Biology), Berkeley CA. 415-642-2531
Carrol, Arthur L, *Dir,* United States Department of Health & Human Services (Parklawn Health Library), Rockville MD. 301-443-2665
Carroll, Bruce, *Circ,* Community College of Baltimore (Harbor Campus), Baltimore MD. 301-396-1860
Carroll, C Edward, *Prof,* University of Missouri-Columbia, School of Library & Informational Science, MO. 314-882-4546
Carroll, Celia, *Media,* Santa Monica Public Library, Santa Monica CA. 213-451-5751
Carroll, Dewey E, *Dean,* North Texas State University, School of Library & Information Sciences, TX. 817-788-2445
Carroll, Diane, *Ref,* University of Minnesota, Duluth (Health Science Library), Duluth MN. 218-726-8585
Carroll, Elizabeth, *Dir,* A Holmes Johnson Memorial Library, Kodiak Public Library, Kodiak AK. 907-486-3312
Carroll, Elizabeth C, *Dir,* Talbot County Free Library, Easton MD. 301-822-1626
Carroll, F Lee, *Dir,* First Presbyterian Church of Charleston Library, Charleston WV. 304-343-8961

Carroll, Frances, *Acq,* Santa Fe Community College Library, Gainesville FL. 904-377-5161, Ext 315
Carroll, Frances C, *ILL,* Rutland Free Library, Rutland VT. 802-773-6880
Carroll, Frank, *Commun Servs,* North Central Kansas Libraries System, Manhattan KS. 913-776-4741
Carroll, Frank, *Librn Blind,* North Central Kansas Libraries System (Subregional Talking Books), Manhattan KS. 913-776-4741
Carroll, George, *Corp Librn,* Associated Spring-Barnes Group Inc, Technical Center Library, Bristol CT. 203-583-1331, Ext 469
Carroll, Hardy, *Assoc Prof,* Western Michigan University, School of Librarianship, MI. 616-383-1849
Carroll, Holly, *Librn,* Geauga County Public Library (Chester), Chesterland OH. 216-729-4250
Carroll, Irene, *Librn,* Madison County Public Library (Hot Springs Branch), Mars Hills NC. 704-649-3741
Carroll, Jack, *Dir,* Brevard Community College, Melbourne Campus Learning Resources Center, Melbourne FL. 305-254-0305, Ext 227, 228
Carroll, Jeanne, *AV & Circ,* Wartburg College, Engelbrecht Library, Waverly IA. 319-352-1200, Ext 244
Carroll, Jerry, *Ref,* Wayne County Public Library, Inc, Goldsboro NC. 919-735-1824
Carroll, Libby, *Librn,* Memphis-Shelby County Public Library & Information Center (Whitehaven), Memphis TN. 901-396-9700
Carroll, Linda J, *Librn,* Population Crisis Committee Library, Washington DC. 202-659-1833
Carroll, Margaret, *Librn,* Brantley Public Library, Brantley AL. 205-527-2931
Carroll, Marty, *Dir,* Hardin County Library, Savannah TN. 901-925-4314
Carroll, Mary, *Doc, Rare Bks & Spec Coll,* Grand Canyon College, Fleming Library, Phoenix AZ. 602-249-3300, Ext 207
Carroll, Mary, *Librn,* Standard & Poor's Compustat Services, Inc, Data Center, Englewood CO. 303-771-6510, Ext 347
Carroll, P, *YA,* Shoreham-Wading River Public Library, Shoreham NY. 516-929-4488
Carroll, Ruth, *Dir,* Saint Francis Hospital & Medical Center (Hospital Library), Hartford CT. 203-548-4746
Carroll, Ruth, *Dir,* Saint Francis Hospital & Medical Center (School of Nursing Library), Hartford CT. 203-247-4441, Ext 244
Carroll, Sally, *Media,* Stephen F Austin State University, Ralph W Steen Library, Nacogdoches TX. 713-569-4109
Carroll, Theresa A, *Dir,* Public Library of Brookline, Brookline MA. 617-734-0100
Carroll, Thomas B, *Park Ranger,* National Park Service, Gran Quivira National Monument Library, Mountainair NM. 505-847-2770
Carroll, Tom, *Librn,* Dayton Daily News, Reference Library, Dayton OH. 513-225-2430
Carroll, Virginia L, *Librn,* Camp, Dresser & Mckee, Herman G Dresser Library, Boston MA. 617-742-5151
Carroon, Robert G, *Curator,* Milwaukee County Historical Society, Library & Archives, Milwaukee WI. 414-273-8288
Carruth, Kathy, *Asst Dir,* Redwood Falls Public Library, Redwood Falls MN. 507-637-8650
Carruth, Louise, *Bus, Sci & Tech,* Worcester Public Library, Worcester MA. 617-752-3751
Carruthers, Joan, *Ref & On-Line Servs,* York University, Scott Library, Downsview ON. 416-667-2235
Carruthers, Mrs E C, *Librn,* Loudoun County Public Library (Purcelville Branch), Purcellville VA. 703-338-7235
Carruthers, R T, *Pres,* Bioproducts, Inc, Columbia Empire Publications Library, Warrenton OR. 503-861-2256
Carry, Jane, *Librn,* San Bernardino Public Library (Coddington), San Bernardino CA. 714-882-8816
Carsch, Judith S, *Librn,* Isaac M Wise Temple, Ralph Cohen Library, Cincinnati OH. 513-793-2556
Carson, Barbara, *Librn,* Fayette County Public Library (Montgomery), Montgomery WV. 304-442-5665

Carson, Barbara H, *Librn,* Middlebury Public Library, Middlebury CT. 203-758-2634
Carson, David, *Instrnl Designer-Producer,* Odessa College, Murry H Fly Learning Resources Center, Odessa TX. 915-337-5381, Ext 299
Carson, Donald, *Chief Librn,* College of Insurance Library, New York NY. 212-962-4111, Ext 277
Carson, Herbert, *Media,* Corning Community College, Arthur A Houghton, Jr Library, Corning NY. 607-962-9251
Carson, Irene, *Librn,* White Pine County Library (Kinnear), McGill NV. 702-235-7220
Carson, J, *Bibliog Instr,* Carleton University, Murdoch Maxwell MacOdrum Library, Ottawa ON. 613-231-4357
Carson, Kate, *Tech Serv,* Bradford Public Library, Bradford ON. 416-775-6482
Carson, Lynn R, *Asst Dir,* Church of Jesus Christ of Latter-Day Saints (Genealogical Society of Utah), Salt Lake City UT. 801-531-2323
Carson, Miss E, *Librn,* Canada Institute for Scientific & Technical Information (Building Research), Ottawa ON. 613-993-1600
Carson, Nancy I, *Librn,* Sacramento Peak Observatory Technical Library, Sunspot NM. 505-434-1390, Ext 224
Carson, Thomas Moore, *Librn,* El Paso County Library, Fabens TX. 915-764-3635
Carson, Thomasine, *Librn,* North Las Vegas Municipal Library, North Las Vegas NV. 702-649-2363
Carstarphen, James, *Cat,* Lenoir-Rhyne College, Carl A Rudisill Library, Hickory NC. 704-328-1741, Ext 221
Carstens, Amanda L, *Librn,* Galva Public Library, Galva IA. 712-282-4400
Carstens, Barbara, *ILL,* University of Manitoba Libraries, Winnipeg MB. 204-474-9881
Carstens, Jane Ellen, *Prof & Coordr,* University of Southwestern Louisiana, Dept of School Librarianship, LA. 318-264-6713
Carstensen, Helen, *Librn,* Miami County Law Library Association, Troy OH. 513-335-8341, Ext 261
Carswell, Mary Alice, *Dir,* Academy of the New Church Library, Bryn Athyn PA. 215-947-0203
Cart, Michael, *City Librn,* Beverly Hills Public Library, Beverly Hills CA. 213-550-4711
Carta, Ann D, *Cat,* Welles-Turner Memorial Library, Glastonbury CT. 203-633-1300
Carte, Mary Sue, *Reader Serv,* George S Houston Memorial Library, Dothan AL. 205-793-9767
Cartemelia, Carolyn, *Librn,* Smith-Welch Memorial Library, Hearne TX. 713-279-5191
Carter, Alberta, *Librn,* Jefferson County Public Library (Columbine High School Public), Littleton CO. 303-979-5124
Carter, Ann, *Librn,* Fayette County Public Library (Patrick C Graney Jr, Library), Mt Hope WV. 304-877-3260
Carter, Ann B, *Librn,* Factoryville Public Library, Factoryville PA. 717-945-5051
Carter, Ann M, *Librn,* Dorsey, Windhorst, Hannaford, Whitney & Halladay Library, Minneapolis MN. 340-2613 & 340-2614
Carter, Bobby R, *Dir,* Texas College of Osteopathic Medicine Library, Fort Worth TX. 817-735-2465
Carter, Caroline, *Librn,* Letts Public Library, Letts IA. 319-726-5121
Carter, Catharine, *Librn,* Central Florida Regional Library (Yankeetown), Ocala FL. 904-629-8551
Carter, Clarence, *Personnel Officer,* University of Minnesota Libraries-Twin Cities, Minneapolis MN. 612-373-3097
Carter, Darline L, *Dir,* West Islip Public Library, West Islip NY. 516-661-7080, 661-7082
Carter, Denise, *Librn,* Maffett Memorial Library, Groesbeck Public Library, Groesbeck TX. 817-729-3667
Carter, Dennis L, *Chief Park Naturalist,* Shenandoah National Park Library, Luray VA. 703-999-2243, Ext 76
Carter, Doris C, *Librn,* Florence County Library (Lake City Public), Lake City SC. 803-394-8071
Carter, Eleanor, *Dir,* State University of New York, Agricultural & Technical College at Cobleskill, Jared van Wagenen, Jr Learning Resource Center, Cobleskill NY. 518-234-5841
Carter, Ellen, *Circ,* Virginia Intermont College, J F Hicks Memorial Library, Bristol VA. 703-669-6101, Ext 26

Carter, Esther M, *Assoc Prof,* Shippensburg State College, Dept of Library Science, PA. 717-532-1472
Carter, Faye T, *Acq,* Lincoln University, Inman E Page Library, Jefferson City MO. 314-751-2325, Ext 326
Carter, Gail N, *Dir,* Pamlico Technical College Library, Grantsboro NC. 919-249-1851, Ext 22
Carter, Georgia Kay, *Dir,* Hercules Inc, Hattiesburg Plant Laboratory Library, Hattiesburg MS. 601-545-3450
Carter, Harriett, *Tech Serv,* Reading Public Library, Reading MA. 617-944-0840
Carter, Helen, *Librn,* Baltimore County Public Library (Cockeysville Branch), Cockeysville MD. 301-666-0447
Carter, Helen, *Librn,* Baltimore County Public Library (Jacksonville Minilibrary), Phoenix MD. 301-667-1292
Carter, Helen, *Legal Research,* University of New Mexico General Library (Law Library), Albuquerque NM. 505-277-6236
Carter, Ida, *Librn,* Gard, Inc Library, Niles IL. 312-647-9000, Ext 275
Carter, Illona, *Librn,* Brighton Public Library, Brighton ON. 613-475-2511
Carter, Jack, *In Charge,* United States Naval Photographic Center (Still Picture Library), Washington DC. 202-545-6700
Carter, Jackson, *Ser,* Eastern New Mexico University Library, Portales NM. 505-562-2624
Carter, Jane Robbins, *Dean,* Louisiana State University, Graduate School of Library Science, LA. 504-388-3158
Carter, Jeannette, *Ref,* Iowa City Public Library, Iowa City IA. 319-354-1265
Carter, Jennelea, *Dir,* Maltman Memorial Library, Wood River Public Library, Wood River NE. 308-583-2349
Carter, Jewell A, *Dir,* Samford University (L R Jordan Library), Birmingham AL. 205-591-2371
Carter, Jim, *Librn,* Sacramento Public Library (Del Paso Heights), Sacramento CA. 916-927-1133
Carter, Joan M, *Librn,* Louisiana Correctional Institute for Women Library, Saint Gabriel LA. 504-642-5529
Carter, John, *ILL,* Louisiana State University (Troy H Middleton Library), Baton Rouge LA. 504-388-2217
Carter, John M, *Media Dir,* Jones County Junior College Memorial Library & Media Center, Ellisville MS. 601-477-9311, Ext 298
Carter, John M, *Head,* Louisiana State University System Interlibrary Network, (SINET), LA. 504-388-2138
Carter, Joyce, *Librn,* Kitsap Regional Library (Silverdale Station), Tracyton WA. 206-377-3571
Carter, Judy J, *Librn,* Palomar Community College (Fine Arts Library), San Marcos CA. 714-744-1150, Ext 275, 276 & 473
Carter, Julia, *Head,* Indiana University at Bloomington (Medical Sciences), Bloomington IN. 812-337-3347
Carter, Karen, *Dir Info Resource Dept,* American Academy of Family Physicians, Information Resource Dept, Kansas City MO. 816-333-9700, Ext 352
Carter, Karen J, *Librn,* Chesapeake Corporation of Virginia Library, West Point VA. 804-843-5000, Ext 321
Carter, Kent, *Chief Archivist,* National Archives & Records Service, Federal Archives & Records Center, Region 7, Fort Worth TX. 817-334-5515
Carter, Leafy, *Librn,* Scott Sebastian Regional Library (Mansfield Library), Mansfield AR. 501-996-2856
Carter, Linda, *Librn Blind & Physically Handicapped,* Central Kansas Library System, Great Bend KS. 316-792-4865
Carter, Mamie, *In Charge,* Eureka-Humboldt County Library (Trinidad Branch), Trinidad CA. 707-445-7284, 445-7513
Carter, Marion L, *YA,* Salt Lake City Public Library, Salt Lake City UT. 801-363-5733
Carter, Maureen, *Anthrop,* University of Waterloo Library, Waterloo ON. 519-885-1211
Carter, Melinda, *Librn,* Palm Beach County Public Library System (North County), Tequesta FL. 305-746-5970
Carter, Mikel-Jon, *AV,* Bentley College, Solomon R Baker Library, Waltham MA. 617-891-2231
Carter, Mrs Dick, *Librn,* Statesboro Regional Library (Franklin Memorial), Swainsboro GA. 912-237-7791
Carter, Mrs Richard, *Acq,* Frankfort Community Public Library, Frankfort IN. 317-654-8746
Carter, Nancy, *Librn,* Open Bible College, Carrie Hardy Memorial Library, Des Moines IA. 515-283-0476
Carter, Nancy Carol, *Dir,* Golden Gate University (School of Law Library), San Francisco CA. 415-442-7260
Carter, Patricia, *ILL,* Dartmouth College, Baker Memorial Library, Hanover NH. 603-646-2235
Carter, Patricia, *Circ,* Kansas City College of Osteopathic Medicine, Mazzacano Hall Library, Kansas City MO. 816-283-2451, 2454
Carter, Philip, *Circ,* Medical Library Center of New York, New York NY. 212-427-1630
Carter, Quentin, *Ref,* Pikes Peak Community College, Learning Materials Center, Colorado Springs CO. 303-576-7711, Ext 536
Carter, Rita A, *Librn,* COMSAT Central Library, (Communications Satellite Corp), Washington DC. 202-554-6658
Carter, Robert, *Instr,* California State University-Los Angeles, Library Services Credential Program, CA. 213-224-3765
Carter, Ross, *Dir,* Vancouver Community College Libraries, Vancouver BC. 604-688-1111
Carter, Sharon C, *Librn,* Worcester Telegram & Gazette Library, Worcester MA. 755-4321
Carter, Steva, *Librn,* Springfield-Greene County Library (Republic Branch), Republic MO. 417-732-2700
Carter, Sue, *Librn,* War Memorial Public Library (Fairview Library), Fairview TN. 615-799-0235
Carter, Thomas G, *Dir,* Wilmington Township Public Library, Wilmington IL. 815-476-6719
Carter, Vera, *Librn,* Prescott Public-Yavapai County Library System (Kirkland Public), Kirkland AZ. 602-442-3356
Carter, Virginia A, *Dir,* Coventry Public Library, Coventry RI. 401-821-5654
Carter, Vivian, *Ch,* Normal Public Library, Normal IL. 309-452-1757
Carter, Wendy N, *Reader Serv & On-Line Servs,* Veterans Administration (Library Division), Washington DC. 202-389-2781
Carter, William E, *Chief, Hispanic Div,* Library of Congress, Washington DC. 202-287-5000
Carter, III, William, *In Charge,* Enoch Pratt Free Library (Washington Village), Baltimore MD. 301-396-5430, 396-5395
Cartey, Betty, *Librn,* Brooklyn Public Library (Stone Avenue), Brooklyn NY. 212-385-3737
Carthel, Sally M, *Bkmobile Coordr,* Abilene Public Library, Abilene TX. 915-677-2474
Cartier, Celine R, *Dir,* Universite Laval Bibliotheque, Quebec PQ. 418-656-3344
Cartledge, Ellen, *Librn,* Connecticut Mutual Life Insurance Co Library, Hartford CT. 203-727-6500, Ext 2473 & 2475
Cartledge, Louisa B, *ILL & Ref,* Furman University Library, Greenville SC. 803-294-2191
Cartmill, Roger E, *Tech Serv,* Pratt Institute Library, Brooklyn NY. 212-636-3684
Cartwright, Bob, *Librn,* Saint Edward's University Library (Social Work Center), Austin TX. 512-444-2621
Cartwright, Martha, *Librn,* Lititz Public Library, Lititz PA. 717-626-2255
Cartwright, Moira C, *Chief Librn,* Kingston Public Library, Kingston ON. 613-549-8888
Cartwright, Phyllis, *Tech Servs Syst Librn,* Broward County Division of Libraries, Broward County Library, Pompano Beach FL. 305-972-1100
Cartwright, Virginia, *Librn,* Kawaiahao Church Library, Honolulu HI. 808-538-6267
Carty, Kevin, *Dir,* Metropolitan Pro & Liability Insurance, Business & Law Library, Warwick RI. 401-827-2658
Caruso, Fern, *Librn,* United States Department of the Interior (US Bureau of Mines, Western Field Operations Center Library), Spokane WA. 509-484-1610
Caruso, Joan, *Chief, Extension Servs,* Queens Borough Public Library, Jamaica NY. 212-990-0700
Caruso, Karin, *Media,* New Hampshire College, Shapiro Library, Manchester NH. 603-668-2211, Ext 211
Caruso, Mary Elsie, *Admin Librn,* United States Army (Medical & Biological Science Library), Presidio of San Francisco CA. 415-561-2465
Caruso, Nicholas, *Librn,* University of Pittsburgh (Graduate School of Public & International Affairs), Pittsburgh PA. 412-624-4737
Caruthers, Judith, *Ref & On-Line Servs,* Louisiana State University Medical Center Library, New Orleans LA. 504-568-6100
Carvalho, Eugene, *Librn,* University of Kansas Libraries (East Asian), Lawrence KS. 913-864-4669
Carver, Chad, *Libr Tech,* Allentown Hospital Association, Health Sciences Library, Allentown PA. 215-821-2263
Carver, Jos E, *Librn,* British Columbia Institute of Technology Library, Burnaby BC. 604-434-5734, Ext 360
Carver, Larry, *Map & Imagery Coll,* University of California, Santa Barbara Library, Santa Barbara CA. 805-961-2741
Carver, Michael A, *Asst Dir,* Bennington College, Crossett Library, Bennington VT. 802-442-5401, Ext 278, 279, 290
Carver, Mildred Roach, *Librn,* Macksville City Library, Macksville KS. 316-348-2002
Carver, Pam, *Cat,* McMurry College, Jay-Rollins Library, Abilene TX. 915-692-4130, Ext 291
Carver, Jr, Ira E, *Libr Asst,* University of Texas Libraries (Collections Deposit Library), Austin TX. 512-471-3051
Cary, Howard B, *Vice President Welding Syst,* Hobart Brothers Co Technical Center, John H Blankenbuehler Memorial Library, Troy OH. 513-339-6011, Ext 4603
Cary, Linda, *Tech Serv,* Elkhart Public Library, Elkhart IN. 219-294-5463
Casady, Joyce, *Asst Librn,* Putnam County Public Library, Unionville MO. 816-947-3192
Casagrande, Barbara, *Librn,* South Hero Community Library, South Hero VT. 802-372-6600
Casamajo, Julia M, *Librn,* URS Company Library, San Mateo CA. 415-574-5000
Casarez, Nora, *Librn,* Chevron Industries, Inc, Chevron Geophysics Co Library, Houston TX. 713-781-3030, Ext 284
Casas, Diana, *Librn,* Tremont Area Free Public Library, Tremont PA. 717-695-3325
Casaubon, Edouard, *Law,* Universite Laval Bibliotheque, Quebec PQ. 418-656-3344
Casazza, Rosa, *Bkmobile Coordr,* Richmond Public Library, Richmond CA. 415-231-2119
Casciero, Albert J, *Dir,* University of the District of Columbia, Learning Resources Division, Washington DC. 202-282-7536
Cascio, Nina, *Media,* State University of New York at Buffalo (Charles B Sears Law Library), Buffalo NY. 716-636-2043
Casco, Natalie C, *Librn,* Middletown Springs Public Library, Middletown Springs VT. 802-235-2435
Cascone, Viola, *Librn,* Paterson Free Public Library (Riverside), Paterson NJ. 201-881-3785
Case, Barbara, *Cat,* California State University, John F Kennedy Memorial Library, Los Angeles CA. 213-224-2201
Case, Candice, *ILL,* Ames Public Library, Ames IA. 515-232-4404
Case, Jane, *Librn,* Wenatchee Valley College, John A Brown Library Media Center, Wenatchee WA. 509-662-1651
Case, Joanna M, *Dir,* Mystic & Noank Library, Inc, Mystic CT. 203-536-7721
Case, Laura, *Librn,* Southeast Arkansas Regional Library (Arkansas City), Monticello AR. 501-367-3336
Case, Lorraine, *Ch,* Watertown Regional Library, Watertown SD. 605-886-8521, 886-8282
Case, Robert N, *Dir,* Lancaster County Library, Lancaster PA. 717-394-2651
Casebier, Janet, *Librn,* California Institute of Technology (Humanities & Social Science Library), Pasadena CA. 213-795-6811, Ext 2418
Casebier, Janet, *Humanities & Social Sci,* California Institute of Technology, Robert A Millikan Memorial Library, Pasadena CA. 213-795-6811
Casella, Roberta, *Librn,* Texas Tech University Library (Core Collection), Lubbock TX. 806-742-2247

Casella, Thomas, *AV,* Cayuga County Community College, Norman F Bourke Memorial Library Learning Resources Center, Auburn NY. 315-255-1743, Ext 296 & 298

Caselton, Ida C, *Librn,* Ord Public Library, Ord Township Library, Ord NE. 308-728-3012

Casey, Betty, *Cat,* Kemp Public Library, Wichita Falls TX. 817-322-5611, Ext 377

Casey, Dennis, *Ref,* Hamline University (School of Law Library), Saint Paul MN. 612-641-2344

Casey, Eva Lyn M, *Librn,* Glendale University, College of Law Library, Glendale CA. 213-247-0770, Ext 23

Casey, Jean, *Ref,* Mason City Public Library, Mason City IA. 515-423-7552

Casey, Joan, *Dir Libr Publications,* National Municipal League, Murray Seasongood Library, New York NY. 212-535-5700

Casey, Kathleen E, *Asst Dir,* Saint Louis University (Divinity Library), Saint Louis MO. 314-658-3082

Casey, Lillian, *Librn,* Public Library of the City of Somerville (East), Somerville MA. 617-776-1118

Casey, Philip, *Librn,* United States Army (Armament Material Readiness Command, Technical Library), Rock Island IL. 309-794-5031

Casey, S, *Librn,* Queen's University at Kingston (Documents Library & Local Government), Kingston ON. 613-547-5767

Casey, Sara, *Per,* Salem College, Benedum Learning Resources Center, Salem WV. 304-782-5238

Casey, Verna, *Librn,* Eastern Kentucky University (Law Enforcement), Richmond KY. 606-622-5234

Casey, William T, *Dir,* Fitchburg State College Library, Fitchburg MA. 617-345-2151, Ext 137

Cash, Michele, *ILL, Ref & Bibliog Instr,* Lewis University Library, Romeoville IL. 815-838-0500, Ext 302

Cash, Pamela J, *Librn,* Johnson Publishing Co Library, Chicago IL. 312-322-9320, 322-9321

Cash, III, William T, *Librn,* Fresno County Free Library (Clovis Branch), Clovis CA. 209-299-9531

Cashin, Janet, *Ch,* Bacon Memorial Public Library, Wyandotte MI. 313-282-7660

Cashman, Lois, *Librn,* Mansfield-Richland County Public Library (Plymouth Branch), Plymouth OH. 419-687-5655

Casier, Bernice M, *Librn,* Saranac Lake Hospital, Montague Memorial Library, Saranac Lake NY. 518-891-3131, Ext 20

Casile, Theresa, *Librn,* New York Public Library (Belmont), New York NY. 212-220-6581

Caskey, Jefferson D, *Prof,* Western Kentucky University, Dept of Library Science & Instructional Media, KY. 502-745-3446

Caskey, Joy, *Cat & On-Line Servs,* Indiana Central University Library, Krannert Memorial Library, Indianapolis IN. 317-788-3268

Caskey, Mary Lou, *Bkmobile Coordr,* Mid-York Library System, Utica NY. 315-735-8328

Caskey, Tamara, *Librn,* Ivy School of Professional Art, Library and Resource Center, Pittsburgh PA. 412-323-3200

Casler, Sally, *Asst Dir,* Boise Art Association Library, Boise ID. 208-345-8330

Casler, Sally, *Asst Dir,* Boise Gallery of Art Association Library, Boise ID. 208-345-8330

Caso, Gasper, *Asst State Librn,* State Library of Massachusetts, Boston MA. 617-727-2590

Cason, Cleo S, *Librn,* Madison County Public Law Library, Huntsville AL. 205-536-5911, Ext 362

Cason, Elizabeth, *Circ,* Oakland Park City Library, Oakland Park FL. 305-561-6287

Cason, Jana Jo, *Librn,* Cynthiana Public Library (Berry Branch), Cynthiana KY. 606-234-4881

Caspari, Sarah B, *Tech Serv,* College of Physicians of Philadelphia Library, Philadelphia PA. 215-561-6050

Casper, Dale, *Pub Servs Coordr,* Saint Clair County Community College, Learning Resources Center, Port Huron MI. 313-984-3881, Ext 278

Casper, Dorothy, *Librn,* Public Library of Charlotte & Mecklenburg County, Inc (Tryon Mall Public), Charlotte NC. 704-374-2469

Casper, Evelyn, *Dir,* Chilton Public Library, Chilton WI. 414-849-4414

Casper, Gordon, *Bus,* Brigham Young University, Harold B Lee Library, Provo UT. 801-378-2905

Casper, Kathy, *Librn,* Ohio State Highway Safety Department, Departmental Professional Library, Columbus OH. 614-466-2550

Casper, Martin A, *Exec Asst,* Kentucky Department of Library & Archives, Frankfort KY. 502-564-7910

Casper, Patricia F, *Tech Serv,* Pitt Community College, Learning Resources Center, Greenville NC. 919-756-3130, Ext 213, 229, 259 & 273

Casper, Roderick J, *Ref,* California Institute of Technology, Robert A Millikan Memorial Library, Pasadena CA. 213-795-6811

Casperson, Dianne, *Librn,* Southern Tier Library System (Mabel D Blodgett Memorial), Rushville NY. 607-962-3141

Cass, Carole, *In Charge,* Nyack Hospital Nursing Library, Nyack NY. 914-358-6200, Ext 2390

Cass, K M, *Tech Serv, Acq & Cat,* West Caldwell Public Library, West Caldwell NJ. 201-226-5441

Cass, Richard, *Dir,* West Caldwell Public Library, West Caldwell NJ. 201-226-5441

Cassedy, David W, *Librn,* Museums at Stony Brook, Kate Strong Historical Library, Stony Brook NY. 516-751-0066

Cassel, Kathy Ann, *Dir,* Potsdam Public Library, Potsdam NY. 315-265-7230

Cassell, Judy A, *Librn,* Coca-Cola Co (Marketing Information Center), Atlanta GA. 404-897-3314

Cassell, Kay A, *Dir,* Bethlehem Public Library, Delmar NY. 518-439-9314

Cassell, Marianne, *Ad,* State of Vermont Department of Libraries, Montpelier VT. 802-828-3261

Cassell, William, *Media,* Santa Monica College Library, Santa Monica CA. 213-450-5150

Cassels-Brown, Rosemary, *Acq,* Episcopal Divinity School, Sherrill Hall Library, Cambridge MA. 617-868-3450, Ext 31

Cassen, Balfour, *Ref,* Woodbury University Library, Los Angeles CA. 482-8491, Ext 25

Casserly, Laurence, *Librn & Acq,* Sauk Centre Public Library, Sauk Centre MN. 612-352-3016

Cassidy, Eileen, *Chief Libm,* Palo Alto Medical Clinic & Medical Research Foundation, Barnett-Hall Library, Palo Alto CA. 415-321-4121, Ext 350

Cassidy, Ellen, *Ch,* Great Neck Library, Great Neck NY. 516-466-8055

Cassidy, Helen, *Cat,* Marianopolis College Library, Montreal PQ. 514-931-8792

Cassidy, Lelia, *Dir,* Mendocino Community College Library, Ukiah CA. 707-468-0677

Cassidy, Michael, *Instr,* Saint Cloud State University, Center for Library & Audiovisual Education, MN. 612-255-2022

Cassidy, Phoebe, *Bibliog Instr,* Sun Co, Library & Information Service, Marcus Hook PA. 215-447-1723

Cassinetto, Betty Jane, *Ref,* Tuolumne County Free Public Library, Sonora CA. 209-532-7842

Cassity, Turner, *Ser,* Emory University Libraries (General Libraries), Atlanta GA. 404-329-6861

Cassmassi, Elsa, *Libm,* Saint Barnabas Hospital for Chronic Diseases (Patients' Library), Bronx NY. 212-960-9000

Casson, Carolyn, *Br Coordr,* Oklahoma State University, Oklahoma City Branch, Technical Institute Library, Oklahoma City OK. 405-947-4421, Ext 251

Castagna, Mary Lou, *Libm,* Linden Free Public Library (Winfield Park School), Winfield NJ. 201-486-7140

Castagna, Mary Lou, *Ch,* Rahway Free Public Library, Rahway NJ. 201-388-0761

Castagnetti, Nancy, *Tech Serv,* Russell Public Library, Middletown CT. 203-347-2528

Castagnozzi, Carol, *Ref,* California State University, Hayward Library, Hayward CA. 415-881-3664

Castaneda, Liliana, *Health Sci Libr Mgr,* Saint Joseph Hospital, Medical Library, Chicago IL. 312-975-3038

Castaneda, Per, *Supv Libm,* Upland Public Library, Upland CA. 714-982-1561

Castaneda, S, *Dir,* General Hospital of Ventura County, Lillian Smolt Memorial Library, Ventura CA. 805-648-6171, Ext 3324

Casteel, Kathleen, *Media,* Case Western Reserve University & Cleveland Medical Library Association, Cleveland Health Sciences Library, Cleveland OH. 216-368-3426

Castelo, Clara, *Libm Blind,* Rolling Prairie Library System, Decatur IL. 217-429-2586

Castelo, Clara F, *Libm,* Rolling Prairie Library System (Talking Book Department), Decatur IL. 217-429-2586

Caster, Lillie D, *Cat,* North Carolina State University, D H Hill Library, Raleigh NC. 919-737-2843, 2595

Caster, Suzanne, *Libm,* San Francisco Chronicle Newspaper Publishing Co Library, San Francisco CA. 415-777-1111

Caster-Riemer, Cyd, *ILL,* Kansas City Kansas Community College Library, Kansas City KS. 913-334-1100, Ext 38

Castiglione, Barbara, *Libm,* Monmouth County Library (Oceanport Branch), Oceanport NJ. 201-229-2626

Castiglione, Mary, *Ref,* Tulare County Library System, Visalia CA. 209-733-8440

Castiglione, Mary, *Libm,* Tulare County Library System (Visalia), Visalia CA. 209-733-8440

Castillo, Connie R, *Libm,* United States Army (Corps of Engineers, Detroit District Technical Library), Detroit MI. 313-226-6413

Castillo, L Del, *Supvr,* Stauffer Chemical Co, de Guigne Technical Center Research Library, Richmond CA. 415-231-1020

Castillo, Max, *Libm,* El Paso Community College, Learning Resources Center, El Paso TX. 915-594-2585

Castillo, Rebecca, *Media,* Whittier Public Library, Whittier CA. 213-698-8949

Castka, Marilyn, *Libm,* Clarkson Memorial Library, Clarkson NE. 402-892-3235

Castle, Florence, *Asst Dir,* Lake County Library, Lakeview OR. 503-947-2321

Castle, Jean, *Libm,* Argonne National Laboratory (High Energy Physics & Preprint Library), Argonne IL. 312-972-6203

Castle, Jewell C, *In Charge,* IBM Corp, Office Products Division, Technical Library, Lexington KY. 606-233-2000

Castle, Mary, *Tech Serv, Acq & Cat,* Piedmont Virginia Community College Library, Charlottesville VA. 804-977-3900, Ext 268

Castle, Sarah, *Ref,* Wilmington College, Sheppard Arthur Watson Library, Wilmington OH. 513-382-6661, Ext 206

Castleman, John J, *Dir,* Brookings Public Library, Brookings SD. 605-692-9407, 692-9408

Castleman, Martha, *Ref,* Jackson-Madison County Library, Jackson TN. 901-423-0225

Castles, Audra, *Asst Libm,* University of Mississippi Library (Austin A Dodge Library), University MS. 601-232-7381

Castner, Frank, *Ref,* College of the Desert Library, Palm Desert CA. 714-346-8041, Ext 258

Castonguay, Andre, *Br Coordr,* Bibliotheque De La Ville De Montreal, Montreal PQ. 514-872-5923

Castonguay, Yves, *Libm,* CEGEP de Valleyfield Bibliotheque, Valleyfield PQ. 514-373-9441

Castro, Geraldine H, *Bkmobile Coordr,* Guam Public Library, Nieves M Flores Memorial Library, Agana, Guam PI. 472-6417

Castro, J M, *Libm,* General Refractories Co, Research Center Library, Baltimore MD. 301-355-3400

Castro, Mary, *Libm,* Wayne County Public Library, Wayne WV. 304-272-3756

Castro, Virginia, *Libm,* California State Legislative Counsel, Bureau Library, Sacramento CA. 916-445-2609

Caswell, Mrs Garnet S, *Libm,* Coon Rapids Public Library, Coon Rapids IA. 712-684-5410

Caswell, Reva E, *Libm,* Wyalusing Public Library, Wyalusing PA. 717-746-1711

Caswell-Pearce, Sara, *Commun Relations,* Atlantic County Library, Pleasantville NJ. 609-646-8699, 645-7121, 625-2776

Caswell-Pearce, Sara, *Libm,* Atlantic County Library (Audio-Visual Center), Mays Landing NJ. 609-625-2007

Catabia, Ronald, *Ref & Bibliog Instr,* Springfield College, Babson Library, Springfield MA. 413-787-2340

Catania, Mem, *Asst Libm,* Beaver Area Memorial Library, Beaver PA. 412-775-1132

Cate, Charlotte W, *Dir,* Rockingham Community College Library, Learning Resources Center, Wentworth NC. 919-342-4261, Ext 245

Cate, Mae B, *Asst Librn,* Mineral County Public Library (Mina-Luning Community), Mina NV. 702-573-2222

Cater, Judy J, *Instr,* Palomar Community College, Library Technology Certificate Program, CA. 714-744-1150, Ext 473 & 480

Cater, Judy J, *Acq,* Palomar Community College, Phil H Putnam Memorial Library, San Marcos CA. 714-744-1150, Ext 275, 276 & 473

Caterino, Joan, *Librn,* Robbins Library (Edith M Fox), Arlington MA. 617-643-7876

Cates, Don, *Librn,* Grays Harbor College, John Spellman Library, Aberdeen WA. 206-532-9020, Ext 201

Cates, Suzanne M, *ILL,* California State University, Fresno Library, Fresno CA. 209-487-2403

Cathcart, Jane, *Head Extens,* Onondaga County Public Library System, Syracuse NY. 315-473-2702

Cathcart, John, *Tech Serv,* Bentley College, Solomon R Baker Library, Waltham MA. 617-891-2231

Cathcart, Starla, *Dir,* Safford City-Graham County Library, Safford AZ. 602-428-1531

Catherman, Shirley, *Librn,* Hazleton Area Public Library (Conyngham), Hazleton PA. 717-788-1339

Cathey, Connie, *Librn,* Coffee County Lannom Memorial Library, Tullahoma TN. 615-455-2460

Cathey, Eva M, *Librn,* United States Army (Missile & Munitions Center & School), Redstone Arsenal AL. 205-876-7425

Cathey, Mary, *Librn,* Columbia-Lafayette-Ouachita-Calhoun Regional Library (Thornton Branch), Thornton AR. 501-234-1991

Catlett, Ana, *Librn,* Morgan County Public Library, Berkeley Springs WV. 304-258-3350

Catlett, Dorothy, *ILL,* North Olympic Library System, Port Angeles WA. 206-457-4464

Catley, G, *On-Line Servs,* Carleton University, Murdoch Maxwell MacOdrum Library, Ottawa ON. 613-231-4357

Cato, Odell, *Librn,* Colquitt-Thomas Regional Library (Monroe Memorial), Doerun GA. 912-782-5507

Catoe, Debra, *Exten,* Orangeburg County Library, Orangeburg SC. 803-534-1429

Caton, Norman, *Librn,* Hawaii State Library System (Waianae Branch), Waianae HI. 808-696-4257

Catone, Florence, *Librn,* Berkeley Public Library (North), Berkeley CA. 714-644-6850

Catron, Patricia D, *Dir,* Springfield Art Association, Springfield Art Center Library, Springfield OH. 513-325-4673

Catt, Marina, *Tech Serv,* Qualla Boundary Public Library, Cherokee NC. 704-497-9023

Catt, Martha E, *Adminr,* Eastern Indiana Area Library Services Authority, IN. 317-378-0216

Catton, Joyce, *Media,* Douglas County Library System, Roseburg OR. 503-673-1111, Ext 310

Cattrell, Betty, *Librn,* Haysville Community Library, Haysville KS. 316-524-5242

Catudal, Marie, *Ch,* Monroe County Public Library, Stroudsburg PA. 717-421-0800

Caturani, Arthur, *Dir,* Madison Area Technical College, Cora Hardy Library & Technical Center, Madison WI. 608-266-5122, 5026

Caucci, David, *Media,* Ball State University, Alexander M Bracken Library, Muncie IN. 317-285-6261

Caudill, Dorothy, *Librn,* United States Navy (Naval Air Station Library, Miramar), San Diego CA. 714-271-3557

Caudle, Rebecca, *Media,* Albany Medical Center College of Union University, Schaffer Library of Health Sciences, Albany NY. 518-445-5534

Cauffman, Betty Lou, *Dir,* Dwight T Parker Public Library, Fennimore WI. 608-822-6294

Caughey, Julie, *Ad,* Twin Falls Public Library, Twin Falls ID. 208-733-2965

Caughran, Rose Marie, *Librn,* McMinnville Public Library, McMinnville OR. 503-472-9371

Caughron, Diane, *Dir & Bibliog Instr,* Eureka College, Melick Library, Eureka IL. 309-467-3721, Ext 219-258

Caulfield, Mrs J B, *Librn,* Blackmur Memorial Library, Water Valley MS. 601-473-2444

Caulk, Margaret, *Librn,* United States Public Health Service (Center for Disease Control Hepatitis Lab Div Library), Phoenix AZ. 602-241-2660

Caulker, Olive S, *Asst Dir Tech Serv,* Marquette University Memorial Library, Milwaukee WI. 414-224-7214

Caulkins, Lorna, *Librn,* Stewart Library, Grinnell IA. 515-236-5717

Causley, Monroe, *Ref,* Morris County Free Library, Whippany NJ. 201-285-6101

Cauthen, Cindy G, *Librn,* Berkeley County Library (Hanahan Branch), Hanahan SC. 803-899-2218

Cavacini, Giovina C, *Libr Tech,* United States Navy (Navy Regional Medical Center, General Library), Philadelphia PA. 215-755-8219

Cavagos, Leopoldo, *Librn,* Houston Public Library (Stanaker), Houston TX. 713-923-8784

Cavallari, Elfrieda L, *Cat,* United States Air Force (Air Force Geophysics Laboratory, Research Library), Hanscom AFB MA. 617-861-4895

Cavallini, Ed, *Librn,* Santa Clara County Free Library (Calaveras Branch), Milpitas CA. 408-262-1171

Cavallini, Ed, *Librn,* Santa Clara County Free Library (Community Center), Milpitas CA. 408-262-0351

Cavallini, Ed, *Librn,* Santa Clara County Free Library (Sunnyhills), Milpitas CA. 408-262-4200

Cavallini, Jeanne, *Librn,* San Jose Public Library (Rosegarden), San Jose CA. 408-998-1511

Cavanagh, Eileen, *Librn,* Hennepin County Library (Minnetonka Branch), Minnetonka MN. 612-473-2788

Cavanagh, G S T, *Hist Coll Curator,* Duke University (Medical Center Library), Durham NC. 919-684-2092

Cavanagh, Jane, *Librn,* Little Company of Mary Hospital, Medical Library, Evergreen Park IL. 312-422-6200

Cavanaugh, Nancy, *Homebound Serv,* Arlington County Department of Libraries, Arlington Public Library, Arlington VA. 703-527-4777

Cavangh, Rita, *Librn,* Oak Park Public Library (Maze), Oak Park IL. 312-386-4751

Cave, Clifford, *Chief Librn,* Orange County Public Library (Laguna Beach Branch), Laguna Beach CA. 714-497-1733

Cave, Ginger, *Dir,* Family Planning Resource Center of Planned Parenthood of San Antonio, Planned Parenthood-World Population South Central Region Library, San Antonio TX. 512-227-2227

Cave, Kathryn, *Media,* Northeast Georgia Regional Library System, Clarkesville GA. 404-754-4413

Caven, Mary, *Media,* Duluth Public Library, Duluth MN. 218-723-3800

Cavender, Eugenia, *Dir,* Dalton Public Library, Inc, Dalton Regional Library, Dalton GA. 404-278-4507, 278-9247, 226-2039

Caver, Helen, *Instr,* Jacksonville State University, College of Library Science, Communications & Instructional Media, AL. 205-435-6390

Caver, Helen, *Home Econ & Tech,* Jacksonville State University Library, Jacksonville AL. 205-435-9820, Ext 213, 214

Caverzan, Sister Pierina, *Librn,* Brescia College Library, London ON. 519-432-8353

Cavett, Jean, *Dir,* Midwest Christian College Library, Oklahoma City OK. 405-478-1326, Ext 13

Caviglia, Karen, *On-Line Servs,* Rochester Institute of Technology, Wallace Memorial Library, Rochester NY. 716-475-2566

Cavner, Patricia, *Librn,* Kent County Library System (Caledonia Branch), Caledonia MI. 616-891-1502

Cawley, Inez, *Govt Doc,* Wilfrid Laurier University Library, Waterloo ON. 519-884-1970

Cawley, Pamela, *Ref,* Jervis Public Library Association, Rome NY. 315-336-4570

Cawthon, June, *Asst Prof,* University of Georgia, Dept of Educational Media & Librarianship, GA. 404-542-3810

Cawthon, Paula, *Asst Dir,* Blue Mound Memorial Public Library, Blue Mound IL. 217-692-2774

Cawthorne, Edythe, *Ch,* Prince George's County Memorial Library System, Hyattsville MD. 301-699-3500

Cayci, Leila W, *Dir,* New Brunswick Free Public Library, New Brunswick NJ. 201-745-5337

Caylor, Lawrence, *Acq,* Arkansas State University, Dean B Ellis Library, Jonesboro AR. 501-972-3078, 972-3079

Caynon, William, *Asst Prof,* Kent State University, School of Library Science, OH. 216-672-2782, 672-7988

Cayton, Robert F, *Librn,* Marietta College, Dawes Memorial Library, Marietta OH. 614-373-4643, Ext 215, 216, 285

Caywood, Carolyn, *Librn,* Department of Public Libraries & Information (Childrens Division), Virginia Beach VA. 804-340-7798

Cazares, Cecilia, *Librn,* Los Angeles Public Library System (R L Stevenson), Los Angeles CA. 213-268-4710

Cazden, Robert E, *Prof,* University of Kentucky, College of Library Science, KY. 606-258-8876

Cazort, Jean, *Assoc Librn Tech Servs,* Fisk University Library & Media Center, Nashville TN. 615-329-8730

Cebula, Emily G, *Librn,* Douglas County Public Library, Ava MO. 417-683-5633

Cebula, Theodore, *Sci, Bus & Homemaking,* Milwaukee Public Library, Milwaukee WI. 414-278-3000

Cecchini, Linda, *Per,* University of Wisconsin-Eau Claire, William D McIntyre Library, Eau Claire WI. 715-836-3715

Cecil, Sister Josephine, *Circ,* Spalding College Library, Louisville KY. 502-585-9411

Cedrone, Patricia, *Librn,* General Foods Corp (Public Relations & Personnel Services Library), White Plains NY. 914-683-2500

Cefaloni, Don, *Media,* West Valley College, Learning Resource Center, Saratoga CA. 408-867-2200, Ext 284

Cegielka, Irene, *Ref,* Mercy College of Detroit Library, Detroit MI. 313-592-6000

Cehovin, Joseph, *Librn,* Saint Mary's Public Library, Saint Mary's PA. 814-834-6141

Celento, Joan S, *ILL & Ref,* Waynesburg College Library, Waynesburg PA. 412-627-8191, Ext 278

Celeya, Rebecca, *Acq,* Ector County Library, Odessa TX. 915-332-0633

Celigoj, Carmen Z, *Dir,* Kent Free Library, Kent OH. 216-673-4414, 673-3384

Cellini, Nicholas, *Rare Bks & Spec Coll,* Beverly Hills Public Library, Beverly Hills CA. 213-550-4711

Celms, Aina, *Librn,* San Diego Public Library (Balboa), San Diego CA. 714-277-4133

Celnik, Max, *Librn,* Touro College Library, New York NY. 212-575-0190

Celsie, Mary-Jane, *ILL,* Seneca College of Applied Arts & Technology, Finch Campus Learning Resource Centre, Willowdale ON. 416-491-5050, Ext 381

Cenedella, Edmund J, *Media,* Saint Petersburg Junior College, Saint Petersburg Campus Library, Saint Petersburg FL. 813-546-0011, Ext 353

Cenedella, Janet E, *ILL & Circ,* Dean Junior College, E Ross Anderson Library, Franklin MA. 617-528-9100, Ext 261

Centeno, Patricia A, *Librn,* Chicago Public Library (Mayfair), Chicago IL. 312-736-1254

Center, Sue L, *Dir,* Criminal Justice Reference & Information Center, Madison WI. 608-262-1499

Centing, Richard, *Librn,* Ohio State University Libraries (English, Communication & Theater Graduate Library), Columbus OH. 614-422-2786

Centola, Mary, *Ref,* J Herman Bosler Memorial Library, Bosler Free Library, Carlisle PA. 717-243-4642

Centorino, Emma L, *Librn,* IBM Corp (Legal Library), Armonk NY. 914-765-4862

Cepak, Larry, *Media,* Ohio Dominican College Library, Columbus OH. 614-253-2741, Ext 258, 210&219

Cepek, Larry, *Dir AV Ctr,* Ohio Dominican College, Dept of Library Science & Educational Media, OH. 614-253-2741

Ceraudo, Frances I, *Asst Dir,* Saint Clair Shores Public Library, Saint Clair Shores MI. 313-771-9020

Cerceo, Dorothy, *Librn,* Hometown Public Library, Jack R Ladwig Memorial Library, Hometown IL. 312-636-0997

Cercsa, Marie, *Librn,* Cresson Public Library, Cresson PA. 814-886-2619

CERESA

Ceresa, Mario A, *Dir,* Detroit College of Law Library, Detroit MI. 313-965-0150
Cerka, Dorothy E, *Librn,* Colo Public Library, Colo IA. 515-377-2900
Cernin, Mary Ann, *Librn,* Valley Public Library, Valley NE. 402-359-2251
Cerny, Carolyn, *Librn,* Arthur County Library, Arthur NE. 308-764-2066
Cerny, Loretta, *Librn,* Oshkosh Public Library, Oshkosh NE. 308-772-4554
Cerrato, Paula, *Ch,* Frederick E Parlin Memorial Library, Everett MA. 617-387-2550
Cerroni, Douglas J, *Dir,* Thiel College, Langenheim Memorial Library, Greenville PA. 412-588-7700, Ext 233
Cerutti, Elsie, *Chief, Info Servs,* National Bureau of Standards (Bureau of Standards Library), Washington DC. 301-921-3405
Cervinsky, Anna, *Librn,* Fresno County Free Library (Reedley Branch), Reedley CA. 209-638-2818
Cesare, Burton L, *Dir,* University of Connecticut, Waterbury Branch, Edward H Kirschbaum Library, Waterbury CT. 203-757-6795, Ext 50
Cessna, Edward, *Media,* Milwaukee County Federated Library System, Milwaukee WI. 414-278-3210
Cessna, Kathleen, *Librn,* Indiana Hospital Library, Indiana PA. 412-357-7049
Cettomai, Phyllis, *Dir,* Reed Memorial Library, Ravenna Public Library, Ravenna OH. 216-296-2827
Cevallos, Elena, *Libr Orientation,* Hofstra University Library, Hempstead NY. 516-560-3475
Chabot, Jean, *ILL,* Free Public Library of Woodbridge, Woodbridge NJ. 201-634-4450
Chabot, Jean-Pierre, *Prof,* College Lionel-Groulx, Techniques de la Documentation, PQ. 514-430-3120, Ext 261
Chabot, Joyce, *YA,* Provo City Public Library, Provo UT. 801-373-1494
Chace, Laura L, *Librn,* Cincinnati Historical Society Library, Cincinnati OH. 513-241-4622
Chace, Loree, *Librn,* Carbon County Public Library (Medicine Bow Branch), Medicine Bow WY. 307-324-4756
Chach, Maryann, *Librn,* Educational Film Library Association, New York NY. 212-246-4533
Chacko, Jacob, *Asst Librn,* Civil Court of the City of New York Library, New York NY. 212-374-8043
Chacon, Joan G, *In Charge,* Alpine County Law Library, Markleeville CA. 916-694-2281
Chadbourne, Erika S, *Curator of Archives,* Harvard University Library (Law School Library), Cambridge MA. 617-495-3170
Chadima, Kitty, *Asst to Ed,* Pacific Travel News, Research Library, San Francisco CA. 415-397-0070
Chadwick, Henrietta, *ILL,* Mendocino County Library, Ukiah CA. 707-468-4491
Chadwick, Merredith, *Librn,* Kern County Library (Greenfield), Bakersfield CA. 805-861-2130
Chadwick, Regina E, *Librn,* California Medical Association, Socioeconomic Library, San Francisco CA. 415-777-2000, Ext 213
Chadwick, Rojeanne, *Librn,* Battlefords Union Hospital, Medical Library, North Battleford SK. 306-445-2411
Chadwick, Shelley, *Asst Dir & Ch,* Geneva Free Library, Geneva NY. 315-789-5303
Chaff, Sandra, *Archives,* Medical College of Pennsylvania, Florence A Moore Library of Medicine, Philadelphia PA. 215-842-6910
Chaffe, Robert, *Media,* Midwestern Regional Library System, Kitchener ON. 519-576-5061
Chaffee, Juanita, *Librn,* Leonardville Library, Leonardville KS. 913-293-5539
Chaffin, William J, *Ref,* Washington College, Clifton M Miller Library, Chestertown MD. 301-778-2800, Ext 242
Chafin, Debbi, *Assoc Dir,* Waco-McLennan County Library, Waco TX. 817-754-4694
Chakirian, Marie, *Librn,* Chelan County Law Library, Wenatchee WA. 509-663-3280
Chalaron, Peggy, *Order,* Louisiana State University (Troy H Middleton Library), Baton Rouge LA. 504-388-2217
Chalfant, Patricia, *Asst Dir,* Delaware Technical & Community College Library, Newark DE. 302-368-6985

Chalfant, Randolph W, *Curator Maritime Mus,* Maryland Historical Society Library, Baltimore MD. 301-685-3750
Chalker, Mary, *Per,* Memorial University of Newfoundland Library, Saint John's NF. 709-753-1200
Challacombe, Elaine M, *Chief Librn,* Margaret Woodbury Strong Museum Library, Rochester NY. 716-381-1818, Ext 23
Challis, A Thomas, *Dir,* Southern Utah State College Library, Cedar City UT. 801-586-4411, Ext 351
Chalmers, Dorothy, *Ref,* Dunedin Public Library, Dunedin FL. 813-733-4115
Chalmers, Kathleen, *Librn,* Good Samaritan Hospital, Health Science Library, Baltimore MD. 301-323-2200, Ext 297
Chamberlain, Claire, *Librn,* Saint Louis County Library (Grand Glaize), Manchester MO. 314-225-6454
Chamberlain, E S, *In Charge,* University of Toronto Libraries (Dept of Botany), Toronto ON. 416-978-3538
Chamberlain, Ellen E, *ILL,* University of South Carolina, Beaufort Regional Campus Library, Beaufort SC. 803-524-6153
Chamberlain, Erna, *Librn,* Union Hospital Library, Terre Haute IN. 812-238-7000, Ext 7641
Chamberlain, Ken, *Head Librn,* Emily Carr College of Art Library, Vancouver BC. 604-681-9525, Ext 26
Chamberlain, Martin, *Librn,* Bibliotheque De L'abbaye Saint-Benoit, Saint Benoit-du-Lac PQ. 819-843-4080
Chamberlain, Mary K, *Dir,* Scott County Library, Scott City KS. 316-872-3855
Chamberlain, Mitchell, *Cat,* Belmont College, Williams Library, Nashville TN. 615-383-7001, Ext 253
Chamberlain, Ruth, *Librn,* Bristol Myers Co, Bristol Laboratories Library & Information Service, Syracuse NY. 315-432-2232
Chamberlain, Ruth Brown, *Dir,* Plymouth Public Library, Russell Memorial Library, Plymouth MA. 617-746-1927
Chamberlain, Sue, *In Charge,* Prescott Historical Society Library & Archives, Prescott AZ. 602-445-3122
Chamberlain, Susan, *Asst Dir,* University of New Mexico General Library (Medical Center Library), Albuquerque NM. 505-277-2311
Chamberlain, Zella, *Librn,* Boise Bible College Library, Boise ID. 208-376-7731
Chamberland, Eleanore, *Librn,* Arapahoe Regional Library District (Sheridan), Denver CO. 303-789-5422
Chamberlin, Edgar W, *Dir,* Kaskaskia Library System, Smithton IL. 618-235-4220
Chamberlin, Richard, *Ref,* Indiana University of Pennsylvania, Rhodes R Stabley Library, Indiana PA. 412-357-2340
Chambers, Angie L, *Dir,* Chesterfield-Marlboro Technical College Library, Cheraw SC. 803-537-5286, Ext 26
Chambers, Betty, *Librn,* Dorion Public Library, Dorion ON. 807-857-2289
Chambers, Dorothy M, *Librn,* Fallsview Psychiatric Hospital, Cuyahoga Falls OH. 216-929-8301
Chambers, Elizabeth, *Asst Prof,* Northern Illinois University, Dept of Library Science, IL. 815-753-1735
Chambers, Eugene, *Dir,* Harris County Law Library, Houston TX. 713-221-5183
Chambers, Joan, *Pub Servs,* University of California, San Diego, University Libraries, La Jolla CA. 714-452-3336
Chambers, Lee Oda, *Librn,* Western Mental Health Institute (Edward M Levy Professional Library), Bolivar TN. 901-658-5141
Chambers, Lee Oda, *Dir,* Western Mental Health Institute (Polk Patient Library), Bolivar TN. 901-658-5141
Chambers, Leola A, *Librn,* Jackson County Library System (Butte Falls Branch), Butte Falls OR. 503-865-3212
Chambers, Marsha, *Asst Librn,* Obion County Public Library, Union City TN. 901-885-9411
Chambers, Martha, *Spec Coll,* State University of New York, College at Oneonta, James M Milne Library, Oneonta NY. 607-431-2723
Chambers, Patricia A, *Asst Librn,* Our Lady of Lourdes Hospital Library, Lafayette LA. 318-234-7381, Ext 2141

Chambers, Paula, *Ch, YA & Acq,* Southwest Georgia Regional Library, Gilbert H Gragg Library, Bainbridge GA. 912-246-3887, 3894, 3895
Chambers, Robert, *Dir,* Wagner Free Institute of Science Library, Philadelphia PA. 215-763-6529
Chambers, Susan, *Bkmobile Coordr,* Champaign Public Library & Information Center, Champaign IL. 217-356-7243
Chamblee, Sherry, *ILL,* Greenwood-Leflore Public Library System, Greenwood MS. 601-453-3634
Chamblee, Virginia, *Asst Dir,* Bedford Public Library, Bedford TX. 817-283-2751
Chambliss, Lynn, *Asst Librn,* Elko County Library (Battle Mountain Library), Battle Mountain NV. 702-635-2534
Chamline, George R, *Chief Librn,* Continental Chemiste Corp, Smo-Cloud Co Library, Chicago IL. 312-226-2134
Champa, V A, *Prof,* Millersville State College, Dept of Library Science, PA. 717-872-5411, Ext 416
Champion, Sharon, *Librn,* Deaf Smith County Library, Hereford TX. 806-364-1206
Champlin, Caroline, *Acq,* Princeton Public Library, Princeton NJ. 609-924-9529
Champlin, Margaret, *On-Line Servs,* California State University, John F Kennedy Memorial Library, Los Angeles CA. 213-224-2201
Champlin, Richard L, *Asst Dir,* Redwood Library & Athenaeum, Newport RI. 401-847-0292
Champlin, Rose, *Librn,* Tom Green County Library System (North Angelo), San Angelo TX. 915-653-8412
Champneys, Weldon, *Librn,* Defense Logistics Agency, Special Services Library, Ogden UT. 801-399-7239
Champneys, Weldon B, *Librn,* United States Air Force (Gerrity Memorial Library), Hill AFB UT. 801-777-1131
Chan, Alice, *Librn,* Price Waterhouse & Co Library, Los Angeles CA. 213-625-4583
Chan, Chi-wai, *Media,* East Carolina University (Health Affairs Library), Greenville NC. 919-757-6961, Ext 261
Chan, Co-Ming, *Cat,* Oklahoma State University Library, Stillwater OK. 405-624-6313
Chan, Florence M, *Head Librn,* Canada College Library, Redwood City CA. 415-364-1212
Chan, Julia, *Librn,* Saint Joseph's Hospital, George Pennal Library, Toronto ON. 416-534-9531, Ext 629
Chan, Kwan, *Cat,* De Anza College, Learning Center, Cupertino CA. 408-996-4761
Chan, Lois M, *Assoc Prof,* University of Kentucky, College of Library Science, KY. 606-258-8876
Chan, Paul F, *Librn,* United States Navy (Station Library), Long Beach CA. 213-547-7349
Chan, Stella, *Bibliog Instr,* Skyline College Library, San Bruno CA. 415-355-7000, Ext 311
Chan, Wing, *ILL & Ref,* Rutgers University (Kilmer Area Library), New Brunswick NJ. 201-932-3610
Chance, Alice, *ILL & Tech Serv,* New River Community College, Learning Resource Center, Dublin VA. 703-674-4121, Ext 303
Chandik, Barbara V, *Supvr Tech Info,* Northwest Industries Inc, Velsicol Chemical Corporation Technical Information Center, Ann Arbor MI. 313-994-8000, Ext 257
Chandler, Ann, *Soc Sci,* Stephen F Austin State University, Ralph W Steen Library, Nacogdoches TX. 713-569-4109
Chandler, Bertha A, *Librn,* Sharon Public Library, Sharon MA. 617-784-5974
Chandler, Clare, *Regional Coordr,* San Diego County Library (Region D), San Diego CA. 714-565-5100
Chandler, Constance P, *Librn,* Massachusetts General Hospital (Palmer Davis Library), Boston MA. 617-726-3175
Chandler, Deborah G, *Res Librn,* Scott Paper Co, S D Warren Co Research Library, Westbrook ME. 207-856-6911, Ext 2235
Chandler, Devon, *Instruction Materials Servs,* University of Montana, Maureen & Mike Mansfield Library, Missoula MT. 406-243-6800
Chandler, Dorothy, *Bibliog Instr,* Biscayne College Library, Opa Locka FL. 305-625-6000, Ext 109
Chandler, Evelyn H, *ILL,* University of New Orleans, Earl K Long Library, New Orleans LA. 504-283-0353

Chandler, Gwen, *Pub Servs,* Florida Junior College at Jacksonville (North Campus Learning Resources Center), Jacksonville FL. 904-757-6311

Chandler, Harold, *Acq,* Memphis Theological Seminary Library, Memphis TN. 901-458-8232

Chandler, Helen, *Librn,* Torrance Public Library (Southeast), Torrance CA. 213-530-5044

Chandler, Lois, *Librn Blind,* Fort Smith Public Library, Fort Smith AR. 501-783-0229

Chandler, Madelene, *Bkmobile Coordr,* Goodnight Memorial Library, Franklin KY. 502-586-8397

Chandler, Marilyn, *Librn,* Brooklyn Public Library (Paerdegat), Brooklyn NY. 212-763-4848

Chandler, Rachel, *Bkmobile Coordr,* Stanly County Public Library, Albemarle NC. 704-982-0115

Chandler, Samuel C, *Librn,* Daly City Public Library, Daly City CA. 415-992-4500, Ext 220

Chandler, Sue P, *Head Pub Servs,* Fisk University Library & Media Center, Nashville TN. 615-329-8730

Chandler, Thomas W, *Dir,* Oglethorpe University Library, Atlanta GA. 404-261-1441, Ext 24

Chandler, Vivian, *Ref & Bibliog Instr,* Atlanta Junior College Library, Atlanta GA. 404-656-6649

Chaney, A Virginia, *Librn,* United States Army (Post Library), Fort Richardson AK. 907-862-9188

Chaney, Charles, *Librn,* Cleveland Public Library (Jefferson), Cleveland OH. 216-241-7527

Chaney, Robin, *Media,* Aquinas College, Learning Resource Center, Grand Rapids MI. 616-459-8281, Ext 234

Chaney, Suzanne F, *Acq,* University of New Brunswick, Harriet Irving Library, Fredericton NB. 506-453-4740

Chang, Albert, *Circ,* Southwest Texas State University, Learning Resources Center, San Marcos TX. 512-245-2132

Chang, C, *Cat,* Medgar Evers College Library, Brooklyn NY. 212-735-1851

Chang, Che Gil, *Cat,* Denison University, William Howard Doane Library, Granville OH. 614-587-0810, Ext 225

Chang, Chia-Ching, *Acq,* Bucknell University, Ellen Clarke Bertrand Library, Lewisburg PA. 717-524-3056

Chang, Chien, *Tech Serv,* State University of New York, State College of Optometry, Harold Kohn Library, New York NY. 212-477-7965

Chang, Chue-Huei, *Cat,* Detroit Institute of Technology, James C Gordon Memorial Library, Detroit MI. 313-962-0830, Ext 301

Chang, Chun Chuan, *Librn,* Grolier Inc, Grolier Library, Danbury CT. 203-797-3500, Ext 3848

Chang, Clement, *AV,* North Hennepin Community College Library, Brooklyn Park MN. 612-425-4541

Chang, Edna, *Librn,* Brooklyn Public Library (Greenpoint), Brooklyn NY. 212-383-6692

Chang, Frances M, *Librn,* United States Department of the Navy, Office of Naval Research Library, Arlington VA. 202-696-4415

Chang, Helen, *ILL & Ref,* Thomas Nelson Community College Library, Hampton VA. 804-825-2868, 825-2876

Chang, Henry C, *Dir,* Bureau of Libraries, Museums & Archaeological Services, Saint Thomas VI. 809-774-3407

Chang, Hoong, *ILL,* Passaic County Community College, Learning Resources Center Library, Paterson NJ. 201-279-5000, Ext 73

Chang, Hsien-Pei, *Librn,* Saint Joseph's Hospital, Health Science Library, Lowell MA. 617-453-1761, Ext 207

Chang, Hsien-Rei, *Head,* Northeast Consortium for Health Information, MA. 617-922-3000

Chang, Hung-yi, *Cat,* Burlington County College Library, Pemberton NJ. 609-894-9311, Ext 222

Chang, Jean, *Acq,* The Medical College of Wisconsin, Inc, Todd Wehr Library, Milwaukee WI. 414-257-8323

Chang, Kyung-za, *Cat,* University of Hartford, Mortensen Library, West Hartford CT. 203-243-4265

Chang, Leo, *Pub Servs & Doc,* Earlham College, Lilly Library, Richmond IN. 317-962-6561, Ext 360

Chang, Maggio, *Tech Serv & Ref,* Pepperdine University, Los Angeles Campus Library, Los Angeles CA. 213-971-7730, Ext 730

Chang, Marilyn, *Libr Technician,* San Diego County Library (Imperial Beach Branch), Imperial Beach CA. 714-424-6981

Chang, Robert, *Dir,* University of Houston (William I Dykes Library), Houston TX. 713-749-1991

Chang, Sherry, *Librn,* State University of New York (Mathematics Physics), Stony Brook NY. 516-246-5666

Chang, Shirley L, *Ref,* Lock Haven State College, George B Stevenson Library, Lock Haven PA. 717-893-2309

Chang, Stella, *Tech Serv,* Weber State College Library, Stewart Library, Ogden UT. 801-626-6403

Chang, Theresa, *Cat,* Brookings Institution Library, Washington DC. 202-797-6240

Chang, Tohsook, *Cat,* University of Alaska, Anchorage Library, Anchorage AK. 907-263-1825

Chang, Virginia S, *Cat,* County College of Morris, Sherman H Masten Learning Resource Center, Randolph Township NJ. 201-361-5000, Ext 470

Chanin, Leah F, *Dir,* Mercer University (Walter F George School of Law Library), Macon GA. 912-745-6811, Ext 345

Chanley, Pat, *Ch,* Bloomingdale Public Library, Bloomingdale IL. 312-529-3120

Channell, Dorothy, *Librn,* Copiah-Jefferson Regional Library (Crystal Springs Branch), Crystal Springs MS. 601-894-1681

Channell, Julia, *Dir,* Millbrook Public Library, Millbrook AL. 205-285-6688

Channing, Rhoda, *Librn,* Boston College Libraries (School of Management Library), Chestnut Hill MA. 617-969-0100, Ext 3216

Chanove, Barbara, *Librn,* Public Library of Cincinnati & Hamilton County (West Fork), Cincinnati OH. 513-661-7244

Chant, Nadine C, *Librn,* First Church of Christ, Scientist, Montreal, Christian Science Reading Room, Montreal PQ. 514-931-5012

Chant, Patty, *Librn,* Contra Costa County Library (Antioch Branch), Antioch CA. 415-757-2100

Chao, Helen, *Cat,* University of Houston (Clear Lake City), Houston TX. 713-488-9280

Chao, Jennifer J, *Librn,* Boston Globe Newspaper Library, Dorchester MA. 617-929-2540

Chao, Paul, *Dir,* King's College, D Leonard Corgan Library, Wilkes-Barre PA. 717-824-9931, Ext 245

Chao, Paul, *Dir,* Northeastern Pennsylvania Bibliographic Center, PA. 717-824-9931

Chapel, Ann E, *Librn,* United States Department of the Interior (Bureau of Mines, Charles William Henderson Memorial Library), Denver CO. 303-234-2817

Chapel, Bob, *Media & Per,* Huntingdon College, Houghton Memorial Library, Montgomery AL. 205-265-0511, Ext 221

Chapel, Dorothy, *Assoc Prof,* Ouachita Baptist University, Dept of Library Media, AR. 501-246-4531, Ext 151

Chapel, Pat, *Circ,* Elmhurst Public Library, Elmhurst IL. 312-279-8696

Chapin, Doris, *Librn,* Denver Public Library (Ross-Broadway), Denver CO. 303-573-5152, Ext 271

Chapin, Joan R, *Ch & YA,* Clark Public Library, Clark NJ. 201-388-5999

Chapin, Richard E, *Dir,* Michigan State University Library, East Lansing MI. 517-355-2344

Chapin, Shirley, *Librn,* New York City Department of Health, William Hallock Park Memorial Library, New York NY. 212-340-4510

Chaplan, Margaret A, *Librn,* University of Illinois Library at Urbana-Champaign (Labor & Industrial Relations), Urbana IL. 217-333-2380

Chaplin, Ruth C, *Dir,* Steep Falls Library, Steep Falls ME. 207-675-3132

Chapman, Abbie, *Research Dir,* Columbia Pictures Corp, Research Department Library, Burbank CA. 213-843-6000

Chapman, Allan D, *Librn,* Metropolitan Museum of Art (Robert Goldwater Library of Primitive Art), New York NY. 212-879-5500, Ext 706

Chapman, Barbara, *Ch,* Phoenixville Public Library, Phoenixville PA. 215-933-3013

Chapman, Bruce, *Pres,* Bruce Chapman Co Library, Grafton VT. 802-843-2321

Chapman, Dorothy, *Spec Coll,* Texas Southern University Library, Houston TX. 713-527-7121

Chapman, Dwight, *Tech Serv, Cat & On-Line Servs,* Truman College, Learning Resources Center, Chicago IL. 312-878-1700, Ext 2230

Chapman, Ellen, *ILL,* University of Hawaii (University of Hawaii Library), Honolulu HI. 808-948-7205

Chapman, Florence, *Asst Dir & Ch,* Avon Free Public Library, Avon CT. 203-678-1262

Chapman, Florence, *Librn,* Boothbay Public Library, Boothbay Harbor ME. 207-633-3112

Chapman, Geoffrey, *Asst Prof,* University of British Columbia, School of Librarianship, BC. 604-228-2404

Chapman, Judith, *Librn,* Gila Pueblo College Library, Globe AZ. 602-425-3151

Chapman, Katherine, *Asst Dir,* Lubbock City-County Library, Lubbock TX. 806-762-6411, Ext 2828

Chapman, Kathleen, *Tech Serv,* Copiah-Jefferson Regional Library (Hazelhurst Branch (Headquarters)), Hazelhurst MS. 601-894-1681

Chapman, Kathy, *Librn,* Tulsa City-County Library (Special Services for the Blind & Physically Handicapped), Tulsa OK. 918-581-5126

Chapman, Kendall P, *Librn,* Copiah-Lincoln Junior College, Evelyn W Oswalt Library, Wesson MS. 601-643-5101, Ext 364 or 365

Chapman, Lugenia, *Librn,* Cabell County Public Library (Cox Landing Public), Lesage WV. 304-523-9451

Chapman, Marcella, *Librn,* Waverly City Library, Waverly KS. 913-733-2615

Chapman, Mary Helen, *Librn,* Houston Public Library (Children's Room), Houston TX. 713-224-5441

Chapman, Mrs L P, *Dir,* Panola Junior College, M P Baker Library, Carthage TX. 214-693-3839

Chapman, Renee, *Tech Serv, Acq & Cat,* Drake University (Drake Law Library), Des Moines IA. 515-271-2141

Chapman, Ronald F, *Chief Librn,* Honolulu Community College Library, Honolulu HI. 808-845-9220

Chapman, Ruth, *Librn,* Wheatland Township Library, Remus MI. 517-967-8271

Chapman, Sarah, *Librn,* Whipple Free Library, New Boston NH. 603-487-3391

Chapman, Shirley, *Librn,* Glencoe Public Library, Glencoe MN. 612-864-3919

Chapman, Shirley, *Librn,* Metropolitan Library System (Warr Acres), Oklahoma City OK. 405-235-0571

Chapman, Susan, *Librn,* Northern New Mexico Community College, Learning Resource Center, Santa Cruz NM. 505-827-2688

Chapman, William, *V Pres,* Bruce Chapman Co Library, Grafton VT. 802-843-2321

Chappel, Doris, *Media & YA,* Santa Maria Public Library, Santa Maria CA. 805-925-0994, Ext 261

Chappell, Alfred, *Librn,* Prince Edward Island Provincial Library (Borden Branch), Borden PE. 902-892-3504, Ext 54

Chappell, Barbara A, *On-Line Servs,* United States Geological Survey Library, Reston VA. 703-860-6671

Chappell, Beth, *ILL,* Emmanuel School of Religion Library, Johnson City TN. 615-926-1186, Ext 49

Chappell, Dick L, *Dir,* University of Texas of the Permian Basin, Learning Resources Center, Odessa TX. 915-367-2114

Chappell, Gordon S, *In Charge,* National Park Service, Western Regional Resources Library, San Francisco CA. 415-556-4165

Chappell, LaDon, *Librn,* Du Quoin Public Library, Du Quoin IL. 618-542-5045

Chappell, Mrs Glenn, *Librn,* Elkhorn Public Library, Elkhorn NE. 402-289-4367

Chappell, Susan, *Librn,* Greenville Hospital System (Medical Library), Greenville SC. 803-242-8628

Chappell, Susan, *Bkmobile Coordr,* Meade County Public Library, Brandenburg KY. 502-422-2094

Chappell, II, Guy D, *Dir,* Ocmulgee Regional Library, Eastman GA. 912-374-4711

Chapple, Cecilia, *In Charge,* Milwaukee Public Library (Finney), Milwaukee WI. 414-278-3066

Chapple, Linda, *Librn,* Convalescent Hospital for Children Library, Rochester NY. 716-436-4442

Chapple, Susan, *Librn,* Timberland Regional Library (North Mason), Belfair WA. 206-275-3232

Char, Lan Hiang, *S Asia Area Specialist*, University of Hawaii (University of Hawaii Library), Honolulu HI. 808-948-7205

Charbonneau, Bernard, *Dept Head*, College de Jonquiere, Techniques de la Documentation, PQ. 418-547-2191, Ext 270

Charbonneau, Helene, *Ch*, Bibliotheque De La Ville De Montreal, Montreal PQ. 514-872-5923

Charbonneau, Jacques, *Librn*, Bibliotheque De La Ville De Montreal (Notre-Dame), Montreal PQ. 872-2879 (Adult); 872-4698 (Children)

Charchalis, Sandra, *ILL*, University of Rochester (Edward G Miner Library, School of Medicine & Dentistry), Rochester NY. 716-275-3364

Chard, Peter, *Media*, University of Wisconsin Center-Fox Valley Library, Menasha WI. 414-734-8731, Ext 32

Charest, Ginette, *AV*, Hospital Sainte-Justine, Centre d'Information Sur La Sante de L'Enfant, Montreal PQ. 514-731-4931, Ext 339

Charette, Marcel, *Libr Tech*, Agriculture Canada (Neatby Library), Ottawa ON. 613-995-2323

Chariton, Helen, *Dir*, Canastota Public Library, Canastota NY. 315-697-7030

Chariton, May, *Librn*, Saint John's Episcopal Hospital Library, Smithtown NY. 516-360-2000, Ext 2289

Chariton, May, *Librn*, Southside Hospital, Medical Library, Bay Shore NY. 516-435-3026

Charlebois, Joyce, *Lectr*, Concordia University, Library Studies Program, PQ. 514-482-0320, Ext 324

Charles, Brian, *Music*, Great Neck Library, Great Neck NY. 516-466-8055

Charles, Frances, *Librn*, Gilbertville Public Library, Gilbertville MA. 413-477-6312

Charles, Jennie, *Chief Librn*, Springfield Art Association, Michael Victor II Library, Springfield IL. 217-523-3507

Charles, John, *Rare Bks & Spec Coll*, University of Alberta (University Libraries), Edmonton AB. 403-432-3790

Charles, Michael, *Ind Learning Ctr Dir*, San Diego City College Library, San Diego CA. 714-238-1181, Ext 250

Charles, Sharon, *Coordr*, Indianhead Federated Library System, Eau Claire WI. 715-839-5082

Charles, Vera, *Dir*, Carnegie Public Library, Carnegie OK. 405-645-1980

Charlie, Grace, *ILL*, Flagstaff City-Coconino County Public Library System, Flagstaff AZ. 602-774-0603

Charlinski, Helen T, *Librn*, Samaritan Hospital, Medical Library, Troy NY. 518-271-3200

Charlson, Kim, *Textbook Coordr*, Oregon State Library Services for the Blind & Physically Handicapped, Salem OR. 503-378-3849

Charlton, Barbara A, *Sci-Tech*, California State University, Sacramento Library, Sacramento CA. 916-454-6466

Charlton, Mary Lou, *Librn*, Health & Welfare Planning Association of Allegheny County Library, Pittsburgh PA. 412-261-6010

Charnow, Elaine, *Librn*, North Shore Synagogue, Charles Cohn Memorial Library, Syosset NY. 516-921-2282

Charon, Susan, *Librn*, Temple Beth El, Max & Anne Goldberg Library, Fargo ND. 701-232-0441

Charpentier, Arthur A, *Librn*, Yale University Library (Law Library), New Haven CT. 203-436-2215

Charron, Sister Irene, *Librn*, Saint Elizabeth Hospital, Health Sciences Library, Yakima WA. 509-575-5000, Ext 5073

Charter, Jody, *Asst Prof*, University of Arkansas, Instructional Resources Education, AR. 501-575-5444

Charters, Margaret L, *Dir*, Clackamas Community College, Marshall N Dana Memorial Library, Oregon City OR. 503-656-2631, Ext 288

Chartier, Mary, *ILL, Ad & Ref*, Prosser Public Library, Bloomfield CT. 203-243-9721

Chartier, Mary, *Librn*, San Bernardino Public Library (Inghram), San Bernardino CA. 714-887-4494

Chartier, Virginia, *Librn*, Huntington Public Library, Huntington VT. 802-434-2271

Chartier-Lapointe, Jacqueline, *Librn*, Bibliotheque Municipale, Saint Romuald PQ. 418-839-6422

Chartz, Ava, *Assoc Dir & Tech Serv*, Flagstaff City-Coconino County Public Library System, Flagstaff AZ. 602-774-0603

Chartz, Ava, *Librn*, Flagstaff City-Coconino County Public Library System (Technical Services), Flagstaff AZ. 602-774-5281, Ext 277, 278

Chase, Beth, *YA*, Marlborough Public Library, Marlborough MA. 617-485-0494

Chase, Betty, *ILL*, Monroe County Library System, Rochester NY. 716-428-7345

Chase, Eleanor L, *Doc*, University of Washington Libraries, Seattle WA. 206-543-1760

Chase, Esther, *Acq*, Rollins College, Mills Memorial Library, Winter Park FL. 305-646-2000, Ext 2676

Chase, Gina, *Tech Proc*, Northeastern University Libraries (School of Law), Boston MA. 617-437-3338

Chase, Hope, *Ch*, Howard County Library, Columbia MD. 301-997-8000

Chase, Jean, *Dir*, Courtland City Library, Courtland KS. 913-374-4260

Chase, Judith Wragg, *Dir*, Old Slave Mart Museum Library, Old Slave Mart Museum Library, Charleston SC. 803-883-3797

Chase, Julie Ann, *Asst Dir*, Northwest Regional Library, Thief River Falls MN. 218-681-4325

Chase, Karen A, *ILL & Ref*, Jackson County Library System, Medford OR. 503-776-7281

Chase, Marcella, *Librn*, Mutual of Omaha-United of Omaha, Employees Library, Omaha NE. 402-342-7600

Chase, Margaret, *Librn*, Evansville Public Library & Vanderburgh County Public Library (McCollough), Evansville IN. 812-425-2621

Chase, Mary Agnes, *Ref & Bibliog Instr*, College of Saint Catherine, Saint Catherine Library, Saint Paul MN. 612-690-6650

Chase, Peter, *Librn*, Old Lyme, Phoebe Griffin Noyes Library, Old Lyme CT. 203-434-1684

Chase, Rory L, *Librn*, Cincinnati Milacron, Inc, Corporate Information Center, Cincinnati OH. 513-841-8879

Chasen, Larry, *Mgr*, General Electric Co, Space-RSD Division Library, Philadelphia PA. 215-962-4700, Ext 4700

Chaski, Geni, *Asst Librn*, Harcum Junior College Library, Bryn Mawr PA. 215-525-4100, Ext 221

Chasse, Lucy, *Cat*, University of Maine at Fort Kent, Blake Library, Fort Kent ME. 207-834-3165, Ext 215

Chasse, M, *Ref*, Cambrian College of Applied Arts & Technology Library, Sudbury ON. 705-566-8101, Ext 320

Chastain, Hazel E, *Librn*, Texas Instruments Inc (Research Bldg Library), Dallas TX. 214-238-2407

Chastain, Robert A, *Gen Coun*, Florida Department of Agriculture & Consumer Services (Legal Section Library), Tallahassee FL. 904-488-2221

Chatfield, Carol A, *Ch*, Rutland Free Library, Rutland VT. 802-773-6800

Chatfield, Mary, *Lectr*, Simmons College, Graduate School of Library & Information Science, MA. 617-738-2225

Chatfield, Mary V, *Librn*, Harvard University Library (Baker Library), Boston MA. 617-495-3650

Chatfield, Robert W, *Dir & Cat*, Franklin Pierce College Library, Rindge NH. 603-899-5111, Ext 215, 216

Chatham, Sarah, *Ref*, Gulfport-Harrison County Library, Gulfport MS. 601-863-6411

Chatiloviez, Margaret, *Acq*, Kenosha Public Library, Kenosha WI. 414-656-6034

Chatterton, Leigh, *Ser*, Boston College Libraries (Bapst (Central Library)), Chestnut Hill MA. 617-969-0100, Ext 3205

Chatton, Mildred, *Asst Prof*, San Jose State University, Division of Library Science, CA. 408-277-2292

Chaudoin, Sheila, *Cat*, Musser Public Library, Muscatine IA. 319-263-3065

Chaudoin, Sheila, *Tech Serv & Cat*, Musser Public Library, Muscatine IA. 319-263-3065

Chauhan, Ram, *Asst Dir*, East Saint Louis Public Library, East Saint Louis IL. 618-874-7280

Chauncey, Donald, *Media*, High Point Public Library, High Point NC. 919-885-8411

Chaussee, Mary Jane, *Asst Dir*, Veterans Memorial Public Library, Bismarck ND. 701-222-6410

Chauvin, Marie, *Media*, Clinton-Essex-Franklin Library System, Plattsburgh NY. 518-563-5190

Chavers, Shirley, *Asst Dir*, Niobrara County Library, Lusk WY. 307-334-3490

Chavez, Rosaline, *Asst Librn*, South Valley Bernalillo County Library, Albuquerque NM. 505-766-4424

Chavis, C, *Dir*, American Standards Testing Bureau, Inc, Sam Tour Memorial Library, New York NY. 212-943-3156

Chaw, Gladys, *Chief Librn*, College of San Mateo Library, San Mateo CA. 415-574-6100

Chaw, Gladys, *Head Librn*, College of San Mateo, Library Technology, CA. 415-574-6100

Chawla, Ashok K, *Chairman & Tech Servs*, Richard J Daley College, Learning Resource Center, Chicago IL. 312-735-3000, Ext 224, 226, 227

Chawner, B, *Asst Librn*, Boreal Institute for Northern Studies Library, Edmonton AB. 403-432-4409

Chayne, Darrell, *Instructional Coordr*, Aurora Public Library, Aurora CO. 303-750-5000, Ext 410

Cheatham, Eunice, *Asst Librn*, Woodruff County Library, Augusta AR. 501-347-5331

Cheatham, Mary L, *Dir*, Hot Spring County Library, Malvern AR. 501-332-6412

Cheatham, Nidra, *Librn*, Louisiana College, Norton Memorial Library, Pineville LA. 318-487-7201

Check, Gloria, *Cat*, Milford Public Library, Milford CT. 203-878-7461

Checke, Roger A, *Dir*, Hackettstown Free Public Library, Hackettstown NJ. 201-852-4936

Checkon, Margaret, *Asst Librn*, Spangler Public Library, Spangler PA. 814-948-8222

Checkovich, Peter G, *Media*, Shenandoah College & Conservatory of Music, Howe Library, Winchester VA. 703-667-8714, Ext 453

Cheek, Edith S, *Dir*, Galveston College, David Glenn Hunt Memorial Library, Galveston TX. 713-763-6551, Ext 247

Cheek, Joseph Emory, *In Charge*, University of Georgia, Georgia Coastal Plain Experiment Station Library, Tifton GA. 912-386-3447

Cheh, Jennie, *Tech Serv*, Burton Public Library, Burton OH. 216-834-4258

Chekon, Terry A, *Ch*, Sacramento Public Library, Sacramento CA. 916-440-5926

Chelette, Catherine, *Libr Asst*, San Bernardino County Library (Joshua Tree Branch), Joshua Tree CA. 714-366-8615

Chelius, Sister M Alberta, *Librn*, Saint Mary Hospital Library, Philadelphia PA. 215-739-1460

Chellis, Carole, *Asst Dir*, Middlesex Public Library, Middlesex NJ. 201-356-6602

Chelton, Mary Kay, *Asst Prof*, Rutgers-The State University of New Jersey, Graduate School of Library & Information Studies, NJ. 201-932-7500

Chen, Barbara, *Japanese*, Long Island University, Brooklyn Center Libraries, Brooklyn NY. 212-834-6060, 834-6064

Chen, Catherine, *Dir*, Northwood Institute, Strosacker Library, Midland MI. 517-631-1600, Ext 271, 274

Chen, Ching-Chih, *Prof*, Simmons College, Graduate School of Library & Information Science, MA. 617-738-2225

Chen, Christina, *Tech Servs Librn*, Los Angeles County-University of Southern California (General Hospital Library), Los Angeles CA. 213-226-2622

Chen, Danny, *Media*, Pensacola Junior College, Learning Resource Center, Pensacola FL. 904-476-5410

Chen, David, *Asst Librn, Tech Serv*, Emory University Libraries (Pitts Theology Library), Atlanta GA. 404-329-4166

Chen, Donna, *ILL*, Ohio University, Vernon R Alden Library, Athens OH. 614-594-5228

Chen, Faustina, *Librn*, Dalhousie University (Institute of Public Affairs Library), Halifax NS. 902-424-2526, Ext 42

Chen, Flora, *Librn*, National Research Council, Prairie Regional Laboratory Library, Saskatoon SK. 306-665-4197

Chen, Frances, *Librn*, Princeton University Library (Urban & Environmental Studies), Princeton NJ. 609-452-3180

Chen, Joanna, *Librn*, Balch, Bingham, Hawthorne, Williams & Ward Library, Birmingham AL. 205-251-8100

Chen, Joanna, *Cat,* Samford University (Cordell Hull Law), Birmingham AL. 205-870-2714
Chen, Johanna Else, *Dir,* Free Public Library of Mountainside, Mountainside NJ. 201-233-0115
Chen, Lilian, *Cat,* University of Saint Thomas, Robert Pace & Ada Mary Doherty Library, Houston TX. 713-522-7911, Ext 325
Chen, M, *Tech Serv,* Queen's University at Kingston (Law), Kingston ON. 613-547-5934
Chen, Mrs A, *Ref,* Stanstead College, John C Colby Memorial Library, Stanstead PQ. 819-876-2702
Chen, Nancy, *Asst Librn,* Robeson Technical Institute Library, Lumberton NC. 919-738-7101, Ext 66
Chen, Olivia, *Librn,* Chicago Public Library (Chinatown), Chicago IL. 312-326-4255
Chen, Sally, *Cat,* Mercer County Library, Trenton NJ. 609-989-6917
Chen, Suzy, *Acq & Ref,* Ann Arbor Public Library, Ann Arbor MI. 313-994-2333
Chen, Tung Chu, *Psychol, Design & Archit,* Drexel University Library, Philadelphia PA. 215-895-2750
Chenery, Frederick, *Tech Serv,* State Library Commission of Iowa, Des Moines IA. 515-281-4102
Chenery, P J, *Dir,* North Carolina Science & Technology Research Center, NC. 919-549-0671
Chenevert, Barbara L, *Tech Serv,* Westbrook College Library, Portland ME. 207-797-7261, Ext 280
Chenevert, Edward V, *Dir,* Portland Public Library, Baxter Library, Portland ME. 207-773-4761
Cheney, M Margaret, *Librn,* Leonard Morse Hospital Library, Natick MA. 617-653-3400, Ext 2255 or 2256
Cheney, Phillip, *Readers & Info Servs,* Florence County Library, Florence SC. 803-662-8424
Cheney, Roberta, *Librn,* Kalamazoo Public Library (Alma Powell), Kalamazoo MI. 616-344-0781
Cheney, Roberta, *Librn,* Kalamazoo Public Library (Eastwood), Kalamazoo MI. 616-343-6311
Cheney, Ronald, *AV,* Town of Caledon Public Libraries, Bolton ON. 416-857-1400
Cheng, Chao-sheng, *Acq,* East Carolina University (Health Affairs Library), Greenville NC. 919-757-6961, Ext 261
Cheng, Daphne, *Cat,* Scarborough Public Library, Scarborough ON. 416-291-1991
Cheng, Emily, *Librn,* United States Department of Energy (United States Dept of Energy Branch Law Library), Germantown MD. 202-353-4301
Cheng, Jennie, *Asst Dir Tech Serv,* Concordia University Library, Montreal PQ. 514-879-2820
Cheng, Juliana, *Librn,* Los Angeles Public Library System (Chinatown), Los Angeles CA. 213-620-0925
Cheng, Mu-chin, *Librn,* Illinois Department of Mental Health & Developmental Disabilities, Herman M Adler Mental Health Center, Professional Library, Champaign IL. 217-333-4993, Ext 47
Cheng, Nancy, *Pub Servs,* University of Utah (Law Library), Salt Lake City UT. 801-581-6438
Cheng, Paul, *East Asia,* Cornell University Libraries (University Libraries), Ithaca NY. 607-256-4144
Cheng, Phyllis S, *Acq,* Wilkes College, Eugene Shedden Farley Library, Wilkes-Barre PA. 717-824-4651, Ext 331 & 332
Chenier, Andre, *Dir,* Universite Du Quebec: Centre d'etudes Universitaires Dans L'ouest Quebecois Bibliotheque, Rouyn PQ. 819-762-0971, Ext 350
Chenier, Andre, *Dir,* University du Quebec: Centre d'Etudes Universitaires Dans L'Ouest Quebecois, Centre de Hull Bibliotheque, Hull PQ. 819-776-8381
Chenier, Therese, *Dir,* Casselman Public Library, Casselman ON. 613-764-5505
Chenoweth, Robert, *Librn,* Institute for Policy Studies Library, Washington DC. 202-234-9382, Ext 59
Chenoweth, Rose, *Ad,* Willard Library of Evansville, Evansville IN. 812-425-4309
Chepesiuk, Ronald, *Archivist,* Winthrop College, Ida Jane Dacus Library, Rock Hill SC. 803-323-2131
Cherellia, Peter P, *Librn,* Citizens Law Library, Greensburg PA. 412-834-2191

Cherg, Jeanette, *Cat,* Madison Public Library, Madison WI. 608-266-6300
Cherington, Reed, *Adminr,* Orleans County Historical Society, Inc, Old Stone House Library, Brownington VT. 802-754-2022
Chernega, Ann, *Librn,* Westinghouse Electric Corp, Advanced Reactors Div Library, Madison PA. 412-722-5301
Chernenkoff, Eleanor, *Librn,* Alberta Transportation Library, Edmonton AB. 403-427-8802
Chernik, Barbara E, *Acq,* Gateway Technical Institute, Learning Resources Center, Kenosha WI. 414-656-6924, 656-6923
Cherniv, Raisa, *Librn,* Lutheran Hospital, Health Sciences Library, Fort Wayne IN. 219-458-2277
Chernoff, Joan, *Ref,* Newburgh Free Library, Newburgh NY. 914-561-1836
Cherry, Cheryl A, *Librn,* Fischer & Porter Co, Engineering Library, Warminster PA. 215-674-6834
Cherry, Pauline, *Librn,* Chester County Public Library, Henderson TN. 901-989-4673
Cherry, Peggy T, *Head Librn,* Martin Community College Library, Williamston NC. 919-792-1521
Cherry, Ronald L, *Librn,* Minnesota State Supreme Court, Minnesota State Law Library, Saint Paul MN. 612-296-2775
Cherry, Ronald L, *Librn,* University of Arizona Library (Law Library), Tucson AZ. 602-626-1413
Cherry, Wendell, *Dir,* Wyandanch Public Library, Wyandanch NY. 516-643-4848
Cheruitz, Solon, *Cat,* Lindenwood Colleges, Margaret L Butler Library, Saint Charles MO. 314-946-6912
Chervin, Shirley, *Librn,* Pomona Valley Community Hospital, Medical Library, Pomona CA. 714-623-8715, Ext 2113
Cheshier, Robert, *Asst Prof,* Case Western Reserve University, School of Library Science, OH. 216-368-3500
Cheshier, Robert G, *Dir,* Case Western Reserve University & Cleveland Medical Library Association, Cleveland Health Sciences Library, Cleveland OH. 216-368-3426
Cheski, Richard M, *Dir,* State Library of Ohio, Columbus OH. 614-466-2693
Chesley, Joan, *Dir,* North Bend Public Library, North Bend NE. 402-652-8356
Chesley, Robert, *Chief,* ERIC - Educational Resources Information Center, (Central ERIC), DC. 202-254-5500
Cheslock, Rosalind P, *Info Spec,* Martin Marietta Corp, Laboratories Library, Baltimore MD. 301-247-0700
Chesney, Alison Scott, *Librn,* Skidaway Institute of Oceanography Library, Savannah GA. 912-356-2474
Chesney, Carolyn E, *Librn,* House Beautiful Magazine, Editorial Service Library, New York NY. 212-935-4098
Chesney, Sandra, *Asst Librn,* Fort Sanders Presbyterian Hospital, Nursing-Medical Library, Knoxville TN. 615-546-2811, Ext 1293
Chesnut, Bonnie, *Librn,* Unity Township Public Library, Atwood IL. 217-578-2727
Chester, Ethel, *Librn,* Okanagan Regional Library District (Canoe Branch), Canoe BC. 604-832-3579
Chester, J K, *Dir,* Saginaw Art Museum Research Library, Saginaw MI. 517-754-2491
Chestnut, Dorothy, *Instr,* Caldwell College, Library Science Program, NJ. 201-228-4424
Chestnut, James D, *Librn,* United States Army (Corps of Engineers-South Atlantic Div, Library & Information Center), Atlanta GA. 404-221-6620
Cheung, Cecilia, *Cat,* State University of New York, College at Old Westbury Library, Old Westbury NY. 516-876-3156, 876-3152
Chevse, Sheldon, *Media,* Borough of Manhattan Community College Library, Martin B Dworkis Library, New York NY. 212-262-3530
Chew, Luther, *Bibliog Instr,* Selkirk College Library, Castlegar BC. 604-365-7292, Ext 216, 223 & 335, 365-5518
Chewning, Margaret, *Librn,* Orange County Public Library, Orange VA. 703-672-3811
Chiang, Katherine, *Sci Librn,* Georgetown University, Joseph Mark Lauinger Library, Washington DC. 202-625-4095

Chiang, Nancy, *Cat,* Hartwick College Library, Oneonta NY. 607-432-4200, Ext 324
Chiang, Win-Shin S, *Dir,* Loyola University Library (School of Law), New Orleans LA. 504-865-3426, 865-3427, 865-3136
Chiang, Yao Po, *Dir Learning Mat Center,* Kearney State College, Calvin T Ryan Library, Kearney NE. 308-236-4218
Chiasson, Gilles, *In Charge,* Coaching Association of Canada, Sport Information Resource Centre, Ottawa ON. 613-746-5357
Chiasson, Gilles, *Dir,* Haut-Saint-Jean Regional Library, Bibliotheque Regionale du Haut-Saint-Jean, Edmundston NB. 506-739-7331
Chiasson, Robert, *Prof,* CEGEP Francois-Xavier Garneau, Techniques de la documentation, PQ. 418-688-8310, Ext 290
Chiaverotti, Betty, *Ad,* Roseville Public Library, Roseville MI. 313-777-6012
Chichura, Edward, *Librn,* United States Court of Appeals, Ninth Circuit Library, San Francisco CA. 415-556-6129
Chicilla, Kay, *ILL,* University of Texas Health Science Center at Dallas Library, Dallas TX. 214-688-3368
Chicka, Metta, *Librn,* San Antonio Public Library (Westfall), San Antonio TX. 512-344-2373
Chickanzeff, S, *Cat,* San Francisco Art Institute, Anne Bremer Memorial Library, San Francisco CA. 415-771-7020, Ext 59
Chickering, F William, *Media,* Columbia University (University Libraries), New York NY. 212-280-2241
Chicoine, Marilyn, *Librn,* Cornwall Free Public Library, Cornwall VT. 802-462-2125
Chicorel, Marietta, *In Charge,* American Library Publishing Co, Inc, New York NY. 212-787-0767
Chiddell, Philip, *Coordr,* Camosun College, Library-Media Centre, Victoria BC. 604-592-1281
Chidester, Carol, *In Charge,* Arizona Training Program at Tucson, Library of Applied Practices, Tucson AZ. 602-882-5345
Chidester, John K, *Dir,* Mount Vernon Public Library, Mount Vernon OH. 614-392-8671
Chier, Jean, *Asst Librn,* Berlin Public Library, Berlin WI. 414-361-2650
Chigi, Rita, *Asst Librn,* Ketchikan Public Library, Ketchikan AK. 907-225-2748
Chilcoat, Nancy, *Librn,* Lake Lanier Regional Library (Mountain Park Public), Stone Mountain GA. 404-921-1299
Child, Betty, *In Charge,* Texas Education Agency (Region XX), San Antonio TX. 512-828-3551
Childers, David, *Asst Dir,* West Virginia Library Commission, Science & Cultural Center, Charleston WV. 304-348-2041
Childers, Joanlee, *Ch,* Ralph Chandler Harrison Memorial Library, Carmel CA. 408-624-4629
Childers, Joy, *Librn,* Denver Public Library (Montclair), Denver CO. 303-573-5152, Ext 271
Childers, Richard, *Librn,* Memphis-Shelby County Public Library & Information Center (Raleigh Libr), Memphis TN. 901-386-5333
Childers, Thomas, *Prof,* Drexel University, School of Library & Information Science, PA. 215-895-2474
Childress, Boyd, *On-Line Servs,* Western Kentucky University, Helm-Cravens Library, Bowling Green KY. 502-745-4875
Childress, Cheryl, *Librn,* Roanoke County Public Library, Roanoke VA. 703-774-1681
Childress, John, *Media,* Hinds Junior College, George M McLendon Library, Raymond MS. 601-857-5261, Ext 253
Childress, Pat, *Circ,* Chattanooga-Hamilton County Bicentennial Library, Chattanooga TN. 615-757-5320
Childress, Peggy, *Br Coordr,* Webster County Public Library, Dixon KY. 502-639-9171
Childress, Peggy, *Librn,* Webster County Public Library (Providence Branch), Providence KY. 502-667-5658
Childs, Bernice, *Librn,* Rensselaer Falls Library, Rensselaer Falls NY. 315-344-2335
Childs, Betty Ann, *Acq,* Creighton University, Alumni Memorial Library, Omaha NE. 402-449-2705
Childs, Eileen, *Bkmobile Coordr,* Polk County Library, Crookston MN. 218-281-4522

Childs, Elizabeth B, *Librn,* Charlotte-Glades Library System (Englewood-Charlotte Public), Englewood FL. 813-474-1881
Childs, Ellen G, *ILL & Ref,* Jefferson Community College, Melvil Dewey Library, Watertown NY. 315-782-5250
Childs, Herbert, *Dir,* Cogswell College Library, San Francisco CA. 415-433-5550
Childs, Leroy C, *Dir,* West Georgia Regional Library, Neva Lomason Memorial Library, Carrollton GA. 404-832-1381
Childs, Margaret, *On-Line Servs,* Tobacco Institute Library, Washington DC. 202-457-4800
Childs, Pauline, *Librn,* Klamath County Library (Bonanza Branch), Bonanza OR. 503-545-6566
Childs, Peter P, *Dir,* Collingswood Free Public Library, Collingswood NJ. 609-858-0649
Childs, Ronald W, *Librn,* Sarah Stewart Bovard Memorial Library, Tionesta PA. 814-755-4454
Childs, Suse C, *Librn,* Metropolitan Museum of Art (Cloisters Library), New York NY. 212-923-3700
Childs, Ward J, *Asst Archivist,* Philadelphia City Archives, Philadelphia PA. 215-686-2276, 686-2249
Chiles, Verdene, *ILL,* California College of Podiatric Medicine, Schmidt Medical Library, San Francisco CA. 415-563-3444, Ext 246
Chilson, Frances, *Acq,* State University of New York College at Potsdam, Frederick W Crumb Memorial Library, Potsdam NY. 315-268-2940
Chilton, Betty, *Librn,* Fairfax County Public Schools, Professional Reference Library in Education, Fairfax VA. 703-591-4514
Chilton, Joan, *Librn,* Community Hospital, Medical Library, Santa Rosa CA. 707-544-3340, Ext 228
Chimenti, Linda, *AV,* Miami Valley Hospital, Memorial Medical Library, Dayton OH. 513-223-6192
Chimney, Lacy, *Acq,* Texas Southern University Library, Houston TX. 713-527-7121
Chin, Cecilia, *Assoc Librn & Ref,* Art Institute of Chicago (Ryerson & Burnham Libraries), Chicago IL. 312-443-6666
Chin, Ellen, *Librn,* Dane County Regional Planning Commission Library, Madison WI. 608-266-4137
Chin, Helen W, *Librn,* New York Public Library (Eastchester), New York NY. 212-653-3292
Chin, Janet, *Ch,* Concord Pike Library, Wilmington DE. 302-478-7961
Chindvall, Marilyn, *Librn,* Muir Library, Winnebago Public Library, Winnebago MN. 507-893-3196
Chinn, Julian, *Libr Asst,* Far West Laboratory, Library for Educational Research & Development, San Francisco CA. 415-565-3000
Chioffi, Barbara, *Librn,* Readfield Community Library, Readfield ME. 207-685-4902
Chiong, Anna F, *Librn,* University of Washington Libraries (Geography), Seattle WA. 206-543-5244
Chisamore, Connie, *Librn,* Rideau Lakes Union Library (Lyndhurst Branch), Lyndhurst ON. 613-359-5315
Chisholm, Alice, *Cat,* Westwood Public Library, Westwood MA. 617-326-7562
Chisholm, Anne M, *Ch,* McArthur Public Library, Biddeford ME. 207-284-4181
Chisholm, John A, *Ad,* McArthur Public Library, Biddeford ME. 207-284-4181
Chism, Betty L, *Dir,* Modoc County Library, Alturas CA. 916-233-2719
Chism, Harriet J, *Librn,* United States Navy (Lemoore Naval Air Station Library), Lemoore AFB CA. 209-998-2211
Chisman, Janet, *Acq,* Kentucky State University, Blazer Library, Frankfort KY. 502-564-5852
Chisum, Emmett D, *Research Historian,* American Heritage Center Library, Laramie WY. 307-766-3279
Chittampalli, Padma, *Librn,* Montefiore-Morrisania Comprehensive, J Lewis Amster Medical Library, Bronx NY. 212-922-9265
Chittenden, Jan, *Coordr,* Cooperating Libraries in Consortium, (CLIC), MN. 612-227-9531
Chittenden, L, *ILL,* Napa City - County Library, Napa CA. 707-253-4241
Chittenden, Nancy, *Ch,* Fremont Public Library, Fremont MI. 616-924-3480
Chittenden, Robert, *Dir,* Hawkeye Institute of Technology Library, Waterloo IA. 319-296-2320, Ext 237

Chittick, Grace, *ILL,* Keene Memorial Library, Fremont Public Library, Fremont NE. 402-721-5084
Chitty, Mary, *Chief Librn,* Environmental Protection Agency (Air Pollution Technical Information Center Library), Research Triangle Park NC. 919-541-2111
Chitty, Mrs M E, *Chief,* Veterans Administration, Supply Depot & Library Technical Processing, NJ. 201-725-2540
Chitwood, Lera, *Ref & Bibliog Instr,* University of Alabama in Huntsville Library, Huntsville AL. 205-895-6540
Chitwood, Martha, *Dir,* McCall Public Library, McCall ID. 208-634-5522
Chiu, Kai-Yun, *Librn,* Library Co of the Baltimore Bar, Baltimore MD. 301-727-0280
Chiu, Liwa, *Librn,* Pan American World Airways, Inc, Corporate Library, New York NY. 212-880-1917
Chiu, Mrs Tung Chen, *Librn,* Ocean County Library (Point Pleasant Branch), Point Pleasant Beach NJ. 201-892-4575
Chiusolo, Josephine, *Circ,* Maywood Public Library, Maywood IL. 312-343-1847
Chivers, Jr, James R, *Librn,* Stark County District Library (East Canton Branch), East Canton OH. 216-488-1501
Chmela, Alois, *Tech Serv & Acq,* Queensborough Community College Library, Bayside NY. 212-631-6226
Chmelir, Lynn, *Tech Serv & Acq,* Linfield College, Northup Library, McMinnville OR. 503-472-4121, Ext 262
Chmielewski, Roy, *Media,* Goddard College, William Shipman Library, Plainfield VT. 802-454-8311, Ext 232
Cho, Nammy M, *Librn,* Logicon Inc Library, San Pedro CA. 213-831-0611, Ext 500
Cho, Stephen, *Tech Serv & Cat,* South Huntington Public Library, Huntington Station NY. 516-549-4411
Cho, Y J, *Librn,* University of Manitoba Libraries (Engineering), Winnipeg MB. 204-474-9445
Choate, Jackie, *Asst Dir,* Vermilion Parish Library, Abbeville LA. 318-893-2655
Choate, Jo Ann, *Librn,* Federal Aviation Administration, Southwest Region Library, Fort Worth TX. 817-624-4911, Ext 246
Chobanian, Peter, *Asst Dir, Ref & Bibliog Instr,* Ripon College Library, Ripon WI. 414-748-8328
Choi, Eunice, *Librn,* Illinois Institute of Natural Resources, Information Services, Chicago IL. 312-793-3870
Choi, Haesan, *Chief Librn,* Orange County Public Library (La Palma Branch), La Palma CA. 714-523-8585, 523-8586
Choice, Nancy, *YA,* Lakewood Public Library, Lakewood OH. 216-228-8275
Chojenski, Peter R, *Ref, On-Line Servs & Bibliog Instr,* Purdue University Calumet Library, Hammond IN. 219-844-0520, Ext 249
Chojnacki, S, *Dir,* University of Sudbury Library, Sudbury ON. 705-673-5661, Ext 35 & 36
Choldin, Marianna, *Slavic Ref,* University of Illinois Library at Urbana-Champaign, Urbana IL. 217-333-0790
Cholod, Ted, *In Charge,* Saskatchewan Telecommunications Library, Regina SK. 306-347-2008
Chomyk, Lee, *Young Adult & Outreach Servs,* East Brunswick Public Library, East Brunswick NJ. 201-254-1220
Chopra, Swaran, *Dir,* Children's Hospital of Philadelphia, Medical Library, Philadelphia PA. 215-596-9673
Choptiany, Linda, *Inter-campus Servs,* Centennial College of Applied Arts & Technology, Resource Centre, Scarborough ON. 416-439-7180
Choquette, Cliff, *Local History & Genealogy,* Adams Library, Chelmsford MA. 617-256-5521
Chororenko, Rita, *ILL,* United States Air Force (Scott Air Force Base Library), Scott AFB IL. 618-256-5100
Chouinard, Germain, *Dir,* Universite De Sherbrooke Bibliotheque (Bibliotheque de Medecine), Sherbrooke PQ. 819-565-2095
Chouinard, Joseph, *Music,* State University of New York College, Daniel A Reed Library, Fredonia NY. 716-673-3183
Chovelak, Elissa, *Media,* Downers Grove Public Library, Downers Grove IL. 312-960-1200

Chow, Dorothy, *Acq,* Towson State University, Albert S Cook Library, Towson MD. 301-321-2450
Chow, Mrs Oi-Yung, *Dir,* Hawaii State Library System (Hawaii State Library), Honolulu HI. 808-548-7501
Chow, Ruey-Hwa, *Librn,* Dayton & Montgomery County Public Library (Wilmington-Stroop), Dayton OH. 513-224-1651, Ext 221
Chow, Tze-Nan, *Cat,* West Orange Free Public Library, West Orange NJ. 201-736-0198
Chowdhury, Mann, *Chief Librn,* Harlem Hospital Medical Center (Louis T Wright Memorial Library), New York NY. 212-694-8261
Chrinside, Mrs E, *Librn,* Grand Valley Public Library, Grand Valley ON. 519-928-5622
Chrisant, Rosemarie, *Librn,* Akron Law Library Association, Akron OH. 216-379-5734
Chrisinger, Richard L, *Librn,* Crook County Library, Prineville OR. 503-447-7978
Chrislock, Dallas Lindgren, *Head Ref Servs,* Minnesota Historical Society (Division of Archives & Manuscripts), Saint Paul MN. 612-296-6980
Chrisman, Diane S, *Deputy Dirs,* Buffalo & Erie County Public Library System, Buffalo NY. 716-856-7525
Chrisman, Larry, *Asst Prof,* University of South Florida, Graduate Department of Library, Media & Information Studies, FL. 813-974-2557
Chrisp, Aileen, *Librn,* Akron-Summit County Public Library (Ellet), Akron OH. 216-784-2019
Christ, Bonnie, *Cat,* Portland Public Library, Baxter Library, Portland ME. 207-773-4761
Christensen, Alvie, *Asst Librn,* Alma Public Library, Alma MI. 517-463-3966
Christensen, Beth, *Librn,* Saint Olaf College (Hall of Music), Northfield MN. 507-663-3209
Christensen, Carol, *Librn,* Jefferson County Public Library (Golden Regional), Golden CO. 303-279-4585
Christensen, Carol, *Head,* University of Minnesota Libraries-Twin Cities (Circulation), Minneapolis MN. 612-373-2885
Christensen, Connie, *Librn,* Deseret News Library, Salt Lake City UT. 801-237-2155
Christensen, Constance, *Librn,* Beacon Falls Public Library, Beacon Falls CT. 203-729-1441
Christensen, Dorothy, *Tech Serv,* Winfield Public Library, Winfield IL. 312-653-7599
Christensen, Evan J, *Dir & Asst Prof,* Weber State College, Instructional Media Program, UT. 801-626-6280
Christensen, Frank, *AV,* Waubonsee Community College, Learning Resources Center, Sugar Grove IL. 312-466-4811, Ext 303
Christensen, James, *In Charge,* Midwest Planning & Research, Inc Library, Minneapolis MN. 612-379-4600
Christensen, Jean, *Librn,* Sno-Isle Regional Library (Stanwood Branch), Stanwood WA. 206-629-3132
Christensen, John E, *Dir,* Washburn University of Topeka (School of Law Library), Topeka KS. 913-295-6688
Christensen, John O, *Librn,* Utah Technical College at Salt Lake, Instructional Media Center, Salt Lake City UT. 801-967-4195
Christensen, Karen, *Librn,* Department of Public Welfare Library, Lincoln NE. 402-471-3121
Christensen, Karl, *Ref & Circ,* Saint John's University Library (Law), Jamaica NY. 212-969-8000, Ext 651, 652 & 653
Christensen, Kent, *Librn,* Philadelphia College of Performing Arts Library, Philadelphia PA. 215-545-6200, Ext 50,51,52
Christensen, Laura A, *Librn,* Amax Exploration, Inc, Engineering & Mine Evaluation Library, Denver CO. 303-433-6151, Ext 264
Christensen, Lenore, *Librn,* Shelley Public Library, Shelley ID. 208-357-7801
Christensen, Marge, *Librn,* Home Township Library, Edmore MI. 517-427-5241
Christensen, Marguerite, *Ref,* University of Wisconsin-Madison, Memorial Library, Madison WI. 608-262-3521
Christensen, Marilyn, *Librn,* Douglas County Library System (Reedsport Public), Reedsport OR. 503-271-3500
Christensen, Mary Ellen, *Librn,* Dow Chemical USA, Western Division Library, Pittsburg CA. 415-432-5199

Christensen, Nora, *Librn,* First Baptist Church Library, Sioux Falls SD. 605-336-0966
Christensen, Phyllis, *Law Libr Chief,* United States General Accounting Office Library System (Office of Information Systems & Services), Washington DC. 275-3691 (Br Mgr), 275-5180 (Audit Ref Servs), 275-2585 (Law), 275-2555 (Tech Servs)
Christensen, Richard, *Circ,* Illinois State University, Milner Library, Normal IL. 309-438-3675
Christensen, Rowena, *Dir,* Ephrata Public Library, Ephrata WA. 509-754-3971
Christensen, Ruth, *Librn,* Oakland Public Library, Oakland NE. 402-685-9279
Christensen, Ruth M, *Librn,* Southwest Museum Library, Los Angeles CA. 213-221-2163
Christenson, Ann, *In Charge,* Texas Education Agency (Region II), Corpus Christi TX. 512-883-9288
Christenson, Bernie, *Training Coord,* South Dakota Division of Criminal Investigation, Training Center Library, Pierre SD. 605-224-3584
Christenson, Helen, *Cat,* Milwaukee Public Library, Milwaukee WI. 414-278-3000
Christenson, Jan, *Librn,* New York Public Library (Port Richmond), New York NY. 212-442-0158
Christenson, John D, *Dir,* Traverse Des Sioux Library System, Mankato MN. 507-625-6169
Christhansen, Alice, *Librn,* San Bernardino County Library (Victorville Branch), Victorville CA. 714-243-4250
Christian, Arthur Munro, *Dir,* H M S Bounty Society, International, Historical & Genealogical Research Library, Tiburon CA. 415-435-9749
Christian, David, *Librn,* Meiklejohn Civil Liberties Institute Library, Berkeley CA. 415-848-0599
Christian, Deborah A, *Librn,* Oakridge Public Library, Oakridge OR. 503-782-2258
Christian, Dorothy, *Acq,* Santa Cruz Public Library, Santa Cruz CA. 408-429-3533
Christiani, Linnea, *On-Line Servs,* University of California, Berkeley (Law Library), Berkeley CA. 415-642-4044
Christiansen, Claire B, *Ref,* Springfield Public Library, Springfield OR. 503-726-3765
Christiansen, Raymond, *Media,* Aurora College, Charles B Phillips Library, Aurora IL. 312-892-6431, Ext 61, 62
Christiansen, William, *Librn,* San Bernardino County Library (Barstow Branch), Barstow CA. 714-256-8481
Christianson, Bernyce, *Cat,* Webster Groves Public Library, Webster Groves MO. 314-961-3784
Christianson, Carlyn, *Asst Librn,* San Miguel County Public Library, Telluride CO. 303-728-4519
Christianson, Charles, *In Charge,* Missouri State Chest Hospital, Medical Library, Mount Vernon MO. 417-466-3711
Christianson, Marilyn, *Bibliog Instr,* Indiana State University, Cunningham Memorial Library, Terre Haute IN. 812-232-6311, Ext 2451
Christianson, Pat, *Central Servs,* Great River Regional Library, Saint Cloud MN. 612-251-7282
Christianson, Vicky, *Librn,* Valley Medical Center of Fresno, Medical Library, Fresno CA. 209-453-5030
Christie, Alberta F, *Dir & Cat,* Howard Whittemore Memorial Library, Naugatuck CT. 203-729-6129
Christie, Bette, *Librn,* West Florida Regional Library (Milton Branch), Milton FL. 904-623-5565
Christie, Joan, *Librn,* Freeport District Library, Freeport MI. 616-865-3134
Christie, Margaret, *Acq,* Oscar Rose Junior College, Learning Resources Center, Midwest City OK. 405-733-7323, 733-7322
Christiensen, Gaye, *Librn,* Windsor Public Library (Wilson), Windsor CT. 203-247-8960
Christin, Bonnie, *Ch,* Greenville Public Library, Greenville IL. 618-664-3115
Christine, Barbara, *Librn,* Louisville Free Public Library (Shelby Park), Louisville KY. 502-634-9231
Christman, Paul S, *Pres,* Schuylkill Haven Free Public Library, Schuylkill Haven PA. 717-385-0542
Christmann, Catherine, *Ad,* Westborough Public Library, Westborough MA. 617-366-2812

Christmas, Patricia E, *Librn,* Victoria Medical Society, Royal Jubilie Hospital Library, Victoria BC. 604-598-1411
Christoff, Mildred C, *Dir,* Greater Canonsburg Public Library, Canonsburg PA. 412-745-1308
Christoph, Peter, *Assoc Librn,* New York State Library (Manuscripts & Special Collections), Albany NY. 518-474-4461
Christopher, Delois, *Bibliog Instr,* Pasadena City College Library, Pasadena CA. 213-578-7221
Christopher, Irene, *Librn,* Boston University Libraries (Alumni Medical Library), Boston MA. 617-247-6187
Christopher, James R, *Dir,* Simpson College, Dunn Library, Indianola IA. 515-961-6251, Ext 663
Christopher, Paul, *Archives,* University of Southern California, Edward L Doheny Memorial Library, Los Angeles CA. 213-743-6050
Christopher, Rachel, *Cat,* Fort Hays State University, Forsyth Library, Hays KS. 913-628-4431
Christopher, Sandra, *Librn,* Burbank Public Library (Buena Vista), Burbank CA. 213-847-9744
Christopher, Sandra, *Librn,* Burbank Public Library (Northwest Park), Burbank CA. 213-847-9744
Christopher, Virginia K, *ILL, Ref & Bibliog Instr,* Elizabethtown College, Zug Memorial Library, Elizabethtown PA. 717-367-1151, Ext 222
Christopherson, Jane, *ILL & Ref,* East Central Regional Library, Cambridge MN. 612-689-1901
Christy, Carol, *Ch,* San Bernardino County Library, San Bernardino CA. 714-383-1734
Christy, Harriett, *Lectr,* University of Wisconsin-Eau Claire, Dept of Library Science & Media Education, WI. 715-836-2635
Christy, Virginia W, *Librn,* Norman Williams Public Library, Woodstock VT. 802-457-2295
Chrunik, J, *Librn,* Willingdon Public Library, Willingdon AB. 403-367-2222
Chrusoskie, Mrs M, *Br Supvr,* Scarborough Public Library (Highland Creek), Scarborough ON. 416-282-7211
Chrysler, Jean O, *Librn,* Chrysler Art Museum, Art Reference Library, Norfolk VA. 804-622-1211
Chu, B, *Librn,* University of Toronto Libraries (Dept of Physics), Toronto ON. 416-978-5188
Chu, Eliza, *Asst Librn,* Blue Cross of Southern California Library, Woodland Hills CA. 213-703-3160
Chu, Ellen M, *Librn,* National Institutes of Health (Div of Computer Research & Technology Library), Bethesda MD. 301-496-1658
Chu, Ellin, *YA,* Monroe County Library System, Rochester NY. 716-428-7345
Chu, Gen Sen, *Coordr,* Northern Virginia Community College Libraries (Alexandria Campus), Alexandria VA. 703-323-4231
Chu, Raymond, *Cat,* Minot State College, Memorial Library, Minot ND. 701-857-3200
Chu, Ruby, *Librn,* Zenith Radio Corp, Research Library, Glenview IL. 312-391-8452, 391-8453
Chu, Theresa, *Librn,* University of Rochester (Education), Rochester NY. 716-275-4481
Chu, Tien Lu, *Media,* Lock Haven State College, George B Stevenson Library, Lock Haven PA. 717-893-2309
Chu, Toung, *Bindery,* University of Southern California, Edward L Doheny Memorial Library, Los Angeles CA. 213-743-6050
Chu, Wendy, *Librn,* RCA Corporation (David Sarnoff Research Center Library), Princeton NJ. 609-734-2608, 734-2610
Chuang, Felicia S, *Librn, On-Line Servs & Bibliog Instr,* Texas Research Institute of Mental Sciences Library, Houston TX. 713-797-1976, Ext 288
Chubak, Pat, *Librn,* Vanderhoof Public Library, Vanderhoof BC. 604-567-4060
Chulski, Marie Duber, *Chief Librn,* Monroe County Library System (Temperance Branch), Temperance MI. 313-847-6747
Chumbley, Janice, *Ref,* Mississippi Gulf Coast Junior College, Perkinston Campus Learning Resource Center, Perkinston MS. 601-928-5211, Ext 286
Chumbley, Janice, *Feminism,* Mississippi Gulf Coast Junior College, Perkinston Campus Learning Resource Center, Perkinston MS. 601-928-5211, Ext 286
Chumbley, Tami, *Ch,* Lincoln Public Library, Lincoln IL. 217-732-8878

Chung, Anthony H, *Dean,* Edgecombe Technical Institute, R M Fountain Learning Resources Center, Tarboro NC. 919-823-5166
Chung, Jay J, *Dir,* Thomas Hackney Braswell Memorial Library, Rocky Mount NC. 442-1937 & 442-1951
Churan, Esther, *Acq,* Lamar University, Mary & John Gray Library, Beaumont TX. 713-838-8313
Church, Irene Wilder, *Librn,* Madison Public Library, Madison ME. 207-696-3616
Church, James, *Media,* Commerce Public Library, Commerce CA. 213-722-6660
Church, Velma, *Librn,* Dayton Children's Psychiatric Hospital for Dayton & Montgomery County Library, Dayton OH. 513-258-0445
Churchill, Barbara, *Acq,* Maine Maritime Academy, Nutting Memorial Library, Castine ME. 207-326-4311, Ext 238
Churchill, Bette, *Librn,* Knoxville-Knox County Public Library (Sequoyah), Knoxville TN. 615-525-1541
Churchill, Charles, *ILL, Tech Serv & Acq,* Massachusetts College of Art Library, Boston MA. 617-731-2340, Ext 26
Churchill, Jane, *Librn,* Galeton Public Library, Galeton PA. 814-435-2321
Churchville, Lida H, *Librn,* National Archives & Records Service (National Archives Library), Washington DC. 202-523-3286
Churchwell, Charles D, *Dean of Libr Servs,* Washington University Libraries, Saint Louis MO. 314-889-5400
Churgay, Lenore, *Ad,* Dearborn Department of Libraries, Henry Ford Centennial Library, Dearborn MI. 313-271-1000
Churgin, Sylvia J, *Bureau Librn,* Smithsonian Institution Libraries (National Museum of Natural History Bureau Library), Washington DC. 202-381-4160
Churney, Sarah, *Cat,* Law Library of Louisiana, New Orleans LA. 504-568-5705
Chussil, Janet, *Librn,* New Haven Free Public Library (Nathan Hale), New Haven CT. 203-787-8676
Ciallella, Jr, Emil A, *Dir,* Central Falls Free Public Library, Adams Library, Central Falls RI. 401-723-6441
Ciancarelli, Anne, *Tech Serv,* Westwood Public Library, Westwood MA. 617-326-7562
Cianciulli, Jeanne A, *Asst Dir & Ad,* Hempstead Public Library, Hempstead NY. 516-481-6990
Ciaramella, Mary A, *Chief Librn,* Lummus Co-Lummus Technical Center, Technical Information Center Library, Bloomfield NJ. 201-893-2251
Ciaravino, Anthony, *Dept Head,* Automation Industries, Inc, Vitro Laboratories Division Library, Silver Spring MD. 301-871-7200
Ciarkowski, Elaine C, *Circ,* Harvard University Library (Francis A Countway Library of Medicine), Boston MA. 617-732-2142
Ciarlo, George, *Ref,* Orange Coast College Library, Costa Mesa CA. 714-556-5885
Ciarpelli, Kathy, *Librn,* General Railway Signal Co Library, Rochester NY. 716-436-2020
Cibulskis, E R, *Librn, On-Line Servs & Bibliog Instr,* Wm Wrigley Jr Co (Research & Development Library), Chicago IL. 312-523-4040, Ext 473
Ciejka, Eleonora, *Per,* New Jersey Institute of Technology, Robert W Van Houten Library, Newark NJ. 201-645-5306
Cieplechowicz, Barbara, *Media,* Mercer County Library, Trenton NJ. 609-989-6917
Ciesielski, Joseph S, *Dir,* University of San Diego (Marvin Kratter Law Library), San Diego CA. 714-293-4541
Cieslicki, Dorothy, *Dir,* Dickinson College, Boyd Lee Spahr Library, Carlisle PA. 717-245-1396
Cieslik, Robert J, *ILL,* Cleveland State University Libraries, Cleveland OH. 216-687-2486
Cieszynski, Iza, *Resources Coordr,* South Central Library System, Madison WI. 608-266-4181
Cikanek, Ann, *Dir,* J H Robbins Memorial Library, City Library, Ellsworth KS. 913-472-3969
Ciko, Anthony, *Sr Med Librn,* Erie County Medical Center, Medical Library, Buffalo NY. 716-898-3939
Cilento, Linda, *Tech Serv,* Haddonfield Public Library, Haddonfield NJ. 609-429-1304

Ciliberti, Anne, *Ref,* William Paterson College of New Jersey, Sarah Byrd Askew Library, Wayne NJ. 201-595-2113
Cilley, Zaida E, *Librn,* Shedd Free Library, Washington NH. 603-495-3592
Cilli, Karen, *Librn,* Western Pennsylvania Hospital (School of Nursing Library), Pittsburgh PA. 412-682-4200
Cimermanis, Ilze V, *Cat,* Public Library of the District of Columbia, Martin Luther King Memorial Library, Washington DC. 202-727-1101
Cimillo, Cathy, *Libr Asst,* Helen Hayes Hospital, Medical Library, West Haverstraw NY. 914-947-3000, Ext 359
Cinnamon, Betty, *Librn,* Toulon Public Library, Toulon IL. 309-286-5791
Cintron, Carmelo Delgado, *Dir,* University of Puerto Rico Library (Law School Library), San Juan PR. 809-764-0000, Ext 2555
Cipolla, Wilma R, *Ser,* State University of New York at Buffalo, University Libraries, Buffalo NY. 716-636-2965
Cipriani, Debra, *Govt Doc,* United States Military Academy Library, West Point NY. 914-938-2230
Cirbus, Maria, *Tech Serv,* Charles H Taylor Memorial Library, Hampton Public Library, Hampton VA. 804-727-6234
Circiello, Jean, *Librn,* Environmental Protection Agency, Region IX Library Information Center, San Francisco CA. 415-556-1840
Cirillo, Susan E, *Circ,* Roger Williams College Library, Bristol RI. 401-255-2361
Cirino, Paul John, *Dir,* Middle Country Public Library, Centereach NY. 516-585-9393
Cisler, Steve, *Librn,* Contra Costa County Library (Pinole Branch), Pinole CA. 415-758-2741
Cisney, Douglas, *Librn,* Nahant Public Library, Nahant MA. 617-581-0306
Cisyk, Donald B, *Librn,* South Beach Psychiatric Center, Library Department of Education & Training, Staten Island NY. 212-390-6144
Citizen, Katherine, *Dir,* Yorba Linda Library District, Yorba Linda CA. 714-528-7039
Citron, H, *Assoc Dir,* Georgia Institute of Technology, Price Gilbert Memorial Library, Atlanta GA. 404-894-4510
Ciucki, Marcella, *Tech Serv,* Lake County Public Library, Merrillville IN. 219-769-3541
Ciulla, Frances, *Tech Serv,* Elmont Public Library, Elmont NY. 516-354-5280, 354-4091
Ciulla, Mary, *Cat,* Gloucester Lyceum & Sawyer Free Library, Gloucester MA. 617-283-0376
Ciurczak, Alexis, *Instr,* Palomar Community College, Library Technology Certificate Program, CA. 714-744-1150, Ext 473 & 480
Ciurczak, Alexis, *Tech Serv,* Palomar Community College, Phil H Putnam Memorial Library, San Marcos CA. 714-744-1150, Ext 275
Claar, Barbara, *Bkmobile Coordr,* Delaware County District Library, Delaware OH. 614-362-3861
Clack, Doris, *Assoc Prof,* Florida State University, School of Library Science, FL. 904-644-5775
Cladek, Anna L, *Dir,* Perth Amboy Free Public Library, Perth Amboy NJ. 201-826-2600
Claflin, Brenda, *Librn,* West Hartford Public Library (Julia Faxon), West Hartford CT. 203-523-5545
Clairmont, Virginia L, *Librn,* Manistique School & Public Library, Manistique MI. 906-341-2195
Clancy, Constance, *Dir,* South Hadley Library System, South Hadley MA. 413-532-1241
Clancy, Jeanne, *Ch,* Abington Free Library, Abington PA. 215-885-5180
Clancy, Jeanne M, *Librn,* Sasaki Associates, Inc Library, Watertown MA. 617-926-3300
Clancy, Patricia, *Librn,* Long Island Lighting Co, Corporate Library, Hicksville NY. 516-733-4264
Clancy, Patricia, *Librn,* York Regional Library (Chatham Public), Chatham NB. 506-773-6274
Clapham, Thomas, *Ch,* Cherry Hill Free Public Library, Cherry Hill NJ. 609-667-0300
Clapp, Laurel R, *Librn,* Samford University (Cordell Hull Law), Birmingham AL. 205-870-2714
Clapp, Linda, *Tech Serv & Cat,* Muskegon County Library, Muskegon MI. 616-724-6248
Clapp, Marilyn M, *Dir,* Golden West College Library, Huntington Beach CA. 714-892-7711, Ext 541

Clapp, Maxine, *Archivist,* University of Minnesota Libraries-Twin Cities (University Archives), Minneapolis MN. 612-373-2891
Clapper, Sara, *Librn,* Muskingum Area Technical College, Herrold Hall Learning Resource Center, Zanesville OH. 614-454-2501, Ext 311, 312
Clare, Marilyn, *Librn,* Mary C Rauchholz Memorial Library, Hemlock MI. 517-642-8621
Clare, Phyllis, *Ch,* San Jose Public Library, San Jose CA. 408-277-4822
Clare, Sister Mary, *Librn,* Saint Francis Hospital (Memorial Medical Library), Evanston IL. 312-492-2000
Claridge, Geoffrey G, *Librn,* Saint Norbert Abbey, Augustine Library, De Pere WI. 414-336-1321
Clarie, Thomas, *ILL, Ref & Bibliog Instr,* Southern Connecticut State College, Hilton C Buley Library, New Haven CT. 203-397-4505
Claris, Nancy, *Librn,* Epsom Public Library, Epsom NH. 603-736-9920
Clark, A, *Librn,* University of Southern California (Architecture & Fine Arts), Los Angeles CA. 213-743-2798
Clark, Alice, *Librn,* Jamaica Free Public Library, Jamaica VT. 802-874-7031
Clark, Alice S, *Reader Serv,* University of New Mexico General Library, Albuquerque NM. 505-277-4241
Clark, Ann, *Librn,* Andover Public Library, Andover NH. 603-735-5752
Clark, Ann M, *Dir,* Rankin Public Library, Rankin TX. 915-693-2881
Clark, Annetta J, *Dir,* Copiah-Jefferson Regional Library, George W Covington Memorial Library, Hazlehurst MS. 601-894-1681
Clark, Artha, *Acq,* Rock Island Public Library, Rock Island IL. 309-788-7627
Clark, Audra, *Librn,* Mid-Mississippi Regional Library System (Walnut Grove Public), Walnut Grove MS. 601-253-2483
Clark, Audrey, *Librn,* Southeast Arkansas Regional Library (Wilmar Public), Wilmar AR. 501-367-3336
Clark, Barbara, *Bkmobile Coordr,* Los Angeles Public Library System, Los Angeles CA. 213-626-7555
Clark, Barbara, *Librn,* Public Library of Columbus & Franklin County (Hilltop), Columbus OH. 614-222-7110
Clark, Barbara C, *Dir,* Pitt Community College, Learning Resources Center, Greenville NC. 919-756-3130, Ext 213, 229, 259 & 273
Clark, Barton, *Librn,* University of Illinois Library at Urbana-Champaign (Education & Social Science), Urbana IL. 217-333-2305
Clark, Betty, *Film Librn,* Birmingham Public & Jefferson County Free Library (Jefferson County Free), Birmingham AL. 205-254-2551
Clark, Betty, *Ad,* Durham County Library, Durham NC. 919-683-2626
Clark, Blanche T, *Bus & Tech,* Silas Bronson Library, Waterbury CT. 203-574-8200
Clark, Bonnie, *Librn,* Kemper-Newton Regional Library (Chunky Branch), Chunky MS. 601-774-9297
Clark, C, *Librn,* Oakland Public Library (Dimond-Rohan Branch), Oakland CA. 415-530-3881
Clark, Calvin L, *Librn,* Public Library of the District of Columbia (Watha T Daniel), Washington DC. 202-727-1228
Clark, Carol, *Historiography,* Amarillo Art Center Library, Amarillo TX. 806-372-8356
Clark, Carol, *On-Line Servs,* Glassboro State College, Savitz Learning Resource Center, Glassboro NJ. 609-445-6101
Clark, Carol, *Ref,* Hammond Public Library, Hammond IN. 219-931-5100
Clark, Carole, *Librn,* Saint Mary's Hospital Library, Rochester MN. 507-285-5647
Clark, Charles M, *Dir,* Mississippi Gulf Coast Junior College, Perkinston Campus Learning Resource Center, Perkinston MS. 601-928-5211, Ext 286
Clark, Charles M, *Libertarian Thought,* Mississippi Gulf Coast Junior College, Perkinston Campus Learning Resource Center, Perkinston MS. 601-928-5211, Ext 286
Clark, Dan, *Music & Dance,* Ohio University, Vernon R Alden Library, Athens OH. 614-594-5228
Clark, Dan O, *Librn,* Ohio University (Music), Athens OH. 614-594-5733

Clark, David S, *Librn,* Harford County Library (Bel Air Branch), Bel Air MD. 301-838-7484
Clark, Deborah, *AV & Commun Servs,* San Bernardino Public Library, San Bernardino CA. 714-889-0264
Clark, Dennis M, *On-Line Servs & Bibliog Instr,* Orem Public Library, Orem UT. 801-224-7050
Clark, Dodie, *Ch,* Madison Public Library, Madison NJ. 201-377-0722
Clark, Donald E, *Exec Vice Pres,* Cooper, Clark & Associates Library, Palo Alto CA. 415-494-7555
Clark, Edna, *ILL & Circ,* Cuyahoga Community College (Eastern Campus Library), Warrensville OH. 216-464-1450, Ext 228, 229
Clark, Elaine M, *Librn,* Springfield Township Library, Springfield PA. 215-543-2113
Clark, Eleanor, *Acq,* Virginia Union University, William J Clarke Library, Richmond VA. 804-359-9331, Ext 256, 257
Clark, Elizabeth, *Lectr,* Boston University, Dept of Instructional Development-Educational Media, MA. 617-353-3176
Clark, Emma, *Ref,* Richmond Public Library, Richmond CA. 415-231-2119
Clark, Evelyn, *ILL,* Dutchess Community College Library, Poughkeepsie NY. 914-471-4500, Ext 388
Clark, Florence, *Supvr,* Greeley Municipal Museum Library, Greeley CO. 303-353-6123, Ext 299
Clark, Florence, *On-Line Servs,* Sun Chemical Corp, Corporate Research Laboratories Library, Carlstadt NJ. 201-933-4500
Clark, Florence, *Librn & On-Line Servs,* Sun Chemical Corp, Corporate Research Laboratories Library, Carlstadt NJ. 201-933-4500
Clark, Forrest S, *Dir of Learning Resource Ctr,* North Country Community College, Learning Resource Center, Saranac Lake NY. 518-891-2915, Ext 222
Clark, George C, *Chief Librn,* Minot State College, Memorial Library, Minot ND. 701-857-3200
Clark, Georgia A, *Head,* Wayne State University Libraries (Arthur Neef Law Library), Detroit MI. 313-577-3925
Clark, Greta, *Librn,* Philadelphia State Hospital, Staff Library, Philadelphia PA. 215-671-4111
Clark, Harriet, *Ch,* Chicago Ridge Public Library, Chicago Ridge IL. 312-423-7753
Clark, Helen S, *Ser,* University of Iowa Libraries, Iowa City IA. 319-353-4450
Clark, J M, *YA,* San Bernardino Public Library, San Bernardino CA. 714-889-0264
Clark, J Terence, *Dir,* Everett Community College, Library-Media Center, Everett WA. 206-259-7151, Ext 260
Clark, James, *Personnel Off,* Denver Public Library, Denver CO. 303-573-5152, Ext 271
Clark, James L, *Librn,* United States Air Force (Pope Base Library), Pope AFB NC. 919-394-0001
Clark, James P, *Chief Librn,* United States Army (Redstone Scientific Information Center), Redstone Arsenal AL. 205-876-3251
Clark, Jane, *Pub Rel,* Ossining Public Library, Ossining NY. 941-2416; 941-9174
Clark, Jane L, *Dir,* Kent State University, Salem Regional Campus Library, Salem OH. 216-332-0361
Clark, Janet, *Hq Librn,* Public Library Services of the Northwest Territories, Hay River NT. 403-874-6531
Clark, Janice, *Asst Dir,* Yale Public Library, Yale OK. 918-387-2135
Clark, Jay, *Chief, Tech Servs,* Houston Public Library, Houston TX. 713-224-5441
Clark, Jean F, *Cat,* Cedar Grove Public Library, Cedar Grove NJ. 609-239-1447
Clark, Jeanette, *Librn,* Southern Tier Library System (Arkport Village Book Center), Arkport NY. 607-962-3141
Clark, Jeff, *ILL,* State University of New York, College at Old Westbury Library, Old Westbury NY. 516-876-3156, 876-3152
Clark, Joan, *Librn,* Frontenac County Library (Sydenham Branch), Sydenham ON. 613-376-3437
Clark, John E, *Dir,* Bay Shore-Brightwaters Public Library, Brightwaters NY. 516-665-4350
Clark, Joyce, *Librn,* Kevex Corporation Library, Foster City CA. 415-573-5866
Clark, Judith M, *City Librn,* Newport Beach Public Library, Newport Beach CA. 714-640-2141

Clark, Judy, *Ch,* Newport Public Library, Newport RI. 401-847-8720
Clark, Kathy, *Librn,* Saint Anthony Public Library, Saint Anthony ID. 208-624-3192
Clark, Laura, *Librn,* Ryegate Corner Public Library, Ryegate VT. 802-584-3494
Clark, Lavinka, *Chief Librn,* Brantford Public Library, Brantford ON. 519-756-2220
Clark, Lenore, *Ref & Spec Coll,* University of Oklahoma MUniversity Libraries, Norman OK. 405-325-2611
Clark, Lois N, *Librn,* Knoxville College, Alumni Library, Knoxville TN. 615-524-6554
Clark, Lois O, *Librn,* Long Beach Community Hospital, Medical Library, Long Beach CA. 213-597-6655, Ext 2351
Clark, Lola, *Librn,* Clarksville Public Library, Clarksville IA. 319-532-3673
Clark, Loretta, *Commun Servs,* Roswell Public Library, Roswell NM. 505-622-7101
Clark, Lynn, *Ch & YA,* Emporia Public Library, Emporia KS. 316-342-6524
Clark, Lynn, *Bkmobile Coordr,* Springfield-Greene County Library, Springfield MO. 417-869-4621
Clark, Lynn, *Librn,* Springfield-Greene County Library (Parkcrest Mini Branch), Springfield MO. 417-887-6486
Clark, Margaret E, *Ad & Ref,* Sheppard Memorial Library, Greenville NC. 919-752-4177
Clark, Margaret P, *Ref,* Vance-Granville Community College, Learning Resources Center, Henderson NC. 919-492-2061, Ext 251
Clark, Marilyn, *Ref,* University of Kansas Libraries, Watson Memorial Library, Lawrence KS. 913-864-3601
Clark, Marilyn G, *Dir,* University of Maine at Presque Isle Library, Presque Isle ME. 207-764-0311, Ext 223
Clark, Marjorie J, *Dir,* North Georgia College, Stewart Library, Dahlonega GA. 404-864-3391, Ext 226, 294
Clark, Martha Fuller, *Actg Librn,* Strawbery Banke, Inc, Thayer Cumings Historical Reference Library, Portsmouth NH. 603-436-8010
Clark, Martha S, *Librn,* Pecatonica Public Library, Pecatonica IL. 815-239-2616
Clark, Maryanne, *Asst Librn,* New York State Judicial Department, Appellate Division Law Library, Rochester NY. 716-428-5480
Clark, Mike, *Librn,* San Bernardino Public Library (Rowe), San Bernardino CA. 714-883-3411
Clark, Mrs Beanie, *Librn,* Dekalb Library System (Tobie Grant Branch), Scottdale GA. 404-292-9382
Clark, Mrs E, *Librn,* Borough of Etobicoke Public Library (Alderwood), Toronto ON. 416-248-5681
Clark, Pam, *Media,* Saint Edward's University Library, Austin TX. 512-444-2621
Clark, Pat, *Bkmobile Coordr,* Kearney Public Library, Kearney NE. 308-237-5133
Clark, Patricia, *On-Line Servs,* International Communication Agency (Agency Library), Washington DC. 202-724-9214
Clark, Patricia S, *Librn,* Franklin Library Association, Franklin VA. 804-562-4801
Clark, Peter K, *Coll Develop,* University of Illinois at Chicago Circle Library, Chicago IL. 312-996-2716
Clark, Phillip, *Asst Librn,* Craft Memorial Library, Mercer County Service Center, Bluefield WV. 304-325-3943
Clark, Phyllis, *Dir,* Lapeer County Library, Lapeer MI. 313-664-9521
Clark, Raymond, *Asst Librn,* Internal Revenue Service Library, Washington DC. 202-566-6342
Clark, Rita M, *Asst Dir,* Cambria County Library System, Johnstown PA. 814-536-5131
Clark, Robert M, *Librn,* Montana Historical Society Library & Archives, Helena MT. 406-449-2681
Clark, Robert R, *Media,* Dekalb Community College, South Campus, Learning Resources Center, Decatur GA. 404-243-3860, Ext 12
Clark, Rosemary, *Ref,* Northwestern University, Chicago (Dental School Library), Chicago IL. 312-649-8332
Clark, Ruth, *Librn,* Gibbs Memorial Library, Mexia TX. 817-562-3231
Clark, Ruth, *Librn,* South Kingstown Public Library (Robert Beverley Hale), Matunuck RI. 401-783-5386

Clark, Samuel A, *Librn,* North Carolina State University (Biltmore Library (Forest Resources)), Raleigh NC. 919-737-2306
Clark, Scott, *Librn,* Moore Memorial Library, Greene NY. 607-656-9349
Clark, Susan, *Acq,* Bentley College, Solomon R Baker Library, Waltham MA. 617-891-2231
Clark, Susan M, *Ch,* Staunton Public Library, Fannie Bayly King Library, Staunton VA. 703-886-7231
Clark, Thomas A, *Circ & Spec Coll,* Valdosta State College Library, Valdosta GA. 912-247-3228
Clark, Verla, *Librn,* Putman Township Library, Cuba IL. 309-785-5386
Clark, Virginia, *Ref,* Great River Regional Library, Saint Cloud MN. 612-251-7282
Clark, Willie F, *Film Librn,* United States Department of Energy, Technical Information Center, Oak Ridge TN. 615-483-8611
Clark, Jr, Robert L, *Dir,* Oklahoma Department of Libraries, Oklahoma City OK. 405-521-2502
Clarke, Alan, *Ad,* Boulder Public Library, Boulder CO. 303-441-3100
Clarke, Arlene A, *Librn,* Fort Stanton Hospital & Training School Library, Fort Stanton NM. 505-354-2211, Ext 222
Clarke, B, *Per,* Carleton University, Murdoch Maxwell MacOdrum Library, Ottawa ON. 613-231-4357
Clarke, Beverley, *Librn,* International Business Machines Corp (Research Library), San Jose CA. 408-256-2562
Clarke, Carolyn K, *Per,* University of Southern Maine, Gorham ME. 207-780-5340, 780-4273
Clarke, Concetta, *Dir,* Hampton Library, Bridgehampton NY. 516-537-0015
Clarke, Danielle, *Ch,* New Milford Public Library, New Milford CT. 203-355-1191
Clarke, Darlene, *Librn,* Combustion Engineering, Inc, C-E Glass Research Laboratory Library, Pennsauken NJ. 609-662-0400
Clarke, Dorothy, *Dir,* College of Boca Raton, Rowley Library, Boca Raton FL. 305-994-0770, Ext 24
Clarke, Edith, *Development Programs,* Seattle Central Community College, Instructional Resource Services, Seattle WA. 206-587-5420
Clarke, Eric, *In Charge,* British Columbia Ministry of Health Library (Film Library), Victoria BC. 604-387-5881
Clarke, Ina J, *Librn,* Schumacher Memorial Library, Schumacher ON. 705-264-3545
Clarke, James P, *Lectr,* Marywood College, Dept of Librarianship, PA. 717-342-6521
Clarke, James P, *Dir,* Marywood College Library, Scranton PA. 717-343-6521, Ext 289
Clarke, Jessica, *Tech Serv,* Rosenberg Library, Galveston TX. 713-763-8854
Clarke, Nancy, *Ref,* Moore Memorial Public Library, Texas City TX. 713-948-3111, Ext 160
Clarke, Norman, *Asst Prof,* Saint Cloud State University, Center for Library & Audiovisual Education, MN. 612-255-2022
Clarke, Polly S, *Coordr,* Northeastern Oklahoma State University, Library Media Dept, OK. 918-456-5511, Ext 413
Clarke, Robert F, *Librn,* National Institutes of Mental Health, Mental Health Study Center Library, Adelphi MD. 301-436-6340
Clarke, Sarah, *Circ & Teachers Resources Ctr,* North Adams State College Library, Eugene L Freel Library, North Adams MA. 413-664-4511, Ext 321
Clarke, Susan, *Br Coordr,* Russell Public Library, Russell NY. 315-347-3210
Clarke, Susan, *Librn,* Russell Public Library (Russell Town Hall), Russell NY. 315-347-2358
Clarke, Tobin deLeon, *Dir,* San Joaquin Delta College, Goleman Library, Stockton CA. 209-478-2011, Ext 277
Clarkin, William, *Lectr,* State University of New York at Albany, School of Library & Information Science, NY. 518-455-6288
Clarkson, John, *Librn,* Del Norte Library, Crescent City CA. 707-464-9616
Clarkson, Mary F, *Education,* Trinity University Library, San Antonio TX. 512-736-8121
Clarkson, Mildred, *Librn,* Preston Public Library, Preston IA. 319-689-3581
Clarkson, Teresa N, *Librn,* Duane, Morris & Heckscher, Philadelphia PA. 215-854-6248

Clary, Ann Roane, *Chief Librn,* Board of Governors of the Federal Reserve System (Research Library), Washington DC. 202-452-3332
Clary, Lillian, *Librn,* Los Angeles Public Library System (West Valley), Los Angeles CA. 213-345-4393
Clasper, James W, *On-Line Servs,* Cincinnati Milacron, Inc, Corporate Information Center, Cincinnati OH. 513-841-8879
Claspy, Lois, *Chief Librn,* Baldwin-Wallace College (Riemenschneider Bach Institute), Berea OH. 216-826-2207
Claspy, Lois, *Librn,* Middleburg Heights Community Church Library, United Church of Christ, Middleburg Heights OH. 216-842-3033
Classen, Joanne, *In Charge,* Denver Public Library (Genealogy), Denver CO. 303-573-5152, Ext 271
Clatanoff, Robert, *Librn & Research Assoc,* International Association of Assessing Officers Library, Chicago IL. 312-947-2050
Clattenburg, Bev, *In Charge,* Nova Scotia Headquarters of Public Works Libraries, Halifax NS. 902-424-5617
Clattenburg, Bev, *Librn,* Public Works Canada (Atlantic Region), Halifax NS. 902-426-2331
Claus, Robert, *Archivist,* Connecticut State Library, Hartford CT. 203-566-4301
Clausen, Elizabeth, *Librn,* Holy Cross Hospital, Health Science Library, Chicago IL. 312-434-6700, Ext 218
Clausen, Esther M, *Librn,* University of Illinois Library at Urbana-Champaign (Commerce), Urbana IL. 217-333-3619
Clausen, Ethel, *Librn,* Kenai Peninsula Community College Library, Soldotna AK. 907-262-5801
Clausen, Nancy M, *Mgr,* Tracy-Locke Advertising & Public Relations, Inc Library, Dallas TX. 214-742-3131, Ext 422
Clausen, Robert V, *Asst Librn,* Centenary College, Taylor Memorial Learning Resource Center, Hackettstown NJ. 201-852-1400, Ext 244
Clausen, Sherry, *Librn,* Westminster Choir College (Westminster Choir Choral), Princeton NJ. 609-921-3659
Clausman, Gilbert J, *Librn,* New York University (Frederick L Ehrman Medical Library), New York NY. 212-340-5397
Clauson, Patricia, *ILL,* Richmond Memorial Library, Batavia NY. 716-343-9550
Claussen, Robert, *Learning Resources Div Chmn,* Tarrant County Junior College System (Northwest Campus Learning Resources Center), Fort Worth TX. 817-232-2900, Ext 208
Claveau, Celine, *Instr,* College de Jonquiere, Techniques de la Documentation, PQ. 418-547-2191, Ext 270
Claveau, Diane T, *Acq,* CEGEP de Chicoutimi, Centre De Documentation, Chicoutimi PQ. 418-549-9520, Ext 212, 312
Clawson, Pearl, *Asst Librn,* Kelso Public Library, Kelso WA. 206-423-8110
Claxton, Lois, *Govt Publications,* University of Waterloo Library, Waterloo ON. 519-885-1211
Clay, Alice, *Ch,* Kenton County Public Library (Erlanger), Covington KY. 606-341-5115
Clay, Causie, *Librn,* Greenwood-Leflore Public Library System (Wilson), Greenwood MS. 601-453-0472
Clay, Clara C, *Per, Ref & Doc,* Dallas Baptist College, Vance Memorial Library, Dallas TX. 214-331-8311, Ext 213
Clay, Mrs E H, *Librn,* Perry United Methodist Church Library, Perry GA. 912-987-1852
Clayman, Ida H, *Cat,* Virginia State College, Johnston Memorial Library, Petersburg VA. 804-520-6171
Claypool, Margaret, *Librn,* Richland County Public Library (Landmark Square), Columbia SC. 803-776-0855
Clayton, Alyce, *Ch,* North Baltimore Public Library, North Baltimore OH. 419-257-2196
Clayton, Beth, *Librn,* Bondurant Community Library, Bondurant IA. 515-967-4790
Clayton, Charlynn, *ILL,* Augusta Regional Library, Augusta-Richmond County Public Library, Augusta GA. 404-724-1871
Clayton, Diane, *Soc Sci,* Hamline University, Bush Memorial Library, Saint Paul MN. 612-641-2373

CLAYTON

Clayton, J Glenwood, *Spec Coll,* Furman University Library, Greenville SC. 803-294-2191

Clayton, John, *Data Processing,* Orlando Public Library, Orlando FL. 305-425-4694

Clayton, Judy, *Cooror Ch,* Northwestern Regional Library, Elkin NC. 919-835-4894

Clayton, Lola, *Actg Librn & Bkmobile Coordr,* County-City Library, Sweetwater TX. 915-235-3532

Clayton, Mary E, *Librn,* Lane County Law Library, Eugene OR. 503-687-4337

Clayton, Mrs Willie, *Librn,* Marshall County Library (Potts Camp Public), Potts Camp MS. 601-252-3823

Clayton, Sheryl, *Dir,* East Saint Louis Public Library, East Saint Louis IL. 618-874-7280

Clayton, Yvonne, *Librn,* United States Department of Agriculture, Science & Education Administration, United States Water Conservation Laboratory Library, Phoenix AZ. 602-261-4356

Cleal, D A, *Ch,* Lloydminster Public Library, Lloydminster SK. 306-825-2618

Cleary, Judith, *ILL,* Johnson State College, John Dewey Library, Johnson VT. 802-635-2356, Ext 248

Cleaver, Margaret, *Ref,* San Francisco Art Institute, Anne Bremer Memorial Library, San Francisco CA. 415-771-7020, Ext 59

Cleaves, Carol, *Budget Officer,* University of Washington Libraries, Seattle WA. 206-543-1760

Clee, June, *Tech Serv,* Dallas County Public Library, Dallas TX. 214-749-8566, 749-8886

Cleland, Mary, *Librn,* Geneva College (Cross Science), Beaver Falls PA. 412-846-5100, Ext 297

Cleland, Mary E, *ILL & Ref,* Geneva College, McCartney Library, Beaver Falls PA. 412-846-5100, Ext 297

Cleland, Monique C, *Librn,* Dartmouth College (Kresge Physical Sciences), Hanover NH. 603-646-3564

Clem, Harriet M, *Dir,* Rodman Public Library, Alliance OH. 216-821-1410

Clem, Helen L, *Librn,* West Frankfort Public Library, West Frankfort IL. 618-932-3313

Clemence, Trudy, *Ref,* Selby Public Library, Sarasota County Federated Library System, Sarasota FL. 814-366-7303

Clemens, Bonnie, *Personnel Librn,* University of Georgia Libraries, Athens GA. 404-542-2716

Clemens, David, *Ref,* Huntington Public Library, Huntington NY. 516-427-5165

Clemens, James R, *Dir,* Goshen College (Harold & Wilma Good Library), Goshen IN. 219-533-3161, Ext 257

Clemens, Joan, *On-Line Servs,* Grumman Aerospace Corp, Technical Information Center, Bethpage NY. 516-575-3912

Clemens, Martha Jo, *Librn,* Lebanon-Wilson County Library (West Wilson), Mt Juliet TN. 615-444-0632

Clement, Bob, *Lit Chemist,* Ferro Corp Library, Independence OH. 216-641-8580, Ext 619

Clement, Brenda, *Librn,* Bethany Baptist Library, Pawtucket RI. 401-724-5520

Clement, Charles, *Tech Serv,* Church of Jesus Christ of Latter-Day Saints (Genealogical Society of Utah), Salt Lake City UT. 801-531-2323

Clement, Emily, *Librn,* Baker & Botts Law Library, Houston TX. 713-229-1412

Clement, Evelyn G, *Chmn,* Memphis State University, Library Science Dept, TN. 901-454-2837

Clement, Hope, *Assoc Nat Librn,* National Library of Canada, Ottawa ON. 613-995-9481

Clement, Lois, *Acq,* Bellingham Public Library, Bellingham WA. 206-676-6860

Clement, Lois, *Acq,* East Baton Rouge Parish Library, Baton Rouge LA. 504-389-3360

Clement, Mrs Robert, *Librn,* Dixie Regional Library (Pontotoc County Library (hq)), Pontotoc MS. 601-489-3522

Clement, Robert, *Dept Head,* Nicholls State University, Library Science Dept, LA. 504-446-8111, Ext 210 or 300

Clement, Russell, *Pacific Islands,* Brigham Young University-Hawaii Campus, Joseph F Smith Library, Laie HI. 808-293-9211, Ext 260, 264

Clement, Susan D, *On-Line Servs & Bibliog Instr,* Detroit Edison Co Information Services, Detroit MI. 313-237-9216

Clement, Wenda, *Media Ctr,* Marion College Library, Marion IN. 317-674-6901, Ext 228

Clement, Yvonne D, *Asst Dir,* Salt Lake County Library System, Whitmore Library, Salt Lake City UT. 801-943-7614

Clement-Sherman, Linda J, *ILL & On-Line Servs,* Fargo Public Library, Fargo ND. 701-241-1490

Clementine, Sister Mary, *Librn,* Saint Mary Hospital, Medical Library, Livonia MI. 313-464-4800, Ext 283

Clements, Anne, *Pub Servs,* Faulkner-Van Buren Regional Library, Conway AR. 501-327-7482

Clements, Cynthia, *Ref,* Richland College, Learning Resources Center, Dallas TX. 214-746-4460

Clements, Hilda S, *Librn,* Jessica L Bramley Free Library, Jordan NY. 315-689-3296

Clements, Lucy E, *Asst Dir,* Suwannee River Regional Library, Seven-County Region, Live Oak FL. 904-362-5779

Clements, Melba, *Librn,* Choctaw County Public Library (Gilbertown Branch), Gilbertown AL. 205-459-2542

Clements, Roger, *Librn,* Anaheim Public Library (Sunkist), Anaheim CA. 714-956-3501

Clemison, Rachael, *Coordr Coop Servs,* Nevada State Library, Carson City NV. 702-885-5130

Clemmen, Jr, Dan O, *Reader Serv,* United States Department of State, Washington DC. 202-632-0372

Clemmensen, Susan, *Ch,* Urbandale Public Library, Urbandale IA. 515-278-3945

Clemmer, Joel G, *Ref, On-Line Servs & Bibliog Instr,* Bucknell University, Ellen Clarke Bertrand Library, Lewisburg PA. 717-524-3056

Clemmons, Nancy W, *ILL,* University of Alabama in Birmingham (Lister Hill Library of the Health Sciences), Birmingham AL. 205-934-5460

Clemons, John E, *Assoc Prof,* Emory University, Div of Librarianship, GA. 404-329-6840

Clemson, Beverly C, *Dir,* Shadelands Ranch Historical Museum, Shadelands History Room Library, Walnut Creek CA. 415-935-7871

Clendaniel, Estella C, *In Charge,* Eastern Shore Hospital Center, Professional Library, Cambridge MD. 301-228-0800, Ext 321

Clermont, Simonne, *Librn,* Universite De Moncton (Law Library), Moncton NB. 506-858-4569

Clespin, Christine Y, *Librn,* Saint Anthony Hospital Systems, Memorial Medical Library, Denver CO. 303-629-3790

Clestre, Marie, *Supvr Inst Libr Servs,* Washington State Library, Olympia WA. 206-753-5592

Cleveland, Agnes, *Librn,* Kensett Public Library, Kensett IA. 515-845-2222

Cleveland, Allison, *Tech Serv & Acq,* Greenwood-Leflore Public Library System, Greenwood MS. 601-453-3634

Cleveland, Ana D, *Asst Prof,* Texas Woman's University, School of Library Science, TX. 817-387-2418 & 566-1455

Cleveland, Donald B, *Instr,* North Texas State University, School of Library & Information Sciences, TX. 817-788-2445

Cleveland, Florence, *Spec Coll,* Hammond Public Library, Hammond IN. 219-931-5100

Cleveland, Granville, *Asst Librn,* University of Notre Dame Library (Law School Library), Notre Dame IN. 219-283-7024

Cleveland, M Berniece, *Librn,* Ketchikan Law Library, Alaska Court System, Ketchikan AK. 907-225-2748

Cleveland, Mary L, *Dir,* Wiley College, Thomas Winston Cole Sr, Library, Marshall TX. 214-938-8341, Ext 70

Cleveland, Mary Louise, *Assoc Prof,* Alabama Agricultural & Mechanical University, School of Library Media, AL. 205-859-7216 or 859-7238

Cleveland, Susan, *Dir,* University of Pennsylvania Libraries (University Hospital, Medical), Philadelphia PA. 215-227-2577

Cleveland, Trudy, *Librn,* Harris County Public Library (Octavia Fields Branch), Humble TX. 713-446-3377

Cleveland, Jr, Cecil E, *Librn,* Lakeland Public Library, Lakeland FL. 813-686-2168

Clevenger, Judy Beth, *Dir,* Scott Sebastian Regional Library, Greenwood AR. 501-996-2856

Clever, Elaine, *Circ,* Temple University of the Commonwealth System of Higher Education, Samuel Paley Library, Philadelphia PA. 215-787-8231

Clever, Shannon, *Ref,* University of South Carolina (School of Medicine Library), Columbia SC. 803-777-4858

Cleverley, Dorothy, *Commun Servs,* Buena Park Library District, Buena Park CA. 714-826-4100

Clevesy, Sandra R, *Dir,* Framingham Union Hospital, Cesare George Tedeschi Library, Framingham MA. 617-879-7111, Ext 531

Clewson, C U, *Librn,* Combustion Engineering, Inc, C-E Refractories Research & Development Library, Paoli PA. 215-647-3440, 337-1100

Click, Connie, *Librn,* Artesia Christian College Library, Artesia NM. 505-748-1236

Click, Helen, *Dir, ILL & Ref,* Texarkana Community College, Palmer Memorial Library, Texarkana TX. 214-838-4541, Ext 215, 231

Clickner, Deborah, *Librn,* Halifax County-South Boston Regional Library (South Boston Public Library), South Boston VA. 804-572-3440

Clifford, Ann T, *Asst Dir,* Pasadena Public Library, Pasadena TX. 713-477-0276

Clifford, John, *Librn,* Southern Illinois University at Carbondale (Social Studies), Carbondale IL. 618-453-2708

Clifford, Naomi, *Librn,* Ernst & Whinney National Office Library, Cleveland OH. 216-861-5000, Ext 240

Clift, Evelyn S, *Curator,* Henry County Historical Society, Reference Room, New Castle IN. 317-529-4028

Clift, Vicki, *Circ,* Memphis-Shelby County Public Library & Information Center (Science, Business, Social Sciences), Memphis TN. 901-528-2950

Clifton, Joe Ann, *In Charge,* Litton Industries, Inc, Data Systems Div, Technical Library, Van Nuys CA. 213-781-8211, Ext 2997

Clifton, Joe Ann, *In Charge,* Litton Industries, Inc, Guidance & Control Systems Div Technical Library, Woodland Hills CA. 213-887-3867

Cline, Betty R, *Librn,* Knoedler Memorial Library, Augusta KY. 606-756-3911

Cline, Carol, *Asst Librn,* Saint Francis Hospital Library, Beech Grove IN. 317-783-8106

Cline, Elva, *Librn,* Morrill Public Library, Morrill NE. 308-247-2611

Cline, Esther, *Librn,* Saint Louis Public Library (Benton), Saint Louis MO. 314-645-2468

Cline, Gloria S, *Pub Servs,* University of Southwestern Louisiana, Dupre Library, Lafayette LA. 318-264-6396

Cline, Joyce L, *Actg Librn,* Wythe-Grayson Regional Library, Independence VA. 703-773-2761

Cline, Margaret, *AV,* Lenoir-Rhyne College, Carl A Rudisill Library, Hickory NC. 704-328-1741, Ext 221

Cline, Nancy M, *Doc,* Pennsylvania State University, Fred Lewis Pattee Library, University Park PA. 814-865-0401

Cline, Ray, *Asst Dir,* Port Arthur Public Library, Port Arthur TX. 713-982-6491

Cline, Sandra S, *Librn,* Newkirk Public Library, Newkirk OK. 405-362-3934

Cline, Sarah J, *Actg Librn,* Gabie Betts Burton Memorial Library, Clarendon TX. 806-874-3685

Cline, Sarah J, *Librn,* Clarendon College Library, Clarendon TX. 806-874-3571

Cline, Shirley, *Librn,* El Dorado County Library (Lake Valley), South Lake Tahoe CA. 916-544-4416

Cline, Jr, Fred A, *Librn,* Asian Art Museum of San Francisco, Avery Brundage Collection Library, San Francisco CA. 415-558-2993

Clingan, Carol H, *Librn,* Cohoes Public Library, Cohoes NY. 518-235-2570, 235-0503

Clingingsmith, Helen, *Librn,* Dunklin County Library (Malden Branch), Malden MO. 314-276-3674

Clinkenbeard, Ellen, *Librn,* Fremont County Library (Shoshoni Branch), Shoshoni WY. 307-876-2780

Clinton, Berthena, *Librn,* Kent County Library System (Gaines Township), Grand Rapids MI. 616-455-1430

Clinton, Janet C, *Chief Libr Servs,* Mercy Catholic Medical Center, Health Science Library, Darby PA. 215-586-5020, Ext 2253

Clinton, Janet C, *Chief Libr Servs,* Mercy Catholic Medical Center, Misericordia Division-Health Sciences Library, Philadelphia PA. 215-747-7600, Ext 293

Clinton, Marsha, *Asst Dir & Spec Coll,* Lincoln Parish Library, Ruston LA. 318-255-1920

Clinton, Marshall, *Asst Librn,* University of New Brunswick, Harriet Irving Library, Fredericton NB. 506-453-4740

Clipperton, Celeste, *Media,* Watonwan County Library, Saint James MN. 507-375-3791

Clise, Eleanore R, *Archivist,* Geneva Historical Society, James D Luckett Memorial Archives, Geneva NY. 315-789-5151

Clise, Josephine L, *Librn,* Fairhill Mental Health Center, Medical Library, Cleveland OH. 216-421-1340

Cloakey, Gladys, *Librn,* John Fluke Manufacturing Co Library, Mountlake Terrace WA. 206-774-2281, Ext 281

Clock, Raymond M, *Librn,* The Citadel (Civil Engineering), Charleston SC. 803-792-7676

Cloherty, Lauretta, *Media,* Cambridge Public Library, Cambridge MA. 617-498-9080

Cloherty, Jr, Patrick J, *Dir,* Salem Public Library, Salem MA. 617-744-0860

Clombor, Susan, *Asst Dir,* Riverside Public Library, Riverside IL. 312-442-6366

Clonts, Mary, *Librn,* Eloy Public Library, Eloy AZ. 602-466-3814

Close, Elizabeth G, *Supervisory Tech Info Spec,* United States Forest Service, Intermountain Forest & Range Experiment Station Library, Ogden UT. 801-399-6370

Clossen, Peg, *Libr Technician,* San Diego County Library (Lemon Grove), Lemon Grove CA. 714-463-9819

Closson, Elizabeth, *Sr Librn,* New York State Library (Education Reference Service), Albany NY. 518-474-5961

Closson, Trudy, *Librn,* Bureau of Land Management Library, Casper WY. 307-265-5550

Closurdo, Janet S, *Head,* Wayne State University Libraries (Science Library), Detroit MI. 313-577-4066

Closz, Jean, *Circ & Per,* Blount County Library, Maryville TN. 615-982-0981

Clotfeller, Mary, *Asst Librn,* Portales Public Library, Portales NM. 505-356-3940

Clotfelter, Cecil, *Asst Dir,* Eastern New Mexico University Library, Portales NM. 505-562-2624

Cloudsley, Donald H, *Deputy Dirs,* Buffalo & Erie County Public Library System, Buffalo NY. 716-856-7525

Clough, Dorothy, *Asst Librn,* Hill Public Library, Hill NH. 603-934-4015

Clough, Elaine B, *Bus,* Ventura County Library Services Agency, Ventura County Library, Ventura CA. 805-654-2627

Clough, M Evalyn, *Asst to Dean,* University of Pittsburgh, School of Library & Information Science, PA. 412-624-5230

Clouse, Loletta H, *Librn,* Knoxville-Knox County Public Library (Burlington), Knoxville TN. 615-525-5431

Clouse, R Wilburn, *Assoc Prof,* George Peabody College for Teachers, Department of Library Science, TN. 615-327-8037

Clouter, K H, *Dir,* Canadian Union College Library, College Heights AB. 403-782-6461

Cloutier, Guy, *Dir,* Universite De Sherbrooke Bibliotheque, Sherbrooke PQ. 819-565-5611

Cloutier, Jacques, *Acq,* University du Quebec: Centre d'Etudes Universitaires Dans L'Ouest Quebecois, Centre de Hull Bibliotheque, Hull PQ. 819-776-8381

Cloutier, Lucien, *Dir,* College De Levis Bibliotheque, Levis PQ. 418-837-7544

Clow, Faye, *Dir,* Bettendorf Public Library & Information Center, Bettendorf IA. 319-359-4427

Clow, Gail, *Commun Servs & YA,* Ossining Public Library, Ossining NY. 941-2416; 941-9174

Clow, Margaret M, *Dir,* Whitman County Library, Colfax WA. 509-397-4366

Clower, Caroline, *Librn,* White Sulphur Springs Public Library, White Sulphur Springs WV. 304-536-1171

Clower, Clement H, *Dir,* Salem College, Clarksburg Center for Continuing Education, Clarksburg WV. 304-782-5011

Clower, Janina, *ILL,* Bexley Public Library, Columbus OH. 614-231-2784

Clowers, Betty J, *Assoc Librn,* Supreme Court of the United States Library, Washington DC. 202-252-3177

Clowers, Francis M, *Dir,* Shoreline Community College, Library/Media Center, Seattle WA. 206-546-4663

Cloyd, Betty, *Circ,* Midland College, Learning Resources Center, Midland TX. 915-684-7851, Ext 214

Cloyd, Julie, *Media,* Midland College, Learning Resources Center, Midland TX. 915-684-7851, Ext 214

Cluff, E Dale, *Dir,* Southern Illinois University at Carbondale, Delyte W Morris Library, Carbondale IL. 618-453-2522

Cluley, Leonard E, *Cat,* Michigan State University Library, East Lansing MI. 517-355-2344

Clum, Audna T, *Librn,* Saint Mary's Hospital, Doctor's Library, Troy NY. 518-272-5000, Ext 210

Clune, Barbara, *ILL & Ref,* College of Saint Rose Library, Albany NY. 518-454-5180

Clune, John, *Chief Librn,* Kingsborough Community College Library, Brooklyn NY. 212-934-5144

Clunie, June A, *Librn,* Veterans Home of California, Lincoln Memorial Library, Yountville CA. 707-944-2422, Ext 279

Clunie, Prue, *Tech Serv,* North York Public Library, Willowdale ON. 416-494-6838

Cluxton, Harriette M, *Dir Medical Libr Servs,* Illinois Masonic Medical Center, Noah VanCleef Medical Memorial Library, Chicago IL. 312-975-1600, Ext 328

Cluxton, Harriette M, *Coordr,* Metropolitan Consortium, IL. 312-975-1600, Ext 328

Clyde, Carol, *Pub Servs,* McAllen Memorial Library, McAllen TX. 512-682-4531

Clymer, Benjamin, *Ref,* Old Dominion University Library, Norfolk VA. 804-440-4141

Clyne, Barbara A, *Librn,* Sullivan & Cromwell Law Library, New York NY. 212-558-3778

Clyne, Rosemarie, *Tech Serv & Acq,* Polk Community College Library, Winter Haven FL. 813-294-7771, Ext 305

Cnor, Evelyn, *Librn,* WSF Industries, Inc Library, Tonawanda NY. 716-692-4930

Cnota, Mitchell, *Librn,* California Department of Justice Library, Sacramento CA. 916-445-9555

Coady, Helen, *Ch,* Taunton Public Library, Subregional Headquarters for Eastern Massachusetts Regional Library System, Taunton MA. 617-823-3570

Coakley, M L, *Libr Supvr,* Bell Telephone Laboratories (Western Electric Technical Library), Allentown PA. 215-439-7648

Coale, Robert, *Acq & Cat,* Olive-Harvey College, City Colleges of Chicago, Olive-Harvey College Library, Chicago IL. 312-568-3700

Coan, Mary L, *Librn,* Mount Vernon Hospital, Medical-Nursing Library, Mount Vernon NY. 914-664-8000, Ext 3218

Coar, John, *Admin Librn,* Rosenman Colin Freund Lewis & Cohen Library, New York NY. 212-940-8726

Coaston, Shirley, *Ref,* Laney College Library-Learning Resources Center, Oakland CA. 415-763-4791

Coates, Marylse, *Asst Librn,* Virginia State Library for the Visually & the Physically Handicapped, Richmond VA. 804-786-8016

Coates, Nilis, *Librn,* Asheville-Buncombe Library System (West Asheville), Asheville NC. 704-252-2047

Coates, Renata G, *ILL,* Carlsbad City Library, Carlsbad CA. 714-438-5614

Coates, Viona, *Librn,* British Columbia Research Council Library, Vancouver BC. 604-224-4331, Ext 245

Coatney, Louis, *Doc,* Alaska State Library, Juneau AK. 907-465-2910

Coats, Arlene, *On-Line Servs,* Sac City Public Library, Sac City IA. 712-662-7276

Coats, Betty, *Librn,* Public Library of Johnston County & Smithfield (Clayton Public), Clayton NC. 919-553-5542

Coats, Jacqueline, *Acq (Acting),* University of Chicago, Joseph Regenstein Library, Chicago IL. 312-753-2977

Coats, Reed, *Librn,* Memphis-Shelby County Public Library & Information Center (Hollywood), Memphis TN. 901-323-6201

Coatsworth, Mary Louise, *Tech Serv,* University of Pittsburgh at Bradford Library, Bradford PA. 814-362-3801, Ext 126

Coatsworth, Patricia, *Chief Librn,* Charles E Merriam Center for Public Administration, Merriam Center Library, Chicago IL. 312-947-2162

Cobb, Barbara, *Off Mgr,* Asgrow Seed Co Library, Twin Falls ID. 208-326-4321

Cobb, Brigida S, *Librn,* American Geological Institute Library, Falls Church VA. 703-379-2480, Ext 221

Cobb, Charles, *Instr Develop,* Jefferson State Junior College, James B Allen Library, Birmingham AL. 205-853-1200, Ext 280

Cobb, Cynthia, *Librn,* Atlanta Public Library (Kirkwood), Atlanta GA. 404-377-6471

Cobb, David, *Librn,* University of Illinois Library at Urbana-Champaign (Map & Geography), Urbana IL. 217-333-0827

Cobb, Eileen, *Pub Info Officer,* Broward County Division of Libraries, Broward County Library, Pompano Beach FL. 305-972-1100

Cobb, Ella, *ILL,* Peabody Institute Library, Danvers Public Library, Danvers MA. 617-774-0554, Ext 0557, 0555

Cobb, Frances, *Librn,* Prince Edward Island Provincial Library (Morell Branch), Morell PE. 902-892-3504, Ext 54

Cobb, Helen R, *Librn,* Plainville Public Library, Plainville MA. 617-695-1784

Cobb, Jean, *ILL & Ref,* School of Theology at Claremont, Theology Library, Claremont CA. 714-626-3521, Ext 263

Cobb, Karen Bosch, *Commun Libr & Bkmobile Coordr,* Fresno County Free Library, Fresno CA. 209-488-3191

Cobb, LaFaye, *Librn,* Memphis-Shelby County Public Library & Information Center (Bartlett Libr), Bartlett TN. 901-386-8968

Cobb, Ruth, *Media,* Normal Public Library, Normal IL. 309-452-1757

Cobb, Sandra, *Music Cat,* Cleveland Institute of Music Library, Cleveland OH. 216-791-5165

Cobb, Steven, *Librn,* LaGrange Township Public Library, Cassopolis MI. 616-445-3400

Cobb, Syble, *Librn,* Claude Public Library, Claude TX. 806-226-7881

Cobb, Sylvia, *Ser,* Oklahoma Baptist University, Mabee Learning Center, Shawnee OK. 405-275-2850, Ext 245

Cobbett, Linda, *Librn,* C-I-L Inc (Central Library), Montreal PQ. 514-874-3921

Cobedesh, J Geraldine, *Acq,* Stark County District Library, Canton OH. 216-452-0665, Ext 31

Coberly, Jean, *Hist, Govt & Biog,* Seattle Public Library, Seattle WA. 206-625-2665

Cobes, Jon P, *Dir & Acq,* Ohio State University-Mansfield Campus, Louis Bromfield Learning Resources Center, Mansfield OH. 419-755-4321

Coble, Gerald M, *Prog Mgr,* United States Navy (General Library Services), Pensacola FL. 904-452-1380

Cobun, Dr Ted, *Instr,* East Tennessee State University, Library Service Division, TN. 615-929-4244

Coburn, Christine, *Librn,* Microwave Associates, Inc Library, Burlington MA. 617-272-3000, Ext 1955

Coburn, Esther, *ILL,* Mark Skinner Library, Manchester VT. 802-362-2607

Coburn, Leonard, *Librn,* University of Illinois Library at Urbana-Champaign (Engineering), Urbana IL. 217-333-3576

Coburn, Morton, *Libr Res & Bldg Planning,* Chicago Public Library, Chicago IL. 312-269-2900

Coburn, Win, *Br Libr Asst,* Ventura County Library Services Agency (Meiners Oaks Branch), Meiners Oaks CA. 805-646-4804

Cocci, Mary Lou, *Ref & On-Line Servs,* Mitre Corp (Corporate Library), Bedford MA. 617-271-4834

Coch, Carla, *Librn,* Southern Tier Library System (Alfred Town Library), Alfred NY. 607-962-3141

Cochran, Alice, *Acq,* Wofford College, Sandor Teszler Library, Spartanburg SC. 803-585-4821, Ext 396

Cochran, Ann M, *Tech Serv,* Patterson Library, Westfield NY. 716-326-2154
Cochran, Barbara, *Media,* Fayetteville Technical Institute, Paul H Thompson Library, Fayetteville NC. 919-323-1961
Cochran, Carolyn, *Librn,* Devry Institute of Technology Library, Dallas TX. 214-638-6480
Cochran, Cindy, *Tech Serv,* Lincoln City Libraries, Lincoln NE. 402-435-2146
Cochran, Doris E, *Dir,* Merced County Library, Merced CA. 209-726-7484
Cochran, Margaret, *Ch,* Jackson City Library, Jackson OH. 614-286-2609
Cochran, Marilyn B, *Ch,* Velma Teague Library, Glendale Public Library, Glendale AZ. 602-931-5576
Cochran, Mary, *Librn,* Highland Park United Methodist Church Library, Dallas TX. 214-521-3111, Ext 60, 61
Cochran, Nellie, *Librn,* Murray Public Library, Murray IA. 515-447-2296
Cochran, Sarah A, *In Charge,* Spokane Public Library (North Hill), Spokane WA. 509-325-3612
Cochran, Willie Mae, *Acq & Ref,* Central Florida Community College, Library Learning Resources Center, Ocala FL. 904-237-2111, Ext 344
Cochrane, Mary, *Librn,* Eldorado Nuclear Ltd, Research & Development Library, Ottawa ON. 613-238-5222, Ext 242
Cocke, John, *Assoc Librn,* College of Insurance Library, New York NY. 212-962-4111, Ext 277
Cocke, Judy, *Ch,* Hobbs Public Library, Hobbs NM. 505-397-2451
Cocke, Peggy F, *Coordr,* Germanna Community College Library, Locust Grove VA. 703-399-1333, Ext 251
Cockhill, Brian, *State Archivist,* Montana Historical Society Library & Archives, Helena MT. 406-449-2681
Cockley, Marguerite L, *Librn,* Meyersdale Public Library, Meyersdale PA. 814-634-0512
Cockrell, Carolyn H, *Ref,* Sinclair Community College, Learning Resources Center, Dayton OH. 513-226-2855
Cockrum, Frances E, *Librn & On-Line Servs,* Trinity Medical Center (Angus L Cameron Medical Library), Minot ND. 701-857-5435
Cockrum, Jean, *Ch,* Dundee Township Library, Dundee IL. 312-428-3661
Cockrum, Virginia, *Asst Librn,* Phoebe Apperson Hearst Free Library, Lead SD. 605-584-2013
Cocks, III, J Fraser, *Spec Coll,* Colby College, Miller Library, Waterville ME. 207-873-1131, Ext 209
Coco, Alfred, *Instr,* University of Denver, Graduate School of Librarianship and Information Management, CO. 303-753-2557
Coco, Alfred J, *Librn,* University of Denver (Westminster Law Library), Denver CO. 303-753-3405
Coco, Madeline, *Chief Librn,* Veterans Administration, Hospital Library, Batavia NY. 716-343-7500, Ext 274
Cocroft, Mary Jo, *Acq,* Mississippi College, Leland Speed Library, Clinton MS. 601-924-5131, Ext 232, 307
Cocron, Fritz, *Dir,* Austrian Institute Library, New York NY. 212-759-5165
Codd, Marie K, *Librn,* Bon Secours Hospital, Health Science Library, Baltimore MD. 301-233-7100, Ext 297
Coder, Anne, *Librn,* Indian Valley Colleges Library, Novato CA. 415-883-2211
Cody, Shirley A, *Dir,* Walla Walla College, Portland Campus, School of Nursing Library, Portland OR. 503-257-2208
Coe, Anne, *Librn,* Sons of the Revolution Library, Glendale CA. 213-240-1775
Coe, Connie, *Tech Serv,* Sir Sandford Fleming College of Applied Arts & Technology Library, Peterborough ON. 705-743-5610, Ext 268
Coe, Gloria, *Ref,* Goldey Beacom College, J Wilbur Hirons Library, Wilmington DE. 302-998-8814, Ext 47
Coe, Joyce, *Tech Serv,* John C Hart Memorial Library, Shrub Oak NY. 914-245-5262
Coe, Marilyn, *Assoc Dir,* Unity School of Christianity Library, Unity Village MO. 816-524-3550, Ext 333
Coe, Mary Jordan, *Asst Dir,* County of Henrico Public Library, Richmond VA. 804-222-1643

Coe, Ngaire, *Librn,* Burnaby Municipal Library (McGill), Burnaby BC. 604-299-8955
Coe, Ralph T, *Dir,* William Rockhill Nelson Gallery of Art & Mary Atkins Museum of Fine Arts Art Reference Library, Kansas City MO. 816-561-4000, Ext 38
Coe, Richard E, *Dir,* Sons of the Revolution Library, Glendale CA. 213-240-1775
Coefield, Otis, *Dir,* Atlantic Christian College, Hackney Library, Wilson NC. 919-237-3161, Ext 330
Coefield, Pearlee A, *Dir,* Barber Scotia College, Sage Memorial Library, Concord NC. 704-786-5171, Ext 437
Coen, James A, *Tech Serv & Cat,* Washington & Jefferson College Library, Washington PA. 412-222-4400, Ext 271
Coene, Nancy, *Ref,* University of Rochester, Rush Rhees Library, Rochester NY. 716-275-4461
Cofer, Diane, *Bkmobile Coordr,* Memphis-Shelby County Public Library & Information Center, Memphis TN. 901-528-2950
Cofer, Linda Landis, *Dir,* Columbus Technical Institute, Educational Resources Center, Columbus OH. 614-227-2463
Cofer, Mary C, *Librn,* Kansas City Public Library (Van Horn), Independence MO. 816-254-8484
Coffee, Guy, *Librn,* Kansas State University (Veterinary Medical), Manhattan KS. 913-532-6006
Coffee, Kathleen, *Cat,* Pittsburg State University Library, Pittsburg KS. 316-231-7000, Ext 431
Coffel, Susie, *Librn,* Darby Public Library, Darby MT. 406-821-3615
Coffey, Barbara E, *Assoc Librn,* Wentworth Institute of Technology Library, Boston MA. 617-442-9010, Ext 344
Coffey, Helen, *Resource Ctr,* Queen's University at Kingston (Education), Kingston ON. 613-547-6286
Coffey, Irene, *Circ,* University of Pennsylvania Libraries, Van Pelt Library, Philadelphia PA. 215-243-7091
Coffey, James, *Acq,* University of Pennsylvania Libraries, Van Pelt Library, Philadelphia PA. 215-243-7091
Coffey, Jeanne M, *Pub Serv,* Jefferson County Public Library, Lakewood CO. 303-238-8411
Coffie, Patricia R, *Dir,* Waverly Public Library, Waverly IA. 319-352-1223
Coffield, Darleen, *Asst Librn,* Lower Arkansas Valley Regional Library, Las Animas CO. 303-456-1770
Coffield, Mike, *Chief Admin Servs,* San Diego County Library, San Diego CA. 714-565-5100
Coffin, Margaret H, *Dir,* Northern Maine Vocational-Technical Institute Library, Presque Isle ME. 207-769-2461, Ext 45
Coffin, Mary, *Librn,* Custer County Library, Custer SD. 605-673-4562
Coffin, Mrs Charles, *Librn,* Historical Society of Early American Decoration, Inc Library, Cooperstown NY. 607-547-2534
Coffman, Fran, *Librn,* Grand County Libraries (Granby Branch), Granby CO. 303-887-2149
Coffman, Glenn, *Asst Dir,* Tufts Library, Public Libraries of Weymouth, Weymouth MA. 617-337-1402
Coffman, Irene, *Librn,* Martin Public Library, Martin TN. 901-587-3148
Coffman, Irene, *Librn,* Memorial General Hospital & Golden Clinic Medical Center Library, Elkins WV. 304-636-2900
Coffman, M Hope, *Librn,* Charles Stark Draper Laboratory Inc, Technical Information Center, Cambridge MA. 617-258-3555
Coffman, Randy, *Ref,* Texas College of Osteopathic Medicine Library, Fort Worth TX. 817-735-2465
Coffman, Terrence James, *Pres,* Maryland College of Art & Design Library, Silver Spring MD. 301-649-4454
Coffman, Jr, Ralph J, *In Charge,* Digital Equipment Corp, Corporate Library, Maynard MA. 617-493-6231, 493-5821
Coffroth, Irene, *Librn,* Somerset County Law Library, Somerset PA. 814-445-5545
Cogan, Allyson, *Ch,* Salem Free Public Library, Salem NJ. 609-935-0526
Cogen, John, *Dir,* Lehigh County Community College, Learning Resources Center Library, Schnecksville PA. 215-799-1150

Coger, Barbara M, *Ch & YA,* Cortland Free Library, Cortland NY. 607-753-1043
Coggeshall, Lucinda, *Dir,* Orange Coast College Library, Costa Mesa CA. 714-556-5885
Coggins, Albert F, *Dir,* Staten Island Zoological Society Library, Staten Island NY. 212-442-3100
Coghlan, Gladys M, *Dir,* Historical Society of Delaware Library, Wilmington DE. 302-655-7161
Cogliano, Betsy, *Cat,* Mitre Corp (Corporate Library), Bedford MA. 617-271-4834
Cogswell, Howard, *Br Coordr,* Saint John Regional Library, Saint John NB. 506-693-1191
Cogswell, James, *Circ,* Princeton University Library, Princeton NJ. 609-452-3180
Cogswell, Robert E, *Cat,* Episcopal Theological Seminary of the Southwest Library, Austin TX. 512-472-4134
Cohagen, Emmett, *Asst Dir IRC,* New Mexico Junior College, Pannell Library & Instructional Resources Center, Hobbs NM. 505-392-6526, Ext 231 & 233
Cohan, Leonard, *Dir,* Polytechnic Institute of New York, Long Island Center Library, Farmingdale NY. 516-
Cohan, Leonard, *Dir,* Polytechnic Institute of New York, Spicer Library, Brooklyn NY. 212-643-5000
Cohan, Lois, *Librn,* Rockland Research Institute, Rockland Health Sciences Library, Orangeburg NY. 914-359-1050, Ext 2315, 2395
Cohea, Gerri, *Ref,* New Martinsville Public Library, New Martinsville WV. 304-455-4545
Cohee, Robert N, *Dir,* Luzerne County Community College Library, Nanticoke PA. 735-8300 or 825-7594, Ext 201
Cohen, Adrea, *Asst Dir,* Free Public Library of the Town of Belleville, Belleville NJ. 201-759-9200
Cohen, Adrienne, *Librn,* Broward County Division of Libraries (Lauderhill Branch), Lauderhill FL. 305-792-8114
Cohen, Anne, *Acq,* Community College of Baltimore, Bard Library, Baltimore MD. 301-396-0432, 0433
Cohen, Anne, *Med Librn,* Sisters of Charity Hospital, Medical Staff Library, Buffalo NY. 716-862-2846
Cohen, Barbara, *Bibliog Instr,* Thomas Jefferson University (Scott Memorial Library), Philadelphia PA. 215-928-8848
Cohen, David, *Acq,* University of Houston (M D Anderson Memorial Library), Houston TX. 713-749-4241
Cohen, Edna, *ILL,* Newton Free Library, Newton MA. 617-527-7700, Ext 24
Cohen, Edward S, *Ref,* Western Carolina University, Hunter Memorial Library, Cullowhee NC. 704-293-7306
Cohen, Elaine, *Librn,* Temple Sinai Library, Cinnaminson NJ. 609-829-0658
Cohen, Elaine, *Librn,* Temple Sinai Library, Dresher PA. 215-548-7400
Cohen, Elise, *Cat,* Equitable Life Assurance Society of the United States (General Library), New York NY. 212-554-2491
Cohen, Gilbert, *Ref,* Rutgers University, the State University of New Jersey, John Cotton Dana Library, Newark NJ. 201-648-5222
Cohen, Harriet V, *Ref, On-Line Servs & Bibliog Instr,* United States Navy (Medical Library), Oakland CA. 415-639-2031
Cohen, Helen, *Circ,* Downers Grove Public Library, Downers Grove IL. 312-960-1200
Cohen, Ilene, *Librn,* Santa Monica Public Library (Ocean Park Branch), Santa Monica CA. 213-396-2741
Cohen, Jackson, *Sci,* Queens College Library, Flushing NY. 212-520-7616
Cohen, Jean, *Dir,* Westminster Public Library, Westminster CO. 303-429-8311
Cohen, Jeannette H, *Librn,* Tobacco Institute Library, Washington DC. 202-457-4800
Cohen, Kathleen F, *Ref,* University of North Florida Library, Jacksonville FL. 904-646-2553
Cohen, Kathleen F, *Asst Prof,* University of North Florida, Library Science Program, FL. 904-646-2553
Cohen, Leonard, *Hist,* State University of New York College, Memorial Library, Cortland NY. 607-753-2525, 753-2221

Cohen, Leonard, *Reader Serv,* State University of New York College, Memorial Library, Cortland NY. 607-753-2525, 753-2221

Cohen, Lila, *Admin Asst,* Mid-Bergen Federation of Free Public Libraries, Emerson NJ. 201-265-5955

Cohen, Linda, *Cat,* State University of New York at Buffalo (Charles B Sears Law Library), Buffalo NY. 716-636-2043

Cohen, Lynne, *YA,* Milton Public Library, Milton MA. 617-698-5707

Cohen, Madeline, *Adminr,* Research Institute of America, Information Services Center, New York NY. 212-755-8900, Exts 454, 456

Cohen, Marcia, *Librn,* Bolster Mills Village Library, Harrison ME. 207-583-4483

Cohen, Margery A, *Librn,* Connecticut State Department of Health, Stanley H Osborn Library, Hartford CT. 203-566-2198

Cohen, Marian V, *Librn,* Payette Public Library, Payette ID. 208-642-3697

Cohen, Mark, *Media,* Georgetown University, Joseph Mark Lauinger Library, Washington DC. 202-625-4095

Cohen, Marlene, *ILL,* Maywood Public Library, Maywood NJ. 201-845-7755

Cohen, Morris L, *Librn,* Harvard University Library (Law School Library), Cambridge MA. 617-495-3170

Cohen, N, *Media,* North Bay Public Library, North Bay ON. 705-474-4830

Cohen, Nancy, *Librn,* Grant Hospital, Medical Library, Columbus OH. 614-461-3467

Cohen, Nancy, *Dir,* Mount Sinai Hospital, Health Sciences Library, Hartford CT. 203-242-4431, Ext 4417

Cohen, Nancy B, *President,* Connecticut Association of Health Sciences Libraries, (CAHSL), CT. 203-242-4431, Ext 4417

Cohen, Phyllis, *Librn,* Ramsey County Public Library (White Bear), Roseville MN. 612-429-0110

Cohen, Robert, *Dir,* University of Arkansas, Area Health Education Center Library, Jonesboro AR. 501-972-2054

Cohen, Rose Jean, *Librn,* Cary Memorial Library (East Lexington), Lexington MA. 617-862-2773

Cohen, Scott, *Ref,* Jackson State Community College Library, Jackson TN. 901-424-3520, Ext 248

Cohen, Sharon, *Dir,* Providence Hospital, Panzner Memorial Library, Southfield MI. 313-424-3294

Cohen, Steven J, *Asst Librn,* Ohio University (Health Sciences Library), Athens OH. 614-594-6581

Cohen, Toba S, *Librn,* Adath Tikvah-Montefiore, Richard Jonathan Cohen Memorial Library, Philadelphia PA. 215-742-9191

Cohens, Ruth B, *Librn,* Bronx-Lebanon Hospital Libraries (Concourse Div), Bronx NY. 212-588-7000, Ext 522

Cohick, Keith B, *Librn,* University of Pittsburgh, Johnstown Campus Library, Johnstown PA. 814-266-9661, Ext 314

Cohler, Patricia, *Librn,* North Suburban Synagogue Beth El, Maxwell Abbell Library, Highland Park IL. 312-432-8900

Cohn, Adele, *Librn,* Temple Emanu-El, William P Engel Library, Birmingham AL. 205-933-8037

Cohn, Alan, *Librn,* Southern Illinois University at Carbondale (Humanities), Carbondale IL. 618-536-3391

Cohn, Anna, *In Charge,* B'nai B'rith Library, Washington DC. 202-857-6600

Cohn, Elizabeth R, *Librn,* URS - Coverdale & Colpitts - URS Madigan Praeger, Inc Library, New York NY. 212-953-8600

Cohn, Jackie, *Ch,* Windsor Locks Public Library, Windsor Locks CT. 203-623-6170

Cohn, John M, *Dir,* County College of Morris, Sherman H Masten Learning Resource Center, Randolph Township NJ. 201-361-5000, Ext 470

Cohn, Mary Sue, *Circ,* University of San Francisco, Richard A Gleeson Library, San Francisco CA. 415-666-6167

Cohn, William L, *Dir,* Nichols College, Conant Library, Dudley MA. 617-943-1560

Cohon, Barbara, *Asst Librn,* PCR Consoer, Townsend, Inc, Library & Information Center, Chicago IL. 312-337-6900, Ext 271

Cohrs, Joyce, *Tech Serv,* Dekalb Library System, Maud M Burrus Library, Decatur GA. 404-378-7569

Cohrs, Joyce, *Tech Serv,* Dekalb Library System (System Headquarter & Processing Center), Decatur GA. 404-294-6641

Coil, Dorothy, *Librn,* University of Notre Dame Library (Life Sciences), Notre Dame IN. 219-283-7209

Coil, Muriel, *ILL & Ref,* Northern Arizona University Libraries, Flagstaff AZ. 602-523-9011

Coil, Pepper, *Dir,* Maryville College, Father Edward Dowling Memorial Library, Saint Louis MO. 314-434-4100, Ext 241

Coile, Nellie, *Librn,* Kinchafoonee Regional Library (Randolph County), Cuthbert GA. 912-995-2902

Coiner, Ann T, *Ser,* Trinity University Library, San Antonio TX. 512-736-8121

Cok, Cindy, *Librn,* Chittenden County Community Correctional Center, Burlington VT. 802-864-0344

Coker, Queenie, *Librn,* Albany Public Library (Arbor Hill), Albany NY. 518-463-7803

Colabrese, Elizabeth, *Librn,* Data Systems Analysts, Technical Library, Pennsauken NJ. 609-665-6088

Colaianni, Lois A, *Librn,* Cedars-Sinai Medical Center, Health Science Information Center, Los Angeles CA. 213-855-2000

Colas, Elisa, *Asst Librn,* Mercantile Library Association, New York NY. 212-755-6710

Colavito, Greta, *Librn,* Boyce Thompson Institute for Plant Research, Ithaca NY. 607-257-2030

Colbert, Bonnie, *Circ,* Elko County Library, Elko NV. 702-738-3066

Colbert, Donnie, *Librn,* Cobb County Public Library System (South Cobb), Mableton GA. 404-948-2274

Colbert, Dudley, *Librn,* Saint Louis Public Library (Barr), Saint Louis MO. 314-771-7040

Colbert, Melissa, *Librn,* Baker & Botts Law Library, Houston TX. 713-229-1412

Colbertson, Lillian, *Tech Serv,* Chicago Transit Authority Library, Chicago IL. 312-664-7200, Ext 754

Colburn, Ann, *Librn,* San Diego Public Library (Mission Hills), San Diego CA. 213-296-2660

Colburn, Virginia, *Dir,* Elmwood Park Public Library, Elmwood Park NJ. 201-796-8888

Colby, Charles C, *Assoc Librn, Boston Med Libr Servs,* Harvard University Library (Francis A Countway Library of Medicine), Boston MA. 617-732-2142

Colby, Doris K, *Dir,* Aurora College, Charles B Phillips Library, Aurora IL. 312-892-6431, Ext 61, 62

Colby, Edmund, *Prof,* Mankato State College, Library Media Education, MN. 507-389-1965

Colby, Marie, *ILL,* Mason City Public Library, Mason City IA. 515-423-7552

Colby, Robert A, *Prof,* Queens College of the City University of New York, Graduate School of Library & Information Studies, NY. 212-520-7194, 520-7195

Colchin, Helen, *Ref,* Public Library of Fort Wayne & Allen County, Fort Wayne IN. 219-424-7241

Cole, Alexandra, *Ref,* Westmont College, Roger John Voskuyl Library, Santa Barbara CA. 805-969-5051, Ext 378

Cole, Alison, *Humanities & Soc Sci,* McGill University Libraries, Montreal PQ. 514-392-4948

Cole, Alison, *Librn,* McGill University Libraries (McLennan Library), Montreal PQ. 514-392-4937

Cole, Anita L, *Librn,* Apalachee Correctional Institution Library, Sneads FL. 904-593-6431, Ext 117

Cole, Anna B, *Librn,* Weinberg & Green Library, Baltimore MD. 202-332-8620

Cole, Arvena, *Librn,* Guildhall Public Library, Guildhall VT. 802-328-4498

Cole, Audrey S, *Librn,* United States Navy (Fleet Combat Training Center, Atlantic Library), Virginia Beach VA. 804-425-4565

Cole, Carol, *Newsp Indexing,* Mideastern Michigan Library Cooperative, Flint MI. 313-232-7119

Cole, Charlene J, *On-Line Servs & Circ,* Tougaloo College, L Zenobia Coleman Library, Tougaloo MS. 601-956-4941, Ext 271

Cole, Christopher, *Tech Serv & Cat,* Cedar Rapids Public Library, Cedar Rapids IA. 319-398-5123

Cole, Claudia, *Librn,* Ohio Education Association, Resource Center, Columbus OH. 614-228-4526

Cole, David H, *Tech Serv,* Great River Regional Library, Saint Cloud MN. 612-251-7282

Cole, Dick, *AV,* Gaston College, Learning Resources Center, Dallas NC. 704-922-3136, Ext 315

Cole, Doris, *Librn,* Fort Scott Public Library, Fort Scott KS. 316-223-2882

Cole, Edna, *Dir,* Pleasantville Free Public Library, Pleasantville NJ. 609-641-1778

Cole, Edyth B, *Dept Head,* Elizabeth City State University, Media Education Program, NC. 919-335-0551, Ext 326

Cole, Elizabeth, *Consult, Fed Programs & Libr Develop,* Georgia Department of Education (Div of Public Library Services), Atlanta GA. 404-656-2461

Cole, Eva D, *Tech Serv,* Odessa College, Murry H Fly Learning Resources Center, Odessa TX. 915-337-5381, Ext 299

Cole, Frances D, *Dir,* West Baton Rouge Parish, Port Allen LA. 504-343-3484

Cole, Gayle, *Librn,* Dallas Public Library (Hampton-Illinois), Dallas TX. 214-337-4796

Cole, Georgina D, *Dir,* Carlsbad City Library, Carlsbad CA. 714-438-5614

Cole, Gladys, *Librn,* Garden City Library, Boise ID. 208-377-2180

Cole, H Ruth, *Br Coordr,* Abilene Public Library, Abilene TX. 915-677-2474

Cole, H Ruth, *Librn,* Abilene Public Library (Eugenia Pickard Memorial Library), Abilene TX. 915-673-0351

Cole, Heather E, *Librn,* Harvard University Library (Hilles Library-Undergraduate), Cambridge MA. 617-495-8720

Cole, Heather E, *Librn,* Harvard University Library (Lamont Library-Undergraduate), Cambridge MA. 617-495-2450

Cole, Howson W, *Librn,* Virginia Historical Society Library, Richmond VA. 804-358-4901

Cole, Irene, *Cat,* Centre County Library & Historical Museum, Bellefonte PA. 814-355-3131

Cole, Jean, *Librn,* Carp Lake Township Library, White Pine MI. 906-885-5888

Cole, Joan, *Dir,* Township of Washington Public Library, Westwood NJ. 201-664-4586

Cole, John Y, *Dir, Ctr for the Book,* Library of Congress, Washington DC. 202-287-5000

Cole, L M, *Info Alerting Servs Suprvr,* Bell Telephone Laboratories (Bell Telephone Laboratories Technical Library), Murray Hill NJ. 582-4612 (Supvr); 582-3740 (Circ); 582-3604 (Info Alerting Servs); 582-3901 (Systs Design Program); 582-3453 (Computing Info Serv); 582-7330 (Computing)

Cole, Leon M, *Chief, Econ Div,* Library of Congress, Washington DC. 202-287-5000

Cole, Lois H, *Librn,* Northern Trust Co Library, Chicago IL. 312-346-5500, Ext 3137

Cole, Lorna, *Librn & On-Line Servs,* Uniroyal Ltd Research Laboratories Library, Guelph ON. 519-822-3790

Cole, Lynn, *Ser,* Cherry Hill Free Public Library, Cherry Hill NJ. 609-667-0300

Cole, Marge, *Librn,* Pikes Peak Regional Library District (Broadmarket Square), Colorado Springs CO. 303-633-6278

Cole, Marsha, *Dir Libr Serv & On-Line Servs,* Midwest Research Institute (C J Patterson Memorial Library), Kansas City MO. 816-753-7600, Ext 251

Cole, Martha F, *Librn,* Beth Israel Hospital, Lassor Agoos Medical Library, Boston MA. 617-735-4225

Cole, Mary E, *Librn,* Rushville Public Library, Rushville IL. 217-322-3030

Cole, Mary Jane, *Librn,* Woodstock Community Correctional Center Library, Woodstock VT. 802-457-2310

Cole, Mrs C C, *Librn,* Martin Curtis Hendersonville Public Library, Hendersonville TN. 615-824-0656

Cole, Mrs T U, *Librn,* Dixie Regional Library (Calhoun City Branch), Calhoun City MS. 601-489-3522

Cole, Nancy, *Supvry Librn,* Ventura County Library Services Agency (Camarillo Branch), Camarillo CA. 805-482-1952

Cole, Nelle, *On-Line Servs & Bibliog Instr,* Marshall County Public Library, Benton KY. 502-527-9969

Cole, Norma, *Librn,* Reber Memorial Library, Raymondville TX. 512-689-2930

Cole, Orin, *Librn,* Reuben McMillan Free Library Free Library Association (Brownlee Woods), Youngstown OH. 216-782-2512

Cole, Patricia N, *Librn,* Florida Hospital (Doctors' Medical Library), Orlando FL. 305-896-6611, Ext 3419

Cole, Pauline, *Coordr,* Hartford Cooperating Libraries, Hartford VT. 802-295-3546

Cole, Robert, *Librn,* Detroit Public Library (Monteith), Detroit MI. 313-833-9175

Cole, Robert Grey, *Assoc Dir,* University of Missouri-Columbia, Elmer Ellis Library, Columbia MO. 314-882-4701

Cole, Ron, *Acq,* Southeastern Louisiana University, Linus A Sims Memorial Library, Hammond LA. 504-549-2234

Cole, S, *Cat,* Kelsey Institute of Applied Arts & Sciences, Learning Resources Center, Saskatoon SK. 306-664-6417

Cole, Sally, *Chairperson,* Illinois Department of Mental Health & Development Disabilities Library Services Network, (LISN), IL. 312-996-1320

Cole, Sally M, *Librn,* Tinley Park Mental Health Center, Instructional Media Library, Tinley Park IL. 312-532-7000

Cole, Sara, *Librn,* Memphis State University Libraries (Law School Library), Memphis TN. 901-454-2426

Cole, Susan, *Sci,* Colby College, Miller Library, Waterville ME. 207-873-1131, Ext 209

Cole, Terry, *Curator,* Saint Petersburg Historical Society Library, Saint Petersburg FL. 813-894-1052

Cole, William P, *Dir,* Saint Louis University, Pius XII Memorial Library, Saint Louis MO. 314-658-3100

Cole, Winifred, *Librn,* Claiborne Parish Library (Haynesville Branch), Haynesville LA. 318-624-0364

Cole, Jr, Herman, *Dir,* Rose-Hulman Institute of Technology Library, Terre Haute IN. 812-877-1511, Ext 200

Colebourn, Claudette, *ILL,* Blue Island Public Library, Blue Island IL. 312-388-1078

Colegrove, Martha, *Librn,* Smethport Public Library, Smethport PA. 814-887-9962

Coleman, Alice, *Dir,* Washington County Library System, William Alexander Percy Memorial Library, Greenville MS. 601-335-2331

Coleman, Alice M, *Librn,* United States Department of the Interior (Office of Public Inquiries Library Geological Survey), Denver CO. 303-837-4169

Coleman, Ann, *Ch,* Anderson County Library, Anderson SC. 803-225-1429

Coleman, Anna, *Librn,* Union Carbide Corp Chemicals & Plastics Research & Development Dept, Technical Information Service, Bound Brook NJ. 201-356-8000, Ext 2732

Coleman, Barbara N, *Librn,* United States Air Force (Peterson Air Force Base Library), Peterson AFB CO. 303-591-7462

Coleman, Betty, *Librn,* Chelsea Public Library, Chelsea IA. 515-489-2525

Coleman, Crenola, *Asst Prof,* University of Mississippi, Graduate School of Library & Information Science, MS. 601-232-7440

Coleman, Crenola, *Librn,* University of Mississippi Library (Library Science), University MS. 601-232-7440

Coleman, Dorothy V, *Cat,* University of West Florida, John C Pace Library, Pensacola FL. 904-476-9500, Ext 261

Coleman, Earle, *Archivist,* Princeton University Library (University Archives), Princeton NJ. 609-452-3180

Coleman, Elinor W, *ILL & Ref,* Roanoke College Library, Salem VA. 703-389-2351, Ext 202

Coleman, Elizabeth, *Librn,* Moore Free Library, Newfane VT. 802-365-7948

Coleman, Ellen, *Librn,* Sexsmith Community Library, Sexsmith AB. 403-568-3681

Coleman, Frances, *Asst Dir,* Jasper Public Library, Jasper TX. 713-384-3791

Coleman, Frances, *Spec Coll,* Kentucky Department of Library & Archives, Frankfort KY. 502-564-7910

Coleman, Frances, *Librn,* Kentucky Department of Library & Archives (Kentucky Collection), Frankfort KY. 502-564-2480

Coleman, Frances N, *Assoc Dir,* Mississippi State University, Mitchell Memorial Library, Mississippi State MS. 601-325-4225

Coleman, Francis, *Asst Dir,* Mercer County Library, Trenton NJ. 609-989-6917

Coleman, Gayla, *Requisitions & Processing,* Oconee Regional Library, Laurens County Library, Dublin GA. 912-272-5710

Coleman, Gloria, *Librn,* Public Library of Nashville & Davidson County (Z Alexander Looby), Nashville TN. 615-255-9503

Coleman, James H, *ILL & Ref,* Suffolk University College Library, Boston MA. 617-723-4700, Ext 241

Coleman, Jean, *Librn,* Washington County Public Library (Lyman Pomeroy Beverly), Marietta OH. 614-984-4060

Coleman, Jeanette, *Librn,* Mid-Continent Public Library (Excelsior Springs Branch), Excelsior Springs MO. 816-637-6721

Coleman, John S, *Media & Ref,* Wingate College, Ethel K Smith Library, Wingate NC. 704-233-4061, Ext 155

Coleman, Joseph, *Librn,* Fairfax County Public Library (Central Library), Fairfax VA. 703-691-3050, 691-2281

Coleman, Judith, *Dir,* Tuscarawas County Public Library, New Philadelphia OH. 216-364-4474

Coleman, Karen, *Librn,* Fairfax County Public Library (Kings Park Branch), Burke VA. 703-978-5600

Coleman, Kenneth, *Pub Servs,* Carnegie Public Library, Clarksdale MS. 601-624-4461

Coleman, Laura M, *Reader Serv & Ref,* Williamsport Area Community College Library, Williamsport PA. 717-326-3761, Ext 211

Coleman, MacDonald, *Librn,* Red Deer Municipal Library, Red Deer AB. 403-346-4576

Coleman, Marie, *ILL,* Bellingham Public Library, Bellingham WA. 206-676-6860

Coleman, Marie, *Librn,* Meade County Public Library, Brandenburg KY. 502-422-2094

Coleman, Marlene, *Reader Serv,* Saint Louis Public Library, Saint Louis MO. 314-241-2288

Coleman, Melanie, *Bkmobile Coordr,* Robert J Kleberg Public Library, Kingsville TX. 512-592-6381

Coleman, Nancy, *Ch,* Stanly County Public Library, Albemarle NC. 704-982-0115

Coleman, R Colleen, *In Charge,* Sheldon Swope Art Gallery Library, Terre Haute IN. 812-238-1676

Coleman, Sandra, *Ref,* University of New Mexico General Library, Albuquerque NM. 505-277-4241

Coleman, Verna, *Librn,* Adams Public Library, Adams NE. 402-988-2225

Coleman, Virginia, *Librn,* Ohev Shalom Synagogue, Ray Doblitz Memorial Library, Wallingford PA. 215-874-1465

Coleman, W Joseph, *Librn,* Fairfax County Public Central Library, Fairfax VA. 703-691-2741

Coleman, Jr, Theodore H, *Proc Servs,* Medical College of Georgia Library, Augusta GA. 404-828-3441

Coles, Allan F, *Per,* New Mexico Highlands University, Donnelly Library, Las Vegas NM. 505-425-7511, Ext 331

Coles, Betty, *Librn,* Spokane County Library (Deer Park Branch), Deer Park WA. 509-276-2985

Coles, Dora J, *Librn,* Saint Marys Public Library, Saint Marys ON. 519-284-3346

Coles, Gloria, *Librn,* Enoch Pratt Free Library (Highlandtown), Baltimore MD. 301-396-5430, 396-5395

Coles, Jayne P, *Librn,* Fort Myers Beach Public Library, Fort Myers Beach FL. 813-463-9691

Coles, Lynne, *Librn,* Mount Clemens General Hospital, Byron H Stuck Medical Library, Mount Clemens MI. 313-466-8147

Coles, Robert, *Rare Bks,* Glen Cove Public Library, Glen Cove NY. 516-676-2130

Coles, Susan Ebershoff, *Tech Serv,* Indianapolis-Marion County Public Library, Indianapolis IN. 317-635-5662

Colesar, Rebecca B, *Archives & Genealogy,* New Jersey State Library, Trenton NJ. 609-292-6200

Coletti, Jeannette D, *Librn,* National Endowment for the Humanities' Library, Washington DC. 202-724-0360

Coley, Betty, *Librn,* Baylor University (Armstrong Browning Library), Waco TX. 817-755-3566

Coley, Mildred S, *Reader Serv,* Alabama Supreme Court, Supreme Court & State Law Library, Montgomery AL. 205-832-6410

Coley, Robert E, *Rare Bks & Spec Coll,* Millersville State College, Helen A Ganser Library, Millersville PA. 717-872-5411, Ext 341

Colfax, Leslie, *Librn,* Homosexual Information Center Library, Los Angeles CA. 213-464-8431

Colgan, Dolores, *Librn,* National Economic Research Associates Inc Library, New York NY. 212-747-3946

Colgrove, Clyde, *Computer Sci,* Indiana Vocational Technical College, Learning Resource Center, Gary IN. 219-981-1111, Ext 28

Collantes, Lourdes, *Acq,* State University of New York, College at Old Westbury Library, Old Westbury NY. 516-876-3156, 876-3152

Collard, Helen, *Assoc Librn,* New York State Library (Documents Processing), Albany NY. 518-474-5563

Collatz, Pauline L, *Dir,* Lansing Community College, Library Media Technology Program, MI. 517-373-9978

Collazo-Davis, Odila, *Asst Dir,* Inter-American University of Puerto Rico, School of Law Library, Santurce PR. 809-754-7215

Collazo-Vidal, Marisol, *Librn,* Lorain Public Library (South Lorain), Lorain OH. 216-277-5672

Coller, Virginia, *Librn,* Lorain Public Library (Sheffield Lake-Domonkas Branch), Sheffield Lake OH. 216-949-7410

Colleran, Tess, *Asst Dir,* Rawlins Municipal Library, Pierre SD. 605-224-7421

Collet, Lois W, *Dir,* D'Arcy, MacManus, Masius, Library-Information Center, Bloomfield Hills MI. 313-646-1000

Collett, Joan, *Librn & Exec Dir,* Saint Louis Public Library, Saint Louis MO. 314-241-2288

Collett, Martie, *Spec Coll,* Weber State College Library, Stewart Library, Ogden UT. 801-626-6403

Collett, Stewart, *Supvr, Info Ctre,* Falconbridge Nickel Mines Ltd Information Centre, Toronto ON. 416-863-7227

Collette, Maria, *Librn,* Saint Luke's Hospital (W L Estes, Jr Memorial Library), Bethlehem PA. 215-691-4227

Colley, Carl W, *Chief Librn,* Veterans Administration, Medical Center Library, Canandaigua NY. 800-462-1130

Colley, Charles C, *Spec Coll,* Arizona State University Library, Tempe AZ. 602-965-3417

Colley, Elizabeth, *Librn,* Mississauga Public Library (Streetsville), Mississauga ON. 416-826-3001

Collier, Cynthia, *Humanities,* Wright State University Library, Dayton OH. 513-873-2380

Collier, Frances, *Ch & Exten,* Neuse Regional Library, Kinston NC. 919-527-7066

Collier, Leona, *Librn,* Greensboro Free Library, Greensboro VT. 802-533-2531

Collier, Natalee, *Fine Arts,* Long Beach Public Library System, Long Beach CA. 213-436-9225

Collier, Ric, *Dir,* Boise Art Association Library, Boise ID. 208-345-8330

Collier, Susan E, *Librn,* Ingersoll-Rand Research, Inc, Technical Library, Skillman NJ. 609-921-9103

Collier, Virginia, *Doc,* Oklahoma Department of Libraries, Oklahoma City OK. 405-521-2502

Collin, Thomas B, *Librn,* Wisconsin Gas Co, Corporate Library, Milwaukee WI. 414-291-6666

Collinge, Alyce, *Librn,* Tucson Public Library (G Freeman Woods), Tucson AZ. 602-791-4548

Collings, Lois W, *Dir,* Nebraska Wesleyan University, Cochrane-Woods Library, Lincoln NE. 402-466-2371, Ext 354

Collings, Lois W, *Dir,* Nebraska Wesleyan University, Library Science Program, NE. 402-466-2371, Ext 354

Collings, Wayne R, *Librn,* University of Nebraska-Lincoln (C Y Thompson), Lincoln NE. 402-472-2802

Collins, Aline, *Ref,* Midland College, Learning Resources Center, Midland TX. 915-684-7851, Ext 214

Collins, Altamese, *Circ,* Tallahassee Community College Library, Tallahassee FL. 904-576-5181

Collins, Anna, *Ref,* Laney College Library-Learning Resources Center, Oakland CA. 415-763-4791

Collins, Audrey W, *Librn,* Ball State University (Library Science), Muncie IN. 317-285-6472

Collins, Barbara, *In Charge,* Seaford District Library, Seaford DE. 302-629-2524

Collins, Barbara, *ILL,* Ventress Memorial Library, Marshfield MA. 617-837-5035

Collins, Bea, *Circ,* Onondaga County Public Library System, Syracuse NY. 315-473-2702

Collins, Betsie, *Librn,* Indianapolis-Marion County Public Library (Broad Ripple), Indianapolis IN. 317-635-5662

Collins, Betty, *Cat,* Acorn Public Library District, Oak Forest IL. 312-687-3700

Collins, Betty, *SOLINET Tech,* Southern Missionary College, McKee Library, Collegedale TN. 615-396-4290

Collins, Billie, *ILL,* Albany Dougherty Public Library, Albany GA. 912-435-2104

Collins, Bonnie, *Librn,* Southern New England Telephone Co (Employees' Library), New Haven CT. 203-771-5200

Collins, Bruce H, *Dir,* University City Public Library, University City MO. 314-727-3150

Collins, Carol A, *Asst Dir,* George Amos Memorial Library, Campbell County Library, Gillette WY. 307-682-3223

Collins, Catharine L, *Cat,* Capital District Library Council Bibliographic Center-Library, Troy NY. 518-272-8834

Collins, Christiane C, *Head Librn,* Parsons School of Design, Adam L Gimbel Library, New York NY. 212-741-8914, 741-8915

Collins, Delia A, *Acq,* Louisville Presbyterian Theological Seminary Library, Louisville KY. 502-895-3413, Ext 52

Collins, Derith, *Dir,* Gas City-Mill Township Public Library, Gas City IN. 317-674-4718

Collins, Diana, *Librn,* Herman Brown Free Library (Marble Falls Branch), Marble Falls TX. 512-756-2328

Collins, Donald E, *Assoc Prof,* East Carolina University, Dept of Library Science, NC. 919-757-6621, 757-6627

Collins, Donna, *Asst Librn,* Lees Junior College Library, Jackson KY. 606-666-7521, Ext 252

Collins, Edward, *Dir,* Kettering College of Medical Arts Library, Learning Resource Center, Kettering OH. 513-296-7201, Ext 5630

Collins, Eugenia, *Dir,* Holmes Junior College, McMorrough Library, Goodman MS. 601-472-2312, Ext 48

Collins, Eugenia A, *Cat,* United States Army (Post Library), White Sands Missile Range NM. 505-678-5820, 3375

Collins, Evron, *Circ,* Bowling Green State University Library, Bowling Green OH. 419-372-2856

Collins, Francis, *Librn,* Cleveland Public Library (Rice), Cleveland OH. 216-231-5062

Collins, Jacquelyn, *Circ,* University of Santa Clara (Heafey Law Library), Santa Clara CA. 408-984-4451

Collins, Jane, *Ch,* Mary Wood Weldon Memorial Library, Glasgow KY. 502-651-2824

Collins, Janet, *Asst Librn,* Kirkland & Ellis Library, Washington DC. 202-857-5000

Collins, Janet, *Librn,* Westbury Memorial Public Library (Robert Bacon Memorial Children's Library), Westbury NY. 516-333-0176

Collins, Jean L, *Asst Librn,* Industrial Health Foundation, Inc Library, Pittsburgh PA. 412-687-2100

Collins, John, *Bibliog Instr,* Boston University Libraries (Mugar Memorial Library), Boston MA. 617-353-3710

Collins, Judith, *ILL,* Bay County Library System, Bay City MI. 517-894-2837

Collins, Lee, *Librn,* Children's Home Society of California, Weltha M Kelley Memorial Library, Los Angeles CA. 213-390-8954

Collins, Linda S, *Librn,* Portsmouth Receiving Hospital (Library Resource Room), Portsmouth OH. 614-354-2804

Collins, Linda S, *Librn,* Portsmouth Receiving Hospital (Medical Library), Portsmouth OH. 614-354-2804

Collins, Lisa, *Media,* Jackson-Madison County Library, Jackson TN. 901-423-0225

Collins, Loretta, *Ref,* Calumet City Public Library, Calumet City IL. 312-862-6220

Collins, Lucille, *Librn,* Brown County Regional Library, Aberdeen SD. 605-225-8580

Collins, M Eileen, *Doc,* United States Army (Natick Research & Development Command, Technical Library), Natick MA. 617-653-1000, Ext 2248

Collins, Mae S, *Librn,* Government Printing Office, Library Div, Washington DC. 703-557-2145

Collins, Marcia, *Art & Music,* University of Missouri-Columbia, Elmer Ellis Library, Columbia MO. 314-882-4701

Collins, Margie V, *Librn,* Brent-Centreville Public Library, Brent AL. 205-926-4643

Collins, Mary Frances, *Pub Servs,* University of Illinois Library at Urbana-Champaign, Urbana IL. 217-333-0790

Collins, Minnie, *Librn,* Kansas City Public Library (Benton), Kansas City MO. 816-231-1600

Collins, Mrs Harry, *Librn,* Statesboro Regional Library (Evans County), Claxton GA. 912-739-1801

Collins, Nora T, *Librn,* Judges' Library Corp, Thorndike Library, Boston MA. 617-725-8036

Collins, Pauline, *Spanish, Portuguese & Latin Am Studies,* University of Massachusetts at Amherst Library, Amherst MA. 413-545-0284

Collins, Reathel, *Librn,* Mountain Regional Library (Fannin County), Blue Ridge GA. 404-632-5263

Collins, Reba, *Dir,* Will Rogers Memorial Library, Claremore OK. 918-341-0719

Collins, Robert, *ILL & Ref,* Chelsea Public Library, Chelsea MA. 617-884-2335

Collins, Rosemary, *Librn,* Association of National Advertisers, Information Center, New York NY. 212-697-5950

Collins, Ruth, *Ref,* Santa Cruz Public Library, Santa Cruz CA. 408-429-3533

Collins, Sandra, *Librn,* Bethlehem Public Library (South Side), Bethlehem PA. 215-867-7852

Collins, Sarah, *ILL & Ref,* Leonia Public Library, Leonia NJ. 201-944-1444

Collins, Sarah, *Ser,* Wells College, Louis Jefferson Long Library, Aurora NY. 315-364-3351

Collins, Sherrill, *Program Librn,* Southern Tier Library System, Corning NY. 607-962-3141

Collins, Susanna A, *Asst Dir & Ch,* Westerly Public Library, Memorial & Library Association of Westerly, Westerly RI. 401-596-2877

Collins, Thomasine, *Cat,* Dekalb Library System, Maud M Burrus Library, Decatur GA. 404-378-7569

Collinsworth, Barbara, *Assoc Dean, Learning Resources,* Macomb County Community College, Center Campus Library, Mount Clemens MI. 313-286-2104

Collinworth, Barbara, *Assoc Dean,* Macomb County Community College-South Campus, Max Thompson Learning Media Center, Warren MI. 313-445-7401

Colliton, Ruth, *YA,* Kelley Library, Salem Public Library, Salem NH. 603-898-7064

Collopy, Deborah, *Tech Serv,* University of Detroit Library (Dental School), Detroit MI. 313-259-6622, Ext 298

Collord, Mrs D F, *Librn,* First United Methodist Church Library, Glen Ellyn IL. 312-469-3510

Collum, Elizabeth, *Librn,* Rainier National Bank Library, Seattle WA. 206-621-4088

Collura, Concetta M, *Ref,* Saint Francis College, Pius XII Memorial Library, Loretto PA. 814-472-7000, Ext 264, 265 & 266

Collver, Gerald, *Librn,* Hamilton Public Library (Kenilworth), Hamilton ON. 416-544-8705

Collver, Mitsuko, *Ser,* State University of New York, Frank Melville Jr Memorial Library, Stony Brook NY. 516-246-5650

Collver, Randall L, *Librn,* College of Great Falls Library, Great Falls MT. 406-761-8210, Ext 280

Collyer, Dolores G, *In Charge,* American Society for Testing & Materials, Information Center, Philadelphia PA. 215-299-5400

Colman, Ronald, *On-Line Servs,* Eastern Michigan University, Center of Educational Resources, Ypsilanti MI. 313-487-0020

Colmar, Mary H, *Chief Librn,* Orange County Public Library (Mary Wilson), Seal Beach CA. 213-431-3584

Colmer, Mary W, *Librn,* University Baptist Church Library, Baton Rouge LA. 504-766-9474

Colom, Isabel L, *Dir,* Inter-American University of Puerto Rico, Ponce Regional College Library, Ponce PR. 809-843-3480

Colon, Felix, *Binding,* University of Puerto Rico Library, Jose M Lazaro Memorial Library, Rio Piedras PR. 809-764-0000, Ext 3296

Colon, Gustavo, *Dir,* Inter-American University of Puerto Rico, Barranquitas Regional College Library, Barranquitas PR. 809-857-2585, 857-3600

Colon, Lucy Doris, *Ref,* Puerto Rico Junior College (Cupey Campus Learning Resources Center), Rio Piedras PR. 809-765-1716

Colon-Ortiz, Madeline, *Acq,* Inter-American University of Puerto Rico, School of Law Library, Santurce PR. 809-754-7215

Colpaert, Nancy, *Ch,* Monroe County Library System, Monroe MI. 313-241-5277

Colpitts, D Corinne, *Ref,* University of Arkansas Libraries, Fayetteville AR. 501-575-4101

Colquette, Richard L, *Asst Dir,* Louisiana State University in Shreveport Library, Shreveport LA. 318-797-7121, Ext 203

Colston, Stephen, *San Diego Hist Ctr,* San Diego State University Library, San Diego CA. 714-286-6014

Colt, Susan E, *Librn,* Utility Research Co Library, Montclair NJ. 201-744-8259

Colter, Carole S, *Librn,* Womans Christian Assoc Hospital, WCA Health Sciences Library, Jamestown NY. 716-487-0141

Coltman, Helen, *Library Tech,* Merrill-Palmer Institute (Kresge Historical Library in Child Development & Family Life), Detroit MI. 313-875-7450

Colton, Margaret, *Librn,* Phoenix Mutual Life Insurance Co Library, Hartford CT. 203-278-1212, Ext 5320

Colton, Jr, W A, *Dir,* Arizona Crippled Children's Services, Hospital Medical Library, Tempe AZ. 602-968-6461

Coltord, Alice, *Per & Bibliog Instr,* West Chicago Public Library, West Chicago IL. 312-231-1552

Coltrain, Jo, *Librn,* Kansas Farm Bureau Mutual Reference Library, Manhattan KS. 913-537-2261, Ext 166

Colure, Gail, *Librn,* Ocean County Library (Brick Town Branch), Brick Town NJ. 201-477-4513

Colvig, R, *Art & Music,* Oakland Public Library, Oakland CA. 415-273-3281

Colvin, Elsie, *Ser,* University of Chicago, Joseph Regenstein Library, Chicago IL. 312-753-2977

Colvin, Martha, *Ch,* Warder Public Library, Springfield OH. 323-8616 & 323-9751

Colvin, R, *Acq,* Central State University, Hallie Q Brown Memorial Library, Wilberforce OH. 513-376-7212

Colwell, David, *Ref,* Susquehanna County Historical Society & Free Library Association, Montrose PA. 717-278-1881

Colwell, Marcia A, *Librn,* Bullard-Sanford Memorial Library, Vassar MI. 517-823-2171

Colwell, Mrs W F, *Librn,* Kyle Community Library, Kyle TX. 512-268-7411

Coman, Elizabeth, *Librn,* Asheville-Buncombe Library System (Swannanoa Branch), Swannanoa NC. 704-686-5516

Comaromi, John P, *Chief, Decimal Classification Div,* Library of Congress, Washington DC. 202-287-5000

Combaz, Clementine, *Librn,* Legislative Library of Manitoba, Winnipeg MB. 204-944-3784

Combe, David, *Librn,* Tulane University of Louisiana (Monte M Lemann Memorial Law Library), New Orleans LA. 504-866-2751

Combee, Norma, *Circ,* Liberal Memorial Library, Liberal KS. 316-624-0148

Combs, Adele W, *Public Serv,* Northwestern University Library, Evanston IL. 312-492-7658

Combs, Doris, *Librn,* Saint Charles City County Library (North County), Portage des Sioux MO. 314-753-3070

Combs, Ferne, *Librn,* Killdeer Public Library, Killdeer ND. 701-764-5805

Combs, Harve, *Bkmobile Coordr,* Knott County Public Library, Hindman KY. 606-785-5412

Combs, Mary, *Librn,* University of Minnesota Libraries-Twin Cities (College Library), Minneapolis MN. 612-373-2826

Combs, Mary De Palma, *Librn,* Mount Airy Public Library, Mount Airy NC. 919-786-7333

Combs, S Edward, *Dir,* Federal Trade Commission, Atlanta Regional Office Library, Atlanta GA. 404-881-4836

Comeaux, Anne, *On-Line Servs,* University of Texas Health Science Center at San Antonio Library, San Antonio TX. 512-691-6271

Comella, Joe, *Electronics Tech,* McHenry County College, Learning Resource Center System, Crystal Lake IL. 815-455-3700, Ext 276

Comer, Cynthia, *Ref, ILL & On-Line Servs,* North Georgia College, Stewart Library, Dahlonega GA. 404-864-3391, Ext 226, 294

Comes, Grace, *Librn,* Lancaster Town Library, Lancaster MA. 617-365-2008

Comes, James F, *Librn,* Ball State University (Science-Health Science), Muncie IN. 317-285-7889

Comey, Dennis J, *In Charge,* Saint Joseph's University Libraries (Comey Institute of Industrial Relations Library), Philadelphia PA. 215-879-7660

Comfort, Frances, *Dir,* Harrisburg Area Community College, McCormick Library, Harrisburg PA. 717-236-9533, Ext 257

Comfort, Hilda, *Librn,* First United Methodist Church Library, Gulfport MS. 601-863-0047

Comins, Rose, *Cat,* Queensborough Community College Library, Bayside NY. 212-631-6226

Comins, Sandy, *Lang & Lit,* Tampa-Hillsborough County Public Library System, Tampa FL. 813-223-8947

Comisky, Gail, *Librn,* San Diego Public Library (Point Loma), San Diego CA. 714-223-1161

Comley, Nancy, *Librn,* Jackson District Library (Springport Branch), Springport MI. 517-857-3833

Commak, Floyd, *Ref,* Leeward Community College Library, Pearl City HI. 808-455-0210

Commerton, Anne, *Dir,* State University of New York, College of Arts & Science at Oswego, Penfield Library, Oswego NY. 315-341-4232

Commons, Roland, *Librn,* Allen Public Library, Allen TX. 214-727-5536

Como, Louis, *Acq,* Slippery Rock State College Library, Slippery Rock PA. 412-794-2510

Compagno, Joan, *Librn,* Kings County Library (Corcoran Branch), Corcoran CA. 209-992-3314

Compan, Marian, *Librn,* Massillon Public Library (Brewster Branch), Brewster OH. 216-767-3913

Compston, Phyllis, *Circ,* Middlesboro-Bell County Public Library, Middlesboro KY. 606-248-4812

Compton, Anne, *Coordr,* Population Information Program Resource Center, The Johns Hopkins University, Baltimore MD. 301-955-8200

Compton, Anne W, *Librn,* Union Memorial Hospital (Library Services), Baltimore MD. 301-235-7200, Ext 2294

Compton, Edwin T, *Dir,* Olathe Public Library, Olathe KS. 913-764-2259

Compton, M K, *Reader Serv,* Liberty Baptist College Library, Lynchburg VA. 804-528-0821

Compton, Marjorie, *Librn,* Reading Public Library (Northeast), Reading PA. 215-373-1614

Compton, Miles S, *Librn,* Simpson College, Start-Kilgour Memorial Library, San Francisco CA. 415-334-7400, Ext 17

Compton, Olga M, *Mgr,* Central Vermont Public Service Corp, Technical Information Center, Rutland VT. 802-773-2711, Ext 266

Comras, Rema, *Librn & Acq,* Hialeah John F Kennedy Library, Hialeah FL. 305-821-2360

Comstock, Edward, *Librn,* Rogers Free Library, Bristol RI. 401-253-6948

Comstock, Ned, *Dir,* Rogers Free Library, Bristol RI. 401-253-6948

Conable, Gordon, *Assoc Dir Commun Servs,* Fort Vancouver Regional Library, Vancouver WA. 206-695-1561

Conahan, Judy C, *Acq,* Lockheed Missiles & Space Company, Inc, Technical Information Center, Palo Alto CA. 415-493-4411, Ext 45041

Conan, Vivian, *Dir,* Port Chester Public Library, Port Chester NY. 914-939-6710, 939-6711

Conant, Ben, *Spec Coll,* Paris Public Library, South Paris ME. 207-743-6994

Conant, Margaret, *Reader Serv & ILL,* College of Saint Catherine, Saint Catherine Library, Saint Paul MN. 612-690-6650

Conar, Hazel, *Librn,* Niota Public Library, Niota TN. 615-568-2532

Conat, Paige, *Librn,* Jackson District Library (West Avenue), Jackson MI. 517-788-4480

Conaway, Charles W, *Asst Prof,* Florida State University, School of Library Science, FL. 904-644-5775

Conaway, Frank, *Hist, Polit Sci & Libr Sci,* University of Chicago, Joseph Regenstein Library, Chicago IL. 312-753-2977

Conaway, Jo Ann, *Circ,* Martins Ferry Public Library, Martins Ferry OH. 614-633-0314

Conaway, Kathleen, *Circ,* Ottumwa Public Library, Ottumwa IA. 515-682-7563

Conaway, Sister M Christine, *Librn,* Saint Joseph Hospital Library, Ottumwa IA. 515-684-4651, Ext 282

Conaway, Tara L, *Librn,* Zeeland Public Library, Zeeland MI. 616-772-2026

Concklin, Betty, *Cat,* Lee County Library System Administrative Office, Fort Myers FL. 813-334-3221

Conde, Lucille, *Librn,* Cleveland Public Library (East 55th), Cleveland OH. 216-361-6232

Conder, Lelia, *Librn,* Parsons Public Library, Parsons TN. 901-847-6988

Condic, Dorena, *Hist, Psychol & Sociol,* Loyola University of Chicago Libraries (Elizabeth M Cudahy Memorial Library), Chicago IL. 312-274-3000, Ext 771

Condini, Marilyn, *Ad,* Bergenfield Free Public Library, Bergenfield NJ. 201-384-2765

Condit, Nancy, *Cat,* University of Arizona Library (Arizona Health Sciences Center Library), Tucson AZ. 602-626-6121

Conditt, Paul C, *Acq,* University of Idaho Library, Moscow ID. 208-885-6534

Condon, Erika M, *Dir,* Mount Saint Mary's College, Charles Willard Coe Memorial Library, Los Angeles CA. 213-476-2237, Ext 233

Condon, William J, *Dir,* Clay County Public Library, Green Cove Springs FL. 904-284-3822

Condron, Jonel, *Libr Sci & Children's Lit,* North Texas State University Library, Denton TX. 817-788-2411

Conduitte, Catherine, *Librn,* Miami-Dade Public Library System (South Dade Regional), Miami FL. 305-233-8140

Cone, Athena, *Ref & Per,* East Lyme Public Library, Inc, Niantic CT. 203-739-6926

Cone, Helen, *Ch,* Haddon Heights Public Library, Haddon Heights NJ. 609-547-7132

Conelly, Jean, *Tech Serv,* University of Massachusetts Medical School, Medical Center Library, Worcester MA. 617-856-2511

Conesa, Lillian, *Tech Serv,* Miami-Dade Public Library System, Miami FL. 305-579-5001

Conescu, Marcia, *Ch,* Glen Cove Public Library, Glen Cove NY. 516-676-2130

Coney, JoAnn, *Librn,* Seminole County Public Library System (Bookmobile), Casselberry FL. 305-339-4012

Coney, Krisann E, *Librn,* Mount Saint Marys Hospital of Niagara Falls, Medical Library, Lewiston NY. 716-297-4800

Confer, Jayne, *ILL,* Pittsburgh Theological Seminary, Clifford E Barbour Library, Pittsburgh PA. 412-362-5610, Ext 280

Confer, Mary, *Tech Serv,* Nampa Public Library, Nampa ID. 208-466-6121

Congdon, D, *Librn,* Redcliff Centennial Library, Redcliff AB. 403-548-3335

Congdon, Nell, *Ref,* New Orleans Public Library, Simon Heinsheim & Fisk Libraries, New Orleans LA. 504-586-4905

Congdon, Rodney H, *Chief Librn,* Federal Reserve Bank of New York (Law Library Division), New York NY. 212-791-5012

Congleton, Caryl, *Librn,* Florida Power & Light Company, Corporate Library, Miami FL. 305-552-3210, 552-3211

Congleton, Patricia, *Librn,* Butler Public Library, Butler NJ. 201-838-3262

Conine, D Dolores, *ILL,* Kaubisch Memorial Public Library, Fostoria OH. 419-435-2813

Conkis, Dixie M, *Ref,* La Grange Park Public Library District, La Grange Park IL. 312-352-0100

Conkle, Marjorie, *Librn,* Delta County Public Library (Hotchkiss Public), Hotchkiss CO. 303-874-9630

Conklin, Betty J, *Librn,* Atlantic Carnegie Public Library, Atlantic IA. 712-243-5466

Conklin, Charlotte, *Librn,* McGean Chemical Co Inc, Plant & Laboratory Library, Cleveland OH. 216-441-4900, Ext 228

Conklin, Curt E, *Cat,* Brigham Young University (Law Library), Provo UT. 801-378-3593

Conklin, Genevieve, *Librn,* Hart Memorial Library, Belle Plaine IA. 319-444-2902

Conklin, Harriet, *Dir,* Kewanee Public Library, Kewanee IL. 309-852-4505

Conklin, Judy, *Cat,* Hinds Junior College, George M McLendon Library, Raymond MS. 601-857-5261, Ext 253

Conklin, Michael, *Ref,* Wells Fargo Bank (Corporate Library), San Francisco CA. 396-3744 or 3745

Conklin, Nancy, *Librn,* Horseheads Free Library, Ruth B Leet Library, Horseheads NY. 607-739-4581

Conklin, Susan, *Librn,* Kent County Library System (Kentwood Branch), Kentwood MI. 616-455-2200

Conkling, Diedre, *Ch & YA,* Yakima Valley Regional Library, Yakima WA. 509-452-8541, Ext 22

Conlan, Ann A, *Librn,* Veterans Administration Center Library, Bay Pines FL. 813-391-9644

Conley, Binford H, *Dir,* Howard University Libraries, Founders Library, Washington DC. 202-636-7253

Conley, Binford H, *Dir,* Howard University Libraries (Moorland-Spingarn Research Center Library), Washington DC. 202-636-7239

Conley, Catherine C, *Librn,* Upper Saint Clair Township Library, Pittsburgh PA. 412-835-5540

Conley, Edna C, *Librn,* Pawhuska Public Library, Pawhuska OK. 918-287-3989

Conley, Helen, *Tech Serv,* Garfield Memorial Library, Clare Public Library, Clare MI. 517-386-7576

Conley, John, *Media,* Parkland College, Learning Resource Center, Champaign IL. 217-351-2241

Conley, Linda, *Cat,* City College of San Francisco Library, San Francisco CA. 415-239-3404

Conley, Margaret, *Librn,* Rosiclare Memorial Public Library, Rosiclare IL. 618-285-6213

Conley, Sandra, *ILL,* Santa Clara City Library, Santa Clara CA. 408-984-3097

Conley, Sharon A, *Librn,* Middlesex Law Library Association, Lowell MA. 617-452-9301

Conley, Shirley, *Pres,* Northern Lights Library Network, MN. 218-299-4640

Conlin, Carrie, *Syst Develop Officer,* Rolling Prairie Library System, Decatur IL. 217-429-2586

Conlin, David B, *Dir,* Frank Carlson Library, Concordia Free Public Library, Concordia KS. 913-243-2250

Conlon, Eileen L, *Librn,* Roaring Spring Community Library, Roaring Spring PA. 814-224-2994

Conlon, Rosa, *Section Manager,* Avon Products, Inc Library, Suffern NY. 914-357-2000

Conn, Debra, *Librn,* Whitehall Public Library, Pittsburgh PA. 412-882-6622

Conn, Elizabeth, *Tech Serv, Cat & On-Line Servs,* Rochester Public Library, Olmsted County Library System, Rochester MN. 507-285-8000

Conn, Richard G, *Curator,* Denver Art Museum Library, F H Douglas Memorial Library, Denver CO. 303-575-2256

Connan, Shere, *Ser,* Stanford University Libraries, Stanford CA. 415-497-2016

Connell, Kathryn, *Ad,* Craven-Pamlico-Carteret Regional Library, New Bern NC. 919-638-2127

Connell, Mary, *Asst Librn,* Mildred G Fields Library, Milan Public Library, Milan TN. 901-686-8268

Connell, Mary E, *Circ,* Louisiana State University at Alexandria Library, Alexandria LA. 318-445-3672, Ext 46

Connell, Michael L, *Dir,* Montclair Free Public Library, Montclair NJ. 201-744-0500

Connell, Patricia, *Dir,* Altoona Area Public Library, Altoona PA. 814-946-0417

Connell, Patricia J, *Dir,* Blair County Library System, Altoona PA. 814-946-0417

Connell, Robert E, *Librn,* Washington & Jefferson College Library, Washington PA. 412-222-4400, Ext 271

Connell, Vivienne, *Ch,* Mount Pleasant Public Library, Pleasantville NY. 914-769-0548

Connell, Wessie, *Dir,* Roddenbery Memorial Library, Cairo GA. 912-377-3632

Connell, III, John J, *Ad,* Ocean County Library, Toms River NJ. 201-349-6200

Connelly, Jo-anne, *Librn,* New Haven Free Public Library (Sweeting Memorial), New Haven CT. 203-787-8877

Connelly, Monica, *Librn,* Fayette Public Library, La Grange TX. 713-968-3765

Connelly, Thomas R, *Ref,* Pace University, Pleasantville-Briarcliff Library, Pleasantville NY. 914-769-3200, Ext 382
Conner, Andress, *Librn,* Vermilion Parish Library (Pecan Island), Kaplan LA. 318-893-2655
Conner, Betty, *Ref,* Hattiesburg Public Library System, Hattiesburg MS. 601-582-4461
Conner, Carol, *Chief Librn,* Veterans Administration, Medical Center Library, Sheridan WY. 307-672-3473, Ext 261
Conner, Elizabeth, *Coordr Educ Develop Servs,* Allegany Community College, Library (Division of Learning Resources), Cumberland MD. 301-724-7700, Ext 35, 36
Conner, Else, *Dir,* Larder Lake Public Library, Larder Lake ON. 705-643-2222
Conner, Hubert, *Media,* Troy State University Library, Troy AL. 205-566-3000, Ext 263
Conner, Jeanne, *Librn,* Canton Public Library, Canton SD. 605-987-5831
Conner, Virginia B, *Librn,* East Providence Public Library (Fuller), East Providence RI. 401-434-2453
Conners, Doris H, *Librn,* Manchester Public Library, Manchester MA. 617-526-7711
Conners, Elizabeth E, *Tech Serv,* Salem Public Library, Salem MA. 617-744-0860
Conners, Margaret S, *Librn,* Good Samaritan Hospital Medical Library, Cincinnati OH. 513-872-1400
Connick, Kathleen D, *Project Coordr,* Tampa Bay Medical Library Network, (TABAMLN), FL. 813-974-2775
Connolly, Ann, *Ref,* Winnetka Public Library District, Winnetka IL. 312-446-5085
Connolly, Betty, *Chief Libr Servs,* Veterans Administration, Medical Center Library, Long Beach CA. 213-498-1313, Ext 2417 & 2593
Connolly, Bruce E, *Cat,* Alfred University (Scholes Library of Ceramics), Alfred NY. 607-871-2492
Connolly, Dorothy M, *Ad,* Salem Public Library, Salem MA. 617-744-0860
Connolly, Elizabeth, *Reader Serv,* United States Military Academy Library, West Point NY. 914-938-2230
Connolly, G Florence, *Fine Arts Cur,* Boston Public Library, Eastern Massachusetts Library System, Boston MA. 617-536-5400
Connolly, Heather, *Librn & ILL,* Atwater Library of Mechanics Institute of Montreal, Montreal PQ. 514-935-7344, 935-1960
Connolly, Jeromy, *YA,* Loutit Library, Grand Haven MI. 616-842-5560
Connolly, John A, *Librn,* Environmental Protection Agency, Solid Waste Information Retrieval System Library, Rockville MD. 202-655-4000
Connolly, Kathryn S, *Actg Librn,* Bronx Psychiatric Center Library, Bronx NY. 212-931-0600, Ext 2572, 2348
Connolly, M A, *Admin Asst,* Warminster Township Free Library, Warminster PA. 215-672-4362
Connolly, Sister Madeline, *Cat,* Saint Francis Xavier University, Angus L Macdonald Library, Antigonish NS. 902-867-2267
Connolly, William, *Instr,* Illinois Valley Community College, Library Technical Assistant Program, IL. 815-224-2720
Connon, Jesse, *Librn,* Kent County Municipal Public Library (Blenheim Public), Blenheim ON. 519-676-3174
Connor, Camille, *Ch,* Fort Worth Public Library, Fort Worth TX. 817-870-7700
Connor, Carol J, *Dir,* Lincoln City Libraries, Lincoln NE. 402-435-2146
Connor, Christine, *Librn,* Saint Barnabas Medical Center, Medical Staff Library, Livingston NJ. 201-533-5050
Connor, Evelyn, *Librn,* Ashby Free Public Library, Ashby MA. 617-386-5377
Connor, Evelyn, *Dir,* Douglas County Public Library, Castle Rock CO. 303-688-5157
Connor, Jerri L, *Librn,* Chicago Public Library (Avalon), Chicago IL. 312-768-5234
Connor, Mary Beth, *Librn,* Auxiliary Law Library of Dade County at Miami Beach, Miami Beach FL. 305-538-0314
Connor, Nellie, *Librn,* Predicasts, Inc, Information Center, Cleveland OH. 216-795-3000
Connor, Patricia, *Librn,* Marian College Library, Indianapolis IN. 317-924-3291
Connor, Richard J, *Dir,* Sandwich Public Library, Sandwich MA. 617-888-0625

Connors, Jean M, *Ad,* South Huntington Public Library, Huntington Station NY. 516-549-4411
Connors, John F, *Chief Librn,* Veterans Administration, Medical Center Library, Albany NY. 518-462-3311, Ext 349
Connors, Linda, *Acq,* Drew University, Rose Memorial Library, Madison NJ. 201-377-3000, Ext 469
Connors, William, *Dir,* State University of New York, College at New Paltz, Sojourner Truth Library, New Paltz NY. 914-257-2204
Conover, Craig, *Dir,* Sussex County Library System, Sussex County Area Reference Library, Newton NJ. 201-948-3660
Conover, Janet, *Dir,* Port Jervis Free Library, Port Jervis NY. 914-856-7313
Conover, Robert W, *Dir,* Pasadena Public Library, Pasadena CA. 213-577-4066
Conoway, Betty, *Acq,* Northeast Regional Library, Corinth MS. 601-287-2441
Conrad, Agnes C, *Librn,* Hawaii State Archives, Honolulu HI. 808-548-2357
Conrad, Ann, *Libr Technician,* San Diego County Library (Del Mar Branch), Del Mar CA. 714-755-1666
Conrad, Augusta, *Librn,* Peotone Public Library District, Peotone IL. 312-258-3400
Conrad, Carolyn, *Asst Librn, Acq & Br Coordr,* Fort Bend County Library, Richmond TX. 713-342-4455
Conrad, Elizabeth, *Libr Tech,* Milwaukee Area Technical College Library, Mequon WI. 414-278-6205
Conrad, Ethel, *Dir,* Massillon Public Library, Massillon OH. 216-832-9831
Conrad, Frances M, *Librn,* Shelter Rock Public Library, Albertson NY. 516-248-7363
Conrad, James, *Univ Archives,* East Texas State University, James Gilliam Gee Library, Commerce TX. 214-886-5717
Conrad, Judy, *Asst Librn,* Henry County Library, Clinton MO. 816-885-2612
Conrad, Kay, *Ref,* Fond Du Lac City-County Library Service, Fond du Lac WI. 414-921-3670
Conrad, Kay, *Ref,* Mid-Wisconsin Federated Library System, Fond du Lac WI. 414-921-3670
Conrad, Mickey, *Tech Serv,* Daniel, Mann, Johnson & Mendenhall Library, Los Angeles CA. 213-381-3663, Ext 126, 127
Conrad, Norma, *Librn,* Earlham Public Library, Earlham IA. 515-758-2121
Conrad, Patricia R, *Ch,* Glenwood Public Library, Glenwood IA. 712-527-3286
Conrow, Jane, *ILL,* Arizona State University Library, Tempe AZ. 602-965-3417
Conroy, Audrey, *Librn, On-Line Servs & Bibliog Instr,* Canadian Department of Fisheries & Oceans (Regional Library), Saint John's NF. 709-737-2022
Conroy, Janice T, *Bibliog Instr,* Factory Mutual Research Corp, Technical Information Center, Norwood MA. 617-762-4300
Conroy, Jule R, *Librn,* Chicago Public Library (Beverly), Chicago IL. 312-445-7715
Conroy, Lisa, *Librn,* Old Saint Mary's Church, Paulist Library, San Francisco CA. 415-362-0959
Conroy, Mrs Robert J, *Dir,* Goshen Library & Historical Society, Goshen NY. 914-294-6606
Conroy, Patricia, *Librn,* East Grand Forks Public Library, East Grand Forks MN. 218-773-9121
Conroy, Ruth, *Curric Libr,* Boston State College Library, Boston MA. 617-731-3300
Conry, Jonny Rose, *Librn,* Tracy City Public Library, Tracy City TN. 615-592-6512
Consales, Judy, *Librn,* Monmouth Medical Center, Dr Frank J Altschul Medical Library, Long Branch NJ. 201-222-5200, Ext 394, 708
Conser, Mary, *ILL, AV & Circ,* Lorain Public Library, Lorain OH. 216-244-1192
Considine, Joseph D, *Reader Serv & Acq,* New England College, H Raymond Danforth Library, Henniker NH. 603-428-2344
Constance, Dorothy, *Ref,* Peter White Public Library, Marquette MI. 906-228-9510
Constant, Sondra, *Librn,* Goodyear Aerospace Corp Library, Akron OH. 216-794-2557
Constantin, Judie, *Commun Servs,* Jacksonville Public Library System, Haydon Burns Library, Jacksonville FL. 904-633-6870
Constantine, Pauline, *Circ,* Ohio State University Libraries (Vocational Education Research Library), Columbus OH. 614-486-3655, Ext 221

Constantini, Kathaleen M, *Instr,* California State University-Los Angeles, Library Services Credential Program, CA. 213-224-3765
Conte, Joyce, *Ad,* East Detroit Memorial Library, East Detroit MI. 313-775-7221
Converse, Mrs Dale, *Librn,* Waynoka Public Library, Waynoka OK. 405-824-4501
Converse, William, *Arts & Humanities Libr,* University of Calgary Library, Calgary AB. 403-284-5954
Conway, Bernard, *Acq,* West Virginia University, University Library, Morgantown WV. 304-293-4040
Conway, Claire, *Ref,* Schwenkfelder Library, Pennsburg PA. 215-679-7175
Conway, Colleen, *ILL,* Grinnell College, Burling Library, Grinnell IA. 515-236-6181, Ext 598
Conway, Florrie, *Dir,* Wayland Baptist College, Van Howeling Memorial Library, Plainview TX. 806-296-5521, Ext 29
Conway, Jeanne, *Ref & Spec Coll,* Gallaudet College, Edward Miner Gallaudet Memorial Library, Washington DC. 202-651-5566
Conway, Judy, *Dir,* Warner Library, Tarrytown NY. 914-631-2189
Conway, Julie, *Acq,* John Carroll University, Grasselli Library, University Heights OH. 491-4233 & 491-4231
Conway, Merrilee, *Ch,* Renton Public Library, Renton WA. 206-235-2610
Conway, Rita, *Asst Librn,* Le Boeuf, Lamb, Leiby & MacRae Library, New York NY. 212-269-1100
Conwell, Mary K, *Librn,* New York Public Library (Hunt's Point), New York NY. 212-542-2996
Conyers, John, *Ser,* University of Texas at San Antonio Library, San Antonio TX. 512-691-4570
Conyne, Rita, *Librn,* Pennwalt Corp, Pharmaceutical Div Research Library, Rochester NY. 716-271-1000, Ext 330
Coogan, Elizabeth C, *ILL, Humanities-Soc Sci,* Brown University (University Library), Providence RI. 401-863-2167
Coogan, Helen M, *Supvr,* Rockwell International, Science Center Library, Thousand Oaks CA. 805-498-4545, Ext 414
Coogan, Inge M, *Dir,* Southold Free Library, Southold NY. 516-765-2077
Cook, Alice, *Librn,* Presque Isle County Library, Rogers City MI. 517-734-2477
Cook, Angie, *Asst Librn, Br Coordr & Flm Coordr,*West Georgia Regional Library, Neva Lomason Memorial Library, Carrollton GA. 404-832-1381
Cook, Catherine, *Ad,* Northland Public Library, Pittsburgh PA. 412-366-8100, 366-8167
Cook, Charles T, *Dir,* Portsmouth Public Library, Portsmouth OH. 614-354-5688
Cook, Christopher C, *Dir,* Addison Gallery of American Art Library, Andover MA. 617-475-7515
Cook, Colleen, *Librn,* Corvallis Public Library (North Albany Branch), Albany OR. 503-926-6073
Cook, Dave, *Doc,* McMaster University, Hamilton ON. 416-525-9140
Cook, Donald C, *Asst Dir Publ Servs,* State University of New York, Frank Melville Jr Memorial Library, Stony Brook NY. 516-246-5650
Cook, Dorothy H, *Librn,* Fryeburg Public Library, Fryeburg ME. 207-935-2731
Cook, Douglas, *Dir,* Lancaster Bible College, Stoll Memorial Library, Lancaster PA. 717-569-7071, Ext 49
Cook, Douglas, *Media,* Messiah College, Murray Learning Resources Center, Grantham PA. 717-766-2511, Ext 380
Cook, Earleen, *Soc Sci,* University of Texas at Arlington Library, Arlington TX. 817-273-3391
Cook, Esther M, *Librn,* Westminster Presbyterian Church Library, Alexandria VA. 703-549-4767
Cook, Florence, *Librn,* Tipp City Public Library, Tipp City OH. 513-667-3826
Cook, Florence, *Cat,* Winebrenner Theological Seminary Library, Findlay OH. 419-422-4824, Ext 6
Cook, Gail F, *Assoc Dir,* California State University Dominguez Hills, Educational Resources Center, Carson CA. 213-515-3700
Cook, Garnetta, *AV,* Illinois State Library, Springfield IL. 217-782-2994

Cook, Gordon, *Dir,* Northern Virginia Community College Libraries (Woodbridge Campus), Woodbridge VA. 703-670-2191, Ext 217

Cook, Gwen, *ILL,* Albany County Public Library, Laramie WY. 307-745-3365

Cook, Hazel, *Librn,* Bloomfield Public Library, Bloomfield IA. 515-664-2209

Cook, Iomogene, *Ch,* United States Air Force (Scott Air Force Base Library), Scott AFB IL. 618-256-5100

Cook, Jealeen, *Librn,* Birmingham Public & Jefferson County Free Library (Slossfield), Birmingham AL. 205-254-2551

Cook, Jean, *Ser,* Iowa State University Library, Ames IA. 515-294-1442

Cook, Jean, *Librn,* Lockport Township Public Library (Crest Hill), Crest Hill IL. 815-725-0234

Cook, Joe L, *Asst Dir,* Texas Christian University, Mary Couts Burnett Library, Fort Worth TX. 817-921-7106

Cook, Juanita, *Instr,* University of Arkansas at Pine Bluff, Educational Media & Services, AR. 501-535-6700, Ext 322

Cook, Julian I, *Dir,* Temple Sinai of North Dade, Hollander-Rachleff Library, North Miami Beach FL. 305-932-9010

Cook, Lana, *Librn,* Southwest Arkansas Regional Library (Polk County), Mena AR. 501-777-4564

Cook, Margaret C, *Mss & Rare Books,* College of William & Mary in Virginia, Earl Gregg Swem Library, Williamsburg VA. 804-253-4404

Cook, Marion E, *Dir,* Meriden Public Library, Meriden CT. 203-238-2344

Cook, Marjorie, *Librn,* West Volusia Memorial Hospital, Medical Library, De Land FL. 904-734-3320, Ext 539

Cook, Mary, *Asst Dir & Ref,* East Texas State University, James Gilliam Gee Library, Commerce TX. 214-886-5717

Cook, Mary Aline, *Dir, Rare Bks & Spec Coll,* Working Men's Institute Library, New Harmony IN. 812-682-4806

Cook, Mary Jo, *Librn,* Cleveland Public Library (Woodhill), Cleveland OH. 216-721-7970

Cook, Mary S, *Librn,* Shrewsbury Borough Public Library, Shrewsbury PA. 717-235-5806

Cook, Meredith, *ILL,* Etta C Ross Memorial Library, Blue Earth Public Library, Blue Earth MN. 507-526-5012

Cook, Merribeth, *Librn,* Saint Louis Public Library (Buder), Saint Louis MO. 314-352-2900

Cook, Miriam, *Bibliog Instr,* Arkansas Tech University, Tomlinson Library, Russellville AR. 501-968-0304

Cook, Mrs Donald C, *Dir,* Emma S Clark Memorial Library, Setauket NY. 516-941-4080

Cook, Mrs E G, *Librn,* Meriden Community Library, Meriden KS. 913-484-2217

Cook, Patricia A, *Librn,* National Marine Fisheries Service, Northwest Fisheries Center Library, Seattle WA. 206-442-4760

Cook, Paul, *Dir,* Vancouver Community College Libraries (King Edward Campus Library), Vancouver BC. 604-731-4614

Cook, Phyllis, *Librn,* Coleraine Public Library, Coleraine MN. 218-245-2315

Cook, Rachel D, *Govt Doc,* United States Army (Morris Swett Library), Fort Sill OK. 405-351-4525, 351-4477

Cook, Richard L, *Librn,* Hinsdale Sanitarium & Hospital, A C Larson Library, Hinsdale IL. 312-887-2868

Cook, Romilda F, *Librn,* Baptist Medical Center, Clyde L Sibley Medical Library, Birmingham AL. 205-783-3078

Cook, Ruth, *In Charge,* Shepherd of the Valley Lutheran Church Library, Phoenix AZ. 602-249-1936

Cook, Ruth A, *Libr Tech,* United States Food & Drug Administration, Winchester Engineering & Analytical Center Library, Winchester MA. 617-729-5700

Cook, Sally, *Ref,* Seymour Library, Auburn NY. 315-252-2571

Cook, Samuel C, *Assoc Dir,* Saint Francis College, McGarry Library, Brooklyn NY. 212-522-2300, Ext 205, 207

Cook, Thomas G, *Dean,* Ferris State College, Library Technology Program & School Media Specialist Program, MI. 616-796-9971, Ext 588

Cook, Wendell, *Librn,* Atlanta Public Library (Sandy Springs Branch), Sandy Springs GA. 404-255-4085

Cooke, Anna L, *Dir & Bibliog Instr,* Lane College, J K Daniels Library, Jackson TN. 901-424-4600, Ext 274

Cooke, Barbara, *ILL,* E C Scranton Memorial Library, Madison CT. 203-245-7365

Cooke, Bette L, *Dept Head,* Central Missouri State University, Dept of Library Science and Instructional Technology, MO. 816-429-4835

Cooke, Constance B, *Dir,* University of Connecticut, Southeastern Branch Library, Groton CT. 203-446-1020, Ext 267

Cooke, Deborah, *Ch,* Lexington County Circulating Library, Batesburg SC. 803-532-9223

Cooke, Dorothy L, *Univ Librn,* Dalhousie University, Izaak Walton Killam Memorial Library (Humanities & Social Sciences), Macdonald Memorial Library (Science), Halifax NS. 902-424-3601

Cooke, Eileen D, *Dir,* American Library Association, Washington Office, Washington DC. 202-547-4440

Cooke, Harry L, *Dir,* Catawba Valley Technical College, Learning Resource Center, Hickory NC. 704-327-9124, Ext 257

Cooke, Helen, *Librn,* Elkhart Public Library (Blind & Physically Handicapped Services), Elkhart IN. 219-295-5463, Ext 23

Cooke, Joan F, *Outreach Servs,* Finger Lakes Library System, Ithaca NY. 607-273-4074

Cooke, Mabel, *Librn,* North-West Regional Library (Benito Branch), Benito MB. 204-539-2446

Cooke, Marcia Lynn, *Librn,* University of Wisconsin-Madison (Woodman Astronomical Library), Madison WI. 608-262-3521

Cooke, Marischa B, *Dir,* Caldwell Community College & Technical Institute Library, Lenoir NC. 704-728-4323

Cooke, Mrs Dudley S, *Librn,* Rocky Hill Historical Society, Academy Hall Museum Library, Rocky Hill CT. 203-563-8710

Cooke, Mrs G A, *Librn,* Boreal Institute for Northern Studies Library, Edmonton AB. 403-432-4409

Cooke, Nita, *Librn,* University of Alberta (Boreal Institute for Northern Studies), Edmonton AB. 403-432-4409

Cooke, O A, *Librn,* Canada Department of National Defense (Directorate of History Library), Ottawa ON. 613-992-7849

Cooke, Sarah, *Archivist,* Tippecanoe County Historical Association, Alameda McCollough Library, Lafayette IN. 317-742-8411

Cookingham, Robert, *Bus-Personnel Mgr,* Massachusetts Board of Library Commissioners, Office for the Development of Library Services, Boston MA. 617-267-9400

Cooklock, Richard A, *Dir,* University of Wisconsin-River Falls, Chalmer Davee Library, River Falls WI. 715-425-3321

Cooks, Clarice, *Ref,* San Mateo Public Library, San Mateo CA. 415-574-6955

Cooksey, Dorothy, *Librn,* Dublin Public Library, Dublin IN. 317-478-6206

Cooksey, Muriel, *Bkmobile Coordr,* Garfield County Free Library, Jordan MT. 406-557-2297

Cooksey, Muriel D, *Dir,* Miles City Public Library, Sagebrush Federation of Libraries, Miles City MT. 406-232-1496

Cookson, Doris M, *Dir,* Rochester Public Library, Rochester PA. 412-774-7783

Cooley, Alice, *Media Librn,* University of California, Los Angeles (Office of Instructional Development, Instructional Media Library), Los Angeles CA. 213-825-0755

Cooley, Betsy, *Librn,* Oliver Wolcott Library, Litchfield Public Library, Litchfield CT. 203-567-8030

Cooley, Daniel R, *Librn,* Stark County District Library (North), Canton OH. 216-456-4356

Cooley, Everett L, *Spec Coll,* University of Utah (Marriott Library), Salt Lake City UT. 801-581-8558

Cooley, Gen, *Tech Serv,* Beaufort County Library, Beaufort SC. 803-524-0762

Cooley, Lillian, *Asst Dir & Tech Serv,* Millsaps College, Millsaps-Wilson Library, Jackson MS. 601-354-5201, Ext 324

Cooley, Margaret, *Librn,* Akron Public Library, Akron CO. 303-345-6543, 345-6818

Cooley, Patricia, *Cat,* Jones County Junior College Memorial Library & Media Center, Ellisville MS. 601-477-9311, Ext 298

Coolidge, Lowell, *Spec Coll,* College of Wooster, Andrews Library, Wooster OH. 216-264-1234, Ext 483

Coolidge, Richard P, *Librn,* South Carolina Department of Corrections, Library Services, Columbia SC. 803-758-6700, 758-6438

Coombe, Jane, *Librn,* Saskatchewan Department of Labour (Women's Division), Regina SK. 306-565-2465

Coombs, Charles, *Media,* Cape Cod Community College, Library-Learning Resource Center, West Barnstable MA. 617-362-2131, Ext 341, 345

Coombs, Elisabeth G, *Tech Serv,* Fairfield University, Gustav & Dagmar Nyselius Library, Fairfield CT. 203-255-5411, Ext 2451

Coombs, Rosemarie, *Librn,* Westfield Athenaeum (North Side), Westfield MA. 413-562-6404

Coomer, Myrna, *Librn,* Lake Cumberland Regional Library, Columbia KY. 502-384-4211

Coomes, Helen, *Librn,* Graves Memorial Public Library, Saint Paul KS. 316-449-2266

Coomes, Kristy, *Chief Spec Servs,* Washington State Library, Olympia WA. 206-753-5592

Coomes, Kristy, *Suprv Institutional Libr Servs,* Washington State Library, Olympia WA. 206-753-5592

Coomes, Kristy L, *Regional Dir,* Larch Mountain Honor Camp, Yacolt WA. 206-696-6341

Coon, Dorothy, *Librn,* Wickenburg Public Library, Wickenburg AZ. 602-684-2665

Coon, Marilyn R, *Asst Librn,* Saint Mary of Nazareth Hospital, Sr Stella Louise Medical Library, Chicago IL. 312-770-2219

Coon, Nancy, *Asst Librn,* New Holland Community Library, New Holland PA. 717-354-0525

Coon, Susan, *Asst Librn,* Washington Adventist Hospital, Medical Library, Takoma Park MD. 301-891-7324, 891-7325

Coones, S, *ILL & Ref,* Sir Sandford Fleming College of Applied Arts & Technology Library, Peterborough ON. 705-743-5610, Ext 268

Cooney, Dorothy, *YA,* Free Public Library of the Borough of Fort Lee, Fort Lee NJ. 201-461-8020

Cooney, Jane, *Mgr & Chief Librn,* Canadian Imperial Bank of Commerce, Information Centre Library, Toronto ON. 416-862-3053

Cooney, Joan, *Bus Ref,* Hofstra University Library, Hempstead NY. 516-560-3475

Cooney, Mary Anne, *Circ,* Marywood College Library, Scranton PA. 717-343-6521, Ext 289

Coons, Daniel E, *Dir,* Delaware State College, William C Jason Library-Learning Ctr, Dover DE. 302-678-5112

Cooper, Alene, *Coordr Libr Develop,* Montana State Library, Helena MT. 406-449-3004

Cooper, Alene, *Coordr Libr Develop,* Montana State Library, Division for the Blind & Physically Handicapped, Helena MT. 406-339-3004

Cooper, Alice, *Interlibr Coop,* Corn Belt Library System, Normal IL. 309-452-4485

Cooper, Aline L, *Mgr,* Celanese Fibers Company, Technical Information Center, Charlotte NC. 704-554-3083

Cooper, Alita, *Commun Servs,* New Hanover County Public Library, Wilmington NC. 919-763-3303

Cooper, Belinda P, *Asst Librn,* Roanoke Bible College, Mary E Griffith Memorial Library, Elizabeth City NC. 919-338-5191

Cooper, Betty P, *Acq & Cat,* Colquitt-Thomas Regional Library, Moultrie-Colquitt County Library, Moultrie GA. 912-985-6540

Cooper, Billy Jean, *Dir,* Southwest Texas Junior College Library, Uvalde TX. 512-278-4401, Ext 251

Cooper, Byron, *Assoc Librn,* Indiana University School of Law, Law Library, Bloomington IN. 812-337-9666

Cooper, Carolyn, *Librn,* Georgia Military College, Sibley-Cone Memorial Library, Milledgeville GA. 912-453-3481, Ext 44

Cooper, Cathy, *Assoc Librn,* Keeneland Association, Keeneland Library, Lexington KY. 606-254-3412, Ext 223

Cooper, Charles, *Media,* Jackson State Community College Library, Jackson TN. 901-424-3520, Ext 248
Cooper, David L, *Dir,* Noblesville Public Library, Noblesville IN. 317-773-1384
Cooper, Debbie, *Br Supvr,* Scarborough Public Library (Guildwood), Scarborough ON. 416-266-4787
Cooper, Deborah, *Librn,* Middletown Township Public Library (Lincroft Branch), Lincroft NJ. 201-747-1140
Cooper, Douglas W, *ILL & Ref,* Randolph-Macon College, Walter Hines Page Library, Ashland VA. 804-798-8372, Ext 256
Cooper, Eileen, *Asst Librn & Acq,* Delaware Law School Library of Widener University, Wilmington DE. 302-478-5280
Cooper, Ellen, *Librn,* Saint Luke's Memorial Hospital Library, Racine WI. 414-636-2200
Cooper, Ginnie, *Dir,* Kenosha Public Library, Kenosha WI. 414-656-6034
Cooper, Ginny, *Ch,* Hillsboro Public Library, Hillsboro OR. 503-648-6669
Cooper, Gwendolyn, *Acq,* University of Arkansas, Pine Bluff, Watson Memorial Library, Pine Bluff AR. 501-541-6825
Cooper, Helen, *Librn,* Boston State Hospital, Medical Library, Dorchester MA. 617-436-6000, Ext 221
Cooper, Hilma F, *Dir,* Cheltenham Township Library System, Glenside PA. 215-885-0457
Cooper, Ilene, *Ch,* Winnetka Public Library District, Winnetka IL. 312-446-5085
Cooper, Inez, *In Charge & Spec Coll,* Utah State Historical Society, Iron County Historical Society Library, Cedar City UT. 801-586-4411, Ext 358
Cooper, J E, *Libr Supvr,* Bell Telephone Laboratories (Bell Telephone Laboratories Technical Library), Holmdel NJ. 949-3912 (Supvr); 949-5966 (Libr Network Support); 949-7986 (Cat); 229-7810 (W Long Branch Info)
Cooper, Jane, *Circ,* University of Toronto Libraries (University Library), Toronto ON. 416-978-2294
Cooper, Jane G, *MEDLINE Analyst,* Maine Medical Center, Health Science Library, Portland ME. 207-871-2201
Cooper, Joanne, *Dir & On-Line Servs,* Mercyhurst College Learning Resource Center, Erie PA. 814-864-0681, Ext 228, 234
Cooper, Karen, *Tech Serv, Cat & Acq,* Rockford College, Howard Colman Library, Rockford IL. 815-226-4035
Cooper, Kathy, *Media,* Kansas City Kansas Community College Library, Kansas City KS. 913-334-1100, Ext 38
Cooper, Kenneth, *ILL,* Fairleigh Dickinson University, Weiner Library, Teaneck NJ. 201-836-6300, Ext 265
Cooper, L M, *Librn,* Manitoba Department of Labour & Manpower, Research Library, Winnipeg MB. 204-944-2211
Cooper, Margaret F, *Librn,* Linton Public Library, Linton IN. 812-847-7802
Cooper, Marguerite, *Librn,* Arizona Division of Behavioral Health Services, Behavioral Health Library & Information Service, Phoenix AZ. 602-244-1331, Ext 278
Cooper, Marianne, *Instr,* Queens College of the City University of New York, Graduate School of Library & Information Studies, NY. 212-520-7194, 520-7195
Cooper, Mary Eva, *Acq,* University of South Florida (Medical Center Library), Tampa FL. 813-974-2399
Cooper, Mary L, *Tech Serv,* University of Virginia (Law Library), Charlottesville VA. 804-924-3384
Cooper, Mrs H C, *Librn,* Eganville Public Library, Eganville ON. 613-628-2400
Cooper, Myrle E, *Librn,* Windham Public Library, Windham ME. 207-892-8086
Cooper, Neloweze, *Ref,* Savannah State College Library, Savannah GA. 912-356-2183, 356-2184
Cooper, Norma, *Librn,* Pacific University (Music), Forest Grove OR. 503-357-6151, Ext 291
Cooper, Regina G, *Ref,* Wheeler Basin Regional Library, Decatur Public Library, Decatur AL. 205-353-2993
Cooper, Richard, *Actg Librn,* University of California, Berkeley (East Asiatic), Berkeley CA. 415-642-2556
Cooper, Rita, *Librn,* Independence Public Library, Independence KS. 316-331-3030
Cooper, Robert G, *Dir, Tech Serv & Cat,* Southwestern Adventist College, Findley Memorial Library, Keene TX. 817-645-3921, Ext 242
Cooper, Robert W, *Exec Secy,* American Federation of Astrologers, Inc Library, Tempe AZ. 602-838-1751
Cooper, Ruby, *Chief Librn,* Watonga Public Library, Watonga OK. 405-623-7748
Cooper, W, *Doc,* NASA, John F Kennedy Space Center Library, Kennedy Space Center FL. 305-867-3600, 3615
Cooper, William, *Acq,* Livingstone College, Andrew Carnegie Library, Salisbury NC. 704-633-7960, Ext 61 & 62
Cooper, William C, *Dir,* Laurens County Library, Laurens SC. 803-984-0596
Coote, Frances M, *Librn,* Lebanon Correctional Institution Library, Lebanon OH. 513-932-1211, Ext 379
Coots, Genny, *Circ & AV,* University of Michigan-Dearborn Library, Dearborn MI. 313-593-5400
Coover, Diane, *On-Line Servs,* Auraria Libraries, Denver CO. 303-629-2805
Coover, J, *Music,* State University of New York at Buffalo, University Libraries, Buffalo NY. 716-636-2965
Coover, James, *Dir,* State University of New York at Buffalo (Music), Buffalo NY. 716-831-5216
Cooze, Christine, *Librn,* Australian Embassy Library, Washington DC. 202-797-3166
Copas, James, *Ref,* Black Hawk College, Learning Resource Center, Moline IL. 309-796-1311, Ext 344
Cope, Charles, *Circ,* Weatherford Public Library, Weatherford TX. 817-594-2767
Cope, Gabriele, *Assoc Dir & On-Line Servs,* Nebraska Wesleyan University, Cochrane-Woods Library, Lincoln NE. 402-466-2371, Ext 354
Cope, Gabriele, *Instr,* Nebraska Wesleyan University, Library Science Program, NE. 402-466-2371, Ext 354
Cope, Johnnye, *Humanities,* North Texas State University Library, Denton TX. 817-788-2411
Cope, Kennison, *Ch,* A Holmes Johnson Memorial Library, Kodiak Public Library, Kodiak AK. 907-486-3312
Cope, Mary M, *Librn,* City College of the City University of New York (Art), New York NY. 212-690-4268
Cope, Sandra, *Librn,* First Baptist Church Library, Waukesha WI. 414-542-7233
Copeland, Alice, *Cat,* Drew University, Rose Memorial Library, Madison NJ. 201-377-3000, Ext 469
Copeland, Barbara, *Tech Serv,* Cheshire Public Library, Cheshire CT. 203-272-2245
Copeland, Cheryl A, *Spec Proj Mgr,* General Microfilm Co, Library Services Div, Cambridge MA. 617-864-2820
Copeland, Delbert H, *Dir & Acq,* Lake-Sumter Community College, Learning Resources Center, Leesburg FL. 904-787-3747, Ext 33
Copeland, Elizabeth H, *Dir,* Sheppard Memorial Library, Greenville NC. 919-752-4177
Copeland, L Griffin, *Dir,* Florida College, Chatlos Library, Temple Terrace FL. 813-988-5131, Ext 37
Copeland, Marge, *Librn,* Miami-Dade Public Library System (Little River), Miami FL. 305-638-6917
Copeland, Nan F, *Asst Dir,* Northeast Louisiana University, Sandel Library, Monroe LA. 318-342-2195
Copeland, Norene, *Librn,* Federal Aviation Administration, Central Regional Library, Kansas City MO. 816-374-3246
Copeland, Patricia, *Ref & Search Coordr,* Tulane University of Louisiana (Matas Medical Library), New Orleans LA. 504-588-5155
Copeland, Robert M, *Chief Librn & Acq,* Kansas Wesleyan, Memorial Library, Salina KS. 913-827-5541, Ext 233
Copeland, Ruth B, *Librn,* Collin Memorial Hospital, Medical Library, McKinney TX. 214-542-2641
Copeley, William N, *Asst Librn,* New Hampshire Historical Society Library, Concord NH. 603-225-3381
Coplen, David Sneed, *Librn,* West Plains Public Library, West Plains MO. 417-256-4775
Coplen, Ron, *Librn, On-Line Servs & Bibliog Instr,* Harcourt Brace Jovanovich, Inc, Editorial Library, New York NY. 212-888-3497
Copler, Judith, *ILL & Ref,* Indiana University Southeast Library, New Albany IN. 812-945-2731
Coppel, Lynn, *Per,* California State University Fullerton Library, Fullerton CA. 714-773-2714
Coppens, Paul, *Media,* University of Lowell Libraries (O'Leary Library), Lowell MA. 617-452-5000, Ext 480
Coppersmith, Virginia, *Librn,* Kane Public & School Libraries (Children's Branch), Kane PA. 814-837-9641
Coppin, Ann S, *Supvr,* Chevron Oil Field Research Co, Technical Information Services Library, La Habra CA. 213-694-7500
Coppinger, John W, *Dir,* Graymoor Ecumenical Institute, Cardinal Spellman Library, Garrison NY. 914-424-3671, Ext 60
Coppinger, Margaret, *Librn,* Timberland Regional Library (Olympia Branch), Olympia WA. 206-352-0595
Coppola, Dominick, *Dir,* College of Staten Island, Saint George Campus Library, Staten Island NY. 212-390-7824
Coppola, Matilda, *Librn,* Ocean County Library (Island Heights Branch), Island Heights NJ. 201-270-6266
Coram, Barbara H, *Librn,* Athens Regional Library (Lavonia-Carnegie), Lavonia GA. 404-356-4307
Coram, Barbara H, *Librn,* Franklin County Library (Lavonia Branch), Lavonia GA. 404-356-4307
Corazza, Lillian, *Asst Librn,* Lehigh County Law Library, Allentown PA. 215-820-3308
Corbacho, Henry, *Chmn,* Eastern Michigan University, Educational Media Div, MI. 313-487-1266
Corbaci, Margarita, *ILL,* South Bend Public Library, South Bend IN. 219-288-4413
Corbaci, Margarita, *Ad & Syst Coordr,* South Bend Public Library, South Bend IN. 219-288-4413
Corbett, Anne G, *Cat & Ref,* Northwestern Connecticut Community College Library, Winsted CT. 203-379-8543, Ext 308
Corbett, Dorothy, *Asst Dir,* Bethel Park Public Library, Bethel Park PA. 412-835-2207
Corbett, Mary Lynn, *Ref,* Natrona County Public Library, Casper WY. 307-235-9272
Corbett, Patti, *Librn,* University of Pittsburgh (Graduate School of Public Health), Pittsburgh PA. 412-624-3016
Corbin, Bill J, *Lectr,* George Peabody College for Teachers, Department of Library Science, TN. 615-327-8037
Corbin, Brenda G, *Librn,* United States Naval Observatory, Matthew Fontaine Maury Memorial Library, Washington DC. 202-254-4525
Corbin, Evelyn D, *Dir,* Lakeview Public Library, Rockville Centre NY. 516-536-3071
Corbin, John B, *Assoc Dir Tech Servs,* Stephen F Austin State University, Ralph W Steen Library, Nacogdoches TX. 713-569-4109
Corbin, Kathleen, *Librn,* Annapolis Valley Regional Library Headquarters (Kentville Branch), Kentville NS. 902-678-3650
Corbin, Linda S, *Cat,* Trinity University Library, San Antonio TX. 512-736-8121
Corbitt, Janet, *AV,* Parkersburg Community College, Learning Resources Center, Parkersburg WV. 304-424-8210
Corbus, Lawrence J, *Asst Dir,* Geauga County Public Library, Chardon OH. 216-285-7601
Corby, Diane, *Librn,* Dames & Moore Technical Library, Cranford NJ. 201-272-8300
Corcoran, Dennis R, *Dir,* Ventress Memorial Library, Marshfield MA. 617-837-5035
Corcoran, Dorothy, *Ad,* Whittier Public Library, Whittier CA. 213-698-8949
Corcoran, Virginia, *On-Line Servs,* Hartford Hospital Health Science Libraries, Hartford CT. 203-524-2971
Corcoran, Virginia, *Librn,* Hartford Hospital Health Science Library (Robinson Library), Hartford CT. 203-524-2230
Cordaro, Barbara, *Dir,* West Milford Library, West Milford NJ. 201-728-3532

Cordasco, Lois, *Cat,* Gulfport Public Library, Gulfport FL. 813-347-0218
Cordell, Howard W, *Dir,* Florida International University, North Miami Campus Library, North Miami FL. 305-940-5730
Cordell, Howard W, *Dir,* Florida International University, Tamiami Campus, Athenaeum, Miami FL. 305-552-2461
Corder, Phyllis, *Asst Librn,* Church Hill Public Library, Church Hill TN. 615-357-4591
Corderoy, P, *Librn,* Calgary Public Library (Chinook), Calgary AB. 403-255-0388
Cordner, Peggy, *In Charge,* Toledo Mental Health Center, Library & Information Center, Toledo OH. 419-381-8349
Cordon, Irma V, *Dir,* Wetmore Public Library, Wetmore KS. 913-866-2250
Cordon, Myrtle, *Outreach Servs,* Stanislaus County Free Library, Modesto CA. 209-526-6821
Cordova, Gregorio, *Reserve Rm,* University of Puerto Rico Library, Jose M Lazaro Memorial Library, Rio Piedras PR. 809-764-0000, Ext 3296
Cordova, Martha, *Ref & On-Line Servs,* Colgate University, Everett Needham Case Library, Hamilton NY. 315-824-1000
Cordovano, Margaret Dineen, *Circ,* Northern Illinois University, College Law Library, Glen Ellyn IL. 312-858-7200
Corella, Pat, *Bus Mgr,* Tucson Public Library, Tucson AZ. 602-791-4391
Corely, Virginia, *Ref & Bibliog Instr,* Drury College, Walker Library, Springfield MO. 417-865-8731, Ext 282
Corey, Constance, *Assoc Librn,* Arizona State University Library, Tempe AZ. 602-965-3417
Corey, Karen M, *AV & Reader Serv,* Purdue University Calumet Library, Hammond IN. 219-844-0520, Ext 249
Corey, Rose, *Outreach,* Golden Plains Library Federation, Glasgow MT. 406-228-2731
Corey, Ross, *Outreach,* Glasgow City County Library, Glasgow MT. 406-228-2731
Corey, Steven, *Rare Bks & Spec Coll,* University of San Francisco, Richard A Gleeson Library, San Francisco CA. 415-666-6167
Corey, Susan, *Librn,* Linn County Law Library, Cedar Rapids IA. 319-326-8677
Corin, Judith, *Asst Univ Librn Planning,* University of California Los Angeles Library, Los Angeles CA. 213-825-1201
Corkill, Ruth E, *Ad Bkmobile & Home Servs,* Pawtucket Public Library & Regional Library Center, Deborah Cook Sayles Memorial Library, Pawtucket RI. 401-725-3714
Corkum, Mrs C, *Ch,* Borough of Etobicoke Public Library, Weston ON. 416-248-5681
Corless, Isabel, *Librn,* Burlington County Historical Society, Delia Biddle Pugh Library, Burlington NJ. 609-386-4773
Corley, Clara L, *Ch,* Biloxi Public Library, Biloxi MS. 601-374-0330
Corley, Sue, *Librn,* Justin Potter Public Library (Alexandria Library), Alexandria TN. 615-529-2171
Corley, Sue, *Circ,* Saint Michael's College, Durick Library, Colchester VT. 802-655-2000, Ext 2400
Corliss, Jack A, *Dir,* Arlington Public Library, Arlington TX. 817-275-2763, 265-3311, Ext 347
Corliss, Stanley W, *Treas,* Fairmount Public Library, Fairmount IN. 317-948-3177
Corman, Marvin, *Dir,* Lahey Clinic Foundation, Medical Library, Boston MA. 617-262-4900, Ext 322
Cormany, Beulah, *ILL & Acq,* Shorter College, Livingston Library, Rome GA. 404-291-2121, Ext 43
Cormier, Elizabeth A, *Dir,* Worcester Industrial Technical Institute, George I Alden Memorial Library, Worcester MA. 617-754-4141
Cormier, John A, *Librn,* Memorial Hospital, Homer Gage Medical Library, Worcester MA. 617-793-6421
Cormier, Susan Draper, *Asst Librn & Ch,* Eisenhower Public Library District, Harwood Heights IL. 312-867-7828, 452-8989
Corn, Joan, *Ch & YA,* Tuxedo Park Library, Tuxedo Park NY. 914-351-2207
Corn, Ruth, *Librn,* Hazelton Environmental Sciences Library, Northbrook IL. 312-564-0700
Cornacchia, R, *Librn,* Public Works Canada, Ontario Region Library, Willowdale ON. 416-367-7708

Cornacchia, Rocco, *Librn,* Public Works Canada (Ontario Region), Willowdale ON. 416-224-4246
Corneau, Andre-Gaetan, *Dir,* Association Des Administrateurs D'hopitaux De La Province De Quebec, Montreal PQ. 514-842-4861
Corneil, Charlotte, *Pub Servs,* Louisiana State University (Law Center Library), Baton Rouge LA. 504-388-8802
Cornelius, Ellen, *Br Coordr,* East Albemarle Regional Library, Elizabeth City NC. 919-335-2511
Cornell, Dorothy, *Dir,* River Vale Public Library, River Vale NJ. 201-391-2323
Cornell, George W, *Dir,* State University of New York College at Brockport, Drake Memorial Library, Brockport NY. 716-395-2140
Cornell, Mrs M, *Librn,* Bryan Public Library (Edon Public), Edon OH. 419-272-2837
Cornell, Richard A, *Asst Prof,* University of Central Florida, Educational Media Programs, FL. 305-275-2426
Cornell, Sylvia, *Tech Serv, Acq & Cat,* Jacksonville Public Library System, Haydon Burns Library, Jacksonville FL. 904-633-6870
Corner, Dean, *Commun Servs,* Binghamton Public Library, Binghamton NY. 607-723-6457
Cornett, Eileen, *Dir,* Hazard Community College Library, Hazard KY. 606-436-5721, Ext 59
Cornett, Lloyd H, *Dir,* United States Air Force (Albert F Simpon Historical Research Center), Maxwell AFB AL. 205-293-5958
Cornett, Martha S, *Tech Serv & Acq,* Carnegie Library, Rome GA. 404-291-7568
Cornett, Wanda, *Librn,* Oakdale Public Library, Oakdale NE. 402-776-2602
Cornick, Donna, *On-Line Servs,* University of North Carolina at Chapel Hill, Louis Round Wilson Academic Affairs Library, Chapel Hill NC. 919-933-1301
Cornick, Ronald, *Librn,* Greeley & Hansen Engineering Library, Chicago IL. 312-648-1155, Ext 300
Cornish, Barbara J, *Dir,* Wareham Free Library, Wareham MA. 617-295-2343
Cornish, Marsha, *Ch,* Lee Memorial Library, Allendale Public Library, Allendale NJ. 201-327-4338
Cornn, Jean, *Librn,* Atlanta Public Library (Hapeville Branch), Hapeville GA. 404-761-5217
Cornwall, Anita M, *Rec Mgt Specialist,* Bureau of Land Management, Burns District Office Library, Burns OR. 503-573-2071
Cornwall, Scot J, *Chief of Prep Production,* Boston Public Library, Eastern Massachusetts Library System, Boston MA. 617-536-5400
Cornwell, Ann, *Librn,* Florida Department of Legal Affairs, Attorney General's Library, Tallahassee FL. 904-488-6040
Cornwell, B R, *Dir,* Halton Hills Public Libraries, Georgetown ON. 416-877-2631
Cornwell, B R, *Librn,* Halton Hills Public Libraries (Halton Hills Public Libraries), Acton ON. 519-853-0301
Cornwell, Charles, *Librn,* Saint Louis Public Library (Municipal Reference Library), Saint Louis MO. 314-453-3548
Cornwell, Charles H, *Municipal Ref,* Saint Louis Public Library, Saint Louis MO. 314-241-2288
Cornwell, Joy, *Cat,* Mayo Foundation (Medical Library), Rochester MN. 507-284-2061
Coro, Frances B, *Librn,* Topsham Public Library, Topsham ME. 207-725-7658
Corontzes, Arthur N, *Assoc Dir & Phys Proc,* The Citadel, Daniel Library, Charleston SC. 803-792-5116
Corral, Elena, *Ser,* Barry College, Monsignor William Barry Memorial Library, Miami Shores FL. 305-758-3392, Ext 263
Corrales, Helen, *Assoc Librn,* Western Electric Co, Inc, Library, Phoenix AZ. 602-261-5351, 261-5216
Corray, Janeth, *ILL,* Oxnard Public Library, Oxnard CA. 805-486-4311
Correa, Genevieve, *Humanities Bibliogr,* University of Hawaii (University of Hawaii Library), Honolulu HI. 808-948-7205
Correll, Ann, *NC Room,* Forsyth County Public Library, Winston-Salem NC. 919-727-2556
Correll, Emily, *Doc,* Public Library of Charlotte & Mecklenburg County, Inc, Charlotte NC. 704-374-2725

Correll, Laraine, *Spec Coll,* George Mason University Libraries, Fairfax VA. 703-323-2616
Corrier, Mary Ann, *Librn,* New York Public Library (Aguilar), New York NY. 212-534-2930
Corrigan, Gary, *Exten Coordr,* Palm Beach County Public Library System, West Palm Beach FL. 305-686-0895
Corrigan, Jerome, *Librn,* Prince George's County Memorial Library System (Oxon Hill Branch), Oxon Hill MD. 301-839-2400
Corrigan, Joanne M, *AV,* Brevard County Library System, Merritt Island FL. 305-453-9509
Corrigan, Maureen, *Librn,* Earl Township Public Library, Earlville IL. 815-246-9465
Corrigan, Ruth R, *Dir,* Carnegie-Mellon University, Hunt Library, Pittsburgh PA. 412-578-2446, 578-2447
Corrigan, Sister John Marie, *Librn,* Dominican College Library, Blauvelt NY. 914-359-8188
Corrin, Nancy, *Mgr,* National Fire Protection Association, Technical Reference Library, Boston MA. 617-482-8755, Ext 136, 137
Corrinni, Laurina, *ILL,* Hudson Public Library, Hudson MA. 617-562-7521, 7522
Corry, Ann Marie, *Librn,* University of Missouri-Kansas City Libraries (Dental), Kansas City MO. 816-221-3500
Corry, Brother Emmett, *Asst Prof,* Saint John's University, Div of Library & Information Science, NY. 212-969-8000, Ext 200
Corry, Ruth L, *Head Librn,* Georgia Department of Archives & History, Central Research Section Library, Atlanta GA. 404-656-2350
Corson, Janet E, *Mgr,* Frederick Cancer Research Center, Scientific Library, Frederick MD. 301-663-7261
Corson, Richard H, *Dir,* State University of New York Maritime College, Stephen B Luce Library, Bronx NY. 212-892-3004, Ext 235
Corston, Christine, *Librn,* Kitchener Public Library (Forest Heights), Kitchener ON. 519-743-0271, Ext 71
Cort, Margaret M, *Librn,* Sperry Rand Corporation, Sperry Microwave Electronics, Engineering Library, Clearwater FL. 813-855-4471
Cortez, Edwin M, *Asst Prof,* University of Michigan, School of Library Science, MI. 313-764-9376
Corum, Gloria, *Librn,* Tacoma Public Library (Anna E McCormick), Tacoma WA. 206-759-3361
Corvey, James, *Assoc Dean,* Mountain View College, Learning Resources Center, Dallas TX. 214-746-4169
Corvillion, Myrna E, *Librn,* Hope United Presbyterian Church Library, Detroit MI. 313-861-7256
Corwin, E Josephine, *Br Coordr,* Caroline County Public Library, Denton MD. 301-479-1343
Corwin, E Josephine, *Librn,* Caroline County Public Library (Federalsburg Branch), Federalsburg MD. 301-754-8397
Cory, John F, *William Hall Librn,* Cranston Public Library, William H Hall Free Library (Administrative & Reference Center), Cranston RI. 401-781-2450, 781-9580
Cory, Kenneth A, *Ch,* Western Montana College, Lucy Carson Memorial Library, Dillon MT. 406-683-7493
Corya, William L, *Cat,* Purdue University Libraries & Audio-Visual Center, West Lafayette IN. 317-749-2571
Coryell, Franklin M, *Dir,* Wickliffe Public Library, Wickliffe OH. 216-944-6010
Cosby, Carol, *Librn,* South Bend Public Library (Western), South Bend IN. 219-287-0800
Cosby, Mrs James, *Geneology Research,* Giles County Public Library, Pulaski TN. 615-363-2720
Cosco, Evelyn, *Ch,* Chelsea Public Library, Chelsea MA. 617-884-2335
Cosgrove, Patricia J, *ILL & Ref,* Immaculata College Library, Immaculata PA. 215-647-4400, Ext 229
Cosley, Norma G, *Dir,* Port Dover Centennial Public Library, Port Dover ON. 519-583-0622
Cosner, Renna, *Acq,* Mary Washington College, E Lee Trinkle Library, Fredericksburg VA. 703-899-4666
Cossalboon, J, *On-Line Servs & Bibliog Instr,* Bolivar Free Library, Bolivar NY. 716-928-2234

Cossar, B, *Docs & Maps,* Trent University, Thomas J Bata Library, Peterborough ON. 705-748-1550
Cossette, Andre, *Ref,* Trois-Rivieres College Library, Trois-Rivieres PQ. 819-376-1721, Ext 286
Cossette, Joseph, *Bibliothecaire,* Bibliotheque De La Societe Historique De Montreal, Montreal PQ. 514-845-2546
Cossitt, Loyce, *Librn,* Henry A Malley Memorial Library, Broadus MT. 406-436-2812
Cossman, Olive, *Asst Librn,* Community Library, Ketchum ID. 208-726-3493
Costa, Joseph J, *Head Librn,* Pennsylvania State University, Schuylkill Campus Library, Schuylkill Haven PA. 717-385-4500
Costa, Robert N, *Dir,* Cambria County Library System, Johnstown PA. 814-536-5131
Costa, Shirley, *Librn,* Hotchkiss Library Association, Sharon CT. 203-364-5041
Costabile, Salvatore L, *Lectr,* University of Maryland, College of Library & Information Services, MD. 301-454-5441
Costanzi, Victoria, *Librn,* Chisholm Public Library, Chisholm MN. 218-254-3350
Costanzo, Anthony J, *Tech Info Supvr,* Atlantic Richfield Co, ARCO Chemical Co, Research & Engineering Library, Glenolden PA. 215-586-4700, Ext 345, 346
Costanzo, Louis, *Instr,* Saint Cloud State University, Center for Library & Audiovisual Education, MN. 612-255-2022
Costello, A Kathleen, *Dir,* Pitkin County Library, Aspen CO. 303-925-7124
Costello, Anne Marie, *Librn,* Cayuga County Community College, Norman F Bourke Memorial Library Learning Resources Center, Auburn NY. 315-255-1743, Ext 296 & 298
Costello, Barbara, *Acq,* Lord Fairfax Community College, Learning Resource Center, Middletown VA. 703-869-1120
Costello, Francene C, *Dir,* Mahopac Library, Mahopac NY. 914-628-2009
Costello, Joan M, *Librn,* Osterhout Free Library, Wilkes-Barre PA. 717-823-0156
Costello, Mary E, *Med Resources Librn,* Intercommunity Memorial Hospital Library, Newfane NY. 716-778-5111
Costello, Robert C, *Dir,* William M Mercer Inc, Library Information Center, Los Angeles CA. 213-386-7840
Costigan, Dorothy Ann, *Librn,* Canada Steamship Lines Library, Montreal PQ. 514-288-0231, Ext 350
Costin, Diane, *Asst Librn,* Garrett Public Library, Garrett IN. 219-357-5485
Costner, Mary S, *Librn,* Rutherford County Library (Mooneyham Public), Forest City NC. 704-245-2281
Coston, L P, *Dir,* Kilgore College, Randolph C Watson Library, Kilgore TX. 214-984-8531, Ext 286
Cote, Catherine A, *Ch,* Belmont Public Library, Belmont MA. 617-489-2000
Cote, Claire, *Dir,* Pointe Claire Public Library, Bibliotheque Publique de Pointe-Claire, Pointe Claire PQ. 514-695-0222
Cote, Donna, *Libr Supvr,* Cary Medical Center, Health Science Library, Caribou ME. 207-498-3131
Cote, Donna, *Asst Dir & Ad,* Central Rappahannock Regional Library, Wallace Memorial Library, Fredericksburg VA. 703-371-3311
Cote, J, *Head, Libr Serv,* Canadian Radio-Television & Telecommunications Commission Library, Ottawa ON. 819-997-0313
Cote, Lois, *Librn,* Saint Peter's Seminary Library, London ON. 519-432-1824
Cote, Susan J, *Assoc Dir,* Massachusetts Institute of Technology Libraries, Cambridge MA. 617-253-5651
Cotellessa, Violette, *Acq,* State University of New York College at Potsdam, Frederick W Crumb Memorial Library, Potsdam NY. 315-268-2940
Cotgrave, Denise, *Librn,* Cochrane Public Library, Cochrane ON. 705-272-4178
Cotham, John M, *Librn,* Mountain Empire Community College Library, Big Stone Gap VA. 703-523-2400, Ext 267
Cothran, Jr, Mrs Jess, *Librn,* Lewis County Public Library, Hohenwald TN. 615-796-5365

Cothren, Mrs Jeff, *Librn,* Columbia-Lafayette-Ouachita-Calhoun Regional Library (Bradley Branch), Bradley AR. 501-234-1991
Cotler, Barbara, *YA,* Maplewood Memorial Library, Maplewood NJ. 201-762-1622
Cotner, Helen L, *Librn,* Ohio Veteran's Orphans' Home Library, Xenia OH. 513-372-6908, Ext 201
Cotner, Pauline, *Asst Librn,* Okmulgee Public Library, Okmulgee OK. 918-756-1448
Cotnoir, Fleurette, *Chief,* College du Nord-Ouest, Techniques de la Documentation, PQ. 819-762-0931, Ext 342
Cotrill, Penny, *Librn,* Putnam County Library (Eleanor Branch), Eleanor WV. 304-755-9166
Cotsordis, Paul C, *Circ,* United States Navy (Naval Education & Training Center), Newport RI. 401-841-3044, 841-4352
Cottam, Keith M, *Asst Dir Pub Servs,* Vanderbilt University Library, Nashville TN. 615-322-2834
Cottell, Bertell, *Librn,* Maryvale Baptist Church Library, Phoenix AZ. 602-973-9290
Cotter, Helen E, *Cont Advr,* Alberta Association of Registered Nurses Library, Edmonton AB. 403-426-0160
Cotter, Marie T, *Librn,* Wheelock College Library, Boston MA. 617-734-5200, Ext 147
Cotter, Michael, *Doc,* East Carolina University, J Y Joyner Library, Greenville NC. 919-757-6514
Cotter, Raymond R, *Librn,* Caltex Petroleum Corp, Planning & Economics Library, New York NY. 212-697-2000
Cottingham, Carl D, *Dir,* John A Logan College, Learning Resources Center, Carterville IL. 618-985-3741
Cottom, Ruth, *Librn,* Reuben McMillan Free Library Free Library Association (North Lima Branch), North Lima OH. 216-549-2255
Cotton, Catherine, *Circ,* East Hampton Public Library, East Hampton CT. 203-267-2635
Cotton, Kenneth W, *Dir,* Westfield State College Library, Westfield MA. 413-568-3311
Cotton, Marguerite, *ILL,* Bishop's University & Champlain Regional College, John Bassett Memorial Library, Lennoxville PQ. 819-569-9551, Ext 341
Cotton, Nina P, *Librn,* Exxon Chemical Co USA (Exxon Research & Development Laboratory Library), Baton Rouge LA. 504-359-7711
Cottrell, A C, *Info Spec,* Air Products & Chemicals, Inc (Corporate Library), Allentown PA. 215-398-7288
Cottrell, Barbara K, *Dir,* Fair Haven Public Library, Fair Haven NJ. 201-747-5031
Cottrell, Steve, *Dir,* Rusk County Memorial Library, Henderson TX. 214-657-8557
Cottrell, Wilma, *Librn,* Birmingham Public & Jefferson County Free Library (East Ensley Branch), Ensley AL. 205-254-2551
Cottrill, Laura, *Librn,* Fairfield County District Library (Bremen-Rushcreek), Bremen OH. 614-569-7246
Couch, Jeanette R, *Librn,* Sutton Free Library, Sutton NH. 603-927-4927
Couch, Susan H, *Librn,* Moss Rehabilitation Hospital Library, Philadelphia PA. 215-329-5715, Ext 2122
Couch, Virginia, *Circ,* Salem College, Dale H Gramley Library, Winston-Salem NC. 919-721-2649
Couchman, Janet P, *Cat,* Mississippi University for Women, John Clayton Fant Memorial Library, Columbus MS. 601-328-4808
Coudyser, Sharon, *Librn,* Contra Costa County Library (Rodeo Branch), Rodeo CA. 415-799-2606
Coughlan, Kathryn B, *Asst Librn,* Woburn Public Library, Woburn MA. 617-933-0148
Coughlan, Nancy L, *Librn,* Ohio County Law Library, Wheeling WV. 304-234-3634
Coughlin, Betty, *Info Serv,* Davenport Public Library, Davenport IA. 319-326-7832
Coughlin, Caroline M, *Asst Dir,* Drew University, Rose Memorial Library, Madison NJ. 201-377-3000, Ext 469
Coughlin, J, *Libr & Supvr,* Sir Sandford Fleming College of Applied Arts & Technology Library, Peterborough ON. 705-743-5610, Ext 268
Coughlin, Joan, *Media,* New Brunswick Free Public Library, New Brunswick NJ. 201-745-5337
Coughlin, June M, *Librn,* Bowling Green State University, Firelands College Library, Huron OH. 419-433-5560, Ext 252

Coughlin, Mike, *AV,* Randolph Technical Institute, Learning Resources Center, Asheboro NC. 919-629-1471, Ext 27
Coughlin, Peggy M, *Librn,* Probe Systems, Inc, Library, Sunnyvale CA. 408-732-6550, Ext 256
Coulson, Barbara, *Ref,* Central Florida Regional Library, Ocala Public Library, Ocala FL. 904-629-8551
Coulson-Graceffa, Peggy, *Librn,* Harvard University Library (Center for European Studies), Cambridge MA. 617-495-3650
Coulston, Craig, *Librn,* International Center of Environmental Safety Library, Albany Medical College, Holloman AFB NM. 505-679-2761
Coultas, John J, *Dir,* White Pine County Library, Ely NV. 702-289-3737
Coulter, Celia, *Ref,* State University of New York, College at New Paltz, Sojourner Truth Library, New Paltz NY. 914-257-2204
Coulter, Joan M, *Lectr,* Concordia University, Library Studies Program, PQ. 514-482-0320, Ext 324
Coulter, Shirley, *Librn,* Nova Scotia Provincial Library (School Libraries), Halifax NS. 902-424-5457
Coulton, Martha J, *Dir,* Milton-Union Public Library, West Milton OH. 513-698-5515
Councill, Ann, *Librn,* Ecological Analysts Inc Library, Middletown NY. 914-692-6706
Cound, Bill, *Dir Colo Libr Network,* Colorado State Library, Colorado Department of Education, Denver CO. 303-839-3695
Countryman, Judy, *Ref,* Fairbanks North Star Borough Public Library & Regional Center, Fairbanks AK. 907-452-5177
Countryman, R W, *Librn Blind,* Birmingham Public & Jefferson County Free Library, Birmingham AL. 205-254-2551
Countryman, Ron, *Librn,* Birmingham Public & Jefferson County Free Library (Service to the Blind & Physically Handicapped), Birmingham AL. 205-254-2529
Counts, Charlotte, *Librn,* Lonesome Pine Regional Library (Dickenson County Public), Clincho VA. 703-835-8147
Coupe, Sandra L, *Assoc Librn,* Federal Bureau of Investigation, FBI Academy Learning Resource Center, Quantico VA. 703-640-6131, Ext 2471
Couper, Richard W, *Pres,* New York Public Library, Astor, Lenox & Tilden Foundations Library, New York NY. 212-790-6262
Coupey, Joyce, *Asst Librn,* Madill City Library, Madill OK. 405-795-2749
Coursen, Florence, *Librn,* City of Altamonte Springs Library & Cultural Center, Altamonte Springs FL. 305-830-6136
Courson, Barbara, *Dir,* Nogales City-Santa Cruz County Library, Nogales Public Library, Nogales AZ. 602-287-3343, 287-6310
Court, Emily, *Librn,* Norwich Hospital, Health Sciences Library, Norwich CT. 203-889-7361, Ext 788
Court, Kathryn, *Librn,* Salt Lake County Library System (South Salt Lake), Salt Lake City UT. 801-466-5631
Court, Mary L, *Ch,* Galion Public Library Association, Galion OH. 419-468-3203
Court, Patricia C, *Fine Arts,* University of Wisconsin-Platteville, Elton S Karrmann Library, Platteville WI. 608-342-1688
Courtemanche, Harold, *Cat,* Hudson Public Library, Hudson MA. 617-562-7521, 7522
Courtis, Shirley, *Librn,* Noranda Research Centre Library, Pointe Claire PQ. 514-697-6640, Ext 204
Courtnage, Kay, *Ref,* Great Falls Public Library, Pathfinder Federation of Libraries Headquarters, Great Falls MT. 406-453-0349
Courtney, John F, *Librn,* New Hampshire State Library (Littleton Branch), Littleton NH. 603-271-2392
Courtney, Mary E, *Librn,* Memorial Hospital, Medical & Nursing Libraries, Cumberland MD. 301-777-4000
Courtney, Mrs Cecil, *Librn,* Livingston Parish Library (Holden Branch), Holden LA. 504-686-2436
Courtney, Vincent, *Tech Serv,* University of Maine at Farmington, Mantor Library, Farmington ME. 207-778-3501, Ext 225
Courtright, Harry R, *Dir,* Dauphin County Library System, Harrisburg PA. 234-4961

Courtright, Shirley, *Acq,* State Library of Ohio, Columbus OH. 614-466-2693

Courtright, Terry, *Cat,* Saddleback Community College Library, Mission Viejo CA. 714-831-4515

Cousineau, Ann, *Librn,* Stockton-San Joaquin County Public Library (Margaret Klausner Troke), Stockton CA. 209-944-8415

Cousins, Lynn M, *Librn,* Confederation Life Insurance Co Library, Toronto ON. 416-967-8326

Cousins, Jr, Paul M, *Assoc Dir,* Emory University Libraries (General Libraries), Atlanta GA. 404-329-6861

Coutin, Jose D, *Dir,* University of Dayton Libraries (Law School Library), Dayton OH. 513-229-2314

Couto, Mary, *Acq,* Fall River Public Library, Fall River MA. 617-676-8541

Couts, Doris V, *Librn,* Tuscarawas County Law Library Association, New Philadelphia OH. 216-364-3703

Coutts, Jane, *Ch,* Vestal Public Library, Vestal NY. 607-754-4243

Coutts, Marjorie E, *Librn,* Dawson Creek Public Library, Dawson Creek BC. 604-782-4661

Couture, Carmen, *Librn,* Bibliotheque Publique De Hearst, Hearst ON. 705-363-4283, Ext 16

Couture, Diane B, *Librn,* Ottawa General Hospital, Medical Library, Ottawa ON. 613-231-3128

Couturier, Fernande, *Math,* City University of New York, Library of Graduate School & University Center, New York NY. 212-790-4541

Couturier, Roger P, *Dir,* Saskatchewan Department of Highways & Transportation, Planning Branch Library, Regina SK. 306-565-2345

Covalesky, Eleanor, *Cat,* University of San Francisco (School of Law), San Francisco CA. 415-666-6679

Covall, Jean, *ILL & Circ,* Long Beach Public Library System, Long Beach CA. 213-436-9225

Covalt, Jeanie, *Res Librn,* Cultural Heritage & Arts Center Library, Kansas Heritage Center, Dodge City KS. 316-227-2823

Coven, Brenda, *On-Line Servs,* State University of New York, Frank Melville Jr Memorial Library, Stony Brook NY. 516-246-5650

Cover, Kathy, *Curator,* Texarkana Museum Research Library, Texarkana TX. 214-793-4831

Cover, Peggy H, *Sci, Tech & Agr,* Clemson University, Robert Muldrow Cooper Library, Clemson SC. 803-656-3026

Coverly, Carol, *ILL & Ref,* Morse Institute Library, Natick MA. 617-653-4252

Coverly, Cyril F, *Cent Servs,* Denver Public Library, Denver CO. 303-573-5152, Ext 271

Covert, David, *Librn,* Durham County Library (North Durham Branch), Durham NC. 919-471-2129

Covey, Alan, *Prof,* University of Wisconsin-Oshkosh, Dept of Library Science, WI. 414-424-2313

Covey, Harriet, *Area Br Supvrs,* Riverside City & County Public Library, Riverside CA. 714-787-7211

Covey, Martha H, *Ref Supvr,* Georgia Department of Education (Div of Public Library Services), Atlanta GA. 404-656-2461

Coville, Gary, *Commun & Outreach Servs,* Dallas Public Library, Dallas OR. 503-623-2633

Covington, Babs, *Circ,* Chesterfield County Library, Chesterfield SC. 803-623-7489

Covington, Barbara A, *Librn,* Resource Management Corp Library, Bethesda MD. 301-656-2700

Covington, Dorothy, *Bkmobile Librns,* Reelfoot Regional Library Center, Martin TN. 901-587-2347

Covington, Ethel, *Tech Serv,* Illinois College of Podiatric Medicine Library, Chicago IL. 312-280-2891

Covington, Louis, *Dir,* Bossier Parish Public Library, Benton LA. 318-965-2751

Covington, Louis, *Librn,* Red River Parish Library, Coushatta LA. 318-932-5614

Covington, Mary W, *Supvr Tech Info,* Copper Development Association Inc, Copper Data Center, New York NY. 212-953-7300

Covington, Tommy, *Librn,* Northeast Regional Library (Ripley Library), Ripley MS. 601-837-7773

Covington, Virginia, *Spec Coll,* Georgetown College, Cooke Memorial Library, Georgetown KY. 502-863-8011

Covington, W, *Librn,* Optikon Laboratories, Research Library, West Cornwall CT. 203-672-6614

Covino, Diane, *ILL,* Manhasset Public Library, Manhasset NY. 516-627-2300

Covino, Joe, *Dir & Acq,* Great Neck Library, Great Neck NY. 516-466-8055

Covley, Theresa, *Ref & ILL,* Saint Bonaventure University, Friedsam Memorial Library & Resource Center, Saint Bonaventure NY. 716-375-2323

Cowan, Anita, *Chief Librn,* Saginaw Public Library, Saginaw TX. 817-232-2100

Cowan, Ann, *In Charge,* Rockwell Hanford Operations (Hanford Science Center), Richland WA. 509-942-6374

Cowan, B, *Acq,* Atlantic Christian College, Hackney Library, Wilson NC. 919-237-3161, Ext 330

Cowan, Barbara, *Ad,* Saint John Regional Library, Saint John NB. 506-693-1191

Cowan, David, *Ref,* University of Arkansas Libraries (Law), Fayetteville AR. 501-575-5604

Cowan, Dorothy S, *ILL & Ref,* Ashtabula County District Library, Ashtabula OH. 216-997-9341

Cowan, George A, *Librn,* Lincoln County Law Library, Wiscasset ME. 207-882-7517

Cowan, J M, *Pres,* American Council-Learned Societies, Spoken Language Services Inc Library, Ithaca NY. 607-257-0500

Cowan, Janet, *Librn,* Stockton-San Joaquin County Public Library (Tracy Branch), Stockton CA. 209-944-8415

Cowan, Joan, *Circ,* Franklin Township Free Public Library, Somerset NJ. 201-545-8032

Cowan, Karen, *Circ,* Ames Public Library, Ames IA. 515-232-4404

Cowan, Lenore, *Librn,* New York Public Library (Picture Collection), New York NY. 212-790-6101, 6102

Cowan, Marie, *Media,* Jackson-George Regional Library System (Pascagoula City Branch), Pascagoula MS. 601-762-3406

Cowan, Natalie J, *Librn,* California Historical Society, Schubert Hall Library, San Francisco CA. 415-567-1848

Coward, Ernestine, *Librn,* Kingsport Public Library (Carver), Kingsport TN. 615-245-6281

Coward, Hester H, *Dir,* Franklin-Johnson County Public Library, Franklin IN. 317-738-2833

Coward, Robert, *Dir, Tech Serv & On-Line Servs,* Franklin College Library, Franklin IN. 317-736-8441, Ext 257

Cowart, Patricia, *Ch,* Liberal Memorial Library, Liberal KS. 316-624-0148

Cowe, Dorothy, *Librn,* ITEK Corp, Optical Systems Division Library, Lexington MA. 617-276-2643

Cowell, Carol, *Librn,* Florida Free Public Library, Florida MA. 413-664-6023

Cowherd, Mary, *Supvr,* Chicago Public Library (Robert Taylor Homes Reading & Study Center), Chicago IL. 312-548-2828

Cowles, Carol E, *Dir,* Madison-Jefferson County Public Library, Madison IN. 812-265-2744

Cowles, Mary, *Spec Coll,* Oberlin College Library, Oberlin OH. 216-775-8285

Cowling, Sandra L, *Acq,* California State University, Fresno Library, Fresno CA. 209-487-2403

Cowper, Dorothy, *Chief Librn,* Toronto General Hospital, Fudger Medical Library, Toronto ON. 416-595-3549

Cowperthwait, Martha, *ILL,* Burlington County Library, Mount Holly NJ. 609-267-9660

Cowsert, Phyllis, *Librn,* Sacramento Public Library (Courtland Branch), Courtland CA. 916-775-1113

Cox, Alice, *Spec Coll,* Mississippi College, Leland Speed Library, Clinton MS. 601-924-5131, Ext 232, 307

Cox, Ann, *Librn,* Public Library of Cincinnati & Hamilton County (Mount Washington), Cincinnati OH. 513-369-6033

Cox, Barbara, *ILL, Ref & Spec Coll,* University of Albuquerque, Center for Learning & Information Resources, Albuquerque NM. 505-831-1111, Ext 230

Cox, Betty, *City Bookmobile Librn,* Hattiesburg Public Library System, Hattiesburg MS. 601-582-4461

Cox, Betty, *Ch,* Willard Memorial Library, Willard OH. 419-933-8564

Cox, Beverly, *Librn & Acq,* Brookhaven College, Learning Resources Center, Farmers Branch TX. 214-746-5250

Cox, Brenda, *Librn,* Howard University Libraries (Social Work Library), Washington DC. 202-636-7316

Cox, Carolyn, *Systs,* Duke University, William R Perkins Library, Durham NC. 684-2034

Cox, Charles B, *Dir,* Andrew College, Pitts Library, Cuthbert GA. 912-732-2171

Cox, D Z, *Supvr,* Rockwell International Corp, Technical Information Center, Columbus OH. 614-239-3131

Cox, Darlene, *Librn,* North Freedom Public Library, North Freedom WI. 608-

Cox, David M, *Media,* Sinclair Community College, Learning Resources Center, Dayton OH. 513-226-2855

Cox, Doris W, *Prof,* Ball State University, Dept of Library Science, IN. 317-285-7180, 285-7189

Cox, Dorothy, *Ref,* Grundy County-Jewett Norris Library, Trenton MO. 816-359-3577

Cox, Dorothy, *Asst Prof,* Southern Illinois University at Carbondale, Educational Media Program, IL. 618-453-5764

Cox, Dorothy W, *Acq,* Loyola University of Chicago Libraries, Chicago IL. 312-274-3000, Ext 771

Cox, Ernestine, *Librn,* Stone County Library, Galena MO. 417-357-6410

Cox, Hilegard, *Librn,* Kinston-Lenoir County Public Library (Plaza Branch), Kinston NC. 919-522-0480

Cox, Irene, *Librn,* Deep River Public Library, Deep River ON. 613-584-4244

Cox, James C, *Librn,* Loyola University of Chicago Libraries (Medical Center), Maywood IL. 312-531-3192

Cox, Judith L, *Acq,* Gallaudet College, Edward Miner Gallaudet Memorial Library, Washington DC. 202-651-5566

Cox, Lynn, *AV,* Maryland Historical Society Library, Baltimore MD. 301-685-3750

Cox, Marcia, *Media,* University of Missouri-Kansas City Libraries (Medical Library), Kansas City MO. 816-474-4100, Ext 280

Cox, Martha, *Ad,* Madison-Jefferson County Public Library, Madison IN. 812-265-2744

Cox, Martha M, *Dir,* Stark County Law Library Association, Canton OH. 216-456-2330

Cox, Mary Frances, *Librn,* Tennessee Valley Authority (Law Library), Knoxville TN. 615-632-4392

Cox, Mrs Sam, *Librn,* Chattanooga-Hamilton County Bicentennial Library (Northgate), Chattanooga TN. 615-875-4872

Cox, Olamae, *Dir,* Pickaway County District Public Library, Circleville OH. 614-477-1644

Cox, Patricia D, *Librn,* Mississippi Chemical Corp, Engineering Services Support Group, Yazoo City MS. 601-746-4131

Cox, Phyllis, *Coll Develop,* Virginia Commonwealth University (Tompkins-McCaw Library), Richmond VA. 804-786-0629

Cox, Scottie W, *Dean,* Wayne Community College, Learning Resource Center, Goldsboro NC. 919-735-5151, Ext 64

Cox, Suzy, *Librn,* City-County Library of Missoula (Swan Valley Community Library), Condon MT. 406-754-2521

Cox, Travis, *Cat,* Harding University, Beaumont Memorial Library, Searcy AR. 501-268-6161, Ext 354

Cox, Vergie, *Chief Consultant,* North Carolina State Department of Public Instruction, Education Information Center, Raleigh NC. 919-733-7904

Cox, William, *Asst Dir-Cent Libr Serv,* Rochester Public Library, Rochester NY. 716-428-7300

Coxe, Carol, *Librn,* Boston Public Library (Allston Branch), Allston MA. 617-782-3332

Coxe, Carol, *Librn,* Boston Public Library (Faneuil), Brighton MA. 617-782-6705

Coxey, Vivian, *Librn,* Dayton Public Library, Dayton TN. 615-775-9063

Coy, Virginia, *Librn,* South Glastonbury Public Library, South Glastonbury CT. 203-633-4793

Coyle, Barbara, *Librn,* Douglas County Library System (Riddle Public), Riddle OR. 503-874-2070

Coyle, Bernadette, *Ref,* Seneca College of Applied Arts & Technology, Finch Campus Learning Resource Centre, Willowdale ON. 416-491-5050, Ext 381

Coyle, Kathryn, *Asst Curator,* Delaware County Historical Society Library, Chester PA. 215-874-6444

Coyle, Mary, *Ref & On-Line Servs,* Mitre Corp Library, McLean VA. 703-827-6481

Coyle, Michael P, *Chief Librn,* Free Library of Philadelphia, Library for the Blind & Physically Handicapped, Philadelphia PA. 215-925-3213

Coyle, Rosalie, *Asst Librn,* Rawle & Henderson, Law Library, Philadelphia PA. 215-569-2500, Ext 260

Coyle, Sandy, *Librn,* Texas Department of Mental Health & Mental Retardation, Central Office Library, Austin TX. 512-454-3761, Ext 277

Coyne, John, *Ref,* Schaumburg Township Public Library, Schaumburg IL. 312-885-3373

Coyne, Joseph G, *In Charge,* United States Department of Energy, Technical Information Center, Oak Ridge TN. 615-483-8611

Coyne, Martin, *ILL,* Case Western Reserve University Libraries (Sears), Cleveland OH. 216-368-3506

Coyne, Mary A, *Librn,* Bigelow Free Public Library, Clinton MA. 617-365-5052

Coyston, Gail, *Librn,* Winnipeg Public Library (Brooklands), Winnipeg MB. 204-633-5668

Cozzie, Anthony F, *Dir,* Roswell P Flower Memorial Library, Watertown NY. 315-788-2352

Cozzolino, Dorothy, *Chief Librn,* United States Court of Appeals, Third Circuit Library, Philadelphia PA. 215-597-2009

Crabb, Al, *Librn,* Kewanna Public Library, Kewanna IN. 219-653-2011

Crabb, Elizabeth, *Coordr,* Northeast Texas Library System, Dallas TX. 214-651-9266

Crabb, Jan, *Tech Serv,* Arlington Public Library, Arlington TX. 817-275-2763

Crabbe, John W, *Mgr, Info Serv,* Science Applications, Inc Library, McLean VA. 703-821-4521

Crabbe, Nancy, *Asst Librn,* Redwood City Public Library, Redwood City CA. 415-369-6251, Ext 288

Crabill, H Kay, *Librn,* Thomas, Taliaferro, Forman, Burr & Murray Library, Birmingham AL. 205-251-3000

Crabtree, Debbie, *Librn,* W E Sears Youth Center Library, Poplar Bluff MO. 314-785-8436

Crabtree, Duane E, *Tech Serv & Cat,* Belmont Public Library, Belmont MA. 617-489-2000

Crabtree, Mrs G E, *Librn,* West Georgia Regional Library (Haralson County Civic), Tallapoosa GA. 404-832-1381

Crabtree, Mrs V, *Librn,* United California Bank (International Library), Los Angeles CA. 213-614-4111

Craddock, George, *Dir,* Roanoke College Library, Salem VA. 703-389-2351, Ext 202

Craddock, Maxine, *Librn,* McIver's Grant Public Library, Dyersburg TN. 901-285-5032

Cradduck, M, *On-Line Servs & Bibliog Instr,* Bolivar Free Public Library, Bolivar NY. 716-928-2234

Crader, Betty, *Circ,* Howard County Library, Columbia MD. 301-997-8000

Crady, Steve, *Asst Dir,* Illinois Central College, Learning Resources Center, East Peoria IL. 309-694-5461

Craft, Beverly, *Librn,* Kinsley Free Public Library, Kinsley KS. 316-659-3341

Craft, Guy C, *Dir,* Albany State College, Margaret Rood Hazard Library, Albany GA. 912-439-4065

Craft, Jack, *Ser,* Victoria College - University of Houston Victoria Campus Library, Victoria TX. 512-575-7436

Craft, Linda, *Librn,* Wyoming County Library System (Mullens Branch), Mullens WV. 304-294-6687

Craft, Mabel, *Librn,* Richland County Public Library (Northway Plaza), Columbia SC. 803-754-7734

Craft, Margaret E, *Librn,* Wyoming Historical & Geological Society, Bishop Memorial Library, Wilkes-Barre PA. 717-823-6244

Craft, Nancy, *Librn, Tech Serv & Cat,* Tompkins-Cortland Community College, Gerald A Barry Memorial Library, Instructional & Learning Resource Div, Dryden NY. 607-844-8211, Ext 354

Craft, Ruth, *Librn,* Stanislaus County Free Library (Patterson Branch), Patterson CA. 209-892-6473

Craft, Sharon L, *Asst Librn,* United States Navy (Pearl Harbor Naval Base Library), Honolulu HI. 808-471-8238

Craft, Susan N, *Librn,* Kenmore Mercy Hospital, Health Sciences Learning Resource Center, Kenmore NY. 716-879-6253

Crage, Thomas J, *Tech Serv,* Fordham University, Duane Library, Bronx NY. 212-933-2233, Ext 230, 259

Crager, John, *YA & Bkmobile Coordr,* Clinton-Essex-Franklin Library System, Plattsburgh NY. 518-563-5190

Cragg, Carole, *Bibliog Instr,* Trinity College Library, Deerfield IL. 312-945-6700, Ext 217

Craggs, Betsy, *Asst Librn,* Middlesex Memorial Hospital, Health Sciences Library, Middletown CT. 203-347-9471, Ext 387

Cragon, Mary Jo, *Cat,* Vestavia Hills Library, Vestavia Hills AL. 205-823-0520, 823-0521

Crahan, Elizabeth S, *Dir Libr Serv,* Los Angeles County Medical Association Library, Los Angeles CA. 213-483-4555

Craig, Alma E, *Librn,* Rogersville Public Library, Rogersville AL. 205-247-0151

Craig, Bruce D, *Middle East,* University of Chicago, Joseph Regenstein Library, Chicago IL. 312-753-2977

Craig, Charlie Mae, *Bkmobile Coordr,* Bryan Public Library, Bryan TX. 713-823-8021

Craig, Dale W, *District Servs,* Erie County Library System, Erie PA. 814-452-2333

Craig, Don, *Dir,* Middle Tennessee State University, Andrew L Todd Library, Murfreesboro TN. 615-898-2622

Craig, Gladys, *Librn,* Ashland Community Library, Ashland ME. 207-435-6532

Craig, H Eugene, *Librn,* Atlanta Historical Society Library, Atlanta GA. 404-261-1837

Craig, J A, *In Charge,* Boy Scouts of Canada National Headquarters Library, Ottawa ON. 613-224-5131

Craig, J Pat, *Librn,* National Center for Toxicological Research Library, Jefferson AR. 501-541-4322

Craig, James D, *Asst Prof,* Middle Tennessee State University, Department of Library Service, TN. 615-898-2740 & 898-5555

Craig, James L, *Librn,* University of Massachusetts at Amherst Library (Biological Sciences), Amherst MA. 413-545-2674

Craig, Janet Aydt, *On-Line Servs,* State Law Library, Frankfort KY. 502-564-4848

Craig, Jessie, *Librn,* Roanoke City Public Library System (Jackson Park), Roanoke VA. 703-981-2640

Craig, John, *ILL & Ref,* Sullivan County Community College, Hermann Memorial Library, Loch Sheldrake NY. 914-434-5750, Ext 223

Craig, Joseph, *Librn,* Augusta Mental Health Institute (Colonel Black Library), Augusta ME. 207-622-6281

Craig, Joseph, *In Charge,* Santa Cruz County Health Services Agency, Medical Library, Santa Cruz CA. 408-425-2025

Craig, Lillian R, *Librn,* Scotland County Public Library, Memphis MO. 816-465-7042

Craig, Mary, *Ch,* Morse Institute Library, Natick MA. 617-653-4252

Craig, May, *Ch,* West Springfield Public Library, West Springfield MA. 413-736-4561

Craig, Myra, *Librn,* United States Army (Corps of Engineers Library), Tulsa OK. 918-581-7395

Craig, Roland, *Cat,* Texas State Library, Austin TX. 512-475-2166

Craig, Sharon A, *Librn,* Erie County Law Library, Erie PA. 814-456-8851

Craig, Sister Agnes Gregory, *AV,* College of Saint Elizabeth, Mahoney Library, Convent Station NJ. 201-539-1600, Ext 365

Craig, Susan L, *Pub Servs,* Hood College of Frederick, Joseph Henry Apple Library, Frederick MD. 301-663-3131, Ext 364, 365

Craig, Susan V, *Art Hist,* University of California, Berkeley (University Library), Berkeley CA. 415-642-3773

Crail, Kay, *On-Line Servs,* Rockwell International, Anaheim Information Center, Anaheim CA. 714-632-3621

Crain, Carolyn, *Librn,* San Bernardino County Library (Yucaipa Branch), Yucaipa CA. 714-797-9316

Crain, Doris, *Ch,* Harborfields Public Library, Greenlawn NY. 516-757-4200

Crain, John W, *Dir,* Dallas Historical Society Research Center, Dallas TX. 214-421-5136

Crain, Leon C, *Dir,* Sachem Public Library, Holbrook NY. 516-588-5024

Crais, Mina L, *Librn,* International House Reference Library, New Orleans LA. 504-522-3591

Crajno, Eleanor, *Librn,* Rosemary Community Library, Rosemary AB. 403-378-4493

Cram, Kendall J, *Dir State Libr,* Tennessee State Library & Archives, Nashville TN. 615-741-2764

Cram, Laura E, *Librn,* Merrimac Public Library, Thomas H Hoyt Memorial, Merrimac MA. 617-346-9441

Cram, Mona, *Librn,* Newfoundland Public Library Services (Provincial Reference Dept), Saint John's NF. 709-737-3964

Cramer, Anne, *Dir,* Eastern Virginia Medical School, Moorman Memorial Library, Norfolk VA. 804-446-5840

Cramer, Claudia, *Librn,* Rock County Health Care Center, Staff Library, Janesville WI. 608-755-2542

Cramer, Jack C, *Librn,* Southeastern Bible College, Mary M Stribling Library, Lakeland FL. 813-665-4406, Ext 45

Cramer, Jane, *In Charge,* Lockport Memorial Hospital, Medical Library, Lockport NY. 716-434-9111

Cramer, Joan, *Ch,* Auburn Public Library, Auburn WA. 206-931-3018

Cramer, Judith, *Librn,* Cleveland Public Library (Clark), Cleveland OH. 216-651-2692

Cramer, Kathleen, *Librn,* Salmon Public Library, Salmon ID. 208-756-2311

Cramer, Kenneth C, *Archives,* Dartmouth College, Baker Memorial Library, Hanover NH. 603-646-2235

Cramer, Marilyn, *ILL,* Grand Rapids Public Library, Grand Rapids MI. 616-456-4400

Cramer, Nancy, *Librn,* Pittsford Public Library, Pittsford MI. 517-523-2565

Cramer, Patricia, *Librn,* City Library (Forest Park), Springfield MA. 413-733-7019

Cramer, William, *Doc,* Oakland University, Kresge Library, Rochester MI. 313-377-2486, 377-2474

Crames, Joel S, *Assoc Dir,* National College of Education, Learning Resources Center, Evanston IL. 312-256-5150, Ext 273

Crammer, Donna, *Cat,* Alabama Public Library Service, Montgomery AL. 205-832-5743

Crampon, Jean, *Ref & On-Line Servs,* Southern Illinois University School of Medicine Library, Springfield IL. 217-782-2658

Crampton, David, *Circ,* University of Scranton, Alumni Memorial Library, Scranton PA. 717-961-7525

Crampton, Frances, *Librn,* Prescott Public-Yavapai County Library System (Yarnell Public), Yarnell AZ. 602-445-8110

Crandall, Anna A, *Dir,* Belmont Free Library, Belmont NY. 716-268-5308

Crandall, B, *Librn,* Borough of Etobicoke Public Library (Long Branch), Toronto ON. 416-248-5681

Crandall, Gloria, *AV,* Traverse City Public Library, Traverse City MI. 616-941-2311

Crandall, Stephen, *Cat,* Alfred University (Herrick Memorial Library), Alfred NY. 607-871-2184

Crandlemere, R Wayne, *Dir,* Briggs Engineering & Testing Co, Inc Library, Norwell MA. 617-773-2780

Crane, Elizabeth, *Ad,* McMillan Memorial Library, Wisconsin Rapids WI. 715-423-1040

Crane, Jane O, *Chief Librn,* Veterans Administration, Hospital Library, Charleston SC. 803-577-5011

Crane, Karen, *Exten Servs,* Fairbanks North Star Borough Public Library & Regional Center, Fairbanks AK. 907-452-5177

Crane, Kay, *Instr,* Highline Community College Library, Library Technician Program, WA. 206-878-3710, Ext 233

Crane, Laura, *Librn,* United States Fish & Wildlife Service, National Fisheries Research Laboratory Library, Columbia MO. 314-442-2271, Ext 3201
Crane, Lois, *Librn,* Wichita Art Museum Library, Wichita KS. 316-268-4621
Crane, Maurice A, *Librn,* Michigan State University Library (Voice Library), East Lansing MI. 517-355-2344
Crane, Michie, *Doc,* Boise Public Library & Information Center, Boise ID. 208-384-4466
Crane, Mrs Bruce, *Librn,* Humphreys County Public Library, Waverly TN. 615-296-2143
Crane, Nancy, *Ref,* University of Vermont & State Agricultural College, Bailey-Howe Memorial Library, Burlington VT. 802-656-2020
Crane, Richard A, *Dir,* Maude Shunk Public Library, Menomonee Falls Public Library, Menomonee Falls WI. 414-251-4030
Crane, Stanley, *Dir, Ref & Rare Bks,* Pequot Library, Southport CT. 203-259-0346, 255-0779
Crane, William, *Doc,* Public Library of Fort Wayne & Allen County, Fort Wayne IN. 219-424-7241
Cranford, Henrietta K, *Librn,* Moore Gardner & Associates, Inc Library, Asheboro NC. 919-625-6111, Ext 42
Cranford, Janet Walsh, *Dir,* Mandan Public Library, Mandan ND. 701-663-3255
Cranford, Judy, *Ch,* Kemp Public Library, Wichita Falls TX. 817-322-5611, Ext 377
Cranford, M E, *Librn,* CIP Research Ltd Library, Hawkesbury ON. 613-632-4122, Ext 233
Cranford, Martha, *Asst Dir,* Central Texas College, Oveta Culp Hobby Memorial Library, Killeen TX. 817-526-1237
Cranford, Nadine, *Acq,* University of Arkansas-Monticello Library, Monticello AR. 501-367-6811
Cranmer, Marie B, *Br Coordr,* Ocean County Library, Toms River NJ. 201-349-6200
Cranor, Alice T, *Librn,* United States Department of the Navy (Naval Intelligence Support Center), Washington DC. 202-763-1479
Cranston, Linda A, *Acq, Cat & Bibliog Instr,* Roger Williams College Library, Bristol RI. 401-255-2361
Cranston, Mary, *Librn,* Free Library of Aston, Aston PA. 215-494-5877
Cranz, Jeanne, *ILL,* Emporia Public Library, Emporia KS. 316-342-6524
Crary, Eleanor, *Tech Serv,* Alameda County Library, Hayward CA. 415-881-6337
Craven, Jayne, *Art & Music,* Public Library of Cincinnati & Hamilton County, Cincinnati Public Library, Cincinnati OH. 513-369-6000
Craven, Rita, *Cat,* University of Manitoba Libraries, Winnipeg MB. 204-474-9881
Craven, Suzanne, *Ref,* Woodstock Public Library & Art Gallery, Woodstock ON. 519-537-4801
Cravens, Barbara E, *Ad,* Pueblo Library District, Pueblo CO. 303-544-1940
Cravets, Bertha, *Librn,* Temple B'rith Kodesh Library, Rochester NY. 716-244-7060
Cravey, Pamela, *Circ,* Georgia State University, William Russell Pullen Library, Atlanta GA. 404-658-2185, 658-2172
Crawell, Merrilee, *Asst Dir,* Manlius Library, Manlius NY. 315-682-6400
Crawford, Ann, *Dir,* Cross' Mills Public Library, Charlestown RI. 401-364-6211
Crawford, Anthony, *On-Line Servs,* Vancouver School of Theology Library, Vancouver BC. 604-228-9031, Ext 53
Crawford, Anthony R, *Asst Dir & Archivist,* Missouri Historical Society Library, Saint Louis MO. 314-361-1424
Crawford, B L, *Librn,* Clow Corp, Water Management Division Library, Pontiac MI. 313-334-4747
Crawford, Beth, *Librn,* Lebanon Public Library, Lebanon IN. 317-482-3460
Crawford, Carter, *Librn,* Oppenheimer & Co, Inc Library, New York NY. 212-825-4264
Crawford, Debbie, *Librn,* Canadian Mental Health Association Library, Toronto ON. 416-484-7750, 487-3651
Crawford, Don L, *Chmn,* Western Illinois University, Dept of Learning Resources, IL. 309-298-1952
Crawford, Doris L, *Dir,* Saint Elizabeth Hospital (School of Nursing Library), Youngstown OH. 216-746-7211, Ext 3308

Crawford, Dorothea, *Tech Serv,* Crown Zellerbach Corp, Central Research Library, Camas WA. 206-834-4444
Crawford, Dorothy, *Acq,* Maryville College, Lamar Memorial Library, Maryville TN. 615-982-1200
Crawford, Dorothy, *Order,* Princeton University Library, Princeton NJ. 609-452-3180
Crawford, Dorothy B, *Librn,* Cameron Public Library, Cameron TX. 817-697-2401
Crawford, Jane, *Acq,* Dalton Junior College, Library Resource Center, Dalton GA. 404-278-3113, Ext 237, 247
Crawford, Judith, *Librn,* Mary P Shelton Library, Georgetown OH. 513-378-3197
Crawford, Judy, *Librn,* Wentworth Library (Sheffield Branch), Sheffield ON. 416-526-4126
Crawford, Kay, *Librn,* Humphreys County Library System (Isola Public), Isola MS. 601-962-3606
Crawford, Kay F, *ILL,* University of Nebraska-Lincoln, University Libraries, Lincoln NE. 402-472-2526
Crawford, Kimberly, *Assoc Librn,* Virginia Intermont College, J F Hicks Memorial Library, Bristol VA. 703-669-6101, Ext 26
Crawford, Marilyn, *Ad & Ch,* Kitchener Public Library, Kitchener ON. 519-743-0271
Crawford, Marjorie, *ILL,* Rutgers University, the State University of New Jersey (School of Law), Newark NJ. 201-648-5675
Crawford, Mary R, *Dir,* Howard College at Big Spring Library, Big Spring TX. 915-267-6311, Ext 67
Crawford, Mrs Francis, *Librn,* Quinter Public Library, Quinter KS. 913-754-3821
Crawford, Mrs Maurice, *Dir,* Atlanta-Jackson Township Public Library, Atlanta IN. 317-292-2521
Crawford, Myrtle, *Librn,* Le Roy Community Library, Le Roy MI. 616-768-4493
Crawford, Pamela, *Assoc Librn,* Naples Public Library, Naples ME. 207-693-6841
Crawford, Paula, *On-Line Servs & Bibliog Instr,* California State College, Stanislaus Library, Turlock CA. 209-633-2232
Crawford, Ruth, *Chief Librn,* Veterans Administration, Hospital Library, Lincoln NE. 402-489-3802
Crawford, Shelby J, *Librn,* Washington County Law Library, Hagerstown MD. 301-791-3116
Crawford, Susan, *Dir,* American Medical Association, Division of Library & Archival Services, Chicago IL. 751-6000; 751-6011
Crawford, Wm, *AV,* Cape Fear Technical Institute, Library Learning Resource Center, Wilmington NC. 919-343-0481, Ext 230
Crawford, Jr, Mrs Hugh, *Librn,* New Providence Presbyterian Church, Alexander-Smith Library, Maryville TN. 615-983-0182
Crawley, Marian, *Librn,* Indianapolis-Marion County Public Library (Broadway), Indianapolis IN. 317-635-5662
Crawshaw, Elizabeth, *Libr Tech,* George Brown College of Applied Arts & Technology Library (Film Library), Toronto ON. 416-967-1212
Crawshaw, Helen, *Ch,* Saratoga Springs Public Library, Saratoga Springs NY. 518-584-7860
Crawshaw, William, *Acq,* Crandall Library, Glens Falls NY. 518-792-6508
Cray, Katherine, *Asst Librn,* Goldman, Sachs & Co Library, New York NY. 212-676-7400
Creager, Gladys, *Librn,* Ingham County Library (Dansville Branch), Dansville MI. 517-623-6511
Creager, Marile, *Asst Dir Pub Servs,* Tacoma Public Library, Tacoma WA. 206-572-2000
Creaghe, Norma, *Dir,* Saint Anselm's College, Geisel Library, Manchester NH. 603-669-1030, Ext 240, 249
Creamer, Geraldine, *Dir,* Sayreville Public Library, Parlin NJ. 201-727-0213
Creamer, Goldie, *Librn,* Adams Library (MacKay), North Chelmsford MA. 617-251-3212
Creasy, Valerie, *Dir,* Picton Public Library, Picton ON. 613-476-5962
Credle, Ellen, *Ch,* Springfield Public Library, Springfield OR. 503-726-3765
Creed, Verna, *Dir & Spec Coll,* Field Library, Peekskill Library, Peekskill NY. 914-737-0010
Creel, Marion, *Librn,* Wood Gundy Inc Library, New York NY. 212-344-0633
Creelan, Marilee, *Dir,* Akron City Hospital, Medical Library, Akron OH. 216-375-3000

Creelman, Mrs G, *Librn,* Mount Allison University (Alfred Whitehead Memorial Music), Sackville NB. 506-536-2040, Ext 326
Creese, Elaine, *Librn,* Garden Grove Public Library, Garden Grove IA. 515-443-2355
Creighton, Elizabeth, *Tech Serv,* Meriden Public Library, Meriden CT. 203-238-2344
Crenshaw, Kari, *Asst Librn,* Wake Technical College Library, Raleigh NC. 919-772-0551, Ext 236
Crenshaw, Linnie, *Librn,* Southwest Arkansas Regional Library (Winthrop Branch), Winthrop AR. 501-777-4564
Crenshaw, Mildred, *Librn,* Statesboro Regional Library (Pembroke Public), Pembroke GA. 912-653-2822
Crenshaw, Tena, *Librn,* University of Florida Libraries (Education), Gainesville FL. 904-392-0707
Creola, Diane, *Librn,* Pittsville Community Library, Pittsville WI. 715-884-6500
Cresap, Marlys F, *Dir,* Mount Pleasant Public Library, Mount Pleasant IA. 319-385-8150
Crescenzi, Jean D, *Acq & Tech Serv,* Rutgers University (Camden Arts & Science Library), Camden NJ. 609-757-6036
Crespi, Betsey, *ILL, Ad & Ref,* West Caldwell Public Library, West Caldwell NJ. 201-226-5441
Cresswell, Tom, *Media,* Albany County Public Library, Laramie WY. 307-745-3365
Cresto, Kathy, *Ser,* Pepperdine University Library, Payson Library, Malibu CA. 213-456-4252
Cretini, Blanche, *ILL & Ref,* Louisiana State Library, Baton Rouge LA. 504-342-4922
Creviston, Susan, *ILL, Ref & Bibliog Instr,* Lander College Library, Larry A Jackson Library, Greenwood SC. 803-229-8366
Crews, B C, *Bibliog,* North Carolina Agricultural & Technical State University, F D Bluford Library, Greensboro NC. 919-379-7782, 379-7783
Crews, Nancy, *Librn,* Colquitt-Thomas Regional Library (Ochlocknee Branch), Ochlocknee GA. 912-574-3241
Crews, Sarah W, *Tech Serv,* Virginia State Library, Richmond VA. 804-786-8929
Cribben, Sister Mary Margaret, *Assoc Prof,* Villanova University, Graduate Dept of Library Science, PA. 215-527-2100, Ext 354, 355
Crichton, Violet, *Librn,* Frontenac County Library (Barriefield Branch), Barriefield ON. 613-542-8222
Crickman, Robin, *Asst Prof,* University of Minnesota, Library School, MN. 612-373-3100
Crider, Carol, *Instr,* Andrews University, Library Science Dept, MI. 616-471-3549
Cridge, Edmund, *Media,* University of Alaska, Fairbanks, Elmer E Rasmuson Library, Fairbanks AK. 907-479-7224
Cridland, Nacy, *Hist,* Indiana University at Bloomington, University Libraries, Bloomington IN. 812-337-3403
Crigger, Ada, *Librn,* Greenfield Public Library, Greenfield IA. 515-743-6120
Crimi, Rose, *Admin Servs,* San Jose Public Library, San Jose CA. 408-277-4822
Crimmin, Wilbur B, *Librn,* Hartford Public Library, Hartford CT. 203-525-9121
Crinklaw, Winifred, *Asst Librn,* Lovett Memorial Library, Pampa TX. 806-665-3981
Criscoe, Ruth, *Librn,* Northeast Regional Library (Hickory Flat Library), Hickory Flat MS. 601-333-6682
Crislip, Marion, *Dir,* Mayfield-Graves County Library, Mayfield KY. 502-247-2911
Crismond, Linda, *Chief Deputy Co Librn,* Los Angeles County Public Library System, South State Cooperative Library System, Los Angeles CA. 213-974-6501
Crismond, Linda, *Asst Dir of Tech Servs,* University of Southern California, Edward L Doheny Memorial Library, Los Angeles CA. 213-743-6050
Crisp, Annette, *Per,* University of North Carolina at Asheville, D Hiden Ramsey Library, Asheville NC. 704-258-0200
Crisp, J, *Dir,* Pharmaceutical Manufacturers Association Library, Washington DC. 202-463-2089
Crispen, Joanne, *Dir,* Lutheran General Hospital Library, Park Ridge IL. 312-696-5494

Crispin, Emelia, *Cat,* American Samoa-Office of Library Services, Pago Pago, Samoa PI. 633-5869
Crissey, Lois L, *Librn,* New York Supreme Court Library, Eighth Judicial District, Buffalo NY. 716-852-0712
Crissinger, John, *Librn,* Virginia Polytechnic Institute & State University Library (Geology), Blacksburg VA. 703-961-6101
Crissman, Lois, *On-Line Servs,* Northwest Missouri State University, Wells Library, Maryville MO. 816-582-7141, Ext 1192
Crissy, Frank, *Librn,* San Antonio Public Library (Landa Library Center), San Antonio TX. 512-732-8369
Crist, Sally J, *Librn,* Frederick County Planning Commission Library, Frederick MD. 301-663-8300
Criswell, Jean, *Librn,* Public Library of Columbus & Franklin County (Gahanna Branch), Gahanna OH. 614-471-5280
Critchfield, Jo, *Librn,* Lord Corp, Information Centers, Erie PA. 814-868-3611, 456-8511
Critchley, Alice, *Mgr,* Western Union Information Center, Upper Saddle River NJ. 201-825-5850
Critchlow, Therese, *Media,* Princeton Public Library, Princeton NJ. 609-924-9529
Crites, Judith, *Librn,* Bernalillo County Mental Health Center Library, Albuquerque NM. 505-843-2800
Crites, Sue Ellen, *Librn & Bibliog Instr,* Dyersburg State Community College Library, Dyersburg TN. 901-285-6910
Crittenden, Sara N, *Dir,* Saint Petersburg Junior College, Saint Petersburg Campus Library, Saint Petersburg FL. 813-546-0011, Ext 353
Croce, Camille, *Librn,* Family Service Association of America Library, New York NY. 212-674-6100, Ext 49, 50
Crocfer, Philip, *Librn,* San Bernardino County Library (Needles Branch), Needles CA. 714-326-2623
Crochet, Wanda, *Librn,* Iberville Parish Library (East Iberville), St Gabriel LA. 504-642-8380
Crock, Mary Ellen, *Media,* Centre County Library & Historical Museum, Bellefonte PA. 814-355-3131
Crocker, Anne, *Librn,* University of New Brunswick (Law), Fredericton NB. 506-453-4669
Crocker, Jane Lopes, *Dir,* Gloucester County College, Library-Media Center, Sewell NJ. 609-468-5000, Ext 294
Crockett, C M, *Dir,* University of Prince Edward Island, Robertson Library, Charlottetown PE. 902-892-1243
Crockett, M, *Acq,* University of Prince Edward Island, Robertson Library, Charlottetown PE. 902-892-1243
Crockett, Monica, *Librn,* Perry County District Library (Junction City Branch), Junction City OH. 614-342-1077
Crockett, Vera, *Ch,* Wellesley Free Library, Subregional Headquarters for Eastern Massachusetts Regional Library System, Wellesley MA. 617-235-1610
Crockett, Verna L, *Librn,* Middle Tennessee State University (Campus School), Murfreesboro TN. 615-898-2960
Crockett, Yvonne, *Cat,* Southern University, Shreveport-Bossier City Campus Library, Shreveport LA. 318-424-6552, Ext 238
Crodian, Catherine, *Exten Librn,* Shawnee Library System, Carterville IL. 618-985-3711
Crofoot, Barbara K, *Librn,* Henika Public Library, Wayland MI. 616-792-2891
Croft, Betty, *Tech Serv,* Northwest Missouri State University, Wells Library, Maryville MO. 816-582-7141, Ext 1192
Croft, Rebecca, *ILL, Ser & Spec Coll,* Lexington Public Library, Lexington KY. 606-252-8871
Croft, Vicki, *Librn,* Washington State University Library (Veterinary Medicine), Pullman WA. 509-335-9556
Croghan, John H, *Chmn,* University of Miami, Instructional Technology & Design, FL. 305-284-2891
Croke, Carolyn, *Dir,* Woodstock Public Library & Art Gallery, Woodstock ON. 519-537-4801
Crombie, Joanne, *Asst Librn,* Resurrection Hospital, Medical Library, Chicago IL. 312-774-8000, Ext 2512

Crombie, Kenneth C, *Librn,* Delco Electronics Div GMC, Santa Barbara Operations, Technical Library, Goleta CA. 805-961-5080
Cromer, Kenneth, *Asst Dir,* Lorain Public Library, Lorain OH. 216-244-1192
Cromer, Kenneth, *Outreach Services,* Lorain Public Library, Lorain OH. 216-244-1192
Crompton, Dianne, *Libr Technician,* Canada Wire & Cable Ltd, Technical Library, Toronto ON. 416-421-0440, Ext 319
Cromwell, Marie, *Dir,* Randolph Township Free Public Library, Randolph NJ. 201-366-0518
Cron, Howard, *Circ,* University of Santa Clara, Michel Orradre Library, Santa Clara CA. 408-984-4415
Crone, Rhoda, *Librn,* Mendocino County Library (Willits Branch), Willits CA. 707-459-5908
Crone, Sherry, *Librn,* Ruth Enlow Library of Garrett County (Accident Branch), Accident MD. 301-862-8792
Croneberger, Robert, *Deputy Dir,* Memphis-Shelby County Public Library & Information Center, Memphis TN. 901-528-2950
Cronin, Cindy, *Librn,* Eldora Public Library, Eldora IA. 515-858-2173
Cronin, Connie, *Librn,* Parke, Davis & Company Research Library, Ann Arbor MI. 313-994-3500
Cronin, Emma, *Ref Coordr,* Eastfield College, Learning Resources Center, Mesquite TX. 214-746-3168
Cronin, Frances T, *Librn,* Newtown Library Co, Newtown PA. 717-968-9928
Cronin, John, *Librn,* Boston Herald American Newspaper Library, Boston MA. 617-426-3000
Cronin, John, *Lectr,* Simmons College, Graduate School of Library & Information Science, MA. 617-738-2225
Cronin, Mary J, *Exec Dir,* Library Council of Metropolitan Milwaukee, Inc, WI. 414-271-8470
Cronk, Alida, *Coordr,* Ericson Public Library (Old Settler's Library), Boone IA. 515-432-3727, 432-7010, 432-3738
Cronmiller, Mary, *Acq,* Institute of Paper Chemistry Library, Appleton WI. 414-734-9251
Cronshaw, Patricia, *Ser,* University of California, Santa Barbara Library, Santa Barbara CA. 805-961-2741
Crook, Barbara, *Asst Dir,* Columbiana Public Library, Columbiana OH. 216-482-2356
Crook, Carol, *Librn,* Arcade Free Library, Arcade NY. 716-492-1297
Crookes, Frank, *Dir,* Kellogg Community College, Emory W Morris Learning Resource Center, Battle Creek MI. 616-965-3931, Ext 333
Crooks, Constance, *In Charge,* Milwaukee Public Library (Forest Home Branch), Milwaukee WI. 414-278-3083
Crooks, James E, *Ref,* University of Michigan Libraries (Medical Center), Ann Arbor MI. 313-764-1210
Crooks, Joyce, *Ref,* Alameda County Library, Hayward CA. 415-881-6337
Crooks, Mrs Hal, *Librn,* Sterling Free Public Library, Sterling KS. 316-278-3191
Crooks, Nancy, *Cat,* Miami-Dade Public Library System, Miami FL. 305-579-5001
Crosby, Barbara A, *Chief Librn,* Lithgow Public Library, Augusta ME. 207-622-6368
Crosby, Connie, *Librn,* South Mississippi Regional Library (Prentiss Public), Prentiss MS. 601-792-5845
Crosby, Elizabeth, *ILL,* Southeast Regional Library, Dummerston VT. 802-254-2961
Crosby, Joan, *Librn,* Rangely Public Library, Rangely CO. 303-675-8811
Crosby, Meredith, *Ch,* Turner Free Library, Randolph MA. 617-963-3000
Crosby, Mrs P, *Librn,* Vulcan Municipal Library, Vulcan AB. 403-485-2571
Crosby, Peter, *Ref,* New England College, H Raymond Danforth Library, Henniker NH. 603-428-2344
Crosby, Ramona C T, *Supvr,* Stauffer Chemical Co, Information Services, Dobbs Ferry NY. 914-693-1200
Crosby-Brown, Corryn, *On-Line Servs,* University of Nevada, Las Vegas, James R Dickinson Library, Las Vegas NV. 702-739-3286
Crose, Michael, *Bus Mgr,* Timberland Regional Library, Olympia WA. 206-943-5001
Croslin, Kenneth, *Dir,* Troy State University Library, Troy AL. 205-566-3000, Ext 263

Crosman, Alexander C, *Librn,* Peoria Public Library, Peoria IL. 309-672-8839
Cross, Adeline, *Librn,* Fishkill Plains Library, Wappingers Falls NY. 914-226-9943
Cross, Bonnie, *Librn,* Hammond Public Library (Jefferson), Hammond IN. 219-931-5100
Cross, Carlyle, *Acq,* Cumberland College, Norma Perkins Hagan Memorial Library, Williamsburg KY. 606-549-0558
Cross, Catharine, *Acq,* Colorado School of Mines, Arthur Lakes Library, Golden CO. 303-279-0300, Ext 2690
Cross, Dorothy, *On-Line Servs & Bibliog Instr,* United States Department of the Army (The Army Library, Pentagon), Washington DC. 202-697-4301, Ext 69-55346
Cross, Douglas, *Asst Dir,* Walters State Community College, Learning Resource Center, Morristown TN. 615-581-2121, Ext 212
Cross, Elizabeth, *ILL,* Cary Memorial Library, Lexington MA. 617-862-6288
Cross, Esther, *Ch,* Reed Memorial Library, Ravenna Public Library, Ravenna OH. 216-296-2827
Cross, Esther, *Librn,* Sylvan Grove Public Library, Sylvan Grove KS. 913-526-3555
Cross, Geraldine P, *Dir,* Mercer University in Atlanta Library, Atlanta GA. 404-451-0331, Ext 47, 66
Cross, Harriet, *Librn,* Peck Memorial Library, Marathon NY. 607-849-6135
Cross, Jennifer, *ILL,* West Liberty State College, Paul N Elbin Library, West Liberty WV. 304-336-8035
Cross, Joseph, *Ref,* University of South Carolina (Coleman Karesh Law Libr), Columbia SC. 803-777-5942
Cross, Lillie, *In Charge,* United States Department of Commerce, Field Services Library, Dallas TX. 214-767-0544
Cross, Linda, *Cat,* University of Arkansas for Medical Sciences Library, Little Rock AR. 501-661-5980
Cross, Mary K, *Outreach Librn,* Albemarle Regional Library, Winton NC. 919-358-7631
Cross, Robert J, *Assoc Dir Pub Serv,* Western Washington University, Mabel Zoe Wilson Library, Bellingham WA. 206-676-3050
Cross, Susan, *Sr Citizens Coordr,* Wheatland Regional Library, Saskatoon SK. 306-652-5077
Crossan, David, *Dir,* Allen County-Fort Wayne Historical Society Library, Fort Wayne IN. 219-743-5776
Crossen, Phyllis, *Asst Dir,* New School of Music, Alice Tully Library, Philadelphia PA. 215-732-3966
Crossett, Dave, *Librn,* Gila County Law Library, Globe AZ. 602-425-3231
Crossey, J M, *Africana,* Yale University Library (Sterling Memorial Library), New Haven CT. 203-436-8335
Crossfield, Nancy, *Librn,* University of Wisconsin-Madison (Geology-Geophysics Library), Madison WI. 608-262-3521
Crossland, Howard, *Librn,* Free Public Library of the City of Trenton (East Trenton), Trenton NJ. 609-392-7188
Crossland, Marilyn, *Dir,* Tarrant County Junior College System (Northwest Campus Learning Resources Center), Fort Worth TX. 817-232-2900, Ext 208
Crossmon, Mary, *Acq,* Stockton-San Joaquin County Public Library, Stockton Public Libr, Stockton CA. 209-944-8415
Crosthwaite, Mrs E, *Media,* Kelsey Institute of Applied Arts & Sciences, Learning Resources Center, Saskatoon SK. 306-664-6417
Croteau, Mary, *Dir,* Huron Valley Library System, Ann Arbor MI. 313-971-6056
Croteau, Mary, *Dir,* Washtenaw County Library, Ann Arbor MI. 313-971-6056
Crothers, Susan, *Librn,* Burgettstown Community Library, Burgettstown PA. 412-947-9780
Crotts, Brenda, *Tech Serv,* Butte County Library, Oroville CA. 916-534-4525
Crotty, Mary, *Cat & Ref,* Marlborough Public Library, Marlborough MA. 617-485-0494
Crouch, Anne, *Bkmobile Coordr,* Loudoun County Public Library, Leesburg VA. 703-777-0368
Crouch, Christine, *ILL & Ref,* Mid-Hudson Library System, Poughkeepsie NY. 914-471-6060

Crouch, James, *Librn,* United States Department of the Navy (Naval Supply Systems Command Library), Washington DC. 202-695-4704

Crouch, Josephine, *Dir,* Aiken-Bamberg-Barnwell-Edgefield Regional Library, Aiken SC. 803-648-8961

Crouch, Judith, *Cat,* Northwestern Oklahoma State University Library, Alva OK. 405-327-1700, Ext 219

Crouch, Keith, *Chief Librn,* Royal Military College of Canada, Massey Arts & Science-Engineering Library, Kingston ON. 613-545-7305

Crouch, Milton, *Reader Serv,* University of Vermont & State Agricultural College, Bailey-Howe Memorial Library, Burlington VT. 802-656-2020

Crouch, Vivian, *Librn,* Dallas County Public Library (Rowlett Branch), Rowlett TX. 214-475-3841

Crouch, Wayne, *Assoc Prof,* Syracuse University, School of Information Studies, NY. 315-423-2911

Croucher, Sharon, *Librn,* Clifton Springs Library, Clifton Springs NY. 315-462-2821

Crough, Carol, *Librn,* Ennismore Township Public Library, Ennismore ON. 705-292-9892

Crouse, Mary L, *Librn,* Thomasville Public Library, Thomasville NC. 919-476-7217

Crouse, Mary Lee, *Asst Dir,* Davidson County Public Library System, Lexington NC. 704-246-2520

Crouse, Moses C, *Curator Jenks Memorial Coll,* Aurora College, Charles B Phillips Library, Aurora IL. 312-892-6431, Ext 61, 62

Crouse, Rick, *Coordr & Media,* Charity Hospital of Louisiana, School Of Nursing Media Center, New Orleans LA. 504-568-6431

Crow, Linda, *Librn,* Courier-News Library, Bridgewater NJ. 201-722-8800, Ext 328

Crow, Lucy, *Cat,* Victoria Public Library, Victoria TX. 512-578-6241

Crow, Rebecca, *Librn,* Dallas Public Library (Audelia Road), Dallas TX. 214-348-6160

Crow, Rochelle, *Tech Serv,* University of Alabama in Birmingham, Mervyn H Sterne Library, Birmingham AL. 205-934-6360

Crow, Sherry, *Ch,* Hays Public Library, Hays KS. 913-625-9014

Crowder, Audrey, *Asst Librn,* Cherryvale Public Library, Cherryvale KS. 316-336-2491

Crowder, Carolyn, *Circ,* Macon Junior College Library, Macon GA. 912-474-2700, Ext 215, 216

Crowder, John, *Acq & Cat,* Fort Lewis College Library, Durango CO. 303-247-7738

Crowder, Nannie A, *Dir,* H Leslie Perry Memorial Library, Henderson NC. 919-438-3316

Crowe, Alberta, *Dir,* Crystal City Public Library, Crystal City MO. 314-937-7166

Crowe, Alice M, *Librn,* Saint Clair County Library (Ashville), Ashville AL. 205-594-4047

Crowe, Deborah, *Ch,* Oshkosh Public Library, Oshkosh WI. 414-424-0473

Crowe, Ione, *Librn,* Moccasin Bend Mental Health Institute (Health Sciences Library), Chattanooga TN. 615-265-2271, Ext 242

Crowe, John, *Bibliog Instr,* Dauphin County Library System, Harrisburg PA. 234-4961

Crowe, Linda, *Systs Develop Officer,* North Suburban Library System, Wheeling IL. 312-459-1300

Crowe, Mary, *ILL & Ref,* Boston University Libraries (Mugar Memorial Library), Boston MA. 617-353-3710

Crowe, Virginia M, *Chmn,* Edinboro State College, Library Science Dept, PA. 814-732-2000, Ext 2766

Crowe, William, *Asst to Dir,* Ohio State University Libraries (William Oxley Thompson Memorial Library), Columbus OH. 614-422-6151

Crowell, David P, *Ref & Doc,* New Jersey Institute of Technology, Robert W Van Houten Library, Newark NJ. 201-645-5306

Crowell, Evelyn, *ILL,* Portland State University, Branford Price Millar Library, Portland OR. 503-229-4424

Crowell, Jo Lynn, *Asst Dir,* Mercer University (Walter F George School of Law Library), Macon GA. 912-745-6811, Ext 345

Crowell, Marilee, *Tech Serv,* Minneapolis Community College Library, Minneapolis MN. 612-341-7089, 341-7059

Crowell, Mary R, *Librn,* National Association of Purchasing Management, Purchasing Information Center, New York NY. 212-267-3677

Crowell, Mrs Livingston, *Librn,* Watertown Historical Society Library, Watertown CT. 203-274-1634

Crowell, Nancy E, *Librn,* Scarborough Public Library, Scarborough ME. 207-883-4723

Crowers, Clifford P, *Head,* Free Library of Philadelphia (Government Publications), Philadelphia PA. 215-686-5322

Crowl, Virginia, *Doc,* Kent State University Libraries, Kent OH. 216-672-2962

Crowley, Alma, *ILL,* Bloomfield College Library, Bloomfield NJ. 201-748-9000, Ext 281

Crowley, Bill, *Continuing Educ,* Alabama Public Library Service, Montgomery AL. 205-832-5743

Crowley, Cecelia, *Asst Dir,* La Grange Public Library, La Grange IL. 312-352-0576, Ext 6

Crowley, Eleanor M, *Dir,* Ipswich Public Library, Ipswich MA. 617-356-4646

Crowley, Elin Hannigan, *Librn,* Rhode Island Occupational Information Coordinating Committee, Career Counseling Service Library, Providence RI. 401-272-0900

Crowley, John A, *Librn,* Seminary of Saint Vincent De Paul Library, Boynton Beach FL. 305-732-4424, Ext 44

Crowley, John V, *Asst Dir,* State University of New York, College at Oneonta, James M Milne Library, Oneonta NY. 607-431-2723

Crowley, Leone, *Librn,* Reuben McMillan Free Library Free Library Association (Canfield Branch), Canfield OH. 216-533-5631

Crowley, Mrs Elmer, *Librn,* Columbia-Lafayette-Ouachita-Calhoun Regional Library (Stamps Branch), Stamps AR. 501-234-1991

Crowley, Ocea, *Librn,* Saguache County Public Library, Saguache CO. 303-655-2551

Crowley, Patience L, *Librn,* Gifford Memorial Hospital, Inc, Health Information Center, Randolph VT. 802-728-3366

Crowley, Patricia, *On-Line Servs & Bibliog Instr,* University of Florida Libraries (J Hillis Miller Health Center), Gainesville FL. 904-392-4011

Crowley, Stephen, *Librn,* Kanawha County Public Library (Dunbar Public), Dunbar WV. 304-766-7161

Crowley, Susan B, *Librn,* Santa Barbara County Law Library, Santa Barbara CA. 805-966-1611, Ext 6501

Crowley, Susan B, *Librn,* Santa Barbara County Law Library, Santa Maria Branch, Santa Maria CA. 805-922-7831

Crowley, Terence, *Assoc Prof,* San Jose State University, Division of Library Science, CA. 408-277-2292

Crowlie, Colleen, *Publicity-Program,* Cochise County Library System, Bisbee AZ. 602-432-5703, Ext 500

Crownover, Harriet, *Librn,* Linden Free Public Library (Sunnyside), Linden NJ. 201-486-1888

Crownover, Margaret, *Asst Librn,* Sandy Public Library, Sandy OR. 503-668-5537

Crowson, Marjorie, *Dir,* Tangipahoa Parish Library, Amite LA. 504-748-9387

Crowther, Karmen, *On-Line Servs,* University of Tennessee, Knoxville, James D Hoskins Library, Knoxville TN. 615-974-0111

Crowther, Mary C, *Spec Coll,* Salina Public Library, Salina KS. 913-825-4624

Croxford, Agnes M, *Librn,* James F Maclaren Ltd Library, Willowdale ON. 416-499-0880, Ext 276

Croxford, Roberta, *Cat,* West Springfield Public Library, West Springfield MA. 413-736-4561

Croxton, F E, *Dir, Automated Systs Off,* Library of Congress, Washington DC. 202-287-5000

Crozier, Ann, *Librn,* Ventura County Library Services Agency (Ojai Branch), Ojai CA. 805-646-1639

Crozier, C Gordon, *Asst Dir,* Rider College, Franklin F Moore Library, Lawrenceville NJ. 609-896-5111

Crozier, Charlene L, *Chief Librn,* Orange County Public Library (Stanton Branch), Stanton CA. 714-898-3302

Crozier, Marcine, *Librn,* Lake Blackshear Regional Library (Dooly County Public), Vienna GA. 912-268-4687

Crozier, Richard J, *Librn,* North Central Bible College, T J Jones Memorial Library, Minneapolis MN. 612-332-3491

Crozier, Ron, *Librn,* Santa Barbara Museum of Art Library, Santa Barbara CA. 805-963-4363, Ext 24

Crozier, Susan, *Cat,* Southern Alberta Institute of Technology, Learning Resources Centre, Calgary AB. 284-8647; 284-8648

Cruddas, Nola, *Circ,* Montgomery County-Norristown Public Library, Norristown PA. 215-277-3355

Cruddas, Nola Beth, *In Charge,* Bay County Historical Society, Museum of the Great Lakes Library, Bay City MI. 517-893-5733, Ext 4

Cruglio, Madeline, *Librn,* Jefferson Township Public Library, Jefferson Township NJ. 201-697-6363

Crugnola, Nella, *Asst Dir & Pub Servs,* Stamford's Public Library, Ferguson Library, Stamford CT. 203-325-4354

Cruikshank, Clara, *Ch,* Douglass Boulevard Christian Church Library, Louisville KY. 502-452-2629

Cruise, Larry, *ILL,* Raleigh County Public Library, Beckley WV. 304-255-0511

Crum, Mark, *Dir,* Kalamazoo Public Library, Kalamazoo MI. 616-342-9837

Crum, Norm, *Lit Searcher,* Lockheed Corporation (Lockheed-California Company Central Library), Burbank CA. 213-847-5646

Crum, Shutta, *Dir,* South Lyon Public Library, South Lyon MI. 313-437-6431

Crum, Virginia, *Asst Librn,* Shelbyville Free Public Library, Shelbyville IL. 217-774-4432

Crumley, Sandie, *Asst Librn,* Dvoracek Memorial Library, Wilber Public Library, Wilber NE. 402-821-2832

Crumlish, Paul W, *Dir,* Hobart & William Smith Colleges, Warren Hunting Smith Library, Geneva NY. 315-789-5500, Ext 224

Crumm, Beverly, *Librn,* Saint Clair County Library System (Saint Clair Public), St Clair MI. 313-329-3951

Crump, M B, *ILL,* Florida Agricultural & Mechanical University, Samuel H Coleman Memorial Library, Tallahassee FL. 904-599-3370

Crump, Mel, *Tech Serv,* Stanislaus County Free Library, Modesto CA. 209-526-6821

Crump, Ruth Mary, *Librn,* Clifton Community Library, Cranberry Lake NY. 315-848-2915

Crumpler, A P, *On-Line Servs & Bibliog Instr,* United States Department of the Army (Office of the Chief of Engineers Library), Washington DC. 202-693-6753

Crumpler, Linda Boysen, *Actg Dir,* Brazoria County Library, Angleton TX. 713-849-0591

Crumpton, Marguerite, *Instr,* Winthrop College, School Librarianship Program, SC. 803-323-2136

Crusz, Rienzi, *Econ,* University of Waterloo Library, Waterloo ON. 519-885-1211

Crutchfield, Benjamin F, *Asst Prof,* West Virginia Wesleyan College, Dept of Library Science, WV. 304-473-8059

Crutchfield, Mary Jane, *Chief Librn,* Veterans Administration, Center Library, Mountain Home TN. 615-926-1171, Ext 273

Crutchfield, Jr, Ben F, *Ref,* West Virginia Wesleyan College, Annie Merner Pfeiffer Library, Buckhannon WV. 304-473-8059

Cruz, Estrella De La, *Librn,* Norwegian American Hospital, Seufert Memorial Library, Chicago IL. 312-278-8800

Cruz, Karen, *Adminr Health, Educ & Nutrition,* Public Health & Social Services Dept Library, Agana, Guam PI. 734-2951, Ext 200 & 202

Cruz, Leslie, *Doc,* Navajo Community College, Naaltsoos Ba'Hooghan Library, Tsaile AZ. 602-724-6132

Cruz, Lucille, *Chief Librn,* Orange County Public Library (Silverado Branch), Silverado CA. 714-649-2216

Cruz, Luisa, *Cat,* Catholic University of Puerto Rico (Encarnacion Valdes Library), Ponce PR. 809-844-4150, Ext 119

Cruz, Luisa, *Librn,* Chicago Public Library (Humboldt), Chicago IL. 312-486-2244

Cruz, Mrs Santa Andino, *In Charge,* Office of Economic Opportunity Library, San Juan PR. 809-725-0220

Cruz, Sonia E, *Ref,* University of Puerto Rico, Cayey University College Library, Cayey PR. 809-738-2161, Ext 221, 738-5651

Cruzat, Gwendolyn S, *Prof,* University of Michigan, School of Library Science, MI. 313-764-9376

Cry, Eva J, *Librn,* Carnegie Public Library, Terrell TX. 214-563-6463

Cryan, Meike, *Dir,* Liberty Public Library, Liberty NY. 914-292-6070

Cryder, George, *Media,* Ohio Wesleyan University, L A Beeghly Library, Delaware OH. 614-369-4431, Ext 509

Crysup, Carolyn, *Asst Librn,* Bastrop Public Library, Bastrop TX. 512-321-5441

Csaky, Susan D, *Dir,* University of Missouri-Columbia (Law), Columbia MO. 314-882-6096

Csatora, Rebecca, *Ref,* Stetson University College of Law, Charles A Dana Law Library, Saint Petersburg FL. 813-345-1335

Csefalvay, Edmund, *Acq,* United States Department of the Treasury Library, Washington DC. 202-566-2777, 566-3279

Cseh, Eugene, *Acq,* University of Connecticut Health Center, Lyman Maynard Stowe Library, Farmington CT. 203-674-2739

Csicsek, Martha J, *In Charge,* Enoch Pratt Free Library (Canton), Baltimore MD. 301-396-5430, 396-5395

Csoke, Ralph, *Librn,* Public Library of the District of Columbia (Mount Pleasant), Washington DC. 202-727-1361

Csoltko, June K, *Librn,* Bridgeport Public Library (Black Rock), Bridgeport CT. 203-576-7427

Csuros, Barna, *Assoc Dir,* Kean College of New Jersey, Nancy Thompson Library, Union NJ. 201-527-2017

Cubbal, Geraldine B, *Librn,* Mental Health Center at Fort Wayne, Inc, CMHC Library, Fort Wayne IN. 219-482-9111, Ext 229

Cubbedge, Frankie H, *Dir,* University of South Carolina at Aiken, Gregg-Graniteville Library, Aiken SC. 803-648-6851, Ext 165

Cubberly, Carol, *Tech Serv & Acq,* University of the South, Jessie Ball duPont Library, Sewanee TN. 615-598-5931, Ext 265, 267

Cubit, James, *Asst Dir,* University of Missouri-Rolla Library, Rolla MO. 314-341-4227

Cubose, Mrs E H, *President,* San Antonio Art League Library, San Antonio TX. 512-732-6048

Cucchiara, Anthony, *Curator,* Bryant Library, Roslyn NY. 516-621-2240

Cuda, Gabrielle, *ILL,* Ledding Library of Milwaukie, Milwaukie Public Library, Milwaukie OR. 503-659-3911

Cuddy, Joan, *Art hist,* Southern Alberta Institute of Technology, Alberta College of Art Library, Calgary AB. 403-284-8665

Cuddy, Joan, *Asst Librn,* Southern Alberta Institute of Technology, Alberta College of Art Library, Calgary AB. 403-284-8665

Cuellar, Nelson, *Librn,* Public Library of the District of Columbia (Palisades), Washington DC. 202-727-1369

Cuesta, Yolanda, *Minority Groups,* California State Library, Sacramento CA. 916-445-2585

Cuff, Mary, *Librn,* Bankers Trust Co Library, New York NY. 212-692-4680, 692-4681

Culbert, Lorraine M, *Librn,* Sohio Petroleum Company Library, Anchorage AK. 907-265-0594

Culbertson, Diana, *Librn & On-Line Servs,* National Dairy Council Library, Rosemont IL. 312-696-1020

Culbertson, Gladys, *Cat,* University of North Carolina at Asheville, D Hiden Ramsey Library, Asheville NC. 704-258-0200

Culbertson, Katheryn C, *Dir,* Tennessee State Library & Archives, Nashville TN. 615-741-2764

Culhoun, John C, *Tech Serv,* Knox College, Henry W Seymour Library, Galesburg IL. 309-343-0112, Ext 246

Culkin, Patricia, *Assoc Librn,* University of Denver, Penrose Library, Denver CO. 303-753-2007

Cullen, Lawrence, *Librn,* North Hennepin Community College Library, Brooklyn Park MN. 612-425-4541

Cullen, Lawrence R, *Librn,* North Hennepin Community College Library, Minneapolis MN. 612-425-4541

Cullen, Linda, *Br Coordr & Bkmobile Coordr,* Augusta Regional Library, Augusta-Richmond County Public Library, Augusta GA. 404-724-1871

Culley, Paul T, *On-Line Servs,* Alfred University (Scholes Library of Ceramics), Alfred NY. 607-871-2492

Culley, Paul T, *Ceramic, Eng & Sci,* Alfred University (Scholes Library of Ceramics), Alfred NY. 607-871-2492

Cullinan, Mary Jo, *Librn,* Brooklyn Public Library (Spring Creek), Brooklyn NY. 212-649-0020

Cullinane, Irenemarie, *Ch,* Boston Public Library, Eastern Massachusetts Library System, Boston MA. 617-536-5400

Cullison, Frankie, *Curator,* Cowley County Historical Museum Library, Winfield KS. 316-221-4141

Culliver, Linda, *Librn,* Clark County Library District (West Las Vegas), Las Vegas NV. 702-648-9421

Culmer, Carita M, *Per,* Phoenix College Library, Phoenix AZ. 602-264-2492, Ext 621

Culmo, Jo Ann, *Tech Serv,* Ansonia Library, Ansonia CT. 203-734-6275

Culotta, Wendy, *Sci-Tech,* California State University, Long Beach, University Library, Long Beach CA. 213-498-4047

Culp, Bonnie Henderson, *Librn,* Rockwell Public Library, Rockwell NC. 704-279-2180

Culp, Evylund, *Librn,* Johnson County Library (DeSoto Branch), DeSoto KS. 913-585-3106

Culp, Jean R, *Dir,* Laurel County Public Library District, London KY. 606-864-5759

Culp, Marion E, *Dir,* Roosevelt Public Library, Roosevelt NY. 516-378-0222

Culp, Robert, *ILL,* Mount Sinai School of Medicine of City University of New York, Gustave L & Janet W Levy Library, New York NY. 212-650-6671

Culp, Sally, *Libr Asst,* Spartanburg County Public Library (Inman Branch), Inman SC. 803-472-8363

Culpepper, David, *Tech Serv,* Washington County Library System, William Alexander Percy Memorial Library, Greenville MS. 601-335-2331

Culpepper, Jane, *ILL, Ref & On-Line Servs,* Georgia Southwestern College, James Earl Carter Library, Americus GA. 912-928-1352

Culpepper, Jetta, *Asst Prof,* Murray State University, Dept of Library Science, KY. 502-762-2291

Culpepper, Jetta, *Acq,* Murray State University, Harry Lee Waterfield Library, Murray KY. 502-762-2291

Culpepper, Lynn, *Circ,* Pearl River County Library System, Margaret Reed Crosby Memorial Library, Picayune MS. 601-798-5081

Culpepper, Ruth C, *ILL,* University of Louisville Library, Louisville KY. 502-588-6745

Culver, Deenie M, *Librn,* Public Library of Anniston & Calhoun County (Library for the Blind & Physically Handicapped), Anniston AL. 205-237-8501

Culver, Patsy, *Commun Relations,* Lewis & Clark Library, Helena MT. 406-442-2380

Culviner, Leslie, *Asst Librn & Tech Serv,* Madison Public Library, Madison NJ. 201-377-0722

Cumbee, David E, *Dir,* Hopkinsville-Christian County Public Library, Hopkinsville KY. 502-886-2341

Cumberland, Donna M, *Asst Dir & YA,* Anderson City-Anderson & Stony Creek Township Public Library, Anderson Public Library, Anderson IN. 317-644-0938

Cumby, Gladys, *Librn,* Forsyth County Public Library (Clemmons Branch), Clemmons NC. 919-766-5122

Cuming, Rachel, *ILL,* Bolivar County Library, Robinson-Carpenter Memorial Library, Cleveland MS. 601-843-2774

Cummer, Janet, *Librn,* Strathroy Public Library, Strathroy ON. 519-245-1290

Cumming, Jerry, *Media,* Spokane Community College, East Mission Campus Library, Spokane WA. 509-455-7699

Cumming, John, *Dir Clark Historical Libr,* Central Michigan University, Charles V Park Library, Mount Pleasant MI. 517-774-3500

Cumming, Lucile, *Asst Librn,* Oshkosh Public Library, Oshkosh NE. 308-772-4554

Cummings, Betty G, *Asst Librn, Ch & YA,* Rockbridge Regional Library, Lexington VA. 703-463-4324

Cummings, Carol, *Slides,* Southeastern Massachusetts University, Library Communications Center, North Dartmouth MA. 617-999-8662

Cummings, Gary J, *Librn,* Henry Carter Hull Library, Inc, Clinton CT. 203-669-2342

Cummings, Gary J, *Librn,* New Hampshire State Prison Library, Concord NH. 603-224-6554

Cummings, Gwendolyn, *Librn,* Augusta Regional Library (Wallace), Augusta GA. 404-722-6275

Cummings, John P, *Assoc Librn,* United States Naval Academy, Nimitz Library, Annapolis MD. 301-267-2194, 267-2800

Cummings, Laura, *Cat & Bibliog Control Div Chief,* Columbia University (University Libraries), New York NY. 212-280-2241

Cummings, Linda, *Librn,* Digital Equipment Corp, Santa Clara Library, Santa Clara CA. 408-727-0200

Cummings, Marilyn, *Ch,* Sandusky Library Association, Sandusky OH. 419-625-3834

Cummings, Martin M, *Dir,* National Library of Medicine, Bethesda MD. 301-496-6308

Cummings, Nancy, *Headquarter Adminr,* Clark County Library District, Las Vegas NV. 702-733-7810

Cummings, Nancy, *Librn,* Clark County Library District (Flamingo Branch (Hq)), Las Vegas NV. 702-733-7810

Cummings, Nancy, *Librn,* Engineering-Science, Inc Library, Arcadia CA. 213-445-7560, Ext 287

Cummings, Patricia K, *Librn,* Ramsey County Law Library, Saint Paul MN. 612-298-5208

Cummings, Peggy, *Special Servs,* Alaska State Library, Juneau AK. 907-465-2910

Cummings, Roberta, *Acq & Tech Serv,* Southern University Library (Law Library), Baton Rouge LA. 504-771-3776

Cummings, Ruth, *Br Coordr,* Albany Public Library, Albany NY. 518-449-3380

Cummings, Sarah, *Ch,* Sweetwater County Library, Green River WY. 307-875-3615

Cummins, A Blair, *Dir,* Wood Library, Canandaigua NY. 716-394-1381

Cummins, Donna, *Librn,* Newport Public Library, Newport NC. 919-223-4749

Cummins, Dorothy, *Librn,* Lawrence Memorial Public Library, Climax MI. 616-746-4125

Cummins, Julie, *Ch,* Monroe County Library System, Rochester NY. 716-428-7345

Cummins, Wilma, *Acq,* State University of New York Agricultural & Technical College at Canton, Southworth Library, Canton NY. 315-386-7229

Cunha, Evano L, *Dir,* United States Air Force (Air Force Geophysics Laboratory, Research Library), Hanscom AFB MA. 617-861-4895

Cunliffe, Mildred, *Librn,* Asheville-Buncombe Library System (Skyland Branch), Skyland NC. 704-252-8701

Cunning, Dorothy, *Per,* Otterbein College, Courtright Memorial Library, Westerville OH. 614-890-3000, Ext 164

Cunningham, Aime, *Librn,* Hartford Public Library, Hartford MI. 616-621-3408

Cunningham, Charles, *ILL,* Framingham Public Library, Framingham MA. 617-879-3570

Cunningham, Dan, *Asst Dir,* Nicholson Memorial Library, Garland TX. 214-494-7187

Cunningham, Diana, *Librn,* Teledyne Energy Systems Library, Timonium MD. 301-252-8220, Ext 219

Cunningham, Jeanette, *Librn,* Hawley Library Association, Hawley PA. 717-226-4620

Cunningham, Julie, *Bibliog Instr,* Saint John's University Library, Jamaica NY. 212-969-8000, Ext 201

Cunningham, Louise, *ILL & Acq,* Portland Public Library, Baxter Library, Portland ME. 207-773-4761

Cunningham, Lynda S, *Acq,* Maryland Department of Legislative Reference Library, Annapolis MD. 301-269-2871

Cunningham, Margaret, *Librn,* Mississauga Public Library (Clarkson-Lorne Park), Mississauga ON. 416-822-1241

Cunningham, Maxine, *Librn,* Alexandria Library, Alexandria KY. 606-635-4527

Cunningham, Mel, *Dir,* Johnson County Community College Library, Overland Park KS. 913-888-8500, Ext 532

Cunningham, Mrs Tom, *Librn,* Jacksboro Public Library, Jacksboro TN. 615-562-3675

Cunningham, Nell, *Ref,* Louisiana State University in Shreveport Library, Shreveport LA. 318-797-7121, Ext 203
Cunningham, Pat, *Librn,* Midwest Research Institute, North Star Research Division Library, Minnetonka MN. 612-933-7880
Cunningham, Sharon, *Media & On-Line Servs,* Georgetown University (Fred O Dennis Law Library), Washington DC. 202-624-8260
Cunningham, Velma, *Librn,* Julia L Butterfield Memorial Library, Cold Spring NY. 914-265-3040
Cunningham, William D, *Lectr,* University of Maryland, College of Library & Information Services, MD. 301-454-5441
Cunnington, Linda J, *Librn,* Clarkson, Gordon & Co Library, Montreal PQ. 514-875-6060
Cunnion, Theodore, *Librn,* Loyola Reference Library, New York NY. 212-841-5134
Cupp, Christian M, *Dir,* Southeastern Community College, Learning Resources Center, Whiteville NC. 919-642-7141, Ext 218
Curd, Bonnie, *Bkmobile Coordr,* Mary Wood Weldon Memorial Library, Glasgow KY. 502-651-2824
Curdiff, Eleanor, *Librn,* Northport Public Library (East Northport Public), East Northport NY. 516-261-2313
Curell, Ed, *Librn,* Terrace Public Library, Terrace BC. 604-638-8177
Curia, Patt, *Ref & On-Line Servs,* San Jose Public Library, San Jose CA. 408-277-4822
Curl, Marjorie, *Cat,* George W Norris Regional Library, McCook Public Library, McCook NE. 308-345-1906
Curley, Arthur, *Deputy Dir,* Detroit Public Library, Detroit Associated Libraries, Detroit MI. 313-833-1000
Curley, Elmer, *Pub Servs,* University of Nevada, Las Vegas, James R Dickinson Library, Las Vegas NV. 702-739-3286
Curley, Estelle, *Cat,* North Carolina Agricultural & Technical State University, F D Bluford Library, Greensboro NC. 919-379-7782, 379-7783
Curley, Mrs Lawrence, *Librn,* Laura Johnson Memorial Library, Stratford NH. 603-636-1526
Curll, Nancy, *Media,* Middlesex Community College, Learning Resources Center, Bedford MA. 617-275-8910
Curnoe, G, *Librn,* London Public Libraries & Museums (Westown), London ON. 519-439-6456
Curnoles, Howard, *Bibliog Instr,* University of Maryland Baltimore County Library, Baltimore MD. 301-455-2457
Curnow, Mary, *In Charge,* Plumas County Law Library, Quincy CA. 916-283-1245
Curral, Vivian, *Br Libr Asst,* Ventura County Library Services Agency (Newbury Park Branch), Newbury Park CA. 805-498-2139
Curran, Donald C, *Assoc Librn of Congress,* Library of Congress, Washington DC. 202-287-5000
Curran, Helen H, *Librn,* Rohm & Haas Co (Spring House Library), Spring House PA. 215-643-0200
Curren, Geraldine M, *Librn,* Brown's River Library, Jericho Corners VT. 802-899-2545
Current, Charles E, *Librn,* Indian Hills Community College Library, Centerville IA. 515-856-2143
Current, Sharon, *Librn,* Weston Public Library (Grand Rapids Branch), Grand Rapids OH. 419-669-3415
Currey, Viola, *Librn,* Carbon County Public Library (Encampment Branch), Encampment WY. 307-327-5775
Currie, Clifford, *Librn,* College of William & Mary in Virginia, Earl Gregg Swem Library, Williamsburg VA. 804-253-4404
Currie, Hildegard I, *Ref,* United States Army (Technical Reference Div), Fort Huachuca AZ. 602-538-6304
Currie, J, *Ch,* Halton Hills Public Libraries, Georgetown ON. 416-877-2631
Currie, June, *Librn,* Canadian Department of Fisheries & Oceans, Arctic Biological Station Library, Sainte Anne de Bellevue PQ. 514-457-3660, Ext 40
Currie, K, *ILL, Acq & Rare Bks,* Mount Saint Vincent University Library, Halifax NS. 902-443-4450, Ext 120, 121, 125

Currier, Janet, *Librn,* Volusia County Public Libraries (Dickinson Memorial), Orange City FL. 904-252-8374
Currin, Miriam, *Tech Serv,* Vance-Granville Community College, Learning Resources Center, Henderson NC. 919-492-2061, Ext 251
Curro, Helen, *Librn,* Washington County Library System (Arcola Library), Arcola MS. 601-827-5262
Curry, Ann, *Prog Head,* Grant MacEwan Community College, Library Technician Program, AB. 403-474-8521
Curry, Anna, *Asst Dir,* Enoch Pratt Free Library, Baltimore MD. 301-396-5430, 396-5395
Curry, D R, *Mgr,* Burroughs Corp (Corporate Information Research Center), Detroit MI. 313-972-7350
Curry, David S, *Librn,* University of Iowa Libraries (Health Sciences), Iowa City IA. 319-353-4137
Curry, Frances, *Librn,* American Academy of Pediatrics Library, Evanston IL. 312-869-4255, Ext 446
Curry, Frances, *Librn,* Southwest Junior College, Simmons Library, Summit MS. 601-684-0065
Curry, Francis, *Librn,* Windsor Star Library, Windsor ON. 819-259-5511
Curry, Genevieve M, *Librn,* Glenwood Public Library, Glenwood IA. 712-527-3286
Curry, H Justine, *Acq,* Emporia State University, William Allen White Library, Emporia KS. 316-343-1200, Ext 205
Curry, Jean, *Acq,* Mundelein College, Learning Resource Center, Chicago IL. 312-262-8100, Ext 301, 302 & 303
Curry, Juanita, *Commun Servs,* Mid-Continent Public Library, Independence MO. 816-836-5200
Curry, Kathleen, *Libr Technician,* San Diego County Library (Borrego Springs Branch), Borrego Springs CA. 714-767-5761
Curry, Maureen E, *Dir,* Olean Public Library, Olean NY. 716-372-0200
Curry, Mildred, *Circ,* Robeson County Public Library, Lumberton NC. 919-738-4859
Curry, Susan, *Commun Servs,* Saint Joseph Public Library, Saint Joseph MO. 816-232-7729, 232-7720
Cursley, Joyce, *Serials Acq,* University of Calgary Library, Calgary AB. 403-284-5954
Curt, Grace, *Tech Serv,* Triton College Library, River Grove IL. 312-456-0300
Curtice, C E, *Librn,* Williams County Law Library Association, Bryan OH. 419-636-4600
Curtin, Elaine M, *Dir,* Beverly Public Library, Beverly NJ. 609-387-1259
Curtin, Mary, *Librn,* Naarden International USA Library, Owings Mills MD. 301-363-2550
Curtin, Raymond W, *Librn,* Eastman Kodak Co (Engineering Library), Rochester NY. 716-722-2356
Curtin-Stevenson, Mary, *Cat,* Emerson College, Abbot Memorial Library, Boston MA. 617-262-2010, Ext 281
Curtis, Alice, *Librn,* Horry County Memorial Library (Grand Strand), North Myrtle Beach SC. 803-272-5975
Curtis, Barbara, *Admin & On-Line Servs,* Johnson Matthey, Inc, Technical Library, West Chester PA. 215-648-8178
Curtis, Betty J L, *Librn,* Veterans Administration, Medical & Patients' Libraries, Lebanon PA. 717-272-6621, Ext 268, 247
Curtis, Charlotte, *Librn,* Peat, Marwick, Mitchell & Co Library, Houston TX. 713-224-4262
Curtis, Charlotte A, *Librn,* Raytheon Co, Electromagnetic Systems Division, Engineering Library, Goleta CA. 805-967-5511, Ext 2237
Curtis, David K, *Dir,* Dickinson County Library, Iron Mountain MI. 906-774-1218
Curtis, Debra A, *Asst Librn,* University of Arkansas for Medical Sciences, Area Health Education Center-Southwest, Texarkana AR. 501-772-0034
Curtis, Doris, *Librn,* Northeast Regional Library (Burnsville Library), Burnsville MS. 601-427-9258
Curtis, Elizabeth, *Librn,* Hampden Public Library, Hampden MA. 413-566-3047
Curtis, Erma, *Dir,* Viola Public Library, Viola WI. 608-627-1831
Curtis, George A, *Dir,* River Bend Library System, Coal Valley IL. 309-799-3131

Curtis, Howard W, *Rare Bks & Spec Coll,* Haverhill Public Library, Haverhill MA. 617-373-1586
Curtis, Jean, *Exten,* Enoch Pratt Free Library, Baltimore MD. 301-396-5430, 396-5395
Curtis, Jean A, *Chmn,* Marycrest College, Dept of Library Science, IA. 319-326-9254
Curtis, Jim, *AV,* East Tennessee State University (Medical Library), Johnson City TN. 615-928-6426, Ext 252
Curtis, Marcella, *In Charge,* Waite Park Library, Waite Park MN. 612-253-9359
Curtis, Margaret, *Librn,* Saint Paul United Methodist Church Library, Springfield MO. 417-886-4326
Curtis, Marilyn D, *Tech Serv,* United States Naval War College Library, Newport RI. 401-841-2641
Curtis, Marion, *Librn,* Winnipeg Public Library (River Heights), Winnipeg MB. 204-489-5303
Curtis, Marjorie B, *Ref,* Mississippi Valley State University, James Herbert White Library, Itta Bena MS. 601-254-9041, Ext 6340
Curtis, Mary E, *Chief Librn,* Veterans Administration (Center Library), Temple TX. 817-778-4811, Ext 529
Curtis, Mary Lynn, *Ref,* La Grange College, William & Evelyn Banks Library, La Grange GA. 404-882-2911, Ext 34
Curtis, P H, *Chief Librn,* State Historical Society of Iowa Library, Iowa City IA. 319-338-5471
Curtis, Pat, *Bkmobile Librn,* Southern Prairie Library System, Altus OK. 405-477-1930
Curtis, Rita, *Librn,* Hansford County Library, Spearman TX. 806-659-2231
Curtis, Ron, *Automation,* Central State University Library, Edmond OK. 405-341-2980, Ext 494, 495 & 496
Curtis, Sandra J, *In Charge,* Archives of American Art, Texas Area Center, Houston TX. 713-526-1361
Curtis, Sharyn, *Librn,* Moscow-Latah County Library System (Juliaetta Branch), Juliaetta ID. 208-276-7071
Curtis, Vicki, *Librn,* Skidmore, Owings & Merrill, Technical Library, Chicago IL. 312-346-6161, Ext 334
Curtis, Yvonne, *Librn,* Elmore Public Library, Elmore MN. 507-943-3338
Curtiss, Carmen, *Librn,* United States Army (Library Number Three), Fort Knox KY. 502-624-4723
Curtiss, Ruth E, *On-Line Servs & Bibliog Instr,* Hercules Inc (Research Center Library), Wilmington DE. 302-995-3484
Curtsinger, Eula B, *Librn,* United States Army (Post Library), White Sands Missile Range NM. 505-678-5820, 3375
Curwen, Doris R, *Acq,* Transylvania County Library, Inc, Brevard NC. 704-883-9880
Cusack, Edythe, *Librn,* London Free Press, Editorial Library, London ON. 519-679-1111, Ext 257
Cusher, Helen, *Librn,* Adams County Library (Reeder Branch), Reeder ND. 701-567-2741
Cushing, John D, *Librn,* Massachusetts Historical Society Library, Boston MA. 617-536-1608
Cushing, Margaret, *ILL & Ref,* West Orange Free Public Library, West Orange NJ. 201-736-0198
Cushing, Stanley E, *Libr Chairman,* Guild of Book Workers Library, New York NY. 212-757-6454
Cushing, Wendal J, *Librn,* North Dakota State University-Bottineau Branch, Institute of Forestry Library, Bottineau ND. 701-228-2277, Ext 54
Cushman, Anne T, *Librn,* Mark Twain Library, Redding CT. 203-938-2240
Cushman, Helen, *Ref,* Contra Costa College Library, San Pablo CA. 415-235-7800, Ext 213
Cushman, Marion, *ILL & Ref,* Los Angeles City College Library, Los Angeles CA. 213-663-9141, Ext 412
Cushman, Marjorie, *Cat,* Windham Public Library, Windham ME. 207-892-8086
Cushman, Winona, *Librn,* Terril Community Library, Terril IA. 712-853-6224
Cushner, Bertha, *Asst Dir,* Chelsea Public Library, Chelsea MA. 617-884-2335
Cusic, Elaine K, *Librn,* Cordova Township Library, Cordova IL. 309-654-2330
Custer, Charles D, *Exec Dir,* Capital District Library Council for Reference & Research Resources, NY. 518-272-8834

Custer, Charles D, *Dir,* Capital District Library Council Bibliographic Center-Library, Troy NY. 518-272-8834

Custer, Deborah, *Librn,* Kent Historical Society Library, Kent CT. 203-927-3761

Custer, Deborah P, *Librn,* Kent Library Association, Kent Memorial Library, Kent CT. 203-927-3761

Custer, Virginia, *Librn,* Western-Southern Life Insurance Library, Cincinnati OH. 513-421-1800

Custons, Marian, *ILL,* Ossining Public Library, Ossining NY. 941-2416; 941-9174

Cutberth, Mildred L, *Librn,* Northeastern Illinois Planning Commission Library, Chicago IL. 312-454-0400

Cutler, C Mae, *Libr Area Coordr Pacific,* Agriculture Canada Library, Vancouver Research Station, Vancouver BC. 604-224-4355

Cutler, Patricia, *Asst Librn,* Montague Public Library, Montague MA. 413-367-2852

Cutler, Phyllis, *Asst Univ Librn,* Brandeis University (Gerstenzang Science Library), Waltham MA. 617-647-2534

Cutlip, Arthur, *Govt Docs,* Miami-Dade Public Library System, Miami FL. 305-579-5001

Cutshall, Dale, *Librn,* Denver Public Library (Montbello), Denver CO. 303-573-5152, Ext 271

Cutshall, Donna, *AV,* Shelton State Community College, Junior College Division, Tuscaloosa AL. 205-759-1583

Cutsinger, Janette, *Acq,* Lindenwood Colleges, Margaret L Butler Library, Saint Charles MO. 314-946-6912

Cutter, Charles, *Judaica,* Brandeis University, Goldfarb Library, Waltham MA. 617-647-2514

Cutter, Margaret S, *Librn,* Lima Memorial Hospital, Health Sciences Library, Lima OH. 419-228-3335, Ext 563

Cutting, Gregory, *Asst Dir,* Hillsboro Public Library, Hillsboro OR. 503-648-6669

Cutting, Winnifred, *Ch,* Saint Johnsbury Athenaeum Inc Library, Saint Johnsbury VT. 802-748-8291

Cveljo, Katherine, *Instr,* North Texas State University, School of Library & Information Sciences, TX. 817-788-2445

Cylc, Ron, *In Charge,* North American Publishing Co, Custom House Guide Library, Philadelphia PA. 215-574-9600

Cylke, F Kurt, *Dir, Nat Libr Servs for Blind & Phys Handicapped,* Library of Congress, Washington DC. 202-287-5000

Cylkowski, Kathleen, *Tech Serv & Cat,* Salem College, Dale H Gramley Library, Winston-Salem NC. 919-721-2649

Cyr, Betty, *Tech Serv,* Mott Community College, C S Mott Library, Flint MI. 313-762-0400

Cyr, Beverly, *ILL,* Thomas Crane Public Library, Subregional Headquarters for Eastern Massachusetts Regional Library System, Quincy MA. 617-471-2400

Cyr, Carol A, *Dir,* Abel J Morneault Memorial Library, Van Buren Public Library, Van Buren ME. 207-868-5076

Cyr, Florine, *Librn,* Sarah Partridge Library, East Middlebury VT. 802-388-7193

Cyr, Helen W, *AV,* Enoch Pratt Free Library, Baltimore MD. 301-396-5430, 396-5395

Cyr, Lucy, *Librn,* Connecticut State Library (Waterbury Branch), Waterbury CT. 203-566-4301

Cyr, Marilyn, *Librn,* Clyde Public Library, Randolph-Decker Library, Clyde KS. 913-446-3563

Czajka, Irene, *Librn,* Wentworth Library (Winona Branch), Winona ON. 416-526-4126

Czarnecki, Emma-Lou, *Tech Serv & Acq,* West Orange Free Public Library, West Orange NJ. 201-736-0198

Czartoryski, Suzanne, *Asst Dir,* Richfield Township Public Library, Saint Helen MI. 517-389-7630

Czech, Erin, *ILL,* University of Wisconsin-Oshkosh, Forrest R Polk Library, Oshkosh WI. 414-424-3333

Czekuc, Rita, *YA,* Hackley Public Library, Muskegon MI. 616-722-7276

Czernicki, Norma, *Librn,* West Virginia School for the Deaf Library, Romney WV. 304-822-3521, Ext 227

Cziffra, Peter, *Librn,* Princeton University Library (Mathematics, Physics & Astronomy), Princeton NJ. 609-452-3180

Czike, Stephen F, *Librn,* Chicago Bar Association Library, Chicago IL. 312-782-7348, Ext 223

Czisny, Julie, *Media,* University of Wisconsin-Milwaukee, Golda Meir Library, Milwaukee WI. 414-963-4785

Czujak, Maureen, *Reader Serv & On-Line Servs,* New York Medical College, Westchester Medical Center Library, Valhalla NY. 914-347-5237

D

D'Abate, Janina, *Librn,* First Unitarian Church of Providence Library, Providence RI. 401-421-7970

D'Abate, Janina, *Librn,* North Scituate Public Library, North Scituate RI. 401-647-5133

D'Aguanno, Brenda, *Ad & Ch,* Cranston Public Library, William H Hall Free Library (Administrative & Reference Center), Cranston RI. 401-781-2450, 781-9580

D'Alesio, Mary Grace, *Head Librn,* Pennsylvania State University, J Clarence Kelly Library, McKeesport PA. 412-678-9501, Ext 228 & 229

D'Alessandro, Paul, *Asst Dir,* Gardiner Public Library, Gardiner ME. 207-582-3312

D'Ambrosio, Deborah, *Info Assts,* Marsteller Inc Library, New York NY. 212-752-6500, Ext 829

D'Ambrosio, Margaret R, *Assoc Librn,* American Numismatic Society Library, New York NY. 212-234-3130, Ext 20

D'Anci, Marjorie, *Librn,* Harford County Library (Edgewood Branch), Edgewood MD. 301-676-3443

D'Andraia, Frank A, *Tech Serv,* University of Southwestern Louisiana, Dupre Library, Lafayette LA. 318-264-6396

D'Andrea, Fiori, *Media,* Lethbridge Community College, Buchanan Resource Centre, Lethbridge AB. 403-327-2141, Ext 350

D'Andrea, Julia, *Cat,* University of Pittsburgh (Maurice & Laura Falk Library of the Health Sciences), Pittsburgh PA. 412-624-2521

D'Andrea, Mary, *Lectr,* Boston University, Dept of Instructional Development-Educational Media, MA. 617-353-3176

D'Aniello, C, *Am Studies-Black Studies & Hist,* State University of New York at Buffalo, University Libraries, Buffalo NY. 716-636-2965

D'Anna, Edward J, *Dir,* Georgia Mental Health Institute (Patient Library), Atlanta GA. 404-894-5662

D'Aoust, J G, *Librn,* Canadian Dental Association, Sydney Wood Bradley Memorial Library, Ottawa ON. 613-523-1770

D'Aoust, Randa J, *Tech Serv,* Sinclair Community College, Learning Resources Center, Dayton OH. 513-226-2855

D'Elia, George, *Asst Prof,* University of Minnesota, Library School, MN. 612-373-3100

D'Estout, Marc, *Asst Dir,* Triton Museum of Art Library, Santa Clara CA. 408-248-4585

d'Hondt, Mary Thadia, *Archivist,* Seattle & King County Historical Society, Sophie Frye Bass Library, Seattle WA. 206-324-1125, Ext 5

D'Onofrio, Sue, *Circ,* Long Branch Public Library, Long Branch NJ. 201-222-3900

D'Ottavio, Susan, *Bkmobile Coordr,* Cumberland County Library, Bridgeton NJ. 609-455-0080

D'Versa, Maria, *Tech Serv,* Moraine Valley Community College, Learning Resources Center, Palos Hills IL. 312-974-4300, Ext 222

D'Zmura, Elizabeth, *Assoc Librn,* Carlow College, Grace Library, Pittsburgh PA. 412-578-6137

Daane, Jeanette, *Instr,* Mesa Community College, Library Technician Program, AZ. 602-833-1261

Daane, Jeanette, *Educ Serv,* Mesa Community College Library, Mesa AZ. 602-833-1261, Ext 291, 201

Daball, Jack, *Asst Dir,* Jackson District Library, Jackson MI. 517-788-4087

DaBanian, Judith, *Dir,* Allen Park Public Library, Allen Park MI. 313-381-2425

Dabbs, Charolette H, *Librn,* NASA, Marshall Library, Marshall Spaceflight Center AL. 205-453-2432

Dabbs, Mary L, *Bibliog Instr,* Callaway Educational Association, Coleman Library, La Grange GA. 404-882-0946

Dabek, Joan, *Circ,* University of Houston (M D Anderson Memorial Library), Houston TX. 713-749-4241

Dabel, Lydia, *Librn,* Lincoln County Library (Afton Branch), Afton WY. 307-886-5590

Dablemont, Maria, *Librn,* International Library, Archives & Museum of Optometry, Saint Louis MO. 314-991-0324

Dacey, Clarissa O, *Librn,* East Berlin Library Association, East Berlin CT. 203-828-3123

Dachs, Jerry, *Librn,* Metropolitan Technical Community College (South Omaha Campus Instructional Resource Center), Omaha NE. 402-457-5100, Ext 277

Dack, Bruce, *Acq,* Arlington County Department of Libraries, Arlington Public Library, Arlington VA. 703-527-4777

Dacres, Bridget, *Instr,* Highline Community College Library, Library Technician Program, WA. 206-878-3710, Ext 233

Dacres, Bridget E, *Librn,* Bogle & Gates Library, Seattle WA. 206-682-5151

Dacus, Helen, *Librn,* White County Public Library (Searcy), Searcy AR. 501-268-2449

Dacus, Ruth, *Dir,* University of North Alabama, Collier Library, Florence AL. 205-766-4100, Ext 241

Dade, Mary J, *Asst Librn,* Pacific Power & Light Co Library, Portland OR. 503-243-4095

Dadovich, Sally, *Librn,* Haverhill Library Association, Haverhill NH. 603-787-6145

Daede, Leona, *Librn,* Stutsman County Library, Jamestown ND. 701-252-1531

Daehler, Russell, *Dir,* Daytona Beach Community College, Mary Karl Memorial Library, Daytona Beach FL. 904-255-8131

Daetsch, Dorothy, *Bibliog Instr,* Ithaca College Library, Ithaca NY. 607-274-3182

Daffron, Mary Ellen, *Librn,* Federal Maritime Commission Library, Washington DC. 202-523-5762

Daffron, Nancy, *Bkmobile Coordr,* Wayne County Public Library, Monticello KY. 606-348-8565

Dagger, Barbara, *Coordr,* Central Arizona Film Cooperative, AZ. 602-965-5073

Daggett, Mary, *Librn,* Pentwater Township Library, Pentwater MI. 616-869-8581

Dagit, Rosemary, *Librn,* Society of Friends, Yearly Meeting Library, Philadelphia PA. 215-241-7220

Dagnall, Irene J, *Librn,* Broadwater County Library, Townsend MT. 406-266-3672

Dagnese, Joseph M, *Dir,* Purdue University Libraries & Audio-Visual Center, West Lafayette IN. 317-749-2571

Dagold, Mary S, *Dir,* Villa Julie College Library, Stevenson MD. 301-486-7000

Dahl, Catherine, *Librn,* Hennepin County Library (Excelsior Branch), Excelsior MN. 612-474-8760

Dahl, Katherine, *ILL,* Northern State College, Williams Library & Learning Resource Center, Aberdeen SD. 605-622-2645

Dahl, Kathy, *Instr,* Northern State College, Library Science Program, SD. 605-622-2645

Dahl, Richard, *Dir,* Arizona State University Library (Law Library), Tempe AZ. 602-965-6141

Dahlby, Deborah, *Tech Serv,* Hawkeye Institute of Technology Library, Waterloo IA. 319-296-2320, Ext 237

Dahlen, Joan, *Dir,* Westby Public Library, Westby WI. 608-634-4419

Dahlen, Michael F, *Court Adminr,* Illinois Appellate Court, Fifth District, Law Library, Mount Vernon IL. 618-242-3120

Dahlgren, Anders C, *Dir,* Roselle Public Library District, Roselle IL. 312-529-1641

Dahlin, Therrin, *Circ,* Brigham Young University, Harold B Lee Library, Provo UT. 801-378-2905

Dahlke, Betty, *Asst Librn,* East Waushara Cooperative Library, Poy Sippi WI. 414-987-5737

Dahlke, Margie, *Librn,* North Arkansas Regional Library (Baxter County), Mountain Home AR. 501-425-3598

Dahlstedt, Marden, *Dir,* Beach Haven Public Library, Beach Haven NJ. 609-494-7081
Dahlstrom, Joe, *Librn,* San Antonio Public Library (Oakwell), San Antonio TX. 512-828-2569
Dahlstrom, Joe F, *Librn,* First Baptist Church Library, San Antonio TX. 512-226-0363
Dahm, Mary E, *Librn,* Saint Louis County Law Library, Clayton MO. 314-889-2512
Dahm, Minnie, *Rare Bks & Spec Coll,* Dordt College Library, Sioux Center IA. 712-722-3771, Ext 139
Daigle, J Robert, *Exten Librn,* Haut-Saint-Jean Regional Library, Bibliotheque Regionale du Haut-Saint-Jean, Edmundston NB. 506-739-7331
Daigneault, Marie-Jeanne, *Librn & Archivist,* La Societe d'histoire Des Cantons De L'est Bibliotheque, Eastern Townships Historical Society Library, Sherbrooke PQ. 819-562-0616
Dailey, Adelle, *Librn,* University of Kentucky (Music), Lexington KY. 606-258-2800
Dailey, Charles, *Dir,* Institute of American Indian Arts Museum Library, Santa Fe NM. 505-988-6291
Dailey, Joanna, *Exec Dir of Found,* Roscoe Pound - American Trial Lawyers Foundation (Roscoe Pound Memorial Library), Washington DC. 202-333-7330
Dailey, Joanne, *Exec Dir,* Roscoe Pound - American Trial Lawyers Foundation (Horovitz Workmen's Compensation Library), Washington DC. 202-333-7330
Dailey, Kazuko M, *Asst Univ Libm Tech Serv & Automation,* University of California at Davis, General Library, Davis CA. 916-752-2110
Dailey, Mary, *Ref,* Bur Oak Library System, Shorewood IL. 815-729-3345, 729-3346
Dailey, Mary, *Ref,* Joliet Public Library, Joliet IL. 815-727-4726
Dailey, Wallace F, *Cat Maintenance Div: Curator of Cat,* Harvard University Library (Harvard College Library (Headquarters in Harry Elkins Widener Memorial Library)), Cambridge MA. 617-495-2401
Daily, Jay, *Prof,* University of Pittsburgh, School of Library & Information Science, PA. 412-624-5230
Dain, Bernice, *AV,* Washington University Libraries, Saint Louis MO. 314-889-5400
Dain, Phyllis, *Prof,* Columbia University in the City of New York, School of Library Service, NY. 212-280-2292
Daines, Bonnie, *Media,* University of Wisconsin - La Crosse, Film Library, La Crosse WI. 608-785-8045
Daiprai, Pamala, *Libm,* Old American Insurance Co Library, Kansas City MO. 816-753-4900
Dairs, Annette, *Ref,* Chattanooga State Technical Community College, Augusta R Kolwyck Instructional Materials Center, Chattanooga TN. 615-622-6262
Daisy, Pati Jo, *Libm,* Lake City Public Library, Lake City IA. 712-464-3413
Dakan, Norman E, *Dir,* United States Department of the Air Force, Manpower & Personnel Center, Directorate of Morale, Welfare & Recreation, Randolph AFB TX. 512-652-3471, 652-3472
Dakshinamurtt, G, *Tech Serv,* Red River Community College, Learning Resources Center, Winnipeg MB. 204-632-2232
Dalby, Barbara M, *Libm,* Church of Jesus Christ of Latter-Day Saints, Tampa Branch Genealogical Library, Tampa FL. 312-971-2869
Dalby, Richard F, *Libm,* Penrose Hospital, Webb Memorial Library, Colorado Springs CO. 303-475-3227
Dale, Doris Cruger, *Prof,* Southern Illinois University at Carbondale, Educational Media Program, IL. 618-453-5764
Dale, J G, *Honorary Libm,* University of Toronto Libraries (Faculty of Dentistry), Toronto ON. 416-978-2796
Dale, Margaret, *Circ,* Lewisville Public Library, Lewisville TX. 214-436-1812
Dale, Rose Hart, *Libm,* Overton County Public Library, Livingston TN. 615-823-5116
Dalen, Adelle, *Libm,* Hennepin County Library (Long Lake Branch), Long Lake MN. 612-473-5600
Daler, Joan, *Microform & Per Reading Room,* University of Houston (M D Anderson Memorial Library), Houston TX. 713-749-4241

Dales, Elizabeth, *Tech Serv, Acq & Cat,* South Bend Public Library, South Bend IN. 219-288-4413
Daley, Betty, *Libm,* Somerdale Public Library, Somerdale NJ. 609-783-4344
Daley, John G, *Asst Dir,* Newton Free Library, Newton MA. 617-527-7700, Ext 24
Daley, Patricia, *Libm,* Newton Free Library (Oak Hill Park Branch), Oak Hill Park MA. 617-527-7700, Ext 24
Daley, Trudy, *Chief Libm,* United States Trust Co, Investment Library, New York NY. 212-425-4500, Ext 496
Dalhaimer, Kim, *On-Line Servs,* Sheboygan County Federated Library System, Sheboygan WI. 414-459-3412
Dallas, Georgia, *Libm,* O'fallon Public Library, O'Fallon IL. 618-632-3783
Dallas, Jean C, *Curator,* Riley County Historical Museum, Seaton Memorial Library, Manhattan KS. 913-537-2210
Dallas, Larayne, *Instr,* Arkansas State University, Dept of Library Science, AR. 501-972-3077
DallaValle, C, *Acq,* Georgia Institute of Technology, Price Gilbert Memorial Library, Atlanta GA. 404-894-4510
Dallman, Glenn R, *Dir,* Saint Petersburg Junior College, Michael M Bennett Library, Clearwater FL. 813-441-0681, Ext 2616
Dallof, Betty, *Circ,* Weber County Library, Ogden UT. 801-399-8516
Dally, Betty, *Admin Libr,* Baudette Public Library, Baudette MN. 218-634-2329
Dalquist, Janet A, *Dir,* Suomi College Library, Hancock MI. 906-482-5300, Ext 252
Dalrymple, Patricia, *Libm,* Hamot Medical Center, Medical Library, Erie PA. 814-455-6711, Ext 272
Dalrymple, Roy, *Exten,* Victoria Public Library, Victoria TX. 512-578-6241
Dalton, Chester A, *Dir,* Cypress College Library, Cypress CA. 714-826-2220, Ext 124, 125
Dalton, Deborah, *Libm,* Mary Imogene Bassett Hospital, Medical Library, Cooperstown NY. 607-547-6481
Dalton, Edyth, *Coordr,* Kansas City Metropolitan Library Network, MO. 816-257-7771
Dalton, Kathleen J, *Ref, On-Line Servs & Bibliog Instr,* Susquehanna University, Roger M Blough Learning Ctr, Selinsgrove PA. 717-374-0101, Ext 329
Dalton, Laura B, *Asst Dir,* Hartford Graduate Center Library, Hartford CT. 203-549-3600, Ext 224
Dalton, Richard, *Asst Libm,* University of Missouri-Kansas City Libraries (Medical Library), Kansas City MO. 816-474-4100, Ext 280
Dalton, Sheila, *Ref,* Richmond Hill Public Library, Richmond Hill ON. 416-884-9288
Dalton, Shirley, *Circ,* Walters State Community College, Learning Resource Center, Morristown TN. 615-581-2121, Ext 212
DaLuiso, F, *Art & Italian,* State University of New York at Buffalo, University Libraries, Buffalo NY. 716-636-2965
Dalum, De, *Ref,* Elisha D Smith Public Library, Menasha WI. 414-729-5166
Dalva, Harry, *Acq & Ref,* Fresno City College, Learning Resources Center, Fresno CA. 209-442-8204
Daly, D E, *Libm,* Ignatius College Library, Guelph ON. 519-824-1250
Daly, Dorothy, *YA,* Meriden Public Library, Meriden CT. 203-238-2344
Daly, James A, *Dir,* Lincoln Public Library, Lincoln MA. 617-259-8465
Daly, John, *Dir,* Illinois State Archives, Springfield IL. 217-782-4682
Daly, Linda, *Ref,* Nepean Public Library, Ottawa ON. 613-224-4338
Daly, Louise L, *Cat,* Marygrove College Library, Detroit MI. 313-862-8000
Daly, Richard, *Cat,* Swarthmore College, McCabe Library, Swarthmore PA. 215-447-7477, 447-7480
Daly, Simeon, *Dir,* Saint Meinrad College & School of Theology, Archabbey Library, Saint Meinrad IN. 812-357-6611, Ext 401
Dalzell, Anne, *Chief, Div Pub Servs,* Montgomery County Department of Public Libraries, Rockville MD. 301-279-1401

Dalzell, Lee B, *ILL,* Williams College, Sawyer Library, Williamstown MA. 413-597-2501
Dam, T T N, *Libm,* Proctor & Redfern Group Library, Toronto ON. 416-486-5225
Damaskos, James C, *Libm,* Harvard University Library (Littauer Library), Cambridge MA. 617-495-2105
Dambergs, I, *On-Line Servs,* Union College, Schaffer Library, Schenectady NY. 518-370-6278
Dame, Fern Shrewsberry, *Libm,* National Geographic Society Library (Illustrations), Washington DC. 202-857-7492
Dameron, Logan, *Circ,* Phoenix College Library, Phoenix AZ. 602-264-2492, Ext 621
Dameron, William T, *Dir,* Kenyon College, Gordon Keith Chalmers Memorial Library, Gambier OH. 614-427-2244, Ext 2186
Dames, Barbara, *ILL,* Harvard University Library (Harvard College Library (Headquarters in Harry Elkins Widener Memorial Library)), Cambridge MA. 617-495-2401
Damico, James, *Assoc Dir,* William Marsh Rice University, Fondren Library, Houston TX. 713-527-4022
Damien, Brian, *Asst Libm,* Captain John Curtis Memorial Library, Brunswick Public Library, Brunswick ME. 207-725-5242
Damien, Yvonne, *Anthropology & Fine Arts,* Loyola University of Chicago Libraries (Elizabeth M Cudahy Memorial Library), Chicago IL. 312-274-3000, Ext 771
Dammann, Arvilla, *Libm,* Carnegie Library, Armour SD. 605-724-2743
Damme, Marjorie Van, *Soc Sci,* Simmons College, Beatley Library, Boston MA. 617-738-2241
Damon, Clara, *Asst Dir,* Goshen Public Library, Goshen MA. 413-268-7856
Damon, Cora M, *Libm,* Mid Maine Medical Center, Health Sciences Library, Waterville ME. 207-873-0621, Ext 332
Damon, Gene, *Systs Libm,* University of Waterloo Library, Waterloo ON. 519-885-1211
Damore, John M, *Business,* University of Miami, Otto G Richter Library, Coral Gables FL. 305-284-3551
Dana, D Brownell, *Tech Serv,* Colgate University, Everett Needham Case Library, Hamilton NY. 315-824-1000
Danahar, Catherine M, *Libm,* Harvard University Library (Harvard Forest Library), Petersham MA. 617-724-3285
Dance, B, *In Charge,* University of Toronto Libraries (Faculty of Management Studies), Toronto ON. 416-978-3421
Dance, James, *Pub Rels,* Detroit Public Library, Detroit Associated Libraries, Detroit MI. 313-833-1000
Dance, Sara E, *Dir,* Salem Public Library, Salem IN. 812-883-5600
Dancy, Sherry, *Media,* Wilkes Community College, Learning Resources Library, Wilkesboro NC. 919-667-7136, Ext 26
Dandridge, Vonita, *Ser,* Virginia State College, Johnston Memorial Library, Petersburg VA. 804-520-6171
Dandridge-Perry, Cheryl, *Libm,* University of California Los Angeles Library (English Reading Room), Los Angeles CA. 213-825-4511
Dane, Sylvia, *Libm,* Chichester Town Library, Chichester NH. 603-798-5350
Daneau, Lise, *Libm,* Hospital Du Sacre Coeur, Pavillion Albert Prevost, Montreal PQ. 514-333-4284
Daneshy, Mrs Rowshan, *Libm,* Halliburton Services, Research Center Library, Duncan OK. 405-251-3080
Danford, Ardath, *Dir,* Toledo-Lucas County Public Library, Toledo OH. 419-255-7055
Danford, Robert E, *Cat,* Washington & Lee University, The University Library, Lexington VA. 703-463-9111, Ext 403
Dangle-Killeen, Kathy, *Asst Libm,* Nichols College, Conant Library, Dudley MA. 617-943-1560
Danhart, Ann, *Dir,* Magnolia Public Library, Magnolia NJ. 609-783-1520
Daniel, Carol, *Libm,* Public Library of Cincinnati & Hamilton County (Mount Healthy), Cincinnati OH. 513-521-6381
Daniel, Eleanor M, *Libm,* Ohio State University Libraries (Black Studies Library), Columbus OH. 614-422-8403

Daniel, Evelyn, *Prof,* Syracuse University, School of Information Studies, NY. 315-423-2911
Daniel, Hildreth, *Librn,* Cornwall Historical Library, Cornwall CT. 203-672-6874
Daniel, Holly, *Circ,* Oklahoma City University (Dulaney-Browne Library), Oklahoma City OK. 405-521-5068
Daniel, Kay, *Librn,* Mid-Continent Public Library (Edgarton Branch), Edgerton MO. 816-227-3569
Daniel, Lee, *Ch,* East Baton Rouge Parish Library, Baton Rouge LA. 504-389-3360
Daniel, Mary Ellen, *Librn,* Saint Mary's Hospital, Medical Library, Rochester NY. 716-328-3300
Daniel, Mrs Lewis, *Librn,* Cornwall Public Library, Cornwall CT. 203-672-6874
Daniel, Sister Edward, *Dean,* Mary Regina College, Library Service Program, NY. 315-474-4891
Daniel, Wendell, *Dir,* Piedmont Virginia Community College Library, Charlottesville VA. 804-977-3900, Ext 268
Daniel, Willa Dean, *Dir,* Carl Elliott Regional Library, Jasper AL. 205-221-2567
Daniells, Lorna M, *Bibliog Instr,* Harvard University Library (Baker Library), Boston MA. 617-495-3650
Daniels, Barbara, *Librn,* Maury County Public Library (Mount Pleasant Branch Library), Mt Pleasant TN. 615-379-3752
Daniels, Bernice, *Dir,* Worthington Public Library, Worthington OH. 614-885-3185
Daniels, Bruce, *Deputy Dir,* Rhode Island Department of State Library Services, Providence RI. 401-277-2726
Daniels, Cecelia, *Asst Librn,* Haston Free Public Library, North Brookfield MA. 617-867-7978
Daniels, Della, *AV & Cat,* Olive-Harvey College, City Colleges of Chicago, Olive-Harvey College Library, Chicago IL. 312-568-3700
Daniels, Elizabeth, *Libr Technician,* San Diego County Library (Solana Beach Branch), Solana Beach CA. 714-755-1404
Daniels, Ida, *Librn,* Peat, Marwick, Mitchell & Co (Tax Library), New York NY. 212-758-9700
Daniels, Jerome P, *Dir,* University of Wisconsin-Platteville, Elton S Karrmann Library, Platteville WI. 608-342-1688
Daniels, Jerome P, *Dir,* University of Wisconsin-Platteville, Program in Library Education, WI. 608-342-1757
Daniels, Judy, *Libr Asst,* United States Army (Huntington District Corps of Engineers Library), Huntington WV. 304-529-5435, 529-5713
Daniels, Lewis, *Librn,* Hamden Library, Miller Memorial, Hamden CT. 203-248-7747
Daniels, Linda Torfin, *Actg Exec Dir,* Midwest Region Library Network, (MIDLNET), WI. 414-465-2750
Daniels, Marilyn, *Librn,* Lakewood Public Library (Madison), Lakewood OH. 216-228-7428
Daniels, Mrs M B, *Librn,* Ness City Library, Ness City KS. 913-798-3415
Daniels, Nancy, *Librn,* Pankhurst Memorial Library, Amboy IL. 815-687-3925
Daniels, Pete, *Br Coordr,* Broward County Division of Libraries, Broward County Library, Pompano Beach FL. 305-972-1100
Daniels, Ronald B, *Asst Dir,* Bucknell University, Ellen Clarke Bertrand Library, Lewisburg PA. 717-524-3056
Daniels-Dixon, Charlene, *Librn,* Mount Sterling Public Library, Mount Sterling IL. 217-773-2013
Danielson, Mildred E, *Librn,* Newell Public Library, Newell IA. 712-272-3688
Danigelis, Anita, *Librn,* Pierson Library, Shelburne VT. 802-985-2040
Danin, Barbara, *Acq,* Philadelphia College of Art Library, Philadelphia PA. 215-893-3126
Danio, Mary, *Asst Librn & Ref,* University of Miami, Rosentiel School of Marine & Atmospheric Sciences, Miami FL. 305-350-7207
Dank, Naomi, *Admnr,* Crisis Intervention Center Library, Norristown PA. 215-631-2000
Danke, Beatrice, *Librn,* Westview Christian Reformed Church Library, Grand Rapids MI. 616-453-3105
Danker, Mrs William, *ILL & Circ,* Christ Seminary-Seminex Library, Saint Louis MO. 314-534-7535

Dankert, Elizabeth, *Circ,* Mercer University, Stetson Memorial Library, Macon GA. 912-745-6811, Ext 284
Dankewych, Michael, *In Charge,* United States Department of the Navy (David W Taylor Naval Ship Research & Development Center), Bethesda MD. 202-277-1309
Dankner, Laura, *Librn,* Loyola University Library (Music), New Orleans LA. 504-865-2774
Danko, Diana M, *Supvr Info Serv,* PPG Industries Research Library, Chemical Division, Barberton OH. 216-848-4161, Exts 551, 550
Dannecker, Joyce, *Acq & Ref,* Bay County Public Library Association, Northwest Regional Library System, Panama City FL. 904-785-3457
Danner, Carolyn, *Bkmobile Coordr,* Sweetwater County Library, Green River WY. 307-875-3615
Danner, Richard, *Assoc Dir,* Duke University (Law School Library), Durham NC. 919-684-2847
Danner, Susan T, *Librn,* John D Archbold Memorial Hospital, Ralph Perkins Memorial Library, Thomasville GA. 912-226-4121, Ext 166
Dannis, Marjorie, *Librn,* Weeks Library, Greenland NH. 603-436-8548
Danoff, Fran, *Librn,* Planned Parenthood Association of Wisconsin, Maurice Ritz Memorial Library & Resource Center, Milwaukee WI. 414-271-8116, Ext 52
Dansker, Shirley E, *Dir,* Lenox Hill Hospital, Health Sciences Library, New York NY. 212-794-4266
Danton, Lois King, *Librn,* Herrick Memorial Hospital (Medical Staff Library), Berkeley CA. 415-845-0130, Ext 491
Dapogny, David, *Coordr,* Columbia College Library (Slide Library), Chicago IL. 312-663-1600, Ext 465
Daptula, Joan Helen, *Librn,* Sacred Heart Hospital, Health Service Library, Allentown PA. 215-821-3280
Darby, Jim L, *Dir,* Brunswick-Glynn County Regional Library, Brunswick GA. 912-264-7360
Darby, Louise, *Librn,* Shepard-Pruden Memorial Library, Edenton NC. 919-482-4112
Darby, William J, *Nutrition,* Vanderbilt University Medical Center Library, Nashville TN. 615-322-2292
Darcangelo, Roseanne, *Cat,* Corning Community College, Arthur A Houghton, Jr Library, Corning NY. 607-962-9251
Darcy, Kathleen, *Libr Develop Off,* Wyoming State Library, Cheyenne WY. 307-777-7281
Darcy, Jr, William E, *Librn,* United States Air Force (Laughlin Air Force Base Library), Laughlin AFB TX. 512-298-5119
Darden, Christina, *Librn,* Ayerst Labs Inc Library, Science Library, Rouses Point NY. 518-297-6611, Ext 293
Darden, Jud, *Media,* University of the Pacific, Irving Martin Library, Stockton CA. 209-946-2431
Darden, Sue, *Dir,* Stanly County Public Library, Albemarle NC. 704-982-0115
Dare, Phillip, *Bibliog Instr,* University of Kentucky, Margaret I King Library, Lexington KY. 606-257-3801
Dargay, Charlotte, *Librn,* Township of Hamilton Free Public Library (Independence Mall), Trenton NJ. 609-890-3783
Dark, James, *Dean,* San Diego City College Library, San Diego CA. 714-238-1181, Ext 250
Dark, Maxine, *Librn,* Tulsa City-County Library (Broken Arrow Branch), Broken Arrow OK. 918-251-3819
Darkus, Jean, *Circ,* Pender County Library, Burgaw NC. 919-259-4521
Darland, Jeanette, *Librn,* Renwick Public Library, Renwick IA. 515-824-3209
Darling, Bernice, *Librn,* Newark Public Library (Utica Branch), Utica OH. 614-892-2400
Darling, Dorette, *Curric Mat,* Northern State College, Williams Library & Learning Resource Center, Aberdeen SD. 605-622-2645
Darling, John, *Librn,* University of North Carolina at Chapel Hill (Zoology), Chapel Hill NC. 919-933-2264
Darling, Linda, *Librn,* Harris County Public Library (Woodforest), Houston TX. 713-453-8188

Darling, Pamela, *Preservation,* Columbia University (University Libraries), New York NY. 212-280-2241
Darling, Richard L, *Dean,* Columbia University in the City of New York, School of Library Service, NY. 212-280-2292
Darnall, Nellie, *Mus Curator,* Butterfield Trail Association & Logan County Historical Society, Inc, Butterfield Trail Museum Library, Russell Springs KS. 913-751-4242
Darnell, Edna, *Dir & Acq,* Three Rivers Community College Library, Poplar Bluff MO. 314-785-7794, Ext 57
Darnell, Linda K, *Librn,* E A Conway Memorial Hosptial, Louisiana Hospital Association, Medical Library, Monroe LA. 318-387-8460, Ext 342
Darnell, Polly C, *Librn,* Sheldon Museum's Swift Research Center Library, Middlebury VT. 802-388-2117
Darnell, Winnie, *Librn,* Washington County Library System (Glen Allan), Glen Allan MS. 601-839-4066
DaRold, Joseph H, *Dir,* Santa Fe Springs City Library, Santa Fe Springs CA. 213-868-7738
Darr, Christi, *Bkmobile Coordr,* Coshocton Public Library, Coshocton OH. 614-622-0956
Darr, William, *Asst Librn,* Grace College & Grace Theological Seminary, Betty Zimmer Morgan Library, Winona Lake IN. 219-267-8191, Ext 182
Darrah, Vernita, *Librn,* Mid-Continent Public Library (Smithville Branch), Smithville MO. 816-873-2252
Darrin, Phyllis, *Sr Clerk,* Buffalo Psychiatric Center (Staff Library), Buffalo NY. 716-885-2261, Ext 462
Darst, Elizabeth, *Curator of Museum,* Rosenberg Library, Galveston TX. 713-763-8854
Darst, Valerie, *Dir,* Little Dixie Regional Libraries, Moberly MO. 816-263-4426
Darte, Lorna C, *Cat,* Wilkes College, Eugene Shedden Farley Library, Wilkes-Barre PA. 717-824-4651, Ext 331 & 332
Dartez, Nettie B, *Librn,* Vermilion Parish Library (Maurice Branch), Maurice LA. 318-893-5583
DasGupta, Krishna, *Tech Serv,* Worcester State College, Learning Resources Center, Worcester MA. 617-752-7700, Ext 132, 135
Daso, Judy, *Doc,* Ohio University, Vernon R Alden Library, Athens OH. 614-594-5228
Datko, Mary Jo, *Bkmobile Coordr,* Saint Paul Public Library, Saint Paul MN. 612-292-6311
Datres, Lorraine, *Tech Serv,* Blue Water Library Federation, Port Huron MI. 313-987-7323
Datres, Lorraine, *Tech Serv,* Saint Clair County Library System, Port Huron MI. 313-987-7323
Daub, Marian, *Tech Serv,* Reading Public Library, Reading Public Library District, Reading PA. 215-374-4548
Daubenspeck, Anita T, *Dir,* Ridgefield Library & Historical Association, Ridgefield CT. 203-438-2282
Daubert, Richard, *Tech Serv,* Michigan City Public Library, Michigan City IN. 219-879-4561
Daubert, Richard R, *Actg Dir,* Purdue University, North Central Campus Library, Westville IN. 219-785-2541
Dauble, Dary, *Circ & Ref,* Eastern Oregon State College, Walter M Pierce Library, La Grande OR. 503-963-2171, Ext 240
Daubs, Judy, *Asst Librn,* Indian Creek Township Library, Norris City IL. 618-378-3171
Daugherty, Betty Jane, *Librn,* Ball Memorial Hospital, Medical Library, Muncie IN. 317-747-3204
Daugherty, Carolyn, *Dir,* Union Memorial Hospital (Nursing School Library), Baltimore MD. 301-235-7200, Ext 2212
Daugherty, Della, *Librn,* Public Library of Columbus & Franklin County (Northside), Columbus OH. 614-222-7133
Daugherty, Dorothy, *Ch,* Ralston Public Library, Ralston NE. 402-331-7636
Daugherty, Josephine, *Asst Dir,* Hemet Public Library, Hemet CA. 714-658-7293
Daugherty, M June, *Librn,* Jackson County Library System (Rogue River Branch), Rogue River OR. 503-582-1714
Daugherty, Robert A, *Circ,* University of Illinois at Chicago Circle Library, Chicago IL. 312-996-2716

Dauphinais, Edward J, *Librn,* University of New Hampshire (Technology), Durham NH. 603-862-1540
Dauphinais, Helaine, *Tech Serv,* South Windsor Public Library, South Windsor CT. 203-644-1541
Dauphinais, Mary, *Acq,* Alexandria Library, Alexandria VA. 703-750-6351
Dauple, Ila, *Dir,* Hanover Town Library, Hanover NH. 603-643-3237
Davalos, Helen, *Dir,* Southwestern Indian Polytechnic Institute, Media Center, Albuquerque NM. 505-766-3266
DaVault, Jewel Wayne, *Ch,* Dunklin County Library, Kennett MO. 314-888-3561
Dave, Barbara, *Librn,* Los Angeles Public Library System (Westchester), Los Angeles CA. 213-645-6082
Davenny, Ena, *Librn,* New Haven Free Public Library (Mitchell), New Haven CT. 203-787-8117
Davenport, Anita, *Media,* Brookdale Community College, Learning Resources Center, Lincroft NJ. 201-842-1900, Ext 392
Davenport, Barbara, *Librn,* Childrens Hospital Medical Center, Medical Library, Oakland CA. 415-654-5600, Ext 210
Davenport, Betty, *Librn,* Anderson County Library (Piedmont Branch), Piedmont SC. 803-845-6534
Davenport, Diane, *Librn,* Alameda County Library (Castro Valley Branch), Castro Valley CA. 415-881-6036
Davenport, Frances, *Librn,* West Salem Public Library, West Salem IL. 618-456-8970
Davenport, Grace, *Cat,* Fullerton College, William T Boyce Library, Fullerton CA. 714-871-8000
Davenport, Helen, *Librn,* Anderson County Library (Lander Memorial), Williamston SC. 803-847-7110
Davenport, Jean Z, *On-Line Servs,* Cleveland Public Library, Cleveland OH. 216-623-2800
Davenport, John, *Rare Bks & Spec Coll,* College of Saint Thomas, O'Shaughnessy Library, Saint Paul MN. 612-647-5720
Davenport, Joyce, *Librn,* Jackson District Library (Michigan Center Branch), Michigan Center MI. 517-764-2550
Davenport, Lawrence B, *Dir,* Warren Public Library, Warren MI. 313-264-8720
Davenport, Margaret, *Librn,* Barrett, Smith, Schapiro, Simon & Armstrong Library, New York NY. 212-422-8180, Ext 222
Davenport, Myra, *YA,* Belmont College, Williams Library, Nashville TN. 615-383-7001, Ext 253
Davenport, Shirley, *Acq,* Kentucky Wesleyan College, Library Learning Center, Owensboro KY. 502-926-3111, Ext 113, 117
Davenport, Stella, *Librn,* Tombstone Reading Station, Tombstone AZ. 602-457-3612
Davern, Dorothy, *Acq,* Saint Lucie County Library Systems, Fort Pierce FL. 305-461-5708
Davey, Beryl P, *Commun Servs,* Omaha Public Library, W Dale Clark Library, Omaha NE. 402-444-4800
Davey, Betty, *Librn,* Victoria County Public Library (Norland Branch), Norland ON. 705-324-3104
Davey, Mary, *Eng,* University of Calgary Library, Calgary AB. 403-284-5954
David, Indra M, *Asst Dean,* Oakland University, Kresge Library, Rochester MI. 313-377-2486, 377-2474
David, Janet, *On-Line Servs,* Community College of Denver, North Campus Learning Materials Center, Westminster CO. 303-466-8811, Ext 500
David, Joe, *Ref,* El Centro College, Learning Resources Center, Dallas TX. 214-746-2292
David, Susan H, *ILL & Ad,* Henderson County Public Library, Hendersonville NC. 704-693-8427
David, Zdenek V, *Librn,* Woodrow Wilson International Center for Scholars Library, Washington DC. 202-381-5850
Davidoff, D, *Ad & Ref,* Bellmore Memorial Library, Bellmore NY. 516-785-2990
Davidoff, Marcia, *Dir,* University of South Alabama (Biomedical Library), Mobile AL. 205-460-7043
Davidosky, Maria, *AV,* Imperial Valley College, Spencer Library Media Center, Imperial CA. 714-352-8320, Ext 270

Davidson, Audrey I, *Librn,* Marshall Public Library, Marshall IL. 217-826-2535
Davidson, B J, *Librn,* United States Department of Energy, Laramie Energy Technology Center Library, Laramie WY. 307-721-2201
Davidson, Beatrice, *Dir,* Carnegie Public Library, East Liverpool OH. 216-385-2048
Davidson, Bonnie, *Librn,* Southeast Arkansas Regional Library (Watson Public), Watson AR. 501-367-3336
Davidson, Carol J, *Librn,* United States Air Force (Wurtsmith Air Force Base Library), Wurtsmith AFB MI. 517-739-6597
Davidson, Chalmers G, *Archivist,* Davidson College, E H Little Library, Davidson NC. 704-892-2000, Ext 331
Davidson, Dorothy B, *Dir,* Mid-South Bible College, Oscar White Memorial Library, Memphis TN. 901-458-7526, Ext 41, 43
Davidson, G, *Head Off Librn,* Steel Company of Canada, Ltd, Corporate Library Services, Hamilton ON. 416-528-2511
Davidson, Gale, *Ref,* Montana College of Mineral Science and Technology Library, Butte MT. 406-792-8321, Ext 371
Davidson, Harold, *Dept Head,* Eastern Montana College, School Library Program, MT. 406-657-2137
Davidson, Helen, *Ref,* Agency for International Development, Development Information Center, Washington DC. 202-632-8571
Davidson, J Maureen, *Instr,* Grant MacEwan Community College, Library Technician Program, AB. 403-474-8521
Davidson, Jeff, *Supervising Librn,* Stanford Research Institute Library, Arlington VA. 703-524-2053
Davidson, Louise S, *Dir,* Ashland Community College Library, Ashland KY. 606-325-8586
Davidson, Martha W, *Tech Serv,* Simmons College, Beatley Library, Boston MA. 617-738-2241
Davidson, Mary, *Music Libr,* Wellesley College, Margaret Clapp Library, Wellesley MA. 617-235-0320, Ext 280
Davidson, Mrs R, *Librn,* Centre for Christian Studies Library, Toronto ON. 416-923-1168
Davidson, Nancy M, *Bibliog Instr,* Winthrop College, Ida Jane Dacus Library, Rock Hill SC. 803-323-2131
Davidson, R B, *R & D Info Specialist,* B F Goodrich Chemical Group, Technical Information Center, Avon Lake OH. 216-933-6181, Ext 1335
Davidson, Rebecca, *On-Line Servs,* University of North Carolina at Chapel Hill (Health Sciences Library), Chapel Hill NC. 919-966-2111
Davidson, Robert, *Circ & Ref,* Florence County Library, Florence SC. 803-662-8424
Davidson, Sara Jane, *Ref,* Paul Sawyier Public Library, Frankfort KY. 502-223-1658
Davidson, Sarah, *Dir,* Farmland Industries Inc Communications Services, J W Cummins Memorial Library, Kansas City MO. 816-459-6606
Davidson, Shirley, *Asst Librn,* Minnedosa Regional Library, Minnedosa MB. 204-867-2585
Davidson, Silvia, *Librn,* Albert Einstein College of Medicine (John Thompson Library), Bronx NY. 212-430-5571
Davidson, Virginia, *Media,* Midland Lutheran College Library, Fremont NE. 402-721-5482, Ext 4
Davidson, Wm T, *Circ & Per,* Roanoke College Library, Salem VA. 703-389-2351, Ext 202
Davie, Judith F, *Instr,* Appalachian State University, Department of Educational Media: Librarianship & Instructional Technology, NC. 704-262-2243
Davies, Anne G, *Head Tech Servs,* Harvard University Library (Gutman Library-Research Center), Cambridge MA. 617-495-4225
Davies, C A, *Librn, On-Line Servs & Bibliog Instr,* Roads & Transportation Association of Canada Library, Ottawa ON. 613-521-4052
Davies, Deborah K, *Gen Serv,* North Babylon Public Library, North Babylon NY. 516-669-4020
Davies, Dorothy, *Dir,* Trenton Memorial Public Library, Trenton ON. 613-394-3381
Davies, Elaine, *Asst Librn,* Hamer Public Library, Hamer ID. 208-662-5275
Davies, Elizabeth E, *Dir,* Wissahickon Valley Public Library, Ambler PA. 215-646-1072

Davies, Grace A, *Acq,* Gannon University, Nash Library, Erie PA. 814-871-7352
Davies, Jean B, *Librn,* Slatington Library, Slatington PA. 215-767-6461
Davies, Jean C, *Asst Dir, Cat & Ref,* Washington University Libraries (School of Dental Medicine Library), Saint Louis MO. 314-454-0385
Davies, June N, *Librn,* Horseshoe Bend Public Library, Horseshoe Bend ID. 208-793-2460
Davies, Margaret, *AV,* Public Library of Columbus & Franklin County, Columbus OH. 614-864-8050
Davila, Daniel, *Dir,* Passaic County Community College, Learning Resources Center Library, Paterson NJ. 201-279-5000, Ext 73
Davini, Thurston, *Librn,* University of Wisconsin-Madison (Social Work Library), Madison WI. 608-262-3521
Davis, Alleyne, *Librn,* Rockcastle County Library, Mount Vernon KY. 606-256-2388
Davis, Alta K, *Asia & Mil Hist,* National Defense University Library, Washington DC. 202-693-8437
Davis, Alyce L, *Librn,* California State Department of Transportation, District Seven Library, Los Angeles CA. 213-620-5500, 620-5553
Davis, Andrith, *Dir,* Rocky Ford Public Library, Rocky Ford CO. 303-254-6641
Davis, Ann Fant, *Librn,* Holmes County Library (Lexington Branch), Lexington MS. 601-834-2571
Davis, Anna M, *Dir,* Bayport-Blue Point Public Library, Blue Point NY. 516-363-6133
Davis, Anne, *Circ,* Old Dominion University Library, Norfolk VA. 804-440-4141
Davis, Anne, *Librn,* Saint Mary's Hospital, Max C Fleischmann Medical Library, Reno NV. 702-323-2041, Ext 3108
Davis, Anne C, *Librn,* University of Michigan (Mental Health Research Institute Library), Ann Arbor MI. 313-764-4202
Davis, Anne L, *In Charge,* Church of the Ascension Library, Montgomery AL. 205-263-5529
Davis, Annie, *Circ,* United States Air Force (Scott Air Force Base Library), Scott AFB IL. 618-256-5100
Davis, Areta B, *Librn,* Spirit Lake Public Library, Spirit Lake ID. 208-623-4791
Davis, Aurora, *Instr,* University of Missouri-Columbia, School of Library & Informational Science, MO. 314-882-4546
Davis, Barbara, *Ch,* Lake Geneva Public Library, Lake Geneva WI. 414-248-8311
Davis, Barbara, *Librn,* Long Beach Public Library System (Alamitos), Long Beach CA. 213-436-6448
Davis, Barbara, *Ser,* Texas Southern University Library, Houston TX. 713-527-7121
Davis, Barbara A, *Assoc Dir, ILL & Ref,* Nazareth College of Rochester Library, Lorette Wilmot Library, Rochester NY. 716-586-2525, Ext 232
Davis, Barbara M, *Tech Serv,* Cabot Corp, Technical Information Center, Billerica MA. 617-272-3500, Ext 412
Davis, Beatrice F, *Asst Librn,* College of Physicians of Philadelphia Library, Philadelphia PA. 215-561-6050
Davis, Betty, *Media,* Downey City Library, Downey CA. 213-923-3256
Davis, Betty Bartlett, *OCLC,* Kansas State University, Farrell Library, Manhattan KS. 913-532-6516
Davis, Billie Sue, *Librn,* Pikeville Public Library, Pikeville KY. 606-432-1285
Davis, Bonnie, *Libr Coop Consult,* Lincoln Trail Libraries System, Champaign IL. 217-352-0047
Davis, Bonnie D, *Librn,* United States Navy (Naval Explosive Ordnance Disposal Facility Technical Library), Indian Head MD. 301-743-4738
Davis, Bruce, *TV Coordr,* San Antonio College Library, San Antonio TX. 512-734-7311, Ext 2480
Davis, Bruce A, *Instr,* San Antonio College, Library Technology Program, TX. 512-734-7311, Ext 2482
Davis, Bryan T, *Dir,* Oskaloosa Public Library, Oskaloosa IA. 515-673-6214
Davis, C Roger, *Bibliogr,* Smith College Library, Northampton MA. 413-584-2700, Ext 501
Davis, Carl, *Bkmobile Coordr,* Morgan County Library, John F Kennedy Memorial Library, West Liberty KY. 606-743-4151

Davis, Carol, *Librn,* Sturgis Public Library, Sturgis SD. 605-347-2740
Davis, Caroline, *Per,* Miami Dade Community College (Medical Center Campus Library), Miami FL. 305-547-1256
Davis, Carolyn, *Dir,* Ada Public Library, Ada OK. 405-332-2320
Davis, Carolyn, *Librn,* Pine Forest Regional Library (Stone County Public), Wiggins MS. 601-928-4993
Davis, Catharine W, *Dir,* Frank L Basloe Library of Herkimer New York, Herkimer NY. 315-866-1733
Davis, Charlene, *Automation,* Kentucky Department of Library & Archives, Frankfort KY. 502-564-7910
Davis, Charles, *Dean,* University of Illinois, Graduate School of Library Science, IL. 217-333-3280
Davis, Charles E, *Dir,* Southern Missionary College, Library Science Program, TN. 615-396-4291
Davis, Charles E, *Dir, Acq & Spec Coll,* Southern Missionary College, McKee Library, Collegedale TN. 615-396-4290
Davis, Charles M, *AV,* Itawamba Junior College Vocational-Technical Center, Itawamba Junior College-Tupelo Branch, Learning Resources Ctr, Tupelo MS. 601-842-5621, Ext 25
Davis, Charlie, *Librn,* University Computing Co, Technical Library, Dallas TX. 214-655-8822
Davis, Christine, *Librn,* Bladen County Public Library (Clarkton Public), Clarkton NC. 919-647-3661
Davis, Clarke S, *Dir,* Nashua Public Library, Nashua NH. 603-883-4141, 883-4142
Davis, Clayla, *Dir,* Saint Helena Public Library, George & Elsie Wood Public Library, Saint Helena CA. 707-963-5244
Davis, Cleda M, *Dir,* Cordelia B Preston Memorial Library, Orleans Public Library, Orleans NE. 308-473-3425
Davis, Clifford, *Asst Librn,* Jarvis Christian College, Ohlin Library & Communication Center, Hawkins TX. 214-769-2174, Ext 154
Davis, Clifton G, *Dir,* Bangor Theological Seminary, Moulton Library, Bangor ME. 207-942-6781
Davis, Connie, *Ref,* Boone County Public Library, Florence KY. 606-371-6222
Davis, Constance, *Exten,* Glendale Public Library, Glendale CA. 213-956-2030
Davis, D, *Librn,* Okanagan Regional Library District (Trout Creek Branch), Trout Creek BC. 604-494-1425
Davis, Dale, *Asst Librn, Cat & Ch,* Franklin Library Association, Franklin PA. 814-432-5062
Davis, Dan, *Dir,* Arizona-Sonora Desert Museum Library, Tucson AZ. 602-883-1380
Davis, David, *AV,* San Diego County Library, San Diego CA. 714-565-5100
Davis, Dennis, *Dir,* Ottumwa Public Library, Ottumwa IA. 515-682-7563
Davis, Donald, *Circ,* Public Library of Des Moines, Des Moines IA. 515-283-4152
Davis, Donna, *Cat,* Darlington County Library, Darlington SC. 803-393-5864
Davis, Donna, *Librn,* Morgantown Public Library (Subregional Library for the Blind & Physically Handicapped), Morgantown WV. 304-291-7427
Davis, Donna L, *Librn,* Baptist Memorial Hospital, John L McGehee Library, Memphis TN. 901-522-5140
Davis, Doris T, *Acq,* University of California Library, San Francisco CA. 415-666-2334
Davis, Dorothy, *Dir,* Mason-Dixon Public Library, Stewartstown PA. 717-993-2404
Davis, Dorothy, *Doc,* University of Michigan-Flint Library, Flint MI. 313-762-3400
Davis, Dorothy W, *Librn,* Whiting Public Library, Chester VT. 802-875-2277
Davis, Douglas, *Circ,* California State University, Northridge, Delmar T Oviatt & South Libraries, Northridge CA. 213-885-2271
Davis, Elisabeth B, *Librn,* University of Illinois Library at Urbana-Champaign (Biology), Urbana IL. 217-333-3654
Davis, Ellen, *Librn,* Jefferson County Public Library, Monticello FL. 904-997-3712
Davis, Emma, *Circ,* Center for Research Libraries, Chicago IL. 312-955-4545
Davis, Erwin, *ILL,* University of Richmond, Boatwright Memorial Library, Richmond VA. 804-285-6452
Davis, Estelle, *Librn,* Donald N Sharp Memorial Community Hospital, Health Science Library, San Diego CA. 714-292-2538
Davis, Eve, *Librn,* Toledo-Lucas County Public Library (Reynolds Corners), Toledo OH. 419-255-7055
Davis, Evelyn, *Librn,* Toronto Public Library, Toronto KS. 316-637-2445
Davis, Fannie M, *Librn,* Sumter Technical College Library, Sumter SC. 803-773-3971
Davis, Faye, *Ad,* Public Library of Enid & Garfield County, Enid Public Library, Enid OK. 405-234-6313
Davis, Frances F, *Librn,* Tuskegee Institute (Engineering), Tuskegee Institute AL. 205-727-8901
Davis, George, *Librn,* Fishkill Correctional Facility, Johnston Hall Library, Beacon NY. 914-831-4800
Davis, George R, *Asst Chief Librn,* Pillsbury, Madison & Sutro, Law Library, San Francisco CA. 415-983-1130
Davis, Gerald F, *Coordr,* Cooperating Libraries of Greater Springfield: A CCGS Agency, MA. 413-787-2341
Davis, Gerald F, *Dir,* Springfield College, Babson Library, Springfield MA. 413-787-2340
Davis, Gertrude C, *Librn,* Woodrow Wilson Birthplace Foundation, Inc, Research Library, Staunton VA. 703-885-0897
Davis, Harry O, *Doc & Maps,* Frostburg State College Library, Frostburg MD. 301-689-4396
Davis, Helaine, *Ref,* Hampshire College, Harold F Johnson Library Center, Amherst MA. 413-549-4600
Davis, Helen, *Librn,* Coors Porcelain Co, Research Library, Golden CO. 303-279-6565, Ext 2943
Davis, Helen M, *Librn,* Baptist Hospital, Medical Library, Beaumont TX. 713-832-5160
Davis, Hillis D, *Dir,* Cooperative College Library Center, Inc, (CCLC), GA. 404-659-6886
Davis, Hiram L, *Dir,* University of the Pacific, Irving Martin Library, Stockton CA. 209-946-2431
Davis, Howard, *Dir,* Artesia Christian College Library, Artesia NM. 505-748-1236
Davis, Ida, *ILL,* Benton Harbor Public Library (Filmco-Cooperative Service Center for Southwest Michigan Library Cooperative), Benton Harbor MI. 616-926-6741
Davis, Ida, *Librn,* Los Angeles Public Library System (Watts), Los Angeles CA. 213-567-2297
Davis, Ilse, *Libr Techn,* University of Oklahoma (Architecture), Norman OK. 405-325-5521
Davis, Jack, *Media,* Washington State University Library, Pullman WA. 509-335-4557
Davis, James, *Ref & Ad,* Clearwater Public Library, Clearwater FL. 813-462-6800
Davis, James, *Media,* Harrisburg Area Community College, McCormick Library, Harrisburg PA. 717-236-9533, Ext 257
Davis, James, *Cat,* Jersey City State College, Forrest A Irwin Library, Jersey City NJ. 201-547-3026
Davis, Jean, *ILL,* Frederick County Public Library, Frederick MD. 301-694-1613
Davis, Jean, *Asst Librn,* Rogers Corp, Lurie Library, Rogers CT. 203-774-9605, Ext 319
Davis, Jean B, *County Librn,* San Mateo County Library, Belmont CA. 415-573-2056
Davis, Jeanette, *Br Asst,* Timberland Regional Library (Winlock Branch), Winlock WA. 206-785-3461
Davis, Jeannette, *Librn,* Fabric Research Library, Albany International Co, Dedham MA. 617-326-5500, Ext 216, 217
Davis, Jim, *Rare Bks,* Idaho State Library, Boise ID. 208-334-2150
Davis, Joan, *Media,* Arizona Western College, Library Learning Center, Yuma AZ. 602-726-1000, Ext 360
Davis, Joan, *Librn,* Huntsville Memorial Hospital, Earnestine Connor Memorial Library, Huntsville TX. 713-291-3411, Ext 142
Davis, Joan, *Assoc Librn,* Petawawa Village & Township Union Public Library, Petawawa ON. 613-687-2227
Davis, Joan, *Asst Librn,* H B Stamps Memorial Library, Hawkins County Rogersville Public Library, Rogersville TN. 615-272-8710
Davis, John H, *Ref,* Gonzaga University (Law Library), Spokane WA. 509-328-4220, Ext 3781
Davis, Joyce, *Asst Librn,* Williamsport-Washington Township Public Library, Williamsport IN. 317-762-6555
Davis, Juanita, *Bkmobile Coordr,* West Georgia Regional Library, Neva Lomason Memorial Library, Carrollton GA. 404-832-1381
Davis, Karen A, *Librn,* Winona Memorial Hospital, Medical Library, Indianapolis IN. 317-927-2248
Davis, Katherine, *Admin,* Lakeland Library Cooperative, Grand Rapids MI. 616-456-4457
Davis, Kathryn, *Ch,* Chatham-Effingham-Liberty Regional Library, Savannah Public Library, Savannah GA. 912-234-5127
Davis, Kathryn, *Doc,* University of the South, Jessie Ball duPont Library, Sewanee TN. 615-598-5931, Ext 265, 267
Davis, Kitty, *Librn,* South Berwick Public Library, South Berwick ME. 207-384-2838
Davis, L, *Librn,* Borough of York Public Library (Evelyn Gregory), Toronto ON. 416-653-6185
Davis, Leola, *Librn,* Northeast Regional Library (George Allen), Booneville MS. 601-335-2331
Davis, Leslie, *Librn,* New York Association for the Blind, Lighthouse Library, New York NY. 212-355-2200, Ext 397
Davis, Linda M, *On-Line Servs & Bibliog Instr,* Norwich-Eaton Pharmaceuticals, Research Library, Norwich NY. 607-335-2539
Davis, Linda M, *Circ,* Southern Illinois University at Carbondale, Delyte W Morris Library, Carbondale IL. 618-453-2522
Davis, Lola M, *Tech Serv,* Allegany County Library, Cumberland MD. 301-777-1200
Davis, Lora Frances, *Librn,* United States Army (Brooke Army Medical Center Library), Fort Sam Houston TX. 512-221-4119, 221-3595
Davis, Lucille, *Librn,* Atkinson Township Library, Atkinson NE. 402-925-2855
Davis, Lynda C, *Ref,* Maryland Department of Legislative Reference Library, Annapolis MD. 301-269-2871
Davis, Lynn, *Asst Librn,* Westminster Theological Seminary Library, Glenside PA. 215-887-5511
Davis, Madelyn, *Per,* Point Loma College, Ryan Library, San Diego CA. 714-222-6474, Ext 355, 338
Davis, Madonna, *Bibliog Instr,* Northwest Missouri State University, Wells Library, Maryville MO. 816-582-7141, Ext 1192
Davis, Marc L, *Librn,* Washington Gas Light Co Library, Washington DC. 202-624-6386, 624-6387
Davis, Margaret C, *Librn,* Southwestern Indian Polytechnic Institute, Media Center, Albuquerque NM. 505-766-3266
Davis, Margaret I, *Librn,* Bessemer Public Library, Bessemer AL. 205-428-7882
Davis, Margaret L, *Dir,* Warsaw Public Library, Warsaw NY. 716-796-5650
Davis, Maribelle, *Dir,* Plano Public Library System, Plano TX. 214-423-6502, 867-1002
Davis, Marie A, *Dep Dir,* Free Library of Philadelphia, Philadelphia PA. 215-686-5322
Davis, Marion, *Ch,* Florida Gulf Coast Art Center Library, Clearwater FL. 813-584-8634
Davis, Marjorie, *Dir,* South Sioux City Public Library, South Sioux City NE. 402-494-4371
Davis, Martha, *Librn,* United States Army (Combined Arms Research Library), Fort Leavenworth KS. 913-684-3282
Davis, Martha H, *Dir,* Rockingham County Public Library, Eden NC. 919-627-1106
Davis, Martin, *Spec Coll,* University of Virginia, Alderman Library, Charlottesville VA. 804-924-3026
Davis, Mary, *Librn,* University of Kentucky (Art), Lexington KY. 606-257-3938
Davis, Mary B, *Librn,* Columbia-Lafayette-Ouachita-Calhoun Regional Library (Stephens Branch), Stephens AR. 501-234-1991
Davis, Mary B, *Librn,* Museum of the American Indian, Huntington Free Library, Bronx NY. 212-829-7770
Davis, Mary C, *Librn,* Flomaton Public Library, Flomaton AL. 205-296-3552
Davis, Mary E, *Librn,* Bridgeport Public Library, Bridgeport TX. 817-683-4412
Davis, Maud, *Media,* Marion Public Library, Marion IN. 317-664-7363
Davis, Melba, *Librn,* Thorsby Public Library, Thorsby AL. 205-646-3575

Davis, Melora, *Ref,* Cape May County Library, Cape May Court House NJ. 609-465-7837

Davis, Michelle, *Ref,* Washington Carnegie Library, Washington Court House OH. 614-335-2540

Davis, Mike, *Dir,* Lincoln Land Community College, Learning Resources Center, Springfield IL. 217-786-2354

Davis, Mildred, *Cat,* Virginia Military Institute, J T L Preston Library, Lexington VA. 703-463-6228

Davis, Mrs Clifton, *Dir,* Salisbury Public Library, Salisbury MA. 617-465-5071

Davis, Mrs D, *Spec Coll,* Southern University Library, Baton Rouge LA. 504-771-4990, 771-4991, 771-4992

Davis, Mrs Otis, *Librn,* West Georgia Regional Library (Douglas County), Douglasville GA. 404-832-1381

Davis, Mrs Troy, *Bkmobile Librn,* Copiah-Jefferson Regional Library, George W Covington Memorial Library, Hazlehurst MS. 601-894-1681

Davis, N K, *Ref,* John McIntire Public Library Public Library, Zanesville OH. 614-453-0391

Davis, Nancy H, *Dir,* Franklin Mint Corp, Information Research Services, Franklin Center PA. 215-459-6374

Davis, Nell, *Actg Librn,* Laurel-Jones County Library, Laurel MS. 601-428-4313

Davis, Oree, *Librn,* East Mississippi Regional Library (Stonewall Public), Stonewall MS. 601-659-9127

Davis, Pat, *Librn,* Craighead County & Jonesboro Public Library (Lake City Branch), Lake City AR. 501-237-4407

Davis, Pat, *Librn,* Crowley Ridge Regional Library (Lake City Public), Lake City AR. 501-237-4407

Davis, Paul, *Chmn,* Worcester State College, Dept of Media, MA. 617-752-7700, Ext 151

Davis, Paula M, *Librn,* Perry County District Library, New Lexington OH. 614-342-1077

Davis, Phil, *Media,* Kansas City Kansas Community College Library, Kansas City KS. 913-334-1100, Ext 38

Davis, Phyllis A, *Librn,* Bendix Corp, Communications Div, Engineering Library, Towson MD. 301-832-2200, Ext 212

Davis, Rachel, *Bkmobile Coordr,* Mayfield-Graves County Library, Mayfield KY. 502-247-2911

Davis, Ramona, *Cat,* Golden West College Library, Huntington Beach CA. 714-892-7711, Ext 541

Davis, Richard A, *Dir,* Butler University, Irwin Library, Indianapolis IN. 317-283-9225

Davis, Rosalie, *ILL & Ref,* Free Public Library of the City of Orange, Orange NJ. 201-673-0153

Davis, Russell L, *Dir,* Utah State Library, Salt Lake City UT. 801-533-5875

Davis, Ruth, *Librn,* Gloucester Public Library (Edward D Jones), Ottawa ON. 613-731-9907

Davis, Ruth A, *Librn,* Bethlehem Evangelical Lutheran Church Library, Saint Charles IL. 312-584-2199

Davis, Sadie, *Librn,* Stanly County Public Library (South Albemarle), Albemarle NC. 704-982-4248

Davis, Sally, *Librn,* University of Wisconsin-Madison (Library School Library), Madison WI. 608-262-3521

Davis, Samuel, *Ref,* Manchester Community College Library, Manchester CT. 203-646-4900, Ext 295

Davis, Sandra, *Librn,* Chicago Public Library (Jeffery Manor), Chicago IL. 312-374-6479

Davis, Sarah V, *Librn,* Charleston County Library (Cooper River Memorial), Charleston Heights SC. 803-744-2489

Davis, Sharon, *Circ,* Champaign Public Library & Information Center, Champaign IL. 217-356-7243

Davis, Sharon, *Asst Dir for Info Servs,* University of Colorado Health Sciences Center (Denison Memorial Library), Denver CO. 303-394-5125

Davis, Sherry, *Librn,* Yolo County Library (Winters Branch), Winters CA. 916-795-4955

Davis, Shirley, *Ch,* Mansfield Library, Mansfield Center CT. 203-423-2501

Davis, Shirley, *Tech Serv,* San Jacinto College, Lee Davis Library, Pasadena TX. 713-476-1850, 476-1501, Ext 241

Davis, Susan, *On-Line Servs,* Lummus Co-Lummus Technical Center, Technical Information Center Library, Bloomfield NJ. 201-893-2251

Davis, Susan, *Bkmobile Librn,* Taylor County Public Library, Campbellsville KY. 502-465-2562

Davis, Susan, *AV,* Treasure Valley Community College Library, Ontario OR. 503-889-6493, Ext 68

Davis, Suzanne S, *Ref,* Queens College, Everett Library, Charlotte NC. 704-332-7121, Ext 278

Davis, Suzanne S, *ILL,* Queens College, Everett Library, Charlotte NC. 704-332-7121, Ext 278

Davis, Thelma T, *Librn,* Oak Hill Public Library, Oak Hill OH. 614-682-6457

Davis, Vetory, *Doc & Spec Coll,* University of Arkansas, Pine Bluff, Watson Memorial Library, Pine Bluff AR. 501-541-6825

Davis, Virginia, *Cat,* University of Houston (Law Library), Houston TX. 713-749-3119

Davis, Virginia M, *Asst Dir,* Washington County Public Library, Abingdon VA. 703-628-2971

Davis, Wendy, *Media,* Dodge City Community College, Learning Resources Center, Dodge City KS. 316-225-1321, Ext 220

Davis, Willard G, *Circ,* University of Michigan Libraries (University Library), Ann Arbor MI. 313-764-9356

Davis, William J, *Librn,* Norfolk & Portsmouth Bar Association Law Library, Norfolk VA. 804-622-3152

Davis, Wylma, *ILL & Ref,* Virginia Military Institute, J T L Preston Library, Lexington VA. 703-463-6228

Davis, Jr, Walter, *Librn,* Austin Public Library (Oak Springs), Austin TX. 512-472-5433

Davis-Millis, Nina, *Dance,* Juilliard School, Lila Acheson Wallace Library, New York NY. 212-799-5000, Ext 265

Davison, Frieda, *Tech Serv,* East Tennessee State University (Medical Library), Johnson City TN. 615-928-6426, Ext 252

Davison, Mary, *Librn,* Madison Public Library (Monroe), Madison WI. 608-266-6390

Davison, Robert L, *Dir,* Library Services Branch, Victoria BC. 604-387-6517, 5277

Davisson, Anna Marie, *Ref,* Monmouth College, Hewes Library, Monmouth IL. 309-457-2031

Davol, Anne, *Librn,* Greenwich Hospital Association, Gray Carter Library, Greenwich CT. 203-869-7000, Ext 379

Davoli, Joyce M, *Librn,* Town of Tonawanda Public Library (Kenilworth), Kenmore NY. 716-873-2861

Davy, Edgar W, *Librn,* Massachusetts Institute of Technology Libraries (Dewey-Business & Management), Cambridge MA. 617-253-5677

Daw, Robert, *Music & Fine Arts,* Topeka Public Library, Topeka KS. 913-233-2040

Dawdy, Clifford G, *Assoc Dir,* Florida International University, Tamiami Campus, Athenaeum, Miami FL. 305-552-2461

Dawe, Janice, *Librn,* Webster Free Public Library, Webster NH. 603-648-2272

Dawkins, Mary S, *Dir & Bkmobile Coordr,* Buffalo Trace Regional Library, Flemingsburg KY. 606-845-9571

Dawkins, Mrs Burton T, *Librn,* Rapides General Hospital, Medical Library, Alexandria LA. 318-487-8111, Ext 269

Dawood, Rosemary, *Asst Chief,* Chicago Public Library (Business, Science & Technology Div), Chicago IL. 312-269-2814, 269-2865

Dawson, Bernice, *Libr Asst,* University of Texas Libraries (Classics), Austin TX. 512-471-5742

Dawson, Eleanor, *YA,* Chippewa Library League, Mount Pleasant MI. 517-773-3242

Dawson, Eleanor, *YA,* Veterans Memorial Library, Mount Pleasant MI. 517-773-3242

Dawson, Joyce, *Librn,* Saint Clair County Library System (Marysville Public), Marysville MI. 313-364-9493

Dawson, Judy, *Ref,* Jefferson State Junior College, James B Allen Library, Birmingham AL. 205-853-1200, Ext 280

Dawson, Loretta, *Ch,* Dallas County Public Library, Dallas TX. 214-749-8566, 749-8886

Dawson, Luther, *Librn,* US News & World Report, Inc Library, Washington DC. 202-861-2350

Dawson, Mary, *Ch,* Bethlehem Public Library, Bethlehem PA. 215-867-3761

Dawson, Meg, *Bibliog Instr,* Pacific Gas & Electric Co (James Hugh Wise Library), San Francisco CA. 415-781-4211, Ext 2573

Dawson, Patricia N, *Pub Servs & On-Line Servs,* Drake University, Cowles Library, Des Moines IA. 515-271-3993

Dawson, Robert MacG, *Assoc Prof,* Dalhousie University, School of Library Service, NS. 902-424-3656

Dawson, Terry, *ILL,* Appleton Public Library, Appleton WI. 414-734-7171

Dawson, Theresa, *Applied Sci,* Saint Louis Public Library, Saint Louis MO. 314-241-2288

Dawson, Val, *Ch,* Sault Sainte Marie Public Library, Sault Sainte Marie ON. 705-949-2152

Dawson, Victoria A, *Librn,* Educational Broadcasting Corp, Thirteen Research Library, New York NY. 212-560-3063, 3064, 3065

Dax, Edward R, *Dir,* Lane Public Library, Hamilton OH. 513-894-7156

Day, Adrian, *Librn,* Raymond Public Library, Raymond MN. 612-967-4226

Day, Bette, *ILL & Acq,* Sioux Falls College, Norman B Mears Library, Sioux Falls SD. 605-331-5000

Day, Billee M, *Dir,* Chickasaw Library System, Ardmore OK. 405-223-3164

Day, Carol, *Librn,* Genesee District Library (Linden Branch), Linden MI. 313-735-7700

Day, Cheryl, *Librn,* Port Colborne Public Library (Janet Street Branch), Port Colborne ON. 416-835-2926

Day, D R, *In Charge,* General Mills Inc (General Office Library), Minneapolis MN. 612-540-3536

Day, Deena, *Cat,* Goodnow Library, Sudbury MA. 617-443-9112

Day, Harriet, *ILL & Ref,* Southern Arkansas University, Magale Library, Magnolia AR. 501-234-5120, Ext 260, 262, 263

Day, Heather, *Librn,* Lilly Endowment Library, Indianapolis IN. 317-924-5471

Day, J Dennis, *Dir,* Salt Lake City Public Library, Salt Lake City UT. 801-363-5733

Day, Jane, *Librn,* Lawrence County Public Library, Moulton AL. 205-974-0883

Day, Janet, *Ad,* Wilton Library Association, Wilton CT. 203-762-3950

Day, Jean, *Librn,* Umatilla County Library (Echo Branch), Echo OR. 503-276-1881

Day, John M, *Dir,* Lake Erie College, James F Lincoln Learning Resource Center, Painesville OH. 216-352-3361, Ext 280

Day, Joy, *Dir,* Hobe Sound Bible College Library, Hobe Sound FL. 305-546-6166

Day, Judith, *Librn,* Racine Public Library (Uptown Branch), Racine WI. 414-636-9258

Day, Louise, *Librn,* Kaufman County Library, Kaufman TX. 214-932-6222

Day, Mrs E B, *Librn,* Lambton County Library (Watford Branch), Watford ON. 519-876-2204

Day, Mrs E H, *Librn,* Good Samaritan Hospital, Richard S Beinecke Medical Library, West Palm Beach FL. 305-655-5511, Ext 4315

Day, Norfleete, *Tech Serv,* Birmingham Public & Jefferson County Free Library, Birmingham AL. 205-254-2551

Day, Robert, *Librn,* The Pas Public Library, The Pas MB. 204-623-2023

Day, Robert S, *Dir,* International Tennis Hall of Fame & Tennis Museum Library, Newport RI. 401-846-4567

Day, Ron, *Asst Librn,* Pineville-Bell County Public Library, Pineville KY. 606-337-3422

Day, Roy, *Librn,* Pamlico County Library, Bayboro NC. 919-745-3515

Day, Roy E C, *Ref,* Craven-Pamlico-Carteret Regional Library, New Bern NC. 919-638-2127

Day, Sandra, *Librn,* Victoria County Public Library (Carden Township), Orillia ON. 705-324-3104

Day, Susan, *Asst Dir,* Royal Roads Military College, Coronel Memorial Library, Victoria BC. 604-388-1483

Day, Teresa A, *Tech Serv,* Bureau of Land Management (Denver Service Center Library), Denver CO. 303-234-4578

Day, Viola N, *Tech Serv & Cat,* Yale University Library (Divinity School), New Haven CT. 203-436-8440

Dayall, Susan, *Pub Servs,* Hampshire College, Harold F Johnson Library Center, Amherst MA. 413-549-4600

Dayhoff, Judy, *Librn,* Ball Aerospace Systems Div, Technical Library, Boulder CO. 303-441-4436

Days, Everett A, *Chief Librn,* Saint Augustine's College, New College Library, Raleigh NC. 919-828-4451, Ext 236

Dayton, Donald W, *Librn,* Bethany & Northern Baptist Theological Seminaries Library, Oak Brook IL. 312-620-2214

Dayton, Jane, *Librn,* Carnegie Library of Pittsburgh (East Liberty), Pittsburgh PA. 412-622-3100

Daze, Colleen J, *Librn,* Schenectady Gazette Library, Schenectady NY. 518-374-4141, Ext 237

De-Rowyn, Solange, *Chief Librn,* Centre Hospitalier Saint-Joseph, Bibliotheque Medicale, Trois-Rivieres PQ. 819-379-8112, Ext 276

Deadrich, Audrey, *Librn,* Kern County Library (Lake Isabella), Isabella CA. 805-861-2130

Deadrich, Dianne, *Librn,* Alpine County Free Library, Markleeville CA. 916-694-2120

Deagle, Joyce, *Libr Asst,* Pictou Antigonish Regional Library (Stellarton Branch), Stellarton NS. 902-752-1638

Deahl, Thomas F, *In Charge,* Microdoc, Technical Library, Philadelphia PA. 215-848-4545

Deahn, Jean, *Asst Dir,* Arapahoe Community College Library, Littleton CO. 303-794-1550, Ext 395

Deakin, Barbara, *Ref,* Golden West College Library, Huntington Beach CA. 714-892-7711, Ext 541

Deakins, Augusta, *Bibliog Instr,* South Georgia Regional Library, Valdosta-Lowndes County Public Library, Valdosta GA. 912-247-3405

Deakins, Maxine, *Acq,* Chattanooga-Hamilton County Bicentennial Library, Chattanooga TN. 615-757-5320

Deakyne, William, *Dir,* East Lyme Public Library, Inc, Niantic CT. 203-739-6926

Deal, Carl, *Latin Am,* University of Illinois Library at Urbana-Champaign, Urbana IL. 217-333-0790

Deal, Mrs James, *Librn,* Faith Library, Faith NC. 704-279-4723

DeAlleaume, William, *Prin Librn, Coll Acq & Proc,* New York State Library, Albany NY. 518-474-5930

Dealy, Ross, *Librn,* University of Wisconsin Center, Marinette County Campus Library, Marinette WI. 715-735-7477, Ext 65

Dean, Carole, *Asst Dir,* Center for Disease Control Library, Atlanta GA. 404-329-3396

Dean, Delight, *Commun Servs,* Shelby Township Library, Utica MI. 313-739-7414

Dean, Donna, *Librn,* Enlow Public Library, West Branch IA. 319-643-2633

Dean, Doris W, *Dir,* Troup Harris Coweta Regional Library, La Grange Memorial Library, La Grange GA. 404-882-7784

Dean, Esther N, *Librn,* Rosebud County Library, Forsyth MT. 406-356-7561

Dean, Linda M, *Librn,* Brevard Community College, Titusville Campus Learning Resource Center, Titusville FL. 305-269-5664

Dean, Louise M, *Librn,* University of Maine at Orono, Ira C Darling Ctr, Walpole ME. 207-563-3146, Ext 46

Dean, Marilyn, *Librn,* A R Gould Memorial Hospital, Health Sciences Library, Presque Isle ME. 207-769-2511, Ext 4182

Dean, Russell W, *Dir,* Snow College, Lucy A Phillips Library, Ephraim UT. 801-283-4201, Ext 204

Dean, Susan M, *Librn,* University of Connecticut, Torrington Branch Library, Torrington CT. 203-482-7635

Dean, Thelma, *Librn,* East Rochester Public Library, Rochester NH. 603-332-8013

Dean, W F, *Soc Sci,* Cleveland State University Libraries, Cleveland OH. 216-687-2486

Dean, Wilma M, *Librn,* Los Angeles Public Library System (Hyde Park), Los Angeles CA. 213-750-7241

Dean-Deibert, Margaret, *Assoc Librn,* Great River Library System, Quincy IL. 217-223-2560

Deane, Andrea, *Dir,* Sierra Nevada College Library, Incline Village NV. 702-831-1314

Deane, Betty G, *Librn,* Public Library of the District of Columbia (Deanwood), Washington DC. 202-724-4162

Deane, Judith, *Chief Librn,* Pembroke Public Library, Pembroke MA. 617-293-6771

Deane, Marie B, *AV,* Georgian Bay Regional Library System, Barrie ON. 705-726-4676, 8251

Deane, Roxanna L, *Washingtoniana,* Public Library of the District of Columbia, Martin Luther King Memorial Library, Washington DC. 202-727-1101

Deane, Shirley P, *Asst Prof,* Eastern Kentucky University, Dept of Library Science, KY. 606-622-2481

DeAngelis, Patrick, *Dir,* Mattatuck Community College, D'Arcy Memorial Library, Waterbury CT. 203-757-9661

DeAngelis, Paul A, *Dir,* Public Library of the City of Somerville, Somerville MA. 617-623-5000

Deans, Joycelyn, *Librn,* Ingham County Library (Okemos Branch), Okemos MI. 517-349-0250

Deany, Patricia, *Per,* Saint Mary-Of-The-Woods College Library, Saint Mary-of-the-Woods IN. 812-535-4141, Ext 223

Dearborn, Susan C, *Librn,* Harvard University Library (Developmental Office Library), Cambridge MA. 617-495-2196

Deardorff, John, *Soc Sci,* Slippery Rock State College Library, Slippery Rock PA. 412-794-2510

Dearing, Enid, *Librn,* North Vancouver District Public Library, North Vancouver BC. 604-984-0286

Dearing, Marjory, *Librn,* Marceline Carnegie Library, Marceline MO. 816-376-3223

Dearing, Mrs Fran P, *Librn,* Reeves County Library, Pecos TX. 915-445-5340

Dearnaley, Carolyn, *Asst Dir,* Colgate University, Everett Needham Case Library, Hamilton NY. 315-824-1000

Deas, Brenda, *Ch,* Upland Public Library, Upland CA. 714-982-1561

Deasey, Mary Alice, *Dir,* East Orange General Hospital Library, East Orange NJ. 201-672-8400, Ext 343, 370

deAsin, Josephine, *ILL,* George Washington University Library (Jacob Burns Law Library), Washington DC. 202-676-6646

Deason, Mary L, *Librn,* Chattahoochee Valley Regional Library (Lumpkin Public), Lumpkin GA. 912-838-6472

Deasy, Veronica, *Libr Asst,* San Bernardino County Library (Crestline Branch), Crestline CA. 714-338-3294

Deatherage, Ermadean, *Librn,* Waverly Public Library, Waverly IL. 217-435-2051

Deaton, Maxine, *Media,* Kellogg Community College, Emory W Morris Learning Resource Center, Battle Creek MI. 616-965-3931, Ext 333

Deatrich, Geneva, *Tech Serv,* Hays Public Library, Hays KS. 913-625-9014

Deats, John W, *County Librn,* Midland County Public Library, Midland TX. 915-683-2708

Deaven, Paul, *Media,* Dakota County Library System, Burnsville MN. 612-435-8111

DeBardeleben, Marian Z, *Librn,* Philip Morris, Inc, Research Center Library, Richmond VA. 804-271-2877

DeBaun, Robert R, *Librn,* United States Air Force (Norton Air Force Base Library), Norton AFB CA. 714-382-7119

deBear, Estelle, *Ref,* Saint John's Provincial Seminary Library, Plymouth MI. 313-453-6200, Ext 37

DeBeaumont, J G, *Users Services,* Public Service Commission Library, Ottawa ON. 613-992-4808, 997-3606

DeBella, Rose Marie, *Librn,* Kaiser-Permanente Medical Center, Medical Library, Redwood City CA. 415-365-4321, Ext 210

Debenham, Roger, *Ad,* Central Massachusetts Regional Library System, Worcester MA. 617-752-3751

Debenham, W Stuart, *Dir,* Colby College, Miller Library, Waterville ME. 207-873-1131, Ext 209

deBenks, Eugene, *Int Coll,* Michigan State University Library, East Lansing MI. 517-355-2344

DeBerry, Linda, *Librn,* Idabel Public Library, Idabel OK. 405-286-6406

Debner, Linda, *Asst Librn,* Marble Rock Public Library, Marble Rock IA. 515-397-4480

DeBoer, Julie Farmar, *Librn,* Sidley & Austin Library, Chicago IL. 312-329-5475

DeBoer, Kee, *Soc-Sci, Bus,* California State University, Long Beach, University Library, Long Beach CA. 213-498-4047

DeBoer, Sue, *Ref,* Prairie State College, Learning Center, Chicago Heights IL. 312-756-3110, Ext 113

DeBois, Mildred, *Asst Librn,* State Technical Institute at Memphis, George E Freeman Library, Memphis TN. 901-377-4106

DeBolt, Doris W, *Librn,* Cheboygan Area Public Library, Cheboygan MI. 616-627-2381

Debons, Anthony, *Prof,* University of Pittsburgh, School of Library & Information Science, PA. 412-624-5230

deBonville, Jean, *Journalism & Info,* Universite Laval Bibliotheque, Quebec PQ. 418-656-3344

deBorhegyi, Suzanne, *Dir,* Museum of Albuquerque Library, Albuquerque NM. 505-766-7878

deBrebeuf, Sister Marie, *Tech Serv,* Immaculata College Library, Immaculata PA. 215-647-4400, Ext 229

DeBrosse, Patricia, *Dir,* Coldwater Public Library, Coldwater OH. 419-678-2431

deBruijn, Elsie, *Librn,* University of British Columbia Library (Marjorie Smith Social Work), Vancouver BC. 604-228-2242

DeBurle, Ann, *Ref & Acq,* Porterville Public Library, Porterville CA. 209-784-0177, 784-1400, Ext 523

DeBuse, Ray, *Wash Libr Network Mgr,* Washington State Library, Olympia WA. 206-753-5592

DeCamp, Laurie, *Ch,* Dickinson County Library, Iron Mountain MI. 906-774-1218

DeCampos, Gabriel, *Asst Librn,* Connecticut State Library, Library for the Blind & Physically Handicapped, Hartford CT. 203-566-3028

DeCandido, Grace Anne, *Tech Serv,* Parsons School of Design, Adam L Gimbel Library, New York NY. 212-741-8914, 741-8915

DeCaprio, Albert, *Asst Librn,* San Bernardino County Library, San Bernardino CA. 714-383-1734

DeCaterina, Marion, *Acq,* Newburgh Free Library, Newburgh NY. 914-561-1836

DeChambeau, Saranell, *Librn,* Sno-Isle Regional Library (Langley Branch), Langley WA. 206-321-4383

DeChant, Kathleen, *Acq,* Detroit Bible College, Farmington Hills MI. 313-553-7200

Dechene, C, *Librn,* Goff-Nelson Memorial Library (Tupper Lake Branch Library), Tupper Lake NY. 518-359-2541

Dechene, Chalice, *Librn,* Goff-Nelson Memorial Library, Tupper Lake Public Library, Tupper Lake NY. 518-359-9421

Dechow, Eileen, *Librn,* Butterworth Hospital (Medical Library), Grand Rapids MI. 616-774-1655

Deck, Margaret, *Dir,* Seward Community Library, Seward AK. 907-224-3646

Deck, Norma L, *Ad,* Racine Public Library, Racine WI. 414-636-9241

Deck, Sharyn, *Cat,* Douglas County Library System, Roseburg OR. 503-673-1111, Ext 310

Decker, Barbara, *Asst Librn,* Eureka Carnegie Library, Eureka KS. 316-583-6222

Decker, Barbara, *Tech Serv,* Jackson District Library, Jackson MI. 517-788-4087

Decker, Charles, *Bkmobile Coordr,* Four County Library System, Binghamton NY. 607-723-8236

Decker, Geri, *Librn,* University of Notre Dame Library (Architecture), Notre Dame IN. 219-283-6654

Decker, Judy J, *Bkmobile Coordr,* Quincy Public Library, Quincy IL. 217-223-1309

Decker, Richard C, *Dir,* Cuyahoga Community College, District Office, Cleveland OH. 216-241-5966, Ext 220

Deckert, Delilah, *Librn,* Hillsboro Public Library, Hillsboro KS. 316-947-3827

Deckert, Eileen, *Tech Serv,* Huron Public Library, Huron SD. 605-352-3778

DeCleene, Clare, *Dir,* Fiske Free Library, Claremont NH. 603-542-4393

DeCora, Lambert, *Asst Dir,* University of Arkansas at Little Rock Library (University of Arkansas at Little Rock School of Law & Pulaski County Law Library), Little Rock AR. 501-371-1071

DeCorso, Deborah, *Pub Servs,* Sacred Heart University Library, Bridgeport CT. 203-374-9441

DeCosin, Manni, *Bibliog Instr,* Leeward Community College Library, Pearl City HI. 808-455-0210

Decoteau, Earline M, *Dir,* Ascension Parish Library, Donaldsonville LA. 504-473-8052

DeCoux, Elizabeth A, *Librn,* United States Air Force (McBride Library), Keesler AFB MS. 601-377-2181, 377-2604

Dedas, Madelyn, *Asst Dir,* Fort Wright College of the Holy Names Library, Spokane WA. 509-328-2970, Ext 20, 456-5087
Dedas, Virgil, *Tech Serv,* Whitworth College, Harriet Cheney Cowles Memorial Library, Spokane WA. 509-466-3260
deDelpin, Anita A, *Asst Librn,* Inter-American University of Puerto Rico, Ponce Regional College Library, Ponce PR. 809-843-3480
Dedman, Leslie, *Librn,* Mercer County Public Library, Harrodsburg KY. 606-734-3680
Dedmon, Joyce, *Spec Coll,* Norfolk State University, Lyman Beecher Brooks Library, Norfolk VA. 804-623-8873
Dee, Cynthia, *Dir,* Corona Public Library, Corona CA. 714-736-2381
Dee, Mathew F, *Dir,* Ohio State University, College of Law Library, Columbus OH. 614-422-6691
Deeble, Ellen, *Librn,* Monmouth County Library (Howell Branch), Howell NJ. 201-938-2300
Deegan, Joyce H, *Mgr,* Rockwell International, Information Center, Richardson TX. 214-690-6022
Deemer, Larry, *Pub Servs,* Gonzaga University (Law Library), Spokane WA. 509-328-4220, Ext 3781
Deere, Kathleen, *Librn,* Carnegie-Schuyler Library, Pana Public Library, Pana IL. 217-562-2326
Deering, James F, *Librn,* United States Navy (Naval Support Activity, Treasure Island), San Francisco CA. 415-765-5809
Deering, Ronald F, *Dir & Bibliog Instr,* Southern Baptist Theological Seminary, James P Boyce Centennial Library, Louisville KY. 502-897-4807
Deering, Ronald F, *Dir,* Theological Education Association of Mid America, (TEAM-A), KY. 606-897-4807
Deerr, Kathleen, *Ch,* Mastics-Moriches-Shirley Community Library, Shirley NY. 516-339-1511
Dees, Anthony R, *Dir,* Georgia Historical Society Library, Savannah GA. 912-944-2128
Dees, Suzanne, *Asst Dir,* Superiorland Library Cooperative, Marquette MI. 906-228-7697
Deese, William P, *ILL & Ref,* Pepperdine University Library, Payson Library, Malibu CA. 213-456-4252
DeFalco, Joan, *Asst Dir & Ref,* Public Library of Steubenville & Jefferson County, Steubenville OH. 614-282-9782
DeFato, Elizabeth, *Librn,* Seattle Art Museum Library, Seattle WA. 206-447-4710
DeFato, Joan, *Librn,* Los Angeles State & County Arboretum, Plant Science Library, Arcadia CA. 213-446-8251, Ext 32
Defato, Linda, *On-Line Servs,* Arizona State University Library, Tempe AZ. 602-965-3417
Defenderfer, Carolyn, *Ch, Tech Serv & Ref,* Calexico Public Library, Calexico CA. 714-357-2605
Deffenbaugh, James, *On-Line Servs,* University of Notre Dame Library, Notre Dame IN. 219-283-7317
Deffenbaugh, Ruth, *Dir,* Estes Park Public Library, Estes Park CO. 303-586-3180
Deffner, Virginia, *Ref,* Rock Island Public Library, Rock Island IL. 309-788-7627
Defoe, Deborah, *Ad,* Kingston Public Library, Kingston ON. 613-549-8888
DeFord, Donna, *Librn,* Spokane County Library (Fairfield Branch), Fairfield WA. 509-283-2512
DeForest, Emily, *Librn,* Kenai Community Library, Kenai AK. 907-283-4378
deForest, Kellam, *Dir,* de Forest Research Service Library, Los Angeles CA. 213-469-2271
DeForest, Marjorie, *Librn,* Montefiore Hospital & Medical Center (Medical Library), Bronx NY. 212-920-4666, 4667
DeForest, Patricia, *Deputy Dir,* Sterling Heights Public Library, Sterling Heights MI. 313-977-6260
DeFrance, Jean, *Ch,* Musser Public Library, Muscatine IA. 319-263-3065
deFrancesco, Laura, *Asst Dir,* Southbury Public Library, Southbury CT. 203-264-0606, Ext 239
Degange, Harriett, *Cat & Ref,* South Georgia Regional Library, Valdosta-Lowndes County Public Library, Valdosta GA. 912-247-3405
Degani, Edith, *Chief Librn, On-Line Servs & Bibliog Instr,* Jewish Theological Seminary of America Library, New York NY. 212-749-8000

deGarin, Maria A Morales, *Dir,* University of the Sacred Heart, Madre Maria Teresa Guevara Library, Santurce PR. 809-727-7800
DeGarmo, Lloyd, *Librn,* Compton College Library, Compton CA. 213-635-8081
DeGennaro, Richard, *Dir,* University of Pennsylvania Libraries, Van Pelt Library, Philadelphia PA. 215-243-7091
DeGeorges, Patricia, *Librn,* Milton Helpern Library of Legal Medicine, New York NY. 212-340-0102
Degere, Lois, *Librn,* Elizabeth Sanford Botsford Memorial Library (White Oaks), Williamstown MA. 413-458-8556
Degerman, Cora, *Ch,* Barron Public Library, Barron WI. 715-537-3881
DeGeus, Marilyn, *Dir & Acq,* Kansas City College of Osteopathic Medicine, Mazzacano Hall Library, Kansas City MO. 816-283-2451, 2454
Degner, Ruth, *Librn,* MacNeill Clinic Library, Saskatoon SK. 306-664-5800
DeGolyer, Christine, *Librn,* Rochester Institute of Technology (Chemistry Research), Rochester NY. 716-475-2520
DeGolyer, Christine, *Sci & Math,* Rochester Institute of Technology, Wallace Memorial Library, Rochester NY. 716-475-2566
deGonzalez, Ana Mercedes Lupianez, *Librn,* Puerto Rico Central Office of Personnel Administration Library, Santurce PR. 809-723-4300, Ext 404
deGonzalez, Olga Alvarez, *Chief Librn,* Commonwealth of Puerto Rico (Supreme Court Library), San Juan PR. 809-722-5219
DeGraaff, Jerome, *Soc Sci,* Portland State University, Branford Price Millar Library, Portland OR. 503-229-4424
DeGraauw, Cleo S, *Dir,* Vermilion Parish Library, Abbeville LA. 318-893-2655
DeGraff, Hattie, *Librn,* United States Navy (Naval Regional Medical Center), San Diego CA. 714-233-2816
deGrant, Nereida Pardo, *Librn,* Biblioteca Departamento De Servicios Sociales, Santurce PR. 809-724-7400, 724-8135
DeGruson, Eugene, *Spec Coll,* Pittsburg State University Library, Pittsburg KS. 316-231-7000, Ext 431
DeHaan, Elva, *Librn,* Carnegie Viersen Public Library, Pella IA. 515-628-4268
DeHart, Carl, *Media,* Blue Ridge Regional Library, Martinsville VA. 703-632-7125
deHaville, Marie, *ILL & Circ,* College of Saint Elizabeth, Mahoney Library, Convent Station NJ. 201-539-1600, Ext 365
Dehn, Mary B, *Asst Dir & Circ,* Great Neck Library, Great Neck NY. 516-466-8055
DeHoff, Julia, *Ch,* Haywood County Public Library, Waynesville NC. 704-452-5169
DeHoogh, Doris, *Librn,* Freeman Junior College Library, Freeman SD. 605-925-4237, Ext 28
DeIallo, N A, *Mgr,* Singer Co, Technical Information Center, State College PA. 814-238-4311, Ext 678
Deibler, Barbara, *Rare Bks,* State Library of Pennsylvania, Harrisburg PA. 717-787-2646
Deich, Ione, *Asst Librn,* Hutchinson Memorial Library, Randolph WI. 414-326-3420
Deily, Carole, *Cat,* Plano Public Library System, Plano TX. 214-423-6502, 867-1002
Deines, Lois Ann, *Librn,* San Marino Public Library, San Marino CA. 213-282-8484
Deinhardt, Nina, *Ch,* Martin County Library, Fairmont MN. 507-238-4207
Deis, Louise, *On-Line Servs,* CPC International, Inc, Best Food Information Center, Union NJ. 201-688-9000
Deiss, William, *Deputy Archivist,* Smithsonian Institution Archives, Washington DC. 202-381-4075
Deistler, Marvel, *Librn,* Lake County Public Library (Forty-First Avenue Public), Gary IN. 219-980-5180
Deiter, Sandra, *Tech Serv,* Princeton Public Library, Princeton NJ. 609-924-9529
Deitrick, Bernard E, *Librn,* Neshaminy-Warwick Presbyterian Church Library, Warminster PA. 215-313-6060
Deitsch, Wilma, *Ch,* Dwyer-Mercer County District Library, Celina OH. 419-586-2314

Deitzer, Margaret, *Head Librn,* Pennsylvania State University, Allentown Campus, Library Learning Resource Center, Fogelsville PA. 215-285-4811
DeJardin, Carole, *Ch,* Appleton Public Library, Appleton WI. 414-734-7171
DeJarnatt, Jim, *Dir,* Georgia Regional Library for the Blind & Physically Handicapped, Atlanta GA. 404-656-2465
DeJohn, William, *Dir,* Pacific Northwest Bibliographic Center, (PNBC), WA. 206-543-1878
DeJong, Mrs Delmar, *Librn,* Hudsonville Public Library, Hudsonville MI. 616-669-1255
DeJung, Janet, *Dir,* Cadott Community Library, Cadott WI. 715-289-4950
deKieffer, Robert E, *Coordr,* University of Colorado, Educational Technology Program, CO. 303-492-5141 & 492-6715
Dekker, Mrs B, *Librn,* Brock Township Public Library, Sunderland ON. 705-357-3109
Dekle, Barbara, *Pub Servs,* Auburn University at Montgomery Library, Montgomery AL. 205-279-9110, Ext 247
Dekle, Liz, *Ser,* Georgia Southwestern College, James Earl Carter Library, Americus GA. 912-928-1352
deKlerk, Ann, *Assoc Dir,* Carnegie-Mellon University, Hunt Library, Pittsburgh PA. 412-578-2446, 578-2447
DeKlerk, Peter, *Asst Dir (Sem),* Calvin College & Seminary Library, Grand Rapids MI. 616-949-4000, Ext 297
Dekoff, Rita, *Librn,* Buffalo & Erie County Public Library System (Erie County Medical Center, Hospital-Patient Library), Buffalo NY. 716-856-7525
DeKrey, June, *Ch,* Valley City Public Library, Valley City ND. 701-845-3821
Delacroix, Scott, *Ref & Law Clerk,* United States Court of Appeals, Fifth Circuit Library, New Orleans LA. 504-589-6510
delaCruz, Emma, *Tech Serv,* Bellingham Public Library, Bellingham WA. 206-676-6860
delaCruz, Emma J, *Tech Serv,* Whatcom County Public Library, Bellingham WA. 206-384-3150
delaCruz, Ernesto, *Coordr,* Oxnard Public Library, Oxnard CA. 805-486-4311
DeLaCruz, Frank, *Librn,* Tucson Public Library (El Rio), Tucson AZ. 602-791-4468
Delahaie, Suzanne, *Systems,* Virginia Commonwealth University (James Branch Cabell Library), Richmond VA. 804-257-1105
Delahanty, Thomas E, *Librn,* Androscoggin County Law Library, Auburn ME. 207-782-3121
delaHerran, Rebeca, *Librn,* Kansas City Kansas Public Library (Argentine), Kansas City KS. 913-831-2242
DeLamar, Nancy, *Visual Arts Asst,* Arkansas Arts Center, Elizabeth Prewitt Taylor Memorial Library, Little Rock AR. 501-372-4000
Delamarter, Ralph, *Libr Develop,* Oregon State Library, Salem OR. 503-378-4243
Delana, Genevieve, *Librn,* Loyola University of Chicago Libraries (Julia Deal Lewis Library), Chicago IL. 312-670-2875
DeLancey, James, *Asst Librn,* Georgetown University, Joseph Mark Lauinger Library, Washington DC. 202-625-4095
Delaney, Annette, *Circ,* Hopkinsville Community College Library, Hopkinsville KY. 502-886-3921, Ext 39
Delaney, Bonnie E, *Librn,* Johnson County Mental Health Center, John R Keach Memorial Library, Mission KS. 913-384-1100, Ext 350
Delaney, Bonnie E, *Librn,* Johnson County Mental Health Center Library, Olathe KS. 913-782-2100
Delaney, Caldwell, *Dir,* Museums of the City of Mobile, Reference Library, Mobile AL. 205-438-7569
Delaney, Claire, *Spec Coll,* Trinity College Library, Burlington VT. 802-658-0337, Ext 343
Delaney, Esther, *Librn,* Safeco Insurance Co Library, Seattle WA. 206-545-5505
Delaney, Helen E, *Librn,* Midland Public Library, Midland ON. 705-526-5811
Delaney, Marie G, *Dir,* Wells College, Louis Jefferson Long Library, Aurora NY. 315-364-3351

Delaney, Mrs L, *Librn,* Canada Institute for Scientific & Technical Information (Aeronautical & Mechanical Engineering), Ottawa ON. 613-993-1600

Delaney, Oliver, *Legis Ref,* Oklahoma Department of Libraries, Oklahoma City OK. 405-521-2502

Delaney, Verlean, *Chief Librn,* Veterans Administration, Hospital Library, Oklahoma City OK. 405-272-9876, Ext 442

Delap, Kay, *Librn,* Indiana Law Enforcement Academy, David F Allen Memorial Learning Resources Ctr, Plainfield IN. 317-839-5191, Ext 54

DeLargy, Ann, *Asst Librn,* Ross Roy Inc Library, Detroit MI. 313-568-6000

deLasa, Conchita, *Tech Serv,* Southern Connecticut State College, Hilton C Buley Library, New Haven CT. 203-397-4505

Delashmit, Mary, *Librn,* Holderness Free Library, Holderness NH. 603-279-5176

DeLashmitt, Eleanor, *Librn,* Monterey County Law Library, Salinas CA. 408-758-6444

DeLauche, Jean, *Acq,* Washburn University of Topeka, Mabee Library, Topeka KS. 913-295-6479

DeLaura, Carole, *Librn,* Troy Free Public Library, Troy PA. 717-297-2745

DeLauriers, Don, *Curator,* Kankakee County Historical Society Library, Kankakee IL. 815-932-5279

DelBane, Lena, *Ref,* Hubbard Public Library, Hubbard OH. 216-534-3512

Delbaum, Judith, *Librn,* Blue Cross of Greater Philadelphia, E A van Steenwyk Memorial Library, Philadelphia PA. 215-448-5400

DelCont, Mary, *Librn,* West Virginia Legislative Reference Library, Charleston WV. 304-348-2153

DeLeo, Pauline M, *Librn,* Chicago Public Library (Edgebrook), Chicago IL. 312-763-8313

Delesdernier, Betsy, *Librn,* M N Spear Memorial Library, Shutesbury MA. 413-256-8171

Delevich, Biljana Billie, *Librn,* General Motors Corp (Design Staff Information Center), Warren MI. 313-575-1957

Delfause, Ellen, *Librn,* Winooski Memorial Library, Winooski VT. 802-655-0401

DelFierro, Julie, *Librn,* ITEK Corp, Applied Technology Division Library, Sunnyvale CA. 408-732-2710, Ext 2604

DelFrate, Adelaide A, *Librn,* NASA, Goddard Space Flight Center Library, Greenbelt MD. 301-344-6244

Delgado, Idalia, *Grad Libr,* University of Puerto Rico Library, Jose M Lazaro Memorial Library, Rio Piedras PR. 809-764-0000, Ext 3296

Delgado, Rafael R, *Dir,* University of Puerto Rico Library, Jose M Lazaro Memorial Library, Rio Piedras PR. 809-764-0000, Ext 3296

Delgado, Trini, *Librn,* El Paso Public Library (Clardy Fox Branch), El Paso TX. 915-543-3847

Delia, Anesia, *Librn,* Guam Public Library (Merizo), Agana, Guam PI. 828-8240

Delisle, Louise, *Appl Sci,* Universite Laval Bibliotheque, Quebec PQ. 418-656-3344

deLissovoy, Reymour, *Slide Curator,* Rhode Island School of Design Library, Providence RI. 401-331-3507, Ext 229

Delius, Betty, *Dir,* Bellarmine College Library, Louisville KY. 502-452-8137

Delkhasteh, Patricia, *Librn,* Los Angeles Public Library System (Cypress Park), Los Angeles CA. 213-225-0989

Delks, Patricia J, *Dir,* Rollins College, Mills Memorial Library, Winter Park FL. 305-646-2000, Ext 2676

Dell, Barbara, *Regional Librn,* Public Library of the District of Columbia (Chevy Chase (Regional)), Washington DC. 202-727-1341

Dell, Geraldine, *Circ,* Creighton University (Health Sciences), Omaha NE. 402-449-2908

Dell, Jane, *Librn,* Clark County Library District (Indian Springs Branch), Indian Springs NV. 702-879-3845

Dellaria, Janet, *Media,* Truman College, Learning Resources Center, Chicago IL. 312-878-1700, Ext 2230

Dellenback, John R, *President,* Christian College Consortium, DC. 202-293-6177

Deller, A Michael, *Dir,* Madison Heights Public Library, Madison Heights MI. 313-588-1200, 588-7763

Dellinger, Bob, *Dir,* United States Wrestling Federation, National Wrestling Hall of Fame Library, Stillwater OK. 405-377-5242

Dellinger, Doris, *Librn,* Borg-Warner Corp, York Div Engineering Library, York PA. 717-846-7890, Ext 2435

Dellinger, Janet, *Asst Dir,* Hawkeye Institute of Technology Library, Waterloo IA. 319-296-2320, Ext 237

Delman, Bruce, *Bibliog Instr,* Veterans Administration, Medical Library, Cleveland OH. 216-791-3800, Ext 7307

DelMar, Patricia, *Tech Serv,* Long Beach Public Library System, Long Beach CA. 213-436-9225

Delmore, Sister Elizabeth, *Dir,* College of Saint Catherine, Saint Catherine Library, Saint Paul MN. 612-690-6650

DeLonais, Edna, *Dir,* Bradley Public Library, Bradley IL. 815-932-6245

Deloney, B, *Librn,* Fulton State Hospital (Patient's Library), Fulton MO. 314-642-3311

DeLong, Douglas, *Ser,* Illinois State University, Milner Library, Normal IL. 309-438-3675

DeLong, Ed, *AV,* Greenville County Library, Greenville SC. 803-242-5000

DeLong, Sharon, *Librn,* Diamond Shamrock Corp, Corporate Library, Cleveland OH. 216-694-6253

DeLong, Trish, *Dir,* Theodore Austin Cutler Memorial Library, Saint Louis Public Library, Saint Louis MI. 517-651-5141

deLopez, Lillian C, *Dir,* University of Puerto Rico, Medical Sciences Campus Library, San Juan PR. 809-767-9626, Ext 438

deLopez, Manuela O Martinez, *ILL,* Library Services Division, Dept of Education, Hato Rey PR. 809-753-9191, 754-0950

Delorey, Arlene, *Librn,* Chester Public Library, Chester NH. 603-887-3636

DeLorme, M M, *Mgr,* International Telephone & Telegraph Corp (Library & Records Unit), New York NY. 212-940-1224

Delorme, Sylvie, *Librn,* La Magnetotheque, Montreal PQ. 514-524-6831

Delorme-toupin, Carmen, *In Charge,* Le Musee D'art De Joliette Bibliotheque, Joliette PQ. 514-756-0311

delosATorres, Maria, *Tech Serv,* Inter-American University of Puerto Rico, Aguadilla Regional College Library, Aguadilla PR. 809-891-0998

Delougaz, Nathalie, *Chief, Shared Cat Div,* Library of Congress, Washington DC. 202-287-5000

Delozier, Lynn F, *Chief Librn,* Veterans Administration, Hospital Library, Perry Point MD. 301-642-2411

delPilar, Giovanna, *Librn,* University of Puerto Rico Library (Graduate School of Natural Sciences), Rio Piedras PR. 809-764-0000, Ext 2359

Delvecchio, Cheryl, *Br Ch Librn,* Fairfield Public Library, Fairfield CT. 203-259-8303

DelVecchio, Valentine, *Ser & Doc,* The Citadel, Daniel Library, Charleston SC. 803-792-5116

DeMaillie, Marjorie, *Ch,* Pittsford Community Library, Pittsford NY. 716-586-1251

DeMan, T, *Librn,* Firestone Tire & Rubber Co (Defense Research Division Library), Akron OH. 216-379-6485

DeMange, Kathryn, *Rare Bks & Spec Coll,* University of Maryland at Baltimore (Health Sciences Library), Baltimore MD. 301-528-7545

DeMarco, Elaine, *Ad,* Stoughton Public Library, Stoughton MA. 617-344-2711

Demaree, Pauline, *Dir,* Lorain Public Library, Lorain OH. 216-244-1192

Demarest, Robert, *Ref,* Collier County Free Public Library, Naples FL. 813-262-4130, 261-8208

Demarest, Rosemary R, *Chief Librn,* Price Waterhouse & Company, National Office Library, New York NY. 212-489-8900

DeMars, Bonnie, *Cat,* West Florida Regional Library, Pensacola Public Library, Pensacola FL. 904-438-5479

DeMatteo, Claudia, *Tech Serv,* Teaneck Public Library, Teaneck NJ. 201-837-4171

DeMayo, John B, *Dir,* Saint Charles Borromeo Seminary, Ryan Memorial Library, Philadelphia PA. 215-839-3760, Ext 275

Dembicki, Diane, *Curator,* Cultural Center Museum Library, Ponca City OK. 405-762-6123

Demchock, Charlotte, *Dir,* Satellite Beach Public Library, Satellite Beach FL. 305-773-9411

deMedina, Awilda Gonzales, *Dir,* Biblioteca Departamento De Servicios Sociales, Santurce PR. 809-724-7400, 724-8135

Dement, Alice, *Tech Serv,* San Bernardino County Library, San Bernardino CA. 714-383-1734

Demeris, Nick C, *Librn,* City of Houston (Legal Dept Library), Houston TX. 713-222-5151

Demers, Henri, *In Charge,* Quebec Ministere de l'Industrie et du Commerce, Centre de Documentation, Quebec PQ. 418-643-5081, 643-5082

Demers, N, *In Charge,* Industrial Life Insurance Co, Personnel Dept Library, Quebec PQ. 418-688-8210

Demers, Ruth J, *Librn,* Ashaway Free Library, Ashaway RI. 401-377-2770

Demes, Stanley B, *Chief Librn,* Hughes Aircraft Co-Fullerton, Technical Library, Fullerton CA. 714-871-3232, Ext 3506

Demidowich, Christine, *Librn,* Rutgers University, the State University of New Jersey, John Cotton Dana Library, Newark NJ. 201-648-5222

Demidowich, Christine R, *Librn,* Parade Publications, Inc, Editorial Library, New York NY. 212-956-7560

Deming, Rosemary, *Bkmobile Coordr,* Sioux City Public Library, Sioux City IA. 712-279-6179

Demiray, A, *Cat,* Barrie Public Library, Barrie ON. 705-728-1010

Demirjean, Hazel, *Cat,* Urbandale Public Library, Urbandale IA. 515-278-3945

Demirtas, Abdullah, *ILL,* Georgetown University, Joseph Mark Lauinger Library, Washington DC. 202-625-4095

Demirtas, Gail, *ILL,* Ventura County Library Services Agency, Ventura County Library, Ventura CA. 805-654-2627

Demlinger, Marlin, *Librn,* City College of the City University of New York (Science), New York NY. 212-690-8243

Demlinger, Marlin, *Librn,* City College of the City University of New York (Engineering), New York NY. 212-690-5324

Demmers, Linda, *Dir,* Newbury Junior College, Mewshaw Library, Boston MA. 617-262-9350, Ext 50

Demmers, Linda, *Chief Librn,* Pine Manor College, Alumnae Library, Chestnut Hill MA. 617-731-7081, 731-7083

Demmitt, Kathy, *Dir,* Grand Prairie Memorial Library, Grand Prairie TX. 214-264-1571

Demo, William J, *Dir,* Allegany Community College, Library (Division of Learning Resources), Cumberland MD. 301-724-7700, Ext 35, 36

DeMontigny, Sister Fernande, *Librn,* Saint Vincent Hospital, Medical Library, Ottawa ON. 613-231-4041, Ext 231

DeMorales, Mickey, *Librn,* Mohave County Library (Bullhead City), Riviera AZ. 602-753-5730

Demorest, Dorothy, *Dir,* Brighton City Library, Brighton MI. 313-229-6571

Demoret, Dona, *Librn,* Gove City Library, Gove KS. 913-938-4480

Demos, John T, *Dean,* University of Louisville Library, Louisville KY. 502-588-6745

DeMoss, Lucille, *Librn,* Mahoning Law Library Association, Youngstown OH. 216-747-2000, Ext 260

Dempsey, Bruce, *Dir,* Jacksonville Art Museum Library, Jacksonville FL. 904-398-8336

Dempsey, Frank J, *Exec Librn,* Arlington Heights Memorial Library, Arlington Heights IL. 312-392-0100

Dempsey, Margie, *Librn,* Cheshire Hospital, Medical Library, Keene NH. 603-352-4111

Dempster, Dora, *Dir,* Seneca College of Applied Arts & Technology, Finch Campus Learning Resource Centre, Willowdale ON. 416-491-5050, Ext 381

DeMund, Mary, *Librn,* Denver Medical Society Library, Denver CO. 303-861-1221

DeMundoLo, Sara, *Librn,* University of Illinois Library at Urbana-Champaign (Modern Languages), Urbana IL. 217-333-0076

DeMuth, Phyllis, *Librn,* Alaska Historical Library, Juneau AK. 907-465-2925

DeMuth, Phyllis, *Reader Serv,* Alaska State Library, Juneau AK. 907-465-2910

DEMYON

Demyon, Hildegarde, *Asst Dir,* Schuylkill Haven Free Public Library, Schuylkill Haven PA. 717-385-0542

DenAdel, Norma, *On-Line Servs,* William Penn College, Wilcox Library, Oskaloosa IA. 515-673-8311, Ext 291

deNarvaez, Martha M, *Curator Mss & Rare Bks,* Hispanic Society of America Library, New York NY. 212-926-2234

DeNatale, Rose Marie, *Librn,* DMS, Inc Library, Greenwich CT. 203-661-7800

Dendy, Adele, *Media,* Indiana University at Bloomington, University Libraries, Bloomington IN. 812-337-3403

Denfeld, Kay, *On-Line Servs,* University of Washington Libraries (Health Sciences), Seattle WA. 206-543-5530

Dengel, Raymond, *Doc,* Edinboro State College, Baron-Forness Library, Edinboro PA. 814-732-2780

Dengler, Eartha, *Asst Librn,* Merrimack Valley Textile Museum Library, North Andover MA. 617-686-0191

Denham, Bernard J, *ILL,* Stanford University Libraries, Stanford CA. 415-497-2016

Denham, Mrs Ralph, *Bkmobile Coordr,* Boone County Public Library, Florence KY. 606-371-6222

Denio, Jean, *Librn,* Provident Mutual Life Insurance Co Library, Philadelphia PA. 215-472-5000, Ext 381

Denis, Leonard Rossiter, *Librn,* Germantown Historical Society Library, Philadelphia PA. 215-844-0514

Deniston, Mary, *Ch,* Fulton County Public Library, Rochester IN. 219-223-2713

Deniston, Patricia S, *Dir,* Polk Community College Library, Winter Haven FL. 813-294-7771, Ext 305

Denkovich, Ethel M, *ILL,* United States Army War College Library, Carlisle Barracks PA. 717-245-4319

Denlinger, Georgette, *Acq,* Scotch Plains Public Library, Scotch Plains NJ. 201-322-5007

Denman, M, *Librn,* ITT-Telecommunications Technology Center, TTC Library, Shelton CT. 203-929-7341

Denman, Margaret W, *Coordr,* Western Maryland College, Media-Library Science, MD. 301-848-7000

Dennard, Dianne, *ILL,* West Georgia College Library, Carrollton GA. 404-834-1370

Dennen, Delores, *ILL,* Miles City Public Library, Sagebrush Federation of Libraries, Miles City MT. 406-232-1496

Dennett, Louise K, *ILL,* Northeastern University Libraries, Boston MA. 617-437-2350

Denney, Christine, *Librn,* Daviess County Library (Jamesport Branch), Jamesport MO. 816-684-6120

Denney, Gloria, *Librn,* Grand County Public Library, Moab UT. 801-259-5421

Denney, Kathryn C, *Librn,* Virginia Department of Corrections Academy for Staff Development Library, Waynesboro VA. 703-943-3141

Dennhardt, Lauren R, *Librn,* American Conservatory of Music Library, Chicago IL. 263-4161 Ext 249

Dennin, Marjorie C, *Dir,* Northern Virginia Community College Libraries (Annandale Campus), Annandale VA. 703-323-3128

Denning, Catherine, *Ref Asst,* Brown University (Annmary Brown Memorial), Providence RI. 401-863-2429

Denning, E Aileen, *ILL & Ad,* Moline Public Library, Moline IL. 309-762-6883

Denning, Julie, *Librn,* Albuquerque Public Library (San Pedro), Albuquerque NM. 505-766-7914

Dennis, Anne, *Asst Librn,* Florence Township Public Library, Roebling NJ. 609-499-0143

Dennis, Betty, *Librn,* Florence Township Public Library, Roebling NJ. 609-499-0143

Dennis, Betty L, *Dir,* Lee Library Association, Lee MA. 413-243-0385

Dennis, Donald, *Systs Analyst,* University of British Columbia Library, Vancouver BC. 604-228-3871

Dennis, Donald D, *Librn,* American University, Jack I & Dorothy G Bender Library & Learning Resources Center, Washington DC. 202-686-2323

Dennis, Elise, *Ref,* West Springfield Public Library, West Springfield MA. 413-736-4561

Dennis, Jo Ellen, *Tech Serv,* Parkersburg & Wood County Public Library, Wood County Service Center, Parkersburg WV. 304-485-6564

Dennis, Martha, *Librn,* Nelson County Public Library (Bloomfield Branch), Bloomfield KY. 502-348-3714

Dennis, Nancy, *Acq & Cat,* Waterville Public Library, Waterville ME. 207-872-5433

Dennis, Rodney G, *Curator of Mss,* Harvard University Library (Houghton Library-Rare Books & Manuscripts), Cambridge MA. 617-495-2441

Dennis, Sandra T, *Librn,* Inforonics, Inc Library, Littleton MA. 617-486-8976

Dennis, Sister Mary, *President,* Tri-State College Library Cooperative, (TCLC), PA. 215-525-0796

Dennis, Willye, *Ch,* Jacksonville Public Library System, Haydon Burns Library, Jacksonville FL. 904-633-6870

Dennison, Addie, *Librn,* Whitneyville Library Association, Inc, Whitneyville ME. 207-255-8077

Dennison, Frances, *Asst Librn & On-Line Servs,* Black & Veatch Consulting Engineers, Central Library, Kansas City MO. 913-967-2223

Dennison, Keith E, *Dir,* Pioneer Museum & Haggin Galleries, Library of California, Stockton CA. 209-462-4116, 462-1566

Dennison, Sam, *Curator,* Free Library of Philadelphia (Edwin A Fleisher Coll of Orchestral Music), Philadelphia PA. 215-686-5322

Denny, Anne, *ILL,* Tucson Public Library, Tucson AZ. 602-791-4391

Denny, Sybil I, *Asst Librn,* Burkburnett Library, Burkburnett TX. 817-569-2991

Denpewolf, Billie, *Admin Asst,* Oklahoma Crime Commission Library, Oklahoma City OK. 405-521-2821

Denslow, Sharon, *Ch,* Porter Public Library, Westlake OH. 216-871-2600

Densmore, Donna, *Asst Librn,* Odell Public Library, Odell IL. 815-998-2012

Densmore, Richard, *ILL,* Baldwin-Wallace College, Ritter Library, Berea OH. 216-826-2204, 2205, Ext 2455

Denson, Elaine, *Librn,* Sunflower County Library System (Kathy June Sheriff Library), Moorhead MS. 601-246-8263

Denson, Janeen, *Circ,* Duke University (Law School Library), Durham NC. 919-684-2847

Denton, A Wayne, *Dir,* Christian Brothers College Library, Memphis TN. 901-278-0100, Ext 220

Denton, Adelyn, *Librn,* West Georgia Regional Library (Paulding County Public), Dallas GA. 404-832-1381

Denton, Ann, *Actg Tech Serv,* Memphis State University Libraries, Memphis TN. 901-454-2201

Denton, Carla, *Librn,* Thomas Hackney Braswell Memorial Library (Middlesex Branch), Middlesex NC. 442-1937 & 442-1951

Denton, Francis D, *Dir,* North Seattle Community College, Instructional Resources Center, Seattle WA. 206-634-4400

Denton, Mrs Spencer, *Librn,* Five Civilized Tribes Museum Library, Muskogee OK. 918-683-1701

Denton, N E, *In Charge,* Mono County Law Library, Bridgeport CA. 714-932-7911, Ext 223

Denton, Ramona, *Resources Librn,* Baptist Sunday School Board of the Southern Baptist Convention, Dargan-Carver Library, Nashville TN. 615-251-2133

Denton, Stella, *Spec Servs,* Newburgh Free Library, Newburgh NY. 914-561-1836

Denton, W R, *Tech Serv,* School of Theology at Claremont, Theology Library, Claremont CA. 714-626-3521, Ext 263

Dentzel, Carl S, *Dir,* Southwest Museum Library, Los Angeles CA. 213-221-2163

Denue, Gary N, *Dir,* University of Detroit Library, Detroit MI. 313-927-1090

deOnis, Johanna R, *Ser,* United States Military Academy Library, West Point NY. 914-938-2230

DeOrpor, Lino S Lipinsky, *Curator Hist,* John Jay Homestead Library, Katonah NY. 914-232-5651

Depaso, Beth, *Ch,* South Park Township Community Library, Library PA. 412-833-5585

DePersiis, Arlene, *Acq,* Pratt Institute Library, Brooklyn NY. 212-636-3684

DePew, John, *Assoc Prof,* Florida State University, School of Library Science, FL. 904-644-5775

DePiesse, Larry, *Bus & Tech,* Wichita Public Library, Wichita KS. 316-262-0611

Depoian, Haig W, *Bus Serv,* Franklin Park Public Library District, Franklin Park IL. 312-455-6016

dePonce, Blanca N Rivera, *Dir,* Library Services Division, Dept of Education, Hato Rey PR. 809-753-9191, 754-0950

DePopolo, Margaret E, *Librn,* Massachusetts Institute of Technology Libraries (Rotch Library-Architecture & Planning), Cambridge MA. 617-253-7052

DeProspo, Jr, Ernest R, *Prof,* Rutgers-The State University of New Jersey, Graduate School of Library & Information Studies, NJ. 201-932-7500

Depta, Pawel, *Ref,* Cambridge Public Library, Cambridge MA. 617-498-9080

DePue, Micheal, *Librn,* Barry-Lawrence Regional Library (Aurora Branch), Aurora MO. 417-678-2036

Dequin, Henry, *Asst Prof,* Northern Illinois University, Dept of Library Science, IL. 815-753-1735

Derby, Catherine, *Librn,* North Hero Public Library, North Hero VT. 802-372-6926

Derbyshire, Joseph J, *Dir,* Bates College, George and Helen Ladd Library, Lewiston ME. 207-784-2949

Derck, K Lynn, *Asst Dir,* Bay County Library System, Bay City MI. 517-894-2837

Derck, Lucille, *Librn & Ad,* Oakfield Public Library, Haxton Memorial Library, Oakfield NY. 716-948-9900

Deredita, Laurie, *Tech Serv,* Free Public Library of the Borough of Fort Lee, Fort Lee NJ. 201-461-8020

DeRemer, Mary, *Librn,* Dimmick Memorial Library, Jim Thorpe PA. 717-325-2131

DeRenzis, Ann, *Sr Librn,* Phillipsburg Free Public Library, Phillipsburg NJ. 201-454-3712

Derenzy, Maureen, *Reader Serv,* White Pine Library Cooperative, Saginaw MI. 517-792-0001

Derer, Bohus, *Dir,* Borough of York Public Library, Toronto ON. 416-781-5208

DeReu, Murriel L, *Librn,* Marion Public Library, Marion NY. 315-926-4933

Derfer, Marlan M, *Supvr Libr & Info Servs,* SCM Corp, Glidden Durkee Div Technical Library, Jacksonville FL. 904-764-1711, Ext 336, 368

Derge, Charlene C, *Librn,* United States Securities & Exchange Commission Library, Washington DC. 202-755-1464

Derla, Mary, *Librn,* Central School District Free Public Library, Watkins Glen Public Library, Watkins Glen NY. 607-535-2346

Dermody, Anna, *Ref,* Johnson State College, John Dewey Library, Johnson VT. 802-635-2356, Ext 248

Dermon, Helene, *Librn,* Tucker Free Library, Henniker NH. 603-428-3471

Dermyer, A L, *Chief Librn,* Union Pacific Railroad Library, Omaha NE. 402-271-4785

Derner, Carol, *Asst Dir,* Lake County Public Library, Merrillville IN. 219-769-3541

Derosier, Ella Mae, *In Charge,* Red Lake Falls Public Library, Red Lake Falls MN. 218-253-2992

Derouchie, Mayo, *Educ,* Mankato State University, Memorial Library, Mankato MN. 507-389-6201

Derr, Richard L, *Prof,* Case Western Reserve University, School of Library Science, OH. 216-368-3500

Derrick, Louise S, *Librn,* Sacred Heart Hospital, Health Science Library, Cumberland MD. 301-759-7229

Derry, Clara, *Librn,* Hood River County Library (Cascade Locks Branch), Cascade Locks OR. 503-374-8388

Dershem, Darlene, *Librn,* Deckerville Public Library, Deckerville MI. 313-376-8015

Dertien, James L, *Dir,* Bellevue Public Library System, Bellevue NE. 402-291-8000

Derting, Anne, *Librn,* Evans Products Co, Corporate Library, Portland OR. 503-222-5592

Derwinski, Alyce, *Asst Dir,* Dickinson County Library, Iron Mountain MI. 906-774-1218

Dery, Jeannine, *In Charge,* Le Centre Hospitalier Sainte-Therese, Bibliotheque Medicale, Shawinigan PQ. 819-537-9351

Dery, Mary A, *Librn,* Harper Grace Hospitals (Grace Hospital, Oscar Le Seure Professional Library), Detroit MI. 313-494-7000

Desai, B M, *Dir,* Natrona County Public Library, Casper WY. 307-235-9272

deSalva, Angelin R, *Dir,* Biblioteca Publica Carnegie, San Juan PR. 809-724-1046

DeSalvo, Barbara, *Librn,* Colorado State Hospital (Hospital Community Library), Pueblo CO. 303-543-1170, Ext 2667

DeSalvo, Patricia, *Dir,* University of Maine at Orono, Bangor Community College Library, Bangor ME. 207-581-7328

DeSantis, Madeline, *Asst Librn,* Rutgers University, the State University of New Jersey, John Cotton Dana Library, Newark NJ. 201-648-5222

DeSantis, Mary, *Librn,* Cabell County Public Library (Gallaher Village), Huntington WV. 304-523-4207

DeSantis, Sylvia, *Chief Librn,* Monson Free Library & Reading Room Association, Horatio Lyon Memorial Library, Monson MA. 413-267-3866

Desaulniers, Marie, *Librn,* Gloucester Public Library (Beriault Branch), Orleans ON. 613-824-1962

DeSautels, Jeanne, *Ch,* Bibliotheque Municipale De Sherbrooke, Sherbrooke Municipal Library, Sherbrooke PQ. 819-565-5860, 565-5861 & 565-5862

Desbman, Hazel M, *Actg Librn,* Mooresville Public Library, Mooresville NC. 704-664-2927

Desch, Carol Ann, *Ad & Ref,* Bethlehem Public Library, Delmar NY. 518-439-9314

Deschamps, Ethel, *Librn,* Washington County Free Library (Hancock War Memorial), Hancock MD. 301-678-5300

Deschamps, Normand, *Librn,* Canadian Broadcasting Corp, Head Office Library, Ottawa ON. 613-731-3111, Ext 561 or 560

DesChene, Dorice, *Head,* University of Cincinnati Libraries (Chemistry-Biology), Cincinnati OH. 513-475-4524

Descheneaux, Mary Ellen, *Librn,* Klamath County Library (Loyd DeLap Law Library), Klamath Falls OR. 503-882-2501, Ext 232

Deschenes, Huguette, *Dir,* Bibliotheque Municipale, Saint Leonard PQ. 514-321-7630

DeSchryver, Victor, *Librn,* University of Detroit Library (Dental School), Detroit MI. 313-259-6622, Ext 298

deSciora, Edward, *Dir,* Port Washington Public Library, Port Washington NY. 516-883-4400

deScossa, C, *Asst Prof,* University of Alberta, Faculty of Library Science, AB. 403-432-4578

DeSerio, Judith, *Actg Dir,* American Council on Education, National Center for Higher Education Library, Washington DC. 202-833-4690

DeShazc, Rebecca, *Librn,* Southwest Georgia Regional Library (Talking Book Center), Bainbridge GA. 912-246-3895

DeShazo, Virginia, *Librn,* Harquahala Public Library, Buckeye AZ. 602-372-4611

DeShields, Ruth, *Librn,* Holdenville Public Library, Holdenville OK. 405-379-3245

DeSimone, Mary, *Librn,* Lynn Hospital, Health Sciences Library, Lynn MA. 617-598-5100, Ext 247

Desjardins, Jacqueline, *Dir,* Bibliotheque Municipale, Saint Jerome PQ. 514-436-1772

Desjardins, Wendy, *Circ,* Lethbridge Community College, Buchanan Resource Centre, Lethbridge AB. 403-327-2141, Ext 350

Desjarlais, Marsha, *Dir,* Durham Public Library, Durham CT. 203-349-9544

Desmarais, Carmen, *Ref,* Bibliotheque De La Ville De Montreal, Montreal PQ. 514-872-5923

Desmarais, Elisabeth, *Dir,* Harold J Patten Public Library, Tewksbury MA. 617-851-6071

Desmarais, Norman, *Dir,* Saint Mary's Seminary & University, School of Theology Library, Baltimore MD. 301-323-3200, Ext 70

DeSmet, Nadine, *Librn,* Yolo County Library (Esparto Branch), Esparto CA. 916-787-3426

Desmond, Winifred S, *Chief, Tech Ref Branch,* National Highway Traffic Safety Administration, Technical Reference Branch, Washington DC. 202-426-2768

DeSoto, Randy A, *Librn,* East Carroll Parish Library, Lake Providence LA. 318-559-2615

DeSouza, Connie, *AV,* Auburn Public Library, Auburn WA. 206-931-3018

Despres, Thomas E, *Librn,* State Library of Ohio (Central Ohio Bookmobile Center), Columbus OH. 614-291-6175

Desreuisseau, M A, *Librn,* Battelle Columbus Laboratories, William F Clapp Laboratories Inc Library, Duxbury MA. 617-934-5682, Ext 43

Desrochers, Edmond, *Dir,* Maison Bellarmin Library, Montreal PQ. 514-387-2541, Ext 75

Desroches, V, *Area Coordr,* Agriculture Canada (Entomology Research Library), Ottawa ON. 613-995-4502

Desrosiers, Fernande, *Ref,* Saint Paul University Library, Ottawa ON. 613-235-1421, Ext 54

Desrosiers, Jeanne, *Dir,* Westfield Memorial Library, Westfield NJ. 201-233-1515

Desrosiers, Shirley, *Librn,* British Columbia-Ministry of Lands, Parks & Housing, Parks Library, Victoria BC. 604-387-1696, Ext 27

Desruisseaux, Irene, *Librn,* Grand Seminaire Des Saints Apotres Library, Sherbrooke PQ. 819-563-9934

Dessaux, Jill, *Libr Asst,* San Bernardino County Library (Lake Arrowhead), Blue Jay CA. 714-337-3118

Dessy, Blane K, *Dir,* Mifflin County Library, Lewistown PA. 717-242-2391

DeStefano, Mary, *Ad,* Antioch Township Library, Antioch IL. 312-395-0874

DeStefano, Rita A, *Cat,* Saint Charles Borromeo Seminary, Ryan Memorial Library, Philadelphia PA. 215-839-3760, Ext 275

DeStreel, Quentin, *Librn,* Easton Area Public Library, Easton PA. 215-258-2917

Detchon, Kathy, *Ch,* Flint River Regional Library, Griffin GA. 404-227-2756

deTemple, Elaine, *Ch,* Ottawa Public Library, Ottawa ON. 613-236-0301

deTemple, Jean, *Asst Dir & Br Coordr,* Ottawa Public Library, Ottawa ON. 613-236-0301

Determan, Susan, *Librn,* Early Public Library, Early IA. 712-273-5334

Dethlefs, Billie, *ILL,* Shasta College Library, Redding CA. 916-241-3523, Ext 377

Detjen, A L, *Dir,* Kiel Public Library, Stoelting Public Library, Kiel WI. 414-894-7122

Detlefs, Ann, *Librn,* Sno-Isle Regional Library (Silvana Branch), Silvana WA. 206-652-8000

Detlefsen, Ellen, *Assoc Prof,* University of Pittsburgh, School of Library & Information Science, PA. 412-624-5230

deTonnancour, P Roger, *Librn,* General Dynamics-Fort Worth Division, Technical Library, Fort Worth TX. 817-732-4811, Ext 4319, 4320

DeTreville, Virginia E, *Ref & Spec Coll,* Augusta College, Reese Library, Augusta GA. 404-828-4566, 828-4066

deTreville, Virginia E, *Asst Curator,* Richmond County Historical Society Library, Augusta GA. 404-828-4566, 828-4801

Detrick, Virginia, *Asst Dir,* Pemberton Community Library Association, Pemberton NJ. 609-894-2516

Detro, Randall A, *Dir,* Nicholls State University, Allen J Ellender Memorial Library, Thibodaux LA. 504-446-8111, Ext 401, 402

Dettle, Roger, *Cat,* Saint Mary's College, Fitzgerald Library, Winona MN. 507-452-4430, Ext 232

Dettmering, Diane, *Librn,* Marathon County Public Library (Brokaw Branch), Brokaw WI. 715-845-7214, Ext 21

DeTurk, Virginia, *Librn,* Duke University (Medical Sciences Library), Durham NC. 919-684-2502

Detweiler, Mary Jo, *Dir,* Prince William Public Library, Manassas VA. 703-361-8211

Detwiler, Doris, *Social & Econ,* Detroit Public Library, Detroit Associated Libraries, Detroit MI. 313-833-1000

Deuel, Marlene, *Dir,* Poplar Creek Public Library District, Streamwood IL. 312-837-6800

Deurell, Anne M, *On-Line Servs,* United States Air Force (Electronics Systems Division, Base Library), Hanscom AFB MA. 617-861-2177

deUsabel, Frances, *Instnl Serv,* Wisconsin Department of Public Instruction (Reference & Loan Library), Madison WI. 608-266-7270

Deuss, Jean, *Chief Librn,* Federal Reserve Bank of New York (Research Library), New York NY. 212-791-5670, 5671

Deutsch, Karen, *Librn,* East Syracuse Free Library, East Syracuse NY. 315-437-4841

Deutsch, Stewart F, *Librn,* Fried, Frank, Harris, Shriver & Jacobson Library, New York NY. 212-964-6500, Ext 350

Dev, Roderick, *Librn,* Colorado Springs Fine Arts Center Library, Colorado Springs CO. 303-634-5581, Ext 22

Devan, Christopher B, *Dir,* Jefferson-Madison Regional Library, McIntire Public Library, Charlottesville VA. 804-296-6157

Devaney, Barbara, *Librn,* Fayette Public Library, Fayette MO. 816-248-3348

Devaney, James M, *Librn,* Joseph Bulova School of Watchmaking Library, Flushing NY. 212-424-2929

DeVaney, Kathleen, *Ref,* Flagler College, Louise Wise Lewis Library, Saint Augustine FL. 904-829-6481, Ext 205 & 206

DeVaul, Florence, *Dir,* Inwood Public Library, Inwood IA. 515-753-4427

Deveau, J Alphone, *Acadiana,* Universite Sainte Anne, Louis R Comeau Bibliotheque, Church Point NS. 902-769-2114, Ext 163

deVelez, Leida Torres, *Librn,* Puerto Rico Regional Library for the Blind & Physically Handicapped, Biblioteca Regional para Ciegos y Fisicamente Impedidos de PR, San Juan PR. 809-723-1519

DeVenney, Lorraine, *Librn,* Samborn, Steketee, Otis & Evans Inc Library, Resource & Information Center, Toledo OH. 419-255-3830

Dever, Laurence A, *Librn,* Montgomery County Library (South), Woodlands TX. 713-367-3939, 756-0412

Devereux, Eleanor, *Ch & YA,* Transylvania County Library, Inc, Brevard NC. 704-883-9880

Devers, Alice, *Br Coordr,* Lancaster County Library, Lancaster PA. 717-394-2651

Devers, Charlotte M, *Dir,* North Castle Public Library, Armonk NY. 914-273-3887

DeVilbiss, Mary Lee, *Arabian Horses,* California State Polytechnic University Library, Pomona CA. 714-598-4671

Deville, Gayle, *Librn,* Kentucky School for the Deaf Library, Danville KY. 606-236-5132

DeVillier, Pat, *Librn,* Sperry Corp, Flight Systems Div Engineering Library, Phoenix AZ. 602-942-2311

Devine, Judith, *Ref,* Saint Paul Public Library, Saint Paul MN. 612-292-6311

Devine, Eileen, *Dir Office of AV Serv,* State Library Commission of Iowa, Des Moines IA. 515-281-4102

Devine, Marie, *Instrnl Servs & On-Line Servs,* University of North Carolina at Asheville, D Hiden Ramsey Library, Asheville NC. 704-258-0200

Devine, Nancy, *Acq & Ref,* Mount Holyoke College, Williston Memorial Library, South Hadley MA. 413-538-2226

Devine, Robert E, *Chief Librn,* United States Nuclear Regulatory Commission Library, Washington DC. 492-7000 & 492-7748

DeVinney, CoraEllen, *Asst Dir,* Macomb County Library, Mount Clemens MI. 313-469-5300

Devinney, Janet W, *Librn,* Carroll County Public Library (Mount Airy), Westminster MD. 301-795-0635

DeVisser, Deb, *Librn,* First Christian Reformed Church Library, Kalamazoo MI. 616-345-4280

DeVito, Patricia L, *Ref,* Mishawaka-Penn Public Library, Mishawaka IN. 219-259-5277

Devlin, Eugene, *Librn,* Peck Memorial Library, Kensington CT. 203-828-4310

Devlin, Margaret, *Reserve Bks,* Temple University of the Commonwealth System of Higher Education, Samuel Paley Library, Philadelphia PA. 215-787-8231

Devlin, Mary K, *Am Lit & English,* University of Portland, Wilson W Clark Memorial Library, Portland OR. 503-283-7111

Devlin, Mary K, *Tech Serv, Cat & On-Line Servs,* University of Portland, Wilson W Clark Memorial Library, Portland OR. 503-283-7111

Devlin, Patricia B, *Librn,* University of Michigan Libraries (Museums), Ann Arbor MI. 313-764-0467

Devlin, Patricia B, *Librn,* University of Michigan Libraries (Natural Science & Natural Resources), Ann Arbor MI. 313-764-1494

Devlin, Pearl, *Asst Librn,* Shedd Free Library, Washington NH. 603-495-3592

Devlin, Rosalie E, *Asst Dir,* San Mateo Public Library, San Mateo CA. 415-574-6955
Devlin, Violet, *Art,* Rider College, Franklin F Moore Library, Lawrenceville NJ. 609-896-5111
DeVoe, Stephen, *Asst Head,* Wayne State University Libraries (Science Library), Detroit MI. 313-577-4066
Devol, Rena, *On-Line Servs & Bibliog Instr,* Sul Ross State University, Bryan Wildenthal Memorial Library, Alpine TX. 915-837-3461
Devore, Ralph E, *Commun Servs,* Western Maryland Public Libraries, Hagerstown MD. 301-739-3250
DeVos, Lawrence, *Continuations,* Ball State University, Alexander M Bracken Library, Muncie IN. 317-285-6261
deVries, Eileen, *Librn,* Culinary Institute of America, Angell Library, Hyde Park NY. 914-452-9600, Ext 270
Devyatkin, Paul, *Actg Librn,* Yeshiva University Libraries (Landowne-Bloom Library), New York NY. 212-790-0238
Dew, Barbara, *Ad,* Ottawa Library, Ottawa KS. 913-242-3080
Dew, Garry W, *Media,* Wilson County Technical Institute, Learning Resource Center, Wilson NC. 919-291-1195, Ext 235
deWaal, Ellen Ora, *Librn,* South Baltimore General Hospital, Medical Staff Library, Baltimore MD. 301-354-1000
DeWaal, Ronald, *Humanities,* Colorado State University, William E Morgan Library, Fort Collins CO. 303-491-5911
Dewald, Elmer J, *Librn,* North Dakota Supreme Court Law Library, Bismarck ND. 701-244-2227
DeWall, Dori, *Ch,* Michigan City Public Library, Michigan City IN. 219-879-4561
Dewar, Jo E, *Dir,* Miami Dade Community College (Niles Trammel Learning Resources), Miami FL. 305-596-1293
DeWeese, Calvin, *Media,* Brunswick Junior College, Clara Wood Gould Memorial Library, Brunswick GA. 912-264-7270
DeWeese, Eldonna, *Dir,* Southwest Baptist College, Estep Library, Bolivar MO. 417-326-5281, Ext 228
Dewey, Betsy, *Ch,* Sussex County Library System, Sussex County Area Reference Library, Newton NJ. 201-948-3660
Dewey, Gene, *Acq,* University of Wisconsin-Madison, Memorial Library, Madison WI. 608-262-3521
Dewey, Patrick, *Librn,* Chicago Public Library (North Austin), Chicago IL. 312-637-7825
Dewey, Wilma J, *Librn,* Los Angeles Public Library System (Municipal Reference), Los Angeles CA. 213-485-3791
DeWitt, Benjamin L, *Mgr Tech Info Serv,* G K Technologies, Edison NJ. 201-225-4780
DeWitt, Kathleen, *Librn,* Center for the Study of the Presidency, New York NY. 212-249-1200
DeWitt, Mrs Kilby A, *Librn,* Royalton College Library, South Royalton VT. 802-763-7766
Dewitt, Pat, *Librn,* George P & Susan Platt Cady Library, Nichols NY. 607-699-3835
Dexon, Leure, *YA,* Muncie-Center Township Public Library, Muncie IN. 317-288-9971
Dexter, Joan, *Librn,* Raytheon Co, Technical Information Center, Sudbury MA. 617-443-9521, Ext 2282
Dexter, Kathy, *In Charge,* Southeast Alabama Medical Center, Medical Library, Dothan AL. 205-794-3131, Ext 540
Dexter, Martha M, *Librn,* United States Office of Technology Assessment, Information Services, Washington DC. 202-224-6994
deYcaza, Francelia, *Ch,* Barrington Public Library District, Barrington IL. 312-382-1300
DeYoung, Barbara, *Asst Dir,* Lawrence Public Library, Lawrence MA. 617-682-1727
DeYoung, Charles D, *Dir,* Michigan City Public Library, Michigan City IN. 219-879-4561
DeYoung, J A, *Eng Serv Librn,* Steel Company of Canada, Ltd, Corporate Library Services, Hamilton ON. 416-528-2511
Dhawan, Sita, *Bkmobile Coordr,* Scarborough Public Library, Scarborough ON. 416-291-1991
Dhuse, Susan, *Asst Ch,* West Chicago Public Library, West Chicago IL. 312-231-1552
Di-Muccio, Mary-Jo, *Admin Libr, Readers Servs,* Sunnyvale Public Library, Sunnyvale CA. 408-738-5585

Dia, Sister, *Dept Head,* Manor Junior College, Library Assistant Technology Program, PA. 215-885-2360
Dial, Carolyn, *Ad,* Holdrege Public Library System, South Central Regional Library, Holdrege NE. 308-995-6556
Dial, David E, *Librn,* New Madison Public Library, New Madison OH. 513-996-1741
Dial, Marshall, *Librn,* New Madrid County Library, Portageville MO. 314-379-3583
Dial, Mildred, *Librn,* Moweaqua Public Library, Moweaqua IL. 217-768-4700
Diambra, Eileen, *Acq,* University of Wisconsin-Eau Claire, William D McIntyre Library, Eau Claire WI. 715-836-3715
Diamond, Ruth, *Dir,* Temple University of the Commonwealth System of Higher Education (Health Science Center), Philadelphia PA. 215-221-4032
Dianne, Marguerite M, *Ch,* Beaman Memorial Public Library, West Boylston MA. 617-835-3711
Dias, Ruth, *Librn,* Kings County Library (Armona Branch), Armona CA. 209-584-6293
Diaz, Aura L, *Librn,* University of Puerto Rico Library (Graduate School of Public Communication), Rio Piedras PR. 809-764-0000, Ext 2398
Diaz, Daniel, *Res,* Montana Legislative Council Library, Helena MT. 406-449-3064, Ext 42
Diaz, Norka, *Foreign Lang,* New Orleans Public Library, Simon Heinsheim & Fisk Libraries, New Orleans LA. 504-586-4905
Dibble, Katherine, *ILL,* Boston Public Library, Eastern Massachusetts Library System, Boston MA. 617-536-5400
Dibble, Katherine, *ILL,* Eastern Massachusetts Regional Library System, Boston MA. 617-536-4010
Dibble, Mary S, *Commun Servs,* Patterson Library, Westfield NY. 716-326-2154
Dibble, Priscilla, *ILL,* Larchmont Public Library, Larchmont NY. 914-834-1960
DiBenedetto, Guy, *Spec Coll,* Auburn University, Ralph Brown Draughton Library, Auburn AL. 205-826-4500
Dice, Frances, *Librn,* Covington Public Library (Veedersburg Public), Veedersburg IN. 317-793-2572
Dice, Marguerite, *Librn,* Marion Public Library (Caledonia Branch), Caledonia OH. 419-845-3666
Dick, Anastasia, *Asst Dir, Acq & Ref,* Manor Junior College, Basileiad Library, Jenkintown PA. 215-885-2360, Ext 9
Dick, Aurora, *Librn,* Zenda Public Library, Zenda KS. 316-243-5171
Dick, Carolyn, *Admin Asst,* Stark County District Library, Canton OH. 216-452-0665, Ext 31
Dick, Daniel, *Ref,* Worcester State College, Learning Resources Center, Worcester MA. 617-752-7700, Ext 132, 135
Dick, Irene, *Bkmobile Coordr,* Thomas Branigan Memorial Library, Las Cruces Public Library, Las Cruces NM. 505-526-0347
Dick, Isabelle, *Libr Asst,* Pennsylvania College of Podiatric Medicine, Charles E Krausz Library, Philadelphia PA. 215-629-0300, Ext 215
Dick, Jacqueline, *Librn,* Miami-Dade Public Library System (South Miami), South Miami FL. 305-667-6121
Dick, Patricia, *Librn,* Fort Stockton Public Library, Fort Stockton TX. 915-336-2732
Dick, Shirley, *Dir,* Keokuk Public Library, Keokuk IA. 319-524-1483
Dick, T Stuart, *Rare Bks & Spec Coll,* University of Delaware, Hugh M Morris Library, Newark DE. 302-738-2231
Dick, Thomas E, *Br Coordr & Bkmobile Coordr,* Stark County District Library, Canton OH. 216-452-0665, Ext 31
Dickau, Norma, *Media,* College of Saint Benedict Library, Saint Joseph MN. 612-363-5011
Dicke, Karen P, *Researcher,* University of Colorado at Boulder (Business Research Division, Travel Reference Center), Boulder CO. 303-492-8227
Dickens, Berkley, *Media,* Rockingham Community College Library, Learning Resources Center, Wentworth NC. 919-342-4261, Ext 245
Dickens, Jr, Mrs Sam, *Librn,* Lampasas Public Library, Lampasas TX. 512-556-3251

Dickenson, Emily, *Spec Coll,* Wake County Department of the Public Library, Raleigh NC. 919-755-6077
Dickenson, Karen, *Librn,* Southwestern College Library, Oklahoma City OK. 405-947-2331, Ext 214
Dicker, Joan, *Media & Ref,* Wayne Public Library, Wayne NJ. 201-694-4272
Dickerman, Bill, *Media,* University of Houston (Clear Lake City), Houston TX. 713-488-9280
Dickerman, W P, *Secy,* Old Colony Historical Society Library, Taunton MA. 617-822-1622
Dickerson, Carole, *Dir,* Newport Public Library, Newport OR. 503-265-2153
Dickerson, Lon R, *Dir,* Lake Agassiz Regional Library, Moorhead MN. 218-233-7594
Dickerson, Mary E, *Info & Ref,* Ontario Legislative Library, Research & Information Services, Toronto ON. 416-965-4545
Dickerson, Maurine, *Dir,* Mid-America Nazarene College Library, Olathe KS. 913-782-3750, Ext 216
Dickerson, Peggy, *Dir,* Shelter Island Public Library, Shelter Island NY. 516-749-0042
Dickerson, Reginald H, *Librn,* Public Library of the District of Columbia (Washington Highlands), Washington DC. 202-727-1393
Dickerson, Virginia, *Br Coordr,* Detroit Public Library, Detroit Associated Libraries, Detroit MI. 313-833-1000
Dickes, Janis, *Tech Serv & Cat,* Mount Mercy College, Catherine McAuley Library, Cedar Rapids IA. 319-363-8213, Ext 244
Dickey, David C, *Ref & Bibliog Instr,* Taylor University, Ayres Alumni Memorial Library, Upland IN. 317-998-2751, Ext 241
Dickey, Jack W, *Librn,* University of Iowa Libraries (Physics), Iowa City IA. 319-353-4762
Dickey, Jack W, *Librn,* University of Iowa Libraries (Zoology), Iowa City IA. 319-353-5419
Dickey, Julia Edwards, *Dir,* Southeastern Indiana Area Library Services Authority, IN. 812-372-0691, 376-8928
Dickey, Laura, *Librn,* Bradford Public Library, Woods Memorial Library, Bradford VT. 802-222-4536
Dickey, Loren L, *Dir,* Ozark Bible College Library, Joplin MO. 417-624-2518, Ext 48
Dickieson, Elizabeth, *Ch,* Detroit Public Library, Detroit Associated Libraries, Detroit MI. 313-833-1000
Dickinson, Brigitte, *Ch,* Mamaroneck Free Library, Mamaroneck NY. 914-698-1250
Dickinson, Candace, *Regional Servs Coordr,* Lake Erie Regional Library System, London ON. 519-453-9100
Dickinson, Charles, *Dir,* Coloma Public Library, Coloma MI. 616-468-3431
Dickinson, Donald C, *Prof,* University of Arizona, Graduate Library School, AZ. 602-626-3565
Dickinson, Dorothy, *Dir, Tech Serv & Cat,* Chestatee Regional Library, Gainesville GA. 404-532-3311
Dickinson, Elizabeth, *Tech Serv,* Stockton-San Joaquin County Public Library, Stockton Public Libr, Stockton CA. 209-944-8415
Dickinson, Fidelia, *Coll Develop,* San Diego State University Library, San Diego CA. 714-286-6014
Dickinson, Helen, *Cat,* North Vancouver District Public Library, North Vancouver BC. 604-984-0286
Dickinson, Isabel, *Librn,* University of California, Riverside (Bioagricultural), Riverside CA. 714-787-3238
Dickinson, Isabel, *Biol-Agr,* University of California, Riverside, University Library, Riverside CA. 714-787-3221
Dickinson, Jean E, *Librn,* United States Air Force (Air Force Flight Test Center Technical Library), Edwards AFB CA. 805-277-3606, Ext 2218
Dickinson, Jo Anne, *Dir,* Harbor Beach Public Library, Harbor Beach MI. 517-479-5284
Dickinson, Lenore M, *Librn,* Harvard University Library (Arnold Arboretum), Cambridge MA. 617-495-2366
Dickinson, Lenore M, *Librn,* Harvard University Library (Gray Herbarium Library), Cambridge MA. 617-495-2366

Dickinson, Luren E, *On-Line Servs, Bibliog Instr & Ref,* Ambassador College Library, Pasadena CA. 213-577-5540

Dickinson, Margaret H, *Librn Supvr,* Newport News Public Library System, Newport News VA. 804-247-8506

Dickinson, Marjorie S, *Librn,* Kingwood Center Library, Mansfield OH. 419-522-0211, Ext 35

Dickinson, Mrs John S, *Librn,* Piedmont Regional Library (Monroe-Walton County Branch), Monroe GA. 404-867-2762

Dickinson, Ruth, *Librn,* Alexandria Library (James M Duncan, Jr), Alexandria VA. 703-750-6343

Dickinson, Vickie, *Bkmobile Librns,* Mercer County Public Library, Harrodsburg KY. 606-734-3680

Dickison, Ray, *Mgr,* Oak Ridge National Laboratory Library, Oak Ridge TN. 615-574-6722

Dickman, Claudia K, *Librn,* McCutchen, Doyle, Brown & Enersen, Law Library, San Francisco CA. 415-393-2198

Dickman, Emma Jane, *Librn,* Public Library of Cincinnati & Hamilton County (Mariemont), Cincinnati OH. 513-271-3268

Dickman, Marutta, *Dir,* Armstrong Public Library, Armstrong IA. 712-864-3353

Dicks, Roy, *Ref,* Wake County Department of the Public Library, Raleigh NC. 919-755-6077

Dickson, Ann, *Librn,* New England Institute of Technology Library, Providence RI. 401-467-7744

Dickson, Barbara, *Acq,* City of Cerritos Public Library, Cerritos CA. 213-924-5775

Dickson, Bobbie, *Asst Dir,* Chesterfield-Marlboro Technical College Library, Cheraw SC. 803-537-5286, Ext 26

Dickson, Elizabeth, *Ref,* United States Army (Morris Swett Library), Fort Sill OK. 405-351-4525, 351-4477

Dickson, Josephine, *Librn,* Rollins College (Crummer Graduate Business), Winter Park FL. 305-646-2000, Ext 2676

Dickson, Lance E, *Dir,* Louisiana State University (Law Center Library), Baton Rouge LA. 504-388-8802

Dickson, Margaret, *Cat,* Texas Tech University Library, Lubbock TX. 806-742-2261

Dickson, Muriel, *Info Serv,* Saskatoon Public Library, Saskatoon SK. 306-664-9555

Dickson, Noe, *Librn,* Coastal Plain Regional Library (Berrien County), Nashville GA. 912-686-2782

Dickson, Robert T, *Librn,* Mason County Library, Scottville MI. 616-757-2588

Dickson, Roland, *Consults,* New York State Library, Albany NY. 518-474-5930

Dickson, Ruth, *Asst Librn,* Luther Rice Seminary, Bertha Smith Library, Jacksonville FL. 904-396-2316

Dickson, Thomas A, *Chief Librn,* California Health & Welfare Agency, Interdepartmental Library, Sacramento CA. 916-445-8975

Dickson, Vivienne, *Instrnl Pub Servs,* Tusculum College Library, Greeneville TN. 615-639-1481

Didden, Margaret, *Ch,* Martinsburg-Berkeley County Public Library, Martinsburg Service Center, Martinsburg WV. 304-267-8933

Didier, E, *Librn,* Trends Publishing Inc, Research Library, Washington DC. 202-393-0031

DiDomenico, Carmela, *Tech Serv,* Rowan Public Library, Salisbury NC. 704-633-5578

Diehl, Alice S, *Cat,* Lebanon Valley College, George D Gossard Memorial Library, Annville PA. 717-867-4411, Ext 217

Diehl, Anna Grace, *Dir,* Boissevain & Morton Regional Library, Boissevain MB. 204-534-6478

Diehl, Beverly, *Tech Serv,* Natrona County Public Library, Casper WY. 307-235-9272

Diehl, David J, *Asst Librn,* TSTI Harlingen Library, Harlingen TX. 512-425-4922, Ext 50

Diehl, June, *Librn,* Wysox Township Library, Milledgeville IL. 815-225-7457

Diener, Margery, *Ref,* Glendora Public Library, Glendora CA. 213-963-4168

Diener, Ronald E, *Exec Dir,* OHIONET, OH. 614-457-1471

Diener, Sister Margaret, *Asst Librn,* Dominican College of San Rafael, Archbishop Alemany Library, San Rafael CA. 415-457-4440, Ext 251

Dienes, Betsy, *Librn,* Louisville Free Public Library (Highland), Louisville KY. 502-451-4646

Dienes, Jennie, *Librn,* University of Kansas Libraries (Engineering), Lawrence KS. 913-864-3866

Dieno, Lesley, *Sr Librn,* Richmond Public Library, Richmond BC. 604-273-6606

Dierauer, Joyce, *Young Adult & Field Servs Librn,* Wisconsin Valley Library Service, System Headquarters, Wausau WI. 715-845-7214, Ext 35, 49, 50 & 51

Dierker, Velda, *Librn,* Friends Creek Township Library, Argenta IL. 217-795-2144

Dierking, Barbara A, *Curator,* Fort Lewis Military Museum Research Library, Fort Lewis WA. 206-967-4796, 967-5524

Dierks, Janet, *Asst Librn,* Wichita County Library, Leoti KS. 316-375-4322

Dierksen, Deane C, *Dir,* Mary Riley Styles Public Library, Falls Church VA. 703-241-5030

Dierlam, Maxine, *Cat,* Queens College Library, Flushing NY. 212-520-7616

Diesen, Betty, *Librn,* Whittier Public Library (Whittwood), Whittier CA. 213-947-5417

Dieteman, Agnes, *Ch,* Allegany Public Library, Allegany NY. 716-373-1056

Dieter, Jean C, *Librn,* Raytheon Service Co Technical Library, Burlington MA. 617-272-9300, Ext 2245

Dieterle, Diane, *Dir,* Genealogical Library for the Blind & Physically Handicapped, Inc, Genealogical Center Library, Atlanta GA. 404-393-9777

Dietkus, Naomi R, *Librn,* Georgetown Public Library, Georgetown IL. 217-662-2164

Dietrich, Bruce L, *Dir,* Reading Public Museum Library, Reading PA. 215-373-1525

Dietrich, Irma, *Ref,* Johnson County Community College Library, Overland Park KS. 913-888-8500, Ext 532

Dietsch, Margaret, *Acq,* Public Library of Fort Wayne & Allen County, Fort Wayne IN. 219-424-7241

Dietterich, Virginia, *Librn,* Ransom Public Library, Ransom KS. 913-731-2220

Dietz, James W, *Acq,* Jackson County Library System, Medford OR. 503-776-7281

Dietz, Sylvia, *Asst Librn,* South Beloit Public Library, South Beloit IL. 815-389-2495

DiFelice, Clara, *AV,* Oakland University, Kresge Library, Rochester MI. 313-377-2486, 377-2474

Differding, Jane, *Librn,* Nielsen Engineering & Research, Inc Library, Mountain View CA. 415-968-9457

DiFrancisco, Annmarie, *Ch,* Franklin Square Public Library, Franklin Square NY. 516-488-3444

DiFranco, Claire, *Librn,* Cranston Public Library (Knightsville), Cranston RI. 401-942-2504

DiFranco, Janice, *Dep Dir,* Warwick Public Library and Regional Center, Warwick RI. 401-739-5440

Diggins, Jean, *Ref,* Rapid City Public Library, Rapid City SD. 605-394-4171

Digianantonio, Barbara, *Tech Serv,* Louisville Public Library, Louisville OH. 216-875-1696

DiGiovanna, Helen, *Librn,* Bristol Public Library (F N Manross Memorial), Forestville CT. 203-584-7790

DiGiulio, Eva M, *Librn,* Amax, Inc, Climax-Molybdenum Co of Michigan Library, Ann Arbor MI. 313-761-2300, Ext 272

DiGregorio, Marcia, *Bus, Indust & Sci,* Providence Public Library, Providence RI. 401-521-7722

DiIorio, A, *Ref,* Canadian Pacific Limited, Corporate Library Information Centre, Montreal PQ. 514-395-6762

Dike, Laurel, *Librn,* Parsons, Brinckerhoff, Quade & Douglas Library, New York NY. 212-239-7900

Dikeman, Robert, *Asst Prof,* San Jose State University, Division of Library Science, CA. 408-277-2292

Dikijian, Armine, *Librn,* National Council on Crime & Delinquency Library, Hackensack NJ. 201-488-0400, Ext 129

Dilan, Awilda, *Acq,* Catholic University of Puerto Rico (Encarnacion Valdes Library), Ponce PR. 809-844-4150, Ext 119

Dilbone, K, *Circ,* Dwyer-Mercer County District Library, Celina OH. 419-586-2314

Dileonardo, Mrs, *Librn,* Southern New England Telephone Co (Engineering Library), New Haven CT. 203-771-5200

diLisio, Roch-Joseph, *Tech Serv & Rare Bks,* Sacred Heart University Library, Bridgeport CT. 203-374-9441

Dillard, Bonita D, *Ref,* Saint Charles City County Library, Saint Peters MO. 314-441-2300

Dillard, Fannie, *YA,* Public Library of Charlotte & Mecklenburg County, Inc, Charlotte NC. 704-374-2725

Dillard, Georgia, *Dir,* Phoenix College Library, Phoenix AZ. 602-264-2492, Ext 621

Dillard, Julia, *Cat,* Troy State University Library, Troy AL. 205-566-3000, Ext 263

Dillard, Kay, *Ad,* West Carroll Parish Library, Oak Grove LA. 318-428-2697

Dillard, Lois, *Ref,* Geological Information Library of Dallas, Dallas TX. 214-363-1078

Dillard, Jr, Thomas W, *ILL & Ref,* Charles A Cannon Memorial Library, Concord NC. 704-788-3167

Dillavou, Joyce, *Librn,* Woodward State Hospital-School (Professional Library), Woodward IA. 515-438-2600

Dillehay, Betty, *Librn,* A H Robins Co, Inc, Research Center Library, Richmond VA. 804-257-2000

Dillehay, Claudia, *Librn,* Smith County Public Library, Carthage TN. 615-735-1326

Dillen, Judith, *Dir,* New Cumberland Public Library, New Cumberland PA. 717-774-0403

Dillenschneider, Patricia, *Asst Dir & Cat,* Camden Free Public Library, Camden NJ. 609-963-4807

Dilley, Richard, *Ser,* Illinois State Library, Springfield IL. 217-782-2994

Dillibe, Anne G, *Librn,* California Hospital Medical Center, Health Sciences Library, Los Angeles CA. 213-742-5588

Dillin, Dorothy, *Librn,* Carnegie Institution of Washington (Dept of Terrestrial Magnetism Library), Washington DC. 202-966-0863

Dillingham, Sr, Mrs Arthur E, *Librn,* Berkley Public Library, Berkley MA. 617-822-3329

Dillion, Katherine, *Asst Librn,* Benton Public Library, Benton IL. 618-438-7511

Dillon, C, *Per,* University of Prince Edward Island, Robertson Library, Charlottetown PE. 902-892-1243

Dillon, David, *Humanities,* University of New Orleans, Earl K Long Library, New Orleans LA. 504-283-0353

Dillon, David, *Bibliog Instr,* University of New Orleans, Earl K Long Library, New Orleans LA. 504-283-0353

Dillon, Eloise, *Acq,* State Library of Florida, Div of Library Services, Dept of State, Tallahassee FL. 904-487-2651

Dillon, Howard W, *Assoc Dir for Pub Serv,* University of Chicago, Joseph Regenstein Library, Chicago IL. 312-753-2977

Dillon, Martin, *Assoc Prof,* University of North Carolina at Chapel Hill, School of Library Science, NC. 919-933-8366

Dillon, Mary P, *Reader Serv,* University of Miami (Louis Calder Memorial Library), Miami FL. 305-547-6441

Dillon, Mrs Richard M, *Librn,* First Presbyterian Church Library, Libertyville IL. 312-362-2174

Dillon, Mrs S E, *Librn,* Burr Oak City Library, Burr Oak KS. 913-587-3111

Dillon, Sue A, *Librn,* Hancock County Law Library Association, Findlay OH. 419-423-1756

Dillon, Virginia, *Librn,* Eau Claire District Library, Eau Claire MI. 616-461-6241

Dillon, Virginia, *Circ,* Wichita Public Library, Wichita KS. 316-262-0611

Dillon, William, *ILL,* Wesleyan University, Olin Memorial Library, Middletown CT. 203-347-9411, Ext 296

Dillon, William A, *Dir,* Jervis Public Library Association, Rome NY. 315-336-4570

Dillow, Helen Ruth, *Cat,* Lincoln Land Community College, Learning Resources Center, Springfield IL. 217-786-2354

Dilmore, Donald, *Ref & On-Line Servs,* Houghton College, Willard J Houghton Library, Houghton NY. 716-567-2211, Ext 227

DiLorenzo, Barbara, *Asst Librn,* Clarksburg Town Library, Clarksburg MA. 413-663-8118

Dils, Elizabeth, *Librn,* United States Navy (Base Library), Groton CT. 203-449-3723

Dilts, Mrs M I, *Librn,* Wainfleet Township Library, Wainfleet ON. 416-899-1277

DiLuigi, Florence, *Dir,* Gibbstown Public Library, Gibbstown NJ. 609-423-0684

DIMACULANGAN

Dimaculangan, Mrs G S, *Librn*, Western Manitoba Regional Library, Brandon MB. 204-727-6648

DiMattia, Jr, Ernest, *Dir*, Stamford's Public Library, Ferguson Library, Stamford CT. 203-325-4354

Dimick, Mary F, *Ref*, Lake Oswego Public Library, Lake Oswego OR. 503-636-7628

Dimick, Vivienne, *Librn*, Bear Lake County Free Library, Montpelier ID. 208-847-1664

Dimmick, Mary L, *On-Line Servs*, University of Pittsburgh, Hillman Library, Pittsburgh PA. 412-624-4400

Dimmitt, Don, *Ref*, Waterloo Public Library, Waterloo IA. 319-291-4521

Dimmock, Claire, *ILL*, Cobb County Public Library System, Marietta GA. 404-427-2462

Dimond, Janene, *Librn*, Lincoln County Library (Cokeville Branch), Cokeville WY. 307-279-3213

Dimsdale, Christine, *Info Servs I*, Bell-Northern Research, Technical Information Center, Ottawa ON. 613-596-2469

DiMuccio, Mary-Jo, *Instr*, Foothill College, Library-Media Technical Assistant Program, CA. 415-948-8590, Ext 390

Din, Munir U, *Librn*, Hospital for Special Surgery, Kim Barrett Memorial Library, New York NY. 212-535-5500, Ext 210

DiNapoli, Christina M, *Librn*, Woburn Public Library, Woburn MA. 617-933-0148

Dindial, F A, *Coll*, University of Prince Edward Island, Robertson Library, Charlottetown PE. 902-892-1243

Dineen, Diane, *Librn*, Mississauga Public Library (Central), Mississauga ON. 416-279-7002

Dines, Frances, *Tech Serv*, Kewanee Public Library, Kewanee IL. 309-852-4505

Dingle-Cliff, Susan, *Librn*, Alberta Alcoholism & Drug Abuse Commission Library, Edmonton AB. 403-427-7303

Dingledy, John F, *Librn*, Edinburg Public Library, Edinburg IN. 812-526-5487

Dingman, Nancy R, *Librn*, Veterans Administration, Hospital Library, Saginaw MI. 517-793-2340

Dingman, Vera M, *Librn*, Scranton Public Library, Scranton IA. 712-652-3453

Dinnan, Leo T, *Librn*, Wayne County Federate Library System Headquarters, Wayne MI. 313-326-8910

Dinnan, Leo T, *Dir*, Wayne Oakland Library Federation, Wayne MI. 313-326-8910

Dinney, Juliana B, *Acq*, Columbia College, J Drake Edens Library, Columbia SC. 803-786-3878

Dinniman, Margo P, *Librn & On-Line Servs*, Roy F Weston Inc Library, West Chester PA. 215-692-3030, Ext 208 & 209

Dinnin, Mildred, *Media*, Kemp Public Library, Wichita Falls TX. 817-322-5611, Ext 377

Dinning, Janet, *Asst Dir*, Bettendorf Public Library & Information Center, Bettendorf IA. 319-359-4427

Dino, Gerald, *Fac Advisor*, Byzantine Catholic Seminary of Saints Cyril & Methodius Library, Pittsburgh PA. 412-321-8383

Dinsmore, Daniel, *Librn*, Lyman Allyn Museum Library, New London CT. 203-443-2545

Dintrone, Charles, *Govt Publications*, San Diego State University Library, San Diego CA. 714-286-6014

Dinwoody, Bryan E, *Librn*, Alma Public Library, Alma MI. 517-463-3966

Diodati, Carmine, *Librn*, New York Public Library (Wakefield), New York NY. 212-652-4663

Dion, Dolores, *Circ*, Windsor Locks Public Library, Windsor Locks CT. 203-623-6170

Dion, Kathleen, *Librn*, Nevada State Prison Library, Carson City NV. 702-882-9202, Ext 278

Dion, Louise, *Geog & Ecol*, Universite Laval Bibliotheque, Quebec PQ. 418-656-3344

Dion, R N, *Supvr*, E I Du Pont De Nemours & Co, Inc (Jackson Laboratory Library), Wilmington DE. 609-299-5000, Ext 486

Dionne, Lucienne J, *Librn*, Fall River Public Library (South End), Fall River MA. 617-678-3800

Dionne, Martha E, *Librn*, Millipore Corp Technical Library, Bedford MA. 617-275-9200

Dionne, Richard, *Librn*, Yale University Library (Kline Science Library), New Haven CT. 203-436-3710

Dipaola, Monica E, *Librn*, Symes Building Law Library, Denver CO. 303-

DiPasquale, Marcia, *Librn*, Parsippany-Troy Hills Public Library (Mount Tabor Libr), Mount Tabor NJ. 201-627-9508

DiPasquale, Renee, *Librn*, Piedmont Technical College, Learning Resources Center, Roxboro NC. 919-599-1181, Ext 266

DiPerna, Ruth, *Ch*, Caldwell County Public Library, Lenoir NC. 704-758-8451

DiPiazza, Anna, *Hist & Travel*, Detroit Public Library, Detroit Associated Libraries, Detroit MI. 313-833-1000

DiPietro, Lawrence N, *Assoc Dir*, Eastfield College, Learning Resources Center, Mesquite TX. 214-746-3168

DiPrete, Robert, *Media*, Bryant College, Edith M Hodgson Memorial Library, Smithfield RI. 401-231-1200, Ext 300

DiRienzo, Alice M, *Librn*, Photographic Sciences Corp Library, Webster NY. 716-265-1600

Dirks, Laura E, *Librn*, Alexander & Alexander Inc, National Production Information Center, Minneapolis MN. 612-546-1628

Dirksen, Jean, *Territorial Librn*, Yukon Territory Government, Library Services Branch, Whitehorse YT. 403-667-5238

Dirlik, Raja, *Librn*, McGill University Libraries (Islamic Studies), Montreal PQ. 514-392-5197

DiRoma, Edward, *Chief*, New York Public Library (Economics & Public Affairs), New York NY. 212-790-6185

Dirtadian, Helen H, *Dir*, Utica Public Library, Utica NY. 315-735-2279

DiRusso, Benedetto, *Deputy Librn & Ref*, York College University, Jamaica NY. 212-969-4026

Disbrow, Nancy, *Instr*, Southern Connecticut State College, Div of Library Science & Instructional Technology, CT. 203-397-4532

Discavage, Carol L, *Librn*, McCarter & English Law Library, Newark NJ. 201-622-4444, Ext 288

Discher, Anne G, *Ad, Acq & Ref*, Jeffersonville Township Public Library, Jeffersonville IN. 812-282-7765

Discount, Linda, *Librn*, Camden County Free Library (Haddon Township), Westmont NJ. 609-854-2752

Dismant, Mary Ann, *Librn*, Ouray Public Library, Ouray CO. 303-325-4616

Dissinger, Eleanor, *Librn*, New Holland Community Library, New Holland PA. 717-354-0525

Distler, Gladys M, *Librn*, Stroock & Stroock & Lavan Library, New York NY. 212-425-5200

Ditch, Jeffery J, *Tech Librn*, Kirkwood Community College, Men's Reformatory Library, Anamosa IA. 319-462-3504, Ext 432

Ditchey, Linnea, *Supvr*, Allied Chemical Corp (Technical Information Service), Morristown NJ. 201-455-3014

Ditlz, Elinor, *Ch*, Coeur D'alene Public Library, Coeur d'Alene ID. 208-667-4676

Ditmar, Mrs Robert, *Media*, Bernardsville Public Library, Bernardsville NJ. 201-766-0118

Dittlinger, Esther, *Genealogy & Local Hist*, Anderson City-Anderson & Stony Creek Township Public Library, Anderson Public Library, Anderson IN. 317-644-0938

Dittman, Maria, *Bibliog Instr*, Marquette University Memorial Library, Milwaukee WI. 414-224-7214

Dittmann, Chrisma, *Cat*, Saint Olaf College, Rolvaag Memorial Library, Northfield MN. 507-663-2222

Dittrich, Eleanor, *Librn*, Hennepin County Library (Saint Bonifacius Branch), St Bonifacius MN. 612-446-1418

Ditzler, Carol, *Ref & On-Line Servs*, East Tennessee State University (Medical Library), Johnson City TN. 615-928-6426, Ext 252

Ditzler, Marianne K, *Coordr*, Armstrong Cork Company (Management Reference Service Library), Lancaster PA. 717-397-0611, Ext 2258,3420

Divan, Linda, *ILL*, Cedarville College Library, Cedarville OH. 513-766-2211, Ext 207

Divel, Leon, *Ref*, Pittsburg State University Library, Pittsburg KS. 316-231-7000, Ext 431

Divelbiss, John E, *Assoc Dir, ILL & Ref*, Westmont College, Roger John Voskuyl Library, Santa Barbara CA. 805-969-5051, Ext 378

Dively, Carolyn, *Librn*, Claysburg Area Public Library, Claysburg PA. 814-239-2782

Diver, Bettie, *Dir & YA*, Dobbs Ferry Public Library, Dobbs Ferry NY. 914-693-6614

Diver, Ethel, *Librn*, Boise Cascade Corp, Corporate Information Center, Boise ID. 208-834-6693

Divilbiss, D A, *Librn*, Missouri Supreme Court Library, Jefferson City MO. 314-751-2636

Divilbiss, J V, *Assoc Prof*, University of Illinois, Graduate School of Library Science, IL. 217-333-3280

Divinsky, Judy, *Librn*, Royal Bank of Canada Library, Vancouver BC. 604-665-4069

Divona, Evelyn, *Dir*, Carroll County District Library (Malvern Branch), Malvern OH. 216-863-0636

Dix, Steve, *Eastern Regional Librn*, Genesee District Library, Flint MI. 313-732-0110

Dixey, Daisy, *Librn*, Shoshone-Bannock Library, Fort Hall Library, Fort Hall ID. 208-237-0405

Dixon, Billie J, *Librn*, Elida Public Library, Elida NM. 505-274-6281

Dixon, Billy, *Chmn*, Southern Illinois University at Carbondale, Educational Media Program, IL. 618-453-5764

Dixon, Brian R, *Asst Dir, Ref & On-Line Servs*, George Washington University Library (Jacob Burns Law Library), Washington DC. 202-676-6646

Dixon, Catherine, *Acq*, New Orleans Public Library, Simon Heinsheim & Fisk Libraries, New Orleans LA. 504-586-4905

Dixon, Cynthia E, *Librn*, Hayden Stone Inc, Research Library, New York NY. 212-350-0685

Dixon, D, *Librn*, Borough of Etobicoke Public Library (Brentwood), Toronto ON. 416-248-5681

Dixon, Dorothy Kay, *Librn*, California Thoroughbred Breeders Association, Carleton F Burke Memorial Library, Arcadia CA. 213-445-7800

Dixon, Gay, *Ref*, Florida State University, Robert Manning Strozier Library, Tallahassee FL. 904-644-5211

Dixon, Gene, *Commun Servs*, Escondido Public Library, Escondido CA. 714-741-4683

Dixon, Gladys, *Librn*, Beaver County Library, Beaver OK. 405-625-3076

Dixon, Jane, *Cat*, Tarleton State University Library, Stephenville TX. 817-968-9246

Dixon, Joe, *Asst Dir*, Catawba Valley Technical College, Learning Resource Center, Hickory NC. 704-327-9124, Ext 257

Dixon, Mildred, *Dir*, Homer Public Library, Homer OH. 614-892-2020, Ext 1

Dixon, Mrs S, *In Charge*, Eastern Counties Regional Library (Canso Branch), Canso NS. 902-747-2597

Dixon, Ruth E, *Librn*, Middletown Hospital Association, Ada Leonard Memorial Library, Middletown OH. 513-422-5411

Dixon, Sandra S, *Librn*, McCune City Library, McCune KS. 316-632-4299

Dize, Margaret A, *Librn*, York County Law Library, York PA. 717-854-0754

Djevalikian, Sonia, *Ad, Acq & Cat*, Saint-Laurent Municipal Library, Saint Laurent PQ. 514-744-6411, Ext 220

Djonovich, Dusan J, *Chief Librn*, Yeshiva University Libraries (Benjamin N Cardozo School of Law Library), New York NY. 212-790-0422

Dlin, E Deborah, *ILL*, Green Gold Library System, Shreveport LA. 318-221-0101

Doak, Genevieve, *Librn*, Garfield County Public Library (Glenwood Springs Branch), Glenwood Springs CO. 303-945-5958

Doan, Carl, *Librn*, Burlington County Library (Evesham Branch), Marlton NJ. 609-983-1444

Doan, Janice Y, *Dir*, Media-Upper Providence Free Library, Media PA. 215-566-1918

Doan, Patricia R, *Dir*, Okmulgee Public Library, Okmulgee OK. 918-756-1448

Doane, Virginia S, *Dir*, Brooks Free Library, Harwich MA. 617-432-1799

Doares, Juanita, *Planning Officer*, New York Public Library (The Research Libraries), New York NY. 212-790-6262

Doares, Wade, *Librn*, Columbia University (Journalism), New York NY. 212-280-2241

Doarn, Patty, *Cat*, Flagstaff City-Coconino County Public Library System, Flagstaff AZ. 602-774-0603

Dobb, Linda, *Cat Media,* City College of San Francisco Library, San Francisco CA. 415-239-3404

Dobb, Theodore C, *Librn,* Simon Fraser University Library, Burnaby BC. 604-291-3265

Dobberfuhl, Alma, *Dir,* Concordia College Library, Portland OR. 503-288-9371, Ext 241

Dobbert, Irene A, *Librn,* Sentry Library, Stevens Point WI. 715-346-6788

Dobbin, Gerry, *Systs Librn,* University of British Columbia Library, Vancouver BC. 604-228-3871

Dobbin, Marion, *Librn,* Rochester General Hospital, Ely & Parnall Memorial Library, Rochester NY. 716-338-4548

Dobbin, Patricia, *Ext Servs,* Montgomery County-Norristown Public Library, Norristown PA. 215-277-3355

Dobbins, Irlene, *Dir,* John C Calhoun State Community College, Albert P Brewer Library, Decatur AL. 205-353-3102

Dobbins, Kay L, *Asst Dir,* Sioux Center Public Library, Sioux Center IA. 712-722-2138

Dobbins, Sara, *Asst Librn,* San Fernando Valley College of Law Library, Sepulveda CA. 213-894-5711

Dobbs, Ann, *Librn,* Adams County Public Library (Northglenn), North Glenn CO. 303-452-7534

Dobbs, Joanne Elliott, *Librn,* Cohen & Uretz Library, Washington DC. 202-293-4740, Ext 40

Dobbs, Mrs Nicklin, *Tech Serv & Cat,* Chattanooga-Hamilton County Bicentennial Library, Chattanooga TN. 615-757-5320

Dobbs, Sister M Kathryn, *Dir,* Holy Family College Library, Philadelphia PA. 215-637-7700, Ext 51

Dobbs, Valentine, *Acq & Doc,* North Georgia College, Stewart Library, Dahlonega GA. 404-864-3391, Ext 226, 294

Dobbs, Vivian Lynn, *Pub Servs & On-Line Servs,* United States Army (Brooke Army Medical Center Library), Fort Sam Houston TX. 512-221-4119, 221-3595

Dobiesz, Robert, *Circ,* Gannon University, Nash Library, Erie PA. 814-871-7352

Dobis, R, *Humanities,* Mount San Antonio College, Learning Resources Center, Walnut CA. 714-594-5611, Ext 260

Dobkin, John H, *Dir,* National Academy of Design Library, New York NY. 212-369-4880

Doblander, Grace, *Librn,* Machlett Laboratories, Inc Library, Springdale CT. 203-348-7511, Ext 375

Doble, Jr, Frank, *Per,* Onondaga Community College, Sidney B Coulter Library, Syracuse NY. 315-469-7741, Ext 5335-5338

Dobling, Betty, *Librn,* Westside Public Library, Westside IA. 712-663-4558

Dobney, Mrs Albert, *Librn,* Churdan City Library, Churdan IA. 712-685-3423

Dobroski, Jr, C H, *Dir,* Lon Morris College, Simon & Louise Henderson Library, Jacksonville TX. 214-586-2471, Ext 52

Dobrosky, Brenda, *Librn,* Oyen Municipal Library, Oyen AB. 403-664-3580

Dobrosky, Patricia M, *Dir,* United States Customs Service Library, Library & Information Service, Washington DC. 202-566-8195

Dobrovolny, John, *Dir,* Central Technical Community College, Nuckolls Study Lounge, Hastings NE. 402-463-9811, Ext 363

Dobrowolski, Joan, *Librn,* New Brunswick Home News Library, New Brunswick NJ. 201-246-5500

Dobrzynski, Sister M Terenita, *Dir,* Villa Maria College of Buffalo Library, Buffalo NY. 716-896-0703

Dobson, Dawn, *Librn,* Canadian Labour Congress Library, Ottawa ON. 613-521-3400, Ext 52

Dobson, Joanna, *Librn,* American Ceramic Society Library, Columbus OH. 614-268-8645

Dobson, John, *Spec Coll,* University of Tennessee, Knoxville, James D Hoskins Library, Knoxville TN. 615-974-0111

Dobson, Nancy, *Librn,* Austin State Hospital, Medical Library, Austin TX. 512-452-0381

Dobur, Olga, *Head,* University of Cincinnati Libraries (Math), Cincinnati OH. 513-475-4449

Docherty, Beverly, *Dir,* Boundary County Free Library, Bonners Ferry ID. 208-267-3750

Dockery, Sherry, *Librn,* Northeast Georgia Regional Library System (Helen Community), Clarkesville GA. 404-754-4413

Dockins, Glenn, *Dir,* Cumberland Trail Library System, Flora IL. 618-662-2679, 622-2741

Dockwiller, Marjorie, *Dir,* Salina Free Library, Mattydale NY. 315-454-4524

Doctoroff, Edward B, *Circ,* Harvard University Library (Harvard College Library (Headquarters in Harry Elkins Widener Memorial Library)), Cambridge MA. 617-495-2401

Doctorow, Erica, *Art,* Adelphi University Library, Garden City NY. 516-294-8700

Doctorow, Erica, *Spec Coll,* Adelphi University Library, Garden City NY. 516-294-8700

Dodd, Debbie, *Circ,* Oregon City Library, Oregon City OR. 503-655-8398, 655-8399

Dodd, Helen R, *Dir, Acq & Cat,* Pine Grove Public Library, Pine Grove WV. 304-889-5988

Dodd, James A, *Dir,* Adrian College, Shipman Library, Adrian MI. 517-265-5161, Ext 220

Dodd, Jean, *Instr,* Seneca College of Applied Arts & Technology, Library Techniques, ON. 416-491-5050

Dodd, L, *Spec Coll,* Whitman College, Penrose Memorial Library, Walla Walla WA. 509-527-5191

Dodd, Mel, *ILL,* Texas A&M University Libraries, College Station TX. 713-845-6111

Dodd, Mel, *ILL Head,* USDA Southwest Regional Document Delivery System, TX. 713-845-5614

Dodd, Opal, *Librn,* Bethalto Public Library, Bethalto IL. 618-377-8141

Dodd, Patricia E, *Librn,* Saskatchewan Department of the Attorney General (Civil Law Library), Regina SK. 306-565-7444

Dodds, Joann L, *Western Hist Coll,* Pueblo Library District, Pueblo CO. 303-544-1940

Dodge, Juliana B, *Librn,* Romeo District Library, Romeo MI. 313-752-2291

Dodge, Kathy, *Ch,* Louis B Goodall Memorial Library, Sanford Public Library, Sanford ME. 207-324-4714

Dodge, Lynn L, *Dir,* Lynchburg Public Library, Lynchburg VA. 804-847-1565

Dodge, Marjorie B, *Librn,* Rockport Public Library, Rockport ME. 207-236-3642

Dodge, Nancy L, *Dir,* New Hampshire Vocational Technical College Library, Portsmouth NH. 603-436-3423

Dodge, William R, *Chief, Fed Res Div,* Library of Congress, Washington DC. 202-287-5000

Dodman, Sister Margaret, *Ref,* Saint Joseph's College (Suffolk Campus), Patchogue NY. 516-231-3054

Dodsen, Ann T, *Mgr,* OCLC, Inc. Library, Columbus OH. 614-486-3661

Dodson, Ann, *ILL,* Louisiana State University School of Medicine in Shreveport, Medical Library, Shreveport LA. 318-226-3447

Dodson, Betty, *Bkmobile Coordr,* Vigo County Public Library, Terre Haute IN. 812-232-1113

Dodson, Fern, *Librn,* Ward County Library, Monahans TX. 915-943-3332

Dodson, James T, *Dir,* University of Texas at Dallas, University Library, Richardson TX. 214-690-2950

Dodson, Linda, *Librn,* Booz Allen & Hamilton, Booz Allen Applied Research Library, Bethesda MD. 301-951-2700

Dodson, Lois B, *Acq,* Mississippi University for Women, John Clayton Fant Memorial Library, Columbus MS. 601-328-4808

Dodson, Marguerite, *Ch,* Brooklyn Public Library, Brooklyn NY. 212-780-7712

Dodson, Maxwell G, *Librn,* United States Court of Appeals, Fifth Circuit Library, New Orleans LA. 504-589-6510

Dodson, Sherry, *Librn,* Group Health Cooperative of Puget Sound, Medical Library, Seattle WA. 206-326-6093

Dodson, Suzanne, *Govt Publications & Microforms,* University of British Columbia Library, Vancouver BC. 604-228-3871

Dodsworth, Joan, *Librn,* Kanata Public Library, Kanata ON. 613-592-2712

Dodwell, Catherine, *Ad,* Wyckoff Public Library, Wyckoff NJ. 201-891-4866

Doe, Linda, *Librn,* Daniel Arthur Rehabilitation Center, Media Center, Oak Ridge TN. 615-482-4081

Doe-Cohen, E J, *Cat,* Massachusetts Maritime Academy, Captain Charles H Hurley Library, Buzzards Bay MA. 617-759-5761, Ext 281

Doebbeling, Mary, *Librn,* Fort Worth Public Library (West Branch), Fort Worth TX. 817-737-6619

Doeden, Janet, *Librn,* Actors' Studio Theatre Library, New York NY. 212-757-0870

Doehle, Anna, *Media,* Clatsop Community College Library, Astoria OR. 503-324-0910

Doelle, Eva, *Librn,* McGill University Libraries (Blackader-Lauterman Library of Architecture & Fine Arts), Montreal PQ. 514-392-4960

Doellinger, Keith E, *Chmn,* Bowling Green State University, Dept of Library & Educational Media, OH. 419-372-2461

Doellman, Michael, *Ref,* Burton Public Library, Burton OH. 216-834-4258

Doennig, David R, *Dir,* Barry-Lawrence Regional Library, Monett MO. 417-235-6646

Doering, Mrs Adolph, *Librn,* Davenport Public Library, Davenport NE. 402-364-2147

Doerrer, David H, *Tech Serv,* University of West Florida, John C Pace Library, Pensacola FL. 904-476-9500, Ext 261

Doesburgh, John, *Librn,* Arthur C Logan Memorial Hospital, L B Dana Memorial Library, New York NY. 212-690-7222

Doesch, Evelyn, *Dir,* Western Bible College Library, Morrison CO. 303-697-8135, Ext 25

Doggett, Leona E, *Dir,* Amherst County Public Library, Amherst VA. 804-946-5260

Doherty, Denis J, *Librn,* Diocese of Fresno Catholic Library, Fresno CA. 209-486-1833

Doherty, Edmond J, *Dir,* Reading Public Library, Reading Public Library District, Reading PA. 215-374-4548

Doherty, Elizabeth, *On-Line Servs,* University of Alabama in Huntsville Library, Huntsville AL. 205-895-6540

Doherty, Evelyn, *Tech Serv,* Wayne Public Library, Wayne NJ. 201-694-4272

Doherty, Grace L, *Librn,* G H Hathaway Library, Freetown MA. 617-644-2385

Doherty, Helen, *Ch,* Lansdowne Public Library, Lansdowne PA. 215-623-0239

Doherty, John J, *Asst Dir,* Boston Public Library, Eastern Massachusetts Library System, Boston MA. 617-536-5400

Doherty, Joseph H, *Dir,* Providence College, Phillips Memorial Library, Providence RI. 401-865-2242

Doherty, Marianne, *Ref & MEDLINE,* Rush-Presbyterian-Saint Luke's Medical Center (Library of Rush University), Chicago IL. 312-942-2271, 942-5950

Doherty, R Austin, *Librn,* Hogan & Hartson Library, Washington DC. 202-331-4500

Doherty, William J, *Ref,* Boston State College Library, Boston MA. 617-731-3300

Dohman, Gloria, *Per,* North Dakota State School of Science, Mildred Johnson Library, Wahpeton ND. 701-671-2298

Doi, Makiko, *Per,* Central Washington University Library, Ellensburg WA. 509-963-1901

Doi, Masako, *Tech Librn,* Hittman Associates, Inc, Technical Information Dept-Library, Columbia MD. 301-730-7800, Ext 358

Doig, Mrs Thomas G, *Librn,* Concord Antiquarian Society, Library of Ralph W Emerson, Concord MA. 617-369-9609

Doikos, Helen, *Librn,* Scudder, Stevens & Clark Library, Boston MA. 617-482-3990

Dolan, Alice, *ILL,* Brockton Public Library System, Brockton MA. 617-587-2515

Dolan, Jane, *Cat,* West Lafayette Public Library, West Lafayette IN. 317-743-2261

Dolan, Jean, *Head Spec Servs to Phys Handicapped & Homebound,* Chillicothe & Ross County Public Library, Chillicothe OH. 614-773-4145

Dolan, Jeanne M, *Librn,* Kollmorgen Corporation, Macbeth Division Library, Newburgh NY. 914-561-7300

Dolan, Mary E, *Cat,* Georgian Court College, Farley Memorial Library, Lakewood NJ. 201-364-2200, Ext 19

Dole, Elizabeth, *Librn,* University of Vermont & State Agricultural College (Physics & Chemistry), Burlington VT. 802-656-2268

Dole, Grace, *Asst Librn,* University of Connecticut at Stamford Library, Stamford Branch Library, Stamford CT. 203-322-3466

Dole, Sandra, *ILL,* Northwest Kansas Library System, Norton KS. 913-877-5148

Dole, Wanda V, *Humanities,* University of Illinois at Chicago Circle Library, Chicago IL. 312-996-2716
Dolenoki, Leo, *Mss,* Bryn Mawr College, Canaday Library, Bryn Mawr PA. 215-645-5279
Dolezal, Helen, *Librn,* Public Library of Steubenville & Jefferson County (Dillonvale Branch), Dillonvale OH. 614-282-9782
Dolgin, Barbara, *Asst Librn,* American Council of Life Insurance Library, Washington DC. 202-862-4050
Dolgin, Jeanne, *Librn,* Mercy College, Yonkers Extension Center, Yonkers NY. 914-693-0372
Doliwa, Zofia J, *Asst Librn,* New York State Department of Labor (Research Library New York City), New York NY. 212-488-6295, 6296
Doll, Jacqueline, *Ref,* Allegan Public Library, Allegan MI. 616-673-4625
Doll, Karen B, *Admin Asst,* Caldwell County Public Library, Lenoir NC. 704-758-8451
Dollard, Peter, *Dir,* Alma College Library, Alma MI. 517-463-2141, Ext 332
Dollerschell, Allen L, *Librn,* Rochester Community College, Goddard Library, Rochester MN. 507-285-7233
Dolleslager, Kathy, *Dir,* Robert R Jones Public Library, Coal Valley IL. 309-799-3047
Dollette, Maureen, *ILL,* Santa Maria Public Library, Santa Maria CA. 805-925-0994, Ext 261
Dollinger, Janie A, *Librn,* Lanark Public Library, Lanark IL. 815-493-2166
Dollison, Ann, *Bkmobile Coordr,* Logan-Hocking County District Library, Logan OH. 614-385-2348
Dolliver, Kathleen, *Librn,* Goodwin Library, Farmington NH. 603-755-2944
Dolman, Jodi, *Ch,* Center Moriches Free Public Library, Center Moriches NY. 516-878-0940
Dolman, Jodi, *Children's Coll,* Center Moriches Free Public Library, Center Moriches NY. 516-878-0940
Dolores, Sister M, *Dir,* Texas Catholic Historical Society, Catholic Archives of Texas Library, Austin TX. 512-476-4888
Doloughty, Barbara, *Serials Librn,* University of Pittsburgh (Maurice & Laura Falk Library of the Health Sciences), Pittsburgh PA. 412-624-2521
Dolphus, Robbie, *Sci,* Public Library of Charlotte & Mecklenburg County, Inc, Charlotte NC. 704-374-2725
Dolven, Mary, *Dir,* Diablo Valley College Library, Pleasant Hill CA. 415-685-1230, Ext 241
Domal, Julia, *Circ,* Pensacola Junior College, Learning Resource Center, Pensacola FL. 904-476-5410
Doman, Shelley C, *Librn,* Veterans Administration, Medical Center Library, Beckley WV. 304-255-2121, Ext 258
Domas, Ralph, *Bibliog Instr,* San Antonio College Library, San Antonio TX. 512-734-7311, Ext 2480
Domas, Ralph E, *Instr,* San Antonio College, Library Technology Program, TX. 512-734-7311, Ext 2482
Dombourian, Sona, *Librn,* Assumption Parish Library, Napoleonville LA. 504-369-7070
Dombrowski, Agnes J, *Asst Librn,* Remington-Carpenter Township Public Library, Remington IN. 219-261-2543
Dombrowski, Mark A, *Dir & On-Line Servs,* Siena Heights College Library, Adrian MI. 517-263-0731, Ext 242
Domek, L Fay, *Librn,* North Dakota State Hospital, Health Science Library, Jamestown ND. 701-253-2679
Domench, William, *Ref,* Inter-American University of Puerto Rico, Aguadilla Regional College Library, Aguadilla PR. 809-891-0998
Domenico, Ida, *Ref,* New York Stock Exchange, Research Library, New York NY. 212-623-5049
Domer, Mary, *Librn,* Lagrange County Library (Topeka Branch), Topeka IN. 219-463-2841
Domine, Kay J, *Archivist,* College of William & Mary in Virginia, Earl Gregg Swem Library, Williamsburg VA. 804-253-4404
Domine, Patricia, *Supvr,* Canadian Standards Association, Information Centre, Rexdale ON. 416-744-4058
Dominques, Larry, *YA,* Robbins Library, Arlington MA. 617-643-0026
Domitz, Gary, *Soc Sci,* Idaho State University Library, Pocatello ID. 208-236-3202

Domney, James M, *Dir,* Arcadia Public Library, Arcadia CA. 213-446-7111
Doms, Keith, *Dir,* Free Library of Philadelphia, Philadelphia PA. 215-686-5322
Domzella, Janet M, *Dir,* Lewiston Public Library, Lewiston NY. 716-754-4720
Donahoe, Barbara, *Asst Dir & Ch,* Shawnee Library System, Carterville IL. 618-985-3711
Donahoe, Barbara, *Librn,* Shawnee Library System (Subregional Library for the Blind & Physically Handicapped), Carterville IL. 618-985-3713
Donahoe, Barbara, *Asst Librn,* La Moille Clarion Library District, La Moille IL. 815-638-2356
Donahue, Janice, *Cat,* Florida Atlantic University, S E Wimberly Library, Boca Raton FL. 305-395-5100, Ext 2448
Donahue, Jeffrey B, *Media,* Newberry College, Wessels Library, Newberry SC. 803-276-5010, Ext 300
Donahue, Karin, *Educ,* Indiana University-Purdue University at Indianapolis, University Library, Indianapolis IN. 317-264-4101
Donahue, Katharine, *Librn,* Natural History Museum of Los Angeles County, Research Library, Los Angeles CA. 213-744-3387, 744-3388
Donahue, Martha, *Ref,* Mansfield State College Library, Mansfield PA. 717-662-4071
Donahue, Mary Ellen, *Asst Dir,* Southeastern Libraries Cooperating, Rochester MN. 507-288-5513
Donahue, Mary Ellen, *Asst Dir,* Southeastern Libraries Cooperating, (SELCO), MN. 507-288-5513
Donahue, Mary Kaye, *Dir,* Hidalgo County Library System, McAllen TX. 512-682-6397
Donahue, Roberta, *ILL,* Dartmouth College (Dana Biomedical), Hanover NH. 603-646-2858
Donahue, Sandra, *Circ,* Illinois Valley Community College, Jacobs Memorial Library, Oglesby IL. 815-224-2720
Donahue, Therese, *Dir,* North Salem Free Library, North Salem NY. 914-669-5161
Donahugh, Robert H, *Dir,* Reuben McMillan Free Library Free Library Association, Public Library of Youngstown & Mahoning County, Youngstown OH. 216-744-8636
Donald, Mrs G, *Librn,* Wasaga Beach Public Library, Wasaga Beach ON. 705-429-5481
Donaldson, Alvin, *Doc,* United States Department of the Navy (Naval Regional Data Automation Center, Technical Library), Washington DC. 202-433-4363, 433-4105
Donaldson, Anna L, *Ad & Ref,* Abilene Public Library, Abilene TX. 915-677-2474
Donaldson, Marion, *AV,* Lake County Public Library, Merrillville IN. 219-769-3541
Donaldson, Martha P, *Dir,* Okefenokee Regional Library, Waycross GA. 912-283-3126
Donaldson, Mary Ann, *Librn,* Mitchell, Silverberg & Knupp, Law Library, Los Angeles CA. 213-553-5000
Donaldson, Maurin C, *Dir,* Saint James Parish Library, Lutcher LA. 504-869-3618
Donaldson, Patrica B, *Librn,* New York Supreme Court Law Library at Watertown, Watertown NY. 315-785-3064
Donaldson, Paul, *Librn,* Spruce Grove Public Library, Spruce Grove AB. 403-962-4423
Donata, Sister M, *Librn,* Nazareth Hospital, Medical Library, Philadelphia PA. 215-331-8000, Ext 479
Donati, Georgia, *Ref,* Mount Vernon Public Library, Mount Vernon NY. 914-668-1840
Donato, Anne K, *Curator,* Medical University of South Carolina Library (Waring Historical), Charleston SC. 803-792-2288
Donato, Carolyn R, *Librn,* Borden Inc, Borden Foods Research Center, Syracuse NY. 315-474-8526
Doncevic, Lois A, *Sr Librn,* Call-Chronicle Library, Allentown PA. 215-820-6523
Donders, Helen, *Librn,* Brainerd Memorial Library, Haddam CT. 203-345-2204
Dondy, Emanuel, *Dir,* Mount Vernon Public Library, Mount Vernon NY. 914-668-1840
Donegan, Lydia, *Librn,* Pike-Amite-Walthall Library System (Gloster Public), Gloster MS. 601-225-4341
Donio, Jennie, *Librn,* Rocky Bay Library, MacDiarmid ON. 807-885-3191

Donkin, Kate, *Curator,* McMaster University (Map Library), Hamilton ON. 416-525-9140, Ext 4152
Donlan, Alberta, *Librn,* Museum of New Mexico (Museum of Fine Arts Library), Santa Fe NM. 505-827-2440
Donley, Albert M, *Assoc Dir, Archivist, Rare Bks & Computer Applications,* Northeastern University Libraries, Boston MA. 617-437-2350
Donley, Mary, *Tech Serv,* University of Wisconsin-Stout, Pierce Library, Menomonie WI. 715-232-1184
Donnan, Elizabeth, *Dir,* East Central Regional Library, Cedar Rapids IA. 319-365-0521
Donnegan, Patricia, *Circ,* Mount Vernon College Library, Washington DC. 202-331-3475
Donnegan, Sister Catherine, *Acq,* Marywood College Library, Scranton PA. 717-343-6521, Ext 289
Donnell, R Janice, *Cat,* University of Oklahoma University Libraries, Norman OK. 405-325-2611
Donnell, Robert M, *Asst Dir,* University of South Alabama (Biomedical Library), Mobile AL. 205-460-7043
Donnelly, A Richard, *Instr,* Georgia College, Education Library Media, GA. 912-453-4047 & 453-5573
Donnelly, Anna, *Ref,* Saint John's University Library, Jamaica NY. 212-969-8000, Ext 201
Donnelly, Arthur R, *Media,* Georgia College, Ina Dillard Russell Library, Milledgeville GA. 912-453-4047, 453-5573
Donnelly, C Gerard, *Dir,* Center Moriches Free Public Library, Center Moriches NY. 516-878-0940
Donnelly, C Gerard, *Jazz,* Center Moriches Free Public Library, Center Moriches NY. 516-878-0940
Donnelly, E, *Br Coordr & Ch,* London Public Libraries & Museums, London ON. 519-432-7166
Donnelly, Helen, *Ref,* Taunton Public Library, Subregional Headquarters for Eastern Massachusetts Regional Library System, Taunton MA. 617-823-3570
Donnelly, Jeanne M, *Supvr Tech Libr,* Cities Service Co, Energy Resources Group Research Library, Tulsa OK. 918-586-2524
Donnelly, Jeannette, *Dir,* Mount Arlington Public Library, Mount Arlington NJ. 201-398-1516
Donnelly, Kevin, *Librn,* Cambridge Public Library (Central Square), Cambridge MA. 617-498-9081
Donnelly, Margaret M, *Librn,* Merck Sharp & Dohme (Marketing Information Center), West Point PA. 215-699-5311
Donnelly, Marie, *Tech Serv & Circ,* White Plains Public Library, White Plains NY. 914-682-4400
Donnelly, Mark, *Librn,* R Dixon Speas Associates Technical Library, Lake Success NY. 516-488-6930
Donnelly, Mary Jane, *Acq & Ser,* King's College, D Leonard Corgan Library, Wilkes-Barre PA. 717-824-9931, Ext 245
Donnelly, Mrs Leo, *Librn,* Garrison Public Library, Garrison IA. 319-477-5531
Donnelly, Ward, *Asst Prof,* Villanova University, Graduate Dept of Library Science, PA. 215-527-2100, Ext 354, 355
Donnelson, Irene, *Librn,* Sno-Isle Regional Library (Arlington Branch), Arlington WA. 206-435-3033
Donner, Carl, *Acq,* General Research Corp, Science & Technology Div Library, Santa Barbara CA. 805-964-7724
Donnocker, Nell, *Bkmobile Coordr,* Massapequa Public Library, Massapequa NY. 516-798-4607
Donofrio, Gary J, *Circ & Per,* California College of Podiatric Medicine, Schmidt Medical Library, San Francisco CA. 415-563-3444, Ext 246
Donofrio, Nancy, *Doc,* Royal Oak Public Library, Royal Oak MI. 313-541-1470
Donoghue, Helen S, *Dir,* Atlantic Highlands Public Library Association, Atlantic Highlands NJ. 201-291-1956
Donoghue, James, *Ref & Bibliog Instr,* Belmont Abbey College, Abbot Vincent Taylor Library, Belmont NC. 704-825-3711, Ext 342
Donoho, Thomas, *Media,* Louisville Free Public Library, Louisville KY. 502-584-4154
Donohoo, Christine, *Librn,* Toledo-Lucas County Public Library (Birmingham), Toledo OH. 419-255-7055

Donohoo, Christine, *Librn,* Toledo-Lucas County Public Library (Lag-Central), Toledo OH. 419-255-7055

Donohoo, Christine, *Librn,* Toledo-Lucas County Public Library (South), Toledo OH. 419-255-7055

Donohue, Deidre, *Librn,* Rhode Island Medical Center (Institute of Mental Health Medical Library), Cranston RI. 401-464-2580

Donohue, Deirdre, *Librn,* Rhode Island Medical Center (Institute of Mental Health, Patient's Library), Cranston RI. 401-464-2580

Donohue, Dorothy, *Graphics,* Carl Sandburg College, Learning Resources Center, Galesburg IL. 309-344-2518, Ext 247 & 257

Donohue, Dorothy E, *Acq,* Cambridge Public Library, Cambridge MA. 617-498-9080

Donor, Mary, *YA & Ref,* Jericho Public Library, Jericho NY. 516-935-6790

Donovan, Aileen M, *Librn,* University of California (Earthquake Engineering Research Ctr Library), Richmond CA. 415-231-9403

Donovan, Catherine, *Librn,* Maple Park Public Library, Maple Park IL. 815-827-3362

Donovan, Elizabeth, *ILL & Ref,* Cocoa Public Library, Cocoa FL. 305-636-3243, 636-7323

Donovan, Ellen A, *Librn,* New York State Department of Correctional Services, Training Academy Library, Albany NY. 518-457-5712

Donovan, Helen, *Circ,* Boston State College Library, Boston MA. 617-731-3300

Donovan, John, *Dir,* Children's Book Council Library, New York NY. 212-254-2666

Donovan, John P, *Dir,* Emanuel Einstein Free Public Library, Pompton Lakes NJ. 201-835-0482

Donovan, Kathryn M, *Mgr,* Pennwalt Corp, Technical Div Library, King of Prussia PA. 215-265-3200

Donovan, Margaret J, *Librn,* Veterans Administration, Hospital Library, Fort Howard MD. 301-477-1800, Ext 309

Donovan, Parmelee, *Asst Dir,* Newark Public Library, Newark OH. 345-1750 & 345-8972

Donovan, Patricia, *Ref,* West Texas State University, Cornette Library, Canyon TX. 806-656-2761

Donovan, Priscilla, *Librn,* Warren Public Library, Warren CT. 203-868-2195

Donovan, R, *Librn,* Canada Institute for Scientific & Technical Information (Sussex Building), Ottawa ON. 613-993-1600

Donovan, Ruth, *Asst Dir,* University of Nevada-Reno, Noble H Getchell Library, Reno NV. 702-784-6533

Donovan, Sandra J, *Dir,* Laramie County Community College Library, Cheyenne WY. 307-634-5853

Donovan, William, *Biol Sci,* Chicago Public Library (Business, Science & Technology Div), Chicago IL. 312-269-2814, 269-2865

Donze, Sara Lee, *Dir,* North Canton Public Library, North Canton OH. 216-499-4712

Dooe, Frederick C, *Ad & Media,* Belmont Public Library, Belmont MA. 617-489-2000

Doolan, Helen M, *Librn,* Providence Public Library (Smith Hill), Providence RI. 401-421-6974

Doolen, Richard M, *Asst Dir,* University of Michigan (Michigan Historical Collections), Ann Arbor MI. 313-764-3482

Dooley, Cynthia, *Librn,* Literary & Historical Society of Quebec Library, Quebec PQ. 418-694-9147

Dooley, Jo Ellen, *ILL,* Riverside City College, Martin Luther King Library, Riverside CA. 714-684-3240, Ext 328

Dooley, John, *Ref,* Bryn Mawr College, Canaday Library, Bryn Mawr PA. 215-645-5279

Dooley, John, *Tech Serv,* Cumberland County Public Library, Anderson Street Library, Frances Brooks Stein Memorial Library, Fayetteville NC. 919-483-1580

Dooley, John, *Tech Serv,* Palo Alto City Library, Palo Alto CA. 415-329-2436

Dooley, Pat, *ILL,* Brevard Community College, Melbourne Campus Learning Resources Center, Melbourne FL. 305-254-0305, Ext 227, 228

Dooley, Ruth, *Asst Dir,* Palm Beach Junior College, North Campus Library, West Palm Beach FL. 305-842-3500

Dooling, Marie, *Mgr,* Special Libraries Association Information Services, New York NY. 212-477-9250

Doolittle, Alan, *Dir,* Iowa Wesleyan College, Chadwick Library, Mount Pleasant IA. 319-385-8021, Ext 131

Door, Ronald, *Pres,* Hussian School of Art Library, Philadelphia PA. 215-563-5726

Dopp, James, *Cat,* Georgia College, Ina Dillard Russell Library, Milledgeville GA. 912-453-4047, 453-5573

Dopp, Norma, *Librn,* Oakite Products Inc, Oakite Chemical Research Library, Berkeley Heights NJ. 201-464-6900, Ext 365

Doran, Jim, *Media,* Saint Lawrence College of Applied Arts & Technology Library Services, Kingston ON. 613-544-5400, Ext 163

Doran, Mildred, *Librn,* Blanco Library, Inc, Blanco TX. 512-833-4525

Doran, Sister Marie Stella, *Librn,* Holy Family Convent Library, Benet Lake WI. 414-862-2010

Dordick, Beverly F, *Librn,* National Association of Realtors, Herbert U Nelson Memorial Library, Chicago IL. 312-440-8070

Dore, Marc, *Dir,* Bibliotheque Municipale De Loretteville, Loretteville PQ. 418-842-1921

Dorey, Sheila, *Librn,* Treat Memorial Library, Livermore Falls ME. 207-897-3631

Dorf, William, *Circ & Ref,* Cheyney State College, Leslie Pinckney Hill Library, Cheyney PA. 215-758-2000, Ext 2203, 2208, 2245

Dorfman, Andrew, *Instr,* Kentucky Wesleyan College, Department of Library Science, KY. 502-926-3111, Ext 112, 113

Dorfman, Andrew R, *AV,* Kentucky Wesleyan College, Library Learning Center, Owensboro KY. 502-926-3111, Ext 113, 117

Dorgant, Mrs Hays, *Librn,* Avoyelles Parish Library (Mansura Branch), Mansura LA. 318-253-7559

Dorham, Barbara, *Librn,* Brookside Hospital, Medical Staff Library, San Pablo CA. 415-235-7000, Ext 2127

Dorigan, M M, *Info Research,* Standard Oil Co (Indiana), Library-Information Center, Chicago IL. 312-856-5961

Dorman, David, *Tech Serv,* Mercy College Libraries, Dobbs Ferry NY. 914-693-4500, Ext 260

Dorman, Louise, *Actg Librn,* Wayne County General Hospital, Medical Library, Eloise MI. 313-274-3000, Ext 6049

Dorman, Phae H, *Librn,* Dow Chemical Co (Business Information Center), Midland MI. 517-636-3779

Dorn, Vivian L, *Dir & ILL,* Huston-Tillotson College, Downs-Jones Library, Austin TX. 512-476-7421, Ext 300

Dorner, Steven, *Mgr Libr Servs,* American Gas Association Library, Arlington VA. 703-841-8415

Dorney, Betty, *Secy to Dir,* Adams State College Library, Alamosa CO. 303-589-7781

Dornfeldt, Jeanne, *Librn,* Fox Lake Correctional Institution Library, Fox Lake WI. 414-928-3151

Dorning, Catherine, *Librn,* Hallstead Public Library, Hallstead PA. 717-879-2227

Dorogi, Ruth, *Dir,* Ahira Hall Memorial Library, Brocton NY. 716-792-9418

Dorosh, Marion, *Librn,* SOHIO Petroleum Company, San Francisco CA. 415-445-9511

Doroski, Shirley, *Tech Serv,* Riverhead Free Library, Riverhead NY. 516-727-3228

Dorothy, Sister M, *Dir & Ref,* Harriman College Library, Harriman NY. 914-782-8136, Ext 16

Dorr, Margaret E, *ILL,* Merced County Library, Merced CA. 209-726-7484

Dorr, Rulze W, *Planning,* University of Louisville Library, Louisville KY. 502-588-6745

Dorsch, Pat, *Ch,* Burton Public Library, Burton OH. 216-834-4258

Dorsch, William, *Pres,* Windham County Law Library, Brattleboro VT. 802-254-9876

Dorsett, Cora Matheny, *Dir,* Public Library of Pine Bluff & Jefferson County, Pine Bluff AR. 501-534-4802, 534-4818

Dorsett, Helen M, *Librn,* Miami-Dade Public Library System (North Dade Regional), Miami FL. 305-625-6424

Dorsey, James E, *Librn,* Emanuel County Junior College Library, Swainsboro GA. 912-237-7831, Ext 251

Dorsey, Margaret, *Supvr,* University of the District of Columbia (Mount Vernon Campus), Washington DC. 202-727-5200, 727-2501

Dort, Donna, *Librn,* Pennsylvania Joint State Government Commission Library, Harrisburg PA. 717-787-6803

Dort, Frances, *Librn,* Texas Instruments Inc (North Building Library), Dallas TX. 214-238-2803

Dorton, Louise, *Dir,* Mayne Williams Public Library, Johnson City TN. 615-928-3116

Dorwart, J, *Librn,* Okanagan Regional Library District (Rutland Branch), Rutland BC. 604-765-8165

Dorzweiler, Adrian N, *Cat,* Western State College of Colorado, Leslie J Savage Library, Gunnison CO. 303-943-2053

Dosa, Marta, *Prof,* Syracuse University, School of Information Studies, NY. 315-423-2911

Dosdall, Ann, *Librn,* Marshall-Lyon County Library (Cottonwood Community), Cottonwood MN. 507-423-6488

Doser, Virginia, *Ref,* Upland Public Library, Upland CA. 714-982-1561

Doshi, Shakuntala, *Tech Serv & Cat,* Montgomery College-Takoma Park Campus Library, Takoma Park MD. 301-587-4090, Ext 242

Doskocil, Mike, *Environ Sci,* Indiana Vocational Technical College, Learning Resource Center, Gary IN. 219-981-1111, Ext 28

Doss, Anita, *Librn,* Buffalo Creek Memorial Library, Man WV. 304-583-7887

Doss, Lois, *Librn,* Mid-Continent Public Library (Kearney Branch), Kearney MO. 816-676-2815

DosSantos, Anthony, *Librn,* Sacramento Public Library (Mabel R Gillis), Sacramento CA. 916-455-2985

Dosser, Dorris, *Librn,* Los Angeles Public Library System (Van Nuys Branch), Van Nuys CA. 213-989-8453

Doten, Dorothy, *Ref,* Kent County Library System, Grand Rapids MI. 616-774-3250

Dothard, Mary, *Librn,* Public Library of Anniston & Calhoun County (Carver Public), Anniston AL. 205-237-8501, Ext 8503

Dotson, James R, *Librn,* Symphony Society of San Antonio, Symphony Library, San Antonio TX. 512-225-6161

Dotter, Mrs B D, *Librn,* Okeene Public Library, Okeene OK. 405-822-3306

Dotterer, Ellen C, *Librn,* Rohm & Haas Co (Home Office Library), Philadelphia PA. 215-592-3000

Dotterer, Kathryn, *Librn,* Bluffton-Wells County Public Library (Ossian Branch), Ossian IN. 219-622-4691

Dotterer, Peggy, *Librn,* Madison County Public Library (Mars Hills Branch), Hot Springs NC. 704-622-3741

Dotterrer, Ellen Castellan, *Librn,* Rohm & Haas Co, Home Office Library, Philadelphia PA. 215-592-3631, 3632

Doty, Constance, *Dir,* Northfield Public Library, Northfield MN. 507-645-7626

Doty, Darla, *AV,* Western Texas College, Learning Resource Center, Snyder TX. 915-573-8511, Ext 265

Doty, Jean S, *Chief Librn,* Eastern Maine Medical Center, Health Sciences Library, Bangor ME. 207-947-3711, Ext 2941

Doucet, J G, *Dir,* Universite Sainte Anne, Louis R Comeau Bibliotheque, Church Point NS. 902-769-2114, Ext 163

Doucet, Mildred, *Librn,* Acadia Parish Library (Evangeline Branch), Evangeline LA. 318-788-1880

Doud, Mary, *Media,* Kent County Library System, Grand Rapids MI. 616-774-3250

Doudna, Eileen B, *Librn,* Memorial Osteopathic Hospital Library, York PA. 717-843-8623, Ext 217

Dougherty, Dolly, *YA,* Central Florida Regional Library, Ocala Public Library, Ocala FL. 904-629-8551

Dougherty, Honora, *Dir,* Larchmont Public Library, Larchmont NY. 914-834-1960

Dougherty, Jane, *ILL & Ref,* Hazleton Area Public Library, Hazleton PA. 717-454-2961, 454-0244

Dougherty, Jeannette, *Librn,* Public Library of Steubenville & Jefferson County (Toronto Branch), Toronto OH. 614-537-1262

Dougherty, June E, *Dir,* North Haledon Free Public Library, North Haledon NJ. 201-427-6213

Dougherty, Linda Anne, *Librn,* Chicago Public Library (Clearing), Chicago IL. 312-767-5657

Dougherty, Lucille, *Librn,* High River Centennial Library, High River AB. 403-652-2917

Dougherty, Nina, *On-Line Servs & Bibliog Instr,* University of Utah (Spencer S Eccles Health Sciences Library), Salt Lake City UT. 801-581-8771

Dougherty, Richard M, *Dir,* University of Michigan Libraries (University Library), Ann Arbor MI. 313-764-9356

Dougherty, Richard M, *Prof,* University of Michigan, School of Library Science, MI. 313-764-9376

Doughtie, Gillis, *Dir,* Montgomery City-County Public Library, Montgomery AL. 205-263-4735

Doughtie, Susan C, *Librn,* Acres American Engineering Library, Buffalo NY. 853-7525 Ext 290

Doughty, Barbara P, *Ref & On-Line Servs,* University of Alabama, Health Sciences Library, Tuscaloosa AL. 205-348-4950, Ext 360

Doughty, Elaine, *Librn,* Shreve Memorial Library (Hamilton), Shreveport LA. 318-631-3675

Doughty, Janice, *Librn,* Central Arkansas Library System (Perryville Branch), Perryville AR. 501-889-2554

Doughty, Marilyn J, *Asst Dir, ILL & Ref,* Neenah Public Library, Neenah WI. 414-729-4728

Doughty, Patricia, *Librn,* Natrona County Public Library (Edgerton Branch), Edgerton WY. 307-437-6617

Douglas, Alice, *Acq,* Wesley College, Parker Library, Dover DE. 302-736-2413

Douglas, Alice, *Dir,* Weston Public Library, Weston MA. 617-893-3312

Douglas, Claudia, *Media,* Southern Alberta Institute of Technology, Learning Resources Centre, Calgary AB. 284-8647; 284-8648

Douglas, Coreen, *Librn,* City of Edmonton Planning Department Library, Edmonton AB. 403-428-2665

Douglas, Elizabeth A, *Dir,* Andes Public Library, Andes NY. 914-676-4632

Douglas, Hugh, *Librn,* Atglen Reading Center, Atglen PA. 215-593-6848

Douglas, Jean, *Asst Librn,* Town of Caledon Public Libraries (Caledon Branch), Caledon ON. 416-857-1400

Douglas, Jeanne, *ILL,* Janesville Public Library, Janesville WI. 608-752-8934, Ext B

Douglas, Jeffrey Alan, *Dir,* Kentucky State Penitentiary Library, Eddyville KY. 502-388-2211

Douglas, Juanita, *Index,* Andalusia Public Library, Andalusia AL. 205-222-6612

Douglas, Kimberly, *Librn,* Maine Department of Marine Resources, Bigelow Laboratory for Ocean Sciences Library, West Boothbay Harbor ME. 207-633-2173, 633-5572

Douglas, Margie, *Librn,* Lincoln-Lawrence-Franklin Regional Library (Lawrence County), Monticello MS. 601-587-2471

Douglas, Mary, *Librn,* Tulare County Library System (Strathmore Branch), Strathmore CA. 209-568-1087

Douglas, Miriam, *Librn,* Carnegie Library of Pittsburgh (Brookline), Pittsburgh PA. 412-622-3100

Douglas, W A B, *Dir,* Canada Department of National Defense (Directorate of History Library), Ottawa ON. 613-992-7849

Douglas, Worth, *Librn,* Boston Public Library (Egleston Square), Roxbury MA. 617-445-4340

Douglas, Worth, *Librn,* Boston Public Library (Grove Hall), Rochester MA. 617-427-3337

Douglass, Ada L, *Dir,* Columbiana Public Library, Columbiana OH. 216-482-2356

Douglass, Adele S, *Chief Librn,* Illinois State Water Survey Library, Urbana IL. 217-333-4956

Douglass, Jim, *Librn,* San Juan County Library, Monticello UT. 801-587-2281

Douglass, John R, *Chief Park Naturalist,* National Park Service, Olympic National Park Library, Port Angeles WA. 206-452-9235

Douglass, Lora, *Librn,* San Juan County Library, Monticello UT. 801-587-2281

Douglass, Mollie E, *Dir,* Penn Hills Library, Pittsburgh PA. 412-793-8049

Douglass, Renee, *Librn,* Buchanan County Law Library, Saint Joseph MO. 816-279-0274

Douglass, Richard, *Assoc Dir,* Ingham County Library, Library Service Center, Mason MI. 517-676-9088

Douglass, Richard A, *Assoc Dir,* Capital Library Cooperative, Mason MI. 517-676-9511

Douglass, Wiley C, *Dir,* Palm Beach Junior College, Library Learning Resources Center, Lake Worth FL. 305-965-8000, Ext 213

Doull, Elaine, *Ad,* East Providence Public Library, Weaver Memorial Library, East Providence RI. 401-434-2453

Doumato, Lamia, *Librn,* University of Colorado at Boulder (Art & Architecture Library), Boulder CO. 303-492-7955

Douthitt, Mildred W, *Librn,* Bicknell-Vigo Township Public Library, Bicknell IN. 812-735-3650

Doutrich, Phyllis I, *Acq & Ref,* Martin Memorial Library, York PA. 717-843-3978

Douville, Judith A, *Tech Serv,* TRC Environmental Consultants, Inc Library, Wethersfield CT. 203-563-1431

Douvlos, Denise, *Ch,* Talbot County Free Library, Easton MD. 301-822-1626

Dove, Elenor, *Librn,* Big Horn County Library (Lovell Library), Lovell WY. 307-548-7228

Dove, Harold R, *Chairperson,* Council of Research & Academic Libraries (Circulation & Interlibrary Loan Group (CIRCILL)), San Antonio TX. 512-734-7311

Dove, Harold R, *Circ,* San Antonio College Library, San Antonio TX. 512-734-7311, Ext 2480

Dove, Harold R, *Asst Prof,* San Antonio College, Library Technology Program, TX. 512-734-7311, Ext 2482

Dove, Mary Lou, *Per,* Missouri Southern State College, George A Spiva Library, Joplin MO. 417-624-8100, Ext 251

Dover, Joseph, *Circ,* University of Utah (Law Library), Salt Lake City UT. 801-581-6438

Dover, Judi, *ILL & On-Line Servs,* Center for Naval Analyses Library, Alexandria VA. 703-998-3580

Dover, Martha, *Librn,* New Orleans Public Library (Gentilly), New Orleans LA. 504-288-4259

Dow, Carolyn, *Media,* East Islip Public Library, East Islip NY. 516-581-9200, 581-9228

Dow, Doris B, *Librn,* Charles M Bailey Library, Winthrop ME. 207-377-8673

Dow, Gail, *Acq,* Denver Public Library, Denver CO. 303-573-5152, Ext 271

Dow, Greta, *ILL & Ref,* Attleboro Public Library, Joseph L Sweet Memorial, Attleboro MA. 617-222-0157

Dow, Mary, *Tech Serv, On-Line Servs & Bibliog Instr,* Everett Public Library, Everett WA. 206-259-8858

Dow, Orrin B, *Dir,* White Plains Public Library, White Plains NY. 914-682-4400

Dow, Ronald F, *Ref,* Dartmouth College (Feldberg Business Administration & Engineering), Hanover NH. 603-646-2191

Dow, Sally, *Ch,* Ossining Public Library, Ossining NY. 941-2416; 941-9174

Dow, Sally C, *Ch,* Helen Kate Furness Free Library, Wallingford PA. 215-566-9331

Dow, Susan, *Doc,* State Library of Massachusetts, Boston MA. 617-727-2590

Dowcet, Angela, *Br Asst,* Saint Charles Parish Library (Hahnville Branch), Hahnville LA. 504-783-2341

Dowd, B, *Librn,* Algonquin College of Applied Arts & Technology (Heron Park Campus), Ottawa ON. 613-731-9441

Dowd, Brother Philip M, *Dir,* Manhattan College, Cardinal Hayes Library, Bronx NY. 212-548-1400, Ext 366 & 367

Dowd, Frank, *Dir,* Maharishi International University Library, Fairfield IA. 515-472-5031, Ext 152, 232

Dowd, Georgette, *Ch,* Georgetown Peabody Library, Georgetown MA. 617-352-8428

Dowd, Judith A, *Dept Head,* Kaiser Permanente Medical Care Program, Medical Library, Los Angeles CA. 213-667-4011

Dowd, Maxine, *Librn,* Graham & Dunn, Law Library, Seattle WA. 206-624-8300

Dowd, Sheila T, *Asst Dir Coll Develop & Ref,* University of California, Berkeley (University Library), Berkeley CA. 415-642-3773

Dowd, Thomas C, *In Charge,* Association of Junior Leagues, Inc, Information Center, New York NY. 212-355-4380, Ext 32

Dowd, W Timothy, *Dir,* Interstate Oil Compact Commission, Hardwick Memorial Library, Oklahoma City OK. 405-525-3556

Dowdell, Gladys, *Librn,* Albany Dougherty Public Library (Carnegie Business), Albany GA. 912-435-2145

Dowdell, Marlene S, *Dir,* Teledyne Inc CAE Engineering Library, Toledo OH. 419-470-3027

Dowden, Keith, *Spec Coll,* Purdue University Libraries & Audio-Visual Center, West Lafayette IN. 317-749-2571

Dowdey, Carolyn D, *Tech Serv & Cat,* Chesterfield County Central Library, Chesterfield VA. 804-748-1601

Dowdy, James W, *Circ, Ser & Spec Coll,* Polk Community College Library, Winter Haven FL. 813-294-7771, Ext 305

Dowell, Connie, *Bibliog Instr,* Morgan State University, Morris A Soper Library, Baltimore MD. 301-444-3488, 444-3489

Dowell, David, *Admin Servs,* Duke University, William R Perkins Library, Durham NC. 684-2034

Dowell, Virginia B, *Dir,* New Britain Public Library, New Britain CT. 203-224-3155

Dowen, Madeline E, *Supvr,* Saint Catherine Hospital, McGuire Memorial Library, East Chicago IN. 219-392-7494

Dowler, Lawrence E, *Assoc Librn Mss & Archives,* Yale University Library (University Library), New Haven CT. 203-436-8335

Dowlin, Kenneth E, *Dir,* Pikes Peak Regional Library District, Penrose Public Library, Colorado Springs CO. 303-473-2080

Dowling, Charles, *Instr,* Quincy College, Library Science Program, IL. 217-222-8020, Ext 225

Dowling, Heather-Belle, *Dir,* County of Strathcona Municipal Library, Sherwood Park AB. 403-467-3513

Dowling, Jane, *ILL,* Pittsford Community Library, Pittsford NY. 716-586-1251

Dowling, Louise, *Dir,* Ellsworth Public Library, Ellsworth WI. 715-273-3209

Dowling, Mary H, *Librn,* Elba Public Library, Elba AL. 205-897-6921

Downen, Mildred, *Librn,* Sparta Public Library, Sparta IL. 618-443-5014

Downen, Thomas W, *Assoc Prof,* University of Michigan, School of Library Science, MI. 313-764-9376

Downer, Edwin J, *Librn,* Springfield Newspapers Library, Springfield MA. 413-787-2411

Downer, Naomi, *Librn,* Texas Department of Corrections Library, Huntsville TX. 713-295-6371, Ext 397

Downer, Sherida, *Circ,* Auburn University, Ralph Brown Draughton Library, Auburn AL. 205-826-4500

Downes, Kathy, *Biomed,* Wichita State University, Library & Media Resources Center, Wichita KS. 316-689-3586

Downes, Marie, *Ch,* West Deptford Public Library, Thorofare NJ. 609-845-5593

Downes, Robin, *Dir,* University of Houston (M D Anderson Memorial Library), Houston TX. 713-749-4241

Downey, Bernard, *Librn,* Rutgers University (Institute of Management & Labor Relations), New Brunswick NJ. 201-932-9513

Downey, Howard R, *Dir,* Bellingham Public Library, Bellingham WA. 206-676-6860

Downey, Janice, *Librn,* Union Congregational Church, Schneidewind Library, Upper Montclair NJ. 201-744-7424

Downey, Lawrence, *Assoc Dir Cent Servs,* Indianapolis-Marion County Public Library, Indianapolis IN. 317-635-5662

Downey, Lynda, *Circ,* Madison County-Canton Public Library, Canton MS. 601-859-3202

Downey, Marcese W, *Librn,* Villanova University, Augustinian Historical Institute Library, Villanova PA. 215-527-2100, Ext 377

Downey, Patricia, *Chief Librn,* Fauquier County Public Library, Warrenton VA. 703-347-3401

Downey, Rita, *ILL,* Melbourne Public Library, Melbourne FL. 305-723-0611

Downey, Roberta, *Circ,* Kellogg-Hubbard Library, Montpelier VT. 802-223-3338

Downie, Trudy, *Librn,* Lambton County Library (Oil Springs Branch), Oil Springs ON. 519-834-2670

Downing, Anthea, *Chief Librn,* Royal Bank of Canada, Head Office Information Resources, Montreal PQ. 514-874-2452

Downing, Bernas, *In Charge,* Eli Lilly & Co, Greenfield Laboratories Library Agricultural Service, Greenfield IN. 317-462-8225
Downing, Corinne W, *Librn,* Sullivan County Public Library, Milan MO. 816-265-3911
Downing, Erin Gail, *Librn,* Huron Company Law Library Association, Norwalk OH. 419-668-5127
Downing, Jeannette, *Librn,* New Orleans Museum of Art, Felix J Dreyfous Library, New Orleans LA. 504-488-2631, Ext 21
Downing, Joan, *Reader Serv,* Idaho State University Library, Pocatello ID. 208-236-3202
Downing, Kathy, *Librn,* Monroe County Library System (Frenchtown-Dixie), Monroe MI. 313-289-1035
Downing, Kenneth, *Rare Bks,* Loras College, Wahlert Memorial Library, Dubuque IA. 319-588-7125
Downing, Margaret, *Librn,* Niagara Falls Public Library (Stamford Centre), Niagara Falls ON. 416-357-0410
Downing, Merle, *Ser,* Youngstown State University Library, William F Maag Library, Youngstown OH. 216-742-3676
Downing, Mildred, *Asst Prof,* University of North Carolina at Chapel Hill, School of Library Science, NC. 919-933-8366
Downing, Naomi, *Librn,* Gary Public Library (W E B Dubois), Gary IN. 219-886-9120
Downing, Naomi, *ILL,* Lincoln Library, Springfield Public Library, Springfield IL. 217-753-4900
Downing, Patricia, *Instr,* Central Missouri State University, Dept of Library Science and Instructional Technology, MO. 816-429-4835
Downing, Sandra, *Doc,* University of Tennessee at Martin, Paul Meek Library, Martin TN. 901-587-7060
Downing, Sister Mary Thomas, *Dir,* Villa Maria College Library, Erie PA. 814-838-1966, Ext 222
Downing, Virginia, *Info Servs,* New Mexico State Library, Santa Fe NM. 505-827-2033
Downs, Elizabeth H, *Dir,* Cyrenius H Booth Library, Newtown CT. 203-426-4533
Downs, Judy, *Librn,* Centennial College of Applied Arts & Technology (Progress Resource Centre), Scarborough ON. 416-439-7180, Ext 230
Downs, Linda, *Librn,* Cairo Public Library, Cairo NY. 518-622-9864
Downs, Matthew P, *Librn,* Valparaiso University (School of Law Library), Valparaiso IN. 219-464-5438
Dowse, Linda, *Librn,* Copeland Public Library, Copeland KS. 316-668-3573
Doyle, Arlene, *Librn,* Sidney Public Library, Sidney NY. 607-563-1200, 563-8021
Doyle, Bonny, *Ch,* Marshall-Lyon County Library, Marshall MN. 532-2646; 532-2849
Doyle, Bridgit, *Librn,* A Barton Hepburn Hospital, Medical Library, Ogdensburg NY. 315-393-3600
Doyle, Cynthia, *Ch,* Providence Athenaeum, Providence RI. 401-421-6970
Doyle, Erin T, *Asst Dir,* Medicine Hat Public Library, Medicine Hat AB. 403-527-5551
Doyle, Frances M, *Librn,* United States Army (TRADOC Technical Library), Fort Monroe VA. 804-727-2111
Doyle, Francis Robert, *Librn,* Loyola University of Chicago Libraries (Law School Library), Chicago IL. 312-670-2952
Doyle, G, *Librn,* Oakland Public Library (Melrose), Oakland CA. 415-532-6800
Doyle, Gregory, *Asst Librn,* Oregon City Library, Oregon City OR. 503-655-8398, 655-8399
Doyle, Ieva, *Acq,* Findlay College, Shafer Library, Findlay OH. 419-422-8313, Ext 327
Doyle, James, *Ref,* Macomb County Community College-South Campus, Max Thompson Learning Media Center, Warren MI. 313-445-7401
Doyle, James, *ILL,* Tri-County Regional Library, Rome GA. 404-291-9360
Doyle, Joanne, *YA,* Wicomico County Free Library, Salisbury MD. 301-749-5171
Doyle, Mary J, *Dir,* Bergenfield Free Public Library, Bergenfield NJ. 201-384-2765
Doyle, Mary Joyce, *In Charge,* Mid-Bergen Federation of Free Public Libraries, Emerson NJ. 201-265-5955
Doyle, Mrs E, *Librn,* Borough of Etobicoke Public Library (Rexdale Branch), Rexdale ON. 416-248-5681
Doyle, Patricia, *Dir,* McKinney Memorial Public Library, McKinney TX. 214-542-7263
Doyle, Patricia C, *Librn,* United States Navy (Naval Air Station Library), Jacksonville FL. 904-772-3415
Doyle, Richard, *Dir & Bibliog Instr,* Coe College, Stewart Memorial Library, Cedar Rapids IA. 319-399-8585, 399-8586
Doyle, Sister Edwarda, *Librn,* Sacred Heart School of Practical Nursing Library, Milwaukee WI. 414-276-6604
Doyle, Vivian A, *Librn,* Frances L Folks Memorial Library, Loogootee Public Library, Loogootee IN. 812-295-3713
Doyton, Gary A, *Archivist,* State University College at Buffalo (Burchfield Resource Center), Buffalo NY. 716-878-6011, Ext 7
Dozier, Lois G, *Asst Dir Gen Libr,* Howard University Libraries, Founders Library, Washington DC. 202-636-7253
Dozoree, Olga, *Librn,* Newbrook Community Library, Newbrook AB. 403-576-3771
Dozoretz, Louis, *Dir,* Binghamton Psychiatric Center (Professional Library), Binghamton NY. 607-724-1391, Ext 450
Drabenstott, Jon, *Acq,* Northern Michigan University, Lydia M Olson Library, Marquette MI. 906-227-2250
Drace, Frances E, *Dir,* Grinnell Library Association, Wappingers Falls NY. 914-297-3428
Drachkovitch, Milorad M, *Archivist,* Hoover Institution on War, Revolution & Peace, Stanford CA. 415-497-2058
Draganski, Donald, *Music,* Roosevelt University, Murray-Green Library, Chicago IL. 312-341-3639
Dragasnki, Donald, *Librn,* Roosevelt University (Music), Chicago IL. 312-341-3651
Drage, Dixie, *Acq,* Utah State University, Merrill Library & Learning Resources Program, Logan UT. 801-750-2637
Drage, Dixie, *Assoc Dir,* Utah State University, Merrill Library & Learning Resources Program, Logan UT. 801-750-2637
Drago, Linda, *Librn,* Carnegie Library of Pittsburgh (Beechview), Pittsburgh PA. 412-622-3100
Dragomir, Florica, *Librn,* University of Montreal Libraries (Botany), Montreal PQ. 514-872-2702
Dragon, Andrea C, *Asst Prof,* Rutgers-The State University of New Jersey, Graduate School of Library & Information Studies, NJ. 201-932-7500
Dragoo, Linda, *Ch,* Kent Free Library, Kent OH. 216-673-4414, 673-3384
Dragotta, L, *Ref,* Air Products & Chemicals, Inc (Corporate Library), Allentown PA. 215-398-7288
Drahmann, Catherine, *Librn,* Perham Public Library, Perham MN. 218-346-4892
Drain, Ann, *Librn,* Case Western Reserve University Libraries (Freiberger), Cleveland OH. 216-368-3506
Drake, Caroline C, *Adminr,* Sterling Drug, Inc, Sterling-Winthrop Research Institute Library, Rensselaer NY. 518-445-8260
Drake, David, *Librn,* Oklahoma State University, Oklahoma City Branch, Technical Institute Library, Oklahoma City OK. 405-947-4421, Ext 251
Drake, Don, *AV,* College of Lake County, Learning Resource Center, Grayslake IL. 312-223-6601, Ext 392
Drake, Grady, *Dir,* Broward Community College, Learning Resources Center, Fort Lauderdale FL. 305-475-6500
Drake, Harold, *Librn,* University of Manitoba Libraries (Saint Paul's College), Winnipeg MB. 204-474-8585
Drake, Jim, *Mgr,* Reed Ltd Technical Information Center, Toronto ON. 416-862-5000
Drake, Linda S, *Actg Dir,* Wilmington Public Library, Wilmington OH. 513-382-2417
Drake, Martha, *Acq,* Saint Bonaventure University, Friedsam Memorial Library & Resource Center, Saint Bonaventure NY. 716-375-2323
Drake, Mayo, *Librn,* Louisiana State University School of Medicine in Shreveport, Medical Library, Shreveport LA. 318-226-3442
Drake, Miriam A, *Asst Dir Admin Servs,* Purdue University Libraries & Audio-Visual Center, West Lafayette IN. 317-749-2571
Drake, Paul, *Ill & Coordr Regional Servs,* Warwick Public Library and Regional Center, Warwick RI. 401-739-5440
Drake, Paul B, *Coordr,* Western Interrelated Library System, Warwick RI. 401-739-1919
Drake, Phyllis, *Asst Librn,* Defense Technical Information Center, Alexandria VA. 202-274-6833, 6834
Drake, Theodore E, *Dir,* Paris Junior College, Learning Center, Paris TX. 214-785-7661
Dralle, Dorothy, *Librn,* Ellis Hospital, Medical-Nursing Library, Schenectady NY. 518-382-4381
Draper, Ann, *Librn,* Mid-Mississippi Regional Library System (Attala County), Kosciusko MS. 601-289-5141
Draper, Hazel, *Bkmobile Coordr,* Kinderhook Regional Library (Waynesville Service Center), Waynesville MO. 417-532-2148
Draper, James, *Librn,* Dekalb Library System (Doraville Branch), Doraville GA. 404-457-4858
Draper, Laura, *Ch,* Colchester-East Hants Regional Library, Truro NS. 902-895-4183
Draper, Patricia, *Assoc Librn,* Fulton-Montgomery Community College Library, Johnstown NY. 518-762-4651, Ext 396
Draper, Rose M, *Librn,* Jackson County Library System (Eagle Point Branch), Eagle Point OR. 503-826-3313
Drapp, Laureen, *Librn,* Akron-Summit County Public Library (Northfield Branch), Northfield OH. 216-762-7621
Draughn, Pearlie, *Librn,* Air Force Association, Research Library, Washington DC. 202-637-3300
Drayson, Pamela Kay, *Librn,* Saint Mary's Hospital Library, Kansas City MO. 816-753-5700, Ext 221
Draz, Peter, *Chief Librn,* State Historical Society of Wisconsin Library, Madison WI. 608-262-3421
Drazan, J, *Acq,* Whitman College, Penrose Memorial Library, Walla Walla WA. 509-527-5191
Drazba, Mary T, *Sr Dir,* Blue Cross & Blue Shield Associations Library, Chicago IL. 312-440-6147
Drazniowsky, R, *Curator,* University of Wisconsin-Milwaukee (American Geographical Society Collection), Milwaukee WI. 414-963-6282
Drazniowsky, Roman, *Am Geographical Society Coll, Curator,* University of Wisconsin-Milwaukee, Golda Meir Library, Milwaukee WI. 414-963-4785
Dreasher, Louise, *Librn,* Sioux City Public Library (North), Sioux City IA. 712-279-6179
Drees, Norma, *Tech Serv & Cat,* Central Kansas Library System, Great Bend KS. 316-792-4865
Dreese, Rebecca, *Librn,* Stephenson Memorial Library, Greenfield Library, Greenfield NH. 603-547-2790
Drefke, Verlea, *Asst Librn,* Williamsburg Community Library, Williamsburg IA. 319-668-1195
Dreger, Leah, *Librn,* General Applied Science Laboratories, Inc Library, Westbury NY. 516-832-2590
Dreher, Cora, *Sci,* Northeast Louisiana University, Sandel Library, Monroe LA. 318-342-2195
Dreher, Judy, *Circ,* Cheshire Public Library, Cheshire CT. 203-272-2245
Dreher, Marjorie, *Dir,* Henderson County District Library, Biggsville IL. 309-627-2450
Dreifuss, Richard, *Bus, Pub Admin & Social Sci,* University of Missouri-Kansas City Libraries, Kansas City MO. 816-276-1531
Drellich, Barbara, *Librn,* United States Navy (Mare Island Naval Shipyard Technical Library), Vallejo CA. 707-646-4306
Drendall, Ethel, *ILL & Media,* Easton Area Public Library, Easton PA. 215-258-2917
Drennan, Sarah, *Librn,* Medford Public Library, Medford OK. 405-395-2342
Drescher, Judith, *Dir,* Champaign Public Library & Information Center, Champaign IL. 217-356-7243
Drescher, Robert A, *Asst Dir,* Illinois Valley Library System, Pekin IL. 309-673-3132

Dresp, Don, *Dir & Commun Servs,* Thomas Branigan Memorial Library, Las Cruces Public Library, Las Cruces NM. 505-526-0347

Dresser, Sylvia L, *Acq,* University of Arkansas at Little Rock Library (University of Arkansas at Little Rock School of Law & Pulaski County Law Library), Little Rock AR. 501-371-1071

Drew, Elliot A, *Tech Serv,* Wilmington Memorial Library, Wilmington MA. 617-658-2967

Drew, Eva, *Librn,* Chattahoochee Valley Regional Library (Richland Public), Richland GA. 912-887-2103

Drew, Harry J, *Dir,* Klamath County Museum, Research Library, Klamath Falls OR. 503-882-2501

Drew, Joyce, *Ch & Media,* Brooks Memorial Library, Brattleboro VT. 802-254-5290

Drew, Laurel E, *Librn,* Albuquerque Public Library (Special Collections), Albuquerque NM. 505-766-5009

Drew, Margaret, *Asst Dir,* Bradford Public Library, Woods Memorial Library, Bradford VT. 802-222-4536

Drew, Marlene L, *Librn,* Mason Library, Great Barrington MA. 413-528-2403

Drew, Ola, *Librn,* Texas County Library (Summersville Branch), Summersville MO. 417-932-5502

Drew, Sally J, *Dir,* Wisconsin Department of Public Instruction (Public & Cooperative Library Service), Madison WI. 608-266-7270

Drewry, Melita, *Librn,* Lakeland Regional Library (Cartwright Branch), Cartwright MB. 204-529-2261

Drews, Margaret A, *Librn,* Henkel Corporation, Technical Information Services, Minneapolis MN. 612-378-8758

Drews, Mary, *Librn,* Palos Community Hospital, Medical Library, Palos Heights IL. 312-361-4500

Dreyer, Ruth, *Ch,* Florence A Williams Public Library, Saint Croix VI. 809-773-5715

Driedger, Irene, *Librn,* Essex County Public Library (Ruthven Branch), Ruthven ON. 519-776-5241

Driesner, Barbara, *Ch,* Edwardsville Public Library, Edwardsville IL. 618-656-4594

Driesschen, T, *Librn,* Town of Pickering Public Library, Pickering ON. 416-284-0623

Driggers, Jeff, *Media,* Jacksonville Public Library System, Haydon Burns Library, Jacksonville FL. 904-633-6870

Driggers, Jeff, *Art & Music,* Jacksonville Public Library System, Haydon Burns Library, Jacksonville FL. 904-633-6870

Drinkwater, Lynne, *In Charge,* Public Library of Pine Bluff & Jefferson County (White Hall), AR. 501-247-5064

Driscoll, Alice, *Ref,* Chatham-Effingham-Liberty Regional Library, Savannah Public Library, Savannah GA. 912-234-5127

Driscoll, Eleanor A, *Dir,* United States Department of the Air Force (Air Force Systems Command, Hq, AFSC/DPSL), Washington DC. 301-981-2598

Driscoll, Loretto, *Dir,* Bradford College, Madaleine Cooney Hemingway Library, Haverhill MA. 617-372-7161, Ext 386

Driscoll, Marjorie G, *Dir,* Shute Memorial Library, Everett MA. 617-387-3612

Driscoll, Nancy, *Records Manager,* Bureau of Land Management Library, Fairbanks AK. 907-356-2025

Driscoll, Sister Loretto, *President,* Haverhill Area Library Resources Consortium, MA. 617-372-7161

Driver, Lottie E, *Dir,* Newport News Public Library System, Newport News VA. 804-247-8506

Driver, Martha, *Planning Develop Supvr,* State Library of Ohio, Columbus OH. 614-466-2693

Drobiarz, Harriet, *Librn,* Aldrich Free Library, Moosup CT. 203-564-8760

Drobny, Daria, *Librn,* Rehabilitation Institute, McPherson Browning Memorial Library, Detroit MI. 313-494-9759

Droescher, Marianna, *Librn,* United States Navy (Long Beach Naval Shipyard Technical Library), Long Beach CA. 213-547-6515

Droessler, W F, *Dir,* University of Arkansas-Monticello Library, Monticello AR. 501-367-6811, Ext 80,81

Drolet, Gaetan, *Soc Sci,* Universite Laval Bibliotheque, Quebec PQ. 418-656-3344

Drolet, Leon, *AV,* Suburban Library System, Burr Ridge IL. 312-325-6640

Drolet, Leon, *Dir,* Suburban Library System (Audio-Visual Service), La Grange Park IL. 312-352-7671

Drone, Jeanette, *Librn,* Memphis State University Libraries (Music), Memphis TN. 901-454-1556

Drone, Lucille, *Librn,* Shawneetown Public Library, Shawneetown IL. 618-269-3761

Drong, Janet, *Bibliogr,* Hoechst-Roussel Pharmaceuticals, Inc Library, Div of American Hoechst Corp Library, Somerville NJ. 201-685-2394

Drong, Josephine V, *Micro, Security & Storage,* Hughes Aircraft Co (Company Technical Document Center Library), Culver City CA. 213-391-0711, Ext 6187

Dronska, Harriet, *Dir,* Child Study Association of America-Wel Met Inc, Alice M Ehrich Memorial Library, New York NY. 212-889-3450

Droscha, Glenna, *Librn,* Ingham County Library (Aurelius), Mason MI. 517-628-2083

Drosehn, Olive, *Librn,* Hinsdale Public Library, Hinsdale MA. 413-655-8186

Droste, Frances, *Librn,* Fort Worth Public Library (Southwest Branch), Fort Worth TX. 817-292-3368

Drought, Carol S, *Ad,* Warwick Public Library and Regional Center, Warwick RI. 401-739-5440

Drouin, Fernand, *Librn,* La Presse, Ltee, Centre de Documentation, Montreal PQ. 514-285-7007

Drown, E A, *Librn,* Aldrich Public Library, Barre VT. 802-476-7550

Drowne, Brother Lawrence, *Dir & Acq,* Saint Francis College, McGarry Library, Brooklyn NY. 212-522-2300, Ext 205, 207

Drozda, Raymond, *Librn,* Greyhound Corp, Patent Law Dept Library, Scottsdale AZ. 602-991-3000, Ext 365

Druck, Kitty, *Translation,* Hoechst-Roussel Pharmaceuticals, Inc Library, Div of American Hoechst Corp Library, Somerville NJ. 201-685-2394

Drucker, Roslyn, *Local Hist,* Yonkers Public Library, Yonkers NY. 914-337-1500

Drucker, Roslyn, *Librn,* Yonkers Public Library (Grinton I Will), Yonkers NY. 914-337-1500

Druehl, Suzanne, *Acq,* Central Arkansas Library System, Little Rock AR. 501-374-7546

Drueke, Jeanetta, *Asst Librn,* Edwardsville Public Library, Edwardsville IL. 618-656-4594

Drueke, John, *Circ,* Southern Illinois University at Edwardsville, Elijah P Lovejoy Library, Edwardsville IL. 618-692-2711

Druesedow, John E, *Librn,* Oberlin College Library (Mary M Vial Music Library), Oberlin OH. 216-775-8280

Drugash, Mary Sue, *Ref & On-Line Servs,* Delaware Technical & Community College, Southern Campus Library, Georgetown DE. 302-856-5438

Druglwall, Alma, *Asst Librn,* Lake Mills Public Library, Lake Mills IA. 515-592-2202

Druhot, Louise, *Librn,* Lorain Public Library (North Ridgeville Branch), North Ridgeville OH. 216-327-8326

Druker, Joyce, *Art & Photography,* Long Island University, Brooklyn Center Libraries, Brooklyn NY. 212-834-6060, 834-6064

Druley, Helen, *Cat,* Miami University, Edgar W King Library, Oxford OH. 513-529-2944

Drum, Carol A, *Librn,* University of Florida Libraries (Chemistry), Gainesville FL. 904-392-0573

Drum, Eunice P, *Tech Serv,* North Carolina Department of Cultural Resources, Division of State Library, North Carolina State Library, Raleigh NC. 919-733-3270

Drumheller, Janet, *Librn,* Knoxville-Knox County Public Library (Farragut), Knoxville TN. 615-693-1191

Drumm, John, *Asst Dir & Commun Servs,* Valparaiso-Porter County Public Library System & Administrative Headquarters, Valparaiso IN. 219-462-0524

Drummond, Donald R, *AV,* San Antonio College Library, San Antonio TX. 512-734-7311, Ext 2480

Drummond, F M, *In Charge,* Amoco Canada Petroleum Co Ltd Library, Calgary AB. 403-233-1451, 233-1867 & 233-1963

Drummond, Forrest S, *Librn,* Los Angeles County Law Library, Los Angeles CA. 213-629-3531

Drummond, Hedy L, *In Charge,* Enoch Pratt Free Library (Kirk Avenue), Baltimore MD. 301-396-5430, 396-5395

Drummond, Jr, Herbert W, *Pub Servs,* California State University, Sacramento Library, Sacramento CA. 916-454-6466

Drury, Cheryl, *Dir,* Dickinson Public Library, Dickinson ND. 701-225-2162

Drury, Donald V, *Dir,* Menlo College & School of Business Administration, Bowman Library, Menlo Park CA. 415-323-6141, Ext 323

Drury, George H, *Info Chief,* Kalmbach Publishing Co, Information Center, Milwaukee WI. 414-272-2060, Ext 46

Drury, M K, *Ch,* South Brunswick Public Library, Monmouth Junction NJ. 201-821-8224, 821-8225

Drury, William Francisco, *Per,* University of Portland, Wilson W Clark Memorial Library, Portland OR. 503-283-7111

Druschel, Joselyn, *Asst Dir for Tech Servs,* Washington State University Library, Pullman WA. 509-335-4557

Druse, Judy, *YA,* Mesa Public Library, Mesa AZ. 602-834-2207

Dry, Lloyd C, *Dir,* Reedley College Library, Reedley CA. 209-638-3641, Ext 239

Dryden, D M, *Librn,* Alberta Teachers' Association Library, Edmonton AB. 403-453-2411

Dryden, Deana, *Librn,* Royal Alexandra Hospital (Medical Library), Edmonton AB. 403-474-3431, Ext 442

Dryden, Donald W, *Dir,* Allendale-Hampton-Jasper Regional Library, Allendale SC. 803-584-3513

Dryden, Margaret S, *Circ,* Hopkinsville-Christian County Public Library, Hopkinsville KY. 502-886-2341

Dryden, Margaret S, *Develop & Special Programming,* Hopkinsville-Christian County Public Library, Hopkinsville KY. 502-886-2341

Dryden, Sherre H, *Librn,* University of South Carolina, Salkehatchie Campus Library, Allendale SC. 803-584-3446

Drye, Jerry, *Bus, Tech & Soc Sci,* Norfolk Public Library, Norfolk VA. 804-441-2887

Drynan, Tom, *Chief Librn,* Mohawk College of Applied Arts & Technology, Library Resource Centre, Hamilton ON. 416-389-5665

Drysdale, Isobel J, *Ch,* Pueblo Library District, Pueblo CO. 303-544-1940

Duarte, Charlotte L, *Librn,* Association for the Preservation of Virginia Antiquities, Richmond VA. 804-359-0239

Dubberly, Ronald A, *City Librn,* Seattle Public Library, Seattle WA. 206-625-2665

Dubin, Eileen, *ILL,* Northern Illinois University, Founders Memorial Library, De Kalb IL. 815-753-1094

Dubois, Florian, *Librn,* Bibliotheque Municipale, Boucherville PQ. 514-655-3131

DuBois, Henry, *Media, Fine Arts & Humanities,* California State University, Long Beach, University Library, Long Beach CA. 213-498-4047

Dubois, Marit, *Br Coordr,* Lubbock City-County Library, Lubbock TX. 806-762-6411, Ext 2828

Dubois, Marit, *Librn,* Lubbock City-County Library (Godeke Branch), Lubbock TX. 806-762-6411, Ext 2828

DuBois, Paul Z, *Dir,* Trenton State College, Roscoe L West Library, Trenton NJ. 609-771-1855

Dubois, Ric, *Bkmobile Coordr,* Crow River Regional Library, Willmar MN. 612-235-3162

DuBois, Russell E, *Dir,* University of Minnesota-Morris, Rodney A Briggs Library, Morris MN. 612-589-2221

DuBois, William, *Lang & Lit,* Northern Illinois University, Founders Memorial Library, De Kalb IL. 815-753-1094

DuBose, Betty, *Librn,* Oconee County Library (Seneca Branch), Seneca SC. 803-882-4855

DuBow, Cathryn, *Cat,* Coca-Cola Co (Business Information Services), Atlanta GA. 404-898-2124

Dubuc, Pierrette, *Head,* Hospital Sainte-Justine, Centre d'Information Sur La Sante de L'Enfant, Montreal PQ. 514-731-4931, Ext 339

DuBuc, Richard, *Asst Librn,* Barreau De Montreal, La Bibliotheque Du Barreau, Montreal PQ. 514-873-3083

Dubus, Mrs A E, *Librn,* Fred Wilson Public Library, Andover KS. 316-733-1303

Ducey, Richard E, *Reader Serv,* New England School of Law Library, Boston MA. 617-267-9655, Ext 50

Duchac, Gretchen N, *Librn,* Lutheran Medical Center, Medical Library, Brooklyn NY. 212-630-7200

Duchac, Joseph, *Per,* Long Island University, Brooklyn Center Libraries, Brooklyn NY. 212-834-6060, 834-6064

Duchac, Joseph, *Music,* Long Island University, Brooklyn Center Libraries, Brooklyn NY. 212-834-6060, 834-6064

Duchac, Kenneth F, *Dir,* Brooklyn Public Library, Brooklyn NY. 212-780-7712

Duchamp, Hazel S, *Dir,* Saint Martin Parish Library, Saint Martinville LA. 318-394-4086

DuCharme, Michael, *Dir,* Grant County Public Library, Milbank SD. 605-432-6543

Ducheneaux, Jane, *Librn,* Dewey County Library, Timber Lake SD. 605-865-3541

Duchesne, Claude, *Librn,* Montreal City Planning Department Library, Montreal PQ. 514-872-1111

Duchesne, Guy, *Dir,* Centrale De L'enseignement Du Quebec, Centre de Documentation, Quebec PQ. 418-658-5711, Ext 165

Duchin, Kathryn, *YA,* Springfield Public Library, Springfield OR. 503-726-3765

Duchon, Maire, *ILL & Acq,* Manhattan College, Cardinal Hayes Library, Bronx NY. 212-548-1400, Ext 366 & 367

Duchow, Sandra R, *Librn,* Royal Victoria Hospital (Medical Library), Montreal PQ. 514-842-1251, Ext 250

Duchowicz, David, *Media,* Kishwaukee College Library, Malta IL. 815-825-2086, Ext 225

Duck, Patricia M, *Librn,* NUS Corp, Northern Environmental Services Division Library, Pittsburgh PA. 412-343-9200, Ext 251

Duckert, Joyce, *Circ,* Janesville Public Library, Janesville WI. 608-752-8934, Ext B

Duckett, Charles, *Libr aid,* Ecorse Public Library, Ecorse MI. 313-381-6630

Duckett, Gaynell, *YA,* Greenville County Library, Greenville SC. 803-242-5000

Duckett, Kenneth, *Spec Coll,* University of Oregon Library, Eugene OR. 503-686-3056

Duckett, Ruby, *Librn,* Tulsa City-County Library (Suburban Acres), Tulsa OK. 918-425-0131

Duckles, Vincent, *Librn,* University of California, Berkeley (Music Library), Berkeley CA. 415-642-2623

Duckwall, Larry, *Librn,* Alameda County Library (Bookmobile & Extension Services), Fremont CA. 415-881-6337

Duckworth, Avis M, *State Librn,* New Hampshire State Library, Concord NH. 603-271-2392

Duckworth, Paul, *ILL & Ref,* Springfield-Greene County Library, Springfield MO. 417-869-4621

Duclow, Geraldine, *In Charge,* Free Library of Philadelphia (Theatre Collection), Philadelphia PA. 215-686-5322

Ducote, Richard L, *Dean,* College of DuPage, Learning Resources Center, Glen Ellyn IL. 312-858-2800, Ext 2351

Duda, Cynthia, *ILL,* Trinity University Library, San Antonio TX. 512-736-8121

Duda, Frederick, *Asst Univ Librn, Personnel,* Columbia University (University Libraries), New York NY. 212-280-2241

Duda, Judi, *ILL,* University of North Carolina at Asheville, D Hiden Ramsey Library, Asheville NC. 704-258-0200

Duda, Judy, *Tech Serv,* Kenrick Seminary, Charles L Souvay Memorial Library, Saint Louis MO. 314-961-4320, Ext 28,29

Duda, S, *Librn,* University of Toronto Libraries (Dept of Pathology), Toronto ON. 416-978-2558

Dudak, Helen L, *Librn,* United States Department of Agriculture, Science & Education Administration, Horticultural Research Laboratory Library, Orlando FL. 305-898-6791, Ext 42

Dudden, Rosalind F, *Librn,* Mercy Medical Center, Library & Media Resources Department, Denver CO. 303-388-6288, Ext 2349

Dudek, Adela, *Librn,* Schuyler Public Library, Schuyler NE. 402-352-2221

Dudey, David, *ILL,* University of Vermont & State Agricultural College (Dana Medical), Burlington VT. 802-656-2200

Dudley, Beverly, *Dir,* York County Public Library, Grafton VA. 804-898-0077

Dudley, Claire, *Media,* Fairleigh Dickinson University, Weiner Library, Teaneck NJ. 201-836-6300, Ext 265

Dudley, Durand S, *Sr Law Librn,* Marathon Oil Co, Law Library, Findlay OH. 419-422-2121, Ext 3376

Dudley, Edmund, *Off Servs,* State Library of Pennsylvania, Harrisburg PA. 717-787-2646

Dudley, Jean, *ILL,* Red Bank Public Library, Eisner Memorial Library, Red Bank NJ. 201-842-0690

Dudley, Laura, *Acq,* Hofstra University Library, Hempstead NY. 516-560-3475

Dudley, Laurie, *Commun Servs,* Abilene Public Library, Abilene TX. 915-677-2474

Dudley, Lola, *Asst Dir,* Mamaroneck Free Library, Mamaroneck NY. 914-698-1250

Dudley, Norman, *Asst Univ Librn Coll Develop,* University of California Los Angeles Library, Los Angeles CA. 213-825-1201

Dudman, Mary, *Librn,* Auburn University, Ralph Brown Draughton Library, Auburn AL. 205-826-4500

Dudman, Mary Elizabeth, *Asst Dir,* Bates College, George and Helen Ladd Library, Lewiston ME. 207-784-2949

Dudman, Sheila E, *Librn,* Nashua Public Library (Chandler Memorial), Nashua NH. 603-882-4461

Dueltgen, Ronald R, *Mgr,* Henkel Corporation, Technical Information Services, Minneapolis MN. 612-378-8758

Duensing, Edward, *Librn,* Rutgers University (Center for Urban Policy Research), New Brunswick NJ. 201-932-3136

Duermyer, Louis, *Librn,* Holland Society of New York Library, New York NY. 212-758-1675

Duesing, Ann, *Librn,* Community Medical Center (School of Nursing Library), Scranton PA. 717-961-6277

Duesterbeck, F, *Cat,* Wascana Institute of Applied Arts & Sciences, Resource & Information Center, Regina SK. 306-565-4321

Duesterbeck, Florence, *Librn,* Wascana Institute of Applied Arts & Sciences, Resource & Information Center, Regina SK. 306-565-4321

Duff, Ann M, *Librn,* Dofasco, Research Information Centre, Hamilton ON. 416-544-3761, Ext 3396

Duff, Elizabeth J, *In Charge,* Illinois State Geological Survey (Map Room), Urbana IL. 217-344-1481, Ext 261

Duff, Kenneth M, *Librn,* University of New Brunswick, Saint John Campus, Ward Chipman Library, Saint John NB. 506-657-7310

Duff, Lucy, *Librn,* Bureau of Social Science Research, Inc Library, Washington DC. 202-223-4300, Ext 220

Duffany, Maureen, *Spec Coll,* Saint John's Seminary, Edward Laurence Doheny Memorial Library, Camarillo CA. 805-482-4697

Duffany, Muriel, *Librn,* Bridport Public Library, Bridport VT. 802-758-2339

Duffett, Gorman, *Asst Dir Pub Serv,* Cleveland State University Libraries, Cleveland OH. 216-687-2486

Duffy, Alma, *Circ,* Jackson State University, Henry Thomas Sampson Library, Jackson MS. 601-968-2123

Duffy, Annette, *Librn,* Metropolitan Library System (Bethany Branch), Bethany OK. 405-235-0571

Duffy, Eleanore, *Ad,* Southington Public Library, Southington CT. 203-628-0947

Duffy, Esther, *Art, Music,* Greenwich Library, Greenwich CT. 203-622-7900

Duffy, Frances L, *Librn,* Stamford Catholic Library, Inc, Stamford CT. 203-348-4422

Duffy, Geraldine, *Chief Librn,* Lehighton Memorial Library, Lehighton PA. 215-377-2750

Duffy, Jacqueline, *Ref,* Porter Public Library, Westlake OH. 216-871-2600

Duffy, Karen Rollin, *Ref Coordr,* South Bay Area Reference Network, CA. 408-294-2345

Duffy, Karen Rollin, *Ref,* South Bay Cooperative Library System, Santa Clara CA. 408-984-3278

Duffy, Mark J, *Archivist,* Episcopal Diocese of Massachusetts Library and Archives, Boston MA. 617-742-4720, Ext 40

Duffy, Mary Anne Burns, *Doc,* West Chester State College, Francis Harvey Green Library, West Chester PA. 215-436-2643

Duffy, Melanie, *Librn,* Wentworth Library (Freelton Branch), Freelton ON. 416-526-4126

Duffy, Ruby, *Dir,* Robert Morris College, Learning Resource Ctr, Carthage IL. 217-357-2121, Ext 35

Duffy, Shawn P, *Librn,* Petoskey Public Library, Petoskey MI. 616-347-4211

Duffy, Valerie, *Admin Asst,* William A Farnsworth Library & Art Museum, Rockland ME. 207-596-6457

DuFore, Thomas, *Flm Bureau,* Akron-Summit County Public Library, Akron OH. 216-762-7621

Dufour, Allen, *Dir,* Bibliotheque Municipale De Sherbrooke, Sherbrooke Municipal Library, Sherbrooke PQ. 819-565-5860, 565-5861 & 565-5862

Dufour, J P, *Librn,* CEGEP de Jonquiere Bibliotheque, Jonquiere PQ. 418-547-2191

Dufresne, Daphne, *Chief Librn,* Universite Du Quebec, Pavillon des Arts Library, Montreal PQ. 514-282-4655

Dufton, J P, *In Charge,* General Telephone & Electronics, GTE Automatic Electric Ltd, Research & Development-Forty Four Library, Brockville ON. 613-342-6621

Dufur, Mary, *Dir,* Dolores Public Library, Dolores CO. 303-882-4127

Dugal, Diane L, *Tech Serv & Cat,* Bridgewater Public Library, Bridgewater MA. 617-697-3331

Dugan, Charlotte, *Librn,* Marengo Public Library, Marengo IA. 319-642-3825

Dugan, Frank, *Doc,* Colgate University, Everett Needham Case Library, Hamilton NY. 315-824-1000

Dugan, Genevieve, *Librn,* Hoesch Memorial Public Library, Alma NE. 308-928-2600

Dugan, Inge, *Librn,* Johnson County Library (Corinth), Prairie Village KS. 913-831-1550

Dugan, Kathy, *Ch & YA,* Crandall Library, Glens Falls NY. 518-792-6508

Dugan, Mary, *Tech Serv,* Burlington Public Library, Burlington IA. 319-753-1649

Dugan, Mike, *Librn,* Albany Dougherty Public Library (Westtown), Albany GA. 912-436-7797

Dugan, Patricia, *Asst Dir & Bibliog Instr,* Utica College of Syracuse University, Frank E Gannett Memorial Library, Utica NY. 315-792-3041

Dugan, Robert E, *Librn,* Boxford Town Library, Boxford MA. 617-887-8022

Dugas, Mildred E, *Head Librn Cat Dept,* Yale University Library (Sterling Memorial Library), New Haven CT. 203-436-8335

Duggan, Ann V, *Dir Libr Serv,* American Foundrymen's Society Library, Des Plaines IL. 312-824-0181, Ext 54

Duggan, Carol, *Ad,* Richland County Public Library, Columbia SC. 803-799-9084

Duggan, Donald, *Asst Dir,* University of Santa Clara, Michel Orradre Library, Santa Clara CA. 408-984-4415

Duggan, Doris, *AV Coordr,* Massachusetts Bay Community College Library, Wellesley MA. 617-237-1100, Ext 193

Duggan, E, *Librn,* Grace General Hospital, School of Nursing Library, Saint John's NF. 709-778-6643

Duggan, Kathleen, *ILL,* Massachusetts Bay Community College Library, Wellesley MA. 617-237-1100, Ext 193

Duggan, Norma, *Dir,* Lincoln Public Library, Lincoln CA. 916-645-8744

Dugger, Linda, *Ser,* Lamar University, Mary & John Gray Library, Beaumont TX. 713-838-8313

Duggin, Merry, *Librn,* Skagit Valley College-Whidbey Branch, Library-Media Center, Oak Harbor WA. 206-675-6656

Duggins, Christine, *Librn,* Kearny Public Library, Arthur E Pomeroy Public Library, Kearny AZ. 602-363-5861

DuGoff, E M, *Librn,* Florida Institute of Technology Library (Medical Research Institute Library), Melbourne FL. 305-723-3701, Ext 252

Duhamel, Louis, *Librn,* Ottawa Public Library (Rideau), Ottawa ON. 613-236-0301, Ext 275

Duhe, Mary, *Circ,* Saint John the Baptist Parish Library, LaPlace LA. 504-652-2144
Duhr, Debra, *Cat & Ref,* Clinton Public Library, Clinton IA. 319-242-8441
Duino, Russell, *Asst Librn,* Cuyahoga Community College (Metropolitan Campus Library), Cleveland OH. 216-241-5966, Ext 217
Dujsik, Gerald, *Coordr,* Chicago & South Consortium, IL. 312-425-8000, Ext 5732
Dujsik, Gerald, *Librn,* Christ Hospital, Medical Library, Oak Lawn IL. 312-425-8000, Ext 5732
Dujsik, Gerald, *Libr Mgr,* Evangelical School of Nursing, Wojniak Memorial Library, Oak Lawn IL. 312-425-8000, Ext 5515
Dukart, David, *Librn,* Edmonson County Public Library, Brownsville KY. 502-597-2146
Dukas, Martha, *Cat Head,* Boston Public Library, Eastern Massachusetts Library System, Boston MA. 617-536-5400
Duke, Barbara, *Librn,* Jefferson County Library System, Madras Public Library, Madras OR. 503-475-3351
Duke, Barbara, *ILL,* Texas State Library, Austin TX. 512-475-2166
Duke, Barbara, *Mgr,* Texas State Library Communications Network, TX. 512-475-3564
Duke, Eleanor C, *Dir,* Bluefield State College, Wendell G Hardway Library, Bluefield WV. 304-325-7102, Ext 230, 334
Duke, Irma, *Librn,* Phenix City-Russell County Library, Phenix AL. 205-297-1139
Duke, Lucy L, *Librn,* Emory University Libraries (Sheppard W Foster Library), Atlanta GA. 404-329-6695
Duke, Mrs E C, *Librn,* Copperhill Public Library, Copperhill TN. 615-496-4324
Dukes, Eugene D, *Librn,* Girard Free Public Library, Girard OH. 216-545-2508
Dukes, William H, *Librn,* Giffels Associates, Inc Library, Southfield MI. 313-355-4600
Dula, Doron A, *Librn,* Physics International Co Library, San Leandro CA. 415-357-4610
Dulaigh, Janet, *Librn,* Mesa County Public Library (Collbran Community), Collbran CO. 303-487-3545
Duley, Rose, *Librn,* Crawford County Library, Grayling MI. 517-348-9214
Dulhanty, Mrs R, *Ch,* Ajax Public Library, Ajax ON. 416-683-6911
Dulka, Michael, *Doc,* Florence A Williams Public Library, Saint Croix VI. 809-773-5715
Dull, P J, *Librn,* Trumbull Memorial Hospital, Wean Medical Library, Warren OH. 216-841-9379
Dulude, Annette, *Librn,* Chicopee Public Library (Chicopee Falls), Chicopee MA. 413-592-0177
Dumaine, Holly Hock, *Librn,* Cumston Free Public Library, Monmouth Library, Monmouth ME. 207-933-4788
Dumais, Ginette, *Librn,* Bibliotheque De La Ville De Montreal (Saint-Michel Adult), Montreal PQ. 514-872-3790
Dumais, Ginette, *Librn,* Bibliotheque De La Ville De Montreal (Saint-Michel Children), Montreal PQ. 514-872-3049
Dumantt, Mary F, *Librn,* University of Puerto Rico, Arecibo Regional College Library, Arecibo PR. 809-878-2830, Ext 332
Dumas, Robert H, *Dir,* Decatur Public Library, Decatur IL. 217-428-6617, Ext 33
Dumbauld, Helen W, *Dir,* Alexandria Public Library, Alexandria OH. 614-924-3561
Dummer, Minnette M, *Dir,* First Presbyterian Church, Thomas E Boswell Memorial Library, Evanston IL. 312-864-1472, Ext 27
Dummett, Sylvia, *Librn,* Dominion Securities Ltd, Research Department Library, Toronto ON. 416-362-5711
Dumond, Marion M, *Dir,* Ellenville Public Library & Museum, Ellenville NY. 914-647-5530
Dumont, Nancy C, *Librn,* United States Army (Cold Regions Research & Engineering Laboratories), Hanover NH. 603-643-3200, Ext 238
Dumont, Rosemary, *Asst Prof,* University of Kentucky, College of Library Science, KY. 606-258-8876
Dumoulin, M Jacques, *Librn,* Bibliotheque Municipale, Victoriaville PQ. 819-758-8441
Dunagan, Marie, *Pub Servs,* Florida Junior College at Jacksonville (South Campus Learning Resources Center), Jacksonville FL. 904-646-2170

Dunavent, Kay M, *Librn,* Saint Jude Children's Research Hospital, Medical Library, Memphis TN. 901-522-0388
Dunaway, Cleta, *Tech Serv & Cat,* Columbia Bible College, Columbia Graduate School of Bible & Missions, Learning Resources Center, Columbia SC. 803-754-4100, Ext 276 & 277
Dunbar, Barbara, *Dir,* McLean County Historical Society Library, Bloomington IL. 309-827-0428
Dunbar, Debra, *Librn,* American Telephone & Telegraph Co (Long Lines Dept General Library), New York NY. 212-393-5538
Dunbar, Eleanore, *Dir,* East Lansdowne Library, East Lansdowne PA. 215-368-3630
Dunbar, Eva Mae, *Librn,* Woodruff County Library (Cotton Plant Public), Cotton Plant AR. 501-459-3680
Dunbar, Gabrielle, *Librn,* Bucksport Memorial Library, Bucksport ME. 207-469-2650
Dunbar, Helen, *Librn,* Alameda County Library (Hayward Business & Government), Hayward CA. 415-881-6328
Dunbar, Helen, *Libr Technician,* San Diego County Library (La Mesa Branch), La Mesa CA. 714-469-2151
Dunbar, Helene S, *Librn,* Cape Cod Museum of Natural History, Clarence L Hay Library, Brewster MA. 617-896-3867
Dunbar, Kathleen, *Tech Serv,* Clackamas Community College, Marshall N Dana Memorial Library, Oregon City OR. 503-656-2631, Ext 288
Dunbar, M Linda, *Libr Tech,* Vancouver Teachers' Professional Library, Vancouver School Board, Vancouver BC. 604-874-2617
Dunbar, Marlene, *Bkmobile Coordr,* Russell County Public Library, Jamestown KY. 502-343-3545
Dunbar, Minnie, *Spec Coll,* Florida International University, Tamiami Campus, Athenaeum, Miami FL. 305-552-2461
Dunbar, Tinker, *ILL,* University of Alabama in Birmingham, Mervyn H Sterne Library, Birmingham AL. 205-934-6360
Duncan, A A, *Dir,* University of Florida, Agricultural Research & Education Center, Institute of Food & Agricultural Sciences Library, Homestead FL. 305-247-4624
Duncan, Ann, *Dir,* Washington Public Library, Washington IA. 319-653-2726
Duncan, Anne S, *Dir,* La Grange Park Public Library District, La Grange Park IL. 312-352-0100
Duncan, Audrey, *Ch,* Algona Public Library, Algona IA. 515-295-5476
Duncan, Cynthia, *Dean,* Old Dominion University Library, Norfolk VA. 804-440-4141
Duncan, Deborah, *Ch,* Coquitlam Public Library, Coquitlam BC. 604-931-2416
Duncan, Don, *Ref,* Washington State Library, Olympia WA. 206-753-5592
Duncan, Donna, *Lectr,* Concordia University, Library Studies Program, PQ. 514-482-0320, Ext 324
Duncan, Dorothy J, *Librn,* Stanstead College, John C Colby Memorial Library, Stanstead PQ. 819-876-2702
Duncan, Edward, *Tech Serv,* Memphis-Shelby County Public Library & Information Center, Memphis TN. 901-528-2950
Duncan, Lester, *Doc,* University of South Carolina, Thomas Cooper Library, Columbia SC. 803-777-3142
Duncan, Lucy, *Cat,* Incarnate Word College, Saint Pius X Library, San Antonio TX. 512-828-1261, Ext 215
Duncan, Lura, *Librn,* Wister Public Library, Wister OK. 918-655-7654
Duncan, Marian, *Librn,* MacLean Hunter Ltd, Toronto ON. 416-596-5244, Ext 311
Duncan, Marion D, *Librn,* Moline Public Hospital, School of Nursing Library, Moline IL. 309-762-3651
Duncan, Michael, *Bkmobile Coordr,* Waco-McLennan County Library, Waco TX. 817-754-4694
Duncan, Mozelle, *Librn,* Upshur County Library, Gilmer TX. 214-843-3582
Duncan, Myrle, *Media,* University of Calgary Library (Faculty of Medicine Medical Library), Calgary AB. 403-284-6858

Duncan, Sandra, *Tech Serv,* Wisconsin Supreme Court, Wisconsin State Law Library, Madison WI. 608-266-1424, 266-1600
Duncan, Shirley T, *Ad,* Harris Electronic Systems Division, Engineering Library, Melbourne FL. 305-727-4677
Duncan, Susan G, *In Charge,* Hallmark Cards, Inc, Creative Research Library, Kansas City MO. 816-274-5525
Duncan, Sylvia, *Librn,* Saint Louis Public Library (Kingshighway), Saint Louis MO. 314-771-5450
Duncan, Vicki, *Librn,* United States Department of Energy, Grand Forks Energy Technology Center Library, Grand Forks ND. 701-795-8132
Duncan, William L, *Soc Sci,* University of New Orleans, Earl K Long Library, New Orleans LA. 504-283-0353
Duncan, William M, *Dir,* Metropolitan Library Service Agency, Saint Paul MN. 612-645-5731
Duncan, Jr, Wesley, *Librn,* Huttonsville Correctional Center Library, Huttonsville WV. 304-335-2291
Duncanson, Blanche, *In Charge,* Acadia University (Engineering), Wolfville NS. 902-542-2201, Ext 206
Dundon, Margo, *Co-Dir,* Grout Museum of History & Science Library, Waterloo IA. 319-234-6357
Dundon, Theresa, *Librn,* University of California, Berkeley, Naval Biosciences Laboratory, Naval Supply Center Library, Oakland CA. 415-832-5217
Dunfee, Aileen, *Librn,* Hammond Public Library (Hansen), Hammond IN. 219-931-5100
Dunford, G, *Media,* Whitchurch-Stouffville Public Library, Stouffville ON. 416-640-2395
Dungan, Creola, *Librn,* Mammoth Public Library, Mammoth AZ. 602-487-2874
Dunham, Della M, *Pub Servs,* Chicago State University, Paul & Emily Douglas Library, Chicago IL. 312-995-2254
Dunham, E, *Libr Tech,* Sheridan College of Applied Arts & Technology Library (Credit Valley Campus), Mississauga ON. 416-845-9430, Ext 166
Dunham, Judith B, *Librn,* Virginia State Library for the Visually & the Physically Handicapped, Richmond VA. 804-786-8016
Dunham, Louise, *Librn,* Western Electric Co, Inc, Library, Phoenix AZ. 602-261-5351, 261-5216
Dunham, Marilyn J, *Asst Syst Coordr,* Texas Trans Pecos Library System, El Paso Public Library, El Paso TX. 915-544-6772
Dunham, Mrs Dennis, *Librn,* Southeast Alabama Cooperative Library System (Rossie Purcell), Columbia AL. 205-696-3345
Dunham, Mrs Gilbert, *Asst Librn,* Frederick Public Library, Frederick OK. 405-335-3601
Dunham, Ruth, *Librn,* Brunswick-Glynn County Regional Library (Long County), Ludowici GA. 912-545-2521
Dunham, Thomas, *Dir,* Marion County Public Library, Fairmont WV. 304-366-4831
Dunigan, Janis M, *Librn,* Consolidated Diesel, Engineering Statistics Library, Old Greenwich CT. 203-637-4341, Ext 353
Dunikoski, Alfred, *AV,* William Rainey Harper College, Harper Learning Resource Ctr, Palatine IL. 312-397-3000
Dunkel, Lisa M, *Ref,* University of California at Davis (Health Sciences Library), Davis CA. 916-752-1214
Dunkin, Gordon H, *Educ,* University of Alabama in Birmingham, Mervyn H Sterne Library, Birmingham AL. 205-934-6360
Dunklau, Dorothy, *Dir,* Arlington Public Library, Arlington NE. 402-478-4545
Dunkle, William, *Librn,* Woods Hole Oceanographic Institution (Data Library), Woods Hole MA. 617-584-1400, Ext 2471
Dunklee, Joanna, *Bibliog Servs,* California State University Dominguez Hills, Educational Resources Center, Carson CA. 213-515-3700
Dunkly, James, *Librn,* Nashotah House Library, Nashotah WI. 414-646-3371, Ext 26
Dunlap, Alice, *Dir,* Caldwell Public Library, Caldwell ID. 208-459-3242
Dunlap, Barbara J, *Librn,* City College of the City University of New York (College Archives & Special Collections), New York NY. 212-690-5367

Dunlap, Connie R, *Librn,* Duke University, William R Perkins Library, Durham NC. 684-2034

Dunlap, Joseph, *Curator,* Allen County Historical Society, Elizabeth M MacDonell Memorial Library, Lima OH. 419-222-9426

Dunlap, Leslie W, *Dean,* University of Iowa Libraries, Iowa City IA. 319-353-4450

Dunlap, Sally, *ILL,* Stevens Memorial Library, North Andover MA. 617-682-6260

Dunlap, Walter, *Tech Serv,* Arrowhead Library System, Virginia MN. 218-741-3840

Dunlavy, Terry, *Librn,* Brooklyn Public Library (Brooklyn Heights), Brooklyn NY. 212-780-7788

Dunleavy, Clara, *Ref & On-Line Servs,* Albert Einstein College of Medicine, D Samuel Gottesman Library, Bronx NY. 212-430-3108

Dunlop, Joan, *Asst Dir,* Greenwood Lake Public Library, Greenwood Lake NY. 914-477-8377

Dunlop, William, *Acq,* University of Vermont & State Agricultural College, Bailey-Howe Memorial Library, Burlington VT. 802-656-2020

Dunmire, Ray, *Dir,* Augustana College, Library Science Program, SD. 605-336-4921

Dunmire, Ray, *Dir,* North Central University Center, SD. 605-336-4921

Dunmire, Raymond, *Dir,* Augustana College, Mikkelsen Library & Learning Resources Center, Sioux Falls SD. 605-336-4921

Dunn, Barbara E, *Librn,* Hawaiian Historical Society Library, Honolulu HI. 808-537-6271

Dunn, Bessie, *Librn,* Waterloo-Grant Township Public Library, Waterloo IN. 219-837-4491

Dunn, Carolyn, *Pure Sci & Spanish Lang,* Austin Public Library, Austin TX. 512-472-5433

Dunn, Cathy H, *Ch,* Pickens County Library, Easley SC. 803-859-9679

Dunn, Charles, *ILL & Ref,* Benedict College, Benjamin F Payton Learning Resources Ctr, Columbia SC. 803-256-4220

Dunn, Cherry, *Ref,* American River College Library, Sacramento CA. 916-484-8293

Dunn, David W, *Dir,* Albany Law School Library, Albany NY. 518-445-2311, 445-2340

Dunn, Donald J, *Dir,* Western New England College (Law Library), Springfield MA. 413-782-3111, Ext 454, 455

Dunn, Dorothy, *Librn,* Hennepin County Library (Edina Branch), Edina MN. 612-922-1611

Dunn, E, *Bkmobile Coordr,* Carnegie-Stout Public Library, Dubuque Public Library, Dubuque IA. 319-583-9197

Dunn, Eloise, *Librn,* Tolland Public Library, Tolland MA. 413-258-4794

Dunn, Glenda, *Ch,* Lake County Public Library, Leadville CO. 303-486-0569

Dunn, JoAnn, *Librn,* Princeton Community Library, Princeton MN. 612-389-3753

Dunn, Linda, *Spec Coll,* Lake County Public Library, Merrillville IN. 219-769-3541

Dunn, Mary Ellen, *Dir,* Shamokin-Coal Township Public Library, Inc, Shamokin PA. 717-648-3202

Dunn, Mrs John, *Librn,* Pleasant Grove Christian Church Library, Dallas TX. 214-391-3159

Dunn, Nancy, *Librn,* Children's Hospital of Pittsburgh, Blaxter Memorial Library, Pittsburgh PA. 412-647-5288

Dunn, Nancy C, *Librn,* Village Library of Cooperstown, Cooperstown NY. 607-547-8344

Dunn, Paula H, *Asst Dir,* Texas Woman's University, Bralley Memorial Library, Denton TX. 817-566-6415

Dunn, Phyllis, *Ch,* Sibley Public Library, Sibley IA. 712-754-2888

Dunn, Phyllis, *Librn,* Vulcan Materials Co, Chemicals Div Research & Development Library, Wichita KS. 316-524-4211

Dunn, R Timothy, *Ad, YA & Ref,* Geauga County Public Library, Chardon OH. 216-285-7601

Dunn, Sandra, *Asst Coordr,* Ontario Crafts Council, Craft Resource Centre, Toronto ON. 416-977-3551

Dunn, William, *Librn,* Hinsdale Public Library, Hinsdale NH. 603-336-7394

Dunn, Willie Mae, *Dir,* Copiah-Lincoln Junior College, Natchez Campus Library, Natchez MS. 601-442-9111, Ext 9

Dunn, Jr, Horton, *Mgr, Research Info,* Lubrizol Corp, Information Center, Wickliffe OH. 216-943-4200, Ext 509

Dunnam, Mary E, *Librn,* Prairie County Library, Terry MT. 406-637-5546

Dunne, Alice, *Libr Asst,* University of Pennsylvania Libraries (Chemistry), Philadelphia PA. 215-243-5627

Dunne, Patrice Norine, *Acq,* Mundelein College, Learning Resource Center, Chicago IL. 312-262-8100, Ext 301, 302 & 303

Dunne, William J, *Librn,* United States Navy (Naval Radio Station Library), Sugar Grove WV. 304-249-7011, Ext 237

Dunnigan, Maureen, *Librn,* Lawyers' Joint Law Library, Minneapolis MN. 612-338-4320

Dunning, Kathleen, *Librn,* United States Navy (Crews Library), Camp Pendleton CA. 714-725-1299

Dunning, M, *ILL,* Santa Ana College, Nealley Library, Santa Ana CA. 714-835-3000, Ext 357

Dunnington, Nancy, *Librn,* Mason General Hospital Library, Shelton WA. 206-426-1611

Dunnum, N, *Librn,* Okanagan Regional Library District (Golden Branch), Golden BC. 604-344-6516

Dunrield, E, *Librn,* University of New Brunswick (Engineering), Fredericton NB. 506-453-4747

Dunton, Joan H, *Asst Librn,* Currituck County Public Library, Coinjock NC. 919-453-8345

Dunwody, Jessie, *Librn,* Anson Public Library, Anson TX. 915-823-2711

Dunwody, M Lynn, *Librn,* Hay Associates Library, Philadelphia PA. 215-875-2300, Ext 2370

Duplaix, Sally, *Dir,* Swampscott Public Library, Swampscott MA. 617-593-8380

Dupont, Elizabeth, *Actg Dir,* George Mercer, Jr School of Theology, Mercer Theological Library, Garden City NY. 516-248-4800, Ext 73

DuPont, France Charbonneau, *Librn,* Imasco Foods Library, Montreal PQ. 514-937-9111, Ext 72

Dupont, Janet, *Ch,* Fall River Public Library, Fall River MA. 617-676-8541

DuPree, Sandy, *Bkmobile Coordr,* Lexington County Circulating Library, Batesburg SC. 803-532-9223

Dupree, Virginia, *Librn,* Lynn Public Library, Lynn AL. 205-893-5250

DuPuis, Alice, *Ref,* Miami-Dade Public Library System, Miami FL. 305-579-5001

Dupuis, Carmen, *Ref,* Hospital Sainte-Justine, Centre d'Information Sur La Sante de L'Enfant, Montreal PQ. 514-731-4931, Ext 339

Dupuis, Mrs M, *Librn,* Penetanguishene Public Library, Penetanguishene ON. 705-549-7164

Duran, Frances, *Per & Doc,* Adams State College Library, Alamosa CO. 303-589-7781

Durance, Cynthia, *Dir, Nat Libr Network Project,* National Library of Canada, Ottawa ON. 613-995-9481

Durand, Barbara, *Librn,* Mutual Life Assurance Co of Canada, Head Office Library, Waterloo ON. 519-888-2262

Durand, Jo Anne, *Ref,* McNeese State University, Lether E Frazar Memorial Library, Lake Charles LA. 318-477-2520, Ext 271

Durand, Joan, *Librn,* Mount Saint Alphonsus Seminary Library, Esopus NY. 914-384-6550, Ext 25

Durand, Marielle, *Librn,* University of Montreal Libraries (Education-Psychology-Communication), Montreal PQ. 514-343-6638

Durant, Bene, *Librn,* Center for Community Economic Development Library, Washington DC. 202-659-3986

Durant, H Lawrence, *Cat,* Boston College Libraries (Bapst (Central Library)), Chestnut Hill MA. 617-969-0100, Ext 3205

Durant, Hazel, *Librn,* Mitchell Carnegie Library, Harrisburg IL. 618-253-7455

Durbin, Tom, *Bkmobile Coordr,* Bowling Green Public Library, Bowling Green KY. 502-781-4882

Durden, Adelle, *Librn,* Houston Public Library (Meyer), Houston TX. 713-723-1630

Durett, Charlene, *Consultant,* Western Mental Health Institute (Edward M Levy Professional Library), Bolivar TN. 901-658-5141

Durgnan, Peter, *Curator Africa Coll,* Hoover Institution on War, Revolution & Peace, Stanford CA. 415-497-2058

Durham, Linda, *Internal Communications,* Coca-Cola Co (Business Information Services), Atlanta GA. 404-898-2124

Durham, Mae, *Asst Dir,* Laurel County Public Library District, London KY. 606-864-5759

Durham, Mary J, *Tech Serv,* Valdosta State College Library, Valdosta GA. 912-247-3228

Durham, Vaida, *Librn,* Harris Hospital Medical Library, Fort Worth TX. 817-334-6474

Durham, Yuki, *ILL,* Battelle-Seattle Research Center, Library Services, Seattle WA. 206-525-3130

Duris, Richard, *Mus,* Temple University of the Commonwealth System of Higher Education, Samuel Paley Library, Philadelphia PA. 215-787-8231

Duris, Richard, *Acting Head Ref,* Temple University of the Commonwealth System of Higher Education, Samuel Paley Library, Philadelphia PA. 215-787-8231

Duris, Sylvia M, *Dir,* Prospect Park Free Library, Prospect Park PA. 215-532-4643

Durivage, Mary Jo, *Librn,* Veterans Administration, Library Service, Allen Park MI. 313-562-6000, Ext 380

Durkan, Michael J, *Librn,* Swarthmore College, McCabe Library, Swarthmore PA. 215-447-7477, 447-7480

Durkcc, Barbara, *Tech Serv, Acq & Cat,* Nova Scotia Agricultural College Library, Truro NS. 902-895-1571, Ext 231, 228 & 291

Durkee, Douglas W, *Dir & Acq,* Green Mountain College Library, Poultney VT. 802-287-9313, Ext 42 & 43

Durkes, Sharon, *Librn,* Pottawatomie-Wabaunsee Regional Library (Eskridge Branch), Eskridge KS. 913-449-2296

Durkin, M L, *Chief Librn,* United States Army (Army Aviation Training Library), Fort Rucker AL. 205-255-6181

Durkin, Margaret, *Ref,* Public Library of the City of Somerville, Somerville MA. 617-623-5000

Durkin, Virginia, *Med Librn & On-Line Servs,* Saint Vincent Hospital & Health Care Center, Garceau Library, Indianapolis IN. 317-871-2095

Durler, Lee, *Librn,* Larned State Hospital (J T Naramore Memorial Library), Larned KS. 316-285-2131, Ext 352

Durnan, Mary, *Dir,* Marshall County Historical Society Library, Plymouth IN. 219-936-2306

Durnell, George, *AV,* Saint Louis County Library, Saint Louis MO. 314-994-3300

Durnell, Jane, *Coordr Libr Instr,* University of Oregon Library, Eugene OR. 503-686-3056

Durocher, George E, *Dir,* University of Alberta (Faculte Saint Jean Bibliotheque), Edmonton AB. 403-466-2196

Durow, Vering, *Asst Librn,* Waverly City Library, Waverly KS. 913-733-2615

Durr, Betty Jean, *Asst Dir,* Ocmulgee Regional Library, Eastman GA. 912-374-4711

Durr, W Theodore, *Dir,* University of Baltimore (Baltimore Region Institutional Studies Center), Baltimore MD. 301-727-6350, Ext 444

Durrance, Joan C, *Lectr,* University of Michigan, School of Library Science, MI. 313-764-9376

Durrance, Raymond E, *Asst Prof,* University of Michigan, School of Library Science, MI. 313-764-9376

Durrant, Jr, William L, *Librn,* Florida Department of Administration, Div of State Planning, Tallahassee FL. 904-488-0630

Durrence, Annelle W, *Admin Asst,* Lake Blackshear Regional Library, Americus GA. 912-924-8091

Durrence, Carol, *Coordr of Ocala Servs,* Central Florida Regional Library, Ocala Public Library, Ocala FL. 904-629-8551

Durso, Angie, *Librn,* Children's Hospital of San Francisco, Emge Medical Library, San Francisco CA. 415-387-8700, Ext 534

Durso, Michael P, *Librn,* United States Department of Energy, Environmental Measurements Lab Library, New York NY. 212-620-3606

Durst, James W, *Curator,* Museum Library, Greenwood SC. 803-229-7093

Durst, Karla, *Librn,* Mason County Library, Mason TX. 915-347-5446

Durst, Leslie, *Librn,* West Virginia School for the Blind Library, Romney WV. 304-822-3521

Duschen, Brigitte C, *Librn,* Bausch & Lomb Corporate Library, Rochester NY. 716-338-6053

Duschenchuk, J, *Librn,* General Instrument Corp, Engineering Library, Hicksville NY. 516-733-3000, Ext 3443, 3514

Dusenbery, Helen, *Ch,* Hood River County Library, Hood River OR. 503-386-2535
Dusenbury, Carolyn, *Bibliog Instr,* University of Utah (Marriott Library), Salt Lake City UT. 801-581-8558
Dusing, Betty, *Acq,* Park College Library, Parkville MO. 816-741-2000, Ext 254
Duss, Edith, *Librn,* Marion Carnegie Library, Marion IA. 319-377-3412
Dusseault, Madeleine, *Librn,* Centre Hospitalier Cote-des-Neiges, Medical Library, Montreal PQ. 514-344-3700
Dussol, Evelyn, *Librn,* Weber County Library (Southwest), Roy UT. 801-773-2556
Dustin, Doris B, *Librn,* Shedd-Porter Memorial Library, Alstead Library, Alstead NH. 603-835-6661
Dustin, John, *Humanities,* Southern Illinois University at Edwardsville, Elijah P Lovejoy Library, Edwardsville IL. 618-692-2711
Dustin, Muriel, *Ref & On-Line Servs,* South Dakota State Library, Pierre SD. 605-773-3131
Duston, Beth, *Librn,* Aerodyne Research Inc, Bedford Research Park Library, Bedford MA. 617-275-9400, Ext 168
Duszkiewicz, Irene A, *Dir,* Hempstead Public Library, Hempstead NY. 516-481-6990
Dutchak, K, *Librn,* Thunder Bay Public Library (Mary J L Black), Thunder Bay ON. 807-623-1529
Dutcher, Harry, *Media,* Lincoln Trail Libraries System, Champaign IL. 217-352-0047
Dutcher, Milton, *Librn,* Baltimore County Public Library (Randallstown Area Branch), Randallstown MD. 301-655-6600
Dutra, Patricia, *Librn,* Binghamton Public Library (South), Binghamton NY. 607-722-8118
Dutton, J E, *Dir,* Calgary Public Library, Calgary AB. 403-268-2880
Dutton, Lee, *Southeast Asia,* Northern Illinois University, Founders Memorial Library, De Kalb IL. 815-753-1094
Duttweiler, Robert, *Ref & Doc,* Augusta College, Reese Library, Augusta GA. 404-828-4566, 828-4066
Duty, Charlotte E, *Tech Serv,* Southwest Virginia Community College Library, Richlands VA. 703-964-2555
Duval, Barbara, *Librn,* Mercy School of Nursing Library, Charlotte NC. 704-372-5100, Ext 286
DuVal, Kate, *Acq & Bibliog Instr,* University of Richmond, Boatwright Memorial Library, Richmond VA. 804-285-6452
Duval, Marjorie A, *Univ Archivist,* University of Southern Maine, Gorham ME. 207-780-5340, 780-4273
Duval, Mary J, *Librn,* Organization Resources Counselors Inc, Information Center Library, New York NY. 212-575-7511
DuVall, Justin, *Asst Dir,* Saint Meinrad College & School of Theology, Archabbey Library, Saint Meinrad IN. 812-357-6611, Ext 401
Duvally, Charlotte, *Eng,* Drexel University Library, Philadelphia PA. 215-895-2750
Duwaldt, Frances, *Ad & Tech Serv,* West Chicago Public Library, West Chicago IL. 312-231-1552
DuWors, Elaine R, *Librn,* Canadian Geriatrics Research Society, J W Crane Memorial Library, Toronto ON. 416-537-6000
Dux, Sherrie, *Outreach & Ref,* Beatrice Public Library, Beatrice NE. 402-223-3584
Duyka, Ann, *Med Cat,* Texas A&m University Libraries (Medical Sciences), College Station TX. 713-845-7427, 845-7428
Duyka, Georgie, *ILL,* Wharton County Library, Wharton TX. 713-532-4822
Duyst, Jo, *Acq,* Calvin College & Seminary Library, Grand Rapids MI. 616-949-4000, Ext 297
Dvarishkis, Kathryn, *Librn,* Park County Library (Meeteetse Branch), Meeteetse WY. 307-868-2248
Dvoracek, Nicholas, *AV,* Knox College, Henry W Seymour Library, Galesburg IL. 309-343-0112, Ext 246
Dvorak, Anna, *Librn,* North Carolina Museum of Art Library, Raleigh NC. 919-733-7568
Dvorak, Robert, *Dir,* Gordon-Conwell Theological Seminary, Burton L Goddard Library, South Hamilton MA. 617-468-7111, Ext 255, 256
Dvorak, Susan L, *Asst Librn & Acq,* American Samoa-Office of Library Services, Pago Pago, Samoa PI. 633-5869

Dvorzak, Marie, *Librn,* University of Minnesota Libraries-Twin Cities (Geology), Minneapolis MN. 612-373-4052
Dwigans, Irene, *Br Supvr,* Buffalo & Erie County Public Library System, Buffalo NY. 716-856-7525
Dwight, Linda Perry, *Supvr,* University of Alaska, Arctic Environmental Information & Data Center Library, Anchorage AK. 907-279-4523
Dworak, Marcia L, *Dir,* College of the Atlantic Library, Bar Harbor ME. 207-288-5015, Ext 4
Dwoskin, Beth, *Librn,* Temple Library, Cleveland OH. 216-791-7755
Dwyer, Claudette, *Dir,* Council of West Suburban Colleges, IL. 312-971-0960
Dwyer, Joseph, *Russian & East European Coll,* Hoover Institution on War, Revolution & Peace, Stanford CA. 415-497-2058
Dwyer, Mary, *In Charge,* Saint Paul Ramsey Hospital & Medical Center, Medical Library, Saint Paul MN. 612-221-3607
Dwyer, Melva, *Fine Arts,* University of British Columbia Library, Vancouver BC. 604-228-3871
Dwyer, Sharon K, *Dir,* Eau Gallie Public Library, Melbourne FL. 305-254-1739
Dwyer-Hirten, Maureen, *Spec Coll,* University of Maryland Baltimore County Library, Baltimore MD. 301-455-2457
Dyal, Don, *Spec Coll,* Texas A&M University Libraries, College Station TX. 713-845-6111
Dyar, Jeanne, *Media,* Pearl River Junior College Library, Poplarville MS. 601-795-4517
Dyas, Gwendolyn, *Librn,* Greene County District Library (Cedarville Branch), Cedarville OH. 513-766-4511
Dybdahl, Russell, *Doc,* Wichita State University, Library & Media Resources Center, Wichita KS. 316-689-3586
Dyck, Marge, *Dir,* Ritzville Public Library, Ritzville WA. 509-659-1222
Dyck, Ron, *Cat, On-Line Servs & Bibliog Instr,* Okanagan Regional Library District, Kelowna BC. 604-860-4033
Dye, Carrie, *Ch,* Nevada County Library, Nevada City CA. 916-265-2461, Ext 244
Dye, Judy, *Tech Serv,* University of South Carolina at Spartanburg Library, Spartanburg SC. 803-578-1800, Exts 410, 411, 420 & 421
Dye, Luella, *Librn,* Craft Memorial Library, Mercer County Service Center, Bluefield WV. 304-325-3943
Dyer, Barbara M, *Dir,* Clinch-Powell Regional Library, Clinton TN. 615-457-0931
Dyer, Carol, *Librn,* Sno-Isle Regional Library (Coupeville Branch), Coupeville WA. 206-678-4461
Dyer, Charles, *AV,* Guilford College Library, Greensboro NC. 919-292-5511, Ext 250
Dyer, Charles R, *Dir,* University of Missouri-Kansas City Libraries (Leon E Bloch Law Library), Kansas City MO. 816-276-1659
Dyer, Charlotte, *Librn,* Mid-Continent Public Library (Buckner Branch), Buckner MO. 816-249-3212
Dyer, Esther R, *Asst Prof,* Rutgers-The State University of New Jersey, Graduate School of Library & Information Studies, NJ. 201-932-7500
Dyer, Ethelwyn, *Librn,* Legion Public Library, Friday Harbor WA. 206-378-2798
Dyer, Jane L, *Ref,* Chapel Hill Public Library, Chapel Hill NC. 919-942-5455
Dyer, Josephine, *Librn,* Grimes County Library, Navasota TX. 713-825-6744
Dyer, Judith C, *Librn,* San Diego Society of Natural History Library, San Diego CA. 714-232-3821
Dyer, Mary F, *Librn,* Owl's Head Village Library Association, Owl's Head ME. 207-594-7646
Dyer, Rosemary, *Cat,* Georgia Department of Education (Div of Public Library Services), Atlanta GA. 404-656-2461
Dyer, Victor E, *Asst Dir,* Abbot Public Library, Marblehead MA. 617-631-1480
Dyer, Virginia, *Librn,* Troup Harris Coweta Regional Library (Harris County), Hamilton GA. 404-628-4685
Dyess, Cynthia, *Librn,* IBM Corp, Technical Library, Austin TX. 512-838-6842
Dyess, Stewart W, *Asst Dir,* Texas Tech University Library, Lubbock TX. 806-742-2261
Dyess, Vance, *Coordr,* Jackson Metropolitan Library (Pearl Library), Pearl MS. 601-352-3677

Dyess, Vance, *Librn,* Rankin County Library, Pearl MS. 601-932-2262
Dygert, Mike, *Admin & Tech Servs,* Eastern Massachusetts Regional Library System, Boston MA. 617-536-4010
Dyke, James, *Dir,* New Mexico State University Library, Las Cruces NM. 505-646-1508
Dyke, Rosemary, *Ch,* Melbourne Public Library, Melbourne FL. 305-723-0611
Dykes, Ann, *Librn,* Battery Power Unit Vehicle Corp Library, Lookout Mountain CO. 303-526-0254
Dykes, Patricia, *On-Line Servs,* Virginia Wesleyan College, Henry Clay Hofheimer II Library, Norfolk VA. 804-461-3232
Dyki, Judy, *Librn,* University of Detroit Library (Business & Administration Evening), Detroit MI. 313-927-1525
Dykins, Jeanne, *Pub Rel,* Reuben McMillan Free Library Free Library Association, Public Library of Youngstown & Mahoning County, Youngstown OH. 216-744-8636
Dyknoff, Cynthia, *Coordr,* Parkersburg & Wood County Public Library (Services for the Blind & Physically Handicapped), Parkersburg WV. 304-485-6564
Dykstra, John, *Librn,* Brooklyn Public Library (De Kalb), Brooklyn NY. 212-452-5678
Dykstra, Mary, *Asst Prof,* Dalhousie University, School of Library Service, NS. 902-424-3656
Dykstra, Stephanie, *Librn,* Agriculture Canada (Animal Disease Research Institute Library), Ottawa ON. 613-825-4521
Dykstra, Stephanie, *Librn,* Agriculture Canada (Animal Research Institute Library), Ottawa ON. 613-995-9477
Dyle, Mary, *Graphics Technician,* Mississippi Gulf Coast Junior College, Jackson County Campus Library, Gautier MS. 601-497-4313, Ext 226, Libr; 497-4313, Ext 255 Media Ctr
Dymek, Mary, *Ch,* Prosser Public Library, Bloomfield CT. 203-243-9721
Dyment, Alan R, *Dir,* Mount Royal College Library, Calgary AB. 403-246-6111
Dysart, Jane, *Librn,* Royal Bank of Canada, Information Resources, Toronto ON. 416-865-2780
Dysinger, Robert E, *Librn,* Auburn Public Library, Auburn ME. 207-782-3191
Dyson, Allan, *Dir,* University of California, University Library, Santa Cruz CA. 408-429-2076
Dyson, Sam A, *Dir,* Louisiana Tech University, Prescott Memorial Library, Ruston LA. 318-257-2577
Dyson, Sam A, *Assoc Prof,* Louisiana Tech University, Teacher Education-Library Science, LA. 318-257-3242
Dyson-Bonter, P, *Dir,* Canadian Film Institute, National Film Library of Canada, Ottawa ON. 613-232-2495
Dyste, Mena, *Commun Servs, West Area,* Hennepin County Library, Edina MN. 612-830-4944
Dytyniak, Olga, *Librn,* FMC Corp, Chemical Research & Development Center, Technical Information Services Library, Princeton NJ. 609-452-2300, Ext 229
Dzida, Mrs B A, *Librn,* Borough of Etobicoke Public Library (New Toronto Libr), Toronto ON. 416-248-5681
Dziedzic, Donna, *Dir,* Chicago Public Library (Illinois Regional Library for the Blind & Physically Handicapped), Chicago IL. 312-738-9210
Dziedzina, Christine A, *Asst Librn,* Cleveland Metropolitan General Hospital, Harold H Brittingham Memorial Library, Cleveland OH. 216-398-6000, Ext 4313
Dziura, Walter T, *Dir,* Hingham Public Library, Hingham MA. 617-749-0907
Dzuira, Walter T, *Lectr,* Simmons College, Graduate School of Library & Information Science, MA. 617-738-2225
Dzwonkoski, Peter, *Rare Bks & Spec Coll,* University of Rochester, Rush Rhees Library, Rochester NY. 716-275-4461

E

Eadie, Tom, *Philos,* University of Waterloo Library, Waterloo ON. 519-885-1211

Eadie, Tom, *Ref & Coll Develop,* University of Waterloo Library. Waterloo ON. 519-885-1211

Eads, Barbara, *Librn, On-Line Servs & Bibliog Instr,* Exxon Co USA (Refinery Library), Baytown TX. 713-427-5711, Ext 2837

Eads, Pauline, *Libr Assts,* Surry Community College, Learning Resources Center, Dobson NC. 919-386-8121, Ext 52

Eady, D, *Librn,* Windsor Public Library (Seminole), Windsor ON. 519-945-6467

Eagan, Deborah, *Librn,* University of New Mexico General Library (Tireman Learning Materials Center), Albuquerque NM. 505-277-3856

Eagen, Marian S, *Librn,* Alberta & Southern Gas Company Ltd Library, Calgary AB. 403-263-8320, Ext 372

Eager, Nancy, *Ch,* Hayward Public Library, Hayward CA. 415-581-2545

Eagle, Harriet, *Librn,* Sandusky Public Library, Sandusky MI. 313-648-2644

Eagle, Peggy, *Ad,* Grandview Heights School District Public Library, Columbus OH. 614-486-2951

Eaglen, Audrey B, *Acq,* Cuyahoga County Public Library, Cleveland OH. 216-398-1800

Eagles, Frank L, *Dean,* Wilson County Technical Institute, Learning Resource Center, Wilson NC. 919-291-1195, Ext 235

Eaglesfield, Jaunette, *Librn,* Massachusetts Institute of Technology Libraries (Lindgren-Earth Sciences), Cambridge MA. 617-253-5679

Eaglesham, Mary, *Librn,* Regina Public Library (Glen Elm), Regina SK. 306-569-7615

Eagleson, Janet A, *Dir,* Flint Memorial Library, North Reading MA. 617-664-4942

Eagleson, Laurie, *Cat,* Eastern New Mexico University Library, Portales NM. 505-562-2624

Eagleson, Laurie, *Music,* Eastern New Mexico University Library, Portales NM. 505-562-2624

Eagleton, Kathy, *Librn,* Brandon General Hospital Library, Brandon MB. 204-728-3321, Ext 399

Eagleton, Lynn, *Librn,* Patoka Public Library, Patoka IL. 618-432-5855

Eagon, B, *Dean,* University of Wisconsin-Stevens Point, Albertson Learning Resources Ctr, Stevens Point WI. 715-346-2540

Eagon, Carrie W, *Librn,* Esso Eastern Inc Library, Houston TX. 713-656-7346

Eakin, Dottie, *Tech Serv,* Houston Academy of Medicine, Texas Medical Center Library, Houston TX. 713-797-1230

Eakin, Laurabelle, *Dir,* University of Pittsburgh (Maurice & Laura Falk Library of the Health Sciences), Pittsburgh PA. 412-624-2521

Eames, Charles B, *Dir,* Willard Memorial Library, Willard OH. 419-933-8564

Eames, Donald, *Chmn, Libr Trustees,* Skowhegan Free Public Library, Skowhegan ME. 207-474-9072

Eamon, Virginia, *Br Coordr,* Western Counties Regional Library, Yarmouth NS. 902-742-2486

Eannarino, Judith C, *Reader Serv,* Mohawk Valley Community College Library, Utica NY. 315-792-5337

Earhart, Joyce, *Ref,* Lord Fairfax Community College, Learning Resource Center, Middletown VA. 703-869-1120

Earhart, Marilyn, *Acq & Cat,* University of Santa Clara (Heafey Law Library), Santa Clara CA. 408-984-4451

Earhart, Shirley, *Librn,* Lieber Public Library, Osage City KS. 913-528-3727

Earl, Jane, *Librn,* Emory John Brady Hospital, Franklin G Ebaugh MD Library, Colorado Springs CO. 303-473-4460

Earl, Marcellus, *Librn,* Abbey of the Genesee Library, Piffard NY. 716-243-0660

Earl, Marjorie, *Librn,* Athens Public Library, Athens OH. 613-924-2048

Earl, Martha M, *Special Projects,* United States Military Academy Library, West Point NY. 914-938-2230

Earle, Elinor, *Librn,* Akron-Summit County Public Library (Kenmore), Akron OH. 216-745-6126

Earles, Christine B, *Librn,* Spencer Hospital Library, Spencer WV. 304-927-2110, Ext 232

Earley, Emily, *Coordr,* University of Wisconsin-Madison, Institute for Environmental Studies Reading Room, Madison WI. 608-263-3185

Earnest, Marcia, *Librn,* Charles E Merrill Publishing Co Library, Columbus OH. 614-258-8441

Earnhard, Maxiene, *Ser,* Greensboro College, James Addison Jones Library, Greensboro NC. 919-272-7102, Ext 234

Easley, Jane, *Librn,* United States Navy (Naval Regional Medical Center Library), Bremerton WA. 206-478-4269

Easley, Janet, *Circ & Bibliog Instr,* University of California Library, Irvine CA. 714-833-5212

Easley, Juanita, *Tech Serv & Cat,* Averett College, Mary B Blount Library, Danville VA. 804-793-7811, Ext 265

Easley, Linda, *Librn,* Library Association of Portland (Holgate), Portland OR. 503-771-3475

Easley, Mrs Cecil, *Dir,* Grainger County Library, Rutledge TN. 615-828-4784

Eason, Betty D, *Dir,* Carnegie Public Library, Bradford PA. 814-362-6527

Eason, Jacklynn, *Bkmobile Coordr,* Brazoria County Library, Angleton TX. 713-849-0591

Eason, Ken, *Asst Librn,* Oklahoma Library for the Blind & Physically Handicapped, Oklahoma City OK. 405-521-3514, 521-3832

Eason, Sister Evelyn, *Dir,* Our Lady of Holy Cross College Library, New Orleans LA. 504-394-7744

Eason, Sister Evelyn, *Dept Head,* Our Lady of Holy Cross College, School Library Program, LA. 504-394-7744

East, Kathy, *Ch & YA,* Public Library of Columbus & Franklin County, Columbus OH. 614-864-8050

East, Mona, *Selection Officer,* University of Michigan Libraries (University Library), Ann Arbor MI. 313-764-9356

Easterbrook, David, *African Studies,* Indiana University at Bloomington, University Libraries, Bloomington IN. 812-337-3403

Easterday, Nancy, *AV,* Worthington Public Library, Worthington OH. 614-885-3185

Easterling, Barbara, *Acq,* Wabash College, Lilly Library, Crawfordsville IN. 317-362-1400, Ext 215, 216

Easterly, Ambrose, *Dir Libr Servs,* William Rainey Harper College, Harper Learning Resource Ctr, Palatine IL. 312-397-3000

Easterly, Grace, *Librn,* Southgate Public Library, Southgate MI. 313-284-3266

Easterwood, Peggy, *Exten,* George S Houston Memorial Library, Dothan AL. 205-793-9767

Eastlick, John, *Instr,* University of Denver, Graduate School of Librarianship and Information Management, CO. 303-753-2557

Eastlund, Janice, *Ch,* Elm Grove Public Library, Elm Grove WI. 414-782-6717

Eastman, Frank, *Acq,* Newport Beach Public Library, Newport Beach CA. 714-640-2141

Eastman, Frank, *Librn,* Newport Beach Public Library (Mariners), Newport Beach CA. 714-640-2141

Eastman, Grace, *Librn,* East Bridgewater Public Library, Washburn Memorial, East Bridgewater MA. 617-378-2821

Eastman, Jane, *Ad,* Watertown Free Public Library, Watertown MA. 617-924-5390

Eastman, Janice, *Cat,* Chapman College, Thurmond Clarke Memorial Library, Orange CA. 714-997-6806

Eastmond, Helen, *Ch,* Provo City Public Library, Provo UT. 801-373-1494

Easton, Shirley L, *Librn,* Coquille Public Library, Coquille OR. 503-396-2410

Easton, Diana, *Tech Serv,* Oconee County Library, Walhalla SC. 803-638-5837

Easton, Patricia, *Dir,* Lancaster Public Library, Lancaster NY. 716-683-1120

Eastwood, Lorraine, *Librn,* Wentworth Library (Waterdown Branch), Waterdown ON. 416-526-4126

Eastwood, Louise, *Tech Serv,* Florida Southern College, Roux Library, Lakeland FL. 813-683-5521, Ext 211

Eatenson, Ervin, *Current Coll,* Dallas Public Library, Dallas TX. 214-748-9071

Eates, Peter J, *Info Spec & On Line Search Coord,* Syncrude Canada Ltd (Research Library), Edmonton AB. 403-464-8400

Eathorne, Gladys, *Librn,* Imlay Township Library, Imlay City MI. 313-724-8043

EBERHARD

Eaton, Andrew J, *Dir Emeritus & Spec Asst to Dean of Libr Servs,* Washington University Libraries, Saint Louis MO. 314-889-5400

Eaton, Barbara, *Librn,* Central Ohio Psychiatric Hospital (Patients' Library), Columbus OH. 614-466-5950, Ext 348

Eaton, Barbara, *Intraloan Coordr,* Chattahoochee Valley Regional Library, W C Bradley Memorial Library, Headquarters, Columbus GA. 404-327-0211

Eaton, Bernice, *Ser,* Fort Valley State College, Henry Alexander Hunt Memorial Library, Fort Valley GA. 912-825-6342

Eaton, Betsy, *Librn,* Littleton Public Library, Littleton NH. 603-444-5741

Eaton, Conrad P, *Librn,* United States Department of State, Washington DC. 202-632-0372

Eaton, E M, *Reader Serv & Bibliog Instr,* Florida Agricultural & Mechanical University, Samuel H Coleman Memorial Library, Tallahassee FL. 904-599-3370

Eaton, Elizabeth Gale, *Ch,* Berkshire Athenaeum, Pittsfield Public Library, Pittsfield MA. 413-442-1559

Eaton, Elizabeth K, *Pub Serv,* University of Texas Medical Branch, Moody Medical Library, Galveston TX. 713-765-1971

Eaton, Eugenia, *Public Affairs Servs,* University of California Los Angeles Library, Los Angeles CA. 213-825-1201

Eaton, Jeanne Miller, *Asst Librn,* University of Michigan (Institute of Gerontology), Ann Arbor MI. 313-763-1325

Eaton, John, *Media,* Texas Christian University, Mary Couts Burnett Library, Fort Worth TX. 817-921-7106

Eaton, John, *Dir,* Texas Christian University (Instructional Services), Fort Worth TX. 817-921-7121

Eaton, Katherine G, *Librn,* University of Oregon Library (Bureau of Governmental Research & Service), Eugene OR. 503-686-3048

Eaton, Lawrence A, *Dir,* Northern Interrelated Library System, Pawtucket RI. 401-723-5350

Eaton, Lawrence A, *Dir,* Pawtucket Public Library & Regional Library Center, Deborah Cook Sayles Memorial Library, Pawtucket RI. 401-725-3714

Eaton, Leona G, *Dir,* Lyons School District Public Library, Lyons NY. 315-946-9262

Eaton, Mrs James T, *Dir,* Carmel United Presbyterian Church, Carmel Memorial Library, Glenside PA. 215-887-1074

Eaton, Nancy, *Tech Serv, On-Line Servs & Bibliog Instr,* Atlanta Public Library, Atlanta GA. 404-688-4636

Eaton, Sally, *Circ,* East Brunswick Public Library, East Brunswick NJ. 201-254-1220

Eaton, III, Edward A, *Asst Prof,* Emory University, Div of Librarianship, GA. 404-329-6840

Eaves, Carolyn, *Dir,* Howard Payne University, Walker Memorial Library, Brownwood TX. 915-646-2502, Ext 352

Eayrs, Beverly, *ILL,* College of Great Falls Library, Great Falls MT. 406-761-8210, Ext 280

Ebbers, Gertrude, *Librn,* DeWitt Public Library, DeWitt NE. 402-683-2145

Ebbers, Susan K, *Tech Serv,* Menlo College & School of Business Administration, Bowman Library, Menlo Park CA. 415-323-6141, Ext 323

Ebbinghouse, Carol L Price, *Librn,* South Bay University College of Law Library, Los Angeles CA. 213-380-5411

Ebbs, C, *Librn,* Algonquin College, Lanark Campus Resource Centre, Perth ON. 613-267-2859

Ebeling, Elinor, *Dir,* Brookdale Community College, Learning Resources Center, Lincroft NJ. 201-842-1900, Ext 392

Ebeling, Grace, *Librn,* Independence Sanitarium & Hospital, Dr Charles F Grabske Sr Library, Independence MO. 816-836-8100, Ext 2388

Eben, Craig, *Media,* Illinois Benedictine College, Theodore Lownik Library, Lisle IL. 312-968-7270, Ext 286

Eben, J P, *Supvr,* Dow Chemical USA, Texas Div Library, Freeport TX. 713-238-3513

Eber, Beryl, *Librn,* New York Public Library (Nathan Straus Young Adult Library), New York NY. 212-790-6471, 6472

Eberhard, Neysa, *Dir,* Newton Public Library, Newton KS. 316-283-2890

Eberhardt, James G, *Dir,* Florida Keys Community College Library, Key West FL. 305-296-9081
Eberhardt, Newman C, *Dir,* Saint John's Seminary, Edward Laurence Doheny Memorial Library, Camarillo CA. 805-482-4697
Eberhart, Arthur, *Media,* Chadron State College Library, Chadron NE. 308-432-4451, Ext 271
Eberhart, George, *Ser,* University of Kansas Libraries (School of Law), Lawrence KS. 913-864-3025
Eberhart, Gwen, *Coordr,* San Antonio Major Resource System, San Antonio TX. 512-223-5538
Eberhart, Gwen, *ILL,* San Antonio Public Library, San Antonio TX. 512-299-7790
Eberhart, Mary, *ILL,* College of Wooster, Andrews Library, Wooster OH. 216-264-1234, Ext 483
Eberhart, W Lyle, *Ad,* Wisconsin Department of Public Instruction, Division of Library Services, Madison WI. 608-266-2205
Ebersale, Brian, *Ref,* Claremont Colleges Libraries (Norman F Sprague Memorial), Claremont CA. 714-621-8000, Ext 3190
Ebert, Mrs Fred H, *Dir,* East Troy Public Library, East Troy WI. 414-642-5979
Ebert, Patrice G, *Person Co Librn,* Hyconeechee Regional Library, Yanceyville NC. 919-694-6241
Ebert, Patrice G, *Librn,* Person County Public Library, Roxboro NC. 919-599-7615
Eble, Mary C, *Adjunct Prof,* Case Western Reserve University, School of Library Science, OH. 216-368-3500
Ebner, William E, *In Charge,* Teledyne Ryan Aeronautical, Technical Information Services, San Diego CA. 714-291-7311, Ext 1067
Ebsen, Paula Nan, *Ref,* McMillan Memorial Library, Wisconsin Rapids WI. 715-423-1040
Ebstein, Ilse M, *Librn,* Temple Israel, Meta Marx Lazarus Memorial Library, Columbus OH. 614-866-0010
Ebster, Deborah, *Ref,* Rock Valley College Educational Resources Center, Rockford IL. 815-226-3762
Eby, Beth, *Coordr,* Patrick Henry Memorial Library, Brookneal VA. 804-376-3363
Eby, Carl, *Media,* Trevecca Nazarene College, Mackey Library, Nashville TN. 615-244-6000, Ext 214
Eby, Harold H, *Dir,* Conoco Inc Research & Development Department, Technical Information Services, Ponca City OK. 405-767-4719
Eby, Joan S, *Ch,* Pottstown Public Library, Pottstown PA. 215-326-2532
Eby, Patricia, *Ch,* Adrian Public Library, Adrian MI. 517-263-2161, Ext 277
Eccell, Sister Raphael, *Tech Serv,* Incarnate Word College, Saint Pius X Library, San Antonio TX. 512-828-1261, Ext 215
Eccles, Ann, *Librn,* Hennepin County Library (Wayzata Branch), Wayzata MN. 612-473-9721
Eccles, Denise, *Librn,* Gridley Library, Gridley KS. 316-836-3145
Echard, Dena, *Actg Librn,* Montana College of Mineral Science and Technology Library, Butte MT. 406-792-8321, Ext 371
Echols, Anne S, *Librn,* Chicago Public Library (Auburn), Chicago IL. 312-783-5927
Echols, Dan, *In Charge,* Tarrant County Junior College System (Northeast Campus Learning Resource Center), Hurst TX. 817-281-7860, Ext 477
Echols, Gail B, *Cat,* Pfeiffer College, Gustavus Adolphus Pfeiffer Library, Misenheimer NC. 704-463-7343, Ext 278
Echols, Ottoleine D, *Librn, Ad & Spec Coll,* Craighead County & Jonesboro Public Library, Jonesboro AR. 501-935-5133
Echols, Ottoleine D, *Asst Dir,* Crowley Ridge Regional Library, Jonesboro AR. 501-935-5133
Echols, Ruth, *Librn,* Athens Regional Library (Lavonia-Carnegie), Danielsville GA. 404-795-2180
Echt, Sandy, *On-Line Servs,* Texas Christian University, Mary Couts Burnett Library, Fort Worth TX. 817-921-7106
Eckard, Gladys, *Dir,* Rutherford Free Public Library, Rutherford NJ. 201-939-8600
Eckard, Louise, *Librn,* De Pue Public Library, De Pue IL. 815-447-2660
Eckard, Rowena, *Dir,* Milford Memorial Library, Milford IA. 712-338-4643

Eckart, Barbara, *Asst Librn,* Johnson County Law Library, Olathe KS. 913-782-5000, Ext 512
Eckburg, Louise, *Actg Librn,* Chevy Chase Presbyterian Church Library, Washington DC. 202-363-2202
Eckel, Virginia E, *Actg Dir,* United States Air Force (Academic Library), Wright-Patterson AFB OH. 513-255-5894
Eckels, Diane D, *Assoc Dir,* Houston Academy of Medicine, Texas Medical Center Library, Houston TX. 713-797-1230
Eckels, Patricia W, *Dir,* Howe Library, Hanover NH. 603-643-4120
Eckenberg, Gary, *Media,* Saint Louis County Health Department Library, Duluth MN. 218-727-8661, Ext 14
Ecker, Melvin, *Asst Dir, Ad & Ref,* Lynbrook Public Library, Lynbrook NY. 516-599-8630
Eckert, Betty A, *ILL & Ref,* Ardmore Public Library, Ardmore OK. 405-223-8290
Eckert, Dan, *Librn,* Holy Family Hospital, Health Sciences Library, Manitowoc WI. 414-684-2260
Eckert, Jeffrey, *Media,* New College of the University of South Florida, Sarasota Campus Library, Sarasota FL. 813-355-7671, Ext 214
Eckes, Harold, *Coordr,* Los Angeles Trade Technical College, Library Media Technical Assistant, CA. 213-746-0800, Ext 494
Eckes, Harold, *Dir,* Los Angeles Trade Technical College Library, Los Angeles CA. 213-746-0800, Ext 217
Eckes, Mark, *Admin Servs Coordr,* Minnesota Interlibrary Telecommunications Exchange, (MINITEX), MN. 612-376-3925, 376-3926
Eckhardt, Vicki, *Tech Serv,* Texas Lutheran College, Blumberg Memorial Library, Seguin TX. 512-379-4161, Ext 90
Eckhouse, Elena, *Chief Librn,* Union Service Corp Library, New York NY. 212-432-4002, 432-4003
Ecklund, Betty, *Librn,* Margaret Shontz Memorial Library, Conneaut Lake Public Library, Conneaut Lake PA. 814-382-6666
Eckman, Charles, *Chief Librn,* Veterans Administration, Hospital Library, Fort Wayne IN. 219-743-5431
Eckman, Dorothy, *Librn,* Foley Public Library, Foley AL. 205-943-7665
Eckman, Elizabeth, *Cat,* Bedford Public Library, Bedford IN. 812-275-4471
Eckman, John, *Librn,* San Joaquin General Hospital, Medical Library, Stockton CA. 209-982-1800, Ext 203
Eckmann, Juliann, *Librn,* Harris County Public Library (Katy Branch), Katy TX. 713-371-3509
Eckwright, Gail Z, *On-Line Servs,* University of Idaho Library, Moscow ID. 208-885-6534
Ecock, Mary, *Librn,* Brooklyn Public Library (Jamaica Bay), Brooklyn NY. 212-531-1602
Economous, Charles, *Assoc Prof,* Clarion State College, School of Library Science, PA. 814-226-2271
Ecton, Martha, *In Charge,* Aluminum Co of America, Alcoa Corporate Library, Pittsburgh PA. 412-552-4481
Ector, Jay, *Librn,* Inyo County Free Library, Independence CA. 714-878-2411, Ext 269
Edberg, J Fyle, *Dir,* Norwalk Community College Library, Norwalk CT. 203-853-2040, Ext 261, 262
Edberg, J Fyle, *Dir Libr Servs & Libr Sch,* Norwalk Community College, Library Technical Assistant Program, CT. 203-853-2040, Ext 261, 262
Eddie, Ann, *Asst Dir,* Scarborough Public Library, Scarborough ON. 416-291-1991
Eddie, Margaret, *Librn,* Talcott Free Public Library, Rockton IL. 815-624-7511
Eddings, Dorothy M, *Librn,* Blue Ridge Township Public Library, Mansfield Public Library, Mansfield IL. 217-489-9033
Eddins, Donna, *Ch,* First Regional Library, DeSoto County Library, Hernando MS. 601-368-4439
Eddison, Stanley T, *Dir,* Plainview-Old Bethpage Public Library, Plainview NY. 516-938-0077
Eddy, Barbara, *Librn,* Memorial University of Newfoundland Library (Education), Saint John's NF. 709-753-1200
Eddy, Beverley D, *Dir,* Central Pennsylvania Consortium, PA. 717-245-1490
Eddy, Donald, *Rare Bks,* Cornell University Libraries (University Libraries), Ithaca NY. 607-256-4144

Eddy, Jack H, *Curator,* Deforest Memorial Archives, Electronics Museum, Los Altos Hills CA. 415-948-8590, Ext 414
Eddy, Joan S, *Dir,* Bloomfield Public Library, East Bloomfield NY. 716-657-6264
Eddy, Julie M, *Ref,* Colorado College, Charles Leaming Tutt Library, Colorado Springs CO. 303-473-2233, Ext 415
Eddy, Leonard M, *Dir,* University of Louisville Library (Kornhauser Health Sciences), Louisville KY. 502-588-5771
Eddy, Leonard M, *Dir,* University of Oklahoma Health Sciences Center Library, Oklahoma City OK. 405-271-2285
Eddy, Warren S, *Dir,* Cortland Free Library, Cortland NY. 607-753-1043
Edel, Betty, *In Charge,* University of Rhode Island, Graduate School of Oceanography (National Sea Grant Depository), Narragansett RI. 401-792-6114
Edelen, Joe, *Cat,* University of South Dakota, I D Weeks Library, Vermillion SD. 605-677-5371
Edelman, Cathy, *Librn,* Mercy Hospital, Medical Staff Library, Miami FL. 305-854-4400, Ext 2160
Edelman, Gayle S, *Tech Serv,* De Paul University Libraries (Law Library), Chicago IL. 312-321-7710
Edelman, Hendrik, *Librn,* Rutgers University (University Libraries), New Brunswick NJ. 201-932-7505
Edelman, Ivan Keith, *Dir,* Kings County Library, Hanford CA. 209-582-0261
Edelman, Maria, *Librn,* Niagara College of Applied Arts & Technology, Resource Center, Welland Vale Campus, Saint Catharines ON. 416-684-4315
Edelson, Arlene, *Acq,* Westchester Community College Library, Valhalla NY. 914-347-6939
Edelstein, Irving, *AV,* Massachusetts Bay Community College Library, Wellesley MA. 617-237-1100, Ext 193
Edelstein, J M, *Chief Librn,* National Gallery of Art Library, Washington DC. 202-737-4215
Eden, David, *Dir,* Cherokee County Public Library, Gaffney SC. 803-489-4381
Eden, John, *Actg Acq,* State University of New York at Buffalo, University Libraries, Buffalo NY. 716-636-2965
Edens, John, *Head, Cent Tech Servs,* State University of New York at Buffalo, University Libraries, Buffalo NY. 716-636-2965
Eder, Annette, *Extension,* Bloomington Public Library, Bloomington IL. 309-828-6091
Eder, Christine, *Supvr,* University of Notre Dame Library (Medieval Institute), Notre Dame IN. 219-283-6603
Edgar, Diane, *Librn,* Atlas Testing Laboratories, Inc Library, Los Angeles CA. 213-722-8810
Edgar, Martha, *Librn,* Melinda Cox Free Library, Doylestown PA. 215-348-4224
Edgar, Shirley, *Coordr,* Fanshawe College of Applied Arts & Technology, Library Technician Programme, ON. 519-452-4369
Edgcombe, Frank B, *Asst Dir Media & Tech Servs,* Christopher Newport College, Captain John Smith Library, Newport News VA. 804-599-7130
Edge, Barbara J, *Cat,* Converse College, Gwathmey Library, Spartanburg SC. 803-585-6421, Ext 260
Edge, Doris, *Librn,* Irwin Management Co, Inc Library, Columbus IN. 812-376-3331
Edge, Sharon M, *Circ,* University of Louisville Library, Louisville KY. 502-588-6745
Edge, Jr, William F, *Asst Dir,* Adams Library, Chelmsford MA. 617-256-5521
Edgerton, Mary, *Ref,* Tompkins-Cortland Community College, Gerald A Barry Memorial Library, Instructional & Learning Resource Div, Dryden NY. 607-844-8211, Ext 354
Edinburg, Gloria L, *Chief Librn,* Oxford Free Library, Oxford MA. 617-987-2882
Edinger, Cathy, *Librn,* Wadena Library, Wadena MN. 218-631-2476
Edkins, Barbara B, *Librn,* Peabody Museum of Salem, Phillips Library, Salem MA. 617-745-1876
Edkins, Margaret, *Librn,* Lakeland Regional Library (Pilot Mound Branch), Pilot Mound MB. 204-825-2035
Edlen, Eileen, *Asst Librn,* M C River Valley Public Library District, Meredosia IL. 217-584-1571

Edlhauser, June, *Fine Arts,* Milwaukee Public Library, Milwaukee WI. 414-278-3000
Edlin, Katherine Chadwick, *Asst Dir,* Greenwich Library, Greenwich CT. 203-622-7900
Edlund, Lucia, *Asst Librn,* Pembroke Public Library, Pembroke MA. 617-293-6771
Edlund, Norma L, *Librn,* Salida Regional Library, Salida CO. 303-539-4826
Edmiston, Dixon, *ILL,* Altoona Area Public Library, Altoona PA. 814-946-0417
Edmond, Beatrice, *Circ,* Westerly Public Library, Memorial & Library Association of Westerly, Westerly RI. 401-596-2877
Edmonds, Anne C, *Dir,* Mount Holyoke College, Williston Memorial Library, South Hadley MA. 413-538-2226
Edmonds, Edmund P, *Assoc Librn,* College of William & Mary in Virginia (Marshall-Wythe Law Library), Williamsburg VA. 804-253-4680
Edmonds, Kathlyn, *Librn,* Cass County Public Library (Drexel Branch), Drexel MO. 816-657-4740
Edmonds, Leslie, *Ch & YA,* Rolling Meadows Library, Rolling Meadows IL. 312-259-6050
Edmonds, Nancy J, *Librn,* Keene Valley Library Association, Keene Valley NY. 518-576-4335
Edmondson, Jr, Clarence, *Librn,* Cook Paint & Varnish Co Library, Kansas City MO. 816-391-6040
Edmonston, Allyson, *Librn,* Art Institute of Boston Library, Boston MA. 617-262-2844
Edmonston, Boyd, *ILL & Reader Serv,* Simmons College, Beatley Library, Boston MA. 617-738-2241
Edmunds, Rita, *YA & Librn Deaf,* Framingham Public Library, Framingham MA. 617-879-3570
Edney, Ramona, *Librn,* Oconee County Library (Salem Branch), Salem SC. 803-638-5837
Edsall, Shirley, *Librn,* Charles S Wilson Memorial Hospital, Learning Resources Department, Johnson City NY. 607-773-6030, 773-6677
Edsill, Norma, *Actg Dir,* College of Osteopathic Medicine & Surgery Library, Des Moines IA. 515-274-4861, Ext 118
Edson, Mary, *Librn,* Yolo County Library (Knights Landing Branch), Knights Landing CA. 916-666-8323
Edson, Mary, *Librn,* Yolo County Library (Yolo Branch), Yolo CA. 916-662-2363
Edson, Wendy B, *Librn,* Phillips, Lytle, Hitchcock, Blaine & Huber Library, Buffalo NY. 716-847-7086
Edward, Ian M, *Acq,* Memphis State University Libraries, Memphis TN. 901-454-2201
Edward, Sharon, *Librn,* Buffalo & Erie County Public Library System (East Clinton), Buffalo NY. 716-823-5626
Edwards, Alice, *ILL,* University of Missouri-Columbia (Medical), Columbia MO. 314-882-8086
Edwards, Anne, *Humanities,* Syracuse University Libraries, Ernest S Bird Library, Syracuse NY. 315-423-2575
Edwards, Anne, *Hist,* University of Missouri-Columbia, Elmer Ellis Library, Columbia MO. 314-882-4701
Edwards, B, *Libr Asst,* Oakland Public Library (North Oakland), Oakland CA. 415-654-0307
Edwards, C E, *Libr Officer,* United States Navy (Naval Facility Pacific Beach Station Library), Pacific Beach WA. 206-276-4414
Edwards, Carletta B, *Ser,* Pembroke State University, Mary Livermore Library, Pembroke NC. 919-521-4214, Ext 238
Edwards, Carol, *Librn,* Mason County Public Library (New Haven Public), New Haven WV. 304-675-2913
Edwards, Carolyn, *Librn,* Stockport Public Library, Stockport IA. 515-796-4681
Edwards, Cecilia, *Ch,* Free Public Library of Roselle Park, Veterans Memorial Library, Roselle Park NJ. 201-245-2456, 245-7171
Edwards, Cecilia C, *Librn,* United States Army (Womack Army Hospital Library), Fort Bragg NC. 919-396-3719
Edwards, Darlene, *Asst Librn,* International University Library, Kansas City MO. 816-931-6374
Edwards, Darlene, *Librn,* United States Department of the Interior, Alaska Power Administration Library, Juneau AK. 907-586-7405

Edwards, Elizabeth, *Librn,* Elizabeth Lund Home Library, Burlington VT. 802-864-7467
Edwards, Ella C, *Asst Dir & Ref,* Centenary College of Louisiana, Magale Library, Shreveport LA. 318-869-5170
Edwards, Fern, *Librn,* Gallaudet College, Edward Miner Gallaudet Memorial Library, Washington DC. 202-651-5566
Edwards, Fran, *In Charge,* Alabama Department of Public Health, Reference Library, Montgomery AL. 205-832-3194
Edwards, Freda, *Librn,* Altamont Public Library, Altamont KS. 316-784-5530
Edwards, Gene, *Cat,* Kings County Library, Hanford CA. 209-582-0261
Edwards, Geraldine, *Cent Circ,* Enoch Pratt Free Library, Baltimore MD. 301-396-5430, 396-5395
Edwards, Gerard, *Librn,* Avoyelles Parish Library, Marksville LA. 318-253-7559
Edwards, Grace, *Bkmobile Coordr,* Sampson-Clinton Public Library, Clinton NC. 919-592-4153
Edwards, Helen, *Librn,* Saint Petersburg Public Library (James Weldon Johnson), Saint Petersburg FL. 813-893-7136
Edwards, Herbert A, *AV Technician,* Pitt Community College, Learning Resources Center, Greenville NC. 919-756-3130, Ext 213, 229, 259 & 273
Edwards, J Duke, *Librn,* Salt Lake County Judges' Law Library, Salt Lake City UT. 801-535-7518
Edwards, Jackie, *Librn,* Baptist Hospital, Medical Library, Nashville TN. 615-329-5373
Edwards, Jan, *Cat,* Thomas Nelson Community College Library, Hampton VA. 804-825-2868, 825-2876
Edwards, Jean, *Spec Coll,* Cumberland County Library, Bridgeton NJ. 609-455-0080
Edwards, John C, *Archivist,* University of Georgia Libraries, Athens GA. 404-542-2716
Edwards, Keith, *Media,* Tulsa City-County Library, Tulsa OK. 918-581-5221
Edwards, Kelley, *Asst Librn,* Imlay Township Library, Imlay City MI. 313-724-8043
Edwards, Leroy, *AV,* Central State University, Hallie Q Brown Memorial Library, Wilberforce OH. 513-376-7212
Edwards, Leslie, *Assoc Dir,* University of Arkansas Libraries, Fayetteville AR. 501-575-4101
Edwards, Lucille, *Assoc Dir, Media & Ref,* College of DuPage, Learning Resources Center, Glen Ellyn IL. 312-858-2800, Ext 2351
Edwards, Mark T, *Librn,* California Air Resources Board Library, Sacramento CA. 916-322-3464
Edwards, Mary, *Librn,* Willington Public Library, West Willington CT. 203-429-3854
Edwards, Mary Jane, *Per,* State Library of Pennsylvania, Harrisburg PA. 717-787-2646
Edwards, Mrs John, *Chief Librn,* Bridgewater Library Association, Burnham Library, Bridgewater CT. 203-354-6937
Edwards, Mrs R L, *Dir,* George Brown College of Applied Arts & Technology Library, Toronto ON. 416-967-1212
Edwards, Mrs Ross, *In Charge,* Oxford County Library (Beachville Library), Beachville ON. 519-423-6302
Edwards, Nina L, *Dir,* Maxwell Memorial Library, Camillus NY. 315-672-3661
Edwards, Olga, *Bkmobile Coordr,* Monroe County Library System, Rochester NY. 716-428-7345
Edwards, Paul, *Spec Coll,* Graceland College, Frederick Madison Smith Library, Lamoni IA. 515-784-3311, Ext 144
Edwards, Ralph M, *Chief, Central Libr,* Dallas Public Library, Dallas TX. 214-748-9071
Edwards, Renee, *Librn,* Iberville Parish Library (E B Schwing), Plaquemine LA. 504-687-4755
Edwards, Ruth Ann, *Dir,* Randolph-Macon Woman's College, Lipscomb Library, Lynchburg VA. 804-846-7392, Ext 242
Edwards, Shirley, *Librn,* SPAR Aerospace Limited, Library, Sainte-Anne-de-Bellevue PQ. 514-457-2150, Ext 259
Edwards, Shirley, *Cat,* Wharton County Junior College, J M Hodges Learning Center, Wharton TX. 713-532-4560, Ext 36
Edwards, Stella, *Spec Coll,* Allegheny College, Lawrence Lee Pelletier Library, Meadville PA. 814-724-3363

Edwards, Sue, *Librn,* Owens-Corning Fiberglas Corp (Toledo Fiberglas Library), Toledo OH. 419-248-8176
Edwards, Susan, *Librn,* Columbia College Library, Chicago IL. 312-663-1600, Ext 465
Edwards, William, *Librn,* Mississauga Public Library (Woodlands), Mississauga ON. 416-275-7087
Edwards, Willie M, *Librn,* University of Michigan (Institute of Gerontology), Ann Arbor MI. 313-763-1325
Effertz, Rose, *Ch,* Hillside Public Library, Hillside IL. 312-449-7510
Efron, Muriel C, *Pub Serv,* Florida International University, Tamiami Campus, Athenaeum, Miami FL. 305-552-2461
Egan, Bessie, *Ch,* Winnipeg Public Library, Winnipeg MB. 204-985-6450
Egan, Doris, *Ad,* Seymour Library, Auburn NY. 315-252-2571
Egan, E, *Ref,* Lisle Library District, Lisle IL. 312-971-1675
Egan, Elizabeth, *Librn,* Indiana University at Bloomington (Optometry), Bloomington IN. 812-337-8629
Egan, Elizabeth, *Dir,* Sparta Public Library, Sparta NJ. 201-729-3101
Egan, Laura C, *Librn,* Saint Joseph State Hospital (Professional Library), Saint Joseph MO. 816-232-8431, Ext 462
Egan, Phyllis, *Libr Tech,* Queen's University at Kingston (Civil Engineering), Kingston ON. 613-547-5546
Egan, Robert, *Tech Serv,* Passaic County Community College, Learning Resources Center Library, Paterson NJ. 201-279-5000, Ext 73
Egan, Sister Kathleen, *Assoc Librn & Media,* Benedictine College (North Campus Library), Atchison KS. 913-367-5340, Ext 290
Egebrecht, Linda, *Tech Serv,* Park Ridge Public Library, Park Ridge IL. 312-825-3123
Egeland, Janet, *Exec Vice Pres,* Bibliographic Retrieval Services, Inc, (BRS), NY. 518-374-5011
Egeland, Robin, *Librn,* Simpson Timber Co, Research Center Library, Redmond WA. 206-885-4181
Egeler, Donna, *Librn,* Hansen Public Library, Hansen ID. 208-423-4122
Eger, Stephany, *Librn,* Museum of New Mexico (History Library), Santa Fe NM. 505-827-2343
Egertson, Yvonne, *Librn,* American Newspaper Publishers Association Library, Reston VA. 703-620-9500, Ext 250
Eggebeen, Richard, *Ref & Media,* Schools of Theology in Dubuque Library, Dubuque IA. 319-589-3100, 556-8151
Eggen, Deloris, *Librn,* Sisseton Library, Sisseton SD. 605-698-7391
Eggers, James, *Info Specialist,* Mitre Corp (Technical Report Center), Bedford MA. 617-271-2351
Eggers, Lolly, *Dir,* Iowa City Public Library, Iowa City IA. 319-354-1265
Eggers, Sara H, *Dir,* Old Bridge Public Library, Old Bridge NJ. 201-679-5622
Eggerss, Anita, *In Charge,* Goodyear Aerospace Corp, Arizona Division Library, Litchfield Park AZ. 602-932-7000
Eggert, Meris Morrison, *Dir,* Brooks Memorial Library, Brattleboro VT. 802-254-5290
Eggleston, Gerald R, *Acq,* State Historical Society of Wisconsin Library, Madison WI. 608-262-3421
Eggleston, Kenneth L, *Asst Dir,* Park College Library, Parkville MO. 816-741-2000, Ext 254
Eggleston, Tom, *Librn,* Ancient Free & Accepted Masons, Grand Lodge of Iowa Masonic Library, Cedar Rapids IA. 319-365-1438
Eggum, Janet, *Librn,* Whitefish Bay Public Library, Milwaukee WI. 414-964-4380
Egloff, Janice, *Librn,* Bio-Dynamics-BMC Library, Technical Information Center, Indianapolis IN. 317-849-6635
Egoff, Sheila, *Prof,* University of British Columbia, School of Librarianship, BC. 604-228-2404
Ehas, Vera, *Librn,* Clermont County Public Library (Union Township), Cincinnati OH. 513-528-1744
Ehinger, Margaret, *Asst Dir, Tech Serv & Acq,* North Tonawanda Public Library, North Tonawanda NY. 716-693-4132

Ehle, Margaret, *Ch,* Nichols Library, Naperville IL. 312-355-1540
Ehlers, Mary, *Ch,* Keene Memorial Library, Fremont Public Library, Fremont NE. 402-721-5084
Ehlert, Arnold D, *Dir,* Christian Heritage College Library, El Cajon CA. 714-440-3043, Ext 156
Ehlert, Phyllis, *Librn,* Sacramento Public Library (Isleton Branch), Isleton CA. 916-777-6638
Ehli, Gerald, *Instr,* Northern State College, Library Science Program, SD. 605-622-2645
Ehli, Gerald, *Educ Servs,* Northern State College, Williams Library & Learning Resource Center, Aberdeen SD. 605-622-2645
Ehnis, Shirley, *ILL & Circ,* Adrian Public Library, Adrian MI. 517-263-2161, Ext 277
Ehr, Patricia H, *Librn,* Northwestern Mutual Life Insurance Co (Reference Library), Milwaukee WI. 414-271-1444, Ext 3381 & 4076
Ehrenberg, Lori, *Asst Librn,* Creighton Public Library, Creighton NE. 402-358-5115
Ehrgott, Gladys, *Librn,* Supreme Court Library at Saratoga Springs, Saratoga Springs NY. 518-584-4862
Ehrhardt, Allyn, *Dir,* Franklin University Library, Columbus OH. 614-224-6237, Ext 52
Ehrhardt, Harryette, *Instrn Design,* Mountain View College, Learning Resources Center, Dallas TX. 214-746-4169
Ehrhorn, Jean R, *Asst to Univ Librn,* University of Hawaii (University of Hawaii Library), Honolulu HI. 808-948-7205
Ehrig, Ellen, *ILL & Ref,* State University of New York, Agricultural & Technical College at Alfred, Walter C Hinkle Memorial Library, Alfred NY. 607-871-6313
Ehrke, Helen, *Per,* The Medical College of Wisconsin, Inc, Todd Wehr Library, Milwaukee WI. 414-257-8323
Ehrlich, Evelyn, *Cat,* Alfred University (Herrick Memorial Library), Alfred NY. 607-871-2184
Ehrlich, Evelyn, *Librn,* National Psychological Association for Psychoanalysis, Inc, George Lawton Memorial Library, New York NY. 212-924-7440
Ehrlich, Nancy M, *Dir,* Jackson County Historical Society Research Library & Archives, Independence MO. 816-252-7454
Ehrmann, Marie, *Librn,* United States Gypsum Co, Research Center Library, Des Plaines IL. 312-299-3381, Ext 210
Eichenhofer, Donald R, *Asst Librn,* Eisenhower College of the Rochester Institute of Technology, Ellis Slater Library, Seneca Falls NY. 315-568-7171
Eicher, Charlaine, *Ref,* Southwestern University, Cody Memorial Library, Georgetown TX. 512-863-6511, Ext 338
Eichfeld, Kathleen M, *Ch,* Southern Maryland Regional Library Association, La Plata MD. 301-934-9442
Eichinger, Ann, *ILL,* South Dakota State Library, Pierre SD. 605-773-3131
Eichmanis, J, *In Charge,* University of Toronto Libraries (Institute of Environmental Studies), Toronto ON. 416-978-7429
Eichstadt, John, *Ref,* University of Denver (Westminster Law Library), Denver CO. 303-753-3405
Eichstedt, Marie, *Acq,* United States Air Force (Air Force Weapons Laboratory Technical Library), Kirtland AFB NM. 505-844-7449
Eichten, Paul, *Media,* University of Wisconsin-Green Bay, Library Learning Center, Green Bay WI. 414-465-2382
Eickhoff, Betty, *Librn,* Washington University Libraries (Pfeiffer Physics), Saint Louis MO. 314-889-6215
Eickmeyer, Alice, *Librn,* Southwestern Baptist Bible College, Dr S R Beal Sr Library, Phoenix AZ. 602-992-6101
Eide, Marge, *Soc Sci,* Eastern Michigan University, Center of Educational Resources, Ypsilanti MI. 313-487-0020
Eidelson, Elizabeth, *Asst Dir,* Lower Merion Library Association, Bryn Mawr PA. 215-527-3889
Eidleman, Mary, *Coordr,* Dundalk Community College Library, Baltimore MD. 301-282-6700, Ext 314

Eifert, P Michael, *Librn,* Dayton & Montgomery County Public Library (Northtown-Shiloh), Dayton OH. 513-224-1651, Ext 249
Eifling, Janice K, *Librn,* United States Department of Agriculture, National Animal Disease Laboratory Library, Ames IA. 515-232-0250, Ext 271
Eifrig, Janice, *Info Analyst,* Digital Equipment Corp, Corporate Library, Maynard MA. 617-493-6231, 493-5821
Eigenrauch, Jane, *Tech Serv, Cat & Ref,* Red Bank Public Library, Eisner Memorial Library, Red Bank NJ. 201-842-0690
Eigher, Beatrice E, *Asst Dir,* Great Falls Public Library, Pathfinder Federation of Libraries Headquarters, Great Falls MT. 406-453-0349
Eigler, Mrs Paul, *Librn,* Fenton Public Library, Fenton IA. 515-889-2333
Eigner, Selma W, *Librn,* Whidden Memorial Hospital, School of Nursing Library, Everett MA. 617-389-6270, Ext 326
Eikel, Sue A, *Librn,* Todd Shipyard Corp, Research & Technical Division Library, Galveston TX. 713-744-4581
Eiland, Joyce, *Actg Dir,* Cahaba Regional Library, Clanton AL. 205-755-2130
Eilers, Pamela J, *Librn, On-Line Servs & Bibliog Instr,* Cambridge Scientific Abstracts, Inc Library, Riverdale MD. 301-864-5753
Eilts, Linda, *Asst Librn,* Massena Public Library, Massena NY. 712-779-2295
Eimer, Marianne, *Acq,* D'Youville College, Library Resources Center, Buffalo NY. 716-886-8100, Ext 304
Einhorn, Judith Meister, *Librn,* South Kingstown Public Library (Kingston Free), Kingston RI. 401-783-8254
Einhorn, Nathan, *Chief,* Library of Congress (Exchange & Gift Division), Washington DC. 202-287-5243
Einsohn, Howard, *Tech Serv,* Middlesex Community College Library, Middletown CT. 203-344-3062, 344-3063, 344-3064
Eisbach, Ramona, *ILL,* Loras College, Wahlert Memorial Library, Dubuque IA. 319-588-7125
Eischied, Katherine, *Librn,* Genesee District Library (Goodrich Branch), Goodrich MI. 313-636-2489
Eisel, Marguerite, *Soc Sci,* Rockford Public Library, Rockford IL. 815-965-6731
Eisele, Anna, *Librn,* Columbia Public Library, Columbia PA. 717-684-2255
Eiselstein, June, *Librn,* Enoch Pratt Free Library (Forest Park), Baltimore MD. 301-396-5430, 396-5395
Eisen, David J, *Asst Dir,* Mishawaka-Penn Public Library, Mishawaka IN. 219-259-5277
Eisen, David J, *Dir,* Newspaper Guild (AFL-CIO), Heywood Broun Memorial Library, Washington DC. 202-296-2990
Eisen, Marc, *Asst Dir,* East Orange Public Library, East Orange NJ. 201-266-5600
Eisenberg, Hermine, *In Charge,* Microform Review Inc Library, Westport CT. 203-226-6967
Eisenberg, Phyllis, *ILL & Ref,* Piedmont Virginia Community College Library, Charlottesville VA. 804-977-3900, Ext 268
Eisenbichler, William, *Ch,* Southeast Regional Library, Weyburn SK. 306-842-4402, 842-3432
Eisenbichler, William, *Br Coordr,* Southeast Regional Library, Weyburn SK. 306-842-4402, 842-3432
Eisenbut, Cheryl, *Librn,* Medtronic, Inc Library, Minneapolis MN. 612-574-3154
Eisenhart, Adelaide, *ILL,* Johns Hopkins University Libraries (Milton S Eisenhower Library), Baltimore MD. 301-338-8325
Eisenhart, Elizabeth J, *Librn,* American Bible Society Library, New York NY. 212-581-7400, Ext 210, 211
Eisenhauer, Jean M, *Tech Serv & Cat,* Washington & Lee University (Wilbur C Hall Library), Lexington VA. 703-463-3157
Eisenman, Jean, *Asst Dir,* University of Missouri-Rolla Library, Rolla MO. 314-341-4227
Eiser, Mary Jo, *Librn,* Sybron Corp, Taylor Instrument Technical Information Center, Rochester NY. 716-235-5000, Ext 3695
Eising, Donald C, *Libr Mgr,* IBM Corp, Federal Systems Div Library, Gaithersburg MD. 301-840-7760
Eisinger, Judith, *Ch,* Santa Clara City Library, Santa Clara CA. 408-984-3097

Eisman, Harriet, *Circuit Librn,* Robert Packer Hospital Library, Sayre PA. 717-888-6666, Ext 220
Eisner, Anne Marie, *Asst Librn,* Rock County Community Library, Luverne MN. 507-283-8569
Eisner, Joseph, *Dir,* Plainedge Public Library, Massapequa NY. 516-735-4133
Eiss, Merle I, *Supvr,* McCormick & Co, Inc, Research & Development Laboratories Technical Information Center, Hunt Valley MD. 301-667-7485
Eital, Sherry, *Tech Serv,* Northeast Missouri State University, Pickler Memorial Library, Kirksville MO. 816-665-5121, Ext 7186
Eitzen, Judy, *Br Coordr (North Region),* Sacramento Public Library, Sacramento CA. 916-440-5926
Eitzman, Mrs Ernest, *Librn,* Byron Public Library, Byron NE. 402-236-8752
Ek, Jacqueline, *Films,* Indianapolis-Marion County Public Library, Indianapolis IN. 317-635-5662
Ekblad, Judith, *YA,* Elmhurst Public Library, Elmhurst IL. 312-279-8696
Ekdahl, Janice, *Art,* Vassar College Library, Poughkeepsie NY. 914-452-7000
Ekechukwu, Myriette, *Librn,* Tucson Public Library (Columbus), Tucson AZ. 602-791-4081
Ekendahl, James E, *Asst Dir,* University of Washington Libraries (Health Sciences), Seattle WA. 206-543-5530
Ekhaml, Leticia, *Ref,* Midland Lutheran College Library, Fremont NE. 402-721-5482, Ext 4
Ekhaus, Margaret, *Instr,* University of Guam, Library Science Program, GU. 734-2921
Ekimov, Rosa, *Librn,* Exxon Co USA (Alaska-Pacific Division Library), Houston TX. 713-656-1598
Eklund, Sara, *YA,* Morley Library, Painesville OH. 216-352-3383
Ekman, Sheila, *Ref,* Bentley College, Solomon R Baker Library, Waltham MA. 617-891-2231
Ekstrand, Nancy, *Clinical Med Librns,* Wake Forest University (Bowman Gray School of Medicine Library), Winston-Salem NC. 919-727-4691
Ekstrom, Donna, *Local Hist & Genealogy,* Tipton County Public Library, Tipton IN. 317-675-2526
Elam, Barbara J, *Dir,* La Grande Public Library, La Grande OR. 503-963-5621
Elam, Craig, *Tech Serv & Acq,* Texas College of Osteopathic Medicine Library, Fort Worth TX. 817-735-2465
Elayan, Betty, *Circ,* Wheeler Basin Regional Library, Decatur Public Library, Decatur AL. 205-353-2993
Elbert, Carol, *Ch,* Ames Public Library, Ames IA. 515-232-4404
Eldelyi, Diane, *Per,* Long Beach Public Library System, Long Beach CA. 213-436-9225
Elder, Beverly, *Circ,* North Iowa Area Community College Library, Mason City IA. 515-421-4232
Elder, Charles, *Librn,* Hunter College of the City University of New York Library (School of Social Work Library), New York NY. 212-570-5071
Elder, David, *Production Coordr,* San Antonio College Library, San Antonio TX. 512-734-7311, Ext 2480
Elder, Eleanor S, *Sci Res,* University of New Orleans, Earl K Long Library, New Orleans LA. 504-283-0353
Elder, Eleanor S, *On-Line Servs,* University of New Orleans, Earl K Long Library, New Orleans LA. 504-283-0353
Elder, Jane, *Asst Librn,* Pennsylvania Historical & Museum Commission, Drake Well Museum Library, Titusville PA. 814-827-2797
Elder, Janet, *Dir,* Mental Hygiene Institute, Peel Center Library, Montreal PQ. 514-844-1947
Elder, K, *Media,* Scarborough Public Library, Scarborough ON. 416-291-1991
Elder, Kathleen, *Librn,* New Alexandria Public Library, New Alexandria PA. 412-668-9901
Elder, S Jean, *Ch,* Lebanon Public Library, Lebanon OR. 503-258-5844
Elder, Valerie, *Librn,* United States Navy (Naval Facility Centerville Beach Station Library), Ferndale CA. 707-786-9531
Elderkin, Terry, *Librn,* Annapolis Valley Regional Library Headquarters (Middleton Branch), Middleton NS. 902-532-2260

Eldevik, Bruce, *Asst Librn,* North American Baptist Seminary, Kaiser-Ramaker Library, Sioux Falls SD. 605-336-6805, Ext 8

Eldot, Eleanor, *Music & Art,* Queensborough Community College Library, Bayside NY. 212-631-6226

Eldred, Heather, *Syst Admin,* Wisconsin Valley Library Service, System Headquarters, Wausau WI. 715-845-7214, Ext 35, 49, 50 & 51

Eldred, Priscilla, *Dir,* Wenham Public Library, Wenham MA. 617-468-4062

Eldredge, Bruce B, *Dir,* Schenectady Museum Library, Schenectady NY. 518-382-7890

Eldredge, Jon, *Ref, On-Line Servs & Bibliog Instr,* Lake Forest College, Donnelley Library, Lake Forest IL. 312-234-3100, Ext 405

Eldridge, Jane A, *Dir,* Eastham Public Library, Eastham MA. 617-255-3070

Eldridge, Leslie, *Librn,* San Francisco Public Library (Communications Center), San Francisco CA. 415-558-5035

Eldridge, Mildred, *Librn,* Essex County Public Library (Essex), Essex ON. 519-776-5241

Eldridge, Paul W, *Personnel Officer,* Cornell University Libraries (University Libraries), Ithaca NY. 607-256-4144

Eleckel, Joan, *Librn,* Umatilla County Library (Helix Branch), Helix OR. 503-276-1881

Elen, Ramon J, *Dir,* Dezign House III Library, Cleveland OH. 216-621-7777

Elenausky, Edward V, *Dir,* Free Public Library of Summit, Summit NJ. 201-273-0350

Elespuru, Rosalie, *ILL, Acq & Bibliog Instr,* Tompkins-Cortland Community College, Gerald A Barry Memorial Library, Instructional & Learning Resource Div, Dryden NY. 607-844-8211, Ext 354

Elevich, Raya, *Br Head,* Lancaster Public Library, Lancaster NY. 716-683-1120

Elfrank, James D, *Librn,* Granville Public Library, Granville OH. 614-587-0196

Elgan, Katie, *Librn,* Lake Mead National Recreation Area Library, Boulder City NV. 702-293-4041

Elgin, Raymond T, *Ad,* Public Library of the District of Columbia, Martin Luther King Memorial Library, Washington DC. 202-727-1101

Elgin, Susan, *Ch,* Santa Cruz Public Library, Santa Cruz CA. 408-429-3533

Elgood, William R, *Dir,* General Motors Institute Library, Flint MI. 313-776-5000

Eliasson, Dale, *Librn,* Memorial Hospital Library, Easton MD. 301-822-1000, Ext 450

Elinoff, Linda, *Librn,* Camp Dresser & Mckee Environmental Library, Wheat Ridge CO. 303-422-0469

Elisee, Bernier, *Librn,* Institut de Technologie Agricole, Centre de Documentation, Kamouraska PQ. 418-856-1110, Ext 233

Elizer, Fran, *Tech Serv,* Emory University, Oxford College Library, Oxford GA. 404-786-7051, Ext 281

Elkin, Betty, *Circ,* State University of New York, Frank Melville Jr Memorial Library, Stony Brook NY. 516-246-5650

Elkins, Carolyn Burns, *In Charge,* Florida Agricultural & Mechanical University (Library of Media Specialization), Tallahassee FL. 904-599-3366

Elkins, Elizabeth A, *Bibliog Instr,* State University of New York, College of Environmental Science & Forestry, F Franklin Moon Library, Syracuse NY. 315-473-8696

Elkins, Sue, *Librn,* Denver Public Library (Athmar Park), Denver CO. 303-573-5152, Ext 271

Elkins, Sue Loew, *Librn,* Georgia Baptist Medical Center (Nursing Library), Atlanta GA. 404-659-4211, Ext 2566

Elkins, Thelma, *Dir,* Baptist College at Charleston, L Mendel Rivers Library, Charleston SC. 803-797-4718

Elkins, Virgie, *Librn,* Chatham-Effingham-Liberty Regional Library (Thunderbolt Branch), Thunderbolt GA. 912-354-5864

Elkouri, Jim, *Tech Serv,* Altadena Library District, Altadena CA. 213-798-0833

Elks, Hazel H, *Dir,* Elizabeth Public Library, Elizabeth NJ. 201-354-6060

Elledge, Dot, *Ref,* Wayne Community College, Learning Resource Center, Goldsboro NC. 919-735-5151, Ext 64

Ellem, K, *Dir,* Putnam Memorial Hospital (Institute for Medical Research of Bennington), Bennington VT. 442-6361 Ext 298

Ellenberg, Ronald, *Librn,* Midland-Ross Corp, Experimental & Research Laboratory Library, Owosso MI. 517-723-7811

Ellenberger, J S, *Librn,* Shearman & Sterling Library, New York NY. 212-483-1000, Ext 356

Eller, James C, *Assoc Dir,* Wichita State University, Library & Media Resources Center, Wichita KS. 316-689-3586

Ellerbeck, Ethel, *Librn,* Lennox & Addington County Public Library (Odessa Branch), Odessa ON. 613-354-2585

Ellerbrock, Pat, *Librn,* Cherokee Public Library, Cherokee IA. 712-225-3498

Ellert, John, *On-Line Servs & Bibliog Instr,* Wichita Public Library, Wichita KS. 316-262-0611

Elliker, Calvin H, *Asst Librn,* Wisconsin Conservatory of Music Library, Milwaukee WI. 414-276-4350

Ellingson, Celia, *Head,* University of Minnesota Libraries-Twin Cities (Education, Psychology & Library Science), Minneapolis MN. 612-373-3841

Ellingson, Jo Ann, *Dir,* Zion-Benton Public Library District, Zion IL. 312-872-4680

Ellingson, John D, *Ref & Bibliog Instr,* Concordia College Library, Ann Arbor MI. 313-665-3691, Ext 197,121&122

Ellingson, Linda, *Cat,* Minot Public Library, Minot ND. 701-852-1045

Ellington, Ann W, *Librn,* Moses H Cone Memorial Hospital, Medical Library, Greensboro NC. 919-379-4484

Ellington, Lillie C, *Ad, Cat & Ref,* Oconee Regional Library, Laurens County Library, Dublin GA. 912-272-5710

Ellingwood, Mrs F, *YA,* Webster Public Library, Webster NY. 872-3251 & 872-0240

Ellingwood, Sue, *Acq,* Saint Paul Public Library, Saint Paul MN. 612-292-6311

Elliot, Judith M, *Librn,* Dayton & Montgomery County Public Library (Kettering-Moraine), Dayton OH. 513-224-1651, Ext 238 & 239

Elliot, M, *Cat,* Calgary Public Library, Calgary AB. 403-268-2880

Elliot, Mrs William, *In Charge,* Oxford County Library (Innerkip Library), Innerkip ON. 519-469-3387

Elliot, Myrtle, *Librn,* Lamont Public Library, Lamont IA. 319-924-2278

Elliott, Aileen F, *Dir,* Bayard Public Library, Bayard NE. 308-586-1144

Elliott, Anne, *Librn,* Indianapolis-Marion County Public Library (Nora), Indianapolis IN. 317-635-5662

Elliott, Annette, *Librn,* Miami-Dade Public Library System (Miami Springs Branch), Miami Springs FL. 305-579-5579

Elliott, Barbara, *Tech Serv,* Baltimore County Public Library, Towson MD. 301-296-8500

Elliott, Barbara, *Cat & Ref,* Bluffton-Wells County Public Library, Bluffton IN. 219-824-1612

Elliott, Barbara, *Librn,* General Dynamics Corp, Public Affairs Library, Saint Louis MO. 314-862-2440

Elliott, Barbara, *In Charge,* Lynchburg Training School & Hospital (General Library), Lynchburg VA. 804-528-6104

Elliott, Bessie C, *Librn,* Sabine Parish Library, Many LA. 318-256-2212

Elliott, Betsy, *Librn,* Harvey Helm Memorial Library, Lincoln County Public Library, Stanford KY. 606-365-7513

Elliott, Betty, *Librn,* Northumberland Union Public Library (Garden Hill Branch), Garden Hill-Campbellcroft ON. 416-797-2465

Elliott, Dena, *Librn,* Monroe Public Library, Monroe OR. 503-847-5175

Elliott, Dorothy S, *Dir,* Saint Joseph Public Library, Saint Joseph MO. 816-232-7729, 232-7720

Elliott, Elizabeth, *Dir,* Lowndes County Library System (Artesia Public), Artesia MS. 601-272-5355

Elliott, Ethel C, *Librn,* Public Library of Fort Wayne & Allen County (Monroeville Branch), Monroeville IN. 219-623-6714

Elliott, Gwen, *Admin Asst,* Bemidji State University, A C Clark Library, Bemidji MN. 218-755-2955

Elliott, James, *Dir,* United States Army (Div of Quality Assurance Technical Library), Lexington KY. 606-293-3011

Elliott, Jan, *Librn,* Barton Public Library, Barton VT. 802-525-6524

Elliott, Jean A, *Public Serv,* Shepherd College, Ruth Scarborough Library, Shepherdstown WV. 304-876-6775

Elliott, Jean A, *Coordr,* Shepherd College, School Library Media, WV. 304-876-2511, Ext 217

Elliott, Joan, *Spec Coll,* Willard Library of Evansville, Evansville IN. 812-425-4309

Elliott, Kay M, *Librn,* Iowa State Department of Public Instruction, Resource Center, Des Moines IA. 515-281-3770

Elliott, L Gene, *Dir,* Bob Jones University, J S Mack Library, Greenville SC. 803-242-5100, Ext 296

Elliott, Linda, *Coll Develop,* Fanshawe College of Applied Arts & Technology Library, London ON. 519-452-4350

Elliott, Linda, *Tech Serv, Cat & Br Coordr,* Santa Maria Public Library, Santa Maria CA. 805-925-0994, Ext 261

Elliott, Lonnie J, *Librn,* Human Resources Research Organization (Hum RRO), Van Evera Library, Alexandria VA. 703-549-3611, Ext 281

Elliott, MaryBell, *Librn,* Georgetown County Memorial Library (Andrews Branch), Andrews SC. 803-264-8785

Elliott, Maxine B, *Librn,* Phoenix Public Library (Acacia), Phoenix AZ. 602-262-6223

Elliott, Maxine B, *Librn,* Phoenix Public Library (Century), Phoenix AZ. 602-262-7411

Elliott, Meredith, *ILL,* Warren Public Library, Warren OH. 216-399-8807

Elliott, Nora, *Ch,* North Bay Public Library, North Bay ON. 705-474-4830

Elliott, Pat, *Media,* Trident Technical College (North Campus Learning Resources Center), Charleston SC. 803-572-6094

Elliott, Pat, *Media,* Trident Technical College (Palmer Campus Learning Resource Center), Charleston SC. 803-792-7135

Elliott, Phyllis, *ILL & AV,* Colby Community College, H F Davis Memorial Library, Colby KS. 913-462-3984, Ext 265

Elliott, Richard G, *Dir,* College of Idaho, Terteling Library, Caldwell ID. 208-459-5505

Elliott, Shirley B, *Librn,* Legislative Library of Nova Scotia, Halifax NS. 902-424-5932

Elliott, Stella, *Librn,* Lake County Law Library Association, Painesville OH. 216-352-6281

Elliott, Susan, *Per,* Odessa College, Murry H Fly Learning Resources Center, Odessa TX. 915-337-5381, Ext 299

Elliott, Thelma, *Clerk,* Oakland City-Columbia Township Public Library, Oakland City IN. 812-749-3559

Elliott, W Winston, *Spec Coll,* Lee College Library, Cleveland TN. 615-472-2111, Ext 329

Elliotte, Kay, *Reader Serv,* Saint Leo College Library, Saint Leo FL. 904-588-8258

Ellis, Bess, *Librn,* Linson Memorial Library, Stanley ND. 701-628-2223

Ellis, Beverly, *Librn,* United Technologies Corp, Pratt & Whitney Aircraft Group Government Products Division Library, West Palm Beach FL. 305-844-7311, Ext 3621

Ellis, Bonnie, *Librn,* New Brunswick Research & Productivity Council Library, Fredericton NB. 506-455-8994, Ext 255 or 256

Ellis, Brenda M, *Librn,* John Umstead Hospital, Learning Resource Center, Butner NC. 919-575-7259, 575-7322

Ellis, Carl E, *Dir,* Everhart Museum of Natural History, Science & Art, Reference Library, Scranton PA. 717-346-7186

Ellis, Christine, *ILL,* Pocatello Public Library, Information and Video Center, Pocatello ID. 208-232-1263

Ellis, Christine L, *Idaho Doc,* Pocatello Public Library, Information and Video Center, Pocatello ID. 208-232-1263

Ellis, Eleanor, *Dir,* Eleanor Ellis Public Library, Phelps WI. 715-545-2887

Ellis, Elizabeth, *Coordr Libr Instruction,* Pennsylvania State University, Fred Lewis Pattee Library, University Park PA. 814-865-0401

Ellis, Elizabeth, *Librn,* Reuben McMillan Free Library Free Library Association (Poland Branch), Poland OH. 216-757-1852

Ellis, Elizabeth, *Librn,* Santa Cruz Public Library (Freedom Branch), Freedom CA. 408-724-6672
Ellis, Frances, *Cat,* University of South Dakota, Christian P Lommen Health Sciences Library, Vermillion SD. 605-677-5347
Ellis, Gen, *Librn,* Mid-Mississippi Regional Library System (Lexington Public), Lexington MS. 601-834-2571
Ellis, Georgia, *Chief Librn,* Statistics Canada Library, Ottawa ON. 613-992-2365
Ellis, Gloria B, *Dir,* Walsh College of Accountancy & Business Administration, James C Gordon Memorial Library, Troy MI. 313-689-8282
Ellis, Jack D, *Chmn,* Morehead State University, Dept of Library Science-Instructional Media, KY. 606-783-2221
Ellis, Jack D, *Dir,* Morehead State University, Johnson Camden-Julian Carroll Library, Morehead KY. 606-783-2250
Ellis, James, *Media,* Saint Paul's College, Russell Memorial Library, Lawrenceville VA. 804-848-3111, Ext 221
Ellis, Janet Louise, *Librn,* United States Marine Corps (Air Station Library), Beaufort SC. 803-846-7682
Ellis, Janice, *ILL,* Buffalo Trace Regional Library, Flemingsburg KY. 606-845-9571
Ellis, Jean, *Asst Librn,* Greensboro Public Library, Greensboro NC. 373-2474; 373-2471
Ellis, Joan, *Ref, On-Line Servs & Bibliog Instr,* University of Lowell Libraries (Alumni-Lydon Library), Lowell MA. 617-452-5000, Ext 378
Ellis, JoAnn, *ILL, Circ & Ref,* Imperial Valley College, Spencer Library Media Center, Imperial CA. 714-352-8320, Ext 270
Ellis, Joyce P, *Dir,* Framingham Public Library, Framingham MA. 617-879-3570
Ellis, Judith A, *Dir,* Davenport Public Library, Davenport IA. 319-326-7832
Ellis, Ken, *Ref,* High Point Public Library, High Point NC. 919-885-8411
Ellis, Lawrence E, *Librn,* Broward Community College, North Campus Library, Pompano Beach FL. 305-972-9100, Ext 2250
Ellis, M Elizabeth, *Ref,* Sandwich Public Library, Sandwich MA. 617-888-0625
Ellis, Madaleen J, *Librn,* Newtown Public Library, Newtown Square PA. 215-353-1022
Ellis, Marie, *Ref,* University of Georgia Libraries, Athens GA. 404-542-2716
Ellis, Mary E, *Librn,* Jonathan Bourne Public Library (Buzzards Bay Branch), Buzzards Bay MA. 617-759-3921
Ellis, Melinda, *Librn,* Evansville Public Library & Vanderburgh County Public Library (West), Evansville IN. 812-425-2621
Ellis, Mrs Ray, *In Charge,* Oxford County Library (Dereham Centre), Mt Elgin ON. 519-485-0387
Ellis, P Levon, *Cat & On-Line Servs,* Central State University, Hallie Q Brown Memorial Library, Wilberforce OH. 513-376-7212
Ellis, Rachel E, *Bkmobile Coordr,* Charleston County Library, Charleston SC. 803-723-1645
Ellis, Richard, *Acq,* Memorial University of Newfoundland Library, Saint John's NF. 709-753-1200
Ellis, Roberta, *Librn,* Chattahoochee Valley Regional Library (Quitman County), Georgetown GA. 404-327-0211
Ellis, Rose Ann, *Librn,* Colusa County Free Library (Grimes Branch), Grimes CA. 916-437-2428
Ellis, Royce M, *In Charge,* Isothermal Community College, Learning Resources Center, Spindale NC. 704-286-3636, Ext 216
Ellis, Virginia, *Tech Serv & Cat,* Free Public Library of Summit, Summit NJ. 201-273-0350
Ellis, Virginia R, *Dir,* Miami University-Middletown, Gardner-Harvey Library, Middletown OH. 513-424-4444, Ext 221, 222
Ellis, Virginia R, *Actg Head Librn & Coordr,* Miami University-Middletown, Library-Media Technical Assistant Program, OH. 513-424-4444, Ext 221
Ellison, Betty, *Dir,* Attalla-Etowah County Public Library, Attalla AL. 205-538-9266
Ellison, Catherine K, *Librn,* Milo Free Public Library, Milo ME. 207-943-2612
Ellison, Frances, *Doc,* Winthrop College, Ida Jane Dacus Library, Rock Hill SC. 803-323-2131
Ellison, Jane, *Librn,* Los Angeles Public Library System (Echo Park), Los Angeles CA. 213-628-5903

Ellison, Jay, *Librn,* United Church of Religious Science Library, Los Angeles CA. 213-388-2181, Ext 26
Ellison, John, *Assoc Prof,* State University of New York at Buffalo, School of Information & Library Studies, NY. 716-636-2412
Ellison, Lucille M, *Librn,* Savonburg Public Library, Savonburg KS. 316-754-3727
Ellison, Martha, *Archivist,* Warren Wilson College Library, Swannanoa NC. 704-298-3325, Ext 45
Ellison, Peggy, *Librn,* University of Arkansas, Area Health Education Center Library, El Dorado AR. 501-863-2381
Ellison, Suzanne, *Cat,* Memorial University of Newfoundland Library, Saint John's NF. 709-753-1200
Ellison, Theresa, *Librn,* Prescott Public-Yavapai County Library System (Camp Verde Public), Camp Verde AZ. 602-567-3414
Ellison, Virginia N, *Tech Serv, Acq & Cat,* Hempstead Public Library, Hempstead NY. 516-481-6990
Elliston, Margaret, *Dir,* Biscayne College Library, Opa Locka FL. 305-625-6000, Ext 109
Ellsworth, Daryl G, *Librn,* Warren State Hospital (Patients' Library), Warren PA. 814-723-5500, Ext 356
Ellsworth, Jeanette M, *Dir,* Hopkinton Public Library, Hopkinton MA. 617-435-3450
Ellsworth, Rudolph C, *Librn, On-Line Servs & Bibliog Instr,* Metropolitan Sanitary District of Greater Chicago Library, Chicago IL. 751-5782; 751-5813
Ellsworth, Shirley, *Cat,* Syracuse University Libraries, Ernest S Bird Library, Syracuse NY. 315-423-2575
Ellwood, Marion, *Librn,* Lambton County Library (Mandaumin), Wyoming ON. 519-337-6810
Ellzey, John, *Ref,* Ricks Memorial Library, Yazoo-Sharkey-Issaquena Library System, Yazoo City MS. 601-746-5557
Elman, Stanley A, *Mgr,* Lockheed Corporation (Lockheed-California Company Central Library), Burbank CA. 213-847-5646
Elmann, Edward P, *Mgr Info Syst,* Pepsico Inc, Technical Information Center, Valhalla NY. 914-683-0500
Elmendorf, Dorothy, *Ad,* Hinsdale Public Library, Hinsdale IL. 312-986-1976
Elmer, Mrs Clayton, *Pres,* Westport Historical Society Library, Westport CT. 203-226-7656
Elmer, Wilma, *Per,* Western Evangelical Seminary, G Hallauer Memorial Library, Portland OR. 503-654-5182
Elmiger, Janet, *Dir,* Purchase Free Library, Purchase NY. 914-948-0550
Elmore, Barbara, *Per,* Waukegan Public Library, Waukegan IL. 312-623-2041
Elmore, Faye, *Librn,* Alameda County Library (Newark Branch), Newark CA. 415-791-4792
Elmore, Faye P, *Actg Librn,* Clayton-Liberty Public Library, Clayton IN. 317-539-2991
Elovich, Alessandra, *Clerk,* Mid-Columbia Regional Library (West Richland Branch), West Richland WA. 509-967-3191
Elrod, Frances, *Ch,* Mount Vernon Public Library, Mount Vernon NY. 914-668-1840
Elrod, Helen, *Librn,* Arkansas School for the Deaf Library, Little Rock AR. 501-371-1555
Elrod, J McRee, *Instr,* Vancouver Community College at Langara Campus, Library Technician Program, BC. 604-324-5418
Elrod, Lorene, *Librn,* Tri-County Regional Library (Sans Souci-Adairsville Branch), Adairsville GA. 404-291-9360
Else, Carolyn J, *Dir,* Pierce County Rural Library District, Tacoma WA. 206-572-6760
Else, James, *Cat,* Graduate Theological Union Library, Berkeley CA. 415-841-9811
Elsen, Marie, *Assoc Prof,* Saint Cloud State University, Center for Library & Audiovisual Education, MN. 612-255-2022
Elser, George C, *Dir,* Inland Library System, Redlands CA. 714-793-0871
Elser, George C, *Dir,* San Bernardino, Inyo, Riverside Counties United Library Services, (SIRCULS), CA. 714-793-0874
Elser, Helen C, *Librn,* Danvers State Hospital, MacDonald Medical Library, Hathorne MA. 617-774-5000, Ext 316
Elsmo, Nancy, *Ch,* Racine Public Library, Racine WI. 414-636-9241

Elsner, Norman, *ILL, Ref & Bibliog Instr,* University of North Alabama, Collier Library, Florence AL. 205-766-4100, Ext 241
Elson, Rita Shelton, *Dir,* Norton Public Library, Norton KS. 913-877-2481
Elstein, Herman, *Dir,* Ocean County Library, Toms River NJ. 201-349-6200
Elston, Charles, *Rare Bks & Spec Coll,* Marquette University Memorial Library, Milwaukee WI. 414-224-7214
Elston, M Elizabeth, *Librn,* First Presbyterian Church Library, Shreveport LA. 318-222-0604
Elsweiler, John, *ILL & On-Line Servs,* West Texas Library System, Lubbock TX. 806-762-5442
Elveson, Leon, *Librn,* Jewish Hospital & Medical Center of Brooklyn (Greenpoint Hospital Affiliation Medical Library), Brooklyn NY. 212-387-3010, Ext 250, 396
Elvidge, Mrs M, *Librn,* Ogilvy, Renault Library, Montreal PQ. 514-875-5424
Elvord, Zhita, *Librn,* Wilshire Boulevard Temple, Sigmund Hecht Library, Los Angeles CA. 213-388-2401
Elwell, Emma G, *Dir,* Cape May City Public Library, Cape May NJ. 609-884-3305
Elwell, Margaret, *Librn,* Humboldt County Library, Winnemucca NV. 702-623-5081, Ext 315 & 316
Elwell, Pamela M, *Dir,* Mount Carmel Medical Center, Mother M Constantine CSC Memorial Library, Columbus OH. 614-225-5214
Elwert, Charlotte, *Media,* Southeast Regional Library, Weyburn SK. 306-842-4402, 842-3432
Ely, Tamson, *Actg Dir,* Springfield Technical Community College Library, Springfield MA. 413-781-7822, Ext 3485
Elzenga, Eve, *Young Adult Librn & Program Coordr,* Henrietta Public Library, Rochester NY. 716-334-3401
Elzy, Almada, *Librn,* Houston Public Library (Hester House), Houston TX. 713-674-8769
Ema, William L, *Asst Dir,* Hyconeechee Regional Library, Yanceyville NC. 919-694-6241
Emal, Le Ann, *Asst Librn,* Dvoracek Memorial Library, Wilber Public Library, Wilber NE. 402-821-2832
Embar, Indrani, *Librn,* World Book-Childcraft International, Inc, Research Library, Chicago IL. 312-341-8777
Emberson, Eileen, *Dir Libr Serv,* Luther Hospital Medical Library, Eau Claire WI. 715-839-3248
Embler, Marion, *Librn,* Saint Luke's Hospital, Medical Library, Newburgh NY. 914-561-4400, Ext 215
Embry, Bernice, *Librn,* Dixie Regional Library (Jesse Yancy Memorial), Bruce MS. 601-489-3522
Embry, Joan, *Librn,* Florida School for the Deaf & Blind (Library for the Deaf), Saint Augustine FL. 904-824-1654, Ext 227
Embs, Ardith, *Asst Prof,* Western Michigan University, School of Librarianship, MI. 616-383-1849
Emele, Russell J, *Dir,* East Stroudsburg State College, Kemp Library, East Stroudsburg PA. 717-424-3467
Emenecker, Richard, *Lectr,* Duquesne University, School of Education, Library Science Program, PA. 412-434-6100
Emens, Helen, *Librn,* Greece Public Library (Paddy Hill), Rochester NY. 716-865-3350
Emerick, Mrs Harold, *Librn,* La Porte County Library (Hanna Branch), Hanna IN. 219-797-4735
Emerick, Ralph S, *Dir,* Trinity College Library, Hartford CT. 203-527-3151, Ext 396
Emerick, Ralph S, *Librn,* Trinity College Library (Watkinson), Hartford CT. 203-527-3151, Ext 307
Emerson, Ann L, *Librn,* Village Library (West End), Unionville CT. 203-673-3584
Emerson, Eileen, *Cat,* Flagler College, Louise Wise Lewis Library, Saint Augustine FL. 904-829-6481, Ext 205 & 206
Emerson, Frederica M, *Librn,* Dorothy Alling Memorial Library, Williston VT. 802-878-4918
Emerson, Marie L, *Ref,* Albany Law School Library, Albany NY. 518-445-2311, 445-2340
Emerson, Mary, *Ch,* Lithgow Public Library, Augusta ME. 207-622-6368
Emerson, Ruth M, *Librn,* American Institute of Baking Library, Manhattan KS. 913-537-4750

Emerson, Susan, *Librn,* Ohio State University Libraries (Agriculture Library), Columbus OH. 614-422-6125

Emerson, Virginia B, *Dir,* New School of Music, Alice Tully Library, Philadelphia PA. 215-732-3966

Emerson, William R, *Dir,* General Services Administration - National Archives & Records Service, Franklin D Roosevelt Library, Hyde Park NY. 914-229-8114

Emery, Barbara E, *Librn,* Kennebunk Free Library, Kennebunk ME. 207-985-2173

Emery, C David, *Assoc Librn for Support Servs,* University of Waterloo Library, Waterloo ON. 519-885-1211

Emery, Dorothy, *Ch,* Westborough Public Library, Westborough MA. 617-366-2812

Emery, Marilyn, *ILL, Ad & Ref,* Waco-McLennan County Library, Waco TX. 817-754-4694

Emery, Mary, *Librn,* University of Santa Clara (Heafey Law Library), Santa Clara CA. 408-984-4451

Emery, Meredith, *YA,* Jacob Edwards Library, Southbridge MA. 617-764-2544

Emery, Sandra A, *Librn,* Cleveland Public Library (Collinwood), Cleveland OH. 216-541-4220

Emery, Shirley, *Librn,* William Fogg Library, Eliot ME. 207-439-9437

Emith, Elinore, *Cat,* Tucson Museum of Art Library, Tucson AZ. 602-623-4881

Emmendorpher, Marie, *Librn,* Ozark Regional Library (Sainte Genevieve Branch), Sainte Genevieve MO. 314-883-3358

Emmenegger, Lydia J, *Dir,* Peninsula Community College, John D Glann Library, Port Angeles WA. 206-452-9277, Ext 216, 217

Emmert, Betty, *Asst Dir,* Klamath County Library, Klamath Falls OR. 503-882-8894

Emmert, Imogene, *Branch Supervisor,* Bartholomew County Library (Hope Branch), Hope IN. 812-546-5310

Emmert, Jerry, *Media,* Northern Oklahoma College Library, Tonkawa OK. 405-628-2581, Ext 48

Emmerton, Elaine, *Librn,* Hammond Public Library (Sawyer), Hammond IN. 219-931-5100

Emmons, Florence, *Librn,* Longlac Public Library, Longlac ON. 807-876-4515

Emmons, Judith, *Films Librn,* Rochester Public Library, Olmsted County Library System, Rochester MN. 507-285-8000

Emmons, Julia V, *Assoc Prof,* Emory University, Div of Librarianship, GA. 404-329-6840

Emmons, M, *Cat,* Georgia Institute of Technology, Price Gilbert Memorial Library, Atlanta GA. 404-894-4510

Emons, Paula J, *Librn,* Mahomet Township Public Library, Mahomet IL. 217-586-2611

Emper, Roseanne, *ILL,* Atlantic County Library, Pleasantville NJ. 609-646-8699, 645-7121, 625-2776

Empey, Verla E, *Librn,* Wellesley Hospital Library, Toronto ON. 416-966-6631

Empringham, Louise, *Tech Serv & Cat,* Raleigh County Public Library, Beckley WV. 304-255-0511

Emslie, Heiress V, *Dir,* Lamoni Public Library, Lamoni IA. 515-784-6686

Encarnacion, Jorge, *Asst Prof,* University of Puerto Rico, Graduate School of Librarianship, PR. 809-764-0000, Ext 3522, 3526

Encinias, Concha, *Librn,* Moise Memorial Library, Santa Rosa NM. 505-472-3101

Encke, Lucille, *Commun Servs, Br Coordr & Bkmobile Coordr,* Wayne Public Library, Wayne NJ. 201-694-4272

Encke, Lucille, *Librn,* Wayne Public Library (Preakness), Wayne NJ. 201-694-7110

Endel, Van Allan, *Cat,* Tarleton State University Library, Stephenville TX. 817-968-9246

Enders, Alice H, *Libr Attendant,* Londe-Parker-Michels, Inc Library, Saint Louis MO. 314-725-5501

Endo, Carolyn, *Tech Serv,* Metropolitan State Hospital (Patients Library), Norwalk CA. 213-863-7011, Ext 3274

Endsley, Mrs Ross, *Librn,* Sweetwater Public Library, Sweetwater TN. 615-337-5274

Endsley, Nancy, *Librn,* Indianapolis-Marion County Public Library (West Indianapolis), Indianapolis IN. 317-635-5662

Enequest, Jacqueline, *Prin Librn, Legislative & Govt Servs,* New York State Library, Albany NY. 518-474-5930

Eng, Robena, *Librn,* University of Florida Libraries (Music), Gainesville FL. 904-392-6678

Engberg, Linda, *Tech Serv,* Hennepin County Library, Edina MN. 612-830-4944

Engebretson, Mary E, *Bus & Econ,* University of Florida Libraries, Gainesville FL. 904-392-0341

Engebretson, Pat Collins, *Librn,* Belle Fourche Public Library, Belle Fourche SD. 605-892-4407

Engel, Carl Thomas, *Librn,* Lake County Historical Society, Percy Kendall Smith Library for Historical Research, Mentor OH. 216-255-8722

Engel, Claire, *Librn,* Montana Supreme Court, State Law Library of Montana, Helena MT. 406-449-3660

Engel, Debbie, *Librn,* Tucson Public Library (Valencia), Tucson AZ. 602-791-4531

Engel, Eleanor, *Dir,* Nevada Public Library, Nevada IA. 515-382-2628

Engel, Joyce, *Circ,* Township of Hamilton Free Public Library, Trenton NJ. 609-890-3460

Engel, Laura, *In Charge,* Cranford United Methodist Church Library, Cranford NJ. 201-276-0936

Engel, Ruth Mary, *Asst Librn,* Orillia Public Library, Orillia ON. 705-325-2338

Engeland, Mrs Bruce, *Librn,* Milverton Public Library, Milverton ON. 519-595-8395

Engelberg, Linda, *Soc Sci Bibliogr,* University of Hawaii (University of Hawaii Library), Honolulu HI. 808-948-7205

Engelbert, Linda D, *Dir,* Central Valley Free Library, Central Valley NY. 914-928-2114

Engelbrecht, Pamela N, *Dir,* Montgomery-Floyd Regional Library, Christiansburg VA. 703-382-3342

Engeldinger, Eugene, *Ref,* University of Wisconsin-Eau Claire, William D McIntyre Library, Eau Claire WI. 715-836-3715

Engelhardt, Aldoris, *Librn,* Carver County Library System (Chaska Branch), Chaska MN. 612-448-3886

Engelhardt, Antoinette, *Books-By-Mail,* Grand Forks Public City-County Library, Grand Forks ND. 701-772-8116

Engelhardt, D LeRoy, *Dir,* New Brunswick Theological Seminary, Gardner A Sage Library, New Brunswick NJ. 201-247-5241, Ext 6

Engelke, Elaine, *In Charge,* Public Service Commission, Legal Div Library, Madison WI. 608-266-1241

Engelke, Hans, *Assoc Dir,* Western Michigan University, Dwight B Waldo Library, Kalamazoo MI. 616-383-4961

Engelking, Ellen, *Asst Dir,* Arabut Ludlow Memorial Library, Monroe WI. 608-325-3331

Engelland, Virginia, *Media,* Dekalb Library System, Maud M Burrus Library, Decatur GA. 404-378-7569

Engelman, Alice H, *Dir,* Lake Geneva Public Library, Lake Geneva WI. 414-248-8311

Engelman, Alice H, *Dir,* Walworth County Library Services, Lake Geneva WI. 414-248-8312

Engelstad, Louise, *Cat & Ref,* Sutter County Free Library, Yuba City CA. 916-673-5773

Engeman, Richard H, *Librn,* Southern Oregon Historical Society, Research Library, Jacksonville OR. 503-899-1847

Engen, Richard B, *Dir,* Alaska State Library, Juneau AK. 907-465-2910

England, Ann D, *Librn,* White County Public Library, Sparta TN. 615-836-3613

England, Beatrice J, *Librn,* United States Air Force (Bolling Air Force Base Library), Bolling AFB MD. 202-767-4251

England, Blanche, *Librn,* Prince Edward Island Provincial Library (Alberton Branch), Alberton PE. 902-892-3504, Ext 54

England, Margie, *Ser & Exchange,* Campbellsville College Library, Campbellsville KY. 502-465-8158, Ext 272

England, Mary, *Librn,* Montgomery County Department of Public Libraries (Chevy Chase Branch), Chevy Chase MD. 301-656-0494

Englander, Evelyn A, *Librn,* United States Marine Corps (Marine Corps Historical Center Library), Washington DC. 202-433-3447, 433-4253

Engle, Emma R, *Librn,* Saint Joseph Hospital, School of Nursing, Lancaster PA. 717-291-8121

Engle, June, *Librn,* Ramsey County Public Library (North Saint Paul), Roseville MN. 612-777-5611

Engle, June L, *Asst Prof,* Emory University, Div of Librarianship, GA. 404-329-6840

Engle, June L, *Librn,* Emory University Libraries (Div of Librarianship Library), Atlanta GA. 404-329-6840

Engle, Lucille, *Librn,* RMI Co, Research & Development Department Library, Niles OH. 216-652-9951

Engle, Michael, *Ref,* Willamette University Library, Salem OR. 503-370-6312

Engle, Robert L, *Pub Bldgs Supt,* Enoch Pratt Free Library, Baltimore MD. 301-396-5430, 396-5395

Engle, Virginia, *Asst Librn,* Pittsburg Public Library, Pittsburg KS. 316-231-8110

Engle, Virginia H, *Librn,* Lancaster General Hospital, Mueller Health Sciences Library, Lancaster PA. 717-299-5511

Englehardt, Sandra, *Micro,* University of Calgary Library, Calgary AB. 403-284-5954

Engler, Lois, *Dir,* Bismarck Junior College Library, Bismarck ND. 701-223-4500, Ext 50

Englerth, Gilbert R, *Dir,* Eastern Baptist Theological Seminary, Austin K De Blois Library, Philadelphia PA. 215-896-5000, Ext 32

Engley, Donald B, *Assoc Librn,* Yale University Library (University Library), New Haven CT. 203-436-8335

English, Alison, *Librn,* Alabama Power Co Library, Birmingham AL. 205-323-5341

English, Dorothy, *Ch,* Seattle Public Library, Seattle WA. 206-625-2665

English, James, *Bibliog,* Quinnipiac College Library, Hamden CT. 203-288-5251, Ext 271

English, Janet L, *Index,* Central State University, Hallie Q Brown Memorial Library, Wilberforce OH. 513-376-7212

English, Linda M, *Librn,* Northeastern University Libraries (Mathematics-Psychology Graduate Research), Boston MA. 617-437-2460

English, Margaret, *ILL,* Monterey Bay Area Cooperative Library System, Salinas CA. 408-758-9818

English, Melda, *Librn,* Cleveland Public Library (Harvard-Lee), Cleveland OH. 216-751-9955

English, Raymond, *Ref, On-Line Servs & Bibliog Instr,* Oberlin College Library, Oberlin OH. 216-775-8285

English, Sara, *Librn,* Warren County Library, Warrenton GA. 404-465-2656

Engman, J D, *Librn,* Dickinson Public Library, Dickinson TX. 713-534-3812

Engstrom, June J, *Librn,* Huntington Memorial Hospital, Health Sciences Information Center, Pasadena CA. 213-440-5161

Engstrom, Ruth Ann, *Librn,* Immanuel - Saint Joseph's Hospital, Health Science Library, Mankato MN. 507-625-4031, Ext 2774

Enis, Alma, *Librn,* All Saints Episcopal Hospital Library, Fort Worth TX. 817-926-2544, Ext 169

Enis, Alma, *Librn,* Dallas-Tarrant County Health Science Consortia, TX. 817-926-2544

Eniti, Barbara, *Media,* Stanislaus County Free Library, Modesto CA. 209-526-6821

Eniti, Barbara, *Media,* The 49-99 Cooperative Library System, Stockton CA. 209-944-8649

Enloe, Jr, Cortez F, *Publisher,* Nutrition Today, Inc Library, Annapolis MD. 301-267-8616

Ennen, Robert, *Dir, On-Line Servs & Bibliog Instr,* Loyola University of Chicago Libraries, Chicago IL. 312-274-3000, Ext 771

Ennerberg, Erik G, *Acq,* California State Polytechnic University Library, Pomona CA. 714-598-4671

Ennis, Joan, *Librn,* Stockton-San Joaquin County Public Library (Escalon Branch), Escalon CA. 209-944-8415

Ennis, Mary Jane, *Librn,* Drackett Company Research & Development Library, Bristol-Myers Co, Cincinnati OH. 513-632-1449

Ennis, Patricia C, *On-Line Servs & Bibliog Instr,* Canisius College, Andrew L Bouwhuis Library, Buffalo NY. 716-883-7000, Ext 253, 254, 290

Eno, Gilbert, *Media,* Lenawee County Library, Adrian MI. 517-263-1011

Eno, Marguerette L, *Dir,* Blessing Hospital, School of Nursing Library, Quincy IL. 217-223-5811, Ext 340

Enoch, June E, *Assoc Prof,* Manchester College, Educational Media Specialist Program, IN. 219-982-2141, Ext 231

Enockson, Mrs Russel, *Librn,* Plover Public Library, Plover IA. 712-857-3938

Enos, Elizabeth, *Libm,* San Francisco Art Institute, Anne Bremer Memorial Library, San Francisco CA. 415-771-7020, Ext 59

Enos, Joan, *Libm,* Fort McDowell Community Library, Fountain Hills AZ. 602-837-9831

Enright, Mary, *Bkmobile Coordr,* Hamilton Public Library, Hamilton ON. 416-529-8111

Enright, Mary, *Libm,* Hamilton Public Library (Extension), Hamilton ON. 416-388-7515

Ensanian, Elisabeth Anahid, *Chief Libm,* Ensanian Physicochemical Institute, Institute Library, Eldred PA. 814-225-3296

Ensey, Thelma, *Ch,* Duncan Public Library, Duncan OK. 405-255-0636

Ensign, David, *ILL,* Topeka Public Library, Topeka KS. 913-233-2040

Ensign, Marie, *Acq & On-Line Servs,* Westmont College, Roger John Voskuyl Library, Santa Barbara CA. 805-969-5051, Ext 378

Ensle, Kay, *Ad,* Oil City Library, Oil City PA. 814-646-8771

Ensminger, Crystal, *Circ,* Fairbanks North Star Borough Public Library & Regional Center, Fairbanks AK. 907-452-5177

Ensminger, Maggie, *Ref,* Tennessee Wesleyan College, Merner-Pfeiffer Library, Athens TN. 615-745-2363

Entman, Christine V, *Doc,* Northern Illinois University, College Law Library, Glen Ellyn IL. 312-858-7200

Enty, Karen R, *Ref,* Morgan State University, Morris A Soper Library, Baltimore MD. 301-444-3488, 444-3489

Enyeart, James, *Dir,* University of Arizona Library (Center for Creative Photography), Tucson AZ. 602-626-4636

Enz, Dimple, *Asst Libm,* Carrier Mills Public Library, Carrier Mills IL. 618-994-2011

Enz, Pat, *Libm,* Red Wing Area Vo-Tech Institute Library, Media Center, Red Wing MN. 612-388-3551

Enz, Philip I, *Libm,* Larue D Carter Memorial Hospital (Medical Library), Indianapolis IN. 317-634-8401, Ext 248, 548

Enzle, Carla S, *Asst Libm,* Guernsey County District Public Library, Cambridge OH. 614-432-5946

Epp, Mary Ann, *Head Libm,* Vancouver Community College at Langara Campus, Library Technician Program, BC. 604-324-5418

Epp, Mary Anne, *Dir,* Vancouver Community College Libraries (Langara Library), Vancouver BC. 604-324-5387

Eppditi, Vittoria G, *Ch,* Melrose Public Library, Melrose MA. 617-665-2313

Eppenberger, Katherine, *Ch & Bkmobile Coordr,* Saint Louis County Library, Saint Louis MO. 314-994-3300

Epperson, Peggy, *Coordr,* Dakota Wesleyan University, Layne Library, Mitchell SD. 605-996-6511, Ext 203

Eppink, Alice J, *Libm,* Center for Applied Linguistics Library, Arlington VA. 703-528-4312, Ext 52

Epps, Donna, *Dir,* Friendship Junior College Library, Rock Hill SC. 803-327-1186

Epstein, Barbara, *Ref,* University of Pittsburgh (Western Psychiatric Institute & Clinic Library), Pittsburgh PA. 412-624-2378

Epstein, Edward, *Ref,* Asheville-Buncombe Library System, Asheville NC. 704-252-8701

Epstein, Jacob S, *Dep Dir,* Public Library of Cincinnati & Hamilton County, Cincinnati Public Library, Cincinnati OH. 513-369-6000

Epstein, Michelle Iuviene, *Libm,* National Audubon Society Library, New York NY. 212-832-3200

Epstein, Rheda, *Libm,* Department of Public Libraries & Information (Library Technical Services Division), Virginia Beach VA. 804-481-6096

Epstein, Sue B, *On-Line Servs,* Los Angeles County Public Library System, South State Cooperative Library System, Los Angeles CA. 213-974-6501

Epstein, Theodore, *Dir,* Rider College, Franklin F Moore Library, Lawrenceville NJ. 609-896-5111

Erani, Karen, *Asst Libm,* Pfizer Inc, Pharmaceuticals Library, New York NY. 212-573-2323

Erb, Peter C, *Dir,* Schwenkfelder Library, Pennsburg PA. 215-679-7175

Erceg, Lynn, *ILL,* Columbia-Greene Community College Library, Hudson NY. 518-828-4181

Ercegovac, Zorana, *Libm,* Transaction Technology, Inc, Technical Library, Los Angeles CA. 213-879-1212, Ext 130

Erdel, Timothy Paul, *Ref,* Trinity Evangelical Divinity School, Rolfing Memorial Library, Deerfield IL. 312-945-6700, Ext 317

Erdhardt, Luise, *Tech Serv & Cat,* Los Angeles Mission College, Learning Resources Center, San Fernando CA. 213-365-8271, Ext 283

Erdman, David, *Ed,* New York Public Library, Astor, Lenox & Tilden Foundations Library, New York NY. 212-790-6262

Erdmann, Christine, *Ser,* Guilford College Library, Greensboro NC. 919-292-5511, Ext 250

Erdmann, Erika, *Libr Asst,* Western Counties Regional Library (Shelburne Branch), Shelburne NS. 902-875-3615

Ereudenberger, Elsie, *Acq,* School of Theology at Claremont, Theology Library, Claremont CA. 714-626-3521, Ext 263

Erganian, Richard, *Libm,* OK Markets, Real Estate Library, Fresno CA. 209-222-0182

Erhart, Debbie, *Tech Serv,* Dodge City Community College, Learning Resources Center, Dodge City KS. 316-225-1321, Ext 220

Ericksen, Jane, *Libm,* Thomasville Public Library, Thomasville AL. 205-636-5343

Erickson, Alan E, *Sci,* Harvard University Library, Cambridge MA. 617-495-3650

Erickson, Alan E, *Sci Specialist,* Harvard University Library (Godfrey Lowell Cabot Science Library), Cambridge MA. 617-495-5351

Erickson, C A, *Libm,* Yakima County Law Library, Yakima WA. 509-457-5452

Erickson, Carol, *Ch,* La Crosse Public Library, La Crosse WI. 608-784-8623

Erickson, Carolyn A, *Libm,* Zoecon Corp Library, Palo Alto CA. 415-329-1130

Erickson, Charles, *Libr Personnel,* Chicago Public Library, Chicago IL. 312-269-2900

Erickson, Cheryl, *Libm,* San Bernardino County Library (Twentynine Palms Branch), Twentynine Palms CA. 714-367-9519

Erickson, Corrine, *Dir,* Cordova Public Library, Cordova AK. 907-424-7444

Erickson, Donald R, *Head, Technical Libr & Head, Libr Documentation Br (Actg),* United States Department of the Navy (Naval Sea Systems Command, Library Documentation Branch), Washington DC. 202-692-3305

Erickson, Donna, *Libm,* Chicago Public Library (Gage Park), Chicago IL. 312-778-1737

Erickson, Erick P, *Dir,* Leesburg Public Library, Leesburg FL. 904-787-6607

Erickson, Evelyn, *Libm,* Fertile Public Library, Fertile MN. 218-945-6137

Erickson, Floyd R, *Dir,* California State University, Hayward Library, Hayward CA. 415-881-3664

Erickson, Genevieve, *Tech Serv,* Medical College of Pennsylvania, Florence A Moore Library of Medicine, Philadelphia PA. 215-842-6910

Erickson, George O, *Asst Prof,* Saint Cloud State University, Center for Library & Audiovisual Education, MN. 612-255-2022

Erickson, Gordon, *Asst Prof,* Western Michigan University, School of Librarianship, MI. 616-383-1849

Erickson, Harold H J, *Dir,* University of Nevada, Las Vegas, James R Dickinson Library, Las Vegas NV. 702-739-3286

Erickson, Joan, *Libm,* Hennepin County Library (Hopkins Branch), Hopkins MN. 612-938-3531

Erickson, JoAnn, *Ch,* Rice Lake Public Library, Rice Lake WI. 715-234-4861

Erickson, Joe, *Libm,* Guam Public Library (Dededo), Agana, Guam PI. 632-5503

Erickson, Judith, *Ref,* University of Maryland at College Park (Chemistry), College Park MD. 301-454-2609

Erickson, June, *Rare Bks & Spec Coll,* Manistee County Library, Manistee MI. 616-723-2519

Erickson, Leif, *Media,* Muskegon County Library, Muskegon MI. 616-724-6248

Erickson, Linda, *Libm,* Westville Correctional Center (Resident Library), Westville IN. 219-785-2511, Ext 397

Erickson, Lucille W, *Dir,* Sidney Public Library, Sidney MT. 406-482-1917

Erickson, Marie K, *Acq,* Loyola University Library (School of Law), New Orleans LA. 504-865-3426, 865-3427, 865-3136

Erickson, Mariliss S, *AV & Circ,* North Central College Library, Naperville IL. 312-355-0597, 420-3425

Erickson, Marilyn, *Libm,* Union Carbide Corp, Metals Division Library, Grand Junction CO. 303-245-3700

Erickson, Marion, *Libm,* Colona Township Library, Green Rock IL. 309-792-0548

Erickson, Marsha, *Ref,* Broadview Public Library, Broadview IL. 312-345-1325

Erickson, Mary E, *Libm,* Windom Public Library, Windom MN. 507-831-2727

Erickson, Patricia A, *Dir,* Stoughton Public Library, Stoughton WI. 608-873-6281

Erickson, Phyllis, *Libm,* Clatskanie Public Library, Clatskanie OR. 503-728-2313

Erickson, Richard N, *Dir,* Baptist Bible College of Pennsylvania (Instructional Materials Center), Clarks Summit PA. 717-587-1172, Ext 220

Erickson, Rickard, *Libm,* San Bernardino County Library (Yucca Valley Branch), Yucca Valley CA. 714-365-2387

Erickson, Robert, *ILL,* Augustana College, Mikkelsen Library & Learning Resources Center, Sioux Falls SD. 605-336-4921

Erickson, Rodney, *Acq,* Moorhead State University, Livingston Lord Library, Moorhead MN. 218-236-2922

Erickson, Rodney, *Comt Chmn,* Trinity Lutheran Church Library, Moorhead MN. 218-236-1333

Erickson, Rolf H, *Circ,* Northwestern University Library, Evanston IL. 312-492-7658

Erickson, Ture, *Libm,* University of British Columbia Library (Sedgewick Undergraduate), Vancouver BC. 604-228-3097

Erickson, Virgie, *Libm,* Austin Public Library (Windsor Village), Austin TX. 512-472-5433

Erickson, W Edwin, *Dir,* Black Hills State College, E Y Berry Library-Learning Center, Spearfish SD. 605-642-6833

Erickson, W Edwin, *Dept Head,* Black Hills State College, Library Media Program, SD. 605-642-6833, Ext 2

Ericson, Christine, *Cat,* Colorado School of Mines, Arthur Lakes Library, Golden CO. 303-279-0300, Ext 2690

Eriksen, Iris, *Asst Libm,* Dows Community Library, Dows IA. 515-852-4326

Erisman, Kathryn, *Doc,* Central Missouri State University, Ward Edwards Library, Warrensburg MO. 816-429-4141

Erland, Virginia, *Cat,* Harris County Public Library, Houston TX. 713-221-5350

Erlandson, Eileen M, *Libm,* Bethesda Lutheran Medical Center, Medical & Nursing Library, Saint Paul MN. 612-221-2291

Erlen, John, *Spec Coll,* University of Texas Health Science Center at Dallas Library, Dallas TX. 214-688-3368

Erlich, Martin, *Dir,* Orange Public Library, Orange CA. 714-532-0391

Ermatinger, Charles J, *Vatican Film Libr,* Saint Louis University, Pius XII Memorial Library, Saint Louis MO. 314-658-3100

Ermel, George F, *Assoc Libm,* Luzerne County Community College Library, Nanticoke PA. 735-8300 or 825-7594, Ext 201

Ermis, Beverly, *Asst Dir & Tech Serv,* Wharton County Library, Wharton TX. 713-532-4822

Ernest, Doug, *Ref,* Missouri Western State College, Hearnes Learning Resources Center, Saint Joseph MO. 816-271-4368

Ernisse, Patricia A, *Ch,* Barberton Public Library, Barberton OH. 216-745-1194

Ernst, Donna, *Libm,* Public Library of Cincinnati & Hamilton County (Institutions, Books-By-Mail), Cincinnati OH. 513-369-6070

Ernst, Margaret, *GAO Doc Serv,* United States General Accounting Office Library System (Office of Information Systems & Services), Washington DC. 275-3691 (Br Mgr), 275-5180 (Audit Ref Servs), 275-2585 (Law), 275-2555 (Tech Servs)

Ernst, William B, *Bus, Econ & Educ,* University of Illinois at Chicago Circle Library, Chicago IL. 312-996-2716

Erovick, Mrs Art, *Dir,* Park River Public Library, Park River ND. 701-284-6116

Errington, P, *Media,* Saint Catharines Public Library, Saint Catharines ON. 416-688-6103

Errion, Jane, *Media,* Weber County Library, Ogden UT. 801-399-8516

Erritt, Joyce, *Librn,* Somers Public Library, Somers IA. 712-467-5522

Erskine, Edward J, *Dean, Learning Resources,* Macomb County Community College, Center Campus Library, Mount Clemens MI. 313-286-2104

Erskine, Edward J, *Dean,* Macomb County Community College-South Campus, Max Thompson Learning Media Center, Warren MI. 313-445-7401

Erskine, Hilary A, *On-Line Servs,* Ciba-Geigy Corp Library, Greensboro NC. 919-292-7100, Ext 2860

Erskine, Stephen C, *Dir,* Seymour Library, Auburn NY. 315-252-2571

Erslev, A, *Librn,* Thomas Jefferson University (Tocantins Memorial Library), Philadelphia PA. 215-928-8474

Ertel, Joyous, *Dir,* Frank L Weyenberg Library, Mequon WI. 414-242-2590

Ertel, Monica, *In Charge,* Memorex Corporation, Technical Information Center, Santa Clara CA. 408-987-3599

Ertell, Irene, *Dir,* Tigard Public Library, Tigard OR. 503-639-9511

Ertl, Elin I, *Ch,* Fox Lake District Library, Fox Lake IL. 312-587-0198

Ertl, Mary, *Acq,* University of Iowa Libraries (Law Library), Iowa City IA. 319-353-5968

Ervin, Colleen S, *Acq,* California Western School of Law, San Diego CA. 714-239-0391, Ext 36

Ervin, Philip E, *Librn,* United Way, Inc Library, Los Angeles CA. 213-736-1300

Ervin, Robert M, *AV,* University of Alabama in Birmingham, Mervyn H Sterne Library, Birmingham AL. 205-934-6360

Erwin, Clarissa, *Librn,* Chicago Public Library (Martin L King Jr), Chicago IL. 312-225-7543

Erwin, Jackye, *ILL & Circ,* Maysville Community College Library, Maysville KY. 606-759-7141, Ext 28

Erwin, Jacqueline, *Librn,* Saint Luke Hospital, Medical Library, Pasadena CA. 213-797-1141

Erwin, Joan, *Commun Relations,* Orlando Public Library, Orlando FL. 305-425-4694

Erwin, Laeuna, *Librn,* Putnam County Library, Hurricane WV. 304-757-7308

Erwin, Mildred M, *Dir,* Nolichucky Regional Library, Morristown TN. 615-586-6251

Erwin, Pat, *Ref & On-Line Servs,* Mayo Foundation (Medical Library), Rochester MN. 507-284-2061

Erwin, Peggy B, *Tech Serv,* Haywood County Public Library, Waynesville NC. 704-452-5169

Esbeck, Verna, *Ch,* Atlantic Carnegie Public Library, Atlantic IA. 712-243-5466

Escalera, Digna C, *Acq,* University of Puerto Rico Library, Jose M Lazaro Memorial Library, Rio Piedras PR. 809-764-0000, Ext 3296

Eschelbach, John, *Tech Serv,* College of Marin Library, Kentfield CA. 415-485-9470

Eschenauer, L A, *In Charge,* University of Toronto Libraries (Dept of Geology), Toronto ON. 416-978-3024

Eschliman, Delores, *Librn,* Minneapolis Public Library, Minneapolis KS. 913-392-3205

Eschner, Laurel, *Librn,* Tewksbury Township Public Library, Oldwick NJ. 201-832-5161

Escobar, Gabriel, *Asst Librn,* Racquet & Tennis Club Library, New York NY. 212-753-9700

Escoffier, Alfred, *Ref,* Burlingame Public Library, Burlingame CA. 415-344-7107

Eshelman, L, *Bibliog Instr,* Parliament of Canada, Library of Parliament, Ottawa ON. 613-995-7113

Eshelman, Larry, *Dir,* Eastern Ontario Library System, Ottawa ON. 613-238-8457

Eskelson, Bonnie, *Chief Librn,* Surveyer, Nenninger & Chenevert, Inc Library, Montreal PQ. 514-282-9551

Eskew, Frances, *Asst Librn,* Carroll County Library, Florine Harbert Maddox Memorial Libray, Huntingdon TN. 901-986-3991

Esling, Mrs L, *Librn,* Borough of Etobicoke Public Library (Eatonville), Islington ON. 416-248-5681

Esper, Elizabeth, *Librn, Acq & Cat,* Brockway Memorial Library, Miami Shores FL. 305-758-8000

Espersen, Susan, *Librn,* Carnegie Free Library, Hayward WI. 715-634-2161

Espino, Iris, *Coordr Exten Servs,* El Paso Public Library, El Paso TX. 915-543-3804

Espino-McGhee, Angelita, *Librn,* Detroit Public Library (Bowen), Detroit MI. 313-833-9717

Esplin, David G, *Assoc Librn,* University of Toronto Libraries (University Library), Toronto ON. 416-978-2294

Esposito, Ellen, *Ch,* Camden County Free Library, Voorhees NJ. 609-772-1636

Esposito, Michael, *Librn,* Buffalo & Erie County Public Library System (Dudley), Buffalo NY. 716-823-1854

Esposito, Michael A, *Librn,* New York State Department of Social Services Library, Albany NY. 518-473-8072

Esquibel, Sandra, *Servs to State Agencies,* New Mexico State Library, Santa Fe NM. 505-827-2033

Esquimaux, Joanne, *Librn,* Sucker Creek Indian Band Public Library, Little Current ON. 705-368-2228

Esquivel, Fern E, *Dir,* Shorewood Public Library, Shorewood WI. 414-332-2498

Esquivel, Ray, *Ref,* Rio Hondo Community College Library, Whittier CA. 213-692-0921, Ext 371

Essary, Kathy, *Pub Servs, On-Line Servs & Bibliog Instr,* University of Arkansas at Little Rock Library, Little Rock AR. 501-569-3120

Esselborn, Albert, *Librn,* Appellate Division of the Supreme Court, Second Judicial Department Library, Brooklyn NY. 212-875-1300

Essick, James F, *Dir,* Western New Mexico University, Miller Library, Silver City NM. 505-538-6731

Essig, Linda, *In Charge,* Denver Public Library (Children's Library), Denver CO. 303-573-5152, Ext 271

Essig, Mildred M, *Spec Coll,* Miami University-Middletown, Gardner-Harvey Library, Middletown OH. 513-424-4444, Ext 221, 222

Esslinger, Guenter, *AV & Doc,* Gustavus Adolphus College, Folke Bernadotte Memorial Library, Saint Peter MN. 507-931-4300, Ext 2301

Essman, Mary Pat, *Librn,* Greene County District Library (Beavercreek Community), Dayton OH. 513-426-4442

Essman, Pat, *Dir,* Mason Public Library, Mason OH. 513-398-2711

Esson, Beverly J, *Librn,* United Technologies Corp, Pratt & Whitney Aircraft Div, Materials Engineering & Research Laboratory Library, Middletown CT. 203-344-5138

Esson, Brenda, *Syst Librn,* Canadian National Railways (Headquarters Library), Montreal PQ. 514-877-4407

Estabrook, Bonnie, *Media,* Musser Public Library, Muscatine IA. 319-263-3065

Estabrook, Leigh, *Assoc Prof,* Syracuse University, School of Information Studies, NY. 315-423-2911

Estelle, Robert, *Head,* University of Minnesota Libraries-Twin Cities (Learning Resource Center), Minneapolis MN. 216-373-2538

Estes, Alice P, *Librn,* Dravo Corp Library, Pittsburgh PA. 412-566-5071

Estes, David E, *Spec Coll,* Emory University Libraries (General Libraries), Atlanta GA. 404-329-6861

Estes, Elaine G, *Dir,* Public Library of Des Moines, Des Moines IA. 515-283-4152

Estes, Glenn E, *Assoc Prof,* University of Tennessee, Knoxville, Graduate School of Library & Information Science, TN. 615-974-2148

Estes, Jessie B, *Librn,* Poultney Public Library, Poultney VT. 802-287-5556

Estes, Maryland A, *Librn,* Congregation Sons of Israel & David, William G Braude Library, Providence RI. 401-331-6070

Estes, Maurine, *Librn,* Oswayo Valley Memorial Library, Shinglehouse PA. 814-697-6691

Estes, Ruth A, *Librn,* Oneonta Public Library, Oneonta AL. 205-274-7641

Estrada, James, *Cat,* University of Connecticut Health Center, Lyman Maynard Stowe Library, Farmington CT. 203-674-2739

Estrada, Margaret, *Media,* Fresno County Free Library, Fresno CA. 209-488-3191

Estrada, Margaret, *Media,* San Joaquin Valley Library System, Fresno CA. 201-488-3185

Estridge, Carolyn, *Librn,* Prince George's County Memorial Library System (Greenbelt Branch), Greenbelt MD. 301-345-5800

Esworthy, Robert, *Dir,* School of the Ozarks (Lois Brownell Research Library), Point Lookout MO. 417-334-6411, Ext 407

Etheredge, Helene K, *Librn,* Portland General Electric Co Library, Portland OR. 503-226-8695

Etheridge, Debbie, *Librn,* Oktibbeha County Library System (Sturgis Branch), Sturgis MS. 601-465-7493

Ethridge, Freda, *Librn,* Central Florida Regional Library (Chiefland), Ocala FL. 904-493-4433

Etimov, Dimiter, *Dir,* Loretto Hospital, Health Sciences Library, Chicago IL. 312-626-4300, Ext 338

Ettelt, Darleene, *Ref,* Dutchess Community College Library, Poughkeepsie NY. 914-471-4500, Ext 388

Ettelt, Harold J, *Dir,* Columbia-Greene Community College Library, Hudson NY. 518-828-4181

Ettl, Lorraine, *Ref,* University of North Dakota (Harley French Medical Library), Grand Forks ND. 701-777-3993

Ettlinger, John R T, *Assoc Prof,* Dalhousie University, School of Library Service, NS. 902-424-3656

Eubank, Ralph L, *Dir,* Winnipeg Bible College & Theological Seminary Library, Otterburne MB. 204-284-2923, Ext 141

Eubank, Tish, *Cat,* Center for Disease Control Library, Atlanta GA. 404-329-3396

Eubanks, Carolyn T, *Cat,* Petersburg Public Library, Petersburg VA. 804-732-3851

Eubanks, Diane, *Bibliog Instr,* Seminole Community College Library, Sanford FL. 305-323-1450, Ext 450

EuDaly, Adeline P, *Acting Chief,* United States Army (Corps of Engineers, Savannah District Technical Library), Savannah GA. 912-233-8822

Euing, Barbara, *Librn,* Meadville City Hosptial, Hummer Library, Meadville PA. 814-336-3121, Ext 308

Eukers, Sharron, *Tech Serv & Cat,* Windsor Public Library, Windsor CT. 203-688-6433

Eure, Susie M, *ILL,* Appomattox Regional Library, Maud Langhorne Nelson Library, Hopewell VA. 804-458-6329

Eury, Jessie C, *Librn,* Lincoln Christian College & Seminary Library, Lincoln IL. 217-732-3168, Ext 234

Eustace, Ann L, *Ref,* Nutley Public Library, Nutley NJ. 201-667-0405

Euster, Joanne R, *Dir,* Loyola University Library, Main Library, New Orleans LA. 504-865-3346

Evalds, Victoria K, *Librn,* Samuel Bellet Library of Law, Medicine & Behavorial Science, Philadelphia PA. 215-662-2848

Evancho, Stephanie, *AV,* Carnegie-Mellon University, Hunt Library, Pittsburgh PA. 412-578-2446, 578-2447

Evanger, Jackie, *Librn,* Industrial Minerals Ventures, Records & Technical Information Library, Golden CO. 303-278-9551

Evankow, Lucy, *Chief Librn,* Scholastic Magazines & Book Services, Editorial Library, New York NY. 212-867-7700, Ext 342, 343

Evans, Al, *AV,* Morehead State University, Johnson Camden-Julian Carroll Library, Morehead KY. 606-783-2250

Evans, Anaclare, *Tech Serv & Cat,* Wayne State University Libraries (Vera P Shiffman Medical Library), Detroit MI. 313-577-1088

Evans, Ann, *Librn,* Montgomery County Department of Public Libraries (White Oak), Silver Spring MD. 301-622-2492

Evans, Ardelia, *Librn,* Harlan Public Library (Rebecca Caudill Branch), Cumberland KY. 606-573-5220

Evans, Bernadette, *Librn,* Mineral County Public Library, Superior MT. 406-822-4562

Evans, Betty, *Bkmobile Librn,* Owsley County Library, Booneville KY. 606-593-5700

Evans, Billie Faye, *Tech Serv,* Pembroke State University, Mary Livermore Library, Pembroke NC. 919-521-4214, Ext 238

Evans, Bruce, *Asst Dir & YA,* Northeast Regional Library, Corinth MS. 601-287-2441

Evans, Calvin, *Pub Servs,* University of Alberta (University Libraries), Edmonton AB. 403-432-3790

Evans, Carol, *Acq,* Georgetown University, Joseph Mark Lauinger Library, Washington DC. 202-625-4095

Evans, Celia, *Librn,* East Coulee Community Library, East Coulee AB. 403-822-3872
Evans, Charles, *Assoc Prof,* University of Mississippi, Graduate School of Library & Information Science, MS. 601-232-7440
Evans, Charlotte, *Librn,* Indianapolis-Marion County Public Library (Lawrence), Indianapolis IN. 317-635-5662
Evans, Christine, *Tech Serv,* Abbot Public Library, Marblehead MA. 617-631-1480
Evans, Connie, *Librn,* Twin Mountain Public Library, Carrol NH. 603-846-5754
Evans, David, *ILL & On-Line Servs,* Armstrong State College, Lane Memorial Library, Savannah GA. 912-927-5332
Evans, David, *Instr,* Armstrong State College, Library Media, GA. 912-927-5332
Evans, David, *Librn,* New Canaan Historical Society Library, New Canaan CT. 203-966-1776
Evans, David G, *Librn,* Ohio State University, Marion Regional Campus Library, Marion OH. 614-389-2361
Evans, David L, *Librn,* Hartford Graduate Center Library, Hartford CT. 203-549-3600, Ext 224
Evans, Dorothy W, *Librn,* Walter Reed Army Institute of Research (WRAIR Library), Washington DC. 202-576-2417
Evans, Douglas L, *Librn,* Harvey G Wolfe Library, Glendale CA. 213-241-7284
Evans, Edith P, *Bkmobile Coordr,* Pasquotank-Camden Library, Elizabeth City NC. 919-335-2473
Evans, Elizabeth, *Ch,* Scarsdale Public Library, Scarsdale NY. 914-723-2005
Evans, Emily, *Librn,* Portland Art Association Library, Portland OR. 503-226-2811, Ext 36
Evans, Estelle W, *Dir,* Baiting Hollow Free Library, Calverton NY. 516-722-3793
Evans, Esther R, *Acq,* Worcester County Library, Snow Hill MD. 301-632-2600
Evans, Gael, *Ser,* University of Massachusetts Medical School, Medical Center Library, Worcester MA. 617-856-2511
Evans, Georgianna, *Librn,* Bemus Point Public Library, Bemus Point NY. 716-386-2274
Evans, Gloria B, *Cat,* Alabama Agricultural & Mechanical University, Joseph F Drake Memorial Learning Resources Center, Normal AL. 205-859-7309
Evans, Glyn T, *Dir,* State University of New York - OCLC Library Network, (SUNY-OCLC), NY. 518-474-1685
Evans, Howard M, *Librn,* Haystack Mountain School of Crafts Library, Deer Isle ME. 207-348-6948
Evans, J David, *Media & Bkmobile Coordr,* Houston County Public Library System, Perry GA. 912-987-3050
Evans, Jean, *Dir,* Del Norte Public Library, Del Norte CO. 657-2633
Evans, Jean, *Archivist,* Urbana Free Library, Urbana IL. 217-367-4057
Evans, Jeanne, *Tech Serv,* Tarkio College, J A Thompson Library, Tarkio MO. 816-736-4131, Ext 433
Evans, Joan F, *Dir,* Greenville Area Public Library, Greenville PA. 412-588-5490
Evans, John, *On-Line Servs,* University of South Dakota, I D Weeks Library, Vermillion SD. 605-677-5371
Evans, John W, *Dir & Spec Coll,* Eastern Oregon State College, Walter M Pierce Library, La Grande OR. 503-963-2171, Ext 240
Evans, Juanita, *Librn,* Dunklin County Library (Clarkton Branch), Clarkton MO. 314-448-3803
Evans, Juanita, *Librn,* Dunklin County Library (Holcomb Branch), Holcomb MO. 314-792-3268
Evans, June, *ILL,* High Point Public Library, High Point NC. 919-885-8411
Evans, Kate, *Librn,* Green County Public Library, Greensburg KY. 502-932-7081
Evans, Kathryn M, *Dir,* Camden Free Public Library, Camden NJ. 609-963-4807
Evans, Kathy, *Outreach,* Marion County Public Library, Fairmont WV. 304-366-4831
Evans, Kenneth, *Librn,* West Virginia State Supreme Court Law Library, Charleston WV. 304-348-2607, 348-3637
Evans, Laura M, *Acq,* Huntingdon County Library, Huntingdon PA. 814-643-0200

Evans, Leona Elouise, *Librn,* Jackson Metropolitan Library (Morton Library), Morton MS. 601-352-3677
Evans, Leta, *Librn,* Parowan Public Library, Parowan UT. 801-477-3491
Evans, Lois, *Librn, On-Line Servs & Bibliog Instr,* J T & E J Crumbaugh Memorial Public Library, Le Roy IL. 309-962-3911
Evans, Louise, *Acq,* North Texas State University Library, Denton TX. 817-788-2411
Evans, Louise S, *Dir,* East Mississippi Regional Library, Quitman MS. 601-776-2492
Evans, Malinda, *Dir,* Vespasian Warner Public Library, Clinton IL. 217-935-5174
Evans, Margaret, *Tech Serv,* Hammond Public Library, Hammond IN. 219-931-5100
Evans, Margaret J, *Librn,* United States Customs Court Library, New York NY. 212-264-2816
Evans, Marilyn A, *Coordr,* Baldwin-Wallace College (Curriculum & Materials Center), Berea OH. 216-826-2206
Evans, Marjorie J, *Dir,* Powell Memorial Library, Troy MO. 314-528-7853
Evans, Mark D, *Dir,* Perry Public Library, Perry NY. 716-237-2243
Evans, Mark D, *Dir,* Wyoming County Library System, Warsaw NY. 716-786-2460
Evans, Mary, *In Charge,* Nebraska Arts Council Library, Omaha NE. 402-554-2122
Evans, Mary, *Librn,* Ohio Valley General Hospital Library, McKees Rocks PA. 412-777-6203
Evans, Mary Lee, *Librn,* Grand County Libraries (Fraser Branch), Fraser CO. 303-726-5689
Evans, Mary-Anne, *Librn,* Lennox & Addington County Public Library (Napanee), Napanee ON. 613-354-2525
Evans, Marybeth, *YA,* Hoyt Library, Kingston PA. 717-287-2013
Evans, Marylin A, *Media & Ref,* Baldwin-Wallace College, Ritter Library, Berea OH. 216-826-2204, 2205, Ext 2455
Evans, Maxine, *Ch,* Carlinville Public Library, Carlinville IL. 217-854-3505
Evans, Micki, *Tech Serv & Cat,* Coalinga District Library, Coalinga CA. 209-935-1676
Evans, Mrs, *Librn,* Tampa-Hillsborough County Public Library System (Sun City Library Station), Sun City FL. 813-634-1315
Evans, Myra, *Librn,* Franklin County Library (Cowan Branch), Cowan TN. 615-967-3706
Evans, Nancy, *Librn,* Vernon Free Public Library, Vernon VT. 802-257-0150
Evans, Patricia, *Librn,* National Naval Dental Center, William L Darnall Library, Bethesda MD. 301-652-6318
Evans, Paula R, *Ch,* Middlesboro-Bell County Public Library, Middlesboro KY. 606-248-4812
Evans, Peter, *Librn,* University of California, Berkeley (Forest Products), Berkeley CA. 415-231-9549
Evans, Richard A, *Librn,* United States Naval Academy, Nimitz Library, Annapolis MD. 301-267-2194, 267-2800
Evans, Robert F, *President,* Del Norte Biosciences Library Consortium, TX. 915-544-1880
Evans, Robert W, *Dir,* State University of New York College at Purchase Library, Purchase NY. 914-253-5085
Evans, Rose, *Ch,* Fort McMurray Public Library, Fort McMurray AB. 403-743-2121
Evans, Rosemary, *Librn,* Chariton Free Public Library, Chariton IA. 515-774-5514
Evans, Rosemary K, *Dir,* Gordon Junior College Library, Barnesville GA. 404-385-1700, Ext 271, 272, 276
Evans, Rosemary W, *Librn,* Village Library, Williamsville IL. 217-566-3520
Evans, Roy, *Assoc Prof,* University of Missouri-Columbia, School of Library & Informational Science, MO. 314-882-4546
Evans, Ruth Anne, *Asst Dir,* Union College, Schaffer Library, Schenectady NY. 518-370-6278
Evans, Sally, *Librn,* Amherst College (Music), Amherst MA. 413-542-2387
Evans, Sally, *Dir,* Somerset Public Library, Somerset MA. 617-675-1505
Evans, Susan, *Librn,* Klamath County Library (Bly Branch), Bly OR. 503-353-2381
Evans, Wylene, *Librn,* Ducktown Public Library, Ducktown TN. 615-496-7212

Evanson, Beth, *Librn,* Boeing Vertol Co, Lydra Rankin Technical Library, Philadelphia PA. 215-522-2536
Evanson, Darell, *Asst Prof,* University of North Dakota, Dept of Library Science & Audiovisual Instruction, ND. 701-777-3003
Evatt, Martha S, *Librn,* Central Wesleyan College, Bridwell Library, Central SC. 803-639-2453
Eveland, Irene, *Ch,* Saint Louis Public Library, Saint Louis MO. 314-241-2288
Eveland, Lilly F, *Librn,* Liberty County Library, Chester MT. 406-759-5445
Eveland, Ruth A, *Dir,* Camas Public Library, Camas WA. 206-834-4692
Evenhuis, James, *Librn,* Detroit Public Library (Duffield), Detroit MI. 313-833-9800
Evensen, Jeanne, *Librn,* Anoka County Library (Ham Lake Branch), Ham Lake MN. 612-434-6542
Evensen, Robert, *Creative Arts,* Brandeis University, Goldfarb Library, Waltham MA. 617-647-2514
Evenson, Jeanne, *Librn,* Anoka County Library (Saint Francis Branch), Saint Francis MN. 612-753-2131
Evenson, Mariellen, *Cat,* Milwaukee Area Technical College, Rasche Memorial Library, Milwaukee WI. 414-278-6205
Evenson, Michaeljohn, *Media,* Emmaus Bible School Library, Oak Park IL. 312-383-7000, Ext 55
Evenson, Noreen, *Pub Servs,* Columbia College Library, Chicago IL. 312-663-1600, Ext 465
Evento, Carrie, *Circ,* Connecticut College Library, New London CT. 203-442-1630
Everett, Bessie B, *Librn,* Washakie County Library (Ten Sleep Branch), Ten Sleep WY. 307-366-2348
Everett, Billye, *Librn,* Jackson Metropolitan Library (D'Lo Library), D'Lo MS. 601-352-3677
Everett, Janice, *Commun Servs,* Albert Lea Public Library, Albert Lea MN. 507-373-8862
Everett, Jennie, *Librn Deaf & Librn Blind,* Middle Georgia Regional Library, Macon GA. 912-745-5813
Everett, Mrs R F, *Librn,* Greenwood-Leflore Public Library System (Sidon Branch), Sidon MS. 601-453-0472
Everett, Patty L, *Librn,* Morgan Community College Library, Fort Morgan CO. 303-867-8872
Everett, Richard, *ILL,* Lafayette College, David Bishop Skillman Library, Easton PA. 215-253-6281, Ext 289
Everhart, Doug, *Dir,* Anacortes Public Library, Anacortes WA. 206-293-2700
Everhart, Elizabeth, *Tech Serv,* Whitworth College, Harriet Cheney Cowles Memorial Library, Spokane WA. 509-466-3260
Everley, Beulah, *Librn,* Douglas County Library System (Yoncalla Public), Yoncalla OR. 503-673-1111, Ext 310
Evers, Jacques J, *Mgr,* Motor Vehicle Manufacturers Association of the United States, Inc (Statistics Information Center), Detroit MI. 313-872-4311, Ext 228
Eversole, Sharon, *Librn,* Saint Rita's Medical Center Library, Lima OH. 419-227-3361, Ext 3332, 3523
Evert, Ruth, *Dir,* South Central Area Library, Edgeley ND. 701-493-2769
Evert, Ruth, *Librn,* South Central Area Library (Edgeley Public), Edgeley ND. 701-493-2769
Everts, Dorothy, *Librn,* Veterans Memorial Library (Rolland Township), Blanchard MI. 517-561-2431
Everts, Helen, *ILL,* Concordia Teachers College, Link Library, Seward NE. 402-643-3651, Ext 258
Everts, Helen L, *Librn,* Lancaster Newspapers, Inc Library, Lancaster PA. 717-291-8773
Everts, Irma D, *Reader Serv,* San Antonio College Library, San Antonio TX. 512-734-7311, Ext 2480
Eves, Judith A, *Librn,* Pennsylvania Economy League, Inc, Western Div Library, Pittsburgh PA. 412-471-1477
Evetts, Rosemary, *Librn,* South Dakota Department of Cultural Affairs, Historical Resource Center, Pierre SD. 605-773-4370

Evetts, Rosemary, *Librn,* South Street Seaport Museum Library, New York NY. 212-766-9047, 766-9089
Evoy, Nancy H, *Librn,* Gladwyne Free Library, Gladwyne PA. 215-642-3957
Ewald, Carlyn, *Spec Projects Librn,* Weil, Gotshal & Manges Library, New York NY. 212-758-7800, Ext 212
Ewald, Susan, *Librn,* Roanoke City Public Library System (Raleigh Court), Roanoke VA. 703-981-2240
Ewalt, Mary Lee, *Tech Serv & Cat,* Arlington Heights Memorial Library, Arlington Heights IL. 312-392-0100
Ewan, Bette, *Chief Librn,* Orange County Public Library (Costa Mesa Branch), Costa Mesa CA. 714-646-8845
Ewart, Mary Beth, *Instr,* Northwest Missouri State University, Library Science Dept, MO. 816-582-7141, Ext 1271
Ewart-Peschel, Susan, *Librn,* Aldrich Chemical Co, Inc Library, Milwaukee WI. 414-237-3850
Ewbank, Eleanor, *Librn,* Lawrenceburg Public Library, Lawrenceburg IN. 812-537-2775
Ewbank, R, *Dir & Theol Specialist,* Winnipeg Bible College-Winnipeg Theological Seminary, Otterburne MB. 204-284-2923, Ext 36
Ewell, Kathleen S, *Dir,* Montgomery County Intermediate Unit Board of School Directors, Regional Resources Center of Eastern Pennsylvania for Special Education Library, King of Prussia PA. 215-265-7321
Ewen, Sylvia S, *Chief Librn,* State University Agricultural & Technical College at Farmingdale, Thomas D Greenley Library, Farmingdale NY. 516-420-2011, 420-2012
Ewens, Wilma, *Cat,* Georgetown University (John Vinton Dahlgren Memorial Library), Washington DC. 202-625-7577
Ewer, Sandra, *Acq & Cat,* Oklahoma Christian College Library, Oklahoma City OK. 405-478-1661, Ext 337
Ewert, Genevieve, *Cat,* Southington Public Library, Southington CT. 203-628-0947
Ewert, Genevieve, *Librn,* Van Buren County Library (Lawrence Branch), Lawrence MI. 616-674-3200
Ewick, Charles Ray, *Dir,* Indiana State Library, Indianapolis IN. 317-232-3675
Ewin, Mildred M, *Dir,* Dandridge Public Library, Dandridge TN. 615-397-7420
Ewing, Barbara, *Ch,* Tell City-Perry County Public Library, Tell City IN. 812-547-2661
Ewing, Elizabeth, *Spec Proj,* Bartholomew County Library, Cleo Rogers Memorial Library, Columbus IN. 812-379-1255
Ewing, Evelyn, *Asst Librn,* Middleport Free Library, Middleport NY. 716-735-3281
Ewing, Jerry, *Doc,* Washington University Libraries, Saint Louis MO. 314-889-5400
Ewing, Laura J, *Librn,* Lassen County Law Library, Susanville CA. 916-257-5534
Ewing, Leslie, *Librn,* De Leuw, Cather & Co Library, Chicago IL. 312-346-0424, Ext 223, 224
Ewing, Linda, *ILL,* Saint Lucie County Library Systems, Fort Pierce FL. 305-461-5708
Ewing, Mrs Harold, *Librn,* Bonner Springs City Library, Bonner Springs KS. 913-441-2665
Ewing, Robert, *Cent Librn,* San Bernardino Public Library, San Bernardino CA. 714-889-0264
Ewing, Stephen D, *Dir,* San Leandro Community Library, San Leandro CA. 415-577-3480
Ewing, Susan, *Media,* Community College of the Finger Lakes Library, Canandaigua NY. 315-394-3500, Ext 127
Ewing, Ula, *Librn,* Central Kansas Medical Library, Great Bend KS. 316-792-2511
Ewy, John, *Radio & TV,* Dodge City Community College, Learning Resources Center, Dodge City KS. 316-225-1321, Ext 220
Eyer, Elizabeth, *Commun Servs,* Bethlehem Public Library, Bethlehem PA. 215-867-3761
Eyler, Carol E, *Asst Librn,* Chatham College, Jennie King Mellon Library, Pittsburgh PA. 412-441-8200, Ext 220 & 221
Eyman, David H, *Dir,* Juniata College, L A Beeghly & O R Myers Science Library, Huntingdon PA. 814-643-4310, Ext 57
Eyzaguirre, Elena, *Tech Serv, Acq & Rare Bks,* University of Utah (Spencer S Eccles Health Sciences Library), Salt Lake City UT. 801-581-8771

Ezell, Charlaine, *Ch,* Daniel Boone Regional Library, Columbia MO. 314-443-3161
Ezell, Francis H, *Librn,* Tennessee Regional Library for the Blind & Physically Handicapped, Nashville TN. 615-741-3915
Ezell, Johanna, *Head Librn,* Pennsylvania State University, Mont Alto Campus Library, Mont Alto PA. 717-749-3111, Ext 113
Ezell, John, *Western Hist,* University of Oklahoma MUniversity Libraries, Norman OK. 405-325-2611
Ezell, Margaret M, *Librn,* W R Grace & Co, Cryovac Division Technical Library, Duncan SC. 803-439-4121
Ezell, Richard T, *Dir,* Conococheague District Library System, Chambersburg PA. 717-263-1054
Ezera, Onuma, *Africa,* Michigan State University Library, East Lansing MI. 517-355-2344
Ezzell, Catherine, *Cat,* Bryan Public Library, Bryan TX. 713-823-8021

F

Faailoilo, Mrs, *Curator,* Jean P Haydon Museum Library, Pago Pago, Samoa PI. 633-4347
Faber, Glen, *Media,* Marymount Manhattan College, Thomas J Shanahan Library, New York NY. 212-472-3800, Ext 460, 461
Faber, Katherine, *On-Line Servs,* Airco Inc, Information Center, Murray Hill NJ. 201-464-2400
Fabian, Karen, *Bkmobile Coordr,* Brockton Public Library System, Brockton MA. 617-587-2515
Fabian, Merle G, *Librn,* Canadian Embassy Library, Washington DC. 202-785-1400, Ext 212 & 366
Fabish, John, *Tech Serv,* Sioux City Public Library, Sioux City IA. 712-279-6179
Fabizio, L L, *Tech Serv,* Charles River Associates Library, Boston MA. 617-266-0500
Fablinger, Virginia, *Ch,* Merritt Island Public Library, Merritt Island FL. 305-452-3834
Fabrizio, N, *Multi-media,* State University of New York at Buffalo, University Libraries, Buffalo NY. 716-636-2965
Fabrizio, Nancy, *Media,* State University of New York at Buffalo (Health Sciences), Buffalo NY. 716-831-5465
Fabro, Anna, *Librn,* Crowsnest Municipal Library (Blairmore Municipal Library), Blourmore AB. 403-562-8393
Fabugais, Violanda, *Asst Librn,* Fulbright & Jaworski Law Library, Houston TX. 713-651-5219, 651-5151
Facer, Kathleen, *Ad,* Richmond Memorial Library, Batavia NY. 716-343-9550
Fackler, June, *Librn,* Paine, Webber, Mitchell, Hutchins Inc, Library, New York NY. 212-437-7465
Fackler, Sandra, *Librn,* Central Florida Regional Library (Williston), Ocala FL. 904-629-8551
Facto, Helen, *Dir,* Mercy Hospital, Nurses' Library, Iowa City IA. 319-337-0660
Fadlalla, Gerald J, *Dir,* Glen Rock Public Library, Glen Rock NJ. 201-445-4222, 445-4223
Fadley, Pauline, *Librn,* Sycamore Community Library, Sycamore OH. 419-927-2407
Fadum, H, *Tech Serv,* Malaspina College, Learning Resources Center, Nanaimo BC. 604-753-3245
Faerber, Esther, *Librn,* Houston Public Library (Institutional Services), Houston TX. 713-869-9046
Fagan, Bertha, *Dir,* Adair Public Library, Adair IA. 515-742-3323
Fagan, George V, *Librn,* Colorado College, Charles Leaming Tutt Library, Colorado Springs CO. 303-473-2233, Ext 415
Fagan, Hewlett, *Acq,* State University of New York, Agricultural & Technical College at Norrisville Library, Morrisville NY. 315-684-7055
Fagan, Nancy, *Librn,* Carroll County Public Library (Northeast), Hampstead MD. 301-374-9000
Fagan, Sister Matilda, *Curric & AV,* Incarnate Word College, Saint Pius X Library, San Antonio TX. 512-828-1261, Ext 215
Fagan, Wanda M, *Librn,* Omaha Public Library (Kellom), Omaha NE. 402-444-4847

Fagen, Diane A, *Librn,* Rockford Memorial Hospital, School of Nursing Library, Rockford IL. 815-968-6861
Fagen, Nancy, *Exec Dir,* Philadelphia Fellowship Commission Library, Philadelphia PA. 215-546-7600
Fagerlie, Joan, *Head,* University of Minnesota Libraries-Twin Cities (Interlibrary Loan), Minneapolis MN. 612-373-3259
Faget, Carolyn, *Media & Acq,* Laney College Library-Learning Resources Center, Oakland CA. 415-763-4791
Faggiani, Irene, *Ch,* East Islip Public Library, East Islip NY. 516-581-9200, 581-9228
Fahey, Barbara, *Doc,* Fond Du Lac City-County Library Service, Fond du Lac WI. 414-921-3670
Fahey, James L, *Librn,* Pope John XXIII National Seminary Library, Weston MA. 617-899-5500, Ext 1
Fahey, Katherine H, *Librn,* Fidelity & Deposit Co of Maryland, Law Library, Baltimore MD. 301-539-0800, Ext 204
Fahey, Marianne, *Tech Serv & On-Line Servs,* Saint Joseph's College, McEntegart Hall Library, Brooklyn NY. 212-789-5383
Fahey, Mary, *Dir,* Harrison Public Library, Harrison NJ. 201-483-2366
Fahnestock, Frank, *Librn,* Hawaii State Library System (Lahaina Branch), Lahaina HI. 808-661-0566
Fahrbach, Helen, *Spec Servs,* Elisha D Smith Public Library, Menasha WI. 414-729-5166
Fahrenbach, Betty, *Ref,* Alhambra Public Library, Alhambra CA. 213-570-5008
Fahrenbach, Jean R, *Dir,* Tomkins Cove Public Library, Tomkins Cove NY. 914-786-3060
Faibisoff, Sylvia G, *Chairperson,* Northern Illinois University, Dept of Library Science, IL. 815-753-1735
Faidley, Charles, *Librn,* Public Library of Cincinnati & Hamilton County (Groesbeck), Cincinnati OH. 513-522-2997
Faigel, Martin, *Dir, Acq & Spec Coll,* University of Alabama, Amelia Gayle Gorgas Library, University AL. 205-348-5298
Faille, F, *Cat,* LaSalle Municipal Library, Bibliotheque Municipale La Salle, La Salle PQ. 514-366-2582
Fain, Elaine F, *Asst Prof,* University of Wisconsin-Milwaukee, School of Library Science, WI. 414-963-4707
Fair, Agnes, *Ref,* Middle Tennessee State University, Andrew L Todd Library, Murfreesboro TN. 615-898-2622
Fair, Agnes H Mills, *Instr,* Middle Tennessee State University, Department of Library Service, TN. 615-898-2740 & 898-5555
Fair, Brenda J, *Tech Serv,* Lane College, J K Daniels Library, Jackson TN. 901-424-4600, Ext 274
Fairbairn, Louise, *Librn,* Carnegie Public, Tekamah Public Library, Tekamah NE. 402-374-2453
Fairbanks, Eleanor, *Librn,* Oberlin College Library (Class of 1904 Science Library), Oberlin OH. 216-775-8310
Fairbanks, Mary, *Librn,* Snow College, Lucy A Phillips Library, Ephraim UT. 801-283-4201, Ext 204
Fairbarn, Sophia, *Librn,* Georgina Public Library Administration (Keswick), Keswick ON. 416-476-5762
Fairbrother, Cynthia, *Ref,* Bernardsville Public Library, Bernardsville NJ. 201-766-0118
Fairchild, Cindy, *Dir,* LaSalle Parish Library, Jena LA. 318-992-5675
Fairchild, Judith, *Asst Dir,* Buhl Public Library, Buhl ID. 208-543-6500
Fairchild, Martha, *Librn,* New Fairfield Free Library, New Fairfield CT. 203-746-9297
Fairchild, Mrs Willie E, *Librn,* Friona Public Library, Friona TX. 806-247-3200
Fairchild, Pat, *Cat,* Albuquerque Technical-Vocational Institute, Instructional Materials Center, Albuquerque NM. 505-843-7250, Ext 243
Fairclough, G Thomas, *Librn,* Burkburnett Library, Burkburnett TX. 817-569-2991
Fairclough, Sharon, *YA,* Nevada County Library, Nevada City CA. 916-265-2461, Ext 244
Faird, Susan L, *Librn,* Parkview Memorial Hospital, Parkview Methodist School of Nursing Library, Fort Wayne IN. 219-484-6636, Ext 2605

FAIRE

Faire, Sandra, *Support Servs,* Upland Public Library, Upland CA. 714-982-1561

Faireloth, Barbara, *Bkmobile Coordr,* Sampson-Clinton Public Library, Clinton NC. 919-592-4153

Faires, Jane, *Cat,* Pomona Public Library, Pomona CA. 714-620-2033

Fairfield, J M, *Librn,* Markham Municipal Public Library, Thornhill ON. 416-881-5668

Fairfield, Marianne, *Librn,* Cuyahoga County Public Library (Brook Park Branch), Brook Park OH. 216-267-5250

Fairley, Mary, *Ch,* North Platte Public Library, Lincoln Keith Perkins Regional Library, North Platte NE. 308-532-6560

Faison, Moses, *Librn,* Albany Dougherty Public Library (Lee), Albany GA. 912-436-5019

Fait, Kathy, *Librn,* Wisconsin State Department of Transportation Libraries (Planning Div Library), Madison WI. 608-266-0724

Faivre, Patricia Le, *YA & Ref,* Sweetwater County Library, Green River WY. 307-875-3615

Fajardo, Lieselotte, *Bibliog Instr,* University of California, Santa Barbara Library, Santa Barbara CA. 805-961-2741

Falato, Kimberly S, *Librn,* Peoria Heights Public Library, Peoria Heights IL. 309-682-5578

Falby, Irene, *Asst Librn,* South Hero Community Library, South Hero VT. 802-372-6600

Falck, P, *Admin Coordr,* Western Behavioral Sciences Institute Library, La Jolla CA. 714-459-3811

Falco, Ruth, *In Charge,* Halcon International Inc, Technical Information Center, New York NY. 212-689-1222

Falconer, Shirley, *Supvr,* Huron County Public Library (Clinton Branch), Clinton ON. 519-482-3673, 482-7513

Fales, Claudine, *Asst Dir,* Rogers Free Library, Bristol RI. 401-253-6948

Falger, David E, *Chief Librn,* Veterans Administration, Medical Library, Philadelphia PA. 215-382-2400

Falgione, Joseph F, *Assoc Dir,* Carnegie Library of Pittsburgh, Pittsburgh PA. 412-622-3100

Faliski, Jean, *Librn,* Bay County Public Library Association (Port Saint Joe Branch), Port Saint Joe FL. 904-229-8879

Falk, Gretchen, *Ref,* Park Forest Public Library, Park Forest IL. 312-748-3731

Falk, Joyce Duncan, *Dir & On-Line Servs,* American Bibliographical Center of ABC-CLIO, Inc, Inge Boehm Library, Santa Barbara CA. 805-963-4221

Falk, Marvin, *Arctic Bibliogr,* University of Alaska, Fairbanks, Elmer E Rasmuson Library, Fairbanks AK. 907-479-7224

Falkenberg, Cora, *Br Coordr & Exten Servs,* Sudbury Public Library, La Bibliotheque Publique de Sudbury, Sudbury ON. 705-673-1155

Falkenstien, Anne, *Librn,* Pottawatomie-Wabaunsee Regional Library (Onaga Branch), Onaga KS. 913-889-4531

Falkner, Etta, *Librn,* Old Sturbridge Village, Research Library, Sturbridge MA. 617-347-3362, Ext 132

Fall, Anna Lou, *Br Coordr,* Fullerton City Library, Fullerton CA. 714-738-6333, Ext 301

Fall, Anna Lou, *Librn,* Fullerton City Library (Hunt Public Library), Fullerton CA. 714-871-9450

Fall, H Cutler, *Librn,* Wilkes College (Wilkes College Music Library), Wilkes-Barre PA. 717-824-4651, Ext 341

Fall, James E, *Technical Support Staff: Dir,* Columbia University (University Libraries), New York NY. 212-280-2241

Fall, Mrs C R, *Librn,* Laurel-Jones County Library (Ellisville Branch), Ellisville MS. 601-428-4313

Fall, Mrs Ernest, *Librn,* Laurel-Jones County Library (Sandersville Branch), Sandersville MS. 601-428-4313

Falla, Bonnie, *Ch,* Sheffield Public Library, Sheffield IL. 815-454-2628

Faller, Martha, *ILL,* Niagara County Community College, Library Learning Center, Sanborn NY. 716-731-3271, Ext 145

Fallert, Florence, *Tech Serv,* Auburn Public Library, Auburn WA. 206-931-3018

Fallerton, Sylvia, *Sci,* Dalhousie University, Izaak Walton Killam Memorial Library (Humanities & Social Sciences), Macdonald Memorial Library (Science), Halifax NS. 902-424-3601

Fallis, Margaret G, *Circ, Ref & On-Line Servs,* Philadelphia College of Pharmacy & Science, Joseph W England Library, Philadelphia PA. 215-386-5800, Ext 296

Fallis, Stuart, *ILL,* Wayne Public Library, Wayne NJ. 201-694-4272

Fallon, Marcia, *Per,* Miami Dade Community College (Niles Trammel Learning Resources), Miami FL. 305-596-1293

Fallon, Phyllis, *Librn,* Montana State Department of Natural Resources & Conservation, Helena MT. 406-449-3712

Fallon, Robert P, *Librn,* Prudential Insurance Co of America (Business Library), Newark NJ. 201-877-6747

Falls, Corrine, *Cat,* Public Library of Steubenville & Jefferson County, Steubenville OH. 614-282-9782

Falsone, Anne Marie, *Deputy State Librn & Asst Commissioner,* Colorado State Library, Colorado Department of Education, Denver CO. 303-839-3695

Falvey, Mary, *Librn,* Technomic Consultant Library, Chicago IL. 312-346-5900

Famera, Karen McNerney, *Librn,* American Music Center, Inc Library, New York NY. 212-247-3121

Famularo, Sabiha, *Cat,* Johns Hopkins University School of Advanced International Studies, Sydney R & Elsa W Mason Library, Washington DC. 202-785-6296

Fancher, Evelyn P, *Dir,* Tennessee State University, Martha M Brown - Lois W Daniel Library, Nashville TN. 615-320-3682, 251-1417

Fancher, Marsha, *Tech Resource Asst,* Alan M Voorhees & Associates Library, Planning Research Corp, McLean VA. 703-893-1440

Fancy, Mrs M, *Spec Coll,* Mount Allison University, Ralph Pickard Bell Library, Sackville NB. 506-536-2040, Ext 375

Fanelli, Michelle, *Acq,* Fairleigh Dickinson University, Weiner Library, Teaneck NJ. 201-836-6300, Ext 265

Fanestil, Richard E, *Librn,* Montana State Library (Warm Springs State Hospital, Patient Library), Warm Springs MT. 406-693-2221, Ext 2447

Fang, Josephine R, *Prof,* Simmons College, Graduate School of Library & Information Science, MA. 617-738-2225

Fangman, Philip, *Coll Develop,* Washoe County Library, Reno NV. 702-785-4039

Fankhauser, Linda M, *Dir,* Toledo Hospital Library, Toledo OH. 419-473-4405

Fankhauser, Marcy R, *Acq,* McAllen Memorial Library, McAllen TX. 512-682-4531

Fannin, Wanda, *Dir,* Iraan Public Library, Iraan TX. 915-639-2235

Fanning, Darlene, *Circ,* Waubonsee Community College, Learning Resources Center, Sugar Grove IL. 312-466-4811, Ext 303

Fanning, Thelma E, *Librn,* Nanton Municipal Library, Nanton AB. 403-486-2858

Fanning, Virginia H, *Chmn,* Concord College, Library Science Dept, WV. 304-384-3115

Fannon, Elizabeth, *In Charge,* Cleveland Public Library (Documents Collection), Cleveland OH. 216-623-2870

Fannon, Lynette, *On-Line Servs,* University of Washington Libraries, Seattle WA. 206-543-1760

Fanoele, Dorothy, *Dir,* Columbus Public Library, Columbus KS. 316-429-2086

Fansher, Virginia, *Librn,* Public Library of Cincinnati & Hamilton County (Parkdale), Cincinnati OH. 513-851-3929

Fant, Katherine, *Ch,* Gulfport-Harrison County Library, Gulfport MS. 601-863-6411

Fanta, David P, *Asst Librn,* Chapman & Cutler, Law Library, Chicago IL. 312-726-6130, Ext 449

Faoro, Madge, *Info Serv,* Davenport Public Library, Davenport IA. 319-326-7832

Farace, Virginia K, *Dir, Ad & Acq,* Boynton Beach City Library, Boynton Beach FL. 732-2624 or 732-8111, Ext 223, 224 & 225

Farand, Lorraine, *Ch,* Emma S Clark Memorial Library, Setauket NY. 516-941-4080

Farber, Ann, *Tech Serv,* Union College, MacKay Library-Learning Resource Center, Cranford NJ. 201-276-2600, Ext 244

Farber, Dorothy, *Librn,* Free Public Library of Independence, Independence IA. 319-334-2470

Farber, Evan Ira, *Dir,* Earlham College, Lilly Library, Richmond IN. 317-962-6561, Ext 360

Farbstein, Ellen, *Librn,* Huntington Beach Library (Banning St Annex), Huntington Beach CA. 714-962-6664

Farbstein, Ellen, *Librn,* Huntington Beach Library (Graham St Annex), Huntington Beach CA. 714-894-1307

Farbstein, Ellen, *Br Coordr,* Huntington Beach Library, Information & Cultural Resource Center, Huntington Beach CA. 714-842-4481

Farbstein, Ellen, *Librn,* Huntington Beach Library (Main St), Huntington Beach CA. 714-960-3344

Farcas, Jane, *Dir,* Saint Matthew's & Saint Timothy's Neighborhood Center, Inc Library, New York NY. 212-362-6750

Fardig, Elsie, *Librn,* University of Miami (Music), Coral Gables FL. 305-284-2429

Farhat, Fred, *Mgr Libr Servs,* Kaiser Aluminum & Chemical Corp, Ctr for Technology, Technical Information Ctr Library, Pleasanton CA. 415-462-1122

Farid, Kamil, *Librn,* Brooklyn Public Library (Ryder), Brooklyn NY. 212-232-5064

Farid, M M, *Librn, On-Line Servs & Bibliog Instr,* Rockwell International (Information Center), Pittsburgh PA. 412-247-3095

Farid, Mona, *Asst Prof,* Syracuse University, School of Information Studies, NY. 315-423-2911

Faris, Mary C, *Doc,* Texas Christian University, Mary Couts Burnett Library, Fort Worth TX. 817-921-7106

Farish, Don E, *Reader Serv,* Texas State Library, Division for the Blind & Physically Handicapped, Austin TX. 512-475-4758

Farish, Terry, *Dir,* Ralston Public Library, Ralston NE. 402-331-7636

Fark, Ronald K, *Head Circ Librn,* Brown University (University Library), Providence RI. 401-863-2167

Farkas, Andrew, *Dir,* University of North Florida Library, Jacksonville FL. 904-646-2553

Farkas, Andrew, *Dir Prof,* University of North Florida, Library Science Program, FL. 904-646-2553

Farkas, Charles R, *Dir,* Briarcliff Manor Public Library, Briarcliff Manor NY. 914-941-7072

Farkas, Elizabeth, *Acq,* Regis College Library, Weston MA. 617-893-1820, Ext 252

Farkas, Eugene, *Chief, Educ Resources Div,* National Agricultural Library, Beltsville MD. 301-344-4248

Farkas, Susan, *Librn,* Atomic Industrial Forum Library, Washington DC. 301-654-9260

Farley, David J, *Asst Dir for Admin,* Marquette University Memorial Library, Milwaukee WI. 414-224-7214

Farley, Earl, *Dir,* University of Kansas Medical Center, College of Health Sciences & Hospital, Clendening Library, Kansas City KS. 913-588-7166

Farley, Elizabeth, *Ch,* North Merrick Public Library, North Merrick NY. 516-378-7474

Farley, Frances, *Asst Librn,* Tecumseh Public Library, Tecumseh NE. 402-335-2060

Farley, Janet L, *Librn,* Warren Memorial Library, Westbrook ME. 207-854-5891

Farley, Janice S, *Dir,* Arrowhead Library System, Janesville WI. 608-755-2490

Farley, Joanne, *Dir,* Federal Reserve Bank of Minneapolis Library, Minneapolis MN. 612-340-2292

Farley, John, *Actg Dir,* State University of New York at Albany Library, Albany NY. 518-457-8542

Farley, John J, *Prof,* State University of New York at Albany, School of Library & Information Science, NY. 518-455-6288

Farley, Laine, *Humanities,* Stephen F Austin State University, Ralph W Steen Library, Nacogdoches TX. 713-569-4109

Farley, Richard, *Chmn,* United States Department of Agriculture Graduate School, Certificate Program for Library Technicians, DC. 202-447-5885

Farley, Richard A, *Dep Dir for Tech Info Systs,* National Agricultural Library, Beltsville MD. 301-344-4248

Farley, Sally, *Librn,* Barton Library (Smackover Branch), Smackover AR. 501-725-3741

Farmann, Kathleen, *Law Librn,* University of Notre Dame Library (Law School Library), Notre Dame IN. 219-283-7024

Farmann, Stanley, *Assoc Librn,* University of Notre Dame Library (Law School Library), Notre Dame IN. 219-283-7024

Farmer, Ann, *Librn,* Spencer Public Library, Spencer NC. 704-636-9072

Farmer, David, *Spec Coll,* University of Tulsa, McFarlin Library, Tulsa OK. 918-592-6000, Ext 351

Farmer, Diana M, *Acq & Ser,* Kansas State University, Farrell Library, Manhattan KS. 913-532-6516

Farmer, Edna, *Acq,* North Carolina Wesleyan College Library, Rocky Mount NC. 919-442-7121, Ext 280, 283

Farmer, Gregory, *Curator,* Connecticut Valley Historical Museum Library, Springfield MA. 413-732-3080

Farmer, Linda G, *Librn,* Jackson-Madison County General Hospital, Learning Center Library, Jackson TN. 901-424-0424

Farmer, M, *ILL & On-Line Servs,* Veterans Administration, Medical Center Library, Milwaukee WI. 414-384-2000, Ext 2354

Farmer, Mabel, *Librn,* College of Fisheries, Navigation, Marine Engineering & Electronics Library, Saint John's NF. 709-726-5272

Farmer, Malcolm F, *Dir,* Whittier College (Learning Resources Center), Whittier CA. 213-693-0771, Ext 266

Farmer, Ruth, *Acq,* University of Central Arkansas, Torreyson Library, Conway AR. 501-329-2931, Ext 449

Farnell, Margaret, *Ref,* University of Alberta (University Libraries), Edmonton AB. 403-432-3790

Farney, Patricia, *Tech Serv,* Rock Valley College Educational Resources Center, Rockford IL. 815-226-3762

Farnsley, Charles P, *Pres,* Filson Club Library, Louisville KY. 502-582-3727

Farnsworth, Mary Lee, *Asst Librn,* Wallowa County Library, Enterprise OR. 503-426-3969

Farquharson, Connie, *Librn,* Sudbury Public Library (W Clarence Sinclair), Sudbury ON. 705-673-1155, Ext 43

Farr, Elisabeth, *Asst Librn,* Charlotte E Hobbs Memorial Library, Lovell ME. 207-925-3025

Farr, Julie, *Librn,* Sweetwater County Library (Reliance Branch), Reliance WY. 307-875-3615

Farrands, Jane E, *Librn,* Organon Inc, Medical Library, West Orange NJ. 201-325-4614

Farrar, Bruce, *Librn,* Ohio County Public Library, Wheeling WV. 304-232-0244

Farrar, David, *Acq,* Mountain View College, Learning Resources Center, Dallas TX. 214-746-4169

Farrar, Florence, *Librn,* Jackson Citizen Patriot Newspaper Library, Jackson MI. 517-787-2300, Ext 37

Farrar, Jennifer K, *Librn,* Stauffer Chemical Co, Corporate Library, Westport CT. 203-226-1511, Ext 2846

Farrar, Ruth, *Library Asst,* Spartanburg County Public Library (Landrum Branch), Landrum SC. 803-457-2218

Farrar, Sarah, *Asst Librn,* Richards Library, Warrensburg NY. 518-623-5611

Farrar-Starkey, Anita M, *Libr Tech,* Madera County Department of Education, School Library, Madera CA. 209-674-4641, Ext 288

Farrell, Barbara, *ILL,* Providence College, Phillips Memorial Library, Providence RI. 401-865-2242

Farrell, Colman, *Circ & Rare Bks,* Benedictine College (North Campus Library), Atchison KS. 913-367-5340, Ext 290

Farrell, Diane, *Ch,* Eastern Massachusetts Regional Library System, Boston MA. 617-536-4010

Farrell, Frances G, *Coordr,* Providence Interrelated Library System, Providence RI. 401-521-7722

Farrell, Frances G, *Coordr Prin Pub Libr,* Providence Public Library, Providence RI. 401-521-7722

Farrell, Lois, *Librn,* University of California, Berkeley (Agriculture), Berkeley CA. 415-642-4493

Farrell, Margaret, *ILL & Ref,* Pierce County Rural Library District, Tacoma WA. 206-572-6760

Farrell, Mary, *Ref,* Union City Free Public Library, Union City NJ. 201-866-7500

Farrell, Maureen, *Ref,* Lynn Public Library, Lynn MA. 617-595-0567

Farrell, Maureen, *Librn,* Washington County Library (Lake Elmo), Lake Elmo MN. 612-777-5002

Farrell, Michele, *ILL, Ref & Bibliog Instr,* D'Youville College, Library Resources Center, Buffalo NY. 716-886-8100, Ext 304

Farrell, Mrs Robert, *Asst Dir,* Frankfort Community Public Library, Frankfort IN. 317-654-8746

Farrell, Patricia C, *Course Support Liaison,* National Defense University Library, Washington DC. 202-693-8437

Farrell, Rhonda, *Librn,* Saginaw Public Libraries (Claytor), Saginaw MI. 517-753-5591

Farrell, Toni, *Librn,* Saint Petersburg Municipal Reference Library, Saint Petersburg FL. 813-893-7547

Farrell, Jr, James L, *Sr Librn,* Great Meadow Correctional Facility Library, Comstock NY. 518-639-5516

Farrell-Duncan, Howartine, *Librn,* Howard University Libraries (Medical-Dental Library), Washington DC. 202-636-6270

Farrelly, Deignan, *AV,* York College of Pennsylvania Library, York PA. 717-846-7788, Ext 353

Farren, Donald, *Spec Coll,* University of New Mexico General Library, Albuquerque NM. 505-277-4241

Farrens, Mary B, *Librn,* University of California at Davis (Agricultural Economics Library), Davis CA. 916-752-1540

Farrens, Mary B, *Agr Econ,* University of California at Davis, General Library, Davis CA. 916-752-2110

Farrer, Doris, *Librn,* Gorham Public Library, Gorham NH. 603-466-2525

Farrier, Margaret A, *Dir,* Old Dominion Library, Globe Public Library, Globe AZ. 602-425-2753

Farrington, Rachael W, *Actg Librn,* Clapp Memorial Library, Belchertown MA. 413-323-6224

Farrior, Grace B, *Acq,* University of North Carolina at Greensboro, Walter Clinton Jackson Library, Greensboro NC. 919-379-5880

Farris, Alice, *Acq,* Memphis-Shelby County Public Library & Information Center, Memphis TN. 901-528-2950

Farris, Donn Michael, *Librn,* Duke University (Divinity School Library), Durham NC. 919-684-3691

Farris, Donna, *Dir,* Jessamine County Public Library District, Withers Memorial Public Library, Nicholasville KY. 606-885-3523

Farris, Faith, *Graphics Coordr,* Eastfield College, Learning Resources Center, Mesquite TX. 214-746-3168

Farris, Jeanne J, *Cat,* Flint River Regional Library, Griffin GA. 404-227-2756

Farris, Mike, *AV,* Southwest Texas State University, Learning Resources Center, San Marcos TX. 512-245-2132

Farris, Miriam, *Librn,* Chaffee Public Library, Chaffee MO. 314-887-3298

Farrugia, A Denise, *Ch,* Woodridge Public Library, Woodridge IL. 312-964-7899

Faruquee, Atauar, *Cert & Training,* State Library of Pennsylvania, Harrisburg PA. 717-787-2646

Fasana, Paul F, *Chief,* New York Public Library (Preparation Services), New York NY. 212-790-6262

Fasko, Marjorie, *Tech Serv,* Lewisville Public Library, Lewisville TX. 214-436-1812

Fasold, Eloise, *Admin Asst,* Arapahoe Regional Library District, Littleton CO. 303-798-2444

Fasold, Eloise, *Librn,* Arapahoe Regional Library District (John V Christensen Library), Littleton CO. 303-798-2441

Fass, Joyce, *Librn,* Bruce Mines & Plummer Additional Union Public Library, Bruce Mines ON. 705-785-3370

Fassler, Joan, *On-Line Servs,* Kansas City Kansas Public Library, Kansas City KS. 913-621-3073

Fast, Anne, *Librn,* Angus Mowat Public Library, Moose Factory Island ON. 705-658-4897

Fast, Daniel, *Coordr,* Stone Hills Area Library Service Authority, IN. 812-829-6014

Fast, Mrs Lee, *Librn,* Winfield State Hospital & Training Center Library, Winfield KS. 316-221-1200, Ext 283

Fasth, Elsa, *Libr Technician,* San Diego County Library (Bonita-Sunnyside Branch), Bonita CA. 714-475-4642

Fatcheric, Jerome, *Senior Info Scientists,* Schering-Plough Pharmaceutical Research Div, Library Information Center, Bloomfield NJ. 201-743-6000, Ext 781

Fatout, Leslie P, *Tech Serv,* University of Texas of the Permian Basin, Learning Resources Center, Odessa TX. 915-367-2114

Fattal, Florence, *Spec Coll,* Geneva College, McCartney Library, Beaver Falls PA. 412-846-5100, Ext 297

Fatula, Martha, *Librn,* South Fork Public Library, South Fork PA. 814-495-4812

Fatzer, Jill, *Acting Ref,* University of Texas Libraries (Perry-Castaneda Library (Main Library)), Austin TX. 512-471-3811

Fauber, Kim, *ILL, Ad & Commun Servs,* Rockbridge Regional Library, Lexington VA. 703-463-4324

Faubert, Michel, *Prof,* College de Maisonneuve, Techniques de la Documentation, PQ. 514-254-7131

Faubion, Anita, *Librn,* Hogg Foundation for Mental Health, Hogg Foundation Library, Austin TX. 512-471-5041

Faucher, Rose-Grace, *Undergrad Librn,* University of Michigan Libraries (University Library), Ann Arbor MI. 313-764-9356

Faucher, Suzanne, *Librn,* Commission Des Ecoles Catholiques De Montreal, Bibliotheque Centrale, Montreal PQ. 514-525-6311

Fauhl, Ruth, *In Charge,* University of Kansas Libraries (Mathematics), Lawrence KS. 913-864-3440

Faul, Carol, *Librn,* University of Pennsylvania Libraries (Geology Map Library), Philadelphia PA. 215-243-5630

Fauley, Judith, *Librn,* Clark County Memorial Hospital Library, Jeffersonville IN. 812-283-2358

Faulhaber, Ardell, *Ch,* Villa Park Public Library, Villa Park IL. 312-834-1164

Faulk, Avis, *Ref,* Sul Ross State University, Bryan Wildenthal Memorial Library, Alpine TX. 915-837-3461

Faulkenbery, Barbara, *Librn,* Northeast Regional Library (Ashland Library), Ashland MS. 601-224-8945

Faulkner, B, *Librn,* Stirling Public Library, Stirling ON. 613-395-2837

Faulkner, Deborah, *Operating Systs,* Hermes Electronics Ltd Library, Dartmouth NS. 902-463-9295

Faulkner, Jamia, *Librn,* Galena Public Library, Galena KS. 316-783-5132

Faull, William T, *Bookmobile,* Walton-De Funiak Library, Walton County Public Library, De Funiak Springs FL. 904-892-3624

Fault, Corliss, *Acq & Cat,* Paramus Public Library, Paramus NJ. 201-265-1800

Faunce, Maria, *Assoc Prof,* University of Puerto Rico, Graduate School of Librarianship, PR. 809-764-0000, Ext 3522, 3526

Faunce, Stella, *Librn,* Plainfield Public Library, Plainfield CT. 203-564-7769

Faupel, David William, *Dir,* Asbury Theological Seminary, B L Fisher Library, Wilmore KY. 606-858-3581, Ext 246

Faurier, Ruth G, *Humanities,* Auburn University, Ralph Brown Draughton Library, Auburn AL. 205-826-4500

Faurot, Margaret, *Sr Librn,* Cornwall Public Library, Cornwall-on-Hudson NY. 914-534-8282

Fausold, Beryl M, *YA,* Peters Township Library, McMurray PA. 412-941-9430

Faust, Julia, *Librn,* West Suburban Hospital, Walter Lawrence Memorial Library, Oak Park IL. 312-383-6200

Faust, Kathy, *Cat,* Lewis & Clark College (Paul L Boley Law Library), Portland OR. 503-244-1181, Ext 685

Faust, Mary, *Acq,* Ball State University, Alexander M Bracken Library, Muncie IN. 317-285-6261

Faust, Mary, *Dir,* North Haven Memorial Library, North Haven CT. 203-239-5803

Faust, Thelma E, *Librn,* Mahanoy City Public Library, Mahanoy City PA. 717-773-1610

Fauteaux, Doris B, *Assoc Dir, Acq & Ref,* Cape Cod Community College, Library-Learning Resource Center, West Barnstable MA. 617-362-2131, Ext 341, 345

Fauteck, Frances M, *ILL, On-Line Servs & Bibliog Instr,* Nicholls State University, Allen J Ellender Memorial Library, Thibodaux LA. 504-446-8111, Ext 401, 402

Favors, Thelma, *Librn,* Linden Free Public Library (East), Linden NJ. 201-486-3994

Fawcett, Braden S, *Librn,* Northwest Bible College, J C Cooke Library, Edmonton AB. 403-452-0808, 452-0954, Ext 9

Fawcett, Carolyn R, *Bk Selection Specialists,* Harvard University Library (Harvard College Library (Headquarters in Harry Elkins Widener Memorial Library)), Cambridge MA. 617-495-2401

Fawcett, Georgene E, *Acq & Ser,* University of Nebraska Medical Center, Library of Medicine, Omaha NE. 402-541-4006

Fawcett, Joan, *Ref,* Oakville Public Library, Oakville ON. 416-845-3405

Fawcett, Patrick, *On-Line Servs,* University of Manitoba Libraries (Medical Library), Winnipeg MB. 204-786-4342

Fawcett, W Peyton, *Librn,* Field Museum of Natural History Library, Chicago IL. 312-922-9410, Ext 282

Fawson, E Curtis, *Dir,* Brigham Young University-Hawaii Campus, Joseph F Smith Library, Laie HI. 808-293-9211, Ext 260, 264

Fawson, Janice Lane, *ILL & Circ,* West Valley College, Learning Resource Center, Saratoga CA. 408-867-2200, Ext 284

Fawson, Ken, *Dir,* Evergreen Valley College Library, San Jose CA. 408-274-7900, Ext 310

Fay, Cora, *Librn,* Mobile Public Library (Cottage Hill), Mobile AL. 205-661-9121

Fay, Evelyn, *Librn,* Cottage Hospital, David L Reeves Medical Library, Santa Barbara CA. 805-682-7393

Fay, Juanita G, *Librn,* Pinecrest Hospital Library, Beckley WV. 304-252-6251, Ext 74

Fay, Rimmon C, *Owner,* Pacific Bio-Marine Laboratories, Inc, Research Library, Venice CA. 213-822-5757

Fayen, Emily, *Systs,* Dartmouth College, Baker Memorial Library, Hanover NH. 603-646-2235

Fealko, Mrs John, *Librn,* Mullan Public Library, Mullan ID. 208-774-1403

Fear, Eleanor, *Librn,* Sidney Community Library, Sidney IL. 217-688-2332

Fear, Flora, *Supvr,* Huron County Public Library (Blyth Branch), Blyth ON. 519-523-9656

Fearnley, Edith, *Acq,* Massachusetts Bay Community College Library, Wellesley MA. 617-237-1100, Ext 193

Fearnley, Henry, *Libr Instr,* College of Marin Library, Kentfield CA. 415-485-9470

Fears, Judy, *Librn,* Pfizer Inc, Vigo Plant Library, Terre Haute IN. 812-299-2121, Ext 417

Feasal, Doris, *Librn,* Mulliken District Library, Mulliken MI. 517-649-8611

Feaster, Helen W, *Librn,* Elkins-Randolph County Public Library, Elkins WV. 304-636-1121

Feaster, Sharon, *In Charge,* Texas Education Agency (Region VII), Kilgore TX. 214-984-3071

Feather, Pamela, *Dir,* Sugar Grove Public Library, Sugar Grove IL. 312-466-4686

Febles, Mary, *Ref,* Compton Advertising Inc Library, New York NY. 212-350-1570

Fecteau, Albert J, *Librn,* United States Air Force (Hancock Field Base Library), Syracuse NY. 315-458-5500, Ext 310

Fedders, Cynthia, *ILL,* Washington University Libraries (School of Medicine Library), Saint Louis MO. 314-454-3711

Feder, Doris R, *Dir,* Elmont Public Library, Elmont NY. 516-354-5280, 354-4091

Feder, Helga, *ILL,* City University of New York, Library of Graduate School & University Center, New York NY. 212-790-4541

Feder, Helga, *Humanities,* City University of New York, Library of Graduate School & University Center, New York NY. 212-790-4541

Feder, Maria, *Bibliog Instr,* Lawrence Berkeley Laboratory Library, Berkeley CA. 415-486-5621

Federgreen, Dorothea, *Librn,* Chicago Public Library (Rogers Park), Chicago IL. 312-764-0156

Federico, Hilda, *Per,* Jacksonville University, Carl S Swisher Library, Jacksonville FL. 904-744-3950, Ext 266, 267

Federico, Josephine, *Tech Serv,* Ladycliff College, Msgr C Hugo Doyle Library, Highland Falls NY. 914-446-4747, Ext 21

Fediuk, Simon, *Librn,* New York State Division of Human Rights, Reference Library, New York NY. 212-488-5372

Fedorowich, Donna, *Librn,* Grant MacEwan Community College, Learning Resource Centres, Edmonton AB. 403-484-7791

Fedors, Carmel, *Librn,* Hall-Brooke Hospital Library, Westport CT. 203-227-1251, Ext 242

Fedorzyn, Susan, *ILL,* Southeastern Massachusetts University, Library Communications Center, North Dartmouth MA. 617-999-8662

Feduff, Anne, *Tech Librn,* Hitco Technical Library, Gardena CA. 213-321-8080, Ext 249, 649

Fedunok, Suzanne, *Librn,* Columbia University (Mathematics-Science), New York NY. 212-280-2241

Feduska, Melanie, *Ref,* Scott & White Memorial Hospital, Medical Library, Temple TX. 817-774-2228

Fee, Audrey, *Librn,* Zearing Public Library, Zearing IA. 515-487-7888

Feehan, Paul G, *Circ,* University of Miami, Otto G Richter Library, Coral Gables FL. 305-284-3551

Feeke, Willa, *Librn,* New York Public Library (Spuyten Duyvil), New York NY. 212-796-1202

Feeley, James, *Dir,* Algonquin College of Applied Arts & Technology, Resource Centers, Ottawa ON. 613-725-7302

Feeley, James, *Librn,* Algonquin College of Applied Arts & Technology (Woodroffe Campus), Ottawa ON. 613-275-7301

Feener, Katherine, *Media,* Endicott College, Fitz Memorial Library, Beverly MA. 617-927-0585, Ext 280

Feener, Loretta, *Supvr,* Huron County Public Library (Cranbrook), Brussels ON. 519-887-6593

Feeney, M Patricia, *Librn,* Burroughs Corp, Mission Viejo Plant Engineering Library, Mission Viejo CA. 714-768-2170

Feeney, Martha, *Processing,* Southern Illinois University at Edwardsville, Elijah P Lovejoy Library, Edwardsville IL. 618-692-2711

Feeney, Mary E, *Librn,* Yale University Library (Medical Library), New Haven CT. 203-436-4784, 436-2961

Feeney, Rosemary, *Librn,* New York Institute of Technology, Commack Center Library, Commack NY. 516-499-8506

Feenker, Cherie, *Librn,* Birmingham Public & Jefferson County Free Library (Woodlawn), Birmingham AL. 205-254-2551

Fees, Gerald, *Bkmobile Coordr,* Barry-Lawrence Regional Library, Monett MO. 417-235-6646

Fegley, Lynda, *Ad,* Rahway Free Public Library, Rahway NJ. 201-388-0761

Fehlner, Peter D, *Dir, Acq & Rare Bks,* Saint Anthony-On-Hudson Library, Rensselaer NY. 518-463-2261

Fehnel, Randi, *Tech Serv,* Northampton Area Public Library, Northampton PA. 215-262-7537

Feil, Paul, *Ad,* Morton Grove Public Library, Morton Grove IL. 312-965-4220

Feinberg, Elizabeth, *Librn,* Haines City Public Library, Haines City FL. 813-422-1749

Feinberg, Hilda, *In Charge,* Revlon Research Center Library, Bronx NY. 212-824-9000, Ext 258

Feinberg, Richard, *Bibliog Instr,* State University of New York, Frank Melville Jr Memorial Library, Stony Brook NY. 516-246-5650

Feinberg, Ruth, *Librn,* Preston Medical Library, Knoxville TN. 615-971-3237

Feinberg, Sandra, *Ch,* Middle Country Public Library, Centereach NY. 516-585-9393

Feindel, Richard, *Instnl Servs,* Kentucky Department of Library & Archives, Frankfort KY. 502-564-7910

Feinsilver, Jeffrey, *On-Line Servs & Bibliog Instr,* New York Institute of Technology Library, Old Westbury NY. 516-686-7657, 686-7658

Feinstein, Ann, *Circ,* New Bedford Free Public Library, Subregional Headquarters for Eastern Massachusetts Regional Library System, New Bedford MA. 617-999-6291

Feinstein, Joanne P, *Librn,* Southeastern Pennsylvania Transportation Authority Library, Philadelphia PA. 215-574-7387

Feir, Mitchell, *Ref & Data Base,* Bankers Trust Co Library, New York NY. 212-692-4680, 692-4681

Feir, Mollie, *Librn,* Brooklyn Public Library (Gerritsen), Brooklyn NY. 212-743-3040

Feister, Barbara, *Materials Selection: Adult Specialist,* Chicago Public Library, Chicago IL. 312-269-2900

Feiszli, Doris M, *Librn,* United Church of Christ Evangelical & Reformed Library, Vermilion OH. 216-967-4539

Feitler, Lila, *Assoc Librn,* Iowa State Department of Social Services Library, Des Moines IA. 515-281-5925

Fekete, Phyllis, *Dir,* Walnut Street Baptist Church, Media Center, Louisville KY. 502-589-5290

Fekete, Terry, *Tech Serv,* Medicine Hat College, Learning Resource Center, Medicine Hat AB. 403-527-7141, Ext 245

Fekety, Peter, *Music & Art,* Richardson Public Library, Richardson TX. 214-238-8251

Felbel, Dennis, *Circ,* University of Manitoba Libraries, Winnipeg MB. 204-474-9881

Felcone, Joseph J, *Librn,* David Library of the American Revolution, Washington Crossing PA. 215-493-6776

Felcone, Joseph J, *Librn,* Historical Society of Princeton Library, Princeton NJ. 609-921-6748

Felder, Charletta P, *Librn,* Veterans Administration, Hospital Library, Columbia SC. 803-776-4000

Felder, Mary, *Spec Coll,* Claflin College, H V Manning Library, Orangeburg SC. 803-534-2710, Ext 56

Feldick, Peggy, *ILL, Ref & On-Line Servs,* Macalester College, Weyerhaeuser Library, Saint Paul MN. 612-647-6346

Feldman, Caryl-Ann, *Librn,* Children's Museum Library, Boston MA. 617-426-6500

Feldman, D H, *Mgr,* Platt Saco Lowell Corporation, Engineering Library, Easley SC. 803-859-3211

Feldman, Felice, *Ch,* Kirkwood Public Library, Kirkwood MO. 314-821-5770

Feldman, Irwin, *Eve Librn,* Mendocino Community College Library, Ukiah CA. 707-468-0677

Feldman, Marjorie, *Dir,* Central Young Men's Christian Association Community College, Stanley G Harris Library, Chicago IL. 312-222-8212

Feldman, Mary, *HQ Servs Br,* United States Department of Transportation, Library Services Div, Washington DC. 202-426-2565, 426-1792

Feldman, Sari, *Dir,* Onondaga Free Library, Syracuse NY. 315-492-1727

Feldman, T K, *Dir,* Jewish Community Center of Greater Washington, Kass Judaic Library, Rockville MD. 301-881-0100, Ext 52

Feldman, William, *Librn,* Dade County Law Library, Hialeah FL. 305-855-1223

Felice, Michael, *Ser,* University of Illinois at the Medical Center, Library of the Health Sciences, Chicago IL. 312-996-8974

Felician, Brother, *Librn,* Union Saint-Jean Baptiste, Bibliotheque Mallet, Woonsocket RI. 401-769-0520

Felix, G Doris, *Dir,* Oelwein Public Library, Oelwein IA. 319-283-1515

Felker, William A, *Head,* Free Library of Philadelphia (General Information), Philadelphia PA. 215-686-5322

Felkey, Leonard, *Ad,* Kokomo Public Library, Kokomo IN. 317-457-5558

Fell, Mary B, *Coordr,* Jerico-Underhill Library Cooperative, Jericho VT. 802-899-2207

Fell-Johnson, Barbara, *Librn,* Hampshire County Law Library, Northampton MA. 413-586-2228, 586-2297

Fellabaum, Marti, *Librn,* Harris County Public Library (Stratford), Highlands TX. 713-426-4214

Feller, Jean, *Librn,* Redfield Public Library, Redfield IA. 515-833-2200

Feller, Judith, *Doc,* East Stroudsburg State College, Kemp Library, East Stroudsburg PA. 717-424-3467

Feller, Siegfried, *Spec Coll,* University of Massachusetts at Amherst Library, Amherst MA. 413-545-0284

Feller, Siegfried, *Germanic Studies,* University of Massachusetts at Amherst Library, Amherst MA. 413-545-0284

Fellers, Bill, *Business Librn,* Weil, Gotshal & Manges Library, New York NY. 212-758-7800, Ext 212

Fellers, Helen B, *Dir,* Beaufort Technical College, Learning Resource Center, Beaufort SC. 803-524-3380, Ext 236 & 241

Fellin, Octavia, *Dir,* Gallup Public Library, Gallup NM. 505-863-3692

Fellows, Barbara, *Bus & Tech,* Public Library of Columbus & Franklin County, Columbus OH. 614-864-8050

Felsted, Carla Martindell, *Librn,* American Airlines Inc Corporate Library, Dallas TX. 214-355-1464

Felt, Margie, *Librn,* Stanislaus County & Stanislaus County Medical Society Medical Library, Modesto CA. 209-526-6132

Feltes, Mary Kay, *Librn,* Independence Public Library, Independence WI. 715-985-3616

Felthaus, Robert, *Rare Bks,* Orange Public Library, Orange CA. 714-532-0391

Felthouse, Patricia, *Spec Coll,* Tehama County Library, Red Bluff CA. 916-527-0604

Feltis, Beverly, *Librn,* Santa Cruz Public Library (Scotts Valley Branch), Scotts Valley CA. 408-438-2855

Felton, Barbara, *Librn,* Indianapolis-Marion County Public Library (Warren), Indianapolis IN. 317-635-5662

Felton, Elmer, *Media,* Grand Canyon College, Fleming Library, Phoenix AZ. 602-249-3300, Ext 207

Felton, John, *Ref & Ad,* Lincoln City Libraries, Lincoln NE. 402-435-2146

Felts, Lucille, *Librn,* Webster Parish Library (Heflin Branch), Heflin LA. 318-377-1411

Felts, Margaret, *Anthrop, Psychol, SPac Studies,* University of California, University Library, Santa Cruz CA. 408-429-2076

Felts, Nancy, *Librn,* Woodbury County Rural Library (Pierson Branch), Pierson IA. 712-873-3322

Felty, Walter C, *Chmn,* Marshall University, Dept of Educational Media, WV. 304-696-2330

Feltz, William, *Resource Specialist,* East-West Center, Culture Learning Institute, Resource Materials Collection, Honolulu HI. 808-948-7081

Fencil, Kathleen H, *Librn,* Hopkinton Village Library, Hopkinton NH. 603-746-4292

Fender, Anna Marie, *Park Technician,* National Park Service, Rocky Mountain National Park Library, Estes Park CO. 586-2371 Ext 227

Fendry, Marie, *Res Librn,* Pabst Brewing Co, P-L Biochemicals, Inc Research Library, Milwaukee WI. 414-347-7448

Feng, Cyril, *Dir,* University of Maryland at Baltimore (Health Sciences Library), Baltimore MD. 301-528-7545

Feng, Grace C, *Librn,* United States Army (Corps of Engineers, Memphis District Library), Memphis TN. 901-521-3618

Feng, Yen-Tsai, *Librn of Harvard Col,* Harvard University Library (Harvard College Library (Headquarters in Harry Elkins Widener Memorial Library)), Cambridge MA. 617-495-2401

Fenichel, Carol H, *Dir,* Philadelphia College of Pharmacy & Science, Joseph W England Library, Philadelphia PA. 215-386-5800, Ext 296

Fenichel, Carol H, *Asst Prof,* University of Kentucky, College of Library Science, KY. 606-258-8876

Fenker, Lois, *Tech Serv,* Fort Vancouver Regional Library, Vancouver WA. 206-695-1561

Fenn, Martha J, *Librn,* Brattleboro Memorial Hospital, Medical Library, Brattleboro VT. 802-257-0341, Ext 257

Fenn, Robin, *Ch & YA,* Beverly Public Library, Beverly MA. 617-922-0310

Fenn, Rosalynn F, *Librn,* Florida State Legislature Joint Legislative Management Committee, Division of Legislative Library Services, Tallahassee FL. 904-488-2812

Fenn, Jr, Dan H, *Dir,* General Services Administration - National Archives & Records Service, John F Kennedy Library, Dorchester MA. 617-929-4500

Fennell, Janice C, *Coordr,* Georgia College, Education Library Media, GA. 912-453-4047 & 453-5573

Fennell, Janice C, *Dir,* Georgia College, Ina Dillard Russell Library, Milledgeville GA. 912-453-4047, 453-5573

Fennell, Judy K, *Asst Librn,* South Georgia College, William S Smith Library, Douglas GA. 912-384-1100, Ext 233, 290

Fenner, Sarah G, *Dir,* Rockville Centre Public Library, Rockville Centre NY. 516-766-6258

Fennessey, Mary D, *Dir,* Northland College, Dexter Library, Ashland WI. 715-682-4531, Ext 297

Fennessy, Kathryn, *Ref,* Alfred University (Herrick Memorial Library), Alfred NY. 607-871-2184

Fennimore, Flora, *Chmn,* Western Washington University, Dept of Education, WA. 206-676-3010

Fennimore, Patricia, *Ch,* Springfield Free Public Library, Springfield NJ. 201-376-4930

Fenning, Kathleen, *Ref,* Franklin Sylvester Library, Medina OH. 216-725-0588

Fenninger, Edward P, *Sound Archives Cur,* Boston Public Library, Eastern Massachusetts Library System, Boston MA. 617-536-5400

Fenske, David, *Librn,* Indiana University at Bloomington (Music), Bloomington IN. 812-337-8541

Fenske, Geanene, *ILL,* Houston Academy of Medicine, Texas Medical Center Library, Houston TX. 713-797-1230

Fensom, Jean, *Librn,* McGill University Libraries (Dentistry), Montreal PQ. 514-392-4926

Fenster, Madeleine, *Librn,* New York County District Attorney's Office Library, New York NY. 212-553-9344

Fenstermaker, Ellen, *Librn,* Montgomery County Department of Public Libraries (Bethesda Branch), Bethesda MD. 301-986-8450

Fenstermaker, Kathleen, *Ch,* West Bridgewater Public Library, West Bridgewater MA. 617-583-2067

Fenstermann, Duane, *Tech Serv & Acq,* Luther College, Preus Library, Decorah IA. 319-387-1163

Fenton, E A, *Librn,* Canadian Telephone Employees' Association Library, Montreal PQ. 514-861-9963

Fenton, Joan, *Ref,* New Brunswick Free Public Library, New Brunswick NJ. 201-745-5337

Fenton, Nancy A, *Asst Librn,* Economics Laboratory Inc, Information Center, Saint Paul MN. 612-451-5651

Fenton, Pat, *On-Line Servs,* Minnesota Department of Education Professional Library, Saint Paul MN. 612-296-6104

Fenton, Peter L, *Dir,* Boston State College Library, Boston MA. 617-731-3300

Fenton, Willaim, *AV,* Blue Mountain Community College Library, Pendleton OR. 503-276-1260, Ext 234

Fentress, Christine, *Librn,* Saint Vincent's Medical Center, Doctors Library, Jacksonville FL. 904-389-7751, Ext 8318

Fenwick, Jean, *Bkmobile Coordr,* Mid-Mississippi Regional Library System, Kosciusko MS. 601-289-5141, 289-5146

Ferch, David L, *Librn,* Mount Mercy College, Catherine McAuley Library, Cedar Rapids IA. 319-363-8213, Ext 244

Fereira, Lynda, *Librn,* South Pekin Public Library, South Pekin IL. 309-348-2464

Ferens, Mariley B, *Librn,* Northwest Federal Regional Council Library, Seattle WA. 206-442-5554

Ferestad, Virginia H, *Librn,* Campbell-Mithun, Inc Creative Library, Minneapolis MN. 612-339-7383

Feret, Ronald E, *Librn,* Pope, Ballard, Uriell, Kennedy, Shepard & Fowle Library, Chicago IL. 312-630-4238

Fergason, Dorinda, *On-Line Servs,* National Fire Protection Association, Technical Reference Library, Boston MA. 617-482-8755, Ext 136, 137

Ferguson, Alana, *Librn,* Ogden Rose Public Library, Ogden IL. 217-582-6085

Ferguson, Anthony, *Soc Sci,* Brigham Young University, Harold B Lee Library, Provo UT. 801-378-2905

Ferguson, Barbara, *Dir & Ch,* Mary Fuller Frazier Memorial School & Community Library, Perryopolis PA. 412-736-4426

Ferguson, C, *Librn,* Blue Cross of Western Pennsylvania, Pittsburgh PA. 412-391-0500, Ext 536

Ferguson, Charles B, *Dir,* New Britain Museum of American Art Library, New Britain CT. 203-229-0257

Ferguson, Charlotte, *Librn,* Ignace Public Library, Ignace ON. 807-934-2548

Ferguson, Chris, *Bibliog Instr,* University of Mississippi Library, University MS. 601-232-7091

Ferguson, Diane A, *Librn,* United States Arms Control & Disarmament Agency Library, Rosslyn VA. 703-235-9550

Ferguson, Donna, *Asst Librn,* Bedford County Library, Bedford PA. 814-623-5010

Ferguson, Dorothy, *Librn,* Lake County Library (Middletown Branch), Middletown CA. 707-987-3674

Ferguson, Earle, *Reader Serv,* University of Manitoba Libraries (Law), Winnipeg MB. 204-474-9773

Ferguson, Helen J, *Librn,* Saint Elizabeth Hospital, Medical & Nursing Library, Elizabeth NJ. 201-527-5371

Ferguson, J Ray, *Acq,* Washington University Libraries (Freund Law Library), Saint Louis MO. 314-889-6459

Ferguson, Jane J, *Librn,* University of South Carolina at Sumter Library, Sumter SC. 803-775-6341, Ext 34

Ferguson, John Philip, *In Charge,* Cleveland Public Library (Popular Library), Cleveland OH. 216-623-2842

Ferguson, John W, *Asst Librn,* Mid-Continent Public Library, Independence MO. 816-836-5200

Ferguson, Lanei, *Acq,* Los Angeles Times Editorial Library, Los Angeles CA. 213-972-7184

Ferguson, Lori, *On-Line Servs,* Hanover College, Duggan Library, Hanover IN. 812-866-2151, Ext 333

Ferguson, Lynn, *Rare Bks,* Greensboro Public Library, Greensboro NC. 373-2474; 373-2471

Ferguson, Margaret, *Asst Librn,* Crafton Public Library, Crafton PA. 412-922-6877

Ferguson, Margaret E, *Librn,* Grace Enterprises Library, Albany GA. 912-883-4908

Ferguson, Marilyn, *Asst Dir,* Whitchurch-Stouffville Public Library, Stouffville ON. 416-640-2395

Ferguson, Mrs Morris H, *Librn,* Hale County Public Library, Greensboro AL. 205-624-3409

Ferguson, Norma, *Librn,* Lonesome Pine Regional Library (Scott County Pub), Pennington Gap VA. 703-546-1141

Ferguson, Pamelyn, *ILL & Ref,* Westfield Memorial Library, Westfield NJ. 201-233-1515

Ferguson, Patricia, *Librn,* Bendix Corp, Avionics Div Library, Fort Lauderdale FL. 305-776-4100

Ferguson, Paul F, *Dir,* Saint Mary's University (School of Law Library), San Antonio TX. 512-436-3435

Ferguson, Sandra, *Librn,* American Microsystems, Inc Information Center, Santa Clara CA. 408-246-0330, Ext 851

Ferguson, Sara, *Dir,* Updata Publications Inc Library, Los Angeles CA. 213-474-5900

Ferguson, Sarah, *Asst Librn, ILL & Ref,* Brookhaven College, Learning Resources Center, Farmers Branch TX. 214-746-5250

Ferguson, Sister Anne, *Asst Prof,* Ohio Dominican College, Dept of Library Science & Educational Media, OH. 614-253-2741

Ferguson, Sister Mary Patrick, *Librn,* Marian College of Fond Du Lac, Cardinal Meyer Library, Fond du Lac WI. 414-921-3900, Ext 237

Ferguson, Yvette, *Librn,* Marshalltown Area Community Hospital, School of Nursing Library, Marshalltown IA. 515-754-5179

Fergusson, David G, *Librn,* Davie County Public Library, Mocksville NC. 704-634-2023

Fergusson, Eden, *Dir,* San Marcos Public Library, San Marcos TX. 512-392-8124

Ferkull, Marion, *Relig & Philos,* Chicago Public Library (Literature & Philosophy Div), Chicago IL. 312-269-2880

FERLAND

Ferland, Ronald J, *Librn,* United States Air Force (Barksdale Air Force Base Library), Barksdale AFB LA. 318-456-4101

Ferlanti, Vita, *Tech Serv & Cat,* Denville Free Public Library, Denville NJ. 201-627-6555

Fern, Alan, *Dir, Spec Coll,* Library of Congress, Washington DC. 202-287-5000

Fernald, Anne Conway, *On-Line Servs,* Warner-Eddison Associates, Inc Library, Cambridge MA. 617-661-8124

Fernandes, Susan R, *Librn,* Radian Corp Library, Austin TX. 512-454-4797

Fernandez, Dot, *Librn,* Bossier Parish Public Library (Henry L Aulds Memorial), Bossier City LA. 318-742-2337

Fernandez, Maria, *Librn,* Alameda County Library (San Lorenzo Branch), San Lorenzo CA. 415-881-0500

Fernandez, Martha, *Librn,* Shreveport Journal Library, Shreveport LA. 318-424-0373

Fernandez, Nell, *Librn,* Monmouth County Board of Social Services Library, Freehold NJ. 201-431-6011

Fernandez, Priscilla, *Ref,* Chaffey College Library, Alta Loma CA. 714-987-1737, Ext 303

Fernandez, Zenaida, *Cat,* Miami Dade Community College (Central Technical Processing), Miami FL. 305-685-4276

Fernandez-Ortiz, Arturo, *Dir,* University of Puerto Rico, Graduate School of Librarianship, PR. 809-764-0000, Ext 3522, 3526

Ferner, Hazel, *Librn,* Parsippany-Troy Hills Public Library (Lake Hiawatha Libr), Lake Hiawatha NJ. 201-398-6120

Ferng, Hou Ran, *Asian Coll,* Saint John's University Library, Jamaica NY. 212-969-8000, Ext 201

Fernsler, Jennilou, *Reader Serv,* Christopher Newport College, Captain John Smith Library, Newport News VA. 804-599-7130

Ferrall, Rebecca T, *Assoc Librn,* Federal Bureau of Investigation, FBI Academy Learning Resource Center, Quantico VA. 703-640-6131, Ext 2471

Ferrante, Karlene, *Curric Media Librn,* Bemidji State University, A C Clark Library, Bemidji MN. 218-755-2955

Ferrante, Karlene, *Instr,* Bemidji State University, Library Science Program, MN. 218-755-2955

Ferrara, A, *Tech Serv,* Public Works Canada, Ontario Region Library, Willowdale ON. 416-367-7708

Ferrara, John, *Media Production,* Wright State University Library (Fordham Library, Cox Heart Institute Library & Fels Research Institute Library), Dayton OH. 513-873-2266

Ferrara, Mark, *Assoc Dir,* Kean College of New Jersey, Nancy Thompson Library, Union NJ. 201-527-2017

Ferrara, Robert, *Librn,* Brooklyn Public Library (Brighton Beach), Brooklyn NY. 212-266-0005

Ferraro, Deborah, *Ch,* Free Public Library of the City of Orange, Orange NJ. 201-673-0153

Ferree, Mrs Origen, *Ref,* Bridgeville Public Library, Bridgeville PA. 412-221-3737

Ferrell, Barbara S, *Dir,* Durham Technical Institute, Learning Resources Center, Durham NC. 919-596-9311, Ext 228

Ferrell, Bruce, *Tech Serv,* Los Angeles City College Library, Los Angeles CA. 213-663-9141, Ext 412

Ferrell, Dorothy P, *Cat,* Mary Baldwin College, Martha S Grafton Library, Staunton VA. 703-885-0811, Ext 382

Ferrell, Elizabeth Davis, *Librn,* Beaufort County Community College, Washington NC. 919-946-6194, Ext 244

Ferrell, Mrs Bernie, *Librn,* Saint Louis Municipal Medical Library, Saint Louis MO. 314-622-5255

Ferrell, Rosalie, *Media & Ser,* Campbell University, Carrie Rich Memorial Library, Buies Creek NC. 919-893-4111, Ext 238

Ferrell, Virgie, *Librn,* Yoakum Public Library, Yoakum TX. 512-293-5001

Ferren, Dorothy, *Cat,* Pacific Union College, W E Nelson Memorial Library, Angwin CA. 707-965-6241

Ferrero, Michael J, *Staff Dea,* San Jose Public Library, San Jose CA. 408-277-4822

Ferrier, Douglas, *Acq,* University of Arkansas at Little Rock Library, Little Rock AR. 501-569-3120

Ferrier, Marion, *Circ,* Valdez Public Library, Valdez AK. 907-835-4632

Ferriero, David, *Lectr,* Simmons College, Graduate School of Library & Information Science, MA. 617-738-2225

Ferriero, David S, *Librn,* Massachusetts Institute of Technology Libraries (Humanities), Cambridge MA. 617-253-5681

Ferrin, Eric, *Computer Servs,* Pennsylvania State University, Fred Lewis Pattee Library, University Park PA. 814-865-0401

Ferrin, Ida, *Librn,* Arizona Community Library, Arizona City AZ. 602-466-5505

Ferrin, J P, *Librn,* Monsanto Industrial Chemicals Co, Research Library, Akron OH. 216-666-4111, Ext 247

Ferris, Barbara, *Librn,* Willoughby-Eastlake Public Library (Willoughby Branch), Willoughby OH. 216-942-3200

Ferris, Brenda, *Ref,* Concord Pike Library, Wilmington DE. 302-478-7961

Ferris, Dolores, *Asst Librn,* Trumbull Library, Trumbull CT. 203-261-6421

Ferris, Jeffrey P, *Librn,* Claymont Public Library, Claymont DE. 302-798-4164

Ferry, Adeline, *Librn,* A C Daugherty Memorial Township Library, Dupo IL. 618-286-4444

Ferry, Mary R, *Head Librn,* Pennsylvania State University, Hazleton Campus Library, Hazleton PA. 717-454-8731, Ext 60

Ferry, S, *Forestry & Industry,* British Columbia Institute of Technology Library, Burnaby BC. 604-434-5734, Ext 360

Ferry, Wilma, *Dir,* Orland City Library, Orland CA. 916-865-3465

Ferstl, Kenneth L, *Instr,* North Texas State University, School of Library & Information Sciences, TX. 817-788-2445

Fersuson, Frank P, *Dir,* J Lewis Crozer Library, Chester PA. 215-494-3454

Fesenmaier, Stephen, *Media,* West Virginia Library Commission, Science & Cultural Center, Charleston WV. 304-348-2041

Fessenden, Ann, *Tech Serv,* University of Mississippi, Law Library, University MS. 601-232-7361

Fessenden, Jane, *Librn,* Marine Biological Laboratory Library, Woods Hole MA. 617-548-3705

Fessenden, Robert, *Hist,* University of California, University Library, Santa Cruz CA. 408-429-2076

Festa, Dan, *Circ,* University of South Carolina (School of Medicine Library), Columbia SC. 803-777-4858

Fetchet, Marilyn, *Librn,* Lorain Public Library (Columbia Branch), Columbia Station OH. 216-236-8751

Fetchison, Connie, *Librn,* London Public Libraries & Museums (Argyle), London ON. 519-451-7600

Fetesoff, Barbara, *Librn,* Sonoma State Hospital (Eldridge Community Library), Eldridge CA. 707-938-6547

Fetherston, Lynn, *Tech Serv & Cat,* New Brunswick Theological Seminary, Gardner A Sage Library, New Brunswick NJ. 201-247-5241, Ext 6

Fetics, Marion, *Info Assts,* Colgate-Palmolive Co, Technical Information Center Library, Piscataway NJ. 201-463-1212, Ext 277

Fetkovich, Malinda, *Librn,* Penn Area Library, Trafford PA. 412-373-3526

Fetkovich, Malinda M, *Dir,* Shadyside Hospital, James Frazer Hillman Health Science Library, Pittsburgh PA. 412-622-2415

Fetkovitch, Malinda M, *Librn,* Penn Area Library (Level Green Reading Station), Trafford PA. 412-373-3526

Fetros, John, *Acq,* San Francisco Public Library, San Francisco CA. 415-558-4235

Fetscher, Virginia, *Ad,* Katonah Village Library, Katonah NY. 914-232-3508

Fetty, Vivian, *Ch,* Timberland Regional Library, Olympia WA. 206-943-5001

Fetvedt, Robert O, *Dir,* University of Wisconsin-Eau Claire, William D McIntyre Library, Eau Claire WI. 715-836-3715

Feuchtwanger, Mrs M, *Curator,* University of Southern California (Feuchtwanger), Los Angeles CA. 213-743-6050

Feuerhelm, Margaret, *Librn,* Waukon Municipal Library, Waukon IA. 319-568-4424

Feverstein, Terri, *Adminr,* Mechanical Technology Inc, Research & Development Library, Latham NY. 518-785-2509

Few, John, *Ref,* City College of San Francisco Library, San Francisco CA. 415-239-3404

Fewell, Madeline, *Librn,* Crosby County Library, Crosbyton TX. 806-675-2673

Fewings, Rose, *Chief Librn,* Southwestern Manitoba Regional Library, Melita MB. 204-522-3923

Feye-Stuka, Janice, *Libr Consult,* Minnesota State Library Agency, Office of Public Libraries & Interlibrary Cooperation, Saint Paul MN. 612-296-2821

Fezell, Nancy, *Tech Serv,* Maurice M Pine Free Public Library, Fair Lawn NJ. 201-796-3400

Fiasconaro, Anita, *Librn,* New Orleans Public Library (Nix), New Orleans LA. 504-586-4905

Fiatte, Enid, *Asst Librn,* Community College of Allegheny County, Boyce Campus Library, Monroeville PA. 412-327-1327, Ext 312

Fiaui, Papa, *Librn,* American Samoa-Office of Library Services (Instructional Resource Center), Utulei Village PI. 633-4357

Fichett, Hilda, *Doc,* Florida Institute of Technology Library, Melbourne FL. 305-723-3701, Ext 270

Fichtelberg, Leo E, *Dir,* Paterson Free Public Library, Danforth Memorial Library, Paterson NJ. 201-881-3770

Fichtenau, Lane, *Asst Librn,* Adams-Pratt Oakland County Law Library, Pontiac MI. 313-858-0011

Ficio, Diane Dellure, *Ch,* Hillside Free Public Library, Hillside NJ. 201-923-4413

Fick, John S, *Interim Dir,* University of Missouri at Columbia, Academic Support Center Film Library, Columbia MO. 314-882-3601

Ficke, Eleanore R, *Exec Dir,* Continuing Library Education Network & Exchange, (CLENE), DC. 202-635-5825

Ficke, Harold A, *Dir,* Leonia Public Library, Leonia NJ. 201-944-1444

Ficker, Kathleen, *Librn,* Public Library of Cincinnati & Hamilton County (Greenhills), Cincinnati OH. 513-825-2353

Fidler, Leah Josephine, *Acq,* Marshall University, James E Morrow Library, Huntington WV. 304-696-3120

Fiedler, Barbara, *Ad & ILL,* Yankton Community Library, Yankton SD. 605-665-4501, Ext 34

Fiedler, Christine, *Ref,* Cedar Crest College, Cressman Library, Allentown PA. 215-437-4471, Ext 264

Fiedler, Christine, *Ref,* Muhlenberg College, John A W Haas Library, Allentown PA. 215-433-3191, Ext 214

Fiegenbaum, Dorothy, *ILL,* Mount Holyoke College, Williston Memorial Library, South Hadley MA. 413-538-2226

Field, Annette, *ILL,* Norfolk Public Library, Norfolk VA. 804-441-2887

Field, Carolyn W, *Ch,* Free Library of Philadelphia, Philadelphia PA. 215-686-5322

Field, Charles L, *Asst Librn,* Northeastern University Libraries (School of Law), Boston MA. 617-437-3338

Field, Dana, *Librn,* Long Island Association of Commerce & Industry Library, Melville NY. 516-752-9600

Field, Dorothy, *Asst Dir & Br Coordr,* Tampa-Hillsborough County Public Library System, Tampa FL. 813-223-8947

Field, Florence P, *Dir,* John G McCullough Free Library, North Bennington VT. 802-447-7121

Field, Harriet, *ILL,* Lakeland Library Cooperative, Grand Rapids MI. 616-456-4457

Field, Hope, *Librn,* Walter T A Hansen Memorial Library, Mars Hill ME. 207-429-9625

Field, Jack, *Head, Hq,* Monmouth County Library, Freehold NJ. 201-431-7220

Field, Jean, *Mgr, Info & Libr Servs,* Honeywell Information Systems Inc, System Technical Library, Waltham MA. 617-890-8400

Field, John, *Hist Consultant,* Niagara Historical Society Library, Niagara on the Lake ON. 416-468-3912

Field, Judith, *Ref,* Flint Public Library, Flint MI. 313-232-7111

Field, Linda, *Asst Librn & Bibliog Instr,* Nebraska Library for the Blind & Physically Handicapped, Lincoln NE. 402-471-2045

Field, Margaret, *Br Coordr,* Monmouth County Library, Freehold NJ. 201-431-7220

Field, Margaret E, *Asst Dir & Ch,* Woodstock Public Library, Woodstock IL. 815-338-0542
Field, Marilee, *Ser,* Colorado State Library, Colorado Department of Education, Denver CO. 303-839-3695
Field, Naomi, *Circ,* Paramus Public Library, Paramus NJ. 201-265-1800
Field, Oliver, *Instr,* University of Denver, Graduate School of Librarianship and Information Management, CO. 303-753-2557
Field, Sister Mary, *Dir,* Rosary College, Rebecca Crown Library, River Forest IL. 312-366-2490, Ext 305
Field, Vivian, *Librn,* Rockford Public Library, Rockford IA. 515-756-3725
Field, William Noe, *Dir, Rare Bks & Spec Coll,* Seton Hall University, McLaughlin Library, South Orange NJ. 201-762-9000, Ext 282, 276
Fielden, S, *Assoc Librn & Tech Serv,* University of Regina Library, Regina SK. 306-584-4132
Fielder, Martha, *Ref,* Angelo State University, Porter Henderson Library, San Angelo TX. 915-942-2222
Fielder, Terry, *Training Specialist,* U S Bancorp Resource Library, Portland OR. 503-225-5816
Fielders, Margaret G, *Chmn,* Ohio Dominican College, Dept of Library Science & Educational Media, OH. 614-253-2741
Fielding, Gail, *Pub Serv & ILL,* Whitworth College, Harriet Cheney Cowles Memorial Library, Spokane WA. 509-466-3260
Fielding, Kenneth R, *Asst Dir,* Steele Memorial Library, Chemung-Southern Tier Library System, Elmira NY. 607-733-9173, 733-9174, 733-9175
Fielding, Ruby, *Ref,* Dalton Junior College, Library Resource Center, Dalton GA. 404-278-3113, Ext 237, 247
Fielding, Susan, *Tech Serv,* Nichols Library, Naperville IL. 312-355-1540
Fields, Arbutus, *Dir,* Perry County Public Library, Hazard KY. 606-436-2475, 436-4747
Fields, Carole, *Librn,* Klamath County Library (Sprague River Branch), Sprague River OR. 503-882-8894
Fields, Dee, *Ref,* South Oklahoma City Junior College, Learning Resources Center, Oklahoma City OK. 405-682-7574
Fields, Dennis, *Prof,* Saint Cloud State University, Center for Library & Audiovisual Education, MN. 612-255-2022
Fields, James C, *Ad,* Cabell County Public Library, Western Counties Regional Library System, Huntington WV. 304-523-9451
Fields, Mildred Sellers, *Dir & Acq,* Essex Community College, James A Newpher Library, Baltimore MD. 301-682-6000, Ext 320
Fields, Patti P, *Cat,* Medical University of South Carolina Library, Charleston SC. 803-792-2374
Fields, Vera D, *Media,* University of Maryland-Eastern Shore, Frederick Douglass Library, Princess Anne MD. 301-651-2200, Ext 229
Fiero, Linda, *Circ,* University of California Los Angeles Library, Los Angeles CA. 213-825-1201
Fierro, Mary, *Librn,* Georgina Public Library Administration (Sutton Centennial Branch), Sutton ON. 416-722-5702
Figatner, Annette, *Per,* City Colleges of Chicago, Kennedy-King College Library, Chicago IL. 312-962-3262
Figgatt, Ruth E, *Tech Serv,* Kanawha County Public Library, Kanawha County Service Center, Charleston WV. 304-343-4646
Figge, Lulu, *Librn,* Northeast Missouri Library Service (Schuyler County), Lancaster MO. 816-457-3731
Figueredo, O, *Per,* Florida Institute of Technology, Jensen Beach Library, Jensen Beach FL. 305-334-4200, Ext 60, 61
Figueroa, Isobel, *Librn,* Stanislaus County Free Library (Salida Branch), Salida CA. 209-545-0319
Figureoa, Rosemary, *Acq,* Palo Alto City Library, Palo Alto CA. 415-329-2436
Fike, Claude, *Dir,* University of Southern Mississippi (William David McCain Library), Hattiesburg MS. 601-266-4172
Fike, Sharon, *Ch,* Mifflin County Library, Lewistown PA. 717-242-2391
Fikes, May, *Librn,* General James Clinton Free Library, East Springfield NY. 607-858-0230

Filbeck, Joe, *Br Coordr,* Mid-Continent Public Library, Independence MO. 816-836-5200
Filbert, Elaine, *Librn,* Santa Clara Public Community Library, Espanola NM. 505-753-7326
Files, Harriet, *ILL,* Trail Blazer Library System, Monroe LA. 318-323-8494
Filgate, Robert M, *Dir,* McArthur Public Library, Biddeford ME. 207-284-4181
Filion, Paul-Emile, *Dir,* Concordia University Library, Montreal PQ. 514-879-2820
Filipelli, Carolyn, *ILL & Ref,* Westark Community College, Holt Library, Fort Smith AR. 501-785-4241, Ext 308
Filipic, Mary A, *Librn,* Cuyahoga County Public Library (Brooklyn Branch), Brooklyn OH. 216-398-4600
Filippelli, Ronald, *Labor Archives,* Pennsylvania State University, Fred Lewis Pattee Library, University Park PA. 814-865-0401
Filkins, Susanne, *Asst Librn,* Tracy Memorial Library, New London NH. 603-526-4656
Filler, Mary Ann, *Ref,* Pennsylvania State University, Capitol Campus Heindel Library, Middletown PA. 717-787-7771
Fillhart, Lin, *Ch,* Scott County Library, Eldridge IA. 319-285-4794
Fillion, Rebecca, *ILL,* Oregon College of Education Library, Monmouth OR. 503-838-1220, Ext 240
Filstrup, E Christian, *Chief,* New York Public Library (Oriental), New York NY. 790-6335 & 790-6509
Filteau, Nicole, *Prof,* College de Maisonneuve, Techniques de la Documentation, PQ. 514-254-7131
Fimbres, Lisa, *Media,* Calexico Public Library, Calexico CA. 714-357-2605
Finan, Howard, *Librn,* Prince Albert Central Institute Library, Prince Albert SK. 306-763-6485
Finan, Marcella S, *Dir,* Bristol Public Library, Bristol CT. 203-584-7787
Finan, Patrick E, *Dir,* Logan-Hocking County District Library, Logan OH. 614-385-2348
Finch, C Herbert, *Asst Univ Librn, Rare Bks, Mss & Archives,* Cornell University Libraries (University Libraries), Ithaca NY. 607-256-4144
Finch, Donna M, *Asst Librn,* Hopkins County-Madisonville Public Library, Madisonville KY. 502-825-2680
Finch, Elizabeth, *Dir,* Brewster Ladies' Library, Brewster MA. 617-896-3913
Finch, Jean, *Res & Develop Librn,* Lewis & Clark College (Paul L Boley Law Library), Portland OR. 503-244-1181, Ext 685
Finch, Leroy, *Librn,* Esco Corp, Technical Resource Library, Portland OR. 503-228-2141
Finch, Lois, *Ch,* Paris Public Library, Paris TX. 214-785-8531
Finch, Lynette, *Librn,* Nash Technical Institute Library, Rocky Mount NC. 919-443-4011, Ext 20
Finch, Lynn H, *Librn,* Franklin Free Library, Franklin NY. 607-829-2941
Finch, Mildred, *Tech Serv,* County of Henrico Public Library, Richmond VA. 804-222-1643
Finch, Mrs R C, *Dir,* Guernsey Memorial Library, Norwich NY. 607-334-4034
Finch, R, *Librn,* University of Toronto Libraries (University of Trinity College), Toronto ON. 416-978-2653
Finch, Rella, *Librn,* Hagerman Public Library, Hagerman ID. 208-837-4530
Finch, Jr, William E, *Curator,* Historical Society of Town of Greenwich, Inc Library, Cos Cob CT. 203-622-9686
Findley, Marcia M, *Dir & Acq,* Spring Hill College, Thomas Byrne Memorial Library, Mobile AL. 205-460-2381
Fine, Arnold, *Consult,* Beth Jacob Synagogue, Berkman Memorial Library, Norwich CT. 203-887-8331
Fine, Debbie, *Ref,* Boonslick Regional Library, Sedalia MO. 816-826-6195
Fine, Gerald, *Librn,* Detroit Public Library (Hubbard), Detroit MI. 313-833-9817
Fine, Martha, *Librn,* Greater Youngwood Area Public Library, Youngwood PA. 412-925-9350
Fine, Sara, *Assoc Prof,* University of Pittsburgh, School of Library & Information Science, PA. 412-624-5230

Fineman, Charles, *Western European Lit & Lang, Latin Am Studies,* University of California, University Library, Santa Cruz CA. 408-429-2076
Finfrock, Lynda, *Librn,* Pretty Prairie Public Library, Pretty Prairie KS. 316-459-6512
Fingeret, Rose W, *Librn,* Veterans Administration, Edward Hines Jr, Hospital Library, Hines IL. 312-343-7200
Fingland, Geoffrey, *Librn,* Christian Science Monitor Library, Boston MA. 617-262-2300, Ext 2680
Finisan, Myrtle H, *Librn,* Easthampton Public Library, Easthampton MA. 413-527-1031
Fink, Ann, *ILL,* Wartburg College, Engelbrecht Library, Waverly IA. 319-352-1200, Ext 244
Fink, Barbara, *Librn,* Siskiyou County Public Library (Fort Jones Branch), Ft Jones CA. 916-468-2383
Fink, Deborah, *On-Line Servs & Bibliog Instr,* University of Dubuque, Ficke-Laird Library, Dubuque IA. 319-589-3218
Fink, Madeleine, *Dir,* Municipal Library, Saint Lambert PQ. 514-465-4508
Fink, Myron, *Librn,* University of New Mexico General Library (Law Library), Albuquerque NM. 505-277-6236
Fink, Norma, *Librn,* Attica Public Library, Attica IN. 317-764-4194
Fink, Norman, *Librn,* Bibliotheque Municipale De Rouyn, Rouyn PQ. 819-762-0944
Fink, Sister Madonna, *AV,* Saint Mary College Library, Leavenworth KS. 913-682-5151, Ext 202
Finkbeiner, Jane, *Dir,* Maitland Public Library, Maitland FL. 305-647-7700
Finkbeiner, Katherine D, *Admin Asst,* Nichols Library, Naperville IL. 312-355-1540
Finke, Betty L, *Librn,* Carrollton Public Library, Carrollton MO. 816-542-0183
Finkel, Emanuel, *ILL,* Nassau Community College Library, Garden City NY. 516-222-7400
Finkelpearl, Katherine, *Art Librn,* Wellesley College, Margaret Clapp Library, Wellesley MA. 617-235-0320, Ext 280
Finkelstein, Dvora, *Libr Asst,* Baltimore Hebrew College, Joseph M Meyerhoff Library, Baltimore MD. 301-466-7900, Ext 307
Finken, Mary L, *Librn,* Harlan Public Library, Harlan IA. 712-755-5934
Finkle, Mariam, *Librn,* Chattahoochee Valley Regional Library (Marion County Public), Buena Vista GA. 912-649-6385
Finkler, Norman, *Dir,* Montgomery County Department of Public Libraries, Rockville MD. 301-279-1401
Finks, Lee W, *Assoc Prof,* North Carolina Central University, School of Library Science, NC. 919-683-6485
Finlay, Dorothy M, *Librn,* Carbondale City Library, Carbondale KS. 913-564-7108
Finlay, Jane, *Ad,* Frederick E Parlin Memorial Library, Everett MA. 617-387-2550
Finlay, M, *Librn,* Department of National Defence, Mobile Command Headquarters Library, Saint Hubert PQ. 514-671-3711, Ext 242
Finlay, Sister M Catherine, *Dir,* Saint Joseph Hospital, Health Sciences Library, Houston TX. 713-757-1000
Finlayson, Janet, *Librn,* McGill University Libraries (Macdonald Campus Library), Saint Anne de Bellevue PQ. 514-457-2000, Ext 297
Finlayson, Mary S, *Librn,* Science Museum of Minnesota, Louis S Headley Memorial Library, Saint Paul MN. 612-222-9430
Finley, Betty Jo, *Cat,* Louisiana State Library, Baton Rouge LA. 504-342-4922
Finley, Doris, *Ref,* Saint Joseph Public Library, Saint Joseph MO. 816-232-7729, 232-7720
Finley, Elliot C, *Chief, Cent Serv Div,* Library of Congress, Washington DC. 202-287-5000
Finley, Sevilla, *Info Specialist,* Appalachia Educational Laboratory, Inc, Reference & Resource Center, Charleston WV. 304-344-8371, Ext 2
Finley, Vera, *Tech Serv,* Harrison County Library System, Gulfport MS. 601-868-1383
Finn, Barbara L, *Dir,* Sinai Hospital of Detroit, Samuel Frank Medical Library, Detroit MI. 313-493-5140
Finn, Bonnie, *Dir,* Bedford Public Library, Bedford TX. 817-283-2751

Finn, Lucille, *In Charge,* Saint Paul Public Library (Arlington Hills), Saint Paul MN. 612-292-6637
Finn, Susanna, *Librn,* Salisbury Free Public Library, Salisbury VT. 802-352-6671
Finn, V, *In Charge,* Pointe Claire Public Library (Stewart Hall), Pointe Claire PQ. 514-695-3330
Finnan, Anne M, *Educ,* Fordham University Library at Lincoln Center, New York NY. 212-841-5130, 841-5133
Finnan, Anne M, *Ref & Bibliog Instr,* Fordham University Library at Lincoln Center, New York NY. 212-841-5130, 841-5133
Finne, Bonnie, *Librn,* Hammer, Siler, George Associates Library, Atlanta GA. 404-524-6441
Finnegan, Maryann, *Dir Libr Serv,* Newton-Wellesley Hospital, Paul Talbot Babson Memorial Library, Newton Lower Falls MA. 617-964-2800, Ext 377
Finnegan, Nancy, *Ref & On-Line Servs,* Columbus Technical Institute, Educational Resources Center, Columbus OH. 614-227-2463
Finnegan, Robert, *Media & Acq,* College of Lake County, Learning Resource Center, Grayslake IL. 312-223-6601, Ext 392
Finnegan, S, *Archivist,* State University of New York at Buffalo (University Archives), Buffalo NY. 716-636-2916
Finnegan, Shonnie M, *Spec Coll,* State University of New York at Buffalo, University Libraries, Buffalo NY. 716-636-2965
Finnel, Soma, *Dir,* Oceanside Free Library, Oceanside NY. 516-766-2360
Finnelly, Cynthia, *Librn,* Wake County Department of the Public Library (Cameron Village), Raleigh NC. 919-755-6098
Finnemore, Alison, *Librn,* Pulp & Paper Research Institute of Canada Library, Pointe-Claire PQ. 514-697-4110, Ext 226
Finneran, Rosemary, *Librn,* Portsmouth Free Library, Portsmouth RI. 401-683-9457
Finnerty, Sandra, *Tech Serv & Cat,* City Library, Springfield MA. 413-739-3871
Finney, Ann, *Dir,* Marion County Memorial Hospital, Medical Staff Library, Marion SC. 803-423-3210, Ext 248
Finney, Bernard, *Consult,* New York State Library, Albany NY. 518-474-5930
Finney, Bonnie, *AV,* Metropolitan Library System, Oklahoma City OK. 405-235-0571
Finney, Jayne, *Circ,* Claremont Colleges Libraries, Claremont CA. 714-621-8000, Ext 3721
Finney, Lance C, *Pub Libr Specialists,* Maryland State Department of Education, Division of Library Development & Services, Baltimore MD. 301-796-8300, Ext 284
Finney, Marah S, *Librn,* Worcester County Library (Pocomoke City Branch), Pocomoke City MD. 301-957-0878
Finney, Nancy, *Per,* College of the Sequoias Library, Visalia CA. 209-733-2050, Ext 314
Finster, Eileen E, *Librn,* Pittsburgh Press Newspaper Library, Pittsburgh PA. 412-263-1480
Finton, Anna, *Librn,* Roanoke County Public Library (Vinton Branch), Vinton VA. 703-345-8153
Finzi, John, *Dir, Coll Develop Off,* Library of Congress, Washington DC. 202-287-5000
Fiore, Jannette C, *Spec Coll,* Michigan State University Library, East Lansing MI. 517-355-2344
Fiore, Lu-Ann, *Ad & Circ,* Canton Public Library, Canton MA. 617-828-0177
Fiorella, Marguerite, *Ch, Tech Serv & Ch,* Juneau Memorial Library, Juneau AK. 907-586-2429
Firestone, Ray, *Dir,* Baker University Library, Baldwin City KS. 913-594-6451, Ext 414
Firich, Mildred, *Bus Mgr & Ch Servs,* Laughlin Memorial Free Library, Ambridge PA. 412-266-3857
Firth, Edith, *Canadian Hist,* Metropolitan Toronto Library Board, Metropolitan Toronto Library, Toronto ON. 416-928-5150
Firth, Fran, *Librn,* Port Isabel Public Library, Port Isabel TX. 512-943-1822
Firth, Margaret A, *Librn,* Beverly Hospital Library, Beverly MA. 617-922-3000, Ext 254
Firth, Pauline, *Asst Dir,* San Jose Public Library, San Jose CA. 408-277-4822
Fischer, Ann, *Asst Librn,* Chandler Public Library, Chandler AZ. 602-963-8111, Ext 390
Fischer, Ann, *Ad,* Chester County Library & District Center, Exton PA. 215-363-0884
Fischer, Anne, *Ch,* Avon Lake Public Library, Avon Lake OH. 216-933-8128
Fischer, B, *Cat,* Muskingum College Library, New Concord OH. 614-826-8152
Fischer, Barbara, *Ch,* Wichita Public Library, Wichita KS. 316-262-0611
Fischer, Cathy, *Dir,* Southeast Community College Library, Fairbury NE. 402-729-6148
Fischer, Dorothy, *ILL,* Philadelphia College of Pharmacy & Science, Joseph W England Library, Philadelphia PA. 215-386-5800, Ext 296
Fischer, Elizabeth, *Librn,* Audubon Hospital, Medical Library, Louisville KY. 502-636-7296
Fischer, Eugene T, *Dir,* Campbell County Public Library, Rustburg VA. 804-847-0961
Fischer, Gloria A, *Dir & ILL,* Sacred Heart College, McCarthy Library, Belmont NC. 704-825-5146
Fischer, Joseph, *Librn,* Baltimore Symphony Orchestra Association, Inc Library, Baltimore MD. 301-837-5691
Fischer, Laural, *Commun Servs,* Akron-Summit County Public Library, Akron OH. 216-762-7621
Fischer, Mabel J, *Dir,* Fort Worth Public Library, Fort Worth TX. 817-870-7700
Fischer, Margaret Mary, *Cat,* King's College, D Leonard Corgan Library, Wilkes-Barre PA. 717-824-9931, Ext 245
Fischer, Marge, *Ch,* Lancaster Town Library, Lancaster MA. 617-365-2008
Fischer, Robert, *Librn,* Jacksonville Public Library System (Willow), Jacksonville FL. 904-633-4668
Fischer, Russ, *Dir,* San Jose City College Library, San Jose CA. 408-298-2181, Ext 410
Fischer, Ruth, *Librn,* College Church in Wheaton Library, Wheaton IL. 312-668-0878
Fischer, Thea, *Librn,* Lankenau Hospital (Medical Library), Philadelphia PA. 215-645-2698
Fischier, Adrienne, *Asst to the Dir,* Mercy College Libraries, Dobbs Ferry NY. 914-693-4500, Ext 260
Fischler, Barbara, *Librn,* Indiana University-Purdue University at Indianapolis (Thirty-Eighth Street Campus), Indianapolis IN. 317-923-1325
Fiscus, Judith A, *Dir,* Bedford Public Library, Bedford IN. 812-275-4471
Fisfis, Ann D, *Ref, On-Line Servs & Bibliog Instr,* California State College, Louis L Manderino Library, California PA. 412-938-4091
Fish, Althea W, *Librn,* Ludden Memorial Library, Dixfield ME. 207-562-8838
Fish, James H, *State Librn,* State Library of Massachusetts, Boston MA. 617-727-2590
Fish, Marie, *Reader Serv,* Glendale Public Library, Glendale CA. 213-956-2030
Fish, Monica, *Librn,* Kasson Public Library, Kasson MN. 507-634-7615
Fish, Vera, *Ch,* Westwood Public Library, Westwood MA. 617-326-7562
Fishback, Janice, *Librn,* Haywood County Public Library (Canton), Canton NC. 704-648-2924
Fishback, Margaret J, *Librn,* Duerson-Oldham County Public Library, La Grange KY. 502-222-1133
Fishbein, Patricia B, *Cat,* Susquehanna University, Roger M Blough Learning Ctr, Selinsgrove PA. 717-374-0101, Ext 329
Fishburn, Frances, *Spec Coll,* Park College Library, Parkville MO. 816-741-2000, Ext 254
Fisher, Alan J, *Coll Develop Librn,* Colorado College, Charles Learning Tutt Library, Colorado Springs CO. 303-473-2233, Ext 415
Fisher, Albert, *Librn,* Killingworth Library, Killingworth CT. 203-663-2000
Fisher, Alma M, *Dir,* Utica Junior College, William H Holtzclaw Library, Utica MS. 601-885-6062, Ext 48
Fisher, Ann H, *Dir,* Radford Public Library, Radford VA. 703-639-2621
Fisher, Anna T, *Librn,* West Fairlee Free Public Library, West Fairlee VT. 802-333-4651
Fisher, Barbara, *Librn,* Bay County Library System (Bay City), Bay City MI. 517-893-9566
Fisher, Beverly S, *Asst Dir & Ch,* Shrewsbury Free Public Library, Shrewsbury MA. 617-842-0081
Fisher, Brenda, *Librn,* New Glarus Public Library, New Glarus WI. 608-527-2003
Fisher, Brittany, *Pub Servs,* Johnson County Library, Shawnee Mission KS. 913-831-1550
Fisher, Carol, *Librn,* Whatcom County Public Library (Glacier Branch), Glacier WA. 206-384-3150
Fisher, Darien, *YA Servs & Inst Libr Consult,* State Library Commission of Iowa, Des Moines IA. 515-281-4102
Fisher, Debra, *Librn,* Southern University Library (Lab School), Baton Rouge LA. 504-771-3490
Fisher, Dema Jean, *Librn,* West Lebanon Pike Township Public Library, West Lebanon IN. 317-893-4014
Fisher, Denise, *Bkmobile Coordr,* Owensboro-Daviess County Public Library, Owensboro KY. 502-684-0211
Fisher, Diana, *ILL,* Dallas Theological Seminary, Mosher Library, Dallas TX. 214-824-3094, Ext 285
Fisher, Dixie Lou, *Acq,* Chesapeake Public Library, Chesapeake VA. 804-547-6579, 547-6592
Fisher, Elmer H, *Supvr Info Servs,* Babcock & Wilcox Research Center Library, Alliance OH. 216-821-9110, Ext 531
Fisher, Esther, *Librn,* Renville City Library, Renville MN. 612-329-8193
Fisher, Eunice M, *Asst Librn,* Winnebago County Law Library, Rockford IL. 815-987-2514
Fisher, Frances, *Circ & Ref,* United States Navy (Technical Library), China Lake CA. 714-939-2507
Fisher, Gladys, *Librn,* Jackson Metropolitan Library (Sebastapol Library), Sebastopol MS. 601-352-3677
Fisher, Gwen, *Librn,* Gallipolis State Institute Library, Gallipolis OH. 614-446-1642
Fisher, Idacna, *Libr Technician,* San Diego County Library (Jacumba Branch), Jacumba CA. 714-766-4608
Fisher, Jane Ellen, *Dir,* North Judson-Wayne Township Public Library, North Judson IN. 219-896-2841
Fisher, Janet, *YA,* Kokomo Public Library, Kokomo IN. 317-457-5558
Fisher, Janet S, *Asst Dean,* East Tennessee State University (Medical Library), Johnson City TN. 615-928-6426, Ext 252
Fisher, Jocelyn, *Dir,* Beyond Baroque Foundation, Small Press Publications Library, Venice CA. 213-822-3006
Fisher, John M, *Dir,* American Security Council Education Foundation, Boston VA. 703-825-1776
Fisher, Katherine P, *Commun Servs,* Worcester County Library, Snow Hill MD. 301-632-2600
Fisher, Katie, *ILL,* Iliff School of Theology, Ira J Taylor Library, Denver CO. 303-744-1287, Ext 30
Fisher, Kyle E, *Librn,* Jackson, Kelly, Holt & O'farrell, Law Library, Charleston WV. 304-347-7500
Fisher, Larry, *Ref & ILL,* American River College Library, Sacramento CA. 916-484-8293
Fisher, Lillian, *Dir, On-Line Servs & Bibliog Instr,* Allegheny General Hospital, Medical Library, Pittsburgh PA. 412-237-3040
Fisher, Louise R, *Asst Dir, ILL & Cat,* Iberia Parish Public Library, New Iberia LA. 318-369-6321
Fisher, Madeleine, *Dir,* Bell Memorial Public Library, Mentone IN. 219-353-7234
Fisher, Margaret, *Bkmobile Coordr,* Caroline County Public Library, Denton MD. 301-479-1343
Fisher, Marian Davis, *Librn,* Saint Louis County Library (Florissant Branch), Florissant MO. 314-921-7200
Fisher, Marion, *Tech Serv,* Belleville Public Library, Belleville ON. 613-968-7536
Fisher, Mary, *Librn,* General Electric Co, Corporate Legal Library, Fairfield CT. 203-373-2485
Fisher, Nancy, *Ref,* Cleveland Heights-University Heights Public Library, Cleveland Heights OH. 216-932-3600
Fisher, Olvena, *Librn,* Columbia-Lafayette-Ouachita-Calhoun Regional Library (Stamps Branch), Camden AR. 501-234-1991
Fisher, Patricia, *Asst Dir & Pub Servs,* University of Denver, Penrose Library, Denver CO. 303-753-2007
Fisher, Perry G, *Librn,* Columbia Historical Society Library, Washington DC. 202-785-2068

Fisher, Roberta, *Librn,* Perry County District Library (Corning Branch), Corning OH. 614-342-1077

Fisher, Ruby, *Librn,* Statesboro Regional Library (Candler County), Metter GA. 912-685-2455

Fisher, Ruth, *Librn,* Fairfax County Public Library (Engleside Branch), Alexandria VA. 703-360-6061

Fisher, Suzanne, *Fine arts, Recreation & Humanities,* Public Library of Columbus & Franklin County, Columbus OH. 614-864-8050

Fisher, W H, *Libr Supvr,* Bell Telephone Laboratories (Western Electric Technical Library), Princeton NJ. 609-639-2512

Fisher, Willie Mae, *In Charge,* Florida Agricultural & Mechanical University (Nursing Reading Room), Tallahassee FL. 904-599-3457

Fishlyn, Fannie, *ILL & Circ,* University of Southern California (Asa V Call Law Library), Los Angeles CA. 213-743-6487

Fishman, Jack, *Asst Dir,* Free Public Library of Woodbridge, Woodbridge NJ. 201-634-4450

Fishman, Joel, *Librn,* Allegheny County Law Library, Pittsburgh PA. 412-355-5353

Fishman, W, *Media,* Eastern Michigan University, Center of Educational Resources, Ypsilanti MI. 313-487-0020

Fisk, Al, *Media,* South Seattle Community College, Instructional Resources Center, Seattle WA. 206-764-5395

Fisk, Alice, *Asst Librn,* Middleport Free Library, Middleport NY. 716-735-3281

Fisk, Dorothy, *Dir,* United States Department of the Army (Office of the Adjutant General, Army Library Management Office), Washington DC. 202-325-9128, 325-9129

Fisk, Linda Fuerle, *Librn,* Berks County Law Library, Reading PA. 215-375-6121, Ext 266

Fiske, Arthur, *Librn,* Cleveland Law Library Association, Cleveland OH. 216-861-5070

Fisler, Lorraine, *Librn,* Mentor Public Library (Headlands), Mentor OH. 216-257-2000

Fisler, Lorraine, *Librn,* Mentor Public Library (Lake), Mentor OH. 216-257-2512

Fitch, Ann, *Librn,* First Baptist Church Library, Saint Paul MN. 612-222-0718

Fitch, Ann, *Librn,* Ramsey County Public Library (Maplewood), Roseville MN. 612-777-8146

Fitch, Donald, *Ref,* University of California, Santa Barbara Library, Santa Barbara CA. 805-961-2741

Fitch, E C, *Asst Dir,* Fairleigh Dickinson University, Friendship Library, Madison NJ. 201-377-4700, Ext 234

Fitch, E C, *Humanities,* Fairleigh Dickinson University, Friendship Library, Madison NJ. 201-377-4700, Ext 234

Fitch, Julia, *Librn,* Atlanta Public Library (Smith Memorial), Roswell GA. 404-993-6511

Fitch, June, *Br Asst,* Morehouse Parish Library (Oak Ridge Branch), Oak Ridge LA. 318-281-3683

Fitch, Mildred, *Librn,* Beebe Hospital, Medical Library, Lewes DE. 302-645-3283

Fitch, Sally Bemont, *Librn,* Baxter Memorial Library, Sharon VT. 802-763-8438

Fitch, Virginia, *Librn,* Guilford Free Library, Guilford VT. 802-254-2608

Fitcmaurice, Annette, *Acq,* University of Santa Clara, Michel Orradre Library, Santa Clara CA. 408-984-4415

Fite, Debra Kay, *Ch,* West Plains Public Library, West Plains MO. 417-256-4775

Fite, Vicki, *Pub Servs,* Tarrant County Junior College System (Northeast Campus Learning Resource Center), Hurst TX. 817-281-7860, Ext 477

Fites, Sandra E, *Media,* West Virginia Institute of Technology, Vining Library, Montgomery WV. 304-442-3141

Fithian, Andrea H, *Dir,* Mercer Free Public Library, Mercer PA. 412-662-4233

Fitschen, Ken, *Learning Lab Instr,* Western Wyoming Community College, Library Learning Resources Center, Rock Springs WY. 307-382-2121, Ext 154

Fitt, Stephen D, *Media,* San Diego State University Library, San Diego CA. 714-286-6014

Fitting, Polly, *Librn,* Douglas Library, Canaan CT. 203-824-7863

Fittro, Terry, *On-Line Servs & Bibliog Instr,* Everett Public Library, Everett WA. 206-259-8858

Fitts, Dorothy, *Librn,* First Regional Library (Lafayette County-Oxford Public), Oxford MS. 601-234-5751

Fitz, Caroline Moul, *Dir,* Amityville Public Library, Amityville NY. 516-264-0567

Fitz, Helen, *Librn,* Baltimore County Public Library (Perry Hall), Baltimore MD. 301-256-5522

Fitz, Tom, *Asst Dir,* University of Wisconsin Center-Barron County Library, Rice Lake WI. 715-234-8176, Ext 20

Fitzgerald, Alison, *Media,* North Central Regional Library System, Sudbury ON. 705-675-6467

Fitzgerald, Bonnie, *YA,* Weber State College Library, Stewart Library, Ogden UT. 801-626-6403

Fitzgerald, Bro A, *Curator,* Catholic University of America (Semitics), Washington DC. 202-635-5084

Fitzgerald, Carol, *Soc Sci,* City University of New York, Library of Graduate School & University Center, New York NY. 212-790-4541

Fitzgerald, Carol H, *Librn,* Delmar Public Library, Delmar DE. 302-846-9894

Fitzgerald, Catherine, *Cat,* Boston College Libraries (Law Library), Chestnut Hill MA. 617-969-0100, Ext 4405

Fitzgerald, Diana K, *Asst Librn,* Free Public Library of Mountainside, Mountainside NJ. 201-233-0115

Fitzgerald, Edna, *Ch,* Rogers Free Library, Bristol RI. 401-253-6948

Fitzgerald, Edward E, *Dir,* Florida Junior College at Jacksonville, Central Technical Services, Jacksonville FL. 904-387-8354

Fitzgerald, Edward E, *Librn,* Florida Junior College at Jacksonville (Kent Campus Learning Resource Center), Jacksonville FL. 904-387-8222

Fitzgerald, Eileen, *Asst Dir,* Girard Township Library, Girard IL. 217-627-2414

Fitzgerald, Frances, *Librn,* Frederic D Barstow Memorial Library, Chittenden VT. 802-773-6926

Fitzgerald, Jo, *Tech Serv & Acq,* Ardmore Public Library, Ardmore OK. 405-223-8290

Fitzgerald, Lizbeth, *Dir,* Broadview Public Library, Broadview IL. 312-345-1325

Fitzgerald, Louise, *Librn,* Valparaiso Community Library, Valparaiso FL. 904-678-7635

Fitzgerald, Mae Isom, *Librn,* Le Moyne-Owen College, Hollis F Price Library, Memphis TN. 901-774-9090

Fitzgerald, Margaret, *Ch,* Rochester Public Library, Rochester NY. 603-332-1428

Fitzgerald, Mary Monica, *Dir,* College of Saint Joseph the Provider Library, Rutland VT. 802-775-0806

Fitzgerald, Mary R, *Librn,* Talihina Public Library, Talihina OK. 918-567-2002

Fitzgerald, May, *Librn,* Whitney Museum of American Art Library, New York NY. 212-570-3649

Fitzgerald, Michael J, *Cat & Ser Div Chief,* Harvard University Library (Harvard College Library (Headquarters in Harry Elkins Widener Memorial Library)), Cambridge MA. 617-495-2401

Fitzgerald, Patricia, *ILL,* Malden Public Library, Malden MA. 617-324-0218

Fitzgerald, Richard W, *Dir,* Jonathan Bourne Public Library, Bourne MA. 617-759-3172

Fitzgerald, Sharron A, *Tech Serv,* Supreme Court of the United States Library, Washington DC. 202-252-3177

Fitzgerald, Sister Marie Annette, *AV,* Saint Mary's Junior College Library, Minneapolis MN. 612-332-5521

Fitzgibbon, Bernadine, *Ref,* Caldwell College Library, Caldwell NJ. 201-228-4424, Ext 34

Fitzgibbon, Marianne, *Librn,* Auld Public Library, Red Cloud NE. 402-746-3352

Fitzgibbons, Shirley A, *Asst Prof,* University of Maryland, College of Library & Information Services, MD. 301-454-5441

Fitzhugh, Della, *Librn,* Jackson Metropolitan Library (Sand Hill Library), Sand Hill MS. 601-352-3677

Fitzhugh, Kenneth W, *Librn,* Davenport College of Business Library, Grand Rapids MI. 616-451-3511, Ext 238

Fitzpatrick, Ann E, *Dir,* Nassau Board of Cooperative Educational Services, Educational Resources Center, Westbury NY. 516-931-8121

Fitzpatrick, Diane, *Hist,* University of Waterloo Library, Waterloo ON. 519-885-1211

Fitzpatrick, Elva, *Tech Serv,* Pitkin County Library, Aspen CO. 303-925-7124

Fitzpatrick, Jane, *Librn,* Jasper Municipal Library, Jasper Public Library, Jasper AB. 403-852-3652

Fitzpatrick, Jean, *Tech Serv,* Saint Peter's College Library, Englewood Cliffs NJ. 201-568-7730

Fitzpatrick, Judy, *Asst Librn,* Howe Memorial Library, Breckenridge MI. 517-842-3202

Fitzpatrick, Kelly, *Dir,* Mount Saint Mary's College & Seminary, Hugh J Phillips Library, Emmitsburg MD. 301-447-6122, Ext 243

Fitzpatrick, Lois A, *Dir,* Carroll College Library, Helena MT. 406-442-3450, Ext 245, 247 & 442-1295

Fitzpatrick, Lucy, *Librn,* Josephine County Library System (Williams Branch), Williams OR. 503-846-6083

Fitzpatrick, M Elaine, *Librn,* C-I-L Paints Inc, Paint Research Laboratory Library, Toronto ON. 416-787-2411, Ext 262

Fitzpatrick, Nora, *Ref,* Cambria County Library System, Johnstown PA. 814-536-5131

Fitzpatrick, R, *Tech Serv,* Florida Institute of Technology, Jensen Beach Library, Jensen Beach FL. 305-334-4200, Ext 60, 61

Fitzpatrick, Robert E, *Media,* Nashua Public Library, Nashua NH. 603-883-4141, 883-4142

Fitzsimmons, Richard, *Head Librn,* Pennsylvania State University, Worthington Scranton Campus Library, Dunmore PA. 717-961-4775

Fivash, Marilyn, *Librn,* Arkansas College, Mabee Learning Resources Center, Batesville AR. 501-793-9813

Flack, Shirley, *Dir,* Scottsbluff Public Library, Scottsbluff NE. 308-632-4424

Flagg, Becky, *ILL,* Martinsburg-Berkeley County Public Library, Martinsburg Service Center, Martinsburg WV. 304-267-8933

Flagg, Cheryl, *Dir,* Vienna Public Library, Vienna WV. 304-295-7771

Flagg, Jo Ellen, *Br Coordr,* Kanawha County Public Library, Kanawha County Service Center, Charleston WV. 304-343-4646

Flagg, Lucy, *Librn,* Agnew State Hospital (Staff Library), San Jose CA. 408-262-2100, Ext 2367

Flagg, Mary, *Rare Bks & Spec Coll,* University of New Brunswick, Harriet Irving Library, Fredericton NB. 506-453-4740

Flaherty, Beverly, *Br Coordr,* Anoka County Library, Blaine MN. 612-784-1100

Flaherty, Beverly, *Librn,* Anoka County Library (Fridley Branch), Fridley MN. 612-571-1934

Flaherty, Chuck, *Asst Dir,* Framingham Public Library, Framingham MA. 617-879-3570

Flaherty, Peggy, *ILL,* Eastern Kentucky University, John Grant Crabbe Library, Richmond KY. 606-622-3606

Flaherty, Susan, *Dir,* South Milwaukee Public Library, South Milwaukee WI. 414-762-8692

Flaim, Anna, *ILL,* Olean Public Library, Olean NY. 716-372-0200

Flake, Chad, *Rare Bks & Spec Coll,* Brigham Young University, Harold B Lee Library, Provo UT. 801-378-2905

Flake, Donna, *ILL & Circ,* East Carolina University (Health Affairs Library), Greenville NC. 919-757-6961, Ext 261

Flaker, Gladys, *Librn,* Electronic Associates, Inc, Library, West Long Branch NJ. 201-229-1100

Flammia, Ruth, *Dir,* East Hanover Township Free Public Library, East Hanover NJ. 201-887-6215

Flanagan, Ann B, *Librn,* Virginia Electric & Power Co Library, Richmond VA. 804-771-3659, 3657

Flanagan, Jerry L, *Dir,* Princeton Public Library, Mercer Memorial Library, Princeton WV. 304-425-3324

Flanagan, Lee, *Coordr,* Region One Cooperating Library Services Unit, Inc, CT. 203-756-6149

Flanagan, Lois, *Homebound Serv,* Dodge City Public Library, Dodge City KS. 316-225-0248

Flanagan, Margaret A, *Librn,* Episcopal Hospital, Medical Library, Philadelphia PA. 215-426-8000

Flanagan, Mary, *Ch,* Prince William Public Library, Manassas VA. 703-361-8211

Flanagan, Robert, *Ad,* Camden County Free Library, Voorhees NJ. 609-772-1636

Flanagan, Rosemary, *Librn,* Saint Elizabeth Hospital, Medical Library, Danville IL. 217-442-6300, Ext 409
Flanders, Bruce, *Ref,* Kansas State Library, Topeka KS. 913-296-3296
Flanders, H Juanita, *Acq,* Florida International University, Tamiami Campus, Athenaeum, Miami FL. 305-552-2461
Flanigan, Ann Jane, *Librn,* Saint Mary's Hospital Library, Streator IL. 815-664-5311
Flann, Viola, *Librn,* Lake Lillian Public Library, Lake Lillian MN. 612-664-4210
Flannery, Louis, *Chief Librn,* Oregon Historical Society Library, Portland OR. 503-222-1741
Flannery, Michael, *Media,* Plymouth State College, Herbert H Lamson Library, Plymouth NH. 603-536-1550, Ext 257
Flannery, Michael J, *ILL,* Plymouth State College, Herbert H Lamson Library, Plymouth NH. 603-536-1550, Ext 257
Flannery, Susan, *YA,* Public Library of the City of Somerville, Somerville MA. 617-623-5000
Flansburg, Deborah, *Libr Technician,* Middleville Free Library, Middleville NY. 315-891-3957
Flasher, Peggy, *Commun Servs,* Jackson Metropolitan Library, Jackson MS. 601-352-3677
Flatness, Gail, *Ref & On-Line Servs,* Georgetown University, Joseph Mark Lauinger Library, Washington DC. 202-625-4095
Flattery, Dorothy, *Head Libr,* Novi Public Library, Novi MI. 313-349-0720
Flaum, Gary, *Dir,* Metromedia Producers Corp, Research Department Library, Los Angeles CA. 213-462-7111
Flautz, Nancy, *Acq,* Cedar Crest College, Cressman Library, Allentown PA. 215-437-4471, Ext 264
Flautz, Nancy, *Acq,* Muhlenberg College, John A W Haas Library, Allentown PA. 215-433-3191, Ext 214
Flavin, Harold J, *ILL,* City Library, Springfield MA. 413-739-3871
Flax, Edwina, *Dir,* Calvary Hospital (Nursing Library), Bronx NY. 212-430-4888
Flayer, Carol, *Librn,* Kent County Library System (Mailbox Library), Grand Rapids MI. 616-774-3250
Fleak, Audrey E, *Librn,* United States Navy (Naval Amphibious School Library), San Diego CA. 714-437-2295
Flechuk, Marge, *Asst Librn,* Vegreville Public Library, Vegreville AB. 403-632-3491
Fleck, Janet, *Librn,* Stockton Township Public Library, Stockton IL. 815-947-2030
Fleck, Jeane, *ILL,* Saint Norbert College, Todd Wehr Library, De Pere WI. 414-337-3280
Fleckenstein, Dolores D, *Librn,* Powers Library, Moravia NY. 315-497-1955
Flecker, Dale P, *Head of Office for Systs Planning & Res,* Harvard University Library, Cambridge MA. 617-495-3650
Fledderus, Helen, *Librn,* Reader's Digest Association (Advertising & Marketing Library), New York NY. 212-972-3730
Fleenor, Elisabeth, *Cat,* United States Air Force Academy Library, United States Air Force Academy CO. 303-472-2590
Fleer, Cherie, *Circ,* Lincolnwood Public Library, Lincolnwood IL. 312-677-5277
Fleet, Frances A, *Librn,* Bliss Memorial Public Library, Bloomville OH. 419-983-4675
Fleet, Jane, *Ref & Tech Serv,* Christian Brothers College Library, Memphis TN. 901-278-0100, Ext 220
Fleetwood, Margaret, *Assistant Chief Librn,* Town of Caledon Public Libraries, Bolton ON. 416-857-1400
Fleetwood, Margaret, *Asst Librn,* Town of Caledon Public Libraries (Albion-Bolton Branch), Bolton ON. 416-857-1400
Fleharty, Janet, *Media,* Colorado School for the Deaf & Blind Library, Colorado Springs CO. 303-636-5186
Fleischer, Miriam, *Librn,* New York Public Library (Fort Washington), New York NY. 212-927-3533
Fleischer, Regina, *Tech Serv,* Wilmette Public Library District, Wilmette IL. 312-256-5025
Fleischman, Donald J, *Media,* Niagara Falls Public Library, Niagara Falls NY. 716-278-8041

Fleischman, Libby, *Asst Archivist,* Judah L Magnes Memorial Museum (Western Jewish History Center), Berkeley CA. 415-849-2710, Ext D & E
Fleischmann, Martha, *Cat,* Birmingham Public & Jefferson County Free Library, Birmingham AL. 205-254-2551
Fleisher, Lisa, *Cat,* Tucson Public Library, Tucson AZ. 602-791-4391
Fleisher, Mary-Louise, *Librn,* Wolf, Block, Schorr & Solis-Cohen Library, Philadelphia PA. 215-569-4000
Fleming, Alice, *Librn,* Mary L Goodrich Public Library, Toppenish WA. 509-865-3600
Fleming, Carrie, *Cat,* University of Calgary Library, Calgary AB. 403-284-5954
Fleming, Charlotte, *Librn,* Chrisman Public Library, Chrisman IL. 217-269-3011
Fleming, Darlene, *Librn,* Alcon Laboratories, Inc, Technical Library, Fort Worth TX. 817-293-0450, Ext 2263
Fleming, Fred, *Librn,* Cherokee Regional Library (Rossville Branch), Rossville GA. 404-866-1368
Fleming, Gail, *Assoc Librn,* University of California, Hastings College of the Law Library, San Francisco CA. 415-557-1354
Fleming, Herman, *In Charge,* National Science Foundation Library, Washington DC. 202-632-4070
Fleming, Jacqueline, *Librn,* Louisville Free Public Library (Taylor Boulevard), Louisville KY. 502-361-4577
Fleming, John, *Spec Coll,* Edinboro State College, Baron-Forness Library, Edinboro PA. 814-732-2780
Fleming, Josephine, *Librn,* Richmond Hill Public Library (Charles Connor Memorial), Richmond Hill ON. 416-773-5533
Fleming, Judith, *Dean,* Odessa College, Murry H Fly Learning Resources Center, Odessa TX. 915-337-5381, Ext 299
Fleming, June, *Dir,* Palo Alto City Library, Palo Alto CA. 415-329-2436
Fleming, Lois D, *Dir,* Leon County Public Library, Leon-Jefferson Library System, Tallahassee FL. 904-487-2665
Fleming, Lynn, *Dir,* Tri-County Public Library District, Augusta IL. 217-392-2211
Fleming, Mary, *Librn,* Ahoskie Public Library, Ahoskie NC. 919-332-5500
Fleming, Mattie, *Librn,* Crowley Ridge Regional Library (Marked Tree Branch), Marked Tree AR. 501-358-3190
Fleming, Mrs A, *Librn,* Michipicoten Township Public Library, Wawa ON. 705-856-2062
Fleming, Pamela, *Media,* North Carolina State University, D H Hill Library, Raleigh NC. 919-737-2843, 2595
Fleming, Pheobe, *Ref & Ser,* Somerset County College Library, Somerville NJ. 201-526-1200, Ext 224, 304
Fleming, Robert, *Bkmobile Coordr,* Kitchener Public Library, Kitchener ON. 519-743-0271
Fleming, William C, *Librn,* Hope Congregational Library, East Providence RI. 401-434-2415
Flemister, Wilson N, *Librn,* Interdenominational Theological Center Library, Atlanta GA. 404-522-1744
Flemming, Bernetha H, *Librn,* Crafts-Farrow State Hospital Library, Columbia SC. 803-758-4864
Flemming, Julie, *Dir,* Fox Lake Public Library, Fox Lake WI. 414-928-3223
Flener, Jane G, *Assoc Dir,* University of Michigan Libraries (University Library), Ann Arbor MI. 313-764-9356
Flentge, Marguerite, *Ch,* Des Plaines Public Library, Des Plaines IL. 312-827-5551
Flesch, Joan, *Librn,* Bristol-Myers Co, International Div Library, New York NY. 212-644-2100
Flesher, Ellen M, *Librn,* Topeka State Hospital Staff Library, Topeka KS. 913-296-4411
Flesher, Lorna J, *Supvr Librn,* California State Department of Transportation (Law Library), Sacramento CA. 916-445-2291
Flesher, Mary, *Librn,* Shodair Crippled Children's Hospital Library, Helena MT. 406-442-1980
Fleshman, Linda, *Doc,* Indiana University at South Bend Library, South Bend IN. 219-237-4440
Flesia, Faye, *Dir & On-Line Servs,* University of Wisconsin Center, Waukesha County Library, Waukesha WI. 414-542-8825, Ext 280
Fleszar, Val, *Acq,* Wayne Oakland Library Federation, Wayne MI. 313-326-8910

Fletcher, Amy L, *Asst Dir,* Carnegie Library, Olney IL. 618-392-3711
Fletcher, Bonnie, *Asst Cat,* Idaho State University Library, Pocatello ID. 208-236-3202
Fletcher, Carolyn J, *Cat,* University of Miami, Otto G Richter Library, Coral Gables FL. 305-284-3551
Fletcher, Charlotte, *Dir & Acq,* Saint John's College, Woodward Hall Library, Annapolis MD. 301-263-2371, Ext 71, 72
Fletcher, Corella M, *Librn,* Walters Public Library, Walters OK. 405-875-2006
Fletcher, Elsa, *Librn,* Gideon Public Library, Gideon MO. 314-448-3554
Fletcher, Homer L, *Dir,* San Jose Public Library, San Jose CA. 408-277-4822
Fletcher, James, *Librn,* Northwest Georgia Regional Hospital, Health Science Library, Rome GA. 404-295-6246
Fletcher, Jane, *Archivist,* Rollins College, Mills Memorial Library, Winter Park FL. 305-646-2000, Ext 2676
Fletcher, Jeff, *Instr,* Appalachian State University, Department of Educational Media: Librarianship & Instructional Technology, NC. 704-262-2243
Fletcher, Katy, *Ad,* Bud Werner Memorial Library, Steamboat Springs CO. 303-879-0240
Fletcher, Kay, *Consultant, Libr Distribution Programs,* Colorado State Library, Colorado Department of Education, Denver CO. 303-839-3695
Fletcher, Lee, *Ref & ILL,* New Albany Floyd County Public Library, New Albany IN. 812-944-8464
Fletcher, Mabel, *Acq,* Miami Dade Community College (North Campus Library), Miami FL. 305-685-4436
Fletcher, Mary, *Librn,* Maywood Public Library (Maywood), Maywood IL. 312-343-0508
Fletcher, Mary, *Pub Servs,* Mission College, Learning Resource Services, Santa Clara CA. 408-988-2200, Ext 1531
Fletcher, Miles A, *Librn,* Vienna Correctional Center Library, Vienna IL. 618-658-2081
Fletcher, Mrs Bruce, *Librn,* Orchard Public Library, Orchard NE. 402-893-4606
Fletcher, Mrs L, *Acq,* Red Deer College, Learning Resources Center, Red Deer AB. 403-346-6450
Fletcher, Nell, *Librn,* Wyoming Public Library, Wyoming IL. 309-695-4831
Fletcher, Ruth, *Spec Coll & Archivist,* Wheaton College Library, Norton MA. 617-285-7722, Ext 518
Fletcher, Shirley, *Acq,* Adams Library, Chelmsford MA. 617-256-5521
Fleure, Nancy, *Chief Librn,* Monroe County Library System (Dorsch), Monroe MI. 313-241-7878
Fleurent, Vernona, *Librn,* Durham Center Museum Inc, Research Library, East Durham NY. 518-239-8461
Fleury, Dorothy, *Head Librn,* South Interlake Regional Library, Stonewall MB. 204-467-8415
Flexner, John, *Tech Serv,* Harwood Foundation Library, Taos NM. 505-758-3063
Flick, Buddy, *Cat,* Lockheed Corporation (Lockheed-California Company Central Library), Burbank CA. 213-847-5646
Flick, Roger, *Genealogy,* Brigham Young University, Harold B Lee Library, Provo UT. 801-378-2905
Flinn, Kathryn, *Dir,* Walters State Community College, Learning Resource Center, Morristown TN. 615-581-2121, Ext 212
Flinner, Bea, *ILL, Ref & Bibliog Instr,* Bethany Nazarene College, R T Williams Memorial Library, Bethany OK. 405-789-6400, Ext 276
Flint, Elaine, *Acq,* Glendale Community College, John F Prince Library, Glendale AZ. 602-934-2211, Ext 239, 242
Flint, Susan, *Asst Librn,* Temple Emanu-El, William P Engel Library, Birmingham AL. 205-933-8037
Flippo, Jennie, *Acq,* First Regional Library, DeSoto County Library, Hernando MS. 601-368-4439
Flodman, Mildred, *Dir,* Stromsburg Public Library, Stromsburg NE. 402-764-7681
Flohr, Sharon, *Circ,* Weld County Library, Greeley CO. 303-330-7691
Flokstra, Jr, Gerard J, *Dir,* Central Bible College Library, Springfield MO. 417-833-2551, Ext 37

Flood, Francis J, *Assoc Prof*, University of Missouri-Columbia, School of Library & Informational Science, MO. 314-882-4546
Flood, Helen, *County Exten*, John McIntire Public Library Public Library, Zanesville OH. 614-453-0391
Flood, Mary K, *Librn*, Buck Library, Portland CT. 203-342-1841
Flook, Carolyn, *Librn*, Bayard Public Library, Bayard IA. 712-651-2238
Flook, Jeff, *Asst Librn*, Aspen Systems Corporation, Library & Information Center, Rockville MD. 301-428-0700
Florence, Mattie Lou, *Librn*, Bay County Public Library Association (Liberty County Branch), Bristol FL. 904-643-8858
Florentino, Barbara, *Commun Servs*, Hamden Library, Miller Memorial, Hamden CT. 203-248-7747
Flores, Anita R, *Spec Coll*, Albany Medical Center College of Union University, Schaffer Library of Health Sciences, Albany NY. 518-445-5534
Flores, Annie T, *Librn*, Catholic University of America (Library Science), Washington DC. 202-635-5092
Flores, Clarita H, *Librn*, American Chemical Society Library, Washington DC. 202-872-4600
Flores, Michael, *Librn*, Colorado River Indian Tribes Public Library, Parker AZ. 602-669-9211
Flores, Robert J, *Bur of Regional Libr Servs: Chief*,New York State Library, Albany NY. 518-474-5930
Flores, Sandra, *Dir*, Jasper Public Library, Jasper TX. 713-384-3791
Florin, Carol C, *Librn*, William Mitchell College of Law, Law Library, Saint Paul MN. 612-227-9171
Florkiewicz, Isle, *Actg Librn*, Manitouwadge Public Library, Manitouwadge ON. 807-826-3913
Flotho, Sally, *ILL & Circ*, Golden West College Library, Huntington Beach CA. 714-892-7711, Ext 541
Flournoy, Donald B, *Cartographer*, United States Air Force, Air University Library, Maxwell AFB AL. 205-293-2888
Flournoy, Nancy, *Ref*, Hinds Junior College, George M McLendon Library, Raymond MS. 601-857-5261, Ext 253
Flower, Kenneth, *Ref*, State Library of Massachusetts, Boston MA. 617-727-2590
Flower, Muriel, *Librn*, McGill University Libraries (Nursing), Montreal PQ. 514-392-5027
Flowers, Ann A , *Ch*, Wayland Free Public Library, Wayland MA. 617-358-2311, 358-2308
Flowers, Bonnie, *Ch*, Kent Free Public Library, Carmel NY. 914-225-8585
Flowers, Eileen S, *Librn*, Wadsworth Public Library, Wadsworth OH. 216-334-5761
Flowers, Emily, *Asst Dir & Cat*, Southwestern at Memphis, Burrow Library, Memphis TN. 901-274-1800, Ext 365, 366
Flowers, Kathryn, *Librn*, Envirodyne Engineers, Inc Library, Saint Louis MO. 314-434-6960, Ext 253
Flowers, Loretta L, *Asst Dir*, Santa Fe Regional Library, Gainesville Public Library Headquarters, Gainesville FL. 904-374-2091
Flowers, Marion E, *Personnel Officer*, Saint Louis Public Library, Saint Louis MO. 314-241-2288
Flowers, Patricia P, *Ref*, Inland Library System, Redlands CA. 714-793-0871
Floyd, Bill, *Soc Sci*, North Texas State University Library, Denton TX. 817-788-2411
Floyd, Joy Marie, *Librn*, Monroe Public Library, Monroe CT. 203-261-3651
Floyd, Sarah, *Librn*, First Baptist Church, Stinceon Ivey Memorial Library, Fairmont NC. 919-628-6371
Fluckiger, Adrienne, *Ch*, Syosset Public Library, Syosset NY. 516-921-7161
Fluegge, Carol, *Ad & AV*, West Florida Regional Library, Pensacola Public Library, Pensacola FL. 904-438-5479
Fluesmeier, Eva, *Ch*, Miami Public Library, Miami OK. 918-542-3064
Flukas, Karen, *In Charge*, Sentry Insurance Library, Scottsdale AZ. 602-994-7000
Flumiani, C M, *Dir*, American Classical College Library, Albuquerque NM. 505-843-7749
Fly, Connie L, *Coordr*, Biomedical Library Program, CA. 209-252-2851
Flynn, Ann M, *Librn*, Framingham Public Library, Framingham MA. 617-879-3570

Flynn, Barbara, *Head, AV Ctr*, Chicago Public Library (Cultural Center), Chicago IL. 312-269-2820
Flynn, Barbara, *Soc Sci & Hist*, Ontario Public Library, Ontario CA. 984-2758 Ext 38
Flynn, Barbara, *Ref, On-Line Servs & Bibliog Instr*,University of Southwestern Louisiana, Dupre Library, Lafayette LA. 318-264-6396
Flynn, Barbara J, *Librn*, Ontario Public Library, Ontario CA. 984-2758 Ext 38
Flynn, Frances, *Librn*, Harvard University Library (Schering Foundation Library of Health Care), Boston MA. 617-732-2103
Flynn, John C, *Librn*, Moose Lake State Hospital Library, Moose Lake MN. 218-485-4411
Flynn, Kathleen M, *Asst Librn*, Western New England College (Law Library), Springfield MA. 413-782-3111, Ext 454, 455
Flynn, Kathryn J, *Dir*, Neenah Public Library, Neenah WI. 414-729-4728
Flynn, Kay, *Librn*, Claiborne Parish Library (Homer Branch), Homer LA. 318-927-3845
Flynn, Lauri, *Asst Librn & Tech Serv*, Lewis & Clark College (Paul L Boley Law Library), Portland OR. 503-244-1181, Ext 685
Flynn, Lawrence E, *Librn*, Racine County Law Library, Racine WI. 414-636-3408
Flynn, Libby, *Tech Serv*, Graduate Theological Union Library, Berkeley CA. 415-841-9811
Flynn, Linda, *Cat*, Blinn College, W L Moody Jr Library, Brenham TX. 713-836-6566
Flynn, Marianne, *Asst Librn*, Glendive Public Library, Dawson County Library, Glendive MT. 406-365-3633
Flynn, Marion C, *Asst Dir*, Greater Hartford Community College Library, Hartford CT. 203-549-4200, Ext 277
Flynn, Mark, *Acq*, Loyola University Library, Main Library, New Orleans LA. 504-865-3346
Flynn, Maureen D, *Librn*, United States Postal Service, Training & Development Institute, Technical Center Library, Norman OK. 405-325-1001
Flynn, Neil, *Dir*, Lake County Public Library, Merrillville IN. 219-769-3541
Flynn, Richard, *Librn*, Federal Bar Foundation Library, Washington DC. 202-638-1956
Flynn, Roger, *Asst Prof*, University of Pittsburgh, School of Library & Information Science, PA. 412-624-5230
Flynn, Sister Marian, *Librn*, Maria College of Albany Library, Albany NY. 518-438-3111
Flynn, Thelma A, *Librn*, Fairmount Community Library, Syracuse NY. 315-487-8933
Flynn, Thomas, *Asst Librn*, Maria College of Albany Library, Albany NY. 518-438-3111
Flynt, Cora, *Librn*, Atlanta Public Library (Dixie Hills), Atlanta GA. 404-799-3266
Foche, Mae, *Librn*, Kings County Library (Grangeville Branch), Grangeville CA. 209-584-4805
Focke, Helen Metcalf, *Emer Prof*, Case Western Reserve University, School of Library Science, OH. 216-368-3500
Fockler, Susan, *Media*, Outagamie Waupaca Counties Federated Library System, Appleton WI. 414-734-8873
Fodor, Elza O, *Librn*, Public Utilities Commission of Ohio, Research & Law Library, Columbus OH. 614-466-5082
Fody, Barbara, *Head Librn*, Paine Webber Jackson & Curtis, Research Library, New York NY. 212-437-2995
Foehl, Audrey, *Librn*, First Congregational Church Library, Cheshire CT. 203-272-5323
Foelgner, Kay S, *Ch*, Cocoa Beach Public Library, Cocoa Beach FL. 305-783-7350
Foell, John F, *Info Specialists*, Conoco Inc Research & Development Department, Technical Information Services, Ponca City OK. 405-767-4719
Foeller, Robert J, *Librn*, Rockingham Community College Library, Learning Resources Center, Wentworth NC. 919-342-4261, Ext 245
Foelster, Alice, *Circ*, Bernardsville Public Library, Bernardsville NJ. 201-766-0118
Foerstel, Herbert, *Librn*, University of Maryland at College Park (Engineering & Physical Science), College Park MD. 301-454-4281
Fogarty, Charlotte, *Librn*, Saint Clair County Library System (G Lynn Campbell), Port Huron MI. 313-982-9171

Fogarty, Elizabeth W, *Tech Serv*, Charleston County Library, Charleston SC. 803-723-1645
Fogarty, Nancy C, *Ref*, University of North Carolina at Greensboro, Walter Clinton Jackson Library, Greensboro NC. 919-379-5880
Fogarty, Nicholas, *YA*, Roxbury Public Library, Succasunna NJ. 201-584-2400, 584-2401
Fogel, Natalee, *Ref*, Ossining Public Library, Ossining NY. 941-2416; 941-9174
Fogelberg, Audrey, *Acq*, Baldwin Public Library, Baldwin NY. 516-223-6228
Fogerson, Nancy, *Dir*, Hillsdale Free Will Baptist College Library, Moore OK. 405-794-6661, Ext 11
Fogerty, James E, *Deputy State Archivist*, Minnesota Historical Society (Division of Archives & Manuscripts), Saint Paul MN. 612-296-6980
Fogg, Elizabeth C, *Dir*, Salem Free Public Library, Salem NJ. 609-935-0526
Fogg, Jean B, *Librn*, Reichhold Chemicals, Inc, Newport Div Research Library, Pensacola FL. 904-433-7621, Ext 313
Fogg, May, *Cat*, Lane Community College Library, Eugene OR. 503-747-4501, Ext 2354
Fogh-Dohmsmidt, Jane, *Lectr*, Lakehead University, School of Library Technology, ON. 807-345-2121, Ext 240
Fogle, Almeada M, *Librn*, Garfield County Free Library, Jordan MT. 406-557-2297
Fogle, Barb, *Librn*, Technology Inc, Instruments & Controls Div Library, Dayton OH. 513-426-2405
Fogleman, Levergne, *Acq*, McNeese State University, Lether E Frazar Memorial Library, Lake Charles LA. 318-477-2520, Ext 271
Fogleman, Marguerite, *Assoc Librn*, Augusta College, Reese Library, Augusta GA. 404-828-4566, 828-4066
Fohl, Roger, *Second Vice President*, Chase Manhattan Bank (Information Center), New York NY. 212-552-8014
Foisy, Aline, *Asst Librn*, Bonfield Public Library, Bonfield ON. 705-776-2641
Folan, Ann, *ILL*, University of Pittsburgh, Johnstown Campus Library, Johnstown PA. 814-266-9661, Ext 314
Folcarelli, Michele R, *Dir*, Cora J Belden Library, Rocky Hill CT. 203-529-2379
Folcarelli, Ralph J, *Dean*, Long Island University, Palmer Graduate Library School, NY. 516-299-2855 & 299-2856
Folda, Linda W, *Tech Serv*, Chapel Hill Public Library, Chapel Hill NC. 919-942-5455
Foldes, Lance J, *Ref*, Berry College, Memorial Library, Mount Berry GA. 404-232-5374, Ext 221, 388
Foley, David, *Tech Serv*, Richland Community College, Learning Resources Center, Decatur IL. 217-875-7200
Foley, Evin A, *Librn*, Massasoit Community College Library, Brockton MA. 617-588-9100, Ext 141
Foley, Gerald, *ILL, Ref & Bibliog Instr*, Springfield Technical Community College Library, Springfield MA. 413-781-7822, Ext 3485
Foley, Hila O, *Librn*, Cincinnati Municipal Reference Library, Cincinnati OH. 513-352-3309
Foley, James, *Tech Serv*, Mohawk Valley Library Association, Schenectady NY. 518-355-2010
Foley, James, *Tech Serv*, Schenectady County Public Library, Schenectady NY. 518-382-3500
Foley, Katherine, *Coordr Data Base*, Missouri State Library, Jefferson City MO. 314-751-4214
Foley, Katherine B, *Bkmobile Coordr*, Mohawk Valley Library Association, Schenectady NY. 518-355-2010
Foley, Kathy, *Librn*, Houston Post Library, Houston TX. 713-840-5830, 840-5835
Foley, Margaret M, *Asst Dir & Ad*, Schenectady County Public Library, Schenectady NY. 518-382-3500
Foley, Mary M, *Librn*, Sullivan County Library, Dushore PA. 717-928-9352
Foley, May, *Asst Prof*, University of Guam, Library Science Program, GU. 734-2921
Foley, Patricia H, *Librn*, University of Iowa Libraries (Business Administration), Iowa City IA. 319-353-5803
Foley, Robert, *ILL*, Fitchburg State College Library, Fitchburg MA. 617-345-2151, Ext 137

Foley, Rose, *Asst Librn,* Chester C Corbin Public Library, Webster Public Library, Webster MA. 617-943-0131

Foley, Wendy, *Commun Servs,* Portland Public Library, Baxter Library, Portland ME. 207-773-4761

Folk, Charlotte, *Librn,* Environmental Protection Agency, Environmental Research Laboratory Library, Athens GA. 404-546-3103

Folk, Charlotte, *Cat,* University of Georgia Libraries, Athens GA. 404-542-2716

Folk, Margaret, *Asst Librn,* Parker Pen Co, Corporate Technical Center Libr, Janesville WI. 608-755-7203

Folk, Mary, *Ref,* Perry County District Library, New Lexington OH. 614-342-1077

Folke, Patricia, *Per,* University of North Dakota (Olaf H Thormodsgard Law Library), Grand Forks ND. 701-777-2204

Folkerts, Mrs H G, *Librn,* Victor Public Library, Victor IA. 319-647-3646

Folkes, Tom, *Librn,* Clarinda Mental Health Institute (Professional Library), Clarinda IA. 712-542-2161

Folkes, Tom, *Librn,* Clarinda Mental Health Institute (Resident's Library), Clarinda IA. 712-542-2161

Folks, Dorotha, *Librn,* Pioneer Multi-County Library (Purcell Public), Purcell OK. 405-527-5546

Follett, Sharron, *Librn,* Reynolds Township Library, Howard City MI. 616-937-5575

Follom, Rebecca, *Librn,* Volga Public Library, Volga IA. 319-767-2465

Follstad, Virginia P, *Dir,* Whitewater Public Library, Whitewater WI. 414-473-3906

Folman, James R, *Reader Serv,* Weber State College Library, Stewart Library, Ogden UT. 801-626-6403

Folsom, Louise D, *Librn,* Vose Library, Union ME. 207-785-4733

Folsom, Retta, *Ch & YA,* Paducah Public Library, Paducah KY. 502-442-2510, 443-2664

Folsom, Roddelle B, *Dir,* South Georgia Regional Library, Valdosta-Lowndes County Public Library, Valdosta GA. 912-247-3405

Foltin, Bela, *Fine Arts,* University of Georgia Libraries, Athens GA. 404-542-2716

Foltz, Faye, *Ser,* Wake Forest University (Bowman Gray School of Medicine Library), Winston-Salem NC. 919-727-4691

Foltz, Meredith, *YA,* Sheppard Memorial Library, Greenville NC. 919-752-4177

Foly, Ruth M, *Dir,* Saint Clair County Community College, Learning Resources Center, Port Huron MI. 313-984-3881, Ext 278

Fomerand, Raissa, *Librn,* Sleepy Hollow Restorations Library, Tarrytown NY. 914-631-8200

Fonda, Dorothy B, *Ch,* Knoxville Public Library, Knoxville IA. 515-842-5512

Fondi, Ruth M, *Dir,* Sewickley Public Library, Sewickley PA. 412-741-6920

Fondren, Yvonne, *Librn,* Sunflower County Library System (Henry M Seymour Library), Indianola MS. 601-887-1672

Fondren, Yvonne B, *Librn,* Henry M Seymour Public Library, Indianola MS. 601-887-1672

Fong, Florence, *Tech Serv,* Holy Names College, Paul J Cushing Library, Oakland CA. 415-436-1332

Fong, Karina, *Per,* Humber College, Learning Resource Centre, Rexdale ON. 416-675-3111, Ext 331

Fong, Liane, *Cat,* Fullerton City Library, Fullerton CA. 714-738-6333, Ext 301

Font, Betty, *Cat,* Northland Pioneer College (District Learning Resources Center), Holbrook AZ. 602-524-6111, Ext 234 & 243

Fontaine, Lorraine, *Librn,* Woonsocket Call, Editorial Department Library, Woonsocket RI. 401-762-3000

Fontaine, Marcel, *Asst Dir,* Bibliotheque Nationale Du Quebec, Montreal PQ. 514-873-4553

Fontaine, Sue, *Pub Info Off,* Washington State Library, Olympia WA. 206-753-5592

Fontaine, William, *Instr,* Northwestern College, Library Science Program, IA. 712-722-4821

Fontaine, William, *Ref, On-Line Servs & Bibliog Instr,* Northwestern College, Ramaker Library, Orange City IA. 712-737-4821, Ext 57, 58

Fontana, Cecilia, *Librn,* Magnavox Government & Industrial Electron Company, Advanced Products Division Library, Torrance CA. 213-328-0770, Ext 2228

Fontana, Mrs Joe, *Librn,* Belt Public Library, Belt MT. 406-277-3621

Fontenette, E J, *Librn,* University of Arkansas, Pine Bluff, Watson Memorial Library, Pine Bluff AR. 501-541-6825

Fontenot, Karen, *Br Asst,* Allen Parish Library (Oakdale Branch), Oakdale LA. 318-335-2690

Fontenot, Mary, *Librn,* Washington County Library System (Torrey Wood Memorial), Hollandale MS. 601-827-2335

Fonvielle, Yvonne, *Dir,* Southern University Library (Law Library), Baton Rouge LA. 504-771-3776

Foote, Cheryl, *ILL & Ref,* Tuscarawas County Public Library, New Philadelphia OH. 216-364-4474

Foote, D S, *Lab Dir,* Remington Arms Company Inc, Research Department Library, Bridgeport CT. 203-333-1112, Ext 464

Foote, Lynne, *Dir,* Colorado Technical Reference Center, CO. 303-492-8774

Foote, Sister Mary Maud, *Ref,* Benedictine College (North Campus Library), Atchison KS. 913-367-5340, Ext 290

Foote, Thomas E, *Asst Dir,* Kuskokwim Consortium Library, Bethel Public Library, Bethel AK. 907-543-2118

Foran, Patricia K, *Librn,* Science Center of Pinellas County Library, Saint Petersburg FL. 813-342-8691

Forbes, Chuck, *Humanities,* University of British Columbia Library, Vancouver BC. 604-228-3871

Forbes, Edith J, *Ch,* Nassau Community College Library, Garden City NY. 516-222-7400

Forbes, Harry, *Tech Serv,* Nicholson Memorial Library, Garland TX. 214-494-7187

Forbes, Jean, *Librn,* Essex County Public Library (LaSalle Branch), LaSalle ON. 519-776-5241

Forbes, Jean, *Acq,* Roseville Public Library, Roseville CA. 916-783-7158

Forbes, John, *Spec Coll,* Morehead State University, Johnson Camden-Julian Carroll Library, Morehead KY. 606-783-2250

Forbes, Mrs F, *Librn,* Keewatin Public Library, Keewatin ON. 807-547-2145

Forbes, Olive G, *Librn,* University of Texas Libraries (Lyndon B Johnson School of Public Affairs Library), Austin TX. 512-471-4962

Forbes, Ruby, *Librn,* Livingston Parish Library (Walker Branch), Walker LA. 504-686-2436

Forbes, Sylbert, *Librn,* Samuel H Wentworth Library, Sandwich NH. 603-284-6665

Forbus, Betty, *ILL & Ref,* George S Houston Memorial Library, Dothan AL. 205-793-9767

Force, Evangeline, *Asst Librn,* Ida Public Library, Belvidere IL. 815-544-3838

Force, Ronald, *Assist Dir for Pub Servs,* Washington State University Library, Pullman WA. 509-335-4557

Forcell, Cora B, *Ref,* Nicholls State University, Allen J Ellender Memorial Library, Thibodaux LA. 504-446-8111, Ext 401, 402

Forcellon, Mary, *Librn,* Cahill Gordon & Reindel Library, New York NY. 212-825-0100, Ext 395, 396

Forcht, Wanda, *Librn,* Washington State School for the Deaf, Learning Resource Center, Vancouver WA. 206-696-6223

Forcier, Ben R, *Librn,* Walla Walla County Law Library, Walla Walla WA. 509-529-2280

Ford, Agnes, *Librn,* Thomas Crane Public Library (Wollaston Branch), Wollaston MA. 617-471-2400

Ford, Barbara J, *Doc,* University of Illinois at Chicago Circle Library, Chicago IL. 312-996-2716

Ford, Ben, *Infor Ser,* Cameron University Library, Lawton OK. 405-248-2200, Ext 410

Ford, Bernard, *Assoc Dir,* University of Pennsylvania Libraries, Van Pelt Library, Philadelphia PA. 215-243-7091

Ford, Carol, *Librn,* Tuskegee Institute (Veterinary Medicine), Tuskegee Institute AL. 205-727-8307

Ford, Carol W, *ILL,* Tuskegee Institute, Hollis Burke Frissell Library, Tuskegee Institute AL. 205-727-8894

Ford, Carolyn, *Dir,* Jefferson Davis Parish Library, Jennings LA. 318-824-1210

Ford, Charlie M, *Librn,* Atlanta Public Library (Dunbar), Atlanta GA. 404-523-2873

Ford, Cidellia R, *Asst Dir Tech Servs,* Flint River Regional Library, Griffin GA. 404-227-2756

Ford, Constance, *Chief Librn,* Union Electric Co Library, Saint Louis MO. 314-622-3222, Ext 2291, 2913

Ford, D'Arlene, *Librn,* United States Navy (Naval Air Station Library), Glenview IL. 312-657-1000

Ford, Emerson, *ILL,* Duke University, William R Perkins Library, Durham NC. 684-2034

Ford, Evelyn C, *Librn,* Energy Research & Generation, Inc Library, Oakland CA. 415-658-9785

Ford, Janet, *Dir,* Clyde Public Library, Clyde OH. 419-547-7174

Ford, Jeanne, *Librn,* Douglas Library Association, Hebron CT. 203-228-9312

Ford, Jennifer, *Librn,* Elgin Mental Health Center, Anton Boisen Professional Library, Elgin IL. 312-742-1040, Ext 3263

Ford, John H, *Exec Dir,* Kentuckiana Metroversity, Inc, KY. 502-897-3374

Ford, Lowell, *Coordr,* Chemeketa Cooperative Regional Library Service, OR. 503-399-3119

Ford, Maria A, *Librn,* Canadian Numismatic Association Library, Collingwood ON. 705-445-3668

Ford, Marjorie M, *Info Specialist,* Filtrol Corp, Information Center, Los Angeles CA. 213-263-5111, Ext 79

Ford, Maudelle, *Cat,* Los Angeles County Public Library System, South State Cooperative Library System, Los Angeles CA. 213-974-6501

Ford, Miriam, *Circ,* Jefferson State Junior College, James B Allen Library, Birmingham AL. 205-853-1200, Ext 280

Ford, Oscar, *Librn,* Nevada State Library, Special Services Division for the Blind, Carson City NV. 702-885-5155

Ford, Oscar W, *Asst State Librn,* Nevada State Library, Carson City NV. 702-885-5130

Ford, Patricia D, *Asst Dir,* Alabama Agricultural & Mechanical University, Joseph F Drake Memorial Learning Resources Center, Normal AL. 205-859-7309

Ford, Ruby Nell, *Librn,* Saint Clair County Library (Ragland), Ragland AL. 205-472-2661

Ford, Stephen, *Dir,* Grand Valley State Colleges, Zumberge Library, Allendale MI. 313-895-6611, Ext 252

Ford, Vicki, *Librn,* Grand Rapids Public Library (Yankee Clipper), Grand Rapids MI. 616-456-4432

Ford, Virginia, *ILL,* New England Conservatory of Music, Harriet M Spaulding Library, Boston MA. 617-262-1120

Ford, Jr, Robert B, *Dir,* Medgar Evers College Library, Brooklyn NY. 212-735-1851

Ford-Foster, Barbara, *Black Studies & Nursing,* Wright State University Library, Dayton OH. 513-873-2380

Fordon, Iris S, *Librn,* Hancock School Public Library, Hancock MI. 906-482-2750

Forehand, Ann, *In Charge,* Texarkana Museum Research Library, Texarkana TX. 214-793-4831

Forehand, Margaret, *Librn Supvr,* Chesapeake Public Library, Chesapeake VA. 804-547-6579, 547-6592

Forehand, Ruth, *Librn,* Sunland Center at Tallahassee Library, Tallahassee FL. 904-877-4161, Ext 231

Foreman, Alma B, *Dir,* Tama Public Library, Tama IA. 515-484-4484

Foreman, Clifton M, *Librn,* Church of Jesus Christ of Latter-Day Saints, Tacoma Branch Genealogy Library, Tacoma WA. 206-564-1103

Foreman, Dorothy H, *Librn,* Lehigh Acres Public Library, Lehigh Acres FL. 813-369-1098

Foreman, Iona, *Asst Librn,* Georgia Regional Library for the Blind & Physically Handicapped, Atlanta GA. 404-656-2465

Foreman, Meriette, *ILL,* Boise Public Library & Information Center, Boise ID. 208-384-4466

Foreman, Robyn, *Reader Serv,* Washington Regional Library for the Blind & Physically Handicapped, Seattle WA. 464-6930. SCAN 576-6930

Foreman, William, *Ref,* Dowagiac Public Library, Dowagiac MI. 616-782-3826, 782-2195 Ext 30

Forer, Daniel, *Coordr,* San Francisco Lighthouse Center for the Blind, Braille Library, San Francisco CA. 415-431-1481

Forest, Eileen, *Ref,* Commodity Futures Trading Commission Library, Washington DC. 202-254-5901

Forest, Monique, *Asst Librn,* National Theatre School of Canada Library, Montreal PQ. 514-842-7954, Ext 38

Forest, Mrs D, *Librn,* Onaping Falls Public Library, Levack ON. 705-966-2291

Forester, James L, *Dir,* Louisiana State University, LeDoux Library, Eunice LA. 318-457-7311, Ext 38

Forester, Jean B, *Asst Librn & Tech Serv,* Louisiana State University, LeDoux Library, Eunice LA. 318-457-7311, Ext 38

Forester, Nancy, *Librn,* Millville Public Library, Millville NJ. 609-825-7087

Forget, Louis, *Dir, Libr Systs Ctr,* National Library of Canada, Ottawa ON. 613-995-9481

Forgione, Nancy, *Cat,* Maryland Institute College of Art, Decker Library, Baltimore MD. 301-669-9200, Ext 27, 28

Forister, Ann, *Media,* Roseville Public Library, Roseville CA. 916-783-7158

Forlow, Kathy, *Acq,* Judson College, Benjamin P Browne Library, Elgin IL. 312-695-2500, Ext 550-553

Forman, Elizabeth, *Cat,* Newark Free Library, Newark DE. 302-731-7550

Forman, Frances, *Ref,* Cincinnati Historical Society Library, Cincinnati OH. 513-241-4622

Formawek, Ellen, *In Charge,* Settlement Music School, Blanche Wolf Kohn Library, Philadelphia PA. 215-336-0400

Formero, Elizabeth, *Dir,* Rutland Community Library, Rutland IL. 815-863-5116

Formica, Cheryl, *Patent Libr,* Providence Public Library, Providence RI. 401-521-7722

Forney, Brian, *Ref & On-Line Servs,* Saint Louis University, Pius XII Memorial Library, Saint Louis MO. 314-658-3100

Forrest, Elaine K, *Librn,* First Presbyterian Church, Pierce Memorial Library, Flint MI. 313-234-8673

Forrest, Fred H, *Dir,* Webb Institute of Naval Architecture, Livingston Library, Glen Cove NY. 516-671-0439

Forrest, Frederick A, *Assoc Prof,* Queens College of the City University of New York, Graduate School of Library & Information Studies, NY. 212-520-7194, 520-7195

Forrest, James, *Dir,* Bradford Brinton Memorial Ranch Library, Big Horn WY. 307-672-3173

Forrest, Joseph, *Asst Dir,* Howard University Libraries, Founders Library, Washington DC. 202-636-7253

Forrest, Kathryn S, *Assoc Dir,* San Jose State University Library, San Jose CA. 408-277-3377

Forrest, Mindy, *Ref,* Brooklyn Law School, Henry L Ughetta Law Library, Brooklyn NY. 212-625-2200, Ext 53 or 55

Forrest, Sally, *ILL,* Cowley County Community College, Renn Memorial Library, Arkansas City KS. 316-442-0430, Ext 57

Forrest, Sue P, *Dir,* West Virginia College of Graduate Studies Library, Institute WV. 304-768-9711, Ext 262

Forsee, Joe B, *Dir,* Mississippi Library Commission, Jackson MS. 601-354-6369

Forseth, Vonda, *Asst Librn,* Rivoli Township Library, New Windsor IL. 309-667-2515

Forson, Barbara, *Librn,* Clasco Inc, Computer Learning Library, Springfield VA. 703-273-7501

Forsstrom, Alice E, *Ch,* Warwick Public Library and Regional Center, Warwick RI. 401-739-5440

Forst, Frederika H, *Admin Sec,* Capital District Library Council for Reference & Research Resources, NY. 518-272-8834

Forstall, Louise, *Hq Librn,* Alexandria Library, Alexandria VA. 703-750-6351

Forstall, Philip L, *Librn,* Rand McNally & Co Library, Skokie IL. 312-673-9100, Ext 565

Forster, Teresa, *Order Clerk,* Lane Public Library, Hamilton OH. 513-894-7156

Forsyth, Genevieve, *Cat,* Hometown Public Library, Jack R Ladwig Memorial Library, Hometown IL. 312-636-0997

Forsyth, J, *Dir,* Alberta Department of Culture (Library Services), Edmonton AB. 403-427-2556

Forsyth, James F, *Ref,* Albany Dougherty Public Library, Albany GA. 912-435-2104

Forsyth, Kenna, *Librn,* Baltimore County Public Library (Rosedale Area), Baltimore MD. 301-866-5650

Forsyth, Pamela, *Dir,* Confederation Centre Library, Charlottetown Public Library, Charlottetown PE. 902-892-7932

Forsythe, Charlotte L, *Librn,* Trinity United Presbyterian Church, Norman Hjorth Memorial Library, Cherry Hill NJ. 609-428-2050

Forsythe, Joan, *Asst Librn,* Brobeck, Phleger & Harrison Library, San Francisco CA. 415-442-1053

Fortado, Robert, *Doc,* Southern Illinois University at Edwardsville, Elijah P Lovejoy Library, Edwardsville IL. 618-692-2711

Forte, Carol, *Cat,* Baldwin Public Library, Baldwin NY. 516-223-6228

Forte, Joseph, *Asst Dir,* Phillips County Community College Library, Helena AR. 501-338-6474, Ext 246

Forte, Loretta, *Librn,* West Haven Public Library (Louis J Piantino Branch), West Haven CT. 203-933-9335

Forte, Thomas A, *Dir,* Glencoe Public Library, Glencoe IL. 312-835-5056

Fortenberry, Ann, *Tech Serv & Cat,* Alaska Court Libraries, Anchorage AK. 907-274-8611, Ext 580

Fortenbery, Bobbie, *Librn,* Amarillo Globe-News Library, Amarillo TX. 806-376-4488

Forth, Stuart, *Dean,* Pennsylvania State University, Fred Lewis Pattee Library, University Park PA. 814-865-0401

Fortier, Andre, *Librn,* Bibliotheque Municipale, Verdun PQ. 514-768-1149

Fortier, Bernard, *Head,* Catholic University of America (Engineering-Architecture & Science Reference), Washington DC. 202-635-5167

Fortier, Debra, *Ref,* Manistee County Library, Manistee MI. 616-723-2519

Fortier, Gilles, *Coordr,* Commission Des Ecoles Catholiques De Quebec, Bibliotheques du Personnel, Quebec PQ. 418-688-3211

Fortier, Jan Marie, *Librn,* Pacific University, Harvey W Scott Memorial Library, Forest Grove OR. 503-357-6151, Ext 301

Fortier, P, *Librn,* Trois-Rivieres College Library, Trois-Rivieres PQ. 819-376-1721, Ext 286

Fortier+015,7 *Tech Serv,* Trois-Rivieres College Library, Trois-Rivieres PQ. 819-376-1721, Ext 286

Fortin, Clifford C, *Assoc Prof,* University of Wisconsin-River Falls, Dept of Education Library Science-Media Program, WI. 715-425-3854

Fortner, Donald D, *Librn,* Veterans Administration, Hospital Library, Big Spring TX. 915-263-7361, Ext 250

Fortney, Lindalee, *ILL & Circ,* Blount County Library, Maryville TN. 615-982-0981

Fortney, Lynn M, *Dir,* University of Alabama, Health Sciences Library, Tuscaloosa AL. 205-348-4950, Ext 360

Fortney, Mary E, *Map Coll,* Northwestern University Library, Evanston IL. 312-492-7658

Fortney, V J, *Head Info Servs Dept,* Bell Telephone Laboratories, Libraries & Information Systems Center, Murray Hill NJ. 582-2854 (General); 582-4466 (Info Systs Dept); 582-6880 (Info Servs Dept); 949-3456 (Libr Operations Dept)

Fortriede, Steven, *Br Coordr,* Public Library of Fort Wayne & Allen County, Fort Wayne IN. 219-424-7241

Fortunato, Paul, *Ad & Ref,* Brockton Public Library System, Brockton MA. 617-587-2515

Fortune, Jennie, *Bkmobile Coordr,* Iosco-Arenac Regional Library, Tawas City MI. 517-362-2651

Forwalter, Lois A, *Librn,* Indiana University School of Medicine & Northwest Center for Medical Education, Medical Resource Center, Gary IN. 219-980-6852, 980-6853

Forys, Jr, John W, *Librn,* University of Iowa Libraries (Engineering), Iowa City IA. 319-353-5224

Forys, Jr, John W, *Librn,* University of Iowa Libraries (Mathematics), Iowa City IA. 319-353-5939

Fosbender, Jule, *Dir,* Adrian Public Library, Adrian MI. 517-263-2161, Ext 277

Fosdick, Emma, *Librn,* Canada Center for Inland Waters Library, Environment Canada, Burlington ON. 416-637-4282

Fosdick, Sidney, *Cat,* Brock University Library, Saint Catharines ON. 416-684-7201

Foshee, Anne, *Genealogy,* Colquitt-Thomas Regional Library, Moultrie-Colquitt County Library, Moultrie GA. 912-985-6540

Foshee, Anne, *Genealogy & Local Hist,* Southwest Georgia Regional Library, Gilbert H Gragg Library, Bainbridge GA. 912-246-3887, 3894, 3895

Fosher, Shirley, *Asst Dir & Ch,* Boone County Public Library, Florence KY. 606-371-6222

Foss, Jo Anne, *Ch,* Lancaster County Library, Lancaster PA. 717-394-2651

Foss, Joyce, *Tech Serv,* Capital Library Cooperative, Mason MI. 517-676-9511

Foss, Joyce, *Tech Serv,* Ingham County Library, Library Service Center, Mason MI. 517-676-9088

Foss, M, *Tech Serv,* Carleton University, Murdoch Maxwell MacOdrum Library, Ottawa ON. 613-231-4357

Foss, Marie, *Librn,* Walnut Township Memorial Library, Walnut IL. 815-379-2159

Fosse, J Alexi, *Dir,* Lewis & Clark Library System, Edwardsville IL. 618-656-3216

Fosselman, Stephen A, *Dir,* Spencer Public Library, Spencer IA. 712-262-2960

Fossum, Dennis, *Monographs,* University of North Dakota (Olaf H Thormodsgard Law Library), Grand Forks ND. 701-777-2204

Foster, Alice, *Ch,* Whiting Public Library, Whiting IN. 219-659-0269, 659-0320

Foster, Anna Grace, *Program Coordr,* Williamsburg Regional Library, Williamsburg VA. 804-229-7326

Foster, Antoinette, *Cat,* Wake County Department of the Public Library, Raleigh NC. 919-755-6077

Foster, Coleen, *Media,* Stockton-San Joaquin County Public Library, Stockton Public Libr, Stockton CA. 209-944-8415

Foster, Dixie, *Asst Dir,* Denison Public Library, Denison TX. 214-465-1797

Foster, Dorothy, *Librn,* Kent County Municipal Public Library (Highgate Public), Highgate ON. 519-678-3313

Foster, Elaine, *Librn,* Carmi Public Library, Carmi IL. 618-382-5277

Foster, Elizabeth, *Tech Serv,* Reuben McMillan Free Library Free Library Association, Public Library of Youngstown & Mahoning County, Youngstown OH. 216-744-8636

Foster, Eloise C, *Dir,* Library of the American Hospital Association, Asa S Bacon Memorial, Chicago IL. 312-280-6263

Foster, Emily, *Ch,* Ritter Memorial Library, Lunenburg MA. 617-582-7817

Foster, Ernestine, *Librn,* Mid-Mississippi Regional Library System (West Public), West MS. 601-967-2510

Foster, Faith D, *Librn,* Havana Public Library, Havana IL. 309-543-4701

Foster, Fay, *Librn,* Nepean Public Library (Centennial), Ottawa ON. 613-828-0515

Foster, Hal D, *Circ,* Palm Beach Junior College, Library Learning Resources Center, Lake Worth FL. 305-965-8000, Ext 213

Foster, Harry E, *Librn,* Anne Arundel Community College, Andrew G Truxal Library, Arnold MD. 301-647-7100

Foster, James, *Res Librn,* Steamship Historical Society of America, Inc, Baltimore MD. 301-727-6350

Foster, James J, *Spec Coll,* University of Baltimore, Langsdale Library, Baltimore MD. 301-727-6350, Ext 444

Foster, Jane, *ILL,* Palo Alto City Library, Palo Alto CA. 415-329-2436

Foster, Jane N, *In Charge,* NASA, Technical Library, Wallops Flight Center, Wallops Island VA. 804-824-3411, Ext 2389

Foster, Janet, *ILL,* Alhambra Public Library, Alhambra CA. 213-570-5008

Foster, Jean, *Librn,* Callier Center for Communication Disorders, Materials Resource Center Library, Dallas TX. 214-783-3143

Foster, Jim, *Dir,* Central Carolina Technical Institute, Learning Resource Center, Sanford NC. 919-775-5401, Ext 244

Foster, Joan, *Librn,* Wilton Library Association, Wilton CT. 203-762-3950

Foster, Joanne, *Cat & On-Line Servs,* Eureka College, Melick Library, Eureka IL. 309-467-3721, Ext 219-258

Foster, Julia A, *ILL, Ref & Bibliog Instr,* Pfeiffer College, Gustavus Adolphus Pfeiffer Library, Misenheimer NC. 704-463-7343, Ext 278

Foster, Katharin, *Ref & On-Line Servs,* Ohio University, Vernon R Alden Library, Athens OH. 614-594-5228

Foster, Keith, *Curator,* Long Beach Public Library System (Los Cerritos Ranch House), Long Beach CA. 213-424-9423

Foster, Kim, *Librn,* Public Library of Nashville & Davidson County (East), Nashville TN. 615-262-0656

Foster, Lee M, *Mgr,* Rockwell International, Inc, Collins Radio Division Information Center, Newport Beach CA. 714-833-4389

Foster, Lois, *Librn,* Mid-Continent Public Library (Dearborn Branch), Dearborn MO. 816-992-3502

Foster, Louis, *Officer, Freedom of Info,* Defense Intelligence Agency, Central Reference Div Library, Washington DC. 202-692-5311

Foster, Marilyn, *Dir,* Art Circle Public Library, Cumberland County, Crossville TN. 615-484-6790

Foster, Marilyn, *Librn,* Swanton Public Library, Swanton VT. 802-868-7656

Foster, Mary Gail, *Librn,* Oklahoma Department of Human Services, Employees Library, Oklahoma City OK. 405-521-3518

Foster, Matoka D, *Ch,* Peninsula Public Library, Lawrence NY. 516-239-3262

Foster, Mrs Richard, *Librn,* Faulkner-Van Buren Regional Library (Fairfield Bay Branch), Fairfield Bay AR. 501-327-7482

Foster, Mrs Robert, *Librn,* Dekalb Library System (Nancy Guinn Branch), Conyers GA. 404-483-7756

Foster, Nancy, *Asst Librn,* Evergreen Park Public Library, Evergreen Park IL. 312-422-8522

Foster, Norma, *Dir,* First Baptist Church Library, Slocomb AL. 205-886-2533

Foster, Paula, *Asst Librn,* Systems Applications, Inc Library, San Rafael CA. 415-472-4011

Foster, Robert, *Librn,* Albany Public Library (Downtown), Albany OR. 503-967-4308

Foster, Russell E, *Dir,* Bay County Public Library Association, Northwest Regional Library System, Panama City FL. 904-785-3457

Foster, Saba L, *Chief Librn,* National Life Insurance Co, Law Library, Montpelier VT. 802-229-3278

Foster, Selma, *Cat,* State University of New York College at Potsdam, Frederick W Crumb Memorial Library, Potsdam NY. 315-268-2940

Foster, Thomas U, *Dir,* Grossmont College, Lewis F Smith Learning Resource Center Library, El Cajon CA. 714-465-1700, Ext 333, 334

Foster, Wanda, *ILL,* Roswell Public Library, Roswell NM. 505-622-7101

Foster, Yancey, *Librn,* Dare County Library (Hatteras Community Center), Hatteras NC. 919-968-2385

Foth, Ellen K, *Librn,* Montclair Free Public Library (Bellevue Ave), Upper Montclair NJ. 201-744-2468

Foth, Nancy, *Dir,* Arabut Ludlow Memorial Library, Monroe WI. 608-325-3331

Foti, Frank, *Media,* New England College, H Raymond Danforth Library, Henniker NH. 603-428-2344

Foti, Tina, *Media,* Cumberland County Public Library, Anderson Street Library, Frances Brooks Stein Memorial Library, Fayetteville NC. 919-483-1580

Foucher, Harriet, *Media,* San Bernardino County Library, San Bernardino CA. 714-383-1734

Fought, Donald F, *Dir,* Ida Rupp Public Library, Port Clinton OH. 419-732-3212

Fought, Joanne, *ILL, Ref & Bibliog Instr,* Illinois Central College, Learning Resources Center, East Peoria IL. 309-694-5461

Foulem, Lorrain, *Cat,* Universite De Moncton, Bibliotheque Champlain, Moncton NB. 506-858-4012

Foulger, Glenda, *Area Br Supvrs,* Riverside City & County Public Library, Riverside CA. 714-787-7211

Foulke, Mary, *Librn,* Sel-Rex Co Library, Nutley NJ. 201-667-5200

Fountain, Marguerite, *Librn,* Arlington City Library, Arlington KS. 316-538-2471

Fourneaux, Yvonne, *Prof,* College de Maisonneuve, Techniques de la Documentation, PQ. 514-254-7131

Fourney, Mrs N, *Librn,* Saint Lawrence College of Applied Arts & Technology Library, Cornwall ON. 613-933-6080

Fournier, Anne-Marie, *Reader Serv,* Francis Bacon Library, Francis Bacon Foundation Inc, Claremont CA. 714-624-6305

Fournier, Edouard, *Asst Librn,* Universite Du Quebec A Trois-Rivieres Bibliotheque, Trois-Rivieres PQ. 819-376-5706

Fournier, Francis J, *Training Officer,* California State Department of Corporations Library, Sacramento CA. 916-445-2298

Fournier, Huguette, *Tech Serv,* Haut-Saint-Jean Regional Library, Bibliotheque Regionale du Haut-Saint-Jean, Edmundston NB. 506-739-7331

Fournier, Michel, *Cat,* Universite Laval Bibliotheque, Quebec PQ. 418-656-3344

Fouse, Betty Keith, *Librn,* Memorial Public Library of the Borough of Alexandria, Alexandria PA. 814-669-4313

Foust, Judith, *Actg Law Librn & Ref,* State Library of Pennsylvania, Harrisburg PA. 717-787-2646

Foutch, Rachelle, *Actg Librn,* Taneyhills Community Library, Branson MO. 417-334-1418

Fouts, Nancy, *Librn,* Saint Clair County Library (Ashville), Ashville AL. 205-594-4047

Foutty, Kitty, *Librn,* NASA (Life Science Library), Moffett Field CA. 415-965-5387

Fouty, Gary, *Ref,* Iowa State University Library, Ames IA. 515-294-1442

Foutz, Chole, *Assoc Librn,* Union College Library, Lincoln NE. 402-488-2331, Ext 316

Foutz, Pauleen C, *Librn,* Church of Jesus Christ of Latter-Day Saints, Genealogical Library, Las Vegas NV. 702-382-9695

Fowells, Fumi, *Cat,* University of San Francisco, Richard A Gleeson Library, San Francisco CA. 415-666-6167

Fowler, Ann, *Info Spec,* North Carolina State Department of Public Instruction, Education Information Center, Raleigh NC. 919-733-7904

Fowler, Barbara, *Dir,* University of Wyoming (Jayne Media Center), Laramie WY. 307-766-6391

Fowler, Barbara, *Instr,* University of Wyoming, Library Media Program, WY. 307-766-2349

Fowler, Bonnie, *Ch,* Forsyth County Public Library, Winston-Salem NC. 919-727-2556

Fowler, Carole F, *Asst Dir,* Jervis Public Library Association, Rome NY. 315-336-4570

Fowler, Evelin, *Librn,* Houston Public Library (Vinson), Houston TX. 713-433-0356

Fowler, Jane, *ILL & Ref,* Bates College, George and Helen Ladd Library, Lewiston ME. 207-784-2949

Fowler, Joseph, *Librn,* Cleveland Public Library (Brooklyn), Cleveland OH. 216-661-6178

Fowler, Joyce, *Librn,* Grace Public Library District, Grace ID. 208-425-3695

Fowler, Karla Fingerson, *Librn,* Olympia Technical Community College Library, Olympia WA. 206-753-3018

Fowler, Kay, *Librn,* Troy State University in Montgomery Library, Montgomery AL. 205-834-2320

Fowler, Linda, *Ch,* Burlington Public Library, Burlington IA. 319-753-1649

Fowler, Mrs Clarence, *Asst Librn,* Muenster Public Library, Muenster TX. 817-759-4291

Fowler, Nelda F, *ILL & Cat,* North Bend Public Library, North Bend OR. 503-756-6712

Fowler, Norma, *Circ & Ref,* Grant County Library, Ulysses KS. 316-356-1433

Fowler, Rena, *Librn,* Colorado Mountain College, Learning Resources Center, Leadville CO. 303-486-2015, Ext 36

Fowler, Zinita, *Ch,* Carrollton Public Library, Carrollton TX. 214-323-5014

Fowlie, Bess, *Tech Serv & Cat,* A K Smiley Public Library, Redlands CA. 714-793-2201

Fowlie, E Les, *Chief Librn,* Toronto Public Library, Toronto ON. 416-484-8015

Fox, Beryl, *Librn,* University of Mississippi Library (Music), University MS. 601-232-7268

Fox, Betty, *Librn,* Ozark Regional Library (Viburnum Branch), Viburnum MO. 314-244-5989

Fox, Betty L, *Chief Librn,* Defense Nuclear Agency, Technical Library Div, Washington DC. 202-325-7780

Fox, Charles, *Special Servs,* North Carolina Department of Cultural Resources, Division of State Library, North Carolina State Library, Raleigh NC. 919-733-2570

Fox, Charles H, *Librn,* North Carolina Regional Library for the Blind & Physically Handicapped, Raleigh NC. 919-733-4376

Fox, Del, *Media,* Brevard Community College, Learning Resources Center, Cocoa FL. 305-632-1111, Ext 295, 298

Fox, Dexter L, *Librn,* United States Army (Environmental Hygiene Agency Library), Aberdeen Proving Ground MD. 301-671-4236

Fox, Don, *On-Line Servs,* McMaster University, Hamilton ON. 416-525-9140

Fox, Dreama C, *Librn,* Westvaco Corp, Covington Research Center Library, Covington VA. 703-962-2111

Fox, Edith, *Librn,* Lancaster County Public Library, Kilmarnock VA. 804-435-1729

Fox, Edna, *Tech Serv,* Sussex County Library System, Sussex County Area Reference Library, Newton NJ. 201-948-3660

Fox, Faye L, *Librn,* Walter A Woodward Memorial Library, Cottage Grove OR. 503-942-3828

Fox, George A, *Dir,* Prairie State College, Learning Center, Chicago Heights IL. 312-756-3110, Ext 113

Fox, H Ronald, *Chief, Libr Serv,* Veterans Administration, Hospital Library, Grand Island NE. 308-382-3660

Fox, Jacqueline, *Pub Servs,* University of Virginia (Law Library), Charlottesville VA. 804-924-3384

Fox, James R, *Librn,* Dickinson School of Law, Sheely-Lee Law Library, Carlisle PA. 717-243-4611, Ext 9

Fox, Jane G, *Librn,* Fox Consulting & Library Service, Special Science Information Center, Swarthmore PA. 215-543-2801

Fox, Janis M, *Librn,* Pontiac Osteopathic Hospital Library, Pontiac MI. 313-338-7271, Ext 433

Fox, Jeanne, *Librn,* Arlington County Department of Libraries (Westover), Arlington VA. 703-538-5070

Fox, Jeff, *Planning Dir,* North Dakota State Library, Bismarck ND. 701-224-2490

Fox, Judith, *Cat,* Washington University Libraries, Saint Louis MO. 314-889-5400

Fox, Judy, *Cat & On-Line Servs,* Marion Public Library, Marion OH. 614-387-0992

Fox, June, *Dir,* Saugatuck-Douglas District Library, Saugatuck MI. 616-857-8241

Fox, Karen C, *Librn,* Ohio Reformatory for Women, Clearview Library, Marysville OH. 513-642-1065

Fox, Karl M, *Consultant,* Fox Consulting & Library Service, Special Science Information Center, Swarthmore PA. 215-543-2801

Fox, Kathy, *Cat & Ref,* San Jose City College Library, San Jose CA. 408-298-2181, Ext 410

Fox, Kay, *Dir,* Keene Public Library, Keene NH. 603-352-0157

Fox, Leandra, *ILL,* Community College of Allegheny County, Allegheny Campus Library, Pittsburgh PA. 412-237-2585

Fox, LeRoy G, *Dir,* Johnson County Library, Shawnee Mission KS. 913-831-1550

Fox, Marjorie N, *Dir,* Egg Harbor City Free Public Library, Egg Harbor City NJ. 609-965-1496

Fox, Mark, *Cat,* Nevada State Library, Carson City NV. 702-885-5130

Fox, Maxine, *Dir,* Midvale Community Library, Midvale ID. 208-355-2213

Fox, Merle U, *Head Librn,* Pennsylvania State University, Du Bois Campus Library, Du Bois PA. 814-371-2800, Ext 11

Fox, Mrs Alex, *Librn,* Stillwater County Library (Park City Smeltzer Memorial), Park City MT. 406-322-5337

Fox, Pam, *Pub Servs,* Kalamazoo Valley Community College, Learning Resources Center, Kalamazoo MI. 616-372-5000, Ext 328

Fox, Patricia, *YA,* West Shore Public Library, Camp Hill PA. 717-761-3900, 761-3901

Fox, Phyllis, *Acq,* Peabody Institute Library, Danvers Public Library, Danvers MA. 617-774-0554, Ext 0557, 0555

Fox, Reba, *Ref,* Davidson County Public Library System, Lexington NC. 704-246-2520

Fox, Susan, *Cat,* American International College, McGown Memorial Library, Springfield MA. 413-737-5331, Ext 225

Fox, Virginia, *Librn,* University of California, Berkeley (Giannini Foundation for Agricultural Economics Research Library), Berkeley CA. 415-642-7121

Foxman, Lois, *Librn,* Euclid Public Library (Upson), Euclid OH. 216-731-1151

Foy, Jacquelyn M, *Librn,* Gilbert Library, Inc, Northfield CT. 203-283-8176

Foy, Kathleen M, *Lectr,* Concordia University, Library Studies Program, PQ. 514-482-0320, Ext 324

Foyle, James, *Instr,* University of Denver, Graduate School of Librarianship and Information Management, CO. 303-753-2557

Fraass, Ruth, *Asst Dir,* Nancy Fawcett Memorial Library, Lodgepole NE. 308-483-5714

Frack, Edna, *Asst Librn,* Macksville City Library, Macksville KS. 316-348-2002

Fraction, Nicolette, *Asst Dir & Tech Serv,* Hostos Community College Library, Bronx NY. 212-960-1093

Fradkin, Bernard, *AV,* Evergreen Valley College Library, San Jose CA. 408-274-7900, Ext 310

Fragale, Jr, John, *Chief Librn,* United States Army (Headquarters Army Materiel Development & Readiness Command Technical Library), Alexandria VA. 202-274-8152

Fragasso, Philip, *Asst Dir,* Lucius Beebe Memorial Library, Wakefield MA. 617-245-0790

Fraley, Raymah, *Dir,* Waverly Free Library, Waverly NY. 607-565-9341

Fraley, Ruth A, *Tech Serv,* Schenectady County Community College Library, Library Resources Center, Schenectady NY. 518-346-6211, Ext 240, 241

Fralick, Beatrice, *Librn,* Putnam County District Library (Leipsic Branch), Leipsic OH. 419-523-3747

Frame, Margaret, *Asst Librn,* Detroit College of Business Library, Dearborn MI. 313-582-6983, Ext 24

Frame, Paul N, *Dir,* Colorado Women's College, Permelia Curtis Porter Library, Denver CO. 303-394-6804

Frampton, Marcia, *AV,* Medical Library of Mecklenburg County, Learning Resource Center of Charlotte AHEC, Charlotte NC. 704-373-3129

France, Bronwyn, *Librn,* Dixie Regional Library, Pontotoc MS. 601-489-3522

France, Grace, *Instr,* Montana State University, Library Science Dept, MT. 406-994-2851, 994-4752

France, Irene, *Instr,* East Tennessee State University, Library Service Division, TN. 615-929-4244

France, Kathryn, *Media,* State University of New York, College at Oneonta, James M Milne Library, Oneonta NY. 607-431-2723

Francell, Larry, *Mus Dir,* Wichita Falls Museum & Art Center Library, Wichita Falls TX. 817-692-0923

Frances, Gloria, *Rare Bks,* Detroit Public Library, Detroit Associated Libraries, Detroit MI. 313-833-1000

Franceschi, J M, *Commun Servs,* Medford Public Library, Medford MA. 617-395-7950

Franceschi, J Michael, *Dir,* Merrill Memorial Library, Yarmouth ME. 207-846-4763

Francis, Bernice, *Circ,* Dodge City Public Library, Dodge City KS. 316-225-0248

Francis, Carol A, *Librn,* Bristol County Law Library, Taunton MA. 617-824-7632

Francis, Diana, *Ref,* Lebanon County Library System, Lebanon PA. 717-273-7624

Francis, Diane, *ILL & Ref,* Lebanon Community Library, H C Grumbine Free Public Library, Lebanon PA. 717-273-7624

Francis, Diane S, *Dir,* New Castle County Public Library System, Wilmington DE. 302-571-7670

Francis, Eileen K, *Ch,* Mary Riley Styles Public Library, Falls Church VA. 703-241-5030

Francis, Ella S, *Dir,* Lake City Community College, G T Melton Learning Resources Center, Lake City FL. 904-752-1822, Ext 260

Francis, Frank, *Gen Mgt,* Rothman's of Pall Mall Canada Ltd, Automotive Reference Library, Toronto ON. 416-789-3432

Francis, Helen C, *Dir,* Springfield Free Public Library, Springfield NJ. 201-376-4930

Francis, Joan, *Supvr,* Huron County Public Library (Kirkton Branch), Kirkton ON. 519-229-6314

Francis, Joan, *ILL,* Portage County District Library, Hiram OH. 216-569-7666

Francis, Kathleen, *Humanities,* University of Richmond, Boatwright Memorial Library, Richmond VA. 804-285-6452

Francis, Lois, *Tech Serv,* Ohio Wesleyan University, L A Beeghly Library, Delaware OH. 614-369-4431, Ext 509

Francis, M, *Spec Coll,* Los Angeles Trade Technical College Library, Los Angeles CA. 213-746-0800, Ext 217

Francis, Nancy E, *Librn,* Kitchener-Waterloo Art Gallery, Eleanor Calvert Memorial Library, Kitchener ON. 519-745-6671

Francis, Sister Rita, *Asst Dir & Ref,* Ladycliff College, Msgr C Hugo Doyle Library, Highland Falls NY. 914-446-4747, Ext 21

Francis, Virginia, *Humanities,* University of Florida Libraries, Gainesville FL. 904-392-0341

Francis, Jr, Frank, *Prof,* Prairie View A & M University, Dept of Library Service Education, TX. 713-857-2012

Francis, Jr, Frank, *Dir,* Prairie View Agricultural & Mechanical University, W R Banks Library, Prairie View TX. 713-857-3311

Franck, Aurela, *Librn,* Hawkeye Public Library, Hawkeye IA. 319-427-5536

Franck, Ilona, *Librn,* Jefferson Community College (Southwest Campus), Louisville KY. 502-584-0181, Ext 305

Franck, Jane P, *Dir,* Teachers College - Columbia University Library, New York NY. 212-678-3022, 678-3020

Franckowiak, Bernard, *Dean,* University of Denver, Graduate School of Librarianship and Information Management, CO. 303-753-2557

Franco, Kathryn, *Bibliog Instr,* State University of New York, College at Oneonta, James M Milne Library, Oneonta NY. 607-431-2723

Franco, Martha, *Ser,* York College Library, Jamaica NY. 212-969-4026

Francoeur, Louise, *ILL,* West Islip Public Library, West Islip NY. 516-661-7080, 661-7082

Francom, Phyllis, *Dir,* Duncan Public Library, Duncan AZ. 602-359-2094

Frandsen, Rex, *Non Print Serv,* Brigham Young University-Hawaii Campus, Joseph F Smith Library, Laie HI. 808-293-9211, Ext 260, 264

Franich, Mary, *Ch,* Watsonville Public Library, Watsonville CA. 408-722-2408

Frank, Agnes T, *Librn,* Saint Vincent's Hospital & Medical Center of New York, Medical Library, New York NY. 212-790-7811

Frank, Amy, *Librn,* Newark Fire Department Historical Association Library, Newark NJ. 201-733-6600

Frank, Bernice, *Music,* Tenafly Public Library, Tenafly NJ. 201-568-8680

Frank, Bernice, *Media,* Tenafly Public Library, Tenafly NJ. 201-568-8680

Frank, Bernice C, *Librn,* Burroughs Corp (Legal Activity Library), Detroit MI. 313-972-7895

Frank, Betty, *Librn,* Marin County Free Library (San Geronimo Valley Branch), Lagunitas CA. 415-488-0430

Frank, Carol, *Librn,* Berlin Public Library, Berlin WI. 414-361-2650

Frank, Conie J, *Librn,* Saint Joseph County Law Library, South Bend IN. 219-284-9657

Frank, Dana, *Librn,* National Museums of Canada Library (Canadian Conservation Institute), Ottawa ON. 613-998-3721

Frank, Darlene, *Librn Blind,* Kimball Public Library, Kimball NE. 308-235-4523

Frank, Edwin, *Librn,* Memphis State University Libraries (Speech & Hearing Center), Memphis TN. 901-525-2682

Frank, Elsie, *Librn,* Hancock Town Library, Hancock NH. 603-525-4411

Frank, Frances, *Librn,* University Hospital-Lgh, Medical Library, Louisville KY. 502-589-4321, Ext 235

Frank, Janice, *Librn,* New York Public Library (Children's Library), New York NY. 212-790-6262

Frank, Janrose, *Librn,* Crestline Public Library, Crestline OH. 419-683-3909

Frank, Joseph E, *Librn,* Chittenden County Law Library, Burlington VT. 802-863-3467

Frank, Kenneth, *Ad,* Des Plaines Public Library, Des Plaines IL. 312-827-5551

Frank, Marion, *Librn,* Industrial Accident Prevention Association Library, Toronto ON. 416-965-8888

Frank, Maureen S, *Ad,* Atlantic City Free Public Library, Atlantic City NJ. 609-345-2269

Frank, Peter, *Germanic Langs,* Stanford University Libraries, Stanford CA. 415-497-2016

Frank, Phyllis, *Librn,* Lompoc Public Library (Village), Lompoc CA. 805-733-3323

Frank, Robyn, *Chief, Food & Nutrition Info Ctr,* National Agricultural Library, Beltsville MD. 301-344-4248

Frank, Virginia, *Reader Serv & Bibliog Instr,* Staley Library, Millikin University, Decatur IL. 217-424-6214

Franke, Beulah, *Librn,* Herndon City Library, Herndon KS. 913-322-5333

Franke, Eileen, *Bk Selection Coordr,* Saint Louis Public Library, Saint Louis MO. 314-241-2288

Frankel, Edith, *Circ & Ref,* State University of New York College at Potsdam, Frederick W Crumb Memorial Library, Potsdam NY. 315-268-2940

Frankel, Gertrude, *ILL,* Alexandria Library, Alexandria VA. 703-750-6351

Frankel, Jean, *Librn,* Communication Workers of America Library, Washington DC. 202-785-6799

Frankel, Norman, *Librn,* Western Michigan University (Library Science), Kalamazoo MI. 616-383-1877

Frankel, Norman, *Asst Prof,* Western Michigan University, School of Librarianship, MI. 616-383-1849

Franken, Carolyn, *Per,* Bentley College, Solomon R Baker Library, Waltham MA. 617-891-2231

Frankenberg, Celestine, *Dir,* Young & Rubicam, Inc Library, New York NY. 212-953-3075

Frankhouse, Dorothy, *Librn,* Stockton Record Library, Stockton CA. 209-466-2652, Ext 238

Frankland, Michelle, *Librn,* Georgina Public Library Administration (Pefferlaw Branch), Pefferlaw ON. 705-437-1514

Frankle, Raymond A, *Dir Libr Serv,* Stockton State College Library, Pomona NJ. 609-652-1776, Ext 343

Franklin, Avis, *ILL & Ad,* Roseville Public Library, Roseville CA. 916-783-7158

Franklin, Brinley, *Librn,* Peat Marwick Mitchell & Co Library, Washington DC. 202-223-9525

Franklin, Carole, *Music,* Pennsylvania State University, Fred Lewis Pattee Library, University Park PA. 814-865-0401

Franklin, Evelyn, *ILL,* Bedford Public Library, Bedford VA. 703-586-8911

Franklin, George, *On-Line Servs,* International Research & Evaluation, Information & Research Resources Library-Data Base, Eagan MN. 612-869-2675

Franklin, Greg, *Assoc Dean Learning Resource Ctr,* Muskegon Community College, Allen G Umbreit Library, Muskegon MI. 616-773-9131, Ext 260

Franklin, Hardy R, *Dir,* Public Library of the District of Columbia, Martin Luther King Memorial Library, Washington DC. 202-727-1101

Franklin, Hugh, *Eng,* Oregon State University, William Jasper Kerr Library, Corvallis OR. 503-754-3411

Franklin, Janice, *Instr,* Alabama State University, Library Educational Media Program, AL. 205-832-6072, Ext 502

Franklin, John, *Ref,* Ocean County Library, Toms River NJ. 201-349-6200

Franklin, Kevin, *Librn,* New Orleans Public Library (Alvar), New Orleans LA. 504-947-5359

Franklin, Laurel, *Cat,* City College of the City University of New York, Morris Raphael Cohen Library, New York NY. 212-690-6612

Franklin, Lora, *Librn,* Osgood Public Library, Osgood IN. 812-689-4011

Franklin, Madeleine L'Engle, *Librn,* Cathedral Church of Saint John the Divine Library, New York NY. 212-678-6910

FRANKLIN

Franklin, Manie M, *Assoc Librn,* Thomas County Community College Library, Thomasville GA. 912-226-1621

Franklin, Marjorie, *Librn,* Carnegie Library of Pittsburgh (Homewood), Pittsburgh PA. 412-622-3100

Franklin, Marsha, *Asst Dir,* Spencer Public-Owen County Contractual Library, Spencer IN. 812-829-3392

Franklin, Martha, *Assoc Librn,* Kalamazoo Institute of Arts Library, Kalamazoo MI. 616-349-7775, Ext 5

Franklin, Mary, *Circ,* Traverse City Public Library, Traverse City MI. 616-941-2311

Franklin, Miriam, *Acq,* Jacksonville State University Library, Jacksonville AL. 205-435-9820, Ext 213, 214

Franklin, Nancy, *Dir,* Marcellus Free Library, Marcellus NY. 315-673-3221

Franklin, Phoebe, *Dir,* Elk Township Library, Peck MI. 313-378-5409

Franklin, Ralph, *Chief Librn,* Whitworth College, Harriet Cheney Cowles Memorial Library, Spokane WA. 509-466-3260

Franklin, Sandra, *Asst Librn,* Mercer University Southern School of Pharmacy, H Custer Naylor Library, Atlanta GA. 404-688-6291, Exts 62, 73

Franklin, Sherrill, *Librn,* Indianapolis-Marion County Public Library (Northeast), Indianapolis IN. 317-635-5662

Franklin, Sister M Lawrence, *Archivist,* Mercyhurst College Learning Resource Center, Erie PA. 814-864-0681, Ext 228, 234

Frankovich, Sister Margaret, *Asst Dir & ILL,* Sacred Heart School of Theology, Leo Dehon Library, Hales Corners WI. 425-8300 & 425-8301, Ext 27

Frankowski, Hazel, *Dir,* Rockland Public Library, Rockland ME. 207-594-5434

Franks, Carolyn J, *Dir, Ad & Commun Servs,* Ardmore Public Library, Ardmore OK. 405-223-8290

Franks, Ethel, *Circ,* Brunswick-Glynn County Regional Library, Brunswick GA. 912-264-7360

Franks, Patricia, *Media,* Noble County Public Library, Albion IN. 219-636-7197

Frantz, Barbara, *Bus, Sci & Tech,* Indianapolis-Marion County Public Library, Indianapolis IN. 317-635-5662

Frantz, John C, *Dir,* San Francisco Public Library, San Francisco CA. 415-558-4235

Frantz, Maxine, *Cat,* Wayne Public Library, Wayne NJ. 201-694-4272

Franz, Carol, *On-Line Servs,* University of Virginia (Law Library), Charlottesville VA. 804-924-3384

Franz, Charlotte, *Librn,* McGregor Public Library, McGregor IA. 319-873-3318

Franz, David A, *Ref,* Vestal Public Library, Vestal NY. 607-754-4243

Franz, Margaret, *Librn,* Canadian Mennonite Bible College Library, Winnipeg MB. 204-888-6781

Franz, Nedra, *Asst Dir,* Waterford Township Public Library, Pontiac MI. 313-674-4831

Franzen, John F, *Circ & Per,* Shelter Rock Public Library, Albertson NY. 516-248-7363

Franzen, Mrs Albert, *Librn,* Cedar Rapids Public Library, Cedar Rapids NE. 308-358-0240

Frappier, Gilles, *Dir,* Ottawa Public Library, Ottawa ON. 613-236-0301

Frappoli, Dianne, *Govt Docs,* East Brunswick Public Library, East Brunswick NJ. 201-254-1220

Frary, Dorothy B, *Dir & Ad,* Edwards Public Library, Southampton Public Library, Southampton MA. 413-527-9480

Fraser, Amanda, *Acq,* Earlham College, Lilly Library, Richmond IN. 317-962-6561, Ext 360

Fraser, C William, *Dir,* College of Physicians & Surgeons of British Columbia, British Columbia Medical Library Services, Vancouver BC. 604-736-5551

Fraser, Carol E, *Dir & Acq,* Stonehill College, Cushing-Martin Library, North Easton MA. 617-238-1081, Ext 328, 329, 313

Fraser, Catherine, *Librn,* Pettes Memorial Library, Lac Brome PQ. 514-243-6128

Fraser, Christine, *Librn,* United States Department of Housing & Urban Development, Boston Regional Office Library, Boston MA. 617-223-4674

Fraser, Edith J, *Dir,* United States Army (Technical Reference Div), Fort Huachuca AZ. 602-538-6304

Fraser, James H, *Dir,* Fairleigh Dickinson University, Friendship Library, Madison NJ. 201-377-4700, Ext 234

Fraser, Jayne, *Br Coordr,* Lynnfield Public Library, Lynnfield MA. 617-334-5411

Fraser, Jean Marie, *On-Line Servs,* University of Missouri-Columbia, Elmer Ellis Library, Columbia MO. 314-882-4701

Fraser, John L, *Photo Div Head,* Harvard University Library (Harvard College Library (Headquarters in Harry Elkins Widener Memorial Library)), Cambridge MA. 617-495-2401

Fraser, M Doreen E, *Asst Prof,* Dalhousie University, School of Library Service, NS. 902-424-3656

Fraser, Mary L, *Dir,* Cape Breton Regional Library, Sydney NS. 902-562-3279

Fraser, Mrs J, *Pub Servs,* University of Victoria (Law), Victoria BC. 604-477-6911

Fraser, Therese M, *Dir,* Des Plaines Historical Society Library, Des Plaines IL. 312-297-4912

Fraser, W, *Acq,* University of Windsor, Leddy Library, Windsor ON. 519-253-4232, Ext 198

Fraser, Walter J, *Systs & Automation,* University of California at Davis, General Library, Davis CA. 916-752-2110

Fraser, Y, *Media,* Medgar Evers College Library, Brooklyn NY. 212-735-1851

Frashier, Anne, *Cat & Spec Coll,* Pepperdine University Library, Payson Library, Malibu CA. 213-456-4252

Frashier, Joyce, *Librn,* Albuquerque Public Library (Prospect Park), Albuquerque NM. 505-766-7922

Frasier, Mary, *Info Serv,* South Dakota State Library, Pierre SD. 605-773-3131

Frater, Ethel, *Dir,* Leon-Saxeville Township Library, Pine River WI. 414-987-5478

Frater, Norma, *Circ,* Richmond Public Library, Richmond CA. 415-231-2119

Frautschi, Mary H, *Dir,* Union County Public Library, Liberty IN. 317-458-5355

Fravel, Mark, *Chmn,* Old Dominion University, Div of Library Science, VA. 804-440-3006 & 440-4177

Fraver, Margaret, *Tech Serv,* Washington County Free Library, Hagerstown MD. 301-739-3250

Frawley, Eleanor M, *Cat,* Fairfax County Public Library, Administrative Offices, Springfield VA. 703-321-9810

Fray, Mary P, *Cat,* Westminster College, McGill Library, New Wilmington PA. 412-946-8761, Ext 342

Frazee, June, *Asst Librn,* Terra Alta Public Library, Terra Alta WV 304-789-2724

Frazee, Mary Louise, *Librn,* Westinghouse Electric Corp (Bettis Atomic Power Laboratory Library), West Mifflin PA. 412-462-5000

Frazee, Mary S, *Librn,* Metropolitan Life Insurance Co (General Library), New York NY. 212-578-3700

Frazelle, Betty, *Librn,* United States Navy (Medical Library, Naval Regional Medical Ctr), Camp Lejeune NC. 919-451-4570

Frazer, Amy, *Circ,* Dare County Library, Manteo NC. 919-473-2372

Frazer, John W, *Exec Dir,* Council of Independent Kentucky Colleges & Universities, KY. 606-236-3533

Frazier, Beverly, *Circ,* Taylor Memorial Public Library, Cuyahoga Falls Public Library, Cuyahoga Falls OH. 216-928-2117

Frazier, Catherine, *English & Soc Studies,* Wayne Community College, Learning Resource Center, Goldsboro NC. 919-735-5151, Ext 64

Frazier, Edna C, *Dir,* Brown County Public Library, Nashville Public Library, Nashville IN. 812-988-2850

Frazier, Edna M, *Librn,* Congressional Quarterly Inc, Editorial Reports Library, Washington DC. 202-296-6800, Ext 262

Frazier, Janet, *Ch,* Martins Ferry Public Library, Martins Ferry OH. 614-633-0314

Frazier, John, Argonne National Laboratory (Chemical Engineering), Argonne IL. 312-972-4481

Frazier, Ruby, *Bkmobile Coordr,* Owen County Public Library, Owenton KY. 502-484-3450

Frazier, Thomas, *Humanities,* Western Washington University, Mabel Zoe Wilson Library, Bellingham WA. 206-676-3050

Frazor, Georgia, *Ref & Bibliog Instr,* Houston Baptist University, Moody Memorial Library, Houston TX. 713-774-7661, Ext 303

Frear, Ruth, *On-Line Servs,* University of Utah (Marriott Library), Salt Lake City UT. 801-581-8558

Freatman, Jane, *Librn,* Enterprise Public Library, Enterprise OR. 503-426-3906

Freburg, Ruth E, *Dir,* Petroleum County Community Library, Winnett MT. 406-429-2271

Frechette, James R, *Tech Serv,* Rhode Island Junior College, Knight Campus Library, Warwick RI. 401-825-2215

Frederick, Edith, *Media,* Claflin College, H V Manning Library, Orangeburg SC. 803-534-2710, Ext 56

Frederick, Franz, *Assoc Prof,* Purdue University, Dept of Education, Library Media & Instructional Development, IN. 317-749-2902

Frederick, Jeanne, *Dir,* Crown Point-Center Public Library, Crown Point IN. 219-663-0270

Frederick, Kathleen A, *Dir,* Easttown Township Public Library, Berwyn PA. 215-644-0138, 644-0170

Frederick, Louise, *Librn,* Richardson Public Library, Richardson TX. 214-238-8251

Frederick, Marie, *Librn,* Allegheny Ludlum Industries, Inc, Research Center Library, Brackenridge PA. 412-226-2000

Frederick, Nadia, *Cat,* Frederick E Parlin Memorial Library, Everett MA. 617-387-2550

Frederick, Pauline, *Librn,* University of California at Davis (California Primate Research Center, Reference Services), Davis CA. 916-752-0424

Frederick, Ronald D, *Dir,* College of Saint Benedict Library, Saint Joseph MN. 612-363-5011

Fredericksen, Grant A, *Dir,* Dunlap Public Library District, Dunlap IL. 309-243-5716

Fredericksen, Richard B, *Dir,* University of Alabama in Birmingham (Lister Hill Library of the Health Sciences), Birmingham AL. 205-934-5460

Frederickson, Dennis, *Info Serv,* Lewis & Clark Library, Helena MT. 406-442-2380

Frederickson, Ethel L, *Librn,* Corning City Library, Corning KS. 913-868-2755

Fredette, Kathy, *Pub Info Offices,* Topeka Public Library, Topeka KS. 913-233-2040

Fredine, Anne, *Librn,* Nashua Public Library, Nashua IA. 515-435-4635

Fredrick, Nancy S, *Chief Librn,* General Dynamics, Pomona Division Library, Pomona CA. 714-629-5111, Ext 4151, 4161

Fredrick, William J, *Librn,* Back Mountain Memorial Library, Dallas PA. 717-675-1182

Fredrickson, Joan M, *Chief Librn,* United States Army (Quartermaster Center & Fort Lee Post Library), Fort Lee VA. 804-734-2322

Fredrickson, Karen, *Chief Librn,* Menlo Park Public Library, Menlo Park CA. 415-326-4421

Fredrickson, Mary, *Dir,* Kidder County Library, Steele ND. 701-475-2855

Fredrickson, Wanita, *Tech Serv & On-Line Servs,* Superior Public Library, Superior WI. 715-394-0248

Free, Barbara, *Ad,* John Packard Library of Yuba County, Marysville CA. 916-674-6241

Free, Doris, *Librn,* Blodgett Memorial Library, Fishkill NY. 914-896-9215

Free, Opal M, *Rare Bks & Spec Coll,* Florida State University, Robert Manning Strozier Library, Tallahassee FL. 904-644-5211

Free, Peggy, *Ref,* De Kalb Public Library, Haish Memorial Building, De Kalb IL. 815-756-4431

Free, Ruth, *Info Serv,* Sunflower County Library System, Indianola MS. 601-887-2153, 887-2298

Freebourn, Carol, *Ch,* Edwards Public Library, Southampton Public Library, Southampton MA. 413-527-9480

Freebury, Mrs W H, *Librn,* Tofield Municipal Library, Tofield AB. 403-662-3838

Freed, Emil, *Dir,* Southern California Library for Social Studies & Research, Los Angeles CA. 213-759-6063

Freed, Fay, *Ad,* Arizona State Library, Dept of Library, Archives & Public Records, Phoenix AZ. 602-255-4035

Freed, J Arthur, *Head Librn,* Los Alamos Scientific Laboratory Libraries, Library Services Group, Los Alamos NM. 505-667-4448

Freed, Wayne S, *Media,* Mohawk Valley Community College Library, Utica NY. 315-792-5337

Freedle, S D, *Dean of Educ,* Mississippi University for Women, School of Education, Div of Library Science, MS. 601-328-9100

Freedman, Arlene L, *Dir,* Beth Israel Medical Center, Medical Library, New York NY. 212-420-2000

Freedman, Janet, *Dir,* Southeastern Massachusetts University, Library Communications Center, North Dartmouth MA. 617-999-8662

Freedman, Lillian, *Ch,* Merrick Library, Merrick NY. 516-379-3476

Freedman, Lynn P, *Administrator,* American Can Co, Business Information Center, Greenwich CT. 203-552-2160, 552-2161 & 552-3685

Freedman, Mary F, *Asst Dir,* Elyria Public Library, Elyria OH. 216-323-5747

Freedman, Maurice, *Assoc Prof,* Columbia University in the City of New York, School of Library Service, NY. 212-280-2292

Freedman, Phyllis D, *Librn,* Orlando Municipal Reference Library, Orlando FL. 305-849-2249

Freedman, Robert, *Tech Serv & Cat,* Bethlehem Public Library, Bethlehem PA. 215-867-3761

Freedman, Robert, *Adjunct Prof,* Northampton County Area Community College, Library Technical Assistant Program, PA. 215-865-5351, Ext 221

Freehling, Leonore, *Librn,* Reiss-Davis Child Study Center, Research Library, Los Angeles CA. 213-204-1666

Freel, Mary Lou, *Lectr,* Concordia University, Library Studies Program, PQ. 514-482-0320, Ext 324

Freeland, Betty, *Tech Serv, Cat & Spec Coll,* Sturgis Public Library, Sturgis MI. 616-651-7907, 651-2321

Freeman, Anita, *Ch, YA & Media,* Denville Free Public Library, Denville NJ. 201-627-6555

Freeman, Benny D, *Dir,* Dunklin County Library, Kennett MO. 314-888-3561

Freeman, Carol Lynne, *Instr,* Southwest Missouri State University, Dept of Library Science, MO. 417-836-5104

Freeman, Corinne A, *Soc Serv,* Fordham University Library at Lincoln Center, New York NY. 212-841-5130, 841-5133

Freeman, Douglas, *Automated Processing,* University of Tennessee, Knoxville, James D Hoskins Library, Knoxville TN. 615-974-0111

Freeman, Frances, *Homebound Project,* Bladen County Public Library, Elizabethtown NC. 919-862-8171

Freeman, George C, *Chief Librn,* University of British Columbia Library (Biomedical Branch), Vancouver BC. 873-5441

Freeman, Helen, *Librn,* United Vintners, Inc, Italian Swiss Colony Research & Development Technical & Information Center, Madera CA. 209-674-5634

Freeman, Isabelle, *Exten Servs,* Elkhart Public Library, Elkhart IN. 219-294-5463

Freeman, Jane, *Librn,* W R Grace & Company, Dallas TX. 214-620-3131

Freeman, Jane L, *Dir,* Belmont Abbey College, Abbot Vincent Taylor Library, Belmont NC. 704-825-3711, Ext 342

Freeman, Janet L, *Dir & ILL,* Wingate College, Ethel K Smith Library, Wingate NC. 704-233-4061, Ext 155

Freeman, John C, *Dir,* Institute for Storm Research, Inc Library, Houston TX. 713-529-4891

Freeman, Joyce A, *Librn,* Whitley County Library, Williamsburg KY. 606-549-0818

Freeman, Larry, *Ref,* Greenville County Library, Greenville SC. 803-242-5000

Freeman, Lester, *Librn,* DeMary Memorial Library, Rupert ID. 208-436-3874

Freeman, Marjorie, *Cat,* Lynchburg College, Knight Memorial & Capron Libraries, Lynchburg VA. 804-845-9071, Ext 271

Freeman, Mary B, *Librn,* American Telephone & Telegraph Co, Long Lines Div, Government Communications Library, Washington DC. 202-457-3038

Freeman, Mary L, *Bkmobile Coordr,* Craft Memorial Library, Mercer County Service Center, Bluefield WV. 304-325-3943

Freeman, Michael, *Ref,* Dartmouth College, Baker Memorial Library, Hanover NH. 603-646-2235

Freeman, Mrs Lawrence, *Librn,* First Baptist Church Library, Murfreesboro TN. 615-893-2514

Freeman, Nancy, *Librn,* SCM Corp, Glidden Pigments Group Library, Baltimore MD. 301-633-6400

Freeman, Paul, *Dir,* Hawaii Loa College, Amos Starr & Juliette Montegue Cooke Academic Center, Kaneohe HI. 808-235-3641, Ext 119,136,137

Freeman, Peter, *Librn,* University of Alberta (Weir Memorial Law Library), Edmonton AB. 403-432-5560

Freeman, Robert G, *Asst Dir & Tech Serv,* Great Neck Library, Great Neck NY. 516-466-8055

Freeman, Ruth, *Librn,* Hobart Public Library, Hobart OK. 405-726-2535

Freeman, Sally, *Librn,* Contra Costa County Library (Martinez Branch), Martinez CA. 415-372-2898

Freeman, Sharon, *Asst Dir,* Lambton County Library, Wyoming ON. 519-845-3324

Freeman, Thelma, *Ch,* Bowling Green Public Library, Bowling Green KY. 502-781-4882

Freeman, Thomas, *Assoc Prof,* Jacksonville State University, College of Library Science, Communications & Instructional Media, AL. 205-435-6390

Freeman, Thomas, *On-Line Servs & Bibliog Instr,* Jacksonville State University Library, Jacksonville AL. 205-435-9820, Ext 213, 214

Freeman, V, *Cat,* Kennebunk Free Library, Kennebunk ME. 207-985-2173

Freeman, William S, *Municipal Govt & Law,* Monmouth County Library, Freehold NJ. 201-431-7220

Freeny, Bonnie, *Librn,* Mid-Mississippi Regional Library System (Carthage-Leake County), Carthage MS. 601-267-7821

Freeny, Maralita, *Librn,* Prince George's County Memorial Library (Beltsville Branch), Beltsville MD. 301-937-0294

Freerksen, Lois, *Librn,* Grand Junction Public Library, Grand Junction IA. 515-738-2506

Freese, Ella R, *Librn,* Avon Grove Free Library, West Grove PA. 215-869-2004

Freese, Kathryn, *Librn,* Southern Tier Library System (Valois-Logan-Hector Library), Hector NY. 607-962-3141

Freese, Lenora, *Dir,* Haworth Munincipal Library, Haworth NJ. 201-384-1020

Freese, Margaret W, *ILL,* Albright College Library, Reading PA. 215-921-2381, Ext 224

Freese, Robert, *Physical Sci & Eng,* McGill University Libraries, Montreal PQ. 514-392-4948

Freese, Robert, *Librn,* McGill University Libraries (Mathematics), Montreal PQ. 514-392-8273

Freese, Robert, *Librn,* McGill University Libraries (Physical Sciences), Montreal PQ. 514-392-5712

Freese, William, *Arts,* University of California, Santa Barbara Library, Santa Barbara CA. 805-961-2741

Frehse, Michael, *Info Systs Supvr,* Milwaukee County Federated Library System, Milwaukee WI. 414-278-3210

Freiband, Susan Jane, *Asst Prof,* Our Lady of the Lake University of San Antonio, Learning Resources Certification, TX. 512-434-6711, Ext 245

Freiburger, Gary, *Ref,* Loyola-Notre Dame Library, Inc, Baltimore MD. 301-532-8787

Freides, Thelma, *Reader Serv, On-Line Servs & Bibliog Instr,* State University of New York College at Purchase Library, Purchase NY. 914-253-5085

Freidman, Kathleen, *Librn,* Third Judicial Circuit Court of Wayne County Library, Detroit MI. 313-224-5265

Freimarck, Fran, *Dir,* Pamunkey Regional Library, Hanover VA. 804-798-6081, Ext 285, 287

Freisner, Vee, *Automation & Info Sci,* Kansas State Library, Topeka KS. 913-296-3296

Freitag, E, *Librn,* Burlington Medical Center, Health Sciences Library, Burlington IA. 319-753-3011

Freitag, Mary Sue, *Ref,* Indiana University at South Bend Library, South Bend IN. 219-237-4440

Freitag, Wolfgang M, *Librn,* Harvard University Library (Fine Arts Library), Cambridge MA. 617-495-3373

Freitas, Helen, *Bkmobile Coordr,* Millicent Library, Fairhaven MA. 617-992-5342

Freitas, John, *Admin Asst,* Fresno County Free Library, Fresno CA. 209-488-3191

Freling, Anne, *ILL,* Chippewa Library League, Mount Pleasant MI. 517-773-3242

Freling, Anne, *Acq,* Veterans Memorial Library, Mount Pleasant MI. 517-773-3242

Fremd, Edward G, *Res Coordr,* Boston Public Library, Eastern Massachusetts Library System, Boston MA. 617-536-5400

Fremier, Allene, *Outreach,* Ralph Chandler Harrison Memorial Library, Carmel CA. 408-624-4629

Fremier, Allene, *Tech Serv,* Ralph Chandler Harrison Memorial Library, Carmel CA. 408-624-4629

Fremin, Karen, *Reader Serv,* LaSalle Parish Library, Jena LA. 318-992-5675

Fremming, Susan, *Librn,* East Alton Public Library, East Alton IL. 618-259-7061

French, A F, *Computing Info Serv Supvr,* Bell Telephone Laboratories (Bell Telephone Laboratories Technical Library), Murray Hill NJ. 582-4612 (Supvr); 582-3740 (Circ); 582-3604 (Info Alerting Servs); 582-3901 (Systs Design Program); 582-3453 (Computing Info Serv); 582-7330 (Computing)

French, Betty, *Librn,* Kalkaska County Library, Kalkaska MI. 616-258-9411

French, Bonnie, *Librn,* Piermont Public Library, Piermont NH. 603-272-4964

French, Charlotte, *Dir,* South Oklahoma City Junior College, Learning Resources Center, Oklahoma City OK. 405-682-7574

French, Doris, *Tech Serv,* Lassen College, Media Center, Susanville CA. 916-257-6181, Ext 261

French, Dorothy M, *Librn,* Centerville Library Association, Centerville MA. 617-775-1787

French, Elsa, *Librn,* Fairfax County Public Library (King's Park), Vienna VA. 703-938-0405

French, Evelyn, *Dir,* American Business Press Inc Library, New York NY. 212-661-6360

French, Gladys, *Bkmobile Coordr,* Union County District Library, Morganfield KY. 502-389-1696

French, James, *Tech Serv & Cat,* Johnson Free Public Library, Hackensack NJ. 201-343-4169

French, Jean, *Chief Librn,* Nationwide Insurance Co Library, Columbus OH. 614-227-6154

French, John, *Librn,* American Institutes for Research in the Behavioral Sciences, Palo Alto CA. 415-493-3550, Ext 289, 286

French, John, *Ref,* Brevard Community College, Learning Resources Center, Cocoa FL. 305-632-1111, Ext 295, 298

French, Joyce, *Ch, Acq & Commun Servs,* South Charleston Public Library, South Charleston WV. 304-744-6561

French, Kay, *Librn,* Houston County Public Library, Erin TN. 615-289-3858

French, Kenneth E, *Dir,* Port Jefferson Free Library Association, Port Jefferson NY. 516-473-0022

French, Mary Jane, *Librn,* Atlanta Public Library (Mobile Information Services), Atlanta GA. 404-261-5860

French, Michael, *Dir,* Rossford Public Library, Rossford OH. 419-666-0924

French, Muriel, *Tech Serv, Acq & On-Line Servs,* New Castle Public Library, New Castle PA. 412-658-6659

French, Randy, *Dir,* Menominee County Library, Stephenson MI. 906-753-6923

French, Robert B, *In Charge,* Louisville Academy of Music Library, Louisville KY. 502-893-7885

French, Sharon, *Librn,* Bank of America (Law Library), San Francisco CA. 415-622-6040

French, Thomas, *Media & Ser,* Xavier University, McDonald Memorial Library, Cincinnati OH. 513-745-3881

Freneta, William, *Departmental Personnel Office,* San Jose Public Library, San Jose CA. 408-277-4822

Frenette, Geraldine, *Philos, Relig & Educ,* Detroit Public Library, Detroit Associated Libraries, Detroit MI. 313-833-1000

Freney, Mary, *YA,* Silas Bronson Library, Waterbury CT. 203-574-8200

Frentzen, Marilee, *Librn,* Colusa County Free Library (Arbuckle), Arbuckle CA. 916-476-2526

Frenzel, Bernice, *Acq,* Saginaw Public Libraries, Hoyt Public Library, Saginaw MI. 517-755-0904

Frese, Anne, *Dir,* Niles Community Library, Niles MI. 616-683-8545, 683-8546

Freshley, Katherine T, *Librn,* Textile Museum, Arthur D Jenkins Library, Washington DC. 202-667-0441

Freshwater, Marjorie, *Cat,* Ohio State University Libraries (Vocational Education Research Library), Columbus OH. 614-486-3655, Ext 221

Fretwell, Gordon, *Pub Servs,* University of Massachusetts at Amherst Library, Amherst MA. 413-545-0284

Fretwell, Verda, *Bkmobile Coordr,* Middlesboro-Bell County Public Library, Middlesboro KY. 606-248-4812

Fretz, Evelyn C, *Dir,* Wyomissing Public Library, Wyomissing PA. 215-374-2385

Freudenthal, Juan R, *Assoc Prof,* Simmons College, Graduate School of Library & Information Science, MA. 617-738-2225

Freund, Alfred L, *Dir,* Ramapo Catskill Library System, Middletown NY. 914-343-1131, 352-4825, 565-3030

Freund, Patsy, *Dir,* Atchison Public Library, Atchison KS. 913-367-1902

Freve, Reay, *Librn,* Colchester-East Hants Regional Library, Truro NS. 902-895-4183

Frevert, Laura, *Librn,* Hammond Public Library (Wilson), Hammond IN. 219-931-5100

Frey, Agnes L, *Reader Serv,* United States Army War College Library, Carlisle Barracks PA. 717-245-4319

Frey, Amy, *ILL,* West Hartford Public Library, Noah Webster Memorial Library, West Hartford CT. 203-236-6286

Frey, Anita, *Ref,* East Islip Public Library, East Islip NY. 516-581-9200, 581-9228

Frey, Emil F, *Chmn,* Houston Area Research Library Consortium, (HARLIC), TX. 713-527-8101, Ext 2642

Frey, Emil F, *Dir,* University of Texas Medical Branch, Moody Medical Library, Galveston TX. 713-765-1971

Frey, Janet, *Librn,* Greene County Public Library, Snow Hill NC. 919-747-3437

Frey, Joan, *Librn,* Kimball Public Library, Randolph VT. 802-728-5073

Frey, Katherine, *Librn,* Tulare County Library System (Farmersville Branch), Farmersville CA. 209-747-0867

Frey, Mrs Walter, *Ch,* Sumter County Library, Sumter SC. 803-773-7273

Frey, Peter, *Asst Dir,* University of Richmond (T C Williams School of Law), Richmond VA. 804-285-6239

Frey, Phyllis B, *Dir,* Kaltreider Memorial Library, Red Lion PA. 717-244-2032

Freyer, Kenneth, *Bibliog Instr,* Queens College Library, Flushing NY. 212-520-7616

Freymuth, Louis, *Circ,* Emporia State University, William Allen White Library, Emporia KS. 316-343-1200, Ext 205

Freynet, Lucile, *Coordr French Lang Servs,* Winnipeg Public Library (Saint Boniface), Winnipeg MB. 204-233-7755

Frick, Claudette, *Librn,* Chicago Public Library (West Belmont), Chicago IL. 312-637-1801

Frick, E, *Bibliog Instr,* University of Colorado at Colorado Springs, Library, Colorado Springs CO. 303-593-3296

Frick, Elizabeth, *Ref,* University of Colorado at Colorado Springs, Library, Colorado Springs CO. 303-593-3296

Frick, Joan, *Librn,* Ford, Bacon & Davis, Inc Library, New York NY. 212-344-3200, Ext 229

Fricke, Nora, *Librn,* Spicer Public Library, Spicer MN. 612-796-5560

Fricks, Mona A, *Dir,* Albertville Public Library, Albertville AL. 205-878-4321

Friday, Bill, *Interlibr Loan & Referral Librn,* Vigo County Public Library, Terre Haute IN. 812-232-1113

Friday, Bonnie, *On-Line Servs,* United States Air Force (Strughold Aeromedical Library), Brooks AFB TX. 512-536-3321

Friday, Sherlyn, *Dir & Media,* Loma Linda University (Jorgensen Memorial Library), Loma Linda CA. 714-796-0141, Ext 207

Friddle, Richard L, *Librn,* Colorado Correctional Facility Library, Canon City CO. 303-275-4181

Friddle, Richard L, *Librn,* Colorado Women's Correctional Facility Library, Canon City CO. 303-275-3311, Ext 411

Fridenberg, Daryl, *Ch,* Canada Public Service Staff Relations Board Library, Ottawa ON. 613-992-3584

Fridie, Stephanie, *Nursing,* Salisbury State College, Blackwell Library, Salisbury MD. 301-546-3261, Ext 351

Fridley, Bonna, *Asst Librn,* Strawberry Point Public Library, Strawberry Point IA. 319-933-4340

Fried, Arthur N, *Supvr,* Lockheed Missiles & Space Company, Inc, Technical Information Center, Palo Alto CA. 415-493-4411, Ext 45041

Friedenstein, Hanna, *Libr Mgr & On-Line Search Coordr,* Cabot Corp, Technical Information Center, Billerica MA. 617-272-3500, Ext 412

Friedland, Rhoda, *Ch,* Elmont Public Library, Elmont NY. 516-354-5280, 354-4091

Friedlander, Florence, *Ch,* Shelter Rock Public Library, Albertson NY. 516-248-7363

Friedli, Mary, *Acq,* Lexington Public Library, Lexington IL. 309-365-7801

Friedline, Ruth, *Archivist,* Shippensburg State College, Ezra Lehman Memorial Library, Shippensburg PA. 717-532-1463

Friedman, Antonia, *Pub Servs,* Saint Mary's College of California, Saint Albert Hall Library, Moraga CA. 415-376-4411, Ext 229, 230

Friedman, B, *Librn,* Tifereth Israel Synagogue Library, Lincoln NE. 402-423-8569

Friedman, Dean, *Instr,* Morningside College, Library Science Dept, IA. 712-277-5125

Friedman, Dean, *Media,* Morningside College, Wilhemina Petersmeyer Library, Sioux City IA. 712-277-5195

Friedman, Estelle, *Librn,* New York Public Library (West Farms), New York NY. 212-367-5376

Friedman, Frances, *YA,* Johnson Free Public Library, Hackensack NJ. 201-343-4169

Friedman, Gary, *Sci, Geog & Photo,* Ontario Public Library, Ontario CA. 984-2758 Ext 38

Friedman, Jane, *ILL & Ref,* University of Houston (William I Dykes Library), Houston TX. 713-749-1991

Friedman, Joan M, *Curator Rare Bks,* Yale University Library (Center for British Art), New Haven CT. 203-432-4594

Friedman, Judy, *Mgr Libr Servs,* National Broadcasting Co (Reference Library), New York NY. 212-664-5307

Friedman, Kathleen, *Librn,* Wayne County Circuit Court Law Library, Detroit MI. 313-224-5265

Friedman, Lee, *Dir,* School for International Training, Donald B Watt Library, Brattleboro VT. 802-257-7751, Ext 216

Friedman, Lydia, *Chief Librn,* Maimonides Medical Center, Medical Library, Brooklyn NY. 212-270-7679, Ext 6253

Friedman, Martha, *Librn,* University of Illinois Library at Urbana-Champaign (History & Philosophy), Urbana IL. 217-333-1091

Friedman, Ruth E, *Ch,* Darien Library, Inc, Darien CT. 203-655-2568

Friedmann, Esther, *Dir,* Johnson School of Technology Library, Scranton PA. 717-342-6404

Friedon, Charles, *Circ,* University of Virginia, Alderman Library, Charlottesville VA. 804-924-3026

Friedrich, Esther B, *Chief Librn,* Orange County Public Library (La Habra Branch), La Habra CA. 714-526-7728, 7729, 7720

Frieling, Thomas J, *Asst Librn,* Bainbridge Junior College Library, Bainbridge GA. 912-246-7646

Friemoth, Viola, *Librn,* Putnam County District Library (Ottoville Branch), Ottoville OH. 419-523-3747

Friend, David S, *Dir & Spec Coll,* Pocatello Public Library, Information and Video Center, Pocatello ID. 208-232-1263

Friend, Janet, *Tech Serv,* Hunterdon County Library, Flemington NJ. 201-788-1444

Friend, Linda, *On-Line Servs,* Pennsylvania State University, Fred Lewis Pattee Library, University Park PA. 814-865-0401

Friend, Robert G, *Librn,* Western Iowa Technical Community College, Instructional Materials Center, Sioux City IA. 712-276-0380, Ext 250

Frierson, Gretchel, *Afro-Am,* Benedict College, Benjamin F Payton Learning Resources Ctr, Columbia SC. 803-256-4220

Fries, Bea Ann, *ILL, Ref & On-Line Servs,* Belleville Area College Library, Belleville IL. 618-235-2700, Ext 236

Friesen, E, *Librn,* Okanagan Regional Library District (Mica Creek Branch), Mica Creek BC. 604-834-7436

Friesen, Eva, *Acq,* Ryerson Polytechnical Institute, Donald Mordell Learning Resources Centre, Toronto ON. 416-595-5331

Friesen, Margaret, *ILL,* University of British Columbia Library, Vancouver BC. 604-228-3871

Friesen, Ruby E, *Asst Dir & Ref,* Salem Public Library, Salem OR. 503-588-6071

Friesen, Susanne, *Cat,* Goshen Public Library, Goshen IN. 219-533-9531

Friesz, Teena, *Asst Librn,* Miles Community College Library, Miles City MT. 406-232-3031

Friis, Harriet, *Librn,* Long Beach Public Library System (Dana), Long Beach CA. 213-424-4828

Frimmel, Stella, *YA,* Watertown Free Public Library, Watertown MA. 617-924-5390

Frink, Marvyl J, *Librn,* New Hampton Public Library, New Hampton IA. 515-394-2184

Frins, Sarah, *Tech Serv,* Alabama Supreme Court, Supreme Court & State Law Library, Montgomery AL. 205-832-6410

Frisbie, Elizabeth, *Spec Servs,* Minneapolis Public Library & Information Center, Minneapolis MN. 612-372-6500

Frisbie, Granville K, *In Charge,* Scottish Rite Bodies Library, San Diego CA. 714-297-0395

Frisbie, Mary Lee, *Librn,* Brentwood Public Library, Brentwood MO. 314-962-4800, Ext 47

Frisby, Carol, *Hist,* Arlington Public Library, Arlington TX. 817-275-2763, 265-3311, Ext 347

Frisby, Glenn, *Ref & ILL,* Nicholson Memorial Library, Garland TX. 214-494-7187

Frisby, Wilfred A, *Dir,* Philadelphia College of Textiles & Science, Senator John O Pastore Library, Philadelphia PA. 215-843-9700

Frisch, Corrine, *Pub Relations,* Lincoln Library, Springfield Public Library, Springfield IL. 217-753-4900

Frisch, Irene, *Dir,* Sterling Drug, Inc, Medical Library, New York NY. 212-972-6256

Frischkorn, Florine, *In Charge,* Saint Paul Public Library (Riverview), Saint Paul MN. 612-292-6626

Frishett, Judy, *YA,* Prince William Public Library, Manassas VA. 703-361-8211

Frishie, J G, *Librn,* Systems Technology Associates Inc Library, Washington DC. 202-471-6633

Frising, Marjanna J, *Dir,* Hopkinsville Community College Library, Hopkinsville KY. 502-886-3921, Ext 39

Frisz, Liz, *Librn,* United States Navy (Fleet Analysis Center Library), Corona CA. 714-736-5000

Frith, Betsy, *Tech Serv,* Yuma City-County Library, Yuma AZ. 602-782-1871

Fritsch, A Frances, *Librn,* Garner Public Library, Garner IA. 515-923-2850

Fritsch, Ardelle, *Librn,* Southeast Arkansas Regional Library (Tillar Public), Tillar AR. 501-367-3336

Fritsch, Helen, *Librn,* Squaw Grove Township Public Library, Hinckley IL. 815-286-3220

Fritsel, Nancy, *Ch,* Palm Springs Public Library, Palm Springs CA. 714-323-8291

Fritter, Joanne, *Librn,* Oak Brook Free Public Library, Oak Brook IL. 312-654-2222

Fritts, Veta, *Librn,* Saint Louis County Library (Weber Rd), St Louis MO. 314-638-2210

Fritz, Dianna, *Librn,* Peoria Public Library (South Side), Peoria IL. 309-672-8839

Fritz, Doris, *Librn,* Niobrara Public Library, Niobrara NE. 402-857-3565

Fritz, Dorothy, *ILL,* Burton Public Library, Burton OH. 216-834-4258

Fritz, Lucile, *Ref,* Lincoln Library, Springfield Public Library, Springfield IL. 217-753-4900

Fritz, Lynda, *Librn,* Long Beach Public Library System (North), Long Beach CA. 213-422-1927

Fritz, Pamela, *Librn,* PPG Industries, Chemical Div US Library, Chicago IL. 312-694-2700

Fritz, Ruth T, *Dir,* Penns Grove-Carney's Point Library, Penns Grove NJ. 609-299-4255

Fritz, Theodore, *Media,* Capital University Library, Columbus OH. 614-236-6614

Fritz, W Richard, *Dir,* Lutheran Theological Southern Seminary, Lineberger Memorial Library, Columbia SC. 803-786-5750

Frizzell, Robert, *Rare Bks & Spec Coll,* Illinois Wesleyan University Library, Bloomington IL. 309-556-3172

Froats, Mrs Willis, *Librn,* Renfrew Public Library, Renfrew ON. 613-432-8151

Frobom, Jerome, *Govt Publications,* Wyoming State Library, Cheyenne WY. 307-777-7281

Froehlich, R H, *In Charge,* General Motors Corp, Pontiac Motor Division, Technical Information Center, Pontiac MI. 313-857-5000

Frohlich, Anne, *Librn,* Detroit Bible College, Farmington Hills MI. 313-553-7200

Frohmberg, Katherine, *Syst Coordr,* Oberlin College Library, Oberlin OH. 216-775-8285

Frohrip, Karen, *Outreach & Volunteers,* Great River Regional Library, Saint Cloud MN. 612-251-7282

Froman, James, *Librn,* Antioch College, Human Ecology Center Library, Columbia MD. 301-730-9175

Frome, Lynda, *Dir,* Longmont United Hospital, Medical Staff Library, Longmont CO. 303-776-1422

Fromm, Esther, *Dir,* Greeley Public Library, Greeley Municipal Library, Greeley CO. 303-353-6123, Ext 392

Fromm, Roger W, *ILL & Ref,* Bloomsburg State College, Harvey A Andruss Library, Bloomsburg PA. 717-389-2716

Fromm, Sunny, *Librn,* Library Association of Portland (Midland), Portland OR. 503-252-1164

Frommeyer, L Ronald, *Acq,* University of Cincinnati Libraries, Central Library, Cincinnati OH. 513-475-2218

Frontz, Stephanie, *Librn,* University of Rochester (Art), Rochester NY. 716-275-4476

Froscher, Jean, *Acq,* Edison Community College, Learning Resources Center, Fort Myers FL. 813-481-2121, Ext 219, 220, 360

Fross, Dorothy, *Librn,* Clayton Township Public Library, Clayton IL. 217-894-6519

Frost, Alice, *Ref,* Amos Memorial Public Library, Sidney Public Library, Sidney OH. 513-492-8354

Frost, Annette K, *Head Libr Serv,* Fanshawe College of Applied Arts & Technology Library, London ON. 519-452-4350

Frost, Carolyn O, *Asst Prof,* University of Michigan, School of Library Science, MI. 313-764-9376

Frost, Charles, *Inter-Branch Loan,* Brooklyn Public Library, Brooklyn NY. 212-780-7712

Frost, J William, *Dir,* Friends Historical Library of Swarthmore College, Swarthmore PA. 215-447-7496

Frost, John F, *Librn,* New York University (Fales Collection), New York NY. 212-598-2484

Frost, Louise, *Ch,* Katonah Village Library, Katonah NY. 914-232-3508

Frost, Robert, *Media Dir,* Tarrant County Junior College System (South Campus Learning Resource Center), Fort Worth TX. 817-534-4861, Ext 223

Frost, Robert C, *Ref,* Nashua Public Library, Nashua NH. 603-883-4141, 883-4142

Frost, Walter, *Dir AV Servs,* Southeastern Massachusetts University, Library Communications Center, North Dartmouth MA. 617-999-8662

Frost, William J, *Ref Coll,* Bloomsburg State College, Harvey A Andruss Library, Bloomsburg PA. 717-389-2716

Frow, Richard, *Urban Affairs,* Miami-Dade Public Library System, Miami FL. 305-579-5001

Frowine, Victoria M, *Chief Librn, On-Line Servs & Bibliog Instr,* Carlow College, Grace Library, Pittsburgh PA. 412-578-6137

Fruchtenicht, Carolyn, *Ref,* Napa Community College Library, Napa CA. 707-255-2100, Ext 311

Frump, John A, *On-Line Servs,* International Minerals & Chemical Corp, R & D Library, Terre Haute IN. 812-232-0121, Ext 349 & 405

Fruth, Alice, *Cat,* Grandview Heights School District Public Library, Columbus OH. 614-486-2951

Fry, Arline, *On-Line Servs,* Spokane Community College, East Mission Campus Library, Spokane WA. 509-455-7699

Fry, Bernard M, *Dean,* Indiana University, Graduate Library School, IN. 812-337-2848

Fry, Geraldine, *Librn,* Dames & Moore Library, Bethesda MD. 301-652-2215, Ext 217

Fry, Hazel, *Librn,* Agriculture Canada (Canadian Grain Commission), Winnipeg MB. 204-949-3360

Fry, Jack, *Dir,* Elisha D Smith Public Library, Menasha WI. 414-729-5166

Fry, James, *Deputy Asst State Librn for Tech Serv,* State Library of Ohio, Columbus OH. 614-466-2693

Fry, Kaia, *Asst Librn,* Deerfield Public Library, Deerfield WI. 608-764-8102

Fry, Mabel C, *Librn,* Yukon Public Library, Yukon OK. 405-354-8232

Fry, Miriam B, *Dir,* Nichols Library, Naperville IL. 312-355-1540

Fry, Morel, *Fed Programs, Planning, Evaluation & Res Coordr,* Nebraska Library Commission, Lincoln NE. 402-471-2045

Fry, Roy, *Pub Servs,* Loyola University of Chicago Libraries, Chicago IL. 312-274-3000, Ext 771

Fry, Roy, *Polit Sci,* Loyola University of Chicago Libraries (Elizabeth M Cudahy Memorial Library), Chicago IL. 312-274-3000, Ext 771

Fry, Stephen, *Librn,* University of California Los Angeles Library (Music), Los Angeles CA. 213-825-4881

Fry, Thomas, *Actg Librn,* University of California Los Angeles Library (College Undergraduate), Los Angeles CA. 213-825-7837

Fry, Warren, *Dir,* Central Arizona Film Cooperative, AZ. 602-965-5073

Fryar, Barbara, *Libr Technician,* San Diego County Library (San Marcos Branch), San Marcos CA. 714-744-0707

Fryar, Linda, *Asst Librn,* United States Air Force (Sheppard Air Force Base Library), Sheppard AFB TX. 817-851-2687

Fryberger, Nancy, *Librn,* Somerset County Library (Warren Township Library), Warren NJ. 201-754-5554

Fryberger, Nancy B, *Dir,* Warren Township Public Library, Warren NJ. 201-754-5554

Frye, Florence, *Librn,* Seattle Post-Intelligencer Library, Seattle WA. 206-628-8000

Frye, Gwendolyn, *Librn,* W R Holley Memorial Library (Cornelia Elmore), Atmore AL. 205-368-5248

Frye, John, *Spec Coll,* Washington County Free Library, Hagerstown MD. 301-739-3250

Frye, John H, *Asst Dean,* Triton College Library, River Grove IL. 312-456-0300

Frye, Larry J, *Dir,* Bethany College, T L Phillips Memorial Library, Bethany WV. 304-829-7000

Frye, Margaret, *Cat,* Northwest College of the Assemblies of God, Hurst Library, Kirkland WA. 206-822-8266, Ext 255

Frye, Marvel, *ILL,* Gail Borden Public Library District, Elgin IL. 312-742-2411

Frye, Rosie, *ILL,* Duluth Public Library, Duluth MN. 218-723-3800

Fryer, Hazel H, *Dir,* Mauney Memorial Library, Kings Mountain Public Library, Kings Mountain NC. 704-739-2371

Fryer, Judith, *Per,* Ursinus College, Myrin Library, Collegeville PA. 215-489-4111, Ext 290

Fryer, Melinda Lane, *Librn,* Financial Accounting Standards Board Library, Stamford CT. 203-329-8401

Frysiak, Sister M Speciose, *AV,* Villa Maria College of Buffalo Library, Buffalo NY. 716-896-0703

Fu, Pao-Jen, *Librn,* Hoke County Library, Raeford NC. 919-875-2502

Fu, Paul, *Tech Serv,* Sandhill Regional Library System, Rockingham NC. 919-997-3388

Fu, Paul S, *Librn,* Supreme Court of Ohio Law Library, Columbus OH. 614-466-2044

Fu, Shirley, *Acq & Cat,* Clark County Community College, Learning Resources Center, North Las Vegas NV. 702-643-6060, Ext 269

Fu, T, *Pub Servs, On-Line Servs & Bibliog Instr,* University of Wisconsin-Oshkosh, Forrest R Polk Library, Oshkosh WI. 414-424-3333

Fuchik, Marie, *Asst Dir,* Euclid Public Library, Euclid OH. 216-261-5300

Fuchs, C, *Librn,* Research & Education Association Library, New York NY. 212-695-9487

Fuchs, JoAnn, *Tech Serv,* Pawtucket Public Library & Regional Library Center, Deborah Cook Sayles Memorial Library, Pawtucket RI. 401-725-3714

Fuchs, Mary H, *Librn,* Humphrey Public Library, Humphrey NE. 402-923-1701

Fuchs, Phyllis, *Ch,* Captain John Curtis Memorial Library, Brunswick Public Library, Brunswick ME. 207-725-5242

Fuchs, Sister Gertrude, *Ad, Tech Serv & Acq,* Tenafly Public Library, Tenafly NJ. 201-568-8680

Fuehring, Dorothy, *Librn,* Mackinaw Township Library, Mackinaw IL. 309-359-8022

Fuerbringer, Jane, *Bkmobile Coordr,* Ingham County Library, Library Service Center, Mason MI. 517-676-9088

Fueston, Michelle, *Circ,* Lebanon Public Library, Lebanon OH. 513-932-4725

Fugate, Elizabeth, *Librn,* University of Washington Libraries (Drama), Seattle WA. 206-543-5148

Fuge, Nancy, *Ch,* Westhampton Free Library, Westhampton Beach NY. 516-288-3335

Fuhro, Laura, *Ch,* Free Public Library of the Township of Berkeley Heights, Berkeley Heights NJ. 201-464-9333

Fujii, Ray, *Librn,* Hawaii State Library System (Kaneohe Regional), Kaneohe HI. 808-247-6691

Fujino, Amy H, *Adminr,* Hawaii State Library System (West Oahu Library District), Pearl City HI. 808-455-9023

Fukami, Marguerite, *Cat,* Chicago Public Library, Chicago IL. 312-269-2900

Fukano, Yasuko T, *Librn,* University of Washington Libraries (Fisheries-Oceanography), Seattle WA. 206-543-4279

Fukumitsu, Pamela, *Librn,* Cumberland County Public Library (Eutaw), Fayetteville NC. 919-485-4214

Fulcher, Jane M, *Librn,* Washington County Law Library, Washington PA. 412-228-6747

Fulcher, Mary, *Ad,* Paducah Public Library, Paducah KY. 502-442-2510, 443-2664

Fulcher, Sophie, *Librn,* Tarpon Springs Public Library, Tarpon Springs FL. 813-937-1462

Fulghum, Elsie C, *Br Coordr,* Lake Blackshear Regional Library, Americus GA. 912-924-8091

Fulghum, Elsie C, *Librn,* Lake Blackshear Regional Library (Cordele Carnegie), Cordele GA. 912-273-2464

Fulghum, Viola R, *Asst Librn,* McIver's Grant Public Library, Dyersburg TN. 901-285-5032

Fulk, Margaret E, *Dean,* Western Piedmont Community College, Learning Resources Center, Morganton NC. 704-437-8688, Ext 234

Fullam, Agatha, *Curator,* Waterville Historical Society Library, Waterville ME. 207-872-9439

Fullam, Paul J, *Dir,* Immaculate Conception Monastery, Passionist Monastic Seminary Library, Jamaica NY. 212-739-6502

Fullbright, Nancy F, *Dir,* Davidson County Public Library System, Lexington NC. 704-246-2520

Fuller, Ann, *Librn,* Montgomery City-County Public Library (Eastern), Montgomery AL. 205-272-5036

Fuller, Brenda, *Doc,* Kentucky Department of Library & Archives, Frankfort KY. 502-564-7910

Fuller, Carolyn, *Tech Serv,* Cass County Public Library, Harrisonville MO. 816-884-3483

Fuller, Clara, *Librn,* Stuart Township Library, Stuart NE. 402-924-3242

Fuller, Donald F, *Dir,* Santa Clara City Library, Santa Clara CA. 408-984-3097

Fuller, Donnie, *Ch,* Woolworth Community Library, Jal NM. 505-395-3268

Fuller, Doris, *Librn,* Stone Memorial Library, Conneautville PA. 814-587-2142

Fuller, Dorothy C, *Pub Libr Develop,* Virginia State Library, Richmond VA. 804-786-8929

Fuller, Dorothy M, *Supervisory Libr Tech,* United States Navy (Pearl Harbor Naval Base Library), Honolulu HI. 808-471-8238

Fuller, Edward, *Spec Coll,* Swarthmore College, McCabe Library, Swarthmore PA. 215-447-7477, 447-7480

Fuller, Fred, *ILL,* Alabama Public Library Service, Montgomery AL. 205-832-5743

Fuller, Harriet, *Ad,* Central Arkansas Library System, Little Rock AR. 501-374-7546

Fuller, Hazel, *Librn,* Bureau of Land Management, Riverside District Office Library, Riverside CA. 714-787-1462

Fuller, J A, *On-Line Servs,* Alberta Research Council Library, Edmonton AB. 403-432-8121

Fuller, J Lorene, *Librn,* Environmental Protection Agency, Robert S Kerr Environmental Research Center, Ada OK. 405-332-8800, Ext 241

Fuller, Jane, *Librn,* Grain Processing Corporation, Technical Library Center, Muscatine IA. 319-264-4389

Fuller, Jane, *On-Line Servs & Bibliog Instr,* Grain Processing Corporation, Technical Library Center, Muscatine IA. 319-264-4389

Fuller, Jean, *Circ,* Athol Public Library, Athol MA. 617-249-9515

Fuller, Jean, *Media,* Charles County Community College, Learning Resource Center, La Plata MD. 301-934-2251, Ext 251

Fuller, Jean, *Librn,* Saint Mary's Hospital, Medical & Nursing Library, Waterbury CT. 203-574-6408

Fuller, Joyce, *AV,* Pierce County Rural Library District, Tacoma WA. 206-572-6760

Fuller, Karen, *Librn,* Nekoosa Public Library, Nekoosa WI. 715-886-3109

Fuller, Martha, *Librn,* Jericho Town Library, Jericho Center VT. 802-899-4436

Fuller, Mary D, *Acq,* Westfield Athenaeum, Westfield MA. 413-568-7833

Fuller, Mary Ellen, *Dir & Ch,* Charlotte-Glades Library System, Port Charlotte FL. 813-629-1715

Fuller, Miriam, *Instr,* University of Missouri-Columbia, School of Library & Informational Science, MO. 314-882-4546

Fuller, Mrs Ray P, *Librn,* Fletcher Memorial Library, Hampton CT. 203-445-9295

Fuller, Mrs Robert, *Asst Dir,* Bixby Memorial Free Library, Vergennes VT. 802-877-2211

Fuller, Nancy, *Tech Serv & Cat,* Lake Superior State College Library, Sault Sainte Marie MI. 906-632-6841, Ext 402

Fuller, Nancy F, *Librn,* University of Mississippi Library (Austin A Dodge Library), University MS. 601-232-7381

Fuller, Nell B, *Tech Serv & Acq,* University of Virginia (Claude Moore Health Sciences Library), Charlottesville VA. 804-924-5444

Fuller, Peter F, *Dir,* East Greenwich Free Library, East Greenwich RI. 401-884-9511

Fuller, Roger A, *Media,* Tidewater Community College, Chesapeake Campus Library, Chesapeake VA. 804-547-9271, Ext 261-269

Fuller, Rose Mary, *Asst Librn,* First Baptist Church & Satsuma Christian School, Satsuma Christian Library, Satsuma AL. 205-675-1280, Ext 21

Fuller, Sara R, *Media,* Paducah Community College Library, Paducah KY. 502-442-6131, Ext 17

Fuller, Susan, *Br Coordr,* San Jose Public Library, San Jose CA. 408-277-4822

Fuller, Susan, *Ch,* Sandpoint-East Bonner County Free Public Library District, Sandpoint ID. 208-263-6930

Fuller, Walline, *Librn,* Fort Vancouver Regional Library (Steveson Community), Stevenson WA. 509-427-5471

Fullerton, Denis, *Librn,* Siskiyou County Public Library (Dorris Branch), Dorris CA. 916-397-4932

Fullerton, Erma E, *Librn,* Prosser City Library, Prosser WA. 509-786-2533

Fullerton, Hilda L, *Librn,* J R Clarke Public Library, Covington OH. 513-473-2226

Fullmer, Sara, *Asst Librn,* Barclay Public Library of Illini Township, Warrensburg IL. 217-672-3621

Fullshire, Lynn C, *Librn,* Tenth Judicial District Supreme Court Law Library, Riverhead NY. 516-727-4700, Ext 407

Fulmer, Bernita, *Br Coordr,* Imperial County Free Library, Imperial CA. 714-355-2260

Fulmer, Constance M, *Librn,* Good Samaritan Hospital, Medical Library, Lexington KY. 606-252-6612

Fulmer, Russell, *Tech Serv,* Jackson Metropolitan Library, Jackson MS. 601-352-3677

Fulmer, William G, *Dir,* Carnegie-Stout Public Library, Dubuque Public Library, Dubuque IA. 319-583-9197

Fulsaas, Barbara, *Circ, Ref & Per,* Spokane Falls Community College, Library Media Services, Spokane WA. 509-456-2860

Fulton, Betty, *Librn,* Farmington Public Library, Farmington IL. 309-245-2175

Fulton, Elizabeth, *Librn,* National Steel Corp, Research Center Library, Weirton WV. 304-797-2837

Fulton, Glenda, *Librn,* Knoxville-Knox County Public Library (East Knoxville), Knoxville TN. 615-522-8052

Fulton, June, *Dir,* Mid-Eastern Regional Medical Library Service, PA. 215-561-6050

Fulton, June M, *Dir,* College of Physicians of Philadelphia Library, Philadelphia PA. 215-561-6050

Fulton, Violet, *Librn,* Stockton-San Joaquin County Public Library (Ripon Branch), Ripon CA. 209-944-8415

Fulton, William R, *Head Librn,* Pennsylvania State University, Beaver Campus Library, Monaca PA. 412-775-8830

Fultz, Marcella, *ILL,* Towson State University, Albert S Cook Library, Towson MD. 301-321-2450

Fulwell, Elizabeth, *Media,* Niagara County Community College, Library Learning Center, Sanborn NY. 716-731-3271, Ext 145

Fundis, Lois A, *Cat,* Mary H Weir Public Library, Weirton WV. 304-748-7070

Fung, Paul, *Ref,* University of Southern Colorado Library, Pueblo CO. 303-549-2361

Fung, Phyllis Lok-ping, *Librn,* Pacific States University Library, Los Angeles CA. 213-731-2383, Ext 7

Funk, Ann, *Films,* Martin Memorial Library, York PA. 717-843-3978

Funk, Carla, *Pub Libr Consult,* Suburban Library System, Burr Ridge IL. 312-325-6640

Funk, Carla, *Dir,* Warren-Newport Public Library District, Gurnee IL. 312-244-5150

Funk, Dorothy S, *Librn,* Springfield Hospital, Information Center Library, Springfield VT. 802-885-2151

Funk, Elizabeth A, *Spec Libr Servs, Librs in State Correctional Insts & State Hospitals, Actg Adv,* State Library of Pennsylvania, Harrisburg PA. 717-787-2646

Funk, Linda M, *Ch,* Granville Public Library, Granville OH. 614-587-0196

Funk, Marie, *Librn,* Washington County Free Library (Smithsburg Branch), Smithsburg MD. 301-824-7722

Funk, Susan, *Librn,* Coopers & Lybrand Audit Library, Chicago IL. 312-648-1133

Funkhouser, Brenda, *Librn,* Eldorado Memorial Library, Eldorado IL. 618-273-7922

Funkhouser, Richard, *Librn,* Purdue University Libraries & Audio-Visual Center (Mathematical Sciences), West Lafayette IN. 317-494-8711

Funnell, Maureen D, *Librn,* Southwest Foundation for Research & Education, Preston G Northrup Memorial Library, San Antonio TX. 512-674-1410, Ext 226

Funston, J Arthur, *Spec Coll,* Earlham College, Lilly Library, Richmond IN. 317-962-6561, Ext 360

Funt, Jerrie, *Librn,* Lewisville Public Library, Lewisville ID. 208-775-4706

Furan, Robert, *Librn,* Western Plains Library System (Graceville Branch), Graceville MN. 612-748-7332

Furbeyre, M, *Librn,* University of Southern California (Library Science), Los Angeles CA. 213-743-2869

Furche, Ann, *Ch,* Irving Public Library System, Irving TX. 214-253-2639

Furer, Sheila, *Coordr,* Alaska State Library (Southcentral Region), Anchorage AK. 907-274-6625

Furlong, Elizabeth J, *Coordr of Automation Procedures for Tech Servs,* Northwestern University Library, Evanston IL. 312-492-7658

Furlong, R E, *Libr Supvr,* Bell Telephone Laboratories (Bell Telephone Laboratories Technical Library), Naperville IL. 312-690-2550

Furman, Hazel, *Asst Prof,* Texas Woman's University, School of Library Science, TX. 817-387-2418 & 566-1455

Furmanik, Helen, *Ad,* Taunton Public Library, Subregional Headquarters for Eastern Massachusetts Regional Library System, Taunton MA. 617-823-3570

Furnas, Gail Abbott, *Librn,* Windsor Public Library, Windsor VT. 802-674-2556

Furnas, John, *Cat & Tech Serv,* Lakeland Community College Library, Mentor OH. 216-951-1000, Ext 226

Furnish, Dorothy J, *Relig Educ Curric Lab,* Garrett-Evangelical Theological Seminary Library, Evanston IL. 312-866-3911

Furnish, Marlene, *Librn,* Forest County Library, Marienville Area Public Library, Marienville PA. 814-927-8552

Furnival, Eleanor, *Librn,* North American Weather Consultants, Technical Library, Salt Lake City UT. 801-261-5660, Ext 20

Furnival, Eleanor K, *Librn,* North American Weather Consultants, Technical Library, Goleta CA. 805-967-1246, Ext 45

Furr, Barbara, *Media & Circ,* University of Cincinnati Libraries (Robert S Marx Law Library), Cincinnati OH. 513-475-3016

Furr, Nancy, *Librn,* Telcom, Inc Library, Vienna VA. 703-893-7700

Furrow, Barbara B, *Tech Serv,* Hastings Public Library, Hastings MI. 616-945-4263

Furst, Kenneth U, *Librn,* State University of New York (Engineering), Stony Brook NY. 516-246-7724

Furst, Kenneth W, *Coordr Sci Librs,* State University of New York, Frank Melville Jr Memorial Library, Stony Brook NY. 516-246-5650

Furumoto, Viola, *Sci-Tech & Ref,* University of Hawaii (University of Hawaii Library), Honolulu HI. 808-948-7205

Fury, Laura D, *Librn,* Madison State Hospital, Cragmont Medical Library, Madison IN. 812-265-2611, Ext 448

Fuscoe, James C, *Librn,* Rohr Industries, Inc, Corporate Library, Chula Vista CA. 714-575-3010

Fuseler, Elizabeth A, *Dir,* Texas A & M University at Galveston, Mitchell Campus Library, Galveston TX. 713-766-3366, 766-3367, 766-3368

Fuson, Elgie M, *Educ & Psychol,* California State University, Sacramento Library, Sacramento CA. 916-454-6466

Fussler, Herman H, *Prof,* University of Chicago, Graduate Library School, IL. 312-753-3482

Fustukjian, Sam, *Info Access,* State University of New York, College of Arts & Science at Oswego, Penfield Library, Oswego NY. 315-341-4232

Futas, Elizabeth, *Asst Prof,* Emory University, Div of Librarianship, GA. 404-329-6840

Futch, Eleanor, *Librn,* Middle Georgia Regional Library (Riverside), Macon GA. 912-745-5813

Futernick, Jennifer, *Librn,* Far West Laboratory, Library for Educational Research & Development, San Francisco CA. 415-565-3000

Futrell, Gene, *Asst Librn, Curric Lab,* East Texas Baptist College Library, Marshall TX. 214-938-0377

Fydenchuk, Marie, *Supvr,* Huron County Public Library (Crediton Branch), Crediton ON. 519-234-6487

G

Gaab, Donna, *Pub Servs,* Cochise County Library System, Bisbee AZ. 602-432-5703, Ext 500

Gaal, M L, *Info Scientist,* C-I-L Inc, Chemicals Research Laboratory Library, McMasterville PQ. 514-467-3314

Gaar, Marcella C, *Mgr Inf Center,* Washington Mutual Savings Bank, Dietrich Schmitz, Seattle WA. 206-464-4501

Gabany, Suzanne A, *Librn,* Mercy Hospital of Pittsburgh (Medical Library), Pittsburgh PA. 412-391-8800

Gabbay, Susan D, *Asst Dir,* Liverpool Public Library, Liverpool NY. 315-457-0310

Gabbert, Gwen, *Librn,* John Mosser Public Library, Abingdon IL. 309-462-3129

Gabel, Deborah, *Librn,* Misericordia Hospital (School of Nursing Library), Bronx NY. 212-920-9825

Gabel, E Margaret, *Asst Dir, Cat & On-Line Servs,* Elizabethtown College, Zug Memorial Library, Elizabethtown PA. 717-367-1151, Ext 222

Gable, June R, *Tech Libr Branch Head,* United States Department of the Navy (Strategic Systems Project Office, Technical Library), Washington DC. 202-697-2852

Gable, Sarah, *Cat,* University of South Carolina (School of Medicine Library), Columbia SC. 803-777-4858

Gaboriault, Paul H, *Dir,* Superior Public Library, Superior WI. 715-394-0248
Gaboury, Grace, *Tech Serv,* North Shore Community College, Learning Resource Center, Beverly MA. 617-927-4850, Ext 195, 199, 237
Gaboury, J D, *Dir,* North Shore Community College, Learning Resource Center, Beverly MA. 617-927-4850, Ext 195, 199, 237
Gabriel, Andrea, *Librn,* Tall Timbers Research Station Library, Tallahassee FL. 904-893-4153
Gabriel, Jennifer, *Dir,* Reconstructionist Rabbinical College, Mordecai M Kaplan Library, Philadelphia PA. 215-223-8121
Gabriel, Joyce, *Ch,* Baker County Public Library, Baker OR. 503-523-6414, 523-6419
Gabriel, Mike, *Govt Publications,* Mankato State University, Memorial Library, Mankato MN. 507-389-6201
Gabriel, Sister, *Librn,* Mount Sacred Heart College Library, Hamden CT. 203-248-4225
Gabriel, Tezeta, *Ref & Spec Coll,* Kentucky State University, Blazer Library, Frankfort KY. 502-564-5852
Gabura, Mrs J, *Tech Serv, Acq & Cat,* Ajax Public Library, Ajax ON. 416-683-6911
Gackle, C, *Dir,* Anoka-Ramsey Community College, Learning Media Center, Coon Rapids MN. 612-427-2600
Gaddie, Myrna, *Librn,* Chicago Urban League, Research & Planning, Chicago IL. 312-285-5800
Gaddipati, Rao, *Hindi, Tamil & Telugu,* Long Island University, Brooklyn Center Libraries, Brooklyn NY. 212-834-6060, 834-6064
Gaddis, Dale, *Asst Dir,* Durham County Library, Durham NC. 919-683-2626
Gaddis, Jane L, *Librn,* Lord, Bissell & Brook, Law Library, Chicago IL. 312-443-0700
Gaddy, Aileen, *Librn,* Hood River County Library, Hood River OR. 503-386-2535
Gade, Evelyn, *Asst Librn,* North-West Regional Library (Benito Branch), Benito MB. 204-539-2446
Gade, M, *Researcher,* Carnegie Foundation for the Advancement of Teaching Library, Washington DC. 202-387-7200
Gade, Rachel, *ILL, On-Line Servs & Bibliog Instr,* Ramsey County Public Library, Roseville MN. 612-631-0494
Gadia, Hariette Huff, *Instr,* Middle Tennessee State University, Department of Library Service, TN. 615-898-2740 & 898-5555
Gadsden, Alice H, *Bibliog Instr,* University of North Carolina at Greensboro, Walter Clinton Jackson Library, Greensboro NC. 919-379-5880
Gadziala, Marian, *Tech Serv & Cat,* Sullivan County Community College, Hermann Memorial Library, Loch Sheldrake NY. 914-434-5750, Ext 223
Gaede, Owen, *Instr,* Georgia Southern College, Library - Media, GA. 912-681-5204
Gaeden, Sister Annela, *Librn,* Mount Angel Public Library, Mount Angel OR. 503-845-6401
Gaertner, Donell J, *Dir,* Saint Louis County Library, Saint Louis MO. 314-994-3300
Gaetzke, Evelyn, *Librn,* Meservey Public Library, Meservey IA. 515-358-6408
Gaff, Lou, *Librn,* Cass County Library (Edwardsburg Branch), Edwardsburg MI. 616-445-8651
Gaffett, Sandra M, *Dir,* Island Free Library, Block Island RI. 401-466-5970
Gaffey, Ruth, *Ad,* Wallingford Public Library, Wallingford CT. 203-265-6754
Gaffield, Charles, *Librn,* New York Public Library (Science Dept), New York NY. 212-790-6578
Gaffney, Jean, *Librn,* Dayton & Montgomery County Public Library (Miamisburg Branch), Miamisburg OH. 513-866-1071
Gaffney, Thelma O, *Librn,* Katy Stricker Library, Calvert TX. 713-369-2563
Gaffney, Thomas L, *Dir,* Maine Historical Society Library, Portland ME. 207-774-1822
Gafford, Jr, Frank Hall, *Dir,* Clark County Community College, Learning Resources Center, North Las Vegas NV. 702-643-6060, Ext 269
Gage, Robert Ivy, *Librn,* McLennan County Law Library, Waco TX. 817-753-7341
Gagen, Cynthia A, *Mgr,* National Broadcasting Co (News Archives Library), New York NY. 212-664-4444

Gagliardi, Frank, *Asst Dir, Rare Bks & Spec Coll,* Central Connecticut State College, Elihu Burritt Library, New Britain CT. 203-827-7531
Gagne, Fern L, *Tech Serv,* Rio Hondo Community College Library, Whittier CA. 213-692-0921, Ext 371
Gagne, Gerard, *Assoc Librn Tech Servs,* Southeastern Massachusetts University, Library Communications Center, North Dartmouth MA. 617-999-8662
Gagne, Jeannette, *Librn,* Stark Public Library, Stark NH. 603-449-6656
Gagne, Joan, *Librn,* McGill University Libraries (Education (incl Curriculum Lab & Physical Educ Reading Room)), Montreal PQ. 514-392-8812
Gagne, Rolande B, *Librn,* Bibliotheque Publique, La Malbaie PQ. 418-665-6027
Gagnier, Elizabeth, *Librn,* Essex County Public Library (Emeryville Branch), Emeryville ON. 519-776-5241
Gagnier, Gertrude, *Dir,* Notre Dame College Library, Manchester NH. 603-669-4298, Ext 20
Gagnon, Louise, *Prof,* College de Jonquiere, Techniques de la Documentation, PQ. 418-547-2191, Ext 270
Gagnon, Patrick, *Instr,* Silver Lake College, School Librarianship Program, WI. 414-684-6691, Ext 34
Gagnon, R, *Acting Departmental Librn,* Public Works Canada, Departmental Library, Ottawa ON. 613-998-4705, 996-8211
Gagnon, Ronald, *Cat,* Peabody Institute Library, Danvers Public Library, Danvers MA. 617-774-0554
Gagnon, Vernon N, *Librn,* Boise Cascade Corp, Pulp & Paper Research Library, Vancouver WA. 206-695-4477, Ext 347
Gahagan, Jr, Steven W, *Acq,* Nicholls State University, Allen J Ellender Memorial Library, Thibodaux LA. 504-446-8111, Ext 401, 402
Gahl, Daniel R, *Dir,* Valparaiso University, Henry F Moellering Memorial Library, Valparaiso IN. 219-464-5364
Gaines, Carol L, *Asst Dir,* Laurens County Library, Laurens SC. 803-984-0596
Gaines, Carol L, *Librn,* Laurens County Library (Clinton Public Branch), Clinton SC. 803-833-1853
Gaines, Cassie, *Librn,* Bloomfield Public Library, Bloomfield MO. 314-568-2729
Gaines, Elaine D, *Actg Librn,* Baptist Bible College & Seminary, Broomfield CO. 303-469-1984
Gaines, Elizabeth, *Librn,* Elkins Park Free Library (La Mott Free Library), Elkins Park PA. 215-635-4419
Gaines, Ervin J, *Dir,* Cleveland Public Library, Cleveland OH. 216-623-2800
Gaines, Robert, *Applied Sci,* Austin Public Library, Austin TX. 512-472-5433
Gaines, William C, *Pub Servs,* Parkland College, Learning Resource Center, Champaign IL. 217-351-2241
Gaines, Jr, James E, *Dir,* Virginia Military Institute, J T L Preston Library, Lexington VA. 703-463-6228
Gains, Ellen, *Government Doc,* Hutchinson Public Library, Hutchinson KS. 316-663-5441
Gair, L, *Librn,* Okanagan Regional Library District (Trout Lake), Ferguson BC. 604-860-4033
Gaiser, Doris, *Librn,* Vanderburgh County Law Library, Evansville IN. 812-426-5171
Gaiser, Rosemary, *Sci & Indust,* Public Library of Cincinnati & Hamilton County, Cincinnati Public Library, Cincinnati OH. 513-369-6000
Gaitenby, Jane, *Actg Librn,* Haskins Laboratories Library, New Haven CT. 203-436-1774
Gaithee, Edmund B, *Dir & Curator,* Museum of National Center of Afro-American Artists, Slide Library, Boston MA. 617-723-8863
Gaither, Verlie A, *ILL & Ref,* Delaware Technical & Community College, Wilmington Campus Learning Resources Center, Wilmington DE. 302-571-2113
Gajewski, Marge, *Librn,* Brown County Library (Pulaski Branch), Pulaski WI. 414-822-3220
Gal, Imre, *Dir,* Bloomfield College Library, Bloomfield NJ. 201-748-9000, Ext 281
Galamgam, Adele, *Asst Librn & Cat,* Imperial Valley College, Spencer Library Media Center, Imperial CA. 714-352-8320, Ext 270

Galano, Jacqueline, *ILL & Ref,* North Merrick Public Library, North Merrick NY. 516-378-7474
Galarza, Monse, *Asst Librn,* Inter-American University of Puerto Rico, Ponce Regional College Library, Ponce PR. 809-843-3480
Galaway, William, *Ad,* Arlington Heights Memorial Library, Arlington Heights IL. 312-392-0100
Galbally, Marjory L, *Ref,* Grossmont College, Lewis F Smith Learning Resource Center Library, El Cajon CA. 714-465-1700, Ext 333, 334
Galban, Victoria S, *Asst Curator,* Metropolitan Museum of Art (Robert Lehman Collection Library), New York NY. 212-879-5500, Ext 656
Galbavy, Jan, *Syst Coord,* Metropolitan Cooperative Library System, Pasadena CA. 213-577-4081
Galbraith, Constance, *Librn,* Carnegie Library of Pittsburgh (West End), Pittsburgh PA. 412-622-3100
Galbraith, Gloria, *Librn,* Trustees of the California State University & Colleges, Chancellor's Office Library, Long Beach CA. 213-590-5758
Galbraith, Jeanne, *Circ,* State University of New York (Health Sciences Center Library), East Setauket NY. 516-246-2512
Galbraith, Les R, *Dir,* Christian Theological Seminary Library, Indianapolis IN. 317-924-1331, Ext 33
Galbraith, Lois Anne, *Bibliog Instr,* Laredo Junior College, Harold R Yeary Library, Laredo TX. 512-724-7544, 722-0521
Galbraith, Lois Anne, *Bibliog Instr,* Laredo State University, Harold R Yeary Library, Laredo TX. 512-722-8001, Ext 42
Galbraith, Marc, *Ref & Doc,* Kansas State Library, Topeka KS. 913-296-3296
Galda, Maria, *Librn,* Mine Safety Appliances Co, MSA Research Division Library, Evans City PA. 412-538-3510, Ext 116
Gale, Florence, *Ch,* Baldwin Public Library, Birmingham MI. 313-647-1700
Gale, Frederick C, *Director of Archives,* Nevada State County Municipal Archives Reference Library, Carson City NV. 702-885-5210
Gale, Helen W, *Asst Dir & Ch,* Saint Charles Public Library District, Saint Charles IL. 312-584-0076
Gale, Janis, *Asst Dir for Exten Servs,* Laramie County Library System, Cheyenne WY. 307-634-3561
Gale, Linda, *Librn,* Emhart Corporation, Hartford Div Library, Windsor CT. 203-688-8551, Ext 329
Gale, Margaret J, *Librn,* British Information Services Library, New York NY. 212-752-8400
Gale, Robert, *Cat,* Newark Public Library, Newark OH. 345-1750 & 345-8972
Gale, Sarah, *Acq,* Indiana State University, Cunningham Memorial Library, Terre Haute IN. 812-232-6311, Ext 2451
Galejs, John E, *Asst Dir, Resources,* Iowa State University Library, Ames IA. 515-294-1442
Galey, Mary, *Librn,* Public Library of Steubenville & Jefferson County (Mingo Junction Branch), Mingo Junction OH. 614-535-1377
Galgan, Mary N, *Tech Serv,* Rockefeller University Library, New York NY. 212-360-1000
Galgoci, Jane, *Dir,* Cliffside Park Free Public Library, Cliffside Park NJ. 201-945-2867
Galiani, Benjamin, *Librn,* Frequency Electronics, Inc Library, New Hyde Park NY. 516-328-0100
Galibois, Paul, *Dir,* Yellowhead Regional Library, Spruce Grove AB. 403-962-2003
Gall, Nancy, *Cat,* Oshkosh Public Library, Oshkosh WI. 414-424-0473
Gall, Nancy, *Tech Serv,* Portage County District Library, Hiram OH. 216-569-7666
Gallaghen, Hieda, *Tech Serv & Doc,* Santa Cruz Public Library, Santa Cruz CA. 408-429-3533
Gallagher, Ada, *Librn,* Shabbona Public Library, Shabbona IL. 815-824-2466
Gallagher, Barbara, *Head Libr Servs,* American Chemical Society Library, Washington DC. 202-872-4600
Gallagher, Connell, *Archivist,* University of Vermont & State Agricultural College, Bailey-Howe Memorial Library, Burlington VT. 802-656-2020
Gallagher, D Nora, *Dir,* Adelphi University Library, Garden City NY. 516-294-8700

Gallagher, Dennis J, *Asst Prof,* Villanova University, Graduate Dept of Library Science, PA. 215-527-2100, Ext 354, 355

Gallagher, Edith, *Per & ILL,* North Kansas City Public Library, North Kansas City MO. 816-221-3360

Gallagher, Eileen, *Asst Librn & Bibliog Instr,* Felician College Library, Chicago IL. 312-539-2328

Gallagher, Helen, *Applied Sci,* Austin Public Library, Austin TX. 512-472-5433

Gallagher, Iris, *Librn,* Paulding County Carnegie Public Library, Paulding OH. 419-399-2032

Gallagher, Jane, *Acq,* University of South Carolina at Aiken, Gregg-Graniteville Library, Aiken SC. 803-648-6851, Ext 165

Gallagher, Joan L, *In Charge,* American Cyanamid Co, Chemical Research Division Library, Bound Brook NJ. 201-356-2000

Gallagher, Joan M, *Per,* Lock Haven State College, George B Stevenson Library, Lock Haven PA. 717-893-2309

Gallagher, June, *Librn,* Washington Township Free Public Library, Long Valley NJ. 201-876-3596

Gallagher, Kathy, *Acq,* Washington University Libraries (School of Medicine Library), Saint Louis MO. 314-454-3711

Gallagher, Lynn, *ILL & Ref,* Thomas Nelson Community College Library, Hampton VA. 804-825-2868, 825-2876

Gallagher, Marian, *Prof,* University of Washington, School of Librarianship, WA. 206-543-1794

Gallagher, Marian G, *Librn,* University of Washington Libraries (Law Library), Seattle WA. 206-543-4089

Gallagher, Martha, *Librn,* Brown County Library (Southwest), Green Bay WI. 414-497-3447

Gallagher, Olive P, *Admin Asst,* Carnegie Library of Pittsburgh, Pittsburgh PA. 412-622-3100

Gallagher, Paul, *Dir,* Johnson State College, John Dewey Library, Johnson VT. 802-635-2356, Ext 248

Gallagher, Philip J, *Librn,* Robert Wood Johnson Foundation Library, Princeton NJ. 609-452-8701, Ext 201 & 202

Gallagher, Sandra, *Librn,* Seminole County Public Library System (Casselberry Branch), Casselberry FL. 305-339-4000

Gallagher, Sister Annette, *ILL, Ref & Bibliog Instr,* Marycrest College, Cone Library, Davenport IA. 319-326-9254

Gallagher, Sister Mary, *Bibliog Instr,* College of Our Lady of the Elms Library, Chicopee MA. 413-598-8351, Ext 80

Gallagher, Susan, *Librn,* Canadian National Railways (Photographic Library Public Affairs), Montreal PQ. 514-877-4834

Gallagher, Suzanne, *Actg Librn,* Lyndon State College, Samuel Read Hall Library, Lyndonville VT. 802-626-3555

Gallagher, W T, *Mgr,* International Business Machines Corp (Research Library), San Jose CA. 408-256-2562

Gallant, Geraldine, *Librn,* Presho Public Library, Presho SD. 605-895-2443

Gallas, Martin, *ILL,* Starved Rock Library System, Ottawa IL. 815-434-7537

Gallego, Terry, *Asst Librn,* Trustees of the California State University & Colleges, Chancellor's Office Library, Long Beach CA. 213-590-5758

Gallegos, Margaret, *Tech Serv,* Laramie County Library System, Cheyenne WY. 307-634-3561

Gallenbeck, Elizabeth, *Librn,* Carbon County Public Library (Dixon Station Branch), Dixon Station WY. 307-383-2583

Gallentine, Ann, *Librn,* Clayton City Library, Clayton KS. 913-693-4476

Gallentine, Ruth, *Exten Servs,* Northwest Kansas Library System, Norton KS. 913-877-5148

Galler, Anne M, *Coordr,* Concordia University, Library Studies Program, PQ. 514-482-0320, Ext 324

Gallery, Joan, *Ref,* Inver Hills Community College, Learning Resource Center, Inver Grove Heights MN. 612-455-9621, Ext 58

Gallery, Joan, *Humanities,* Inver Hills Community College, Learning Resource Center, Inver Grove Heights MN. 612-455-9621, Ext 58

Gallicchio, Carol, *Librn, Servs to Phys Handicapped,* Montgomery County Department of Public Libraries, Rockville MD. 301-279-1401

Gallicchio, Virginia, *Supvr,* B F Goodrich Co, Akron Information Center, Akron OH. 216-379-4368

Galligan, Regina, *On-Line Servs,* First Boston Corp Library, New York NY. 212-825-7781

Galligan, Sara, *Ref,* University of Michigan-Dearborn Library, Dearborn MI. 313-593-5400

Gallimore, C R, *Chief Librn,* Veterans Administration, Hospital Library Service, Palo Alto CA. 415-493-5000

Gallimore, Howard, *Supvr,* Baptist Sunday School Board of the Southern Baptist Convention, Dargan-Carver Library, Nashville TN. 615-251-2133

Gallinger, Janice, *Dir & Spec Coll,* Plymouth State College, Herbert H Lamson Library, Plymouth NH. 603-536-1550, Ext 257

Gallinger, Susan, *Ad,* Nicholson Memorial Library, Garland TX. 214-494-7187

Gallis, Caroline C, *Dir,* Warminster Township Free Library, Warminster PA. 215-672-4362

Gallivan, B A, *Librn,* University of Toronto Libraries (Faculty of Pharmacy), Toronto ON. 416-978-2872

Gallmeyer, Ann E, *Dir,* Adams Library, Chelmsford MA. 617-256-5521

Gallo, Bela, *Librn,* Stanford University Libraries (J Hugh Jackson Business), Stanford CA. 415-497-2161

Gallo, Jeanne, *Ref,* Highland Park Public Library, Highland Park NJ. 201-572-2750

Gallo, Nancy V, *Dir,* Free Public Library of the Borough of Fort Lee, Fort Lee NJ. 201-461-8020

Gallo, Phyllis, *Dir,* Way Public Library, Perrysburg OH. 419-874-3135

Gallo, Jr, Raymond, *Librn,* State Library of Ohio (Northwest Bookmobile Center), Bowling Green OH. 419-352-9131

Galloway, Barbara, *Reader Serv,* Miami Dade Community College (Niles Trammel Learning Resources), Miami FL. 305-596-1293

Galloway, Delfina C, *Chief Librn,* United States Army (Air Defense School Library), Fort Bliss TX. 915-568-5781, 568-5010

Galloway, Elise S, *ILL,* Darlington County Library, Darlington SC. 803-393-5864

Galloway, James, *Ref & On-Line Servs,* Texas Woman's University, Bralley Memorial Library, Denton TX. 817-566-6415

Galloway, Louise, *Media,* University of Louisville Library, Louisville KY. 502-588-6745

Galloway, Lucille, *Dir,* Burlington Public Library, Burlington ON. 416-639-3611

Galloway, Mary Alyce, *Ref,* Mid-America Nazarene College Library, Olathe KS. 913-782-3750, Ext 216

Galloway, R Dean, *Dir,* California State College, Stanislaus Library, Turlock CA. 209-633-2232

Galloway, Randy, *Librn,* General Telephone & Electronics, GTE Sylvania Library, Mountain View CA. 415-966-3082

Galloway, Sarah Beth, *Reader Serv,* Davis County Library, Farmington UT. 801-867-2322

Galloway, Susan, *Ch,* Eastern Shore Regional Library, Salisbury MD. 301-742-1537

Galloway, Vinita, *YA,* Elk City Carnegie Library, Elk City OK. 405-225-0136

Gallowich, Pauline, *Librn,* Gunnison County Library (Crested Butte Branch), Crested Butte CO. 303-349-6535

Gallucci, Robert, *Asst Dir,* Watertown Library Association, Watertown CT. 203-274-6729

Gallucci, Robert R, *Librn,* Prospect Public Library, Prospect CT. 203-758-6625, 758-6626

Gallucci, Ronald, *Asst Librn,* Tulare Public Library, Tulare CA. 209-688-2001

Gallup, Deborah, *Librn,* William H & Lucy F Rand Memorial Library, North Troy VT. 802-988-4752

Gallup, Jr, William, *Bibliog Instr,* Regis College Library, Weston MA. 617-893-1820, Ext 252

Galneder, Mary, *Librn,* University of Wisconsin-Madison (Map & Air Photo Library), Madison WI. 608-262-3521

Galt, Alfreda S, *In Charge,* Lifwynn Foundation Library, Westport CT. 203-227-4139

Galt, Francis E, *In Charge,* Saint Paul Public Library (Hayden Heights), Saint Paul MN. 612-292-6646

Galtere, Mary, *Dir,* Sally Strech Keen Memorial Library, Vincentown NJ. 609-895-3598

Galvin, Elizabeth A, *Librn,* UOP, Inc, Bostrom Division Engineering Library, Milwaukee WI. 414-271-4122

Galvin, Thomas J, *Dean,* University of Pittsburgh, School of Library & Information Science, PA. 412-624-5230

Galvin, Verna, *Librn,* Lime Springs Public Library, Lime Springs IA. 319-566-4419

Galway, Helen, *Librn,* Rideau Lakes Union Library (Delta Branch), Delta ON. 613-359-5315

Galyon, Betty, *Librn,* Washington University Libraries (Biology), Saint Louis MO. 314-889-5405

Gamache, Earleen P, *Dir,* Lincoln Public Library, Appleby Memorial Library, Lincoln RI. 401-724-5470

Gamache, Georges H, *Librn,* College Des Jesuits Bibliotheque, Quebec PQ. 418-681-0107

Gamache, Rose Ann, *Librn,* Environmental Protection Agency, Environmental Research Laboratory Library, Narragansett RI. 401-789-1071, Ext 265

Gamage, Alvin F, *Ref, On-Line Servs & Bibliog Instr,* Skidmore College, Lucy Scribner Library, Saratoga Springs NY. 518-584-5000, Ext 234

Gamaluddin, Ahmad, *Prof,* Clarion State College, School of Library Science, PA. 814-226-2271

Gambee, Bud, *Prof,* University of North Carolina at Chapel Hill, School of Library Science, NC. 919-933-8366

Gambell, Kay, *Circ,* Findlay College, Shafer Library, Findlay OH. 419-422-8313, Ext 327

Gamble, Jeanne, *On-Line Servs & Bibliog Instr,* Urbana College, Swedenborg Memorial Library, Urbana OH. 513-652-1301

Gamble, Lynne, *Acq & Coll Develop,* California Polytechnic State University Library, San Luis Obispo CA. 805-546-2345

Gamble, Marian, *Asst Dir,* Genesee District Library, Flint MI. 313-732-0110

Gamble, Robert, *Archivist,* University of Texas at Arlington Library, Arlington TX. 817-273-3391

Gambrell, Carole, *Ref,* Emma S Clark Memorial Library, Setauket NY. 516-941-4080

Gambrell, Debbie, *Media Processing,* Tri-County Technical College, Learning Resource Center, Pendleton SC. 803-646-3227

Gamelin, Francis C, *Dir,* Higher Education Center of Saint Louis, MO. 314-534-2700

Gamez, Jose, *Media,* McAllen Memorial Library, McAllen TX. 512-682-4531

Gammill, Dora, *Librn,* National Clearinghouse for Alcohol Information Library, Rockville MD. 301-468-2600

Gammon, Donald B, *Area Coordr-Atlantic,* Agriculture Canada, Research Station Library, Fredericton NB. 506-455-9931, Ext 239, 290

Gamson, Arthur L, *Librn,* Gillette Research Institute, Technical Library, Rockville MD. 301-424-2000

Gamson, Ruth, *Librn,* Fall River Herald News Library, Fall River MA. 617-676-8211

Gandron, Marie L, *Dir,* Hudson Falls Free Library, Hudson Falls NY. 518-747-6406

Ganju, Autar K, *Dir,* Simcoe Public Library, Simcoe ON. 519-426-3506

Gann, L H, *Curator Africa Coll,* Hoover Institution on War, Revolution & Peace, Stanford CA. 415-497-2058

Gann, Paul W, *Mgr, Libr Systs,* Monsanto Textiles Company, Technical Library, Pensacola FL. 904-968-8248

Gannaway, Paula, *Ref,* Lubbock Christian College, Moody Library, Lubbock TX. 806-792-3221, Ext, 241, 242

Gannon, Barbara, *Ref,* Saint Anselm's College, Geisel Library, Manchester NH. 603-669-1030, Ext 240, 249

Gannon, Catherine, *Ad, Acq & Commun Servs,* Jones Library, Inc, Amherst MA. 413-256-0246

Gannon, Eleanor, *Cat,* Newburyport Public Library, Newburyport MA. 617-462-4031

Gannon, Elsa, *Cat,* Prince George's County Memorial Library System, Hyattsville MD. 301-699-3500

Gannon, Marian, *Librn,* Clarion Public Library, Clarion IA. 515-532-3673

Ganser, Mrs Muriel K, *Actg Librn,* Christ Church Cathedral, Margaret Ridgely Memorial Library, Indianapolis IN. 317-636-4577

Gant, Annette, *Librn,* Palm Beach County Public Library System (Palm Beach Gardens), Palm Beach Gardens FL. 305-626-6133

Gantt, John G, *Photoduplication Servs,* University of Michigan Libraries (University Library), Ann Arbor MI. 313-764-9356

Gantt, Mary Jane, *Info Scientist,* American Type Culture Collection Library, Rockville MD. 301-881-2600

Gantz, Ethel, *Tech Serv & Cat,* Lansing Public Library, Lansing MI. 517-374-4600

Gantz, Joan, *Librn,* Carnegie Institution of Washington, Hale Observatories Library, Pasadena CA. 213-577-1122

Ganus, Norma, *Acq,* McMurry College, Jay-Rollins Library, Abilene TX. 915-692-4130, Ext 291

Ganz, Stacia, *Desk Supvr,* Evergreen Park Public Library, Evergreen Park IL. 312-422-8522

Gapen, D Kaye, *Asst Dir, Tech Serv,* Iowa State University Library, Ames IA. 515-294-1442

Gapsewicz, Linda, *Dir,* Sauk Village Public Library District, Sauk Village IL. 312-757-4771

Gara, Otto G, *Dir,* Maricopa County Law Library, Phoenix AZ. 602-262-3461

Garabrant, Judith, *Ref,* Peterborough Town Library, Peterborough NH. 603-924-6401

Garbe, Kathryn, *Librn,* Roosevelt County Library (Culbertson Public), Culbertson MT. 406-653-2411

Garbee, Julie, *ILL,* Northeastern Ohio Universities College of Medicine, Basic Medical Sciences Library, Rootstown OH. 216-325-2511

Garber, Jack, *Asst Prof,* University of Wisconsin-Eau Claire, Dept of Library Science & Media Education, WI. 715-836-2635

Garber, Nora, *Librn,* Tuscarawas County Public Library (Emma Huber Memorial), Strasburg OH. 216-878-5711

Garbon, Nancy J, *Librn,* Ontario Ministry of the Attorney General Library, Toronto ON. 416-965-2831

Garbor, Marion H, *In Charge & On-Line Servs,* Oak Ridge Associated Universities (Medical Library), Oak Ridge TN. 615-576-3070

Garcia, Ann, *Dir,* Keeseville Free Library, Keeseville NY. 518-834-9054

Garcia, Brenda, *Tech Serv,* Saint Edward's University Library, Austin TX. 512-444-2621

Garcia, Ceil, *Technical Indexer,* GAF Corp, Technical Information Services Library, Wayne NJ. 201-628-3320

Garcia, Della, *Dir,* Costilla County Library, San Luis CO. 303-672-3309

Garcia, Donna M, *Adminr,* Hawaii State Library System (Kauai Library District), Lihue HI. 808-245-3617

Garcia, June, *Librn,* Phoenix Public Library (Cholla), Phoenix AZ. 602-262-4776

Garcia, Margaret, *Librn,* Tulare County Library System (Goshen Branch), Goshen CA. 209-733-8440

Garcia, Nora, *Dir,* Catholic University of Puerto Rico, Arecibo Branch Library, Arecibo PR. 809-878-4060

Garcia-Ginn, Gladys, *Librn,* Austin Public Library (Govalle), Austin TX. 512-472-5433

Gard, Betty, *ILL & Ref,* University of North Dakota, Chester Fritz Library, Grand Forks ND. 701-777-2617

Gard, Delpha G, *Asst Dir,* West Texas State University, Cornette Library, Canyon TX. 806-656-2761

Gard, Virginia, *Ch,* Marion Public Library, Marion IN. 317-664-7363

Garden, Joan, *Tech Serv & Cat,* Boynton Beach City Library, Boynton Beach FL. 732-2624 or 732-8111, Ext 223, 224 & 225

Gardener, Margaret, *Ref,* Blauvelt Free Library, Blauvelt NY. 914-359-2811

Gardener, R L, *In Charge,* Wascana Institute of Applied Arts & Sciences Library, Moose Jaw SK. 306-692-6491

Gardimer, Catherine, *Librn,* Worcester Public Library (Main South), Worcester MA. 617-755-5398

Gardine, Peter C, *Acq,* Plymouth State College, Herbert H Lamson Library, Plymouth NH. 603-536-1550, Ext 257

Gardiner, Allen, *Fed Programs,* Kansas State Library, Topeka KS. 913-296-3296

Gardiner, George L, *Dean,* Oakland University, Kresge Library, Rochester MI. 313-377-2486, 377-2474

Gardiner, L, *Librn,* Okanagan Regional Library District (Kaleden Branch), Kaleden BC. 604-497-5453

Gardiner, Marilyn, *Ch & YA,* North Bend Public Library, North Bend OR. 503-756-6712

Gardiner, Marion, *Ad,* Borough of Etobicoke Public Library, Weston ON. 416-248-5681

Gardiner, Maxine, *Librn,* Kent County Municipal Public Library (Tilbury Public), Tilbury ON. 519-682-0100

Gardiner, Peggy, *Librn,* Manitoba Hydro Library, Winnipeg MB. 204-474-1471

Gardiner, Ruth, *Librn,* American Indian Bible Institute, Dorothy L Cummings Memorial Library, Phoenix AZ. 602-944-3335

Gardner, Bryan, *Librn,* Utah Technical College at Salt Lake (Downtown Campus), Salt Lake City UT. 801-328-8521

Gardner, C Hugh, *Assoc Prof,* University of Georgia, Dept of Educational Media & Librarianship, GA. 404-542-3810

Gardner, Carol McDonald, *Art,* Saint Louis Public Library, Saint Louis MO. 314-241-2288

Gardner, Carolyn, *Dir,* Craig Public Library, Craig AK. 907-826-3281

Gardner, Carroll S, *Dir,* Boulder City Library, Boulder City NV. 702-293-1281

Gardner, Charles A, *Dir,* Hastings College, Perkins Library, Hastings NE. 402-463-2402, Ext 230

Gardner, Donna, *Librn,* Wheatland Regional Library, Saskatoon SK. 306-652-5077

Gardner, Dorothy, *Librn,* Preble County District Library (West Alexandria), Eaton OH. 513-839-4915

Gardner, E Helen, *Librn,* First Church in Albany (Reformed) Library, Albany NY. 518-463-4449

Gardner, Ellen S, *Dir,* Elroy Public Library, Elroy WI. 608-462-5191

Gardner, Essie, *Librn,* Northeast Missouri Library Service (Knox County), Edina MO. 816-397-2460

Gardner, Frances, *Librn,* Mid-Mississippi Regional Library System (Winona-Montgomery County), Winona MS. 601-283-3443

Gardner, Francis, *Librn,* Barry-Lawrence Regional Library (Miller Branch), Miller MO. 417-452-3466

Gardner, Gladys, *Librn,* Chesley Memorial Library, Northwood NH. 603-942-5472

Gardner, Helen M, *Librn,* Muhlenberg County Libraries (Harbin Memorial), Greenville KY. 502-338-4760

Gardner, Jack, *Librn,* Clark County Library District (Las Vegas), Las Vegas NV. 702-382-3493

Gardner, Jacqueline, *Dir,* Centralia Public Library, Centralia IL. 618-532-5222

Gardner, Jane, *Ch,* South Carolina State Library, Columbia SC. 803-758-3181

Gardner, Joan, *Librn,* Los Angeles Public Library System (Mar Vista), Los Angeles CA. 213-390-3454

Gardner, John R, *Dir,* Morley Library, Painesville OH. 216-352-3383

Gardner, Juanita, *Librn,* Terra Alta Public Library, Terra Alta WV. 304-789-2724

Gardner, Martha, *Ch,* Washington Carnegie Library, Washington Court House OH. 614-335-2540

Gardner, Mrs John C, *Librn,* First Presbyterian Church Library, Colorado Springs CO. 303-471-3763

Gardner, Pamela Ann, *Librn,* Sun Life Assurance Co of Canada, Reference Library, Wellesley Hills MA. 617-237-6030, Ext 2298

Gardner, Ronald, *Circuit Librn,* Robert Packer Hospital Library, Sayre PA. 717-888-6666, Ext 220

Gardner, Ruth, *Librn,* San Diego Public Library (San Carlos), San Diego CA. 415-461-4480

Gardner, Shelley, *Ch,* Cecil County Public Library, Elkton MD. 301-398-0914

Gardner, Stan, *Librn Blind,* Kansas City Kansas Public Library, Kansas City KS. 913-621-3073

Gardner, Telza, *Librn,* New York Public Library (George Bruce Branch), New York NY. 212-662-9727

Gardner, Trudy, *Instr,* University of Missouri-Columbia, School of Library & Informational Science, MO. 314-882-4546

Gardner, Valerie, *In Charge,* Charles H Taylor Memorial Library (Pine Chapel Library Station), Hampton VA. 804-838-2311

Gardner, William M, *Dir,* Marquette University Memorial Library, Milwaukee WI. 414-224-7214

Gardon, Shirley, *Librn,* Financial World Library, New York NY. 212-826-4360

Gardos, Susan Jo, *Librn,* Harvard University Library (Russian Research Center Library), Cambridge MA. 617-495-4030

Gardy, Barbara, *Asst Dir,* Wicksteed Public Library, Hornepayne ON. 807-868-2332

Garelick, Alexander, *Libr Serv Coordr & Cat,* Ocean County College, Learning Resources Center, Toms River NJ. 201-255-4298

Garen, Robert, *Film Dept,* Detroit Public Library, Detroit Associated Libraries, Detroit MI. 313-833-1000

Gares, Pamela, *Ch,* Edison Free Public Library, Edison NJ. 201-287-2298

Garey, Carol, *Music,* Grand Valley State Colleges, Zumberge Library, Allendale MI. 313-895-6611, Ext 252

Garfoot, Rosemary, *Dir,* Cross Plains Public Library, Cross Plains WI. 608-798-3881

Garganta, Narciso M, *Dir,* Burbank Community Hospital, Medical Library, Burbank CA. 213-846-3135, Ext 318

Garland, Barbara, *Ref,* Mott Community College, C S Mott Library, Flint MI. 313-762-0400

Garland, C, *Ad,* Lisle Library District, Lisle IL. 312-971-1675

Garland, Colleen, *Librn,* Burnside Library, Burnside KY. 606-561-5287

Garland, Jean, *Librn,* Bartlett Public Library, Bartlett NH. 603-374-2755

Garland, Judith S, *Librn,* Memorial Hospital of Martinsville & Henry County, Medical Library, Martinsville VA. 703-632-2911, Ext 137

Garland, Mrs M, *Librn,* Canadian Department of Communications, Communications Research Centre Library, Ottawa ON. 613-995-8883

Garland, Peter J, *Cat,* Vanderbilt University School of Law Library, Nashville TN. 615-322-2568

Garland, Robert, *Ref,* University of Detroit Library, Detroit MI. 313-927-1090

Garland, Valerie, *Librn,* Whitby Public Library (Brooklin Branch), Brooklin ON. 416-655-3191

Garlock, Gayle, *Tech Serv,* Dalhousie University, Izaak Walton Killam Memorial Library (Humanities & Social Sciences), Macdonald Memorial Library (Science), Halifax NS. 902-424-3601

Garman, Mrs Bonner, *Librn,* First National Bank of Fort Worth Library, Fort Worth TX. 817-390-6161

Garn, Nancy W, *Dir,* University of Health Sciences-Chicago Medical School Library, Chicago IL. 312-942-2859

Garnaas, Helen, *Govt Doc,* Minneapolis Public Library & Information Center, Minneapolis MN. 612-372-6500

Garnar, William H, *Asst Dir,* Louisville Free Public Library, Louisville KY. 502-584-4154

Garneau, Francine, *Chief Librn,* Centre Hospitalier Regional De Lanaudiere Pavillon Saint Charles Bibliotheque, Medical Library, Joliette PQ. 514-756-1681, Ext 404

Garneau, Pat, *Librn,* Edmonton Journal Library, Edmonton AB. 403-420-1919

Garneau, Patricia, *Asst Librn,* Immaculate Conception Monastery, Passionist Monastic Seminary Library, Jamaica NY. 212-739-6502

Garner, Carolyn, *Govt Doc,* Arcadia Public Library, Arcadia CA. 213-446-7111

Garner, D, *Librn,* Okanagan Regional Library District (Enderby Branch), Enderby BC. 604-838-6488

Garner, David L, *Admin Off,* Ventura County Library Services Agency, Ventura County Library, Ventura CA. 805-654-2627

Garner, E, *Librn,* Simcoe County Law Association, Law Library, Barrie ON. 705-728-1221, Ext 54

Garner, Frank, *Educ & Training Aids Consult,* Oklahoma Department of Human Services, Employees Library, Oklahoma City OK. 405-521-3518

Garner, Hazel, *Librn,* North Arkansas Regional Library (Boone County), Harrison AR. 501-741-3665

Garner, Holly W, *Librn,* William M Mercer Inc, Library-Information Center, Boston MA. 617-421-0340

Garner, Jo, *Librn,* Kern County Library (Arvin Branch), Arvin CA. 805-861-2130

Garner, Kathleen, *Cat & Tech Serv,* Southeast Kansas Library System, Iola KS. 316-365-3833

Garner, Nancy, *Ch,* Parkland Community Library, Guthsville PA. 215-398-1361
Garner, Nancy, *Dir,* Whitehall Township Public Library, Whitehall PA. 215-432-4339
Garner, Paula, *Dir,* North Manchester Public Library, North Manchester IN. 219-982-4773
Garner, Sharon K, *Cat,* Huntingdon County Library, Huntingdon PA. 814-643-0200
Garner, Warren K, *Dir,* Manchester College, Educational Media Specialist Program, IN. 219-982-2141, Ext 231
Garnes, Carolyn, *Librn,* Atlanta Public Library (Georgia Hill), Atlanta GA. 404-658-6738
Garnes, Glennis S, *ILL,* Conococheague District Library System, Chambersburg PA. 717-263-1054
Garnett, C R, *Librn,* Canadian Department of Fisheries & Oceans, Biological Station Library, Saint Andrews NB. 506-529-8854
Garnett, Elyda, *Local Hist Project Dir,* Madison County-Canton Public Library, Canton MS. 601-859-3202
Garnjost, Phoebe, *Ch,* Holliston Public Library, Holliston MA. 617-429-6070
Garnsey, Alice M, *Librn,* Mayville District Public Library, Mayville MI. 517-843-6522
Garoian, Catherine, *Ad,* Newton Free Library, Newton MA. 617-527-7700, Ext 24
Garon, Agathe, *ILL,* Universite Laval Bibliotheque, Quebec PQ. 418-656-3344
Garralda, John, *Dir & Acq,* Western State College of Colorado, Leslie J Savage Library, Gunnison CO. 303-943-2053
Garrell, Lillian B, *Dir,* United States District Court Library, Eastern District of New York, Brooklyn NY. 212-330-7483
Garren, Alice K, *Librn,* Gracewood State School & Hospital, Hospital Library, Gracewood GA. 404-790-2183
Garretson, George, *Dir,* Roanoke County Public Library, Roanoke VA. 703-774-1681
Garretson, Juanita, *Actg Dir Libr & Archives,* American Psychiatric Association Library, Washington DC. 202-797-4955
Garrett, Betty E, *Dir,* Chetopa City Library, Chetopa KS. 316-236-7194
Garrett, Beverly, *ILL,* Willard Library, Battle Creek MI. 616-968-8166
Garrett, Dianne, *Librn,* Owensville Public Library, Owensville IN. 812-724-3335
Garrett, Jann, *Librn,* Saint Louis County Library (Bridgeton Trails), Bridgeton MO. 314-291-7570
Garrett, Laura, *Librn,* State Farm Insurance Co Library, Bloomington IL. 309-662-6025
Garrett, Lynda, *Librn,* United States Fish & Wildlife Service, Patuxent Wildlife Research Center Library, Laurel MD. 301-776-4880, Ext 235
Garrett, Mary Leone, *Librn,* Roane County Public Library, Spencer WV. 304-927-1130
Garrett, Melinda, *Commun Relations,* Mansfield-Richland County Public Library, Mansfield OH. 419-524-1041
Garrett, Nadene G, *Chief Librn,* Royal Canadian Mounted Police Library, Ottawa ON. 613-993-3225
Garrett, Pat, *Ref, On-Line Servs & Bibliog Instr,* University of Houston (Clear Lake City), Houston TX. 713-488-9280
Garrett, Paul D, *Librn,* Saint Vladimir's Orthodox Theological Seminary Library, Father Georges Florovsky Library, Yonkers NY. 914-961-8313, Ext 10
Garrett, Roberta S, *Librn,* Ohio State University Libraries (Veterinary Medicine Library), Columbus OH. 614-422-6107
Garrett, Stuart, *Cat,* University of Tennessee, Knoxville, James D Hoskins Library, Knoxville TN. 615-974-0111
Garrett, Susanne, *Spec Coll,* Sarah Lawrence College, Esther Raushenbush Library, Bronxville NY. 914-337-0700, Ext 479
Garrey, Mary Ellen, *Circ,* Lewis University Library, Romeoville IL. 815-838-0500, Ext 302
Garrison, Barbara, *Ref,* Public Library of Johnston County & Smithfield, Smithfield NC. 919-934-8146
Garrison, Guy, *Dean,* Drexel University, School of Library & Information Science, PA. 215-895-2474
Garrison, Jacqueline A, *Librn,* Eastern Arizona College, Learning Resources Center, Thatcher AZ. 602-428-1133, Ext 305, 306, 307

Garrison, Joan, *Ad & Ref,* Caldwell Public Library, Caldwell NJ. 201-226-2837
Garrison, Margaret, *Ser,* Letourneau College, Margaret Estes Library, Longview TX. 214-753-0231, Ext 230
Garrison, Marilee, *On-Line Servs & Bibliog Instr,* Evansville Public Library & Vanderburgh County Public Library, Evansville IN. 812-425-2621
Garrison, Michael G, *Dir,* Quincy Public Library, Quincy IL. 217-223-1309
Garrity, Frances, *ILL,* Orange County Public Library, Orange CA. 714-634-7841
Garrolds, John, *On-Line Servs,* Western State College of Colorado, Leslie J Savage Library, Gunnison CO. 303-943-2053
Garrot, Leslie, *Tech Serv,* Wauwatosa Public Library, Wauwatosa WI. 414-258-5700
Garry, Loraine Spencer, *Librn,* Registered Nurses Association of Ontario Library, Toronto ON. 416-923-3523, Ext 49
Garstka, Katharine, *Assoc Librn,* Massachusetts General Hospital (Palmer Davis Library), Boston MA. 617-726-3175
Garten, Edward D, *Dir,* Northern State College, Library Science Program, SD. 605-622-2645
Garten, Edward D, *Dir,* Northern State College, Williams Library & Learning Resource Center, Aberdeen SD. 605-622-2645
Gartenfeld, Ellen, *Coordr,* Community Health Information Network, MA. 617-492-3500, Ext 1772, 1788
Garthwait, Carolyn, *On-Line Servs,* Housatonic Community College, Library Learning Resource Center, Bridgeport CT. 203-579-6465
Gartland, Joan W, *Librn,* Edison Institute (Greenfield Village & Henry Ford Museum), Robert Hudson Tannahill Research Library, Dearborn MI. 313-271-1620
Gartner, Eva, *Librn,* Randolph Public Library, Randolph NE. 402-625-3561
Gartner, Janet, *Librn,* Sausalito Public Library, Sausalito CA. 415-332-2325
Gartner, Karen, *Ad & Acq,* Easton Area Public Library, Easton PA. 215-258-2917
Gartner, Martha, *YA,* Edison Free Public Library, Edison NJ. 201-287-2298
Garton, William W, *Dir,* Slippery Rock State College Library, Slippery Rock PA. 412-794-2510
Garver, Elizabeth, *Ch & YA,* Kent County Library System, Grand Rapids MI. 616-774-3250
Garver, Martha S, *Ad & Circ,* Quincy Public Library, Quincy IL. 217-223-1309
Garver, Naomi, *Rd Adv,* Reuben McMillan Free Library Free Library Association, Public Library of Youngstown & Mahoning County, Youngstown OH. 216-744-8636
Garverick, Eunice B, *Asst Chief Libr,* United States Air Force (Strughold Aeromedical Library), Brooks AFB TX. 512-536-3321
Garvey, Eleanor M, *Curator of Printing & Graphic Arts,* Harvard University Library (Houghton Library-Rare Books & Manuscripts), Cambridge MA. 617-495-2441
Garvey, Gerald T, *Chief, Bldgs Mgt Div,* Library of Congress, Washington DC. 202-287-5000
Garvey, Helen, *Librn,* Cresap, McCormick & Paget Library, New York NY. 212-953-7000
Garvey, J, *Librn,* Syncrude Canada Ltd (Technical Information Service), Edmonton AB. 403-429-9110
Garvey, Jeffrey M, *Librn,* Mercy Hospital Library, Watertown NY. 315-785-2152
Garvey, Nancy G, *Librn,* Automatic Switch Co, ASCO Library, Florham Park NJ. 201-966-2479
Garvin, Gordon, *Bkmobile Coordr,* Cherokee Regional Library, LaFayette-Walker County Library, LaFayette GA. 404-638-2992
Garvin, Lavonia S, *Asst Librn,* University of South Carolina, Salkehatchie Campus Library, Allendale SC. 803-584-3446
Garvin, Virginia, *ILL,* Case Western Reserve University & Cleveland Medical Library Association, Cleveland Health Sciences Library, Cleveland OH. 216-368-3426
Garwig, Paul L, *Tech Info Mgr,* FMC Corp, Chemical Research & Development Center, Technical Information Services Library, Princeton NJ. 609-452-2300, Ext 229
Garwood, Alfred N, *Dir,* Tenafly Public Library, Tenafly NJ. 201-568-8680

Garwood, Rosemary, *Ch,* Pequannock Township Public Library, Pompton Plains NJ. 201-835-7460
Gary, Carlotta, *Spec Coll,* New York Public Library (Dance & Drama), New York NY. 212-790-6262
Gary, E, *Ref,* Richard J Daley College, Learning Resource Center, Chicago IL. 312-735-3000, Ext 224, 226, 227
Gary, Frankie, *Librn,* Chattahoochee Valley Regional Library (Twelfth Street), Columbus GA. 404-322-7277
Gary, Joe, *AV,* Lake Land College, Virgil H Judge Learning Resource Center, Mattoon IL. 217-235-3131, Ext 267
Garypie, Renwick, *Dir,* Oxford Public Library, Oxford MI. 313-628-3034
Garza, Antoinette, *Ref & Main Libr Dir,* Our Lady of the Lake University Libraries, San Antonio TX. 512-434-6711, Ext 272
Garza, Gregoria, *Tech Serv,* Weslaco Public Library, Porter Doss Memorial Library, Weslaco TX. 512-968-4533
Garza, Meliss, *Cat & Ref,* Santa Barbara City College Library, Santa Barbara CA. 805-965-0581, Ext 242
Garza, Raul R, *Libr Tech In-Charge,* United States Navy (Naval Air Station Library), Beeville TX. 512-354-2706
Garza, Teri, *Chief Librn,* Orange County Public Library (Mission Viejo Branch), Mission Viejo CA. 714-830-7100
Gasaway, Laura Nell, *Dir,* University of Oklahoma (Law Library), Norman OK. 405-325-4311
Gasche, Francita, *Dir,* Wauseon Exempted School District Library, Wauseon Public Library, Wauseon OH. 419-335-6626
Gaschler, Lois A, *Librn,* Ellis Public Library, Ellis KS. 913-726-3464
Gash, Anne Gail, *Librn,* Queens County Supreme Court Library, Jamaica NY. 212-520-3140
Gaskell, Carolyn, *Circ,* Walla Walla College, Peterson Memorial Library, College Place WA. 509-527-2133
Gaskill, Lula Mae, *Dir,* Allerton Public Library, Monticello IL. 217-762-4676
Gaskin, Ann, *Ch,* Shaker Heights Public Library, Shaker Heights OH. 216-991-2030
Gaspar, N J, *Chief Librn,* Imperial Oil Limited, Research Dept Library, Sarnia ON. 519-339-2471
Gasper, Linda, *Ch & YA,* Pearl River County Library System, Margaret Reed Crosby Memorial Library, Picayune MS. 601-798-5081
Gasperini, Bonnie A, *Librn,* Ypsilanti Regional Psychiatric Hospital (Medical Library), Ypsilanti MI. 313-434-3400, Ext 226
Gasque, Marge, *Librn,* Marion County Library (Mullin Branch), Mullins SC. 803-464-9621
Gass, A Beverley, *ILL, Ref & Bibliog Instr,* Guilford Technical Institute, Learning Resource Center, Jamestown NC. 919-292-1101, 454-1126
Gass, Fern L, *Librn,* Westinghouse Electric Corp, East Pittsburgh Division Library, East Pittsburgh PA. 412-256-2414
Gassett, Inez, *Chief Librn,* Holmes Public Library, Halifax MA. 617-293-2271
Gassiott, Nancy Diane, *Librn,* Silsbee Public Library, Silsbee TX. 713-385-4831
Gasson, Grace, *Dir & Acq,* Sweetwater County Library, Green River WY. 307-875-3615
Gast, Marie, *Maps, Microtexts & Newsp,* Cornell University Libraries (University Libraries), Ithaca NY. 607-256-4144
Gastaldy, Suzanne, *Asst Prof,* University of Montreal, Ecole de Bibliteconomie, PQ. 514-343-6044
Gastl, LeRoy F, *Ref,* Chadron State College Library, Chadron NE. 308-432-4451, Ext 271
Gaston, Mable, *Ref,* Mississippi College, Leland Speed Library, Clinton MS. 601-924-5131, Ext 232, 307
Gaston, Michael K, *Librn,* Florence Public Library, Florence OR. 503-997-3132
Gately, Charles F, *Librn,* United States Department of Health & Human Services, Departmental Library, Washington DC. 202-245-6339
Gately, Frank, *Chief Librn,* Veterans Administration, Main Library (142D), Bath NY. 607-776-2111, Ext 223

Gater, Helen L, *Assoc Librn,* Arizona State University Library, Tempe AZ. 602-965-3417

Gaterud, Dorothy D, *Dir,* Flemington Free Public Library, Flemington NJ. 201-782-5733

Gates, A D, *Meteorologist, Sci Servs,* Environment Canada, Atmospheric Environment Service, Bedford NS. 902-835-3709

Gates, Barbara A, *Head Cat Librn,* Brown University (University Library), Providence RI. 401-863-2167

Gates, Christine, *Librn,* Siskiyou County Public Library (Happy Camp Branch), Happy Camp CA. 916-493-3964

Gates, Diana, *ILL,* Gallaudet College, Edward Miner Gallaudet Memorial Library, Washington DC. 202-651-5566

Gates, Earl, *Librn,* University of Kansas Libraries (Music), Lawrence KS. 913-864-3496

Gates, Francis, *Librn,* Columbia University (Law Library), New York NY. 212-280-2241

Gates, Harry, *Media,* Southern Oregon State College Library, Ashland OR. 503-482-6445

Gates, Helen, *Dir,* Marcus Public Library, W L Gund Memorial Library, Marcus IA. 712-376-2328

Gates, Jane, *Chief Librn,* Strybing Arboretum Society of Golden Gate Park, Helen Crocker Russell Library of Horticulture, San Francisco CA. 415-661-1316

Gates, Jean, *Assoc Prof,* University of South Florida, Graduate Department of Library, Media & Information Studies, FL. 813-974-2557

Gates, Joseph E, *Tech Serv,* Delaware Technical & Community College, Terry Campus Learning Resources Center, Dover DE. 302-678-5404

Gates, Linda, *Asst Dir,* Mississippi Library Commission, Jackson MS. 601-354-6369

Gates, Lorena, *Circ,* University of Arkansas-Monticello Library, Monticello AR. 501-367-6811, Ext 80

Gates, Lorraine K, *Librn,* Calumet City Public Library, Calumet City IL. 312-862-6220

Gates, Margaret, *Dir,* Manhattan Public Library, Manhattan KS. 913-776-4741

Gates, Margaret, *Dir,* North Central Kansas Libraries System, Manhattan KS. 913-776-4741

Gates , Mary, *Ch,* Deerfield Public Library, Deerfield IL. 312-945-3311

Gates, Mary D, *Dir,* Dwight Foster Public Library, Fort Atkinson WI. 414-563-5124

Gates, Mrs Johnnie, *Tech Serv,* Saint Mary Parish Library, Franklin LA. 318-828-5364

Gates, Rosemary, *YA,* Ocmulgee Regional Library, Eastman GA. 912-374-4711

Gatesman, Julie A, *Dir,* Eccles-Lesher Memorial Library, Rimersburg PA. 814-473-3800

Gatewood, Wynema, *Librn,* Florida School for the Deaf & Blind (Library for the Blind), Saint Augustine FL. 904-824-1654, Ext 419

Gathings, Thresa, *ILL,* Graham Public Library, Graham TX. 817-549-0600

Gathright, Vera P, *Ref,* United Nations Information Center, Washington DC. 202-296-5370

Gatlin, Nancy, *Dir,* Southern College of Optometry, William P MacCracken Jr Memorial Library, Memphis TN. 901-725-0180, Ext 280

Gatner, Elliott, *Eng, Am Lit, Higher Educ,* Long Island University, Brooklyn Center Libraries, Brooklyn NY. 212-834-6060, 834-6064

Gatner, Elliott, *Dir, Spec Coll & Br Coordr,* Long Island University, Brooklyn Center Libraries, Brooklyn NY. 212-834-6060, 834-6064

Gattin, Jr, Leroy M, *Dir,* Saline County Public Library, Benton AR. 501-778-4766

Gattinger, F Eugene, *Librn,* Toronto Board of Education, Education Center Library, Toronto ON. 416-598-4931

Gattis, Betty, *Tech Serv,* Kentucky Department of Library & Archives, Frankfort KY. 502-564-7910

Gatton, Neil, *Films,* Lansing Public Library, Lansing MI. 517-374-4600

Gattone, Dean, *Circ,* University of Maryland at College Park (Undergraduate), College Park MD. 301-454-4743

Gauch, M Lois, *Librn,* Eastman Kodak Co (Business Library), Rochester NY. 716-724-3041

Gauchay, Helen, *Librn,* Clark County District Free Library, Dubois ID. 208-374-5267

Gaucher, Elaine M, *Librn,* United States Navy (Medical Library), Groton CT. 203-449-3629

Gaughan, Florence, *Librn,* Osterhout Free Library (South), Wilkes-Barre PA. 717-823-5544

Gault, Billie M, *Librn,* F M Richards Memorial Library, Brady TX. 915-597-2617

Gault, Constance B, *Librn,* Ashland Public School District Library, Ashland OH. 419-289-8188

Gault, David, *Librn,* San Diego Public Library (East San Diego), San Diego CA. 714-283-3632

Gault, James E, *Media,* University of California, Berkeley (University Library), Berkeley CA. 415-642-3773

Gault, Jean, *Govt Docs,* Humber College, Learning Resource Centre, Rexdale ON. 416-675-3111, Ext 331

Gault, Mary, *Librn,* Harrie P Woodson Memorial Library, Caldwell City Library, Caldwell TX. 713-567-4111

Gault, Robin R, *Circ,* Florida State University (Law Library), Tallahassee FL. 904-644-1004

Gaunce, Patricia, *Librn,* Kansas City Kansas Public Library (Wyandotte Plaza), Kansas City KS. 913-788-5400

Gaunee, Pat, *Spec Coll,* Kansas City Kansas Public Library, Kansas City KS. 913-621-3073

Gauri, Kul, *Tech Serv,* Case Western Reserve University Libraries, Cleveland OH. 216-368-3506

Gause, George, *ILL,* Pan American University, Learning Resource Center, Edinburg TX. 512-381-2751

Gause, Sharon, *Media & Circ,* University of Colorado at Boulder (University Libraries), Boulder CO. 303-492-7511

Gauthier, Anita M, *Dean of Learning Resources,* Southern Vermont College Library, Bennington VT. 802-442-5427

Gauthier, Betty, *Acq,* University of Michigan-Dearborn Library, Dearborn MI. 313-593-5400

Gauthier, Ghislaine, *In Charge,* Bell-Northern Research, Technical Information Center, Verdun PQ. 514-761-5831, Ext 257

Gauthier, Real, *Educ,* Universite Laval Bibliotheque, Quebec PQ. 418-656-3344

Gauvreau, Lorraine, *Ref,* Middle Country Public Library, Centereach NY. 516-585-9393

Gavalis, Amy, *Ch,* Swampscott Public Library, Swampscott MA. 617-593-8380

Gaven, Maureta, *Ch,* Mesquite Public Library, Mesquite TX. 214-285-6369

Gaver, Bruce, *Librn,* United States Air Force (Altus Air Force Base Library), Altus AFB OK. 405-482-8670

Gaver, Eleanore, *Librn,* Gibbes Art Gallery Library, Charleston SC. 803-722-2706

Gavin, Christine B, *Instructional Media Specialist,* Arlington Developmental Center, Staff Library, Arlington TN. 901-867-2921, Ext 380

Gavora, E, *Librn,* Agriculture Canada (Plant Research Library), Ottawa ON. 613-995-9461

Gavrish, Diane Arrato, *Librn,* Derry Public Library, Derry NH. 603-432-3901

Gawienowski, Wanda, *ILL,* Rutgers University, the State University of New Jersey, John Cotton Dana Library, Newark NJ. 201-648-5222

Gawler, Ann C, *Dir,* LaFayette Public Library, LaFayette NY. 315-677-3782

Gawron, Carol, *Bkmobile Coordr,* Miami-Dade Public Library System, Miami FL. 305-579-5001

Gay, Alma, *Librn,* Pittsylvania County Public Library (Gretna), Chatham VA. 804-656-2579

Gay, Ann H, *Librn,* Choctaw County Public Library, James S & Bessie F Dearmon Foundation, Butler AL. 205-459-2542

Gay, Barbara, *Cat,* University of Vermont & State Agricultural College, Bailey-Howe Memorial Library, Burlington VT. 802-656-2020

Gay, Hazel, *Ch,* Franklin Library, Ray Memorial Library, Franklin MA. 617-528-0371

Gay, Kay, *Bkmobile Coordr,* Jackson County Public Library, McKee KY. 606-287-8113

Gay, Mildred S, *Librn,* Oklahoma School for the Deaf Library, Sulphur OK. 405-622-3186

Gaydosh, Mary E, *Librn,* San Luis Obispo County Law Library, San Luis Obispo CA. 805-549-5855

Gaylor, Robert, *Coll Develop & Ref,* Oakland University, Kresge Library, Rochester MI. 313-377-2486, 377-2474

Gaylord, C, *Circ,* Atlantic Christian College, Hackney Library, Wilson NC. 919-237-3161, Ext 330

Gaylord, Mary E, *Asst Dir,* Balsam Lake Public Library, Balsam Lake WI. 715-485-3215

Gayman, Jonnie, *Librn,* Tulsa City-County Library (Sperry Branch), Sperry OK. 918-288-6167

Gaymon, Nicholas E, *Dir,* Florida Agricultural & Mechanical University, Samuel H Coleman Memorial Library, Tallahassee FL. 904-599-3370

Gaynor, David, *Archivist,* Northeast Minnesota Historical Center, Duluth MN. 218-726-8526

Gazess, Paula H, *Ch,* Roosevelt Public Library, Roosevelt NY. 516-378-0222

Gazetteers, Hemenway, *Rare Bks,* Lanpher Memorial Library, Hyde Park VT. 802-888-4628

Gazillo, Mark J, *Librn,* Massachusetts College of Pharmacy-Hampden Campus, Alumni Library, Springfield MA. 413-532-1955, 532-9398, Ext 3

Gbala, Helen, *Cat & On-Line Servs,* College of Saint Catherine, Saint Catherine Library, Saint Paul MN. 612-690-6650

Gear, Elnor, *ILL,* Boulder City Library, Boulder City NV. 702-293-1281

Gearhart, Carol A, *Asst Prof,* Kutztown State College, Dept of Library Science, PA. 215-683-4300, 683-4301

Gearhart, Jane, *Asst Librn,* Arcanum Public Library, Arcanum OH. 513-692-8484

Geary, James, *Archivist,* Kent State University Libraries, Kent OH. 216-672-2962

Geary, Kathleen A, *Dir,* Fletcher Free Library, Burlington VT. 802-863-3403

Gebeau, Jane, *Tech Serv,* Wilbraham Public Library, Wilbraham MA. 413-596-6142

Gebele, Dorothy, *Librn,* Wittenberg University (Music), Springfield OH. 513-327-7038

Geberer, Tobia, *Librn,* Broward County Division of Libraries (Tamarac Branch), Tamarac FL. 305-722-0710

Gebhard, Patricia, *Bibliog Instr,* University of California, Santa Barbara Library, Santa Barbara CA. 805-961-2741

Gebhard, Ruth E, *Librn,* Xerox Corp (Law Library), Rochester NY. 716-423-4064

Gebhardt, Nan, *Asst Librn & Per,* Ringling School of Art Library, Sarasota FL. 813-355-1232

Gebhart, Karen, *Librn,* Saint Mary's Hospital, Health Science Library, Decatur IL. 217-429-2966

Gecas, Judith, *Head Pub Servs,* University of Chicago (Law Library), Chicago IL. 312-753-3425

Geckle, Justine, *Librn,* Richland County Public Library (John Hughes Cooper Branch), Columbia SC. 803-787-3462

Geddes, A Bruce, *Dir,* Lennox & Addington County Public Library, Napanee ON. 613-354-2585

Geddes, Andrew, *Dir,* Nassau Library System, Uniondale NY. 516-292-8920

Geddes, Anne, *YA,* Middle Country Public Library, Centereach NY. 516-585-9393

Geddes, Charles L, *Dir,* American Institute of Islamic Studies Library, Denver CO. 303-936-0108

Geddie, Leonard, *Asst Dir, Proc,* University of Western Ontario, A B Weldon Library, London ON. 519-679-6191

Geddis-Meakin, Catherine, *ILL & Media,* Columbia University (Barnard College), New York NY. 212-280-3846

Gee, Fred, *Librn,* New York Public Library (Jerome Park), New York NY. 212-549-5200

Gee, J, *Librn,* Fluor Ocean Services Library, Houston TX. 713-776-4369

Gee, Mary W, *Librn,* Aiken-Bamberg-Barnwell-Edgefield Regional Library (Denmark Branch), Denmark SC. 803-648-8961

Gee, Sharon, *Librn,* Alberta Research Council Library, Edmonton AB. 403-432-8121

Gee, Virginia, *Librn,* Monroe County Library System (Petersburg Branch), Petersburg MI. 313-279-1025

Geehan, Blanche, *Librn,* Proctor Library, Ascutney VT. 802-674-2863

Geentiens, Mrs Leonard, *Asst Librn,* Catherine Dickson Hofman Library, Blairstown NJ. 201-362-8376

Geer, Eileen T, *Librn,* Belden Library Association, Cromwell CT. 203-635-4433

Geer, Martha, *Librn,* Colquitt-Thomas Regional Library (Boston Carnegie Branch), Boston GA. 912-498-5101

Geering, Margaret B, *Librn,* Monticello Medical Center Library, Longview WA. 206-423-5850

GEERS

Geers, Elmer, *Librn,* Cincinnati Post Library, Cincinnati OH. 513-352-2786

Geery, Barbara S, *Librn,* Burlington Public Library, Burlington KS. 316-364-5333

Geesey, Barry, *Commun Servs,* Kanawha County Public Library, Kanawha County Service Center, Charleston WV. 304-343-4646

Geesey, Mae, *Librn,* Pioneer Public Library, Montpelier OH. 419-737-2833

Geffner, Linda, *Ser,* Saint Joseph College, Pope Pius XII Library, West Hartford CT. 203-232-4571, Ext 208

Gegelys, Mary, *Dir Info Center,* J Walter Thompson Co, Information Center, New York NY. 212-867-1000

Gehler, Ann, *Ad Continuing Educ,* Forsyth County Public Library, Winston-Salem NC. 919-727-2556

Gehman, Carolyn, *Ch,* Wissahickon Valley Public Library, Ambler PA. 215-646-1072

Gehman, Daniel, *Dir,* Montana Institute of the Bible Library, Lewistown MT. 406-538-3452, Ext 60

Gehman, Louise A, *Dir,* Wolfeboro Public Library, Wolfeboro NH. 603-569-2428

Gehres, Eleanor, *In Charge,* Denver Public Library (Western History), Denver CO. 303-573-5152, Ext 271

Gehring, Adrian, *Librn,* Toronto Transit Commission Library, Toronto ON. 416-481-4252, Ext 1231

Gehring, Donna, *Supvr,* University of Notre Dame Library (Mathematics-Computing), Notre Dame IN. 219-283-7278

Gehringer, Michael E, *Research & On-Line Search Coordr,* Supreme Court of the United States Library, Washington DC. 202-252-3177

Gehrman, Gloria, *Dir & Ad,* Moscow-Latah County Library System, Moscow ID. 208-882-3925

Geib, Eileen, *Asst Dir,* Ault Public Library, Ault CO. 303-834-1259

Geiger, Gene, *Asst Univ Librn Circ Serv,* Auburn University, Ralph Brown Draughton Library, Auburn AL. 205-826-4500

Geiger, Rita, *Tech Serv,* Pottsville Free Public Library, Pottsville Library District Center, Pottsville PA. 622-8105; 622-8880

Geiger, Susan, *YA,* Hayward Public Library, Hayward CA. 415-581-2545

Geil, Marian, *Asst Dir & Ref,* Hearst Free Library, Anaconda MT. 406-563-9990

Geiman, Robert, *Dir,* University of Alaska, Fairbanks, Elmer E Rasmuson Library, Fairbanks AK. 907-479-7224

Geiman, Robert H, *Dir,* Ferris State College Library, Big Rapids MI. 616-796-9494, 796-9971, Ext 323

Geisbert, Molly, *Acq,* Montgomery County Department of Public Libraries, Rockville MD. 301-279-1401

Geisel, Ann M, *Dir,* Peterborough Town Library, Peterborough NH. 603-924-6401

Geisel, Etta, *Cat,* Cranford Public Library, Cranford NJ. 201-276-1826

Geiser, Cherie, *Post-harvest Documentation,* Kansas State University, Farrell Library, Manhattan KS. 913-532-6516

Geisheimer, Eleanor, *Acq,* Connecticut College Library, New London CT. 203-442-1630

Gelarden, Diane, *Librn,* National Institute on Drug Abuse, Addiction Research Center Library, Lexington KY. 606-255-6812, Ext 7111

Gelarden, Diane, *On-Line Servs,* Veterans Administration, Medical Center Library, Lexington KY. 606-233-4511, Ext 323

Gelber, Robert, *Asst Librn,* Supreme Court, Appellate Div, First Dept Law Library, New York NY. 212-340-0478

Gelecke, Betty, *Librn,* Hometown Public Library, Jack R Ladwig Memorial Library, Hometown IL. 312-636-0997

Gelfand, Melvyn, *Ser,* Temple University of the Commonwealth System of Higher Education, Samuel Paley Library, Philadelphia PA. 215-787-8231

Gelfius, Larry W, *Dir, Media & Commun Servs,* Homewood Public Library, Homewood IL. 312-798-0121

Gelhausen, Michael J, *Dir,* Duerrwaechter Memorial Library, Germantown WI. 414-251-5730

Gelinas, Jeanne, *Librn,* Hennepin County Library (Golden Valley Branch), Golden Valley MN. 612-545-2761

Gelinas, Michele, *Librn,* Bibliotheque De La Ville De Montreal (Centrale Children), Montreal PQ. 514-872-5923

Gelinas, Patricia, *Acq,* Great Lakes Historical Society, Clarence S Metcalf Research Library, Vermilion OH. 216-967-3467

Gelletly, Alayne, *Doc,* Schoolcraft College, Eric J Bradner Library, Livonia MI. 313-591-6400, Ext 412

Gellman, Sally, *Dir,* Ethelbert B Crawford Memorial Library, Monticello NY. 914-794-4660

Geltz, Elizabeth G, *Librn,* American Institute of Banking, Herbert W Trecartin Finance & Bank Management Library, New York NY. 212-349-8440, Ext 6

Gelven, M Olga, *Cat,* Cardinal Ritter Library, Saint Louis MO. 314-544-0455, Ext 56

Gelzer, Francina, *Librn,* Boston Public Library (Dudley), Roxbury MA. 617-442-6186

Genaway, David C, *Assoc Dir,* Eastern Kentucky University, John Grant Crabbe Library, Richmond KY. 606-622-3606

Genaway, Inez, *Dir,* Council of State Governments, States Information Center, Lexington KY. 606-252-2291, Ext 274

Genco, Carol M E, *Lectr,* University of Michigan, School of Library Science, MI. 313-764-9376

Gendler, Carol, *Librn,* Douglas County Law Library, Omaha NE. 402-444-7174

Gendron, Billie, *ILL,* Graduate Theological Union Library, Berkeley CA. 415-841-9811

Gendron, Danielle, *Ref,* Gouvernement Du Quebec Ministere De L'immigration, Centre de Documentation, Montreal PQ. 514-873-3255

Generao, Clarita M, *Librn,* Management Consulting Library, Lester B Knight & Associates, Inc, Chicago IL. 312-346-2100, Ext 550

Genesen, Judith, *Ref,* Chicago Transit Authority Library, Chicago IL. 312-664-7200, Ext 754

Genest, Sister Marie-Paule, *Librn,* Hospital Saint Francois D'assise, Medico-Administrative Library, Quebec PQ. 418-529-7311, Ext 305

Genetti, Raynna Bowlby, *Librn,* Central Maine Medical Center, Gerrish-True Health Science Library, Lewiston ME. 207-795-2376

Gengler, Rita A, *Tech Serv, On-Line Servs & Bibliog Instr,* Spokane Public Library, Comstock Building Library, Spokane WA. 509-838-3361, Ext 65

Genier, G, *Chief Librn,* Ottawa Board of Education, Library Service Center, Ottawa ON. 613-563-2211

Gennett, Robert G, *Assoc Librn, Rare Bks & Spec Coll,* Lafayette College, David Bishop Skillman Library, Easton PA. 215-253-6281, Ext 289

Genova, Bissy, *Assoc Prof,* Syracuse University, School of Information Studies, NY. 315-423-2911

Gensel, Susan, *Chief Librn,* Cold Spring Harbor Laboratory Library, Cold Spring Harbor NY. 516-692-6660, Ext 750

Gensel, Susan, *Librn,* Performing Arts Foundation, Arts-In-Education Resource Center, Huntington Station NY. 516-549-0050

Gensler, Faith I, *Librn,* G & W Natural Resources, Zerbe Research Library, Bethlehem PA. 215-866-9249

Genson, Thomas, *Asst Dir,* Grand Rapids Public Library, Grand Rapids MI. 616-456-4400

Genson, Thomas, *Dir,* Woodlands Library Cooperative, Albion MI. 517-629-9469, 629-9460

Gentert, Sister Alice Marie, *Circ,* Our Lady of Angels College Library, Aston PA. 215-449-0905, Ext 10

Gentile, Annette, *Br Coordr,* Ashtabula County District Library, Ashtabula OH. 216-997-9341

Gentile, Annette, *Librn,* Ashtabula County District Library (Geneva Public), Geneva OH. 216-466-4521

Gentry, Eleanor, *Librn,* Orlando Public Library (Saint Cloud Branch), Saint Cloud FL. 305-892-3954

Gentry, Eleanore, *Librn,* Orlando Public Library (Kissimmee Branch), Kissimmee FL. 305-847-5829

Gentry, Elna H, *Ch & Media,* Washington County Library, Saint George UT. 801-673-2562

Gentry, Janie, *Acq,* Austin Peay State University, Felix G Woodward Library, Clarksville TN. 615-648-7346

Gentry, Lloyd, *Dir,* Belleville Area College Library, Belleville IL. 618-235-2700, Ext 236

Gentry, Mark, *Ref,* Central Bible College Library, Springfield MO. 417-833-2551, Ext 37

Gentry, Peggy, *ILL,* Glendora Public Library, Glendora CA. 213-963-4168

Genuchi, Kathleen, *Assoc Dir,* Western Texas College, Learning Resource Center, Snyder TX. 915-573-8511, Ext 265

Genus, Arnold, *Cat,* Hostos Community College Library, Bronx NY. 212-960-1093

Genzoli, Marilyn, *In Charge,* Eureka-Humboldt County Library (Ferndale), Ferndale CA. 707-786-9559

Geoffroy, Melba Y, *Librn,* Winchester Community Library, Winchester IN. 317-584-4824

George, Aubrey, *Info Servs,* Corpus Christi Public Libraries, La Retama Public Library, Corpus Christi TX. 512-882-1937

George, Barbara, *Librn,* Richard Sugden Public Library, Spencer MA. 617-885-3336

George, Clara, *ILL & Ref,* Lenoir Community College, Learning Resources Center, Kinston NC. 919-527-6223, Ext 235

George, Doris, *Librn, On-Line Servs & Bibliog Instr,* Falconbridge Nickel Mines Ltd, Metallurgical Laboratories Library, Thornhill ON. 416-889-6221

George, Edna, *Librn,* Western Electric Co, Inc (General Business Library), New York NY. 212-571-4884

George, Edward R, *Chief Librn,* Essex County Public Library, Essex ON. 519-776-5241

George, Emily, *Librn,* Pillsbury Free Library, Warner NH. 603-456-2289

George, Harvey F, *Dir,* Gravure Research Institute Library, Manor Haven NY. 516-883-6670

George, Helen, *Librn,* Anderson County Library (Pendleton Branch), Pendleton SC. 803-646-3923

George, Henrene, *Supvr,* American Baptist Churches in the United States of America (Library & Records Management Center), Valley Forge PA. 215-768-2383

George, Marguerite, *Librn,* Blairsville Public Library, Blairsville PA. 412-459-6077

George, Melvin R, *Univ Librn & Dir of Learning Servs,* Northeastern Illinois University Library, Chicago IL. 312-583-4050, Ext 469, 470, 471, 472

George, Nadine F, *Ref,* Kenyon College, Gordon Keith Chalmers Memorial Library, Gambier OH. 614-427-2244, Ext 2186

George, Nancy, *Librn,* Phillips Petroleum Co (Engineering Library), Bartlesville OK. 918-661-5911

George, Paulette, *Consult Info Retrieval,* Colorado State Library, Colorado Department of Education, Denver CO. 303-839-3695

George, Rachel, *Dir,* Reformed Presbyterian Theological Seminary Library, Pittsburgh PA. 412-731-8690

George, Roselyn, *Librn,* Quitman Public Library, Quitman TX. 214-763-4191

George, Rosemary, *Pub Serv,* Canada College Library, Redwood City CA. 415-364-1212

George, Rosemary, *Librn,* Winnipeg Public Library (Charleswood), Winnipeg MB. 204-837-3267

George, Shirley, *Dir,* Maywood Public Library, Maywood IL. 312-343-1847

George, Virginia, *Cat,* Seattle Public Library, Seattle WA. 206-625-2665

Georgeff, Lucille, *Cat,* Granite City Public Library, Granite City IL. 618-876-0550

Georgeson, Patricia, *Tech Serv,* Madison Public Library, Madison WI. 608-266-6300

Georgi, Charlotte, *Librn,* University of California Los Angeles Library (Management), Los Angeles CA. 213-825-4871

Georgia, Jean, *Librn,* Delevan-Yorkshire Public Library, Delevan NY. 716-492-1961

Gephart, Carolyn, *Ch,* Riverdale Public Library District, Riverdale IL. 312-841-3311

Geppert, Alida, *Dir,* Southwest Michigan Library Cooperative, Kalamazoo MI. 616-375-8842

Gera, Lynn, *On-Line Servs,* Walter Reed Army Institute of Research (WRAIR Library), Washington DC. 202-576-2417

Gerads, Marjorie, *On-Line Servs & Bibliog Instr,* Veterans Administration, Medical Center Learning Resources Center, Saint Cloud MN. 252-1670 Ext 270

Gerain-Lajoie, Henri, *Librn,* Montreal City Hall, Municipal Archives Reference Library, Montreal PQ. 514-872-2678

Gerard, Frances, *Ref,* Kanawha County Public Library, Kanawha County Service Center, Charleston WV. 304-343-4646

Gerard, G, *Librn,* Currie, Coopers & Lybrand Ltd Library, Toronto ON. 416-366-1921, Ext 545

Gerard, Helen J, *Ch,* New Brunswick Free Public Library, New Brunswick NJ. 201-745-5337

Gerard, Tobe Lynn, *Dir,* Insurance Library Association of Boston, Boston MA. 617-227-2087

Gerardi, Florence, *Librn,* Otis Elevator Co, North American Operations Engineering Center Library, Mahwah NJ. 201-825-4400

Gerbens, Martin, *Media & Tech Serv,* Ringling School of Art Library, Sarasota FL. 813-355-1232

Gerber, Gloria, *Media,* Charles S Wilson Memorial Hospital, Learning Resources Department, Johnson City NY. 607-773-6030, 773-6677

Gerber, Martha, *On-Line Servs & Bibliog Instr,* Cheltenham Township Library System, Glenside PA. 215-885-0457

Gerber, Martha, *Librn,* Glenside Free Library, Glenside PA. 215-885-0455

Gerber, Mary A, *Tech Serv,* Miami University-Middletown, Gardner-Harvey Library, Middletown OH. 513-424-4444, Ext 221, 222

Gerber, Norine, *Ref,* Berkeley Public Library, Berkeley CA. 415-644-6095

Gerbereux, Robert, *Dir & Acq,* Southampton College Library of Long Island University, Southampton NY. 516-283-4000, Ext 264

Gerberg, Eugene J, *Librn,* Insect Control & Research Inc Library, Baltimore MD. 301-747-4500

Gerbracht, Charles, *Tech Serv & Acq,* Niagara County Community College, Library Learning Center, Sanborn NY. 716-731-3271, Ext 145

Gercken, Richard, *Dir,* Great Falls Public Library, Pathfinder Federation of Libraries Headquarters, Great Falls MT. 406-453-0349

Gerdes, Doris, *Dir,* Manly Public Library, Manly IA. 515-454-2219

Gerdes, Neil W, *Dir,* Chicago Cluster of Theological Schools, IL. 312-667-3550, Ext 266, 267

Gerdes, Neil W, *Dir,* Meadville-Lombard Theological School Library, Chicago IL. 312-753-3195, 753-3196

Gerdes, Sharman, *Ch,* Prescott Public-Yavapai County Library System, Prescott AZ. 602-445-8110

Gereaux, Jacque, *Dir, Acq & Cat,* Manistee County Library, Manistee MI. 616-723-2519

Gergely, Emma, *Librn,* Allied Chemical Corp (Corporate Medical Affairs Library), Morristown NJ. 201-455-2283

Gergen, Genevieve, *Librn,* Smith Memorial Library, Dawson NE. 402-855-2555

Gerhan, D, *Bibliog Instr,* Union College, Schaffer Library, Schenectady NY. 518-370-6278

Gerhardt, Jean, *Talking Bks Serv,* Fairfax County Public Library (John Marshall), Alexandria VA. 703-971-0010

Gerhardt, Robert, *Science,* Southern Illinois University at Edwardsville, Elijah P Lovejoy Library, Edwardsville IL. 618-692-2711

Gerhart, Marian, *Dir,* Joint Free Public Library of Morristown & Morris Township, Morristown NJ. 201-538-6161

Gerhart, Susan M, *Dir,* Benzonia Public Library, Benzonia MI. 616-882-4111

Gericke, Paul, *Dir,* New Orleans Baptist Theological Seminary Library, New Orleans LA. 504-282-4455, Ext 289

Gerity, Louise P, *Ref,* Lewis & Clark College, Aubrey R Watzek Library, Portland OR. 503-244-6161, Ext 400

Gerity, Thomas W, *Bus & Econ,* Portland State University, Branford Price Millar Library, Portland OR. 503-229-4424

Gerke, Carol, *Librn,* Erdco Engineering Corp Library, Addison IL. 312-543-6733

Gerken, Bonnie, *Ch,* Pikes Peak Regional Library District, Penrose Public Library, Colorado Springs CO. 303-473-2080

Gerko, Elizabeth, *Librn,* Beaverdale Community Library, Beaverdale PA. 814-487-7742

Gerl, Brian Jonathan, *Chief Librn,* Wisconsin Conservatory of Music Library, Milwaukee WI. 414-276-4350

Gerlach, Ann, *Librn,* Edward U Demmer Memorial Library, Three Lakes WI. 715-546-3391

Gerlach, Donald E, *Coll Develop,* University of Wisconsin-Platteville, Elton S Karrmann Library, Platteville WI. 608-342-1688

Gerlach, Georgette, *ILL,* Midwestern State University, George Moffett Library, Wichita Falls TX. 817-692-6611, Ext 204

Gerling, Sally M, *Ch,* Genesee Hospital, Stabins Health Sciences Library, Rochester NY. 716-263-6305

Germain, Claire, *Ref,* Duke University (Law School Library), Durham NC. 919-684-2847

Germain, Jean-Pierre, *Dir,* Bibliotheque Centrale De Pret De L'outaouais Et Des Laurentides Inc, Hull PQ. 819-771-7345

German, Barbara, *Librn,* Traphagen School of Fashion, Ethel Traphagen Memorial Library, New York NY. 212-673-0300, Ext 5

German, Clara Nell, *Dir,* Miami County Public Library, Louisburg Library, Louisburg KS. 913-837-2217

German, Roy E, *Librn,* United States Navy (Naval Regional Medical Center General Library), Corpus Christi TX. 512-385-4100

Germovnik, Francis, *Librn,* De Andreis Seminary Library, Lemont IL. 312-257-5454, Ext 28

Germy, Joanne, *Asst Dir,* Ford City Public Library, Ford City PA. 412-762-3091

Gernes, William D, *Dir,* Winona County Historical Society, Laird Lucas Memorial Library, Winona MN. 507-454-2723

Gernot, Nebel, *Prof,* CEGEP Francois-Xavier Garneau, Techniques de la documentation, PQ. 418-688-8310, Ext 290

Geron, Cary Ann, *Librn,* Foreign Mission Board of the Southern Baptist Convention, Missionary Orientation Library, Pine Mountain GA. 404-663-2235

Geron, Charles W, *Librn,* Greene County Law Library, Xenia OH. 513-376-5115

Geroux, Madeleine, *Librn,* Kent County Municipal Public Library (Ridgetown Public), Ridgetown ON. 519-674-3121

Gerow, Jerry, *Instr,* Lansing Community College, Library Media Technology Program, MI. 517-373-9978

Gerrard, Philip, *Librn,* New York Public Library (Jefferson Market), New York NY. 212-243-4334

Gerriets, Gladys, *Dir,* Webster Public Library, Webster SD. 605-345-3263

Gerritts, Judy, *Librn,* San Francisco Examiner Library, San Francisco CA. 415-777-7845

Gerry, Elizabeth, *Librn,* Milford Public Library (Woodmont), Woodmont CT. 203-874-5675

Gers, Muriel L, *Librn,* Walters Art Gallery Library, Baltimore MD. 301-547-9000, Ext 20

Gers, Jr, Ralph E, *Pub Libr Specialists,* Maryland State Department of Education, Division of Library Development & Services, Baltimore MD. 301-796-8300, Ext 284

Gersh, Jonas, *Ref,* Rockville Centre Public Library, Rockville Centre NY. 516-766-6258

Gerstner, Noella, *Librn,* Warren Public Library, Warren MI. 313-264-8720

Gerstner, Noella, *Librn,* Warren Public Library (Arthur J Miller), Warren MI. 313-751-5370

Gerstner, Patsy, *Archivist,* Case Western Reserve University & Cleveland Medical Library Association, Cleveland Health Sciences Library, Cleveland OH. 216-368-3426

Gerstner, Patsy, *Adjunct Prof,* Case Western Reserve University, School of Library Science, OH. 216-368-3500

Gertler, Isadora, *Asst Librn,* Yeshiva University Libraries (Benjamin N Cardozo School of Law Library), New York NY. 212-790-0422

Gertner, Marcia, *Tech Serv,* Worthington Community College, Learning Resource Center, Worthington MN. 507-372-2107, Ext 50

Gertz, Jay, *Doc,* University of North Carolina at Asheville, D Hiden Ramsey Library, Asheville NC. 704-258-0200

Gertzog, Alice, *Dir,* Meadville Library Art & Historical Association, Meadville PA. 814-336-1773

Gervais, Marie, *Tech Serv,* Chateauguay Municipal Library, Chateauguay PQ. 514-691-1934

Gervino, Joan, *Dir,* American Bankers Association Library, Washington DC. 202-467-4180

Gerwing, H B, *Rare Bks & Spec Coll,* University of Victoria, McPherson Library, Victoria BC. 604-477-6911, Ext 4466

Gery, Nina, *Resource Librn,* Greater Portland Landmarks, Inc, Resource Library, Portland ME. 207-774-5561

Gery, Nina, *Preservation Educ,* Greater Portland Landmarks, Inc, Resource Library, Portland ME. 207-774-5561

Gesch, Arthur, *Supvr Admin,* Milwaukee Public Library, Milwaukee WI. 414-278-3000

Geschwindt, John, *Govt Pubs,* State Library of Pennsylvania, Harrisburg PA. 717-787-2646

Geschwindt, John, *Govt Publications,* State Library of Pennsylvania, Harrisburg PA. 717-787-2646

Gesell, Garry, *Tech Serv,* Southeast Regional Library, Weyburn SK. 306-842-4402, 842-3432

Geske, Aina S, *Chief Librn,* Kenyon & Eckhardt Inc Library, New York NY. 212-973-7894

Geske, Dulcie, *Libr Techn,* United States Air Force (Luke Air Force Base Library), Luke AFB AZ. 602-935-6301, 935-7191

Gesler, Sara, *Librn,* Knight Publishing Co Library, Charlotte NC. 704-374-7307

Gess, Catherine, *Asst Librn,* Tampa Tribune Library, Tampa FL. 813-272-7665

Gessell, Judy, *Spec Coll,* Sussex County Library System, Sussex County Area Reference Library, Newton NJ. 201-948-3660

Gessner, Robert, *Media,* Cook Christian Training School, Mary M McCarthy Library, Tempe AZ. 602-968-9354

Gesterfield, Kathryn J, *Dir ILL,* Illinois Library & Information Network, (ILLINET), IL. 217-782-7848

Gestrine, Jane, *ILL,* Mohave County Library, Kingman AZ. 602-753-5730

Getch, K, *Librn,* Carbone Lorraine Industries Corp Library, Boonton NJ. 201-334-0700

Gettelman, John, *Media,* Wauwatosa Public Library, Wauwatosa WI. 414-258-5700

Gettelman-Johnson, Robin, *Dir,* Franklin Ferguson Memorial Library, Cripple Creek CO. 303-689-2800

Gettone, Vernon G, *Dir,* Benedict College, Benjamin F Payton Learning Resources Ctr, Columbia SC. 803-256-4220

Getz, Richard, *Tech Serv,* Texas State Library, Austin TX. 512-475-2166

Gevirtz, Maureen, *Librn,* Wilshire Boulevard Temple, Sigmund Hecht Library, Los Angeles CA. 213-388-2401

Gewirtzman, Mrs T, *Tech Serv,* Albany Medical Center College of Union University, Schaffer Library of Health Sciences, Albany NY. 518-445-5534

Gex, Robert, *Librn,* Stanford University Libraries (Linear Accelerator Center), Stanford CA. 415-498-2411

Geyer, Della, *Librn,* Baylor University (Law), Waco TX. 817-755-2168

Geyer, Enid, *Cat,* Albany Medical Center College of Union University, Schaffer Library of Health Sciences, Albany NY. 518-445-5534

Geyer, John, *Dir,* Coast Area Library Cooperative, CA. 213-420-4231

Geyger, Barbara F, *Children's Div,* Public Library of the District of Columbia, Martin Luther King Memorial Library, Washington DC. 202-727-1101

Ghannoum, Magdalynne, *Asst Librn,* Carnegie Library, Fitzgerald-Ben Hill County Library, Fitzgerald GA. 912-423-3642

Gharst, Willie Dee, *Res Specialist,* Mississippi Library Commission, Jackson MS. 601-354-6369

Ghattas, Mina B, *Learning Resources,* Northeastern University Libraries, Boston MA. 617-437-2350

Ghearing, Carol, *Asst Librn,* Mary L Cook Public Library, Waynesville OH. 513-897-4826

Gheesling, Lynda, *Librn,* Bartram Trail Regional Library (McDuffie County), Thomson GA. 404-678-7736

Ghent, Gretchen, *Soc Sci Libr,* University of Calgary Library, Calgary AB. 403-284-5954

Ghering, Sister M Virgil, *Librn,* Saint Thomas Institute Library, Cincinnati OH. 513-861-3460

Gherman, Paul M, *Asst Dir, Admin Serv,* Iowa State University Library, Ames IA. 515-294-1442

Ghigo, Helen, *Tech Serv & Cat,* Hutchinson County Library, Borger TX. 806-274-6221

Ghikas, Mary W, *Asst Commissioner for Cent Libr & Cultural Ctr,* Chicago Public Library, Chicago IL. 312-269-2900

Gholston, H D, *Librn,* Chevron Research Co, Technical Information Center, Richmond CA. 415-237-4411

Ghorpade, Lotus, *ILL,* Denison University, William Howard Doane Library, Granville OH. 614-587-0810, Ext 225

Giacalone, Donna, *Asst Librn,* Continental Chemiste Corp, Smo-Cloud Co Library, Chicago IL. 312-226-2134

Giagni, Annamary, *Librn,* Los Angeles Public Library System (Venice Branch), Venice CA. 213-821-1769

Giannella, Anita, *Ch,* Glen Rock Public Library, Glen Rock NJ. 201-445-4222, 445-4223

Giannetti, Emma M, *Librn,* Arkansas Co, Inc Library, Newark NJ. 201-589-0516

Giannini, Evelyn, *Librn,* Kemper Insurance Companies Library, Long Grove IL. 312-540-2229

Giard, E M, *Dir,* Skagit County Historical Museum Library, La Conner WA. 206-466-3365

Giardina, Joyce, *ILL,* Southern Illinois University at Edwardsville, Elijah P Lovejoy Library, Edwardsville IL. 618-692-2711

Giardina, Mrs Joseph, *Acq,* Saint Mary's Dominican College, John XXIII Library, New Orleans LA. 504-865-7761, Ext 225

Giasi, Marie G, *Librn,* Brooklyn Botanical Garden Library, Brooklyn NY. 212-622-4433

Gibb, B, *ILL,* University of Victoria, McPherson Library, Victoria BC. 604-477-6911, Ext 4466

Gibb, Elizabeth, *Librn,* Appleby College Library, Oakville ON. 416-845-4681

Gibbing, Naomi, *Dir,* Utica Public Library, Utica MI. 313-731-4141

Gibbins, Margaret E, *Librn,* Dupont Canada Inc (Central Library), Montreal PQ. 514-861-3861, Ext 7781

Gibbons, Andrew H, *Asst Prof,* University of Northern Colorado, Department of Educational Media, CO. 303-351-2807

Gibbons, Barbara, *Librn,* Bureau of Land Management, Ukiah District Office Library, Ukiah CA. 707-462-3873

Gibbons, Douglas, *Librn,* Museum of Broadcasting Library, New York NY. 212-752-4690

Gibbons, Gayle G, *Librn,* Smyrna Public Library, Smyrna DE. 302-653-4579

Gibbons, Marjorie, *Supv of Br,* Boston Public Library, Eastern Massachusetts Library System, Boston MA. 617-536-5400

Gibbons, Shirley, *Librn,* Cascade Public Library, Cascade ID. 208-382-4757

Gibbons, Susan, *Librn,* Dechert, Price & Rhoads Library, Philadelphia PA. 215-972-3452

Gibbs, Anne, *Librn,* Smith County Public Library (Gordonsville Library), Gordonsville TN. 615-683-8063

Gibbs, Bertha, *Sci-tech,* Chicago Public Library (Woodson Regional), Chicago IL. 312-881-6900

Gibbs, Betty S, *Librn,* Menifee County Public Library, Frenchburg KY. 606-768-2212

Gibbs, Donald T, *Dir,* Redwood Library & Athenaeum, Newport RI. 401-847-0292

Gibbs, Marilyn O, *Med Librn,* Dekalb General Hospital, Medical Library, Decatur GA. 404-292-4444, Ext 5084

Gibbs, Mary, *Librn,* Purdue University Libraries & Audio-Visual Center (Consumer & Family Sciences), West Lafayette IN. 317-749-2520

Gibbs, Robert, *Asst Univ Librn Ref Serv,* Auburn University, Ralph Brown Draughton Library, Auburn AL. 205-826-4500

Gibbs, Ruth, *Assoc Univ Librn for Res & Instrnl Servs,* University of California Los Angeles Library, Los Angeles CA. 213-825-1201

Gibbs, Willie M, *Media,* Sheppard Memorial Library, Greenville NC. 919-752-4177

Gibian, Germaine L, *Librn,* Cleveland Public Library (Martin Luther King Jr Regional), Cleveland OH. 216-795-4117

Giblin, Carol, *Librn,* Hummelstown Community Library, Hummelstown PA. 717-566-0949

Giblin, Robert, *Asst Dir,* University of Houston (Law Library), Houston TX. 713-749-3119

Giblon, Charlie, *Tech Serv & Cat,* Tallahassee Community College Library, Tallahassee FL. 904-576-5181

Gibney, Patricia, *Ser,* Princeton University Library, Princeton NJ. 609-452-3180

Gibout, Betty, *Books-by-Mail,* Grand Rapids Public Library, Grand Rapids MI. 616-456-4400

Gibson, Ann, *Ch,* Henrietta Public Library, Rochester NY. 716-334-3401

Gibson, Barbara H, *Dir,* Village Library, Farmington CT. 203-677-1529

Gibson, Betty, *Libr Asst,* Rusk County Memorial Library (Tatum Branch), Tatum TX. 214-657-8557

Gibson, Betty J, *Librn,* Wenatchee Valley College, John A Brown Library Media Center, Wenatchee WA. 509-662-1651

Gibson, C Catherine, *Ad,* Indianapolis-Marion County Public Library, Indianapolis IN. 317-635-5662

Gibson, Carol, *Coordr,* Manitowoc-Calumet Counties Federated Library System, Manitowoc WI. 414-682-6861

Gibson, Carolyn, *Librn,* South Central Bell Telephone Co, Public Relations Library, Birmingham AL. 205-321-2064

Gibson, Charles, *Circ & Systs,* William Marsh Rice University, Fondren Library, Houston TX. 713-527-4022

Gibson, Dennis A, *Spec Coll,* University of Southwestern Louisiana, Dupre Library, Lafayette LA. 318-264-6396

Gibson, Frank E, *Dir,* Omaha Public Library, W Dale Clark Library, Omaha NE. 402-444-4800

Gibson, Gladys, *Librn,* Atomic Energy of Canada Ltd, Whiteshell Nuclear Research Establishment Library, Pinawa MB. 204-753-2311, Ext 244

Gibson, Harold R, *Dir,* University of the Pacific & Pacific Medical Center, Health Sciences Library, San Francisco CA. 415-563-4321, Ext 2751

Gibson, Harriet, *Circ,* Marlboro County Library, Bennettsville SC. 803-479-6201

Gibson, Imogene, *Dir & On-Line Servs,* Austin College, Hopkins Library, Sherman TX. 214-892-9101, Ext 237

Gibson, Jean L, *Librn,* Livingston Public Library, Livingston MT. 406-222-0862

Gibson, Kay, *Librn,* Saint Mary's Hospital, Medical Library, Huntington WV. 304-696-6807

Gibson, Linda, *Librn,* Athol City Library, Athol KS. 913-695-2314

Gibson, Linda, *Librn,* Memphis-Shelby County Public Library & Information Center (Cherokee), Memphis TN. 901-743-3655

Gibson, Linda, *Media Coordr,* Toronto Institute of Medical Technology Library, Toronto ON. 416-596-3123

Gibson, Mary, *Per,* Columbia College, J Drake Edens Library, Columbia SC. 803-786-3878

Gibson, Mary Beth, *Librn,* Victoria County Public Library, Lindsay ON. 705-324-3104

Gibson, Mrs Stuart B, *Librn,* Valentine Museum Library, Richmond VA. 804-649-0711

Gibson, Neva Y, *Dir,* Clinch Valley College of the University of Virginia, John Cook Wyllie Library, Wise VA. 703-328-2431, Ext 255

Gibson, Pamela, *Eaton Room Librn,* Manatee County Public Library System, Bradenton FL. 813-748-5555

Gibson, Phillip W, *Media,* Northwest Christian College, Learning Resource Center, Eugene OR. 503-343-1641, Ext 35

Gibson, Robert S, *Coordr,* Radford University, Library Science Program, VA. 703-731-5364

Gibson, Robert Sherrill, *Tech Serv & Cat,* Mayne Williams Public Library, Johnson City TN. 615-928-3116

Gibson, Roger, *Librn,* Wichita Public Library (Minisa), Wichita KS. 316-262-0611

Gibson, Ruth, *Asst Dir,* Tuscarawas County Public Library, New Philadelphia OH. 216-364-4474

Gibson, Sarah S, *Asst Prof,* Case Western Reserve University, School of Library Science, OH. 216-368-3500

Gibson, Theda F, *Dir,* Lonesome Pine Regional Library, Wise VA. 703-328-8061

Gibson, Theda F, *Dir,* Lonesome Pine Regional Library (Wise County Public), Wise VA. 703-328-8061

Gibson, Jr, Robert W, *Chief Librn,* General Motors Corp (Research Laboratories Library), Warren MI. 313-575-2731

Gibson-MacDonald, N, *Librn,* Canada Department of Agriculture, Harrow Research Station Library, Harrow ON. 519-738-2251

Gicker, Mary Louise, *Librn,* Delaware City Library, Delaware City DE. 302-834-4148

Giddens, Margaret, *Librn,* South Georgia Regional Library (Lakeland Branch), Lakeland GA. 912-482-3966

Giddens, Nancy C, *Ref,* Golden Gate Baptist Theological Seminary Library, Mill Valley CA. 415-388-8080, Ext 37

Giddings, Carolyn, *Librn,* Tulare County Library System (Springville Branch), Springville CA. 209-539-2624

Giddings, Mrs Oliver, *Librn,* Prince Edward Island Provincial Library (Murray River Branch), Murray River PE. 902-892-3504, Ext 54

Giddings, Ruth L, *Asst Dir,* West Hartford Public Library, Noah Webster Memorial Library, West Hartford CT. 203-236-6286

Giddy, Sarah, *Asst Librn,* NASA, Goddard Institute For Space Studies, New York NY. 212-678-5613

Gideon, Mrs T B, *Librn,* Leola Roberts Public Library, Whiteville TN. 901-254-8834

Gidney, M, *Bibliog Instr,* Warren Wilson College Library, Swannanoa NC. 704-298-3325, Ext 45

Gidney, Margaret, *Tech Serv & Acq,* Warren Wilson College Library, Swannanoa NC. 704-298-3325, Ext 45

Giebel, Miriam, *Tech Serv,* Crestwood Public Library District, Crestwood IL. 312-371-4090

Gieck, Susan, *Librn,* Imperial County Law Library, El Centro CA. 714-352-3610

Giedrys, Ilona M, *Librn,* Merck & Co, Inc (Research Library), Rahway NJ. 574-6046/574-6059

Giefer, Gerald, *Librn,* University of California, Berkeley (Water Resources Center Archives), Berkeley CA. 415-642-2666

Gieger, Geraldine, *Librn,* Exxon Co USA (Exxon Research & Engineering Co Library), Baytown TX. 713-428-5100

Giehl, Rose, *Acq,* Mastics-Moriches-Shirley Community Library, Shirley NY. 516-339-1511

Gierasimowicz, Helena, *Librn,* University of North Carolina at Chapel Hill (Planning), Chapel Hill NC. 919-933-3733

Gierok, Anne, *Ch,* Winona Public Library, Winona MN. 507-452-4582

Gieryic, Michael, *Dir,* State University of New York, Agricultural & Technical College at Norrisville Library, Morrisville NY. 315-684-7055

Giesbrecht, Gene, *Br Librn,* EG&G Idaho, Inc, INEL Technical Library, Idaho Falls ID. 208-526-1185

Giesbrecht, Herbert, *Dir,* Mennonite Brethren Bible College Library, Winnipeg MB. 204-667-9560, Ext 29

Giesbrecht, J, *Area Coordr,* Canada Agriculture, Research Institute Library, London ON. 519-679-4452

Giesbrecht, John W, *Asst Librn,* Manitoba Department of Economic Development & Tourism Library, Winnipeg MB. 204-944-2036

Giese, Karen, *Librn,* Reed City Public Library, Reed City MI. 616-832-2131

Giese, Theodore L, *Ref & Doc,* Minot State College, Memorial Library, Minot ND. 701-857-3200

Giesecke, Joan, *North Campus,* George Mason University Libraries, Fairfax VA. 703-323-2616

Gifford, Curtis, *Forestry & Agr Sci,* Colorado State University, William E Morgan Library, Fort Collins CO. 303-491-5911

Gifford, Lulu F, *Librn,* Jamestown City Library, Jamestown KS. 913-439-6258

Gifford, Roger G, *Acq,* Michigan State University Library, East Lansing MI. 517-355-2344

Gifford, Ruby, *Per,* Houston Baptist University, Moody Memorial Library, Houston TX. 713-774-7661, Ext 303

Gifford, Virginia J, *Librn,* Vassar College Library (George Sherman Dickenson Music Library), Poughkeepsie NY. 914-312-3057

Gigante, Marianne, *Librn,* Ohio Attorney General, Law Library, Columbus OH. 614-466-2465

Gignac, Luisa, *Librn,* Albuquerque Public Library (Los Griegos Branch), Albuquerque NM. 505-766-7889

Gignac, Solange G, *Librn,* Denver Botanic Gardens, Helen Fowler Library, Denver CO. 303-575-2547, Exts 24, 26

Giguere, Marcella, *Dir,* Niagara Public Library, Niagara WI. 715-251-3236

Giguere, Pierre, *Lit & Lang,* Universite Laval Bibliotheque, Quebec PQ. 418-656-3344

Gil-Passolas, Diana, *Doc,* Ventura County Library Services Agency, Ventura County Library, Ventura CA. 805-654-2627
Gilbert, Adah, *Acq,* Pittsburg State University Library, Pittsburg KS. 316-231-7000, Ext 431
Gilbert, Annie May, *Chief, Mat Proc,* Dallas Public Library, Dallas TX. 214-748-9071
Gilbert, B, *Supvr,* Bendix Corp, Electrical Components Div, Engineering Library, Sidney NY. 607-563-5605, Ext 437
Gilbert, Bennett, *Bibliog Instr,* Philosophical Research Society Library, Los Angeles CA. 213-663-2167
Gilbert, Carl, *Bibliog Instr,* Hampshire College, Harold F Johnson Library Center, Amherst MA. 413-549-4600
Gilbert, Catherine, *Dir,* Scottsville Free Library, Scottsville NY. 716-889-2023
Gilbert, Cynthia L, *Librn,* Milton Public Library, Milton PA. 717-742-7111
Gilbert, Deborah D, *Chief Librn,* Children's Hospital National Medical Center, Medical Library, Washington DC. 202-745-3195
Gilbert, Don, *Ch,* Harlan Public Library, Harlan KY. 606-573-5220
Gilbert, Elizabeth, *AV,* Richardson Public Library, Richardson TX. 214-238-8251
Gilbert, Elizabeth X, *In Charge,* Gem Village Museum, Green Memorial Library, Bayfield CO. 303-884-2811
Gilbert, Elsie, *Librn,* Frankfort City Library, Frankfort MI. 616-352-4671
Gilbert, Gail R, *Librn,* University of Louisville Library (Art), Louisville KY. 502-588-6741
Gilbert, Greg, *Graphics,* Cerro Coso Community College, Learning Resources Center, Ridgecrest CA. 714-375-5001, Ext 47
Gilbert, Harry, *Librn,* University of Kentucky (Architecture), Lexington KY. 606-257-1533
Gilbert, Helen, *Cat,* Pittsburg State University Library, Pittsburg KS. 316-231-7000, Ext 431
Gilbert, Helen E, *Dir,* McKendree College, Holman Library, Lebanon IL. 618-537-4481, Ext 166, 168
Gilbert, Iris, *Asst Librn,* California Public Library, California PA. 412-938-2907
Gilbert, Jane C, *In Charge,* Herkimer County Law Library, Herkimer NY. 315-867-1172
Gilbert, Janet M, *Acq,* Chipola Junior College Library, Marianna FL. 904-526-2761, Ext 122
Gilbert, Jean, *Tech Serv,* Ponca City Library, Ponca City OK. 405-762-6311
Gilbert, Jean E, *Asst Librn,* United States Department of Defense, Defense Communications Agency, Command & Control Technical Center Library, Washington DC. 202-697-6469
Gilbert, Jim, *Media,* Gordon Junior College Library, Barnesville GA. 404-385-1700, Ext 271, 272, 276
Gilbert, Joan, *Reader Serv & Ref,* Walters State Community College, Learning Resource Center, Morristown TN. 615-581-2121, Ext 212
Gilbert, Larry C, *Media,* College of William & Mary in Virginia, Earl Gregg Swem Library, Williamsburg VA. 804-253-4404
Gilbert, Luanne, *Pub Servs,* Alameda County Library, Hayward CA. 415-881-6337
Gilbert, Marianne, *Ref,* Elmira College, Gannett-Tripp Learning Ctr, Elmira NY. 607-734-3911, Ext 287
Gilbert, Ophelia, *Librn,* Central Missouri State University (Laboratory School), Warrensburg MO. 816-429-4508
Gilbert, Ruth E, *Librn,* Veterans Administration, Hospital Library, Denver CO. 303-399-8020, Ext 351
Gilbert, Thomas, *Cat,* University of the South, Jessie Ball duPont Library, Sewanee TN. 615-598-5931, Ext 265, 267
Gilbert, Thomas F, *Cat,* University of the South (School of Theology), Sewanee TN. 615-698-5931, Ext 281
Gilbert, Virginia, *Dir,* Derby Public Library, Derby KS. 316-788-0760
Gilbert, Virginia, *Soc Sci Bibliog,* University of Alabama, Amelia Gayle Gorgas Library, University AL. 205-348-5298
Gilbertson, Barbara, *Ch,* Mount Lebanon Public Library, Pittsburgh PA. 412-531-1912
Gilbertson, Mary Edith, *Acq,* Willamette University Library (College of Law Library), Salem OR. 503-370-6387

Gilbreath, Jean, *Librn,* Northeast Georgia Regional Library System (Cleveland), Clarkesville GA. 404-754-4413
Gilbreath, Ruby M, *Librn,* Guntersville Public Library, Guntersville AL. 205-582-3837
Gilbride, Irene L, *Librn,* Sierracin Corp Library, Sylmar CA. 213-367-6184
Gilchrist, Betty J, *Dir,* Gibbsboro Public Library, Gibbsboro NJ. 609-783-5589
Gilchrist, Frances, *Asst Dir & Cat,* Taunton Public Library, Subregional Headquarters for Eastern Massachusetts Regional Library System, Taunton MA. 617-823-3570
Gilchrist, Mary Jane, *Librn,* General Motors Overseas Operations Library, New York NY. 212-486-3464
Gilden, William K, *Tech Serv,* California State University, Sacramento Library, Sacramento CA. 916-454-6466
Gildersleeve, Pat, *Coordr,* NEBASE, NE. 402-471-2045
Gildersleeve, Robert, *Cat,* Port Authority of New York & New Jersey Library, New York NY. 212-466-4067, 4068
Giles, Arlo W, *Dir,* Springfield Public Library, Springfield OR. 503-726-3765
Giles, Charles E, *Chief Librn,* General Dynamics Corp, Electric Boat Division Library, Groton CT. 203-446-3481
Giles, Elsa, *Librn,* Wallace Public Library, Wallace ID. 208-752-4571
Giles, Esther L, *Librn,* Trans World Airlines, Inc, Corporate Library, New York NY. 212-557-6055
Giles, James T, *Syst Dir,* Cranston Public Library, William H Hall Free Library (Administrative & Reference Center), Cranston RI. 401-781-2450, 781-9580
Giles, Jane, *Cat,* Nolichucky Regional Library, Morristown TN. 615-586-6251
Giles, Janice, *Ch,* Pekin Public Library, Pekin IL. 309-347-7111
Giles, Margaret, *AV,* Erie Community College-North, Library Resources Center, Buffalo NY. 716-634-0800
Giles, Martha Ann, *Asst Dir,* Kennesaw College Library, Marietta GA. 404-422-8770, Ext 250
Giles, Sondra, *Ref,* Providence College, Phillips Memorial Library, Providence RI. 401-865-2242
Giles, Sue, *Coordr Info Servs & Libr Servs,* Ryerson Polytechnical Institute, Donald Mordell Learning Resources Centre, Toronto ON. 416-595-5331
Giles, Jr, Clifton F, *Univ Librn,* University of Southern Maine, Gorham ME. 207-780-5340, 780-4273
Gilheany, Rosary S, *Dir,* United Hospitals of Newark (Library & Information Services), Newark NJ. 201-268-8774, 268-8776
Gilkerson, Sue, *Dir,* Montreat-Anderson College, L Nelson Bell Library, Montreat NC. 704-669-2382
Gilkes, Thelma, *Cat,* Connecticut College Library, New London CT. 203-442-1630
Gill, Barbara, *Asst Dir,* Priest Lake Community Library, Priest River ID. 208-443-2454
Gill, Dorothy B, *Dir,* Jefferson County Library, Nederland TX. 713-727-2735, 727-2736
Gill, Elizabeth, *Ref & On-Line Servs,* S R I International Library, Research Information Services, Menlo Park CA. 415-326-6200, Ext 2634
Gill, Gail P, *Librn,* Delaware Academy of Medicine, Inc Library, Wilmington DE. 302-656-1629
Gill, Gail P, *Pres,* Wilmington Area Biomedical Library Consortium, (WABLC), DE. 302-656-1629
Gill, Jane, *Info,* Bethlehem Public Library, Bethlehem PA. 215-867-3761
Gill, Jean, *Br Asst,* Timberland Regional Library (Cosmopolis Branch), Cosmopolis WA. 206-532-4961
Gill, Johnoween, *ILL,* Texas Christian University, Mary Couts Burnett Library, Fort Worth TX. 817-921-7106
Gill, Karen, *Cat,* Reed College, E V Hauser Memorial Library, Portland OR. 503-771-1112, Ext 260
Gill, LaZelle, *Librn,* Kent County Library System (Krause Memorial), Rockford MI. 616-866-2352

Gill, Linda, *Asst Prof,* Middle Tennessee State University, Department of Library Service, TN. 615-898-2740 & 898-5555
Gill, Linda S, *Per,* Middle Tennessee State University, Andrew L Todd Library, Murfreesboro TN. 615-898-2622
Gill, Louis J, *Dir,* Waycross Junior College Library, Waycross GA. 912-285-6136
Gill, Lynne, *Tech Processes,* Connecticut State Library, Hartford CT. 203-566-4301
Gill, Marcia, *Dir,* Indian Valley Public Library, Telford PA. 215-723-9109
Gill, Norman N, *Dir,* Citizens' Governmental Research Bureau Library, Milwaukee WI. 414-276-8240
Gill, Suzanne, *Instr,* Saint Louis Community College at Florissant Valley, Library Technical Assistant Program, MO. 314-595-4494
Gillan, Dennis, *Tech Serv,* Bloomfield College Library, Bloomfield NJ. 201-748-9000, Ext 281
Gilland, Patricia, *Asst Librn,* Marrowbone Township Library, Bethany IL. 217-665-3014
Gillard, Betty, *Ref,* Orlando Public Library, Orlando FL. 305-425-4694
Gillard, Peter McCann, *Actg Dir,* Smithtown Library, Smithtown NY. 516-265-2072
Gillen, Betty, *YA & Circ,* Nichols Library, Naperville IL. 312-355-1540
Gillen, Mary F, *Dir,* Joseph Hooper Free Library, Lebanon Springs NY. 518-794-8844
Gillen, Thomas, *Ref,* Smithtown Library, Smithtown NY. 516-265-2072
Gillentine, Jane P, *Develop,* New Mexico State Library, Santa Fe NM. 505-827-2033
Gilleran, Elaine, *Supvr,* Wells Fargo Bank (History Room), San Francisco CA. 415-396-2619
Gillespie, David M, *Dir & Acq,* Glenville State College, Robert F Kidd Library, Glenville WV. 304-462-7361, Ext 291
Gillespie, David M, *Head Librn,* Glenville State College, Library Science Program, WV. 304-462-7361, Ext 291, 292
Gillespie, Eileen, *In Charge,* Simi Valley Adventist Hospital, Medical Library, Simi Valley CA. 805-527-2472, Ext 172 & 351
Gillespie, Ellamae, *Librn,* Esther Washburn Public Library, Tremont IL. 309-925-5432
Gillespie, Harriet, *Librn,* Dresser Industries, Inc, Harbison-Walker Refractories Div Library, Pittsburgh PA. 412-562-6200
Gillespie, Harriett, *Librn,* Dresser Industries, Inc, Harbison-Walker Refractories Co, Garber Research Center Library, West Mifflin PA. 412-562-6200
Gillespie, J, *Coordr,* Thunder Bay Public Library (Technical Services Department), Thunder Bay ON. 807-623-3112
Gillespie, Janet, *Ch,* Anderson City-Anderson & Stony Creek Township Public Library, Anderson Public Library, Anderson IN. 317-644-0938
Gillespie, John T, *Prof,* Long Island University, Palmer Graduate Library School, NY. 516-299-2855 & 299-2856
Gillespie, M, *Circ,* University of Saskatchewan Library, Saskatoon SK. 306-343-4216
Gillespie, Mrs J M, *Librn,* Aluminum Co of Canada, Ltd, Research Center Library, Kingston ON. 613-549-4500, Ext 245
Gillette, Catherine Hall, *Pub Serv,* Cleveland State University Libraries (Joseph W Bartunek III Law Library), Cleveland OH. 216-687-2250
Gillette, Kate, *Bibliog Instr,* Case Western Reserve University Libraries (Sears), Cleveland OH. 216-368-3506
Gillette, Kay J, *Dir,* Douglas Public Library, Douglas AZ. 602-364-3851
Gillette, Mary, *Librn,* Mather Memorial Library, Inc, Ulster PA. 717-358-3595
Gilley, Sharon, *Dir,* Lucius Beebe Memorial Library, Wakefield MA. 617-245-0790
Gillham, Peggy, *ILL,* Bossier Parish Public Library, Benton LA. 318-965-2751
Gilliam, Dorothy, *Cat,* Union Theological Seminary in Virginia Library, Richmond VA. 804-355-0671, Ext 311
Gilliam, Jack, *Cat,* Brevard Community College, Melbourne Campus Learning Resources Center, Melbourne FL. 305-254-0305, Ext 227, 228
Gilliam, Muriel, *Librn,* North Arkansas Regional Library (Madison County), Huntsville AR. 501-738-2754

Gilliam, Renee P, *Media,* Kentucky State University, Blazer Library, Frankfort KY. 502-564-5852

Gilliam, Robert, *ILL,* State University of New York College at Brockport, Drake Memorial Library, Brockport NY. 716-395-2140

Gilliana, Zia Solomon, *Librn,* Ravenswood Hospital Medical Center, Medical-Nursing Library, Chicago IL. 312-878-4300, Ext 547

Gillies, Catharine, *Librn,* Essex County Public Library (Tecumseh Branch), Tecumseh ON. 519-776-5241

Gillies, Elizabeth W, *Librn,* S S Huebner Foundation for Insurance Education Library, Philadelphia PA. 215-243-7620

Gillies, Ellen, *Librn,* University of Vermont & State Agricultural College (Dana Medical), Burlington VT. 802-656-2200

Gillies, Thomas D, *Dir,* Linda Hall Library, Kansas City MO. 816-363-4600

Gilligan, J Joseph, *Librn,* Essex County Law Library Association, Hon James J Ronan Library, Salem MA. 617-744-1240

Gilligan, Wilhelmina, *Tech Serv,* Dutchess Community College Library, Poughkeepsie NY. 914-471-4500, Ext 388

Gilliland, Ernestine, *Dir,* Kansas State Library, Topeka KS. 913-296-3296

Gilliland, Melvin W, *Tech Serv,* Walla Walla College, Peterson Memorial Library, College Place WA. 509-527-2133

Gilliland, Shirley, *Librn,* Houston County Public Library System (Centerville-Houston County Branch), Centerville GA. 912-953-4500

Gillio, Marie B, *Librn,* Deaconess Hospital, Medical-Nursing Library, Spokane WA. 509-624-0171, Ext 2209

Gillis, Aurea, *In Charge,* Eastern Counties Regional Library (Coady & Tompkins Memorial Branch), Margaree Forks NS. 902-747-2597

Gillis, Eileen W, *Librn,* Mercy Hospital Inc (McGlannon Memorial Library), Baltimore MD. 301-332-9189

Gillis, Jenny, *Asst Dir,* Kent Free Library, Kent OH. 216-673-4414, 673-3384

Gillis, Mary Alice L, *Librn,* Easton Library, North Easton NY. 518-692-2253

Gillis, Mrs Robert, *Librn,* Montana School for the Deaf and Blind, Great Falls MT. 406-453-1401

Gillis, Patsy, *Acq,* Albany Dougherty Public Library, Albany GA. 912-435-2104

Gillis, Susan, *Cat,* Fond Du Lac City-County Library Service, Fond du Lac WI. 414-921-3670

Gillis, Susan, *Cat,* Mid-Wisconsin Federated Library System, Fond du Lac WI. 414-921-3670

Gillis, Virginia, *Librn,* Monmouth Library, Monmouth OR. 503-838-1932

Gilliss, Geraldine Channon, *Dir,* Canadian Teachers' Federation, George G Croskery Memorial Library, Ottawa ON. 613-232-1505

Gillock, Jr, Oliver P, *Coordr Libr Planning & Develop,* New Jersey State Library, Trenton NJ. 609-292-6200

Gillord, Peter M, *Librn Blind,* Northland Library Cooperative, Alpena MI. 517-356-4444

Gillott, Doris, *Ch,* Baldwin Public Library, Baldwin NY. 516-223-6228

Gills, Coral, *Pub Info,* County of Henrico Public Library, Richmond VA. 804-222-1643

Gillson, Lyn, *Librn,* Newport Beach Public Library (Corona del Mar Branch), Corona del Mar CA. 714-640-2191

Gillum, Gary, *Lang,* Brigham Young University, Harold B Lee Library, Provo UT. 801-378-2905

Gilman, Betty, *Asst Dir,* Matilda J Gibson Memorial Library, Creston IA. 515-782-2277

Gilman, Esther, *Dir,* Trails Regional Library, Johnson County-Lafayette County Library, Warrensburg MO. 816-747-9177

Gilman, Gail, *Ch,* Saginaw Public Libraries, Hoyt Public Library, Saginaw MI. 517-755-0904

Gilman, Grace A, *Librn,* Shasta County Library, Redding CA. 916-246-5756

Gilman, Helen, *Librn,* Laramie County Library System (Burns Branch), Burns WY. 307-547-2249

Gilman, Lynn, *Librn,* San Bernardino County Medical Center Library, San Bernardino CA. 714-383-3367

Gilman, Marie, *Circ,* Ralph Chandler Harrison Memorial Library, Carmel CA. 408-624-4629

Gilman, Nelson J, *Dir,* University of Southern California (Norris Medical Library), Los Angeles CA. 213-226-2231

Gilman, Phyllis, *Dir,* Holliston Public Library, Holliston MA. 617-429-6070

Gilman, Richard, *Acq,* University of Bridgeport, Magnus Wahlstrom Library, Bridgeport CT. 203-576-4740

Gilmer, Alice O, *Librn,* Russell County Public Library, Lebanon VA. 703-889-2881

Gilmer, Jr, Wesley, *Librn,* State Law Library, Frankfort KY. 502-564-4848

Gilmore, Ann, *Acq,* Springfield-Greene County Library, Springfield MO. 417-869-4621

Gilmore, Catharine, *ILL & Ad,* Haddon Heights Public Library, Haddon Heights NJ. 609-547-7132

Gilmore, Ellen, *Librn,* Sacred Heart Hospital, Medical Library, Hanford CA. 209-582-2551, Ext 362

Gilmore, Helen A, *Librn,* Five Rivers Public Library, Parsons WV. 304-478-3880

Gilmore, Louise, *Librn,* Oktibbeha County Library System (Starkville Branch (Headquarters)), Starkville MS. 601-323-2766

Gilmore, Mary Joanne, *Tech Serv,* Troup Harris Coweta Regional Library, La Grange Memorial Library, La Grange GA. 404-882-7784

Gilmore, Orlena, *Librn,* Cass County Public Library (Belton Branch), Belton MO. 816-331-0049

Gilmore, Peggy S, *Ser,* Georgia Southern College Library, Statesboro GA. 912-681-5115

Gilmore, Vera, *ILL & Circ,* Maryville College, Lamar Memorial Library, Maryville TN. 615-982-1200

Gilmore, Willard H, *Asst Librn & Cat,* Maine Maritime Academy, Nutting Memorial Library, Castine ME. 207-326-4311, Ext 238

Gilmore-Forczak, Cherie, *Anglo-Am Law,* University of Michigan (Law Library), Ann Arbor MI. 313-764-9322

Gilpatrick, Brenda, *Asst Librn,* Red Bud Public Library, Red Bud IL. 618-282-2255

Gilpin, Lois, *Asst Dir,* Taylor County Public Library, Campbellsville KY. 502-465-2562

Gilpin, Risa, *ILL,* Rhode Island School of Design Library, Providence RI. 401-331-3507, Ext 229

Gilreath, Jean, *Circ,* Princeton Public Library, Mercer Memorial Library, Princeton WV. 304-425-3324

Gilroy, Dorothy, *Librn,* University Affiliated Cincinnati Center for Developmental Disorders, Research Library, Cincinnati OH. 513-559-4626

Gilroy, Marilyn, *AV,* Mercer County Community College Library, Trenton NJ. 609-586-4800, Ext 358

Gilroy, Marilyn, *Instr,* Mercer County Community College, Library-Media Center Technical Assistant Program, NJ. 609-586-4800, Ext 360

Gilroy, Pauline, *Librn,* Eudora Public Library, Eudora KS. 913-542-2496

Gilroy, Robert, *Librn,* Upper Arlington Public Library (Lane Road Branch), Upper Arlington OH. 614-459-0273

Gilroy, Rupert, *Assoc Librn,* Brandeis University, Goldfarb Library, Waltham MA. 617-647-2514

Gilroy, Susan, *Dir,* Santiago Library System, Orange CA. 714-634-7137

Gilson, Christine, *Dir,* Lincoln Public Library, Lincoln IL. 217-732-8878

Gilson, Preston, *Dir,* Lincoln College, McKinstry Library, Lincoln IL. 217-732-3155, Ext 277

Giltinam, Mary J, *Reader Serv,* Saint Charles Borromeo Seminary, Ryan Memorial Library, Philadelphia PA. 215-839-3760, Ext 275

Giltinan, Eleanor B, *Cat & Ref,* Conococheague District Library System, Chambersburg PA. 717-263-1054

Gilwood, Katherine, *Librn,* Mercy College, Miami Center for Bilingual Education, Miami FL. 305-545-9881

Gilzinger, Jr, Donald M, *Librn,* Suffolk County Community College, Eastern Campus Library, Riverhead NY. 516-369-2600, Ext 228

Gima, Marguerite, *Librn,* Saint Margaret Hospital, Memorial Medical Library, Hammond IN. 219-932-2300

Gimbel, Christa, *Coordr,* Heritage Hills Area Library Services Authority, IN. 812-944-8464

Gimmi, Robert, *Cat,* Shippensburg State College, Ezra Lehman Memorial Library, Shippensburg PA. 717-532-1463

Ginalski, Sister Marianna, *Cat,* Marywood College Library, Scranton PA. 717-343-6521, Ext 289

Gindin, Susan E, *Librn,* E I Du Pont De Nemours & Co, Inc (Legal Dept Library), Wilmington DE. 302-774-1000

Ginger, Ann Fagan, *Dir,* Meiklejohn Civil Liberties Institute Library, Berkeley CA. 415-848-0599

Gingras, Yolande, *Librn,* Centre D'etude Et De Cooperation Internationale Bibliotheque, Montreal PQ. 514-735-3618

Gingrich, Mary J, *Circ,* Saginaw Valley State College Library & Learning Resources Center, University Center MI. 517-790-4237

Ginn, Bess, *Per,* Agnes Scott College, McCain Library, Decatur GA. 404-373-2571, Ext 220

Ginn, Christine M, *Librn,* Dow Badische Co Library, Williamsburg VA. 804-887-6335

Ginn, Louise, *Librn,* Trimble County Library, Bedford KY. 502-255-7362

Ginn, Marjorie, *Acq,* Mayo Foundation (Medical Library), Rochester MN. 507-284-2061

Ginnis, Carla, *Acq,* Battelle-Seattle Research Center, Library Services, Seattle WA. 206-525-3130

Ginsburg, Mary Lou, *Ref,* Abington Free Library, Abington PA. 215-885-5180

Ginter, Charles, *Dir,* Indianola Public Library, Indianola IA. 515-961-2162

Ginter, Lucia, *Asst Librn,* Levi E Coe Library, Middlefield CT. 203-349-3857

Gioffre, Betty Jo, *Librn,* Huron Public Library, Huron OH. 419-433-5009

Gioia, Diane, *ILL,* North Country Community College, Learning Resource Center, Saranac Lake NY. 518-891-2915, Ext 222

Gionfriddo, Jacqueline, *Librn,* Saint Joseph's Hospital, Jerome Medical Library, Saint Paul MN. 612-291-3193

Gionfriddo, Jan, *Pub Servs,* Boston College Libraries (Law Library), Chestnut Hill MA. 617-969-0100, Ext 4405

Giop, John, *Librn,* Butte Vocational Technical Center Library, Butte MT. 406-792-4256

Giordano, Frederick, *Librn,* New York Public Library (Allerton), New York NY. 212-881-4240

Giordano, Joan, *Acq,* Bloomfield College Library, Bloomfield NJ. 201-748-9000, Ext 281

Giordano, Joan, *Librn,* Westchester County Medical Center, Health Sciences Library, Valhalla NY. 914-347-7033

Giosia, Pat, *Librn,* Mount Ephraim Public Library, Mount Ephraim NJ. 609-931-6606

Giovanoni, Rita, *Reader Serv,* West Bridgewater Public Library, West Bridgewater MA. 617-583-2067

Gipson, Wanda Lee, *Librn,* Tulare County Library System (Woodlake Branch), Woodlake CA. 209-564-8424

Giral, Angela, *Librn,* Harvard University Library (Frances L Loeb Library), Cambridge MA. 617-495-2574

Giralico, John A, *Dir,* Elting Memorial Library, New Paltz NY. 914-255-5030

Girard, Louise, *Tech Serv,* University of Toronto Libraries (University of Saint Michael's College), Toronto ON. 416-921-3151

Girard, Renee, *Prof,* CEGEP Francois-Xavier Garneau, Techniques de la Documentation, PQ. 418-688-8310, Ext 290

Girard, Roland, *Dept Head,* CEGEP de Trois-Rivieres, Technologie de la Documentation, PQ. 819-376-1721, Ext 274

Girotti, Mary M, *Librn,* City Library (Liberty), Springfield MA. 413-732-1033

Giroux, Loretta, *Asst Dir,* Notre Dame College Library, Manchester NH. 603-669-4298, Ext 20

Girshick, David, *Cat,* Montana Historical Society Library & Archives, Helena MT. 406-449-2681

Gishler, J, *Soc Sci,* Calgary Public Library, Calgary AB. 403-268-2880

Gisselquist, Borghild, *Librn,* Story City Public Library, Story City IA. 515-733-2685

Gisselquist, Kathleen, *Media & Bkmobile Coordr,* Washington County Library, Lake Elmo MN. 612-777-8143

Gitchell, Penny, *Asst Librn,* Nickerson City Library, Nickerson KS. 316-422-3361

Githens, Elizabeth, *Dir,* Barrington Public Library, Barrington NJ. 609-546-9666

Gitisetan, D Darrin, *Cat,* Clarkson College of Technology, Harriet Call Burnap Memorial Library, Potsdam NY. 315-268-6645

Gitner, Fred J, *Librn,* French Institute-Alliance Francaise Library, New York NY. 212-355-6100

Gittelsohn, I Marc, *Librn,* University of California, San Diego (Cluster Undergraduate), La Jolla CA. 714-452-3065

Gittings, Dan, *Librn,* National Marine Fisheries Service, Southwest Fisheries Center Library, La Jolla CA. 714-453-2820, Ext 243

Gittings, Jeanne, *Librn,* Lutheran Hospital, Medical Staff & School for Nurses Library, Moline IL. 309-797-7912

Gittleman, Helen, *ILL, Ad & Ref,* Baldwin Public Library, Baldwin NY. 516-223-6228

Gittleman, Jerome, *Dir,* Sullivan County Community College, Hermann Memorial Library, Loch Sheldrake NY. 914-434-5750, Ext 223

Gittlen, Betty, *Librn,* Birmingham Temple Library, Farmington MI. 313-477-0177

Giuffrida, Irene, *Librn,* Aetna Life & Casualty (Engineering Research & Development Library) Hartford CT. 203-273-2406

Giuliano, Lillian C, *Dir,* Marlborough Public Library, Marlborough MA. 617-485-0494

Giusti, Mildred T, *Ref & Reader Adv,* Providence Public Library, Providence RI. 401-521-7722

Giustino, Emily, *Med Librn,* Memorial Hospital Medical Center, Medical Library, Long Beach CA. 213-595-3841

Given, Elinor, *Supvr,* Elgin County Public Library (Aylmer Branch), Aylmer ON. 519-633-0815

Givens, Beth, *Coordr Libr Servs & On-Line Servs,* Montana State Library, Helena MT. 406-449-3004

Givens, Marjorie, *Librn,* Polk Public Museum Library, Lakeland FL. 813-688-7744

Givens, Sibyl, *Librn,* Butler County Library, Morgantown KY. 502-526-4722

Gjelstad, Alice, *Librn,* Kalama Public Library, Kalama WA. 206-673-3060

Gjettum, Pamela, *Dir,* Exeter Public Library, Exeter NH. 603-772-3101

Glad, Beverly J, *Dir,* Salomon Brothers Library, New York NY. 212-747-7932, 747-6146

Gladhill, A Paul, *Rare Bks,* Manhattan College, Cardinal Hayes Library, Bronx NY. 212-548-1400, Ext 366 & 367

Gladieus, Mary Beth, *Librn,* Cardinal Glennon College Library, Saint Louis MO. 314-644-0728

Gladieux, Patricia, *Ch,* Rossford Public Library, Rossford OH. 419-666-0924

Gladish, Christine, *ILL,* University of Southern California, Edward L Doheny Memorial Library, Los Angeles CA. 213-743-6050

Gladish, Mary Louise, *On-Line Servs,* Vanderbilt University Medical Center Library, Nashville TN. 615-322-2292

Gladish, Wayne, *Acq,* University of Southern California, Edward L Doheny Memorial Library, Los Angeles CA. 213-743-6050

Glancy, Jean, *Dir,* Lovington Township Public Library, Lovington IL. 217-873-4468

Glannon, Helen, *Ad,* Bryant Library, Roslyn NY. 516-621-2240

Glasco, Ingrid, *ILL,* University of Pittsburgh, Hillman Library, Pittsburgh PA. 412-624-4400

Glascock, Mary A, *Librn,* Salvation Army Education Department (Archive & Research Center), New York NY. 212-620-4392

Glascoff, Elisabeth, *Doc,* Governors State University, University Library, Park Forest South IL. 312-534-5000, Ext 2231

Glaser, June L, *Librn,* Eastman Dental Center, Basil G Bibby Library, Rochester NY. 716-275-5010

Glasgow, Jean, *Spec Coll,* Texas Woman's University, Bralley Memorial Library, Denton TX. 817-566-6415

Glasgow, Marion, *Librn,* United States Public Health Service Hospital, Medical Library, Boston MA. 617-782-3400, Ext 235

Glasgow, Mrs John, *Librn,* Southwest Arkansas Regional Library (DeQueen Branch), DeQueen AR. 501-777-4564

Glaski, Vlasta, *Asst Librn & Sub,* Colby Public Library, Colby WI. 715-223-2000

Glass, Catherine, *Cat,* Millersville State College, Helen A Ganser Library, Millersville PA. 717-872-5411, Ext 341

Glass, Fred, *Asst Librn,* Pacific Telephone Company Library, San Francisco CA. 415-542-2896

Glass, Gertrude, *Bibliog Instr,* State University Agricultural & Technical College at Farmingdale, Thomas D Greenley Library, Farmingdale NY. 516-420-2011, 420-2012

Glass, Robert E, *Cat & Rare Bks,* Centre College of Kentucky, Grace Doherty Library, Danville KY. 606-236-5211, Ext 237

Glass, Velvet, *Librn,* Baker & Botts Law Library, Houston TX. 713-229-1412

Glasser, Dorothy, *Librn,* Houston Public Library (Texas & Local History), Houston TX. 713-224-5441

Glasser, Robin, *Librn,* Congregation Beth Yeshurun, Cantor Rubin Kaplan Memorial Library, Houston TX. 713-666-1884

Glassman, Jerome, *Pres,* Mitchell Museum Library, Mount Vernon IL. 618-242-1236

Glassmeyer, Anita T, *Media,* University of Arizona Library (Arizona Health Sciences Center Library), Tucson AZ. 602-626-6121

Glassmeyer, Mrs Herb, *Asst Librn,* Moore County Public Library, Lynchburg TN. 615-759-7285

Glasson, Mabel E, *Librn,* Wheeler Memorial Library, Orange MA. 617-544-2295

Glatfelter, Charles H, *Dir,* Adams County Historical Society Library, Gettysburg PA. 717-334-4723

Glatt, Carol R, *Librn,* Council of Jewish Federations Library, New York NY. 212-751-1311

Glatthaar, Nancy, *Ref,* Mount Vernon Public Library, Mount Vernon IL. 618-242-6322

Glaub, Alvin F, *Dir,* Illinois Prairie District Public Library, Metamora IL. 309-367-4594

Glauber, Leni, *Ad & Ref,* Harrison Public Library, Harrison NY. 914-835-0324

Glauner, Mary M, *Ad,* Columbia Heights Public Library, Columbia Heights MN. 612-788-3924

Glaus, Irene, *Assoc Dir,* Tennessee State University, Martha M Brown - Lois W Daniel Library, Nashville TN. 615-320-3682, 251-1417

Glaviano, John C, *Cat,* Colgate University, Everett Needham Case Library, Hamilton NY. 315-824-1000

Glaze, Evelyn, *Librn,* Saint Louis County Library (Natural Bridge), St Louis MO. 314-382-3116

Glaze, Ruth, *Librn,* Jackson Metropolitan Library (Polkville Library), Morton MS. 601-352-3677

Glazener, Shirley, *Acq,* George Mason University Libraries, Fairfax VA. 703-323-2616

Glazener, Willa, *Librn,* Rob & Bessie Welder Wildlife Foundation Library, Sinton TX. 512-364-2643

Glazer, Aileen, *Librn,* Newcomerstown Public Library, Newcomerstown OH. 614-498-8228

Glazer, Frederic J, *Dir,* West Virginia Library Commission, Science & Cultural Center, Charleston WV. 304-348-2041

Glazer, Sylvia, *Ch,* Milford Public Library, Milford CT. 203-878-7461

Glazier, Joan W, *Chief Librn,* Marine Midland Bank, Research Library, New York NY. 212-797-6473

Gleason, Dorothy, *Circ,* Park Ridge Public Library, Park Ridge IL. 312-825-3123

Gleason, Edith M, *Dir,* Heath Public Library, Heath MA. 413-337-4934, Ext 2

Gleason, Joan, *Cat,* Burlington County Library, Mount Holly NJ. 609-267-9660

Gleason, John, *AV,* Lansing Public Library, Lansing MI. 517-374-4600

Gleason, Joy, *Newsp & Gen Per,* Chicago Public Library (General Information Service Div), Chicago IL. 312-269-2800

Gleason, Judith M, *Librn,* Norton Co Library, Worcester MA. 617-853-1000, Ext 2278

Gleason, Linda, *On-Line Servs,* Memorial Sloan-Kettering Cancer Center, Lee Coombe Memorial Library, New York NY. 212-794-7440

Gleason, Marianne, *Cat,* College of Saint Mary Library, Omaha NE. 402-393-8800, Ext 234, 235

Gleason, Patricia, *Librn,* Chicago Public Library (Lincoln Park), Chicago IL. 312-935-0286

Gleason, Ronald R, *Librn,* Tyler Museum of Art Library, Tyler TX. 214-595-1001

Gleason, Sister Mary Joan, *Faculty Servs & Bibliog Instr,* Nazareth College of Rochester Library, Lorette Wilmot Library, Rochester NY. 716-586-2525, Ext 232

Gleason, Virginia, *Librn,* Saint Paul United Methodist Church Library, Springfield MO. 417-886-4326

Gleason, Virginia, *Ch,* Springfield-Greene County Library, Springfield MO. 417-869-4621

Gleaves, Edwin S, *Dir,* George Peabody College for Teachers, Department of Library Science, TN. 615-327-8037

Gleeson, Margot U, *Ad,* Genealogical Society of Pennsylvania Library, Philadelphia PA. 215-545-0391

Glein, Marilyn, *ILL,* Alexandria Public Library, Alexandria MN. 612-763-4640

Glendy, Stella B, *Librn,* Lewis-Gale Hospital, Inc, Medical Library, Salem VA. 703-989-4261, Ext 247

Glenister, Peter, *Cat,* Mount Saint Vincent University Library, Halifax NS. 902-443-4450, Ext 120, 121, 125

Glenn, Beatrice, *Ref,* Winnetka Public Library District, Winnetka IL. 312-446-5085

Glenn, Jerry, *Ref,* Ricks College, David O McKay Learning Resources Center, Rexburg ID. 208-356-2351

Glenn, Leila E, *Cat,* University of Miami (Law), Coral Gables FL. 305-284-2230

Glenn, Linda, *Librn,* First Plymouth Congregational Church Library, Englewood CO. 303-789-0535

Glenn, Luci, *Commun Servs,* New City Free Library, New City NY. 914-634-4997

Glenn, Margaret, *Tech Serv & Acq,* Oakville Public Library, Oakville ON. 416-845-3405

Glenn, Suzanne, *Br Coordr,* Camden County Free Library, Voorhees NJ. 609-772-1636

Glennon, Irene, *Instr,* United States Department of Agriculture Graduate School, Certificate Program for Library Technicians, DC. 202-447-5885

Glessner, Mary-Louise, *Librn,* Narberth Community Library, Narberth PA. 215-664-2878

Glick, Jackie, *ILL,* The Medical College of Wisconsin, Inc, Todd Wehr Library, Milwaukee WI. 414-257-8323

Glick, Ruth I, *Librn,* Huntington Hospital, Medical Library, Huntington NY. 516-351-2283

Glickman, Linda S, *Librn,* System Planning Corp, Research Library, Arlington VA. 703-841-2878

Glidden, Benjaman C, *Dir,* United States Air Force Academy Library, United States Air Force Academy CO. 303-472-2590

Glidden, Irene B, *Librn,* Eldredge Public Library, Chatham MA. 617-945-0274

Glindining, Robin, *Librn,* Dodge County Library Service (Lowell Public), Lowell WI. 414-927-3371

Glines, Elsa, *Acq,* California State University, Hayward Library, Hayward CA. 415-881-3664

Glinka, John L, *Assoc Deans,* University of Kansas Libraries, Watson Memorial Library, Lawrence KS. 913-864-3601

Globus, Sheila, *Librn,* Molson Breweries of Canada Ltd, Research & Development Dept, Information Center, Montreal PQ. 514-527-5151, Ext 347

Glock, Diane C, *Cat,* General Electric Co (Main Library), Schenectady NY. 518-385-2117

Glock, Jennie, *Librn,* Saint Mary's Hospital, Medical Library, West Palm Beach FL. 305-844-6300, Ext 286

Glodek, C J, *Chief Librn,* Michigan Cancer Foundation Research Library, Detroit MI. 313-833-0710, Ext 239

Glodkowski, Susan, *Ad & Ref,* Grande Prairie Public Library District, Hazel Crest IL. 312-798-5563

Gloeckner, Paul B, *Chief Librn,* Paul, Weiss, Rifkind, Wharton & Garrison Library, New York NY. 212-644-8235

Gloin, Valerie, *Supvr,* Middlesex County Library (Komoka Branch), Komoka ON. 519-438-8368

Glosson, Virginia, *Dir,* King City Public Library, King City CA. 408-385-3677

Glover, Carol, *Main Libr Supvr,* Rockwell International, Anaheim Information Center, Anaheim CA. 714-632-3621

Glover, Carol, *Librn,* Tatum Community Library, Tatum NM. 505-398-4822

Glover, Charlotte L, *Librn,* Carrier Corp, Elliott Company Engineering Library, Jeannette PA. 412-527-2811, Ext 557

Glover, Gwen, *Librn,* Central Carolina Technical Institute, Learning Resource Center, Sanford NC. 919-775-5401, Ext 244

Glover, Jane E, *Librn,* Knoxville Public Library, Knoxville PA. 814-326-4448

Glover, Linda, *Librn,* Ideal Basic Industries, Cement Division Research Library, Fort Collins CO. 303-482-5600

Glover, Nancy, *Cat,* Charles A Cannon Memorial Library, Concord NC. 704-788-3167

Glover, Peggy, *Ad & YA,* Free Library of Philadelphia, Philadelphia PA. 215-686-5322

Glowacka, Maria T, *Librn,* New York State Office of Mental Retardation & Developmental Disabilities, Medical Library, West Seneca NY. 716-674-6300, Ext 425

Glowacki, Jeanne, *Asst Librn,* Justice Public Library District, Justice IL. 312-496-1790

Glowacki, Sheila, *Ref,* Coshocton Public Library, Coshocton OH. 614-622-0956

Glowcheski, Mrs Fred, *Dir,* Galesville Public Library, Galesville WI. 608-582-2552

Glowgowski, Mary Ruth, *On-Line Servs,* State University College at Buffalo, Edward H Butler Library, Buffalo NY. 716-878-6302

Gluck, Marc, *Bkmobile Coordr,* Public Library of Annapolis & Anne Arundel County Inc, Annapolis MD. 301-224-7371

Glueckert, John P, *Libr Use Instr,* University of Southern California (School of Dentistry), Los Angeles CA. 312-743-2884, 743-2870

Glueckert, John P, *On-line Ref Servs,* University of Southern California (School of Dentistry), Los Angeles CA. 312-743-2884, 743-2870

Glunz, Diana L, *Ref,* University of Southern California (Norris Medical Library), Los Angeles CA. 213-226-2231

Glushakow, Mildred, *Dir,* Spring Garden College Library, Philadelphia PA. 215-242-3700

Gluz, Janet, *Admin Secy,* Film Cooperative of Connecticut, Inc, CT. 203-888-5558

Glynn, Camilla, *Bibliog Instr,* Salem State College Library, Salem MA. 617-745-0556, Ext 474, 475

Glynn, Georgia R, *Librn,* Pontiac Public Library, Pontiac IL. 815-844-7229

Glynn, Joann, *Dir,* Tripp Memorial Library, Prairie du Sac WI. 608-643-8318

Gmeiner, Timothy, *Music,* Belmont College, Williams Library, Nashville TN. 615-383-7001, Ext 253

Gnat, Jean, *Tech Serv,* Indiana University-Purdue University at Indianapolis, University Library, Indianapolis IN. 317-264-4101

Gnat, Raymond E, *Dir,* Indianapolis-Marion County Public Library, Indianapolis IN. 317-635-5662

Gniechwicz, Chrisann, *Librn,* Marin County Free Library (Bolinas Branch), Bolinas CA. 415-868-1171

Gniechwicz, Chrisann, *Librn,* Marin County Free Library (Stinson Beach Branch), Stinson Beach CA. 415-868-0252

Gnnn, June, *Librn,* Beaumont Public Library (Central Park), Beaumont TX. 713-838-0784

Gnoza, Edmond, *Humanities,* Portland State University, Branford Price Millar Library, Portland OR. 503-229-4424

Go, Ivonne K, *Librn,* Governor Bacon Health Center, School Library, Delaware City DE. 302-834-9201, Ext 229

Goad, Kimberly R, *Librn,* Carlton Public Library, Carlton MN. 218-384-4229

Gobber, Carol, *Librn,* Cook Public Library, Cook NE. 402-864-5302

Gobble, Rachael C, *Ch & Br Coordr,* Brunswick-Greensville Regional Library, Lawrenceville VA. 804-848-2418

Gobble, Rachael C, *Librn,* Brunswick-Greensville Regional Library (William E Richardson Jr Memorial Library), Emporia VA. 804-634-2539

Gobble, Richard L, *Dir,* Fort Lewis College Library, Durango CO. 303-247-7738

Gobel, Rosalyn K, *Librn,* Cornelius Public Library, Cornelius OR. 503-357-9112

Goble, Bonnie C McGill, *Chief Librn,* Murrysville Community Library, Murrysville PA. 412-327-1102

Gocek, Matilda A, *Dir,* Suffern Free Library, Suffern NY. 914-357-1237

Gocken, Colleen, *Tech Serv,* Waubonsee Community College, Learning Resources Center, Sugar Grove IL. 312-466-4811, Ext 303

Godbout, Luce, *Librn,* Bibliotheque Publique, Asbestos PQ. 819-879-4363

Goddard, Joan, *Librn,* San Jose Public Library (Evergreen), San Jose CA. 408-238-4433

Goddard, John, *Asst Cat,* University of Tennessee at Martin, Paul Meek Library, Martin TN. 901-587-7060

Goddard, Mrs B Frank, *Dir,* Elberon Library, Elberon NJ. 201-229-9409

Goddard, Rosalind, *Librn,* Los Angeles Public Library System (Robertson), Los Angeles CA. 213-837-1239

Goddard, Susan, *Librn,* University of Toronto Libraries (Faculty of Dentistry), Toronto ON. 416-978-2796

Goderwis, Cherie, *Librn,* Rutland Hospital Health Information Center, Rutland VT. 802-775-7111

Godfrey, Eleanor, *Media,* Union Theological Seminary in Virginia Library, Richmond VA. 804-355-0671, Ext 311

Godfrey, Florence, *Ad,* Cherry Hill Free Public Library, Cherry Hill NJ. 609-667-0300

Godfrey, Georgiana, *Media,* Maine Maritime Academy, Nutting Memorial Library, Castine ME. 207-326-4311, Ext 238

Godfrey, Lois E, *Asst Head Librn,* Los Alamos Scientific Laboratory Libraries, Library Services Group, Los Alamos NM. 505-667-4448

Godfrey, Margaret, *Librn,* Scranton Public Library (Hyde Park), Scranton PA. 717-347-5514

Godfrey, Stuart, *AV,* Salem College, Benedum Learning Resources Center, Salem WV. 304-782-5238

Godin, Roger A, *Dir,* United States Hockey Hall of Fame Library, Eveleth MN. 218-749-5167

Godin, Sally, *Librn,* Kent County Library System (East Grand Rapids), East Grand Rapids MI. 616-363-2855

Godlewski, Susan Glover, *Spec Coll,* Providence Public Library, Providence RI. 401-521-7722

Godley, Larry B, *Adminr,* Oklahoma State Department of Education, Instructional Media, Oklahoma City OK. 405-521-3103

Godog, Luis Anthony, *Librn,* Puerto Rican Family Institute, Maria Pintado Rahn Library, New York NY. 212-924-6320

Godown, Ruth E, *Librn,* Milford Public Library, Milford NJ. 201-995-4072

Godoy, Alicia, *Foreign Lang,* Miami-Dade Public Library System, Miami FL. 305-579-5001

Godsey, Jim, *Dir,* Huntington City Township Public Library, Huntington IN. 219-356-0824

Godsmark, Linda, *Acq,* Occidental Research Corp Library, Irvine CA. 714-957-7450

Goduti, Louise, *Ch, Acq & Cat,* Fairfield Public Library, Fairfield NJ. 201-227-3575

Godwin, Ermie, *Actg Librn,* Harnett County Library (Erwin Public), Erwin NC. 919-897-7485

Godwin, Mary Jo P, *Dir,* Edgecombe County Memorial Library, Tarboro NC. 919-823-1141

Goebel, Florence, *Librn,* Minnesota Valley Regional Library (Arlington), Mankato MN. 612-964-2490

Goebel, Rosemary, *Librn,* Ovid Public Library, Ovid MI. 517-834-5800

Goecke, Wanda, *Librn,* United States Air Force (Holloman Air Force Base Library), Holloman AFB NM. 505-479-6266, Ext 3939

Goeckler, Jane, *Librn,* Silver Lake Library, Silver Lake KS. 913-582-5141

Goeddeke, Sister Ann Fernard, *Coordr,* Barry College, Monsignor William Barry Memorial Library, Miami Shores FL. 305-758-3392, Ext 263

Goehlert, Robert, *Econ, Forensic Sci & Polit Sci,* Indiana University at Bloomington, University Libraries, Bloomington IN. 812-337-3403

Goehner, Donna, *Acq,* Western Illinois University Libraries, Macomb IL. 309-298-2411

Goehring, Sue, *Circ,* Luling Public Library, Luling TX. 512-875-2813

Goekermann, Judy, *Librn,* Legion Memorial Library, Mellen WI. 715-274-8331

Goerig, Janet, *Dir Libr Serv,* Saint Vincent's Medical Center, Daniel T Banks Health Science Library, Bridgeport CT. 203-576-5336

Goering, Jan, *Bus,* Wichita State University, Library & Media Resources Center, Wichita KS. 316-689-3586

Goerler, Raimund, *Univ Archivist,* Ohio State University Libraries (William Oxley Thompson Memorial Library), Columbus OH. 614-422-6151

Goers, Janet, *Ch,* Clinton Public Library, Clinton IA. 319-242-8441

Goertzen, Norma S, *Dir,* North Park College & Theological Seminary (Mellander Library), Chicago IL. 312-583-2700, Ext 264 & 288

Goerz, Richard, *Media,* Northwestern Michigan College, Mark Osterlin Library, Traverse City MI. 616-946-5650, Ext 541

Goethert, Gay D, *Supvr,* ARO Inc, Arnold Engineering Development Center Technical Library, Arnold AFS TN. 615-455-2611, Ext 431

Goethert, Gay D, *Librn,* United States Air Force (Arnold Engineering Development Center Library), Arnold AFS TN. 615-455-2611

Goetz, Arthur H, *Dir,* Wicomico County Free Library, Salisbury MD. 301-749-5171

Goetz, Ruth, *Ch,* Middle Island Public Library, Middle Island NY. 516-924-4160

Goetze, P R, *Info Spec,* Intertechnology-Solar Corp Library, Warrenton VA. 703-347-7900

Goff, Betty, *ILL, Ref & Bibliog Instr,* Mesa College, Learning Resource Services, Lowell Heiny Library, Grand Junction CO. 303-248-1436

Goff, Betty J, *Librn,* Forked Deer Regional Library Center, Trimble TN. 901-297-5810

Goff, Carolyn B, *Dir,* B B Comer Memorial Library, Sylacauga AL. 205-249-0961

Goff, Jean, *Librn,* Jackson-George Regional Library System (East Central Public), Hurley MS. 601-588-6263

Goff, Karen, *Ref,* West Virginia Library Commission, Science & Cultural Center, Charleston WV. 304-348-2041

Goff, Marilyn, *Orientation,* Incarnate Word College, Saint Pius X Library, San Antonio TX. 512-828-1261, Ext 215

Goff, Sister Dorothy, *Librn,* Lutheran Deaconess Community Library, Gladwyne PA. 215-642-8838

Goff, William J, *Librn,* University of California, San Diego (Scripps Institution of Oceanography), La Jolla CA. 714-452-3274

Goffman, William, *Prof,* Case Western Reserve University, School of Library Science, OH. 216-368-3500

Goforth, Jean, *Tech Serv,* Lee College Library, Cleveland TN. 615-472-2111, Ext 329

Goggin, Margaret, *Instr,* University of Denver, Graduate School of Librarianship and Information Management, CO. 303-753-2557

Goguen, Fernande, *Pub Serv,* Universite De Moncton, Bibliotheque Champlain, Moncton NB. 506-858-4012

Goheen, Patricia, *Pub Servs,* Florida State University, Robert Manning Strozier Library, Tallahassee FL. 904-644-5211

Gohlke, Ramon, *Dir,* Westfield Public Library, Ethel Everhard Memorial Library, Westfield WI. 608-296-2544

Gohmann, Myron, *Dir,* Kenrick Seminary, Charles L Souvay Memorial Library, Saint Louis MO. 314-961-4320, Ext 28,29

Goin, Sanford, *Bibliog Instr,* Mercy College Libraries, Dobbs Ferry NY. 914-693-4500, Ext 260

Going, Patricia A, *Librn,* Broken Bow Delphian Library, Broken Bow OK. 405-584-2815

Goins, Doris, *Asst Dir,* Plymouth Public Library, Plymouth IN. 219-936-2324

Golanka, Mary, *Instr,* Highline Community College Library, Library Technician Program, WA. 206-878-3710, Ext 233

Gold, A M, *Librn,* Oakland Public Library (Temescal), Oakland CA. 415-652-2504

Gold, Betty, *Librn,* National Council on Alcoholism, Inc, Yvelin Gardner Alcoholism Library, New York NY. 212-986-4433

Gold, Ethel, *Ref, On-Line Servs & Bibliog Instr,* New York Institute of Technology Library, Old Westbury NY. 516-686-7657, 686-7658

Gold, Gerald, *Bus Mgr,* New York Public Library, Astor, Lenox & Tilden Foundations Library, New York NY. 212-790-6262

Gold, Leonard, *Chief,* New York Public Library (Jewish), New York NY. 212-790-6347

Gold, Sandra S, *Librn,* Keck, Mahin & Cate Library, Chicago IL. 312-876-3575

Goldasser, Meg, *Librn,* Josephine County Library System (Illinois Valley), Cave Junction OR. 503-592-4101

Goldberg, A, *Acq,* Charles River Associates Library, Boston MA. 617-266-0500

Goldberg, Elizabeth D, *Librn,* Overseas Private Investment Corporation Library, Washington DC. 202-632-0146

Goldberg, Ettie, *Cat,* Westwood Free Public Library, Westwood NJ. 201-664-0583

Goldberg, Joan E, *Librn,* Betz Laboratories, Inc Library, Trevose PA. 215-355-3300, Ext 507

Goldberg, Kenneth P, *Pub Servs & Bibliog Instr,* Cleveland Institute of Art, Jessica Gund Memorial Library, Cleveland OH. 216-421-4322, Ext 30

Goldberg, Louise, *Ref & Rare Bks,* University of Rochester (Sibley Music Library), Rochester NY. 716-275-3018

Goldberg, R L, *Dir,* William Paterson College of New Jersey, Sarah Byrd Askew Library, Wayne NJ. 201-595-2113

Goldberg, Rhoda L, *Asst Dir,* Harris County Public Library, Houston TX. 713-221-5350

Goldberg, Rochelle, *Head Readers' Servs,* Art Institute of Chicago (Art School Library), Chicago IL. 312-443-3748

Goldberg, Ronnie, *On-Line Servs,* State University of New York at Binghamton Library, Binghamton NY. 607-798-2194

Goldberg, Susan, *Ad & YA,* Tucson Public Library, Tucson AZ. 602-791-4391

Goldberg, Thresa, *Librn,* Toledo-Lucas County Public Library (Sanger), Toledo OH. 419-255-7055

Goldblatt, Margaret, *Ser,* Washington University Libraries (Freund Law Library), Saint Louis MO. 314-889-6459

Goldcamp, Alice, *Dir of Educ,* Butler Institute of American Art Library, Youngstown OH. 216-743-1711

Golden, Beatrice, *Circ,* Morris College, Pinson Memorial Library, Sumter SC. 803-775-9371, Ext 216

Golden, Bruce G, *Dir,* Edmonds Community College Library-Media Center, Lynnwood WA. 206-771-1529

Golden, Fay Ann, *Dir,* Liverpool Public Library, Liverpool NY. 315-457-0310

Golden, Helene, *Ch,* Bibliotheque Municipale Des Sources, Sources Public Library, Roxboro PQ. 514-684-8247, 684-8260

Golden, Judith A, *Dir,* Houston County Public Library System, Perry GA. 912-987-3050

Golden, Judy, *Dir,* Clark County Library, Arkadelphia AR. 501-246-2271

Golden, Lois, *ILL,* Wake Forest University (Bowman Gray School of Medicine Library), Winston-Salem NC. 919-727-4691

Golden, Mary K, *ILL,* Ector County Library, Odessa TX. 915-332-0633

Golden, Ruth, *Librn,* Ponca Public Library, Ponca NE. 402-755-2739

Golden, Urla, *Dir,* De Kalb Public Library, Haish Memorial Building, De Kalb IL. 815-756-4431

Goldfarb, Elizabeth, *Librn,* New York Public Library (West New Brighton), New York NY. 212-442-1416

Goldfarb, Jacqueline, *Doc,* University of Virginia (Law Library), Charlottesville VA. 804-924-3384

Goldhawk, Mrs M, *Librn,* Lambton County Library (Warwick), Watford ON. 519-876-5533

Goldhor, Herbert, *Prof,* University of Illinois, Graduate School of Library Science, IL. 217-333-3280

Goldie, Mary, *Librn,* Library Association of Portland (Montavilla), Portland OR. 503-253-8176

Goldin, Lillian, *Commun Servs,* North Shore Community College, Learning Resource Center, Beverly MA. 617-927-4850, Ext 195, 199, 237

Goldman, Irene, *On-Line Servs,* Connecticut General Life Insurance Co Library, Bloomfield CT. 203-726-4239, 726-4327

Goldman, Janet, *On-Line Servs,* United States Navy (Naval Training Equipment Center Technical Information Center), Orlando FL. 305-646-4797

Goldman, Linda, *Librn,* Burlington County Library (Cinnaminson Branch), Cinnaminson NJ. 609-829-9340

Goldman, Maurice S, *Dir,* Willingboro Public Library, Willingboro NJ. 609-877-6668

Goldman, Paul E, *Dir,* Kankakee Community College, Learning Resource Center, Kankakee IL. 815-933-0260

Goldman, Phyllis, *Coordr Adult Educ & Ext Servs,* North York Public Library, Willowdale ON. 416-494-6838

Goldman, Terry, *Media,* University of Richmond, Boatwright Memorial Library, Richmond VA. 804-285-6452

Goldmann, Jack B, *Tech Serv & Cat,* Chabot College, Learning Resource Center, Hayward CA. 415-786-6762

Goldner, Matthew, *Cat,* Asbury Theological Seminary, B L Fisher Library, Wilmore KY. 606-858-3581, Ext 246

Goldschmid, Johanna, *Rare Bks & Spec Coll,* San Francisco Public Library, San Francisco CA. 415-558-4235

Goldschmidt, Eric N, *Dir,* Endo Laboratories, Inc Library, Garden City NY. 516-832-2002

Goldsmith, Marina F, *Librn,* Kawecki Berylco Industries, Inc Library, Metallurgical Research & Development Library, Reading PA. 215-921-5262

Goldsmith, Mrs William, *Librn,* Agudas Achim Synagogue, Stein Memorial Library, Columbus OH. 614-237-2747

Goldson, Doris, *Acq,* Columbia College Library, Columbia CA. 209-532-3141, Ext 228

Goldstaub, Curt, *Cat,* Kutztown State College, Rohrbach Library, Kutztown PA. 215-683-4480

Goldstein, Cynthia, *Tech Serv,* Tulane University of Louisiana (Matas Medical Library), New Orleans LA. 504-588-5155

Goldstein, Doris, *Librn,* Kennedy Institute (Center for Bioethics Library), Washington DC. 202-625-0100

Goldstein, Doris R, *Librn,* Wixom Public Library, Wixom MI. 313-624-2512

Goldstein, Harold, *Dean,* Florida State University, School of Library Science, FL. 904-644-5775

Goldstein, Julia S, *Librn,* Florida Department of Labor & Employment Security, Research Library, Tallahassee FL. 488-4295 & 488-4332

Goldstein, Larry, *Spec Coll,* Leeward Community College Library, Pearl City HI. 808-455-0210

Goldstein, Linda, *Ref,* Chappaqua Central School District Public Library, Chappaqua Library, Chappaqua NY. 914-238-4779

Goldstein, M, *German, Judaic Studies, Portuguese, Spanish & Philos,* State University of New York at Buffalo, University Libraries, Buffalo NY. 716-636-2965

Goldstein, Pauline, *Acq,* Carnegie-Mellon University, Hunt Library, Pittsburgh PA. 412-578-2446, 578-2447

Goldstein, Rachael, *Librn,* Columbia University (Health Sciences Library), New York NY. 212-694-3688

Goldstein, Roger, *Asst Librn,* Creare Engineering Research Library, Hanover NH. 603-643-3800

Goldstein, S, *Bibliog Instr,* Mount Royal College Library, Calgary AB. 403-246-6111

Goldstein, Samuel, *Adjunct Asst Prof,* Simmons College, Graduate School of Library & Information Science, MA. 617-738-2225

Goldstein, Selma, *Librn,* Naples Public Library, Naples ME. 207-693-6841

Goldstein, Wendy, *Doc,* Northeastern Illinois University Library, Chicago IL. 312-583-4050, Ext 469

Goldthwaite, Leila, *Br Librn,* Newburgh Free Library, Newburgh NY. 914-561-1836

Goldthwaite, Leila, *Librn,* Newburgh Free Library (West Street), Newburgh NY. 914-561-9110

Goldwyn, A J, *Prof,* Case Western Reserve University, School of Library Science, OH. 216-368-3500

Goldzweig, Arthur, *Ref,* Hunter College of the City University of New York Library, New York NY. 212-570-5511

Goldzwig, Jeanne B, *Librn,* Temple Israel, Rabbi Louis Witt Memorial Library, Dayton OH. 513-277-6070

Gole, Lydia, *Cat,* Ladycliff College, Msgr C Hugo Doyle Library, Highland Falls NY. 914-446-4747, Ext 21

Goleb, Lynn, *Asst Librn,* Federal Reserve Bank of Cleveland Research Library, Cleveland OH. 216-241-2800, Ext 288

Golembiewski, Terri, *Ref,* Chicago Sun-Times, Editorial Library, Chicago IL. 312-321-2594

Goley, Elaine, *Juvenile Spec,* Houston Public Library, Houston TX. 713-224-5441

Golgart, Patricia, *ILL,* New Castle Public Library, New Castle PA. 412-658-6659

Goliath, Jacquie, *Dir,* Wapiti Regional Library, Prince Albert SK. 306-764-0712

Gollata, James A, *Dir,* Mount Senario College Library, Ladysmith WI. 715-532-5511, Ext 259

Golliff, Ruth, *Librn,* Lima Public Library (Spencerville Branch), Spencerville OH. 419-228-5113

Gollop, Claudia J, *In Charge,* Earl G Graves Publishing Co, Minority Business Information Institute, New York NY. 212-889-8220

Gollub, George A, *Librn,* Northampton County Court, Law Library, Easton PA. 215-253-4111, Ext 336

Golob, Mimi, *Information Scientist,* Avon Products, Inc Library, Suffern NY. 914-357-2000

Golosh, Marilyn, *Acq,* Greenfield Community College, Library-Learning Resources Center, Greenfield MA. 413-774-3131, Ext 285

Golphin, Sylvania, *Ad,* Florence A Williams Public Library, Saint Croix VI. 809-773-5715

Golter, Robert, *Librn,* Mills College Library, Oakland CA. 415-632-2700, Ext 260

Goltz, Cheryl, *Asst Dir,* Western Plains Library System, Montevideo MN. 612-269-5644

Goltz, Eileen, *Doc,* Laurentian University Library, Bibliotheque de l'Universite Laurentienne, Sudbury ON. 705-675-1151, Ext 251 & 252

Golub, Andrew, *Kresge Ctr for Teaching Resources,* Lesley College Library, Cambridge MA. 617-868-9600, Ext 170, 171

Golub, Melinda, *Pub Servs Dept Asst Librn,* Harvard University Library (Law School Library), Cambridge MA. 617-495-3170

Golumb, Bernard M, *Ad,* Hayward Public Library, Hayward CA. 415-581-2545

Goman, LaVern, *Adjunct Assoc Prof,* University of Puget Sound, School Librarianship Program, WA. 206-756-3391

Goman, Lora, *Librn,* Wayne County Public Library (Doylestown Branch), Doylestown OH. 216-658-4677

Gomes, Libby, *Librn,* Zion Bible Institute Library, East Providence RI. 401-438-2680

Gomes, Lorraine, *Librn,* Colusa County Free Library (Princeton), Princeton CA. 916-439-2235

Gomez, Isidro, *Ch,* Bureau of Libraries, Museums & Archaeological Services (Enid M Baa Library & Archives), Charlotte Amalie VI. 809-774-0630

Gomez, Martin, *Regional Coordr,* San Diego County Library (Region A), San Diego CA. 714-565-5100

Gomez, Osborne L, *Dir,* Florida, State University System, Extension Library, Saint Petersburg FL. 813-893-9120

Gomez, Robert, *AV,* Inter-American University of Puerto Rico, Aguadilla Regional College Branch Library, Ramey AFB PR. 809-890-5118

Gomez, Seida, *Librn,* Chesterfield County Central Library (La Prade), Richmond VA. 804-276-7755

Gomez, Thomas Allen, *Tech Serv,* Wisconsin Conservatory of Music Library, Milwaukee WI. 414-276-4350

Goncar, John, *Supvr, Main Libr,* United Technologies Corp Library, East Hartford CT. 203-727-7120

Gonce, Nancy, *Tech Serv,* University of Maryland Baltimore County Library, Baltimore MD. 301-455-2457

Gong, James G, *Circ,* Seattle-First National Bank Library, Seattle WA. 206-583-4056

Gongloff, Ann, *Librn,* Nanty Glo Public Library, Nanty Glo PA. 814-749-0111

Gongoll, Ward E, *Dir,* De Sales Hall School of Theology Library, Hyattsville MD. 301-559-4022

Gonin, Jean-Paul, *Asst Prof,* University of Montreal, Ecole de Bibliotheconomie, PQ. 514-343-6044

Gonneville, Priscilla R, *Tech Serv, Cat & Ref,* Assumption College Library, Worcester MA. 617-752-5615, Ext 272

Gonsalves, Alfred, *Dir,* Immaculate Heart College Library, Los Angeles CA. 213-462-1301, Ext 271

GONSHOROWSKI

Gonshorowski, Gladys, *In Charge,* Greenbush Public Library, Greenbush MN. 218-782-2218

Gontrum, Barbara, *Exec Librn,* University of Maryland at Baltimore (School of Law Library), Baltimore MD. 301-528-7270

Gonyon, Sister Jeanne M, *Librn,* Carmelite Monastery Library, Barre VT. 802-476-8362

Gonzales, Alice, *Librn,* Aberdeen Public Library, Aberdeen ID. 208-397-4427

Gonzales, Carmen C, *Librn,* Elsa Public Library, Elsa TX. 512-262-3061

Gonzales, Harriette, *Librn,* Aurora Public Library (Northwest), Aurora CO. 303-341-4173

Gonzales, Lydia, *Tech Serv,* Woodbury University Library, Los Angeles CA. 482-8491, Ext 25

Gonzales, Rose, *Puerto Rican Coll,* University of Puerto Rico, Cayey University College Library, Cayey PR. 809-738-2161, Ext 221

Gonzalez, Daniel, *Doc,* University of Puerto Rico, Cayey University College Library, Cayey PR. 809-738-2161, Ext 221

Gonzalez, Daniel, *Music,* University of Puerto Rico, Cayey University College Library, Cayey PR. 809-738-2161, Ext 221

Gonzalez, Emma, *Assoc Prof,* University of Puerto Rico, Graduate School of Librarianship, PR. 809-764-0000, Ext 3522, 3526

Gonzalez, Esther, *Env & Urban,* Florida International University, Tamiami Campus, Athenaeum, Miami FL. 305-552-2461

Gonzalez, Jesus, *Media,* University of Puerto Rico - Bayamon Regional College, Learning Resources Center, Bayamon PR. 809-786-5225

Gonzalez, Julia, *Cat,* University of Tampa, Merl Kelce Library, Tampa FL. 813-253-8861, Ext 385

Gonzalez, Ondina, *Dir,* Berry College, Memorial Library, Mount Berry GA. 404-232-5374, Ext 221, 388

Gonzalez, Rafael, *Media,* Florida International University, North Miami Campus Library, North Miami FL. 305-940-5730

Gonzalez, Victoria, *Librn,* Bergen Pines County Hospital, Medical Library, Paramus NJ. 201-261-9000, Ext 201

Gonzalez-Camacho, Valentin, *Cat,* Inter-American University of Puerto Rico, School of Law Library, Santurce PR. 809-754-7215

Gooch, G Ann, *Asst Dir,* Navarro College, Gaston T Gooch Library, Corsicana TX. 214-874-6501, Ext 257

Gooch, Hope, *Ch,* Greensboro Public Library, Greensboro NC. 373-2474; 373-2471

Gooch, Margaret, *ILL,* Tufts University, Nils Yngve Wessell Library, Medford MA. 617-628-5000, Ext 235

Gooch, Peggy, *Librn,* Park Cities Baptist Church Library, Dallas TX. 214-369-8211

Gooch, Richard E, *Dir,* Birchard Public Library of Sandusky County, Fremont OH. 419-332-1121

Gooch, Rita, *Asst Supervisor,* University of Texas Libraries (Film Library), Austin TX. 512-471-3573

Gooch, Ruth, *Acq,* Culver-Stockton College, Carl Johann Memorial Library, Canton MO. 314-288-5221, Ext 21

Gooch, William D, *Asst Dir,* Texas State Library, Austin TX. 512-475-2166

Good, Julanne, *Ch Lit,* Saint Louis Public Library, Saint Louis MO. 314-241-2288

Good, L, *Assoc Librn,* Queen's University at Kingston, Douglas Library, Kingston ON. 547-5950 (Admin); 547-6992 (Chief Librn)

Good, Linda, *Librn,* American Color & Chemicals Corp, Research & Development Laboratory Library, Lock Haven PA. 717-748-6747

Good, Ruth, *Dir,* Toccoa Falls College, Seby Jones Library, Toccoa Falls GA. 404-886-6831, Ext 229

Good, Ruth, *Area Head,* Winnipeg Public Library (West Kildonan Branch), Winnipeg MB. 204-589-5359

Good, Stella, *Asst Librn,* Lake View Medical Center, Medical & Nursing Library, Danville IL. 217-443-5000, Ext 394

Goodale, Leslie, *Dir,* Children's Memorial Hospital, Joseph Brennemann Library, Chicago IL. 312-649-4000

Goodchild, Eleanor, *Dir Libr Servs,* Los Angeles County Harbor General Hospital, Medical Library, Torrance CA. 213-533-2372

Goode, Allan, *AV,* Oklahoma Department of Libraries, Oklahoma City OK. 405-521-2502

Goode, Frances B, *Ch & YA,* Chesterfield County Central Library, Chesterfield VA. 804-748-1601

Goode, Geneva, *Cat,* Southeast Community College, Learning Resources Center, Cumberland KY. 606-589-2145, Ext 25

Goode, Paul K, *Dir,* Texas A&I University, James C Jernigan Library, Kingsville TX. 512-595-2111

Goode, Ruby, *Asst Librn,* Mahomet Township Public Library, Mahomet IL. 217-586-2611

Goodell, Lela, *Asst Librn,* Hawaiian Mission Children's Society Library, Honolulu HI. 808-531-0481

Goodemote, Rita L, *Assoc Dir,* Schering-Plough Pharmaceutical Research Div, Library Information Center, Bloomfield NJ. 201-743-6000, Ext 781

Gooden, Elizabeth, *Librn,* Long Beach Public Library System (Mark Twain Branch), Long Beach CA. 213-591-7412

Gooden, Gerald L, *Librn,* Biola College & Talbot Theological Seminary, Rosemead Graduate School of Professional Psychology, Rose Memorial Library, La Mirada CA. 213-944-0351, Ext 3255

Goodfellow, Patricia, *Librn,* East York Public Library (Leaside), Toronto ON. 416-425-1044

Goodfellow, William, *Fine Arts & Lit,* Oak Lawn Public Library, Oak Lawn IL. 312-422-4990

Goodger-Hill, Carol, *ILL,* Bozeman Public Library, Bozeman MT. 406-586-2148

Goodgion, Laurel, *Ch,* New Britain Public Library, New Britain CT. 203-224-3155

Goodhand, Shirley, *Librn,* Toronto Sun Publishing Co Library, Toronto ON. 416-868-2257

Goodhartz, Gerald, *Librn & On-Line Servs,* Kaye, Scholer, Fierman, Hays & Handler Law Library, New York NY. 212-759-8400, Ext 312

Goodhope, Jeanie, *YA,* Contra Costa County Library, Pleasant Hill CA. 415-944-3423

Goodhouse, Barbara A, *Librn,* York Research Corp Library, Stamford CT. 203-325-1371

Goodhue, Katherine, *Librn,* Hawaii State Library System (Kailua Branch), Kailua HI. 808-261-4611

Goodier, Kathryn, *Librn,* Sayre Public Library Inc, Sayre PA. 717-888-2256

Goodin, Barbara, *Acq,* Athens State College Library, Athens AL. 205-232-1802, Ext 291

Gooding, Martha C, *Dir,* Saint Joseph State Hospital (Professional Library), Saint Joseph MO. 816-232-8431, Ext 462

Goodlett, Doris, *Ad, On-Line Servs & Bibliog Instr,*Stamford's Public Library, Ferguson Library, Stamford CT. 203-325-4354

Goodman, Anita Sue, *Asst Dir,* Mobile College, J L Bedsole Library, Mobile AL. 205-675-5990

Goodman, Barbara W, *Librn,* Thiele Kaolin Co, Research & Development Library, Sandersville GA. 912-552-2421

Goodman, Bro Dennis, *Asst Dir,* Saint Mary's College of California, Saint Albert Hall Library, Moraga CA. 415-376-4411, Ext 229, 230

Goodman, Clara, *Bkmobile Coordr,* Rowan County Public Library, Morehead KY. 606-784-7137

Goodman, David, *Librn,* Princeton University Library (Chemistry & Biochemistry), Princeton NJ. 609-452-3180

Goodman, Delena, *Dir,* Anderson College (Byrd Memorial Library), Anderson IN. 317-649-9071, Ext 2077

Goodman, Diane L, *Dir,* If Every Fool...Inc, Performing Arts Library, New York NY. 212-964-7240

Goodman, Diane L, *Ser,* State University of New York College, Daniel A Reed Library, Fredonia NY. 716-673-3183

Goodman, Donna, *Ch,* Alva Public Library, Alva OK. 405-327-1833

Goodman, Gwynette, *Circ,* Jefferson Parish Library Division, Metairie LA. 504-834-5850

Goodman, Lewis E, *Librn,* Dayton & Montgomery County Public Library (West Carrollton Branch), West Carrollton OH. 513-859-4011

Goodman, Lois, *Pub Servs,* Rochester Institute of Technology, Wallace Memorial Library, Rochester NY. 716-475-2566

Goodman, Marion, *Librn,* Maryland-National Capital Park & Planning Commission Library, Silver Spring MD. 301-565-7507, 565-7508

Goodman, Mrs Herman, *Librn,* B'nai Zion Temple Library, Shreveport LA. 318-861-2122

Goodmundson, Phyllis, *Librn,* Dutton Public Library, Dutton MT. 406-476-3382

Goodness, Jeanne M, *Librn,* Eastern Maine Vocational Technical Institute Library, Bangor ME. 207-942-5217, Ext 34

Goodpaster, Howard, *Arch & Records,* Kentucky Department of Library & Archives, Frankfort KY. 502-564-7910

Goodpasture, Maenette, *ILL,* University of Oklahoma (Law Library), Norman OK. 405-325-4311

Goodrich, Ann, *Ref & Doc,* Rosary College, Rebecca Crown Library, River Forest IL. 312-366-2490, Ext 305

Goodrich, Jeanne G, *Dir Libr Develop,* Nevada State Library, Carson City NV. 702-885-5130

Goodrich, Jim, *Reader Serv,* State University of New York, College at New Paltz, Sojourner Truth Library, New Paltz NY. 914-257-2204

Goodrich, Klara, *Librn,* Resurrection Hospital, Medical Library, Chicago IL. 312-774-8000, Ext 2512

Goodrich, Mrs Herbert, *Librn,* Plains Public Library, Plains MT. 406-826-3411

Goodrich, Mrs R W, *Dir,* Durand Free Library, Durand WI. 715-672-8730

Goodrick, Edith, *Ch,* South Plainfield Free Public Library, South Plainfield NJ. 201-754-7885

Goodson, Jeanne, *Tech Serv,* Middle Georgia Regional Library, Macon GA. 912-745-5813

Goodson, Steve, *Dir,* Fresno County Department of Education, Instructional Materials Center, Fresno CA. 209-488-3999

Goodstein, Judith R, *Archivist,* California Institute of Technology, Robert A Millikan Memorial Library, Pasadena CA. 213-795-6811

Goodwin, Carol F, *Asst Dir,* Library Cooperative of Macomb, Mount Clemens MI. 313-286-5750

Goodwin, Doris, *In Charge,* Calhoun County Historical Library, Rockwell City IA. 712-297-8307

Goodwin, Edythe, *Ch,* South Pasadena Public Library, South Pasadena CA. 213-799-9108

Goodwin, Eric, *Dir Support Servs,* Fairfax County Public Library, Administrative Offices, Springfield VA. 703-321-9810

Goodwin, Jack H, *Librn,* Virginia Theological Seminary, Bishop Payne Library, Alexandria VA. 703-370-6602

Goodwin, Julia B, *Clerk,* United States Bureau of Mines, Salt Lake City Research Center Library, Salt Lake City UT. 801-524-5379

Goodwin, Marilyn, *Cat & Doc,* Southern Baptist College, Felix Goodson Library, Walnut Ridge AR. 501-886-6741, Ext 130

Goodwin, Mary, *Ch,* Alexandrian Free Public Library, Mount Vernon IN. 812-838-3286

Goodwin, Peggy, *Humanities,* Nicholson Memorial Library, Garland TX. 214-494-7187

Goodwin, Vania, *ILL,* Indiana University-Purdue University at Indianapolis, University Library, Indianapolis IN. 317-264-4101

Goodwin, Virginia, *Bibliog Instr,* Ferrum College, Thomas Stanley Library, Ferrum VA. 703-365-2121, Ext 161

Goodwin, Virginia, *Librn,* Letcher County Public Library, Whitesburg KY. 606-633-7547

Goodwin, Jr, George H, *Chief Librn,* United States Geological Survey Library, Reston VA. 703-860-6671

Goodyear, Judith, *Librn,* Maryland Department of State Planning Library, Baltimore MD. 301-383-2439

Goodyear, Mary Lou, *On-Line Servs,* Stephens College, Hugh Stephens Library, Columbia MO. 314-442-2211, Ext 428

Goold, Karla, *Librn,* Carnegie-Mellon University (Engineering & Science), Pittsburgh PA. 412-578-2426, 578-2427

Goolian, Alice, *Asst Dir,* Adrian Public Library, Adrian MI. 517-263-2161, Ext 277

Goolsby, Josephine B, *Asst Dir,* Carnegie Public Library, Clarksdale MS. 601-624-4461

Goolsby, Lyndell, *Librn,* Kotzebue Public Library, Kotzebue AK. 907-442-3816

Goorough, Gary, *Dir,* University of Wisconsin - La Crosse, Film Library, La Crosse WI. 608-785-8045

Goosey, Edna C, *Librn,* Carnegie Public Library, Big Timber MT. 406-932-2871

Gorbold, Dianne, *Cat,* Bur Oak Library System, Shorewood IL. 815-729-3345, 729-3346

Gorchels, Clarence, *Dir,* Oregon College of Education Library, Monmouth OR. 503-838-1220, Ext 240

Gorchels, Clarence, *Dir,* Oregon College of Education, Library Science Program, OR. 503-838-1220, Ext 240

Gordan, Diane M, *Librn,* United States Air Force (Scott Air Force Base Library), Scott AFB IL. 618-256-5100

Gordon, Anne, *Media,* Mount Lebanon Public Library, Pittsburgh PA. 412-531-1912

Gordon, Anne M, *Librn,* Long Island Historical Society Library, Brooklyn NY. 212-624-0890

Gordon, Annetta, *Librn,* Newton Free Library (Newton Upper Falls Branch), Newton Upper Falls MA. 617-527-7700, Ext 24

Gordon, Archer S, *Dir,* Statham Instruments Library, Oxnard CA. 805-487-8511

Gordon, Barbara B, *Librn,* University of Washington Libraries (Forest Resources), Seattle WA. 206-543-2758

Gordon, Betty, *Circ,* Frank Hughes Memorial Library, Liberty MO. 816-781-3611

Gordon, Bonnie, *Librn,* William Underwood Co Library, Westwood MA. 617-329-5300

Gordon, Catherine, *Librn,* University of California, Berkeley (Education-Psychology), Berkeley CA. 415-642-4208

Gordon, Christine, *Br Coordr,* Ottumwa Public Library, Ottumwa IA. 515-682-7563

Gordon, Clara B, *Dir,* Morris College, Pinson Memorial Library, Sumter SC. 803-775-9371, Ext 216

Gordon, Dorothy, *Actg Librn,* Saint Barnabas Hospital for Chronic Diseases (Medical Library), Bronx NY. 212-960-9000

Gordon, Elaine, *Cat,* Saint Mary's University (Academic Library), San Antonio TX. 512-436-3441

Gordon, Eloise B, *Tech Serv & Cat,* Columbia College, J Drake Edens Library, Columbia SC. 803-786-3878

Gordon, Elsie, *Dir,* Rantoul Public Library, Rantoul IL. 217-893-3955

Gordon, Gerald, *Instr,* Arkansas State University, Dept of Library Science, AR. 501-972-3077

Gordon, Harold D, *Dir,* Paul Sawyier Public Library, Frankfort KY. 502-223-1658

Gordon, Harriet S, *Librn,* Yonkers Public Library (Main), Yonkers NY. 914-337-1500

Gordon, Helen, *Asst Librn,* Planned Parenthood Association of Wisconsin, Maurice Ritz Memorial Library & Resource Center, Milwaukee WI. 414-271-8116, Ext 52

Gordon, Helen M, *Dir,* Wamego Public Library, Wamego KS. 913-456-7339

Gordon, Homa F, *Librn,* Ahoskie Public Library (Murfreesboro Library), Murfreesboro NC. 919-332-5500

Gordon, Ines Mora, *Dir,* Conservatory of Music of Puerto Rico Library, San Juan PR. 809-763-8015

Gordon, Irving, *Mgr,* Hooker Chemical Co, Technical Information Center, Grand Island NY. 716-773-8531

Gordon, J G, *Librn,* Trinity College School Library, Port Hope ON. 416-885-2842

Gordon, J G, *Librn,* Trinity College School Library (History), Port Hope ON. 416-885-2842

Gordon, Janet, *Librn,* Tuscarawas County Public Library (Bolivar Branch), Bolivar OH. 216-874-2720

Gordon, Jean, *Asst Dir,* Motlow State Community College, Library-Learning Resources Center, Tullahoma TN. 615-455-8511, Ext 225

Gordon, Jean P, *Tech Serv,* Dominican College of San Rafael, Archbishop Alemany Library, San Rafael CA. 415-457-4440, Ext 251

Gordon, Judith M, *Ref,* New Castle-Henry County Public Library, New Castle IN. 317-529-0362

Gordon, June, *Dir,* Saint Clair County Library, Osceola MO. 417-646-2214

Gordon, Kathleen Fuller & Miriam, *Lit Analysts,* B F Goodrich Chemical Co Library, Cleveland OH. 216-524-0200

Gordon, Keith, *Tech Serv, Acq & Cat,* Altoona Area Public Library, Altoona PA. 814-946-0417

Gordon, Leonard, *Acq,* California State University, John F Kennedy Memorial Library, Los Angeles CA. 213-224-2201

Gordon, Lucille, *Dir,* Hamilton Public Library, Hamilton MT. 406-363-1670

Gordon, M Charleen, *On-Line Servs,* United States Army (The Army Logistics Library), Fort Lee VA. 804-734-1797, 734-4286

Gordon, Marceline, *Librn,* Argonne National Laboratory (Physics-Mathematics), Argonne IL. 312-972-4224

Gordon, Marjorie, *Librn,* American Council of Life Insurance Library, Washington DC. 202-862-4050

Gordon, Marsha, *Librn,* First Regional Library (Sardis Public), Sardis MS. 601-487-2126

Gordon, Martin, *Per,* Franklin & Marshall College Library, Lancaster PA. 717-291-4223

Gordon, Maureen M, *Librn,* Kendall Co, Research Div Library, Charlotte NC. 704-366-5221

Gordon, Mrs E, *Librn,* Schreiber Public Library, Schreiber ON. 807-824-2477

Gordon, Page R, *AV Dir,* Richmond Area Film Library Cooperative, VA. 804-257-1098

Gordon, Patricia Hinckley, *Asst Librn,* Kaye, Scholer, Fierman, Hays & Handler Law Library, New York NY. 212-759-8400, Ext 312

Gordon, Paul R, *Chief Interpreter,* Bighorn Canyon National Recreation Area Library, Fort Smith MT. 406-666-2412

Gordon, Rachael, *Asst Law Librn,* Bank of America, Law Library, Los Angeles CA. 213-683-3101

Gordon, Robert N, *Exec Dir,* Braille Circulating Library, Inc, Richmond VA. 804-359-3743

Gordon, Vesta Lee, *Dir,* Saint Johns River Community College, B C Pearce Learning Resources Center, Palatka FL. 904-328-1571, Ext 216

Gordon, Vondale, *Sr Libr Asst,* Madera County Library (Chowchilla Branch), Chowchilla CA. 209-665-2630

Gordon, William B, *Ser,* University of South Carolina, Thomas Cooper Library, Columbia SC. 803-777-3142

Gordon, William R, *Dir,* Prince George's County Memorial Library System, Hyattsville MD. 301-699-3500

Gordon, Willie H, *Circ,* North Georgia College, Stewart Library, Dahlonega GA. 404-864-3391, Ext 226, 294

Gore, Atrice, *Librn,* Livingston Parish Library (Frenchsettlement Branch), Frenchsettlement LA. 504-686-2436

Gore, Daniel, *Dir,* Lewis & Clark College, Aubrey R Watzek Library, Portland OR. 503-244-6161, Ext 400

Gore, Herbert, *Acq,* Pepperdine University Library, Payson Library, Malibu CA. 213-456-4252

Gore, Mary L, *Librn,* Grafton Free Public Library, Grafton NH. 603-523-7161

Gore, Tom, *In Charge,* Open Space Gallery, Secession Photography Library, Victoria BC. 604-383-8833

Gorecki, Sister Maria Tiburtia, *Librn,* Hilbert College, McGrath Library, Hamburg NY. 716-649-7900, Ext 237

Goren, Morton S, *Librn,* Drug Enforcement Administration Library, Washington DC. 202-633-1369

Goren, Sheila, *Librn,* American Express Co, Card Division, Systems Library, Fort Lauderdale FL. 305-473-3750

Goren, Simon L, *Dir,* Case Western Reserve University Libraries (School of Law Library), Cleveland OH. 216-368-2792

Goren, Simon L, *Prof,* Case Western Reserve University, School of Library Science, OH. 216-368-3500

Gores, Sister Dorothy Marie, *Dir,* College of Saint Mary Library, Omaha NE. 402-393-8800, Ext 234, 235

Gorey, Marie C, *Ref,* Port Authority of New York & New Jersey Library, New York NY. 212-466-4067, 4068

Gorghan, Ann, *Librn,* Saint Joseph's Hospital, Medical Library, Yonkers NY. 914-965-6700

Gorin, M, *Cat,* Shoreham-Wading River Public Library, Shoreham NY. 516-929-4488

Gorman, Evelyn S, *Dir,* Saint Joseph's Hospital & Medical Center Library, Phoenix AZ. 602-277-6611, Ext 3362

Gorman, Judith, *Ch,* Old Lyme, Phoebe Griffin Noyes Library, Old Lyme CT. 203-434-1684

Gorman, Mary R, *Lib Traffic Mgr,* Boston State College Library, Boston MA. 617-731-3300

Gorman, Michael, *Tech Serv,* University of Illinois Library at Urbana-Champaign, Urbana IL. 217-333-0790

Gorman, Michael J, *Librn,* Erie Community College-South Campus, Library Learning Resources Center, Orchard Park NY. 716-648-5400, Ext 270, 274

Gorman, Nancy, *Cat,* College of Medicine & Dentistry of New Jersey, George F Smith Library of the Health Sciences, Newark NJ. 201-456-4580

Gorman, Patricia, *Asst Dir & Ch,* Cora J Belden Library, Rocky Hill CT. 203-529-2379

Gorman, Robert M, *Dir,* Kansas Newman College, Ryan Library, Wichita KS. 316-942-4291, Ext 40

Gorman, Vera, *Ad,* Greece Public Library, Rochester NY. 716-225-8930, 225-8951

Gormish, Eloise M, *Asst Librn,* Barnesboro Public Library, Barnesboro PA. 814-948-7820

Gormley, Ann, *Librn,* Millerton Free Library, Millerton NY. 518-789-3340

Gormley, Dennis M, *Coordr,* Channeled Arizona Information Network, (CHAIN), AZ. 602-255-5841

Gormley, Mary T, *Supvr,* American Can Co, Barrington Technical Center, Barrington IL. 312-381-1900

Gorsegner, Ronald H, *Dir,* Nicolet Federated Library System, Green Bay WI. 414-497-3443

Gorshe, Susan, *Librn,* Henderson County Public Library (Fletcher Branch), Fletcher NC. 704-684-9446

Gorski, Lorraine, *Per,* College of Saint Elizabeth, Mahoney Library, Convent Station NJ. 201-539-1600, Ext 365

Gorsline, Sr, Robert A, *Dir,* Dawson County Public Library, Lamesa TX. 806-872-7042

Gorson, Pamela, *Ch & YA,* Clarksburg-Harrison Public Library, Clarksburg WV. 304-624-6512, 624-6513

Gorson, Pamela, *Dir,* Webster-Addison Public Library, Webster Springs WV. 304-847-5764

Gort, Dale, *Tech Serv,* Manitowoc Public Library, Manitowoc WI. 414-682-6861

Gosch, Janet, *Reader Serv,* Scott Sebastian Regional Library, Greenwood AR. 501-996-2856

Gosch, Janet, *Librn,* Scott Sebastian Regional Library (Sebastain County), Greenwood AR. 501-996-2856

Gosden, Carmella, *On-Line Servs,* Andco Technical Services, Inc Library, Cheektowaga NY. 716-681-7400

Gosier, Doris, *Pub Servs,* Fort Valley State College, Henry Alexander Hunt Memorial Library, Fort Valley GA. 912-825-6342

Gosier, L James, *Dir,* Harford County Library, Bel Air MD. 301-838-7484

Gosik, Pamela, *Ad & Ref,* Royal Oak Public Library, Royal Oak MI. 313-541-1470

Gosling, Marilyn, *Dir,* Glen Oaks Community College, Learning Resources Center, Centreville MI. 616-467-9945, Ext 212

Gosling, William, *Tech Serv,* Duke University, William R Perkins Library, Durham NC. 684-2034 (Main).

Goslinga, Marian, *Latin Amer & Caribbean,* Florida International University, Tamiami Campus, Athenaeum, Miami FL. 305-552-2461

Gosman, Ruth, *Cat,* Congregation B'nai David, Isadore Gruskin Library, Southfield MI. 313-557-8211

Gosnell, Jessie, *Librn,* Anderson County Library (Pelzer Branch), Pelzer SC. 803-947-9735

Gosner, Pamela, *Ch,* Maplewood Memorial Library, Maplewood NJ. 201-762-1622

Gospodarek, F, *Ch,* Bellmore Memorial Library, Bellmore NY. 516-785-2990

Goss, Anne, *Health Sci,* Ohio University, Vernon R Alden Library, Athens OH. 614-594-5228

Goss, Anne, *Librn,* Ohio University (Health Sciences Library), Athens OH. 614-594-6581

Goss, Brigitte, *Asst Librn,* Black River Falls Public Library, Black River Falls WI. 715-284-4112

Goss, Dorothy K, *Chief Librn,* Summa Corp, Hughes Helicopters Library, Culver City CA. 213-930-4451

Goss, Jessica S, *Librn,* Worcester Historical Museum Library, Worcester MA. 617-753-8278

Goss, Peggy L, *Librn,* American States Insurance Co Library, Indianapolis IN. 317-262-6560

Goss, Theresa C, *Per,* Saint Petersburg Junior College, Michael M Bennett Library, Clearwater FL. 813-441-0681, Ext 2616

Gossack, Ben J, *Librn,* Choteau County Free Library (Highwood Library Station), Highwood MT. 406-733-2551

Gossage, Wayne, *Dir,* Bank Street College of Education Library, New York NY. 212-663-7200, Ext 245

Gossard, Cody, *Supvr,* American Telephone & Telegraph Co, Training Center Library, Baltimore MD. 301-752-2350

Gossard, Diane, *Reader Serv,* University of Virginia (Claude Moore Health Sciences Library), Charlottesville VA. 804-924-5444

Gosse, Betty, *Asst Dir,* Muehl Public Library, Seymour Public Library, Seymour WI. 414-833-2725

Gosse, Catherine, *Librn,* Superior Public Library (East End), Superior WI. 715-398-3145

Gossett, Dona J, *Librn,* Geoscience Limited Library, Solana Beach CA. 714-755-9396

Gosson, John F, *Curator,* Marine Museum at Fall River, Inc Library, Fall River MA. 617-674-3533

Gostely, Martha, *Asst Dir,* Delaware County District Library, Delaware OH. 614-362-3861

Gosz, Kathleen M, *Dir,* T B Scott Free Library, Merrill Public Library, Merrill WI. 715-536-7191

Gotanda, Masae, *In Charge,* Hawaii State Library System (Research & Evaluation), Honolulu HI. 808-548-7503

Gothard, Gene, *AV,* Lake Erie College, James F Lincoln Learning Resource Center, Painesville OH. 216-352-3361, Ext 280

Gothberg, Helen M, *Asst Prof,* University of Arizona, Graduate Library School, AZ. 602-626-3565

Gothberg, Loren A, *Dir,* Saint Luke's Memorial Hospital, A M Johnson Memorial Library, Spokane WA. 509-838-4771, Ext 2291

Gotlieb, Howard B, *Spec Coll,* Boston University Libraries (Mugar Memorial Library), Boston MA. 617-353-3710

Gotliebson, R, *Manager,* Madison Public Library (INFO-Community Information & Referral Service), Madison WI. 608-266-6366

Gotlobe, Jack L, *Assoc Dir for pub Servs & On-Line Search Coordr,* Temple University of the Commonwealth System of Higher Education, Samuel Paley Library, Philadelphia PA. 215-787-8231

Gott, Delmar D, *Librn,* Dixie College Library, Saint George UT. 801-673-4811, Ext 230

Gott, Gary, *Media,* Brigham Young University (Law Library), Provo UT. 801-378-3593

Gottesman, Barbara, *YA,* Wayne Public Library, Wayne NJ. 201-694-4272

Gottesman, Magda, *ILL,* Hunter College of the City University of New York Library, New York NY. 212-570-5511

Gottfried, Claire, *Librn,* Brooklyn Public Library (McKinley Park), Brooklyn NY. 212-748-5800

Gottleib, Ann K, *Librn,* Schering-Plough Corp Library, Business Information Center, Kenilworth NJ. 201-931-3121

Gottlieb, Dan, *ILL,* University of Cincinnati Libraries, Central Library, Cincinnati OH. 513-475-2218

Gottlob, Carol, *Librn,* Arapahoe Regional Library District (Byers Library), Byers CO. 303-822-5238

Gottlober, Helen R, *Coordr,* Monterey Bay Area Cooperative Library System, Salinas CA. 408-758-9818

Gottschalk, Laura, *Ch,* Danbury Public Library, Danbury CT. 203-797-4505

Gottschlich, Lotte O, *Librn,* University of Pennsylvania Law School, Health Law Project Library, Philadelphia PA. 215-243-6951

Gottselig, Leonard J, *Librn,* Glenbow-Alberta Institute Historical Library & Archives, Calgary AB. 403-264-8300

Gotwals, Joan, *Assoc Dir,* University of Pennsylvania Libraries, Van Pelt Library, Philadelphia PA. 215-243-7091

Goudeau, John M, *Prof,* Florida State University, School of Library Science, FL. 904-644-5775

Goudy, Frances, *Spec Coll,* Vassar College Library, Poughkeepsie NY. 914-452-7000

Gough, Carolyn, *Dir & Bibliog Instr,* Cabrini College, Holy Spirit Library, Radnor PA. 215-687-2100, Ext 60

Gough, Margaret E, *Dir,* Saint Louis Community College (Meramec Campus), Saint Louis MO. 314-966-7623

Gough, Paul, *Librn,* Connecticut Agricultural Experiment Station, Thomas B Osborne Library, New Haven CT. 203-789-7214

Gouker, David, *Ref,* North Central Regional Library System, Mason City IA. 515-423-6917

Gould, Anna Mae, *Librn,* Fairview Public Library, Fairview OK. 405-227-2190

Gould, Joan, *Librn,* Hazen Memorial Library, Shirley MA. 617-425-9645

Gould, Linda J, *Coll Develop,* University of Washington Libraries, Seattle WA. 206-543-1760

Gould, Linda J, *Librn,* University of Washington Libraries (Political Science), Seattle WA. 206-543-2389

Gould, Lydia M, *Librn,* Brown Library, Seabrook NH. 603-474-2044

Gould, Martha B, *Asst Dir,* Washoe County Library, Reno NV. 702-785-4039

Gould, Theodore F, *Bibliog Instr,* University of California at Davis, General Library, Davis CA. 916-752-2110

Goulden, D R, *Librn,* Federal Aviation Administration (Civil Aeromedical Institute Library), Oklahoma City OK. 405-686-4398

Goulding, Mary, *Ad,* Elmhurst Public Library, Elmhurst IL. 312-279-8696

Goulet, Pamela, *Librn,* North-West Regional Library, Swan River MB. 204-734-3880

Gouner, Rita, *Librn,* Iberia Parish Public Library (Jeanerette Branch), Jeanerette LA. 318-276-4014

Gourlay, J W Gordon, *Dir,* Clemson University, Robert Muldrow Cooper Library, Clemson SC. 803-656-3026

Gourley, Elinor, *Asst Librn,* Brighton Public Library, Brighton ON. 613-475-2511

Gourley, Janet H, *Ch & YA,* Welles-Turner Memorial Library, Glastonbury CT. 203-633-1300

Gouy, Sharon, *Librn,* Southeast Arkansas Regional Library, Monticello AR. 501-367-3336

Govaars, Inga, *Librn,* Crocker National Bank Library, San Francisco CA. 415-983-3581

Govan, James F, *Dir,* University of North Carolina at Chapel Hill, Louis Round Wilson Academic Affairs Library, Chapel Hill NC. 919-933-1301

Gove, Esther, *Tech Serv & Cat,* Fitchburg State College Library, Fitchburg MA. 617-345-2151, Ext 137

Gove, Katharine M, *Dir,* G A R Memorial Library, West Newbury MA. 617-363-2952

Gover, Harvey R, *ILL & Ref,* Tarleton State University Library, Stephenville TX. 817-968-9246

Govig, Ramona, *Librn,* Griswold Public Library, Griswold IA. 712-778-4130

Gowan, Sam, *Assist Dir Spec Resources,* University of Florida Libraries, Gainesville FL. 904-392-0341

Goward, Louise, *Librn,* Vernon District Public Library, Vernon MI. 517-288-6486

Gower, Frances K, *Admin Asst,* Albany Law School Library, Albany NY. 518-445-2311, 445-2340

Gower, Helene, *Exten Servs,* Spokane Falls Community College, Library Media Services, Spokane WA. 509-456-2860

Gower, Leslie M, *Dir,* Pan American University, Learning Resource Center, Edinburg TX. 512-381-2751

Gowerluk, Eleanor, *Libr Technician,* Manitoba Association of Registered Nurses Library, Winnipeg MB. 204-774-3477

Goyer, Doreen S, *Librn,* University of Texas Libraries (Population Research Center Library), Austin TX. 512-471-5514

Goyette, Jr, William D, *Librn,* Bay Path Junior College, Frank & Marian Hatch Library, Longmeadow MA. 413-567-0621, Ext 444

Goza, Cheryl, *Asst Pub Servs,* Fisk University Library & Media Center, Nashville TN. 615-329-8730

Gozesky, Max, *Librn,* San Diego Public Library (La Jolla Branch), La Jolla CA. 714-459-5174

Gozzi, Cynthia, *Acq,* Syracuse University Libraries, Ernest S Bird Library, Syracuse NY. 315-423-2575

Grabe, Lauralee, *ILL,* Creighton University, Alumni Memorial Library, Omaha NE. 402-449-2705

Graber, Lynne, *Librn,* Valley General Hospital Library, Renton WA. 206-228-3450

Graber, Reta, *Tech Serv,* Hutchinson Public Library, Hutchinson KS. 316-663-5441

Graber, Reta, *Librn,* South Central Kansas Library System (Book Processing Center), Hutchinson KS. 316-669-9651

Grabert, Marla M, *Librn & On-Line Servs,* Swedish Medical Center Library, Englewood CO. 303-789-6616

Grable, Janet, *Circ,* Huntingdon College, Houghton Memorial Library, Montgomery AL. 205-265-0511, Ext 221

Grable, Susan, *Librn,* Mid-Continent Public Library (Weston Branch), Weston MO. 816-386-2874

Grabout, Mary, *Ch & YA,* West Caldwell Public Library, West Caldwell NJ. 201-226-5441

Graboyes, Betty, *Librn,* Main Line Reform Temple, Beth Elohim Library, Wynnewood PA. 215-649-7800

Grace, Bro Michael, *Archives & Spec Coll,* Loyola University of Chicago Libraries, Chicago IL. 312-274-3000, Ext 771

Grace, Brother Michael, *Church Hist & Jesuitica,* Loyola University of Chicago Libraries (Elizabeth M Cudahy Memorial Library), Chicago IL. 312-274-3000, Ext 771

Grace, Lorann, *Asst Prof,* Southern Missionary College, Library Science Program, TN. 615-396-4291

Grace, Lorann, *Per,* Southern Missionary College, McKee Library, Collegedale TN. 615-396-4290

Grace, Monica, *Cat,* Tufts Library, Public Libraries of Weymouth, Weymouth MA. 617-337-1402

Gracy, David, *Archivist,* Texas State Library, Austin TX. 512-475-2166

Gradess, Ella, *Librn,* Waldemar Medical Research Foundation, Generoso Pope Library, Woodbury NY. 516-433-2500

Gradinger, Christina, *Ref,* Kansas City Public Library, Kansas City MO. 816-221-2685

Grady, Eley D, *Asst Librn,* Pine Forest Regional Library (Collins Public), Collins MS. 601-765-8582

Grady, Grace, *Acq,* Washington County Library, Lake Elmo MN. 612-777-8143

Grady, Grace Mary, *Librn,* Washington County Library (Marine Branch), Marine-on-St Croix MN. 612-433-2820

Grady, Mamie, *Human Servs Libr Program,* Chicago Public Library, Chicago IL. 312-269-2900

Grady, Mary, *Ch,* Reading Public Library, Reading Public Library District, Reading PA. 215-374-4548

Graeber, K, *In Charge,* Los Angeles Area Chamber of Commerce, Economic Information & Research Department Library, Los Angeles CA. 213-629-0673

Graening, Paige, *Ref,* Jackson District Library, Jackson MI. 517-788-4087

Graf, Ellen, *Asst Librn,* Bleyhl Community Library, Grandview Public Library, Grandview WA. 509-882-2807

Graf, Fran, *Coll Develop,* University of Connecticut Health Center, Lyman Maynard Stowe Library, Farmington CT. 203-674-2739

Graff, Doris M, *In Charge,* Administrative Management Society, Management Information Center Library, Willow Grove PA. 215-659-4300

Graff, Linda, *Ad,* Flagstaff City-Coconino County Public Library System, Flagstaff AZ. 602-774-0603

Graff, Ruth, *Acq,* Oberlin College Library, Oberlin OH. 216-775-8285

Graffagnino, J Kevin, *Curator of Wilbur Coll,* University of Vermont & State Agricultural College, Bailey-Howe Memorial Library, Burlington VT. 802-656-2020

Graffe, Betty, *Librn,* Glenns Ferry Public Library, Glenns Ferry ID. 208-366-7418

Grafton, John W, *Asst to President,* Dover Publications, Inc Library, New York NY. 212-255-3755

Grafton, Mona, *Librn,* Mattoon Public Library, Mattoon IL. 217-234-2621

Graham, Alice, *Librn,* Markdale Public Library, Markdale ON. 519-986-3436
Graham, Ann, *Asst Librn,* University of Texas Libraries (Nettie Lee Benson Latin American Collection), Austin TX. 512-471-3818
Graham, Anne, *Circ & Per,* Gardner-Webb College, Dover Memorial Library, Boiling Springs NC. 704-434-2361
Graham, Anne, *Ch,* New Castle Public Library, New Castle PA. 412-658-6659
Graham, Audrey R, *Dir,* College of Saint Rose Library, Albany NY. 518-454-5180
Graham, Bess Althaus, *Librn,* Corpus Christi Museum Library, Corpus Christi TX. 512-883-2862
Graham, Betty, *Librn,* Sun Ship, Inc Library, Chester PA. 215-876-9121, Ext 788
Graham, Carolyn, *Tech Serv & Commun Servs,* Palliser Regional Library, Moose Jaw SK. 306-693-3669
Graham, Deborah, *Librn,* Tucson Medical Center Library, Tucson AZ. 602-327-5461, Ext 5140
Graham, Doris, *Librn,* Brooklyn Public Library (Crown Heights), Brooklyn NY. 212-773-1223
Graham, Doris, *Librn,* Southern University Library (Art-Architecture), Baton Rouge LA. 504-771-3290
Graham, Dorothy M, *Librn,* California Legislature Assembly, Office of Research Library, Sacramento CA. 916-445-3551
Graham, Edna, *Librn,* Pinawa Public Library, Pinawa MB. 204-753-2496
Graham, Elaine, *Librn & On-Line Servs,* Kaiser Permanente Medical Center, Health Science Library, Panorama City CA. 213-908-2239
Graham, Frieda, *Librn,* Harrington Public Library, Harrington WA. 509-253-4345
Graham, Garth, *Dir,* Yukon Territory Government, Library Services Branch, Whitehorse YT. 403-667-5238
Graham, Gary N, *Dir,* Samuels Public Library, Front Royal VA. 703-635-2941
Graham, Gayle, *Librn,* Brown & Root, Inc, Technical Library, Houston TX. 713-679-1966
Graham, Grace, *Acq,* Quinnipiac College Library, Hamden CT. 203-288-5251, Ext 271
Graham, Heather, *Area Head,* Winnipeg Public Library (Henderson Branch), Winnipeg MB. 204-339-4286
Graham, Helen, *Asst Dir & ILL,* Sheridan County Fulmer Public Library, Sheridan WY. 307-674-8585, 674-9898
Graham, Holt, *Dir,* United Theological Seminary of the Twin Cities Library, New Brighton MN. 612-633-4311
Graham, Irene, *Dir,* University of Mississippi Medical Center, Rowland Medical Library, Jackson MS. 601-968-4620
Graham, Isabel, *Asst Librn,* Town of Caledon Public Libraries (Inglewood Branch), Inglewood ON. 416-857-1400
Graham, Jim, *Circ,* Pikes Peak Regional Library District, Penrose Public Library, Colorado Springs CO. 303-473-2080
Graham, Joy, *Cat & Bibliog Instr,* University of Alabama in Huntsville Library, Huntsville AL. 205-895-6540
Graham, Judith, *Libr Tech,* Hawaii State Library System (Holualoa Branch), Holualoa HI. 808-324-6881
Graham, Karen, *Acq,* Maple Woods Community College Library, Kansas City MO. 816-436-6500, Ext 73, 74
Graham, Kenneth, *Librn,* California Institute of Technology (Earthquake Engineering Research Library), Pasadena CA. 213-795-6811, Ext 1227
Graham, Lillian G, *Librn,* United States Army (Hospital Medical Library), Fort Campbell KY. 502-798-6620
Graham, M, *In Charge,* Pointe Claire Public Library (Valois), Pointe Claire PQ. 514-697-1347
Graham, Margaret H, *Mgr,* Exxon Research & Engineering Company, Research & Engineering Information Services, Linden NJ. 201-474-3108
Graham, Margaret H, *Librn,* North Collins Library Association, North Collins NY. 716-337-3211
Graham, Marianna, *Librn,* National Council for United States - China Trade, Washington DC. 202-331-0290
Graham, Marilyn, *Librn,* Greece Public Library (Dewey-Stone Branch), Rochester NY. 716-225-8930, 225-8951

Graham, Marilyn, *Ch,* Township of Shaler North Hills Library, Glenshaw PA. 412-486-0211, 486-0212
Graham, Mary E, *Librn,* Heard Museum of Anthropology & Primitive Art Library, Phoenix AZ. 602-252-8848
Graham, Mary K, *Dir,* Westchester Public Library, Westchester IL. 312-562-3573
Graham, Mary Ruth, *Librn,* Bronson Public Library, Bronson KS. 316-939-4578
Graham, Norman F, *Dir,* Harrison County Library System, Gulfport MS. 601-868-1383
Graham, Pamela, *Tech Serv,* University of Miami (Law), Coral Gables FL. 305-284-2250
Graham, Patricia, *Librn,* Scott Sebastian Regional Library (Lavaca Library), Lavaca AR. 501-996-2856
Graham, Paul, *Tech Serv & Cat,* University of Arkansas-Monticello Library, Monticello AR. 501-367-6811, Ext 80
Graham, Pauline A, *Dir,* Bethel Park Public Library, Bethel Park PA. 412-835-2207
Graham, Robert, *Media,* Lancaster County Library, Lancaster PA. 717-394-2651
Graham, Sheena, *Librn,* Boulder River School and Hospital, Habilitation Dept Library, Boulder MT. 406-225-3311, Ext 316
Graham, Sister Rosalie, *Per,* Ohio Dominican College Library, Columbus OH. 614-253-2741, Ext 258
Graham, Tauni, *Asst Librn,* Anchor Hocking Corp, Corporate Library, Lancaster OH. 614-687-2403
Graham, William, *Librn,* United States Department of Energy, Grand Junction Office Technical Library, Grand Junction CO. 303-242-8621, Ext 278
Graham, Yvonne, *Librn,* Salem Public Library (West Salem Branch), Salem OR. 503-588-6301
Grahame, Viola, *Librn,* Armite Laboratories Library, Los Angeles CA. 213-587-7737, 587-7744
Grahner, Richard, *Chief Librn,* Floating Points Systems, Inc Library, Portland OR. 503-297-5531, Ext 212
Graiebing, Virginia J, *Librn,* Meldrum & Fewsmith Inc, Business Information Library, Cleveland OH. 216-241-2141
Grainger, Claudia, *On-Line Servs,* Saint Vincent Hospital & Medical Center, Health Science Library, Toledo OH. 419-259-4324
Grainger, Gale, *Librn,* Winnipeg Public Library (Munroe), Winnipeg MB. 204-667-0956
Grainger, Shirley J, *Librn,* Dartmouth College (Dana Biomedical), Hanover NH. 603-646-2858
Grainger, William K, *Dir,* Pasadena City College Library, Pasadena CA. 213-578-7221
Gralapp, Marcelee, *Dir,* Boulder Public Library, Boulder CO. 303-441-3100
Gralow, Elenora, *Dir,* Judge George W Armstrong Library, Homochitto Valley Regional Library, Natchez MS. 601-445-8862
Gralow, Elenora, *Librn,* Wilkinson County Library System, Woodville MS. 601-888-6712
Gram, Dorothy, *Librn,* Belmond Public Library, Belmond IA. 515-444-4160
Gramka, B J, *Cat,* University of South Alabama (Biomedical Library), Mobile AL. 205-460-7043
Gramlich, Charles, *Librn,* Erie County Library System (Liberty), Erie PA. 814-864-9527
Gramlich, Charles, *Head,* Erie County Library System (Presque Isle), Erie PA. 814-453-5763
Gramling, Mary, *AV,* Southeast Alabama Cooperative Library System, Dothan AL. 205-793-9767
Grams, Bea, *Genealogy,* Laramie County Library System, Cheyenne WY. 307-634-3561
Grams, Theodore C W, *Tech Serv,* Portland State University, Branford Price Millar Library, Portland OR. 503-229-4424
Gramse, Erna L, *Chief Librn,* FMC Corp, Technical Library, Philadelphia PA. 215-299-6000
Granados, Rose, *Librn,* California Office of the State Architect, Architectural-Engineering Library, Sacramento CA. 916-445-2163
Grande, Anne W, *Librn,* Hennepin County Law Library, Minneapolis MN. 612-348-3022
Grande, Dolores, *Tech Serv,* John Jay College of Criminal Justice Library, New York NY. 212-489-5169
Grandits, Joanne, *Ch,* Peru Public Library, Peru IL. 815-223-0229

Grandstaff, Judy, *Librn,* Blue Hill Public Library, Blue Hill NE. 402-756-2701
Granese, Mary A, *Doc,* Massachusetts Institute of Technology, Lincoln Laboratory Library, Lexington MA. 617-862-5500, Ext 7195
Granger, Betty, *Librn,* Bellevue Township Library, Bellevue MI. 616-763-3369
Granger, Carole Ann, *Librn,* University of Montana (Law School Library), Missoula MT. 406-243-5603
Granger, Catherine, *Librn,* Chicago Public Library (McKinley Park), Chicago IL. 312-523-6082
Granger, Ralph H, *Chmn,* University of Maine at Farmington, Instructional Media Technology Program, ME. 207-778-3501, Ext 291
Granges, Marcelle Des, *Librn,* Bell Canada (Law Library), Montreal PQ. 514-870-2683
Granier, Jacqueline, *Doc,* Vanderbilt University School of Law Library, Nashville TN. 615-322-2568
Granis, Linn, *ILL & Circ,* Columbia College Library, Columbia CA. 209-532-3141, Ext 228
Granston, Carolyn, *Librn,* Altoona Public Library, Altoona IA. 515-967-3881
Granstrom, Jane E, *Ch,* Thomas Crane Public Library, Subregional Headquarters for Eastern Massachusetts Regional Library System, Quincy MA. 617-471-2400
Grant, Barbara, *Ch,* Cass County Library, Cassopolis MI. 616-445-8651
Grant, Bernice, *Consultant,* Big Country Library System, Abilene TX. 915-673-2311
Grant, Charlene, *Librn,* Non-Linear Systems, Inc, Library, Del Mar CA. 714-755-1134
Grant, G E, *Libr Network Support Supvr,* Bell Telephone Laboratories (Bell Telephone Laboratories Technical Library), Holmdel NJ. 949-3912 (Supvr); 949-5966 (Libr Network Support); 949-7986 (Cat); 229-7810 (W Long Branch Info)
Grant, George C, *Dir,* Morgan State University, Morris A Soper Library, Baltimore MD. 301-444-3488, 444-3489
Grant, Jeri Ann, *Librn,* Remsen Public Library, Remsen IA. 712-786-2911
Grant, Joan, *Exten Servs,* New York University, Elmer Holmes Bobst Library, New York NY. 212-598-2484
Grant, Juanita G, *Dir & Acq,* Averett College, Mary B Blount Library, Danville VA. 804-793-7811, Ext 265
Grant, Juanita S, *Tech Serv,* Pearl River County Library System, Margaret Reed Crosby Memorial Library, Picayune MS. 601-798-5081
Grant, Kathalee H, *Librn,* Cuyahoga County Public Library (Independence Branch), Independence OH. 216-447-0160
Grant, Marilyn, *Ref & On-Line Servs,* Boston College Libraries (Science & Geophysics Library), Chestnut Hill MA. 617-969-0100, Ext 3230
Grant, Marilyn L, *Dir,* Mississippi County Library District, Charleston MO. 314-683-6748
Grant, Marion, *Librn,* Solano County Law Library, Fairfield CA. 707-429-6655
Grant, Mary, *ILL,* University of Louisville Library (Kornhauser Health Sciences), Louisville KY. 502-588-5771
Grant, Mattie, *ILL,* Texas Southern University Library, Houston TX. 713-527-7121
Grant, Mildred, *Ref,* Fort Valley State College, Henry Alexander Hunt Memorial Library, Fort Valley GA. 912-825-6342
Grant, Mrs James, *Librn,* Dickson County Public Library, Dickson TN. 615-446-8293
Grant, Mrs Jessie, *Librn,* Public Library of Johnston County & Smithfield (Four Oaks Public), Four Oaks NC. 919-934-8146
Grant, Ruth Ann, *Acq,* Jackson Metropolitan Library, Jackson MS. 601-352-3677
Grant, Sally, *In Charge,* Northside Free Library District, Wallace ID. 208-752-4571
Grant, Sue, *Commun Servs,* Brookings Public Library, Brookings SD. 605-692-9407, 692-9408
Grant, Thomas, *AV,* Jefferson Community College, Melvil Dewey Library, Watertown NY. 315-782-5250
Grant, Virginia, *Bkmobile Coordr,* Cedar Rapids Public Library, Cedar Rapids IA. 319-398-5123
Grant, Virginia, *Librn,* Cedar Rapids Public Library (Edgewood), Cedar Rapids IA. 319-398-5123

GRANT

Grant, III, Jason C, *Dir,* Hampton Institute, Huntington P Collis Library, Hampton VA. 804-727-5371

Grant, Jr, Frederic, *Librn,* Foley, Hoag & Eliot Library, Boston MA. 617-482-1390

Grantham, Blanche, *Librn,* Dunn Public Library, Dunn NC. 919-892-7830

Grantham, Elizabeth, *Acq,* Waycross Junior College Library, Waycross GA. 912-285-6136

Grantham, Eva Mae, *Dir,* Laurel-Jones County Library, Laurel MS. 601-428-4313

Grantham, Walter, *Asst Chief,* Chicago Public Library (Social Sciences & History Div), Chicago IL. 312-269-2830

Grasberg, Gabriel, *Chief Bibliographer,* University of Massachusetts at Boston Library, Boston MA. 617-287-1900, Ext 2224

Grasing, Kathleen, *Deputy State Librn,* Oregon State Library, Salem OR. 503-378-4243

Grasing, Kay, *Asst State Librn,* Oregon State Library Network, OR. 503-378-4239

Grasmick, Brenda, *ILL, Cat & Ser,* Metropolitan Technical Community College, Instructional Resource Center, Omaha NE. 402-457-5100

Grasmick, Charles, *Librn,* Metropolitan Technical Community College (Fort Omaha Campus Instructional Resource Center), Omaha NE. 402-457-5100, Ext 185

Grass, Edith, *Librn,* Monsour Medical Center, Health Sciences Library, Jeannette PA. 412-527-1511, Ext 351

Grass, Gene, *ILL & YA,* Cranford Public Library, Cranford NJ. 201-276-1826

Grass, Sister Mary Winifred, *Dir,* Saint Joseph's College, McEntegart Hall Library, Brooklyn NY. 212-789-5385

Grassby, Margaret M, *Asst Dir,* Marlborough Public Library, Marlborough MA. 617-485-0494

Grassl, Victoire, *Ref,* Everett Public Library, Everett WA. 206-259-8858

Grasso, Marion, *Librn,* Upper Arlington Public Library (Miller Park Branch), Upper Arlington OH. 614-488-5710

Grasso, Maryann, *Spec Coll,* Burbank Public Library, Burbank CA. 213-847-9744

Gratacus, Lucidia, *Spec Coll,* Inter-American University of Puerto Rico, Metropolitan Campus Library, Hato Rey PR. 809-754-7215, Ext 246, 245, 256

Gration, Selby U, *Dir,* State University of New York College, Memorial Library, Cortland NY. 607-753-2525, 753-2221

Grattan, III, Robert, *Coordr & On-Line Servs,* J Sargeant Reynolds Community College (Parham Campus Learning Resources Center), Richmond VA. 804-264-3220

Gratz, Delbert, *Librn,* Bluffton College, Musselman Library, Bluffton OH. 419-358-8015, Ext 114

Grau, Ellen M, *Librn,* Oscar Foss Memorial Library, Barnstead NH. 603-269-3900

Graubart, Marilyn, *Libr Supvr,* Diamond Shamrock Corp, Corporate Library, Cleveland OH. 216-694-6253

Gravel, Mable, *Bkmobile Coordr,* Barrhead Elementary School Public Library, Barrhead AB. 403-674-2160

Graves, Alison, *Spec Coll,* Saint Joseph Public Library, Saint Joseph MO. 816-232-7729, 232-7720

Graves, Carolyn A, *Librn,* United States Army (Morale Support Activity Division, Library Branch), Fort Dix NJ. 609-562-4858

Graves, Charles, *Br Coordr,* McDowell Public Library, Welch WV. 304-436-3070

Graves, Dan W, *Dir,* Clarion State College, Rena M Carlson Library, Clarion PA. 814-226-2343

Graves, Deborah, *Librn,* Cleveland Heights-University Heights Public Library (Coventry Village), Cleveland Heights OH. 216-932-3600

Graves, Deborah A, *Librn,* Church of the Covenant Library, Cleveland OH. 216-421-0482

Graves, Donna L, *Actg Dir & Curator,* Wyandotte County Museum, Trowbridge Research Library, Bonner Springs KS. 913-721-1078

Graves, Elizabeth, *Ch,* Irvington Public Library, Guiteau Foundation, Irvington NY. 914-591-7840

Graves, Elizabeth, *Tech Serv,* Tampa-Hillsborough County Public Library System, Tampa FL. 813-223-8947

Graves, Evelyn, *Dir,* Matthias M Hoffman Public Library, Dyersville IA. 319-875-9812

Graves, Fairy Lou, *Librn,* Southwest Arkansas Regional Library (Mineral Springs Branch), Mineral Springs AR. 501-777-4564

Graves, Frances, *Actg Coordr,* Sacramento State University, Library Services Credential Program, CA. 916-454-7028

Graves, Gail T, *Librn,* University of Alabama (Education), University AL. 205-348-6055

Graves, Geraldine N, *Librn,* Kaiser Permanente Medical Center, Health Sciences Library, Bellflower CA. 213-920-4247

Graves, Helen, *Librn,* Paterson Free Public Library (Eastside), Paterson NJ. 201-881-3779

Graves, Howard, *Cat,* Hofstra University Library, Hempstead NY. 516-560-3475

Graves, Jane, *Art,* Skidmore College, Lucy Scribner Library, Saratoga Springs NY. 518-584-5000, Ext 234

Graves, Karen, *Educ Servs & Bibliog Servs,* University of Tennessee Center for the Health Sciences Library, Memphis TN. 901-528-5638

Graves, Kay, *Librn,* University of Wyoming (Film), Laramie WY. 307-766-3184

Graves, Lewis, *Librn,* Newark Public Library (Springfield), Newark NJ. 201-733-7736

Graves, Linda, *Ch,* Houston County Public Library System, Perry GA. 912-987-3050

Graves, Margaret, *Librn,* Glenwood & Souris Regional Library, Souris MB. 204-483-2757

Graves, Marie, *Bkmobile Coordr,* Akron-Summit County Public Library, Akron OH. 216-762-7621

Graves, Mary D Sanders, *Librn,* Livingston Parish Library (Watson Branch), Watson LA. 504-686-2436

Graves, Mildred, *Ch,* Seymour Public Library, Seymour IN. 812-522-3412

Graves, Rita A, *Librn,* Chillicothe & Ross County Public Library (Richmond Dale Branch), Richmond Dale OH. 614-884-4990

Graves, Sheila, *Librn,* Wenatchee Daily World Library, Wenatchee WA. 509-663-5161

Graves, Shirley, *Per,* Walla Walla College, Peterson Memorial Library, College Place WA. 509-527-2133

Graves, Jr, Sid F, *Dir,* Carnegie Public Library, Clarksdale MS. 601-624-4461

Gray, Allan, *Dir,* Northwest Library District, (NORWELD), OH. 419-352-2903

Gray, Annie Rae, *Dir,* Jefferson College Library, Hillsboro MO. 314-789-3951

Gray, Barbara, *In Charge,* Dunning-Hough Public Library, Plymouth MI. 313-453-0750

Gray, Barbara, *Pub Serv,* Wayne Oakland Library Federation, Wayne MI. 313-326-8910

Gray, Bernadine, *Librn,* Fredonia Public Library, Fredonia KS. 316-378-2863

Gray, Beth, *Dir,* East Hampton Free Library, East Hampton NY. 516-324-0222, Ext 0243

Gray, Bonnie, *Commun Servs,* Lake Erie Regional Library System, London ON. 519-453-9100

Gray, Bonny G, *Librn,* Jonathan Bourne Public Library (Sagamore Branch), Sagamore MA. 617-888-0003

Gray, C, *Ch,* Shoreham-Wading River Public Library, Shoreham NY. 516-929-4488

Gray, Carol, *Asst Dir,* Washington University Libraries (GWB School of Social Work), Saint Louis MO. 314-889-6616

Gray, Catherine, *Librn,* Monmouth County Library (Marlboro Branch), Marlboro NJ. 201-536-9406

Gray, Connie M, *Doc,* University of Louisville Library, Louisville KY. 502-588-6745

Gray, Deanna, *Librn,* Cochranton Area Public Library, Cochranton PA. 814-425-3996

Gray, Donald, *Asst Dir & Pub Serv,* University of Northern Iowa Library, Cedar Falls IA. 319-273-2737

Gray, Donna, *Cat,* Monroeville Public Library, Monroeville PA. 412-372-0500

Gray, Dorothy, *Librn,* Bureau of Land Management, Craig District Office Library, Craig CO. 303-824-3417

Gray, Dorothy A, *Ref,* University of Louisville Library, Louisville KY. 502-588-6745

Gray, Elisabeth A, *Librn,* Warner & Swasey Co, Research Division Library, Solon OH. 216-368-6144

Gray, Ellen, *Ad,* Wilmette Public Library District, Wilmette IL. 312-256-5025

Gray, Gary B, *Asst Librn,* Methodist Hospital of Indiana, Inc, Library Department, Indianapolis IN. 317-924-8021

Gray, James D, *Dir & Acq,* Elmira College, Gannett-Tripp Learning Ctr, Elmira NY. 607-734-3911, Ext 287

Gray, James E, *Librn,* Wake Technical College Library, Raleigh NC. 919-772-0551, Ext 236

Gray, Jane, *Dir Office of Libr Develop,* State Library Commission of Iowa, Des Moines IA. 515-281-4102

Gray, Jean, *Dir,* Chanute Public Library, Chanute KS. 316-431-3820

Gray, John, *Instr,* United States Department of Agriculture Graduate School, Certificate Program for Library Technicians, DC. 202-447-5885

Gray, Josephine D, *Asst Librn,* Watertown Regional Library, Watertown SD. 605-886-8521, 886-8282

Gray, Karen, *Cat,* Caldwell Public Library, Caldwell ID. 208-459-3242

Gray, Karen, *Syst Coordr,* Great River Library System, Quincy IL. 217-223-2560

Gray, Karen, *Librn,* Great River Library System (Talking Book Library), Quincy IL. 217-223-2560

Gray, Kent, *Asst Librn,* State of Vermont Department of Libraries, Montpelier VT. 802-828-3261

Gray, Linda, *Bkmobile Coordr,* Uncle Remus Regional Library, Madison GA. 404-342-1206, 342-2955

Gray, Lollie, *Dir,* Festus Public Library, Festus MO. 314-937-2017

Gray, Margaret, *Librn,* Weimar Public Library, Weimar TX. 713-725-6608

Gray, Marilyn, *Librn,* Anoka County Library (Coon Rapids East Branch), Coon Rapids MN. 612-755-4290

Gray, Marjo, *Per,* University of San Diego, James S Copley Library, San Diego CA. 714-291-6480, Ext 4312, 4313, 4314

Gray, Martha, *Librn,* Paw Paw Public Library, Paw Paw MI. 616-657-3800

Gray, Marthajane, *Ch,* Jacksonville Public Library, Jacksonville IL. 217-243-5435

Gray, Mary, *Spec Coll,* Tusculum College Library, Greeneville TN. 615-639-1481

Gray, Mary Clare, *Librn,* Smithsonian Institution Libraries, Chesapeake Bay Center for Environmental Studies, Edgewater MD. 301-261-4190

Gray, Mary Clare, *Librn,* Smithsonian Institution Libraries (National Zoological Park Library), Washington DC. 202-381-7271

Gray, Maurine, *Dir,* Beaumont Public Library, Beaumont TX. 713-838-0812

Gray, Mildred, *Librn,* Riceville Public Library, Riceville IA. 515-985-2273

Gray, Pat, *Librn,* Dillon County Library, Latta Library, Latta SC. 803-752-5389

Gray, Patricia, *Librn,* Indiana Women's Prison Library, Indianapolis IN. 317-639-2671

Gray, Patsy, *Librn,* Norfolk Public Library (Barron F Black), Norfolk VA. 804-855-5111

Gray, Phyllis A, *Librn,* Miami Beach Public Library, Miami Beach FL. 305-673-7535

Gray, Phyllis J, *Librn,* Royal Center-Boone Township Public Library, Royal Center IN. 219-643-3185

Gray, Randall, *Librn,* Adams, Duque & Hazeltine Library, La Verne CA. 714-620-1240

Gray, Robert G, *Dir Pub Servs,* Nevada State Library, Carson City NV. 702-885-5130

Gray, Sabin H, *Dir,* Tulare County Educational Resource Center, Visalia CA. 209-733-6433

Gray, Sarah C, *Librn,* Livermore Public Library, Livermore CA. 415-447-2376

Gray, Sarah V, *Per,* College of William & Mary in Virginia, Earl Gregg Swem Library, Williamsburg VA. 804-253-4404

Gray, Sharlene, *Commun Servs,* Owen Sound Public Library, Owen Sound ON. 519-376-6623

Gray, Susan, *Ch & Cat,* Long Branch Public Library, Long Branch NJ. 201-222-3900

Gray, Suzanne K, *Sci-Tech Coordr,* Boston Public Library, Eastern Massachusetts Library System, Boston MA. 617-536-5400

Gray, Thomas, *Dir,* Museum of Early Southern Decorative Arts Library, Winston-Salem NC. 919-722-6148

Gray, Vickie D, *Librn,* Shorter College, A W Young Library, North Little Rock AR. 501-374-6305

Gray, Walter, *Commun Servs,* Metropolitan Library System, Oklahoma City OK. 405-235-0571
Gray, Walter, *Librn,* Polk County Public Library, Columbus NC. 704-894-8721
Gray, Wayne D, *Ref,* Dallas Public Library, Dallas TX. 214-748-9071
Graybeal, June A, *Cat,* Virginia Western Community College, Brown Library, Roanoke VA. 703-982-7303
Graydon, Elizabeth, *Librn,* Princeton University Library (Plasma Physics), Princeton NJ. 609-452-3180
Grayson, Bessie Rivers, *Asst Prof,* Alabama Agricultural & Mechanical University, School of Library Media, AL. 205-859-7216 or 859-7238
Grayson, C, *Librn,* Calgary Public Library (Southwood), Calgary AB. 403-252-2948
Grazaitis, Mariana, *Ser,* Orange Coast College Library, Costa Mesa CA. 714-556-5885
Graziano, Eugene E, *Asst Dir Servs,* University of California, Santa Barbara Library, Santa Barbara CA. 805-961-2741
Grazier, Guy W, *Librn,* Dow Chemical Co, Human Health Research & Development Library, Indianapolis IN. 317-266-2000
Grazier, Michael, *Dir,* Moses Greeley Parker Memorial Library, Dracut MA. 617-454-5474
Grazier, Robert T, *Assoc Dir,* Wayne State University Libraries, Detroit MI. 313-557-4020
Grazier, Virginia, *Librn,* Jacksonville Public Library System (Fernandiana Beach), Fernandina Beach FL. 904-261-6921
Grazioli, Margaret, *Dir,* Secaucus Free Public Library, Secaucus NJ. 201-863-9201
Grazioli, Margaret, *Dir,* Weehawken Free Public Library, Weehawken NJ. 201-863-7823
Grazvlis, T Lili, *Librn,* John F Kennedy Jr Library, Dearborn Heights MI. 313-292-2975
Greason, Irene, *In Charge,* Oxford County Library (Uniondale Branch), Uniondale ON. 519-537-3322
Greathouse, Mrs Walser, *Pres,* Charles & Emma Frye Art Museum Library, Seattle WA. 206-622-9250
Greathouse, Patricia, *Asst Dir,* Thomas Branigan Memorial Library, Las Cruces Public Library, Las Cruces NM. 505-526-0347
Greaves, Anna P, *Librn,* Cabot Public Library, Cabot VT. 802-563-2721
Greaves, F Landon, *Dept Head,* Southeastern Louisiana University, Department of Education, LA. 504-549-2221
Greaves, F Landon, *Dir,* Southeastern Louisiana University, Linus A Sims Memorial Library, Hammond LA. 504-549-2234
Greaves, Harold P, *Librn,* Board of Education for the City of North York, F W Minkler Library, Willowdale ON. 416-225-4661, Ext 395
Grebles, Shelley, *Bibliog Instr,* University of Texas at San Antonio Library, San Antonio TX. 512-691-4570
Grech, Anthony P, *Librn,* Association of the Bar of the City of New York Library, New York NY. 212-840-3550
Greco, Fran M, *Librn,* Maplewood Public Library, Maplewood MO. 314-781-2174
Greco, Gloria T, *Dir,* College of New Rochelle, Gill Library, New Rochelle NY. 914-632-5300, Ext 347
Grede, Lillian, *ILL,* Madison Public Library, Madison WI. 608-266-6300
Grediagin, Mary Jane, *Dir,* Fern Ridge Community Library, Veneta OR. 503-935-7512
Greear, Yvonne E, *Asst Dir,* University of Texas at El Paso Library, El Paso TX. 747-5683; 747-5684
Greehey, Barbara, *Cat,* Massachusetts College of Pharmacy & Allied Health Sciences, Sheppard Library, Boston MA. 732-2810 (Gen info), 732-2813 (Ref)
Greekmore, Pollyanna, *Local Hist & Genealogy,* East Tennessee State University, Sherrod Library, Johnson City TN. 615-929-4338
Greeley, Bill, *Br Coordr,* San Bernardino Public Library, San Bernardino CA. 714-889-0264
Greeley, Joyce E, *Librn,* Clinton Township Public Library, Waterman IL. 815-264-3339
Greemore, Barbara, *Librn,* Vermont College Division of Norwich University, Gary Memorial Library, Montpelier VT. 802-229-0522, Ext 53
Green, Alice, *Dir,* Amarillo Public Library, Amarillo TX. 806-378-3000, Ext 2250

Green, Amelia, *Librn,* Suttons Bay Area Library, Suttons Bay MI. 616-271-3512
Green, Ann, *Dir,* Pictou Antigonish Regional Library, New Glasgow NS. 902-752-6217
Green, Ann H, *Ref,* University of Baltimore, Langsdale Library, Baltimore MD. 301-727-6350, Ext 444
Green, Anna, *Regional Adminr,* Gateway Regional Library System, Pocatello ID. 208-237-2192
Green, Anna, *Dir,* Portneuf District Library, Pocatello ID. 208-237-2192
Green, Bernice, *Libr Asst,* Evansdale Public Library, Evansdale IA. 319-232-5367
Green, Blanche, *Publications Mgr,* National Civil Service League Library, Chevy Chase MD. 301-654-8664
Green, Carol, *Librn,* Idaho Legislative Council, Legislative Library, Boise ID. 208-334-2475
Green, Carolyn, *Librn,* Omaha Public Library (North), Omaha NE. 402-444-4849
Green, Claude, *Dir,* Elizabeth City State University, G R Little Library, Elizabeth City NC. 919-335-0551, Ext 332
Green, David, *Assoc Libr for Collection Develop,* Graduate Theological Union Library, Berkeley CA. 415-841-9811
Green, David A, *Dir,* Rhode Island Library Film Cooperative, RI. 401-739-2278
Green, Donald, *Asst Librn,* Combs College of Music Library, Philadelphia PA. 215-848-7500
Green, Dorothy F, *Librn,* Center for Naval Analyses Library, Alexandria VA. 703-998-3580
Green, Douglas, *Dir,* Ambassador College, Roy Hammer Memorial Learning Resources Center, Big Sandy TX. 214-636-4311, Ext 230
Green, Edith, *Librn,* California Missionary Baptist Institute & Seminary Library, Bellflower CA. 213-925-4082
Green, Eleanor, *Librn,* Salt Lake County Library System (South Jordan Branch), South Jordan UT. 801-943-7614
Green, Ellen, *Librn,* Veterans Administration Center (Wadsworth Medical Library), Los Angeles CA. 213-478-3711, Ext 6271
Green, Frank L, *Librn,* Washington State Historical Society, Henry Hewitt Jr Memorial Library, Tacoma WA. 206-593-2830
Green, G Patrick, *Deputy Commissioner for Mgt Servs,* Chicago Public Library, Chicago IL. 312-269-2900
Green, Genevieve, *Commun Servs,* Portage County District Library, Hiram OH. 216-569-7666
Green, Geraldine, *Bkmobile Coordr,* Logan-Helm Woodford County Public Library, Versailles KY. 606-873-5191, 873-9703
Green, Helen I, *Librn,* Cleveland Public Library (Memorial), Cleveland OH. 216-531-5860
Green, Hope, *Librn,* Wesleyan University (Psychology), Middletown CT. 203-347-9411, Ext 426
Green, Jana, *ILL,* Kansas State Library, Topeka KS. 913-296-3296
Green, Jane, *Librn,* University of Southwestern Louisiana (Horticulture), Lafayette LA. 318-264-6064
Green, Joseph H, *Dir,* Atlantic County Library, Pleasantville NJ. 609-646-8699, 645-7121, 625-2776
Green, Joyce D, *Librn,* Vicksburg Community Library, Vicksburg MI. 616-694-1648
Green, Judith, *Bk Selection & Acq,* Timberland Regional Library, Olympia WA. 206-943-5001
Green, Judy, *Ref,* Honeywell Information Systems Inc, System Technical Library, Waltham MA. 617-890-8400
Green, Julian, *Librn,* Harvard University Library (Geological Sciences Library), Cambridge MA. 617-495-2029
Green, Kerry, *Media,* William Paterson College of New Jersey, Sarah Byrd Askew Library, Wayne NJ. 201-595-2113
Green, Kim, *Librn,* West Coast Technical Service, Inc, Library, Cerritos CA. 213-921-9831
Green, L, *Librn,* Inco Metals Co, J Roy Gordon Research Lab Library, Mississauga ON. 416-822-3322, Ext 249
Green, Leon C, *Tech Serv & Cat,* Moline Public Library, Moline IL. 309-762-6883
Green, Leroy A, *Prof,* University of Northern Colorado, Department of Educational Media, CO. 303-351-2807

Green, Lois R, *Bk Selection Coordr,* Troy State University Library, Troy AL. 205-566-3000, Ext 263
Green, Louise, *Librn Blind,* Southwest Kansas Library System (Subregional Talking Books Library), Dodge City KS. 316-225-1231
Green, Mabel, *Librn,* First Baptist Church Library, Melrose MA. 617-665-4470
Green, Margie, *Librn,* Carver County Library System (Young America Branch), Young America MN. 612-467-2665
Green, Marguerite, *Librn,* Webb City Free Public Library, Webb City MO. 417-673-4326
Green, Marilyn V, *Project Librarian,* South Bay Cooperative Library System, Santa Clara CA. 408-984-3278
Green, Marion, *Chief Med Ed,* United States Air Force (Strughold Aeromedical Library), Brooks AFB TX. 512-536-3321
Green, Martha, *Cat,* Huntington Beach Library, Information & Cultural Resource Center, Huntington Beach CA. 714-842-4481
Green, Mary, *Librn,* Prince Rupert Municipal Library, Prince Rupert BC. 604-627-1345
Green, Mrs Eddie, *Asst Librn & Cat,* Village Library, Wimberley TX. 512-847-2188
Green, Paula, *Ref,* Boise Public Library & Information Center, Boise ID. 208-384-4466
Green, Phyllis, *Librn,* Brownell Public Library, Brownell KS. 913-481-2325
Green, Roberta, *Asst Librn,* Phillips County Public Library, Malta MT. 406-654-2407
Green, Rodeane, *Dir & On-Line Servs,* Nebraska Library for the Blind & Physically Handicapped, Lincoln NE. 402-471-2045
Green, Rosemary A, *Tech Serv,* Handley Library, Winchester VA. 703-662-9041
Green, Sue, *Ch,* George S Houston Memorial Library, Dothan AL. 205-793-9767
Green, Sylvie, *Selection Servs Librns,* Dallas Public Library, Dallas TX. 214-748-9071
Green, Thomas A, *Librn,* Austin Public Library, Austin MN. 507-433-2391
Green, Tonya, *Librn,* Ingham County Library (Delhi), Holt MI. 517-694-9351
Green, Virginia T, *Dir,* Middlesboro-Bell County Public Library, Middlesboro KY. 606-248-4812
Green, Virginia T, *Librn,* Pineville-Bell County Public Library, Pineville KY. 606-337-3422
Green, Jr, Bill, *In Charge,* Allegany County Museum Library, Belmont NY. 716-268-7612, Ext 244
Green, Jr, Walter H, *Per,* Southwest Missouri State University Library, Springfield MO. 417-836-5104
Greenamoyer, Alma, *Librn,* Lehighton Memorial Library, Lehighton PA. 215-377-2750
Greenawalt, Mary, *Ch,* Gail Borden Public Library District, Elgin IL. 312-742-2411
Greenbank, John, *Actg Librn,* Baptist Bible College Library (Music), Springfield MO. 417-869-9811, Ext 307
Greenbaum, Dale, *Media,* Geauga County Public Library, Chardon OH. 216-285-7601
Greenbaum, Diane, *Librn,* Midland-Ross Corp Library, Cleveland OH. 216-491-8400, Ext 288
Greenberg, Adele, *Librn,* New York Public Library (Reader's Adviser's Office), New York NY. 212-790-6576
Greenberg, Adele, *Reader's Advisor,* New York Public Library (The Branch Libraries), New York NY. 212-790-6262
Greenberg, Alan, *Cat,* College of Charleston, Robert Scott Small Library, Charleston SC. 803-792-5530
Greenberg, Arlene, *Librn & On-Line Servs,* Sir Mortimer B Davis Jewish General Hospital, Medical Library, Montreal PQ. 514-342-3111, Ext 325, 376
Greenberg, Bette, *ILL & Ref,* Yale University Library (Medical Library), New Haven CT. 203-436-4784, 436-2961
Greenberg, Carolyn R, *Ref,* Massachusetts Institute of Technology, Lincoln Laboratory Library, Lexington MA. 617-862-5500, Ext 7195
Greenberg, Emily, *Librn,* University of Baltimore (Law Library), Baltimore MD. 301-727-6350, Ext 328
Greenberg, Herman, *Personnel,* Free Library of Philadelphia, Philadelphia PA. 215-686-5322
Greenberg, Janet, *Circ,* Rutgers University (Archibald Stevens Alexander Library), New Brunswick NJ. 201-932-7129

Greenberg, Kaija, *Ref,* Mercer County Library, Trenton NJ. 609-989-6917
Greenberg, Lenore R, *Librn,* Human Resources Center, Ina Mend Research Library, Albertson NY. 516-747-5400
Greenberg, Marilyn W, *Coordr,* California State University-Los Angeles, Library Services Credential Program, CA. 213-224-3765
Greenberg, Rayma, *Dir,* Los Angeles Mission College, Learning Resources Center, San Fernando CA. 213-365-8271, Ext 283
Greenberg, Ruth, *Librn,* Mercer County Library (Highstown Memorial), Hightstown NJ. 609-448-1474
Greenberg, Stanley, *Asst Dir & Ref,* Forbes Library, Northampton MA. 413-584-8399
Greenbie, Vlasta K, *Librn,* University of Massachusetts at Amherst Library (Physical Sciences), Amherst MA. 413-545-1370
Greenblatt, Judith S, *Librn,* Temple B'nai Israel, Michael Lichtenstein Memorial Library, Toledo OH. 419-531-1677
Greenblatt, Ruth, *Librn,* Beth Israel Synagogue, Beth Israel Congregation Library, Vineland NJ. 609-691-0852
Greenblatt, Stella, *Librn,* Palm Beach County Public Library System (Mid-County), Lake Worth FL. 305-964-2525
Greenburg, Alice, *Librn,* Indianapolis-Marion County Public Library (Brightwood), Indianapolis IN. 317-635-5662
Greene, Adell, *Librn,* Massachusetts Department of Commerce & Development Library, Boston MA. 617-727-3215
Greene, B P, *Librn,* Conway County Library, Morrilton AR. 501-354-5204
Greene, Beverly A, *Ref,* Middlesboro-Bell County Public Library, Middlesboro KY. 606-248-4812
Greene, Christine, *Librn,* Carrier Corp, Logan Lewis Library, Syracuse NY. 315-432-6306
Greene, Ellin, *Assoc Prof,* University of Chicago, Graduate Library School, IL. 312-753-3482
Greene, Faith, *Tech Serv & Cat,* Ashland College Library, Ashland OH. 419-289-4067
Greene, Frances G, *Librn,* Baird Corp, Technical Library, Bedford MA. 617-276-6000
Greene, Fred, *AV,* Walters State Community College, Learning Resource Center, Morristown TN. 615-581-2121, Ext 212
Greene, Gladys, *Librn,* Nelson County Public Library (Boston Branch), Boston KY. 502-348-3714
Greene, Glenda-mae, *Librn,* Kingsway College Library, Oshawa ON. 416-725-6557, Ext 21
Greene, Grace, *Ch,* Robbins Library, Arlington MA. 617-643-0026
Greene, Gwendolyn, *Tech Serv,* Miracosta College Learning Resource Center, Oceanside CA. 714-757-2121, Ext 250
Greene, Irene B, *Dir,* Berlin Free Town Library, Berlin NY. 518-658-2231
Greene, James T, *Librn,* New York Public Library (Epiphany), New York NY. 212-683-9845
Greene, Jane, *Art & Music,* Birmingham Public & Jefferson County Free Library, Birmingham AL. 205-254-2551
Greene, Jane, *Dir,* Door County Library, Sturgeon Bay WI. 414-743-6578
Greene, Joan, *Librn,* Onslow County Public Library (Swansboro Branch), Swansboro NC. 919-347-2592, 347-5495
Greene, Jon S, *Librn,* University of California Los Angeles Library (Architecture & Urban Planning), Los Angeles CA. 213-825-2747
Greene, K Richard, *Tech Serv,* Free Public Library of Woodbridge, Woodbridge NJ. 201-634-4450
Greene, Katherine, *Commun Servs,* Lexington Public Library, Lexington KY. 606-252-8871
Greene, Kingsley W, *On-Line Servs,* Rensselaer Polytechnic Institute, Folsom Library, Troy NY. 518-270-6673
Greene, Larosa, *Librn,* Memphis-Shelby County Public Library & Information Center (Levi), Memphis TN. 901-789-3140
Greene, Lois B, *Dir,* James H Johnson Memorial Library, Deptford NJ. 609-227-4424
Greene, Lucy R, *On-Line Servs,* United States Army (The Army Logistics Library), Fort Lee VA. 804-734-1797, 734-4286
Greene, Margaret, *Librn,* Pettee Memorial Library, Wilmington VT. 802-464-3764
Greene, Martha, *Acq,* Santa Monica Public Library, Santa Monica CA. 213-451-5751

Greene, Minnie L, *Reader Serv,* University of Arkansas, Pine Bluff, Watson Memorial Library, Pine Bluff AR. 501-541-6825
Greene, Nancy, *Ref,* Lee Memorial Library, Allendale Public Library, Allendale NJ. 201-327-4338
Greene, Nancy, *Asst Dir,* Elisha D Smith Public Library, Menasha WI. 414-729-5166
Greene, Orenn, *Librn,* Durham County Library (Forest Hills), Durham NC. 919-489-3010
Greene, Phyllis C, *Acq,* Winthrop Public Library, Frost Public Library, Winthrop MA. 617-846-1703
Greene, Richard, *Librn,* University of Montreal Libraries (Humanities & Social Sciences), Montreal PQ. 514-343-7424
Greene, Richard O, *Dir,* Mid-Mississippi Regional Library System, Kosciusko MS. 601-289-5141, 289-5146
Greene, Robert J, *Dir,* Kennesaw College Library, Marietta GA. 404-422-8770, Ext 250
Greene, Roberta, *On-Line Servs,* Lewis Cooper Junior Memorial Library & Arts Center, Opelika AL. 205-749-1426
Greene, Rose, *Librn,* Skene Memorial Library, Fleischmanns NY. 914-254-5514
Greene, Thomas, *Tech Serv & On-Line Servs,* United States Army (Army Engineer Center & Fort Belvoir Van Noy Library), Fort Belvoir VA. 703-664-6255
Greene, William T, *Supvr,* 3M (Engineering Information Services), Saint Paul MN. 612-778-4264
Greene, Wilma, *Librn,* Lewisburg Library, Lewisburg KY. 502-755-5071
Greener, Barbara, *Music,* Queens College Library, Flushing NY. 212-520-7616
Greeney, Joan, *Tech Serv,* Adriance Memorial Library, Poughkeepsie NY. 914-485-4790
Greenfeder, Paul, *In Charge,* New York Times (Reference Library), New York NY. 212-556-7428
Greenfeld, R, *On-Line Servs & Bibliog Instr,* Bell Canada (Information Resource Centre), Montreal PQ. 514-870-8922
Greenfeldt, Eric, *Ref,* Princeton Public Library, Princeton NJ. 609-924-9529
Greenfield, Anne L, *Assoc Librn,* Travenol Labs, Inc, Business & Law Library, Deerfield IL. 312-948-3880
Greenfield, Coralyn, *Ch,* Eckhart Public Library, Auburn IN. 219-925-2414
Greenfield, Gloria, *Librn,* Deseronto Public Library, Deseronto ON. 613-396-2744
Greenfield, Hilary, *Media,* Township of Hamilton Free Public Library, Trenton NJ. 609-890-3460
Greenfield, Jane, *Asst Dir, ILL & Ad,* Evanston Public Library, Evanston IL. 312-866-0300
Greenfield, Katharine, *Rare Bks & Spec Coll,* Hamilton Public Library, Hamilton ON. 416-529-8111
Greenfield, Marjorie, *Librn,* Metropolitan Hospital Library, Philadelphia PA. 215-238-2312
Greenfield, Mary E, *Head Conserv Studio,* Yale University Library (Sterling Memorial Library), New Haven CT. 203-436-8335
Greenfield, Patricia J, *Librn,* Touro Infirmary (Hospital Library), New Orleans LA. 504-897-8102, 897-8502
Greenfield, Robert, *Librn,* Baltimore County Public Library (Woodlawn), Baltimore MD. 301-265-7766
Greenhalgh, James A, *Librn,* United States Department of Labor, Mine Safety & Health Administration Informational Service Library, Lakewood CO. 303-234-4961
Greenhalgh, Kathleen, *Librn,* Indian & Colonial Research Center, Inc, Butler Library, Old Mystic CT. 203-536-9771
Greenhall, Margaret, *Librn,* New York Public Library (Record Libraries), New York NY. 212-790-6402
Greenholz, Carol, *Tech Serv & Cat,* State University Agricultural & Technical College at Farmingdale, Thomas D Greenley Library, Farmingdale NY. 516-420-2011, 420-2012
Greeniaus, Barbara, *Lectr,* Concordia University, Library Studies Program, PQ. 514-482-0320, Ext 324
Greeniaus, Barbara, *Librn,* Montreal General Hospital, Medical Library, Montreal PQ. 514-937-6011, Ext 775

Greenick, Betty, *Acq,* Mansfield-Richland County Public Library, Mansfield OH. 419-524-1041
Greening, Betty, *Asst Librn,* Howe Memorial Library, Breckenridge MI. 517-842-3202
Greening, David, *Media,* Gordon College, Winn Library, Wenham MA. 617-927-2300, Ext 233
Greening, Monica, *Ad, Acq & Ref,* Monrovia Public Library, Monrovia CA. 213-358-0174
Greening, Walter, *Chief Librn,* Stockton State Hospital, Professional Library, Stockton CA. 209-948-7181
Greenlee, Donna, *ILL,* Pioneer Memorial Library, Colby KS. 913-462-3881
Greenlee, Margaret, *Reader Serv,* Belmont College, Williams Library, Nashville TN. 615-383-7001, Ext 253
Greenley, Maude, *Supvr,* Huron County Public Library (Lakelet), Clifford ON. 519-327-8533
Greenmun, Janet, *Spec Coll,* Broome Community College, Cecil C Tyrrell Learning Resources Center, Binghamton NY. 607-772-5020
Greenshields, Eleanor, *Cat,* Park College Library, Parkville MO. 816-741-2000, Ext 254
Greenshields, Harry, *Chief Librn,* Atomic Energy of Canada Limited, Chalk River Nuclear Laboratories Main Library, Chalk River ON. 613-584-3311
Greenslade, Thomas B, *Archivist,* Kenyon College, Gordon Keith Chalmers Memorial Library, Gambier OH. 614-427-2244, Ext 2186
Greenspun, Joanne, *Dir,* Vineland Free Public Library, Vineland NJ. 609-696-1100
Greenstein, Bee, *Librn,* Congregation Kins of West Rogers Park, Jordan E Feuer Library, Chicago IL. 312-761-4000
Greenup, Nadine, *Ref,* Black Gold Cooperative Library System, Ventura CA. 805-654-2643
Greenwald, Evelyn, *On-Line Servs,* Los Angeles Public Library System, Los Angeles CA. 213-626-7555
Greenwald, Evelyn, *Dir,* Southern California Answering Network, (SCAN), CA. 213-626-7555
Greenwald, Mary, *Media,* Adrian Public Library, Adrian MI. 517-263-2161, Ext 277
Greenwell, Marilyn F, *Librn,* Middleport Free Library, Middleport NY. 716-735-3281
Greenwood, Alma, *Ref,* Timberland Regional Library, Olympia WA. 206-943-5001
Greenwood, Donna, *Librn,* Holland College Royalty Centre Library, West Royalty PE. 902-892-2401
Greenwood, Larry, *Circ,* University of Kentucky, Margaret I King Library, Lexington KY. 606-257-3801
Greenwood, M D, *Librn,* Burndy Library, Norwalk CT. 203-838-4444
Greenwood, Mary, *Chief Librn,* Imperial Oil Ltd, Business Library, Toronto ON. 416-924-9111, Ext 345
Greenwood, Ralph, *Consult,* Cambria County Library System, Johnstown PA. 814-536-5131
Greenwood, Ralph H, *Librn,* Barnesboro Public Library, Barnesboro PA. 814-948-7820
Greer, Anna, *Dir,* Yoakum County Library, Denver City TX. 806-592-2754
Greer, Barbara F, *Librn,* Fivco Regional Library, Louisa KY. 606-638-4797
Greer, Brian J, *Dir,* Palmer College of Chiropractic, Davenport IA. 319-324-1611, Ext 242
Greer, Cora A, *Dir,* Palliser Regional Library, Moose Jaw SK. 306-693-3669
Greer, Kathleen M, *Asst Librn,* Polk County Historical & Genealogical Library, Bartow FL. 813-533-5146
Greer, Nancy, *Bkmobile Coordr,* Lancaster County Library, Lancaster PA. 717-394-2651
Greer, Natalia, *Librn,* Jefferson County Public Library (Villa Regional), Lakewood CO. 303-936-7407
Greer, Patricia L, *Librn,* United States International Trade Commission Library (Law Library), Washington DC. 202-523-0333
Greer, Roger C, *Dean,* University of Southern California, School of Library Science, CA. 213-741-2548
Greer, V, *Cat,* Queen's University at Kingston (Bracken Library), Kingston ON. 613-547-5753
Greeson, Georgianna W, *Librn,* Saint Charles Parish Library, Luling LA. 504-785-8471
Greeson, Judy, *Coordr,* Wabash Valley Area Library Services Authority, IN. 317-362-4235

Greeson, Nancy, *Librn,* Durand Memorial Library, Durand MI. 517-288-3743
Greeson, Tamra, *Asst Dir & Ch,* Uncle Remus Regional Library, Madison GA. 404-342-1206, 342-2955
Greey, Kathleen, *Educ & Psychol,* Portland State University, Branford Price Millar Library, Portland OR. 503-229-4424
Gref, Beverley, *Instruction Servs,* University of Calgary Library, Calgary AB. 403-284-5954
Grefrath, Richard, *ILL & Ref,* University of Nevada-Reno, Noble H Getchell Library, Reno NV. 702-784-6533
Grefsheim, Suzanne, *Access Servs,* George Washington University Library (Paul Himmelfarb Health Sciences Library), Washington DC. 202-676-2850
Gregath, Ann, *Asst Regional Dir,* Cullman County Public Library, Cullman AL. 205-734-2720
Gregg, Alice E, *Assoc Librn, Tech Serv & Acq,* Loma Linda University, Vernier Radcliffe Memorial Library, Loma Linda CA. 714-796-7311, Ext 2916
Gregg, Elizabeth L, *ILL & Ref,* Bridgewater Public Library, Bridgewater MA. 617-697-3331
Gregg, Joseph, *Acq,* Northeastern Illinois University Library, Chicago IL. 312-583-4050, Ext 469, 470, 471, 472
Gregg, Mary, *Librn,* Library Association of Portland (Sellwood), Portland OR. 503-236-4014
Gregg, Mrs K, *Librn,* Cosby, Mason & Martland Township Public Library, Noelville ON. 705-898-2965
Grego, Noel R, *Dept Chmn & Circ,* City Colleges of Chicago, Kennedy-King College Library, Chicago IL. 312-962-3262
Grego, Noel R, *Lectr,* Felician College, Dept of Library Science, IL. 312-539-2328
Gregoire, Carol, *Ref,* Windsor Locks Public Library, Windsor Locks CT. 203-623-6170
Gregoire, Parker, *Dean,* San Jacinto College, Lee Davis Library, Pasadena TX. 713-476-1850, 476-1501, Ext 241
Gregor, Janet, *Tech Serv,* Union College, Schaffer Library, Schenectady NY. 518-370-6278
Gregor, Margaret A, *Dir,* J Sargeant Reynolds Community College (Parham Campus Learning Resources Center), Richmond VA. 804-264-3220
Gregory, Anita, *Assoc Librn,* Immaculate Heart College Library, Los Angeles CA. 213-462-1301, Ext 271
Gregory, Barbara K, *YA,* Mount Vernon Public Library, Mount Vernon NY. 914-668-1840
Gregory, Barbara L, *Librn,* Richmond Public Library (West End), Richmond VA. 804-285-8820
Gregory, Cris, *Librn,* Sons of Norway, North Star Library, Minneapolis MN. 612-827-3611
Gregory, Dean W, *Librn,* Folsom State Prison Library, Represa CA. 916-985-2561
Gregory, Doris, *Asst Librn,* Barclay Public Library of Illini Township, Warrensburg IL. 217-672-3621
Gregory, Freda, *Coordr,* Merced College, Library Technology Program, CA. 209-723-4321, Ext 274
Gregory, Helen, *Ch,* Albion Public Library, Albion MI. 517-629-5571
Gregory, Laurel, *Ref,* Pacific University, Harvey W Scott Memorial Library, Forest Grove OR. 503-357-6151, Ext 301
Gregory, Lorraine, *In Charge,* Kimball Library, Kimball MN. 612-398-3915
Gregory, Mae, *Librn,* Chicago Public Library (Whitney M Young Jr), Chicago IL. 312-723-2133
Gregory, Pamela J, *Librn,* Prince George's County Circuit Court Law Library, Upper Marlboro MD. 301-952-3438
Gregory, Patricia, *Humanities,* University of Richmond, Boatwright Memorial Library, Richmond VA. 804-285-6452
Gregory, Sara M, *Librn,* Emory University, Oxford College Library, Oxford GA. 404-786-7051, Ext 281
Gregory, Timothy P, *Tech Serv,* Newport Beach Public Library, Newport Beach CA. 714-640-2141
Gregory, Vickie, *Tech Serv,* Auburn University at Montgomery Library, Montgomery AL. 205-279-9110, Ext 247

Greif, Lorene, *Librn,* Slater Public Library, Slater IA. 515-685-3558
Greife, Mrs Frederick, *Dir,* Lenora Blackmore Public Library, Windsor MO. 816-647-2298
Greig, P A, *Pub Servs,* University of Saskatchewan Library, Saskatoon SK. 306-343-4216
Greil, Barbara, *Ser,* State University of New York, Agricultural & Technical College at Alfred, Walter C Hinkle Memorial Library, Alfred NY. 607-871-6313
Greiner, Blanche, *Librn,* Richland Public Library, Richland IA. 515-688-6541
Greiner, Eileen, *Librn,* Cary Public Library, Cary IL. 312-639-4210
Greiner, Jerilyn, *Librn,* Dodge County Library Service (Iron Ridge Public), Iron Ridge WI. 414-885-4571, 885-5134
Greisch, Elizabeth, *Coord Libr Spec Servs,* Palo Alto City Library, Palo Alto CA. 415-329-2436
Grele, Gaile, *Asst Dir,* Old Bridge Public Library, Old Bridge NJ. 201-679-5622
Gremling, Richard, *On-Line Servs & Bibliog Instr,* Ortho Pharmaceutical Corp, Hartman Library, Raritan NJ. 201-524-2240
Grenda, Johanna, *On-Line Servs,* Raytheon Co (Research Division Library), Waltham MA. 617-899-8400, Ext 2196
Grennon, Candace, *Librn,* New Haven Public Library, New Haven VT. 802-545-2426
Grenrich, Fran, *Librn,* Sundstrand Aviation, Engineering Library, Rockford IL. 815-226-6753
Grenville, Sally, *On-Line Servs,* Memorial University of Newfoundland Library, Saint John's NF. 709-753-1200
Grenz, Jeanette, *Librn,* Wagner Public Library, Wagner SD. 605-384-5248
Gresack, Barbara, *Librn,* Central Synagogue Nassau County, Helen Blau Memorial Library, Rockville Centre NY. 516-766-4300
Gresehover, Beverly, *Circ,* University of Maryland at Baltimore (Health Sciences Library), Baltimore MD. 301-528-7545
Gresehover, Robert, *Assoc Dir,* Johns Hopkins University Libraries (William H Welch Medical Library), Baltimore MD. 301-955-3411
Gresham, Catherine, *Asst Dir,* Collinsville Memorial Public Library, Collinsville IL. 618-344-1112
Gresham, Cubie P, *Librn,* Memphis Pink Palace Museum Library, Memphis TN. 901-454-5601
Greskovic, Cheryle, *Librn,* Gould Inc, Chesapeake Instrument Division Engineering Technical Library, Glen Burnie MD. 301-867-2151, Ext 310
Gresser, Marylyn, *Chief Librn,* Veterans Administration, Hospital Library Service, Gainesville FL. 904-376-1611, Ext 6313
Gresseth, Dale, *Dept Chmn,* University of Wisconsin-La Crosse, Murphy Library, La Crosse WI. 608-785-8505
Gressley, Gene M, *Dir,* American Heritage Center Library, Laramie WY. 307-766-3279
Gretz, Dolores, *In Charge,* Herald-News Library, Joliet IL. 815-729-6161
Greve, Clyde L, *Coordr,* University of Wisconsin-LaCrosse, Educational Media Dept, WI. 608-784-8134
Greve, Edward, *ILL & Bibliog Instr,* University of Wisconsin-Superior, Jim Dan Hill Library, Superior WI. 715-392-8101, Ext 346
Greve, Edward F, *Instr,* University of Wisconsin-Superior, Library Science Program, WI. 715-392-8101, Ext 346, 347
Greve, Lana, *Bkmobile Coordr,* Fort Dodge Public Library, Fort Dodge IA. 515-573-8167
Greve, Lana, *Librn,* Fort Dodge Public Library (South East), Fort Dodge IA. 515-573-4631
Grewal, Bonnie, *AV,* Kansas City College of Osteopathic Medicine, Mazzacano Hall Library, Kansas City MO. 816-283-2451, 2454
Grey, Suanne, *Learning Ctr,* Lincoln Christian College & Seminary Library, Lincoln IL. 217-732-3168, Ext 234
Gribbin, John H, *Dir,* University of Missouri-Columbia, Elmer Ellis Library, Columbia MO. 314-882-4701
Gribble, Stokely, *Asst Dir,* West Virginia University, University Library, Morgantown WV. 304-293-4040
Grider, Patty B, *Asst Librn,* Hart County Public Library, Munfordville KY. 502-524-9953
Grieb, Sherry, *Librn,* Dallas Public Library (Park Forest), Dallas TX. 214-241-1434

Griebenow, Leona, *Librn,* Clermont Public Library, Clermont IA. 319-423-5262
Grieder, Theodore, *Asst Librn,* New York University (Fales Collection), New York NY. 212-598-2484
Grief, Violetta, *Librn,* Marshall County Public Library (Calvert City Branch), Calvert City KY. 502-395-5745
Grieger, Sharon, *Ad,* Mount Prospect Public Library, Mount Prospect IL. 312-253-5675
Griehshammer, Louisa, *Br Coordr,* San Jose Public Library, San Jose CA. 408-277-4822
Griener, J, *Ch,* Saint Thomas Public Library, Saint Thomas ON. 519-631-6050
Griener, J, *Acq,* Saint Thomas Public Library, Saint Thomas ON. 519-631-6050
Grier, Margaret, *Ref,* Otis Library, Norwich CT. 203-889-2365
Grier, Martha, *Bkmobile Coordr,* Collier County Free Public Library, Naples FL. 813-262-4130, 261-8208
Grier, Mary, *Librn,* San Diego Public Library (Claremont), San Diego CA. 714-276-1140
Gries, Norma, *Librn,* Cameron Iron Works Inc Library, Houston TX. 713-939-3789
Griest, Lois, *ILL,* Vanderbilt University Library (Central-Science), Nashville TN. 615-322-6603
Grieve, D, *On-Line Servs,* University of Victoria, McPherson Library, Victoria BC. 604-477-6911, Ext 4466
Griffel, Eugene B, *Dir,* Mideastern Michigan Library Cooperative, Flint MI. 313-232-7119
Griffen, Agnes M, *Deputy Dir,* Tucson Public Library, Tucson AZ. 602-791-4391
Griffen, Charles S, *Bus, Sci & Tech,* Hartford Public Library, Hartford CT. 203-525-9121
Griffen, Charles S, *Coordr Central Servs,* Hartford Public Library, Hartford CT. 203-525-9121
Griffeth, Elaine O, *Circ,* Piedmont Regional Library, Winder GA. 404-867-2762
Griffin, Alberta, *Librn,* Chattahoochee Valley Regional Library (Baker Village), Columbus GA. 404-689-7352
Griffin, Bill, *Librn,* Kentucky Rural Electric Cooperative Corp Library, Louisville KY. 502-582-2453
Griffin, Brian, *Spec Coll,* Elmont Public Library, Elmont NY. 516-354-5280, 354-4091
Griffin, Clifton, *Librn,* Austin Public Library (Carver), Austin TX. 512-472-5433
Griffin, Constance, *Asst Dir,* Moses Greeley Parker Memorial Library, Dracut MA. 617-454-5474
Griffin, Diane, *Media,* Warder Public Library, Springfield OH. 323-8616 & 323-9751
Griffin, Doris, *Spec Coll,* Free Public Library of Roselle Park, Veterans Memorial Library, Roselle Park NJ. 201-245-2456, 245-7171
Griffin, Edith M, *Chmn,* University of the District of Columbia-Mount Vernon Square Campus, Dept of Library Science & Instructional Systems Technology, DC. 202-727-2756, 727-2757 & 727-2758
Griffin, Elna, *Librn,* Worcester County Library (Ocean City Branch), Ocean City MD. 301-289-7297
Griffin, Evelyn, *Asst Dir,* Crowley Ridge Regional Library, Jonesboro AR. 501-935-5133
Griffin, Evelyn, *Librn,* Poinsett County Library, Harrisburg AR. 501-578-5666
Griffin, Gerald T, *Chief Librn Br, MWR Div,* United States Air Force (Electronics Systems Division, Base Library), Hanscom AFB MA. 617-861-2177
Griffin, Gerald T, *Librn,* United States Air Force (Loring Air Force Base Library), Loring AFB ME. 207-999-1110
Griffin, Hillis L, *Dir,* Argonne National Laboratory, Technical Information Services Dept, Argonne IL. 312-972-2000
Griffin, Ida, *Librn,* Cumberland County Public Library (Cumberland County Law Library), Fayetteville NC. 919-323-5618
Griffin, Ima, *Dir,* United States Forest Service, Southern Forest Experimental Station Library, Gulfport MS. 601-864-3461
Griffin, J M, *Librn,* United States Navy (Naval Regional Medical Center, General Library), Charleston SC. 803-743-5130
Griffin, Jane D, *Dir,* Lexington County Circulating Library, Batesburg SC. 803-532-9223
Griffin, Janette, *Cat,* New Orleans Baptist Theological Seminary Library, New Orleans LA. 504-282-4455, Ext 289

Griffin, John L, *Media* Pitt Community College, Learning Resources Center, Greenville NC. 919-756-3130, Ext 213

Griffin, June, *Ad,* Portland Public Library, Baxter Library, Portland ME. 207-773-4761

Griffin, Karen, *Ref,* International University Library, Kansas City MO. 816-931-6374

Griffin, Marie, *Media,* Lassen College, Media Center, Susanville CA. 916-257-6181, Ext 261

Griffin, Martha, *Cat,* University of North Alabama, Collier Library, Florence AL. 205-766-4100, Ext 241

Griffin, Mary, *Librn,* Library Association of Portland (North Portland), Portland OR. 503-284-5622

Griffin, Mary Ann, *Dir,* Xavier University, McDonald Memorial Library, Cincinnati OH. 513-745-3881

Griffin, Mary C, *Librn,* Bellevue Public Library, Bellevue ID. 208-788-3692

Griffin, Mary T, *Librn,* Omaha Public Library (Swanson), Omaha NE. 402-444-4852

Griffin, P, *ILL & Spec Coll,* South Carolina Wildlife & Marine Resources Department, Marine Resources Div Library, Charleston SC. 803-795-6350, Ext 205

Griffin, Pamela B, *Asst Dir,* University of Calgary Library (Faculty of Medicine Medical Library), Calgary AB. 403-284-6858

Griffin, Patricia S, *Dir,* Roanoke Bible College, Mary E Griffith Memorial Library, Elizabeth City NC. 919-338-5191

Griffin, Peggy, *Ad & Acq,* Ridgewood Public Library, Ridgewood NJ. 201-652-5200

Griffin, Pope, *Dir,* Florida Junior College at Jacksonville (Downtown Campus Learning Resource Center), Jacksonville FL. 904-633-8330

Griffin, Rita, *In Charge,* Eastern Counties Regional Library (Port Hawkesbury Branch), Port Hawkesbury NS. 902-747-2597

Griffin, Stephanie, *Cat,* Bentley College, Solomon R Baker Library, Waltham MA. 617-891-2231

Griffin, William H, *Tech Serv,* Southwest Texas State University, Learning Resources Center, San Marcos TX. 512-245-2132

Griffing, Sister Dorothy, *Dir,* Sisters, Servants of the Immaculate Heart of Mary, College Library, Monroe MI. 313-241-3660, Ext 233

Griffis, Barbara A, *ILL,* Union Theological Seminary Library, New York NY. 212-662-7100, Ext 274

Griffis, Kathy, *Librn,* Polk County Law Library, Bartow FL. 813-533-0411, Ext 218

Griffiss, Keating, *AV,* Chattanooga-Hamilton County Bicentennial Library, Chattanooga TN. 615-757-5320

Griffith, Alice B, *Dir,* Mohawk Valley Community College Library, Utica NY. 315-792-5337

Griffith, Barbara, *Librn,* Willett Free Library, Saunderstown RI. 401-294-2081

Griffith, Belver, *Prof,* Drexel University, School of Library & Information Science, PA. 215-895-2474

Griffith, Dorothy K, *Dir,* Greenup County Public Libraries, Greenup KY. 606-473-6514

Griffith, Frances J, *Librn,* Mills-Petrie Memorial Library, Ashton IL. 815-453-2213

Griffith, Jack, *Librn,* Veterans Administration, Health Sciences Library, North Little Rock AR. 501-372-8361, Ext 7586

Griffith, Janet, *Acq,* Eureka College, Melick Library, Eureka IL. 309-467-3721, Ext 219-258

Griffith, Jean, *Librn,* Chandler Public Library, Chandler AZ. 602-963-8111, Ext 390

Griffith, Johnnie, *Asst Librn,* Seminole Junior College, David L Boren Library, Seminole OK. 405-382-9950, Ext 243

Griffith, M, *Librn,* Ontario Workmans Compensation Board, Public Services & Information Div Library, Toronto ON. 416-965-8725

Griffith, Mary E, *Ad,* Trails Regional Library, Johnson County-Lafayette County Library, Warrensburg MO. 816-747-9177

Griffith, Mona C, *Librn,* Martin Marietta Aerospace, Orlando Division, Technical Information Center Library, Orlando FL. 305-352-2051

Griffith, Ruth, *Ch & YA,* Arlington Heights Memorial Library, Arlington Heights IL. 312-392-0100

Griffith, William J, *Dir,* Anaheim Public Library, Anaheim CA. 714-533-5221

Griffith, Winifred, *Cat,* Eastern Montana College Library, Billings MT. 406-657-2320

Griffiths, Alice, *Dir,* Hancock County Library, Hawesville KY. 502-927-6760

Griffiths, Evelyn, *Librn,* Morrisville Library, Morrisville NY. 315-684-3808

Griffiths, Marian, *Dir,* Carnegie Library, Olney IL. 618-392-3711

Griffiths, Suzanne, *Librn,* University of Illinois Library at Urbana-Champaign (Classics), Urbana IL. 217-333-1124

Griffitt, Luella, *Librn,* Little River Community Library, Little River KS. 316-897-6610

Griffitts, Donna, *Instr,* United States Department of Agriculture Graduate School, Certificate Program for Library Technicians, DC. 202-447-5885

Griffitts, Donna K, *Admin Librn,* Offices of the Surgeons General United States Army-United States Air Force, Joint Medical Library, Washington DC. 202-695-5752

Griffitts, Michael, *Librn,* Morgan County Library, John F Kennedy Memorial Library, West Liberty KY. 606-743-4151

Griffler, Carl G, *Librn,* Norfolk Public Library (Little Creek), Norfolk VA. 804-480-1309

Grigg, Virginia C, *Bureau of Library Development: Chief,* State Library of Florida, Div of Library Services, Dept of State, Tallahassee FL. 904-487-2651

Griggs, Bessie T, *Librn,* Aetna Life & Casualty (Company Library), Hartford CT. 203-273-2946

Griggs, Doris, *Librn,* Victoria County Public Library (Little Britain Branch), Little Britain ON. 705-324-3104

Griggs, Fosteene E, *Dir,* Woodrow Wilson College of Law School, Joseph B Kilbride Library, Atlanta GA. 404-881-1457, Ext 21

Griggs, Glenda, *Circ,* University of North Alabama, Collier Library, Florence AL. 205-766-4100, Ext 241

Griggs, John B, *Librn,* Lloyd Library & Museum, Cincinnati OH. 513-721-3707

Griggs, Marian L, *Librn,* Pope Memorial Library, Danville VT. 802-684-2256

Grigsby, Earline, *Librn,* Birmingham Public & Jefferson County Free Library (Parke Memorial), Birmingham AL. 205-254-2551

Grilikhes, Sandra, *Librn,* University of Pennsylvania Libraries (Annenberg School of Communications), Philadelphia PA. 215-243-7027

Grilikhes, Sandra B, *Librn,* Annenberg School of Communications Library, Philadelphia PA. 215-243-7027, 243-7028

Grill, Emogene O, *Librn,* Dittlinger Memorial Library, New Braunfels TX. 512-625-8919

Grill, Laura, *Ch,* Harrison Public Library, Harrison NY. 914-835-0324

Grill, Stanley, *Librn,* Program Planners Inc, Library Information Center, New York NY. 212-840-2600, Ext 52

Grills, Russell A, *In Charge,* New York State Div for Historic Preservation, Lorenzo State Historic Site Archives & Library, Cazenovia NY. 315-655-3200

Grim, Eugene C, *Dir,* South Jersey Regional Film Library, Inc, Voorhees NJ. 609-772-1642

Grim, Joyce, *Tech Serv,* Western Theological Seminary, Beardslee Library, Holland MI. 616-392-8555, Ext 37 & 38

Grim, Pat, *Asst Dir,* Onslow County Public Library, Jacksonville NC. 919-347-2592, 347-5495

Grimaldi, Angelina, *Asst Librn,* Saint Thomas Hospital, Medical Library, Akron OH. 216-379-1111, Ext 7505

Grimason, Mrs D, *Dir,* Bedford Free Library, Bedford NY. 914-234-3570

Grimes, Alice M, *Librn,* Jackson County Library System (White City Branch), White City OR. 503-826-3615

Grimes, Deborah, *Dir,* Shelton State Community College, Junior College Division, Tuscaloosa AL. 205-759-1583

Grimes, Deirdre, *Asst Librn,* Royal Bank of Canada, Information Resources, Toronto ON. 416-865-2780

Grimes, Doris, *Asst Librn,* Fort Wayne Bible College, S A Lehman Memorial Library, Fort Wayne IN. 219-456-2111, Ext 223

Grimes, Gloria, *Pub Servs,* Palos Verdes Library District, Palos Verdes Peninsula CA. 213-541-2559, 2550

Grimes, Janet, *Librn,* Commonwealth Life Insurance Co, Louisville KY. 502-587-7371

Grimes, Kathleen J, *Librn,* Willowbrook State School, Learning Resource Center, Staten Island NY. 212-698-1440, Ext 596

Grimes, Marcia, *ILL,* James Madison University, Madison Memorial Library, Harrisonburg VA. 703-433-6150

Grimes, Martha, *Tech Serv,* Rockhurst College, Greenlease Library, Kansas City MO. 816-363-4010, Ext 253

Grimes, Maxyne M, *Tech Serv,* University of South Florida (Medical Center Library), Tampa FL. 813-974-2399

Grimes, Nancy, *Librn,* Hagerstown Public Library, Hagerstown IN. 317-489-5632

Grimes, Theodore, *Pub Servs,* Florida Junior College at Jacksonville (South Campus Learning Resources Center), Jacksonville FL. 904-646-2170

Grimley, Arlene, *Circ,* Central Michigan University, Charles V Park Library, Mount Pleasant MI. 517-774-3500

Grimley, Susan, *Bkmobile Coordr & Br Coordr,* Spartanburg County Public Library, Spartanburg SC. 582-4123 & 585-2441

Grimm, Ann, *ILL & Ref,* Grand Canyon College, Fleming Library, Phoenix AZ. 602-249-3300, Ext 207

Grimm, Ann, *Librn,* University of Michigan (Highway Safety Research Institute Library), Ann Arbor MI. 313-764-2171

Grimm, Ben E, *Dir,* Jersey City Public Library, Jersey City NJ. 201-547-4500

Grimm, Dorothy, *Soc Sci,* San Diego Public Library, San Diego CA. 714-236-5800

Grimm, Emily, *Staff Servs,* University of Cincinnati Libraries, Central Library, Cincinnati OH. 513-475-2218

Grimm, Erna F, *Librn,* Waveland Public Library, Waveland IN. 317-435-2700

Grimm, Mary, *Librn,* Tazewell County Public Library (Bluefield Branch), Bluefield VA. 703-326-1214

Grimme, Carol, *Librn,* Chadron Public Library, Chadron NE. 308-432-2891

Grimshaw, Polly, *Sociol, Folklore, Anthropology & Women's Studies,* Indiana University at Bloomington, University Libraries, Bloomington IN. 812-337-3403

Grimson, Heather A, *Librn,* Federation of Saskatchewan Indians, Saskatchewan Indian Cultural College Library, Saskatoon SK. 306-244-1146, Ext 41

Grinch, Mary L, *Chief Librn,* Altoona Hospital, Glover Memorial Library, Altoona PA. 814-946-2308, 946-2318, 946-2319

Griner, Janet, *Librn,* Wake County Department of the Public Library (North Hills), Raleigh NC. 919-782-0281

Griner, Lilly, *Librn,* American Institute for Research in the Behavioral Sciences, Washington Office Library, Washington DC. 202-342-5000

Griner, Louise B, *Dir,* Hoopeston Public Library, Hoopeston IL. 217-283-6711

Griner, Marina, *Librn,* United States Army (School Center Library), Fort Benjamin Harrison IN. 317-542-3101

Grinnell, Gennett, *Tech Serv,* James Blackstone Memorial Library, Branford CT. 203-488-1441

Grinnell, Margaret, *Librn,* Washington State Library (Fircrest School Staff Library), Seattle WA. 206-364-0300, Ext 405

Grinnell, Margaret, *Librn,* Washington State Library (Fircrest School Resident Library), Seattle WA. 206-364-0300, Ext 227

Griparis, Bess, *Acq,* Bur Oak Library System, Shorewood IL. 815-729-3345, 729-3346

Grippe, Barbara, *Biblioq Instruc,* Edinboro State College, Baron-Forness Library, Edinboro PA. 814-732-2780

Grisak, Garry, *Coord Libr Services,* Olds College Library, Olds AB. 403-556-8243

Grise, Anne S, *Librn,* Industrial Risk Insurers, Engineering Library, Hartford CT. 203-525-2601

Grisham, Connie, *Ref,* Sherman Public Library, Sherman TX. 214-892-4545, Ext 242

Grisham, Frank P, *Dir,* Vanderbilt University Library, Nashville TN. 615-322-2834
Grissett, Margaret, *Tech Serv,* Andalusia Public Library, Andalusia AL. 205-222-6612
Grisso, Alene, *Ad,* Craft Memorial Library, Mercer County Service Center, Bluefield WV. 304-325-3943
Grissom, Janice, *Librn,* Houston Public Library (Bracewell), Houston TX. 713-941-3130
Grissom, Jean, *Serv to Disadvantaged,* Southwest Georgia Regional Library, Gilbert H Gragg Library, Bainbridge GA. 912-246-3887, 3894, 3895
Grissom, John, *In Charge,* Welex Division Halliburton Co, R & E Library, Houston TX. 713-496-8100, Ext 266
Grist, Donna, *Tech Serv,* Princeton Public Library, Mercer Memorial Library, Princeton WV. 304-425-3324
Griswold, Agnes, *Librn,* Shawano City-County Library (Tigerton Public), Tigerton WI. 715-535-2194
Griswold, William H, *Librn,* South Congregational Church Library, Granby CT. 203-653-3390
Gritten, Mary, *Librn,* Bird City Public Library, Bird City KS. 913-734-2616
Grittner, Dorothy, *Dir,* Westboro Public Library, Westboro WI. 715-427-5864
Gritton, James H, *Librn,* State Library Commission of Iowa (State Law Library), Des Moines IA. 515-281-5124
Gritz, Ruby, *Asst Librn,* Tuolumne County Free Public Library, Sonora CA. 209-532-7842
Grnel, Fred, *Dir,* Leo Baeck Institute Inc Library, New York NY. 212-744-6400
Grobar, Bonnie, *Ref,* Texas State Library, Austin TX. 512-475-2166
Grobe, Kathleen, *Librn,* Austin Public Library (Old Quarry), Austin TX. 512-472-5433
Grochmal, Helen, *Per & On-Line Servs,* Monmouth College, Guggenheim Library, West Long Branch NJ. 201-222-6600, Ext 264
Grod, Joe, *Acq,* Thornton Community College, Learning Resources Center, South Holland IL. 312-596-2000, Ext 240
Groden, Daniel M, *Dir, Ad & Ref,* West Hempstead Public Library, West Hempstead NY. 516-481-6591
Grodin, Erica, *Librn,* New Haven Free Public Library (Davenport), New Haven CT. 203-787-8112
Grodzicki, Bess L, *Dir,* Mill Memorial Library, Nanticoke PA. 717-735-3030
Grodzicky, R R, *Dir,* Marianopolis College Library, Montreal PQ. 514-931-8792
Groeb, Lee, *Asst Dir,* Lenawee County Library, Adrian MI. 517-263-1011
Groen, Frances, *Life Sci,* McGill University Libraries, Montreal PQ. 514-392-4948
Groen, Frances, *Librn,* McGill University Libraries (Medical), Montreal PQ. 514-392-3059
Groen, Paulette, *Librn,* Society of Manufacturing Engineers Library, Dearborn MI. 313-271-1500
Groenewold, Ettie, *Dir,* Everly Public Library, Everly IA. 712-834-2691
Groesbeck, Margaret, *Bibliog Instr,* Amherst College, Robert Frost Library, Amherst MA. 413-542-2212
Groesch, Dorthada, *Dir,* Saint John's Hospital (Health Science Library), Springfield IL. 217-544-6464, Ext 4566, 4567
Grof, Andrew, *Rare Bks & Spec Coll,* Fordham University, Duane Library, Bronx NY. 212-933-2233, Ext 230, 259
Grogan, Dorothy, *Asst Chief,* Veterans Administration, Medical & Regional Office Center Library Service, Augusta ME. 207-623-8411, Ext 275, 504
Grogan, Florence, *Librn,* Troup Harris Coweta Regional Library (Newnan-Coweta Carnegie), Newnan GA. 404-253-3625
Groh, Dianne V, *Librn,* Environmental Protection Agency, Region VIII Library, 8M-ASL, Denver CO. 303-837-2560
Groher, Maxine, *Commun Servs,* Downey City Library, Downey CA. 213-923-3256
Grohman, Jean, *Ref,* Butler Public Library, Butler PA. 412-287-5576
Gromala-Schoenborn, Rita, *Librn,* Elmcrest Psychiatric Institute Professional Library, Portland CT. 203-342-0480, Ext 301
Gronau, Sharon, *Librn,* Whitewater Public Library, Whitewater KS. 316-799-2568

Grondin, Lucie, *Librn,* Centre Hospitalier Sainte-Marie, Bibliotheque Medicale, Trois-Rivieres PQ. 819-379-4130
Groom, Wilma, *Librn,* Warren Township Public Library, Warren IL. 815-745-2076
Groome, Trudy, *Librn,* Iroquois Falls Public Library, Iroquois Falls ON. 705-232-5722
Grooms, Janet, *Librn,* Sikeston Regional Center for the Developmentally Disabled Library, Sikeston MO. 314-471-9455
Grooms, L Jean, *Dir,* Marysville Public Library, Marysville OH. 513-642-1876
Grooms, Martha, *AV,* Carl Elliott Regional Library, Jasper AL. 205-221-2567
Groone, Sandra, *Tech Serv, Acq & Cat,* Buena Park Library District, Buena Park CA. 714-826-4100
Groose, Mrs Alfred C, *Librn,* East Dallas Christian Church, Haggard Memorial Library, Dallas TX. 214-824-8185
Groot, Elizabeth H, *Librn, On-Line Servs & Bibliog Instr,* Schenectady Chemicals Inc, W Howard Wright Research Center Library, Schenectady NY. 518-346-8711, Ext 572
Grooters, Lyle, *AV,* Saint Clair County Community College, Learning Resources Center, Port Huron MI. 313-984-3881, Ext 278
Groover, Mary Glenn, *Acq,* Augusta Regional Library, Augusta-Richmond County Public Library, Augusta GA. 404-724-1871
Groppe, Jeanette, *Librn,* Scribner Public Library, Scribner NE. 402-664-3540
Grosclaude, Ollie J, *Librn,* Sallisaw City Library, Sallisaw OK. 918-775-2791
Grose, B Donald, *Dir,* Indiana University-Purdue University at Fort Wayne Library, Walter E Helmke Library, Fort Wayne IN. 219-482-5456
Grose, Erma, *Acq,* West Virginia Institute of Technology, Vining Library, Montgomery WV. 304-442-3141
Grose, Ruth, *Librn,* Almena City Library, Almena KS. 913-669-3425
Groseck, Pat, *Commun Servs,* Public Library of Columbus & Franklin County, Columbus OH. 614-864-8050
Grosjean, Margaretta, *Cat,* Baptist Bible College of Pennsylvania, Richard J Murphy Memorial Library, Clarks Summit PA. 717-587-1172, Ext 280
Groskopf, Helen, *Librn,* Kemptville Public Library, Kemptville ON. 613-258-5577
Groskurth, Bonnie, *Librn,* House Memorial Library, Pender NE. 402-385-2521
Gross, Alice, *Librn,* Joseph E Seagram & Sons Inc Library, New York NY. 212-572-7871
Gross, Betty, *Librn,* University of the Pacific (Curriculum Library), Stockton CA. 209-946-2287
Gross, Brenda, *Librn,* Jefferson Public Library, Jefferson NH. 603-586-7791
Gross, Carol E, *Librn,* Institute of Internal Auditors Library, Altamonte Springs FL. 305-830-7600
Gross, Dean C, *Dir,* Norfolk Public Library, Norfolk VA. 804-441-2887
Gross, Dorothy-Ellen, *Dir,* Barat College Library, Lake Forest IL. 312-234-3000, Ext 237
Gross, Evelyn, *Ch,* W Leslie Rogers Library, Pennsauken Public Library, Pennsauken NJ. 609-665-5959
Gross, Harriet, *Ad,* John C Hart Memorial Library, Shrub Oak NY. 914-245-5262
Gross, Jean, *Head Librn,* Vineyard Haven Public Library, Vineyard Haven MA. 617-693-9721
Gross, Joan, *Ch,* Morton Grove Public Library, Morton Grove IL. 312-965-4220
Gross, John, *Dir,* Salinas Public Library, John Steinbeck Library, Salinas CA. 408-758-7311
Gross, K Frederick, *Librn,* Brooklyn Bar Association Library, Brooklyn NY. 212-624-0675
Gross, Katie, *Ch,* Central Rappahannock Regional Library, Wallace Memorial Library, Fredericksburg VA. 703-371-3311
Gross, Kenneth L, *Libr Servs Dir,* Northwest Municipal Conference, Government Information Center, Mount Prospect IL. 312-398-6460
Gross, Laura, *Ch,* Falmouth Public Library, Subregional Headquarters for Eastern Massachusetts Regional System, Falmouth MA. 617-548-0280

Gross, Mary S, *Asst Librn,* Francesville-Salem Township Public Library, Francesville IN. 219-567-9433
Gross, Minnie, *Ch,* Carnegie City Library, Little Falls MN. 612-632-9676
Gross, N, *Librn,* Rummel, Klepper & Kahl Library, Baltimore MD. 301-685-3105
Gross, Norma, *Asst Librn,* Saginaw Public Library, Saginaw TX. 817-232-2100
Gross, Norma L, *Librn,* Church Hospital Corp, Hunner-Morgan Library, Baltimore MD. 301-732-4730, Ext 259
Gross, Patty, *Librn,* Council Valley Library District, Council ID. 208-253-6004
Gross, Richard F, *Dir,* Lewiston Public Library, Lewiston ME. 207-784-0135
Gross, Robbie W, *Librn,* Aiken-Bamberg-Barnwell-Edgefield Regional Library (North Augusta Branch), North Augusta SC. 803-648-8961
Gross, Ruth, *Ad & Ref,* Covina Public Library, Covina CA. 213-967-3935
Gross, Sandra Y, *Asst Dir,* Petersham Memorial Library, Petersham MA. 617-724-3405
Grossardt, Sharon, *Spec Coll,* Hutchinson Public Library, Hutchinson KS. 316-663-5441
Grossberudt, Jo Ann, *Librn,* General Host Corporation Library, Stamford CT. 203-357-9900
Grosshans, Maxine, *Ref,* University of Maryland at Baltimore (School of Law Library), Baltimore MD. 301-528-7270
Grosshuesch, Susan, *Dir,* Kewaunee Public Library, Kewaunee WI. 414-388-3331
Grossman, Alta, *Librn,* Bourbon Public Library, Bourbon IN. 219-342-5655
Grossman, Elaine, *Acq,* Abington Free Library, Abington PA. 215-885-5180
Grossman, George S, *Dir,* Northwestern University, Chicago (School of Law Library), Chicago IL. 312-649-8450
Grossman, Harriet, *Media,* Emerson College, Abbot Memorial Library, Boston MA. 617-262-2010, Ext 281
Grossman, James, *Media & YA,* Mesquite Public Library, Mesquite TX. 214-285-6369
Grossman, Martha, *ILL,* Bayouland Library System, Lafayette LA. 318-233-7548
Grossmann, Maria, *Librn,* Harvard University Library (Andover-Harvard Theological Library), Cambridge MA. 617-495-5788
Grossmann, Walter, *Dir,* University of Massachusetts at Boston Library, Boston MA. 617-287-1900, Ext 2224
Grosso, Katharine, *Tech Serv & Cat,* Ela Area Public Library District, Lake Zurich IL. 312-438-3433
Grosso, Margaret, *Dir,* Raritan Free Public Library, Raritan NJ. 201-725-0413
Grosvenor, Elizabeth, *Librn,* Georgia Retardation Center Library, Atlanta GA. 404-393-7076
Grosvenor, Linda, *Librn,* United States Marine Corps (MCAS (H) Station Library), Jacksonville NC. 919-455-6715
Grosvold, June, *Libr Asst,* Pictou Antigonish Regional Library (Pictou Branch), Pictou NS. 902-485-5021
Grot-Zakrzewski, Zena C, *Mgr,* Combustion Engineering, Inc, Power Systems Group Library Services, Windsor CT. 203-688-1911, Ext 5603, 5619 & 2477
Grota, Susan, *Librn,* Badger Meter Inc Library, Milwaukee WI. 414-355-0400, Ext 554
Grote, Jewel, *Librn,* Hawley Library Association, Hawley PA. 717-226-4620
Grotevant, Winifred, *Ref,* Cazenovia College, Daniel W Terry Library, Cazenovia NY. 315-655-3466, Ext 240
Groth, Tanis, *Librn,* Sacramento Public Library (Arden), Sacramento CA. 916-483-6361
Grothaus, Jewell, *Music Librn,* Olivet Nazarene College, Benner Library & Resource Center, Bourbonnais IL. 815-939-5354
Grothaus, Mary Alice, *ILL,* Clermont County Public Library, Batavia OH. 513-732-2128
Grothe, Bernice, *Librn,* Wisner Public Library, Wisner NE. 402-529-6018
Grothjan, Kent, *Librn,* El Dorado County Library (El Dorado Hills Branch), El Dorado Hills CA. 916-933-6449
Grothjan, Kent, *Librn,* El Dorado County Library (Shingle Springs Branch), Shingle Springs CA. 916-677-2460

GROTSKY

Grotsky, Stephen R, *Librn,* Supreme Court, Appellate Div, First Dept Law Library, New York NY. 212-340-0478

Grott, Geraldine, *Librn,* La Porte County Library (Union Hills Branch), Union Mills IN. 219-767-2604

Grott, Mildred, *Ad,* West Nyack Free Library, West Nyack NY. 914-358-6081

Grotyohann, Susan, *Bkmobile Coordr,* New Brunswick Free Public Library, New Brunswick NJ. 201-745-5337

Groulx, Jean, *Librn,* Stanislaus County Free Library (David F Bush Library), Oakdale CA. 209-847-4204

Grout, Barbara S, *Coordr,* Areawide Hospital Library Consortium of Southwestern Illinois, (AHLC), IL. 618-233-7750, Ext 5343

Grovdahl, Elba C, *Circ,* University of Central Florida Library, Orlando FL. 305-275-2564

Grove, Carolyn, *Dir,* Milford Public Library, Milford IN. 219-658-4312

Grove, Genevieve, *Doc,* University of Washington Libraries (Law Library), Seattle WA. 206-543-4089

Grove, Joann, *Librn,* Marrowbone Township Library, Bethany IL. 217-665-3014

Grove, Judith, *Cat,* Villa Park Public Library, Villa Park IL. 312-834-1164

Grove, Lynn A, *Tech Serv & Spec Coll,* Wilmington College, Sheppard Arthur Watson Library, Wilmington OH. 513-382-6661, Ext 206

Grove, Pearce S, *Dir,* Western Illinois University Libraries, Macomb IL. 309-298-2411

Grove, Shari T, *Librn for Pub Servs,* Harvard University Library (Tozzer Library), Cambridge MA. 617-495-2253

Grover, Arlene, *Librn,* Errol Public Library, Errol NH. 603-482-3243

Grover, Bill, *Media,* Polk Community College Library, Winter Haven FL. 813-294-7771, Ext 305

Grover, Connie, *Librn,* Shiawassee County Library (Morrice Village), Morrice MI. 517-625-3430

Grover, Elna F, *Librn,* Salem School Community Library, Sugar City ID. 208-356-4437

Grover, Iva Sue, *Coordr, Cat & Acq,* Whatcom Community College, Learning Resources Center, Bellingham WA. 206-676-2139

Grover, Monica, *Section Head,* Colgate-Palmolive Co, Technical Information Center Library, Piscataway NJ. 201-463-1212, Ext 277

Grover, Sister Nona, *Ref,* Viterbo College Library, La Crosse WI. 608-784-0040, Ext 429

Groves, Doris, *Dir Learning Resource Center,* Southern Connecticut State College, Hilton C Buley Library, New Haven CT. 203-397-4505

Groves, Imogene, *Librn,* Van Buren County Public Library, Spencer TN. 615-946-2575

Groves, Mrs M, *Tech Serv,* College of Trades & Technology Library, Saint John's NF. 709-753-9360, Ext 318

Groves, Trudy, *Ch,* Noblesville Public Library, Noblesville IN. 317-773-1384

Grubb, Alpha, *Bkmobile Coordr,* Laurel County Public Library District, London KY. 606-864-5759

Grubbs, Alyce, *Dir,* Laughlin Memorial Free Library, Ambridge PA. 412-266-3857

Grubbs, Charles, *Bus Sci & Local Info,* Greenville County Library, Greenville SC. 803-242-5000

Grubbs, Margaret, *Librn,* Logan County District Library (East Liberty Branch), Bellefontaine OH. 513-599-4189

Grubbs, Phyllis, *Asst Librn,* Brandon Township Public Library, Ortonville MI. 313-627-2804, Ext 44

Grubbs, Shirley, *Asst Dir,* Martin County Public Library, Stuart FL. 305-287-2257

Gruben, Karl T, *Librn,* Vinson & Elkins, Law Library, Houston TX. 713-651-2678

Gruber, Dottie, *Librn,* Institute for Medical Research Library, Camden NJ. 609-966-7377, Ext 100

Gruby, Rose Marie, *Cat,* American River College Library, Sacramento CA. 916-484-8293

Grudzien, Pamela, *Ch,* Loutit Library, Grand Haven MI. 616-842-5560

Gruenbeck, Laurie, *Librn,* San Antonio Public Library (Bazan), San Antonio TX. 512-225-1614

Gruenberg, Eden J, *Dir,* Crouse-Irving Memorial Hospital Library, Syracuse NY. 315-424-6380

Gruenberg, Patricia, *Tech Serv,* Hamden Library, Miller Memorial, Hamden CT. 203-248-7747

Gruenewald, Helen, *Circ,* Messiah College, Murray Learning Resources Center, Grantham PA. 717-766-2511, Ext 380

Gruis, Gail, *Librn,* Park Rapids Public Library, Park Rapids MN. 218-732-4853

Grunberger, Michael, *Librn,* Gratz College Library, Philadelphia PA. 215-329-3363

Grunczewski, Frieda, *Ref,* Weld County Library, Greeley CO. 303-330-7691

Grunder, Barbara, *Acq,* Bethlehem Public Library, Bethlehem PA. 215-867-3761

Grundish, Elizabeth S, *Librn,* School of Fine Arts Library, Willoughby OH. 216-951-7500

Grundke, Patricia J, *Librn,* Community Memorial General Hospital, Medical Library, La Grange IL. 312-352-1200

Grundt, Leonard, *Dir,* Nassau Community College Library, Garden City NY. 516-222-7400

Grundy, Diane, *Dir,* Grove City College, Henry Buhl Library, Grove City PA. 412-458-6600, Ext 270

Grundy, Ruth, *Librn,* University of Texas, Port Aransas Marine Laboratory Library, Port Aransas TX. 512-749-6723

Grunow, Millie, *Librn,* Deaconess Hospital, Grace Hahn Health Science Library, Evansville IN. 812-426-3385

Grupe, Fritz H, *Exec Dir,* Associated Colleges of the Saint Lawrence Valley, NY. 315-265-2790

Grushkin, Jean, *ILL,* Englewood Library, Englewood NJ. 201-568-2215

Gruver, Eileen, *Ref,* Capital University Library (Law School Library), Columbus OH. 614-445-8634

Grzesiakowski, Linda, *Librn,* Wm Wrigley Jr Co (Company Library), Chicago IL. 312-644-2121, Ext 216

Grzyb, Alexander, *Finance,* Chicago Public Library, Chicago IL. 312-269-2900

Grzyb, Marion, *Asst Librn,* Watertown Township Library, Fostoria MI. 517-795-2127

Guagliardo, Dennis, *Media,* Jefferson Community College, Learning Resources Center, Louisville KY. 502-584-0181, Ext 305

Guajardo, Luciano, *Dir,* Laredo Public Library, Laredo TX. 512-722-2435

Gualtieri, Joseph P, *Dir,* Slater Memorial Museum Library, Norwich CT. 203-887-2505, Ext 218

Guarducci, Elizabeth B, *Librn,* Essex County Hospital Center, Hamilton Memorial Library, Cedar Grove NJ. 201-239-1900, Ext 485

Guarino, Charmian, *Librn,* Pasadena Public Library (San Rafael), Pasadena CA. 213-795-7974

Guarneri, Ruth, *Librn,* Satterlee & Stephens Library, New York NY. 212-826-6200

Guarrera, Joseph A, *Dir Commun Servs,* Azusa City Library, Azusa CA. 213-334-0338

Guay, Andre, *Tech Serv & Acq,* Acadia University, Harold Campbell Vaughan Memorial Library, Wolfville NS. 902-542-2201, Ext 215

Guay-Gagnon, Gisele, *Librn,* Bibliotheque Municipale, Saint Felicien PQ. 418-679-0251

Gubb, Barbara, *Media,* Laboure Junior College Library, Boston MA. 617-296-8300, Ext 418

Gubman, Nancy, *Librn,* New York University (Courant Institute of Mathematical Sciences), New York NY. 212-460-7301

Gude, Gilbert, *Dir, Cong Res Serv,* Library of Congress, Washington DC. 202-287-5000

Gudeit, D, *Librn,* Okanagan Regional Library District (Lumby Branch), Lumby BC. 604-547-9528

Gudenick, Josephine, *Tech Serv,* Villa Park Public Library, Villa Park IL. 312-834-1164

Guderjahn, Jilde, *Librn,* Cassiar Public Library, Recreation Center, Cassiar BC. 604-778-7753

Gudgen, Gretta, *Circ,* Pittsburg State University Library, Pittsburg KS. 316-231-7000, Ext 431

Gudzinlaas, Wayne, *Asst Librn,* Inter-American University of Puerto Rico, Aguadilla Regional College Branch Library, Ramey AFB PR. 809-890-5118

Guebert, G A, *ILL,* Concordia College, Klinck Memorial Library, River Forest IL. 312-771-8300, Ext 450

Guebert, Lois, *Tech Serv,* Concordia College Library, Ann Arbor MI. 313-665-3691, Ext 197

Guedderti, Kathryn, *Curator,* Sacramento City Museum & History Department Library, Sacramento CA. 916-447-2958

Guedon, Mary, *Spec Coll,* University of Santa Clara, Michel Orradre Library, Santa Clara CA. 408-984-4415

Guengerich, Elsie, *Librn,* Wellman Scofield Library, Wellman IA. 319-646-2145

Guenter, Bruce, *Librn,* American Druggist Magazine, New York NY. 212-262-4258

Guenther, Eleanor, *Dir,* Bluefield College, Easley Library, Bluefield VA. 304-327-7137

Guenther, Sue, *Librn,* Denver Public Library (Dahlia Libr), Denver CO. 303-573-5152, Ext 271

Guentner, Geraldine C, *Dir,* Burlington Public Library, Burlington MA. 617-272-2520

Guerena, Sal, *In Charge,* Santa Barbara Public Library (Eastside), Santa Barbara CA. 805-963-3727

Guerette, Normand, *Dir,* Bibliotheque Du Ministere De L'energie Et Des Ressources, Quebec PQ. 418-643-4624

Guerin-Place, Rosemary, *Librn,* Girl Scouts of the United States Library & Archives, New York NY. 212-940-7500

Guernsey, Betty, *Cat,* Williamsburg Regional Library, Williamsburg VA. 804-229-7326

Guerra, Noe, *Librn,* Del Mar College Library (Technical Branch), Corpus Christi TX. 512-881-6308

Guerrero, Felicito C, *Dir,* United States Department of Commerce, Houston Field Office Library, Houston TX. 713-226-4231

Guerrero, Nancy, *Librn,* Elsie & Hogan Public Library, Willcox AZ. 602-384-4271

Guerrette, Mona, *Librn,* York Regional Library (Bibliotheque du Centre Scholaire-Communautaire), Fredericton NB. 506-455-1740

Guerri, Doris, *In Charge,* Clemson University (College of Industrial Management & Textile Science), Clemson SC. 803-656-3026

Guess, Laurel, *Librn,* Buffalo & Erie County Public Library System (Kensington), Buffalo NY. 716-833-7278

Guest, Francis, *Archivist-Librn,* Santa Barbara Mission Archive Library, Santa Barbara CA. 805-682-4713

Guest, Joanne, *ILL & Ref,* Burlington Public Library, Burlington IA. 319-753-1649

Guida, Pat, *Bibliog Instr,* Booz Allen & Hamilton Inc, Foster D Snell Inc Information Center, Florham Park NJ. 201-377-6700, Ext 211

Guida, Patricia, *Mgr,* Booz Allen & Hamilton Inc, Foster D Snell Inc Information Center, Florham Park NJ. 201-377-6700, Ext 211

Guidinger, Delmar, *Dir,* Liberal Memorial Library, Liberal KS. 316-624-0148

Guido, John, *Archives, Mss, Spec Coll,* Washington State University Library, Pullman WA. 509-335-4557

Guidotti, Annetta C, *Librn,* Whitman, Ransom & Coulson Library, New York NY. 212-575-5800

Guidry, Nancy, *YA,* Santa Monica Public Library, Santa Monica CA. 213-451-5751

Guidry, Susan, *Asst Librn,* Avoyelles Parish Library, Marksville LA. 318-253-7559

Guidry, Jr, George J, *Dir,* Louisiana State University (Troy H Middleton Library), Baton Rouge LA. 504-388-2217

Guilbault, Oscar R, *Dir,* Rockville Public Library, George Maxwell Memorial Library, Vernon CT. 203-875-5892

Guilfoil, Elizabeth J, *Dir,* Sacred Heart Medical Center, Health Sciences Library, Spokane WA. 509-455-3094

Guilford, II, Ben J, *Asst Dir,* Miami-Dade Public Library System, Miami FL. 305-579-5001

Guilfoyle, Marvin, *Ref,* University of Evansville, Clifford Memorial Library & Learning Resources, Evansville IN. 812-479-2462

Guillaume, Marilyn, *Libr Instruction,* University of Wisconsin-La Crosse, Murphy Library, La Crosse WI. 608-785-8505

Guillemette, M Michel, *Librn,* Bibliotheque Municipale, Schefferville PQ. 418-585-3461

Guillet, Nancy M, *Chief Librn,* Veterans Administration, General Library, Alexandria LA. 318-442-0251

Guillette, Edna, *Ch,* Attleboro Public Library, Joseph L Sweet Memorial, Attleboro MA. 617-222-0157

Guilliams, Don, *Dir,* Western Wyoming Community College, Library Learning Resources Center, Rock Springs WY. 307-382-2121, Ext 154

Guilliams, Nellie, *Librn,* Coshocton Public Library (West Lafayette Branch), West Lafayette OH. 614-545-6672

Guilmette, Pierre, *Soc Sci,* Universite Laval Bibliotheque, Quebec PQ. 418-656-3344

Guin, Marilyn, *Marine Sci,* Oregon State University, William Jasper Kerr Library, Corvallis OR. 503-754-3411

Guinan, Betty, *Librn,* East Granby Public Library, East Granby CT. 203-653-3002

Guinn, Betty, *Financial Secretary,* Eastern Oklahoma District Library System, Muskogee OK. 918-683-2846

Guinther, Carol, *Librn,* Hamburg Public Library, Hamburg PA. 215-562-2843

Guion, Kathleen, *Coordr,* Department of Public Libraries & Information (Municipal Reference Division), Virginia Beach VA. 804-427-4644

Guirin, Maxine, *Librn,* Iberville Parish Library (Rosedale Branch), Rosedale LA. 504-648-2213

Guirlinger, Annette, *Librn,* Bay County Library System (South Side), Bay City MI. 517-893-1287

Guise, Ben, *Asst Prof,* Western Michigan University, School of Librarianship, MI. 616-383-1849

Guitard, Mary, *Libr Asst II,* Chaleur Regional Library (Dalhousie Centennial Public), Dalhousie NB. 506-684-2068

Guiu, Elizabeth, *Dir,* New England Baptist Hospital (Helene Fuld Library), Boston MA. 617-738-5800, Ext 349

Guiu, Rafael, *Mgr,* Swedenborgian Library, Massachusetts New-Church Union, Boston MA. 617-262-5918

Guiven, Cesar, *Ref,* Inter-American University of Puerto Rico, Library-Metropolitan Campus Bayamon Unit, Bayamon PR. 809-780-4040, Ext 16

Gukeisen, Lois, *Librn,* Platte Public Library, Platte SD. 605-337-3436

Gulack, Marian, *Librn & On-Line Servs,* American Can Co, Operations Technology Engineering Library, Fair Lawn NJ. 201-797-8200, Ext 322

Gulam, Elaine, *Librn,* Jackson-George Regional Library System (St Martin Public), Biloxi MS. 601-435-2013

Gulati, Kailash, *Librn,* Saint Vincent's Medical Center of Richmond, Medical Library, Staten Island NY. 212-390-1327

Guldner, Becky, *Asst Dir,* Hamilton County Library, Syracuse KS. 316-384-5622

Guleff, Chris, *Librn,* Auraria Libraries (Environmental Design Library), Denver CO. 303-629-2805

Guleff, Chris, *Librn,* Auraria Libraries (Vocational-Technical Library), Denver CO. 303-629-2805

Guleke, Kay S, *Librn,* Austin American Statesman Library, Austin TX. 512-397-1212, Ext 1297

Gulick, Dorothy, *Tech Serv,* Haddon Heights Public Library, Haddon Heights NJ. 609-547-7132

Gulick, Joan, *Librn,* Susquehanna County Historical Society & Free Library Association (Susquehanna Branch), Susquehanna PA. 717-853-4106

Gulley, Jean, *Librn,* Dekalb Library System (Avis Williams Branch), Decatur GA. 404-633-2387

Gullick, M G, *ILL,* Whitman College, Penrose Memorial Library, Walla Walla WA. 509-527-5191

Gulliver, J V, *Librn,* Middlesex Law Association, Law Library, London ON. 519-679-7046

Gullo, Robert J, *Dir,* Saint John Fisher College, Lavery Library, Pittsford NY. 716-586-4140, Ext 222

Gully, Susan, *Librn,* Little Dixie Regional Libraries (Huntsville Branch), Huntsville MO. 816-277-4518

Gulrajani, Inju, *Cat,* Marion County Library, Marion SC. 803-423-2244

Gumeson, Warren, *Tech Serv,* Bemidji State University, A C Clark Library, Bemidji MN. 218-755-2955

Gumeson, Warren, *Instr,* Bemidji State University, Library Science Program, MN. 218-755-2955

Gumm, Bob, *Media,* University of Wisconsin Center, Washington County Library, West Bend WI. 414-338-8753, Ext 60

Gundaker, Martha J, *Ref,* University of Tennessee at Chattanooga Library, Chattanooga TN. 615-755-4701

Gunderman, Joyce L, *Librn,* Commonwealth Court Library, Harrisburg PA. 717-787-5884

Gunderman, Pat, *Assoc Dir,* Merced College, Lesher Library, Merced CA. 209-723-4321, Ext 274

Gundersen, Dolly, *Dir,* Willoughby-Eastlake Public Library, Willowick OH. 216-944-6900

Gunderson, LeRue, *Librn,* Wauneta Public Library, Wauneta NE. 308-394-5247

Gunderson, Marion, *Librn,* Rolfe Public Library, Rolfe IA. 712-848-3143

Gundlach, Alyne, *Bus Servs,* Public Library of Nashville & Davidson County, Nashville TN. 615-244-4700

Gundlah, William, *Librn,* Eastern College, Frank Warner Memorial Library, Saint Davids PA. 215-688-3300, Ext 210

Gundry, L D, *Chief Librn,* Bryn Mawr Hospital, Medical Library, Bryn Mawr PA. 215-896-3160

Gunn, Gertrude E, *Dir,* University of New Brunswick, Harriet Irving Library, Fredericton NB. 506-453-4740

Gunn, Gladys, *Librn,* Eldorado Public Library, Eldorado TX. 915-853-2783

Gunn, Jim, *Dir,* Elko County Library, Elko NV. 702-738-3066

Gunn, Lee, *Acq,* University of Michigan (Law Library), Ann Arbor MI. 313-764-9322

Gunn, Margaret, *Asst Prof,* Delta State University, Dept of Media & Library Science, MS. 601-843-8638

Gunn, Parker, *Media,* Phillips County Community College Library, Helena AR. 501-338-6474, Ext 246

Gunn, Thomas H, *Dir,* Jacksonville University, Carl S Swisher Library, Jacksonville FL. 904-744-3950, Ext 266, 267

Gunnells, Danny C, *Dir,* Bowling Green Public Library, Bowling Green KY. 502-781-4882

Gunning, C, *Asst Dir,* Canadore College of Applied Arts & Technology Library, North Bay ON. 705-474-7600

Gunning, Jan, *Acq,* Public Library of Anniston & Calhoun County, Liles Memorial Library, Anniston AL. 205-237-8501, Ext 8503

Gunning, Kathleen, *Head Ref Librn,* Brown University (University Library), Providence RI. 401-863-2167

Gunning, Ruth, *In Charge,* Rockwell International (Business Research Center), Pittsburgh PA. 412-565-5880

Gunnoe, Elizabeth, *Ad,* Martinsburg-Berkeley County Public Library, Martinsburg Service Center, Martinsburg WV. 304-267-8933

Gunoy, Jayne Van, *Librn,* Miami-Dade Public Library System (Fairlawn), Miami FL. 305-261-1571

Gunsaulis, Judy, *Asst Dir,* Fayette County Public Library, Oakhill WV. 304-465-0121, 465-0311

Gunson, Linda, *Librn,* Vancouver Community College at Langara Campus, Library Technician Program, BC. 604-324-5418

Gunter, Betty, *Asst Librn,* Todd County Public Library, Elkton KY. 502-265-9071

Gunter, Judy, *Ad & YA,* Jefferson County Library, Nederland TX. 713-727-2735, 727-2736

Gunter, Marvin, *Media,* Southwestern Adventist College, Findley Memorial Library, Keene TX. 817-645-3921, Ext 242

Gunter, Mary Lou, *Librn,* Amarillo Speech & Hearing Learning Center Library, Amarillo TX. 806-359-7681

Gunter, Wayne L, *Asst Dir & ILL,* Sandpoint-East Bonner County Free Public Library District, Sandpoint ID. 208-263-6930

Gunther, Barbara, *Lang Ctr,* Metropolitan Toronto Library Board, Metropolitan Toronto Library, Toronto ON. 416-928-5150

Gunther, Ellen P, *Librn,* Alberto-Culver Co, Research Library, Melrose Park IL. 312-531-2328

Gunzenhauser, Dorothy, *Asst Dir & Commun Servs,* Franklin Square Public Library, Franklin Square NY. 516-488-3444

Gupta, Cheryl, *Librn,* Ancora Psychiatric Hospital (Health Sciences Library), Hammonton NJ. 609-561-1700, Ext 228

Gupta, Marianne V, *Chief Librn,* American Telephone & Telegraph Co (Corporate Research Library), New York NY. 212-393-3714

Guptill, Barbara, *Librn,* Seattle Public Library (Governmental Research Assistance Library), Seattle WA. 206-625-2853

Gureeri, Lorenzo, *Ref,* Pikes Peak Community College, Learning Materials Center, Colorado Springs CO. 303-576-7711, Ext 536

Gurganus, Julia, *Reserve Rm,* East Carolina University, J Y Joyner Library, Greenville NC. 919-757-6514

Gurklis, Ann V, *Asst Dir,* Lake Worth Public Library, Lake Worth FL. 305-585-9882

Gurley, Mary Scott, *Dir,* Lee County Library, Sanford NC. 919-776-3133

Gurn, Robert M, *Media,* Buffalo & Erie County Public Library System, Buffalo NY. 716-856-7525

Gurnee, R, *Phys Sci,* Mount San Antonio College, Learning Resources Center, Walnut CA. 714-594-5611, Ext 260

Gurnett, Julia, *Ad,* Tufts Library, Public Libraries of Weymouth, Weymouth MA. 617-337-1402

Gurney, Ellen, *ILL & Ad,* Lewiston Public Library, Lewiston ME. 207-784-0135

Gurubatham, Gladstone P, *Dept Chmn & Prof,* Columbia Union College, Library Science Dept, MD. 301-270-9200, Ext 231

Gurubatham, Gladstone P, *Ref,* Columbia Union College, Theofield G Weis Library, Takoma Park MD. 301-270-4999

Gushee, David E, *Chief, Environ Natural Resources Policy Div,* Library of Congress, Washington DC. 202-287-5000

Gushikuma, Nathalie, *Librn,* San Diego Public Library (Serra Mesa), San Diego CA. 714-278-0640

Gushue, Rhoda M, *Dir,* Bedford Hills Free Library, Bedford Hills NY. 914-666-6472

Guss, Emily, *Librn,* Chicago Public Library (Sherman Park), Chicago IL. 312-268-1753

Gustafson, Angelet, *Librn,* Cook Public Library, Cook MN. 218-666-2200

Gustafson, Berdella, *Librn,* Edgewater Baptist Church Library, Minneapolis MN. 612-827-3803

Gustafson, Beverly, *Librn,* Beech Aircraft Corp, Engineering Library, Boulder CO. 303-443-1650

Gustafson, Carmen S, *In Charge,* English Lutheran Church Library, La Crosse WI. 608-784-9335

Gustafson, Charles, *Media,* Lake Superior State College Library, Sault Sainte Marie MI. 906-632-6841, Ext 402

Gustafson, Doris, *Librn,* Brooklyn Public Library (New Lots), Brooklyn NY. 212-649-3700

Gustafson, Eleanor, *Tech Serv,* Monmouth College, Hewes Library, Monmouth IL. 309-457-2031

Gustafson, Eleanor, *Assoc Librn & Tech Serv,* Wellesley College, Margaret Clapp Library, Wellesley MA. 617-235-0320, Ext 280

Gustafson, Helen H, *Asst Dir,* Coventry Public Library, Coventry RI. 401-821-5654

Gustafson, Jean B, *Dir,* Chemeketa Community College Library, Salem OR. 503-399-5043

Gustafson, Mattie E, *Dir,* Tiverton Library Services, Tiverton RI. 401-624-8079

Gustafson, Maxine, *Librn,* United States Air Force (United States Air Force Regional Hospital Medical Library), Sheppard AFB TX. 817-851-6647

Gustafsson, Olof, *Librn,* SKF Industries, Inc, SKF Technology Service Library, King of Prussia PA. 215-265-1900

Gustavson, J, *Asst Librn,* Methodist Medical Center of Illinois (Learning Resource Center-School of Nursing Library & Audio Visual), Peoria IL. 309-672-5570

Gustavson, Nancy, *Dir,* Juneau Memorial Library, Juneau AK. 907-586-2429

Gustin, Deborah, *On-Line Servs,* Veterans Administration, Medical & Regional Office Center Library Service, Augusta ME. 207-623-8411, Ext 275, 504

Gustow, Hazel, *Dir,* Philadelphia College of Art Library, Philadelphia PA. 215-893-3126

Gustufson, Sandra, *Librn,* Western Plains Library System (Maynard Branch), Maynard MN. 612-269-5644

Gusukuma, Sherie, *ILL & On-Line Servs,* University of Hawaii at Hilo Libraries, Hilo HI. 808-961-9344

Gutekunst, Betty, *Librn,* Catholic University of America (Humanities), Washington DC. 202-635-5075

Gutekunst, Eugenia S, *ILL*, Saint John Fisher College, Lavery Library, Pittsford NY. 716-586-4140, Ext 222
Gutenberger, Marion, *Tech Serv*, Sandpoint-East Bonner County Free Public Library District, Sandpoint ID. 208-263-6930
Gutglass, Judy, *Ref*, Washington University Libraries (Freund Law Library), Saint Louis MO. 314-889-6459
Guth, Doris, *Librn*, Sno-Isle Regional Library (Lynnwood Branch), Lynnwood WA. 206-778-2148
Guthrie, Beverly, *Asst Librn*, Noble County Public Library, Albion IN. 219-636-7197
Guthrie, Cynthia, *Asst Dir, Tech Serv & Cat*, Attleboro Public Library, Joseph L Sweet Memorial, Attleboro MA. 617-222-0157
Guthrie, Cynthia, *Asst Dir & Ch*, Middletown Free Library, Middletown RI. 846-1573 & 846-1584
Guthrie, Donald, *Bkmobile Coordr*, Holmes County District Public Library, Millersburg OH. 216-674-5972
Guthrie, Dorothy, *Dir*, Gibbon Public Library, Gibbon NE. 308-468-5889
Guthrie, Gerry, *Budget*, Ohio State University Libraries (William Oxley Thompson Memorial Library), Columbus OH. 614-422-6151
Guthrie, Mary, *Librn*, Calhoun Public Library, Calhoun TN. 615-336-2348
Guthrie, Nina, *Librn*, Jim Lucas Memorial Library, Checotah OK. 918-473-6715
Guthrie, Vera G, *Dept Head*, Western Kentucky University, Dept of Library Science & Instructional Media, KY. 502-745-3446
Guthrie, Virginia, *Librn*, Birmingham Public & Jefferson County Free Library (Ensley Branch), Ensley AL. 205-254-2551
Gutierrez, Carolyn, *Librn*, Dancer-Fitzgerald-Sample, Inc Library, New York NY. 212-661-0800, Ext 2838
Gutierrez, Sally, *Librn*, Citizens Savings Athletic Foundation Library, Los Angeles CA. 213-642-0200
Gutierrez-Witt, Laura, *Librn*, University of Texas Libraries (Nettie Lee Benson Latin American Collection), Austin TX. 512-471-3818
Gutke, Audrey, *Ad*, Webster Groves Public Library, Webster Groves MO. 314-961-3784
Gutkowski, Arnold, *Librn*, West Allis Public Library (East), West Allis WI. 414-543-5110
Gutshell, Thelma, *Librn*, Texas County Library (Cabool Branch), Cabool MO. 417-962-3722
Gutteridge, Mary, *Cat & Ref*, Sheldon Jackson College, Stratton Library, Sitka AK. 907-747-5235, 747-5259
Guttman, Michael, *Librn*, Illinois Department of Labor, Statistics Programs & Publications Library, Chicago IL. 312-793-2817
Guttridge, Mrs B, *Librn*, Vaughan Public Libraries (Gallanough Public), Thornhill ON. 416-881-2828
Gutz, Robert R, *Asst Librn*, New York State Judicial Department, Appellate Division Law Library, Rochester NY. 716-428-5480
Guy, Carol, *Librn*, Cities Service Co (Chemicals & Minerals Group Market Research Library), Tulsa OK. 918-586-4889
Guy, E Katherine, *Librn*, Auld-Doudna Public Library, Guide Rock NE. 402-257-3655
Guy, Nancy A, *Librn*, Humboldt County Law Library, Eureka CA. 707-445-7201
Guy, Wilma, *Librn*, Pinckneyville Public Library, Pinckneyville IL. 618-357-2410, Ext 618
Guydon, Janet, *Cat*, Gary Public Library, Gary IN. 219-886-2484
Guyer, Mark, *Spec Coll*, Anderson College (Byrd Memorial Library), Anderson IN. 317-649-9071, Ext 2077
Guyett, Virginia, *Librn*, United States Navy (Supply Dept Technical Library), Portsmouth NH. 207-439-1000, Ext 1670
Guyette, Patricia, *ILL*, East Carolina University, J Y Joyner Library, Greenville NC. 919-757-6514
Guyitt, Keith, *Asst Librn & ILL*, Huron College, Silcox Memorial Library, London ON. 519-438-7224, Ext 13
Guyot, Karen, *Info Serv*, Seattle University, A A Lemieux Library, Seattle WA. 206-626-6859
Guyotte, Linda, *ILL*, Oakland University, Kresge Library, Rochester MI. 313-377-2486, 377-2474
Guzelis, Evangeline, *Ch*, San Bruno Public Library, San Bruno CA. 415-877-8878

Guzman, Diane, *Librn*, Brooklyn Museum (Wilbour Library of Eqyptology), Brooklyn NY. 212-638-5000, Ext 215
Guzman, Isidro, *Cat & On-Line Servs*, Corpus Christi State University Library, Corpus Christi TX. 512-991-6810, Ext 242
Guzman, Lupe, *Commun Servs*, Edinburg Public Library, Edinburg TX. 512-383-6246, 383-6247
Guzman, Melva, *Dir*, Loyal Public Library, Loyal WI. 715-255-8189
Guzman, Reina, *Librn*, Trunkline Gas Co, General Library, Houston TX. 713-664-3401, Ext 507
Guzo, Audrey, *Ch*, Stickney-Forest View Library District, Stickney IL. 312-749-1050
Guzowski, Mary, *Dir*, West Iron District Library, Iron River MI. 906-265-2831
Guzzetta, Beatrice, *In Charge*, Morgan City Public Library, Morgan City LA. 504-385-1666
Guzzetta, Blanche J, *Librn*, Weil, Gotshal & Manges Library, New York NY. 212-758-7800, Ext 212
Guzzo, Carol, *Librn*, Toledo-Lucas County Public Library (Maumee Branch), Maumee OH. 419-255-7055
Gwaltney, B Mildred, *Asst Prof*, Western Kentucky University, Dept of Library Science & Instructional Media, KY. 502-745-3446
Gwaltney, Mildred, *Librn*, Geary Public Library, Geary OK. 405-884-5466
Gwin, James, *Cat*, University of Richmond, Boatwright Memorial Library, Richmond VA. 804-285-6452
Gwinn, Irys J, *Dir*, Hurst Public Library, Hurst TX. 817-485-5320
Gwinn, Mary Jane, *Librn*, Washington University Libraries (Chemistry), Saint Louis MO. 314-889-6591
Gwinn, Maureen, *ILL*, Tarkio College, J A Thompson Library, Tarkio MO. 816-736-4131, Ext 433
Gwosch, Mary M, *Librn*, Nesmith Library, Windham NH. 603-432-7154
Gwyn, Ann S, *Rare Bks & Spec Coll*, Tulane University of Louisiana, Howard-Tilton Memorial Library, New Orleans LA. 504-865-5131
Gwyn, Patricia, *Outreach Coordr*, Rockingham County Public Library, Eden NC. 919-627-1106
Gygi, Leland R, *Dir*, Stevens Henager College Library, Ogden UT. 801-394-7791
Gyorgyey, Ferenc A, *Rare Bks & Spec Coll*, Yale University Library (Medical Library), New Haven CT. 203-436-4784, 436-2961
Gysbers, Derk, *Media*, Fullerton College, William T Boyce Library, Fullerton CA. 714-871-8000

H

Haab, Nancy J, *Librn*, Winthrop, Stimson, Putnam & Roberts Library, New York NY. 212-943-0700
Haabala, Sylvia, *Ref*, Mayo Foundation (Medical Library), Rochester MN. 507-284-2061
Haacker, Daniel D, *Librn*, Milton Public Library (East Milton), Milton MA. 617-698-1733
Haaf, Angela, *Acq*, Vancouver Community College Libraries, Vancouver BC. 604-688-1111
Haag, Enid, *Educ*, Western Washington University, Mabel Zoe Wilson Library, Bellingham WA. 206-676-3050
Haag, Margaret, *Ref & Bibliog Instr*, Sarah Lawrence College, Esther Raushenbush Library, Bronxville NY. 914-337-0700, Ext 479
Haaland, Ardis, *Librn*, Dakota Hospital Library, Fargo ND. 701-280-4187
Haan, Ralph, *Genealogy*, Herrick Public Library, Holland MI. 616-392-3114
Haapala, Edith S, *Dir*, Grand Rapids Public Library, Grand Rapids MN. 218-326-3081
Haar, Gail, *Commun Servs*, Prosser Public Library, Bloomfield CT. 203-243-9721
Haas, Andrine J, *Librn*, Dawson College Library, Glendive MT. 406-365-3396, Ext 25
Haas, Connie, *Cat*, Lake Worth Public Library, Lake Worth FL. 305-585-9882
Haas, David, *Media*, Mount Vernon College Library, Washington DC. 202-331-3475
Haas, Edward F, *Dir & Archivist*, Louisiana State Museum, Louisiana Historical Center Library, New Orleans LA. 504-568-6970, 568-6979, 568-6982

Haas, Elsie D, *Dir*, Plain Public Library, Plain WI. 608-546-4201
Haas, Janice L, *Spec Coll*, Rutherford B Hayes Library, Fremont OH. 419-332-2081
Haas, M, *Ref*, State University of New York at Buffalo, University Libraries, Buffalo NY. 716-636-2965
Haas, M, *Anthropology & Linguistics*, State University of New York at Buffalo, University Libraries, Buffalo NY. 716-636-2965
Haas, Margaret, *Librn*, Nauvoo Public Library, Nauvoo IL. 217-453-2707
Haas, Marjorie V, *Librn*, Florence Public Library, Florence KS. 316-878-4378
Haas, Pamela, *Photog Coll*, American Museum of Natural History Library, New York NY. 212-873-1300, Ext 494
Haas, S, *Religion & Classical Studies*, Bloomfield College Library, Bloomfield NJ. 201-748-9000, Ext 281
Haas, Shirley, *Pub Info*, Chicago Public Library, Chicago IL. 312-269-2900
Haas, Stephen, *Soc Sci*, Wright State University Library, Dayton OH. 513-873-2380
Haase, Gretchen, *Librn*, Oppenheimer Law Firm Library, Saint Paul MN. 612-227-7271, Ext 622
Haase, Jane, *Librn*, Austen Riggs Center, Inc, Austen Fox Riggs Library, Stockbridge MA. 413-298-5511, Ext 259
Haase, Marion, *Librn*, American Can Co Library, Rothschild WI. 715-359-6544, Ext O
Haban, Mary F, *Dean*, James Madison University, Madison Memorial Library, Harrisonburg VA. 703-433-6150
Haben, Dorothy, *Vol Coordr*, Oregon State Library Services for the Blind & Physically Handicapped, Salem OR. 503-378-3849
Haber, Barbara, *Curator of Printed Bks*, Radcliffe College, Arthur & Elizabeth Schlesinger Library on the History of Women in America, Cambridge MA. 617-495-8647
Haber, Walter, *Dir & Commun Servs*, Baldwin Public Library, Baldwin NY. 516-223-6228
Haberer, Vera, *Librn*, Library Association of Portland (Rockwood), Portland OR. 503-665-9440
Haberkorn, Elaine, *Librn*, Aitkin Public Library, Aitkin MN. 218-927-2339
Haberland, Jean, *Fiction & Fine Arts*, Arlington County Department of Libraries, Arlington Public Library, Arlington VA. 703-527-4777
Haberman, Lynabelle, *Dir*, Brillion Public Library, Brillion WI. 414-756-3215
Habib, Marsie, *Acq*, Saddleback Community College Library, Mission Viejo CA. 714-831-4515
Hablitzel, Erna, *Dir*, Eustis Public Library, Eustis NE. 308-486-2651
Habousha, Racheline, *Ref*, Albert Einstein College of Medicine, D Samuel Gottesman Library, Bronx NY. 212-430-3108
Hachey, Peg, *Commun Servs*, Macomb County Library, Mount Clemens MI. 313-469-5300
Hack, Kristine A, *In Charge*, Bodine Electric Co Library, Chicago IL. 312-478-3515, Ext 385
Hack, Leo, *Librn*, Black & Veatch Consulting Engineers, Central Library, Kansas City MO. 913-967-2223
Hack, Rosalinda I, *Music*, Chicago Public Library (Fine Arts Div), Chicago IL. 312-269-2839
Hacker, Lois, *Tech Serv*, City University of New York, Library of Graduate School & University Center, New York NY. 212-790-4541
Hacker, Ray K, *Ref*, Millersville State College, Helen A Ganser Library, Millersville PA. 717-872-5411, Ext 341
Hackett, Alice, *ILL*, Lima Public Library, Lima OH. 419-228-5113
Hackett, Marguerite, *Order*, Southern Illinois University at Edwardsville, Elijah P Lovejoy Library, Edwardsville IL. 618-692-2711
Hackett, N J, *Librn*, Fountaindale Public Library District (Fountaindale), Romeoville IL. 815-886-2030
Hackett, Peggy, *In Charge*, Phelps Dodge Exploration East Library, Reston VA. 703-437-6655
Hacking, Gene, *Librn*, San Juan County Library (Blanding Branch), Blanding UT. 801-587-2281678-2335
Hackler, Evaughn, *Librn*, Abernathy Public Library, Abernathy TX. 806-298-2241

Hackney, Carrie, *Librn,* Howard University Libraries (Fine Arts Library), Washington DC. 202-636-7071
Hackney, Judith, *Asst Dir,* Galloway Township Library, Cologne NJ. 609-965-2791
Hackstatt, Mrs Larry, *Ref,* Crawfordsville District Public Library, Crawfordsville IN. 317-362-2242
Hacthoun, Isabel, *Chief Libm,* Mount Sinai Medical Center Library, Audiovisual Services, Miami Beach FL. 305-674-2840
Hadaller, Ruth R, *Dir,* Covington Public Library, Covington IN. 317-793-2572
Hadar, Elizabeth, *Ch,* Humboldt Free Public Library, Humboldt IA. 515-332-1925
Hadd, Arnold S, *Librn,* United Society of Shakers Library, Poland Spring ME. 207-926-4865
Haddad, Ann M, *Dir,* Falmouth Public Library, Subregional Headquarters for Eastern Massachusetts Regional System, Falmouth MA. 617-548-0280
Hadden, Linda W, *YA,* Edgecombe County Memorial Library, Tarboro NC. 919-823-1141
Hadderman, Margaret L, *Dir,* John F Kennedy University Library, Orinda CA. 415-254-0200, Ext 36
Haddick, Vern, *Dir,* California Institute of Asian Studies Library, San Francisco CA. 415-648-1489
Haddock, Jr, Mrs Walter, *Librn,* South Windham Public Library, Windham ME. 207-892-8086
Hadgis, Diana, *ILL,* Bronx Community College Library, Bronx NY. 212-367-7300, Ext 315
Hadidian, Dikran Y, *Dir,* Pittsburgh Theological Seminary, Clifford E Barbour Library, Pittsburgh PA. 412-362-5610, Ext 280
Hadley, Cornelia, *Cat,* Decatur Public Library, Decatur IL. 217-428-6617, Ext 33
Hadley, Kay, *Circ,* Dowagiac Public Library, Dowagiac MI. 616-782-3826, 782-2195 Ext 30
Hadley, M, *Librn,* Newcastle Public Library (Clarke), Orono ON. 416-983-5507
Hadley, Mary K, *Librn,* Billerica Public Library, Billerica MA. 617-663-3183
Hadley, Thelma, *Librn,* Mariposa County Historical Society Research Library, Mariposa CA. 209-966-2924
Hadlock, Robert L, *Per,* University of Maryland at Baltimore (Health Sciences Library), Baltimore MD. 301-528-7545
Hadlow, Ruth, *Ch,* Cleveland Public Library, Cleveland OH. 216-623-2800
Haefner, Phyllis, *Librn,* Ocean County Library (Long Beach Island), Ship Bottom NJ. 609-494-2480
Haegele, Linda, *Librn,* Rock Rapids Public Library, Rock Rapids IA. 712-472-3541
Haertjens, Albert J, *Acq,* Santa Monica College Library, Santa Monica CA. 213-450-5150
Haertle, Robert J, *Head, Coll Develop,* Marquette University Memorial Library, Milwaukee WI. 414-224-7214
Haeuser, Michael, *Librn,* Linfield College, Northup Library, McMinnville OR. 503-472-4121, Ext 262
Hafer, Helen, *ILL,* Curry College, Louis R Levin Memorial Library, Milton MA. 617-333-0500, Ext 177
Hafer, James, *Dir,* Newark Public Library, Newark OH. 345-1750 & 345-8972
Hafer, Lonnie, *Librn,* Psychiatric Institutes of America Library, Washington DC. 202-337-5600
Haffey, Sharon, *Dir,* Port Carbon Public Library, Port Carbon PA. 717-622-5120
Haffner, Barbara, *Librn,* Bedford Park Public Library District, Argo IL. 312-458-6826
Hafner, William, *Humanities,* Florida Atlantic University, S E Wimberly Library, Boca Raton FL. 305-395-5100, Ext 2448
Hafner, Naomi, *Librn,* Scenic Regional Library of Franklin, Gasconade & Warren Counties (Warrenton Service Center), Warrenton MO. 314-456-3321
Hafner, Ruth, *Ref,* College of Saint Scholastica Library, Duluth MN. 218-723-6143
Hafner, Ruth, *Instr,* College of Saint Scholastica, Library Science Program, MN. 218-723-6143
Hafner, V Kay, *Librn,* United States Air Force (David Grant Medical Center Library), Travis AFB CA. 707-438-3257
Hafter, Ruth, *Dir,* Sonoma State University, Ruben Salazar Library, Rohnert Park CA. 707-664-2397

Hag, Sylvia S, *Librn,* Munson-Williams-Proctor Institute, Art Reference Library, Utica NY. 315-797-0000, Ext 23
Hagaman, W Hugh, *Assoc Prof,* University of North Carolina at Greensboro, Library Science-Educational Technology Div, NC. 919-379-5710
Hagan, Jane, *Librn,* Glendale Public Library (Brand Art & Music), Glendale CA. 213-956-2051
Hagan, Jean, *Librn,* Sullivan County Public Library (Colonial Heights Branch), Kinsport TN. 615-239-6930
Hagan, Michael, *Librn,* Perrot Memorial Library, Old Greenwich CT. 203-637-1066
Hagberg, Betty, *Mgr,* Deere & Co Library, Moline IL. 309-752-4442
Hagdu, S, *ILL, Ref & Rare Bks,* Lakehead University Library, Thunder Bay ON. 807-345-2121
Hage, Christine, *Dir,* Shelby Township Library, Utica MI. 313-739-7414
Hage, Elizabeth, *Ch & YA,* Minnesota Valley Regional Library, Mankato MN. 507-387-1856
Hagedorn, Dorothy, *Sci & Eng,* Tulane University of Louisiana, Howard-Tilton Memorial Library, New Orleans LA. 504-865-5131
Hagedorn, Jane, *Doc,* Skokie Public Library, Skokie IL. 312-673-7774
Hagelin, Daniel W, *Ref,* Lakewood Public Library, Lakewood OH. 216-226-8275
Hagelstein, Gail, *Librn,* American Falls Free Library District, American Falls ID. 208-226-2335
Hageman, Vicki, *Ch,* Park Forest Public Library, Park Forest IL. 312-748-3731
Hagemann, Althea, *ILL, Ad & Commun Servs,* Alameda Free Library, Alameda CA. 415-522-5413, 522-3578
Hagemeister, Leslie, *Ch,* Fargo Public Library, Fargo ND. 701-241-1490
Hagemeyer, Alice, *Librn Deaf,* Public Library of the District of Columbia, Martin Luther King Memorial Library, Washington DC. 202-727-1101
Hagen, Beverly, *Librn,* Saint Luke's Hospital Medical Center, Health-Sciences Reference Library, Phoenix AZ. 602-258-7373, Ext 226
Hagen, Carlos G, *Librn,* University of California Los Angeles Library (Map), Los Angeles CA. 213-825-3526
Hagen, Elayne, *Tech Serv,* Southern Adirondack Library System, Saratoga Springs NY. 518-584-7300, 792-3343, 885-1073
Hagen, Jeanne, *Asst Librn,* Union Carnegie Library, Union SC. 803-427-7140
Hagen, Miriam, *Tech Serv,* Appleton Public Library, Appleton WI. 414-734-7171
Hagen, Mrs Alton, *Dir,* Strum Public Library, Strum WI. 715-695-3513
Hagen, Raeburn, *Asst Dean & Media,* Grays Harbor College, John Spellman Library, Aberdeen WA. 206-532-9020, Ext 201
Hagen, Walter, *Ref,* Adirondack Community College Library, Glens Falls NY. 518-793-4491, Ext 60
Hagen, William H, *Librn,* United States Department of the Navy (Naval Regional Data Automation Center, Technical Library), Washington DC. 202-433-4363, 433-4105
Hagen, Winifred, *Cat,* Otis Library, Norwich CT. 203-889-2365
Hagenow, Sally Ann, *Librn,* Westville Public Library, Westville IN. 219-785-2015
Hager, Catherine, *Librn,* Flat River Public Library, Flat River MO. 314-431-4842
Hager, Charles, *Instr,* Illinois Valley Community College, Library Technical Assistant Program, IL. 815-224-2720
Hager, Dorothy, *Librn,* Public Library of Charlotte & Mecklenburg County, Inc (Cornelius Branch), Cornelius NC. 704-892-8581
Hager, Georgie, *ILL,* Minot State College, Memorial Library, Minot ND. 701-857-3200
Hager, Lucille, *Dir,* Christ Seminary-Seminex Library, Saint Louis MO. 314-534-7535
Hagerstrandt, M A, *Exec Vice Pres,* Cherokee National Historical Society, Inc Library, Tahlequah OK. 918-456-6007
Hagerty, Ann, *Ref,* Saddleback Community College Library, Mission Viejo CA. 714-831-4515
Hagerty, Charles, *AV,* Liberty Baptist College Library, Lynchburg VA. 804-528-0821
Hagerty, Fredericka A, *Dir,* Peninsula Library & Historical Society, Peninsula OH. 216-657-2291

Hagerty, Judy, *AV,* Southern Prairie Library System, Altus OK. 405-477-1930
Haggard, Barbara, *Asst Dir,* Algona Public Library, Algona IA. 515-295-5476
Haggard, Candy, *Chief Librn,* Orange County Public Library (San Clemente Branch), San Clemente CA. 714-492-3493
Haggard, Lynn, *ILL & Ref,* McMurry College, Jay-Rollins Library, Abilene TX. 915-692-4130, Ext 291
Haggerty, Gar, *Asst Librn,* Berklee College of Music Library, Boston MA. 617-266-1400, Ext 158
Haggerty, Marguerite B, *Librn,* Bradley, Arant, Rose & White Law Library, Birmingham AL. 205-252-4500
Haggerty, Ruth M, *Librn,* Armed Forces Institute of Pathology, Ash Library, Washington DC. 202-576-2983
Haggin, June D, *Librn,* El Paso County Law Library, El Paso TX. 915-543-2917
Haggstrom, David, *Media,* State University of New York, Agricultural & Technical College at Alfred, Walter C Hinkle Memorial Library, Alfred NY. 607-871-6313
Hagin, Ida Mae, *Ch,* Central Arkansas Library System, Little Rock AR. 501-374-7546
Hagle, Mildred, *Librn,* Millington Township Library, Millington MI. 517-871-2003
Hagler, Betty, *Librn,* West Georgia Regional Library (Lithia Springs Public), Lithia Springs GA. 404-832-1381
Hagles, Ronald, *Prof,* University of British Columbia, School of Librarianship, BC. 604-228-2404
Hagloch, Susan, *Br Coordr,* Tuscarawas County Public Library, New Philadelphia OH. 216-364-4474
Haglund, Doris, *Librn,* United States Air Force (Tinker Air Force Base Library), Tinker AFB OK. 405-732-7321, Ext 2626
Hagman, Joan, *Curriculum Matls,* Concordia College, Buenger Memorial Library, Saint Paul MN. 612-641-8240
Hagn, Margaret, *ILL & Ref,* Yonkers Public Library, Yonkers NY. 914-337-1500
Hagopian, Viola L, *Dir,* San Francisco Conservatory of Music Library, San Francisco CA. 415-564-8086
Hague, Mary G, *Librn,* Wewoka Public Library, Wewoka OK. 405-257-3225
Hagum, Gertrude, *Libr Asst,* San Bernardino County Library (Mentone Branch), Mentone CA. 714-794-2657
Hahlo, Helen M, *Dir,* Waterbury State Technical College Library, Waterbury CT. 203-756-7035, Ext 33
Hahn, Anne, *Ref, On-Line Servs & Bibliog Instr,* Virginia Military Institute, J T L Preston Library, Lexington VA. 703-463-6228
Hahn, Bessie K, *Reader Serv,* Johns Hopkins University Libraries (Milton S Eisenhower Library), Baltimore MD. 301-338-8325
Hahn, Betty Jean, *Cat,* Minneapolis Public Library & Information Center, Minneapolis MN. 612-372-6500
Hahn, Ellen Z, *Chief, Gen Reading Rooms Div,* Library of Congress, Washington DC. 202-287-5000
Hahn, Ermina, *Tech Serv,* Rutgers University, the State University of New Jersey (School of Law), Newark NJ. 201-648-5675
Hahn, Harvey, *Tech Serv,* Addison Public Library, Addison IL. 312-543-3617
Hahn, James H, *Acting Chief, Libr Div,* Veterans Administration (Library Division), Washington DC. 202-389-2781
Hahn, Maureen, *Ch,* Wilkinsburg Public Library, Pittsburgh PA. 412-244-2940
Hahn, Robert, *Curator,* Illinois Benedictine College, Theodore Lownik Library, Lisle IL. 312-968-7270, Ext 286
Hahn, Robert, *Librn,* University of Missouri-Columbia (Journalism), Columbia MO. 314-882-7502
Hahn, Ruth N, *Reader Serv,* Indiana State University, Evansville Library, Evansville IN. 812-464-1824
Hahn, Stephan, *Ref,* Washington & Lee University, The University Library, Lexington VA. 703-463-9111, Ext 403
Hahn, Susanne, *Librn,* Schnader, Harrison, Segal & Lewis Library, Philadelphia PA. 215-988-2111

HAHN

Hahn, Susanne, *On-Line Servs & Bibliog Instr,* Schnader, Harrison, Segal & Lewis Library, Philadelphia PA. 215-988-2111

Hahne, Mary, *Asst Librn,* Peru Public Library, Peru IL. 815-223-0229

Haigh, Eileen, *Asst Dir,* Hill Junior College Library, Hillsboro TX. 817-582-2555, Ext 40

Haigh, Ellen, *Librn,* Toledo-Lucas County Public Library (West Toledo), Toledo OH. 419-255-7055

Haight, Audrey, *Acq,* Montana State University, Roland R Renne Library, Bozeman MT. 406-994-3119

Haight, Larry, *Ref,* Assemblies of God Graduate School Library, Cordas C Burnett Library, Springfield MO. 417-862-2781, Ext 5505

Haigis, Joanne, *Dept Libr Univ Vt Access Off, Burlington,* State of Vermont Department of Libraries, Montpelier VT. 802-828-3261

Hail, Christopher, *Asst Librn & Ref,* Harvard University Library (Frances L Loeb Library), Cambridge MA. 617-495-2574

Haile, Marjorie, *Librn,* Southern Methodist College Library, Orangeburg SC. 803-534-7826

Haile, Nancy, *Acq,* University of Maryland at Baltimore (School of Law Library), Baltimore MD. 301-528-7270

Hailes, Donald, *Outreach,* District of Columbia Library for the Blind & Physically Handicapped, Washington DC. 212-727-2142

Hain, Gloria, *Asst Librn,* Sinking Spring Public Library, Sinking Spring PA. 215-678-4311

Haines, Alyce, *Librn,* Maui Memorial Hospital, Medical Library, Wailuku HI. 808-244-9056

Haines, Carol L, *ILL,* Public Library of Brookline, Brookline MA. 617-734-0100

Haines, Delight, *Dir,* Petersham Memorial Library, Petersham MA. 617-724-3405

Haines, Delight G, *Librn,* Petersham Historical Society Library, Petersham MA. 617-724-3380

Haines, L, *Librn,* Okanagan Regional Library District (Silver Creek Branch), Silver Creek BC. 604-832-4347

Haines, Maria, *Bkmobile Coordr,* Chattahoochee Valley Regional Library, W C Bradley Memorial Library, Headquarters, Columbus GA. 404-327-0211

Haines, Mrs Richard D, *Actg Dir,* Railroad & Pioneer Museum Inc Library, Temple TX. 817-778-6873

Haines, Nancy S, *Chief Librn,* Veterans Administration, Medical Library, Cleveland OH. 216-791-3800, Ext 7307

Haines, Patricia Ann, *Librn,* Westfield Public Library, Westfield PA. 814-367-5411

Haines, Sharon, *Librn,* Flatwoods Public Library, Flatwoods KY. 606-836-3771

Haines, Sharon, *Asst Dir,* Greenup County Public Libraries, Greenup KY. 606-473-6514

Hainess, Joyce, *Asst Librn,* Esther Washburn Public Library, Tremont IL. 309-925-5432

Hains, Peggy, *YA,* Oakville Public Library, Oakville ON. 416-845-3405

Haire, Gloria, *On-Line Servs,* Lawrence Berkeley Laboratory Library, Berkeley CA. 415-486-5621

Haire, Paul, *Librn,* Temple Junior College, Hubert M Dawson Library, Temple TX. 817-773-9961, Ext 42

Haizlip, Claire, *Dir,* Mechanicville District Public Library, Mechanicville NY. 518-664-4646

Haizman, Vivian, *Cat,* Clermont County Public Library, Batavia OH. 513-732-2128

Hajas, S, *On-Line Servs,* Ventura College, D R Henry Library, Ventura CA. 805-642-3211, Ext 201

Haji, Janet, *Chief Librn,* Tacoma Community College, Pearl A Wanamaker Library & Instructional Resource Center, Tacoma WA. 206-756-5087

Hajjar, Felicity, *Acq,* Albany County Public Library, Laramie WY. 307-745-3365

Haka, Cliff, *Circ,* University of Kansas Libraries, Watson Memorial Library, Lawrence KS. 913-864-3601

Hakala, William T, *Dir,* American Swedish Institute Library, Minneapolis MN. 612-871-4907

Hakel, Arthur A, *Librn,* Tribune Publishing Co, Oakland Tribune Library, Oakland CA. 415-645-2000

Hakim, Arlene, *Librn,* Alabama State Department of Pensions & Security Library, Montgomery AL. 205-832-5916

Halasz, Etelka, *Tech Serv, Acq & Cat,* West New York Public Library, Philip A Payne Memorial Library, West New York NJ. 201-854-1028

Halberstadt, Don, *Librn,* Crozer-Chester Medical Center Library, Chester PA. 215-874-9611, Ext 279

Halbrook, Anne-Mieke, *Librn,* J Paul Getty Museum Library, Malibu CA. 213-459-2306

Halbrook, Barbara, *Asst Dir,* Washington University Libraries (School of Medicine Library), Saint Louis MO. 314-454-3711

Halbrook, Ida, *Tech Serv,* Bryan Public Library, Bryan TX. 713-823-8021

Halby, William, *Media,* Los Angeles Pierce College Library, Woodland Hills CA. 213-347-0551, Ext 267

Halcli, Albert, *Asst Dir Pub Servs,* Illinois State Library, Springfield IL. 217-782-2994

Halcums, Robert, *Librn,* Department of Public Libraries & Information (Kempsville), Virginia Beach VA. 804-420-2270

Haldane, Frances, *Circ,* Raleigh County Public Library, Beckley WV. 304-255-0511

Haldeman, Amy, *Tech Serv,* Free Public Library of the Township of Berkeley Heights, Berkeley Heights NJ. 201-464-9333

Hale, Adelene B, *Pres,* International Biomedical Laboratories Inc Library, Boston MA. 617-227-5040

Hale, Charles E, *Dir,* Staley Library, Millikin University, Decatur IL. 217-424-6214

Hale, Edna, *Ch,* Lawrence Public Library, Fairfield ME. 207-453-6867

Hale, Elizabeth F, *Libr Consult,* Society of the Montreal Military & Maritime Museum, Macdonald Stewart Library, Montreal PQ. 514-861-6738

Hale, Ellen, *Acq,* Birmingham Public & Jefferson County Free Library, Birmingham AL. 205-254-2551

Hale, Janice, *Asst Librn,* Middlesex Community College, Learning Resources Center, Bedford MA. 617-275-8910

Hale, Judy E, *In Charge,* Goodyear Tire & Rubber Co, Technical Information Center, Akron OH. 216-794-2121

Hale, Katherine, *Dir,* Southern Prairie Library System, Altus OK. 405-477-1930

Hale, Kay K, *On-Line Servs,* University of New Brunswick, Harriet Irving Library, Fredericton NB. 506-453-4740

Hale, Kay K, *Librn,* University of New Brunswick (Science), Fredericton NB. 506-453-3566, 453-3577

Hale, Marie L, *ILL,* Belmont Public Library, Belmont MA. 617-489-2000

Hale, Mrs J D, *Project Dir,* Rotan Public Library, Rotan TX. 915-735-3362

Hale, R, *On-Line Servs,* Georgia Institute of Technology, Price Gilbert Memorial Library, Atlanta GA. 404-894-4510

Hale, Relda, *Librn,* Memphis-Shelby County Public Library & Information Center (Millington Libr), Millington TN. 901-872-1585

Hale, Stephen, *Librn,* Jackson-George Regional Library System (Moss Point City), Moss Point MS. 601-475-7462

Hale, Syliva, *Libr Asst,* Pictou Antigonish Regional Library (Westville Branch), Westville NS. 902-396-5022

Hale, Vivian, *Media,* Cass County Library, Cassopolis MI. 616-445-8651

Hales, David A, *Ref,* University of Alaska, Fairbanks, Elmer E Rasmuson Library, Fairbanks AK. 907-479-7224

Hales, Dorothy G, *Dir,* Sequoyah Regional Library, R T Jones Memorial Library, Canton GA. 404-479-3090

Hales, Jr, John D, *Dir,* Suwannee River Regional Library, Seven-County Region, Live Oak FL. 904-362-5779

Halette, L, *Librn,* Cache Bay Public Library, Cache Bay ON. 705-753-3505

Halevy, Balfour J, *Librn,* York University (Osgoode Hall Law School Library), Downsview ON. 416-667-3939

Haley, Anne, *Dir,* Walla Walla Public Library, Walla Walla WA. 509-525-5353

Haley, Barbara, *ILL, Cat, Ref & On-Line Servs,* Mount Marty College Library, Yankton SD. 605-668-1555

Haley, Brian, *Tech Serv,* Ursinus College, Myrin Library, Collegeville PA. 215-489-4111, Ext 290

Haley, David Boulter, *Librn,* Maine State Prison Library, Thomaston ME. 207-354-2535, Ext 274

Haley, Edna, *Librn,* Phillips Free Public Library, Phillipston MA. 617-249-6828

Haley, John, *ILL,* Philadelphia College of Art Library, Philadelphia PA. 215-893-3126

Haley, June, *Librn,* Atlantic Council of the United States Library, Washington DC. 202-347-9353

Haley, Mary, *Cat,* Marian College of Fond Du Lac, Cardinal Meyer Library, Fond du Lac WI. 414-921-3900, Ext 237

Haley, Mrs Wallace, *Dir,* Dannemora Free Library, Dannemora NY. 518-492-7005

Haley, Nancy, *Bkmobile Coordr,* Wareham Free Library, Wareham MA. 617-295-2343

Haley, Roger K, *Librn,* United States Senate Library, Washington DC. 202-224-7106

Haley, Wilda M, *ILL & Ref,* Bureau of Land Management (Denver Service Center Library), Denver CO. 303-234-4578

Halferty, JoAnne, *Dir,* Schreiner Memorial Library, Lancaster Public Library, Lancaster WI. 608-723-7304

Halfpenny, Lucille S, *Librn,* Saint Thomas Seminary Library, Bloomfield CT. 203-242-5573, Ext 57

Halgren, Joanne, *ILL,* University of Oregon Library, Eugene OR. 503-686-3056

Halgrimson, Andrea H, *Librn,* Forum Publishing Company Library, Fargo ND. 701-235-7311

Haliburton, Edith, *Rare Bks & Spec Coll,* Acadia University, Harold Campbell Vaughan Memorial Library, Wolfville NS. 902-542-2201, Ext 215

Halicki, Kenneth G, *Librn,* Seyfarth, Shaw, Fairweather & Geraldson Library, Chicago IL. 312-346-8000, Ext 318

Halicki, Lillian, *Librn,* Maroa Township Library, Maroa IL. 217-794-5111

Hall, A, *Dir,* New Brunswick Library Service, Department of Youth, Recreation & Cultural Resources, Fredericton NB. 506-453-2354

Hall, Alan C, *Dir,* Delphos Public Library, Delphos OH. 419-692-1339

Hall, Alexandra, *Media,* College of Marin Library, Kentfield CA. 415-485-9470

Hall, Alice, *Ch,* Zion-Benton Public Library District, Zion IL. 312-872-4680

Hall, Alice M, *Cat,* Lafayette College, David Bishop Skillman Library, Easton PA. 215-253-6281, Ext 289

Hall, Ann, *Librn,* Bureau of Land Management, Eastern States Office Library, Silver Spring MD. 301-427-7500

Hall, Ann Bowman, *Librn, On-Line Servs & Bibliog Instr,* National Marine Fisheries Service, Southeast Fisheries Center, Beaufort Laboratory Library, Beaufort NC. 919-728-4595, Ext 231

Hall, Barbara, *Librn,* Jones College Library, Orlando FL. 305-896-2407, Ext 24

Hall, Barbara, *Dir,* River Forest Public Library, River Forest IL. 312-366-5205

Hall, Barbara, *Slide Cat,* Margaret Woodbury Strong Museum Library, Rochester NY. 716-381-1818, Ext 23

Hall, Berdella, *Librn,* Carthage Free Library (West Carthage Branch), West Carthage NY. 315-493-0454

Hall, Bernita, *Librn,* Saint Clair County Library System (Yale Public), Yale MI. 313-387-2940

Hall, Beth, *Librn,* Haltom City Public Library, Haltom City TX. 817-834-7341

Hall, Blaine, *Lit,* Brigham Young University, Harold B Lee Library, Provo UT. 801-378-2905

Hall, Bonnie, *Librn,* University of Richmond (Music), Richmond VA. 804-285-6398

Hall, Bonnlyn, *Music,* University of Richmond, Boatwright Memorial Library, Richmond VA. 804-285-6452

Hall, Brent, *ILL,* Maine Maritime Academy, Nutting Memorial Library, Castine ME. 207-326-4311, Ext 238

Hall, Bro James M, *Librn,* MSC Center Library, Shelby OH. 419-342-2886

Hall, Caroline, *Ad,* Southbury Public Library, Southbury CT. 203-264-0606, Ext 239

Hall, Carolyn, *Librn,* Florida Department of Health & Rehabilitative Services, Resource Center, Jacksonville FL. 904-354-3961, Ext 332 & 230

Hall, Catharine, *Ref,* Mary Washington College, E Lee Trinkle Library, Fredericksburg VA. 703-899-4666

Hall, Catherine, *Tech Serv,* Christ the King Seminary Library, East Aurora NY. 716-652-8959

Hall, Craige S, *Dir & Prof,* Weber State College, Instructional Media Program, UT. 801-626-6280

Hall, Craige S, *Dir,* Weber State College Library, Stewart Library, Ogden UT. 801-626-6403

Hall, Danelle, *Doc,* Oklahoma City University (Dulaney-Browne Library), Oklahoma City OK. 405-521-5068

Hall, David, *Librn,* Milwaukee Legislative Reference Bureau Library, Milwaukee WI. 414-278-2295

Hall, Deborah A, *Librn,* Milwaukee County Mental Health Center, Michael Kasak Library, Milwaukee WI. 414-257-7381

Hall, Debra, *Asst Dir,* Art Circle Public Library, Cumberland County, Crossville TN. 615-484-6790

Hall, Donald S, *Dir,* Rochester Museum & Science Center (Strassenburgh Planetarium, Todd Library), Rochester NY. 716-244-6060

Hall, Dorothy, *Assistant,* Cambridge City Public Library, Cambridge City IN. 317-478-3335

Hall, Dorothy, *Dir,* Oklahoma State Department of Health Library, Oklahoma City OK. 271-4725; 271-5724

Hall, Edna J, *Ch Outreach Librn,* Hyconeechee Regional Library, Yanceyville NC. 919-694-6241

Hall, Edna W, *Acq & Cat,* Berkshire Athenaeum, Pittsfield Public Library, Pittsfield MA. 413-442-1559

Hall, Edward B, *Dir,* Public Library of Annapolis & Anne Arundel County Inc, Annapolis MD. 301-224-7371

Hall, Elede (Toppy), *Librn,* Addison-Wesley Publishing Co, School Division Library, Menlo Park CA. 415-854-0300, Ext 225

Hall, Elisabeth, *Cat,* Willamette University Library (College of Law Library), Salem OR. 503-370-6387

Hall, Elizabeth R, *Librn,* Monroe County Public Library, William B Harland Memorial Library, Tompkinsville KY. 502-487-5301

Hall, Ellen, *Libr Clerk,* Mohave County Library (Mohave Ranchos), Dolan Springs AZ. 602-753-5730

Hall, Ellen F, *Dir,* Presentation College Library, Aberdeen SD. 605-225-0420, Ext 368

Hall, Erna, *Librn,* Buffalo & Erie County Public Library System (Niagara Branch), Niagara NY. 716-882-1537

Hall, Esther, *Librn,* Show Low Public Library, Show Low AZ. 602-537-2447

Hall, Florence M, *ILL & Ref,* Melrose Public Library, Melrose MA. 617-665-2313

Hall, Frances H, *Librn,* North Carolina Supreme Court Library, Raleigh NC. 919-733-3425

Hall, George, *Music,* University of Calgary Library, Calgary AB. 403-284-5954

Hall, Grace, *Librn,* Montgomery Public Library, Montgomery MA. 413-862-3226

Hall, H Janet, *Librn,* Chester Springs Library, Chester Springs PA. 215-827-9212

Hall, H Palmer, *Dir,* Saint Mary's University (Academic Library), San Antonio TX. 512-436-3441

Hall, Hal, *Microtext,* Texas A&m University Libraries, College Station TX. 713-845-6111

Hall, Hazel, *Librn,* Towanda Public Library, Towanda KS. 316-536-2554

Hall, Helen, *Librn,* Yarmouth County Historical Society Research Library, Yarmouth NS. 902-742-5539

Hall, Henry L, *Dir,* Scotland County Memorial Library, Laurinburg NC. 919-276-0563

Hall, Holly, *Rare Bks,* Washington University Libraries, Saint Louis MO. 314-889-5400

Hall, Homer L, *Librn,* Big Sandy Regional Library, Prestonsburg KY. 606-886-6311

Hall, Hugh, *Ref,* West Valley College, Learning Resource Center, Saratoga CA. 408-867-2200, Ext 284

Hall, Irene, *Dir,* Norwalk Public Library, Norwalk OH. 419-668-6063

Hall, Jane, *Cat,* Chesapeake Public Library, Chesapeake VA. 804-547-6579, 547-6592

Hall, Janice M, *Circ,* Saint Petersburg Junior College, Michael M Bennett Library, Clearwater FL. 813-441-0681, Ext 2616

Hall, Joan A, *Librn,* Rockwell International of Canada Ltd, Collins Canada Division Library, Toronto ON. 416-747-1101, Ext 320

Hall, John, *Asst Prof,* Drexel University, School of Library & Information Science, PA. 215-895-2474

Hall, John B, *Librn,* Putnam Memorial Hospital (Hospital Library), Bennington VT. 802-442-6361, Ext 298

Hall, John G, *Coordr of Libr Prog,* Interuniversity Council of the North Texas Area, (IUC), TX. 214-231-7211

Hall, Joseph H, *Librn,* Covenant Theological Seminary, J Oliver Buswell Jr Library, Saint Louis MO. 314-434-4044

Hall, Juanita, *Tech Serv,* Morehead State University, Johnson Camden-Julian Carroll Library, Morehead KY. 606-783-2250

Hall, June V, *Librn,* Montgomery Area Public Library, Montgomery PA. 717-547-6212

Hall, Kay, *Clerk,* John McIntire Public Library Public Library (Dresden Branch), Dresden OH. 614-754-1003

Hall, L, *Librn,* Bendix Corp, Electrical Components Div, Engineering Library, Sidney NY. 607-563-5605, Ext 437

Hall, Lawrence, *Doc,* Alma College Library, Alma MI. 517-463-2141, Ext 332

Hall, Libby, *Librn,* Forsyth County Public Library (Rural Hall Branch), Rural Hall NC. 919-969-6340

Hall, Lillie W, *Per,* Alabama State University, Library & Learning Resources, Montgomery AL. 205-832-6072

Hall, Lois, *Librn,* Newman Center Library, Minneapolis MN. 612-331-3437

Hall, Lois, *Br Coordr,* Pembroke Public Library, Pembroke MA. 617-293-6771

Hall, Louise, *Ref,* University of North Carolina at Chapel Hill, Louis Round Wilson Academic Affairs Library, Chapel Hill NC. 919-933-1301

Hall, Louise, *Humanities,* University of North Carolina at Chapel Hill, Louis Round Wilson Academic Affairs Library, Chapel Hill NC. 919-933-1301

Hall, Lucile, *Librn,* Mid-Continent Public Library (Antioch), Kansas City North MO. 816-454-1306

Hall, Lynda, *Sci,* University of Calgary Library, Calgary AB. 403-284-5954

Hall, M E, *AV,* Florida Agricultural & Mechanical University, Samuel H Coleman Memorial Library, Tallahassee FL. 904-599-3370

Hall, M S, *Per,* Florida Agricultural & Mechanical University, Samuel H Coleman Memorial Library, Tallahassee FL. 904-599-3370

Hall, Margery, *Ref,* Bala Cynwyd Library, Bala-Cynwyd PA. 215-664-1196

Hall, Marianne, *Librn,* Chetwynd Public Library, Chetwynd BC. 604-788-2559

Hall, Marion, *Librn,* Gilsum Public Library, Gilsum NH. 603-357-0320

Hall, Martha, *Reader Serv & Bibliog Instr,* Philadelphia College of Art Library, Philadelphia PA. 215-893-3126

Hall, Mary, *ILL & Ref,* Delta State University, W B Roberts Library, Cleveland MS. 601-843-2483

Hall, Mary, *Librn,* Powassan & District Union Public Library, Powassan ON. 705-724-3618

Hall, Mary, *Cat,* State University College at Buffalo, Edward H Butler Library, Buffalo NY. 716-878-6302

Hall, Mary A, *Asst Dir Pub Servs,* Prince George's County Memorial Library System, Hyattsville MD. 301-699-3500

Hall, Mary Catherine, *Bkmobile Coordr,* Seymour Public Library, Seymour IN. 812-522-3412

Hall, Mary Joan, *Librn,* Solomon R Guggenheim Museum Library, New York NY. 212-860-1338

Hall, Mrs B, *Librn,* Thornbury Public Library, Thornbury ON. 519-599-3681

Hall, Mrs John, *Librn,* Landis Library, Landis NC. 704-857-2411

Hall, Nan C, *Librn,* Oxford Memorial Library, Oxford NY. 607-843-4021

Hall, Nancy M, *Librn,* Borough of Etobicoke Public Library, Weston ON. 416-248-5681

Hall, Nancy O, *YA,* Public Library of Annapolis & Anne Arundel County Inc, Annapolis MD. 301-224-7371

Hall, Phyllis A, *Librn,* Judith Basin County Free Library, Stanford MT. 406-566-2389

Hall, Richard B, *Consult, Facilities & Pub Libr Film Serv,* Georgia Department of Education (Div of Public Library Services), Atlanta GA. 404-656-2461

Hall, Richard V, *In Charge,* Texas Education Agency (Region III), Victoria TX. 512-575-1471

Hall, Robert B, *Cat,* Stonehill College, Cushing-Martin Library, North Easton MA. 617-238-1081, Ext 328, 329, 313

Hall, Robin, *ILL,* Perry County District Library, New Lexington OH. 614-342-1077

Hall, Ruby, *Librn,* Texas County Library (Licking Branch), Licking MO. 314-674-3811

Hall, Ruth, *Librn,* Orleans Public Library, Orleans IN. 812-865-3270

Hall, S L, *Librn,* Aurora Public Library, Aurora ON. 416-727-9493

Hall, Sally, *Circ,* Maywood Public Library, Maywood NJ. 201-845-7755

Hall, Sharon, *Area Head,* Winnipeg Public Library (Fort Garry Branch), Winnipeg MB. 204-452-3201

Hall, Sister Barnabas, *Dir,* Ladycliff College, Msgr C Hugo Doyle Library, Highland Falls NY. 914-446-4747, Ext 21

Hall, Sylvia D, *Asst Dir,* Southern Tier Library System, Corning NY. 607-962-3141

Hall, Thelma R, *Librn,* United States Air Force (March Air Force Base Library), March AFB CA. 714-655-5234

Hall, V Ruth, *Acq,* Palmer College of Chiropractic, Davenport IA. 319-324-1611, Ext 242

Hall, Virginia, *Head, Tech Servs (Acq & Cat),* George S Houston Memorial Library, Dothan AL. 205-793-9767

Hall, Virginia B, *Librn,* Ohio State University Libraries (Pharmacy Library), Columbus OH. 614-422-8026

Hall, Vivian, *Librn,* University of Kentucky (Geology), Lexington KY. 606-258-5730

Hall, Wanda, *Librn,* Mangum City Library, Mangum OK. 405-782-3185

Hall, William, *Ch,* Durango Public Library, Durango CO. 303-247-2492

Hallahan, John J, *Dir,* Manchester City Library, Manchester NH. 603-625-6485

Hallam, Arlita W, *Tech Serv & Acq,* Abilene Public Library, Abilene TX. 915-677-2474

Hallam, Norman E, *Dir & Br Coordr,* Mendocino County Library, Ukiah CA. 707-468-4491

Hallbauer, Arthur, *Instr,* Morningside College, Library Science Dept, IA. 712-277-5125

Hallberg, Darlene, *Spec Servs,* Watertown Regional Library, Watertown SD. 605-886-8521, 886-8282

Hallblade, Shirley, *Mgr,* Mississippi Research & Development Center, Information Services Divison, Jackson MS. 601-982-6324

Hallborg, Dorothy, *Curriculum Mat,* Hofstra University Library, Hempstead NY. 516-560-3475

Halldorson, Jeanette, *Acq,* Shawnee Library System, Carterville IL. 618-985-3711

Hallemann, Harriett, *Librn,* Scenic Regional Library of Franklin, Gasconade & Warren Counties (New Haven Service Center), New Haven MO. 314-237-2189

Hallenbeck, Vern, *Tech Serv,* Central College, Geisler Learning Resource Center, Pella IA. 515-628-4151, Ext 233

Haller, Blanche W, *Dir,* Montclair State College, Harry A Sprague Library, Upper Montclair NJ. 201-893-4291

Haller, Naomi, *Asst Prof,* Augustana College, Library Science Program, SD. 605-336-4921

Haller, Naomi, *Per,* Augustana College, Mikkelsen Library & Learning Resources Center, Sioux Falls SD. 605-336-4921

Hallerberg, Gretchen, *Adjunct Prof,* Case Western Reserve University, School of Library Science, OH. 216-368-3500

Hallett, Dessie M, *Librn,* Mount Vernon Place United Methodist Church, Dessie M Hallett Library, Washington DC. 202-347-9620

Halliday, Helen, *Pub Servs,* Wilmington College, Sheppard Arthur Watson Library, Wilmington OH. 513-382-6661, Ext 206

Halliday, Jane S, *Librn,* Veterans Administration, Hospital Library, Livermore CA. 415-447-2560, Ext 325

HALLIDAY

Halliday, John, *Dir,* Prescott Public-Yavapai County Library System, Prescott AZ. 602-445-8110

Halligan, Gerald J, *Dir,* Woodward Memorial Library, LeRoy NY. 716-768-8300

Halligan, Shirley, *Ch,* Fairfield Public Library, Fairfield CT. 203-259-8303

Halling, Ingrid, *Tech Serv,* University of Michigan-Flint Library, Flint MI. 313-762-3400

Hallisey, Carol, *YA & Cat,* Frederick E Parlin Memorial Library, Everett MA. 617-387-2550

Halliwell, D W, *Dir,* University of Victoria, McPherson Library, Victoria BC. 604-477-6911, Ext 4466

Hallo, William W, *Curator,* Yale University Library (Babylonian), New Haven CT. 203-432-4725

Hallock, Genevieve, *Acq & Circ,* Bryant Library, Roslyn NY. 516-621-2240

Hallock, Sister Martha, *Dir,* Nazareth College, David Metzger Library, Nazareth MI. 616-349-7783, Ext 270

Hallock, Sister Mary, *Ref,* Nazareth College, David Metzger Library, Nazareth MI. 616-349-7783, Ext 270

Halloran, Dorothy, *Dir,* Gays Mills Public Library, Gays Mills WI. 608-735-4766

Halloran, Helen, *Librn,* San Antonio Public Library (Literature, Philosophy & Religion), San Antonio TX. 512-299-7817, 299-7818

Halloran, JoAnn, *Asst Dir,* Morris Public Library, Morris CT. 203-567-0160

Halloran, Joseph G, *Dir,* Syosset Public Library, Syosset NY. 516-921-7161

Hallowitz, M, *Hist of Med,* State University of New York at Buffalo, University Libraries, Buffalo NY. 716-636-2965

Hallowitz, Mildred, *Rare Bks,* State University of New York at Buffalo (Health Sciences), Buffalo NY. 716-831-5465

Hallstrom, Curtis H, *On-Line Servs,* General Mills Inc (James Ford Bell Technical Information Services), Minneapolis MN. 612-540-3464

Hallstrom, Harlan, *ILL, Ref & Media,* Dakota State College, Karl E Mundt Library, Madison SD. 605-256-3551, Ext 226

Hallsworth, Peter, *Dir,* Sudbury Public Library, La Bibliotheque Publique de Sudbury, Sudbury ON. 705-673-1155

Hallum, Elizabeth Ann, *Librn,* Lassen County Free Library, Susanville CA. 916-257-5547

Halm, Velma, *Librn,* Johnson City Library, Johnson City TX. 512-868-4469

Halma, Linda, *ILL & Ref,* Kutztown State College, Rohrbach Library, Kutztown PA. 215-683-4480

Halma, Sidney, *Dir,* Catawba County Historical Museum Library, Newton NC. 704-465-0383

Halman, Ruth B, *Ref,* University of California, Riverside, University Library, Riverside CA. 714-787-3221

Halperin, Michael, *Ref & On-Line Servs,* Drexel University Library, Philadelphia PA. 215-895-2750

Halpern, Henry, *Acq,* Rider College, Franklin F Moore Library, Lawrenceville NJ. 609-896-5111

Halpern, Meyer William, *Librn,* Marin County Law Library, San Rafael CA. 415-479-1100, Ext 2078; 479-4908

Halpin, James R, *Ref,* Newburgh Free Library, Newburgh NY. 914-561-1836

Halpin, Keum, *Soc Sci,* Seattle Central Community College, Instructional Resource Services, Seattle WA. 206-587-5420

Halpin, Jr, Jerome H, *Cat,* Adams State College Library, Alamosa CO. 303-589-7781

Halpin, Jr, Jerome H, *Instr,* Adams State College, Masters in Educational Media with the University of Northern Colorado, CO. 303-589-7781

Halporn, Barbara, *Classics, Philos, Psychol & Hist, Philos of Sci,* Indiana University at Bloomington, University Libraries, Bloomington IN. 812-337-3403

Halsey, Richard S, *Dean,* State University of New York at Albany, School of Library & Information Science, NY. 518-455-6288

Halsey, Wanda, *Librn,* Enquirer & News, Editorial Dept Library, Battle Creek MI. 616-964-7161

Halstead, Bruce W, *Librn,* World Life Research Institute Library, Colton CA. 714-825-4773

Halstead, Olive, *Local Hist,* Portage Public Library, Portage MI. 616-327-6725

Halstead, Sally, *Acq,* Sandpoint-East Bonner County Free Public Library District, Sandpoint ID. 208-263-6930

Halter, Claudine, *Librn,* Carroll County Library, Florine Harbert Maddox Memorial Libray, Huntingdon TN. 901-986-3991

Halter, E J, *In Charge,* Burgess Industries, Engineering Library, Dallas TX. 214-631-1410

Halter, Sam, *Librn,* Melbourne Public Library, Melbourne IA. 515-482-3115

Halterman, Betty, *ILL,* Santa Cruz Public Library, Santa Cruz CA. 408-429-3533

Haltiwangert, Anna, *Librn,* Midlands Technical College (Airport Campus), Columbia SC. 803-782-5471, Ext 265

Halttunen, Lisa M, *Ref,* Mystic Seaport Museum, G W Blunt White Library, Mystic CT. 203-536-2631, Ext 261

Haluoison, Betty, *Librn,* Western Plains Library System (Madison Branch), Madison MN. 612-598-7938

Halverson, Helen, *ILL, Ref & On-Line Servs,* Anoka County Library, Blaine MN. 612-784-1100

Halverson, Keith, *Librn,* Sioux Falls Park & Recreation Department, Great Plains Zoo Library, Sioux Falls SD. 605-339-7059

Halverson, Sally D, *Asst Librn,* Touro Infirmary (Hospital Library), New Orleans LA. 504-897-8102, 897-8502

Halvorsen, Carol L, *Affiliate Coordr & Bkmobile Coordr,* Warren Library Association, Warren Library, Warren PA. 814-723-4650

Halvorsen, Jeanette, *Circ,* Crystal Lake Public Library, Crystal Lake IL. 815-459-1687

Halvorson, Dorothy, *Librn,* Plainview Public Library, Plainview MN. 507-534-3425

Ham, Deborah, *Tech Serv,* Sacred Heart College, McCarthy Library, Belmont NC. 704-825-5146

Ham, Janet L, *Ch,* Mark Twain Library, Redding CT. 203-938-2240

Hamaker, Chuck, *Coll Develop,* University of Missouri Saint Louis, Thomas Jefferson Library, Saint Louis MO. 314-453-5221

Hamann, Edmund X, *Librn,* Suffolk University College Library, Boston MA. 617-723-4700, Ext 241

Hamann, Erma, *Cat,* Dr Martin Luther College Library, New Ulm MN. 507-354-8221, Ext 242

Hamarzt, Bagdasar, *Circ,* Mercy College Libraries, Dobbs Ferry NY. 914-693-4500, Ext 260

Hamberg, Cheryl, *Bibliog Instr,* Meharry Medical College Library, Kresge Learning Resource Center, Nashville TN. 615-327-6319

Hambley, Susan L, *Asst Librn,* Baldwin-Wallace College (Fern Patterson Jones Memorial Music Library), Berea OH. 216-826-2366

Hamblin, Carol J, *Dir,* Guilderland Free Library, Albany NY. 518-456-2400

Hambridge, Sally, *Tech Serv,* Xerox Corporation, Technical Library, El Segundo CA. 213-679-4511, Ext 2222

Hamburger, Roberta, *Assoc Prof,* Phillips University, Education & Library Science Study Area, OK. 405-237-4433, Ext 417

Hamburger, Roberta, *Asst Dir & Bibliog Instr,* Phillips University (John Rogers Graduate Seminary Library), Enid OK. 405-237-4433, Ext 227

Hamburger, Susan, *Librn,* R T Vanderbilt Co, Inc, Corporate Library, Norwalk CT. 203-853-1400, Ext 430

Hamby, C David, *Media,* Frederick Community College, Learning Resource Center, Frederick MD. 301-694-1242

Hamby, Sharon, *Librn,* Boston College Libraries (Law Library), Chestnut Hill MA. 617-969-0100, Ext 4405

Hamdy, Mohamed, *Instr,* University of Denver, Graduate School of Librarianship and Information Management, CO. 303-753-2557

Hamel, Andre, *Dir,* La Magnetotheque, Montreal PQ. 514-524-6831

Hamelberg, Eileen, *Radio Program,* Washington Regional Library for the Blind & Physically Handicapped, Seattle WA. 464-6930. SCAN 576-6930

Hamelin, Jean B, *Dir,* Georgetown Peabody Library, Georgetown MA. 617-352-8428

Hamer, Allegra, *Asst in Zool,* New York Zoological Society Library, Bronx NY. 212-220-5124

Hamer, Jeanne, *Librn,* Denver Public Library (Field), Denver CO. 303-573-5152, Ext 271

Hamer, Kay, *Ad & Ref,* Washington County Library System, William Alexander Percy Memorial Library, Greenville MS. 601-335-2331

Hamer, Jr, Collin B, *Rare Bks & Spec Coll,* New Orleans Public Library, Simon Heinsheim & Fisk Libraries, New Orleans LA. 504-586-4905

Hamerlinck, Donald, *Librn,* Saint Cloud Area Vo-Tech Institute Library, Resource Center, Saint Cloud MN. 612-252-0101

Hamerski, Louise, *Librn,* East Jordan Public Library, East Jordan MI. 616-536-7131

Hamil, Mary A, *Learning Resources Librn,* Davidson County Community College, Grady E Love Learning Resources Center, Lexington NC. 704-249-8186, Ext 270

Hamill, Allardyce, *Ref,* Saint Lucie County Library Systems, Fort Pierce FL. 305-461-5708

Hamill, Geneva, *Cat,* Boston University Libraries (School of Theology Library), Boston MA. 617-353-3034

Hamilton, Alice, *Librn,* Ralph M Parsons Co, Central Library, Pasadena CA. 213-440-3997

Hamilton, Altamesa, *Libr Chairperson,* Hillsborough Community College Library, Tampa FL. 813-247-6641, Ext 261

Hamilton, Anne, *Dir,* Kentucky Department of Education Materials Center Library, Frankfort KY. 502-564-5513

Hamilton, Annie Mae, *Librn,* Oktibbeha County Library System (Maben Branch), Maben MS. 601-263-5619

Hamilton, Arloene, *Tech Serv,* Redwood City Public Library, Redwood City CA. 415-369-6251, Ext 288

Hamilton, Art, *Librn,* Stillwater County Library (Fishtail Branch), Fishtail MT. 406-322-5337

Hamilton, Barbara, *Librn,* Security Public Library, Security CO. 303-392-8912

Hamilton, Beryl, *Librn,* Lennox & Addington County Public Library (Sandhurst), Bath ON. 613-354-2585

Hamilton, Beth A, *Sr Info Sci,* Triodyne Incorporated Consulting Engineers, Information Center, Skokie IL. 312-677-4730

Hamilton, Betsy, *AV & YA,* Sampson-Clinton Public Library, Clinton NC. 919-592-4153

Hamilton, Brian C, *Librn,* Greystone Park Psychiatric Hospital, Medical Library, Greystone Park NJ. 201-538-1800

Hamilton, Carol, *Ref,* Delaware Technical & Community College Library, Newark DE. 302-368-6985

Hamilton, Carol R, *Librn,* University of Michigan Libraries (North Engineering), Ann Arbor MI. 313-764-5298

Hamilton, Catherine, *ILL,* Holdrege Public Library System, South Central Regional Library, Holdrege NE. 308-995-6556

Hamilton, D E, *Educ,* University of Victoria, McPherson Library, Victoria BC. 604-477-6911, Ext 4466

Hamilton, Donald, *Educ Librn,* University of Victoria, Library Education-Faculty of Education, BC. 604-477-6911

Hamilton, Eleanor E, *Librn,* Saint Paul Fire and Marine Insurance Co, Saint Paul MN. 612-221-8226

Hamilton, Fred, *Acq,* Louisiana Tech University, Prescott Memorial Library, Ruston LA. 318-257-2577

Hamilton, Jane, *Librn,* Hayden H Donahue Mental Health Institute, Medical Library, Norman OK. 405-321-4880, Ext 2613

Hamilton, Janet, *Actg Head Tech Serv,* Alabama Public Library Service, Montgomery AL. 205-832-5743

Hamilton, Joan, *Cat,* Wisconsin Valley Library Service, System Headquarters, Wausau WI. 715-845-7214, Ext 35

Hamilton, Judy, *Dir,* La Porte County Library, La Porte IN. 219-362-6156

Hamilton, Judy, *Dir,* La Porte Public Library, La Porte IN. 219-362-6156

Hamilton, Katherine, *Librn,* Bauder Fashion College Library, Arlington TX. 817-277-6666

Hamilton, L, *Librn,* Wetaskiwin Public Library, Wetaskiwin AB. 403-352-4055

Hamilton, Linda, *Ch,* Holdrege Public Library System, South Central Regional Library, Holdrege NE. 308-995-6556

Hamilton, Ludovine, *Librn,* Lynn Historical Society Museum Library, Lynn MA. 617-592-2465
Hamilton, Malcolm C, *Librn,* Harvard University Library (John Fitzgerald Kennedy School of Government Library), Cambridge MA. 617-495-1302
Hamilton, Margaret, *Librn,* Annapolis Valley Regional Library Headquarters (Windsor Branch), Windsor NS. 902-532-2260
Hamilton, Margaret, *Ch,* Haverstraw Kings Daughters Public Library, Haverstraw NY. 914-429-3445
Hamilton, Margaret L, *Dir,* Shelbyville-Shelby County Public Library, Shelbyville IN. 317-398-7121
Hamilton, Marie, *Librn,* McCoy Memorial Library, McLeansboro IL. 618-643-2125
Hamilton, Martha O, *Librn,* Chebeague Island Library, Chebeague Island ME. 207-846-4162
Hamilton, Mary, *Ch,* Grand Rapids Public Library, Grand Rapids MI. 616-456-4400
Hamilton, Mary Jane, *Cat & Ref,* Ardmore Public Library, Ardmore OK. 405-223-8290
Hamilton, Myra, *Librn,* Williamsport-Washington Township Public Library, Williamsport IN. 317-762-6555
Hamilton, Paula, *Librn,* Marylhurst Education Center, Shoen Library, Marylhurst OR. 503-636-8141, Ext 56 & 61
Hamilton, Phil, *Dir,* Kokomo Public Library, Kokomo IN. 317-457-5558
Hamilton, Phyllis, *Asst Ch Dept,* West Lafayette Public Library, West Lafayette IN. 317-743-2261
Hamilton, Prudence Harvey, *Librn,* Peninsula Hospital & Medical Center, Carl Hoag Library, Burlingame CA. 415-697-4061
Hamilton, Simone, *Librn,* Laurentian Hospital, Medical Library, Sudbury ON. 705-522-2200, Ext 215
Hamilton, Thelma J, *Librn,* Geneva Public Library, Geneva NE. 402-759-3416
Hamilton, Jr, William F, *Dir,* Brewton-Parker College, H Terry Parker Library, Mount Vernon GA. 912-583-2241, Ext 29
Hamlett, Joy, *YA & Commun Servs,* Great Falls Public Library, Pathfinder Federation of Libraries Headquarters, Great Falls MT. 406-453-0349
Hamlett, Timothy, *Bkmobile Coordr,* White River Regional Library, Batesville AR. 501-793-7347
Hamlin, Constance M, *Dir,* Glenside Public Library District, Glendale Heights IL. 618-858-0840
Hamlin, Inez, *Librn,* Berlin Public Library, Berlin NH. 603-752-5210
Hamlin, Jean Boyer, *Librn,* Rutgers University, the State University of New Jersey, John Cotton Dana Library, Newark NJ. 201-648-5222
Hamlin, Marilyn, *ILL,* Duncan Public Library, Duncan OK. 405-255-0636
Hamlin, Nancy, *Librn,* Omaha Public Library (Florence), Omaha NE. 402-444-5299
Hamlin, Jr, Omer, *Dir,* University of Kentucky (Medical Center Library), Lexington KY. 606-233-5300
Hamlin-Morin, Elizabeth, *Librn & ILL,* New Hampshire Vocational Technical College Library, Manchester NH. 603-668-6706
Hamlyn, Grace, *Librn,* Montreal Chest Hospital Center Library, Hopital Thoracique de Montreal, Montreal PQ. 514-849-5201
Hamm, Joyce, *Librn,* Rockingham County Public Library (Madison Branch), Madison NC. 919-548-6553
Hamm, Joyce, *Librn,* Rockingham County Public Library (Mayodan Branch), Mayodan NC. 919-548-6951
Hamm, Joyce, *Librn,* Rockingham County Public Library (Stoneville Branch), Stoneville NC. 919-573-9040
Hamm, Mary Ann, *Librn,* Public Service Company of Colorado Library, Denver CO. 303-571-7084
Hamm, Russell, *Chmn,* College of Lake County, Library Science Program, IL. 312-223-6601
Hammarskjold, Carolyn, *Librn,* Michigan State University Library (Kellogg Biological Station), Hickory Corners MI. 517-355-2344
Hamme, Suzanne, *Cat,* Martin Memorial Library, York PA. 717-843-3978
Hammell, Kathryn, *Doc,* University of Illinois at the Medical Center, Library of the Health Sciences, Chicago IL. 312-996-8974

Hammer, Elaine, *Dir,* Colfax Public Library, Colfax WI. 715-962-3311
Hammer, Leonard, *Dir,* Steele Memorial Library, Chemung-Southern Tier Library System, Elmira NY. 607-733-9173, 733-9174, 733-9175
Hammer, Ruth, *Librn,* Bedford County Library, Bedford PA. 814-623-5010
Hammer, Sharon A, *Asst Dir,* University of Washington Libraries, Seattle WA. 206-543-1760
Hammer, Sharon A, *Librn,* University of Washington Libraries (Odegaard Undergraduate Library), Seattle WA. 206-543-1947
Hammerlund, Barbara, *Librn,* Cooper School of Art Library, Cleveland OH. 216-241-1486
Hammersley, Sherry, *Library Assoc,* Indiana University at Bloomington (Medical Sciences), Bloomington IN. 812-337-3347
Hammersmith, Ruth K, *Mgr,* National Safety Council Library, Chicago IL. 312-527-4800, Ext 312
Hammerstein, Gretchen, *Dir,* Groton Public Library, Groton CT. 203-448-1552, 445-8551
Hammill, Roseann K, *Librn,* Michigan State University Library (Music), East Lansing MI. 517-355-2344
Hammock, Janice, *Cat,* Washington State Library, Olympia WA. 206-753-5592
Hammond, Bonnie, *Librn,* Staples Public Library, Staples MN. 218-894-2550
Hammond, Carol, *Ref,* Mount Clemens Public Library, Mount Clemens MI. 313-465-1906
Hammond, Dorothy S, *Dir,* First Baptist Church Library, Gainesville FL. 904-376-2131
Hammond, Ellen, *Librn,* University of Wisconsin-Madison (Nieman Grant Journalism Reading Room), Madison WI. 608-262-3521
Hammond, Harold, *Cat,* University of Bridgeport, Magnus Wahlstrom Library, Bridgeport CT. 203-576-4740
Hammond, Harriette C, *AV,* Brunswick-Glynn County Regional Library, Brunswick GA. 912-264-7360
Hammond, Harvey, *Librn,* Children's Hospital of Los Angeles, Medical Library, Los Angeles CA. 213-660-2454
Hammond, Jane L, *Librn,* Cornell University Libraries (Law Library), Ithaca NY. 607-256-7236
Hammond, John J, *Dir,* Ledyard Public Libraries, Gales Ferry Library & Bill Library, Ledyard CT. 203-464-9917
Hammond, Lois D, *Chief Librn,* Cincinnati Electronics Corp, Technical Library, Cincinnati OH. 513-563-6000
Hammond, Lyn Smith, *Librn,* Parkview Episcopal Hospital, Medical Library, Pueblo CO. 303-542-8680, Ext 782
Hammond, M A, *Assoc Librn & Pub Servs,* University of Regina Library, Regina SK. 306-584-4132
Hammond, Margaret, *Librn,* Detroit Public Library (Wilder), Detroit MI. 313-833-9159
Hammond, Mildred A, *Chief Librn,* Federal Aviation Administration, Eastern Region Library, Jamaica NY. 212-995-3325
Hammond, Pat, *Doc,* Western Carolina University (Documents), Cullowhee NC. 704-293-7306
Hammond, Samuel, *Librn,* Duke University (Music), Durham NC. 919-684-6449
Hammond, Shannon, *Librn,* Lincoln County Library, Pioche NV. 702-962-5244
Hammond, Wayne G, *Asst Librn,* Williams College (Chapin Library), Williamstown MA. 413-597-2462
Hammons, Reginald, *In Charge,* Thiokol Corp, Clearfield Job Corps Center Library, Clearfield UT. 801-773-1433, Ext 291
Hammontree, Christine, *Librn,* Archer County Public Library, Archer City TX. 817-574-4570
Hamner, N E, *Librn,* National Association of Corrosion Engineers Library, Barker TX. 713-492-0535
Hamnett, Kay, *Librn,* Ohio Township Library, Ohio IL. 815-376-5422
Hamon, Eunice E, *Dir,* Aransas County Public Library, Rockport TX. 512-729-2390
Hamon, Peter, *Dir,* Wisconsin Department of Public Instruction (Reference & Loan Library), Madison WI. 608-266-1053
Hampe, Nancy, *Librn,* Alden Public Library, Alden IA. 515-859-3820

Hampson, Josephine, *Math, Sci,* West Chester State College, Francis Harvey Green Library, West Chester PA. 215-436-2643
Hampton, Alice, *Asst Librn,* Shelbyville Free Public Library, Shelbyville IL. 217-774-4432
Hampton, Corrine, *Librn,* Frederick Eugene Lykes Jr Memorial County Library (Istachatta Branch), Istachatta FL. 904-796-3480
Hampton, Dean, *Adult Print Mat,* Pierce County Rural Library District, Tacoma WA. 206-572-6760
Hampton, Don, *Dir,* Royal Oak Public Library, Royal Oak MI. 313-541-1470
Hampton, Janet C, *Head Acq Librn,* Brown University (University Library), Providence RI. 401-863-2167
Hampton, Laurelle, *Cat,* Kennesaw College Library, Marietta GA. 404-422-8770, Ext 250
Hampton, Marcia W, *Librn,* United States Army (Intelligence School Library/Learning Center), Fort Devens MA. 617-796-3911
Hampton, Martha, *Tech Serv,* Gordon Junior College Library, Barnesville GA. 404-385-1700, Ext 271, 272, 276
Hampton, Mary Faye, *Librn,* Mesa County Public Library (Palisade Public), Palisade CO. 303-464-7557
Hampton, Patricia G, *Librn,* United States Department of Housing & Urban Development Library, Camden NJ. 609-757-5081
Hampton, Regina, *In Charge,* Catlin Public Library District, Catlin IL. 217-427-2550
Hampton, Robert, *Circ,* United States Army (Gaffey Hall Library), Fort Knox KY. 502-624-5449
Hampton, Robert L, *Dir,* Allen County Community Junior College Library, Iola KS. 316-365-5116
Hampton, William, *Media,* Jarvis Christian College, Ohlin Library & Communication Center, Hawkins TX. 214-769-2174, Ext 154
Hamrell, Larry, *Films,* Tampa-Hillsborough County Public Library System, Tampa FL. 813-223-8947
Hamrell, Susan, *Librn,* Duke University (School of Engineering), Durham NC. 919-684-2371
Hamrick, Clifford, *Ref,* West Virginia University, University Library, Morgantown WV. 304-293-4040
Hamrick, Jean T, *Asst Dir for Automation & Bibliog Control,* University of Texas Libraries (General), Austin TX. 512-471-3811
Hamrick, Ruth, *Librn,* Sequoyah Regional Library (Gilmer County Public), Ellijay GA. 404-635-4528
Hamrick, Sarah, *Librn,* Rutherford County Library (Haynes Public), Henrietta NC. 704-657-9110
Hamrick, Sharon, *Libr Supvr,* Dynapol Library, Palo Alto CA. 415-493-5611
Hamsa, Charles F, *Acq,* University of Southwestern Louisiana, Dupre Library, Lafayette LA. 318-264-6396
Hamud, Mark A, *In Charge,* Southern California Association of Governments, Information Resource Center, Los Angeles CA. 213-385-1000
Han, Chin-Soon, *Librn,* Bon Secours Hospital, Health Sciences Library, Methuen MA. 617-687-0151, Ext 2392
Han, Hien Thi, *Librn,* ISS Sperry Univac Corp, Library Department, Santa Clara CA. 408-496-3333, Ext 358
Han, Janet, *Librn,* Akron-Summit County Public Library (McDowell), Akron OH. 216-666-4888
Hanafee, Valerie, *Librn,* Dickinson, Wright, McKean, Cudlip & Moon Law Library, Detroit MI. 313-223-3500
Hanafi, W E, *Dir,* Fraser Valley College, Learning Resource Centres, Abbotsford BC. 604-853-7441
Hanaway, Barbara L, *Dir,* Monona Public Library, Monona WI. 608-222-6127
Hance, Elizabeth, *Spec Coll,* Olivet College Burrage Library, Olivet MI. 616-749-7608
Hancher, Eleanor, *ILL & Ref,* Pickaway County District Public Library, Circleville OH. 614-477-1644
Hanchett, Catherine, *Cat,* State University of New York College, Memorial Library, Cortland NY. 607-753-2525, 753-2221
Hanchett, Esther, *Actg Librn,* Maternity Center Association Library, New York NY. 212-369-7300

Hanclosky, Walt, *Media,* Ursuline College Library, Cleveland OH. 216-449-4200, Ext 276

Hancock, Carol, *Librn,* Houston County Public Library System (Perry-Houston County Branch), Perry GA. 912-987-3050

Hancock, Dan, *Pub Servs,* Community College of Baltimore (Harbor Campus), Baltimore MD. 301-396-1860

Hancock, Georgia, *Tech Serv & Acq,* Central Wyoming College Library, Riverton WY. 307-856-9291, Ext 33

Hancock, Kay, *Dir & Bibliog Instr,* Pequannock Township Public Library, Pompton Plains NJ. 201-835-7460

Hancock, Mabel E, *Librn,* Teledyne Wah Chang Albany Library, Albany OR. 503-926-4211

Hancock, Ray J, *Librn,* Delaware Correctional Center Library, Smyrna DE. 302-653-9261, Ext 340

Hancock, Susan, *Ref & Bibliog Instr,* Pan American University, Learning Resource Center, Edinburg TX. 512-381-2751

Hand, Doris, *Ch,* Collingswood Free Public Library, Collingswood NJ. 609-858-0649

Hand, Dorothy, *Librn,* Edinboro State College (Miller Learning Center), Edinboro PA. 814-732-2569

Hand, Jean, *Tech Serv,* Willamette University Library, Salem OR. 503-370-6312

Hand, Linda M, *Librn,* Jefferson County Law Library, Birmingham AL. 205-325-5628, 325-5629

Hand, Patricia, *Dir,* Abbott Library, Sunapee NH. 603-763-5513

Handel, Lloyd, *Tech Serv & Cat,* Santa Monica College Library, Santa Monica CA. 213-450-5150

Handelman, Lilly, *ILL,* Nassau Library System, Uniondale NY. 516-292-8920

Handfield, Patricia R, *Syst Librn,* Indiana Information Retrieval System, (INDIRS), IN. 317-633-6730

Handley, Lee T, *Actg Dir,* Southeastern Library Network, (SOLINET), GA. 404-892-0943

Handley, William, *Head,* Free Library of Philadelphia (Social Science & History), Philadelphia PA. 215-686-5322

Handlin, Oscar, *Dir,* Harvard University Library, Cambridge MA. 617-495-3650

Handloff, Joy, *Asst Dir & ILL,* Bud Werner Memorial Library, Steamboat Springs CO. 303-879-0240

Handran, Lois, *Librn,* General Telephone Co of the Northwest Inc, Alfred J Barran Library, Everett WA. 206-258-9511

Handrea, Mihai H, *Librn,* Carl and Lily Pforzheimer Foundation, Inc, Carl H Pforzheimer Library, New York NY. 212-697-7217

Handrick, Dorothy, *Dir,* Mount Horeb Public Library, Mount Horeb WI. 608-437-5021

Hands, Jr, Mrs Edgar, *Cat,* Webster Parish Library, Minden LA. 318-377-1411

Handville, S, *Tech Serv,* Patten Free Library, Bath ME. 207-443-5141

Handy, Hayward O, *Prof,* Alabama Agricultural & Mechanical University, School of Library Media, AL. 205-859-7216 or 859-7238

Handy, Riley, *Librn,* Western Kentucky University (Kentucky Library), Bowling Green KY. 502-745-2592

Hane, Paula, *ILL,* State University of New York College at Purchase Library, Purchase NY. 914-253-5085

Hanegraaf, Mary, *Librn,* Riverside Community Memorial Hospital, Health Science Library, Waupaca WI. 715-258-5533, Ext 240

Hanes, Alice C, *Curator,* Portsmouth Naval Shipyard Museum, Marshall W Butt Library, Portsmouth VA. 804-393-8591

Hanes, Fred W, *Dir,* University of Texas at El Paso Library, El Paso TX. 747-5683; 747-5684

Hanes, Geneva, *Librn,* Stokes County Public Library, Danbury NC. 919-593-8720

Hanes, Tena, *Learning Skills Center,* Sheridan College, Kooi Library, Instructional Resource Center, Sheridan WY. 307-674-6446, Ext 170

Haney, Judi, *Media,* McCook Community College, Learning Resource Center, McCook NE. 308-345-6303, Exts 40&41

Haney, Louise, *Librn,* Benton Public Library, Benton TN. 615-338-2841, Ext 233

Haney, Mrs Norman, *Librn,* New Salem Public Library, New Salem MA. 617-544-6437

Haney, Nancy, *Ch,* Mandan Public Library, Mandan ND. 701-663-3255

Haney, Stanley F, *Librn,* Westborough Public Library, Westborough MA. 617-366-2812

Hanf, Betty, *Librn,* Crompton & Knowles Corp, Gibralter Library, Reading PA. 215-582-8765

Hanfelder, Nancy, *Librn,* Stein Roe & Farnham Library, Chicago IL. 312-368-7840

Hanford, Barbara, *Librn,* University of Nevada, Las Vegas (Learning Materials Center), Las Vegas NV. 702-739-3593

Hanger, Myrtle F, *Librn,* E I Du Pont De Nemours & Co, Inc, Benger Library, Waynesboro VA. 703-942-8141

Hangett, Ella M, *ILL, Reader Serv & Ref,* Livingstone College, Andrew Carnegie Library, Salisbury NC. 704-633-7960, Ext 61 & 62

Hanifan, Thomas, *Learning Resources Dir,* Muscatine Community College Library, Muscatine IA. 319-263-8250, Ext 112

Hanifan, Thomas, *On-Line Servs & Bibliog Instr,* Muscatine Community College Library, Muscatine IA. 319-263-8250, Ext 112

Hanig, M W, *Librn,* Congregation Solel Library, Highland Park IL. 312-433-3555

Hankamer, Roberta A, *Librn,* Grand Lodge of Massachusetts Ancient Free & Accepted Masons Library, Boston MA. 617-426-6040, Ext 31

Hanke, Maxine K, *Dir,* Mid-Atlantic Regional Medical Library Program, National Library of Medicine, MD. 301-496-5955

Hankel, Doris, *Dir,* Oakes Public Library, Oakes ND. 701-742-3234

Hankins, Frank D, *Dir,* Del Mar College Library, Corpus Christi TX. 512-881-6308

Hankins, Mrs Frank D, *Dir,* Nueces County Library, Robstown TX. 512-387-1032

Hankins, Verna M, *Dir,* Hopedale Medical Complex Library, Hopedale IL. 309-449-3321

Hanks, Gretchen, *ILL & Ref,* Centre County Library & Historical Museum, Bellefonte PA. 814-355-3131

Hanks, Priscilla, *ILL,* Wellesley Free Library, Subregional Headquarters for Eastern Massachusetts Regional Library System, Wellesley MA. 617-235-1610

Hanks, Sara, *ILL,* Florida Southern College, Roux Library, Lakeland FL. 813-683-5521, Ext 211

Hanley, Patricia, *Librn,* Kaiser Foundation Hospital (Medical Library), Portland OR. 503-285-9321

Hanley, Thomas L, *Asst Librn,* University of Missouri-Columbia (Law), Columbia MO. 314-882-6096

Hanley, Yvonne, *Asst Prof,* University of North Dakota, Dept of Library Science & Audiovisual Instruction, ND. 701-777-3003

Hanlin, Ardith, *Asst Librn,* Millington Township Library, Millington MI. 517-871-2003

Hanlin, Frank S, *Bibliog,* University of Iowa Libraries, Iowa City IA. 319-353-4450

Hanlon, Kathleen, *Librn & On-Line Servs,* W Alton Jones Cell Science Center, George & Margaret Gey Library, Lake Placid NY. 518-523-2427, Ext 30

Hanlon, Mary, *Librn,* Roseland Community Hospital, Health Science Library, Chicago IL. 312-995-3191

Hann, Ella Grace, *Ch,* Grundy County-Jewett Norris Library, Trenton MO. 816-359-3577

Hann, Janet, *Tech Serv,* Westhampton Free Library, Westhampton Beach NY. 516-288-3335

Hann, Katherine, *Admin Librn,* University of Maryland Baltimore County Library, Baltimore MD. 301-455-2457

Hann, Marlene, *Librn,* Baker, Lovick Ltd Library, Information Retrieval Center, Toronto ON. 416-924-6861

Hanna, Alfreda H, *Admin Librn,* Bethany Nazarene College, R T Williams Memorial Library, Bethany OK. 405-789-6400, Ext 276

Hanna, David R, *Librn,* United States Navy (Naval Underwater Systems Center, New London Laboratory), New London CT. 203-447-4276

Hanna, George, *Acq,* New York University, Elmer Holmes Bobst Library, New York NY. 212-598-2484

Hanna, Joan, *Librn,* Bibliotheque Publique, Baie d'Urfe PQ. 514-457-3274

Hanna, Mark, *Ref, Rare Bks & Spec Coll,* Amarillo Public Library, Amarillo TX. 806-378-3000, Ext 2250

Hanna, Sheriden E, *Librn,* Morgan Memorial Library, Suffolk VA. 804-539-3175

Hanna, Sybil, *Ch,* Jackson Metropolitan Library, Jackson MS. 601-352-3677

Hanna, Jr, Archibald, *Curator Western Americana Coll,* Yale University Library (Beinecke Rare Book & Manuscript), New Haven CT. 203-436-0234

Hannaford, William, *Acq,* Middlebury College, Egbert Starr Library, Middlebury VT. 802-388-7621

Hannah, H R, *Pres,* Suffolk County Historical Society Library, Riverhead NY. 516-727-2881

Hannah, Katherine, *Dir,* Taft Museum Library, Cincinnati OH. 513-241-0343

Hannah, Kathy, *Tech Serv & Bkmobile Coordr,* Scotland County Memorial Library, Laurinburg NC. 919-276-0563

Hannan, Edward J, *Ref,* Saint John Fisher College, Lavery Library, Pittsford NY. 716-586-4140, Ext 222

Hannan, Mark, *Dir,* Washington Post Library, Washington DC. 202-334-6000

Hannant, Esther, *Librn,* Griggsville Public Library, Griggsville IL. 217-833-2633

Hannaway, Frank L, *Personnel Officer,* Providence Public Library, Providence RI. 401-521-7722

Hannay, Ruth, *Cat,* Colonie Town Library, Loudonville NY. 518-458-9274

Hanne, Sister Anna Rose, *Dir & Acq,* Saint Mary College Library, Leavenworth KS. 913-682-5151, Ext 202

Hanneman, Linda H, *Dir,* Ballston Community Public Library, Community Library of Burnt Hills, Burnt Hills NY. 518-399-8174

Hanners, Ruth, *Librn,* Casey Township Library, Casey IL. 217-932-2105

Hannigan, Jane, *Prof,* Columbia University in the City of New York, School of Library Service, NY. 212-280-2292

Hannigan, Matthew, *ILL,* Butler University, Irwin Library, Indianapolis IN. 317-283-9225

Hannon, Bea, *Librn,* Jackson Metropolitan Library (Raymond Library), Raymond MS. 601-352-3677

Hannon, John P, *Dir,* Bryant College, Edith M Hodgson Memorial Library, Smithfield RI. 401-231-1200, Ext 300

Hannon, Kathryn M, *Librn,* Grandview Heights School District Public Library, Columbus OH. 614-486-2951

Hannon, Michael, *Ser,* New York University, Elmer Holmes Bobst Library, New York NY. 212-598-2484

Hannon, Patricia A, *Dir,* Wood-Ridge Memorial Library, Wood-Ridge NJ. 201-438-2455

Hanns, Stephen, *Librn,* Hanover Public Library, Hanover ON. 519-364-1420

Hannsen, Keith, *Librn,* Palomar Community College (Learning Resource Center), San Marcos CA. 714-744-1150, Ext 275, 276 & 473

Hanover, Genevieve, *Librn,* Mason City Public Library, Mason City IL. 217-482-3799

Hanrahan, Mary, *Librn,* Lemmon Public Library, Lemmon SD. 605-374-5611

Hansard, Bill, *Chmn,* Arkansas State University, Dept of Library Science, AR. 501-972-3077

Hansberry, Phyllis, *Bkmobile Coordr,* Weld County Library, Greeley CO. 303-330-7691

Hansberry, Verda, *Asst City Librn Central,* Seattle Public Library, Seattle WA. 206-625-2665

Hanschu, Steve, *ILL,* Emporia State University, William Allen White Library, Emporia KS. 316-343-1200, Ext 205

Hansee, Jeanette A, *Librn,* White Pines College Library, Chester NH. 887-4401 & 887-4402

Hanseen, Nancy E, *Doc,* Williams College, Sawyer Library, Williamstown MA. 413-597-2501

Hansel, Patsy J, *Dir,* Onslow County Public Library, Jacksonville NC. 919-347-2592, 347-5495

Hansell, Ruth, *Acq & Cat,* Indian River Community College, Charles S Miley Learning Resources Center, Fort Pierce FL. 305-464-2000, Ext 347

Hansen, Ada S, *Librn,* Preston Public Library, Preston ID. 208-852-0175

Hansen, Alice E, *Librn,* Winter Park Memorial Hospital, Medical Staff Library, Winter Park FL. 305-646-7049

Hansen, Bernice M, *Librn,* Stubbs Public Library, Holstein IA. 712-368-4563
Hansen, Beth, *Ch,* Roselle Public Library District, Roselle IL. 312-529-1641
Hansen, Bruce N, *Dir,* Colonial Heights Public Library, Colonial Heights VA. 804-526-7341
Hansen, Carol, *Librn,* Avondale Public Library, Avondale AZ. 602-932-1270
Hansen, Carol, *ILL & Ref,* Bethel College, Learning Resource Center, Saint Paul MN. 612-641-6222
Hansen, Dolores, *Librn,* Brown Memorial Library, Bradford NH. 603-938-5562
Hansen, Doris, *Librn,* Barron Library, La Belle FL. 813-675-0833
Hansen, Eleonore, *Librn,* Bradley University (Music), Peoria IL. 309-676-7611
Hansen, Erika M, *Librn,* Hollywood Presbyterian Medical Center, Health Sciences Library, Los Angeles CA. 213-660-3530, Ext 20658
Hansen, Eva, *Librn,* Shepard's-Mcgraw-Hill, Law Library, Colorado Springs CO. 303-475-7230
Hansen, Gladys, *San Francisco Coll,* San Francisco Public Library, San Francisco CA. 415-558-4235
Hansen, James L, *Reader Serv,* State Historical Society of Wisconsin Library, Madison WI. 608-262-3421
Hansen, Janet H, *Circ & Br Coordr,* Whatcom County Public Library, Bellingham WA. 206-384-3150
Hansen, Jean, *Dir,* Saint Croix County Library, New Richmond WI. 715-246-6330
Hansen, Joanne, *ILL,* Eastern Michigan University, Center of Educational Resources, Ypsilanti MI. 313-487-0020
Hansen, Joanne, *Sci-Tech,* Eastern Michigan University, Center of Educational Resources, Ypsilanti MI. 313-487-0020
Hansen, Ken, *Head Librn,* Peru Public Library, Peru IL. 815-223-0229
Hansen, Linda, *Librn,* Baltimore County Public Library (Arbutus), Baltimore MD. 301-242-3010
Hansen, Linda, *Librn,* Baltimore County Public Library (Lansdowne), Baltimore MD. 301-247-1121
Hansen, Linda, *Cat,* University of Southern California, Edward L Doheny Memorial Library, Los Angeles CA. 213-743-6050
Hansen, Lois, *Circ,* Idaho State University Library, Pocatello ID. 208-236-3202
Hansen, Margaret, *Librn,* Kern County Library (Shafter Branch), Shafter CA. 805-861-2130
Hansen, Mary, *Ch,* Brigham City Library, Brigham City UT. 801-723-5850
Hansen, Mildred M, *Librn,* Anita Public Library, Anita IA. 712-762-3639
Hansen, Miriam E, *Dir,* West Des Moines Public Library, West Des Moines IA. 515-223-1575
Hansen, Mrs B, *ILL,* Vaughan Public Libraries, Maple ON. 416-832-1432
Hansen, Mrs B, *Librn,* Vaughan Public Libraries (Maple Public), Maple ON. 416-832-1432
Hansen, Mrs James, *Librn,* Blair Public Library, Blair NE. 402-426-3617
Hansen, Myrna, *Librn,* Dunlap Public Library, Dunlap IA. 712-643-5311
Hansen, Oda Bali, *Librn,* Fireman's Fund Insurance Library, San Francisco CA. 415-929-2871
Hansen, Opal, *Librn,* Apache Junction Public Library, Apache Junction AZ. 602-982-1253
Hansen, Orval, *Dir,* Green River Community College, Holman Library, Auburn WA. 206-833-9111
Hansen, Robert, *Rare Bks & Spec Coll,* Galena Public Library, Galena IL. 815-777-0200
Hansen, Teresa, *Librn,* James E Wickson Memorial Library, Frankenmuth MI. 517-652-8323
Hansen, Thelma, *Librn,* Santa Monica Public Library (Fairview Branch), Santa Monica CA. 213-450-0443
Hansen, Thelma, *Librn,* Santa Monica Public Library (Montana Avenue Branch), Santa Monica CA. 213-394-7081
Hansen, Victoria, *Librn,* Coopers & Lybrand Los Angeles Library, Los Angeles CA. 213-481-1000
Hansen, W H, *Asst Librn, On-Line Servs & Bibliog Instr,* United States Army (Gaffey Hall Library), Fort Knox KY. 502-624-5449
Hansford, Linda, *Librn,* Spokane Public Library (Shadle Branch), Spokane WA. 509-327-7731

Hanson, Andy, *Assoc Prof,* California State University, Chico, Dept of Education, Librarianship Program, CA. 916-895-6421
Hanson, Audrey M, *In Charge,* Trinity Lutheran Parish Library, Saint Peter MN. 507-931-4786
Hanson, Barbara C, *Dir,* Allegan Public Library, Allegan MI. 616-673-4625
Hanson, Charles D, *Dir,* North Baltimore Public Library, North Baltimore OH. 419-257-2196
Hanson, Christina, *Librn,* Los Angeles Public Library System (Granada Hills Branch), Granada Hills CA. 213-368-5687
Hanson, Christina, *ILL,* University of Texas Libraries (Perry-Castaneda Library (Main Library)), Austin TX. 512-471-3811
Hanson, Diane H, *Librn,* Barristers' Society of New Brunswick, Law Library, Fredericton NB. 506-453-2500
Hanson, Eugene R, *Prof,* Shippensburg State College, Dept of Library Science, PA. 717-532-1472
Hanson, Eugene W, *Bus Mgr,* Kern County Library, Bakersfield CA. 805-861-2130
Hanson, Faye E, *Dir,* De Witt Public Library, De Witt MI. 517-669-3156
Hanson, Fred, *Libr Sci,* University of Missouri-Columbia, Elmer Ellis Library, Columbia MO. 314-882-4701
Hanson, George, *Dir & Acq,* Truman College, Learning Resources Center, Chicago IL. 312-878-1700, Ext 2230
Hanson, Gertrude, *ILL & Ref,* Texas Lutheran College, Blumberg Memorial Library, Seguin TX. 512-379-4161, Ext 90
Hanson, Gladys, *Librn,* Oxford Public Library, Oxford AL. 205-831-1750
Hanson, Jean, *Cat & Ref,* North Adams Public Library, North Adams MA. 413-662-2545, 663-3317
Hanson, Joel T, *Dir,* University of South Dakota at Springfield, Carl G Lawrence Library, Springfield SD. 605-369-2296
Hanson, Kate, *Ch,* Graham Public Library, Union Grove WI. 414-878-2910
Hanson, Leona, *Librn,* Lyon County Library, Yerington NV. 702-463-3717
Hanson, Marilyn, *Tech Serv,* Elmhurst Public Library, Elmhurst IL. 312-279-8696
Hanson, Mary A, *Librn,* Saint Mary's Hospital Library, Grand Rapids MI. 616-774-6260
Hanson, Mildred, *Librn,* Whitman Public Library, Whitman MA. 617-447-2052
Hanson, Mrs Eugene, *Librn,* Paige Memorial Library, Hardwick MA. 413-477-6051
Hanson, Nancy L, *Librn,* Del Monte Corp, Research Center Technical Library, Walnut Creek CA. 415-933-8000, Ext 235
Hanson, Pauline M, *Dir,* Whatcom County Public Library, Bellingham WA. 206-384-3150
Hanson, Peter P, *Supvr,* E I Du Pont De Nemours & Co, Inc, Photo Products Dept, Information Center Library, Parlin NJ. 201-257-4600, Ext 513, 512
Hanson, Roger K, *Dir,* University of Utah (Marriott Library), Salt Lake City UT. 801-581-8558
Hanson, Stephen, *English Lit,* University of Southern California, Edward L Doheny Memorial Library, Los Angeles CA. 213-743-6050
Hanson, Thomas A, *Librn,* Medical Center Hospital of Oroville Library, Oroville CA. 916-533-8500, Ext 25
Hansotte, Lea, *ILL & Ad,* East Chicago Public Library, East Chicago IN. 219-397-2453
Hanssen, Keith, *Instr,* Palomar Community College, Library Technology Certificate Program, CA. 714-744-1150, Ext 473 & 480
Hanssen, Keith, *Media,* Palomar Community College, Phil H Putnam Memorial Library, San Marcos CA. 714-744-1150, Ext 275, 276 & 473
Hanton, Rena C, *Librn,* Tulsa County Law Library, Tulsa OK. 918-584-0471, Ext 300, 301
Hanus, E J, *Asst Dir,* University of Prince Edward Island, Robertson Library, Charlottetown PE. 902-892-1243
Hanway, Wayne, *Dir,* Cattermole Memorial Library, Fort Madison IA. 319-372-5721
Hanza, Norbetta, *Instr,* Our Lady of the Lake University of San Antonio, Learning Resources Certification, TX. 512-434-6711, Ext 245

Hanzas, Barbara, *Dir,* Woodruff Memorial Library, City Library of La Junta, La Junta CO. 303-384-4612
Hape, Ellen M, *Librn,* Rush Springs Public Library, Rush Springs OK. 405-476-2108
Hapeman, Jean, *Librn,* Scranton Public Library (Green Ridge Branch), Scranton PA. 717-347-5513
Hapke, Phyllis L, *Librn,* Minocqua Public Library, Minocqua WI. 715-356-3830
Happ, George J, *Dir,* Salem Public Library, Salem OR. 503-588-6071
Happer, Alexandra, *Cat,* Iliff School of Theology, Ira J Taylor Library, Denver CO. 303-744-1287, Ext 30
Happy, Susan, *Dir,* United States Department of Transportation-Transportation Systems Center, Technical Reference Center, Cambridge MA. 617-494-2783
Haq, S Farid-ul, *Dir,* Herkimer County Community College Library, Herkimer NY. 315-866-0300, Ext 55
Harahan, Kit, *Librn,* United States League of Savings Associations, Library, Washington DC. 202-637-8910
Haraldson, Alice, *Ch & Ref,* Le Sueur-Waseca Regional Library, Waseca MN. 507-835-2910
Haraschuk, Justin, *Br Coordr,* Burlington Public Library, Burlington ON. 416-639-3611
Haraway, Susan, *Librn,* First Regional Library (B J Chain Library), Olive Branch MS. 601-368-4439
Harbach, Ann, *AV,* Pomona Public Library, Pomona CA. 714-620-2033
Harbach, Nancy Lee, *Tech Serv & Cat,* Roswell Public Library, Roswell NM. 505-622-7101
Harbaugh, Margaret, *Cat,* McLennan Community College Library, Waco TX. 817-756-6551, Ext 264
Harber, Frances, *Tech Serv,* Kitchener Public Library, Kitchener ON. 519-743-0271
Harber, Patty S, *YA,* Colquitt-Thomas Regional Library, Moultrie-Colquitt County Library, Moultrie GA. 912-985-6540
Harbert, Cathy, *ILL,* George Washington University Library (Paul Himmelfarb Health Sciences Library), Washington DC. 202-676-2850
Harbeson, Eloise L, *Dir & Acq,* Tallahassee Community College Library, Tallahassee FL. 904-576-5181
Harbison, Ann, *Librn,* Newton Free Library (Newton Centre Branch), Newton Centre MA. 617-527-7700, Ext 24
Harbison, Zelda W, *Asst Librn,* Colusa County Free Library, Colusa CA. 916-458-7671
Harbold, Mary Jo, *Chief Librn,* Veterans Administration, Medical Center Library, Walla Walla WA. 509-525-5200, Ext 253
Harbord, Heather, *Chief Librn,* Coquitlam Public Library, Coquitlam BC. 604-931-2416
Harbour, Judy, *Librn,* Cobb County Public Library System (Gritters), Marietta GA. 404-427-8428
Harburn, Audrey, *Librn,* Western Manitoba Regional Library (Carberry Branch), Carberry MB. 204-834-3043
Hardacre, Elizabeth, *Librn,* Canada Health & Welfare, Health Protection Branch Library, Vancouver BC. 604-666-3147
Hardaman, Marilyn, *Librn,* Goodwater Public Library, Goodwater AL. 205-839-5741
Hardaway, Laurie, *Librn,* Dallas Public Library (Oak Lawn), Dallas TX. 214-528-6269
Hardcastle, Joyce E, *Head Pub Servs & ILL,* Okanagan College, Muriel Ffoulkes Learning Resource Center, Kelowna BC. 604-762-5445, Ext 293
Hardcastle, Sammie, *Librn,* Houston Public Library (Moody), Houston TX. 713-697-2745
Hardee, M G, *Librn,* Avco Corp, Aerostructures Division Engineering Library, Nashville TN. 615-361-2472
Hardegree, Louette C, *Librn,* Atlanta Newspapers Inc, Reference Department, Atlanta GA. 404-572-5151
Harden, Margaret, *Librn,* Memorial Hospital, Medical Library, Danville VA. 804-799-4418
Harden, William, *On-Line Servs,* Case Western Reserve University Libraries (Freiberger), Cleveland OH. 216-368-3506
Harders, Faith, *Admin Servs,* University of Kentucky, Margaret I King Library, Lexington KY. 606-257-3801

Hardestry, Pamela, *ILL,* Ruth Enlow Library of Garrett County, Oakland MD. 301-334-3996

Hardesty, Larry L, *Ref & Bibliog Instr,* Depauw University, Roy O West Library, Greencastle IN. 317-653-9721, Ext 250

Hardie, Frances, *Asst Dir Coll,* Vanderbilt University Library, Nashville TN. 615-322-2834

Hardie, Susan, *Librn,* Tualatin Public Library, Tualatin OR. 503-638-6730

Hardies, Roderick R, *Sci Tech,* University of Idaho Library, Moscow ID. 208-885-6534

Hardiman, Mary Ellen, *Librn,* North Providence Union Free Library, North Providence RI. 231-5300 & 231-5301

Hardin, Al, *Librn,* United States Department of the Army (Army Library Law Section), Washington DC. 202-695-2957

Hardin, Ethel, *Per,* Southwestern Adventist College, Findley Memorial Library, Keene TX. 817-645-3921, Ext 242

Hardin, Helen, *Librn,* Nelson County Public Library (Chaplin Branch), Chaplin KY. 502-348-3714

Hardin, Irma, *Dir,* Long Beach Public Library, Long Beach MS. 601-863-0711

Hardin, Margaret F, *Dir,* United States Army (Nye Library), Fort Sill OK. 405-351-8111

Hardin, Mary, *OTIS, Info Servs & On-Line Servs,* Oklahoma Department of Libraries, Oklahoma City OK. 405-521-2502

Hardin, Mary, *Head,* Oklahoma Telecommunications Interlibrary System, (OTIS), OK. 405-521-2502

Hardin, Nancy E, *Librn,* United States Department of Energy, Technical Information Center, Oak Ridge TN. 615-483-8611

Hardin, Patricia A, *Librn,* Rutherford County Library (Norris Public), Rutherfordton NC. 704-287-4981

Hardin, Willie, *ILL,* University of Central Arkansas, Torreyson Library, Conway AR. 501-329-2931, Ext 449

Harding, Arlyne L, *Bkmobile Coordr,* Aiken-Bamberg-Barnwell-Edgefield Regional Library, Aiken SC. 803-648-8961

Harding, Barbara, *Ad,* Ringwood Public Library, Ringwood NJ. 201-962-6256

Harding, Bruce A, *Coordr,* Rappahannock Community College, North Campus Learning Resource Center, Warsaw VA. 804-333-4024, Ext 208, 209

Harding, Carol, *Asst Librn,* Agriculture Canada (Canadian Grain Commission), Winnipeg MB. 204-949-3360

Harding, Dianne, *Librn,* Transport Canada Training Institute, Technical Information Centre, Cornwall ON. 613-938-4411

Harding, Edna I, *Ch,* Joseph Mann Library, Two Rivers WI. 414-794-7121

Harding, G J, *ILL, On-Line Servs & Bibliog Instr,* Malaspina College, Learning Resources Center, Nanaimo BC. 604-753-3245

Harding, Helen S, *Dir,* Gale Free Library, Holden MA. 617-829-4988

Harding, Jean, *Media,* Ryerson Polytechnical Institute, Donald Mordell Learning Resources Centre, Toronto ON. 416-595-5331

Harding, Margaret, *ILL & Cat,* Doane College, Perkins Library, Crete NE. 402-826-2161, Ext 224, 287

Harding, Mary, *Ref,* Ford Foundation Library, New York NY. 212-573-5155

Harding, Nancy E, *Dir,* Warren County Library, Belvidere NJ. 201-475-5361, Ext 114

Harding, Richard, *Librn,* Pendleton County Public Library, Franklin WV. 304-358-7038

Harding, Yvonne, *Librn,* Aurora Public Library (South), Aurora CO. 303-693-1440

Hardison, Neal F, *Dir,* Sampson Technical College Library, Clinton NC. 919-592-8081, Ext 250

Hardison, Jr, O B, *Dir,* Folger Shakespeare Library, Washington DC. 202-546-4800

Hardman, Nina, *Actg Librn,* Lewis County War Memorial & Lewis Bennet Public Library, Weston WV. 304-260-5151

Hardman, Regina, *Ad,* Clarksburg-Harrison Public Library, Clarksburg WV. 304-624-6512, 624-6513

Hardnett, Carolyn J, *Librn,* Chicago Tribune Press Service Library, Washington DC. 202-785-9430

Hardsog, Ellen L, *Asst Dir & Cat,* Peterborough Town Library, Peterborough NH. 603-924-6401

Hardt, John P, *Assoc Dir Sr Specialists,* Library of Congress, Washington DC. 202-287-5000

Hardt, Jon, *Ref,* Loma Linda University Library, Riverside CA. 714-785-2022

Hardwick, John F, *In Charge,* Diocese of Pennsylvania Library, Philadelphia PA. 215-567-6650

Hardy, Bette, *Librn,* Anselmo Public Library, Anselmo NE. 308-749-2466

Hardy, Carol L, *Media,* California State University, Chico Library, Chico CA. 916-895-6212

Hardy, Chlorene, *Acq,* Nebraska Library Commission, Lincoln NE. 402-471-2045

Hardy, D Clive, *Archivist,* University of New Orleans, Earl K Long Library, New Orleans LA. 504-283-0353

Hardy, Debra, *Librn,* United States Navy (Naval Security Group), Chesapeake VA. 804-421-8000

Hardy, Frances W, *Dir,* Meridian Junior College Library, Meridian MS. 601-483-8241, Ext 240

Hardy, Gloria, *Librn,* South Shore Regional Library, Bridgewater NS. 902-543-2548

Hardy, John, *Archivist,* George Brown College of Applied Arts & Technology Library (Archives), Toronto ON. 416-967-1212

Hardy, Joyce H, *ILL,* Weston Public Library, Weston MA. 617-893-3312

Hardy, Linda, *ILL,* Alfred University (Herrick Memorial Library), Alfred NY. 607-871-2184

Hardy, Lynne, *ILL,* Castroville Public Library, Castroville TX. 512-538-2656

Hardy, Margaret C, *Librn,* Miami Valley Hospital, Memorial Medical Library, Dayton OH. 513-223-6192

Hardy, Mary A, *Dir,* Newark Public Library, Newark NY. 315-331-4370

Hardy, Mrs John, *ILL & Ref,* Lowndes County Library System, Columbus Public Library, Columbus MS. 601-328-1056

Hardy, Patricia F, *Librn,* Columbus Ledger-Enquirer Newspaper Library, Columbus GA. 404-324-5526

Hardy, Sandra, *Ch,* Anselmo Public Library, Anselmo NE. 308-749-2466

Hardy, Susan, *Ad,* Brainerd Public Library, Brainerd MN. 218-829-5574

Hardy-Davis, G, *Circ,* State University of New York at Buffalo (Lockwood Library), Buffalo NY. 716-636-2816

Hare, Ann T, *Dir,* Lander College Library, Larry A Jackson Library, Greenwood SC. 803-229-8366

Hare, Judy Thomas, *Librn,* Nepean Public Library (Merivale Rd), Ottawa ON. 613-224-7874

Hare, Wm John, *Dir,* New Hampshire Technical Institute, Farnum Library, Concord NH. 603-271-2584

Harens, Lola, *Ch & YA,* Yankton Community Library, Yankton SD. 605-665-4501, Ext 34

Hargis, Patricia L, *Librn,* Warren County Law Library Association, Lebanon OH. 614-932-4040, Ext 150

Hargleroad, Bobbi Wells, *Dir,* Institute on the Church in Urban-Industrial Society Library, Chicago IL. 312-643-7111

Hargraves, Juanita, *Librn,* Chambers County Library (Winnie Stowell), Winnie TX. 713-296-2443

Hargreaves, Mrs Zaidee, *Librn,* New Vineyard Public Library, New Vineyard ME. 207-652-2474

Hargrove, Dorothy, *Commun Servs,* Longmont Public Library, Longmont CO. 303-776-2236

Harig, Katherine J, *Librn,* Enoch Pratt Free Library (Light Street), Baltimore MD. 301-396-5430, 396-5395

Haring, Betty, *Librn,* Hawley Public Library, Hawley MN. 218-483-4549

Harken, Shelby, *Cat,* University of North Dakota, Chester Fritz Library, Grand Forks ND. 701-777-2617

Harker, Carol, *ILL, Ref & Doc,* University of New Haven, Marvin K Peterson Library, West Haven CT. 203-934-6321

Harkink, Judith, *Librn,* Wyoming Industrial Institute Library, Worland WY. 307-347-6144

Harkins, James, *ILL,* Memphis-Shelby County Public Library & Information Center, Memphis TN. 901-528-2950

Harkins, Marjory V, *Librn,* Bridgeport Public Library (East), Bridgeport CT. 203-576-8431

Harkins, Sister Eleanore, *Cat,* Cardinal Stritch College Library, Milwaukee WI. 414-352-5400, Ext 356

Harkins, Sister Sarah, *Dir,* Aquinas Junior College Library, Newton MA. 617-244-8134

Harkness, Mary Lou, *Dir,* University of South Florida (University Library), Tampa FL. 813-974-2721

Harkness, Vanessa, *Tech Serv,* Woodstock Public Library & Art Gallery, Woodstock ON. 519-537-4801

Harlan, Donna, *Ref,* Indiana University at South Bend Library, South Bend IN. 219-237-4440

Harlan, Irma, *Dir,* Chatham-Effingham-Liberty Regional Library, Savannah Public Library, Savannah GA. 912-234-5127

Harlan, James H, *Librn,* San Pedro Peninsula Hospital, Medical Library, San Pedro CA. 213-832-3311, Ext 3273

Harlan, Ronald J, *Music,* California State University, Fresno Library, Fresno CA. 209-487-2403

Harland, Phyllis, *Circ,* Ball State University, Alexander M Bracken Library, Muncie IN. 317-285-6261

Harland, S, *Librn,* University of Regina Library, Regina SK. 306-584-4132

Harling, Darlene, *ILL,* Yolo County Library, Woodland CA. 916-666-8323

Harlock, P, *Librn,* Okanagan Regional Library District (Westbench Branch), Westbench BC. 604-492-3947

Harlow, Ann K, *Ref,* United States Military Academy Library, West Point NY. 914-938-2230

Harlow, Ethelyn, *Librn,* Ontario Ministry of Culture & Recreation, Archives of Ontario Library, Toronto ON. 416-965-4039

Harlow, Ila, *Librn,* Redfield Carnegie Library, Redfield SD. 605-472-1710

Harlow, Linda, *Asst Dir,* Kentucky Department of Education Materials Center Library, Frankfort KY. 502-564-5513

Harlow, Mary H, *Librn,* Abilene State School, Special Library, Abilene TX. 915-692-4053, Ext 437

Harlow, Thompson R, *Dir,* Connecticut Historical Society Library, Hartford CT. 203-236-5621

Harman, Anne L, *Tech Serv,* Georgia College, Ina Dillard Russell Library, Milledgeville GA. 912-453-4047, 453-5573

Harman, Susan, *Bibliog Instr,* Medical & Chirurgical Faculty of the State of Maryland Library, Baltimore MD. 301-539-0872

Harman, Susan, *Asst Cat,* University of Maryland-Eastern Shore, Frederick Douglass Library, Princess Anne MD. 301-651-2200, Ext 229

Harman, Susan H, *Librn,* Drinker, Biddle & Reath Law Library, Philadelphia PA. 215-988-2951

Harmon, Angelina, *Dir,* Memorial Sloan-Kettering Cancer Center, Lee Coombe Memorial Library, New York NY. 212-794-7440

Harmon, Bertha, *Librn,* Norcatur Free Public Library, Norcatur KS. 913-693-4461

Harmon, Coy, *Acq,* Purdue University Libraries & Audio-Visual Center, West Lafayette IN. 317-749-2571

Harmon, Dorothy, *African Studies,* University of California Los Angeles Library, Los Angeles CA. 213-825-1201

Harmon, Floreada, *ILL & Ref,* Millsaps College, Millsaps-Wilson Library, Jackson MS. 601-354-5201, Ext 324

Harmon, Gayle, *Librn,* Volusia County Public Libraries (Edgewater Branch), Edgewater FL. 904-252-8374

Harmon, Jacqueline, *Dir,* Williamsport School of Commerce Library, Williamsport PA. 717-323-3138

Harmon, Linda, *Librn,* Dixie Regional Library (Houlka Public), Houlka MS. 601-489-3522

Harmon, Patricia Ann, *Librn,* Uniroyal Inc, Uniroyal Chemical Div, Information Center Library, Naugatuck CT. 203-723-3252

Harmon, Sarah, *Librn,* Florida Mental Health Institute, Learning Resources Center, Tampa FL. 312-974-4471

Harms, Alan, *Bibliog Instr,* McNeese State University, Lether E Frazar Memorial Library, Lake Charles LA. 318-477-2520, Ext 271

Harms, Betty, *Librn,* Culbertson Public Library, Culbertson NE. 308-278-2341

Harms, Elsie, *Ad,* Sussex County Library System, Sussex County Area Reference Library, Newton NJ. 201-948-3660

Harms, Herbert, *Librn,* Emmaus Lutheran Church Library, Denver CO. 303-477-5358
Harms, Louise I, *Dir & Bibliog Instr,* Tennessee Wesleyan College, Merner-Pfeiffer Library, Athens TN. 615-745-2363
Harms, Marianne, *Librn,* Hesston Public Library, Hesston KS. 316-327-4666
Harms, Patricia T, *Librn,* Laurens Public Library, Laurens IA. 712-845-4612
Harms, Sally, *Librn,* Saint Luke's Methodist Hospital, Health Science Library, Cedar Rapids IA. 319-398-7358
Harmsen, Tyrus G, *Dir,* Occidental College, Mary Norton Clapp Library, Los Angeles CA. 213-259-2640
Harnden, Donna J, *Librn,* Peat, Marwick, Mitchell & Co Library, Minneapolis MN. 612-341-2222, Ext 180
Harned, Olene, *Dir,* University of Texas at Tyler, Tyler TX. 214-566-1471
Harner, Becky, *Ad,* Warder Public Library, Springfield OH. 323-8616 & 323-9751
Harness, Mary Ann, *Librn,* Birmingham Public Library, Birmingham IA. 515-698-4452
Harney, Mary V, *Librn,* Watertown Free Public Library (East), Watertown MA. 617-924-3728
Harney, Nancy L, *In Charge,* Hartford Seminary Foundation, Case Memorial Library, Hartford CT. 203-232-4451, Ext 260 & 261
Harnish, Charlotte, *Tech Serv & Cat,* Winona Public Library, Winona MN. 507-452-4582
Harokopus, W P, *Dir,* Bendix Corp, Communications Div, Engineering Library, Towson MD. 301-832-2200, Ext 212
Harold, Sheila K, *Asst Dir,* Ramsey Free Public Library, Ramsey NJ. 201-327-1445
Harold, Sister Mary Jane, *Circ,* Marylhurst Education Center, Shoen Library, Marylhurst OR. 503-636-8141, Ext 56 & 61
Haroldson, Hilda, *Librn,* Elbow Lake Public Library, Thorsen Memorial Library, Elbow Lake MN. 218-685-4830
Harp, Carol, *Librn,* Santa Maria Public Library (Cuyama Station), New Cuyama CA. 805-766-2490
Harp, Marlene, *Ad,* Lubbock City-County Library, Lubbock TX. 806-762-6411, Ext 2828
Harp, Polly, *Habilitation Tech II,* Arizona Training Program at Coolidge Library (Client Library), Coolidge AZ. 602-723-4151
Harper, Anne, *Asst Dir & Tech Serv,* York County Library, Headquarters Rock Hill Public Library, Rock Hill SC. 803-328-8402
Harper, Annie, *Ref & Circ,* Utica Junior College, William H Holtzclaw Library, Utica MS. 601-885-6062, Ext 48
Harper, Carol Anne, *Librn,* Riverview Hospital, Library Services, Port Coquitlam BC. 604-521-1911
Harper, Cathy, *Asst Dir & Ch,* Pataskala Public Library, Pataskala OH. 614-927-9986
Harper, Charles M, *Librn,* Upper Peninsula Blind & Physically Handicapped Library, Escanaba MI. 906-786-6055
Harper, Denise M, *Librn,* Reynolds Metals Co (Technical Information Services Library), Richmond VA. 804-788-7409, 788-7735
Harper, Donald R, *Supvr,* National Park Service, Scotts Bluff National Monument, Oregon Trail Museum Association Library, Gering NE. 308-436-4340
Harper, Jane, *Librn,* Sacramento Public Library (Folsom Branch), Folsom CA. 916-985-2780
Harper, Judith, *Librn,* University of Manitoba Libraries (Agriculture), Winnipeg MB. 204-474-9457
Harper, Kathryn, *Librn,* Medford Mail Tribune Library, Medford OR. 503-779-1411, Ext 30
Harper, Laura, *On-Line Servs,* University of Mississippi Library, University MS. 601-232-7091
Harper, Lynn, *Ref,* Salisbury State College, Blackwell Library, Salisbury MD. 301-546-3261, Ext 351
Harper, Mamie Jean, *Librn,* Clarksville-Montgomery County Public Library, Clarksville TN. 615-648-8826
Harper, Margaret, *Cat & Tech Serv,* Southeast Kansas Library System, Iola KS. 316-365-3833
Harper, Margaret, *On-Line Servs,* United States Department of Labor Library, Washington DC. 202-523-6988
Harper, Margaret, *Circ,* Wayland Free Public Library, Wayland MA. 617-358-2311, 358-2308
Harper, Mary H, *Doc,* Abilene Public Library, Abilene TX. 915-677-2474
Harper, Mrs Preston, *Media & Bibliog Instr,* Abilene Christian University, Margarett & Herman Brown Library, Abilene TX. 915-677-1911, Ext 2344
Harper, Nancy, *Librn,* E Jack Sharpe Public Library, White Cloud MI. 616-689-1709
Harper, Rebecca P, *Librn,* Charles P Jones Memorial Library, Covington VA. 703-962-3321
Harper, Robert L, *Librn,* California College of Arts and Crafts, Meyer Library, Oakland CA. 415-653-8118, Ext 32
Harper, Rose, *Librn,* Bay Ridge Christian College Library, Kendleton TX. 713-532-3982
Harper, Sally, *Spec Coll,* Tyler Public Library, Tyler TX. 214-595-4267
Harper, Shirley, *Librn,* Cornell University Libraries (M C Catherwood Library of Industrial & Labor Relations), Ithaca NY. 607-256-5435
Harper, Shirley, *Librn,* Saint Mary Corwin Hospital, Dr Finney Memorial Library, Pueblo CO. 303-561-5119
Harper, Viola, *Ref,* University of South Alabama (University Library), Mobile AL. 205-460-7021
Harpole, Patricia C, *Chief of Ref Libr,* Minnesota Historical Society (Minnesota Society Library), Saint Paul MN. 296-2150 (Off), 296-2143 (Ref)
Harpool, Lynn, *Dir,* Pemberton Community Library Association, Pemberton NJ. 609-894-2516
Harpst, Elizabeth, *Librn,* Winebrenner Theological Seminary Library, Findlay OH. 419-422-4824, Ext 6
Harr, Thomas, *Librn,* Montgomery County Department of Public Libraries (Twinbrook), Rockville MD. 301-279-1980
Harral, Jessie L, *Librn,* Gonzales Public Library, Gonzales TX. 512-672-6315
Harrar, H Joanne, *Dir,* University of Maryland at College Park (University Libraries), College Park MD. 301-454-3011
Harre, Henrietta, *Librn,* Exeter Public Library, Exeter NE. 402-266-5331
Harrell, Alfonso, *Rec Storage Cnt Supvr,* Philadelphia City Archives, Philadelphia PA. 215-686-2276, 686-2249
Harrell, Charles, *Assoc Dir,* University of Texas at Arlington Library, Arlington TX. 817-273-3391
Harrell, George F, *Dir,* Floral Park Public Library, Floral Park NY. 516-354-0666
Harrell, Helen, *Librn,* Hermann Hospital, School of Vocational Nursing Library, Houston TX. 713-797-4080
Harrell, Lois, *Media,* La Porte Public Library, La Porte IN. 219-362-6156
Harrell, Robert, *Media,* Clayton Junior College Library, Morrow GA. 404-961-3520
Harren, Judie, *Doc & ILL,* Albany Law School Library, Albany NY. 518-445-2311, 445-2340
Harrer, Gustave A, *Dir,* University of Florida Libraries, Gainesville FL. 904-392-0341
Harrer, Suzanne, *Librn,* Midwest College of Engineering Library, Lombard IL. 312-627-6850
Harri, W, *On-Line Servs,* Moorhead State University, Livingston Lord Library, Moorhead MN. 218-236-2922
Harrick, Rosemary, *Ref,* Kent State University Libraries, Kent OH. 216-672-2962
Harrick, Rosemary, *Bibliog Instr,* Kent State University Libraries, Kent OH. 216-672-2962
Harriff, Nanita, *ILL,* Roberts Wesleyan College, Kenneth B Keating Library, Rochester NY. 716-594-9471, Ext 133
Harrigan, Ann, *Librn,* Lake Circuit Court Library, Crown Point IN. 219-738-2020, Ext 434
Harrigan, Anne, *Librn,* Woodward-Clyde Consultants Library-ESD, San Francisco CA. 415-956-7070, Ext 375
Harriman, Beverly, *Librn,* Hollis Center Library (Salmon Falls Village Library), Hollis ME. 207-929-5452
Harrington, Awona, *Sci,* San Diego State University Library, San Diego CA. 714-286-6014
Harrington, Drew, *Librn,* Farmington Public Library, Farmington NM. 505-327-7701, Ext 1270
Harrington, Edith, *Acq,* Bentley College, Solomon R Baker Library, Waltham MA. 617-891-2231
Harrington, Elaine R, *Chief Librn,* Canada Department of Consumer & Corporate Affairs, Departmental Library, Ottawa ON. 613-997-1632
Harrington, Ellen, *Librn,* Frankfort City Library, Frankfort KS. 913-292-4427
Harrington, Jean, *Dir,* Public Library of Enid & Garfield County, Enid Public Library, Enid OK. 405-234-6313
Harrington, Margaret V, *Librn,* United States District Court, Theodore Levin Memorial Library, Detroit MI. 313-226-6986
Harrington, Patricia, *Librn & Ad,* Southampton Free Library, Southampton PA. 215-322-1415
Harrington, Robert D, *Dir,* San Mateo County Law Library, Redwood City CA. 415-364-5600, Ext 2883
Harrington, Sandra, *Librn,* Binghamton Public Library (West), Binghamton NY. 607-797-4921
Harrington, Sue, *Ser,* University of Oklahoma MUniversity Libraries, Norman OK. 405-325-2611
Harrington, Thomas R, *Media,* Gallaudet College, Edward Miner Gallaudet Memorial Library, Washington DC. 202-651-5566
Harrington, Timothy, *Librn,* Blue Cross-Blue Shield, Research Library, Boston MA. 617-956-2000
Harrington, Walter, *Acq,* University of British Columbia Library, Vancouver BC. 604-228-3871
Harris, Agnes A, *Librn,* Ouachita Parish Public Library, Monroe LA. 318-387-1950
Harris, Alice, *Librn,* Dow Chemical USA, E&CS Information Ctr, Houston TX. 713-978-2971
Harris, Alice D, *In Charge,* East-West Population Institute, Resource Materials Collection, Honolulu HI. 808-948-7684
Harris, Andrea, *Librn,* Dallas Public Library (Preston Royal), Dallas TX. 214-363-5479
Harris, Angela, *Librn,* Schlumberger Limited, EMR Photoelectric Research Library, Princeton Junction NJ. 609-799-1000
Harris, Anna L, *In Charge,* Cleveland Psychiatric Institute, Karnosh Library, Cleveland OH. 216-661-6200, Ext 509
Harris, Anne, *Chief Librn,* Prairie Crocus Regional Library, Rivers MB. 204-328-7613
Harris, Annie B, *Dir,* Camden County College Library, Charles Wolverton Learning Resource Center, Blackwood NJ. 609-227-7200
Harris, Annie V, *Asst Dir,* Tallahatchie County Library, Charleston MS. 601-647-2638
Harris, Barbara, *Librn,* Control Data Corp, Eastern Programs Library, Arlington VA. 703-998-4606
Harris, Barbara, *Per & VF,* Philadelphia College of Art Library, Philadelphia PA. 215-893-3126
Harris, Bernardine, *On-Line Servs,* Gladstone Area School & Public Library, Gladstone MI. 906-428-4224
Harris, Beverly, *Tech Serv,* Westchester Library System, Hartsdale NY. 914-761-7620
Harris, Carol, *Floridiana,* Jacksonville Public Library System, Haydon Burns Library, Jacksonville FL. 904-633-6870
Harris, Carol, *Rare Bks & Spec Coll,* Jacksonville Public Library System, Haydon Burns Library, Jacksonville FL. 904-633-6870
Harris, Carol, *Librn,* Miracle Valley Regional Library (Sand Hill Public), Moundsville WV. 304-845-6911
Harris, Carol, *Librn,* Wisconsin State Department of Natural Resources (Bureau of Legal Services Library), Madison WI. 608-266-2621
Harris, Carol A, *Librn,* Deborah Heart & Lung Center, Medical Library, Browns Mills NJ. 609-893-6611, Ext 205, 203
Harris, Carolyn M, *Dir,* College of the Ozarks, Dobson Memorial Library, Clarksville AR. 501-754-3964
Harris, Charles W, *Deputy Dir,* Indiana Legislative Council, Code Revision Library, Indianapolis IN. 317-269-3440
Harris, Charlotte Ann, *Per,* Eastfield College, Learning Resources Center, Mesquite TX. 214-746-3168
Harris, Cheryl, *Health Sciences,* Veterans Administration, Health Sciences Library, Dayton OH. 513-268-6511, Ext 335
Harris, Colleen, *Librn,* Cobb County Public Library System (Merchant's Walk), Marietta GA. 404-977-7333

Harris, Cora, *Libr Technician,* San Diego County Library (Potrero Branch), Potrero CA. 714-478-5978
Harris, Deborah, *Dir,* Tecumseh Public Library, Tecumseh MI. 517-423-2238
Harris, Dorothy, *Chief Librn,* Brooklyn Public Library (Central Library), Brooklyn NY. 212-780-7712
Harris, Dorothy, *Librn,* Brooklyn Public Library (Mapleton), Brooklyn NY. 212-232-0346
Harris, Dorothy, *Librn,* Houston Public Library (Acres Homes), Houston TX. 713-448-9841
Harris, Edith, *Fine Arts,* New Rochelle Public Library, New Rochelle NY. 914-632-7878
Harris, Edward, *Dir,* Central Missouri State University, Ward Edwards Library, Warrensburg MO. 816-429-4141
Harris, Elazer, *Cat,* Essex County College, Learning Resources Center, Newark NJ. 201-877-3233
Harris, Elizabeth, *Librn,* Howard University Libraries (Nursing-Allied Health Sciences Library), Washington DC. 202-636-7472
Harris, Ella, *Librn,* Port Elizabeth Public Library, Port Elizabeth NJ. 609-825-4113
Harris, Eulala, *Librn,* Larned State Hospital (Patients' Library), Larned KS. 316-285-2131, Ext 352
Harris, Evelyn A, *Dir,* Pacific Oaks College, Andrew Norman Library, Pasadena CA. 213-795-9161, Ext 17, 27
Harris, Frances, *Dir,* Crownsville Hospital Center, Medical Staff Library, Crownsville MD. 301-987-6200, Ext 561
Harris, Freda, *Librn,* Ministry of the Solicitor General Library - Crimdoc Centre, Ottawa ON. 613-995-6898
Harris, George, *Librn,* Circle Seal Corp, Products Division Library, Anaheim CA. 914-774-6110
Harris, Geraldine L, *Dir & Cat,* Chowan College, Whitaker Library, Murfreesboro NC. 919-398-4101, Ext 241
Harris, Gertrude G, *Librn,* Wells Village Library, Wells VT. 802-645-0125
Harris, Grace, *Librn,* Modoc County Library (Likely), Likely CA. 916-233-2719
Harris, Gwendolyn, *Instr,* Jacksonville State University, College of Library Science, Communications & Instructional Media, AL. 205-435-6390
Harris, Helen Y, *Librn,* Semmes, Bowen & Semmes Library, Baltimore MD. 301-539-5040, Ext 606
Harris, Hilda G, *Assoc Dir & Commun Servs,* University of Alabama in Birmingham (Lister Hill Library of the Health Sciences), Birmingham AL. 205-934-5460
Harris, Inez, *Librn,* Lawrence County Library, Walnut Ridge AR. 501-886-3222
Harris, Inez W, *Ch,* Merced County Library, Merced CA. 209-726-7484
Harris, Ira W, *Dean,* University of Hawaii, Graduate School of Library Studies, HI. 808-948-7321
Harris, Jane, *Librn,* Palm Beach County Public Library System (Okeechobee Boulevard), West Palm Beach FL. 305-683-2381
Harris, Jewel, *Ad,* Harford County Library, Bel Air MD. 301-838-7484
Harris, Joan, *Dir,* Winnetka Public Library District, Winnetka IL. 312-446-5085
Harris, John, *AV,* Pennsylvania College of Podiatric Medicine, Charles E Krausz Library, Philadelphia PA. 215-629-0300, Ext 215
Harris, John, *Librn,* Pennsylvania College of Podiatric Medicine (Audio-Visual Library), Philadelphia PA. 215-629-0300, Ext 215
Harris, Karren, *Assoc Prof,* University of New Orleans, College of Education, LA. 504-282-0607
Harris, Kathleen, *Per,* Smithtown Library, Smithtown NY. 516-265-2072
Harris, Kathryn, *Exten,* Southern Illinois University School of Medicine Library, Springfield IL. 217-782-2658
Harris, Kenneth, *English Modern Lang & Theatre,* Loyola University of Chicago Libraries (Elizabeth M Cudahy Memorial Library), Chicago IL. 312-274-3000, Ext 771
Harris, Letha, *Tech Serv,* Emmanuel School of Religion Library, Johnson City TN. 615-926-1186, Ext 49
Harris, Linda S, *Circ,* Wake Forest University (Law Library), Winston-Salem NC. 919-761-5438

Harris, Lois, *Spec Coll,* Vigo County Public Library, Terre Haute IN. 812-232-1113
Harris, Lois E, *Librn,* Pacific Hospital of Long Beach, Medical Library, Long Beach CA. 213-595-1911, Ext 2291
Harris, Lou Ann, *Media & On-Line Servs,* Orange Coast College Library, Costa Mesa CA. 714-556-5885
Harris, Lu Ann, *Librn,* Sacramento Public Library (Carmichael Regional Branch), Carmichael CA. 916-483-6055
Harris, M, *Ref,* Queen's University at Kingston (Education), Kingston ON. 613-547-6286
Harris, M B, *Info Servs Dir,* University of Prince Edward Island, Robertson Library, Charlottetown PE. 902-892-1243
Harris, Madlynne, *Ref,* University of Pittsburgh (Maurice & Laura Falk Library of the Health Sciences), Pittsburgh PA. 412-624-2521
Harris, Margaret, *Ser,* Oklahoma City University (Dulaney-Browne Library), Oklahoma City OK. 405-521-5068
Harris, Margaret J, *Librn,* Cuyahoga County Public Library (Mayfield Regional), Mayfield Village OH. 216-473-0350
Harris, Margaretta, *Asst Librn,* Earl Township Public Library, Earlville IL. 815-246-9465
Harris, Marinella, *Ser,* Southwestern Oklahoma State University, Al Harris Library, Weatherford OK. 405-772-6611, Ext 5311
Harris, Martha T, *ILL & On-Line Servs,* Augustana College, Denkman Memorial Library, Rock Island IL. 309-794-7266
Harris, Mary Frances, *Petroleum Tech,* Midland County Public Library, Midland TX. 915-683-2708
Harris, Mary R, *Librn,* Reynolds Metals Co (Technical Information Services Library), Richmond VA. 804-788-7409, 788-7735
Harris, Michael H, *Prof,* University of Kentucky, College of Library Science, KY. 606-258-8876
Harris, Mollie S, *Librn,* Jewish Community Center of San Diego, Samuel & Rebecca Astor Judaica Library, San Diego CA. 714-583-3300
Harris, Mrs E S, *Librn,* Florida Institute of Technology, Jensen Beach Library, Jensen Beach FL. 305-334-4200, Ext 60, 61
Harris, Mrs F B, *Librn,* Canada Ministry of Solicitor General Library, Ottawa ON. 613-995-1032
Harris, Nancy, *Librn,* Marshall, Melhorn, Cole, Hummer & Spitzer Law Library, Toledo OH. 419-243-4200
Harris, Nancy S, *Librn,* Virginia Associated Research Campus of the College of William & Mary, Newport News VA. 804-877-9231, Ext 224
Harris, Patricia, *Librn,* Greene County District Library (Fairborn Branch), Fairborn OH. 513-878-9383
Harris, Patricia M, *Assoc Dir,* Public Library of Annapolis & Anne Arundel County Inc, Annapolis MD. 301-224-7371
Harris, Paula, *Dir,* Herman Brown Free Library, Burnet TX. 512-756-2328
Harris, Peggy, *Acq,* Flagstaff City-Coconino County Public Library System, Flagstaff AZ. 602-774-0603
Harris, Peggy Jean, *Librn,* Logetronics Inc Library, Springfield VA. 703-971-1400, Ext 215
Harris, R B, *Chmn,* Harris Laboratories, Inc, Library, Lincoln NE. 402-432-2811
Harris, Richard, *Tech Serv,* Eastern Virginia Medical School, Moorman Memorial Library, Norfolk VA. 804-446-5840
Harris, Richard W, *Dir,* Chattanooga State Technical Community College, Augusta R Kolwyck Instructional Materials Center, Chattanooga TN. 615-622-6262
Harris, Rita B, *AV Asst,* Pitt Community College, Learning Resources Center, Greenville NC. 919-756-3130, Ext 213
Harris, Robert A, *Dir,* Bartlett Public Library, Bartlett IL. 312-837-2855
Harris, Robert L, *Ref,* Southwest Texas State University, Learning Resources Center, San Marcos TX. 512-245-2132
Harris, Rodger, *Cat,* University of North Carolina at Chapel Hill, Louis Round Wilson Academic Affairs Library, Chapel Hill NC. 919-933-1301
Harris, Ron, *Librn,* Larimer County Vocational Technical Center Library, Fort Collins CO. 303-226-2500

Harris, Rosemary, *Librn,* E & J Gallo Winery Library, Modesto CA. 209-521-3230
Harris, Ruth, *Librn,* White County Public Library (Baldwin Memorial), Judsonia AR. 501-729-3995
Harris, Sally, *Ref,* Pioneer Multi-County Library, Norman OK. 405-321-1481
Harris, Sandra, *Librn,* Sacramento Public Library (Martin Luther King Regional), Sacramento CA. 916-421-3151
Harris, Sarah Lucille, *Asst Dir,* Salt Lake City Public Library, Salt Lake City UT. 801-363-5733
Harris, Selma, *Rare Bks,* Montclair State College, Harry A Sprague Library, Upper Montclair NJ. 201-893-4291
Harris, Susan, *Asst Dir,* Greenwood-Leflore Public Library System, Greenwood MS. 601-453-3634
Harris, T, *Librn,* Johnston Technical Institute Library, Smithfield NC. 919-934-3051
Harris, Thomas Joe, *Asst Dir & Media,* Cumberland Trail Library System, Flora IL. 618-662-2679, 622-2741
Harris, Virginia, *Media,* University of Arkansas, Pine Bluff, Watson Memorial Library, Pine Bluff AR. 501-541-6825
Harris, Vivian, *Tech Serv,* Cleveland Heights-University Heights Public Library, Cleveland Heights OH. 216-932-3600
Harris, Wilhelmina S, *Librn,* United States Department of the Interior, Adams National Historic Site, Stone Library, Quincy MA. 617-773-1177
Harrison, Alice W, *Dir,* Atlantic School of Theology Library, Halifax NS. 902-423-6801
Harrison, Alice W, *Adjunct Lectr,* Dalhousie University, School of Library Service, NS. 902-424-3656
Harrison, Amalia, *Ref,* Alabama Public Library Service, Montgomery AL. 205-832-5743
Harrison, Annie, *Bibliog Instr,* Kentucky Department of Library & Archives, Frankfort KY. 502-564-7910
Harrison, Annie, *Librn,* Saint Paul's College, Russell Memorial Library, Lawrenceville VA. 804-848-3111, Ext 221
Harrison, Barbara, *Librn,* Milchem, Inc, Research Library, Houston TX. 713-965-8305
Harrison, Ben, *Media,* East Orange Public Library, East Orange NJ. 201-266-5600
Harrison, Betty, *Asst Dir,* Saint Charles City County Library, Saint Peters MO. 314-441-2300
Harrison, Betty, *Librn,* Saint Charles City County Library (Spencer Road), Saint Peters MO. 314-278-3400
Harrison, Betty J, *Librn,* Marshalltown Community College, Learning Resource Center, Marshalltown IA. 515-752-7106
Harrison, Catherine, *Supvr,* Middlesex County Library (Ilderton Branch), Ilderton ON. 519-438-8368
Harrison, Doris, *Dir,* Wilton Public Library, Wilton WI. 608-385-6666
Harrison, Edith, *In Charge,* Oxford County Library (Norwich Library), Norwich ON. 519-863-3113
Harrison, Edward E, *Pres,* Fairfield Historical Society Library, Fairfield CT. 203-259-1598
Harrison, Gail, *ILL,* Tuolumne County Free Public Library, Sonora CA. 209-532-7842
Harrison, Geraldine, *Tech Serv,* Mississippi Library Commission, Jackson MS. 601-354-6369
Harrison, J Orion, *Ref & Bibliog Instr,* Georgia Southern College Library, Statesboro GA. 912-681-5115
Harrison, John A, *Assoc Librn Pub Servs,* Yale University Library (University Library), New Haven CT. 203-436-8335
Harrison, John P, *On-Line Servs,* Boston Athenaeum, Boston MA. 617-227-0270
Harrison, Jon, *Doc,* Missouri State Library, Jefferson City MO. 314-751-4214
Harrison, Karen, *Librn,* Township of Delhi Public Library, Delhi ON. 519-582-1791
Harrison, Lucille, *Acq,* Fort Worth Public Library, Fort Worth TX. 817-870-7700
Harrison, Marcia, *Cat,* Swampscott Public Library, Swampscott MA. 617-593-8380
Harrison, Margaret, *Ch,* Meridian Public Library, Meridian MS. 601-693-6771, 693-4913
Harrison, Marjorie, *Asst Librn & On-Line Servs,* Maine Maritime Academy, Nutting Memorial Library, Castine ME. 207-326-4311, Ext 238

Harrison, Marsha, *Librn,* East Baton Rouge Parish Library (Scotlandville), Baton Rouge LA. 504-778-0618
Harrison, Mary, *Librn,* Kern County Library (South Bakersfield), Bakersfield CA. 805-861-2130
Harrison, Mary, *Librn,* Northeast Regional Library (Walnut Library), Walnut MS. 601-223-6768
Harrison, Mrs John, *Librn,* Selmer Public Library, Selmer TN. 901-645-5571
Harrison, Mrs Melvin, *Librn,* Temple Judea, Mel Harrison Memorial Library, Coral Gables FL. 305-667-5657
Harrison, Mrs R G, *Librn,* New Jersey Bell Telephone, Law Library, Newark NJ. 201-649-9900
Harrison, Mrs T, *Acq,* Kelsey Institute of Applied Arts & Sciences, Learning Resources Center, Saskatoon SK. 306-664-6417
Harrison, Mrs Teddy, *Asst Librn,* Minnedosa Regional Library, Minnedosa MB. 204-867-2585
Harrison, Nannette C, *Coordr Libr Blind & Physically Handicapped,* Oconee Regional Library, Laurens County Library, Dublin GA. 912-272-5710
Harrison, Pamela, *Per,* Rand Corp Library, Santa Monica CA. 213-393-0411, Ext 369
Harrison, Patrick, *Chmn,* San Diego State University, Dept of Educational Technology & Librarianship, CA. 714-265-6718
Harrison, Rayma, *Librn,* California Institute of Technology (Environmental Engineering Library), Pasadena CA. 213-795-6811, Ext 1381
Harrison, Rose, *ILL,* Connecticut State Library, Hartford CT. 203-566-4301
Harrison, Ruth, *Dir,* Arcadia Free Public Library, Arcadia WI. 608-323-7505
Harrison, Sandra J, *Dir,* Qualla Boundary Public Library, Cherokee NC. 704-497-9023
Harrison, Shirley J, *Librn,* West Falmouth Library, West Falmouth MA. 617-548-4709
Harrison, Susan, *Acq,* Free Library of Philadelphia, Philadelphia PA. 215-686-5322
Harrison, Susan, *Librn,* Public Library of Columbus & Franklin County (Franklinton), Columbus OH. 614-222-7101
Harrison, Thomas J, *Coordr,* Gettysburg National Military Park Library, Gettysburg PA. 334-1124 Ext 28
Harrison, Tom, *Mgr,* Kerr-McGee Corp (McGee Library), Oklahoma City OK. 405-270-3358
Harrison, Veronica C, *Librn,* Mercy Hospital of Pittsburgh (School of Nursing Library), Pittsburgh PA. 412-232-7963
Harrison, William L, *Dir,* Lord Fairfax Community College, Learning Resource Center, Middletown VA. 703-869-1120
Harrison, Jr, James G, *Dir,* Converse College, Gwathmey Library, Spartanburg SC. 803-585-6421, Ext 260
Harrod, Etainne, *Asst Librn,* Live Oak County Library, George West TX. 512-449-1124
Harrod, Paula, *Asst Librn,* Edgemont Public Library, Edgemont SD. 605-662-7712
Harrod, Ruth, *ILL,* Indiana University-Purdue University at Fort Wayne Library, Walter E Helmke Library, Fort Wayne IN. 219-482-5456
Harrsch, Reid, *Acq,* Wisconsin Department of Public Instruction (Reference & Loan Library), Madison WI. 608-266-1053
Harry, Ann, *Bkmobile Coordr,* Tiffin-Seneca Public Library, Tiffin OH. 419-447-3751
Harry, J Diann, *In Charge,* Office of the Ombudsman Library, Edmonton AB. 403-427-2756
Harry, Martha, *Extension,* Cherokee County Public Library, Gaffney SC. 803-489-4381
Harry, Martha, *Librn,* Cherokee County Public Library (Blacksburg Branch), Blacksburg SC. 803-839-2630
Harry, Ruth, *Librn,* Louisville Free Public Library (Western), Louisville KY. 502-584-5526
Harsanyi, Nancy, *Librn,* Fort Erie Public Library, Centennial Library, Fort Erie ON. 416-871-2546
Harshbarger, Jane, *Ch,* North Manchester Public Library, North Manchester IN. 219-982-4773
Harshe, Florence E, *Dir,* Southern Adirondack Library System, Saratoga Springs NY. 518-584-7300, 792-3343, 885-1073

Harshman, Cheryl, *Asst Ref Librn,* Miracle Valley Regional Library, City-County Public Library, Moundsville WV. 304-845-6911
Harsted, Pauline, *Librn,* Bond Library, Wenona IL. 815-853-4665
Hart, Alice, *Librn,* Fremont County Library (Dubois Branch), Dubois WY. 307-455-2992
Hart, Betty, *ILL & AV,* Citizens Library, Washington PA. 412-222-2400
Hart, Carroll, *Dir,* Georgia Department of Archives & History, Central Research Section Library, Atlanta GA. 404-656-2350
Hart, Carroll A, *Lectr,* Emory University, Div of Librarianship, GA. 404-329-6840
Hart, David, *AV,* University of Michigan-Flint Library, Flint MI. 313-762-3400
Hart, Diane, *Librn,* Drumheller Municipal Library, Drumheller AB. 403-823-5382
Hart, Don, *Info Systs Mgr,* Alabama Public Library Service, Montgomery AL. 205-832-5743
Hart, Dorothy B, *Librn,* United States Air Force (Nellis Air Force Base Library), Nellis AFB NV. 702-643-2280
Hart, Earl D, *Dir & Assoc Prof,* University of New Orleans, College of Education, LA. 504-282-0607
Hart, Elizabeth, *Asst Admin,* Charles County Public Library, La Plata MD. 301-934-9001
Hart, Evelyn L, *Peabody,* Enoch Pratt Free Library, Baltimore MD. 301-396-5430, 396-5395
Hart, James, *Bibliog Instr,* Southeast Missouri State University, Kent Library, Cape Girardeau MO. 314-651-2235
Hart, James D, *Librn,* University of California, Berkeley (Bancroft Library), Berkeley CA. 415-642-3781
Hart, James D, *Spec Coll,* University of California, Berkeley (University Library), Berkeley CA. 415-642-3773
Hart, Jean F, *Dir,* Greater Hartford Community College Library, Hartford CT. 203-549-4200, Ext 277
Hart, John, *ILL, Ref & Commun Servs,* Bristol Public Library, Bristol VA. 703-669-9444
Hart, Johnetta, *Librn,* Louisville Free Public Library (Harris), Louisville KY. 502-778-7067
Hart, Julia, *Cat,* Jackson-Madison County Library, Jackson TN. 901-423-0225
Hart, Katherine M, *Commun Servs,* West Hartford Public Library, Noah Webster Memorial Library, West Hartford CT. 203-236-6286
Hart, Lenora, *ILL,* Fort Bend County Library, Richmond TX. 713-342-4455
Hart, Lydia, *Librn,* Bartley Public Library, Bartley NE. 308-692-3313
Hart, Marguerite, *Media,* Troy Public Library, Troy MI. 313-689-5665
Hart, Marion L, *Asst Vice Pres, Info Serv,* United Virginia Bankshares Library, Richmond VA. 804-782-7452
Hart, Martha, *ILL,* Olivet College Burrage Library, Olivet MI. 616-749-7608
Hart, Mary, *Info Spec,* Alberta Information Retrieval Association, AB. 403-432-8059
Hart, Maurine, *Ser,* Northeast Missouri State University, Pickler Memorial Library, Kirksville MO. 816-665-5121, Ext 7186
Hart, Mildred, *Librn,* East Cleveland Public Library (North Branch), East Cleveland OH. 216-451-1575
Hart, Mrs H, *Librn,* Hinton Municipal Library, Hinton AB. 403-865-2363
Hart, Nellie A, *Librn,* Camden Public Library, Camden ME. 207-236-3440
Hart, Peter, *Tech Serv,* Ball State University, Alexander M Bracken Library, Muncie IN. 317-285-6261
Hart, Robert, *Dir,* Santa Barbara Public Library, Santa Barbara CA. 805-962-7653
Hart, Robert, *Dir,* Santa Barbara Public Library (Central Library), Santa Barbara CA. 805-962-7653
Hart, Robert, *Instr,* University of Georgia, Dept of Educational Media & Librarianship, GA. 404-542-3810
Hart, Robert W, *Librn,* Indiana Vocational Technical College Library, Fort Wayne IN. 219-482-9171
Hart, Rose, *Librn,* Nora Springs Public Library, Nora Springs IA. 515-749-5569

Hart, Sheila K, *Pub Servs Dept Head & Chief Ref Librn,* Harvard University Library (Harvard College Library (Headquarters in Harry Elkins Widener Memorial Library)), Cambridge MA. 617-495-2401
Hart, Sister Maure, *Dir,* Bethany Hospital, Health Science Library, Framingham MA. 617-872-6750
Hart, Thomas L, *Assoc Prof,* Florida State University, School of Library Science, FL. 904-644-5775
Hart, William E, *Librn,* Hartford Medical Society Library, Hartford CT. 203-236-5613, Ext 25
Hart, William W, *Librn,* United States Army (Corps Of Engineers, Albuquerque District), Albuquerque NM. 505-766-2781
Hart, Wyatt, *Librn,* Orange County Jail Library, Santa Ana CA. 714-834-4523
Hartbank, Betty, *Ref,* Eastern Illinois University, Booth Library, Charleston IL. 217-581-2210
Harte, Margaret S Bret, *Librn,* Arizona Historical Society, Research Library, Tucson AZ. 602-882-5774
Hartenstein, Jeanne L, *Dir,* Bronson Methodist Hospital, Health Science Library, Kalamazoo MI. 616-383-6318
Harter, Esther, *Librn,* Preble County District Library (New Paris), Eaton OH. 513-437-8352
Harter, Stephen, *Assoc Prof,* University of South Florida, Graduate Department of Library, Media & Information Studies, FL. 813-974-2557
Harter, Vivan, *Asst Dir,* Mount Arlington Public Library, Mount Arlington NJ. 201-398-1516
Hartford, Sue, *Librn,* Monroe County Library System (Maybee Branch), Maybee MI. 313-587-3680
Harthan, Phyllis, *Cat,* Grand Rapids Public Library, Grand Rapids MN. 218-326-3081
Harthan, Stephen, *Tech Serv & Cat,* Dallas Theological Seminary, Mosher Library, Dallas TX. 214-824-3094, Ext 285
Hartin, J S, *Prof,* University of Mississippi, Graduate School of Library & Information Science, MS. 601-232-7440
Hartje, George N, *Dept Head,* Northeast Missouri State University, Div of Libraries & Museums, MO. 816-665-5121, Ext 7186
Hartje, George N, *Dir,* Northeast Missouri State University, Pickler Memorial Library, Kirksville MO. 816-665-5121, Ext 7186
Hartke, Phyllis, *Ref,* Squire, Sanders & Dempsey, Law Library, Cleveland OH. 216-696-9200
Hartl, Kathleen, *Librn,* Northeast Iowa Technical Institute Library, Calmar IA. 319-562-3263
Hartley, Alice, *Librn,* Highland County District (Greenfield Branch), Greenfield OH. 513-981-3772
Hartley, Debra, *Ref & On-Line Servs,* Wartburg College, Engelbrecht Library, Waverly IA. 319-352-1200, Ext 244
Hartley, Frances, *Tech Serv & Cat,* Tacoma Public Library, Tacoma WA. 206-572-2000
Hartley, Gloria R, *Librn,* Lukens Steel Co, Technical Library, Coatesville PA. 215-383-2674
Hartley, Patty Y, *Dir,* Bethesda Hospital, Medical & Allied Health Sciences Library, Zanesville OH. 614-454-4220
Hartley, Susan, *Ch,* Hamden Library, Miller Memorial, Hamden CT. 203-248-7747
Hartline, Janet, *Librn,* Livingston County Memorial Library, Chillicothe MO. 816-646-0547
Hartline, Kenneth, *Librn,* Detroit Public Library (Chase), Detroit MI. 313-833-9820
Hartman, Ann, *Pub Servs,* National City Public Library, National City CA. 714-474-8211
Hartman, Delores, *Asst Librn,* Norfolk Regional Center Staff Library (Resident Library), Norfolk NE. 402-371-4343, Ext 322
Hartman, Doris, *Librn,* Hatch Public Library, Hatch NM. 505-267-5132
Hartman, Eleanor C, *Librn,* Los Angeles County Museum of Art, Art Research Library, Los Angeles CA. 213-937-4250, Ext 219
Hartman, Elizabeth, *Asst Dir, ILL & Acq,* Richard Bland College Library, Petersburg VA. 804-732-0111, Ext 226
Hartman, Ethel B, *Librn,* Mounds Public Library, Mounds IL. 618-745-6610
Hartman, Gwen, *Librn,* Delavan Corporation, Delavan Engineering Library, West Des Moines IA. 515-274-1561

Hartman, Ieva, *Ref,* McCowan Memorial Library, Pitman Library, Pitman NJ. 609-589-1656
Hartman, Julieann, *Commun Servs,* Bacon Memorial Public Library, Wyandotte MI. 313-282-7660
Hartman, Mary M, *Pub Servs,* Clark University, Robert Hutchings Goddard Library, Worcester MA. 617-793-7573
Hartman, Mrs C S, *Asst Dir,* Wolfeboro Public Library, Wolfeboro NH. 603-569-2428
Hartman, Mrs Ralph A, *Librn,* Newport Free Library, Newport NY. 315-845-8533
Hartman, Nancy, *Rare Bks,* Northeast Regional Library, Corinth MS. 601-287-2441
Hartman, Paula, *Librn,* Luzerne County Medical Society Library, Wilkes-Barre PA. 717-823-0917
Hartman, Ruth, *Doc,* Central Washington University Library, Ellensburg WA. 509-963-1901
Hartman, Sherry, *Ref,* Albany Medical Center College of Union University, Schaffer Library of Health Sciences, Albany NY. 518-445-5534
Hartman, Susan, *Ref,* Rolling Meadows Library, Rolling Meadows IL. 312-259-6050
Hartman, Susan, *Ch,* San Bernardino Public Library, San Bernardino CA. 714-889-0264
Hartman, Wilma, *Pub Servs,* Linda Hall Library, Kansas City MO. 816-363-4600
Hartmann, Frances, *Librn,* Yorktown Public Library, Yorktown TX. 512-564-3232
Hartmann, Susan, *Circ & Reserve,* Barat College Library, Lake Forest IL. 312-234-3000, Ext 237
Hartmere, Anne, *Librn,* Architects Collaborative Inc Library, Cambridge MA. 617-868-4200
Hartmetz, Walter J, *Librn,* North Kansas City Public Library, North Kansas City MO. 816-221-3360
Hartnett, Thomas, *Ref,* Lucy Robbins Welles Library, Newington CT. 203-666-9350
Hartough, Joanne, *ILL,* University of Toledo, William S Carlson Library, Toledo OH. 419-537-2324
Hartsell, Lynaire, *Librn Blind,* Ozarks Regional Library, Fayetteville AR. 501-442-6253
Hartung, David D, *Dir,* Indianhead Technical Institute, New Richmond Campus Learning Resources Center, New Richmond WI. 715-246-6561, Ext 274
Hartung, Mary Kay, *ILL,* University of South Florida (University Library), Tampa FL. 813-974-2721
Hartung, Mrs Carl, *Ch,* Chattanooga-Hamilton County Bicentennial Library, Chattanooga TN. 615-757-5320
Hartung, Richard P, *Dir,* Rock County Historical Society, Research Library, Janesville WI. 608-752-4519
Hartwell, Eugenie, *Br Asst,* Jefferson Davis Parish Library (Lake Arthur Branch), Lake Arthur LA. 318-774-3661
Hartwell, Glen, *Oregoniana,* Oregon State Library, Salem OR. 503-378-4243
Hartwell, S, *Librn,* Mote Marine Laboratory Library, Arthur Vining Davis Library, Sarasota FL. 813-388-4441
Hartwick, Arlene W, *Dir,* Springfield Public Library, Springfield MN. 507-723-9922
Hartwick, Jule F, *Librn,* Alpena Community College Library, Alpena MI. 517-356-9021, Ext 249
Harty, Rose Marie, *Dir, Ad & Acq,* Albert Lea Public Library, Albert Lea MN. 507-373-8862
Hartz, Frederic R, *Librn,* Warren State Hospital (Medical Library), Warren PA. 814-723-5500, Ext 223
Hartz, Lee, *Media,* Richmond Public Library, Richmond CA. 415-231-2119
Hartz, Mary K, *Librn & Asst Librn,* Bureau of Social Science Research, Inc Library, Washington DC. 202-223-4300, Ext 220
Hartzel, Mrs Gerald F, *Chmn Libr Comm,* Zion Mennonite Church Library, Souderton PA. 215-723-3592
Hartzell, Alyce C, *Librn,* Marengo County Public Library, Linden AL. 205-295-5797
Hartzell, Nina, *Librn,* Edison State Community College Library, Piqua OH. 513-778-8600
Hartzler, Mary, *Cat,* Indiana State Library, Indianapolis IN. 317-232-3675
Harvan, Christine, *Librn,* Lancaster County Law Library, Lancaster PA. 717-299-8090
Harvath, John, *Librn,* Houston Public Library (Fine Arts & Recreation), Houston TX. 713-224-5441

Harvell, Gloria, *Media,* Virginia State College (Instructional Materials Laboratory), Petersburg VA. 804-520-6171
Harvell, Larametta R, *Librn,* United States Navy (Naval Air Station, Whiting Library), Milton FL. 904-623-7274
Harvey, A, *Ref,* Bell Telephone Laboratories (Western Electric Technical Library), Reading PA. 929-7493 (Supvr); 929-7250 (Ref)
Harvey, Brenda K, *Adminr Asst,* L E Phillips Memorial Public Library, Eau Claire WI. 715-839-5002
Harvey, C G, *Librn,* Hudson's Bay Oil & Gas Co Ltd, Corporate Library, Calgary AB. 403-231-6052
Harvey, Charlie R, *Dir,* Villanova University (Pulling Law Library), Villanova PA. 215-527-2100, Ext 702, 703, 704
Harvey, Dorothy, *Bus & Municipal,* Sacramento Public Library, Sacramento CA. 916-440-5926
Harvey, Dorothy B, *Librn,* Loula V York Memorial Library, Pahokee FL. 305-924-5928
Harvey, Dwight, *Commun Servs & Bkmobile Coordr,* Ruth Enlow Library of Garrett County, Oakland MD. 301-334-3996
Harvey, Elaine, *Acq,* Webster College, Eden Theological Seminary, Eden-Webster Libraries, Saint Louis MO. 314-968-0500, Ext 235
Harvey, Elizabeth R, *Dir,* Schlow Memorial Library, State College PA. 814-237-6236
Harvey, Eloise, *Cat,* Somerville Free Public Library, Somerville NJ. 201-725-1336
Harvey, J, *Librn,* University of Southern California (Education), Los Angeles CA. 213-743-6249
Harvey, Jane, *Order,* Metropolitan Toronto Library Board, Metropolitan Toronto Library, Toronto ON. 416-928-5150
Harvey, Karen, *Librn,* Smith College Library (Hillyer Art Library), Northampton MA. 413-584-2700, Ext 743
Harvey, Linda, *Head Info Serv,* Dalhousie University (W K Kellogg Health Sciences Library), Halifax NS. 902-424-2458
Harvey, M F, *Dir,* Instrument Society of America, Albert F Sperry Library, Pittsburgh PA. 412-281-3171
Harvey, Mabel E, *Librn,* South Florida State Hospital (Medical Library), Hollywood FL. 305-983-4321
Harvey, Marguerite, *Dir,* Pearl River Junior College Library, Poplarville MS. 601-795-4517
Harvey, Marjorie A, *Chief Librn,* Guernsey County District Public Library, Cambridge OH. 614-432-5946
Harvey, Mary Alice, *Librn,* Grand Marais Public Library, Grand Marais MN. 218-387-1140
Harvey, Mary Alice, *Dir,* High Bridge Public Library, High Bridge NJ. 201-638-6455
Harvey, Mrs Leslie, *Librn,* Bolton Public Library, Bolton MA. 617-779-2839
Harvey, Nancy E, *Asst Chief,* Chicago Public Library (Fine Arts Div), Chicago IL. 312-269-2839
Harvey, Paul W, *Tech Serv,* Dedham Public Library, Dedham MA. 617-326-0583
Harvey, Robert, *Archives,* Knoxville-Knox County Public Library, Lawson McGhee Library, Knoxville TN. 615-523-0781
Harvey, Robert D, *Dept Head,* Southwest Missouri State University, Dept of Library Science, MO. 417-836-5104
Harvey, Robert D, *Dir,* Southwest Missouri State University Library, Springfield MO. 417-836-5104
Harvey, Serge, *Dir,* CEGEP de Chicoutimi, Centre De Documentation, Chicoutimi PQ. 418-549-9520, Ext 212, 312
Harvey, Sheryl, *Librn,* Dalton Public Library, Dalton NE. 308-376-2413
Harvey, Sister Norma, *Media,* Nazareth College, David Metzger Library, Nazareth MI. 616-349-7783, Ext 270
Harvey, Stephen, *Media,* Rosary College, Rebecca Crown Library, River Forest IL. 312-366-2490, Ext 305
Harvey, Susan, *Librn,* Metcut Research Associates, Machinability Data Center Library, Cincinnati OH. 513-271-9510
Harvey, Suzanne, *Cat,* University of Puget Sound (Law Library), Tacoma WA. 206-756-3322
Harvie, Patrick, *Dir,* Wellington County Public Library, Fergus ON. 519-846-5761

Harvill, Melba S, *Dir,* Midwestern State University, George Moffett Library, Wichita Falls TX. 817-692-6611, Ext 204
Harville, Martha, *Br Coordr,* Petersburg Public Library, Petersburg VA. 804-732-3851
Harvin, Marie, *Dir,* University of Texas (M D Anderson Hospital & Tumor Institute), Houston TX. 713-792-2282
Harwas, Roman, *Librn,* Carnegie Library of Pittsburgh (Woods Run), Pittsburgh PA. 412-622-3100
Harwell, Edalee, *Publications Asst,* Zoological Society of San Diego, Ernst Schwarz Library, San Diego CA. 714-231-1515
Harwell, Edith, *Librn,* Birmingham Public & Jefferson County Free Library (Inglenook), Birmingham AL. 205-254-2551
Harwell, June R, *Librn,* Alamogordo Public Library, Alamogordo NM. 505-437-9058
Harwell, Richard B, *Rare Bks & Mss,* University of Georgia Libraries, Athens GA. 404-542-2716
Harwell, Rolly, *Bibliog Instr,* East Tennessee State University, Sherrod Library, Johnson City TN. 615-929-4338
Harwood, Dorothy, *Librn,* Hammond Public Library (Rupp), Whiting IN. 219-931-5100
Harwood, Judith, *Librn,* Southern Illinois University at Carbondale (Undergraduate), Carbondale IL. 618-453-2818
Harwood, Karen, *Asst Prof,* College of Saint Catherine, Dept of Library Science, MN. 612-690-6651
Harwood, Kay F, *Librn,* Richland Memorial Hospital, Josey Memorial Medical Library, Columbia SC. 803-765-6312
Harwood, Richard, *ILL,* Hardin-Simmons University, Richardson Library, Abilene TX. 915-677-7281, Ext 236
Harwood, Rodene, *Librn,* Adams County Public Library (Commerce City), North Glenn CO. 303-287-0063
Hary, Edith L, *Librn,* State of Maine Law & Legislative Reference Library, Augusta ME. 207-289-2648
Hary, Nicoletta, *Cat,* University of Dayton Libraries, Roesch Library, Dayton OH. 513-229-4221
Hasbrouck, Marjorie, *Dir,* Stone Ridge Library, Stone Ridge NY. 914-687-7023
Hasbury, S, *Art Documentalist,* National Gallery of Canada Library, Ottawa ON. 613-995-6245
Hasegawa, Raymond K, *Librn,* Carlsmith, Carlsmith, Wichman & Case Library, Honolulu HI. 808-523-2500
Hasegawat, Kay, *Librn,* Sioux Valley Hospital Medical Library, Sioux Falls SD. 605-336-3440
Haselbauer, Kathleen, *Sci,* Western Washington University, Mabel Zoe Wilson Library, Bellingham WA. 206-676-3050
Haselden, Clyde L, *Dir,* Lafayette College, David Bishop Skillman Library, Easton PA. 215-253-6281, Ext 289
Haselwood, E L, *Dir,* University of Nebraska at Omaha, Library Media Program, NE. 402-554-2211
Hasemeier, Alfred C, *Dir,* Mid-York Library System, Utica NY. 315-735-8328
Haseo, Romi, *Librn,* Fort Saint John Public Library, Fort Saint John BC. 604-785-3731
Hasfjord, Nellie N, *Dir,* Adams State College Library, Alamosa CO. 303-589-7781
Hasfjord, Nellie N, *Dir,* Adams State College, Masters in Educational Media with the University of Northern Colorado, CO. 303-589-7781
Hashim, Elinor M, *Dir,* Welles-Turner Memorial Library, Glastonbury CT. 203-633-1300
Hasija, Gian C, *Librn,* Jersey Shore Medical Center, Medical Library, Neptune NJ. 201-775-5500, Ext 346, 474
Haskamp, Eileen, *Asst Librn,* Glasgow Public Library, Glasgow MO. 816-338-2395
Haske, Ida Marie, *Librn,* Richard J Trolley Library, Taylor MI. 313-291-5080
Haskell, Elsie, *Asst Dir,* Dartmouth Public Libraries, Southworth Library, South Dartmouth MA. 617-997-1252
Haskell, Inez, *Acq,* Library Association of Portland, Multnomah County Library, Portland OR. 503-223-7201, Ext 40
Haskell, Peter C, *Dir,* Franklin & Marshall College Library, Lancaster PA. 717-291-4223

Haskell, Jr, John D, *Assoc Librn,* College of William & Mary in Virginia, Earl Gregg Swem Library, Williamsburg VA. 804-253-4404

Haskins, Charles D, *Asst Librn,* United States Army (Fort McPherson Library System), Fort McPherson GA. 404-752-2528, 752-3045

Haskins, Mrs V, *Librn,* Lincoln Public Library (Jordan Branch), Jordan ON. 416-562-5895

Haskins, Norma W, *Chief Librn,* Veterans Administration, Medical & Patients' Libraries, Lebanon PA. 717-272-6621, Ext 268, 247

Haskins, Vivian, *Librn,* New Haven Free Public Library (Brook-view), New Haven CT. 203-787-8122

Haskins, Williamena W, *Librn,* Hamilton Public Library, Hamilton IL. 217-847-2219

Haslett, Lenora, *Asst Dir,* Public Library of Northfield, Northfield NJ. 609-646-4476

Haslip, Cleopatra, *Dir,* Roosevelt City Public Library, Roosevelt AL. 205-426-1261, Ext 1

Haslrouch, Kenneth E, *Dir,* Huguenot Historical Society Library, New Paltz NY. 914-255-8445

Hass, Marilyn, *Librn,* Doon Public Library, Doon IA. 712-726-3277

Hass, William, *Instr,* Mercer County Community College, Library-Media Center Technical Assistant Program, NJ. 609-586-4800, Ext 360

Hass, William S, *Ref, Per & Bibliog Instr,* Mercer County Community College Library, Trenton NJ. 609-586-4800, Ext 358

Hassan, Hazel, *Tech Serv,* Rockford Public Library, Rockford IL. 815-965-6731

Hassan, Khan, *AV,* Idaho State University Library, Pocatello ID. 208-236-3202

Hassan, Mohammad Z, *Tech Info,* Stauffer Chemical Co, Information Services, Dobbs Ferry NY. 914-693-1200

Hasse, Glenn, *Chief Librn,* Veterans Administration, Medical Library, Fargo ND. 701-232-3241, Ext 280, 375

Hassebrock, Erna, *Tech Serv,* National Center for Toxicological Research Library, Jefferson AR. 501-541-4322

Hassel, Sheila, *Acq & Per,* Cuyahoga Community College (Eastern Campus Library), Warrensville OH. 216-464-1450, Ext 228, 229

Hassell, L, *Librn,* University of Toronto Libraries (Wycliffe College), Toronto ON. 416-923-6411

Hassell, Willa, *Librn,* Saint Elizabeth Community Health Center, Medical Library, Lincoln NE. 402-489-7181, Ext 233

Hassert, Judith, *Res Librn,* Johnson & Johnson (Chicopee Research Div Library), Milltown NJ. 201-524-7872

Hassibe, Wendy, *Librn,* United States Geological Survey, Public Inquiries Office Library, Salt Lake City UT. 801-524-5652

Hasskarl, Mark P, *Librn,* Brookfield Library, Brookfield Center CT. 203-775-6241

Hassler, Bert G, *Med Staff Libr Chmn,* Methodist Hospital of California, Medical Staff Library, Arcadia CA. 213-445-4441

Hassler, William B, *Librn,* United States Navy (Barbers Point Station Library), Barbers Point HI. 684-4222 & 684-5217

Hassler, William B, *Librn,* United States Navy (Station Library), Barbers Point HI. 808-999-0497

Hasten, Dorris, *Librn,* Alpha Municipal Library, Robstown TX. 512-387-2341

Hastie, Marie T, *Asst Librn,* Boston College, Weston Observatory, Catherine B O'Connor Library, Weston MA. 617-899-9050

Hastings, Annabell, *Librn,* Taylor Library, Derry NH. 603-432-7186

Hastings, Barbara, *Ch,* Allegany Public Library, Allegany NY. 716-373-1056

Hastings, Carolyn, *Tech Serv,* Framingham Public Library, Framingham MA. 617-879-3570

Hastings, Diane, *Cat,* Little Rock Township Public Library, Plano IL. 312-552-3310

Hastings, Henry, *Ref,* Gary Public Library, Gary IN. 219-886-2484

Hastings, John P, *Dir,* Paris Public Library, Paris TX. 214-785-8531

Hastings, Joy, *Mgr, Info Ctr, On-Line Search Coordr & Bibliog Instr,* Hunt Wesson Foods, Information Center, Fullerton CA. 714-871-2100

Hastings, Lois, *Asst Dir,* Keene Public Library, Keene NH. 603-352-0157

Hastings, M E, *Asst Librn,* British Columbia Government, Legislative Library, Victoria BC. 604-387-6500

Hastings, Mazie, *Independent Study Ctr,* Chabot College, Learning Resource Center, Hayward CA. 415-786-6762

Hastings, Mrs Pat, *Librn,* Argie Cooper Public Library, Shelbyville TN. 615-684-7323

Hastings, Pamela, *Librn,* Gillette Co, Personal Care Div, Boston MA. 617-463-2800

Hastings, Richard, *Librn,* Tuolumne County Free Public Library, Sonora CA. 209-532-7842

Hastings, Richard, *Cat,* Winona State University, Maxwell Library, Winona MN. 507-457-2040

Hastings, Virginia, *Asst Librn,* Plainville Public Library, Plainville MA. 617-695-1784

Hastreiter, Jamie, *Librn,* Amherst Public Library (Clearfield), Williamsville NY. 716-688-4955

Hasty, Sharon, *In Charge,* Texas Education Agency (Region X), Richardson TX. 214-231-6301

Haswell, Hollee, *Librn,* Worcester Art Museum Library, Worcester MA. 617-799-4406

Haszel, Marcia, *ILL & Ref,* Marshfield Free Library, Marshfield WI. 715-384-2929, 387-1302

Hatch, Benton, *Spec Coll,* University of Massachusetts at Amherst Library, Amherst MA. 413-545-0284

Hatch, Ednamae, *Asst Dir,* Converse County Library, Douglas WY. 307-358-3644

Hatch, Elizabeth, *Librn,* Walden Public Library, Walden VT. 802-563-2472

Hatch, Eugene, *Media,* Lakewood Public Library, Lakewood OH. 216-226-8275

Hatch, Jane, *Dir,* Dodge City Public Library, Dodge City KS. 316-225-0248

Hatch, Lucile, *Instr,* University of Denver, Graduate School of Librarianship and Information Management, CO. 303-753-2557

Hatch, Orin, *Dir,* New Mexico Junior College, Pannell Library & Instructional Resources Center, Hobbs NM. 505-392-6526, Ext 231 & 233

Hatch, Wendalyn R, *Ad,* Greenfield Public Library, Greenfield MA. 413-772-0989, 772-6305

Hatcher, Danny R, *Dir,* Country Music Foundation Inc Library & Media Center, Nashville TN. 615-256-7008

Hatcher, Evelyn, *ILL,* Hurst Public Library, Hurst TX. 817-485-5320

Hatcher, Joanne, *On-Line Servs,* Clarke College Library, Dubuque IA. 319-588-6320

Hatcher, Kitty, *Admin Asst,* Petersburg Public Library, Petersburg VA. 804-732-3851

Hatchkiss, Flora, *Librn,* Minerva Free Library, Sherman NY. 716-761-6378

Hatfield, Betty K, *Assoc Prof,* Eastern Kentucky University, Dept of Library Science, KY. 606-622-2481

Hatfield, Charlotte, *Librn,* Kodiak Community College Library, Kodiak AK. 907-486-4161

Hatfield, Theda, *Bkmobile Coordr,* Norfolk Public Library, Norfolk VA. 804-441-2887

Hathaway, Anna R, *Actg Librn & ILL,* Shaw Memorial Library, Plainfield MA. 413-634-2252

Hathaway, Clara, *Librn,* Katahdin Public Library, Island Falls ME. 207-463-2478

Hathaway, James C, *Dir,* Leavenworth Public Library, Leavenworth KS. 913-682-5666

Hathaway, Janet, *Instr,* Dalhousie University, School of Library Service, NS. 902-424-3656

Hathaway, Kay, *Asst Librn,* JHK & Associates Technical Library (East), Alexandria VA. 703-370-2411

Hathaway, Kent, *Media,* Northland Pioneer College, Winslow Center Library, Winslow AZ. 602-289-5082

Hathaway, Nicola, *Libr Technician,* United States Army (Post Library), Watertown NY. 315-782-6900, Ext 2929

Hathaway, Richard, *Librn,* Dallas Christian College, C C Crawford Memorial Library, Dallas TX. 214-241-3371

Hathaway, Ruth C, *Bkmobile Coordr,* Edgecombe County Memorial Library, Tarboro NC. 919-823-1141

Hathaway, Theresa, *Cat,* Fiske Free Library, Claremont NH. 603-542-4393

Hathaway, Walter M, *Dir,* Columbia Museums of Art & Science Library, Columbia SC. 803-799-2810

Hathorn, Isabel V, *Librn, On-Line Servs & Bibliog Instr,* Suffolk Academy of Medicine Library, Hauppauge NY. 516-724-7970

Hatke, Rose M, *ILL,* Lewiston City Library, Lewiston ID. 208-743-6519

Hatt, Barbara, *ILL,* University of Calgary Library (Faculty of Medicine Medical Library), Calgary AB. 403-284-6858

Hattasch, Maureen, *Tech Serv,* Greenwich Library, Greenwich CT. 203-622-7900

Hatten, B G, *Librn,* Chevron USA Inc, Eastern Region, Petroleum Technical Library, New Orleans LA. 504-521-6369

Hatten, Cathy, *Librn,* Monroe County Library System (Newport Branch), Newport MI. 313-586-2120

Hatten, Judith, *Reader Serv,* San Jacinto College, Lee Davis Library, Pasadena TX. 713-476-1850, 476-1501, Ext 241

Hatten, V, *Librn,* Manitoba Museum of Man & Nature Library, Winnipeg MB. 204-956-2830, Ext 162

Hattersley, Marjorie, *Ch,* Bancroft Memorial Library, Hopedale MA. 617-473-7692

Hattie, Jean O, *Chief Librn,* Maritime School of Social Work Library, Halifax NS. 902-424-3760

Hatton, Rebecca, *Area Consult,* South Central Kansas Library System (Subregional Talking Book Library), Hutchinson KS. 316-663-5441, Ext 6

Hatton, William, *Sci,* Idaho State University Library, Pocatello ID. 208-236-3202

Haubrich, Jeanette, *In Charge,* Hallock Public Library, Hallock MN. 218-843-2401

Hauch, Monika, *Asst Dir,* Barrhead Elementary School Public Library, Barrhead AB. 403-674-2160

Hauck, Helen, *In Charge,* Cleveland Public Library (Science & Technology), Cleveland OH. 216-623-2935

Hauer, Barb, *Librn,* Western Plains Library System (Ortonville Branch), Ortonville MN. 612-839-2494

Hauer, Barbara E, *Librn,* Ortonville Public Library, Ortonville MN. 612-839-2494

Hauer, Liz, *ILL,* Westminster College, Reeves Memorial Library, Fulton MO. 314-642-6793

Hauer, Margaret L, *Dir,* Dayton & Montgomery County Public Library (New Lebanon Branch), New Lebanon OH. 513-687-2311

Hauer, Margaret L, *Librn,* Dayton & Montgomery County Public Library (Trotwood Branch), Trotwood OH. 513-837-1252

Hauer, Mathilda, *Librn,* Calmar Public Library, Calmar IA. 319-562-3010

Hauet, Gail, *Acq,* Ontario Public Library, Ontario CA. 984-2758 Ext 38

Hauet, Gail, *ILL,* Ontario Public Library, Ontario CA. 984-2758 Ext 38

Haug, Barbara, *Spec Coll,* Smith Memorial Library, Chautauqua Institution, Chautauqua NY. 716-357-5844

Haugaard, Anne, *Asst Dir, ILL & Ref,* Valley City State College, Allen Memorial Library, Valley City ND. 701-845-7276

Haugard, Dorothy, *Librn,* Van Buren County Library (Lawrence Branch), Lawrence MI. 616-674-3200

Hauge, Harris, *Dir,* Monmouth College, Hewes Library, Monmouth IL. 309-457-2031

Hauge, Marcia, *Ref,* Mesa Community College Library, Mesa AZ. 602-833-1261, Ext 291, 201

Hauge, Marcia, *Instr,* Mesa Community College, Library Technician Program, AZ. 602-833-1261

Haugen, Marjorie, *Govt Doc,* Winona State University, Maxwell Library, Winona MN. 507-457-2040

Haught, Alberta, *Ad & Ref,* Altoona Area Public Library, Altoona PA. 814-946-0417

Haughton, Claribel D, *Tech Serv & Cat,* Glencoe Public Library, Glencoe IL. 312-835-5056

Haugland, Palmer I, *Librn,* National Marine Fisheries Service, Fisheries Research Library, Auke Bay AK. 907-789-7231

Hauman, Bro Xavier, *Per,* Belmont Abbey College, Abbot Vincent Taylor Library, Belmont NC. 704-825-3711, Ext 342

Haumont, Corinne, *Librn,* University of Montreal Libraries (Chemistry), Montreal PQ. 514-343-6459

Haun, Barbara A, *Librn,* Illinois Department of Mental Health, George A Zeller Mental Health Ctr, Peoria IL. 309-691-2200, Ext 465

Hauptman, Leo, *Librn,* Jewish Community Center Library, Bridgeport CT. 203-372-6567
Hause, Aaron, *Dir, Doc & Ser,* Eastern Montana College Library, Billings MT. 406-657-2320
Hauser, Chris, *Acq,* University of Calgary Library (Faculty of Medicine Medical Library), Calgary AB. 403-284-6858
Hauser, Mildred, *Doc,* Central State University Library, Edmond OK. 405-341-2980, Ext 494, 495 & 496
Hauser, Sister Bernadette, *Asst Dir, Ref & Rare Bks,* Sacred Heart School of Theology, Leo Dehon Library, Hales Corners WI. 425-8300 & 425-8301, Ext 27
Hausman, Albert, *Tech Serv,* Wallingford Public Library, Wallingford CT. 203-265-6754
Hausman, Patricia R, *ILL,* University of North Carolina at Greensboro, Walter Clinton Jackson Library, Greensboro NC. 919-379-5880
Hauth, Allan, *Ref,* Jackson Metropolitan Library, Jackson MS. 601-352-3677
Hauw, Katherine, *Librn,* Toronto East General & Orthopedic Hospital, Doctors' Library, Toronto ON. 416-461-8272, Ext 275, 276
Havecker, Marilyn, *Dir,* Little Ferry Free Public Library, Little Ferry NJ. 201-641-3721
Havelka, Melissa, *Ad,* Marshalltown Public Library, Marshalltown IA. 515-754-5738
Haven, Gertrude A, *Librn,* Porter Library Association, Coventry CT. 203-742-8416
Havener, J Michael, *On-Line Servs,* University of South Carolina, Thomas Cooper Library, Columbia SC. 803-777-3142
Havener, Jacqueline, *Libr Technician,* San Diego County Library (Santee Branch), Santee CA. 714-448-1863
Havens, Alice, *Librn,* Snake River Community Library, Blackfoot ID. 208-684-3063
Havens, Linda, *Librn,* Borgess Medical Center Library, Kalamazoo MI. 616-383-7000
Havens, Linda, *Librn,* Detroit Osteopathic Hospital Corp, Medical Library, Detroit MI. 313-869-1200, Ext 380
Havens, Marlene, *Circ,* Clearwater Public Library, Clearwater FL. 813-462-6800
Havenstein, Rebecca, *YA,* Royal Oak Public Library, Royal Oak MI. 313-541-1470
Haverstock, William W, *Cat,* California State University, Chico Library, Chico CA. 916-895-6212
Havey, Sallie A, *Librn,* Russell Memorial Library, Monkton VT. 802-453-2041
Haviaras, Stratis, *Curator of Farnsworth & Poetry Rooms,* Harvard University Library (Lamont Library-Undergraduate), Cambridge MA. 617-495-2450
Haviland, Virginia, *Chief, Children's Lit Ctr,* Library of Congress, Washington DC. 202-287-5000
Havill, Karen, *Librn,* Arlington County Department of Libraries (Columbia Pike), Arlington VA. 703-920-6440
Havist, Marjorie, *Chief Librn,* Seattle Central Community College, Instructional Resource Services, Seattle WA. 206-587-5420
Havlena, Betty W, *Ch,* Evening News Association, George B Catlin Memorial Library, Detroit News, Detroit MI. 313-222-2467
Havlik, Robert, *On-Line Servs,* University of Notre Dame Library, Notre Dame IN. 219-283-7317
Havlik, Robert J, *Librn,* University of Notre Dame Library (Engineering), Notre Dame IN. 219-283-6665
Havlin, Karen L, *ILL,* Jacksonville Public Library, Jacksonville IL. 217-243-5435
Havner, Michael, *Librn,* Brooklyn Public Library (Saratoga), Brooklyn NY. 212-455-3078
Hawbaker, Darrel, *Ch & YA,* Hastings Public Library, Hastings MI. 616-945-4263
Hawes, Vincent L, *Dean,* Salem State College, School Library Service Program, MA. 617-745-0556
Hawk, Miriam, *Librn,* Forsyth County Public Library (Reynolda Manor), Winston-Salem NC. 919-727-2948
Hawk, Steven, *Asst Dir Personnel & Br Coordr,* Akron-Summit County Public Library, Akron OH. 216-762-7621
Hawk, Wendy Ann, *Librn,* Youngstown Hospital Association, Health Sciences Library, Youngstown OH. 216-747-0751

Hawken, H A, *Librn,* Salmon Brook Historical Society, Reference & Educational Center, Granby CT. 203-653-2700
Hawkes, Alfred L, *Librn,* Audubon Society of Rhode Island, Hathaway Library of Conservation & Natural Resources, Providence RI. 401-521-1670
Hawkes, Elouise A, *Librn,* United States Navy (Naval Weapons Station Library), Concord CA. 415-671-5498
Hawkes, Sally, *Ch,* Bensenville Community Public Library, Bensenville IL. 312-766-4642
Hawkes, Warren, *Asst Librn,* New York State Nurses Association Library, Guilderland NY. 518-456-9352, 456-9354
Hawkesworth, Phyllis, *Librn,* Charlotte E Hobbs Memorial Library, Lovell ME. 207-925-3025
Hawkey, Teresa, *Librn,* Lexington Public Library (Emrath Lansdowne), Lexington KY. 606-269-6605
Hawkins, Andrea, *Dir,* Joplin Public Library, Joplin MO. 417-623-7953
Hawkins, Annelle R, *Acq,* University of Oklahoma MUniversity Libraries, Norman OK. 405-325-2611
Hawkins, Barbara, *Ad,* Burlington Public Library, Burlington IA. 319-753-1649
Hawkins, Cornelia, *Coordr,* Cottey College, Blanche Skiff Ross Memorial Library, Nevada MO. 417-667-5831
Hawkins, D, *Librn,* Scarborough Borough, Resource Center Library, Scarborough ON. 416-438-7215
Hawkins, Dorothy, *Librn,* Chicot Public Library, Lake Village AR. 501-265-5150
Hawkins, E G, *Bus Adminr,* London Public Libraries & Museums, London ON. 519-432-7166
Hawkins, Earlene, *Librn,* Scott County Public Library, Georgetown KY. 502-863-3566
Hawkins, Elinor D, *Dir,* Cove City Public Library, Cove City NC. 919-638-6363
Hawkins, Elinor D, *Dir,* Craven-Pamlico-Carteret Regional Library, New Bern NC. 919-638-2127
Hawkins, Elinor D, *Dir,* New Bern-Craven County Public Library, New Bern NC. 919-638-2127
Hawkins, Ellen, *Supvr,* Middlesex County Library (Lambeth Branch), Lambeth ON. 519-652-2951
Hawkins, Esther, *Acq,* Crawfordsville District Public Library, Crawfordsville IN. 317-362-2242
Hawkins, Jean V, *Librn,* Waukesha Memorial Hospital, Medical Library, Waukesha WI. 414-544-2150
Hawkins, Jo Anne, *Circ,* University of Texas Libraries (Perry-Castaneda Library (Main Library)), Austin TX. 512-471-3811
Hawkins, Laura, *Acq & Cat,* American Arbitration Association, Eastman Arbitration Library, New York NY. 212-484-4127
Hawkins, Linda, *Ad,* Bloomington Public Library, Bloomington IL. 309-828-6091
Hawkins, Maria, *Per,* Maryville College, Lamar Memorial Library, Maryville TN. 615-982-1200
Hawkins, Mary, *Asst Dean,* University of Kansas Libraries, Watson Memorial Library, Lawrence KS. 913-864-3601
Hawkins, Mrs S, *Librn,* Bureau of Municipal Research Library, Toronto ON. 416-363-9265
Hawkins, Ora, *Librn,* Pilger Public Library, Pilger NE. 402-329-6324
Hawkins, Patricia, *Librn,* Arapahoe Regional Library District (Walnut Hills), Englewood CO. 303-771-3197
Hawkins, Phyllis, *Librn,* Western Township Public Library, Orion IL. 309-526-8375
Hawkins, Phyllis D, *ILL,* Opelousas-Eunice Public Library, Opelousas LA. 318-948-3693
Hawkins, Roberta, *Ref,* College of the Desert Library, Palm Desert CA. 714-346-8041, Ext 258
Hawkins, Ronald A, *Cat,* United Theological Seminary Library, Dayton OH. 513-278-5817
Hawkins, Suzan, *Librn,* Mid-State Business School Library, Auburn ME. 207-783-1478, 783-1479
Hawkins, Verda M, *Librn,* Kennedy-Jenks Engineers, Inc, San Francisco CA. 415-362-6065
Hawkins, Verna, *Libr Specialist,* Washington Public Power Supply System Library, Richland WA. 509-375-5559
Hawks, Beverly, *ILL,* New Mexico Institute of Mining & Technology, Martin Speare Memorial Library, Socorro NM. 505-835-5614

Hawley, Brenda, *Asst Dir Non Public Serv,* Pikes Peak Regional Library District, Penrose Public Library, Colorado Springs CO. 303-473-2080
Hawley, Inez, *Br Libr Asst,* Ventura County Library Services Agency (Oak View Branch), Oak View CA. 805-649-1523
Hawley, Inez, *Br Libr Asst,* Ventura County Library Services Agency (Saticoy Branch), Saticoy CA. 805-647-1623
Hawley, Mary, *Acq,* Berea College, Hutchins Library, Berea KY. 606-986-9341, Ext 289
Hawley, Robert A, *Director, Libr & Archives,* Simsbury Historical Society Inc Library, Simsbury CT. 203-658-2500
Hawley-Williams, J, *Librn,* Madison Public Library (Sequoya), Madison WI. 608-266-6385
Hawn, Bertha E, *Dir,* Minerva Public Library, Minerva OH. 216-868-4101
Hawryliuk, Donald M, *Librn,* Sudbury General Hospital Library, Sudbury ON. 705-674-3181, Ext 238
Hawse, Bernice, *Librn,* Arpin Public Library, Arpin WI. 715-652-2660
Hawthorne, Donna, *Ad,* Charles H Taylor Memorial Library, Hampton Public Library, Hampton VA. 804-727-6234
Hawthorne, Flora L, *Librn,* John J Madden Mental Health Center, Hines IL. 312-345-9870
Hawthorne, Judy A, *Librn,* United States Army (TRADOC Systems Analysis Activity Technical Library), White Sands Missile Range NM. 505-678-3135, 678-1467
Hawthorne, June C, *Doc,* Michigan Technological University Library, Houghton MI. 906-487-2500
Hawthorne, Susan, *Cat,* Yolo County Library, Woodland CA. 916-666-8323
Haxton, Lynn, *Dir,* Ecology Information Center, Sacramento CA. 916-444-3174
Hay, Audry, *Asst Librn,* Carnegie Free Public Library, Rockwell City IA. 712-297-8422
Hay, Betsy, *Librn,* Bud Werner Memorial Library (Oak Creek Public), Oak Creek CO. 303-879-0240
Hay, E P, *Librn,* Ontario Legislative Library, Research & Information Services, Toronto ON. 416-965-4545
Hay, Gerald M, *Librn,* ITT North Electric Co Technical Library, Delaware OH. 614-548-4301, Ext 127
Hay, Henrietta, *Tech Serv & Cat,* Mesa County Public Library, Grand Junction CO. 303-243-4442
Hay, Isabel, *Librn,* Thorold Public Library (Allanburg Deposit Branch), Allanburg ON. 416-227-2042
Hay, Linda, *Asst Dir,* Shiloh Regional Library, Jackson TN. 901-668-0710
Hay, Linda, *Dir,* Springfield Town Library, Springfield VT. 802-885-3108
Hay, Pat, *Supvr,* Huron County Public Library (Wingham Branch), Wingham ON. 519-357-3312
Haycock, Laurel A, *Acq,* University of Minnesota, Duluth (Health Science Library), Duluth MN. 218-726-8585
Hayden, Ann, *Ch,* Ventress Memorial Library, Marshfield MA. 617-837-5035
Hayden, Ardith, *Asst Librn,* Elk Rapids District Library, Elk Rapids MI. 616-264-9979
Hayden, Arline L, *Admin Librn,* United States Navy (Naval Air Station Library), Moffett Field CA. 415-965-5000
Hayden, Carla, *YA,* Chicago Public Library, Chicago IL. 312-269-2900
Hayden, Dolores, *Ref & On-Line Servs,* Wayne Oakland Library Federation, Wayne MI. 313-326-8910
Hayden, Elizabeth, *Pub Servs,* Lansing Public Library, Lansing MI. 517-374-4600
Hayden, Elizabeth, *Adult Basic Educ,* Lansing Public Library, Lansing MI. 517-374-4600
Hayden, Frances, *Librn,* Hollis Social Library, Hollis NH. 603-465-7721
Hayden, Lee, *YA,* Madison Public Library, Madison WI. 608-266-6300
Hayden, Mabel B, *Librn,* Cumberland County Public Library, Burkesville KY. 502-864-2207
Hayden, Mae N, *Librn,* Taycheedah Correctional Institution Library, Taycheedah WI. 414-923-0440, Ext 83
Hayden, Maxine, *Acq,* Idaho State University Library, Pocatello ID. 208-236-3202

Hayden, Ron, *Pub Servs,* Huntington Beach Library, Information & Cultural Resource Center, Huntington Beach CA. 714-842-4481

Hayden, Sharon A, *Librn,* Nixon, Hargrave, Devans & Doyle Library, Rochester NY. 716-546-8000

Hayden, Sister Benita, *Librn,* College of Saint Scholastica Library (Instruction Material Center), Duluth MN. 218-723-6138

Haydon, Martha, *Librn,* Washington County Public Library, Springfield KY. 606-336-7655

Haydu, Mark, *AV,* University of Scranton, Alumni Memorial Library, Scranton PA. 717-961-7525

Hayduk, Duke, *Media,* Skagit Valley College, Library Media Center, Mount Vernon WA. 206-424-1031, Ext 111

Hayes, Bernice, *Librn,* Washington County Public Library (Belpre), Marietta OH. 614-423-8381

Hayes, Bonaventure, *Dir & Acq,* Christ the King Seminary Library, East Aurora NY. 716-652-8959

Hayes, Donnie, *Circ,* University of Maine at Farmington, Mantor Library, Farmington ME. 207-778-3501, Ext 225

Hayes, Carley P, *Librn,* City Library (East Springfield), Springfield MA. 413-733-6731

Hayes, Catherine D, *Asst Dir, Budget & Develop,* University of Rochester, Rush Rhees Library, Rochester NY. 716-275-4461

Hayes, Claudia, *Librn,* Argyle Free Library, Argyle NY. 518-638-8911

Hayes, Cynthia, *Librn,* Buffalo Courier-Express Library, Buffalo NY. 716-847-5380

Hayes, Dale P, *Chmn Educ Admin,* University of Nebraska-Lincoln, School Media Specialist Program, NE. 402-472-3726

Hayes, Deanne, *Librn,* Southern Prairie Library System, Altus OK. 405-477-1930

Hayes, Donatus, *Acq,* Northern Virginia Community College Libraries (Loudoun Campus), Sterling VA. 703-323-4657

Hayes, Donna, *Asst Prof,* Southern Arkansas University, School of Education Library Science Program, AR. 501-234-5120, Ext 260

Hayes, Edna S, *Librn,* Smithton Public Library, Smithton PA. 412-872-7398

Hayes, Eleanor, *Librn,* Mount Sinai Hospital, Sidney Liswood Library, Toronto ON. 416-596-4614

Hayes, Elizabeth, *In Charge,* Yale University Library (Engineering & Applied Science), New Haven CT. 203-432-4539

Hayes, Florence, *Librn,* Saint Charles Public Library, Saint Charles MN. 507-932-3227

Hayes, Frances, *Ch,* Dallas Public Library, Dallas OR. 503-623-2633

Hayes, Frank, *Per,* Harding University, Beaumont Memorial Library, Searcy AR. 501-268-6161, Ext 354

Hayes, George, *ILL & Ad,* Rodman Public Library, Alliance OH. 216-821-1410

Hayes, Gloria, *Librn,* Louisville Free Public Library (Parkland), Louisville KY. 502-772-1212

Hayes, Helen, *Bibliog Instr,* Chestnut Hill College, Logue Library, Philadelphia PA. 215-247-4210, Ext 238

Hayes, Hope, *Commun Servs,* Carbondale Public Library, Carbondale IL. 618-457-0354

Hayes, Jean E, *ILL,* Assumption College Library, Worcester MA. 617-752-5615, Ext 272

Hayes, Jeanne, *Asst Dir,* Byron Public Library District, Byron IL. 815-234-5107

Hayes, Joanne, *Asst Dir & ILL,* Marlboro College, Howard & Amy Rice Library, Marlboro VT. 802-257-4333, Ext 51

Hayes, John, *Media,* De Paul University Libraries (Frank J Lewis Center Library), Chicago IL. 312-321-7619

Hayes, June T, *Circ,* Winthrop College, Ida Jane Dacus Library, Rock Hill SC. 803-323-2131

Hayes, Katharine, *In Charge,* United States Army (Corps of Engineers, District Library Saint Louis), Saint Louis MO. 314-263-5675

Hayes, Kathern J, *Librn,* Economics Laboratory Inc, Information Center, Saint Paul MN. 612-451-5651

Hayes, L Susan, *Info Specialist,* Systems Engineering Laboratories, Development Technical Information Center, Fort Lauderdale FL. 305-587-2900

Hayes, Laura, *Curator,* Wyoming State Archives & Historical Department, Art Gallery Library, Cheyenne WY. 307-777-7518

Hayes, Louise, *Librn,* Clay County Public Library, Celina TN. 615-243-3442

Hayes, Lynn, *Dir,* Oakfield Public Library, Oakfield WI. 414-583-4400

Hayes, Mary, *Librn,* Reagan County Library, Big Lake TX. 915-884-2854

Hayes, Mary E, *Ref,* University of Detroit Library (Law), Detroit MI. 313-961-5444, Ext 239, 240 & 241

Hayes, Mary Ellen, *Librn,* Wray Public Library, Wray CO. 303-332-4744

Hayes, Mrs Philip, *Librn,* Ashland Public Library, Ashland NE. 402-944-7430

Hayes, Oliver R, *Dir,* Eastern Connecticut State College, J Eugene Smith Library, Willimantic CT. 203-456-2231, Ext 374, 422

Hayes, R M, *Dean,* University of California at Los Angeles, Graduate School of Library & Information Science, CA. 213-825-4351

Hayes, Richard E, *Dir,* Paul Pratt, Memorial Library, Cohasset MA. 617-383-1348

Hayes, Robert, *ILL,* Norwich University, Henry Prescott Chaplin Memorial Library, Northfield VT. 802-485-5011, Ext 48

Hayes, Rose Marie, *Librn,* Los Angeles Public Library System (North Hollywood Branch), North Hollywood CA. 213-766-7185

Hayes, Sherman, *Asst to the Dir,* University of North Dakota, Chester Fritz Library, Grand Forks ND. 701-777-2617

Hayes, Stephen M, *Doc,* University of Notre Dame Library, Notre Dame IN. 219-283-7317

Hayes, Susan, *ILL,* Auburn University at Montgomery Library, Montgomery AL. 205-279-9110, Ext 247

Hayes, William F, *Dir,* Boise Public Library & Information Center, Boise ID. 208-384-4466

Hayes, William F, *Regional Dir,* Southwestern Idaho Regional Library System, Boise ID. 208-384-4269

Hayman, Maude, *Librn,* New York Public Library (Van Nest), New York NY. 212-829-5864

Hayman, Mrs D F, *Dir,* Shelton Township Library, Shelton NE. 308-647-5182

Haymond, Jay M, *Coordr,* Utah State Historical Society Library, Salt Lake City UT. 801-533-5808, 533-5809

Haymond, Phillip M, *Chief Field Servs,* United States Department of the Interior, Natural Resources Library, Washington DC. 202-343-5821

Haynes, Charlotte, *Dir,* Whiting Public Library, Whiting IN. 219-659-0269, 659-0320

Haynes, Donald, *State Librn,* Virginia State Library, Richmond VA. 804-786-8929

Haynes, Kathleen, *Cat,* University of Oklahoma Health Sciences Center Library, Oklahoma City OK. 405-271-2285

Haynes, Linda C, *Asst Dir,* Wilkinsburg Public Library, Pittsburgh PA. 412-244-2940

Haynes, Margaret C, *Ch,* Laurens County Library, Laurens SC. 803-984-0596

Haynes, Michael J, *Librn,* Parsons State Hospital & Training Center Libraries (Medical Library), Parsons KS. 316-421-6550

Haynes, Pat, *Instr,* University of Georgia, Dept of Educational Media & Librarianship, GA. 404-542-3810

Haynes, Pervy, *Librn,* Virginian-Pilot & Ledger-Star Library, Norfolk VA. 804-446-2243

Haynes, Roberta, *Librn,* Camden Township Public Library, Camden MI. 517-368-5554

Haynie, Opal, *Librn,* Robert L Williams Public Library, Durant OK. 405-924-3486

Haynie, Violet, *Librn,* Bedford Public Library, Bedford IA. 712-523-2828

Haynie, Virginia, *Cat & On-Line Servs,* Pan American University, Learning Resource Center, Edinburg TX. 512-381-2751

Haynsworth, Joanne, *Acq,* Lake Worth Public Library, Lake Worth FL. 305-585-9882

Hayre, Wanda S, *Ch,* Deer Park Public Library, Deer Park TX. 713-479-5276

Hays, Annie M, *Librn,* Texas Woman's University (Curriculum Materials Center), Denton TX. 817-382-1558

Hays, Carl, *Tech Serv,* University of Maryland at College Park (University Libraries), College Park MD. 301-454-3011

Hays, Carol, *Circ,* Indiana University at Bloomington, University Libraries, Bloomington IN. 812-337-3403

Hays, Celia, *Librn,* Rockwall County Library, Rockwall TX. 214-722-6027

Hays, Dorothy, *Librn,* Mobile Press Register, Inc Library, Mobile AL. 205-433-1551

Hays, Edwina P, *Asst Dir & Cat,* Emmet O'neal Library, Mountain Brook AL. 205-879-0459

Hays, Lynne M, *Librn,* Santa Cruz County Law Library, Santa Cruz CA. 408-425-2211

Hays, Mary J, *Librn,* Cooley, Godward, Castro, Huddleson & Tatum Library, San Francisco CA. 415-981-5252

Hays, Patricia L, *Librn,* Monroeville Public Library, Monroeville PA. 412-372-0500

Hays, Patsy, *Cat,* Alamogordo Public Library, Alamogordo NM. 505-437-9058

Hays, Robert M, *Dir,* Austin Public Library, Austin MN. 507-433-2391

Hays, Timothy, *Chief Librn, On-Line Servs & Bibliog Instr,* United States Army (Corps of Engineers; NED Technical Library), Waltham MA. 617-894-2400, Ext 349

Haysley, Frances, *Librn,* United States Air Force (George Air Force Base Library), George AFB CA. 714-269-1110

Hayslip, H, *Librn,* Fort Erie Public Library (Stevensville Branch), Stevensville ON. 416-382-2051

Hayslip, Paula, *Ch,* Little Dixie Regional Libraries, Moberly MO. 816-263-4426

Hayter, Ursula, *Librn,* Immaculate Heart of Mary Parish Library, Los Alamos NM. 505-662-6193, 672-9061

Haythorn, J Denny, *Dir,* Whittier College School of Law Library, Los Angeles CA. 213-938-3621, Ext 24

Hayton, Elise, *Circ,* McMaster University, Hamilton ON. 416-525-9140

Hayward, Edward B, *Dir,* Hammond Public Library, Hammond IN. 219-931-5100

Hayward, Mattie, *Librn,* Carnegie Public Library (Tabor Memorial Library), South Fork CO. 303-852-3931

Hayward, Olga, *Hist,* Southern University Library, Baton Rouge LA. 504-771-4990, 771-4991, 771-4992

Hayward, Susan, *Tech Serv,* Maryland Institute College of Art, Decker Library, Baltimore MD. 301-669-9200, Ext 27, 28

Hayward, Thomas A, *Humanities,* Bates College, George and Helen Ladd Library, Lewiston ME. 207-784-2949

Haywood, Eleanor, *Lit,* Jacksonville State University Library, Jacksonville AL. 205-435-9820, Ext 213, 214

Haywood, Frances, *Librn,* Ferndale Public Library, Ferndale CA. 707-786-9559

Haywood, Henry, *Ref,* New York Law Institute, New York NY. 212-732-8720

Haywood, Madie, *Librn,* Montgomery County Public Library (Star Branch), Star NC. 919-428-2338

Hazel, Betty, *Librn,* San Jose Public Library (Almaden), San Jose CA. 408-268-7600

Hazel, Kathleen, *Librn,* Dunkerton Public Library, Dunkerton IA. 319-822-4610

Hazelett, Barbara W, *Admin Librn,* National Labor Relations Board Library, Washington DC. 202-254-9055

Hazelton, George, *Librn,* Chesterfield County Central Library (Bon Air Branch), Bon Air VA. 804-320-2461

Hazelton, Penny A, *Librn,* University of Maine School of Law, Donald L Garbrecht Library, Portland ME. 207-780-4350

Hazelwood, Audrey, *Asst Librn,* Ear Falls Public Library, Ear Falls ON. 807-222-3209

Hazelwood, Frances, *Librn,* Alice Public Library (Premont Public Library), Premont TX. 512-348-3815

Hazelwood, Sue, *Br Coordr,* Seymour Public Library, Seymour IN. 812-522-3412

Hazen, Dan, *Latin Am,* Cornell University Libraries (University Libraries), Ithaca NY. 607-256-4144

Hazen, Diane, *Librn,* Romulus Public Library, Romulus MI. 313-941-0775

Hazlett, Esther E, *Ch,* Parsons Public Library, Parsons KS. 316-421-5920

Hazlett, Florence, *Librn,* Memorial Presbyterian Church Library, Midland MI. 517-835-6759

Hazlett, Gwendolyn C, *Librn,* Warnock Hersey Professional Services Limited Library, La Salle PQ. 514-366-3100, Ext 246

Hazlett, Janet, *Art & Photog,* Rochester Institute of Technology, Wallace Memorial Library, Rochester NY. 716-475-2566
Hazlewood, Judith, *Dir,* Lambuth College, Luther L Gobbel Library, Jackson TN. 901-427-6743, Ext 14
Hazlewood, Judith, *Librn,* Lambuth College, Library Science Program, TN. 901-427-6743
Haznedari, Ismael, *Doc,* United States Army (Armament R & D Command, Scientific & Technical Information Div), Dover NJ. 201-328-2914
Hazzard, Rose, *Librn,* Kent County Library System (Plainfield), Grand Rapids MI. 616-361-0611
He'mond, Mary Catherine, *Planning Asst,* Shiawassee County Library, Corunna MI. 517-743-3421, Ext 278
Head, Anita K, *Dir,* University of Kansas Libraries (School of Law), Lawrence KS. 913-864-3025
Head, Clara, *Librn,* Concord Baptist Church Library, Clermont GA. 404-983-7272
Head, Jeanne M, *Acq,* Quaker Oats Co, John Stuart Research Laboratories-Research Library, Barrington IL. 312-381-1980
Head, John, *Assoc Prof,* Clarion State College, School of Library Science, PA. 814-226-2271
Head, Judith, *Librn,* University of Manitoba Libraries (Administrative Studies), Winnipeg MB. 204-474-8440
Head, Lavinia, *Ch,* Chestatee Regional Library, Gainesville GA. 404-532-3311
Head, Myrtle, *Librn,* Kendrick Memorial Library, Brownfield TX. 806-637-3848
Head, Suzie Nisson, *AV,* American River College Library, Sacramento CA. 916-484-8293
Head, Wylene, *Librn,* Central Florida Regional Library (Homosassa), Ocala FL. 904-629-8551
Headd, Sandra, *Librn,* Colonial Fiber Co Library, Manchester CT. 203-646-1233
Headley, Ava Dell, *Librn,* United States Department of the Army, Office of the Chief of Staff, Operational Test & Evaluation Agency, Technical Library, Falls Church VA. 703-756-2234
Headley, Charles, *On-Line Servs,* Teachers College - Columbia University Library, New York NY. 212-678-3022, 678-3020
Headley, Marston, *On-Line Servs & Bibliog Instr,* Northfield Public Library, Northfield MN. 507-645-7626
Headly, Doris, *Ad,* Contra Costa County Library, Pleasant Hill CA. 415-944-3423
Headly, Jacqueline, *Ad & YA,* Lake County Public Library, Merrillville IN. 219-769-3541
Headspeth, Dorothy W, *Librn,* Connecticut State Department of Education, Charles D Hine Research Library, Hartford CT. 203-566-2676
Healey, Charles F, *Asst Dir,* New Jersey Institute of Technology, Robert W Van Houten Library, Newark NJ. 201-645-5306
Healey, James S, *Dir,* University of Oklahoma, School of Library Science, OK. 405-325-0311
Healion, Sister Mary Stephen, *Ref,* Incarnate Word College, Saint Pius X Library, San Antonio TX. 512-828-1261, Ext 215
Healy, Barbara, *Librn,* University of Rochester (Management), Rochester NY. 716-275-4482
Healy, Dorothy, *Spec Coll,* Westbrook College Library, Portland ME. 207-797-7261, Ext 280
Healy, Eleanor F, *Exten Servs,* Henderson County Public Library, Hendersonville NC. 704-693-8427
Healy, Esther, *Librn,* Lisle Free Library, Lisle NY. 607-692-3115
Healy, Kathleen J, *Dir,* Ina Pullen Smallwood Memorial Library, Chickasaw AL. 205-452-3912
Healy, Sister Frances, *Dir,* Providence Hospital, Health Sciences Library, Washington DC. 202-269-4546
Healy, V M, *Dir,* Kemptville College of Agricultural Technology Library, Kemptville ON. 613-258-3414, Ext 256
Heaman, Ellen, *Ch,* Olean Public Library, Olean NY. 716-372-0200
Heaney, Howell J, *Librn,* Free Library of Philadelphia (Rare Book), Philadelphia PA. 215-686-5322
Heaphy, Mary Anne, *Dir,* Solvay Public Library, Solvay NY. 315-468-2441
Heaps, Irene D, *Dir,* Hershey Public Library, Hershey PA. 717-534-3406

Heard, Anita W, *Bus Mgr,* Orlando Public Library, Orlando FL. 305-425-4694
Heard, Charlene, *Librn,* Alton Telegraph, Editorial Department Library, Alton IL. 618-463-2573
Heard, Ernest, *Dir,* Belmont College, Williams Library, Nashville TN. 615-383-7001, Ext 253
Heard, Margaret, *Spec Proj,* Amarillo Art Center Library, Amarillo TX. 806-372-8356
Heard, Virginia, *Librn,* Madison Town & School Library, Madison NH. 603-367-8545
Heard, W G, *Dir,* Royal Canadian Military Institute Library, Toronto ON. 416-597-0286
Hearder-Moan, Wendy, *Librn,* Hamilton Law Association Library, Hamilton ON. 416-522-1563
Hearn, Beverly, *Acq,* Union University, Emma Waters Summar Library, Jackson TN. 901-668-1818, Ext 269
Hearn, Carolyn B, *ILL & Regional Coordr,* Westerly Public Library, Memorial & Library Association of Westerly, Westerly RI. 401-596-2877
Hearn, Elinor S, *Asst Librn,* Episcopal Church Historical Society Library, Austin TX. 512-472-4133
Hearn, Kay, *Syst Coordr,* South County Interrelated Library System, Westerly RI. 401-596-2877
Hearn, Linda, *Librn,* Jonesville-Arlington Public Library, Jonesville NC. 919-835-7604
Hearn, Mary, *Ch,* North Scituate Public Library, North Scituate RI. 401-647-5133
Hearne, Mary Glenn, *Rare Bks,* Public Library of Nashville & Davidson County, Nashville TN. 615-244-4700
Hearne, Mary Glenn, *Local Hist,* Public Library of Nashville & Davidson County, Nashville TN. 615-244-4700
Hearne, Phillip T, *Bkmobile Coordr,* Appomattox Regional Library, Maud Langhorne Nelson Library, Hopewell VA. 804-458-6329
Hearon, Pamela K, *Asst Librn,* University of Florida, Institute of Food & Agriculture Science, Agricultural Research Library, Lake Alfred FL. 813-956-1151, Ext 226
Hearst, Mrs Y, *Librn,* West Hill Collegiate Institute, H A C Farrow Library, West Hill ON. 416-282-1166, Ext 30
Hearst, Nancy, *Librn,* Harvard University Library (Fairbank (East Asian) Research Center), Cambridge MA. 617-495-3650
Hearth, Fred, *Reader Serv,* San Francisco State University, J Paul Leonard Library, San Francisco CA. 415-469-1681
Heartwell, Alison, *Exten Librn,* Central Rappahannock Regional Library, Wallace Memorial Library, Fredericksburg VA. 703-371-3311
Heasley, Leila L, *AV,* Cuyahoga County Public Library, Cleveland OH. 216-398-1800
Heater, Ann, *Asst Dir,* College of the Sequoias Library, Visalia CA. 209-733-2050, Ext 314
Heath, Claire, *Librn,* Atlanta Public Library (Adams Park), Atlanta GA. 404-755-4559
Heath, Dixie, *Pub Servs,* Tarrant County Junior College Library System (South Campus Learning Resource Center), Fort Worth TX. 817-534-4861, Ext 223
Heath, Fred, *Asst Dir,* Radford University, John Preston McConnell Library, Radford VA. 703-731-5471, 5472
Heath, Mrs William, *Dir,* Monmouth Beach Library, Monmouth Beach NJ. 201-229-1187
Heath, Rebekah, *Cat,* Jefferson Community College, Learning Resources Center, Louisville KY. 502-584-0181, Ext 305
Heath, Susan L, *Ref,* Nicolet College & Technical Institute, Learning Resources Center, Rhinelander WI. 715-369-4429
Heath, Thomas, *Tech Serv & Cat,* Lexington Public Library, Lexington KY. 606-252-8871
Heatherly-Kelo, Babbette, *Bus Mgr,* DuPage Library System, Geneva IL. 312-232-8457
Heaton, John, *Acq,* Appalachian State University, Carol Grotnes Belk Library, Boone NC. 704-262-2186
Heaton, Mary, *On-Line Servs,* Sun Co, Library & Information Service, Marcus Hook PA. 215-447-1723
Heavenrich, D, *Asst Librn,* Gillette Research Institute, Technical Library, Rockville MD. 301-424-2000

Hebblethwaite, Norman, *Dir,* Cambridge Municipal Public Library, Cambridge ON. 519-621-0460
Hebeisen, Louise, *In Charge,* Swanville Library, Swanville MN. 612-547-2246
Hebel, John, *Ad,* Danbury Public Library, Danbury CT. 203-797-4505
Hebel, Vera, *Dir,* Holden Public Library, Holden MO. 816-732-4545
Heber, Violet, *ILL,* Medical College of Pennsylvania, Florence A Moore Library of Medicine, Philadelphia PA. 215-842-6910
Hebert, Carolyn, *Ch,* Montgomery County Library, Conroe TX. 713-756-4486
Hebert, Fernande, *Librn,* Maricopa County General Hospital, Medical Library, Phoenix AZ. 602-267-5197
Hebert, Frances, *Librn,* Hooksett Public Library, Hooksett NH. 603-668-1888
Hebert, Francoise, *Librn,* Canadian National Institute for the Blind Library, Toronto ON. 416-486-2579
Hebert, J Andre, *Librn,* Vanier Public Library, Vanier ON. 613-745-0861, 745-4908
Hebert, Janice, *Librn,* Consort Public Library, Consort AB. 403-577-3654
Hebert, Mary, *Librn,* Blue Cross Hospital Service Library, Saint Louis MO. 314-658-4444
Hebert, Mrs Martin, *Librn,* Meekins Library, Williamsburg MA. 413-268-7472
Hebert, R Vivian, *Librn,* United States Department of the Army, Judge Advocate General's School Law Library, Charlottesville VA. 804-293-9824
Hebner, James, *Media,* Clark Technical College, Learning Resource Center, Springfield OH. 513-325-0691, Ext 66
Hebron, Katherine, *Librn,* Tillamook County Public Library (Pacific City-Woods Branch), Pacific City OR. 503-965-6163
Hecht, James, *Hist,* Austin Public Library, Austin TX. 512-472-5433
Hecht, James M, *Dir,* Hoyt Library, Kingston PA. 717-287-2013
Hecht, Joseph A, *Ref,* Denison University, William Howard Doane Library, Granville OH. 614-587-0810, Ext 225
Hecht, Rachel, *Librn,* United States Department of Justice Library (Tax Division), Washington DC. 202-633-2819
Heck, Helen A, *Librn,* Delmont Public Library, Delmont PA. 412-468-5329
Heck, Mildred, *Circ & Doc,* Mary H Weir Public Library, Weirton WV. 304-748-7070
Heck, Ruth S, *Librn,* Mercer Township Free Public Library, Aledo IL. 309-582-2032
Heck, Thomas, *Librn,* Ohio State University Libraries (Music Library), Columbus OH. 614-422-2319
Heckard, David C, *Mgr Patents & Tech Info Servs,* Armco, Inc, Technical Information Services, Middletown OH. 513-425-2596
Heckel, Alice, *Dir,* Prescott Public Library, Prescott WI. 715-262-5544
Heckel, Florence, *Dir,* River Edge Free Public Library, River Edge NJ. 201-261-1663
Heckel, John W, *Librn,* Santa Clara County Law Library, San Jose CA. 408-299-3567
Hecker, Frances, *Librn,* Tulane University of Louisiana (Architecture), New Orleans LA. 504-865-4409
Heckman, A M, *Ref,* Stratford Public Library, Stratford ON. 519-271-0220
Heckman, Marlin L, *Librn,* University of La Verne, W I T Hoover Memorial Library, La Verne CA. 714-593-3511
Hedberg, Hilding, *Ref,* Fall River Public Library, Fall River MA. 617-676-8541
Hedden, Dorothy, *Asst Dir,* Allegany Public Library, Allegany NY. 716-373-1056
Hedderick, Alice Marie, *Librn,* Anglican Church of Canada Library, Toronto ON. 416-924-9192, Ext 291
Hedetniemi, Linda, *ILL,* Lynn Public Library, Lynn MA. 617-595-0567
Hedges, J, *Librn,* London Public Libraries & Museums (Northland), London ON. 519-451-8140
Hedges, Lois, *Tech Serv,* Phoenix College Library, Phoenix AZ. 602-264-2492, Ext 621
Hedges, Martha, *Ref,* Shelby County Library District, Shelbyville KY. 502-633-3803
Hedges, Michael, *AV,* Timberland Regional Library, Olympia WA. 206-943-5001

Hedin, Bonnie, *Instr,* Saint Cloud State University, Center for Library & Audiovisual Education, MN. 612-255-2022

Hedinar, Dagmar, *In Charge,* Becton, Dickinson & Co, R & D Information Services Library, Rutherford NJ. 201-460-3001

Hedler, Julie, *YA,* Palm Springs Public Library, Palm Springs CA. 714-323-8291

Hedley, Helen P, *Dir,* Mountain Lakes Public Library, Mountain Lakes NJ. 201-334-5095

Hedlund, Janet, *Librn,* Los Angeles County-University of Southern California (Women's Hospital Medical Library), Los Angeles CA. 213-226-3234

Hedlund, Jo, *Librn,* Ceresco Community Library, Ceresco NE. 402-665-2391

Hedman, Kenneth W, *Asst Dir,* University of Texas at El Paso Library, El Paso TX. 747-5683; 747-5684

Hedrick, David T, *Media,* Gettysburg College, Schmucker Memorial Library, Gettysburg PA. 717-334-3131, Ext 366

Hedrick, Donna, *Outreach,* Charles H Taylor Memorial Library, Hampton Public Library, Hampton VA. 804-727-6234

Hedrick, Donna M, *Librn,* Charles H Taylor Memorial Library (Phoebus Branch Library), Hampton VA. 804-727-6299

Hedrick, Dorine, *Librn,* California Energy Commission Library, Sacramento CA. 916-920-6468

Hedrick, Floyd D, *Chief, Procurement & Supply Div,* Library of Congress, Washington DC. 202-287-5000

Hedrick, Jane, *Librn,* Clermont County Public Library (Milford Branch), Milford OH. 513-831-0117

Hedrick, Lila F, *ILL & Circ,* Dallas Baptist College, Vance Memorial Library, Dallas TX. 214-331-8311, Ext 213

Hedrick, Margie, *Librn,* Dominy Memorial Library, Fairbury IL. 815-692-3231

Hedrick, Mrs P H, *Librn,* Schaller Public Library, Schaller IA. 712-275-4741

Hedstrom, Gladys, *Chief, Div Tech Servs,* Montgomery County Department of Public Libraries, Rockville MD. 301-279-1401

Heemstra, Linda, *Dir,* Bay County Library System, Bay City MI. 517-894-2837

Heeney, Brian, *Dir,* Trent University, Thomas J Bata Library, Peterborough ON. 705-748-1550

Heer, Lynn, *Ref,* State Library of Ohio, Columbus OH. 614-466-2693

Heezen, Ronald, *Librn,* Davis County Library (North), Clearfield UT. 801-825-6662

Hefferman, Sarah T, *Dir,* Somers Point Public Library, Somers Point NJ. 609-927-7113

Heffernan, Steve, *Librn,* Campbell-Mithun, Inc, Research Library, Chicago IL. 312-565-3968

Heffernan, T L, *Supvr,* Texas State Parks & Wildlife Department, Marine Laboratory Library, Rockport TX. 512-729-2328

Heffernan, Virginia, *Dir,* Scituate Town Library, Scituate MA. 617-545-6600

Heffington, Carl, *Br Coordr,* Horry County Memorial Library, Conway SC. 803-248-4898

Heffron, Paul T, *Actg Chief, Mss Div,* Library of Congress, Washington DC. 202-287-5000

Hefley, Mary Lu, *Asst Dir & Acq,* Saint Mary Parish Library, Franklin LA. 318-828-5364

Heflin, Betty, *Librn,* Montgomery County Department of Public Libraries (Wheaton Branch), Wheaton MD. 301-949-4773

Heflin, Evelyn P, *Librn,* Case-Halstead Public Library, Carlyle IL. 618-594-3309

Hefzallah, Mona, *Cat,* Fairfield University, Gustav & Dagmar Nyselius Library, Fairfield CT. 203-255-5411, Ext 2451

Hegarty, Kathleen G, *Staff Off for Prog,* Boston Public Library, Eastern Massachusetts Library System, Boston MA. 617-536-5400

Hegarty, Kevin, *Dir,* Tacoma Public Library, Tacoma WA. 206-572-2000

Hege, Mrs Norman, *Librn,* Oxford Public Library, Oxford KS. 316-455-2222

Hegel, Richard, *Dir,* Southern Connecticut State College, Hilton C Buley Library, New Haven CT. 203-397-4505

Hegenwald, Shirley B, *Chief Librn,* Veterans Administration, Medical Center Library, Shreveport LA. 318-221-8411, Ext 382

Heggie, Grace, *Bibliog Instr,* York University, Scott Library, Downsview ON. 416-667-2235

Heggland, Christine, *Ch,* Killeen Public Library, Killeen TX. 817-526-6527

Heginbotham, Stanley J, *Chief, Foreign Affairs & Nat Defense Div,* Library of Congress, Washington DC. 202-287-5000

Heglund, Harry, *Librn,* Brainerd Community College Library, Brainerd MN. 218-828-2520

Hehl, Walter, *Minister,* Central Christian Church Library, Lexington KY. 606-233-1551

Hehr, Brenda, *Librn,* Muhlenberg Community Library, Laureldale PA. 215-929-0589

Heibeck, Jean, *Librn,* Johnson Matthey, Inc, Technical Library, West Chester PA. 215-648-8178

Heid, Greg, *Pub Info,* Chattahoochee Valley Regional Library, W C Bradley Memorial Library, Headquarters, Columbus GA. 404-327-0211

Heidamos, Betty, *ILL,* Delray Beach Public Library Association, Inc, Delray Beach FL. 305-276-6482

Heidbrink, Leora, *Librn,* Chester Public Library, Chester NE. 402-324-5202

Heideman, Carol, *Librn,* Public Library of Cincinnati & Hamilton County (Saint Bernard), Cincinnati OH. 513-641-3335

Heideman, Carol, *Librn,* Public Library of Cincinnati & Hamilton County (Elmwood Place), Cincinnati OH. 513-242-3790

Heideman, Mary Beth, *Librn,* Big Springs Public Library, Big Springs NE. 308-889-3482

Heidenblad, Carl, *Librn,* Putnam County Library, Hennepin IL. 815-925-7020

Heidenreich, Fred, *On-Line Servs,* University of Arizona Library (Arizona Health Sciences Center Library), Tucson AZ. 602-626-6121

Heidenreich, Ralph, *Librn,* Hawaii State Library System (Manoa), Honolulu HI. 808-988-6655

Heidgerd, Lloyd H, *Librn,* University of New Hampshire (Biology), Durham NH. 603-862-1540

Heidkamp, Mary K, *Librn,* Willow Branch Township Library, Cisco IL. 217-669-2312

Heidle, John, *ILL & Per,* Erie Community College-North, Library Resources Center, Buffalo NY. 716-634-0800

Heidler, Louise, *Dir,* Miami University-Hamilton Campus, Rentschler Learning Resources Center, Hamilton OH. 513-863-8833, Ext 232

Heidrick, Patricia A, *Dir,* Port Library, Beloit City Library, Beloit KS. 913-738-3936

Heidt, Donald P, *Tech Serv & Cat,* Livingstone College, Andrew Carnegie Library, Salisbury NC. 704-633-7960, Ext 61 & 62

Heiges, Mary J, *Dir,* Carver County Library System, Chaska MN. 612-448-2782

Heigh, Wilma, *Librn,* Grant County Library, Hyannis NE. 308-458-2218

Heikes, Joyce, *Librn,* Warren County Library (Smithshire Branch), Monmouth IL. 309-325-6691

Heikkila, Helen, *Ad,* Fairport Public Library, Fairport Harbor OH. 216-354-8191

Heilakka, Edwin, *Librn,* Curtis Institute of Music Library, Philadelphia PA. 215-893-5265

Heiland, Catherine, *Librn,* Bucklin Public Library, Bucklin KS. 316-826-3223

Heilbronn, Addie, *Assoc Librn,* Saginaw Health Sciences Library, Saginaw MI. 517-771-6846

Heilbronner, Florence K, *Ad,* Bloomfield Public Library, Northwest Essex Area Library, Bloomfield NJ. 201-429-9292

Heileman, Gene, *Tech Serv,* Whirlpool Corporation Technical Information Center Library, Benton Harbor MI. 616-926-5323

Heiles, Ruth, *Cat,* Lindenhurst Memorial Library, Lindenhurst NY. 516-888-7575

Heilman, Marilyn, *Instr,* Morningside College, Library Science Dept, IA. 712-277-5125

Heilman, Tom, *Cat,* Morgantown Public Library, Morgantown Service Center, Morgantown WV. 304-296-4425

Heilmann, Caroline, *Ch,* State of Vermont Department of Libraries, Montpelier VT. 802-828-3261

Heilprin, Laurence B, *Emer Prof,* University of Maryland, College of Library & Information Services, MD. 301-454-5441

Heim, Carrie, *In Charge,* Texas Education Agency (Region XIII), Austin TX. 512-458-9131

Heim, Fern, *Libr Develp & Metrop Network Coordr,* Nebraska Library Commission, Lincoln NE. 402-471-2045

Heim, Kathleen, *Lectr,* University of Illinois, Graduate School of Library Science, IL. 217-333-3280

Heim, Keith, *Coordr,* Murray State University (Pogue Special Collections), Murray KY. 502-762-2291

Heimburger, Bruce, *Exten Librn,* Anderson County Library, Anderson SC. 803-225-1429

Heimer, Alice, *Librn,* Gypsum Public Library, Gypsum KS. 913-536-4296

Heimer, Delphine, *Librn,* Sperry Rand Corp, Sperry New Holland Marketing Research Library, New Holland PA. 717-354-1707

Hein, Elaine, *ILL,* Scott County Library, Eldridge IA. 319-285-4794

Hein, John M, *Tech Serv,* University of North Florida Library, Jacksonville FL. 904-646-2553

Hein, Mabel, *Dir,* Columbus Public Library, Columbus WI. 414-623-2940

Hein, Mary, *Librn,* Northeast Wisconsin Technical Institute, Learning Resources Center, Green Bay WI. 414-497-3190

Heinan, Kathleen, *Ch,* Upper Saddle River Public Library, Upper Saddle River NJ. 201-326-2583

Heinbokel, Mary, *Librn,* Sacred Heart Hospital Medical Library, Yankton SD. 605-665-9371, Ext 284

Heindel, Allan J, *Librn,* Columbia Gulf Transmission Co, Engineering Library, Houston TX. 713-621-1200, Ext 333

Heindel, Marjorie, *Asst Librn,* Grafton Public Library, Grafton VT. 802-843-2404

Heinecke, Margaret, *Asst Librn,* San Diego County Library, San Diego CA. 714-565-5100

Heineman, Stephanie, *Asst Dir & ILL,* Middle Country Public Library, Centereach NY. 516-585-9393

Heinemann, Barbara, *Librn,* Lagrange County Library (Howe Branch), Howe IN. 219-463-2841

Heinemann, Beverly J, *Ch,* Blue Island Public Library, Blue Island IL. 312-388-1078

Heinemann, Kathaleen, *Instr,* California State University-Los Angeles, Library Services Credential Program, CA. 213-224-3765

Heinemann, Luba, *Cat,* Alma College Library, Alma MI. 517-463-2141, Ext 332

Heinemann, Margaret, *Tech Serv,* Rockville Centre Public Library, Rockville Centre NY. 516-766-6258

Heinemann, Sandra W, *Cat,* Hampden Sydney College, Eggleston Library, Hampden Sydney VA. 804-223-4381, Ext 190

Heinen, Bernadette, *Ch,* Dakota County Library System, Burnsville MN. 612-435-8111

Heinen, Margaret, *ILL,* Wayne State University Libraries (Arthur Neef Law Library), Detroit MI. 313-577-3925

Heinick, Barbara, *Circ,* Wofford College, Sandor Teszler Library, Spartanburg SC. 803-585-4821, Ext 396

Heinlein, A Randolph, *Dir,* Neptune Public Library, Neptune NJ. 201-775-8241

Heinlein, Doris, *Mgr Info Bank,* National Broadcasting Co (Reference Library), New York NY. 212-664-5307

Heinlen, William F, *Ref,* California State University, Fresno Library, Fresno CA. 209-487-2403

Heinoldt, Margaret, *Dir,* Galloway Township Library, Cologne NJ. 609-965-2791

Heinrich, Dorothy, *Spec Coll,* University of Wisconsin-Green Bay, Library Learning Center, Green Bay WI. 414-465-2382

Heinrichs, Bethal, *Librn,* Heppner Public Library, Heppner OR. 503-676-9964

Heinrichs, Jay, *Librn,* American Forestry Association Library, Washington DC. 202-467-5810

Heinritz, Fred, *Prof,* Southern Connecticut State College, Div of Library Science & Instructional Technology, CT. 203-397-4532

Heinritz, Mrs Robert, *Librn,* Prince of Peace Lutheran Church Library, Milwaukee WI. 414-483-3828

Heintzberger, Elizabeth A, *Librn,* Reddy Communications, Inc Library, Greenwich CT. 203-661-4800

Heintze, James R, *Librn,* American University (Record-Score, Music Department Library), Washington DC. 202-686-2162

Heintzelman, Susan, *Acting Head, Instrnl Support Servs,* Teachers College - Columbia University Library, New York NY. 212-678-3022, 678-3020

Heinz, Catharine, *Dir,* Broadcast Pioneers Library, Washington DC. 202-223-0088

Heinz, Joan, *Librn,* Minnesota Valley Regional Library (Henderson), Mankato MN. 612-248-3880

Heinzkill, Richard, *Humanities,* University of Oregon Library, Eugene OR. 503-686-3056

Heinzl, Gloria, *Librn,* San Jose Public Library (Alviso), San Jose CA. 408-263-3626

Heisch, Alice, *Librn,* Bellville Public Library, Bellville TX. 713-865-3731

Heisch, John, *Dir,* Oklahoma Historical Society (Division of Library Resources), Oklahoma City OK. 405-521-2491

Heiser, Lois, *Actg Librn,* Indiana University at Bloomington (Geology), Bloomington IN. 812-337-7170

Heiser, W Charles, *Dir,* Saint Louis University (Divinity Library), Saint Louis MO. 314-658-3082

Heisey, Leona H, *Spec Coll,* Lock Haven State College, George B Stevenson Library, Lock Haven PA. 717-893-2309

Heisey, Terry, *Librn,* Evangelical School of Theology Library, Myerstown PA. 717-866-5775, Ext 5

Heishman, Eleanor L, *Dir, Central Libr,* University of Cincinnati Libraries, Central Library, Cincinnati OH. 513-475-2218

Heisler, Helen P, *Librn,* Sargent & Lundy Engineers, Technical Library, Chicago IL. 312-269-3526

Heisser, David, *Doc,* Tufts University, Nils Yngve Wessell Library, Medford MA. 617-628-5000, Ext 235

Heiter, Patricia, *Ref,* Dawson College Library, Montreal PQ. 514-525-2501, Ext 297

Heitkemper, Elsie M, *Dir,* Joseph Mann Library, Two Rivers WI. 414-794-7121

Heitman, Elizabeth, *Asst Dir,* Norton Public Library, Norton KS. 913-877-2481

Heitman, Sheri, *Asst Librn,* Cameron Public Library, Cameron TX. 817-697-2401

Heitner, Anne S, *Mgr,* Batten, Barton, Durstine & Osborn, Inc, Information Retrieval Center, New York NY. 212-355-5800, Ext 101

Heitz, Ann, *Librn,* Joseph Patch Library, Warren NH. 603-764-5565

Held, Charles, *Dir,* Albion College, Stockwell Memorial Library, Albion MI. 517-629-5511, Ext 285

Held, F Jean, *Chmn,* Pittsburgh-East Hospital Library Cooperative, PA. 412-682-4200, Ext 373, 388

Held, F Jean, *Librn,* Western Pennsylvania Hospital, Medical Library, Pittsburgh PA. 412-682-4200

Held, Jonathan, *TV,* Mid-York Library System, Utica NY. 315-735-8328

Held, Patricia, *Per,* Western Pocono Community Library, Brodheadville PA. 717-992-7934

Held, Rosalie H, *Librn,* United States Air Force (Ellsworth Air Force Base Library), Ellsworth AFB SD. 605-342-2400

Helde, Joan P, *Librn,* Kennedy Institute (Center for Population Research Library), Washington DC. 202-625-4333

Heleine, Naomi, *Librn,* Saint Charles City County Library (Wentzville Branch), Wentzville MO. 314-327-4010

Helfand, Esther, *Asst County Librn,* Contra Costa County Library, Pleasant Hill CA. 415-944-3423

Helff, Peter A, *Librn,* Bergen Community College, Learning Resources Center Library, Paramus NJ. 201-447-1500, Ext 405

Helfman, Alyce, *Librn,* West Bloomfield Township Public Library (Westacres), Orchard Lake MI. 313-363-4022

Helfman, Richard, *ILL,* Cooper Union for Advancement of Science & Art Library, New York NY. 212-254-6300, Ext 323

Helfman, Richard, *Local Hist,* Cooper Union for Advancement of Science & Art Library, New York NY. 212-254-6300, Ext 323

Helfman, Sally, *Coordr,* New York Public Library (Donnell Library Center), Manhattan NY. 212-790-6447

Helfrich, Shirley, *Librn,* Southern Maine Library District, Portland ME. 207-773-4761

Helge, Brian L, *Assoc Librn,* Lutheran School of Theology at Chicago, Krauss Library, Chicago IL. 312-667-3500, Ext 226

Helgeson, Duane M, *Librn,* California Institute of Technology (Engineering Library), Pasadena CA. 213-795-6811, Ext 2421

Helgeson, Duane M, *Librn,* California Institute of Technology (Mathematics Library), Pasadena CA. 213-795-6811, Ext 2422

Helgeson, Duane M, *Physical Sci,* California Institute of Technology, Robert A Millikan Memorial Library, Pasadena CA. 213-795-6811

Helgeson, Duane M, *Librn,* California Institute of Technology (Physics Library), Pasadena CA. 213-795-6811, Ext 2422

Helgeson, Elzoe, *Ch,* Alexandria Public Library, Alexandria MN. 612-763-4640

Helgoe, Gayle, *Circ,* Bellingham Public Library, Bellingham WA. 206-676-6860

Helicher, Karl, *Dir,* Wolfsohn Memorial Library, King of Prussia PA. 215-265-5151

Hellard, Dorothy C, *Dir,* Maysville-Mason County Public Library, Maysville KY. 606-564-3286

Hellard, Ellen, *Field Servs,* Kentucky Department of Library & Archives, Frankfort KY. 502-564-7910

Helleloid, Nancy A, *Dir,* Rainy River Community College Library, International Falls MN. 218-283-8491, Ext 17

Hellen, Joan E, *Dir,* Museum of the Southwest Library, Midland TX. 915-683-2882

Heller, Louise A, *Librn,* Tri-State Regional Planning Commission Library, New York NY. 212-938-3313, 938-3314

Heller, Lynda R, *Chief Librn & Ad,* Medway Public Library System, Medway MA. 617-533-2461

Heller, Lynda R, *Librn,* Medway Public Library System (Dean Library), Medway MA. 617-533-2202

Heller, Paul, *Asst Dir, Ref & Bibliog Instr,* Norwich University, Henry Prescott Chaplin Memorial Library, Northfield VT. 802-485-5011, Ext 48

Heller, Susan, *Librn,* United States Department of Housing & Urban Development, Region II Library, New York NY. 212-264-8175, 264-1739

Hellerich, Janet, *Ch,* Richmond Public Library, Richmond CA. 415-231-2119

Helling, Jim, *Librn,* Iowa State Penitentiary Library, Fort Madison IA. 319-372-5432

Helling, Madelyn, *Syst Chmn,* Mountain-Valley Library System, Sacramento CA. 916-444-0926

Helling, Madelyn, *Librn,* Nevada County Library, Nevada City CA. 916-265-2461, Ext 244

Hellstrom, Kathleen, *YA,* Weber County Library, Ogden UT. 801-399-8516

Helm, Chris, *Ad & YA,* Brookfield Public Library, Brookfield WI. 414-782-4140

Helm, Helen, *Asst Dir,* Mount Vernon Public Library, Mount Vernon WA. 206-336-2418

Helm, Rebecca J, *Ref,* Marion Public Library, Marion IN. 317-664-7363

Helm, Thomas, *Head,* Erie County Library System (Lawrence Park), Erie PA. 814-889-0657

Helm, William, *Librn,* New York Public Library (Mosholu), New York NY. 212-882-8239

Helmbold, F Wilbur, *Dir,* Samford University, Harwell Goodwin Davis Library, Birmingham AL. 205-870-2748

Helmer, Catherine O'Connell, *Asst Librn,* Washington County Free Library, Hagerstown MD. 301-739-3250

Helmer, Nancy, *Asst Librn,* Binghamton Psychiatric Center (Professional Library), Binghamton NY. 607-724-1391, Ext 450

Helmick, Aileen, *Instr,* Central Missouri State University, Dept of Library Science and Instructional Technology, MO. 816-429-4835

Helmick, Catherine, *ILL & Ref,* Butte County Library, Oroville CA. 916-534-4525

Helmle, Isabelle, *Librn,* Life Bible College Library, Los Angeles CA. 213-413-1234

Helms, Faye, *Librn,* Western Plains Library System (Kerkhoven Branch), Kerkhoven MN. 612-269-5644

Helms, Frank Q, *Chmn,* Council of Pennsylvania State College & University Library Directors, PA. 215-436-2643

Helms, Frank Q, *Dir,* West Chester State College, Francis Harvey Green Library, West Chester PA. 215-436-2643

Helms, Mrs Leon J, *Librn,* Calhoun County Library (Sea Drift Branch), Seadrift TX. 512-785-4241

Helms, Susan J, *Tech Serv,* Veterans Administration, Medical Center Library, Montgomery AL. 205-272-4670, Ext 260, 261

Helmuth, Ruth W, *Adjunct Prof,* Case Western Reserve University, School of Library Science, OH. 216-368-3500

Helmuth, Vinita, *Ref,* Western Plains Library System, Clinton OK. 405-323-0974

Helquera, Byrd S, *Assoc Dir,* Vanderbilt University Medical Center Library, Nashville TN. 615-322-2292

Helsabeck, Rosemary E, *Librn,* Florida Third District Court of Appeal Law Library, Miami FL. 305-552-2900

Helsabeck, Wyat, *Lit,* Public Library of Charlotte & Mecklenburg County, Inc, Charlotte NC. 704-374-2725

Helser, Fred, *Asst Dir,* Franklin University Library, Columbus OH. 614-224-6237, Ext 52

Helton, Betty, *Librn,* Metropolis Public Library, Metropolis IL. 618-524-4312

Helton, Edith, *Librn,* Three Hills Municipal Library, Three Hills AB. 403-443-5140

Helton, Helen L, *Ch & Tech Serv,* United States Air Force (Academic Library), Wright-Patterson AFB OH. 513-255-5894

Helton, Sallie, *Librn,* Wayne County Public Library, Waynesboro TN. 615-722-5537

Heltsley, Gina, *Ref,* Hopkinsville Community College Library, Hopkinsville KY. 502-886-3921, Ext 39

Heltsley, Mary K, *Librn,* Faribault State Hospital Library, Faribault MN. 507-332-3274

Heltzel, Maggie, *Librn,* Fort Vancouver Regional Library (Washougal Community), Washougal WA. 206-835-5393

Helverson, Louis G, *In Charge,* Free Library of Philadelphia (Automobile Reference Coll (McKean, Snyder & Fahnestock)), Philadelphia PA. 215-686-5322

Helvey, Mary Sewell, *Cat,* Davidson College, E H Little Library, Davidson NC. 704-892-2000, Ext 331

Helzer, Charles A, *Head, Coll Develop,* University of Chicago, Joseph Regenstein Library, Chicago IL. 312-753-2977

Hemesath, James B, *Dir,* Huron College, Ella McIntire Library, Huron SD. 605-352-8721, Ext 231

Heminger, Carol, *Media,* Wood Junior College, Wood Memorial Library, Mathiston MS. 601-263-5352

Hemingway, Maurine O, *Cat,* George Washington University Library (Jacob Burns Law Library), Washington DC. 202-676-6646

Hemmer, Avis, *Librn,* Metropolitan Library System (Midwest City Branch), Midwest City OK. 405-235-0571

Hemming, Terry, *Circ,* Brigham Young University (Law Library), Provo UT. 801-378-3593

Hemmingsen, Louise B, *Dir,* Manlius Library, Manlius NY. 315-682-6400

Hemmingson, Robert, *Dir,* Fergus Falls Public Library, Fergus Falls MN. 218-739-9387

Hemmingway, Nancy, *Librn,* Marin County Free Library (Inverness Branch), Inverness CA. 415-669-1288

Hemphill, Frank, *Phys Fac,* Baltimore County Public Library, Towson MD. 301-296-8500

Hemphill, Frank, *Dir,* Portage Public Library, Portage MI. 616-327-6725

Hemphill, Jean F, *Assoc Dir,* Auraria Libraries, Denver CO. 303-629-2805

Hemphill, Lia, *ILL & Ref,* Ludington Public Library, Bryn Mawr PA. 215-527-1550, 525-1776

Hemphill, Mabel, *Cat,* Louisiana Tech University, Prescott Memorial Library, Ruston LA. 318-257-2577

Hemphill, Margaret, *Librn,* Gutekunst Public Library, State Center Public Library, State Center IA. 515-483-2741

Hemphill, Marjorie, *Asst Librn,* Marissa Public Library, Marissa IL. 618-295-2825

Hemphill, Phyllis, *Librn,* George H Stowell Free Library, Cornish NH. 603-543-3644

Hempleman, Barbara, *Dir,* Warren Wilson College Library, Swannanoa NC. 704-298-3325, Ext 45
Henberg, Agnes, *Ref & Spec Coll,* Albany County Public Library, Laramie WY. 307-745-3365
Hench, Joan M, *Ref,* United States Army War College Library, Carlisle Barracks PA. 717-245-4319
Henchey, Mary, *Librn,* Worcester Public Library (Billings Square), Worcester MA. 617-753-0114
Henderer, Carolyn, *Librn,* Bahai Reference Library of Peoria, Illinois, Peoria IL. 309-691-9311
Henderer, Edmond, *Librn,* Takoma Park Presbyterian Church Library, Takoma Park MD. 301-270-9831
Hendershot, Doris, *Librn,* Riverdale Presbyterian Church Library, Hyattsville MD. 301-927-0477
Hendershot, Jean, *Librn,* Mid-Continent Public Library (Robandee), Kansas City MO. 816-761-3382
Hendershott, Carmen, *ILL,* New School for Social Research, Raymond Fogelman Library, New York NY. 212-741-7906
Henderson, A L, *Systs Analyst,* Brandon Mental Health Centre, Reference & Lending Library, Brandon MB. 204-728-7110, Ext 231
Henderson, B, *Prof,* University of Alberta, Faculty of Library Science, AB. 403-432-4578
Henderson, Barbara, *Asst Librn,* Dillon County Library, Latta Library, Latta SC. 803-752-5389
Henderson, Beatrice, *Asst Librn,* Tulsa County Law Library, Tulsa OK. 918-584-0471, Ext 300, 301
Henderson, Betty, *Librn,* Barry-Lawrence Regional Library (Monett Branch), Monett MO. 417-235-7350
Henderson, Bob, *Br Coordr,* Richmond Hill Public Library, Richmond Hill ON. 416-884-9288
Henderson, Charles, *In Charge,* Texas Education Agency (Region IV), Houston TX. 713-868-1051
Henderson, D, *Librn,* University of Toronto Libraries (Faculty of Library Science), Toronto ON. 416-978-7060
Henderson, David, *ILL & Reader Serv,* Eckerd College, William Luther Cobb Library, Saint Petersburg FL. 813-867-1166, Ext 336
Henderson, Donald C, *Hispanic,* Pennsylvania State University, Fred Lewis Pattee Library, University Park PA. 814-865-0401
Henderson, Dorothy, *Librn,* New York Public Library (Westchester Square), New York NY. 212-863-0436
Henderson, Douglas, *Humanities,* Seattle Central Community College, Instructional Resource Services, Seattle WA. 206-587-5420
Henderson, Edith G, *Curator, Treasure Room,* Harvard University Library (Law School Library), Cambridge MA. 617-495-3170
Henderson, Elise, *Librn, Acq & Cat,* Macomb City Public Library, Macomb IL. 309-833-2714
Henderson, Ena, *Spec Coll,* Florence A Williams Public Library, Saint Croix VI. 809-773-5715
Henderson, Fay J, *Librn, On-Line Servs & Bibliog Instr,* Spartanburg General Hospital, Health Sciences Library, Spartanburg SC. 803-573-6220
Henderson, Floyd L, *Librn,* United States Forest Service, North Central Forest Experiment Station Library, Saint Paul MN. 612-642-5200
Henderson, Gail, *Ch,* Vicksburg-Warren County Public Library, Vicksburg MS. 601-636-6411
Henderson, Harriet, *Dir,* Tyler Public Library, Tyler TX. 214-595-4267
Henderson, Helen H, *On-Line Servs,* Veterans Administration, Hospital Library, Saint Louis MO. 314-652-4100
Henderson, James, *Librn,* University of British Columbia Library (Mathematics), Vancouver BC. 604-228-2667
Henderson, Janice E, *Librn,* Morgan, Lewis & Bockius Library, New York NY. 212-980-4562
Henderson, Jean K, *Librn,* Columbia Public Library, Columbia IL. 618-281-4237
Henderson, Joan, *Ch,* Nicholson Memorial Library, Garland TX. 214-494-7187
Henderson, John E, *Chief Librn,* Community Library of Castle Shannon, Castle Shannon PA. 412-563-4552
Henderson, Karen, *Librn,* Muskegon County Library (Montague Branch), Montague MI. 616-893-2675
Henderson, Katherine Slocum, *Dir,* Clark County Law Library, Las Vegas NV. 702-386-4011, Ext 4696

Henderson, Leonard, *Dir,* Great Western Sugar Co, Agricultural Research Center, Longmont CO. 303-776-5070
Henderson, Lynne, *Ref,* Meredith College, Carlyle Campbell Library, Raleigh NC. 919-833-6461, Ext 231
Henderson, Marie, *Dir,* John C Clegg Public Library, Central City IA. 319-438-6685
Henderson, Marie, *Bkmobile Coordr,* Lawrence County Library, Louisa KY. 606-638-4497
Henderson, Marjorie, *Mgr,* Xerox Corp, Xerox Office Products Division, Dallas TX. 214-689-6027
Henderson, Mary, *Librn,* Sutter County Free Library (Pleasant Grove Branch), Pleasant Grove CA. 916-655-3484
Henderson, Mary Emma S, *Dir,* Abraham Baldwin Agricultural College, Baldwin Library, Tifton GA. 912-386-3223
Henderson, Meg, *Librn,* Nicholson Memorial Library (Ridgewood Branch), Garland TX. 214-494-7103
Henderson, Mrs Earline T, *Acq,* Alabama Agricultural & Mechanical University, Joseph F Drake Memorial Learning Resources Center, Normal AL. 205-859-7309
Henderson, Mrs F M, *Librn,* Curtis Memorial Library, Wheatland IA. 319-374-5341
Henderson, Mrs S H, *Librn,* Travis Avenue Baptist Church Library, Fort Worth TX. 817-924-4266
Henderson, Myrna, *Ch,* New Hanover County Public Library, Wilmington NC. 919-763-3303
Henderson, Olga, *Asst Librn,* Merchantville School & Public Library, Merchantville NJ. 609-663-1097
Henderson, Pearl, *Librn,* Eagle County Public Library (Red Cliff Community), Red Cliff CO. 303-328-7311, Ext 255, 256
Henderson, Peggy, *Chief Librn,* Thompson Public Library, Thompson MB. 204-677-3717
Henderson, Robbie, *ILL & Ref,* Central Kansas Library System, Great Bend KS. 316-792-4865
Henderson, Robbye R, *Chief Librn,* Mississippi Valley State University, James Herbert White Library, Itta Bena MS. 601-254-9041, Ext 6340
Henderson, Robert M, *Chief,* New York Public Library (General Library & Museum of The Performing Arts (Lincoln Center)), New York NY. 212-799-2200
Henderson, Robert M, *Librn,* New York Public Library (Lincoln Center for the Performing Arts), New York NY. 212-799-2000
Henderson, Roberta, *Instr,* Northern Michigan University, Dept of Library Science, MI. 906-227-2250
Henderson, Roberta, *Ref & Bibliog Instr,* Northern Michigan University, Lydia M Olson Library, Marquette MI. 906-227-2250
Henderson, Rosemary, *Dir,* Coffeyville Community College Library, Coffeyville KS. 316-251-7700, Ext 32
Henderson, Ross, *Dir,* Vancouver Community College Libraries (Vancouver Vocational Institute Library), Vancouver BC. 604-681-8111, Ext 297
Henderson, Sallie, *Dir,* Scenic Regional Library of Franklin, Gasconade & Warren Counties, Union MO. 314-583-3224
Henderson, Sallie, *Librn,* Scenic Regional Library of Franklin, Gasconade & Warren Counties (Union Service Center), Union MO. 314-583-3224
Henderson, Sarah W D, *Dir,* Foster Public Library, Foster Center Library, Foster RI. 401-397-7930
Henderson, Sarah W D, *Dir,* Tyler Free Library, Foster RI. 401-397-7930
Henderson, Shannon J, *Asst Dir & ILL,* Arkansas Tech University, Tomlinson Library, Russellville AR. 501-968-0304
Henderson, Sister Joan, *Asst Librn,* Holy Family College Library, Fremont CA. 415-651-1764
Henderson, Sourya, *Librn,* American Cancer Society, Inc, Medical Library, New York NY. 212-371-2900, Ext 329-332
Henderson, Sue, *Librn,* Public Library of Columbus & Franklin County (Whitehall Branch), Whitehall OH. 614-231-6552
Henderson, Susan E, *Dir,* Parma Public Library, Hilton Public Library, Hilton NY. 716-392-8350
Henderson, Tom, *Librn,* Mississippi State University (Architecture), Mississippi State MS. 601-325-5370

Henderson, Vincent, *Ref,* Ventress Memorial Library, Marshfield MA. 617-837-5035
Henderson, Virginia, *Libr Technician,* San Diego County Library (Rancho Santa Fe Branch), Rancho Santa Fe CA. 714-756-2512
Henderson, Vivian, *Ch,* Ligonier Valley Library Association, Inc, Ligonier PA. 412-238-6451
Henderson, W R, *Dir,* Phoenix Public Library, Phoenix AZ. 602-262-6451
Hendeson, Kathryn L, *Assoc Prof,* University of Illinois, Graduate School of Library Science, IL. 217-333-3280
Hendey, Margery, *Dir,* Free Public Library of Hasbrouck Heights, Hasbrouck Heights NJ. 201-288-0488
Hendl, Valerie, *Librn,* Oregon State Hospital (Patients' Library), Salem OR. 503-378-2370
Hendley, David D, *Librn,* Bethlehem Steel Corp (Bernard D Broeker Law Library), Bethlehem PA. 215-694-2424
Hendon, Pamela, *Librn & On-Line Servs,* Reynolds Metals Co, Reduction Research Library, Sheffield AL. 205-383-7141, Ext 242
Hendrick, Marja, *Cat,* Olivet College Burrage Library, Olivet MI. 616-749-7608
Hendrick, Marlene, *Librn Blind,* Topeka Public Library (Subregional Library for the Blind & Physically Handicapped), Topeka KS. 913-233-2040, Ext 50
Hendrick, Mrs Ross, *Librn,* Carnegie City-County Library, Vernon TX. 817-552-2462
Hendrick, Paden, *Librn,* Piedmont Regional Library (Commerce Branch), Commerce GA. 404-867-2762
Hendrick, Susan K, *Librn,* Oklahoma State Department of Vocational-Technical Education, Curriculum & Instructional Materials Resource Center, Stillwater OK. 405-377-2000, Ext 260
Hendricks, Alice C, *Asst Librn,* Auburn-Placer County Library, Auburn CA. 916-823-4391
Hendricks, Avyce, *Ch,* Franklin-Johnson County Public Library, Franklin IN. 317-738-2833
Hendricks, Donald D, *Dir,* University of New Orleans, Earl K Long Library, New Orleans LA. 504-283-0353
Hendricks, Donnetta, *Bkmobile Coordr,* Portage County District Library, Hiram OH. 216-569-7666
Hendricks, Doris K, *Librn,* Young Men's Institute Library, New Haven CT. 203-562-4045
Hendricks, Dwight T, *Assoc Dir & Pub Servs,* Hiram College, Teachout-Price Memorial Library, Hiram OH. 216-569-3211, Ext 220
Hendricks, Epsy Y, *Librn,* Alcorn State University, Boyd Library, Lorman MS. 601-877-3711, Ext 221
Hendricks, James, *Doc,* Anoka County Library, Blaine MN. 612-784-1100
Hendricks, Leroy, *In Charge,* Texas Education Agency (Region VIII), Mount Pleasant TX. 214-572-6676
Hendricks, R H, *Tech Dir,* Singer Co, Link Division Technical Library, Binghamton NY. 607-772-3011
Hendricks, William, *Bus, Sci & Tech,* Tampa-Hillsborough County Public Library System, Tampa FL. 813-223-8947
Hendricks, Yoshi, *Cat,* University of Nevada-Reno, Noble H Getchell Library, Reno NV. 702-784-6533
Hendrickson, Charles, *Dir,* Mesa College, Learning Resource Services, Lowell Heiny Library, Grand Junction CO. 303-248-1436
Hendrickson, Doris, *Acq,* Radford University, John Preston McConnell Library, Radford VA. 703-731-5471, 5472
Hendrickson, Edna, *Librn,* Pasadena Star-News Library, Pasadena CA. 213-579-6300
Hendrickson, Faye, *Rare Bks & Spec Coll,* West Texas State University, Cornette Library, Canyon TX. 806-656-2761
Hendrickson, Mildred, *Ch,* Carleton A Friday Memorial Library, New Richmond Public Library, New Richmond WI. 715-246-2364
Hendriksma, Lois, *Librn,* Dorr Township Library, Dorr MI. 616-681-9678
Hendrix, Arthur, *Acq,* East Texas State University, James Gilliam Gee Library, Commerce TX. 214-886-5717
Hendrix, Carla, *Ref, On-Line Servs & Bibliog Instr,* Lesley College Library, Cambridge MA. 617-868-9600, Ext 170, 171

Hendrix, Jane, *Circ,* Georgia Department of Education (Div of Public Library Services), Atlanta GA. 404-656-2461

Hendrix, Mary, *Media,* Benedict College, Benjamin F Payton Learning Resources Ctr, Columbia SC. 803-256-4220

Hendrix, Ray, *Instr,* Wake Technical College, Library Technical Assistant Program, NC. 919-772-0551

Hendrix, T Cal, *Dir,* Kingsport Public Library, J Fred Johnson Memorial Library, Kingsport TN. 615-245-3141

Hendrix, Verne W, *Librn,* Grand Lodge F & AM Library & Museum, San Francisco CA. 415-776-7000

Hendrix, Wilma P, *Pub Servs,* Memphis State University Libraries, Memphis TN. 901-454-2201

Hendry, Helen I, *Librn,* Nova Scotia Research Foundation Corp Library, Dartmouth NS. 902-424-8670, Ext 176 or 177

Hendry, L, *Tech Serv,* City of Brampton Public Library & Art Gallery, Brampton ON. 416-453-2444

Hendry, Richard, *AV,* Southwest Georgia Regional Library, Gilbert H Gragg Library, Bainbridge GA. 912-246-3887, 3894, 3895

Hendsey, Susanne, *Dir,* Federal Trade Commission Library, Washington DC. 202-523-3871

Henebry, Agnes C, *Librn,* Decatur Herald & Review Library, Decatur IL. 217-422-7395

Heneger, Sharon, *Ch,* Douglas County Library System, Roseburg OR. 503-673-1111, Ext 310

Heneghan, James P, *Librn,* New York County Surrogate's Court Library, New York NY. 212-374-8275

Heneghan, Mary, *Regional Admin,* Boston Public Library, Eastern Massachusetts Library System, Boston MA. 617-536-5400

Heneghan, Mary A, *Regional Adminr,* Eastern Massachusetts Regional Library System, Boston MA. 617-536-4010

Henehan, Jr, Alva D, *Dir,* Saint Lucie County Library Systems, Fort Pierce FL. 305-461-5708

Heneisen, Jane, *In Charge,* Saint Paul's United Church of Christ, Educational Resource Center, Evansville IN. 812-425-1522

Henera, Maria H, *Librn,* Speer Memorial Library, Mission TX. 512-581-2136

Henfling, Erika, *Cat,* Okanagan College, Muriel Ffoulkes Learning Resource Center, Kelowna BC. 604-762-5445, Ext 293

Hengen, Jamie Lynn, *Asst Dir,* Biloxi Public Library, Biloxi MS. 601-374-0330

Henige, David, *Africa,* University of Wisconsin-Madison, Memorial Library, Madison WI. 608-262-3521

Heninger, Irene C, *Dir,* Kitsap Regional Library, Bremerton WA. 206-377-7601

Henington, David, *Dir,* Houston Area Library System, Houston TX. 713-222-4704

Henington, David M, *Dir,* Houston Public Library, Houston TX. 713-224-5441

Henke, Dan F, *Dir,* University of California, Hastings College of the Law Library, San Francisco CA. 415-557-1354

Henke, Esther Mae, *Head Libr Servs,* Oklahoma Department of Libraries, Oklahoma City OK. 405-521-2502

Henley, Carol, *Librn,* Texas Christian University (Acquisitions Division), Fort Worth TX. 817-921-7106, Ext 6126

Henley, Louise, *Librn,* Auburn University (Veterinary Medicine), Auburn AL. 205-826-4780

Henndon, Bonnie, *Librn,* Shreve Memorial Library (Atkins), Shreveport LA. 318-635-6222

Henne, Elva M, *Librn,* Roxbury Public Library, Roxbury KS. 913-254-7811

Henner, Ruthanne T, *On-Line Servs,* College of Physicians of Philadelphia Library, Philadelphia PA. 215-561-6050

Hennessey, Barbara, *Librn,* Milton Public Library (Kidder), Milton MA. 617-698-5299

Hennessey, Dorothy U, *Dir,* Wharton Public Library, Wharton NJ. 201-361-1333

Hennessy, Charlene C, *Coordr,* Delaware County Library Services Department, Media PA. 215-891-2625

Hennessy, Colm, *Ref & MEDLINE,* Rush-Presbyterian-Saint Luke's Medical Center (Library of Rush University), Chicago IL. 312-942-2271, 942-5950

Hennessy, David C, *Dir,* Le Sueur-Waseca Regional Library, Waseca MN. 507-835-2910

Hennessy, William D, *Tech Serv,* Louisville Presbyterian Theological Seminary Library, Louisville KY. 502-895-3413, Ext 52

Hennesy, Janet, *Asst Librn,* Minneapolis College of Art & Design Library, Minneapolis MN. 612-870-3291

Hennig, Florence, *ILL,* Mississauga Public Library, Mississauga ON. 416-625-8681

Hennig, Helen E, *Librn,* Alberta RCMP Century Library, Beaverlodge AB. 403-354-2569

Henning, Betty, *YA,* Public Library of Fort Wayne & Allen County, Fort Wayne IN. 219-424-7241

Henning, Joanne, *Ref,* Chabot College, Learning Resource Center, Hayward CA. 415-786-6762

Henning, Louise, *Ref,* University of Wisconsin-Madison (Kohler Art Library), Madison WI. 608-263-2256

Henning, Mrs Carl, *Spec Coll,* Martha Canfield Memorial Free Library, Arlington Library, Arlington VT. 802-375-6153

Henninge, Rose, *Dir,* Fairport Public Library, Fairport Harbor OH. 216-354-8191

Henninge, Rose, *Media,* Lake Erie College, James F Lincoln Learning Resource Center, Painesville OH. 216-352-3361, Ext 280

Henninger, Linda, *ILL & Govt Doc,* King College, E W King Library, Bristol TN. 615-968-1187, Ext 215

Hennings, Jr, LeRoy, *Dir,* Martin County Public Library, Stuart FL. 305-287-2257

Hennington, Betty, *Librn,* Fort Worth Public Library (North Branch), Fort Worth TX. 817-626-8241

Hennip, Susan, *ILL & Ref,* Edinboro State College, Baron-Forness Library, Edinboro PA. 814-732-2780

Henny, Jo Ann, *Librn,* Acadia Parish Library (Ross), Crowley LA. 318-788-1880

Henri, Muriel, *Librn,* Ogilvie Flour Mills Co Ltd, Food Research & Development Library, Montreal PQ. 514-866-7961, Ext 328

Henrich, F, *Doc,* State University of New York at Buffalo (Lockwood Library), Buffalo NY. 716-636-2816

Henrichs, Judy, *Admin Assts,* Southeast Kansas Library System, Iola KS. 316-365-3833

Henricks, Allen, *Coordr,* North Central Technical Institute, Holm Memorial Library, Wausau WI. 715-675-3331, Ext 293

Henrikson, Ellen A, *Librn,* Southwest Texas State University (Music Department), San Marcos TX. 512-245-2651

Henrikson, Jean M, *Spec Servs,* Navajo Community College, Naaltsoos Ba'Hooghan Library, Tsaile AZ. 602-724-6132

Henritze, Charles, *Cat,* Bristol Public Library, Bristol VA. 703-669-9444

Henritze, Wayne, *Librn,* Richard H Thornton Library, Oxford NC. 919-693-1121

Henrotte, Gayle A, *Librn,* Mississippi University for Women (Music), Columbus MS. 601-328-6202

Henry, Alice C, *Librn,* Community Relations-Social Development Commission, Office of Planning, Research & Evaluation Library, Milwaukee WI. 414-272-5600, Ext 335

Henry, Anita, *Cat & Ser,* Brigham Young University-Hawaii Campus, Joseph F Smith Library, Laie HI. 808-293-9211, Ext 260, 264

Henry, Betty, *Tech Serv,* Royal Oak Public Library, Royal Oak MI. 313-541-1470

Henry, Carol, *Per,* Grand Rapids Public Library, Grand Rapids MI. 616-456-4400

Henry, Charlene, *Asst Librn,* Chicago Board of Trade Library, Chicago IL. 312-435-3552

Henry, Diane V, *AV,* Public Library of the District of Columbia, Martin Luther King Memorial Library, Washington DC. 202-727-1101

Henry, Dorothy, *Dir,* Lamar Public Library, Lamar CO. 303-336-4632

Henry, Ellen, *Librn,* Loudoun County Public Library (Thomas Balch), Leesburg VA. 703-777-0323

Henry, Ginette, *Prof,* College de Maisonneuve, Techniques de la Documentation, PQ. 514-254-7131

Henry, Jean, *Tech Serv,* University of Alaska, Juneau Library, Juneau AK. 907-789-2101, Ext 126, 127 & 128

Henry, Jean B, *In Charge,* Alaska Legislative Affairs Agency, Reference Library, Juneau AK. 907-465-3808

Henry, Jerry, *AV,* Kokomo Public Library, Kokomo IN. 317-457-5558

Henry, Judy G, *Librn,* Saint Joseph's Hospital, Medical Library, Savannah GA. 912-925-4100, Ext 360

Henry, LaVieve, *Secy,* Fort Saint James Village Library, Fort Saint James BC. 604-996-7431

Henry, Lillian M, *Librn,* Brooklyn Library Association, Brooklyn CT. 203-774-0649

Henry, Margaret, *Librn,* Jonesboro-Washington County Library, Jonesboro TN. 615-753-4841

Henry, Marilyn, *Data Processing,* Vanderbilt University Library, Nashville TN. 615-322-2834

Henry, Paula M, *Acq,* State University of New York College at Geneseo, Milne Library, Geneseo NY. 716-245-5591

Henry, Peggy, *Librn,* Mid-Continent Public Library (North Independence Branch), Independence MO. 816-252-0950

Henry, Ruth, *Br Asst,* Timberland Regional Library (North Beach), Hoquiam WA. 206-289-3368

Henry, Shirley J, *Dir,* Hiawatha Public Library, Hiawatha IA. 319-393-1414

Henry, Theresa, *Res Librn,* Tracy-Locke Advertising & Public Relations, Inc Library, Dallas TX. 214-742-3131, Ext 422

Henry, Jr, Eugene B, *Dir,* Newport Public Library, Newport RI. 401-847-8720

Henry-Rousseau, Yvette, *Lectr,* University of Montreal, Ecole de Bibliotheconomie, PQ. 514-343-6044

Hensak, Nancy, *Asst Librn,* University of Colorado at Boulder (Institute of Arctic & Alpine Research Library), Boulder CO. 303-492-6387

Henschel, Clarice, *Commun Servs,* Scarborough Public Library, Scarborough ON. 416-291-1991

Henschel, David, *Philos & Relig,* Austin Public Library, Austin TX. 512-472-5433

Henschel, Susan M, *YA,* Middletown Township Public Library, Middletown NJ. 201-671-3700

Hensel, Janet, *Tech Serv & Cat,* New Brunswick Free Public Library, New Brunswick NJ. 201-745-5337

Hensel, Marliss, *Dir,* Wautoma Public Library, Wautoma WI. 414-787-2988

Hensel, Martha, *Sr Dir,* Citizens Library, Washington PA. 412-222-2400

Hensel, Mary L, *YA,* Allegany County Library, Cumberland MD. 301-777-1200

Hensel, Susan, *ILL & Circ,* Monessen Public Library, Monessen PA. 412-684-4750

Henseler, Barbara, *On-Line Servs,* National Defense University Library, Washington DC. 202-693-8437

Henseler, Barbara, *Econ & Energy,* National Defense University Library, Washington DC. 202-693-8437

Henshaw, Ernstlee, *Libr Technician,* San Diego County Library (Poway Branch), Poway C/.. 714-748-2411

Henshaw, Judith, *Librn,* Dedham Public Library (Endicott), Dedham MA. 617-326-5339

Henshaw, Mary, *Librn,* Exxon Chemical Co USA (B R Plastics Plant Library), Baton Rouge LA. 504-359-5296

Henshaw, Mildred G, *Librn,* Boynton Public Library, Templeton MA. 617-939-5582

Hensley, Charlotta, *Ser,* University of Colorado at Boulder (University Libraries), Boulder CO. 303-492-7511

Hensley, Eleanor M, *Dir,* Towanda Township Public Library, Towanda IL. 309-728-2176

Hensley, Jennifer, *Chief Librn,* Monroe County Library System (Lillian Stewart Navarre), Monroe MI. 313-241-5577

Hensley, Michael, *Media,* Western Wyoming Community College, Library Learning Resources Center, Rock Springs WY. 307-382-2121, Ext 154

Hensley, Paul B, *Archivist,* Mariners Museum Library, Newport News VA. 804-595-0368

Hensley, Peggy, *Librn,* Jonesboro-Washington County Library (Gray), Jonesboro TN. 615-477-3221

Hensley, Ruth, *Dir,* Julesburg Public Library, Julesburg CO. 303-474-2608

Henson, L L, *Dir,* Florida Institute of Technology Library, Melbourne FL. 305-723-3701, Ext 270

Henson, Muriel, *Librn,* Jeudevine Memorial Library, Hardwick VT. 802-472-5948

Henson, Patricia, *Cat,* Albany Dougherty Public Library, Albany GA. 912-435-2104
Henson, Patricia, *Librn,* Albany Dougherty Public Library (Tallulah Massey), Albany GA. 912-435-6105
Henson, S, *Librn,* Okanagan Regional Library District (Princeton Branch), Princeton BC. 604-295-6495
Henson, Virginia, *ILL,* Mid-Continent Public Library, Independence MO. 816-836-5200
Henthorn, Dorothy, *Cat,* Phillips University, Zollars Memorial Library, Enid OK. 405-237-4433, Ext 251
Henthorn, Mary Alice, *Librn,* Killgore Memorial Library (Britain Memorial), Sunray TX. 806-948-5501
Henthorn, Mary Alice, *Dir,* Killgore Memorial Library, Moore County Library, Dumas TX. 806-935-4941
Henton, Helen, *Librn,* Carnegie Public Library, Albany MO. 816-726-5615
Hentzel, Dorothy, *Librn,* New Athens Township Public Library, New Athens IL. 618-475-3255
Henwood, Marylyn, *Librn,* Wentworth Library (Carlisle Branch), Carlisle ON. 416-526-4126
Henze, Ronald, *Librn,* Evansville Public Library & Vanderburgh County Public Library (North), Evansville IN. 812-425-2621
Henzler, Martha, *Cat,* Luther College, Preus Library, Decorah IA. 319-387-1163
Hepler, Susan J, *In Charge,* Petrified Forest National Park Library, Petrified Forest National Park AZ. 602-524-6228
Hepner, Gwen, *Cat & Spec Coll,* Gettysburg College, Schmucker Memorial Library, Gettysburg PA. 717-334-3131, Ext 366
Hepp, Laurel, *Librn,* Pacific Science Center Library, Seattle WA. 206-625-9333, Ext 216
Hepp, Thomas, *Circ,* Grossmont College, Lewis F Smith Learning Resource Center Library, El Cajon CA. 714-465-1700, Ext 333, 334
Heppell, Shirley, *Librn,* Cortland County Historical Society Library, Cortland NY. 607-756-6071
Hepworth, Bobbee, *Librn,* Salt Lake County Library System (Holladay), Salt Lake City UT. 801-278-2808
Herald, Elsa L, *Librn,* California State Department of Rehabilitation, Rehabilitation Library, Sacramento CA. 916-445-9122
Herbel, Patricia, *Libr Servs & Elem Curric Coordr,* North Dakota Department of Public Instruction Library, Bismarck ND. 701-224-2281
Herber, Ann, *Librn,* Indianapolis-Marion County Public Library (Haughville), Indianapolis IN. 317-635-5662
Herbers, Janet L, *Asst Dir,* Saint Charles District Library, Hartley Memorial Library, Saint Charles MI. 517-865-9451
Herbert, Annette F, *Librn,* Kidder, Peabody & Co Inc, Reference Library, New York NY. 212-747-2504, 747-2505, 747-2506
Herbert, Bertie, *ILL & Ref,* Jacksonville State University Library, Jacksonville AL. 205-435-9820, Ext 213, 214
Herbert, Candace, *Ref,* Fergus Falls Public Library, Fergus Falls MN. 218-739-9387
Herbert, Dorothy, *Ref, On-Line Servs & Bibliog Instr,* Minneapolis Community College Library, Minneapolis MN. 612-341-7089, 341-7059
Herbert, Ella, *Libr Technician,* San Diego County Library (Woodlawn Park), Chula Vista CA. 714-426-3677
Herbison, Michael R, *Librn,* University of Colorado at Colorado Springs, Library, Colorado Springs CO. 303-593-3296
Herbrand, Dolly, *In Charge,* Foley Library, Foley MN. 612-968-6612
Herbst, Doris, *Librn,* Kohler School & Public Library, Kohler WI. 414-457-9401
Herbst, Jr, John F, *Dir,* Penn Valley Community College Library, Kansas City MO. 816-756-2800, Ext 428
Herch, Frank A, *Asst Librn & Bibliog Instr,* Georgetown University (Fred O Dennis Law Library), Washington DC. 202-624-8260
Herche, Karen M, *Dir,* University of Michigan (Business Administration Library), Ann Arbor MI. 313-764-1375
Herder, Vonda, *Dir,* Yates Center Public Library, Yates Center KS. 316-625-3341
Herdman, Deborah, *Ch,* Danville Public Library, Danville IL. 217-446-7420

Hereld, Gaby, *Asst Dir,* Bergenfield Free Public Library, Bergenfield NJ. 201-384-2765
Hergonson, Ruth, *Ch,* Commerce Public Library, Commerce CA. 213-722-6660
Heringer, Patricia G, *Dir,* Driftwood Library of Lincoln City, Lincoln City OR. 503-996-2277
Heriot, Caroline C, *Law Librn,* College of William & Mary in Virginia (Marshall-Wythe Law Library), Williamsburg VA. 804-253-4680
Heriot, Ruthanne, *Ref,* Mary H Weir Public Library, Weirton WV. 304-748-7070
Herkner, Donna, *On-Line Servs,* SCM Corporation, Dwight P Joyce Research Center, Technical Info Services, Strongsville OH. 216-771-5121, Ext 2260
Herl, Vickie, *Admin Asst,* Great Bend Public Library, Great Bend KS. 316-792-2409
Herling, John P, *Chief Librn,* Brooklyn College Library, Brooklyn NY. 212-780-5342
Herlinger, Margaret R, *Lectr,* Concordia University, Library Studies Program, PQ. 514-482-0320, Ext 324
Hermalyn, Gary, *Exec Dir,* Museum of Bronx History, The Bronx County Historical Society Library, Bronx NY. 212-881-8900
Herman, Alma, *Librn,* Free Library of New Hope & Solebury, New Hope PA. 215-862-2330
Herman, Barbara, *Ch,* Tuscarawas County Public Library, New Philadelphia OH. 216-364-4474
Herman, Claudene, *Librn,* Choctawhatchee Regional Library (Dale County War Memorial), Ozark AL. 205-774-5480
Herman, Gail, *Asst Librn,* Deseronto Public Library, Deseronto ON. 613-396-2744
Herman, Linda E, *Spec Coll,* California State University Fullerton Library, Fullerton CA. 714-773-2714
Herman, Linda M, *Librn,* Lakeland College, Vermilion Campus Resource Center, Vermilion AB. 403-853-2971, Ext 240
Herman, M, *In Charge,* University of Toronto Libraries (Institute of Child Study), Toronto ON. 416-978-3456
Herman, Margaret, *Asst Dir Tech Servs & Coll Develop,* Illinois State Library, Springfield IL. 217-782-2994
Herman, Sally Edwards, *Asst Dir,* Ormsby Public Library, Carson City NV. 702-882-5665
Herman, Steven, *Chief, Coll Management Div,* Library of Congress, Washington DC. 202-287-5000
Herman, Thelma, *Mgr Tech Info,* United Mineral & Chemical Corp, High Purity Materials Div Library, New York NY. 212-966-4330
Herman, Vivian, *Librn,* Bristow Public Library, Bristow OK. 918-367-6562
Hermann, Geraldine, *Actg Dir,* Belleville Public Library, Belleville IL. 618-234-0441
Hermann, Geraldine, *Librn,* Belleville Public Library (West Branch), Belleville IL. 618-233-4366
Hermann, Gretchen, *Soc Sci,* State University of New York College, Memorial Library, Cortland NY. 607-753-2525, 753-2221
Hermann, Jacquelyn, *Acq,* Ohio University, Vernon R Alden Library, Athens OH. 614-594-5228
Hermes, Thelma, *Librn,* West Acton Citizen's Library, Acton MA. 617-263-9222
Hermesch, Monica, *Librn,* Baxter-Travenol Laboratories, Hyland Research Library, Costa Mesa CA. 714-641-3536
Hermsen, Ann, *Ad,* Carroll Public Library, Carroll IA. 712-792-3432
Hernandez, Carmen M, *Cat,* University of Puerto Rico Library, Jose M Lazaro Memorial Library, Rio Piedras PR. 809-764-0000, Ext 3296
Hernandez, Carole, *Librn,* Aviation Electric Limited, Engineering Library, Montreal PQ. 514-744-2811, Ext 424
Hernandez, Carolina, *Cat,* University of New Orleans, Earl K Long Library, New Orleans LA. 504-283-0353
Hernandez, Isabel, *ILL,* Miami Dade Community College (Medical Center Campus Library), Miami FL. 305-547-1256
Hernandez, Jo Farb, *Dir,* Triton Museum of Art Library, Santa Clara CA. 408-248-4585
Hernandez, Marilyn J, *Librn,* Manitoba Department of Health Library, Winnipeg MB. 204-786-5867, 786-5868
Hernandez, Mary, *Dir,* College of Mount Saint Vincent, Elizabeth Seton Library, Bronx NY. 212-549-8000, Ext 239

Hernandez, Ramon R, *Dir,* McMillan Memorial Library, Wisconsin Rapids WI. 715-423-1040
Hernandez, Yolanda, *Ad,* Prairie Trails Public Library District, Burbank IL. 312-430-3688
Herne, Etha, *Librn,* Colonial Library, Richburg NY. 716-928-1457
Hernon, Peter, *Asst Prof,* Simmons College, Graduate School of Library & Information Science, MA. 617-738-2225
Heron, Judith, *In Charge,* New Brunswick Association of Registered Nurses Library, Fredericton NB. 506-454-5591, Ext 22
Heron, Sheila, *ILL,* Burlington Public Library, Burlington MA. 617-272-2520
Herr, Marcianne, *Curator of Educ,* Akron Art Institute Library, Akron OH. 216-376-9185, Ext 21
Herr, Marion, *Bibliog Instr,* Fairleigh Dickinson University, Friendship Library, Madison NJ. 201-377-4700, Ext 234
Herre, Mary Jane, *Asst Dir & Ad,* West Shore Public Library, Camp Hill PA. 717-761-3900, 761-3901
Herren, Penny, *Librn,* Platteville Public Library, Platteville CO. 303-785-2231
Herrera, A J, *Assoc Dean,* Fresno City College, Learning Resources Center, Fresno CA. 209-442-8204
Herrera, A J, *Assoc Dean,* Fresno City College, Library Technician Program, CA. 209-442-4600
Herrera, Mariana, *ILL,* Chicago State University, Paul & Emily Douglas Library, Chicago IL. 312-995-2254
Herrera, Raul C, *Dir,* New Mexico Highlands University, Donnelly Library, Las Vegas NM. 505-425-7511, Ext 331
Herret, Helen, *Asst Librn,* Belle Fourche Public Library, Belle Fourche SD. 605-892-4407
Herrgesell, Barbara, *Ch,* Liverpool Public Library, Liverpool NY. 315-457-0310
Herrgesell, Ron, *Librn,* Agway, Inc, Corporate Library, DeWitt NY. 315-477-6408
Herrick, Charles C, *Dir,* Helen M Plum Memorial Library, Lombard Public Library, Lombard IL. 312-627-0316
Herrick, Geraldine, *Asst Supvr of Br,* Boston Public Library, Eastern Massachusetts Library System, Boston MA. 617-536-5400
Herrick, Kay, *Institutional Librs Consult,* New Hampshire State Library, Concord NH. 603-271-2392
Herrick, Kenneth, *Dir,* University of Hawaii at Hilo Libraries, Hilo HI. 808-961-9344
Herrick, Mrs Fred R, *Dir,* Springfield Art & Historical Society Library, Springfield VT. 802-885-2415
Herrick, Susan, *Mgr, Libr Servs,* Geisinger Medical Center (Medical Library), Danville PA. 717-275-6463, 275-6346
Herrick, Susan, *Chmn,* Susquehanna Library Cooperative, PA. 717-275-6463
Herrig, Inez R, *Librn,* Lincoln County Free Library, Libby MT. 406-293-4346
Herriges, Melanie, *Librn,* Milwaukee School of the Arts Library, Milwaukee WI. 414-276-7889
Herrin, Barbara, *Librn,* Emporia State University (Curriculum & Instruction Resource Center), Emporia KS. 316-343-1200, Ext 360
Herrin, Donna, *Asst Librn,* Martin Township Public Library, Colfax IL. 309-723-2541
Herrin, Molly, *Tech Serv,* Lewis & Clark Library, Helena MT. 406-442-2380
Herring, Beverly, *Dir,* Madison County-Canton Public Library, Canton MS. 601-859-3202
Herring, Doris B, *Media,* Chipola Junior College Library, Marianna FL. 904-526-2761, Ext 122
Herring, Mary Ruth, *Bkmobile Coordr,* Chesterfield County Central Library, Chesterfield VA. 804-748-1601
Herring, Mary Y, *Dir,* King College, E W King Library, Bristol TN. 615-968-1187, Ext 215
Herring, Rose, *Homebound Project,* Bladen County Public Library, Elizabethtown NC. 919-862-8171
Herring, Ruby C, *Dir,* Jackson County Library, W A Billingsley Memorial Library, Newport AR. 501-523-2952
Herring, Virginia, *Media,* College of Charleston, Robert Scott Small Library, Charleston SC. 803-792-5530
Herrington, James E, *Archives Asst II,* Nevada State County Municipal Archives Reference Library, Carson City NV. 702-885-5210

Herrington, Ruth, *Assoc Dir & Per,* University of Tulsa, McFarlin Library, Tulsa OK. 918-592-6000, Ext 351
Herrington, Susan S, *Librn,* Brandon Free Public Library, Brandon VT. 802-247-8230
Herrman, Jeannette, *Dir,* Lakewood Public Library, Lakewood NJ. 201-363-1435
Herrman, Lillian, *Librn,* South Bay Hospital, Medical Library, Redondo Beach CA. 213-376-9474, Ext 4125
Herrmann, Edith, *Tech Serv,* Hillside Free Public Library, Hillside NJ. 201-923-4413
Herrmann, Johanna, *Dir,* North English Public Library, North English IA. 319-664-3725
Herrmann, Loretta, *Librn,* Newmont Mining Corp, Engineering Library, New York NY. 212-753-4800, Ext 215
Herrmann, Melba, *Librn,* George W Norris Regional Library, McCook Public Library, McCook NE. 308-345-1906
Herron, Adrienne, *Mgt,* QL Systems Limited (Ottawa Branch), Ottawa ON. 613-238-3499
Herron, Margie E, *Field Servs Dir,* South Carolina State Library, Columbia SC. 803-758-3181
Herron, Patricia, *ILL & Ref,* Petersburg Public Library, Petersburg VA. 804-732-3851
Herron, Sharon, *Dir,* Bennett County Public Library, Martin SD. 605-685-6556
Herron, Vivian T, *Librn,* Douglas Township Public Library, Gilman IL. 815-265-7522
Herrschaft, Marjorie, *Reader Serv & Circ,* Trumbull Library, Trumbull CT. 203-261-6421
Hersberger, Julie, *Dir,* Batesville Memorial Public Library, Batesville IN. 812-934-4706
Hersberger, Rodney M, *Asst to Dean Admin Servs,*University of Oklahoma MUniversity Libraries, Norman OK. 405-325-2611
Hersch, Gisela, *Rare Bks,* Butler University, Irwin Library, Indianapolis IN. 317-283-9225
Hersch, Robert C, *Dir,* Methodist College, Davis Memorial Library, Fayetteville NC. 919-488-7110, Ext 227
Herscher, Eugene, *Asst Dir for Tech Servs,* Southern Illinois University at Edwardsville, Elijah P Lovejoy Library, Edwardsville IL. 618-692-2711
Herseth, Avis, *Cat,* Rosary College, Rebecca Crown Library, River Forest IL. 312-366-2490, Ext 305
Hersey, David F, *Pres,* Smithsonian Science Information Exchange, DC. 202-745-4600
Hersh, Richard, *ILL,* Lancaster County Library, Lancaster PA. 717-394-2651
Hershberger, Mable, *Cat,* Otterbein College, Courtright Memorial Library, Westerville OH. 614-890-3000, Ext 164
Hershcop, Richard D, *Assoc Dir,* Colorado State University, William E Morgan Library, Fort Collins CO. 303-491-5911
Hershcopf, Marianne W, *Librn,* Colorado Division of Wildlife, Research Center Library, Fort Collins CO. 303-484-2836, Ext 57
Hersher, Hilda, *Librn,* Onondaga County Public Library System (Reference), Syracuse NY. 315-473-2702
Hersher, Trenaeus, *Art,* Saint Bonaventure University, Friedsam Memorial Library & Resource Center, Saint Bonaventure NY. 716-375-2323
Hershoff, Marcia, *Ref,* Woonsocket Harris Public Library, Woonsocket RI. 401-769-9044
Herskowitz, Paula, *Librn,* Saint Joseph Hospital, Health Science Library, Kansas City MO. 816-942-4400
Hersom, Bessie H, *Librn,* FMC Corp, Marine Colloids Division Library, Rockland ME. 207-594-4436
Herstand, Jo, *ILL,* University of Oklahoma MUniversity Libraries, Norman OK. 405-325-2611
Herstein, Sheila, *Ref,* City College of the City University of New York, Morris Raphael Cohen Library, New York NY. 212-690-6612
Hert, Floral A, *Acq,* Manhattanville College Library, Purchase NY. 914-946-9600, Ext 274
Hertel, Betty, *Librn,* Michael, Best & Friedrich, Law Library, Milwaukee WI. 414-271-6560
Hervey, Norma, *Tech Serv,* Saint Bonaventure University, Friedsam Memorial Library & Resource Center, Saint Bonaventure NY. 716-375-2323

Herz, Michael John, *Librn,* Bureau of Libraries, Museums & Archaeological Services (Regional Library for the Blind and Physically Handicapped), Saint Thomas VI. 809-774-6770
Herzlich, Carol, *ILL,* Quinnipiac College Library, Hamden CT. 203-288-5251, Ext 271
Herzog, Diana E, *Librn,* R M Smythe & Co, Inc, Inactive & Obsolete Securities Library, New York NY. 212-349-1116
Herzog, Dianne, *Ch,* Free Public Library, Council Bluffs IA. 712-323-7553
Herzog, Kate, *Librn,* Massachusetts Institute of Technology Libraries (Aeronautics & Astronautics), Cambridge MA. 617-253-5665
Heseltine, Inez, *Asst Dir,* Canada Institute for Scientific & Technical Information, Ottawa ON. 613-993-1600
Hesler, June, *YA & Ref,* Larchmont Public Library, Larchmont NY. 914-834-1960
Heslin, Catherine, *Librn,* William H Rorer Inc, Research Library, Fort Washington PA. 215-628-6358
Hess, Anne, *Personnel,* California State University, John F Kennedy Memorial Library, Los Angeles CA. 213-224-2201
Hess, Clare Marie, *In Charge,* Oxford University Press, Inc Library, New York NY. 212-679-7300
Hess, Ed, *Asst Dir Pub Servs,* University of Southern California, Edward L Doheny Memorial Library, Los Angeles CA. 213-743-6050
Hess, Esther G, *Librn,* Canton Repository Library, Canton OH. 216-454-5611, Ext 275
Hess, Gail Ann, *Librn,* Montrose Baptist Church Library, Rockville MD. 301-770-5335
Hess, Grace, *Circ,* Coffeyville Public Library, Coffeyville KS. 316-251-1370
Hess, Jayne L, *Dir,* Phillipsburg Free Public Library, Phillipsburg NJ. 201-454-3712
Hess, Jean, *Exten,* West Hills Community College Library, Coalinga CA. 209-935-0801, Ext 47
Hess, Josephine, *Special Servs Consult,* State of Vermont Department of Libraries, Montpelier VT. 802-828-3261
Hess, Josephine, *Librn,* Vermont Regional Library for the Blind & Physically Handicapped, Montpelier VT. 802-828-3273
Hess, Joyce, *Art Librn,* University of Texas Libraries (Fine Arts), Austin TX. 512-471-4777
Hess, Jr, Edward, *Librn,* University of Illinois Library at Urbana-Champaign (Law), Champaign IL. 217-333-2913
Hesse, Lydia, *Librn,* Roscoe Free Library, Roscoe NY. 607-498-5574
Hessel, William, *Instr,* Andrews University, Library Science Dept, MI. 616-471-3549
Hessel, William, *Dir,* Lake Michigan College Library, Benton Harbor MI. 616-927-3571, Ext 261
Hessel, William, *Ch Lit,* Lake Michigan College Library, Benton Harbor MI. 616-927-3571, Ext 261
Hessenauer, Jean, *Doc,* University of Maryland at Baltimore (School of Law Library), Baltimore MD. 301-528-7270
Hesser, Christine N, *Bkmobile Coordr,* Huntingdon County Public Library, Huntingdon PA. 814-643-0200
Hesser, Christine N, *Librn,* Huntingdon County Library, Orbisonia PA. 814-447-3796
Hesser, Christine N, *Librn,* Huntingdon County Library (Mount Union Branch), Mount Union PA. 814-542-4572
Hession, William J, *Librn,* Central State Hospital Library, Waupun WI. 414-324-5571, Ext 262
Hesskew, Anne, *Libr Tech,* Celanese Corp, Celanese Chemical Company, Inc-Technical Center-Library, Corpus Christi TX. 512-241-2343
Hesslein, S, *Assoc Dir,* State University of New York at Buffalo (Health Sciences), Buffalo NY. 716-831-5465
Hesslein, S, *Med & Dent,* State University of New York at Buffalo (Health Sciences), Buffalo NY. 716-831-5465
Hesslein, S, *Gen Med & Dentistry,* State University of New York at Buffalo, University Libraries, Buffalo NY. 716-636-2965
Hessler, David W, *Prof,* University of Michigan, School of Library Science, MI. 313-764-9376
Hessler, Nancy, *Circ,* Moraine Valley Community College, Learning Resources Center, Palos Hills IL. 312-974-4300, Ext 222

Hester, Becky, *ILL,* Evergreen State College, Daniel J Evans Library, Olympia WA. 206-866-6262
Hester, Beth, *Bkmobile Coordr,* Allen County Public Library, Scottsville KY. 502-237-3861
Hester, Gloria, *Acq,* Jackson State Community College Library, Jackson TN. 901-424-3520, Ext 248
Hester, Helen, *Librn,* Merck & Co, Inc (Merck Institute Library), Rahway NJ. 201-574-5773
Hesz, Bianka M, *Librn,* Presbyterian-University Hospital, Medical Library, Pittsburgh PA. 412-647-3287
Hethcoat, Lucille, *Librn,* Birmingham Public & Jefferson County Free Library (Wylam), Wylam AL. 205-254-2551
Hetley, Margaret, *Librn,* New York Public Library (Webster), New York NY. 212-288-5049
Hetrick, Karen, *Librn,* Allegheny Wesleyan College Library, Salem OH. 216-337-6403
Hetzel, Viola H, *Dir,* West Shore Public Library, Camp Hill PA. 717-761-3900, 761-3901
Hetzler, Doris, *Local History,* Cherokee Regional Library, LaFayette-Walker County Library, LaFayette GA. 404-638-2992
Hetzler, Rosemary, *Historian,* Pioneers' Museum, Reference Library & Archives, Colorado Springs CO. 303-471-6650
Hetzner, Bernice M, *Spec Coll,* University of Nebraska Medical Center, Library of Medicine, Omaha NE. 402-541-4006
Heuer, William J, *Dir,* Fremont County Library, Lander WY. 307-332-5194
Heureux, G L, *Librn,* Canadian Pulp & Paper Association Library, Montreal PQ. 514-866-6621
Heuschkel, Harry, *Asst Dir, ILL & Ref,* Saint Francis College, McGarry Library, Brooklyn NY. 212-522-2300, Ext 205, 207
Heuser, Brenda, *Librn,* General Motors Corp (Inland Manufacturing Div Engineering Library), Dayton OH. 513-227-5000
Heuser, G, *Patent Liasion,* Engelhard Minerals & Chemicals Corp, Technical Information Center, Edison NJ. 201-321-5271
Heusinkveld, Emma Lou, *Per,* Central College, Geisler Learning Resource Center, Pella IA. 515-628-4151, Ext 233
Heussman, John W, *Dir,* Pacific Lutheran University, Robert A L Mortvedt Library, Tacoma WA. 206-531-6900, Ext 301
Heusted, Harry, *Ref,* Jacksonville Public Library, Jacksonville IL. 217-243-5435
Heverly, Leonard S, *Ser,* West Chester State College, Francis Harvey Green Library, West Chester PA. 215-436-2643
Hewey, Dell, *Ref,* Oscar Rose Junior College, Learning Resources Center, Midwest City OK. 405-733-7323, 733-7322
Hewey, Edwina, *Librn,* Springvale Public Library, Sanford ME. 207-324-4624
Hewings, Margot, *Municipal Ref,* Metropolitan Toronto Library Board, Metropolitan Toronto Library, Toronto ON. 416-928-5150
Hewins, Louise P, *Librn,* Nichols Memorial Library, Center Harbor NH. 603-253-6950
Hewison, Nancy, *Ref,* University of Oregon Health Sciences Center (Health Sciences Library), Portland OR. 503-225-8026
Hewison, Nancy S, *Ref,* Tufts University, Medical-Dental Library, Boston MA. 617-956-6707
Hewitt, Ann, *Dir,* Long Branch Public Library, Long Branch NJ. 201-222-3900
Hewitt, Gay, *Librn,* Farmland-Far-Mar-Co, Research Center Library, Hutchinson KS. 316-663-5711
Hewitt, Joan, *Circ,* Washington University Libraries, Saint Louis MO. 314-889-5400
Hewitt, Joe, *Tech Serv,* University of North Carolina at Chapel Hill, Louis Round Wilson Academic Affairs Library, Chapel Hill NC. 919-933-1301
Hewitt, John H, *Librn,* Massachusetts Institute of Technology Libraries (Research Laboratory of Electronics), Cambridge MA. 617-253-2566
Hewitt, Julia, *Mgr,* General Electric Co (Main Library), Schenectady NY. 518-385-2117
Hewitt, Margaret W, *Dir, Rare Bks & Spec Coll,* Northwest Christian College, Learning Resource Center, Eugene OR. 503-343-1641, Ext 35
Hewitt, Mary, *Librn,* Kemper-Newton Regional Library (Newton Public), Newton MS. 601-683-3367

Hewitt, Vivian D, *Librn,* Carnegie Endowment for International Peace, James Thomson Shotwell Library, New York NY. 212-572-8208, 557-8209, 557-8210

Hewlett, Lou, *Asst Dir,* Jackson-George Regional Library System, Pascagoula MS. 601-762-3406

Hewlings, Charlotte H, *Librn,* Delaware County Law Library, Media PA. 215-891-2380

Hey, Constance C, *In Charge,* Cumberland County Library System, Carlisle PA. 717-243-6108

Hey, Constance C, *Librn,* Amelia S Givin Free Library, Mount Holly Springs PA. 717-486-3688

Heyd, Michael, *Dir,* Williamsport Hospital, Learning Resources Center, Williamsport PA. 717-322-7861, Ext 2168

Heyer, Terry L, *Librn & Bibliog Instr,* LDS Hospital, Medical Library, Salt Lake City UT. 801-350-1054

Heyer, Warren C, *Dir,* San Diego Mesa College Library, San Diego CA. 714-279-2300, Ext 385

Heyman, Berna L, *Bibliog Instr,* College of William & Mary in Virginia, Earl Gregg Swem Library, Williamsburg VA. 804-253-4404

Heyman, Sister Jerome, *Dir,* Edgewood College of the Sacred Heart Library, Madison WI. 608-257-4861, Ext 226

Heyum, Renee, *Pacific Curator,* University of Hawaii (University of Hawaii Library), Honolulu HI. 808-948-7205

Hiatt, Jean, *Cat,* Greenwood Public Library, Greenwood IN. 317-881-1953

Hiatt, Joada, *Librn,* Greenville County Library (Greer), Greenville SC. 803-877-8722

Hiatt, Peter, *Dir,* University of Washington, School of Librarianship, WA. 206-543-1794

Hiatt, Valentina, *Actg Librn,* Barton Rees Pogue Memorial Library, Upland IN. 317-998-2971

Hiatt, Virginia M, *Dir,* Union City Public Library, Union City IN. 317-964-4748

Hibbard, R Ashley, *Asst Librn,* New York State Department of Labor (Labor Staff Academy Library), New York NY. 212-488-2689

Hibbs, A C, *In Charge,* Adams Advertising Agency, Inc Library, Chicago IL. 312-930-9446

Hibbs, William E, *Chmn,* National Ecumenical Coalition, Inc Library, Arlington VA. 202-833-2516

Hibler, James P, *Dir,* Independence Township Library, Clarkston MI. 313-625-2212

Hickenbottom, Barbara, *Librn,* Elwood Public Library, Elwood NE. 308-785-2035

Hickerson, Beulah, *Librn,* Perry County Public Library, Linden TN. 615-589-2130

Hickerson, H Thomas, *Librn,* Cornell University Libraries (Manuscripts & University Archives), Ithaca NY. 607-256-3530

Hickerson, H Thomas, *Mss & Archives,* Cornell University Libraries (University Libraries), Ithaca NY. 607-256-4144

Hickerson, Wanda, *Asst Librn,* New Orleans Museum of Art, Felix J Dreyfous Library, New Orleans LA. 504-488-2631, Ext 21

Hickey, Colleen, *Assoc Dir,* University of Detroit Library (Law), Detroit MI. 313-961-5444, Ext 239, 240 & 241

Hickey, Damon, *Asst Dir, Pub Servs,* Guilford College Library, Greensboro NC. 919-292-5511, Ext 250

Hickey, Doralyn J, *Instr,* North Texas State University, School of Library & Information Sciences, TX. 817-788-2445

Hickey, Eileen, *Chief Librn,* Veterans Administration, Center Library, Hampton VA. 804-722-9961, Ext 326

Hickey, Elaine, *Acq,* Wellesley Free Library, Subregional Headquarters for Eastern Massachusetts Regional Library System, Wellesley MA. 617-235-1610

Hickey, Gerard R, *Dir,* Free Public Library of the Town of Belleville, Belleville NJ. 201-759-9200

Hickey, Gloria, *Librn,* Keuffel & Esser Co, Chemical Research & Development Library, Morristown NJ. 201-285-5530

Hickey, Jane, *Tech Serv,* Messiah College, Murray Learning Resources Center, Grantham PA. 717-766-2511, Ext 380

Hickey, Kate D, *Libr Technician,* United States Fish & Wildlife Service, National Fishery Research & Development Laboratory Library, Wellsboro PA. 717-724-3322

Hickey, Lynne, *Librn,* Florida Department of Agriculture & Consumer Services, Division of Animal Industry, Bureau of Diagnostic Labs Library, Kissimmee FL. 305-847-3185

Hickey, Margaret, *Librn,* Small Business Administration Reference Library, Washington DC. 202-655-4000

Hickey, Mary, *Asst Librn,* Palatka Public Library, Palatka FL. 904-328-2385

Hickle, Margaret, *Exten Librn,* Craven-Pamlico-Carteret Regional Library, New Bern NC. 919-638-2127

Hickman, Elizabeth, *Librn,* Litton Industries Inc, Amecom Division Library, College Park MD. 301-864-5600

Hickman, Faye, *Librn,* McKenzie Memorial Library, McKenzie TN. 901-352-5741

Hickman, Katherine, *Tech Serv & Acq,* Southwestern College, Memorial Library, Winfield KS. 316-221-4150, Ext 25

Hickman, Marlene B, *Librn,* Southern Forest Products Association Library, Kenner LA. 504-443-4464

Hickman, Theresa, *Librn,* Art Museum of the Palm Beaches, Inc, Norton Gallery & School of Art Library, West Palm Beach FL. 305-832-5194

Hickman, Traphene, *Dir,* Dallas County Public Library, Dallas TX. 214-749-8566, 749-8886

Hickok, Beverly, *Librn,* University of California, Berkeley (Institute of Transportation Studies Library), Berkeley CA. 415-642-3604

Hickok, Florence F, *Ref,* Michigan State University Library, East Lansing MI. 517-355-2344

Hickox, Charles, *Asst Dir,* Tarrant County Junior College System (Northeast Campus Learning Resource Center), Hurst TX. 817-281-7860, Ext 477

Hicks, Anita, *Tech Serv,* Whittier College School of Law Library, Los Angeles CA. 213-938-3621, Ext 24

Hicks, Anne, *Dir,* Chetco Community Public Library, Brookings OR. 503-469-3517

Hicks, Barbara, *Librn,* Worcester Public Library (Tatnuck), Worcester MA. 617-755-9843

Hicks, Barbara L, *Librn,* General Electric Co, Aircraft Engine Group, Technical Information Center, Lynn MA. 617-594-5363

Hicks, Betty Lou, *Ch,* Bay County Library System, Bay City MI. 517-894-2837

Hicks, Charles L, *Acq,* University of Miami, Otto G Richter Library, Coral Gables FL. 305-284-3551

Hicks, Clifford W, *Assoc Dir,* Texas Tech University Library, Lubbock TX. 806-742-2261

Hicks, Donna, *Popular Services,* Northbrook Public Library, Northbrook IL. 312-272-6224

Hicks, Dorothy, *Cat,* Western Evangelical Seminary, G Hallauer Memorial Library, Portland OR. 503-654-5182

Hicks, Dyan, *Librn,* Stanislaus County Free Library (Newman Branch), Newman CA. 209-862-2010

Hicks, Jack, *Ref,* Deerfield Public Library, Deerfield IL. 312-945-3311

Hicks, Jean, *Librn,* Trenton Memorial Public Library (J F Cox), Trenton ON. 613-392-4656

Hicks, Jim, *Ref,* Central Arkansas Library System, Little Rock AR. 501-374-7546

Hicks, Julie J, *ILL,* Sheppard Memorial Library, Greenville NC. 919-752-4177

Hicks, June I, *Assoc Dir, Reader Serv,* Dartmouth College, Baker Memorial Library, Hanover NH. 603-646-2235

Hicks, Linda, *Learning Resources Coord,* Rowan Memorial Hospital Area Health Education Center, Whitehead McKenzie Memorial Library, Salisbury NC. 704-636-3311, Ext 274

Hicks, Maggie, *Librn,* Lake Lanier Regional Library (Snellville Public), Snellville GA. 404-972-0988

Hicks, Marilyn, *Librn,* University of Wisconsin-Madison (School of Business Library), Madison WI. 608-262-3521

Hicks, Paul R, *Doc,* Indiana University of Pennsylvania, Rhodes R Stabley Library, Indiana PA. 412-357-2340

Hicks, Richard H, *Tech Serv,* Drake University, Cowles Library, Des Moines IA. 515-271-3993

Hicks, Valerie, *Ref,* Chabot College, Learning Resource Center, Hayward CA. 415-786-6762

Hicks, Warren B, *Assoc Dean,* Chabot College, Learning Resource Center, Hayward CA. 415-786-6762

Hickson, Charlotte, *Acq,* Texas Tech University Library, Lubbock TX. 806-742-2261

Hickson, Howard, *Dir,* Northeastern Nevada Historical Society, Museum Research Library, Elko NV. 702-738-3418

Hickson, Sarah A, *Dir & Acq,* George M Jones Library Association, Jones Memorial Library, Lynchburg VA. 804-846-0501

Hicok, Paul, *Asst Dir & Ref,* Saginaw Public Libraries, Hoyt Public Library, Saginaw MI. 517-755-0904

Hidalgo, Marty, *Asst for Admin,* William Marsh Rice University, Fondren Library, Houston TX. 713-527-4022

Hieb, Linda, *Ref,* Miles City Public Library, Sagebrush Federation of Libraries, Miles City MT. 406-232-1496

Hieb, Louis A, *Spec Coll,* University of Arizona Library, Tucson AZ. 602-626-2101

Hieb, Louis A, *Librn,* University of Arizona Library (Special Collections Dept), Tucson AZ. 602-626-3435

Hieber, Douglas, *Circ,* University of Northern Iowa Library, Cedar Falls IA. 319-273-2737

Hiebert, Harvey, *Assoc Dir & Tech Serv,* Bluffton College, Musselman Library, Bluffton OH. 419-358-8015, Ext 114

Hiebert, Rachel, *Archivist,* Fresno Pacific College, Hiebert Library, Fresno CA. 209-251-7194, Ext 51

Hiebing, Dorothea, *Continuing Educ,* Wisconsin Department of Public Instruction (Public & Cooperative Library Service), Madison WI. 608-266-7270

Hielkema, Arthur, *Dir,* Northwestern College, Ramaker Library, Orange City IA. 712-737-4821, Ext 57, 58

Hifner, William, *Librn,* Washington Post Library, Washington DC. 202-334-6000

Higbie, Robert, *Circ,* Supreme Court of the United States Library, Washington DC. 202-252-3177

Higby, Helen E, *Geology,* Fremont County Library, Lander WY. 307-332-5194

Higdon, Bettina P, *Regional Dir,* Cullman County Public Library, Cullman AL. 205-734-2720

Higdon, Brother Maron, *Librn,* Capuchin College Library, Washington DC. 202-529-2188

Higdon, Catheryn, *Dir,* Grundy County-Jewett Norris Library, Trenton MO. 816-359-3577

Higdon, Emily, *Acq,* Northeast Louisiana University, Sandel Library, Monroe LA. 318-342-2195

Higdon, Thomas D, *Librn,* University of Arizona Library (Arizona Health Sciences Center Library), Tucson AZ. 602-626-6121

Higginbotham, Barbra, *Orig Cat,* Columbia University (University Libraries), New York NY. 212-280-2241

Higginbotham, Jay, *Local Hist,* Mobile Public Library, Mobile AL. 205-438-7073

Higginbotham, Richard, *Bibliog Instr,* Northeastern Illinois University Library, Chicago IL. 312-583-4050, Ext 469

Higginbotham, Shirley, *Actg Dir,* Minnesota Valley Regional Library, Mankato MN. 507-387-1856

Higginbotham, Susan B, *Librn,* Lutheran Medical Center, Medical Library, Wheat Ridge CO. 303-423-4200, Ext 662

Higginbottom, A, *Librn,* Erin Township Public Library, Hillsburgh ON. 519-855-4010

Higgins, Audrea, *Librn, On-Line Servs & Bibliog Instr,* Villisca Public Library, Villisca IA. 712-826-2184

Higgins, Bertha, *Librn,* Nova Scotia Provincial Library (Technical Services), Halifax NS. 902-424-5471

Higgins, Clare, *Sci & Tech,* Pratt Institute Library, Brooklyn NY. 212-636-3684

Higgins, Ethel, *Circ,* Marion College Library, Marion IN. 317-674-6901, Ext 228

Higgins, Hazel M, *Librn,* Raytheon Data Systems Co, Norwood Library, Norwood MA. 617-762-6700

Higgins, James J, *In Charge,* Packaging Corporation of America, Research Library, Grand Rapids MI. 616-459-4581

Higgins, Katherine, *Tech Serv,* Westfield State College Library, Westfield MA. 413-568-3311

Higgins, Marguerite, *Librn,* United States Department of Commerce, Field Services Library, Boston MA. 617-223-2381

Higgins, Matthew, *Chief, Div of Planning & Develop,* Rhode Island Department of State Library Services, Providence RI. 401-277-2726

Higgins, Norma, *Spec Coll,* Alfred University (Herrick Memorial Library), Alfred NY. 607-871-2184

Higgins, Norman C, *Chmn,* Arizona State University, Dept of Educational Technology, AZ. 602-965-7191

Higgins, Ruby, *Librn,* Comstock Township Library, Comstock NE. 308-628-2703

Higgins, Thomas C, *Dir,* Middlesex Community College, Learning Resources Center, Bedford MA. 617-275-8910

Higgs, E Lucille, *Asst Dir,* Florida State University, Robert Manning Strozier Library, Tallahassee FL. 904-644-5211

Higgs, M A, *Ref,* Canadian Land Forces Command Staff College & National Defence College of Canada, Fort Frontenac Library, Kingston ON. 613-545-5829

Higgs, Mary, *Supvr,* Middlesex County Library (Coldstream Library), Ilderton ON. 519-438-8368

Higham, Cheryl, *On-Line Servs,* Embry-Riddle Aeronautical University, Learning Resource Center, Daytona Beach FL. 904-252-5561, Ext 360

Highfield, Betty Jane, *Dir,* North Park College & Theological Seminary (Wallgren Library), Chicago IL. 312-583-2700

Highfill, Carroll, *Dir,* Converse County Library, Douglas WY. 307-358-3644

Highgas, Jr, William, *Librn,* Middlesex County Law Library at Cambridge, Cambridge MA. 617-494-4148

Highland, Kristeen, *ILL & Ref,* Yankton College, James M Lloyd Library, Yankton SD. 605-665-4662

Highley, Theresa, *Cat,* State University of New York College, Daniel A Reed Library, Fredonia NY. 716-673-3183

Highsmith, June E, *Librn,* Countryside United Methodist Church Library, Urbana IL. 217-688-2422, 684-2422

Highsmith, June E, *Librn,* Philo Township Public Library, Philo IL. 217-684-2896

Hight, Nola, *Librn,* Contra Costa County Library (Pittsburg (Vincent A Davi)), Pittsburg CA. 415-439-5302

Hightower, Monteria, *Br & Exten Supvr,* Public Library of the District of Columbia, Martin Luther King Memorial Library, Washington DC. 202-727-1101

Hightower, Raymon, *Soc sci,* Chicago Public Library (Woodson Regional), Chicago IL. 312-881-6900

Highum, Clayton, *Dir & On-Line Servs,* Illinois Wesleyan University Library, Bloomington IL. 309-556-3172

Highum, Karen, *AV,* College of Saint Teresa, Mary A Molloy Library, Winona MN. 507-454-2930, Ext 210

Hignett, Joan, *ILL & Acq,* Ashland College Library, Ashland OH. 419-289-4067

Hikory, Julia I, *Librn,* Chelsea Public Library, Alden Speare Memorial Library, Chelsea VT. 802-685-4460

Hiland, Leah F, *Asst Prof,* University of Northern Iowa, Dept of Library Science, IA. 319-273-2050

Hildebran, Shirley, *Librn,* Hartford Public Library, Hartford AL. 205-588-2384

Hildebrand, Anne, *Librn,* Wake County Department of the Public Library (Knightdale Public), Knightdale NC. 919-266-3190

Hildebrand, Carol I, *Librn,* Lake Oswego Public Library, Lake Oswego OR. 503-636-7628

Hildebrand, Jane, *Br Coordr,* Brunswick-Glynn County Regional Library, Brunswick GA. 912-264-7360

Hildebrand, Karen, *Librn,* California School of Professional Psychology, Berkeley Campus Library, Berkeley CA. 415-548-5415

Hildebrand, Linda, *Ref,* Oakland University, Kresge Library, Rochester MI. 313-377-2486, 377-2474

Hildebrand, Marion, *Reader Serv,* State University of New York, Agricultural & Technical College at Norrisville Library, Morrisville NY. 315-684-7055

Hildebrandt, Mary, *ILL & Ref,* Memorial Library of Radnor Township, Wayne PA. 215-687-1124

Hildebrandt, Phyllis, *Ad,* Chippewa Library League, Mount Pleasant MI. 517-773-3242

Hildebrandt, Phyllis, *Ad,* Veterans Memorial Library, Mount Pleasant MI. 517-773-3242

Hildebrant, Darrell, *Program Coordr,* Veterans Memorial Public Library, Bismarck ND. 701-222-6410

Hilden, Sherry, *ILL,* Cass County Library, Cassopolis MI. 616-445-8651

Hildenbrand, D Jane, *Librn,* Carnegie Library of Pittsburgh (Mount Washington), Pittsburgh PA. 412-622-3100

Hildenbrand, Suzanne, *Asst Prof,* State University of New York, College of Arts & Science, School of Library & Information Science, NY. 716-245-5322

Hildesheim, Theresa, *ILL, Ad & Ref,* Mastics-Moriches-Shirley Community Library, Shirley NY. 516-339-1511

Hildlebrand, Janice, *Librn,* Sheboygan Press Library, Sheboygan WI. 414-457-7711, Ext 47

Hildner, Susan, *Cat,* Autauga-Prattville Public Library, Prattville AL. 205-365-3396

Hildner, Susan, *Cat,* Autauga-Prattville Public Library System, Prattville AL. 205-365-3396

Hildreth, John, *Librn,* New York Public Library (Recordings), New York NY. 212-790-6262

Hildreth, Laurie, *Instr,* Alderson-Broaddus College, Media Education Program, WV. 304-457-1700, Ext 258

Hildreth, Mildred L, *ILL, Rare Bks & Ref,* Alderson-Broaddus College, Pickett Library Media Center, Philippi WV. 304-457-1700, Ext 229, 258

Hildreth, Patricia, *Librn,* Thayer Public Library, Winchester NH. 603-239-6589

Hildreth, Stella, *Librn,* Acadia Parish Library (Rayne Branch), Rayne LA. 318-788-1880

Hile, Marjorie J, *Dir,* Rush Public Library, Rush NY. 716-533-1370

Hileman, Helen Bowen, *Librn,* San Luis Obispo City-County Library, San Luis Obispo CA. 805-549-5775

Hileman, Margaret, *Dir,* Bozeman Public Library, Bozeman MT. 406-586-2148

Hileman, Margaret, *Librn,* Broad Valleys Federation of Libraries, Bozeman MT. 406-586-2148

Hiler, Angela, *Librn,* Jackson District Library (Spring Arbor Branch), Spring Arbor MI. 517-750-2030

Hilford, Janet, *Librn,* Orange County Environmental Management Agency, Development Library, Santa Ana CA. 714-834-2300

Hilger, Mrs Urban, *ILL, Circ & Ref,* Christian Brothers College Library, Memphis TN. 901-278-0100, Ext 220

Hilker, Emerson W, *Librn,* Franklin Institute Library, Philadelphia PA. 215-448-1224

Hill, Alice, *Librn,* Chicago Public Library (Bridgeport), Chicago IL. 312-927-8990

Hill, Alice, *ILL, On-Line Servs & Bibliog Instr,* Mohawk Valley Library Association, Schenectady NY. 518-355-2010

Hill, Ann, *Librn,* Colborne Public Library, Colborne ON. 416-355-3430

Hill, Anna, *Librn,* Glendale Public Library (Chevy Chase), Glendale CA. 213-956-2030

Hill, Arden, *Librn,* United States Air Force (Malmstrom Air Force Base Library), Malmstrom AFB MT. 406-731-9990

Hill, Barbara, *Librn,* Veterans Administration, Hospital Library, Battle Creek MI. 616-965-3281

Hill, Barbara M, *Dir,* Massachusetts College of Pharmacy & Allied Health Sciences, Sheppard Library, Boston MA. 732-2810 (Gen info), 732-2813 (Ref)

Hill, Betsy, *Ch,* Greenwood-Leflore Public Library System, Greenwood MS. 601-453-3634

Hill, Brian, *Ref,* Muskogee Public Library, Muskogee OK. 918-682-6657

Hill, Carol J, *Dir,* Pennsville Public Library, Pennsville NJ. 609-678-5473

Hill, Cilia R, *Librn,* Salem Public Library, Hamlin PA. 717-689-9260

Hill, Claire J, *Dir,* Mansfield Free Public Library, Mansfield PA. 717-662-3850

Hill, Connie, *Librn,* Garrett Corporation, Airesearch Manufacturing Company of California, Technical Library, Torrance CA. 213-323-9500, Ext 2255

Hill, Connie, *Cat,* University of Wisconsin-Stout, Pierce Library, Menomonie WI. 715-232-1184

Hill, Deborah C, *Librn,* Lonesome Pine Regional Library (Haysi Public), Haysi VA. 703-865-4851

Hill, Donna, *Ch,* Eugene Public Library, Eugene OR. 503-687-5450

Hill, Dorothy, *Acq,* Mount Sinai School of Medicine of City University of New York, Gustave L & Janet W Levy Library, New York NY. 212-650-6671

Hill, Dorothy, *Asst Librn,* Roscoe Free Library, Roscoe NY. 607-498-5574

Hill, Dorothy C, *Actg Dir,* General Telephone & Electronics-Sylvania, Systems Group Main Library, Needham Heights MA. 617-449-2000

Hill, Dorothy G, *Ch,* Gunn Memorial Library, Washington CT. 203-868-7586, 868-2310

Hill, Dorothy J, *Asst Dir & Ch,* Silver City Public Library, Silver City NM. 505-538-3672

Hill, Ed, *Librn,* Tampa-Hillsborough County Public Library System (Peninsular Public), Tampa FL. 813-253-3768

Hill, Edwin, *Rare Bks & Spec Coll,* University of Wisconsin-La Crosse, Murphy Library, La Crosse WI. 608-785-8505

Hill, Elizabeth J, *Ref, On-Line Servs & Bibliog Instr,* Marshall University, James E Morrow Library, Huntington WV. 304-696-3120

Hill, Esther L, *Dir,* Inter-American University of Puerto Rico, Library-Metropolitan Campus Bayamon Unit, Bayamon PR. 809-780-4040, Ext 16

Hill, Florence, *Ch & YA,* Brockway Memorial Library, Miami Shores FL. 305-758-8000

Hill, Fred, *Asst Prof,* Saint Cloud State University, Center for Library & Audiovisual Education, MN. 612-255-2022

Hill, Graham R, *Librn,* McMaster University, Hamilton ON. 416-525-9140

Hill, Harriett M, *Librn,* Hampton Institute (Architecture), Hampton VA. 804-727-5471

Hill, Hazel C, *Acq,* John Marshall Law School Library, Chicago IL. 312-427-2737, Ext 254

Hill, Howard, *Cat,* Oregon College of Education Library, Monmouth OR. 503-838-1220, Ext 240

Hill, Janet Swan, *Cat,* Northwestern University Library, Evanston IL. 312-492-7658

Hill, Jeanne D, *Dir,* Norfolk Public Library, Norfolk MA. 617-528-3380

Hill, Joylyn, *Librn,* Colorado State Division of Highways, Technical Library, Denver CO. 303-757-9308

Hill, Keith, *Ref,* Appalachian State University, Carol Grotnes Belk Library, Boone NC. 704-262-2186

Hill, Kenneth, *AV,* Clark County Community College, Learning Resources Center, North Las Vegas NV. 702-643-6060, Ext 269

Hill, Lawrence H, *Ref & Per,* Saint Vincent College & Archabbey Libraries, Latrobe PA. 412-539-9761, Ext 378

Hill, Leonard E, *Assoc Prof,* Andrews University, Library Science Dept, MI. 616-471-3549

Hill, Linda, *Tech Serv,* Cities Service Co, Energy Resources Group Research Library, Tulsa OK. 918-586-2524

Hill, Linda, *Bkmobile Coordr,* Menifee County Public Library, Frenchburg KY. 606-768-2212

Hill, Lucy, *Librn,* Chicago Public Library (Independence), Chicago IL. 312-463-3620

Hill, M, *Librn,* Paul Rosenberg Associates Library, Pelham NY. 914-738-2266

Hill, Mabel, *Cat,* Jackson Community College Library, Jackson MI. 517-787-0800, Ext 294, 295

Hill, Malcolm K, *Dir,* Pottsville Free Public Library, Pottsville Library District Center, Pottsville PA. 622-8105; 622-8880

Hill, Margaret, *Ref,* Cooke County Library, Gainesville TX. 817-665-2401

Hill, Margaret, *Librn,* Henderson Advertising Inc Library, Greenville SC. 803-271-6000

Hill, Marilyn, *Ch,* East Alton Public Library, East Alton IL. 618-259-7061

Hill, Marion T, *YA,* Woodward Memorial Library, LeRoy NY. 716-768-8300

Hill, Marnesba D, *Chief Librn,* Herbert H Lehman College Library, Bronx NY. 212-960-8577, 960-8582

Hill, Mrs H, *Librn,* Society of Management Accountants of Canada, Resource Centre, Hamilton ON. 416-525-4100, Ext 46

Hill, Mrs Ronald, *Librn,* Lake Mills Public Library, Lake Mills IA. 515-592-2202

Hill, Paul, *Ref,* Creighton University (Klutznick Law Library), Omaha NE. 402-449-2875

Hill, Phyllis M, *Librn,* Washington County Board of Education Resource Center Library, Hagerstown MD. 301-791-4213

Hill, Richard L, *Head,* New York Public Library (Annex Section), New York NY. 212-790-7351

Hill, Sandra, *Circ,* Villa Park Public Library, Villa Park IL. 312-834-1164

Hill, Sara I, *Dir,* Saint Luke's Hospital, Spencer Center for Education Medical Library, Kansas City MO. 816-932-2333

Hill, Sarah V, *Librn,* Agness Community Library, Agness OR. 503-247-6083

Hill, Shirley M, *Librn,* Saint Ignace City Public Library, Saint Ignace MI. 906-643-8318

Hill, Susan, *Dir,* White Pine Library Cooperative, Saginaw MI. 517-792-0001

Hill, Susan M, *Librn,* National Association of Broadcasters Library, Washington DC. 202-293-3578

Hill, Suzanne, *Asst Dir,* Catonsville Community College, Learning Resources Div, Baltimore MD. 301-455-4586

Hill, Veronica, *Librn,* Marion County Public Library, Lebanon KY. 502-692-4698

Hill, Wanda, *Ref,* Frederick County Public Library, Frederick MD. 301-694-1613

Hill, William, *Librn,* Norfolk Public Library (Pretlow), Norfolk VA. 804-480-1279

Hillard, Ernest, *Doc,* Westminster College, Reeves Memorial Library, Fulton MO. 314-642-6793

Hillard, James M, *Dir,* The Citadel, Daniel Library, Charleston SC. 803-792-5116

Hillario, Gloria E, *Asst Dir Media Servs,* Saint Mary's University (Academic Library), San Antonio TX. 512-436-3441

Hillbruner, Fred, *Head Tech Servs,* Art Institute of Chicago (Art School Library), Chicago IL. 312-443-3748

Hille, Michael, *Dir & Br Coordr,* Shawano City-County Library, Shawano WI. 715-526-3829

Hille, Tansill, *Acq,* Southwestern at Memphis, Burrow Library, Memphis TN. 901-274-1800, Ext 365, 366

Hillemeier, Edwinna C, *Curator,* Windsor Historical Society Library, Windsor CT. 203-688-3813

Hillen, Glenis, *Librn,* Albany Public Library (Delaware), Albany NY. 518-463-0254

Hillengas, Paul, *ILL & Ref,* New York State Office of Mental Health Library, Albany NY. 518-474-7165

Hiller, Steven Z, *Maps,* University of Washington Libraries, Seattle WA. 206-543-1760

Hilley, Jeanelle, *Commun Servs & Bkmobile Coordr,* Elbert County Library, Elberton GA. 404-283-5375

Hillhouse, Rowena, *Librn,* Brazoria County Library (Alvin Branch), Alvin TX. 713-585-4884

Hilliard, Jessie, *Curator,* Bureau County Historical Society Museum & Library, Princeton IL. 815-875-2184

Hilliard, Ruth, *Video,* Lansing Public Library, Lansing MI. 517-374-4600

Hilliard, Ruth, *Ad & Ref,* Lansing Public Library, Lansing MI. 517-374-4600

Hillier, Carol M, *Americas & Mil Policy,* National Defense University Library, Washington DC. 202-693-8437

Hilligoss, Martha M, *Art,* Saint Louis Public Library, Saint Louis MO. 314-241-2288

Hilliker, Patricia, *Chief Librn,* Angola Public Library, Angola NY. 716-549-1271

Hillis, John B, *Dir,* West Palm Beach Public Library, West Palm Beach FL. 203-659-0810

Hillis, Patricia M, *Doc,* Washington University Libraries (Freund Law Library), Saint Louis MO. 314-889-6459

Hillman, David L, *Dir,* Virginia Western Community College, Brown Library, Roanoke VA. 703-982-7303

Hillman, Marnell, *ILL,* Cabrillo College, Robert E Swenson Library, Aptos CA. 408-425-6473, 688-6458

Hillman, Marnell, *Asst Librn,* Cabrillo College, Robert E Swenson Library, Aptos CA. 408-425-6473, 688-6458

Hillman, Raymond W, *Curator of History,* Pioneer Museum & Haggin Galleries, Library of California, Stockton CA. 209-462-4116, 462-1566

Hillman, Stephanie, *Asst Dir & Bibliog Instr,* California State University, Fresno Library, Fresno CA. 209-487-2403

Hillmer, Patricia, *Ref,* Tiffin-Seneca Public Library, Tiffin OH. 419-447-3751

Hills, Margarette, *Cat,* Christian Heritage College Library, El Cajon CA. 714-440-3043, Ext 156&172

Hills, Virginia Carter, *Librn,* National Geographic Society Library, Washington DC. 202-857-7787

Hillsbeck, Barbara, *Librn,* Adriance Memorial Library (La Grange), Pleasant Valley NY. 914-485-4796

Hillson, Muriel, *Librn,* Norfolk Regional Center Staff Library (Resident Library), Norfolk NE. 402-371-4343, Ext 322

Hillson, Muriel V, *Librn,* Norfolk Regional Center Staff Library, Norfolk NE. 402-371-4343, Ext 290

Hillyer, Georgiana, *Chief Librn,* United States Air Force (Air Force Weapons Laboratory Technical Library), Kirtland AFB NM. 505-844-7449

Hillyer, Lila N, *Librn,* Wisconsin Alumni Research Foundation, Madison WI. 608-263-2848

Hillyers, Marcia, *Librn,* Washington Library, Washington KS. 913-325-2114

Hilscher, Arthur, *Dir,* Carter-Wallace Inc, Wallace Laboratory Div Library, Cranbury NJ. 609-655-1100

Hilscher, Patricia, *In Charge,* Cobb County Public Library System (Lewis A Ray), Smyrna GA. 404-436-9501

Hilt, Lyda, *Genealogist,* Tippecanoe County Historical Association, Alameda McCollough Library, Lafayette IN. 317-742-8411

Hilton, Arlie, *Librn,* Lonesome Pine Regional Library (Saint Paul Public), Saint Paul VA. 703-762-9702

Hilton, Gail, *Librn,* Hartford Insurance Group (Loss Control Library), Hartford CT. 547-5000 Ext 3099

Hilton, John, *Media,* Mineral Area College, Instructional Resources Center, Flat River MO. 314-431-4593, Ext 38

Hilton, Kenneth L, *Librn,* Pitt Community College, Learning Resources Center, Greenville NC. 919-756-3130, Ext 213

Hilton, Margaret L, *Dir,* Gleason Public Library, Carlisle MA. 617-369-4898

Hilton, Robert C, *Dir,* Cary Memorial Library, Lexington MA. 617-862-6288

Hilton, Ruth, *Music,* New York University, Elmer Holmes Bobst Library, New York NY. 212-598-2484

Hilton, Stillman P, *Dir & Acq,* Gloucester Lyceum & Sawyer Free Library, Gloucester MA. 617-283-0376

Hiltz, Carl, *Mgr, Educ Resources,* Conestoga College of Applied Arts & Technology, Waterloo Campus, Educational Resources, Waterloo ON. 519-885-0300, Ext 59

Hilyard, Stevens W, *Dir,* Pittsburg State University Library, Pittsburg KS. 316-231-7000, Ext 431

Hime, Gary, *Asst Dir,* Wichita Public Library, Wichita KS. 316-262-0611

Himelfarb, Laurence, *Librn,* Metropolitan Washington Council of Governments Library, Washington DC. 202-223-6800, Ext 232

Himes, Dorothy, *YA,* North Kansas City Public Library, North Kansas City MO. 816-221-3360

Himes, James B, *In Charge,* Richardson Co, Research & Development Library, Melrose Park IL. 312-344-4300, Ext 336

Himes, Jean, *Ad,* Kewanee Public Library, Kewanee IL. 309-852-4505

Himmel, Ethel, *Ad,* La Crosse Public Library, La Crosse WI. 608-784-8623

Himmel, Ned, *ILL, Ad & Ref,* Redwood City Public Library, Redwood City CA. 415-369-6251, Ext 288

Himmelberger, Dorothy, *Rare Bks,* University of Michigan-Flint Library, Flint MI. 313-762-3400

Himmelsbach, Carl J, *Dir,* Morrill Memorial Library, Norwood MA. 617-769-0200

Himmelsteib, Carol, *Ch,* Cleveland Heights-University Heights Public Library, Cleveland Heights OH. 216-932-3600

Himrich, Debra, *Librn,* Sandstone Public Library, Sandstone MN. 612-245-2270

Himrod, David, *Reader Serv,* Garrett-Evangelical Theological Seminary Library, Evanston IL. 312-866-3911

Hinchliffe, Louise M, *In Charge,* National Park Service, Grand Canyon National Park Research Library, Grand Canyon AZ. 602-638-2411, Ext 231

Hinckley, Ann, *Ref,* University of California Los Angeles Library, Los Angeles CA. 213-825-1201

Hinckley, Malcom, *Ref,* Oklahoma Christian College Library, Oklahoma City OK. 405-478-1661, Ext 337

Hinckley, Margaret F, *ILL & Ref,* Winthrop Public Library, Frost Public Library, Winthrop MA. 617-846-1703

Hindeleh, Nitsa, *Librn,* Baptist Bible College Library, G B Vick Memorial Library, Springfield MO. 417-869-9811, Ext 375, 376

Hinden, Judith A, *Mgr Adv & Sales Promotion,* Micropublishers Library, Div of Bell & Howell Co, Wooster OH. 216-264-6666

Hinding, Andrea, *Dir,* University of Minnesota Libraries-Twin Cities (Walter Library), Minneapolis MN. 612-376-2931

Hindle, Florence R, *Circ,* Providence Public Library, Providence RI. 401-521-7722

Hindley, Dierdre, *Librn,* Free Public Library of the City of Trenton (Briggs), Trenton NJ. 609-392-7188

Hindman, Thomas, *Bkmobile Coordr,* Beverly Public Library, Beverly MA. 617-922-0310

Hindmarsh, Doug, *Ref,* Utah State Library, Salt Lake City UT. 801-533-5875

Hinds, Isabelle P, *Asst Dir,* Lapeer County Library, Lapeer MI. 313-664-9521

Hinds, Lillian A, *Librn,* Kent State University, Tuscarawas Campus Library, New Philadelphia OH. 216-339-3391, Ext 256

Hinds, Mrs J, *Br Supvr,* Scarborough Public Library (Cliffcrest), Scarborough ON. 416-266-5697

Hinds, Vira, *Librn,* City College of the City University of New York (Education-Psychology), New York NY. 212-690-4148

Hine, Elizabeth N, *Librn,* Centerville & Center Township Library, Centerville IN. 317-855-5223

Hine, Lela M, *Curator,* Hermitage Foundation Library, Norfolk VA. 804-423-2052

Hines, Billie, *Librn,* Athens Regional Library (Winterville Branch), Winterville GA. 404-742-8600

Hines, Cordie H, *Librn for Community Servs,* Dallas Public Library, Dallas TX. 214-748-9071

Hines, David, *Sr Librn,* IBM Corp, Information Center Library, Rochester MN. 507-286-4462

Hines, Geraldine T, *Dir,* Samuel W Smith Memorial Public Library, Port Allegany PA. 814-642-7294

Hines, Helen, *Librn,* Larue County Public Library, Hodgenville KY. 502-358-3851

Hines, Jeanne C, *Acq,* Woburn Public Library, Woburn MA. 617-933-0148

Hines, L Joy, *Librn,* Mountain Home Public Library, Mountain Home ID. 208-587-4716

Hines, Loren, *ILL,* University of New Mexico General Library (Law Library), Albuquerque NM. 505-277-6236

Hines, Melva, *Librn,* Hoya Memorial Library, Nacogdoches TX. 713-564-4693, Ext 122

Hines, Nicola, *Dir,* Sweet Home Public Library, Sweet Home OR. 503-367-5007

Hines, Nora, *Librn,* Atlantic City Free Public Library (Richmond Ave), Atlantic City NJ. 609-347-1902

Hines, Norma, *Librn,* Volusia County Public Libraries (De Bary Branch), De Bary FL. 904-252-8374

Hines, Patricia, *Circ,* Elizabeth City State University, G R Little Library, Elizabeth City NC. 919-335-0551, Ext 332

Hines, Susie M, *Librn,* National Marine Fisheries Service, Northeast Fisheries Center, Oxford Laboratory Library, Oxford MD. 301-226-5193

Hines, Theodore C, *Chmn & Prof,* University of North Carolina at Greensboro, Library Science-Educational Technology Div, NC. 919-379-5710

Hingers, Edward, *Media,* Nassau Library System, Uniondale NY. 516-292-8920

Hingley, Eleanor, *ILL,* Southampton Free Library, Southampton PA. 215-322-1415

Hinkle, John, *Continuing Educ Coordr,* Oklahoma Department of Libraries, Oklahoma City OK. 405-521-2502

Hinkle, Kristina, *Tech Serv,* A Holmes Johnson Memorial Library, Kodiak Public Library, Kodiak AK. 907-486-3312

Hinkle, Regina A, *Librn,* Southern Natural Gas Co, Corporate Library, Birmingham AL. 205-325-7409

Hinkley, Louise, *Librn,* Fiber Materials Inc Library, Biddeford ME. 207-282-5911, Ext 370

Hinks, Yvonne, *Librn,* University of Calgary Library (Gallagher Geology), Calgary AB. 403-284-6042

Hinman, Marjory B, *Librn,* Broome County Historical Society Library & Archives, Binghamton NY. 607-772-0660

Hinman, Rhonda, *Readers' Advisor Supvr,* South Dakota State Library for the Handicapped, Pierre SD. 605-773-3514

Hinners, Linda J, *Asst Librn,* Kent Library Association, Kent Memorial Library, Kent CT. 203-927-3761

Hinnov, Ann, *Librn,* Allendale Mutual Insurance Co Library, Johnston RI. 401-275-4500

Hinrichs, Donald F, *Librn,* Los Angeles Public Library System (Water & Power), Los Angeles CA. 213-481-4611

Hinrichs, Linda, *Archives & Spec Coll,* University of Dayton Libraries, Roesch Library, Dayton OH. 513-229-4221

Hinsberger, Ralph, *Ref, Rare Bks & Spec Coll,* Alameda Free Library, Alameda CA. 415-522-5413, 522-3578

Hinshaw, Marilyn, *Assoc Dir,* Daniel Boone Regional Library, Columbia MO. 314-443-3161

Hinshaw, Martha, *Librn,* Arnolds Park Municipal Public Library, Arnolds Park IA. 712-332-2033

Hinson, Ann J, *Acq,* Florida Agricultural & Mechanical University, Samuel H Coleman Memorial Library, Tallahassee FL. 904-599-3370

Hinson, Lottie, *Librn,* Shreve Memorial Library (Rodessa Branch), Rodessa LA. 318-221-2614

Hinson, Mary, *Librn,* York County Library (Fort Mill Public), Fort Mill SC. 803-547-4114

Hintmer, Jo, *Bibl Control,* University of New Mexico General Library, Albuquerque NM. 505-277-4241

Hinton, Bertha, *Librn,* Paterson Free Public Library (First Ward), Paterson NJ. 201-881-3782

Hinton, Cheryl, *Asst Librn,* Mississippi Gulf Coast Junior College, Jackson County Campus Library, Gautier MS. 601-497-4313, Ext 226, Libr; 497-4313, Ext 255 Media Ctr

Hinton, Eugene, *Dir,* North Carolina Department of Community Colleges, NC. 919-733-7714

Hinton, Frances, *Proc Servs,* Free Library of Philadelphia, Philadelphia PA. 215-686-5322

Hinton, James, *Tech Serv,* Grandview Heights School District Public Library, Columbus OH. 614-486-2951

Hinton, John, *Dean Media Mat,* Cabrillo College, Robert E Swenson Library, Aptos CA. 408-425-6473, 688-6458

Hinton, Lloyd G, *Mgr Process Develop,* Fraser Inc, Central Technical Library, Edmundston NB. 506-735-5551

Hinton, Mrs Waudell, *Librn,* Pine Forest Regional Library (McLain Public), McLain MS. 601-788-6539

Hinton, Pam, *Media,* Fort Dodge Public Library, Fort Dodge IA. 515-573-8167

Hinton, Rebekah G, *Admin Librn,* United States Public Health Service (Phoenix Indian Medical Center Library), Phoenix AZ. 602-263-1200, Ext 335

Hintz, Jeanne, *Ad & On-Line Servs,* Gail Borden Public Library District, Elgin IL. 312-742-2411

Hintz, Joann, *Tech Serv,* Mid Michigan Community College, Charles A Amble Library, Harrison MI. 517-386-7792, Ext 258

Hintz, Lois, *Librn,* Olin Corporation, Lake Charles Technical Information Ctr Library, Lake Charles LA. 318-491-3000

Hinz, Fredda, *Librn,* Manning Public Library, Manning IA. 712-653-8861

Hinz, James, *Humanities,* Swarthmore College, McCabe Library, Swarthmore PA. 215-447-7477, 447-7480

Hinz, Joan, *Ref, On-Line Servs & Bibliog Instr,* Kalamazoo College, Upjohn Library, Kalamazoo MI. 616-383-8481

Hinz, Robert D, *Dir,* Jacksonville Health Educational Program, James L Borland Medical Library, Jacksonville FL. 904-353-9696

Hinze, Adrien C, *Librn,* Emory University Libraries (Lamar School of Law Library), Atlanta GA. 404-329-6823

Hipp, Joseph, *Spec Coll,* Tampa-Hillsborough County Public Library System, Tampa FL. 813-223-8947

Hipp, Joseph, *Local Hist,* Tampa-Hillsborough County Public Library System, Tampa FL. 813-223-8947

Hippe, Erwin L, *Librn,* King County Masonic Library Association Inc Library, Seattle WA. 206-234-0110

Hippenhammer, Craighton, *Ch,* Decatur Public Library, Decatur IL. 217-428-6617, Ext 33

Hippensteel, Doloris, *Asst Dir,* Peru Public Library, Peru IN. 317-473-3069

Hipsher, Janice, *Librn,* Santa Anna City Library, Santa Anna TX. 915-348-3395

Hipson, Nancy B, *Dir,* University of Sarasota Library, Sarasota FL. 813-955-4228

Hire, Janet B, *Librn,* Milan-Berlin Township Public Library, Milan OH. 419-499-4117

Hires, Mary E, *Librn,* Sunland Hospital at Orlando, Medical Library, Orlando FL. 305-293-1421, Ext 339

Hirnickle, Mrs C, *Dir,* Maple Shade Public Library, Maple Shade NJ. 609-779-9767

Hirsch, Brian, *Develop Servs,* Manitoba Department of Cultural Affairs & Historical Resources, Public Library Services Branch, Winnipeg MB. 204-453-7549

Hirsch, Deborah, *Librn,* New York Public Library (Tompkins Square), New York NY. 212-228-4747

Hirsch, Evelyn, *Cat & Commun Servs,* Long Beach Public Library, Long Beach NY. 516-432-7201

Hirsch, Ingrid, *Rare Bks & Spec Coll,* Fairleigh Dickinson University, Friendship Library, Madison NJ. 201-377-4700, Ext 234

Hirsch, Irving, *Librn,* Heed University Library, Hollywood FL. 305-925-1600

Hirsch, Jane, *Ad,* Montgomery County Department of Public Libraries, Rockville MD. 301-279-1401

Hirsch, Miriam, *Librn,* San Francisco General Hospital, Barnett-Briggs Library, San Francisco CA. 415-821-8553, 821-8554

Hirsch, Molly, *Chief Librn,* Central Mortgage & Housing Corp, Canadian Housing Information Centre, Ottawa ON. 613-996-8211, 225-6771

Hirsch, Muriel, *Librn,* Kimball Public Library, Atkinson NH. 603-362-5234

Hirsch, Patricia R, *Librn,* Review & Herald Editorial Library, Washington DC. 202-723-3700, Ext 219

Hirschel, Aimee A, *Dir,* Asotin County Rural Library, Clarkston WA. 509-758-5454

Hirschenburger, Shirley, *Media,* Bayliss Public Library, Sault Sainte Marie MI. 906-632-9331

Hirschenburger, Shirley, *Media,* Hiawathaland Library Cooperative, Sault Sainte Marie MI. 906-632-9331

Hirschfeld, Harriett, *Dir,* Logan College of Chiropractic Library, Chesterfield MO. 314-227-2100

Hirschy, Christine, *Ser,* Emmanuel College, Cardinal Cushing Library, Boston MA. 617-277-9340, Ext 126

Hirsekorn, Patricia, *ILL,* Gloucester County College, Library-Media Center, Sewell NJ. 609-468-5000, Ext 294

Hirst, Donna, *Tech Serv,* University of Iowa Libraries (Law Library), Iowa City IA. 319-353-5968

Hirst, Ruth, *Ch,* Atlantic County Library, Pleasantville NJ. 609-646-8699, 645-7121, 625-2776

Hirtle, Jr, Eugene G, *Curator,* Hayward Area Historical Society Museum Library, Hayward CA. 415-581-0223

Hirtz, Carrie, *Librn,* Skadden, Arps, Slate, Meagher & Flom Library, New York NY. 212-371-6000

Hirtz, Sophie, *Librn,* United States Bureau of Reclamation Library, Sacramento CA. 916-484-4491

Hiser, Karen F, *Dir,* Keyser-Mineral County Public Library, Potomac Valley Regional Library, Keyser WV. 304-788-3222

Hisle, Wendell Lee, *Dir,* Lexington Technical Institute Library, Lexington KY. 606-258-4919

Hiss, Sheila, *Media,* North Florida Junior College Library, Madison FL. 904-973-2288, Ext 52

Hissong, Barbara, *Librn,* Fulton County Public Library (Aubbee), Leiters Ford IN. 219-542-4859

Hitchcock, N L, *Librn,* Friend Memorial Public Library, Brooklin ME. 207-359-2276

Hitchcock-Mort, Karen A, *Coll Develop,* University of Central Florida Library, Orlando FL. 305-275-2564

Hitchens, Susan, *Media,* Kanawha County Public Library, Kanawha County Service Center, Charleston WV. 304-343-4646

Hitchingham, Eileen, *Research & Analysis,* Oakland University, Kresge Library, Rochester MI. 313-377-2486, 377-2474

Hitchings, Gladys M, *Librn,* Davenport Municipal Art Gallery, Art Reference Library, Davenport IA. 319-326-7804

Hitchings, Sinclair H, *Keeper of Prints,* Boston Public Library, Eastern Massachusetts Library System, Boston MA. 617-536-5400

Hitchins, Adella, *Cat,* Clearwater Christian College Library, Clearwater FL. 813-726-1153, Ext 20

Hite, Charles L, *In Charge,* H Carl Rowland Memorial Library, Charlotte NC. 704-376-0291

Hite, Marilyn, *Ch & Commun Servs,* Bluffton-Wells County Public Library, Bluffton IN. 219-824-1612

Hite, Jr, Francis S, *Cat,* South Carolina State Library, Columbia SC. 803-758-3181

Hitt, Ione T, *Librn,* Veterans Administration, Hospital Library, Murfreesboro TN. 615-893-1360

Hitt, Samuel, *Dir,* University of North Carolina at Chapel Hill (Health Sciences Library), Chapel Hill NC. 919-966-2111

Hivale, K R, *Asst Dir, On-Line Servs & Bibliog Instr,* Humber College, Learning Resource Centre, Rexdale ON. 416-675-3111, Ext 331

Hixon, Jeffrey S, *Dir,* Clay Center Carnegie Library, Clay Center KS. 913-632-3889

Hixson, Catherine, *Circ,* New York University, Elmer Holmes Bobst Library, New York NY. 212-598-2484

Hixson, Cheryl, *AV,* Whitehall Township Public Library, Whitehall PA. 215-432-4339

Hizny, Annette, *Per,* Marywood College Library, Scranton PA. 717-343-6521, Ext 289

Hlavac, Ruth Ann, *Librn,* Louisville Public Library, Louisville NE. 402-234-6265

Hlavka, Gailyn, *Librn,* Fairfax County Public Library (Reston Regional), Reston VA. 703-860-2600

Hluchany, Gladyne, *On-Line Servs & Bibliog Instr,* Letourneau College, Margaret Estes Library, Longview TX. 214-753-0231, Ext 230

Ho, Agnes, *ILL & Ref,* Neuse Regional Library, Kinston NC. 919-527-7066

Ho, Alan, *Cat,* George Mason University Libraries, Fairfax VA. 703-323-2616

Ho, Angie, *Cat,* University of Houston (William I Dykes Library), Houston TX. 713-749-1991

Ho, Cora, *Tech Serv,* Tufts University, Medical-Dental Library, Boston MA. 617-956-6707

Ho, D T, *Libr Supvr,* Bell Telephone Laboratories (Bell Telephone Laboratories Technical Library), Piscataway NJ. 981-6500 (Supvr); 561-2587 (South Plainfield)

Ho, Ena, *Tech Serv,* Lansing Community College Library, Lansing MI. 517-373-9978

Ho, Ena, *Instr,* Lansing Community College, Library Media Technology Program, MI. 517-373-9978

Ho, G, *Cat,* University of Missouri-Rolla Library, Rolla MO. 314-341-4227

Ho, Herbert L, *Librn,* Legal Assistance Foundation of Chicago Library, Chicago IL. 312-341-1070, Ext 237

Ho, J, *Tech Serv,* Canada Department of Energy, Mines & Resources (Canada Center for Mineral & Energy Technology Library), Ottawa ON. 613-995-4132

Ho, James K K, *Actg Asst Dir for Tech Servs,* Howard University Libraries, Founders Library, Washington DC. 202-636-7253

Ho, James K K, *Asst Dir,* Howard University Libraries (Social Work Library), Washington DC. 202-636-7253

Ho, Rosa, *Dir,* Saint Andrew's College Library, Saskatoon SK. 306-343-5145

Hoad, Carol, *Librn,* Oswego City Library, Oswego NY. 315-341-5867

Hoadley, Irene B, *Dir,* Texas A&m University Libraries, College Station TX. 713-845-6111
Hoag, Catherine, *Librn,* Jackson District Library (Liberty), Clarklake MI. 517-529-4374
Hoag, Judith, *Ref,* Central North Carolina Regional Library, Burlington NC. 919-227-2096
Hoag, Susie, *Librn,* Detroit Public Library (Richard), Detroit MI. 313-833-9763
Hoage, Elizabeth, *Librn,* Los Angeles Public Library System (Exposition Park, Mary McLeod Bethune), Los Angeles CA. 213-732-0169
Hoagland, Joan, *In Charge,* Cleveland Public Library (Fine Arts), Cleveland OH. 216-623-2848
Hoagland, Maria, *Asst Librn,* Ridgway Memorial Library, Bullitt County Library, Shepherdsville KY. 502-543-7675
Hoare, C G D, *In Charge,* Hoffmann-La Roche Ltd, Medical Information Library, Vaudreuil PQ. 514-487-8425
Hoare, V E, *Librn,* Canada Department of Energy, Mines & Resources (Surveys & Mapping Branch), Ottawa ON. 613-995-4071
Hoats, Margaret, *Librn,* Hazleton Area Public Library (McAdoo), Hazleton PA. 717-929-1120
Hobart, Helen L, *Librn,* Laingsburg Public Library, Laingsburg MI. 517-651-6282
Hobbins, Joan, *Lectr,* Concordia University, Library Studies Program, PQ. 514-482-0320, Ext 324
Hobbins, Ruthann, *Librn,* Public Library of Columbus & Franklin County (South High), Columbus OH. 614-497-9588
Hobble, Florence, *Librn,* Oregon State Hospital (Medical Library), Salem OR. 503-378-2266
Hobbs, Barbara, *Librn,* Veterans Administration, Hospital Medical Library, Waco TX. 817-752-6581
Hobbs, Brian, *AV,* Pembroke Public Library, Pembroke ON. 613-732-8844
Hobbs, Jane, *Librn,* Wilkes County Public Library, North Wilkesboro NC. 919-838-2818
Hobbs, Mary, *Trade Spec,* United States Department of Commerce, Minneapolis District Office Library, Minneapolis MN. 617-725-2134
Hobbs, Marylou, *Librn,* Fairfax County Public Library (Dolly Madison), McLean VA. 703-356-0770
Hobbs, Molly, *Librn,* Waurika Library, Waurika OK. 405-228-3308
Hobbs, Nola, *Acq,* University of Tennessee at Martin, Paul Meek Library, Martin TN. 901-587-7060
Hobbs, Thomas C, *Asst Librn,* Prestonsburg Community College Library, Prestonsburg KY. 606-886-3863
Hobbs, Wylma, *Librn,* Woodbury County Rural Library (Hornick Branch), Hornick IA. 712-873-3322
Hobday, Barbara Fenrich, *Librn,* Enoch Pratt Free Library (Bookmobile Headquarters), Baltimore MD. 301-396-5430, 396-5395
Hobeika, George, *Tech Serv,* Florence County Library, Florence SC. 803-662-8424
Hobert, Edith, *Librn,* City County Library, Munday TX. 512-422-4877
Hobgood, Katherine, *Circ,* Chicago State University, Paul & Emily Douglas Library, Chicago IL. 312-995-2254
Hobin, James R, *Librn,* Albany Institute of History & Art, McKinney Library, Albany NY. 518-463-4478
Hobrock, Brice G, *Asst Dean, Planning & Res,* University of Nebraska-Lincoln, University Libraries, Lincoln NE. 402-472-2526
Hobson, Gladys, *Librn,* Cleveland County Library, Rison AR. 501-325-7270
Hobson, Jane, *ILL,* Georgia State University, William Russell Pullen Library, Atlanta GA. 404-658-2185, 658-2172
Hobson, Kitty A, *Archivist,* Oshkosh Public Museum Library, Oshkosh WI. 414-424-0452
Hobson, Mary, *ILL,* Chula Vista Public Library, Chula Vista CA. 714-427-1151
Hobson, Pam, *Tech Serv,* Florida Institute of Technology Library, Melbourne FL. 305-723-3701, Ext 270
Hocamp, Dianne Sample, *Librn,* Milton Roy Company, Applied Research Library, Saint Petersburg FL. 813-544-2581, Ext 325
Hoch, Flora Jeanne, *Librn,* Downingtown Library Co, Downingtown PA. 215-269-2741

Hoch, Janet W, *Librn,* Kate Love Simpson Library, McConnelsville OH. 614-962-2533
Hoch, Minnie B, *Dir,* Community College of Baltimore, Bard Library, Baltimore MD. 301-396-0432, 0433
Hochberg, Alan C, *Asst Head Librn & Ref,* State University Agricultural & Technical College at Farmingdale, Thomas D Greenley Library, Farmingdale NY. 516-420-2011, 420-2012
Hochberg, Barbara, *Librn,* Berkshire Community College, Jonathan Edwards Library, Pittsfield MA. 413-499-4660, Ext 201, 202, 203
Hochberg, Barbara, *Bibliog Instr,* Berkshire Community College, Jonathan Edwards Library, Pittsfield MA. 413-499-4660, Ext 201, 202, 203
Hochschild, Susan, *Asst Dir & Ad,* William Jeanes Memorial Library, Lafayette Hill PA. 215-828-0441
Hochsprung, Loretta, *Librn,* Brownton Public Library, Brownton MN. 612-328-5900
Hock, Paula C, *Librn,* Salt Lake City Public Library (Chapman), Salt Lake City UT. 801-363-5733
Hockenberry, Velma, *Asst Dir,* John Graham Newville Public Library, Newville PA. 717-776-5900
Hocker, Justine L, *Librn,* Haverford Township Free Library, Havertown PA. 215-446-3082
Hockersmith, Charles E, *Dir,* Cecil Community College, Learning Resource Center, North East MD. 301-287-6060, Ext 217
Hockett, Jane, *Ref & Bibliog Instr,* Whittier College (Bonnie Bell Wardman Library), Whittier CA. 213-693-0771, Ext 223
Hocking, Evelyn, *Asst Dir,* South Haven Memorial Library, South Haven MI. 616-637-2403
Hodapp, Gladys, *Asst Librn,* College of Insurance Library, New York NY. 212-962-4111, Ext 277
Hodge, Ruth E, *Cat,* United States Army War College Library, Carlisle Barracks PA. 717-245-4319
Hodge, Linda, *AV & Media,* Bellingham Public Library, Bellingham WA. 206-676-6860
Hodge, Lyla M, *Librn,* Roodhouse Public Library, Roodhouse IL. 217-589-5123
Hodge, Muriel, *Archivist,* Hobart & William Smith Colleges, Warren Hunting Smith Library, Geneva NY. 315-789-5500, Ext 224
Hodge, Patricia, *Librn,* Exxon Co USA, Medical Department, Linden NJ. 201-474-2506
Hodge, Sister Patricia A, *Dir,* Trinity College Library, Burlington VT. 802-658-0337, Ext 343
Hodge, Stanley P, *Resource Develop,* Texas A&M University Libraries, College Station TX. 713-845-6111
Hodgeman, Suzanne I, *Hispanic,* University of Wisconsin-Madison, Memorial Library, Madison WI. 608-262-3521
Hodges, Anne E, *Ref,* Converse College, Gwathmey Library, Spartanburg SC. 803-585-6421, Ext 260
Hodges, Deborah, *Asst Dir,* Hutchinson Community Junior College, John F Kennedy Library & Learning Resources Center, Hutchinson KS. 316-663-5781, Ext 125
Hodges, Gerald G, *Asst Prof,* University of North Carolina at Greensboro, Library Science-Educational Technology Div, NC. 919-379-5710
Hodges, Janice, *Librn,* Greensboro Public Librar (Pomona), Greensboro NC. 919-852-0053
Hodges, Jessie K, *Librn,* Sherman County Public Library, Stratford TX. 806-396-2200
Hodges, Jo, *Per,* Grand Canyon College, Fleming Library, Phoenix AZ. 602-249-3300, Ext 207
Hodges, John S, *Librn,* Fiske Public Library, Wrentham MA. 617-384-2761
Hodges, Judith, *Librn,* Tennessee Hospital Association, Inc Library, Nashville TN. 615-256-8240
Hodges, Kathy, *Sr Librn,* Johns-Manville Corporation (Corporate Information Center), Denver CO. 979-1000 Ext 3440, 3448
Hodges, Kathy, *Librn,* Regional Transportation District Library, Denver CO. 303-759-1000, Ext 467
Hodges, Linda, *Dir,* Humanistic Psychology Institute, Abraham H Maslow Memorial Library, San Francisco CA. 415-626-4494
Hodges, Lois F, *Ch,* Schenectady County Public Library, Schenectady NY. 518-382-3500
Hodges, Lottie, *Exten Coordr,* Pine Mountain Regional Library, Manchester GA. 404-846-2186

Hodges, Louise, *ILL,* Amherst County Public Library, Amherst VA. 804-946-5260
Hodges, Louise, *Tech Serv & Br Coordr,* Kings County Library, Hanford CA. 209-582-0261
Hodges, Marcia, *Ref,* Brunswick-Glynn County Regional Library, Brunswick GA. 912-264-7360
Hodges, Margaret, *Emer Prof,* University of Pittsburgh, School of Library & Information Science, PA. 412-624-5230
Hodges, Mrs Bill, *Circ,* Kurth Memorial Library, Lufkin TX. 713-634-7923
Hodges, Richard, *Dir,* University of Puget Sound, School Librarianship Program, WA. 206-756-3391
Hodges, Susan, *ILL,* Bangor Public Library, Bangor ME. 207-947-8336
Hodges, T Mark, *Dir,* Vanderbilt University Medical Center Library, Nashville TN. 615-322-2292
Hodgin, Ellis, *Dir,* College of Charleston, Robert Scott Small Library, Charleston SC. 803-792-5530
Hodgin, Sue, *Circ,* Rockingham Community College Library, Learning Resources Center, Wentworth NC. 919-342-4261, Ext 245
Hodgkin, Helen S, *Dir,* Oneida Library, Oneida NY. 315-363-3050
Hodgkinson, Sharon, *Librn,* Perth Public Library, Perth ON. 613-267-1224
Hodgson, Joan, *ILL,* University of California, University Library, Santa Cruz CA. 408-429-2076
Hodgson, Verda, *Cat,* Lethbridge Public Library, Lethbridge AB. 403-329-3233
Hodina, Alfred, *Sci & Eng,* University of California, Santa Barbara Library, Santa Barbara CA. 805-961-2741
Hodos, Susan, *Librn,* Broward County Division of Libraries (Lauderdale Lakes Branch), Lauderdale Lakes FL. 305-731-2424
Hodowanec, George V, *Dir,* Emporia State University, William Allen White Library, Emporia KS. 316-343-1200, Ext 205
Hodson, Janet, *Br Coordr,* Bryan Public Library, Bryan OH. 419-636-2937
Hodson, Maradee, *Acq,* A K Smiley Public Library, Redlands CA. 714-793-2201
Hodson, Ruby J, *Librn,* Britt Public Library, Britt IA. 515-843-4245
Hoe, William S, *Librn,* Ogunquit Memorial Library, Wells ME. 207-646-9024
Hoeber, Mary, *Cat,* Mission College, Learning Resource Services, Santa Clara CA. 408-988-2200, Ext 1531
Hoefler, Barbara Burton, *Chief Librn,* Hawaii Pacific College, Meader Library, Honolulu HI. 808-521-3881
Hoeft, Marjorie, *Cat,* Blue Mountain Community College Library, Pendleton OR. 503-276-1260, Ext 234
Hoegh, Gloria C, *Asst Dir,* Winnefox Library System, Oshkosh WI. 414-424-0486
Hoehl, Mary D, *Cat,* Robert Morris College Library, Coraopolis PA. 412-264-9300
Hoehle, Frances, *Per & Ser,* North Dakota State University Library, Fargo ND. 701-237-8876
Hoehn, Marie, *Bkmobile Coordr,* Stamford's Public Library, Ferguson Library, Stamford CT. 203-325-4354
Hoehn, Mary Ann, *Tech Serv,* East Central Regional Library, Cambridge MN. 612-689-1901
Hoekman, Dixie, *Consultant,* Davis, Hockenberg, Wine, Brown & Koehn Library, Des Moines IA. 515-243-2300
Hoekstra, Ruth, *Asst Librn,* Ocheyedan Public Library, Ocheyedan IA. 712-758-3352
Hoelle, Delores, *Librn,* Princeton University Library (Engineering), Princeton NJ. 609-452-3180
Hoelle, Edith, *Librn,* Gloucester County Historical Society Library, Woodbury NJ. 609-845-4771
Hoelting, Leona, *Volunteer Servs,* Chicago Public Library, Chicago IL. 312-269-2900
Hoelzl, Mary L, *Librn,* Cuyahoga County Public Library (Middleburg Heights Branch), Middleburg Heights OH. 216-234-3600
Hoeper, Sharon, *Librn,* Mercy Medical Center, Health Sciences Library, Oshkosh WI. 414-231-3300, Ext 285
Hoepfner, Jean, *Corp Files,* Donaldson, Lufkin & Jenrette Securities Corp, Corporate Library, New York NY. 212-943-0300, Ext 1356-9

Hoerl, Laone, *YA,* Marshfield Free Library, Marshfield WI. 715-384-2929, 387-1302

Hoerter, Eleanor, *Libr Clerk,* Mid-State Technical Institute, Stevens Point Campus Library, Stevens Point WI. 715-344-3063

Hoey, Evelyn, *Dir,* State University of New York, Upstate Medical Center Library, Syracuse NY. 315-473-4580

Hof, Marianna, *YA & Ref,* Oyster Bay-East Norwich Public Library, Oyster Bay NY. 516-922-1212

Hofbauer, Jenna, *Librn,* Canadian Association in Support of the Native People, Toronto Library & Information Centre, Toronto ON. 416-964-0169

Hofer, Louise, *Librn,* Broward County Division of Libraries (Hollywood Branch), Hollywood FL. 305-921-3418

Hofer, Sherry, *Circ,* University of Wisconsin-Whitewater, Library & Learning Resources, Whitewater WI. 414-472-1000

Hoff, Anne, *Ref,* Pike-Amite-Walthall Library System, McComb Public Library (Headquaters), McComb MS. 601-684-7034

Hoff, Carole, *On-Line Servs & Bibliog Instr,* McGaw Laboratories Technical Information, Irvine CA. 714-754-2066

Hoff, Janette, *Librn,* Hood River County Library (Parkdale Branch), Parkdale OR. 503-352-2562

Hoffacker, Michael P N, *Librn,* Ardmore Free Library, Ardmore PA. 215-642-5187

Hoffeld, Sheila, *Librn,* Albany Public Library (New Scotland), Albany NY. 518-482-6661

Hoffer, Beth, *Ch,* Lynnfield Public Library, Lynnfield MA. 617-334-5411

Hoffer, F B, *Librn,* Virginia Division of Mineral Resources Library, Charlottesville VA. 804-293-5121

Hoffert, Marvin, *Media,* Mount Vernon Nazarene College Library, Mount Vernon OH. 614-397-1244

Hoffman, Andrea, *Asst Dir, Head Resources & Res Dir,* Teachers College - Columbia University Library, New York NY. 212-678-3022, 678-3020

Hoffman, Barbara, *YA,* Connetquot Public Library, Bohemia NY. 516-567-5115

Hoffman, Barbara, *Ch,* John Mosser Public Library, Abingdon IL. 309-462-3129

Hoffman, Catherine, *Cat,* Warren County Library, Belvidere NJ. 201-475-5361, Ext 114

Hoffman, Claire, *Info Specialist,* World Data Center-A for Glaciology Library, Boulder CO. 303-492-5171

Hoffman, Daphne T, *On-Line Servs,* Portland State University, Branford Price Millar Library, Portland OR. 503-229-4424

Hoffman, David R, *LSCA, Title III, Interlibr Coop, Acad & Spec Libr Servs,* State Library of Pennsylvania, Harrisburg PA. 717-787-2646

Hoffman, Frances, *Tech Serv,* Saint Mary's University (Academic Library), San Antonio TX. 512-436-3441

Hoffman, Frank, *Asst Prof,* Sam Houston State University, Library Science Department, TX. 713-295-6211, Ext 1151

Hoffman, Gertrude C, *Dir,* Joshua Hyde Public Library, Sturbridge MA. 617-347-3735

Hoffman, Helen, *Librn,* Rutgers University (Waksman Institute of Microbiology), Piscataway NJ. 201-932-2907

Hoffman, Herbert, *Tech Serv & Ref,* Santa Ana College, Nealley Library, Santa Ana CA. 714-835-3000, Ext 357

Hoffman, Kathy, *Cat,* Houston Academy of Medicine, Texas Medical Center Library, Houston TX. 713-797-1230

Hoffman, Marcia, *Librn,* Crowsnest Municipal Library (Coleman Municipal Library), Coleman AB. 403-563-3757

Hoffman, Martha E, *Dir,* Flora-Monroe Public Library, Flora IN. 219-967-3912

Hoffman, Mary Ann, *Librn,* Saint Elizabeth Medical Center, Health Sciences Library, Dayton OH. 513-223-3141, Ext 564

Hoffman, Mary Ann, *Spec Coll,* Wright State University Library (Fordham Library, Cox Heart Institute Library & Fels Research Institute Library), Dayton OH. 513-873-2266

Hoffman, Maurine W, *Dir,* Matteson Public Library, Matteson IL. 312-748-4431

Hoffman, Nancy, *Cat,* Southern Methodist University Libraries (Central University Libraries), Dallas TX. 214-692-2400

Hoffman, Paul, *Computer,* Rockford Public Library, Rockford IL. 815-965-6731

Hoffman, Raphaela, *Librn,* Bethel-Tulpehocken Free Public Library, Bethel PA. 717-933-5169

Hoffman, Rich, *Cat & Bibliog Instr,* Biola College & Talbot Theological Seminary, Rosemead Graduate School of Professional Psychology, Rose Memorial Library, La Mirada CA. 213-944-0351, Ext 3255

Hoffman, Sandra, *Lectr,* Concordia University, Library Studies Program, PQ. 514-482-0320, Ext 324

Hoffman, Sidney, *Librn,* Inkster Public Library, Inkster MI. 313-563-1144

Hoffman, Sister M Anne Lucy, *Librn,* Mount Mary College Library, Milwaukee WI. 414-258-4810, Ext 234

Hoffman, Sylvia, *Librn,* Nossaman Krueger & Marsh Library, Los Angeles CA. 213-628-5221

Hoffman, Veronica E, *In Charge,* Irvington Public Library (Baillet), Irvington NJ. 201-372-6403

Hoffman, Wallace, *Acq,* Fullerton College, William T Boyce Library, Fullerton CA. 714-871-8000

Hoffman, Wallace, *Prof,* Fullerton College, Library Technician Program, CA. 714-871-8000, Ext 244

Hoffman, William, *Bus,* Tacoma Public Library, Tacoma WA. 206-572-2000

Hoffman, William J, *Dir,* Mount San Antonio College, Learning Resources Center, Walnut CA. 714-594-5611, Ext 260

Hoffman, Winona, *Librn,* Waterbury Public Library, Waterbury VT. 802-244-7036

Hoffmann, Carole, *ILL,* Vermont Technical College, Hartness Library, Randolph Center VT. 802-728-3391, Ext 32

Hoffmann, Ellen, *Asst Dir Special Servs,* York University, Scott Library, Downsview ON. 416-667-2235

Hoffmann, Lydia M, *Dir,* Town of Hamburg Public Library, Hamburg NY. 716-649-4415

Hoffmeister, Fran, *Media,* Saint Paul Technical Vocational Library, Saint Paul MN. 612-221-1410

Hoffschneider, Dale W, *Dir,* Carnegie Public Library, Ironwood MI. 906-932-0203

Hoffsis, Wallis D, *Acq,* Florida State University (Law Library), Tallahassee FL. 904-644-1004

Hoffsommer, Alene, *Acq,* Saint Joseph Public Library, Saint Joseph MO. 816-232-7729, 232-7720

Hofmann, Anne, *Librn,* New York Public Library (Clason's Point), New York NY. 212-842-1235

Hofmann, Catherine N, *Central Servs,* Ventura County Library Services Agency, Ventura County Library, Ventura CA. 805-654-2627

Hofmann, Dolores, *Cat,* University of Detroit Library, Detroit MI. 313-927-1090

Hofmann, William, *Microforms,* State University of New York, Frank Melville Jr Memorial Library, Stony Brook NY. 516-246-5650

Hofstad, Richard J, *Athenaeum Librn & Bk Selection,* Minneapolis Public Library & Information Center, Minneapolis MN. 612-372-6500

Hofstetter, Eleanore O, *Assoc Dir Pub Serv,* Towson State University, Albert S Cook Library, Towson MD. 301-321-2450

Hofstetter, Jo, *Librn,* Harris County Public Library (La Porte Branch), La Porte TX. 713-471-4022

Hogan, Alan D, *Asst Dir,* University of Toledo, William S Carlson Library, Toledo OH. 419-537-2324

Hogan, C J, *In Charge,* International Federation of Petroleum & Chemical Workers, IFPCW Library, Denver CO. 303-388-9237

Hogan, Carol, *Media,* Chabot College, Learning Resource Center, Hayward CA. 415-786-6762

Hogan, Debra K, *Librn,* Sheppard, Mullin, Richter & Hampton Library, Los Angeles CA. 213-620-1780, Ext 266

Hogan, Edmund, *Librn,* International Silver Co Library, Meriden CT. 203-634-2500

Hogan, Elaine, *Asst Librn,* Emmaus Bible School Library, Oak Park IL. 312-383-7000, Ext 55

Hogan, Fannie, *Librn,* Clark College, Marquis L Harris Library, Atlanta GA. 404-681-3080

Hogan, James, *Dir,* Brock University Library, Saint Catharines ON. 416-684-7201

Hogan, Louise G, *Dir,* Seneca Public Library, Seneca IL. 815-357-6566

Hogan, Mary, *Outreach,* George Amos Memorial Library, Campbell County Library, Gillette WY. 307-682-3223

Hogan, Patricia M, *Info Librn & Computer Coordr,* North Suburban Library System, Wheeling IL. 312-459-1300

Hogan, Peggy, *Librn,* Calgary Herald Library, Calgary AB. 403-269-6361

Hogan, Rev Ernest A, *Librn,* Providence College, Phillips Memorial Library, Providence RI. 401-865-2242

Hogan, Rose, *Dir,* University of Arkansas for Medical Sciences Library, Little Rock AR. 501-661-5980

Hogan, Sarah, *Cat,* North Texas State University Library, Denton TX. 817-788-2411

Hogan, Sharon A, *Asst to Dir,* University of Michigan Libraries (University Library), Ann Arbor MI. 313-764-9356

Hogan, Virginia C, *Ch & Syst Coordr,* Oconee Regional Library, Laurens County Library, Dublin GA. 912-272-5710

Hoganson, Mary, *Asst Dir,* Park County Public Library, Bailey CO. 303-838-5539

Hogarty, Inez, *Librn,* Leber Katz Partners Inc, Marketing Information Center, New York NY. 212-826-3900

Hoge, Robert W, *Dir,* Sanford Museum & Planetarium, Reference Library, Cherokee IA. 712-225-3922

Hogen, Mrs Lowell, *Librn,* Beresford Public Library, Beresford SD. 605-763-2782

Hogeveen, Eunice, *Librn,* Touche Ross-P S Ross & Partners, Library-Information Center, Toronto ON. 416-364-4242, Ext 350; 366-6521, Ext 248

Hogg, Jerry L, *Librn,* Standard Oil Co (Indiana), Amoco Production Co, Exploration Library, Houston TX. 713-652-5222

Hogg, Marjorie, *Dir,* Caroline Kennedy Library, Dearborn Heights MI. 313-278-1464

Hogg, Muriel, *Librn,* Stauffer Chemical Co, Information Services, Dobbs Ferry NY. 914-693-1200

Hoggard, Frances, *Librn,* Lawrence Memorial Public Library, Windsor NC. 919-794-2244

Hogue, Betty, *Ch,* Palo Alto City Library, Palo Alto CA. 415-329-2436

Hogue, Betty, *Librn,* Palo Alto City Library (Children's), Palo Alto CA. 415-329-2134

Hogwood, Flo, *Asst Dir,* Duncan Public Library, Duncan OK. 405-255-0636

Hohenstein, Margaret, *Govt Publications,* University of Wisconsin-Platteville, Elton S Karrmann Library, Platteville WI. 608-342-1688

Hohhof, Bonnie, *Libr Mgr,* Motorola, Inc, Communications Group Library, Schaumburg IL. 312-576-5949

Hohl, Robert, *Ref & Bibliog Instr,* Saint Mary's College, Alumnae Centennial Library, Notre Dame IN. 219-284-4242

Hohlmayer, Arthur F, *Librn,* Springfield Bar & Law Library Association, Springfield OH. 513-324-5871, Ext 256

Hohman, Carolyn, *Media,* Hayner Public Library District, Alton IL. 618-462-0651

Hohmeister, Catharine, *ILL,* State Library of Florida, Div of Library Services, Dept of State, Tallahassee FL. 904-487-2651

Hohmeister, Catherine G, *Head of Loans Section,* Florida Library Information Network, FL. 904-487-2651

Hohn, Dianne, *Chief Librn,* Veterans Administration, Hospital Medical Library, Butler PA. 412-287-4781

Hoijer, Linda, *Tech Serv,* Menominee County Library, Stephenson MI. 906-753-6923

Hoistman, Helen, *Rare Bks & Spec Coll,* Jennings County Public Library, North Vernon IN. 812-346-2091

Hokanson, Sherry Ann, *Head of Field Servs,* Florida Regional Library for the Blind & Physically Handicapped, Daytona Beach FL. 904-252-4722

Hoke, Elizabeth, *Ch,* Montgomery County Department of Public Libraries, Rockville MD. 301-279-1401

Hoke, Elizabeth G, *Librn,* Wadsworth Atheneum, Auerbach Art Library, Hartford CT. 203-278-2670, Ext 257

Hoke, Grace, *Ref,* Haverstraw Kings Daughters Public Library, Haverstraw NY. 914-429-3445

Hoke, Jerry, *Asst Librn,* Wharton County Junior College, J M Hodges Learning Center, Wharton TX. 713-532-4560, Ext 36

Hoke, Pavey, *Media,* Lord Fairfax Community College, Learning Resource Center, Middletown VA. 703-869-1120

Hoke, Sheila Wilder, *Dir,* Southwestern Oklahoma State University, Al Harris Library, Weatherford OK. 405-772-6611, Ext 5311

Hoke, Susan B, *Ch,* Emmaus Public Library, Emmaus PA. 215-965-9284

Holab-Abelman, Robin, *Librn,* Fabric Research Library, Albany International Co, Dedham MA. 617-326-5500, Ext 216, 217

Holab-Ableman, Robin, *Asst Librn,* Camp, Dresser & Mckee, Herman G Dresser Library, Boston MA. 617-742-5151

Holahan, Jane, *Selection Servs Librns,* Dallas Public Library, Dallas TX. 214-748-9071

Holben, Dorothy, *Librn,* Moscow-Latah County Library System (Genesee Branch), Genesee ID 208-285-1398

Holbert, Sue E, *State Archivist,* Minnesota Historical Society (Division of Archives & Manuscripts), Saint Paul MN. 612-296-6980

Holbert, Zella J, *Curr Libr,* Columbia Union College, Theofield G Weis Library, Takoma Park MD. 301-270-4999

Holbrook, Betty J, *Ch,* Pocatello Public Library, Information and Video Center, Pocatello ID. 208-232-1263

Holcomb, Charlotte, *Acq,* Rochester Institute of Technology, Wallace Memorial Library, Rochester NY. 716-475-2566

Holcomb, J, *Med Librn,* Veterans Administration, Medical Center Library, Milwaukee WI. 414-384-2000, Ext 2354

Holcomb, Janet, *Librn,* Historic Saint Augustine Preservation Board, Hispanic Research Library, Saint Augustine FL. 904-824-3355

Holcomb, Joyce, *Tech Serv,* Midland College, Learning Resources Center, Midland TX. 915-684-7851, Ext 214

Holcomb, Kay, *Ad,* Champaign County Library, Urbana OH. 513-653-3811

Holcomb, Virginia, *Spec Coll,* Lee College, Learning Resources Center, Baytown TX. 713-427-5611, Ext 279, 277

Holcombe, Alice K, *Dir,* Taylor University, Ayres Alumni Memorial Library, Upland IN. 317-998-2751, Ext 241

Holcumb, Janice, *Librn,* Modoc County Library (Lookout), Lookout CA. 916-233-2719

Holdeman, Elizabeth H, *Asst Dir,* Keystone Junior College, Miller Library, La Plume PA. 717-945-5141, Ext 275

Holdeman, Menno, *Dir,* Cloud County Community College, Learning Resources Center, Concordia KS. 913-243-1435

Holden, Chris, *ILL,* Wilbraham Public Library, Wilbraham MA. 413-596-6142

Holden, Eileen, *Circ,* Itasca Community Library, Itasca IL. 312-773-1699

Holden, Elizabeth F, *Librn,* First Presbyterian Church Library, Phoenixville PA. 215-933-8816

Holden, Enid, *Librn,* Sudbury Public Library (Copper Cliff Centennial), Copper Cliff ON. 705-673-1155, Ext 45

Holden, Harley P, *Curator Univ Archives,* Harvard University Library, Cambridge MA. 617-495-3650

Holden, Myretta, *Dir,* Horseshoe Bend Regional Library, Dadeville AL. 205-825-9232

Holden, Nancy, *Circ,* University of Maryland at Baltimore (School of Law Library), Baltimore MD. 301-528-7270

Holden, Sandee, *Ch,* Oil City Library, Oil City PA. 814-646-8771

Holden, Valentine, *ILL,* Kelso Public Library, Kelso WA. 206-423-8110

Holden, Wendy C, *In Charge,* Saint Mary's Hospital, Doctors Library, East Saint Louis IL. 618-274-1900

Holden, Winifred, *Admin Asst,* Chippewa Falls Public Library, Chippewa County Library Service, Chippewa Falls WI. 715-723-1147

Holder, Nell T, *Librn,* Combustion Engineering, Inc, Metallurgical & Materials Library, Chattanooga TN. 615-265-4631, Ext 3132

Holder, Paul, *Sci & Tech,* Hamilton Public Library, Hamilton ON. 416-529-8111

Holder, Priscilla D, *Acq,* University of Charleston, Andrew S Thomas Memorial Library, Charleston WV. 304-346-1400

Holder, Wanda C, *Librn,* United States Army (Post Library), Fort Leavenworth KS. 913-684-4021

Holdorf, John, *Assoc Librn,* Union College, MacKay Library-Learning Resource Center, Cranford NJ. 201-276-2600, Ext 244

Holdredge, Faith A, *Dir,* Sevier County Public Library, Sevierville TN. 615-453-3532

Holdridge, Robert E, *Instr,* Illinois State University, Department of Information Sciences, IL. 309-438-3671

Hole, Carol, *Bkmobile Coordr,* Santa Fe Regional Library, Gainesville Public Library Headquarters, Gainesville FL. 904-374-2091

Holian, Lydia, *Assoc Librn,* Case Western Reserve University & Cleveland Medical Library Association, Cleveland Health Sciences Library, Cleveland OH. 216-368-3426

Holian, Lydia T, *Adjunct Prof,* Case Western Reserve University, School of Library Science, OH. 216-368-3500

Holibaugh, Ralph, *Music,* William Marsh Rice University, Fondren Library, Houston TX. 713-527-4022

Holicky, Bernard H, *Dir,* Purdue University Calumet Library, Hammond IN. 219-844-0520, Ext 249

Holiday, Ann, *Cat,* Tulane University of Louisiana (Matas Medical Library), New Orleans LA. 504-588-5155

Holl, Deborah G, *ILL, On-Line Servs & Bibliog Instr,* Rosemont College, Gertrude Kistler Memorial Library, Rosemont PA. 215-527-0200, Ext 226

Hollaar, Hester M, *Dir,* Dordt College Library, Sioux Center IA. 712-722-3771, Ext 139

Hollaar, Hester M, *Head,* Dordt College, Library Science Minor Program, IA. 712-722-3771, Ext 139

Holland, Barron G, *ILL & Ref,* Monterey Institute of International Studies, William Tell Coleman Library, Monterey CA. 408-649-3113, Ext 50&52

Holland, Debra, *Ref,* Colonie Town Library, Loudonville NY. 518-458-9274

Holland, Edna, *Dir,* Gail Borden Public Library District, Elgin IL. 312-742-2411

Holland, Gloria J, *Chief Librn,* United States Army (Mobility Equipment Research & Development Command Technical Library), Fort Belvoir VA. 703-664-5179

Holland, Harold, *Assoc Prof,* University of Missouri-Columbia, School of Library & Informational Science, MO. 314-882-4546

Holland, Helen, *Tech Serv & Cat,* Corvallis Public Library, Corvallis-Benton County Library, Corvallis OR. 503-757-6928

Holland, Hester, *Media,* Rockbridge Regional Library, Lexington VA. 703-463-4324

Holland, Jane, *Librn,* Fulbright & Jaworski Law Library, Houston TX. 713-651-5219, 651-5151

Holland, Jeannie, *Librn,* Chatham-Effingham-Liberty Regional Library (Pooler Branch), Pooler GA. 912-748-0471

Holland, Karine, *Asst Librn,* Warren Township Public Library, Warren IL. 815-745-2076

Holland, Lawrence, *Spec Coll,* Jersey City State College, Forrest A Irwin Library, Jersey City NJ. 201-547-3026

Holland, M A, *ILL,* Huron Valley Library System, Ann Arbor MI. 313-971-6056

Holland, M A, *ILL,* Washtenaw County Library, Ann Arbor MI. 313-971-6056

Holland, Margaret, *Librn,* Bison Community Library, Bison KS. 913-356-4608

Holland, Martha, *Circ,* Lamar University, Mary & John Gray Library, Beaumont TX. 713-838-8313

Holland, Mary K, *Dir,* College of Alameda Library & Resources Center, Alameda CA. 415-522-7221, Ext 365

Holland, Maurita P, *Librn,* University of Michigan Libraries (Engineering-Transportation), Ann Arbor MI. 313-764-7494

Holland, P F, *Librn,* E I Du Pont De Nemours & Co, Inc, Plastic Department, Research & Development Library, Orange TX. 713-886-6418

Holland, Robert D, *Supvr,* Goodyear Atomic Corp, Technical Library, Piketon OH. 614-289-2331, Ext 2177

Hollander, Gail, *Asst Librn & Cat,* Commodity Futures Trading Commission Library, Washington DC. 202-254-5901

Hollander, P, *Dir,* Catskill Public Library, Catskill NY. 518-943-4230

Hollands, N, *Librn,* American Standard Library, Toronto ON. 416-534-3521, Ext 121

Hollar, Robyn, *Ref,* Georgia Department of Education (Div of Public Library Services), Atlanta GA. 404-656-2461

Hollars, Gene, *Reproduction,* Tennessee State Library & Archives, Nashville TN. 615-741-2764

Hollaway, Esther, *Asst Librn,* Broadwater County Library, Townsend MT. 406-266-3672

Holleman, Curt, *Coll Develop,* Southern Methodist University Libraries (Fondren Humanities & Social Sciences), Dallas TX. 214-692-2323

Holleman, John, *Librn,* Los Angeles Public Library System (Sherman Oaks Branch), Sherman Oaks CA. 213-981-7850

Holleman, Margaret, *Facilitator,* Pima Community College, Library Technology Program, AZ. 602-884-6821

Holleman, Margaret, *Dir Libr Serv,* Pima Community College, West Campus Learning Resource Center, Tucson AZ. 602-884-6821

Holleman, Marian, *Dir & Spec Coll,* University of San Diego, James S Copley Library, San Diego CA. 714-291-6480, Ext 4312, 4313, 4314

Holleman, Marian, *Assoc Prof,* University of San Diego, Dept of Library Science, CA. 714-291-6480, Ext 4315

Hollenbach, Paulena, *Librn,* Midstate Regional Library, Berlin VT. 802-828-2320

Hollenhors, Sister Bernice, *Dir,* Saint Mary's College, Alumnae Centennial Library, Notre Dame IN. 219-284-4242

Hollenhorst, Kathryn, *Doc,* North Dakota State University Library, Fargo ND. 701-237-8876

Holler, Fred, *Polit Sci,* California State University, Northridge, Delmar T Oviatt & South Libraries, Northridge CA. 213-885-2271

Holler, Suzanne E, *On-Line Servs,* Winthrop College, Ida Jane Dacus Library, Rock Hill SC. 803-323-2131

Hollerich, Kathryn, *Dir,* Spring Valley Public Library, Spring Valley IL. 815-663-4741

Holley, Beth, *Cat,* Greenville Technical College, Learning Resources Center, Greenville SC. 803-242-3170, Ext 321

Holley, Edward G, *Dean,* University of North Carolina at Chapel Hill, School of Library Science, NC. 919-933-8366

Holley, James, *Librn,* Binghamton Public Library (Emma Brown First Ward), Binghamton NY. 607-722-1904

Holley, Janice, *Supv,* Procter & Gamble Co Buckeye Cellulose Corp, Cellulose & Specialties Technical Information Service, Memphis TN. 901-454-8310

Holley, Robert E, *Tech Serv,* University of Utah (Marriott Library), Salt Lake City UT. 801-581-8558

Holley, Shara, *Librn,* Northeast Regional Library (Belmont Library), Belmont MS. 601-454-7841

Holliday, Barbara, *Pharmacy,* Texas Southern University Library, Houston TX. 713-527-7121

Holliday, Judith, *Librn,* Cornell University Libraries (College of Architecture-Art), Ithaca NY. 607-256-3710

Hollifield, Lucille, *Librn,* Spruce Pine Public Library, Spruce Pine NC. 704-765-4673

Holling, Constance G, *Librn,* Brewer Public Library, Brewer ME. 207-989-7943

Hollinger, Paul, *Librn,* Lawrence University (Conservatory of Music Library), Appleton WI. 414-739-3681

Hollingsworth, Ann, *Media,* Texas State Library, Austin TX. 512-475-2166

Hollingsworth, Janis, *ILL & Ref,* Laramie County Library System, Cheyenne WY. 307-634-3561

Hollingsworth, Ken, *Spec Coll,* Roddenbery Memorial Library, Cairo GA. 912-377-3632

Hollingsworth, Rudene, *Ref, Cat & Spec Coll,* West Georgia Regional Library, Neva Lomason Memorial Library, Carrollton GA. 404-832-1381

Hollingsworth, Rudene B, *Dir,* Oak Grove Baptist Church Library, Carrollton GA. 404-834-7019

Hollis, Thomas W, *Librn,* Henderson District Public Library, Henderson NV. 702-565-8402

Hollis, Tricia, *Info Specialist,* Mississippi Library Commission, Jackson MS. 601-354-6369
Hollis, Vida, *Librn,* Northeastern Regional Library, Cimarron NM. 505-376-2474
Hollman, Edward, *Soc Sci & Educ,* Oklahoma State University Library, Stillwater OK. 405-624-6313
Hollmann, Pauline V, *Dir, Info Servs,* Geomet Technologies Inc, Information Center Library, Rockville MD. 301-770-1500
Holloman, Martha, *Librn,* Halifax County Library, Halifax NC. 919-583-3631
Hollon, Josephine, *Bkmobile Coordr,* Wolfe County Library, Campton KY. 606-668-6571
Holloway, Bobby E, *Asst Univ Librn Tech Serv,* Auburn University, Ralph Brown Draughton Library, Auburn AL. 205-826-4500
Holloway, Jean, *Asst Dir,* Brown Deer Public Library, Brown Deer WI. 414-354-3440
Holloway, Mary, *Librn,* Lebo Public Library, Lebo KS. 316-256-6828
Holloway, Marye, *Libr Tech,* United States Air Force (Beale Air Force Base Library), Beale AFB CA. 916-634-2706
Holloway, Ralph, *Asst Dir (ID),* Eastfield College, Learning Resources Center, Mesquite TX. 214-746-3168
Holloway, Sue L, *Librn,* Beatty Community Library, Beatty NV. 702-553-2257
Holloway, Jr, Joaquin M, *Media,* University of South Alabama (University Library), Mobile AL. 205-460-7021
Hollowell, Edith, *Librn,* Wichita Public Library (Sweetbriar), Wichita KS. 316-262-0611
Holly, Philip, *Acq,* Angelo State University, Porter Henderson Library, San Angelo TX. 915-942-2222
Hollyfield, Diane, *Media,* George Washington University Library, Washington DC. 202-676-6455
Holm, Alice G, *Librn,* Odessa Public Library, Odessa WA. 509-982-2654
Holm, Edla, *ILL,* University of Massachusetts at Amherst Library, Amherst MA. 413-545-0284
Holman, Alberta, *Ref & ILL,* Oakwood College, Eva B Dykes Library, Huntsville AL. 205-837-1630, Ext 275
Holman, Anna, *Librn,* University of Western Ontario (Education), London ON. 519-679-6307
Holman, Emily, *Ch,* Ocean County Library, Toms River NJ. 201-349-6200
Holman, Judy, *Dir,* Tell City-Perry County Public Library, Tell City IN. 812-547-2661
Holman, Matilda L, *Librn,* Roger Williams Technical & Economic Services, Inc Library, Princeton Junction NJ. 609-799-1200
Holman, Norman, *Personnel,* Cleveland Public Library, Cleveland OH. 216-623-2800
Holmberg, Helen, *Media,* Yorba Linda Library District, Yorba Linda CA. 714-528-7039
Holmberg, Tom, *Media,* Schaumburg Township Public Library, Schaumburg IL. 312-885-3373
Holmen, Ginny, *Librn,* Mendocino County Law Library, Ukiah CA. 707-468-4481
Holmer, Eileen, *Cat,* Deere & Co Library, Moline IL. 309-752-4442
Holmes, Barbara, *Librn,* LuVerne Public Library, LuVerne IA. 515-882-3436
Holmes, Bettie S, *Librn,* Baltimore County General Hospital, Medical Staff Library, Randallstown MD. 301-922-5700
Holmes, Beverly, *Coordr,* El Centro College, Learning Resources Center, Dallas TX. 214-746-2292
Holmes, Carmen, *Librn,* United States Navy (Naval Sea Support Center, Pacific Library), San Diego CA. 714-225-4654
Holmes, Christian, *Bibliog Instr,* Bay De Noc Community College, Learning Resources Center, Escanaba MI. 906-786-5802, Ext 31
Holmes, Connie Lee, *Circ,* United States Army (Morris Swett Library), Fort Sill OK. 405-351-4525, 351-4477
Holmes, D, *Librn,* Canada Institute for Scientific & Technical Information (Energy), Ottawa ON. 613-993-1600
Holmes, D, *Librn,* Canada Institute for Scientific & Technical Information (National Aeronautical Establishment), Uplands ON. 613-993-1600
Holmes, Dixie, *Librn,* Coastal Plain Regional Library (Cook County), Adel GA. 912-896-3652

Holmes, Dorothy, *Dir, Tech Serv & Spec Coll,* Socorro Public Library, Socorro NM. 505-835-1114
Holmes, Elizabeth, *Dir, On-Line Servs & Bibliog Instr,* Saint Andrews Presbyterian College, DeTamble Library, Laurinburg NC. 919-276-3652, Ext 307, 289
Holmes, Harvey, *Mgr,* New York Times (New York Times Index), New York NY. 212-556-1418
Holmes, Hazel, *Tech Serv,* Madison County-Canton Public Library, Canton MS. 601-859-3202
Holmes, Hilda, *Librn,* Prudential Insurance Co of America, Western Home Office Business Library, Los Angeles CA. 213-857-4372
Holmes, J, *Supvr,* Huron County Public Library (Molesworth), Listowel ON. 519-291-1335
Holmes, Jimie, *YA,* Albany Dougherty Public Library, Albany GA. 912-435-2104
Holmes, Joel H, *Dir,* Columbus College, Simon Schwob Memorial Library, Columbus GA. 404-568-2042
Holmes, John L, *Dir,* Auburn Public Library, Auburn WA. 206-931-3018
Holmes, Judith, *Cat,* Kitchener Public Library, Kitchener ON. 519-743-0271
Holmes, Julia, *Ref,* Jackson-George Regional Library System, Pascagoula MS. 601-762-3406
Holmes, Julia, *Ref,* Jackson-George Regional Library System (Pascagoula City Branch), Pascagoula MS. 601-762-3406
Holmes, Kathleen, *Librn,* Hudson Community Library, Hudson IA. 319-825-3600
Holmes, L, *ILL,* North Castle Public Library, Armonk NY. 914-273-3887
Holmes, Linda, *Reader Serv,* Pace University, School of Law Library, White Plains NY. 914-682-7272
Holmes, Lois L, *Librn,* Elberta Public Library, Elberta MI. 616-352-4351
Holmes, Marie, *Librn,* Stuart Public Library, Stuart IA. 515-523-2152
Holmes, Marion C, *Archivist,* San Mateo County Historical Association, Museum Library, San Mateo CA. 415-574-6441
Holmes, Mary, *Asst Dir & Ref,* Greenfield Public Library, Greenfield MA. 413-772-0989, 772-6305
Holmes, Maxine, *Circ,* Eldora Public Library, Eldora IA. 515-858-2173
Holmes, Nancy, *Librn,* Buchanan Public Library, Buchanan MI. 616-695-3681
Holmes, Peggy, *Main Libr,* Long Beach Public Library System, Long Beach CA. 213-436-9225
Holmes, Richard, *Ser,* Central Missouri State University, Ward Edwards Library, Warrensburg MO. 816-429-4141
Holmes, Ruth, *Librn,* Greig Memorial Library, Oneida IL. 309-483-3482
Holmes, Sue Ellen, *Ch,* Stevens Memorial Library, North Andover MA. 617-682-6260
Holmes, Timothy, *Librn,* Cobleskill Public Library, Cobleskill NY. 518-234-7897
Holmgren, Edwin S, *Dir Br Libr,* New York Public Library, Astor, Lenox & Tilden Foundations Library, New York NY. 212-790-6262
Holmgren, Edwin S, *Dir,* New York Public Library (The Branch Libraries), New York NY. 212-790-6262
Holmgren, L Norma, *Dir,* Locust Valley Library, Locust Valley NY. 516-671-1837
Holmquist, Carolyn, *Art & Music,* Seattle Public Library, Seattle WA. 206-625-2665
Holmquist, Norma, *Ref,* Central Connecticut State College, Elihu Burritt Library, New Britain CT. 203-827-7531
Holobeck, Noel, *Hist & Genealogy,* Saint Louis Public Library, Saint Louis MO. 314-241-2288
Holoch, Alan, *Asst Dir,* University of Southern California (Asa V Call Law Library), Los Angeles CA. 213-743-6487
Holoch, June, *Ch,* Vermillion Public Library, Vermillion SD. 605-624-2741
Holohan, John, *Media,* Tufts University, Medical-Dental Library, Boston MA. 617-956-6707
Holoman, Israel, *Bkmobile Coordr,* Laramie County Library System, Cheyenne WY. 307-634-3561
Holopigian, Jill, *Media & YA,* Bensenville Community Public Library, Bensenville IL. 312-766-4642

Holowaychuk, D, *Librn,* Camrose Public Library, Camrose AB. 403-672-4214
Holpert, Betty, *Librn,* Tucson Public Library (Main), Tucson AZ. 602-791-4391
Holscher, Peter, *Librn,* First Presbyterian Church Library, Providence RI. 401-781-4665
Holsclaw, Jr, Mrs Roy, *Librn,* Etowah Public Library, Etowah TN. 615-263-9475
Holst, Jerome A, *Librn,* Good Samaritan Hospital, Medical Library, Anaheim CA. 714-533-6220, Ext 213
Holst, Kathryn S, *Librn,* Berne Public Library, Berne IN. 219-589-2809
Holst, Ruth, *Librn,* Columbia Hospital (Medical Library), Milwaukee WI. 414-961-3858
Holste, Belle, *Librn,* Massena Public Library, Massena IA. 712-779-2295
Holstein, Lucille, *Librn,* Tracy Public Library, Tracy MN. 507-629-4011
Holstrom, Evelyn, *Librn,* Western Manitoba Regional Library (Neepawa Branch), Neepawa MB. 204-476-5648
Holsworth, Patricia A, *Librn,* Cuyahoga County Public Library (Fairview Park Regional), Fairview Park OH. 216-333-4700
Holt, Agnes M, *Librn,* Los Angeles Baptist College, Robert L Powell Memorial Library, Newhall CA. 805-259-3540
Holt, Alison, *ILL & Ref,* Simon's Rock Early College Library, Great Barrington MA. 413-528-0771, Ext 273
Holt, Barbara, *Instr,* Highline Community College Library, Library Technician Program, WA. 206-878-3710, Ext 233
Holt, Barbara C, *Librn,* Perkins, Coie, Stone, Olsen & Williams Library, Seattle WA. 206-682-8770, Ext 444
Holt, David Earl, *Dir,* Austin Public Library, Austin TX. 512-472-5433
Holt, Janet, *Ad,* River Forest Public Library, River Forest IL. 312-366-5205
Holt, Janice C, *Chief Librn,* Maryland-National Capital Park & Planning Commission Library, Silver Spring MD. 301-565-7507, 565-7508
Holt, Jean, *Dir,* Oakland Public Library, Oakland ME. 207-465-7533
Holt, June C, *Librn,* Massachusetts Rehabilitation Commission Library, Boston MA. 617-727-1140
Holt, Laura, *Librn,* Museum of New Mexico (Laboratory of Anthropology Library), Santa Fe NM. 505-827-3241
Holt, Louise, *Librn,* Jefferson-Madison Regional Library (Scottsville Branch), Scottsville VA. 804-286-3541
Holt, Mabel H, *Ad & Ref,* Chesterfield County Central Library, Chesterfield VA. 804-748-1601
Holt, Mrs, *Librn,* Fort Vermillion Public Library, Fort Vermilion AB. 403-927-3393
Holt, Mrs Graham, *Librn,* Public Library of Johnston County & Smithfield (Princeton Public), Princeton NC. 919-934-8146
Holt, Mrs C B, *Librn,* Grainger County Library (Bean Station Public Library), Bean Station TN. 615-587-0908
Holt, Omeda, *Librn,* Sullivan County Public Library (Bloomingdale Branch), Kingsport TN. 615-288-3835
Holt, Suzy, *Coll Mgr,* Lewis & Clark Library, Helena MT. 406-442-2380
Holter, Ian C, *Dir,* Port Moody Public Library, Port Moody BC. 604-939-1588
Holtman, Eugene, *Asst Dir & Tech Serv,* Eastern Michigan University, Center of Educational Resources, Ypsilanti MI. 313-487-0020
Holtman, Prue, *Acq,* College of Wooster, Andrews Library, Wooster OH. 216-264-1234, Ext 483
Holton, Arthur, *Librn,* Arizona-Sonora Desert Museum Library, Tucson AZ. 602-883-1380
Holton, Charlotte P, *Librn,* American Museum of Natural History Library (Osborn Library), New York NY. 212-873-1300, Ext 328
Holton, Edwin L, *Coordr,* Hillsborough Community College Plant City Center, Learning Resources Center, Plant City FL. 813-223-1761
Holton, James, *Archivist,* Lewis & Clark College, Aubrey R Watzek Library, Portland OR. 503-244-6161, Ext 400
Holton, Susan C, *Librn,* American Institute of Architects Library, Washington DC. 202-785-7300
Holton, Tommy, *Media,* Dillard University, Will W Alexander Library, New Orleans LA. 504-949-2123, Ext 256, 257

Holtrey, Trevelyn, *Asst Librn,* Selover Public Library, Chesterville OH. 419-768-3431
Holtum, Edwin, *Adjunct Asst Prof,* University of Iowa, School of Library Science, IA. 319-353-3644
Holtz, Jerry, *Bibliog Control,* Teachers College - Columbia University Library, New York NY. 212-678-3022, 678-3020
Holtz, Myron, *Dir Res & Info Bur,* New York State Division of Housing & Community Renewal, Reference Room, New York NY. 212-488-4968
Holtz, Virginia, *Librn,* University of Wisconsin-Madison (William S Middleton Health Sciences Library), Madison WI. 608-262-3521
Holtzman, Susan, *AV,* Cambria County Library System, Johnstown PA. 814-536-5131
Holubik, Regina, *Librn,* Lenawee County Library (Roberts-Ingold Memorial), Deerfield MI. 517-447-3400
Holubowicz, Vincent B, *Dir,* Campbellsport Public Library, Campbellsport WI. 414-533-8534
Holum, Katherine, *Librn,* University of Minnesota Libraries-Twin Cities (Music), Minneapolis MN. 612-373-3438
Holz, Carole, *Asst Librn,* Sun Life Assurance Co of Canada, Reference Library, Wellesley Hills MA. 617-237-6030, Ext 2298
Holz, Sandra, *Librn,* Whitefield Public Library, Whitefield NH. 603-837-2030
Holzbauer, H, *Librn,* Defense Intelligence Agency, Central Reference Div Library, Washington DC. 202-692-5311
Holzbaur, Rita, *ILL,* Maurice M Pine Free Public Library, Fair Lawn NJ. 201-796-3400
Holzberlein, Deanne B, *Asst Prof,* Ball State University, Dept of Library Science, IN. 317-285-7180, 285-7189
Holzer, Anna, *Asst Dir,* Tarrant County Junior College System (Northwest Campus Learning Resources Center), Fort Worth TX. 817-232-2900, Ext 208
Holzer, Mary, *Circ,* Howard Whittemore Memorial Library, Naugatuck CT. 203-729-6129
Holzinger, Phyllis, *Tech Serv,* Monroe County Library System, Monroe MI. 313-241-5277
Holzman, Thomas, *Librn,* Princeton University Library (Population Research), Princeton NJ. 609-452-3180
Hom, Kimiyo, *Librn,* University of California, Berkeley (Astronomy-Mathematics & Statistics-Computer Science), Berkeley CA. 415-642-3381
Hom, Lily W, *Chief Librn,* Veterans Administration (Office of Technology Transfer-Reference Collection), New York NY. 212-620-6659
Hom, Sharon, *Cat,* First Regional Library, DeSoto County Library, Hernando MS. 601-368-4439
Homan, Bonnie L, *Librn,* Cooper Memorial Library, Clermont FL. 904-394-4265
Homan, Michael, *Head, Info Serv,* Upjohn Company (Corporate Technical Library), Kalamazoo MI. 616-385-6414
Homan, Rebecca, *Librn,* Graysville Public Library, Graysville AL. 205-674-3040
Homans, Phoebe, *Tech Serv,* Wayland Free Public Library, Wayland MA. 617-358-2311, 358-2308
Homans, Phoebe, *Tech Serv, On-Line Servs & Bibliog Instr,* Wayland Free Public Library, Wayland MA. 617-358-2311, 358-2308
Homblette, Kathryn, *Ch,* Middleton Public Library, Middleton WI. 608-831-5564
Home, Pauline, *Asst Dir,* Halifax City Regional Library, Halifax NS. 902-426-6980
Homer, David, *Inst Aid Resources,* York University, Scott Library, Downsview ON. 416-667-2235
Homer, Garth, *Dir & Acq,* Okanagan College, Muriel Ffoulkes Learning Resource Center, Kelowna BC. 604-762-5445, Ext 293
Homer, Marlene, *Ref & Bibliog Instr,* Saint Mary's College of Maryland Library, Saint Mary's City MD. 301-994-1600, Ext 216
Homer, Patricia J, *Librn,* Enoch Pratt Free Library (Roland Park), Baltimore MD. 301-396-5430, 396-5395
Homer, Virginia K, *Dir Libr Serv,* Brandywine College Library, Wilmington DE. 302-478-3000
Homewood, Donna V, *Chief, Libr Serv,* Veterans Administration, Hospital Library Services, Roseburg OR. 503-672-4411
Homewood, Inez, *Librn,* Big Horn County Library (Frannie Branch), Frannie WY. 307-568-2388

Homeyard, Marjorie, *Mat Selection,* United States Navy (General Library Services), Pensacola FL. 904-452-1380
Homeyer, Jr, Mrs Charles W, *Librn,* First Congregational Church of Wellesley Hills Library, Wellesley Hills MA. 617-235-4424
Homiller, Carol, *Ref,* Reinhardt College, Hill Freeman Library, Waleska GA. 404-479-1454, Ext 27, 43
Homm, Joyce, *Librn,* Oakley City Library, Oakley KS. 913-672-4776
Hommel, Justine, *Dir,* Haines Falls Free Library, Haines Falls NY. 518-589-5707
Homoki, Claudia, *YA,* South Brunswick Public Library, Monmouth Junction NJ. 201-821-8224, 821-8225
Homola, Barbara, *Ch,* Manhasset Public Library, Manhasset NY. 516-627-2300
Homrighausen, Carol L, *Librn,* Woodside Receiving Hospital, Staff Resource Library & Patients' Library, Youngstown OH. 216-788-8712, Ext 267
Homsey, S, *Librn,* Delaware Museum of Natural History, Greenville DE. 302-658-9111
Honchul, Quava S, *Librn,* Murray State University (Legal), Murray KY. 502-762-2291
Honebrink, Andrea, *Ref Servs Coordr,* Minnesota Interlibrary Telecommunications Exchange, (MINITEX), MN. 612-376-3925, 376-3926
Honey, Rose Ann, *Librn,* Atkins Public Library, Atkins IA. 319-446-7676
Honey, W J, *Librn,* Percy Township Public Library, Warkworth ON. 705-924-2931
Honeycutt, Doretta, *Dir,* Riverside Public Library Association, Inc, Riverside NJ. 609-461-6922
Honeycutt, Sue K, *Dir,* Northeast Mississippi Junior College, Eula Dees Memorial Library, Booneville MS. 601-728-7751, Ext 237
Honeyman, Carrie, *Librn,* Madison Public Library, Madison KS. 316-437-2634
Honeyman, Erma, *In Charge,* Santa Barbara Public Library (Solvang Branch), Solvang CA. 805-688-4214
Hong, Rita, *Resource Mat Spec,* East-West Center Resource Systems Institute, Resource Materials Collection, Honolulu HI. 808-948-8728
Honig, Dale, *Librn,* Congregation Keneseth Israel Library, Allentown PA. 435-9074 or 435-9075
Honjo, Tatsuko, *Dir,* Chamber of Commerce of Hawaii, Reference Library, Honolulu HI. 808-531-4111
Honks, Elsie, *Librn,* Tallahatchie County Library (Webb Branch), Webb MS. 601-375-8787
Honore, Mildred, *Librn,* Dallas Public Library (Dallas West), Dallas TX. 214-637-1204
Honsa, Vlasta, *Ref,* Clark County Library District, Las Vegas NV. 702-733-7810
Honychurch-Matz, Maureen, *Librn,* Daland Memorial Library, Mont Vernon NH. 603-673-7888
Honza, Sister Julian, *Librn,* Our Lady of the Lake University Libraries (Departmental Library Science), San Antonio TX. 512-434-6711, Ext 273
Honza, Sister Norberta, *Ref,* Our Lady of the Lake University Libraries, San Antonio TX. 512-434-6711, Ext 272
Hood, Dale A, *Dir,* Robert L F Sikes Public Library, Crestview FL. 904-682-4432
Hood, Faye R, *Dir,* Jackson Parish Library, Jonesboro LA. 318-259-2069
Hood, Howard A, *Ref,* Vanderbilt University School of Law Library, Nashville TN. 615-322-2568
Hood, Kate W, *Librn,* Georgetown County Memorial Library, Georgetown SC. 803-546-2521
Hood, Lawrence, *Acq,* Brigham Young University (Law Library), Provo UT. 801-378-3593
Hood, Marrion G, *Dir,* Lanpher Memorial Library, Hyde Park VT. 802-888-4628
Hood, Mary D, *Pub Serv,* University of Santa Clara (Heafey Law Library), Santa Clara CA. 408-984-4451
Hood, Mary E, *Tech Serv, Cat & Rare Bks,* North Georgia College, Stewart Library, Dahlonega GA. 404-864-3391, Ext 226, 294
Hood, Nelma, *Ch,* York County Library, Headquarters Rock Hill Public Library, Rock Hill SC. 803-328-8402
Hood, Willa, *Bibliog Instr,* Leslie County Library, Hyden KY. 606-672-2460

Hooge, Orpha, *Cat,* Kearney State College, Calvin T Ryan Library, Kearney NE. 308-236-4218
Hoogenboom, Dennis, *Cat,* Phoenix Public Library, Phoenix AZ. 602-262-6451
Hoogland, Sandra, *Librn,* Motorola Inc, Systems Division Library, Franklin Park IL. 312-451-1000
Hook, Carolyn, *Librn,* Washington State University Library (Education), Pullman WA. 509-335-1591
Hook, Nancy, *Asst Dir,* Pierce Free Public Library, Pierce ID. 208-464-2823
Hook, Pamela, *ILL & Ref,* Santa Clara County Free Library, San Jose CA. 408-293-2326
Hook, Robert D, *ILL & Circ,* University of Idaho Library, Moscow ID. 208-885-6534
Hooker, Catherine J, *Br Coordr & Bkmobile Coordr,* Anaheim Public Library, Anaheim CA. 714-533-5221
Hooker, Catherine J, *Librn,* Anaheim Public Library (Euclid), Anaheim CA. 714-533-0160
Hooker, Gertrude, *Ch,* Red Bank Public Library, Eisner Memorial Library, Red Bank NJ. 201-842-0690
Hooker, Ida M, *Librn,* Mountain Bell Telephone Co Library, Denver CO. 303-624-4607
Hooker, Joan, *YA,* Township of Hamilton Free Public Library, Trenton NJ. 609-890-3460
Hooker, Lloyd W, *Librn,* Federal Bureau of Prisons Library, Washington DC. 202-724-3029
Hooker, Marjory, *Librn,* Tulsa City-County Library (Martin East Regional), Tulsa OK. 918-581-5221
Hooker, Mary, *Ref,* Gulfport-Harrison County Library, Gulfport MS. 601-863-6411
Hooks, Eleanor, *Ad,* Public Library of Johnston County & Smithfield, Smithfield NC. 919-934-8146
Hooks, James D, *Dir,* Indiana University of Pennsylvania, Armstrong County Campus Library, Kittanning PA. 412-543-1078, Ext 19, 20
Hoolihan, Christopher, *Rare Bks,* Washington University Libraries (School of Medicine Library), Saint Louis MO. 314-454-3711
Hoomes, Virginia, *Asst Dir,* W R Holley Memorial Library, Atmore AL. 205-368-3052
Hoon, Marion, *Asst Librn,* Nashua Public Library, Nashua IA. 515-435-4635
Hoopai, Lorelei, *Clerk,* Belt, Collins-Lyon Associates, Information Services, Honolulu HI. 808-521-5361
Hooper, Barbara L, *In Charge,* Bisbee Council on the Arts & Humanities, Lemuel C Shattuck Memorial Archival Library, Bisbee AZ. 602-432-7071
Hooper, Dorothy L, *Chief Librn,* First United Methodist Church Library, Alhambra CA. 213-289-4258
Hooper, Glenda, *Dir,* Bay Area Reference Center, (BARC), CA. 415-558-2941
Hooper, Hanna, *Librn,* United States Army (Language Training Facility Library), Fort Hood TX. 817-685-6392
Hooper, James E, *Dir,* Young Harris College, Henry & J Lon Duckworth Memorial Libraries, Young Harris GA. 404-379-3526
Hooper, Robert, *Librn,* Graham County Public Library, Hill City KS. 913-674-2722
Hoornbeck, Lynda C, *Ref,* Franklin Park Public Library District, Franklin Park IL. 312-455-6016
Hoose, David C, *Librn,* University of Wisconsin-Milwaukee (School of Nursing Media Library), Milwaukee WI. 414-963-5507
Hoose, Esther, *Asst Librn,* Baldwin-Wallace College (Riemenschneider Bach Institute), Berea OH. 216-826-2207
Hooser, Mary Van, *Librn,* Orena Humphrey Public Library, Whitwell TN. 901-658-6134
Hooten, Ruth, *Asst Dir,* Memorial Hall Library, (Subregional Headquarters for Eastern Massachusetts Regional System), Andover MA. 617-475-6960
Hootkin, Neil, *Rare Bks & Spec Coll,* The Medical College of Wisconsin, Inc, Todd Wehr Library, Milwaukee WI. 414-257-8323
Hoover, Alice, *Bkmobile Coordr,* Lane Public Library, Hamilton OH. 513-894-7156
Hoover, Anna R, *ILL & Ch,* Piedmont Regional Library, Winder GA. 404-867-2762

Hoover, Barbara, *ILL & Ref,* Anderson City-Anderson & Stony Creek Township Public Library, Anderson Public Library, Anderson IN. 317-644-0938

Hoover, Dolly B, *Cat,* Indiana State University, Cunningham Memorial Library, Terre Haute IN. 812-232-6311, Ext 2451

Hoover, Edris E, *Administrator,* American College of Obstetricians & Gynecologists Resource Center, Chicago IL. 312-222-1600

Hoover, Ellen L, *Librn,* Spangler Public Library, Spangler PA. 814-948-8222

Hoover, Evelyn, *Ad & Ref,* Kings County Library, Hanford CA. 209-582-0261

Hoover, John, *Assist Dir, Coll Develop,* University of Western Ontario, A B Weldon Library, London ON. 519-679-6191

Hoover, Leona, *Librn,* Livingston Parish Library (Maurepas), Springfield LA. 504-686-2436

Hoover, Onnalee D, *Librn,* Burlington Township Library, Burlington MI. 517-765-2323

Hoover, Peggy, *Asst Librn,* Petersburg Public Library (A P Hill), Petersburg VA. 804-861-6290

Hoover, Peter R, *Dir,* Paleontological Research Institution Library, Ithaca NY. 607-273-6623

Hoover, Priscilla W, *Librn,* Watts Hospital, School of Nursing Library, Durham NC. 919-286-5456, 286-5558

Hope, Ann, *YA,* Cleveland Heights-University Heights Public Library, Cleveland Heights OH. 216-932-3600

Hope, Dorothy, *Cat,* University of Louisville Library (Kornhauser Health Sciences), Louisville KY. 502-588-5771

Hope, Nelson W, *Librn,* Airesearch Manufacturing Co, Engineering Library, Phoenix AZ. 602-267-2062

Hope-Brown, A, *Dir & Ad,* Whitby Public Library, Whitby ON. 416-668-6531, 668-6541

Hopkins, Benjamin, *Chief Librn,* Massachusetts College of Art Library, Boston MA. 617-731-2340, Ext 26

Hopkins, Betty, *Doc,* Wayne State University Libraries (G Flint Purdy Library), Detroit MI. 313-577-4032

Hopkins, Billye, *Librn,* Tulsa City-County Library (Prattville), Sand Springs OK. 918-245-3553

Hopkins, Edith, *Media,* Oakville Public Library, Oakville ON. 416-845-3405

Hopkins, Frances, *Bibliog Instr,* Franklin & Marshall College Library, Lancaster PA. 717-291-4223

Hopkins, James W, *Asst Dir & Tech Servs,* United States Air Force Academy Library, United States Air Force Academy CO. 303-472-2590

Hopkins, Jane, *Regional Coordr,* San Diego County Library (Region G), San Diego CA. 714-565-5100

Hopkins, Jean, *Librn,* Consolidated Hospitals of Idaho Falls Library, Idaho Falls ID. 208-592-6111

Hopkins, Joan A, *Dir,* Selby Public Library, Sarasota County Federated Library System, Sarasota FL. 814-366-7303

Hopkins, Joan M, *ILL, Ref & Bibliog Instr,* Illinois Benedictine College, Theodore Lownik Library, Lisle IL. 312-968-7270, Ext 286

Hopkins, John, *Lit & Fine Arts,* Orlando Public Library, Orlando FL. 305-425-4694

Hopkins, Joseph S, *Chief Librn,* Worcester Public Library, Worcester MA. 617-752-3751

Hopkins, Karen, *Librn,* Converse County Library (Glenrock Branch), Glenrock WY. 307-436-2573

Hopkins, Linda Mitro, *Mgr,* Abbott Laboratories, Ross Laboratories Library, Columbus OH. 614-227-3503, 227-3204

Hopkins, Marjorie, *Librn,* Franklin County Library, Winchester TN. 615-967-3706

Hopkins, Marjorie A, *Librn,* Corry Public Library, Corry PA. 814-664-7611

Hopkins, Monroe, *Dir,* William Woods College, Dulany Memorial Library, Fulton MO. 314-642-3269

Hopkins, Mrs Bama, *Librn,* Duncanville Public Library, Duncanville TX. 214-298-5400

Hopkins, Nita, *Clerk,* Burley Public Library, Burley ID. 208-678-7708

Hopkins, Pauline, *Librn,* Fultondale Public Library, Fultondale AL. 205-849-6335

Hopkins, Rosalind, *Librn,* Fidelity Mutual Life Insurance Co Library & Archives, Philadelphia PA. 215-585-8093

Hopkins, William, *Tech Serv,* Community College of the Finger Lakes Library, Canandaigua NY. 315-394-3500, Ext 127

Hopkinson, Shirley, *Prof,* San Jose State University, Division of Library Science, CA. 408-277-2292

Hopp, Ralph H, *Dir,* University of Minnesota Libraries-Twin Cities (Institute of Technology Libraries), Minneapolis MN. 612-376-2932

Hoppe, Anita, *Asst Librn,* Lincoln First Bank, Library Services, Rochester NY. 716-262-2306, 262-2307

Hoppe, David, *Media,* Michigan City Public Library, Michigan City IN. 219-879-4561

Hoppe, Hazel, *Dir,* Sturm Public Library, Manawa Public Library, Manawa WI. 414-596-2252

Hoppe, Patrica, *Ch,* Shorewood Public Library, Shorewood WI. 414-332-2495

Hopper, Johanne, *Librn,* University of Montreal Libraries (Paramedical), Montreal PQ. 514-343-7490

Hopper, June, *Librn,* Jefferson County Library (Family Memorial), Wrens GA. 404-547-3484

Hopper, Katherine D, *Asst Librn,* Garden City Library, Boise ID. 208-377-2180

Hopper, Mildry S, *Classified,* National Defense University Library, Washington DC. 202-693-8437

Hopper, S, *Librn,* Kaman Corp Library, Bloomfield CT. 203-242-4461

Hoppes, Muriel, *Librn,* California State Library (Law Library), Sacramento CA. 916-445-8833

Hopson, Jean, *Librn,* Wake Forest University (Charles H Babcock Graduate School of Management Library), Winston-Salem NC. 919-761-5414

Horacek, Louis, *Tech Serv,* Miracle Valley Regional Library, City-County Public Library, Moundsville WV. 304-845-6911

Horak, Robert, *Cat,* Linden Free Public Library, Linden NJ. 201-486-3888

Horan, James, *Ch,* Starved Rock Library System, Ottawa IL. 815-434-7537

Horan, Patricia, *Doc,* University of Portland, Wilson W Clark Memorial Library, Portland OR. 503-283-7111

Horan, Susan Hartman, *Spec Servs,* DuPage Library System, Geneva IL. 312-232-8457

Horan, Susan Hartman, *Librn,* DuPage Library System (Subregional Library for the Blind & Physically Handicapped), Geneva IL. 312-232-8457

Hord, Jean, *Supvr,* Middlesex County Library (Ilderton Branch), Ilderton ON. 519-438-8368

Hord, Patricia S, *Librn,* International Labor Office Library, Washington DC. 202-376-2315

Hordusky, Clyde, *Doc,* State Library of Ohio, Columbus OH. 614-466-2693

Horgan, Maureen, *Ch,* Newburyport Public Library, Newburyport MA. 617-462-4031

Hori, Ruby, *Cat,* Los Angeles Public Library System, Los Angeles CA. 213-626-7555

Horikawa, Emi, *Librn,* Swarthmore College (Dupont Science), Swarthmore PA. 215-447-7261

Horikawa, Emi, *Sci,* Swarthmore College, McCabe Library, Swarthmore PA. 215-447-7477, 447-7480

Horinek, Mary C, *Dir,* Phillipsburg City Library, Phillipsburg KS. 913-543-5325

Horio, Nina, *Ref & ILL,* Illinois Institute of Technology, James S Kemper Library, Chicago IL. 312-567-3355

Horkel, Jane, *Info Serv,* Victoria Public Library, Victoria TX. 512-578-6241

Horn, Anna E, *Mgr, Main Libr,* Saint Louis Public Library, Saint Louis MO. 314-241-2288

Horn, Barbara J, *Dir,* United States Navy (Naval School, Civil Engineer Corps Officers, Moreell Library), Port Hueneme CA. 805-982-3241, 3242

Horn, Betty, *Librn,* United States Air Force (Duluth International Airport Base Library), Duluth MN. 218-727-8211

Horn, David E, *Spec Coll,* Depauw University, Roy O West Library, Greencastle IN. 317-653-9721, Ext 250

Horn, Helen, *Librn,* Carroll County Public Library (Eldersburg), Sykesville MD. 301-795-3520

Horn, Janice, *Cat,* Clarion State College, Rena M Carlson Library, Clarion PA. 814-226-2343

Horn, Jerry, *Ref, Cat & Bkmobile Coordr,* Elbert County Library, Elberton GA. 404-283-5375

Horn, Judy, *Govt Pubs,* University of California Library, Irvine CA. 714-833-5212

Horn, Margaret, *Cat,* Concordia College, Buenger Memorial Library, Saint Paul MN. 612-641-8240

Horn, Miriam C, *Librn,* Stroud Public Library, Stroud OK. 918-968-2567

Horn, Mrs Theo, *Librn,* Washakie County Library, Worland WY. 307-347-2231

Horn, Nancy D, *Librn,* Malvern Public Library, Malvern PA. 215-644-7259

Horn, Roberta, *Asst Librn,* Cherry Valley Village Library, Cherry Valley IL. 815-332-5161

Horn, Roger, *Circ,* Clarion State College, Rena M Carlson Library, Clarion PA. 814-226-2343

Horn, W Richard, *Asst Librn,* Avila College, Hooley-Bundschu Library, Kansas City MO. 816-942-8400, Ext 220

Hornaday, Ellen R, *Librn,* Central Baptist College, J E Cobb Library, Conway AR. 501-329-6872

Hornaday, Heidi H, *Ch,* Saint Joseph Public Library, Saint Joseph MO. 816-232-7729, 232-7720

Hornak, Ann, *Asst Dir,* Houston Area Library System, Houston TX. 713-222-4704

Hornak, Ann, *Asst Dir,* Houston Public Library, Houston TX. 713-224-5441

Hornbach, Ruth, *Chief Librn,* Kendall School of Design Library, Grand Rapids MI. 616-451-2787

Hornbeck, J, *ILL,* Georgia Institute of Technology, Price Gilbert Memorial Library, Atlanta GA. 404-894-4510

Hornberger, Frances, *Ch,* Floral Park Public Library, Floral Park NY. 516-354-0666

Hornburg, Howard, *Librn,* Orlando Public Library (Eastland), Orlando FL. 305-277-0021

Hornburg, Martine A, *Librn,* Colton Public Library, Colton CA. 714-825-1585

Hornby, Carol, *Librn,* Edmonton Separate School Board, Professional Library, Edmonton AB. 403-429-7631, Ext 226

Hornby, Doris J, *Data Proc,* Providence Public Library, Providence RI. 401-521-7722

Horne, Alan J, *Asst Librn,* University of Toronto Libraries (University Library), Toronto ON. 416-978-2294

Horne, Carla M, *Dir,* Ralpho Township Public Library, Elysburg PA. 717-672-9449

Horne, Kenneth, *Librn,* Public Library of Cincinnati & Hamilton County (Cheviot), Cincinnati OH. 513-369-6015

Horner, John W, *Dir,* Contra Costa College Library, San Pablo CA. 415-235-7800, Ext 213

Horner, Margaret, *Asst Dir,* Onondaga County Public Library System, Syracuse NY. 315-473-2702

Hornet, Daniel, *Outreach Librn,* Peninsula Library Systems, Daly City CA. 415-878-5577

Horney, Joyce, *ILL,* Illinois State Library, Springfield IL. 217-782-2994

Hornick-Lockard, Barbara, *Bibliog Instr,* University of North Carolina at Chapel Hill, Louis Round Wilson Academic Affairs Library, Chapel Hill NC. 919-933-1301

Horning, Alis, *AV,* Arcadia Public Library, Arcadia CA. 213-446-7111

Hornsby, Betty, *Librn,* Fayette County Public Library (Fayetteville), Fayetteville WV. 304-574-0070

Hornsby, Vickey, *Librn,* Fayette County Public Library (Manion), Ansted WV. 304-658-5472

Hornstra, Betty, *Librn,* Dorr Township Library (Salem Township Library), Burnips MI. 616-896-8170

Hornung, Susan, *Ref,* Minnesota Valley Regional Library, Mankato MN. 507-387-1856

Hornung, Y, *Librn,* American Acrylic Corp Library, Farmingdale NY. 516-249-1129

Horny, Karen L, *Tech Serv,* Northwestern University Library, Evanston IL. 312-492-7658

Horowitz, Cyma M, *Dir,* American Jewish Committee, Blaustein Library, New York NY. 212-751-4000

Horowitz, Harvey P, *Librn,* Hebrew Union College, Jewish Institute of Religion, Frances-Henry Library, Los Angeles CA. 213-749-3424

Horowitz, Katrin, *On-Line Servs,* Ontario Legislative Library, Research & Information Services, Toronto ON. 416-965-4545

Horr, Sharon, *Librn,* Fairfax Community Library, Fairfax VT. 802-849-6711
Horrell, Carol, *Indiana Hist Project Coordr,* Indiana State Library, Division for the Blind & Physically Handicapped, Indianapolis IN. 317-232-3684
Horrell, Laird J, *Librn,* Public Library of the District of Columbia (West End), Washington DC. 202-727-1397
Horres, Mary, *Assoc Dir,* University of North Carolina at Chapel Hill (Health Sciences Library), Chapel Hill NC. 919-966-2111
Horrigan, Joseph, *Curator & Researcher,* Pro Football Hall of Fame Library, Research Center, Canton OH. 216-456-8207
Horrmann-Pinther, Elizabeth, *Cat,* Ohio University, Vernon R Alden Library, Athens OH. 614-594-5228
Horrocks, Jane, *Ad & Acq,* Richmond Hill Public Library, Richmond Hill ON. 416-884-9288
Horrocks, Norman, *Dir,* Dalhousie University, School of Library Service, NS. 902-424-3656
Horsley, Mary Lou, *ILL & Ref,* Montgomery County Library, Conroe TX. 713-756-4486
Horst, Karen, *Asst Librn,* Saint Luke's Hospital, Spencer Center for Education Medical Library, Kansas City MO. 816-932-2333
Horst, Mona, *Librn,* Marysville-Rye Library, Marysville PA. 717-957-2851
Horst, Stanley E, *Assoc Librn,* Northern Illinois University, College Law Library, Glen Ellyn IL. 312-858-7200
Hortin, Larry L, *Dir,* Provo City Public Library, Provo UT. 801-373-1494
Hortman, Pat, *Librn,* Frederick County Public Library (Brunswick), Frederick MD. 301-694-1613
Horton, Anne, *Dir,* Webster Groves Public Library, Webster Groves MO. 314-961-3784
Horton, Barbara, *Assoc Dir, Tech Serv & Cat,* Ector County Library, Odessa TX. 915-332-0633
Horton, Bernice, *Ad,* Pine Mountain Regional Library, Manchester GA. 404-846-2186
Horton, Edward K, *Dir,* Seaford Public Library, Seaford NY. 516-221-1334
Horton, Elliott R, *Dir,* Morgantown Public Library, Morgantown Service Center, Morgantown WV. 304-296-4425
Horton, Gerry, *On-Line Servs,* Quaker Oats Co, John Stuart Research Laboratories-Research Library, Barrington IL. 312-381-1980
Horton, Irene, *Librn,* Winhall Memorial Library, Bondville VT. 802-297-1961
Horton, Isobel, *Dir,* Acadia University, Harold Campbell Vaughan Memorial Library, Wolfville NS. 902-542-2201, Ext 215
Horton, Janet S, *Asst Prof,* Indiana State University, Dept of Library Science, IN. 812-232-6311, Ext 2834
Horton, Judy, *Librn,* Los Angeles Public Library System (West Los Angeles), Los Angeles CA. 213-477-9546
Horton, Kathleen, *Asst Librn,* University of Connecticut, Southeastern Branch Library, Groton CT. 203-446-1020, Ext 267
Horton, Kathy Lynne, *Dir,* Muskego Public Library, Muskego WI. 414-679-1220
Horton, Michael, *Asst Librn,* Plymouth Public Library, Plymouth NH. 603-536-2616
Horton, Shirley, *Librn,* Los Angeles Public Library System (Panorama City Branch), Panorama City CA. 213-894-4071
Horton, Stanley W, *Dir,* Colorado Northwestern Community College, Learning Resources & Media Center, Rangely CO. 303-675-2261
Horton, Steve, *Tech Serv,* Jarvis Christian College, Ohlin Library & Communication Center, Hawkins TX. 214-769-2174, Ext 154
Horton, Weldon J, *Dir,* Midland College, Learning Resources Center, Midland TX. 915-684-7851, Ext 214
Horuath, Sandor, *Cat,* Daemen College, Marian Library, Amherst NY. 716-839-3600, Ext 243
Horvath, Donna, *Head Ref Coll,* Bethlehem Public Library, Bethlehem PA. 215-867-3761
Horvath, Helen S, *Cat,* Oregon State University, William Jasper Kerr Library, Corvallis OR. 503-754-3411
Horvath, Mary Ann E, *Librn,* Avon Products, Inc Library, Suffern NY. 914-357-2000
Horvay, Gloria, *Ch,* Glassboro Public Library, Glassboro NJ. 609-881-0001

Horwath, Dan, *Asst Librn,* Clinton Public Library, Clinton IA. 319-242-8441
Horwath, Dorothy, *Asst Dir & Media,* Saginaw Valley State College Library & Learning Resources Center, University Center MI. 517-790-4237
Horwitz, Marsha V, *Tech Serv,* City College of the City University of New York, Morris Raphael Cohen Library, New York NY. 212-690-6612
Horwitz, Ruth, *AV,* Bentley College, Solomon R Baker Library, Waltham MA. 617-891-2231
Horwitz, Sharon, *Librn,* Akron-Summit County Public Library (Green Branch), Greensburg OH. 216-896-9074
Horwood, Ruby, *Librn,* Eastern Pennsylvania Psychiatric Institute Library, Philadelphia PA. 215-842-4508, 842-4509 & 842-4510
Hoscheid, Marie A, *Ref & Spec Coll,* Moline Public Library, Moline IL. 309-762-6883
Hoschouer, Fannie, *Dir,* Burlington Public Library, Burlington CO. 303-346-8109
Hosek, Marjorie, *Librn,* United States Marine Corps (Air Station Library), Yuma AZ. 602-726-2011
Hosford, Mari, *Librn,* Albion Public Library, Albion NE. 402-395-2021
Hoshiko, Patsy-Rose, *ILL Coop Librn,* Shawnee Library System, Carterville IL. 618-985-3711
Hoskin, Adele, *In Charge,* Eli Lilly & Co (Scientific Library), Indianapolis IN. 317-261-4452
Hoskins, Pat S, *Chief Librn,* Conoco Inc Research & Development Department, Technical Information Services, Ponca City OK. 405-767-4719
Hoskinson, Marsha, *Media,* Mid Michigan Community College, Charles A Amble Library, Harrison MI. 517-386-7792, Ext 258
Hosler, Doris, *Bibliog Instr,* Millersville State College, Helen A Ganser Library, Millersville PA. 717-872-5411, Ext 341
Hosler, Robert M, *Dir,* Great Lakes Historical Society, Clarence S Metcalf Research Library, Vermilion OH. 216-967-3467
Hospodka, Vera, *Head Librn,* Pennsylvania State University, Radner Center for Graduate Studies & Continuing Education Library, Radnor PA. 215-293-9860
Hoss, Suzanne, *Cat,* Cobb County Public Library System, Marietta GA. 404-427-2462
Hostetler, Karen, *Per,* Moody Bible Institute Library, Chicago IL. 312-329-4138
Hostetler, Lela, *Per & Acq,* Messiah College, Murray Learning Resources Center, Grantham PA. 717-766-2511, Ext 380
Hostetler, Machelle, *Ref,* Valparaiso-Porter County Public Library System & Administrative Headquarters, Valparaiso IN. 219-462-0524
Hostetter, Alice W, *Assoc Prof,* Millersville State College, Dept of Library Science, PA. 717-872-5411, Ext 416
Hostetter, David, *Tech Serv & Cat,* Mount San Antonio College, Learning Resources Center, Walnut CA. 714-594-5611, Ext 260
Hostetter, Robert G, *Media,* Millersville State College, Helen A Ganser Library, Millersville PA. 717-872-5411, Ext 341
Hotchkiss, Patricia, *Asst Dir,* Cochise College, Cochise Sierra Vista Learning Resources Center, Sierra Vista AZ. 602-458-7110
Hotchkiss, Patricia, *Librn,* Cochise College, Learning Resources Center, Douglas AZ. 602-364-7943, Ext 280
Hoth, LaDell, *AV,* Utah State University, Merrill Library & Learning Resources Program, Logan UT. 801-750-2637
Hotra, Barbara, *Acq & Cat,* Fairfield Public Library, Fairfield NJ. 201-227-3575
Hotta, Ann, *Asst Librn,* International Business Machines Corp (Research Library), San Jose CA. 408-256-2562
Hotze, Angela, *Tech Serv,* Southeastern Community College Library-North Campus, West Burlington IA. 319-752-2731, Ext 55
Houck, Michael, *Librn, On-Line Servs & Bibliog Instr,* Greater Baltimore Medical Center, John E Savage Medical Staff Library, Baltimore MD. 301-828-2530
Houdek, Frank G, *Librn,* Lawler, Felix & Hall Library, Los Angeles CA. 213-629-9513
Hougas, Alyce, *Librn,* Saint Joseph Public Library (Washington Park), Saint Joseph MO. 816-232-2052

Hough, Carolyn, *Corp Librn,* Osteopathic Hospitals of Detroit, Inc, West Unit Library, Detroit MI. 313-897-6400, Ext 245
Hough, Leslie, *Archivist,* Georgia State University, William Russell Pullen Library, Atlanta GA. 404-658-2185, 658-2172
Hough, Marianne, *Dir,* Tampa General Hospital, Medical Library, Tampa FL. 813-251-7328
Hough, Samuel J, *Curator,* Brown University (Annmary Brown Memorial), Providence RI. 401-863-2429
Hough, Samuel J, *Asst Librn,* Brown University (John Carter Brown Library), Providence RI. 401-863-2725
Hough, Suzanne, *Tech Serv,* Boulder Public Library, Boulder CO. 303-441-3100
Hough, III, William E, *Dir,* Lebanon Valley College, George D Gossard Memorial Library, Annville PA. 717-867-4411, Ext 217
Houghland, Nola, *Ch,* Rawlins Municipal Library, Pierre SD. 605-224-7421
Houghtaling, Cathy, *Asst Librn,* British Columbia Law Library Foundation, Kamloops Court House Library, Kamloops BC. 604-374-7415
Houghton, Elizabeth, *ILL,* Cheshire Public Library, Cheshire CT. 203-272-2245
Houghton, Elizajane, *Ad,* Concord Public Library, Concord NH. 603-225-2743
Houghton, George G, *Librn,* Faith Baptist Bible College Library, Ankeny IA. 515-964-0601, Ext 53
Houghton, Maxine J, *Librn,* IBM Canada Limited, Central Library, Toronto ON. 416-443-2043
Houk, Judy, *Supvr, Libr Servs to State Agencies,* Colorado State Library, Colorado Department of Education, Denver CO. 303-839-3695
Houk, Martha, *Librn,* Los Angeles Public Library System (Sunland-Tujunga Branch), Tujunga CA. 213-352-4481
Houk, Vickie J, *Librn,* News-Journal Library, Wilmington DE. 302-573-2038
Houk, Wallace E, *Dir,* Alvin Community College Library, Alvin TX. 713-331-6111, Ext 245
Houk, Wallace E, *Entomology, Horticulture, Plant Pathology & Libr Sci,* Alvin Community College Library, Alvin TX. 713-331-6111, Ext 245
Houk, William, *Correctional Insts Servs,* San Joaquin Valley Library System, Fresno CA. 201-488-3185
Houkes, John, *Librn,* Purdue University Libraries & Audio-Visual Center (Management & Economics), West Lafayette IN. 317-749-2027
Houlahan, John M, *Dir,* Northwest Regional Library System, Sioux City IA. 712-279-6186
Houle, Donna L, *Tech Serv,* Cherokee County Public Library, Gaffney SC. 803-489-4381
Houle, Francine, *Ad,* Bibliotheque Municipale De Montreal-Est, Montreal-Est PQ. 514-645-7431, Ext 272
Houle, Marcel, *Dir,* College Marie-Victorin Bibliotheque, Montreal PQ. 514-325-0150, Ext 231
Houle, Mariette, *Librn,* Bibliotheque De La Ville De Montreal (Hochelaga Children), Montreal PQ. 514-872-3666
Houpt, Louise, *Asst Librn,* Coyle Free Library, Chambersburg PA. 717-263-8409
House, Barbara, *Instr,* Atlanta University, School of Library & Information Studies, GA. 404-681-0251, Ext 312
House, Charletta, *Rare Bks & Spec Coll,* University of Maryland-Eastern Shore, Frederick Douglass Library, Princess Anne MD. 301-651-2200, Ext 229
House, Dorothy A, *Librn,* Museum of Northern Arizona Library, Flagstaff AZ. 602-774-5211, Ext 56
House, Emelyn, *Govt Doc,* University of Michigan (Law Library), Ann Arbor MI. 313-764-9322
House, Gary, *Instructional Materials Center Coordr,* Albuquerque Technical-Vocational Institute, Instructional Materials Center, Albuquerque NM. 505-843-7250, Ext 243
House, Glenn, *Asst Prof,* University of Alabama, Graduate School of Library Service, AL. 205-348-4610
House, Linda, *Librn,* First Regional Library (Robert C Irwin Library), Tunica MS. 601-363-2162
House, Robbie, *Ser,* East Texas State University, James Gilliam Gee Library, Commerce TX. 214-886-5717

217

House, Roseanne, *Cat,* Amarillo Public Library, Amarillo TX. 806-378-3000, Ext 2250

Householder, Carolyn, *Dir,* Nashville State Technical Institute, Educational Resource Center, Nashville TN. 615-741-1245

Householder, Marjorie, *Librn,* Holland Township Free Public Library, Milford NJ. 201-995-4767

Housel, James, *Psychol & Parapsychol,* Ontario Public Library, Ontario CA. 984-2758 Ext 38

Housel, James R, *Dir,* Ontario Public Library, Ontario CA. 984-2758 Ext 38

Houseman, Marilyn M, *Dir,* Rio Hondo Community College Library, Whittier CA. 213-692-0921, Ext 371

Housen, Mylo, *Exec Dir,* French Library in Boston Inc, Boston MA. 617-266-4351

Houser, Doris, *ILL,* Everett Public Library, Everett WA. 206-259-8858

Houser, Florence, *Acq & Ref,* Kingsborough Community College Library, Brooklyn NY. 212-934-5144

Houser, Heather, *Tech Serv,* Central North Carolina Regional Library, Burlington NC. 919-227-2096

Houser, Jan, *Fed Doc,* Northwestern Oklahoma State University Library, Alva OK. 405-327-1700, Ext 219

Houser, Kay, *Librn,* Crook Community Library, Crook CO. 303-886-2222

Houser, Mary Jane, *Librn,* Honeywell Inc Library, Saint Petersburg FL. 813-531-4611, Ext 3256

Houser, Nell, *Librn,* Havelock-Craven County Library, Havelock NC. 919-447-7509

Housley, Mrs Glenn, *Asst Dir,* Weslaco Public Library, Porter Doss Memorial Library, Weslaco TX. 512-968-4533

Housman, Fern E, *Asst Librn,* Mediapolis Public Library, Mediapolis IA. 319-394-3895

Houston, Blanche V, *Cat,* Frick Art Reference Library, New York NY. 212-288-8700

Houston, Guyla, *Acq,* Oklahoma State University Library, Stillwater OK. 405-624-6313

Houston, Mary, *Librn,* Wilkes Community College, Learning Resources Library, Wilkesboro NC. 919-667-7136, Ext 26

Houston, Merle Z, *Dir,* Chipola Junior College Library, Marianna FL. 904-526-2761, Ext 122

Houston, Ruth, *Circ,* Amarillo Art Center Library, Amarillo TX. 806-372-8356

Houts, C F X, *In Charge,* Hawaii State Library System (Library Promotional Services), Honolulu HI. 808-548-3967

Houze, Robert A, *Dir,* Trinity University Library, San Antonio TX. 512-736-8121

Hovde, Ann, *ILL,* University of Minnesota, Duluth (Health Science Library), Duluth MN. 218-726-8585

Hovde, Oivind, *Rare Bks,* Luther College, Preus Library, Decorah IA. 319-387-1163

Hovdebot, Allen, *AV,* Wascana Institute of Applied Arts & Sciences, Resource & Information Center, Regina SK. 306-565-4321

Hover, Leila M, *Dir,* Holy Name Hospital, School of Nursing Library, Teaneck NJ. 201-833-3015

Hoverson, Martha, *Librn,* Hawaii State Library System (Koloa Community-School), Koloa HI. 808-742-1635

Hovik, Gloria, *Librn,* Sno-Isle Regional Library (Marysville Branch), Marysville WA. 206-659-2364

Hovius, Beth, *Librn,* Hamilton Public Library (Picton), Hamilton ON. 416-529-8111

Hovorka, Diana, *Circ,* State University of New York, Agricultural & Technical College at Alfred, Walter C Hinkle Memorial Library, Alfred NY. 607-871-6313

Hovorka, Marjorie, *Cat,* Brandeis University, Goldfarb Library, Waltham MA. 617-647-2514

Hovorka, Rae, *Librn,* Health Sciences Centre School of Nursing Library, Winnipeg MB. 204-787-3316

Howard, Ada M, *Coordr,* Big Country Library System, Abilene TX. 915-673-2311

Howard, Albert A, *Spec Coll,* University of Southern Maine, Gorham ME. 207-780-5340, 780-4273

Howard, Alison, *Librn,* University of California, Berkeley (Optometry), Berkeley CA. 415-642-1020

Howard, Ann, *Cat,* Ursuline College Library, Cleveland OH. 216-449-4200, Ext 276

Howard, B D, *Chief Librn,* United States Navy (Naval Station Library), San Diego CA. 714-235-1403

Howard, Barbara, *Media,* Cedar Crest College, Cressman Library, Allentown PA. 215-437-4471, Ext 264

Howard, Bernadette, *Librn,* Delaporte Memorial Public Library, Underhill Center VT. 802-899-4434

Howard, Betty, *Dir,* Potomac State College Library, Keyser WV. 304-788-3011, Ext 40, 72

Howard, Carlie M, *Ad & Ref,* Killeen Public Library, Killeen TX. 817-526-6527

Howard, Catherine, *Ch,* Wake County Department of the Public Library, Raleigh NC. 919-755-6077

Howard, Clint, *Acq,* University of Kansas Libraries, Watson Memorial Library, Lawrence KS. 913-864-3601

Howard, Cordelia, *Librn,* Long Beach Public Library System (El Dorado), Long Beach CA. 213-429-1814

Howard, David, *Per,* David Lipscomb College, Crisman Memorial Library, Nashville TN. 615-385-3855, Ext 282, 283

Howard, Dianne, *Librn,* Lord Corp, Information Centers, Erie PA. 814-868-3611, 456-8511

Howard, Don, *Hist, Relig & Philos,* Brigham Young University, Harold B Lee Library, Provo UT. 801-378-2905

Howard, Edward Allen, *Dir,* Evansville Public Library & Vanderburgh County Public Library, Evansville IN. 812-425-2621

Howard, Edward N, *Dir,* Vigo County Public Library, Terre Haute IN. 812-232-1113

Howard, Eleanor, *Librn,* Haverhill Municipal (HALE) Hospital, Medical Library, Haverhill MA. 617-372-7141, Ext 239

Howard, Elizabeth, *Librn,* University of Kentucky (Biological Sciences), Lexington KY. 606-258-5889

Howard, Elizabeth F, *Asst Prof,* West Virginia University, Dept of Library Science, WV. 304-293-3540

Howard, Elizabeth Hicks, *Librn,* Honeywell, Inc (Residential Engineering Library), Minneapolis MN. 612-870-2120

Howard, Elizabeth M, *Librn,* Veterans Administration, Hospital Library Service, Brockton MA. 617-583-4500, Ext 338, 321

Howard, Ellen J, *Ref,* University of Washington Libraries (Health Sciences), Seattle WA. 206-543-5530

Howard, Glenda, *Br Coordr,* Hardin County Public Library, Elizabethtown KY. 502-769-6337

Howard, Helen, *Asst Librn,* Eugene Public Library, Eugene OR. 503-687-5450

Howard, Jean, *Librn,* Gering Public Library, Gering NE. 308-436-7433

Howard, Jeanne, *Librn,* University of Oklahoma (Chemistry-Mathematics), Norman OK. 405-325-5628

Howard, Jeanne, *Librn,* University of Oklahoma (Physics), Norman OK. 405-325-2611

Howard, Joseph H, *Asst Librn, Processing Servs,* Library of Congress, Washington DC. 202-287-5000

Howard, Judy, *ILL & Ref,* Mitchell Public Library, Mitchell SD. 605-996-6693

Howard, Karen, *Librn,* Spokane County Library (North Spokane), Spokane WA. 509-489-8610

Howard, Laurie, *YA,* Brooks Memorial Library, Brattleboro VT. 802-254-5290

Howard, Lin, *Libr Tech,* Queen's University at Kingston (Physics), Kingston ON. 613-547-2739

Howard, Lois F, *ILL & Ref,* Saint Petersburg Junior College, Saint Petersburg Campus Library, Saint Petersburg FL. 813-546-0011, Ext 353

Howard, Lynette, *Librn,* Sno-Isle Regional Library (Granite Falls), Granite Falls WA. 206-691-6087

Howard, M, *Librn,* Okanagan Regional Library District (Falkland Branch), Falkland BC. 604-379-2381

Howard, Margaret, *Librn,* Hamlin-Lincoln County Public Library (Branchland Branch), Branchland WV. 304 824 5481

Howard, Margery, *Ref,* Cary Memorial Library, Lexington MA. 617-862-6288

Howard, Marion, *Dir,* Darlington Public Library, Darlington WI. 608-776-4171

Howard, Marion, *Librn,* Louisville Free Public Library (Newman), Louisville KY. 502-448-6325

Howard, Mary, *Dir,* Waukesha County Technical Institute Library, Pewaukee WI. 414-691-3200, Ext 311

Howard, Morton, *Cat,* Virginia Highlands Community College Library, Abingdon VA. 628-6094, Ext 268

Howard, Mrs Willie, *Librn,* Grant County Library, Ulysses KS. 316-356-1433

Howard, Nora, *Librn,* National Planning Association, Gerhard Colm Memorial Library, Washington DC. 202-265-7685

Howard, Patricia A, *Librn,* Siskiyou County Law Library, Yreka CA. 916-842-3531, Ext 60

Howard, Pauline, *Dir,* Southwest Technical Institute Library, East Camden AR. 501-574-0741, Ext 26

Howard, Rachel, *Librn,* Emmanuel College Library, Franklin Springs GA. 404-245-7226, Ext 32

Howard, Richard C, *Actg Chief, Asian Div,* Library of Congress, Washington DC. 202-287-5000

Howard, Roberta L, *Librn,* E I Du Pont De Nemours & Co, Inc, Elastomers Chemical Department, Research & Development Library, Beaumont TX. 713-722-3451

Howard, Sandra L, *Dir,* H B Stamps Memorial Library, Hawkins County Rogersville Public Library, Rogersville TN. 615-272-8710

Howard, Sharon, *Librn,* Scottsdale Community College Library, Scottsdale AZ. 602-941-0999

Howard, Sheila, *Ref & Bibliog Instr,* Okanagan College, Muriel Ffoulkes Learning Resource Center, Kelowna BC. 604-762-5445, Ext 293

Howard, Shermon, *Librn,* Ocean County Library (New Egypt Branch), New Egypt NJ. 201-758-7888

Howard, Sophy, *Asst Dir,* McCall Public Library, McCall ID. 208-634-5522

Howard, Theresa A, *Asst Librn,* Hornell Public Library, Hornell NY. 607-324-1210

Howard, Vivian S, *Admin Libr,* United States Army (Infantry School Library), Fort Benning GA. 404-544-4053

Howard, Wanda, *Bkmobile Coordr,* Cherokee County Public Library, Gaffney SC. 803-489-4381

Howard, Jr Milo B, *Dir,* Alabama Department of Archives & History Library, Montgomery AL. 205-832-6510

Howarth, Meribah, *Asst Dir,* Upper Arlington Public Library, Upper Arlington OH. 614-486-9621

Howarth, Shirley, *Dir,* Tampa Museum Library, Tampa FL. 813-223-8128

Howatt, Sister Helen Clare, *Dir,* Holy Names College, Paul J Cushing Library, Oakland CA. 415-436-1332

Howden, Norman, *Asst Prof,* Louisiana State University, Graduate School of Library Science, LA. 504-388-3158

Howdle, Susan, *Librn,* Quarles & Brady, Law Library, Milwaukee WI. 414-277-5000

Howe, Andrea, *Asst Librn,* Farmington Public Library, Farmington NM. 505-327-7701, Ext 1270

Howe, Ellen M, *Dir,* Princeton Public Library, Princeton MA. 617-464-2839

Howe, Harriet S, *Chief Librn,* Sanibel Island Public Library, Sanibel Island FL. 813-472-2483

Howe, Helen E, *Librn,* School District of Philadelphia, Pedagogical Library, Philadelphia PA. 215-299-7783

Howe, Judith, *Dir,* Itasca Community Library, Itasca IL. 312-773-1699

Howe, Lucy Y, *Dir,* Hamilton Public Library, Hamilton NY. 315-824-3060

Howe, Patricia, *Librn,* Chesterfield County Central Library (Midlothian Branch), Midlothian VA. 804-748-1601

Howe, Robert, *Asst Librn,* University of Florida Libraries (Latin American Collection), Gainesville FL. 904-392-0359, 392-0360

Howel, Sara, *Librn,* Tri-County Regional Library (Cave Spring Branch), Cave Spring GA. 404-291-9360

Howell, Alan G, *Acq,* Bridgewater State College, Clement C Maxwell Library, Bridgewater MA. 617-697-8321, Ext 441, 442

Howell, Alibeth, *Librn,* East Orange Public Library (Ampere), East Orange NJ. 201-266-5610

Howell, Alibeth, *Librn,* East Orange Public Library (Franklin), East Orange NJ. 201-266-5630
Howell, David B, *Pub Servs,* Nicholls State University, Allen J Ellender Memorial Library, Thibodaux LA. 504-446-8111, Ext 401, 402
Howell, Doris, *Shut-In Serv,* Dartmouth Regional Library, Dartmouth NS. 902-466-7623
Howell, Emory, *Dir,* University of Southern Mississippi (Teaching-Learning Resources Center), Hattiesburg MS. 601-266-7307
Howell, G, *Asst Librn,* Supreme Court of Canada Library, Ottawa ON. 995-6354-55-56
Howell, J B, *Dir,* Mississippi College, Leland Speed Library, Clinton MS. 601-924-5131, Ext 232, 307
Howell, Janet, *Librn,* Public Library of Charlotte & Mecklenburg County, Inc (Mint Hill Branch), Mint Hill Station NC. 704-545-3932
Howell, Josephine, *Librn,* Marsh & McLennan, Inc Information Center, New York NY. 212-997-7800
Howell, Katherine, *Dir,* New Hanover County Public Library, Wilmington NC. 919-763-3303
Howell, Lilith, *Asst Dir & Ch,* Somerset County Library, Somerville NJ. 201-725-4700, Ext 234
Howell, Lynette N, *Librn & Acq,* Daemen College, Marian Library, Amherst NY. 716-839-3600, Ext 243
Howell, Margaret, *Spec Coll,* University of Missouri-Columbia, Elmer Ellis Library, Columbia MO. 314-882-4701
Howell, Marie, *Asst Dir,* Rhoads Memorial Library, Dimmitt TX. 806-647-3532
Howell, Mrs Joseph, *Librn,* Zanesville Art Center Library, Zanesville OH. 614-452-0741
Howell, Raymond C, *Chief Librn,* Brockville Public Library, Brockville ON. 613-342-3936
Howell, Rebecca, *Bibliog Instr,* Troy State University Library, Troy AL. 205-566-3000, Ext 263
Howell, Ruth, *Asst Librn,* Bridgeport Public Library, Bridgeport TX. 817-683-4412
Howell, Sarah, *Ch,* Bay County Public Library Association, Northwest Regional Library System, Panama City FL. 904-785-3457
Howell, Susan, *Pub Serv,* Orange Public Library, Orange TX. 713-883-7323
Howells, James, *Ad & Acq,* Salt Lake County Library System, Whitmore Library, Salt Lake City UT. 801-943-7614
Howerton, Betty, *Librn,* Waddell & Reed, Inc, Investment Management Div Research Library, Kansas City MO. 816-283-4072
Howery, Doris, *Bkmobile Coordr,* Ward County Public Library, Minot ND. 701-852-1045
Howes, Bonnie, *Librn,* Henry F Schricker Library, Knox Public Library, Knox IN. 219-772-4207
Howes, Pat, *Librn,* Dames & Moore Library, Houston TX. 713-688-4541
Howes, Susan G, *Cat,* Nashua Public Library, Nashua NH. 603-883-4141, 883-4142
Howey, Joseph I, *Dir,* Troy Public Library, Troy MI. 313-689-5665
Howey, Marion, *Doc,* University of Kansas Libraries, Watson Memorial Library, Lawrence KS. 913-864-3601
Howick, Muriel, *Asst Prof,* Northern Illinois University, Dept of Library Science, IL. 815-753-1735
Howie, Dalene, *Circ,* Boise Public Library & Information Center, Boise ID. 208-384-4466
Howie, Margaret, *Tech Serv,* Stephens College, Hugh Stephens Library, Columbia MO. 314-442-2211, Ext 428
Howie, Jr, Robert L, *Register & Historiographer,* Episcopal Diocese of Massachusetts Library and Archives, Boston MA. 617-742-4720, Ext 40
Howieson, A Carleen, *Librn,* Horton Free Public Library, Horton KS. 913-486-3326
Howington, Lee, *Asst Dir Pub Servs,* Flint River Regional Library, Griffin GA. 404-227-2756
Howington, Lee, *Librn,* Flint River Regional Library (Griffin-Spalding County Branch), Griffin GA. 404-227-2756
Howitson, Brenda C, *Ad,* Malden Public Library, Malden MA. 617-324-0218
Howland, Cecil, *Bio-Sci,* Oklahoma State University Library, Stillwater OK. 405-624-6313
Howland, Eleanor J, *Librn,* Temple Terrace Public Library, Temple Terrace FL. 813-988-4731
Howland, Joan, *On-Line Servs,* Stanford University Libraries (Law Library), Stanford CA. 415-497-2721
Howland, Libby, *Res Asst,* Urban Land Institute Library, Washington DC. 202-331-8500
Howland, Margaret E C, *Dir,* Greenfield Community College, Library-Learning Resources Center, Greenfield MA. 413-774-3131, Ext 285
Howlett, Amy W, *Dir,* Southeast Regional Library, Dummerston VT. 802-254-2961
Howlett, Barbara, *On-Line Servs,* Rome Historical Society, William E & Elaine Scripture Memorial Library, Rome NY. 315-336-5870
Howlett, JoAnn M, *Librn,* State of Wisconsin Department of Administration Library, Madison WI. 608-266-0035
Howley, Helen, *Assoc Librn,* Saginaw Health Sciences Library, Saginaw MI. 517-771-6846
Howling, Bernice, *Ch,* Wayne Public Library, Wayne NJ. 201-694-4272
Howrish, Cathy, *Librn,* Spirit River Municipal Library, Spirit River AB. 403-864-3543
Howse, Beth, *Spec Coll,* Fisk University Library & Media Center, Nashville TN. 615-329-8730
Howser, Ray E, *Dir,* Illinois Valley Library System, Pekin IL. 309-673-3132
Howser, Wilma, *Librn,* Atlanta Public Library, Atlanta IL. 217-648-2112
Hoy, Eileen, *Tech Serv,* Hamilton Public Library, Hamilton ON. 416-529-8111
Hoy, Isabel M, *Dir,* Goshen County Library, Torrington WY. 307-532-3411
Hoyer, Edward, *Circ,* Southern Connecticut State College, Hilton C Buley Library, New Haven CT. 203-397-4505
Hoyle, Jean, *Supvr,* Middlesex County Library (Avon Library), Springfield ON. 519-438-8368
Hoyle, Karen Nelson, *Curator,* University of Minnesota Libraries-Twin Cities (Children's Literature Research Collections), Minneapolis MN. 612-373-9731
Hoyle, Norman E, *Assoc Prof,* State University of New York at Albany, School of Library & Information Science, NY. 518-455-6288
Hoyle, Ruth, *Asst Librn,* Methodist College, Davis Memorial Library, Fayetteville NC. 919-488-7110, Ext 227
Hoyle, Stephen J, *Ref,* United States Department of Labor, National Mine Health & Safety Academy Learning Resource Center, Beckley WV. 304-255-0451, Ext 266
Hoyman, Lisa, *Ch,* Mason City Public Library, Mason City IA. 515-423-7552
Hoynes, Emmet E, *Dir & Acq,* Olympic College, Learning Resources Center, Bremerton WA. 206-478-4609
Hoyt, Anne, *Curric Mat Lab,* Oklahoma State University Library, Stillwater OK. 405-624-6313
Hoyt, Arabelle, *Admin Asst,* Valparaiso-Porter County Public Library System & Administrative Headquarters, Valparaiso IN. 219-462-0524
Hoyt, Beryl, *Editorial & Training Libr,* Wisconsin Department of Public Instruction, Division of Library Services, Madison WI. 608-266-2205
Hoyt, Dolores, *Acq,* Indiana University-Purdue University at Indianapolis, University Library, Indianapolis IN. 317-264-4101
Hoyt, Helen, *Dir,* Rapid City Public Library, Rapid City SD. 605-394-4171
Hoyt, Jan, *Librn,* Denver Public Library (Virginia Village), Denver CO. 303-573-5152, Ext 271
Hoyt, Jan, *Librn,* Lake Lanier Regional Library (Duluth Public), Duluth GA. 404-476-1992
Hoyt, Lillian, *Librn,* Jones Memorial Library, Orleans VT. 802-754-6606
Hoyt, Rebecca, *Librn,* United States Air Force Institute of Technology Library, Grand Forks AFB ND. 701-594-6366, Ext 4
Hoytt, Eleanor H, *Asst Prof,* Atlanta University, School of Library & Information Studies, GA. 404-681-0251, Ext 312
Hrabak, Dorothy, *Librn,* Willoughby-Eastlake Public Library (Willowick Branch), Willowick OH. 216-943-4151
Hraban, Joan, *Tech Serv & Cat,* Ossining Public Library, Ossining NY. 941-2416; 941-9174
Hrachovy, Anita, *Circ,* San Jacinto College, Lee Davis Library, Pasadena TX. 713-476-1850, 476-1501, Ext 241
Hreha, Sheryl M, *Librn,* Bentleyville Public Library, Bentleyville PA. 412-239-5122
Hronek, Sally, *Doc,* Arizona State Library, Dept of Library, Archives & Public Records, Phoenix AZ. 602-255-4035
Hrybinsky, B, *Dir,* Vaughan Public Libraries, Maple ON. 416-832-1432
Hsia, Gloria H, *Chief, Cat Publ Div,* Library of Congress, Washington DC. 202-287-5000
Hsia, Tao-tai, *Chief, Far Eastern Law Div,* Library of Congress, Washington DC. 202-287-5000
Hsiao, Kathleen, *Asst Prof,* University of Guam, Library Science Program, GU. 734-2921
Hsieh, Rosemary, *Ref & On-Line Servs,* Saint Joseph's University Libraries (Drexel Library), Philadelphia PA. 215-879-7559
Hsiung, L, *Tech Serv,* Memorial University of Newfoundland Library (Health Sciences Library), Saint John's NF. 709-737-6670
Hsu, Hsiu-hsiang, *Tech Serv,* Cape May County Library, Cape May Court House NJ. 609-465-7837
Hsu, Kuang-Liang, *Prof,* Ball State University, Dept of Library Science, IN. 317-285-7180, 285-7189
Hsu, Patrick, *Tech Serv & On-Line Servs,* Ripon College Library, Ripon WI. 414-748-8328
Hsu, Raymond Chen-Huan, *Orientalia,* University of Miami, Otto G Richter Library, Coral Gables FL. 305-284-3551
Hsu, Veronica, *Librn,* RCA Corp, Government & Commercial Systems/Aerospace Systems Div, Engineering Library, Burlington MA. 617-272-4000
Hu, Bete, *Libr Asst,* Hawaii Department of Health, H H Walker Medical Library, Honolulu HI. 808-734-0221, Ext 314
Hu, Chia-yaung, *Chinese Bibliogr,* Harvard University Library (Harvard-Yenching Library), Cambridge MA. 617-495-3327
Hu, Janet Nai-Chen, *Chief Librn,* Hospital of Saint Raphael, Medical Library, New Haven CT. 203-789-3330
Hu, Mei Ming, *Cat,* Muscle Shoals Regional Library System, Florence AL. 205-764-6563
Hu, Shih Sheng, *Librn,* University of Toronto Libraries (Faculty of Law), Toronto ON. 416-978-3719
Hu, Shu Chao, *Acq,* Saint Francis College, Pius XII Memorial Library, Loretto PA. 814-472-7000, Ext 264, 265 & 266
Hu, Susan, *Cat,* Saint Francis College, Pius XII Memorial Library, Loretto PA. 814-472-7000, Ext 264, 265 & 266
Huacuja, Yvonne T, *Ref,* Neptune Public Library, Neptune NJ. 201-775-8241
Huang, C K, *Dir,* State University of New York at Buffalo (Health Sciences), Buffalo NY. 716-831-5465
Huang, Dora, *Librn,* United States Naval Air Development Center (Technical Information Branch Library), Warminster PA. 215-441-2541
Huang, Eileen W, *Bus & Human Resources Mgt,* National Defense University Library, Washington DC. 202-693-8437
Huang, Felicia, *Librn,* Metropolitan Library System (Belle Isle), Oklahoma City OK. 405-235-0571
Huang, George W, *Coordr & Prof,* California State University, Chico, Dept of Education, Librarianship Program, CA. 916-895-6421
Huang, Liza, *ILL,* Sloan-Kettering Institute for Cancer Research, Donald S Walker Laboratory, C P Rhoads Memorial Library, Rye NY. 914-698-1100, Ext 277
Huang, Maxine, *Cat,* Albuquerque Public Library, Albuquerque NM. 505-766-7882
Huang, Sam, *Acq,* University of South Dakota (McKusick Law Library), Vermillion SD. 605-677-5259
Huang, Steve, *Asst Dir,* University of South Carolina (Coleman Karesh Law Libr), Columbia SC. 803-777-5942
Huang, Theodore S, *Dir,* Fairleigh Dickinson University, Weiner Library, Teaneck NJ. 201-836-6300, Ext 265
Huang, Vicky, *Librn,* Hughes Aircraft Co, El Segundo Library, Los Angeles CA. 213-648-4668
Huang, Winnie S, *Ref,* Miami Dade Community College (New World Center Campus), Miami FL. 305-577-6890
Hubacek, Lois, *Librn,* Kern County Library (Wofford Heights Branch), Wofford Heights CA. 805-861-2130
Huband, Jenny, *Tech Serv & Cat,* Fort McMurray Public Library, Fort McMurray AB. 403-743-2121
Hubbard, Brother Bede, *Librn,* Saint Peter's Abbey & College Library, Muenster SK. 306-682-3373

Hubbard, Cynthia, *Librn,* Peabody Institute Library (South), Peabody MA. 617-531-3380

Hubbard, Edwina M, *Librn,* Veterans Administration, Medical Center Library, Cheyenne WY. 307-778-7550, Ext 236

Hubbard, Hazel C, *Humanities,* Virginia Polytechnic Institute & State University Library, Blacksburg VA. 703-961-5593

Hubbard, Howard W, *Pub Relations,* Enoch Pratt Free Library, Baltimore MD. 301-396-5430, 396-5395

Hubbard, Joan, *Acq,* University of North Dakota, Chester Fritz Library, Grand Forks ND. 701-777-2617

Hubbard, M, *Librn,* Canada Institute for Scientific & Technical Information (Electrical Engineering), Ottawa ON. 613-993-1600

Hubbard, Margaret, *Librn,* Goddard Public Library, Goddard KS. 316-794-8771

Hubbard, Marguerite, *Curator,* General Services Administration - National Archives & Records Service, Franklin D Roosevelt Library, Hyde Park NY. 914-229-8114

Hubbard, Marian E, *Librn,* Chaminade University of Honolulu Library, Honolulu HI. 808-732-1471

Hubbard, Mary Kathryn, *Librn,* Turner Collie & Braden, Inc, Library, Houston TX. 713-780-4100, Ext 3804

Hubbard, Michael, *ILL,* Library Association of Portland, Multnomah County Library, Portland OR. 503-223-7201, Ext 40

Hubbard, Paula, *Ref,* Maryville College, Father Edward Dowling Memorial Library, Saint Louis MO. 314-434-4100, Ext 241

Hubbard, Stephen, *Ref,* Fargo Public Library, Fargo ND. 701-241-1490

Hubbard, Susan, *Librn,* Greater Saint Louis Health System Agency Library, Saint Louis MO. 314-241-5810

Hubbard, Terry, *Soc Sci,* Colorado State University, William E Morgan Library, Fort Collins CO. 303-491-5911

Hubbard, Virginia F, *Librn,* Town of Tonawanda Public Library (Greenhaven), Tonawanda NY. 716-873-2861

Hubbard, William, *Dir Libr Serv,* Virginia State Library, Richmond VA. 804-786-8929

Hubbard, William J, *Bibliog Instr,* Virginia Polytechnic Institute & State University Library, Blacksburg VA. 703-961-5593

Hubbard, Willis M, *Dir,* Stephens College, Hugh Stephens Library, Columbia MO. 314-442-2211, Ext 428

Hubbell, Carol, *Librn,* Traverse City Public Library (Subregional Library for Blind & Physically Handicapped), Traverse City MI. 616-941-0144

Hubbers, Mrs D, *Librn,* Tyendinaga Township Public Library, Shannonville ON. 613-962-3303

Hubbert, Jane, *Asst Librn,* Greenville Public Library, Greenville IL. 618-664-3115

Hubble, Gerald B, *Dir,* Rockhurst College, Greenlease Library, Kansas City MO. 816-363-4010, Ext 253

Hubbs, Betty, *ILL,* Mitchell Public Library, Mitchell NE. 308-623-2222

Hubbs, Ronald B, *Dir,* Windsor Locks Public Library, Windsor Locks CT. 203-623-6170

Huber, Betty, *Tech Serv,* Dickinson Public Library, Dickinson ND. 701-225-2162

Huber, C, *Librn,* Okanagan Regional Library District (Armstrong Branch), Armstrong BC. 604-546-8311

Huber, C Edward, *Dir,* Radford University, John Preston McConnell Library, Radford VA. 703-731-5471, 5472

Huber, Celia R, *Librn,* Temple Beth Sholom Library, Miami Beach FL. 305-538-7231, Ext 22

Huber, Donald L, *Dir,* Trinity Lutheran Seminary Library, Columbus OH. 614-236-7116

Huber, George, *Librn,* Swarthmore College (Daniel Underhill Music), Swarthmore PA. 215-447-7231

Huber, Lawrence, *Dir,* Rio Grande College, Jeanette Albiez Davis Library, Rio Grande OH. 614-245-5353

Huber, M Violet, *Librn,* Government of Canada Department of Indian Affairs & Northern Development Library, Yellowknife NT. 403-920-8110

Huber, Mary Ann, *Librn,* Public Library of Columbus & Franklin County (Channingway Branch), Columbus OH. 614-864-1305

Huber, Maxine, *Librn,* Muskegon County Library (Egelston), Muskegon MI. 616-788-4811

Huber, Mildred, *Asst Dir,* Westmoreland Hospital Association (Health Education Center Library), Greensburg PA. 412-837-0100, Ext 380

Huber, Pearl, *Librn,* Container Testing Laboratory, Inc Library, New York NY. 212-677-5775

Huber, William E, *Librn,* Auglaize County Law Library, Wapakoneta OH. 419-738-3124

Hubert, Evelyn, *Cat,* Port Arthur Public Library, Port Arthur TX. 713-982-6491

Hubert, Mary, *ILL & Circ,* University of Washington Libraries (Law Library), Seattle WA. 206-543-4089

Hubert, Nora, *Librn,* Gould Inc, NavCom Systems, Engineering Library, El Monte CA. 213-442-0123, Ext 300

Hubing, Nancy, *Dir,* Neillsville Free Library, Neillsville WI. 715-743-2558

Hubler, Grace, *Arts,* Bridgeport Public Library, Bridgeport CT. 203-576-7777

Huchting, Mary, *Ref,* Mundelein College, Learning Resource Center, Chicago IL. 312-262-8100, Ext 301, 302 & 303

Huck, Sherry, *ILL,* University of Alaska, Anchorage Library, Anchorage AK. 907-263-1825

Huckabee, Dwan, *Ch,* Cabell County Public Library, Western Counties Regional Library System, Huntington WV. 304-523-9451

Huckabee, E H, *Librn,* Prudential Insurance Co of America, Business Library, Houston TX. 713-663-5909

Hucke, S, *Ref,* LaSalle Municipal Library, Bibliotheque Municipale La Salle, La Salle PQ. 514-366-2582

Huckins, Barbara, *On-Line Servs,* Veterans Administration Medical Center, Library Service, Dallas TX. 214-376-5451, Ext 214

Hucks, Jr, Herbert, *Col Archives,* Wofford College, Sandor Teszler Library, Spartanburg SC. 803-585-4821, Ext 396

Hucksoll, A C, *Dir,* Abbie Greenleaf Memorial Library, Franconia NH. 603-823-8424

Huddle, Annette, *Business & Science,* Mobile Public Library, Mobile AL. 205-438-7073

Huddleston, Charlotte, *Tech Serv,* Carnegie Public Library, Clarksdale MS. 601-624-4461

Huddleston, Don, *Media,* University of Hawaii (University of Hawaii Library), Honolulu HI. 808-948-7205

Huddleston, Kathy, *Bkmobile Coordr,* Dare County Library, Manteo NC. 919-473-2372

Huddleston, Pamela, *Humanities, Soc Sci & Ref,* University of Hawaii (University of Hawaii Library), Honolulu HI. 808-948-7205

Huddleston, Shirley, *Dir,* Clearwater Public Library, Clearwater KS. 316-584-6474

Hudgens, Jan, *Art,* Long Island University, Brooklyn Center Libraries, Brooklyn NY. 212-834-6060, 834-6064

Hudgins, Mildred S, *Librn,* Mathews Memorial Library, Mathews VA. 804-725-5747

Hudgins, Miriam, *Tech Serv & Ref,* Mercer University, Stetson Memorial Library, Macon GA. 912-745-6811, Ext 284

Hudnall, Carole, *Librn,* Columbia-Lafayette-Ouachita-Calhoun Regional Library (Taylor Branch), Taylor AR. 501-234-1991

Hudon, Marcel, *Rare Bks,* Universite Laval Bibliotheque, Quebec PQ. 418-656-3344

Hudon, Michele, *Cat,* University du Quebec: Centre d'Etudes Universitaires Dans L'Ouest Quebecois, Centre de Hull Bibliotheque, Hull PQ. 819-776-8381

Hudson, Alice, *Librn,* Victoria County Public Library (Dalton Township), Sebright ON. 705-324-3104

Hudson, Anita, *Asst Dir,* Springfield Town Library, Springfield VT. 802-885-3108

Hudson, Dale L, *Librn,* Florida State University (Music), Tallahassee FL. 904-644-5028

Hudson, Donna M, *Dir,* West Virginia School of Osteopathic Medicine Library, Lewisburg WV. 304-645-6270, Ext 213, 261

Hudson, Earline, *Acq & Tech Serv,* Tennessee State University, Martha M Brown - Lois W Daniel Library, Nashville TN. 615-320-3682, 251-1417

Hudson, Gary, *Acq,* South Dakota State University, Hilton M Briggs Library, Brookings SD. 605-688-5106

Hudson, Grace, *Sch Librn,* Pamlico County Library, Bayboro NC. 919-745-3515

Hudson, Hallie E, *Librn,* Maury County Public Library, Columbia TN. 615-388-6332

Hudson, Janet, *Librn,* Ligonier Valley Library Association, Inc, Ligonier PA. 412-238-6451

Hudson, Jean, *Tech Serv,* Schering-Plough Pharmaceutical Research Div, Library Information Center, Bloomfield NJ. 201-743-6000, Ext 781

Hudson, John A, *Dir,* University of Texas at Arlington Library, Arlington TX. 817-273-3391

Hudson, Mary, *Librn,* Montrose County Regional District Library (Naturita Branch), Naturita CO. 303-865-2848

Hudson, Nancy, *Asst Dir,* Clark County Library District, Las Vegas NV. 702-733-7810

Hudson, Patricia, *Librn,* East Moline Public Library, East Moline IL. 309-755-9614

Hudson, Paul, *Govt & Bus,* Public Library of Cincinnati & Hamilton County, Cincinnati Public Library, Cincinnati OH. 513-369-6000

Hudson, Phyllis, *Bibliog Instr,* University of Central Florida Library, Orlando FL. 305-275-2564

Hudson, Richard, *Chmn,* Alderson-Broaddus College, Media Education Program, WV. 304-457-1700, Ext 258

Hudson, Richard, *Media,* Alderson-Broaddus College, Pickett Library Media Center, Philippi WV. 304-457-1700, Ext 229, 258

Hudson, Robert O, *Dir,* Bladen Technical Institute Library, Dublin NC. 919-862-2164

Hudson, Roberta L, *Bks Librn,* Rutherford B Hayes Library, Fremont OH. 419-332-2081

Hudson, Roger, *Chief Med Examiner,* Medical Examiner, Forensic Library, Chapel Hill NC. 919-966-2253

Hudson, Saundra, *On-Line Servs & Bibliog Instr,* Missouri Institute of Psychiatry Library, Saint Louis MO. 314-644-8838

Hudson, Sharon, *Asst Librn,* Quarles & Brady, Law Library, Milwaukee WI. 414-277-5000

Hudson, Sophie, *Librn,* Taunton Public Library (East Taunten), East Taunton MA. 617-823-3570

Hudson, Thomas, *Coordr,* Pennhurst Center, Staff Library & Pennhurst Clients' Library, Spring City PA. 215-948-3500, Ext 209, 270

Hudson, Jr, Mrs John, *Librn,* Pine Forest Regional Library (Purvis Public), Purvis MS. 601-794-8171

Hudspeth, Marilyn, *Librn,* Geneva Public Library, Geneva AL. 205-684-2459

Huebner, Orma, *Librn,* Marvin Memorial Library, Shelby OH. 419-347-5576

Huebsch, Virginia, *Librn,* Samuel Roberts Noble Foundation, Inc, Biomedical Library, Ardmore OK. 405-223-5810, Ext 230

Huepers, Jenice, *Asst Librn,* Vidor Public Library, Vidor TX. 713-769-7148

Huesemann, Tom, *Acq,* University of New Mexico General Library (Law Library), Albuquerque NM. 505-277-6236

Hueste, Leoba, *Adminr,* Library Services Center of Missouri, MO. 314-635-6412

Huet, Francois, *Librn,* Bibliotheque Municipale, Marieville PQ. 514-460-4988

Hueter, Eike, *Dir & Acq,* Richard Bland College Library, Petersburg VA. 804-732-0111, Ext 226

Huey, Dorothy, *Librn,* Ibm Corp, Systems Communications Div Library, Research Triangle Park NC. 919-549-5221

Huey, Elisabeth, *Librn,* Natchitoches Parish Library, Natchitoches LA. 318-352-2415

Huey, Paula, *Asst Dir,* Viking Library System, Fergus Falls MN. 218-739-2896

Huff, Barbara, *Ref,* Loyola Marymount University (Loyola Law School Library), Los Angeles CA. 213-642-2934

Huff, Dorothy, *Cat,* Grundy County-Jewett Norris Library, Trenton MO. 816-359-3577

Huff, Helen, *Librn,* Boise State University Library (Vo-Tech Learning Center), Boise ID. 208-385-3484

Huff, James, *Assoc Prof,* California State University, Chico, Dept of Education, Librarianship Program, CA. 916-895-6421

Huff, Kitty, *Asst Librn,* Disciples of Christ Historical Society Library, Nashville TN. 615-327-1444

Huff, Margaret F, *Dean,* Orangeburg-Calhoun Technical College, Gressette Learning Resources Center, Orangeburg SC. 803-536-0311, Ext 296

Huff, Martha, *Ref & Bibliog Instr,* Odessa College, Murry H Fly Learning Resources Center, Odessa TX. 915-337-5381, Ext 299

Huff, Mary, *Cat,* Appalachian State University, Carol Grotnes Belk Library, Boone NC. 704-262-2186

Huff, May, *Librn,* Parrottsville Public Library, Parrottsville TN. 615-623-2688

Huff, Mrs A W, *Librn,* Madison County Public Library (Mars Hill Branch), Mars Hill NC. 704-649-3741

Huff, Phyllis, *Guided Studies Coordr,* Central Carolina Technical Institute, Learning Resource Center, Sanford NC. 919-775-5401, Ext 244

Huff, Roland K, *President,* Disciples of Christ Historical Society Library, Nashville TN. 615-327-1444

Huff, Rose, *Librn,* Pickens County Library (Allen Community), Central SC. 803-639-2711

Huff, Rose Marie, *Acq & Cat,* Trident Technical College (North Campus Learning Resources Center), Charleston SC. 803-572-6094

Huff, William, *Coll Develop,* University of Illinois Library at Urbana-Champaign, Urbana IL. 217-333-0790

Huff, Jr, Mrs W D, *Librn,* Corrales Community Library, Corrales NM. 505-897-0733

Huffer, Mary A, *Dir,* National Natural Resources Library & Information System, DC. 202-343-5821

Huffer, Mary A, *Dir,* United States Department of the Interior, Natural Resources Library, Washington DC. 202-343-5821

Huffman, Carol P, *Librn,* Evans Public Library, Vandalia IL. 618-283-2824

Huffman, Edna M, *Librn,* Nassau Hospital, Seaman Memorial Library, Mineola NY. 516-663-2280

Huffman, George, *Dir,* Amarillo College, Learning Resource Center, Amarillo TX. 806-376-5111, Ext 2420

Huffman, Margie, *Dir,* Hollifield Memorial Library, Auburn Public Library, Auburn AL. 205-887-8497

Huffman, Mrs Gary, *Librn,* Dixie Regional Library (Houston Carnegie), Houston MS. 601-489-3522

Huffman, Rebecca, *ILL,* Grandview Heights School District Public Library, Columbus OH. 614-486-2951

Huffman, Robert, *Educ-Psychol,* University of Missouri-Columbia, Elmer Ellis Library, Columbia MO. 314-882-4701

Huffman, Sharon, *Dir,* Reginald J P Dawson Library, Bibliotheque de Ville Mont Royal, Mount Royal PQ. 514-342-1892

Huffman, Winifred, *Dir,* Greenville Public Library, Greenville IL. 618-664-3115

Huffnagle, Beth, *Librn,* Dillsburg Area Public Library, Dillsburg PA. 717-432-5613

Hufford, Bernadette, *Interpreter for the Deaf,* Suburban Library System (Blind & Physically Handicapped Services), Burr Ridge IL. 312-325-6640

Hufford, G Lynn, *Pub Servs,* Miami University-Middletown, Gardner-Harvey Library, Middletown OH. 513-424-4444, Ext 221, 222

Hufford, Jon, *Cat,* Middle Georgia College, Roberts Memorial Library, Cochran GA. 912-934-6221, Ext 274

Huffstetler, Kathleen, *Acq,* Gaston-Lincoln Regional Library, Gastonia NC. 704-866-3756

Huffstutler, Rickey, *Media,* Alexander City State Junior College, Thomas D Russell Library, Alexander City AL. 205-234-6346, Ext 290

Hug, William E, *Chmn,* University of Georgia, Dept of Educational Media & Librarianship, GA. 404-542-3810

Huggett, Janice, *Br Coordr & Bkmobile Coordr,* Eureka-Humboldt County Library, Eureka CA. 707-445-7284, 445-7513

Huggins, Mildred, *Librn,* Clarke County Public Library, Grove Hill AL. 205-275-8157

Huggins, Minnie M, *Doc,* Wake Forest University, Z Smith Reynolds Library, Winston-Salem NC. 919-761-5480

Huggins, Una D, *Chief of Acq,* United States Department of the Army (Office of the Adjutant General, Morale Support Directorate, Library Activities Division), Washington DC. 202-325-9700

Huggins-Chan, June, *Br Coordr,* Parkland Regional Library, Yorkton SK. 306-783-2876

Huggins-Chan, Kathleen, *Business,* Hamilton Public Library, Hamilton ON. 416-529-8111

Hughes, Gwynne, *Librn,* Albert-Westmorland-Kent Regional Library (Moncton Public), Moncton NB. 506-389-2631

Hughes, Allan R, *Dir,* University of Pittsburgh at Titusville, Haskell Memorial Library, Titusville PA. 814-827-2702, Ext 239

Hughes, Alphia, *Tech Serv & Cat,* Armstrong State College, Lane Memorial Library, Savannah GA. 912-927-5332

Hughes, Amanda, *ILL,* Utica Junior College, William H Holtzclaw Library, Utica MS. 601-885-6062, Ext 48

Hughes, Ann, *ILL,* Canton Public Library, Canton MA. 617-828-0177

Hughes, Anne, *Librn,* Belmont Public Library (Waverly Reading Room), Belmont MA. 617-489-2000

Hughes, Annette, *Librn,* Arab Public Library, Arab AL. 205-586-3366

Hughes, Barbara, *Librn,* Gray Public Library, Gray ME. 207-657-4110

Hughes, Barbara, *Cat, On-Line Servs & Bibliog Instr,* Marin County Free Library, San Rafael CA. 415-479-1100, Ext 2577

Hughes, Betty L, *Dir,* James Memorial Library, Saint James MO. 314-265-7211

Hughes, Brenda, *Librn,* Library of Spiritual Frontiers Fellowship, Independence MO. 816-254-8585

Hughes, Carolyn C, *Coordr,* Tidewater Community College, Virginia Beach Campus Library, Virginia Beach VA. 804-427-3070, Ext 123, 126

Hughes, Cleo H, *Dir Program Develop & Eval,* Tennessee State Library & Archives, Nashville TN. 615-741-2764

Hughes, David, *On-Line Servs,* Elmira College, Gannett-Tripp Learning Ctr, Elmira NY. 607-734-3911, Ext 287

Hughes, Dick, *Librn,* Florida Audubon Society Headquarters Library, Maitland FL. 305-647-7700

Hughes, Doris K, *Actg Librn,* Abbeville-Greenwood Regional Library (Abbeville County), Abbeville SC. 803-459-4009

Hughes, Edwin J, *Dir,* Oxnard Public Library, Oxnard CA. 805-486-4311

Hughes, Elaine, *On-Line Servs,* Atlanta University, Trevor Arnett Library, Atlanta GA. 404-681-0251, Ext 225

Hughes, Erskine D, *Dir,* Pratt Community College Library, Pratt KS. 316-672-5641, Ext 127

Hughes, Geraldine, *Dir,* Sheridan College of Applied Arts & Technology, Library Techniques Program, ON. 416-845-9430, Ext 270

Hughes, Glenda, *Cat,* Georgia Department of Education (Div of Public Library Services), Atlanta GA. 404-656-2461

Hughes, Ivan W, *Actg Dir,* Saint Maur Theological Center Library, Indianapolis IN. 317-925-9095

Hughes, Jane, *Dir,* South Dakota Department of Transportation, Technical Library, Pierre SD. 605-224-3454

Hughes, Jane E, *Librn,* Fayette County Public Library, Oakhill WV. 304-465-0121, 465-0311

Hughes, Jean, *Ref,* Lake Lanier Regional Library, Lawrenceville GA. 404-963-5231

Hughes, Joe, *Media,* William Jewell College, Curry Library, Liberty MO. 816-781-3806

Hughes, Joyce, *Tech Serv & Cat,* Edison Community College, Learning Resources Center, Fort Myers FL. 813-481-2121, Ext 219, 220, 360

Hughes, Judy L, *Librn,* First Baptist Church of Lakewood Library, Long Beach CA. 213-420-1471

Hughes, Kerry, *Librn,* Rumrill-Hoyt Inc, Library, Rochester NY. 716-271-2150

Hughes, Lealer, *Librn,* United States Army (Applied Technology Labs, Technical Library), Fort Eustis VA. 804-878-2963

Hughes, Lillie, *Circ,* Meridian Public Library, Meridian MS. 601-693-6771, 693-4913

Hughes, Lois J, *Dean of Learning Reasources,* Antelope Valley College, Roy A Knapp Library, Lancaster CA. 805-943-3241, Ext 234

Hughes, Mabel, *Librn,* Southwest Arkansas Regional Library (Southwest Regional), Nashville AR. 501-777-4564

Hughes, Marija M, *Chief Librn,* United States Commission on Civil Rights, National Clearinghouse Library, Washington DC. 202-254-6636

Hughes, Mary, *Spec Coll,* Bowdoin College Library, Brunswick ME. 207-725-8731, Ext 281

Hughes, Mary, *Tech Serv,* Calaveras County Library, San Andreas CA. 209-754-4266

Hughes, MaryAnn, *Librn,* Mound City Public Library, Mound City IL. 618-748-9427

Hughes, Mrs Odell, *Librn,* Southwest Arkansas Regional Library (Delight Branch), Delight AR. 501-777-4564

Hughes, Norma, *Librn,* Mohave County Historical Society, Mohave Museum of History & Arts Library, Kingman AZ. 602-753-3195

Hughes, Pearl, *Ch,* Village Library, Wimberley TX. 512-847-2188

Hughes, Phyllis, *Ref & Bibliog Instr,* Berea College, Hutchins Library, Berea KY. 606-986-9341, Ext 289

Hughes, Richard, *Head,* University of Toledo (Learning Resources Center), Toledo OH. 419-537-3188

Hughes, Rita A, *Chief Librn,* Merrill Lynch, Pierce, Fenner & Smith Inc, Securities Research Library, New York NY. 212-766-7414

Hughes, Ruth, *Librn,* Bonita Springs Free Public Library, Inc, Bonita Springs FL. 813-992-0101

Hughes, Sue, *Librn,* Minor Hill Public Library, Minor Hill TN. 615-565-3699

Hughes, Sue Margaret, *Dir,* Baylor University, Moody Memorial Library, Waco TX. 817-755-2111, 2112

Hughes, Susan Kutscher, *Info Resources Coordr,* Mobil Producing Texas & New Mexico, Inc, Information Resource Center, Houston TX. 713-871-5621

Hughes, Suzanne, *Librn,* Louisiana Legislative Council Library, Baton Rouge LA. 504-392-2358

Hughes, Virginia, *Librn,* Hazleton Laboratories, Inc Library, Vienna VA. 703-893-5400

Hughes, Virginia, *Librn,* Martins Ferry Public Library (Shadyside Public), Shadyside OH. 614-676-0506

Hughes, Virginia, *ILL,* Normal Public Library, Normal IL. 309-452-1757

Hughes, Yvonne, *Librn,* Thomas Public Library (Gano Childrens Reading Center), Fort Valley GA. 912-825-8540

Hughes, II, J Marshal, *Librn,* United States Navy (Dahlgren Laboratory, General Library), Dahlgren VA. 703-663-8531

Hugo, Carita, *Commun Servs,* Mason City Public Library, Mason City IA. 515-423-7552

Hugo, Joan, *Librn,* Otis Art Institute of Parsons School of Design, Los Angeles CA. 213-387-5288

Hugo, Sandra L, *Librn,* Woden Public Library, Woden IA. 515-926-5716

Huguelet, Eugene W, *Dir,* University of North Carolina at Wilmington, William Madison Randall Library, Wilmington NC. 919-791-4330, Ext 2270

Huijgen, Diane, *Librn,* Bancroft, Avery & McAlister Library, San Francisco CA. 415-788-8855, Ext 301

Huisman, Gary B, *Dir,* Covenant College, Anna Emma Kresge Memorial Library, Lookout Mountain TN. 615-820-1560, Ext 216

Huisman, Linda B, *Librn,* Plainfield Public Library, Plainfield IA. 319-276-4461

Hukill, Jane E, *Dir,* Brandywine College Library, Wilmington DE. 302-478-3000

Hulbert, Doris J, *Circ,* University of Delaware, Hugh M Morris Library, Newark DE. 302-738-2231

Hulbert, Mary, *Librn,* Woods Memorial Library, Falls City NE. 402-245-2913

Hulburt, Jeanette, *Tech Serv,* Seattle University, A A Lemieux Library, Seattle WA. 206-626-6859

Hulbush, Dorothy L, *Librn,* United States Air Force (McChord Air Force Base Library), McChord AFB WA. 206-984-2126

Huleatt, Richard S, *Mgr, Libr Servs,* Armour & Co & Greyhound Corp, Armour Research Center Library, Scottsdale AZ. 602-991-3000, Ext 420, 422

Hulek, Mary Lou, *Librn,* Castleton Public Library, Castleton-on-Hudson NY. 518-732-2211

Hulen, Nancy, *Circ,* Northeast Missouri State University, Pickler Memorial Library, Kirksville MO. 816-665-5121, Ext 7186

Huling, Nancy, *Bibliog Instr,* State University of New York at Binghamton Library, Binghamton NY. 607-798-2194

Hulkonen, David A, *Clinical Med,* University of Texas Medical Branch, Moody Medical Library, Galveston TX. 713-765-1971

Hull, David, *Chief Librn,* National Maritime Museum, J Porter Shaw Library, San Francisco CA. 415-556-8177

Hull, Dorothy, *Librn,* Windsor Township Library, Dimondale MI. 517-646-0633

Hull, Joan, *Asst Dir,* Owen Sound Public Library, Owen Sound ON. 519-376-6623

Hull, Melicent, *ILL,* Pasadena Public Library, Pasadena TX. 713-477-0276

Hull, Robert V, *Librn,* North Branford Library System, North Branford CT. 203-488-7205

Hull, Thomas V, *Librn,* American Legion National Headquarters Library, Indianapolis IN. 317-635-8411

Hull, Vernelle, *Librn,* Mexico-Audrain County Library (Farber Branch), Farber MO. 314-249-2012

Hull, Yvonne, *Librn,* Xavier University of Louisiana Library (Pharmacy), New Orleans LA. 504-486-7411, Ext 296

Hullihan, Ann, *Librn,* Arthur Meyerhoff Associates, Inc, Research Library, Chicago IL. 312-337-7860

Hullinger, Jim, *Librn,* Women's Reformatory, The Tomorrow Center Library, Rockwell City IA. 712-297-7521

Hulsart, Dorothy, *In Charge,* Presbyterian Church Library, Westfield NJ. 201-232-7123

Hulse, Jeanne, *Libr Clerk,* Cornwall Public Library (Mountainville Branch), Mountainville NY. 914-534-8282

Hulsey, Judy, *Librn,* San Jacinto Baptist Church Library, Amarillo TX. 806-376-5951

Hulsey, Richard, *Asst Dir,* Willard Library, Battle Creek MI. 616-968-8166

Hulsizer, Bernice L, *Librn,* University of Illinois Library at Urbana-Champaign (Physics-Astronomy), Urbana IL. 217-333-2101

Hulst, Carolyn, *Bus Mgr,* Herrick Public Library, Holland MI. 616-392-3114

Hulst, Louise, *Ref & ,* Dordt College Library, Sioux Center IA. 712-722-3771, Ext 139

Hulton, Clara, *Librn,* Florida Department of Offender Rehabilitation, Florida Correctional Institution Library, Lowell FL. 904-622-5151, Ext 271

Hulton, Jr, John G, *Dir,* Central Florida Community College, Library Learning Resources Center, Ocala FL. 904-237-2111, Ext 344

Hulzenga, Bill, *Circ,* Essex County College, Learning Resources Center, Newark NJ. 201-877-3233

Humbert, Karen L, *Media,* Cheyney State College, Leslie Pinckney Hill Library, Cheyney PA. 215-758-2000, Ext 2203, 2208, 2245

Humbertson, Jane V, *Librn,* Hagerstown Junior College Library, Hagerstown MD. 301-790-2800, Ext 237

Humble, Sharron L, *In Charge,* Atlanta Regional Commission Library, Atlanta GA. 404-656-7715

Hume, Kathleen, *Cat & On-Line Servs,* University of Albuquerque, Center for Learning & Information Resources, Albuquerque NM. 505-831-1111, Ext 230

Hume, Valda, *Librn,* Prince Edward Island Provincial Library (Murray Harbour Branch), Murray Harbour PE. 902-892-3504, Ext 54

Hume, Jr, Howard N, *Acq,* National Defense University Library, Washington DC. 202-693-8437

Humes, Aileen W, *Librn,* New Brunswick Electric Power Commission Library, Fredericton NB. 506-453-4353, 453-4215

Humes, B, *Librn,* Oakland Public Library (Glenview), Oakland CA. 415-530-5770

Hummel, Janice, *Ref,* Southern Maryland Regional Library Association, La Plata MD. 301-934-9442

Hummel, Margaret, *Librn,* South Central Area Library (Gackle Public), Gackle ND. 701-483-3331

Hummel, Patricia, *Doc,* University of Utah (Law Library), Salt Lake City UT. 801-581-6438

Hummel, Patti, *Cat,* Lincoln Parish Library, Ruston LA. 318-255-1920

Hummel, Rosalie, *Librn,* Mid-Continent Public Library (Red Bridge), Kansas City MO. 816-942-1780

Hummel, Wilma L, *Librn,* Summerville Public Library, Summerville PA. 814-856-2384

Hummer, Kathryn, *Res Librn,* Johnson & Johnson (Personal Products), Milltown NJ. 201-524-7544

Humnickey, Virginia, *ILL,* Indiana University (School of Medicine Library), Indianapolis IN. 317-264-7182

Humphrey, Adeline, *Librn,* Onslow County Public Library (Richlands Branch), Richlands NC. 919-347-2592, 347-5495

Humphrey, David H, *V Pres,* Urban Research & Development Corp Library, Bethlehem PA. 215-865-0701

Humphrey, Ellen, *Asst to Dir,* University of Calgary Library, Calgary AB. 403-284-5954

Humphrey, J Steven, *Dir,* City of Easton Hugh Moore Park & Pennsylvania Canal Society, Canal Museum Library, Easton PA. 215-258-7155

Humphrey, Kathleen Ann, *Asst Librn,* Marylhurst Education Center, Shoen Library, Marylhurst OR. 503-636-8141, Ext 56 & 61

Humphrey, Linda, *Librn,* San Bernardino County Library (Montclair Branch), Montclair CA. 714-624-4671

Humphrey, M Moss, *Sr Med Librn,* Martin Luther King Jr General Hospital, Medical Library, Los Angeles CA. 213-603-4321

Humphrey, Sandi, *Ch,* Wasilla Public Library, Wasilla AK. 907-376-5913

Humphrey, Thomas W, *Dir,* Central Wyoming College Library, Riverton WY. 307-856-9291, Ext 33

Humphrey, Virginia Shea, *Dir,* Johnstown Public Library, Johnstown NY. 518-762-8317

Humphrey, Jr, Graham H, *Dir,* Escondido Public Library, Escondido CA. 714-741-4683

Humphreys, Jo Ann, *Asst Librn,* University of Missouri-Columbia (Law), Columbia MO. 314-882-6096

Humphreys, Nancy, *Ref,* University of Wisconsin-La Crosse, Murphy Library, La Crosse WI. 608-785-8505

Humphreys, Richard H, *Librn,* Delaware Law School Library of Widener University, Wilmington DE. 302-478-5280

Humphreys, Shannon, *Jail Program,* Norfolk Public Library, Norfolk VA. 804-441-2887

Humphries, Beth F, *Librn,* Hurricane City Library, Hurricane UT. 801-635-4542

Humphries, Beverly H, *Dept Head,* Lewis & Clark Community College, Library Technology Program, IL. 618-466-3411, Ext 348

Humphries, Beverly H, *Librn,* Lewis & Clark Community College, Reid Memorial Library, Godfrey IL. 618-466-3411, Ext 350

Humphries, Lyla, *Bkmobile Librn,* Buffalo Trace Regional Library, Flemingsburg KY. 606-845-9571

Humphries, Lyla L, *Librn,* Fleming County Public Library, Flemingsburg KY. 606-845-7851

Humphris, Jeannine, *Asst Dir & Ad,* Kemp Public Library, Wichita Falls TX. 817-322-5611, Ext 377

Humsey, Marjorie, *Librn,* Warren Public Library (Dorothy M Busch), Warren MI. 313-755-5750

Hundertmark, Barbara, *Circ,* Messiah College, Murray Learning Resources Center, Grantham PA. 717-766-2511, Ext 380

Hung, Elaine, *Tech Serv, Cat & On-Line Servs,* Alameda Free Library, Alameda CA. 415-522-5413, 522-3578

Hung, Esther C H, *Cat,* Columbia Theological Seminary, John Bulow Campbell Library, Decatur GA. 404-378-8821, Ext 67

Hunger, Charles H, *Dir,* Kent State University Libraries (Audio-Visual Services), Kent OH. 216-672-3456

Hungerford, Anthos, *Dir,* Hurley Medical Center, Michael H Hamady Health Sciences Library, Flint MI. 313-766-0427

Hunn, Marvin, *Ref,* Dallas Theological Seminary, Mosher Library, Dallas TX. 214-824-3094, Ext 285

Hunneyman, Norman, *Media,* Jefferson Community College, Melvil Dewey Library, Watertown NY. 315-782-5250

Hunsaker, Leland, *Cat,* Ricks College, David O McKay Learning Resources Center, Rexburg ID. 208-356-2351

Hunsberger, Barbara, *Acq,* Millersville State College, Helen A Ganser Library, Millersville PA. 717-872-5411, Ext 341

Hunsberger, Charles, *Dir,* Clark County Library District, Las Vegas NV. 702-733-7810

Hunsberger, Katherine, *Asst Supvr,* Waterloo Regional Library (St Jacobs), St Jacobs ON. 519-664-3443

Hunsberger, W D, *Asst Dir,* Indiana University-Purdue University at Fort Wayne Library, Walter E Helmke Library, Fort Wayne IN. 219-482-5456

Hunsecker, Helen L, *Acq,* United States Army War College Library, Carlisle Barracks PA. 717-245-4319

Hunsicker, Marya, *Dir,* New Jersey Library for the Blind & Handicapped, Trenton NJ. 609-292-6450

Hunsperger, Madeline, *Librn,* Philadelphia National Bank Library, Philadelphia PA. 215-629-4152

Hunsucker, Alice, *Librn & Ch,* Wells Fargo Bank (Corporate Library), San Francisco CA. 396-3744 or 3745

Hunsucker, Coy, *Exceptional Children,* Public Library of Cincinnati & Hamilton County, Cincinnati Public Library, Cincinnati OH. 513-369-6000

Hunsucker, David L, *Dir,* Gaston College, Learning Resources Center, Dallas NC. 704-922-3136, Ext 315

Hunt, Alta N, *Librn,* United States Air Force (Gunter Air Force Station Library), Gunter AFB AL. 205-279-3179, 279-4732

Hunt, Ann, *Librn,* Tulsa City-County Library (Jenks Branch), Jenks OK. 918-299-5932

Hunt, Ann C, *Librn,* TransAmerica DeLaval Inc, Research & Advanced Product Development Library, Trenton NJ. 609-890-5445

Hunt, Barbara, *Asst Librn,* Dade County Law Library, Miami FL. 305-579-5422

Hunt, Ben B, *Librn,* Saint Paul's College Library, Washington DC. 202-832-6262, Ext 27

Hunt, Betty, *Librn,* Mifflin County Library (Milroy Branch), Milroy PA. 717-667-2866

Hunt, Betty J, *Asst Librn,* Doddridge County Public Library, West Union WV. 304-873-1941

Hunt, Beverly, *Asst Dir,* Fremont Public Library, Fremont MI. 616-924-3480

Hunt, Carlotta, *AV,* Sutter County Free Library, Yuba City CA. 916-673-5773

Hunt, Carol, *In Charge,* Putnam Museum Library, Davenport IA. 319-324-1933

Hunt, Charles D, *Librn,* Lycoming County Law Library, Williamsport PA. 717-323-9811, Ext 2475

Hunt, Clara, *Reserve,* University of Mississippi Library, University MS. 601-232-7091

Hunt, Deborah, *Govt Pub,* University of Nevada-Reno, Noble H Getchell Library, Reno NV. 702-784-6533

Hunt, Diana, *Librn,* McCarthy & McCarthy Library, Toronto ON. 416-362-1812, Ext 362

Hunt, Donald R, *Dir,* University of Tennessee, Knoxville, James D Hoskins Library, Knoxville TN. 615-974-0111

Hunt, Elizabeth, *Librn,* Calef Memorial Library, Washington VT. 802-883-2210

Hunt, Florine E, *Corporate Librn,* Public Service Electric & Gas Company Library, Newark NJ. 201-430-7333

Hunt, Gary, *Rare Bks, Spec Coll & Archivist,* Ohio University, Vernon R Alden Library, Athens OH. 614-594-5228

Hunt, Hester, *Librn,* Elkhorn City Public Library, Elkhorn KY. 606-754-5451

Hunt, Hester, *Librn,* Stone Public Library (Elkhorn Branch), Elkhorn KY. 606-754-5451

Hunt, James R, *Dir,* Public Library of Cincinnati & Hamilton County, Cincinnati Public Library, Cincinnati OH. 513-369-6000

Hunt, Janet M, *ILL,* University of King's College Library, Halifax NS. 902-422-1271

Hunt, Jonathan, *Librn,* Massillon State Hospital, Patients Library, Massillon OH. 216-833-3135, Ext 363

Hunt, Judith Lin, *Dir,* University of Bridgeport, Magnus Wahlstrom Library, Bridgeport CT. 203-576-4740

Hunt, June, *Per,* Antillian College Library, Mayaguez PR. 809-832-9595, Ext 209

Hunt, Kathleen, *Circ,* East Lyme Public Library, Inc, Niantic CT. 203-739-6926

Hunt, Kathleen, *Ref,* West Georgia College Library, Carrollton GA. 404-834-1370

Hunt, Lori A, *Librn,* Shook, Hardy & Bacon, Law Library, Kansas City MO. 816-474-6550

Hunt, Mary, *Spec Coll,* Township of Hamilton Free Public Library, Trenton NJ. 609-890-3460

Hunt, Mary A, *Assoc Prof,* Florida State University, School of Library Science, FL. 904-644-5775

Hunt, Mildred, *ILL,* East Islip Public Library, East Islip NY. 516-581-9200, 581-9228

Hunt, Myrtle M, *Librn,* Normandy Osteopathic Hospital, Medical Library, Saint Louis MO. 314-389-0015

Hunt, Nancy, *Program Servs,* South Bend Public Library, South Bend IN. 219-288-4413

Hunt, Pearl, *Rotation,* Southeast Kansas Library System, Iola KS. 316-365-3833

Hunt, Roger, *Dir,* Antillian College Library, Mayaguez PR. 809-832-9595, Ext 209

Hunt, Suellyn, *Personnel & Training,* Monroe County Library System, Rochester NY. 716-428-7345

Hunt, Susan, *Dir,* Colchester City Library, Colchester IL. 309-776-4861

Hunt, Tom, *Media,* River Bend Library System, Coal Valley IL. 309-799-3131

Hunt, Tommie, *Tech Serv & Cat,* Houston County Public Library System, Perry GA. 912-987-3050

Hunt, Wanda B, *Librn,* United States Army (Corps of Engineers Sacramento District-Technical Information Center), Sacramento CA. 916-440-3404

Hunt-McCain, Pearl, *Librn,* Boston Redevelopment Authority Library, Boston MA. 617-722-4300, Ext 315, 407

Hunter, Ann, *Librn,* Anheuser-Busch, Inc, Corporate Library, Saint Louis MO. 314-577-3492, 577-2669

Hunter, Beryl M, *Librn,* Commissioner of Official Languages Library, Ottawa ON. 613-995-7717

Hunter, Bonnie, *Tech Serv & Cat,* Maine State Library, Augusta ME. 207-289-3561

Hunter, Bonnie I, *Bkmobile Coordr,* Moline Public Library, Moline IL. 309-762-6883

Hunter, Brenda, *Librn,* Atlanta Public Library (Uncle Remus), Atlanta GA. 404-753-5109

Hunter, Carolyn, *Art,* Public Library of Charlotte & Mecklenburg County, Inc, Charlotte NC. 704-374-2725

Hunter, David A, *Ref,* United States Army Medical Center (Post-Patients' Library), Washington DC. 202-576-1314

Hunter, Don, *In Charge,* United States Bureau of Mines, Metallurgy Research Laboratory Library, Boulder City NV. 702-293-1033, Ext 214

Hunter, Dorothy, *Ref,* Taylor Memorial Public Library, Cuyahoga Falls Public Library, Cuyahoga Falls OH. 216-928-2117

Hunter, Elizabeth, *Media,* Kirkwood Public Library, Kirkwood MO. 314-821-5770

Hunter, Frances, *Instr,* Middle Tennessee State University, Department of Library Service, TN. 615-898-2740 & 898-5555

Hunter, Frances, *ILL,* Middle Tennessee State University, Andrew L Todd Library, Murfreesboro TN. 615-898-2622

Hunter, Gail, *Librn,* Saint Clair County Library (Steele), Steele AL. 205-884-1685

Hunter, Isabel, *Librn,* Memorial University of Newfoundland Library (Health Sciences Library), Saint John's NF. 709-737-6670

Hunter, J, *Actg Librn,* National Gallery of Canada Library, Ottawa ON. 613-995-6245

Hunter, James, *Librn,* Columbus Dispatch Library, Columbus OH. 614-461-5016

Hunter, John H, *Asst Dir Tech Serv,* Auraria Libraries, Denver CO. 303-629-2805

Hunter, Josephine R, *Asst Librn,* Human Resources Research Organization (Hum RRO), Van Evera Library, Alexandria VA. 703-549-3611, Ext 281

Hunter, Judy, *Dir,* Huntsville Public Library, Huntsville TX. 713-295-6471

Hunter, Julie, *Lectr,* Atlanta University, School of Library & Information Studies, GA. 404-681-0251, Ext 312

Hunter, Julie V, *Actg Dir,* Atlanta University, Trevor Arnett Library, Atlanta GA. 404-681-0251, Ext 225

Hunter, June, *Librn,* Victoria County Public Library (Burnt River Branch), Burnt River ON. 705-324-3104

Hunter, Linette A, *Dir,* American Samoa-Office of Library Services, Pago Pago, Samoa PI. 633-5869

Hunter, Lola, *In Charge,* Cobb County Public Library System (Marietta Place), Marietta GA. 404-428-2836

Hunter, Lora C, *Acq,* Saint Petersburg Junior College, Saint Petersburg Campus Library, Saint Petersburg FL. 813-546-0011, Ext 353

Hunter, Lynn S, *Ch,* Piscataway Township Free Public Library, John F Kennedy Memorial Library, Piscataway NJ. 201-463-1633

Hunter, M Edward, *Librn,* On-Line Servs & Bibliog Instr, Methodist Theological School in Ohio Library, Delaware OH. 614-363-1146, Ext 242

Hunter, Marian, *Ad,* Avon Free Public Library, Avon CT. 203-678-1262

Hunter, Martha, *Acq,* Plaquemines Parish Library, Buras LA. 504-657-7121

Hunter, Mary, *Asst Librn,* Jerseyville Free Library, Jerseyville IL. 618-498-4511

Hunter, Patricia, *Dir,* Virginia Highlands Community College Library, Abingdon VA. 628-6094, Ext 268

Hunter, Robert J, *Dir,* Haddon Heights Public Library, Haddon Heights NJ. 609-547-7132

Hunter, Robin, *Ch,* El Segundo Public Library, El Segundo CA. 213-322-4121

Hunting, Susan, *Ref,* Sioux City Public Library, Sioux City IA. 712-279-6179

Huntington, Barbara, *Ch,* Platteville Public Library, Platteville WI. 608-348-7441

Huntington, Claire, *Librn,* Geisinger Medical Center (School of Nursing Library), Danville PA. 717-275-6288

Huntington, Mary, *Dir,* Canyon Public Library, Canyon TX. 806-655-9271

Huntington, Nancy J, *Admin Asst,* United Society of Shakers Library, Poland Spring ME. 207-926-4865

Huntley, Jill Perry, *Dir,* Southern Seminary & Junior College, Von Canon Library, Buena Vista VA. 703-261-6181, Ext 241

Huntley, Mary Deane, *Dir & Commun Servs,* Hayner Public Library District, Alton IL. 618-462-0651

Huntley, Nancy, *Pub Servs,* Lincoln Library, Springfield Public Library, Springfield IL. 217-753-4900

Huntoon, Elizabeth, *Serv Specialists: Children,* Chicago Public Library, Chicago IL. 312-269-2900

Huntsman, Lona, *Librn,* Fillmore City Library, Fillmore UT. 801-743-5314

Hupp, Gloria, *Bkmobile Coordr,* Toledo-Lucas County Public Library, Toledo OH. 419-255-7055

Hupp, Gloria, *Librn,* Toledo-Lucas County Public Library (Special Services), Maumee OH. 419-255-7055

Hupp, Mary A, *Coordr,* Fairmont State College, Library Science Program, WV. 304-367-4121

Hupp, Sherry Winn, *Regional Coordr,* Southern Connecticut Library Council, CT. 203-387-3690

Huppert, Ramona R, *Librn,* 3M (The 251 Technical Library), Saint Paul MN. 612-733-5236

Hurd, Albert E, *Dir,* Chicago Theological Seminary, Hammond Library, Chicago IL. 312-752-5757, Ext 55 & 56

Hurd, Ange, *Asst Dir & Br Coordr,* Wayne County Public Library, Wooster OH. 216-262-0916

Hurd, Chris, *Dist Librn,* United States Army (Corps of Engineers, Portland District Library), Portland OR. 503-221-6016

Hurd, Hellen, *Dir,* Green River Regional Library District, Owensboro KY. 502-685-4514

Hurd, Karen, *Bibliog Instr,* University of Wisconsin Center, Waukesha County Library, Waukesha WI. 414-542-8825, Ext 280

Hurd, Louise O, *Librn,* Merrill Public Library, Merrill IA. 712-938-9305

Hurd, Marilyn L, *Librn,* Redondo Beach Public Library, Redondo Beach CA. 213-376-8723

Hurd, Sandra, *ILL & Cat,* Plymouth Public Library, Russell Memorial Library, Plymouth MA. 617-746-1927

Hurd, Sister Naomi, *Librn,* Saint Joseph Medical Center, Health Science Library, Burbank CA. 213-843-5111, Ext 2522

Hurd, Stephen, *Librn,* Dekalb Library System (Brookhaven), Atlanta GA. 404-261-4719

Hurd, Wenona, *In Charge,* Rockwell International, Technical Information Center, Tulsa OK. 918-835-3111

Hurdle, Jr, James R, *Dir,* Coastal Carolina Community College Library, Jacksonville NC. 919-455-1221

Hurkett, Jack W, *Asst Dir,* State Library Commission of Iowa, Des Moines IA. 515-281-4102

Hurl, Thelma, *Asst Librn,* High River Centennial Library, High River AB. 403-652-2917

Hurlbert, Agatha L, *Asst Librn,* Richmond Public Library, Richmond VA. 804-780-4256

Hurlbert, Betty E, *Librn,* ASARCO Inc Library, South Plainfield NJ. 201-756-4800, Ext 226

Hurlbert, Bruce M, *Asst Dir,* Virginia Commonwealth University (James Branch Cabell Library), Richmond VA. 804-257-1105

Hurley, Carol R, *Librn,* Ford Aerospace & Communications Corp, Western Development Laboratories Library, Palo Alto CA. 415-494-7400

Hurley, Carolyn, *Ref,* Northbrook Public Library, Northbrook IL. 312-272-6224

Hurley, Donna, *On-Line Servs & Bibliog Instr,* United States Naval Academy, Nimitz Library, Annapolis MD. 301-267-2194, 267-2800

Hurley, Gileen M, *Ch,* Osterville Free Library, Osterville MA. 617-428-2565

Hurley, Hazel, *Librn,* New Mexico Department of Hospitals & Institutions, Ella P Kief Memorial Library, Las Vegas NM. 505-425-6711, Ext 380

Hurley, John, *Ref,* Moorpark College Library, Moorpark CA. 805-529-2321, Ext 270

Hurley, Leo, *Libr Program Officer (Europe),* International Communication Agency (Education & Cultural Affairs), Washington DC. 202-632-5346, 632-6752

Hurley, Suzanne, *Archivist,* National City Public Library, National City CA. 714-474-8211

Hurley, Trudy, *Doc,* Southwest Texas State University, Learning Resources Center, San Marcos TX. 512-245-2132

Hurnard, Shirley A, *Supvr,* Law Society of Saskatchewan Libraries, Regina SK. 306-569-8020

Hurr, Doris, *Asst Dir,* Cumberland County Public Library, Anderson Street Library, Frances Brooks Stein Memorial Library, Fayetteville NC. 919-483-1580

Hurrey, Katharine C, *Librn,* Charles County Public Library, La Plata MD. 301-934-9001

Hurrey, Katharine C, *Adminr,* Southern Maryland Regional Library Association, La Plata MD. 301-934-9442

Hurrey, Katherine, *Ad,* Calvert County Public Library, Prince Frederick MD. 301-535-0291

Hurrey, Katherine, *Admin,* Saint Mary's County Memorial Library, Leonardtown MD. 301-475-2846

Hurst, Anne, *ILL & Circ,* Stetson University, duPont-Ball Library, De Land FL. 904-734-4121, Ext 220

Hurst, Bernice, *Librn,* Houston Public Library (Young), Houston TX. 713-643-8556

Hurst, Cindi, *Librn,* Chevron Industries, Inc, Chevron Geophysics Co Library, Houston TX. 713-781-3030, Ext 284

Hurst, Don, *On-Line Servs,* East Tennessee State University, Sherrod Library, Johnson City TN. 615-929-4338

Hurst, Earlene, *Doc,* Stetson University College of Law, Charles A Dana Law Library, Saint Petersburg FL. 813-345-1335

Hurst, Frances, *Tech Serv & Cat,* Jefferson State Junior College, James B Allen Library, Birmingham AL. 205-853-1200, Ext 280

Hurst, Kathleen, *Media,* Saint Joseph Public Library, Saint Joseph MO. 816-232-7729, 232-7720

Hurst, Pauline, *Librn,* Opp Public Library, Opp AL. 205-493-6423

Hurt, Anne P, *Librn,* Nottoway County Library, Nottoway VA. 804-645-9310

Hurt, Byrnice, *Librn,* Saint Francis Hospital, Medical Library, Roslyn NY. 516-627-6200, Ext 1659

Hurt, Charlene, *Dir,* Washburn University of Topeka, Mabee Library, Topeka KS. 913-295-6479

Hurt, Howard, *Librn,* University of British Columbia Library (Education Curriculum Laboratory), Vancouver BC. 604-228-5378

Hurter, Collen, *On-Line Servs,* Woods Hole Oceanographic Institution (General Library), Woods Hole MA. 617-548-1400, Ext 2512, 2708

Hurtes, R, *Librn,* University of Miami (Opthalmology Branch Library, Bascom Palmer Eye Institute & Anne Bates Leach Eye Hospital), Miami FL. 305-547-6023

Hurtt, Sandra L, *Publicity Spec,* Norfolk Public Library, Norfolk VA. 804-441-2887

Hurtubise, Gisele, *Tech Serv,* Bibliotheque De Quebec, Quebec PQ. 418-694-6356

Hurwitz, Jack, *Librn,* Hinsdale Public Library, Hinsdale IL. 312-986-1976

Hurwitz, Sue, *YA & Media,* Memorial Hall Library, (Subregional Headquarters for Eastern Massachusetts Regional System), Andover MA. 617-475-6960

Hurwood, Gilbert Arthur, *Librn,* State of Ohio Department of Corrections, London Correctional Institute Library, London OH. 614-852-2454

Hurych, Jitka, *On-Line Servs,* Northern Illinois University, Founders Memorial Library, De Kalb IL. 815-753-1094

Husa, Suzanne, *Tech Serv & Cat,* Harrisburg Area Community College, McCormick Library, Harrisburg PA. 717-236-9533, Ext 257

Husband, Dolores, *Librn,* Tahquamenon Area Public Library, Newberry MI. 906-293-5662

Husband, Janet G, *Acq,* Thomas Crane Public Library, Subregional Headquarters for Eastern Massachusetts Regional Library System, Quincy MA. 617-471-2400

Husband, Jonathan F, *Chief Bibliogr,* Boston State College Library, Boston MA. 617-731-3300

Huse, Ruth, *Librn,* Weatherford College Library, Weatherford TX. 817-594-5471, Ext 51

Huseman, Dwight, *Ser & Doc,* Gettysburg College, Schmucker Memorial Library, Gettysburg PA. 717-334-3131, Ext 366

Husier, Richard P, *Asst Librn,* Snow College, Lucy A Phillips Library, Ephraim UT. 801-283-4201, Ext 204

Huslig, Dennis, *Librn Deaf & Librn Blind,* Illinois Valley Library System, Pekin IL. 309-673-3132

Huslig, Dennis, *Special Servs Consult,* Illinois Valley Library System (Special Services Department), Pekin IL. 309-353-4115

Huslig, Mary Ann, *Cat,* Illinois Central College, Learning Resources Center, East Peoria IL. 309-694-5461

Hussain, M Riaz, *Dir & On-Line Servs,* Nova Scotia Technical College Library, Halifax NS. 902-429-8300, Ext 254

Husselman, Grace, *Dir,* Lee Memorial Library, Allendale Public Library, Allendale NJ. 201-327-4338

Hust, Carolyn R, *Cat,* Drake University, Cowles Library, Des Moines IA. 515-271-3993

Hustad, Aldora, *Librn,* Elkader Public Library, Elkader IA. 319-245-1446

Hustad, Sandra, *Dir,* METRONET, MN. 612-645-5731

Husted, Grace S, *Librn,* Hockessin Public Library, Hockessin DE. 302-239-5160

Husted, Rhonda, *Librn,* Ida Grove Public Library, Ida Grove IA. 712-364-2306

Husted, Thom, *ILL & Circ,* Saint Louis University (Omer Poos Law Library), Saint Louis MO. 314-658-2755

Huston, Bryan, *Asst Dir,* Lethbridge Public Library, Lethbridge AB. 403-329-3233

Huston, Jim, *Arts & Recreation,* Lincoln Library, Springfield Public Library, Springfield IL. 217-753-4900

Huston, Timothy, *Ref,* Sonoma State University, Ruben Salazar Library, Rohnert Park CA. 707-664-2397

Hustuft, Dean, *Instr,* Illinois State University, Department of Information Sciences, IL. 309-438-3671

Hutch, Janet, *Librn,* Cleveland Public Library (Sterling), Cleveland OH. 216-621-5766

Hutchason, Clark, *Supvr,* Coen Company Library, Burlingame CA. 415-697-0440, Ext 247

Hutcheson, Barbara, *Librn,* Winnipeg Public Library (William Avenue), Winnipeg MB. 204-985-6487

Hutcheson, S, *Asst Librn Res,* Toronto Public Library, Toronto ON. 416-484-8015

Hutcheson, Sandra, *Librn,* Mississippi County Library District (Mitchell Memorial), East Prairie MO. 314-649-2131

Hutcheson, Shirley, *Cat,* Niles Community Library, Niles MI. 616-683-8545, 683-8546

Hutchings, Carol, *Ch,* Morris Public Library, Morris IL. 815-942-6880

Hutchings, Mary Jo, *Dir,* Mount Prospect Public Library, Mount Prospect IL. 312-253-5675

Hutchins, Jeanette, *Librn,* Northwest Regional Library (Russellville Branch), Russellville AL. 205-332-1535

Hutchins, Martha, *Reader Serv,* Beverly Public Library, Beverly MA. 617-922-0310

Hutchins, Meredith, *Dir,* Southwest Harbor Public Library, Southwest Harbor ME. 207-244-7065

Hutchins, Pat, *Librn,* Indiana Vocational Technical College, Terre Haute IN. 812-299-1121, Ext 22

Hutchins, Paul R, *Dir,* Dowagiac Public Library, Dowagiac MI. 616-782-3826, 782-2195 Ext 30

Hutchins, Richard G, *Librn,* University of Miami (Law), Coral Gables FL. 305-284-2250

Hutchins, Thelma J, *Dir,* South Georgia College, William S Smith Library, Douglas GA. 912-384-1100, Ext 233, 290

Hutchinson, Ann P, *Dir,* Roswell Park Memorial Institute, Medical & Scientific Library, Buffalo NY. 716-845-5966

Hutchinson, Barbara, *Librn,* Rawson Memorial Library, Cass City MI. 517-872-2856

Hutchinson, Carol, *Ad & Ref,* Fairfield Public Library, Fairfield CT. 203-259-8303

Hutchinson, Cindy, *Chief Librn,* Acurex Corp, Technical Library, Mountain View CA. 415-964-3200, Ext 3221

Hutchinson, Clinton, *Per,* Trinity College Library, Burlington VT. 802-658-0337, Ext 343

Hutchinson, E, *Librn,* McGarry Township Public Library, Virginiatown ON. 705-634-2145

Hutchinson, Irene, *Librn,* Harvey-Mitchell Memorial Library, Epping NH. 603-679-5944

Hutchinson, June, *Cat,* Lynnfield Public Library, Lynnfield MA. 617-334-5411

Hutchinson, Loraine, *Dir,* Orchard Park Public Library, Orchard Park NY. 716-662-9851

Hutchinson, Maureen, *Assoc Librn,* University of Toronto Libraries (University Library), Toronto ON. 416-978-2294

Hutchinson, Susan, *Dir,* Lawrence Memorial Hospital, Health Sciences Library, Medford MA. 617-396-9250, Ext 240

Hutchinson, William L, *Librn,* Pacific Power & Light Co Library, Portland OR. 503-243-4095

Hutchison, Dorothy, *ILL,* San Diego Public Library, San Diego CA. 714-236-5800

Hutchison, Liza, *Media,* Vancouver Community College Libraries, Vancouver BC. 604-688-1111

Hutchison, Mrs R L, *Librn,* Westminster Presbyterian Church Library, Pittsburgh PA. 412-835-6630

Hutsell, Terry, *Media,* Washington County Library System, William Alexander Percy Memorial Library, Greenville MS. 601-335-2331

Hutson, Dorothy A, *Mgr Tech Servs,* General Electric Co, Advanced Reactor Systems Department Library, Sunnyvale CA. 408-738-7177

Hutson, Jean B, *Chief,* New York Public Library (Schomburg Center for Research in Black Culture (Harlem)), New York NY. 212-862-4000

Hutt, Lucyle M, *Librn,* Ralph Memorial Library, Belhaven NC. 919-943-2993

Hutter, Jane, *Ch,* Wilmette Public Library District, Wilmette IL. 312-256-5025

Huttner, Marian, *Asst Dir,* Cleveland Public Library, Cleveland OH. 216-623-2800

Huttner, Sydney F, *George Arents Res Libr for Spec Coll,* Syracuse University Libraries, Ernest S Bird Library, Syracuse NY. 315-423-2575

Hutton, Bette, *ILL,* Owen Sound Public Library, Owen Sound ON. 519-376-6623

Hutton, Betty Jean, *Acq,* Southern Illinois University at Carbondale, Delyte W Morris Library, Carbondale IL. 618-453-2522

Hutton, Charlotte M, *Librn,* Lane Memorial Library, Hampton NH. 603-926-3368

Hutton, M A, *Librn,* Canadian Association for the Mentally Retarded, John Orr Foster Memorial Library, Downsview ON. 416-661-9611

Hutton, Randy, *Librn,* Memphis-Shelby County Public Library & Information Center (Popular Library), Memphis TN. 901-528-2950

Huwa, Elaine, *Asst Librn,* Gates Rubber Co, Technical Information Center, Denver CO. 303-744-4150

Huwar, Linda, *Asst Librn,* Mary Fuller Frazier Memorial School & Community Library, Perryopolis PA. 412-736-4426

Huwiler, Paul, *Asst Prof,* Southern Connecticut State College, Div of Library Science & Instructional Technology, CT. 203-397-4532

Hux, Roger K, *ILL & Spec Coll,* Francis Marion College, James A Rogers Library, Florence SC. 803-669-4121, Ext 321

Huyke, Ena C, *Per,* University of Puerto Rico Library, Jose M Lazaro Memorial Library, Rio Piedras PR. 809-764-0000, Ext 3296

Huzzard, Sarah, *Asst Dir,* Royersford Free Public Library, Royersford PA. 215-948-7277

Hwang, Aileen A, *Dir,* Bound Brook Memorial Library, Bound Brook NJ. 201-356-0043

Hyatt, Dennis R, *Assoc Librn,* University of Oregon Library (Law), Eugene OR. 503-686-3088

Hyatt, James, *Librn,* Mary Wood Weldon Memorial Library, Glasgow KY. 502-651-2824

Hyatt, James, *Genealogy,* Mary Wood Weldon Memorial Library, Glasgow KY. 502-651-2824

Hyatt, John D, *Head Librn,* Rosenberg Library, Galveston TX. 713-763-8854

Hybell, Kay, *YA,* Somers Library, Somers NY. 914-277-3420

Hyde, Dennis, *Coll Develop,* University of Pennsylvania Libraries, Van Pelt Library, Philadelphia PA. 215-243-7091

Hyde, Elizabeth S, *Librn,* Pomfret Free Public Library, Pomfret CT. 203-928-3475

Hyde, Gail L, *Librn,* Cornell University, New York State Agricultural Experiment Station Library, Geneva NY. 315-787-2214

Hyde, Hugh C, *Media,* Southwestern College Library, Chula Vista CA. 714-421-6700, Ext 237

Hyde, Irena, *Librn,* H F Brigham Free Library, Bakersfield VT. 802-827-6675

Hyde, Mary Lynn, *Instr,* Grossmont College, Library Technology Program, CA. 714-465-1700, Ext 319

Hyde, Mary Lynn, *Tech Serv & Doc,* University of San Diego (Marvin Kratter Law Library), San Diego CA. 714-293-4541

Hyde, Maxine, *Supvr,* Huron County Public Library (Huron Park Branch), Huron Park ON. 519-524-7751

Hyde, Wilma, *Acq,* San Jose Public Library, San Jose CA. 408-277-4822

Hyer, Susan, *Asst Librn,* Newspaper Advertising Bureau, Inc, Information Center, New York NY. 212-557-1822, 557-1823

Hyland, Elizabeth, *Tech Serv,* Center Moriches Free Public Library, Center Moriches NY. 516-878-0940

Hyland, Rosemary, *Ad,* Ridley Township Public Library, Folsom PA. 215-583-0593

Hylton, Ellen, *Tech Serv,* Roanoke County Public Library, Roanoke VA. 703-774-1681

Hylton, Kenny, *Asst Librn,* Jennings Public Library, Jennings LA. 318-824-4367

Hyman, Arnold, *Librn,* New York Public Library (Morrisania), New York NY. 212-589-9268

Hyman, Ferne, *Coll Develop,* William Marsh Rice University, Fondren Library, Houston TX. 713-527-4022

Hyman, Karen, *Ref,* Cherry Hill Free Public Library, Cherry Hill NJ. 609-667-0300

Hyman, Richard J, *Dir,* Queens College of the City University of New York, Graduate School of Library & Information Studies, NY. 212-520-7194, 520-7195

Hyman, Rita, *Ad,* South Windsor Public Library, South Windsor CT. 203-644-1541

Hyman, Toby A, *Dir,* Copiague Memorial Public Library, Copiague NY. 516-842-0032

Hymas, June, *Librn,* Santa Clara County Free Library (Gilroy Public), Gilroy CA. 408-842-8207

Hymel, Betty, *Librn,* Pointe Coupee Parish Library (Innis Library), Innis LA. 504-638-7593

Hymes, Judith, *Tech Serv,* University of Puerto Rico - Bayamon Regional College, Learning Resources Center, Bayamon PR. 809-786-5225

Hyndman, R E, *In Charge,* United Church of Canada, Knox-Metropolitan United Church Library, Edmonton AB. 403-439-1718

Hynes, Arleen, *Libm,* Saint Elizabeth's Hospital (Circulating Library), Washington DC. 202-574-7274

Hynes, Edward, *ILL, Ref & Bibliog Instr,* Stonehill College, Cushing-Martin Library, North Easton MA. 617-238-1081, Ext 328, 329, 313

Hypio, Mike, *Libm,* West Shore Community College, Instructional Media Center, Scottville MI. 616-845-6211, Ext 228

Hyslop, Mary, *Asst Dir, Acq & Br Coordr,* Branch County Library, Coldwater MI. 517-278-2341

Hyslop, Shirley W, *Cat & Ref,* Field Library, Peekskill Library, Peekskill NY. 914-737-0010

Hyson, Gay, *YA,* Medford Public Library, Medford MA. 617-395-7950

Hyvarien, Virginia, *Commun Servs,* Duluth Public Library, Duluth MN. 218-723-3800

I

Iacono, Frank P, *Ref,* Rhode Island Department of State Library Services, Providence RI. 401-277-2726

Iacovantuno, Yolanda, *YA & Acq,* Nutley Public Library, Nutley NJ. 201-667-0405

Iannitto, Deborah, *ILL & Materials Coordr,* County of Henrico Public Library, Richmond VA. 804-222-1643

Iarusso, Marilyn, *Storytelling,* New York Public Library (The Branch Libraries), New York NY. 212-790-6262

Ibach, Doris L, *In Charge,* Spokane Public Library (East Side), Spokane WA. 509-534-3030

Ibach, Robert, *Dir,* Grace College & Grace Theological Seminary, Betty Zimmer Morgan Library, Winona Lake IN. 219-267-8191, Ext 182

Iber, Elizabeth, *Ad & Ref,* Harborfields Public Library, Greenlawn NY. 516-757-4200

Ibey, Maria, *Acq,* Goddard College, William Shipman Library, Plainfield VT. 802-454-8311, Ext 232

Ibrahim, Saad M, *Assoc Prof,* University of Wisconsin-Milwaukee, School of Library Science, WI. 414-963-4707

Ice, Nolamae S, *Libm,* Holly Public Library, Holly CO. 303-537-6520

Ice, Priscilla, *Libm,* Spokane County Library (Valley), Spokane WA. 509-926-6783

Ichl, Ron, *Acq,* California State University, Northridge, Delmar T Oviatt & South Libraries, Northridge CA. 213-885-2271

Ickes, Clark, *Chief Libm,* Baltimore News American Library, Baltimore MD. 301-752-1212

Iddings, Joy, *ILL,* Wright State University Library, Dayton OH. 513-873-2380

Iddins, Mildred, *Dir & Acq,* Carson-Newman College Library, Jefferson City TN. 615-475-9061, Ext 247

Idema, Celene, *Mich & Genealogy,* Grand Rapids Public Library, Grand Rapids MI. 616-456-4400

Ierley, Edna, *Commun Servs,* Madison Public Library, Madison NJ. 201-377-0722

Iffland, Carol, *Interlibr Coop Coordr,* Bur Oak Library System, Shorewood IL. 815-729-3345, 729-3346

Ifshin, Steven, *Pub Servs,* University of Illinois at the Medical Center, Library of the Health Sciences, Chicago IL. 312-996-8974

Iglar, Jon J, *Dir,* Calumet College, Mary Gorman Specker Memorial Library, Hammond IN. 219-473-4373

Ignasiak, Janet, *Tech Serv & Cat,* Downey City Library, Downey CA. 213-923-3256

Ignatius, Doris, *Libm,* College of Saint Scholastica Library (Science), Duluth MN. 218-723-6178

Ignon, Olga S, *Asst Dir Coll Develop,* University of California, Santa Barbara Library, Santa Barbara CA. 805-961-2741

Iheanacho, Morris, *Tech Serv & Cat,* Oakwood College, Eva B Dykes Library, Huntsville AL. 205-837-1630, Ext 275

Ihlenfeldt, Kay, *Head,* Chicago Public Library (Government Publications), Chicago IL. 312-269-3002

Ihrig, Robert, *Cat,* Monroe County Library System, Rochester NY. 716-428-7345

Ike, Alice, *Ref,* Santa Ana College, Nealley Library, Santa Ana CA. 714-835-3000, Ext 357

Ikeda, Susan, *Libm,* Los Angeles Public Library System (Wilshire), Los Angeles CA. 213-467-7343

Ikeda, Virginia, *Cat,* University of Hawaii at Hilo Libraries, Hilo HI. 808-961-9344

Ikehara, Hide, *Cat,* Eastern Michigan University, Center of Educational Resources, Ypsilanti MI. 313-487-0020

Ikemoto, Karen, *Libm,* Hawaii State Library System (Kauai Regional), Lihue HI. 808-245-3617

Ilic, Ursula D, *Western European Lang & Lit,* University of Chicago, Joseph Regenstein Library, Chicago IL. 312-753-2977

Ilisevich, Robert, *Rare Bks,* Meadville Library Art & Historical Association, Meadville PA. 814-336-1773

Ilisevich, Robert D, *Libm,* Crawford County Historical Society Library, Meadville PA. 814-724-6080

Illes, Doris, *MUSAT (AID) Project Libm,* University of California, Riverside (Bioagricultural), Riverside CA. 714-787-3238

Illingworth, Nancie, *Ch,* Rockingham Free Public Library, Bellows Falls VT. 802-463-4270

Illinik, Barbara, *Ad,* Howell Carnegie Library, Howell MI. 517-546-0720

Illsley, Barbara, *Asst Dir,* Westminster Public Library, Westminster CO. 303-429-8311

Imber, Scott, *Libm,* Salt Lake County Library System (Kearns Branch), Kearns UT. 801-298-4441

Imbrie, Agnes, *Libm,* Los Angeles County Preventative & Public Health Service, John L Pomeroy Memorial Library, Los Angeles CA. 213-974-7780

Imhof, Peter H, *Libm,* Naval Research Laboratory, Ruth H Hooker Technical Library, Washington DC. 202-545-6700

Imhoff, Edith, *Libm,* Presbyterian Church of the Covenant, Port Arthur TX. 713-983-1675

Imhoff, Elizabeth, *Libm,* Ashton Public Library, Ashton IA. 712-724-6426

Imhoff, Kathleen, *Dir,* Chattahoochee Valley Regional Library, W C Bradley Memorial Library, Headquarters, Columbus GA. 404-327-0211

Imlay, Terri, *Tech Processing & Extens,* Sandusky Library Association, Sandusky OH. 419-625-3834

Imlay, Wilma, *Actg Libm,* United States Geological Survey Library, Golden CO. 303-234-4133

Immerman, Virginia, *Libm,* Louisville Free Public Library (Iroquois), Louisville KY. 502-367-1236

Impastato, David J, *Libm,* Salmagundi Club Library, New York NY. 212-255-7740

Inabinett, E L, *Libm,* University of South Carolina (South Caroliniana), Columbia SC. 803-777-3131

Ince, David, *Dir,* Valdosta State College Library, Valdosta GA. 912-247-3228

Indig, Shirley, *Acq,* Catonsville Community College, Learning Resources Div, Baltimore MD. 301-455-4586

Infantino, Cynthia, *Ch,* Warren-Newport Public Library District, Gurnee IL. 312-244-5150

Infortuna, Victor C, *In Charge,* Valley Forge Military Junior College Library, Wayne PA. 215-688-1800

Ingalls, Anne C, *Ad,* San Jose Public Library, San Jose CA. 408-277-4822

Ingalls, Flora S, *Dir,* Middlesex Public Library, Middlesex NJ. 201-356-6602

Ingalls, Janice, *Music,* University of Lowell Libraries (O'Leary Library), Lowell MA. 617-452-5000, Ext 480

Ingalls, Joan V, *Libm,* Wine Institute Library, San Francisco CA. 415-986-0878

Ingber, Ellen Oberman, *Libm,* Purdue Frederick Library, Norwalk CT. 203-853-0123, Ext 253, 254

Ingebritsen, Ann S, *Acq & Ref,* Menlo College & School of Business Administration, Bowman Library, Menlo Park CA. 415-323-6141, Ext 323

Ingersoll, Ann, *In Charge,* Eureka-Humboldt County Library (Rio Dell), Rio Dell CA. 707-764-3436

Ingersoll, Diane, *Tech Serv & Acq,* Iowa City Public Library, Iowa City IA. 319-354-1265

Ingersoll, Joan, *Libm,* United States Navy (Naval Ocean Systems Center), San Diego CA. 714-225-6623

Ingersoll, Lyn, *Libm,* Prince William Public Library (Potomac), Woodbridge VA. 703-494-8126

Ingibergsson, Asgeir, *Libm,* Camrose Lutheran College Library, Camrose AB. 403-672-3381, Ext 244

Inglaur, Carol, *On-Line Servs,* University of North Carolina at Charlotte, J Murrey Atkins Library, Charlotte NC. 704-597-2221

Ingle, Irene, *Libm,* Wrangell Public Library, Wrangell AK. 907-874-3535

Ingle, Neelima, *Libm,* Moraine Park Technical Institute Library, Fond du Lac WI. 414-922-8611, Ext 360

Ingle, Roma, *Libm,* Woodruff County Library, Augusta AR. 501-347-5331

Ingles, Anne, *Cat,* University of Calgary Library, Calgary AB. 403-284-5954

Ingles, Vera, *Dir, Acq & Cat,* Creve Coeur Public Library, Creve Coeur IL. 309-699-7921

Ingmire, Mary, *Libm,* Silver Cross Hospital, Medical Library, Joliet IL. 815-729-7811

Ingmire, Wanda, *Chief Libm,* Kaiser Engineers Library, Oakland CA. 415-271-4357

Ingraham, Beverly, *Dir,* Owyhee County Historical Society, Museum & Library Complex, Murphy ID. 208-495-2319

Ingraham, Gerald, *Audio Lab,* Our Lady of the Lake University Libraries, San Antonio TX. 512-434-6711, Ext 272

Ingram, Ada, *Dir,* Central State University Library, Edmond OK. 405-341-2980, Ext 494, 495 & 496

Ingram, Alice L, *Actg Libm,* Wilson College, John Stewart Memorial Library, Chambersburg PA. 717-264-4141, Ext 344

Ingram, Anne, *Adm Asst,* Wake Forest University (Bowman Gray School of Medicine Library), Winston-Salem NC. 919-727-4691

Ingram, Brian, *Co-chairpersons,* Sault Area International Library Association, MI. 906-632-6841, Ext 402

Ingram, Brian R, *Dir,* Sault Sainte Marie Public Library, Sault Sainte Marie ON. 705-949-2152

Ingram, Carolyn, *Ref,* Alexander City State Junior College, Thomas D Russell Library, Alexander City AL. 205-234-6346, Ext 290

Ingram, Charles, *Acq,* Southwestern Oklahoma State University, Al Harris Library, Weatherford OK. 405-772-6611, Ext 5311

Ingram, Frances, *Asst Dir,* Northport Public Library, Northport NY. 516-261-6930

Ingram, John E, *Archivist,* Colonial Williamsburg (Research Archives), Williamsburg VA. 804-229-1000, Ext 2282

Ingram, Lois M, *Libm,* Deep River Public Library, Deep River CT. 203-526-5674

Ingram, LouElla, *Libm,* United States Court of Claims & United States Court of Customs & Patent Appeals Library, Washington DC. 202-633-7291

Ingram, Marie, *Libm,* Manatee County Bar Association Law Library, Bradenton FL. 813-748-5408

Ingram, Saralyn, *In Charge,* Marsteller Inc Library, New York NY. 212-752-6500, Ext 829

Ingrim, Sharon, *Tech Serv,* Manhattan Public Library, Manhattan KS. 913-776-4741

Ingroia, Joanne, *Circ,* Smithtown Library, Smithtown NY. 516-265-2072

Ingrum, Barbara, *Libm,* Sno-Isle Regional Library (North Creek), Bothell WA. 206-481-4501

Ingui, Bette Jean, *Ref,* State University of New York (Health Sciences Center Library), East Setauket NY. 516-246-2512

Iniguez, Eva R, *Spec Projects,* University of Puerto Rico Library, Jose M Lazaro Memorial Library, Rio Piedras PR. 809-764-0000, Ext 3296

Inlow, Ruth, *Libm,* Ohio Valley Local District Free Public Library (Peebles), Manchester OH. 513-587-2085

Inman, Ruth, *Libm,* Warren County Library (Berwick Branch), Berwick IL. 309-462-3187

Inman, Susan A, *Asst Libm,* Park Forest South Public Library District, Park Forest South IL. 312-534-2580

Innella, Louise W, *Tech Serv & Cat,* Ocean County Library, Toms River NJ. 201-349-6200

Innes, Lila K, *Libm,* Frederick H Cossitt Library, North Granby CT. 203-653-3689

Innes, Shirley, *Acq,* Reginald J P Dawson Library, Bibliotheque de Ville Mont Royal, Mount Royal PQ. 514-342-1892

Innes, Wanda, *Librn,* Elyria Memorial Hospital, M B Johnson School of Nursing Library, Elyria OH. 216-323-3221, Ext 387

Innes-Taylor, Catherine, *Acq,* University of Alaska, Anchorage Library, Anchorage AK. 907-263-1825

Innis, Helen, *Librn,* Litchfield District Library, Litchfield MI. 517-542-3887

Innis, Wendy, *Libr Tech,* Queen's University at Kingston (Chemistry), Kingston ON. 613-547-2636

Inouye, Judy, *Tech Serv,* Fraser Valley College, Learning Resource Centres, Abbotsford BC. 604-853-7441

Inrig, Mrs S, *Librn,* Vaughan Public Libraries (Woodbridge Public), Woodbridge ON. 416-851-1296

Insabella, Peter, *Asst Librn,* Mercy College, Yorktown Heights Branch Campus, Yorktown Heights NY. 914-962-9486

Insero, Donna, *AV,* University of Tulsa, McFarlin Library, Tulsa OK. 918-592-6000, Ext 351

Inskeep, Lois J, *Chief Librn,* Veterans Administration, Medical Library, Omaha NE. 402-346-8800, Ext 359, 372

Intner, Sheila, *On-Line Servs,* Great Neck Library, Great Neck NY. 516-466-8055

Inwood, Jeanne, *Dir,* Monterey Peninsula College Library, Monterey CA. 408-649-1150, Ext 278

Ioanes, Shirley, *Librn,* Franklin Sylvester Library (Hinckley Branch), Hinckley OH. 216-278-4271

Iobst, Barbara J, *Librn & On-Line Servs,* Allentown Hospital Association, Health Sciences Library, Allentown PA. 215-821-2263

Iodice, Marcell, *Ad & Ref,* Brockway Memorial Library, Miami Shores FL. 305-758-8000

Iorio, Dorothy, *ILL, Per & Bibliog Instr,* University of Tampa, Merl Kelce Library, Tampa FL. 813-253-8861, Ext 385

Iorio, Edward J, *Dir,* Marine Products Library, Boston MA. 617-268-0758

Ip, Susan, *Head, Billings Libr & MEDLINE Analyst,* University of Chicago (Billings Library), Chicago IL. 312-947-5442

Ip, Susan, *On-Line Servs,* University of Chicago, Joseph Regenstein Library, Chicago IL. 312-753-2977

Ipock, Mary, *Librn,* Pollosksville Public Library, Pollosksville NC. 919-224-5011

Ippolito, Andrew, *Dir Libr & Res,* Newsday Library, Garden City NY. 516-222-5090

Irby, Martha, *ILL,* Mississippi State University, Mitchell Memorial Library, Mississippi State MS. 601-325-4225

Irby, Jr, Charles, *Asst Librn & Media,* Corpus Christi State University Library, Corpus Christi TX. 512-991-6810, Ext 242

Iredell, Patricia, *Asst Dir,* Tarrant County Junior College System (South Campus Learning Resource Center), Fort Worth TX. 817-534-4861, Ext 223

Ireland, J, *Librn,* Prudential Insurance Co of America, Business Library, Toronto ON. 416-366-6971

Ireland, Joe, *Librn,* New Orleans Public Library (Algiers Regional), New Orleans LA. 504-393-6565

Ireland, Lee, *Dir,* Holdrege Public Library System, South Central Regional Library, Holdrege NE. 308-995-6556

Ireland, Martha, *Curator,* Princeton Antiques Bookservice, Art Marketing Reference Library, Atlantic City NJ. 609-344-1943

Ireland, Melody, *Circ,* Millinocket Memorial Library, Millinocket ME. 207-723-9610

Ireland, Pamela, *Asst Librn,* Brookline Public Library, Brookline NH. 603-673-3330

Ireland, T, *In Charge,* University of Toronto Libraries (Dept of Anthropology), Toronto ON. 416-978-3296

Irish, Kathleen A, *Ad & Ref,* Center Moriches Free Public Library, Center Moriches NY. 516-878-0940

Irizarry, Franklin, *Dir,* Universidad Central De Bayamon Library, Bayamon PR. 809-786-3030

Irizarry, Jose G, *Librn,* Memorial Hospital, Medical Library, Hollywood FL. 305-987-2000, Ext 5340

Irlan, Ciara, *Librn,* Moravia Public Library, Moravia IA. 515-724-3458

Irshay, Phyllis, *Dir,* A K Smiley Public Library, Redlands CA. 714-793-2201

Irvin, Alise R, *Asst Dir,* East Albemarle Regional Library, Elizabeth City NC. 919-335-2511

Irvin, Alise R, *Dir,* Pasquotank-Camden Library, Elizabeth City NC. 919-335-2473

Irvin, Betty W, *ILL & Spec Coll,* Laurens County Library, Laurens SC. 803-984-0596

Irvin, Charles, *Asst Dir,* Bartram Trail Regional Library, Mary Willis Library Headquarters, Washington GA. 404-678-7736

Irvin, Kenneth, *Coordr of Ctr for Individualized Instruction,* Middlesex Community College, Learning Resources Center, Bedford MA. 617-275-8910

Irvine, Anne, *Ch,* Pembroke Public Library, Pembroke ON. 613-732-8844

Irvine, Betty Jo, *Librn,* Indiana University at Bloomington (Fine Arts), Bloomington IN. 812-337-3314

Irvine, Terry, *Acq,* Wascana Institute of Applied Arts & Sciences, Resource & Information Center, Regina SK. 306-565-4321

Irvine, W, *Libr Tech,* Ontario Ministry of Correctional Services, Guelph Correctional Center Library, Guelph ON. 519-822-0020, Ext 313

Irving, Elizabeth, *Librn,* Buffalo & Erie County Public Library System (Northwest), Buffalo NY. 716-885-8345

Irving, Jon, *Ch,* Stewart Library, Grinnell IA. 515-236-5717

Irving, Madeline R, *Dir Admin,* New Hampshire State Library, Concord NH. 603-271-2392

Irwin, Barbara S, *Librn,* New Jersey Historical Society Library, Newark NJ. 201-483-3939

Irwin, Gail J, *Librn,* Alder Public Library, Ainsworth Public Library, Ainsworth NE. 402-387-2032

Irwin, John, *Rare Bks & Spec Coll,* Northern Arizona University Libraries, Flagstaff AZ. 602-523-9011

Irwin, Lorna, *Ref,* Orillia Public Library, Orillia ON. 705-325-2338

Irwin, Phyllis, *Librn,* Ramsey County Public Library (Arden Hills), Roseville MN. 612-636-1790

Irwin, Ruth Ann, *Librn,* Delaware State Hospital, Medical Library, New Castle DE. 302-421-6368

Irzebiatowski, Elaine, *Ref,* Staley Library, Millikin University, Decatur IL. 217-424-6214

Isa, Jacqueline, *Acq,* Central Connecticut State College, Elihu Burritt Library, New Britain CT. 203-827-7531

Isaac, Frederick, *Acq,* Loyola-Notre Dame Library, Inc, Baltimore MD. 301-532-8787

Isaac, James, *Librn,* Denver Public Library (County Jail), Denver CO. 303-573-5152, Ext 271

Isaac, Karen, *Br Coordr,* Torrance Public Library, Torrance CA. 213-328-2251

Isaac, Torrey, *Dir,* Smith Memorial Library, Chautauqua Institution, Chautauqua NY. 716-357-5844

Isaac, Vicki, *Librn,* Lambton County Library (Walpole Island), Wallaceburg ON. 519-627-3442

Isaacs, B D, *Dir,* News-Record Library, Greensboro NC. 919-373-1000

Isaacs, Heide, *Librn,* Hamilton Public Library (Concession), Hamilton ON. 416-383-2322

Isaacs, Jacquelyn, *Acq,* Salem College, Benedum Learning Resources Center, Salem WV. 304-782-5238

Isaacs, Nancy B, *Dir,* Lasell Junior College, Jessie Shepherd Brennan Library, Auburndale MA. 617-243-2242

Isaacson, Ann C, *Dir,* Chamberlayne Junior College Library, Boston MA. 617-536-4500, Ext 47

Isaacson, Katherine Jones, *Librn,* Robert Gore Rifkind Foundation, Art Library & Graphics Collection, Beverly Hills CA. 213-278-0970, Ext 323

Isaacson, Kathy, *Ref,* Lawrence University, Seeley G Mudd Library, Appleton WI. 414-739-3681, Ext 264

Isaacson, Marion, *Librn,* Mercy School of Nursing of Detroit, Pontiac Unit Library, Pontiac MI. 313-858-6040

Isaacson, Richard T, *Librn,* Garden Center of Greater Cleveland, Eleanor Squire Library, Cleveland OH. 216-721-1600

Isabelle, Lucille, *Ch,* Saint-Laurent Municipal Library, Saint Laurent PQ. 514-744-6411, Ext 220

Isabelle, Margot, *Ref,* Hingham Public Library, Hingham MA. 617-749-0907

Isacco, Julia, *Asst Dir,* Pontiac Free Library Association, Warwick RI. 401-737-3292

Isadore, Harold, *Ref,* Southern University Library (Law Library), Baton Rouge LA. 504-771-3776

Isaksen, Bonnie, *Cat,* Central Rappahannock Regional Library, Wallace Memorial Library, Fredericksburg VA. 703-371-3311

Isbell, Frances, *Dir,* Weslaco Public Library, Porter Doss Memorial Library, Weslaco TX. 512-968-4533

Ische, John P, *Dir,* Louisiana State University Medical Center Library, New Orleans LA. 504-568-6100

Iseman, Patricia C, *Dir & Ad,* Millis Public Library, Millis MA. 617-376-8282

Isensee, Karen, *Librn,* Rush City Public Library, Rush City MN. 612-358-3948

Isensee, Mrs George W, *Librn,* Schulenburg Public Library, Schulenburg TX. 713-743-3345

Isern, Tom, *Archivist,* Adams County Historical Society Archives, Hastings NE. 402-463-5838

Isetts, Charles, *Head,* University of Cincinnati Medical Center Libraries (History of Health Sciences Library & Museum), Cincinnati OH. 513-872-5120

Isherwood, Helen C, *Dir,* New York Institute for the Education of the Blind, Walter Brooks Library, Bronx NY. 212-547-1234, Ext 236

Isherwood-Lemos, Jane, *Asst Dir,* Tiverton Library Services, Tiverton RI. 401-624-8079

Ishii, Frances, *Dir,* Memorial Hospital Medical Center, Medical Library, Long Beach CA. 213-595-3841

Ishimoto, Carol F, *Cat & Proc Dept: Head,* Harvard University Library (Harvard College Library (Headquarters in Harry Elkins Widener Memorial Library)), Cambridge MA. 617-495-2401

Isler, Sharon Louise, *Librn & On-Line Servs,* Richland Hills Public Library, Fort Worth TX. 817-284-4991

Isler, Sharon Louise, *Librn,* John Peter Smith Hospital, Medical Library, Fort Worth TX. 817-921-3431

Isler, Sharon Louise, *On-Line Servs & Bibliog Instr,* John Peter Smith Hospital, Medical Library, Fort Worth TX. 817-921-3431

Isley, Natelle, *In Charge,* Mississippi Research & Development Center, Information Services Divison, Jackson MS. 601-982-6324

Isley, Virginia, *Commun Servs,* Crown Point-Center Public Library, Crown Point IN. 219-663-0270

Ismail, F, *Librn,* International Civil Aviation Organization Library, Montreal PQ. 514-285-8207, 285-8208

Ismarin, Corazon O'S, *Librn,* Saint Luke's Hospital, Medical-Nursing Library, San Francisco CA. 415-647-8600, Ext 6949

Isnardi, Patti, *Librn,* Waldoboro Public Library, Waldoboro ME. 207-832-4484

Isom, Bill, *Circ,* Eastern Illinois University, Booth Library, Charleston IL. 217-581-2210

Isom, Dorothy, *Librn,* Carroll Public Library, Carroll NE. 402-585-4841

Isom, Gayle, *Ch,* Bradford Memorial Library, El Dorado KS. 316-321-3363

Ison, Donna, *Ad,* Madison-Jefferson County Public Library, Madison IN. 812-265-2744

Ison, Ferceyna, *Cat,* Kent County Library System, Grand Rapids MI. 616-774-3250

Ison, John E, *Dir,* Durango Public Library, Durango CO. 303-247-2492

Ison, Shirley, *Ch,* Scott County Public Library, Georgetown KY. 502-863-3566

Isphording, Betsy, *Processing,* Toledo-Lucas County Public Library, Toledo OH. 419-255-7055

Israel, Dorothy, *Tech Serv,* Hinds Junior College, George M McLendon Library, Raymond MS. 601-857-5261, Ext 253

Israel, Fred C, *Dir,* Windsor Public Library, Windsor ON. 519-258-8111

Israel, Judith, *Dir,* Dare County Library, Manteo NC. 919-473-2372

Israel, Judith, *Ad,* East Albemarle Regional Library, Elizabeth City NC. 919-335-2511

Israel, Kenneth E, *Dir,* Marion Public Library, Marion IN. 317-664-7363
Israel, Marie, *Bkmobile Coordr,* Kinchafoonee Regional Library, Dawson GA. 912-995-2902
Israel, Richard, *Librn,* Chicago Public Library (Near North), Chicago IL. 312-664-6575
Issette, S, *Ref,* Atlantic Christian College, Hackney Library, Wilson NC. 919-237-3161, Ext 330
Istre, Rebecca E, *Librn,* Vermilion Parish Library (Gueydan Branch), Gueydan LA. 318-536-6781
Italia, Patrick, *Librn,* Melrose Park Public Library, Melrose Park IL. 312-343-3391
Itamura, Ruth S, *Asst Supvr & State Librn,* Hawaii State Library System, Honolulu HI. 808-548-2430
Itesco, Victor, *Chief Librn,* Montreal Urban Community Transit Commission Library, Montreal PQ. 514-877-6046
Ithen, Thelma, *Librn,* Grove City Community Library, Grove City PA. 412-458-7320
Itkin, Stanley L, *Dir,* Hillside Public Library, New Hyde Park NY. 516-488-3316, 488-3317
Ittner, Dwight, *Librn,* University of Alaska, Fairbanks (Biomedical Library), Fairbanks AK. 907-479-7442
Ivanisevic, Vlatka, *Librn,* Case Western Reserve University Libraries (School of Applied Social Science), Cleveland OH. 216-368-3506
Ivanoff, Evelyn I, *Assoc Prof,* New Mexico Highlands University, Library Science Program, NM. 505-425-7511, Ext 517
Ivers, Linda M, *Librn,* Boston Public Library (Codman Square), Dorchester MA. 617-436-8214
Ivers, Linda M, *Asst Supvr of Br,* Boston Public Library, Eastern Massachusetts Library System, Boston MA. 617-536-5400
Ivers, Virginia M, *Librn,* Columbus Hospital Medical Library, Chicago IL. 312-883-7341
Iverson, Deborah, *Librn,* Sheridan College, Kooi Library, Instructional Resource Center, Sheridan WY. 307-674-6446, Ext 170
Iverson, DiAnn, *Tech Serv, On-Line Servs & Bibliog Instr,* Starved Rock Library System, Ottawa IL. 815-434-7537
Iverson, Gladys, *Librn,* Rushford Public Library, Rushford MN. 507-864-7600
Iverson, Herman A, *Dir,* Saint Joseph's Hospital, Medical Library, Eureka CA. 707-443-8051
Iverson, June, *Librn,* Manistee County Library (Bear Lake-Pleasanton Branch), Bear Lake MI. 616-723-2519
Ives, Carol, *Br Supvr,* Scarborough Public Library (Bendale), Scarborough ON. 416-431-9141
Ives, Eleanor, *ILL,* Cerro Coso Community College, Learning Resources Center, Ridgecrest CA. 714-375-5001, Ext 47
Ives, Harriet G, *Dir,* Elsie Quirk Public Library, Englewood FL. 813-474-3515
Ives, Sidney, *Rare Bks,* University of Florida Libraries, Gainesville FL. 904-392-0341
Ivey, Barbara M, *Acq,* United States Air Force Academy Library, United States Air Force Academy CO. 303-472-2590
Ivey, Donna M, *Librn,* Consumers' Gas Co Library, Willowdale ON. 416-492-5490
Ivey, Janet, *Tech Serv,* Selby Public Library, Sarasota County Federated Library System, Sarasota FL. 814-366-7303
Ivey, Juanita, *Tech Serv,* Montreat-Anderson College, L Nelson Bell Library, Montreat NC. 704-669-2382
Ivey, Marva, *Librn,* Atlanta Public Library (West Hunter), Atlanta GA. 404-758-0811
Ivey, Peggy, *Librn,* Saint Pauls Public Library, Saint Pauls NC. 919-865-4002
Ivey, Robert, *Tech Serv,* Richard H Thornton Library, Oxford NC. 919-693-1121
Ivey, Robert G, *Librn,* Louisiana Training Institute Library, De Quincy LA. 318-789-1563
Ivey, Roma, *Circ,* Gary Public Library, Gary IN. 219-886-2484
Ivey, Jr, G Frank, *President,* Arkansas Foundation of Associated Colleges, AR. 501-378-0843
Ivin, Kathryn E, *Librn,* Sherwood Music School Library, Chicago IL. 312-427-6267
Ivy, Barbara, *Instr,* Alderson-Broaddus College, Media Education Program, WV. 304-457-1700, Ext 258
Ivy, Barbara Anne, *Dir & Acq,* Alderson-Broaddus College, Pickett Library Media Center, Philippi WV. 304-457-1700, Ext 229, 258

Ivy, Karen E, *Librn,* Coopers & Lybrand Library, San Francisco CA. 415-445-1342
Iyer, Gargi, *Tech Serv & Cat,* Mishawaka-Penn Public Library, Mishawaka IN. 219-259-5277
Izbicki, Walter J, *Librn,* Howard Bracken Memorial Library, Woodstock CT. 203-928-0046

J

Jaap, Karilyn B, *Dir,* Gulf Beaches Public Library, Madeira Beach FL. 813-391-2828
Jabbour, Alan, *Dir, Am Folklife Ctr,* Library of Congress, Washington DC. 202-287-5000
Jablanofsky, Cornelia A, *Tech Serv,* West Deptford Public Library, Thorofare NJ. 609-845-5593
Jablonowski, Christina, *Librn,* Chandler-Evans Inc Co Library, West Hartford CT. 203-236-0651
Jacinto, Julia, *Govt Publns,* Claremont Colleges Libraries, Claremont CA. 714-621-8000, Ext 3721
Jacka, David, *Ref,* Columbus Public Library, Pawnee Regional Library, Columbus NE. 402-564-7116
Jackimcyzk, Elaine, *Librn,* Camden County Free Library (Gloucester Township), Blackwood NJ. 609-228-0022
Jackimczyk, Elaine, *Librn,* Gloucester Township Library, Blackwood NJ. 609-228-0022
Jacklyn, Connie, *Libr Asst,* Western Counties Regional Library (Clark's Harbour Branch), Clark's Harbour NS. 902-745-2885
Jackman, Caroline, *Dir,* Monon Town & Township Library, Monon Public Library, Monon IN. 219-253-6517
Jackman, Flora M, *Asst Librn,* Huachuca City Public Library, Huachuca City AZ. 602-456-1553
Jackman, Harvey, *AV,* Ricks College, David O McKay Learning Resources Center, Rexburg ID. 208-356-2351
Jacknowitz, Linda, *Media,* West Virginia University (Medical Center Library), Morgantown WV. 304-293-2113
Jacks, Gerald, *Dir,* Mercy College of Detroit Library, Detroit MI. 313-592-6000
Jackson, Ada E, *Librn,* New York Public Library (Bloomingdale), New York NY. 212-222-8030
Jackson, Adele M, *Assoc Dir,* Southern University Library, Baton Rouge LA. 504-771-4990, 771-4991, 771-4992
Jackson, Agnes M, *Librn,* V B Cook Co Ltd Library, Thunder Bay ON. 807-623-0461, Ext 34
Jackson, Allene, *ILL,* Spring Arbor College, Hugh A White Library, Spring Arbor MI. 517-750-1200, Ext 234
Jackson, Alonzo, *Chief Southeast District Br,* Chicago Public Library, Chicago IL. 312-269-2900
Jackson, Aurelia, *Consult,* Northwest Kansas Library System (Western Kansas Sub-Regional Library for the Blind & Physically Handicapped), Norton KS. 913-877-5148
Jackson, Barbara B, *Librn,* Chesterfield County Central Library (Chester Branch), Chester VA. 804-748-6314
Jackson, Bernice, *Dir,* Lawton Public Library, Lawton OK. 405-248-6287
Jackson, Bernice, *Spec Coll,* University of Kansas Medical Center, College of Health Sciences & Hospital, Clendening Library, Kansas City KS. 913-588-7166
Jackson, Betty B, *Dir,* Caldwell Parish Library, Columbia LA. 318-649-2259
Jackson, Betty B, *Librn,* Franklin Parish Library, Winnsboro LA. 318-724-7399
Jackson, Betty Jean, *Cat,* Mount Holyoke College, Williston Memorial Library, South Hadley MA. 413-538-2226
Jackson, Beverly Jo, *Librn,* San Antonio Public Library (McCreless), San Antonio TX. 512-532-4254
Jackson, Bobbie, *Asst Librn,* Neshoba County Public Library, Philadelphia MS. 601-656-4911
Jackson, Brenda, *ILL,* Shreve Memorial Library, Shreveport LA. 318-221-2614
Jackson, Brenda J, *Librn,* State Street Bank & Trust Co Library, Boston MA. 617-786-3572
Jackson, Brinton, *Drama,* Juilliard School, Lila Acheson Wallace Library, New York NY. 212-799-5000, Ext 265

Jackson, Bryant H, *Assoc Dir,* Illinois State University, Milner Library, Normal IL. 309-438-3675
Jackson, Carolyn, *Librn,* Blackwater Community Library, Coolidge AZ. 602-723-4471
Jackson, Carolyn, *Asst Librn, Tech Servs,* East Texas Baptist College Library, Marshall TX. 214-938-0377
Jackson, Claire, *Librn,* Acme Community Library, Acme AB. 403-546-3845
Jackson, Clara, *Assoc Prof,* Kent State University, School of Library Science, OH. 216-672-2782, 672-7988
Jackson, Claudine, *YA,* Kansas City Public Library, Kansas City MO. 816-221-2685
Jackson, Claudine, *Librn,* Kansas City Public Library (East), Kansas City MO. 816-231-5481
Jackson, Donna, *Librn,* Frito-Lay Inc Library, Dallas TX. 214-351-7298
Jackson, Dorothy, *Asst Dir,* Media-Upper Providence Free Library, Media PA. 215-566-1918
Jackson, Edward S, *Librn,* Central Oregon Community College Learning Resources Center, Bend OR. 503-382-6112, Ext 240, 241
Jackson, Elisabeth, *Assoc Librn,* Georgetown University (Fred O Dennis Law Library), Washington DC. 202-624-8260
Jackson, Elisabeth, *Librn,* Westinghouse Canada Ltd, Electronics Systems Div Library, Burlington ON. 416-528-8811, Ext 4226
Jackson, Elizabeth Christian, *Dir,* Mercer University Southern School of Pharmacy, H Custer Naylor Library, Atlanta GA. 404-688-6291, Exts 62, 73
Jackson, Elnora, *Librn,* New York Public Library (Soundview), New York NY. 212-589-0880
Jackson, Ervin, *Ch,* Wakulla County Public Library, Crawfordville FL. 904-926-7415
Jackson, Evangeline N, *Admin Librn, On-line Search Coord & Biblio Instr,* Commodity Futures Trading Commission Library, Washington DC. 202-254-5901
Jackson, Florrie, *Educ,* University of Georgia Libraries, Athens GA. 404-542-2716
Jackson, Frances, *Bkmobile Coordr,* Cumberland County Public Library, Anderson Street Library, Frances Brooks Stein Memorial Library, Fayetteville NC. 919-483-1580
Jackson, G Diane, *On-Line Servs & Bibliog Instr,* University of Akron (McDowell Library), Akron OH. 216-375-7330
Jackson, Gene, *AV,* Wayne County Public Library, Inc, Goldsboro NC. 919-735-1824
Jackson, Gloria, *Asst Librn,* Museum of Our National Heritage, Scottish Rite Masonic Museum & Library, Lexington MA. 617-861-6559
Jackson, Hannah, *Dir,* Kingsdown Library, Kingsdown KS. 316-369-2370
Jackson, Harriet, *Librn,* Memphis-Shelby County Public Library & Information Center (Parkway Village), Memphis TN. 901-363-8923
Jackson, Harvey G, *Dir,* Brevard Community College, Learning Resources Center, Cocoa FL. 305-632-1111, Ext 295, 298
Jackson, J M, *Librn,* British Columbia Teachers' Federation Resources Center, Vancouver BC. 604-731-8121, Ext 260
Jackson, Jacqueline A, *Sci & Tech Coordr,* San Antonio College Library, San Antonio TX. 512-734-7311, Ext 2480
Jackson, James, *Sci,* Long Beach Public Library System, Long Beach CA. 213-436-9225
Jackson, James, *On-Line Servs,* Long Beach Public Library System, Long Beach CA. 213-436-9225
Jackson, James, *Soc Sci,* University of Richmond, Boatwright Memorial Library, Richmond VA. 804-285-6452
Jackson, James H, *Librn,* American Medical Association Library, Washington DC. 202-857-1336
Jackson, James J, *Librn,* Central Courts' Library, Brooklyn NY. 212-643-2843
Jackson, James W, *Media,* Lincoln Land Community College, Learning Resources Center, Springfield IL. 217-786-2354
Jackson, Jane, *Librn,* Dorr Township Library (Moline Public Library), Moline MI. 616-877-4143
Jackson, Jean R, *Librn,* GAI Consultants, Inc Library, Monroeville PA. 412-242-6530

Jackson, Jeanne, *Librn,* Flint River Regional Library (Monroe County), Forsyth GA. 404-994-6444

Jackson, Jeffrey, *Librn,* University of Pittsburgh (Afro-American Collection), Pittsburgh PA. 412-624-4447

Jackson, Joan, *Bibliog Searching,* Columbia University (University Libraries), New York NY. 212-280-2241

Jackson, Joan, *Librn,* Gilbert Hart Library, Wallingford VT. 802-446-2685

Jackson, Joel, *Media,* Wake County Department of the Public Library, Raleigh NC. 919-755-6077

Jackson, John, *Librn,* Washington Veterans Home Staff Library, Retsil WA. 206-876-7605

Jackson, John F, *Dir,* Manchester Public Library, Mary Cheney Library, Manchester CT. 203-643-2471

Jackson, John W, *Chief Librn,* Solano College Library, Vallejo CA. 707-864-7000

Jackson, Johnny W, *Asst Librn & Tech Serv,* Central State University, Hallie Q Brown Memorial Library, Wilberforce OH. 513-376-7212

Jackson, Johnny W, *Dir,* Rust College, Leontyne Price Library, Holly Springs MS. 601-252-4661, Ext 250

Jackson, Joseph Abram, *Dir,* University of Tennessee at Chattanooga Library, Chattanooga TN. 615-755-4701

Jackson, Joseph B, *Dir,* Oklahoma School of Business, Accountancy, Law & Finance Library, Tulsa OK. 918-582-9111

Jackson, Joyce, *Librn,* Brooklyn Public Library (Red Hook), Brooklyn NY. 212-875-4412

Jackson, Kathryn E, *Librn,* New York State Department of State, Community Affairs Library, Albany NY. 518-474-7144

Jackson, Kathy, *Ref,* Texas A&m University Libraries, College Station TX. 713-845-6111

Jackson, Kim, *AV & Circ,* Rutgers University (Kilmer Area Library), New Brunswick NJ. 201-932-3610

Jackson, Lauren, *Cat,* Pace University, Pleasantville-Briarcliff Library, Pleasantville NY. 914-769-3200, Ext 382

Jackson, Leila, *Instr,* United States Department of Agriculture Graduate School, Certificate Program for Library Technicians, DC. 202-447-5885

Jackson, Lila E, *Librn,* Chicago Public Library (Brighton Park), Chicago IL. 312-523-0666

Jackson, Lois, *ILL, Tech Serv & Acq,* Kellogg Community College, Emory W Morris Learning Resource Center, Battle Creek MI. 616-965-3931, Ext 333

Jackson, Lois B, *Librn,* Pleasant Hills Public Library, Pleasant Hills PA. 412-655-2424

Jackson, Lorraine, *Dir,* South Brunswick Public Library, Monmouth Junction NJ. 201-821-8224, 821-8225

Jackson, Lorraine E, *Ch,* Salem Public Library, Salem MA. 617-744-0860

Jackson, Lorraine M, *Librn,* R P Scherer Corp Library, Detroit MI. 313-571-6100

Jackson, Louise, *Doc,* University of North Carolina at Wilmington, William Madison Randall Library, Wilmington NC. 919-791-4330, Ext 2270

Jackson, M Virginia, *Sci & Eng,* University of Alabama in Birmingham, Mervyn H Sterne Library, Birmingham AL. 205-934-6360

Jackson, Marceil, *Librn,* New York Public Library (Harlem), New York NY. 212-348-5620

Jackson, Margaret, *Tech Serv,* University of Missouri-Columbia, Elmer Ellis Library, Columbia MO. 314-882-4701

Jackson, Marianne, *Librn,* Corpus Christi Caller-Times Library, Corpus Christi TX. 512-884-2011, Ext 242

Jackson, Marie, *Asst Librn,* Kershaw County Library, Camden SC. 803-432-5183

Jackson, Marie, *AV & Ch,* North Kansas City Public Library, North Kansas City MO. 816-221-3360

Jackson, Martha, *Librn,* Caswell Public Library, Harrison ME. 207-583-2970

Jackson, Mary, *ILL,* University of Pennsylvania Libraries, Van Pelt Library, Philadelphia PA. 215-243-7091

Jackson, Mary C, *Librn,* Lane Public Library (Fairfield Branch), Fairfield OH. 513-895-7148

Jackson, Mattye, *Dir,* Forked Deer Regional Library Center, Trimble TN. 901-297-5810

Jackson, Melinda I, *Dir,* Jackson County Public Library, Marianna FL. 904-482-2415

Jackson, Michael, *ILL,* University of California, Riverside, University Library, Riverside CA. 714-787-3221

Jackson, Mildred R, *Librn,* United States Army (Galveston District Corps of Engineers Technical Library), Galveston TX. 713-763-1211, Ext 414

Jackson, Miles, *Prof,* University of Hawaii, Graduate School of Library Studies, HI. 808-948-7321

Jackson, Mrs Alvin, *Asst Librn,* Ruby Pickens Tartt Public Library, Livingston Public Library, Livingston AL. 205-652-2349

Jackson, Mrs M, *Supvr,* Edmonton Public Library (Sprucewood), Edmonton AB. 403-477-6752

Jackson, Nancy, *Media,* Olean Public Library, Olean NY. 716-372-0200

Jackson, Nancy, *Dir,* South Salem Library, South Salem NY. 914-763-3857

Jackson, Patience K, *Dir,* Daniel Webster College Library, Nashua NH. 603-883-3556

Jackson, Patricia A, *Librn,* East Texas State University, Metroplex Center Library, Dallas TX. 214-341-8575

Jackson, Patricia M, *Dir,* Berkeley County Library, Moncks Corner SC. 803-899-2218

Jackson, Paulette, *Acq,* Saint Edward's University Library, Austin TX. 512-444-2621

Jackson, Phyllis, *Librn,* Pocahontas County Free Library (Marlinton Branch), Marlinton WV. 304-799-4165

Jackson, R, *Secy,* Rossland Public Library Association, Rossland BC. 604-362-7611

Jackson, Randall E, *Media,* Roosevelt University, Murray-Green Library, Chicago IL. 312-341-3639

Jackson, Robert D, *Librn,* Mount Carmel Public Library, Mount Carmel IL. 618-262-4639

Jackson, Ruth, *Ref,* Plumas County Library, Quincy CA. 916-283-0780

Jackson, S, *Doc,* Carleton University, Murdoch Maxwell MacOdrum Library, Ottawa ON. 613-231-4357

Jackson, Sandra, *Ch,* Greeley Public Library, Greeley Municipal Library, Greeley CO. 303-353-6123, Ext 392

Jackson, Sara Jean, *Pub Servs,* Houston Academy of Medicine, Texas Medical Center Library, Houston TX. 713-797-1230

Jackson, Sheila, *Librn,* Martins Ferry Public Library (Neffs Public), Neffs OH. 614-633-0314

Jackson, Sister Mary Mercita, *Asst Dir, Tech Serv & Cat,* Saint Mary College Library, Leavenworth KS. 913-682-5151, Ext 202

Jackson, Stewart P, *Librn,* Garrett Community College, Learning Resource Center, McHenry MD. 301-387-6666, Ext 36

Jackson, Susan K, *Librn,* American Can Co, Princeton Research Center, Princeton NJ. 609-921-2510, Ext 245

Jackson, Susan M, *Dir,* Alpha Park Public Library District, Bartonville IL. 309-697-3822

Jackson, Therese A, *YA & Tech Serv,* San Bruno Public Library, San Bruno CA. 415-877-8878

Jackson, Victor L, *Chief Park Naturalist,* National Park Service, Zion National Park Library, Springdale UT. 801-772-3256, Ext 46

Jackson, Virginia, *Librn,* Frederick Eugene Lykes Jr Memorial County Library (Rock Cannery), Brooksville FL. 904-796-9244

Jackson, Virginia, *Extension Serv,* San Diego Public Library, San Diego CA. 714-236-5800

Jackson, Virginia, *Cat,* Upsala College Library, East Orange NJ. 201-266-7295

Jackson, W Carl, *Dean,* Indiana University at Bloomington, University Libraries, Bloomington IN. 812-337-3403

Jackson, William, *Media,* Hardin-Simmons University, Richardson Library, Abilene TX. 915-677-7281, Ext 236

Jackson, Jr, James E, *Asst Librn,* California Academy of Sciences, J W Mailliard, Jr Library, San Francisco CA. 415-221-4214, 221-5100, Ext 275

Jackson, Jr, William, *Ser,* Clearwater Public Library, Clearwater FL. 813-462-6800

Jacob, Diane, *Rare Bks & Spec Coll,* Virginia Military Institute, J T L Preston Library, Lexington VA. 703-463-6228

Jacob, Dorothy, *Ref & Bibliog Instr,* Idaho State University Library, Pocatello ID. 208-236-3202

Jacob, Helen, *Ch,* Glencoe Public Library, Glencoe IL. 312-835-5056

Jacob, Jean, *Librn,* United States Air Force (MacDill Air Force Base Library), MacDill AFB FL. 813-830-3607

Jacob, Jean L, *Librn,* United States Air Force (Wright Patterson Air Force Base General Library), Wright-Patterson AFB OH. 513-257-4815

Jacob, Lila, *Dean,* Children's Theatre Company Library, Minneapolis MN. 612-874-0500, Ext 43

Jacob, Merle, *Reader Serv & YA,* Skokie Public Library, Skokie IL. 312-673-7774

Jacob, Norman, *Librn,* Prince George's County Memorial Library System (Hyattsville), Hyattsville MD. 301-779-9330

Jacob, Roz, *Govt Publications,* Saint Paul Public Library, Saint Paul MN. 612-292-6311

Jacober, Sheryl, *Librn,* Shaker-Heights Public Library, Shaker Heights OH. 216-991-2030

Jacobs, Alma S, *State Librn,* Montana Information Network & Exchange, (MINE), MT. 406-449-3004

Jacobs, Alma S, *State Librn,* Montana State Library, Helena MT. 406-449-3004

Jacobs, Anita M, *Patient Servs Technician,* Veterans Administration, Hospital Library, Cincinnati OH. 513-861-3100

Jacobs, Arlene M, *Librn,* Public Library of Brookline (Coolidge Corner), Brookline MA. 617-277-0579

Jacobs, Barbara, *Acq,* Los Angeles Public Library System, Los Angeles CA. 213-626-7555

Jacobs, Deborah, *Br Coordr & Bkmobile Coordr,* Corvallis Public Library, Corvallis-Benton County Library, Corvallis OR. 503-757-6928

Jacobs, Eugene, *Dir,* C G Jung Institute of Los Angeles, Library & Information Center, Los Angeles CA. 213-556-1193

Jacobs, Geraldine M, *Dir,* Madison County Library District, Rexburg ID. 208-356-3461

Jacobs, James, *Micro,* University of San Diego (Marvin Kratter Law Library), San Diego CA. 714-293-4541

Jacobs, Jane, *Bkmobile Coordr,* Pickaway County District Public Library, Circleville OH. 614-477-1644

Jacobs, Margaret I, *Bus Sci & Tech,* Enoch Pratt Free Library, Baltimore MD. 301-396-5430, 396-5395

Jacobs, Margaret M, *Librn,* Akwesasne Library & Culture Center, Hogansburg NY. 518-358-2240

Jacobs, Mary S, *Dir,* David A Howe Public Library, Wellsville NY. 716-593-3410

Jacobs, Mina, *Spec Coll,* University of Alaska, Anchorage Library, Anchorage AK. 907-263-1825

Jacobs, Nina, *Librn,* United States Air Force (Mitchell Memorial Library), Travis AFB CA. 707-438-5254

Jacobs, Roger E, *Librn,* Supreme Court of the United States Library, Washington DC. 202-252-3177

Jacobs, Rosamond, *Ad,* Ashtabula County District Library, Ashtabula OH. 216-997-9341

Jacobs, Sue, *Asst Dir,* Toledo Hospital Library, Toledo OH. 419-473-4405

Jacobs, Susan, *Ref,* La Grange Public Library, La Grange IL. 312-352-0576, Ext 6

Jacobsen, Brent, *Users Serv,* EG&G Idaho, Inc, INEL Technical Library, Idaho Falls ID. 208-526-1185

Jacobsen, Donald, *Dir,* New City Free Library, New City NY. 914-634-4997

Jacobsen, Edward T, *Dir,* Winona State University, Maxwell Library, Winona MN. 507-457-2040

Jacobsen, Jessie, *Librn,* Coulter Public Library, Coulter IA. 515-866-6942

Jacobsen, Larry, *Librn,* University of Wisconsin-Madison (Primate Center Library), Madison WI. 608-263-3512

Jacobsen, Teresa L, *Tech Serv & Ref,* Mount Saint Mary's College, Charles Willard Coe Memorial Library, Los Angeles CA. 213-476-2237, Ext 233

Jacobskind, Ruth, *Librn,* Temple Beth-El, Arnold & Marie Schwartz Library, Great Neck NY. 516-497-0900

Jacobson, Benjamin H, *Asst Univ Librn for Admin Servs & Br Librs,* Northwestern University Library, Evanston IL. 312-492-7658
Jacobson, Eileen, *Asst Librn,* Ely Public Library, Ely IA. 319-848-9197
Jacobson, Frances, *Circ,* Western State College of Colorado, Leslie J Savage Library, Gunnison CO. 303-943-2053
Jacobson, Gary, *Librn,* Pierce County Rural Library District (Tenzler), Tacoma WA. 206-582-6040
Jacobson, Gerald J, *Librn,* Dr Martin Luther College Library, New Ulm MN. 507-354-8221, Ext 242
Jacobson, Gertrude, *Libr Instruction,* Iowa State University Library, Ames IA. 515-294-1442
Jacobson, Jeanette, *Asst Librn & Cat,* Westminster Choir College, Talbott Library, Princeton NJ. 921-3658 (Dir), 921-7826 (Publ Servs), 921-3659 (Choral Libr), 921-7148 (Media Servs)
Jacobson, June B, *Librn,* Florida Department of Agriculture & Consumer Services, Division of Plant Industry Library, Gainesville FL. 904-372-3505, Ext 131
Jacobson, Lillian, *Dir & Acq,* Valley City State College, Allen Memorial Library, Valley City ND. 701-845-7276
Jacobson, Lillian, *Librn,* Valley City State College, Library Science Program, ND. 701-845-7276
Jacobson, Marie, *Asst Librn,* Caledonia Public Library, Caledonia MN. 507-724-2671
Jacobson, Mrs Gordon, *Tech Serv,* Bernardsville Public Library, Bernardsville NJ. 201-766-0118
Jacobson, Nancy C, *Dir,* Memorial Hall Library, (Subregional Headquarters for Eastern Massachusetts Regional System), Andover MA. 617-475-6960
Jacobson, Patricia, *Librn,* Madison Public Library (Hawthorne), Madison WI. 608-266-6340
Jacobson, Paul, *Librn,* Salt Lake County Library System (Granger Branch), Granger UT. 801-298-3517
Jacobson, Paulene H, *Co Dir,* Miriam Hospital (Patients' Library), Providence RI. 401-274-3700, Ext 279
Jacobson, Sabina, *Tech Serv,* United States Department of Labor Library, Washington DC. 202-523-6988
Jacobson, Selma, *Curator,* Swedish Pioneer Archives, Chicago IL. 312-583-5722
Jacobson, Solomon, *In Charge,* Municipal Reference & Research Center, New York NY. 212-566-4285
Jacobson, Susan, *Acq,* Youngstown State University Library, William F Maag Library, Youngstown OH. 216-742-3676
Jacobson, Wendy, *Librn,* Crossfield Municipal Library, Crossfield AB. 403-946-4232
Jacobstein, J Myron, *Librn,* Stanford University Libraries (Law Library), Stanford CA. 415-497-2721
Jacoby, Karen P, *Asst Map Librn,* National Geographic Society Map Library, Gaithersburg MD. 202-857-7000, Ext 1401
Jacoby, Kathryn, *Asst Librn,* Farmington Community Library (Oakland County Library for Blind & Physically Handicapped), Farmington Hills MI. 313-553-0300, Ext 39
Jacoby, Matthew, *Cat,* Divine Word College, Mat Jacoby Library, Epworth IA. 319-876-3354
Jacoby, Mrs Melvin, *Librn,* Spencer Public Library, Spencer NE. 402-589-1311
Jacoby, Thomas, *Art & Design,* University of Connecticut Library, Storrs CT. 203-486-2219
Jacocks, Jean P, *Popular Libr,* Enoch Pratt Free Library, Baltimore MD. 301-396-5430, 396-5395
Jacolev, Leon, *Dir,* Associated Technical Services Inc, Science & Technology Library, Glen Ridge NJ. 201-748-5673
Jacquest, Cindy, *Ch,* Largo Library, Largo FL. 813-584-8671, Ext 281, 282
Jacquette, Janet, *Librn,* Manoff, Geers, Grass, Inc, Advertising Library, New York NY. 212-350-9234
Jacquin, Mary Louise, *Librn,* Peoria County Law Library, Peoria IL. 309-672-6084
Jaech, Carol, *ILL & Ad,* Santa Clara County Free Library, San Jose CA. 408-293-2326
Jaeger, Doris, *Ser,* Mount Sinai School of Medicine of City University of New York, Gustave L & Janet W Levy Library, New York NY. 212-650-6671

Jaeger, Elsie, *Librn,* Clay Center Public Library, Clay Center NE. 402-762-3861
Jaeger, Margaret, *Librn,* Brown County Library (Subregional Special Services Division), Green Bay WI. 414-497-3473
Jaeger, Sally, *Librn,* Flint Public Library (West Flint Branch), Flint MI. 313-238-3637
Jaeggli, Evelyn, *Librn,* Butt-Holdsworth Memorial Library, Kerrville TX. 512-257-8422, 257-8420
Jaffe, John, *Acq,* Sweet Briar College Library, Sweet Briar VA. 804-381-5541
Jaffe, Steven, *Librn,* Consolidated Edison Co of New York, Technical Library, New York NY. 212-460-4228
Jaffee, Cyrisse, *YA,* Morse Institute Library, Natick MA. 617-653-4252
Jaggers, Carleen, *Librn,* American Air Filter Co, Inc, Research Library, Louisville KY. 502-637-0251
Jaggers, Jeane, *Acq,* San Diego Public Library, San Diego CA. 714-236-5800
Jaggers, Karen, *Reader Serv,* Western New Mexico University, Miller Library, Silver City NM. 505-538-6731
Jagoe, Katherine P, *Texas & Dallas,* Dallas Public Library, Dallas TX. 214-748-9071
Jahncke, Maude W, *Dir,* Kirkwood Community College, Learning Resource Center, Cedar Rapids IA. 319-398-5553
Jahnke, B J, *Asst Librn, Ch & Br Coordr,* Evanston Public Library, Evanston IL. 312-866-0300
Jahnke, Ruth, *Librn,* Hyster Co, Technical Information Service Library, Portland OR. 503-280-7403
Jahns, Karan L, *Librn,* Compton Advertising Inc Library, New York NY. 212-350-1570
Jahns, Rolland, *Cat,* McHenry County College, Learning Resource Center System, Crystal Lake IL. 815-455-3700, Ext 276
Jahoda, Gerald, *Prof,* Florida State University, School of Library Science, FL. 904-644-5775
Jaillite, Joyce Ann, *Ref, On-Line Servs & Bibliog Instr,* Northeast Missouri State University, Pickler Memorial Library, Kirksville MO. 816-665-5121, Ext 7186
Jaimes, Rene, *Dir,* International Planned Parenthood Federation, Documentation & Publications Center, New York NY. 212-679-2230, Ext 50
Jain, Betty, *Librn,* Pioneer Multi-County Library (Moore Public), Moore OK. 405-799-3326
Jain, Nirmal, *Librn,* Acadia University (Science), Wolfville NS. 902-542-2201, Ext 403
Jain, Nirmal, *On-Line Servs,* Acadia University, Harold Campbell Vaughan Memorial Library, Wolfville NS. 902-542-2201, Ext 215
Jajko, Edward A, *Librn,* Yale University Library (American Oriental Society), New Haven CT. 203-436-1040
Jajko, Pamela, *Librn,* Saint Francis Hospital & Medical Center (School of Nursing Library), Hartford CT. 203-247-4441, Ext 244
Jakobe, Lucie S, *Librn,* Bonne Terre Memorial Library, Bonne Terre MO. 314-358-2260
Jakubczak, Dorothy K, *Librn,* Duro-Test Corporation, Technical Library, North Bergen NJ. 201-867-7000, Ext 204
Jakus, Florence I, *Librn,* Sunrise Hospital, Medical Library, Las Vegas NV. 702-731-8210
Jala, Susan O, *Librn,* Marion Laboratories, Inc, Research Library, Kansas City MO. 816-363-1800
Jalbert, Betty, *Cat,* Auburn Public Library, Auburn ME. 207-782-3191
Jambrek, William, *Tech Serv,* Kenosha Public Library, Kenosha WI. 414-656-6034
Jamerino, Camilla, *Ch,* Roseville Public Library, Roseville MI. 313-777-6012
James, Alice, *Librn,* Detroit Public Library (Mark Twain), Detroit MI. 313-833-9150
James, Ann, *Librn,* Export Development Corporation Library, Ottawa ON. 613-237-2570, Ext 266
James, Anna, *Librn,* Texas Southern University Library (Law Library), Houston TX. 713-527-7125
James, Bernice, *Ad,* Anderson City-Anderson & Stony Creek Township Public Library, Anderson Public Library, Anderson IN. 317-644-0938
James, Betsye, *Dir Classification,* North Park Baptist Church Library, Sherman TX. 214-892-8429

James, Billy Michael, *Dir,* United States Public Health Service Hospital, Health Science Library, New Orleans LA. 504-899-3441, Ext 278
James, Brenda, *Asst Dir,* Cobb County Public Library System, Marietta GA. 404-427-2462
James, Brenda, *ILL,* Davidson County Community College, Grady E Love Learning Resources Center, Lexington NC. 704-249-8186, Ext 270
James, Christina, *ILL,* University of Alberta (University Libraries), Edmonton AB. 403-432-3790
James, Darlene, *Librn,* Polacca Community Library, Polacca AZ. 602-737-2670
James, Donna D, *Asst Dir,* Paducah Community College Library, Paducah KY. 502-442-6131, Ext 17
James, Eleanor, *Asst Chief Librn,* Oakville Public Library, Oakville ON. 416-845-3405
James, Elisha, *Instr,* University of the District of Columbia-Mount Vernon Square Campus, Dept of Library Science & Instructional Systems Technology, DC. 202-727-2756, 727-2757 & 727-2758
James, Ethel, *Acq,* Louisiana State Library, Baton Rouge LA. 504-342-4922
James, Florence, *Commun Servs,* Fullerton City Library, Fullerton CA. 714-738-6333, Ext 301
James, Geraldine R, *Librn,* PQ Corp, Research Library, Lafayette Hill PA. 215-825-5000, Ext 63
James, J, *Librn,* University of Saskatchewan Library (Western College of Veterinary Medicine), Saskatoon SK. 306-343-3249
James, Jan, *Asst Dir,* New Mexico State Supreme Court Law Library, Santa Fe NM. 505-827-2515
James, Jean, *Librn,* Marlboro County Library, Bennettsville SC. 803-479-6201
James, Jerry, *Anglo-American Lit & Lang, Philos, Classics, Religious Studies, Theater,* University of California, University Library, Santa Cruz CA. 408-429-2076
James, John, *Cat,* Shoreline Community College, Library/Media Center, Seattle WA. 206-546-4663
James, John E, *Supvr of Libr Servs,* American Home Products, Wyeth Laboratories Technical Library, Radnor PA. 215-688-4400, Ext 336, 337
James, John R, *Head,* University of Washington Libraries (Serials Division), Seattle WA. 206-543-1760
James, June, *Librn,* Eaton Rapids Public Library, Eaton Rapids MI. 517-663-8744
James, Mary, *Librn,* Nicholson Memorial Public Library (Broughton Branch), Longview TX. 214-753-9074
James, Mary, *Br Asst,* Timberland Regional Library (McCleary Branch), McCleary WA. 206-495-3368
James, Marylou, *YA,* Syosset Public Library, Syosset NY. 516-921-7161
James, Maxine D, *Librn,* Unicoi County Public Library, Erwin TN. 615-743-6533
James, Mildred, *Librn,* Pearl River County Library System (Poplarville Public), Poplarville MS. 601-795-8411
James, Mildred, *Librn,* Poplarville Public Library, Poplarville MS. 601-795-8411
James, Nicola, *Media,* College of New Rochelle, Gill Library, New Rochelle NY. 914-632-5300, Ext 347
James, Olive, *Ref,* Stanford University Libraries, Stanford CA. 415-497-2016
James, Pauline, *Librn,* Selover Public Library, Chesterville OH. 419-768-3431
James, Stephen, *Asst Prof,* Atlanta University, School of Library & Information Studies, GA. 404-681-0251, Ext 312
James, Teresa, *Commun Servs,* North Vancouver District Public Library, North Vancouver BC. 604-984-0286
James, Toni, *Asst Dir,* Pike-Amite-Walthall Library System, McComb Public Library (Headquaters), McComb MS. 601-684-7034
James, Toni, *Librn,* Pike-Amite-Walthall Library System (Summit Public), Summit MS. 601-276-5611
James, Valerie, *Librn,* Chicago Public Library (Bezazian), Chicago IL. 312-561-1864
James, Wendell E, *Librn & Media,* Northeast Iowa Technical Institute, South Center Library, Peosta IA. 319-556-5110

James, William, *Librn,* University of Kentucky (Law), Lexington KY. 606-258-8686
James, William I, *Librn,* Harlandale United Methodist Church Library, San Antonio TX. 512-922-7773
James, Jr, Henry, *Dir,* Sweet Briar College Library, Sweet Briar VA. 804-381-5541
Jameson, E M, *Librn,* Southwest Arkansas Regional Library (Gillham Branch), Gillham AR. 501-777-4564
Jameson, Harriet C, *Rare Bks,* University of Michigan Libraries (University Library), Ann Arbor MI. 313-764-9356
Jameson, Phillip, *Ref,* Ohio State University Libraries (Vocational Education Research Library), Columbus OH. 614-486-3655, Ext 221
Jameson, V Lloyd, *Govt Docs, Microtext, Newspaper,* Boston Public Library, Eastern Massachusetts Library System, Boston MA. 617-536-5400
Jamieson, E M, *Dir,* Glenrose Provincial General Hospital Library, Edmonton AB. 403-474-5451, Ext 265
Jamieson, Grace, *Librn,* Douglas County Public Library (Lake Tahoe), Zephyr Cove NV. 702-588-6411
Jamison, Barbara, *Dir,* Kemp Public Library, Wichita Falls TX. 817-322-5611, Ext 377
Jamison, Hal, *Librn,* Southeastern Community College, South Campus Library, Keokuk IA. 319-524-3221
Jamison, L Gladys, *Librn,* New Castle Public Library, New Castle DE. 302-328-1995
Jamison, Linda L, *Asst Librn,* Holmes Junior College, McMorrough Library, Goodman MS. 601-472-2312, Ext 48
Jamison, Susan C, *Librn,* Corbit-Calloway Memorial Library, Odessa DE. 302-378-8838
Jamison, Tanya, *Coordr,* West Texas Library System, Lubbock TX. 806-762-5442
Janak, Sandra Z, *Librn,* E I Du Pont De Nemours & Co, Inc, Victoria Plant Technical Library, Victoria TX. 512-573-3211, Ext 349
Janda, Marylou, *Librn,* Le Sueur-Waseca Regional Library (Le Center Public), Le Center MN. 612-357-6792
Jandl, N, *Librn, On-Line Servs & Bibliog Instr,* Charles River Associates Library, Boston MA. 617-266-0500
Jandreau, Leslie, *ILL,* Prince William Public Library, Manassas VA. 703-361-8211
Jane, Sister Frances, *Librn,* Sainte Therese Hospital Medical Library, Waukegan IL. 312-688-5969
Janecek, Kilbourn L, *Dir,* North Dakota State University Library, Fargo ND. 701-237-8876
Janes, Annette, *Librn,* Hamilton Public Library, South Hamilton MA. 617-468-2202
Janes, Connie, *Librn,* Tacoma Public Library (South Tacoma), Tacoma WA. 206-472-7354
Janeway, R C, *Libr Servs Dir,* Texas Tech University Library, Lubbock TX. 806-742-2261
Jang, Stephanie, *Librn,* Signetics Corp Library, Sunnyvale CA. 408-739-7700
Jangula, Teddy, *Librn,* New Plymouth Community Library, New Plymouth ID. 208-278-5881
Janiak, Jane M, *Chief Librn,* Port Authority of New York & New Jersey Library, New York NY. 212-466-4067, 4068
Janis, Jane, *Circ,* Lewis & Clark Library, Helena MT. 406-442-2380
Janisse, John, *Dir,* Saint Joseph's College Library, Edmonton AB. 403-433-1569
Janke, Dorothy, *Librn,* Butterfield Trail Association & Logan County Historical Society, Inc, Butterfield Trail Museum Library, Russell Springs KS. 913-751-4242
Janke, Leslie H, *Dir,* San Jose State University, Division of Library Science, CA. 408-277-2292
Janky, Donna, *Ch,* Findlay-Hancock County Public Library, Findlay OH. 419-422-1712
Janowski, Bronislaw, *Dir,* Evangeline Parish Library, Ville Platte LA. 318-363-1369
Janowski, Mary T, *Dir,* Allen Parish Library, Oberlin LA. 318-639-4338
Jansen, Harris, *Dir of Research Serv,* Assemblies of God Graduate School Library, Cordas C Burnett Library, Springfield MO. 417-862-2781, Ext 5505
Jansen, Janet, *Dir,* Grafton Public Library, Grafton WI. 414-377-5740
Jansen, Kathleen, *Dir,* Lake County Library, Lakeport Library, Lakeport CA. 707-263-2291

Janson, Patricia, *Reader Serv,* Suffolk County Community College, Western Campus Library, Brentwood NY. 516-348-4522
Janssen, Amy, *AV,* Central Kansas Library System, Great Bend KS. 316-792-4865
Januskis, Lola, *Latin Am,* Temple University of the Commonwealth System of Higher Education, Samuel Paley Library, Philadelphia PA. 215-787-8231
Januszkiewicz, Phillip J, *Asst Coordr for Res,* Boston Public Library, Eastern Massachusetts Library System, Boston MA. 617-536-5400
Janzen, Deborah K, *Dir & Bibliog Instr,* Hesston College, Mary Miller Library, Hesston KS. 316-327-4221, Ext 242
Jaquay, Robert, *Circ,* Colonie Town Library, Loudonville NY. 518-458-9274
Jaques, Jennifer, *Circ,* Central Washington University Library, Ellensburg WA. 509-963-1901
Jaques, Thomas F, *State Librn,* Louisiana State Library, Baton Rouge LA. 504-342-4922
Jaramillo, Carmen, *Librn,* Los Lunas Community Public Library, Los Lunas NM. 505-865-6779
Jarbor, Linda, *Tech Serv,* Burbank Public Library, Burbank CA. 213-847-9744
Jardin, Patricia, *Librn,* United States Air Force (Tyndall Air Force Base Library), Tyndall AFB FL. 904-283-1130
Jardine, Barbara, *Asst Librn,* Conference Board in Canada, Information Div Library, Ottawa ON. 613-746-1261
Jardine, Barbara, *ILL,* Ricks College, David O McKay Learning Resources Center, Rexburg ID. 208-356-2351
Jardine, Myrtle U, *Librn,* Washburn Memorial Library, Washburn ME. 207-445-4814
Jarett, Nella, *Librn,* Loeb & Loeb, Law Library, Los Angeles CA. 213-629-0418
Jarmak, Sandra, *Librn,* Pittsfield Public Library, Pittsfield ME. 207-487-5880
Jarnot, Marie, *Librn,* Buffalo & Erie County Public Library System (Fronczak), Buffalo NY. 716-892-3941
Jaros, Emily, *Ad,* Dearborn Department of Libraries, Henry Ford Centennial Library, Dearborn MI. 313-271-1000
Jaroslow, Sylvia, *AV,* Paterson Free Public Library, Danforth Memorial Library, Paterson NJ. 201-881-3770
Jarosz, Jean, *Ref,* Northeastern Ohio Universities College of Medicine, Basic Medical Sciences Library, Rootstown OH. 216-325-2511
Jarred, Ada D, *Librn,* Louisiana State University at Alexandria Library, Alexandria LA. 318-445-3672, Ext 46
Jarrell, Helen J, *Dir,* Capitol Institute of Technology Library, Kensington MD. 301-933-2599
Jarrell, Howard, *Bus,* Wright State University Library, Dayton OH. 513-873-2380
Jarrett, Gladys W, *Chief Librn,* York College Library, Jamaica NY. 212-969-4026
Jarrett, Lottie, *AV & Per,* Saint Mary's College of O'fallon Library, O'Fallon MO. 314-272-3420, Ext 224
Jarrett, M, *ILL,* Chatham Public Library, Chatham ON. 519-354-2940
Jarrett, Merrick, *Librn,* Kitchener Public Library (Stanley Park), Kitchener ON. 519-743-0271, Ext 72
Jarvis, D, *Circ,* University of Southern California, Edward L Doheny Memorial Library, Los Angeles CA. 213-743-6050
Jarvis, Frances, *Librn,* Chateaugay Memorial Library, Chateaugay NY. 518-497-6931
Jasken, Eloise, *Librn,* 3M (Health Care Library), Saint Paul MN. 612-733-1703
Jasnich, Adrienne, *On-Line Servs,* Quaker Oats Co, John Stuart Research Laboratories-Research Library, Barrington IL. 312-381-1980
Jaspal, Lelita, *ILL & Ref,* Bank Street College of Education Library, New York NY. 212-663-7200, Ext 245
Jasper, James, *Tech Serv,* Oxnard Public Library, Oxnard CA. 805-486-4311
Jassman, Sherrida, *Search Coordr,* Auburn University, Ralph Brown Draughton Library, Auburn AL. 205-826-4500
Jauquet, Barbara, *Asst Dir,* Mid-Peninsula Library Cooperative, Iron Mountain MI. 906-774-1218

Jauquet, Barbara, *Per,* University of Wisconsin-Superior, Jim Dan Hill Library, Superior WI. 715-392-8101, Ext 346
Jauquet, Barbara J, *Instr,* University of Wisconsin-Superior, Library Science Program, WI. 715-392-8101, Ext 346, 347
Jawitz, Jane, *Ch,* Port Jefferson Free Library Association, Port Jefferson NY. 516-473-0022
Jaworski, Mrs T M, *Librn,* J P Stevens & Co Inc, Technical Center Library, Garfield NJ. 201-772-7100, Ext 315
Jax, John J, *Dir,* University of Wisconsin-Stout, Pierce Library, Menomonie WI. 715-232-1184
Jaxa-Debicki, Stanislaus, *Per,* Saint Charles Borromeo Seminary, Ryan Memorial Library, Philadelphia PA. 215-839-3760, Ext 275
Jay, Donald E, *Chief,* New York Public Library (Humanities/Social Sciences Research Center (Central Bldg)), New York NY. 212-790-6262
Jayne, JoAnn, *Tech Serv & Cat,* Academy of Aeronautics Library, East Elmhurst NY. 212-429-6600
Jaynes, Phyllis E, *Librn,* Dartmouth College (Feldberg Business Administration & Engineering), Hanover NH. 603-646-2191
Jean, Jill, *Ch,* Portage Public Library, Portage MI. 616-327-6725
Jeansonne, Henrietta W, *Ref,* Nicholls State University, Allen J Ellender Memorial Library, Thibodaux LA. 504-446-8111, Ext 401, 402
Jebb, Marcia, *Asst Univ Librn, Pub Servs,* Cornell University Libraries (University Libraries), Ithaca NY. 607-256-4144
Jedeka, Julianne, *Librn,* Tektronix, Inc Library, Beaverton OR. 503-644-0161, Ext 5388
Jedlicka, Janet, *Librn,* Society of Automotive Engineers Library, Warrendale PA. 412-776-4841
Jeffcoat, A, *Acq, Ref & Per,* South Carolina Wildlife & Marine Resources Department, Marine Resources Div Library, Charleston SC. 803-795-6350, Ext 205
Jeffcott, Janet, *On-Line Servs,* Madison Area Technical College, Cora Hardy Library & Technical Center, Madison WI. 608-266-5122, 5026
Jefferies, Mrs George A, *Librn,* Cummer Gallery of Art Library, Jacksonville FL. 904-356-6857
Jeffers, J Ruth, *Librn,* Burroughs Corp, Electronic Components Div, Engineering Library, Plainfield NJ. 201-757-5000, Ext 219
Jeffers, Linden, *Asst Librn,* American Water Works Association, Library & Technical Information Center, Denver CO. 303-794-7711
Jefferson, Gene, *AV,* Maysville Community College Library, Maysville KY. 606-759-7141, Ext 28
Jefferson, Henry, *AV,* Maysville Community College Library, Maysville KY. 606-759-7141, Ext 28
Jefferson, Lila, *ILL,* Big Country Library System, Abilene TX. 915-673-2311
Jefferson, Lila R, *ILL,* Abilene Public Library, Abilene TX. 915-677-2474
Jefferson, Mary E, *Asst Dir, ILL & Bibliog Instr,* Averett College, Mary B Blount Library, Danville VA. 804-793-7811, Ext 265
Jefferson, Velma, *In Charge,* Miami-Dade Public Library System (Edison Center), Miami FL. 305-638-6907
Jeffery, Jonathan, *On-Line Servs,* University of Delaware, Hugh M Morris Library, Newark DE. 302-738-2231
Jeffery, Marjorie, *Librn,* Oskaloosa Public Library, Oskaloosa KS. 913-863-2651
Jefferys, Gretchen, *Tech Serv,* Rodman Public Library, Alliance OH. 216-821-1410
Jeffress, Victor C, *Dir,* McLennan Community College Library, Waco TX. 817-756-6551, Ext 264
Jeffrey, Frances, *Tech Serv,* Warder Public Library, Springfield OH. 323-8616 & 323-9751
Jeffrey, Gail, *Librn,* Oxford County Library (Ingersoll Branch), Ingersoll ON. 519-485-2505
Jeffries, Carolyn M, *Ref,* Winter Park Public Library, Winter Park FL. 305-647-1638
Jeffries, Mary W, *Tech Serv,* Lorain County Community College Library, Elyria OH. 216-365-4191, Ext 201
Jeffs, Joseph E, *Dir,* Georgetown University, Joseph Mark Lauinger Library, Washington DC. 202-625-4095

Jegant, Karen, *Video-Tape,* Southwest Georgia Regional Library, Gilbert H Gragg Library, Bainbridge GA. 912-246-3887, 3894, 3895

Jehle, MaryJane, *Librn,* Gaylord-Otsego County Library, Gaylord MI. 517-732-5841

Jelalian, Sona, *Librn,* Cambridge Public Library (Mount Auburn), Cambridge MA. 617-498-9085

Jelen, Edward, *Librn,* Brooklyn Public Library (Dyker), Brooklyn NY. 212-748-1395

Jelley, David, *Chief Librn,* General Telephone & Electronics Laboratories, Inc, Waltham Research Center Library, Waltham MA. 617-890-8460

Jellous, Ruth, *In Charge,* Oxford County Library (Foldens), Ingersoll ON. 519-537-5145

Jemelka, Peggy, *Ch & Outreach Consult,* Central Texas Library System, Austin TX. 512-474-5355

Jemison, Keith, *Librn,* Tulsa City-County Library (North Regional Library & Social Services Center), Tulsa OK. 918-582-8654

Jen, Albert, *Cat,* Northeastern Illinois University Library, Chicago IL. 312-583-4050, Ext 469, 470, 471, 472

Jen, Neil, *Cat,* Salisbury State College, Blackwell Library, Salisbury MD. 301-546-3261, Ext 351

Jendyk, G B, *Librn,* Sangudo Junior Senior High School and Public Library, Sangudo AB. 403-785-2212

Jeng, Helene, *Librn,* Maryland Department of Health & Mental Hygiene (Thomas Wilson Center, Patient), Mount Wilson MD. 301-486-7676, Ext 266

Jeng, Helene, *Librn,* Maryland Department of Health & Mental Hygiene (Thomas Wilson Center, Medical & Professional), Mount Wilson MD. 301-486-7676, Ext 266

Jenkins, Aileen Mc C, *Librn,* Bill Communications, Inc, Sales & Marketing Management Library, New York NY. 212-986-4800, Ext 248

Jenkins, Ann A, *Librn,* Kelco Division of Merck Library, San Diego CA. 714-292-4900

Jenkins, Barbara Williams, *Dir,* South Carolina State College, Miller F Whittaker Library, Orangeburg SC. 803-536-7045, 536-7046

Jenkins, Betty L, *Ref,* Teachers College - Columbia University Library, New York NY. 212-678-3022, 678-3020

Jenkins, Brunette B, *Librn,* United States Air Force (Department of Social Actions Training Library), Lackland AFB TX. 512-671-1110

Jenkins, Carol G, *Assoc Dir,* University of Virginia (Claude Moore Health Sciences Library), Charlottesville VA. 804-924-5444

Jenkins, Connie, *Asst Librn,* Noblesville Public Library, Noblesville IN. 317-773-1384

Jenkins, Constance, *Commun Servs,* Taylor Memorial Public Library, Cuyahoga Falls Public Library, Cuyahoga Falls OH. 216-928-2117

Jenkins, Curtis, *ILL & Ref,* Linden Free Public Library, Linden NJ. 201-486-3888

Jenkins, Darrell L, *Admin Servs,* Southern Illinois University at Carbondale, Delyte W Morris Library, Carbondale IL. 618-453-2522

Jenkins, David, *Tech Serv & Circ,* Bergen Community College, Learning Resources Center Library, Paramus NJ. 201-447-1500, Ext 405

Jenkins, Deena, *Ch,* North Chicago Public Library, North Chicago IL. 312-689-0125

Jenkins, Elaine, *Librn,* Chestatee Regional Library (Flowery Branch Library), Flowery Branch GA. 404-967-6911

Jenkins, Elizabeth C, *Tech Serv & Acq,* Alliance College Library, Cambridge Springs PA. 814-398-4611, Ext 283

Jenkins, Ellen B, *Librn,* Aiken-Bamberg-Barnwell-Edgefield Regional Library (Barnwell County), Barnwell SC. 803-259-3612

Jenkins, Florence, *Librn,* Belmont Technical College Library, Saint Clairsville OH. 304-695-9500, Ext 36

Jenkins, Geraldine, *Dir,* Hutchinson Memorial Library, Randolph WI. 414-326-3420

Jenkins, Glen, *Rare Bks,* Case Western Reserve University & Cleveland Medical Library Association, Cleveland Health Sciences Library, Cleveland OH. 216-368-3426

Jenkins, Glen, *Adjunct Prof,* Case Western Reserve University, School of Library Science, OH. 216-368-3500

Jenkins, Harold R, *Dir,* Kansas City Public Library, Kansas City MO. 816-221-2685

Jenkins, Helen, *Librn,* Cass County Public Library (Garden City Branch), Garden City MO. 816-862-6611

Jenkins, Janelle, *Librn,* Uniontown Public Library, Uniontown KY. 502-822-4244

Jenkins, Joyce, *Reader & Advisory,* Howard County Library, Columbia MD. 301-997-8000

Jenkins, Joyce, *Librn,* Petersburg Public Library, Petersburg AK. 907-772-3349

Jenkins, Katherine A, *Asst Dir,* University of Texas (M D Anderson Hospital & Tumor Institute), Houston TX. 713-792-2282

Jenkins, Katherine I, *Acq,* Queens College, Everett Library, Charlotte NC. 704-332-7121, Ext 278

Jenkins, Larry, *Media,* Broome Community College, Cecil C Tyrrell Learning Resources Center, Binghamton NY. 607-772-5020

Jenkins, Mary M, *Librn,* West Virginia Department of Culture & History, Archives & History Library, Charleston WV. 304-348-0230, 0231, 0232

Jenkins, Maureen, *Commun Servs,* Chickasaw Library System, Ardmore OK. 405-223-3164

Jenkins, Melody S, *Dir,* Colquitt-Thomas Regional Library, Moultrie-Colquitt County Library, Moultrie GA. 912-985-6540

Jenkins, Nancy A, *Dir,* Newburgh-Ohio Township Public Library, Newburgh IN. 812-853-5468

Jenkins, Norma, *Librn,* Corning Museum of Glass Library, Corning NY. 607-937-5371

Jenkins, Pat, *Coodr Info Servs,* North York Public Library, Willowdale ON. 416-494-6838

Jenkins, Phillip, *Dir,* Detroit Community Music School Library, Detroit MI. 313-831-2870

Jenkins, Robert, *Librn,* Prescott Public-Yavapai County Library System (Crown King Public), Crown King AZ. 602-445-8110

Jenkins, Sadie, *Librn,* Tri-County Regional Library (Talking Book Center), Rome GA. 404-291-6030

Jenkins, Sadie J, *Librn Deaf & Librn Blind,* Tri-County Regional Library, Rome GA. 404-291-9360

Jenkins, Sallie, *Media,* Central Piedmont Community College Library, Charlotte NC. 704-373-6883

Jenkins, Sarah, *Librn,* Cerritos College Library, Learning Materials Center, Norwalk CA. 213-860-2451, Ext 286

Jenkins, Sarah, *Librn,* Tallahatchie County Library (Sumner Branch), Sumner MS. 601-375-8901

Jenkins, Susan, *Tech Serv,* Perry County District Library, New Lexington OH. 614-342-1077

Jenkins, Sylvia, *ILL & Ref,* Virginia Union University, William J Clarke Library, Richmond VA. 804-359-9331, Ext 256, 257

Jenkins, Victoria W, *Chief Librn,* Morris Brown College, Jordan-Thomas Library, Atlanta GA. 404-525-7831, Ext 37

Jenkins, Wink, *Res Mat,* Tyler Junior College, Edgar H Vaughn Memorial Library, Tyler TX. 214-592-5993, 593-3342

Jenks, Annette R, *Librn,* Elizabeth Sanford Botsford Memorial Library, Williamstown Public Library, Williamstown MA. 413-458-5369

Jenks, George M, *Dir,* Bucknell University, Ellen Clarke Bertrand Library, Lewisburg PA. 717-524-3056

Jenks, Ginny, *Librn,* Meloy Laboratories, Inc Library, Springfield VA. 703-354-2600

Jenks, Margaret, *Cat,* Moscow-Latah County Library System, Moscow ID. 208-882-3925

Jenks, Susan, *ILL & Ref,* Marshall-Lyon County Library, Marshall MN. 532-2646; 532-2849

Jenner, Barbara M, *Ref,* Staunton Public Library, Fannie Bayly King Library, Staunton VA. 703-886-7231

Jenner, Elizabeth, *In Charge,* Canadian Broadcasting Corp (Reference Library), Toronto ON. 416-925-3311, Ext 2097

Jenner, L, *Librn,* Okanagan Regional Library District (Cawston Branch), Cawston BC. 604-499-2629

Jennerich, Edward J, *Chmn,* Baylor University, Dept of Library Science, TX. 817-755-2410

Jennigs, Phyllis, *Librn,* Public Affairs Research Council of Louisiana Inc, Library, Baton Rouge LA. 504-343-9204

Jennings, Barbara, *Dir,* Baker Junior College of Business Library, Flint MI. 313-744-4040

Jennings, Beatrice, *Acq,* Grambling State University, A C Lewis Memorial Library, Grambling LA. 318-247-6941, Ext 220

Jennings, Billie Joe, *Bkmobile Coordr,* Acadia Parish Library, Crowley LA. 318-788-1880

Jennings, Catherine, *Circ,* Hanover College, Duggan Library, Hanover IN. 812-866-2151, Ext 333

Jennings, Diane Richmond, *Dir,* Franklin County Library, Rocky Mount VA. 703-483-5163, 5164

Jennings, Francis, *Dir, Ctr Hist of Am Indian,* Newberry Library, Chicago IL. 312-943-9090

Jennings, Hoyland, *ILL & Ref,* Robeson County Public Library, Lumberton NC. 919-738-4859

Jennings, Hoyland, *Local Hist,* Robeson County Public Library, Lumberton NC. 919-738-4859

Jennings, Ida, *Librn,* Portsmouth Public Library (New Boston Branch), New Boston OH. 614-456-4412

Jennings, Linda L, *Acq,* Wilkinsburg Public Library, Pittsburgh PA. 412-244-2940

Jennings, Lois, *clerk,* Burley Public Library, Burley ID. 208-678-7708

Jennings, M, *Librn,* Algonquin College of Applied Arts & Technology (Byron Campus), Ottawa ON. 613-728-4945

Jennings, Mae, *Librn,* Choctaw Nation Multi-County Library, Poteau OK. 918-426-0456

Jennings, Mae, *Dir,* McAlester Public Library, McAlester OK. 918-426-0456

Jennings, Margaret, *Info Spec,* American Society for Information Science Library, Washington DC. 202-659-3644

Jennings, Marie D, *Librn,* United States Air Force (Patrick Air Force Base Library), Patrick AFB FL. 305-494-1110

Jennings, Mary, *Librn,* Alaska Regional Library for the Blind & Physically Handicapped, Anchorage AK. 907-274-6625

Jennings, Minnie, *In Charge,* Monroe County Public Library (Marathon Branch), Marathon FL. 305-743-5156

Jennings, Mrs E, *Commun Servs,* Algonquin Regional Library System, Parry Sound ON. 705-746-9161

Jennings, Rebecca, *Ch & YA,* Amos Memorial Public Library, Sidney Public Library, Sidney OH. 513-492-8354

Jennings, S, *Cat,* Essex Library Association, Inc, Essex CT. 203-767-1560

Jennings, Theresa A, *Librn,* Hull Corp, Thinco, Inc Library, Hatboro PA. 215-675-5000

Jennings, Vera, *Librn,* Butterick Patterns Archives Library, New York NY. 212-620-2555

Jennings, Vincent, *Govt Docs & Maps,* Hofstra University Library, Hempstead NY. 516-560-3475

Jensen, Alta, *Librn,* Garwin Public Library, Garwin IA. 515-499-2024

Jensen, Betty J, *Librn,* Saint Luke's Hospital-Saint Joseph Hospital-Whatcom County Medical Society, Whatcom-Island Health Services Library, Bellingham WA. 206-734-5400, Ext 438 & 734-8300, Ext 241

Jensen, Bonnie, *Librn,* Chamberlain Manufacturing Corp, Research & Development Technical Library, Waterloo IA. 319-291-1600, Ext 334

Jensen, Dale, *Media,* Salt Lake County Library System, Whitmore Library, Salt Lake City UT. 801-943-7614

Jensen, David, *Coordr,* Southern Utah State College, School of Education-Instructional Media Endorsement, UT. 801-586-4411, Ext 301

Jensen, David P, *Dir,* Greensboro College, James Addison Jones Library, Greensboro NC. 919-272-7102, Ext 234

Jensen, Delores, *ILL & Ad Asst,* Auburn Public Library, Auburn WA. 206-931-3018

Jensen, Dennis F, *Libr Mgr,* Standard & Poor's Corp Library, New York NY. 212-248-3940

Jensen, Elaine, *Circ,* Coshocton Public Library, Coshocton OH. 614-622-0956

Jensen, Eloise, *Librn,* Exira Public Library, Exira IA. 712-268-5489

Jensen, Florence, *Asst Librn,* Scappoose Public Library, Scappoose OR. 503-543-7123

Jensen, Gunvor, *ILL,* Wagner College, Horrmann Library, Staten Island NY. 212-390-3001

Jensen, Gunvor, *Science,* Wagner College, Horrmann Library, Staten Island NY. 212-390-3001

Jensen, Harlan, *Asst Prof,* Saint Cloud State University, Center for Library & Audiovisual Education, MN. 612-255-2022

Jensen, Harriet, *Ref,* Long Branch Public Library, Long Branch NJ. 201-222-3900
Jensen, Ida Marie, *Assoc Librn,* Utah State University, Merrill Library & Learning Resources Program, Logan UT. 801-750-2637
Jensen, Jill, *Media,* North Iowa Area Community College Library, Mason City IA. 515-421-4232
Jensen, Joan, *Ref,* University of Connecticut Library, Storrs CT. 203-486-2219
Jensen, Joan R, *Librn,* Hudson Engineering Corp Technical Library, Houston TX. 713-782-4400, Ext 309
Jensen, Joanne, *Libr Admin,* Mount Olivet Lutheran Church Library, Minneapolis MN. 612-926-7651
Jensen, Joanne C, *Dir,* Lewis O Flom - Lansing Public Library, Lansing IL. 312-474-2447
Jensen, Joseph E, *Librn,* Medical & Chirurgical Faculty of the State of Maryland Library, Baltimore MD. 301-539-0872
Jensen, Judith Bourgeois, *Librn & On-Line Servs,* Agnes Scott College, McCain Library, Decatur GA. 404-373-2571, Ext 220
Jensen, Judy, *In Charge,* Godel Memorial Library, Warren MN. 218-745-5465
Jensen, Ken, *Asst Dir,* Regina Public Library, Regina SK. 306-569-7615
Jensen, Kenneth O, *Acq & Cat,* University of Virginia, Alderman Library, Charlottesville VA. 804-924-3026
Jensen, Leona, *Dir,* Blaine County Library, Chinook MT. 406-357-2932
Jensen, Lorraine, *Librn,* Hayward Public Library (Weekes), Hayward CA. 415-782-2155
Jensen, Mary Ann, *Curator,* Princeton University Library (Theatre Collection), Princeton NJ. 609-452-3180
Jensen, Mary E, *Dean,* West Valley College, Learning Resource Center, Saratoga CA. 408-867-2200, Ext 284
Jensen, Mrs S, *In Charge,* Oxford County Library (Harrington Branch), Harrington ON. 519-349-2738
Jensen, Mrs Verner, *Librn,* Dike Public Library, Dike IA. 319-989-2608
Jensen, Norine, *Librn,* Richfield City Library, Richfield UT. 801-896-5169
Jensen, Norm, *Instr,* Highline Community College Library, Library Technician Program, WA. 206-878-3710, Ext 233
Jensen, Patricia, *Asst Prof,* University of Rhode Island, Graduate Library School, RI. 401-792-2878 or 792-2947
Jensen, Richard, *Sci,* Brigham Young University, Harold B Lee Library, Provo UT. 801-378-2905
Jensen, Richard, *Dir, Family & Community Hist Ctr,* Newberry Library, Chicago IL. 312-943-9090
Jensen, Roberta, *Cat,* McMillan Memorial Library, Wisconsin Rapids WI. 715-423-1040
Jensen, Sonia, *Librn,* Big Horn County Library, Basin WY. 307-568-2388
Jensen, Thomas, *Chmn,* Dickinson State College, ND. 701-227-2542, 227-2322
Jensen, Yvette M, *Librn,* Massachusetts Mutual Life Insurance Co Library, Springfield MA. 413-788-8411
Jensent, Hans W, *Asst Dir,* Sun Prairie Public Library, Sun Prairie WI. 608-837-5644
Jenson, David L, *Librn,* Minneapolis Technical Institute Library, Minneapolis MN. 612-348-4100
Jenson, Florence, *Librn,* United States Air Force (PACAF Library Service Center), Wheeler AFB HI. 808-471-7411
Jenson, Janet, *Systs Consult,* Winding Rivers Library System, La Crosse WI. 608-784-3151
Jenson, Judy, *Tech Serv,* Iowa Western Community College, Hoover Media Library, Council Bluffs IA. 712-325-3247
Jenson, Linda, *Pub Servs & On-Line Servs,* Tarrant County Junior College System (South Campus Learning Resource Center), Fort Worth TX. 817-534-4861, Ext 223
Jepkes, Judi T, *Dir,* Gowrie Public Library, Gowrie IA. 515-352-3315
Jeppesen, E Carol, *Librn,* Ruskin Public Library, Ruskin NE. 402-226-2341
Jepps, Sheila J, *Librn,* Shell Canada Resources Ltd, Technical Library, Calgary AB. 403-232-3512
Jepson, Mabel, *Tech Serv,* State University of New York at Buffalo (Charles B Sears Law Library), Buffalo NY. 716-636-2043

Jerashen, Antonette Joan, *Corp Libr Mgr,* Liggett Group, Inc (Liggett Group, Inc, Corporate Library), Durham NC. 919-471-7511, Ext 7343
Jergens, Clara, *Librn,* National Oceanic & Atmospheric Administration, Environmental Data Service, Coral Gables Center Library, Coral Gables FL. 305-350-4498
Jerkovich, George, *Slavic Curator,* University of Kansas Libraries, Watson Memorial Library, Lawrence KS. 913-864-3601
Jerman, Orpha, *Ref,* Morningside College, Wilhemina Petersmeyer Library, Sioux City IA. 712-277-5195
Jernigan, Faith E, *Dir,* Hartford City Public Library, Hartford City IN. 317-348-1720
Jernigan, Marilyn Jean, *Ref,* Cleveland Public Library, Cleveland TN. 615-476-8431
Jernigan, Norva, *Librn,* Hamlet Public Library, Hamlet NC. 919-582-3477
Jernigan, Shelley, *Librn,* Knoxville-Knox County Public Library (North Knoxville), Knoxville TN. 615-525-7036
Jerome, Frank, *Media,* Oscar Rose Junior College, Learning Resources Center, Midwest City OK. 405-733-7323, 733-7322
Jerome, Julia M, *Dir,* Eveleth Public Library, Eveleth MN. 218-741-4913
Jersey, Patricia, *ILL & Ref,* East Stroudsburg State College, Kemp Library, East Stroudsburg PA. 717-424-3467
Jervis, Frances A, *Tech Serv,* Cumberland County Library, Bridgeton NJ. 609-455-0080
Jerwick, Vera I, *Ref,* Nassau Community College Library, Garden City NY. 516-222-7400
Jerwick, Vera I, *Govt Docs,* Nassau Community College Library, Garden City NY. 516-222-7400
Jeryn, Irene, *Librn,* Hospital for Sick Children, Hospital Library, Toronto ON. 416-597-1500, Ext 1446
Jeschke, Channing R, *Librn,* Emory University Libraries (Pitts Theology Library), Atlanta GA. 404-329-4166
Jeschke, Freya, *Librn,* Goethe Institute, Munich, Goethe House Library, New York NY. 212-744-8310
Jeser, Sharlee, *Ref,* Richland College, Learning Resources Center, Dallas TX. 214-746-4460
Jesh, Genevieve, *In Charge,* Albany Public Library, Albany MN. 612-845-4244
Jespersen, B, *Librn,* Campbell Soup Co, Campbell Institute for Food Research, Food Science & Technology Library, Camden NJ. 609-964-4000, Ext 2023
Jespersen, Helene, *Dir,* Williston Park Public Library, Williston Park NY. 516-742-1820
Jessee, LaVerne, *Librn,* Lake Cumberland Regional Library, Columbia KY. 502-384-4211
Jessup, Doris, *Guidance & Counseling,* Greensboro Public Library, Greensboro NC. 373-2474; 373-2471
Jessup, Gladys, *Asst Librn,* Knightstown Public Library, Knightstown IN. 317-345-5095
Jessup, Helen C, *Librn,* Potomac Electric Power Company Library, Washington DC. 202-872-2361
Jessup, Libby F, *Librn,* New York State Supreme Court Library, Brooklyn, Brooklyn NY. 212-643-8080, 643-8081, 643-8082
Jesswein, Edith, *Monograph Acq,* University of Calgary Library, Calgary AB. 403-284-5954
Jester, Melinda, *Ref,* Indiana University School of Law, Law Library, Bloomington IN. 812-337-9666
Jestes, Edward C, *Geology & Physics,* University of California at Davis, General Library, Davis CA. 916-752-2110
Jesus, A M de, *Librn,* Union Carbide Canada Ltd, Technical Centre Library, Pointe-Aux-Trembles PQ. 514-645-5311
Jett, Don, *Librn,* University of Tennessee, Knoxville (Science-Engineering), Knoxville TN. 615-974-3270
Jette, Jean-Paul, *Librn,* University of Montreal Libraries (Veterinary Medicine), Montreal PQ. 514-773-8521
Jette, Jean-Paul, *Librn,* University of Montreal, Veterinary Medical Library, Saint Hyacinthe PQ. 514-773-8521, Ext 258
Jetter, Chrystal, *Librn,* Anchorage Municipal Libraries (Spenard Community), Anchorage AK. 907-276-8086

Jetter, Margaret, *Assoc Prof,* Clarion State College, School of Library Science, PA. 814-226-2271
Jewell, John, *Ref & On-Line Servs,* Fresno County Free Library, Fresno CA. 209-488-3191
Jewell, Mary Ellen, *Librn,* Huron Road Hospital Library & Audiovisual Center, Library & Audiovisual Center, Cleveland OH. 216-761-3300, Ext 3206
Jewell, Mona D, *Libr Supervisor,* Ingersoll-Rand Co, Engineering Library, Nashua NH. 603-882-2711
Jewell, Thomas N, *Librn,* Waltham Public Library, Waltham MA. 617-893-1750
Jewell, Timothy, *Ref,* Bowling Green State University Library, Bowling Green OH. 419-372-2856
Jewkes, Peggy, *Ref & Doc,* Bloomsburg State College, Harvey A Andruss Library, Bloomsburg PA. 717-389-2716
Jimenez, Ivonne, *Librn,* Houston Public Library (Cliff Tuttle), Houston TX. 713-675-4656
Jimerson, Peggy, *ILL,* Jackson-Madison County Library, Jackson TN. 901-423-0225
Jimerson, Randall, *Archivist,* University of Connecticut Library, Storrs CT. 203-486-2219
Jio, Rachael, *Circ,* Maui Community College, Learning Resource Center, Kahului HI. 808-242-5433, 242-5498
Jiran, Mila, *Foreign Law,* University of Michigan (Law Library), Ann Arbor MI. 313-764-9322
Jiranek, June, *Librn,* Farmington Public Library, Farmington IA. 319-878-3702
Jiron, Sharon, *Librn,* Carnegie Public Library, Las Vegas NM. 505-454-1403
Juliano, Margaret C, *Librn,* Andrew Carnegie Free Library, Carnegie PA. 412-276-3456
Jo, Julitta, *Ser,* State University of New York (Health Sciences Center Library), East Setauket NY. 516-246-2512
Joachim, Martin, *Cat,* Indiana University at Bloomington, University Libraries, Bloomington IN. 812-337-3403
Job, Amy, *Cat,* William Paterson College of New Jersey, Sarah Byrd Askew Library, Wayne NJ. 201-595-2113
Job, Maris, *Ad,* Merrick Library, Merrick NY. 516-379-3476
Job, Susan, *Fine Arts & Humanities,* Hamline University, Bush Memorial Library, Saint Paul MN. 612-641-2373
Joba, Barbara, *Librn,* Adriance Memorial Library (Red Oak Mills), Poughkeepsie NY. 914-485-4797
Jobe, Ruth, *Ch,* Blount County Library, Maryville TN. 615-982-0981
Jobe, Shirley A, *Librn,* General Services Administration - National Archives & Records Service, John F Kennedy Library, Dorchester MA. 617-929-4500
Jobin, Odette, *Librn,* Winnipeg Public Library (Westwood), Winnipeg MB. 204-837-3136
Joback, Avis, *Ch,* Elisha D Smith Public Library, Menasha WI. 414-729-5166
Jobson, Betty, *Tech Serv & Acq,* West Georgia College Library, Carrollton GA. 404-834-1370
Jocelyn, Babette E, *Librn,* Pine Hill Public Library, Morton Memorial Library, Pine Hill NY. 914-254-4222
Jochim, Jack, *Bus & Urban Studies,* Loyola University of Chicago Libraries (Julia Deal Lewis Library), Chicago IL. 312-670-2875
Jochimson, Betty, *California & Local Hist,* San Bernardino Public Library, San Bernardino CA. 714-889-0264
Jockell, Mary-Lou, *Librn,* Grafton Public Library, Grafton VT. 802-843-2404
Joder, Richard F, *Dir,* Collier County Free Public Library, Naples FL. 813-262-4130, 261-8208
Joe, Linda, *Cat Products,* University of British Columbia Library, Vancouver BC. 604-228-3871
Joergensen, B, *District Librn,* Scarborough Public Library, Scarborough ON. 416-291-1991
Joergensen, B, *Librn,* Scarborough Public Library (Cedarbrae District), Scarborough ON. 416-431-2222
Johannessen, Joanne, *Librn,* Wertheim & Co Inc, Research Library, New York NY. 212-578-0200
Johanns, Donald L, *Dir,* Butte Community College Library, Oroville CA. 916-895-2541
Johansen, Kathleen, *Per,* Massachusetts Bay Community College Library, Wellesley MA. 617-237-1100, Ext 193

Johansen, Priscilla P, *Dir,* Lincoln-Lawrence-Franklin Regional Library, Brookhaven MS. 601-833-3369

Johansen, Saran, *Ref,* West Chicago Public Library, West Chicago IL. 312-231-1552

Johansen, Tove, *Ch,* Linden Free Public Library, Linden NJ. 201-486-3888

Johanson, Nancy, *Librn,* Prince George's County Memorial Library System (Surratts-Clinton Branch), Clinton MD. 301-868-9200

Johansonas, Irena, *Librn,* Acme-Cleveland Development Co Library, Cleveland OH. 216-473-0300

Johmann, Nancy, *Ref,* Bridgeport Public Library, Bridgeport CT. 203-576-7777

John, Annette, *Acq,* Washington & Lee University, The University Library, Lexington VA. 703-463-9111, Ext 403

John, Margaret D, *Tech Info,* Scott Paper Co (Research Library & Technical Information Service), Philadelphia PA. 215-521-5000, Ext 2416

John, Nancy R, *Asst Librn, Coll Control & Delivery Servs,* University of Illinois at Chicago Circle Library, Chicago IL. 312-996-2716

John, Ruth A, *Actg Librn,* Fairmount Public Library, Fairmount IN. 317-948-3177

Johns, Cecily, *Ref,* University of Cincinnati Libraries, Central Library, Cincinnati OH. 513-475-2218

Johns, Fabienne, *Librn,* Payne Theological Seminary, Reverdy C Ransom Memorial Library, Wilberforce OH. 513-376-2946

Johns, Frank, *Training Specialist,* Blue Cross & Blue Shield of Virginia Library, Richmond VA. 804-359-7000

Johns, Glenna, *Librn,* Southwest Arkansas Regional Library (Glenwood Branch), Glenwood AR. 501-777-4564

Johns, Gloria F L, *Librn,* Canada Life Assurance Co Library, Toronto ON. 416-597-1456

Johns, Helen, *Librn,* Belmont Public Library, Belmont NC. 704-825-5426

Johns, Jacqueline, *Librn,* Akron-Summit County Public Library (Maple Valley), Akron OH. 216-864-5721

Johns, Jean J, *Per,* University of Cincinnati Libraries, Central Library, Cincinnati OH. 513-475-2218

Johns, Mary, *Ad,* Kearney Public Library, Kearney NE. 308-237-5133

Johns, Mary M, *Dir,* Iowa Methodist Medical Center (Marjorie Gertrude Morrow Library), Des Moines IA. 515-283-6378

Johns, Michele, *Ref,* University of Illinois, Peoria Campus Library of the Health Sciences, Peoria IL. 309-671-3095

Johns, Mozelle, *Librn,* Hickman Public Library, Hickman KY. 502-236-2464

Johns, Mrs Doyle, *Librn,* Fulton Public Library (Hickman Public), Hickman KY. 502-236-2464

Johns, Verna, *Librn,* Davenport Public Library, Davenport WA. 509-725-4355

Johns, Jr, Claude J, *Dir,* University of Northern Colorado, James A Michener Library, Greeley CO. 303-351-2601

Johnsen, Marietta, *Librn,* Willmar Community College Library, Willmar MN. 612-235-2131, Ext 26

Johnsen, Ursula E, *Librn,* Penick Corp, Research Library, Orange NJ. 201-673-1335

Johnson, Alice, *Acq & Ref,* Ramsey County Public Library, Roseville MN. 612-631-0494

Johnson, Alice H, *Cat,* North Suburban District Library, Loves Park IL. 815-633-4247, 633-4248

Johnson, Alice K, *Librn,* PPG Industries, Inc, Chemical Division Library, New Martinsville WV. 304-455-2200, Ext 344

Johnson, Alice L, *Librn,* San Antonio Conservation Society Library, San Antonio TX. 512-224-6163

Johnson, Alice V, *Shut-in serv,* Salem Public Library, Salem MA. 617-744-0860

Johnson, Allan R, *Dir,* Briercrest Bible Institute, Archibald Library, Caronport SK. 306-756-2321, Ext 41

Johnson, Angie, *Librn,* Cato Township Public Library, Lakeview MI. 517-352-6274

Johnson, Anita K, *Dir,* Notre Dame College, Clara Fritzsche Library, Cleveland OH. 216-381-1680, Ext 59

Johnson, Anne, *Per,* Saint Mary's College, Alumnae Centennial Library, Notre Dame IN. 219-284-4242

Johnson, Antoinette, *Systs Develop,* Dallas Public Library, Dallas TX. 214-748-9071

Johnson, Arlene, *Dir,* Balmertown Public Library, Balmertown ON. 807-735-2110

Johnson, Audrey, *Acq,* Hoyt Library, Kingston PA. 717-287-2013

Johnson, Audrey, *Librn,* Lakeside Public Library, Wallace H Larson Memorial Library, Lakeside AZ. 602-336-2288

Johnson, Barbara, *Media & Cat,* Way Public Library, Perrysburg OH. 419-874-3135

Johnson, Barbara Coe, *Librn,* Harper Grace Hospitals (Harper Hospital Department of Libraries), Detroit MI. 313-494-8264

Johnson, Barbara M, *Dir,* Union County Public Library, Monroe NC. 704-282-8184

Johnson, Barry, *Syst Coordr,* Oakland University, Kresge Library, Rochester MI. 313-377-2486, 377-2474

Johnson, Bernice W, *Librn,* Brockton Enterprise-Times Library, Brockton MA. 617-586-6200

Johnson, Bessie, *Librn,* Sumpter Township Library, Toledo IL. 217-849-2072

Johnson, Bethry, *Cat,* Stearns-Roger Engineering Corp, Technical Library, Denver CO. 303-758-1122, Ext 2943

Johnson, Betty, *Librn,* Bridgeville Public Library, Bridgeville DE. 302-337-7401

Johnson, Betty D, *Tech Serv,* Stetson University, duPont-Ball Library, De Land FL. 904-734-4121, Ext 220

Johnson, Betty R, *Librn,* United States Army (Mississippi River Commission Technical Library), Vicksburg MS. 601-634-5880

Johnson, Bill, *Actg Dir,* Hart County Library, Hartwell GA. 404-376-4655

Johnson, Bruce, *Ref,* University of Michigan (Law Library), Ann Arbor MI. 313-764-9322

Johnson, C, *YA & Ref,* Ipswich Public Library, Ipswich MA. 617-356-4646

Johnson, Candice M, *Librn,* Sybron Corp, Pfaudler Division Technical Library, Henrietta NY. 716-334-1600, Ext 18

Johnson, Carol, *Acq & On-Line Servs,* Metropolitan Library System, Oklahoma City OK. 405-235-0571

Johnson, Carol, *Ch,* Mitchell Public Library, Mitchell SD. 605-996-6693

Johnson, Carol, *Chief, Analysis,* National Agricultural Library, Beltsville MD. 301-344-4248

Johnson, Carol, *Ser,* Saint John's University, Alcuin Library, Collegeville MN. 612-363-2119

Johnson, Carol, *Co-Dir,* South Saint Paul Public Library, South Saint Paul MN. 612-451-1093

Johnson, Carol, *Instr,* United States Department of Agriculture Graduate School, Certificate Program for Library Technicians, DC. 202-447-5885

Johnson, Carole, *Dir,* Richland College, Learning Resources Center, Dallas TX. 214-746-4460

Johnson, Carolyn, *Ch,* Fullerton City Library, Fullerton CA. 714-738-6333, Ext 301

Johnson, Carolyn E, *Dir,* Pearl River Public Library, Pearl River NY. 914-735-4084

Johnson, Cathy, *Librn,* TV Guide Library, Radnor PA. 215-293-8947

Johnson, Charles, *Media,* State University of New York Agricultural & Technical College at Canton, Southworth Library, Canton NY. 315-386-7229

Johnson, Charles B, *Dir,* Saint Thomas Seminary Library, Bloomfield CT. 203-242-5573, Ext 57

Johnson, Charlie, *Media,* Elizabeth City State University, G R Little Library, Elizabeth City NC. 919-335-0551, Ext 332

Johnson, Chris, *Librn,* Coca-Cola Co (Law Library), Atlanta GA. 404-898-2096

Johnson, Clifton, *Dir,* Amistad Research Center Library, New Orleans LA. 504-940-0239

Johnson, Corinne, *Actg Dir,* Southwestern Ohio Rural Libraries, (SWORL), OH. 513-382-2503

Johnson, Corlan Dokken, *Librn,* Napa State Hospital, Wrenshall A Oliver Professional Library, Imola CA. 707-255-6600, Ext 477

Johnson, Cynthia, *Ch,* Norfolk Public Library, Lewis & Clark Regional Library, Norfolk NE. 402-371-4590

Johnson, D R, *Librn & On-Line Servs,* Anoka-Ramsey Community College, Learning Media Center, Coon Rapids MN. 612-427-2600

Johnson, D Ronald, *Acq, Rare Bks & Spec Coll,* University of North Carolina at Wilmington, William Madison Randall Library, Wilmington NC. 919-791-4330, Ext 2270

Johnson, Dale, *Archivist & Special Coll,* University of Montana, Maureen & Mike Mansfield Library, Missoula MT. 406-243-6800

Johnson, David L, *Dir,* Parkland College, Learning Resource Center, Champaign IL. 217-351-2241

Johnson, Debra W, *Ad,* Arrowhead Library System, Janesville WI. 608-755-2490

Johnson, Della, *Librn,* Stanton Community Library, Stanton IA. 712-829-2290

Johnson, Delois D, *Assoc Dir,* University of Arkansas, Pine Bluff, Watson Memorial Library, Pine Bluff AR. 501-541-6825

Johnson, Derryl, *Librn,* Providence Public Library (Washington Park), Providence RI. 401-461-7348

Johnson, Diana, *Tech Serv,* Kirtland Community College Library, Roscommon MI. 517-275-5121

Johnson, Diana, *ILL,* Worcester Polytechnic Institute, George C Gordon Library, Worcester MA. 617-753-1411, Ext 410

Johnson, Diane, *Tech Serv & Cat,* Calloway County Public Library, Murray KY. 502-753-2288

Johnson, Diane, *Assoc Librn,* Frederick Cancer Research Center, Scientific Library, Frederick MD. 301-663-7261

Johnson, Diane, *Librn,* Olivet College Burrage Library (Barker Cawood Education & Media Center), Olivet MI. 616-749-7677

Johnson, Diane, *Info Servs,* State Library Commission of Iowa, Des Moines IA. 515-281-4102

Johnson, Donald, *Reader Serv,* College of William & Mary in Virginia, Earl Gregg Swem Library, Williamsburg VA. 804-253-4404

Johnson, Donald C, *Dir,* Valparaiso-Porter County Public Library System & Administrative Headquarters, Valparaiso IN. 219-462-0524

Johnson, Donna, *Dir,* Abbott-Northwestern Hospital, Health Sciences Library, Minneapolis MN. 612-874-4312

Johnson, Donna, *Librn,* Dallas Public Library (Martin Luther King Jr Library-Learning Center), Dallas TX. 214-421-4171

Johnson, Donna, *Librn,* Lamotte Township Library, Palestine IL. 618-586-5317

Johnson, Donna, *Dir,* Sister Kenny Institute Library, Minneapolis MN. 612-874-4312

Johnson, Doris, *Ref,* Adelphi University Library, Garden City NY. 516-294-8700

Johnson, Doris, *Librn,* Emmett Public Library, Emmett ID. 208-365-3941

Johnson, Doris, *Librn,* Southwestern Christian College Library, Hogan-Steward Learning Center, Terrell TX. 214-563-3341

Johnson, Dorothea A, *Media,* Saint Thomas Aquinas College Library, Sparkill NY. 359-9500 Ext 246, 245

Johnson, Dorothy, *Ref,* Mount Pleasant Public Library, Pleasantville NY. 914-769-0548

Johnson, Dorothy E, *Asst Dir & Area Coordr,* Bloomfield Public Library, Northwest Essex Area Library, Bloomfield NJ. 201-429-9292

Johnson, Dorothy E, *Librn,* Rowayton Free Public Library, Rowayton CT. 203-838-5038

Johnson, Dorothy J, *Librn,* Allen University, J S Flipper Library, Columbia SC. 803-254-4165, Ext 355

Johnson, Dorothy P, *Librn,* Mose Hudson Tapia Public Library, Bayou La Batre AL. 205-824-4213

Johnson, Dorothy T, *Program Head,* Cuyahoga Community College, Library-Media Technology, OH. 216-241-5966, Ext 223

Johnson, Duane F, *Dir,* Hutchinson Public Library, Hutchinson KS. 316-663-5441

Johnson, Duane F, *Librn,* South Central Kansas Library System, Hutchinson KS. 316-663-5441

Johnson, Edward, *Dir,* North Texas State University Library, Denton TX. 817-788-2411

Johnson, Edwin, *Asst Dir, ILL & Ref,* Valparaiso University, Henry F Moellering Memorial Library, Valparaiso IN. 219-464-5364

Johnson, Eileen, *Ch,* Sandhill Regional Library System, Rockingham NC. 919-997-3388

Johnson, Elaine B, *Librn,* Baltimore Police Department, Education & Training Division Library, Baltimore MD. 301-396-2518

JOHNSON

Johnson, Elaine D, *Asst Dir,* Danville Public Library, Danville VA. 804-799-5195

Johnson, Eleanor, *Doc,* Muncie-Center Township Public Library, Muncie IN. 317-288-9971

Johnson, Eleanor, *Field Librn,* University of Arizona Library (Arizona Health Sciences Center Library), Tucson AZ. 602-626-6121

Johnson, Eleanor G, *Librn,* Myers Memorial Library, Frewsburg NY. 716-569-5515

Johnson, Eleanor M, *Dir,* Rochester Public Library, Rochester WI. 414-534-3533

Johnson, Elizabeth, *Lit & Hist,* Library Association of Portland, Multnomah County Library, Portland OR. 503-223-7201, Ext 40

Johnson, Elizabeth, *Librn,* Northwest Alabama State Junior College Library, Phil Campbell AL. 205-993-5331

Johnson, Elizabeth, *Librn,* Sioux City Public Library (Smith Villa), Sioux City IA. 712-279-6179

Johnson, Elizabeth S, *Librn,* Fiduciary Trust Co of New York, Research Library, New York NY. 212-466-4100

Johnson, Ellen M, *Librn,* Federal Reserve Bank of Kansas City, Research Library, Kansas City MO. 816-881-2676

Johnson, Elsa L, *Librn,* Boys' Club of New York, Paul Morton Library, New York NY. 212-534-2661

Johnson, Emily, *Circ,* Hinsdale Public Library, Hinsdale IL. 312-986-1976

Johnson, Emily, *Ref,* West Florida Regional Library, Pensacola Public Library, Pensacola FL. 904-438-5479

Johnson, Emma, *Librn,* North Haverhill Town Library, Haverhill NH. 603-787-6204

Johnson, Eric, *Assoc Librn & Pub Servs,* University of New Haven, Marvin K Peterson Library, West Haven CT. 203-934-6321

Johnson, Erma, *Librn,* Ruthven Public Library, Ruthven IA. 712-837-4820

Johnson, Esther, *Librn,* University of California, Berkeley (Forestry), Berkeley CA. 415-642-2936

Johnson, Ethel, *Ch,* Public Library of Fort Wayne & Allen County, Fort Wayne IN. 219-424-7241

Johnson, Ethel, *Librn,* Southwest Arkansas Regional Library (Lockesburg Branch), Lockesburg AR. 501-777-4564

Johnson, Eunice, *Head,* University of Minnesota Libraries-Twin Cities (Public Administration), Minneapolis MN. 612-373-2892

Johnson, Evelyn, *Librn,* La Conner Memorial Library, La Conner WA. 206-466-3352

Johnson, Evelyn, *Bibliog Instr,* North Carolina Agricultural & Technical State University, F D Bluford Library, Greensboro NC. 919-379-7782, 379-7783

Johnson, Fannie, *Circ, Rare Bks & Spec Coll,* Lincoln University, Inman E Page Library, Jefferson City MO. 314-751-2325, Ext 326

Johnson, Floy, *Librn,* Greenville County Library (Berea), Greenville SC. 803-246-1695

Johnson, Fran, *Librn,* Maricopa Technical Community College, Library Resource Center, Phoenix AZ. 602-258-7251, Ext 313

Johnson, Gail W, *Librn,* New York Life Insurance Co (Reference Library), New York NY. 212-576-6737, 576-6738

Johnson, Gary, *Librn,* Birmingham Public & Jefferson County Free Library (Parke Memorial), Birmingham AL. 205-254-2551

Johnson, George, *Instr,* University of the District of Columbia-Mount Vernon Square Campus, Dept of Library Science & Instructional Systems Technology, DC. 202-727-2756, 727-2757 & 727-2758

Johnson, George C, *Dir,* Cross Trails Regional Library Service, Opp AL. 205-493-6423

Johnson, George T, *Librn,* Central State University, Hallie Q Brown Memorial Library, Wilberforce OH. 513-376-7212

Johnson, Georgina, *Librn,* Tabor College Library, Hillsboro KS. 316-947-3121

Johnson, Gerald, *Librn,* University of Maryland-Eastern Shore (Music Learning Resources), Princess Anne MD. 301-651-2200, Ext 304

Johnson, Geraldine, *Circ,* Free Public Library of Summit, Summit NJ. 201-273-0350

Johnson, Geraldine, *Tech Serv,* New City Free Library, New City NY. 914-634-4997

Johnson, Geraldine, *Dir,* United States Tongue Point-Job Corps, Instructional Media Center, Astoria OR. 503-325-2131, Ext 387, 388

Johnson, Glenn H, *Librn,* Western New England College, John D Churchill Library, Springfield MA. 413-782-3111, Ext 457

Johnson, Gloria, *Asst Librs,* East Central Junior College, Burton Library, Decatur MS. 601-635-2111, Ext 219

Johnson, Gloria B, *Librn,* Eastern Shore Public Library (Northampton Memorial Library), Cape Charles VA. 804-331-1300

Johnson, Guela M, *Librn,* University of Washington Libraries (Social Work), Seattle WA. 206-543-5742

Johnson, H Joan, *Instr,* McPherson College, Audiovisual Communications Program, KS. 316-241-5156

Johnson, H Thayne, *Assoc Prof,* Brigham Young University, School of Library & Information Sciences, UT. 801-378-2976

Johnson, Harry A, *Chairperson,* Virginia State College, Dept of Library Science & Educational Media, VA. 804-520-5000

Johnson, Hazel, *Librn,* Columbia-Lafayette-Ouachita-Calhoun Regional Library (Lewisville Branch), Lewisville AR. 501-234-1991

Johnson, Hazel M, *Librn,* Choctawhatchee Regional Library (Abbeville Memorial), Abbeville AL. 205-585-2818

Johnson, Helen, *Librn,* Kenilworth Historical Society, Kilner Library, Kenilworth IL. 312-251-2565

Johnson, Helen, *Librn,* Saint Martin's Evangelical Lutheran Church Library, Austin TX. 512-476-6757

Johnson, Herbert, *Dir Media Ctr,* McPherson College, Audiovisual Communications Program, KS. 316-241-5156

Johnson, Herbert, *Media,* McPherson College, Miller Library, McPherson KS. 316-241-0731, Ext 67

Johnson, Herbert F, *Dir,* Emory University Libraries (General Libraries), Atlanta GA. 404-329-6861

Johnson, Hilary, *Ser,* College of Physicians of Philadelphia Library, Philadelphia PA. 215-561-6050

Johnson, Irene, *ILL,* Logan-Hocking County District Library, Logan OH. 614-385-2348

Johnson, Irma Y, *Librn,* Massachusetts Institute of Technology Libraries (Science), Cambridge MA. 617-253-5685

Johnson, Iva, *Br Coordr,* Cooke County Library, Gainesville TX. 817-665-2401

Johnson, Iva S, *Librn,* Everett Free Library, Everett PA. 814-652-5922

Johnson, J, *Librn,* University of Southern California (Government Documents), Los Angeles CA. 213-743-5192

Johnson, J Peter, *Dir,* Middle Island Public Library, Middle Island NY. 516-924-4160

Johnson, J W H, *Commun Servs,* Queen's University at Kingston (Law), Kingston ON. 613-547-5934

Johnson, Jacqueline, *Br Coordr,* Kansas City Public Library, Kansas City MO. 816-221-2685

Johnson, Jacqueline, *Librn,* Kansas City Public Library (Boys Club), Kansas City MO. 816-861-6300

Johnson, Jacqueline, *Librn,* Kansas City Public Library (Clymer), Kansas City MO. 816-471-2076

Johnson, Jacqueline, *Librn,* Kansas City Public Library (Linwood Multi-Purpose), Kansas City MO. 816-924-6900

Johnson, Jacquelyn, *Librn,* Nicholson Memorial Public Library (Broughton Branch), Longview TX. 214-753-9074

Johnson, James, *Spec Coll,* Memphis-Shelby County Public Library & Information Center, Memphis TN. 901-528-2950

Johnson, James, *Librn,* Memphis-Shelby County Public Library & Information Center (History & Travel), Memphis TN. 901-528-2950

Johnson, James P, *Chief Librn,* Howard University Libraries (Moorland-Spingarn Research Center Library), Washington DC. 202-636-7239

Johnson, Jan, *Librn,* Daviess County Library, Gallatin MO. 816-663-3222

Johnson, Jan, *Secy,* Lynchburg Area Library Cooperative, VA. 804-846-7392, Ext 242

Johnson, Jan, *Acq,* Randolph-Macon Woman's College, Lipscomb Library, Lynchburg VA. 804-846-7392, Ext 242

Johnson, Jane, *ILL,* California State College, Stanislaus Library, Turlock CA. 209-633-2232

Johnson, Jane G, *Acq,* Georgia Southern College Library, Statesboro GA. 912-681-5115

Johnson, Janice Sims, *Ref & Bibliog Instr,* Tidewater Community College, Virginia Beach Campus Library, Virginia Beach VA. 804-427-3070, Ext 123, 126

Johnson, Jean, *Librn,* Bath County Memorial Library, Owingsville KY. 606-674-2531

Johnson, Jean, *Ref,* Laurel-Jones County Library, Laurel MS. 601-428-4313

Johnson, Jean S, *Assoc Dir for Admin Servs,* University of Wyoming, William Robertson Coe Library, Laramie WY. 307-766-3279

Johnson, Jeanette, *Coordr,* Court of Civil Appeals, Fifth Supreme Judicial District Law Library, Dallas TX. 214-749-8381

Johnson, Jeannette, *YA,* Augusta Regional Library, Augusta-Richmond County Public Library, Augusta GA. 404-724-1871

Johnson, Jeannie Honhart, *Librn,* Zumbrota Public Library, Carnegie Public Library, Zumbrota MN. 507-732-5211

Johnson, Jerry, *Ch,* Frederick County Public Library, Frederick MD. 301-694-1613

Johnson, Jerry, *Librn,* University of South Dakota (School of Business, Business Research Bureau), Vermillion SD. 605-677-5287

Johnson, Joan, *Asst Librn,* McPherson College, Miller Library, McPherson KS. 316-241-0731, Ext 67

Johnson, JoAnn, *Chief Librn,* Environmental Protection Agency, Environmental Research Center Library, Cincinnati OH. 513-684-7701

Johnson, Joanne D, *Dir,* Sandwich Township Public Library, Sandwich IL. 815-786-8308

Johnson, John, *Doc,* Kansas State University, Farrell Library, Manhattan KS. 913-532-6516

Johnson, Joy A, *Dir,* Community Public Library, Saint Marys OH. 419-394-4209

Johnson, Joyce, *AV,* Clermont County Public Library, Batavia OH. 513-732-2128

Johnson, Joyce, *Librn,* Mary E Seymour Memorial Free Library (Cassadaga Branch), Cassadaga NY. 716-595-3323

Johnson, Juanita, *Librn,* Eastern Oklahoma State College, Raymond Gary Library, Wilburton OK. 918-465-2361

Johnson, Juanita B, *Reader Serv,* Miami Dade Community College (New World Center Campus), Miami FL. 305-577-6890

Johnson, Judy, *ILL,* Albion College, Stockwell Memorial Library, Albion MI. 517-629-5511, Ext 285

Johnson, Judy, *ILL,* Panhandle Regional Library System, Coeur d'Alene ID. 208-772-7456

Johnson, Julia, *Librn,* Marsh & McLennan, Inc Information Center, New York NY. 212-997-7800

Johnson, Julie M, *Assoc Med Libr,* University of South Carolina (School of Medicine Library), Columbia SC. 803-777-4858

Johnson, Justine, *Asst Dir,* Olathe Public Library, Olathe KS. 913-764-2259

Johnson, K, *Archives,* Trent University, Thomas J Bata Library, Peterborough ON. 705-748-1550

Johnson, K E, *Supvr Libr Servs,* Varian Associates, Technical Library, Palo Alto CA. 415-493-4000, Ext 2824

Johnson, K Paul, *Librn,* Chesapeake Public Library (Hillard), Chesapeake VA. 804-485-1543

Johnson, K Suzanne, *Librn,* Colorado State University (Veterinary Teaching Hospital Branch Library), Fort Collins CO. 303-491-7101

Johnson, Karen, *Librn,* Grand Isle Free Library, Grand Isle VT. 802-372-8816

Johnson, Karl, *Coordr,* Pima Community College (East Education Center), Tucson AZ. 602-884-6590

Johnson, Karla, *Tech Serv,* Helen Matthes Library, Effingham IL. 217-342-2464

Johnson, Katharine E, *Cat,* Christopher Newport College, Captain John Smith Library, Newport News VA. 804-599-7130

Johnson, Kathleen, *African Anthrop & Ethnomusicology,* Kelso Public Library, Kelso WA. 206-423-8110

Johnson, Kathleen A, *Librn,* Kelso Public Library, Kelso WA. 206-423-8110

Johnson, Kathryn, *Acq,* Southern University Library, Baton Rouge LA. 504-771-4990, 771-4991, 771-4992

Johnson, Kerry A, *Asst Prof,* University of Maryland, College of Library & Information Services, MD. 301-454-5441

Johnson, Kordillia C, *Rare Bks,* University of Wisconsin-Platteville, Elton S Karrmann Library, Platteville WI. 608-342-1688

Johnson, Kordillia C, *Soc Sci & Humanities,* University of Wisconsin-Platteville, Elton S Karrmann Library, Platteville WI. 608-342-1688

Johnson, Kris, *Librn,* University of Minnesota Libraries-Twin Cities (Architecture), Minneapolis MN. 612-373-2203

Johnson, L Louise, *Librn,* De Soto County Public Library, Arcadia FL. 813-494-2305

Johnson, Laura, *Extension,* Indiana State Library, Indianapolis IN. 317-232-3675

Johnson, Lawrence W, *Dir,* Frederick County Planning Commission Library, Frederick MD. 301-663-8300

Johnson, Leonard R, *Dir,* Suffolk County Community College (Central Library & AV Technical Services), Selden NY. 516-233-5181

Johnson, Lillian, *ILL & Ref,* Salem Free Public Library, Salem NJ. 609-935-0526

Johnson, Linda, *Ch,* Alsip-Merrionette Park Library, Alsip IL. 312-371-5666

Johnson, Linda, *Librn, On-Line Servs & Bibliog Instr,* Raltech Scientific Services, Inc Library, Madison WI. 608-241-4471, Ext 397

Johnson, Linea, *Per,* Judson College, Benjamin P Browne Library, Elgin IL. 312-695-2500, Ext 550-553

Johnson, Liz, *Librn,* Energy Resources Conservation Board Library, Calgary AB. 403-261-8242

Johnson, Lorraine, *Ch,* Evergreen Park Public Library, Evergreen Park IL. 312-422-8522

Johnson, Louise, *Librn,* Texas County Library, Houston MO. 417-967-2258

Johnson, Lyle C, *Librn,* Acadia Parish Library, Crowley LA. 318-788-1880

Johnson, M Douglas, *On-Line Servs,* United States Air Force Academy Library, United States Air Force Academy CO. 303-472-2590

Johnson, M Jean, *Librn,* Action for Children's Television Resource Library, Newtonville MA. 617-527-7870

Johnson, M Malinda, *Admin Librn,* United States Army (Fort Stewart - Hunter Army Airfield Library System), Fort Stewart GA. 912-767-2260, 767-2828

Johnson, Mable, *Librn,* Public Library of Johnston County & Smithfield (Mary Duncan Public), Benson NC. 919-894-3724

Johnson, Maggie, *Doc,* Missouri State Library, Jefferson City MO. 314-751-4214

Johnson, Marcella, *Asst Librn,* Lakota Public Library, Lakota IA. 515-886-2312

Johnson, Margaret, *Coll Proc Div,* University of Minnesota, Saint Paul Campus Libraries, Saint Paul MN. 612-373-0904

Johnson, Margaret, *Librn,* Van Buren County Library (Bangor Branch), Bangor MI. 616-427-8810

Johnson, Margaret Ann, *ILL,* University of Arkansas for Medical Sciences Library, Little Rock AR. 501-661-5980

Johnson, Margaret L, *Assoc Univ Librn & Tech Servs,* University of Hawaii (University of Hawaii Library), Honolulu HI. 808-948-7205

Johnson, Margery, *Media & Bibliog Instr,* Clarion State College, Rena M Carlson Library, Clarion PA. 814-226-2343

Johnson, Margery, *Ref,* Eisenhower College of the Rochester Institute of Technology, Ellis Slater Library, Seneca Falls NY. 315-568-7171

Johnson, Margot, *Tech Serv & Acq,* Franklin Pierce College Library, Rindge NH. 603-899-5111, Ext 215, 216

Johnson, Marguerite H, *Librn,* Palm Beach County Law Library, West Palm Beach FL. 305-837-2928

Johnson, Marianne, *AV,* State University of New York, College at Old Westbury Library, Old Westbury NY. 516-876-3156, 876-3152

Johnson, Marie, *Librn,* Marysville Public Library (Raymond Public), Raymond OH. 513-246-5155

Johnson, Marilyn, *Librn,* Shell Oil Co, Information & Library Services, Houston TX. 713-241-5433

Johnson, Marilyn S, *Acq & Br Coordr,* Muscle Shoals Regional Library System, Florence AL. 205-764-6563

Johnson, Marion, *Exhibits & Libr Asns Laison,* Gustavus Adolphus College, Folke Bernadotte Memorial Library, Saint Peter MN. 507-931-4300, Ext 2301

Johnson, Marion, *Asst Librn,* West Point Public Library, West Point NE. 402-372-3831

Johnson, Marion E, *Librn,* Environment Canada, Forest Research, Vancouver BC. 604-666-8941

Johnson, Marion M, *Libr Develop,* North Carolina Department of Cultural Resources, Division of State Library, North Carolina State Library, Raleigh NC. 919-733-2570

Johnson, Marjorie, *Dir,* New Castle-Henry County Public Library, New Castle IN. 317-529-0362

Johnson, Marjorie J, *Cat,* Waynesboro Public Library, Waynesboro VA. 703-942-6173

Johnson, Marlys J, *Librn,* Fluidyne Engineering Corp Library, Minneapolis MN. 612-544-2721, Ext 269

Johnson, Martha, *On-Line Servs,* New Bedford Free Public Library, Subregional Headquarters for Eastern Massachusetts Regional Library System, New Bedford MA. 617-999-6291

Johnson, Mary, *Librn,* Aurora Memorial Library, Aurora OH. 216-562-6502

Johnson, Mary, *Librn,* Corpus Christi Public Libraries (Parkdale), Corpus Christi TX. 512-853-9961

Johnson, Mary, *Br Coordr,* Kitsap Regional Library, Bremerton WA. 206-377-7601

Johnson, Mary, *Librn,* Portage County District Library (Aurora), Hiram OH. 216-562-6502

Johnson, Mary, *Librn,* Public Library of Nashville & Davidson County (Old Hickory Branch), Old Hickory TN. 615-847-5207

Johnson, Mary, *Librn,* Varina Public Library, Varina IA. 712-288-6233

Johnson, Mary Ann, *Dir,* Baldwin County Library System, Robertsdale AL. 205-947-7632

Johnson, Mary E, *Librn,* Forest History Society Library, Santa Cruz CA. 408-426-3770

Johnson, Mary E, *Asst Librn & Ref,* Midwestern State University, George Moffett Library, Wichita Falls TX. 817-692-6611, Ext 204

Johnson, Mary Frances, *Spanish Lang, Children's Bks,* Redwood City Public Library, Redwood City CA. 415-369-6251, Ext 288

Johnson, Mary Frances, *Librn,* Redwood City Public Library (Fair Oaks), Redwood City CA. 415-364-5050

Johnson, Mary G, *Librn,* Cold Spring Harbor Library, Cold Spring Harbor NY. 516-692-6820

Johnson, Mary H, *Librn,* Mental Health Association of Westchester County Library, White Plains NY. 914-949-6741

Johnson, Mary Lee C, *Librn,* Milltown Public Library, Milltown WI. 715-825-3258

Johnson, Mary P, *Librn,* Brown County Library (Fort Howard), Green Bay WI. 414-497-3446

Johnson, Maurine, *Librn,* Manti City Library, Manti UT. 801-835-2201

Johnson, Merrill, *Ref,* Klamath County Library, Klamath Falls OR. 503-882-8894

Johnson, Michelle, *Librn,* Digital Equipment Corp, Marlboro Library, Marlborough MA. 617-481-9511, Ext 5040

Johnson, Mildred, *Librn,* Holmes County Library (Pickens Public), Pickens MS. 601-468-2391

Johnson, Mildred, *Librn,* Mid-Mississippi Regional Library System (Linda Farabee Library), Pickens MS. 601-468-2391

Johnson, Mildred, *Rare Bks,* San Bernardino Public Library, San Bernardino CA. 714-889-0264

Johnson, Mrs Charles, *Librn,* Marshall Community Library, Marshall WI. 414-655-3123

Johnson, Mrs Elton, *Librn,* Commerce Public Library, Commerce TX. 214-886-6858

Johnson, Myrtle I, *Librn,* Gordon Public Library, Gordon NE. 308-282-1198

Johnson, Nan, *Librn,* Nelson County Public Library (New Haven Branch), New Haven KY. 502-348-3714

Johnson, Nan A, *Librn,* Tufts University (Edwin Ginn Library), Medford MA. 617-628-5000, Ext 235

Johnson, Nancy, *Ser,* George S Houston Memorial Library, Dothan AL. 205-793-9767

Johnson, Naomi, *Ad,* Sumter County Library, Sumter SC. 803-773-7273

Johnson, Neal, *Dir & Media,* Cedar Falls Public Library, Cedar Falls IA. 319-266-2629

Johnson, Nell, *Tech Serv, Acq & Cat,* Ottawa University, Myers Library, Ottawa KS. 913-242-5200, Ext 317

Johnson, Noel W, *Research Rpts,* Naval Postgraduate School, Dudley Knox Library, Monterey CA. 408-646-2341

Johnson, Oneita, *Dir,* Pratt Public Library, Pratt KS. 316-672-3041

Johnson, Pat, *Asst Dir, Media & Tech Serv,* Butler Carnegie Library, Butler IN. 219-868-2351

Johnson, Pat M, *Librn, On-Line Servs & Bibliog Instr,* McClelland Engineers, Corporate Library, Houston TX. 713-772-3701, Ext 252

Johnson, Patricia, *ILL,* Arapahoe Regional Library District, Littleton CO. 303-798-2444

Johnson, Patricia, *Cat,* Gonzaga University (Law Library), Spokane WA. 509-328-4220, Ext 3781

Johnson, Patricia, *Tech Serv,* Middle Island Public Library, Middle Island NY. 516-924-4160

Johnson, Patricia, *Ref & ILL,* Sioux Falls Public Library, Sioux Falls SD. 605 339 7081

Johnson, Patricia, *Br Coordr,* Waterford Township Public Library, Pontiac MI. 313-674-4831

Johnson, Patricia, *Librn,* Waterford Township Public Library (Waterford Township Branch), Drayton Plains MI. 313-673-6220

Johnson, Patricia A, *Librn,* Pueblo Library District (Belmont), Pueblo CO. 303-544-5040

Johnson, Patricia J, *Asst Librn,* Northwestern Mutual Life Insurance Co (Reference Library), Milwaukee WI. 414-271-1444, Ext 3381 & 4076

Johnson, Patrick, *Head,* University of Minnesota Libraries-Twin Cities (Walter Reserve & Storage), Minneapolis MN. 612-373-2889

Johnson, Patti J, *Assoc Dir,* Georgia Association of Educators, Materials Center, Decatur GA. 404-289-5867, Ext 145

Johnson, Paul, *Info Servs Dir,* Rolling Prairie Library System, Decatur IL. 217-429-2586

Johnson, Paul H, *Librn,* United States Coast Guard Academy Library, New London CT. 203-443-8463, Ext 292

Johnson, Paula, *ILL,* National Marine Fisheries Service, Fisheries Research Library, Auke Bay AK. 907-789-7231

Johnson, Paula, *Librn,* Poland Public Library, Poland NY. 315-826-3112

Johnson, Peter, *Latin Am, Spain & Portugal,* Princeton University Library, Princeton NJ. 609-452-3180

Johnson, Phillip, *Librn,* Muskegon County Library (Muskegon Heights), Muskegon Heights MI. 616-733-4160

Johnson, Priscilla, *Librn,* Westwood Public Library (Islington), Westwood MA. 617-326-5914

Johnson, R, *Asst Dir,* Lisle Library District, Lisle IL. 312-971-1675

Johnson, R M, *Librn,* Canada Cement La Farge Ltd, Advertising Dept Library, Montreal PQ. 514-861-1411

Johnson, Rae Dell S, *Librn,* Richmond City Library, Richmond UT. 801-258-2092

Johnson, Raymond, *Asst Prof,* Mankato State College, Library Media Education, MN. 507-389-1965

Johnson, Rebecca, *Librn,* Texas Advisory Commission on Intergovernmental Relations, Information Center, Austin TX. 512-475-3728

Johnson, Reta, *Deputy Librn,* Nebraska State Library, Lincoln NE. 402-432-2922

Johnson, Richard C, *Bibliogr Am Hist & Lit,* Newberry Library, Chicago IL. 312-943-9090

Johnson, Richard D, *Dir,* State University of New York, College at Oneonta, James M Milne Library, Oneonta NY. 607-431-2723

Johnson, Richard L, *Tech Serv, Acq & Cat,* Grossmont College, Lewis F Smith Learning Resource Center Library, El Cajon CA. 714-465-1700, Ext 333, 334

Johnson, Richardia S, *Librn,* Staunton Public Library, Fannie Bayly King Library, Staunton VA. 703-886-7231

Johnson, Robert, *Head,* University of Cincinnati Libraries (College-Conservatory of Music), Cincinnati OH. 513-475-4471

Johnson, Robert K, *Prof,* University of Arizona, Graduate Library School, AZ. 602-626-3565

Johnson, Roger M, *In Charge,* Cleveland Public Library (Children's Literature), Cleveland OH. 216-623-2835

Johnson, Ronald D, *Dir,* Dana College, C A Dana-Life Library, Blair NE. 402-426-4101, Ext 119

JOHNSON

Johnson, Rose, *In Charge,* Albert-Westmorland-Kent Regional Library (Port Elgin Public), Port Elgin NB. 506-389-2631

Johnson, Rose, *ILL,* Center Moriches Free Public Library, Center Moriches NY. 516-878-0940

Johnson, Roy C, *Librn,* New York University (John & Bertha E Waldman Memorial Library), New York NY. 212-481-5874

Johnson, Rudy, *Ref,* University of Minnesota, Duluth, Duluth MN. 218-726-8100

Johnson, Ruth, *Ref,* Amarillo College, Learning Resource Center, Amarillo TX. 806-376-5111, Ext 2420

Johnson, Ruth, *Dir,* Amarillo College, Library Technical Assistant Program, TX. 806-376-5111, Ext 2424

Johnson, Ruth, *Librn,* Dyckman Free Library, Sleepy Eye MN. 507-794-7655

Johnson, Ruth, *Chief Comm Librs,* Minneapolis Public Library & Information Center, Minneapolis MN. 612-372-6500

Johnson, Ruth Ann, *Dir,* Cushing Public Library, Cushing OK. 918-225-4188

Johnson, Ruth E, *Dir,* MacKenzie Memorial Public Library, Madison OH. 216-428-2189

Johnson, Ruth H, *Librn,* Babcock & Wilcox Co, Nuclear Power Generation Division Technical Library, Lynchburg VA. 804-384-5111, Ext 2475

Johnson, Ruth R, *School Servs,* Burlington County Library, Mount Holly NJ. 609-267-9660

Johnson, Sallie, *Librn,* Memphis-Shelby County Public Library & Information Center (Science, Business, Social Sciences), Memphis TN. 901-528-2950

Johnson, Sandra, *Tech Serv,* Bossier Parish Public Library, Benton LA. 318-965-2751

Johnson, Sandra, *Librn,* Crowley Ridge Regional Library (Library for the Blind & Physically Handicapped), Jonesboro AR. 501-935-5133

Johnson, Sandra K, *Clerk,* Lawrence County Bar & Law Library Association, Ironton OH. 614-532-0582

Johnson, Sharon, *Chief Librn,* Veterans Administration, General & Medical Library, Albuquerque NM. 505-265-1711, Ext 2248

Johnson, Shirley, *Acq,* Illinois Wesleyan University Library, Bloomington IL. 309-556-3172

Johnson, Shirley, *In Charge,* Norfolk Public Library (Blyden), Norfolk VA. 804-441-2852

Johnson, Shirley, *State Doc Dep,* State Library Commission of Iowa, Des Moines IA. 515-281-4102

Johnson, Shirley A, *Acq,* Toledo-Lucas County Public Library, Toledo OH. 419-255-7055

Johnson, Sigrid, *Icelandic,* University of Manitoba Libraries, Winnipeg MB. 204-474-9881

Johnson, Sister Dorothy, *Dir,* Saint Francis Seminary, Salzmann Library, Milwaukee WI. 414-483-1979

Johnson, Sister Marie Inez, *Tech Serv & Acq,* College of Saint Catherine, Saint Catherine Library, Saint Paul MN. 612-690-6650

Johnson, Stella, *Librn,* Moscow-Latah County Library System (Troy Branch), Troy ID. 208-835-4311

Johnson, Stephen C, *Instr,* Illinois State University, Department of Information Sciences, IL. 309-438-3671

Johnson, Sue, *Non-Print Tech Serv & On-Line Servs,* Atlantic Community College, Daniel Leeds Learning Resources Center, Mays Landing NJ. 625-1111 & 646-4950

Johnson, Susan, *ILL & Ref,* Fort McMurray Public Library, Fort McMurray AB. 403-743-2121

Johnson, Susan, *Asst Dir,* Multnomah School of the Bible, John & Mary Mitchell Library, Portland OR. 503-255-0332, Ext 362

Johnson, Susan, *Bibliog Instr,* Pillsbury Company (Main Office Library), Minneapolis MN. 612-330-4047

Johnson, Susan, *Librn,* Saskatchewan Department of Labour (Occupational Health & Safety Division Library), Regina SK. 306-565-4494

Johnson, Susan, *Personnel Officer,* Washington State Library, Olympia WA. 206-753-5592

Johnson, Suzanne, *Ch,* Bryan Public Library, Bryan OH. 419-636-2937

Johnson, Suzanne, *Biomed Sci,* Colorado State University, William E Morgan Library, Fort Collins CO. 303-491-5911

Johnson, Theodora L, *Dir,* Richmond Public Library, Richmond CA. 415-231-2119

Johnson, Theodore E, *Dir,* United Society of Shakers Library, Poland Spring ME. 207-926-4865

Johnson, Timothy V, *African-Am Studies,* Northwestern University Library, Evanston IL. 312-492-7658

Johnson, Tom, *AV,* Northeastern Oklahoma State University, John Vaughan Library-Learning Resource Center, Tahlequah OK. 918-456-5511, Ext 385

Johnson, Velma, *Circ,* Sturgis Library, Barnstable MA. 617-362-6636

Johnson, Vera, *Pub Servs,* Victoria College - University of Houston Victoria Campus Library, Victoria TX. 512-575-7436

Johnson, Vernon, *Librn,* School for the Deaf Library, Devils Lake ND. 701-662-5113

Johnson, Veronica, *Librn,* Argonne National Laboratory (Materials Science), Argonne IL. 312-972-4936

Johnson, Vickie, *Circ,* Bentley College, Solomon R Baker Library, Waltham MA. 617-891-2231

Johnson, Viola, *Librn,* Fort Vancouver Regional Library (North Bonneville Community), North Bonneville WA. 509-427-8182

Johnson, Viola, *ILL, Circ & Per,* Rockford Public Library, Rockford IL. 815-965-6731

Johnson, Violet, *Librn,* Sewickley Township Library, Herminie PA. 412-446-9940

Johnson, Virginia, *Tech Serv,* Taunton Public Library, Subregional Headquarters for Eastern Massachusetts Regional Library System, Taunton MA. 617-823-3570

Johnson, Vivian A, *Dir,* Buhl-Henderson Community Library, Sharon PA. 412-981-4360

Johnson, W Duane, *Asst Prof,* University of Northern Iowa, Dept of Library Science, IA. 319-273-2050

Johnson, W Duane, *Librn,* Walden University, Institute for Advanced Studies Library, Naples FL. 813-261-7277

Johnson, W Howard, *Dir,* Divine Word Seminary, Saint Augustine's Library, Bay Saint Louis MS. 601-467-4322

Johnson, Walter, *Dir,* Huntington Beach Library, Information & Cultural Resource Center, Huntington Beach CA. 714-842-4481

Johnson, Walter C, *Asst Dir,* Rosenbach Museum & Library, Philadelphia PA. 215-732-1600

Johnson, Walter J, *Pres,* Walter J Johnson Inc Library, Norwood NJ. 201-767-1303

Johnson, Wanda, *Librn,* Los Angeles Public Library System (Mark Twain), Los Angeles CA. 213-755-4088

Johnson, Wayne H, *State Librn,* Wyoming State Library, Cheyenne WY. 307-777-7281

Johnson, William, *Bus, Labor, Govt,* Akron-Summit County Public Library, Akron OH. 216-762-7621

Johnson, William R, *Art & Music,* Brooklyn Public Library (Central Library), Brooklyn NY. 212-780-7712

Johnson, Yvonne, *Asst Librn,* Morgan, Lewis & Bockius Library, New York NY. 212-980-4562

Johnson, Jr, James B, *Asst Dir,* South Carolina State Library, Columbia SC. 803-758-3181

Johnson, Jr, Mrs Sam E, *Actg Librn,* Saint Matthews Episcopal Cathedral Library, Dallas TX. 214-823-8134

Johnson-Lally, Mary, *Ch,* Medford Public Library, Medford MA. 617-395-7950

Johnsson, Gilford, *Dir,* Nobles County Library & Information Center, Worthington MN. 507-372-2981

Johnston, A W, *Librn,* Addiction Research Foundation Library, Toronto ON. 416-595-6144

Johnston, Agnes, *Ch,* Roscoe Free Library, Roscoe NY. 607-498-5574

Johnston, Betty, *Librn,* Muskegon County Library (Dalton), Twin Lake MI. 616-828-4188

Johnston, Bruce, *Librn,* Eye & Ear Hospital of Pittsburgh, Blair-Lippincott Library, Pittsburgh PA. 412-647-2287, 647-2288

Johnston, Cecil, *Rare Bks,* International University Library, Kansas City MO. 816-931-6374

Johnston, Charles R, *Asst Dir Admin Servs,* Vanderbilt University Library, Nashville TN. 615-322-2834

Johnston, Cora, *Librn,* Moss Memorial Library, Hayesville NC. 704-389-8401

Johnston, Dinnie K, *Librn,* Vicksburg Hospital Medical Library, Vicksburg MS. 601-636-2611, Ext 158

Johnston, Drynda, *Librn,* University of Pittsburgh (Langley Life Sciences), Pittsburgh PA. 412-642-4489

Johnston, E Lee, *ILL & Ref,* Walla Walla College, Peterson Memorial Library, College Place WA. 509-527-2133

Johnston, Ellen A, *Ch,* Alcan Aluminum Ltd, Group Information Centre, Montreal PQ. 514-877-2610

Johnston, Gail, *ILL,* Nevada County Library, Nevada City CA. 916-265-2461, Ext 244

Johnston, Gail W, *Dir,* Rehoboth Beach Public Library, Rehoboth Beach DE. 302-227-8044

Johnston, George F, *Asst Librn,* Covenant Theological Seminary, J Oliver Buswell Jr Library, Saint Louis MO. 314-434-4044

Johnston, Gladys, *Librn,* New Mexico Rehabilitation Center Library, Roswell NM. 505-347-5491

Johnston, H G, *Dir,* Baldwin Public Library, Birmingham MI. 313-647-1700

Johnston, H G, *Dir,* Bloomfield Township Public Library, Bloomfield Hills MI. 313-642-5800

Johnston, J, *On-Line Servs,* Calgary Public Library, Calgary AB. 403-268-2880

Johnston, James R, *Dir,* Joliet Public Library, Joliet IL. 815-727-4726

Johnston, Janet, *Ch,* Denison Public Library, Denison TX. 214-465-1797

Johnston, Janet, *Asst Dir,* Oceanside Public Library, Oceanside CA. 714-439-7330

Johnston, John Wayne, *Acq,* International University Library, Kansas City MO. 816-931-6374

Johnston, Joyce, *Librn,* Bruce County Public Library, Port Elgin ON. 519-832-2181

Johnston, Katherine, *Libr Clerk,* Cornwall Public Library (Cornwall), Cornwall NY. 914-534-8232

Johnston, Leta, *Librn,* Wellsville Public Library, Wellsville MO. 314-684-2090

Johnston, Marliss M, *Librn,* Mankato Area Vocational-Technical Institute Library, Mankato MN. 507-625-3441, Ext 45

Johnston, Maxine, *Dir,* Lamar University, Mary & John Gray Library, Beaumont TX. 713-838-8313

Johnston, Midge, *Bus Mgr, Badland Natural Hist Asn,* Badlands National Monument Library, Badlands Natural History Association, Interior SD. 605-433-5361

Johnston, Nancy B, *Ch,* Stark County District Library, Canton OH. 216-452-0665, Ext 31

Johnston, Norma, *Librn,* McGill University Libraries (Religious Studies), Montreal PQ. 514-392-4832

Johnston, Rebecca, *Cat,* Wake Forest University (Bowman Gray School of Medicine Library), Winston-Salem NC. 919-727-4691

Johnston, Robert, *Ref,* Allan Hancock Joint Community College Library, Santa Maria CA. 805-922-6966, Ext 215, 242

Johnston, Robert C, *Ref & Commun Servs,* Warren Library Association, Warren Library, Warren PA. 814-723-4650

Johnston, Ron, *Bkmobile Coordr,* Oakville Public Library, Oakville ON. 416-845-3405

Johnston, Ruby B, *Librn,* Pearisburg Public Library, Pearisburg VA. 703-921-2556

Johnston, S, *Librn,* University of Toronto Libraries (Dept of Computer Science), Toronto ON. 416-978-2987

Johnston, Thomas W, *Librn,* BASF Wyandotte Corp, Corporate Library, Wyandotte MI. 313-282-3300, Ext 6015

Johnston, Walter T, *Dir,* Coastal Plain Regional Library, Tifton GA. 912-386-3400

Johnston, Wanda K, *Media,* Emory University Libraries (General Libraries), Atlanta GA. 404-329-6861

Johnston, Wayne, *Media,* Selby Public Library, Sarasota County Federated Library System, Sarasota FL. 814-366-7303

Johnstone, Betty Lu, *Asst Librn,* Western Conservative Baptist Seminary, Cline-Tunnell Library, Portland OR. 503-233-8561, Ext 23

Johnstone, Hazel, *Librn,* Beardsley & Memorial Library, Winsted CT. 203-379-6043

Johnstone, James C, *Media,* New Mexico State Library, Santa Fe NM. 505-827-2033

Johnting, Wendell, *Tech Serv,* Indiana University (School of Law Library), Indianapolis IN. 317-264-4028

Johson, Charles H, *Supvr,* Spring Grove Hospital Center, Sulzbacher Memorial Library, Catonsville MD. 301-747-4400

Joines, Kenneth L, *Libn,* First Baptist Library, Pawtucket RI. 401-725-7225

Joldersma, Dan, *Dir,* Hillsdale College, Mossey Learning Resources Center, Hillsdale MI. 517-437-7341, Ext 225

Joles, Hilma, *Dir,* Maquoketa Free Public Library, Boardmen Reference Library, Maquoketa IA. 319-652-3874

Jolibois, Mildred, *Br Asst,* Timberland Regional Library (Amanda Park Branch), Amanda Park WA. 206-288-2725

Jolicoeur, Louis-Phillipe, *Sci Admin,* Universite Laval Bibliotheque, Quebec PQ. 418-656-3344

Jolliff, Edna Lee, *On-Line Servs & Bibliog Instr,* Harper Grace Hospitals (Harper Hospital Department of Libraries), Detroit MI. 313-494-8264

Jolly, Becky, *Bkmobile Coordr,* Vicksburg-Warren County Public Library, Vicksburg MS. 601-636-6411

Jolly, John, *Dir,* Glendora Public Library, Glendora CA. 213-963-4168

Jolly, Laurel, *Libn,* Arapahoe Regional Library District (Deer Trail Library), Deer Trail CO. 303-769-4421

Jolly, Mrs William, *Libn,* Norris Community Library, Norris TN. 615-494-7645

Jolly, Wanda, *Bkmobile Coordr,* Hart County Public Library, Munfordville KY. 502-524-9953

Joly, Mariette, *ILL,* Ottawa Public Library, Ottawa ON. 613-236-0301

Jonas, Catherine, *Libn,* Runge Public Library, Runge TX. 512-239-4192

Jonas, Donna, *Libn,* Kendalia Public Library, Kendalia TX. 512-336-2473

Jonas, Dorothy, *Dir,* Hoisington City Library, Hoisington KS. 316-653-4128

Jonas, Eva, *Libn,* Harvard University Library (Museum of Comparative Zoology Library), Cambridge MA. 617-495-2475

Jonas, Mrs Bill, *Libn,* Crescent Heights Baptist Church Library, Abilene TX. 915-677-3749

Jonas, Nellie G, *Libn,* United States Department of the Interior, Rolla Metallurgy Research Center, Technical Library, Rolla MO. 314-364-3169

Jonassen, David H, *Asst Prof,* University of North Carolina at Greensboro, Library Science-Educational Technology Div, NC. 919-379-5710

Jonathan, Edith, *Tech Serv,* Lake Lanier Regional Library, Lawrenceville GA. 404-963-5231

Jones, A Kathleen, *Dir & Ref,* Port Colborne Public Library, Arabella Williams Memorial Library, Port Colborne ON. 416-834-6512

Jones, Adelfa, *ILL,* Salina Public Library, Salina KS. 913-825-4624

Jones, Adrian, *Dir,* Roosevelt University, Murray-Green Library, Chicago IL. 312-341-3639

Jones, Albert B, *Dir,* University Center in Georgia, Inc, GA. 404-542-3715

Jones, Alberta, *Supvr,* Elgin County Public Library (West Lorne Branch), West Lorne ON. 519-633-0815

Jones, Alfred, *Libn,* University of Missouri-Columbia (Engineering), Columbia MO. 314-882-2379

Jones, Alice, *Libn,* Hills Memorial Library, Hudson NH. 603-882-8621

Jones, Alice, *Co-Dir,* South Saint Paul Public Library, South Saint Paul MN. 612-451-1093

Jones, Alston, *Dir,* North Carolina Wesleyan College Library, Rocky Mount NC. 919-442-7121, Ext 280, 283

Jones, Anice, *Libn,* First Regional Library (M R Davis Public), Southaven MS. 601-342-0102

Jones, Anita, *Bkmobile Coordr,* Estill County Public Library, Irvine KY. 606-723-3030

Jones, Ann, *Cat,* Mercer University (Walter F George School of Law Library), Macon GA. 912-745-6811, Ext 345

Jones, Anna E, *Asst Dir,* Burlington County Library, Mount Holly NJ. 609-267-9660

Jones, Anna M, *Libn,* Spring City Public Library, Spring City TN. 615-365-9757

Jones, Anne, *Libn,* Public Library of Cincinnati & Hamilton County (Pleasant Ridge), Cincinnati OH. 513-631-6480

Jones, Barbara, *Libn,* Denver Public Library (Woodbury), Denver CO. 303-573-5152, Ext 271

Jones, Barbara A, *Libn,* Bethany United Methodist Church Library, Wauwatosa WI. 414-258-2868

Jones, Barry, *Libn,* Parker Pen Co, Corporate Technical Center Libr, Janesville WI. 608-755-7203

Jones, Bernadette, *Per,* Saint Michael's College, Durick Library, Colchester VT. 802-655-2000, Ext 2400

Jones, Bernice, *Bus Admin,* Rutgers University, the State University of New Jersey, John Cotton Dana Library, Newark NJ. 201-648-5222

Jones, Bernice, *Libn,* Southeast Arkansas Regional Library (McGehee Public), McGehee AR. 501-222-4097

Jones, Bertha, *Circ,* Jackson District Library, Jackson MI. 517-788-4087

Jones, Betty, *Asst Libn,* Cerritos College Library, Learning Materials Center, Norwalk CA. 213-860-2451, Ext 286

Jones, Betty, *Libn,* Jackson Metropolitan Library (Puckett Library), Puckett MS. 601-352-3677

Jones, Betty, *Circ,* Nederland Public Library, Nederland TX. 713-722-1255

Jones, Beverly, *Network Coordr,* Oklahoma Department of Libraries, Oklahoma City OK. 405-521-2502

Jones, Carol, *Instr,* Kentucky Wesleyan College, Department of Library Science, KY. 502-926-3111, Ext 112, 113

Jones, Carol, *Cat,* Kentucky Wesleyan College, Library Learning Center, Owensboro KY. 502-926-3111, Ext 113, 117

Jones, Carol, *Libn,* Roanoke Public Library, Roanoke AL. 205-863-2632

Jones, Carol, *ILL,* Southeast Kansas Library System, Iola KS. 316-365-3833

Jones, Carol Y, *Asst Dir,* Northwestern College of Chiropractic Library, Saint Paul MN. 612-690-1735, Ext 22

Jones, Carole M, *Libn,* Laboratory Institute of Merchandising Library, New York NY. 212-752-1530

Jones, Carolyn, *On-Line Servs,* Gallaudet College, Edward Miner Gallaudet Memorial Library, Washington DC. 202-651-5566

Jones, Carolyn, *Deafness, Speech & Hearing,* Gallaudet College, Edward Miner Gallaudet Memorial Library, Washington DC. 202-651-5566

Jones, Catherine, *ILL,* University of Alabama, Amelia Gayle Gorgas Library, University AL. 205-348-5298

Jones, Catherine Ann, *Chief, Cong Ref Div,* Library of Congress, Washington DC. 202-287-5000

Jones, Celia B, *Libn,* Volusia County Public Libraries (De Land Branch), De Land FL. 904-252-8374

Jones, Charlene, *Circ,* Illinois Institute of Technology, James S Kemper Library, Chicago IL. 312-567-3355

Jones, Charlene, *Libn,* Poplar Bluff Public Library (Karen West), Poplar Bluff MO. 314-785-8721

Jones, Charlotte, *Libn,* Samford University (School of Education Curriculum), Birmingham AL. 205-870-2746

Jones, Charlotte, *Neighborhood Servs,* Spokane Public Library, Comstock Building Library, Spokane WA. 509-838-3361, Ext 65

Jones, Charlotte, *Libn,* United States Trademark Association Library, New York NY. 212-986-5880

Jones, Charlotte W, *Libn,* Spokane Public Library (Manito), Spokane WA. 509-747-8388

Jones, Cheryl, *Coordr,* University of Kentucky (Law), Lexington KY. 606-258-8686

Jones, Christine, *Graphic Design,* Chicago Public Library, Chicago IL. 312-269-2900

Jones, Christine, *Spec Coll,* Tennessee Technological University, Jere Whitson Memorial Library, Cookeville TN. 615-528-3408

Jones, Chuck, *Libn,* Boeing Military Airplane Company Library, Wichita KS. 316-687-3801

Jones, Clifton H, *Spec Coll,* Southern Methodist University Libraries (Fikes Hall of Special Collections (incl DeGolyer)), Dallas TX. 214-692-2253

Jones, Creba, *Libn,* Sunflower County Library System (Inverness Public), Inverness MS. 601-265-5179

Jones, Daisy, *Libn,* Los Angeles Public Library System (Eagle Rock), Los Angeles CA. 213-255-6315

Jones, Danny, *Interlibrary Loan Libn,* University of Texas Health Science Center at San Antonio Library, San Antonio TX. 512-691-6271

Jones, David, *Acq,* Dawson College Library, Montreal PQ. 514-525-2501, Ext 297

Jones, David, *Tech Serv,* Harris County Public Library, Houston TX. 713-221-5350

Jones, David, *Ref,* Humber College, Learning Resource Centre, Rexdale ON. 416-675-3111, Ext 331

Jones, David, *Bus Mgr,* University of Georgia Libraries, Athens GA. 404-542-2716

Jones, David E, *Cat,* County College of Morris, Sherman H Masten Learning Resource Center, Randolph Township NJ. 201-361-5000, Ext 470

Jones, David E, *ILL,* Montgomery County Community College, Learning Resources Center, Blue Bell PA. 215-643-6000, Ext 340

Jones, Deborah, *Libn,* Institute of Polar Studies, Goldthwait Polar Library, Columbus OH. 614-422-6531

Jones, Debra, *Reader Serv,* Dickinson School of Law, Sheely-Lee Law Library, Carlisle PA. 717-243-4611, Ext 9

Jones, DeElla, *Libn,* Pike-Amite-Walthall Library System (Liberty Public), Liberty MS. 601-657-8781

Jones, Dena, *Bkmobile Coordr,* George Coon Memorial Library, Princeton KY. 502-365-2884

Jones, Diana, *Syst Consult,* Northwest Kansas Library System, Norton KS. 913-877-5148

Jones, Diana, *Cat,* Oklahoma City University (Dulaney-Browne Library), Oklahoma City OK. 405-521-5068

Jones, Donald, *Dept Head,* Community College of Philadelphia, Division of Educational Resources, Philadelphia PA. 215-972-7250

Jones, Donald B, *Libn,* College of Saint Catherine (Performing Arts), Saint Paul MN. 612-690-6696

Jones, Donna R, *Dir,* Pioneer Memorial Library, Colby KS. 913-462-3881

Jones, Dorothy, *Libn,* Butler Memorial Library, Cambridge NE. 308-697-3836

Jones, Dorothy, *Libn,* IBM Corp, Information Retrieval & Library Services, Owego NY. 607-687-2121, Ext 2720

Jones, Dorothy, *Libn,* Pine Forest Regional Library (Richton Public), Richton MS. 601-788-6539

Jones, Dorothy K, *Chief Libr Servs,* Veterans Administration, Hospital Library, Augusta GA. 404-733-4471, Ext 680

Jones, Dorothy S, *Dir,* East Orange Public Library, East Orange NJ. 201-266-5600

Jones, Dorothy S, *In Charge,* Southwest Essex Area Reference Center, NJ. 201-266-5600

Jones, E, *Cat,* University of Western Ontario (Law Library), London ON. 519-679-2857

Jones, E Frances, *Chief Consult Field Servs,* West Virginia Library Commission, Science & Cultural Center, Charleston WV. 304-348-2041

Jones, E Paul, *Business & Tech,* Bridgeport Public Library, Bridgeport CT. 203-576-7777

Jones, Earline, *Libn,* Crockett County Library, Ozona TX. 915-392-2185

Jones, Ebba, *Ch,* Blount County Library, Maryville TN. 615-982-0981

Jones, Edlea, *Libn,* Baltimore City Hospitals, Harold E Harrison Medical Library, Baltimore MD. 301-396-9030

Jones, Edward S, *Media Servs, Assoc Dir,* University of the District of Columbia, Learning Resources Division, Washington DC. 202-282-7536

Jones, Eleanor, *Ch,* Marlborough Public Library, Marlborough MA. 617-485-0494

Jones, Elizabeth, *Libn,* Axtell Public Library, Axtell KS. 913-736-2834

Jones, Elizabeth I, *Asst Libn,* Haysville Community Library, Haysville KS. 316-524-5242

Jones, Erma, *Libn,* Emerson Public Library, Emerson NE. 402-695-2495

Jones, Esther, *ILL & Ref,* University of Florida Libraries (J Hillis Miller Health Center), Gainesville FL. 904-392-4011

Jones, Ethel, *Asst Libn,* Carbarrus Memorial Hospital Library, Concord NC. 704-786-2111, Ext 367

Jones, Eula, *Asst Librn,* Stewart Library, Grinnell IA. 515-236-5717

Jones, Everlee, *Asst Dir,* Talladega College, Savery Library, Talladega AL. 205-362-2046

Jones, Faustina W, *Coordr Tech Serv & Cat,* Alabama State University, Library & Learning Resources, Montgomery AL. 205-832-6072

Jones, Faye, *Tech Serv,* Nova University Libraries (Law Center Library), Fort Lauderdale FL. 522-2300 Ext 113

Jones, Flora, *Reader Serv,* Gustavus Adolphus College, Folke Bernadotte Memorial Library, Saint Peter MN. 507-931-4300, Ext 2301

Jones, Florence, *Librn,* Pawlet Public Library, Pawlet VT. 802-325-3123

Jones, Florence S, *Circ,* Saint Petersburg Junior College, Saint Petersburg Campus Library, Saint Petersburg FL. 813-546-0011, Ext 353

Jones, Fran, *Librn,* Alaska Department of Natural Resources, Division of Oil & Gas Conservation Library, Anchorage AK. 907-277-6615

Jones, Fran, *Librn,* Hennepin County Library (Brooklyn Park Branch), Brooklyn Park MN. 612-425-9000

Jones, Fran, *Librn,* Hennepin County Library (Osseo Branch), Osseo MN. 612-425-3837

Jones, Frances H, *Librn,* Nottoway County Library (Blackstone Branch), Blackstone VA. 804-292-3587

Jones, Frederick, *Acq,* Tufts University, Nils Yngve Wessell Library, Medford MA. 617-628-5000, Ext 235

Jones, Geneva, *Librn,* Mitchell County Public Library, Colorado City TX. 915-728-3968

Jones, Gladys, *Tech Serv,* Lake Worth Public Library, Lake Worth FL. 305-585-9882

Jones, Grace, *Actg Librn,* Southwestern University, Cody Memorial Library, Georgetown TX. 512-863-6511, Ext 338

Jones, Gwendolyn, *Librn,* St Regis Paper Co, Corp Library, New York NY. 212-573-6265

Jones, H, *Mgr,* Northrop Corp, Aircraft Group Library Services, Hawthorne CA. 213-970-2000

Jones, H G, *N Caroliniana,* University of North Carolina at Chapel Hill, Louis Round Wilson Academic Affairs Library, Chapel Hill NC. 919-933-1301

Jones, H Kathy, *Ref,* University of Alabama in Birmingham (Lister Hill Library of the Health Sciences), Birmingham AL. 205-934-5460

Jones, Heberle H, *Mgr,* Procter & Gamble Co (Technical Information Services), Cincinnati OH. 513-562-1100

Jones, Helen, *Librn,* Kaneville Free Public Library, Kaneville IL. 312-557-2441

Jones, Helen, *Acq,* Norfolk State University, Lyman Beecher Brooks Library, Norfolk VA. 804-623-8873

Jones, Helen I, *Chief Librn,* Veterans Administration, Medical Center Library, Memphis TN. 901-523-8990, Ext 5360

Jones, Helen M, *Librn,* Elburn Public Library, Elburn IL. 312-365-6530

Jones, Hilda, *Librn,* Clearwater Public Library, Clearwater NE. 402-485-2365

Jones, Holway R, *Soc Sci,* University of Oregon Library, Eugene OR. 503-686-3056

Jones, Iola, *Librn,* Fayette County Public Library (Patrick C Graney Jr, Library), Mt Hope WV. 304-877-3260

Jones, Irene, *Librn,* Mid-Continent Public Library (Riverside Branch), Riverside MO. 816-741-6288

Jones, J Elias, *Rare Bks & Spec Coll,* Drake University, Cowles Library, Des Moines IA. 515-271-3993

Jones, J Fred, *Tech Serv,* Florida State University, Robert Manning Strozier Library, Tallahassee FL. 904-644-5211

Jones, James V, *Dir,* Case Western Reserve University Libraries, Cleveland OH. 216-368-3506

Jones, James V, *Prof,* Case Western Reserve University, School of Library Science, OH. 216-368-3500

Jones, Jana, *Librn,* Garrett Corporation, Airesearch Manufacturing Company of California, Technical Library, Torrance CA. 213-323-9500, Ext 2255

Jones, Jay M, *Librn,* Clinton Public Library, A E Wood Memorial Library, Clinton MS. 601-924-5684

Jones, Jean, *Asst Librn,* Edgewood College of the Sacred Heart Library, Madison WI. 608-257-4861, Ext 226

Jones, Jean, *Tech Serv & Acq,* Fullerton City Library, Fullerton CA. 714-738-6333, Ext 301

Jones, Jean, *Librn,* South Pasadena Public Library, South Pasadena CA. 213-799-9108

Jones, Jean S, *Dir,* Edward Waters College, H Y Tookes Library, Jacksonville FL. 904-353-5053

Jones, Jennifer, *Librn,* General American Investors Co, Inc Library, New York NY. 212-949-1763, 949-1764

Jones, Jennifer, *Tech Serv,* Veterans Memorial Public Library, Bismarck ND. 701-222-6410

Jones, Joanne E, *Ser,* Boston State College Library, Boston MA. 617-731-3300

Jones, JoEllen, *Asst Dir,* Bellevue Public Library, Bellevue OH. 419-483-4769

Jones, John W, *Bus Sci,* Forsyth County Public Library, Winston-Salem NC. 919-727-2556

Jones, Joy, *Librn,* Jackson Metropolitan Library (Clinton), Jackson MS. 601-352-3677

Jones, Joy B, *Librn,* West Virginia Department of Welfare Library, Charleston WV. 304-348-8834

Jones, Juanita, *Librn,* Environmental Protection Agency (Division of Meteorology Library), Research Triangle Park NC. 919-541-4536

Jones, Juanita, *Dir,* University of Mary Hardin-Baylor, Townsend Memorial Library, Belton TX. 817-939-5811, Ext 256

Jones, Judith A, *Librn,* Semmes-Murphey Clinic Library, Memphis TN. 901-525-8431, Ext 29

Jones, Kathryn, *ILL,* University of South Alabama (University Library), Mobile AL. 205-460-7021

Jones, Kathryn H, *Librn,* Smyrna Public Library, Smyrna GA. 404-436-2370

Jones, Kathy, *Cat,* Barberton Public Library, Barberton OH. 216-745-1194

Jones, Kay, *Ref,* Arizona State University Library, Tempe AZ. 602-965-3417

Jones, Kenneth W, *Dir,* Hardin-Simmons University, Richardson Library, Abilene TX. 915-677-7281, Ext 236

Jones, Kohar, *Soc Sci,* Public Library of Charlotte & Mecklenburg County, Inc, Charlotte NC. 704-374-2725

Jones, LaVerne, *Librn,* Oklahoma State University Library (Architecture), Stillwater OK. 405-624-6047

Jones, Lawrence E, *Librn,* Detroit Edison Co Information Services, Detroit MI. 313-237-9216

Jones, Lee P, *State Doc,* University of Florida Libraries (Agriculture), Gainesville FL. 904-392-1934

Jones, Leigh R, *Dir,* New York State Office of Parks & Recreation, Palisades Interstate Park Commission, Senate House State Historic Site Research Library, Kingston NY. 914-338-2786

Jones, Leota, *Librn,* York Regional Library (Stanley Public), Stanley NB. 506-367-2187

Jones, Linda, *ILL,* Kansas City Public Library, Kansas City MO. 816-221-2685

Jones, Linda, *Acq,* Samford University (Cordell Hull Law), Birmingham AL. 205-870-2714

Jones, Lizbeth Ann, *Librn,* United States Army (Corps of Engineers, Walla Walla District Library), Walla Walla WA. 509-525-5500, Ext 118

Jones, Lois W, *Dir,* Berkshire Christian College, Dr Linden J Carter Library, Lenox MA. 413-673-0838, Ext 77

Jones, Louise M, *Bkmobile Coordr,* Washington County Public Library, Abingdon VA. 703-628-2971

Jones, Lucille, *Ad,* Drexel University Library, Philadelphia PA. 215-895-2750

Jones, Lynn, *Cat & Rare Bks,* North Kingstown Free Library, North Kingstown RI. 401-294-2521

Jones, M B, *Coordr,* Phillips Fibers Corp, Technical Library, Greenville SC. 803-242-6600

Jones, M Frances, *Asst Dir,* West Texas State University, Cornette Library, Canyon TX. 806-656-2761

Jones, Mae B, *Bkmobile Coordr,* Forked Deer Regional Library Center, Trimble TN. 901-297-5810

Jones, Margaret, *Ref,* East Chicago Public Library, East Chicago IN. 219-397-2453

Jones, Margaret, *Lectr,* North Carolina Central University, School of Library Science, NC. 919-683-6485

Jones, Margaret, *Per,* Public Library of the City of Somerville, Somerville MA. 617-623-5000

Jones, Margaret L, *Ad,* New Castle-Henry County Public Library, New Castle IN. 317-529-0362

Jones, Margaret M, *Cat,* University of Maryland at Baltimore (Health Sciences Library), Baltimore MD. 301-528-7545

Jones, Marian, *Librn,* Geological Survey of Canada, Institute of Sedimentary & Petroleum Geology Library, Calgary AB. 403-284-0110

Jones, Marianne, *Circ,* University of Kansas Medical Center, College of Health Sciences & Hospital, Clendening Library, Kansas City KS. 913-588-7166

Jones, Marie R, *Chief Librn,* United States Public Health Service Hospital, Charles Ferguson Medical Library, Staten Island NY. 212-447-3010, Ext 505 & 584

Jones, Marilyn, *Ch,* Frank Hughes Memorial Library, Liberty MO. 816-781-3611

Jones, Marion, *Coll Develop,* Henderson State University, Huie Library, Arkadelphia AR. 501-246-5511, Ext 200

Jones, Martha, *Local Hist,* Bensenville Community Public Library, Bensenville IL. 312-766-4642

Jones, Martha, *Cat,* Morse Institute Library, Natick MA. 617-653-4252

Jones, Martha R, *Librn,* Middletown Public Library, Middletown IN. 317-354-2913

Jones, Mary, *Tech Serv,* Claflin College, H V Manning Library, Orangeburg SC. 803-534-2710, Ext 56

Jones, Mary, *Chief Librn,* Newfoundland Public Library Services (A C Hunter Memorial Library), Saint John's NF. 709-737-3964

Jones, Mary K, *Ref,* Louisiana State University at Alexandria Library, Alexandria LA. 318-445-3672, Ext 46

Jones, Maude, *Cat & Govt Doc,* Cheyney State College, Leslie Pinckney Hill Library, Cheyney PA. 215-758-2000, Ext 2203, 2208, 2245

Jones, Maureen, *Asst Librn,* Schlumberger-Dall Research Center Library, Ridgefield CT. 203-438-2631, Ext 325, 342

Jones, Mildred R, *Librn,* First Wisconsin National Bank Library, Milwaukee WI. 414-765-4928

Jones, Mildred S, *Librn,* University of Miami, Lowe Art Museum Library, Coral Gables FL. 305-284-3535

Jones, Miriam, *Dir,* Oak Hills Bible Institute Library, Bemidji MN. 218-751-8670, Ext 46

Jones, Miriam E, *Actg Dir,* Brevard College, James Addison Jones Library, Brevard NC. 704-883-8292, Ext 68

Jones, Mrs A D, *Librn,* Paragould Public Library (Corning Branch), Corning AR. 501-857-3453

Jones, Mrs G B, *Librn,* Hillsborough County Historical Commission Museum Library, Tampa FL. 813-272-5919

Jones, Mrs J F, *Dir,* Grandin Library, Clinton NJ. 201-735-4812

Jones, Nancy, *Asst Dir,* LaVista Public, LaVista NE. 402-331-9519

Jones, Nedra D, *Librn,* Celanese Corp (Law Library), New York NY. 212-764-8652

Jones, Nellie, *Ad,* Elsie Quirk Public Library, Englewood FL. 813-474-3515

Jones, Nola Y, *Librn,* Karnes City Public Library, Karnes City TX. 512-780-2539

Jones, Norah, *Tech Serv,* University of California Los Angeles Library, Los Angeles CA. 213-825-1201

Jones, Norma L, *Prof,* University of Wisconsin-Oshkosh, Dept of Library Science, WI. 414-424-2313

Jones, Norma S, *Asst Dir,* Clay County Public Library, Green Cove Springs FL. 904-284-3822

Jones, Patricia A, *Librn,* Bennington Public Library, Bennington NE. 402-238-2375

Jones, Patricia B, *Librn,* Libbey Owens Ford Co (Corporate Library), Toledo OH. 419-247-4862

Jones, Paula O, *Librn,* Springville Public Library, Springville UT. 801-489-5937

Jones, Phyllis, *ILL,* Public Library of Nashville & Davidson County, Nashville TN. 615-244-4700

Jones, Pyddney K, *Regional Librn,* Bluegrass (South) Library District, Nicholasville KY. 606-885-3612

Jones, Rachel, *Sci & Math,* Jacksonville State University Library, Jacksonville AL. 205-435-9820, Ext 213, 214

Jones, Ray, *Soc Sci,* University of Florida Libraries, Gainesville FL. 904-392-0341

Jones, Reen, *Cat,* Fort Worth Public Library, Fort Worth TX. 817-870-7700

Jones, Richard, *Dir,* North Central Regional Library System, Sudbury ON. 705-675-6467

Jones, Richard E, *Music,* University of Wisconsin-Milwaukee, Golda Meir Library, Milwaukee WI. 414-963-4785

Jones, Rita, *Acq,* City College of San Francisco Library, San Francisco CA. 415-239-3404

Jones, Robert, *Admin Serv,* Central Washington University Library, Ellensburg WA. 509-963-1901

Jones, Robert, *Ad,* Weatherford Public Library, Weatherford TX. 817-594-2767

Jones, Robert A, *Dir,* Bradley University, Cullom-Davis Library, Peoria IL. 309-676-7611

Jones, Robert C, *Librn,* Mercer County Community College Library (James Kerney Center), Trenton NJ. 609-586-4800, Ext 503

Jones, Robert M, *Dir,* Putnam County District Library, Ottawa OH. 419-523-3747

Jones, Robert P, *ILL,* University of North Florida Library, Jacksonville FL. 904-646-2553

Jones, Robert T, *Dir,* Worcester State College, Learning Resources Center, Worcester MA. 617-752-7700, Ext 132, 135

Jones, Roger M, *Dir,* Paramus Public Library, Paramus NJ. 201-265-1800

Jones, Rosalie, *Librn,* Piedmont Regional Library (Banks County Public), Homer GA. 404-867-2762

Jones, Rosalyn, *Dir,* Syracuse Public Library, Syracuse IN. 219-457-3022

Jones, Roxanne, *Acq,* Victoria College - University of Houston Victoria Campus Library, Victoria TX. 512-575-7436

Jones, Ruth, *Librn,* Wyoming Free Library, Wyoming PA. 717-693-1364

Jones, Ruth A, *Chief Librn,* Veterans Administration, Hospital Library, Spokane WA. 509-328-4521, Ext 257

Jones, Sandi, *Asst Librn,* Valparaiso Public Library, Valparaiso NE. 402-784-6141

Jones, Sarah C, *Dir of Libr Servs,* Morgan Stanley & Co, Inc Library, New York NY. 212-974-4369

Jones, Sarah D, *Dir,* Goucher College, Julia Rogers Library, Towson MD. 301-825-3300, Ext 360

Jones, Sheila, *Dir,* Fawcett Community Library, Fawcett AB. 403-954-3827

Jones, Sheila, *Ch,* Maywood Public Library, Maywood IL. 312-343-1847

Jones, Shirley, *Ser,* Benedict College, Benjamin F Payton Learning Resources Ctr, Columbia SC. 803-256-4220

Jones, Shirley, *Librn,* Sedgwick Public Library, Lillian Tear Library, Sedgwick KS. 316-772-5727

Jones, Shirley, *Acq & Ser,* Washington University Libraries, Saint Louis MO. 314-889-5400

Jones, Shirley L, *Dir,* Welland Public Library, Welland ON. 416-734-6210

Jones, Shirley T, *Dir,* Craven Community College, R C Godwin Memorial Library, New Bern NC. 919-638-4131, Ext 54

Jones, Sister Eleanor, *Asst Dir,* Villa Maria College Library, Erie PA. 814-838-1966, Ext 222

Jones, Sister Marjorie, *Tech Serv & Cat,* Saint Mary's College, Alumnae Centennial Library, Notre Dame IN. 219-284-4242

Jones, Sister Martin Joseph, *Spec Coll & Archivist,* State University College at Buffalo, Edward H Butler Library, Buffalo NY. 716-878-6302

Jones, Suad, *Librn,* United States Navy (Medical Library), Portsmouth VA. 804-444-1521

Jones, Susan, *Asst Librn,* Amargosa Valley Community Library, Lathrop Wells NV. 702-372-5340

Jones, Susan, *Librn,* Union Oil of Canada, Ltd Library, Calgary AB. 403-268-0493, 268-0176

Jones, Thomas, *Acq,* Blue Ridge Regional Library, Martinsville VA. 703-632-7125

Jones, Thomas T, *Dir,* Veterans Memorial Public Library, Bismarck ND. 701-222-6410

Jones, Tina, *ILL,* Chillicothe & Ross County Public Library, Chillicothe OH. 614-773-4145

Jones, Trevelyn, *Ch,* Garden City Public Library, Garden City NY. 516-742-8405

Jones, Vance Harper, *Asst Dir,* Craven Community College, R C Godwin Memorial Library, New Bern NC. 919-638-4131, Ext 54

Jones, Venola, *Cat,* Dillard University, Will W Alexander Library, New Orleans LA. 504-949-2123, Ext 256, 257

Jones, Versie, *Asst Librns,* Northeast Mississippi Junior College, Eula Dees Memorial Library, Booneville MS. 601-728-7751, Ext 237

Jones, Viney, *Librn,* Florence Public Library, Florence AZ. 602-868-5557

Jones, Virgil L, *Ref,* University of Oklahoma Health Sciences Center Library, Oklahoma City OK. 405-271-2285

Jones, Virginia, *Ad, YA & AV,* Stonewall Jackson Regional Library, Buckhannon WV. 304-472-5475, 472-5581

Jones, Virginia Lacy, *Dean,* Atlanta University, School of Library & Information Studies, GA. 404-681-0251, Ext 312

Jones, W Marshall, *Dir,* Instructional Materials Center, Billings MT. 406-259-0291

Jones, Walter R, *Dir,* Uinta County Library, Evanston WY. 307-789-2770

Jones, Wanda, *Lectr,* Lambuth College, Library Science Program, TN. 901-427-6743

Jones, William A, *Spec Coll,* California State University, Chico Library, Chico CA. 916-895-6212

Jones, William G, *Librn,* Northwestern University Library (Science-Engineering), Evanston IL. 312-492-3362

Jones, William G, *Asst Librn, Coll Develop & Info Servs,* University of Illinois at Chicago Circle Library, Chicago IL. 312-996-2716

Jones, Wilson, *Music,* Johnson Free Public Library, Hackensack NJ. 201-343-4169

Jones, Wyman, *Dir,* Los Angeles Public Library System, Los Angeles CA. 213-626-7555

Jones, Zolz, *Ad,* South Georgia Regional Library, Valdosta-Lowndes County Public Library, Valdosta GA. 912-247-3405

Jones, II, Horace, *Commun Servs,* Roseville Public Library, Roseville CA. 916-783-7158

Jones, Jr, Arthur E, *Dir,* Drew University, Rose Memorial Library, Madison NJ. 201-377-3000, Ext 469

Jones, Jr, William W, *Librn,* Radiation Management Corporation Library, Philadelphia PA. 215-243-2950

Jonish, A D, *Dir,* Whitman College, Penrose Memorial Library, Walla Walla WA. 509-527-5191

Jonke, Grace, *Librn,* Baltimore County Public Library (Parkville-Carney), Baltimore MD. 301-668-1313

Jonovich, Tina, *Asst Librn,* Gila County Law Library, Globe AZ. 602-425-3231

Joorfetz, Clara, *Librn,* Saint Dominic-Jackson Memorial Hospital, Luther Manship Medical Library, Jackson MS. 601-982-0121, Ext 2760

Joray, Charles N, *Dir,* Bluffton-Wells County Public Library, Bluffton IN. 219-824-1612

Jorbin, Lesley, *Media,* Cleveland State University Libraries, Cleveland OH. 216-687-2486

Jordahl, Leigh D, *Librn,* Luther College, Preus Library, Decorah IA. 319-387-1163

Jordahl, Neil R, *Humanities,* Enoch Pratt Free Library, Baltimore MD. 301-396-5430, 396-5395

Jordahl, Ron, *Librn,* Prairie Bible Institute Library, Three Hills AB. 403-443-5511, Ext 45

Jordan, Barbara B, *Librn Blind,* Tuscaloosa Public Library, Tuscaloosa AL. 205-345-5820

Jordan, Casper, *Cent Librn,* Atlanta Public Library, Atlanta GA. 404-688-4636

Jordan, Dorothy, *Circ,* Pearl River Junior College Library, Poplarville MS. 601-795-4517

Jordan, Harold, *On-Line Servs,* Principia College, Marshall Brooks Library, Elsah IL. 618-374-2131, Ext 325

Jordan, Helen L, *Dir,* Columbia College, J Drake Edens Library, Columbia SC. 803-786-3878

Jordan, Helen L, *Asst Prof,* Columbia College, Library Services Program, SC. 803-786-3012

Jordan, J, *Dir,* Northeastern University, University College Library Science Program, MA. 617-437-2400

Jordan, Joyce, *Librn, On-Line Servs & Bibliog Instr,* Delaware River Basin Commission Library, West Trenton NJ. 609-883-9500, Ext 292

Jordan, June, *Actg Librn,* Tripp County Library, Winner SD. 605-842-0330

Jordan, K Paul, *Tech Serv,* Brigham Young University, Harold B Lee Library, Provo UT. 801-378-2905

Jordan, Kay, *Circ,* College of Lake County, Learning Resource Center, Grayslake IL. 312-223-6601, Ext 392

Jordan, Linda, *Br Coordr,* Cass County Public Library, Harrisonville MO. 816-884-3483

Jordan, Mary K, *Librn,* American Association of University Women Educational Foundation Library, Washington DC. 202-785-7763

Jordan, Melbourne, *Acq,* University of Texas Libraries (General), Austin TX. 512-471-3811

Jordan, Melissa, *Media,* Cecil County Public Library, Elkton MD. 301-398-0914

Jordan, Nancy L, *Librn,* New Britain Public Library (East Street), New Britain CT. 203-223-3832

Jordan, Pamela C, *In Charge,* Yale University Library (Drama), New Haven CT. 203-436-2213

Jordan, Patricia G, *Librn,* Norfolk State University, Lyman Beecher Brooks Library, Norfolk VA. 804-623-8873

Jordan, Patti L, *Supvr Libr Servs,* TRW Defense & Space Systems Group, Technical Information Center, Redondo Beach CA. 213-536-2631

Jordan, Ray, *Per,* Stetson University, duPont-Ball Library, De Land FL. 904-734-4121, Ext 220

Jordan, Robert, *Instr,* University of the District of Columbia-Mount Vernon Square Campus, Dept of Library Science & Instructional Systems Technology, DC. 202-727-2756, 727-2757 & 727-2758

Jordan, Rosemary, *Sr Citizens & Serv to Handicapped,* Norfolk Public Library, Norfolk VA. 804-441-2887

Jordan, Shelley, *Librn,* Bellin Memorial Hospital, Health Sciences Library, Green Bay WI. 414-468-3693

Jordan, Stephen, *Mgr,* Association for Research & Enlightenment, Edgar Cayce Memorial Library, Virginia Beach VA. 804-428-3588, Ext 178

Jordan, Thecla, *Asst Librn,* Smiths Falls Public Library, Smiths Falls ON. 613-283-2911

Jordan, W Rene, *Br Coordr,* Knoxville-Knox County Public Library, Lawson McGhee Library, Knoxville TN. 615-523-0781

Jordon, Alberta, *Asst Dir,* Baker County Public Library, Baker OR. 503-523-6414, 523-6419

Jordon, Eleanor F, *Asst Dir,* Flint Memorial Library, North Reading MA. 617-664-4942

Jordon, Mary, *ILL, Ref & Bibliog Instr,* Auburn Public Library, Auburn ME. 207-782-3191

Jordon, Mrs Jerry, *Librn,* Tonkawa Public Library, Tonkawa OK. 405-628-3366

Jorgensen, Ada P, *Librn,* United Presbyterian Church of the Atonement Library, Silver Spring MD. 301-649-4131

Jorgensen, Alice, *Per,* Huntington Public Library, Huntington NY. 516-427-5165

Jorgensen, Blythe M, *Dir,* Toledo Public Library, Toledo OR. 503-336-3132

Jorgensen, Dorothy G, *Dir,* Fayetteville Free Library, Fayetteville NY. 315-637-6374

Jorgensen, Nina, *Librn,* University of Minnesota (Plant Pathology), Saint Paul MN. 612-373-1669

Jorgenson, Alan, *Asst Dir,* Waushara-Green Lake Cooperative Library Service, Berlin WI. 414-361-1916

Jorgenson, Marilyn, *Librn,* Jackson County Library (Wanblee Branch), Wanblee SD. 605-837-2689

Jorns, Eileen, *Librn,* Turon City Library, Turon KS. 316-497-6443

Jorve, Ronald M, *Tech Serv,* Amarillo College, Learning Resource Center, Amarillo TX. 806-376-5111, Ext 2420

Jose, Jean, *Asst Dir,* Indiana State Library, Indianapolis IN. 317-232-3675

Jose, Phyllis, *Librn,* Oakland County Governmental Reference Library, Pontiac MI. 313-858-0738

Josel, Jr, Nathan A, *Dir,* El Paso Public Library, El Paso TX. 915-543-3804

Joselyn, Tom, *Librn,* Timberland Regional Library (Chehalis Branch), Chehalis WA. 206-748-3301

Joseph, Alice, *Librn,* Provincetown Public Library, Provincetown MA. 617-487-0850

Joseph, Andrea, *ILL,* University of Connecticut at Hartford (Law Library), West Hartford CT. 203-523-4841, Ext 347, 370

Joseph, Eleanor, *Ref,* East Baton Rouge Parish Library, Baton Rouge LA. 504-389-3360

JOSEPH

Joseph, Margaret, *Schools,* Detroit Public Library, Detroit Associated Libraries, Detroit MI. 313-833-1000

Joseph, Margaret A, *Ref,* University of Texas at San Antonio Library, San Antonio TX. 512-691-4570

Joseph, Marjorie, *Asst Librn,* University of Tennessee Space Institute Library, Tullahoma TN. 615-455-0631, Ext 315

Joseph, Nancy G, *Cat,* New York Law Institute, New York NY. 212-732-8720

Joseph, Sister Edmund, *Dir,* Assumption College for Sisters Library, Mendham NJ. 201-543-6528

Joseph, Sister Mary, *Dir,* Mater Dei College, Augsbury Memorial Library, Ogdensburg NY. 315-393-5940, Ext 27

Joseph, Sister Miriam, *Spec Coll,* Our Lady of Angels College Library, Aston PA. 215-449-0905, Ext 10

Joseph, Sister Veronica, *Instr,* Caldwell College, Library Science Program, NJ. 201-228-4424

Josephs, Cynthia A, *Ad,* Joint Free Public Library of the Chathams, Chatham NJ. 201-635-0603

Josephs, Elmer, *Librn,* National Publications Library, Minneapolis MN. 612-861-2162

Josephs, Myra A, *Librn,* Institute for Rational Living Library, New York NY. 212-535-0822

Josephson, Richard, *Instr,* Saint Cloud State University, Center for Library & Audiovisual Education, MN. 612-255-2022

Josey, E J, *Bur of Specialist Libr Servs: Chief,* New York State Library, Albany NY. 518-474-5930

Josh, Margaret, *Bkmobile Coordr,* Rodman Public Library, Alliance OH. 216-821-1410

Joshi, Irene M, *South Asia,* University of Washington Libraries, Seattle WA. 206-543-1760

Josi, Marilyn, *Govt Doc,* Wisconsin Supreme Court, Wisconsin State Law Library, Madison WI. 608-266-1424, 266-1600

Josiek, Julianne, *Librn,* National Marine Fisheries Service, Southeast Fisheries Center-Miami Laboratory Library, Miami FL. 305-361-5761, Ext 239

Joslin, Ann, *Br Coordr,* Erie County Library System, Erie PA. 814-452-2333

Joslin, Ann, *On-Line Servs,* Idaho State Library, Boise ID. 208-334-2150

Joslin, Elizabeth, *Ad,* Bundy Foundation, Inc, Bundy Art Gallery Library, Waitsfield VT. 802-496-3882

Joslin, Juanita, *Ch,* Public Library of Enid & Garfield County, Enid Public Library, Enid OK. 405-234-6313

Joslin, Madeleine, *Librn,* Allendale-Hampton-Jasper Regional Library (Ridgeland), Allendale SC. 803-584-3513

Joslin, Richard, *Ch,* Lakewood Public Library, Lakewood OH. 216-226-8275

Joslow, Betty, *Cat,* Pine Manor College, Alumnae Library, Chestnut Hill MA. 617-731-7081, 731-7083

Joslyn, Jean, *Tech Serv,* Lincoln Library, Springfield Public Library, Springfield IL. 217-753-4900

Joss, Carolyn Leslie, *Librn,* Ferro Corp Library, Independence OH. 216-641-8580, Ext 619

Joss, Mrs Virgil, *Librn,* Shawano City-County Library (Bonduel Public), Bonduel WI. 715-758-2267

Jossens, Sandy, *Librn,* George Amos Memorial Library (Recluse Branch), Recluse WY. 307-682-3223

Josslin, Dan, *Chief Librn,* Orange County Public Library (Garden Grove Regional), Garden Grove CA. 714-530-0711, 530-0713

Jost, Bob, *Mgr,* Human Resources Center Library, Daytona Beach FL. 904-252-6550

Jourdan, Anne, *Librn,* Brooklyn Public Library (Kings Bay), Brooklyn NY. 212-332-5656

Journey, Susan, *Acq,* Wheeler Basin Regional Library, Decatur Public Library, Decatur AL. 205-353-2993

Jovanovic, Bogoljub, *Tech Serv,* Public Library of the District of Columbia, Martin Luther King Memorial Library, Washington DC. 202-727-1101

Jowers, George, *Asst Prof,* Fort Valley State College, Library Science Dept, GA. 912-825-6250

Joy, Elizabeth, *Chief Librn,* Cleveland Clinic Educational Foundation, Medical Library, Cleveland OH. 216-444-5698

Joy, Ned V, *Actg Dir,* San Diego State University Library, San Diego CA. 714-286-6014

Joy, Patricia, *Ref,* Silas Bronson Library, Waterbury CT. 203-574-8200

Joy, Patricia, *Genealogy,* Silas Bronson Library, Waterbury CT. 203-574-8200

Joyce, Alice, *Doc,* Colorado State Library, Colorado Department of Education, Denver CO. 303-839-3695

Joyce, B, *Bibliog Instr,* University of Oklahoma MUniversity Libraries, Norman OK. 405-325-2611

Joyce, Bertha, *Librn,* North Haven Public Library, North Haven ME. 207-867-4661

Joyce, Charles, *Dir,* Kansas City Kansas Public Library, Kansas City KS. 913-621-3073

Joyce, Donald, *Cur, Harsh Coll of Afro-Am Hist & Lit,* Chicago Public Library (Woodson Regional), Chicago IL. 312-881-6900

Joyce, Irene, *Librn,* Northumberland Union Public Library (Centreton), Baltimore ON. 613-392-1400

Joyce, Janet, *Tech Serv,* Auburn Public Library, Auburn ME. 207-782-3191

Joyce, Mrs Cicely R, *Librn,* Missouri Division of Corrections Libraries (Missouri Intermediate Reformatory Library), Jefferson City MO. 314-751-3050

Joyce, Sharon, *Libr Personal Training,* Chicago Public Library, Chicago IL. 312-269-2900

Joyner, Betty, *Librn,* Thomas Hackney Braswell Memorial Library (Spring Hope Branch), Spring Hope NC. 442-1937 & 442-1951

Joyner, Joan, *Acq,* Merced College, Lesher Library, Merced CA. 209-723-4321, Ext 274

Joyner, Kathryn, *ILL,* Tennessee State Library & Archives, Nashville TN. 615-741-2764

Joyner, Marcia, *ILL,* Nantahala Regional Library, Murphy NC. 704-837-2025

Joyner, Marjorie, *Librn,* Ball State University (Architecture), Muncie IN. 317-285-4760

Joyner, Russell, *Executive Dir,* International Society for General Semantics Library, San Francisco CA. 415-543-1747

Joyner, Vallie, *Per,* Florida Institute of Technology Library, Melbourne FL. 305-723-3701, Ext 270

Jubinski, Sarah B, *Dept Head,* Northampton County Area Community College, Library Technical Assistant Program, PA. 215-865-5351, Ext 221

Jubinski, Sarah B, *Dean,* Northampton County Area Community College, Learning Resources Center, Bethlehem PA. 215-865-5351, Ext 220

Jubinsky, Walter, *Librn,* Volusia County Public Libraries (City Island Public), Daytona Beach FL. 904-252-8374

Juchimek, Vincent, *Chief Librn,* Saint Joseph's Hospital Health Center, School of Nursing & Medical Library, Syracuse NY. 315-424-5053

Judah, Marjorie, *Librn,* McGill University Libraries (Howard Ross Library of Management), Montreal PQ. 514-392-5795

Juday, Barbara, *Librn,* Indianapolis-Marion County Public Library (Southport), Indianapolis IN. 317-635-5662

Judd, Cicely T, *Dir,* Delaware County District Library, Delaware OH. 614-362-3861

Judd, Donna, *Librn,* Lake View Medical Center, Medical & Nursing Library, Danville IL. 217-443-5000, Ext 394

Judd, E Maren, *Acq Dept Head,* Harvard University Library (Baker Library), Boston MA. 617-495-3650

Judd, J Van der veer, *Principal Librn,* New York State Interlibrary Loan Network, (NYSILL), NY. 518-474-5129; Data 474-5784 & 474-5786

Judd, J Vanderveer, *Prin Librn, Coll Mgt & Network Servs,* New York State Library, Albany NY. 518-474-5930

Judd, Julie, *Ch,* Bryan Public Library, Bryan TX. 713-823-8021

Judd, Marjorie, *Ch,* Stoughton Public Library, Stoughton MA. 617-344-2711

Judd, Phyllis, *Ref,* Ansonia Library, Ansonia CT. 203-734-6275

Judd, Ruth, *Librn,* Birchard Public Library of Sandusky County (Woodville Village Branch), Woodville OH. 419-332-1121

Judd, Ruth, *Tech Serv,* Black Hawk College, Learning Resource Center, Moline IL. 309-796-1311, Ext 344

Judd, Theodore, *Librn,* Smithtown Library (Commack Branch), Commack NY. 516-543-0998

Judge, Grace, *Librn,* Penticton Public Library, Penticton BC. 604-492-0024

Judge, Joseph M, *In Charge,* Armstrong Cork Company (Research & Development Center Library), Lancaster PA. 717-397-0611, Ext 7213, 7214

Judge, Mrs Stanley, *Librn,* Shelburne Public Library, Shelburne NH. 603-466-3986

Judith, Sister Mary, *Instr,* Caldwell College, Library Science Program, NJ. 201-228-4424

Judman, Mark, *Librn &* , Colgate-Palmolive Co, Technical Information Center Library, Piscataway NJ. 201-463-1212, Ext 277

Judson, Jean, *Librn,* University of Chicago (Harper Library), Chicago IL. 312-753-3429

Judson, Mildred, *ILL,* Franklin Library Association, Franklin PA. 814-432-5062

Judy, Patricia E, *Tech Serv & Cat,* Hayner Public Library District, Alton IL. 618-462-0651

Juergens, Bonnie, *Data Proc,* Austin Public Library, Austin TX. 512-472-5433

Juffer, Margaret, *Dir,* Northwestern College, Library Science Program, IA. 712-722-4821

Jugovic, Maria, *Ch,* East Chicago Public Library, East Chicago IN. 219-397-2453

Juhl, Berniece, *Librn,* Walnut Public Library, Walnut IA. 712-784-3533

Juhl, Marilyn, *Ref,* Grand View College Library, Des Moines IA. 515-266-2651

Julaphongs, Martha, *Br Coordr,* Library Association of Portland, Multnomah County Library, Portland OR. 503-223-7201, Ext 40

Julian, Cathy, *Librn,* Jackson District Library (Concord Branch), Concord MI. 517-524-6970

Julian, Charles, *Media,* Glenville State College, Robert F Kidd Library, Glenville WV. 304-462-7361, Ext 291

Julian, Charles, *Instr,* Glenville State College, Library Science Program, WV. 304-462-7361, Ext 291, 292

Julian, Meredith, *Librn,* Phoenix Public Library (Mesquite), Phoenix AZ. 602-262-7298

Juliano, Vincent, *Dir,* Waterford Public Library, Waterford CT. 203-442-8551

Julien, Lorraine, *Ref,* Universite De Moncton, Bibliotheque Champlain, Moncton NB. 506-858-4012

Julien, Wilma, *Librn,* Mid-Continent Public Library (Raytown Branch), Raytown MO. 816-353-2052

Julius, Jerry, *Librn,* Temple Emanu-El Library, Tucson AZ. 602-327-4501, Ext 24

Julliard, Joanna, *Ch,* Lane Public Library, Hamilton OH. 513-894-7156

Jumonville, Florence, *Librn,* Historic New Orleans Collection Library, New Orleans LA. 504-523-7146

Junaid, Igbal, *Tech Serv,* Pikes Peak Community College, Learning Materials Center, Colorado Springs CO. 303-576-7711, Ext 536

June, Carolyn H, *Dir,* Moffat Library Association, Washingtonville NY. 914-496-4392

Juneau, Ann, *Librn,* National Agricultural Library (US National Aboretum), Washington DC. 202-399-5400

Juneau, Barbara, *Dir,* Winona Public Library, Winona MN. 507-452-4582

Juneau, Gerard, *Librn,* Bibliotheque Deschatelets Library, Ottawa ON. 613-237-0580

Juneau, Montez, *Librn,* Avoyelles Parish Library (Cottonport Branch), Cottonport LA. 318-253-7559

Juneau, Sister M Theophane, *Assoc Librn,* Saint Mary's Dominican College, John XXIII Library, New Orleans LA. 504-865-7761, Ext 225

Juneja, Derry, *Cat,* Cleveland Public Library, Cleveland OH. 216-623-2800

Jung, Jennifer, *Librn,* Bay View Hospital, Charles J & Anna N Archbold Medical Library, Bay Village OH. 216-331-2500, Ext 23

Jung, Norman, *Dir,* State University of New York, College at Old Westbury Library, Old Westbury NY. 516-876-3156, 876-3152

Jung, Suzanne, *Ch,* Chula Vista Public Library, Chula Vista CA. 714-427-1151

Jung, Walker, *Dir,* Dundalk Community College Library, Baltimore MD. 301-282-6700, Ext 314

Jung, Zing, *Librn,* American Psychological Association, Arthur W Melton Library, Arlington VA. 202-833-7590

Jungclaus, Jackie, *Tech Serv,* Collingswood Free Public Library, Collingswood NJ. 609-858-0649
Junge, Al, *Ref & Pub Servs,* Pepperdine University, Los Angeles Campus Library, Los Angeles CA. 213-971-7730, Ext 730
Junier, Artemisie J, *Chief Librn,* Veterans Administration, Hospital Library, Tuskegee AL. 205-727-0550, Ext 647
Junker, Janice L, *Spec Coll,* Merced County Library, Merced CA. 209-726-7484
Junker, Karen, *Tech Serv,* Saint John Fisher College, Lavery Library, Pittsford NY. 716-586-4140, Ext 222
Junkin, Betty, *Librn,* Gordo Public Library, Gordo AL. 205-364-7111
Junkin, Elaine, *Librn,* Northwest Regional Library (MCHS Community Library), Guin AL. 205-468-3378
Junkins, Bobby M, *Dir,* Gadsden-Etowah County Library, Gadsden Public Library, Gadsden AL. 205-547-1611
Junkins, Nellie, *Librn,* Ruth Enlow Library of Garrett County (Kitzmiller Community Ctr), Kitzmiller MD. 301-453-3368
Jurale, Joan, *Ref,* Wesleyan University, Olin Memorial Library, Middletown CT. 203-347-9411, Ext 296
Jurco, Vlasta L, *Mgr,* Standard Oil Co (Indiana), Library-Information Center, Chicago IL. 312-856-5961
Jurden, Johnetta, *Librn,* Jackson Metropolitan Library (Delta Drive), Jackson MS. 601-352-3677
Jurgens, Elsie, *Librn,* Madison County-Canton Public Library (Ridgeland Public), Ridgeland MS. 601-856-4536
Jurgens, Lann, *Cent Libr Head,* Sacramento Public Library, Sacramento CA. 916-440-5926
Jurgens, Lann, *Librn,* Sacramento Public Library (Central Library), Sacramento CA. 916-449-5203
Jurkins, Jacquelyn, *Librn,* Multnomah Law Library, Portland OR. 503-248-3394
Jurkus, Vida, *Tech Serv,* Queens College Library, Flushing NY. 212-520-7616
Jurries, Elaine, *Ref,* Missouri Western State College, Hearnes Learning Resources Center, Saint Joseph MO. 816-271-4368
Jurrist, Blanche, *Librn,* Surf-Bal-Bay Library, Surfside FL. 305-865-2409
Jursik, Katherine, *Librn,* Urban Land Institute Library, Washington DC. 202-331-8500
Jury, Joan D, *Asst Librn,* Eastern Nazarene College, Nease Library, Wollaston MA. 617-773-6350, Ext 251
Jussin, Estelle, *Prof,* Simmons College, Graduate School of Library & Information Science, MA. 617-738-2225
Just, Judith, *Librn,* Lompoc Public Library (Buellton Branch), Buellton CA. 805-688-3115
Justice, Dema, *Asst Librn,* Gabie Betts Burton Memorial Library, Clarendon TX. 806-874-3685
Justice, Edwina, *Librn,* Coleman Public Library, Mrs J A B Miller Memorial Library, Coleman TX. 915-625-5638
Justice, Hermia, *Librn,* Los Angeles Public Library System (Felipe deNeve), Los Angeles CA. 213-384-7676
Justice, Ila T, *Instr,* Appalachian State University, Department of Educational Media: Librarianship & Instructional Technology, NC. 704-262-2243
Justice, Jeannie R, *Librn,* Judson Baptist College Library, The-Dalles OR. 503-298-4455
Justice, La Donna H, *Librn,* Callaway County Public Library, Fulton MO. 314-642-7261
Justice, LaDonna, *Librn,* Daniel Boone Regional Library (Fulton Service Center), Fulton MO. 314-642-7261
Justice, Sharon, *Tech Serv,* Austin Public Library, Austin TX. 512-472-5433
Justis, Jo, *Librn,* Central Rappahannock Regional Library (Colonial Beach Branch), Colonial Beach VA. 703-371-3311
Justiss, Larry D, *Dir & Br Coordr,* Tom Green County Library System, San Angelo TX. 915-655-7321
Juth-Gavasso, Carol, *ILL & Ref,* Hope College, Van Zoeren Library, Holland MI. 392-5111, Ext 2130
Jwaideh, Zuhair E, *Near Eastern & African Law Div,* Library of Congress, Washington DC. 202-287-5000

Jyurovat, Doris, *Dir,* Stow Public Library, Stow OH. 216-688-3295

K

Kaag, Betty, *Per,* Hanover College, Duggan Library, Hanover IN. 812-866-2151, Ext 333
Kaback, Susann, *Ch,* James H Johnson Memorial Library, Deptford NJ. 609-227-4424
Kabalen, Mladen, *Sci,* Michigan State University Library, East Lansing MI. 517-355-2344
Kabalin, Mladen, *Librn,* Michigan State University Library (Science), East Lansing MI. 517-355-2344
Kabat, Diane, *Tech Serv,* Northbrook Public Library, Northbrook IL. 312-272-6224
Kabell, Christine, *Librn,* Metropolitan Library System (Capitol Hill), Oklahoma City OK. 405-235-0571
Kabler, Anne W, *Assoc Dir,* Medical University of South Carolina Library, Charleston SC. 803-792-2374
Kabler, Sarah, *Cat,* Randolph-Macon Woman's College, Lipscomb Library, Lynchburg VA. 804-846-7392, Ext 242
Kacena, Carolyn A, *Cat,* University of Arizona Library, Tucson AZ. 602-626-2101
Kachkowski, A S, *Librn,* Mohyla Institute Library, Saskatoon SK. 306-653-1944
Kachline, Clifford, *Historian,* National Baseball Hall of Fame & Museum Inc, National Baseball Library, Cooperstown NY. 607-547-9988
Kaczmarek, Mary F, *Tech Librn,* Johnson Controls, Inc, Technical Library, Milwaukee WI. 414-276-9200, Ext 4687
Kaczmarski, Dolores, *Librn,* Witco Chemical Corp, Clearing Library, Chicago IL. 312-767-8771
Kaczynski, Danuta, *Romance,* University of California, Berkeley (University Library), Berkeley CA. 415-642-3773
Kadinger, Sharon, *Librn,* United States Geological Survey, Don Lee Kulow Memorial Library, Sioux Falls SD. 605-594-6511, Ext 114
Kadoich, William, *Adjunct Prof,* Northampton County Area Community College, Library Technical Assistant Program, PA. 215-865-5351, Ext 221
Kaeding, Joan, *ILL,* Oshkosh Public Library, Oshkosh WI. 414-424-0473
Kaegi, Merle, *Librn for the Arts,* Public Library of the District of Columbia, Martin Luther King Memorial Library, Washington DC. 202-727-1101
Kaehr, Robert E, *Asst Prof,* Huntington College, Library Science Minor, IN. 219-356-6000
Kaehr, Robert E, *Asst Prof of Libr Sci,* Huntington College, Loew-Alumni Library, Huntington IN. 219-356-6000
KaFarski, Rosemary, *Librn,* Fair Haven Free Public Library, Fair Haven VT. 802-265-8011
Kafes, Frederick, *Dir,* Our Lady of Lourdes (Hospital Library), Camden NJ. 609-757-3548
Kaften-Minkel, Walter, *Librn,* Library Association of Portland (Albina), Portland OR. 503-287-7147
Kagan, Ilse, *Librn,* W J Levy Consultants Corp Library, New York NY. 212-586-5263
Kagann, Laurie K, *Librn,* Woodridge Public Library, Woodridge IL. 312-964-7899
Kaganoff, Nathan M, *Librn,* American Jewish Historical Society, Lee M Friedman Memorial Library, Waltham MA. 617-891-8110
Kagels, Karen, *Librn,* Buffalo & Erie County Public Library System (Genesee), Buffalo NY. 716-892-8170
Kager, John, *Dir,* Westchester Community College Library, Valhalla NY. 914-347-6939
Kahara, Lynda, *Dir,* Wicksteed Public Library, Hornepayne ON. 807-868-2332
Kahkonen, Laura, *Acq & Spec Coll,* Windsor Public Library, Windsor CT. 203-688-6433
Kahl, Judith, *Acq,* Wellesley College, Margaret Clapp Library, Wellesley MA. 617-235-0320, Ext 280
Kahl, Virginia, *Coord Pub Serv,* Alexandria Library, Alexandria VA. 703-750-6351
Kahle, Larry L, *On-Line Servs,* University of Nebraska-Lincoln, University Libraries, Lincoln NE. 402-472-2526
Kahler, Betty, *Librn,* Graham Bible College Library, Bristol TN. 615-764-8831

Kahn, Jeffrey, *Dir,* Weber County Library, Ogden UT. 801-399-8516
Kahn, Karen, *Ref,* Bentley College, Solomon R Baker Library, Waltham MA. 617-891-2231
Kahn, Leybl, *Librn,* New York City Planning Department, Interdepartmental Planning & Housing Library, New York NY. 212-566-7600
Kahn, Marilyn, *Librn,* William Douglas McAdams Medical Library Medical Library, New York NY. 212-759-6300, Ext 276
Kahn, Nina, *Law,* General Services Administration Library, Washington DC. 202-566-0420
Kahn, Sam, *Korean Area Specialist,* University of Hawaii (University of Hawaii Library), Honolulu HI. 808-948-7205
Kahrar, Janice, *Librn,* United States Testing Co Inc Library, Hoboken NJ. 201-792-2400
Kai, Michele K, *Libr Aid,* United States Navy (Pearl Harbor Naval Base Library), Honolulu HI. 808-471-8238
Kaighn, Anna Lee, *Librn,* EG&G Inc, Technical Library, Las Vegas NV. 702-739-0660
Kaimowitz, Jeffery H, *Rare Bks,* Trinity College Library, Hartford CT. 203-527-3151, Ext 396
Kaimowitz, Jeffrey H, *Curator,* Trinity College Library (Watkinson), Hartford CT. 203-527-3151, Ext 307
Kain, Joan, *Sr Librn,* New York State Department of Law Library, New York NY. 212-488-7445, 7446
Kain-Breese, April, *Dir,* University of Wisconsin Center-Fox Valley Library, Menasha WI. 414-734-8731, Ext 32
Kaipio, T, *Admin Servs Coordr,* Thunder Bay Public Library, Thunder Bay ON. 807-344-3585
Kaiser, Anna G, *Librn,* Long Island Community Library, Long Island KS. 913-854-7453
Kaiser, Betty, *Chief Librn,* Highland Park Community College Library, Highland Park MI. 313-956-0587
Kaiser, Carole, *Bkmobile Coordr,* Baldwin County Library System, Robertsdale AL. 205-947-7632
Kaiser, Diane, *Bkmobile Coordr,* Baldwin County Library System, Robertsdale AL. 205-947-7632
Kaiser, F, *Bibliog Instr,* Georgia Institute of Technology, Price Gilbert Memorial Library, Atlanta GA. 404-894-4510
Kaiser, John R, *Coordr, Coll,* Pennsylvania State University, Fred Lewis Pattee Library, University Park PA. 814-865-0401
Kaiser, Judith, *Librn,* Carver Memorial Library, Searsport ME. 207-548-6682
Kaiser, Margaret, *Librn,* Elk Rapids District Library, Elk Rapids MI. 616-264-9979
Kaiser, Nancy, *Ref,* State University of New York College of Technology, Utica-Rome Library, Utica NY. 315-792-3420
Kaiser, Sister Dolores, *Acq,* Mount Marty College Library, Yankton SD. 605-668-1555
Kakalicik, Judy, *Acq,* College of Great Falls Library, Great Falls MT. 406-761-8210, Ext 280
Kalaf, Lailan N, *Librn,* South Florida Regional Planning Council Library, Miami FL. 305-621-5871
Kalangis, George P, *Dir, Rare Bks & Spec Coll,* Okaloosa-Walton Junior College, Learning Resources Center, Niceville FL. 904-678-5111, Ext 351
Kalb, Margaret, *Tech Serv & Cat,* Madison-Jefferson County Public Library, Madison IN. 812-265-2744
Kalbfell, Mollie B, *Librn,* Instruments Inc, Library, San Diego CA. 714-571-1111
Kaldenburg, Kathy, *Pub Servs,* Alpha Park Public Library District, Bartonville IL. 309-697-3822
Kaldor, Ivan L, *Dean,* State University of New York, College of Arts & Science, School of Library & Information Science, NY. 716-245-5322
Kalen, Bernadine, *Asst Librn & Ref,* Harlan Public Library, Harlan KY. 606-573-5220
Kalikow, Nancy Wise, *Libr Info Specialist,* Massachusetts Board of Library Commissioners, Office for the Development of Library Services, Boston MA. 617-267-9400
Kalionzes, Carole, *Per,* Los Angeles Pierce College Library, Woodland Hills CA. 213-347-0551, Ext 267
Kalisz, Andrew, *ILL,* Goddard College, William Shipman Library, Plainfield VT. 802-454-8311, Ext 232
Kalk, Carol, *Librn,* Clinton Corn Processing Co, Research Library, Clinton IA. 319-242-1121

Kalk, Daniel S, *Dir,* Enfield Central Library, Enfield CT. 203-749-0766

Kalkanis, Agatha, *Music & Performing Arts,* Detroit Public Library, Detroit Associated Libraries, Detroit MI. 313-833-1000

Kalkus, Stanley, *Dir,* United States Department of the Navy (Navy Dept Library), Washington DC. 202-433-4131

Kallaway, William D, *Librn,* Dorr-Oliver Inc, Central Technical Library, Stamford CT. 203-358-3200

Kallay, Ernest, *Commun Servs, Br Coordr & Bkmobile Coordr,* Clarksburg-Harrison Public Library, Clarksburg WV. 304-624-6512, 624-6513

Kallem, Susan, *Librn,* American Pharmaceutical Association Foundation Library, Washington DC. 202-628-4410, Ext 37

Kallenbach, Susan, *Cat,* University of Pennsylvania Libraries, Van Pelt Library, Philadelphia PA. 215-243-7091

Kallenback, Jessamine, *Humanities,* Eastern Michigan University, Center of Educational Resources, Ypsilanti MI. 313-487-0020

Kallenberg, John K, *Librn,* Fresno County Free Library, Fresno CA. 209-488-3191

Kallenberg, John K, *Librn,* San Joaquin Valley Library System, Fresno CA. 201-488-3185

Kallestad, Rena, *Librn,* Rake Public Library, Rake IA. 515-566-3388

Kallfisch, Doreen, *Tech Serv,* Middletown Township Public Library, Middletown NJ. 201-671-3700

Kallmann, H M, *Chief, Music Div,* National Library of Canada, Ottawa ON. 613-995-9481

Kallmann, Mrs Fred, *Librn,* Stanford Free Library, Stanfordville NY. 914-868-1341

Kallner, Esther, *YA,* Baldwin Public Library, Baldwin NY. 516-223-6228

Kalloch, Phillip C, *In Charge,* Union Mutual Life Insurance Co, Information Center, Portland ME. 207-780-2347

Kalloch, Jr, Phillip C, *In Charge,* State Street Church Library, Portland ME. 207-774-6396

Kall,c *In Charge,* Union Mutual Life Insurance Co, Information Center, Portland ME. 207-780-2347

Kalloo, Linnie, *Librn,* Ottawa Public Library (Elmvale Acres), Ottawa ON. 613-236-0301, Ext 276

Kallop, Sharon M, *Librn,* Bigham, Englar, Jones & Houston, Law Library, New York NY. 212-732-4646, Ext 158

Kalman, Georgia, *Librn,* Temple Israel Library, Minneapolis MN. 612-377-9157

Kalmring, Eleanore, *Librn,* Amalgamated Clothing & Textile Workers Union, Research Dept Library, New York NY. 212-255-7800, 777-3600, Ext 368

Kalra, Bhupinder S, *Librn,* Niles Public Library (Niles Pub), Niles IL. 312-297-6266

Kalsch, Alvina, *Tech Serv & Acq,* State University of New York Maritime College, Stephen B Luce Library, Bronx NY. 212-892-3004, Ext 235

Kaltenbach, Margaret, *Emer Assoc Prof,* Case Western Reserve University, School of Library Science, OH. 216-368-3500

Kaltenborn, Helen P, *Tech Serv,* Towson State University, Albert S Cook Library, Towson MD. 301-321-2450

Kaluzsa, Louis S, *Librn,* Cuyahoga County Public Library (Parma-Snow Branch), Parma OH. 216-661-4240

Kalvelage, Rosalind, *Ch & YA,* East Detroit Memorial Library, East Detroit MI. 313-775-7221

Kalvonjian, Araxie, *Cat,* Gateway Technical Institute, Learning Resources Center, Kenosha WI. 414-656-6924, 656-6923

Kam, Tom, *Sci-Tech,* Redwood City Public Library, Redwood City CA. 415-369-6251, Ext 288

Kamaras, Deborah, *Librn,* Kennecott Copper Corporation, Exploration Library, New York NY. 212-687-5800

Kamat, Alison, *Ref & Pub Servs,* University of Texas Health Science Center at Houston, School of Public Health Library, Houston TX. 713-792-4350

Kameen, Karen, *AV,* University of Pittsburgh (Western Psychiatric Institute & Clinic Library), Pittsburgh PA. 412-624-2378

Kamego, Claire, *Ch,* Arlington Public Library, Arlington TX. 817-275-2763, 265-3311, Ext 347

Kamenoff, Lovisa, *Librn,* Brockton Hospital Library, Brockton MA. 617-586-2600, Ext 375

Kaminski, Edward, *On-Line Servs,* American Society for Metals Library, Metals Park OH. 216-338-5151, Ext 557

Kaminski, Jean, *Librn,* Garden Valley District Library, Garden Valley ID. 208-462-3735

Kaminski, Ron, *Librn,* Fairfax County Public Library (Carter Glass Branch), Reston VA. 703-437-8484

Kaminsky, Alan S, *Bus Mgr,* Emory Medical Television Network, GA. 404-659-5307

Kaminsky, Gertrude, *Ad,* Joseph Mann Library, Two Rivers WI. 414-794-7121

Kamm, Dorothy, *Librn,* Paxtang-Swatara Area Community Library, Harrisburg PA. 717-564-0385

Kamm, Keith A, *Bibliog,* Athenaeum of Philadelphia, Philadelphia PA. 215-925-2688

Kammer, F David, *Librn,* United States Army (Corps of Engineers, Baltimore District Library), Baltimore MD. 301-962-3425

Kammer, Patricia, *Librn,* Winfield Public Library, Winfield IL. 312-653-7599

Kammerer, James, *Bkmobile Coordr,* Brunswick-Glynn County Regional Library, Brunswick GA. 912-264-7360

Kammerer, Kathryn, *Librn,* Alta Bates Hospital, Stuart Memorial Health Sciences Library, Berkeley CA. 415-845-7110, Ext 2359

Kamp, Mrs Ben Doren, *Asst Dir,* Alexander Public Library, Alexander IA. 515-692-3228

Kampas, Irene, *Circ,* Bergenfield Free Public Library, Bergenfield NJ. 201-384-2765

Kampen, Jeanette, *Ad, Acq & Ref,* Granite City Public Library, Granite City IL. 618-876-0550

Kamper, Albert F, *Coordr, Tech Servs,* Carnegie Library of Pittsburgh, Pittsburgh PA. 412-622-3100

Kamps, Donald, *Dir,* North Iowa Area Community College Library, Mason City IA. 515-421-4232

Kampworth, Mary Lou, *Librn,* Lewis & Clark Library System (Talking Book Department), Edwardsville IL. 618-656-3216

Kamrud, Sylvia, *Librn,* American Hardware Mutual Insurance Co Library, Minneapolis MN. 612-920-1400

Kamykoski, J David, *Dir,* Waldwick Public Library, Waldwick NJ. 201-652-5104

Kan, Halina, *Assoc Librn,* RCA Corporation (David Sarnoff Research Center Library), Princeton NJ. 609-734-2608, 734-2610

Kanabrodski, Christina C, *Librn,* Motor Vehicle Manufacturers Association of the United States, Inc (Communications Library), Detroit MI. 313-872-4311, Ext 370

Kanady, Catherine, *Librn,* Jackson-George Regional Library System (Ocean Springs Municipal), Ocean Springs MS. 601-875-1193

Kanaley, Daniel, *Cat,* State University of New York College of Technology, Utica-Rome Library, Utica NY. 315-792-3420

Kanalley, William, *Acq,* Siena College, Jerome Dawson Memorial Library, Loudonville NY. 518-783-2522

Kanarek, Evelyn S, *Librn,* Morton Norwich Library, Chicago IL. 312-621-5244

Kanasky, William F, *Assoc Prof,* Kutztown State College, Dept of Library Science, PA. 215-683-4300, 683-4301

Kanbara, Jack, *Tech Serv,* Cuesta College, Library Learning Center, San Luis Obispo CA. 805-544-2943, Ext 280

Kanders, Herman, *Sr Librns,* New York State Library (Monographic Processing), Albany NY. 518-474-5948, 474-7866

Kane, Ann, *Reader Serv,* Monroe County Public Library, Stroudsburg PA. 717-421-0800

Kane, Barbara, *Commun Servs,* Jervis Public Library Association, Rome NY. 315-336-4570

Kane, Charles C, *Librn,* Rand Corporation Library, Washington DC. 202-296-5000, Ext 329

Kane, Dennis, *Librn,* Denver Public Library (Park Hill), Denver CO. 303-573-5152, Ext 271

Kane, Dolores M, *Librn,* Chicago Public Library (Edgewater), Chicago IL. 312-262-3166

Kane, Hilarie, *YA,* New Berlin Public Library, New Berlin WI. 414-786-2990

Kane, James, *Librn,* Nova University Libraries (Oceanography), Dania FL. 305-587-6660, Ext 289

Kane, Kathy, *Ref,* University of Tulsa, McFarlin Library, Tulsa OK. 918-592-6000, Ext 351

Kane, Linda, *Librn,* Shriver (Eunice Kennedy) Center for Mental Retardation, Inc Library, Waltham MA. 617-893-3500

Kane, Lois, *Spec Serv,* Arlington County Department of Libraries, Arlington Public Library, Arlington VA. 703-527-4777

Kane, Marie, *Librn,* Marschalk Co, Inc Library, Cleveland OH. 216-687-8800

Kane, Matthew, *District Serv,* Altoona Area Public Library, Altoona PA. 814-946-0417

Kane, Nancy J, *Librn,* General Electric Co (Ordnance Systems, Engineering Library), Pittsfield MA. 413-494-4145

Kane, Pauline, *Librn,* Richland Township Library, Vestaburg MI. 517-268-5286

Kane, Sister M Edith, *Curric Mat,* Marycrest College, Cone Library, Davenport IA. 319-326-9254

Kane, Virginia, *Ref,* Calcasieu Parish Public Library System, Lake Charles LA. 318-433-1045

Kane, William E, *Chief Librn,* Veterans Administration, Medical Center Library, Castle Point NY. 914-831-2000

Kaneko, Hideo, *Curator E Asian Coll,* Yale University Library (Sterling Memorial Library), New Haven CT. 203-436-8335

Kanell, Richard W, *Librn,* Carnegie Library of Pittsburgh (Knoxville), Pittsburgh PA. 412-622-3100

Kanen, Ronald A, *Bureau of Library Services: Chief,* State Library of Florida, Div of Library Services, Dept of State, Tallahassee FL. 904-487-2651

Kanezo, Marilyn W, *Dir,* Mount Carmel Public Library, Mount Carmel PA. 717-339-0703

Kang, Chung-Sook, *Librn,* Carnegie Library of Pittsburgh (Squirrel Hill), Pittsburgh PA. 412-622-3100

Kang, NamHee, *Info Specialists,* Occidental Research Corp Library, Irvine CA. 714-957-7450

Kang, Un Hi, *Dir,* Westmar College, Charles A Mock Library, Le Mars IA. 712-546-7081, Ext 217

Kangley, Monica, *Asst Librn & Ch,* East Hampton Public Library, East Hampton CT. 203-267-2635

Kanive, Fern, *ILL,* North Platte Public Library, Lincoln Keith Perkins Regional Library, North Platte NE. 308-532-6560

Kanner, Elliott E, *Resources Coordr,* North Suburban Library System, Wheeling IL. 312-459-1300

Kanner, Madeline, *Librn,* Lake County Forest Preserve District, Ryerson Nature Library, Libertyville IL. 312-367-6640

Kanner, Ruth C, *Dir,* Moore-Cottrell Subscription Agencies, Inc, Serials Reference Library, North Cohocton NY. 716-534-5221, Ext 35

Kanocz, Otto, *Chief Librn,* Federation Employment & Guidance Service, Richard J Bernhard Memorial Library, New York NY. 212-777-4900, Ext 155

Kanous, Melva, *Librn,* Lenawee County Library (Britton Branch), Britton MI. 517-451-2860

Kanowicz, Dina McDonald, *Curator,* High Plains Museum Library, McCook NE. 308-345-3661

Kansfield, Norman J, *Librn,* Western Theological Seminary, Beardslee Library, Holland MI. 616-392-8555, Ext 37 & 38

Kantor, David, *Dir,* Volusia County Public Libraries, Daytona Beach FL. 904-252-8374

Kantor, Judith, *Librn,* University of California Los Angeles Library (University Elementary School), Los Angeles CA. 213-825-4928

Kantrowitz, Rosalind, *Info,* Robbins Library, Arlington MA. 617-643-0026

Kanus, Louise, *Nonprint Media Servs Consult,* Massachusetts Board of Library Commissioners, Office for the Development of Library Services, Boston MA. 617-267-9400

Kanzler, George, *Dir,* Rutgers University (Archibald Stevens Alexander Library), New Brunswick NJ. 201-932-7129

Kao, Angela, *Orientalia,* United States Military Academy Library, West Point NY. 914-938-2230

Kao, Anita S, *Cat,* Capital University Library, Columbus OH. 614-236-6614

Kao, Bernice, *Librn,* Dames & Moore Chicago Library, Park Ridge IL. 312-297-6120, Ext 388

Kao, Joyce, *Per,* Mayo Foundation (Medical Library), Rochester MN. 507-284-2061

Kao, Mary Liu, *Coordr,* Mohegan Community College Library, Norwich CT. 203-886-1931

Kao, Rose, *Tech Serv,* Englewood Library, Englewood NJ. 201-568-2215

Kaohi, Aletha, *Libr Tech,* Hawaii State Library System (Waimea Branch), Waimea HI. 808-338-1738

Kapecky, Michele Ann, *Dir,* Detroit Free Press Library, Detroit MI. 313-222-6897

Kapenstein, Henry, *Cent Pub Servs,* Free Library of Philadelphia, Philadelphia PA. 215-686-5322

Kaplan, Amy, *Librn,* Cherry Hill Medical Center, Medical Library, Cherry Hill NJ. 609-665-2000, Ext 363

Kaplan, Bess D, *Mat Coord,* Foundation for Blind Children Library, Scottsdale AZ. 602-947-3744

Kaplan, Dorothy, *Libm,* H Kohnstamm & Co, Inc, Technical Dept Library, New York NY. 212-620-4800

Kaplan, Henriette, *Dept Head,* Butler University, AV Library Science, IN. 317-283-9208

Kaplan, Janice, *Ref,* University of Massachusetts Medical School, Medical Center Library, Worcester MA. 617-856-2511

Kaplan, Judith M, *Head Librn,* American Foundation for the Blind, M C Migel Memorial Library, New York NY. 212-620-2161

Kaplan, Leslie, *Media,* University of Lowell Libraries (Alumni-Lydon Library), Lowell MA. 617-452-5000, Ext 378

Kaplowitz, Dorothy, *Libm,* New York Public Library (Baychester), New York NY. 212-379-6700

Kapnick, Laura B, *Libm,* C B S Inc, CBS News Reference Library, New York NY. 212-975-2877

Kapp, David L, *Pub Serv,* University of Connecticut Library, Storrs CT. 203-486-2219

Kapp, Elizabeth R, *Dir & Cat,* Transylvania County Library, Inc, Brevard NC. 704-883-9880

Kappenberg, Alice W, *Archivist,* Suffolk County Historical Society Library, Riverhead NY. 516-727-2881

Karacius, Lois, *Libm,* Sutton Free Public Library, Sutton MA. 617-865-6939

Karaczewski, Oksana, *Dir,* New York College of Podiatric Medicine, Dr Sidney Druskin Memorial Library, New York NY. 212-427-8400, Ext 26

Karakehian, Lois, *Coordr of Volunteers,* Colorado State Library - Services for the Blind & Physically Handicapped, Denver CO. 303-839-2081

Karalles, Dorothy, *Cat,* Lenoir-Rhyne College, Carl A Rudisill Library, Hickory NC. 704-328-1741, Ext 221

Karas, Margaret, *Libm,* McHenry Nunda Public Library District, McHenry IL. 815-385-6303

Karbal, Albert E, *Dir,* Congregation Shaarey Zedek Library, Southfield MI. 313-357-5544

Karch, Linda, *Libm,* Mercy Hospital, Medical Library, Buffalo NY. 826-7000 Ext 323

Karcher, Carolyn L, *Libm,* Carnegie Free Library, Midland PA. 412-643-8980

Karczag, Edna R, *Dir,* Klamath County Library, Klamath Falls OR. 503-882-8894

Kardokas, Christine, *Branch & Exten,* Worcester Public Library, Worcester MA. 617-752-3751

Kareckas, Agnes, *Ch,* Lawrence Public Library, Lawrence MA. 617-682-1727

Kares, Gale C, *Libm,* Main Lafrentz & Co, National Office Library, New York NY. 212-269-5800

Karesh, Susan, *Libm,* Wake County Department of the Public Library (Glenwood Towers Neighborhood), Raleigh NC. 919-755-6122

Kareta, Sophie, *Assoc Dir,* Westfield Athenaeum, Westfield MA. 413-568-7833

Karetnikova, Inga, *Lectr,* Simmons College, Graduate School of Library & Information Science, MA. 617-738-2225

Karges, Joann, *Tech Serv,* Texas Christian University, Mary Couts Burnett Library, Fort Worth TX. 817-921-7106

Kari, Randy, *Libm,* Sinte Gleska College Library, Mission SD. 605-856-4550

Karim, Zarina, *Libm,* Pakistan Embassy Library, Washington DC. 202-332-8330, Ext 65

Karimkhani, Denise, *Acq,* University of Mary Hardin-Baylor, Townsend Memorial Library, Belton TX. 817-939-5811, Ext 256

Karisky, U Alta, *Libm,* NRC, Inc Library, Newton MA. 617-969-7690

Karkhanis, Sharad, *ILL,* Kingsborough Community College Library, Brooklyn NY. 212-934-5144

Karl, Geneva, *Br Asst,* La Crosse County Library (Campbell), La Crosse WI. 608-785-1478

Karl, Helen, *Dir,* New Lenox Township Library, New Lenox IL. 815-485-2605

Karl, Roger, *Libm,* Public Library of Nashville & Davidson County (Inglewood), Nashville TN. 615-227-9102

Karlen, Ann, *Libm,* Washington County Law Library, Hillsboro OR. 503-648-8880

Karlin, Estelle, *Libm,* Harvard University Library (John G Wolbach Library), Cambridge MA. 617-495-5488

Karlin, Martin, *Chief Br of Info & Advisory Servs,* United States Department of Labor, Bureau of Labor Statistics, New York NY. 212-944-3121

Karling, Geraldine, *Libm,* Chicago Public Library (Portage-Cragin), Chicago IL. 312-736-2577

Karlinsky, Linda Leff, *Libm,* Campion College Library, Regina SK. 306-586-4242, Ext 34

Karlo, Rita, *Libm,* Akron-Summit County Public Library (Norton Branch), Norton OH. 216-825-4724

Karlson, Marjorie, *Ref,* University of Massachusetts at Amherst Library, Amherst MA. 413-545-0284

Karlstrom, Paul, *Libm,* Archives of American Art, West Coast Area Center, San Francisco CA. 414-556-2530

Karmazin, Gretchen, *Libm,* Broward County Division of Libraries (Mirama Branch), Miramar FL. 305-963-5646

Karmazin, Sharon, *Public Relations,* East Brunswick Public Library, East Brunswick NJ. 201-254-1220

Karmazin, Sharon, *Asst Librn & Pub Servs,* East Brunswick Public Library, East Brunswick NJ. 201-254-1220

Karmiller, Dorothy, *Spec Coll & Ref,* Union City Free Public Library, Union City NJ. 201-866-7500

Karn, Betty, *Asst Librn,* Flesherton Public Library, Flesherton ON. 519-924-2241

Karns, Joyce, *Libm,* Indianapolis-Marion County Public Library (Wayne), Indianapolis IN. 317-635-5662

Karns, Thelma R, *Libm,* Leon Public Library, Leon IA. 515-446-6332

Karoblis, Dalija P, *Asst Dir,* Public Library of Brookline, Brookline MA. 617-734-0100

Karow, Betty, *Libm,* Milwaukee Art Center Library, Milwaukee WI. 414-271-9508, Ext 210

Karow, Lee, *Circ,* Moline Public Library, Moline IL. 309-762-6883

Karp, Margot, *Libr Sci,* Pratt Institute Library, Brooklyn NY. 212-636-3684

Karpe, Margaret, *Bibliog Instr,* Center for Biblical Studies, Inc Library, Modesto CA. 209-527-4271

Karpevych, Christine, *Chief Libm,* Avon Products, Inc, Central Library, New York NY. 212-593-5375

Karpicke, Jean, *AV,* Kirtland Community College Library, Roscommon MI. 517-275-5121

Karpiel, Sharon, *Ref,* Roselle Public Library District, Roselle IL. 312-529-1641

Karpinski, Helen, *Media,* Memphis-Shelby County Public Library & Information Center, Memphis TN. 901-528-2950

Karr, Juanita R, *Dir,* Northern Nevada Community College, Learning Resources Center, Elko NV. 702-738-8493, Ext 225

Karre, David, *Ref,* Niagara Falls Public Library, Niagara Falls NY. 716-278-8041

Karre, Mary Anne, *Libm,* Town of Hamburg Public Library (Blasdell Branch), Blasdell NY. 716-823-4220

Karren, Judith, *Libm,* Prince George's County Memorial Library System (Bladensburg Branch), Bladensburg MD. 301-927-4916

Karrow, Robert W, *Curator of Maps,* Newberry Library, Chicago IL. 312-943-9090

Karry, Catherine, *Bks-by-Mail,* Flagstaff City-Coconino County Public Library System, Flagstaff AZ. 602-774-0603

Karson, Phyllis, *Acq,* Miami Dade Community College (Medical Center Campus Library), Miami FL. 305-547-1256

Karsten, Eileen, *Tech Serv,* Barat College Library, Lake Forest IL. 312-234-3000, Ext 237

Karukin, Mildred, *Assoc Libm,* Mount Sinai Medical Center Library, Audiovisual Services, Miami Beach FL. 305-674-2840

Kasabian, Janet, *Libm,* Cox, Castle & Nicholson Library, Los Angeles CA. 213-277-4222

Kasakitis, Jurgis, *Chief Libm,* Balzekas Museum of Lithuanian Culture, Library & Information Center, Chicago IL. 312-847-2441

Kasalko, Sally, *Ref, On-Line Servs & Bibliog Instr,* University of Arkansas for Medical Sciences Library, Little Rock AR. 501-661-5980

Kaschins, E, *Ref,* Luther College, Preus Library, Decorah IA. 319-387-1163

Kase, Shery L, *Libm,* Biotechnology Inc Library, Falls Church VA. 703-573-3700

Kashiki, Elaine, *Dir,* Inner City Cultural Center, Langston Hughes Memorial Library, Los Angeles CA. 213-387-1161

Kashmere, Sister Carmela, *Acq,* College Misericordia Library, Dallas PA. 717-675-2181, Ext 225

Kashyap, Meera, *Tech Serv,* Howard University Libraries (Allen Mercer Daniel Law Library), Washington DC. 202-686-6684

Kasinec, Edward, *Libm,* Harvard University Library (Ukranian Research Institute Reference Library), Cambridge MA. 617-495-3650

Kasling, Theresa, *Cat,* Saint John's University, Alcuin Library, Collegeville MN. 612-363-2119

Kasman, Dorothy, *Chief Libm,* Coopers & Lybrand Library, New York NY. 212-489-1100

Kasner, Betsie, *Info Servs,* Data Bank bureau of Business & Economic Research, Institute for Applied Research Services, Albuquerque NM. 505-277-2216

Kasner, Lynn, *Dir,* New York & New Jersey Regional Medical Library, NY. 212-876-8763

Kasparian, Lucy, *ILL & Ref,* Clark County Community College, Learning Resources Center, North Las Vegas NV. 702-643-6060, Ext 269

Kaspark, Craig W, *AV,* Providence Public Library, Providence RI. 401-521-7722

Kasper, Patricia L, *Libm,* Santa Barbara Botanic Garden Library, Santa Barbara CA. 805-682-4726

Kasper, Ruth, *Ref,* Emmaus Public Library, Emmaus PA. 215-965-9284

Kaspik, Arlene, *Ref,* Mount Prospect Public Library, Mount Prospect IL. 312-253-5675

Kasprowicz, III, Frank W, *Dir,* Claiborne Parish Library, Homer LA. 318-927-3845

Kasputis, Christine, *Tech Serv,* Western Regional Public Library System, Springfield MA. 413-732-3115

Kassinger, Timothy, *Libm,* Geauga County Public Library (Bainbridge), Chagrin Falls OH. 216-543-5611

Kasson, Shirley A, *Dir & Acq,* Comstock Township Library, Comstock MI. 616-345-0136

Kast, Gloria, *Head Ser,* American River College Library, Sacramento CA. 916-484-8293

Kastanis, Terry, *Asst Dean,* Cosumnes River College, Learning Resources Center, Sacramento CA. 916-421-1000, Ext 266

Kasten, Seth, *Ref,* Union Theological Seminary Library, New York NY. 212-662-7100, Ext 274

Kastigar, Sharon, *Libm,* Paden City Public Library, Paden City WV. 304-337-9333

Kastner, James, *Chief Libm,* Veterans Administration, Hospital Library, Louisville KY. 502-895-3401

Kastner, Margaret, *Index,* Time, Inc (Main Library), New York NY. 212-841-3745

Kasuba, Jayne, *Ad,* Mount Clemens Public Library, Mount Clemens MI. 313-465-1906

Kasulanis, Betty, *Libm,* West Pittston Library, West Pittston PA. 717-654-9847

Kasunich, Mary Anne, *Media,* Carlow College, Grace Library, Pittsburgh PA. 412-578-6137

Kaszynski, Tadeusz, *Cat,* Edison Free Public Library, Edison NJ. 201-287-2298

Katagiri, George, *Learning Resource Specialist,* Oregon State Department of Education, Resource Dissemination Center, Salem OR. 503-378-4974

Katan, James, *Libm,* Chaleur Regional Library (Campbellton Centennial Public), Campbellton NB. 506-753-5253

Katana, Ruth, *Asst Librn, ILL & Ad,* Sweetwater County Library, Green River WY. 307-875-3615

Katayama, Jane H, *Librn,* Massachusetts Institute of Technology, Lincoln Laboratory Library, Lexington MA. 617-862-5500, Ext 7195
Kateley, Margaret A, *Dir,* New Canaan Library, New Canaan CT. 203-966-1985
Katelko, Mrs V, *Librn,* Hairy Hill Municipal Library, Hairy Hill AB. 403-768-3800
Kates, Edith, *Ad,* Big Horn County Public Library, Hardin MT. 406-665-1808
Kates, Jacqueline R, *Librn,* Instrumentation Laboratory, Inc Library, Lexington MA. 617-861-0710, Ext 316
Kates, Mary, *Ref,* Holyoke Public Library, Holyoke MA. 413-534-3357
Kather, Jan, *Media,* Elmira College, Gannett-Tripp Learning Ctr, Elmira NY. 607-734-3911, Ext 287
Kathman, Michael D, *Dir,* Saint John's University, Alcuin Library, Collegeville MN. 612-363-2119
Katka, Matt, *Librn,* San Diego Public Library (Ocean Beach), San Diego CA. 714-223-8757
Kato, Steve, *Media,* Union College, MacKay Library-Learning Resource Center, Cranford NJ. 201-276-2600, Ext 244
Katona, Florence C, *Librn,* Cuyahoga County Public Library (Bedford Branch), Bedford OH. 216-439-4997
Katre, Helen, *Acq & On-Line Servs,* Hellenic College & Holy Cross Greek Orthodox School of Theology, Cotsidas-Tonna Library, Brookline MA. 617-731-3500, Ext 43, 44, 45
Katte, Vista, *Librn,* Mercer County Library (Washington), Robbinsville NJ. 609-259-2151
Katter, Yvonne, *Ref,* Deschutes County Library, Bend OR. 503-382-5191
Katti, Susan Nagar, *Librn,* Mount Sinai Medical Center, Medical Library, Milwaukee WI. 414-289-8200, Ext 2582
Kattlove, Rose W, *Chief Librn,* Xerox Corporation, Technical Library, El Segundo CA. 213-679-4511, Ext 2222
Katusz, Brother Christian M, *Librn,* Saint Hyacinth College & Seminary, Kolbe Memorial Library, Granby MA. 413-467-7191
Katz, Annelise, *Librn,* Harvard University Library (Psychology Library), Cambridge MA. 617-495-3858
Katz, Barbara, *Ch,* Milton Public Library, Milton MA. 617-698-5707
Katz, Bonnie, *Ch,* Upper Dublin Public Library, Dresher PA. 215-885-5320
Katz, Doris B, *Admin,* National Broadcasting Co (Information-Unit Research Department), New York NY. 212-664-4243
Katz, Helen, *Ref & On-Line Servs,* Canadian Imperial Bank of Commerce, Information Centre Library, Toronto ON. 416-862-3053
Katz, Janet, *Ref,* Suffolk University College Library (Law), Boston MA. 617-723-4700, Ext 176
Katz, Linda, *Archivist,* Albert Einstein College of Medicine, D Samuel Gottesman Library, Bronx NY. 212-430-3108
Katz, Lorraine, *Ad & Ref,* Shelter Rock Public Library, Albertson NY. 516-248-7363
Katz, Marilyn, *Librn,* Child Welfare League of America, Dorothy L Berhard Library, New York NY. 212-254-7410, Ext 419, 224
Katz, Mrs Henry, *Librn,* Temple Judah Library, Cedar Rapids IA. 319-362-1261
Katz, Nancy, *ILL,* Tulane University of Louisiana (Matas Medical Library), New Orleans LA. 504-588-5155
Katz, Robert, *Media,* Albany Public Library, Albany NY. 518-449-3380
Katz, Toni, *Librn,* Beal College Library, Bangor ME. 207-947-7905
Katz, William A, *Prof,* State University of New York at Albany, School of Library & Information Science, NY. 518-455-6288
Katzen, Andrew, *Assoc Librn,* Stoughton Public Library, Stoughton MA. 617-344-2711
Katzenberg, Avis, *Dir,* Genoa City Public Library, Genoa City WI. 414-279-6188
Katzer, Jeffrey, *Assoc Prof,* Syracuse University, School of Information Studies, NY. 315-423-2911
Katzung, Judith, *Librn,* Saint Paul Dispatch & Saint Paul Pioneer Press Library, Northwest Publications, Inc, Saint Paul MN. 612-222-5011
Kaubris-Kowalzyk, Sally A, *Asst Dir,* Bangor Theological Seminary, Moulton Library, Bangor ME. 207-942-6781

Kauderer, Charles, *Dir,* Regis College, Dayton Memorial Library, Denver CO. 303-458-4030
Kaufer, Sheila V, *Ch,* Township of Washington Public Library, Westwood NJ. 201-664-4586
Kauff, Joan L, *Chief Librn,* Long Island Jewish-Hillside Medical Center, Hillside Division Health Sciences Library, Glen Oaks NY. 516-470-4406
Kauffman, Betty, *Librn,* American Telephone & Telegraph Co, Morristown Corporation Human Resources, Morristown NJ. 201-540-6439
Kauffman, Betty G, *Librn,* American Telephone & Telegraph, Business & Technical Resources Center, Piscataway NJ. 201-699-2169
Kauffman, Blair, *Dir,* National Judicial College, Law Library, Reno NV. 702-784-6747
Kauffman, Bruce, *Dir & Spec Coll,* Boca Raton Public Library, Boca Raton FL. 395-2980 & 395-1110, Ext 285, 286, 336
Kauffman, Inge, *Dir,* California School of Professional Psychology, Fresno Campus Library, Fresno CA. 209-486-8420, Ext 30
Kauffman, Kathy A, *Ref,* Colorado College, Charles Leaming Tutt Library, Colorado Springs CO. 303-473-2233, Ext 415
Kauffman, Linda, *Librn,* Iosco-Arenac Regional Library (Au Gres Library), Au Gres MI. 517-362-2651
Kaufhold, Eleanor, *Dir,* North Merrick Public Library, North Merrick NY. 516-378-7474
Kaufhold, O G, *Dir,* Bellmore Memorial Library, Bellmore NY. 516-785-2990
Kaufman, Billie Jo, *Dir,* Brownsburg Public Library, Brownsburg IN. 317-852-3167
Kaufman, David, *ILL,* Indiana University of Pennsylvania, Rhodes R Stabley Library, Indiana PA. 412-357-2340
Kaufman, Diane W, *Tech Serv, Acq & Cat,* North Olympic Library System, Port Angeles WA. 206-457-4464
Kaufman, Ivy, *Librn,* Marshall, Bratter, Greene, Allison & Tucker, Law Library, New York NY. 212-421-7200, Ext 281
Kaufman, Jay, *Media,* Ramapo College of New Jersey Library, Mahwah NJ. 201-825-2800, Ext 260
Kaufman, JoAnn, *Educ,* State University of New York College, Daniel A Reed Library, Fredonia NY. 716-673-3183
Kaufman, John R, *Dir,* N W Ayer ABH International, Ayer Information Center, New York NY. 212-974-6411
Kaufman, Judith, *Assoc Librn,* State University of New York (Music), Stony Brook NY. 516-246-5660
Kaufman, Leah, *Librn,* New York Public Library (Woodlawn Heights), New York NY. 212-324-0791
Kaufman, Louise L, *Dir,* Cherryvale Public Library, Cherryvale KS. 316-336-2491
Kaufman, Lynn, *Asst Librn,* Environmental Law Institute Library, Washington DC. 202-452-9600, Ext 206
Kaufman, Oxanna, *Libr Resources Coordr,* University of Pittsburgh, Hillman Library, Pittsburgh PA. 412-624-4400
Kaufman, Paula, *Librn,* Columbia University (Business-Economics), New York NY. 212-280-2241
Kaufmann, Lois W, *Librn,* Warren Public Library, Warren VT. 802-496-3913
Kaufmann, Robert, *Librn,* Smithsonian Institution Libraries, Cooper-Hewitt Museum Library, New York NY. 212-860-6883
Kaufmann, Ruth M, *Bkmobile Coordr,* Mount Vernon Public Library, Mount Vernon NY. 914-668-1840
Kaul, K L, *Head,* Wayne State University Libraries (G Flint Purdy Library), Detroit MI. 313-577-4032
Kaulfuss, Carol B, *Librn,* Highwood Public Library, Highwood IL. 312-432-5404
Kaup, Jerry, *Dir,* Minot Public Library, Minot ND. 701-852-1045
Kaupa, Joyce, *Librn,* Veterans Administration, Hospital Library Service, Buffalo NY. 716-834-9200
Kaushagen, B A, *Libr Suprv,* Bell Telephone Laboratories (Western Electric Technical Library), Columbus OH. 614-868-3696
Kauvadias, Virginia, *Librn,* Omaha Public Library (Sorensen), Omaha NE. 402-444-5274

Kavanagh, Helen, *Dir,* Holmes County District Public Library, Millersburg OH. 216-674-5972
Kavanagh, Rosemary, *Syst Coordr,* Central Ontario Regional Library, Richmond Hill ON. 416-884-4395
Kavanagh, Sister Clarencia, *Rare Bks,* Incarnate Word College, Saint Pius X Library, San Antonio TX. 512-828-1261, Ext 215
Kavanaugh, Irene, *Cat,* University of Massachusetts at Amherst Library, Amherst MA. 413-545-0284
Kavass, Igor I, *Dir,* Vanderbilt University School of Law Library, Nashville TN. 615-322-2568
Kavulich, Linda, *Per,* Georgian Court College, Farley Memorial Library, Lakewood NJ. 201-364-2200, Ext 19
Kawa, Paula, *Librn,* Bureau of Land Management, Utah State Office, Records Office Library, Salt Lake City UT. 801-524-5337
Kawakami, Toyo S, *Librn,* Ohio State University Libraries (Social Work Library), Columbus OH. 614-422-6627
Kawano, Kei, *Cat,* W Leslie Rogers Library, Pennsauken Public Library, Pennsauken NJ. 609-665-5959
Kawaquchi, Miyako, *Tech Serv,* Liberty Baptist College Library, Lynchburg VA. 804-528-0821
Kawar, Harriet, *Librn,* Marion County Library, Marion SC. 803-423-2244
Kay, Debra A, *Acq & Media,* Converse College, Gwathmey Library, Spartanburg SC. 803-585-6421, Ext 260
Kay, Dennis, *Librn,* Clark County Library District (Sunrise), Las Vegas NV. 702-453-1104
Kay, Kathryn L, *Dir,* Tiffin University, Richard C Pfeiffer Library, Tiffin OH. 419-447-6442, Ext 44
Kay, Mary, *ILL,* University of Kansas Libraries, Watson Memorial Library, Lawrence KS. 913-864-3601
Kay, Mrs Sidney R, *Librns,* Temple B'nai Israel, Lasker Memorial Library, Galveston TX. 713-765-5796
Kay, Wendy, *Librn,* San Jose Public Library (Seventrees), San Jose CA. 408-629-4535
Kaya, Beatrice, *Chief Librn,* Hawaii Newspaper Agency, Inc Library, Honolulu HI. 808-525-7669
Kaya, Mariko, *Tech Serv & Acq,* Los Angeles County Public Library System, South State Cooperative Library System, Los Angeles CA. 213-974-6501
Kaye, Alan, *Acq,* Clayton Junior College Library, Morrow GA. 404-961-3520
Kaye, Doug, *Librn,* University of British Columbia Library (Wilson Recordings Collection), Vancouver BC. 604-228-2534
Kaye, Geraldine C, *Librn,* Harvard University Library (Farlow Reference Library), Cambridge MA. 617-495-2369
Kaye, Sheldon, *Dir,* Marshfield Free Library, Marshfield WI. 715-384-2929, 387-1302
Kaylo, Susen, *Asst Librn,* Prescott Public Library, Prescott ON. 613-925-4340
Kaylor, Ann, *Librn,* Chetek Public Library, Chetek WI. 715-924-3195
Kays, Mary, *Asst Dir,* Bell Public Library, Portland TX. 512-643-6527
Kayser, Sandra, *Librn,* Prince George's County Memorial Library System (Suitland Branch), Suitland MD. 301-736-6262
Kazadi, Camille, *Dir,* Art Center College of Design, Fogg Memorial Library, Pasadena CA. 213-577-1700, Ext 265
Kazan, Camille, *Media,* Beverly Hills Public Library, Beverly Hills CA. 213-550-4711
Kazlauskas, Diane, *Circ,* Southern Illinois University School of Medicine Library, Springfield IL. 217-782-2658
Kazmierski, Dan, *Dir,* International Correspondence Schools Library, Scranton PA. 717-342-7701, Ext 268
Kazymyra, B, *Archivist,* University of Regina Library, Regina SK. 306-584-4132
Keable, Doreen, *Instr,* Saint Cloud State University, Center for Library & Audiovisual Education, MN. 612-255-2022
Keall, M, *Librn,* Georgian Bay Township Library, MacTier ON. 705-375-5430
Keane, Jane, *Librn,* Brockton Public Library System (West), Brockton MA. 617-584-1265
Keane, Margaret, *Cat,* John Marshall Law School Library, Chicago IL. 312-427-2737, Ext 254

Keane, Patricia, *Art,* Chicago Public Library (Fine Arts Div), Chicago IL. 312-269-2839

Keaney, Kevin, *Instr,* United States Department of Agriculture Graduate School, Certificate Program for Library Technicians, DC. 202-447-5885

Kear, Becky, *Librn,* Dames & Moore Atlanta Library, Atlanta GA. 404-262-2915, Ext 49

Kearl, Biruta, *Cent Tex Libr Syst Coordr,* Austin Public Library, Austin TX. 512-472-5433

Kearl, Biruta, *Coordr,* Central Texas Library System, Austin TX. 512-474-5355

Kearley, David A, *Librn,* Vanderbilt University Library (Education), Nashville TN. 615-327-8184

Kearnes, James, *Exec Asst,* Herbert H Lehman College Library, Bronx NY. 212-960-8577, 960-8582

Kearney, Ann M, *Ser,* University of Miami (Louis Calder Memorial Library), Miami FL. 305-547-6441

Kearney, Eileen, *Tech Processes,* Saint Charles Borromeo Seminary, Ryan Memorial Library, Philadelphia PA. 215-839-3760, Ext 275

Kearney, Lorraine, *Coordr,* District One Technical Institute Library, Eau Claire WI. 715-836-3971

Kearney, Robert D, *Asst Dir, Media & On-Line Servs,* California College of Podiatric Medicine, Schmidt Medical Library, San Francisco CA. 415-563-3444, Ext 246

Kearns, Richard, *Circ,* University of Tulsa, McFarlin Library, Tulsa OK. 918-592-6000, Ext 351

Kearns, Viola B, *Tech Serv & Acq,* Eau Gallie Public Library, Melbourne FL. 305-254-1739

Keaschuk, Michael, *Librn,* Chinook Regional Library, Swift Current SK. 306-773-3186

Keaser, Daisy, *Ch,* Elsie Quirk Public Library, Englewood FL. 813-474-3515

Keasler, Donna S, *Librn,* Northern Petrochemical Co, Polymer Technical Center Library, Morris IL. 815-942-7400

Keasler, Wally, *Doc,* Chattanooga-Hamilton County Bicentennial Library, Chattanooga TN. 615-757-5320

Keates, Marjorie, *Librn,* Rideau Lakes Union Library (Elgin), Elgin ON. 613-359-5315

Keathley, Katherine, *Dir,* Arkansas River Valley Regional Library, Dardanelle AR. 501-229-4418

Keating, Anne, *Librn,* Thomas Crane Public Library (Adams Shore), Quincy MA. 617-471-2400

Keating, Barbara, *Chief Librn,* Register Newspaper Library, Santa Ana CA. 714-835-1234, Ext 237

Keating, Benjamin, *Regional Servs,* Maine State Library, Augusta ME. 207-289-3561

Keating, Evelyn, *Librn,* Argonne National Laboratory, Argonne-West Technical Library, Idaho Falls ID. 208-526-7237

Keating, Faith D, *Asst Dir, Acq & Cat,* West Islip Public Library, West Islip NY. 516-661-7080, 661-7082

Keating, H J, *Librn,* Cross City Correctional Institution Library, Cross City FL. 904-498-5576

Keating, John, *Cat,* Boston State College Library, Boston MA. 617-731-3300

Keating, Judith, *Ref,* University of Southern Maine, Gorham ME. 207-780-5340, 780-4273

Keating, Nancy, *Asst Librn,* Gilsum Public Library, Gilsum NH. 603-357-0320

Keating, Pamela, *Librn,* New York University (Institute of Judicial Administration), New York NY. 212-598-7723

Keaton, Carolyn, *Bkmobile Coordr,* Raleigh County Public Library, Beckley WV. 304-255-0511

Keator, Carol, *Librn,* Santa Barbara Public Library (Goleta Branch), Goleta CA. 805-964-7878

Keatts, Rowena W, *Librn,* Paul Quinn College, Sherman-Abington Library, Waco TX. 817-753-6415

Keaveney, Sydney S, *Art & Archit,* Pratt Institute Library, Brooklyn NY. 212-636-3684

Kebabian, Paul B, *Dir,* University of Vermont & State Agricultural College, Bailey-Howe Memorial Library, Burlington VT. 802-656-2020

Kebildis, Melba, *Librn,* United Automobile Workers Research Library, Detroit MI. 313-926-5388

Kebodeaux, Mary, *ILL,* Jefferson Davis Parish Library, Jennings LA. 318-824-1210

Kebschull, Anita B, *Asst Librn,* New Rochelle Hospital Medical Center, J M Perley Health Science Library, New Rochelle NY. 914-632-5000, Ext 257

Keck, Delores, *Media,* George Williams College Library, Downers Grove IL. 312-964-3100, Ext 242

Keck, Janice, *Librn,* War Memorial Public Library, Williamson County Public Library, Franklin TN. 615-794-3105

Keck, Mary Ellen, *Acq,* United States Department of the Interior, Natural Resources Library, Washington DC. 202-343-5821

Keckler, Jane E, *Librn,* Kent State University, Stark Campus Learning Resource Center, Canton OH. 216-499-9602

Keddle, David G, *Dir,* Ingham Medical Center, John W Chi Memorial Medical Library, Lansing MI. 517-374-2270

Keder, Janice K, *Pub Serv,* University of Pittsburgh at Bradford Library, Bradford PA. 814-362-3801, Ext 126

Kedl, Aloysius, *Librn,* Saint Charles Scholasticate Library, Battleford SK. 306-937-2355

Kee, Leslie, *Exten,* Mansfield-Richland County Public Library, Mansfield OH. 419-524-1041

Keech, Ann M, *Librn,* Newport News Public Library System (Subregional Library for the Blind & Physically Handicapped), Newport News VA. 804-877-9488

Keefe, M, *Ref,* University of Rhode Island Library, Kingston RI. 401-792-1000

Keefe, Margaret, *Ref,* Oak Park Public Library, Scoville Institute, Oak Park IL. 312-383-8200

Keefe, Tanya, *Circ & Per,* Fresno City College, Learning Resources Center, Fresno CA. 209-442-8204

Keefer, Elaine, *Search Librn,* University of South Alabama (Biomedical Library), Mobile AL. 205-460-7043

Keefer, Joan, *Spec Coll,* Huntington City Township Public Library, Huntington IN. 219-356-0824

Keefer, Ruth, *On-Line Servs,* Mobil Research & Development Corp, Field Research Laboratory, Technical Information Services Library, Dallas TX. 214-333-6531

Keegstra, Cora Mae, *Librn,* Eastern Avenue Christian Reformed Church Library, Grand Rapids MI. 454-48888

Keelan, Mary F, *Librn,* Great-West Life Assurance Co Library, Winnipeg MB. 204-946-9225

Keeler, Anne, *Exten,* Orlando Public Library, Orlando FL. 305-425-4694

Keeler, Ronald F, *Librn,* Intermountain Bible College Library, Grand Junction CO. 303-243-3870

Keeler, Rose, *Graphics,* Centre County Library & Historical Museum, Bellefonte PA. 814-355-3131

Keeley, Barbara, *Cat,* Oakton Community College, Learning Resource Center, Morton Grove IL. 312-967-5120, Ext 331

Keeley, Kurt M, *Librn,* American Water Works Association, Library & Technical Information Center, Denver CO. 303-794-7711

Keelin, Irene, *Circ,* Ottawa Library, Ottawa KS. 913-242-3080

Keeling, Alfreida G, *On-Line Servs,* Veterans Administration, Hospital Library, Saint Louis MO. 314-652-4100

Keeling, Celia, *Asst Librn,* Nelson County Public Library, Bardstown KY. 502-348-3714

Keeling, Geneva, *Bkmobile Coordr,* Washington County Public Library, Springfield KY. 606-336-7655

Keeling, Michael, *Media,* Medicine Hat College, Learning Resource Center, Medicine Hat AB. 403-527-7141, Ext 245

Keels, Nancy M, *Mgr, Publishing Servs,* Dallas Public Library, Dallas TX. 214-748-9071

Keen, Barbara, *Science & Government,* Battelle-Seattle Research Center, Library Services, Seattle WA. 206-525-3130

Keen, Beverly, *Librn,* Saint Lucie County Law Library, Fort Pierce FL. 305-461-5708

Keen, John, *Librn,* Dr Eugene Clark Library, Lockhart TX. 512-398-3223

Keen, Reba, *Films,* Oklahoma State Department of Health Library, Oklahoma City OK. 271-4725; 271-5724

Keenan, Eleanor M, *Librn,* West Virginia Commission on Aging Library, Charleston WV. 304-348-2241

Keenan, Gloria, *Clerk,* Long Beach Public Library (West End), Long Beach NY. 516-432-8949

Keenan, Gloria E, *Chief Librn,* Gannett Newspapers, Press & Sunday-Sun Bulletin Library, Binghamton NY. 607-798-1159

Keenan, K, *Tech Serv,* Carnegie-Stout Public Library, Dubuque Public Library, Dubuque IA. 319-583-9197

Keenan, Linda, *ILL,* Cornell University Libraries (University Libraries), Ithaca NY. 607-256-4144

Keenan, Mae, *ILL,* Lucius Beebe Memorial Library, Wakefield MA. 617-245-0790

Keenan, Sue, *Ch,* Larchmont Public Library, Larchmont NY. 914-834-1960

Keene, Gloria, *Ch,* El Dorado County Library, Placerville CA. 916-626-2561

Keene, Jan, *Asst Dir Non-Pub Serv,* Tulsa City-County Library, Tulsa OK. 918-581-5221

Keene, Shelagh, *Assoc Librn,* Dalhousie University, Izaak Walton Killam Memorial Library (Humanities & Social Sciences), Macdonald Memorial Library (Science), Halifax NS. 902-424-3601

Keener, Donald S, *Asst Dir,* North Carolina State University, D H Hill Library, Raleigh NC. 919-737-2843

Keener, Frances L, *Ad,* Sapulpa Public Library, Sapulpa OK. 918-224-5624

Keeney, Al, *Art,* Rock Springs Public Library, Rock Springs WY. 307-362-6212

Keeney, Ann, *Librn,* Fresno Community Hospital, Medical Library, Fresno CA. 442-6000 Ext 5370

Keeney, Barbara, *Cat,* County-City Library, Sweetwater TX. 915-235-3532

Keeney, Bruce, *Dir,* State University of New York College of Technology, Utica-Rome Library, Utica NY. 315-792-3420

Keeney, Frances Z, *Librn,* Noxell Corp Library, Baltimore MD. 301-666-2662

Keeney, Mary, *Librn,* United States District Court Library, Anchorage AK. 907-271-5568

Keeney, W Robert, *Dir,* Eastern Shore Public Library, Accomac VA. 804-787-3400

Keepers, Mary, *AV & YA,* Neenah Public Library, Neenah WI. 414-729-4728

Keepper, Michael, *Dir,* Shelbyville Free Public Library, Shelbyville IL. 217-774-4432

Kees, Stephen J, *Librn,* Niagara College of Applied Arts & Technology, Tecumseh Resource Centre, Welland ON. 416-735-2211, Ext 297

Keesee, Larry B, *Dir Libr Serv,* High Point College, Wrenn Memorial Library, High Point NC. 919-885-5101

Keesey, Marjorie P, *Librn,* Rappahannock County Library, Washington VA. 703-675-3780

Keeth, John, *Acq,* University of South Florida (University Library), Tampa FL. 813-974-2721

Keeth, Kent, *Librn,* Baylor University (Texas Collection), Waco TX. 817-755-1268

Keever, Ellen, *Reader Serv,* College of Wooster, Andrews Library, Wooster OH. 216-264-1234, Ext 483

Kegg, Janet, *Librn,* American Association for the Advancement of Science Library, Washington DC. 202-467-4428

Kegley, Jay, *Doc,* Otterbein College, Courtright Memorial Library, Westerville OH. 614-890-3000, Ext 164

Keguardt, Cynthia Horsburgh, *Mss,* Maryland Historical Society Library, Baltimore MD. 301-685-3750

Kehl, Vida, *Librn,* Leelanau Township Public Library, Northport MI. 616-386-5131

Kehoe, H, *Archivist & Local Hist,* Paterson Free Public Library, Danforth Memorial Library, Paterson NJ. 201-881-3770

Kehoe, Patrick E, *Librn,* American University (Washington College of Law Library), Washington DC. 202-686-2625

Kehoe, Vincent J R, *Curator,* Society for the Preservation of Colonial Culture Library, Lowell MA. 617-459-9864

Kehrer, Shelby J, *Asst Librn,* Cincinnati Electronics Corp, Technical Library, Cincinnati OH. 513-563-6000

Keifer, Genevieve, *Office Mgt,* Howard County Library, Columbia MD. 301-997-8000

Keiffer, Joan, *ILL & Tech Serv,* Ramapo Catskill Library System, Middletown NY. 914-343-1131, 352-4825, 565-3030

Keil, Doreen, *Cat & Bibliog Instr,* Caldwell College Library, Caldwell NJ. 201-228-4424, Ext 34

Keil, Doreen, *Instr,* Caldwell College, Library Science Program, NJ. 201-228-4424
Keim, Eileen, *Librn,* New Hampshire State Library, Services To Handicapped Division, Concord NH. 603-271-3429
Keim, Nancy, *Acq,* Oyster Bay-East Norwich Public Library, Oyster Bay NY. 516-922-1212
Keim, Peter, *Ref,* Emma S Clark Memorial Library, Setauket NY. 516-941-4080
Keindel, G E, *Librn,* Saint Gerard's Roman Catholic Parish Library, Yorkton SK. 306-782-2449
Keip, Ellen, *Librn,* Western Illinois Library System (Talking Books Library), Monmouth IL. 309-734-7141
Keiser, Barbara J, *Dir,* Monroe County Public Library, Stroudsburg PA. 717-421-0800
Keister, Martha, *ILL,* Pace University, School of Law Library, White Plains NY. 914-682-7272
Keiter, Linda S, *Librn,* University of Wyoming (Science/Technology), Laramie WY. 307-766-5165
Keith, Dianna, *Doc,* Kearney State College, Calvin T Ryan Library, Kearney NE. 308-236-4218
Keith, Eugenie, *Librn,* Sussex County Library System (Franklin-Eastern District), Franklin NJ. 201-827-6555
Keith, Howard D, *Librn,* Yale University Library (Cross Campus), New Haven CT. 203-436-0318
Keith, Marie C, *Asst Librn,* Frick Art Reference Library, New York NY. 212-288-8700
Keith, Maye, *Dir,* Yuma City-County Library, Yuma AZ. 602-782-1871
Keith, Mrs Harry L, *Librn,* Caruthersville Public Library, Caruthersville MO. 314-333-2480
Keith, Nora, *Tech Serv,* Pender County Library, Burgaw NC. 919-259-4521
Keith, Virginia F, *Acq,* City Library, Springfield MA. 413-739-3871
Keithan, Margaret, *Cat,* California State University Fullerton Library, Fullerton CA. 714-773-2714
Keithly, Karin M, *Librn,* State Fair Community College, Learning Resources Center, Sedalia MO. 816-826-7100, Ext 28
Keizer, Ina C, *Librn,* Thomaston Public Library, Thomaston ME. 207-354-2453
Keklock, Donna, *Ref,* Medical Library of Mecklenburg County, Learning Resource Center of Charlotte AHEC, Charlotte NC. 704-373-3129
Kelenson, Dora, *Librn,* American Federation of Labor & Congress of Industrial Organizations Library, Washington DC. 202-637-5297
Kelker, Signe, *Ill, Ref & Actg Head,* Shippensburg State College, Ezra Lehman Memorial Library, Shippensburg PA. 717-532-1463
Kell, Annette, *Post Librn,* United States Army (Morale Support Activities Division Library), Fort Hood TX. 817-685-6011
Kell, Bea, *Ref,* Golden West College Library, Huntington Beach CA. 714-892-7711, Ext 541
Kell, Mary Kate, *Ref & Commun Servs,* University of Houston (Law Library), Houston TX. 713-749-3119
Kell, Patricia, *Ad & Acq,* Wayne Public Library, Wayne NJ. 201-694-4272
Kell, Ruth, *Dir,* Superiorland Library Cooperative, Marquette MI. 906-228-7697
Kell, Ruth S, *Librn,* Peter White Public Library, Marquette MI. 906-228-9510
Kelleher, Denise, *Ref,* Arlington County Department of Libraries, Arlington Public Library, Arlington VA. 703-527-4777
Kelleher, Elizabeth G, *Commun Servs,* Albright College Library, Reading PA. 215-921-2381, Ext 224
Kelleher, Kathleen, *Librn,* Teachers Insurance & Annuity Association of America, Business Library, New York NY. 212-490-9000, Ext 2592
Kelleher, Mary, *Ref,* Falmouth Public Library, Subregional Headquarters for Eastern Massachusetts Regional System, Falmouth MA. 617-548-0280
Kelleher, Mary, *Bkmobile Coordr,* Newburyport Public Library, Newburyport MA. 617-462-4031
Kellen, Jim, *Cat,* College of Saint Thomas, O'Shaughnessy Library, Saint Paul MN. 612-647-5720
Keller, A, *Ch,* North York Public Library, Willowdale ON. 416-494-6838

Keller, Arlene, *Librn,* Temple University of the Commonwealth System of Higher Education (College of Engineering Technology), Philadelphia PA. 215-787-7828
Keller, Claire, *On-Line Servs,* Allentown College of Saint Francis De Sales Library, Center Valley PA. 215-282-1100, Ext 266
Keller, Dean H, *Rare Bks & Spec Coll,* Kent State University Libraries, Kent OH. 216-672-2962
Keller, Dorothy, *Dir,* Goodall City Library, Ogallala Public Library, Ogallala NE. 308-284-4354
Keller, Imogene, *Actg Librn,* Corydon Public Library, Corydon IN. 812-738-4110
Keller, Jan K, *Dir,* College of the Canyons, William G Bonelli Instructional Resource Center, Valencia CA. 805-259-7800, Ext 381, 382
Keller, Jan K, *Actg Dir,* College of the Canyons, Library-Media Technology, CA. 805-259-7800
Keller, Jean I, *Asst Librn,* H J Heinz Co, Research & Development Laboratory Library, Pittsburgh PA. 412-237-5948, 237-5949
Keller, Judith, *Deputy Dir Extended Libr Serv,* Rochester Public Library, Olmsted County Library System, Rochester MN. 507-285-8000
Keller, Lela, *YA,* Lafayette Parish Public Library, Lafayette LA. 318-233-0587
Keller, Lois, *Librn,* Cass County Library (Edwardsburg Branch), Edwardsburg MI. 616-445-8651
Keller, Marcia, *Librn,* San Anselmo Public Library, San Anselmo CA. 415-456-4419
Keller, Mary Ann, *Librn,* Saint Charles City County Library (K Linnemann), Saint Charles MO. 314-724-6366, 946-7988
Keller, Mary Ann, *Librn,* Saint Charles City County Library (Merrill), Saint Charles MO. 314-723-0232
Keller, Michael, *Librn,* Cornell University Libraries (Music), Ithaca NY. 607-256-4011
Keller, Mike, *Media,* Claremore Junior College, Thunderbird Library, Claremore OK. 918-341-7510, Ext 278
Keller, Mildred, *Dir,* P R Mallory Co, Technical Information Center, Burlington MA. 617-272-4100, Ext 45
Keller, Mrs Lewis, *ILL,* Tombigbee Regional Library, Bryan Public Library, West Point MS. 601-494-4872
Keller, Patricia E, *Acq,* University of Cincinnati Libraries (Robert S Marx Law Library), Cincinnati OH. 513-475-3016
Keller, Paul F G, *Asst Prof,* University of Maryland, College of Library & Information Services, MD. 301-454-5441
Keller, Sandra, *Cat,* Converse County Library, Douglas WY. 307-358-3644
Keller, Sharon, *Librn,* Wellston Public Library, Wellston OH. 614-384-6660
Keller, Thomas E, *Res Coordr,* J J Keller & Associates, Inc, Library Research Center, Neenah WI. 414-722-2848, Ext 308
Keller, Wanda, *Librn,* Allegany County Bar Association Library, Cumberland MD. 301-724-8995
Kellett, Mark Wm, *Librn & Bibliog Instr,* Joslyn Art Museum Art Reference Library, Omaha NE. 402-342-3300, Ext 41
Kelley, Alice K, *Librn,* Kountze Public Library, Kountze TX. 713-246-2826
Kelley, Ann, *Librn,* Witco Chemical Corp Library, Houston TX. 713-433-7281
Kelley, Anne, *Bkmobile Coordr,* Rapid City Public Library, Rapid City SD. 605-394-4171
Kelley, Ava M, *Librn,* Jewell Public Library, Jewell KS. 913-428-3630
Kelley, Betty H, *Dir,* Farmers Branch Public Library, Farmers Branch TX. 214-247-3131, Ext 60, 61
Kelley, David, *Dept Head,* Northern Essex Community College, Learning Resource Center, MA. 617-374-0721, Ext 231, 234
Kelley, Dennis J, *Dir,* Melrose Public Library, Melrose MA. 617-665-2313
Kelley, Elizabeth, *Librn,* Hamline University (School of Law Library), Saint Paul MN. 612-641-2344
Kelley, Elizabeth M, *Ch,* Schuylkill Haven Free Public Library, Schuylkill Haven PA. 717-385-0542
Kelley, Esther, *Archives Manager,* American Heritage Center Library, Laramie WY. 307-766-3279

Kelley, Gaylen B, *Chmn & Prof,* Boston University, Dept of Instructional Development-Educational Media, MA. 617-353-3176
Kelley, Gloria, *Asst Librn,* Farmington Public Library, Farmington IL. 309-245-2175
Kelley, Grace P, *Librn,* Norfolk General Hospital, Health Sciences Library, Norfolk VA. 804-628-3000
Kelley, Helen, *Ref,* University of Scranton, Alumni Memorial Library, Scranton PA. 717-961-7525
Kelley, John, *Circ,* Auburn Public Library, Auburn ME. 207-782-3191
Kelley, John, *Media,* University of California, Riverside, University Library, Riverside CA. 714-787-3221
Kelley, Judy, *YA,* Iowa City Public Library, Iowa City IA. 319-354-1265
Kelley, Karen, *Ch,* Englewood Public Library, Englewood CO. 303-761-4376
Kelley, Marianne, *Search Analyst,* Abbott-Northwestern Hospital, Health Sciences Library, Minneapolis MN. 612-874-4312
Kelley, Marianne, *On-Line Servs,* Sister Kenny Institute Library, Minneapolis MN. 612-874-4312
Kelley, Marilyn, *Asst Librn,* Sturgis Library, Barnstable MA. 617-362-6636
Kelley, Mary E, *Cat,* College of New Rochelle, Gill Library, New Rochelle NY. 914-632-5300, Ext 347
Kelley, Mary E, *Cat,* Dunklin County Library, Kennett MO. 314-888-3561
Kelley, Maxine, *Librn,* Faulkner-Van Buren Regional Library (Van Buren County), Clinton AR. 501-745-2100
Kelley, Pat, *ILL & Ref,* Shoreline Community College, Library/Media Center, Seattle WA. 206-546-4663
Kelley, Patricia, *Bibliog Instr,* American University, Jack I & Dorothy G Bender Library & Learning Resources Center, Washington DC. 202-686-2323
Kelley, Patrick, *Actg Chmn,* Georgia Institute of Technology, School of Information & Computer Science, GA. 404-894-2000
Kelley, Rosemary, *Librn,* University of New England (New England College of Osteopathic Medicine Library), Biddeford ME. 207-282-1515, Ext 38
Kelley, Sarah, *Bkmobile Coordr,* Kanawha County Public Library, Kanawha County Service Center, Charleston WV. 304-343-4646
Kelley, Timothy A, *Librn,* Pearle L Crawford Memorial Library, Dudley MA. 617-943-5333
Kellman, Amy, *Ch,* Carnegie Library of Pittsburgh, Pittsburgh PA. 412-622-3100
Kellner, Hazel, *Tech Serv,* Grande Prairie Regional College Library, Grande Prairie AB. 403-532-8830, Ext 302
Kellog, Jo Ann, *Librn,* Hominy Public Library, Hominy OK. 918-885-4486
Kellogg, Dale M, *Librn,* Thompson-Hickman Free County Library, Madison County Library, Virginia City MT. 406-843-5346
Kellogg, J E, *Librn,* Washington Avenue Presbyterian Church Library, Terre Haute IN. 812-232-1638
Kellogg, Judith G, *Librn,* Salt Lake City Public Library (Rose Park), Salt Lake City UT. 801-363-5733
Kellogg, Marya S, *Cat,* Katonah Village Library, Katonah NY. 914-232-3508
Kellogg, Mercy, *Librn,* New York Public Library (Seward Park), New York NY. 212-477-6770
Kellogg, Rebecca, *Head Cent Ref,* University of Arizona Library, Tucson AZ. 602-626-2101
Kells, Herbert R, *Prof,* Rutgers-The State University of New Jersey, Graduate School of Library & Information Studies, NJ. 201-932-7500
Kelly, Agnes V, *Ref,* Donaldson, Lufkin & Jenrette Securities Corp, Corporate Library, New York NY. 212-943-0300, Ext 1356-9
Kelly, Alex, *ILL,* Eugene Public Library, Eugene OR. 503-687-5450
Kelly, Alice, *Extension Spec,* Manitowoc Public Library, Manitowoc WI. 414-682-6861
Kelly, Ann, *On-Line Servs,* Cutchogue Free Library, Cutchogue NY. 516-734-6360
Kelly, Ann, *Librn,* Muskegon County Library (Blind & Physically Handicapped Library), Muskegon MI. 616-724-6257

Kelly, Ardie L, *Librn,* Mariners Museum Library, Newport News VA. 804-595-0368
Kelly, Barbara F, *Dir,* Manitowoc Public Library, Manitowoc WI. 414-682-6861
Kelly, Barbara F, *Dir,* Manitowoc-Calumet Counties Federated Library System, Manitowoc WI. 414-682-6861
Kelly, Beth, *Ad,* Duluth Public Library, Duluth MN. 218-723-3800
Kelly, Betty, *Assoc Dir,* Midwestern Baptist Theological Seminary Library, Kansas City MO. 816-453-4600, Ext 248
Kelly, Burt, *TV,* Moraine Valley Community College, Learning Resources Center, Palos Hills IL. 312-974-4300, Ext 222
Kelly, Cheryl C, *Librn,* South Carolina State Hospital, Horger Library, Columbia SC. 803-758-7357
Kelly, Claire B, *Librn,* Merck-Frosst Laboratories, Research Library, Kirkland PQ. 514-695-7920, Ext 463
Kelly, Donald, *Asst Dir & Tech Serv,* Adelphi University Library, Garden City NY. 516-294-8700
Kelly, Donalda, *Dir,* Zephyrhills Public Library, Zephyrhills FL. 813-782-1451
Kelly, Donna, *Librn,* Clearwater Public Library (East Twig), Clearwater FL. 813-462-6893
Kelly, Dorothy B, *Assoc Librn,* San Benito County Free Library, Hollister CA. 408-637-2013
Kelly, Elaine, *Circ,* Florida Atlantic University, S E Wimberly Library, Boca Raton FL. 305-395-5100, Ext 2448
Kelly, Eleanor M, *Librn,* Our Lady of Lourdes (School of Nursing Library), Camden NJ. 609-757-3722
Kelly, Elinor C, *Librn,* Eastern Washington State Historical Society Library, Spokane WA. 509-456-3931
Kelly, Elizabeth, *Librn,* Middle Georgia Regional Library (Mary Vinson Memorial), Milledgeville GA. 912-452-2021
Kelly, Elizabeth C, *Dir,* United States Department of Health & Human Services (Food & Drug Administration, Medical Library), Rockville MD. 301-443-1538
Kelly, Elizabeth M, *Librn,* Amherst College (Fine Arts), Amherst MA. 413-542-2335
Kelly, Elizabeth Monaco, *Asst Dir,* Creighton University (Klutznick Law Library), Omaha NE. 402-449-2875
Kelly, Else M, *Dir,* Gladwin County Library, Gladwin MI. 517-426-8221
Kelly, Florence, *Librn,* Trenton Psychiatric Hospital (Patients Library), Trenton NJ. 609-396-8261, Ext 245
Kelly, Glen, *Acq,* Laurentian University Library, Bibliotheque de l'Universite Laurentienne, Sudbury ON. 705-675-1151, Ext 251 & 252
Kelly, Harold, *Dir,* Jamestown College, Raugust Library, Jamestown ND. 701-253-2525
Kelly, Harold, *Cat,* University of South Carolina at Spartanburg Library, Spartanburg SC. 803-578-1800, Exts 410, 411, 420 & 421
Kelly, Hazel, *Librn,* Dekalb Library System (Chamblee Branch), Chamblee GA. 404-457-8764
Kelly, Helen R, *ILL,* Port Chester Public Library, Port Chester NY. 914-939-6710, 939-6711
Kelly, James, *Cat,* Saint Anthony-On-Hudson Library, Rensselaer NY. 518-463-2261
Kelly, Jane Y, *Automated Serv,* Pueblo Library District, Pueblo CO. 303-544-1940
Kelly, Janice, *Librn,* Olympia Fields Osteopathic Medical Center Library, Olympia Fields IL. 747-4000 Ext 1190
Kelly, Jean M, *Librn,* Vegreville Public Library, Vegreville AB. 403-632-3491
Kelly, Jeanne B, *Bkmobile Coordr,* Fargo Public Library, Fargo ND. 701-241-1490
Kelly, John, *Asst Curator for Spec Coll,* University of Southern Mississippi (William David McCain Library), Hattiesburg MS. 601-266-4172
Kelly, John J, *Librn,* Hampden County Law Library, Springfield MA. 413-781-8100, Ext 3078
Kelly, Karon M, *Dir,* Western Interstate Commission for Higher Education Library, Boulder CO. 303-497-0284
Kelly, Kathy, *Tech Serv,* Laboure Junior College Library, Boston MA. 617-296-8300, Ext 418

Kelly, Kay, *Librn,* Northern Michigan Hospitals Inc & Burns Clinic Medical Center, Pc, Dean C Burns Health Science Library, Petoskey MI. 616-347-7000, Ext 500
Kelly, Kay, *Librn,* Odell Public Library, Odell IL. 815-998-2012
Kelly, Liam M, *Asst Dir & Clerk of Corp,* Boston Public Library, Eastern Massachusetts Library System, Boston MA. 617-536-5400
Kelly, Lorraine P, *Librn,* Saint Olaf Lutheran Church Library, Minneapolis MN. 612-529-7726
Kelly, Louise R, *Librn,* Edward Ward Carmack Public Library, Gallatin TN. 615-452-1722
Kelly, Lucille M, *Librn,* Warner Lambert Research Library, Detroit MI. 313-567-5300, Ext 5165
Kelly, Margaret A, *Ser,* Bloomsburg State College, Harvey A Andruss Library, Bloomsburg PA. 717-389-2716
Kelly, Martin, *Pub Info Dir,* Maternity Center Association Library, New York NY. 212-369-7300
Kelly, Mary, *Ch,* Mesa Public Library, Mesa AZ. 602-834-2207
Kelly, Mary M, *Asst Librn & Ch,* Holbrook Public Library, Holbrook MA. 617-767-3644
Kelly, Mary Margaret, *Librn,* Barrett Memorial Library, Petersburg IN. 812-354-6257
Kelly, Mary R, *Librn,* Albuquerque Public Library (Erna Fergusson), Albuquerque NM. 505-766-7925
Kelly, Michael F, *President,* Council of Research & Academic Libraries, (CORAL), TX. 512-691-4570
Kelly, Michael F, *Dir,* Texas Council of State University Librarians, TX. 512-691-4570
Kelly, Michael F, *Dir,* University of Texas at San Antonio Library, San Antonio TX. 512-691-4570
Kelly, Noella, *Librn,* Beardmore Public Library, Beardmore ON. 807-875-2075
Keily, Patricia, *Dir,* Victor Free Library, Victor NY. 716-924-2637
Kelly, Patricia A, *Librn,* Addison Public Library, Addison IL. 312-543-3617
Kelly, Patrick, *ILL, Ref & Bibliog Instr,* Bryant College, Edith M Hodgson Memorial Library, Smithfield RI. 401-231-1200, Ext 300
Kelly, Robert, *Dir,* Creighton University (Klutznick Law Library), Omaha NE. 402-449-2875
Kelly, Robert J, *Librn,* Indiana University of Pennsylvania, Punxsutawney Center Library, Punxsutawney PA. 814-938-6711
Kelly, Ruth, *Asst Dir & Ref,* Monterey Public Library, Monterey CA. 408-646-3930
Kelly, Ruth N, *Librn,* Jewish Hospital of Saint Louis (Rothschild Medical Library), Saint Louis MO. 314-454-7208
Kelly, Sister Cecil, *Media,* Mundelein College, Learning Resource Center, Chicago IL. 312-262-8100, Ext 301, 302 & 303
Kelly, Sister Mary Clarentia, *Librn,* Dominican Education Center Library, Sinsinawa WI. 608-748-4411, Ext 276
Kelly, Sister Maryclare, *Librn,* College of Saint Gertrude Library, Cottonwood ID. 208-962-3224
Kelly, Sister Thomas Aquin, *Acq & Archivist,* Ohio Dominican College Library, Columbus OH. 614-253-2741, Ext 258, 210&219
Kelly, T, *Bus,* British Columbia Institute of Technology Library, Burnaby BC. 604-434-5734, Ext 360
Kelly, Veronica D, *Dir,* Seymour Public Library, Seymour CT. 203-888-3903
Kelly, William R, *Librn,* San Francisco Law Library (Mills), San Francisco CA. 415-558-4627
Kelly-Bercu, Lenore, *Ch,* Avon Township Public Library, Rochester MI. 313-651-1426
Kelmer, Leona, *Br Coordr,* Prosser Public Library, Bloomfield CT. 203-243-9721
Kelmer, Leona, *Librn,* Prosser Public Library (Wintonbury), Bloomfield CT. 203-243-9721
Kelner, Barbara, *Librn,* John F Kennedy Institute, Interdisciplinary Multi-Media Library, Baltimore MD. 301-955-4240
Kelner, Evelyn, *Librn,* Dwyer-Mercer County District Library (Mendon Branch), Mendon OH. 419-586-2314
Kelner, Loretta, *Ref & Loan,* Indiana State Library, Indianapolis IN. 317-232-3675

Kelsay, Maria Thiesen, *Librn,* Roann Public Library, Roann IN. 317-833-5231
Kelsey, Barbara, *Commun Servs,* Geauga County Public Library, Chardon OH. 216-285-7601
Kelsey, Donald, *Libr Space Officer,* University of Minnesota Libraries-Twin Cities, Minneapolis MN. 612-373-3097
Kelsey, Janet, *Dir,* Litchfield Free Public Library, Hudson NH. 603-424-4044
Kelsey, Marie, *Cat,* College of Saint Scholastica Library, Duluth MN. 218-723-6143
Kelsey, Marie, *Instr,* College of Saint Scholastica, Library Science Program, MN. 218-723-6143
Kelsey, Maude Q, *Librn,* Cleveland County Memorial Library, Shelby NC. 704-487-9069
Kelsey, Ruby, *Rare Bks,* Troy-Miami County Public Library, Troy OH. 513-339-0502
Kelso, Barbara B, *Ref,* University of Texas Medical Branch, Moody Medical Library, Galveston TX. 713-765-1971
Kelso, Dorothy, *Asst Librn,* Gilbert Memorial Library, Friend NE. 402-947-5081
Kelso, Elmer, *Libr Chmn,* Grand Prairie Community Hospital, Dr Phil R Russell Library, Grand Prairie TX. 214-264-1651
Kelso, Ruth, *Asst Librn,* Maquon Township Library, Maquon IL. 309-875-3573
Kelterborn, Nancy, *Pub Servs,* Flint River Regional Library, Griffin GA. 404-227-2756
Kelton, Allen, *Bus Bibliographer,* University of Alabama, Amelia Gayle Gorgas Library, University AL. 205-348-5298
Kelty, Daniel, *Asst Librn & Ch,* Polk County Library, Crookston MN. 218-281-4522
Kelver, Ann E, *Dir,* Arapahoe Regional Library District, Littleton CO. 303-798-2444
Kemmit, Patricia, *Asst Librn,* Marion Military Institute, Baer Memorial Library, Marion AL. 205-683-9593
Kemp, Betty, *Dir,* Lee-Itawamba Library System, Lee County Library, Tupelo MS. 601-844-2377
Kemp, Edward C, *Gifts,* University of Oregon Library, Eugene OR. 503-686-3056
Kemp, Elaine A, *Cat,* University of Oregon Library, Eugene OR. 503-686-3056
Kemp, Emma, *Librn,* Chicago Public Library (Blackstone), Chicago IL. 312-624-0511
Kemp, Erle P, *Resources Group: Dir & Assoc Univ Libr,* Columbia University (University Libraries), New York NY. 212-280-2241
Kemp, Gregg, *Media,* Catawba College, Corriher-Linn-Black Library, Salisbury NC. 704-637-4448, 637-4449
Kemp, Joanne, *Librn,* Alberta Consumer & Corporate Affairs Resource Center Library, Edmonton AB. 403-427-5215
Kemp, Joanne, *Asst Librn,* Ashe County Public Library, West Jefferson NC. 919-246-2041
Kemp, Karl, *Acq,* Brooklyn Public Library, Brooklyn NY. 212-780-7712
Kemp, L Helen, *Librn,* Rucker Products Library, Emeryville CA. 415-635-6200
Kemp, Leatrice, *Asst Librn,* Rochester Museum & Science Center, Museum Library, Rochester NY. 716-271-4320, Ext 30
Kemp, Lenore, *Tech Serv,* State University College at Buffalo, Edward H Butler Library, Buffalo NY. 716-878-6302
Kemp, Louise, *Ch,* William D Himmelreich Memorial Library, Lewisburg PA. 717-523-8562
Kemp, Margaret W, *Librn,* Public Library of the District of Columbia (Anacostia), Washington DC. 202-727-1329
Kemp, Thomas, *Genealogy,* Stamford's Public Library, Ferguson Library, Stamford CT. 203-325-4354
Kempe, John A, *Librn,* Olin Water Services Library, Kansas City KS. 913-621-2021
Kempeivich, Pat, *Librn,* Baudette Public Library, Baudette MN. 218-634-2329
Kempel, Peter M, *Dir,* Thomas M Cooley Law School Library, Lansing MI. 517-371-5140
Kempel, Suzanne, *Ref,* Pine Manor College, Alumnae Library, Chestnut Hill MA. 617-731-7081, 731-7083
Kemper, Kaye, *Ch,* Granite City Public Library, Granite City IL. 618-876-0550
Kemper, Robert E, *Dir,* Northern Arizona University Libraries, Flagstaff AZ. 602-523-9011
Kemper, Suzanne W, *Acq & Ref,* North Adams State College Library, Eugene L Freel Library, North Adams MA. 413-664-4511, Ext 321

Kemppinen, Nancy S, *Consult to Franklin Co Branches,* Athens Regional Library, Athens GA. 404-543-0134

Kenagy, Beth A, *Asst Dir & Pub Servs,* Indiana University at South Bend Library, South Bend IN. 219-237-4440

Kenamore, Jane, *Archivist,* Rosenberg Library, Galveston TX. 713-763-8854

Kendall, Betty C, *Pub Servs & Bibliog Instr,* Carthage College, John Mosheim Ruthrauff Library, Kenosha WI. 414-551-8500, Ext 530

Kendall, Charles, *Ref,* Starved Rock Library System, Ottawa IL. 815-434-7537

Kendall, Ellen, *Librn,* Wayne County Regional Library for the Blind & Physically Handicapped, Wayne MI. 313-274-2600

Kendall, Inez S, *Librn,* Dormont Public Library, Pittsburgh PA. 412-531-8754

Kendall, John, *English & Am Studies,* University of Massachusetts at Amherst Library, Amherst MA. 413-545-0284

Kendall, Mrs Aubyn, *Curator,* Fort Worth Museum of Science & History Library, Fort Worth TX. 817-732-1631

Kendall, Priscilla, *AV,* Sussex County Library System, Sussex County Area Reference Library, Newton NJ. 201-948-3660

Kendig, Barbara, *Asst Librn,* Bolt Beranek & Newman Inc Library, Cambridge MA. 617-491-1850, Ext 3277

Kendle, Irene, *Librn,* Holmes County District Public Library (Walnut Creek Branch), Walnut Creek OH. 216-674-5972

Kendrick, Betty, *Asst Librn,* Crockett Public Library, Crockett TX. 713-544-3089

Kendrick, Jane T, *Dir,* Thomaston Public Library, Thomaston CT. 203-283-4339

Kendrick, Ruth, *Branch Asst,* Cumberland Regional Library (Parrsboro Branch), Amherst NS. 902-254-2046

Kendrick, Sister Clarice M, *Tech Serv,* Fontbonne College Library, Saint Louis MO. 314-862-3456, Ext 352

Kendrick, Susan, *Asst Librn,* Baylor University (Law), Waco TX. 817-755-2168

Kenealy, Edmund, *Ref,* Canton Public Library, Canton MA. 617-828-0177

Kenefick, Colleen, *ILL,* University of North Dakota (Harley French Medical Library), Grand Forks ND. 701-777-3993

Keng, Hsiu-Yun, *Chief Librn,* South Carolina Department of Mental Retardation, Whitten Center Library & Media Resource Services, Clinton SC. 803-833-2736

Kenin, Milton, *Librn,* Union League of Philadelphia Library, Philadelphia PA. 215-563-6500, Ext 368

Keniston, Virginia D, *Librn,* Bethel Library Association, Bethel ME. 207-824-2520

Kenna, Catherine, *Assoc Librn,* Maria Regina College Library-Media Center, Syracuse NY. 315-474-4891, Ext 28

Kennard, Mrs Spencer P, *Dir,* Lenox Library Association, Lenox MA. 413-637-0197

Kenneally, Louise, *Spec Coll,* Stonehill College, Cushing-Martin Library, North Easton MA. 617-238-1081, Ext 328, 329, 313

Kennedy, Anne, *Librn,* Marin County Free Library (Belvedere-Tiburon Branch), Tiburon CA. 415-435-1361

Kennedy, Barbara Jean, *Dir,* Seward Public Library, Seward NE. 402-643-3318

Kennedy, Betty, *Librn,* Tulsa City-County Library (Red Fork), Tulsa OK. 918-446-7627

Kennedy, Beverly, *Librn,* Scappoose Public Library, Scappoose OR. 503-543-7123

Kennedy, Dan, *ILL,* Orlando Public Library, Orlando FL. 305-425-4694

Kennedy, Donna, *Tech Serv & Cat,* Northeastern University, Suburban Campus Library, Burlington MA. 617-272-5500, Ext 55

Kennedy, Doris A, *Librn,* Christian Church (Disciples of Christ) Library, Indianapolis IN. 317-353-1491, Ext 256

Kennedy, Gail, *Acq,* University of Kentucky, Margaret I King Library, Lexington KY. 606-257-3801

Kennedy, Imogene, *Genealogy,* Montgomery County Library, Conroe TX. 713-756-4486

Kennedy, James, *Librn,* Ohio Regional Library for the Blind & Physically Handicapped, Cincinnati OH. 513-369-6074, 369-6075

Kennedy, James R, *Dir,* Lawrence Public Library, Lawrence MA. 617-682-1727

Kennedy, Jane F, *Librn,* United States Postal Service Library, Washington DC. 202-245-4023

Kennedy, Jean A, *Dir Libr Serv,* Veterans Administration (Hospital Library), Salem VA. 703-982-2463, Ext 358

Kennedy, Joan, *Acq,* Orange County Community College Library, Middletown NY. 914-343-1121

Kennedy, Joanne, *Librn,* Saint John's Hospital, Health Sciences Library, Oxnard CA. 805-487-7861, Ext 2191, 2169

Kennedy, Johnnye, *Ref,* Tyler Junior College, Edgar H Vaughn Memorial Library, Tyler TX. 214-592-5993, 593-3342

Kennedy, Josephine, *Curric Librn,* Chadron State College Library, Chadron NE. 308-432-4451, Ext 271

Kennedy, Joy, *Ref,* Arlington Heights Memorial Library, Arlington Heights IL. 312-392-0100

Kennedy, Judith, *Librn,* Sheppard & Enoch Pratt Hospital (Patients' Library), Towson MD. 301-823-8200

Kennedy, Kathy K, *Dir,* Peoples Library, New Kensington PA. 412-339-1021

Kennedy, Larry, *Asst Librn,* Kanawha County Public Library (Library for the Blind & Physically Handicapped), Charleston WV. 304-343-4061, 348-4062

Kennedy, Linda P, *Librn,* Lansdowne Public Library, Lansdowne PA. 215-623-0239

Kennedy, M R, *Dir,* Nevins Memorial Library, Methuen MA. 617-686-4080

Kennedy, Madeline, *Librn,* Cardinal Public Library, Cardinal ON. 613-657-3340

Kennedy, Marie, *Cat,* Fayetteville State University, Charles W Chesnutt Library, Fayetteville NC. 919-486-1232

Kennedy, Mary C, *Librn,* California Highway Patrol, Headquarters Library, Sacramento CA. 916-445-1951

Kennedy, Mary C, *Librn,* Oxford Public Library, Oxford CT. 203-888-6944

Kennedy, Mary E, *Instr,* Glenville State College, Library Science Program, WV. 304-462-7361, Ext 291, 292

Kennedy, Mary Ellen, *Ref,* Glenville State College, Robert F Kidd Library, Glenville WV. 304-462-7361, Ext 291

Kennedy, Nella, *Archivist,* Northwestern College, Ramaker Library, Orange City IA. 712-737-4821, Ext 57, 58

Kennedy, R A, *Dir,* Bell Telephone Laboratories, Libraries & Information Systems Center, Murray Hill NJ. 582-2854 (General); 582-4466 (Info Systs Dept); 582-6880 (Info Servs Dept); 949-3456 (Libr Operations Dept)

Kennedy, Robert, *Librn,* Arizona Division of Behavioral Health Services (Cholla Unit), Phoenix AZ. 602-244-1331

Kennedy, Roger, *Media,* University of Toledo, William S Carlson Library, Toledo OH. 419-537-2324

Kennedy, Rose-Marie, *Librn,* Contra Costa County Library (Ygnacio Valley (Thurman G Casey Memorial)), Walnut Creek CA. 415-938-1481

Kennedy, Rosemary, *Cat,* Saint Louis University, Pius XII Memorial Library, Saint Louis MO. 314-658-3100

Kennedy, Ruth, *Ad,* Mississauga Public Library, Mississauga ON. 416-625-8681

Kennedy, Scott, *Phys Sci Librn,* University of California at Davis, General Library, Davis CA. 916-752-2110

Kennedy, Scott, *Librn,* University of California at Davis (Physical Sciences Library), Davis CA. 916-752-0459

Kennedy, Ted C, *Librn,* United States Air Force (Goodfellow Air Force Base Morale, Welfare & Recreation Div Base Library), Goodfellow AFB TX. 915-653-3231, Ext 2412

Kennedy, William, *Librn,* Edgemont Public Library, Edgemont SD. 605-662-7712

Kennedy, Jr, James R, *Ref,* Earlham College, Lilly Library, Richmond IN. 317-962-6561, Ext 360

Kennell, Johanna, *Ref,* Riverhead Free Library, Riverhead NY. 516-727-3228

Kenner, Mona, *Asst Librn,* Burley Public Library, Burley ID. 208-678-7708

Kenneson, Muriel, *Librn,* Byron G Merrill Library, Rumney NH. 603-786-9520

Kennet, Elsie, *Asst Prof,* Kutztown State College, Dept of Library Science, PA. 215-683-4300, 683-4301

Kenneth, Lawrence, *Media,* Mississippi Delta Junior College, Stanny Sanders Library, Moorhead MS. 601-243-8672

Kenneth, Marsha, *Tech Serv,* Mississippi Delta Junior College, Stanny Sanders Library, Moorhead MS. 601-243-8672

Kennewig, Margaret, *Tech Serv,* Lewisville Public Library, Lewisville TX. 214-436-1812

Kenney, Edward D, *Librn,* Federal Bureau of Investigation, FBI Academy Learning Resource Center, Quantico VA. 703-640-6131, Ext 2471

Kenney, Jo Ellen, *Ch,* Carnegie Free Library, McKeesport PA. 412-672-0625

Kenney, Joan M, *On-Line Servs,* Factory Mutual Research Corp, Technical Information Center, Norwood MA. 617-762-4300

Kenney, Margaret, *Dir,* Hopewell Public Library, Hopewell NJ. 609-466-1625

Kenney, Noreen M, *Librn,* Broadview Developmental Center Staff Library, Cleveland OH. 216-526-5000, Ext 271

Kenney, Patricia, *Tech Serv & Cat,* Butler County Community College Library, Butler PA. 412-287-8711, Ext 198

Kenney, Sue, *Instr,* University of Georgia, Dept of Educational Media & Librarianship, GA. 404-542-3810

Kenney, W J, *Librn,* Canada Department of National Defense (Judge Advocate General Library), Ottawa ON. 613-992-4813

Kennison, James, *Librn,* Florida Division of Adult Corrections, Sumter Correctional Institution Library, Bushnell FL. 904-793-2525

Kennon, Sister Mary Fleurette, *Librn,* Saint Joseph's College Library, North Windham ME. 207-892-6766, Ext 24

Kenny, Margaret, *Actg Librn,* City College of the City University of New York, Morris Raphael Cohen Library, New York NY. 212-690-6612

Kenny, Patricia, *Pub Support Dir,* American Red Cross, Film Library, Madison WI. 608-255-0021

Kenny, Patricia, *Librn,* New York Public Library (Saint George Library Center), Staten Island NY. 212-442-8560

Kenny, William, *Librn, Media & Acq,* Fort McMurray Public Library, Fort McMurray AB. 403-743-2121

Kenrich, Patrick, *Bibliog Instr & Reader Serv,* Indiana University Southeast Library, New Albany IN. 812-945-2731

Kensmoe, Christine L, *Librn,* Zimpro Inc Library, Rothschild WI. 715-359-7211, Ext 293

Kent, Allen, *Dir,* University of Pittsburgh (Knowledge Availability Systems Center), Pittsburgh PA. 412-624-5216

Kent, Allen, *Instr,* University of Pittsburgh, School of Library & Information Science, PA. 412-624-5230

Kent, Beverly, *Librn,* Bank of Nova Scotia Library, Toronto ON. 416-866-6257

Kent, Carl, *Coordr School Libr,* Kansas City Kansas Public Library, Kansas City KS. 913-621-3073

Kent, Charles R, *Archives,* Lock Haven State College, George B Stevenson Library, Lock Haven PA. 717-893-2309

Kent, Ethel Mae, *Dir,* Lisbon Public Library, Lisbon IA. 319-455-2800

Kent, Eunice, *Librn,* Los Angeles Public Library System (Chatsworth Branch), Chatsworth CA. 213-341-4276

Kent, Frederick, *Head,* Free Library of Philadelphia (Music), Philadelphia PA. 215-686-5322

Kent, Hilda, *Chief Librn,* Virden-Elkhorn Regional Library, Virden MB. 204-748-3862

Kent, Joel S, *Mem Servs Coordr,* OHIONET, OH. 614-457-1471

Kent, Renee, *Art Slide Libr,* Sarah Lawrence College, Esther Raushenbush Library, Bronxville NY. 914-337-0700, Ext 479

Kent, Susan H, *Dir,* Methodist Hospital, Health Science Libraries, Gary IN. 219-886-4554

Kent, Theresa, *Librn,* Tangipahoa Parish Library (Chesbrough Branch), Chesbourg LA. 504-229-7379

Kenworthy, Eleanora M, *Dir,* Hahnemann Medical College & Hospital of Philadelphia, Warren H Fake Library, Philadelphia PA. 215-448-7186

Kenyon, Carleton, *Law Librn,* Library of Congress, Washington DC. 202-287-5000

Kenyon, Fern, *Rare Bks,* Library Association of Portland, Multnomah County Library, Portland OR. 503-223-7201, Ext 40
Kenyon, Kenneth, *In Charge,* Twentieth Century-Fox Film Corp, Research Library, Los Angeles CA. 213-277-2211, Ext 2782
Kenyon, Mary, *Librn,* West Hartford Library, West Hartford VT. 802-295-2338
Keogh, Jeanne M, *Librn,* Libbey Owens Ford Co (Technical Center Library), Toledo OH. 419-247-4367
Keogh, Judy, *Exten & Bkmobile Coordr,* Chester County Library & District Center, Exton PA. 215-363-0884
Keogh, Richard P, *Asst Librn,* Johnson & Wales College Library, Providence RI. 401-456-1098, 456-1076
Keough, Vera, *Chief Librn,* Mother Whiteside Memorial Library, Grants NM. 505-287-4793
Keown, Lenore A, *Librn,* Grand Lodge of Masons Library, Helena MT. 406-442-7774
Keown, Mary Ann, *Librn,* Klamath County Library (Gilchrist Branch), Gilchrist OR. 503-882-8894
Kepferle, Duane, *Librn,* Stillwater County Library (Molt Branch), Molt MT. 406-322-5337
Kephart, John E, *Prof,* State University of New York, College of Arts & Science, School of Library & Information Science, NY. 716-245-5322
Kepler, Twylah, *Local Hist,* Brewer Public Library, Richland Center WI. 608-647-6444
Kepner, Mary Jane, *Librn,* Lincoln Library (West), Springfield IL. 217-753-4985
Kepper, Judy, *In Charge,* United States Navy (Naval Air Facility General Library), El Centro CA. 714-339-2461
Kepple, Elizabeth C, *Dir,* Stonington Library, Stonington CT. 203-535-0658
Kepple, Robert J, *Dir,* Westminster Theological Seminary Library, Glenside PA. 215-887-5511
Kepple, Robert R, *Librn,* Johns Hopkins University, Applied Physics Laboratory, R E Gibson Library, Laurel MD. 301-953-7100, Ext 601
Kerchner, Joan, *Doc,* Nevada State Library, Carson City NV. 702-885-5130
Kereth, Daniel, *Cat,* Concord College, J Frank Marsh Library, Athens WV. 304-384-3115, Ext 247
Kerley, Daphane, *Cat,* University of Mary Hardin-Baylor, Townsend Memorial Library, Belton TX. 817-939-5811, Ext 256
Kerman, Edwin, *Dir,* Fremont Public Library, Fremont MI. 616-924-3480
Kern, Bernice, *Librn,* Riverside Regional Library (Center 2), Benton MO. 314-545-3581
Kern, Carol H, *In Charge,* Western Pocono Community Library, Brodheadville PA. 717-992-7934
Kern, Helen, *Librn,* Barry's Bay Public Library, Barry's Bay ON. 613-756-2000
Kern, Louise, *Librn,* Madison Public Library, Madison IL. 618-876-8448
Kern, Marsha, *Media,* Mishawaka-Penn Public Library, Mishawaka IN. 219-259-5277
Kern, Mary S, *Commun Servs,* Mount Vernon Public Library, Mount Vernon NY. 914-668-1840
Kern, Pat, *Ch,* Scenic Regional Library of Franklin, Gasconade & Warren Counties, Union MO. 314-583-3224
Kern, Sara, *Asst Librn,* Rebecca M Arthurs Memorial Library, Brookville PA. 814-849-5512
Kern, Stella, *Pub Relations,* Ocean County Library, Toms River NJ. 201-349-6200
Kern, Susan K, *Librn,* Providence Public Library (South Providence), Providence RI. 401-941-2660
Kerndt, Miriam, *Librn,* University of Wisconsin-Madison (Geography Library), Madison WI. 608-262-3521
Kerns, Patricia, *Ch & Media,* Winter Park Public Library, Winter Park FL. 305-647-1638
Kerns, Ruth, *Humanities,* George Mason University Libraries, Fairfax VA. 703-323-2616
Keroack, Isabelle A, *Librn,* New Hampshire Vocational Technical College Library, Berlin NH. 603-752-1113
Kerr, Agnes, *Cat,* Luther-Northwestern Seminary Library, Saint Paul MN. 612-641-3225
Kerr, Ann, *Librn,* Mercer County Library (Ewing Headquarters), Trenton NJ. 609-989-6919

Kerr, Anne, *Dir,* Dunellen Free Public Library, Dunellen NJ. 201-968-4585
Kerr, Anne, *Librn,* Marks-Quitman County Library, Marks MS. 601-326-7141
Kerr, Audrey, *Librn,* University of Manitoba Libraries (Medical Library), Winnipeg MB. 204-786-4342
Kerr, C Jeanne, *Ch,* Grand Forks Public City-County Library, Grand Forks ND. 701-772-8116
Kerr, Donald, *Asst Dir & Tech Serv,* East Texas State University, James Gilliam Gee Library, Commerce TX. 214-886-5717
Kerr, Donna, *AV & Rare Bks,* Niles Community Library, Niles MI. 616-683-8545, 683-8546
Kerr, Dr Stephen, *Instr,* University of Puget Sound, School Librarianship Program, WA. 206-756-3391
Kerr, Eileen, *Government,* Morley Library, Painesville OH. 216-352-3383
Kerr, G Robert, *Exec Dir,* Georgia Conservancy Library, Atlanta GA. 404-262-1967
Kerr, Jane, *Librn,* Hamden Library (Community), Hamden CT. 203-248-7285
Kerr, Jeannette A, *Librn,* United States Navy (Marine Corps Air Station Library), Santa Ana CA. 714-559-2569, 3474
Kerr, Judith, *Librn,* Hazelton District Public Library, Hazelton BC. 604-842-5961
Kerr, Karen, *ILL,* University of South Dakota, Christian P Lommen Health Sciences Library, Vermillion SD. 605-677-5347
Kerr, Linda, *Librn,* Kansas City Public Library (Westport), Kansas City MO. 816-531-6161
Kerr, Loralee, *Head,* University of Minnesota Libraries-Twin Cities (Periodicals), Minneapolis MN. 612-373-2887
Kerr, Margaret, *Adjunct Asst Prof,* Emory University, Div of Librarianship, GA. 404-329-6840
Kerr, Marilynn, *Tech Serv,* Eastern Ontario Library System, Ottawa ON. 613-238-8457
Kerr, Marjorie, *Supvr,* Waterloo Regional Library (Ayr), Ayr ON. 519-632-7298
Kerr, Martha, *Cat,* Mount Lebanon Public Library, Pittsburgh PA. 412-531-1912
Kerr, Miriam, *Librn,* Union College, Department of Nursing Library, Denver CO. 303-778-1955, Ext 1864
Kerr, William A, *ILL,* University of New Brunswick, Saint John Campus, Ward Chipman Library, Saint John NB. 506-657-7310
Kerr, William G, *Librn,* Eisenhower College of the Rochester Institute of Technology, Ellis Slater Library, Seneca Falls NY. 315-568-7171
Kerridge, K, *On-Line Servs,* Bristol Myers Co, Bristol Laboratories Library & Information Service, Syracuse NY. 315-432-2232
Kerrigan, Esther, *Librn,* Bronx County Bar Association, Law Library, Bronx NY. 212-293-5600
Kerrigan, Margaret, *YA,* Elmont Public Library, Elmont NY. 516-354-5280, 354-4091
Kerrigan, Patricia, *Actg Coordr,* Beaver County Federated Library System, Aliquippa PA. 412-378-0585
Kersey, Barbara J, *Tech Serv,* University of Oklahoma Health Sciences Center Library, Oklahoma City OK. 405-271-2285
Kersey, Evelyn, *Librn,* Ocmulgee Regional Library (Telfair County), McRae GA. 912-868-2978
Kershaw, Helen, *Librn,* Pilgrim Church of United Church of Christ Memorial Library, Toledo OH. 419-478-6012
Kershner, Bruce S, *Dir,* Fairfield Public Library, Fairfield CT. 203-259-8303
Kershner, Stephen A, *Dir,* Geauga County Public Library, Chardon OH. 216-285-7601
Kerstein, Margaret, *Ch,* Waukesha Public Library, Waukesha WI. 414-542-4297
Kerstetter, Donald B, *Librn,* United States Air Force (USAF Hospital Medical Library), Laughlin AFB TX. 512-298-2311
Kerstetter, John, *Media Supvrs,* Kent State University Libraries (Audio-Visual Services), Kent OH. 216-672-3456
Kertiles, Marietta F, *Librn,* Delaware Division of Libraries, Handicapped Services, Dover DE. 302-678-4523
Kertland, Diana, *Chief Librn,* Lakehead University Library, Thunder Bay ON. 807-345-2121
Kerwin, Nancy A, *Ch,* Carroll Public Library, Carroll IA. 712-792-3432

Kesarwani, Malti, *Cat,* Nepean Public Library, Ottawa ON. 613-224-4338
Keshavjee, Valerie, *Librn,* Canadian Memorial Chiropractic College & Clinic Library, Toronto ON. 416-482-2340
Kesler, Joan, *Tech Serv,* Poplar Creek Public Library District, Streamwood IL. 312-837-6800
Kesner, Richard M, *Archives of Appalachia,* East Tennessee State University, Sherrod Library, Johnson City TN. 615-929-4338
Kesner, Susan Nayer, *Librn,* Legal Services of Upper East Tennessee Library, Johnson City TN. 615-928-8311
Kesper, Jeffrey, *Librn,* Free Public Library of Woodbridge (Fords Branch), Fords NJ. 201-738-0250
Kess, Patricia J, *Librn,* Nelson Public Library, Nelson NE. 402-225-7111
Kessinger, David, *Ref & Bibliog Instr,* Belmont Abbey College, Abbot Vincent Taylor Library, Belmont NC. 704-825-3711, Ext 342
Kessler, Bernice, *Ch,* Berlin Public Library, Berlin MA. 617-838-2812
Kessler, Margaret H, *Librn,* Town of Tonawanda Public Library (Kenmore), Kenmore NY. 716-873-2861
Kessling, Vicki, *Librn,* Salt Lake County Library System (Arthur E Peterson Branch), Sandy UT. 801-943-7614
Kessner, Nancy, *Librn,* Massachusetts General Hospital (Warren Patients' Library), Boston MA. 617-726-2000
Kester, Daphne, *Librn,* Davis Community Church, Resource Center Library, Davis CA. 916-753-2894
Kestler, Helen E, *Librn,* Dr W B Konkle Memorial Library, Montoursville PA. 717-368-1840
Kestner, Kathy, *Librn,* Kansas Neurological Institute, Professional Library, Topeka KS. 913-256-5389
Ketcham, Marjorie, *Librn,* Concrete Public Library, Concrete WA. 206-826-3198
Ketcham, Roule, *Librn,* Cosmos Public Library, Cosmos MN. 612-877-7345
Ketcham, Sarah, *Librn,* Plainfield Public Library, Plainfield WI. 715-335-4523
Ketchell, Debra, *Ref,* Eastern Virginia Medical School, Moorman Memorial Library, Norfolk VA. 804-446-5840
Ketcherid, Arthur, *Tech Serv,* University of South Florida (University Library), Tampa FL. 813-974-2721
Ketchins, Jewell, *AV,* Dekalb Library System, Maud M Burrus Library, Decatur GA. 404-378-7569
Ketchum, Molly, *Librn,* Rowan Public Library, Rowan IA. 515-853-2327
Kethley, Sue, *Spec Coll,* Waco-McLennan County Library, Waco TX. 817-754-4694
Kettering, Florence, *Dir,* Lewistown City Library, Lewistown MT. 406-538-5212
Kettle, Mrs Ralph, *Librn,* Monroe City Public Library, Monroe City MO. 314-735-2665
Kettner, Dorothy Hagen, *Librn,* Fergus Falls Community College Library, Fergus Falls MN. 218-736-7544
Ketton, Beverly, *Acq & Cat,* Oneonta Public Library, Oneonta AL. 205-274-7641
Ketzer, Sister M Barbara, *Ref,* Brescia College Library, Owensboro KY. 502-685-3131, Ext 213
Keuck, Louise F, *Dir,* Franklin Park Public Library District, Franklin Park IL. 312-455-6016
Keuker, Susan L, *Librn,* Insurance School of Chicago Library, Chicago IL. 312-427-2520
Kevin, Doris, *Asst Dir,* Gulfport Public Library, Gulfport FL. 813-347-0218
Kevorkian, Kathy, *Librn,* Ann Arbor Public Library (Nellie S Loving), Ann Arbor MI. 313-994-2353
Key, Addee, *Libr Asst,* San Bernardino County Library (Running Springs Branch), Running Springs CA. 714-867-2554
Key, Betty McKeever, *Oral hist,* Maryland Historical Society Library, Baltimore MD. 301-685-3750
Key, Jack D, *Librn,* Mayo Foundation (Medical Library), Rochester MN. 507-284-2061
Key, Margaret, *Mus Registrar,* Bowers Museum Library, Santa Ana CA. 714-972-1900
Key, Mary P, *Cat,* Ohio State University Libraries (William Oxley Thompson Memorial Library), Columbus OH. 614-422-6151
Key, Polly, *Asst Librn, Acq & Cat,* Haines City Public Library, Haines City FL. 813-422-1749

KEY

Key, Sara, *Ch,* Citizens Library, Washington PA. 412-222-2400

Key, Virginia M, *Librn,* Choctawhatchee Regional Library (Troy Public), Troy AL. 205-566-1314

Keyes, Ethel, *Asst Librn,* Littlefield Library, Tyngsboro MA. 617-649-7361

Keyes, Karen Canova, *On-Line Servs,* George Mason University Libraries, Fairfax VA. 703-323-2616

Keyes, Karen Canova, *Soc Sci & Nursing,* George Mason University Libraries, Fairfax VA. 703-323-2616

Keyes, Margaret N, *Dir,* University of Iowa, Old Capitol Library, Iowa City IA. 319-353-7293

Keyes, Molline, *Librn,* Pine Forest Regional Library (Collins Public), Collins MS. 601-765-8582

Keys, Edith, *ILL & Ref,* East Tennessee State University, Sherrod Library, Johnson City TN. 615-929-4338

Keys, Marshall, *Circ & Reader Serv,* Curry College, Louis R Levin Memorial Library, Milton MA. 617-333-0500, Ext 177

Keys, Nettie, *Asst Dir,* Oconee County Library, Walhalla SC. 803-638-5837

Khairallah, Lois M, *Librn,* Middle East Institute, George Camp Keiser Library, Washington DC. 202-785-1141

Khalatbari, Adel, *Librn,* Public Library of the District of Columbia (Capitol View), Washington DC. 202-727-1337

Khan, Munawwar, *Librn,* University of Toledo (Learning Resources Center), Toledo OH. 419-537-3188

Khan, Sallie, *Librn,* Fairfax County Public Library (Martha Washington), Alexandria VA. 703-768-6700

Kharbas, Judith N, *Tech Serv,* University of Rochester, Rush Rhees Library, Rochester NY. 716-275-4461

Kheel, Susan, *Ref,* East Brunswick Public Library, East Brunswick NJ. 201-254-1220

Kho, Barbara, *Librn,* Mississauga Public Library (Burnhamthorpe), Mississauga ON. 416-625-4314

Kho, Joyce, *Per,* University of San Francisco, Richard A Gleeson Library, San Francisco CA. 415-666-6167

Khoury, Fawzi, *Near East,* University of Washington Libraries, Seattle WA. 206-543-1760

Khoury, Nancy, *Ser,* McNeese State University, Lether E Frazar Memorial Library, Lake Charles LA. 318-477-2520, Ext 271

Kibben, Elna, *Dir,* Curtis Public Library, Curtis NE. 308-367-4148

Kibbey, Mark, *Librn,* Columbia University (Chemistry), New York NY. 212-280-2241

Kibler, Dorothy M, *Librn,* University of Iowa Libraries (Education-Psychology), Iowa City IA. 319-353-5345

Kibler, W J, *Dir,* Tonawanda City Public Library, Tonawanda NY. 716-693-5043

Kick, Elaine, *Assoc Dir & Ad,* Urbana Free Library, Urbana IL. 217-367-4057

Kickbusch, Marion, *Librn,* Marathon County Public Library (Little Chicago), Marathon WI. 715-842-5929

Kidd, Arvilla M, *Librn,* Weston Public Library, Weston OH. 419-669-3415

Kidd, Carole, *Ch,* Allentown Public Library, Allentown PA. 215-820-2400

Kidd, Claren, *Librn,* University of Oklahoma (Geology), Norman OK. 405-325-6451

Kidd, Gordon L, *Dir,* Ulster County Community College, Macdonald DeWitt Library, Stone Ridge NY. 914-687-7621, Ext 250

Kidd, Jerry S, *Prof,* University of Maryland, College of Library & Information Services, MD. 301-454-5441

Kidd, Mary, *Tech Serv,* Antioch College, Olive Kettering Memorial Library, Yellow Springs OH. 513-767-7331, Ext 229

Kidder, Audrey, *Asst Dir,* Southern Illinois University School of Medicine Library, Springfield IL. 217-782-2658

Kidman, Roy, *Dir,* University of Southern California, Edward L Doheny Memorial Library, Los Angeles CA. 213-743-6050

Kidney, Sister Olivia, *Librn,* Regis College Library, Weston MA. 617-893-1820, Ext 252

Kidorf, Bernice, *YA,* Millville Public Library, Millville NJ. 609-825-7087

Kidwell, Eva, *ILL,* Illinois Wesleyan University Library, Bloomington IL. 309-556-3172

Kidwell, Mrs James, *Bkmobile Coordr,* Chattanooga-Hamilton County Bicentennial Library, Chattanooga TN. 615-757-5320

Kiefer, Karel, *Outreach Libr,* Haywood County Public Library, Waynesville NC. 704-452-5169

Kiefer, Lawrence, *Librn,* University of Maryland at Baltimore (School of Law Library), Baltimore MD. 301-528-7270

Kiefer, Lawrence L, *Lectr,* University of Maryland, College of Library & Information Services, MD. 301-454-5441

Kiefer, Michael P, *Librn,* Amarillo Art Center Library, Amarillo TX. 806-372-8356

Kiefer, Patricia, *Librn,* Space Vector Corp Library, Northridge CA. 213-886-6500

Kiefer, Shirley E, *YA,* Hartford Public Library, Hartford CT. 203-525-9121

Kieffer, Lawrence, *Ref,* University of Northern Iowa Library, Cedar Falls IA. 319-273-2737

Kieffer, Suzanne, *Exec Dir,* Indiana Library Film Service, IN. 812-422-3537

Kiehl, Barbara, *Librn,* Santa Cruz Public Library (Felton Branch), Felton CA. 408-335-4052

Kiehn, Betty, *Film Librn,* Western Plains Library System, Clinton OK. 405-323-0974

Kiehne, Gloria, *Librn,* Jackson Public Library, Jackson MO. 314-243-5150

Kiek, Rose, *Librn,* Hopkins Public Library, Hopkins MI. 616-793-7516

Kiel, Mary, *Cat,* Washtenaw County Library, Ann Arbor MI. 313-971-6056

Kielas, Sandra, *ILL & Ad,* Eager Free Public Library, Evansville WI. 608-882-4230

Kielly, Marion, *Librn,* Prince Edward Island Department of Education, Planning Library, Charlottetown PE. 902-892-3504, Ext 29

Kienitz, LaDonna T, *Dir,* Lincolnwood Public Library, Lincolnwood IL. 312-677-5277

Kier, Martha, *Asst Librn,* Alvan Bolster Ricker Memorial Library, Poland ME. 207-998-4390

Kiersky, Loretta J, *Supvr,* Airco Inc, Information Center, Murray Hill NJ. 201-464-2400

Kierstead, Marilyn, *On-Line Servs & Bibliog Instr,* Reed College, E V Hauser Memorial Library, Portland OR. 503-771-1112, Ext 260

Kierstead, Rosemary, *Librn,* Mintz, Levin, Cohn, Glovsky & Popeo, Law Library, Boston MA. 617-742-5800

Kies, Cosette N, *Assoc Prof,* George Peabody College for Teachers, Department of Library Science, TN. 615-327-8037

Kiesling, Lee, *Librn,* Saint Louis County Library (Rock Road), Saint Ann MO. 314-429-5116

Kiesners, Mrs B, *Br Supvr,* Scarborough Public Library (Eglinton Square), Scarborough ON. 416-755-3986

Kiessling, Highla Ellen, *Info Servs Asst,* Lincoln National Life Insurance Co (Law Library), Fort Wayne IN. 219-424-5421, Ext 7492

Kietzer, Jane, *Dir,* Lomira Public Library, Lomira WI. 414-269-4115

Kietzman, William, *Slides,* Plymouth State College, Herbert H Lamson Library, Plymouth NH. 603-536-1550, Ext 257

Kiewitt, Eva, *Librn,* Indiana University at Bloomington (Graduate Library School), Bloomington IN. 812-337-5968

Kigar, Lorraine, *Librn,* Grand Rapids Baptist College & Seminary, Ketcham Library, Grand Rapids MI. 616-949-5300, Ext 228

Kiger, James A, *Librn,* Fayette County Law Library, Washington Court House OH. 614-335-6371

Kight, Barbara, *Librn,* United States Geological Survey, Water Resources Div Library, Boise ID. 208-334-2217

Kight, Myra L, *Art & Music,* Richmond Public Library, Richmond VA. 804-780-4256

Kightlinger, Margaret, *Lang Lab Technician,* United States Army (Language Training Facility Library), Fort George G Meade MD. 301-677-7255

Kijanka, Dorothy M, *Asst Dir,* Fairfield University, Gustav & Dagmar Nyselius Library, Fairfield CT. 203-255-5411, Ext 2451

Kiker, Fiona M, *Ref,* Lebanon Public Library, Lebanon OR. 503-258-5844

Kilbourne, John D, *Dir,* Society of the Cincinnati Library, Washington DC. 202-785-2040

Kilbourne, Richard A, *Librn,* Larkspur Public Library, Larkspur CA. 415-924-2405

Kilbridge, Rosemary, *Ref,* Chippewa Falls Public Library, Chippewa County Library Service, Chippewa Falls WI. 715-723-1147

Kilburn, Irmeli, *Librn,* Glover Memorial Hospital Library, Needham MA. 617-444-5600

Kilby, Clyde, *Curator,* Wheaton College Library, Wheaton IL. 312-682-5101

Kilby, Vera V, *Dir,* Lenox Public Library, Lenox IA. 515-333-2838

Kildea, Helen, *ILL,* Drexel University Library, Philadelphia PA. 215-895-2750

Kile, Barbara, *Govt Doc,* William Marsh Rice University, Fondren Library, Houston TX. 713-527-4022

Kile, Jean E, *Librn,* Kiowa County Library, Greensburg KS. 316-723-2683

Kiley, Carol, *Librn,* Lucius Beebe Memorial Library (Greenwood), Wakefield MA. 617-245-6130

Kiley, David, *Circ,* University of California, Santa Barbara Library, Santa Barbara CA. 805-961-2741

Kiley, Mrs F A, *Dir,* West Stockbridge Public Library, West Stockbridge MA. 413-232-7080

Kilfoil, Thomas F, *Ref,* West Hartford Public Library, Noah Webster Memorial Library, West Hartford CT. 203-236-6286

Kilgour, Alison, *Cat,* Willamette University Library, Salem OR. 503-370-6312

Kilgour, Frederick G, *President & Exec Dir,* OCLC, Inc, OH. 614-486-3661

Kilianski, Patricia, *Dir,* New Milford Public Library, New Milford NJ. 201-262-1221

Kilkenny, Angela, *Asst Librn,* Canadian Embassy Library, Washington DC. 202-785-1400, Ext 212 & 366

Kilkenny, Eugene F, *Librn,* Montgomery County Public Service Training Academy Library, Rockville MD. 301-279-8235

Killam, Frances H, *Librn,* Charles B Danforth Public Library, Barnard VT. 802-234-9579

Killam, Melanie, *Tech Serv,* Hawaii Loa College, Amos Starr & Juliette Montegue Cooke Academic Center, Kaneohe HI. 808-235-3641, Ext 119

Killebrew, Al, *Media,* Ambassador College Library, Pasadena CA. 213-577-5540

Killeen, Jean N, *Librn,* Bellaire Public Library, Bellaire MI. 616-533-8814

Killian, Daniel R, *Dir,* North Tonawanda Public Library, North Tonawanda NY. 716-693-4132

Killian, Gertrude, *Acq,* Petersburg Public Library, Petersburg VA. 804-732-3851

Killian, Gertrude, *Librn,* Petersburg Public Library (Rodof Sholom), Petersburg VA. 804-733-3363

Killian, Glenda, *Librn,* Roosevelt Public Library, Roosevelt UT. 801-722-4441

Killian, Mary, *Librn,* Wayne Oakland Library Federation (Audio-Visual), Wayne MI. 313-722-8012

Killian, Michael, *Bibliog Instr,* Morehead State University, Johnson Camden-Julian Carroll Library, Morehead KY. 606-783-2250

Killian, Naomi, *Librn,* Elbert Ivey Memorial Library (Ridgeview Public), Hickory NC. 704-327-2972

Killian, Thomas R, *Librn,* City of Detroit Law Department Library, Detroit MI. 313-224-4550

Killick, B, *Humanities,* Calgary Public Library, Calgary AB. 403-268-2880

Killie, Louise, *President,* Ridge Historical Society Library, Chicago IL. 312-881-1675

Killinger, Hope, *Librn,* Fowlerville Public Library, Fowlerville MI. 517-223-9089

Killingsworth, Amy, *Librn,* Northwest Missouri State University (Horace Mann Learning Center Library), Maryville MO. 816-582-7141, Ext 233

Killingsworth, Ruth, *Chmn,* Northwest Missouri State University, Library Science Dept, MO. 816-582-7141, Ext 1271

Killmon, Charles W, *AV,* Eastern Shore Community College, Learning Resources Center, Melfa VA. 804-787-3972

Kilman, Robert R, *Media,* Northeastern Oklahoma A&m College, Learning Resources Center, Miami OK. 918-542-8441, Ext 220

Kilminster, Catherine, *Librn,* Harford County Library (Darlington Branch), Darlington MD. 301-457-5566

Kilpatric, Patricia, *Ch,* Martinsburg-Berkeley County Public Library, Martinsburg Service Center, Martinsburg WV. 304-267-8933

Kilpatrick, Gabriel W, *Librn,* Augusta Mental Health Institute (Medical Library), Augusta ME. 207-623-4711, Ext 210

Kilpatrick, Lynn, *Commun Servs,* Chestatee Regional Library, Gainesville GA. 404-532-3311

Kilpatrick, Lynn, *Commun Servs,* Northeast Georgia Regional Library System, Clarkesville GA. 404-754-4413

Kilpatrick, Thomas L, *ILL,* Southern Illinois University at Carbondale, Delyte W Morris Library, Carbondale IL. 618-453-2522

Kilroy, Ed, *Librn,* Miami-Dade Public Library System (Coral Gables Branch), Coral Gables FL. 305-442-8706

Kiltun, Elizabeth, *Librn,* Park Avenue Synagogue, Cohen Library, New York NY. 212-369-2600

Kim, Bang, *Doc,* South Dakota State University, Hilton M Briggs Library, Brookings SD. 605-688-5106

Kim, C, *Librn,* Ryerson Polytechnical Institute (Architecture), Toronto ON. 416-595-5161

Kim, Chai, *Assoc Prof,* State University of New York at Buffalo, School of Information & Library Studies, NY. 716-636-2412

Kim, Chang Ho, *Tech Serv,* Community College of Baltimore, Bard Library, Baltimore MD. 301-396-0432, 0433

Kim, Chi Su, *Docs & Maps,* California Polytechnic State University Library, San Luis Obispo CA. 805-546-2345

Kim, Chin, *Dir,* California Western School of Law, San Diego CA. 714-239-0391, Ext 36

Kim, Choong Han, *Prof,* Indiana State University, Dept of Library Science, IN. 812-232-6311, Ext 2834

Kim, David, *Head, Tech Servs,* University of Lowell Libraries (O'Leary Library), Lowell MA. 617-452-5000, Ext 480

Kim, Helen, *Librn,* Munger, Tolles & Rickershauser, Law Library, Los Angeles CA. 213-683-9100

Kim, Ik-Sam, *Librn,* University of California Los Angeles Library (Oriental), Los Angeles CA. 213-825-4836

Kim, Jei, *Assoc Librn,* Howard University Libraries (Pharmacy Library), Washington DC. 202-636-6530

Kim, Joong Suk, *Dir,* C W Post Center, Saint Joseph's College Coordinate Campus Library, Brentwood NY. 516-273-5112

Kim, Moon H, *Librn,* Nissan Motor Corp in United States of America, Corp Library, Carson CA. 213-532-3111, Ext 2743

Kim, Mrs Tae-Ock, *Librn,* University of Santa Clara (Frank Gentles Science), Santa Clara CA. 408-984-4415

Kim, Nancy, *Acq,* Northwest Christian College, Learning Resource Center, Eugene OR. 503-343-1641, Ext 35

Kim, Sangyol, *Tech Serv,* Essex County College, Learning Resources Center, Newark NJ. 201-877-3233

Kim, Stella, *Tech Serv & On-Line Servs,* Biola College & Talbot Theological Seminary, Rosemead Graduate School of Professional Psychology, Rose Memorial Library, La Mirada CA. 213-944-0351, Ext 3255

Kim, Sue, *Tech Serv,* Palatine Public Library District, Palatine IL. 312-358-5881

Kim, Sungha, *Asst Librn,* Harvard University Library (Harvard-Yenching Library), Cambridge MA. 617-495-3327

Kim, Young, *Cat,* Saint Joseph's University Libraries (Drexel Library), Philadelphia PA. 215-879-7559

Kimball, Jane A, *Entomology,* University of California at Davis, General Library, Davis CA. 916-752-2110

Kimball, Judith, *Librn,* New Hampshire State Library (Concord), Concord NH. 603-271-2392

Kimball, Lee, *Coordr,* Art Gallery of Ontario, Edward P Taylor Reference Library, Toronto ON. 416-977-0414, Ext 339, 340 & 390

Kimball, Merle, *Ser,* College of William & Mary in Virginia, Earl Gregg Swem Library, Williamsburg VA. 804-253-4404

Kimball, Richard H, *Dir,* North Country Reference & Research Resources Council, NY. 315-386-4569

Kimball, Tevis, *Assoc Librn & Systs Analyst,* Southeastern Massachusetts University, Library Communications Center, North Dartmouth MA. 617-999-8662

Kimball, Thomas, *Dir,* Barstow College Library, Barstow CA. 714-252-2411, Ext 220

Kimble, Mary, *Adminr,* Mary Riley Styles Public Library, Falls Church VA. 703-241-5030

Kimble, Mrs M W, *Dir,* Morton College Library, Cicero IL. 312-656-8000, Ext 271, 320 & 321

Kimbrell, Beth, *Circ,* Wingate College, Ethel K Smith Library, Wingate NC. 704-233-4061, Ext 155

Kimbrough, J Marion, *Assoc Prof,* George Peabody College for Teachers, Department of Library Science, TN. 615-327-8037

Kimbrough, Jane, *Librn,* Pioneer Multi-County Library (Blanchard Public), Blanchard OK. 405-485-2275

Kimbrough, Joseph, *Dir,* Minneapolis Public Library & Information Center, Minneapolis MN. 612-372-6500

Kimerer, Sally, *Librn,* Sutter County Free Library (Sutter Branch), Sutter CA. 916-755-0485

Kimmage, Dennis, *Bibliog Instr,* State University of New York College at Plattsburgh, Benjamin F Feinberg Library, Plattsburgh NY. 518-564-3180

Kimmel, Margaret, *Assoc Prof,* University of Pittsburgh, School of Library & Information Science, PA. 412-624-5230

Kimmel, Ruth N, *Dir,* West Nyack Free Library, West Nyack NY. 914-358-6081

Kimsey, Hellen H, *Dir,* Mountain Regional Library, Young Harris GA. 404-379-3732

Kimzey, Ann, *Instr,* University of Houston at Clear Lake City, Learning Resources Specialist Program, TX. 713-488-9405

Kinard, John R, *Dir,* Anacostia Neighborhood Museum Library, Washington DC. 202-357-1300

Kincaid, Anne, *Ad,* San Francisco Public Library, San Francisco CA. 415-558-4235

Kincaid, Barbara, *Dir,* Western Counties Regional Library, Yarmouth NS. 902-742-2486

Kincaid, Cecille G, *Librn,* Valier Public Library, Valier MT. 406-279-3366

Kinch, Camilla, *Librn,* Tulare County Library System (Panorama Heights), Posey CA. 805-536-8816

Kinch, Michael, *Agr-Forestry,* Oregon State University, William Jasper Kerr Library, Corvallis OR. 503-754-3411

Kincheloe, Frances D, *Librn,* Toole County Free Library, Shelby MT. 406-434-5411

Kinchen, Robert P, *Dir,* Onondaga County Public Library System, Syracuse NY. 315-473-2702

Kinchen, Robert P, *Dir,* Queens Borough Public Library, Jamaica NY. 212-990-0700

Kinchen, Weeda, *Librn,* Satilla Regional Library (Hazlehurst Public), Hazlehurst GA. 912-375-2386

Kindle, Odis B, *Dir,* Navarro College, Gaston T Gooch Library, Corsicana TX. 214-874-6501, Ext 257

Kindlin, Jean, *Librn,* University of Pittsburgh (Graduate School of Library & Information Sciences), Pittsburgh PA. 412-624-5238

Kindred, Louise, *Librn,* Middletown Fine Arts Center Library, Middletown OH. 513-424-2416

Kindrick, Julie J, *Librn,* Fresno County Free Library (Blind & Handicapped Services), Fresno CA. 209-488-3217

Kindt, LaVerne, *Librn,* Mansfield-Richland County Public Library (Butler Branch), Butler OH. 419-883-2220

Kindzerske, Marcia, *Librn,* Arthur D Little Inc, Burlington Library, Burlington MA. 617-864-5770, Ext 2186

Kiney, Doris, *Bkmobile Coordr,* Franklin Township Free Public Library, Somerset NJ. 201-545-8032

King, Ann, *Local Hist,* Saint Charles City County Library, Saint Peters MO. 314-441-2300

King, Ann H, *Acq,* University of Florida Libraries (Agriculture), Gainesville FL. 904-392-1934

King, Annie G, *Librn,* Tuskegee Institute, Hollis Burke Frissell Library, Tuskegee Institute AL. 205-727-8894

King, Arline, *Librn,* Josephine County Library System (Wolf Creek Branch), Wolf Creek OR. 503-866-2640

King, Artie Mae, *Dir,* Clayton Public Library, Albert W Thompson Memorial Library, Clayton NM. 505-374-9423

King, Audre, *Librn,* Frontenac County Library (Hartington Branch), Hartington ON. 613-372-2524

King, Betty, *Librn,* Rockwell Hanford Operations (Basalt Waste Isolation Project Library), Richland WA. 509-942-6898

King, Betty, *Librn,* San Antonio Public Library (Hertzberg Circus), San Antonio TX. 512-299-7810

King, Beverley, *Br Coordr,* Monroe County Library System, Monroe MI. 313-241-5277

King, Blanche L, *Dir,* Old Town Public Library, Old Town ME. 207-827-5985

King, Bonita, *Libr Techn,* Gaston College, Learning Resources Center, Dallas NC. 704-922-3136, Ext 315

King, Bonnie, *Librn,* Lima Public Library (Cairo Branch), Cairo OH. 419-228-5113

King, Bonnie, *Bus & Econ,* University of Toledo, William S Carlson Library, Toledo OH. 419-537-2324

King, Bonnie Jean, *Librn,* Anta Corp Library, Oklahoma City OK. 405-272-9321, Ext 212

King, Brenda, *Librn,* Corhart Refractories Co, Inc Library, Div of Corning Glass Works, Louisville KY. 502-778-3311

King, C, *Librn,* Canada Department of National Defense, Scientific Information Center, Defense & Civil Institute of Environmental Medicine Library, Downsview ON. 416-633-4240, Ext 209

King, Carol S, *Per,* Southwest Texas State University, Learning Resources Center, San Marcos TX. 512-245-2132

King, Carole, *Ch,* Chesapeake Public Library, Chesapeake VA. 804-547-6579, 547-6592

King, Catharine, *Ref,* Milton Public Library, Milton MA. 617-698-5707

King, Chery, *Children's Outreach,* Bladen County Public Library, Elizabethtown NC. 919-862-8171

King, Christobel, *Librn,* I B Turner Library, Washington NC. 919-946-3579

King, Coline, *Media,* Tyler Junior College, Edgar H Vaughn Memorial Library, Tyler TX. 214-592-5993, 593-3342

King, Cynthia, *Ch,* Fresno County Free Library, Fresno CA. 209-488-3191

King, Cyrus B, *Asst Dir & Tech Serv,* North Carolina State University, D H Hill Library, Raleigh NC. 919-737-2843, 2595

King, Dan M, *Prof,* Kentucky Wesleyan College, Department of Library Science, KY. 502-926-3111, Ext 112, 113

King, Dan M, *Chief Librn,* Kentucky Wesleyan College, Library Learning Center, Owensboro KY. 502-926-3111, Ext 113, 117

King, David A, *ILL & Ref,* San Joaquin Delta College, Goleman Library, Stockton CA. 209-478-2011, Ext 277

King, David E, *Librn,* Standard Educational Corp, Editorial Library, Chicago IL. 312-346-7440, Ext 107

King, Dawn, *Librn,* Keystone Public Library, Keystone IA. 319-442-3329

King, Dennis W, *Dir,* Island Trees Public Library, Levittown NY. 516-731-2211, 731-2213

King, Diana R, *Librn,* Witherle Memorial Library, Castine ME. 207-326-4375

King, Dixie, *Librn,* San Augustine Public Library, San Augustine TX. 713-275-5367

King, Donald Ross, *Assoc Prof,* Rutgers-The State University of New Jersey, Graduate School of Library & Information Studies, NJ. 201-932-7500

King, Donna J, *Dir,* South Charleston Public Library, South Charleston WV. 304-744-6561

King, Dorothy, *Long Island Coll,* East Hampton Free Library, East Hampton NY. 516-324-0222, Ext 0243

King, Edna, *Reader Serv,* Slippery Rock State College Library, Slippery Rock PA. 412-794-2510

King, Elizabeth, *Circ,* Henry Ford Community College, Eshleman Library, Dearborn MI. 313-271-2750, Ext 378

King, Ellen, *Ch,* Grace A Dow Memorial Library, Midland Public Library, Midland MI. 517-835-7151

King, Ethel, *Ad & Ref,* Elmont Public Library, Elmont NY. 516-354-5280, 354-4091

King, Eveline, *Cat,* Mid-America Nazarene College Library, Olathe KS. 913-782-3750, Ext 216

King, Evelyn M, *Asst Dir Coll Interp,* Texas A&M University Libraries, College Station TX. 713-845-6111

251

KING

King, Frances, *Dir,* Huerfano County Public Library, Walsenburg CO. 303-738-2774

King, Franklin, *Assoc Prof,* Jacksonville State University, College of Library Science, Communications & Instructional Media, AL. 205-435-6390

King, Franklin, *Dir Nonprint Media,* Jacksonville State University Library, Jacksonville AL. 205-435-9820, Ext 213, 214

King, Gail, *Librn,* North Arkansas Regional Library (Searcy County), Yellville AR. 501-449-6015

King, Geraldine, *Pub Serv,* Ramsey County Public Library, Roseville MN. 612-631-0494

King, Hannah M, *Librn,* University of Nebraska Medical Center (Eppley Institute for Cancer Research Library), Omaha NE. 402-541-7669

King, J, *Dir,* Canadian Council on Social Development Documentation Centre Library, Ottawa ON. 613-728-1865

King, Jack B, *Librn,* Hamline University, Bush Memorial Library, Saint Paul MN. 612-641-2373

King, James M, *Asst Prof,* University of Georgia, Dept of Educational Media & Librarianship, GA. 404-542-3810

King, Jane, *Ser,* Arlington Public Library, Arlington TX. 817-275-2763, 265-3311, Ext 347

King, Jeanette, *Asst Dir,* Hardin County Library, Savannah TN. 901-925-4314

King, Joan, *Librn,* Englehart Public Library, Englehart ON. 705-544-2100

King, JoAnn, *Media,* Thomas Jefferson University (Scott Memorial Library), Philadelphia PA. 215-928-8848

King, Joe, *Tech Serv & Cat,* City-County Library of Missoula, Missoula MT. 406-728-5900

King, Josephine, *Circ,* Haysville Community Library, Haysville KS. 316-524-5242

King, Joyce, *Librn,* Dekalb Library System (Sue Kellogg Branch), Stone Mountain GA. 404-469-3069

King, Katharine, *Librn,* Tenney Memorial Library, Inc, Newbury VT. 802-866-5955

King, Katherine S, *Librn,* American Public Power Association Library, Washington DC. 202-333-9200, Ext 67

King, Kathryn, *Asst Librn,* Natural History Museum of Los Angeles County, Research Library, Los Angeles CA. 213-744-3387, 744-3388

King, Kathryn, *On-Line Servs,* South Dakota State University, Hilton M Briggs Library, Brookings SD. 605-688-5106

King, Kathyrn, *ILL,* California State University, Sacramento Library, Sacramento CA. 916-454-6466

King, Kenneth, *Dir,* Mount Clemens Public Library, Mount Clemens MI. 313-465-1906

King, Leon, *Cat,* Lakewood Community College Library, White Bear Lake MN. 612-770-1331, Ext 129

King, Lynne, *On-Line Servs,* State University of New York College at Plattsburgh, Benjamin F Feinberg Library, Plattsburgh NY. 518-564-3180

King, M F, *Mgr,* General Electric Co (Whitney Library), Schenectady NY. 518-385-8791

King, Margot, *Dir,* Saint Thomas More College, Shannon Library, Saskatoon SK. 306-343-4561

King, Mark, *In Charge,* Santa Barbara Public Library (Carpinteria Branch), Carpinteria CA. 805-684-4314

King, Marvel, *Librn,* Mathis Public Library, Mathis TX. 512-547-6201

King, Mary, *On-Line Servs & Bibliog Instr,* System Development Corp, Information Retrieval Center, Santa Monica CA. 213-829-7511, Ext 3433

King, Mavis, *Dir,* Carnegie Public Library, Dell Rapids Public Library, Dell Rapids SD. 605-428-3280

King, Maxine, *Librn,* Randolph Public Library (John W Clark Public), Franklinville NC. 919-824-2604

King, Mrs Roy, *Librn,* Tombigbee Regional Library (Weir Public), Weir MS. 601-541-6747

King, Mrs Wade, *Librn,* Anna Porter Memorial Public Library, Gatlinburg TN. 615-436-5588

King, Muriel, *Tech Serv & Cat,* Leeward Community College Library, Pearl City HI. 808-455-0210

King, Pat, *Bkmobile Coordr,* Southeast Arkansas Regional Library, Monticello AR. 501-367-3336

King, Patricia Miller, *Dir,* Radcliffe College, Arthur & Elizabeth Schlesinger Library on the History of Women in America, Cambridge MA. 617-495-8647

King, Paul F, *Dir,* Peace College, Lucy Cooper Finch Library, Raleigh NC. 919-832-2881

King, Peggy D, *Librn,* Legislative Research Commission Library, Frankfort KY. 502-564-8100, Ext 341, 342

King, Phyllis, *Librn,* Golconda Public Library, Golconda IL. 618-683-6531

King, Polly, *Librn,* Leighton Public Library, Leighton AL. 205-446-5380

King, Polly C, *Librn,* Forsyth Technical Institute Library (Allied Health), Winston-Salem NC. 919-723-0371

King, Reta, *Dir,* Chadron State College, Educational Media Program, NE. 308-432-4451, Ext 271

King, Reta, *Dir Libr Serv,* Chadron State College Library, Chadron NE. 308-432-4451, Ext 271

King, Sally M, *Asst Librn,* Rappahannock Community College, North Campus Learning Resource Center, Warsaw VA. 804-333-4024, Ext 208, 209

King, Sandra, *Asst Librn,* Daviess County Library, Gallatin MO. 816-663-3222

King, Sandra, *Dir,* Lurleen B Wallace State Junior College Library, Andalusia AL. 205-222-6591, Ext 265

King, Sharon, *Bibliog Instr,* International Research & Evaluation, Information & Research Resources Library-Data Base, Eagan MN. 612-869-2675

King, Shelden S, *Librn,* Westinghouse Electric Corp, Engineering Library, Horseheads NY. 607-796-3207

King, Sherry, *Librn,* East Baton Rouge Parish Library (Zachary Branch), Zachary LA. 504-654-5086

King, Viola E, *Dir,* Worcester Junior College, Harrington Library, Worcester MA. 617-755-4314

King, Virginia, *Asst Librn,* Alamosa Southern Peaks Public Library, Alamosa CO. 303-589-6592

King, Virginia, *Fine Arts,* Azusa Pacific College, Marshburn Memorial Library, Azusa CA. 213-969-3434, Ext 198

King, Walter, *Acq,* Southwest Missouri State University Library, Springfield MO. 417-836-5104

King, Jr, Charles H, *Cat,* Smithsonian Institution Libraries (Library of the National Collection of Fine Arts & the National Portrait Gallery), Washington DC. 202-357-1886

Kingery, Victor, *Dir,* Quincy College Library, Quincy IL. 217-222-8020, Ext 225

Kingery, Victor, *Instr,* Quincy College, Library Science Program, IL. 217-222-8020, Ext 225

Kinghorn, Helen, *Asst Librn,* Jewish Hospital (Medical Library), Cincinnati OH. 513-872-3136

Kingman, Elizabeth Y, *Librn,* School of American Research Library, Santa Fe NM. 505-982-3583

Kingman, Nancy M, *Supvr,* 3M (Business Information Service), Saint Paul MN. 612-733-9057

Kingsbury, Armelle, *Librn,* Bonfield Public Library, Bonfield ON. 705-776-2641

Kingsbury, Mary, *Assoc Prof,* University of North Carolina at Chapel Hill, School of Library Science, NC. 919-933-8366

Kingsbury, Norma, *Librn,* Moretown Memorial Library, Moretown VT. 802-496-3624

Kingsley, Marcia S, *On-Line Servs,* University of North Carolina at Greensboro, Walter Clinton Jackson Library, Greensboro NC. 919-379-5880

Kingsley, Thomas, *Librn,* Syracuse University Libraries (William C Ruger Law Library), Syracuse NY. 315-423-2527

Kingston, JoAnn, *Librn,* Flint Public Library (Freeman), Flint MI. 313-743-6360

Kingston, Margaret, *Librn,* Olive G Pettis Library, Goshen NH. 603-863-4013

Kingston, Sara B, *Asst Librn,* Hartland Public Library, Hartland WI. 414-367-3350

Kinkel, Zerma D, *Dir,* Montrose County Regional District Library, Montrose CO. 303-249-9656

Kinman, William R, *Dir,* Alhambra Public Library, Alhambra CA. 213-570-5008

Kinna, Keith, *Ad,* Jervis Public Library Association, Rome NY. 315-336-4570

Kinnaird, Ann, *Cat, ILL & Ref,* Spalding College Library, Louisville KY. 502-585-9411

Kinnaman, Mary, *Clerk,* Mid-Columbia Regional Library (Pasco Branch), Pasco WA. 509-545-3451

Kinnan, Marjorie, *Clerk,* John McIntire Public Library Public Library (Roseville Branch), Roseville OH. 614-697-0237

Kinney, Lillie C, *Ref,* Onondaga Community College, Sidney B Coulter Library, Syracuse NY. 315-469-7741, Ext 5335-5338

Kinney, Lisa, *Dir,* Albany County Public Library, Laramie WY. 307-745-3365

Kinney, Margaret, *ILL & Ref,* Mid-Mississippi Regional Library System, Kosciusko MS. 601-289-5141, 289-5146

Kinney, Margaret M, *Librn,* Veterans Administration, Medical Center Library Service, Bronx NY. 212-584-9000, Ext 435, 641

Kinney, Marjorie, *Missouri Valley Hist,* Kansas City Public Library, Kansas City MO. 816-221-2685

Kinney, Marnelle, *Branch Libr Supvr,* Rockwell International, Anaheim Information Center, Anaheim CA. 714-632-3621

Kinney, Jr, Paul W, *ILL,* County College of Morris, Sherman H Masten Learning Resource Center, Randolph Township NJ. 201-361-5000, Ext 470

Kinney-Moede, Mary, *Media,* Lawrence University, Seeley G Mudd Library, Appleton WI. 414-739-3681, Ext 264

Kinnison, Luella, *Asst Dir,* Weld County Library, Greeley CO. 303-330-7691

Kinsella, Eileen, *Acq,* Glen Cove Public Library, Glen Cove NY. 516-676-2130

Kinsella, May H, *Librn,* General Accident Group Library, Philadelphia PA. 215-238-5000

Kinsella, Peggy, *Rare Bks,* Ryerson Polytechnical Institute, Donald Mordell Learning Resources Centre, Toronto ON. 416-595-5331

Kinsella, Peggy, *Arts & Lit,* Ryerson Polytechnical Institute, Donald Mordell Learning Resources Centre, Toronto ON. 416-595-5331

Kinsey, Betty, *Librn,* Wayne Public Library, Wayne OH. 419-288-2708

Kinsey, David, *Media,* Kettering College of Medical Arts Library, Learning Resource Center, Kettering OH. 513-296-7201, Ext 5630

Kinsky, Katherine, *ILL,* Binghamton Public Library, Binghamton NY. 607-723-6457

Kinslow, Barbara A, *Librn,* Kaman Sciences Corporation Library, Colorado Springs CO. 303-599-1777

Kintner, Anne, *Archives,* Grinnell College, Burling Library, Grinnell IA. 515-236-6181, Ext 598

Kintner, Keith, *AV,* Los Angeles Mission College, Learning Resources Center, San Fernando CA. 213-365-8271, Ext 283

Kintz, Nancy L, *Librn,* Mellon National Corp Library, Pittsburgh PA. 412-232-4100

Kinzel, Mary, *Librn,* Lutheran Theological Seminary, Otto Olson Memorial Library, Saskatoon SK. 306-343-8204, Ext 01

Kinzer, Jacqueline, *Music & Art,* Carnegie Library, Rome GA. 404-291-7568

Kinzer, Kathryn, *ILL & Ref,* Saint John's College, Woodward Hall Library, Annapolis MD. 301-263-2371, Ext 71, 72

Kinzy, Louise, *Librn,* Appalachia Educational Laboratory, Inc, Reference & Resource Center, Charleston WV. 304-344-8371, Ext 47

Kiohe, Anastasia, *Librn,* Northeastern Regional Library System (Moonsonee Public), Moonsonee ON. 705-567-7043

Kious, Mary, *Librn,* Lansing Public Library, Lansing IA. 515-533-4713

Kipp, E, *ILL & Ref,* Northern Montana College Library, Havre MT. 406-265-7821, Ext 3306, 3307

Kipp, Eileen, *Librn,* Ossian Public Library, Ossian IA. 319-532-9461

Kipping, Karen, *Tech Serv,* Bibliotheque Municipale De Dorval, Dorval PQ. 514-631-3575

Kipple, Ruth, *Dir,* Long Island Community Library, Long Island KS. 913-854-7453

Kiprick, Joan, *Librn,* Alberta Department of Attorney General & Law Society of Alberta Library, Lethbridge AB. 403-329-3266

Kiraldi, Louis, *Doc,* Western Michigan University, Dwight B Waldo Library, Kalamazoo MI. 616-383-4961

Kirbawy, Barbara, *Dir,* Barberton Public Library, Barberton OH. 216-745-1194

Kirby, Algee G, *Prof,* University of Arkansas at Pine Bluff, Educational Media & Services, AR. 501-535-6700, Ext 322

Kirby, Ami, *Ch,* Santa Monica Public Library, Santa Monica CA. 213-451-5751

Kirby, Barbara L, *Dir,* El Segundo Public Library, El Segundo CA. 213-322-4121

Kirby, Christine, *Special Clientele,* State Library of Florida, Div of Library Services, Dept of State, Tallahassee FL. 904-487-2651

Kirby, Douglas, *Librn,* Prince Edward Island Provincial Library (Kinkora Branch), Kinkora PE. 902-892-3504, Ext 54

Kirby, Elizabeth, *Extension Specialist,* Coastal Plain Regional Library, Tifton GA. 912-386-3400

Kirby, Helen R, *Asst Prof,* Ball State University, Dept of Library Science, IN. 317-285-7180, 285-7189

Kirby, Mable, *Librn,* Shreve Memorial Library (Hosston Branch), Hosston LA. 318-221-2614

Kirchen, Terri, *Automation Coordr,* Elon College, Iris Holt McEwen Library, Elon College NC. 919-584-9711, Ext 230 or 242

Kirchenberger, Felicitas, *Actg Librn,* Allan Memorial Institute of Psychiatry Library, Montreal PQ. 514-842-1251, Ext 269

Kircher, Roland E, *Librn,* Wesley Theological Seminary Library, Washington DC. 202-363-0922

Kirchfeld, Friedhelm, *Librn,* National College of Naturopathic Medicine Library, Portland OR. 503-226-3745

Kirchgraber, Nancy B, *Cat,* Belleville Public Library, Belleville IL. 618-234-0441

Kirchhoff, Ursula, *Media,* Bluffton-Wells County Public Library, Bluffton IN. 219-824-1612

Kirchmann, Jennifer, *Ref,* Peru State College Library, Peru NE. 402-872-3815, Ext 218

Kirchner, Andras K, *Dir,* University of Calgary Library (Faculty of Medicine Medical Library), Calgary AB. 403-284-6858

Kirchner, Elizabeth, *Librn,* Calgary General Hospital, Library Services, Calgary AB. 403-268-9234

Kirchner, Elizabeth, *Chief Librn,* Saint Louis Mercantile Library Association, Saint Louis MO. 314-621-0670

Kirchner, Judith, *Tech Serv,* University of Dubuque, Ficke-Laird Library, Dubuque IA. 319-589-3218

Kirchner, William N, *Dir,* Cherokee Regional Library, LaFayette-Walker County Library, LaFayette GA. 404-638-2992

Kirchoff, Lori, *Processor,* George Amos Memorial Library, Campbell County Library, Gillette WY. 307-682-3223

Kirghgassner, Eleanor, *Asst Librn,* Oaklyn Memorial Library, Oaklyn NJ. 609-858-8226

Kirk, Artemis, *Dir,* Simmons College, Beatley Library, Boston MA. 617-738-2241

Kirk, Artemis, *Lectr,* Simmons College, Graduate School of Library & Information Science, MA. 617-738-2225

Kirk, Irving C, *Adjunct Lectr,* Dalhousie University, School of Library Service, NS. 902-424-3656

Kirk, Jay, *Sci,* Marquette University Memorial Library, Milwaukee WI. 414-224-7214

Kirk, Muriel S, *Coordr,* Museum of Fine Arts, Reference Library, Saint Petersburg FL. 813-896-2667

Kirk, Patricia A, *Librn,* Oregon State Library Services for the Blind & Physically Handicapped, Salem OR. 503-378-3849

Kirk, Ruth, *ILL,* University of Washington Libraries, Seattle WA. 206-543-1760

Kirk, Sherwood, *Assoc Dir Libr Operations,* Illinois State Library, Springfield IL. 217-782-2994

Kirk, Thomas G, *Actg Dir,* University of Wisconsin-Parkside Library, Kenosha WI. 414-553-2221

Kirk, Tom L, *Librn,* United States Air Force (Vance Air Force Base Library), Vance AFB OK. 405-237-2121, Ext 7368

Kirkbridge, Rebecca, *Librn,* Oklahoma State University, School of Technical Training Learning Resources Center, Okmulgee OK. 918-756-6211

Kirkby, Arthur M, *Librn,* Mary Ball Washington Museum & Library Inc, Lancaster VA. 804-462-7280

Kirkeberg, Inez, *Librn,* Murphy Memorial Library, Monona IA. 319-539-2356

Kirkegard, P, *Librn,* Teledyne, Inc, Teledyne McCormick Selph Library, Hollister CA. 408-637-3731

Kirkendall, James, *Cat,* Eureka-Humboldt County Library, Eureka CA. 707-445-7284, 445-7513

Kirkes, Stephanie, *Commun Servs,* Chattahoochee Valley Regional Library, W C Bradley Memorial Library, Headquarters, Columbus GA. 404-327-0211

Kirkham, Phebe, *Asst Prof,* Phillips University, Education & Library Science Study Area, OK. 405-237-4433, Ext 417

Kirkham, Phebe, *Ref & Bibliog Instr,* Phillips University, Zollars Memorial Library, Enid OK. 405-237-4433, Ext 251

Kirking, Clayton, *Fine Arts,* Tacoma Public Library, Tacoma WA. 206-572-2000

Kirkland, J, *Ref,* Georgia Institute of Technology, Price Gilbert Memorial Library, Atlanta GA. 404-894-4510

Kirkland, James A, *Librn,* Texas Baptist Institute, Seminary Library, Henderson TX. 214-657-6543

Kirkland, N L, *Librn,* Tacoma News Tribune Library, Tacoma WA. 206-597-8629

Kirkland, Ruth, *ILL & Ref,* Hackley Public Library, Muskegon MI. 616-722-7276

Kirkland, Theolia, *Librn,* Chatham-Effingham-Liberty Regional Library (Yamacraw), Savannah GA. 912-236-2062

Kirkley, Lynn, *Librn,* Lee County Public Library, Woodward Memorial Library, Bishopville SC. 803-484-5921

Kirkman, Catherine, *Librn,* Public Library of Columbus & Franklin County (Reynoldsburg Branch), Reynoldsburg OH. 614-866-0075

Kirkman, Jaqueline N, *Librn,* Martin Marietta Chemicals, Technical Library, Charlotte NC. 704-827-4351

Kirkpatrick, Brett A, *Librn,* New York Academy of Medicine Library, New York NY. 212-876-8200

Kirkpatrick, Marcia, *Librn,* Sacramento Public Library (Fair Oaks-Orangevale Branch), Fair Oaks CA. 916-966-5740

Kirkpatrick, Mel, *Librn,* Investors Diversified Services, Investment Library, Minneapolis MN. 612-372-3429

Kirkpatrick, Melba, *Librn,* Metropolitan Library System (Del City Branch), Del City OK. 405-235-0571

Kirkpatrick, Mrs James, *Dir,* Marlin Public Library, Marlin TX. 817-883-6602

Kirkpatrick, Nancy, *Pub Servs,* Yavapi College Learning Resources Center, Prescott AZ. 602-445-7300, Ext 272

Kirkpatrick, Oliver, *Librn,* Brooklyn Public Library (Bushwick), Brooklyn NY. 212-443-1078

Kirkpatrick, Stephen, *Circ & Per,* State University of New York, College at Old Westbury Library, Old Westbury NY. 516-876-3156, RD 3152

Kirks, James H, *Coordr,* North State Cooperative Library System, Willows CA. 916-934-2173

Kirksey, Mary Bess, *Southern History & Lit,* Birmingham Public & Jefferson County Free Library, Birmingham AL. 205-254-2551

Kirkwood, Alexa, *Weed Br,* Stamford's Public Library, Ferguson Library, Stamford CT. 203-325-4354

Kirkwood, Alexa, *In Charge,* Stamford's Public Library (Weed Memorial), Stamford CT. 203-322-5844

Kirkwood, Charles C, *Librn,* University of Notre Dame Library (Law School Library), Notre Dame IN. 219-283-7024

Kirkwood, Mildred, *Ind Learning Ctr Asst Dir,* San Diego City College Library, San Diego CA. 714-238-1181, Ext 250

Kirkwood, Richard E, *Dir,* Hollins College, Fishburn Library, Hollins College VA. 703-362-6592

Kirkwood, Sonya A, *ILL,* Sinclair Community College, Learning Resources Center, Dayton OH. 513-226-2855

Kirmss, Carolyn, *Tech Serv,* Henry Carter Hull Library, Inc, Clinton CT. 203-669-2342

Kirn, Judith, *Acq, Cat & Spec Coll,* Saint Mary's Seminary College, Saint Mary's of the Barrens Library, Perryville MO. 314-547-6300

Kirol, Jean T, *Dir,* Teton County Library, Huff Memorial Library, Jackson WY. 307-733-2164

Kirsch, Anne, *Librn,* Central Suffolk Hospital, Medical Library, Riverhead NY. 516-369-6000, Ext 6088

Kirsch, Carol, *Cat,* Upper Arlington Public Library, Upper Arlington OH. 614-486-9621

Kirsch, Debra, *ILL,* Russell Sage College, James Wheelock Clark Library, Troy NY. 518-270-2249

Kirsch, Mary, *Spec Projects,* Hudson Valley Community College Learning Resources Center, Dwight Marvin Library, Troy NY. 518-283-1100, Ext 629

Kirsch, Olive, *Librn,* Herrin City Library, Herrin IL. 618-942-6109

Kirschner, Mary, *Dir,* Sauk City Public Library, Sauk City WI. 608-643-8346

Kirschner, Ruth, *Librn,* Essex County Law Library, Newark NJ. 201-961-7293

Kirsh, Julie, *Librn,* Toronto Sun Publishing Co Library, Toronto ON. 416-868-2257

Kirshenbaum, Larry, *ILL,* Montclair State College, Harry A Sprague Library, Upper Montclair NJ. 201-893-4291

Kirshenbaum, Mrs Nelson, *Librn,* Temple Beth El Library, Rochester NY. 716-473-1770, Ext 24

Kirtley, Ladine, *Asst Librn,* Tonkawa Public Library, Tonkawa OK. 405-628-3366

Kirtley, Marjorie D, *Librn,* Supreme Court of Virginia, Virginia State Law Library, Richmond VA. 804-786-2075

Kirton, Robena, *Dir,* Gravenhurst Municipal Public Library, Gravenhurst ON. 705-687-3382

Kirven, Marian, *Dir,* Swedenborg School of Religion, Newton MA. 617-244-0504

Kirwan, John, *Dir,* Monticello Union Township Public Library, Monticello IN. 219-583-5643

Kirwan, William J, *Dir,* Western Carolina University, Hunter Memorial Library, Cullowhee NC. 704-293-7306

Kirwin, Florence M, *Librn,* Aspen Institute for Humanistic Studies, David Mayer Library, Aspen CO. 303-925-7010

Kisch, Sister Angelinda, *ILL,* Viterbo College Library, La Crosse WI. 608-784-0040, Ext 429

Kise, Harle, *Librn,* United States Navy (Marine Corps Recruit Depot Library), San Diego CA. 714-225-4011

Kish, C, *Bibliog Instr,* Monroe County Community College, Learning Resources Center, Monroe MI. 313-242-7300

Kish, Irene, *Supvr,* Mohawk College of Applied Arts & Technology (Stony Creek (Saltfleet) Campus), Hamilton ON. 416-389-4461

Kishel, Deane, *Coll Develop,* Bemidji State University, A C Clark Library, Bemidji MN. 218-755-2955

Kishel, Deane, *Instr,* Bemidji State University, Library Science Program, MN. 218-755-2955

Kishi, Gloria, *Per,* Free Public Library of the City of Trenton, Trenton NJ. 609-392-7188

Kisley, Dawn, *Librn,* Shiawassee County Library, Corunna MI. 517-743-3421, Ext 278

Kissee, Elaine, *Librn,* Barry-Lawrence Regional Library (Marionville Branch), Marionville MO. 417-463-2675

Kissel, Fern, *Librn,* Yuma City-County Library (Wellton), Wellton AZ. 602-782-1871

Kissel, Paul, *Ref,* University of the South, Jessie Ball duPont Library, Sewanee TN. 615-598-5931, Ext 265, 267

Kissel, Sharon, *Librn,* Board of Governors of the Federal Reserve System (Law Library), Washington DC. 202-452-3284

Kissner, Arthur J, *Dir,* Fitchburg Public Library, Fitchburg MA. 617-343-3096

Kissner, Joan G, *Dir,* Forbush Memorial Library, Westminster MA. 617-874-2172

Kister, Suzon O, *Dir,* Jefferson Community College, Melvil Dewey Library, Watertown NY. 315-782-5250

Kistler, Mrs David, *Librn,* White Pigeon Township Library, White Pigeon MI. 616-483-7409

Kistler, Wilma, *Dir,* Greentown & Eastern Howard School & Public Library, Greentown Library, Greentown IN. 317-628-3534

Kistler, Winifred, *Health Sci,* University of California at Davis, General Library, Davis CA. 916-752-2110

Kistler, Winifred E, *Public Servs,* University of California at Davis (Health Sciences Library), Davis CA. 916-752-1214

Kistner, Glen, *Circ,* Northeastern Illinois University Library, Chicago IL. 312-583-4050, Ext 469

Kitajo, Gary, *Ref,* Alameda County Law Library, Oakland CA. 415-874-5823

Kitchel, Barbara, *Circ,* University of Oregon Library, Eugene OR. 503-686-3056

Kitchen, Luella, *Librn,* Lagrange County Library (Wolcottville Branch), Wolcottville IN. 219-463-2841

Kitchen, Ruthene, *Librn,* Ozark Regional Library (Bourbon Branch), Bourbon MO. 314-732-5313

Kitchens, Larry, *Assoc Dean,* Richland College, Learning Resources Center, Dallas TX. 214-746-4460

Kitchens, Phil, *Librn,* University of Alabama (Engineering), University AL. 205-348-6551

Kitchin, Carl, *Circ,* Mid-America Nazarene College Library, Olathe KS. 913-782-3750, Ext 216

Kitchings, Vivian I, *Tech Serv,* Shrewsbury Free Public Library, Shrewsbury MA. 617-842-0081

Kitelinger, Gay M, *Dir,* Cuba City Public Library, Cuba City WI. 608-744-2613

Kitko, Robert, *Ref,* Bloomfield College Library, Bloomfield NJ. 201-748-9000, Ext 281

Kitsen, Robert K, *Dir,* Blue Ridge Talc Co Inc Library, Henry VA. 703-629-5325

Kitt, Sandra, *Librn,* American Museum of Natural History Library (Hayden Planetarium), New York NY. 212-873-1300, Ext 478

Kittams, Susan, *Librn,* Leadore Community Library, Leadore ID. 208-768-2571

Kittelson, David, *Hawaiian Curator,* University of Hawaii (University of Hawaii Library), Honolulu HI. 808-948-7205

Kittle, A T, *Assoc Dir,* Georgia Institute of Technology, Price Gilbert Memorial Library, Atlanta GA. 404-894-4510

Kittle, Barbara, *Librn,* University of Arizona Library (Museum of Art Library), Tucson AZ. 602-626-2389

Kittleson, Ila, *Dir,* Nissen Public Library, Saint Ansgar Public Library, Saint Ansgar IA. 515-736-4921

Kittner, Dorothy, *Ad,* Cape May County Library, Cape May Court House NJ. 609-465-7837

Kittrell, Kay, *Dir,* Williams Brothers Engineering Co, Technical Information Center, Tulsa OK. 918-496-5020

Kittrell, Mrs Gene, *Cat,* Public Library of Nashville & Davidson County, Nashville TN. 615-244-4700

Kitzrow, Cindy, *Librn,* Kent County Library System (Walker), Grand Rapids MI. 616-453-9843

Kitzrow, Helen, *Librn,* Chicago Public Library (Oriole Park), Chicago IL. 312-774-4544

Kivi, Marcia, *Asst Librn,* Montezuma Public Library, Montezuma IA. 515-623-3417

Kivilvoma, Lynne, *Asst Head,* Chicago Public Library (Government Publications), Chicago IL. 312-269-3002

Kizer, Kathryn, *Librn,* Pleasant Mount Public Library, Pleasant Mount PA. 717-448-2573

Kizis, Carol A, *Info Spec,* American Sterilizer Co Library, Erie PA. 452-3100 Ext 2467

Kjellberg, Betty J, *Librn & On-Line Servs,* Good Samaritan Hospital, Health Science Library, Phoenix AZ. 602-257-4353

Kjoss, Anna D, *Dir,* Wadleigh Memorial Library, Milford NH. 603-673-2408

Klaaren, Donna, *Instr,* Miami University-Middletown, Library-Media Technical Assistant Program, OH. 513-424-4444, Ext 221

Klahn, Tanemi, *Librn,* Placer County Law Library, Auburn CA. 916-823-4391

Klamm, Jacquelyn B, *ILL, Ref & Ad,* Edgecombe County Memorial Library, Tarboro NC. 919-823-1141

Klammer, Werner, *Media,* Concordia Teachers College, Link Library, Seward NE. 402-643-3651, Ext 258

Klanian, Mary, *Libr Mgr,* IBM Corp (Business Reference Library), Armonk NY. 914-765-1900, Ext 6021

Klapper, Carla S, *Dir,* Bayouland Library System, Lafayette LA. 318-233-7548

Klapproth, Judy, *Dir,* Eureka-Humboldt County Library, Eureka CA. 707-445-7284, 445-7513

Klapthor, Bob, *On-Line Servs,* Western Illinois University Libraries, Macomb IL. 309-298-2411

Klasek, Charles, *Assoc Prof,* Southern Illinois University at Carbondale, Educational Media Program, IL. 618-453-5764

Klass, Winifred, *Bus Mgr,* New City Free Library, New City NY. 914-634-4997

Klassen, Carolyn, *Tech Serv,* Yukon Territory Government, Library Services Branch, Whitehorse YT. 403-667-5238

Klassen, David, *Acting Curator,* University of Minnesota Libraries-Twin Cities (Social Welfare History Archives), Minneapolis MN. 612-373-4420

Klath, Nancy, *Asst Librn for Tech Servs,* Princeton University Library, Princeton NJ. 609-452-3180

Klatt, Melvin, *Dir,* Elmhurst College, A C Buehler Library, Elmhurst IL. 312-279-4100, Ext 255

Klauber, Julie, *Asst Dir & Ad,* Great Neck Library, Great Neck NY. 516-466-8055

Klauck, Karl D, *Librn,* Foreign Claims Settlement Co, Law Library, Washington DC. 202-653-6166

Klaue, Mary L, *Dir,* Snyder County Library, Selinsgrove PA. 717-374-7163

Klaue, Mary L, *Librn,* Snyder County Library (Selingsgrove Community Center (hq)), Selinsgrove PA. 717-374-7163

Klaus, Evelyn, *Ch,* Caldwell Public Library, Caldwell NJ. 201-226-2837

Klave, Mary, *Circ,* University of North Dakota, Chester Fritz Library, Grand Forks ND. 701-777-2617

Klawitter, Alice L, *Librn,* East Waushara Cooperative Library, Poy Sippi WI. 414-987-5737

Kleban, June R, *Librn,* Adas Kodesch Shel Emeth Congregation, Eleanor Bell Kursh Library, Wilmington DE. 302-762-2705

Klecker, Anita N, *Librn & On-Line Servs,* Torrance Memorial Hospital, Medical Library, Torrance CA. 213-325-9110

Kleckner, Barry, *Media,* Roger Williams College Library, Bristol RI. 401-255-2361

Kleckner, Simone-Marie, *Librn,* United Nations (Legal and Political Reference), New York NY. 212-754-5372, 754-5373

Klee, Ed, *Librn,* Bluegrass North Regional Library, Frankfort KY. 502-227-7842

Klee, Rosita, *Tech Serv,* Navajo Community College, Naaltsoos Ba'Hooghan Library, Tsaile AZ. 602-724-6132

Kleeberger, Patricia, *Asst Dir,* Reed Memorial Library, Ravenna Public Library, Ravenna OH. 216-296-2827

Klein, A, *Librn,* Yeshiva University of Los Angeles Library, Los Angeles CA. 213-553-9036

Klein, Alice, *Ext,* Minnesota Valley Regional Library, Mankato MN. 507-387-1856

Klein, Bernard, *Librn,* B Klein Publications Library, Coral Springs FL. 305-752-1708

Klein, Betty, *Media & Commun Servs,* Merrick Library, Merrick NY. 516-379-3476

Klein, Geraldine, *Asst Librn,* Pigeon District Library, Pigeon MI. 517-453-2341

Klein, Jeanne E, *Dir,* Streator Public Library, Streator IL. 815-672-2729

Klein, Joanne S, *Librn,* Jones & Laughlin Steel Corp (Technical Library), Pittsburgh PA. 412-884-1000, Ext 225, 226

Klein, Kathleen, *Commun Servs,* Ellensburg Public Library, Ellensburg WA. 509-962-9863, Ext 250

Klein, Leanne A, *Librn,* Minnesota Museum of Art Library, Saint Paul MN. 612-224-7431

Klein, Leonard E, *Librn,* University of Pittsburgh (School of Law), Pittsburgh PA. 412-624-6214

Klein, Linda, *Ad & Acq,* Linden Free Public Library, Linden NJ. 201-486-3888

Klein, Lynn, *Librn,* Sno-Isle Regional Library (Snohomish Branch), Snohomish WA. 206-568-2898

Klein, Martha, *Librn,* Public Library of Columbus & Franklin County (Livingston Branch), Columbus OH. 614-237-9423

Klein, Mary S, *In Charge,* E R Squibb & Sons, Inc, Research Laboratories Library, New Brunswick NJ. 201-545-1300

Klein, Michele G S, *Librn,* Children's Hospital of Michigan, Kresge Center for Medical Education Library, Detroit MI. 313-494-5322

Klein, Mindy, *ILL,* University of Houston (M D Anderson Memorial Library), Houston TX. 713-749-4241

Klein, Mrs Bernard, *Librn,* Temple on the Heights, Jack Jacobson Memorial Library, Cleveland Heights OH. 216-932-6060

Klein, Phyllis, *Libr Asst,* Helen Hayes Hospital, Medical Library, West Haverstraw NY. 914-947-3000, Ext 359

Klein, Phyllis, *Cat & Ref,* Skagit Valley College, Library Media Center, Mount Vernon WA. 206-424-1031, Ext 111

Klein, Regina, *Bus & Econ,* Central Missouri State University, Ward Edwards Library, Warrensburg MO. 816-429-4141

Klein, Richard S, *Dir,* Illinois College of Podiatric Medicine Library, Chicago IL. 312-280-2891

Klein, Richard S, *Librn,* Saint Elizabeth Hospital, Luken Health Science Library, Chicago IL. 312-278-2000

Klein, Robert, *Dir,* Tri-College Cooperative Effort, IA. 319-588-7125

Klein, Robert F, *Librn & On-Line Servs,* Loras College, Wahlert Memorial Library, Dubuque IA. 319-588-7125

Klein, Sami W, *Librn,* Environmental Protection Agency, Headquarters Library, Washington DC. 202-755-0308

Klein, Shelagh, *Dir,* Sterling Heights Public Library, Sterling Heights MI. 313-977-6260

Klein, Stanley, *Ref,* Yeshiva University Libraries (Mendel Gottesman Library of Hebraica-Judaica), New York NY. 212-960-5382

Klein, Stephanie, *Cat,* Public Library of Columbus & Franklin County, Columbus OH. 614-864-8050

Klein, Stephen C, *Dir,* Sutter County Free Library, Yuba City CA. 916-673-5773

Klein, Susan, *On-Line Servs,* Austin Peay State University, Felix G Woodward Library, Clarksville TN. 615-648-7346

Klein, Sylvia, *ILL,* East Orange Public Library, East Orange NJ. 201-266-5600

Kleiner, Joseph, *Circ,* Free Public Library of the City of Trenton, Trenton NJ. 609-392-7188

Kleinert, Ruth, *Ad,* Saginaw Public Libraries, Hoyt Public Library, Saginaw MI. 517-755-0904

Kleinke, Joyce, *Librn,* Winnebago Mental Health Institute (Instructional Materials Center Library), Winnebago WI. 414-235-4910, Ext 473

Kleinmailer, Judy, *Pub Info,* South Central Library System, Madison WI. 608-266-4181

Kleinman, Elsa C, *Librn,* California School for the Deaf Library, Berkeley CA. 415-845-4629, Ext 39

Kleinmuntz, Dalia, *Dir,* Grant Hospital of Chicago, Medical Library, Chicago IL. 312-883-2230

Kleinmuntz, Dalia, *Dep Coordr,* Metropolitan Consortium, IL. 312-975-1600, Ext 328

Kleinpeter, Maragret, *Librn,* Iberia Parish Public Library (New Iberia), New Iberia LA. 318-369-6321

Kleinpeter, Margaret, *Circ,* Iberia Parish Public Library, New Iberia LA. 318-369-6321

Kleinschmidt, Anthony, *Theology,* Pontifical College Josephinum, Wehrle Memorial Library, Worthington OH. 614-885-2376

Kleinsckmidt, Lynnea, *On-Line Servs & Bibliog Instr,* Richmond Public Library, Richmond CA. 415-231-2119

Kleinwachter, Patricia, *ILL,* Northwest Regional Library, Thief River Falls MN. 218-681-4325

Klem, Elizabeth, *Librn,* Calumet Park Public Library, Calumet Park IL. 312-385-5768

Kleman, Bonnie, *Ser,* Hamline University (School of Law Library), Saint Paul MN. 612-641-2344

Kleman, Eleanor, *Librn,* Prince George's General Hospital & Medical Center, Saul Schwartzbach Memorial Library, Cheverly MD. 301-341-4077

Klement, Kaye, *Asst Librn,* Saint Mary's Hospital, Medical Library, Duluth MN. 218-727-4551

Klement, Sharon H, *Librn,* Berwick Public Library, Berwick PA. 717-752-2241

Klemme, Virginia, *Librn,* Drexel Burnham Lambert Inc (Corporate Finance Library), New York NY. 212-480-6051

Klempner, Irving M, *Prof,* State University of New York at Albany, School of Library & Information Science, NY. 518-455-6288

Klemt, Calvin, *Librn,* Austin Presbyterian Theological Seminary, Stitt Library, Austin TX. 512-472-6736

Klene, Joanne, *Support Servs Dir,* Suburban Library System, Burr Ridge IL. 312-325-6640

Klenow, Shirley, *Librn,* Iosco-Arenac Regional Library (Tawas City), Tawas City MI. 517-362-6557

Klensch, Helen, *Asst Librn,* Daniel Freeman Hospital, Victor J Wacha Medical Library, Inglewood CA. 213-674-7050, Ext 3230, 3235

Klepeis, Eleanor, *Librn,* Seattle Public Library (Mobile Services), Seattle WA. 206-625-4913

Klepich, Dave, *Tech Serv,* EG&G Idaho, Inc, INEL Technical Library, Idaho Falls ID. 208-526-1185

Klepper, Michael, *Media,* University of Virginia (Law Library), Charlottesville VA. 804-924-3384

Kleppinger, Ed, *Acq,* Mission College, Learning Resource Services, Santa Clara CA. 408-988-2200, Ext 1531

Klepser, Gerry, *Librn,* Second Congregational Church Library, Grand Rapids MI. 616-361-2629

Kleptach, Sharon M, *Assoc Librn,* Shenandoah College & Conservatory of Music, Howe Library, Winchester VA. 703-667-8714, Ext 453

Klestzick, Karen, *In Charge,* Bramson ORT School, Learning Resource Center, New York NY. 212-677-7420

Klett, Rex, *Librn,* Anson County Library, Wadesboro NC. 704-694-5177

Klett, Rex, *Tech Serv,* Sandhill Regional Library System, Rockingham NC. 919-997-3388

Klice, Mary Lou, *Per,* Canisius College, Andrew L Bouwhuis Library, Buffalo NY. 716-883-7000, Ext 253, 254, 290

Klieman, Janet, *Librn,* Saint Mary of Nazareth Hospital, Sr Stella Louise Medical Library, Chicago IL. 312-770-2219

Klimek, Sister Monica, *Librn,* Saint Francis Center for Christian Renewal Library, Oklahoma City OK. 405-721-5651

Klimiades, Mario Nick, *Librn,* Amerind Foundation, Inc, Fulton-Hayden Memorial Library, Dragoon AZ. 602-586-3003

Klimley, Susan, *Librn,* Columbia University (Geology), New York NY. 212-280-2241

Klinck, Cindi, *Dir,* Washington Township Public Libraries, Centerville OH. 513-433-8091

Klinck, Patricia E, *State Librn,* State of Vermont Department of Libraries, Montpelier VT. 802-828-3261

Kline, Barbara, *Cat,* New York University, Elmer Holmes Bobst Library, New York NY. 212-598-2484

Kline, Barbara, *Ref,* Wayne State University Libraries (Vera P Shiffman Medical Library), Detroit MI. 313-577-1088

Kline, Catherine, *Librn,* Pleasants County Public Library, Saint Marys WV. 304-684-7494

Kline, Eve, *Dir,* Somerset County Medical Library Consortium, PA. 814-455-6501, Ext 216

Kline, Eve, *Librn,* Somerset State Hospital Library, Somerset PA. 814-445-6501, Ext 216

Kline, Karen, *Librn,* Fayette County Public Library (Manion), Ansted WV. 304-658-5472

Kline, Larry, *Cat,* Duke University, William R Perkins Library, Durham NC. 684-2034

Kline, Lisa, *Bkmobile Coordr,* Noble County Public Library, Albion IN. 219-636-7197

Kline, Norman, *Theatre Mgr,* Mamaroneck Free Library, Mamaroneck NY. 914-698-1250

Kline, Patricia, *Ch,* Lebanon Community Library, H C Grumbine Free Public Library, Lebanon PA. 717-273-7624

Kline, Patricia, *Ch,* Lebanon County Library System, Lebanon PA. 717-273-7624

Kline, Peggy S, *Cat,* Emory University Libraries (General Libraries), Atlanta GA. 404-329-6861

Kline, Sims D, *Ref,* Stetson University, duPont-Ball Library, De Land FL. 904-734-4121, Ext 220

Kline, Susan A, *Librn,* Pennsylvania Legislative Reference Bureau Library, Harrisburg PA. 717-787-4910

Kling, Harriet, *Librn,* Quain & Ramstad Clinic Medical Library, Bismarck ND. 701-222-5390

Kling, Joseph, *Bkmobile Coordr,* Library Association of Portland, Multnomah County Library, Portland OR. 503-223-7201, Ext 40

Kling, Susan, *Ref & Info,* Nebraska Library Commission, Lincoln NE. 402-471-2045

Klingbeil, Nancy A, *Dir,* Lake Linden-Hubbell Public Library, Lake Linden MI. 906-296-0698

Klingberg, Susan, *Ref,* University of Lowell Libraries (O'Leary Library), Lowell MA. 617-452-5000, Ext 480

Klingensmith, Margaret, *Acq,* Alfred University (Herrick Memorial Library), Alfred NY. 607-871-2184

Klinger, E J, *Dir,* Miami-Jacobs Junior College of Business Library, Dayton OH. 513-461-5174

Klinger, Fran, *Librn,* Southwestern Indiana Mental Health Center Library, Evansville IN. 812-423-7791, Ext 251

Klingerman, Ethel, *Dir,* Moorestown Free Public Library, Moorestown NJ. 609-234-0333

Klingerman, Mary Jo, *Ch & Syst Coordr,* South Bend Public Library, South Bend IN. 219-288-4413

Klingle, Philip, *ILL,* John Jay College of Criminal Justice Library, New York NY. 212-489-5169

Klingle, Shelley, *Librn & Bibliog Instr,* Advertising Research Foundation Library, New York NY. 212-751-5656

Klingler, Laird, *Ref & Doc,* Rutgers University (Kilmer Area Library), New Brunswick NJ. 201-932-3610

Klingman, Mrs George B, *Asst Librn,* Jane I & Annetta M Herr Memorial Library, Mifflinburg PA. 717-966-0831

Klink, Joan, *Asst Dir,* Arcadia Free Public Library, Arcadia WI. 608-323-7505

Klink, Scott, *Ad,* Bellwood Public Library, Bellwood IL. 312-547-7393

Klinkroth, Margaret M, *On-Line Servs,* University of California, San Diego (Biomedical), La Jolla CA. 714-452-3253

Klipper, Phyllis, *Librn,* Hanna Muncipal Library, Hanna AB. 403-854-4433

Kliss, Claire, *Asst Librn,* Mercy Medical Center, Health Sciences Library, Oshkosh WI. 414-231-3300, Ext 285

Klobe, Elaine, *Fiction,* Nicholson Memorial Library, Garland TX. 214-494-7187

Klocek, Carole A, *Librn,* Mount Pleasant Free Public Library, Mount Pleasant PA. 412-547-3850

Klompstra, Gayle, *Librn,* Lambton County Library (Sombra Branch), Sombra ON. 519-892-3711

Klonis, Steward, *Dir,* Art Students League of New York Library, New York NY. 212-247-4510

Klopfer, Karen L, *Bkmobile Librn,* Berkshire Athenaeum, Pittsfield Public Library, Pittsfield MA. 413-442-1559

Klopp, Eleanor, *Ch,* Berkley Public Library, Berkley MI. 313-542-3393

Klose, Michelle, *Ch,* Niles Community Library, Niles MI. 616-683-8545, 683-8546

Klosek, Chester, *Dir,* Boyden Library, Foxboro MA. 617-543-8882

Klosky, Patricia W, *Librn,* International Food Policy, Research Institute Library, Washington DC. 202-862-5614

Klossner, Michael J, *Tech Serv,* L E Phillips Memorial Public Library, Eau Claire WI. 715-839-5002

Klostermann, Helen, *Govt Doc,* Emporia State University, William Allen White Library, Emporia KS. 316-343-1200, Ext 205

Kloth, Violet J, *Librn,* National Park Service, Southwest Regional Office Library, Santa Fe NM. 505-988-6383

Klotz, Edna, *ILL & Circ,* Capital University Library, Columbus OH. 614-236-6614

Kluever, Connie L, *Librn,* Brown, Wood, Ivey, Mitchell & Petty Library, New York NY. 212-349-7500, Ext 297

Kluger, J A, *Librn,* GAF Corp, Research Library, Binghamton NY. 607-774-3138

Klump, Barbara, *Librn,* Lenawee County Library (Schultz-Holmes Memorial), Blissfield MI. 517-486-2858

Klusek, Louise, *Psych-Educ,* Rutgers University (Camden Arts & Science Library), Camden NJ. 609-757-6036

Kluttz, Arletta M, *Librn,* Cone Mills Corp Library, Greensboro NC. 919-379-6215

Klymowycz, Oksana, *Cat & On-Line Servs,* Bronx Community College Library, Bronx NY. 212-367-7300, Ext 315

Kmepler, Dorothy, *Librn,* Agnew State Hospital (Reading & Listening Center), San Jose CA. 408-262-2100

Kmetz, Olga, *Acq,* Garfield Free Public Library, Garfield NJ. 201-478-3800

Knaapen, Juliana J, *Ch,* Superior Public Library, Superior WI. 715-394-0248

Knapik, R, *Librn,* United Technologies, Sikorsky Aircraft Div Library, Stratford CT. 203-386-4713

Knapke, Beth, *Ref,* Salisbury State College, Blackwell Library, Salisbury MD. 301-546-3261, Ext 351

Knapp, Carol, *Librn,* First Lutheran Church Library, Sioux Falls SD. 605-336-3735

Knapp, Dee, *YA, Tech Serv & Circ,* Branch County Library, Coldwater MI. 517-278-2341

Knapp, Ethel, *ILL,* Mount Kisco Public Library, Mount Kisco NY. 914-666-8041

Knapp, Jean, *Librn,* Bala Cynwyd Library, Bala-Cynwyd PA. 215-664-1196

Knapp, Jeanette, *ILL & Ref,* Southern Adirondack Library System, Saratoga Springs NY. 518-584-7300, 792-3343, 885-1073

Knapp, Jim, *Media,* Tulsa Junior College, Learning Resource Center, Tulsa OK. 918-587-6561, Ext 363

Knapp, Leila, *Rare Bks,* Brooks Memorial Library, Brattleboro VT. 802-254-5290

Knapp, Leslie C, *Librn,* Woonsocket Hospital, Medical Library, Woonsocket RI. 401-767-3211

Knapp, Lucille, *Tech Serv,* Lindenhurst Memorial Library, Lindenhurst NY. 516-888-7575

Knapp, Marjorie, *Library Chairman,* Los Angeles Valley College Library, Van Nuys CA. 213-781-1200, Ext 426

Knapp, Paul, *Librn,* Northern Illinois University (Faraday Chemistry & Physics), De Kalb IL. 815-753-1257

Knapp, Paul, *Sci,* Northern Illinois University, Founders Memorial Library, De Kalb IL. 815-753-1094

Knapp, Peter J, *Ref & Bibliog Instr,* Trinity College Library, Hartford CT. 203-527-3151, Ext 396

Knapp, Sara, *On-Line Servs,* State University of New York at Albany Library, Albany NY. 518-457-8542

Knapp, Victoria, *Asst Dir,* Salisbury Public Library, Salisbury MA. 617-465-5071

Knarr, Bruce A, *Dir,* Population Reference Bureau Library, Washington DC. 202-785-4664

Knarr, Linda, *Coordr,* Johns Hopkins University Libraries (Depts of Maternal & Child Health, Population Dynamics Library), Baltimore MD. 301-955-3573

Knauff, Elisabeth S, *Mgr Info Servs Div,* United States Department of the Treasury Library, Washington DC. 202-566-2777, 566-3279

Knauff, Mrs E, *Dir,* Terrace Bay Public Library, Terrace Bay ON. 807-825-3819

Knauss, Bonnie, *Ref,* William Jewell College, Curry Library, Liberty MO. 816-781-3806

Knauth, Sally, *Librn,* Public Library of Charlotte & Mecklenburg County, Inc (East), Charlotte NC. 704-374-2982

Kneale, Ida E, *Tech Serv, Acq & Cat,* Bloomfield Public Library, Northwest Essex Area Library, Bloomfield NJ. 201-429-9292

Kneale, Rosemary, *Librn,* Cuyahoga County Public Library (Lyndhurst), Cleveland OH. 216-442-4088

Kneale, Rosemary, *Librn,* Cuyahoga County Public Library (South Euclid Branch), South Euclid OH. 216-382-4880

Kneas, Katherine, *ILL,* Ursinus College, Myrin Library, Collegeville PA. 215-489-4111, Ext 290

Kneeland, Joanne, *Librn,* Middle Haddam Public Library, Middle Haddam CT. 203-267-9093

Kneeland, Marjorie H, *Dir,* South Burlington Community Library, South Burlington VT. 802-658-3385

Knego, John, *Assoc Prof,* University of South Florida, Graduate Department of Library, Media & Information Studies, FL. 813-974-2557

Kneiss, Kathy, *Commun Servs,* Allentown Public Library, Allentown PA. 215-820-2400

Kneppe, Margaret, *Librn,* Kothe Memorial Library, Parkersburg IA. 319-346-2442

Knepper, Edith, *Ref,* University of South Florida (University Library), Tampa FL. 813-974-2721

Knerr, Christine, *Asst Librn,* Air Products & Chemicals, Inc (Business Library), Allentown PA. 215-398-7442

Knerr, Valerie, *Dir,* Appalachian Regional Library, North Wilkesboro NC. 919-838-2818

Knes, Ann, *Librn,* Detroit Public Library (Downtown), Detroit MI. 313-833-9800

Knetel, Mary Anne, *Circ & Per,* University of Illinois, Woodruff L Crawford Branch Library of Health Sciences, Rockford IL. 815-987-7382

Knezek, Jana, *Librn,* Olney Community Library & Arts Center, Olney TX. 817-564-5513
Knickerbocker, Jean, *Ch,* Roscoe Free Library, Roscoe NY. 607-498-5574
Knickerbocker, Mary H, *Librn,* Juneau Memorial Library (Floyd Dryden Community), Juneau AK. 907-789-0125
Knier, Timothy, *On-Line Servs & Bibliog Instr,* Marquette University Memorial Library (Legal Research Center), Milwaukee WI. 414-224-7031
Knierim, Dorothy, *Spec Coll,* Kingsport Public Library, J Fred Johnson Memorial Library, Kingsport TN. 615-245-3141
Kniesner, Dan L, *Librn,* Ohio Institute of Technology Library, Columbus OH. 614-253-7291
Knievel, Helen, *Traveling Librn-Consult,* Northeastern Iowa Regional Library System, Waterloo IA. 319-233-1200
Knievel, Michael, *Librn,* Cloquet Public Library, Cloquet MN. 218-879-7336
Knight, Barbara, *Libr Media Coordr,* Saint Luke's Medical Center, School of Nursing Library, Sioux City IA. 712-279-3156
Knight, Bessie, *Librn,* Lambton County Library (Grand Bend Branch), Grand Bend ON. 519-238-2067
Knight, C Raymond, *V Pres & Gen Mgr,* Arinc Research Corp Library, Annapolis MD. 301-266-4000
Knight, Carole, *Tech Serv,* Tusculum College Library, Greeneville TN. 615-639-1481
Knight, Dorthy H, *Coordr,* Passavant Memorial Area Hospital Association, Sibert Library, Jacksonville IL. 217-245-9541, Ext 298
Knight, Ina E, *Librn,* White Hall Township Library, White Hall IL. 217-374-6014
Knight, James, *On-Line Servs & Bibliog Instr,* United States Army (Quartermaster Center & Fort Lee Post Library), Fort Lee VA. 804-734-2322
Knight, Jean M, *Librn,* Thetford Town Library, Latham Memorial Library, Thetford VT. 802-785-4361
Knight, JoAnn, *Librn,* Kentucky State Reformatory Library, La Grange KY. 502-222-9441
Knight, Jym, *Chief Librn,* Tennessee Botanical Gardens & Fine Arts Center Library, Minnie Ritchey & Joel Owsley Cheek Library, Nashville TN. 615-356-3306, Ext 4
Knight, Katherine, *Librn,* Hawaii State Library System (Waikiki-Kapahulu), Honolulu HI. 808-732-2777
Knight, Marie, *Librn,* Lockheed Electronics Co, Inc, Technical Documentation Center & Library, Watchung NJ. 201-757-1600, Ext 2200
Knight, Mary Jane, *Librn,* Hawaiian Mission Children's Society Library, Honolulu HI. 808-531-0481
Knight, Novella S, *Librn,* Englewood Christian Church Library, Indianapolis IN. 317-639-1541
Knight, Shurl, *Librn,* Berkeley County Library (Saint Stephen Branch), Saint Stephen SC. 803-899-2218
Knight, Tanith, *Librn,* Jefferson-Madison Regional Library (Nelson County), Lovingston VA. 804-263-5904
Knighten, Thelma S, *Asst Librn,* Claiborne Parish Library, Homer LA. 318-927-3845
Knighton, Phyllis R, *Commun Servs,* Laurens County Library, Laurens SC. 803-984-0596
Knipe, Nancy, *Tech Serv,* Colorado College, Charles Leaming Tutt Library, Colorado Springs CO. 303-473-2233, Ext 415
Knoblauch, Carol, *Librn,* Public Library of Columbus & Franklin County (Hilliard Branch), Hilliard OH. 614-876-4204
Knoblauch, Mark, *Acq,* Chicago Public Library, Chicago IL. 312-269-2900
Knobler, Herbert, *Ref,* Queensborough Community College Library, Bayside NY. 212-631-6226
Knoblich, Paul L, *Dir,* George Amos Memorial Library, Campbell County Library, Gillette WY. 307-682-3223
Knobloch, Earl T, *Media,* Somerset County College Library, Somerville NJ. 201-526-1200, Ext 224, 304
Knoch, Daniel, *Tech Serv,* Hillsdale College, Mossey Learning Resources Center, Hillsdale MI. 517-437-7341, Ext 225
Knoche, Grace F, *Theory & Philos,* Theosophical University Library, Altadena CA. 213-798-8020, Ext 5

Knock, Bee, *Librn,* Muskingum County Genealogical Society Library, Zanesville OH. 614-453-0762, Ext 76; 454-2501, Ext 312
Knode, M Kathleen, *Librn,* Washington County Free Library (Williamsport Memorial), Williamsport MD. 301-223-7027
Knodel, Jane, *Librn,* Brazoria County Library (Lake Jackson Branch), Lake Jackson TX. 713-297-1271
Knodle, Shirley, *Dir,* Verona Public Library, Verona WI. 608-845-7180
Knoebel, Miriam, *Ad,* Shelbyville-Shelby County Public Library, Shelbyville IN. 317-398-7121
Knoepfle, Clara, *Ch,* Wheaton Public Library, Wheaton IL. 312-668-1374
Knoop, Mrs Gene Harrison, *Dir,* Chesterfield County Central Library, Chesterfield VA. 804-748-1601
Knoop, Pearl, *Librn,* Marble Rock Public Library, Marble Rock IA. 515-397-4480
Knopp, Mary, *Cat,* Saint Paul Seminary, John Ireland Memorial Library, Saint Paul MN. 612-690-4355
Knopp, Ruth K, *Librn,* Cripple Creek Public Library, Victor CO. 303-689-2011
Knor, Frank, *Media & Systs,* British Columbia Institute of Technology Library, Burnaby BC. 604-434-5734, Ext 360
Knorr, Martin, *Dir Libr Serv & Media,* Harris-Stowe State College Library, Saint Louis MO. 314-533-3366, Ext 36
Knoten, Doris, *Librn,* Tulsa City-County Library (Collinsville Branch), Collinsville OK. 918-371-3268
Knott, Joan, *Ch & YA,* Jackson District Library, Jackson MI. 517-788-4087
Knott, Judith, *Asst Librn,* American Home Products, Wyeth Laboratories Technical Library, Radnor PA. 215-688-4400, Ext 336, 337
Knott, Kathleen, *Librn,* George Gamble Library, Danbury NH. 603-768-3447
Knott, Laura A, *Librn,* Naval Surface Weapons Center, White Oak Library, Silver Spring MD. 301-545-6700
Knott, Sandra, *Bus & Law,* Florida Atlantic University, S E Wimberly Library, Boca Raton FL. 305-395-5100, Ext 2448
Knott, William A, *Dir,* Jefferson County Public Library, Lakewood CO. 303-238-8411
Knotts, Barbara, *Dir,* Mabel Tainter Memorial Free Library, Menomonie WI. 715-235-7366
Knotts, Mary Ann, *Chief Librn,* Veterans Administration, Hospital Library, Birmingham AL. 205-933-8101, Ext 264
Knouse, Jr, E R, *Librn,* Carpenter Technology Corp Research & Development Center Library, Reading PA. 215-372-4511, Ext 695, 583
Knower, R S, *Librn,* Avco Corp, Systems Division Library, Wilmington MA. 617-657-2632
Knowles, Caroline, *Lectr,* Concordia University, Library Studies Program, PQ. 514-482-0320, Ext 324
Knowles, Elaine, *Cat,* New Milford Public Library, New Milford NJ. 201-262-1221
Knowles, Jane, *Archivist,* Radcliffe College, Arthur & Elizabeth Schlesinger Library on the History of Women in America, Cambridge MA. 617-495-8647
Knowles, Marjorie, *Librn,* Plaistow Public Library, Plaistow NH. 603-382-6011
Knowles, Melissa, *Media,* Snead State Junior College, Virgil B McCain Learning Resource Center, Boaz AL. 205-593-5120, Ext 274
Knowles, Mrs Burton, *Librn,* Centralia Public Library, Centralia MO. 314-682-2036
Knowles, Pamela, *Ref,* Guilford Free Library, Guilford CT. 203-453-6561
Knowlton, Carol, *Librn,* Muskegon County Library (Walker), Muskegon MI. 616-744-9500
Knowlton, David L, *Dir,* New Jersey Optometric Association, Dr E C Nurock Library, Trenton NJ. 609-695-3456
Knowlton, Deborah, *Librn,* Hawaiian Electric Co, Inc (Corporate Library), Honolulu HI. 808-548-7915
Knowlton, Deborah, *Librn,* Hawaiian Electric Co, Inc (Engineering Library), Honolulu HI. 808-548-7915
Knowlton, Doris, *Tech Serv & Cat,* West Haven Public Library, West Haven CT. 203-932-2221

Knowlton, Suzanne L, *Assoc Univ Librn & Tech Servs,* University of Southern Maine, Gorham ME. 207-780-5340, 780-4273
Knox, Beth, *Librn,* Lansing General Hospital, K M Baker Memorial Library, Lansing MI. 517-377-8389
Knox, Elizabeth B, *Curator,* New London County Historical Society, New London CT. 203-443-1209
Knox, Marjorie, *Librn,* Wadena Public Library, Wadena IA. 319-774-2875
Knox, Merle, *Librn,* Barton Library (Strong Branch), Strong AR. 501-863-5447
Knox, Susan, *Dir,* Spartanburg Methodist College, Marie Blair Burgess Library, Spartanburg SC. 803-576-3911, Ext 49
Knudsen, Astrid, *Librn,* Perry County Library, Marion AL. 205-683-6411
Knudsen, Carmelle, *Librn,* American Baptist Seminary of the West Library, Berkeley CA. 415-848-0501
Knudsen, Helen, *Librn,* California Institute of Technology (Astrophysics Library), Pasadena CA. 213-795-6811, Ext 1008
Knudsen, Lawrence, *Dir,* Elmhurst Public Library, Elmhurst IL. 312-279-8696
Knudsen, Patricia, *Deputy Dir & Ref,* University of Maryland at Baltimore (Health Sciences Library), Baltimore MD. 301-528-7545
Knudson, Evelyn, *Librn,* Fertile Public Library, Fertile IA. 515-797-2787
Knudson, Frances, *Librn,* Norton Co, Chamberlain Laboratories Library, Stow OH. 216-673-5860, Ext 3601
Knudson, June M, *Dir,* Hood River County Library, Hood River OR. 503-386-2535
Knudson, Rod, *Librn,* Crook County Library (Hulett Library), Hulett WY. 307-283-1006
Knudtson, Gail, *Librn,* Los Angeles Public Library System (Wilmington), Los Angeles CA. 213-834-1082
Knuebel, Virginia, *Dir,* Maywood Public Library, Maywood NJ. 201-845-7755
Knup, Marie, *Tech Serv,* United Engineers & Constructors, Inc Library, Philadelphia PA. 215-422-3374
Knupp, Valerie, *In Charge & Tech Serv,* McKinsey & Co, Inc Library, New York NY. 212-692-6000
Knutson, A C, *In Charge,* United States Navy (Naval Facility Station Library), Big Sur CA. 408-624-2761
Knutson, Linda, *Syst Coordr,* Bay Area Library & Information System, Hayward CA. 415-881-6337
Knutson, Maurice, *Librn,* Veterans Administration, Center Library, Fort Harrison MT. 406-442-6410, Ext 259
Knutson, Robert, *Spec Coll,* University of Southern California, Edward L Doheny Memorial Library, Los Angeles CA. 213-743-6050
Ko, Gertrude, *Ad,* Zion-Benton Public Library District, Zion IL. 312-872-4680
Ko, Jean, *Chief Librn,* Bibliotheque Municipale De Montreal-Est, Montreal-Est PQ. 514-645-7431, Ext 272
Koba, Thomas, *Media,* Bowling Green State University, Firelands College Library, Huron OH. 419-433-5560, Ext 252, 281 & 211
Kobasa, Paul A, *Librn,* Greenwood Press Library, Westport CT. 203-226-3571
Kobayashi, Deanna H, *Ref,* Merced County Library, Merced CA. 209-726-7484
Kobayashi, George, *Spec Coll,* San Jose Public Library, San Jose CA. 408-277-4822
Kobayashi, Hanako, *Librn,* Legislative Reference Bureau Library, Honolulu HI. 808-548-7853
Kobelski, P, *Chem,* State University of New York at Buffalo, University Libraries, Buffalo NY. 716-636-2965
Kober, Mary J, *Librn,* Catalytic Inc, Engineering Library, Philadelphia PA. 215-864-8559
Kobes, Marjorie, *Dir,* Dvoracek Memorial Library, Wilber Public Library, Wilber NE. 402-821-2832
Koblenz, Esther, *Exten Servs,* South Central Library System, Madison WI. 608-266-4181
Koblenz, Esther, *Librn,* South Central Library System (Extension Services), Prairie Du Sac WI. 608-266-4181
Kobrin, Etta, *Circ & Spec Coll,* Manhattan College, Cardinal Hayes Library, Bronx NY. 212-548-1400, Ext 366 & 367

Kobulnicky, Michael, *Ref,* West Virginia Northern Community College, Weirton Campus Library, Weirton WV. 304-723-2210

Kobulnicky, Paul, *Librn,* University of Pittsburgh (Allegheny Observatory), Pittsburgh PA. 412-321-2400

Kobulnicky, Paul, *Librn,* University of Pittsburgh (Chemistry), Pittsburgh PA. 412-624-5026

Kobulnicky, Paul, *Librn,* University of Pittsburgh (Computer Science), Pittsburgh PA. 412-624-6699

Kobulnicky, Paul, *Librn,* University of Pittsburgh (Physics), Pittsburgh PA. 412-624-4482

Kobus, Julia, *Doc,* Southern Connecticut State College, Hilton C Buley Library, New Haven CT. 203-397-4505

Koch, Charles W, *Dir,* Northwest Missouri State University, Wells Library, Maryville MO. 816-582-7141, Ext 1192

Koch, David V, *Spec Coll,* Southern Illinois University at Carbondale, Delyte W Morris Library, Carbondale IL. 618-453-2522

Koch, Dolores, *Librn,* Institute for Defense Analyses Library, Princeton NJ. 609-924-4600, Ext 300

Koch, Henry C, *Assoc Dir,* Michigan State University Library, East Lansing MI. 517-355-2344

Koch, Josephine, *Pub Servs,* Whatcom Community College, Learning Resources Center, Bellingham WA. 206-676-2139

Koch, June V, *Librn,* Enoch Pratt Free Library (Northwood), Baltimore MD. 301-396-5430, 396-5395

Koch, Loretta, *Ad,* Carbondale Public Library, Carbondale IL. 618-457-0354

Koch, Patrica E, *Dir,* New Hartford Free Public Library, New Hartford CT. 203-379-8121

Koch, Patricia A, *Librn,* Advisory Commission on Intergovernmental Relations Library, Washington DC. 202-653-5034

Koch, Patricia J, *Libr Techician,* Bureau of Land Management Library, Billings MT. 406-657-6671

Koch, Paul G, *Librn,* University of Wisconsin Center, Fond du Lac Library, Fond du Lac WI. 414-922-8440, Ext 23

Koch, Rose, *Ref,* Carnegie Free Library, McKeesport PA. 412-672-0625

Kochan, Roman, *Tech Serv,* California State University, Long Beach, University Library, Long Beach CA. 213-498-4047

Kocher, E G, *Exec Dir,* West Bend Gallery of Fine Arts, West Bend WI. 414-334-9638

Kocher, Evelyn, *Cat,* West Virginia University, University Library, Morgantown WV. 304-293-4040

Kochoff, Stephen I, *Libr Develop,* Providence Public Library, Providence RI. 401-521-7722

Kochtanek, Tom, *Asst Prof,* University of Missouri-Columbia, School of Library & Informational Science, MO. 314-882-4546

Kockinos, Jean, *Ch,* San Diego Public Library, San Diego CA. 714-236-5800

Kocsis, Jean, *Soc Sci,* University of Massachusetts at Amherst Library, Amherst MA. 413-545-0284

Kocsis, Lois, *In Charge,* Oxford County Library (Mount Elgin Library), Mt Elgin ON. 519-485-3059

Koda, Paul, *Rare Bks,* University of North Carolina at Chapel Hill, Louis Round Wilson Academic Affairs Library, Chapel Hill NC. 919-933-1301

Kodanko, Joan, *Reader Serv,* Villa Park Public Library, Villa Park IL. 312-834-1164

Koder, Sister Alma, *Librn,* Lankenau Hospital (School of Nursing Library), Philadelphia PA. 215-642-3931

Koefod, Marion, *Librn,* Olivia Public Library, Olivia MN. 612-523-1738

Koehler, Boyd, *ILL,* Augsburg College, George Sverdrup Library, Minneapolis MN. 612-330-1014

Koehler, Boyd, *Ref,* Augsburg College, George Sverdrup Library, Minneapolis MN. 612-330-1014

Koehler, Helen, *Librn,* Perry County District Library (Thornville Branch), Thornville OH. 614-246-5133

Koehler, Theodore, *Dir,* University of Dayton, Marian Library, Dayton OH. 513-229-4221

Koehmstedt, Maria, *Per,* Clatsop Community College Library, Astoria OR. 503-324-0910

Koehn, Constance, *Ad Book Selector,* Cleveland Public Library, Cleveland OH. 216-623-2800

Koehn, Louise, *Ref,* Bethel College Library, North Newton KS. 316-283-2500, Ext 377

Koel, Ake I, *Assoc Librn Tech Servs,* Yale University Library (University Library), New Haven CT. 203-436-8335

Koel, Ottilia, *Librn & Curator,* New Haven Colony Historical Society Library, New Haven CT. 203-562-4183

Koelewyn, Arie, *Ref,* Mansfield-Richland County Public Library, Mansfield OH. 419-524-1041

Koelker, June, *Serials,* Tucson Public Library, Tucson AZ. 602-791-4391

Koeller, Janet, *Librn,* Reardan Public Library, Reardan WA. 509-796-2862

Koelln, Joann, *Ref,* Duluth Public Library, Duluth MN. 218-723-3800

Koenig, Dan, *Dir,* Piedmont Technical College Library, Greenwood SC. 803-223-8357, Ext 282

Koenig, Dorothy, *Librn,* University of California, Berkeley (Anthropology), Berkeley CA. 415-642-2400

Koenig, Edward, *Syst Coordr,* University of Lowell Libraries (O'Leary Library), Lowell MA. 617-452-5000, Ext 480

Koenig, Roman T, *Librn,* Fritzsche, Dodge & Olcott, Inc Library, New York NY. 212-929-4100

Koenigsberg, Allen, *Dir,* Antique Phonograph Monthly, Library of Recorded Sound, Brooklyn NY. 212-941-6835

Koeninger, Patty, *Fiction,* Austin Public Library, Austin TX. 512-472-5433

Koepke, Susan, *Librn,* Monroe County Library System (Rasey Memorial), Luna Pier MI. 313-848-4572

Koepp, Donald W, *Librn,* Princeton University Library, Princeton NJ. 609-452-3180

Koeppel, Betty, *Asst Librn,* Waterbury Hospital, Health Center Library, Waterbury CT. 203-573-6148

Koepsel, Sue, *Dir,* Fontana Public Library, Fontana WI. 414-275-5107

Koert, Katherine, *ILL,* Bridgeport Public Library, Bridgeport CT. 203-576-7777

Koetitz, Edward, *Ref,* Bethany Bible College Library, Scotts Valley CA. 408-438-3800, Ext 441

Koferl, Mary, *YA & Commun Servs,* South Huntington Public Library, Huntington Station NY. 516-549-4411

Koford, Camilla, *Librn,* East Texas Chamber of Commerce, Research Department Library, Longview TX. 214-757-4444

Kofron, Viola, *Librn,* Janesville Public Library, Janesville IA. 319-987-2925

Kofsky, Charna, *On-Line Servs,* Scarborough Public Library, Scarborough ON. 416-291-1991

Koft, Betty, *Cat,* Spotswood Public Library, Spotswood NJ. 201-251-1515

Koger, Ellen, *Cat,* Nampa Public Library, Nampa ID. 208-466-6121

Koger, Grove, *Commun Servs,* Boise Public Library & Information Center, Boise ID. 208-384-4466

Kohl, Barbara H, *Ad,* Public Library of Brookline, Brookline MA. 617-734-0100

Kohler, Barbara, *Librn,* Great Lakes Basin Commission Library, Ann Arbor MI. 313-668-2322

Kohler, Betty G, *Librn,* Central Rappahannock Regional Library, Wallace Memorial Library, Fredericksburg VA. 703-371-3311

Kohler, Carolyn W, *Govt Publications,* University of Iowa Libraries, Iowa City IA. 319-353-4450

Kohler, Emil, *Cat,* Manhattan College, Cardinal Hayes Library, Bronx NY. 212-548-1400, Ext 366 & 367

Kohler, Karen M, *Dir, Med Rec Dept,* Saint Mary's Hospital Medical Center (Medical Library), Green Bay WI. 414-494-3474, Ext 236, 237

Kohler, Ruth, *Dir,* John Michael Kohler Arts Center Library, Sheboygan WI. 414-458-6144

Kohlhorst, Gail L, *Librn,* General Services Administration Library, Washington DC. 202-566-0420

Kohn, Mickey, *Instr,* Foothill College, Library-Media Technical Assistant Program, CA. 415-948-8590, Ext 390

Kohn, Rita, *Pub Info Officer,* Corn Belt Library System, Normal IL. 309-452-4485

Kohut, Joseph, *Sci,* Portland State University, Branford Price Millar Library, Portland OR. 503-229-4424

Kohut, Taras, *Bkmobile Coordr,* Saint Clair Shores Public Library, Saint Clair Shores MI. 313-771-9020

Kojelis, Daina, *Media,* University of Illinois at the Medical Center, Library of the Health Sciences, Chicago IL. 312-996-8974

Kok, Bede, *Librn,* Gethsemani, Abbey Library, Trappist KY. 502-549-3117

Kok, John, *Dir,* Foote, Cone & Belding Advertising, Inc, Information Center, Chicago IL. 312-467-9200

Kok, Victoria T, *On-Line Servs,* Virginia Polytechnic Institute & State University Library, Blacksburg VA. 703-961-5593

Kokeko, Elizabeth L, *Librn,* Christ United Methodist Church Library, Bethel Park PA. 412-835-6621

Kokiko, Elizabeth, *Ch,* Upper Saint Clair Township Library, Pittsburgh PA. 412-835-5540

Kolady, Nancy, *AV, YA & Ref,* Sturgis Public Library, Sturgis MI. 616-651-7907, 651-2321

Kolar, Irene, *Tech Serv,* Yankton Community Library, Yankton SD. 605-665-4501, Ext 34

Kolb, Audrey, *Coordr,* Alaska State Library (Northern Region), Fairbanks AK. 907-452-2999

Kolb, Carol, *Ad, Acq & Ref,* Somerset County Library, Somerville NJ. 201-725-4700, Ext 234

Kolb, Charles, *Librn,* Public Library of Des Moines (South Side), Des Moines IA. 515-283-4940

Kolbe, H K, *Co-Dir, Population Info Program,* Population Information Program Resource Center, The Johns Hopkins University, Baltimore MD. 301-955-8200

Kolbe, Jane, *Dir,* Colleges of Mid-America Inc, (CMA), SD. 605-332-5951

Kolbe, Jane, *Librn,* Sioux Falls College, SD. 605-336-2850, Ext 123

Kolbe, Jane, *Dir,* Sioux Falls College, Norman B Mears Library, Sioux Falls SD. 605-331-5000

Kolberg, Judy, *Asst Librn,* Pitkin County Library, Aspen CO. 303-925-7124

Kolbet, Richard M, *Tech Serv,* University of Iowa Libraries, Iowa City IA. 319-353-4450

Kolehmainen, Laura, *Librn,* Oakland Community College, Highland Lakes Campus Library, Union Lake MI. 313-363-7191, Ext 335

Kolenbrander, Nancy, *Ch,* Longmont Public Library, Longmont CO. 303-776-2236

Kolk, Carol, *Librn,* Standard Brands, Inc, Clinton Corn Processing Co Research Library, Clinton IA. 319-242-1121, Ext 314

Kolkow, Amy, *Librn,* Klamath County Library (Malin Branch), Malin OR. 503-723-2772

Koll, Nancy, *Librn,* Dodge County Library Service (Theresa Public), Theresa WI. 414-488-2032, 488-2342

Kollar, Rose Marie, *Cat & Ref,* Free Public Library of Oakland, Oakland NJ. 201-337-3742

Kollath, Violet, *Dir,* Muehl Public Library, Seymour Public Library, Seymour WI. 414-833-2725

Koller, Judy, *Dir,* Brodhead Memorial Public Library, Brodhead WI. 608-897-4070

Koller, Sharon, *Librn,* Veterans Administration, Medical Center Library, Iron Mountain MI. 906-774-3300, Ext 250

Kolliner, Jean, *Asst Dir, Ref & Bibliog Instr,* Bronx Community College Library, Bronx NY. 212-367-7300, Ext 315

Kollmorgen, Ann, *Curriculum Mat,* Midwestern State University, George Moffett Library, Wichita Falls TX. 817-692-6611, Ext 204

Kollmorgen, Rose M, *Dir,* Roseville Public Library, Roseville MI. 313-777-6012

Kolloae, Sandra, *ILL,* Hawaii State Library System (Hawaii State Library), Honolulu HI. 808-548-7501

Kolman, Judith, *Librn,* Municipal Reference Library (Police Library), Chicago IL. 312-744-4992

Kolman, Roberta, *Ref,* University of Connecticut Health Center, Lyman Maynard Stowe Library, Farmington CT. 203-674-2739

Kolner, Stuart J, *Librn,* University of Illinois, Woodruff L Crawford Branch Library of Health Sciences, Rockford IL. 815-987-7382

Kolp, Jane, *Ch,* Greenville Public Library, Carnegie Library, Greenville OH. 513-548-3915

Kolstrom, Yvette, *Ad,* Lawton Public Library, Lawton OK. 405-248-6287

Komadina, Kristi, *Bibliog Instr,* Illinois State Geological Survey (Library), Urbana IL. 217-344-1481, Ext 252

Komai, Lois, *Librn,* Wisconsin State Department of Natural Resources (Technical Library), Madison WI. 608-266-9725

Komidar, Joseph S, *Librn,* Tufts University, Nils Yngve Wessell Library, Medford MA. 617-628-5000, Ext 235

Kominski, John J, *Gen Counsel,* Library of Congress, Washington DC. 202-287-5000

Koncewicz, Belle, *ILL,* Erie County Library System, Erie PA. 814-452-2333

Kondayan, Betty, *Rare Bks & Spec Coll,* Washington & Lee University, The University Library, Lexington VA. 703-463-9111, Ext 403

Kondelik, John P, *Dir,* Olivet College Burrage Library, Olivet MI. 616-749-7608

Kondelik, Marlene, *Ref & Bibliog Instr,* Olivet College Burrage Library, Olivet MI. 616-749-7608

Kondo, Gail, *Asst Librn,* Peat Marwick Mitchell & Co Library, Washington DC. 202-223-9525

Kondratie, Dale, *Librn,* Charleroi Public Library, Charleroi PA. 412-483-8282

Konecey, Joseph, *Media,* Wesley College, Parker Library, Dover DE. 302-736-2413

Konerding, Erhard, *Doc,* Wesleyan University, Olin Memorial Library, Middletown CT. 203-347-9411, Ext 296

Konetsco, Kaight, *Ch,* West Shore Public Library, Camp Hill PA. 717-761-3900, 761-3901

Kongwa, Francis S, *Dir,* Vermont Law School Library, South Royalton VT. 802-763-8307

Konitzer, Barbara G, *Librn,* Lake Villa District Library, Lake Villa IL. 312-356-7711

Konlande, Jean, *Ch,* Plano Public Library System, Plano TX. 214-423-6502, 867-1002

Konold, Marilyn, *Ch,* Reedsburg Public Library, Reedsburg WI. 608-524-3316

Konop, Arthur J, *Dir,* Saint Francis College (James A Kelly Institute for Local Historical Studies), Brooklyn NY. 212-522-2300, Ext 202

Konoshima, Sumiye, *In Charge,* East West Communication Institute, East West Center, Resource Materials Collection, Honolulu HI. 808-948-8624

Konoski, Robert, *Ref,* Sayville Library, Sayville NY. 516-589-4440

Konowitch, Beatrice, *Ch,* Cape May County Library, Cape May Court House NJ. 609-465-7837

Konrath, Rose E, *Ref,* Hughes Aircraft Co (Technical Library), Culver City CA. 213-391-0711, Ext 2615

Koo, S, *Librn,* Firestone Tire & Rubber Co (Central Research Library), Akron OH. 216-379-7430

Koob, Mary E, *Ch,* Wood-Ridge Memorial Library, Wood-Ridge NJ. 201-438-2455

Kooken, Sue Gale, *Per,* San Jacinto College, Lee Davis Library, Pasadena TX. 713-476-1850, 476-1501, Ext 241

Koons, Elizabeth, *Ch,* Decatur Public Library, Decatur IN. 219-724-2605

Koontz, Barbara, *Cat,* Racine Public Library, Racine WI. 414-636-9241

Koontz, Franklin, *Assoc Dir,* University of Toledo (University Television Services), Toledo OH. 419-537-3386

Koontz, Mrs John E, *Librn,* Aguila Public Library, Aguila AZ. 602-685-2295

Koontz, Philip E, *MEDLINE Analyst,* Veterans Administration, Medical Center Libraries, Leavenworth KS. 913-682-2000, Ext 223, 224

Koontz, Sharon, *ILL,* Dodge City Public Library, Dodge City KS. 316-225-0248

Koontz, Sondra, *Flm,* Wichita Public Library, Wichita KS. 316-262-0611

Koontz, Sondra B, *Dir,* Kansas State Audiovisual Center, KS. 316-262-0611

Koontz, Una, *Ref,* College of Great Falls Library, Great Falls MT. 406-761-8210, Ext 280

Koos, Greg, *Archivist,* McLean County Historical Society Library, Bloomington IL. 309-827-0428

Koozer, Don, *Libr Techn,* University of Oklahoma (Art), Norman OK. 405-325-2841

Kopec, Grace B, *Chief Librn,* Kenora Public Library, Kenora ON. 807-468-7091, 468-7408

Koper, Daniel R, *Dir,* Carnegie Public Library, Devils Lake Public Library, Devils Lake ND. 701-662-2220

Kopischke, John, *Dir,* Nebraska Library Commission, Lincoln NE. 402-471-2045

Kopkin, T J, *Rep,* Government-Industry Data Exchange Program, (GIDEP), GA. 404-424-2522

Kopkin, T J, *On-Line Servs,* Lockheed-Georgia Company, Technical Information Dept Library, Marietta GA. 404-424-2928

Kopkin, Theodore, *Lectr,* Atlanta University, School of Library & Information Studies, GA. 404-681-0251, Ext 312

Koplan, Margarette, *Librn,* Erlanger Medical Center (Medical Library), Chattanooga TN. 615-755-7246, 755-7247, 755-7166

Koplan, Stephen M, *Assoc Dir,* Georgia Mental Health Institute, Addison M Duval Library, Atlanta GA. 404-894-5663

Koplin, Julia, *Librn,* Caney City Library, Caney KS. 316-879-5341

Kopp, Eileen, *Circ,* Southwest Missouri State University Library, Springfield MO. 417-836-5104

Kopp, Emma Lue, *Assoc Dir,* University of Kansas Medical Center, College of Health Sciences & Hospital, Clendening Library, Kansas City KS. 913-588-7166

Kopp, Patti, *Librn,* Grimes Public Library, Grimes IA. 515-986-9032

Koppelman, Jan, *Media,* Viterbo College Library, La Crosse WI. 608-784-0040, Ext 429

Koppenhaver, Barbara K, *In Charge,* Thunder Bay Public Library (Brodie Resource Library), Thunder Bay ON. 807-622-6446

Kopper, Carolyn, *Librn,* Eskaton American River Healthcare Center, Erle M Blunden Memorial Library, Carmichael CA. 916-486-2128

Kopper, John, *Tech Serv,* Mayo Foundation (Medical Library), Rochester MN. 507-284-2061

Kopplin, Barbara A, *Dir,* Flagg Township Library, Rochelle IL. 815-562-6767

Kopren, Eileen, *ILL & Circ,* Dickinson State College, Stoxen Library, Dickinson ND. 701-227-2135

Kopycinski, Joseph V, *Dir,* University of Lowell Libraries (Alumni-Lydon Library), Lowell MA. 617-452-5000, Ext 378

Koran, Adolph A, *Librn,* United States Navy (Navy Personnel Research & Development Center), San Diego CA. 714-225-7971

Koranda, Hazel, *Dir,* Wreigie Memorial Library, Oxford Junction IA. 319-486-2400

Korb, Linda A, *Librn,* United States Forest Service, Southern Forest Experiment Station Library, New Orleans LA. 504-589-6798

Korbein, Stewart, *Asst Dir,* University of Wisconsin - La Crosse, Film Library, La Crosse WI. 608-785-8045

Korbel, Albert, *Librn,* Bellwood Public Library, Bellwood IL. 312-547-7393

Korber, Nancy J, *Bus-Municipal,* Nashua Public Library, Nashua NH. 603-883-4141, 883-4142

Korchow, Lydia, *Local Hist,* Cooper Union for Advancement of Science & Art Library, New York NY. 212-254-6300, Ext 323

Korda, Marion, *Librn,* University of Louisville Library (Music), Louisville KY. 502-588-5659

Kordalewski, A J, *On-Line Servs,* Motorola, Inc, Government Electronics Div, Technical Library, Scottsdale AZ. 602-949-3471

Kordish, Heike, *Syst Planning,* Columbia University (University Libraries), New York NY. 212-280-2241

Kordoski, Donna, *Librn,* National Paint & Coatings Association, Technical Library, Washington DC. 202-462-6272

Korea, Jean U, *Dir,* Metropolitan Club Library, New York NY. 212-838-7400

Koren, Stefania A, *Ref,* Manhattanville College Library, Purchase NY. 914-946-9600, Ext 274

Koressaar, Viktor, *Chief,* New York Public Library (Slavonic), New York NY. 212-790-6336

Korey, Marie E, *Curator, Printed Books,* Library Co of Philadelphia, Philadelphia PA. 215-546-3181

Korfhage, Anna, *Librn,* Louisville Free Public Library (Fern Creek), Louisville KY. 502-584-4154

Koritnik, Mary, *ILL,* Rock Springs Public Library, Rock Springs WY. 307-362-6212

Korkmas, Carolyn Crawford, *Dir,* Medical Group Management Association, Information Service, Denver CO. 303-753-1111

Korman, Adrienne, *Acq,* William Paterson College of New Jersey, Sarah Byrd Askew Library, Wayne NJ. 201-595-2113

Korman, Frank, *Media,* Mountain View College, Learning Resources Center, Dallas TX. 214-746-4169

Korman, M, *YA & Ref,* Bellmore Memorial Library, Bellmore NY. 516-785-2990

Kormelink, Barbara, *Librn,* Bay Medical Center Library, Bay City MI. 517-894-3782

Korn, Margaret, *Dir,* Northern Oklahoma College Library, Tonkawa OK. 405-628-2581, Ext 48

Kornegay, Mrs Bobbie, *Librn,* Jackson County Library, Edna TX. 512-782-2162

Kornfeld, Carol, *Bibliog Instr,* Thomas J Lipton Inc, Technical Research Library, Englewood Cliffs NJ. 201-567-8000

Kornfeld, Carol E, *Librn,* Thomas J Lipton Inc, Technical Research Library, Englewood Cliffs NJ. 201-567-8000

Kornstein, Barbara, *Actg Librn,* University of California, Berkeley (Undergraduate Library), Berkeley CA. 415-642-5070

Korob, Michele A, *Research Mgr,* Hayes-Hill Incorporated Library, Chicago IL. 312-984-5250

Korpan, Ann, *Asst Librn,* Runnemede Public Library, Runnemede NJ. 609-939-4688

Korsmeyer, Joan, *Asst Dir Tech Servs,* University of Wisconsin-Milwaukee, Golda Meir Library, Milwaukee WI. 414-963-4785

Korstev, Irene, *Ref,* Maple Woods Community College Library, Kansas City MO. 816-436-6500, Ext 73, 74

Korstredt, Cheri, *Librn,* Wyoming Mineral Corp, Exploration Library, Denver CO. 303-988-8530

Kort, Rita, *Librn,* Los Angeles Public Library System (Fairfax), Los Angeles CA. 213-936-6191

Korte, Connie, *Circ,* Columbus Public Library, Pawnee Regional Library, Columbus NE. 402-564-7116

Korth, Dorothy A, *Dir,* Juneau Public Library, Juneau WI. 414-386-2746

Korthaus, Betty, *AV,* Scott County Library, Eldridge IA. 319-285-4794

Korty, Margaret, *AV,* Riverdale Presbyterian Church Library, Hyattsville MD. 301-927-0477

Korzelius, Candy, *Ch,* Graham Public Library, Union Grove WI. 414-878-2910

Kos, Roman, *Bibliog Instr,* Balch Institute for Ethnic Studies Library, Philadelphia PA. 215-925-8090

Kosaka, Emi, *Tech Serv,* Memorial Hospital Medical Center, Medical Library, Long Beach CA. 213-595-3841

Kosakowski, David, *On-Line Servs & Bibliog Instr,* California State College, Bakersfield Library, Bakersfield CA. 805-833-2151

Kosanke, Connie, *Off Mgr,* Blue Water Library Federation, Port Huron MI. 313-987-7323

Kosanke, Joanne, *Info & Ref,* Oshkosh Public Library, Oshkosh WI. 414-424-0473

Kosanovic, Virginia, *Librn,* Stanford University Libraries (Physics), Stanford CA. 415-497-4342

Kosche, Ludwig, *Librn,* National Museums of Canada Library (Canadian War Museum Library), Ottawa ON. 613-996-4708

Koschik, Douglas, *Librn,* Delta College, Learning Resources Center, University Center MI. 517-686-9000

Kosciusko, Adrienne, *Librn,* Republican National Committee Library, Washington DC. 202-484-6500

Kosek, Reynold, *Ref,* Mercer University (Walter F George School of Law Library), Macon GA. 912-745-6811, Ext 345

Koshil, Larysa, *Librn,* Mississauga Public Library (Mississauga Valley), Mississauga ON. 416-276-6890

Koshute, Joseph, *Art Dir,* Patterson Library, Westfield NY. 716-326-2154

Kosinski, Nancy, *Librn,* Montgomery County Department of Public Libraries (Long), Silver Spring MD. 301-565-7410

Koski, Charlotte, *Tech Serv,* Hibbing Public Library, Hibbing MN. 218-262-1038

Koski, M, *President,* Cambrian College of Applied Arts & Technology, Library Techniques Program-Programme en Bibliotechniques, ON. 705-566-8101

Koslov, Marcia J, *Librn,* Wisconsin Supreme Court, Wisconsin State Law Library, Madison WI. 608-266-1424, 266-1600

Koslovsky, Mary, *ILL,* Lansing Public Library, Lansing MI. 517-374-4600

Koslow, Donald M, *Asst Dir,* United States Military Academy Library, West Point NY. 914-938-2230

Koslow, Helen, *AV,* Shelter Rock Public Library, Albertson NY. 516-248-7363

Kosman, Thomas, *Librn & Acq,* Labouré Junior College Library, Boston MA. 617-296-8300, Ext 418

Kosowski, Helen, *In Charge,* Squibb Institute for Medical Research Library, Princeton NJ. 609-921-4844

Koss, Dr Helen, *Asst Prof,* Southern Connecticut State College, Div of Library Science & Instructional Technology, CT. 203-397-4532

Koss, Helen, *Spec Coll & Rare Bks,* Southeastern Massachusetts University, Library Communications Center, North Dartmouth MA. 617-999-8662

Kosseim, Hoda, *Cat,* Mount Pleasant Public Library, Pleasantville NY. 914-769-0540

Kosta, Pearl, *Dir,* Woodburn Public Library, Woodburn OR. 503-982-2665

Kostarides, Ariadne, *Bkmobile Coordr,* Newport Public Library, Newport RI. 401-847-8720

Kostel, Mary Lou, *Librn,* South Dakota Human Service Center (Medical Library), Yankton SD. 605-665-3671

Koster, Desmond, *Ref,* Medical University of South Carolina Library, Charleston SC. 803-792-2374

Koster, Gregory, *Asst Librn,* Pace University, School of Law Library, White Plains NY. 914-682-7272

Kostick, Marie, *Librn,* Withee Public Library, Withee WI. 715-229-4132

Kostopolus, Nancy, *Librn,* Pullman Inc, Pullman-Standard Division Library, Chicago IL. 312-322-7070

Kostroski, Sharon, *Librn,* Marathon County Public Library (Marathon City Branch), Marathon WI. 715-443-2133

Kosuda, Kathleen L, *Dir,* Gloversville Free Library, Gloversville NY. 518-725-2819

Kotcher, Betty G, *Librn,* National Geographic Society Library (Film), Washington DC. 202-857-7659

Kothe, Linda, *Librn,* EIMCO PMD Technology & Development, Technical Library, Salt Lake City UT. 801-521-2000, Ext 2635

Kothe, Natalie, *Librn,* United States Army (Engineer Topographic Laboratories Scientific & Technical Information (STINFO) Center), Fort Belvoir VA. 703-664-6071

Kotlarz, Claudia Stanwick, *Librn,* Chicago Public Library (Northwest), Chicago IL. 312-235-2727

Kotlarz, Susan, *In Charge,* Warroad Public Library, Warroad MN. 218-386-1283

Kotler, Elizabeth, *Librn,* Blaisdell Memorial Library, Nottingham NH. 603-679-8484

Kott, Katherine, *Cat,* Duke University (Law School Library), Durham NC. 919-684-2847

Kottkamp, Gretchen, *Ch,* Grande Prairie Public Library District, Hazel Crest IL. 312-798-5563

Kottkamp, Trarie, *Tech Serv,* Erie County Library System, Erie PA. 814-452-2333

Kottmamp, Trarie, *Coordr,* Northern Virginia Community College Libraries (Media Processing Services), Springfield VA. 703-323-3294

Kotulis, Judy, *Ch,* Sterling Heights Public Library, Sterling Heights MI. 313-977-6260

Kotun, H Paul, *Dir,* Washington County Museum of Fine Arts Library, Hagerstown MD. 301-739-5727

Kotzen, Sanford, *Dir,* Franklin Square Hospital, Medical Library, Baltimore MD. 301-391-3900

Koukol, Winifred, *Librn,* Lyons Public Library, Lyons IL. 312-447-3577

Kouris, Pat, *Circ,* George Amos Memorial Library, Campbell County Library, Gillette WY. 307-682-3223

Kovacs, Lazlo, *Humanities,* Purdue University Libraries & Audio-Visual Center (General), West Lafayette IN. 317-749-2577, 494-8516

Kovalan, Mary E, *Dir,* Public Library of Steubenville & Jefferson County, Steubenville OH. 614-282-9782

Kovalik, Gus T, *Info Spec,* University of Florida Libraries (Agriculture), Gainesville FL. 904-392-1934

Koven, Barbara, *Media,* Harvard University Library (Gutman Library-Research Center), Cambridge MA. 617-495-4225

Kovic, Annette E, *Ad,* Plattsburgh Public Library, Plattsburgh NY. 518-563-0921

Kowal, Daphne A Tkachuk, *Librn,* Manitoba Health Services Commission Library, Winnipeg MB. 204-786-7398

Kowaleski, Beth, *Ad,* Bacon Memorial Public Library, Wyandotte MI. 313-282-7660

Kowalewski, Denis S, *Assoc Librn,* Chapman & Cutler, Law Library, Chicago IL. 312-726-6130, Ext 449

Kowalewski, Rosanna, *Circ, On-Line Servs & Bibliog Instr,* University of Lowell Libraries (O'Leary Library), Lowell MA. 617-452-5000, Ext 480

Kowalewski, Thadeus L, *Librn,* FMC Corp, Agriculture Chemical Division, Research, Development & Technical Library, Middleport NY. 716-735-3761

Kowall, Mary C, *Dir,* Oswego Public Library District, Oswego IL. 312-554-3150

Kowalski, Jean Hurd, *Sr Info Systs Specialist,* Honeywell Inc, Process Controls Div, Information Center, Fort Washington PA. 215-641-3982

Kowitz, Aletha, *Dir,* American Dental Association, Bureau of Library Services, Chicago IL. 312-440-2653

Koyama, Janice, *Libr Instruction & Ref,* California State University, Long Beach, University Library, Long Beach CA. 213-498-4047

Koyne, Margaret, *Media,* Morgan State University, Morris A Soper Library, Baltimore MD. 301-444-3488, 444-3489

Koz, Coreen, *Asst Librn,* University of Winnipeg Library, Winnipeg MB. 204-786-7811, Ext 520

Kozachenko, Jane, *Libr Asst,* San Bernardino County Library (Trona Branch), Trona CA. 714-372-5847

Kozaczka, Stanley J, *Librn & Rare Bks,* Alliance College Library, Cambridge Springs PA. 814-398-4611, Ext 283

Kozak, Anne, *Ch School Consult,* Suburban Library System, Burr Ridge IL. 312-325-6640

Kozak, Karen, *Cat,* Creighton University, Alumni Memorial Library, Omaha NE. 402-449-2705

Kozak-Budd, Sylvia, *Librn,* Mendocino County Library (Fort Bragg Branch), Fort Bragg CA. 707-964-2020

Kozel, Marie, *Circ,* Wesley College, Parker Library, Dover DE. 302-736-2413

Koziol, Jeanette R, *Librn,* Singer Co, SPG Engineering Library, Elizabeth NJ. 201-527-6884

Kozlovsky, Sonia, *Spec Coll,* Baltimore Hebrew College, Joseph M Meyerhoff Library, Baltimore MD. 301-466-7900, Ext 307

Kozlowski, Yvonne, *Soc Sci,* Auburn University, Ralph Brown Draughton Library, Auburn AL. 205-826-4500

Kozlowski, Anne, *In Charge,* Catholic Social Services Library, Milwaukee WI. 414-271-2881, Ext 82

Kozlowski, B A, *Ad,* Fountaindale Public Library District, Bolingbrook IL. 312-759-2102

Kozlowski, Marianne, *Fine Arts,* Southern Illinois University at Edwardsville, Elijah P Lovejoy Library, Edwardsville IL. 618-692-2711

Kozlowski, Ronald S, *Dir,* Louisville Free Public Library, Louisville KY. 502-584-4154

Kozlowski, Yvonne, *Ad,* Auburn University (Architecture), Auburn AL. 205-826-4510

Kozuch, Julianna, *Instr,* Our Lady of the Lake University of San Antonio, Learning Resources Certification, TX. 512-434-6711, Ext 245

Kozuch, Sister Julianna, *Ref,* Our Lady of the Lake University Libraries, San Antonio TX. 512-434-6711, Ext 272

Kozup, Kathleen, *Ch,* Warren Public Library, Warren OH. 216-399-8807

Kraav, Marju, *Assoc Librn & Tech Serv,* McMaster University, Hamilton ON. 416-525-9140

Kraayenbrink, Jeanette, *Outreach,* Stockton-San Joaquin County Public Library, Stockton Public Libr, Stockton CA. 209-944-8415

Kraemer, Joanne, *Librn,* Hamilton Public Library (Sherwood), Hamilton ON. 416-389-8977

Kraenow, Marvin, *Assoc Dean Learning Resources,* Platte Technical Community College, Resource Center, Columbus NE. 402-564-7132

Kraeuter, David W, *ILL & Ref,* Washington & Jefferson College Library, Washington PA. 412-222-4400, Ext 271

Krafka, Ernestine, *Librn,* Carlisle Public Library, Carlisle IA. 515-989-0909

Kraft, Cecelia, *Librn,* Perth Amboy General Hospital, Charles E Gregory School of Nursing Library, Perth Amboy NJ. 201-442-3700, Ext 469

Kraft, Connie, *Librn,* Hope Public Library, Hope ND. 701-945-2461

Kraft, Connie, *Asst Dir,* Roseville Public Library, Roseville MI. 313-777-6012

Kraft, Kaye, *Librn,* Newport Public Library, Newport MN. 612-459-9631

Kraft, Linda, *ILL,* East Baton Rouge Parish Library, Baton Rouge LA. 504-389-3360

Kraft, Myrtle, *In Charge,* Cochise County Library System (Portal Public Library), Portal AZ. 602-558-9291

Kraft, Nancy, *Librn,* Sioux Empire College Library, Hawarden IA. 712-552-9900

Kraft, Nancy, *Librn,* Sioux Empire College, Resource Center, IA. 712-552-9900

Kraft, Sandy, *Librn,* Young Radiator Co Technical Library, Racine WI. 414-639-1010, Ext 227

Krahl, Celeste, *Ch,* Plumb Memorial Library, Shelton CT. 203-734-3386

Krahn, Allan, *Automation Librn,* Luther-Northwestern Seminary Library, Saint Paul MN. 612-641-3225

Kraig, Alfred R, *Dir,* San Mateo Public Library, San Mateo CA. 415-574-6955

Krakauer, Eleanor, *Librn,* American Cancer Research Center & Hospital, Grace & Philip Lichtenstein Scientific Library, Lakewood CO. 303-233-6501, Ext 239

Kralisz, Patricia, *Commun Servs,* Northeast Texas Library System, Dallas TX. 214-651-9266

Kralisz, Victor F, *Admin Mgr, Flm Libr,* Dallas Public Library, Dallas TX. 214-748-9071

Kralisz, Victor F, *Librn for Media Develop,* Dallas Public Library, Dallas TX. 214-748-9071

Krall, Pauline, *Librn,* Ely Public Library, Ely MN. 218-365-5140

Kraman, Alma, *YA,* Shelter Rock Public Library, Albertson NY. 516-248-7363

Kramer, Cecile E, *Librn,* Northwestern University, Chicago (Archibald Church Library), Chicago IL. 312-649-8126

Kramer, Deborah, *Librn,* Houston Public Library (Oak Forest), Houston TX. 713-688-2251

Kramer, Dorothy, *Librn,* Reading Community Library, Reading MI. 517-283-2344

Kramer, Helen, *Ref,* Pittsburg State University Library, Pittsburg KS. 316-231-7000, Ext 431

Kramer, Janice, *Tech Serv, Cat & Bibliog Instr,* Belleville Area College Library, Belleville IL. 618-235-2700, Ext 236

Kramer, Karen, *Asst Librn,* Jackson Public Library, Jackson MO. 314-243-5150

Kramer, Laurel, *Ad,* Way Public Library, Perrysburg OH. 419-874-3135

Kramer, Lloyd A, *Assoc Dir,* California State University, Long Beach, University Library, Long Beach CA. 213-498-4047

Kramer, Margaret, *Dir,* Bristol-Washington Township Public Library, Bristol Public Library, Bristol IN. 219-848-7214

Kramer, Margy, *Dir,* Hocking Technical College Library, Nelsonville OH. 614-753-3591, Ext 254

Kramer, Martin, *Asst Prof,* Augustana College, Library Science Program, SD. 605-336-4921

Kramer, Wendy, *Asst Librn,* United States Forest Service, Forest Products Laboratory Library, Madison WI. 608-264-5713

Kramer, William, *Dir,* Glen Cove Public Library, Glen Cove NY. 516-676-2130

Kramp, Carole, *Asst Dir & ILL,* Acton Memorial Library, Acton MA. 617-263-2232, 263-9109

Kranack, Pat, *Librn,* Westinghouse Electric Corp (Advanced Energy Systems Div Library), Pittsburgh PA. 412-892-5600

Kraner, Debra, *AV,* Manatee County Public Library System, Bradenton FL. 813-748-5555

Kranich, Nancy, *Research & Develop,* New York University, Elmer Holmes Bobst Library, New York NY. 212-598-2484

Krans, Lida, *ILL,* Natrona County Public Library, Casper WY. 307-235-9272

Krantz, Linda L, *Dir & Ref,* Rockbridge Regional Library, Lexington VA. 703-463-4324

Kranz, Kirker, *Media Tech,* Saginaw Valley State College Library & Learning Resources Center, University Center MI. 517-790-4237

Kranzler, David, *Soc Sci,* Queensborough Community College Library, Bayside NY. 212-631-6226

Krash, Ronald D, *Dir,* University of Missouri Saint Louis, Thomas Jefferson Library, Saint Louis MO. 314-453-5221

Krasik, Margaret K, *Librn,* Duquesne University Library (School of Law), Pittsburgh PA. 412-434-6293

Krasner, F, *Librn,* Miller-Dwan Hospital, Medical Library, Duluth MN. 218-727-8762

Krasner, Faye M, *Coordr,* Arrowhead Professional Libraries Association, MN. 218-727-8762

Krasner, Joan K, *Librn,* Kenneth Leventhal & Co Library, Los Angeles CA. 213-277-0880, Ext 203

Krasnick, Shirlee, *Librn,* Independence Public Library, Independence OR. 503-838-1811

Krastel, Joseph, *Librn,* Saint Alphonsus College, Ligouri Library, Suffield CT. 203-668-7393

Kratz, Catherine, *Librn,* Vermont Law Enforcement Training Academy Library, Pittsford VT. 802-483-6228

Kratz, Charles, *Bibliog Instr,* University of Missouri-Kansas City Libraries, Kansas City MO. 816-276-1531

Kratz, Eva, *Dir,* Saint Francis Medical Center, Mother Macaria Health Science Library, Lynwood CA. 213-603-6045

Krau, Harold, *Adminr Clayton County Libr,* Flint River Regional Library, Griffin GA. 404-227-2756

Krau, Harold, *Librn,* Flint River Regional Library (Jonesboro Branch), Jonesboro GA. 404-478-7120

Kraulio, Ruth L, *Librn,* Central Baptist Seminary Library, Toronto ON. 416-752-1976

Kraus, Anne, *Dir,* INFO, OH. 216-244-1733

Kraus, D, *Scripture,* Blue Cloud Abbey Library, Marvin SD. 605-432-5528, Ext 904

Kraus, Darla Jean, *Librn,* Random Lake Public Library, Random Lake WI. 414-994-4825

Kraus, David H, *Actg Chief, European Div,* Library of Congress, Washington DC. 202-287-5000

Kraus, Eleanor, *Librn,* Scripture Press Publications, Inc Library, Wheaton IL. 312-668-6000, Ext 280

Kraus, Elizabeth, *Chief Librn,* Eastman Kodak Co (Research Library), Rochester NY. 716-722-2723

Kraus, Irwin, *Librn,* New York Public Library (Record Library), New York NY. 212-790-6262

Kraus, Joe W, *Dir,* Illinois State University, Milner Library, Normal IL. 309-438-3675

Kraus, Marilyn, *Chief Librn & On-Line Servs,* Veterans Administration, Hospital Library, Iowa City IA. 319-338-0581, Ext 274

Kraus, Rita M, *Reader Serv,* Flathead County Free Library, Kalispell MT. 406-755-5300, Ext 357

Kraus-Kissam, Elaine, *Ch,* Mahopac Library, Mahopac NY. 914-628-2009

Krause, Elizabeth, *Librn,* Washington University Libraries (Gaylord Music), Saint Louis MO. 314-889-5560

Krause, Eric, *Hist Rec Supvr,* Environment Canada & Parks Canada, Fortress of Louisbourg Library, Louisbourg NS. 902-733-2280

Krause, Lois, *Asst Dir,* Jefferson Public Library, Jefferson IA. 515-386-2836

Krauss, Dina R, *Librn,* Cushing Hospital (Medical Library), Framingham MA. 617-872-4301, Ext 281

Krauss, Dina R, *Librn,* Cushing Hospital (Patient's Library), Framingham MA. 617-872-4301, Ext 277

Krauss, Linda, *Librn,* Teachers Insurance & Annuity Association of America (College Retirement Equities Fund, Research Library), New York NY. 490-9000 Ext 2839

Krauss, Sandra, *ILL,* Huntingdon Valley Library, Huntingdon Valley PA. 215-947-5138

Krausse, S, *ILL,* University of Rhode Island Library, Kingston RI. 401-792-1000

Krautblatt, Eugene, *Acq,* Hillside Free Public Library, Hillside NJ. 201-923-4413

Krawulski, Janet H, *Librn,* Detroit Institute of Technology, James C Gordon Memorial Library, Detroit MI. 313-962-0830, Ext 301

Krchmar, Sandy, *Admin Asst,* Lincoln Trail Libraries System, Champaign IL. 217-352-0047

Kreager, Sister Kathryn, *Circ,* Marycrest College, Cone Library, Davenport IA. 319-326-9254

Kreamer, Katherine A, *Librn,* Hawaii State Prison Library, Honolulu HI. 808-841-8711

Krebs, Jeanette, *Ch,* Jackson-George Regional Library System (Pascagoula City Branch), Pascagoula MS. 601-762-3406

Krecidlo, Janine C, *Dir,* Dunham Public Library, Whitesboro NY. 315-736-9734

Kreckman, Ellen, *Cat,* Houghton College, Willard J Houghton Library, Houghton NY. 716-567-2211, Ext 227

Kredel, Olivia, *Mgr,* National League of Cities, Muncipal Reference Service, Washington DC. 293-5878; Ref 293-2631; ILL 293-2356

Kredel, Stephen, *On-Line Servs,* United States Air Force (Rome Air Development Center Technical Library), Griffiss AFB NY. 315-330-7607

Kreeber, Lillian, *Asst Librn,* Kinderhook Memorial Library, Kinderhook NY. 518-758-6192

Kregar, Martha, *Ch,* Girard Free Public Library, Girard OH. 216-545-2508

Kregel, Jr, Charles E, *Info Mgr,* Kirkland & Ellis Library, Washington DC. 202-857-5000

Kreger, Joyce, *Librn,* Franklin Grove Public Library, Franklin Grove IL. 815-456-2823

Kreger, Louise Parker, *Dir,* Darien Library, Inc, Darien CT. 203-655-2568

Kregstein, Phyllis L, *Librn,* Rocky Mountain Hospital, C Loyd Peterson Memorial Library, Denver CO. 303-388-5588, Ext 608

Kreh, David, *Teaching Mat Ctr,* State University of New York College, Memorial Library, Cortland NY. 607-753-2525, 753-2221

Krehbiel, Kathryn, *Librn,* Moundridge Public Library, Moundridge KS. 316-345-6355

Kreiberg, H, *Dir,* Sunbury Shores Arts of Nature Centre Inc Library, Saint Andrews NB. 506-529-3386

Kreider, Robert, *Dir,* Bethel College Library (Mennonite Library & Archives), North Newton KS. 316-283-2500, Ext 310

Kreigh, Helen, *Ch & YA,* Wisconsin Department of Public Instruction (Public & Cooperative Library Service), Madison WI. 608-266-7270

Kreil, Lydia, *Librn,* Central Ohio Psychiatric Hospital (Marlin R Wedemeyer Memorial Library), Columbus OH. 614-466-5950

Kreilick, Kristine R, *Assoc Librn,* Saint Louis University (Omer Poos Law Library), Saint Louis MO. 314-658-2755

Kreilkamp, H D, *Asst Dir, Ref & Bibliog Instr,* Saint Joseph's College Library, Rensselaer IN. 219-866-7111, Ext 187

Kreimeyer, Vicki R, *Asst Dir,* Lewis & Clark College, Aubrey R Watzek Library, Portland OR. 503-244-6161, Ext 400

Kreinbring, Mary, *Ad,* Dolton Public Library District, Dolton IL. 312-849-2385

Kreiner, Connie, *Cat,* Chippewa Library League, Mount Pleasant MI. 517-773-3242

Kreiner, Connie, *Cat,* Veterans Memorial Library, Mount Pleasant MI. 517-773-3242

Kreis, Arlene, *Asst Librn;* Richfield Springs Public Library, Richfield Springs NY. 315-858-0230

Kreischer, Gloria, *ILL,* Massapequa Public Library, Massapequa NY. 516-798-4607

Kreissmann, Bernard, *Dir,* University of California at Davis, General Library, Davis CA. 916-752-2110

Kreissman, Jane, *Acq,* Stanislaus County Free Library, Modesto CA. 209-526-6821

Kreiter, Marion A, *Librn,* University of Pennsylvania Libraries (Math-Physics-Astronomy Library), Philadelphia PA. 215-243-8173

Kreitz, Sister Marie Angela, *Dir,* Sisters, Servants of the Immaculate Heart of Mary, College Library, Monroe MI. 313-241-3660, Ext 233

Kreitz, Sister Theresa, *Dir,* Sisters, Servants of the Immaculate Heart of Mary, College Library, Monroe MI. 313-241-3660, Ext 233

Kreitzburg, M J, *Ref,* University of Pittsburgh, Johnstown Campus Library, Johnstown PA. 814-266-9661, Ext 314

Kreitzer, Sonja, *Ch,* Porterville Public Library, Porterville CA. 209-784-0177, 784-1400, Ext 523

Krekel, Beverly, *Asst Dir & Ref,* Longview Community College Library, Lee's Summit MO. 816-763-7777, Ext 266, 267, 268

Krell, Eleanor H, *Dir,* Temple Sinai Library, Washington DC. 202-363-6394

Krell, H Barbara, *Librn,* Strayer College, Wilkes Library, Washington DC. 202-783-5180, Ext 48

Kremen, Dorothy, *Librn,* Chicago Public Library (Northtown), Chicago IL. 312-465-2292

Kremer, Jill L, *Dir,* Theodore F Jenkins Memorial Law Library, Philadelphia PA. 215-686-5692

Kremer, Lynn, *Librn,* Chatham-Effingham-Liberty Regional Library (Oglethorpe Mall Branch), Savannah GA. 912-234-5127

Kremer, Teresa, *Librn,* Jewish Hospital & Medical Center of Brooklyn (Medical & Nursing Library), Brooklyn NY. 212-240-1795

Krenson, Leonora, *Ch,* Kinchafoonee Regional Library, Dawson GA. 912-995-2902

Krenta, Alicja, *Acq,* Yale University Library (Medical Library), New Haven CT. 203-436-4784, 436-2961

Krenzer-Norman, Barbara, *Librn,* Yadkin County Public Library, Yadkinville NC. 919-679-8792

Kreshka, Eva, *Tech Serv,* Mills College Library, Oakland CA. 415-632-2700, Ext 260, 261, 262

Kreshka, Eva, *Librn,* Mills College Library (Margaret Prall Music), Oakland CA. 415-632-2700, Ext 260, 261, 262

Kresner, F, *On-Line Servs,* Miller-Dwan Hospital, Medical Library, Duluth MN. 218-727-8762

Kress, Betsy, *Tech Serv & Circ,* Cayuga County Community College, Norman F Bourke Memorial Library Learning Resources Center, Auburn NY. 315-255-1743, Ext 296 & 298

Kress, Frances, *Librn,* Golden Valley County Library, Beach ND. 701-872-4627

Kress, Virginia, *Librn,* Alexandria Library (Ellen Coolidge Burke), Alexandria VA. 703-370-6051

Kretschman, Addie, *Librn,* Otterbein Public Library, Otterbein IN. 317-583-2107

Kretser, Shiela, *Ch,* Greenville Area Public Library, Greenville PA. 412-588-5490

Kreyenbuhl, Jeannine, *Dir,* College of Steubenville, Starvaggi Memorial Library, Steubenville OH. 614-283-3771, Ext 318

Krezminski, Lois, *Librn,* McClester-Nimmons Free Public Library, Plainfield IL. 815-436-6639

Krezowski, Patricia, *In Charge,* Saint Paul Public Library (Merriam Park), Saint Paul MN. 612-292-6624

Krichbaum, Mary, *Librn,* Huron Road Hospital Library & Audiovisual Center, Library & Audiovisual Center, Cleveland OH. 216-761-3300, Ext 3206

Krick, Mary, *Librn,* Illinois State Geological Survey (Library), Urbana IL. 217-344-1481, Ext 252

Krick, Mary, *Librn,* University of Illinois Library at Urbana-Champaign (Geological Survey-State), Urbana IL. 217-344-1481, Ext 252

Krick, R K, *In Charge,* Fredericksburg & Spotsylvania National Military Park Library, Fredericksburg VA. 703-373-4461

Krieger, Janet, *Librn,* University of Minnesota Libraries-Twin Cities (Pharmacy Library), Minneapolis MN. 612-373-2193

Krieger, Leslie A, *On-Line Servs,* Xerox Corp, Technical Information Center, Webster NY. 716-422-3505

Krieger, Michael T, *Asst Librn,* Miami University-Hamilton Campus, Rentschler Learning Resources Center, Hamilton OH. 513-863-8833, Ext 232

Krieger, Susan, *Media,* Old Bridge Public Library, Old Bridge NJ. 201-679-5622

Krier, Maureen, *Acq,* Framingham State College, Henry Whittemore Library, Framingham MA. 617-620-1220, Ext 273

Kriesel, Ronald, *Tech Serv,* California Maritime Academy Library, Vallejo CA. 707-644-5601, Ext 265

Kriigel, Barbara, *Instr,* Andrews University, Library Science Dept, MI. 616-471-3549

Kriplani, Pramila, *Librn,* Sacramento Public Library (Arcade), Sacramento CA. 916-483-5061

Kris, Edward J, *Dir,* Buffalo Testing Laboratories Inc Library, Buffalo NY. 716-873-2303

Krischel, Cheryl, *Cat,* International University Library, Kansas City MO. 816-931-6374

Krisciunas, Kathy P, *Tech Serv & Cat,* University of Detroit Library (Law), Detroit MI. 313-961-5444, Ext 239, 240 & 241

Kristensen, Calista, *Br Coordr,* Brooks Memorial Library, Brattleboro VT. 802-254-5290

Kristensen, Calista, *Librn,* Brooks Memorial Library (West Brattleboro Branch), West Brattleboro VT. 802-254-4023

Kristofferson, Judith, *Librn,* San Jose Public Library (West Valley), San Jose CA. 408-244-4747
Kritch, Joseph, *Ref,* Englewood Library, Englewood NJ. 201-568-2215
Kritzer, Hyman W, *Dir,* Kent State University Libraries, Kent OH. 216-672-2962
Krivanek, Judy M, *Librn,* United States Army (Dwight David Eisenhower Army Medical Center), Fort Gordon GA. 404-791-4238
Krivi, Vida, *Librn,* Mount Olive Public Library, Mount Olive IL. 217-999-7311
Krivonak, Paul, *ILL & Ref,* Cumberland County College Library, Vineland NJ. 609-691-8600, Ext 44, 45
Kriz, Harry M, *Sci & Tech,* Virginia Polytechnic Institute & State University Library, Blacksburg VA. 703-961-5593
Krizman, Geraine, *Base Librn,* United States Air Force (Andersen Air Force Base Library), APO San Francisco CA. 415-366-4294, 4291
Kroah, Larry A, *Dir,* Wilmington College, Sheppard Arthur Watson Library, Wilmington OH. 513-382-6661, Ext 206
Krober, Alfred, *Dir,* Roberts Wesleyan College, Kenneth B Keating Library, Rochester NY. 716-594-9471, Ext 133
Krochman, Kay, *Fine Arts,* Dallas Public Library, Dallas TX. 214-748-9071
Krodshen, Breta M, *Librn,* United Bank Center Law Library, Denver CO. 303-861-4304
Kroeger, Esther, *Ad,* Monroe County Library System, Rochester NY. 716-428-7345
Kroeger, Evelyn, *Dir,* Bogota Public Library, Bogota NJ. 201-488-7185
Kroeger, Karl, *Dir,* Moravian Music Foundation, Peter Memorial Library, Winston-Salem NC. 919-725-0651
Kroeger, Marie, *Music,* North Carolina School of the Arts, Semans Library, Winston-Salem NC. 919-784-7170, Ext 2566
Kroeker, Hilda, *Dir,* Calvary Bible College, Hilda Kroeker Library, Kansas City MO. 816-753-4511, Ext 256
Kroeker, Rena, *Librn,* Grace Hospital Library, Winnipeg MB. 204-837-8311, Ext 457
Kroesche, Bettie, *Librn,* Austin County Library System (Sealy Public), Sealy TX. 713-885-6341
Kroffe, Marguerite, *Librn,* Long Beach Public Library System (Los Altos), Long Beach CA. 213-596-7370
Krog, Laura, *ILL & Ref,* Southwest Baptist College, Estep Library, Bolivar MO. 417-326-5281, Ext 228
Krogstad, Roland, *Research Consult,* Wisconsin Board of Vocational-Technical & Adult Education, Research Coordination Unit Library, Madison WI. 608-266-3705
Krohle, Frederick J, *ILL & Ref,* Wilkes College, Eugene Shedden Farley Library, Wilkes-Barre PA. 717-824-4651, Ext 331 & 332
Krohmer, Gladys, *Librn,* Roosevelt County Library (Froid Public), Froid MT. 406-653-2411
Krohn, Steven, *Media,* North Dakota State School of Science, Mildred Johnson Library, Wahpeton ND. 701-671-2298
Krohnke, Margaret, *Librn,* Charter Oak Public Library, Charter Oak IA. 712-678-3425
Krol, Rosemary, *Librn,* Montague Public Library, Montague MA. 413-367-2852
Krol, Rosemary, *Librn,* Turners Falls Carnegie Public Library, Turners Falls MA. 413-863-4484
Kroll, Mark A, *Tech Serv & On-Line Servs,* Illinois Benedictine College, Theodore Lownik Library, Lisle IL. 312-968-7270, Ext 286
Kroll, Michael, *Librn,* McDonnell Douglas Corp (Corporate Library), Saint Louis MO. 314-232-8515
Kroll, R, *ILL,* State University of New York at Buffalo (Lockwood Library), Buffalo NY. 716-636-2816
Kromar, Jan, *Librn,* Bunker Ramo Corp Library, Westlake Village CA. 805-889-2211, Ext 2357, 2358
Kromer, Edith, *Asst Prof,* College of Saint Catherine, Dept of Library Science, MN. 612-690-6651
Krompart, Janet, *Coll Develop & Ref,* Oakland University, Kresge Library, Rochester MI. 313-377-2486, 377-2474
Krompf, Steven Scott, *Librn,* Willard Psychiatric Center (Professional Health Sciences Medical Library), Willard NY. 607-869-3111, Ext 3286

Kron, Irvin, *Doc,* State University of New York, Frank Melville Jr Memorial Library, Stony Brook NY. 516-246-5650
Kroneberger, Jeanne, *Acq,* Loyola Marymount University, Charles Von Der Ahe Library, Los Angeles CA. 213-642-2788
Kroner, Linda, *Personnel Officer,* Los Angeles Public Library System, Los Angeles CA. 213-626-7555
Kronick, David A, *Dir,* University of Texas Health Science Center at San Antonio Library, San Antonio TX. 512-691-6271
Kronmiller, Ruth, *Librn,* New York Public Library (Great Kills), New York NY. 212-984-6670
Kronsbein, Roy O, *Librn,* Concordia College Library, Ann Arbor MI. 313-665-3691, Ext 197
Kronstedt, Richard, *Dir,* Minneapolis College of Art & Design Library, Minneapolis MN. 612-870-3291
Kroon, Monique, *Librn,* Environment Canada (Bibliotheque de la Faune et des Eaux Interieures), Sainte Foy PQ. 418-694-7062
Kroon, Monique, *Librn,* Environment Canada, Centre de Recherches Forestieres des Laurentides, Sainte Foy PQ. 418-694-4428
Kropp, Rhonda, *Librn,* Abilene Reporter News Library, Abilene TX. 915-673-4271
Kropp, Sylvia, *Librn,* Green Free Library, Wellsboro PA. 717-724-4876
Kroshus, Mary, *Tech Serv,* North Dakota State School of Science, Mildred Johnson Library, Wahpeton ND. 701-671-2298
Kroshus, Mrs E, *Librn,* Central Collegiate Institute Library, Moose Jaw SK. 306-693-4691
Kross, Dora, *Asst Dir,* Chicago Ridge Public Library, Chicago Ridge IL. 312-423-7753
Krost, Mary, *Librn,* Florida Department of Natural Resources, Marine Research Laboratory Library, Saint Petersburg FL. 813-896-8626, Ext 43
Krotiak, Elizabeth, *Librn,* Atlantic Richfield Co, Research Division Library, Harvey IL. 312-468-9300
Krouse, Philip E, *Technical Information Specialist,* ESB Technology Co, Technical Information Services, Yardley PA. 215-493-7053
Krouskop, Constance, *Librn,* Carnegie Library of Pittsburgh (Carrick), Pittsburgh PA. 412-622-3100
Krout, Doris L, *Librn,* United States Department of the Interior, Office of Hearings & Appeals Library, Arlington VA. 703-557-1143
Krubeck, Dorothy, *Librn,* Longview Daily News Library, Longview WA. 206-577-2508
Kruckman, Virginia, *Librn,* Sioux Rapids Memorial Library, Sioux Rapids IA. 712-283-2064
Krucoff, Ella, *Chief Ref & Documentation,* European Community Information Service Library, Commission of the European Communities, Washington DC. 202-862-9500
Kruegel, Leslie, *YA & Ref,* Free Public Library of Hasbrouck Heights, Hasbrouck Heights NJ. 201-288-0488
Krueger, Frederick W, *Librn,* Public Library of Fort Wayne & Allen County (Waynedale), Fort Wayne IN. 219-747-9821
Krueger, Gerald, *Govt Doc,* University of Wisconsin-Oshkosh, Forrest R Polk Library, Oshkosh WI. 414-424-3333
Krueger, Joan, *Exhibitions/Publications,* John Michael Kohler Arts Center Library, Sheboygan WI. 414-458-6144
Krueger, Lise, *Librn,* National Film Board-Phototheque, Ottawa ON. 613-593-5826
Krueger, Mabre, *Dir,* Jackson Community College Library, Jackson MI. 517-787-0800, Ext 294, 295
Krueger, Marlene, *Lectr,* University of Wisconsin-Oshkosh, Dept of Library Science, WI. 414-424-2313
Krueger, Phyllis, *Tech Serv & Cat,* Neenah Public Library, Neenah WI. 414-729-4728
Krueger, Robert, *Instr,* University of Wisconsin-River Falls, Dept of Education Library Science-Media Program, WI. 715-425-3854
Krueger, Virginia, *Ref,* Findlay-Hancock County Public Library, Findlay OH. 419-422-1712
Krug, John C, *Dir & Cat,* Wabash Valley College, Bauer Media Center, Mount Carmel IL. 618-262-8641, Ext 225, 226
Krug, Sue, *Librn,* Deerfield Public Library, Deerfield WI. 608-764-8102

Krug, Tony, *Coordr,* Wabash Valley College, Library Media Technology Program, IL. 618-262-8641, Ext 225
Kruger, Karen, *Doc,* University of Cincinnati Libraries, Central Library, Cincinnati OH. 513-475-2218
Kruger, Sy, *Dir,* Millburn Free Public Library, Millburn NJ. 201-376-1006
Krugerud, Mary, *Librn,* Western Plains Library System (Dawson Branch), Dawson MN. 612-769-2069
Kruk, Valerie, *In Charge,* Cook County State's Attorney's Library, Chicago IL. 312-443-8723
Krull, Charles F, *In Charge,* De Kalb Agresearch, Inc, Corn Research Center Library, De Kalb IL. 815-758-3461
Krull, Fred, *Librn,* Texhoma Public Library, Texhoma OK. 405-423-7155
Krull, Jeffrey R, *Dir,* Mansfield-Richland County Public Library, Mansfield OH. 419-524-1041
Krum, Anne, *Petroleum, Geol, Energy,* Natrona County Public Library, Casper WY. 307-235-9272
Krum, Janelle, *Acq,* Spokane County Library, Spokane WA. 509-924-4122
Krumland, Elaine, *Cat,* Columbus Public Library, Pawnee Regional Library, Columbus NE. 402-564-7116
Krumm, Roger, *Librn,* University of Florida Libraries (Engineering & Physics), Gainesville FL. 904-392-0987
Krummel, Donald W, *Prof,* University of Illinois, Graduate School of Library Science, IL. 217-333-3280
Krumwiede, Richard, *Dir,* Outagamie Waupaca Counties Federated Library System, Appleton WI. 414-734-8873
Krupp, E C, *Dir,* Griffith Observatory Library, Los Angeles CA. 213-664-1181
Krupp, Mary F, *Librn,* Getty Oil Co, Corporate Library, Los Angeles CA. 213-381-7151, Ext 275
Krupp, Robert G, *Chief,* New York Public Library (Science & Technology Research Center (Cent Bldg)), New York NY. 212-790-6294, 790-6295
Krusback, Harold, *Dir,* Southwest Wisconsin Vocational-Technical Institute, Learning Resources Center, Fennimore WI. 608-822-3262, Ext 142
Kruse, Anne A, *ILL,* Tuxedo Park Library, Tuxedo Park NY. 914-351-2207
Kruse, Bonnie, *Dir, On-Line Servs & Bibliog Instr,* Baptist Memorial Hospital, Learning Resources Center, Kansas City MO. 816-361-3500, Ext 7863
Kruse, Cathy, *Circ,* Lake Michigan College Library, Benton Harbor MI. 616-927-3571, Ext 261
Kruse, Cindy, *ILL,* Wabash Valley College, Bauer Media Center, Mount Carmel IL. 618-262-8641, Ext 225, 226
Kruse, Ethna E, *Librn,* Royal Public Library, Royal IA. 712-933-2421
Kruse, Eula M, *Librn,* Winters Public Library, Winters TX. 915-754-4251
Kruse, Gerald, *Dir,* Research Medical Center, Lockwood Memorial Library, Kansas City MO. 816-276-4159
Kruse, Ginny Moore, *Librn,* Wisconsin Department of Public Instruction (Cooperative Children's Book Center), Madison WI. 608-263-3720
Kruse, Harriet, *Librn,* United Theological Seminary of the Twin Cities Library, New Brighton MN. 612-633-4311
Kruse, Kathryn W, *On-Line Servs,* Duke University (Medical Center Library), Durham NC. 919-684-2092
Kruse, Marina, *Librn,* Warren Public Library (Edgar A Guest), Warren MI. 313-772-0240
Kruse, Martha, *Librn,* Evansville Public Library & Vanderburgh County Public Library (Oaklyn), Evansville IN. 812-425-2621
Kruse, Paul, *Media,* Peru State College Library, Peru NE. 402-872-3815, Ext 218
Kruse, Robert K, *Cat,* Hobart & William Smith Colleges, Warren Hunting Smith Library, Geneva NY. 315-789-5500, Ext 224
Kruse, Thelma, *Circ,* Anchorage Municipal Libraries (Z J Loussac Public Library), Anchorage AK. 907-264-4481
Krust, Katherine, *Asst Dir,* Jasper Public Library, Jasper IN. 812-482-2712

Kruus, Alan, *Acting Bk Order,* New York Public Library (The Branch Libraries), New York NY. 212-790-6262

Kruut, Evald, *Dir,* Chippewa Library League, Mount Pleasant MI. 517-773-3242

Kruut, Evald, *Librn,* Veterans Memorial Library, Mount Pleasant MI. 517-773-3242

Krymkowski, Brother Joseph, *Librn,* Franciscan Friars, Assumption Friary Library, Pulaski WI. 414-822-3291

Krynicki, Marguerite J, *Librn,* Illinois Bell Telephone Co Library, Chicago IL. 312-727-2668

Krynycky, Tatiana, *Languages Coll,* Ottawa Public Library, Ottawa ON. 613-236-0301

Krysa, Cathy, *Tech Serv & Cat,* Trinity College Library, Deerfield IL. 312-945-6700, Ext 217

Krysak, Wayne D, *Bus, Econ & Vacation,* Public Library of the District of Columbia, Martin Luther King Memorial Library, Washington DC. 202-727-1101

Krzyminski, Cathleen, *Coordr,* Alverno College, Dept of Library Science, WI. 414-671-5400, Ext 213

Krzyminski, Cathleen, *Dir,* Alverno College, Library Media Center, Milwaukee WI. 414-671-5400, Ext 419

Krzys, Richard, *Prof,* University of Pittsburgh, School of Library & Information Science, PA. 412-624-5230

Krzyzak, George, *Dir,* Norwalk Public Library (South Norwalk Libr), South Norwalk CT. 203-866-6240

Ku, Gloria, *Tech Serv,* Greenfield Community College, Library-Learning Resources Center, Greenfield MA. 413-774-3131, Ext 285

Ku, Joyce, *ILL & Ref,* South Plainfield Free Public Library, South Plainfield NJ. 201-754-7885

Ku, Peter, *Per,* Niagara University Library, Niagara University NY. 716-285-1212, Ext 376

Ku, Peter C, *Dir,* Howard Community College Library, Columbia MD. 301-992-4812

Kuammen, Suzanne, *Librn,* CTL Engineering, Inc, Library, Columbus OH. 614-276-8123

Kuan, Jenny W, *Librn,* Day & Zimmermann, Inc Library, Philadelphia PA. 215-299-8222

Kuba, Patricia H, *Librn,* Bingham, Dana & Gould, Law Library, Boston MA. 617-357-9300, Ext 312

Kubala, Jean, *Ad,* Temple Public Library, Temple TX. 817-778-5555

Kubas, Anne P, *In Charge,* Hawaiian Agronomics Company (International) Library, Honolulu HI. 808-524-3906

Kubiak, Janice, *Head,* Free Library of Philadelphia (Northwest Regional Library), Philadelphia PA. 215-843-9805

Kubiak, Matthew C, *Asst Dir,* Mary H Weir Public Library, Weirton WV. 304-748-7070

Kubic, Jennifer, *Circ,* Mount Vernon Public Library, Mount Vernon WA. 206-336-2418

Kubicki, Arthur, *Asst Chief Operating Engineer,* Chicago Public Library, Chicago IL. 312-269-2900

Kubik, K, *Tech Serv,* Stauffer Chemical Co, de Guigne Technical Center Research Library, Richmond CA. 415-231-1020

Kubinec, Janet, *Curator, Hist Coll,* University of Pittsburgh (Maurice & Laura Falk Library of the Health Sciences), Pittsburgh PA. 412-624-2521

Kubiniec, Sister M Joyce, *ILL,* Hilbert College, McGrath Library, Hamburg NY. 716-649-7900, Ext 237

Kubjas, A, *Librn,* Scarborough General Hospital Library, Scarborough ON. 416-438-2911

Kubota, Wanda, *Librn,* Reuben McMillan Free Library Free Library Association (Struthers Branch), Struthers OH. 612-755-3322

Kucera, Lucille, *ILL,* North Suburban District Library, Loves Park IL. 815-633-4247, 633-4248

Kucharski, Jane, *Commun Servs,* Piscataway Township Free Public Library, John F Kennedy Memorial Library, Piscataway NJ. 201-463-1633

Kuchinsky, Saul, *Librn,* Brooklyn Hospital, Medical & Nursing Library, Brooklyn NY. 212-270-4411

Kuchta, Carol, *Per,* Royal Oak Public Library, Royal Oak MI. 313-541-1470

Kuck, Freda, *Librn,* Auglaize County District Library (New Knoxville Library), New Knoxville OH. 419-753-2724

Kuck, Mary Shaw, *Librn,* United States Court of Military Appeals Library, Washington DC. 202-693-7100, Ext 47

Kuczka, Jessamine, *Dir,* Glen Ellyn Public Library, Glen Ellyn IL. 312-469-0879

Kuczynski, Kathleen, *Dir,* Helen Hayes Hospital, Medical Library, West Haverstraw NY. 914-947-3000, Ext 359

Kudiesy, Norma M, *Pub Servs Librn,* United States Army (Air Defense School Library), Fort Bliss TX. 915-568-5781, 568-5010

Kudlaty, Ruth, *Tech Serv,* Minneapolis Community College Library, Minneapolis MN. 612-341-7089, 341-7059

Kudryk, Oleg, *Acq,* Indiana University at Bloomington, University Libraries, Bloomington IN. 812-337-3403

Kuehling, Mary A, *Librn,* Methodist Hospital Library, Madison WI. 608-251-2371, Ext 3691

Kuehn, Katherine, *Librn,* Memphis-Shelby County Public Library & Information Center (South), Memphis TN. 901-396-9700

Kuehn, Melody, *Asst Dir & Ref,* Minot Public Library, Minot ND. 701-852-1045

Kuehn, Virginia, *Cat,* Florida State University, Robert Manning Strozier Library, Tallahassee FL. 904-644-5211

Kuehne, Patsy, *Libr Mgr,* Western Evangelical Seminary, G Hallauer Memorial Library, Portland OR. 503-654-5182

Kueny, Suzanne, *Ref,* United States Army, Concepts Analysis Agency, Information Center, Bethesda MD. 301-295-1530

Kuenzer, Ardys, *Librn,* Manistee County Library (Kaleva Branch), Kaleva MI. 616-362-3178

Kuenzer, Ardys, *Librn,* Manistee County Library (Onekama Branch), Onekama MI. 616-889-4041

Kugle, Paula, *Librn,* Hill Junior College Library, Hillsboro TX. 817-582-2555, Ext 40

Kugle, Vivian M, *Librn,* York Haven Free Library, York Haven PA. 717-266-4712

Kugler, Richard C, *Dir,* Old Dartmouth Historical Society Library, New Bedford MA. 617-997-0046

Kugler, Ruth, *Asst Librn,* Eustis Public Library, Eustis NE. 308-486-2651

Kuhl, Dorothy B, *In Charge,* Sea-Land Service, Inc Library, Elizabeth NJ. 201-558-6000

Kuhlman, Jim, *Bibliog Instr,* University of Georgia Libraries, Athens GA. 404-542-2716

Kuhlmann, Florence A, *Librn,* Cuyahoga County Public Library (Orange), Pepper Pike Village OH. 316-831-4282

Kuhlmann, Jessie S, *Tech Serv,* Blue Island Public Library, Blue Island IL. 312-388-1078

Kuhn, Annamae, *Librn,* Manteno District Library, Manteno IL. 815-468-3323

Kuhn, Carol, *Mich Coll Libr,* Traverse City Public Library, Traverse City MI. 616-941-2311

Kuhn, Hannah R, *Librn,* House of the Book, Brandeis-Bardin Institute, Brandeis CA. 213-526-1131, 213-348-7201

Kuhn, John, *Syst Coordr,* Onondaga County Public Library System, Syracuse NY. 315-473-2702

Kuhn, Lee Ann, *Librn,* West Virginia Department of Highways (Reference Library), Charleston WV. 304-348-3525

Kuhn, Luvada L, *Sch Servs,* Chillicothe & Ross County Public Library, Chillicothe OH. 614-773-4145

Kuhn, Lydia, *Acq,* Fresno County Free Library, Fresno CA. 209-488-3191

Kuhn, Margaret, *Ad,* Petersburg Public Library, Petersburg VA. 804-732-3851

Kuhn, Mark, *ILL,* Kent County Library System, Grand Rapids MI. 616-774-3250

Kuhn, Warren B, *Dir,* Iowa State University Library, Ames IA. 515-294-1442

Kuhner, David, *Asst Dir Sci,* Claremont Colleges Libraries, Claremont CA. 714-621-8000, Ext 3721

Kuhner, David, *Dir,* Claremont Colleges Libraries (Norman F Sprague Memorial), Claremont CA. 714-621-8000, Ext 3920

Kuhner, David, *Librn,* Claremont Colleges Libraries (Norman F Sprague Memorial), Claremont CA. 714-621-8000, Ext 3190

Kuhner, Robert, *Pub Servs,* City College of the City University of New York, Morris Raphael Cohen Library, New York NY. 212-690-6612

Kuhns, Charles L, *On-Line Servs,* Hood College of Frederick, Joseph Henry Apple Library, Frederick MD. 301-663-3131, Ext 364, 365

Kuiper, Marilyn, *Librn,* Newton Free Library (Newtonville Branch), Newtonville MA. 617-527-7700, Ext 24

Kuipers, M, *ILL,* British Columbia Institute of Technology Library, Burnaby BC. 604-434-5734, Ext 360

Kujawa, Dianna, *Librn,* Sunland Training Center, Suntown Library, Marianna FL. 904-526-2123, Ext 310

Kukla, Jon K, *Publications,* Virginia State Library, Richmond VA. 804-786-8929

Kuklin, Susan Beverly, *Dir,* De Paul University Libraries (Law Library), Chicago IL. 312-321-7710

Kuklo, Iris Ann, *Librn,* Loxley Public Library, Loxley AL. 205-964-5695

Kulberg, Gretchen S, *Dir,* West Bloomfield Township Public Library, West Bloomfield MI. 313-682-2120

Kulberg, Raoul, *Supvr,* University of the District of Columbia (Georgia Harvard Campus), Washington DC. 202-673-7188

Kulchar, A G, *Med Librn,* Bryn Mawr Hospital, Medical Library, Bryn Mawr PA. 215-896-3160

Kulhawy, Gloria, *Librn,* Paleontological Research Institution Library, Ithaca NY. 607-273-6623

Kulibert, Marie, *Cat,* Traverse City Public Library, Traverse City MI. 616-941-2311

Kulkarni, Janardan, *Librn,* University of Louisville Library (Life Sciences), Louisville KY. 502-588-5945

Kulkarni, Janardan, *Librn,* University of Louisville Library (Natural Sci), Louisville KY. 502-588-5986

Kullas, Gertrude, *Librn,* Timmins Public Library (Whitney Public), Porcupine ON. 705-235-5185

Kulleseid, Eleanor R, *Asst Dir & Sch Librn,* Bank Street College of Education Library, New York NY. 212-663-7200, Ext 245

Kulow, June D, *Dir,* Seymour Public Library, Seymour IN. 812-522-3412

Kulp, Leslie, *Chief, Acq,* National Agricultural Library, Beltsville MD. 301-344-4248

Kulp, Leslie, *Instr,* United States Department of Agriculture Graduate School, Certificate Program for Library Technicians, DC. 202-447-5885

Kulpa, Lorraine A, *Librn,* General Motors Corp (Legal Staff Library), Detroit MI. 313-556-4010

Kulyckyj, Irene, *Cat,* Reader's Digest Association, General Books Division Library, New York NY. 212-972-8452

Kumar, Vijay, *Cat,* University of Western Ontario (Health Sciences Library), London ON. 519-679-6175

Kumatz, Tad G, *Treas,* Academic Libraries of Brooklyn, NY. 212-636-3545

Kumatz, Tad G, *Asst Dir,* Pratt Institute Library, Brooklyn NY. 212-636-3684

Kumor, Charlotte, *Librn,* Hastings Memorial Library, Grant City Library, Grant NE. 308-352-4894

Kumor, Mary A, *Librn,* Saint Luke's Hospital, Medical Staff Library, Cleveland OH. 216-368-7691

Kumsha, Mary Jane, *Dir,* College of Saint Scholastica Library, Duluth MN. 218-723-6143

Kumsha, Mary Jane, *Dept Head,* College of Saint Scholastica, Library Science Program, MN. 218-723-6143

Kuncaitis, Yadwiga, *Ref & Bibliog Instr,* Case Western Reserve University Libraries (Freiberger), Cleveland OH. 216-368-3506

Kundzins, Ilga, *Tech Info Specialist,* United States Department of Commerce, New York District Office Library, New York NY. 212-264-0630

Kunen, Eleanor, *Dir,* Marlborough Hospital, Health Science Library, Marlborough MA. 617-485-1121, Ext 248

Kunert, E R, *Dir,* Mead Public Library, Sheboygan WI. 414-459-3400

Kunert, Ernest R, *Dir,* Sheboygan County Federated Library System, Sheboygan WI. 414-459-3412

Kunitz, Don, *Spec Coll,* University of California at Davis, General Library, Davis CA. 916-752-2110

Kunkel, Ida, *Librn,* Mound City Public Library, Mound City MO. 816-442-3434

Kunkle, Hannah J, *Prof,* Texas Woman's University, School of Library Science, TX. 817-387-2418 & 566-1455

Kunkler, Marion, *Libr Technician,* San Diego County Library (Vista Branch), Vista CA. 714-724-5507

Kunoff, Hugo, *Modern European Langs,* Indiana University at Bloomington, University Libraries, Bloomington IN. 812-337-3403

Kunsemiller, Lucille, *Acq,* California State University, Chico Library, Chico CA. 916-895-6212

Kunstler, Jane, *Librn,* New York Public Library (High Bridge), New York NY. 212-293-7800

Kunstler, Phyllis, *Ch,* Port Chester Public Library, Port Chester NY. 914-939-6710, 939-6711

Kuntz, Janice, *Librn,* Saskatchewan Department of Social Services Library, Regina SK. 306-565-2345

Kuntz, L S, *Supvry Librn,* United States Army (Aviation Center Library), Fort Rucker AL. 205-255-5010, 6093

Kuntz, Lenore, *Librn,* Regina Public Library (Prince of Wales), Regina SK. 306-569-7615

Kunze, Miriam, *ILL,* Somerset County Library, Somerville NJ. 201-725-4700, Ext 234

Kuo, Frank, *AV,* Portland State University, Branford Price Millar Library, Portland OR. 503-229-4424

Kuo, Margaret, *Librn,* Schlumberger Well Services, Engineering Library, Houston TX. 713-928-4411

Kuo, Thomas, *Librn,* University of Pittsburgh (East Asian), Pittsburgh PA. 412-624-4457

Kupferman, Norman, *Ad & Ref,* Long Beach Public Library, Long Beach NY. 516-432-7201

Kupper, Ronald J, *Dir,* Colorado Mountain College-West Campus, Learning Center, Glenwood Springs CO. 303-945-7481, Ext 66

Kupstas, Kathryn, *Head, Tech Proc,* American Bankers Association Library, Washington DC. 202-467-4180

Kuramoto, Mary I, *Librn,* First Hawaiian Bank, Research Division Library, Honolulu HI. 808-525-7000

Kurbjun, Virginia, *Librn,* United States Army (Applied Technology Labs, Technical Library), Fort Eustis VA. 804-878-2963

Kurceba, Kathy, *Ref,* University of Calgary Library (Faculty of Medicine Medical Library), Calgary AB. 403-284-6858

Kurland, Mildred, *Librn,* Congregation Rodeph Shalom Library, Philadelphia PA. 215-627-6747

Kurland, Roslyn, *Librn,* Temple Beth El, Billie Davis Rodenberg Memorial Library, Hollywood FL. 305-920-8225

Kurmey, W J, *Dean & Prof,* University of Alberta, Faculty of Library Science, AB. 403-432-4578

Kurrier, Michael, *ILL,* Hampshire College, Harold F Johnson Library Center, Amherst MA. 413-549-4600

Kursinsky, Jeanette, *Librn,* Deckerville Public Library, Deckerville MI. 313-376-8015

Kurtenbach, Dorothy E, *Librn,* Piper City Public Library, Piper City IL. 815-686-9234

Kurtt, Mildred, *Librn,* Denver Public Library, Denver IA. 319-984-5140

Kurtz, Betty W, *Librn,* Bellwood-Antis Public Library, Bellwood PA. 814-742-8234

Kurtz, Mary, *Librn,* Ephrata Public Library, Ephrata PA. 717-733-4411

Kurtz, Mike, *Classified Information Center,* Rand Corp Library, Santa Monica CA. 213-393-0411, Ext 369

Kurtz, Willa, *Librn,* Los Angeles Public Library System (Encino-Tarzana Branch), Tarzana CA. 213-343-1983

Kurutz, Gary F, *Librn,* Sutro Library, San Francisco CA. 415-557-0374

Kurzig, Carol M, *Pub Servs,* Foundation Center Library, New York NY. 212-975-1120

Kurzman, Cal, *Dir,* College of Marin Library, Kentfield CA. 415-485-9470

Kusack, James, *Instr,* University of Iowa, School of Library Science, IA. 319-353-3644

Kusche, Genevieve, *Librn,* Kankakee County Historical Society Library, Kankakee IL. 815-932-5279

Kuschel, Olive G, *Tech Serv & Acq,* Floral Park Public Library, Floral Park NY. 516-354-0666

Kuse, Margret, *Dir,* Medford Free Public Library, Medford WI. 715-748-2505

Kush, Catherine, *Librn,* Lexington County Circulating Library (Lexington Branch), Lexington SC. 803-532-9223

Kushin, Robert M, *Librn,* Erie Community College-North (City Campus Library Resource Center), Buffalo NY. 716-881-4200, Ext 320

Kushinka, Kerry, *Info Specialist,* Knoll Pharmaceutical Co, Research Library, Whippany NJ. 201-887-8300, Ext 168

Kushon, Susan, *Tech Serv, Acq & Cat,* Point Park College Library, Helen-Jean Moore Library, Pittsburgh PA. 412-391-4100, Ext 361

Kuske, Mariellyn, *Librn,* Kent County Library System (Kent City Branch), Kent City MI. 616-678-4571

Kuskowski, Jerome, *Dir,* Pallottine Provincialate Library, Milwaukee WI. 414-258-0653

Kusler, Alan, *Pub Rel,* Monroe County Library System, Rochester NY. 716-428-7345

Kusmik, C J, *Tech Serv & Spec Coll,* Concordia College, Klinck Memorial Library, River Forest IL. 312-771-8300, Ext 450

Kusner, Patricia, *Librn,* Ada Public School District Library, Ada OH. 419-634-5246

Kusnerz, P A, *Librn,* University of Michigan, Detroit Library, Detroit MI. 313-832-7400

Kusnerz, Peggy A, *Librn,* University of Michigan Libraries (Library Extension), Ann Arbor MI. 313-764-9364

Kuta, Celeste, *Asst Librn,* Stein Roe & Farnham Library, Chicago IL. 312-368-7840

Kuther, Patricia A, *Librn,* United States Air Force (Professional Medical Library), Maxwell AFB AL. 205-293-6206

Kutolowski, Terry, *Librn,* Cuyahoga County Public Library (Bay Village Branch), Bay Village OH. 216-871-6392

Kutsagoitz, Andrea K, *Asst Librn,* AVCO Corp, Lycoming Division Library & Information Center, Stratford CT. 203-378-8211

Kutzelnig, Eve, *Librn,* Ontario Ministry of Industry and Tourism Library, Toronto ON. 416-965-3365

Kuuskmae, Mati, *AV,* Suffolk County Community College, Eastern Campus Library, Riverhead NY. 516-369-2600, Ext 228

Kuykendall, Francis, *Librn,* Barton Library (Parker Chapel), El Dorado AR. 501-862-2360

Kuykendall, Judith A, *Dir & Acq,* Temple Public Library, Temple TX. 817-778-5555

Kuykendall, Susan H, *Acq,* Furman University Library, Greenville SC. 803-294-2191

Kuykendall, Thomas, *Librn,* San Antonio College Library (Southwest Center, SACCD), San Antonio TX. 512-734-7311, Ext 2480

Kuykendell, Billie, *Librn,* H B Zachry Co, Central Records & Library, San Antonio TX. 512-922-1213, Ext 371

Kuzara, Elizabeth, *Bkmobile Coordr,* Bloomfield Public Library, Northwest Essex Area Library, Bloomfield NJ. 201-429-9292

Kuzaro, Frances, *Librn,* East Haddam Public Library, East Haddam CT. 203-873-8248

Kuzma, Toni, *Dir,* Somerset County College Library, Somerville NJ. 201-526-1200, Ext 224, 304

Kvill, S, *Librn,* Mayerthorpe Library, Mayerthorpe AB. 403-786-2404

Kwan, Anna, *Librn,* City of Brampton Public Library & Art Gallery (Chinguacousy), Bramalea ON. 416-793-4636

Kwan, Barbara, *ILL,* California State University, Hayward Library, Hayward CA. 415-881-3664

Kwanten, Luc, *Far Eastern Libr,* University of Chicago, Joseph Regenstein Library, Chicago IL. 312-753-2977

Kwarcinski, Deborah, *Librn,* Mercy School of Nursing of Detroit Library, Detroit MI. 313-923-5700

Kwiatkowski, J, *Librn,* Taylor Public Library, Taylor PA. 717-562-3180

Kwiecinski, JoAnne M, *Ch,* Peabody Institute Library, Peabody MA. 617-531-0100

Kwitkowsky, Marta, *Ch,* Saint Clair Shores Public Library, Saint Clair Shores MI. 313-771-9020

Kwok, Maureen, *Librn,* San Jose Public Library (Educational Park), San Jose CA. 408-272-3662

Kwok, Mrs Tzu-Wen, *Asst Librn,* Kinston-Lenoir County Public Library, Kinston NC. 919-527-7066

Kwok, Mrs Tzu-Wen, *Actg Dir,* Neuse Regional Library, Kinston NC. 919-527-7066

Kwok, Rosita, *Tech Serv,* Pepperdine University Library, Payson Library, Malibu CA. 213-456-4252

Kwon, Ella, *Tech Serv,* Moraine Valley Community College, Learning Resources Center, Palos Hills IL. 312-974-4300, Ext 222

Kwon, Hidong, *Tech Serv,* William Paterson College of New Jersey, Sarah Byrd Askew Library, Wayne NJ. 201-595-2113

Kwon, Sang H, *Tech Serv,* Chicago State University, Paul & Emily Douglas Library, Chicago IL. 312-995-2254

Kwon, Veong, *Cat,* Fairleigh Dickinson University, Weiner Library, Teaneck NJ. 201-836-6300, Ext 265

Kyed, James M, *Librn,* Massachusetts Institute of Technology Libraries (Barker-Engineering), Cambridge MA. 617-253-5663

Kyle, Arlene, *Cat,* Texarkana Community College, Palmer Memorial Library, Texarkana TX. 214-838-4541, Ext 215, 231

Kyle, Deborah Nolan, *Chief Librn, AV & Circ,* Cuyahoga Community College (Western Campus Library), Parma OH. 216-845-4000, Ext 278

Kyle, Deborah Nolan, *Dir,* Cuyahoga Community College-Western Campus Library, Parma OH. 216-845-4000

Kyle, Hazel E, *Librn,* Rolla Public Library, Rolla ND. 701-477-6634

Kyle, Linda H, *Ch,* Wilton Library Association, Wilton CT. 203-762-3950

Kyle, Margaret J, *Asst Dir, Ad & Br Coordr,* Evansville Public Library & Vanderburgh County Public Library, Evansville IN. 812-425-2621

Kyle, Peggy, *Librn,* Asheville-Buncombe Technical Institute Library, Asheville NC. 704-254-1921, Ext 63

Kyllo, Y M, *Librn,* Alberta Government Telephones, Commission Library, Edmonton AB. 403-425-3653

Kynerd, Wanda, *ILL,* Hinds Junior College, George M McLendon Library, Raymond MS. 601-857-5261, Ext 253

Kysely, Elizabeth, *Ref,* United States Air Force Academy Library, United States Air Force Academy CO. 303-472-2590

Kyser, Glenda J, *Librn,* Ennis Public Library, Ennis TX. 214-875-2675

Kyzar, Mary, *Asst Librn,* Andalusia Public Library, Andalusia AL. 205-222-6612

L

L'Esperance, Marcelle, *Chief Librn,* Notre-Dame Hospital, Medical Library, Montreal PQ. 514-876-6862

L'Herault, Pierre, *Dir,* Bibliotheque Centrale De Pret De La Mauricie, Trois-Rivieres PQ. 819-375-9623

Laabe, Joan, *Asst Dir,* East Central College, Library Services, Union MO. 314-583-5193, Ext 244

Laack, Jean, *Dir & Ad,* Plymouth Public Library, Plymouth WI. 414-892-4416

Laasko, L, *Librn,* University of Toronto Libraries (E J Pratt Library), Toronto ON. 416-978-3825

Laats, Armilda, *Asst Librn & Tech Serv,* Port Authority of New York & New Jersey Library, New York NY. 212-466-4067, 4068

Laatz, Mary J, *Dir,* Indiana University (School of Medicine Library), Indianapolis IN. 317-264-7182

Labahn, Wilma, *Tech Serv & On-Line Servs,* Arkansas Tech University, Tomlinson Library, Russellville AR. 501-968-0304

LaBarge, Diane, *Librn,* Richville Free Library, Richville NY. 315-287-1481

LaBarr, Clair, *ILL,* Oregon State Library, Salem OR. 503-378-4243

LaBarr, Mona, *Librn,* Harvard Public Library, Harvard NE. 402-772-7101

Labato, Theresa, *Tech Serv & Cat,* Holyoke Community College Library, Holyoke MA. 413-538-7000, Ext 261

LaBaugh, Ross, *Bibliog Instr,* Southeastern Massachusetts University, Library Communications Center, North Dartmouth MA. 617-999-8662

Laben, Dorothy, *Librn,* Davis Community Church, Resource Center Library, Davis CA. 916-753-2894

LaBere, Marilyn, *Actg Librn,* Walkerton-Lincoln Township Public Library, Walkerton IN. 219-586-2933

Laberge, Leo, *Dir,* Bibliotheque Deschatelets Library, Ottawa ON. 613-237-0580
LaBissoniere, William, *Head,* University of Minnesota Libraries-Twin Cities (Government Publications), Minneapolis MN. 612-373-7813
LaBonte, P, *Media & Systs,* British Columbia Institute of Technology Library, Burnaby BC. 604-434-5734, Ext 360
Laborde, Andrea, *Librn,* Community General Osteopathic Hospital Library, Harrisburg PA. 717-652-3000, Ext 185
Laborie, Timothy, *Libr & Info Sci,* Drexel University Library, Philadelphia PA. 215-895-2750
Labott, Judith, *Dir,* Hales Corners Library, Hales Corners WI. 414-425-8050
Labovitz, Judy, *In Charge,* McGaw Laboratories Technical Information, Irvine CA. 714-754-2066
Labovitz, Marsha, *Planning & Analysis,* Sussex County Library System, Sussex County Area Reference Library, Newton NJ. 201-948-3660
LaBrake, Orlyn B, *Acting Chief Librn,* United States Navy (Naval Training Equipment Center Technical Information Center), Orlando FL. 305-646-4797
LaBrake, Orlyn B, *Assoc Dir,* University of Central Florida Library, Orlando FL. 305-275-2564
LaBranche, Joyce, *Librn,* Iberville Parish Library (White Castle), White Castle LA. 504-545-8424
Labrie, Janine, *Librn,* University of Montreal Libraries (Physics), Montreal PQ. 514-343-6613
Labrie, Marie, *Librn,* Chicopee Public Library (Fairview), Chicopee MA. 413-533-8218
LaBudde, Kenneth J, *Dir,* University of Missouri-Kansas City Libraries, Kansas City MO. 816-276-1531
Lacasse, Francine, *Instr,* College Lionel-Groulx, Techniques de la Documentation, PQ. 514-430-3120, Ext 261
LaCerte, Robert, *Pub Servs,* Whitworth College, Harriet Cheney Cowles Memorial Library, Spokane WA. 509-466-3260
Lacey, Rosalie, *Librn,* East Providence Public Library (Riverside), East Providence RI. 401-434-2453
Lach, Michael, *Circ,* Dartmouth College, Baker Memorial Library, Hanover NH. 603-646-2235
Lachance, Andree, *Asst Dir,* Francois-Xavier Garneau College Library, Quebec PQ. 418-688-8310, Ext 256
Lacharite, L, *Ref,* Bibliotheque Municipale De Lachine, Lachine PQ. 514-637-2568
Lachat, Georgette, *Librn,* New York Public Library (Saint Agnes), New York NY. 212-877-4380
Lachendro, Leonard L, *Dir,* Lodi Public Library, Lodi CA. 209-334-3973
Lachner, Elizabeth, *Librn,* New York Public Library (Cathedral), New York NY. 212-753-3066
Lachowicz, Connie, *Dir,* South Kingstown Public Library, Peace Dale RI. 401-789-1555
Lachowicz, Connie, *Librn,* South Kingstown Public Library (Peace Dale), Peace Dale RI. 401-783-4085
Lackey, Jewel, *Librn,* Shackelford County Library, Albany TX. 915-762-2477, 762-2672
Lackey, Lois, *Circ,* John C Hart Memorial Library, Shrub Oak NY. 914-245-5262
Lackey, Polly, *Acq,* Wayland Baptist College, Van Howeling Memorial Library, Plainview TX. 806-296-5521, Ext 29
Lackie, Kaye, *Librn,* Front of Leeds & Lansdowne District Public Library, Lansdowne ON. 613-659-3885
Lackner, Irene, *Librn,* Economic Council of Canada Library, Ottawa ON. 613-993-1914
Lacks, Bernice K, *Reader Serv,* Vassar College Library, Poughkeepsie NY. 914-452-7000
LaClair, Linda, *Ch,* West Bloomfield Township Public Library, West Bloomfield MI. 313-682-2120
Lacock, Leona, *Dir,* Jefferson Public Library, Jefferson IA. 515-386-2836
Lacomis, Dorothy, *Librn,* Pittston Memorial Library, Pittston PA. 717-654-9565
LaCosse, Victoria, *Dir,* Alexandria Public Library, Alexandria MN. 612-763-4640
LaCour, Verdel, *YA,* Altadena Library District, Altadena CA. 213-798-0833
Lacroix, Denise, *Librn,* University of Montreal Libraries (Optometry), Montreal PQ. 514-343-7674

LaCroix, Michael, *Tech Serv,* Wright State University Library (Fordham Library, Cox Heart Institute Library & Fels Research Institute Library), Dayton OH. 513-873-2266
LaCroix, Pauline, *Asst Librn,* Merriam-Gilbert Public Library, West Brookfield MA. 617-867-8784
LaCroix, Sister M Martina, *Ref,* Saint Anthony-On-Hudson Library, Rensselaer NY. 518-463-2261
Lacy, Doug, *Ref,* Cumberland County Public Library, Anderson Street Library, Frances Brooks Stein Memorial Library, Fayetteville NC. 919-483-1580
Lacy, Jack, *AV,* University of Mississippi Library, University MS. 601-232-7091
Lacy, Linda, *Acq & Cat,* Downers Grove Public Library, Downers Grove IL. 312-960-1200
Lacy, Melissa Bauer, *Asst Dir, Tech Serv & Ref,* Arkansas State University, Beebe Branch, Abington Memorial Library, Beebe AR. 501-882-3393, Ext 33
Lacy, Samuel A, *Deputy Dir,* Queens Borough Public Library, Jamaica NY. 212-990-0700
Lada, Elaine, *Librn,* Northville Public Library, Northville MI. 313-349-3020
Lada, Lynn, *Ch,* Ericson Public Library, Boone IA. 515-432-3727, 432-7010, 432-3738
Ladak, Zofia, *ILL,* Warren Public Library, Warren MI. 313-264-8720
Ladd, Charlotte J, *Dir,* Valentine Public Library, Valentine NE. 402-376-3160
Ladd, David L, *Register of Copyrights,* Library of Congress (Order Division), Washington DC. 202-287-5000
Ladd, Diana, *Librn,* Platt Memorial Library, Shoreham VT. 802-897-2647
Ladd, Dorothy P, *Assoc Dir,* Boston University Libraries (Mugar Memorial Library), Boston MA. 617-353-3710
Ladd, Frances R, *Cat,* University of Rochester, Rush Rhees Library, Rochester NY. 716-275-4461
Ladd, Jay, *Dept Librn,* Ohio State University Libraries (William Oxley Thompson Memorial Library), Columbus OH. 614-422-6151
Ladd, Marcia, *Bibliog Instr,* Bentley College, Solomon R Baker Library, Waltham MA. 617-891-2231
Ladd, Martha W, *Ad,* Winchester Public Library, Winchester MA. 617-729-3770
Ladely, Ardis, *Librn,* Jackson County Library (Long Valley Branch), Long Valley SD. 605-837-2689
Ladion, Gertrudes J, *Librn,* San Joaquin County Law Library, Stockton CA. 209-944-2208
Ladley, Janet, *Asst Librn,* Prospect Park Free Library, Prospect Park PA. 215-532-4643
Ladley, John, *Ref,* Bowdoin College Library, Brunswick ME. 207-725-8731, Ext 281
Ladner, Mary H, *Librn,* Harrison County Law Library, Gulfport MS. 601-864-5161, Ext 336
Ladof, Nina S, *Dir,* Camden County Free Library, Voorhees NJ. 609-772-1636
Ladrach, Linda, *Librn,* Tuscarawas County Public Library (Sugarcreek Branch), Sugarcreek OH. 216-852-2813
Ladwig, Jo, *Librn,* Stephens College (Child Study), Columbia MO. 314-442-2211, Ext 428
Laeuchli, Ann, *Acq,* Temple University of the Commonwealth System of Higher Education (Law), Philadelphia PA. 215-787-7891
Lafaye, Cary, *Ref,* Midlands Technical College, Beltline Campus Library, Columbia SC. 803-782-5471, Ext 265
LaFayette, Grace, *ILL,* Moorhead State University, Livingston Lord Library, Moorhead MN. 218-236-2922
Lafayette, Patricia, *Librn,* Trenton Veterans Memorial Library, Trenton MI. 313-676-9777
Lafferty, George, *Ref,* Chester County Library & District Center, Exton PA. 215-363-0884
Laffey, Eleanor F, *Librn,* Allegany County Library (Frostburg Public), Frostburg MD. 301-689-6830
Laflamme, Sister Simonne, *Cat,* Saint Joseph's College Library, North Windham ME. 207-892-6766, Ext 24
LaFleur, Judy, *Chief Librn,* Monroe County Library System (South Rockwood Branch), South Rockwood MI. 313-379-3333
LaFleur, Thomas, *Ref,* Providence College, Phillips Memorial Library, Providence RI. 401-865-2242

LaFon, S E, *Div Head,* United States Navy (Technical Library), China Lake CA. 714-939-2507
LaFond, T, *Librn,* Field Public Library, Field ON. 705-758-6659
Lafontaine, Louise, *Librn,* Bibliotheque De Casimir, Jennings Et Appley Public Library, Saint Charles Public Library, Saint Charles ON. 705-867-5332
LaForce, Joy, *Acq,* Phillips University (John Rogers Graduate Seminary Library), Enid OK. 405-237-4433, Ext 227
LaForte, Robert, *Univ Archivist,* North Texas State University Library (University Archives), Denton TX. 817-788-2411
LaFortune, Francois, *Librn,* Musee Du Quebec, Bibliotheque des Arts, Quebec PQ. 418-643-7134
LaFortune, Madeleine F, *Librn,* Bibliotheque Municipale, Saint Jacques-de-Montcalm PQ. 514-839-3926
LaFountaine, Marian, *Ch,* Royal Oak Public Library, Royal Oak MI. 313-541-1470
LaFrance, Dorothy R, *Librn,* Newburyport Public Library, Newburyport MA. 617-462-4031
LaFrance, Pierre, *Dir,* Universite De Sherbrooke Bibliotheque (Bibliotheque Generale), Sherbrooke PQ. 819-565-5507
Lafranchi, William E, *Dir,* Indiana University of Pennsylvania, Rhodes R Stabley Library, Indiana PA. 412-357-2340
Lagano, Vincent, *Librn,* Kaiser-Permanente Medical Center, Medical Library, San Francisco CA. 415-929-4100
Lagasse, Ronald L, *Dir,* Schenectady County Public Library, Schenectady NY. 518-382-3500
Lagattuta, Joe Ann, *Librn,* Tangipahoa Parish Library (Independence Branch), Independence LA. 504-878-4109
Lage, Neva, *Asst Librn,* Elko County Library (Tuscarora Library), Tuscarora NV. 702-738-3066
Lager, Edna B, *Librn,* North Kingstown Free Library, North Kingstown RI. 401-294-2521
Lagerbloom, Mary, *Ad,* T B Scott Free Library, Merrill Public Library, Merrill WI. 715-536-7191
Lagier, Jennifer, *Librn,* Stockton-San Joaquin County Public Library (Tracy Branch), Stockton CA. 209-944-8415
Lagoo, Edna, *Librn,* Boyden Public Library, Boyden IA. 712-725-2281
LaGow, Robert, *Head Instructional Design,* University of Nebraska-Lincoln, School Media Specialist Program, NE. 402-472-3726
LaGrange, Charlene, *ILL,* Albany Medical Center College of Union University, Schaffer Library of Health Sciences, Albany NY. 518-445-5534
Lagrowe, Mary, *Bkmobile Coordr,* Lafayette Parish Public Library, Lafayette LA. 318-233-0587
LaGrutta, Charles, *Coordr,* Urban Investment & Development Co, Information Center, Chicago IL. 312-440-3296
Lague, Mark, *Media & Tech Serv,* Canton Public Library, Canton MA. 617-828-0177
Lagunowich, Dorothy, *Tech Serv,* York College of Pennsylvania Library, York PA. 717-846-7788, Ext 353
LaHatte, Greg, *Instr,* University of Georgia, Dept of Educational Media & Librarianship, GA. 404-542-3810
Lahey, Anitra, *Librn,* Psychological Service of Pittsburgh Library, Pittsburgh PA. 412-261-1333, Ext 19
Lahey, Judith A, *Assoc Librn,* University of Connecticut at Hartford (Law Library), West Hartford CT. 203-523-4841, Ext 347, 370
Lahey, Marion, *Ch,* River Forest Public Library, River Forest IL. 312-366-5205
Lahm, Craig A, *Dir,* Kaukauna Public Library, Kaukauna WI. 414-766-1812
Lahn, Sally, *Cat,* Chadron State College Library, Chadron NE. 308-432-4451, Ext 271
Lahr, Mildred A, *In Charge,* Rockwell International, Collins Division Information Center, Cedar Rapids IA. 319-395-2138
Lahti, Joyce, *Ch & Circ,* Hibbing Public Library, Hibbing MN. 218-262-1038
Lai, Janet, *Ser & Doc,* Loyola Marymount University, Charles Von Der Ahe Library, Los Angeles CA. 213-642-2788

Lai, Sheila, *Cat,* California State University, Sacramento Library, Sacramento CA. 916-454-6466

Lai, Violet L, *Librn,* Hawaii Chinese History Center Library, Honolulu HI. 808-521-5948

Lai, Yung-hsiang, *Assoc Librn,* Harvard University Library (Harvard-Yenching Library), Cambridge MA. 617-495-3327

Laidlaw, Sheila, *Sigmund Samuel Librn,* University of Toronto Libraries (University Library), Toronto ON. 416-978-2294

Lail, Dean, *Librn,* Southern Regional Education Board Library, Atlanta GA. 404-875-9211

Lain, Christine R, *Librn,* United States Air Force (Carswell Air Force Base Library), Carswell AFB TX. 817-735-5230

Lain, Virginia, *Commun Servs, Br Coordr & Bkmobile Coordr,* Warder Public Library, Springfield OH. 323-8616 & 323-9751

Laine, Esther, *Librn,* University of California, Berkeley (Entomology), Berkeley CA. 415-642-2030

Laing, A, *Sci,* Queen's University at Kingston, Douglas Library, Kingston ON. 547-5950 (Admin); 547-6992 (Chief Librn)

Laing, Harry M, *Librn,* Region V Educational Service Agency, Parkersburg WV. 304-485-6513

Laing, S, *Librn,* Okanagan Regional Library District (Keremeos Branch), Keremeos BC. 604-499-2313

Lair, Zovinar, *Media,* Malone College, Everett L Cattell Library, Canton OH. 216-454-3011, Ext 311

Laird, Ferne, *In Charge,* Calhoun County Historical Society, Museum Library, Rockwell City IA. 712-297-8307

Laird, Gertrude L, *Asst Dir & Ad,* Finger Lakes Library System, Ithaca NY. 607-273-4074

Laird, Marilyn P, *Librn,* South Suburban Genealogical & Historical Society Library, South Holland IL. 312-333-9474

Laird, Mary, *Librn,* Yuma City-County Library (Quartzsite), Quartzsite AZ. 602-782-1871

Laird, Roland, *Librn,* Brooklyn Public Library (Arlington), Brooklyn NY. 212-277-0160

Laird, Susan, *Librn,* Alza Inc, Research Library, Palo Alto CA. 415-494-5271

Laird, W David, *Dir,* University of Arizona Library, Tucson AZ. 602-626-2101

Laite, Berkeley, *Med-Currie,* Shippensburg State College, Ezra Lehman Memorial Library, Shippensburg PA. 717-532-1463

Laite, Carol, *Circ,* Shippensburg State College, Ezra Lehman Memorial Library, Shippensburg PA. 717-532-1463

Laiten, Anne, *Ch,* East Rockaway Public Library, East Rockaway NY. 516-599-1664

Laizure, David, *Syst Specialist,* Defense Intelligence Agency, Central Reference Div Library, Washington DC. 202-692-5311

LaJeunesse, Jessie, *Tech Serv,* Jacob Edwards Library, Southbridge MA. 617-764-2544

Lajeunesse, Marcel, *Assoc Prof,* University of Montreal, Ecole de Bibliotheconomie, PQ. 514-343-6044

Lajewski, Jean, *Tech Serv,* Arlington County Department of Libraries, Arlington Public Library, Arlington VA. 703-527-4777

LaJoie, Diane, *Acq,* Auburn Public Library, Auburn ME. 207-782-3191

Lake, B, *Librn,* Calgary Public Library (Shaganappi), Calgary AB. 403-249-9572

Lake, Don, *ILL & Ref,* Eastern Washington University, John F Kennedy Memorial Library, Cheney WA. 509-359-2261

Lake, Don, *On-Line Servs,* Eastern Washington University, John F Kennedy Memorial Library, Cheney WA. 509-359-2261

Lake, Dorothy, *Media,* Fisk University Library & Media Center, Nashville TN. 615-329-8730

Lake, E, *Cat,* Trent University, Thomas J Bata Library, Peterborough ON. 705-748-1550

Lake, Iris, *Librn,* Brunswick-Glynn County Regional Library (Charlton County), Nahunta GA. 912-462-5454

Lake, Patricia, *AV,* Anderson City-Anderson & Stony Creek Township Public Library, Anderson Public Library, Anderson IN. 317-644-0938

Lake, Velma, *Dir,* Duncan Public Library, Duncan OK. 405-255-0636

Lakey, Jacqueline, *Librn,* Salt Lake County Library System (Extension Div), Salt Lake City UT. 801-943-7614

Lakey, Jacqueline, *Bkmobile Coordr,* Salt Lake County Library System, Whitmore Library, Salt Lake City UT. 801-943-7614

Lakios, Andrea, *Per,* Rutgers University, the State University of New Jersey, John Cotton Dana Library, Newark NJ. 201-648-5222

Lakos, Amos, *Can Studies & Polit Sci,* University of Waterloo Library, Waterloo ON. 519-885-1211

LaLande, Wenda, *Librn,* Lennox & Addington County Public Library (Camden East Public), Camden East ON. 613-354-2585

Laliotes, Ann B, *Dir,* Franklin County Library, Louisburg NC. 919-496-4942

Lalley, John B, *Acq,* East Stroudsburg State College, Kemp Library, East Stroudsburg PA. 717-424-3467

Lally, John, *Dir,* Grand Rapids Junior College, Arthur Andrews Memorial Library, Grand Rapids MI. 616-456-4841

Lam, Silvio, *Cat,* Fairleigh Dickinson University, Friendship Library, Madison NJ. 201-377-4700, Ext 234

Lamagra, Mary, *ILL,* West New York Public Library, Philip A Payne Memorial Library, West New York NJ. 201-854-1028

Lamance, Andrew, *Librn,* Stanislaus County Free Library (Turlock Branch), Turlock CA. 209-667-1667

LaManna, Fred, *Acq,* Northbrook Public Library, Northbrook IL. 312-272-6224

LaManna, Joan M, *Librn,* Foremost Foods Co, Research & Development Library, Dublin CA. 415-828-1440, Ext 34

Lamanno, Suzanne M, *Librn,* United States Navy (Station Library), Virginia Beach VA. 804-425-2401

Lamar, Carol R, *Librn,* Poseyville Public Library, Poseyville IN. 812-874-3418

Lamar, Doris M, *Mngr Info Servs,* McKinsey & Company Library, Los Angeles CA. 213-624-1414

Lamb, Alberta C, *Librn,* Canadian Indian Rights Commission, Ottawa ON. 613-995-9585

Lamb, Anne L, *Ch,* Mystic & Noank Library, Inc, Mystic CT. 203-536-7721

Lamb, Autie, *Librn,* Crowley Ridge Regional Library (Lepanto Branch), Lepanto AR. 501-475-2713

Lamb, Beverly, *Librn,* Episcopal Church Center, Bishops Library, Burlington VT. 802-862-2411

Lamb, Beverly, *Librn,* Port Townsend Public Library, Port Townsend WA. 206-385-3181

Lamb, Cheryl, *Librn,* American Can Co, Neenah Technical Center, Research & Development Library, Neenah WI. 414-729-8169

Lamb, Connie, *On-Line Servs,* Brigham Young University, Harold B Lee Library, Provo UT. 801-378-2905

Lamb, Daryle, *Librn,* Greensboro Public Librar (Benjamin), Greensboro NC. 919-288-1956

Lamb, David J, *Circ & Reserved Bks,* University of Wisconsin-Platteville, Elton S Karrmann Library, Platteville WI. 608-342-1688

Lamb, David J, *Engineering, Sci & Tech,* University of Wisconsin-Platteville, Elton S Karrmann Library, Platteville WI. 608-342-1688

Lamb, Dee Anne, *Dir,* Clark Memorial Library, Shannock RI. 401-364-6100

Lamb, Donald K, *Coordr,* Dane County Library Service, Madison WI. 608-266-6388

Lamb, Gail, *Libr Technician,* San Diego County Library (Valley Center Branch), Valley Center CA. 714-749-1305

Lamb, Gertrude, *Dir & Bibliog Instr,* Hartford Hospital Health Science Libraries, Hartford CT. 203-524-2971

Lamb, Harriet, *YA,* Timberland Regional Library, Olympia WA. 206-943-5001

Lamb, Jerome D, *Asst Dir,* Fargo Public Library, Fargo ND. 701-241-1490

Lamb, John, *ILL & Pub Serv,* Episcopal Divinity School, Sherrill Hall Library, Cambridge MA. 617-868-3450, Ext 31

Lamb, John, *Pub Servs,* Weston School of Theology Library, Cambridge MA. 617-868-3450, Ext 31

Lamb, Jolaine, *Librn,* United States Air Force (Beale Air Force Base Library), Beale AFB CA. 916-634-2706

Lamb, Kathleen, *On-Line Servs,* Fluor Engineers & Constructors, Design Engineering Library, Irvine CA. 714-975-3238

Lamb, Lillian, *Ch,* Nelson County Public Library, Bardstown KY. 502-348-3714

Lamb, Norma, *Dir,* Gulfport Public Library, Gulfport FL. 813-347-0218

Lamb, Norma Jean, *Music,* Buffalo & Erie County Public Library System, Buffalo NY. 716-856-7525

Lamb, Opal D, *Librn,* Mankato City Library, Mankato KS. 913-378-3885

Lamb, Sara G, *Librn,* C F Industries Inc Library, Long Grove IL. 312-438-9500

Lamb, Susan, *Vice Pres for Develop & External Affairs,* New York Public Library, Astor, Lenox & Tilden Foundations Library, New York NY. 212-790-6262

Lambers, Stephen, *Ref,* Calvin College & Seminary Library, Grand Rapids MI. 616-949-4000, Ext 297

Lambert, Barbara, *Tech Serv,* Somers Library, Somers NY. 914-277-3420

Lambert, Beverly, *Librn,* Portland Public Library (Talking Books Department), Portland ME. 207-773-4761

Lambert, Carol, *Media,* Anna Maria College Library, Paxton MA. 617-757-4586, Ext 56

Lambert, Claire, *Librn,* Jesup Memorial Library, Bar Harbor ME. 207-288-4245

Lambert, Eleanor N, *Librn,* Taylorville Public Library, Taylorville IL. 217-824-4736

Lambert, Guy R, *Assoc Librn & Bibliog Instr,* Elon College, Iris Holt McEwen Library, Elon College NC. 919-584-9711, Ext 230 or 242

Lambert, Helene D, *Librn,* New Rochelle Hospital Medical Center, J M Perley Health Science Library, New Rochelle NY. 914-632-5000, Ext 257

Lambert, Irma, *Cat,* Burbank Public Library, Burbank CA. 213-847-9744

Lambert, Lois, *Librn,* Pacific Telephone Company Library, San Francisco CA. 415-542-2896

Lambert, Madeline C, *Tech Serv,* Hospital Sainte-Justine, Centre d'Information Sur La Sante de L'Enfant, Montreal PQ. 514-731-4931, Ext 339

Lambert, Nancy, *Supvr,* 3M (Patents & Profiles), Saint Paul MN. 612-733-7670

Lambert, Nancy S, *Librn,* Yale University Library (Art), New Haven CT. 203-436-0307

Lambert, Pattie, *Acq,* Thomas Hackney Braswell Memorial Library, Rocky Mount NC. 442-1937 & 442-1951

Lambert, Peggy B, *Librn,* Duke Power Co, David Nabow Library, Charlotte NC. 704-373-4095

Lambert, Toni, *Ch,* League City Public Library, League City TX. 713-554-6612

Lambert, Jr, Alloyd P, *Librn,* William Carey College (Mather Library), New Orleans LA. 601-582-5051, Ext 245 & 246

Lambert, Jr, Alloyd P, *Regional Librn,* William Carey College, School of Nursing Library, New Orleans LA. 504-899-9311, Ext 1402

Lambert, Jr, Fred L, *Tech Serv & Acq,* Augusta College, Reese Library, Augusta GA. 404-828-4566, 828-4066

Lamberts, Irina, *Librn,* United States Navy (Medical Library), Long Beach CA. 213-420-5287

Lambkin, Claire A, *Chief Librn,* American Management Associations Library, New York NY. 212-586-8100, Ext 173, 174

Lambremont, Jane A, *Librn,* Earl K Long Hospital, Medical Library, Baton Rouge LA. 504-356-3361, Ext 400

Lambright, Maxie J, *Dir,* Defiance College, Anthony Wayne Library & Instructional Resource Ctr, Defiance OH. 419-784-4010, Ext 132-135

Lambrix, Dorothy, *Asst Librn,* Eden Free Library, Eden NY. 716-992-4028

Lambros, Nicholas, *Librn,* Annunciation Greek Orthodox Church Library, Cranston RI. 401-942-4188

Lambson, Annette, *Dir,* Clark College Library, Vancouver WA. 206-699-0251

Lameier, Carole, *Ad,* Riviera Beach Public Library, Riviera Beach FL. 305-845-4194, 845-4195, 845-4196

Lamers, Claire, *Librn,* New York Genealogical & Biographical Society Library, New York NY. 212-755-8532

Lamirande, Armand, *Dir,* College Militaire Royal De Saint-Jean Library, Saint Jean PQ. 514-346-2131, Ext 606; 878-1962 Ext 606

Lamm, Charlot, *Dir,* Morris Plains Library, Morris Plains NJ. 201-538-2599

Lamm, Kathryn, *Tech Serv,* Scottsdale Community College Library, Scottsdale AZ. 602-941-0999

Lamm, Peggy, *Dir,* Wilson County Public Library (Lucama Branch), Lucama NC. 919-237-3818

Lammers, Alice, *Rare Bks,* Central College, Geisler Learning Resource Center, Pella IA. 515-628-4151, Ext 233

Lammers, Beatrice, *Actg Librn,* Dwyer-Mercer County District Library (Saint Henry & Granville Township Branch), St Henry OH. 419-586-2314

Lammers, Dorothy, *Librn,* Public Library of Columbus & Franklin County (Clintonville), Columbus OH. 614-262-3955

Lamonde, Francine, *Ref,* Bibliotheque Nationale Du Quebec, Montreal PQ. 514-873-4553

Lamonde, Yvon, *In Charge,* Centre D'etudes Canadiennes Francaises, Bibliotheque, Montreal PQ. 514-392-5200

LaMont, Barbara, *Librn,* Vassar College Library, Poughkeepsie NY. 914-452-7000

Lamont, Bridget, *Assoc Dir Libr Develop,* Illinois State Library, Springfield IL. 217-782-2994

Lamont, Joyce H, *Spec Coll & Rare Bks,* University of Alabama, Amelia Gayle Gorgas Library, University AL. 205-348-5298

Lamont, Martha, *Librn,* Kirkland Public Library, Kirkland IL. 815-522-6260

Lamont, Mary Lou, *Tech Serv,* Centennial College of Applied Arts & Technology, Resource Centre, Scarborough ON. 416-439-7180

Lamont, Ruth, *Homebound & Outreach Servs,* Shelter Rock Public Library, Albertson NY. 516-248-7363

Lamont, Sylvia, *Dir,* Los Angeles Harbor College Library, Wilmington CA. 213-518-1000, Ext 292 & 293

Lamontagne, Don L, *Librn,* Pineland Center Library, Pownal ME. 207-688-4811, Ext 205

Lamoreaux, Shirley, *Asst Librn,* Community College of Allegheny County, Boyce Campus Library, Monroeville PA. 412-327-1327, Ext 312

LaMothe, Louise, *Librn,* New Orleans Public Library (Algiers Point), New Orleans LA. 504-366-8527

LaMourea, Jeanette, *Librn,* Jackson Public Library, Jackson MN. 507-847-4748

Lamoureux, Jacquelyn, *Librn,* Hope Library, Hope RI. 401-821-7910

Lampe, Saundra, *Librn,* Pikes Peak Regional Library District (Ute Pass), Cascade CO. 303-684-9342

Lampel, Ruth R, *Librn,* Jamestown Public Library, Jamestown RI. 401-423-0436

Lampel, Ruth R, *Librn,* Jamestown Public Library (Jamestown Museum), Jamestown RI. 401-423-0784

Lamphere, Dawn M, *Dir,* Margaret Reaney Memorial Library, Saint Johnsville NY. 518-568-7822

Lampshire, Laura, *Librn,* Mesa County Public Library (Clifton Branch), Clifton CO. 303-434-9936

Lamrey, Helen, *Supv Info Serv,* PPG Industries Inc (Coatings & Resins Research Center Library), Allison Park PA. 412-487-4500

Lamsback, Sheila, *Librn,* Kern County Library (Mohave Branch), Mohave CA. 805-861-2130

Lamson, Merle E, *Assoc Prof,* Brigham Young University, School of Library & Information Sciences, UT. 801-378-2976

Lana, Jr, A W, *Dir,* Fansteel Inc Library, North Chicago IL. 312-689-4900

Lancaster, Edith, *Dir,* Northwest Nazarene College, Riley Library, Nampa ID. 208-467-8605

Lancaster, Elizabeth, *Librn,* Howard County Library (Wilde Lake), Columbia MD. 301-730-8848

Lancaster, F W, *Prof,* University of Illinois, Graduate School of Library Science, IL. 217-333-3280

Lancaster, Jane, *Librn,* Winfield Public Library, Winfield KS. 316-221-4460

Lancaster, Jo Ann, *Asst Librn,* Seguin-Guadalupe County Public Library, Seguin TX. 512-379-1531

Lancaster, John, *Spec Coll & Archivist,* Amherst College, Robert Frost Library, Amherst MA. 413-542-2212

Lancaster, Kay J, *Dir,* Burr Oak Public Library, Burr Oak MI. 616-489-2906

Lancaster, Kevin, *Librn,* New Mexico State Supreme Court Law Library, Santa Fe NM. 505-827-2515

Lancaster, Marianne, *Ext Librn,* Monroe County Public Library, Key West FL. 305-294-7100

Lancaster, Olive, *Librn,* Fairview College Learning Resources Centre, Fairview AB. 403-835-2213, Ext 28

Lancaster, Richard F, *Coordr,* John Tyler Community College Library, Chester VA. 804-748-6481, Ext 251

Lancaster, Serena, *Acq,* Colgate University, Everett Needham Case Library, Hamilton NY. 315-824-1000

Lance, David I, *Dir,* Linden Free Public Library, Linden NJ. 201-486-3888

Lancier, Kathryn, *Librn,* Babcock & Wilcox Co, Corporate Library, New York NY. 212-687-6700, Ext 236

Land, Iris L, *Chief Librn,* Air Canada Library, Montreal PQ. 514-874-4841

Land, Mary, *Librn,* Saint Catharines Public Library (Pen Centre), Saint Catharines ON. 416-682-3568

Land, Phyllis M, *Dir,* Department of Public Instruction, Professional Library, Indianapolis IN. 317-927-0295

Land, R B, *Dir,* Ontario Legislative Library, Research & Information Services, Toronto ON. 416-965-4545

Land, Rosabelle, *Dir & Bibliog Instr,* Wood Junior College, Wood Memorial Library, Mathiston MS. 601-263-5352

Landau, Edith, *Tech Serv,* Pacific Lutheran University, Robert A L Mortvedt Library, Tacoma WA. 206-531-6900, Ext 301

Landau, Elaine, *Dir,* Tuckahoe Public Library, Tuckahoe NY. 914-961-2121

Landau, Elvita, *ILL & Circ,* Kansas Wesleyan, Memorial Library, Salina KS. 913-827-5541, Ext 233

Landau, Elvita, *Tech Serv,* Salina Public Library, Salina KS. 913-825-4624

Landau, Rebecca, *Librn,* Toronto Jewish Congress, Jewish Public Library of Toronto, Toronto ON. 416-781-6282, 781-8065

Landau, Zuki, *Chief Librn,* School of Visual Arts Library, New York NY. 679-7350 Ext 67, 68

Lande, Barbara, *Librn,* Porter Medical Center Inc, Medical Library & Information Service, Middlebury VT. 802-388-7901, Ext 215

Landeck, Mary, *Ref,* Milwaukee Area Technical College, Rasche Memorial Library, Milwaukee WI. 414-278-6205

Landeen, Jane, *Commun Servs,* Rock Springs Public Library, Rock Springs WY. 307-362-6212

Landenberger, Paul, *Acq,* Central Michigan University, Charles V Park Library, Mount Pleasant MI. 517-774-3500

Lander, Dorothy J, *Dir,* Ossining Public Library, Ossining NY. 941-2416; 941-9174

Lander, Dorothy M, *Order,* Public Library of the District of Columbia, Martin Luther King Memorial Library, Washington DC. 202-727-1101

Lander, James H, *Libr Mgr,* Dubuque (Iowa) Area Library Consortium, IA. 319-588-8140

Lander, James H, *In Charge,* Mercy Health Center, Anthony C Pfohl Health Science Library, Dubuque IA. 319-588-8140

Lander, Sarah S, *Asst Dir & Collection Develop,* Pickens County Library, Easley SC. 803-859-9679

Landergan, Kathe, *Librn,* Lynn Public Library (Shute Branch), Lynn MA. 617-593-5539

Landers, Alison B, *Talking Books Librn,* Orlando Public Library, Orlando FL. 305-425-4694

Landers, Doris W, *Librn,* Jonathan Bourne Public Library (Pocasset Branch), Pocasset MA. 617-563-6577

Landers, Katherine, *Librn,* Church of the Holy Faith, Episcopal, Parish Library, Santa Fe NM. 505-982-4447

Landers, Lora, *Dep Dir,* Hennepin County Library, Edina MN. 612-830-4944

Landers, Patty, *Ad,* Irving Public Library System, Irving TX. 214-253-2639

Landers, Susan, *Librn,* Claremore Junior College, Thunderbird Library, Claremore OK. 918-341-7510, Ext 278

Landes, Edythe M, *Dir,* Stratford Library Association, Stratford CT. 203-378-7345

Landfield, Jean, *Asst Librn,* Veterans Administration, Hospital Library, Lincoln NE. 402-489-3802

Landgraf, Elizabeth, *Ad,* Kirkwood Public Library, Kirkwood MO. 314-821-5770

Landis, Lois, *Acq,* Dickinson College, Boyd Lee Spahr Library, Carlisle PA. 717-245-1396

Landis, Marjorie W, *Librn,* United States Department of Health & Human Services, Region VIII Library, Denver CO. 303-837-5949

Landis, Mary, *Librn,* Newport Public Library, Newport PA. 717-567-6860

Landon, Richard, *Rare Bks,* University of Toronto Libraries (University Library), Toronto ON. 416-978-2294

Landram, Christina L, *Cat,* Georgia State University, William Russell Pullen Library, Atlanta GA. 404-658-2185, 658-2172

Landress, Sylvia, *Dir,* Zionist Archives & Library, New York NY. 212-753-2167

Landreville, L P, *Librn,* Canada Department of Supply & Services Library, Ottawa ON. 613-997-6363

Landriault, R, *French Lang Servs,* Algonquin Regional Library System, Parry Sound ON. 705-746-9161

Landrum, Carolyn, *Ch,* Spartanburg County Public Library, Spartanburg SC. 582-4123 & 585-2441

Landrum, John H, *Reader Serv,* South Carolina State Library, Columbia SC. 803-758-3181

Landry, Anne, *Ch,* Saugus Public Library, Saugus MA. 617-233-0530

Landry, Frances G, *Librn,* New Liskeard Public Library, New Liskeard ON. 705-647-4215

Landry, Muriel, *YA,* Lewiston Public Library, Lewiston ME. 207-784-0135

Landry, Muriel, *Librn,* Lewiston Public Library (Subregional Library for the Blind & Physically Handicapped), Lewiston ME. 207-783-2331

Landsverk, Jan, *Dir,* Austin Community College Library, Austin MN. 507-437-6691

Landtroop, Ann, *Coordr, Spec Admin Project,* Houston Public Library, Houston TX. 713-224-5441

Landweber, Martin, *Media,* Peninsula Public Library, Lawrence NY. 516-239-3262

Landwehr, Lois E, *Librn,* Americus Township Library, Americus KS. 316-884-5503

Landwirth, Trudy, *Librn,* Methodist Medical Center of Illinois (Medical Library), Peoria IL. 309-672-4937

Lane, A, *Circ & Per,* Northern Montana College Library, Havre MT. 406-265-7821, Ext 3306, 3307

Lane, Alfred, *Gifts & Exchange,* Columbia University (University Libraries), New York NY. 212-280-2241

Lane, Anna R, *Librn,* Pontiac Public Library, Pontiac MI. 313-857-7767

Lane, Billie Jean, *Tech Serv,* Craft Memorial Library, Mercer County Service Center, Bluefield WV. 304-325-3943

Lane, Carol, *Librn,* Burnaby Municipal Library (Crest Neighbourhood), Burnaby BC. 604-522-4115

Lane, Carol, *Ch,* Plant City Public Library, Plant City FL. 813-752-8685, 752-7942

Lane, Catherine, *Cat,* Baltimore Museum of Art Library, Baltimore MD. 301-396-6317

Lane, Christine, *ILL, Media & Tech Serv,* Oyster Bay-East Norwich Public Library, Oyster Bay NY. 516-922-1212

Lane, David O, *Dir,* Hunter College of the City University of New York Library, New York NY. 212-570-5511

Lane, David T, *Bibliog Instr,* New York State Office of Mental Health, Psychiatric Institute Research Library, New York NY. 212-568-4000

Lane, Eileen L, *Librn,* General Motors Corp, AC Spark Plug Div, Engineering Library, Flint MI. 313-766-2655

Lane, Elizabeth J, *Assoc Dean Learning Resource Center,* Genesee Community College, Alfred C O'Connell Library, Batavia NY. 716-343-0055, Ext 350

Lane, Elizabeth L, *Librn,* United States Navy (Naval Air Station Library), Alameda CA. 415-869-2519

Lane, Helen I, *Actg Librn,* Lewis County Law Library, Chehalis WA. 206-748-9121, Ext 171

Lane, Joyce, *Librn,* United States Department of the Navy (Naval Military Personnel Command, Technical Library), Washington DC. 202-694-2073, Code 11, Ext 42073

Lane, Judith, *ILL & Ref,* Mountain-Valley Library System, Sacramento CA. 916-444-0926

Lane, Laura, *Librn,* American Heritage Publishing Co Library, New York NY. 212-399-8930

Lane, Mrs Byron S, *Dir,* Roxbury Public Library, Succasunna NJ. 201-584-2400, 584-2401

Lane, Mrs J E, *Dir,* University of King's College Library, Halifax NS. 902-422-1271

Lane, Nina M, *Dir,* Group Health Association of America, Gertrude Sturges Memorial Library, Washington DC. 202-483-4012

Lane, Robert B, *Dir,* United States Air Force, Air University Library, Maxwell AFB AL. 205-293-2888

Lane, Rosemary, *Dir,* Albuquerque Public Library, Albuquerque NM. 505-766-7882

Lane, Sister Mary B, *Librn,* Historical Foundation of the Presbyterian & Reformed Churches Library, Montreat NC. 704-669-7061

Lane, Walker, *ILL,* Corpus Christi State University Library, Corpus Christi TX. 512-991-6810, Ext 242

Lane, William T, *Ref & Bibliog Instr,* State University of New York College at Geneseo, Milne Library, Geneseo NY. 716-245-5591

Lane, Jr, C Gardner, *Dir,* Penobscot Marine Museum, Lincoln Colcord Memorial Library, Searsport ME. 207-548-6634

Lanerhass, Ludwig, *Latin American Studies,* University of California Los Angeles Library, Los Angeles CA. 213-825-1201

Laners, Dolores, *Librn,* Clark College Library, Vancouver WA. 206-699-0251

Lanese, Lewis L, *Asst Librn,* Bridgeport Public Library, Bridgeport CT. 203-576-7777

Laney, Mary, *Librn,* Chesterfield County Library (Matheson Memorial), Cheraw SC. 803-623-7489

Lang, Anita, *Librn,* Our Lady of the Lake University Libraries (Saint Martin Hall), San Antonio TX. 512-434-6711, Ext 283

Lang, Anna Mary, *Librn,* Combs College of Music Library, Philadelphia PA. 215-848-7500

Lang, Curtis E, *Ref,* San Diego City College Library, San Diego CA. 714-238-1181, Ext 250

Lang, David W, *Librn,* Wilkes & Artis, Chartered, Law Library, Washington DC. 202-457-7872

Lang, Delores, *In Charge,* Howard Lake Library, Howard Lake MN. 612-543-2020

Lang, George W, *Admin,* North American Baptist Seminary, Kaiser-Ramaker Library, Sioux Falls SD. 605-336-6805, Ext 8

Lang, Georgy, *Ref,* Boston College Libraries (Law Library), Chestnut Hill MA. 617-969-0100, Ext 4405

Lang, Helen C, *Chief Librn,* Free Public Library, Rowley MA. 617-948-2850

Lang, Hilda, *Librn,* Suffolk County Community College (Selden Campus Library), Selden NY. 516-233-5181

Lang, Isa, *Asst Librn & On-Line Servs,* University of Utah (Law Library), Salt Lake City UT. 801-581-6438

Lang, Janice, *Tech Serv,* Wisconsin Department of Public Instruction (Reference & Loan Library), Madison WI. 608-266-1053

Lang, Jean, *Spec Coll,* State University of New York, Agricultural & Technical College at Alfred, Walter C Hinkle Memorial Library, Alfred NY. 607-871-6313

Lang, Jovian P, *Assoc Prof,* Saint John's University, Div of Library & Information Science, NY. 212-969-8000, Ext 200

Lang, Juanita, *Librn,* Broken Bow Public Library, Broken Bow NE. 308-872-2927

Lang, Lebby, *Bus Coll,* Greensboro Public Library, Greensboro NC. 373-2474; 373-2471

Lang, Leona, *Librn,* Pasqua Hospital Library, Regina SK. 306-527-9641

Lang, Martha, *Ad,* Monroeville Public Library, Monroeville PA. 412-372-0500

Lang, Nancy, *Ch,* Kenton County Public Library, Covington KY. 606-292-2363

Lang, Norman, *Tech Serv & Per,* Quinnipiac College Library, Hamden CT. 203-288-5251, Ext 271

Lang, Rosalie A, *Supv of Gen Libr,* Boston Public Library, Eastern Massachusetts Library System, Boston MA. 617-536-5400

Lang, Sister Franz, *Dir,* Barry College, Monsignor William Barry Memorial Library, Miami Shores FL. 305-758-3392, Ext 263

Lang, Sister Regine, *Librn,* Saint Francis Hospital, Health Sciences Library, La Crosse WI. 608-785-0940, Ext 2685

Langan, Damasus, *ILL,* Saint Meinrad College & School of Theology, Archabbey Library, Saint Meinrad IN. 812-357-6611, Ext 401

Langan, Diane, *Cat,* A Holmes Johnson Memorial Library, Kodiak Public Library, Kodiak AK. 907-486-3312

Langan, Sister M Florence, *Lectr,* Marywood College, Dept of Librarianship, PA. 717-342-6521

Langdon, Bruce E, *Dir,* Palos Verdes Library District, Palos Verdes Peninsula CA. 213-541-2559, 2550

Langdon, James H, *Acq,* University of Alabama in Birmingham, Mervyn H Sterne Library, Birmingham AL. 205-934-6360

Langdon, Jean, *Instr,* Saint Mary of the Plains College, Library Science Program, KS. 316-225-4171, Ext 68

Lange, Clifford E, *State Librn,* New Mexico State Library, Santa Fe NM. 505-827-2033

Lange, Cora, *Ch,* Newfoundland Area Public Library, Newfoundland PA. 717-676-4518

Lange, Elizabeth A, *Asst Dir & Tech Serv,* University of South Carolina, Thomas Cooper Library, Columbia SC. 803-777-3142

Lange, John, *Media,* College of Saint Catherine, Saint Catherine Library, Saint Paul MN. 612-690-6650

Lange, Linda, *Tech Serv & Cat,* Clearwater Public Library, Clearwater FL. 813-462-6800

Lange, Margaret, *ILL,* Wheeler Basin Regional Library, Decatur Public Library, Decatur AL. 205-353-2993

Lange, R Thomas, *Chief Med Libr,* University of South Carolina (School of Medicine Library), Columbia SC. 803-777-4858

Langelan, Severine L, *Librn,* United States Army Medical Center (Post-Patients' Library), Washington DC. 202-576-1314

Langen, John S, *Librn,* University of Alabama (Science), University AL. 205-348-5959

Langenkamp, Stephanie, *Pub Servs,* San Marcos Public Library, San Marcos TX. 512-392-8124

Langer, Esme, *Librn,* Winnipeg Free Press Library, Winnipeg MB. 204-943-9361

Langer, Frank, *Acq & Cat,* Clarksburg-Harrison Public Library, Clarksburg WV. 304-624-6512, 624-6513

Langford, Bill, *Media,* Southwestern Baptist Theological Seminary, Fleming Library, Fort Worth TX. 817-923-1921, Ext 277

Langford, Kay, *Bkmobile Coordr,* Lowndes County Library System, Columbus Public Library, Columbus MS. 601-328-1056

Langille, Mrs G, *Branch Assistant,* Cumberland Regional Library (Springhill Branch), Springhill NS. 902-597-2211

Langiotti, Sister M Edith, *Per,* Mercyhurst College Learning Resource Center, Erie PA. 814-864-0681, Ext 228, 234

Langkabel, Carol, *Ch,* Plymouth Public Library, Plymouth WI. 414-892-4416

Langkau, Claire Marie, *Librn,* Union Carbide Corp, Battery Products Div Technical Information Center, Cleveland OH. 216-631-3100, Ext 367

Langley, Sam, *Librn,* First Christian Church, Adult Library, Columbia MO. 314-443-3317

Langlois, Lorraine, *Librn,* Newark Public Library (Emerson R Miller Branch), Newark OH. 614-344-2858

Langlois, Nancy R, *Librn,* McIntosh Junior College, Dover NH. 603-742-3518

Langsdorf, Betty G, *Dir,* Upper Moreland Free Public Library, Willow Grove PA. 215-659-3638

Langsley, Arleta, *Librn,* Baker County Public Library (Huntington Branch), Huntington OR. 503-523-6414, 523-6419

Langston, Carol, *Asst Librn,* Kimberley Public Library, Kimberley BC. 604-427-3112

Langston, Helen, *Librn,* Springfield-Greene County Library (Brentwood Branch), Springfield MO. 417-881-2840

Langston, Nancy, *Actg Dir, Acq & Ref,* Roswell Public Library, Roswell NM. 505-622-7101

Langston, Pamela, *ILL,* Rock Island Public Library, Rock Island IL. 309-788-7627

Langston, Patsy, *Br Asst,* Morehouse Parish Library (Collinston Branch), Collinston LA. 318-281-3683

Langton, Mary G, *Librn,* Boston Public Library (Hospital Library Services), Boston MA. 617-424-4578

Langworthy, Donald, *Dir,* Inver Hills Community College, Learning Resource Center, Inver Grove Heights MN. 612-455-9621, Ext 58

Langworthy, Donald, *Sciences,* Inver Hills Community College, Learning Resource Center, Inver Grove Heights MN. 612-455-9621, Ext 58

Lanier, Bob R, *Dir,* Graham Public Library, Graham TX. 817-549-0600

Lanier, Delores, *Librn,* Colorado Legislative Council Library, Denver CO. 303-839-3521

Lanier, Gene D, *Chmn,* East Carolina University, Dept of Library Science, NC. 919-757-6621, 757-6627

Lanier, Glenna, *Librn,* Surry County-Dobson Library, Dobson NC. 919-386-8208

Lanier, Ruby B, *Librn,* Tallassee Community Library, Tallassee AL. 205-283-2732

Lanktree, Mrs B, *Dir,* Saint Jerome's College Library, Waterloo ON. 519-884-8110, Ext 52

Lanman, Ella, *Librn,* Gulf-Coast Bible College, Charles Ewing Brown Library, Houston TX. 713-862-3800

Lanmon, Linda F, *Instrnl Develop & Graphics Supv,* University of Southern Mississippi (Teaching-Learning Resources Center), Hattiesburg MS. 601-266-7307

Lannan, Paul A, *Dir,* Catholic Information Centre Library, Toronto ON. 416-534-2326

Lanning, Dixie M, *Librn,* Bethany College, Wallerstedt Library, Lindsborg KS. 913-227-3311, Ext 165

Lanning, Glendora, *ILL,* Webster Groves Public Library, Webster Groves MO. 314-961-3784

Lannom, Patricia H, *Chief Librn,* Lindsey Hopkins Technical Education Center Library, Miami FL. 305-350-3431

Lannon, Geneva, *Librn,* Kansas City Public Library (Blue Valley), Kansas City MO. 816-231-5924

Lano, Joan, *In Charge,* Long Prairie Library, Long Prairie MN. 612-732-2332

Lanou, Janice, *Asst Librn,* Wheeler Memorial Library, Orange MA. 617-544-2295

Lanphear, Lucy M, *Coordr,* Saint Petersburg Junior College, Michael M Bennett Library Processing Center, Pinellas Park FL. 813-546-0021

Lanphere, Alyce, *ILL,* Gloversville Free Library, Gloversville NY. 518-725-2819

Lanphier, Margaret, *Media,* City College of San Francisco Library, San Francisco CA. 415-239-3404

Lansberg, Helen R, *Librn,* Institute of Living, Medical Library, Hartford CT. 203-278-7950, Ext 412

Lansdale, Mary Ann, *YA,* Greenburgh Public Library, Elmsford NY. 914-682-5265

Lansdale, Metta T, *Librn,* Saint Joseph Mercy Hospital, Riecker Memorial Library, Ann Arbor MI. 313-572-3045

Lansing, Lurline, *Librn,* Pike-Amite-Walthall Library System (Magnolia Public), Magnolia MS. 601-783-3212

Lantelme, Claudia, *ILL,* Adelphi University Library, Garden City NY. 516-294-8700

Lantis, Barbara, *Ch,* Great River Regional Library, Saint Cloud MN. 612-251-7282

Lanto, Enid G, *On-Line Servs & Bibliog Instr,* San Bernardino Valley College, Samuel E Andrews Memorial Library, San Bernardino CA. 714-888-6511, Ext 237

Lantz, Conni, *Commun Servs,* Pottsville Free Public Library, Pottsville Library District Center, Pottsville PA. 622-8105; 622-8880

Lanum, Maxine, *Br Coordr,* Albany County Public Library, Laramie WY. 307-745-3365

Lanzim, Acq, Ocean County Library, Toms River NJ. 201-349-6200

Lanzino, Catherine, *Librn,* Dauphin County Law Library, Harrisburg PA. 717-234-7001

Lanzisera, Frances, *Librn,* Adria Laboratories, Inc, Library Research Center, Plain City OH. 614-889-9759

Lapaglia, Anne, *Librn,* Lum, Biunno & Tompkins Law Library, Newark NJ. 201-622-2300

Lapalme, Suzette, *Asst Librn,* Bibliotheque De Casimir, Jennings Et Appley Public Library, Saint Charles Public Library, Saint Charles ON. 705-867-5332

Lape, Jane M, *Librn,* Fort Ticonderoga Association, Inc Library, Ticonderoga NY. 518-585-2821

Lapensee, Judith, *Librn,* Frontenac County Library (Arden Branch), Arden ON. 613-335-2511

LaPerla, Susan, *Librn,* National Institute of Justice Library, Washington DC. 202-862-2900

Laperriere, Jerome, *Dir,* Seminaire Saint Joseph Library, Trois Rivieres PQ. 819-378-5167

Lapham, Tonia, *Librn,* Boston Educational Research Inc, Boston MA. 617-227-4200

Lapicola, Valerie, *Dir,* Matheson Memorial Library, Elkhorn WI. 414-723-2678

Lapidus, Cecelia L, *Librn,* Sinai Temple, Blumenthal Library, Los Angeles CA. 213-474-1518

Lapierre, Maurice E, *Asst Dean,* University of Alabama, Amelia Gayle Gorgas Library, University AL. 205-348-5298

LaPlante, A S, *Dir,* Mattapoisett Free Public Library, Mattapoisett MA. 617-758-2213

LaPlante, Mrs Leroy H, *In Charge,* First Congregational Church Library, Auburn MA. 617-832-2845

LaPlante, Ola, *Librn,* Lowell Public Library, Lowell VT. 802-744-2488

LaPlume, Sister Mary Kathleen, *Lectr,* Felician College, Dept of Library Science, IL. 312-539-2328

Lapointe, Ginette, *Librn,* Bibliotheque Municipale, Terrebonne PQ. 514-471-4042

LaPointe, Madeleine, *Libr Tech,* Sheridan College of Applied Arts & Technology Library (School of Crafts & Design), Mississauga ON. 416-845-9430, Ext 166

LaPointe, Ruth M, *Librn,* United States Army (Groninger Library), Fort Eustis VA. 804-878-5251

LaPorte, Sister Margaret, *Librn & Pub Servs,* Columbus Hospital, Health Science Library, Great Falls MT. 406-727-3333, Ext 541

Lapow, Beth, *Acq,* College of Medicine & Dentistry of New Jersey, George F Smith Library of the Health Sciences, Newark NJ. 201-456-4580

Lapp, Mrs D, *Libr Tech,* Canada Department of the Environment, Wildlife Service, Prairie Migratory Bird Research Centre Library, Saskatoon SK. 306-665-4096

Lapp, Natalie, *Dir, Tech Serv & Cat,* Lynbrook Public Library, Lynbrook NY. 516-599-8630

LaQuay, Edwin G, *Librn,* Mobay Chemical Corp, Research Center Library, Pittsburgh PA. 412-923-2700

Laramy, Ercel, *Librn,* Jackson District Library (Brooklyn Branch), Brooklyn MI. 517-592-8031

Larason, Larry D, *Dir,* Northeast Louisiana University, Sandel Library, Monroe LA. 318-342-2195

Laraway, Nell, *Govt Doc,* West Virginia Library Commission, Science & Cultural Center, Charleston WV. 304-348-2041

Larcom, Leslie A, *Librn,* Green Free Library, Canton PA. 717-673-5744

Lardieri, Anthony, *Librn,* Newark Public Library (North End), Newark NJ. 201-733-7766

Lareau, Carolyn, *Librn,* Piper & Marbury, Law Library, Baltimore MD. 301-539-2530

Large, Alfred P, *AV,* Indiana University at South Bend Library, South Bend IN. 219-237-4440

Large, Anna, *Acq,* Jacksonville University, Carl S Swisher Library, Jacksonville FL. 904-744-3950, Ext 266, 267

Largent, Millie, *Librn,* West Coast Bible College, McBrayer Library, Fresno CA. 209-299-7205

LaRiccia, Louise, *Librn,* Goodyear Aerospace Corp Library, Akron OH. 216-794-2557

Larin, C, *Dir,* Des Moines Area Community College, Boone Campus Library, Boone IA. 515-432-7203, Ext 34

Larison, Phyllis, *Media, Ref & Spec Coll,* Edwin A Bemis Public Library, Littleton Public Library, Littleton CO. 303-795-3826

Larison, Ruth A, *Librn,* National Park Service Library, Lakewood CO. 303-234-4443

Lark, Gary, *Asst Dir & Tech Serv,* North Bend Public Library, North Bend OR. 503-756-6712

Larkin, Mary, *Librn,* McDowell Public Library (Kimball Branch), Kimball WV. 304-436-3070

Larkin, Mary, *Librn,* Prince Edward Island Provincial Library (Saint Peters Branch), Saint Peters PE. 902-892-3504, Ext 54

Larkin, Olive, *Tech Serv, Acq & Cat,* Barry-Lawrence Regional Library, Monett MO. 417-235-6646

Larkin, Patrick J, *Librn,* Iona College, Ryan Library, New Rochelle NY. 914-636-2100

Larkin, Sheila A, *Librn,* Fitchburg Law Library, Fitchburg MA. 617-345-6726

Larkins, Rosemary M, *Librn,* Ohio Industrial Commission (Reference Library), Columbus OH. 614-466-7388

LaRoache, Roger J, *Librn,* United States Department of Commerce, Miami District Office Library, Miami FL. 305-350-5267

LaRocca, Regina, *District Consult,* New Castle Public Library, New Castle PA. 412-658-6659

LaRocco, August, *Special Projects,* University of Miami (Louis Calder Memorial Library), Miami FL. 305-547-6441

LaRoche, Sara, *Librn,* Kentuckiana Regional Library, Eminence KY. 502-845-7059

Laroche, Therese, *Librn,* Bibliotheque De La Ville De Montreal (Bois-de-Boulogne Children), Montreal PQ. 514-872-4438

Larochelle, Andre, *Per,* Bibliotheque De Quebec, Quebec PQ. 418-694-6356

LaRochelle, Fabien, *Dir,* Bibliotheque Municipale De Shawinigan, Shawnigan Municipal Library, Shawinigan PQ. 819-537-0021

Larochelle, Nicole, *Cat,* Bibliotheque Nationale Du Quebec, Montreal PQ. 514-873-4553

Larose, Luanne, *Librn,* Canada Department of Insurance Library, Ottawa ON. 613-996-5162

LaRose, Margaret, *Assoc Dir Personnel,* Detroit Public Library, Detroit Associated Libraries, Detroit MI. 313-833-1000

LaRosee, Georgianna, *Circ,* Milton Public Library, Milton MA. 617-698-5707

Larouche, Monique, *Ad,* Chateauguay Municipal Library, Chateauguay PQ. 514-691-1934

Laroussini, Donna H, *Cat,* Wake Forest University (Law Library), Winston-Salem NC. 919-761-5438

Larrabee, Patricia S, *Librn,* Portsmouth Public Library (Manor), Portsmouth VA. 804-488-3104

Larrabee, II, Don M, *Law,* Lycoming County Law Library, Williamsport PA. 717-323-9811, Ext 2475

Larrea, Catherine, *Asst Dir,* Riverside Public Library Association, Inc, Riverside NJ. 609-461-6922

Larrere, Francesca, *Dir,* J V Fletcher Library, Westford MA. 617-692-6263

Larrey, Camilla B, *Librn,* Woods Hole Library, Woods Hole MA. 617-548-8961

Larrington, Betty, *Librn,* Potter County Free Public Library, Gettysburg SD. 605-765-9518

Larsen, A Dean, *Asst Dir, Coll Develop,* Brigham Young University, Harold B Lee Library, Provo UT. 801-378-2905

Larsen, Claire J, *Dir Libr Serv,* Bakersfield College, Grace Van Dyke Bird Library, Bakersfield CA. 805-395-4461

Larsen, Eileen, *Librn,* Stratford Public Library, Stratford IA. 515-838-2131

Larsen, Hans L, *Dir,* Ohlone College, Blanchard Learning Resources Center, Fremont CA. 415-657-2100, Ext 317

Larsen, John, *Assoc Prof,* Northern Illinois University, Dept of Library Science, IL. 815-753-1735

Larsen, Linda, *Ch,* A K Smiley Public Library, Redlands CA. 714-793-2201

Larsen, Lotte, *Ser,* Oregon College of Education Library, Monmouth OR. 503-838-1220, Ext 240

Larsen, Margaret B, *ILL,* Omaha Public Library, W Dale Clark Library, Omaha NE. 402-444-4800

Larsen, Mrs William, *Dir,* Southwest Craft Center Library, San Antonio TX. 512-224-1848

Larsen, Sister Mary Jude, *Per,* Saint Joseph Memorial Hospital, Health Science Library, Kokomo IN. 317-456-5344

Larsen, Suzanne, *Librn,* Wisconsin Indianhead Technical Institute, Rice Lake Campus Library, Rice Lake WI. 715-234-7082

Larsen, Suzanne T, *Librn,* United States Department of Energy, Grand Junction Office Technical Library, Grand Junction CO. 303-242-8621, Ext 278

Larsgaard, Mary, *Maps,* Colorado School of Mines, Arthur Lakes Library, Golden CO. 303-279-0300, Ext 2690

Larson, Arlene, *Librn,* Western Plains Library System (Milan Branch), Milan MN. 612-269-5644

Larson, Barbara, *Librn,* Barnes Reading Room, Everest KS. 913-548-7733

Larson, Barbara, *Librn,* Kent County Library System (Comstock Park Branch), Comstock Park MI. 616-363-2855

Larson, Carol, *Dir,* Humboldt Free Public Library, Humboldt IA. 515-332-1925

Larson, Carol, *ILL, Tech Serv & Cat,* Washington County Library, Lake Elmo MN. 612-777-8143

Larson, Carole, *Ref,* Kearney State College, Calvin T Ryan Library, Kearney NE. 308-236-4218

Larson, Cindi, *Ref & Outreach,* Veterans Memorial Public Library, Bismarck ND. 701-222-6410

Larson, Cora, *Librn,* Dearborn Department of Libraries (Esper), Dearborn MI. 313-581-0300

Larson, Cynthia, *Asst Librn,* Nipigon Township Public Library, Nipigon ON. 807-887-3142

Larson, D, *Librn,* Madison Public Library (Pinney), Madison WI. 608-266-6371

Larson, Donna R, *Doc,* Arizona State University Library, Tempe AZ. 602-965-3417

Larson, Eugene F, *Dir,* Oakland Community College, Auburn Hills Campus Learning Resources Center, Auburn Heights MI. 313-852-1000, Ext 222

Larson, Evva L, *Asst Dir & Ch,* Idaho State Library, Boise ID. 208-334-2150

Larson, Evva L, *In Charge,* Idaho State Library - Blind & Physically Handicapped Services, Boise ID. 208-334-2150

Larson, Genevieve, *Ch,* Ringwood Public Library, Ringwood NJ. 201-962-6256

Larson, Gertrude, *ILL & Ad,* Escondido Public Library, Escondido CA. 714-741-4683

Larson, Janet, *Br Coordr (South Region),* Sacramento Public Library, Sacramento CA. 916-440-5926

Larson, Janice, *Librn,* Ransom Memorial Public Library, Altona IL. 309-484-6193

Larson, Joan, *Ref,* Peninsula Library Systems, Daly City CA. 415-878-5577

Larson, Joan, *Circ,* South Dakota State University, Hilton M Briggs Library, Brookings SD. 605-688-5106

Larson, Karen, *Asst Dir & Tech Serv,* Atlantic County Library, Pleasantville NJ. 609-646-8699, 645-7121, 625-2776

Larson, Linda, *AV,* Mesa Community College Library, Mesa AZ. 602-833-1261, Ext 291, 201

Larson, Linda, *Instr,* Mesa Community College, Library Technician Program, AZ. 602-833-1261

Larson, Linda, *Tech Serv,* Saint Mary's Junior College Library, Minneapolis MN. 612-332-5521

Larson, Lola M, *Dir,* Tomah Public Library, Tomah WI. 608-372-4569

Larson, Maria, *Personnel,* Princeton University Library, Princeton NJ. 609-452-3180

Larson, Marilyn, *Librn,* Ashton Public Library, Ashton ID. 208-652-7280

Larson, Marjorie, *Librn,* Griggs County Library, Cooperstown ND. 701-797-2214

Larson, Melba, *Librn,* Bureau of Land Management, Bakersfield District Office Library, Bakersfield CA. 805-861-4191

Larson, Mildred, *AV,* L E Phillips Memorial Public Library, Eau Claire WI. 715-839-5002

Larson, Mildred, *Art & Music,* L E Phillips Memorial Public Library, Eau Claire WI. 715-839-5002

Larson, Mrs Clyde, *Librn,* Burns Public Library, Burns KS. 316-726-5574

Larson, Mrs Donn, *Librn,* Enderlin Municipal Library, Enderlin ND. 701-437-4911

Larson, Rachel, *Librn,* Northwood Public Library, Northwood IA. 515-324-1340

Larson, Robert, *Acq,* Georgetown University (John Vinton Dahlgren Memorial Library), Washington DC. 202-625-7577

Larson, Ronald D, *Librn,* Graves Public Library, Wakefield Public Library, Wakefield NE. 402-287-2334

Larson, Ronald J, *Librn,* Wisconsin State Journal Library, Madison WI. 608-252-6112

Larson, Rose Ann, *Librn,* Kimballton Public Library, Kimballton IA. 712-773-2052

Larson, Sandra L, *Tech Serv,* Northwest Regional Library, Belle Fourche SD. 605-892-4420

Larson, Signe, *Media,* United States Department of the Interior, Natural Resources Library, Washington DC. 202-343-5821

Larson, Suzanne, *Ch,* Charles City Public Library, Charles City IA. 515-228-5532

Larson, W L Larry, *Dir,* North Arkansas Regional Library, Harrison AR. 501-741-3665

Larson, Jr, Peter D, *Dir,* Caldwell County Public Library, Lenoir NC. 704-758-8451

Larsson, Anita, *Librn,* Fairleigh Dickinson University (Edward Williams College), Hackensack NJ. 201-836-6300, Ext 517

Larsson, Betty, *Acq,* Framingham Public Library, Framingham MA. 617-879-3570

Larsson, Laura G, *Supervisor,* University of Washington Libraries (Mathematics Research), Seattle WA. 206-543-7296

Larter, Cynthia A, *Asst Librn,* Reed, Smith, Shaw & McClay, Law Library, Pittsburgh PA. 412-288-3340

Larue, Ginette, *Librn,* International Institute of Stress, Library and Documentation Service, Montreal PQ. 514-288-2707, 288-6665

Larue, Marge, *Coordr,* Southwest New Jersey Consortium for Health Information Services, NJ. 609-964-0140

Larue, Norah, *ILL & Ad,* Bibliotheque Municipale Des Sources, Sources Public Library, Roxboro PQ. 514-684-8247, 684-8260

Lary, Marilyn, *Asst Prof,* University of South Florida, Graduate Department of Library, Media & Information Studies, FL. 813-974-2557

Larzelere, David W, *Chief Librn,* Flint Journal, Editorial Library, Flint MI. 313-767-0660, Ext 192-197

LaSalle, Daniel, *Librn,* College Edouard-Montpetit Bibliotheque, Longueuil PQ. 514-679-2630, Ext 324

LaSalle, Lise, *Head Librn,* Sidbec-Dosco Corp, Service de Documentation, Montreal PQ. 514-875-7070

LaSalle, Marilynn, *Librn,* Portland Cement Association, Research Library, Skokie IL. 312-966-6200, Ext 534

Laschinger, Carol, *Librn,* Buffalo Color Corporation, Technical Library, Buffalo NY. 716-827-4500

Laseter, Ernest, *Federal Program & State Aid,* Alabama Public Library Service, Montgomery AL. 205-832-5743

Laseter, Shirley, *Librn,* Autauga-Prattville Public Library, Prattville AL. 205-365-3396

Laseter, Shirley Brooks, *Dir,* Autauga-Prattville Public Library System, Prattville AL. 205-365-3396

Lash, Barry, *Chief Librn,* State University of New York, Agricultural & Technical College at Alfred, Walter C Hinkle Memorial Library, Alfred NY. 607-871-6313

Lashbrook, John, *Tech Serv,* Mount Vernon Nazarene College Library, Mount Vernon OH. 614-397-1244

Lasher, Lu, *Ad & Ref,* Greenwood Public Library, Greenwood IN. 317-881-1953

Laska, Vaclav, *Slavic & Linguistics,* University of Chicago, Joseph Regenstein Library, Chicago IL. 312-753-2977

Laskaris, Joan, *Head, BPH Services,* Shawnee Library System (Subregional Library for the Blind & Physically Handicapped), Carterville IL. 618-985-3713

Laskovski, Peter, *Dir,* Shaker Museum, Emma B King Library, Old Chatham NY. 518-794-9100

Laskowski, Seno, *Cat,* University of Alberta (University Libraries), Edmonton AB. 403-432-3790

Lasky, Sylvia C, *Ch,* Guam Public Library, Nieves M Flores Memorial Library, Agana, Guam PI. 472-6417

Lasley, Norma, *Ref,* Muncie-Center Township Public Library, Muncie IN. 317-288-9971

Lasman, E, *Acq,* Northeastern University, Suburban Campus Library, Burlington MA. 617-272-5500, Ext 55

Lasnier, Jean, *Librn,* Bibliotheque Municipale, Beloeil PQ. 514-467-7872

Lass, Marilyn, *Ctr for Minn Studies,* Mankato State University, Memorial Library, Mankato MN. 507-389-6201

Lastrapes, Blanca J, *Librn,* Louisiana State Library, Section for the Blind & Physically Handicapped, Baton Rouge LA. 504-342-4922

Laszcz, Joan, *Ref,* Euclid Public Library, Euclid OH. 216-261-5300

Laszlo, George A, *Librn,* Ayerst Laboratories (Medical Information Center), New York NY. 212-878-5970

Latal, Mary, *Librn,* United States Court of Appeals, Eighth Circuit Law Library, Saint Louis MO. 314-622-4930

Lataniotis, Dolores, *Librn,* Forbes, Inc Library, New York NY. 212-675-7500

Latch, Patricia, *Librn,* Cobb County Public Library System (Sibley), Marietta GA. 404-422-6070

Latendresse, Raymond, *Info Spec,* International Flavors & Fragrances, Inc, IFF Research & Development Laboratory, Technical Information Center, Union Beach NJ. 201-264-4500, Ext 521

Latham, Ann, *Cat,* Southeastern Oklahoma State University Library, Durant OK. 405-924-0121, Ext 245

Latham, Bonita, *Ch & Cat,* Miles City Public Library, Sagebrush Federation of Libraries, Miles City MT. 406-232-1496

Latham, Dorothy M, *Coordr,* University of Oregon, Educational Media Endorsement Program, OR. 503-686-3468

Latham, Helen, *Ref & Bibliog Instr,* Austin College, Hopkins Library, Sherman TX. 214-892-9101, Ext 237

Latham, Joyce, *Acq,* Community College of Baltimore (Harbor Campus), Baltimore MD. 301-396-1860

Latham, Ronald, *Dir,* Athol Public Library, Athol MA. 617-249-9515

Lathem, Margaret S, *Assoc Dir,* Sequoyah Regional Library, R T Jones Memorial Library, Canton GA. 404-479-3090

Lathrop, Alan, *Curator,* University of Minnesota Libraries-Twin Cities (Manuscripts Collection), Minneapolis MN. 612-376-7271

Lathrop, Irene, *Lectr,* Simmons College, Graduate School of Library & Information Science, MA. 617-738-2225

Lathrop, Irene M, *Dir,* Rhode Island Hospital, Peters Memorial Library, Providence RI. 401-277-4671

Latiak, Dorothy, *Librn,* Chicago Public Library (South Chicago), Chicago IL. 312-721-8065

Latimer, Adrienne G, *Ref,* Cape Cod Community College, Library-Learning Resource Center, West Barnstable MA. 617-362-2131, Ext 341, 345

Latimer, Bruce T, *Doc,* University of North Florida Library, Jacksonville FL. 904-646-2553

Latimer, Nancy, *Ch & YA,* Murray Public Library, Murray UT. 801-266-1137

Latimer, Sister Francisanne, *Tech Serv,* Sacred Heart School of Theology, Leo Dehon Library, Hales Corners WI. 425-8300 & 425-8301, Ext 27

LaTourette, Joanne D, *Cat,* Allegheny College, Lawrence Lee Pelletier Library, Meadville PA. 814-724-3363

Latsis, Carol, *Ref,* Young & Rubicam, Inc Library, New York NY. 212-953-3075

Latta, Barbara, *Dir,* Cerebral Palsy Research Foundation of Kansas, Inc, Resource Center & Library, Wichita KS. 316-688-1888, Ext 217

Lattimer, Sarah, *In Charge,* Pennsylvania State University (Mathematics), University Park PA. 814-865-6822

Lattimore, Clare, *Ser,* Southern Methodist University Libraries (Central University Libraries), Dallas TX. 214-692-2400

Latus, Jane Keating, *Dir,* Boston City Hospital (Morse-Slanger Library), Boston MA. 617-424-4771

Latus, Marjorie, *Librn,* Hurdman & Cranstoun Library, New York NY. 212-269-5800

Latus, Sheila, *Librn,* Kaiser Permanente Medical Center, Health Sciences Library, San Diego CA. 714-563-2190

Latzke, H R, *Dir,* Concordia College, Klinck Memorial Library, River Forest IL. 312-771-8300, Ext 450

Lau, Chau Mun, *Chinese Area Specialist,* University of Hawaii (University of Hawaii Library), Honolulu HI. 808-948-7205

Lau, Lily, *Librn,* H J Nugen Public Library, New London Public Library, New London IA. 319-367-5512

Lau, Ray D, *Libr Dir & Dept Chmn,* Northwestern Oklahoma State University, Dept of Library Science, OK. 405-327-1700, Ext 219

Lau, Ray D, *Dir & Acq,* Northwestern Oklahoma State University Library, Alva OK. 405-327-1700, Ext 219

Laub, Barbara, *Instrnl & Liaison Librn,* Stevens Institute of Technology, Samuel C Williams Library, Hoboken NJ. 201-420-5198

Laubach, Dena, *Librn,* Essex Free Library, Essex VT. 802-879-0313

Laubacker, Ann, *Librn,* Elma Public Library, Elma NY. 716-652-2719

Laubenthal, Charles, *Ref,* Spring Hill College, Thomas Byrne Memorial Library, Mobile AL. 205-460-2381

Lauber, Karen, *Ch,* Ogdensburg Public Library, Ogdensburg NY. 315-393-4325

Lauber, Louise, *Chief Librn,* Newfield Free Public Library, Newfield NJ. 609-697-0415

Laubersheimer, Susan, *Ref,* Texas Medical Association, Memorial Library, Austin TX. 512-477-6704, Ext 191

Laucius, Ilona, *Ch,* Prairie Trails Public Library District, Burbank IL. 312-430-3688

Laucks, Cami L, *Dir,* Trinity Lutheran Hospital, Florence L Nelson Memorial Library, Kansas City MO. 816-753-4600, Ext 637

Laucus, John, *Univ Librn,* Boston University Libraries (Mugar Memorial Library), Boston MA. 617-353-3710

Laudati, Geri, *Librn,* Fairleigh Dickinson University (Music), Rutherford NJ. 201-933-5000, Ext 327

Laudati, Gerri, *Librn,* University of Wisconsin-Madison (Mills Music Library), Madison WI. 608-262-3521

Laudenslager, Elaine, *Asst Librn,* Longwood Gardens Inc Library, Kennett Square PA. 215-388-6741, Ext 510

Lauderdale, Kenneth, *Librn,* General Electric Co (William Stanley Library), Pittsfield MA. 413-494-3764

Lauderdale, Mrs Alfred A, *Librn,* Trousdale County Public Library, Fred A Vaught Memorial Library, Hartsville TN. 615-374-3677

Lauen, Les, *Dir,* Oklahoma Christian College Library, Oklahoma City OK. 405-478-1661, Ext 337

Lauer, Anita R, *ILL & Cat,* Manhattanville College Library, Purchase NY. 914-946-9600, Ext 274

Lauer, Carl, *On-Line Servs & Bibliog Instr,* McDonnell Douglas Corp (McDonnell Aircraft Library), Saint Louis MO. 314-232-6134

Lauer, Joseph, *Sahil Africana,* Michigan State University Library, East Lansing MI. 517-355-2344

Lauer, Kenneth, *Librn,* Public Library of Fort Wayne & Allen County (Shawnee), Fort Wayne IN. 219-456-5864

Lauer, Marjorie, *Asst Librn,* IBM Canada Limited, Central Library, Toronto ON. 416-443-2043

Lauer, Virginia, *ILL,* Huntington Beach Library, Information & Cultural Resource Center, Huntington Beach CA. 714-842-4481

Lauerman, Joanne, *ILL,* Free Public Library of Roselle Park, Veterans Memorial Library, Roselle Park NJ. 201-245-2456, 245-7171

Laufer, Janice, *Librn, On-Line Servs & Bibliog Instr,* Nova Scotia Department of the Environment, Halifax NS. 902-424-8600

Laufer, Laura, *Ad,* West Bloomfield Township Public Library, West Bloomfield MI. 313-682-2120

Laufer, Linda, *Tech Serv & Cat,* Somerset County Library, Somerville NJ. 201-725-4700, Ext 234

Lauffer, Donna, *On-Line Servs,* Johnson County Library, Shawnee Mission KS. 913-831-1550

Lauffer, Susan, *Librn,* Fairview General Hospital (Health Media Center), Cleveland OH. 216-252-1222, Ext 487

Laufle, Gail, *Community Liaison,* Library Cooperative of Macomb, Mount Clemens MI. 313-286-5750

Laughlin, Evelyn, *Asst Librn,* Town of Caledon Public Libraries (Belfountain Branch), Belfountain ON. 416-857-1400

Laughlin, Mary, *Cat,* Baldwin County Library System, Robertsdale AL. 205-947-7632

Laughlin, Mary C, *Librn*, IDS Life Insurance Company Library, Minneapolis MN. 612-372-3747

Laughlin, Sara B, *Dir*, Vermont Institute of Natural Science Library, Woodstock VT. 802-457-1207

Laughlin, Steven, *Bus & Spec Studies*, University of Alabama in Birmingham, Mervyn H Sterne Library, Birmingham AL. 205-934-6360

Laurent, Celine, *Info Servs Consult*, Kaskaskia Library System, Smithton IL. 618-235-4220

Laurey, Patricia, *Bibliog Instr*, University of Central Arkansas, Torreyson Library, Conway AR. 501-329-2931, Ext 449

Lauria, Elaine, *Librn*, Deaconess Hospital, Medical Library, Buffalo NY. 716-886-4400

Laurin, Mala, *In Charge*, Gould Inc, Gould Information Center, Rolling Meadows IL. 312-640-4423

Laurin-Conway, S, *Librn*, Algonquin College of Applied Arts & Technology (Colonel By Campus), Ottawa ON. 613-237-5257

Lauritsen, David, *ILL*, Western Plains Library System, Montevideo MN. 612-269-5644

Lauritsen, Ella, *Librn*, Sioux City Public Library (Morningside), Sioux City IA. 712-279-6179

Lauritsen, Ella L, *Ch*, Sioux City Public Library, Sioux City IA. 712-279-6179

Lauritzen, Robert L, *Tech Serv*, San Jose State University Library, San Jose CA. 408-277-3377

Lauritzen, Shirley, *AV*, Snow College, Lucy A Phillips Library, Ephraim UT. 801-283-4201, Ext 204

Laursen, Irene, *Sci Libr*, Wellesley College, Margaret Clapp Library, Wellesley MA. 617-235-0320, Ext 280

Lautaret, Ronald, *Reader Serv*, University of Alaska, Anchorage Library, Anchorage AK. 907-263-1825

Lautenschlager, E, *Info Scientist*, William H Rorer Inc, Research Library, Fort Washington PA. 215-628-6358

Lauterman, Freida, *Librn*, Agudath Israel Congregation, Malca Pass Library, Ottawa ON. 613-728-1750

Lauver, Marvin E, *Librn*, Northern Natural Gas Company (Company Library), Omaha NE. 402-348-4000

Laux, Barbara, *Cat*, Christ the King Seminary Library, East Aurora NY. 716-652-8959

Laux, Peter J, *Dir*, Canisius College, Andrew L Bouwhuis Library, Buffalo NY. 716-883-7000, Ext 253, 254, 290

Lauzon, Helene, *Librn*, Montreal Association for Mentally Retarded Library, Montreal PQ. 514-336-0684

Lauzon, Janice, *Sr Consult*, Central Massachusetts Regional Library System, Worcester MA. 617-752-3751

Lauzon, Maurice G, *Librn*, Standard Times Publishing Co Library, New Bedford MA. 617-997-7411, Ext 270

Lavallee, David, *AV*, Central Massachusetts Regional Library System, Worcester MA. 617-752-3751

LaValley, Marianne, *Ch*, Upper Moreland Free Public Library, Willow Grove PA. 215-659-3638

laVega, Amalia de, *ILL*, University of Miami (Louis Calder Memorial Library), Miami FL. 305-547-6441

Lavendel, Giuliana, *Mgr*, Xerox Corp, Palo Alto Research Center's Technical Information Center, Palo Alto CA. 415-494-4042

Lavender, Jane M, *Librn*, Choctawhatchee Regional Library (Ariton Public), Ariton AL. 205-762-2323

Lavender, Kay, *Bkmobile Coordr*, Judge George W Armstrong Library, Homochitto Valley Regional Library, Natchez MS. 601-445-8862

Lavender, Kenneth, *Collection Development*, Victoria College - University of Houston Victoria Campus Library, Victoria TX. 512-575-7436

LaVerdi, Adelaide, *Cat*, State University of New York College at Geneseo, Milne Library, Geneseo NY. 716-245-5591

Laverdiere, Guy, *Librn*, Bibliotheque Municipale, Outremont PQ. 514-274-9451, Poste 12

Lavergne, Rodolphe, *Dir*, Ecole Des Hautes Etudes Commerciales De Montreal Bibliotheque, Montreal PQ. 514-343-4481

Lavery, Joseph, *Deputy Chief Librn*, Newfoundland Public Library Services, Saint John's NF. 709-737-3964

Lavigne, Doris, *Librn*, East Brookfield Public Library, East Brookfield MA. 617-867-7928

Lavigueur, Lucile, *Librn*, Saint Mary's Hospital, Medical Library, Montreal PQ. 514-344-3317

Lavilla, Sonia, *ILL*, Hahnemann Medical College & Hospital of Philadelphia, Warren H Fake Library, Philadelphia PA. 215-448-7186

Lavinder, Elva B, *Bkmobile Coordr*, Blue Ridge Regional Library, Martinsville VA. 703-632-7125

Lavine, Frank, *Dir*, Medford Public Library, Medford MA. 617-395-7950

Lavoie, Gerard, *Chief Librn*, Centre Universitaire Saint-Louis-Maillet, Students Library, Edmundston NB. 506-735-8804

LaVoie, Madeline, *Asst Librn*, Jones Memorial Library, Orleans VT. 802-754-6606

Lavoie, Monique, *Dir*, Dawson College Library, Montreal PQ. 514-525-2501, Ext 297

Lavoie, Mrs, *Librn*, Windsor Public Library (Emma K Hatheway), Windsor CT. 203-688-4604

Lavorini, Amy E, *Librn*, Butler County Traveling Library, Butler PA. 412-285-3260

Law, Dan, *Co-Director*, Regional Information & Communication Exchange, TX. 713-528-3553

Law, Edna C, *Dir*, New York University (Graduate Library of Business Administration), New York NY. 212-285-6230

Law, James B, *Ref*, Elizabeth City State University, G R Little Library, Elizabeth City NC. 919-335-0551, Ext 332

Law, John W, *Librn*, Decatur Memorial Hospital, Medical Staff & School of Nursing Library, Decatur IL. 217-877-8121, Ext 662

Law, Leanne, *Steno-Librn*, Manitoba Department of Health & Social Development, Selkirk Health Sciences Library, Selkirk MB. 204-482-4511

Law, Margaret, *Asst Prof*, University of Georgia, Dept of Educational Media & Librarianship, GA. 404-542-3810

Law, Ruth, *Tech Serv*, Grand Ledge Public Library, Grand Ledge MI. 517-627-7014

Law, Terri J, *Librn*, Southeastern Wisconsin Regional Planning Commission, Reference Library, Waukesha WI. 414-547-6721, Ext 216

Lawford, Hugh, *President*, QL Systems Limited, ON. 613-549-4611

Lawhead, Terry, *Bkmobile Coordr*, Moscow-Latah County Library System, Moscow ID. 208-882-3925

Lawhon, Betty, *Librn*, Doniphan Public Library, Doniphan MO. 314-996-2616

Lawhorn, Velma Rose, *ILL*, Safford City-Graham County Library, Safford AZ. 602-428-1531

Lawhun, Kathryn, *ILL*, Mill Valley Public Library, Mill Valley CA. 415-388-4245

Lawin, Betty, *Dir*, Bloomer Public Library, Bloomer WI. 715-568-2384

Lawler, Elizabeth, *Ch*, Cheshire Public Library, Cheshire CT. 203-272-2245

Lawler, Jeanne, *Librn*, Kalamazoo Public Library (Oshtemo), Kalamazoo MI. 616-375-5662

Lawler, Jeanne, *Librn*, Kalamazoo Public Library (Washington Square), Kalamazoo MI. 616-343-6933

Lawless, Donna, *Ref*, Union College, MacKay Library-Learning Resource Center, Cranford NJ. 201-276-2600, Ext 244

Lawless, Jane, *Media*, Malden Public Library, Malden MA. 617-324-0218

Lawless, Paul, *Dir*, Wesley College, Parker Library, Dover DE. 302-736-2413

Lawlor, C, *Librn*, United States Navy (Correctional Center Library), Newport RI. 401-841-3044

Lawlor, Geraldine, *Asst Librn*, Town of Caledon Public Libraries (Caledon East Branch), Caledon ON. 416-857-1400

Lawlor, Martha, *Doc*, University of Wyoming, William Robertson Coe Library, Laramie WY. 307-766-3279

Lawrance, Margaret W, *Librn*, Merced County Law Library, Merced CA. 209-723-3101

Lawrence, Betty, *Librn*, Denver Public Library (Ford-Warren), Denver CO. 303-573-5152, Ext 271

Lawrence, Betty A, *Asst to Dir*, Pioneer Library System, Rochester NY. 716-428-7345

Lawrence, Brian D, *Media*, Lewis & Clark College, Aubrey R Watzek Library, Portland OR. 503-244-6161, Ext 400

Lawrence, Cheryl, *Admin Asst*, Triton Museum of Art Library, Santa Clara CA. 408-248-4585

Lawrence, David, *Dir*, Reading Area Community College, Learning Resources Center, Reading PA. 215-372-4721

Lawrence, Doris, *Bkmobile Coordr*, Ashtabula County District Library, Ashtabula OH. 216-997-9341

Lawrence, Eileen, *Librn*, Chicago Public Library (South Shore), Chicago IL. 312-734-4780

Lawrence, Elizabeth, *Circ*, Ann Arbor Public Library, Ann Arbor MI. 313-994-2333

Lawrence, Mary L, *Order*, Providence Public Library, Providence RI. 401-521-7722

Lawrence, Mrs James W, *Dir*, Service League Library, Carthage TX. 214-693-6741

Lawrence, Patricia, *Asst Dir*, Napa City - County Library, Napa CA. 707-253-4241

Lawrence, Phyllis, *ILL*, Indiana University at South Bend Library, South Bend IN. 219-237-4440

Lawrence, Robert, *Biol Sci*, Oregon State University, William Jasper Kerr Library, Corvallis OR. 503-754-3411

Lawrence, Rose, *Acq*, Rockefeller University Library, New York NY. 212-360-1000

Lawrence, Sharon, *Ch*, Bedford Free Public Library, Bedford MA. 617-275-9440

Lawrence, Steven T, *Pub Info Officer*, Denver Public Library, Denver CO. 303-573-5152, Ext 271

Lawrence, Stuart E, *Dir*, Kirtland Community College Library, Roscommon MI. 517-275-5121

Lawrence, Jr, Philip D, *Librn & On-Line Servs*, West Point-Pepperell Inc, Research Center Library, Shawmut AL. 205-756-7111, Ext 2135

Lawrey, Roberta, *Dir*, Edith Abbott Memorial Library, Grand Island Public Library, Grand Island NE. 308-382-4894

Lawry, Martha, *Librn*, Ohio State University Libraries (Women's Studies), Columbus OH. 614-422-3035

Lawrynovicz, Florence, *ILL*, Ridgefield Library & Historical Association, Ridgefield CT. 203-438-2282

Laws, Julie, *Tech Serv*, Golden Gate Baptist Theological Seminary Library, Mill Valley CA. 415-388-8080, Ext 37

Laws, Marian, *Librn*, Austin Public Library (Howson), Austin TX. 512-472-5433

Laws, Melzetta, *Librn*, Atlanta Public Library (Dogwood), Atlanta GA. 404-794-8261

Lawson, A Venable, *Dir*, Emory University, Div of Librarianship, GA. 404-329-6840

Lawson, Anne-Marie, *Librn*, Saint Catharines Public Library (Port Dalhousie), Saint Catharines ON. 416-934-2621

Lawson, Bennett F, *Librn*, Veterans Administration, Hospital Library, Kansas City MO. 816-861-4700

Lawson, C D, *Dir*, Midwestern Regional Library System, Kitchener ON. 519-576-5061

Lawson, Deedy A, *Librn*, Newport News Public Library System (Main Street), Newport News VA. 804-596-5723

Lawson, Dennis, *Librn*, Tipton County Public Library, Tipton IN. 317-675-2526

Lawson, Diane, *Ch*, Albert A Wells Memorial Library, Tippecanoe County Contractual Library, Lafayette IN. 317-423-2602

Lawson, Dorothy, *ILL & Ref*, Malone College, Everett L Cattell Library, Canton OH. 216-454-3011, Ext 311

Lawson, Frances, *Asst Dir*, Belmar Public Library, Belmar NJ. 201-681-0775

Lawson, George, *Asst Dir*, Ames Public Library, Ames IA. 515-232-4404

Lawson, Gladys, *Librn*, Crowley Ridge Regional Library (Weiner Branch), Weiner AR. 501-684-2235

Lawson, Harriet G, *Dir*, West Deptford Public Library, Thorofare NJ. 609-845-5593

Lawson, J, *Librn*, Manzanola Public Library, Manzanola CO. 303-462-5671

Lawson, Judith, *Asst Librn*, Congregation Beth Achim, Joseph Katkowsky Library, Southfield MI. 313-352-8670

Lawson, Karen, *Librn*, Cass County Public Library (Archie Branch), Archie MO. 816-293-5579

Lawson, Lonnie, *Sci*, Central Missouri State University, Ward Edwards Library, Warrensburg MO. 816-429-4141

Lawson, Mrs O, *Asst Librn*, Frankford Public Library, Frankford ON. 613-398-7572

Lawson, Norma R, *Librn,* Union Carbide Corp (Research & Development Department Building 740 Library), South Charleston WV. 304-747-4308

Lawson, Rhea, *In Charge,* Enoch Pratt Free Library (Lafayette Square), Baltimore MD. 301-396-5430, 396-5395

Lawson, Rosylind, *Librn,* Sheffield Public Library, Sheffield AL. 205-383-6857

Lawson, Ruth, *Dir,* Mountain View Public Library, Mountain View CA. 415-968-6595

Lawton, Amelia G, *Dir,* Free Library of Northampton Township, Richboro PA. 215-357-3050

Lawton, J Kevin, *Dir,* Swansea Free Public Library, Swansea MA. 617-674-9609

Lawton, Natalie V, *Librn,* Westerly Hospital, Medical Library, Westerly RI. 401-596-4961, Ext 280

Lawver, Marien, *Dir,* Manson Public Library, Manson IA. 712-469-2237

Lawyer, W Robert, *Dir,* Western Washington University, Mabel Zoe Wilson Library, Bellingham WA. 206-676-3050

Lax, Jill, *Librn,* Montgomery County Public Library (Candor Branch), Candor NC. 919-974-4033

Laxer, Carol, *Dental Librn,* University of Oregon Health Sciences Center (Health Sciences Library), Portland OR. 503-225-8026

Laxon, Joanne, *Librn,* Ruth Suckow Memorial Library, Earlville IA. 319-923-5235

Lay, Douglas, *Dir Libr Servs,* Wausau Insurance Companies Library, Wausau WI. 715-847-8504

Lay, Jr, William, *Curator,* Tioga County Historical Society Museum Library, Owego NY. 607-687-2460

Layaout, Cora, *Ser & Doc,* Ohio Northern University, Heterick Memorial Library, Ada OH. 419-634-9921, Ext 370, 490

Laycock, Anitra, *Librn,* Halifax Infirmary, Health Services Library, Halifax NS. 902-428-3058

Layell, Sam, *AV,* Robeson Technical Institute Library, Lumberton NC. 919-738-7101, Ext 66

Layland, Deen, *Br Asst,* La Crosse County Library (Holmen), La Crosse WI. 608-536-4336

Layman, Lois, *Admin Servs,* Anderson City-Anderson & Stony Creek Township Public Library, Anderson Public Library, Anderson IN. 317-644-0938

Layman, Mary F, *Librn,* United States Department of the Interior (Fish & Wildlife Service, Denver Wildlife Research Center Library), Denver CO. 303-234-4919

Layne, Mrs C L, *Librn,* Lebanon-Wilson County Library, Lebanon TN. 615-444-0632

Laythe, Rosamond, *Asst Dir for Pub Servs,* Southern Illinois University at Edwardsville, Elijah P Lovejoy Library, Edwardsville IL. 618-692-2711

Layton, Anna, *Librn,* Clark County Library District (Blue Diamond Branch), Blue Diamond NV. 702-875-4295

Layton, Jeanne, *Dir,* Davis County Library, Farmington UT. 801-867-2322

Layton, Kathy, *Librn,* Lancer Division-Sherwood Medical Industries Library, Foster City CA. 415-573-1343

Layton, Mrs S A, *Librn,* Peat, Marwick & Partners Library, Toronto ON. 416-863-3440, 863-3441

Layton, Rose, *Librn,* Lawrence Township Public Library, Cedarville NJ. 609-447-4554

Layvas, Sue D, *Librn,* Kaiser Foundation Hospital, Medical Library, Fontana CA. 714-829-5085

Lazar, David, *In Charge,* Oheb Zedeck Synagogue Center Library, Pottsville PA. 717-622-5890

Lazar, Jon, *Order,* Buffalo & Erie County Public Library System, Buffalo NY. 716-856-7525

Lazar, Nancy, *Librn,* United States Court of Appeals, District of Columbia Circuit Court, Judges' Library, Washington DC. 202-426-7187

Lazar, Shirley, *Ch & Br Coordr,* Paterson Free Public Library, Danforth Memorial Library, Paterson NJ. 201-881-3770

Lazarevic, Martha, *Tech Serv,* Ford Foundation Library, New York NY. 212-573-5155

Lazaroff, Rebecca, *Bkmobile Coordr,* Jackson District Library, Jackson MI. 517-788-4087

Lazenby, Gail, *Syst Coordr,* Dekalb Library System, Maud M Burrus Library, Decatur GA. 404-378-7569

Lazewski, Barbara A, *Librn,* Ray-O-Vac Corp, Engineering & Development Center Library, Madison WI. 608-252-7400, Ext 344

Lazo, Marilyn M, *Librn,* National Park Service, Glacier National Park, George C Ruble Library, West Glacier MT. 406-888-5441, Ext 31

Lazorchak, Tula, *Cat,* Richardson Public Library, Richardson TX. 214-238-8251

Lea, Edna Mae, *Librn,* Dallas County Library (Carthage Branch), Carthage AR. 501-352-3592

Lea, K, *Libr Supvr & Cat,* Lethbridge Community College, Buchanan Resource Centre, Lethbridge AB. 403-327-2141, Ext 350

Lea, Lucile, *Rare Bks & Spec Coll,* Central Missouri State University, Ward Edwards Library, Warrensburg MO. 816-429-4141

Lea, Marcia J, *Asst Dir,* Brigham City Library, Brigham City UT. 801-723-5850

Lea, Ruth, *Librn,* Marshall County Library (Byhalia Public), Byhalia MS. 601-252-3823

Lea, Shirley, *Librn,* Alberta Mental Health Services Library, Edmonton AB. 403-427-4444

Lea, Stephanie R, *Media,* Community College of Baltimore (Harbor Campus), Baltimore MD. 301-396-1860

Leach, Barbara, *Librn,* Adriance Memorial Library (Uptown), Poughkeepsie NY. 914-485-4795

Leach, Dorothy M, *Dir,* Pontiac Free Library Association, Warwick RI. 401-737-3292

Leach, Helen, *Cat,* Saginaw Public Libraries, Hoyt Public Library, Saginaw MI. 517-755-0904

Leach, Joan Riordan, *Ch,* Burlingame Public Library, Burlingame CA. 415-344-7107

Leach, Lois V, *Librn,* Armed Forces Staff College Library, Norfolk VA. 804-444-5155

Leach, Martha, *Librn,* Scotland Neck Memorial Library, Scotland Neck NC. 919-826-5578

Leach, Mrs J Lawrence, *Dir,* Woodbridge Town Library, Clark Memorial Library, Woodbridge CT. 203-387-8681

Leach, Richard G, *Dir,* McGregor Public Library, Highland Park Library, Highland Park MI. 313-252-0288

Leach, Ronald G, *Assoc Dir,* Central Michigan University, Charles V Park Library, Mount Pleasant MI. 517-774-3500

Leach, Sally, *Tech Serv, Acq & Cat,* East Orange Public Library, East Orange NJ. 201-266-5600

Leach, Sally S, *Actg Librn,* University of Texas Libraries (Humanities Research Center), Austin TX. 512-471-1833

Leach, Virginia, *Rare Bks,* Episcopal Divinity School, Sherrill Hall Library, Cambridge MA. 617-868-3450, Ext 31

Leach, Jr, Maurice D, *Dir,* Washington & Lee University, The University Library, Lexington VA. 703-463-9111, Ext 403

Leachman, Roger, *Ref,* University of Virginia, Alderman Library, Charlottesville VA. 804-924-3026

Leadbeater, Dave S, *Librn,* Canadian Broadcasting Corp, Music & Record Library, Halifax NS. 902-422-8311, Ext 863, 864

Leadenham, Carol, *Actg Slavic & E European Langs,* Indiana University at Bloomington, University Libraries, Bloomington IN. 812-337-3403

Leadenham, Douglas, *Librn,* Indiana University at Bloomington (Swain Library (Astronomy, Computer Science, Physics, Math)), Bloomington IN. 812-337-2758

Leaf, Ivoline, *Librn,* Michael J Owens Technical College Library, Perrysburg OH. 419-666-0580, Exts 221 & 251

Leaf, Lorraine, *Asst Librn,* Republic-Michigamme Public Library, Republic MI. 906-376-8401

Leahong, Nancy, *Coordr,* Ecology Center Library, Berkeley CA. 415-548-2220

Leahy, Lynda, *Ref,* Brandeis University, Goldfarb Library, Waltham MA. 617-647-2514

Leahy, Margaret T, *Librn,* Canadian Government Expositions Centre, Supply & Service Canada, Technical Library, Ottawa ON. 613-993-9732

Leahy, Margaret T, *In Charge,* Supply & Services Canada, Canadian Government Expositions Centre Library, Ottawa ON. 613-993-9732

Leahy, Mary, *Rare Bks,* Bryn Mawr College, Canaday Library, Bryn Mawr PA. 215-645-5279

Leahy, Mary F, *Supvr & Librn,* Mitre Corp (Corporate Library), Bedford MA. 617-271-4834

Leahy, Suzanne, *Ref,* Lynchburg College, Knight Memorial & Capron Libraries, Lynchburg VA. 804-845-9071, Ext 271

Leak, J, *Librn,* Newcastle Public Library (Main Branch), Bowmanville ON. 416-623-7322

Leal, Andrea, *Asst Librn,* Cathedral Church of Saint John the Divine Library, New York NY. 212-678-6910

Leal, Cheney, *Asst Dir,* Casa Grande City Library, Casa Grande AZ. 602-836-7242

Leamon, David, *Dir,* Jackson District Library, Jackson MI. 517-788-4087

Leamon, Lois, *Librn,* Indianapolis-Marion County Public Library (Brown), Indianapolis IN. 317-635-5662

Leapley, Glennis, *Librn,* Lincoln Regional Center (Medical Library), Lincoln NE. 402-477-3971

Leapley, Glennis, *Librn,* Lincoln Regional Center (Patients' Library), Lincoln NE. 402-477-3971

Lear, Marc, *Asst Dir Pub Servs,* American Merchant Marine Library Association, New York NY. 212-775-1038

Lear, Martha, *Ref & On-Line Servs,* Mid-Continent Public Library, Independence MO. 816-836-5200

Lear, Winston R, *Media,* Western Piedmont Community College, Learning Resources Center, Morganton NC. 704-437-8688, Ext 234

Learnard, Joyce, *Ch,* Colonial Heights Public Library, Colonial Heights VA. 804-526-7341

Learned, Margaret, *Librn,* Andover Public Library, Andover ME. 207-392-3321

Leary, Dorothy D, *Ad,* Brunswick-Greensville Regional Library, Lawrenceville VA. 804-848-2418

Leary, Margaret A, *Asst Dir,* University of Michigan (Law Library), Ann Arbor MI. 313-764-9322

Leary, Margaret A, *Lectr,* University of Michigan, School of Library Science, MI. 313-764-9376

Leary, Marilyn, *Librn,* Lee-Itawamba Library System (Itawamba County), Fulton MS. 601-862-4926

Lease, Joan, *Media,* Fulton County Public Library, Rochester IN. 219-223-2713

Leasher, Evelyn, *Social,* Oregon State University, William Jasper Kerr Library, Corvallis OR. 503-754-3411

Leask, Mary, *Actg Dir,* Ministry of Provincial Secretary and Government Services, Library Services Branch, Dawson Creek BC. 604-782-2814

Leath, Louise, *Librn,* Enoch Pratt Free Library (Reisterstown Road), Baltimore MD. 301-396-5430, 396-5395

Leather, Victoria, *Librn,* Chattanooga-Hamilton County Bicentennial Library (Eastgate), Chattanooga TN. 615-899-9249

Leathers, Barbara, *Librn,* Woodland Public Library, Woodland WA. 206-225-8631

Leathers, James A, *Dir,* Mid-Continent Public Library, Independence MO. 816-836-5200

Leathers, Jean, *Per & Doc,* Findlay College, Shafer Library, Findlay OH. 419-422-8313, Ext 327

Leathers, Mary, *Cat,* Frank Hughes Memorial Library, Liberty MO. 816-781-3611

Leavens, Bill, *Chief Librn,* Veterans Administration, Library Service, Allen Park MI. 313-562-6000, Ext 380

Leaver, Winnie, *Ch,* Peters Township Library, McMurray PA. 412-941-9430

Leavitt, Donald, *Chief, Music Div,* Library of Congress, Washington DC. 202-287-5000

Leavitt, Edward P, *Librn,* Tufts University, Medical-Dental Library, Boston MA. 617-956-6707

Leavitt, Eleanor, *ILL,* Paul Smiths College of Arts & Sciences, Frank L Cubley Library, Paul Smiths NY. 518-327-6313

Leavitt, Jane M, *Asst Dir,* Dickinson Memorial Library, Northfield Library, Northfield MA. 413-498-2455

Leavy, Marvin, *Behavioral Sci,* Wichita State University, Library & Media Resources Center, Wichita KS. 316-689-3586

LeBaron, Joy M, *Librn,* Fairfax Community Library, Fairfax VT. 802-849-6711

LeBaron, Louisa, *Circ,* Reading Public Library, Reading MA. 617-944-0840

Lebbin, Josephine, *ILL,* Arlington Heights Memorial Library, Arlington Heights IL. 312-392-0100

Lebbin, Lee, *Librn,* Eckerd College, William Luther Cobb Library, Saint Petersburg FL. 813-867-1166, Ext 336
Lebbin, Lee, *Dir,* New Mexico Institute of Mining & Technology, Martin Speare Memorial Library, Socorro NM. 505-835-5614
Lebda, Anna, *Librn,* Somerset County Library, Somerset PA. 814-445-4011
Lebda, Anna N, *Librn,* Mary S Biesecker Public Library, Somerset PA. 814-445-4011
LeBeau, Constance J, *Librn,* Ginn & Co Library, Lexington MA. 617-861-1670
LeBeau, Kay, *Ch,* Norton Public Library, Norton KS. 913-877-2481
Lebeau, Marcia, *Per,* Nichols Library, Naperville IL. 312-355-1540
Lebel, H, *Dir,* Monastere Des Peres Redemptoristes, Bibliotheque, Sherbrooke PQ. 819-562-2677
LeBel, Jocelyne, *Dir,* New Brunswick Legislative Library, Fredericton NB. 506-453-2338
Leber, Michele, *Librn,* Fairfax County Public Library (John Marshall), Alexandria VA. 703-971-0010
LeBlanc, Alida L, *Librn,* Our Lady of Lourdes Hospital Library, Lafayette LA. 318-234-7381, Ext 2141
Leblanc, Amedee, *Acq,* Universite De Moncton, Bibliotheque Champlain, Moncton NB. 506-858-4012
LeBlanc, Claudette, *Sub-Regional Librn,* Chaleur Regional Library (Nepisiguit Centennial), Bathurst NB. 506-546-9825, 548-9562
LeBlanc, Diane, *Instr,* Grant MacEwan Community College, Library Technician Program, AB. 403-474-8521
LeBlanc, Eric S, *Librn,* National Research Council of Canada, Dominion Astrophysical Observatory Library, Victoria BC. 604-388-0298
LeBlanc, Peggy B, *Librn,* Vermilion Parish Library (Erath Branch), Erath LA. 318-937-5628
LeBlanc, Ronald, *Librn,* Universite De Moncton (Centre d'Etudes Acadeciennes), Moncton NB. 506-858-4076
Leblond, M P, *Info Officer,* Bio-Research Ltd Library, Sainte-Anne-de-Bellevue PQ. 514-457-2280
Lebreton, Leonie, *Tech Serv & Cat,* CEGEP de Chicoutimi, Centre De Documentation, Chicoutimi PQ. 418-549-9520, Ext 212, 312
Lebron, Mariano Morales, *Dir,* University of Puerto Rico, Cayey University College Library, Cayey PR. 809-738-2161, Ext 221
Lebrun, Shirley A, *Librn,* Ontario Cancer Foundation Ottawa Clinic, Beattie Library, Ottawa ON. 613-725-4361
LeBus, Lou, *Coordr,* Medical Center Hospital, Bell-Marsh Memorial Library, Tyler TX. 214-597-0531, Ext 269
LeButt, Katherine, *Dir & Acq,* York Regional Library, Fredericton NB. 506-454-4481
Lechiaro, Marguerite, *Asst Dir,* Cambridge Public Library, Cambridge MA. 617-498-9080
Lechner, Marian G, *Corp Librn,* Connecticut General Life Insurance Co Library, Bloomfield CT. 203-726-4239, 726-4327
Lechner, Marie, *Librn,* Haskell Public Library, Haskell OK. 918-482-3614
Leckie, Rosemary, *Librn,* Crum & Forster Insurance Co, Morristown NJ. 201-285-3973
Leckrone, Joyce, *Instr,* Manchester College, Educational Media Specialist Program, IN. 219-982-2141, Ext 231
Leckrone, Joyce, *Acq,* Manchester College, Funderburg Library, North Manchester IN. 219-982-2141, Ext 231
Leckrone, Naomi, *Librn,* Hammond Public Library (Lincoln), Hammond IN. 219-931-5100
Leclair, Micheline, *Asst Librn,* Hotel-Dieu d'Arthabaska, Medical Library, Arthabaska PQ. 819-357-2031, Ext 216
LeClaire, Ann, *Dir, On-Line Servs & Bibliog Instr,* Miriam Hospital (Medical Library), Providence RI. 401-274-3700
LeClercq, Anne, *Librn,* University of Tennessee, Knoxville (John C Hodges Undergraduate Library), Knoxville TN. 615-974-4273
Lecompte, Louis-Luc, *Behav Sci,* Hospital Sainte-Justine, Centre d'Information Sur La Sante de L'Enfant, Montreal PQ. 514-731-4931, Ext 339
LeConte, Dianne, *Asst Librn,* Walker Memorial Library, Westbrook ME. 207-854-2391

LeCroissette, Jill, *Tech Serv,* California State University, John F Kennedy Memorial Library, Los Angeles CA. 213-224-2201
Ledbetter, Bonnie M, *Soc Sci,* University of Alabama in Birmingham, Mervyn H Sterne Library, Birmingham AL. 205-934-6360
Ledden, Mildred, *Assoc Librn,* New York State Library (Humanities Reference Service), Albany NY. 518-474-6837
Ledder, Susan, *Ch,* North Tonawanda Public Library, North Tonawanda NY. 716-693-4132
LeDell, Betty, *Librn,* Grace Lutheran Church Library, Wayzata MN. 612-473-2362
Ledet, Henry J, *Asst Dir,* Lincoln-Lawrence-Franklin Regional Library, Brookhaven MS. 601-833-3369
Ledford, Carole L, *Librn,* University of Georgia, Georgia Experiment Station Library, Experiment GA. 404-228-7238
Ledford, Elizabeth, *Librn,* Charlotte Law Library, Charlotte NC. 704-334-4912
Ledford, Gayle, *Librn,* Q B Boydstun Library, Fort Gibson OK. 918-478-3587
Ledford, Jean, *Actg Librn,* Carroll County District Library, Carrollton OH. 216-627-2613
Ledhetter, Fraser L, *Librn,* Saint Simons Public Library, Saint Simons Island GA. 912-638-8234
Ledicauskas, Alice B, *Librn,* Wyman-Gordon Co Library, North Grafton MA. 617-839-4441, Ext 657
Ledley, Ida, *Librn,* Auglaize County District Library (Waynesfield Public), Waynesfield OH. 419-568-5851
Ledlie, Mary Elizabeth, *Ch,* Milwaukee Public Library, Milwaukee WI. 414-278-3000
LeDuc, Carol, *Outreach Servs,* Hennepin County Library, Edina MN. 612-830-4944
Leduc, Lise, *Ref,* Hospital Sainte-Justine, Centre d'Information Sur La Sante de L'Enfant, Montreal PQ. 514-731-4931, Ext 339
Leduc, Richard G, *Librn,* Rhode Island Regional Library for the Blind & Physically Handicapped, Providence RI. 401-277-2726
Ledward, Kay, *Librn,* Silverton Public Library, Gladys Hoyt Memorial Library, Silverton OR. 503-873-5173
Ledwell, W A, *Media,* Prince Edward Island Provincial Library, Charlottetown PE. 902-892-3504, Ext 54
Ledwell, William, *Librn,* Prince Edward Island Provincial Library (Film Library, Media Center), Charlottetown PE. 902-894-3786
Ledwidge, Jean F, *Dir,* Tri-Lakes Regional Library, Hot Springs AR. 501-623-4161
Lee, Alice T, *Librn,* United States Air Force (Kirtland Air Force Base Library), Kirtland AFB NM. 505-264-1086, 247-1711
Lee, Alice T, *Librn,* United States Air Force (Medical Library), Kirtland AFB NM. 505-844-1086
Lee, Amy C, *Librn,* Federal Deposit Insurance Corp Library, Washington DC. 202-389-4314, Exts 314&315
Lee, Angel, *ILL,* Mount Vernon Public Library, Mount Vernon WA. 206-336-2418
Lee, Beverly, *Librn,* University of Minnesota Libraries-Twin Cities (Chemistry), Minneapolis MN. 612-373-2375
Lee, Carolyn, *Librn,* Catholic University of America (Theology-Philosophy), Washington DC. 202-635-5055
Lee, Carolyn, *Librn,* Charlotte-Glades Library System (Glades County Branch), Moore Haven FL. 813-946-0744
Lee, Carolyn T, *Rare Bks & Spec Coll,* Catholic University of America, John K Mullen of Denver Memorial Library, Washington DC. 202-635-5055
Lee, Carrie, *Br Asst,* Saint Charles Parish Library (Norco Branch), Norco LA. 504-764-6581
Lee, Celia, *Cat,* San Bernardino County Library, San Bernardino CA. 714-383-1734
Lee, Cenetta, *Commun Servs,* Stamford's Public Library, Ferguson Library, Stamford CT. 203-325-4354
Lee, Chang C, *Head Librn,* Pennsylvania State University, Behrend College Library, Erie PA. 814-898-1511, Ext 273, 259
Lee, Charles Donald, *Dir,* College of the Albemarle, Whitehurst Library, Elizabeth City NC. 919-335-0821, Ext 287

Lee, Charles W, *Librn,* Lima State Hospital, Forensic Psychiatric Library, Lima OH. 419-227-4631, Ext 224
Lee, Chen-Li, *Asst Dir,* Villa Julie College Library, Stevenson MD. 301-486-7000
Lee, Chui-Chun, *ILL,* State University of New York, College at New Paltz, Sojourner Truth Library, New Paltz NY. 914-257-2204
Lee, Chui-Chun, *Asian,* State University of New York, College at New Paltz, Sojourner Truth Library, New Paltz NY. 914-257-2204
Lee, Dae, *Asst Prof,* Saint Cloud State University, Center for Library & Audiovisual Education, MN. 612-255-2022
Lee, Dennis, *Tech Serv,* Northwest College of the Assemblies of God, Hurst Library, Kirkland WA. 206-822-8266, Ext 255
Lee, Edward, *Tech Serv & Cat,* Wayne State University Libraries (Arthur Neef Law Library), Detroit MI. 313-577-3925
Lee, Ethel B, *Circ,* Southeastern Baptist Theological Seminary Library, Wake Forest NC. 919-556-3101, Ext 225, 250
Lee, Ethel M, *Head Doc Librn,* Brown University (University Library), Providence RI. 401-863-2167
Lee, Felicia, *Librn,* Midrex Corp Library, Charlotte NC. 704-373-1600, Ext 279
Lee, Frances, *Tech Serv,* San Diego Public Library, San Diego CA. 714-236-5800
Lee, Frances, *Librn,* Warren Public Library (Walt Whitman), Warren MI. 313-751-0770
Lee, Frank S, *ILL,* Dallas Public Library, Dallas TX. 214-748-9071
Lee, Fred, *Librn,* Dow Corning Corp (Business Information Center), Midland MI. 517-496-4961
Lee, Grant, *Asst to Dean,* University of Pittsburgh, School of Library & Information Science, PA. 412-624-5230
Lee, Helen, *Librn,* Union Camp Corp, Research & Development Library, Princeton NJ. 609-896-1200, Ext 713
Lee, Hwa-Wei, *Dir,* Ohio University, Vernon R Alden Library, Athens OH. 614-594-5228
Lee, Hwa-Wei, *Adjunct Prof,* Ohio University, Educational Media Program, OH. 614-594-5404
Lee, Hyosoo, *Tech Serv & On-Line Servs,* Cleveland Institute of Art, Jessica Gund Memorial Library, Cleveland OH. 216-421-4322, Ext 30
Lee, Inn Sook, *Cat,* Herrick Public Library, Holland MI. 616-392-3114
Lee, James, *Cat,* Cumberland County Public Library, Anderson Street Library, Frances Brooks Stein Memorial Library, Fayetteville NC. 919-483-1580
Lee, James, *Ad & Ref,* Olean Public Library, Olean NY. 716-372-0200
Lee, James D, *Ref,* University of North Carolina at Asheville, D Hiden Ramsey Library, Asheville NC. 704-258-0200
Lee, Jane Yu, *Librn,* General Telephone & Electronics, GTE Automatic Electric Laboratories, Inc Library, Northlake IL. 312-681-7118
Lee, Joann H, *Ref, On-Line Servs & Bibliog Instr,* Lake Forest College, Donnelley Library, Lake Forest IL. 312-234-3100, Ext 405
Lee, Joe B, *Librn,* Angelo State University, Porter Henderson Library, San Angelo TX. 915-942-2222
Lee, Joe Y, *Assoc Dir,* Public Library of the District of Columbia, Martin Luther King Memorial Library, Washington DC. 202-727-1101
Lee, Joel M, *Librn,* American Library Association, Headquarters Library, Chicago IL. 312-944-6780, Ext 338
Lee, John, *Ref,* State University of New York Maritime College, Stephen B Luce Library, Bronx NY. 212-892-3004, Ext 235
Lee, John, *Librn,* West Virginia State Penitentiary Library, Moundsville WV. 304-845-2363
Lee, Jonathan K, *Ref,* Northeastern Regional Library System, Kirkland Lake ON. 705-567-7043
Lee, Joyce C, *Ref,* Nevada State Library, Carson City NV. 702-885-5130
Lee, June, *Asst Dir & Ad,* Farmington Community Library, Farmington Hills MI. 313-553-0300
Lee, June, *Dir,* Mississippi State Hospital, Medical Library, Whitfield MS. 601-939-1221, Ext 441

Lee, Jung Won, *Librn,* Missouri Training Center for Men, James O Datson School Library, Moberly MO. 816-263-3778

Lee, Katherine A, *Librn,* Bolivar County Library (Field Memorial), Shaw MS. 601-754-6381

Lee, Kathryn, *Reader Serv,* Tulsa City-County Library, Tulsa OK. 918-581-5221

Lee, Kay Won, *Oriental Mat,* Georgetown University, Joseph Mark Lauinger Library, Washington DC. 202-625-4095

Lee, Lauren, *Ad,* Cobb County Public Library System, Marietta GA. 404-427-2462

Lee, Lila, *Librn,* Mendocino County Historical Society, Held-Poage Memorial Home & Research Library, Ukiah CA. 707-462-6969

Lee, Lillian J, *Librn,* Northwestern University Library (Geology), Evanston IL. 312-492-5525

Lee, Loree, *Librn,* Rigby City Library, Rigby ID. 208-745-8231

Lee, Lydia H, *Librn,* Exxon Co USA, Exxon Nuclear Co, Richland WA. 509-375-7386

Lee, Lynda M, *Dir,* Calcasieu Parish Public Library System, Lake Charles LA. 318-433-1045

Lee, Malinda C, *Asst Dir & Tech Serv,* George Washington University Library (Jacob Burns Law Library), Washington DC. 202-676-6646

Lee, Margaret, *Serv to Local Govt,* Fresno County Free Library, Fresno CA. 209-488-3191

Lee, Margaret, *Spec Coll,* Public Library of Johnston County & Smithfield, Smithfield NC. 919-934-8146

Lee, Margaret L, *Dir,* Miles Laboratories, Inc, Library Resources & Services, Elkhart IN. 219-264-8341

Lee, Margaret S, *Dir,* Reinhardt College, Hill Freeman Library, Waleska GA. 404-479-1454, Ext 27, 43

Lee, Marilyn, *Dir,* San Manuel Public Library, San Manuel AZ. 602-385-4470

Lee, Marilyn M, *Librn,* Franklin County Law Library, Greenfield MA. 413-772-6580

Lee, Marlene, *Ch,* Oakland Park City Library, Oakland Park FL. 305-561-6287

Lee, Marlyce, *Librn,* Washington County Library (Wildwood), Willernie MN. 612-426-2042

Lee, Martha Ann, *Ref,* Mississippi Research & Development Center, Information Services Divison, Jackson MS. 601-982-6324

Lee, Mary, *ILL,* Gavilan College Library, Gilroy CA. 408-847-1400, Ext 312

Lee, Maureen, *Ser,* University of Toronto Libraries (University Library), Toronto ON. 416-978-2294

Lee, Mei Moi, *Ref,* Benton & Bowles Inc Library, New York NY. 212-758-6200, Ext 3156

Lee, Michael, *Dir,* Saginaw Valley State College Library & Learning Resources Center, University Center MI. 517-790-4237

Lee, Mildred, *Cat & Ref,* North Haledon Free Public Library, North Haledon NJ. 201-427-6213

Lee, Mrs Helmer, *Librn,* Sheridan County Free Library, Plentywood MT. 406-765-1282

Lee, Mrs Jung Won, *Librn,* Missouri Division of Corrections Libraries (Missouri Training Center for Men), Jefferson City MO. 314-751-3050

Lee, Nadean, *Instr,* Arkansas State University, Dept of Library Science, AR. 501-972-3077

Lee, Nancy, *Tech Serv,* University of Louisville Library (Kornhauser Health Sciences), Louisville KY. 502-588-5771

Lee, P, *Cat,* Union Carbide Corp (Research & Development Department Building 740 Library), South Charleston WV. 304-747-4308

Lee, Pauline, *Coordr,* Grambling State University, Library Education Program, LA. 318-247-6941, Ext 220

Lee, Pauline W, *Dir,* Grambling State University, A C Lewis Memorial Library, Grambling LA. 318-247-6941, Ext 220

Lee, Peggy, *On-Line Servs & Bibliog Instr,* J P Stevens & Co Inc, Learning Resources Center, Charlotte NC. 704-366-3221

Lee, Pier M, *Dir,* Peters Township Library, McMurray PA. 412-941-9430

Lee, R A, *Head Research Dept,* Universal City Studios, Research Dept Library, Universal City CA. 508-2493 & 508-2494

Lee, Robert, *Librn,* University of Western Ontario, A B Weldon Library, London ON. 519-679-6191

Lee, Robert P, *Cat,* Thomas Jefferson University (Scott Memorial Library), Philadelphia PA. 215-928-8848

Lee, Rosalie, *Librn,* South Mississippi Regional Library (Bassfield Public), Bassfield MS. 601-943-5424

Lee, Ruby, *Librn,* Tri-County Regional Library (Rockmart Branch), Rockmart GA. 404-291-9360

Lee, Ruth, *Bkmobile Coordr,* Superiorland Library Cooperative, Marquette MI. 906-228-7697

Lee, Sang C, *Cat,* Herbert H Lehman College Library, Bronx NY. 212-960-8577, 960-8582

Lee, Sara, *Librn,* Dillon County Library (Dunbar Memorial), Dillon SC. 803-774-9601

Lee, Sara J, *Librn,* Texas Instruments, Inc, Austin Library, Austin TX. 512-258-7421

Lee, Shirley, *Ref,* Rand Corp Library, Santa Monica CA. 213-393-0411, Ext 369

Lee, Shirley T, *Librn,* Cleveland Public Library (Mount Pleasant), Cleveland OH. 216-561-4790

Lee, Silva, *Dir,* South Huntington Public Library, Huntington Station NY. 516-549-4411

Lee, Soo, *Assoc Dir,* Wake Forest University (Bowman Gray School of Medicine Library), Winston-Salem NC. 919-727-4691

Lee, Sul H, *Dean,* University of Oklahoma University Libraries, Norman OK. 405-325-2611

Lee, Susan, *Dir,* American International College, McGown Memorial Library, Springfield MA. 413-737-5331, Ext 225

Lee, Susie, *Comparative Law,* University of Washington Libraries (Law Library), Seattle WA. 206-543-4089

Lee, Tsun Hai, *Dir,* Kern County Health Department, Myrnie A Gifford Public Health Library, Bakersfield CA. 805-861-3631

Lee, William, *Phys Sci & Eng,* Iowa State University Library, Ames IA. 515-294-1442

Lee, William M, *Pub Serv,* University of West Florida, John C Pace Library, Pensacola FL. 904-476-9500, Ext 261

Lee, Young S, *Dir & Acq,* William Carey College, I E Rouse Library, Hattiesburg MS. 601-582-5051, Ext 245 & 246

Lee, Yvonne, *Cat & Bibliog Instr,* Linn-Benton Community College, Learning Resource Center, Albany OR. 503-928-2361, Ext 330

Leece, Gordon, *Adjunct Lectr,* Dalhousie University, School of Library Service, NS. 902-424-3656

Leech, Linda, *Media,* University of Pittsburgh, Johnstown Campus Library, Johnstown PA. 814-266-9661, Ext 314

Leech, Sara, *Assoc Dir,* University of Kentucky (Medical Center Library), Lexington KY. 606-233-5300

Leedale, Joan, *Librn,* Dupont Canada Inc (Legal Library), Mississauga ON. 416-821-3300, Ext 504

Leedale, Joan, *Librn,* DuPont Canada Inc, Legal Library, Mississauga ON. 416-821-3300, Ext 504

Leeds, Doris M, *Librn,* National Cash Register Co, Research Library, San Diego CA. 714-485-3291

Leeds, Edith H, *Librn,* Friends Meeting of Washington Library, Washington DC. 202-483-3310

Leeds, Pauline, *Librn,* New England Nuclear Corp Library, Boston MA. 617-482-9595, Ext 2662, 2663

Leehey, H R, *Librn,* John Deere Product Engineering Center Library, Waterloo IA. 319-235-4668

Leen, Mary, *Librn,* Bostonian Society Library, Boston MA. 617-523-7033

Leenders, Penny, *Librn,* Whatcom County Public Library (Sumas Branch), Sumas WA. 206-988-2501

Leeper, Blanche M, *Librn,* Marion Koogler McNay Art Institute Art Institute Library, San Antonio TX. 512-824-5368

Leeper, Dennis, *Asst Prof,* Drexel University, School of Library & Information Science, PA. 215-895-2474

Leeper, Mary Frances, *Librn,* Perry County Public Library (Lobelville Branch), Lobelville TN. 615-593-2302

Leeper, Mrs Jacque, *Librn,* Wayne Presbyterian Church (Resource Center), Wayne PA. 215-688-8700

Leeper, Regina, *Asst Dir, AV & Tech Serv,* North Kingstown Free Library, North Kingstown RI. 401-294-2521

Leeper, Yvette, *Librn,* Maryland State Department of Health & Mental Hygiene Library, Baltimore MD. 301-383-2683

Leerhoff, Ruth, *Tech Serv,* San Diego State University Library, San Diego CA. 714-286-6014

Lees, Sandra, *Ad,* Noblesville Public Library, Noblesville IN. 317-773-1384

Leese, Laura, *Librn,* Elizabeth A Horton Memorial Hospital, Medical Library, Middletown NY. 914-343-2424

Leeson, Joanne, *Supvr,* Middlesex County Library (Putnam Branch), Putnam ON. 519-485-4946

Leet, Richard E, *Dir,* Charles H MacNider Museum Library, Mason City IA. 515-423-9563

Lefaivre, Paula, *Ref,* Red Deer Municipal Library, Red Deer AB. 403-346-4576

LeFeber, Janet, *Librn,* Richmond Township Public Library, Palmer MI. 906-475-5241

LeFebvre, Gilbert, *Actg Librn,* College D'enseignement General & Professionnel De Limoilou Bibliotheque, Quebec PQ. 418-694-7400

LeFebyre, Margaret, *Librn,* Mapleton Public Library, Mapleton IA. 712-882-1312

Lefere, Mari Beth, *Head,* Chicago Public Library (Chicago Library Service for the Blind & Physically Handicapped (Subregional)), Chicago IL. 312-738-9200

LeFevre, Geraldine, *Asst Dir,* San Antonio Public Library, San Antonio TX. 512-299-7790

Leff, Barbara, *Librn,* Stephen S Wise Temple, Jack Diener Memorial Library, Los Angeles CA. 213-272-7831

Leffel, Rick, *Media,* Elmira College, Gannett-Tripp Learning Ctr, Elmira NY. 607-734-3911, Ext 287

Leffers, Mary Jeanne, *Librn,* Public Library of Fort Wayne & Allen County (Tecumseh), Fort Wayne IN. 219-483-8975

Leffingwell, Alta, *Librn,* Huachuca City Public Library, Huachuca City AZ. 602-456-1553

Leffler, Nadine E, *Chief, Bibliog & Tech Servs,* Orange County Public Library, Orange CA. 714-634-7841

Lefkovits, Ruth, *Dir,* Iberia Parish Public Library, New Iberia LA. 318-369-6321

Lefkowitz, Mark, *Librn,* Visual Information Systems, Physicians Radio Network, New York NY. 212-541-8384, Ext 198

Lefkowitz, Robert J, *Librn,* Saint Anthony Hospital, M O'Donoghue Medical Library, Oklahoma City OK. 405-231-1811, Ext 2197

Lefkowski, Mary, *Doc,* Dickinson School of Law, Sheely-Lee Law Library, Carlisle PA. 717-243-4611, Ext 9

Lefler, Margaret S, *Librn,* Roanoke-Chowan Technical Institute, Learning Resource Center, Ahoskie NC. 919-332-5921

Lefleur, J C, *Exec Secy,* Quebec Ministere Des Affaires Sociales Informatheque, Quebec PQ. 418-643-6392

Lefrancois, Guy, *Ref,* Centre Universitaire Saint-Louis-Maillet, Students Library, Edmundston NB. 506-735-8804

LeFree, Thomas O, *Planning & Evaluation Servs,* Denver Public Library, Denver CO. 303-573-5152, Ext 271

Leftwich, June, *Libr Assoc for Gifts,* Dallas Public Library, Dallas TX. 214-748-9071

Legate, Lynn T, *Ref,* Ottawa Public Library, Ottawa ON. 613-236-0301

Legault, Lucille, *Librn,* Bibliotheqe Publique De Russell, Embrun ON. 613-443-3636

Legault, Therese, *Librn,* Hawkesbury Public Library, Hawkesbury ON. 613-632-6656

Legeault, J, *Ch,* Bibliotheque Municipale De Lachine, Lachine PQ. 514-637-2568

Legendre, Beatrice, *In Charge,* Albert-Westmorland-Kent Regional Library (Saint Joseph Public), Saint Joseph NB. 506-389-2631

LeGendre, Elaine U, *Health Sci Librn,* Lawrence Memorial Hospital, Health Sciences Library, Medford MA. 617-396-9250, Ext 240

Legere, Monique, *Dir,* Canadian International Development Agency Library, Hull PQ. 819-997-5456

Leget, Max, *Ref,* University of South Dakota, I D Weeks Library, Vermillion SD. 605-677-5371

LeGette, Louise, *Chief Librn,* Tampa Tribune Library, Tampa FL. 813-272-7665

Legg, Georgia, *Librn,* Carnegie Public Library, Grayville IL. 618-375-7121

Leggett, Mark, *Bus Info Serv,* Milwaukee Public Library, Milwaukee WI. 414-278-3000
Leggett, Mary G, *Ad,* Clinton-Essex-Franklin Library System, Plattsburgh NY. 518-563-5190
Leggett, Patrick, *Regional Librn,* United States Department of Housing & Urban Development, Region-Area VIII Library, Denver CO. 303-837-3431
Lego, Jane B, *Circ,* Norfolk Public Library, Norfolk VA. 804-441-2887
Lego, Jane B, *Fiction,* Norfolk Public Library, Norfolk VA. 804-441-2887
Legott, S, *Librn,* Kahl Scientific Instrument Corp Library, El Cajon CA. 714-444-2158
Lehan, Dorothy, *Librn,* Dammasch State Hospital Library, Wilsonville OR. 503-682-3111
Lehan, Theresa, *Librn,* Santa Clara County Free Library (Morgan Hill Public), Morgan Hill CA. 408-779-3196
Lehe, Mardelle, *Asst Librn,* Darlington Public Library, Darlington IN. 312-794-4813
Lehman, Arnold L, *Dir,* Metropolitan Museum & Art Center Library, Coral Gables FL. 305-442-1448
Lehman, Betty, *Coordr,* Estherville Public Library, Estherville IA. 712-362-3869
Lehman, Clifford, *Media,* Oklahoma Baptist University, Mabee Learning Center, Shawnee OK. 405-275-2850, Ext 245
Lehman, Diane, *Dir,* Elliot Lake Public Library, Elliot Lake ON. 705-848-7454
Lehman, Doris, *Commun Servs,* Columbiana Public Library, Columbiana OH. 216-482-2356
Lehman, James O, *Dir,* Eastern Mennonite College & Seminary Library, Harrisonburg VA. 703-433-2771, Ext 171
Lehman, Lois, *Acting Asst Dir Tech Servs,* Indiana University at Bloomington, University Libraries, Bloomington IN. 812-337-3403
Lehman, Lois J, *Librn,* Pennsylvania State University, Milton S Hershey Medical Center, George T Harrell Library, Hershey PA. 717-534-8626
Lehmann, Bernice, *Librn,* Scenic Regional Library of Franklin, Gasconade & Warren Counties (Owensville Service Center), Owensville MO. 314-437-2188
Lehmann, Eric, *Per,* Johnson Free Public Library, Hackensack NJ. 201-343-4169
Lehmann, Lucile, *Archivist,* Coastal Engineering Archives, Gainesville FL. 904-392-1436
Lehmann, Lucile, *Archivist,* University of Florida Libraries (Coastal Engineering Archives), Gainesville FL. 904-392-1436
Lehnert, Mabel, *Ch,* Warren County Library, Belvidere NJ. 201-475-5361, Ext 114
Lehnert, Sharon, *Librn,* Hamilton Public Library (Terryberry), Hamilton ON. 416-388-7515
Lehnig, Katharine P, *Librn,* Bucks County Law Library, Doylestown PA. 215-348-2911, Ext 268
Lehnus, Donald J, *Assoc Prof,* University of Mississippi, Graduate School of Library & Information Science, MS. 601-232-7440
Lehocky, Barbara, *Ref,* University of Missouri Saint Louis, Thomas Jefferson Library, Saint Louis MO. 314-453-5221
Lehoux, Bernard, *Librn,* Bibliotheque Municipale, Gatineau PQ. 819-663-9254
Lehovec, Gisela, *Ch & YA,* Bennington Free Library, Bennington VT. 802-442-9051
Lehr, Milt, *Dir,* Northwestern Oklahoma State University Library (Instructional Media Center), Alva OK. 405-327-1700, Ext 316
Lehr, Robert M, *Cat,* University of Nebraska Medical Center, Library of Medicine, Omaha NE. 402-541-4006
Lehtinen, Mary, *Librn,* Lowell General Hospital Library, Lowell MA. 617-454-0411, Ext 242
Leibiger, I, *Chief Librn,* O W Leibiger Research Laboratories, Inc, Technical Library, Hoosick Falls NY. 518-686-5841
Leible, Shirley, *Lectr,* University of Wisconsin-Oshkosh, Dept of Library Science, WI. 414-424-2313
Leibman, Roy, *Media,* California State University, John F Kennedy Memorial Library, Los Angeles CA. 213-224-2201
Leibouici, Martin M, *Librn,* Goldwater Memorial Hospital, Medical Library, New York NY. 212-750-6749
Leibowitz, Margaret, *Deputy Dir,* Alaska State Library, Juneau AK. 907-465-2910

Leibowitz, Shirley, *ILL & Ref,* Willingboro Public Library, Willingboro NJ. 609-877-6668
Leich, Elizabeth L, *Dir,* Thomas E Ryan Public Library, East Williston NY. 516-741-1213
Leichter, Janice, *Librn,* Mount Zion Temple, Joseph & Charlotte Melamed Bloom Library, Saint Paul MN. 612-698-3881
Leide, John, *Asst Prof,* University of Hawaii, Graduate School of Library Studies, HI. 808-948-7321
Leiden, Mary, *Librn,* Austin Public Library (Montopolis), Austin TX. 512-472-5433
Leidinger, Claudia, *Librn,* Elkins Public Library, Canterbury NH. 603-783-4386
Leidy, Dean, *Media,* College of Wooster, Andrews Library, Wooster OH. 216-264-1234, Ext 483
Leif, Mary D, *Dir,* Washington Hospital-School of Nursing, Medical Nurses Library, Washington PA. 412-225-7000, Ext 306
Leigh, Bob, *Bus & Indust,* Stockton-San Joaquin County Public Library, Stockton Public Libr, Stockton CA. 209-944-8415
Leigh, Jaroslava, *Librn,* Smithtown Library (Kings Park Branch), Kings Park NY. 516-269-9191
Leigh, Joan H, *Asst Prof,* University of Minnesota, Library School, MN. 612-373-3100
Leigh, Kathleen A, *Librn,* Germantown Dispensary & Hospital (School of Nursing Library), Philadelphia PA. 215-438-9700
Leigh, Robert, *Asst Dir,* Prince George Public Library, Prince George BC. 604-563-9251
Leigh, Sharon, *On-Line Servs,* Southern Utah State College Library, Cedar City UT. 801-586-4411, Ext 351
Leighton, David T S, *Librn,* Dean Junior College, E Ross Anderson Library, Franklin MA. 617-528-9100, Ext 261
Leighton, Elizabeth, *Cat,* Huron College, Silcox Memorial Library, London ON. 519-438-7224, Ext 13
Leighton, Helene, *Head Computer Search Servs,* Massachusetts General Hospital (Treadwell Library), Boston MA. 617-726-8600
Leighton, Judith, *Librn,* Bangor Public Library (Subregional Library for the Blind & Physically Handicapped), Bangor ME. 207-947-8336
Leighton, Muriel, *Tech Serv,* South Portland Public Library, South Portland ME. 207-799-2204
Leighton, Virginia, *Librn,* Easton Free Public Library, Easton NH. 603-823-5238
Leightty, Virginia, *Acq,* University of Louisville Library (Kornhauser Health Sciences), Louisville KY. 502-588-5771
Leighty, Dorothy, *Librn,* Kendallville Public Library (Orange Township), Kendallville IN. 219-854-2775
Leilich, Nita, *Librn,* Norman, Craig & Kummel Inc, Marketing Research Department Library, New York NY. 212-751-0900
Leinbach, Philip E, *Asst Univ Librn for Personnel,* Harvard University Library, Cambridge MA. 617-495-3650
Leiner, Alverta, *Librn,* Riverside Regional Library (Center 1), Illmo MO. 314-263-2413
Leininger, Roberta, *Librn,* Friends Bible College, Worden Memorial Library, Haviland KS. 316-862-5274
Leinoff, Thelma, *Asst Dir,* Greenburgh Public Library, Elmsford NY. 914-682-5265
Leinweber, Jan, *Acq,* Southern Alberta Institute of Technology, Learning Resources Centre, Calgary AB. 284-8647; 284-8648
Leiserson, Alice, *Bkmobile Coordr & Ch,* John Packard Library of Yuba County, Marysville CA. 916-674-6241
Leishman, Sara, *Curator,* Cambria County Historical Society Library, Ebensburg PA. 814-472-6674
Leister, Jack, *Librn,* University of California, Berkeley (Institute of Governmental Studies Library), Berkeley CA. 415-642-1472
Leitch, Carolyn, *Head of Volunteer Utilization,* Florida Regional Library for the Blind & Physically Handicapped, Daytona Beach FL. 904-252-4722
Leitch, Jean, *Asst Dir,* Grand Ledge Public Library, Grand Ledge MI. 517-627-7014
Leitch, Ruth, *Librn,* Lambton County Library (Alvinston Branch), Alvinston ON. 519-898-2921
Leith, Anna, *Librn,* University of British Columbia Library (Woodward Biomedical), Vancouver BC. 604-228-2762

Leith, Marian P, *Asst Librn,* North Carolina Department of Cultural Resources, Division of State Library, North Carolina State Library, Raleigh NC. 919-733-2570
Leitman, Margaret C, *Dir,* Forbes Health System Libraries (Pittsburgh Skilled Nursing Center Library), Pittsburgh PA. 412-665-3050
Leitner, LaVonne, *Librn,* Rampart Regional Library, Woodland Park CO. 303-687-9616
Leitner, Ramona, *Dir,* New Albany Floyd County Public Library, New Albany IN. 812-944-8464
Leitzel, Susan, *Librn,* Dauphin County Library System (Northern Dauphin), Lykens PA. 717-453-9315
Leitzke, Nowell D, *Libr Consult,* Minnesota State Library Agency, Office of Public Libraries & Interlibrary Cooperation, Saint Paul MN. 612-296-2821
Leive, Mildred, *Cat,* Carnegie Free Library, McKeesport PA. 412-672-0625
Leja, Ilga, *Asst Librn,* Legislative Library of Nova Scotia, Halifax NS. 902-424-5932
LeKernec, William J, *Dir,* Middletown Township Public Library, Middletown NJ. 201-671-3700
Lem, Nancy E, *Librn,* Hewlett-Packard Co (H-P Laboratories Library), Palo Alto CA. 415-857-5206
Leman, Amy, *Librn,* Sussex County Library System (Vernon-Northeastern District), Vernon NJ. 201-764-7140
Lemann, Harriet M, *Librn,* Law Library of Louisiana, New Orleans LA. 504-568-5705
LeMaster, Charles, *Chmn & Asst Prof,* Morningside College, Library Science Dept, IA. 712-277-5125
LeMaster, Charles, *Dir,* Morningside College, Wilhemina Petersmeyer Library, Sioux City IA. 712-277-5195
Lemaster, Gloria S, *Librn,* Library for the Blind & Physically Handicapped, Department of Adult Blind & Deaf, Talladega AL. 205-362-1050, Ext 401, 402
LeMaster, Phil, *Librn,* Hurdman & Cranstoun Library, San Francisco CA. 415-981-7720
LeMay, Denis, *Law,* Universite Laval Bibliotheque, Quebec PQ. 418-656-3344
Lemay, Philippe, *Sci,* Universite Laval Bibliotheque, Quebec PQ. 418-656-3344
LeMay, Phyllis, *Librn,* Tidewater Psychiatric Institute Library, Norfolk VA. 804-481-4565
LeMay, Susan, *Librn,* Streetsboro Library, Streetsboro OH. 216-626-4458
Lemee, Loretta F, *Librn,* Ralston Purina Co, Corporate Library, Saint Louis MO. 314-982-2150, 2181
Lemelin, Eva, *Librn,* Connecticut State Library (Litchfield Branch), Litchfield CT. 203-566-4301
Lemieux, Jean-Claude, *Dir,* College De Sainte-Foy, Centre des Medias, Sainte Foy PQ. 418-657-3624
Lemieux, Marcel, *Assoc Librn,* College Universitaire De Saint-Boniface Bibliotheque, Winnipeg MB. 204-233-0210, Ext 130
Lemieux, Real, *On-Line Servs,* Ecole Des Hautes Etudes Commerciales De Montreal Bibliotheque, Montreal PQ. 514-343-4481
Leming, Betty J, *Librn,* Winthrop Public Library, Winthrop IA. 319-935-3374
Leming, Margaret, *Librn,* Knoxville-Knox County Public Library (Corryton Branch), Corryton TN. 615-523-0781
Lemire, Camil, *Chief Librn,* Louis H LaFontane Hospital, Personnel Library, Montreal PQ. 514-253-8200, Ext 740
Lemire, Lise, *Dir,* College Jean-de-Brebeuf, Bibliotheque de Pavillon Lalemant, Montreal PQ. 514-342-1320
Lemkau, Jr, Henry L, *Dir,* University of Miami (Louis Calder Memorial Library), Miami FL. 305-547-6441
Lemke, Antje, *Prof,* Syracuse University, School of Information Studies, NY. 315-423-2911
Lemke, Darrell H, *Coordr Libr Program,* Consortium of Universities of the Washington Metropolitan Area, DC. 202-667-4416
Lemke, Dorothy, *ILL,* University of Minnesota, Duluth, Duluth MN. 218-726-8100
Lemke, Lucille, *Librn,* Battle Creek Public Library, Battle Creek NE. 402-675-6934
Lemke, Susan K, *Rare Bks,* United States Military Academy Library, West Point NY. 914-938-2230

Lemmon, Helen, *Dir,* Johnson Bible College, Glass Memorial Library, Knoxville TN. 615-573-4517, Ext 55

Lemmons, Louise, *Doc,* Pittsburg State University Library, Pittsburg KS. 316-231-7000, Ext 431

LeMoine, Claude, *Chief Ref & Circ Div,* National Library of Canada, Ottawa ON. 613-995-9481

Lemon, Margaret S, *Dir,* Tivoli Free Library, Tivoli NY. 914-757-3771

Lemon, Mrs J, *Librn,* Holmes County District Public Library (Holmesville Branch), Holmesville OH. 216-674-5972

Lemon, Mrs James, *Dir,* Art Association of Richmond Library, Richmond IN. 317-966-0256

LeMosy, Joan, *Ref & Bibliog Instr,* Florida Institute of Technology Library, Melbourne FL. 305-723-3701, Ext 270

Lenarz, Leona, *Librn,* Lincoln County Free Library (Eureka Branch), Eureka MT. 406-296-2613

Lenderman, Doris, *Ad,* Hutchinson County Library, Borger TX. 806-274-6221

Lengnick, Marcia E, *Acq,* Siena Heights College Library, Adrian MI. 517-263-0731, Ext 242

Lenig, Wayne, *Dir,* Mohawk-Caughnawaga Museum Library, Fonda NY. 518-853-3646

Lenkowsky, Dorothy, *Librn,* Edith Belle Libby Memorial Library, Old Orchard Beach ME. 207-934-4351

Lennard, Martha, *Media,* Louisiana State University School of Medicine in Shreveport, Medical Library, Shreveport LA. 318-226-3442

Lennenberg, Hans, *Music,* University of Chicago, Joseph Regenstein Library, Chicago IL. 312-753-2977

Lennerton, Joan F, *Librn,* Leicester Public Library, Leicester MA. 617-892-8236

Lennier, Nora, *Asst Librn,* Mount Pleasant Municipal Library, Mount Pleasant TX. 214-572-2705

Lennon, Donald, *Manuscripts,* East Carolina University, J Y Joyner Library, Greenville NC. 919-757-6514

Lennstrom, Nancy, *Reader Serv,* Highline Community College Library, Midway WA. 206-878-3710, Ext 230

Lenox, Gary J, *Librn, Acq & Ref,* University of Wisconsin Center-Rock County Library, Janesville WI. 608-755-2831

Lenox, Mary, *Assoc Prof,* University of Missouri-Columbia, School of Library & Informational Science, MO. 314-882-4546

Lenser, Ruth D, *Librn,* Tilden Public Library, Tilden NE. 402-368-5306

Lent, Emily I, *Dir,* Highland Free Library, Highland NY. 914-691-2275

Lentfer, Pearl, *Dir,* Bennett Public Library, Bennett IA. 319-893-2361

Lentz, Robert T, *Rare Bks & Spec Coll,* Thomas Jefferson University (Scott Memorial Library), Philadelphia PA. 215-928-8848

Lentz, Rosemary, *Tech Serv,* Emmaus Public Library, Emmaus PA. 215-965-9284

Lenz, Barbara, *Circ,* Southwest Wisconsin Library System, Fennimore WI. 608-822-3393

Lenz, Jim, *AV,* Wisconsin Indianhead Technical Institute, Rice Lake Campus Library, Rice Lake WI. 715-234-7082

Lenz, Sharon, *Acq,* Oshkosh Public Library, Oshkosh WI. 414-424-0473

Leo, Karen A, *Public Servs Dir,* Pomona Public Library, Pomona CA. 714-620-2033

Leo, May K, *Dir,* Nyack College Library, Nyack NY. 914-358-1710, Ext 270, 271

Leon, Judith Mae, *Asst Librn,* Reed, Smith, Shaw & McClay, Law Library, Pittsburgh PA. 412-288-3340

Leon, Maurice, *Librn,* University of Wisconsin-Madison (Law School Library), Madison WI. 608-262-3521

Leon, Solomon J, *NE Area Adminr,* Free Library of Philadelphia, Philadelphia PA. 215-686-5322

Leon-Guerrero, Joe, *Librn,* National Steel & Shipbuilding Co, Engineering Library, San Diego CA. 714-232-4011, Ext 661

Leonarczyk, Norman, *Dir,* Consumers Union of the United States Inc Library, Mount Vernon NY. 914-664-6400

Leonard, Berthe, *Librn,* Northeastern Regional Library System (Bibliotheque Publique de Moonbeam), Moonbeam ON. 705-567-7043

Leonard, Bradley, *Ad,* Flint Public Library, Flint MI. 313-232-7111

Leonard, Charlene, *Ref,* Rochester Public Library, Rochester NH. 603-332-1428

Leonard, Charlotte, *Ch,* Dayton & Montgomery County Public Library, Dayton OH. 513-224-1651

Leonard, Christine, *Tech,* International Nickel Co of Canada Ltd, Technical Library, Toronto ON. 416-361-7641

Leonard, Doris, *ILL, Tech Serv & Bibliog Instr,* Becker Junior College at Leicester, Paul Swan Library, Leicester MA. 617-892-3784

Leonard, Dorothy J, *Librn,* Shawinigan Engineering Co Ltd Library, Montreal PQ. 514-878-9311, Ext 229

Leonard, Edward W, *Librn & Commun Servs,* Otis Library, Norwich CT. 203-889-2365

Leonard, Elsie A, *Educ Libr Specialist,* Maryland State Department of Education, Division of Library Development & Services, Baltimore MD. 301-796-8300, Ext 284

Leonard, Frances, *Librn,* Walnut Cove Public Library, Walnut Cove NC. 919-591-7496

Leonard, Gene W, *Librn,* North Carolina Central University (Fine Arts), Durham NC. 919-683-6475

Leonard, Helen, *Commun Servs,* Grosse Pointe Public Library, Grosse Pointe MI. 313-343-2074

Leonard, James W, *In Charge,* IBM Corp, Thomas J Watson Research Ctr Library, Yorktown Heights NY. 914-945-1415

Leonard, Julia, *ILL,* Nathaniel Hawthorne College, Silver Library, Antrim NH. 603-588-6341, Ext 235

Leonard, Kathleen, *Librn,* C P Hall Co Library, Chicago IL. 312-767-4600

Leonard, Lawrence, *Tech Proc Br,* United States Department of Transportation, Library Services Div, Washington DC. 202-426-2565, 426-1792

Leonard, Lucinda, *Network Coordr,* FEDLINK, DC. 202-287-6454

Leonard, May, *Librn,* Shreve Memorial Library (Cedar Grove), Shreveport LA. 318-868-3890

Leonard, Michael, *Ch,* Onslow County Public Library, Jacksonville NC. 919-347-2592, 347-5495

Leonard, Michael, *Info Analyst,* Tracy-Locke Advertising & Public Relations, Inc Library, Dallas TX. 214-742-3131, Ext 422

Leonard, Mrs Luke, *Librn,* James White Memorial Library, East Freetown MA. 617-763-5344

Leonard, Patricia, *Ch & AV,* Walker Memorial Library, Westbrook ME. 207-854-2391

Leonard, Peter H, *Supv Eng Rec & Publ Sect,* Metco Inc, Engineering Library, Westbury NY. 516-334-1300

Leonard, Rosalita J, *Librn,* National Woman's Christian Temperance Union, Frances E Willard Memorial Research Library, Evanston IL. 312-864-1396, Ext 24

Leonard, Thomas, *Dir,* Cape May County Library, Cape May Court House NJ. 609-465-7837

Leonard, W Patrick, *Dean,* Chicago State University, Paul & Emily Douglas Library, Chicago IL. 312-995-2254

Leondar, Judith C, *Mgr Tech Info Servs,* American Cyanamid Co, Agricultural Div Library, Princeton NJ. 609-799-0400, Ext 2514

Leong, Elaine B, *Librn,* Lockheed Missiles & Space Company, Inc, Technical Information Center, Palo Alto CA. 415-493-4411, Ext 45041

Leonhardt, Margaret, *Ref,* Schenectady County Public Library, Schenectady NY. 518-382-3500

Leonhardt, Tom, *Acq,* Duke University, William R Perkins Library, Durham NC. 684-2034

Leopard, Spencer H, *Res Analyst,* American Legion National Organization, National Security-Foreign Relations Div Library, Washington DC. 202-393-4811, Ext 18

Leow, Anthony, *Circ,* Antillian College Library, Mayaguez PR. 809-832-9595, Ext 209

LePage, Francoise, *Ref,* Bibliotheque Municipale de Hull, Hull PQ. 819-777-4341

LePage, Mary K, *Librn,* Baltimore County Public Library (Loch Raven), Baltimore MD. 301-821-5410

Lepage, Suzanne, *Asst Librn,* National Indian Brotherhood, Indian Resource Information Centre, Ottawa ON. 613-236-0673

LePere, Evelyn, *ILL,* Richards Memorial Library, North Attleboro Public Library, North Attleboro MA. 617-695-6411

Lepine, Pierre, *Cartography,* Bibliotheque Nationale Du Quebec, Montreal PQ. 514-873-4553

Lepke, John, *Circ,* Valparaiso University, Henry F Moellering Memorial Library, Valparaiso IN. 219-464-5364

Lepley, Virginia, *Ch,* South Georgia Regional Library, Valdosta-Lowndes County Public Library, Valdosta GA. 912-247-3405

Lepore, Jacqueline, *Ad,* West Orange Free Public Library, West Orange NJ. 201-736-0198

Lepore, Wilma J, *Asst Dir,* Reading Public Library, Reading MA. 617-944-0840

Leppan, Mary, *Ad & Ref,* North Bay Public Library, North Bay ON. 705-474-4830

Lepper, Maurice, *Govt Publications,* University of Calgary Library, Calgary AB. 403-284-5954

Leppert, Elaine, *Ref,* Caldwell Public Library, Caldwell ID. 208-459-3242

Leppla, Mrs P, *Librn,* Holmes County District Public Library (Nashville Branch), Nashville OH. 216-674-5972

Lepponen, Eileen, *Librn,* Jackson County Public Library, Walden CO. 303-723-4602

Lerch, Barbara, *Asst Dir,* Saint Anselm's College, Geisel Library, Manchester NH. 603-669-1030, Ext 240, 249

Lerch, Miriam, *Librn,* Carnegie Library of Pittsburgh (Business Branch), Pittsburgh PA. 412-622-3100

Lerner, Adele, *Pub Servs,* Cornell University Medical College, Samuel J Wood Library, New York NY. 212-472-5300

Lerner, Helene, *Cat,* Hebrew Theological College, Saul Silber Memorial Library, Skokie IL. 312-267-9800

Leroux, Madeleine, *Asst Dir,* Bibliotheque De La Ville De Montreal, Montreal PQ. 514-872-5923

LeRoy, Jean L, *In Charge,* Saint Paul's Episcopal Church Library, Richmond VA. 804-643-3589

Lesh, Nancy, *Tech Serv,* University of Alaska, Anchorage Library, Anchorage AK. 907-263-1825

Lesieur, Denis J, *Local Hist & Lit,* Berkshire Athenaeum, Pittsfield Public Library, Pittsfield MA. 413-442-1559

Leskiw, Sophie, *Librn,* Smoky Lake Municipal Library, Smoky Lake AB. 403-656-3674

Lesley, J Ingrid, *Librn,* Chicago Public Library (Lake View), Chicago IL. 312-281-7565

Lesley, Miriam, *Librn,* Free Library of Philadelphia (Art), Philadelphia PA. 215-686-5322

Leslie, Frances, *Librn,* Big Horn County Library (Byron Branch), Byron WY. 307-568-2388

Leslie, Mrs G, *Processing,* NASA, John F Kennedy Space Center Library, Kennedy Space Center FL. 305-867-3600, 3615

Leslie, Mrs Ronald, *Librn,* Croydon Town Library, Croydon NH. 603-863-3422

Leslie, Robert L, *Dir,* Typophiles Inc, Typographic Reference Library, Brooklyn NY. 212-462-2017

Lesly, Ruth, *Dir,* Hastings-On-Hudson Public Library, Hastings-on-Hudson NY. 914-478-3307

Lesnak, Mary, *Librn,* Patton Public Library, Patton PA. 814-674-8231

Lesnak, Stephen, *Asst Dir-Comm Libr Serv,* Rochester Public Library, Rochester NY. 716-428-7300

Lesniak, Benjamin A, *Librn,* Carbon County Law Library, Jim Thorpe PA. 717-325-3111

Lesnick, Sheila, *Local Hist,* Jericho Public Library, Jericho NY. 516-935-6790

LeSourd, Margaret, *Urban Doc,* University of Florida Libraries, Gainesville FL. 904-392-0341

Lessard, Elizabeth, *Librn,* Manchester Historic Association Library, Manchester NH. 603-622-7531

Lessard, R, *Libr Tech,* Queen's University at Kingston (Electrical Engineering), Kingston ON. 613-547-6697

Lessard-Durrant, Wendy, *Cat,* Bishop's University & Champlain Regional College, John Bassett Memorial Library, Lennoxville PQ. 819-569-9551, Ext 341

Lesser, Ann, *Dir,* Warren Library Association, Warren Library, Warren PA. 814-723-4650

Lesser, Barbara, *Librn,* Temple Beth Zion Library, Buffalo NY. 716-886-7151

Lesser, Mary Lou, *Chief Librn,* United States Marine Corps (Special Services Library), Quantico VA. 703-640-2414

Lessin, Bart, *Asst Dir,* Central Michigan University, Charles V Park Library, Mount Pleasant MI. 517-774-3500

Lessun, Walter, *Librn,* Ohio State Reformatory Library, Mansfield OH. 419-526-2000, Ext 323

LESTAGE

LeStage, Mrs Chester, *Librn,* Clarksburg Town Library, Clarksburg MA. 413-663-8118

Lester, Daniel W, *Tech Serv,* University of New Mexico General Library, Albuquerque NM. 505-277-4241

Lester, Elizabeth, *Ad,* High Point Public Library, High Point NC. 919-885-8411

Lester, Gail L, *Librn,* Avon Public Library, Avon IL. 309-465-3907

Lester, Lorraine E, *Tech Serv,* University of New Mexico General Library (Law Library), Albuquerque NM. 505-277-6236

Lester, Marilyn A, *Assoc Dir & On-Line Servs,* National College of Education, Learning Resources Center, Evanston IL. 312-256-5150, Ext 273

Lester, Roger, *Instr,* Concord College, Library Science Dept, WV. 304-384-3115

Lester, Roger, *Media,* Concord College, J Frank Marsh Library, Athens WV. 304-384-3115, Ext 247

Lestishen, Nancy, *Ref,* Manhattan Public Library, Manhattan KS. 913-776-4741

Lestor, Dorothy, *Librn,* Glendale Public Library (Casa Verdugo), Glendale CA. 213-956-2030

LeStourgeon, Martha H, *Dir,* Longwood College, Dabney S Lancaster Library, Farmville VA. 804-392-9376

LeStourgeon, Zethyl, *In Charge,* Episcopal Diocese of West Texas, Cathedral Library, San Antonio TX. 512-824-5387

LeSuer, Jack A, *Librn,* Racine Public Library, Racine WI. 414-636-9241

LeSueur, C R, *Librn,* New England Regional Medical Library Service, MA. 617-732-2128

LeSueur, C Robin, *Librn,* Harvard University Library (Francis A Countway Library of Medicine), Boston MA. 617-732-2142

Leta, Kathy, *Librn,* Hanson Public Library, Hanson MA. 617-293-2151

Letcher, Tisha, *Librn,* Nicolet Scientific Corp Library, Northvale NJ. 201-767-7100

LeTellier, Cecile, *Info Specialist,* Union Mutual Life Insurance Co, Information Center, Portland ME. 207-780-2347

Letendre, Anita, *Librn,* Allenstown Public Library, Allenstown NH. 603-485-7651

Letendre, James, *Librn,* Chicago Public Library (Austin), Chicago IL. 312-287-0667

Lethaw, Ellen, *Librn,* O Hommel Co Research Library, Carnegie PA. 412-923-2233

Lethbridge, Mary C, *Info Officer,* Library of Congress, Washington DC. 202-287-5000

Letherland, Lillian, *Supvr,* Huron County Public Library (Auburn Branch), Auburn ON. 519-526-7560

LeTourneau, Janet, *Asst Librn,* Saint Albans Free Library, Saint Albans VT. 802-524-3804

Letson, Jane, *Tech Serv & Cat,* Dakota County Library System, Burnsville MN. 612-435-8111

Letson, Ruth S, *Librn,* Tennessee Department of Transportation Library, Nashville TN. 615-741-2330

Letton, Lucille, *YA,* University of Northern Iowa Library, Cedar Falls IA. 319-273-2737

Leung, Joyce, *ILL & Ref,* Bridgewater State College, Clement C Maxwell Library, Bridgewater MA. 617-697-8321, Ext 441, 442

Leung, Kai, *Cat,* Youngstown State University Library, William F Maag Library, Youngstown OH. 216-742-3676

Leung, Shirley, *Tech Serv,* University of California, Riverside, University Library, Riverside CA. 714-787-3221

Leung, Shuet-Keung, *Asian Lang & Lit,* University of California at Davis, General Library, Davis CA. 916-752-2110

Leung, Terry, *Asst Librn, ILL & On-Line Servs,* Pepperdine University, Los Angeles Campus Library, Los Angeles CA. 213-971-7730, Ext 730

Leutenegger, Benedict, *Librn,* San Jose Mission, Old Spanish Mission Historical Research Library, San Antonio TX. 512-922-0543

Lev, Norma, *Librn,* Lake Park Public Library, Lake Park IA. 712-832-9505

Levalley, Avis M, *Librn,* Dayton Public Library, Dayton IA. 515-547-2700

Levan, Lonella, *Asst Librn,* Marion Public Library, Marion NY. 315-926-4933

Levas, Irene, *Librn,* Veterans Administration, Hospital Library, New York NY. 212-686-7500, Ext 445, 279

Leve, Arless, *Manager,* Union Carbide Corp (Corp Business Library), New York NY. 212-551-4301

Leveau, Marie-Claude, *Librn,* Bibliotheque Municipale De Dorval (Surrey Gardens), Dorval PQ. 514-631-6912

LeVeille, Linda L, *Info Specialist,* Rexnord, Inc, Research Library, Milwaukee WI. 414-643-2725

Leveille, Lizette, *Tech Serv, Cat & Ref,* Lewiston Public Library, Lewiston ME. 207-784-0135

LeVeille, Pam, *Libr Tech,* Saint Luke's Memorial Hospital Library, Racine WI. 414-636-2200

Levene, Lee-Allison, *On-Line Servs,* University of Kansas Medical Center, College of Health Sciences & Hospital, Clendening Library, Kansas City KS. 913-588-7166

Leventhal, Lou, *On-Line Servs,* Vernon Area Public Library, Prairie View IL. 312-634-3650

Leventhal, Phyllis, *Media,* Mobile Public Library, Mobile AL. 205-438-7073

Leveridge, Jennie, *Asst Librn,* Grant Hospital of Chicago, Medical Library, Chicago IL. 312-883-2230

Levering, Philip, *AV,* Suffolk Cooperative Library System, Bellport NY. 516-286-1600

Leverton, Melinda, *Commun Servs,* Tri-County Public Library District, Augusta IL. 217-392-2211

Levesay, Mary Kay, *Librn,* Public Library of Cincinnati & Hamilton County (Roselawn), Cincinnati OH. 513-369-6045

Levesque, Albert, *Dir,* Universite De Moncton, Bibliotheque Champlain, Moncton NB. 506-858-4012

Levesque, C, *Dir,* Port-Alfred Ville La Baie Municipal Library, Port-Alfred PQ. 418-544-1151

Levesque, Janet, *Librn,* Greenville Public Library, Greenville RI. 401-949-3630

Levesque, Janet, *Media,* Taunton Public Library, Subregional Headquarters for Eastern Massachusetts Regional Library System, Taunton MA. 617-823-3570

Levesque, John, *Cat,* Bentley College, Solomon R Baker Library, Waltham MA. 617-891-2231

Levesque, Lyn, *Ch,* Richards Memorial Library, North Attleboro Public Library, North Attleboro MA. 617-695-6411

Levesque, M Michel, *Librn,* Bibliotheque Municipale, Amos PQ. 819-732-6070

Levesque, Margaret, *Librn,* Canadair Ltd, Co Library, Montreal PQ. 514-744-1511, Ext 263

Levesque, Raymond, *Ref,* Trois-Rivieres College Library, Trois-Rivieres PQ. 819-376-1721, Ext 286

Levett, Willie L G, *Librn,* United States Army (Stinfo & Reference Library Branch), Saint Louis MO. 314-263-0703

Levey, Jennie, *On-Line Servs,* Case Western Reserve University Libraries (Sears), Cleveland OH. 216-368-3506

Levi, Dennis L, *Chief Librn,* Veterans Administration, Medical Center, Medical & General Libraries, Tacoma WA. 206-582-8440, Ext 226, 410

Levi, Preston, *ILL & Ref,* Shawnee Library System, Carterville IL. 618-985-3711

Levie, Donna E, *Librn,* International Swimming Hall of Fame Library, Fort Lauderdale FL. 305-462-6536

Levie, Pauline K, *Libr Adminr & Media Servs,* Bureau of Jewish Education, Jewish Community Library, San Francisco CA. 415-751-6983, Ext 12

Levien, Ruth, *Ch,* Rockville Centre Public Library, Rockville Centre NY. 516-766-6258

Levin, Ann, *Librn,* Peninsula Temple Beth El Library, San Mateo CA. 415-341-7701

Levin, Rhoda, *Acq,* John C Hart Memorial Library, Shrub Oak NY. 914-245-5262

Levin, Sylvia, *Asst Dir,* Manhasset Public Library, Manhasset NY. 516-627-2300

Levine, Amy M, *Dir,* USV Pharmaceutical Corp, Information Services Department, Tuckahoe NY. 914-779-6300, Ext 2592

Levine, Beryl, *Coordr,* Grossmont College, Library Technology Program, CA. 714-465-1700, Ext 319

Levine, Elaine, *Librn,* Harris County Public Library (Aldine), Houston TX. 713-445-5560

Levine, Fay, *Cat,* Memphis-Shelby County Public Library & Information Center, Memphis TN. 901-528-2950

Levine, Judith L, *Dir,* Shenendehowa Free Library, Clifton Park NY. 518-371-9698

Levine, Judy, *ILL & Ref,* Sir Mortimer B Davis Jewish General Hospital, Medical Library, Montreal PQ. 514-342-3111, Ext 325, 376

Levine, L, *Tech Serv,* Dow Chemical USA, Texas Div Library, Freeport TX. 713-238-3513

Levine, Margaret, *Cat,* Bloomfield College Library, Bloomfield NJ. 201-748-9000, Ext 281

Levine, Marion H, *Head, Ref Dept,* Harvard University Library (Francis A Countway Library of Medicine), Boston MA. 617-732-2142

Levine, Michael, *ILL & Ref,* Lake Agassiz Regional Library, Moorhead MN. 218-233-7594

Levine, Michael, *Librn,* Moorhead Public Library, Moorhead MN. 218-233-7594

Levine, Muriel, *Ch,* North Merrick Public Library, North Merrick NY. 516-378-7474

Levine, Robert, *Reader Serv,* Pennsylvania State University, Capitol Campus Heindel Library, Middletown PA. 717-787-7771

Levine, Sandra, *Dir,* Somers Library, Somers NY. 914-277-3420

Levinson, F, *Librn,* Thomas International Corp Library, Chicago IL. 312-647-0770

Levinson, Leona G, *Dir,* Missouri Valley Public Library, Missouri Valley IA. 712-642-4111

Levinson, Mary, *Tech Serv & Circ,* University of Redlands, George & Verda Armacost Library, Redlands CA. 714-793-2121, Ext 472

Levinton, Juliette, *Mgr Libr Servs,* Lionel D Edie & Co Inc Library, New York NY. 212-575-4211

Levis, Joel, *Librn,* Newfoundland Public Library Services (Central Region), Grand Falls NF. 709-489-9001

Leviton, Lillian, *Librn,* South Hadley Library System (Maylord Memorial), South Hadley MA. 413-532-0108

Levitt, Andrea, *Dir,* Armstrong College Library, Berkeley CA. 415-848-2500, Ext 22

Levitt, Carole, *Ser,* John Marshall Law School Library, Chicago IL. 312-427-2737, Ext 254

Levitt, Irene S, *Info Ctr Coordr,* Charles V Hogan Regional Center, Staff Library, Hathorne MA. 617-774-5000, Ext 146

Levitt, Theodore, *YA,* Alameda Free Library, Alameda CA. 415-522-5413, 522-3578

Levkovitz, Susan, *Cat,* City University of New York, Library of Graduate School & University Center, New York NY. 212-790-4541

Levonick, Deborah, *Asst Librn,* Jefferson Township Public Library, Jefferson Township NJ. 201-697-6363

Levy, Annette R, *Librn,* Jewish Federation Libraries (Akiva Library), Nashville TN. 615-292-6614

Levy, Annette R, *Librn,* Jewish Federation Libraries (Jewish Community Center Library), Nashville TN. 615-297-3588

Levy, Annette R, *Librn,* Jewish Federation Libraries (Temple Library), Nashville TN. 615-352-7620

Levy, Annette R, *Librn,* Jewish Federation Libraries (West End Synagogue Library), Nashville TN. 615-269-4592

Levy, Charlotte L, *Dir,* Brooklyn Law School, Henry L Ughetta Law Library, Brooklyn NY. 212-625-2200, Ext 53 or 55

Levy, Dorothy, *Dir,* Berkley Public Library, Berkley MI. 313-542-3393

Levy, Evelyn, *Librn,* Los Angeles Public Library System (West Hollywood), Los Angeles CA. 213-876-2741

Levy, James, *Dir,* Harwood Foundation Library, Taos NM. 505-758-3063

Levy, Jane, *Ch,* Bureau of Jewish Education, Jewish Community Library, San Francisco CA. 415-751-6983, Ext 12

Levy, Janell, *Cat,* Oglethorpe University Library, Atlanta GA. 404-261-1441, Ext 24

Levy, Judith, *Librn,* San Mateo County Department of Health & Welfare Library, San Mateo CA. 415-573-2520

Levy, Mary Jo, *Adminr Libr Syst Activities,* Palo Alto City Library, Palo Alto CA. 415-329-2436

Levy, Nancy W, *Dir,* Irvington Public Library, Guiteau Foundation, Irvington NY. 914-591-7840

Levy, Sarah, *Per & ILL,* Yeshiva University Libraries (Mendel Gottesman Library of Hebraica-Judaica), New York NY. 212-960-5382

Levy, Susan M, *Librn,* Donors Forum of Chicago Library, Chicago IL. 312-726-4877
Levy, Willa Mae, *Ref,* Hillsdale Free Public Library, Hillsdale NJ. 201-664-0020
Lew, Susan, *Tech Serv & Cat,* Greenburgh Public Library, Elmsford NY. 914-682-5265
Lewallen, David, *Librn,* Alameda County Library (Oakland Business & Government Library), Oakland CA. 415-874-5178
Lewandowski, Thomas, *Librn, Media & Acq,* Oakland Community College, Royal Oak Campus Learning Resources Center, Royal Oak MI. 313-548-1252, Ext 15, 16 & 17
Lewandowski, Thomas, *Librn,* Oakland Community College, Southeast Campus Library, Southfield MI. 313-548-1252
Lewandowski, Virginia, *Librn,* Harlem Valley Psychiatric Center, Interdisciplinary Library, Wingdale NY. 914-832-6611, Ext 471 & 575
Lewek, June B, *Librn,* Sonoma County Law Library, Santa Rosa CA. 707-527-2668
Lewin, Elizabeth, *Ad & Ref,* North Tonawanda Public Library, North Tonawanda NY. 716-693-4132
Lewin, Julia, *Librn,* Greene County District Library (Yellow Springs), Yellow Springs OH. 513-767-7661
Lewin, Martin, *Commun Relations,* Buffalo & Erie County Public Library System, Buffalo NY. 716-856-7525
Lewis, Aileen, *Chief Librn,* Dartmouth Regional Library, Dartmouth NS. 902-466-7623
Lewis, Alan D, *Asst Dir,* Minnesota State Library Agency, Office of Public Libraries & Interlibrary Cooperation, Saint Paul MN. 612-296-2821
Lewis, Alan M, *Head, Documentation Section (Actg),* United States Department of the Navy (Naval Sea Systems Command, Library Documentation Branch), Washington DC. 202-692-3305
Lewis, Alfred, *Asst Librn Public Servs,* University of California at Davis (Law Library), Davis CA. 916-752-3322
Lewis, Alice G, *Librn,* Owensboro-Daviess County Public Library, Owensboro KY. 502-684-0211
Lewis, Annie, *Librn,* University of California, Berkeley (Biochemistry), Berkeley CA. 415-642-5112
Lewis, Annie May Alston, *Librn,* Harding College Graduate School of Religion, L M Graves Memorial Library, Memphis TN. 901-761-1354
Lewis, Arlayne, *Librn,* Livonia Public Library (Vest Pocket), Livonia MI. 313-421-6219
Lewis, Barbara B, *Librn,* Delaware Supreme Court Library, Delhi NY. 607-746-2603
Lewis, Benjamin M, *Dir,* Ohio Wesleyan University, L A Beeghly Library, Delaware OH. 614-369-4431, Ext 509
Lewis, Betty K, *Librn,* United States Army (Kenner Army Hospital Library), Fort Lee VA. 804-734-2989
Lewis, Betty Mae, *Curator,* Foundation Historical Association, Inc, Library, Auburn NY. 315-252-1283
Lewis, Beverly, *Librn,* Tulare County Library System (Dinuba Branch), Dinuba CA. 209-591-0778
Lewis, Brian, *Dir,* Brigham City Library, Brigham City UT. 801-723-5850
Lewis, Carla E, *Librn,* Rockwell International Reference Center, Troy MI. 313-435-1668
Lewis, Carol, *Ref,* Vanderbilt University Medical Center Library, Nashville TN. 615-322-2292
Lewis, Catherine H, *Dir,* Horry County Memorial Library, Conway SC. 803-248-4898
Lewis, Charles S, *Cat,* J Sargeant Reynolds Community College (Media Processing Center), Richmond VA. 804-257-0208
Lewis, Cheryl, *Ch,* Saint Mary Parish Library, Franklin LA. 318-828-5364
Lewis, David, *Circ,* Davenport Public Library, Davenport IA. 319-326-7832
Lewis, David, *Ref,* Franklin & Marshall College Library, Lancaster PA. 717-291-4223
Lewis, David V, *Ad,* Franklin-Johnson County Public Library, Franklin IN. 317-738-2833
Lewis, Debra, *Children's Outreach,* Bladen County Public Library, Elizabethtown NC. 919-862-8171
Lewis, Demetria, *Librn,* Roanoke City Public Library System (Melrose), Roanoke VA. 703-981-2648

Lewis, E R, *Librn,* United States House of Representatives Library, Washington DC. 202-225-0462
Lewis, Edith, *Asst Librn,* District of Columbia Library for the Blind & Physically Handicapped, Washington DC. 212-727-2142
Lewis, Elizabeth, *Institutional Librn,* Virginia State Library, Richmond VA. 804-786-8929
Lewis, Eloise, *Librn,* Ross Roy Inc Library, Detroit MI. 313-568-6000
Lewis, Ethel M, *Librn,* New York Supreme Court, Seventh Judicial District Law Library, Bath NY. 607-776-7126
Lewis, Florence, *Bibliog Instr,* Sangamon State University, Norris L Brookens Library, Springfield IL. 217-786-6597
Lewis, Frank R, *Dir,* La Grange College, William & Evelyn Banks Library, La Grange GA. 404-882-2911, Ext 34
Lewis, Gary, *Tech Serv,* Radford University, John Preston McConnell Library, Radford VA. 703-731-5471, 5472
Lewis, George R, *Dir,* Mississippi State University, Mitchell Memorial Library, Mississippi State MS. 601-325-4225
Lewis, Gloria, *Asst Librn,* Angelina College Library, Lufkin TX. 713-639-1301
Lewis, Gwen, *Librn,* Vermilion Public Library, Vermilion AB. 403-853-4288
Lewis, Helen, *Librn,* Stauffer-Wacker Silicone Corp, Technical Library, Adrian MI. 517-263-5711
Lewis, James, *Ref,* Carolina Population Center Library, Chapel Hill NC. 919-933-3081
Lewis, Janet, *Librn,* New Port Richey Public Library, New Port Richey FL. 813-849-2179
Lewis, Janice B, *Chief Librn,* Chicago Sun-Times, Editorial Library, Chicago IL. 312-321-2594
Lewis, Jannith L, *Librn,* Oakwood College, Eva B Dykes Library, Huntsville AL. 205-837-1630, Ext 275
Lewis, Jean, *Ref,* Kirksville College of Osteopathic Medicine, A T Still Memorial Library, Kirksville MO. 816-626-2345
Lewis, Jean, *ILL,* Longmont Public Library, Longmont CO. 303-776-2236
Lewis, Jill, *Commun Servs,* Avon Township Public Library, Rochester MI. 313-651-1426
Lewis, John, *AV,* Eastern New Mexico University Library, Portales NM. 505-562-2624
Lewis, John, *Librn,* Eastern New Mexico University Library (Instructional Resources Center), Portales NM. 505-562-2258
Lewis, June, *Acq,* Foster Wheeler Development Corp, Research Information Center & Library, Livingston NJ. 201-533-3663, 533-3670
Lewis, Karen, *Non-Print,* Azusa Pacific College, Marshburn Memorial Library, Azusa CA. 213-969-3434, Ext 198
Lewis, Katheryn, *Cat & On-Line Servs,* Saginaw Valley State College Library & Learning Resources Center, University Center MI. 517-790-4237
Lewis, Kathryn L, *Dir,* Loudonville Public Library, Loudonville OH. 419-994-3395
Lewis, Larry, *Librn,* University of Western Ontario (Health Sciences Library), London ON. 519-679-6175
Lewis, Laura S, *Asst Dir & Media,* Troup Harris Coweta Regional Library, La Grange Memorial Library, La Grange GA. 404-882-7784
Lewis, Lileth, *On-Line Servs,* Modoc County Library, Alturas CA. 916-233-2719
Lewis, Louise, *Pub Servs & On-Line Servs,* Center for Disease Control Library, Atlanta GA. 404-329-3396
Lewis, Lucille, *Librn,* Omaha Public Library (Benson), Omaha NE. 402-444-4846
Lewis, Marcia, *Ref,* City Library, Springfield MA. 413-739-3871
Lewis, Marcia M, *Librn,* Hobbs Public Library, Hobbs NM. 505-397-2451
Lewis, Margaret, *Ad,* State University of New York, State College of Optometry, Harold Kohn Library, New York NY. 212-477-7965
Lewis, Marge, *Librn,* Howard County Library (Long Reach), Columbia MD. 301-997-7222
Lewis, Marie, *ILL,* Lincoln Parish Library, Ruston LA. 318-255-1920
Lewis, Marilyn, *Bkmobile Coordr,* Natrona County Public Library, Casper WY. 307-235-9272

Lewis, Martha, *Acq,* University of South Carolina (Coleman Karesh Law Libr), Columbia SC. 803-777-5942
Lewis, Mary, *Librn,* Buffalo & Erie County Public Library System (Martin Luther King), Buffalo NY. 716-854-2070
Lewis, Mary, *Librn,* United States Army & Air Force Exchange Service, Central Library, Dallas TX. 214-330-3337
Lewis, Mary E, *Chief Librn,* Pratt & Whitney Aircraft Canada Ltd Library, Longueuil PQ. 514-677-9411, Ext 7209
Lewis, Mary J, *Librn,* Environmental Protection Agency, National Water Quality Laboratory Library, Duluth MN. 218-727-6692
Lewis, Melba H, *Librn,* New York State Electric & Gas Corp, Corporate Technical Library, Binghamton NY. 607-729-2551
Lewis, Merwin, *Librn,* University of Western Ontario (Music), London ON. 519-679-2466
Lewis, Patricia, *Acq,* Saint Olaf College, Rolvaag Memorial Library, Northfield MN. 507-663-2222
Lewis, Patricia, *Br Coordr,* Toledo-Lucas County Public Library, Toledo OH. 419-255-7055
Lewis, Ralph, *Chief Librn,* NASA (Technical Library), Moffett Field CA. 415-965-5157
Lewis, Renata, *Tech Serv,* New Albany Floyd County Public Library, New Albany IN. 812-944-8464
Lewis, Robert F, *Librn,* University of California, San Diego (Biomedical), La Jolla CA. 714-452-3253
Lewis, Robert G, *Librn & On-Line Servs,* Cominco Ltd, Central Technical Library, Trail BC. 604-364-4409
Lewis, Roger, *Cat,* California Polytechnic State University Library, San Luis Obispo CA. 805-546-2345
Lewis, Ronald A, *Dir,* Saint Mary's University, Patrick Power Library, Halifax NS. 902-422-7361
Lewis, Rosalyn, *Librn,* United Methodist Publishing House Library, Nashville TN. 615-749-6437
Lewis, Rosemary, *ILL, Ref & On-Line Servs,* College of New Rochelle, Gill Library, New Rochelle NY. 914-632-5300, Ext 347
Lewis, Shirley, *Asst Librn,* City of Brampton Public Library & Art Gallery, Brampton ON. 416-453-2444
Lewis, Shirley, *Librn,* General Hospital, Health Sciences Library, Everett WA. 206-258-6300
Lewis, Shirley, *Media,* University of Minnesota, Duluth, Duluth MN. 218-726-8100
Lewis, Shirley, *Outreach Coordr,* Yakima Valley Regional Library, Yakima WA. 509-452-8541, Ext 22
Lewis, Shirley C, *Dir,* Providence Hospital of Everett, Health Sciences Library, Everett WA. 206-258-7550
Lewis, Stanley T, *Prof,* Queens College of the City University of New York, Graduate School of Library & Information Studies, NY. 212-520-7194, 520-7195
Lewis, Susan, *Chief Librn,* Boston Architectural Center Library, Boston MA. 617-536-9018
Lewis, Susan, *Librn,* Central Collegiate Library, Regina SK. 306-525-9592
Lewis, Susan, *Tech Serv,* Saint Louis Community College (Administrative Center), Saint Louis MO. 314-644-9589
Lewis, Veronica, *Ad,* Oregon City Library, Oregon City OR. 503-655-8398, 655-8399
Lewis, William P, *Dir,* Lackawanna Historical Society Library, Scranton PA. 717-344-3841
Lewis, William R, *Soc Sci Coordr,* Boston Public Library, Eastern Massachusetts Library System, Boston MA. 617-536-5400
Lewis, Jr, G Gordon, *Dir,* Farmington Community Library, Farmington Hills MI. 313-553-0300
Lewter, Rachel, *Librn,* Wake County Department of the Public Library (Apex Public), Apex NC. 919-362-8252
Ley, Kathryn, *Asst Head Librn,* Rosenberg Library, Galveston TX. 713-763-8854
Ley, Pamela, *Librn,* Public Library of Columbus & Franklin County (Northern Lights), Columbus OH. 614-267-3366
Leyda, Mabel, *Spec Coll,* Beaumont Public Library, Beaumont TX. 713-838-0812
Leyda, Mabel, *Librn,* Beaumont Public Library (Tyrrell Historical), Beaumont TX. 713-838-0780

Leyden, Annette, *Librn,* Medical Letter Inc Library, New Rochelle NY. 914-235-0500
Leyman, Jean, *Ref,* Wheaton Public Library, Wheaton IL. 312-668-1374
Leysath, Nell, *Asst Librn,* Red River Parish Library, Coushatta LA. 318-932-5614
Leyshon, Myra, *Br Coordr,* Chinook Regional Library, Swift Current SK. 306-773-3186
Lhota, Robert, *Assoc Dean & Dir LRC,* Eastfield College, Learning Resources Center, Mesquite TX. 214-746-3168
Lhota, Robert L, *Dir,* Dodge City Community College, Learning Resources Center, Dodge City KS. 316-225-1321, Ext 220
Li, Caroline C, *Tech Serv & Cat,* University of Idaho Library (College of Law), Moscow ID. 208-885-6521
Li, Dorothy, *Tech Serv,* Oak Park Public Library, Scoville Institute, Oak Park IL. 312-383-8200
Li, Francis, *Librn,* Lutheran Deaconess Hospital Library, Minneapolis MN. 612-721-2933, Ext 278
Li, Grace, *Tech Serv,* Waukegan Public Library, Waukegan IL. 312-623-2041
Li, Ming-yu, *Librn,* University of California at Davis (Environmental Toxicology Library), Davis CA. 916-752-2562
Liao, Helen, *Librn,* Bethany Medical Center, Medical Library, Kansas City KS. 913-281-8400
Liau, Tom, *Tech Serv,* Ricks College, David O McKay Learning Resources Center, Rexburg ID. 208-356-2351
Liaw, Barbara, *Cat,* Alabama Agricultural & Mechanical University, Joseph F Drake Memorial Learning Resources Center, Normal AL. 205-859-7309
Libbey, David, *Assoc Prof,* Southern Connecticut State College, Div of Library Science & Instructional Technology, CT. 203-397-4532
Libbey, Elizabeth M, *Librn,* Catholic University of America (Music), Washington DC. 202-635-5424
Libbey, Frances, *Sci,* University of Hartford, Mortensen Library, West Hartford CT. 203-243-4265
Libbey, Maurice, *Acq,* Eastern Illinois University, Booth Library, Charleston IL. 217-581-2210
Libbey, Miriam H, *Lectr,* Emory University, Div of Librarianship, GA. 404-329-6840
Libbey, Miriam H, *Librn,* Emory University Libraries (A W Calhoun Medical Library), Atlanta GA. 404-329-5810
Libbey, Miriam H, *Dir,* Southeastern Regional Medical Library Program, (SERMLP), GA. 404-329-5818
Libby, Eileen, *Librn,* University of Chicago (Social Service Administration), Chicago IL. 312-753-3426
Libby, George, *Hist,* Temple University of the Commonwealth System of Higher Education, Samuel Paley Library, Philadelphia PA. 215-787-8231
Libby, George, *Bibliog Instr,* Temple University of the Commonwealth System of Higher Education, Samuel Paley Library, Philadelphia PA. 215-787-8231
Libby, Ruth R, *Librn,* Boerne Public Library, Boerne TX. 512-249-3053
Libersky, Barbara, *Librn,* Public Library of the District of Columbia (Tenley Friendship), Washington DC. 202-727-1389
Libertini, Arleen, *Librn,* Everett A Gladman Memorial Hospital, Medical Library, Oakland CA. 415-536-8111
Liby, Ruby K, *Dir,* Manitou Springs Public Library, Manitou Springs CO. 303-685-5206
Licari, Lena, *Librn,* Specialty Chemical & Product Group, Parker Division Library, Madison Heights MI. 313-583-9300
Licht, Juanita, *Librn,* Shapiro Developmental Center, Resident & Staff Library, Kankakee IL. 815-939-8419
Lichtenberg, Elsa R, *Acq,* Villanova University (Pulling Law Library), Villanova PA. 215-527-2100, Ext 702, 703, 704
Lichtenfels, Dave, *Media,* Saint Petersburg Junior College, Michael M Bennett Library, Clearwater FL. 813-441-0681, Ext 2616
Lichtenstein, Aniela, *Librn,* Millard Fillmore Hospital, Kideney Health Sciences Library, Buffalo NY. 716-848-4600

Lichtenstein, Kineret, *Chief Librn,* Illinois State Psychiatric Institute, Professional Library, Chicago IL. 312-996-1320
Lichty, Phyllis, *ILL,* Marion College Library, Marion IN. 317-674-6901, Ext 228
Licitis, Margot B, *Translator,* Rohm & Haas Co, Research Div, Information Services Dept, Spring House PA. 215-643-0200
Lidd, Frank J, *Librn,* Vapor Corp, Technical Library, Niles IL. 312-967-8300
Liddiard, Karen, *Librn,* Winnipeg Tribune Library, Winnipeg MB. 204-985-4600
Liddiard, Leola D, *Libr Tech,* United States Army (Post Library), Dugway UT. 801-522-2178
Liddle, Carol, *Pub Servs,* Janesville Public Library, Janesville WI. 608-752-8934, Ext B
Liddle, Ernest V, *Dir,* Liberty Baptist College Library, Lynchburg VA. 804-528-0821
Liddle, Yonne, *Librn,* Kent County Municipal Public Library (Wheatley Public), Wheatley ON. 519-825-7131
Liddy, Elizabeth D, *ILL & Ref,* Onondaga Community College, Sidney B Coulter Library, Syracuse NY. 315-469-7741, Ext 5335-5338
Lidgren, A, *Librn,* Calgary Public Library (Forest Lawn), Calgary AB. 403-272-1212
Lidle, Judy, *Librn,* Sweetwater County Library (Superior Branch), Superior WY. 307-875-3615
Lidsky, Ella, *Tech Serv,* Fairleigh Dickinson University, Friendship Library, Madison NJ. 201-377-4700, Ext 234
Liebenberg, Irene, *Head, Reader Servs,* Riverside City & County Public Library, Riverside CA. 714-787-7211
Lieber, Elsie, *Asst Dir,* Garden City Public Library, Garden City NY. 516-742-8405
Lieber, Winifred, *Librn,* Roosevelt Hospital, Medical Library, New York NY. 212-554-6872
Lieberman, Hedi, *Commun Servs,* Alexandria Library, Alexandria VA. 703-750-6351
Lieberman, Janice, *Lectr,* San Jose State University, Division of Library Science, CA. 408-277-2292
Lieberman, Judith, *Librn,* Boston Public Library (Adams Street), Dorchester MA. 617-436-6900
Lieberman, Louise, *Dir,* Mount Ida Junior College, Hallden Library, Newton Centre MA. 617-969-7000, Ext 152
Lieberman, Susan, *Circ,* Mount Sinai School of Medicine of City University of New York, Gustave L & Janet W Levy Library, New York NY. 212-650-6671
Liebert, Martha, *Dir,* Bernalillo County Library, Bernalillo NM. 505-766-4424
Liebert, Roberta, *Librn,* Jefferson County Public Library (Conifer Library), Conifer CO. 303-238-8411
Liebesbind, Eileen, *On-Line Servs & Bibliog Instr,* Iona College, Ryan Library, New Rochelle NY. 914-636-2100
Liebett, Mrs Harold, *Librn,* Oostburg Public Library, Oostburg WI. 414-364-2934
Liebhaber, Arthur, *Asst Librn,* Dade County Law Library, Miami FL. 305-579-5422
Liecyn, Nancy, *Dir of Publ,* Community Council of Greater New York, Agency Resources Services Library, New York NY. 212-777-5000
Lied, James L, *Dir, Media Servs,* University of Cincinnati Libraries, Central Library, Cincinnati OH. 513-475-2218
Liegl, Dorothy M, *Pub Libr Coordr,* South Dakota State Library, Pierre SD. 605-773-3131
Liem, Frieda, *Cat,* Eastern Pennsylvania Psychiatric Institute Library, Philadelphia PA. 215-842-4508, 842-4509 & 842-4510
Lien, Dennis, *In Charge,* Minnesota Science Fiction Society Library, Minneapolis MN. 612-722-5217
Lien, Viola M, *Librn,* Stillwater County Library, Columbus MT. 406-322-5337
Liening, Patricia A, *Librn,* Eden Free Library, Eden NY. 716-992-4028
Liepina, Rita G, *Librn,* Insurance Institute for Highway Safety Library, Washington DC. 202-333-0770
Liesen, Rosemary, *Librn,* Genesee District Library (Johnson Memorial), Genesee MI. 313-640-1410
Liesener, James W, *Prof,* University of Maryland, College of Library & Information Services, MD. 301-454-5441

Liever-Mackay, Gerry, *Asso Dean,* Cerritos College Library, Learning Materials Center, Norwalk CA. 213-860-2451, Ext 286
Lifland, Donna, *Librn,* Temple Israel Library, Lawrence NY. 516-239-9213
Lifson, Sue, *ILL,* Cornell College, Russell D Cole Library, Mount Vernon IA. 319-895-8811, Ext 117
Liggett, Chris, *Librn,* Community Library, Roundup MT. 406-323-1802
Liggett, Julie, *Librn,* Mary Esther Public Library, Mary Esther FL. 904-243-5731
Liggett, Kathleen, *YA,* Muskogee Public Library, Muskogee OK. 918-682-6657
Liggett, Thomas Joe, *Instr,* Appalachian State University, Department of Educational Media: Librarianship & Instructional Technology, NC. 704-262-2243
Liggio, Rita, *Dir,* Brewster Public Library, Brewster NY. 914-279-6421
Light, A Jeanette, *Acq,* University of West Florida, John C Pace Library, Pensacola FL. 904-476-9500, Ext 261
Light, Barbara, *Librn,* Fresno County Free Library (Sanger Branch), Sanger CA. 209-875-2435
Light, Carol L, *Coordr,* Lebanon County Historical Society Library, Lebanon PA. 717-272-1473
Light, Christine S, *Res Dir,* Oliver & Rozner Associates Library, New York NY. 212-688-1850
Light, Goddard, *Librn,* Rye Historical Society Library, Rye NY. 914-967-7588
Light, Jane, *Dir,* Peninsula Library Systems, Daly City CA. 415-878-5577
Light, Karen, *Ref & Tech Serv,* Westerly Public Library, Memorial & Library Association of Westerly, Westerly RI. 401-596-2877
Lightbody, Debbie, *Off Mgr,* Wheatland Regional Library, Saskatoon SK. 306-652-5077
Lightman, Benjamin, *Chief Librn,* Time, Inc (Main Library), New York NY. 212-841-3745
Lightsey, Katie Lee, *Librn,* East Mississippi Regional Library (Pachuta Public), Pachuta MS. 601-776-2492
Lightsey, Lanelle, *Tech Serv,* Shelton State Community College, Junior College Division, Tuscaloosa AL. 205-759-1583
Lightsey, Norma, *Extension,* Greenville County Library, Greenville SC. 803-242-5000
Lightsey, Virginia Ann, *Asst Dir & Pub Servs,* Public Library of Pine Bluff & Jefferson County, Pine Bluff AR. 501-534-4802, 534-4818
Lignell, Ellen, *Dir,* Kansas City Art Institute, Jessie Burnham Downing Library, Kansas City MO. 816-561-4852, Ext 24
Liivak, Arno, *Librn,* Rutgers University (Camden School of Law Library), Camden NJ. 609-757-6173, 757-6172
Likins, John, *Tech Serv,* Wellesley Free Library, Subregional Headquarters for Eastern Massachusetts Regional Library System, Wellesley MA. 617-235-1610
Likness, Craig S, *On-Line Servs,* Trinity University Library, San Antonio TX. 512-736-8121
Lilek, Sharon, *Librn,* Chicago Bridge & Iron Co, Research Library, Plainfield IL. 815-436-2912
Liles, Martha, *Librn,* Systems Control Inc Technical Library, Palo Alto CA. 415-494-1165, Ext 201
Liljequist, Orval, *Humanities,* Milwaukee Public Library, Milwaukee WI. 414-278-3000
Liljequist, Orval, *Rare Bks & Spec Coll,* Milwaukee Public Library, Milwaukee WI. 414-278-3000
Lillard, Stewart, *Admin Librn,* Queens College, Everett Library, Charlotte NC. 704-332-7121, Ext 278
Lilley, Keith, *Learning Ctr,* Cuesta College, Library Learning Center, San Luis Obispo CA. 805-544-2943, Ext 280
Lilley, Phyllis J, *Dir,* Belle Glade Municipal Library, Belle Glade FL. 305-996-3453, 996-0445
Lillian, Mrs A W, *Librn,* Hartford Public Library, Hartford KS. 316-392-5518
Lilly, David, *Ref,* Huntsville-Madison County Public Library, Huntsville AL. 205-536-0021
Lilly, Lee, *Ref,* Oscar Rose Junior College, Learning Resources Center, Midwest City OK. 405-733-7323, 733-7322
Lilly, Martha E, *Actg Librn,* Palestine Carnegie Library, Palestine TX. 214-729-4121
Lilly, Vera, *Librn,* Southeast Arkansas Regional Library (Dumas), Monticello AR. 501-382-5763

Lim, Josefina, *Tech Serv & Acq,* Cornell University Medical College, Samuel J Wood Library, New York NY. 212-472-5300

Lim, Lourdes P, *Librn,* General Motors Corp (Public Relations Library), New York NY. 212-486-5092

Lim, Sue C, *Actg Cat,* California State Polytechnic University Library, Pomona CA. 714-598-4671

Lim, Young Sook, *Tech Serv,* Worthington Public Library, Worthington OH. 614-885-3185

Lima, Constance M, *Librn,* Exxon Co USA (Medical Library), New York NY. 212-398-3000

Limbach, Paul, *Librn,* Huron Valley Public Library, Flat Rock MI. 313-782-2430

Limbacher, James, *Media,* Dearborn Department of Libraries, Henry Ford Centennial Library, Dearborn MI. 313-271-1000

Limmer, M Annette, *Circ,* Deer Park Public Library, Deer Park TX. 713-479-5276

Limpert, T M, *In Charge,* Union Carbide Corp Chemicals & Plastics Div, Training Department Library, Port Lavaca TX. 512-552-7511

Limuere, Karl, *Dir,* North Dakota Farmers Union Research Library, Jamestown ND. 701-252-2340

Lin, Agnes, *Tech Serv & Cat,* New York Institute of Technology Library, Old Westbury NY. 516-686-7657, 686-7658

Lin, Caroline, *Ad,* Yorba Linda Library District, Yorba Linda CA. 714-528-7039

Lin, Che-Hwei, *Asian-Am Studies,* University of California Los Angeles Library, Los Angeles CA. 213-825-1201

Lin, James, *Coordr,* State Community College of East Saint Louis, Learning Resource Center, East Saint Louis IL. 618-875-9100, Ext 238, 378

Lin, Janney, *Librn,* Onondaga County Public Library System (Mundy), Syracuse NY. 315-473-4395

Lin, Jiann I, *Chinese,* Oberlin College Library, Oberlin OH. 216-775-8285

Lin, John T, *Coordr,* Tidewater Community College, Frederick Campus Library, Portsmouth VA. 804-484-2121, Ext 226

Lin, Katy, *Per & Doc,* Capital University Library, Columbus OH. 614-236-6614

Lin, Kevin, *Librn,* University of Texas Libraries (Asian), Austin TX. 512-471-3135

Lin, Laura, *Ref,* McGregor Public Library, Highland Park Library, Highland Park MI. 313-252-0288

Lin, Raymond, *Tech Serv,* Springfield College, Babson Library, Springfield MA. 413-787-2340

Lin, Shu-Fang, *Govt Doc,* Saint John's University Library, Jamaica NY. 212-969-8000, Ext 201

Lin, Stanley, *Tech Serv,* Edinboro State College, Baron-Forness Library, Edinboro PA. 814-732-2780

Lin, Susan Tu, *Librn,* United States Army (Corps of Engineers, Rock Island District Library), Rock Island IL. 309-788-6361, Ext 300

Linam, Doris, *Acq,* Waco-McLennan County Library, Waco TX. 817-754-4694

Linard, J Labon, *Librn,* Fairfax County Comprehensive Planning Library, Fairfax VA. 703-691-2641, Ext 20

Linard, Stephanie, *Tech Serv,* Alexandria Library, Alexandria VA. 703-750-6351

Lincer, C A, *Dir,* Cochise College, Cochise Sierra Vista Learning Resources Center, Sierra Vista AZ. 602-458-7110

Lincer, Catherin A, *Acq,* Cochise College, Learning Resources Center, Douglas AZ. 602-364-7943, Ext 280

Lincoln, Carol, *Librn,* Newmarket Public Library, Newmarket NH. 603-659-5311

Lincoln, John, *Asst Librn,* Lakeland Community College Library, Mentor OH. 216-951-1000, Ext 226

Lincoln, Robert, *Acq,* University of Manitoba Libraries, Winnipeg MB. 204-474-9881

Lincoln, Shirley, *Tech Serv,* Bureau of Libraries, Museums & Archaeological Services, Saint Thomas VI. 809-774-3407

Lind, Anda, *Ad,* Prince William Public Library, Manassas VA. 703-361-8211

Lind, Beverly, *Dir,* Northeastern Iowa Regional Library System, Waterloo IA. 319-233-1200

Lind, Leon, *Media,* University of Idaho Library, Moscow ID. 208-885-6534

Lind, Mary, *Bkmobile Coordr,* Kansas City Kansas Public Library, Kansas City KS. 913-621-3073

Lindahl, Charles, *Assoc Librn,* University of Rochester (Sibley Music Library), Rochester NY. 716-275-3018

Lindahl, John, *Curator,* Nebraska State Historical Society, John G Neihardt Center Research Library, Bancroft NE. 402-648-3388

Lindaman, Shirley, *Librn,* Aplington Legion Memorial Library, Aplington IA. 319-347-2432

Lindamood, Marti, *Librn,* Hamilton City Library, Hamilton KS. 316-678-3646

Lindars, William Arthur, *Librn,* General Drafting Co Inc, Map Library, Convent Station NJ. 201-538-7600, Ext 66

Lindauer, George, *Librn,* University of Louisville Library (Speed School), Louisville KY. 502-588-6297

Lindauer, Robert H, *Actg State Librn,* Connecticut State Library, Hartford CT. 203-566-4301

Lindberg, Helen, *Dir,* Leach Public Library, Wahpeton ND. 701-642-5732

Lindberg, Henna Mae, *Dir,* Hurley Public Library, Hurley WI. 715-561-5707

Lindberg, Lois A, *Cat,* Oberlin College Library, Oberlin OH. 216-775-8285

Lindberg, Mary, *Librn,* Presbyterian Medical Center (School of Nursing Library), Denver CO. 303-839-6081

Lindblom, Freda, *Acq,* Providence College, Phillips Memorial Library, Providence RI. 401-865-2242

Lindblom, Joseph H, *Dir,* Church of Jesus Christ of Latter Day Saints, Arizona Branch Genealogical Library, Mesa AZ. 602-964-1200

Lindelein, Johnabell, *Librn,* Austin Public Library (Grand Meadow Public), Grand Meadow MN. 507-754-5859

Lindell, Linda, *Ref,* Texas State Library, Division for the Blind & Physically Handicapped, Austin TX. 512-475-4758

Lindemon, Agnes M, *Librn,* Baltimore Gas & Electric Co Library, Baltimore MD. 301-234-5000

Lindemuth, Mary, *Cat,* Brockway Public Library, Glenn Mengle Memorial Library, Brockway PA. 814-265-8245

Linden, Joan, *Librn,* Great Neck Library (Station), Great Neck NY. 516-466-8055, Ext 232

Linden, M, *Cat,* University of Toronto Libraries (Victoria College), Toronto ON. 416-978-3821

Linden, Margaret J, *Librn,* Standard Oil Co of California Library, San Francisco CA. 415-894-2945

Linden, Michael, *Dir,* Motion Picture Association of America, Inc, Research Department Library, New York NY. 212-840-6161

Lindenfeld, Joe, *Librn,* Memphis-Shelby County Public Library & Information Center (Shelby State Community College Libr), Memphis TN. 901-528-6743

Lindenfeld, Joseph F, *Dir,* Shelby State Community College Library, Memphis TN. 901-528-6743

Lindeqvist, Ingrid, *ILL,* Elmira College, Gannett-Tripp Learning Ctr, Elmira NY. 607-734-3911, Ext 287

Linder, George R, *Dir,* Durham County Library, Durham NC. 919-683-2626

Linder, L H, *Mgr Tech Info Servs,* Ford Aerospace & Communications Corp, Technical Information Services, Newport Beach CA. 714-759-5367

Linder, Mrs William, *Librn,* Lindsborg Community Library, Lindsborg KS. 913-227-2710

Linderman, Jim, *Acq,* Upjohn Company (Corporate Technical Library), Kalamazoo MI. 616-385-6414

Linderman, Marion, *Assoc Prof,* Southern Missionary College, Library Science Program, TN. 615-396-4291

Linderman, Marion, *ILL, On-Line Servs & Bibliog Instr,* Southern Missionary College, McKee Library, Collegedale TN. 615-396-4290

Lindgren, Arla, *Acq,* Teachers College - Columbia University Library, New York NY. 212-678-3022, 678-3020

Lindgren, Jon, *Ref,* Saint Lawrence University, Owen D Young Library, Canton NY. 315-379-5451

Lindgren, Mary, *Librn,* Minnesota Society for Crippled Children & Adults, Courage Center Library, Golden Valley MN. 612-588-0811, Ext 244

Lindgren, Miriam, *Dir,* Axtell Public Library, Axtell NE. 308-743-2592

Lindgren, William, *Cat,* Colorado State University, William E Morgan Library, Fort Collins CO. 303-491-5911

Lindgren, William, *Dir,* Illinois Central College, Learning Resources Center, East Peoria IL. 309-694-5461

Lindgren, William, *Dir,* Illinois Central College, Library Technical Assistant Program, IL. 309-694-5461

Lindley, Edith, *Librn,* Parkersburg & Wood County Public Library (Williamstown Public), Williamstown WV. 304-485-6564

Lindley, Patricia J, *Dir,* Herrick Memorial Library, Wellington Public Library, Wellington OH. 216-647-2120

Lindley, Samuel, *Asst Librn & Ref,* Honolulu Community College Library, Honolulu HI. 808-845-9220

Lindloff, Kay, *Librn,* Texas Institute for Rehabilitation & Research, Information Services Center Library, Houston TX. 713-797-1440, Ext 220

Lindner, Alden, *Acq,* Capital University Library, Columbus OH. 614-236-6614

Lindner, Charlotte, *Libr Technician,* San Diego County Library (Cardiff Branch), Cardiff CA. 714-753-4027

Lindner, Charlotte K, *Dir,* Albert Einstein College of Medicine, D Samuel Gottesman Library, Bronx NY. 212-430-3108

Lindner, Katherine, *Librn,* Englewood Hospital, Medical Library, Englewood NJ. 201-568-3400, Ext 583

Lindquist, Frances, *Asst Librn,* Carnegie City Library, Little Falls MN. 612-632-9676

Lindquist, Georgia, *Ch,* Monticello Union Township Public Library, Monticello IN. 219-583-5643

Lindquist, Jeanne, *ILL,* Anna Maria College Library, Paxton MA. 617-757-4586, Ext 56

Lindquist, June A V, *Spec Coll,* Bureau of Libraries, Museums & Archaeological Services, Saint Thomas VI. 809-774-3407

Lindquist, Karen, *Dir,* Lenawee County Library, Adrian MI. 517-263-1011

Lindquist, R Marie, *Dir,* Southeastern Library Services, Southeast Iowa Regional Library, Davenport IA. 319-324-0019

Lindquist, Verna, *Librn,* Cambridge Township Library, Cambridge IL. 309-937-2233

Lindsay, Angie W, *Asst Librn,* Tooele Public Library, Tooele UT. 801-882-2182

Lindsay, Carol, *Chief Librn,* Toronto Star Newspapers Ltd Library, Toronto ON. 416-367-2420

Lindsay, Marion, *Librn,* York Regional Library (L P Fischer), Woodstock NB. 506-328-6880

Lindsay, Muriel, *Librn,* Automobile Club of Missouri, Information Resource Center, Saint Louis MO. 314-576-7350, Ext 378, 379

Lindsay, Noah, *Ref,* Lake City Community College, G T Melton Learning Resources Center, Lake City FL. 904-752-1822, Ext 260

Lindsay, Ruth, *Librn,* Richwood North Union Public Library, Richwood OH. 614-943-3054

Lindsay, Sharon, *Librn,* Rockbridge Regional Library (Bath County), Warm Springs VA. 703-839-2472

Lindsay, Zona H, *Asst Dir,* Brandywine College Library, Wilmington DE. 302-478-3000

Lindsey, Christopher Baar, *Ch,* Henderson County Public Library, Hendersonville NC. 704-693-8427

Lindsey, George, *Circ,* Brooks Memorial Library, Brattleboro VT. 802-254-5290

Lindsey, Ivylyn, *Acq,* Coastal Plain Regional Library, Tifton GA. 912-386-3400

Lindsey, John M, *Librn,* Temple University of the Commonwealth System of Higher Education (Law), Philadelphia PA. 215-787-7891

Lindsey, John R, *Librn,* Public Library of the District of Columbia (Barry Farms), Washington DC. 202-767-7198

Lindsey, Jonathan A, *Librn,* Meredith College, Carlyle Campbell Library, Raleigh NC. 919-833-6461, Ext 231

Lindsey, Lowell L, *Dir,* Nicholson Memorial Library, Garland TX. 214-494-7187

Lindsey, Margaret A, *Librn,* Clearwater Public Library (Beach), Clearwater Beach FL. 813-462-6890

Lindsey, Marie J, *Chief Librn,* United States Army (Grandstaff Memorial Library), Fort Lewis WA. 206-967-4934

Lindsey, Mary Lee, *Cat,* Wayne County Public Library, Inc, Goldsboro NC. 919-735-1824

Lindsey, Ruthie P, *In Charge,* Bendix Guidance Systems Div, Technical Library, Mishawaka IN. 219-255-2111, Ext 212

Lindsley, Ellen J, *Tech Serv & Cat,* College of Saint Rose Library, Albany NY. 518-454-5180

Lindsley, Lavina, *Librn,* Slayton Public Library, Slayton MN. 507-836-8778

Lindsley, Robert E, *Dir,* West Paterson Free Public Library, West Paterson NJ. 201-345-8120

Lindsten, Rosetta, *Asst Librn,* Goodland Public Library, Goodland KS. 913-899-5461

Lindstrand, Margaret A, *Librn,* Saint James Hospital, Medical Library, Chicago Heights IL. 312-756-1000, Ext 6150

Lindstrom, Elizabeth, *Cat,* Nicolet College & Technical Institute, Learning Resources Center, Rhinelander WI. 715-369-4429

Lindstrom, William E, *Dir,* Maui Community College, Learning Resource Center, Kahului HI. 808-242-5433, 242-5498

Lindt, Theodora L D, *Dir,* Jewish Memorial Hospital Library, New York NY. 212-569-4700, Ext 69, 70

Line, Bryant, *Librn,* Arlington County Department of Libraries (Central Library), Arlington VA. 703-527-4777

Lineback, Corrie T, *Librn,* Scientific-Atlanta, Inc Library, Atlanta GA. 404-449-2000, Ext 2256

Lineham, Jr, Thomas U, *Cat,* Rollins College, Mills Memorial Library, Winter Park FL. 305-646-2000, Ext 2676

Linehan, Janice, *Bus & Econ,* Rochester Institute of Technology, Wallace Memorial Library, Rochester NY. 716-475-2566

Linehan, Vivien B, *ILL,* Suffolk County Community College, Eastern Campus Library, Riverhead NY. 516-369-2600, Ext 228

Linepensel, Kenneth, *Librn,* Great Lakes Chemical Corporation, Corporate & Research Library, West Lafayette IN. 317-463-2511, Ext 207

Lines, Wesley, *Media,* Inver Hills Community College, Learning Resource Center, Inver Grove Heights MN. 612-455-9621, Ext 58

Linford, John, *Exec Dir,* NELINET, MA. 969-0400

Linford, Mary G, *Librn,* Garland Public Library, Garland UT. 801-257-3118

Ling, Larie, *Chief Librn,* Elko Clinic Library, Elko NV. 702-738-3111

Ling, Mrs Robert E, *Librn,* High Street Christian Church, H A Valentine Memorial Library, Akron OH. 216-434-1039

Lingbloom, Pamela, *Circ,* Rock Springs Public Library, Rock Springs WY. 307-362-6212

Lingelbach, Lorene, *Librn,* Berlex Laboratories, Science & Technology Library, Cedar Knolls NJ. 201-540-8700, Ext 229

Linger, Neil, *Ref,* Broward Community College, Learning Resources Center, Fort Lauderdale FL. 305-475-6500

Link, Margaret M, *Dir,* Vanderbilt University Library (Management), Nashville TN. 615-322-2534

Link, Noreen, *Librn,* Foley & Lardner, Law Library, Milwaukee WI. 414-271-2400

Link, Phoebe A, *Cat,* Mount Aloysius Junior College Library, Cresson PA. 814-886-4131, Ext 70

Link, Sarah Dean, *Dir,* Mendham Township Public Library, Brookside NJ. 201-543-4018

Link, Terry, *Ref,* Aquinas College, Learning Resource Center, Grand Rapids MI. 616-459-8281, Ext 234

Linke, Frances Baur, *Librn,* Blue Cross of Southern California Library, Woodland Hills CA. 213-703-3160

Linker, Pat, *Asst Librn,* Carbarrus Memorial Hospital Library, Concord NC. 704-786-2111, Ext 367

Linker, Rita, *Bus,* Tri-County Regional Library, Rome GA. 404-291-9360

Linkes, Nancy, *Librn,* Apollo Memorial Library, Apollo PA. 412-478-4214

Linkhart, Edward, *Librn,* Nez Perce County Law Library, Lewiston ID. 208-743-2561

Linkhart, Edward, *Admnr & Regional Dir,* North Central Idaho Regional Library System, Lewiston ID. 208-743-2561

Linkhart, Edward G, *Dir,* Nez Perce County Free Library District, Lewiston ID. 208-743-2561

Linkins, Germaine C, *Ser,* Virginia Polytechnic Institute & State University Library, Blacksburg VA. 703-961-5593

Linklater, Elizabeth, *Librn,* Oshawa Public Library (North Simcoe), Oshawa ON. 416-576-6040

Linkletter, Esther, *Librn,* State University of New York (Chemistry), Stony Brook NY. 516-246-5664

Linn, Carol, *Librn,* Debevoise, Plimpton, Lyons & Gates Law Library, New York NY. 212-752-6400, Ext 278

Linn, Dorotha C, *Librn,* Veterans Administration, Hospital Library Service, Asheville NC. 704-298-7911

Linn, James J, *Dir,* Tulane University of Louisiana (Norman Mayer Library), New Orleans LA. 504-865-6111

Linn, Loren E, *On-Line Servs & Bibliog Instr,* Hercules Inc (Research Center Library), Wilmington DE. 302-995-3484

Linn, Mary L, *Librn,* Boston Public Library (Mattapan Branch), Mattapan MA. 617-298-9218

Linn, Mary L, *Librn,* Boston Public Library (Uphams Corner), Dorchester MA. 617-265-0139

Linn, Sarah, *Ref,* Middleton Public Library, Middleton WI. 608-831-5564

Linn, Suellen, *Librn,* Lake Placid School of Art, Nettie Marie Jones Fine Arts Library, Association for Music, Drama & Art, Lake Placid NY. 518-523-2591, 523-2592, Ext 31

Linnamaa, Mari, *Cat,* New Jersey Institute of Technology, Robert W Van Houten Library, Newark NJ. 201-645-5306

Linnane, Mary Lu, *Cat,* De Paul University Libraries (Law Library), Chicago IL. 312-321-7710

Linneman, Mark A, *Ref,* University of Iowa Libraries (Law Library), Iowa City IA. 319-353-5968

Linsley, Laurie H, *ILL,* University of Central Florida Library, Orlando FL. 305-275-2564

Linstrom, Olive C, *Librn,* Veterans Administration, Medical Library, Fort Meade SD. 605-347-2511

Linthicum, Ruth, *Librn,* Randolph Public Library (Randleman Branch), Randleman NC. 919-498-2604

Lintner, Barbara, *Ch,* Allerton Public Library, Monticello IL. 217-762-4676

Linton, Barbara, *Asst Librn,* National Audubon Society Library, New York NY. 212-832-3200

Linton, Carol, *ILL,* College of William & Mary in Virginia, Earl Gregg Swem Library, Williamsburg VA. 804-253-4404

Linton, Linda, *Ref,* Howard County Library, Columbia MD. 301-997-8000

Linton, Mary Lou, *Media,* Brevard Community College, Learning Resources Center, Cocoa FL. 305-632-1111, Ext 295, 298

Linton, Teresa, *Ref,* Washington & Lee University, The University Library, Lexington VA. 703-463-9111, Ext 403

Linville, Bettye, *Acq & Accounts,* Maysville Community College Library, Maysville KY. 606-759-7141, Ext 28

Linville, Herbert, *Govt Publications,* University of California, Santa Barbara Library, Santa Barbara CA. 805-961-2741

Linzmayer, Ferdinand, *Dep Librn, Systs,* University of Calgary Library, Calgary AB. 403-284-5954

Lipan, Leslie, *Reader Serv,* Mary H Weir Public Library, Weirton WV. 304-748-7070

Lipes, Dorothy, *ILL,* Pathfinder Library System, Montrose CO. 303-249-9656

Lipetz, Ben-Ami, *Prof,* State University of New York at Albany, School of Library & Information Science, NY. 518-455-6288

Lipford, Mary Ann, *Dir Educ Media & Tech,* Grayson County Junior College Library, Denison TX. 214-465-6030, Ext 237

Lipkin, Hilda, *Actg Dir,* Teaneck Public Library, Teaneck NJ. 201-837-4171

Lipkind, Rochelle, *Ad,* Middle Country Public Library, Centereach NY. 516-585-9393

Lipman, Paula, *Asst Librn,* United States Department of Energy (Law Library), Washington DC. 202-666-8922

Lipman, Penny, *Librn,* Rio Algom Ltd Library, Toronto ON. 416-367-4299, 367-4249

Lipman, Peter, *Asst Univ Librn-Systs & Cir,* Brown University (University Library), Providence RI. 401-863-2167

Lipnik, Ruth, *ILL,* Roanoke County Public Library, Roanoke VA. 703-774-1681

Lipow, Anne, *ILL,* University of California, Berkeley (University Library), Berkeley CA. 415-642-3773

Lippert, Edna, *Asst Dir & Cat,* Northland College, Dexter Library, Ashland WI. 715-682-4531, Ext 297

Lippert, Marianne, *Ref,* North Suburban District Library, Loves Park IL. 815-633-4247, 633-4248

Lippincott, Joan, *Bibliog Instr,* Georgetown University, Joseph Mark Lauinger Library, Washington DC. 202-625-4095

Lippitt, Louise G, *Librn,* Twentieth Century Trends Institute Inc, Source Library, Darien CT. 203-655-8344

Lippitt, Ruth, *Tech Serv,* Chester County Library & District Center, Exton PA. 215-363-0884

Lippke, Margaret, *Dir,* Barbara Sanborn Public Library, Pewaukee WI. 414-691-1300

Lippman, Anne F, *Ref,* Boston College Libraries (School of Nursing Library), Chestnut Hill MA. 617-969-0100, Ext 3235

Lippman, Marc, *Rare Bks,* University Club Library, New York NY. 212-572-3418

Lippman, Murray, *Per,* Elmont Public Library, Elmont NY. 516-354-5280, 354-4091

Lippmann, Susan B, *Librn,* Newman Catholic Student Center, Timothy Parkman Memorial Library, Tucson AZ. 602-327-6662

Lipps, Ilo, *Librn,* Franklin Public Library, Franklin NE. 308-425-3162

Lipschutz, Eleanor, *Librn,* A G Holley State Hospital, Patients Library, Lantana FL. 305-582-5666, Ext 234

Lipscomb, Barbara, *Reader Serv & Bibliog Instr,* Louisiana Tech University, Prescott Memorial Library, Ruston LA. 318-257-2577

Lipscomb, Carolyn, *ILL & Circ,* University of North Carolina at Chapel Hill (Health Sciences Library), Chapel Hill NC. 919-966-2111

Lipscomb, Robert, *County Librn,* Saint Johns County Library, Saint Augustine FL. 904-824-3992

Lipsett, V, *Librn,* Okanagan Regional Library District (Seymour Arm), Sicamous BC. 604-860-4033

Lipsitz, Jeanne, *Librn,* Old York Road Temple Beth Am Library, Abington PA. 215-886-8000

Lipsky, Orah, *Librn,* Temple Beth Sholom, Herbert Goldberg Memorial Library, Haddon Heights NJ. 609-547-6113

Lipton, Ilise, *YA,* Montclair Free Public Library, Montclair NJ. 201-744-0500

Lipton, Saundra, *Humanities,* University of Calgary Library, Calgary AB. 403-284-5954

Lisefski, Alice, *Librn,* Hazleton Area Public Library (Nuremberg), Hazleton PA. 717-384-4101

Lisker, Carol, *Ser,* Indiana University School of Law, Law Library, Bloomington IN. 812-337-9666

Liskov, Judith L, *Ad,* Waterford Public Library, Waterford CT. 203-442-8551

Liskowiak, Zara, *Librn,* Champaign County Library, Urbana OH. 513-653-3811

Lisowski, Andrew, *Cat,* George Washington University Library, Washington DC. 202-676-6455

Lissak, Debra Jo, *Librn,* Burnham City Hospital Library, Champaign IL. 217-337-2591

Lissel, Bonnie, *Tech Serv,* Grande Prairie Public Library, Grande Prairie AB. 403-532-3580

List, Mary Ann, *Librn,* Peabody Institute Library (West), Peabody MA. 617-535-3354

Lister, Mrs J, *Group Leader,* George Brown College of Applied Arts & Technology Library (Saint James Campus), Toronto ON. 416-967-1212

Listi, Christopher, *Circ,* Lake County Public Library, Leadville CO. 303-486-0569

Listoe, Philip, *Librn,* Nutana Collegiate Institute, Memorial Library & Art Gallery, Saskatoon SK. 306-653-1677

Lit, Estelle, *Instr,* California State University-Los Angeles, Library Services Credential Program, CA. 213-224-3765

Litchauer, Frances, *Librn,* Curtiss-Wright Corp, Information Services, Wood-Ridge NJ. 201-777-2900, Ext 2077

Litchfield, Ann, *Librn,* Taunton Public Library (Weir), Taunton MA. 617-823-3570
Litchfield, Meredith C, *Asst Dir,* Kansas State University, Farrell Library, Manhattan KS. 913-532-6516
Litoff, Leslie, *Media & Ref,* Western New England College (Law Library), Springfield MA. 413-782-3111, Ext 454, 455
Litt, Ethel, *Librn,* Temple Beth Sholom, Esther Swinkin Memorial Library, Hamden CT. 203-288-7748
Litterst, Mary, *Planning & Res Servs Consult,* Massachusetts Board of Library Commissioners, Office for the Development of Library Services, Boston MA. 617-267-9400
Littier, Thomas A, *Librn,* Brooklyn Children's Museum Library, Brooklyn NY. 212-735-4400
Little, Agnes E, *Head Pembroke Librn,* Brown University (University Library), Providence RI. 401-863-2167
Little, Ann, *Librn,* Manufacturers Hanover Trust Co, Corporate Library. Financial Library Division, New York NY. 212-350-4733
Little, Beth, *Ch,* Beaumont Public Library, Beaumont TX. 713-838-0812
Little, Doris P, *Librn,* Federal Aviation Administration, Southern Region Library, East Point GA. 404-763-7527
Little, Gelynn, *Librn,* Barton Library (Huttig Branch), Huttig AR. 501-943-2222
Little, Hilda, *Librn,* Carrollton Public Library, Carrollton IL. 217-942-6715
Little, Howard, *Acq,* Morgan State University, Morris A Soper Library, Baltimore MD. 301-444-3488, 444-3489
Little, Jonathan J, *Dir,* John Packard Library of Yuba County, Marysville CA. 916-674-6241
Little, Joyce, *ILL,* Tangipahoa Parish Library, Amite LA. 504-748-9387
Little, Karen, *Dir,* Health Information Retrieval Center, ID. 208-386-2222
Little, Karen, *Dir,* Saint Luke's Hospital, Medical Library, Boise ID. 208-386-2222, Ext 2277
Little, Linda, *Tech Serv,* Davenport Public Library, Davenport IA. 319-326-7832
Little, Margaret, *Binding,* Mayo Foundation (Medical Library), Rochester MN. 507-284-2061
Little, Mary, *Dir,* Caney Fork Regional Library, Sparta TN. 615-836-3335
Little, Nancy C, *Librn,* M Knoedler & Co Inc, Art Library, New York NY. 212-794-0550
Little, Patricia, *Coordr,* Rideau Lakes Union Library, Elgin ON. 613-359-5315
Little, Paul, *Exten Chief,* Metropolitan Library System, Oklahoma City OK. 405-235-0571
Little, Robert D, *Chmn,* Indiana State University, Dept of Library Science, IN. 812-232-6311, Ext 2834
Little, Robin, *Circ,* Ashe County Public Library, West Jefferson NC. 919-246-2041
Little, Rosemary, *Librn,* Princeton University Library (Public Administration), Princeton NJ. 609-452-3180
Littlefield, Audrey, *Ref,* Middletown Free Library, Middletown RI. 846-1573 & 846-1584
Littlefield, Judy, *Libr Tech,* Veterans Administration, Medical & Regional Office Center Library Service, Augusta ME. 207-623-8411, Ext 275, 504
Littlejohn, Quinette, *Librn,* Union County Library System (Blue Springs Public), Blue Springs MS. 601-534-6942
Littlepage, Sue, *Librn,* Ensco Inc Library, Springfield VA. 703-321-9000, Ext 204
Littler, June D, *Dir,* Santa Fe Community College Library, Gainesville FL. 904-377-5161, Ext 315
Littleton, Alice, *Librn,* Marin County Free Library (Marin City Branch), Marin City CA. 415-332-1128
Littleton, Harold J, *President,* Lombardy Hall Foundation Library, Wilmington DE. 302-772-4286
Littleton, Isaac T, *Dir,* North Carolina State University, D H Hill Library, Raleigh NC. 919-737-2843, 2595
Littleton, Vera, *Librn,* Badin Branch Library, Badin NC. 704-422-3218
Littman, Rosette, *Cat,* Villanova University (Pulling Law Library), Villanova PA. 215-527-2100, Ext 702, 703, 704
Litton, Jocelan, *Tech Serv,* Coquitlam Public Library, Coquitlam BC. 604-931-2416

Litton, Karen, *Ch,* Confederation Centre Library, Charlottetown Public Library, Charlottetown PE. 902-892-7932
Litton, Linda, *Cat,* Dalton Public Library, Inc, Dalton Regional Library, Dalton GA. 404-278-4507, 278-9247, 226-2039
Litton, Sally, *Bus, Sci & Indust,* Jacksonville Public Library System, Haydon Burns Library, Jacksonville FL. 904-633-6870
Litvinoff, Ana D, *Acq,* Louisiana State University (Law Center Library), Baton Rouge LA. 504-388-8802
Litwinowicz, Mrs L, *Spec Librarian,* Holy Trinity Orthodox Seminary Library, Jordanville NY. 315-858-1332
Litzenberger, Mary Margaret, *Asst Librn,* Buffalo Psychiatric Center (Rehabilitation Services Library), Buffalo NY. 716-885-2261, Ext 256
Litzinger, Linda, *ILL, AV & Ref,* Grove City Public Library, Grove City OH. 614-875-6716
Liu, Agnete, *Cat,* McAllen Memorial Library, McAllen TX. 512-682-4531
Liu, Albert, *Cat,* Old Dominion University Library, Norfolk VA. 804-440-4141
Liu, David Y, *Librn,* Pharr Memorial Library, Pharr TX. 512-787-3966, 787-3301, 787-1491 (Dir off)
Liu, Ellen, *Monographs Acq Librn,* University of Arkansas for Medical Sciences Library, Little Rock AR. 501-661-5980
Liu, Frank, *Asst Librn,* Villanova University (Pulling Law Library), Villanova PA. 215-527-2100, Ext 702, 703, 704
Liu, Shari S, *Librn,* Ballard, Spahr, Andrews & Ingersoll Library, Philadelphia PA. 215-564-1800
Liu, Susanna, *Per,* San Jose State University Library, San Jose CA. 408-277-3377
Lively, Eileen T, *Librn,* Southwest Texas Methodist Hospital, Medical Nursing & Patient Library, San Antonio TX. 512-696-1200
Livermore, Chad M, *Media,* Wentworth Institute of Technology Library, Boston MA. 617-442-9010, Ext 344
Livermore, Elaine D, *Acq,* University of Arizona Library, Tucson AZ. 602-626-2101
Livermore, Elaine D, *Librn,* University of Arizona Library (Acquisitions), Tucson AZ. 602-626-3713
Livermore, Jane M, *Librn,* Science Service, Inc Library, Washington DC. 202-785-2255
Livesay, Mary L, *Librn,* Carroll County Public Library, Carrollton KY. 502-732-6352
Livingston, Debra, *Librn & On-Line Servs,* Systems Applications, Inc Library, San Rafael CA. 415-472-4011
Livingston, Frances G, *Dir & Spec Coll,* Indiana University Southeast Library, New Albany IN. 812-945-2731
Livingston, Lois, *Librn,* Sno-Isle Regional Library (Mukilteo Branch), Mukilteo WA. 206-355-2542
Livingston, Louise, *Librn,* Kingfisher Memorial Library, Kingfisher OK. 405-375-3384
Livingston, Lyn, *Librn,* Southwest Missouri State University Library (Greenwood Laboratory School), Springfield MO. 417-836-5958
Livingston, Mrs Leon E, *Librn,* New Ipswich Public Library, New Ipswich NH. 603-878-2772
Livingston, R W, *Dir,* Duval Corp, Process Development Library, Tucson AZ. 602-881-6200
Livingston, Susan H, *Acq,* Skidmore College, Lucy Scribner Library, Saratoga Springs NY. 518-584-5000, Ext 234
Livingston, William O, *ILL & Ref,* Spring Hill College, Thomas Byrne Memorial Library, Mobile AL. 205-460-2381
Livingstone, Ardith, *ILL & Ref,* Homewood Public Library, Homewood IL. 312-798-0121
Livingstone, Bertha, *Librn,* Duke University (Biology-Forestry), Durham NC. 919-684-2381
Livingstone, Julia, *Tech Serv,* Cambria County Library System, Johnstown PA. 814-536-5131
Livingstone, Jr, John H, *Dir,* Monmouth County Library, Freehold NJ. 201-431-7220
Liwag, Crisencia, *Bibliog Instr,* UOP, Inc (Research Library), Des Plaines IL. 312-391-3361
Lizer, Bonnie, *Ad,* Washington County Free Library, Hagerstown MD. 301-739-3250
Llerandi, Patricia, *Ad,* Schaumburg Township Public Library, Schaumburg IL. 312-885-3373
Llewellyn, Fredrick, *Dir,* Forest Lawn Museum Library, Glendale CA. 213-254-3131

Llewellyn, Mary Emma, *Asst Prof,* Millersville State College, Dept of Library Science, PA. 717-872-5411, Ext 416
Llorens, Ana M R, *Librn,* Ohio State University Libraries (Foreign Languages Graduate Library), Columbus OH. 614-422-2594
Lloyd, Betty G, *Dir,* Arthur Johnson Memorial Library, Raton Public Library, Raton NM. 505-445-9711
Lloyd, Diane, *AV,* Spokane Falls Community College, Library Media Services, Spokane WA. 509-456-2860
Lloyd, Ellen, *Assoc Librn,* Arizona Training Program at Coolidge Library (Client Library), Coolidge AZ. 602-723-4151
Lloyd, Ellen W, *In Charge,* Arizona Training Program at Coolidge Library, Coolidge AZ. 602-723-4151
Lloyd, Heather, *Ref & Bibliog Instr,* Oklahoma State University Library, Stillwater OK. 405-624-6313
Lloyd, Janice, *Librn,* Graphic Arts Technical Foundation, E H Wadewitz Memorial Library, Pittsburgh PA. 412-621-6941, Ext 255
Lloyd, Jayne, *Media,* Vigo County Public Library, Terre Haute IN. 812-232-1113
Lloyd, Joe, *Govt Info,* Mobile Public Library, Mobile AL. 205-438-7073
Lloyd, Lynn, *Asst Librn,* Veterans Administration, Hospital Library, Providence RI. 401-521-1700, Ext 537, 539
Lloyd, Patricia, *Coll Develop,* Grant MacEwan Community College, Learning Resource Centres, Edmonton AB. 403-484-7791
Lloyd, Renee D, *Librn,* West Virginia Northern Community College Library, Learning Resources Center, Wheeling WV. 304-233-5900, Ext 240
Lloyd, Sylvia, *Acq,* Clermont County Public Library, Batavia OH. 513-732-2128
Lloyd, Warren F, *Dir,* Darlington County Library, Darlington SC. 803-393-5864
Llull, Harry, *Librn,* Stanford University Libraries (Mathematical & Computer Sciences), Stanford CA. 415-497-4672
Lo, Henry, *Dir,* Lindenhurst Memorial Library, Lindenhurst NY. 516-888-7575
Lo, Karl K, *Librn,* University of Washington Libraries (East Asia), Seattle WA. 206-543-4490
Lo, Lisa, *Chief Librn,* Newmarket Public Library, Newmarket ON. 416-895-5196
Lo, Lydia, *Actg Dir,* Shasta College Library, Redding CA. 916-241-3523, Ext 377
Lo, Mary, *Asst Librn,* University of Tennessee Space Institute Library, Tullahoma TN. 615-455-0631, Ext 315
Lo, Mei Yiao, *Cat,* University of Maryland-Eastern Shore, Frederick Douglass Library, Princess Anne MD. 301-651-2200, Ext 229
Loader, Rebecca, *Dir,* Columbia Heights Public Library, Columbia Heights MN. 612-788-3924
Loar, Barbara, *Asst Dir, Exten,* Dekalb Library System, Maud M Burrus Library, Decatur GA. 404-378-7569
Loar, Barbara, *Asst Dir Exten,* Dekalb Library System (System Headquarter & Processing Center), Decatur GA. 404-294-6641
Loar, Frances E, *Asst Acq Librn,* United States Department of the Army (Office of the Adjutant General, Morale Support Directorate, Library Activities Division), Washington DC. 202-325-9700
Loar, Harriet, *Dir,* Metamora Public School District Library, Metamora OH. 419-644-2771
Lobaza, Cynthia, *Tech Serv,* Warren-Newport Public Library District, Gurnee IL. 312-244-5150
Loberg, Alice, *Dir,* Amherst Public Library, Amherst WI. 715-824-5510
Lobert, Robin, *Dir,* Los Angeles College of Chiropractic, Library & Audiovisual Media Center, Glendale CA. 213-244-7686, Ext 216
LoBue, Ben, *Ref,* University of Colorado at Boulder (University Libraries), Boulder CO. 303-492-7511
Locascio, John, *Dir,* Freeport Public Library, Freeport IL. 815-232-7187
Locascio, Patricia, *Tech Serv,* Loudoun County Public Library, Leesburg VA. 703-777-0368
Locatelli, Janet, *ILL,* Michigan Technological University Library, Houghton MI. 906-487-2500
Locher, Annie, *Asst Dir,* Monticello Public Library, Monticello IA. 319-465-3354

LOCHER

Locher, Cornelia, *Asst Librn & On-Line Servs,* Skadden, Arps, Slate, Meagher & Flom Library, New York NY. 212-371-6000

Locher, Karen, *Spec Coll,* Victoria Public Library, Victoria TX. 512-578-6241

Lochner, Pamela J, *Librn,* Yardney Electric Corp, Technical Information Center, Pawcatuck CT. 203-599-1100, Ext 315

Lock, Hazel, *Asst Librn,* Yellowhead Regional Library, Spruce Grove AB. 403-962-2003

Lockard, Karen S, *Librn,* Montgomery County Circuit Court, Law Library, Rockville MD. 301-279-8293

Lockary, Ruth, *Ser,* Bloomfield College Library, Bloomfield NJ. 201-748-9000, Ext 281

Locke, Avys, *In Charge,* Texas Education Agency (Region VI), Huntsville TX. 713-295-9161

Locke, Edward, *Dir,* Milton Public Library, Milton MA. 617-698-5707

Locke, Ernestine L, *Dir,* Morrisville Free Library Association, Morrisville PA. 215-295-4850

Locke, Germaine, *Librn,* A H Brown Public Library, Mobridge SD. 605-845-2808

Locke, Josephine D, *Actg Librn,* Charlotte County Free Library, Charlotte Court House VA. 804-542-5247

Locke, Mary E, *Librn,* Walpole Public Library, Walpole MA. 617-668-0232

Locke, Patricia, *Librn,* Worcester Public Library (South Worcester), Worcester MA. 617-752-3203

Locke, S Judson, *Dir,* George F Johnson Memorial Library, Endicott NY. 607-754-1746

Locke, Ula May, *Librn,* Lebanon City Library, Lebanon KS. 913-389-7703

Locken, Mary Ann, *Bibliog Instr,* Northwest Missouri State University, Wells Library, Maryville MO. 816-582-7141, Ext 1192

Locker, Frank J, *Supvr,* Travenol Labs, Inc, Business & Law Library, Deerfield IL. 312-948-3880

Lockerby, Robin, *Ref,* Point Loma College, Ryan Library, San Diego CA. 714-222-6474, Ext 355, 338

Lockerman, Ellen C, *Rare Bks & Spec Coll,* Averett College, Mary B Blount Library, Danville VA. 804-793-7811, Ext 265

Lockert, Clinton, *Southeast Asia,* Michigan State University Library, East Lansing MI. 517-355-2344

Lockett, Lenora C, *Dir,* Delgado College, Moss Memorial Library, New Orleans LA. 504-486-7393

Lockett, Mary, *Ref,* Marshall County Library, Holly Springs MS. 601-252-3823

Lockett, Sandra, *Doc,* University of Iowa Libraries (Law Library), Iowa City IA. 319-353-5968

Lockhart, Deborah R, *Librn,* Public Library of the District of Columbia (Takoma Park), Washington DC. 202-727-1385

Lockhart, H, *Librn,* Law Society of British Columbia, Victoria Library, Victoria BC. 604-387-5239

Lockhart, Helen, *Commun Servs,* Memphis-Shelby County Public Library & Information Center, Memphis TN. 901-528-2950

Lockhart, J, *Dir,* Grande Prairie General Hospital, Medical Library, Grande Prairie AB. 403-532-7711, Ext 40

Locking, Ruby, *Librn,* Wellington County Public Library (Clifford Branch), Clifford ON. 519-327-8328

Lockington, Jeanette K, *Asst Librn,* Missouri Department of Natural Resources, Division of Geology & Land Survey Library, Rolla MO. 314-364-1752

Lockwood, Anita, *Ch,* Randolph Township Free Public Library, Randolph NJ. 201-366-0518

Lockwood, Julie, *Librn,* Chicago Public Library (Legler), Chicago IL. 312-638-7730

Lockwood, Linda, *Librn,* Winston & Strawn Library, Chicago IL. 312-786-5740

Lockwood, Patricia M, *Ch,* Bloomfield Public Library, Northwest Essex Area Library, Bloomfield NJ. 201-429-9292

Lockwood, Phyllis, *AV,* Principia College, Marshall Brooks Library, Elsah IL. 618-374-2131, Ext 325

Lockwood, Sherry A, *Doc,* Superior Public Library, Superior WI. 715-394-0248

Lodden, Anneliese, *Librn,* Walled Lake City Library, Walled Lake MI. 313-624-3772

Loder, Michael Westcott, *Asst Librn,* College of Ganado Library, Ganado AZ. 602-755-3442

Lodge, Patricia O, *Asst Librn,* Riverside Hospital Library, Wilmington DE. 302-764-6120, Ext 402

Loe, Nancy, *Local hist,* Pikes Peak Regional Library District, Penrose Public Library, Colorado Springs CO. 303-473-2080

Loe, Sharon, *Ref-Info Servs,* Northern Illinois Library System, Rockford IL. 815-229-0330

Loepfe, Mrs G, *Dir,* Cedarburg Public Library, Cedarburg WI. 414-377-1730

Loerke, Jean Penn, *Dir,* Waukesha County Museum Research Center Library, Waukesha WI. 414-544-8430

Loertscher, David V, *Assoc Prof,* University of Arkansas, Instructional Resources Education, AR. 501-575-5444

Loesch, B, *Circ,* Shoreham-Wading River Public Library, Shoreham NY. 516-929-4488

Loesch, Susan, *Librn,* Arkansas School for the Blind Library, Little Rock AR. 501-663-4185, Ext 34

Loesel, Louise K, *Librn,* Church of the Covenant, Brittain Library, Erie PA. 814-456-4243

Loewen, Mrs I, *Librn,* South Central Regional Library, Morden MB. 204-822-4092

Loewen, Mrs K, *Librn,* Evergreen Regional Library (Riverton Branch), Riverton MB. 204-378-5592

Loewenberg, Nancy, *Acq,* Mercantile Library Association, New York NY. 212-755-6710

Loewenkamp, Lucille, *Librn,* Evansville Press Library, Evansville IN. 812-464-7455

Lofquist, Joanne, *Tech Serv,* Eckerd College, William Luther Cobb Library, Saint Petersburg FL. 813-867-1166, Ext 336

Loften, Mary, *Asst Librn,* Sage Public Library, Osage IA. 515-732-3323

Loftis, Loraine, *Cat,* East Saint Louis Public Library, East Saint Louis IL. 618-874-7280

Loftis, Pattie, *Librn,* Boyce Ditto Municipal Library, Mineral Wells TX. 817-325-3488

Lofts, W Peter, *Dir,* Okanagan Regional Library District, Kelowna BC. 604-860-4033

Loftus, Helen, *Dept Head,* Eli Lilly & Co (Business Library), Indianapolis IN. 317-261-3241

Loftus, Leslie, *ILL,* University of Missouri-Kansas City Libraries, Kansas City MO. 816-276-1531

Loftus, Leslie, *Educ & Psychology,* University of Missouri-Kansas City Libraries, Kansas City MO. 816-276-1531

Loftus, Leslie Wayne, *Librn,* University of Missouri-Kansas City Libraries (Truman Campus Library), Independence MO. 816-276-1531

Loftus, Mrs William, *Librn,* Rockcliffe Park Public Library, Rockcliffe ON. 613-745-2562

LoGalbo, Brother Anthony, *Librn,* Holy Name College Library, Washington DC. 202-526-9310

Logan, Anne-Marie, *Librn & Photog Archivist,* Yale University Library (Center for British Art), New Haven CT. 203-432-4594

Logan, Catharine, *Librn,* Illinois Prairie District Public Library (Washburn Branch), Washburn IL. 309-248-7429

Logan, Darryl, *Librn,* Saint Francis Hospital, Health Sciences Library, Tulsa OK. 918-494-1210

Logan, Florence, *Dir,* Edison Free Public Library, Edison NJ. 201-287-2298

Logan, G Allen, *Mgr Student & Faculty Servs,* Conestoga College of Applied Arts & Technology Library, Kitchener ON. 519-653-2511

Logan, Liz, *ILL,* Stephen F Austin State University, Ralph W Steen Library, Nacogdoches TX. 713-569-4109

Logan, Lou, *Tech Serv,* Sun Prairie Public Library, Sun Prairie WI. 608-837-5644

Logan, Marie V, *Librn,* Atascadero State Hospital (Patients' Library), Atascadero CA. 805-466-2200

Logan, Marie V, *Librn,* Atascadero State Hospital (Professional Library), Atascadero CA. 805-466-2200

Logan, Mary, *Librn,* Regional Planning Council Library, Baltimore MD. 301-383-5864

Logan, Mrs Richard, *Asst Librn,* Iowa Park Library, Iowa Park TX. 817-592-4981

Logan, Ruth, *Librn,* Formoso Community Library, Formoso KS. 913-794-2473

Loggie, Ann, *ILL,* Kemp Public Library, Wichita Falls TX. 817-322-5611, Ext 377

Loggins, Ann, *Dir,* Cleburne Public Library, Cleburne TX. 817-645-2798

Lognion, Patricia, *Librn,* Hawaii State Library System (Wahiawa Branch), Wahiawa HI. 808-621-6331

Logsdon, Guy, *Dir,* University of Tulsa, McFarlin Library, Tulsa OK. 918-592-6000, Ext 351

Logsdon, Paul, *ILL, Rare Bks & Bibliog Instr,* Ohio Northern University, Heterick Memorial Library, Ada OH. 419-634-9921, Ext 370, 490

Logsdon, Robert, *Ref,* Indiana State Library, Division for the Blind & Physically Handicapped, Indianapolis IN. 317-232-3684

Logue, Carol, *Tech Serv,* De Kalb Public Library, Haish Memorial Building, De Kalb IL. 815-756-4431

Logue, Sally, *Asst Librn,* Cecil Community College, Learning Resource Center, North East MD. 301-287-6060, Ext 217

Lohbright, Mrs Peter, *Librn,* Page Memorial Library, Aberdeen NC. 919-944-9897

Lohf, Kenneth, *Rare Bks,* Columbia University (University Libraries), New York NY. 212-280-2241

Lohf, Kenneth A, *Librn,* Columbia University (Rare Book & Manuscript Library), New York NY. 212-280-2241

Lohman, Kathleen, *Librn,* Greenville Public Library, Greenville MI. 616-754-6359

Lohman, Toni, *Dir,* Georgetown Township Public Library, Jenison MI. 616-457-9620, 457-9140

Lohman-Pinkerton, Maura, *Ch,* Chillicothe & Ross County Public Library, Chillicothe OH. 614-773-4145

Lohmann, Lenore, *Acq,* Union Theological Seminary in Virginia Library, Richmond VA. 804-355-0671, Ext 311

Lohness, Kay, *Librn,* Jonesville District Library, Jonesville MI. 517-849-9701

Lohoefener, Sharon, *ILL,* North Platte Public Library, Lincoln Keith Perkins Regional Library, North Platte NE. 308-532-6560

Lohr, Adrienne Louise, *Librn,* Stauffer Chemical Co, Sunnyvale CA. 408-739-0511, Ext 171, 172

Lohr, Jacklyn J, *Ad,* Nicolet Federated Library System, Green Bay WI. 414-497-3443

Lohr, Jane, *Ch,* Adams Memorial Library, Latrobe PA. 412-537-2821

Lohr, John, *AV,* Seminole Community College Library, Sanford FL. 305-323-1450, Ext 450

Lohr, Judith, *In Charge,* Our Lady of Victory Hospital, Hospital Library, Lackawanna NY. 716-825-8000

Lohr, Mary E, *Ref,* Allegany County Library, Cumberland MD. 301-777-1200

Lohr, Sally V, *Dir,* Reed Memorial Library, Carmel NY. 914-225-2439

Lohrer, Fred E, *Librn,* Archbold Expeditions Inc, Biological Station Library, Lake Placid FL. 813-465-2571

Lohrmann, Henry T, *Dir & Acq,* Tarleton State University Library, Stephenville TX. 817-968-9246

Lohrmeyer, Janice, *Librn,* Logan Public Library, Logan KS. 913-689-4865

Lohrstorfer, John K, *Ya & Institution Libr Coordr,* DuPage Library System, Geneva IL. 312-232-8457

Lohse, Alice L, *Librn,* Nevada Mental Health Institute Library, Sparks NV. 702-322-6961, Ext 227

Lohse, Louise Waldrop, *Clerk,* Court of Civil Appeals Sixth District, Law Library, Texarkana TX. 214-794-2576

Loiselle, Gisele, *Ad,* Bibliotheque Municipale Des Trois-Rivieres, Trois-Rivieres PQ. 819-374-3521, Ext 71

Loke, Lesley, *Research & Grants Coordr,* Detroit Public Library, Detroit Associated Libraries, Detroit MI. 313-833-1000

Loken, Sally F, *Asst Dir for Central Servs,* Timberland Regional Library, Olympia WA. 206-943-5001

Loker, Donald E, *Local Hist,* Niagara Falls Public Library, Niagara Falls NY. 716-278-8041

Lokey, Patricia, *Librn,* Denver Botanic Gardens, Helen Fowler Library, Denver CO. 303-575-2547, Exts 24, 26

Lokk, A, *Librn,* London Public Libraries & Museums (Fred Landon Branch), London ON. 519-439-6240

Lokke, M Jean, *Librn,* University of Illinois Library at Urbana-Champaign (Applied Life Studies), Urbana IL. 217-333-3615

Lola, Judith A, *Librn,* University of Chicago, Yerkes Observatory Library, Williams Bay WI. 414-245-5555, Ext 30

Lollathin, Anna D, *Librn,* Naval Ordnance Systems Command, Technical Library, Louisville KY. 502-361-2641

Lolley, John, *Dir,* Tarrant County Junior College System (South Campus Learning Resource Center), Fort Worth TX. 817-534-4861, Ext 223

Lollis, William F, *Dir,* Westbury Memorial Public Library, Westbury NY. 516-333-0176

Lomasson, Barbara, *Commun Servs,* Long Branch Public Library, Long Branch NJ. 201-222-3900

Lomax, Mary Helen, *Ser,* Sul Ross State University, Bryan Wildenthal Memorial Library, Alpine TX. 915-837-3461

Lomax, Ronald, *Ref,* Alameda County Law Library, Oakland CA. 415-874-5823

Lomax, William E, *Asst Librn,* Interstate Commerce Commission Library, Washington DC. 275-7327; 275-7328

Lombard, Janet, *Fine Arts,* Tucson Public Library, Tucson AZ. 602-791-4391

Lombardi, Ralph, *Assoc Librn,* Shearman & Sterling Library, New York NY. 212-483-1000, Ext 356

Lombardo, Daniel, *Art & Music,* Forbes Library, Northampton MA. 413-584-8399

Lomen, Nancy L, *Actg Librn,* Veterans Administration, Medical Center, Medical & Patients Library, Des Moines IA. 515-255-2173, Ext 218

Lonberger, Rose E, *Librn,* University of Pennsylvania Libraries (Towne Scientific), Philadelphia PA. 215-243-7266

Loncaric, Inge, *In Charge,* Atlantic Richfield Co, Research & Development Library, Plano TX. 214-424-3511

London, Eleanor, *Dir,* Cote Saint-Luc Public Library, Cote Saint-Luc PQ. 514-481-5676

London, Ellen, *Librn,* Soda Springs Public Library, Soda Springs ID. 208-547-3759

London, Frank M, *Librn,* United States Army (DARCOM Intern Training Center, Technical Library), Texarkana TX. 214-838-2141

London, Jean, *ILL,* State University of New York, College at Oneonta, James M Milne Library, Oneonta NY. 607-431-2723

London, Jill, *Media,* Long Beach Public Library, Long Beach NY. 516-432-7201

Lone, Naomia D, *Librn,* Forsyth Memorial Hospital (PNE Library), Winston-Salem NC. 919-768-2200, Ext 219

Lone, Naomia S, *Librn,* Forsyth Memorial Hospital, John C Whitaker Library, Winston-Salem NC. 919-768-2200, Ext 219

Loner, Anne S, *Librn, On-Line Servs & Bibliog Instr,* Wheeling Hospital Medical Library, Wheeling WV. 304-243-3000

Lonergan, Jean, *Tech Serv,* Nichols College, Conant Library, Dudley MA. 617-943-1560

Lonergan, Lawrence A, *Dir,* Saint John's University Library, Jamaica NY. 212-969-8000, Ext 201

Long, A M, *Librn,* Ottawa Public Library (Alta Vista), Ottawa ON. 613-236-0301, Ext 272, 278

Long, Adrienne, *Ref,* Claremont Colleges Libraries (Ella Strong Denison Library), Claremont CA. 714-621-8000, Ext 3941

Long, Alice, *Librn,* Eureka Carnegie Library, Eureka KS. 316-583-6222

Long, Avis, *In Charge,* Southeast Iowa Academic Libraries, (SIAL), IA. 319-752-2731

Long, Avis, *Pub Servs,* Southeastern Community College Library-North Campus, West Burlington IA. 319-752-2731, Ext 55

Long, Barbara, *Ad & Ref,* A K Smiley Public Library, Redlands CA. 714-793-2201

Long, Betty, *Librn,* Amarillo Public Library (East), Amarillo TX. 806-378-3058, 378-3059

Long, Calverta, *On-Line Servs & Bibliog Instr,* South Carolina State College, Miller F Whittaker Library, Orangeburg SC. 803-536-7045, 536-7046

Long, Catherine D, *Tech Serv & Cat,* Lincoln University, Inman E Page Library, Jefferson City MO. 314-751-2325, Ext 326

Long, Charles R, *Librn,* New York Botanical Garden Library, Bronx NY. 212-220-8749

Long, Doris, *Librn,* Dauphin County Library System (Hub), Harrisburg PA. 717-232-7286

Long, Eleanor G, *Librn,* East Blue Hill Public Library, East Blue Hill ME. 207-374-5515

Long, Elizabeth, *Dir,* Hamden Library, Miller Memorial, Hamden CT. 203-248-7747

Long, F Ray, *Med Libr Dir,* University of California Library, Irvine CA. 714-833-5212

Long, Glenn A, *Exec Dir,* Sunrise Foundation, Inc Library, Charleston WV. 304-344-8035

Long, Hank, *Staff Servs,* Aurora Public Library, Aurora CO. 303-750-5000, Ext 410

Long, Harriet Geneva, *Emer Prof,* Case Western Reserve University, School of Library Science, OH. 216-368-3500

Long, Janis L, *Admin Asst,* Appomattox Regional Library, Maud Langhorne Nelson Library, Hopewell VA. 804-458-6329

Long, Jean, *Librn,* Newington Children's Hospital, Professional Library, Newington CT. 203-666-2461, Ext 309

Long, Joan C, *On-Line Servs,* Union Carbide Corp-Parma Technical Center, Technical Information Service, Parma OH. 216-676-2263

Long, Judith A, *Art & Music,* Public Library of Brookline, Brookline MA. 617-734-0100

Long, Kathleen A, *On-Line Servs,* Arthur D Little Inc, Research Library, Cambridge MA. 617-864-5770, Ext 3019

Long, Kathleen J, *Ref,* Cayuga County Community College, Norman F Bourke Memorial Library Learning Resources Center, Auburn NY. 315-255-1743, Ext 296 & 298

Long, Luella C, *Librn,* Salina Public Library, Salina UT. 801-529-3651

Long, Margaret, *Ch,* Public Library of Cincinnati & Hamilton County, Cincinnati Public Library, Cincinnati OH. 513-369-6000

Long, Marguerite, *Librn,* Thornton Public Library, Thornton IA. 515-998-2416

Long, Marie, *Librn,* Vigo County Public Library (Plaza North Libr), Terre Haute IN. 812-466-3638

Long, Mary Ann, *Branch Librns,* Hinds Junior College, George M McLendon Library, Raymond MS. 601-857-5261, Ext 253

Long, Nancy, *ILL,* Orange Public Library, Orange CA. 714-532-0391

Long, Rosalie A, *Asst Dir,* Annie Halenbake Ross Library, Lock Haven PA. 717-748-3321

Long, Russell, *Coll Management Coordr,* Orange County Public Library, Orange CA. 714-634-7841

Long, Sally, *Ch,* Worcester County Library, Snow Hill MD. 301-632-2600

Long, Sandra Kay, *Cat,* Davis County Library, Farmington UT. 801-867-2322

Long, Sarah Ann, *Dir,* Fairfield County District Library, Lancaster OH. 614-653-2745

Long, Susan, *Librn,* Kalispell Regional Hospital, Medical Library, Kalispell MT. 406-755-5111, Ext 660

Long, Walter K, *Dir,* Cayuga Museum of History & Art Library, Auburn NY. 315-253-8051

Longacker, Nancy, *Media,* Hudson Valley Community College Learning Resources Center, Dwight Marvin Library, Troy NY. 518-283-1100, Ext 629

Longan, Louise, *Dir,* Tulare Public Library, Tulare CA. 209-688-2001

Longenecker, Ellen, *Tech Serv,* Scott County Library, Eldridge IA. 319-285-4794

Longenecker, Susan L, *Chief Librn,* Vermont State Hospital (Agency Of Human Services Library), Waterbury VT. 802-241-2248

Longin, Germaine, *Asst Librns,* Stamford Village Library, Stamford NY. 607-652-5001

Longinia, Sister Mary, *Tech Serv,* Ancilla College, Ancilla Domini Library, Donaldson IN. 219-936-8898, Ext 123

Longino, Charline, *Librn,* Knoxville-Knox County Public Library (South Knoxville), Knoxville TN. 615-573-1772

Longland, Jean R, *Curator,* Hispanic Society of America Library, New York NY. 212-926-2234

Longley, Patricia S, *Librn,* Fayette Community Library, Fayette IA. 319-425-3344

Longmoor, Caroline G, *Dir,* Kansas State Library, Division for the Blind & Physically Handicapped, Topeka KS. 913-296-3642

Longnecker, Joan, *Ad,* Iberville Parish Library, Plaquemine LA. 504-687-2520

Longnecker, Joan, *Librn,* Iberville Parish Library (Plaquemine (Headquarters)), Plaquemine LA. 504-687-2520

Longo, Beverly, *Librn,* Blake Memorial Library, East Corinth VT. 802-439-5338

Longo, Estela, *Librn,* Cuba Library, Cuba NY. 716-968-1668

Longo, John, *On-Line Servs & Bibliog Instr,* Suffolk County Community College (Central Library & AV Technical Services), Selden NY. 516-233-5181

Longo, Joy, *Librn,* Key Bank NA Library, Albany NY. 518-447-3594

Longoria, Ester, *Librn,* United States Navy (Naval Air Station Library), Kingsville TX. 512-595-6212

Longstreet, Charline, *On-Line Servs & Bibliog Instr,* Scottsdale Public Library, Scottsdale AZ. 602-994-2471

Longstreet, J, *Tech Serv,* Brockway Memorial Library, Miami Shores FL. 305-758-8000

Longstreet, Josephine, *Librn,* Wellington County Public Library (Erin Branch), Erin ON. 519-833-2216

Longstreth, Emma, *Librn,* Elma Public Library, Elma IA. 515-393-2543

Longstreth, Jean, *Asst Librn,* United States Department of Defense, DISAM Library, Wright-Patterson AFB OH. 513-255-5567

Longton, Marvin, *Librn,* Brooklyn Public Library (Washington Irving), Brooklyn NY. 212-386-6212

Longwell, Helen, *Librn,* Upjohn Company (Patent Law Library), Kalamazoo MI. 616-385-7569

Longworth, Carolyn, *Ch,* Millicent Library, Fairhaven MA. 617-992-5342

Longworth, Lola E, *Librn,* Hawley Library Association, Hawley PA. 717-226-4620

Lonie, C Ann, *Ref,* University of Notre Dame Library, Notre Dame IN. 219-283-7317

Lonnberg, Charles M, *Cat,* Indiana State University, Evansville Library, Evansville IN. 812-464-1824

Lonnberg, Julia M, *Librn Asst,* College Center of the Finger Lakes Library, Corning NY. 607-962-3134

Lonney, J, *Section Chief,* Western Electric Co Inc, Corporate Education Center Library, Hopewell NJ. 609-639-4451

Lonsak, John A, *Librn,* Cuyahoga County Public Library (Parma Regional), Parma OH. 216-885-5362

Looker, Zoe S, *Graphic Artist,* County College of Morris, Sherman H Masten Learning Resource Center, Randolph Township NJ. 201-361-5000, Ext 470

Lookhart, Isla, *Asst Librn,* North Platte Public Library (Library for the Blind & Physically Handicapped), North Platte NE. 308-532-6560

Loomis, Barbara, *Command Libr Dir,* United States Air Force (Alaska Air Command), Elmendorf AFB AK. 907-752-3787

Loomis, Betty, *Ad,* Warren County Library, Monmouth IL. 309-734-6412

Loomis, Frances L, *Librn,* City Library (Indian Orchard Branch), Indian Orchard MA. 413-543-3918

Loomis, L W, *Librn,* Port Leyden Community Library, Port Leyden NY. 315-348-6077

Loomis, Laura A, *Tech Serv & Cat,* Warren Library Association, Warren Library, Warren PA. 814-723-4650

Loomis, Opal, *Ch,* Goodland Public Library, Goodland KS. 913-899-5461

Looney, Jim, *Librn,* British Columbia Library Services Branch, Audiobook Service to the Handicapped, Burnaby BC. 604-298-0322

Looney, Julia, *Librn,* Tri-County Regional Library (Cartersville-Bartow Branch), Cartersville GA. 404-291-9360

Looney, Nancy, *Exten Librn,* Kershaw County Library, Camden SC. 803-432-5183

Looney, Pat, *Librn,* Merchants National Bank of Mobile, Employees Library, Mobile AL. 205-690-1212

Looney, Robert F, *Head,* Free Library of Philadelphia (Print & Picture), Philadelphia PA. 215-686-5322

Loop, Jacqueline, *Librn,* Energy Inc, Technical Library, Idaho Falls ID. 208-524-1000

Loos, Patricia, *Librn,* Journal-Star Printing Co Library, Lincoln NE. 402-473-7375

Loos, William H, *Rare Bks,* Buffalo & Erie County Public Library System, Buffalo NY. 716-856-7525

Loose, Rhonda, *Secy,* Hudson's Hope Public Library, Hudson's Hope BC. 604-783-9414

Loovis, Virginia, *ILL,* University of Maryland Baltimore County Library, Baltimore MD. 301-455-2457

Lopas, Martha, *Ref & Bibliog Instr,* East Carolina University, J Y Joyner Library, Greenville NC. 919-757-6514

LoPatriello, Susan, *Librn,* Buffalo & Erie County Public Library System (Cazenovia), Buffalo NY. 716-822-2436

Loper, Alma, *Acq,* Lower Merion Library Association, Bryn Mawr PA. 215-527-3889

Loper, Larry D, *Off Mgr,* Medical Arts Publishing Foundation Library, Houston TX. 713-529-7371

Loper, Vivian, *Librn,* Livingston Parish Library (Springfield Branch), Springfield LA. 504-686-2436

Lopes, Sol, *In Charge,* Manlabs, Inc Library, Cambridge MA. 617-491-2900

Lopez, Anita, *Acq,* New Mexico State Library, Santa Fe NM. 505-827-2033

Lopez, Deborah, *Tech Serv,* Ohoopee Regional Library, Vidalia-Toombs County Library Headquarters, Vidalia GA. 912-537-9283

Lopez, Donna Stephenson, *Librn,* Tolleson Public Library, Tolleson AZ. 602-936-7111

Lopez, Eugene V, *Librn,* United States Navy (Naval Air Station Library), Corpus Christi TX. 512-385-4100

Lopez, Flora, *Acq,* Herrick Public Library, Holland MI. 616-392-3114

Lopez, Heriberto, *Dir,* University of Puerto Rico, Humacao University College Library, Humacao PR. 809-852-2525, Ext 200

Lopez, Joanne, *Librn,* Jefferson-Madison Regional Library (Gordon Ave), Charlottesville VA. 804-296-5544

Lopez, Lillian, *Acting Borough Coordr Bronx,* New York Public Library (The Branch Libraries), New York NY. 212-790-6262

Lopez, M, *Sociology, Social Work & Political Sci,* State University of New York at Buffalo, University Libraries, Buffalo NY. 716-636-2965

Lopez, Marlena, *Asst Librn,* Kearny County Library, Lakin KS. 316-355-6674

Lopez, Mildred, *Ref,* Catholic University of Puerto Rico (Encarnacion Valdes Library), Ponce PR. 809-844-4150, Ext 119

Lopez, Molly, *Outreach,* Mesa Public Library, Mesa AZ. 602-834-2207

Lopez, Robert, *Librn,* Minneapolis Star & Tribune Library, Minneapolis MN. 612-372-4374

Lopez, Valentin, *Libr Tech,* United States Air Force (Kelly Air Force Base Library), Kelly AFB TX. 512-925-4116

Lopez, Yvette, *ILL,* University of Arkansas, Pine Bluff, Watson Memorial Library, Pine Bluff AR. 501-541-6825

Lopiano, Rosemary, *ILL,* Art Institute of Chicago (Ryerson & Burnham Libraries), Chicago IL. 312-443-6666

Lopinot, M Loretta, *Librn,* Cahokia Public Library, Cahokia IL. 618-332-1491

Lopker, Betty, *Actg Librn,* California Department of Transportation, Highways Div Library, San Diego CA. 714-294-5030

LoPresti, George, *ILL,* State University Agricultural & Technical College at Farmingdale, Thomas D Greenley Library, Farmingdale NY. 516-420-2011, 420-2012

LoPresti, Maryellen, *Librn,* North Carolina State University (Harrye B Lyons Design Library), Raleigh NC. 919-737-2207

Lopresti, Robert, *Govt Doc,* Wayne Public Library, Wayne NJ. 201-694-4272

Lora, Mary P, *Visual Serv,* Toledo-Lucas County Public Library, Toledo OH. 419-255-7055

Loranth, Alice, *Rare Bks,* Cleveland Public Library, Cleveland OH. 216-623-2800

Loranth, Alice N, *In Charge,* Cleveland Public Library (John G White Department of Orientalia, Folklore & Chess), Cleveland OH. 216-623-2818

Loranth, Leslie Z, *Dir,* Lorain County Community College Library, Elyria OH. 216-365-4191, Ext 201

Loranz, Claire, *Doc,* Wellesley College, Margaret Clapp Library, Wellesley MA. 617-235-0320, Ext 280

Lorber, Carl, *Per,* Lincoln Library, Springfield Public Library, Springfield IL. 217-753-4900

Lorber, Ula F, *Asst Librn,* Urbanna Public Library, Urbanna VA. 804-758-5717

Lord, Anne, *Libr Tech,* California School for the Blind, Library Media Center, Berkeley CA. 415-843-5944

Lord, Barbara H, *Dir,* Avon Free Public Library, Avon CT. 203-678-1262

Lord, Caryle, *Ch,* Charlotte Public Library, Carnegie Library, Charlotte MI. 517-543-1300

Lord, Christine, *Librn,* Wentworth Library (Saltfleet), Hamilton ON. 416-526-4126

Lord, Gary, *Colonial Hist,* Norwich University, Henry Prescott Chaplin Memorial Library, Northfield VT. 802-485-5011, Ext 48

Lord, Marion, *Tech Serv,* Adams Library, Chelmsford MA. 617-256-5521

Lord, Marjorie, *ILL,* State University College at Buffalo, Edward H Butler Library, Buffalo NY. 716-878-6302

Lord, Robert, *Ref,* New York Academy of Medicine Library, New York NY. 212-876-8200

Lordi, Joseph A, *Dir,* Bayard Taylor Memorial Library, Kennett Square PA. 215-444-2702

Lordi, Michael, *Dir,* New School for Social Research, Raymond Fogelman Library, New York NY. 212-741-7906

Loreen, Lola, *Librn,* Whatcom County Public Library (Point Roberts Branch), Point Roberts WA. 206-384-3150

Lorentowicz, Genia, *Lectr,* Concordia University, Library Studies Program, PQ. 514-482-0320, Ext 324

Lorentz, Ann R, *Ref,* Parkersburg & Wood County Public Library, Wood County Service Center, Parkersburg WV. 304-485-6564

Lorenz, Denis M, *Dir,* West Hartford Public Library, Noah Webster Memorial Library, West Hartford CT. 203-236-6286

Lorenz, Frank K, *Ref & Spec Coll,* Hamilton College, Burke Library, Clinton NY. 315-859-4478

Lorenz, Gladys M, *Dir,* Rhinelander Public Library, Rhinelander WI. 715-369-1070

Lorenz, Harriet, *Ch & YA,* South Windsor Public Library, South Windsor CT. 203-644-1541

Lorenz, Stella, *Librn,* American Appraisal Co Library, Milwaukee WI. 414-271-7240, Ext 247

Lorenzen, Elaine, *Librn,* Townsend Public Library, Townsend MA. 617-597-2817

Lorenzi, Nancy, *Dir,* University of Cincinnati Medical Center Libraries, Cincinnati OH. 513-872-5627

Lorenzo, Gladys, *Chief Librn,* Orange County Public Library (Los Alimitus-Rossmoor), Seal Beach CA. 213-343-4211, 343-4216

Lorenzo, Miriam, *Dir,* Inter-American University of Puerto Rico, Aguadilla Regional College Library, Aguadilla PR. 809-891-0998

Lorenzo, Miriam, *Dir,* Inter-American University of Puerto Rico, Aguadilla Regional College Branch Library, Ramey AFB PR. 809-890-5118

Loretta, Sister, *Librn,* Mallinckrodt College, Independent Library Program, IL. 312-256-1094

Loretta, Sister, *Dir,* Mallinckrodt College Library, Wilmette IL. 312-256-1094

Lorimer, James, *Lectr,* Dalhousie University, School of Library Service, NS. 902-424-3656

Lorimer, Nicholas, *Librn,* New Zealand Consulate General Library, New York NY. 212-586-0060

Loring, Phillip, *Librn,* Sacramento Public Library (Galt Branch), Galt CA. 209-745-2066

Lorio, Edith, *Librn,* Pointe Coupee Parish Library (Julian Poydras), Rougon LA. 504-638-7593

Lorkovic, Tatjana B, *Cat,* University of Iowa Libraries, Iowa City IA. 319-353-4450

Lorne, Lorraine K, *Tech Serv,* Detroit College of Law Library, Detroit MI. 313-965-0150

Lorona, Lionel, *Chief,* New York Public Library (General Research & Humanities), New York NY. 212-790-6362

Lorrig, Judy, *Learning Resource Center Supr,* Mayo Foundation (Medical Library), Rochester MN. 507-284-2061

Lorriman, Alice, *Librn,* East York Public Library (S Walter Stewart), Toronto ON. 416-425-8222

Lorschied, M, *Tech Serv,* Blue Cloud Abbey Library, Marvin SD. 605-432-5528, Ext 904

Lortz, Marilyn, *Librn,* Dorcas Carey Public Library, Carey OH. 419-396-7921

Losee, Madeleine W, *Program Coordr,* NASA Library Network, (NALNET), DC. 202-755-3544

Losey, Doris, *Librn,* Tampa-Hillsborough County Public Library System (Seminole Public), Tampa FL. 813-232-9271

Loshaek, Laurie, *Librn,* Dawson, Nagel, Sherman & Howard Law Library, Denver CO. 303-893-2900, Ext 448

Losher, Susan, *Tech Serv,* Trumbull Library, Trumbull CT. 203-261-6421

Losick, Merill, *Ad & Ref,* West New York Public Library, Philip A Payne Memorial Library, West New York NJ. 201-854-1028

Losinski, Julia, *YA,* Prince George's County Memorial Library System, Hyattsville MD. 301-699-3500

Lospinuso, Margaret, *Librn,* University of North Carolina at Chapel Hill (Music), Chapel Hill NC. 919-933-1030

Loss, Susan, *Librn,* Colorado State Department of Social Services Library, Region Eight Adoption Resource Center Library, Denver CO. 303-839-2253

Losse, Kathy, *In Charge,* Roseau Public Library, Roseau MN. 218-463-2825

Lostra, Mercedes, *ILL,* Elko County Library, Elko NV. 702-738-3066

Lothrop, Jean K, *Ad,* Burton L Wales Public Library, North Abington MA. 617-878-1239

Lothyan, Phillip E, *In Charge,* General Services Administration - National Archives & Records Service, Seattle Federal Archives & Records Center, Seattle WA. 206-442-4500

Lotman, Orrell, *Dir,* College of the Southwest, Scarborough Memorial Library, Hobbs NM. 505-392-6561, Ext 35

Lotreck, Annelaine, *Dir,* Willoughby Wallace Memorial Library, Stony Creek CT. 203-488-8702

Lott, Barbara, *Handicapped Servs,* University of Connecticut Library, Storrs CT. 203-486-2219

Lott, Mary, *Librn,* Peterson City Library, Peterson IA. 712-295-6401

Lott, Odell B, *Librn,* Southeastern Baptist College, A R Reddir Memorial Library, Laurel MS. 601-426-6346

Lott, Sue, *Bkmobile Coordr,* Ricks Memorial Library, Yazoo-Sharkey-Issaquena Library System, Yazoo City MS. 601-746-5557

Loubiere, Sue, *Librn,* Louisiana State University (School of Veterinary Medicine Library), Baton Rouge LA. 504-346-3172

Louch, Jan, *Asst Dir,* Douglas County Public Library, Minden NV. 702-782-3023

Loucka, Patricia A, *Librn,* General Electric Co (Refractory Metal Products Department Library), Cleveland OH. 216-266-3736

Loucks, Kathy, *ILL,* Public Library of Columbus & Franklin County, Columbus OH. 614-864-8050

Loucks, Kathy, *Fiction,* Public Library of Columbus & Franklin County, Columbus OH. 614-864-8050

Loud, Dana, *Asst Librn,* Lake Placid School of Art, Nettie Marie Jones Fine Arts Library, Association for Music, Drama & Art, Lake Placid NY. 518-523-2591, 523-2592, Ext 31

Louden, Jonathan E, *Dir,* Dr Samuel L Bossard Memorial Library, Gallipolis OH. 614-446-7323

Louden, Kristin, *Circ,* University of Colorado Health Sciences Center (Denison Memorial Library), Denver CO. 303-394-5125

Louden, Richard, *Dir,* Merritt Island Public Library, Merritt Island FL. 305-452-3834

Louet, Sandra, *Librn,* Ministry of Natural Resources, Research Library, Maple ON. 416-832-2761, Ext 205, 213

Lough, Barbara, *Librn,* Toledo-Lucas County Public Library (Kent), Toledo OH. 419-255-7055

Loughlin, Beverly A, *Spec Coll,* Hartford Public Library, Hartford CT. 203-525-9121

Loughlin, Lorraine, *Dir,* West Yarmouth Library, West Yarmouth MA. 617-775-5206

Loughridge, Nancy, *Dir, Coll,* University of Cincinnati Libraries, Central Library, Cincinnati OH. 513-475-2218

Louie, Ruby Ling, *Instr,* California State University-Los Angeles, Library Services Credential Program, CA. 213-224-3765

Louise, Sister Mary, *Librn,* Saint Joseph's Hospital, School of Nursing Library, Philadelphia PA. 215-236-3700

Lounberg, Joyce, *Cat,* University of Utah (Spencer S Eccles Health Sciences Library), Salt Lake City UT. 801-581-8771
Lounsbury, Loretta, *Actg Librn,* Stiefel Laboratories Inc, Stiefel Research Institute Inc Library, Oak Hill NY. 518-239-6901, Ext 257
Loup, Jean L, *Librn,* University of Michigan Libraries (Library Science), Ann Arbor MI. 313-764-9375
Loupe, Mary E, *Librn,* Pointe Coupee Parish Library, New Roads LA. 504-638-7593
Lourwood, Marion, *ILL,* Parks College Library, Cahokia IL. 618-337-7500, Ext 244, 274
Louton, Arlene, *Librn,* Donaldson Co, Inc, Technical Information Center, Minneapolis MN. 612-887-3019
Louviere, Mel, *Ad & Ref,* Ector County Library, Odessa TX. 915-332-0633
Louzin, Brenna A, *Librn,* Battelle-Seattle Research Center, Library Services, Seattle WA. 206-525-3130
Lovallo, Janet, *Circ,* Satellite Beach Public Library, Satellite Beach FL. 305-773-9411
Lovas, Paula M, *Dir,* National Gerontology Resource Center, National Retired Teachers Asn-American Asn of Retired Persons, Washington DC. 202-872-4844
Love, Alice, *Cat,* Fern Ridge Community Library, Veneta OR. 503-935-7512
Love, Amelia, *Librn,* Thacher, Proffitt & Wood, Law Library, New York NY. 212-483-5843
Love, Barbara, *ILL & Ref,* Saint Lawrence College of Applied Arts & Technology Library Services, Kingston ON. 613-544-5400, Ext 163
Love, D Stanley, *Dir,* Kansas City Regional Council for Higher Education, MO. 816-361-4143
Love, Dorothy, *Librn,* Orford Free Library, Orford NH. 603-353-9093
Love, Erika, *Dir,* University of New Mexico General Library (Medical Center Library), Albuquerque NM. 505-277-2311
Love, J, *Librn,* Gananoque Public Library, Gananoque ON. 613-382-2436
Love, M J, *Librn,* Ministry of Human Resources Library, Victoria BC. 604-658-5215
Love, Robert, *Cat,* Slippery Rock State College Library, Slippery Rock PA. 412-794-2510
Love, Ruth, *Asst Librn,* Gibson County Memorial Library, Trenton TN. 901-855-1991
Love, Wayne, *Dir,* George S Houston Memorial Library, Dothan AL. 205-793-9767
Love, Wayne, *Admin,* Southeast Alabama Cooperative Library System, Dothan AL. 205-793-9767
Lovelace, Frances, *Ch,* Northern Illinois Library System, Rockford IL. 815-229-0330
Lovelace, Julianne, *Supvr Pub Servs,* Richardson Public Library, Richardson TX. 214-238-8251
Loveless, Janet, *Bibliog Instr,* Radford University, John Preston McConnell Library, Radford VA. 703-731-5471, 5472
Lovell, Marianne, *Reader Serv,* Autauga-Prattville Public Library, Prattville AL. 205-365-3396
Lovell, Marianne, *Reader Serv,* Autauga-Prattville Public Library System, Prattville AL. 205-365-3396
Lovell, Philip, *V Pres,* John Lovell & Son Ltd Library, Montreal PQ. 514-849-2321
Lovelock, Marty H, *Chief Librn,* Canadian Transport Commission Library, Ottawa ON. 819-997-7160
Lovely, Louise P, *Dir,* San Diego State University, Imperial Valley Campus Library, Calexico CA. 714-357-4747
Lovely, Norman, *Ref & Res,* Worcester Public Library, Worcester MA. 617-752-3751
Lovett, Carol B, *Archivist,* Marshall Historical Society Archives, Marshall MI. 616-781-8544
Lovett, Dana, *Librn,* Stanislaus County Law Library, Modesto CA. 209-526-6302
Lovett, Mary, *Librn,* Randolph Public Library (Liberty Branch), Liberty NC. 919-622-4605
Lovett, Valerie, *Librn,* Wake County Department of the Public Library (Olivia Raney), Raleigh NC. 919-755-6085
Lovett, Valerie W, *Asst Dir,* Wake County Department of the Public Library, Raleigh NC. 919-755-6077
Lovett, Vivian, *Librn,* Burke County Library (Sardis Branch), Sardis GA. 912-554-3277
Lovgren, Phyllis, *Ch & Media,* Greenwood Public Library, Greenwood IN. 317-881-1953

Lovgren, Ruth, *Librn,* Hinckley Public Library, Hinckley MN. 612-384-6351
Loving, Betty, *Librn,* Yavapai County Law Library, Prescott AZ. 602-445-7450, Ext 250
Loving, Patricia, *Librn, Acq & Ref,* Lakewood Community College Library, White Bear Lake MN. 612-770-1331, Ext 129
Lovolo, Mary, *Cat,* Burlington County Library, Mount Holly NJ. 609-267-9660
Lovshin, Marlyn G, *Dir,* Tomahawk Public Library, Tomahawk WI. 715-453-2455
Lovvorn, Jean S, *Librn,* Floyd Medical Center Library, Rome GA. 404-295-5500
Low, Edmon, *Dir,* New College of the University of South Florida, Sarasota Campus Library, Sarasota FL. 813-355-7671, Ext 214
Low, Erick Baker, *Assoc Librn,* National Center for State Courts Library, Williamsburg VA. 804-253-2000
Low, Wendy, *Ch,* Kingston Public Library, Kingston ON. 613-549-8888
Lowden, Arlene, *Librn,* Searle Radiographics Inc, Research Library, Des Plaines IL. 312-635-3100
Lowe, Al, *Instructional Development,* Richland College, Learning Resources Center, Dallas TX. 214-746-4460
Lowe, Ann G, *Librn,* Hardeman County Public Library, Quanah TX. 817-663-8149
Lowe, Della Mae, *Librn,* Lake County Library (Silver Lake Branch), Silver Lake OR. 503-576-2146
Lowe, Doris, *Ref,* Cornell University Medical College, Samuel J Wood Library, New York NY. 212-472-5300
Lowe, Jane, *Asst Dir,* Kellogg-Hubbard Library, Montpelier VT. 802-223-3338
Lowe, Joy L, *Asst Prof,* Louisiana Tech University, Teacher Education-Library Science, LA. 318-257-3242
Lowe, Mary L, *Librn,* Louisville Public Library, Louisville OH. 216-875-1696
Lowe, May E, *Librn,* Mobile County Public Law Library, Mobile AL. 205-690-8436
Lowe, Mildred, *Actg Dir,* Saint John's University, Div of Library & Information Science, NY. 212-969-8000, Ext 200
Lowe, Mrs Edwin, *Librn,* Magnolia Library Center, Gloucester MA. 617-525-3343
Lowe, Nancy, *In Charge,* Texas Education Agency (Region XV), San Angelo TX. 915-655-6551
Lowe, William C, *Asst Dir,* North Carolina State University, D H Hill Library, Raleigh NC. 919-737-2843, 2595
Lowell, Felice K, *Dir,* Miami Dade Community College (Central Technical Processing), Miami FL. 305-685-4276
Lowell, Marcia, *State Librn,* Oregon State Library, Salem OR. 503-378-4243
Lowell, Natalie S, *Dir,* Whelden Memorial Library, West Barnstable MA. 617-362-2262
Lowell, Virginia, *Tech Serv,* Cuyahoga County Public Library, Cleveland OH. 216-398-1800
Lowenfels, Doris B, *Dir,* Chappaqua Central School District Public Library, Chappaqua Library, Chappaqua NY. 914-238-4779
Lowenthal, Eric, *Librn,* Associated Synagogues of Massachusetts, Jacob Rabinovitz Library, Boston MA. 617-426-1832
Lowenthal, Helen, *Librn,* Goodnow Library, Sudbury MA. 617-443-9112
Lowenthal, Ruth H, *Dir & On-Line Servs,* Colby Community College, H F Davis Memorial Library, Colby KS. 913-462-3984, Ext 265
Lowenthal, Sallie, *Circ,* Arizona State University Library, Tempe AZ. 602-965-3417
Lower, Dorothy, *Genealogy,* Public Library of Fort Wayne & Allen County, Fort Wayne IN. 219-424-7241
Lower, Jonathan D, *Circ,* Hardin-Simmons University, Richardson Library, Abilene TX. 915-677-7281, Ext 236
Lowery, James, *Microforms,* Michigan State University Library, East Lansing MI. 517-355-2344
Lowery, Jennifer, *Librn,* Singer Co, Education Systems Library, Rochester NY. 716-586-2020, Ext 364
Lowman, Shirley, *Cat,* Oregon State Library, Salem OR. 503-378-4243
Lowrey, Anna Mary, *Asst Prof,* State University of New York at Buffalo, School of Information & Library Studies, NY. 716-636-2412

Lowrie, Betty, *Cat,* Oscar Rose Junior College, Learning Resources Center, Midwest City OK. 405-733-7323, 733-7322
Lowrie, Harriette, *Ad,* Allentown Public Library, Allentown PA. 215-820-2400
Lowrie, Jean E, *Dir,* Western Michigan University, School of Librarianship, MI. 616-383-1849
Lowrie, Richard, *Librn,* Pemberville Public Library, Pemberville OH. 419-287-4012
Lowry, Andree F, *Librn,* Environmental Protection Agency, Environmental Research Laboratory Library, Gulf Breeze FL. 904-932-5311, Ext 218
Lowry, Charles B, *Chief Librn,* Elon College, Iris Holt McEwen Library, Elon College NC. 919-584-9711, Ext 230 or 242
Lowry, Dana, *Dir,* Jamaica Public Library, Jamaica IA. 515-429-3362
Lowry, H Maynard, *Assoc Dir,* Loma Linda University Library, Riverside CA. 714-785-2022
Lowry, Kay, *Ref,* Albany Junior College, Library-Learning Resources Ctr, Albany GA. 912-439-4332
Lowry, Lina M, *Asst Librn,* Borough of Manhattan Community College Library, Martin B Dworkis Library, New York NY. 212-262-3530
Lowry, Patricia, *Librn,* Akron-Summit County Public Library (Chamberlain), Akron OH. 216-724-2126
Lowry, William H, *Dir,* Pioneer Multi-County Library, Norman OK. 405-321-1481
Lowry, William H, *Librn,* Pioneer Multi-County Library (Norman Public), Norman OK. 405-321-1481
Lowy, Beverly R, *Dir,* North Bellmore Public Library, North Bellmore NY. 516-785-6260
Lowy, George, *Chief Librn,* Columbia University (Psychology), New York NY. 212-280-2241
Lowy, George, *Dir,* Pratt Institute Library, Brooklyn NY. 212-636-3684
Loy, Ursula F, *Dir,* George H & Laura E Brown Library, Washington NC. 919-946-4300
Loyd, Marie, *Acq,* Amarillo Public Library, Amarillo TX. 806-378-3000, Ext 2250
Lozano, Eduardo, *Latin Am Studies,* University of Pittsburgh, Hillman Library, Pittsburgh PA. 412-624-4400
Lozano, Mrs Richard, *Librn,* Ordway Public Library, Ordway CO. 303-267-3823
Lozano, Richard, *Per,* Merced College, Lesher Library, Merced CA. 209-723-4321, Ext 274
Lozen, Sally, *Librn,* Saint Clair County Library System (Ira Township), Fair Haven MI. 313-725-9081
Lu, James, *Humanities & Soc Sci,* Kansas State University, Farrell Library, Manhattan KS. 913-532-6516
Lu, Janet, *Ref,* Nebraska Wesleyan University, Cochrane-Woods Library, Lincoln NE. 402-466-2371, Ext 354
Lu, Janet, *Instr,* Nebraska Wesleyan University, Library Science Program, NE. 402-466-2371, Ext 354
Lu, Joseph, *Doc,* Idaho State University Library, Pocatello ID. 208-236-3202
Lubac, Faye, *Ref,* Washington County Cooperative Library Services, Portland OR. 503-645-5112
Lubans, John, *Bibliog Instr,* University of Houston (William I Dykes Library), Houston TX. 713-749-1991
Lubelski, Gregory, *Librn,* Saginaw Public Libraries (Butman-Fish), Saginaw MI. 517-799-9160
Lubetski, Edith, *Librn,* Yeshiva University Libraries (Hedi Steinberg Library), New York NY. 212-481-0570
Lubetsky, Elaine B, *Asst Librn,* United States Customs Court Library, New York NY. 212-264-2046
Lubiak, C J, *Dir,* Gannon University, Nash Library, Erie PA. 814-871-7352
Lubin, Richard, *Media,* Jervis Public Library Association, Rome NY. 315-336-4570
Lubitz, Lorna, *Ser,* Lethbridge Community College, Buchanan Resource Centre, Lethbridge AB. 403-327-2141, Ext 350
Lubitz, Shirley, *Librn,* Lexington County Circulating Library (Irmo), Columbia SC. 803-532-9223
Lubojacky, Betha, *Ch, YA & Ref,* Fort Bend County Library, Richmond TX. 713-342-4455
Lucas, Barbara, *Pub Servs,* University of Kentucky (Medical Center Library), Lexington KY. 606-233-5300

LUCAS

Lucas, Billie Ann, *Librn,* Tombigbee Regional Library (Hamilton Public), Hamilton MS. 601-343-8962

Lucas, Catherine E, *Librn,* San Diego County Library, San Diego CA. 714-565-5100

Lucas, Charlotte K, *Librn,* University of Pennsylvania Libraries (Moore School of Electrical Engineering), Philadelphia PA. 215-243-8135

Lucas, Colin R, *Librn,* Bruggemeyer Memorial Library, Monterey Park Public Library, Monterey Park CA. 213-573-1411

Lucas, Dorothy B, *Librn,* American Baptist Theological Seminary, College of the Bible, T L Holcomb Library, Nashville TN. 615-228-7877

Lucas, Frank, *Outreach Servs,* Anderson City-Anderson & Stony Creek Township Public Library, Anderson Public Library, Anderson IN. 317-644-0938

Lucas, Janice, *Librn,* Prentiss Normal & Industrial Institute Library, Prentiss MS. 601-792-5899

Lucas, Jean, *Circ,* Crockett Public Library, Crockett TX. 713-544-3089

Lucas, Jean M, *Instr,* Miami University-Middletown, Library-Media Technical Assistant Program, OH. 513-424-4444, Ext 221

Lucas, Joyce, *Librn,* Carus Chemical Company Library, LaSalle IL. 815-223-1500

Lucas, Leonard, *Soc Sci & Hist,* Worcester Public Library, Worcester MA. 617-752-3751

Lucas, Leora, *Teaching Mat,* State University of New York, College at Oneonta, James M Milne Library, Oneonta NY. 607-431-2723

Lucas, Linda, *Ch,* Tehama County Library, Red Bluff CA. 916-527-0604

Lucas, Lydia, *Head of Tech Servs,* Minnesota Historical Society (Division of Archives & Manuscripts), Saint Paul MN. 612-296-6980

Lucas, Lynne, *Librn,* Indiana University of Pennsylvania (University School), Indiana PA. 412-357-2434

Lucas, Marjorie, *Br Coordr,* Yakima Valley Regional Library, Yakima WA. 509-452-8541, Ext 22

Lucas, Patricia, *Librn,* Chicago Public Library (Hamilton Park), Chicago IL. 312-846-7491

Lucas, Patricia, *Librn,* Logan General Hospital, Medical Library, Logan WV. 304-752-1101, Ext 144

Lucas, Patricia, *Assoc Librn,* Portland Cement Association, Research Library, Skokie IL. 312-966-6200, Ext 534

Lucas, Robert, *Dean Learning Resources,* Thornton Community College, Learning Resources Center, South Holland IL. 312-596-2000, Ext 240

Lucas, Willie, *Pub Servs,* Florida Junior College at Jacksonville (North Campus Learning Resources Center), Jacksonville FL. 904-757-6311

Lucchetti, Stephen C, *Librn,* University of Michigan Libraries (Chemistry-Pharmacy), Ann Arbor MI. 313-764-7337

Lucco, Susan, *Dir,* Edwardsville Public Library, Edwardsville IL. 618-656-4594

Luce, Gordon, *Librn,* University of Wisconsin-Madison (Biology Library), Madison WI. 608-262-3521

Luce, Margaret, *Librn,* East Calais Public Library, East Calais VT. 802-456-8809

Luce, Richard, *Admin Servs,* Boulder Public Library, Boulder CO. 303-441-3100

Luce, Richard W, *Spec Projects,* Montana State University, Roland R Renne Library, Bozeman MT. 406-994-3119

Lucero, Emma, *Dir,* Pine River Public Library, Bayfield Public Library, Bayfield CO. 303-884-2222

Luchechko, John, *Asst Librn,* Jersey City State College, Forrest A Irwin Library, Jersey City NJ. 201-547-3026

Lucher, Janice, *Librn,* Harris County Public Library (South Houston Branch), South Houston TX. 713-941-2385

Luchessi, Robert, *Media,* San Jose Public Library, San Jose CA. 408-277-4822

Luchkiw, Vasyl, *Dir,* Rockland Community College, Library Media Center, Suffern NY. 914-356-4650, Ext 409

Luchsinger, Arlene, *Biol Sci,* University of Georgia Libraries, Athens GA. 404-542-2716

Lucht, Irma, *Dir Metrop Per Serv,* North Suburban Library System, Wheeling IL. 312-459-1300

Lucht, Irma M, *Dir,* Metropolitan Periodical Service, IL. 312-664-9366

Lucia, Sister M, *In Charge,* Medical Mission Sisters Library, Philadelphia PA. 215-742-6100

Lucien, Helen, *Circ,* University of Iowa Libraries (Law Library), Iowa City IA. 319-353-5968

Luciw, Wasyl O, *Slavic,* Pennsylvania State University, Fred Lewis Pattee Library, University Park PA. 814-865-0401

Luck, Beverly, *Dir,* Cranbury Public Library, Cranbury NJ. 609-655-0555

Luck, Carolyn, *ILL & Ref,* Memphis-Shelby County Public Library & Information Center (Science, Business, Social Sciences), Memphis TN. 901-528-2950

Luck, Donald, *Assoc Dir, Tech Servs,* Rutgers University (University Libraries), New Brunswick NJ. 201-932-7505

Lucker, Jay K, *Dir,* Massachusetts Institute of Technology Libraries, Cambridge MA. 617-253-5651

Luckett, Betty, *Bkmobile Coordr,* Duerson-Oldham County Public Library, La Grange KY. 502-222-1133

Luckham, Becky, *AV,* Rappahannock Community College, South Campus Library, Glenns VA. 804-758-5324, Ext 208

Lucy, Mary Lou, *Librn,* Columbia University (Nicholas Murray Butler Memorial Library), New York NY. 212-280-2241

Ludden, Bennet, *Music,* Juilliard School, Lila Acheson Wallace Library, New York NY. 212-799-5000, Ext 265

Ludden, Bennet, *Dir, Acq & Ref,* Juilliard School, Lila Acheson Wallace Library, New York NY. 212-799-5000, Ext 265

Ludden, Donald, *Librn,* Grand Rapids Public Library (Seymour Square), Grand Rapids MI. 616-456-4435

Luddy, Ann, *Librn,* Connecticut State Library (Hartford Branch), Hartford CT. 203-566-4301

Ludewig, Bernice R, *Librn,* Saint Joseph Memorial Hospital, Health Science Library, Kokomo IN. 317-456-5344

Ludlam, Elaine, *ILL,* Cape May County Library, Cape May Court House NJ. 609-465-7837

Ludloff, Margaret E, *Librn,* Bay State Junior College of Business Library, Boston MA. 617-266-0220

Ludlow, Jean, *Dir,* Medaille College, Scholastica Library, Buffalo NY. 716-884-3281, Ext 238

Ludlow, Joan E, *Asst Dir,* Hazel Park Memorial Library, Hazel Park MI. 313-542-0940

Ludlow, Roberta, *Librn,* Northeast Regional Library (Blue Mountain Library), Blue Mountain MS. 601-685-5041

Ludlum, Mary, *Circ,* Otterbein College, Courtright Memorial Library, Westerville OH. 614-890-3000, Ext 164

Ludmer, Joyce, *Librn,* University of California Los Angeles Library (Art), Los Angeles CA. 213-825-3817

Ludovici, Ann, *Ref & On-Line Servs,* Temple University of the Commonwealth System of Higher Education (Health Science Center), Philadelphia PA. 215-221-4032

Ludwick, Paula, *Media & Ref,* Northeast Missouri Library Service, Kahoka MO. 816-727-2327

Ludwick, Paula, *Librn,* Northeast Missouri Library Service (H E Sever Memorial), Kahoka MO. 816-727-3262

Ludwig, Deborah, *Sci,* Rutgers University, the State University of New Jersey, John Cotton Dana Library, Newark NJ. 201-648-5222

Ludwig, Laura W, *Cat,* Athens Regional Library, Athens GA. 404-543-0134

Ludwig, Laurie, *YA,* Jacksonville Public Library System, Haydon Burns Library, Jacksonville FL. 904-633-6870

Ludwig, Marion, *Librn,* Bridgeport Public Library (Newfield), Bridgeport CT. 203-576-7428

Ludwig, Mildred A, *Ref,* Tuxedo Park Library, Tuxedo Park NY. 914-351-2207

Ludwig, Paula, *Asst Librn for Rare Bks & Spec Coll,* Princeton University Library, Princeton NJ. 609-452-3180

Ludwig, Stephen, *Circ,* Jacksonville Public Library System, Haydon Burns Library, Jacksonville FL. 904-633-6870

Ludwikowski, Stella E, *Librn,* United States Air Force (Eielson Air Force Base Library), Eielson AFB AK. 907-372-4184

Ludwin, V, *Ref,* Queen's University at Kingston (Bracken Library), Kingston ON. 613-547-5753

Lueb, Miriam Dorothy, *Dir & Assoc Prof,* Our Lady of the Lake University of San Antonio, Learning Resources Certification, TX. 512-434-6711, Ext 245

Lueb, Sister Miriam Dorothy, *Dir,* Our Lady of the Lake University Libraries, San Antonio TX. 512-434-6711, Ext 272

Luebbers, Martina, *Librn,* Independent Township Library, Claflin KS. 316-587-3488

Luebbert, Karen, *Dir Webster,* Webster College, Eden Theological Seminary, Eden-Webster Libraries, Saint Louis MO. 314-968-0500, Ext 235

Luebbing, M, *Librn,* MacCormac College Library, Chicago IL. 312-922-1884

Luebeck, Isla, *Asst Librn,* De Witt Public Library (Cleon Collier Memorial Library), Gillett AR. 501-548-2821

Luebke, Grace, *Librn,* Harris-Elmore Public Library, Elmore OH. 419-862-2482

Lueck, Antoinette, *Phys Sci,* Colorado State University, William E Morgan Library, Fort Collins CO. 303-491-5911

Lueck, Barbara, *Govt Doc,* Oshkosh Public Library, Oshkosh WI. 414-424-0473

Luedeking, Christine, *ILL & Ref,* Umatilla County Library, Pendleton OR. 503-276-1881

Lueders, Mildred D, *Tech Serv,* United States Air Force (Human Resources Laboratory Library), Brooks AFB TX. 512-536-1110

Luedtke, Patricia, *Librn,* Town of Ulster Library, Town of Ulster NY. 914-336-5767

Luehs, Jeanne M, *Dir,* Cedar Grove Public Library, Cedar Grove NJ. 609-239-1447

Luertzing, Walter, *Media,* Cumberland County Library, Bridgeton NJ. 609-455-0080

Luesing, Lois, *ILL, Ref & Bibliog Instr,* Asbury College, Morrison-Kenyon Library, Wilmore KY. 606-858-3511

Luevano, Susan, *Commun Servs,* Santiago Library System, Orange CA. 714-634-7137

Luff, Peggy, *Media,* Asbury College, Morrison-Kenyon Library, Wilmore KY. 606-858-3511

Lufkin, Beatrice, *Regional Pub Libr Systs Consult,* Massachusetts Board of Library Commissioners, Office for the Development of Library Services, Boston MA. 617-267-9400

Lufkin, Patricia L, *Librn,* Ecology & Environment Inc, Library, Buffalo NY. 716-632-4491

Luft, Grace, *Librn,* Wernersville Public Library, Wernersville PA. 215-678-1486

Luft, William, *ILL & Ref,* Macomb County Library, Mount Clemens MI. 313-469-5300

Luger, Herbert, *Regional Librn,* Environmental Protection Agency, Region II Library, New York NY. 212-264-2881

Lugo, Lelah, *Ref,* Saint Francis College Library, Fort Wayne IN. 219-432-3551, Ext 263

Luhde, Jutta, *Librn,* Berkshire Medical Center, Medical Library, Pittsfield MA. 413-499-4161, Ext 2734

Luhrsen, Gloria, *Acq,* Aurora College, Charles B Phillips Library, Aurora IL. 312-892-6431, Ext 61, 62

Luich, Rita M, *Librn,* Vernon Public Library, Vernon CA. 213-583-8811

Luik, A, *Librn,* University of Toronto Libraries (Institute of Aerospace Studies), Toronto ON. 416-635-2823

Luiken, Lois, *Librn,* Steamboat Rock Public Library, Steamboat Rock IA. 515-868-2300

Lukac, Jenko, *Cat & On-Line Servs,* Lewis & Clark College, Aubrey R Watzek Library, Portland OR. 503-244-6161, Ext 400

Lukac, Milan, *Multi-Lang Coll,* Suffolk Cooperative Library System, Bellport NY. 516-286-1600

Lukas, Carla, *Librn,* Yale University Library (Classics), New Haven CT. 203-436-1130

Lukas, Marilyn, *Info Specialist,* Marsteller Inc Library, New York NY. 212-752-6500, Ext 829

Lukasiewicz, Barbara, *On-Line Servs,* University of Michigan-Dearborn Library, Dearborn MI. 313-593-5400

Lukasiewicz, Paul, *In Charge,* Yale University Library (Mathematics), New Haven CT. 203-436-0725

Luke, Keye L, *Librn,* FMC Corp, CEL Library, Santa Clara CA. 408-289-2529

Luke, Lisbeth L, *Librn,* Appalachian Regional Commission Library, Washington DC. 202-673-7845

Lukens, Beatrice, *Librn,* University of California, Berkeley (Earth Sciences), Berkeley CA. 415-642-2997
Lukes, Frank, *Librn,* Baker & McKenzie Library, Chicago IL. 312-565-0025
Lukkarila, Mary, *Librn,* Buhl Public Library, Buhl MN. 218-258-3391
Luks, Lewis F, *Dir,* Marist College Library, Washington DC. 202-832-0076
Luksic, Joseph, *ILL, Ref & Ser,* College Misericordia Library, Dallas PA. 717-675-2181, Ext 225
Luksik, Joan, *Dir,* Mount Carmel Mercy Hospital & Medical Center, Medical Library, Detroit MI. 313-864-5400
Lull, David, *Cat & On-Line Servs,* University of Wisconsin-Superior, Jim Dan Hill Library, Superior WI. 715-392-8101, Ext 346
Lull, David H, *Instr,* University of Wisconsin-Superior, Library Science Program, WI. 715-392-8101, Ext 346, 347
Lull, Patricia T, *ILL & Ref,* Superior Public Library, Superior WI. 715-394-0248
Lulves, Carolanne, *Librn,* Village Library, Morgantown PA. 215-286-6169
Lum, Raymond D, *Bk Selection Specialists,* Harvard University Library (Headquarters in Harry Elkins Widener Memorial Library)), Cambridge MA. 617-495-2401
Lum, Wanza Sue, *Dir,* Mount Pleasant Municipal Library, Mount Pleasant TX. 214-572-2705
Luman, Patricia, *Ch,* Rockingham County Public Library, Eden NC. 919-627-1106
Lumb, Sue K, *Cat,* Cincinnati Historical Society Library, Cincinnati OH. 513-241-4622
Lumetta, Joann, *Librn,* Detroit Public Library (Lothrop), Detroit MI. 313-833-9710
Lumley, S, *Tech Serv & Cat,* Saint Thomas Public Library, Saint Thomas ON. 519-631-6050
Lummer, Florence, *Librn,* Anti-Defamation League of B'Nai B'Rith, Jacob Alson Memorial Library, New York NY. 212-689-7400, Ext 288
Lumpkin, Carolyn, *Librn,* Cheaha Regional Library, Anniston AL. 205-238-1581
Lumpkin, Hazel, *Acq,* North Carolina Central University (School of Law), Durham NC. 919-683-6244
Lumpkins, Charles, *Acq & Cat,* Beverly Public Library, Beverly MA. 617-922-0310
Lumsden, Mrs S E, *Librn,* De Witt Public Library (Cleon Collier Memorial Library), Gillett AR. 501-548-2821
Lumsden, S E, *Librn,* De Witt Public Library, De Witt AR. 501-946-1151
Lunak, Louise T, *Librn,* Chicago Academy of Sciences, Matthew Laughlin Memorial Library, Chicago IL. 312-439-0606
Lunceford, Lucinda, *Dir,* Ray County Library, Richmond MO. 816-776-3291
Lund, Chris, *Photog Ed,* National Film Board-Phototheque, Ottawa ON. 613-593-5826
Lund, Gene, *Ch,* Ridgway Public Library, Ridgway PA. 814-777-7573
Lund, Mrs Jerry, *Librn,* Martin Luther Hospital, Medical Library, Anaheim CA. 714-772-1200, Ext 2955
Lund, Nathan, *Per & On-Line Servs,* Western State College of Colorado, Leslie J Savage Library, Gunnison CO. 303-943-2053
Lund, Shirley, *Librn,* Delta County Public Library (Paonia Public), Paonia CO. 303-874-9630
Lundahl, Margaret A, *Librn,* Isham, Lincoln & Beale, Law Library, Chicago IL. 312-558-7488
Lundberg, Elinor, *Asst Librn,* Grace Lutheran Church Library, Wayzata MN. 612-473-2362
Lundberg, Erveen C, *Librn,* John Woodman Higgins Memorial Library, Worcester MA. 617-853-6015
Lundberg, Kathleen, *Librn,* Toledo-Lucas County Public Library (Heatherdowns), Toledo OH. 419-255-7055
Lundberg, Patsy, *Librn,* Kishwaukee College Library, Malta IL. 815-825-2086, Ext 225
Lundblad, Nell, *Cat,* Rock Island Public Library, Rock Island IL. 309-788-7627
Lunde, Joyce E, *Ref,* Northeastern University Libraries, Boston MA. 617-437-2350
Lunde, Ruth, *Local Hist,* Rockford Public Library, Rockford IL. 815-965-6731
Lundeen, Dorothy, *Cat,* Augustana College, Denkman Memorial Library, Rock Island IL. 309-794-7266

Lundeen, Gerald, *Asst Prof,* University of Hawaii, Graduate School of Library Studies, HI. 808-948-7321
Lundeen, Majorie, *In Charge,* Buffalo Library, Buffalo MN. 612-682-2753
Lunden, Elizabeth, *Asst Librn, Ad & Tech Serv,* Bensenville Community Public Library, Bensenville IL. 312-766-4642
Lunden, Elizabeth, *Asst Admin Librn,* Palatine Public Library District, Palatine IL. 312-358-5881
Lunderman, Dorothy, *Circ,* Sinte Gleska College Library, Mission SD. 605-856-4550
Lundford, Theresa, *Orig Cat,* Louisiana State University (Troy H Middleton Library), Baton Rouge LA. 504-388-2217
Lundholm, Eugene T, *Dir,* University of Wisconsin-Superior, Jim Dan Hill Library, Superior WI. 715-392-8101, Ext 346
Lundholm, Eugene T, *Head Librn,* University of Wisconsin-Superior, Library Science Program, WI. 715-392-8101, Ext 346, 347
Lundin, Gary, *Chairperson,* Mankato State University, Memorial Library, Mankato MN. 507-389-6201
Lundin, Janet, *ILL,* Bay De Noc Community College, Learning Resources Center, Escanaba MI. 906-786-5802, Ext 31
Lundquist, Barbara, *Dir,* United States Fire Administration Library, Washington DC. 202-634-7654
Lundquist, Barbara C, *Sci-Tech,* Public Library of the District of Columbia, Martin Luther King Memorial Library, Washington DC. 202-727-1101
Lundquist, Mary Ann, *Dir,* Kula Hospital, Occupational Therapy Dept Library, Kula HI. 808-878-1221
Lundquist, Mrs Duane, *Librn,* Woodlake Lutheran Church Library, Richfield MN. 612-866-8449
Lundquisto, Donna, *Librn,* Legion Memorial Library, Mellen WI. 715-274-8331
Lundwall, Helen, *Dir,* Silver City Public Library, Silver City NM. 505-538-3672
Lundy, Ruth, *Dir,* Tillamook County Public Library, Tillamook OR. 503-842-4792
Lundy, III, Mack A, *AV,* Trident Technical College (North Campus Learning Resources Center), Charleston SC. 803-572-6094
Lung, Vivian W, *Librn,* Bell Canada, Ontario Region Information Resource Center, Toronto ON. 416-599-4230
Lungys, Julia, *Rare Bks,* Balzekas Museum of Lithuanian Culture, Library & Information Center, Chicago IL. 312-847-2441
Lunn, Niki, *Asst Dir,* Grangeville Centennial Library, Grangeville ID. 208-983-0951
Lunn, Rowena, *Br Coordr,* Chinook Regional Library, Swift Current SK. 306-773-3186
Lunsford, Caroll, *Librn,* Drumright Public Library, Drumright OK. 918-352-2228
Lunsford, Dorothy, *Librn,* Alaska Department of Fish & Game Library, Juneau AK. 907-465-4119
Lunskis, Michael, *YA,* Manatee County Public Library System, Bradenton FL. 813-748-5555
Lunt, Peter C, *Ref,* Arthur D Little Inc (Life Sciences Library), Cambridge MA. 617-864-5770, Ext 2030
Lunt, Ruth, *Criminal Justice & Social Work,* Rochester Institute of Technology, Wallace Memorial Library, Rochester NY. 716-475-2566
Luoma, Karen, *Librn,* Mountain Iron Public Library, Mountain Iron MN. 218-735-8625
Luoma, Lily, *Cat,* Sault Sainte Marie Public Library, Sault Sainte Marie ON. 705-949-2152
LuPack, Walter, *Bkmobile Coordr,* Johnson County Public Library, Paintsville KY. 606-789-4355
Lupianen, Sonia, *ILL,* Inter-American University of Puerto Rico, Metropolitan Campus Library, Hato Rey PR. 809-754-7215, Ext 246, 245, 256
Lupo, Becky, *Ch,* Wheeler Basin Regional Library, Decatur Public Library, Decatur AL. 205-353-2993
Lupo, Mona C, *Librn,* Reynolds Electrical & Engineering Co, Inc, Technical Library, Mercury NV. 702-986-0796
Lupo, Pamela Sheppard, *Librn,* Habitat Inc, Institute for the Environment Library, Belmont MA. 617-489-3850
Lupp, Denise, *Librn,* Washington County Hospital Library, Hagerstown MD. 301-797-2355

Lupp, Robert, *NJ Ref Supvr,* New Jersey State Library, Trenton NJ. 609-292-6200
Luquire, Wilson, *Assoc Dir,* East Carolina University, J Y Joyner Library, Greenville NC. 919-757-6514
Lura, Kathryn, *Librn,* Paynesville Public Library, Paynesville MN. 612-243-4645
Lurie, Nancy, *Ad,* Gates Public Library, Gates Robert Abbott Memorial Library, Rochester NY. 716-247-6446
Lurie, Nancy, *In Charge,* Gates Public Library (Dunn Tower Library Station), Gates NY. 716-247-6446
Lurie, Rick, *Ch,* National City Public Library, National City CA. 714-474-8211
Lurye, Joan B, *Librn,* Arthur Anderson & Co Library, New York NY. 212-956-2815
Lusak, Richard, *Dir,* Comsewogue Public Library, Port Jefferson Station NY. 516-928-1212
Luscombe, Virginia, *Ch,* Canajoharie Library & Art Gallery, Canajoharie NY. 518-673-2314
Luoh, Chuolt, *Librn,* Los Angeles Public Library System (Northridge Branch), Northridge CA. 213-886-3640
Lushington, Nolan, *Dir,* Greenwich Library, Greenwich CT. 203-622-7900
Lusk, Eva-Marie, *On-Line Servs & Bibliog Instr,* Lewis-Clark State College Library, Lewiston ID. 208-746-2341, Ext 236
Lusk, Glenna K, *Dir,* Iberville Parish Library, Plaquemine LA. 504-687-2520
Lusk, Jean, *Info Assts,* Colgate-Palmolive Co, Technical Information Center Library, Piscataway NJ. 201-463-1212, Ext 277
Lusk, Marie N, *Chief Librn,* United States Army (Air Defense Center & Fort Bliss Morale Support Activities), Fort Bliss TX. 915-568-2494
Lusk, Sandra, *Librn,* Houston Public Library (Dixon), Houston TX. 713-633-2147
Lusk, Shirley, *YA,* Simsbury Public Library, Simsbury CT. 203-658-5382
Luskay, Jack, *Asst Prof,* Clarion State College, School of Library Science, PA. 814-226-2271
Lussier, Celine, *Ch,* Chateauguay Municipal Library, Chateauguay PQ. 514-691-1934
Lussier, Claudine, *Regional Librn,* Commission De L Emploi Et De L Immigration, Bibliotheque Regionale, Montreal PQ. 514-283-4695
Lussier, Jean-Pierre, *Dir,* College Andre-Grasset Library, Montreal PQ. 514-381-4293
Lussier, Jean-Pierre, *Dir,* College De Montreal Bibliotheque, Montreal PQ. 514-933-7397, Ext 29
Lussky, Warren, *Dir & Acq,* Texas Lutheran College, Blumberg Memorial Library, Seguin TX. 512-379-4161, Ext 90
Lust, Helen, *YA & Ref,* Merrick Library, Merrick NY. 516-379-3476
Lust, Vernon G, *Coll Develp,* University of California at Davis, General Library, Davis CA. 916-752-2110
Lustig, John, *Dir,* Monrovia Public Library, Monrovia CA. 213-358-0174
Lustig, Marilyn, *Librn,* Crime Control Planning Board Library, Saint Paul MN. 612-296-2771
Lutes, Virgil C, *Dir,* Eastchester Public Library, Eastchester NY. 914-793-5055
Lutgen, Tom, *Ref,* Los Angeles Times Editorial Library, Los Angeles CA. 213-972-7184
Luther, James, *Dir,* Cumberland County College Library, Vineland NJ. 609-691-8600, Ext 44, 45
Luther, M Judy, *Dir,* Embry-Riddle Aeronautical University, Learning Resource Center, Daytona Beach FL. 904-252-5561, Ext 360
Luther, Mary, *Bkmobile Coordr,* Mendocino County Library, Ukiah CA. 707-468-4491
Luther, Mary, *ILL,* Norfolk Public Library, Lewis & Clark Regional Library, Norfolk NE. 402-371-4590
Luthi, Rosemary, *Librn,* Houston Public Library (Hillendahl), Houston TX. 713-467-9090
Luthin, Pat, *Cat,* Westchester Library System, Hartsdale NY. 914-761-7620
Luthy, J, *Librn,* Calgary Public Library (Georgina Thomson), Calgary AB. 403-289-6794
Luton, Barbara, *Dir,* Shaker Heights Public Library, Shaker Heights OH. 216-991-2030
Lutovsky, Margaret, *Spec Coll,* Milwaukee Area Technical College, Rasche Memorial Library, Milwaukee WI. 414-278-6205
Lutrin, Debe, *YA,* North Merrick Public Library, North Merrick NY. 516-378-7474

LUTSCH

Lutsch, Marie, *Bus,* Arlington County Department of Libraries, Arlington Public Library, Arlington VA. 703-527-4777
Lutz, Linda, *Acq,* Chapman College, Thurmond Clarke Memorial Library, Orange CA. 714-997-6806
Lutz, Linda, *Librn,* Texas Instruments Inc (S/C Bldg Library), Dallas TX. 214-238-2511
Lutz, Margaret R, *Actg Librn,* Hartland Public Library, West Hartland CT. 203-379-0048
Lutz, Nola, *Dir,* Sheridan County Fulmer Public Library, Sheridan WY. 307-674-8585, 674-9898
Lutz, Susan E, *Librn,* Oklahoma Water Resources Board Library, Oklahoma City OK. 405-271-2555
Lutzker, Marilyn, *Ref, On-Line Servs & Bibliog Instr,* John Jay College of Criminal Justice Library, New York NY. 212-489-5169
Lux, Mrs James, *ILL & Ref,* Lowndes County Library System, Columbus Public Library, Columbus MS. 601-328-1056
Luxenberg, Alan, *Librn,* Foreign Policy Research Institute Library, Philadelphia PA. 215-382-2054
Luxner, Ann, *Dir,* Free Public Library of Closter, Closter NJ. 201-768-4197
Luzader, Joann, *Pub Servs,* Columbus Technical Institute, Educational Resources Center, Columbus OH. 614-227-2463
Lwanga, KoKuleeba, *Librn,* Robbins Public Library District, Robbins IL. 312-597-2760
Lyas, Nancy L, *Librn,* Richardson-Merrell, Inc, Vick Chemical Co Div Research Library, Mount Vernon NY. 914-664-5000, Ext 230
Lybarger, Cathy, *Librn,* Arcadia Township Library, Arcadia NE. 308-789-4302
Lyberger, Marilyn, *Ch,* Muncie-Center Township Public Library, Muncie IN. 317-288-9971
Lyda, Doris, *Librn,* Brooklyn Public Library (Clinton Hill), Brooklyn NY. 212-857-8038
Lyddane, David, *Data Control,* Columbia University (University Libraries), New York NY. 212-280-2241
Lyder, Eric, *Ad,* Lake County Library, Lakeport Library, Lakeport CA. 707-263-2291
Lyders, Richard A, *Dir,* Houston Academy of Medicine, Texas Medical Center Library, Houston TX. 713-797-1230
Lydia, Sister Mary, *Dir,* Madonna College Library, Livonia MI. 313-591-1200
Lydic, Laura, *Librn,* Thorndike, Doran, Paine & Lewis Library, Atlanta GA. 404-688-2782
Lydic, Patricia, *Asst Librn,* Girard Free Public Library, Girard OH. 216-545-2508
Lydigsen, Mildred, *Librn,* MacNeal Memorial Hospital Association, Frank C Becht Memorial Library, Berwyn IL. 312-795-9100, Ext 3089
Lydon, M E, *In Charge,* Metcalf & Eddy, Inc Library, Boston MA. 617-367-4087, 367-4088
Lydon, Pamela, *Librn,* Connecticut Veterans Home & Hospital, Medical Library, Rocky Hill CT. 203-529-2571, Ext 261
Lydzinski, Margaret, *ILL,* Outagamie Waupaca Counties Federated Library System, Appleton WI. 414-734-8873
Lye, Laurie, *ILL,* Casper College, Goodstein Foundation Library, Casper WY. 307-268-2269
Lyerla, Gloria, *ILL,* Texas Tech University Library, Lubbock TX. 806-742-2261
Lyerla, Shirley A, *Librn,* Hillsboro Public Library, Hillsboro IL. 217-532-3055
Lyke, Elizabeth, *Asst Dir,* Danbury Public Library, Danbury CT. 203-797-4505
Lyle, Katherine C, *Librn,* Population Council Bio-Medical Library, New York NY. 212-360-1707
Lyle, L N, *Librn,* Babcock & Wilcox Co, Power Generation Group Technical Library, Barberton OH. 216-753-4511, Ext 2267
Lyle, Robert S, *On-Line Servs,* Veterans Administration, Medical Center Library, Coatesville PA. 215-384-7711, Ext 333
Lyman, Evelyn L, *Dir,* Swan Library, Albion NY. 716-589-4246
Lyman, June E, *Librn,* William K Kohrs Memorial Library, Deer Lodge MT. 406-846-2622
Lyman, Norma Jane, *Asst Librn,* New Hampshire State Library (Law Division), Concord NH. 603-271-3777
Lyman, Sue, *Librn,* Frances E Kennard Public Library, Meshoppen PA. 717-833-5060
Lymburner, Florence, *Librn,* Wentworth Library (Stoney Creek), Hamilton ON. 416-526-4126

Lynas, L, *On-Line Servs,* New York Botanical Garden Library, Bronx NY. 212-220-8749
Lynch, Anne, *Librn,* University of Southern California (College), Los Angeles CA. 213-743-6057
Lynch, Augusta, *Ch & YA,* Sandwich Public Library, Sandwich MA. 617-888-0625
Lynch, Barbara, *On-Line Servs,* United States Department of the Navy (Navy Dept Library), Washington DC. 202-433-4131
Lynch, Betty H, *Librn,* Frankford Public Library, Frankford DE. 302-732-9351
Lynch, Beverly, *Ad & Acq,* Brooks Memorial Library, Brattleboro VT. 802-254-5290
Lynch, Beverly P, *Librn,* University of Illinois at Chicago Circle Library, Chicago IL. 312-996-2716
Lynch, Catharine, *Librn,* American Broadcasting Co, Inc, ABC General Library, New York NY. 212-887-7777
Lynch, Cheryl, *Librn,* Lawrence Eagle Tribune Editorial Library, North Andover MA. 617-685-1000, Ext 219
Lynch, Divina, *Per,* Pace University, Pleasantville-Briarcliff Library, Pleasantville NY. 914-769-3200, Ext 382
Lynch, Ellen, *Dir,* Hartland Public Libraries, Hartland VT. 802-436-2473
Lynch, Elsie, *Librn,* Ottawa Public Library (Carlingwood), Ottawa ON. 613-236-0301, Ext 267, 268
Lynch, Evangeline, *Rare Bks,* Louisiana State University (Troy H Middleton Library), Baton Rouge LA. 504-388-2217
Lynch, Frances, *Asst Dir Tech Servs,* Vanderbilt University Medical Center Library, Nashville TN. 615-322-2292
Lynch, Gerard F, *Librn,* Trinitarian College Library, Baltimore MD. 301-486-5171, Ext 36
Lynch, James R, *Archivist,* Church of the Brethren General Board, Brethren Historical Library & Archives, Elgin IL. 312-742-5100, Ext. 294
Lynch, Linda, *Librn,* Marketing Corporation of America Library, Westport CT. 203-226-1061, Ext 313
Lynch, Lois, *Librn,* Kern County Library (Edwards Branch), Edwards CA. 805-861-2130
Lynch, Margie R, *Dir,* Hattiesburg Public Library System, Hattiesburg MS. 601-582-4461
Lynch, Marilyn, *Ch,* Lewistown Carnegie Public Library, Lewistown IL. 309-547-2860
Lynch, Mary, *Dir,* Colebrook Public Library, Colebrook NH. 603-237-4808
Lynch, Michael P, *Dir,* North Central Regional Library, Wenatchee WA. 509-663-1117
Lynch, Mollie S, *Dir,* Saint Joseph Mercy Hospital, Educational Resources, Pontiac MI. 313-858-3495
Lynch, Robert, *Tech Serv,* University of Massachusetts at Amherst Library, Amherst MA. 413-545-0284
Lynch, Shawn, *Librn,* Buffalo & Erie County Public Library System (University Heights), Buffalo NY. 716-832-7762
Lynch, Sister Cecelia, *Librn,* Aquinas Junior College Library, Nashville TN. 615-297-7545
Lynch, Sister M Dennis, *Dir,* Rosemont College, Gertrude Kistler Memorial Library, Rosemont PA. 215-527-0200, Ext 226
Lynch, Sister M Wilma, *Librn,* Albertus Magnus College Library, New Haven CT. 203-777-6631, Ext 227
Lynch, Suzanne, *Bkmobile Coordr,* Newport News Public Library System, Newport News VA. 804-247-8506
Lynch, Terence R, *Dir,* Saint Tammany Parish Library, Covington LA. 504-892-2456
Lynch, III, William F, *Dir,* John C Hart Memorial Library, Shrub Oak NY. 914-245-5262
Lynchy, Jerri, *Media,* Milford Public Library, Milford CT. 203-878-7461
Lynde, Arlene, *Librn,* Newton Free Library (Waban Branch), Waban MA. 617-527-7700, Ext 24
Lynden, Frederick C, *Asst Univ Librn-Tech Servs,* Brown University (University Library), Providence RI. 401-863-2167
Lyndgaard, Sophie, *Librn,* Le Sueur-Waseca Regional Library (New Richland Public), New Richland MN. 507-465-3708
Lynema, Karen, *Tech Serv & Cat,* Campbellsville College Library, Campbellsville KY. 502-465-8158, Ext 272

Lynn, Carol, *Librn,* Anclote Psychiatric Center, Medical Library, Tarpon Springs FL. 813-937-4211, Ext 223
Lynn, Daphne, *Librn & On-Line Servs,* McKeesport Hospital, Health Service Library, McKeesport PA. 412-664-2364
Lynn, Dorothy, *Librn,* Bessemer City Public Library, Bessemer City NC. 704-629-3321
Lynn, Harriet K, *Dir,* Jacob Sears Memorial Library, East Dennis Library, East Dennis MA. 617-385-8151
Lynn, Ruby J, *Librn,* Tucumcari Public Library, Tucumcari NM. 505-461-0295
Lynn, Vanessa, *Art & Archit,* Pratt Institute Library, Brooklyn NY. 212-636-3684
Lyon, Douglas, *Assoc Dir,* New Hampshire College & University Council, NH. 603-669-3432
Lyon, Eunice M, *Med Librn,* United States Air Force (Malcolm Grow United States Air Force Medical Center Library), Andrews AFB MD. 301-981-2354
Lyon, G, *Theology,* Blue Cloud Abbey Library, Marvin SD. 605-432-5528, Ext 904
Lyon, Grace B, *Librn,* New Castle Business College Library, New Castle PA. 412-658-9066
Lyon, Jacquelyn, *Librn,* Harris County Public Library (Freeman), Houston TX. 713-488-1906
Lyon, Joan, *Librn,* Mineral-Gold Public Library District, Mineral IL. 309-288-3971
Lyon, Nina, *Ch,* Public Library of Charlotte & Mecklenburg County, Inc, Charlotte NC. 704-374-2725
Lyon, Sherry, *Librn,* Two Hills Municipal Library, Two Hills AB. 403-657-3553
Lyon, Shirley A, *Ancient Near East & Classics,* University of Chicago, Joseph Regenstein Library, Chicago IL. 312-753-2977
Lyon, Tracey, *Librn,* Monmouth County Library (Holmdel Branch), Holmdel NJ. 201-946-4118
Lyon, IV, David A, *Dir,* York County Library, Headquarters Rock Hill Public Library, Rock Hill SC. 803-328-8402
Lyon-Hartmann, Becky, *Asst for Network Develop,* Veterans Administration (Library Division), Washington DC. 202-389-2781
Lyons, A, *Allied Health,* State University of New York at Buffalo (Health Sciences), Buffalo NY. 716-831-5465
Lyons, A, *Health Related Professions,* State University of New York at Buffalo, University Libraries, Buffalo NY. 716-636-2965
Lyons, A James, *Adult Educ,* Saint Louis Public Library, Saint Louis MO. 314-241-2288
Lyons, Donald W, *Dir,* Kentucky State University, Blazer Library, Frankfort KY. 502-564-5852
Lyons, Donald W, *Head,* Kentucky State University, Library Technology Program, KY. 502-564-5852
Lyons, Ellen, *Asst Librn & Ch,* Howell Carnegie Library, Howell MI. 517-546-0720
Lyons, Emily, *Ch,* Oxnard Public Library, Oxnard CA. 805-486-4311
Lyons, Evelyn, *ILL & On-Line Servs,* Millersville State College, Helen A Ganser Library, Millersville PA. 717-872-5411, Ext 341
Lyons, Frances, *Librn,* Roberts County Library, Miami TX. 806-868-3721
Lyons, Grace J, *Chief Librn,* District of Columbia Library for the Blind & Physically Handicapped, Washington DC. 212-727-2142
Lyons, Grace J, *Librn Blind,* Public Library of the District of Columbia, Martin Luther King Memorial Library, Washington DC. 202-727-1101
Lyons, Janet, *Doc,* Illinois State Library, Springfield IL. 217-782-2994
Lyons, Janet R, *Libm,* Trussville Public Library, Trussville AL. 205-655-2022
Lyons, Joan, *ILL,* Free Public Library, Rowley MA. 617-948-2850
Lyons, Kaarina, *Asst Librn,* Aetna Life & Casualty (Company Library), Hartford CT. 203-273-2946
Lyons, Kathleen, *Ch & YA,* Plymouth Public Library, Russell Memorial Library, Plymouth MA. 617-746-1927
Lyons, Lawrence R, *Libm,* Clinton County Law Library, Wilmington OH. 513-382-2428
Lyons, Leo, *Media,* University of Saint Thomas, Robert Pace & Ada Mary Doherty Library, Houston TX. 713-522-7911, Ext 325
Lyons, Lois, *Cat,* University of Wisconsin-Whitewater, Library & Learning Resources, Whitewater WI. 414-472-1000

Lyons, Margaret, *Ref,* Central Texas College, Oveta Culp Hobby Memorial Library, Killeen TX. 817-526-1237

Lyons, Marian, *Asst Dir,* Jackson Metropolitan Library, Jackson MS. 601-352-3677

Lyons, Martha, *Chief Librn,* Orange County Public Library (Mesa Verde Branch), Costa Mesa CA. 714-546-5274

Lyons, Molly M, *Dir,* Saint Patrick's College-Saint Joseph High School Library, Los Altos CA. 415-967-9501, Ext 41

Lyons, Mrs Dean, *Librn,* Albert F Totman Library, Phippsburg ME. 207-389-2560

Lyons, Mrs L, *Librn,* Flos-Elmvale Public Library, Elmvale ON. 705-322-1482

Lyons, Patricia L, *Librn,* Walsh College Library, Canton OH. 216-499-7090, Ext 40

Lyons, Pauline, *Librn,* Lincoln Memorial Library, Lincoln ME. 207-794-2765

Lyons, Rosemary, *Tech Serv,* University of Calgary Library, Calgary AB. 403-284-5954

Lyons, Sarah, *Dir,* Conservative Baptist Theological Seminary, Carey S Thomas Library, Englewood CO. 303-781-8691

Lyons, Susan E, *Dir,* Burlington County Lyceum of History & Natural Sciences, Mount Holly Library, Mount Holly NJ. 609-267-7111

Lyons, Thomas H, *Dir,* Mid Michigan Community College, Charles A Amble Library, Harrison MI. 517-386-7792, Ext 258

Lystad, Muriel, *Librn,* Arne Bob Sanford Library, Watford City ND. 701-842-3785

Lytal, Bill D, *Media,* Mississippi College, Leland Speed Library, Clinton MS. 601-924-5131, Ext 232, 307

Lytell, Delphine, *Librn,* Summit-Argo Public Library, Summit IL. 312-458-1545

Lytle, Edith, *Librn,* Stockton Public Library, Stockton KS. 913-425-6372

Lytle, Judy K, *Librn,* Mathews, Nowlin, MacFarlane & Barrett, Law Library, San Antonio TX. 512-226-4211

Lytle, Marsha, *Ref,* Albert A Wells Memorial Library, Tippecanoe County Contractual Library, Lafayette IN. 317-423-2602

Lytle, Patricia, *Librn,* Lilly-Washington Public Library, Lilly PA. 814-886-7543

Lytle, Richard H, *Archivist,* Smithsonian Institution Archives, Washington DC. 202-381-4075

Lytle, Susan, *Maps & Multi Media,* Texas A&m University Libraries, College Station TX. 713-845-6111

Lytton, Lita, *Pub Servs,* Lake Lanier Regional Library, Lawrenceville GA. 404-963-5231

Lytton, Lita, *Librn,* Lake Lanier Regional Library (Gwinnett County (headquarters)), Lawrenceville GA. 404-963-5231

Lyzotte, Jeanette, *Per,* City-County Library of Missoula, Missoula MT. 406-728-5900

M

Ma, Charles, *Media,* Lakeshore Technical Institute, Educational Resources Center, Cleveland WI. 414-693-8211, 684-4408, Ext 150

Ma, Fred, *Cat,* University of Northern Iowa Library, Cedar Falls IA. 319-273-2737

Ma, Helen, *Librn,* Detroit Public Library (Elmwood Park), Detroit MI. 313-833-9766

Ma, Vilia, *Librn,* International Business Machines Corp (Research Library), San Jose CA. 408-256-2562

Maack, Mary N, *Asst Prof,* University of Minnesota, Library School, MN. 612-373-3100

Maag, Albert F, *Dir,* Capital University Library, Columbus OH. 614-236-6614

Maas, Marian, *Librn,* Dwight Library, Dwight KS. 913-482-3202

Maas, Norman, *Info & Referral,* Detroit Public Library, Detroit Associated Libraries, Detroit MI. 313-833-1000

Maasen, Orlys, *Librn,* Bode Public Library, Bode IA. 515-379-1149

Mabe, Nanette, *Processing,* Blount County Library, Maryville TN. 615-982-0981

Mabley, Elwood, *Dir,* Walla Walla College, Peterson Memorial Library, College Place WA. 509-527-2133

Mabra, Lois, *Librn,* Dallas County Public Library (Hutchins-Atwell Branch), Hutchins TX. 214-225-4711

Mabrey, Helen, *Ch,* L E Phillips Memorial Public Library, Eau Claire WI. 715-839-5002

Mabry, Ann, *Librn,* Mary S Gray Library, Williamston NC. 919-792-5966

Mabry, Shirley, *Chief Librn,* Veterans Administration, Medical Center Library, Lake City FL. 904-752-1400, Ext 272

MacAdam, Bonnie, *Curator,* Lyme Historical Society Library, Old Lyme CT. 203-434-5542

MacAllister, Edith, *Dir,* Old Manse Library, Newcastle NB. 506-622-0453

MacAran, E, *Librn,* Numax Electronics Inc Library, Hauppauge NY. 516-582-3311

Macaree, Mary, *Librn,* University of British Columbia Library (MacMillan Forestry & Agriculture), Vancouver BC. 604-228-3609

MacArthur, Donna, *ILL & Circ,* Nova Scotia Agricultural College Library, Truro NS. 902-895-1571, Ext 231, 228 & 291

MacArthur, Jr, William J, *Spec Coll,* Knoxville-Knox County Public Library, Lawson McGhee Library, Knoxville TN. 615-523-0781

Macat, Marlene, *Librn,* Austin County Library System (West End Branch), Industry TX. 713-357-4434

Macaulay, J, *ILL,* Canada Department of Energy, Mines & Resources (Canada Center for Mineral & Energy Technology Library), Ottawa ON. 613-995-4132

Macauslan, Sally, *Librn,* Bridgton Public Library, Dalton Holmes Davis Memorial Library, Bridgton ME. 207-647-2472

Macbeth, Eileen M, *Librn,* Chester County Law Library, West Chester PA. 215-696-1316

MacBeth, In Cheung Sak, *Instr,* Middle Tennessee State University, Department of Library Service, TN. 615-898-2740 & 898-5555

Macbeth, R A, *Librn,* National Cancer Institute of Canada Library, Toronto ON. 416-961-7223

MacCallum, Alice, *Librn,* Detroit Public Library (Knapp), Detroit MI. 313-833-9156

MacCallum, Barbara, *Librn,* Peapack-Gladstone Library, Gladstone NJ. 201-234-0598

MacCampbell, James C, *Dir,* University of Maine at Orono, Raymond H Fogler Library, Orono ME. 207-581-7328

MacCleave, Mrs E, *Branch Assistant,* Cumberland Regional Library (Oxford Branch), Amherst NS. 902-447-2440

MacConnell, Elizabeth, *Media,* Somerset County Library, Somerville NJ. 201-725-4700, Ext 234

MacCorkle, Gwendolyn B, *On-Line Servs,* University of Miami, Otto G Richter Library, Coral Gables FL. 305-284-3551

MacCready, Mary, *Media & Tech Serv,* Lake County Library, Lakeport Library, Lakeport CA. 707-263-2291

Maccubbin, Patricia G, *Audiovisual Librn,* Colonial Williamsburg (Audiovisual Library), Williamsburg VA. 804-229-1000, Ext 2286

MacDonald, Alan H, *Lectr,* Dalhousie University, School of Library Service, NS. 902-424-3656

MacDonald, Alan H, *Dir,* University of Calgary Library, Calgary AB. 403-284-5954

MacDonald, Allan J, *Dir,* Scott Community College Library, Bettendorf IA. 319-359-7531, Ext 215

MacDonald, B, *Bkmobile Coordr,* Calgary Public Library, Calgary AB. 403-268-2800

MacDonald, Barbara, *Ref,* Colorado School of Mines, Arthur Lakes Library, Golden CO. 303-279-0300, Ext 2690

MacDonald, Bernice, *Assoc Dir,* New York Public Library (The Branch Libraries), New York NY. 212-790-6262

Macdonald, Beverly, *Ch,* Millinocket Memorial Library, Millinocket ME. 207-723-9610

MacDonald, Bonnie, *Commun Servs,* Shiawassee County Library, Corunna MI. 517-743-3421, Ext 278

MacDonald, Christine, *Librn,* Citadel Assurance Co, Information Centre, Toronto ON. 416-928-8540

MacDonald, Christine, *Librn,* Legislative Library of Saskatchewan, Regina SK. 306-565-2277, 565-2276

MacDonald, Dorcas, *ILL,* Syracuse University Libraries, Ernest S Bird Library, Syracuse NY. 315-423-2575

Macdonald, Doreen, *ILL,* Oakville Public Library, Oakville ON. 416-845-3405

MacDonald, Elizabeth, *Librn,* Nova Scotia Provincial Library (Public Libraries), Halifax NS. 902-424-5431

Macdonald, Ernestine, *Ad,* Lynnfield Public Library, Lynnfield MA. 617-334-5411

MacDonald, Gary W, *Program Suprv,* Southern Alberta Institute of Technology, Library Arts Program, AB. 403-284-8328

MacDonald, Goldie, *Librn,* Prince Edward Island Provincial Library (Summerside Branch), Summerside PE. 902-892-3504, Ext 54

MacDonald, Helen D, *Librn,* Lee Public Library, Lee NH. 603-659-2626

Macdonald, Hugh, *Ref,* Texas Christian University, Mary Couts Burnett Library, Fort Worth TX. 817-921-7106

MacDonald, Janet, *Outreach,* Ames Public Library, Ames IA. 515-232-4404

Macdonald, Janet, *AV,* North York Public Library, Willowdale ON. 416-494-6838

MacDonald, Joyce, *ILL,* Arlington County Department of Libraries, Arlington Public Library, Arlington VA. 703-527-4777

MacDonald, M, *Librn,* Calgary Public Library (Crescent Heights), Calgary AB. 403-277-2655

MacDonald, Maggie, *Ref & On-Line Servs,* Southern Alberta Institute of Technology, Learning Resources Centre, Calgary AB. 284-8647; 284-8648

MacDonald, Marjorie, *ILL & Spec Coll,* Nova Scotia Technical College Library, Halifax NS. 902-429-8300, Ext 254

MacDonald, Mary, *Cat,* College of Cape Breton Library, Sydney NS. 902-539-5300

MacDonald, Mary, *YA,* Mamaroneck Free Library, Mamaroneck NY. 914-698-1250

MacDonald, Minna L, *ILL,* Bloomfield Public Library, Northwest Essex Area Library, Bloomfield NJ. 201-429-9292

MacDonald, Robin, *Asst Librn,* University of British Columbia Library, Vancouver BC. 604-228-3871

MacDonald, Roderick, *Dir,* Dakota County Library System, Burnsville MN. 612-435-8111

MacDonald, Ruth, *Actg Dir,* Mount Allison University, Ralph Pickard Bell Library, Sackville NB. 506-536-2040, Ext 375

MacDonald, W James, *Ref & Bibliog Instr,* Connecticut College Library, New London CT. 203-442-1630

MacDonnald, Mary Jane, *On-Line Servs,* Sangamon State University, Norris L Brookens Library, Springfield IL. 217-786-6597

MacDougall, Frank C, *Librn,* Michigan State University Library (Continuing Education), East Lansing MI. 517-355-2344

Macdougall, Judith, *Asst Librn,* Milo Free Public Library, Milo ME. 207-943-2612

MacDougall, Nathalie, *Ch,* Lansing Public Library, Lansing MI. 517-374-4600

MacDowall, Traszha, *Tech Serv,* Nepean Public Library, Ottawa ON. 613-224-4338

Mace, Angela M, *ILL,* Staunton Public Library, Fannie Bayly King Library, Staunton VA. 703-886-7231

Mace, Catherine, *Ch,* Leavenworth Public Library, Leavenworth KS. 913-682-5666

Mace, Mary B, *Librn,* Sprague Electric Company Library, North Adams MA. 413-664-4411, Ext 2355

MacEachern, J, *Doc,* British Columbia Government, Legislative Library, Victoria BC. 604-387-6500

Macek, Carol, *Ref,* Dearborn Department of Libraries, Henry Ford Centennial Library, Dearborn MI. 313-271-1000

Macek, Ruth M, *Librn,* IBM Corp, Burlington Technical Information Center, Essex Junction VT. 802-769-3931

MacEllven, Douglass T, *Dir,* Law Society of Saskatchewan Libraries, Regina SK. 306-569-8020

MacElwee, Andea, *Librn,* Kapuskasing Public Library, Kapuskasing ON. 705-335-3363

MacEwan, Bonnie, *Humanities,* Central Missouri State University, Ward Edwards Library, Warrensburg MO. 816-429-4141

Macey, John F, *Cat & On-Line Servs,* Saint Vincent College & Archabbey Libraries, Latrobe PA. 412-539-9761, Ext 378

MacFadyen, Helen, *ILL,* Digital Equipment Corp, Corporate Library, Maynard MA. 617-493-6231, 493-5821
MacFarlane, Lena, *Librn,* Sedan Public Library, Sedan KS. 316-725-3405
MacFarlane, Mabel, *Dir,* D R Moon Memorial Library, Stanley WI. 715-644-2004
MacFate, Ann, *Ref,* Needham Free Public Library, Needham MA. 617-444-0087, 444-0090
MacGregor, Katherine, *Librn,* Varian Research Library, Beverly MA. 617-922-6000
MacGregor, Lois, *Libr Officer,* United States Navy (Naval Security Group Activity Station Library), Winter Harbor ME. 207-963-5534, Ext 224
MacGregor, Margaret E, *Bibliog Instr,* United States Army War College Library, Carlisle Barracks PA. 717-245-4319
Machin, Marian, *Br Asst,* Timberland Regional Library (Oakville Branch), Oakville WA. 206-273-5305
Machinski, Robert C, *Dir,* James V Brown Library of Williamsport & Lycoming County, Williamsport PA. 717-326-0536
Machintosh, Dona P, *AV,* Dean Junior College, E Ross Anderson Library, Franklin MA. 617-528-9100, Ext 261
Machovec, Charles A, *Librn,* University of Miami (Undergraduate Library), Coral Gables FL. 305-284-3455
Machovec, George, *On-Line Servs,* Arizona State University Library, Tempe AZ. 602-965-3417
Machowski, Ruth, *Interim Adminr,* Niles Public Library, Niles IL. 312-967-8554
Machus, Josephine M, *Dir,* Oconomowoc Public Library, Oconomowoc WI. 414-567-4631
Maciejewski, Richard, *Municipal Ref,* Detroit Public Library, Detroit Associated Libraries, Detroit MI. 313-833-1000
Maciejewski, Richard, *Chief Librn,* Detroit Public Library (Municipal Reference), Detroit MI. 313-224-3885
Macik, John A, *Chief Librn,* Saint Bonaventure University, Friedsam Memorial Library & Resource Center, Saint Bonaventure NY. 716-375-2323
MacIlroy, Dorene L, *Cat,* Brewer Public Library, Brewer ME. 207-989-7943
MacInnes, M J, *Personnel Dir,* University of California Library, Irvine CA. 714-833-5212
MacInnes, Mary Ann, *Per,* Okanagan College, Muriel Ffoulkes Learning Resource Center, Kelowna BC. 604-762-5445, Ext 293
MacInnis, Deborah A, *Ch,* Edgartown Free Public Library, Edgartown MA. 617-627-4221
MacInnis, Sister Rita, *Librn,* College of Cape Breton Library, Sydney NS. 902-539-5300
MacIntosh, Helen, *Tech Serv, Acq & Cat,* Mississauga Public Library, Mississauga ON. 416-625-8681
Maciorkoski, Sunya, *Librn,* Tunkhannock Public Library, Tunkhannock PA. 717-836-1677
Macioroski, Shannon, *Ref, On-Line Servs & Bibliog Instr,* Catholic University of America, John K Mullen of Denver Memorial Library, Washington DC. 202-635-5055
Macioroski, Shannon K, *Coordr,* Catholic University of America (Reference-Social Sciences-Social Service Div), Washington DC. 202-635-5074
Maciuszko, Kathleen L, *Librn,* Baldwin-Wallace College (Fern Patterson Jones Memorial Music Library), Berea OH. 216-826-2366
Mack, Anne, *Gen Ref,* Metropolitan Toronto Library Board, Metropolitan Toronto Library, Toronto ON. 416-928-5150
Mack, Barbara C, *Librn,* Friends World College Library, Huntington NY. 516-549-5000
Mack, Bonnie, *Librn & On-Line Servs,* Rapid City Regional Hospital, Health Science Library, Rapid City SD. 605-341-7108
Mack, Cheryl, *Tech Serv,* Des Plaines Public Library, Des Plaines IL. 312-827-5551
Mack, Forrest, *Tech Serv, Acq & Cat,* Watertown Free Public Library, Watertown MA. 617-924-5390
Mack, Francis, *Librn,* Hutchinson County Library (Fritch Branch), Fritch TX. 806-857-3752
Mack, Gertrude W, *Librn,* Cardington Public Library, Cardington OH. 419-864-2488
Mack, Gloria, *ILL,* John C Hart Memorial Library, Shrub Oak NY. 914-245-5262

Mack, Kevin D, *Acting Admin,* Hartford Insurance Group (Advancement Center Library), Hartford CT. 203-547-3426
Mack, Lenore F, *Music,* Converse College, Gwathmey Library, Spartanburg SC. 803-585-6421, Ext 260
Mack, Marge, *Librn,* Blackduck Library, Blackduck MN. 218-835-6600
Mack, Marie, *Librn,* Santa Fe Regional Library (Micanopy Branch), Micanopy FL. 904-466-3122
Mack, Marilyn, *Librn,* Needham, Harper & Steers Advertising, Inc Library, Chicago IL. 312-861-0100
Mack, Phyllis, *Librn,* New York Public Library (Hamilton Grange), New York NY. 212-926-2147
Mack, Sara R, *Chairperson,* Kutztown State College, Dept of Library Science, PA. 215-683-4300, 683-4301
Mack, Sister Theron, *Cat,* Marywood College Library, Scranton PA. 717-343-6521, Ext 289
Mack, Susan, *Librn,* Saint Joseph's Hospital Medical Library, Fort Wayne IN. 219-423-2614, Ext 2358
Mack, Theodore, *Dir,* Paul Smiths College of Arts & Sciences, Frank L Cubley Library, Paul Smiths NY. 518-327-6313
MacKay, Cynthia B, *Librn,* Melvin & Melvin Library, Syracuse NY. 315-422-1311
MacKay, Jane M, *Doc,* Trinity University Library, San Antonio TX. 512-736-8121
Mackay, Vicki, *In Charge,* Oxford County Library (Hickson Branch), Hickson ON. 519-462-2428
Mackay-Smith, A, *Curator,* National Sporting Library Inc, Middleburg VA. 703-687-6542
MacKelvey, Martha, *Res Info Retrieval Librn,* University of Dayton Libraries (Law School Library), Dayton OH. 513-229-2314
MacKelvie, Vernon S, *Chief Librn,* Labour Canada Library, Ottawa ON. 819-997-3540
MacKenzie, Alberta, *ILL & Ref,* Otterbein College, Courtright Memorial Library, Westerville OH. 614-890-3000, Ext 164
Mackenzie, Barbara N, *Librn,* Nova Scotia Power Corp Library, Halifax NS. 902-424-2928
MacKenzie, Blair, *AV,* Tidewater Community College, Virginia Beach Campus Library, Virginia Beach VA. 804-427-3070, Ext 123, 126
MacKenzie, Dawn, *Librn,* Saint Albans Correctional Facility Library, Saint Albans VT. 802-524-6771
MacKenzie, Donald N, *Dir,* Northwestern State University of Louisiana, Eugene P Watson Memorial Library, Natchitoches LA. 318-357-4403
MacKenzie, Dorothy, *Librn,* Ingham County Library (Williamston Branch), Williamston MI. 517-655-1191
MacKenzie, Lois, *Commun Servs,* San Diego Public Library, San Diego CA. 714-236-5800
MacKenzie, Margaret, *Librn,* Lawrence Memorial Hospitals, Health Science Library, New London CT. 203-442-0711, Ext 238
MacKenzie, Pamela, *Librn,* Civic Garden Centre Library, Don Mills ON. 416-445-1552
Mackenzie, Ronald J, *Dir,* Georgian Bay Regional Library System, Barrie ON. 705-726-4676
MacKenzie, Vincent, *Chief Librn,* Regis College Library, Toronto ON. 416-922-5474, Ext 7
Mackevicius, Aldona, *Head, Tech Proc,* Queens Borough Public Library, Jamaica NY. 212-990-0700
Mackey, James, *Librn,* Trumbull Library (Fairchild Nichols Memorial), Trumbull CT. 203-378-7972
Mackey, Jean, *Cat,* University of Tulsa, McFarlin Library, Tulsa OK. 918-592-6000, Ext 351
Mackey, John T, *Asst Librn,* Public Library of the City of Somerville, Somerville MA. 617-623-5000
Mackey, Neosha, *Librn,* Ohio State University Libraries (Home Economics Library), Columbus OH. 614-422-4220
Mackey, Patricia, *AV,* Monroe County Library System, Rochester NY. 716-428-7345
Mackey, Patricia E, *Asst to Librn,* Rockefeller University Library, New York NY. 212-360-1000
Mackey, Sister Berthold, *Librn,* Saint Francis Xavier University (Marie Michael Library), Antigonish NS. 902-867-3964

Mackie, Duane O, *Tech Serv,* Roosevelt University, Murray-Green Library, Chicago IL. 312-341-3639
Mackie, James, *ILL,* University of California Library, San Francisco CA. 415-666-2334
Mackin, Robert H, *Media,* Onondaga Community College, Sidney B Coulter Library, Syracuse NY. 315-469-7741, Ext 5335-5338
Mackinaw, Rosemary, *Ch,* Mansfield-Richland County Public Library, Mansfield OH. 419-524-1041
MacKinnon, Grace, *Libr Asst,* Pictou Antigonish Regional Library (Antigonish Branch), Antigonish NS. 902-863-4276
MacKinnon, Joan, *Tech Serv & Cat,* Piscataway Township Free Public Library, John F Kennedy Memorial Library, Piscataway NJ. 201-463-1633
MacKinnon, Marcelline, *Librn,* Ecumenical Forum of Canada Library, Toronto ON. 416-924-9351, Ext 4
MacKinnon, Mary, *Librn,* Domglas Ltee, Technical Centre Library, Mississauga ON. 416-823-3860, Ext 236
MacKinnon, Stuart, *Drama & Eng,* University of Waterloo Library, Waterloo ON. 519-885-1211
MacKinnon, Sue, *Asst Librn,* Litchfield Free Public Library, Hudson NH. 603-429-4044
MacKintosh, Mary, *Librn,* California Institute of Technology (Management Library), Pasadena CA. 213-795-6811, Ext 1043
Mackler, Lee, *Librn,* Postgraduate Center for Mental Health, Emil A Gutheil Memorial Library, New York NY. 212-689-7700, Ext 710
Macklin, James R, *Dir,* Macon Junior College Library, Macon GA. 912-474-2700, Ext 215, 216
Macko, Lucinda, *Librn,* Saint Mary Medical Center, Medical Staff Library, Gary IN. 219-882-9411
Macko, Rhonda, *Librn,* Chase Manhattan Bank (Systems Library), New York NY. 212-676-3629
Mackov, Alice O, *Ref,* Thomas Jefferson University (Scott Memorial Library), Philadelphia PA. 215-928-8848
Macksam, David, *Extension,* Central Arkansas Library System, Little Rock AR. 501-374-7546
Macksam, Gilda, *Librn,* Arkansas Legislative Council Library, Little Rock AR. 501-371-1937
Mackzum, Mary F, *Dir,* Clermont County Public Library, Batavia OH. 513-732-2128
MacLachlan, Colleen, *Librn,* Environment Council of Alberta Library, Edmonton AB. 403-427-5792
MacLaren, Grant, *Assoc Dean,* Saint Louis Community College (Meramec Campus), Saint Louis MO. 314-966-7623
Maclaren, Hamish, *Asst Librn,* Naropa Institute Library, Boulder CO. 303-444-0202
MacLaughlin, Barbara, *Librn,* Annapolis Valley Regional Library Headquarters (Kingston Branch), Kingston NS. 902-532-2260
Maclay, Eleanor, *Librn,* DeGolyer & MacNaughton Library, Dallas TX. 214-368-6391
MacLean, Barbara, *Librn,* Anchorage Municipal Libraries (Samson-Dimond Library), Anchorage AK. 907-349-4629
MacLean, Eleanor, *Librn,* McGill University Libraries (Blacker-Wood Library of Zoology & Ornithology), Montreal PQ. 514-392-4955
MacLean, Ellen G, *Librn,* Bureau of Libraries, Museums & Archaeological Services (Enid M Baa Library & Archives), Charlotte Amalie VI. 809-774-0630
MacLean, Judith S, *Coordr,* Tunxis Community College Library, Farmington CT. 203-677-7701, Ext 44
MacLean, Lois, *Chief Librn,* New Mexico State Library for the Blind & Physically Handicapped, Santa Fe NM. 505-827-2033
MacLean, Shelley, *Libr Asst,* Pictou Antigonish Regional Library (Trenton), New Glasgow NS. 902-752-5181
MacLellan, A, *Dir,* Humber College, Learning Resource Centre, Rexdale ON. 416-675-3111, Ext 331
MacLennan, Bernadette, *Circ,* College of Cape Breton Library, Sydney NS. 902-539-5300
Macleod, Anne, *Librn,* Canadian Forces Base Cold Lake, Medley Public Library, Base Cold Lake AB. 403-594-4254

MacLeod, Anne S, *Assoc Prof,* University of Maryland, College of Library & Information Services, MD. 301-454-5441
MacLeod, Joan, *Info Officer,* Eastern Ontario Library System, Ottawa ON. 613-238-8457
MacLeod, June F, *Librn,* Gray, Cary, Ames & Frye, Law Library, San Diego CA. 714-236-1661
MacLeod, Ronald K, *Asst Librn,* Canadian Tax Foundation Library, Toronto ON. 416-368-4657
MacIver, A M, *Librn,* County of York Law Association Library, Toronto ON. 416-965-7488
MacMahon, Judith, *Dir,* Logan Library, Logan UT. 801-752-2365
Macmahon, Maureen, *Asst Librn,* Santa Barbara County Law Library, Santa Maria Branch, Santa Maria CA. 805-922-7831
MacMaster, Maxwell, *Librn,* Giles County Public Library, Pulaski TN. 615-363-2720
MacMillan, Gary D, *Dir,* Rochester Institute of Technology, Wallace Memorial Library, Rochester NY. 716-475-2566
MacMillan, Margaret, *In Charge,* Albert-Westmorland-Kent Regional Library (Riverview Public), Riverview NB. 506-389-2631
MacMillan, Martha C, *Librn, On-Line Servs & Bibliog Instr,* United Church of Los Alamos Library, Los Alamos NM. 505-662-2221
MacMorran, Tom, *Rare Bks & Spec Coll,* Transylvania University, Frances Carrick Thomas Library, Lexington KY. 606-233-8225
MacMullen, Barry, *Info Spec,* Institute for Scientific Information, Literature-Search Service Reference Library, Philadelphia PA. 215-386-0100, Ext 1274
MacMullen, Charmaine, *Cat,* Northeastern Bible College, Lincoln Memorial Library, Essex Fells NJ. 201-226-1074, Ext 29, 50
MacMullen, Kenneth E, *Librn,* Plymouth County Law Library Association, Brockton MA. 617-583-8250
MacMullin, Margaret, *Librn,* Environment Canada & Parks Canada, Fortress of Louisbourg Library, Louisbourg NS. 902-733-2280
MacMurray, Christine, *Librn,* Animal Medical Center Library, New York NY. 212-838-8100
MacMurray, Gwen, *Tech Serv,* Hahnemann Medical College & Hospital of Philadelphia, Warren H Fake Library, Philadelphia PA. 215-448-7186
MacNeil, Bruce, *Reader Serv,* University of Waterloo Library, Waterloo ON. 519-885-1211
MacNeil, Katherine, *Librn,* Oklahoma State University Library (Veterinary Medicine Library), Stillwater OK. 405-624-6655
MacNeil, Linda, *Librn,* Eaton Public Library, Eaton CO. 303-454-2189
MacNeill, Daniel S, *Dir,* Charles A Cannon Memorial Library, Concord NC. 704-788-3167
MacNeill, Grace, *Librn,* Contra Costa County Library (El Cerrito Branch), El Cerrito CA. 415-526-7512
MacNeill, Lila, *Librn,* Prince Edward Island Provincial Library (O'Leary Branch), O'Leary PE. 902-892-3504, Ext 54
Macomber, Ann H, *Assoc Dir, Tech Serv & Acq,* Louisiana State University Medical Center Library, New Orleans LA. 504-568-6100
Macomber, Mary M, *Librn,* Berean Bible College Library, Calgary AB. 403-277-5616
Macon, Deborah, *Ch, YA & Media,* Dalton Public Library, Inc, Dalton Regional Library, Dalton GA. 404-278-4507, 278-9247, 226-2039
Macon, Myra, *Assoc Prof,* University of Mississippi, Graduate School of Library & Information Science, MS. 601-232-7440
MacPhail, Ian, *Librn,* Morton Arboretum, Sterling Morton Library, Lisle IL. 312-968-0074
MacPhail, Jessica, *Tech Serv,* Winnetka Public Library District, Winnetka IL. 312-446-5085
MacPherson, A, *Librn,* Okanagan Regional Library District (Winfield Branch), Winfield BC. 604-766-3141
Macpherson, John, *Librn,* Cabrillo College, Library, CA. 408-425-6473
Macpherson, John, *Librn,* Cabrillo College, Robert E Swenson Library, Aptos CA. 408-425-6473, 688-6458
MacPherson, John, *Librn,* University of Western Ontario (Natural Sciences), London ON. 519-679-6601

Macpherson, John, *Asst Dir, Pub Serv,* University of Western Ontario, A B Weldon Library, London ON. 519-679-6191
MacPherson, Lillian, *Asst Librn,* University of Alberta (Weir Memorial Law Library), Edmonton AB. 403-432-5560
MacPherson, Mary, *Media,* Mid-Continent Public Library, Independence MO. 816-836-5200
MacPherson, Sheila, *Supvr,* Huron County Public Library (Walton Branch), Walton ON. 519-887-6633
Macpherson, Wendy, *Math,* University of Waterloo Library, Waterloo ON. 519-885-1211
MacQuarrie, Diane, *Dir,* Halifax City Regional Library, Halifax NS. 902-426-6980
MacQuown, Vivian, *ILL,* University of Kentucky, Margaret I King Library, Lexington KY. 606-257-3801
Macrae, Georgia, *Asst Librn,* University of Calgary Library (Law), Calgary AB. 403-284-5090
MacSween, David, *Dir,* Canada Ministry of Transport, Canadian Coast Guard College Library, Sydney NS. 902-539-2115, Ext 29
Mactavish, Krista, *Ref,* Wicomico County Free Library, Salisbury MD. 301-749-5171
Macumber, Ann, *Dir,* Manilla Public Library, Manilla IA. 712-654-2632
MacVeam, William, *Librn,* Emmanuel & Saint Chad College Library, Saskatoon SK. 306-343-5216
MacVean, Don, *Ref,* Western Illinois University Libraries, Macomb IL. 309-298-2411
MacWatt, Tamsen R, *Dir,* Conference Board, Inc, Information Service Library, New York NY. 212-759-0900
MacWilliams, Mary, *Assoc Dir,* San Francisco State University, J Paul Leonard Library, San Francisco CA. 415-469-1681
MacWilliams, Sylvia E, *Librn,* Southwest Washington Hospitals, Inc (Saint Josephs Community Hospital Medical Library), Vancouver WA. 206-256-2020
MacWilliams, Sylvia E, *Librn,* Southwest Washington Hospitals, Inc (Vancouver Memorial Hospital, R D Wiswall Memorial Library), Vancouver WA. 206-696-5145
Macy, Catherine, *Librn,* Del Norte Public Library, Del Norte CO. 657-2633
Macy, Rebecca, *Ch,* Azusa City Library, Azusa CA. 213-334-0338
MacYeal, Bettina, *Librn,* Case Western Reserve University Libraries (School of Library Science), Cleveland OH. 216-368-3524
Madan, Raj, *Acq,* State University of New York College at Brockport, Drake Memorial Library, Brockport NY. 716-395-2140
Madaus, J Richard, *Assoc Dir, Libr Develop,* Arkansas Library Commission, Arkansas State Library, Little Rock AR. 501-371-1524
Maddalena, Betty, *Librn & On-Line Servs,* Merced Community Medical Center, Medical Library, Merced CA. 209-383-7058
Maddaus, Elsie M, *Librn,* Ballston Spa Public Library, Ballston Spa NY. 518-885-5022
Madden, Carolyn, *Flm,* Silas Bronson Library, Waterbury CT. 203-574-8200
Madden, Charlotte, *Librn,* Alice Lloyd College, Ethel Mueller Barrat Memorial Library, Pippa Passes KY. 606-368-3111
Madden, Doreitha R, *Libr Outreach Servs Supvr,* New Jersey State Library, Trenton NJ. 609-292-6200
Madden, Florice T, *Librn,* Factory Mutual Research Corp, Technical Information Center, Norwood MA. 617-762-4300
Madden, Kay, *Dir,* Columbia College, Kirtley Library, Columbia MO. 314-449-0531, Ext 221
Madden, Margaret E, *Supvr Rpts Libr,* Monsanto Co, Information Center Library, Saint Louis MO. 694-4736
Madden, Michael J, *Bus,* Schaumburg Township Public Library, Schaumburg IL. 312-885-3373
Madden, Michael J, *Dir & Spec Coll,* Schaumburg Township Public Library, Schaumburg IL. 312-885-3373
Madden, Pam, *Tech Serv,* Euclid Public Library, Euclid OH. 216-261-5300
Madden, Sheila J, Texas Christian University (Music), Fort Worth TX. 817-921-7106
Madden, Sister Mary R, *Dir,* Seton Hill College, Reeves Memorial Library, Greensburg PA. 412-834-2200, Ext 357

Madden, William, *Dir,* Los Angeles Pierce College Library, Woodland Hills CA. 213-347-0551, Ext 267
Maddick, Ann, *Librn,* Panora Public Library, Panora IA. 515-755-2529
Maddix, Jeanne, *Chief Librn,* Haut-Saint-Jean Regional Library (Edmundston Public), Edmundston NB. 506-735-4713
Maddocks, Jane F, *Actg Librn,* Maryland Department of Legislative Reference Library, Annapolis MD. 301-269-2871
Maddox, Bennie F, *Librn,* United States Army (United States Army Coastal Engineering Research Center), Fort Belvoir VA. 202-325-7375
Maddox, Lucy J, *Dir,* Spring Arbor College, Hugh A White Library, Spring Arbor MI. 517-750-1200, Ext 234
Maddox, Nova C, *Librn,* United States Air Force (Brooks Air Force Base Library), Brooks AFB TX. 512-536-2634
Maddux, Karen, *Ref & Ch,* Orange Public Library, Orange TX. 713-883-7323
Madera, Milagros, *Librn,* Ponce Public Library, Ponce PR. 809-843-4820
Madigan, Amy, *Librn,* Schweppe, Doolittle, Krug, Tausend & Beezer Library, Seattle WA. 206-223-1600
Madison, Gertrude, *Librn,* Hughesville Area Public Library, Hughesville PA. 717-584-3762
Madisso, Mrs L, *Librn,* Canadian General Electric Co Ltd, Engineering Library, Peterborough ON. 613-742-7711, Ext 439
Madlock, Ida Mae, *Librn,* Southeast Arkansas Regional Library (Charles Dante), Dumas AR. 501-382-5674
Mador, Harriet S, *Librn,* Dallas Public Library (Casa View), Dallas TX. 214-328-4113
Madore, Odette, *Librn,* Bibliotheque Municipale, Chicoutimi PQ. 418-543-6881
Madrid, Josephine, *Librn,* El Mirage Public Library, El Mirage AZ. 602-933-8407
Madrigal, Blanca, *Librn,* San Bernardino Public Library (Villasenor), San Bernardino CA. 714-884-9696
Madrigal, Dana, *Tech Serv,* Colorado State Library, Colorado Department of Education, Denver CO. 303-839-3695
Madru, Helen A, *Librn,* Huntington Public Library, Huntington MA. 413-667-3018
Madsen, Carol, *Tech Serv,* Elko County Library, Elko NV. 702-738-3066
Madsen, Leza, *Librn,* University of Alaska, Matanuska-Susitna Community College Library, Palmer AK. 907-745-4256
Madson, Judy I, *Dir,* Saint Joseph Mercy Hospital, Medical Library, Mason City IA. 515-424-7699
Mady, Johan, *Librn,* Currie, Coopers & Lybrand Ltd Library, Montreal PQ. 514-866-3721, Ext 225
Maeda, Lorraine, *Libr Tech,* Hawaii State Library System (Bond Memorial), Kapaau HI. 808-889-6729
Maedo, Thomas, *Dir,* State Department of Corrections, Kulani Honor Camp Library, Hilo HI. 808-935-2280, Ext 3
Mael, Elaine, *Asst Librn,* Baltimore Hebrew College, Joseph M Meyerhoff Library, Baltimore MD. 301-466-7900, Ext 307
Maeland, Inger F, *ILL,* Schenectady County Public Library, Schenectady NY. 518-382-3500
Maes, William, *Northern Studies,* University of Calgary Library, Calgary AB. 403-284-5954
Maes, William R, *Librn,* Arctic Institute of North America Library, Calgary AB. 403-284-5966
Maez, Susan, *Dir,* Aram Public Library, Delavan WI. 414-728-3111
Maffett, Ann, *English,* Wilkes Community College, Learning Resources Library, Wilkesboro NC. 919-667-7136, Ext 26
Magariel, Dale, *Librn,* Morrison, Hecker, Curtis, Kuder & Parrish, Law Library, Kansas City MO. 816-842-5910
Magaro, John D, *Dir,* Shippensburg State College, Dept of Library Science, PA. 717-532-1472
Magarrell, Betty, *Librn,* Spokane County Library (Medical Lake Branch), Medical Lake WA. 509-299-4891
Magavero, Filomena, *ILL,* State University of New York Maritime College, Stephen B Luce Library, Bronx NY. 212-892-3004, Ext 235
Magee, Clara, *Librn,* Orlando Public Library (Pine Hills), Orlando FL. 305-295-3223

Magee, E, *Librn,* Windsor Public Library (Riverside), Windsor ON. 519-945-7568

Magee, Kim, *Asst Dir,* Prescott Public Library, Prescott WI. 715-262-5544

Magelssen, Gerald, *Media,* Shoreline Community College, Library/Media Center, Seattle WA. 206-546-4663

Mager, Elizabeth K, *Librn,* Merchantville School & Public Library, Merchantville NJ. 609-663-1097

Magers, Odessa L, *Librn,* Howard City Library, Howard KS. 316-374-2039

Maggeroli, Phyllis, *Coordr,* Black Gold Cooperative Library System, Ventura CA. 805-654-2643

Maggeroli, Phyllis, *Coordr,* Total Interlibrary Exchange, (TIE), CA. 805-654-2643

Maggio, Maria Tama, *Librn,* Johns Hopkins University Libraries (Jonas S Friedenwald Library), Baltimore MD. 301-955-3127

Maggrett, Katherine, *Acq,* College of Saint Mary Library, Omaha NE. 402-393-8800, Ext 234, 235

Maggs, Margaret, *Assoc Librn & Reader Serv,* McMaster University, Hamilton ON. 416-525-9140

Maghrabi, Syed Ahsan, *Librn,* Jackson Park Hospital Foundation, Medical Library, Chicago IL. 312-947-7653

Magill, Margaret, *Dir,* Woodbury Public Library, Woodbury NJ. 609-845-2611

Maginnis, Ann, *Student Services,* Newberry College, Wessels Library, Newberry SC. 803-276-5010, Ext 300

Maginnity, Gerald, *Librn,* Solano County Library (John F Kennedy), Vallejo CA. 707-553-5274

Maginnity, Mary Ann, *Ch,* Upper Arlington Public Library, Upper Arlington OH. 614-486-9621

Magistrate, L A, *Mgr,* Olin Corp, Business Information Center, Stamford CT. 203-356-2498

Magladry, George, *Acq,* Humboldt State University Library, Arcata CA. 707-826-3441

Maglione, Louise Cole, *Librn,* Massachusetts Audubon Society, Hathaway Environmental Education Institute Library, Lincoln MA. 617-259-9500, Ext 255

Magnaghi, Russell M, *Archivist-Hist,* National Ski Hall of Fame Research Library, Ishpeming MI. 906-486-9281

Magnan, Overton, *Librn,* Troup Harris Coweta Regional Library (Hogansville Public), Hogansville GA. 404-637-6230

Magner, Mary Jo, *Librn,* Lakeland Community College Library, Mentor OH. 216-951-1000, Ext 226

Magnolia, L R, *Mgr,* TRW Defense & Space Systems Group, Technical Information Center, Redondo Beach CA. 213-536-2631

Magnuson, Maxine G, *Librn,* Ashland Oil, Inc, Executive Headquarters Library, Ashland KY. 606-329-3333

Magnuson, Norris, *Dir,* Bethel Theological Seminary Library, Arden Hills MN. 612-641-6180

Magochy, Jeanne, *Ch,* Northampton Area Public Library, Northampton PA. 215-262-7537

Magoon, Coralie, *Librn,* Chittenden County Regional Planning Commission Library, Essex Junction VT. 802-658-3004

Magrath, Lynn, *Pub Servs,* Pikes Peak Regional Library District, Penrose Public Library, Colorado Springs CO. 303-473-2080

Magri, Kathy, *ILL,* University of San Francisco, Richard A Gleeson Library, San Francisco CA. 415-666-6167

Magrill, Rose Mary, *Prof,* University of Michigan, School of Library Science, MI. 313-764-9376

Magrish, June, *Asst Librn,* A M Kinney, Inc Library, Cincinnati OH. 513-281-2900

Magruder, Kay, *Asst Librn,* Seminole Public Library, Seminole OK. 405-382-4221

Magruder, Marjorie, *Commun Servs,* Fairfield Public Library, Fairfield CT. 203-259-8303

Maguire, James, *Media,* University of Wisconsin-Parkside Library, Kenosha WI. 414-553-2221

Maguire, Jean, *Dir,* Venice Area Public Library, Venice FL. 813-488-9628

Maguire, Mary M, *Dir,* Yeadon Public Library, Yeadon PA. 215-623-4090

Maguire, Rita A, *Librn,* Inmont Corp, Central Research Laboratories, Clifton NJ. 201-365-3400

Mahaffey, Laurie, *Coll Coordr,* Austin Public Library, Austin TX. 512-472-5433

Mahaffey, Patricia, *Librn,* Montezuma Public Library, Montezuma IA. 515-623-3417

Mahalingham, V, *Asst Chief Librn Branches,* Queen's University at Kingston, Douglas Library, Kingston ON. 547-5950 (Admin); 547-6992 (Chief Librn)

Mahan, Peggy, *Librn,* San Antonio Public Library (Carver), San Antonio TX. 512-225-7801

Mahan, Ruth, *Ref,* North Dakota State Library, Bismarck ND. 701-224-2490

Mahanand, Marilyn, *Theatre,* Howard University Libraries, Founders Library, Washington DC. 202-636-7253

Mahaney, Denise R, *Librn,* Vedder, Price, Kaufman & Kammholz, Law Library, Chicago IL. 312-781-2270

Mahaney, Jeffrey P, *Dir,* Town of Tonawanda Public Library, Kenmore NY. 716-873-2861

Mahar, E P, *Librn,* Covington & Burling, Law Library, Washington DC. 202-452-6000, Ext 6150

Maharaj, Kay, *Ser,* Sir Mortimer B Davis Jewish General Hospital, Medical Library, Montreal PQ. 514-342-3111, Ext 325, 376

Maharaj, Subhash, *Librn,* Harrison Memorial Library, Moose Jaw SK. 306-692-6491

Mahardy, Alice, *Librn,* Richfield Springs Public Library, Richfield Springs NY. 315-858-0230

Mahdi, Johnni, *Librn,* Durham County Library (Bragtown), Durham NC. 919-477-6136

Mahe, Carol, *Area Head,* Winnipeg Public Library, Winnipeg MB. 204-985-6450

Mahe, Jean-Claude, *In Charge,* National Film Board of Canada, Edmonton Office Library, Edmonton AB. 403-420-3010

Maher, Catherine A, *Sr Law Librn,* New York State Supreme Court, Ninth Judicial District, Poughkeepsie NY. 914-485-9874

Maher, James, *Librn,* Brooks Institute, School of Photography Library, Santa Barbara CA. 805-969-2291

Maher, Marlys, *Dir,* Hartnell College, Learning Resources Center, Salinas CA. 408-758-8211, Ext 400

Maher, Marlys, *Dir,* Hartnell College, Library-Media Technology, CA. 408-758-8211, Ext 400

Maher, Ruth, *Librn,* Mount Gilead Free Public Library, Mount Gilead OH. 419-946-4046

Maher, Sister Rita, *Asst Librn,* Carlow College, Grace Library, Pittsburgh PA. 412-578-6137

Maher, Sister Walter, *Per,* Incarnate Word College, Saint Pius X Library, San Antonio TX. 512-828-1261, Ext 215

Maher, William, *Librn,* University of Illinois Library at Urbana-Champaign (Newspaper), Urbana IL. 217-333-1509

Mahin, Joyce, *Tech Serv,* Colby Community College, H F Davis Memorial Library, Colby KS. 913-462-3984, Ext 265

Mahin, Joyce, *Bibliog Instr,* Colby Community College, H F Davis Memorial Library, Colby KS. 913-462-3984, Ext 265

Mahler, Mary E, *Bkmobile Coordr,* Hartford Public Library, Hartford CT. 203-525-9121

Mahler, Virginia, *Librn,* Kimble County Library, Junction TX. 915-446-2342

Mahmoodi, Suzanne, *Educ & Res,* Minnesota State Library Agency, Office of Public Libraries & Interlibrary Cooperation, Saint Paul MN. 612-296-2821

Mahon, Cornelia, *Librn,* New York Telephone Co, Legal Department Library, New York NY. 212-395-6158

Mahon, Patricia, *Acq,* Smithtown Library, Smithtown NY. 516-265-2072

Mahon, Sister Noreen, *Tech Serv & Acq,* Saint Xavier College, Byrne Memorial Library, Chicago IL. 312-779-3300, Ext 217

Mahoney, Barbara A, *Dir,* Oxford Public Library, Oxford IN. 317-385-2177

Mahoney, Barbara L, *Librn,* Saint Francis Memorial Hospital, Walter F Schaller Memorial Library, San Francisco CA. 415-775-4321, Ext 226

Mahoney, Diane, *Librn,* Hooker Chemical Corp, Durez Division Library, North Tonawanda NY. 716-696-6314

Mahoney, Ellen J, *ILL & Cat,* Seymour Library, Auburn NY. 315-252-2571

Mahoney, James J, *Asst Dir & ILL,* Saint Joseph's Seminary, Corrigan Memorial Library, Yonkers NY. 914-969-0794

Mahoney, James M, *Dir,* College of the Holy Cross, Dinand Library, Worcester MA. 617-793-3373

Mahoney, Kay, *Dir,* Tolland Public Library, Tolland CT. 203-872-0138

Mahoney, Laura, *Cat,* University of Washington Libraries (Law Library), Seattle WA. 206-543-4089

Mahoney, Murrelle, *Dir,* Murray State Agriculture College Library, Tishomingo OK. 405-371-2371

Mahoney, Ronald J, *Spec Coll,* California State University, Fresno Library, Fresno CA. 209-487-2403

Mahoney, Sue, *Librn,* Genoa City Library, Genoa NE. 402-993-2943

Mahsem, Frances J, *In Charge,* Saint Francis De Sales College Library, Milwaukee WI. 414-744-5026

Maida, Kathy, *ILL,* University of Detroit Library, Detroit MI. 313-927-1090

Maidrano, Carol, *Ref,* Warder Public Library, Springfield OH. 323-8616 & 323-9751

Maier, Catherine, *Librn,* Glacier County Library, Cut Bank MT. 406-873-4572

Maier, Debra L, *Ad,* Addison Public Library, Addison IL. 312-543-3617

Maier, Frances, *Librn,* Reform Temple of East Brunswick Library, East Brunswick NJ. 201-251-9881

Maier, Grace, *Librn,* Littleport Public Library, Littleport IA. 319-245-2148

Maier, Joan M, *Chief Librn,* National Oceanic & Atmospheric Administration, Environmental Research Laboratories Library, Boulder CO. 303-499-1000, Ext 3271

Maier, Rita, *Librn,* Booth Memorial Center, Medical Library, Flushing NY. 212-670-1118

Maier, Rita, *Librn,* Chenango Memorial Hospital, Medical Library, Norwich NY. 607-335-4159

Maier, Robert C, *Dir,* Bedford Free Public Library, Bedford MA. 617-275-9440

Maier, Virginia L, *Librn,* E I Du Pont De Nemours & Co, Inc, Marshall Laboratory Library, Philadelphia PA. 339-6314 & 339-6541

Maihot, Denise, *Librn,* Ordre Des Infirmieres: Infirmiers Du Quebec, Bibliotheque Memoriale Hersey-Upton, Montreal PQ. 514-935-2501, Ext 253

Maillard, Josephine, *Asst Librn & Tech Serv,* Solano County Library, Fairfield-Suisun Community, Fairfield CA. 707-429-6601

Maillard, Margaret, *Librn,* Sainte Rose Regional Library, Sainte Rose du Lac MB. 204-447-2527

Maillet, Lucienne, *Asst Prof,* Long Island University, Palmer Graduate Library School, NY. 516-299-2855 & 299-2856

Maillet, Phyllis, *AV,* Central Massachusetts Regional Library System, Worcester MA. 617-752-3751

Mailloux, Elizabeth, *Librn,* Mobil Research & Development Corp, Central Research Div Library, Princeton NJ. 609-737-3000, Ext 2324

Mailloux, Elizabeth N, *Librn,* Mobil Chemical Co, Plastics Div Library, Macedon NY. 315-986-6375

Mailloux, Heloise, *Librn,* Mercer County Library (Twin Rivers Branch), Twin Rivers NJ. 609-443-1880

Mailloux, Janice, *Bkmobile Coordr,* Morse Institute Library, Natick MA. 617-653-4252

Mailloux, Monique, *Hist,* Universite Laval Bibliotheque, Quebec PQ. 418-656-3344

Mailman, Rosalie, *ILL & Reader Serv,* Kellogg-Hubbard Library, Montpelier VT. 802-223-3338

Maina, William, *Asst Dir Pub Servs,* University of Texas Health Science Center at Dallas Library, Dallas TX. 214-688-3368

Maine, Henry E, *Librn,* Lee County Law Library, Fort Myers FL. 813-334-2111, Ext 230

Maine, John S, *Dir,* Millersville State College, Helen A Ganser Library, Millersville PA. 717-872-5411, Ext 341

Mainelli, Karen, *Librn,* Climax Molybdenum Co, Technical Library, Climax CO. 303-486-2150, Ext 437

Mainland, Loretta, *Ch,* La Porte Public Library, La Porte IN. 219-362-6156

Mainock, Loretta, *Asst Librn,* Adams County Public Library (Thornton), North Glenn CO. 303-287-2514

Mains, Alice, *Librn,* Hay River Library, Hay River NT. 403-874-6531

Maio, Anne, *Ref,* University of Hartford, Mortensen Library, West Hartford CT. 203-243-4265

Maio, Jack C, *Lectr,* Concordia University, Library Studies Program, PQ. 514-482-0320, Ext 324

Maiocca, Claire, *Librn,* Bridgeport Public Library (North), Bridgeport CT. 203-576-7423

Maisonneuve, Nicole, *Librn,* Bibliotheque De La Ville De Montreal (Rosemount), Montreal PQ. 872-4880 (Adult); 872-4881 (Children)

Maistrelli, Gloria, *Librn,* Bibliotheque De La Ville De Montreal (Acadie), Montreal PQ. 514-872-4566

Maitland, Marie, *In Charge,* Miami-Dade Public Library System (Allapattah), Miami FL. 305-638-6086

Maitlen, Jean, *In Charge,* First Presbyterian Church Library, Yakima WA. 509-248-7940

Maiwurm, Virginia, *Librn,* Wayne County Public Library (Dean & Donald Bonnet Memorial), Shreve OH. 216-567-2219

Maizel, Gloria, *Librn,* Bay College of Maryland Library, Baltimore MD. 301-332-1200, Ext 39

Maizell, R E, *In Charge,* Olin Corp, Business & Scientific Technical Information Services, New Haven CT. 203-789-6041

Maizen, Arnold, *Librn,* North Bay Public Library, North Bay ON. 705-474-4830

Majcher, Micheal D, *Mgr,* Xerox Corp, Technical Information Center, Webster NY. 716-422-3505

Majette, Joanne, *Ad,* Morris County Free Library, Whippany NJ. 201-285-6101

Major, Deborah, *Librn,* African American Historical & Cultural Society Library, San Francisco CA. 415-864-1010

Major, Jean A, *Dir,* Northern Illinois University, Founders Memorial Library, De Kalb IL. 815-753-1094

Major, Jean K, *Treasurer,* Conference of Directors of State University Librarians of Illinois, (CODSULI), IL. 815-753-1094

Majure, William, *Dir,* Kemper-Newton Regional Library, Union MS. 601-774-9297

Mak, Betty, *Asst Dir,* Montvale Free Public Library, Montvale NJ. 201-391-5090

Mak, Loretta, *Librn,* Heller, Ehrman, White & McCauliffe Library, San Francisco CA. 415-772-6105

Makar, Ragai, *Librn,* Adelphi University Library (Social Work), Garden City NY. 516-560-8040

Makasone, Hideo, *Bailiff-Librn,* State Supreme Court, Third Circuit Court-Law Library, Hilo HI. 808-961-7337

Makelen, Ben, *Dir,* Financial Executives Research Foundation Library, New York NY. 212-953-0500

Makepeace, Peggy A, *Librn,* Murphy Oil Corp Library, El Dorado AR. 501-862-6411, Ext 371

Maker, M A, *Librn,* Ohio Semitronics, Inc Library, Columbus OH. 614-486-9561

Maker, Mary, *ILL & Ref,* Martins Ferry Public Library, Martins Ferry OH. 614-633-0314

Maki, Gerry, *Librn,* Confederation College of Applied Arts & Technology, Challis Resource Center, Thunder Bay ON. 807-475-6218

Maki, Linda, *Ser,* Jackson-George Regional Library System (Pascagoula City Branch), Pascagoula MS. 601-762-3406

Maki, Marguerite, *Librn,* Mesabi State Junior College Library, Virginia MN. 218-741-9200

Makin, Carol, *Bkmobile Coordr,* Carroll County Public Library, Carrollton KY. 502-732-6352

Makinen, Ruth, *Head,* University of Minnesota Libraries-Twin Cities (Technical Services), Minneapolis MN. 612-373-9975

Makonnen, Linda, *Info Servs Dept,* Ferris State College Library, Big Rapids MI. 616-796-9494, 796-9971, Ext 323

Makosky, Martha M, *Dir,* Carroll County Public Library, Davis Memorial Library, Westminster MD. 301-848-4250, 876-6008

Makray, Jeannine, *Acq,* Santa Barbara Public Library, Santa Barbara CA. 805-962-7653

Makris, Gregory, *Media,* Stetson University, duPont-Ball Library, De Land FL. 904-734-4121, Ext 220

Maksymec, B, *Librn,* Leduc Public Library, Leduc AB. 403-986-2637

MaKsymovych, Anna, *Spec Coll,* Manor Junior College, Basileiad Library, Jenkintown PA. 215-885-2360, Ext 9

Makuc, Anne Marie, *Dir,* Monterey Library, Monterey MA. 413-528-3795

Malach, J, *Tech Serv,* Canadian Land Forces Command Staff College & National Defence College of Canada, Fort Frontenac Library, Kingston ON. 613-545-5829

Malagiere, Mary Otchy, *Area Coordr,* Johnson Free Public Library, Hackensack NJ. 201-343-4169

Malak, Gregory, *Curator,* Will Rogers Memorial Library, Claremore OK. 918-341-0719

Malakoff, Diane, *Librn,* Wilputte Corp Technical Library, Murray Hill NJ. 201-464-5900, Ext 256

Malamud, Edith A, *Circ,* World Affairs Council of Northern California Library, San Francisco CA. 415-982-2541, Ext 21

Malamud, Ida, *Ref,* Yeshiva University Libraries (Hedi Steinberg Library), New York NY. 212-481-0570

Malamud, Judie, *Librn,* University of Pennsylvania Libraries (Veterinary School), Philadelphia PA. 215-243-8895

Malan, H, *Hist & Lit,* Oakland Public Library, Oakland CA. 415-273-3281

Malaney, Sita, *Dir,* Wanaque Public Library, Wanaque NJ. 201-839-4434

Malarky, Mary Claire, *Dir,* Montville Township Public Library, Montville NJ. 201-334-2333

Malatesta, Vivian A, *Librn,* Bolivar County Library (Shelby Public), Shelby MS. 601-398-7748

Malburg, Helen, *Librn,* Buffalo Township Free Public Library, Polo Public Library, Polo IL. 815-946-2713

Malchow, Beatrice, *Dir,* Longmont Public Library, Longmont CO. 303-776-2236

Malcolm, Barbara, *Ref,* Saint John Regional Library, Saint John NB. 506-693-1191

Malcolm, Janet A, *Librn,* Gulf Oil Chemicals Co, Research Library, Merriam KS. 913-722-3200, Ext 236

Malcom, Wilberta M, *Librn,* A E Ames & Co Ltd Library, Toronto ON. 416-867-4057

Malden, Joyce, *Librn,* Municipal Reference Library, Chicago IL. 312-744-4992

Maldonado, Andrea, *Media,* Inter-American University-Fajardo Regional College, Centro de Recursos para el Aprendizaje, Fajardo PR. 809-863-2390

Male, Ilene, *Ad,* Oakville Public Library, Oakville ON. 416-845-3405

Malecki, Clement, *Librn,* Volusia County Public Libraries (Brannon Memorial), New Smyrna Beach FL. 904-252-8374

Malecki, Paul, *Librn,* Southern Tier Library System, Corning NY. 607-962-3141

Malecki, Paul M, *Dir,* Corning Public Library, Corning NY. 607-936-3713

Malecki, Virginia, *Librn,* Utica Observer-Dispatch & Daily Press Library, Utica NY. 315-797-9150

Malek, Barbara, *Librn,* Reuben McMillan Free Library Free Library Association (Austintown), Youngstown OH. 216-792-6982

Malenfant, Nicole, *Libr Asst,* Haut-Saint-Jean Regional Library (Saint Leonard Public), Saint Leonard NB. 506-423-7787

Males, Patricia, *Librn,* Anderson City-Anderson & Stony Creek Township Public Library (Lapel Public), Lapel IN. 317-534-4654

Malesevich, Jacqueline, *Dir,* Mayville Public Library, Mayville WI. 414-387-5400

Malesky, Eunice A, *Librn,* Worcester Hahnemann Hospital (School of Nursing Library), Worcester MA. 617-757-7751, Ext 328

Malette, Frances M, *Librn,* Nashua Corp, Technical Library, Nashua NH. 603-880-2537

Maley, S, *Chief Librn,* Barrie Public Library, Barrie ON. 705-728-1010

Malfer, Mara U, *Librn,* Texas Chiropractic College, Mae Hilty Memorial Library, Pasadena TX. 713-487-1170

Malgeri, Dina G, *Dir,* Malden Public Library, Malden MA. 617-324-0218

Malick, Pat, *Ref,* Charles M White Memorial Public Library, Stevens Point WI. 715-346-2841

Malik, Janet, *Ref,* Peoples Library, New Kensington PA. 412-339-1021

Malik, Nailah, *Librn,* Burroughs Corp Library, Goleta CA. 805-964-6881, Ext 222

Malikyar, Rahella, *Asst Librn,* Safeco Insurance Co Library, Seattle WA. 206-545-5505

Malin, Wanda, *Librn,* Hubbard Public Library, Hubbard OH. 216-534-3512

Malinconico, S Michael, *Coordr Tech Servs,* New York Public Library (The Branch Libraries), New York NY. 212-790-6262

Malinowsky, H Robert, *Assoc Deans,* University of Kansas Libraries, Watson Memorial Library, Lawrence KS. 913-864-3601

Malizia, Betsey, *Cat,* Mayo Foundation (Medical Library), Rochester MN. 507-284-2061

Malkamus, June, *Librn,* Times Library, San Mateo CA. 415-348-4321

Malkin, Audree, *Librn,* University of California Los Angeles Library (Theater Arts), Los Angeles CA. 213-825-4880

Malkin, Mary Ann O'Brian, *Librn,* AB Bookman's Weekly & Yearbook, AB Reference Library, Clifton NJ. 201-772-0020

Malkus, Hubert P, *Chief Librn,* Veterans Administration, Medical Center Library Service, Richmond VA. 804-233-9631, Ext 458

Mallach, Stanley T, *Fromkin Bibliog,* University of Wisconsin Milwaukee, Golda Meir Library, Milwaukee WI. 414-963-4785

Mallard, Emily, *Librn,* Trenton Public Library, Trenton NC. 919-448-4261

Mallard, Lexie, *Ref,* Texas College, D R Glass Library, Tyler TX. 214-593-8311, Ext 37

Mallery, Edith, *Librn,* Albany County Public Library (Rock River Branch), Rock River WY. 307-745-3365

Mallery, Eula I, *Librn,* United States Army (Post Library), Fort Benjamin Harrison IN. 317-542-3101

Mallery, Mary S, *Dir,* Western Maryland Public Libraries, Hagerstown MD. 301-739-3250

Mallett, Bobbie Jean, *Librn,* University of Southern Mississippi (Music Resources Center), Hattiesburg MS. 601-266-4272

Mallett, Miriam, *Ref,* Islip Public Library, Islip NY. 516-581-5933

Mallette, Mildred H, *Dir,* Shaw University, Learning Resources Center, Raleigh NC. 919-755-4930

Malley, Catherine, *Librn,* Wilson Memorial Library, Keota IA. 515-636-3850

Mallino, Katheryne, *Per,* Indiana University of Pennsylvania, Rhodes R Stabley Library, Indiana PA. 412-357-2340

Mallon, Jane, *Acq,* Tucson Public Library, Tucson AZ. 602-791-4391

Mallory, Carlyle, *Ref,* Cabell County Public Library, Western Counties Regional Library System, Huntington WV. 304-523-9451

Mallory, Naomi, *Librn,* Somerset Hospital Library, Somerset NJ. 201-725-4000

Malloy, Dorothea, *ILL,* University of Dallas, William A Blakley Library, Irving TX. 214-438-1123, Ext 328

Malloy, Luke Joseph, *Dir,* University of South Carolina, Beaufort Regional Campus Library, Beaufort SC. 803-524-6153

Mallozzi, Joan, *Librn,* Zotos International Library, Darien CT. 203-655-8911, Ext 304

Malm, Harry, *Librn,* San Jose Public Library (Cambrian), San Jose CA. 408-269-5062

Malmberg, Carol, *Ref & Bibliog Instr,* Los Alamos Scientific Laboratory Libraries, Library Services Group, Los Alamos NM. 505-667-4448

Malmgren, Linda, *Librn,* Holabird & Root Information Center, Chicago IL. 312-726-5960, Ext 357

Malmgren, Terri L, *Librn,* University of California at Davis (Medical Library), Sacramento CA. 916-453-3529

Malmgren, Terri L, *Librn,* University of California, Davis, UC Davis Medical Center Library, Sacramento CA. 916-453-3529

Malnati, Nancy, *Acq,* Elmira College, Gannett-Tripp Learning Ctr, Elmira NY. 607-734-3911, Ext 287

Malo, Agathe, *Librn,* Quebec Ministere Des Affaires Sociales, Informatheque-Montreal, Montreal PQ. 514-873-3695

Malone, Alzada B, *Curator,* Presidential Museum, John Ben Shepperd Jr Memorial Library of the Presidents, Odessa TX. 915-332-7123

Malone, Brad, *Libr Supvr,* Richmond County Library, Rockingham NC. 919-895-4343

Malone, Christy, *Asst Dir,* La Marque Public Library, La Marque TX. 713-935-5821

Malone, J, *Rare Bks & Spec Coll,* University of Windsor, Leddy Library, Windsor ON. 519-253-4232, Ext 198

Malone, Jackie, *Cat,* Fullerton College, William T Boyce Library, Fullerton CA. 714-871-8000
Malone, Jackie, *Assoc Prof,* Fullerton College, Library Technician Program, CA. 714-871-8000, Ext 244
Malone, Janice, *In Charge,* University Presbyterian Church, Ann Inglett Library, Tuscaloosa AL. 205-758-5422
Malone, Margaret, *Asst Librn, ILL & Ch,* Centerville & Center Township Library, Centerville IN. 317-855-5223
Malone, Mrs David, *Br Coordr & Bkmobile Coordr,* Tombigbee Regional Library, Bryan Public Library, West Point MS. 601-494-4872
Malone, Noreen, *Circ Asst,* North Central College Library, Naperville IL. 312-355-0597, 420-3425
Malone, Robert, *Outreach Servs,* North Brunswick Free Public Library, North Brunswick NJ. 201-246-3545
Malone, Rose Mary, *Rare Bks & Spec Coll,* Casper College, Goodstein Foundation Library, Casper WY. 307-268-2269
Malone, Rose Mary, *History of Casper & Natrona County,* Casper College, Goodstein Foundation Library, Casper WY. 307-268-2269
Malone, Sabrina, *ILL,* Jackson District Library, Jackson MI. 517-788-4087
Malone, Virginia, *ILL,* Holyoke Community College Library, Holyoke MA. 413-538-7000, Ext 261
Maloney, Anne V, *Asst Librn,* Saint Louis University (Omer Poos Law Library), Saint Louis MO. 314-658-2755
Maloney, Edmund P, *Librn,* Fordham University (Biology), Bronx NY. 212-933-2233, Ext 309
Maloney, Edmund P, *Librn,* Fordham University (Chemistry, Physics, Mathematics), Bronx NY. 212-933-2233, Ext 523
Maloney, Edmund P, *Circ,* Fordham University, Duane Library, Bronx NY. 212-933-2233, Ext 230, 259
Maloney, Rosemarie, *Acq,* Heidelberg College, Beeghly Library, Tiffin OH. 419-448-2104
Malott, Judy, *YA & Br Coordr,* Mount Pleasant Public Library, Pleasantville NY. 914-769-0548
Malott, Judy, *Librn,* Mount Pleasant Public Library (Valhalla Branch), Valhalla NY. 914-948-2455
Maloy, Darlene, *Librn,* Burlington Public Library, Burlington WA. 206-755-0760
Maloy, Robert, *Dir,* Smithsonian Institution Libraries, Washington DC. 202-381-5496, 381-5421
Malskis, Joseph, *Librn,* Pfizer Inc, Technical Library, Brooklyn NY. 212-573-1242
Malson, Grace H, *Librn,* Pettit & Martin Library, San Francisco CA. 415-434-4000
Maltby, Florence H, *Asst Prof,* Southwest Missouri State University, Dept of Library Science, MO. 417-836-5104
Maltese, Susan Miller, *Libr Serv,* Oakton Community College, Learning Resource Center, Morton Grove IL. 312-967-5120, Ext 331
Maltz, Vivian, *Librn,* Wendell Public Library, Wendell ID. 208-536-6195
Malzer, Marietta, *Archives & Rec,* Oklahoma Department of Libraries, Oklahoma City OK. 405-521-2502
Mamchur, Natalie J, *Librn,* RCA Corp Missile & Surface Radar Div, Harry R Wege Library, Moorestown NJ. 609-541-7000
Mamick, Helen, *Librn,* Stevens Clinic Hospital Library, Welch WV. 304-436-3161
Maminski, Dolores, *Librn,* Enoch Pratt Free Library (Govans), Baltimore MD. 301-396-5430, 396-5395
Mamoulides, Aphrodite, *Supvr Libr,* Shell Development Co, Bellaire Research Center Library, Houston TX. 713-663-2293
Mamrack, Marion, *Dir,* Chartiers-Houston Community Library, Houston PA. 412-745-4300
Manago, Phyllis, *Dir,* Peabody Library, Columbia City IN. 219-244-5541
Manahan, Martin, *Librn,* San Bernardino County Library (Chino Branch), Chino CA. 714-628-1604
Manakos, Peter G, *Dir, Ad & YA,* Lansdale Public Library, Lansdale PA. 215-855-3228
Manaley, Shirley K, *Librn,* IBM Corp System Products Division Library, Endicott NY. 607-755-3223
Manarin, Louis A, *Archivist,* Virginia State Library, Richmond VA. 804-786-8929

Manbach, Carolyn, *Librn,* Jamaica Hospital Medical Library, Jamaica NY. 212-657-1800, Ext 1527
Manbeck, John, *Archivist,* Kingsborough Historical Society Library, Brooklyn NY. 212-934-5122
Manbeck, Virginia, *Librn,* Brooklyn Public Library (Sunset Park), Brooklyn NY. 212-439-8846
Mancall, Jacqueline, *Asst Prof,* Drexel University, School of Library & Information Science, PA. 215-895-2474
Mance, A Florine, *Ref,* Norwin Public Library Association Inc, Irwin PA. 412-863-4700
Mancebo, Olga, *Librn,* Becton, Dickinson Immunodiagnostics, Schwarz-Mann Division Library, Orangeburg NY. 914-359-2700, Ext 32
Mancevice, Mark F, *Admin Supvr,* New England Telephone Learning Center-Resource Center, Marlborough MA. 617-480-1000
Manchak, Barbara, *Ref & On-Line Servs,* Suburban Library System, Burr Ridge IL. 312-325-6640
Manchak, Barbara, *Dir,* Suburban Library System (Information Service), Oak Lawn IL. 312-423-0843
Manchester, Hugh, *Bkmobile Coordr,* Centre County Library & Historical Museum, Bellefonte PA. 814-355-3131
Manchester, Lenore, *Librn,* Rutland Heights Hospital Library, Rutland MA. 617-886-4711
Manchester, Penny Forsyth, *Commun Servs,* North Vancouver District Public Library, North Vancouver BC. 604-984-0286
Mancini, Dorothy, *Bkmobile Coordr,* Schenectady County Public Library, Schenectady NY. 518-382-3500
Mancini, Dorothy, *Librn,* Schenectady County Public Library (Extension (Bookmobile)), Schenectady NY. 518-382-3503
Mancini, Mary, *Ad,* Chula Vista Public Library, Chula Vista CA. 714-427-1151
Mancuso, Jean B, *Archives,* Nassau Community College Library, Garden City NY. 516-222-7400
Mancuyas, Natividad, *Doc,* Chicago State University, Paul & Emily Douglas Library, Chicago IL. 312-995-2254
Mandel, Claire, *Acq & Ref & On-Line Servs,* San Jose City College Library, San Jose CA. 408-298-2181, Ext 410
Mandel, Marie, *Librn,* Teledyne Isotopes, Research Library, Westwood NJ. 201-664-7070
Mandel, Tobyann, *Librn,* Hughes Research Laboratories, Division of Hughes Aircraft Co Research Library, Malibu CA. 213-456-6411, Ext 373
Mandell, Dorothy, *Librn,* Congregation B'nai Jacob, Sisterhood B'nai Jacob Library, Phoenixville PA. 215-933-5550
Mandell, Edward, *Br Coordr,* Fort Worth Public Library, Fort Worth TX. 817-870-7700
Mander, Chris, *Commun Servs,* Oakville Public Library, Oakville ON. 416-845-3405
Manders, R, *Libr Tech,* Queen's University at Kingston (Geography), Kingston ON. 613-547-6193
Mandeville, Joanne, *Librn,* Crane Co, Hydro-Aire Engineering Library, Burbank CA. 213-842-6121, Ext 393
Mandle, Barbara, *Asst Librn,* Emanuel Einstein Free Public Library, Pompton Lakes NJ. 201-835-0482
Mandros, Jean, *Ref,* Satellite Beach Public Library, Satellite Beach FL. 305-773-9411
Mandy, Elsie, *Asst Librn,* Bovey Public Library, Bovey MN. 218-245-3691
Manes, Louise, *Cat,* Tulsa Junior College, Learning Resource Center, Tulsa OK. 918-587-6561, Ext 363
Maness, Bernice, *Librn,* Lexington-Henderson County Public Library, Lexington TN. 901-968-3239
Maneval, Mrs S, *Librn,* Bryan Public Library (West Unity Public), West Unity OH. 419-924-5237
Maney, James, *Asst Librn,* Seminary of Saint Vincent De Paul Library, Boynton Beach FL. 305-732-4424, Ext 44
Manfredi, Jean, *Librn,* Jones Library, Inc (Munson Memorial), South Amherst MA. 413-253-3839
Mangan, Rita A, *Dir,* Stephenson Public Library, Marinette WI. 715-735-5621
Mangan, Shirley, *Librn,* HTB, Inc, Technical Information Center, Oklahoma City OK. 405-525-7451, Ext 304

Mangeim, David S, *Hist & Internal Combustion Tech,* Spotswood Public Library, Spotswood NJ. 201-251-1515
Mangen, Jane, *Librn,* Bradford Public Library, Bradford OH. 513-448-2612
Mangion, Barbara E, *Librn,* Bird Machine Co Library, South Walpole MA. 617-668-0400, Ext 261
Mangion, Marion, *Ref,* Richland County Public Library, Columbia SC. 803-799-9084
Mangrum, Marita, *Cat,* Richardson Public Library, Richardson TX. 214-238-8251
Mangum, Sheila A, *Acq,* University of North Florida Library, Jacksonville FL. 904-646-2553
Mangus, Florence, *Ch,* Boca Raton Public Library, Boca Raton FL. 395-2980 & 395-1110, Ext 285, 286, 336
Manguson, Bev, *Librn,* Marshall-Lyon County Library (Balaton Community), Balaton MN. 507-734-5461
Manheim, Barbara, *Librn,* Suwannee River Regional Library, Seven-County Region (Jasper (Hamilton County)), Live Oak FL. 904-792-2285
Manheim, Theodore, *Head,* Wayne State University Libraries (Kresge Library), Detroit MI. 313-577-4035
Manheimer, Martha, *Prof,* University of Pittsburgh, School of Library & Information Science, PA. 412-624-5230
Maniadis, Helen, *Librn,* Boston Public Library (Orient Heights), East Boston MA. 617-567-2516
Maniadis, Helen C, *Librn,* Boston Public Library (East Boston Branch), East Boston MA. 617-569-0271
Maniece, Olivia S, *Librn & On-Line Servs,* Veterans Administration, Hospital Medical Library, Tuscaloosa AL. 205-553-3760, Ext 263-265
Manifold, Jana, *Librn,* Heavener Public Library, Heavener OK. 918-653-2870
Manikas, Jennifer K, *Librn,* Bainbridge Junior College Library, Bainbridge GA. 912-246-7646
Manikowski, R, *ILL,* Wayne State University Libraries (Science Library), Detroit MI. 313-577-4066
Manitto, Yvonne, *Librn,* San Juan Bautista City Library, San Juan Bautista CA. 408-623-4687
Manix, Teresa, *Librn,* Los Angeles Public Library System (Pacoima Branch), Pacoima CA. 213-899-5203
Mankin, Carole, *Res Projects Librn,* Massachusetts General Hospital (Treadwell Library), Boston MA. 617-726-8600
Mankowitz, Murray, *Dir,* Motion Picture Services Library, Livingston NJ. 201-992-8194
Manley, Charles, *Ref,* Washoe County Library, Reno NV. 702-785-4039
Manley, Cynthia, *Asst Librn,* Seekonk Public Libraries, Seekonk MA. 617-761-6424
Manley, Irwin G, *Dir,* Gibson, Dunn & Crutcher, Law Library, Los Angeles CA. 213-488-7216
Manley, Karin, *Dir,* Waterloo Regional Library, Waterloo ON. 519-885-9590
Manley, Sharri, *Libr Techn,* Oklahoma Department of Human Services, Employees Library, Oklahoma City OK. 405-521-3518
Manley, Will, *Librn,* Galesburg Public Library, Galesburg IL. 309-343-6118
Manlove, Harriet, *Ch,* Tipton County Public Library, Tipton IN. 317-675-2526
Manlove, Patricia A, *Librn,* Western Montana Clinic Library, Missoula MT. 406-721-5600, Ext 343
Mann, Alice, *Librn,* Riverside Congregational Library, Riverside RI. 401-433-2039
Mann, Amy, *Asst Librn,* Skadden, Arps, Slate, Meagher & Flom Library, New York NY. 212-371-6000
Mann, Carolyn, *Asst Consult,* Southwest Iowa Regional Library System, Missouri Valley IA. 712-642-4131
Mann, Cathy, *Asst Librn,* Canon City Public Library, Canon City CO. 303-275-3669
Mann, Darlene C, *Acq,* Western Maryland Public Libraries, Hagerstown MD. 301-739-3250
Mann, Elaine E, *Dir,* National Museum of Racing Inc Library, Saratoga Springs NY. 518-584-0400
Mann, Elizabeth, *Asst Prof,* Florida State University, School of Library Science, FL. 904-644-5775

Mann, Ellen, *Ref,* Boynton Beach City Library, Boynton Beach FL. 732-2624 or 732-8111, Ext 223, 224 & 225

Mann, Jane E, *Bibliog Spec,* Dallas Public Library, Dallas TX. 214-748-9071

Mann, Janice, *Librn,* Michael J Owens Technical College Library, Perrysburg OH. 419-666-0580, Exts 221 & 251

Mann, Joan, *Br Asst,* Timberland Regional Library (Ilwaco Branch), Ilwaco WA. 206-642-3908

Mann, John B, *Media,* Guilford Technical Institute, Learning Resource Center, Jamestown NC. 919-292-1101, 454-1126

Mann, Joyce A, *Librn,* United States Fish & Wildlife Service, National Fisheries Center Library, Kearneysville WV. 304-725-8461

Mann, Kathleen A, *Dir,* Bartow Public Library, Bartow FL. 813-533-4985

Mann, Kathy, *Acq,* Fort Vancouver Regional Library, Vancouver WA. 206-695-1561

Mann, Linda K, *Mus Dir,* J K Ralston Museum and Art Center, Willo Ralston Memorial Library for Historical Research, Sidney MT. 406-482-3500

Mann, Lorne C, *In Charge,* West Canadian Graphic Industries Ltd, Commonwealth Microfilm Library, Willowdale ON. 416-497-9473

Mann, Mary Jane, *Libr Technician,* San Diego County Library (Encinitas Branch), Encinitas CA. 714-753-7376

Mann, Peggy K, *Admin Librn,* United States Marine Corps (Air Station Library), Cherry Point NC. 919-466-3571, 466-3552

Mann, Ruth, *Rare Bks,* Mayo Foundation (Medical Library), Rochester MN. 507-284-2061

Mann, Sallie E, *Acq,* East Carolina University, J Y Joyner Library, Greenville NC. 919-757-6514

Mann, Shirley, *Librn,* Development Engineering Inc Library, Rifle CO. 303-625-2100

Mann, Thomas L, *Slavic & Soc Sci,* Northwestern University Library, Evanston IL. 312-492-7658

Mann, Walter, *Ref & Bibliog Instr,* Hanover College, Duggan Library, Hanover IN. 812-866-2151, Ext 333

Mann, Jr, Charles W, *Spec Coll,* Pennsylvania State University, Fred Lewis Pattee Library, University Park PA. 814-865-0401

Mann, Jr, Thomas, *Asst Dir,* California State University, Long Beach, University Library, Long Beach CA. 213-498-4047

Mannan, Susan, *Chairperson,* Indiana Vocational Technical College, Library Resource Aide Program, IN. 317-635-6100, Ext 41

Mannan, Susan, *Dir,* Indiana Vocational Technical College, Indianapolis, Learning Resources Center, Indianapolis IN. 317-635-6100, Ext 41

Manner, Kathy, *ILL,* SCM Corporation, Dwight P Joyce Research Center, Technical Info Services, Strongsville OH. 216-771-5121, Ext 2260

Mannes, Kathy A, *Ref,* Kansas Newman College, Ryan Library, Wichita KS. 316-942-4291, Ext 40

Manninen, Nancy, *Librn,* Portage View Hospital, Health Science Library, Hancock MI. 906-482-1122, Ext 253

Manning, Beverly, *Univ Libr,* University of Connecticut at Hartford (Undergratuate Library), West Hartford CT. 203-523-4841, Ext 317

Manning, Dorothy, *Tech Serv & Cat,* Chatham-Effingham-Liberty Regional Library, Savannah Public Library, Savannah GA. 912-234-5127

Manning, Dorothy C, *Dir & Acq,* Keuka College, Lightner Library, Keuka Park NY. 315-536-4411, Ext 224, 248 & 338

Manning, Eleanor, *Librn,* Thomas County Library, Thedford NE. 308-645-2237

Manning, Glen, *Dir,* Periodical Audio Library, Toronto ON. 416-960-1177

Manning, Gordon, *Asst Librn,* Oregon Historical Society Library, Portland OR. 503-222-1741

Manning, Helen, *On-Line Servs,* Florida State University, Robert Manning Strozier Library, Tallahassee FL. 904-644-5211

Manning, Helen, *Asst Librn,* Waverly Free Library, Waverly NY. 607-565-9341

Manning, James F, *Circ,* Salem Public Library, Salem MA. 617-744-0860

Manning, Jeannene, *Commun Relations,* Louisville Free Public Library, Louisville KY. 502-584-4154

Manning, Jo, *Librn,* Reader's Digest Association, General Books Division Library, New York NY. 212-972-8452

Manning, John, *Media,* Columbus Technical Institute, Educational Resources Center, Columbus OH. 614-227-2463

Manning, Kathryn, *Librn,* Wadley Institutes of Molecular Medicine, Research Institute Library, Dallas TX. 214-251-8111

Manning, Leslie A, *Tech Serv,* University of Colorado at Colorado Springs, Library, Colorado Springs CO. 303-593-3296

Manning, M, *Pharmacy,* State University of New York at Buffalo (Health Sciences), Buffalo NY. 716-831-5465

Manning, M, *Pharm,* State University of New York at Buffalo, University Libraries, Buffalo NY. 716-636-2965

Manning, Martha, *Ref,* State University of New York at Buffalo (Health Sciences), Buffalo NY. 716-831-5465

Manning, Mary J, *Ref,* Rhode Island Junior College, Knight Campus Library, Warwick RI. 401-825-2215

Manning, Robert L, *Librn,* Cherokee Regional Library (Talking Book Center), LaFayette GA. 404-638-2992

Manning, Robert N, *Mgr Tech Info Serv,* Hercules Inc (Research Center Library), Wilmington DE. 302-995-3484

Manning, Rosalie, *Librn,* American Institute of Crop Ecology Library, Silver Spring MD. 301-589-4185

Manning, Suzanne, *Asst Dir,* North Chicago Public Library, North Chicago IL. 312-689-0125

Mannion, Mary, *Asst Librn,* Manufacturers Hanover Trust Co, Corporate Library: Financial Library Division, New York NY. 212-350-4733

Manns, Elizabeth, *Librn,* Wallingford Public Library (Childrens Library), Yalesville CT. 203-269-3688

Manocchio, Rita F, *Librn,* Leesona Corp Library, Warwick RI. 401-739-7100

Manojlovich, S, *On-Line Servs,* University of Saskatchewan Library, Saskatoon SK. 306-343-4216

Manor, Blanche, *Librn,* Castle Junior College Library, Windham NH. 603-893-6111

Manos, Eleanor, *Librn,* United States Navy (Naval Construction Battalion Center Library), Port Hueneme CA. 805-982-4411

Manougian, Joy, *Regional Coordr,* San Diego County Library (Region C), San Diego CA. 714-565-5100

Manovill, S, *Circ,* University of Prince Edward Island, Robertson Library, Charlottetown PE. 902-892-1243

Mansbridge, John, *Dir,* Selkirk College Library, Castlegar BC. 604-365-7121, Ext 216

Manseau, Pierre, *Prof,* College de Maisonneuve, Techniques de la Documentation, PQ. 514-254-7131

Mansell, Jean E, *Librn,* Lebanon Public Library, Lebanon NH. 603-448-2459

Mansfield, Doug, *TV Technician,* Mississippi Gulf Coast Junior College, Jackson County Campus Library, Gautier MS. 601-497-4313, Ext 226, Libr; 497-4313, Ext 255 Media Ctr

Mansfield, Juliet I, *Librn,* Sturdy Memorial Hospital, Health Sciences Library, Attleboro MA. 617-222-5200, Ext 3167

Mansfield, Lola, *Assoc Librn,* Culbertson Public Library, Culbertson NE. 308-278-2341

Mansfield, Mrs R R, *Dir,* Blanding Public Library, Rehoboth MA. 617-252-4236

Manson, B, *Asst Dir,* Calgary Public Library, Calgary AB. 403-268-2880

Manson, Connie J, *Sr Librn,* Washington State Department of Natural Resources, Division of Geology & Earth Resources Library, Olympia WA. 206-753-6183

Manson, Elaine, *Librn,* Volusia County Public Libraries (Hopkins Memorial), Lake Helen FL. 904-252-8374

Manson-Smith, P, *Librn,* University of Toronto Libraries (Faculty of Architecture), Toronto ON. 416-978-2649

Mansur, Lena, *Librn,* Wilder Memorial Library, Weston VT. 802-824-6687

Mantell, Nancy, *Librn,* Westchester Reform Temple Library, Scarsdale NY. 914-723-7727

Manthorne, Katherine F, *Cat,* Framingham State College, Henry Whittemore Library, Framingham MA. 617-620-1220, Ext 273

Manthorne, M Jane, *Staff Off for Special Projects,* Boston Public Library, Eastern Massachusetts Library System, Boston MA. 617-536-5400

Mantz, Joan, *Asst Librn,* Bayard Public Library, Bayard IA. 712-651-2238

Mantzell, Lois B, *Librn,* Texaco, Inc, Jefferson Chemical Co, Inc Technical Literature Section Library, Austin TX. 512-465-6543

Mantzoros, Tessie, *Librn,* McGraw-Hill, Inc (Business Week Magazine Library), New York NY. 212-997-1221

Manuel, Frances, *Libr Tech,* Hawaii State Library System (Molokai Branch), Molokai HI. 808-553-5483

Manuel, Melbarose, *Assoc Librn & Cat,* Southern University Library (Law Library), Baton Rouge LA. 504-771-3776

Manuma, Eddie, *Media,* American Samoa-Office of Library Services, Pago Pago, Samoa PI. 633 5869

Manville, Sarah, *Bkmobile Coordr,* Russell Public Library, Middletown CT. 203-347-2528

Manwaring, Stanley, *Librn,* Church of the Redeemer, King Library, Andalusia PA. 215-639-4387

Manwarren, Verl L, *Dir,* Ida Long Goodman Memorial Library, Saint John Public Library, Saint John KS. 316-549-3227

Manwiller, Linda, *Dir,* Whitmoyer Community Library, Myerstown PA. 717-866-2800

Many, Douglas, *On-Line Servs,* Rockefeller University Library, New York NY. 212-360-1000

Manz, Mary C, *Ch,* Norwin Public Library Association Inc, Irwin PA. 412-863-4700

Manzano, Perla, *Libr Technician,* San Diego County Library (Lincoln Acres), National City CA. 714-477-3386

Maounis, John, *Photog,* National Maritime Museum, J Porter Shaw Library, San Francisco CA. 415-556-8177

Mapes, Dorothy, *Librn,* Young Men's Library Association, Ware MA. 413-967-5491

Maples, Carol, *Asst Librn,* United States Air Force (Air Force Flight Test Center Technical Library), Edwards AFB CA. 805-277-3606, Ext 2218

Maples, Cheryl, *Librn,* Stanhope Public Library, Stanhope IA. 515-826-3259

Maples, Esther, *Librn,* Northumberland Union Public Library (Grafton Branch), Trenton ON. 613-392-9445

Mar, Norma B, *Librn,* Chemists' Club Library, New York NY. 212-679-6383, Ext 81

Marafioti, Armida, *Librn,* Emory A Chase Memorial Law Library, Catskill NY. 518-943-3130

Marasco, Bernadette, *Info Specialist,* International Paper Co, Corp Research Center, Technical Information Center, Tuxedo Park NY. 914-351-2101, Ext 207

Maratos, Daniel, *Ref,* Herbert H Lehman College Library, Bronx NY. 212-960-8577, 960-8582

Marattay, Catherine, *Librn,* Spencer County Library, Taylorsville KY. 502-477-8137

Maravilla, Virginia, *Ch,* Crown Point-Center Public Library, Crown Point IN. 219-663-0270

Marble, Bea, *Librn,* Onondaga County Public Library System (Art & Music), Syracuse NY. 315-473-2702

Marble, Carol, *Mgt,* QL Systems Limited (Toronto Branch), Toronto ON. 416-862-7656

Marble, Lawrence, *Educ,* Temple University of the Commonwealth System of Higher Education, Samuel Paley Library, Philadelphia PA. 215-787-8231

Marble, Mrs Welcome S, *Librn,* Alma M Carpenter Public Library, Sour Lake TX. 713-287-3592

Marburger, Linda L, *Tech Serv,* United States Army (Morris Swett Library), Fort Sill OK. 405-351-4525, 351-4477

Marcantel, Marie, *Librn,* Marseilles Public Library, Marseilles IL. 815-795-4437

Marcellus, June, *Dir,* Central College Library, McPherson KS. 316-241-0723

Marcellus, Rhea, *Librn,* Marathon Centennial Public Library, Marathon ON. 807-229-0740

March, Freida, *Librn,* Idaho State Historical Society Libraries (Genealogical Library), Boise ID. 208-334-2305

MARCH

March, Maria, *Librn,* Middleton Public Library, Cowden Memorial Library, Middleton ID. 208-585-3931

Marchant, Hilda, *Tech Serv,* Municipal Reference Library, Chicago IL. 312-744-4992

Marchant, Maurice P, *Dir,* Brigham Young University, School of Library & Information Sciences, UT. 801-378-2976

Marchbanks, Rose, *ILL,* Lompoc Public Library, Lompoc CA. 805-736-3477

Marchi, Marcy, *Librn,* Playboy Enterprises Inc Library, Chicago IL. 312-751-8000, Ext 2796

Marchi, Margaret M, *Dir,* Woodstock Public Library, Woodstock IL. 815-338-0542

Marchiafava, Anna, *Asst Dir, Ch & Bkmobile Coordr,* West Baton Rouge Parish, Port Allen LA. 504-343-3484

Marchive, Ina C, *Librn,* Avoyelles Parish Library (Bunkie Branch), Bunkie LA. 318-253-7559

Marchman, Mary, *Librn,* Nicholas P Sims Library, Waxahachie TX. 214-937-2671

Marchman, Watt P, *Dir,* Rutherford B Hayes Library, Fremont OH. 419-332-2081

Marciano, Marjorie, *Librn,* New York Public Library (Woodstock), New York NY. 212-665-6255

Marcil, Thomas, *Circ,* University of South Carolina, Thomas Cooper Library, Columbia SC. 803-777-3142

Marciniak, Lorraine, *ILL,* Villa Maria College of Buffalo Library, Buffalo NY. 716-896-0703

Marcinko, Dorothy, *Acq,* Auburn University, Ralph Brown Draughton Library, Auburn AL. 205-826-4500

Marcolina, Ruth, *Dir,* State University of New York (Health Sciences Center Library), East Setauket NY. 516-246-2512

Marconi, Barbara, *Acq & Co-op Librn,* Hiawathaland Library Cooperative, Sault Sainte Marie MI. 906-632-9331

Marconi, Joseph V, *Dir & Spec Coll,* Bayliss Public Library, Sault Sainte Marie MI. 906-632-9331

Marconi, Joseph V, *Dir,* Wayne County Public Library, Wooster OH. 216-262-0916

Marcos, Hortensia, *Circ,* University of Kansas Libraries (School of Law), Lawrence KS. 913-864-3025

Marcott, Lawrence E, *Dir,* Hot Springs County Library, Thermopolis WY. 307-864-3663

Marcotte, Fred, *Dir,* University of Cincinnati Libraries (Clermont General & Technical College Library), Batavia OH. 513-732-2990, Ext 13

Marcoux, Catherine L, *Librn,* Sperry-Rand Corp, Sperry Division Engineering Library, Lake Success NY. 516-574-1001

Marcoux, Jean-Marie, *Ch,* Bibliotheque De La Ville De Montreal (Gatineau), Montreal PQ. 514-872-2136

Marcum, Joyce, *Librn,* Owsley County Library, Booneville KY. 606-593-5700

Marcum, Julie, *Librn,* Tiskilwa Township Library, Tiskilwa IL. 815-646-4511

Marcum, Louise, *Dir,* Oconee County Library, Walhalla SC. 803-638-5837

Marcus, Richard W, *Dir,* Spertus College of Judaica, Norman & Helen Asher Library, Chicago IL. 312-922-9012, Ext 50

Marcus, Ronald, *Librn,* Stamford Historical Society Library, Stamford CT. 203-323-1975

Marcus, Terry, *Librn,* Wisconsin Department of Transportation, Research Center Library, Milwaukee WI. 414-224-4889

Marcy, Jean F, *Dir,* Saint Johnsbury Athenaeum Inc Library, Saint Johnsbury VT. 802-748-8291

Marden, Mary Jane, *Ref,* Saint Petersburg Junior College, Michael M Bennett Library, Clearwater FL. 813-441-0681, Ext 2616

Marden, Nancy J, *Librn,* Gale Library, Newton NH. 603-382-4691

Mardfin, Jean Kadooka, *Dir,* Municipal Reference & Records Center, Honolulu HI. 808-523-4577, 523-4578

Mardorf, Helen, *Asst Dir & Ch,* Webster Groves Public Library, Webster Groves MO. 314-961-3784

Marek, Stephen P, *Newspaper & Microtext,* Northwestern University Library, Evanston IL. 312-492-7658

Marek, Vivian, *Cat,* Scotch Plains Public Library, Scotch Plains NJ. 201-322-5007

Marengo, Patricia, *Librn,* Otego Free Library, Otego NY. 607-988-6661

Maret, Lucy, *Librn,* Texaco Inc, Law-Tax Library, White Plains NY. 914-253-4000, Ext 3383

Maret, Lyn, *Librn,* United States Air Force (Base Library), Blytheville AFB AR. 501-763-3931, Ext 7286

Margeton, Steve, *Librn, On-Line Servs & Bibliog Instr,* Steptoe & Johnson Library, Washington DC. 202-862-2606

Margo, Madeline J, *Ch,* Reuben McMillan Free Library Free Library Association, Public Library of Youngstown & Mahoning County, Youngstown OH. 216-744-8636

Margoles, Pat, *Acq,* Long Beach Public Library System, Long Beach CA. 213-436-9225

Margolis, Bernard A, *Dir,* Monroe County Library System, Monroe MI. 313-241-5277

Margolis, Bernard A, *Dir,* Southeast Michigan Regional Film Library, Monroe MI. 313-241-5277

Margolis, Ralph, *Librn,* Community College of Allegheny County, Boyce Campus Library, Monroeville PA. 412-327-1327, Ext 312

Margoshes, Miriam, *Librn,* Pergamon Press Inc Research Library, Elmsford NY. 914-592-9141, Ext 7, 8

Maria, Sister Regina, *Dir,* Chestnut Hill College, Logue Library, Philadelphia PA. 215-247-4210, Ext 238

Marie, Sister Bernice, *Librn,* Gwynedd-Mercy College, Lourdes Library, Gwynedd Valley PA. 215-646-7300, Ext 244

Marie, Sister Florence, *Dir,* Immaculata College Library, Immaculata PA. 215-647-4400, Ext 229

Marie, Sister Francis, *Librn,* Saint Joseph Hospital (Medical Library), Baltimore MD. 301-828-5800

Marie, Sister Sally, *Dir,* De Lourdes College Library, Des Plaines IL. 312-298-6760

Marier, Linda, *Media,* Letourneau College, Margaret Estes Library, Longview TX. 214-753-0231, Ext 230

Marifke, Linda, *Asst Librn,* Quarles & Brady, Law Library, Milwaukee WI. 414-277-5000

Marin, Irwin, *Asst Prof,* University of Pittsburgh, School of Library & Information Science, PA. 412-624-5230

Marin, Regina F, *Doc,* University of Puerto Rico Library, Jose M Lazaro Memorial Library, Rio Piedras PR. 809-764-0000, Ext 3296

Marine, Barbara R, *Librn,* Washington Public Library, Washington IL. 309-444-2241

Marinella, Dorothy, *Acq,* Carnegie Library of Pittsburgh, Pittsburgh PA. 412-622-3100

Marini, Miriam, *Ch,* Baraboo Public Library, Baraboo WI. 608-356-6166

Marinus, Kim, *Dir,* Bryant Free Library, Cummington MA. 413-634-8884

Marinus, Kim, *ILL,* Smith College Library, Northampton MA. 413-584-2700, Ext 501

Marion, C, *Librn,* Sturgeon Falls Public Library, Sturgeon Falls ON. 705-753-2620

Marion, Donald, *Librn,* University of Minnesota Libraries-Twin Cities (Physics), Minneapolis MN. 612-373-3362

Marion, Mrs Claude, *Dir,* Adams County Library, Minnie Erlandson Library, Hettinger ND. 701-567-2741

Maripuu, Reet, *Int Orgns Doc,* University of Michigan (Law Library), Ann Arbor MI. 313-764-9322

Maris, Mrs Shelby, *Librn,* Acadia Parish Library (Mermentau Branch), Mermentau LA. 318-788-1880

Marish, Thelma, *Coordr & Chief Cataloger,* Grambling State University, A C Lewis Memorial Library, Grambling LA. 318-247-6941, Ext 220

Maritz, Cynthia A, *Librn,* Krupnik & Associates, Inc, Information Center, Saint Louis MO. 314-862-9393

Mark, Audrey, *Tech Serv & Cat,* North Central Regional Library System, Sudbury ON. 705-675-6467

Mark, Dorothy, *Librn,* Aurelia Public Library, Aurelia IA. 712-434-5330

Mark, Karen, *AV,* Newmarket Public Library, Newmarket ON. 416-895-5196

Mark, Ruth, *In Charge,* California Department of Industrial Relations, Division of Labor Statistics & Research Library, San Francisco CA. 415-557-2184

Mark, Timothy, *Librn,* York Regional Library (Fredericton Public), Fredericton NB. 506-454-2431

Markarian, Rita, *Literacy Volunteers Project Coordr,* Mid-Hudson Library System, Poughkeepsie NY. 914-471-6060

Markcom, Jimmy, *Librn,* Chicago Public Library (Tuley Park), Chicago IL. 312-846-7608

Marke, Julius J, *Librn,* New York University (Library of the School of Law), New York NY. 212-598-3040

Markel, J Louise, *Librn,* Oak Ridge Associated Universities (Institute for Energy Analysis), Oak Ridge TN. 615-576-3199

Markette, Anne E, *Tech Serv,* Appomattox Regional Library, Maud Langhorne Nelson Library, Hopewell VA. 804-458-6329

Marketti, Diane, *Asst Dir,* Eckhart Public Library, Auburn IN. 219-925-2414

Markey, Raymond, *Librn,* New York Public Library (Melrose), New York NY. 212-588-0110

Markey, Sister Joan, *ILL & Ref,* University of Saint Thomas, Robert Pace & Ada Mary Doherty Library, Houston TX. 713-522-7911, Ext 325

Markey, William, *Performing Arts, Fine Arts & French & Italian Studies,* University of Massachusetts at Amherst Library, Amherst MA. 413-545-0284

Markham, Ann, *Librn,* Illinois Masonic Medical Center School of Nursing, Nursing Education Library, Chicago IL. 312-975-1600, Ext 798

Markham, Charlotte, *Program & Tech Servs,* East Hampton Public Library, East Hampton CT. 203-267-2635

Markham, Dewey, *Librn,* Weinstein Library, New York NY. 212-598-3303

Markham, Susan D, *Libr Technician,* United States Bureau of Mines, Tuscaloosa Metallurgy Research Center Library, University AL. 205-758-0491, Ext 26

Markiewicz, James, *On-Line Servs,* University of Northern Iowa Library, Cedar Falls IA. 319-273-2737

Markin, Donald, *Librn,* United States Department of Labor Library (Main Law Library), Washington DC. 202-523-6988

Markley, Dorothy, *Librn,* United States Navy (Naval Training Center Library), San Diego CA. 714-225-5470

Marklund, Aili, *ILL,* Seattle Public Library, Seattle WA. 206-625-2665

Marko, Lynn F, *Asst, Personnel & Staff Develop,* University of Michigan Libraries (University Library), Ann Arbor MI. 313-764-9356

Markoe, Ronny, *Dir,* Cooperative Information Network, (CIN), CA. 415-329-8287

Markowitz, Marianne, *Asst Dir,* University of Wisconsin-Milwaukee, Golda Meir Library, Milwaukee WI. 414-963-4785

Markowitz, Shelley D, *Asst Librn,* General Motors Corp (Legal Staff Library), New York NY. 212-486-5090

Markowsky, Juliet, *Ch,* Greenburgh Public Library, Elmsford NY. 914-682-5265

Marks, Bruce J, *Exhibits Librn,* Nashua Public Library, Nashua NH. 603-883-4141, 883-4142

Marks, Cicely P, *Tech Servs Specialist,* Veterans Administration (Library Division), Washington DC. 202-389-2781

Marks, Coralyn, *Dir,* Northwest General Hospital, Health Science Library, Milwaukee WI. 414-447-8599, 447-8600

Marks, Eunice, *Librn,* South Beloit Public Library, South Beloit IL. 815-389-2495

Marks, J Lynn, *Orientations,* Phoenix College Library, Phoenix AZ. 602-264-2492, Ext 621

Marks, Kenneth, *Publ Serv,* University of Tennessee, Knoxville, James D Hoskins Library, Knoxville TN. 615-974-0111

Marks, Rose, *Librn,* Sacramento Public Library (Oak Park), Sacramento CA. 916-455-8522

Marks, Ruth, *Anthrop, Archaeol & Relig,* Ector County Library, Odessa TX. 915-332-0633

Marks, Ruth, *Acq,* Waldwick Public Library, Waldwick NJ. 201-652-5104

Marks, Sarajean, *Video,* Tucson Public Library, Tucson AZ. 602-791-4391

Marks, Susan, *Circ,* University of Iowa Libraries, Iowa City IA. 319-353-4450

Marks, III, George P, *Dir,* Union College, MacKay Library-Learning Resource Center, Cranford NJ. 201-276-2600, Ext 244

Markson, Eileen, *Art & Archaeol,* Bryn Mawr College, Canaday Library, Bryn Mawr PA. 215-645-5279

Markush, Catherine, *ILL,* Hebrew Union College-Jewish Institute of Religion, The Klau Library, New York NY. 212-674-5300
Markuson, Barbara Evans, *Exec Dir,* Indiana Cooperative Library Services Authority, (INCOLSA), IN. 317-926-3361, 923-7936
Markwood, Carolyn K, *Librn,* E I Du Pont De Nemours & Co, Inc, Spruance Research Laboratory Library, Richmond VA. 804-743-2616
Marler, Lynn, *Librn,* Alberta Department of Municipal Affairs Library, Edmonton AB. 403-427-4829
Marley, Bonita C, *Dir,* Mooresville Public Library, Mooresville IN. 317-831-3820
Marley, Carol Anne, *Lectr,* Concordia University, Library Studies Program, PQ. 514-482-0320, Ext 324
Marley, Marie, *Cent Pub Serv & ILL,* Fresno County Free Library, Fresno CA. 209-488-3191
Marley, Marie, *Supvr,* Fresno County Free Library (Central), Fresno CA. 204-488-3191
Marlin, Joyce, *Librn,* Contra Costa County Library (Concord Branch), Concord CA. 415-685-7041
Marling, Betty A, *Acq,* Maryville College, Father Edward Dowling Memorial Library, Saint Louis MO. 314-434-4100, Ext 241
Marlow, Grace L, *Librn,* Scott County Public Library, Oneida TN. 615-569-8634
Marlow, Hazel, *Librn,* Foard County Library, Crowell TX. 817-684-4421
Marlow, Marcie, *Librn,* Louisville Free Public Library (Okolona), Louisville KY. 502-964-3515
Marlowe, Carol, *Spec Coll,* Rahway Free Public Library, Rahway NJ. 201-388-0761
Marlowe, Constance, *Outreach Librn,* Wilson County Public Library, Wilson NC. 919-237-3818
Marlowe, Michael, *Librn,* West Virginia State Planning Library, Charleston WV. 304-348-2246
Marney, Dean, *Ch & YA,* North Central Regional Library, Wenatchee WA. 509-663-1117
Maronde, Doreen, *Dept Head,* Kirkwood Community College, Library Services, IA. 319-398-5538
Maroney, Patricia, *Asst Dir & Ref,* Chattanooga-Hamilton County Bicentennial Library, Chattanooga TN. 615-757-5320
Maroon, Ellie, *Dir,* Altamont Public Library, Altamont IL. 618-483-5457
Maroon, Lois, *ILL,* Clearwater Public Library, Clearwater FL. 813-462-6800
Marose, Doris, *Librn,* Memorial Hospital, Medical Library, Sarasota FL. 813-953-1238
Marose, Georgianne, *Cat,* Hometown Public Library, Jack R Ladwig Memorial Library, Hometown IL. 312-636-0997
Marousek, Kathy, *Ref,* Fairleigh Dickinson University (School of Dentistry), Hackensack NJ. 201-836-6300, Ext 578
Maroush, Anne, *Librn,* Geauga County Public Library (Middlefield Branch), Middlefield OH. 216-632-1961
Marovich, Ida, *Tech Serv,* Linn-Benton Community College, Learning Resource Center, Albany OR. 503-928-2361, Ext 330
Marowitz, Eunice, *Dir,* Highland Park Public Library, Highland Park NJ. 201-572-2750
Marple, Elmer, *Chmn,* United Presbyterian Church, First Meridian Heights Library, Indianapolis IN. 317-283-1305
Marqua, Nancy, *Librn,* Public Library of Annapolis & Anne Arundel County Inc (Odenton), Odenton MD. 301-674-6871
Marquardt, Jack, *In Charge,* Smithsonian Institution Libraries (Access Services), Washington DC. 202-381-5382
Marquardt, Steve, *Tech Serv,* Ohio University, Vernon R Alden Library, Athens OH. 614-594-5228
Marquardt, W E, *Dir,* Westminster College, Reeves Memorial Library, Fulton MO. 314-642-6793
Marquardt, William E, *Dir,* Winston Churchill Memorial Library, Fulton MO. 314-642-6648
Marquart, Dorothy C, *Dir,* John Graham Newville Public Library, Newville PA. 717-776-5900
Marquart, Margaret M, *Cat,* Enoch Pratt Free Library, Baltimore MD. 301-396-5430, 396-5395
Marquess, Barbara, *Librn,* Orlando Public Library (West Orange), Winter Garden FL. 305-656-4582

Marquez, Myriam, *Circ,* Puerto Rico Junior College (Cupey Campus Learning Resources Center), Rio Piedras PR. 809-765-1716
Marquis, Julien, *Tech Serv,* College de Rimouski (CEGEP) Bibliotheque, Rimouski PQ. 418-723-1880
Marquis, Rollin P, *Dir,* Dearborn Department of Libraries, Henry Ford Centennial Library, Dearborn MI. 313-271-1000
Marr, Jan, *Talking Bk Librn,* Prescott Public-Yavapai County Library System, Prescott AZ. 602-445-8110
Marr, Judy, *Info Specialist & Online Search Coordr,* Babcock & Wilcox Research Center Library, Alliance OH. 216-821-9110, Ext 531
Marr, Lisa, *Cat,* Southern Connecticut State College, Hilton C Buley Library, New Haven CT. 203-397-4505
Marr, Lottie, *Bkmobile Coordr,* Green County Public Library, Greensburg KY. 502-932-7081
Marr, Ruth C, *Librn,* McCuistion Regional Medical Center, L P McCuistion Library, Paris TX. 214-785-7621, Ext 150
Marraffino, Patricia, *Ch & YA,* Medway Public Library System, Medway MA. 617-533-2461
Marredeth, Gail, *Circ,* Cleveland State University Libraries, Cleveland OH. 216-687-2486
Marrer, Kenneth P, *Media,* Franklin Pierce College Library, Rindge NH. 603-899-5111, Ext 215, 216
Marriott, Lois I, *Dir,* Southwestern College Library, Chula Vista CA. 714-421-6700, Ext 237
Marris, Alice, *Serials Cataloging,* University of Wyoming, William Robertson Coe Library, Laramie WY. 307-766-3279
Marris, Jeanell, *Librn,* Hood County Public Library, Granbury TX. 817-573-3569
Marron, Dot, *Librn,* Collier County Free Public Library (Collier North), Naples FL. 813-262-4130, 261-8208
Marrus, Regina, *Dir,* National Design Center, IDAC Microfiche System Library, New York NY. 212-688-5200
Marsala, Kathryn, *Tech Info Specialist,* Equitable Life Assurance Society of the United States (Technical Information Center-Library Services), New York NY. 212-554-4064
Marschner, Margaret, *Dir,* Conway Public Library, Conway NH. 603-447-5552
Marsden, Thomas, *Info Servs Librn,* Stevens Institute of Technology, Samuel C Williams Library, Hoboken NJ. 201-420-5198
Marsh, Agnes, *Tech Serv,* Orange Public Library, Orange CA. 714-532-0391
Marsh, Eleanor H, *Tech Serv & Cat,* Green Mountain College Library, Poultney VT. 802-287-9313, Ext 42 & 43
Marsh, Helen A, *Commun Servs,* Westerly Public Library, Memorial & Library Association of Westerly, Westerly RI. 401-596-2877
Marsh, Janet, *In Charge,* Elk River Library, Elk River MN. 612-441-1641
Marsh, Jean, *In Charge,* Acadia University (Secretarial Science), Wolfville NS. 902-542-2201, Ext 227
Marsh, John S, *Librn,* Simpson, Thacher & Bartlett, Law Library, New York NY. 212-483-9000, Ext 537
Marsh, Joyce, *Librn,* Winnebago Mental Health Institute (Patients' Library), Winnebago WI. 414-235-4910, Ext 373
Marsh, Judith, *ILL,* Patterson Library, Westfield NY. 716-326-2154
Marsh, Marie, *Librn,* New Baltimore Public Library, New Baltimore MI. 313-725-0273
Marsh, Mildred, *Cat,* Detroit Bible College, Farmington Hills MI. 313-553-7200
Marsh, Paul, *Instr,* Montana State University, Library Science Dept, MT. 406-994-2851, 994-4752
Marsh, Rhonda, *Br Librn,* Jefferson Davis Parish Library (Elton Branch), Elton LA. 318-584-2640
Marsh, Rosemarie, *Dir,* Daniel Pierce Library, Grahamsville Library, Grahamsville NY. 914-985-7233
Marsh, Sheila J, *Media,* California State University, Sacramento Library, Sacramento CA. 916-454-6466
Marshall, A P, *Actg Dir,* Eastern Michigan University, Center of Educational Resources, Ypsilanti MI. 313-487-0020

Marshall, Agnes, *Librn,* Fairfield County District Library (West Side), Lancaster OH. 614-653-2512
Marshall, Arlene, *Bus & Sci,* Madison Public Library, Madison WI. 608-266-6300
Marshall, Audrey, *Dir,* Montreal Public Library, Montreal WI. 715-561-4955
Marshall, Audrey B, *Dir,* Sierra Vista Public Library, Sierra Vista AZ. 602-458-4225
Marshall, Betty, *Librn,* Randolph Public Library, Randolph IA. 712-625-2241
Marshall, Blanche, *Librn,* Acadia Parish Library (Egan Branch), Egan LA. 318-788-1880
Marshall, David, *Librn,* Public Library of Annapolis & Anne Arundel County Inc (Annapolis Area), Annapolis MD. 301-224-7501
Marshall, Denis, *Dir,* University of Manitoba Libraries (Law), Winnipeg MB. 204-474-9773
Marshall, Don, *Media,* Southern Arkansas University, Magale Library, Magnolia AR. 501-234-5120, Ext 260, 262, 263
Marshall, Don, *Asst Prof,* Southern Arkansas University, School of Education Library Science Program, AR. 501-234-5120, Ext 260
Marshall, Dorothy B, *Actg Librn,* Mitchell Community Public Library, Mitchell IN. 812-849-2412
Marshall, E, *Supvr,* Edmonton Public Library (Jasper Place), Edmonton AB. 403-489-0310
Marshall, Elizabeth, *Ch,* Capital Library Cooperative, Mason MI. 517-676-9511
Marshall, Elizabeth, *Ch,* Ingham County Library, Library Service Center, Mason MI. 517-676-9088
Marshall, Elizabeth, *ILL,* Morley Library, Painesville OH. 216-352-3383
Marshall, Elizabeth C, *Dir,* Henderson County Public Library, Hendersonville NC. 704-693-8427
Marshall, Elva, *Librn,* Choctawhatchee Regional Library (Mary Berry Brown Public), Midland City AL. 205-983-3511
Marshall, Eugene, *Dir,* Saint Gregory's College Library, Shawnee OK. 405-273-9870, Ext 309
Marshall, Frances, *Ref, Rare Bks & Spec Coll,* Saint Clair County Library System, Port Huron MI. 313-987-7323
Marshall, Gerald L, *Dir,* Luther Rice Seminary, Bertha Smith Library, Jacksonville FL. 904-396-2316
Marshall, Gordon M, *Asst Librn,* Library Co of Philadelphia, Philadelphia PA. 215-546-3181
Marshall, Gwen, *Librn,* Massey & Townships Public Library, Massey ON. 705-865-2641
Marshall, Hazel B, *Librn,* Bailey H Dunlap Memorial Library, La Feria TX. 512-797-1242
Marshall, James, *Librn,* Hennepin Technical Center South Library, Eden Prairie MN. 612-944-2222
Marshall, James, *Librn,* Toledo-Lucas County Public Library (Sylvania Branch), Sylvania OH. 419-882-2089, 882-2080
Marshall, Jane, *Librn,* Northwestern Mutual Life Insurance Co (Law Library), Milwaukee WI. 414-271-1444, Ext 4460
Marshall, Jane E, *Personnel,* University of Chicago, Joseph Regenstein Library, Chicago IL. 312-753-2977
Marshall, Joan K, *Tech Serv,* Brooklyn College Library, Brooklyn NY. 212-780-5342
Marshall, John David, *Assoc Prof,* Middle Tennessee State University, Department of Library Service, TN. 615-898-2740 & 898-5555
Marshall, Joseph W, *Supvry Libr,* General Services Administration - National Archives & Records Service, Franklin D Roosevelt Library, Hyde Park NY. 914-229-8114
Marshall, K Eric, *Dir Libr Serv & On-Line Servs,* Canadian Department of Fisheries & Oceans, Freshwater Institute Library, Winnipeg MB. 204-269-7379, Ext 156
Marshall, Laelle B, *Exec Secy,* Electro-Mechanics Co Library, Austin TX. 512-451-8273
Marshall, Margaret, *Dir,* Pelham Public Library, Pelham NH. 603-635-7581
Marshall, Marie, *Dir,* Carnegie Public Library, Superior City Library, Superior NE. 402-879-4200
Marshall, Marion, *Librn,* Tax Foundation, Inc Library, Washington DC. 202-328-4565
Marshall, Mary Anne, *Ch,* Trails Regional Library, Johnson County-Lafayette County Library, Warrensburg MO. 816-747-9177

MARSHALL

Marshall, Mrs M N, *Librn,* Lions Gate Hospital, Carson Memorial Library, North Vancouver BC. 604-988-3131, Ext 265

Marshall, Mrs Wilbur, *Librn,* Leon Public Library, Leon KS. 316-745-3428

Marshall, Nancy H, *Dir,* Council of Wisconsin Librarians, Inc, (COWL), WI. 608-263-4962

Marshall, Nancy H, *Assoc Dir Pub Servs,* University of Wisconsin-Madison, Memorial Library, Madison WI. 608-262-3521

Marshall, Nancy H, *Dir,* Wisconsin Interlibrary Loan Service, (WILS), WI. 608-263-4962

Marshall, Nancy H, *Dir,* Wisconsin Library Consortium, (WLC), WI. 608-263-5051

Marshall, Patricia, *Chief Librn,* American Institute of Aeronautics & Astronautics, Technical Information Service, New York NY. 212-247-6500

Marshall, Patricia K, *Mgr Analytic Res Serv,* Mobil Oil Corp, Secretariat Library, New York NY. 212-883-2454

Marshall, Penny L, *Ref & Spec Coll,* Stark County District Library, Canton OH. 216-452-0665, Ext 31

Marshall, Robert, *Ref,* Kirkwood Highway Library, Wilmington DE. 302-999-0161

Marshall, Robert D, *Spec Coll,* California State Polytechnic University Library, Pomona CA. 714-598-4671

Marshall, Rosita, *Acq,* Marycrest College, Cone Library, Davenport IA. 319-326-9254

Marshall, Ruth, *Librn,* Emmaus Bible School Library, Oak Park IL. 312-383-7000, Ext 55

Marshall, Ruth Ann, *Tech Serv & Cat,* Carnegie-Mellon University, Hunt Library, Pittsburgh PA. 412-578-2446, 578-2447

Marshall, Ruth L, *Librn,* Lisbon Public Library, Lisbon NH. 603-838-6615

Marshall, Ruth T, *Dir, Ad & Acq,* Southwest Georgia Regional Library, Gilbert H Gragg Library, Bainbridge GA. 912-246-3887, 3894, 3895

Marshall, Shirley, *Librn,* Auburn Public Library, Auburn IL. 217-438-6211

Marshall, Sister Mary Alacoque, *Librn,* College of White Plains of Pace University, Hates Library, White Plains NY. 914-949-2950

Marshall, Susan K, *Ref,* Pocatello Public Library, Information and Video Center, Pocatello ID. 208-232-1263

Marshall, Theodore, *Spec Coll,* Loyola Marymount University, Charles Von Der Ahe Library, Los Angeles CA. 213-642-2788

Marshall, Thomas A, *Librn,* Jesuit Provincial Residence, Los Gatos CA. 408-354-6140

Marshall, Vicki, *AV,* Flint River Regional Library, Griffin GA. 404-227-2756

Marshall, Virginia, *Dir,* Lewes Public Library, Lewes DE. 302-645-2733

Marshall, William, *Spec Coll,* University of Kentucky, Margaret I King Library, Lexington KY. 606-257-3801

Marshall, III, John R, *Librn,* United States Department of Commerce, Economic Reference Library, Jacksonville Area, Jacksonville FL. 904-791-2796

Marshburn, A Lawrence, *Asst Librn,* University of Redlands, George & Verda Armacost Library, Redlands CA. 714-793-2121, Ext 472

Marshik, Cecelia, *In Charge,* Pierz Library, Pierz MN. 612-468-6486

Marson, Joyce, *Librn & On-Line Servs,* White Memorial Medical Center, Courville-Abbott Memorial Library, Los Angeles CA. 213-269-9131, Ext 1215

Marsteller, Ann L, *Librn,* Alfred A Yee & Associates Inc Library, Honolulu HI. 808-946-3161, Ext 48

Marszalek, Kathleen, *Librn,* Los Angeles Public Library System (Brentwood), Los Angeles CA. 213-826-6579

Mart, Jackie, *Ch,* Deschutes County Library, Bend OR. 503-382-5191

Marte, Gail, *ILL & YA,* Mishawaka-Penn Public Library, Mishawaka IN. 219-259-5277

Martel, Anne, *Librn,* University of Illinois Library at Urbana-Champaign (Illini Union Browsing Room), Urbana IL. 217-333-2475

Martell, Barbara, *Ch,* Waupaca Free Public Library, Waupaca WI. 715-258-3393

Martell, Joyce, *Librn,* San Bernardino County Library (Rialto Branch), Rialto CA. 714-875-0144

Martelle, Jr, Harold D, *Dir,* Sacramento Public Library, Sacramento CA. 916-440-5926

Marten, L, *Area Head,* Winnipeg Public Library (Saint James-Assiniboia Branch), Winnipeg MB. 204-888-0880

Martens, Kathryn I, *Asst Librn,* Montgomery-Floyd Regional Library, Christiansburg VA. 703-382-3342

Martenson, Robert D, *Dir,* Housatonic Community College, Library Learning Resource Center, Bridgeport CT. 203-579-6465

Martha, Sister, *Librn,* Sacred Heart Hospital, Health Science Library, Cumberland MD. 301-759-7229

Martin, Ange-Aimee, *Dir,* Ilsley Library, Middlebury VT. 802-388-2977

Martin, Ann, *Cat,* J Herman Bosler Memorial Library, Bosler Free Library, Carlisle PA. 717-243-4642

Martin, Ann F, *Librn,* Paso Robles Public Library, Paso Robles CA. 805-238-0315

Martin, Anne, *Ch,* Newfoundland Public Library Services (A C Hunter Memorial Library), Saint John's NF. 709-737-3964

Martin, Anthony A, *Dir,* Carnegie Library of Pittsburgh, Pittsburgh PA. 412-622-3100

Martin, Arthur H, *Ref & Bibliog Instr,* Hood College of Frederick, Joseph Henry Apple Library, Frederick MD. 301-663-3131, Ext 364, 365

Martin, Barbara, *Librn,* Pioneer Multi-County Library (Tecumseh Public), Tecumseh OK. 405-598-5955

Martin, Barbara, *Circ,* University of Lowell Libraries (O'Leary Library), Lowell MA. 617-452-5000, Ext 480

Martin, Barbara A, *Commun Servs, Br Coordr & Bkmobile Coordr,* Greenwich Library, Greenwich CT. 203-622-7900

Martin, Barbara H S, *Cat,* Morehouse College School of Medicine, Multi-Media Center, Atlanta GA. 404-681-2800, Ext 202

Martin, Betty, *Librn,* Vermilion Parish Library (Abbeville), Abbeville LA. 318-893-2674

Martin, Betty C, *Asst Dir,* Vigo County Public Library, Terre Haute IN. 812-232-1113

Martin, Betty J, *Dir,* Cowley County Community College, Renn Memorial Library, Arkansas City KS. 316-442-0430, Ext 57

Martin, Beverly, *Librn,* Indianapolis-Marion County Public Library (Eagle), Indianapolis IN. 317-635-5662

Martin, Beverly, *Librn, On-Line Servs & Bibliog Instr,* Jewish Vocational Services Library, Chicago IL. 312-346-6700

Martin, Brenda, *Librn,* Jackson Metropolitan Library (Lake Library), Lake MS. 601-352-3677

Martin, Carmen, *Librn,* Utica Library Association, Utica KS. 913-391-2254

Martin, Carol, *Lit,* Austin Public Library, Austin TX. 512-472-5433

Martin, Carol, *Bkmobile Coordr,* Lancaster County Library, Lancaster SC. 803-285-1502

Martin, Carol, *Librn,* McDonald Public Library, McDonald KS. 913-538-2400

Martin, Carol P, *Head Librn,* Saint Louis Community College (Meramec Campus), Saint Louis MO. 314-966-7623

Martin, Celia, *Br Coordr,* Gulfport-Harrison County Library, Gulfport MS. 601-863-6411

Martin, Charice, *Dial Access,* Tyler Junior College, Edgar H Vaughn Memorial Library, Tyler TX. 214-592-5993, 593-3342

Martin, Charlene, *Acq,* Hutchinson County Library, Borger TX. 806-274-6221

Martin, Charles J, *Dir,* Cooperative Libraries in Central Connecticut, (CLICC), CT. 203-757-0535

Martin, Corinne, *On-Line Servs & Bibliog Instr,* Combustion Engineering, Inc, Power Systems Group Library Services, Windsor CT. 203-688-1911, Ext 5603, 5619 & 2477

Martin, David, *Learning Skills Ctr,* Cayuga County Community College, Norman F Bourke Memorial Library Learning Resources Center, Auburn NY. 315-255-1743, Ext 296 & 298

Martin, David, *Instr,* University of Missouri-Columbia, School of Library & Informational Science, MO. 314-882-4546

Martin, David, *Pub Libr Support Servs,* West Virginia Library Commission, Science & Cultural Center, Charleston WV. 304-348-2041

Martin, Debbie, *Ref,* Judge George W Armstrong Library, Homochitto Valley Regional Library, Natchez MS. 601-445-8862

Martin, Debra, *Bkmobile Coordr,* Norfolk Public Library, Lewis & Clark Regional Library, Norfolk NE. 402-371-4590

Martin, Delores, *Librn,* Cabot Corp, Research & Development Library, Pampa TX. 806-669-2581

Martin, Donald D, *Librn,* James Peter Warbasse Memorial Library, New York NY. 212-673-3900

Martin, Dorothy, *Librn,* Boston Public Library (Fields Corner), Dorchester MA. 617-436-2155

Martin, Dorothy A, *Librn,* American Baptist Churches in the United States of America (Editorial Library), Valley Forge PA. 215-768-2378

Martin, Douglas, *Librn,* North Carolina Central University (School of Law), Durham NC. 919-683-6244

Martin, E J, *In Charge,* General Electric Co, Tempo Dasiac Library, Santa Barbara CA. 805-965-0551, Ext 200

Martin, Earvie, *Librn,* Shreve Memorial Library (Lakeside), Shreveport LA. 318-425-3630

Martin, Elaine, *Bkmobile Coordr,* Laurens County Library, Laurens SC. 803-984-0596

Martin, Elizabeth A, *Dept Head,* University of Northern Iowa, Dept of Library Science, IA. 319-273-2050

Martin, Elizabeth J, *Librn,* Wolcott Community Library, Wolcott VT. 802-888-2401

Martin, Ellen A, *Clerk of Courts,* Ozaukee County Law Library, Port Washington WI. 414-284-9411

Martin, Evalena, *Tech Serv,* North Arkansas Regional Library, Harrison AR. 501-741-3665

Martin, Evelyn, *Librn,* Abilene Public Library (Merkel Public), Merkel TX. 915-677-2474

Martin, Faye, *Commun Servs,* Mount Vernon Public Library, Mount Vernon WA. 206-336-2418

Martin, Frances, *Tech Serv,* South Georgia Regional Library, Valdosta-Lowndes County Public Library, Valdosta GA. 912-247-3405

Martin, Frances S, *Librn,* Lanesborough Public Library, Lanesborough MA. 413-442-0222

Martin, Francis P, *Res Curator,* Evansville Museum of Arts & Science Library, Evansville IN. 812-425-2406

Martin, Frank, *Librn,* Brentwood College Library, Mill Bay BC. 604-743-5521

Martin, Gail, *Ad,* Carnegie Library, Rome GA. 404-291-7568

Martin, Gene, *Dir,* Daniel Boone Regional Library, Columbia MO. 314-443-3161

Martin, George, *Soc Sci,* Howard University Libraries, Founders Library, Washington DC. 202-636-7253

Martin, Georgiana, *Librn,* Schroon Lake Public Library, Schroon Lake NY. 518-532-7903

Martin, Gordon P, *Librn,* California State University, Sacramento Library, Sacramento CA. 916-454-6466

Martin, Harrold B, *Librn,* Philadelphia City Planning Commission Library, Philadelphia PA. 215-686-4637

Martin, Harry, *Librn,* Georgetown University (Fred O Dennis Law Library), Washington DC. 202-624-8260

Martin, Hazel L, *Librn,* Las Animas Public Library, Las Animas CO. 303-456-0509

Martin, Helen, *Librn,* Central Florida Regional Library (Lecanto-Beverly Hills), Ocala FL. 904-746-3489

Martin, Helen, *Asst Librn,* Wadhams Hall Seminary-College Library, Ogdensburg NY. 315-393-4231, Ext 20

Martin, Irene, *Librn,* Skamokawa Library, Skamokawa WA. 206-795-3920

Martin, Irene, *YA,* Villa Park Public Library, Villa Park IL. 312-834-1164

Martin, Irene M, *Ch,* Veterans Administration Center (Brentwood Library Service), Los Angeles CA. 213-879-1303

Martin, Irmgarde D, *Supvr Tech Info Servs,* Anderson Clayton Foods Co, Technical Research Library, Richardson TX. 214-231-6121, Ext 218, 219

Martin, J, *Librn,* Cambridge Municipal Public Library (Hespeler), Cambridge ON. 519-658-4412

Martin, J, *Canadiana,* Trent University, Thomas J Bata Library, Peterborough ON. 705-748-1550

Martin, Jana, *Librn,* Hospital for Joint Diseases, Medical Library, New York NY. 212-650-4475

Martin, Jane, *Acq,* Saint Mary's College, Sarah Graham Kenan Library, Raleigh NC. 919-828-2521, Ext 313, 314

Martin, Jane C, *Librn,* Conway Research, Inc Library, Atlanta GA. 404-458-6026

Martin, Jean, *Librn,* Vancouver Art Gallery Library, Vancouver BC. 604-682-5621, Ext 41

Martin, Jeanette, *Librn,* Tampa-Hillsborough County Public Library System (West Gate Public), Tampa FL. 813-885-4500

Martin, Jess A, *Dir,* University of Tennessee Center for the Health Sciences Library, Memphis TN. 901-528-5638

Martin, Jo, *Librn,* Brazoria County Library (Clute Branch), Clute TX. 713-265-4582

Martin, John, *Special Servs,* Orlando Public Library, Orlando FL. 305-425-4694

Martin, John, *Dir Inst Media,* Tarrant County Junior College System (Northwest Campus Learning Resources Center), Fort Worth TX. 817-232-2900, Ext 208

Martin, John D, *Dir,* Carthage Public Library, Carthage MO. 417-358-2939

Martin, John H, *Dir,* Corning Museum of Glass Library, Corning NY. 607-937-5371

Martin, Judith R, *Asst Prof,* West Virginia Wesleyan College, Dept of Library Science, WV. 304-473-8059

Martin, Judith R, *Cat,* West Virginia Wesleyan College, Annie Merner Pfeiffer Library, Buckhannon WV. 304-473-8059

Martin, Julia G, *Librn,* Warioto Regional Library Center, Clarksville TN. 615-645-9531

Martin, June R, *ILL,* Kanawha County Public Library, Kanawha County Service Center, Charleston WV. 304-343-4646

Martin, Karin F, *Librn,* First Presbyterian Church Library, Upland CA. 714-982-8811

Martin, Katherine, *Librn,* Parsippany-Troy Hills Public Library (Parsippany Libr), Parsippany NJ. 201-887-5150

Martin, Katherine, *Librn,* Timmins Public Library (Charles M Shields Centennial Library), South Porcupine ON. 705-235-4974

Martin, Kathleen, *Asst Librn,* Tarrant City Public Library, Tarrant AL. 205-841-3292

Martin, Kathy, *Ref,* Richardson Public Library, Richardson TX. 214-238-8251

Martin, Kendall, *Bibliog Instr,* United States Air Force (Electronics Systems Division, Base Library), Hanscom AFB MA. 617-861-2177

Martin, Kenneth R, *Dir,* Kendall Whaling Museum, Sharon MA. 617-784-5642

Martin, Lawrence, *Historical-Archival,* Ferris State College Library, Big Rapids MI. 616-796-9494, 796-9971, Ext 323

Martin, Lenore, *Asst Librn,* Washington University Libraries (School of Dental Medicine Library), Saint Louis MO. 314-454-0385

Martin, Lillian M, *Librn,* Lewis-Clark State College Library, Lewiston ID. 208-746-2341, Ext 236

Martin, Linda, *Librn,* Placer Development Ltd Library, Vancouver BC. 604-682-7082, Ext 133

Martin, Loretta, *Librn,* East Brewton Public Library, East Brewton AL. 205-867-9446

Martin, Louis E, *Univ Librn,* Cornell University Libraries (University Libraries), Ithaca NY. 607-256-4144

Martin, M E, *Ad & Ch,* Scarborough Public Library, Scarborough ON. 416-291-1991

Martin, Marcia, *Spec Coll,* Alabama State University, Library & Learning Resources, Montgomery AL. 205-832-6072

Martin, Margaret, *Asst Dir, Tech Serv & Cat,* Sudbury Public Library, La Bibliotheque Publique de Sudbury, Sudbury ON. 705-673-1155

Martin, Margaret B, *Librn,* Hawkins, Delafield & Wood, Law Library, New York NY. 212-952-4772

Martin, Marguerite, *Librn,* Cleveland Public Library (South Brooklyn), Cleveland OH. 216-661-5700

Martin, Margy E, *Dir,* Nebraska Western College Library, Scottsbluff NE. 308-635-3606, Ext 35

Martin, Marie A, *In Charge,* Bishop's Mill Historical Institute, Sol Feinstone Library, Edgemont PA. 215-353-1777

Martin, Marietta, *Asst Dir,* Smith Memorial Library, Chautauqua Institution, Chautauqua NY. 716-357-5844

Martin, Marion, *Circ,* Iberville Parish Library, Plaquemine LA. 504-687-2520

Martin, Marion, *Reserve Librn,* San Jacinto College, Lee Davis Library, Pasadena TX. 713-476-1850, 476-1501, Ext 241

Martin, Marion C, *Dir,* Clay County Library, Manchester KY. 606-598-2617

Martin, Marjorie, *Librn,* Ormond Beach Public Library, Ormond Beach FL. 904-677-0328, Ext 270-243

Martin, Mary, *Librn,* Cobb County Public Library System (Stratton), Marietta GA. 404-422-7328

Martin, Mary H, *Librn,* General Motors Institute Library, Flint MI. 313-776-5000

Martin, Mary W, *Librn,* Choctawhatchee Regional Library (Eufaula Carnegie), Eufaula AL. 205-687-2337

Martin, Max, *AV Dir,* Oklahoma School for the Deaf Library, Sulphur OK. 405-622-3186

Martin, Michael, *Genealogy,* San Francisco Public Library, San Francisco CA. 415-558-4235

Martin, Mikki, *Librn,* Sperry Rand Corp (Engineering Central File Library), New Holland PA. 717-354-1707

Martin, Mildred, *Librn,* Black Creek Public Library, Black Creek WI. 414-984-3295

Martin, Mildred E, *Librn,* Springfield Academy of Medicine, Medical Library, Springfield MA. 413-734-5445

Martin, Morris, *Music,* North Texas State University Library, Denton TX. 817-788-2411

Martin, Mrs Frank, *Librn,* Stewart County Public Library, Dover TN. 615-232-5839

Martin, Mrs Kenneth, *Librn,* Bradley County Library, Warren AR. 501-226-3363

Martin, Murray S, *Assoc Dean,* Pennsylvania State University, Fred Lewis Pattee Library, University Park PA. 814-865-0401

Martin, N, *Ser,* Northeastern University, Suburban Campus Library, Burlington MA. 617-272-5500, Ext 55

Martin, Nannette P, *Ref,* Emporia State University, William Allen White Library, Emporia KS. 316-343-1200, Ext 205

Martin, Neal A, *Ref & Bibliog Instr,* Francis Marion College, James A Rogers Library, Florence SC. 803-669-4121, Ext 321

Martin, Nina N, *Assoc Prof,* University of Alabama, Graduate School of Library Service, AL. 205-348-4610

Martin, Noelene P, *ILL,* Pennsylvania State University, Fred Lewis Pattee Library, University Park PA. 814-865-0401

Martin, Norma Jean, *Bkmobile Coordr,* Lincoln Parish Library, Ruston LA. 318-255-1920

Martin, Norman D, *Cat, Ref & On-Line Servs,* University of Wisconsin-Whitewater, Library & Learning Resources, Whitewater WI. 414-472-1000

Martin, P J, *Dir,* National Presbyterian Church & Center, William S Culbertson Library, Washington DC. 202-537-2800

Martin, P W, *Dir,* Levittown Public Library, Levittown NY. 516-731-5728

Martin, Peggy, *Librn,* Fulton County Law Library, Atlanta GA. 404-572-2330

Martin, Phyllis J, *Librn,* Cleveland Public Library (East 131st Street), Cleveland OH. 216-561-6133

Martin, Phyllis R, *Dir,* Priestley-Forsyth Memorial Library, Northumberland PA. 717-473-8201

Martin, Putzie, *Librn,* Bastrop Public Library, Bastrop TX. 512-321-5441

Martin, Rachel S, *Dir,* Furman University Library, Greenville SC. 803-294-2191

Martin, Rebecca R, *Chief Librn,* Veterans Administration, Hospital Medical Library, San Francisco CA. 415-221-4810, Ext 230

Martin, Richard T, *Assoc Librn,* Coastal Carolina Community College Library, Jacksonville NC. 919-455-1221

Martin, Robert, *Spec Coll,* University of Texas at Arlington Library, Arlington TX. 817-273-3391

Martin, Robin, *Actg Dir, On-Line Servs & Bibliog Instr,* Central College, Geisler Learning Resource Center, Pella IA. 515-628-4151, Ext 233

Martin, Roger M, *Reader Serv, On-Line Servs & Bibliog Instr,* Naval Postgraduate School, Dudley Knox Library, Monterey CA. 408-646-2341

Martin, Ron, *Curr Lab,* Florida International University, Tamiami Campus, Athenaeum, Miami FL. 305-552-2461

Martin, Ron, *Bibliog Instr,* Kansas State University, Farrell Library, Manhattan KS. 913-532-6516

Martin, Rosemary S, *Dir,* Central Arkansas Library System, Little Rock AR. 501-374-7546

Martin, Ruth, *Librn,* Memphis-Shelby County Public Library & Information Center (Art-Music-Recreation), Memphis TN. 901-528-2950

Martin, Ruth, *Asst Librn,* Shearson Loeb Rhoades, Inc Library, New York NY. 212-577-5253

Martin, Sarah S, *Librn,* National Radio Astronomy Observatory Library, Charlottesville VA. 804-296-0211, Ext 254

Martin, Sarah S, *Librn,* National Radio Astronomy Observatory Library, Green Bank WV. 304-456-2011, Ext 310

Martin, Shelby A, *Cat,* Montgomery County Community College, Learning Resources Center, Blue Bell PA. 215-643-6000, Ext 340

Martin, Shirley, *Dir,* Colorado State Reformatory Library, Buena Vista CO. 303-395-2418, Ext 294

Martin, Shirley A, *ILL & Ref,* University of Maine at Farmington, Mantor Library, Farmington ME. 207-778-3501, Ext 225

Martin, Sister Rose Marie, *Tech Serv,* Aquinas College, Learning Resource Center, Grand Rapids MI. 616-459-8281, Ext 234

Martin, Sue, *Dir,* North Fond du Lac Public Library, North Fond du Lac WI. 414-923-1466

Martin, Susan K, *Dir,* Johns Hopkins University Libraries (Milton S Eisenhower Library), Baltimore MD. 301-338-8325

Martin, Teresa B, *Librn,* Porter Memorial Hospital, Medical Library, Denver CO. 303-778-1955, Ext 656

Martin, Tom, *Librn,* Andersen Laboratories, Inc Library, Bloomfield CT. 203-242-0761, Ext 301

Martin, Vera, *Librn,* Bureau of Land Management, Roswell District Office Library, Roswell NM. 505-622-7670

Martin, Vernon E, *Art & Music,* Hartford Public Library, Hartford CT. 203-525-9121

Martin, Virginia M, *Librn,* Inolex Pharmaceutical, Division of Wilson Pharmaceutical & Chemical Corp, Research Library, Park Forest IL. 312-534-3281

Martin, W Terry, *Tech Serv,* Southeastern Baptist Theological Seminary Library, Wake Forest NC. 919-556-3101, Ext 225, 250

Martin, Ware, *Asst Librn, Media & Ref,* Sumter County Library, Sumter SC. 803-773-7273

Martin, Ware G, *Art, Hist,* Sumter County Library, Sumter SC. 803-773-7273

Martin, William, *Media,* Wenatchee Valley College, John A Brown Library Media Center, Wenatchee WA. 509-662-1651

Martin, Z, *ILL,* Georgia Mental Health Institute, Addison M Duval Library, Atlanta GA. 404-894-5663

Martin, Jr, Homer E, *Librn,* Bergen Evening Record Corp Library, Hackensack NJ. 201-646-4092

Martin, Jr, William A, *Dir,* University of Science & Arts of Oklahoma, Nash Library, Chickasha OK. 405-224-3140, Ext 260

Martindale, James A, *Dir,* Depauw University, Roy O West Library, Greencastle IN. 317-653-9721, Ext 250

Martinek, Joan, *Sci,* University of Texas at Arlington Library, Arlington TX. 817-273-3391

Martinello, Gilda, *On-Line Servs,* Canadian National Railways (Headquarters Library), Montreal PQ. 514-877-4407

Martinez, Alice, *Media,* Beaumont Public Library, Beaumont TX. 713-838-0812

Martinez, Angelina, *Actg Dir,* California Polytechnic State University Library, San Luis Obispo CA. 805-546-2345

Martinez, Anna, *Lit & Lang,* San Diego Public Library, San Diego CA. 714-236-5800

Martinez, Antonio, *Librn,* Corpus Christi Public Libraries (Greenwood), Corpus Christi TX. 512-854-2356

Martinez, Arlene, *Asst Librn,* Mescalero Community Library, Mescalero NM. 505-671-4494, Ext 205 & 206

Martinez, Beverly, *Librn,* San Jose Public Library (Empire), San Jose CA. 408-286-5627

Martinez, Carmen, *Librn,* San Jose Public Library (Hillview), San Jose CA. 408-272-3100

Martinez, Carole, *Mgr,* Southeast Metropolitan Board of Cooperative Services, Professional Information Center, Denver CO. 303-757-6201

Martinez, Cecilia, *Tech Serv,* Chandler Public Library, Chandler AZ. 602-963-8111, Ext 390

Martinez, Donna, *Asst Librn,* Brobeck, Phleger & Harrison Library, San Francisco CA. 415-442-1053

Martinez, Georgiana, *Librn,* Bureau of Land Management, New Mexico State Office Library, Santa Fe NM. 505-988-6243

Martinez, Grace M, *Actg Librn,* Espanola Public Library, Espanola NM. 505-753-3860

Martinez, Jane, *Ref,* Newport Beach Public Library, Newport Beach CA. 714-640-2141

Martinez, Jane, *Librn,* Newport Beach Public Library (Newport Center), Newport Beach CA. 714-640-2141640-2246

Martinez, Jo Anne Bourguard, *Librn,* Aerospace Corp, Washington Library, Washington DC. 202-488-6154

Martinez, Joan, *Ref Coordr,* Riverside City & County Public Library, Riverside CA. 714-787-7211

Martinez, Luis Angel Flores, *Acq,* Inter-American University of Puerto Rico, Metropolitan Campus Library, Hato Rey PR. 809-754-7215, Ext 246, 245, 256

Martinez, Nora, *Circ,* Allan Hancock Joint Community College Library, Santa Maria CA. 805-922-6966, Ext 215, 242

Martinez, Robert O, *Librn,* Albuquerque Public Library (Esperanza Branch), Albuquerque NM. 505-766-7899

Martinez-Vidal, Vivian, *Dir,* William Jeanes Memorial Library, Lafayette Hill PA. 215-828-0441

Martinian, Sister Mary, *Per,* Marylhurst Education Center, Shoen Library, Marylhurst OR. 503-636-8141, Ext 56 & 61

Martinke, Thomas L, *Librn,* Hercules Inc (Research Center Library), Wilmington DE. 302-995-3484

Martino, Bernice, *Librn,* Herald News Editorial Library, Passaic NJ. 201-365-3107

Martinoff, Zoia, *Librn,* American Russian Institute, San Francisco CA. 415-861-3813

Martinsen, Elizabeth A, *In Charge,* United States Department of Health & Human Services, Parklawn Health Library, Hyattsville MD. 301-436-6147

Martinson, C E, *Pres,* C E Martinson & Associates, Science Press, Princeton NJ. 609-924-1055

Martinson, Gayle, *Archivist,* University of Wisconsin-Stout, Pierce Library, Menomonie WI. 715-232-1184

Martinson, Sheila, *Supervisor,* Otter Tail Power Co Library, Fergus Falls MN. 218-736-5411

Martz, Frederick M, *Head Circ Dept,* Yale University Library (Sterling Memorial Library), New Haven CT. 203-436-8335

Martz, Jim, *Asst Dir, Acq & Ref,* Dickinson State College, Stoxen Library, Dickinson ND. 701-227-2135

Martz, Ruby, *Ref & Bibliog Instr,* Waubonsee Community College, Learning Resources Center, Sugar Grove IL. 312-466-4811, Ext 303

Martz, Jr, David J, *Coll Coordr & Bibliog Instr,* Colonial Williamsburg (Research Center Library), Williamsburg VA. 804-229-1000, Ext 2275

Maru, O, *Librn,* American Bar Foundation, Cromwell Library, Chicago IL. 312-667-4700

Marullo, Filippa, *Librn,* Cambridge Public Library (Cambridge Field), Cambridge MA. 617-498-9083

Marullo, Filippa, *Librn,* Cambridge Public Library (East Cambridge), Cambridge MA. 617-498-9082

Maruskin, Albert F, *Tech Serv,* California State College, Louis L Manderino Library, California PA. 412-938-4091

Marvel, Catherine, *Librn,* Pendleton & Fall Creek Township Public Library, Pendleton IN. 317-778-2046

Marvel, Zelda A, *Librn,* Goose Creek Township Carnegie Library, De Land IL. 217-664-3572

Marvin, James C, *Librn,* Topeka Public Library, Topeka KS. 913-233-2040

Marvin, Mary, *Asst Librn,* Chrisman Public Library, Chrisman IL. 217-269-3011

Marvin, Stephen, *Bus,* Ridley Township Public Library, Folsom PA. 215-583-0593

Marwood, Alice, *Librn,* British Columbia Genealogical Society Library, Richmond BC. 604-274-3659

Marx, Amy, *On-Line Servs,* University of Georgia Libraries, Athens GA. 404-542-2716

Marx, Charles, *Cat,* University of Wisconsin-La Crosse, Murphy Library, La Crosse WI. 608-785-8505

Marx, Karen, *Libr Asst,* Brookhaven Memorial Hospital, Medical Library, Patchogue NY. 516-654-7074

Marx, Marjorie, *Librn,* Iosco-Arenac Regional Library (East Tawas Library), East Tawas MI. 517-362-6162

Marx, Victor, *Ref, On-Line Servs & Bibliog Instr,* Central Washington University Library, Ellensburg WA. 509-963-1901

Marye, Frances, *ILL & Ref,* Auraria Libraries, Denver CO. 303-629-2805

Maryott, Margaret, *Librn,* East Providence Public Library (Rumford), East Providence RI. 401-434-2453

Marz, Sandra, *Pub Servs & On-Line Servs,* Washoe County Law Library, Reno NV. 702-785-4188

Marzillier, Helen, *Tech Info Specialist,* Merck & Co, Inc (Reference Room Animal Science Research), Rahway NJ. 201-574-6310

Marzolf, Marsha LeClair, *Ch & YA,* Salt Lake County Library System, Whitmore Library, Salt Lake City UT. 801-943-7614

Masak, P J, *Cat & Ref,* Concordia College, Klinck Memorial Library, River Forest IL. 312-771-8300, Ext 450

Mascari, Walter, *Librn,* New Orleans Public Library (Latter), New Orleans LA. 504-899-6021

Mascher, Janet, *On-Line Servs,* Mead Johnson Research Library, Evansville IN. 812-426-6546

Maschin, Harold F, *Curator,* Westfield Athenaeum, Westfield MA. 413-568-7833

Masciotra, Shirley, *Librn,* Thornton Public Library, Thornton IL. 312-877-2579

Mash, Evelyn, *Librn,* Saltsburg Free Library, Saltsburg PA. 412-639-9763

Mashbaum, Jesse, *Dir,* Baltimore Hebrew College, Joseph M Meyerhoff Library, Baltimore MD. 301-466-7900, Ext 307

Mashburn, B C, *Librn,* Iowa Park Library, Iowa Park TX. 817-592-4981

Mashburn, Gloria, *Dir,* Skagit Valley College, Library Media Center, Mount Vernon WA. 206-424-1031, Ext 111

Mashe, Katherine, *Librn,* Oxford Public Library, Oxford IA. 319-628-4378

Masia, Phyliss, *Coodr Volunteer Servs,* New Jersey Library for the Blind & Handicapped, Trenton NJ. 609-292-6450

Masich, Andrew E, *Curator,* Yuma County Historical Society Library, Yuma AZ. 602-783-8020

Masiello, Dennis R, *Dir,* Tempe Public Library, Tempe AZ. 602-968-8231

Masih, Ranjani, *Ad,* Dartmouth Regional Library, Dartmouth NS. 902-466-7623

Masin, Anton, *Spec Coll & Rare Bks,* University of Notre Dame Library, Notre Dame IN. 219-283-7317

Masirovits, Susan, *Dir,* Henderson Memorial Public Library, Jefferson OH. 216-576-3761

Maskel, Jane, *On-Line Servs & Bibliog Instr,* Kokomo Public Library, Kokomo IN. 317-457-5558

Maslansky, Hannah V, *Asst Librn,* Union Carbide Corp (Library & Technical Information Serv), Tarrytown NY. 914-789-3700

Masling, Annette, *Librn,* Albright-Knox Art Gallery, Art Reference Library, Buffalo NY. 716-882-8700, Ext 25

Masling, Charles, *Librn,* Houston Public Library (Neighborhood Information Center, (Information & Referral Service)), Houston TX. 713-224-5441, Ext 206

Mason, Alexandra, *Librn,* University of Kansas Libraries (Special Collections), Lawrence KS. 913-864-4334

Mason, Ann, *ILL,* Frankfort Community Public Library, Frankfort IN. 317-654-8746

Mason, Ann V, *Supvr of Libr Servs,* Mobil Chemical Corp, Research & Development Laboratories Library, Edison NJ. 201-321-6000

Mason, Bernice, *Ch,* York Public Library, York NE. 402-362-3039

Mason, Carolyn S, *Librn,* United States Navy (Marine Corps Base Library), Camp Lejeune NC. 919-451-5724

Mason, Charlene, *Central Admin Servs,* University of Minnesota Libraries-Twin Cities, Minneapolis MN. 612-373-3097

Mason, Charles, *Librn,* East Chicago Public Library (Grand Boulevard), East Chicago IN. 219-397-2453

Mason, David B, *Chief Archives & Libr Program,* Provincial Archives of British Columbia, Northwest Collection Library, Victoria BC. 604-387-5885

Mason, Douglas, *Cat,* Orange Coast College Library, Costa Mesa CA. 714-556-5885

Mason, E, *Acq,* Los Angeles Trade Technical College Library, Los Angeles CA. 213-746-0800, Ext 217

Mason, Eileen, *Tech Serv,* Citizens Library, Washington PA. 412-222-2400

Mason, Elaine, *Librn,* Kern County Library (Taft Branch), Taft CA. 805-861-2130

Mason, Elizabeth A, *Ch,* Ashland Public School District Library, Ashland OH. 419-289-8188

Mason, Elizabeth A, *Librn,* Edith Evans Public & School Library, Laona WI. 715-674-4751

Mason, Ellsworth, *Rare Bks & Spec Coll,* University of Colorado at Boulder (University Libraries), Boulder CO. 303-492-7511

Mason, Frank, *Dir,* University of Southern California (School of Dentistry), Los Angeles CA. 312-743-2884, 743-2870

Mason, Geraldine, *Circ,* Richardson Public Library, Richardson TX. 214-238-8251

Mason, Helen B, *Librn,* University of Tennessee Space Institute Library, Tullahoma TN. 615-455-0631, Ext 315

Mason, Helen F, *Ad & Commun Servs,* Warren Library Association, Warren Library, Warren PA. 814-723-4650

Mason, I, *Mgr,* Ministry of Education Library, Toronto ON. 416-965-1451

Mason, Iris, *Mgr Libr Serv,* Ontario Ministry of Colleges and Universities Library, Toronto ON. 416-965-4537

Mason, Jane, *Tech Serv,* Richland County Public Library, Columbia SC. 803-799-9084

Mason, Jo Ann, *Librn,* Hancock County Library (Lewisport Branch), Lewisport KY. 502-295-3765

Mason, Joan H, *Admin Sec,* Atlantic City Free Public Library, Atlantic City NJ. 609-345-2269

Mason, Julia, *Librn,* Colusa County Free Library (Williams), Williams CA. 916-473-5955

Mason, Laurie, *Ch,* Middletown Township Public Library, Middletown NJ. 201-671-3700

Mason, Lori, *Acq,* Shelton State Community College, Junior College Division, Tuscaloosa AL. 205-759-1583

Mason, Louise H, *Librn,* Russell Public Library, Russell MA. 413-862-4554

Mason, Mae, *Tech Serv,* Seneca College of Applied Arts & Technology, Finch Campus Learning Resource Centre, Willowdale ON. 416-491-5050, Ext 381

Mason, Margaret, *Actg Librn,* Trail Municipal Library, Trail BC. 604-364-1731

Mason, Margaret C, *Dir,* Central Oregon Community College Learning Resources Center, Bend OR. 503-382-6112, Ext 240, 241

Mason, Marion, *Asst Librn,* Motorola, Inc, Communications Group Library, Schaumburg IL. 312-576-5949

Mason, Martha, *Librn,* Binghamton Psychiatric Center (Professional Library), Binghamton NY. 607-724-1391, Ext 450

Mason, Martha, *Librn,* Northwest Regional Library (Red Bay Public), Red Bay AL. 205-356-9255

Mason, Martha A, *Librn,* Binghamton Psychiatric Center (Rehabilitation Library), Binghamton NY. 607-724-1391, Ext 614

Mason, Mary, *Lectr,* Concordia University, Library Studies Program, PQ. 514-482-0320, Ext 324

Mason, Pauline M, *Librn,* Veterans Administration (Hospital Library), Pittsburgh PA. 412-363-4900

Mason, Philip P, *Dir,* Wayne State University Libraries (Walter P Reuther Library of Labor & Urban Affairs), Detroit MI. 313-577-4024

Mason, Rebecca, *Librn,* Department of Public Libraries & Information (Reference Division), Virginia Beach VA. 804-464-9485
Mason, Sally, *Ref,* Emmaus Public Library, Emmaus PA. 215-965-9284
Mason, Sally, *Librn,* Powers Memorial Library, Palmyra WI. 414-495-4605
Mason, Tim, *Cat,* Texas College of Osteopathic Medicine Library, Fort Worth TX. 817-735-2465
Mason, Virginia, *Librn,* Franklin Sylvester Library (Seville Branch), Seville OH. 216-769-2852
Mason, Wallace L, *Dir & ILL,* Richards Memorial Library, North Attleboro Public Library, North Attleboro MA. 617-695-6411
Mason, Wendy, *Ch,* Sherborn Library, Sherborn MA. 617-653-0770
Masoni, Daniel, *Dir & Acq,* Emporia Public Library, Emporia KS. 316-342-6524
Masse, Lillian, *Librn,* Saint Paul Municipal Library, Saint Paul AD. 403-645-4904
Masseau, Barbara A, *Acq,* Centenary College, Taylor Memorial Learning Resource Center, Hackettstown NJ. 201-852-1400, Ext 244
Masselink, W, *Br Coordr,* Prince Edward Island Provincial Library, Charlottetown PE. 902-892-3504, Ext 54
Massello, Barbara, *ILL, Ref & On-Line Servs,* Southwest Missouri State University Library, Springfield MO. 417-836-5104
Massen, Dorothy, *Ad,* Connetquot Public Library, Bohemia NY. 516-567-5115
Massenburg, Phyllis, *Cat,* Gadsden-Etowah County Library, Gadsden Public Library, Gadsden AL. 205-547-1611
Massengale, R Glenn, *Dir & Acq,* Huntingdon College, Houghton Memorial Library, Montgomery AL. 205-265-0511, Ext 221
Massey, Don, *Dir, Tech Serv & Acq,* Haywood Technical Institute, A L Freedlander Learning Resource Center, Clyde NC. 704-627-2821, Ext 16, 20
Massey, Jim, *Media,* Harford County Library, Bel Air MD. 301-838-7484
Massey, Judith, *Dir,* Cresskill Public Library, Cresskill NJ. 201-567-3521
Massey, Katha D, *Non-Book,* University of Georgia Libraries, Athens GA. 404-542-2716
Massey, Kay, *Librn,* Newton Public Library, Newton IL. 618-783-8141
Massey, Lucile, *Librn,* Bartram Trail Regional Library (Greene County), Greensboro GA. 404-678-7736
Massey, Thelma, *Librn,* Frontenac County Library (Ompah Branch), Ompah ON. 613-479-2281
Massey, William Clayton, *Dir,* South Windsor Public Library, South Windsor CT. 203-644-1541
Massie, Juanita J, *Librn, On-Line Servs & Bibliog Instr,* Evansville Psychiatric Children's Center Library, Evansville IN. 812-477-6436
Massie, Laura, *Dir,* Farmington Public Library, Farmington MO. 314-756-5241
Massie, Paul, *AV,* Saint Michael's College, Durick Library, Colchester VT. 802-655-2000, Ext 2400
Massingill, Katy, *Ref,* Grady C Hogue Library, Learning Resource Center, Beeville TX. 512-358-7032
Massis, Bruce Edward, *Dir,* Jewish Guild for the Blind, Cassette Library, New York NY. 212-595-2000, Ext 331&332
Massman, Virgil F, *In Charge,* James Jerome Hill Reference Library, Saint Paul MN. 612-227-9531
Massmann, Robert, *Dir,* Central Connecticut State College, Elihu Burritt Library, New Britain CT. 203-827-7531
Massnick, Nancy, *Dir,* Delafield Public Library, Delafield WI. 414-646-8506
Masson, Sandra, *Librn,* CNA Financial Corporation Library, Chicago IL. 312-822-7630
Masson, Sandra K, *Librn,* Albuquerque Public Library (Ernie Pyle), Albuquerque NM. 505-766-7921
Massonneau, Suzanne, *Tech Serv,* University of Vermont & State Agricultural College, Bailey-Howe Memorial Library, Burlington VT. 802-656-2020
Mast, Jane E, *Librn,* Parsons Public Library, Parsons KS. 316-421-5920
Mast, Mary M, *Librn,* Fairfield Public Library, Fairfield MT. 406-467-2477

Mast, Susan, *Librn,* Sandown Public Library, Sandown NH. 603-887-3428
Mastalir, Janet, *Asst Librn,* National College Library, Rapid City SD. 605-394-4943
Masters, Ila, *Librn,* Bowerston School District Public Library, Bowerston OH. 614-269-8531
Masters, Richard, *Dir,* Munising School-Public Library, Munising MI. 906-387-2125
Masters, Robert, *Instr,* Fairmont State College, Library Science Program, WV. 304-367-4121
Masters, Robert G, *Dir,* Fairmont State College Library, Fairmont WV. 304-367-4121
Masters, Suzann, *Ch & YA,* Saint Lucie County Library Systems, Fort Pierce FL. 305-461-5708
Masters, Jr, Fred N, *Librn,* Dexter Corp, C H Dexter Division Technical Library, Windsor Locks CT. 203-623-9801, Ext 557
Masterson, Greg, *Dir,* Cape Cod Community College, Library-Learning Resource Center, West Barnstable MA. 617-362-2131, Ext 341, 345
Masterson, Ingrid, *Bkmobile Coordr,* Mississauga Public Library, Mississauga ON. 416-625-8681
Masterson, Joan, *Dir,* Morgan County Public Library, Martinsville IN. 317-342-3451
Masterson, Leona, *Cat,* Willard Memorial Library, Willard OH. 419-933-8564
Masterson, William, *Librn,* Prince George's County Memorial Library System (College Park Branch), College Park MD. 301-927-1694
Masterson, William, *Librn,* Prince George's County Memorial Library System (Mount Rainier Branch), Mount Rainier MD. 301-864-8937
Masterton, Mary, *Browsing Libr,* Detroit Public Library, Detroit Associated Libraries, Detroit MI. 313-833-1000
Masterton, Phyllis, *ILL,* Wilmette Public Library District, Wilmette IL. 312-256-5025
Masthay, Elizabeth, *Ch,* Southington Public Library, Southington CT. 203-628-0947
Mastin, Charles, *Acq,* College of Marin Library, Kentfield CA. 415-485-9470
Maston, Donna, *Bkmobile Coordr,* Veterans Memorial Public Library, Bismarck ND. 701-222-6410
Mastro, Cherie, *Librn,* Washington State Library (Purdy Treatment Center Library), Gig Harbor WA. 206-858-9101, Ext 230
Mastropierro, Rae, *Librn,* Volusia County Law Library, Daytona Beach FL. 904-258-7000
Mastrovita, Frank, *Cat,* Mitre Corp (Technical Report Center), Bedford MA. 617-271-2351
Matarazzo, James M, *Assoc Prof,* Simmons College, Graduate School of Library & Information Science, MA. 617-738-2225
Matas, G P, *Admin Supvr,* Illinois Power Co, Generation Engineering Department Library, Decatur IL. 217-424-6600, 424-6992
Matcher, Rita, *Dir, On-Line Servs & Bibliog Instr,* Sinai Hospital of Baltimore, Staff Library, Baltimore MD. 301-367-7800, Ext 8551
Matchett, Katherine, *Cat,* Whiteriver Public Library, Whiteriver AZ. 602-338-4884
Matchinski, William L, *Inst Libr Program specialist,* Wyoming State Hospital Library, Evanston WY. 307-789-3464, Ext 279
Mate, A V, *Info Servs,* University of Windsor, Leddy Library, Windsor ON. 519-253-4232, Ext 198
Mate, A V, *Actg Librn,* University of Windsor, Leddy Library, Windsor ON. 519-253-4232, Ext 198
Mateer, Carolyn S, *Ref,* University of Washington Libraries, Seattle WA. 206-543-1760
Matejka, Marcella, *In Charge,* Cleveland Public Library (Business & Economics), Cleveland OH. 216-623-2930
Matera, Marylouise, *Librn,* Nassau County Museum Reference Library, East Meadow NY. 516-292-4292
Matern, Dorothy, *Librn,* Live Oak County Library (Three Rivers Branch), Three Rivers TX. 512-786-3037
Maternowski, Lee, *Ad,* Elk Grove Village Public Library, Elk Grove Village IL. 312-439-0447
Materson, June, *Ref,* Miami Beach Public Library, Miami Beach FL. 305-673-7535
Mates, Barbara, *Librn,* Cleveland Public Library (Union), Cleveland OH. 216-641-4961
Mathany, Sue, *Librn,* Jackson-George Regional Library System (Pascagoula City Branch), Pascagoula MS. 601-762-3406

Matheke, Margaret, *Tech Serv,* Upsala College Library, East Orange NJ. 201-266-7295
Matheny, Jr, James C, *Dir,* Holyoke Public Library, Holyoke MA. 413-534-3357
Matheny-White, Pat, *Reader Serv,* Evergreen State College, Daniel J Evans Library, Olympia WA. 206-866-6262
Mather, Dan, *Assoc Dir Tech Serv,* Western Washington University, Mabel Zoe Wilson Library, Bellingham WA. 206-676-3050
Mather, Florence, *Cat,* Erie Community College-North, Library Resources Center, Buffalo NY. 716-634-0800
Mather, Marjorie, *Librn,* Chocorua Public Library, Chocorua NH. 603-323-8610
Matherne, Brenda, *Librn,* Iberville Parish Library (Maringouin Branch), Maringouin LA. 504-625-2743
Mathes, Elizabeth, *Tech Serv,* Crystal Lake Public Library, Crystal Lake IL. 815-459-1687
Matheson, Arden, *Instr,* Southern Alberta Institute of Technology, Library Arts Program, AB. 403-284-8328
Matheson, Del, *Dir,* Lane Community College Library, Eugene OR. 503-747-4501, Ext 2354
Matheson, Joyce, *Librn,* Haverford State Hospital, Medical Library, Haverford PA. 215-252-9620
Matheson, Mrs Tom, *In Charge,* Oxford County Library (Brooksdale Sunday School), Embro ON. 519-475-4429
Matheson, Nina W, *Dir,* George Washington University Library (Paul Himmelfarb Health Sciences Library), Washington DC. 202-676-2850
Matheson, William, *Chief, Rare Bks & Spec Coll Div,* Library of Congress, Washington DC. 202-287-5000
Mathew, Alice, *Librn,* International College, Honolulu HI. 808-595-2408
Mathews, Faye, *Librn,* Henry Laird Library, Belpre KS. 316-995-3202
Mathews, Florence, *Librn,* San Diego Public Library (University Community), San Diego CA. 714-453-5722
Mathews, Irene, *Music,* University of Redlands, George & Verda Armacost Library, Redlands CA. 714-793-2121, Ext 472
Mathews, James C, *Acq,* University of Wisconsin-Whitewater, Library & Learning Resources, Whitewater WI. 414-472-1000
Mathews, Janet B, *Dir,* Albany Business College Library, Albany NY. 518-449-7163
Mathews, Karen L, *Syst Analyst,* Los Alamos Scientific Laboratory Libraries, Library Services Group, Los Alamos NM. 505-667-4448
Mathews, Karlotta, *Asst Dir & Ad,* Glenview Public Library, Glenview IL. 312-724-5200
Mathews, Kathleen, *Librn,* Hamilton Public Library (Barton), Hamilton ON. 416-527-8122
Mathews, Leita L, *Dir,* Salem Township Free Public Library, Jaquith-Corbin Memorial Library, Yates City IL. 309-358-1678
Mathews, Marilyn, *Librn,* Saint Mary's General Hospital, Medical Library, Kitchener ON. 519-744-3311, Ext 453
Mathews, Mary Ann, *Librn,* Thorntown Public Library, Thorntown IN. 317-436-7348
Mathews, Sidney E, *Asst Dir,* Southern Illinois University at Carbondale, Delyte W Morris Library, Carbondale IL. 618-453-2522
Mathews, Susan, *Dir,* League City Public Library, League City TX. 713-554-6612
Mathewson, Ann, *Librn,* Madison County Law Library, London OH. 614-852-9515
Mathewson, Betty, *Librn,* Rebecca M Arthurs Memorial Library, Brookville PA. 814-849-5512
Mathewson, Sara, *Librn,* Kanawha County Public Library (Cross Lanes), Charleston WV. 304-776-5999
Matheys, Joan M, *Tech Serv,* Northeastern University Libraries (School of Law), Boston MA. 617-437-3338
Mathias, Barbara, *Librn,* Ontario Ministry of Labour (Ontario Labour Relations Board Library), Toronto ON. 416-965-0206
Mathies, Dr Bonnie K, *Coordr,* Wright State University, Div of Library & Communication Science, OH. 513-873-2182
Mathies, Lorraine, *Librn,* University of California Los Angeles Library (Education & Psychology), Los Angeles CA. 213-825-4081

Mathieson, Marion, *Media,* Sheridan College, Kooi Library, Instructional Resource Center, Sheridan WY. 307-674-6446, Ext 170

Mathieu, Maurice, *Theol,* Universite Laval Bibliotheque, Quebec PQ. 418-656-3344

Mathis, Ann, *Ref,* Freed-Hardeman College, Loden-Daniel Library, Henderson TN. 901-989-4611, Ext 133

Mathis, Margaret, *Asst Dir,* El Paso Public Library, El Paso TX. 915-543-3804

Mathis, Treva W, *Assoc Dir & Curator Quaker Coll,* Guilford College Library, Greensboro NC. 919-292-5511, Ext 250

Mathys, Nel, *Librn,* United States Air Force (Rome Air Development Center Technical Library), Griffiss AFB NY. 315-330-7607

Matina, Charles, *Media,* Nazareth College of Rochester Library, Lorette Wilmot Library, Rochester NY. 716-586-2525, Ext 232

Matirne, Nancy, *Librn,* Iberville Parish Library (Grosse Tete), Plaquemine LA. 504-687-2520

Matis, Gregg, *Librn,* Camden County Free Library (Winslow Township), Sicklerville NJ. 609-629-3141

Matis, Sarah, *Asst to the Dir,* Plattsburgh Public Library, Plattsburgh NY. 518-563-0921

Matise, Geraldine A, *Asst RML Librn,* New York & New Jersey Regional Medical Library, NY. 212-876-8763

Matlock, Ann, *Librn,* Bay County Public Library Association (Wewahitchka Branch), Wewahitchka FL. 904-639-2419

Matlock, Mary G, *Asst Prof,* Alverno College, Dept of Library Science, WI. 414-671-5400, Ext 213

Matlock, Mary G, *Bibliog Instr,* Alverno College, Library Media Center, Milwaukee WI. 414-671-5400, Ext 419

Matlock, Sarah, *Circ,* University of the South, Jessie Ball duPont Library, Sewanee TN. 615-598-5931, Ext 265, 267

Matos, Antonio, *Dir,* Catholic University of Puerto Rico (Encarnacion Valdes Library), Ponce PR. 809-844-4150, Ext 119

Matos, Maria, *Librn,* Inter-American University of Puerto Rico, San German Campus Library, San German PR. 809-892-1095

Matovich, Richard M, *ILL,* California State College, Louis L Manderino Library, California PA. 412-938-4091

Matson, Constance, *Dir,* City & County Library, Ladysmith Public Library, Ladysmith WI. 715-532-6275

Matson, Esther, *Librn,* D R Evarts Library, Athens NY. 518-945-1417

Matson, Kathy, *Asst Dir & Ch,* Crow River Regional Library, Willmar MN. 612-235-3162

Matson, Lucile, *Ch,* Fort Dodge Public Library, Fort Dodge IA. 515-573-8167

Matson, Madeline, *Coordr Publ,* Missouri State Library, Jefferson City MO. 314-751-4214

Matson, Molly, *Pub Servs,* University of Massachusetts at Boston Library, Boston MA. 617-287-1900, Ext 2224

Matsuda, Shizue, *Asia & Far East Coll,* Indiana University at Bloomington, University Libraries, Bloomington IN. 812-337-3403

Matsui, Masato, *Japanese Area Specialties,* University of Hawaii (University of Hawaii Library), Honolulu HI. 808-948-7205

Matsumiya, Hisao, *Librn,* Hughes Aircraft Co (Publications Clearance Unit), Culver City CA. 213-391-0711, Ext 3474

Matsumura, Wilma, *Librn,* Hawaii State Library System (Hawaii Regional), Hilo HI. 808-935-5407

Matsuoka, Mary, *Librn,* Hawaiian Sugar Planters' Association, Experiment Station Library, Aiea HI. 808-487-5561, Ext 270-1

Matt, Salinda M, *Librn,* Lancaster County Historical Society Library, Lancaster PA. 717-392-4633

Matta, Paula J, *Librn,* Princeton Library in New York, New York NY. 212-682-6400

Mattas, Frank, *Admin Dir,* San Mateo Educational Resources Center, CA. 415-364-5600, Ext 4401

Matte, Lise, *Librn,* Bibliotheque Municipale, Chibougamau PQ. 819-276-2688, Poste 22

Matte, Pierre, *Dir,* Service Des Bibliotheques Publiques, Ministere des Affaires Culturelles, Quebec PQ. 418-643-2140

Matteo, Christine, *Librn,* Ocean County Library (Jackson Township), Jackson NJ. 201-928-4400

Matter, Donna, *Librn,* Lake Region Junior College, Paul Hoghaug Library, Devils Lake ND. 701-662-4951, Ext 42

Mattes, Jean, *Librn,* Clarinda Public Library, Clarinda IA. 712-542-2416

Mattes, Lillian, *Librn,* Congregation B'nai Moshe, Isaac & Helen Liebson Library, Oak Park MI. 313-548-9000

Matteson, James, *Librn,* Grand Rapids Public Library (West Side), Grand Rapids MI. 616-456-4436

Matteson, Mary Bliss, *Librn,* Cambridge Public Library (Observatory Hill), Cambridge MA. 617-498-9084

Matteucig, Catherine, *Dir,* Heald Engineering College Library, San Francisco CA. 415-441-5562

Matteucig, Iole L, *Dir,* City College of San Francisco Library, San Francisco CA. 415-239-3404

Matthew, Jeannette, *Spec Coll,* Indiana University-Purdue University at Indianapolis, University Library, Indianapolis IN. 317-264-4101

Matthewman, Anne, *Librn,* Essex County Law Association Library, Windsor ON. 519-252-8418

Matthews, Ann, *Asst Dir,* Franklin Sylvester Library, Medina OH. 216-725-0588

Matthews, Anne, *Instr,* University of Denver, Graduate School of Librarianship and Information Management, CO. 303-753-2557

Matthews, Barbara, *Cat,* Saint Mary's Dominican College, John XXIII Library, New Orleans LA. 504-865-7761, Ext 225

Matthews, C, *Librn,* University of Toronto Libraries (Centre of Criminology), Toronto ON. 416-978-7068

Matthews, Charles, *Tech Librn,* Digital Equipment Corp, Salem Library, Salem NH. 603-893-9011, Ext 2254

Matthews, Christine, *Acq,* Campbell University, Carrie Rich Memorial Library, Buies Creek NC. 919-893-4111, Ext 238

Matthews, Christine, *Reader Serv,* Jarvis Christian College, Ohlin Library & Communication Center, Hawkins TX. 214-769-2174, Ext 154

Matthews, Donald N, *Librn,* Lutheran Theological Seminary, A R Wentz Library, Gettysburg PA. 717-334-6286

Matthews, Eileen, *Librn,* Sterling Drug, Inc, Lehn & Fink Products Co Library, Montvale NJ. 201-391-8500, Ext 231

Matthews, Felicia, *ILL,* Ponca City Library, Ponca City OK. 405-762-6311

Matthews, Frederick W, *Assoc Prof,* Dalhousie University, School of Library Service, NS. 902-424-3656

Matthews, Jaxon, *Librn,* Control Data Library, Sunnyvale CA. 408-734-7873

Matthews, Linda, *Dir,* African Bibliographic Center, Inc, Research Library, Washington DC. 202-223-1392

Matthews, Lynn, *Dir,* Kitchener Public Library, Kitchener ON. 519-743-0271

Matthews, Majorie, *Librn,* Haines Borough Public Library, Haines AK. 907-766-2545

Matthews, Martha F, *Librn,* Veterans Administration, Hospital Library, Birmingham AL. 205-933-8101, Ext 264

Matthews, Mrs Raymond, *Librn,* First Baptist Church, E F Walker Memorial Library, Luling TX. 512-875-2227

Matthews, Myrtle W, *Librn,* Bolivar County Library (Thelma Rayner Memorial), Merigold MS. 601-748-3201

Matthews, Pat, *Librn,* Times-World Corp Library, Roanoke VA. 703-981-3279

Matthews, Paula, *Librn,* Lubec Memorial Library, Lubec ME. 207-733-2491

Matthews, Regenia, *Cat,* New Orleans Public Library, Simon Heinsheim & Fisk Libraries, New Orleans LA. 504-586-4905

Matthews, Robert O, *Superintendent,* Norfolk Botanical Gardens Library, Norfolk VA. 804-855-0194

Matthews, Sandra S, *On-Line Servs,* Armed Forces Radiobiology Research Institute, Bethesda MD. 301-295-0428

Matthews, Sister Linda M, *Rare Bks,* Emory University Libraries (General Libraries), Atlanta GA. 404-329-6861

Matthews-Granshaw, Carole L, *Librn,* San Jose Medical Clinic Library, San Jose CA. 408-998-5551, Ext 300

Matthewson, Elsie, *Acq,* Mount Vernon Public Library, Mount Vernon WA. 206-336-2418

Matthias, Rita, *Librn,* Siskiyou County Public Library (Dunsmuir Branch), Dunsmuir CA. 916-235-2035

Matthis, Mildred B, *Dir,* Lenoir Community College, Learning Resources Center, Kinston NC. 919-527-6223, Ext 235

Matthis, Raimund, *Tech Serv,* University of Puget Sound, Collins Memorial Library, Tacoma WA. 206-756-3257

Mattice, Virginia, *Asst Librn,* RCA Corp, Government Communications Systems Library, Camden NJ. 609-338-3488

Mattimore, Maryanne, *Librn,* Binghamton General Hospital, Stuart B Blakely Memorial Library, Binghamton NY. 607-772-1100, Ext 220

Mattingly, John F, *Dir,* Saint Patrick's Seminary, McKeon Memorial Library, Menlo Park CA. 415-322-2224

Mattingly, Marilyn, *ILL,* Bowling Green Public Library, Bowling Green KY. 502-781-4882

Mattison, Gloria, *Acq,* Claflin College, H V Manning Library, Orangeburg SC. 803-534-2710, Ext 56

Mattison, Marguerite, *Librn,* Art League of Manatee County, McKelvey Memorial Library, Bradenton FL. 813-746-2862

Mattox, Ethel, *Ch,* Whittier Public Library, Whittier CA. 213-698-8949

Mattson, Bonnie, *Librn,* Municipality of Metropolitan Seattle (Metro) Library, Seattle WA. 206-447-6770

Mattson, Margaret J, *Librn,* United States Bureau of Mines Library, Juneau AK. 907-364-2111

Mattson, Marguerite E, *Dir,* Canadian Bible College-Canadian Theological College, Archibald Foundation Library, Regina SK. 306-545-1515

Mattson, Mrs Orville, *Librn,* Casselton Public Library, Casselton ND. 701-347-4861

Mattson, Rosalee, *Librn,* Bandera County Library, Bandera TX. 512-796-4213

Matulich, Shirley A, *Librn,* Oceanographic Services, Inc, Technical Library, Goleta CA. 805-685-4521

Matulka, Carol, *Librn,* Saint Joseph Medical Center Library, Wichita KS. 316-685-1111, Ext 2588

Matusak, Susan, *Chief Librn,* Institute for Sex Research, Research Collections & Information Services, Bloomington IN. 812-337-7686

Matwey, Lidia, *In Charge,* Carnegie Library of Pittsburgh (Sheraden), Pittsburgh PA. 412-622-3100

Matz, Ruth G, *Chief Librn,* Commonwealth of Massachusetts, Department of the Attorney General Library, Boston MA. 617-727-1036

Matz, Sandra A, *Asst Dir,* Sinai Hospital of Detroit, Samuel Frank Medical Library, Detroit MI. 313-493-5140

Matzek, Richard, *Dir,* Nazareth College of Rochester Library, Lorette Wilmot Library, Rochester NY. 716-586-2525, Ext 232

Matzen, Caroline B, *Dir,* Kingston Area Library, Kingston NY. 914-331-0507

Matzka, Liselotte, *Librn,* Adelphi University Library (Science), Garden City NY. 516-294-8700, Ext 7522

Mau, Marian, *Librn,* Paullina Free Public Library, Paullina IA. 712-448-3941

Maud, Pam, *Librn,* Lake County Public Library (Griffith Public), Griffith IN. 219-838-2825

Maudlin, S, *Indian Studies,* Blue Cloud Abbey Library, Marvin SD. 605-432-5528, Ext 904

Mauer, Bradley, *Librn,* Davis County Library (South), Bountiful UT. 801-295-8732

Mauerhoff, Joy, *Coll Develp Librn,* Ontario Legislative Library, Research & Information Services, Toronto ON. 416-965-4545

Maughan, Patricia, *Librn,* Columbia University (Engineering), New York NY. 212-280-2241

Maul, Helen, *Librn,* Cochise County Library System, Bisbee AZ. 602-432-5703, Ext 500

Maul, Shirley, *ILL,* Vassar College Library, Poughkeepsie NY. 914-452-7000

Mauldin, Ellen, *Ser,* Mississippi State University, Mitchell Memorial Library, Mississippi State MS. 601-325-4225

Mauldin, Eugenia, *Prof,* University of Tennessee, Knoxville, Graduate School of Library & Information Science, TN. 615-974-2148

Mauldin, Evelyn, *Dir,* Ault Public Library, Ault CO. 303-834-1259

Mauldin, Glynon, *Dir,* Ingleside Public Library, Ingleside TX. 512-776-2517

Maulsby, Helen, *Librn,* Fairfax County Public Library (Thomas Jefferson), Falls Church VA. 703-573-1060

Maunsell, Kay, *ILL,* Crawfordsville District Public Library, Crawfordsville IN. 317-362-2242

Maupin, Alfred J, *Asst Dir,* Reuben McMillan Free Library Free Library Association, Public Library of Youngstown & Mahoning County, Youngstown OH. 216-744-8636

Maupin, Ann, *Librn,* Los Angeles Public Library System (Studio City Branch), Studio City CA. 213-769-5212

Maupin, Vewa, *Commun Servs,* Calloway County Public Library, Murray KY. 502-753-2288

Maurer, Barbara S, *Circ,* Franklin & Marshall College Library, Lancaster PA. 717-291-4223

Maurer, Carol, *Chief Librn,* Veterans Administration Hospital Library, Seattle WA. 206-762-1010

Maurer, Charles B, *Dir,* Denison University, William Howard Doane Library, Granville OH. 614-587-0810, Ext 225

Maurer, Charles D, *Dir,* Rutland Free Library, Rutland VT. 802-773-6880

Maurer, Esther J, *Head,* Free Library of Philadelphia (Education, Philosophy & Religion), Philadelphia PA. 215-686-5322

Maurer, Linda, *Libr Technician,* Department of Northern Saskatchewan, Research Library, La Ronge SK. 306-425-2033, Ext 210

Maurer, Linda M, *Librn,* Skagway Public Library, Skagway AK. 907-983-2665

Maurer, Thomas, *Librn,* Allen County Law Library Association, Lima OH. 419-223-1426

Mauri, Carla, *Librn,* Hawaii State Library System (Makawao Branch), Makawao HI. 808-572-8094

Maurice, Francoise, *Dir,* Bibliotheque Municipale, Coaticook PQ. 819-849-4013

Maurich, Christine, *Tech Serv,* Yakima Valley Regional Library, Yakima WA. 509-452-8541, Ext 22

Maurin, Mrs Robert, *Librn,* Cornell City Library, Cornell WI. 715-239-6041

Maurin, Raissa, *Chief Librn,* Veterans Administration (Medical Library), Miami FL. 305-344-4455, Ext 3461 or 3462, 324-3187

Mauro, Elsi, *Personnel,* Stanford University Libraries, Stanford CA. 415-497-2016

Maurushat, Joan, *Librn,* Cleveland Public Library (Lorain), Cleveland OH. 216-631-4962

Maus, Carol R, *Asst Librn,* Saint Peter's College Library, Englewood Cliffs NJ. 201-568-7730

Mauseth, Barbara J, *Librn,* Homer Public Library, Homer AK. 907-235-7660

Mauseth, James, *Instr,* Northern State College, Library Science Program, SD. 605-622-2645

Mauseth, James, *Tech Serv,* Northern State College, Williams Library & Learning Resource Center, Aberdeen SD. 605-622-2645

Mauter, George A, *Chief Librn,* Fairchild Industries, Fairchild Republic Co, Engineering Library, Farmingdale NY. 516-531-3497

Maw, Bertha, *Tech Serv,* Pickens County Library, Easley SC. 803-859-9679

Mawdsley, Katherine F, *Doc,* University of California at Davis, General Library, Davis CA. 916-752-2110

Max, Jean, *Librn,* Jackson Metropolitan Library (Brandon Library), Brandon MS. 601-352-3677

Max, Patrick, *Bibliog Instr,* University of Notre Dame Library, Notre Dame IN. 219-283-7317

Maxey, Annie Bell, *Asst,* Sabine Parish Library (Noble Branch), Noble LA. 318-256-2212

Maxey, Trudy, *Tech Serv,* Monterey Public Library, Monterey CA. 408-646-3930

Maxey, Victor L, *Dir,* Cincinnati Bible Seminary Library, Cincinnati OH. 513-471-4800, Ext 49

Maxey, Vivian, *Librn,* Winn Parish Library, Winnfield LA. 318-628-4478

Maxfield, Phillip L, *Asst Dir Mgt Servs,* Tacoma Public Library, Tacoma WA. 206-572-2000

Maxian, M Bruce, *Asst Prof,* Long Island University, Palmer Graduate Library School, NY. 516-299-2855 & 299-2856

Maxim, Carol, *Ch,* Colonie Town Library, Loudonville NY. 518-458-9274

Maxin, Jacqueline A, *Librn,* PPG Industries Inc (Fiberglass Technical Center Library), Pittsburgh PA. 412-782-5130, Ext 218

Maxon, William, *Taxation,* Georgetown University (Fred O Dennis Law Library), Washington DC. 202-624-8260

Maxon, William, *ILL & Ref,* Georgetown University (Fred O Dennis Law Library), Washington DC. 202-624-8260

Maxson, Wayne, *ILL,* Temple University of the Commonwealth System of Higher Education, Samuel Paley Library, Philadelphia PA. 215-787-8231

Maxton, Pauline, *Asst Dir,* Reading Public Library, Reading Public Library District, Reading PA. 215-374-4548

Maxwell, Barbara A, *Tech Serv,* Shepherd College, Ruth Scarborough Library, Shepherdstown WV. 304-876-6775

Maxwell, Laura, *Acq,* Circleville Bible College Library, Circleville OH. 614-474-8896

Maxwell, Littleton, *Bus,* University of Richmond, Boatwright Memorial Library, Richmond VA. 804-285-6452

Maxwell, Littleton, *On-Line Servs,* University of Richmond, Boatwright Memorial Library, Richmond VA. 804-285-6452

Maxwell, Margaret F, *Prof,* University of Arizona, Graduate Library School, AZ. 602-626-3565

Maxwell, Marjo, *On-Line Servs,* University of Dayton Libraries, Roesch Library, Dayton OH. 513-229-4221

Maxwell, Martha Ann, *Dir,* Cape Girardeau Public Library, Cape Girardeau MO. 314-334-5279

Maxwell, Monty M, *Dir,* Eastern Oklahoma District Library System, Muskogee OK. 918-683-2846

Maxwell, N K, *Dir,* Copperas Cove Public Library, Copperas Cove TX. 817-547-3826

Maxwell, Nancy, *Ref,* Henrietta Public Library, Rochester NY. 716-334-3401

Maxwell, Roberta, *Librn,* Texas Instruments Inc Library, Houston TX. 713-494-5115, Ext 3244

Maxwell, Rosemary, *Librn,* United States Air Force (Seymour Johnson Air Force Base Library), Seymour Johnson AFB NC. 919-736-5707

Maxwell, Sara, *Asst Dir,* Elbert County Library, Elberton GA. 404-283-5375

Maxwell, Vera J, *Chief Librn,* Thomas County Community College Library, Thomasville GA. 912-226-1621

Maxworthy, Lucille, *Acq,* Beloit College, Col Robert H Morse Library, Beloit WI. 608-365-3391, Ext 230

May, Arlee, *Dir, New England Regional Med Libr Serv,* Harvard University Library (Francis A Countway Library of Medicine), Boston MA. 617-732-2142

May, Arlee, *Dir,* New England Regional Medical Library Service, MA. 617-732-2128

May, Barbara C, *Ref Ed,* Dallas Morning News Reference Department, Dallas TX. 214-745-8302

May, Bob, *Asst City Librn Commun Servs,* Seattle Public Library, Seattle WA. 206-625-2665

May, Cornelia E, *Dir,* Greenville College, Ruby E Dare Library, Greenville IL. 618-664-1840, Ext 237

May, Curtis, *Dir of Libr Servs,* San Mateo Educational Resources Center, CA. 415-364-5600, Ext 4401

May, Dolores A, *Ref,* Ebasco Services, Inc Library, New York NY. 212-785-5895

May, Dorothy R, *Ad,* Mill Memorial Library, Nanticoke PA. 717-735-3030

May, Elizabeth, *Cat,* Millville Public Library, Millville NJ. 609-825-7087

May, Eric, *Dir,* Capuchin Fathers - Capuchin Seminary Library, Garrison NY. 914-424-3069

May, Frank J, *Librn,* Wrightsville Marine Bio-Medical Library, Wilmington NC. 919-791-4330

May, James, *Asst Prof,* Saint Cloud State University, Center for Library & Audiovisual Education, MN. 612-255-2022

May, James H, *Assoc Dir,* Sonoma State University, Ruben Salazar Library, Rohnert Park CA. 707-664-2397

May, Jill, *Asst Prof,* Purdue University, Dept of Education, Library Media & Instructional Development, IN. 317-749-2902

May, Joanne M, *Librn,* United States Navy (Naval Environmental Prediction Research Facility), Monterey CA. 408-646-2813

May, John R, *Dir,* Centre College of Kentucky, Grace Doherty Library, Danville KY. 606-236-5211, Ext 237

May, Kathy, *Bus Ref,* High Point Public Library, High Point NC. 919-885-8411

May, Loydene, *Librn,* Aurora Public Library, Aurora MN. 218-229-2021

May, Lucinda, *Reader Serv,* John C Calhoun State Community College, Albert P Brewer Library, Decatur AL. 205-353-3102

May, Mabel, *Circ,* Vanderbilt University Library (Central-Science), Nashville TN. 615-322-6603

May, Maija B, *Librn,* Erikson Institute for Early Education Library, Chicago IL. 312-493-0200

May, Margery, *Circ,* Wesleyan University, Olin Memorial Library, Middletown CT. 203-347-9411, Ext 296

May, Mrs Edwin, *Librn,* Silverton Library, Silverton TX. 806-823-2325

May, Nadine, *Librn,* Kentucky School for the Deaf Library, Danville KY. 606-236-5132

May, Patricia, *YA,* Albany Public Library, Albany NY. 518-449-3380

May, Ruby S, *Assoc Regional Med Libr Dir,* Midwest Health Science Library Network, (MHSLN), IL. 312-996-2464

May, Ruby S, *Assoc Dir,* University of Illinois at the Medical Center, Library of the Health Sciences, Chicago IL. 312-996-8974

May, Ruth, *Bibliography,* University of Manitoba Libraries, Winnipeg MB. 204-474-9881

May, Sue, *ILL,* Talbot County Free Library, Easton MD. 301-822-1626

May, W David, *Dir,* Patrick Henry Community College Library, Martinsville VA. 703-638-8777, Ext 51

May, Jr, Lynn E, *Exec Dir,* Baptist Information Retrieval System, (BIRS), TN. 615-251-2660

Maya, Yolanda, *Health Sci Libr Tech,* Saint Joseph Hospital, Medical Library, Chicago IL. 312-975-3038

Mayberry, Merrill, *Librn,* Kansas City Public Library (Central), Kansas City MO. 816-923-1555

Mayden, Priscilla M, *Dir,* University of Utah (Spencer S Eccles Health Sciences Library), Salt Lake City UT. 801-581-8771

Mayer, Betty, *Soc Sci,* University of Bridgeport, Magnus Wahlstrom Library, Bridgeport CT. 203-576-4740

Mayer, Clara, *Librn,* Brooklyn Public Library (Carroll Gardens), Brooklyn NY. 212-625-5838

Mayer, Dinah, *Librn,* Addison Public Library, Addison NY. 607-359-3888

Mayer, Dorothy, *Dir,* Opelousas-Eunice Public Library, Opelousas LA. 318-948-3693

Mayer, Dorothy, *Librn,* Opelousas-Eunice Public Library (Eunice Public), Eunice LA. 318-457-7120

Mayer, Elizabeth C, *Librn,* Wender, Murase & White, Law Library, New York NY. 212-832-3333, Ext 525

Mayer, Eric, *Librn,* Hudson County Law Library, Jersey City NJ. 201-792-3737, Ext 271

Mayer, George, *Librn,* New York Public Library (General Library (Circulating & Information Collections)), New York NY. 212-790-6262

Mayer, George, *Librn,* New York Public Library (Music), New York NY. 212-790-6262

Mayer, Louise, *Librn,* Sno-Isle Regional Library (Darrington Branch), Darrington WA. 206-436-1600

Mayer, M, *AV,* Richard J Daley College, Learning Resource Center, Chicago IL. 312-735-3000, Ext 224, 226, 227

Mayer, Mary, *Librn,* Department of Public Libraries & Information (Bayside), Virginia Beach VA. 804-464-9280

Mayer, Mary, *Librn,* Portsmouth Public Library (Churchland), Portsmouth VA. 804-484-5584

Mayer, Nancy, *Acq,* Rockhurst College, Greenlease Library, Kansas City MO. 816-363-4010, Ext 253

Mayer, Tom, *Personnel Dir,* Timberland Regional Library, Olympia WA. 206-943-5001

Mayer, Vera, *Vice President, Info & Archives,* National Broadcasting Co (Reference Library), New York NY. 212-664-5307

Mayer, William J, *Mgr Tech Info Serv,* General Mills Inc (James Ford Bell Technical Information Services), Minneapolis MN. 612-540-3464

Mayers, Bernard J, *Librn,* International Flavors & Fragrances, Inc, IFF Research & Development Laboratory, Technical Information Center, Union Beach NJ. 201-264-4500, Ext 521

Mayers, Irwin, *Librn,* Merritt College Learning Resources Center, Oakland CA. 415-531-4911, Ext 330

Mayes, Deanne, *Librn,* Hollis Public Library, Hollis OK. 405-688-2744

Mayes, Milton, *Dir,* Rappahannock Community College, South Campus Library, Glenns VA. 804-758-5324, Ext 208

Mayeski, John, *Dir,* Kearney State College, Calvin T Ryan Library, Kearney NE. 308-236-4218

Mayeski, John, *Personnel,* University of Washington Libraries, Seattle WA. 206-543-1760

Mayeux, Pauline, *Librn,* Avoyelles Parish Library (Moreauville Branch), Moreauville LA. 318-253-7559

Mayfield, Doris W, *Ad,* Omaha Public Library, W Dale Clark Library, Omaha NE. 402-444-4800

Mayfield, John S, *Librn,* Army & Navy Club Library, Washington DC. 202-628-8400, Ext 216

Mayfield, Lynn, *Cat,* Northeast Regional Library, Corinth MS. 601-287-2441

Mayfield, Mary Jane, *Librn,* Marquette Community Library, Marquette KS. 913-546-2561

Mayfield, Vada, *Media,* Madison Public Library, Madison WI. 608-266-6300

Mayhew, Jean, *Librn,* United Technologies, Hamilton Standard Library, Windsor Locks CT. 203-623-1621

Mayhle, Conni, *Asst Librn,* Allegheny Wesleyan College Library, Salem OH. 216-337-6403

Maylan, Betsey Brown, *Librn,* Bellante, Clauss, Miller & Nolan Co Library, Scranton PA. 717-346-8771, Ext 333

Maylender, Becky, *Media,* Walla Walla Public Library, Walla Walla WA. 509-525-5353

Mayles, William, *Ref,* Indiana University-Purdue University at Indianapolis (Thirty-Eighth Street Campus), Indianapolis IN. 317-923-1325

Maylone, R Russell, *Spec Coll,* Northwestern University Library, Evanston IL. 312-492-7658

Maynard, Almeda, *Librn,* Chicago Public Library (Hamlin Park), Chicago IL. 312-281-0838

Maynard, Althea, *Librn,* Savoy Hollow Public Library, Savoy MA. 413-743-3675

Maynard, Barbara, *Librn,* Port Ewen Library Association, Port Ewen NY. 914-338-5580

Maynard, D D, *Asst Librn,* Pima County Law Library, Tucson AZ. 602-792-8456

Maynard, Edna, *Librn,* Westport Public Library, Westport CT. 203-273-3223

Maynard, Elizabeth, *Librn,* Federal Reserve Bank of Cleveland Research Library, Cleveland OH. 216-241-2800, Ext 288

Maynard, Helen J, *Librn,* Groton Public Library, Groton MA. 617-448-6761

Maynard, J Edward, *Circ,* The Citadel, Daniel Library, Charleston SC. 803-792-5116

Maynard, James W, *Dir,* Auglaize County District Library, Wapakoneta OH. 419-738-2921

Maynard, Joanne, *ILL,* University of Dayton Libraries, Roesch Library, Dayton OH. 513-229-4221

Maynard, Marvis, *Asst Librn,* Paris Public Library, South Paris ME. 207-743-6994

Maynard, Mary, *Librn,* Chatham Public Library, Chatham NY. 518-392-3666

Maynard, Nancy Bowden, *Librn,* Hartford Public Library, Hartford VT. 802-295-6080

Maynard, Robert, *Circ,* College of Alameda Library & Resources Center, Alameda CA. 415-522-7221, Ext 365

Mayo, Deborah, *Ref,* Elizabeth City State University, G R Little Library, Elizabeth City NC. 919-335-0551, Ext 332

Mayo, Donald S, *Asst Dean,* Chabot College, Learning Resource Center, Hayward CA. 415-786-6762

Mayo, Harriett E, *Tech Serv, Acq & Cat,* Abraham Baldwin Agricultural College, Baldwin Library, Tifton GA. 912-386-3223

Mayo, Hope, *Curator of Rare Bks,* Saint John's University, Alcuin Library, Collegeville MN. 612-363-2119

Mayo, Julia, *Mgt Sci & Info Systs,* National Defense University Library, Washington DC. 202-693-8437

Mayo, Kathleen, *Inst,* State Library of Florida, Div of Library Services, Dept of State, Tallahassee FL. 904-487-2651

Mayo, Lynn, *Acq,* Transylvania University, Frances Carrick Thomas Library, Lexington KY. 606-233-8225

Mayo, Marjorie, *Curric Ctr,* Olivet Nazarene College, Benner Library & Resource Center, Bourbonnais IL. 815-939-5354

Mayo, Mary, *Ch,* York Regional Library, Fredericton NB. 506-454-4481

Mayo, Wayne, *Dir,* Lawrence Public Library, Lawrence KS. 913-843-3833

Mayol, Isabel, *ILL,* Catholic University of Puerto Rico (Encarnacion Valdes Library), Ponce PR. 809-844-4150, Ext 119

Mayol, Josefina, *Acq,* Saint Petersburg Junior College, Michael M Bennett Library, Clearwater FL. 813-441-0681, Ext 2616

Mayos, Mrs George, *In Charge,* Oxford County Library (Brownsville Library), Brownsville ON. 519-877-2928

Mayover, Steven, *Head,* Free Library of Philadelphia (Films), Philadelphia PA. 215-686-5367

Mayrand, Lisa, *Librn,* University of Montreal Libraries (Physical Education), Montreal PQ. 514-343-6714

Mays, Brenda, *Cat,* Macon Junior College Library, Macon GA. 912-474-2700, Ext 215, 216

Mays, Charlotte, *Librn,* Atlanta Public Library (Martin Luther King, Jr), Atlanta GA. 404-658-7064

Mays, Lynnabeth, *Ch,* Henry Carter Hull Library, Inc, Clinton CT. 203-669-2342

Mays, Martha, *Spec Coll,* University of Lowell Libraries (Alumni-Lydon Library), Lowell MA. 617-452-5000, Ext 378

Mays, Mary, *Librn,* Public Technology, Inc, Information Center, Washington DC. 202-452-7700

Mayson, Joanne, *Librn,* Plymouth Congregational United Church of Christ Library, Burlington WI. 414-763-6890

Mayson, M, *Libr Tech,* Queen's University at Kingston (Geological Sciences), Kingston ON. 613-547-2653

Maythan, Thomas N, *Dir,* Denver Art Museum Library, F H Douglas Memorial Library, Denver CO. 303-575-2256

Mazareas, Helen, *Librn,* New England Merchants National Bank Library, Boston MA. 617-742-4000, Ext 2464

Mazerall, Anne, *On-Line Servs,* Canada Department Fisheries & Oceans, Bedford Institute of Oceanography Library, Dartmouth NS. 902-426-3675

Mazor, Armo, *Librn,* Warder Public Library (Indian Mound), Enon OH. 513-864-2502

Mazorol, Louise N, *Librn,* News & Courier & Evening Post Publishing Co, Post-Courier Library, Charleston SC. 803-577-7111

Mazsick, Bro Frank, *ILL & Ref,* Thomas More College, Learning Resources Center, Fort Mitchell KY. 606-341-5800, Ext 61

Mazur, Marjorie, *Tech Serv,* South Carolina State Library, Columbia SC. 803-758-3181

Mazur, Rebecca, *On-Line Servs,* State University of New York, College of Arts & Science at Oswego, Penfield Library, Oswego NY. 315-341-4232

Mazura, Irene C, *Ref,* Azusa City Library, Azusa CA. 213-334-0338

Mazurek, Adam, *Librn,* Public Library of Annapolis & Anne Arundel County Inc (Brooklyn Park), Baltimore MD. 301-789-3030

Mazzaferri, Janice, *Librn,* Massillon Public Library (Navarre Branch), Navarre OH. 216-879-2113

Mazzei, June, *ILL,* Central Connecticut State College, Elihu Burritt Library, New Britain CT. 203-827-7531

Mazzone, Mrs John R, *Dir,* Amsterdam Free Library, Amsterdam NY. 518-842-1080

McAdam, Pat, *Ref,* Arcadia Public Library, Arcadia CA. 213-446-7171

McAdoo, Karen, *Librn,* Public Library of the District of Columbia (Petworth), Washington DC. 202-727-1373

McAfee, Alberta, *Inst Mat Ctr,* West Chester State College, Francis Harvey Green Library, West Chester PA. 215-436-2643

McAfee, Mary, *Commun Servs,* Richland County Public Library, Columbia SC. 803-799-9084

McAlice, Sister Edith, *Dir,* College of Our Lady of the Elms Library, Chicopee MA. 413-598-8351, Ext 80

McAlister, Annette, *Libr Develop Asst,* State Library of Pennsylvania, Harrisburg PA. 717-787-2646

McAlister, Burgess E, *Librn,* Aiken-Bamberg-Barnwell-Edgefield Regional Library (Williston Branch), Williston SC. 803-648-8961

McAlister, George L, *Assoc Dir,* Loma Linda University, Vernier Radcliffe Memorial Library, Loma Linda CA. 714-796-7311, Ext 2916

McAlister, J A, *Mgr Environ Affairs,* Georgia Kraft Co, Technical Library, Rome GA. 404-291-6920

McAlister, John, *Librn,* Toole County Free Library (Sunburst Branch), Sunburst MT. 406-434-5411

McAlister, Larry, *Media,* Cochise College, Learning Resources Center, Douglas AZ. 602-364-7943, Ext 280

McAllister, Desretta V, *Asst Prof,* North Carolina Central University, School of Library Science, NC. 919-683-6485

McAllister, John K, *Dir,* Melbourne Public Library, Melbourne FL. 305-723-0611

McAllister, Marianne, *Ch,* Valparaiso-Porter County Public Library System & Administrative Headquarters, Valparaiso IN. 219-462-0524

McAllister, Wayne, *Asst Prof,* San Diego State University, Dept of Educational Technology & Librarianship, CA. 714-265-6718

McAlpine, Barbara, *In Charge,* Oakville Public Library (White Oaks), Oakville ON. 416-844-8464

McAnallen, Harry W, *Librn,* United States Air Force (Davis-Monthan Air Force Base Library), Davis Monthan AFB AZ. 602-748-3900

McAnanama, Judith, *Chief Librn,* Hamilton Public Library, Hamilton ON. 416-529-8111

McAndrew, Elizabeth, *Asst Dir, ILL & Ref,* Crandall Library, Glens Falls NY. 518-792-6508

McAndrew, Pat, *Ref,* Wake Forest University (Bowman Gray School of Medicine Library), Winston-Salem NC. 919-727-4691

McAninch, Sandra, *Doc,* University of Georgia Libraries, Athens GA. 404-542-2716

McAninch, Sherry, *AV,* Martins Ferry Public Library, Martins Ferry OH. 614-633-0314

McArdle, David, *Personnel,* Cambridge Public Library, Cambridge MA. 617-498-9080

McArdle, James J, *Librn,* King County Law Library, Seattle WA. 206-344-3940

McArthur, Judith, *Circ,* Loras College, Wahlert Memorial Library, Dubuque IA. 319-588-7125

McArthur, Patricia, *Librn,* Orland Park Public Library, Orland Park IL. 312-349-8138

McAskill, John, *Cat,* Washburn University of Topeka, Mabee Library, Topeka KS. 913-295-6479

McAulay, Tammy, *Bkmobile Coordr,* Monterey Public Library, Monterey CA. 408-646-3930

McAuliffe, James R, *Chief Librn,* Pierce Junior College Library, Philadelphia PA. 215-545-6400, Ext 270

McAuliffe, Nancy, *Asst Dir, Tech Serv & Cat,* Springfield Technical Community College Library, Springfield MA. 413-781-7822, Ext 3485

McAuliffe, Nicholas, *Ref,* Peabody Institute Library, Danvers Public Library, Danvers MA. 617-774-0554, Ext 0557, 0555

McAvey, Mora F, *Librn,* Worcester City Hospital (Isabel Girling Hunt Memorial Library), Worcester MA. 617-756-1551, Ext 346

McAvin, John, *Consults,* New York State Library, Albany NY. 518-474-5930

McAvoy, Kathleen, *Librn,* Saint Joseph Hospital, Health Science Library, North Providence RI. 401-456-3060

McBane, Marian, *Librn,* Atlanta-Jackson Township Public Library (Arcadia Branch), Arcadia IN. 317-292-2521

McBee, David, *Ser,* University of the South, Jessie Ball duPont Library, Sewanee TN. 615-598-5931, Ext 265, 267

McBee, Wenona H, *Dir,* Parrott-Wood Memorial Library, Strawberry Plains TN. 615-933-1311

McBeth, Marilynn, *Librn,* Garden City Public Library, Garden City MI. 313-421-5080

McBrady, Cindy, *ILL,* College of Lake County, Learning Resource Center, Grayslake IL. 312-223-6601, Ext 392

McBreen, Sister Grace Roberta, *Cat,* College of Saint Elizabeth, Mahoney Library, Convent Station NJ. 201-539-1600, Ext 365

McBride, Annie, *Ref,* Marion County Library, Marion SC. 803-423-2244

McBride, Betty, *Acq,* Williamsburg Regional Library, Williamsburg VA. 804-229-7326

McBride, Carolyn, *Ser,* State University of New York College at Brockport, Drake Memorial Library, Brockport NY. 716-395-2140

McBride, Cheryl, *Ref,* North Brunswick Free Public Library, North Brunswick NJ. 201-246-3545

McBride, E Harry, *Dir,* United States Department of Housing & Urban Development, Region III Library, Philadelphia PA. 215-597-2685

McBride, Frances, *Tech Serv,* Crown Point-Center Public Library, Crown Point IN. 219-663-0270

McBride, Francis R, *Dir,* Hornell Public Library, Hornell NY. 607-324-1210

McBride, Jean, *Librn,* Niagara Falls Public Library (Drummond), Niagara Falls ON. 416-354-2633

McBride, June Qualls, *Tech Serv,* Findlay College, Shafer Library, Findlay OH. 419-422-8313, Ext 327

McBride, Margaret, *Ch,* Pioneer Memorial Library, Colby KS. 913-462-3881

McBride, Margaret G, *Dir & Acq,* Pacific Grove Public Library, Pacific Grove CA. 408-373-0603

McBride, Nell, *Librn,* Forsyth County Public Library (Lewisville Branch), Lewisville NC. 919-945-3786

McBride, Pat Shaw, *Librn,* Saint Albans Free Library, Saint Albans VT. 802-524-3804

McBride, Patricia, *Tech Processing & Cat,* Free Public Library, Council Bluffs IA. 712-323-7553

McBride, Ron, *Media,* Dalton Junior College, Library Resource Center, Dalton GA. 404-278-3113, Ext 237, 247

McBrien, Helen C, *Librn,* Staunton Public Library, Staunton IL. 618-635-3852

McBurney, M B, *Chief Librn,* Queen's University at Kingston, Douglas Library, Kingston ON. 547-5950 (Admin); 547-6992 (Chief Librn)

McCabe, Carol, *Asst Dir,* Juneau Memorial Library, Juneau AK. 907-586-2429

McCabe, Emma R, *Dir,* Millsboro Public Library, Millsboro DE. 302-934-8743

McCabe, Gerard B, *Dir,* Virginia Commonwealth University (James Branch Cabell Library), Richmond VA. 804-257-1105

McCabe, Gerard B, *Dir,* Virginia Commonwealth University (Tompkins-McCaw Library), Richmond VA. 804-786-0629

McCabe, James P, *Librn,* Allentown College of Saint Francis De Sales Library, Center Valley PA. 215-282-1100, Ext 266

McCabe, Jean, *Chief Librn,* Smiths Falls Public Library, Smiths Falls ON. 613-283-2911

McCabe, Linda, *Coordr,* Fox River Valley Area Library Cooperative, WI. 414-693-8211

McCabe, Linda, *Acq & Ref,* Lakeshore Technical Institute, Educational Resources Center, Cleveland WI. 414-693-8211, 684-4408, Ext 150

McCabe, Margaret M, *Info Scientist,* Morton-Norwich Products, Inc, Research Library, Woodstock IL. 815-338-1800, Ext 240

McCabe, Michael, *Acq,* Kingsport Public Library, J Fred Johnson Memorial Library, Kingsport TN. 615-245-3141

McCabe, Pat, *Tech Serv,* Kansas City Kansas Community College Library, Kansas City KS. 913-334-1100, Ext 38

McCabe, Patrick P, *Dir,* United States Department of Commerce, Industry & Trade Administration Library, Philadelphia PA. 215-597-2850

McCabe, Peggy, *Ad,* Deerfield Public Library, Deerfield IL. 312-945-3311

McCabe, Ronald B, *Dir,* LeMars Public Library, Le Mars IA. 712-546-5004

McCabe, Timothy J, *Cat,* Edgecliff College, Brennan Memorial Library, Cincinnati OH. 513-961-3770

McCabe, Jr, R Edward, *Dir,* Ohoopee Regional Library, Vidalia-Toombs County Library Headquarters, Vidalia GA. 912-537-9283

McCafferty, Carol, *Ref,* Wayne Township Library, Morrisson-Reeves Library, Richmond IN. 317-966-8291

McCafferty, Helen, *Librn,* Mattawamkeag Public Library, Mattawamkeag ME. 207-736-3244

McCaffrey, Anne, *Pa Doc & YA,* Cambria County Library System, Johnstown PA. 814-536-5131

McCaghy, Dawn, *ILL,* Bowling Green State University Library, Bowling Green OH. 419-372-2856

McCahey, Kathleen, *Librn,* Providence Public Library (Olneyville), Providence RI. 401-861-1909

McCahill, Michael J, *Spec Projects,* University of Toronto Libraries (University Library), Toronto ON. 416-978-2294

McCain, Charles, *Computer Assisted Instruction-Instrn Design,* Mountain View College, Learning Resources Center, Dallas TX. 214-746-4169

McCain, Diana, *Cat,* Connecticut Historical Society Library, Hartford CT. 203-236-5621

McCain, Lois, *Librn,* Southwest Arkansas Regional Library (Nevada County), Prescott AR. 501-777-4564

McCall, Lea, *On-Line Servs,* Morton Public Library, Morton IL. 309-264-6401

McCall, Maureen, *Per,* Holy Names College, Paul J Cushing Library, Oakland CA. 415-436-1332

McCall, Mrs Talley, *Librn,* Kurth Memorial Library, Lufkin TX. 713-634-7923

McCall, Theresa, *ILL,* Syosset Public Library, Syosset NY. 516-921-7161

McCall, William J, *Sr Tech Librn,* New England Power Service Company, Technical Information Center, Westborough MA. 617-366-9011, Ext 2696, 2697

McCall, William J, *On-Line Servs & Bibliog Instr,* New England Power Service Company, Technical Information Center, Westborough MA. 617-366-9011, Ext 2696, 2697

McCalla, A, *Acq & Ser,* Trent University, Thomas J Bata Library, Peterborough ON. 705-748-1550

McCallan, Norma, *Extension Servs,* New Mexico State Library, Santa Fe NM. 505-827-2033

McCallips, Cheryl, *Asst Dir,* Mifflin County Library, Lewistown PA. 717-242-2391

McCallister, Ellen, *Librn,* Mount Vernon Ladies' Association of the Union, Research & Reference Library, Mount Vernon VA. 703-780-2000

McCallum, Heather, *Theatre,* Metropolitan Toronto Library Board, Metropolitan Toronto Library, Toronto ON. 416-928-5150

McCallum, John, *Librn,* Missouri Valley College, Murrell Memorial Library, Marshall MO. 816-886-6924

McCallum, Lee, *Acq,* Trinity College Library, Hartford CT. 203-527-3151, Ext 396

McCallum, Tracy, *ILL,* Harwood Foundation Library, Taos NM. 505-758-3063

McCalmant, Glenda, *Asst Librn,* Boundary County Free Library, Bonners Ferry ID. 208-267-3750

McCambridge, William, *Asst Librn,* Kenyon & Eckhardt Inc Library, New York NY. 212-973-7894

McCance, John, *Tech Serv,* College of the Southwest, Scarborough Memorial Library, Hobbs NM. 505-392-6561, Ext 35&38

McCandless, Nancy P, *Librn,* Tracor, Inc, Technical Library, Austin TX. 512-926-2800, Ext 139

McCann, Gary, *ILL & Ref,* American University (Washington College of Law Library), Washington DC. 202-686-2625

McCann, Jeff, *Ser,* East Carolina University (Health Affairs Library), Greenville NC. 919-757-6961, Ext 261

McCann, Katherine T, *Acq,* Cleveland Public Library, Cleveland OH. 216-623-2800

McCann, Susan, *Asst Dir,* Portsmouth Public Library, Portsmouth NH. 603-431-2000, Ext 252

McCanon, Marilyn, *Assoc Dir Ext Servs,* Indianapolis-Marion County Public Library, Indianapolis IN. 317-635-5662

McCard, Laurel, *Asst Librn,* Junction City Public Library, Junction City OR. 503-998-8942

McCardic, Mickie, *In Charge,* Eureka-Humboldt County Library (Hoopa), Hoopa CA. 707-445-7284, 445-7513

McCardy, Trudy, *Tech Serv,* Tom Green County Library System, San Angelo TX. 915-655-7321

McCarron, Judith, *Librn,* Kent State University Libraries (Music Library), Kent OH. 216-672-2004

McCarron, Mary M, *Librn,* Sears, Roebuck & Co, Merchandise Development & Testing Lab Library, Chicago IL. 312-875-5991

McCartan, Eleanor, *Librn,* Olin Corp, Public Relations Library, New York NY. 212-486-7200

McCarter, Bobbye L, *Librn,* Bethel College Library, McKenzie TN. 901-352-5321

McCarthy, Audrey, *Librn,* Portage County District Library (Streetsboro), Hiram OH. 216-626-4458

McCarthy, Carole A, *Librn,* South Hampton Free Public Library, South Hampton NH. 603-394-7696

McCarthy, Catherine, *Prof Libr Ref-Info Servs,* Massachusetts Board of Library Commissioners, Office for the Development of Library Services, Boston MA. 617-267-9400

McCarthy, Cecile, *Commun Servs,* Danville Public Library, Danville IL. 217-446-7420

McCarthy, Clare, *Tech Serv & Cat,* Port Chester Public Library, Port Chester NY. 914-939-6710, 939-6711

McCarthy, Constance, *Acq,* George Washington University Library, Washington DC. 202-676-6455

McCarthy, Dortha, *Dir,* Southwestern Oregon Community College, Learning Resource Center, Coos Bay OR. 503-888-3234, Ext 250

McCarthy, Fran, *Commun Servs,* Durango Public Library, Durango CO. 303-247-2492

McCarthy, Frank, *Tech Serv,* Aspen Systems Corporation, Library & Information Center, Rockville MD. 301-428-0700

McCarthy, Jacqueline, *Res,* Dillon, Read & Co, Inc Library, New York NY. 212-285-5690

McCarthy, Jane, *Ch,* Grandview Heights School District Public Library, Columbus OH. 614-486-2951

McCarthy, Jane, *Librn,* Muhlenberg Hospital, E Gordon Glass MD Memorial Library, Plainfield NJ. 201-668-2005

McCarthy, Joseph F, *Chief Librn,* New York Daily News Library, New York NY. 212-682-1234

McCarthy, Juanita, *Librn,* Mallinckrodt, Inc, Corporate Library, Saint Louis MO. 314-895-5514

McCarthy, Leo, *Dir,* Carmelitana Collection Library, Washington DC. 202-526-1221

McCarthy, Malachy, *Media,* Saint Anselm's College, Geisel Library, Manchester NH. 603-669-1030, Ext 240, 249

McCarthy, Mrs R G, *Dir,* Turner Free Library, Randolph MA. 617-963-3000

McCarthy, Paul, *Archives & Mss,* University of Alaska, Fairbanks, Elmer E Rasmuson Library, Fairbanks AK. 907-479-7224

McCarthy, Philip R, *Dir,* Highland Community College Library, Freeport IL. 815-235-6121, Ext 256

McCarthy, Ruth L, *Dir,* Emerson Public Library, Emerson NJ. 201-261-5604

McCarthy, Ruth P, *Librn,* Upper Dublin Public Library, Dresher PA. 215-885-5320

McCarthy, William G, *In Charge,* Minnesota Department of Public Welfare Library, Saint Paul MN. 612-296-6117

McCartin, Kathleen, *Ref,* Orangeburg Public Library, Orangeburg NY. 914-359-2244

McCartney, Betty S, *Librn,* Grant County Library, Petersburg WV. 304-257-4122

McCartney, Molly, *Tech Serv,* Elmhurst College, A C Buehler Library, Elmhurst IL. 312-279-4100, Ext 255

McCartney, Robert W, *Acq,* Virginia Polytechnic Institute & State University Library, Blacksburg VA. 703-961-5593

McCarty, Adelle McMillan, *Dir,* Riverdale Public Library District, Riverdale IL. 312-841-3311

McCarty, Barbara, *Ref,* John Packard Library of Yuba County, Marysville CA. 916-674-6241

McCarty, Daniel J, *Consultant,* Federal-Mogul Corporation, Materials Research Library, Ann Arbor MI. 313-761-4200

McCarty, Julie, *Cat,* Bound Brook Memorial Library, Bound Brook NJ. 201-356-0043

McCarty, Mary Lou, *Librn,* Sno-Isle Regional Library (Sultan Branch), Sultan WA. 206-793-1695

McCarty, Rosa, *Librn,* Illinois Prairie District Public Library (Springbay Branch), Springbay IL. 309-566-8257

McCarville, Sarah, *Ch,* Ottumwa Public Library, Ottumwa IA. 515-682-7563

McCaslin, Michael E, *Info Servs,* DuPage Library System, Geneva IL. 312-232-8457

McCaslin, Sharon, *Cat,* Peru State College Library, Peru NE. 402-872-3815, Ext 218

McCaud, Charles, *Assoc Prof,* Middle Tennessee State University, Department of Library Service, TN. 615-898-2740 & 898-5555

McCaughrin, Ellenor, *ILL & Ref,* University of South Carolina at Spartanburg Library, Spartanburg SC. 803-578-1800, Exts 410, 411, 420 & 421

McCaughtry, Dorothy, *Librn,* Travelers Insurance Co Library, Hartford CT. 203-277-5048

McCauley, Betty M, *Librn,* Environmental Protection Agency, Corvallis Environmental Research Laboratory Library, Corvallis OR. 503-757-4731

McCauley, Cynthia, *Librn, On-Line Servs & Bibliog Instr,* United States Fish & Wildlife Service, Van Oosten Library, Great Lakes Fishery Laboratory, Ann Arbor MI. 313-994-3331, Ext 210

McCauley, Gladys, *Dir,* Ohio County Public Library, Hartford KY. 502-298-3790

McCauley, Hannah, *Dir,* Ohio University-Lancaster Library, Lancaster OH. 614-654-6711, Ext 221

McCauley, Hannah, *Instr,* Ohio University-Lancaster, Library Media Technology, OH. 614-654-6711

McCauley, Harriet, *Dir,* Finney Public Library, Clintonville Public Library, Clintonville WI. 715-823-4563

McCauley, Jean, *Chief Inf Br,* National Archives & Records Service (National Audiovisual Center), Washington DC. 301-763-1896

McCauley, Joan, *Cat,* California State University, Long Beach, University Library, Long Beach CA. 213-498-4047

McCauley, Mrs B, *Librn,* Vaughan Public Libraries (Concord Public), Concord ON. 416-669-2528

McCauley, Philip F, *Spec Coll, Archivist & On-Line Servs,* South Dakota School of Mines & Technology, Devereaux Library, Rapid City SD. 605-394-2418

McCawley, Christina, *Cat, Non-print,* West Chester State College, Francis Harvey Green Library, West Chester PA. 215-436-2643

McCawley, Clemma, *Acq,* Central State University Library, Edmond OK. 405-341-2980, Ext 494, 495 & 496

McChesney, Kathryn, *Asst Prof,* Kent State University, School of Library Science, OH. 216-672-2782, 672-7988

McClain, Alice, *Dir,* Montana State University, Roland R Renne Library, Bozeman MT. 406-994-3119

McClain, Ann J, *Librn,* Andrew Bayne Memorial Library, Bellevue PA. 412-761-2967

McClain, Ardina M, *Librn,* United States Navy (Naval Air Station Library), Key West FL. 305-296-3561, Ext 2116

McClain, Arnold G, *In Charge,* Cleveland Public Library (Audiovisual), Cleveland OH. 216-623-2942

McClain, Christeen, *ILL,* Flint River Regional Library, Griffin GA. 404-227-2756

McClain, David C, *Dir & Acq,* Baptist Bible College of Pennsylvania, Richard J Murphy Memorial Library, Clarks Summit PA. 717-587-1172, Ext 280

McClain, Gerald M, *Librn,* Citizens Law Library, Greensburg PA. 412-834-2191

McClain, Helen, *Librn,* Carnegie Library of Pittsburgh (Wylie Avenue Branch), Pittsburgh PA. 412-622-3100

McClain, Juanita, *Dir,* Macon County-Tuskegee Public Library, Tuskegee AL. 205-727-5192

McClanahan, Annalee, *Librn,* Jasonville Public Library, Jasonville IN. 812-665-3366

McClang, Janice, *Librn,* Greenbrier County Library, Lewisburg WV. 304-645-2350

McClannahan, Joyce, *Librn,* Eunice Public Library, Eunice NM. 505-394-2336

McClarren, Robert R, *Dir,* North Suburban Library System, Wheeling IL. 312-459-1300

McClary, Gayla, *Librn,* Goodnight Memorial Library, Franklin KY. 502-586-8397

McClary, Jane, *Local Hist,* Lansing Public Library, Lansing MI. 517-374-4600

McClary, Nancy, *Librn,* Library Association of Portland (Hollywood), Portland OR. 503-281-0826

McClaskey, Harris C, *Assoc Prof,* University of Minnesota, Library School, MN. 612-373-3100

McClatchey, Helen E, *Librn,* Fred C fischer Memorial Library, Belleville MI. 313-699-3291

McClaughry, Helen C, *Librn,* United States Air Force (Base Library FL 3059), Lowry AFB CO. 303-370-3093, 370-3836

McClean, Ann, *Law Libr Clerk,* Ninth Judicial District Law Library, Goshen NY. 914-294-5151, Ext 287

McClean, Ann, *Law Libr Clerk,* Ninth Judicial District Law Library, Newburgh NY. 914-565-9874

McClear, Mary Ellen, *Ch,* Midwestern Regional Library System, Kitchener ON. 519-576-5061

McCleary, G Louise, *Ref,* Gulf Oil Corp (Gulf Science & Technology Co Library), Pittsburgh PA. 412-665-5576

McCleery, Rose, *Exten Dept,* Ector County Library, Odessa TX. 915-332-0633

McClellan, Gabrielle W, *Librn,* Enoch Pratt Free Library (Dundalk Ave), Baltimore MD. 301-396-5430, 396-5395

McClellan, Marsha, *Librn,* Mount Carmel Public Library, Church Hill TN. 615-357-4011

McClellan, Mike, *Librn,* Honeywell Corporate Technology Center Library, Bloomington MN. 612-887-4321

McClellan, William M, *Librn,* University of Illinois Library at Urbana-Champaign (Music), Urbana IL. 217-333-6161

McClenaghan, Norma, *Acq,* Wilfrid Laurier University Library, Waterloo ON. 519-884-1970

McClendon, Ida, *Fiction,* Library Association of Portland, Multnomah County Library, Portland OR. 503-223-7201, Ext 40

McClendon, Mildred, *Librn,* Benton Public Library, Benton IL. 618-438-7511

McClendon, Selina, *Librn,* Tri-County Regional Library (Bartow County), Cartersville GA. 404-291-9360

McClennahan, Nancy, *Librn,* Bronx-Lebanon Hospital Libraries (Fulton Div), Bronx NY. 212-588-7000, Ext 308

McClintock, Alice, *Acq,* Grandview Heights School District Public Library, Columbus OH. 614-486-2951

McClintock, Brandon C, *Dir,* Woodland Public Library, Woodland CA. 916-662-6616

McClish, Ellen, *Librn,* Morley Library (Concord), Painesville OH. 216-357-6003

McClish, Lois, *Dir,* Commerce Public Library, Commerce CA. 213-722-6660

McCloskey, Alice, *Librn,* Ridgway Public Library, Ridgway PA. 814-773-7573

McCloskey, Christine, *Dir,* Irvington Public Library, Irvington NJ. 201-372-6400

McCloskey, Terry, *Dir,* Holy Redeemer College Library, Waterford WI. 414-534-3191, Ext 51

McCloskey, Terry, *Redemptonist Order Mat,* Holy Redeemer College Library, Waterford WI. 414-534-3191, Ext 51

McCloskey, William H, *Dir,* Sinte Gleska College Library, Mission SD. 605-856-4550

McCloud, Darlene, *Dir,* The Municipal Art Society of New York, The Information Exchange, New York NY. 212-935-3960

McCloud, Janet P, *In Charge,* Enoch Pratt Free Library (Highlandtown), Baltimore MD. 301-396-5430, 396-5395

McClous, Beatrice, *Circ,* West Lafayette Public Library, West Lafayette IN. 317-743-2261

McCloy, C, *Librn,* Calgary Public Library (Thorn-Hill), Calgary AB. 403-274-6315

McCloy, N, *ILL, Ref & On-Line Servs,* Mount Allison University, Ralph Pickard Bell Library, Sackville NB. 506-536-2040, Ext 375

McCloy, William, *Spec Lang Cat,* Indiana University at Bloomington, University Libraries, Bloomington IN. 812-337-3403

McClung, Carol, *Cat,* San Marcos Public Library, San Marcos TX. 512-392-8124

McClung, Cloyd, *Ser,* Eckerd College, William Luther Cobb Library, Saint Petersburg FL. 813-867-1166, Ext 336

McClung, Edith, *Librn,* Daviess County Library (Pattonsburg Branch), Pattonsburg MO. 816-367-2216

McClure, Alan, *Media,* Temple Junior College, Hubert M Dawson Library, Temple TX. 817-773-9961, Ext 42

McClure, Cynthia, *Resource Librn,* Ida Long Goodman Memorial Library, Saint John Public Library, Saint John KS. 316-549-3227

McClure, Frances, *Supvr Exten Servs,* Montgomery County Department of Public Libraries, Rockville MD. 301-279-1401

McClure, Georgia, *Librn,* Veterans Administration (Medical Library), Lyons NJ. 201-647-0180, Ext 317

McClure, Joan, *Librn,* South Bend Public Library (River Park), South Bend IN. 219-288-6311

McClure, John D, *Soc Sci & Bus Admin,* California State University, Sacramento Library, Sacramento CA. 916-454-6466

McClure, Lola, *Librn,* Huntington Alloys, Inc, Technology Library, Huntington WV. 304-696-6260

McClure, Lola, *Librn,* Toluca City Library, Toluca IL. 815-452-2211

McClure, Lucretia, *Dir,* University of Rochester (Edward G Miner Library, School of Medicine & Dentistry), Rochester NY. 716-275-3364

McClure, Margaret, *Librn,* Arlington Public Library (North), Arlington TX. 817-277-5573

McClure, Margaret, *Librn,* Michigan Department of Natural Resources, Institute for Fisheries Research Library, Ann Arbor MI. 313-663-3554

McClure, Margaret, *Tech Serv,* Roseville Public Library, Roseville CA. 916-783-7158

McClure, Mary L, *Librn,* Decatur Public Library, Decatur TX. 817-627-5512

McClure, Velma, *Libr Asst,* Rusk County Memorial Library (Mount Enterprise Branch), Mount Enterprise TX. 214-657-8557

McClurg, Roger A, *Librn,* Oregon City Library, Oregon City OR. 503-655-8398, 655-8399

McCobb, Charlotte, *Librn,* Oaklyn Memorial Library, Oaklyn NJ. 609-858-8226

McCollester, Mrs Glover C, *Dir,* Wood Place Community Library, California MO. 314-796-2642

McCollum, Sue, *Access Servs,* University of Missouri-Columbia, Elmer Ellis Library, Columbia MO. 314-882-4701

McColm, Mrs D, *Librn,* Canada Institute for Scientific & Technical Information (Administration Building), Ottawa ON. 613-993-1600

McComb, Ronald G, *Librn,* Cornish School of Allied Arts, Poncho Library, Seattle WA. 206-323-1400

McCombs, Donna, *Ch,* Mississauga Public Library, Mississauga ON. 416-625-8681

McCombs, Mrs J W, *Librn,* China Grove Library, China Grove NC. 704-857-9945

McConkey, Thomas W, *Admin Servs,* Free Library of Philadelphia, Philadelphia PA. 215-686-5322

McConn, Marjory, *Librn,* Reuben McMillan Free Library Free Library Association (Campbell Branch), Campbell OH. 216-755-4227

McConnel, Jean, *Tech Serv,* Wayne County Public Library, Wooster OH. 216-262-0916

McConnell, Anne Y, *Assoc Prof,* University of Kentucky, College of Library Science, KY. 606-258-8876

McConnell, Carol, *Librn,* Southern Tier Library System (Prattsburg Library), Prattsburg NY. 607-962-3141

McConnell, Dorothy D, *Librn,* Louisiana Office of Public Works, Technical Library, Baton Rouge LA. 504-342-7580

McConnell, Elaine H, *Dir Libr Serv,* Piscataway Township Free Public Library, John F Kennedy Memorial Library, Piscataway NJ. 201-463-1633

McConnell, Fraiser, *Asst Librn,* California College of Arts and Crafts, Meyer Library, Oakland CA. 415-653-8118, Ext 32

McConnell, Karen S, *Librn,* Gulf States Utilities Company Library, Beaumont TX. 713-838-6631, Ext 3541

McConnell, Loretta U, *Librn,* American Law Institute, Philadelphia PA. 215-243-1658

McConnell, Lori, *Asst Librn,* Hamburg Township Library, Hamburg MI. 313-231-1771

McConnell, Mary A, *Librn,* Campus Crusade for Christ International, Arrowhead Springs Library, San Bernardino CA. 714-886-5224, Ext 113

McConnell, Odell, *Librn,* Pepperdine University Library (School of Law), Malibu CA. 213-456-4252

McConnell, Pamela, *Librn,* University of Missouri-Columbia (Dalton Research Center), Columbia MO. 314-882-3527

McConnell, Pauline, *Librn,* Mountain Regional Library (Towns County), Hiawasee GA. 404-379-3732

McConnell, Sharon, *Spec Coll,* Eastern Kentucky University, John Grant Crabbe Library, Richmond KY. 606-622-3606

McConnell, Shirley May, *Ad Libr,* South Central Library System, Madison WI. 608-266-4181

McConnell, Tamara, *Librn,* East Baton Rouge Parish Library (North Baton Rouge), Baton Rouge LA. 504-356-2790

McConnell, W P, *Ref,* City of Cerritos Public Library, Cerritos CA. 213-924-5775

McCool, Betty, *Ser,* Rhode Island Junior College, William F Flanagan Campus Library, Lincoln RI. 401-333-7053

McCool, Donna, *Asst Dir for Admin Servs,* Washington State University Library, Pullman WA. 509-335-4557

McCool, Gary, *Curriculum Laboratory,* Plymouth State College, Herbert H Lamson Library, Plymouth NH. 603-536-1550, Ext 257

McCord, Cecilia A, *Librn,* Sulphur Institute Library, Washington DC. 202-331-9660

McCord, John G W, *Ref Servs,* Lake County Public Library, Merrillville IN. 219-769-3541

McCord, Mary, *Librn,* Northeast Regional Library (Rienzi Library), Rienzi MS. 601-462-9320

McCord, Mary G, *Dir,* Abbeville-Greenwood Regional Library, Greenwood SC. 803-223-4515

McCord, S Joe, *Dir,* Victoria College - University of Houston Victoria Campus Library, Victoria TX. 512-575-7436

McCorison, Marcus, *Dir,* American Antiquarian Society Library, Worcester MA. 617-755-5221

McCorkle, Barbara, *Map Librn,* Yale University Library (Sterling Memorial Library), New Haven CT. 203-436-8335

McCormack, Ardyce, *Dir,* General N B Baker Public Library, Sutherland Public Library, Sutherland IA. 712-446-3839

McCormack, Claire, *Ad & YA,* Lima Public Library, Lima OH. 419-228-5113

McCormack, Margaret, *Cat,* Smithtown Library, Smithtown NY. 516-265-2072

McCormally, Susan, *Librn,* Wichita Public Library (Planeview), Wichita KS. 316-262-0611

McCormick, Adoreen M, *Legis Liaison Officer,* Library of Congress, Washington DC. 202-287-5000

McCormick, Ardis, *Asst Librn,* Jackson County Library, Kadoka SD. 605-837-2689

McCormick, Ardis, *Asst Librn,* Jackson County Library (Kadoka Library), Kadoka SD. 605-837-2689

McCormick, Bernice E, *Tech Serv & Cat,* Deer Park Public Library, Deer Park TX. 713-479-5276

McCormick, Dianne, *Librn,* Montgomery House Library, McEwensville PA. 717-538-1381

McCormick, Dorcas M C, *Librn,* Northwestern State University of Louisiana, Shreveport Div Library, Shreveport LA. 318-424-1827

McCormick, Doris, *Ref & Bibliog Instr,* Fullerton College, William T Boyce Library, Fullerton CA. 714-871-8000

McCormick, George H, *Librn,* Annie Halenbake Ross Library, Lock Haven PA. 717-748-3321

McCormick, Lisa L, *Med Res Librn,* Christ Hospital Institute of Medical Research, Research Library, Cincinnati OH. 513-369-2540

McCormick, Margie, *Cat,* Marion County Public Library, Fairmont WV. 304-366-4831

McCormick, Polly, *Circ,* Florida Southern College, Roux Library, Lakeland FL. 813-683-5521, Ext 211

McCormick, Regina, *Librn,* Social Science Education Consortium Resource & Demonstration Center Library, Boulder CO. 303-492-8155

McCormick, Rosemary, *Librn,* Law Society of Upper Canada, Great Library, Toronto ON. 416-362-5811, Ext 268

McCormick, Shirley, *ILL,* Lindenwood Colleges, Margaret L Butler Library, Saint Charles MO. 314-946-6912

McCormick, Tamsie, *Ext Dir,* Charlestown Township Public Library, Charlestown IN. 812-256-5974

McCormick, Virginia, *Librn,* Middletown Township Public Library (Bayshore), Port Monmouth NJ. 201-787-4050

McCormick, Yolanda, *Outreach,* Dillon County Library, Latta Library, Latta SC. 803-752-5389

McCort, Ramona, *Librn,* New Buffalo Public Library, New Buffalo MI. 616-469-2933

McCoskey, Patricia, *Acq,* Texas State Library, Division for the Blind & Physically Handicapped, Austin TX. 512-475-4758

McCoskey, Veva, *ILL,* Ball State University, Alexander M Bracken Library, Muncie IN. 317-285-6261

McCoul, Billie, *Librn,* Carbon County Public Library (Elk Mountain Branch), Elk Mountain WY. 307-324-4756

McCourt, Ferne, *Librn,* Bay County Library System (Pinconning Branch), Pinconning MI. 517-879-3283

McCourt, Laura, *ILL,* Bowdoin College Library, Brunswick ME. 207-725-8731, Ext 281

McCourt, Mrs R C, *Librn,* Lee Public Library, Gladewater TX. 214-845-2498

McCowan, Eva, *Librn,* Wichita County Library, Leoti KS. 316-375-4322

McCown, Leonard J, *Dir,* Dallas Baptist College, Vance Memorial Library, Dallas TX. 214-331-8311, Ext 213

McCoy, Arcada J, *Branch Librn,* Dorchester County Library (Summerville Branch), Summerville SC. 803-871-5075

McCoy, Barbara S, *Librn,* RCA Corp, Solid State Div Library, Somerville NJ. 201-685-6017

McCoy, Betty, *Tech Serv,* Public Library of Cincinnati & Hamilton County, Cincinnati Public Library, Cincinnati OH. 513-369-6000

McCoy, Carolyn, *Librn,* Mid-Mississippi Regional Library System (Kilmichael Public), Kilmichael MS. 601-262-7615

McCoy, Cheryl, *Asst Dir,* Montclair Free Public Library, Montclair NJ. 201-744-0500

McCoy, David, *Asst Dir (CRS),* Eastfield College, Learning Resources Center, Mesquite TX. 214-746-3168

McCoy, DeLores T, *Actg Librn,* Florida State University (Developmental Research School), Tallahassee FL. 904-644-3498

McCoy, Donna Stone, *Librn,* Sinton Public Library, Sinton TX. 512-364-4545

McCoy, Duncan R, *Dir,* Hays Public Library, Hays KS. 913-625-9014

McCoy, Evelyn, *Dir,* Arkansas Arts Center, Elizabeth Prewitt Taylor Memorial Library, Little Rock AR. 501-372-4000

McCoy, Garnett, *Sr Curator,* Archives of American Art, National Headquarters, New York NY. 212-826-5722

McCoy, James, *Librn,* Aransas Pass Public Library, Aransas Pass TX. 512-758-2350

McCoy, James F, *Dir,* Hudson Valley Community College Learning Resources Center, Dwight Marvin Library, Troy NY. 518-283-1100, Ext 629

McCoy, Janet, *Pub Servs,* Aurora Public Library, Aurora CO. 303-750-5000, Ext 410

McCoy, Lenior, *Tech Serv,* Pitt Community College, Learning Resources Center, Greenville NC. 919-756-3130, Ext 213, 229, 259 & 273

McCoy, Mabel S, *In Charge,* Cochise County Library System (Sunizona Valley Public Library), Pearce AZ. 602-824-3514

McCoy, Mrs R, *Librn,* Marmora, Delora, Marmora & Lake Townships Union Public Library, Marmora ON. 613-472-3122

McCoy, Pressley C, *President,* Dayton-Miami Valley Consortium, OH. 513-278-9105

McCoy, Ralph E, *Actg Exec Dir,* Association of Research Libraries, DC. 202-232-2466

McCoy, Sharron, *Ref,* Morton Grove Public Library, Morton Grove IL. 312-965-4220

McCoy, Warren, *Actg Librn,* California Department of Corrections, California Institution for Women Library, Frontera CA. 714-597-1771

McCoy, William F, *Assoc Univ Librn,* University of California at Davis, General Library, Davis CA. 916-752-2110

McCracken, Barbara, *Dir,* Arizona Western College, Library Learning Center, Yuma AZ. 602-726-1000, Ext 360

McCracken, Cathye, *Ch,* Howard County Library, Big Spring TX. 915-267-5295

McCracken, Linda, *ILL,* Yakima Valley Regional Library, Yakima WA. 509-452-8541, Ext 22

McCracken, Tom, *Media,* Armstrong State College, Lane Memorial Library, Savannah GA. 912-927-5332

McCrank, Lawrence, *Asst Prof,* University of Maryland, College of Library & Information Services, MD. 301-454-5441

McCrann, Joan, *In Charge,* United States Navy (Naval Weapons Station, MenRiv Library), Charleston SC. 803-743-7900

McCrary, Alma, *Librn,* Greenville County Library (Travelers Rest), Travelers Rest SC. 803-834-3650

McCrary, Martha, *Librn,* Baptist Memorial Hospital, Medical Library, Gadsden AL. 205-492-1240, Ext 281

McCraw, John, *Librn,* National Park Service, Western Archeological Center Library, Tucson AZ. 602-792-6896

McCray, Jeanette C, *Pub Servs,* University of Arizona Library (Arizona Health Sciences Center Library), Tucson AZ. 602-626-6121

McCray, Jimmie, *Librn,* Atlantic Richfield Co, Research & Development Library, Plano TX. 214-424-3511

McCray, Marilyn, *Librn,* Cabell County Public Library (Barboursville Branch), Barboursville WV. 304-736-4621

McCrea, Graydon, *In Charge,* National Film Board of Canada, Edmonton Office Library, Edmonton AB. 403-420-3010

McCrea, Katherine L, *Chmn,* Health Information Library Network of Northeastern Pennsylvania, PA. 717-288-1411, Ext 258

McCrea, Katherine L, *Librn,* Nesbitt Memorial Hospital Library, Kingston PA. 717-288-1411, Ext 258

McCreadie, Maureen, *Mat Develop,* Bucks County Community College Library, Newtown PA. 215-968-5861, Ext 306, 307

McCready, Jean, *Med Libr Asst,* Washoe Medical Center Library, Reno NV. 702-785-5693

McCready, Reyburn R, *Librn,* University of Oregon Library (Architecture & Allied Arts), Eugene OR. 503-686-3637

McCreary, Diane M, *Librn,* Environmental Protection Agency, Region III Library, Philadelphia PA. 215-597-0580

McCreary, Mary Louise, *Librn,* Legislative Reference Bureau Library, Springfield IL. 217-782-6625

McCree, Mary L, *Mss,* University of Illinois at Chicago Circle Library, Chicago IL. 312-996-2716

McCree, O'Nell, *Mgr,* Hattiesburg Public Library System (Hattiesburg), Hattiesburg MS. 601-583-3691

McCreedy, Justin, *In Charge,* Assumption Church, Parish Library, Seattle WA. 206-523-2636

McCreery, Sharolyn, *Librn,* Attica Public Library, Attica KS. 316-254-7767

McCreless, Susan, *Asst Librn,* Wesleyan College, Willet Memorial Library, Macon GA. 912-477-1110, Ext 200

McCrink, D, *Asst Dir,* North Castle Public Library, Armonk NY. 914-273-3887

McCrosky, Janet, *Acq,* Warder Public Library, Springfield OH. 323-8616 & 323-9751

McCrossan, John A, *Chmn & Assoc Prof,* University of South Florida, Graduate Department of Library, Media & Information Studies, FL. 813-974-2557

McCue, Michael, *Dir,* Upper Saddle River Public Library, Upper Saddle River NJ. 201-326-2583

McCuistion, Thomas M, *Dir,* Clark Technical College, Learning Resource Center, Springfield OH. 513-325-0691, Ext 66

McCuiston, Burl, *ILL, Acq & Ref,* Lenoir-Rhyne College, Carl A Rudisill Library, Hickory NC. 704-328-1741, Ext 221

McCullers, Kathy, *Tech Serv,* Elizabeth City State University, G R Little Library, Elizabeth City NC. 919-335-0551, Ext 332

McCulley, Patricia, *ILL & Circ,* Bridgeton Free Public Library, Bridgeton NJ. 609-451-2620

McCulloch, Gini, *Ch, YA & Circ,* Bell Public Library, Portland TX. 512-643-6527

McCulloch, Meredith, *Asst Dir,* Bedford Free Public Library, Bedford MA. 617-275-9440

McCulloch, Mrs M, *YA,* Ottawa Public Library, Ottawa ON. 613-236-0301

McCulloch, Winifred, *Dir,* American Teilhard Association for the Future of Man, Inc Library, Bronx NY. 212-548-1400

McCullock, Eva, *Librn,* White County Public Library (Beebe), Searcy AR. 501-882-3235
McCulloh, Amelia, *Tech Serv,* Mount Pleasant Public Library, Pleasantville NY. 914-769-0548
McCullough, Barbara, *Librn,* Escambia County Health Department Library, Pensacola FL. 904-438-8571
McCullough, Barbara, *Ref,* Lee College Library, Cleveland TN. 615-472-2111, Ext 329
McCullough, Deborah, *Librn,* Reuben McMillan Free Library Free Library Association (North Branch), Youngstown OH. 216-747-3719
McCullough, Ethel, *Librn,* Jefferson County Library (Bedingfield-Prichard), Wadley GA. 912-252-1366
McCullough, Frances, *Librn,* Mercy Hospital, Health Science Library, Hamilton OH. 513-868-2000
McCullough, Gary, *Head, Talking Bks,* Chatham-Effingham-Liberty Regional Library, Savannah Public Library, Savannah GA. 912-234-5127
McCullough, Gina, *Circ,* Merced College, Lesher Library, Merced CA. 209-723-4321, Ext 274
McCullough, Helen, *Librn,* Nairobi College Library, Palo Alto CA. 415-323-8501
McCullough, James M, *Chief, Sci Policy Res Div,* Library of Congress, Washington DC. 202-287-5000
McCullough, John, *Librn,* Divine Word Seminary Library, Bordentown NJ. 609-298-0549, Ext 9
McCullough, Mabel, *Chief Librn,* United States Navy (Naval Air Station Library), Pensacola FL. 904-452-4362
McCullough, Mary, *Dir,* Halifax County Regional Library, Halifax NS. 902-477-6265
McCullough, Mireille, *Asst Librn,* Canada Labour Relations Board Library, Ottawa ON. 613-995-0895
McCullough, Pat, *Asst Librn,* Fredonia Public Library, Fredonia AZ. 643-5395
McCullough, Ruth R, *Supvr,* Westinghouse Electric Corp, Defense & Electronic Systems Center Library, Baltimore MD. 301-765-2858
McCully, Nancy, *On-Line Servs & Bibliog Instr,* Caterpillar Tractor Co (Business Library), Peoria IL. 309-675-4622
McCully, Jr, William C, *Dir,* Pekin Public Library, Pekin IL. 309-347-7111
McCurdle, Rachel, *Dir,* Hardy Wilson Memorial Hospital Library, Hazlehurst MS. 601-894-4541
McCurdy, Fran, *Ch,* Pittsburg Public Library, Pittsburg KS. 316-231-8110
McCurley, Marsha, *Cat,* Augusta College, Reese Library, Augusta GA. 404-828-4566, 828-4066
McCurnin, Debra, *Tech Serv,* Marshalltown Public Library, Marshalltown IA. 515-754-5738
McCurry, Allan, *Archivist,* Southern Illinois University at Edwardsville, Elijah P Lovejoy Library, Edwardsville IL. 618-692-2711
McCusker, Andrew, *Acq,* Lawrence Public Library, Lawrence MA. 617-682-1727
McCusker, Sister Lauretta, *Dean,* Rosary College, Graduate School of Library Science, IL. 312-366-2490, Ext 324
McCuskey, Jean, *Librn,* Canton Art Institute Library, Purdy Memorial Library, Canton OH. 216-453-7666, Ext 8
McCutchan, Sims, *Librn,* Houston Public Library (Heights), Houston TX. 713-861-4149
McCutchen, Peggy, *Librn,* Scottsboro Public Library, Scottsboro AL. 205-574-4335
McCutcheon, Ethel J, *Curator,* Texas Confederate Museum Library, Austin TX. 512-472-2596
McCutcheon, Hazel J, *Head Librn,* Pennsylvania State University, Ogontz Campus Library, Abington PA. 215-886-9400, Ext 311 & 312
McCutcheon, Mrs M, *Librn,* Vaughan Public Libraries (Kleinburg Branch), Maple ON. 416-893-1248
McDade, Evy S, *Dir Libr Serv,* Lawrence General Hospital, Health Sciences Library, Lawrence MA. 617-683-4000, Ext 257
McDaniel, Constance, *Librn,* Saint Lawrence Psychiatric Center Library, Ogdensburg NY. 315-393-3000
McDaniel, Evelyn, *Dir & Ref,* Blount County Library, Maryville TN. 615-982-0981
McDaniel, Gretchen, *Laboratory Instr,* Samford University (L R Jordan Library), Birmingham AL. 205-591-2371
McDaniel, Jean, *Librn,* Saint Mary's Hospital, Medical Library, Enid OK. 405-233-6100, Ext 439

McDaniel, Karen, *Cat,* Kentucky State University, Blazer Library, Frankfort KY. 502-564-5852
McDaniel, Lisa, *Cat,* Montgomery County Library, Conroe TX. 713-756-4486
McDaniel, Patricia L, *Ref,* Mississippi University for Women, John Clayton Fant Memorial Library, Columbus MS. 601-328-4808
McDaniel, Sharon, *Librn,* Delta County Public Library, Delta CO. 303-874-9630
McDaniel, Sharon, *Librn,* Delta County Public Library (Delta Public), Delta CO. 303-874-9630
McDaniel, Susan L Jewell, *Librn,* Washington Carnegie Library, Washington Court House OH. 614-335-2540
McDavid, Doug, *Ref,* Palo Alto City Library, Palo Alto CA. 415-329-2436
McDavid, Leslie, *Librn,* Portsmouth Public Library (Cradock), Portsmouth VA. 804-393-8759
McDavid, Michael, *Librn,* Equifax Inc Library, Atlanta GA. 404-885-8320
McDavid, Sara June, *Librn,* Federal Reserve Bank of Atlanta, Research Library, Atlanta GA. 404-586-8829
McDeering, Marjorie, *Librn,* Newport Public Library, Newport ME. 207-368-5074
McDermand, Robert V, *Ref, On-Line Servs & Bibliog Instr,* Plymouth State College, Herbert H Lamson Library, Plymouth NH. 603-536-1550, Ext 257
McDermott, Marilyn, *Supvr,* Mohawk College of Applied Arts & Technology (Braneida Campus), Brantford ON. 519-759-7200
McDermott, Ann Day, *Rare Bks & Spec Coll,* Texas Christian University, Mary Couts Burnett Library, Fort Worth TX. 817-921-7106
McDermott, Ellen, *ILL &,* Ridgewood Public Library, Ridgewood NJ. 201-652-5200
McDermott, Grace G, *Librn,* Library Association of Warehouse Point, Warehouse Point CT. 203-623-5482
McDermott, Kathryn, *Librn,* Hyde County Library, Highmore SD. 605-652-2514
McDermott, Mary, *Circ,* Old Bridge Public Library, Old Bridge NJ. 201-679-5622
McDermott, Molly E, *Cent Serv,* Sonoma County Library, Santa Rosa CA. 707-545-0831
McDermott, Patricia, *Asst Librn,* Internal Revenue Service Library, Washington DC. 202-566-6342
McDermott, W S, *Dir,* Keene Memorial Library, Fremont Public Library, Fremont NE. 402-721-5084
McDiffitt, Marie L, *Actg Librn,* Galion Public Library Association, Galion OH. 419-468-3203
McDiffitt, Sharon, *Librn,* Borg-Warner Corp, Chemicals Library, Washington WV. 304-863-7335, Ext 335
McDill, Edwin B, *Acq,* Guilford Technical Institute, Learning Resource Center, Jamestown NC. 919-292-1101, 454-1126
McDill, Ruth, *Librn,* Jackson Metropolitan Library (Forest Library), Forest MS. 601-352-3677
McDivitt, Robert, *ILL & Media,* Our Lady of Angels College Library, Aston PA. 215-449-0905, Ext 10
McDonald, Alice, *Librn,* National Food Processors Association Library, Washington DC. 202-331-5900
McDonald, Alice P, *Librn,* Sacramento County Law Library, Sacramento CA. 916-444-5910
McDonald, Ann M, *Librn,* Liberty Mutual Insurance Co (Business Reference Library), Boston MA. 617-357-3359
McDonald, Arlys, *Librn,* Arizona State University Library (Music), Tempe AZ. 602-965-3513
McDonald, Barbara M, *Librn,* Westvaco Corp, Charleston Research Center, North Charleston SC. 803-744-8231
McDonald, Baxter, *Cat,* Northeast Louisiana University, Sandel Library, Monroe LA. 318-342-2195
McDonald, Betty E, *Media,* Columbia College, J Drake Edens Library, Columbia SC. 803-786-3878
McDonald, Beverly, *Librn,* Othello Public Library, Othello WA. 509-488-9683
McDonald, Christine, *Dir,* Crandall Library, Glens Falls NY. 518-792-6508
McDonald, Daisy, *Librn,* Cumberland County Public Library (Gillespie Street), Fayetteville NC. 919-483-5022
McDonald, Daisy, *Acq,* Monroe County Public Library, Key West FL. 305-294-7100

McDonald, Dana, *Dir,* Southern Illinois University School of Medicine Library, Springfield IL. 217-782-2658
McDonald, Diana, *Librn,* Annapolis Valley Regional Library Headquarters (Hantsport Branch), Hantsport NS. 902-532-2260
McDonald, Ethel Q, *Info Specialist,* EG&G Ortec Technical Library, Oak Ridge TN. 615-482-4411, Ext 351
McDonald, Evelyn, *Ad,* Satilla Regional Library, Douglas GA. 912-384-4667, 384-1172
McDonald, Frances, *Asst Prof,* Mankato State College, Library Media Education, MN. 507-389-1965
McDonald, Frances L, *Dir,* Chester Public Library, Chester IL. 618-826-3711
McDonald, Hazel, *Inst,* Mississippi Library Commission, Jackson MS. 601-354-6369
McDonald, Isabel, *Librn,* Oregon Regional Primate Research Center Library, Beaverton OR. 503-645-1141
McDonald, Jeannette S, *Dir & Acq,* Canton Public Library, Canton MA. 617-828-0177
McDonald, Joan, *Supvr,* Middlesex County Library (Ailsa Craig Branch), Ailsa Craig ON. 519-293-3441
McDonald, John P, *Dir,* University of Connecticut Library, Storrs CT. 203-486-2219
McDonald, Judy, *Dean,* Bemidji State University, A C Clark Library, Bemidji MN. 218-755-2955
McDonald, Judy, *Dir,* Bemidji State University, Library Science Program, MN. 218-755-2955
McDonald, Kay, *Librn,* Wentworth Library (Beverly Rockton Branch), Rockton ON. 416-526-4126
McDonald, Lany, *Bibliog Instr,* Sandhills Community College Library, Carthage NC. 919-692-6185, Ext 221, 223
McDonald, Marilyn L, *Cat,* Dean Junior College, E Ross Anderson Library, Franklin MA. 617-528-9100, Ext 261
McDonald, Marybelle, *ILL,* Upper Iowa University, Henderson-Wilder Library, Fayette IA. 319-425-3311, Ext 270
McDonald, Moss, *Librn,* Morgan County Library, Versailles MO. 314-378-5319
McDonald, Murray F, *Librn,* Dedham Public Library, Dedham MA. 617-326-0583
McDonald, Nathan, *Tech Serv,* Mississippi Valley State University, James Herbert White Library, Itta Bena MS. 601-254-9041, Ext 6340
McDonald, Norene, *Tech Serv,* Johnson County Library, Shawnee Mission KS. 913-831-1550
McDonald, Patricia, *Dir,* Yankton College, James M Lloyd Library, Yankton SD. 605-665-4662
McDonald, Susan J, *ILL & Ref,* Pacific Lutheran University, Robert A L Mortvedt Library, Tacoma WA. 206-531-6900, Ext 301
McDonald, Velma, *Librn,* Pine Forest Regional Library (Seminary Public), Seminary MS. 601-788-6539
McDonald, Jr, Stanley M, *Dir,* Framingham State College, Henry Whittemore Library, Framingham MA. 617-620-1220, Ext 273
McDonell, Edwin D, *Librn,* Kirklin Public Library, Kirklin IN. 317-279-9876
McDonell, Ellen, *Cat,* University of Tennessee Center for the Health Sciences Library, Memphis TN. 901-528-5638
McDonnell, Anne, *Librn,* Kentucky Historical Society Library, Frankfort KY. 502-564-3016
McDonnell, Anthony, *Tech Serv,* Prince George's County Memorial Library System, Hyattsville MD. 301-699-3500
McDonnell, Claire R, *Manager,* Johnson & Johnson, Research Center Library, New Brunswick NJ. 201-524-5563
McDonnell, Janice, *Cat,* Temple University of the Commonwealth System of Higher Education (Law), Philadelphia PA. 215-787-7891
McDonnell, Janice P, *Librn,* Tennessee Valley Authority, Forestry Technical Library, Norris TN. 615-632-6450
McDonnell, Julia, *Cat & Rare Bks,* Belmont Abbey College, Abbot Vincent Taylor Library, Belmont NC. 704-825-3711, Ext 342
McDonnell, Latrell, *Dir,* Yoakum County Library, Plains TX. 806-456-8725
McDonough, Bette, *Librn,* Fresno County Free Library (Selma Branch), Selma CA. 209-896-3393
McDonough, Douglas, *Librn,* Portland Public Library (Riverton), Portland ME. 207-773-4761

McDonough, George E, *Dir*, Seattle Pacific University, Weter Memorial Library, Seattle WA. 206-284-2000

McDonough, Marie, *Cat*, Bangor Public Library, Bangor ME. 207-947-8336

McDonough, Terrence, *Ser*, University of Connecticut Library, Storrs CT. 203-486-2219

McDougal, Bee, *Per*, Bryant Library, Roslyn NY. 516-621-2240

McDougal, Joan, *Librn*, Dillon City Library, Dillon MT. 406-683-4544

McDougal, Nathalie, *Instr*, Lansing Community College, Library Media Technology Program, MI. 517-373-9978

McDougall, D B, *Librn*, Legislative Assembly of Alberta, Legislature Library, Edmonton AB. 403-427-2473

McDougall, Kathy, *Media*, Owen Sound Public Library, Owen Sound ON. 519-376-6623

McDougall, Stanley M, *Librn*, Haliburton County Public Library, Haliburton ON. 705-457-2241

McDowell, Barbara, *Ch*, Horseheads Free Library, Ruth B Leet Library, Horseheads NY. 607-739-4581

McDowell, Barbara, *Chief Librn & Bibliog Instr*, Veterans Administration, Center Library, Sioux Falls SD. 605-336-3230, Ext 272

McDowell, Bernadette, *Br Libr Asst*, Ventura County Library Services Agency (Moorpark Branch), Moorpark CA. 805-529-0440

McDowell, Catherine, *Librn*, Daughters of the Republic of Texas Library, San Antonio TX. 512-225-1071

McDowell, D J, *Asst Librn*, Truth or Consequences Public Library, Truth or Consequences NM. 505-894-3027

McDowell, Elizabeth H, *Librn*, Cannon Free Library, Delhi NY. 607-746-2662

McDowell, Ida L, *Exec Dir*, Four Rivers Area Library Services Authority, IN. 812-425-2521

McDowell, Julie H, *Librn*, Supreme Court Library, Elmira NY. 607-737-2983

McDowell, Lucile, *Librn*, Sidell District Library, Sidell IL. 217-288-9031

McDowell, Marie, *On-Line Servs & Bibliog Instr*, United States Navy (Navy Personnel Research & Development Center), San Diego CA. 714-225-7971

McDowell, Robert, *Asst Librn*, Pan American University, Learning Resource Center, Edinburg TX. 512-381-2751

McDowell, Sylvia A, *Librn*, Massachusetts Institute of Technology Libraries (Student Center), Cambridge MA. 617-253-7050

McDuff, Rebecca, *Dir*, Edinburg Public Library, Edinburg TX. 512-383-6246, 383-6247

McDuffie, Jean S, *ILL*, Central Piedmont Community College Library, Charlotte NC. 704-373-6883

McDuffie, Patsy R, *Librn*, Bureau of Land Management Library, Reno NV. 702-784-5452

McEachern, Mrs J E, *Librn*, South River - Mauchar Public Library, South River ON. 705-386-0222

McEachern, Virginia S, *Librn*, G Werber Bryan Psychiatric Hospital Library, Columbia SC. 803-758-4839

McElderry, Stanley, *Dir*, University of Chicago, Joseph Regenstein Library, Chicago IL. 312-753-2977

McElfresh, Melvin P, *Librn*, United States Air Force (Kelly Air Force Base Library), Kelly AFB TX. 512-925-4116

McElhaney, William E, *Dir*, Jackson City Library, Jackson OH. 614-286-2609

McElhinney, Helen, *Tech Serv*, Troy Public Library, Troy MI. 313-689-5665

McElhinney, P J, *Dir*, Bur Oak Library System, Shorewood IL. 815-729-3345, 729-3346

McElligott, Jean F, *On-Line Servs*, Catholic University of America (Nursing), Washington DC. 202-635-5411

McElrath, Sara L, *Dir*, Woodbury County Rural Library, Moville IA. 712-873-3322

McElravy, Linda, *Ref*, Lethbridge Public Library, Lethbridge AB. 403-329-3233

McElroy, Audrey, *Br Coordr*, East Baton Rouge Parish Library, Baton Rouge LA. 504-389-3360

McElroy, Elizabeth, *Librn*, University of Maryland at College Park (Chemistry), College Park MD. 301-454-2609

McElroy, F Clifford, *Librn*, Boston College Libraries (Science & Geophysics Library), Chestnut Hill MA. 617-969-0100, Ext 3230

McElroy, F Clifford, *Librn*, Boston College, Weston Observatory, Catherine B O'Connor Library, Weston MA. 617-899-9050

McElroy, Joseph, *Asst Dir*, Ontario Cooperative Library System, Newark NY. 315-331-2176

McElroy, Joseph, *Asst Dir*, Wayne County Library System, Newark NY. 315-331-2176

McElroy, Mary, *Librn*, Cornell University Libraries (College of Engineering), Ithaca NY. 607-256-4318

McElroy, Mary Joe, *Librn*, Kasilof Public Library, Tustumena School Library, Kasilof AK. 906-262-4844

McElroy, Meleja, *Patients' Librn*, University of Pittsburgh (Western Psychiatric Institute & Clinic Library), Pittsburgh PA. 412-624-2378

McElroy, Mildred, *Librn*, Tallahatchie County Library (Tutwiler Branch), Tutwiler MS. 601-345-8475

McElwain, Katherine, *Ad*, Hunterdon County Library, Flemington NJ. 201-788-1444

McElwain, Maryhardy, *Librn*, Elizabeth Jones Library, Grenada MS. 601-226-2072

McElwain, Minnie, *Supvr*, Huron County Public Library (Fordwich Branch), Fordwich ON. 519-335-3367

McEnaney, Barbara, *Cat*, Niagara University Library, Niagara University NY. 716-285-1212, Ext 376

McEndarfer, Ann, *Librn*, Sojourners Public Library, Kirksville MO. 816-665-6038

McEntire, Gerrye, *Bibliog Instr*, University of Texas at Dallas, University Library, Richardson TX. 214-690-2950

McEntire, Madge, *Librn*, Kimberly Public Library, Kimberly ID. 208-423-4556

McEntire, P, *Librn*, United States Navy (NRMC-Patients Library), Newport RI. 401-841-3044

McEntyre, Roy A, *Librn*, United States Navy (Charleston Naval Shipyard Technical Library), Charleston SC. 803-743-3843

McEven, Joddy, *Librn*, Coolidge Public Library, Coolidge AZ. 602-723-4538

McEvers, Mike, *Micro-Per Supvr*, Kansas City Public Library, Kansas City MO. 816-221-2685

McEvily, Michele, *Ref*, George Washington University Library (Paul Himmelfarb Health Sciences Library), Washington DC. 202-676-2850

McEvoy, Rita A, *Librn*, Derby Neck Library, Derby CT. 203-734-1492

McEwan, Jodie, *Librn*, Monroe County Library System (Carleton Branch), Carleton MI. 313-654-2180

McEwan, Linda, *Tech Serv*, Elgin Community College, Renner Learning Resources Center, Elgin IL. 312-697-1000, Ext 258

McEwen, Barney, *Librn Blind*, Indiana State Library, Indianapolis IN. 317-232-3675

McEwen, Barney, *Librn*, Indiana State Library, Division for the Blind & Physically Handicapped, Indianapolis IN. 317-232-3684

McFadden, Charles A, *Acq*, Kutztown State College, Rohrbach Library, Kutztown PA. 215-683-4480

McFadden, Linda C, *Asst Librn*, Tekonsha Public Library, Tekonsha MI. 517-767-4769

McFadden, Marilyn, *Tech Serv*, Murray State University, Harry Lee Waterfield Library, Murray KY. 502-762-2291

McFadden, Mrs I, *Acq*, Ottawa Public Library, Ottawa ON. 613-236-0301

McFadden, Mrs Wilmot C, *Librn*, Rock Springs Public Library, Rock Springs WY. 307-362-6212

McFadden, Sue, *Bus & Econ*, Louisiana Tech University, Prescott Memorial Library, Ruston LA. 318-257-2577

McFadden, Tom, *Eng & Computer Sci & Printing*, Rochester Institute of Technology, Wallace Memorial Library, Rochester NY. 716-475-2566

McFaden, Marion, *Librn*, Public Library of Annapolis & Anne Arundel County Inc (Severna Park), Severna Park MD. 301-647-5522

McFadyen, Jolynn, *Librn*, Patterson, Belknap, Webb & Tyler Library, New York NY. 212-541-4000

McFadyen, Margaret, *Info Serv Coordr*, Central Ontario Regional Library, Richmond Hill ON. 416-884-4395

McFarland, Betty, *Librn*, Collingdale Public Library, Collingdale PA. 215-583-2214

McFarland, Betty, *Librn*, Elizabethtown Community College, Media Center Library, Elizabethtown KY. 502-769-2371, Ext 287

McFarland, Bob, *Instr*, Appalachian State University, Department of Educational Media: Librarianship & Instructional Technology, NC. 704-262-2243

McFarland, Carol, *Ref*, North Central Regional Library, Wenatchee WA. 509-663-1117

McFarland, Carolyn, *Ref*, Rollins College, Mills Memorial Library, Winter Park FL. 305-646-2000, Ext 2676

McFarland, Clara, *Doc*, Public Library of Enid & Garfield County, Enid Public Library, Enid OK. 405-234-6313

McFarland, Doris H, *Asst Dir*, Paris-Bourbon County Library, Paris KY. 606-987-4419

McFarland, George S, *Ch*, Brevard County Library System, Merritt Island FL. 305-453-9509

McFarland, Jerry, *Dir*, Florida Parole & Probation Commission Library, Tallahassee FL. 904-488-3415

McFarland, M H, *Librn*, Santa Rosa Medical Center, Health Science Library, San Antonio TX. 512-228-2284

McFarland, Mary Jane, *Librn*, Gregory Public Library, Gregory TX. 512-643-6562

McFarland, Phyllis, *Librn*, Friendship Public Library, Friendship ME. 207-832-4244

McFarland, Roger, *Media*, Mount San Antonio College, Learning Resources Center, Walnut CA. 714-594-5611, Ext 260

McFarland, Sarah C, *Ref*, Williams College, Sawyer Library, Williamstown MA. 413-597-2501

McFarland, Thomas A, *Dir*, Cocoa Public Library, Cocoa FL. 305-636-3243, 636-7323

McFarland, Wilma L, *Dir & Cat*, North Platte Public Library, Lincoln Keith Perkins Regional Library, North Platte NE. 308-532-6560

McFarlane, Agnes, *Chief Librn*, Gazette Library, Montreal PQ. 514-861-1111

McFarlane, Jane, *Librn*, Saint Louis Public Library (Lashly), Saint Louis MO. 314-367-4120

McFarlane, Linda, *Librn & On-Line Servs*, Sunnybrook Hospital, Health Sciences Library, Toronto ON. 416-486-3880

McFarlane, Ruth, *Librn*, Fort Erie Public Library (Bertie), Ridgeway ON. 416-894-1281

McFee, Doris, *Librn*, Chappell Memorial Library & Art Gallery, Chappell NE. 308-874-2626

McFeely, Mary D, *Ref, On-Line Servs & Bibliog Instr*, Smith College Library, Northampton MA. 413-584-2700, Ext 501

McFerran, Warren, *Dir & Ad*, Muskegon County Library, Muskegon MI. 616-724-6248

McFerren, Priscilla Greco, *Dir*, Hanover Public Library, Hanover PA. 717-632-5183

McFerrin, James B, *Dir*, Union College, Abigail E Weeks Memorial Library, Barbourville KY. 606-546-4151, Ext 137

McGahee, Betty B, *Bkmobile Coordr*, Jefferson County Library, Louisville GA. 912-625-3751

McGalliard, Mary Lou, *Asst Dir*, Yakima Valley Regional Library, Yakima WA. 509-452-8541, Ext 22

McGammon, Leslie, *Acq*, Florida International University, North Miami Campus Library, North Miami FL. 305-940-5730

McGarity, Mary Sue, *Dir*, University of Alabama in Birmingham, School Library Media Program, School of Education, AL. 205-934-3250

McGarr, Sheila, *ILL*, Mary Washington College, E Lee Trinkle Library, Fredericksburg VA. 703-899-4666

McGarth, L W, *Dir*, Saint John's Seminary Library, Brighton MA. 617-254-2610, Ext 79

McGarty, Jean, *Cat*, Saint John's Provincial Seminary Library, Plymouth MI. 313-453-6200, Ext 37

McGarvey, Jane, *ILL*, Adriance Memorial Library, Poughkeepsie NY. 914-485-4790

McGaughey, Betty J, *Librn*, Wellington Public Library, Wellington KS. 316-326-2011

McGaughey, Susan, *Ch*, Apollo Memorial Library, Apollo PA. 412-478-4214

McGaughran, Roberta, *Ref*, Williamsburg Regional Library, Williamsburg VA. 804-229-7326

McGavern, John H, *Dir*, University of Hartford, Mortensen Library, West Hartford CT. 203-243-4265

MCGEE

McGee, Ann, *Assoc Dean LRC,* El Centro College, Learning Resources Center, Dallas TX. 214-746-2292

McGee, Carol, *Librn,* Central Louisiana State Hospital (Medical & Professional Library), Pineville LA. 318-445-2421, Ext 429

McGee, Elsie, *Librn,* Haskell County Library, Haskell TX. 817-864-2747

McGee, Faye W, *Circ,* Santa Fe Community College Library, Gainesville FL. 904-377-5161, Ext 315

McGee, Gregg, *Br Coordr,* Granite City Public Library, Granite City IL. 618-876-0550

McGee, Mabel, *Librn,* First Regional Library (Coldwater Public), Coldwater MS. 601-622-4511

McGee, Mary Louise, *Ref & Bibliog Instr,* Saint Joseph's College, McEntegart Hall Library, Brooklyn NY. 212-789-5385

McGee, Ruby, *Tech Serv,* Honeywell Information Systems Inc, System Technical Library, Waltham MA. 617-890-8400

McGee, Sara H, *Media,* Athens Regional Library, Athens GA. 404-543-0134

McGee, Sue, *Per,* Southwestern College Library, Oklahoma City OK. 405-947-2331, Ext 214

McGeean, Jim, *Video,* Seneca College of Applied Arts & Technology, Finch Campus Learning Resource Centre, Willowdale ON. 416-491-5050, Ext 381

McGhan, Dorothy, *Librn,* Plaquemines Parish Library (Belle Chasse Branch), Belle Chasse LA. 504-394-3570

McGhee, Elizabeth, *Librn,* Troup Harris Coweta Regional Library (Union St), LaGrange GA. 404-882-2694

McGhee, Frances, *Librn,* Knoxville-Knox County Public Library (Mascot Branch), Mascot TN. 615-933-2620

McGhee, Mrs Theo, *Ch,* Belton City Library, Belton TX. 817-939-1161

McGhee, Ruth, *Librn,* Legislative Service Bureau Library, Des Moines IA. 515-281-3566

McGhie, Vecelia, *Dir,* Westchester County Historical Society Library, Tuckahoe NY. 914-337-1753

McGiboney, Mattie, *Librn,* Shelby County Regional Library (Columbiana), Columbiana AL. 205-669-7851

McGill, Mike, *Assoc Prof,* Syracuse University, School of Information Studies, NY. 315-423-2911

McGill, Priscilla, *Libr Technician,* United States Air Force (George Air Force Base Library), George AFB CA. 714-269-1110

McGill, Theodora, *Librn,* Export-Import Bank of the United States, Eximbank Library, Washington DC. 202-566-8320, 566-8897

McGilvery, Sharon, *Ad & Commun Servs,* Auburn Public Library, Auburn ME. 207-782-3191

McGilvray, Caroline, *Dir,* Foundation Center-San Francisco Library, San Francisco CA. 415-397-0902

McGilvrey, Marie, *Librn,* Mount Ayr Public Library, Mount Ayr IA. 515-464-2159

McGinley, Mary, *Per,* Cambria County Library System, Johnstown PA. 814-536-5131

McGinn, Judy, *Librn,* Athens Mental Health & Mental Retardation Center (Staff Library), Athens OH. 614-592-3031, Ext 262

McGinnis, Barbara, *Ref, On-Line Servs & Bibliog Instr,* University of Minnesota-Morris, Rodney A Briggs Library, Morris MN. 612-589-2221

McGinnis, Callie B, *Cat,* Columbus College, Simon Schwob Memorial Library, Columbus GA. 404-568-2042

McGinnis, Daniel W, *Dir,* Kaubisch Memorial Public Library, Fostoria OH. 419-435-2813

McGinnis, Gary R, *Media,* South Georgia College, William S Smith Library, Douglas GA. 912-384-1100, Ext 233, 290

McGinnis, Kay W, *Librn,* Gulf South Research Institute Library, Baton Rouge LA. 504-766-3300, Ext 300

McGinnis, Lila, *Ch,* Elyria Public Library, Elyria OH. 216-323-5747

McGinnis, Michael M, *Librn,* Itasca Community College Library, Grand Rapids MN. 218-326-0311, Ext 257

McGinnis, Ted, *Librn,* Susquehanna County Historical Society & Free Library Association (Forest City Branch), Montrose PA. 717-785-5590

McGinniss, Dorothy A, *Dir,* Chilmark Library, Chilmark MA. 617-645-3360

McGinniss, Frank, *AV,* Rockville Centre Public Library, Rockville Centre NY. 516-766-6258

McGinty, James, *Dir,* Ocean County College, Learning Resources Center, Toms River NJ. 201-255-4298

McGinty, John, *ILL,* University of Connecticut Health Center, Lyman Maynard Stowe Library, Farmington CT. 203-674-2739

McGinty, Kathryn S, *Librn,* Rochester Academy of Medicine Library, Rochester NY. 716-271-1313

McGinty, T P, *Chief Librn,* Vought Advanced Technology Center Library, Grand Prairie TX. 214-266-5168

McGinty, Thomas P, *Chief Librn,* Vought Corp, Technical Information Services Library, Dallas TX. 214-266-5168, 266-4660

McGirt, Jacquelyn G, *ILL & Ref,* Bennett College, Thomas F Holgate Library, Greensboro NC. 919-273-4431, Ext 139

McGiverin, Rolland, *Media,* Frostburg State College Library, Frostburg MD. 301-689-4396

McGlinn, Eileen A, *Librn,* Ann Arbor Public Library (West Branch), Ann Arbor MI. 313-994-1674

McGlinn, Susan L, *Librn,* Squamish Public Library, Squamish BC. 604-892-3110

McGlohon, Brenda, *Humanities,* Chicago Public Library (Woodson Regional), Chicago IL. 312-881-6900

McGloin, James, *Librn,* Lemont Public Library, Lemont IL. 312-257-6541

McGlynn, Barbara, *Dir,* Soldiers Grove Public Library, Soldiers Grove WI. 608-624-3264

McGlynn, Daniel J, *Mgr,* New York Times (Corporate Records Library), New York NY. 212-556-1958

McGlynn, Nan E, *Dir,* Remington-Carpenter Township Public Library, Remington IN. 219-261-2543

McGorray, John, *Librn,* State University of New York at Buffalo (Main Street), Buffalo NY. 716-831-4413

McGorty, Jacqueline, *Librn,* Ocean County Library (Tuckerton Branch), Tuckerton NJ. 201-296-1470

McGouey, Elaine, *AV,* Hastings-On-Hudson Public Library, Hastings-on-Hudson NY. 914-478-3307

McGough, Peggy, *YA,* Hays Public Library, Hays KS. 913-625-9014

McGough, Jr, Willie B, *Chief Librn,* Cape Fear Technical Institute, Library Learning Resource Center, Wilmington NC. 919-343-0481, Ext 230

McGovern, Cassandra, *Ref,* College of Lake County, Learning Resource Center, Grayslake IL. 312-223-6601, Ext 392

McGovern, Eleanor, *Librn,* Universal Technical Testing Laboratories Library, Collingdale PA. 215-586-3070

McGovern, Kathleen, *YA,* Pittsford Community Library, Pittsford NY. 716-586-1251

McGovern, Mrs A, *Circ,* NASA, John F Kennedy Space Center Library, Kennedy Space Center FL. 305-867-3600, 3615

McGowan, Anne W, *Librn,* Wyoming Department of Economic Planning & Development Library, Cheyenne WY. 307-777-7284, Ext 31

McGowan, Dolores, *Librn,* Pine Forest Regional Library (New Augusta Public), New Augusta MS. 601-964-3710

McGowan, Frank M, *Dir Acq & Overseas Opers,* Library of Congress, Washington DC. 202-287-5000

McGowan, Jay, *ILL,* Topeka Public Library, Topeka KS. 913-233-2040

McGowan, John P, *Univ Librn,* Northwestern University Library, Evanston IL. 312-492-7658

McGowan, Kathleen, *On-Line Servs,* State University of New York College at Geneseo, Milne Library, Geneseo NY. 716-245-5591

McGowan, Margaret, *Ad,* Wauwatosa Public Library, Wauwatosa WI. 414-258-5700

McGowan, Nancy, *Librn,* Norwood Public Library, Norwood PA. 215-534-0693

McGowan, Owen T P, *Dir,* Bridgewater State College, Clement C Maxwell Library, Bridgewater MA. 617-697-8321, Ext 441, 442

McGowan, Owen T P, *Chmn,* Southeastern Massachusetts Cooperating Libraries, (SMCL), MA. 617-697-8321

McGowan, Rebecca, *Microforms,* East Carolina University, J Y Joyner Library, Greenville NC. 919-757-6514

McGowan, Sarah, *Ref,* Arkansas State University, Dean B Ellis Library, Jonesboro AR. 501-972-3078, 972-3079

McGowan, Sarah M, *Dir & Acq,* Ripon College Library, Ripon WI. 414-748-8328

McGowen, C, *ILL,* Shoreham-Wading River Public Library, Shoreham NY. 516-929-4488

McGowon, Dorothy, *Mgr,* Magazine Publishers Association, Information Center, New York NY. 212-752-0055

McGrail, Elizabeth, *Asst Librn,* Sonnenschein, Carlin, Nath & Rosenthal, Law Library, Chicago IL. 312-876-7906

McGrane, Jane, *Dir,* Ionia Community Library, Ionia IA. 515-394-4010

McGrath, Anna, *Tech Serv,* University of Maine at Presque Isle Library, Presque Isle ME. 207-764-0311, Ext 223

McGrath, Catherine, *Librn,* Silas Bronson Library (East End), Waterbury CT. 203-574-8220

McGrath, E, *Librn,* General Hospital Corp Medical Library, Saint John's NF. 709-737-6300

McGrath, Eileen, *Staff,* Wabash College, Lilly Library, Crawfordsville IN. 317-362-1400, Ext 215, 216

McGrath, Kathleen, *Asst Librn,* Arthur Andersen & Co Library, Chicago IL. 312-580-0033

McGrath, Lucy S, *Dir,* Carteret Technical College Library, Morehead City NC. 919-726-2811, Ext 54

McGrath, Marsha, *Ad & YA,* Dunedin Public Library, Dunedin FL. 813-733-4115

McGrath, Mary, *Circ,* Loyola University of Chicago Libraries, Chicago IL. 312-274-3000, Ext 771

McGrath, Patricia, *Med Librn,* Veterans Administration, Medical Center Library Service, Boston MA. 617-232-9500, Ext 634

McGrath, Richard, *Librn,* Crosier Seminary Library, Onamia MN. 612-532-3103

McGrath, Shirley, *Ad & Ref,* Memorial Hall Library, (Subregional Headquarters for Eastern Massachusetts Regional System), Andover MA. 617-475-6960

McGraw, Carol, *Librn,* Yolo County Law Library, Woodland CA. 916-666-8011

McGraw, Dorothy, *Librn,* Black Mountain Public Library, Black Mountain NC. 704-669-2652

McGraw, Jane, *Dir,* East Detroit Memorial Library, East Detroit MI. 313-775-7221

McGree, Shirley, *Dir,* Hudson Public Library, Hudson WI. 715-386-3101

McGreevy, Kathleen, *On-Line Servs,* Pasadena City College Library, Pasadena CA. 213-578-7221

McGreevy, Susan, *Dir,* Wheelwright Museum, Mary Cabot Wheelwright Research Library, Santa Fe NM. 505-982-4636

McGregor, Abby, *Librn,* Sarah Carpenter Memorial Library, Hinesburg Public Library, Hinesburg VT. 802-482-2878

McGregor, Colleen Boshell, *Dir,* Buena Park Library District, Buena Park CA. 714-826-4100

McGregor, George, *Media,* Northeast Mississippi Junior College, Eula Dees Memorial Library, Booneville MS. 601-728-7751, Ext 237

McGregor, James W, *Asst Univ Librn for Tech Servs,* Northeastern Illinois University Library, Chicago IL. 312-583-4050, Ext 469, 470, 471, 472

McGregor, Rebecca, *Bkmobile Coordr,* Marshall County Public Library, Benton KY. 502-527-9969

McGregor, Virginia, *Ad,* Girard Free Public Library, Girard OH. 216-545-2508

McGrew, Dorothy, *Cat,* Marshalltown Public Library, Marshalltown IA. 515-754-5738

McGrew, M F, *Dir,* Association of American Railroads, Pittsburgh PA. 412-281-4074

McGrew, Mary Lou, *Asst Prof,* University of Northern Iowa, Dept of Library Science, IA. 319-273-2050

McGriff, Kay, *Bus,* University of Central Arkansas, Torreyson Library, Conway AR. 501-329-2931, Ext 449

McGriff, Ronald I, *Asst Dir,* East Central Regional Library, Cambridge MN. 612-689-1901

McGue, Mary L, *Commun Servs,* Sturgis Public Library, Sturgis MI. 616-651-7907, 651-2321

McGuiggan, T, *Librn,* High Voltage Engineering Corp, Ion Physics Co Technical Library, Burlington MA. 617-272-1313

McGuinn, Marion George, *Dir,* Rutherford County Library, Rutherfordton NC. 704-286-9776

McGuire, Carol, *Ser,* Colby Community College, H F Davis Memorial Library, Colby KS. 913-462-3984, Ext 265

McGuire, Carol, *Pub Servs,* Colby Community College, H F Davis Memorial Library, Colby KS. 913-462-3984, Ext 265

McGuire, Catherine A, *Librn,* United States Court of Appeals, Branch Library, Wilmington DE. 302-573-6178

McGuire, David S, *Librn,* Canadian Mental Health Association Library, Edmonton AB. 403-426-6665

McGuire, Dorothy, *Librn,* Asheville-Buncombe Library System (Black Mountain Branch), Black Mountain NC. 704-669-2652

McGuire, John E, *Dir,* Jefferson Technical College Library, Steubenville OH. 614-264-5591

McGuire, Laura, *Govt Doc,* Eastern New Mexico University Library, Portales NM. 505-562-2624

McGuire, M Genevieve, *Dir,* Lowville Free Library, Lowville NY. 315-376-2131

McGuire, Margaret, *Ch,* Gadsden-Etowah County Library, Gadsden Public Library, Gadsden AL. 205-547-1611

McGuire, Mark M, *Asst Librn,* Williams & Connolly Library, Washington DC. 202-331-5519

McGuire, Maureen, *Librn,* Shanley & Fisher Law Library, Newark NJ. 201-643-1220

McGuire, Michael, *Dir,* Traverse City Public Library, Traverse City MI. 616-941-2311

McGuire, Virginia, *Dir,* Truro Public Libraries, Pilgrim Memorial Library & Cobb Memorial Library, North Truro MA. 617-487-1125

McGuirl, Marlene C, *Chief, Am-British Law Div,* Library of Congress, Washington DC. 202-287-5000

McHale, Thomas J, *Dir,* Scranton Public Library, Albright Memorial Library, Scranton PA. 717-961-2451

McHatten, Sheila, *Librn,* Fresno County Department of Mental Health Services Library, Fresno CA. 209-488-3781

McHenry, J E, *Librn,* California State Prison, San Quentin (Legal), San Quentin CA. 415-454-1460

McHenry, James E, *Chief Librn,* California Department of Corrections, California Institution for Men Library, Chino CA. 714-597-1861

McHenry, Jerome G, *Tech Serv,* Kingston Public Library, Kingston ON. 613-549-8888

McHenry, Linda, *Ad,* Oswego City Library, Oswego NY. 315-341-5867

McHenry, Margaret, *Ref,* Henry Ford Community College, Eshleman Library, Dearborn MI. 313-271-2750, Ext 378

McHollin, Mattie, *Ref & Spec Coll,* Tennessee State University, Martha M Brown - Lois W Daniel Library, Nashville TN. 615-320-3682, 251-1417

McHugh, Alicia, *Librn,* Oakland Park City Library, Oakland Park FL. 305-561-6287

McHugh, Marjorie, *Librn,* Afton Free Library, Afton NY. 607-639-1212

McIlmoyl, V, *Librn,* Okanagan Regional Library District (Oliver Branch), Oliver BC. 604-498-2242

McIlroy, N J, *Librn,* Ontario Ministry of the Environment Library, Toronto ON. 416-965-7978

McIlroy, William R, *Head,* Free Library of Philadelphia (Fiction), Philadelphia PA. 215-686-5322

McIlvain, Bill, *Librn,* Oklahoma Library for the Blind & Physically Handicapped, Oklahoma City OK. 405-521-3514, 521-3832

McIlvaine, Betsy, *Librn,* North American Philips Corp, Philips Laboratories Research Library, Briarcliff Manor NY. 914-762-0300, Ext 421

McIlvaine, Betty, *Librn,* Wayne County Public Library (Creston Branch), Creston OH. 216-435-4204

McIlvaine, Paul M, *Assoc Librn,* Ciba-Geigy Corp, Corporate Library, Ardsley NY. 914-478-3131, Ext 2397

McIlwain, Doris, *Media,* Central Carolina Technical Institute, Learning Resource Center, Sanford NC. 919-775-5401, Ext 244

McIlwain, Kathleen, *Dir,* Jackson-George Regional Library System, Pascagoula MS. 601-762-3406

McInnes, Cynthia, *Ser,* East Central State University, Linscheid Library, Ada OK. 405-332-8000

McInnes, Douglas, *Asst Librn,* University of British Columbia Library, Vancouver BC. 604-228-3871

McInnis, Raymond, *ILL & Ref,* Western Washington University, Mabel Zoe Wilson Library, Bellingham WA. 206-676-3050

McInroy, Moira, *Media,* Texas College of Osteopathic Medicine Library, Fort Worth TX. 817-735-2465

McIntire, Susan, *Ad & Cat,* Comstock Township Library, Comstock MI. 616-345-0136

McIntosh, Alma, *Supvr,* Elgin County Public Library (Dutton Branch), Dutton ON. 519-633-0815

McIntosh, Cam, *Librn,* Puget Sound Council of Governments, Council Library, Seattle WA. 206-464-7090

McIntosh, Carolyn, *Hist,* University of Southern California, Edward L Doheny Memorial Library, Los Angeles CA. 213-743-6050

McIntosh, Ethylene, *Librn,* Jackson Metropolitan Library (Pineville Library), Pineville MS. 601-352-3677

McIntosh, F H, *Actg Dir,* Lakehead University, School of Library Technology, ON. 807-345-2121, Ext 240

McIntosh, George W, *Ref,* Beaufort Technical College, Learning Resource Center, Beaufort SC. 803-524-3380, Ext 236 & 241

McIntosh, Gertrude, *Librn,* Hudson Library, Highlands NC. 704-526-3031

McIntosh, Karen F, *ILL & Cat,* Amarillo College, Learning Resource Center, Amarillo TX. 806-376-5111, Ext 2420

McIntosh, Linda, *Librn,* Fairview Community Hospital, Health Science Library, Minneapolis MN. 612-371-6545

McIntosh, Melinda, *Microforms,* University of Massachusetts at Amherst Library, Amherst MA. 413-545-0284

McIntosh, Mildred, *Local Hist,* Given Memorial Library, Pinehurst NC. 919-295-6022

McIntosh, Mrs R S, *Librn,* Missisquoi Museum Library, Stanbridge East PQ. 514-248-3153

McIntosh, Wanda, *Librn,* Edna Zybell Memorial Library, Clarence IA. 319-452-3734

McInturff, Mary Jane, *Librn,* Schick's Shadel Hospital, Medical Library, Seattle WA. 206-244-8100

McIntyre, Burnelle, *Bibliog Instr,* Gallaudet College, Edward Miner Gallaudet Memorial Library, Washington DC. 202-651-5566

McIntyre, H, *Librn,* London Public Libraries & Museums (William O Carson Branch), London ON. 519-432-7166

McIntyre, Jane, *Ref,* Robert J Kleberg Public Library, Kingsville TX. 512-592-6381

McIntyre, Marion, *Librn,* Gilmanton Corner Public Library, Gilmanton NH. 603-267-6308

McIntyre, Mary, *Dir,* Detroit College of Business Library, Dearborn MI. 313-582-6983, Ext 24

McIntyre, Patrick F, *Librn,* North Country Community College, Learning Resource Center, Saranac Lake NY. 518-891-2915, Ext 222

McIntyre, Paula, *Cat,* Jacksonville University, Carl S Swisher Library, Jacksonville FL. 904-744-3950, Ext 266, 267

McIntyre, Ronald, *Media,* Upsala College Library, East Orange NJ. 201-266-7295

McIntyre, S V, *Mgr,* Boeing Co (Kent Technical Library), Seattle WA. 206-773-0590

McIntyre, Sharon, *Librn,* Iosco-Arenac Regional Library (Oscoda Library), Oscoda MI. 517-739-9581

McIntyre, Sharon R, *Librn,* Jones, Day, Reavis & Pogue Library, Cleveland OH. 216-696-3939, Ext 533

McIntyre, Susan J, *Librn,* Mount Sinai Hospital, Medical Library, Minneapolis MN. 612-871-3700, Ext 1769

McIntyre, William A, *Dir,* New Hampshire Vocational Technical College Library, Nashua NH. 603-882-6923

McIsaac, Charles A, *Dir Libr Serv,* North Adams State College Library, Eugene L Freel Library, North Adams MA. 413-664-4511, Ext 321

McIver, Aline, *Librn,* Winkler County Library (Wink Branch), Wink TX. 915-527-3691

McIver, Minna, *Acting Acq,* Clemson University, Robert Muldrow Cooper Library, Clemson SC. 803-656-3026

McIver, Miss, *Librn,* Norwalk Hospital (Wilcox Library), Norwalk CT. 203-838-3611, Ext 530

McIver, Vivian D, *Dir,* Needham Free Public Library, Needham MA. 617-444-0087, 444-0090

McIvor, R M, *Dir,* Penticton Public Library, Penticton BC. 604-492-0024

McKain, Adelaide R, *Librn,* Methodist Hospital Library, Philadelphia PA. 215-339-5133

McKain, Celia H, *Dir,* Kittanning Free Library, Kittanning PA. 412-543-1383

McKann, Helen, *Librn,* County of Henrico Public Library (Varina), Richmond VA. 804-222-8686

McKann, Michael, *Assoc State Librn for Readers & Tech Servs,* Louisiana State Library, Baton Rouge LA. 504-342-4922

McKay, Ann H, *Librn,* Acres Consulting Services Ltd Library, Niagara Falls ON. 416-354-3831, Ext 247

McKay, Bernice, *Librn,* Batchawana Community Library, Batchawana Bay ON. 705-882-2460

McKay, David N, *Dir,* North Carolina Department of Cultural Resources, Division of State Library, North Carolina State Library, Raleigh NC. 919-733-2570

McKay, Eleanor, *Spec Coll,* Memphis State University Libraries, Memphis TN. 901-454-2201

McKay, Jeri, *Bkmobile Coordr,* Madison-Jefferson County Public Library, Madison IN. 812-265-2744

McKay, John P, *Dir,* Malverne Public Library, Malverne NY. 516-599-0750

McKay, Michael, *Grants Mgt Consult,* Massachusetts Board of Library Commissioners, Office for the Development of Library Services, Boston MA. 617-267-9400

McKay, Pamela, *Per,* Worcester State College, Learning Resources Center, Worcester MA. 617-752-7700, Ext 132, 135

McKay, Patricia W, *Librn,* Richmond Public Library (Broad Rock), Richmond VA. 804-233-3651

McKay, Robert, *Actg Dir,* Ohio Valley Area Libraries, (OVAL), OH. 614-384-2103

McKean, Jean, *Shut-In Serv,* Richmond Hill Public Library, Richmond Hill ON. 416-884-9288

McKean, Jean, *Librn,* Richmond Hill Public Library (Richvale), Richmond Hill ON. 416-889-2847

McKechnie, Eleanor, *Circ,* Gloucester Lyceum & Sawyer Free Library, Gloucester MA. 617-283-0376

McKedy, Diane L, *Pub Info Consult,* Massachusetts Board of Library Commissioners, Office for the Development of Library Services, Boston MA. 617-267-9400

McKee, Allyson, *Tech Serv,* West Virginia University (Medical Center Library), Morgantown WV. 304-293-2113

McKee, Beth, *Tech Serv,* Okanagan Regional Library District, Kelowna BC. 604-860-4033

McKee, Bonnie, *Dir,* Western Oklahoma State College, Learning Resources Center, Altus OK. 405-477-2000, Ext 69

McKee, Christopher, *Dir,* Grinnell College, Burling Library, Grinnell IA. 515-236-6181, Ext 598

McKee, David, *Librn,* Western Michigan University (Business), Kalamazoo MI. 616-383-1926

McKee, Elizabeth A, *In Charge,* Atlantic Richfield Co, ARCO Chemical Co Library, Philadelphia PA. 215-577-2000

McKee, Genie, *Tech Serv, Cat & On-Line Servs,* Maryville College, Father Edward Dowling Memorial Library, Saint Louis MO. 314-434-4100, Ext 241

McKee, George, *Librn,* Museum of Contemporary Art Library, Chicago IL. 312-943-7755

McKee, Jay R, *Librn,* Martin Marietta Aerospace, Research Library, Denver CO. 303-973-5512

McKee, Jeanette L, *Ref,* Dedham Public Library, Dedham MA. 617-326-0583

McKee, Jimmy D, *Dir,* Bladen County Public Library, Elizabethtown NC. 919-862-8171

McKee, Joel, *Librn,* Clark County Library District (Charleston Heights), Las Vegas NV. 702-878-3682

McKee, Mary, *Tech Serv,* Fordham University, School of Law Library, New York NY. 212-841-5223

McKee, Miriam, *Librn,* Nelsonville Public Library (Athens Branch), Athens OH. 614-593-6845

McKee, N Ruth, *Actg Librn,* Odon Winkelpleck Memorial Library, Odon IN. 812-636-4949

McKee, Nancy, *Asst Librn,* Immaculate Conception Seminary Library, Mahwah NJ. 201-327-0300

McKee, Nancy S, *ILL, Ref & On-Line Servs,* Clarion State College, Rena M Carlson Library, Clarion PA. 814-226-2343

McKee, Phillipa, *Asst Librn,* Wernersville Public Library, Wernersville PA. 215-678-1486

McKee, R, *Dir,* Music & Arts Institute of San Francisco, College Library, San Francisco CA. 415-567-1445

McKeehan, Nancy C, *Tech Serv,* Medical University of South Carolina Library, Charleston SC. 803-792-2374

McKeen, Jill, *ILL,* Palliser Regional Library, Moose Jaw SK. 306-693-3669

McKeen, M, *Librn,* Calgary Public Library (Memorial Park), Calgary AB. 403-232-0254

McKeen, Richard B, *Coordr,* Maine Correctional Center Library, South Windham ME. 207-892-6716, Ext 254

McKeen, V, *Media & Tech Serv,* Powell River District Libraries, Powell River BC. 604-485-4796

McKeever, Sister Estelle M, *Librn,* Mount Saint Mary College, Curtin Memorial Library, Newburgh NY. 914-561-0800, Ext 248

McKellar, Carole, *Ch,* Van Buren County Library, Webster Memorial Library, Decatur MI. 616-423-4771

McKellar, Norma S, *Asst Dir & Ch,* Colquitt-Thomas Regional Library, Moultrie-Colquitt County Library, Moultrie GA. 912-985-6540

McKelvey, Josephine, *YA,* Chappaqua Central School District Public Library, Chappaqua Library, Chappaqua NY. 914-238-4779

McKenna, Dee J, *Librn,* Kegoayah Kozga Public Library, Nome AK. 907-443-5242

McKenna, Eloise M, *Dir, Cat & Ref,* Briggs-Lawrence County Public Library, Ironton OH. 614-532-1124

McKenna, Florence, *Proc Coordr,* University of Pittsburgh, Hillman Library, Pittsburgh PA. 412-624-4400

McKenna, Gerald, *Librn,* Cumberland County Public Library (Bordeaux), Fayetteville NC. 919-485-1425

McKenna, Janet, *Ad & Ref,* North Tonawanda Public Library, North Tonawanda NY. 716-693-4132

McKenna, Jennifer, *Librn,* Burlington Public Library (Aldershot), Burlington ON. 416-639-3611, Ext 58

McKenna, L, *On-Line Servs & Bibliog Instr,* Canada Ministry of Transport, Canadian Coast Guard College Library, Sydney NS. 902-539-2115, Ext 29

McKenna, Liesje, *Ref,* Durham College of Applied Arts & Technology Library, Oshawa ON. 416-576-0210, Ext 214

McKenna, Mary, *Librn,* Porter Memorial Library, Blandford MA. 413-848-2853

McKenna, Mary E, *Librn,* Providence Public Library (Mount Pleasant), Providence RI. 401-861-1962

McKenna, Sheila, *District Consult,* Central Maine Library District, Augusta ME. 207-289-3561

McKenna, Sister Virginia, *Dir,* Marymount College, Gloria Gaines Memorial Library, Tarrytown NY. 914-631-3200

McKenna, Thomas, *Media & Acq,* State University of New York College of Technology, Utica-Rome Library, Utica NY. 315-792-3420

McKennan, Harriet, *Librn,* Oregon State Department of Human Resources, Children's Services Division, Staff Development Library, Salem OR. 503-378-3033

McKenney, Louise, *Ref,* Menominee County Library, Stephenson MI. 906-753-6923

McKenney, Nancy, *Dir & Acq,* Campbellsville College Library, Campbellsville KY. 502-465-8158, Ext 272

McKennon, Mrs D H, *Librn,* Jackson Metropolitan Library (Mendenhall Library), Mendenhall MS. 601-352-3677

McKenzie, Alice, *Librn,* Brobeck, Phleger & Harrison Library, San Francisco CA. 415-442-1053

McKenzie, Cheryl L, *Dir,* Brenau College, Lessie Southgate Simmons Memorial Library, Gainesville GA. 404-534-6113

McKenzie, Connie, *Libr Tech,* Environmental Protection Agency, Region VII Library, Kansas City MO. 816-374-3497

McKenzie, Donald, *Chief Librn,* Town of Caledon Public Libraries, Bolton ON. 416-857-1400

McKenzie, Jeanne, *Correctional Libr Servs Librn,* Shawnee Library System, Carterville IL. 618-985-3711

McKenzie, Joseph, *Ch,* Salina Public Library, Salina KS. 913-825-4624

McKenzie, Karen, *Sr Cat,* Art Gallery of Ontario, Edward P Taylor Reference Library, Toronto ON. 416-977-0414, Ext 339, 340 & 390

McKenzie, Margaret, *Tech Serv & Cat,* Huntsville-Madison County Public Library, Huntsville AL. 205-536-0021

McKenzie, Marjorie, *Dir,* Pine Mountain Regional Library, Manchester GA. 404-846-2186

McKenzie, Mary, *Librn,* Indian Creek Township Library, Norris City IL. 618-378-3171

McKenzie, Michael, *Dir,* Paul D Camp Community College Library, Franklin VA. 804-562-2171, Ext 234

McKeogh, Claire, *Librn,* Canadian Nurses Association Library, Ottawa ON. 613-237-2133, Ext 49

McKeon, Isabel, *Librn,* West Warren Library Association, West Warren MA. 413-436-5506

McKeough, Dolores, *Dir,* Aberdeen-Matawan Public Library, Matawan NJ. 201-583-9100

McKeown, Tricia, *On-Line Servs,* University of Texas Health Science Center at Dallas Library, Dallas TX. 214-688-3368

McKibben, Eloise, *Librn,* Faulkner-Van Buren Regional Library (Helen Lever Memorial), Conway AR. 501-327-7482

McKie, Barbara, *Media,* Benton Harbor Public Library, Benton Harbor MI. 616-926-6139

McKie, Barbara, *Media,* Benton Harbor Public Library (Filmco-Cooperative Service Center for Southwest Michigan Library Cooperative), Benton Harbor MI. 616-926-6741

McKiernan, Lester, *Dir,* Choctaw Nation Multi-County Library System, McAlester OK. 918-426-0456

McKillen, Kathryn Garfield, *Librn,* Dexter District Library, Dexter MI. 313-426-4477

McKillip, Dorothy M, *Dir,* Land O'Lakes Public Library, Land O'Lakes WI. 715-547-3255

McKillips, Rebecca, *Ser,* Northeast Louisiana University, Sandel Library, Monroe LA. 318-342-2195

McKillop, D, *Pub Servs,* Red River Community College, Learning Resources Center, Winnipeg MB. 204-632-2232

McKillop, Wm E, *Pub Serv,* Richard J Daley College, Learning Resource Center, Chicago IL. 312-735-3000, Ext 224, 226, 227

McKinin, Emma Jean, *Ref,* University of Missouri-Columbia (Medical), Columbia MO. 314-882-8086

McKinlay, Bessie J, *Librn,* Hamilton Academy of Medicine Library, Hamilton ON. 416-528-1611

McKinley, Alice E, *Dir,* DuPage Library System, Geneva IL. 312-232-8457

McKinley, Gail, *Br Coordr,* Noble County Public Library, Albion IN. 219-636-7197

McKinley, Gail, *Librn,* Noble County Public Library (Avilla Branch), Avilla IN. 219-897-3900

McKinley, Margaret, *Ser,* University of California Los Angeles Library, Los Angeles CA. 213-825-1201

McKinley, Martha, *Bkmobile Coordr,* Muncie-Center Township Public Library, Muncie IN. 317-288-9971

McKinley, Martha, *Librn,* Muncie-Center Township Public Library (Extension Service), Muncie IN. 317-289-3444

McKinnerney, Maxine, *Librn,* Oracle Public Library, Oracle AZ. 602-896-2121

McKinney, Betty, *Librn,* Princeton Community Hospital Library, Princeton WV. 304-487-1515, Ext 246

McKinney, Eleanor, *Assoc Prof,* Western Michigan University, School of Librarianship, MI. 616-383-1849

McKinney, Florence, *Librn,* Youngsville Public Library, Youngsville PA. 814-563-7670

McKinney, Frances, *Librn,* United States Air Force (Reese Air Force Base Library), Reese AFB TX. 806-885-4511

McKinney, Gayle, *On-Line Servs,* Georgia State University, William Russell Pullen Library, Atlanta GA. 404-658-2185, 658-2172

McKinney, Helen, *Librn,* Society of the Four Arts Library, Palm Beach FL. 305-655-2766

McKinney, Joanne, *In Charge,* Avery International, Research Center Technical Library, Pasadena CA. 213-799-0881

McKinney, Juanita, *Ch,* Homewood Public Library, Homewood AL. 205-871-7342

McKinney, Kerry, *Chief Librn,* World Affairs Council of Northern California Library, San Francisco CA. 415-982-2541, Ext 21

McKinney, Margot, *ILL, Ref & Bibliog Instr,* Green Mountain College Library, Poultney VT. 802-287-9313, Ext 42 & 43

McKinney, Nancy, *Asst Dir,* Midwestern Baptist College, B R Lakin Library, Pontiac MI. 313-334-0961

McKinney, Rose, *Regist & Circ,* Saint Louis Public Library, Saint Louis MO. 314-241-2288

McKinney, Venora, *In Charge,* Milwaukee Public Library (Martin L King), Milwaukee WI. 414-278-3098

McKinnon, Katherine, *Chief Librn,* Orillia Public Library, Orillia ON. 705-325-2338

Mckinnon, Marjorie G, *Libr Technician,* Brandon Mental Health Centre, Reference & Lending Library, Brandon MB. 204-728-7110, Ext 287

McKinnon, Sister Marie M, *Librn,* Saint Augustine's Seminary Library, Scarborough ON. 416-261-7207, Ext 36

McKinstry, Shirley, *Librn,* Public Library of Steubenville & Jefferson County (Brilliant Branch), Brilliant OH. 614-598-4028

McKinzie-Beene, Holly, *ILL, Circ & Per,* Glendale Community College, John F Prince Library, Glendale AZ. 602-934-2211, Ext 239, 242

McKirdy, Colin, *Info Systs Mgr,* University of Lowell Libraries (O'Leary Library), Lowell MA. 617-452-5000, Ext 480

McKissic, Thelma, *Librn,* Memphis-Shelby County Public Library & Information Center (North), Memphis TN. 901-276-6631

McKitrick, Patricia, *AV,* Elkhart Public Library, Elkhart IN. 219-294-5463

McKitterick, Mrs, *Librn,* Darien Historical Society Inc Library, Darien CT. 203-655-9233

McKnight, Joanne, *Ref,* Mount Union College Library, Alliance OH. 216-821-5320, Ext 260

McKnight, Joyce, *Sci-Tech,* Akron-Summit County Public Library, Akron OH. 216-762-7621

McKnight, Norma, *Cat,* Southampton Free Library, Southampton PA. 215-322-1415

McKnown, Muriel, *Librn,* Suwannee River Regional Library, Seven-County Region (Greenville (Madison County)), Live Oak FL. 904-362-5779

McKone, Catherine, *Librn,* Blandinsville-Hire District Library, Blandinsville IL. 309-652-3166

McKown, Cornelius, *Librn,* Pennsylvania State University (Physical Science), University Park PA. 814-865-7616

McKoy, W Keith, *Per,* East Brunswick Public Library, East Brunswick NJ. 201-254-1220

McKula, Kathleen, *Librn,* Hartford Courant News Library, Hartford CT. 203-249-6411, Ext 229

McKune, Muriel, *Asst Librn,* Beatrice Foods Co, Research Center Library, Chicago IL. 312-791-8292

McLachlan, Elizabeth, *Supvr,* Middlesex County Library (Beechwood Library), Ailsa Craig ON. 519-438-8368

McLain, Mrs Era, *Librn,* Shelby County Regional Library (Calera), Calera AL. 205-669-7851

McLain, Mrs J A, *Librn,* Malakoff Public Library, Malakoff TX. 214-489-1818

McLain, Wanda, *Dir,* Watervliet Public Library, Watervliet MI. 616-463-6382

McLaird, Lee N, *Curator of Coll,* Siouxland Heritage Museums, Pettigrew Museum Library, Sioux Falls SD. 605-339-7097

McLallen, Ruth S, *Info Mgr,* Procter & Gamble Co Buckeye Cellulose Corp, Cellulose & Specialties Technical Information Service, Memphis TN. 901-454-8310

McLane, Eugene G, *Dir,* Fond Du Lac City-County Library Service, Fond du Lac WI. 414-921-3670

McLane, Eugene G, *Dir,* Mid-Wisconsin Federated Library System, Fond du Lac WI. 414-921-3670

McLaren, Bruce, *Dir,* New Mexico Military Institute, Learning Resource Center, Roswell NM. 505-622-6250, Ext 227, 213

McLaren, Dorothy, *Media,* Del·Mar College Library, Corpus Christi TX. 512-881-6308

McLaren, Mary K, *Dir,* Lees Junior College Library, Jackson KY. 606-666-7521, Ext 252

McLaren, Susan, *Dir,* Barrhead Elementary School Public Library, Barrhead AB. 403-674-2160

McLaughlin, Ann E, *Ad,* Thomas Crane Public Library, Subregional Headquarters for Eastern Massachusetts Regional Library System, Quincy MA. 617-471-2400

McLaughlin, Betty, *In Charge,* Hillcrest Baptist Hospital, Medical Reference Library, Waco TX. 817-756-8011

McLaughlin, Denis, *Librn,* Mercy College, White Plains Extension Center, White Plains NY. 914-948-3666

McLaughlin, Dorothy, *Librn,* Atlantic Richfield Co, ARCO Chemical Co, Research & Engineering Library, Glenolden PA. 215-586-4700, Ext 345, 346

McLaughlin, Dorothy, *Librn,* Thiokol Corp, Specialty Chemicals Division Library, Trenton NJ. 609-396-4001, Ext 316, 317

McLaughlin, Duffy, *Librn,* Montgomery County Planning Commission Library, Norristown PA. 215-275-5000

McLaughlin, Eleanor, *Br Coordr,* Miami-Dade Public Library System, Miami FL. 305-579-5001

McLaughlin, Elizabeth, *Librn,* Breckinridge Public Library, Breckenridge MN. 218-643-2113

McLaughlin, Evelyn, *Asst Librn,* Martins Ferry Public Library, Martins Ferry OH. 614-633-0314

McLaughlin, Jean E, *Librn,* Saint Joseph Hospital, Health Sciences Library, Reading PA. 215-378-2389

McLaughlin, Joy, *Dir,* Rock Creek Public Library, Rock Creek OH. 216-563-3340

McLaughlin, Kathleen, *Librn,* Perkins School for the Blind (School Libraries), Watertown MA. 617-924-3434, Ext 240

McLaughlin, LaVerne, *Tech Serv,* Georgia Southwestern College, James Earl Carter Library, Americus GA. 912-928-1352

McLaughlin, Malie, *Admin Asst,* State Library of Pennsylvania, Harrisburg PA. 717-787-2646

McLaughlin, Mary T, *Librn,* Ciba-Geigy Corp, Corporate Library, Ardsley NY. 914-478-3131, Ext 2397

McLaughlin, Maxine, *Asst Dir,* Millinocket Memorial Library, Millinocket ME. 207-723-9610

McLaughlin, Mildred, *Librn,* Lynn Public Library (Houghton Branch), Lynn MA. 617-592-4632

McLaughlin, P J, *Pres,* Union Camp Corp Library, Wayne NJ. 201-628-9000

McLaughlin, Shirley, *Dir,* Asheville-Buncombe Technical Institute Library, Asheville NC. 704-254-1921, Ext 63

McLaughlin, Terry L, *Dir,* Ashtabula County District Library, Ashtabula OH. 216-997-9341

McLaughlin, Vivian, *Spec Coll,* Carnegie Free Library, Beaver Falls PA. 412-846-4340

McLaurine, Mattie, *Librn,* Lake City Public Library, Lake City TN. 615-426-6762

McLean, Austin, *Head,* University of Minnesota Libraries-Twin Cities (Special Collections & Rare Books), Minneapolis MN. 612-373-2897

McLean, Carol, *Circ,* Sir Mortimer B Davis Jewish General Hospital, Medical Library, Montreal PQ. 514-342-3111, Ext 325, 376

McLean, Edward J, *Librn,* Catholic Lending Library of Hartford, Hartford CT. 203-246-5628

McLean, Emma Ruth, *Librn,* Scotland County Memorial Library (McGirt's Bridge Road), Laurinburg NC. 919-276-2638

McLean, Grace, *Librn,* Northumberland Union Public Library (Codrington Branch), Codrington ON. 613-475-2124

McLean, J, *Librn,* Windsor Public Library (Tecumseh Mall), Windsor ON. 519-945-7323

McLean, J Craig, *Asst Dir,* Virginia Commonwealth University (Tompkins-McCaw Library), Richmond VA. 804-786-0629

McLean, Janice, *Asst Librn,* National Society of the Daughters of the American Revolution Library, Washington DC. 202-628-1776, Ext 226

McLean, John H, *Dir,* National Archives & Records Service (National Audiovisual Center), Washington DC. 301-763-1896

McLean, Mavis, *Librn,* Alliance Public Library, Alliance NE. 308-762-1387

McLean, P, *Librn,* London Public Libraries & Museums (Northridge), London ON. 519-439-4331

McLean, Sue, *Asst Librn,* Mackinaw Area Public Library, Mackinaw City MI. 616-436-5451

McLean, Susan, *Librn,* Halifax City Regional Library (Halifax North), Halifax NS. 902-426-6987

McLean, Virginia, *Admin Asst,* Vineyard Haven Public Library, Vineyard Haven MA. 617-693-9721

McLeese, Karen, *Acq,* University of Utah (Law Library), Salt Lake City UT. 801-581-6438

McLellan, Arnold, *Dir,* Bethany Bible College Library, Scotts Valley CA. 408-438-3800, Ext 441

McLellan, Bonnie, *Ad & Acq,* Dakota County Library System, Burnsville MN. 612-435-8111

McLellan, Mary, *Legis Ref,* State Library of Massachusetts, Boston MA. 617-727-2590

McLelland, Karen, *Head Clerk,* Coalinga District Library (Huron), Coalinga CA. 209-945-2284

McLemore, A J, *Dir,* Savannah State College Library, Savannah GA. 912-356-2183, 356-2184

McLemore, Joan, *Librn,* Lincoln-Lawrence-Franklin Regional Library (Franklin County), Meadville MS. 601-384-5208

McLendon, Bobbye, *Librn,* Pine Forest Regional Library (Mt Olive Public), Mt Olive MS. 601-788-6539

McLendon, June, *Acq,* Delta State University, W B Roberts Library, Cleveland MS. 601-843-2483

McLendon, Wallace, *Acq & Ser,* University of North Carolina at Chapel Hill (Health Sciences Library), Chapel Hill NC. 919-966-2111

McLennon, Doris, *In Charge,* Old Bridge Public Library (Old Bridge Branch), Old Bridge NJ. 201-254-5477

McLeod, A D, *Dir,* Saskatchewan Wheat Pool Research Division Library, Regina SK. 306-569-4480

McLeod, Barbara, *Librn,* Law Society of Newfoundland Library, Saint John's NF. 709-753-7770

McLeod, Cora, *Librn,* Winterport Memorial Library, Winterport ME. 207-223-5540

McLeod, Dwight, *Dir,* Manhattan School of Music, Frances Hall Ballard Library, New York NY. 212-749-2802, Ext 507, 510, 511, 512

McLeod, H Eugene, *Librn,* Southeastern Baptist Theological Seminary Library, Wake Forest NC. 919-556-3101, Ext 225, 250

McLeod, John, *Librn,* Association of American Railroads, Economics & Finance Dept Library, Washington DC. 202-293-4068

McLeod, Louise M, *Dir,* Robert A Frost Memorial Library, Limestone ME. 207-325-7271

McLeod, Lynn, *Librn,* Mississauga Public Library (Sheridan Mall), Mississauga ON. 416-823-4106

McLeod, M, *Health,* British Columbia Institute of Technology Library, Burnaby BC. 604-434-5734, Ext 360

McLeod, Norman C, *Librn,* Guelph Public Library, Guelph ON. 519-824-6220

McLeod, Priscilla, *Librn,* Phoenix Public Library (Yucca), Phoenix AZ. 602-262-6787

McLeod, Sheila, *Ref,* Whitchurch-Stouffville Public Library, Stouffville ON. 416-640-2395

McLeod, Sherry, *Chmn,* Southern Oregon State College, Dept of Library Science, OR. 503-482-6445

McLeod, Walter H, *Dir & Acq,* University of Idaho Library (College of Law), Moscow ID. 208-885-6521

McLindeon, Alice M, *Librn,* Shearson Haydon Stone Inc, Research Department Library, Garden City NY. 516-248-8600

McMahan, Elnor, *Cat,* Austin Peay State University, Felix G Woodward Library, Clarksville TN. 615-648-7346

McMahan, Jean, *Dir,* Dodgeville Memorial Public Library, Dodgeville WI. 608-935-3728

McMahan, Jennie J, *Dir,* Dorchester County Library, Saint George SC. 803-563-9189

McMahan, Maude, *Librn,* Brownstown Public Library, Brownstown IN. 812-358-2853

McMahon, J, *Ref,* Oakland Community College, Highland Lakes Campus Library, Union Lake MI. 313-363-7191, Ext 335

McMahon, Jan, *Librn,* McCall Memorial Hospital Library, McCall ID. 208-634-2221

McMahon, Judith, *Ch,* Calumet City Public Library, Calumet City IL. 312-862-6220

McMahon, Lucille, *Ref,* Wellesley Free Library, Subregional Headquarters for Eastern Massachusetts Regional Library System, Wellesley MA. 617-235-1610

McMahon, Mary, *Lit,* Metropolitan Toronto Library Board, Metropolitan Toronto Library, Toronto ON. 416-928-5150

McMahon, Mary W, *Librn,* Eustis Memorial Library, Eustis FL. 904-357-6991, Ext 19

McMahon, Nathalie, *Asst,* United States Department of the Air Force, Manpower & Personnel Center, Directorate of Morale, Welfare & Recreation, Randolph AFB TX. 512-652-3471, 652-3472

McMahon, Rosemary, *Cat,* Columbus Technical Institute, Educational Resources Center, Columbus OH. 614-227-2463

McMains, R, *Asst Librn,* United States Army (Post Library System), Fort Huachuca AZ. 602-538-3041

McManimon, M Frances, *Librn,* Saint Joseph's Hospital, Samuel Rosenthal Memorial Library, Milwaukee WI. 414-447-2194

McManman, Mary, *Ref,* Bay County Library System, Bay City MI. 517-894-2837

McManus, Evelyn, *Dir,* Tyler Junior College, Edgar H Vaughn Memorial Library, Tyler TX. 214-592-5993, 593-3342

McManus, Joeann S, *Dir,* Charlestown Township Public Library, Charlestown IN. 812-256-5974

McManus, Mark, *Cat,* Berry College, Memorial Library, Mount Berry GA. 404-232-5374, Ext 221, 388

McManus, Nancy Carmichael, *Librn,* Social Science Research Council, Center for Coordinator of Research on Social Indicators Library, Washington DC. 202-667-8884

McManus, Sister Mary Ann, *Librn,* Saint Francis College Library, Fort Wayne IN. 219-432-3551, Ext 263

McMartin, Nora, *AV,* Chula Vista Public Library, Chula Vista CA. 714-427-1151

McMaster, Beverly, *Librn,* United States Navy (Naval Air Station Library), Meridian MS. 601-679-2211

McMaster, Deborah, *Pub Servs Coordr,* Wake Forest University (Bowman Gray School of Medicine Library), Winston-Salem NC. 919-727-4691

McMaster, Gert, *Librn,* Kent County Municipal Public Library (Bothwell Public), Bothwell ON. 519-695-2844

McMaster, Mary Ann, *Librn,* Richmond Free Library, Richmond VT. 802-434-3036

McMaster, Nina, *Librn,* Harvard University Library (Physics Research Library), Cambridge MA. 617-495-2878

McMaster, Sarah D, *Dir,* Fairfield County Library, Winnsboro SC. 803-635-4971

McMechan, Mrs R, *Librn,* Dunnville Public Library, Dunnville ON. 416-774-4240

McMeen, Eva M, *Librn,* Gregory Public Library, Gregory SD. 605-835-9346

McMeen, Gretchen, *Ch,* Three Rivers Public Library, Three Rivers MI. 616-279-2245

McMillan, Ataloa O, *Asst Dir,* Sapulpa Public Library, Sapulpa OK. 918-224-5624

McMillan, Barbara, *Asst Dir,* Carver County Library System, Chaska MN. 612-448-2782

McMillan, Carnette, *Acq,* Mississippi College (Law Library), Clinton MS. 601-924-5131, Ext 280

McMillan, Joann, *Reader Serv,* Hendrix College, Olin C Bailey Library, Conway AR. 501-329-9323

McMillan, Lenora W, *Reader Serv,* United States Commission on Civil Rights, National Clearinghouse Library, Washington DC. 202-254-6636

McMillan, Mary, *Librn,* Plainfield Public Library, Plainfield IN. 317-839-6602

McMillan, Nancy C, *Librn,* McMillan Science Associates, Inc Library, Los Angeles CA. 213-473-6541

MCMILLAN

McMillan, Pat, *Tech Serv,* Shreve Memorial Library, Shreveport LA. 318-221-2614

McMillen, Carolyn J, *Asst Dir,* Michigan State University Library, East Lansing MI. 517-355-2344

McMillen, Genevieve, *Ref,* Indian River Community College, Charles S Miley Learning Resources Center, Fort Pierce FL. 305-464-2000, Ext 347

McMillian, Patricia, *Educ,* Northern Illinois University, Founders Memorial Library, De Kalb IL. 815-753-1094

McMinn, Ann, *ILL,* Lincoln Land Community College, Learning Resources Center, Springfield IL. 217-786-2354

McMonigal, Elizabeth, *In Charge,* Saint Paul Public Library (Highland Park), Saint Paul MN. 612-292-6622

McMorran, Charles E, *Dir,* Boone-Madison Public Library, Madison WV. 304-369-4675

McMorrow, K, *Librn,* University of Toronto Libraries (Faculty of Music), Toronto ON. 416-978-3734

McMullan, Jr, Mrs William, *In Charge,* Oxford County Library (Otterville Branch), Otterville ON. 519-879-6907

Mcmullen, Becky, *ILL, Ref & Bibliog Instr,* Illinois Central College, Learning Resources Center, East Peoria IL. 309-694-5461

McMullen, Eleanor, *Librn,* Ingalls Memorial Library, Rindge NH. 603-899-3303

McMullen, Elizabeth, *Librn,* Saint Peter's Medical Center, Medical Center Library, New Brunswick NJ. 201-745-8600, Ext 8355

McMullen, Haynes, *Prof,* University of North Carolina at Chapel Hill, School of Library Science, NC. 919-933-8366

McMullen, John, *Librn,* Blue Cloud Abbey Library, Marvin SD. 605-432-5528, Ext 904

McMullen, L E, *Librn,* Uarco, Inc, Engineering & Research Library, Barrington IL. 312-381-7000

McMullen, Marilyn, *Dir,* Gerrish-Higgins School District Public Library, Roscommon Public Library, Roscommon MI. 517-275-5723

McMullen, Patricia, *Librn,* Vivitar Product Development & Manufacturing Division, Technical Library, Los Angeles CA. 213-477-0481

McMullen, Winifred E, *Acq,* Dowling College Library, Oakdale NY. 516-589-6100, Ext 218 or 219

McMullin, Philip W, *Exec Dir,* Institute of Family Research, Who Am I Library, Salt Lake City UT. 801-532-4000

McMullin, Velma, *Librn,* Scenic Regional Library of Franklin, Gasconade & Warren Counties (Saint Clair Service Center), St Clair MO. 314-629-2546

McMullin, William, *Media, Cat & Spec Coll,* Northeast Regional Library, Corinth MS. 601-287-2441

McNabb, Carol, *In Charge,* Saskatchewan Industry & Commerce Library, Regina SK. 306-565-2254

McNabb, Diane, *Ch,* Public Library of Nashville & Davidson County, Nashville TN. 615-244-4700

McNair, Janet, *ILL,* Emmaus Public Library, Emmaus PA. 215-965-9284

McNair, Marian B, *Librn,* Westwood First Presbyterian Church Library, Cincinnati OH. 513-661-6846

McNally, Mary D, *Dir,* Dorchester County Public Library, Cambridge MD. 301-228-7331

McNally, Mary Jane, *Adjunct Instr,* Kean College of New Jersey, Library-Media Program, NJ. 201-527-2626, 527-2071

McNally, Robert F, *In Charge,* Special Metals Corp Library, Technical Library, New Hartford NY. 315-798-2936

McNally, Tom, *Asst Dir & Ref,* Ohio State University-Mansfield Campus, Louis Bromfield Learning Resources Center, Mansfield OH. 419-755-4321

McNamara, Coletta, *Actg Librn,* Case Western Reserve University Libraries (Music House), Cleveland OH. 216-368-3506

McNamara, Darrell, *Commun Servs,* North Dakota State Library, Bismarck ND. 701-224-2490

McNamara, Evelyn, *Circ,* Oyster Bay-East Norwich Public Library, Oyster Bay NY. 516-922-1212

McNamara, Frances, *Tech Serv,* State Library of Massachusetts, Boston MA. 617-727-2590

McNamara, G A, *Librn,* Memorial Hospital, Medical Library, Albany NY. 518-471-3264

McNamara, Joane, *Tech Serv,* Wolfsohn Memorial Library, King of Prussia PA. 215-265-5151

McNamara, John N, *Librn,* United States Circuit Court of Appeals, Tenth Circuit Law Library, Denver CO. 303-837-3591

McNamara, Martha, *ILL,* Boston College Libraries (Bapst (Central Library)), Chestnut Hill MA. 617-969-0100, Ext 3205

McNamara, Mary Jane, *Dial Access,* Tyler Junior College, Edgar H Vaughn Memorial Library, Tyler TX. 214-592-5993, 593-3342

McNamara, Mrs Thomas, *Librn,* Tinton Falls Public Library, Tinton Falls NJ. 201-542-3110

McNamara, Patricia, *Asst Librn,* Livonia Public Library, Livonia NY. 716-346-3450

McNamara, Rebecca, *Asst Dir,* Hardin County Public Library, Elizabethtown KY. 502-769-6337

McNamee, Alice, *Asst Librn,* Marin County Free Library, San Rafael CA. 415-479-1100, Ext 2577

McNamee, Donald, *Cat,* California Institute of Technology, Robert A Millikan Memorial Library, Pasadena CA. 213-795-6811

McNames, Jaci, *Processing,* Saint Charles City County Library, Saint Peters MO. 314-441-2300

McNatt, Suzanne, *ILL,* Princeton University Library, Princeton NJ. 609-452-3180

McNaught, J E, *Mgr,* Mitre Corp (Corporate Library), Bedford MA. 617-271-4834

McNaught, Joan, *Mgr,* Mitre Corp (Technical Report Center), Bedford MA. 617-271-2351

McNaught, William, *Dir,* Archives of American Art (New York Area Center), New York NY. 212-826-5722

McNaughton, Janet, *Librn,* United States Fish & Wildlife Service Library, Anchorage AK. 907-276-3800

McNaughton, Milicent, *ILL, Tech Serv & Cat,* Caldwell Public Library, Caldwell NJ. 201-226-2837

McNeal, Anita, *Librn,* Cuyahoga County Public Library (Berea Branch), Berea OH. 216-234-5475

McNealy, Terry A, *Dir,* Bucks County Historical Society, Spruance Library, Doylestown PA. 215-345-0210

McNee, John, *Asst Dir, Pub Serv,* Iowa State University Library, Ames IA. 515-294-1442

McNeece, Judy, *Media,* Delta State University, W B Roberts Library, Cleveland MS. 601-843-2483

McNeel, Nina, *Cat,* Garfield County Public Library, New Castle CO. 303-984-2346

McNeely, Betty, *Librn,* Union County Library System (Myrtle Public), Myrtle MS. 601-988-2895

McNeely, Kathleen V, *Librn,* Mobil Oil Canada Ltd Library, Calgary AB. 403-268-7785

McNees, Ada Mae, *Librn,* New Market Public Library, New Market IA. 712-585-3467

McNeff, Marie, *Chairperson,* Augsburg College, Dept of Education, MN. 612-330-1130

McNeice, Beverly, *Dir,* Theosophical Society in America, Olcott Library & Research Center, Wheaton IL. 312-668-1571

McNeice, J, *Librn,* Georgian College of Applied Arts & Technology Library, Barrie ON. 705-728-1951

McNeil, Audrey, *Librn,* Wilkes Community College, Learning Resources Library, Wilkesboro NC. 919-667-7136, Ext 26

McNeil, Deborah, *Librn,* Seattle Public Library (Northeast Region), Seattle WA. 206-625-4915

McNeil, Don W, *Dir,* Leeward Community College Library, Pearl City HI. 808-455-0210

McNeil, Gary, *Equipment Tech,* Wilkes Community College, Learning Resources Library, Wilkesboro NC. 919-667-7136, Ext 26

McNeil, Hazel, *Librn,* Clark County Library District (Bunkerville Branch), Bunkerville NV. 702-346-3419

McNeil, Heather, *Ch,* Edwin A Bemis Public Library, Littleton Public Library, Littleton CO. 303-795-3826

McNeil, Janet, *ILL,* Hamilton Public Library, Hamilton ON. 416-529-8111

McNeil, Janet, *Coll Develop,* Virginia Commonwealth University (James Branch Cabell Library), Richmond VA. 804-257-1105

McNeil, Marguerite, *Cat,* Public Library of Cincinnati & Hamilton County, Cincinnati Public Library, Cincinnati OH. 513-369-6000

McNeil, Mary E, *Librn,* United States Department of the Navy, Naval Support Activity Library, Seattle WA. 206-527-0111, Ext 527

McNeil, Sharon, *Librn,* Security Pacific National Bank, Corporate Library, Los Angeles CA. 213-613-8623

McNeil, Susan, *ILL & Ref,* Community College of the Finger Lakes Library, Canandaigua NY. 315-394-3500, Ext 127

McNeill, Joseph P, *Cat,* Midwestern State University, George Moffett Library, Wichita Falls TX. 817-692-6611, Ext 204

McNeill, Margaret, *Coordr,* Area Library Services Authority Region 2, IN. 219-773-3641

McNeill, Joseph, *Cat,* Midwestern State University, George Moffett Library, Wichita Falls TX. 817-692-6611, Ext 204

McNeilly, David, *Librn,* Real Estate Research Corp Library, Chicago IL. 312-346-5885

McNeisch, Lorraine, *Asst Librn,* Black Creek Public Library, Black Creek WI. 414-984-3295

McNerlin, Elizabeth, *Librn,* Dechert, Price & Rhoads Library, Philadelphia PA. 215-972-3452

McNicholas, William, *Asst Directors: Libr Finance,* Chicago Public Library, Chicago IL. 312-269-2900

McNichols, Genette, *Dir,* George Fox College, Shambaugh Library, Newberg OR. 503-538-8383, Ext 303

McNiff, Philip J, *Dir,* Boston Public Library, Eastern Massachusetts Library System, Boston MA. 617-536-5400

McNinch, Frances A, *Librn,* Abbeville-Greenwood Regional Library (Greenwood County), Greenwood SC. 803-223-4515

McNinch, Francis A, *Asst Dir,* Abbeville-Greenwood Regional Library, Greenwood SC. 803-223-4515

McNinch, Thomas C, *Librn,* Holland & Hart Law Library, Denver CO. 303-575-8000

McNown, Mildred, *Ad, Tech Serv & Cat,* Huntington City Township Public Library, Huntington IN. 219-356-0824

McNulty, Pamela A, *Cat,* Mystic Seaport Museum, G W Blunt White Library, Mystic CT. 203-536-2631, Ext 261

McNulty, Patricia J, *Supvr & Librn,* Mitre Corp (Technical Report Center), Bedford MA. 617-271-2351

McNutt, Eleanor M, *Asst Dir,* Albany Medical Center College of Union University, Schaffer Library of Health Sciences, Albany NY. 518-445-5534

McPartland, Regina A, *Head Librn Acq Dept,* Yale University Library (Sterling Memorial Library), New Haven CT. 203-436-8335

McPeak, James J, *Librn,* Lepper Library, Lisbon OH. 216-424-3117

McPeak, Katherine, *Ref & Ser,* College of Saint Rose Library, Albany NY. 518-454-5180

McPeek, Maurice, *Media,* Richland College, Learning Resources Center, Dallas TX. 214-746-4460

McPhail, Dorothy, *Librn,* Sampson-Clinton Public Library (Miriam B Lamb Memorial), Garland NC. 919-529-4141

McPhail, Linda, *Secy,* Fort Nelson Public Library, Fort Nelson BC. 604-774-6777

McPhail, Sunny, *Libr Supvr,* Stearns-Roger Engineering Corp, Technical Library, Denver CO. 303-758-1122, Ext 2943

McPheeters, Roger, *Ref,* Ricks College, David O McKay Learning Resources Center, Rexburg ID. 208-356-2351

McPheron, Elaine, *Libr Instruction,* University of Cincinnati Libraries, Central Library, Cincinnati OH. 513-475-2218

McPheron, William, *English,* University of Cincinnati Libraries, Central Library, Cincinnati OH. 513-475-2218

McPherson, Atha T, *Librn,* Anderson Memorial Hospital Libraries, Anderson SC. 803-224-3411

McPherson, Christine, *ILL,* Woonsocket Harris Public Library, Woonsocket RI. 401-769-9044

McPherson, Claire, *On-Line Servs,* Canadian Department of Fisheries & Oceans, Maritimes Regional Library, Halifax NS. 902-426-3972

McPherson, Donald, *Law Enforcement,* Lewis & Clark Library System, Edwardsville IL. 618-656-3216

McPherson, Flora, *Dir,* Middlesex County Library, Arva ON. 519-438-8368
McPherson, Frances, *Tech Serv,* Allegan Public Library, Allegan MI. 616-673-4625
McPherson, Joy, *Libr Sci,* Simmons College, Beatley Library, Boston MA. 617-738-2241
McPherson, Kenneth B, *Librn,* County of Simcoe Library, Midhurst ON. 705-726-9300
McPherson, Kenneth F, *Dir,* Morris County Free Library, Whippany NJ. 201-285-6101
McPherson, Margaret, *Asst Librn & Cat,* Emory University, Oxford College Library, Oxford GA. 404-786-7051, Ext 281
McPherson, Marjorie, *Extension,* Deschutes County Library, Bend OR. 503-382-5191
McPherson, Maxine, *Librn,* Johnson County Library (Gardner Branch), Gardner KS. 913-884-7223
McPherson, R, *Librn,* Couchiching Reserve Library, Fort Frances ON. 807-274-9607
McQuarie, Robert J, *Dir,* Littleton Historical Museum Library, Littleton CO. 303-795-3850
McQueen, Lorraine, *Librn,* Nova Scotia Provincial Library (Information Services), Halifax NS. 902-424-5432
McQueen, Marge, *Asst Dir,* Alvah N Belding Library, Belding MI. 616-794-1450
McQueen, Patricia, *Ad,* Free Public Library of Summit, Summit NJ. 201-273-0350
McQueen, William F, *Librn,* Metropolitan Hospital, Medical Library, Detroit MI. 313-869-3600
McQuerry, Jean, *Librn,* Parker Public Library, Parker AZ. 602-669-2622
McQuerry, Jean, *Librn,* Yuma City-County Library (Parker), Parker AZ. 602-782-1871
McQueston, Helen, *Librn,* Goodwin Memorial Library, Hadley MA. 413-584-7451
McQuillan, David C, *Librn,* University of South Carolina (Map Depository), Columbia SC. 803-777-2802
McQuillan, Nancy, *Ch,* City of Cerritos Public Library, Cerritos CA. 213-924-5775
McQuillen, Mary, *Librn,* Woodbury County Bar Association Library, Sioux City IA. 712-279-6609
McQuire, Mary, *Librn,* La France Manufacturing Co, Library, Saint Louis MO. 314-426-2567
McQuitty, David, *Librn,* Southwestern Baptist Theological Seminary (Curriculum Laboratory), Fort Worth TX. 817-923-1921, Ext 277
McQuitty, Jeanette, *Librn,* Muskogee Public Library, Muskogee OK. 918-682-6657
McRae, Donaldine, *Librn,* Santa Cruz Public Library (Garfield Park), Santa Cruz CA. 408-423-4338
McRae, Jane, *Pub Relations,* Northwestern Regional Library, Elkin NC. 919-835-4894
McRae, Laura, *Cat & On-Line Servs,* San Jose Public Library, San Jose CA. 408-277-4822
McRae, Lois, *Librn,* Eramosa Community Library, Rockwood ON. 519-856-4851
McRae, Pat, *Librn,* Coaldale Municipal Library, Coaldale AB. 403-345-2920
McRae, Patricia, *Librn,* Bovey Public Library, Bovey MN. 218-245-3691
McRae, Patricia, *Librn,* Keewatin Public Library, Keewatin MN. 218-778-6480
McReynolds, Joe, *Ref & Bibliog Instr,* Harding University, Beaumont Memorial Library, Searcy AR. 501-268-6161, Ext 354
McRory, Mary, *Fla,* State Library of Florida, Div of Library Services, Dept of State, Tallahassee FL. 904-487-2651
McShane, Betsy L, *Librn,* Spencer, Stuart & Associates, Research Department Library, Chicago IL. 312-822-0080
McShane, Gail, *Ch,* Lake Blackshear Regional Library, Americus GA. 912-924-8091
McShane, Tim, *Ref,* Monroe County Public Library, Key West FL. 305-294-7100
McSheeby, Bruce, *Ref,* Fitchburg State College Library, Fitchburg MA. 617-345-2151, Ext 137
McSorley, Aidan, *Media, Cat & Ref,* Conception Abbey & Conception Seminary College Library, Conception MO. 816-944-2211
McSpadden, Michael, *Media,* International University Library, Kansas City MO. 816-931-6374
McSparren, Christine, *Northern Regional Librn,* Orange County Public Library, Orange CA. 714-634-7841

McSpedon, Frances M, *Librn,* White Haven Center (Resident Library), White Haven PA. 717-443-9564, Ext 251
McSpedon, Frances M, *Librn,* White Haven Center (Staff Library), White Haven PA. 717-443-9564, Ext 381
McSpiritt, M L, *Circ Supvr,* Bell Telephone Laboratories (Bell Telephone Laboratories Technical Library), Murray Hill NJ. 582-4612 (Supvr); 582-3740 (Circ); 582-3604 (Info Alerting Servs); 582-3901 (Systs Design Program); 582-3453 (Computing Info Serv); 582-7330 (Computing)
McSweeney, Bonnie, *Librn,* Madison County Library, Madisonville TX. 713-348-6118
McSweeney, Josephine, *Ref,* Pratt Institute Library, Brooklyn NY. 212-636-3684
McSweeney, Maria Jones, *Supvr,* SCM Corporation, Dwight P Joyce Research Center, Technical Info Services, Strongsville OH. 216-771-5121, Ext 2260
McSweeney, Marion, *Acq,* Chabot College, Learning Resource Center, Hayward CA. 415-786-6762
McSweeney, Priscilla, *Ch,* New Milford Public Library, New Milford NJ. 201-262-1221
McSweeney, Thomas J, *Media,* Gannon University, Nash Library, Erie PA. 814-871-7352
McSweeny, Virginia M, *Asst Ref Librn,* Worcester State Hospital, General Library, Worcester MA. 617-752-4681, Ext 331
McSweeny, Marilee, *Asst Dir,* Morgantown Public Library, Morgantown Service Center, Morgantown WV. 304-296-4425
McTaggart, Conni, *Bkmobile Coordr,* Douglas County Library System, Roseburg OR. 503-673-1111, Ext 310
McTaggart, John B, *Dir,* Methodist Theological School in Ohio Library, Delaware OH. 614-363-1146, Ext 242
McTyre, J, *Cat,* Los Angeles Trade Technical College Library, Los Angeles CA. 213-746-0800, Ext 217
McVarish, Maureen, *Ad & Ref,* Ajax Public Library, Ajax ON. 416-683-6911
McVeigh, Roberta, *In Charge,* American Podiatry Association, William J Stickel Memorial Library, Washington DC. 202-537-4900
McVey, Susan, *Actg Dir,* Oklahoma City University (Dulaney-Browne Library), Oklahoma City OK. 405-521-5068
McVicar, Ann, *Librn,* Boy Scouts of America Library, Irving TX. 201-249-6000, Ext 265
McVoy, Jean, *Resource Coordr Specialist,* Veterans Administration (Library Division), Washington DC. 202-389-2781
McWeeney, Mark, *Instr,* University of Colorado, Educational Technology Program, CO. 303-492-5141 & 492-6715
McWhinney, Russell, *Dir,* Beaver College, Eugenia Fuller Atwood Library, Glenside PA. 215-884-3500, Ext 222
McWhirter, David I, *Librn,* Disciples of Christ Historical Society Library, Nashville TN. 615-327-1444
McWhorter, Ann, *Ch,* Danville-Boyle County Public Library, Danville KY. 606-236-8466
McWhorter, George, *Rare Bks & Spec Coll,* University of Louisville Library, Louisville KY. 502-588-6745
McWhorter, Gerald, *In Charge,* Southern Union Co Library, Dallas TX. 214-748-8511, Ext 230
McWhorter, Jimmie, *Br Coordr,* Mobile Public Library, Mobile AL. 205-438-7073
McWilliam, D, *Coordr,* Columbus Area Library & Information Council of Ohio, (CALICO), OH. 614-882-0221
McWilliams, Ann G, *Dir,* Anderson Public Library, Lawrenceburg KY. 502-839-6420
McWilliams, Annie, *Ad,* Cherokee Regional Library, LaFayette-Walker County Library, LaFayette GA. 404-638-2992
McWilliams, Annie Y, *Ad,* Tri-County Regional Library, Rome GA. 404-291-9360
McWilliams, David Jackson, *Dir,* La Casa Del Libro, San Juan PR. 809-723-0354
McWilliams, Emilie, *Librn,* Pennsylvania State University (Earth & Mineral Science), University Park PA. 814-865-9517
Meacham, Amy, *Librn,* Little Wood River Library District, Carey ID. 208-823-4479
Meacham, Kathy, *Ch,* Arcadia Public Library, Arcadia CA. 213-446-7111

Meacham, Vivian, *Librn,* Brownsville Public Library, Brownsville OR. 503-466-5454
Mead, Billie, *Librn,* Loudon City Library, Loudon TN. 615-458-3161
Mead, Catherine, *Asst State Librn for Info Resources,* State Library of Ohio, Columbus OH. 614-466-2693
Mead, John H, *Dir,* Bear Mountain Trailside Museum Library, Bear Mountain NY. 914-786-2701, Ext 25
Mead, Karla, *Librn,* Anoka County Library (Centennial Branch), Circle Pines MN. 612-786-5120
Mead, Ken, *On-Line Servs,* Fish Memorial Hospital, Medical Library, De Land FL. 904-734-2323
Mead, Ken, *Dir,* Halifax Hospital, Medical Library, Daytona Beach FL. 904-258-1611, Ext 2058
Mead, Ken, *On-Line Servs & Bibliog Instr,* West Volusia Memorial Hospital, Medical Library, De Land FL. 904-734-3320, Ext 539
Mead-Donaldson, Susan, *Circ,* Florida International University, North Miami Campus Library, North Miami FL. 305-940-5730
Meade, B R, *Supvr,* Singer Co, Kearfott Div, Technical Information Center Library, Wayne NJ. 201-256-4000, Ext 3749
Meade, Joan, *Librn,* Montgomery County Department of Public Libraries (Damascus Branch), Damascus MD. 301-253-5100
Meade, Leslie, *Librn,* Denver Post Library, Denver CO. 303-297-1523
Meade, Margaret, *Media,* Saint Ambrose College, Learning Resource Center, Davenport IA. 319-324-1681, Ext 241
Meade, Margaret M, *Librn,* Ames Free Library of Easton, Inc, North Easton MA. 617-238-2000
Meade, Robert, *On-Line Servs,* Rockwell International (Business Research Center), Pittsburgh PA. 412-565-5880
Meade, Sister Maura, *Dir,* Emmanuel College, Cardinal Cushing Library, Boston MA. 617-277-9340, Ext 126
Meader, Robert F W, *Librn,* Shaker Community Inc Library, Pittsfield MA. 413-447-7284
Meador, Joan, *Ref,* Tulsa City-County Library, Tulsa OK. 918-581-5221
Meador, John, *Ref & Doc,* Georgia Department of Education (Div of Public Library Services), Atlanta GA. 404-656-2461
Meador, John, *Gen Ref & Soc Sci,* University of Houston (M D Anderson Memorial Library), Houston TX. 713-749-4241
Meador, Nancy, *Asst Dir & Cat,* Lee College, Learning Resources Center, Baytown TX. 713-427-5611, Ext 279, 277
Meador, Patricia, *Spec Coll,* Louisiana State University in Shreveport Library, Shreveport LA. 318-797-7121, Ext 203
Meadow, Charles, *Prof,* Drexel University, School of Library & Information Science, PA. 215-895-2474
Meadow, Cyril, *Dir,* Center for Modern Psychoanalytic Studies Library, New York NY. 212-260-7052
Meadows, Barbara A, *Chief Librn,* Veterans Administration, Hospital Library, Nashville TN. 615-327-4751, Ext 7615
Meadows, Donald F, *Librn,* Saskatchewan Provincial Library, Regina SK. 306-565-2976
Meadows, Mark D, *Cat,* Arkansas State University, Dean B Ellis Library, Jonesboro AR. 501-972-3078, 972-3079
Meadows, Sammie D, *Librn,* Lewis Cooper Junior Memorial Library & Arts Center, Opelika AL. 205-749-1426
Meadows, Susan, *Actg Coordr,* Northeast Missouri Library Network, MO. 816-665-5121, Ext 7230
Meadows, Theresa, *Librn,* Public Library of Fort Wayne & Allen County (Hessen Cassel), Fort Wayne IN. 219-447-6511
Meadows, Vada B, *Asst Librn,* Clayton Public Library, Albert W Thompson Memorial Library, Clayton NM. 505-374-9423
Meagher, Janet H, *Dir,* Holbrook Public Library, Holbrook MA. 617-767-3644
Meagher, Joyce M, *Dir,* Saranac Lake Free Library, Saranac Lake NY. 518-891-4190
Meagher, Sister Agnes, *Assoc Librn,* Saint Joseph's College (Suffolk Campus), Patchogue NY. 516-231-3054

MEAHL

Meahl, D Darren, *Media,* Michigan State University Library, East Lansing MI. 517-355-2344

Meahl, D Darren, *Librn,* Michigan State University Library (Audio-Visual), East Lansing MI. 517-355-2344

Mealey, Catherine, *Librn,* University of Wyoming (Law), Laramie WY. 307-766-5175

Meals, Doris, *Asst Librn,* Carroll County Library, Florine Harbert Maddox Memorial Library, Huntingdon TN. 901-986-3991

Means, Beverley H, *Librn,* Columbia Museums of Art & Science Library, Columbia SC. 803-799-2810

Means, Frances C, *Acq,* Francis Marion College, James A Rogers Library, Florence SC. 803-669-4121, Ext 321

Means, Mildred, *Librn,* City-County Public Library (Waveland), Waveland MS. 601-467-9240

Means, R B, *Dir,* Creighton University, Alumni Memorial Library, Omaha NE. 402-449-2705

Meany, Iva M, *Chief Librn,* Evansdale Public Library, Evansdale IA. 319-232-5367

Meany, Philip, *Media,* Centralia College Library, Centralia WA. 206-736-9391, Ext 241

Mears, Marian, *Librn,* Library Association of Portland (Lombard), Portland OR. 503-289-7336

Mears, Tiny, *Librn,* Mid-Mississippi Regional Library System (Duck Hill Public), Duck Hill MS. 601-565-2391

Mears, William, *President,* Council of Research & Academic Libraries (Audiovisual-Instructional Media Services Group (AIMS)), San Marcos TX. 512-245-2133

Mears, William B, *Assoc Dir,* Southwest Texas State University, Learning Resources Center, San Marcos TX. 512-245-2132

Mears, Zula, *Librn,* Jaquith Public Library, Marshfield VT. 802-426-3581

Mecca, Raymond G, *Dir,* Bulletin Library, Philadelphia PA. 215-662-7630

Mecera, Ruth, *Chief Librn,* Flenniken Memorial Public Library, Carmichaels PA. 412-966-5263

Mech, Terrence, *Instrnl Pub Servs,* Tusculum College Library, Greeneville TN. 615-639-1481

Mecham, Bette, *Librn,* Morgan County Library, Morgan UT. 801-829-3481

Mechanic, Sylvia, *Librn,* Brooklyn Public Library (Business Library), Brooklyn NY. 212-780-7800

Mechtenberg, Paul, *Dir,* Dundee Township Library, Dundee IL. 312-428-3661

Mecinski, Isabella, *Bd & Preparation,* Enoch Pratt Free Library, Baltimore MD. 301-396-5430, 396-5395

Meckley, E P, *In Charge,* Koppers Co, Engineering & Construction Division Information Service Library, Pittsburgh PA. 412-227-3033

Meckly, E P, *Librn,* Koppers Co, Inc, Monroeville Research Center Library, Monroeville PA. 412-327-3000

Mecray, Frieda, *Info Spec,* Philadelphia Quartz Co, Marketing & Engineering Information Service, Valley Forge PA. 215-293-7200

Medaris, Linda, *ILL & Ref,* Central Missouri State University, Ward Edwards Library, Warrensburg MO. 816-429-4141

Medder, Susan, *Librn,* Wayne City Public Library, Wayne City IL. 618-895-2661

Medders, Mary Diane, *Tech Serv,* Lake Blackshear Regional Library, Americus GA. 912-924-8091

Medeiros, Annmarie, *Librn,* Taunton State Hospital Medical Library, Taunton MA. 617-824-7551

Medeiros, Joseph, *Librn,* United States Department of the Air Force (Air Force Systems Command, Hqs Tech Info Center), Andrews AFB DC. 301-981-3551

Medeiros, Rosemary, *Dir,* Dartmouth Public Libraries, Southworth Library, South Dartmouth MA. 617-997-1252

Meder, Stephen A, *Librn,* Colombiere College, Dinan Library, Clarkston MI. 313-625-5611

Medici, Margaret, *ILL,* Tappan Library, Tappan NY. 914-359-3877

Medigovich, Stella A, *Dir,* McDonnell-Douglas Corp, Actron Division Technical Library, Monrovia CA. 213-359-8216, Ext 257

Medina, Carlos H, *Dir, Educ Tech Dept,* Puerto Rico Junior College (Cupey Campus Learning Resources Center), Rio Piedras PR. 809-765-1716

Medina, Jane V, *Asst Librn,* Tooele Public Library, Tooele UT. 801-882-2182

Medina, Kay, *Kansas Coll,* Kansas City Kansas Public Library, Kansas City KS. 913-621-3073

Medina, Rubens, *Chief, Hispanic Law Div,* Library of Congress, Washington DC. 202-287-5000

Medina, Sue, *Planning & Research,* Alabama Public Library Service, Montgomery AL. 205-832-5743

Medley, Cindy, *Tech Serv,* Dare County Library, Manteo NC. 919-473-2372

Medley, L D, *Librn,* A O Smith Corp Library, Milwaukee WI. 414-447-4683

Medley, Nora, *On-Line Servs,* Miami Herald Library, Reference Herald Plaza, Miami FL. 305-350-2419

Medley, Paul, *Circ,* Corpus Christi State University Library, Corpus Christi TX. 512-991-6810, Ext 242

Medlicott, Mary Alice, *Spec Coll,* Franklin College Library, Franklin IN. 317-736-8441, Ext 257

Medlin, Debbie, *ILL,* Southern Baptist College, Felix Goodson Library, Walnut Ridge AR. 501-886-6741, Ext 130

Medrinos, Roxanne, *ILL, Circ & Per,* Hellenic College & Holy Cross Greek Orthodox School of Theology, Cotsidas-Tonna Library, Brookline MA. 617-731-3500, Ext 43, 44, 45

Meehan, Carolyn Isaak, *Librn,* Westmoreland Public Library, Westmoreland NH. 603-399-7750

Meehan, Charles, *Dir,* University of Lowell Libraries (O'Leary Library), Lowell MA. 617-452-5000, Ext 480

Meehan, Margaret, *Info Specialists,* Digital Equipment Corp, Corporate Library, Maynard MA. 617-493-6231, 493-5821

Meehan-Black, Elizabeth, *Ref,* Pennsylvania State University, Ogontz Campus Library, Abington PA. 215-886-9400, Ext 311 & 312

Meek, Fern, *Dir,* Longview Community College Library, Lee's Summit MO. 816-763-7777, Ext 266, 267, 268

Meek, Lyn, *Consult,* Cambria County Library System, Johnstown PA. 814-536-5131

Meek, Peggy, *Bibliog Instr,* Stephen F Austin State University, Ralph W Steen Library, Nacogdoches TX. 713-569-4109

Meeks, David, *ILL & Ref,* Saint Johns River Community College, B C Pearce Learning Resources Center, Palatka FL. 904-328-1571, Ext 216

Meeks, James D, *Dir,* Eugene Public Library, Eugene OR. 503-687-5450

Meerdink, Richard, *Dir,* Milwaukee Area Technical College, Rasche Memorial Library, Milwaukee WI. 414-278-6205

Meernik, Mary, *Librn,* Ann Arbor News Library, Ann Arbor MI. 313-994-6953

Meers, Mary J, *Librn,* Blackstone Public Library, Blackstone MA. 617-883-1931

Meese, Francess M, *Librn,* Memorial Hospital, Medical-Nursing Library, Colorado Springs CO. 303-634-7701

Meeting, Sally, *ILL,* Mansfield-Richland County Public Library, Mansfield OH. 419-524-1041

Mefford, Phyllis, *Ch,* Valparaiso-Porter County Public Library System & Administrative Headquarters, Valparaiso IN. 219-462-0524

Mefford, Phyllis, *Geneology,* Valparaiso-Porter County Public Library System & Administrative Headquarters, Valparaiso IN. 219-462-0524

Megaw, Jeanie, *Ad,* Homer Public Library, Homer OH. 614-892-2020, Ext 1

Megehee, Josephine, *Br Coordr,* Pearl River County Library System, Margaret Reed Crosby Memorial Library, Picayune MS. 601-798-5081

Megehee, Josephine, *Librn,* Pearl River County Library System (W A Zeltner), McNeill MS. 601-798-6096

Megerian, Mrs Gene, *Librn,* New York Public Library (Dongan Hills), New York NY. 212-351-1444

Meglis, Anne Llewellyn, *Librn,* District of Columbia Department of Housing & Community Development Library, Washington DC. 202-724-8709

Mehaffey, Kathleen E, *Dir,* Downers Grove Public Library, Downers Grove IL. 312-960-1200

Mehalick, Joan, *Librn,* East Orange General Hospital Library (School of Nursing Library), East Orange NJ. 201-672-8400, Ext 343, 370

Mehes, Shiela, *Ch,* Waterloo Regional Library, Waterloo ON. 519-885-9590

Meheula, Barbara F, *Librn,* Hawaii Foundation for History & the Humanities, Multi-Cultural Center Library, Honolulu HI. 808-548-2070

Mehl, Warren, *Dir Eden,* Webster College, Eden Theological Seminary, Eden-Webster Libraries, Saint Louis MO. 314-968-0500, Ext 235

Mehlhaff, Bruce, *Cat & On-Line Servs,* Rapid City Public Library, Rapid City SD. 605-394-4171

Mehlin, Peter, *ILL,* Brooklyn Public Library, Brooklyn NY. 212-780-7712

Mehlinger, Howard, *Develop Ctr Dir,* Indiana University Social Studies Development Center, Curriculum Resource Center, Bloomington IN. 812-337-3584

Mehlman, Janice, *ILL,* Millinocket Memorial Library, Millinocket ME. 207-723-9610

Mehmel, Donna, *Librn,* Winnipeg Public Library (McPhillips), Winnipeg MB. 204-586-4642

Mehr, Joseph O, *Librn,* Providence Journal Co, News Library, Providence RI. 401-277-7393

Mehta, Subhash, *Dir,* Pembroke Public Library, Pembroke ON. 613-732-8844

Meiboom, Esther, *Clinical Libr,* College of Medicine & Dentistry of New Jersey, George F Smith Library of the Health Sciences, Newark NJ. 201-456-4580

Meide, JoAnn, *ILL & Ref,* Eastern Montana College Library, Billings MT. 406-657-2320

Meier, Glennis, *Librn,* Readlyn Community Library, Readlyn IA. 319-279-3432

Meier, Kathleen, *Cat,* Hunter College of the City University of New York Library, New York NY. 212-570-5511

Meier, Margaret, *Ch & YA,* Willard Library of Evansville, Evansville IN. 812-425-4309

Meierhenry, Wes, *Chmn Adult Educ,* University of Nebraska-Lincoln, School Media Specialist Program, NE. 402-472-3726

Meigs, Catherine, *Librn,* Swink Public Library, Swink CO. 303-384-8083

Meigs, Deborah S, *Librn,* Colby Memorial Library, Danville NH. 603-382-6733

Meinhardt, Cynthia, *Librn,* Outboard Marine Corp, Research Center Library, Milwaukee WI. 414-445-9134, Ext 52

Meinhold, Janet, *Tech Serv & Cat,* Augusta Regional Library, Augusta-Richmond County Public Library, Augusta GA. 404-724-1871

Meinhold, Leonard J, *Dir,* North Country Library System, Watertown NY. 315-782-5540

Meinke, Darrel M, *Dir,* Moorhead State University, Livingston Lord Library, Moorhead MN. 218-236-2922

Meinke, Darrel M, *Coordr,* Tri-College University Libraries Consortium, MN. 218-236-2922

Meirose, Leo H, *Dir,* Tampa-Hillsborough County Public Library System, Tampa FL. 813-223-8947

Meirose, Leo H, *Dir,* Tampa-Hillsborough County Public Library System (Subregional Library for the Blind & Physically Handicapped), Tampa FL. 813-223-8851

Meischeid, Richard C, *Librn,* Kollsman Instrument Company Library, Merrimack NH. 603-889-2500, Ext 2083

Meisels, Henry R, *Dir,* Corn Belt Library System, Normal IL. 309-452-4485

Meisels, Sarah, *Dir,* Wheaton Public Library, Wheaton IL. 312-668-1374

Meiss, Harriet, *On-Line Servs,* Mount Sinai School of Medicine of City University of New York, Gustave L & Janet W Levy Library, New York NY. 212-650-6671

Meissner, Edith, *In Charge,* Saint Paul Public Library (Lexington), Saint Paul MN. 612-292-6620

Meissner, Lana, *Ref,* Alfred University (Herrick Memorial Library), Alfred NY. 607-871-2184

Meister, Ruby, *Librn,* Tecumseh Public Library, Tecumseh NE. 402-335-2060

Mekkawi, Mod, *Librn,* Howard University Libraries (Architecture & City Planning Library), Washington DC. 202-636-7773, 636-7774

Mekos, Katherine F, *Librn,* Arnot-Ogden Memorial Hospital, Wey Memorial Library, Elmira NY. 607-737-4101

Mela, Doris K, *Librn,* National Biomedical Research Foundation Library, Washington DC. 202-625-2121

Melanson, Robert, *Ref,* Chesapeake Public Library, Chesapeake VA. 804-547-6579, 547-6592

Melbinger, Joyce, *Asst Librn,* Harvey Public Library, Harvey IL. 312-331-0757

Melbourne, Gertrude, *Ad,* Bradford Public Library, Bradford ON. 416-775-6482

Melcher, Carolyn, *Ch,* Wyckoff Public Library, Wyckoff NJ. 201-891-4866

Melchiorre, Rosemarie, *ILL,* West Chester State College, Francis Harvey Green Library, West Chester PA. 215-436-2643

Meldrom, Richard B, *Dir,* Roanoke Rapids Public Library, Roanoke Rapids NC. 919-537-6457

Melegrito, Jon, *Circ,* George Washington University Library, Washington DC. 202-676-6455

Melendez, Luisa, *Asst Librn,* Inter American University-Fajardo Regional College, Centro de Recursos para el Aprendizaje, Fajardo PR. 809-863-2390

Melendy, Antoinette, *Acq,* Sonoma State University, Ruben Salazar Library, Rohnert Park CA. 707-664-2397

Melesh, R, *Ref,* Shoreham-Wading River Public Library, Shoreham NY. 516-929-4488

Melick, Audrey, *Br Coordr,* West Orange Free Public Library, West Orange NJ. 201-736-0198

Melick, Audrey, *Librn,* West Orange Free Public Library (Tory Corner), West Orange NJ. 201-736-0452

Melikian, Michael, *Bus Mgr,* Providence Public Library, Providence RI. 401-521-7722

Melius, Charlotte B, *ILL,* Louisiana State University (Law Center Library), Baton Rouge LA. 504-388-8802

Melkus, Lisi, *Librn,* Alameda Contra Costa Medical Association Library, Oakland CA. 415-534-8055, Ext 257

Mellen, Lois, *Bkmobile Coordr,* Cook Memorial Public Library District, Libertyville IL. 312-362-2330

Mellett, Elizabeth, *Acq,* Simmons College, Beatley Library, Boston MA. 617-738-2241

Mellette, Susan, *Ref,* Palm Beach County Public Library System, West Palm Beach FL. 305-686-0895

Mellican, Nancy, *Ch,* Glen Ellyn Public Library, Glen Ellyn IL. 312-469-0879

Mellichamp, Catherine, *In Charge,* Cobb County Public Library System (Powder Springs Branch), Powder Springs GA. 404-943-6752

Mellichamp, Freddie Ann, *Bureau of Library Support Services: Chief,* State Library of Florida, Div of Library Services, Dept of State, Tallahassee FL. 904-487-2651

Mellin, Ruth, *Dept Chairperson & Cat,* Colby-Sawyer College, Fernald Library, New London NH. 603-526-2010, Ext 245

Mellinger, Sydney S, *Dir,* Lake Forest Library, Lake Forest IL. 312-234-0636

Mello, Catherine, *Cat,* East Providence Public Library, Weaver Memorial Library, East Providence RI. 401-434-2453

Mello, Dennis, *ILL,* San Jose Public Library, San Jose CA. 408-277-4822

Mellon, Constance, *Bibliog Instr,* University of Tennessee at Chattanooga Library, Chattanooga TN. 615-755-4701

Mellon, Georganne, *ILL,* University of New Mexico, Gallup Branch, Learning Resources Center, Gallup NM. 505-863-9327

Mellon, Jeanne F, *Librn,* Arthur Young & Co Library, New York NY. 212-922-4880

Mellon, Richard M, *On-Line Servs,* Martin Marietta Aerospace, Orlando Division, Technical Information Center Library, Orlando FL. 305-352-2051

Mellott, Constance, *Asst Prof,* Kent State University, School of Library Science, OH. 216-672-2782, 672-7988

Mellown, Richard H, *Per,* University of Georgia Libraries, Athens GA. 404-542-2716

Melnick, Ralph, *Spec Coll,* College of Charleston, Robert Scott Small Library, Charleston SC. 803-792-5530

Melnychuk, Dianne, *Ser,* Cedar Crest College, Cressman Library, Allentown PA. 215-437-4471, Ext 264

Melnychuk, Dianne, *Ser,* Muhlenberg College, John A W Haas Library, Allentown PA. 215-433-3191, Ext 214

Melnyk, Christine, *Cat & On-Line Servs,* Yale University Library (Ira V Hiscock Library), New Haven CT. 203-436-3148

Meloy, Aldona, *Dir Libr Serv,* Tinley Park Public Library, Tinley Park IL. 312-532-0160

Meloy, Ann, *Libr Technician,* Veterans Administration, General & Medical Library, Albuquerque NM. 505-265-1711, Ext 2248

Meloy, Patricia, *Ad,* Dundee Township Library, Dundee IL. 312-428-3661

Melroy, Virginia, *Cat,* University of Iowa Libraries (Law Library), Iowa City IA. 319-353-5968

Melton, Becky, *Libr Mgr,* Driscoll Foundation Children's Hospital Library, Corpus Christi TX. 512-854-5341

Melton, Carolyn, *Ch & YA,* Madison-Jefferson County Public Library, Madison IN. 812-265-2744

Melton, Doris, *Tech Serv,* Long Beach Public Library, Long Beach MS. 601-863-0711

Melton, Helen, *Librn,* Carlsbad Public Library, Carlsbad NM. 505-885-6776

Melton, Janet Crain, *Librn,* Grand Lodge of Texas AF&AM Library, Waco TX. 817-753-7395

Melton, Lois G, *Librn,* Research Triangle Institute, Technical Library, Research Triangle Park NC. 919-541-6000

Melton, Lynn J, *Dir,* Burlington Public Library, Burlington WI. 414-763-7623

Melton, Sister Marie, *Asst Dir,* Saint John's University Library, Jamaica NY. 212-969-8000, Ext 201

Meltzer, Lester, *Librn,* Phillips Petroleum Co (Research & Development Library), Bartlesville OK. 918-661-3435

Meltzer, Morton F, *Mgr Tech Info Ctr,* Martin Marietta Aerospace, Orlando Division, Technical Information Center Library, Orlando FL. 305-352-2051

Meltzer, S, *Per & Doc,* Muskingum College Library, New Concord OH. 614-826-8152

Melvin, Lucy, *Media,* Grambling State University, A C Lewis Memorial Library, Grambling LA. 318-247-6941, Ext 220

Melvin, Margaret, *Asst Librn,* University of Wisconsin-Milwaukee School of Social Welfare, Region V Child Abuse & Neglect Resource Center, Milwaukee WI. 414-963-6010

Melvin, Rachel, *Asst Librn,* University of Nevada Desert Research Institute, Water Resources Collection, Sparks NV. 702-673-4750, Ext 338

Melvoin, Linda, *Instr,* Highline Community College Library, Library Technician Program, WA. 206-878-3710, Ext 233

Memming, Rolf, *Dir, DMS, Inc* Library (Deadline Data on World Affairs Library), Greenwich CT. 203-661-7800

Menack, Marilyn, *Ref,* Westchester Community College Library, Valhalla NY. 914-347-6939

Menanteaux, Bob, *Circ,* University of Puget Sound (Law Library), Tacoma WA. 206-756-3322

Menard, Michael J, *Archivist,* Museum of Western Colorado, Museum Archives, Grand Junction CO. 303-242-0971

Menard, Real, *Ch,* Defence Research Establishment Valcartier Library, Valcartier PQ. 418-844-4271, 844-4262

Menasco, Geraldine, *Librn,* Lake County Library (Redbud Branch), Clearlake Highlands CA. 707-994-5115

Menashi, Ann, *Librn,* Boston Psychoanalytic Society & Institute Inc Library, Boston MA. 617-266-0953

Mencer, Fred, *Syst Coordr, Dodge County,* Mid-Wisconsin Federated Library System, Fond du Lac WI. 414-921-3670

Mencer, Fred J, *Dir,* Dodge County Library Service, Beaver Dam WI. 414-885-4571, 885-5134

Mendall, Florence S, *Dir,* Plympton Public Library, Plympton MA. 617-585-4551

Mendel, Robin, *YA,* Port Chester Public Library, Port Chester NY. 914-939-6710, 939-6711

Mendel, Roger, *Dir,* Alpena County Library, Alpena MI. 517-356-0505

Mendel, Roger, *Dir,* Northland Library Cooperative, Alpena MI. 517-356-4444

Mendenhall, Bethany, *Assoc Librn,* J Paul Getty Museum Library, Malibu CA. 213-459-2306

Mendenhall, Mary, *Learning Mat Coll Assoc,* Kearney State College, Calvin T Ryan Library, Kearney NE. 308-236-4218

Mendez, Ann, *Ref,* Edinburg Public Library, Edinburg TX. 512-383-6246, 383-6247

Mendez, Elda, *Librn,* Corpus Christi State School Library, Corpus Christi TX. 512-888-5301

Menditto, Joseph, *Tech Serv,* Russell Sage College, James Wheelock Clark Library, Troy NY. 518-270-2249

Mendola, James, *Librn,* Veterans Administration, Hospital Library Service, Buffalo NY. 716-834-9200

Mendoza, Gonzalo, *Pub Servs & ILL,* Hostos Community College Library, Bronx NY. 212-960-1093

Mendoza, Jorge, *Doc,* Laredo Junior College, Harold R Yeary Library, Laredo TX. 512-724-7541, 722-0521

Mendoza, Jorge, *Doc,* Laredo State University, Harold R Yeary Library, Laredo TX. 512-722-8001, Ext 42

Mendoza, Toni, *Librn,* Hayden Public Library, Hayden AZ. 602-356-7031

Mendrinos, Jolene, *Dir,* Rockmont College, Clifton L Fowler Library, Denver CO. 303-238-5386, Ext 45

Menear, William H, *Dir,* Hewlett-Woodmere Public Library, Hewlett NY. 516-374-1967

Menefee, Waiva, *Dir,* International Falls Public Library, International Falls MN. 218-283-8051

Menegaux, Edmond A, *Exec Dir,* South Central Research Library Council, NY. 607-273-9106

Menendez, Miguel, *Ref & On-Line Servs,* Florida International University, North Miami Campus Library, North Miami FL. 305-940-5730

Menendez, Shirley, *Asst to Dir,* Westchester Library System, Hartsdale NY. 914-761-7620

Meneses, Lisa, *Ch,* Jervis Public Library Association, Rome NY. 315-336-4570

Menewitch, Myron E, *Librn,* Malcolm Pirnie Inc Library, White Plains NY. 914-694-2100, Ext 333

Menewitch, Wendy, *Librn,* Greenwich Library (Cos Cob Branch), Cos Cob CT. 203-622-7955

Menge, Geneva, *Librn,* Lyme Town Library, Lyme NH. 603-795-2661

Menges, Gary L, *Assoc Dir Pub Servs,* University of Washington Libraries, Seattle WA. 206-543-1760

Menkal, Janina, *Supvr,* Waterloo Regional Library (Wellesley), Wellesley ON. 519-656-2001

Menke, Nancy, *Librn,* South County Public Library District, Brussels IL. 618-883-2522

Menken, Nancy, *Librn,* Chabot College Valley Campus, Learning Resources Center, Livermore CA. 415-455-5300, Ext 15

Mennard, Barbara, *Dir,* Dickinson Memorial Library, Northfield Library, Northfield MA. 413-498-2455

Mennie, Elizabeth, *Ref Librn,* Quebec Association for Children With Learning Disabilities Library, Montreal PQ. 514-392-8849

Menser, June, *In Charge,* Texas Education Agency (Region XIX), El Paso TX. 915-779-3737

Mensinger, Katherine, *Tech Serv,* Kelley Library, Salem Public Library, Salem NH. 603-898-7064

Menta, Sudesh, *Ad,* Minot Public Library, Minot ND. 701-852-1045

Menthe, Melissa, *Ref & Per,* Rutgers University (Kilmer Area Library), New Brunswick NJ. 201-932-3610

Menzel, John, *Acq,* Morris County Free Library, Whippany NJ. 201-285-6101

Menzemer, Linda S, *Librn,* Ontonagon Township Library, Ontonagon MI. 906-884-4411

Menzies, Neal, *Asst Librn,* Otis Art Institute of Parsons School of Design, Los Angeles CA. 213-387-5288

Meola, Mary, *Ref & On-Line Servs,* Georgian Court College, Farley Memorial Library, Lakewood NJ. 201-364-2200, Ext 19

Mequiar, Jessie, *Librn,* Auburn Library, Auburn KY. 502-542-4721

Merala, Marjan, *Health Sci,* University of California at Davis, General Library, Davis CA. 916-752-2110

Merala, Marjan, *Asst Univ Librn Health Sci,* University of California at Davis, General Library, Davis CA. 916-752-2110

MERALA

Merala, Marjan, *Dir & Media,* University of California at Davis (Health Sciences Library), Davis CA. 916-752-1214

Merbaum, Mark, *Ser,* University of Southern California, Edward L Doheny Memorial Library, Los Angeles CA. 213-743-6050

Mercado, Heidi, *Librn,* University of Washington Libraries (Friday Harbor), Friday Harbor WA. 206-543-1760

Mercado, Nora, *Cat,* Auraria Libraries, Denver CO. 303-629-2805

Mercay, Jessie, *Media,* Maharishi International University Library, Fairfield IA. 515-472-5031, Ext 152, 232

Mercer, Dellene, *Librn,* Barnes-Hind Pharmaceuticals Inc, Technical Library, Sunnyvale CA. 408-736-5462

Mercer, Elizabeth, *Librn,* Springfield Hospital Center, Medical Library, Sykesville MD. 301-795-2100, Ext 481

Mercer, Elizabeth A, *Librn,* Palmerton Library Association, Palmerton PA. 215-826-3424

Mercer, Harriet, *Ad,* Newfoundland Public Library Services (A C Hunter Memorial Library), Saint John's NF. 709-737-3964

Mercer, John, *Ref,* Acadia University, Harold Campbell Vaughan Memorial Library, Wolfville NS. 902-542-2201, Ext 215

Mercer, Mrs Jessie L, *Librn,* River Oaks Public Library, River Oaks TX. 817-626-5421

Merchant, Gertrude, *Cat,* Danville Public Library, Danville VA. 804-799-5195

Merchant, JoAnn, *Librn,* Nus Corp Library, Rockville MD. 301-948-7010, Ext 236

Merchant, Peter, *AV,* Public Library of the City of Somerville, Somerville MA. 617-623-5000

Merchant, Priscilla, *Ref & Bibliog Instr,* Trevecca Nazarene College, Mackey Library, Nashville TN. 615-244-6000, Ext 214

Merchant, Rosemary, *Cat,* Georgetown College, Cooke Memorial Library, Georgetown KY. 502-863-8011

Merchant, Shirley, *ILL,* North Florida Junior College Library, Madison FL. 904-973-2288, Ext 52

Merchant, Thomas L, *Historian,* Seventh Day Baptist Historical Society, Plainfield NJ. 201-561-8700

Mercieca, Charles, *In Charge,* International Association of Educators for World Peace, Research Center of Intercultural Information, Huntsville AL. 205-539-7205

Mercier, Christina, *Librn,* Chester C Corbin Public Library, Webster Public Library, Webster MA. 617-943-0131

Mercier, Sylvia A, *ILL,* Rhode Island Junior College, Knight Campus Library, Warwick RI. 401-825-2215

Mercure, Rosemary P, *ILL, Ref & Spec Coll,* Clinch Valley College of the University of Virginia, John Cook Wyllie Library, Wise VA. 703-328-2431, Ext 255

Mercurio, Carolyn, *Assoc Dean,* Saint Louis Community College at Florissant Valley, Library Technical Assistant Program, MO. 314-595-4494

Mercurio, Carolyn, *Libr Serv,* Saint Louis Community College (Florissant Valley Campus), Saint Louis MO. 314-595-4494

Meredith, Mrs M M, *Librn,* Gibsons Public Library Association, Gibsons BC. 604-886-2130

Meredith, Ruth, *Circ,* United States Army (Armament R & D Command, Scientific & Technical Information Div), Dover NJ. 201-328-2914

Meredith, Susan, *Ch,* Benton Harbor Public Library, Benton Harbor MI. 616-926-6139

Meredith, William, *Coordr Region Two,* Denver Public Library, Denver CO. 303-573-5152, Ext 271

Meredith, William B, *Assoc Dir, Acq & Tech Serv,* Dartmouth College, Baker Memorial Library, Hanover NH. 603-646-2235

Meredith, Willis C, *Librn,* Nathaniel Hawthorne College, Silver Library, Antrim NH. 603-588-6341, Ext 235

Meriam, Philip W, *Dir,* Wilmington Memorial Library, Wilmington MA. 617-658-2967

Mericia, Sister Mary, *Dir,* Felician College Library, Lodi NJ. 201-778-1190, Ext 70

Mericle, Rebecca, *Asst Dir,* Northwestern Michigan College, Mark Osterlin Library, Traverse City MI. 616-946-5650, Ext 541

Merighi, Suzanne, *Asst Dir & Ref,* Millville Public Library, Millville NJ. 609-825-7087

Meringolo, Anne, *Supvr,* Manufacturers Hanover Trust Co (Investment Library Division), New York NY. 212-957-1356

Meringolo, Saluatore, *Bus Ref,* University of Massachusetts at Amherst Library, Amherst MA. 413-545-0284

Merk, P Evelyn, *Librn,* Houston County Public Library System (Warner Robins-Houston County Branch), Warner Robins GA. 912-923-0128

Merkl, Anthony E, *Dir,* South Orange Public Library, South Orange NJ. 201-762-0230

Merkl, Jeanette B, *Librn,* Hospital Center at Orange, William Pierson Medical Library, Orange NJ. 201-678-1100, Ext 310

Merkle, Thomas, *Pub Serv,* Miracosta College Learning Resource Center, Oceanside CA. 714-757-2121, Ext 250

Merkley, John, *Dir & Acq,* Calexico Public Library, Calexico CA. 714-357-2605

Meroff, Debbie, *Librn,* Lisbon Community Library Association, Lisbon ME. 207-353-6564

Meroff, Debbie, *Dir,* Lisbon Falls Community Library, Lisbon Falls ME. 207-353-6564

Meronek, Theodora, *Asst Librn,* Superior Public Library (South Superior Station), Superior WI. 715-394-0249

Merrell, Bruce, *Librn,* Anchorage Municipal Libraries (Grandview Gardens), Anchorage AK. 907-276-8083

Merrell, Mary K, *Ch,* Idaho Falls Public Library, Idaho Falls ID. 208-529-1450

Merrell, Muriel L, *Librn,* United States Attorney's Office Library, Los Angeles CA. 213-688-2434

Merrell, Sheila, *Coordr,* Saint Louis Regional Library Network, MO. 314-878-8750

Merrett, Marilyn, *Cat,* Louisiana State University in Shreveport Library, Shreveport LA. 318-797-7121, Ext 203

Merriam, Betsy, *Interlibrary Coop,* Wisconsin Department of Public Instruction (Public & Cooperative Library Service), Madison WI. 608-266-7270

Merrick, Janet, *Dir,* Nichols Memorial Library, Kingston NH. 603-642-3521

Merrick, Jerald, *Ad,* Salina Public Library, Salina KS. 913-825-4624

Merrick, Mildred, *Ref,* University of Miami, Otto G Richter Library, Coral Gables FL. 305-284-3551

Merrick, Shirlie L, *Tech Serv,* Allegany Community College, Library (Division of Learning Resources), Cumberland MD. 301-724-7700, Ext 35, 36

Merrick, Thomas W, *Dir,* Kennedy Institute (Center for Population Research Library), Washington DC. 202-625-4333

Merrifield, Mary Ann, *Dir,* Lagrange County Library, Lagrange IN. 219-463-2841

Merrigan, Paul G, *Dir,* Nassau County Medical Center Library, East Meadow NY. 516-542-3542

Merril, Mary G, *Asst Dir & Ad,* Cora J Belden Library, Rocky Hill CT. 203-529-2379

Merrill, Barbara, *Circ,* Jones County Junior College Memorial Library & Media Center, Ellisville MS. 601-477-9311, Ext 298

Merrill, Dawn, *Librn,* Binghamton Public Library (Benjamin Franklin), Binghamton NY. 607-722-8587

Merrill, Lucille, *Asst Dir & ILL,* Briggs-Lawrence County Public Library, Ironton OH. 614-532-1124

Merrill, Marjorie, *Asst Librn,* New Carlisle & Olive Township Public Library, New Carlisle IN. 219-654-3046

Merrill, Martha, *Soc Sci,* Jacksonville State University Library, Jacksonville AL. 205-435-9820, Ext 213, 214

Merrill, Max, *Librn,* Veterans Administration, Medical Center Libraries, Grand Junction CO. 303-243-0731, Ext 220

Merrill, Ruth, *Off Mgr,* High Plains Regional Library System, Greeley CO. 303-330-7691

Merriman, Audrey, *ILL & Cat,* Saint Joseph's College Library, Rensselaer IN. 219-866-7111, Ext 187

Merriman, Elaine W, *Media,* Green Mountain College Library, Poultney VT. 802-287-9313, Ext 42 & 43

Merriman, Evelyn, *Asst Dean & Acq,* Blount County Library, Maryville TN. 615-982-0981

Merritt, Anne C, *Asst Librn,* Cannon Free Library, Delhi NY. 607-746-2662

Merritt, Betty, *Librn,* Harris County Law Library, Houston TX. 713-221-5183

Merritt, Cheryl, *Asst Librn,* Buffalo Creek Memorial Library, Man WV. 304-583-7887

Merritt, Clinton E, *Chief Librn,* Hughes Aircraft Co, Information Resources Section, Culver City CA. 213-391-0711, Ext 3474

Merritt, Eleanor, *ILL,* Tulane University of Louisiana, Howard-Tilton Memorial Library, New Orleans LA. 504-865-5131

Merritt, Floyd, *Ref,* Amherst College, Robert Frost Library, Amherst MA. 413-542-2212

Merritt, Lynette M, *On-Line Servs,* Lovelace Biomedical & Environmental Research Institute, Inhalation Toxicology Research Institute Library, Albuquerque NM. 505-844-2600

Merry, Sue, *Tech Serv,* Canadian Imperial Bank of Commerce, Information Centre Library, Toronto ON. 416-862-3053

Merryman, John, *Audit Ref Servs,* United States General Accounting Office Library System (Office of Information Systems & Services), Washington DC. 275-3691 (Br Mgr), 275-5180 (Audit Ref Servs), 275-2585 (Law), 275-2555 (Tech Servs)

Merryman, Virginia, *Librn,* CH2M Hill, Information Center, Redding CA. 916-243-5831, Ext 283

Merryweather, Elva, *Tech Serv,* Cooper Memorial Library, Clermont FL. 904-394-4265

Mersereau, Joseph E, *Media,* Fairfax County Public Library, Administrative Offices, Springfield VA. 703-321-9810

Mershon, Nancy, *Reader Serv,* Upsala College Library, East Orange NJ. 201-266-7295

Mersing, Sally, *Librn,* Mansfield-Richland County Public Library (Lexington Branch), Lexington OH. 419-884-2500

Merskey, Marie G, *Dir,* Harrison Public Library, Harrison NY. 914-835-0324

Mersky, Roy M, *Dir of Res,* University of Texas Libraries (Tarlton Law Library), Austin TX. 512-471-7726

Mertens, Harriet, *Librn,* Pacific Scientific Co, Gardner Laboratory Inc Library, Bethesda MD. 301-656-3600

Mertens, John F, *Dir,* Ozark Regional Library, Ironton MO. 314-546-2615

Mertins, Barbara, *Asst Prof,* West Virginia University, Dept of Library Science, WV. 304-293-3540

Mertons, Mrs M A, *Dir,* Jewish Hospital of Saint Louis (Rothschild Medical Library), Saint Louis MO. 314-454-7208

Meryman, Charles Dale, *In Charge,* Fish Doctor Clinical Center, Inc, Meryman Library of Aquatic Research, Riverview FL. 813-626-1805

Mesa, Rosa Q, *Librn,* University of Florida Libraries (Latin American Collection), Gainesville FL. 904-392-0359, 392-0360

Mesa, Zoe, *Ch,* Sheridan County Fulmer Public Library, Sheridan WY. 307-674-8585, 674-9898

Mesch, JoAnn, *Dir,* Hopkinton Public Library, Hopkinton IA. 319-962-2625

Meschel, Susan, *On-Line Servs,* University of Chicago, Joseph Regenstein Library, Chicago IL. 312-753-2977

Meserve, Beverly, *Circ,* Scotch Plains Public Library, Scotch Plains NJ. 201-322-5007

Mesic, Heidi, *Librn,* Borromeo Seminary of Ohio Library, Wickliffe OH. 216-943-3888

Mesina, Irene, *Asst Librn & Ref,* Honolulu Community College Library, Honolulu HI. 808-845-9220

Mesmer, Gerald, *Librn,* Benedictine College, Library Science Department, KS. 913-367-6110, Ext 204

Mesmer, Gerald J, *Librn & Acq,* Benedictine College (North Campus Library), Atchison KS. 913-367-5340, Ext 290

Mesplay, Debbie, *Librn,* Union County District Library, Morganfield KY. 502-389-1696

Mesre, Josephine, *Ch & YA,* John McIntire Public Library Public Library, Zanesville OH. 614-453-0391

Messenger, Emeline S, *Librn,* North Aurora Public Library, North Aurora IL. 312-896-0240

Messer, Marguerite M, *Librn,* City Library (Sixteen Acres), Springfield MA. 413-783-2161

Messerla, Janet E, *Dir,* Valley Park Community Library, Valley Park MO. 314-225-5608
Messerle, J, *Coordr,* Saint Joseph Hospital, Information Services, Alton IL. 618-463-5282
Messersmith, Susan, *Librn,* Myrtle Point Library, Myrtle Point OR. 503-572-2591
Messier, Elaine, *Librn,* Mission Research Corp Library, Santa Barbara CA. 805-963-8761
Messimer, Jean, *Librn,* University of Colorado at Boulder (Engineering Library), Boulder CO. 303-492-7120
Messimer, Nell, *Librn,* Atlanta Christian College, James A Burns Memorial Library, East Point GA. 404-761-8861, Ext 25
Messineo, Anthony, *Dir,* Mohawk Valley Library Association, Schenectady NY. 518-355-2010
Messineo, Leonard, *Art & Music,* Wichita Public Library, Wichita KS. 316-262-0611
Messingschlager, Jane, *Actg Librn,* Franklin Public Library, Franklin OH. 513-746-2896
Messmann, Irmgard, *Asst Librn & Ref,* Kirkwood Public Library, Kirkwood MO. 314-821-5770
Messmer, George, *Consult,* New York State Library, Albany NY. 518-474-5930
Mest, Belle, *Mgr Info Serv,* Needham, Harper & Steers Advertising, Inc Library, Chicago IL. 312-861-0100
Meszaros, Imre, *Librn,* Washington University Libraries (Art & Architecture), Saint Louis MO. 314-889-5268
Metcalf, Abbie, *Librn,* Norwich Public Library, Norwich VT. 802-649-1184
Metcalf, Harriet, *Librn,* Douglas County Public Library (Parker Branch), Parker CO. 303-841-3503
Metcalf, Jane, *Librn,* United States Army (Hawley Army Hospital Library), Fort Benjamin Harrison IN. 317-542-3101
Metcalf, Joanne, *Med Librn & On Line Search Coordr,* Veterans Administration Medical Center, Library Service, San Diego CA. 714-453-7500, Ext 3421
Metcalf, Judy, *Asst Ref Ed,* Dallas Morning News Reference Department, Dallas TX. 214-745-8302
Metcalf, Kent E, *Librn,* Jefferson County Public Law Library, Louisville KY. 502-581-5943
Metcalf, Louisa S, *Sr Rd & Info Librn,* Boston Public Library, Eastern Massachusetts Library System, Boston MA. 617-536-5400
Metcalf, Marjorie, *Librn,* W R Grace & Co Library, Cambridge MA. 617-876-1400, Ext 436 & 437
Metcalf, Mrs Nelson, *Librn,* Amenia Free Library, Amenia NY. 914-373-8273
Metcalf, Ruth, *Circ,* University of Texas at Arlington Library, Arlington TX. 817-273-3391
Metcalfe, Helen M, *Librn,* Underwood - Memorial Hospital, Medical Library, Woodbury NJ. 609-845-0100
Metcalfe, Mrs L, *Librn,* Essa Centennial Public Library, Angus ON. 705-424-6531
Metcalfe, Shirley, *Librn,* Minnedosa Regional Library, Minnedosa MB. 204-867-2585
Metivier, Irene, *Librn,* Reed Free Library, Surry NH. 603-352-1761
Metrost, Teri, *Ad,* Englewood Public Library, Englewood CO. 303-761-4376
Metsker, Alice P, *Dir,* Montrose Public Library, Montrose IA. 319-463-5532
Mettham, Lorraine, *Librn,* Southwestern Public Service Co Library, Amarillo TX. 806-378-2741
Metts, Jr, Daniel, *Dir,* Mercer University, Stetson Memorial Library, Macon GA. 912-745-6811, Ext 284
Metz, Janice R, *Asst Librn,* Illinois Agricultural Association, IAA & Affiliated Companies Library, Bloomington IL. 309-557-2552
Metz, Lynn, *Acq,* Knox College, Henry W Seymour Library, Galesburg IL. 309-343-0112, Ext 246
Metz, Ray, *Circ,* Northern Michigan University, Lydia M Olson Library, Marquette MI. 906-227-2260
Metz, Rebecca, *Ref,* Marion Public Library, Marion OH. 614-387-0992
Metz, T John, *Librn,* Carleton College Library, Northfield MN. 507-645-4431
Metzenbacher, Gary, *Circ,* Western Evangelical Seminary, G Hallauer Memorial Library, Portland OR. 503-654-5182
Metzgar, Erv, *Chmn,* California Library Authority for Systems & Services, (CLASS), CA. 408-289-1756

Metzger, Bernice, *Librn,* Warren County Library (Roseville Branch), Roseville IL. 309-426-2336
Metzger, Hazel, *Librn,* Palmer Public Library, Palmer IA. 712-359-2296
Metzger, Janet, *Ch,* Louisville Public Library, Louisville OH. 216-875-1696
Metzger, Janice M, *Librn,* Conoco Coal Development Co, Research Division, Technical Library, Library PA. 412-831-6688
Metzger, Jo, *Tech Serv,* Marymount Palos Verdes College Library, Rancho Palos Verdes CA. 213-377-5501, Ext 29
Metzger, Kristen L, *Librn,* Harbor Branch Foundation, Inc Library, Fort Pierce FL. 305-465-2400
Metzger, Kristen L, *On-Line Servs,* Harbor Branch Foundation, Inc Library, Fort Pierce FL. 305-465-2400
Metzger, Ludwig, *Acq,* Johnson Free Public Library, Hackensack NJ. 201-343-4169
Metzger, Oscar F, *Ref,* San Antonio College Library, San Antonio TX. 512-734-7311, Ext 2480
Metzler, Alice, *Dir,* Charles Cook Memorial Library, Oconto Falls WI. 414-846-2673
Metzler, Lorraine, *Librn,* Fremont County Library (Lysite Branch), Lysite WY. 307-332-5194
Meunier, Pierre, *Librn,* Bibliotheque Municipale, Drummondville PQ. 819-472-7679
Meurer, Sonia, *Librn,* Nabisco Inc Research Center Library, Fair Lawn NJ. 201-797-6800, Ext 338
Meury, Janet S, *Asst Librn,* Lamar Community College, Learning Resources Center, Lamar CO. 303-336-2733
Mews, Alison, *Librn,* Memorial University of Newfoundland Library (Curriculum Materials Centre), Saint John's NF. 709-753-1200
Mewshaw, Robyn, *Asst Economist,* Data Bank bureau of Business & Economic Research, Institute for Applied Research Services, Albuquerque NM. 505-277-2216
Meyenson, M, *Librn,* Queens Hospital Center Auxiliary Inc, Elsie K Sanborn Memorial Library, Jamaica NY. 212-990-3152
Meyer, Anne, *Librn,* Carnegie Library of Pittsburgh (Allegheny Regional), Pittsburgh PA. 412-622-3100
Meyer, Annette, *Librn,* Tucson Public Library (Mission), Tucson AZ. 602-791-4811
Meyer, Barbara, *Ch,* Free Public Library of Oakland, Oakland NJ. 201-337-3742
Meyer, Bettina, *ILL,* Western Michigan University, Dwight B Waldo Library, Kalamazoo MI. 616-383-4961
Meyer, Betty J, *Tech Serv,* Ohio State University Libraries (William Oxley Thompson Memorial Library), Columbus OH. 614-422-6151
Meyer, Carol Elaine, *Librn,* Cincinnati Law Library Association, Cincinnati OH. 513-632-8371
Meyer, Cynthia K, *Chief Librn,* Veterans Administration, Medical Center Library, Prescott AZ. 602-445-4860, Ext 271, 349
Meyer, Della, *Asst Librn,* Linn Grove Public Library, Linn Grove IA. 712-296-3919
Meyer, Dorothy, *Librn,* Paddock Publications, Editorial Department Library, Arlington Heights IL. 312-870-3600
Meyer, Evelyn, *Ref & Bibliog Instr,* Drew University, Rose Memorial Library, Madison NJ. 201-377-3000, Ext 469
Meyer, Frances E, *Librn,* Madison Business College Library, Madison WI. 608-256-7794
Meyer, Ingrid, *Ref,* Free Public Library of the City of Orange, Orange NJ. 201-673-0153
Meyer, Ingrid, *Local Hist,* Free Public Library of the City of Orange, Orange NJ. 201-673-0153
Meyer, J G, *Librn,* Anderson Development Company Library, Adrian MI. 517-263-2121
Meyer, Jerry, *Tech Serv,* Klamath County Library, Klamath Falls OR. 503-882-8894
Meyer, Jerry, *Ad,* National Naval Medical Center, E R Stitt Library, Bethesda MD. 301-545-6700
Meyer, Joan, *Librn,* Niagera on the Lake Public Library (Quennston Public), Queenston ON. 416-262-5173
Meyer, Joan L, *Tech Serv,* Springfield Free Public Library, Springfield NJ. 201-376-4930
Meyer, Karen, *Librn,* Caplin & Drysdale Library, Washington DC. 202-862-5000
Mcyer, Marsha, *Ch,* Sturgis Public Library, Sturgis MI. 616-651-7907, 651-2321

Meyer, Mary K, *Genealogical Librn,* Maryland Historical Society Library, Baltimore MD. 301-685-3750
Meyer, Mary Louise, *Ad & Ref,* Township of Hamilton Free Public Library, Trenton NJ. 609-890-3460
Meyer, Mona, *Asst Librn,* Henderson Community College Library, Henderson KY. 502-827-1867
Meyer, R W, *Assoc Dir,* Clemson University, Robert Muldrow Cooper Library, Clemson SC. 803-656-3026
Meyer, Richard, *Ref,* Bettendorf Public Library & Information Center, Bettendorf IA. 319-359-4427
Meyer, Roger L, *Mgr Tech Info Servs,* Engelhard Minerals & Chemicals Corp, Technical Information Center, Edison NJ. 201-321-5271
Meyer, Sandra, *Tech Serv,* University of New Mexico General Library (Medical Center Library), Albuquerque NM. 505-277-2311
Meyer, Sharon, *Asst Librn,* University of Health Sciences-Chicago Medical School Library (North Chicago), Chicago IL. 312-942-2859
Meyer, Sharon I, *Librn,* American Hospital Supply Organization, Corporate Library, Evanston IL. 312-866-4000
Meyer, Ursula, *Dir,* Stockton-San Joaquin County Public Library, Stockton Public Libr, Stockton CA. 209-944-8415
Meyer, Valerie D, *Librn,* University of Michigan Libraries (Fine Arts), Ann Arbor MI. 313-764-5405
Meyer, Valerie L, *Librn,* Lewiston City Library (Tsceminicum), Lewiston ID. 208-743-6519
Meyerend, Maude H, *Dir,* Chestnut Hill Hospital, School of Nursing Library, Philadelphia PA. 215-248-8397
Meyerhoff, Cathy, *ILL,* Waterloo Public Library, Waterloo IA. 319-291-4521
Meyerhoff, Erich, *Dir,* Cornell University Medical College, Samuel J Wood Library, New York NY. 212-472-5300
Meyerhoff, Laurel D, *Librn,* Cutler-Hammer, Inc, AIL Division Library, Melville NY. 516-595-4400
Meyers, Alice, *Ch,* David A Howe Public Library, Wellsville NY. 716-593-3410
Meyers, Arthur S, *Librn,* Muncie-Center Township Public Library, Muncie IN. 317-288-9971
Meyers, Barbara, *Librn,* Thornton Community College, Learning Resources Center, South Holland IL. 312-596-2000, Ext 240
Meyers, Beatrice, *Ch,* Emo Public Library, Emo ON. 807-482-2575
Meyers, Duane H, *Assoc Dir,* Metropolitan Library System, Oklahoma City OK. 405-235-0571
Meyers, Evelyn, *Ref,* Verona Free Public Library, Verona NJ. 201-239-0050
Meyers, James C, *Bkmobile Coordr,* Salem Free Public Library, Salem NJ. 609-935-0526
Meyers, Leslie, *Ref,* New School for Social Research, Raymond Fogelman Library, New York NY. 212-741-7906
Meyers, Lois, *Commun Servs,* Everett Public Library, Everett WA. 206-259-8858
Meyers, Martha, *Rare Bks,* Mid-Continent Public Library, Independence MO. 816-836-5200
Meyers, Martha, *Librn,* Tangipahoa Parish Library (Roseland Branch), Roseland LA. 504-748-9387
Meyers, Maxine, *Asst,* Sabine Parish Library (Zwolle Branch), Zwolle LA. 318-256-2212
Meyers, Patty J, *Asst Dir Public Serv,* Tucson Public Library, Tucson AZ. 602-791-4391
Meyers, Rose, *Librn,* East Baton Rouge Parish Library (Centroplex), Baton Rouge LA. 504-389-4967
Meyers, Stanna, *Dir,* Silverton Public Library, Silverton CO. 303-387-5770
Meyers, Thomas B, *Dir,* Santa Fe Regional Library, Gainesville Public Library Headquarters, Gainesville FL. 904-374-2091
Meyerson, Flora, *Ref,* University of Washington Libraries (Law Library), Seattle WA. 206-543-4089
Meyn, Ann, *Librn,* Ethel L Whipple Memorial Library, Los Fresnos TX. 512-233-5330
Meyn, Margaret, *Dir,* Sacred Heart General Hospital Library Services, Eugene OR. 503-686-6837
Meynard, Roch, *Dir,* Universite Du Quebec A Montreal Bibliotheque, Montreal PQ. 514-282-3116

Meza, Barbara, *Tech Serv,* Merced College, Lesher Library, Merced CA. 209-723-4321, Ext 274
Mezera, Sister Frances Claire, *Dir,* Viterbo College Library, La Crosse WI. 608-784-0040, Ext 429
Mezgar, Lajos, *Dir,* Tompkins County Public Library, Ithaca NY. 607-272-4555
Miah, Abdul J, *Dir,* J Sargeant Reynolds Community College (Downtown Campus-Learning Resources Center), Richmond VA. 804-786-6249
Miasek, Meryl A, *Librn,* Michigan State University Library (Veterinary Clinic), East Lansing MI. 517-355-2344
Miaskoff, Leah, *District Consult,* Easton Area Public Library, Easton PA. 215-258-2917
Miceli, Corinne, *Doc,* University of Connecticut at Hartford (Law Library), West Hartford CT. 203-523-4841, Ext 347, 370
Michael, Ann, *Chief Librn,* Johns-Manville Corporation (Corporate Information Center), Denver CO. 979-1000 Ext 3440, 3448
Michael, Anna, *Librn,* Sacramento Bee Editorial Library, Sacramento CA. 916-446-9611
Michael, Douglas O, *Dir,* Cayuga County Community College, Norman F Bourke Memorial Library Learning Resources Center, Auburn NY. 315-255-1743, Ext 296 & 298
Michael, Kay M, *Tech Serv,* San Joaquin Delta College, Goleman Library, Stockton CA. 209-478-2011, Ext 277
Michael, Mrs David, *Ref,* Frankfort Community Public Library, Frankfort IN. 317-654-8746
Michael, Patricia, *Museum Dir,* Kalamazoo Public Library, Kalamazoo MI. 616-342-9837
Michael, Shirley, *AV,* Free Public Library of the City of Trenton, Trenton NJ. 609-392-7188
Michael, Shirley, *Librn,* Free Public Library of the City of Trenton (North Trenton), Trenton NJ. 609-392-7188
Michaels, Carolyn Leopold, *Librn,* National Society of the Daughters of the American Revolution Library, Washington DC. 202-628-1776, Ext 226
Michaels, Jacqueline, *Ch,* Grosse Pointe Public Library, Grosse Pointe MI. 313-343-2074
Michaels, Rebecca, *Chief Librn,* United States Army (Fort Jackson Morale Support Activities Library), Fort Jackson SC. 803-751-4816, 751-5589
Michaelson, Judy, *Commun Servs,* Worthington Public Library, Worthington OH. 614-885-3185
Michalak, Jo-Ann, *Librn,* Columbia University (School of Library Service Library), New York NY. 212-280-2241
Michalak, Joe, *Ref,* University of California, University Library, Santa Cruz CA. 408-429-2076
Michalak, Sarah, *Librn,* University of Washington Libraries (Natural Sciences), Seattle WA. 206-543-1243
Michalak, Sarah C, *Sci,* University of Washington Libraries, Seattle WA. 206-543-1760
Michalak, Thomas, *On-Line Servs,* Columbia University (University Libraries), New York NY. 212-280-2241
Michalova, Dagmar, *Dir,* New York State Department of Health Research Library, Albany NY. 518-474-6172
Michalski, Cathy, *Librn,* Learning Exchange Library, Evanston IL. 312-864-4133
Michaud, Charles, *Dir,* Topsfield Town Library, Topsfield MA. 617-887-2914
Michaud, Germaine, *Librn,* Dubreuilville Public Library, Dubreuilville ON. 705-884-2284
Michaud, Jeannine, *Cat,* Centre Universitaire Saint-Louis-Maillet, Students Library, Edmundston NB. 506-735-8804
Michaud, John, *Evening Librn,* Durham Technical Institute, Learning Resources Center, Durham NC. 919-596-9311, Ext 228
Michaud, Marcelle, *Librn,* Hopital L'hotel-Dieu De Quebec, Medical Library, Quebec PQ. 418-694-5151
Michaud, Margaret, *Tech Serv & On-Line Servs,* Andover Newton Theological School, Franklin Trask Library, Newton Centre MA. 617-964-1100, Ext 140
Michel, Betty, *Librn,* Saint Louis Public Library (Machacek), Saint Louis MO. 314-718-2948
Michel, Hedwig, *Pres,* Koreshan Unity Research Library, Estero FL. 813-992-2184

Michel, Maurice, *Librn,* University of Montana (Law School Library), Missoula MT. 406-243-5603
Michelak, Naomi, *Patient Librn,* Veterans Administration, Medical Center Library Service, Boston MA. 617-232-9500, Ext 634
Michels, Fredrick, *Dir,* Lake Superior State College Library, Sault Sainte Marie MI. 906-632-6841, Ext 402
Michels, Timothy I, *In Charge,* Londe-Parker-Michels, Inc Library, Saint Louis MO. 314-725-5501
Michelsen, Michel, *Ref,* Danbury Public Library, Danbury CT. 203-797-4505
Michelsen, Michel, *Librn,* Federal Correctional Institution, Dept of Justice Centralized Library, Danbury CT. 203-746-2444
Michelson, Aaron I, *Dir,* University of South Alabama (University Library), Mobile AL. 205-460-7021
Michelson-Thiery, Marybeth, *Cat,* Dutchess Community College Library, Poughkeepsie NY. 914-471-4500, Ext 388
Michener, David H, *Cat,* University of Louisville Library, Louisville KY. 502-588-6745
Michie, Jean, *Dir,* Richards Free Library, Newport NH. 603-863-3430
Michler, Mrs M, *Bibliog Instr,* Fish Memorial Hospital, Medical Library, De Land FL. 904-734-2323
Michna, James T, *Dir,* Rockford College, Howard Colman Library, Rockford IL. 815-226-4035, 226-4036
Michniewski, Henry J, *Libr Develop Bur Head,* New Jersey State Library, Trenton NJ. 609-292-6200
Mick, Minnie, *Dir,* San Jose Bible College, Memorial Library, San Jose CA. 408-293-9058
Mickel, Muriel, *Librn,* Montgomery County Department of Public Libraries (Rockville), Rockville MD. 301-279-1953
Mickelsen, Nadine, *Librn,* Battle Creek Public Library, Battle Creek IA. 712-365-4646
Mickelson, Mary P, *Acq,* South Dakota School of Mines & Technology, Devereaux Library, Rapid City SD. 605-394-2418
Mickelson, Peter, *Ref,* California Lutheran College Library, Thousand Oaks CA. 805-492-2411, Ext 205
Mickelson, Shirley, *Doc,* University of Missouri-Kansas City Libraries, Kansas City MO. 816-276-1531
Mickens, Evelyn, *Librn,* Cleveland Public Library (Woodland (Bookmobile Services)), Cleveland OH. 216-361-7255
Mickens, Joseph, *In Charge,* Western Center Library, Canonsburg PA. 412-745-0700
Mickey, Gloria, *Dir,* Swisher County Library, Tulia TX. 806-995-3447
Mickey, Melissa, *Librn,* Kraft, Inc (Corporate Library), Glenview IL. 312-998-2465
Mickley, Cathye, *Circ,* Oak Lawn Public Library, Oak Lawn IL. 312-422-4990
Mickus, Agnes O, *Dir Libr Serv,* Veterans Administration, Hospital Library, Miles City MT. 406-232-3060, Ext 305
Micuda, Vladimir, *Sci & Tech,* Pennsylvania State University, Fred Lewis Pattee Library, University Park PA. 814-865-0401
Mida, Mrs, *Br Supvr,* Scarborough Public Library (McGregor Park), Scarborough ON. 416-759-6757
Middendorf, Jack L, *Dir,* Wayne State College, U S Conn Library, Wayne NE. 402-375-3157, Ext 243
Middendorf, Jack L, *Dir,* Wayne State College, Library Science & Educational Media Program, NE. 402-375-2200, Ext 243
Middleswart, Melissa, *Librn,* Rolling Hills Consolidated Library (Savanna Branch), Savannah MO. 816-324-4569
Middleton, Ada, *Librn,* Joseph E Seagram & Sons, Inc, Research & Development Library, Louisville KY. 502-634-1551, Ext 297
Middleton, Bernice B, *Chmn,* South Carolina State College, Dept of Library Service, SC. 803-536-7020
Middleton, Cheryl, *Asst Dir,* Colorado Mountain College-West Campus, Learning Center, Glenwood Springs CO. 303-945-7481, Ext 66
Middleton, Dale R, *Assoc Dir,* University of Washington Libraries (Health Sciences), Seattle WA. 206-543-5530

Middleton, Harry J, *Dir,* General Services Administration - National Archives & Records Service, Lyndon Baines Johnson Library, Austin TX. 512-397-5137
Middleton, Kent, *Info Serv,* Austin Public Library, Austin TX. 512-472-5433
Middleton, Marie D, *Dir,* Fort Loudoun Regional Library Center, Athens TN. 615-745-5194
Middleton, Mildred T, *Disabled Servs & Outreach Coordr,* Neenah Public Library, Neenah WI. 414-729-4728
Middleton, Nancy E, *Acq,* Centenary College of Louisiana, Magale Library, Shreveport LA. 318-869-5170
Middleton, Robert L, *Head,* Free Library of Philadelphia (Interlibrary Loan), Philadelphia PA. 215-686-5360
Middleton, Roxanne, *Librn,* Champion Municipal Library, Champion AB. 403-897-3833
Middleton, Susan, *Tech Rep,* Texas A&m University Libraries, College Station TX. 713-845-6111
Middletow, Carol, *ILL,* Whitchurch-Stouffville Public Library, Stouffville ON. 416-640-2395
Midgett, Otis, *Spec Coll,* College of Saint Catherine, Saint Catherine Library, Saint Paul MN. 612-690-6650
Midgley, Dale, *Dir,* Northern Essex Community College Library, Haverhill MA. 617-374-0721, Ext 231
Midgley, John, *Asst Librn,* Arthur Young & Co Library, New York NY. 212-922-4880
Midkiff, Teresa Durhamm, *ILL & Acq,* Shawnee State College Library, Portsmouth OH. 614-354-3205, Ext 29
Miele, Anthony W, *Dir,* Alabama Public Library Service, Montgomery AL. 205-832-5743
Miele, Cecilia M, *Dir,* Palisades Park Free Public Library, Palisades Park NJ. 201-947-5909
Mielke, Kathleen, *Dir,* New London Community Hospital Health Science Library, New London WI. 414-982-5330, Ext 240
Mielke, Linda, *Pub Libr Specialists,* Maryland State Department of Education, Division of Library Development & Services, Baltimore MD. 301-796-8300, Ext 284
Mielke, Thelma, *Ref, Rare Bks & Bibliog Instr,* Long Island University, Brooklyn Center Libraries, Brooklyn NY. 212-834-6060, 834-6064
Mielke, Thelma, *German, Latin Am, Political Sci & Tropical Hort,* Long Island University, Brooklyn Center Libraries, Brooklyn NY. 212-834-6060, 834-6064
Mier, Guadalupe, *Br Coordr & Circ,* Corpus Christi Public Libraries, La Retama Public Library, Corpus Christi TX. 512-882-1937
Miervaldis, Liga, *Info Spec,* Upjohn Company (Corporate Technical Library), Kalamazoo MI. 616-385-6414
Mierzwinski, Barbara J, *Dir,* Bethlehem Public Library, Bethlehem CT. 203-266-7792
Might, Mamie, *Librn,* Detroit Public Library (Lincoln), Detroit MI. 313-833-9813
Migliacci, Jeanne, *Sr Libr Asst,* Medfield State Hospital, Medical Library, Medfield MA. 617-359-7312, Ext 221
Migliacci, Jeanne M, *Sr Librn,* Medfield State Hospital (General Library), Medfield MA. 617-539-7312, Ext 221
Migliore, Lucy N, *Librn,* Salem Township Public Library, Slickville PA. 412-468-4492
Miglorino, Isabelle, *Asst Librn,* Dudley-Tucker Library, Raymond NH. 603-895-2633
Mignault, Marcel, *In Charge,* College De Sainte Anne De La Pocatiere Bibliotheque, La Pocatiere PQ. 418-856-3082
Migneault, Robert, *Tech Serv & Spec Coll,* San Francisco State University, J Paul Leonard Library, San Francisco CA. 415-469-1681
Mignery, Gertrude, *Archivist,* University of the South, Jessie Ball duPont Library, Sewanee TN. 615-598-5931, Ext 265, 267
Mignon, Edmond, *Assoc Prof,* University of Washington, School of Librarianship, WA. 206-543-1794
Mihalyi, Mrs Ernest J, *Cat,* Bridgeville Public Library, Bridgeville PA. 412-221-3737
Mijares, Mary, *Commun Relations,* Sacramento Public Library, Sacramento CA. 916-440-5926
Mikail, Jackie, *Assoc Dir,* Mid-Atlantic Regional Medical Library Program, National Library of Medicine, MD. 301-496-5955

Mikel, Hazel P, *Dir,* Kendall Young Library, Webster City IA. 515-832-2565
Mikel, Sarah A, *Librn,* United States Department of the Army (Office of the Chief of Engineers Library), Washington DC. 202-693-6753
Mikell, Clorinda, *Librn,* Richland County Public Library (Eastover Branch), Eastover SC. 803-353-8584
Mikkelsen, June, *Librn,* Library Association of Portland (Gresham Branch), Gresham OR. 503-665-2222
Mikkonen, Donna, *Librn,* Geraldton Centennial Public Library, Geraldton ON. 807-854-1490
Mikler, Marylou, *On-Line Servs & Bibliog Instr,* West Volusia Memorial Hospital, Medical Library, De Land FL. 904-734-3320, Ext 539
Mikol, Kathryn, *Librn,* Gates Rubber Co, Technical Information Center, Denver CO. 303-744-4150
Mikolajczyk, Janet, *Ch,* Patterson Library, Westfield NY. 716-326-2154
Mikrut, Elsie, *Dir,* Bridgeview Public Library, Bridgeview IL. 312-458-2880
Miksa, Francis L, *Assoc Prof,* Louisiana State University, Graduate School of Library Science, LA. 504-388-3158
Miksa, Mary S, *Librn,* Louisiana Association of Business & Industry Library, Baton Rouge LA. 504-387-5372
Mikulak, Shelagh, *Soc Sci,* University of Calgary Library, Calgary AB. 403-284-5954
Milac, Metod M, *Asst Dir for Coll,* Syracuse University Libraries, Ernest S Bird Library, Syracuse NY. 315-423-2575
Milam, Margaret, *Tech Serv & Acq,* American University (Washington College of Law Library), Washington DC. 202-686-2625
Milam, Vicki, *Acq,* University of Colorado Health Sciences Center (Denison Memorial Library), Denver CO. 303-394-5125
Milanof, Ann, *Librn,* Mount Joy Library Center, Mount Joy PA. 717-653-1510
Milazzo, Carol, *Ref,* James Prendergast Library Association, Jamestown NY. 716-484-7135
Milbry, Cheryl, *Asst Librn,* Macon County-Tuskegee Public Library, Tuskegee AL. 205-727-5192
Milburn, Richard, *Pub Servs,* Ontario College of Art Library, Toronto ON. 416-977-5311, Ext 54 & 55
Milburn, Rosemary, *Br Coordr,* Santa Cruz Public Library, Santa Cruz CA. 408-429-3533
Mildrum, Betty, *Librn,* Choctawhatchee Regional Library (Clayton-Town & County), Clayton AL. 205-775-3506
Miles, Cheryl, *Talking Bk Librn,* Bartholomew County Library, Cleo Rogers Memorial Library, Columbus IN. 812-379-1255
Miles, Cynthia, *Librn,* Library Association of Portland (Gregory Heights), Portland OR. 503-284-1611
Miles, Don, *Librn,* Milliken Research Library, Spartanburg SC. 803-573-2340
Miles, Dorothy, *Librn,* Rockwood Public Library, Rockwood TN. 615-354-1281
Miles, Georgiana, *Librn,* Broward County Division of Libraries (Sunrise Branch), Sunrise FL. 305-742-8585
Miles, Gerson, *Prison Media,* Alexander City State Junior College, Thomas D Russell Library, Alexander City AL. 205-234-6346, Ext 290
Miles, Gertrude, *Circ,* Bucknell University, Ellen Clarke Bertrand Library, Lewisburg PA. 717-524-3056
Miles, Jesker, *Tech Serv,* Itawamba Junior College, Learning Resource Center, Fulton MS. 601-862-3101, Ext 237
Miles, Karen, *Librn,* United States Navy (Naval Ammunition Disposal Library), Colts Neck NJ. 201-462-9500
Miles, Lois E, *Ch,* East Orange Public Library, East Orange NJ. 201-266-5600
Miles, Lois E, *Librn,* East Orange Public Library (Elmwood), East Orange NJ. 201-266-5620
Miles, Lyman, *Admin Asst,* Cerritos College Library, Learning Materials Center, Norwalk CA. 213-860-2451, Ext 286
Miles, Mary C, *Acq,* Vanderbilt University School of Law Library, Nashville TN. 615-322-2568
Miles, Michele L, *Librn,* Acres Consulting Services Ltd Toronto Library, Toronto ON. 416-595-2000
Miles, Robert, *Asst Dir & Acq,* Medgar Evers College Library, Brooklyn NY. 212-735-1851

Miles, Susan, *Librn,* Central Michigan University (Instructional Materials Center), Mount Pleasant MI. 517-774-3549
Miles, William, *Dir,* Leslie R Foss Public Library, Center Line MI. 313-757-7454
Miles, William A, *Spec Servs,* Buffalo & Erie County Public Library System, Buffalo NY. 716-856-7525
Milet, Lynn, *Media,* Lehigh University Libraries, Bethlehem PA. 861-3026 (Dir), 861-3050 (Ref), 861-3030 (Circ), 861-3055 (ILL)
Miletic, Ivan, *Librn,* Cleveland Public Library (South), Cleveland OH. 216-781-1690
Milewski, Robert, *Head, Network Support Servs,* Chicago Public Library (Illinois Regional Library for the Blind & Physically Handicapped), Chicago IL. 312-738-9210
Miley, Delma, *Asst Librn,* Owensville Public Library, Owensville IN. 812-724-3335
Miley, James A, *Librn,* Kendallville Public Library, Kendallville IN. 219-347-3554
Miley, Rachel, *Acq Librn,* East Texas Higher Education Library Information Exchange, TX. 214-753-0231, Ext 230
Milford, Charles C, *Librn,* Stanford University Libraries (Food Research Institute), Stanford CA. 415-497-3943
Milhorne, Deborah S, *Ch,* Washington County Public Library, Abingdon VA. 703-628-2971
Milich, Ricki C, *Librn,* Cleveland Public Library (Broadway), Cleveland OH. 216-883-8692
Milikien, Norma L, *Dir,* Killeen Public Library, Killeen TX. 817-526-6527
Milinovich, Michele, *Librn,* Duluth Bar Library Association, Duluth MN. 218-723-3563
Miljinovic, Susan, *Asst Librn,* Baker & Hostetler Library, Cleveland OH. 216-621-0200
Milkins, Ronald J, *In Charge,* New York Supreme Court Appellate Div, Third Dept Library, Albany NY. 518-474-3632
Milkovic, Milian, *Asst Librn,* Cuyahoga Community College (Metropolitan Campus Library), Cleveland OH. 216-241-5966, Ext 217
Milkovich, Michael, *Dir,* Dixon Gallery & Gardens Library, Memphis TN. 901-761-5250
Millar, Barbara, *Cat,* University of Illinois at the Medical Center, Library of the Health Sciences, Chicago IL. 312-996-8974
Millar, Louise, *Assoc Dir,* Grand Rapids Public Library, Grand Rapids MI. 616-456-4400
Millard, Bradley, *Ref,* University of Puget Sound, Collins Memorial Library, Tacoma WA. 206-756-3257
Millard, Joyce, *Br Asst,* La Crosse County Library (West Salem), West Salem WI. 608-786-1505
Millard, Pamela Anne, *Dir,* Gaston County Public Library, Gastonia NC. 704-866-3756
Millard, Pamela Anne, *Dir,* Gaston-Lincoln Regional Library, Gastonia NC. 704-866-3756
Millard, Sandra, *Bibliog Instr,* Yale University Library (Medical Library), New Haven CT. 203-436-4784, 436-2961
Mille, Martha, *Cat,* University of Santa Clara (Heafey Law Library), Santa Clara CA. 408-984-4451
Millen, George, *Cat,* Central Missouri State University, Ward Edwards Library, Warrensburg MO. 816-429-4141
Miller, Albert J, *Head Librn,* Pennsylvania State University, New Kensington Campus Library, New Kensington PA. 412-339-7561
Miller, Alice, *Librn,* Fairgrove Township Library, Fairgrove MI. 517-693-6050
Miller, Alice, *Dir,* Raynham Public Library, Raynham MA. 617-823-1344
Miller, Alice, *Librn,* Sloan Public Library, Sloan IA. 712-428-6297
Miller, Alice, *Librn,* Vizcaya Guides Library, Miami FL. 305-579-2808
Miller, Ann, *Fiction,* Buffalo & Erie County Public Library System, Buffalo NY. 716-856-7525
Miller, Ann, *Ref,* College of the Mainland, Learning Resources Center, Texas City TX. 713-938-1211, Ext 447
Miller, Ann H, *Tech Serv,* Darlington County Library, Darlington SC. 803-393-5864
Miller, Annie, *Librn,* Chicago Public Library (Woodson Community), Chicago IL. 312-881-6918
Miller, Arleen, *Librn,* Sheridan Public Library, Sheridan OR. 503-843-3420

Miller, Arline, *Circ,* New York Medical College, Westchester Medical Center Library, Valhalla NY. 914-347-5237
Miller, Arthur, *President,* LIBRAS, IL. 312-234-3100, Ext 406
Miller, Ava F, *Circ,* Free Library of Springfield Township, Philadelphia PA. 215-836-5300
Miller, Barbara, *Cat,* Pembroke State University, Mary Livermore Library, Pembroke NC. 919-521-4214, Ext 238
Miller, Barbara, *Librn,* Salinas Public Library (El Gabilan), Salinas CA. 408-758-7302
Miller, Barbara, *Asst Dir & ILL,* Wheeling College, Bishop Hodges Learning Center, Wheeling WV. 304-243-2226
Miller, Barbara G, *Librn,* Weeks Memorial Library, Lancaster NH. 603-788-4911
Miller, Barbara J, *Librn,* Dayton Hudson Corp Library, Minneapolis MN. 612-370-6769
Miller, Barbara R, *ILL,* Saint Vincent College & Archabbey Libraries, Latrobe PA. 412-339-9761, Ext 378
Miller, Barry, *Spec Coll,* Wake Forest University (Bowman Gray School of Medicine Library), Winston-Salem NC. 919-727-4691
Miller, Beth, *Spec Coll,* University of Western Ontario, A B Weldon Library, London ON. 519-679-6191
Miller, Betty, *Libr Supvr,* Calspan Corp Technical Library, Buffalo NY. 716-632-7500, Ext 531
Miller, Betty, *Commun Servs,* Springfield-Greene County Library, Springfield MO. 417-869-4621
Miller, Betty B, *Ch,* Kaubisch Memorial Public Library, Fostoria OH. 419-435-2813
Miller, Betty C, *Librn,* Milo Public Library, Milo IA. 515-942-6557
Miller, Betty D, *Ch & YA,* State Library of Florida, Div of Library Services, Dept of State, Tallahassee FL. 904-487-2651
Miller, Bruce, *Theol & Human,* Catholic University of America, John K Mullen of Denver Memorial Library, Washington DC. 202-635-5055
Miller, Byron B, *Chief Librn,* Veterans Administration, Hospital Library, Houston TX. 713-747-3000
Miller, C Robert, *Asst Dir,* Southern Illinois University at Edwardsville (Audio Visual Services), Edwardsville IL. 618-692-3050
Miller, Carol, *Asst Librn,* Larchwood Public Library, Larchwood IA. 712-477-2583
Miller, Carol, *Librn,* Waltham Hospital Library, Waltham MA. 617-899-3300, Ext 261
Miller, Carol H, *Dir,* Carnegie Free Library of Swissvale, Swissvale Library, Swissvale PA. 412-731-2300
Miller, Carolyn, *Ref,* Pennsylvania State University, Capitol Campus Heindel Library, Middletown PA. 717-787-7771
Miller, Carolyn, *Librn,* University of California (Science), Santa Cruz CA. 408-429-2050
Miller, Carolyn, *Sci,* University of California, University Library, Santa Cruz CA. 408-429-2076
Miller, Carolyn, *Sci,* University of Missouri-Columbia, Elmer Ellis Library, Columbia MO. 314-882-4701
Miller, Carolynne, *Genealogy,* Indiana State Library, Indianapolis IN. 317-232-3675
Miller, Carroll, *Librn,* Public Library of Nashville & Davidson County (Green Hills), Nashville TN. 615-292-8322
Miller, Casimera, *Ch,* Hamtramck Public Library, Albert J Zak Memorial Library, Hamtramck MI. 313-365-7050
Miller, Cedric, *Media,* Washington University Libraries (GWB School of Social Work), Saint Louis MO. 314-889-6616
Miller, Charles E, *Dir,* Florida State University, Robert Manning Strozier Library, Tallahassee FL. 904-644-5211
Miller, Charlotte, *Dir,* Mount Pleasant Public Library, Pleasantville NY. 914-769-0548
Miller, Christina, *Tech Serv,* Santa Clara County Free Library, San Jose CA. 408-293-2326
Miller, Clara, *Librn,* United States Marine Corps (Technical Library), Washington DC. 202-545-6700
Miller, Colleen, *Dir,* Jasper Public Library, Jasper AL. 205-221-2567
Miller, Connie, *Asst Supvr,* Waterloo Regional Library (Baden), Baden ON. 519-634-8933

Miller, Constance, *Bibliog Instr,* Saint John's University, Alcuin Library, Collegeville MN. 612-363-2119

Miller, Daniel, *Media,* University of Texas at El Paso Library, El Paso TX. 747-5683; 747-5684

Miller, Darlene, *Dir,* Anderson College (Instructional Materials Center), Anderson IN. 317-649-9071, Ext 2312

Miller, Debra J, *Coordr,* Serra Cooperative Library System, San Diego CA. 714-278-8090

Miller, Delores, *Librn,* Sto-Rox Free Lending Library, McKees Rocks PA. 412-771-6460

Miller, Diane, *Chief Librn,* Daily Pantagraph-Newspaper Library, Bloomington IL. 309-829-9411, Ext 222

Miller, Dick, *Tech Serv,* Northeastern Ohio Universities College of Medicine, Basic Medical Sciences Library, Rootstown OH. 216-325-2511

Miller, Dona, *Acq,* Mid-Continent Public Library, Independence MO. 816-836-5200

Miller, Donald W, *Dir,* Greater Victoria Municipal Library, Victoria BC. 604-382-7241

Miller, Donna, *Bkmobile Coordr,* Public Library of Columbus & Franklin County, Columbus OH. 614-864-8050

Miller, Doris, *ILL,* University of Alaska, Fairbanks, Elmer E Rasmuson Library, Fairbanks AK. 907-479-7224

Miller, Doris, *Librn,* Washington County Public Library (New Matamoras), Marietta OH. 614-865-3386

Miller, Doris J, *Dir,* Sullivan County Public Library, Sullivan IN. 812-268-4957

Miller, Dorothea, *Ch,* Acton Memorial Library, Acton MA. 617-263-2232, 263-9109

Miller, Dorothy, *Reader Serv,* Warren County Library, Belvidere NJ. 201-475-5361, Ext 114

Miller, Dwight, *Media,* Brigham Young University-Hawaii Campus, Joseph F Smith Library, Laie HI. 808-293-9211, Ext 260, 264

Miller, Edith, *Librn,* Miami University (Music Library), Oxford OH. 513-529-2017

Miller, Edward P, *Dean,* University of Missouri-Columbia, School of Library & Informational Science, MO. 314-882-4546

Miller, Eleanor, *Librn,* Jacksonville Public Library System (Southside), Jacksonville FL. 904-633-4877

Miller, Eleanor, *Ch,* Mount Prospect Public Library, Mount Prospect IL. 312-253-5675

Miller, Elizabeth, *Librn,* Tucson Public Library (South Tucson), Tucson AZ. 602-791-4791

Miller, Ellen L, *Mgr,* Booz, Allen & Hamilton, Inc Library, New York NY. 212-697-1900, Ext 607

Miller, Ellen L, *Librn,* White, Weld & Co Inc Library, New York NY. 212-285-2000

Miller, Elsa, *Acq,* Southern Baptist Theological Seminary, James P Boyce Centennial Library, Louisville KY. 502-897-4807

Miller, Elwood, *Instr,* University of Colorado, Educational Technology Program, CO. 303-492-5141 & 492-6715

Miller, Emma, *Pub Servs,* Huntsville-Madison County Public Library, Huntsville AL. 205-536-0021

Miller, Ethel, *Ref & Bibliog Instr,* Armstrong State College, Lane Memorial Library, Savannah GA. 912-927-5332

Miller, Ethel, *Instr,* Armstrong State College, Library Media, GA. 912-927-5332

Miller, Ethelbert, *In Charge,* Howard University Libraries (Afro-American Studies Resource Center), Washington DC. 202-636-7242

Miller, Florence, *Ch,* Briggs-Lawrence County Public Library, Ironton OH. 614-532-1124

Miller, Floyd W, *Dir,* Shepherd College, Ruth Scarborough Library, Shepherdstown WV. 304-876-6775

Miller, Frances, *Librn,* Miracle Valley Regional Library (Saint Joseph Public), Moundsville WV. 304-845-6911

Miller, Frances, *Circ,* Albert A Wells Memorial Library, Tippecanoe County Contractual Library, Lafayette IN. 317-423-2602

Miller, Frances Ashton, *Librn,* New York State Department of Motor Vehicles, Research Library, Albany NY. 518-474-0684, 474-0685

Miller, G, *Librn,* Fisheries & Oceans Canada, Pacific Biological Station Library, Nanaimo BC. 604-758-1015

Miller, Geoffrey, *Librn,* Richmond Public Library (West Side Branch), Richmond CA. 415-232-7169

Miller, George, *Librn,* Canadian Wildlife Service, Department of Environment Library, Edmonton AB. 403-425-5891

Miller, Gleda, *Librn,* Carrier Mills Public Library, Carrier Mills IL. 618-994-2011

Miller, Glenn, *Librn,* Chicago Institute for Psychoanalysis, McLean Library, Chicago IL. 312-726-6300, Ext 38, 60 & 63

Miller, Glenn, *Librn,* Institute for Psychoanalysis, McLean Library, Chicago IL. 312-726-6300, Ext 63 & 38

Miller, Glenn, *Dir,* Orlando Public Library, Orlando FL. 305-425-4694

Miller, Gordon, *Info Servs,* James Madison University, Madison Memorial Library, Harrisonburg VA. 703-433-6150

Miller, Gordon, *Librn,* Parkersburg & Wood County Public Library (South Parkersburg), Parkersburg WV. 304-485-6564428-7041

Miller, Gwendolyn L, *Librn,* Timken Mercy Medical Center (Medical Library), Canton OH. 216-489-1462

Miller, Hannelore, *Cat,* University of South Alabama (University Library), Mobile AL. 205-460-7021

Miller, Heather S, *Dir,* Massachusetts Horticultural Society Library, Boston MA. 617-536-9280

Miller, Helen, *W Phila Area Adminr,* Free Library of Philadelphia, Philadelphia PA. 215-686-5322

Miller, Helen, *Librn,* George C Wallace State Technical Junior College, Phillip J Hamm Library, Dothan AL. 205-983-3521

Miller, Helen, *Librn,* Kanawha County Public Library (Saint Albans Branch), Saint Albans WV. 304-722-4244

Miller, Helen, *Circ & Ref,* Letourneau College, Margaret Estes Library, Longview TX. 214-753-0231, Ext 230

Miller, Helen, *Dir,* Mineral County Public Library, Mira-Luning Community, Hawthorne NV. 702-945-2778

Miller, Helen C, *Librn,* Roachdale-Franklin Township Public Library, Roachdale IN. 317-596-5052

Miller, Helen M, *Dir,* Idaho State Library, Boise ID. 208-334-2150

Miller, Helen P, *Dir,* Dixon Public Library, Dixon IL. 815-284-7261

Miller, Helena, *Librn,* Elbert County Library, Kiowa CO. 303-621-2041

Miller, Hope, *Librn,* Martinsburg-Berkeley County Public Library (Naylor Memorial), Hedgesville WV. 304-754-3949

Miller, Hope, *Librn,* Martinsburg-Berkeley County Public Library (North Berkeley), Marlowe WV. 304-267-8933

Miller, Howard E, *Dir,* Westwood Public Library, Westwood MA. 617-326-7562

Miller, Inabeth, *Librn,* Harvard University Library (Gutman Library-Research Center), Cambridge MA. 617-495-4225

Miller, Irene, *Librn,* Grove City Public Library (Harrisburg Branch), Harrisburg OH. 614-877-4065

Miller, Irene, *Librn,* Warnaco Inc, Market Research Library, Bridgeport CT. 203-579-8272

Miller, Irene K, *Librn,* Fairfield Historical Society Library, Fairfield CT. 203-259-1598

Miller, J G K, *Exec Dir,* Pittsburgh Council on Higher Education, (PCHE), PA. 412-683-7905

Miller, Jackie, *Ch,* Bellevue Public Library System, Bellevue NE. 402-291-8000

Miller, Jacqueline, *ILL,* Earlham College, Lilly Library, Richmond IN. 317-962-6561, Ext 360

Miller, Jacqueline E, *Dir,* Yonkers Public Library, Yonkers NY. 914-337-1500

Miller, James P, *Librn,* Somerset Community College Library, Somerset KY. 606-678-8174, Ext 238

Miller, Jane, *Dir, ILL & Acq,* Freed-Hardeman College, Loden-Daniel Library, Henderson TN. 901-989-4611, Ext 133

Miller, Jane, *Per,* University of Tennessee at Martin, Paul Meek Library, Martin TN. 901-587-7060

Miller, Jane E, *Librn,* Walton-De Funiak Library, Walton County Public Library, De Funiak Springs FL. 904-892-3624

Miller, Janet, *Librn,* Arizona State School for the Deaf & Blind Library, Tucson AZ. 602-882-5723

Miller, Janet, *Librn,* Copley Hospital, Inc, Information Center, Morrisville VT. 802-888-4231, Ext 213

Miller, Janet, *Circ,* North Dakota State University Library, Fargo ND. 701-237-8876

Miller, Janette, *Bkmobile Coordr,* Lyon County Public Library, Eddyville KY. 502-388-7720

Miller, Jean, *Librn & On-Line Servs,* Beckman Instruments, Inc, Research Library, Fullerton CA. 714-871-4848, Ext 8958

Miller, Jean, *Acq,* Franklin Library, Ray Memorial Library, Franklin MA. 617-528-0371

Miller, Jean, *ILL,* Linn-Benton Community College, Learning Resource Center, Albany OR. 503-928-2361, Ext 330

Miller, Jean, *Art,* University of Hartford, Mortensen Library, West Hartford CT. 203-243-4265

Miller, Jean K, *Dir,* University of Texas Health Science Center at Dallas Library, Dallas TX. 214-688-3368

Miller, Jean L, *Librn,* Haston Free Public Library, North Brookfield MA. 617-867-7978

Miller, Jeannine, *Dir,* First Baptist Church Media Center, Roswell NM. 505-623-2640

Miller, Jerome K, *Asst Prof,* University of Illinois, Graduate School of Library Science, IL. 217-333-3280

Miller, Jewel, *Asst Librn,* University of South Dakota (McKusick Law Library), Vermillion SD. 605-677-5259

Miller, JoAnn, *Librn,* New Orleans Public Library (East New Orleans Regional), New Orleans LA. 504-242-0709

Miller, Joanne, *Acq,* Lethbridge Community College, Buchanan Resource Centre, Lethbridge AB. 403-327-2141, Ext 350

Miller, John, *Librn,* New York Public Library (American History), New York NY. 212-790-6203

Miller, John, *Librn,* Public Library of Cincinnati & Hamilton County (Bookmobile), Cincinnati OH. 513-369-6060

Miller, Joseph, *Librn,* Yale University Library (Forestry & Environmental Studies), New Haven CT. 203-436-0577

Miller, Judith, *Librn,* Minnesota Valley Regional Library (Saint Peter), Mankato MN. 507-931-1228

Miller, Judith, *Ser,* Valparaiso University, Henry F Moellering Memorial Library, Valparaiso IN. 219-464-5364

Miller, Julia, *Asst Librn,* International Foundation of Employee Benefit Plans, Information Center, Brookfield WI. 414-786-6700

Miller, Julia E, *Librn,* Museum of Transportation Library, Boston MA. 617-421-6633

Miller, K, *Nursing,* State University of New York at Buffalo (Health Sciences), Buffalo NY. 716-831-5465

Miller, K, *Nursing,* State University of New York at Buffalo, University Libraries, Buffalo NY. 716-636-2965

Miller, Karen, *Librn,* Carver Public Library, Carver MA. 617-866-4038

Miller, Karen, *ILL,* State University of New York at Buffalo (Health Sciences), Buffalo NY. 716-831-5465

Miller, Karen K, *Librn,* Cleveland Institute of Music Library, Cleveland OH. 216-791-5165

Miller, Kathryn, *Librn,* Pamunkey Regional Library (Ashland Branch), Ashland VA. 804-798-4072

Miller, Kay, *Pub Servs,* University of Southern Mississippi, Cook Memorial Library, Hattiesburg MS. 601-266-7301

Miller, Kent, *Ser,* University of Kansas Libraries, Watson Memorial Library, Lawrence KS. 913-864-3601

Miller, Larry, *Ref,* Moraine Valley Community College, Learning Resources Center, Palos Hills IL. 312-974-4300, Ext 222

Miller, Laura, *Actg Librn,* College for Human Services Library, Oakland CA. 415-451-6203

Miller, Laurence, *Dir,* East Texas State University, James Gilliam Gee Library, Commerce TX. 214-886-5717

Miller, Laurence, *Slavic & East European,* University of Illinois Library at Urbana-Champaign, Urbana IL. 217-333-0790

Miller, LaVonne, *Librn,* Indiana Vocational Technical College Southwest, Learning Resource Center, Evansville IN. 812-426-2865, Ext 26

Miller, Lewis R, *Librn,* Mars Hill College Memorial Library, Mars Hill NC. 704-689-1244

Miller, Lidie, *Librn,* United Presbyterian Church Program Agency, Ghost Ranch Library, Abiquiu NM. 505-685-4333, Ext 134

Miller, Lillie, *Ref,* Arlington Public Library, Arlington TX. 817-275-2763, 265-3311, Ext 347

Miller, Linda, *Consult,* Colorado State Library - Services for the Blind & Physically Handicapped, Denver CO. 303-839-2081

Miller, Linda, *Librn,* Manistee County Library (Wellston Branch), Wellston MI. 616-848-2491

Miller, Lois, *Librn,* Brockway Public Library, Glenn Mengle Memorial Library, Brockway PA. 814-265-8245

Miller, Lydia, *Librn,* Huntingburg Public Library, Huntingburg IN. 812-683-2052

Miller, Lynn, *Librn,* Herman Miller Inc, Resource Center, Zeeland MI. 616-772-3629

Miller, M Charles, *Dir,* Binghamton Public Library, Binghamton NY. 607-723-6457

Miller, M J, *Libr Supvr,* Bell Telephone Laboratories (Bell Telephone Laboratories Technical Library), Whippany NJ. 386-2604 (Supvr); 386-5769 (Tech Rpts)

Miller, Mande S, *Librn,* Athens Public Library, Athens AL. 205-232-1233

Miller, Marcia M, *Instr,* Alabama State University, Library Educational Media Program, AL. 205-832-6072, Ext 502

Miller, Marcy, *Librn,* Fowler Public Library, Fowler KS. 316-646-5772

Miller, Margaret, *Ch,* Centre County Library & Historical Museum, Bellefonte PA. 814-355-3131

Miller, Margaret A, *Librn,* Arthur D Little Inc (Life Sciences Library), Cambridge MA. 617-864-5770, Ext 2030

Miller, Margaret E, *Asst Librn,* General Atomic Company Library, La Jolla CA. 714-455-3322

Miller, Margaret R, *Librn,* Eastern State Hospital, Medical Library, Williamsburg VA. 804-253-5457, 253-5387

Miller, Margery, *Librn,* Prince George's County Memorial Library System (Public Documents Reference Library), Upper Malboro MD. 301-952-3904

Miller, Marilyn, *Cat,* Connecticut State Library, Hartford CT. 203-566-4301

Miller, Marilyn, *AV,* Franklin College Library, Franklin IN. 317-736-8441, Ext 257

Miller, Marilyn, *Ref & Bibliog Instr,* Louisiana State University School of Medicine in Shreveport, Medical Library, Shreveport LA. 318-226-3442

Miller, Marilyn, *Asst Librn,* Montgomery Memorial Library, Jewell IA. 515-827-5112

Miller, Marilyn, *Assoc Prof,* University of North Carolina at Chapel Hill, School of Library Science, NC. 919-933-8366

Miller, Marjorie, *Art ref,* Fashion Institute of Technology, Library-Media Services Dept, New York NY. 212-760-7695

Miller, Marjorie M, *Rare Bks & Spec Coll,* Augustana College, Denkman Memorial Library, Rock Island IL. 309-794-7266

Miller, Martha, *Librn,* La Harpe Carnegie Public Library, La Harpe IL. 217-659-7729

Miller, Martin, *Soc Sci,* Miami University, Edgar W King Library, Oxford OH. 513-529-2944

Miller, Mary, *Librn,* Duluth Public Library (Lester Park), Duluth MN. 218-525-3746

Miller, Mary, *Asst Librn,* Knightstown Public Library, Knightstown IN. 317-345-5095

Miller, Mary B, *Asst Librn,* Corydon Public Library, Corydon IN. 812-738-4110

Miller, Mary B, *Doc,* University of Pittsburgh, Hillman Library, Pittsburgh PA. 412-624-4400

Miller, Mary Celine, *Dir, Learning Resources,* Robert Morris College Library, Coraopolis PA. 412-264-9300

Miller, Mary Celine, *Dir,* Robert Morris College Library, Pittsburgh PA. 412-227-6839

Miller, Mary Leon, *Librn,* Wisconsin Regional Library for the Blind & Physically Handicapped, Milwaukee WI. 414-278-3045

Miller, Mary M, *Librn,* Public Library of Steubenville & Jefferson County (Tiltonsville Branch), Tiltonsville OH. 614-282-9782

Miller, Mary M, *Librn,* Springfield Art Association, Springfield Art Center Library, Springfield OH. 513-325-4673

Miller, Mary R, *Librn,* New Britain Public Library (Thomas Jefferson), New Britain CT. 203-225-4700

Miller, Merrill, *Librn,* Nova University Libraries (George W English Library), Fort Lauderdale FL. 305-475-8300, Ext 245, 248

Miller, Michael, *AV,* Mid-Hudson Library System, Poughkeepsie NY. 914-471-6060

Miller, Michael S, *Dir,* Maryland State Law Library, Annapolis MD. 301-269-3395

Miller, Mildred V, *Asst Dir,* Rockingham Public Library, Harrisonburg VA. 703-434-4475

Miller, Miriam, *Librn,* Rockdale Temple, Sidney G Rose Library, Cincinnati OH. 513-891-9900

Miller, Mrs Clayton, *Librn,* Rockford Public Library, Rockford AL. 205-377-4911

Miller, Mrs J H, *Librn,* White County Public Library (Bald Knob), Searcy AR. 501-724-5452

Miller, Mrs James L, *Librn,* Institutes of Religion & Health Library, New York NY. 212-725-7842

Miller, Mrs Lou, *Librn,* Arizona Division of Behavioral Health Services (Patient's Library), Phoenix AZ. 602-244-1331

Miller, Mrs Namiko, *Librn,* Southwest Georgia Regional Library (Seminole County), Donalsonville GA. 912-246-3887, 3894, 3895

Miller, Mrs Paul H, *Librn,* Saint John's Evangelical United Church of Christ Library, Collinsville IL. 618-344-2740

Miller, Mrs Robert, *Librn,* Primitive Methodist of Lonsdale Library, Cumberland RI. 401-722-7365

Miller, Mrs Ronald E, *Librn,* Williamson Free Public Library, Williamson NY. 315-589-2048

Miller, Nancy, *Dir,* United States Department of the Interior, Vicksburg National Military Park Library, Vicksburg MS. 601-636-0583

Miller, Norma, *Ad,* Lexington Public Library, Lexington KY. 606-252-8871

Miller, Opal, *Librn,* Lenawee County Library (Ridgeway Branch), Ridgeway MI. 517-263-1011

Miller, Opal, *Librn,* Live Oak County Library, George West TX. 512-449-1124

Miller, Orma, *Librn,* Babbitt Public Library, Babbitt MN. 218-827-3345

Miller, Oscar J, *Dir,* University of Colorado at Boulder (Law Library), Boulder CO. 303-492-7534

Miller, Pam, *Asst Librn,* Stone, Marraccini & Patterson Library, San Francisco CA. 415-775-7300

Miller, Patricia, *Dir,* J Herman Bosler Memorial Library, Bosler Free Library, Carlisle PA. 717-243-4642

Miller, Paul F, *Dir,* Verona Free Public Library, Verona NJ. 201-239-0050

Miller, Pauline, *Librn,* Syracuse University Libraries (Engineering & Life Sciences), Syracuse NY. 315-423-2834

Miller, Pauline N, *Sci & Tech,* Syracuse University Libraries, Ernest S Bird Library, Syracuse NY. 315-423-2575

Miller, Pearl, *Dir,* Conrad Public Library, Conrad IA. 515-366-2583

Miller, Peggy, *Tech Serv & Cat,* Ohio Dominican College Library, Columbus OH. 614-253-2741, Ext 258, 210&219

Miller, Philip E, *Librn,* Hebrew Union College-Jewish Institute of Religion, The Klau Library, New York NY. 212-674-5300

Miller, R B, *Supervisor,* Esso Resources Canada Ltd (Technical Information Services), Calgary AB. 403-267-1494

Miller, Rae, *Librn,* Meadows Valley Community Library, New Meadows ID. 208-347-2458

Miller, Richard, *ILL, Ref & On-Line Servs,* Carleton College Library, Northfield MN. 507-645-4431

Miller, Richard, *Coordr Spec Servs,* Missouri State Library, Jefferson City MO. 314-751-4214

Miller, Richard A, *Mat Proc Depts: Acq,* Dallas Public Library, Dallas TX. 214-748-9071

Miller, Richard A, *Librn,* Handley Library, Winchester VA. 703-662-9041

Miller, Richard E, *Librn,* Oshkosh Public Library, Oshkosh WI. 414-424-0473

Miller, Richard E, *Dir,* Winnefox Library System, Oshkosh WI. 414-424-0486

Miller, Robert A, *Librn,* Santa Barbara Historical Society Library, Santa Barbara CA. 805-966-1601

Miller, Robert C, *Dir,* University of Notre Dame Library, Notre Dame IN. 219-283-7317

Miller, Roger C, *Coordr,* Associated College Libraries of Central Pennsylvania, PA. 717-766-2511, Ext 380

Miller, Roger C, *Dir & Bibliog Instr,* Messiah College, Murray Learning Resources Center, Grantham PA. 717-766-2511, Ext 380

Miller, Roger M, *Librn,* United States Army (Fort Carson Recreation Div Libraries), Fort Carson CO. 303-579-2350, 579-2842

Miller, Ron, *Dir,* World Archaeological Society, Information Center, Hollister MO. 417-334-2377

Miller, Ronald, *Dir,* California Library Authority for Systems & Services, (CLASS), CA. 408-289-1756

Miller, Rosalind, *Assoc Prof,* Georgia State University, Library-Media Program, GA. 404-658-2458

Miller, Rosalyn, *Ad,* Jericho Public Library, Jericho NY. 516-935-6790

Miller, Rose M, *Librn,* Eye Research Institute of Retina Foundation, Research Library, Boston MA. 617-742-3140

Miller, Ross E, *Head, Lending Dept,* Hartford Public Library, Hartford CT. 203-525-9121

Miller, Ruby B, *Asst Dir Tech Serv,* Trinity University Library, San Antonio TX. 512-736-8121

Miller, Rudolph P, *Asst Prof,* Ohio University, Educational Media Program, OH. 614-594-5404

Miller, Rush G, *Asst Prof,* Delta State University, Dept of Media & Library Science, MS. 601-843-8638

Miller, Rush G, *Dir,* Delta State University, W B Roberts Library, Cleveland MS. 601-843-2483

Miller, Rush G, *Chmn,* Mississippi Delta Library Council, MS. 601-843-2483

Miller, Russell E, *Univ Archivist,* Tufts University, Nils Yngve Wessell Library, Medford MA. 617-628-5000, Ext 235

Miller, Ruth, *Asst Dir,* Greenwood Lake Public Library, Greenwood Lake NY. 914-477-8377

Miller, Ruth, *Acq,* Hartwick College Library, Oneonta NY. 607-432-4200, Ext 324

Miller, Ruth, *Acq,* University of Evansville, Clifford Memorial Library & Learning Resources, Evansville IN. 812-479-2462

Miller, Ruth C, *Dir & Acq,* Downey City Library, Downey CA. 213-923-3256

Miller, Sara, *Ch,* White Plains Public Library, White Plains NY. 914-682-4400

Miller, Sarah J, *Asst Prof,* Rutgers-The State University of New Jersey, Graduate School of Library & Information Studies, NJ. 201-932-7500

Miller, Scott E, *Reader Serv,* Bloomsburg State College, Harvey A Andruss Library, Bloomsburg PA. 717-389-2716

Miller, Sharon, *Librn,* Gloucester Public Library (Ogilvie Road), Ottawa ON. 613-749-5321

Miller, Sheila, *Asst Librn,* Wayne Public Library (Bloomdale Branch), Bloomdale OH. 419-454-3021

Miller, Shelby, *ILL,* University of Hartford, Mortensen Library, West Hartford CT. 203-243-4265

Miller, Sister Carlos Maria, *Ref,* Mount Aloysius Junior College Library, Cresson PA. 814-886-4131, Ext 70

Miller, Sister Joy, *Librn,* Saint John's Provincial Seminary Library, Plymouth MI. 313-453-6200, Ext 37

Miller, Sister Marilyn, *ILL,* Fontbonne College Library, Saint Louis MO. 314-862-3456, Ext 352

Miller, Sister Mary Elsie, *Chairperson,* Marywood College, Dept of Librarianship, PA. 717-342-6521

Miller, Stephen, *Econ,* Oregon State University, William Jasper Kerr Library, Corvallis OR. 503-754-3411

Miller, Stephen R, *Asst Dir,* Wellesley Free Library, Subregional Headquarters for Eastern Massachusetts Regional Library System, Wellesley MA. 617-235-1610

Miller, Stuart, *Info Specialist,* International Association of Assessing Officers Library, Chicago IL. 312-947-2050

Miller, Sue, *Librn,* Prince George's County Memorial Library System (District Heights Branch), District Heights MD. 301-736-7702

Miller, Sue N, *On-Line Servs,* United Virginia Bankshares Library, Richmond VA. 804-782-7452

Miller, Susan, *AV,* Huntsville-Madison County Public Library, Huntsville AL. 205-536-0021

Miller, Susan, *Asst Librn & Acq,* Lebanon Community Library, H C Grumbine Free Public Library, Lebanon PA. 717-273-7624

Miller, Susan, *Asst Dir,* Lebanon County Library System, Lebanon PA. 717-273-7624

Miller, Susan, *Automation,* Ohio State University Libraries (William Oxley Thompson Memorial Library), Columbus OH. 614-422-6151

Miller, Suzanne, *Actg Librn,* University of La Verne (College of Law Library), La Verne CA. 714-593-7184

Miller, Tamara, *WLC,* University of Wisconsin-Madison, Memorial Library, Madison WI. 608-262-3521

Miller, Tamara, *Coordr,* Wisconsin Library Consortium, (WLC), WI. 608-263-5051

Miller, Terry, *Librn,* Encyclopaedia Britannica, Editorial Library, Chicago IL. 312-321-7221

Miller, Terry, *Tech Serv,* Western Wyoming Community College, Library Learning Resources Center, Rock Springs WY. 307-382-2121, Ext 154

Miller, Thomas E, *Assoc Prof,* Auburn University, Dept of Educational Media, AL. 205-826-4529

Miller, Toby, *Interlibr Coop Consult,* State Library Commission of Iowa, Des Moines IA. 515-281-4102

Miller, Tracy, *Librn,* University of Colorado at Boulder (Business Library), Boulder CO. 303-492-8367

Miller, Virginia, *On-Line Servs,* Medical University of South Carolina Library, Charleston SC. 803-792-2374

Miller, Virginia, *ILL,* Albert A Wells Memorial Library, Tippecanoe County Contractual Library, Lafayette IN. 317-423-2602

Miller, Virginia B, *Cat,* Oskaloosa Public Library, Oskaloosa IA. 515-673-6214

Miller, Wellington Everett, *Librn,* Library of Vehicles, Garden Grove CA. 714-636-9517

Miller, Wharton H, *Ref,* Cuyahoga Community College (Western Campus Library), Parma OH. 216-845-4000, Ext 278

Miller, William B, *Mgr,* United Presbyterian Church in the United States of America, Presbyterian Historical Society Library, Philadelphia PA. 215-627-1852

Miller, William C, *Librn,* Nazarene Theological Seminary, Broadhurst Library, Kansas City MO. 816-333-6254, Ext 29

Miller, Wilma, *Librn,* Indianapolis-Marion County Public Library (Flanner House), Indianapolis IN. 317-635-5662

Miller, Zelpha, *Cat,* Noblesville Public Library, Noblesville IN. 317-773-1384

Miller, Jr, Arthur H, *Dir,* Lake Forest College, Donnelley Library, Lake Forest IL. 312-234-3100, Ext 405

Miller, Jr, Arthur H, *Librn,* Lake Forest College (Freeman Science), Lake Forest IL. 312-234-3100, Ext 340

Miller, Jr, Edwin F, *Ad,* Binghamton Public Library, Binghamton NY. 607-723-6457

Miller, Jr, Lester L, *Supv Librn,* United States Army (Morris Swett Library), Fort Sill OK. 405-351-4525, 351-4477

Miller, Jr, Roy D, *Ad,* Brooklyn Public Library, Brooklyn NY. 212-780-7712

Millet, Grace, *Dir,* Dumont Public Library, Dixon Homestead Library, Dumont NJ. 201-384-2030

Millhauser, Frances, *Virginiana,* Arlington County Department of Libraries, Arlington Public Library, Arlington VA. 703-527-4777

Millhouse, Vera, *Dir,* Galena Public Library, Galena IL. 815-777-0200

Millican, Alta, *Dean,* Jacksonville State University, College of Library Science, Communications & Instructional Media, AL. 205-435-6390

Millican, Alta, *Dean,* Jacksonville State University Library, Jacksonville AL. 205-435-9820, Ext 213, 214

Millican, Beatrice, *Spec Coll,* Carnegie Library, Rome GA. 404-291-7568

Millican, Beatrice, *Genealogy & Local Hist,* Carnegie Library, Rome GA. 404-291-7568

Millich, Eugene, *Ref,* University of Wisconsin-La Crosse, Murphy Library, La Crosse WI. 608-785-8505

Milligan, Edna H, *Librn,* Forbes Health System Libraries (Columbia Health Center Library), Pittsburgh PA. 412-247-2451

Milligan, Patricia M, *Cat,* University of Maine School of Law, Donald L Garbrecht Library, Portland ME. 207-780-4350

Milligan, Stuart, *Micro Spec & Circ,* University of Rochester (Sibley Music Library), Rochester NY. 716-275-3018

Millikan, Donna, *ILL,* Noblesville Public Library, Noblesville IN. 317-773-1384

Milliken, Callie Faye, *Assoc Dir,* Abilene Christian University, Margarett & Herman Brown Library, Abilene TX. 915-677-1911, Ext 2344

Milliken, Ruth L, *Dir,* Cocoa Beach Public Library, Cocoa Beach FL. 305-783-7350

Milliken, Stephen, *Librn,* Florida State Department of Criminal Law Enforcement (Crime Laboratory Bureau Library), Tallahassee FL. 904-487-2500

Milling, Chapman J, *Art, Hist,* Sumter County Library, Sumter SC. 803-773-7273

Milling, Jr, Chapman J, *Dir, Commun Servs & Spec Coll,* Sumter County Library, Sumter SC. 803-773-7273

Milliron, Annette M, *Dir,* Basalt Regional Library, Basalt CO. 303-927-4311

Millis, Marilyn, *Librn,* Contra Costa County Library (Moraga Branch), Moraga CA. 415-376-6852

Millman-Wilson, Doreen, *Lectr,* Concordia University, Library Studies Program, PQ. 514-482-0320, Ext 324

Mills, Ann, *Media,* Danville Public Library, Danville IL. 217-446-7420

Mills, Annie, *Doc,* University of Mississippi Library, University MS. 601-232-7091

Mills, Beth, *Reader Serv,* New Rochelle Public Library, New Rochelle NY. 914-632-7878

Mills, Cecil, *Librn,* Childress Public Library, Childress TX. 817-937-8421

Mills, Cynthia, *ILL,* Falmouth Public Library, Subregional Headquarters for Eastern Massachusetts Regional System, Falmouth MA. 617-548-0280

Mills, Don, *Chief Librn,* West Vancouver Memorial Library, West Vancouver BC. 604-926-3291

Mills, Dorothy J M, *Dir,* Jericho Public Library, Jericho NY. 516-935-6790

Mills, Douglas, *Tech Serv,* University of Montana, Maureen & Mike Mansfield Library, Missoula MT. 406-243-6800

Mills, Elsie, *Librn,* Willis Irving Lewis Memorial Library, Ulysses KS. 814-848-7226

Mills, Emilie, *Spec Coll,* University of North Carolina at Greensboro, Walter Clinton Jackson Library, Greensboro NC. 919-379-5880

Mills, Floyd Ray, *Librn,* Hartford Public Library, Hartford IL. 618-254-9394

Mills, Gladys A, *Librn,* Education Commission of the States, Resource Center, Denver CO. 303-861-4917

Mills, Heather, *Ad,* Cote Saint-Luc Public Library, Cote Saint-Luc PQ. 514-481-5676

Mills, Helen, *Librn,* Hussey Memorial Library, Zionsville IN. 317-873-3149

Mills, Jamie S, *Librn,* Mississippi University for Women (Library Science), Columbus MS. 601-328-9100

Mills, Jeanne M, *Curator,* Pilgrim Society, Pilgrim Hall Library, Plymouth MA. 617-746-1620

Mills, Jesse C, *Chief Librn,* Tennessee Valley Authority (Technical Library Central Staff), Knoxville TN. 615-632-3466

Mills, Josephine A, *Assoc Prof,* State University of New York, College of Arts & Science, School of Library & Information Science, NY. 716-245-5322

Mills, Joyce W, *Asst Prof,* Atlanta University, School of Library & Information Studies, GA. 404-681-0251, Ext 312

Mills, Lila, *Librn,* Booz, Allen & Hamilton Inc Library, Chicago IL. 312-346-1900, Ext 212 & 213

Mills, Luticia, *Commun Servs,* John McIntire Public Library Public Library, Zanesville OH. 614-453-0391

Mills, Mary Alice, *Dir,* Center for Disease Control Library, Atlanta GA. 404-329-3396

Mills, Maxine, *Bkmobile Librn,* Knox County Public Library, Barbourville KY. 606-546-5339

Mills, Melanie, *Instr,* Highline Community College Library, Library Technician Program, WA. 206-878-3710, Ext 233

Mills, Norene, *Librn,* Finch Memorial Library, Arnold NE. 308-848-2219

Mills, Olga A, *Librn,* Ohio University, Belmont County Campus Library, Saint Clairsville OH. 614-695-1720, Ext 30

Mills, Opal, *Librn,* Moundville Public Library, Moundville AL. 205-371-2283

Mills, Robert E, *Chmn,* Central Michigan University, Dept of Library Science, MI. 517-774-3841

Mills, Robin K, *Dir,* University of South Carolina (Coleman Karesh Law Libr), Columbia SC. 803-777-5942

Mills, Susan, *Commun Servs,* Ector County Library, Odessa TX. 915-332-0633

Mills, Sylvia, *Dir,* Stuttgart Public Library, Stuttgart AR. 501-673-1966

Mills, Thelma, *Librn,* Ozark Regional Library (Steelville Branch), Steelville MO. 314-775-2338

Mills, Theresa C, *Inst Libr Consult,* South Carolina State Library, Columbia SC. 803-758-3181

Mills, Tom, *Librn,* Frederick News-Post Library, Frederick MD. 301-662-1177

Mills, Verla, *Cat,* Canon City Public Library, Canon City CO. 303-275-3669

Mills, Jr, William W, *Librn,* United States Department of Defense, Defense Communications Agency, Engineering Center Technical Library, Reston VA. 703-545-6700

Millsap, Gina, *YA,* Daniel Boone Regional Library, Columbia MO. 314-443-3161

Millsap, Larry, *Cat,* University of California, University Library, Santa Cruz CA. 408-429-2076

Millson-Martula, C, *Social Sciences,* Saint Xavier College, Byrne Memorial Library, Chicago IL. 312-779-3300, Ext 217

Millson-Martula, Christopher, *Dir,* Saint Xavier College, Byrne Memorial Library, Chicago IL. 312-779-3300, Ext 217

Millsun, Mrs D, *Librn,* Bangor, Wicklow, McClure & Monteagle Union Public Library, Maynooth ON. 613-338-2811

Millward, Arthur, *Librn,* University of Manitoba Libraries (Saint John's College), Winnipeg MB. 204-474-8542

Milne, Grace A, *Librn,* Scugog Public Library, Port Perry ON. 416-985-7686

Milner, Devin, *Ref,* University of San Diego, James S Copley Library, San Diego CA. 714-291-6480, Ext 4312, 4313, 4314

Milner, Gail, *Librn,* Public Library of Columbus & Franklin County (Shepard), Columbus OH. 614-222-7135

Milner, Leigh, *Librn,* Capital Times Library, Madison WI. 608-252-6412

Milner, Linda, *Exten Servs,* Mid-Mississippi Regional Library System, Kosciusko MS. 601-289-5141, 289-5146

Milord, Shirley, *Acting Coordr Spec Servs,* New York Public Library (The Branch Libraries), New York NY. 212-790-6262

Miloserny, Ginger, *Asst Librn,* Oak Lawn Public Library, Oak Lawn IL. 312-422-4990

Milot, Richard, *In Charge,* La Societe d'histoire Des Cantons De L'est Bibliotheque, Eastern Townships Historical Society Library, Sherbrooke PQ. 819-562-0616

Milota, Marcella, *Actg Dir,* John Carroll University, Grasselli Library, University Heights OH. 491-4233 & 491-4231

Milsaps, David, *Asst Dir,* Fort Loudoun Regional Library Center, Athens TN. 615-745-5194

Milstead, Agnes M, *Dept Head,* University of Wyoming, Library Media Program, WY. 307-766-2349

Milstead, Lois, *Librn,* Pine Forest Regional Library (State Line Public), State Line MS. 601-788-6539

Milton, Ardyce A, *Asst Librn,* Eaton Corp, Cutler-Hammer Library, Milwaukee WI. 414-442-7800, Ext 3679

Milton, Eleanor Silvis, *Asst Librn,* University of Pittsburgh at Greensburg, Powers Hall Library, Greensburg PA. 412-837-7040, Ext 133

Milton, Elsie, *Dir,* Clairton Public Library, Clairton PA. 412-233-7966

Mimkin, Judith, *Librn,* University of Alaska, Fairbanks (Geophysical Institute), Fairbanks AK. 907-479-7503

Mimms, Francenia, *Tech Serv,* Indian River Community College, Charles S Miley Learning Resources Center, Fort Pierce FL. 305-464-2000, Ext 347

Mims, Dorothy H, *Rare Bks & Spec Coll,* Medical College of Georgia Library, Augusta GA. 404-828-3441

Mims, Gloria, *Spec Coll,* Atlanta University, Trevor Arnett Library, Atlanta GA. 404-681-0251, Ext 225

Mims, Marie, *Ref,* Charleston County Library, Charleston SC. 803-723-1645

Mims, Nancy C, *Librn,* Aiken-Bamberg-Barnwell-Edgefield Regional Library (Edgefield County), Edgefield SC. 803-637-6347

Minadakis, Nicholas J, *Dir,* Chelsea Public Library, Chelsea MA. 617-884-2335

Minami, Atsumi, *Oriental Med,* University of California Library, San Francisco CA. 415-666-2334

Minar, Sister Kathryn, *Librn & AV,* Huron College, Ella McIntire Library, Huron SD. 605-352-8721, Ext 231

Mincey, Edith, *Librn,* Horry County Memorial Library (Loris Branch), Loris SC. 803-756-8101

Minchen, Norma A, *Librn-Secy,* Conoco Inc (Continental Carbon Technical Library), Houston TX. 713-965-5226

Minckler, Irene, *Librn,* Sinclairville Free Library, Sinclairville NY. 716-962-5885

Minckler, Jane, *Librn,* Ethicon, Inc, Scientific Information Services, Somerville NJ. 201-524-3402

Minder, Thomas, *Assoc Prof,* University of Alabama, Graduate School of Library Service, AL. 205-348-4610

Minear, Mrs Jay, *Librn,* Belle Plaine City Library, Belle Plaine KS. 316-488-3431

Miner, Afton, *Educ,* Brigham Young University, Harold B Lee Library, Provo UT. 801-378-2905

Miner, Elizabeth D, *Chief Librn,* Arizona Daily Star Library, Tucson AZ. 602-294-4433, Ext 345

Miner, M Gabrielle, *Reader Serv & Ref,* Central State University, Hallie Q Brown Memorial Library, Wilberforce OH. 513-376-7212

Minerva, Jane, *Dir,* Cutchogue Free Library, Cutchogue NY. 516-734-6360

Mines, Denise, *Librn,* Alston, Miller & Gaines, Law Library, Atlanta GA. 404-586-1500, Ext 1508, 1509

Mines, Florence, *Librn,* Sweetwater County Library (Farson Branch), Farson WY. 307-875-3615

Minesinger, Joan, *Librn,* Press-Enterprise Company Library, Riverside CA. 714-684-1200, Ext 301, 396

Minett, E E, *Dir, Libr Automation Systs,* University of Toronto Libraries (University Library), Toronto ON. 416-978-2294

Minett, E E, *Dir,* University of Toronto Library Automation Systems, (UTLAS), ON. 416-978-7171

Minges, James, *Coordr,* Northwest Missouri Library Network, MO. 816-364-3386

Minick, Eleanor, *Administrator,* York County Library System, York PA. 717-846-6017

Minick, Martha J, *Asst Dir & Acq,* Monessen Public Library, Monessen PA. 412-684-4750

Minik, Ruth, *Libr Mgr,* International Business Machines Corp (General Products Division Library), San Jose CA. 408-256-2908

Minimmi, Linda, *Chief Librn,* Medical Library of Mecklenburg County, Learning Resource Center of Charlotte AHEC, Charlotte NC. 704-373-3129

Miniter, John J, *Assoc Prof,* Texas Woman's University, School of Library Science, TX. 817-387-2418 & 566-1455

Mink, Elaine, *Senior Serv,* Monroe County Library System, Monroe MI. 313-241-5277

Mink, James V, *Spec Coll,* University of California Los Angeles Library, Los Angeles CA. 213-825-1201

Mink, Phyllis A, *Circ & Ref,* New River Community College, Learning Resource Center, Dublin VA. 703-674-4121, Ext 303

Minkel, Vera, *Acq,* Honeywell Information Systems Computer Operations Library, Phoenix AZ. 602-866-2639

Minks, Agnes, *Librn,* Wharton County Library (East Bernard Branch), East Bernard TX. 713-335-6142

Minn, Tae, *Govt Doc,* University of Hawaii at Hilo Libraries, Hilo HI. 808-961-9344

Minnerath, Gary R, *Dir,* Rehabilitative School Authority, State Farm Correctional Centers Library, State Farm VA. 804-784-3551, Ext 226

Minnerath, Janet, *Librn,* Alton Ochsner Medical Foundation Library, New Orleans LA. 504-837-3000, Ext 5801

Minnich, D W, *Dir,* Wead Library, Malone Central School District Public Library, Malone NY. 518-483-5251

Minnich, Imogene, *Librn,* United States Army (Research Library), Corpus Christi TX. 512-939-3324

Minnick, Edith, *Librn,* La Moille Clarion Library District, La Moille IL. 815-638-2356

Minnick, Eleanore, *Acq,* Clark Technical College, Learning Resource Center, Springfield OH. 513-325-0691, Ext 66

Minnick, Nelle F, *Asst Librn,* Fresno County Free Library, Fresno CA. 209-488-3191

Minnigh, Joel D, *Dir,* Wilkinsburg Public Library, Pittsburgh PA. 412-244-2940

Minnis, June, *Cat,* Saint Joseph Public Library, Saint Joseph MO. 816-232-7729, 232-7720

Minock, M, *Bibliog Instr,* Lansing Community College Library, Lansing MI. 517-373-9978

Minock, Mary, *Instr,* Lansing Community College, Library Media Technology Program, MI. 517-373-9978

Minogue, Eileen, *YA,* Northport Public Library, Northport NY. 516-261-6930

Minor, Carol, *Librn,* United Bank of Denver, Information Center-Library, Denver CO. 303-861-8811, Ext 2703

Minor, Charlotte, *Collection Development,* Embry-Riddle Aeronautical University, Learning Resource Center, Daytona Beach FL. 904-252-5561, Ext 360

Minor, Denise, *Librn,* Metcalf County Public Library, Edmonton KY. 502-432-4981

Minor, Donna, *Ch,* Minneola City Library, Minneola KS. 316-885-4749

Minor, Huey P, *Tech Serv,* Veterans Administration, General Library, Alexandria LA. 318-442-0251

Minor, John T, *Info Specialists,* Conoco Inc Research & Development Department, Technical Information Services, Ponca City OK. 405-767-4719

Minor, John T, *Asst Dir,* University of North Carolina at Greensboro, Walter Clinton Jackson Library, Greensboro NC. 919-379-5880

Minott, Laurel, *Librn,* Michigan Department of Mental Health, Lansing MI. 517-373-0408

Minster, Bernadette, *Bkmobile Coordr,* Waukegan Public Library, Waukegan IL. 312-623-2041

Mintel, Richard H, *Cat & Ref,* Trinity Lutheran Seminary Library, Columbus OH. 614-236-7116

Minter, Lyle W, *Librn,* United States Army (Intelligence & Security Command, Post Library), Warrenton VA. 703-347-6466

Minton, Ann, *Sci & Tech,* North Texas State University Library, Denton TX. 817-788-2411

Minton, Mary, *Cat,* Mill Valley Public Library, Mill Valley CA. 415-388-4245

Mintz, Graham, *Bkmobile Coordr,* Hopkins County-Madisonville Public Library, Madisonville KY. 502-825-2680

Mintz, Louis, *Chief,* New York Public Library (Stack Maintenance & Delivery), New York NY. 212-790-6262

Minudri, Regina U, *Dir,* Berkeley Public Library, Berkeley CA. 415-644-6095

Minzghor, Evelyn, *Librn,* Cass Lake Library, Cass Lake MN. 218-335-8865

Miracle, Laura J, *Librn,* Chicago Board of Trade Library, Chicago IL. 312-435-3552

Miraldi, Patricia, *Librn,* Burlington County Library (Pinelands Branch), Medford NJ. 609-654-6113

Miranda, Magda, *Ch,* University of Puerto Rico, Cayey University College Library, Cayey PR. 809-738-2161, Ext 221, 738-5651

Miras, Edwardo, *Librn,* Catholic University-Santa Maria, Aguadilla Branch Library, Aguadilla PR. 809-844-4150

Mire, Ann, *Acq,* Acadia Parish Library, Crowley LA. 318-788-1880

Mirell, Sandee, *Librn,* City Attorney Law Library, Los Angeles CA. 213-485-5400

Miriam, Mother, *In Charge,* Our Lady of the Rock Library, Shaw Island WA. 206-468-2321

Mirly, Joann, *Asst Dir,* Concordia Seminary Library, Ludwig E Fuerbringer Hall Library, Saint Louis MO. 314-721-5934, Ext 293

Miron, Leah Rae, *Librn,* Brazosport College Library, Lake Jackson TX. 713-265-6131, Ext 62

Mirsky, Phyllis, *Librn,* Temple Adath Israel, Ruben Library, Merion PA. 215-664-3241

Mirsky, Sonya Wohl, *Librn,* Rockefeller University Library, New York NY. 212-360-1000

Mirth, Karlo J, *Mgr,* Foster Wheeler Development Corp, Research Information Center & Library, Livingston NJ. 201-533-3663, 533-3670

Misch, Carol, *Ch,* Frankfort Community Public Library, Frankfort IN. 317-654-8746

Mischke, Peter, *Librn,* Illinois Department of Mental Health, Professional Library, Dixon IL. 815-288-5561

Misek, Florence, *Librn,* Marathon County Public Library (Spencer Branch), Spencer WI. 715-659-5423

Mishaga, Paula, *Cat & Ref,* Ledding Library of Milwaukie, Milwaukie Public Library, Milwaukie OR. 503-659-3911

Mishkin, Leah C, *Librn,* Hebrew Theological College, Saul Silber Memorial Library, Skokie IL. 312-267-9800

Mishkoff, Adina, *Librn,* Find-SVP Library, New York NY. 212-354-2424

Mishler, Mary, *ILL,* Washington County Free Library, Hagerstown MD. 301-739-3250

Mishler, Miriam, *Ch,* W E Walter Memorial Library, Bremen Public Library, Bremen IN. 219-546-2849

Mishra, Mary, *Librn,* Burnaby Municipal Library (Central Park), Burnaby BC. 604-438-3455

Miska, John P, *Coordr,* Agriculture Canada, Research Station Library, Lethbridge AB. 403-327-4561, Ext 222

Miskall, Ellen B, *Ser Bibliogr,* Northwestern University Library, Evanston IL. 312-492-7658

Miskin, Rose, *Librn,* Toronto Jewish Congress, Jewish Public Library of Toronto, Toronto ON. 416-781-6282, 781-8065

Missar, Charles D, *Librn,* National Institute of Education, Educational Research Library, Washington DC. 202-254-5800

Missonis, George E, *Asst Dir,* Albright College Library, Reading PA. 215-921-2381, Ext 224

Mistaras, Evangeline, *Ref,* Northeastern Illinois University Library, Chicago IL. 312-583-4050, Ext 469, 470, 471, 472

Mistrik, Marion, *Librn,* Air Transport Association of America Library, Washington DC. 872-4184; 872-4185

Mitcham, Fred, *Dir,* Dallas Museum of Fine Arts Library, Dallas TX. 214-421-4187

Mitchel, Marguerite, *Bibliog Instr & ILL,* Stephens College, Hugh Stephens Library, Columbia MO. 314-442-2211, Ext 428

Mitchell, Adeline, *Asst Librn,* Hebron Public Library, Hebron NE. 402-768-6701

Mitchell, Annette, *Dir,* University of Palm Beach Library, West Palm Beach FL. 305-833-5575

Mitchell, Anzella J, *Librn,* United States Department of the Navy (Office of the General Counsel, Law Library), Washington DC. 202-692-7378

Mitchell, Aubrey, *Librn,* University of Tennessee, Knoxville (Agriculture-Veterinary Medicine), Knoxville TN. 615-974-7338

Mitchell, Barbara, *Acq,* Medford Public Library, Medford MA. 617-395-7950

Mitchell, Basil, *Dir,* Siena College, Jerome Dawson Memorial Library, Loudonville NY. 518-783-2522

Mitchell, Bede, *Circ,* Montana State University, Roland R Renne Library, Bozeman MT. 406-994-3119

Mitchell, Betty J, *Assoc Dir,* California State University, Northridge, Delmar T Oviatt & South Libraries, Northridge CA. 213-885-2271

Mitchell, Bill, *Br Coordr,* Halifax County Regional Library, Halifax NS. 902-477-6265

Mitchell, Billie, *Librn,* El Dorado County Law Library, Placerville CA. 916-626-2431

Mitchell, Bonnie Beth, *Head, LSCA,* State Library of Ohio, Columbus OH. 614-466-2693

Mitchell, Bonnie J, *Circ,* Mohawk Valley Community College Library, Utica NY. 315-792-5337

Mitchell, Carolyn, *Librn,* Environmental Protection Agency, Region 4 Library, Atlanta GA. 404-881-4216

Mitchell, Carolyn, *Librn,* Medical Planning Associates Library, Malibu CA. 213-456-2084

Mitchell, Cindy, *Bibliog Instr,* Auburn University, Ralph Brown Draughton Library, Auburn AL. 205-826-4500

Mitchell, Constance J, *Librn,* Union Carbide Agricultural Products Company, Product Development Library, Ambler PA. 215-628-1465

Mitchell, David L, *Asst Prof,* State University of New York at Albany, School of Library & Information Science, NY. 518-455-6288

Mitchell, Deborah, *Asst Librn,* Vicksburg-Warren County Public Library, Vicksburg MS. 601-636-6411

Mitchell, Denise, *Acq,* College De Maisonneuve Bibliotheque, Montreal PQ. 514-254-7131, 254-4035

Mitchell, Doris, *Ref,* Richardson Public Library, Richardson TX. 214-238-8251

Mitchell, Dorothy, *Librn,* Reading Public Library (Northwest), Reading PA. 215-372-2230

Mitchell, Edna M, *Librn,* Hebron Public Library, Hebron NE. 402-768-6701

Mitchell, Elaine, *Dir of Info Servs,* Wilmer & Pickering Library, Washington DC. 202-872-6183

Mitchell, Elaine R, *Librn,* Mexico Free Public Library, Mexico ME. 207-364-2530

Mitchell, Elizabeth, *Ref,* Belleville Public Library, Belleville ON. 613-968-7536

Mitchell, Esther Rose, *Librn,* Washington County Library, Potosi MO. 314-438-4691

Mitchell, Eugene, *Asst Dir,* William Paterson College of New Jersey, Sarah Byrd Askew Library, Wayne NJ. 201-595-2113

Mitchell, G R, *Librn,* Monogram Industries Inc, Glastic Co Library, Cleveland OH. 216-486-0100

Mitchell, Gail, *Ch,* Boonslick Regional Library, Sedalia MO. 816-826-6195

Mitchell, George, *Media,* North Texas State University Library, Denton TX. 817-788-2411

Mitchell, George D, *Librn,* North Texas State University Library (Media), Denton TX. 817-788-2411

Mitchell, George R, *Dir,* De Soto Trail Regional Library, Camilla GA. 912-336-8372

Mitchell, Georgene, *Dir,* Moyer Library, Gibson City IL. 217-784-5343

Mitchell, Hazel, *Librn,* York County Library (York Public), York SC. 803-684-3751

Mitchell, Helen, *On-Line Servs,* University of Nevada-Reno, Noble H Getchell Library, Reno NV. 702-784-6533

Mitchell, Hester L, *Corp Librn,* Addison-Wesley Publishing Co, Inc, A-W Library, Reading MA. 617-944-3700, Ext 429

Mitchell, J G, *Librn,* British Columbia Government, Legislative Library, Victoria BC. 604-387-6500

Mitchell, J G, *Legis Librn,* British Columbia Government, Legislative Library, Victoria BC. 604-387-6500

Mitchell, J G, *Librn,* Getty Refining & Marketing Co, Technical Library, Delaware City DE. 302-629-8470

Mitchell, Janice Aid, *Dir,* Carnegie Public Library, Monte Vista CO. 303-852-3931

Mitchell, Jean, *Librn,* Henry Public Library, Henry IL. 309-364-2516

Mitchell, Jean, *Tech Librn,* Kerr-McGee Corp (Technical Center Library), Oklahoma City OK. 405-341-8551, Ext 271

Mitchell, Joan, *ILL, Media & Ref,* Butler County Community College Library, Butler PA. 412-287-8711, Ext 198

Mitchell, Joan, *Bibliog Searching,* Wilfrid Laurier University Library, Waterloo ON. 519-884-1970

Mitchell, Joe B, *Dir,* Ferrum College, Thomas Stanley Library, Ferrum VA. 703-365-2121, Ext 161

Mitchell, Joyce P, *Ad,* L E Phillips Memorial Public Library, Eau Claire WI. 715-839-5002

Mitchell, Judy, *Dir,* Southern Bible College, McDonald Library, Houston TX. 713-675-2351

Mitchell, June M, *Chief, Libr Servs,* Veterans Administration, Hospital Library, Syracuse NY. 315-476-7461, Ext 284 & 285

Mitchell, Kathleen, *Ch,* Finney Public Library, Clintonville Public Library, Clintonville WI. 715-823-4563

Mitchell, Kathleen, *Librn,* Franklin County Library, Chambersburg PA. 717-264-9663

Mitchell, Laura, *Ref,* Saint Mary-Of-The-Woods College Library, Saint Mary-of-the-Woods IN. 812-535-4141, Ext 223

Mitchell, Lois, *Dir,* Reading Room Association Library, Gouverneur NY. 315-287-0191

Mitchell, Lorna, *Ref & Bibliog Instr,* Westminster College, Reeves Memorial Library, Fulton MO. 314-642-6793

Mitchell, Margaret, *Librn,* New York State Library, Museum & Science Service Library, Albany NY. 518-474-5830

Mitchell, Margaret, *Assoc Librn,* Toronto Institute of Medical Technology Library, Toronto ON. 416-596-3123

Mitchell, Marilyn, *Circ,* Bowling Green Public Library, Bowling Green KY. 502-781-4882

Mitchell, Martha, *Ref,* Bainbridge Junior College Library, Bainbridge GA. 912-246-7646

Mitchell, Martha M, *Librn,* Chemed Corp, Dearborn Chemical Library, Lake Zurich IL. 312-438-8241, Ext 338

Mitchell, Martin L, *Dir,* Avon Lake Public Library, Avon Lake OH. 216-933-8128

Mitchell, Mary Ann, *Bibliog Instr,* Saint Louis Community College (Forest Park Campus), Saint Louis MO. 314-644-9209

Mitchell, Mary Jane, *Instr,* Andrews University, Library Science Dept, MI. 616-471-3549

Mitchell, Mary Jane, *Dir,* Andrews University, James White Library, Berrien Springs MI. 616-471-3264, 471-3275

Mitchell, Milton E, *Dir,* Indianhead Federated Library System, Eau Claire WI. 715-839-5082

Mitchell, Mrs F, *Libr Supvr,* Dauphin Public Library, Dauphin MB. 204-638-3055

Mitchell, Mrs J B, *Librn,* Taft Public Library, Taft TX. 512-528-2900

Mitchell, Nonie, *Librn,* Texas Aeronautics Commission Library, Austin TX. 512-475-4768

Mitchell, Patricia Ann, *Librn,* National Park Service, Midwest Archeological Center Library, Lincoln NE. 402-471-5392

Mitchell, Penelope M, *Actg Dir,* MacMurray College, Henry Pfeiffer Library, Jacksonville IL. 217-245-6151, Ext 285 & 334

Mitchell, Peter D, *Dir,* King's College Library, London ON. 519-433-3491, Ext 44

Mitchell, Quita, *Librn,* Jim Hogg County Public Library, Hebbronville TX. 512-527-3421

Mitchell, Ruby, *ILL, Ad & Ref,* Tyler Public Library, Tyler TX. 214-595-4267

Mitchell, Ruth E, *Dir,* Laurel Public Library, Laurel DE. 302-875-3184

Mitchell, Ruth K, *Chief Librn,* Veterans Administration, Medical Center Library, Milwaukee WI. 414-384-2000, Ext 2354

Mitchell, Selma, *Cat,* Watertown Regional Library, Watertown SD. 605-886-8521, 886-8282

Mitchell, Shirley, *Pres,* Dexter Free Library, Dexter NY. 315-639-6785

Mitchell, T A, *Librn,* Brandon University, John E Robbins Library, Brandon MB. 204-728-9520

Mitchell, Wanda, *Ad,* La Grange Public Library, La Grange IL. 312-352-0576, Ext 6

Mitchell, Zeta, *Bus,* Seattle Central Community College, Instructional Resource Services, Seattle WA. 206-587-5420

Mitchell, Jr, Edward S, *Librn,* Augusta Chronicle-Herald Library, Augusta GA. 404-724-0851, Ext 229

Mitchell-Kerran, Claudia, *Dir,* University of California, Los Angeles (Center for Afro-American Studies), Los Angeles CA. 213-825-6060

Miterry, Mally, *Librn,* Centre County Law Library, Bellefonte PA. 814-355-2861

Mitlin, Laurance R, *Asst Dir & Pub Serv,* Winthrop College, Ida Jane Dacus Library, Rock Hill SC. 803-323-2131

Mitra, H, *Assoc Dir, Tech Serv & Acq,* Mount Allison University, Ralph Pickard Bell Library, Sackville NB. 506-536-2040, Ext 375

Mitsch, Beatrice, *Supvr,* International Paper Co, Corp Research Center, Technical Information Center, Tuxedo Park NY. 914-351-2101, Ext 207

Mittelberger, Ernest G, *Dir,* Wine Museum of San Francisco, Alfred Fromm Rare Wine Books Library, San Francisco CA. 415-673-6990, Ext 177 & 189

Mittelgluck, Eugene L, *Dir,* New Rochelle Public Library, New Rochelle NY. 914-632-7878

Mittelstaedt, Gerard E, *Asst Dir & Tech Serv,* McAllen Memorial Library, McAllen TX. 512-682-4531

Mitten, Rose Marie, *Dir,* Concord Free Public Library, Concord MA. 617-369-5324

Mitton, Halina, *Tech Serv,* Vancouver Community College Libraries, Vancouver BC. 604-688-1111

Miu, Anna, *Cat,* Texas Southern University Library, Houston TX. 713-527-7121

Mixon, Susan, *Tech Serv,* Wayne Community College, Learning Resource Center, Goldsboro NC. 919-735-5151, Ext 64

Mixson, Adrian, *Ext Servs,* Collier County Free Public Library, Naples FL. 813-262-4130, 261-8208

Mixson, Sharon, *Media,* Central Florida Community College, Library Learning Resources Center, Ocala FL. 904-237-2111, Ext 344

Mixter, Janet, *Med,* Loyola University of Chicago Libraries (Medical Center), Maywood IL. 312-531-3192

Mixter, Janet, *On-Line Servs,* Loyola University of Chicago Libraries (Medical Center), Maywood IL. 312-531-3192

Miyashiro, Fusako, *Librn,* Hawaii State Library System (Keaau Community School), Keaau HI. 808-966-8181

Miyauchi, Phyllis, *Cat,* Crandall Library, Glens Falls NY. 518-792-6508

Mize, Barbara Jean, *Asst Librn,* Midway College, Marrs Library, Midway KY. 606-846-4421, Ext 38

Mize, Jamie Nell, *Librn,* Saint Clair County Library (Odenville), Odenville AL. 205-884-1685

Mize, June, *Librn,* Northeast Georgia Regional Library System (Toccoa), Clarkesville GA. 404-754-4413

Mize, Patrica J, *Pub Servs & Bibliog Instr,* Kentucky Wesleyan College, Library Learning Center, Owensboro KY. 502-926-3111, Ext 113, 117

Mize, Patricia, *Asst Prof,* Kentucky Wesleyan College, Department of Library Science, KY. 502-926-3111, Ext 112, 113

Mize, Teresa, *Asst Librn,* Post Falls Public Library, Post Falls ID. 208-773-3511

Mizener, David, *Asst Dir,* Sioux City Public Library, Sioux City IA. 712-279-6179

Mizener, Warren, *Chief Adminr & Treasurer,* Nepean Public Library, Ottawa ON. 613-224-4338

Mjaaland, Jr, Kenneth A, *Dir,* Carrollton Public Library, Carrollton TX. 214-323-5014

Mlott, Luthera W, *Dir,* Wimodaughsian Free Library, Canisteo Library, Canisteo NY. 607-698-4445

Moak, John F, *Dir,* Peabody Institute Library, Danvers Public Library, Danvers MA. 617-774-0554, Ext 0557, 0555

Moake, Virginia H, *Librn,* Veterans Administration, Hospital Library, Marion IL. 618-997-5311, Ext 242

Moberg, F Alden, *Instnl Libr Servs,* Oregon State Library, Salem OR. 503-378-4243

Mobley, Cordelia, *Librn,* Garfield County Public Library (Rifle Branch), Rifle CO. 303-625-3471

Mobley, Emily R, *On-Line Servs & Bibliog Instr,* General Motors Corp (Research Laboratories Library), Warren MI. 313-575-2731

Mobley, Richard, *Librn,* Mobile Public Library (Monte L Moore), Mobile AL. 205-342-2655

Mobley, Robert, *Media,* Savannah State College Library, Savannah GA. 912-356-2183, 356-2184

Mobley, Sara M, *Asst Librn, Reader's Serv,* Emory University Libraries (Pitts Theology Library), Atlanta GA. 404-329-4166

Mochizuki, Tomie, *Librn,* Japan Society Inc Library, New York NY. 212-832-1155

Mochizuki, Tracy, *Librn,* Los Angeles Public Library System (Pio Pico), Los Angeles CA. 213-734-9851

Mock, Donna, *Librn,* Asheville-Buncombe Library System (Beech Community), Weaverville NC. 704-252-8701

Mock, Jerome T, *Learning Resources,* West Georgia College Library, Carrollton GA. 404-834-1370

Mock, Joseph E, *Librn,* Cleveland Public Library (Miles Park), Cleveland OH. 216-641-4990

Mock, Lucille, *Librn,* Trails Regional Library (Warrensburg Branch), Warrensburg MO. 816-747-9177

Mock, Richard, *Dir,* Porterville Public Library, Porterville CA. 209-784-0177, 784-1400, Ext 523

Mocker, Carole, *Librn,* Cass County Public Library (Raymore Branch), Raymore MO. 816-331-8024

Modde, Sally, *Librn,* Riverside Regional Library (Center 3), Perryville MO. 314-547-6508

Mode, Dolores, *Librn,* Grays Harbor County, Law Library, Montesano WA. 206-249-4211

Modeen, J H, *Librn,* Dow Chemical USA, Research & Development Library, Plaquemine LA. 504-389-1626

Model, Velda M, *ILL & Ref,* Reading Public Library, Reading MA. 617-944-0840

Modemann, Harritt, *Assoc Dir,* William Paterson College of New Jersey, Sarah Byrd Askew Library, Wayne NJ. 201-595-2113

Modin, Val, *Asst Librn,* Dorion Public Library, Dorion ON. 807-857-2289

Modlin, Cynthia, *Ad,* Fontana Regional Library, Bryson City NC. 704-488-2382

Modlin, Cynthia, *Librn,* Macon County Public Library, Franklin NC. 704-524-3600

Modlin, Wayne, *Dir,* Fontana Regional Library, Bryson City NC. 704-488-2382

Modscheidler, Christa, *Biol,* University of Chicago, Joseph Regenstein Library, Chicago IL. 312-753-2977

Moe, Cheryl, *Librn,* Baldwin Public Library, Baldwin WI. 715-684-3813

Moe, Cindy, *Instr,* University of Northern Colorado, Department of Educational Media, CO. 303-351-2807

Moe, Georgiana, *Asst Librn,* Pacific School of Religion, Charles Holbrook Library, Berkeley CA. 415-848-0528

Moe, Louise, *ILL & Ref,* Rochester Public Library, Olmsted County Library System, Rochester MN. 507-285-8000

Moedritzer, Anne, *ILL, On-Line Servs & Bibliog Instr,* Webster College, Eden Theological Seminary, Eden-Webster Libraries, Saint Louis MO. 314-968-0500, Ext 235

Moeglein, Margaret, *Bkmobile Coordr,* Northwest Regional Library, Thief River Falls MN. 218-681-4325

Moeller, Bernice, *Librn,* Schleswig Public Library, Schleswig IA. 712-676-3470

Moeller, Henry R, *Dir & Cat,* Central Baptist Theological Seminary Library, Kansas City KS. 913-371-1544

Moeller, Rhonda, *Ch,* Ottawa Library, Ottawa KS. 913-242-3080

Moeller, Vera H, *ILL,* Municipal Library Cooperative of Saint Louis County, MO. 314-966-5568

Moeller-Pfieffer, Kathleen, *Librn,* Confederate Memorial Library, Hillsborough NC. 919-732-2491

Moelter, Joel, *Librn,* Mount Carmel College, Toelle Memorial Library, Niagara Falls ON. 416-356-4113

Moen, Mrs Marcus, *Librn,* Mayville Public Library, Mayville ND. 701-786-3388

Moenning, Carolyn, *Asst Librn,* Scribner Public Library, Scribner NE. 402-664-3540

Moeny, Christine E, *Spec Coll,* Adams State College Library, Alamosa CO. 303-589-7781

Moeny, Christine E, *Instr,* Adams State College, Masters in Educational Media with the University of Northern Colorado, CO. 303-589-7781

Moeny, Donald G, *Media,* Adams State College Library, Alamosa CO. 303-589-7781

Moffa, Monica, *Pub Servs,* Indiana University (School of Dentistry Library), Indianapolis IN. 317-264-7204

Moffat, Edward S, *Assoc Prof,* Long Island University, Palmer Graduate Library School, NY. 516-299-2855 & 299-2856

Moffat, Maureen, *In Charge,* De Graff Memorial Hospital, Health Sciences Library, North Tonawanda NY. 716-694-4500, Ext 3737

Moffat, Maureen, *Librn,* Sheehan Memorial Emergency Hospital, Health Sciences Library, Buffalo NY. 716-842-2200

Moffat, Patricia F, *Librn,* Beneficial Management Corp Library, Morristown NJ. 201-538-5500

Moffatt, Pattie, *Per,* University of Arkansas-Monticello Library, Monticello AR. 501-367-6811, Ext 80

Moffeit, Tony, *Tech Serv & Acq,* University of Southern Colorado Library, Pueblo CO. 303-549-2361

Moffett, Ann W, *Librn,* United States Air Force (Dover Air Force Base Library), Dover AFB DE. 302-678-7011

Moffett, B A, *Pre-Columbian America,* Theosophical University Library, Altadena CA. 213-798-8020, Ext 5

Moffett, Kenneth, *Instr,* East Tennessee State University, Library Service Division, TN. 615-929-4244

Moffett, Martha, *Librn,* National Enquirer, Research Department Library, Lantana FL. 305-586-1111

Moffett, Mary Belle, *AV,* Cass County Public Library, Harrisonville MO. 816-884-3483

Moffett, William A, *Dir,* Oberlin College Library, Oberlin OH. 216-775-8285

Moffit, Kay, *Asst Librn,* Treasure Valley Community College Library, Ontario OR. 503-889-6493, Ext 68

Moffit, Mary, *Librn,* Washington State School for the Deaf, Learning Resource Center, Vancouver WA. 206-696-6223

Moga, Margaret, *ILL,* Barat College Library, Lake Forest IL. 312-234-3000, Ext 237

Mogan, Morlene, *Librn,* Ottawa Public Library (Saint Laurent), Ottawa ON. 613-236-0301, Ext 274

Mogenson, Shirley, *Asst Librn,* Saskatoon Public Library (Sutherland), Saskatoon SK. 306-664-9593

Mogle, Dawn, *Librn,* Lake County Public Library (Black Oak Only), Gary IN. 219-844-8809

Mogle, Dawn, *Librn,* Lake County Public Library (Schererville Public), Schererville IN. 219-322-4731

Mohajerin, Kathryn S, *Asst Prof,* Auburn University, Dept of Educational Media, AL. 205-826-4529

Mohansingh, Lois, *Librn,* Monroeton Public Library, Monroeton PA. 717-265-3365

Mohl, Ines, *Librn,* Southern California Gas Co Library, Los Angeles CA. 213-620-1440

Mohlke, Catherine, *In Charge,* La Porte, Porter, Starke Health Science Library Consortium, IN. 219-785-2511, Ext 397

Mohlke, Catherine M, *Librn,* Westville Correctional Center (Staff Library), Westville IN. 219-785-2511, Ext 397

Mohn, Doris, *Cat,* Bryn Mawr Hospital, Medical Library, Bryn Mawr PA. 215-896-3160

Mohn, Marcia D, *Dir,* Biloxi Public Library, Biloxi MS. 601-374-0330

Mohn, Wallace D, *Tech Serv,* Buffalo & Erie County Public Library System, Buffalo NY. 716-856-7525

Moholt, Mary, *Tech Serv,* Carroll College Library, Helena MT. 406-442-3450, Ext 245, 247 & 442-1295

Mohr, Caroline, *Librn,* Holmes County District Public Library (Winesburg Branch), Winesburg OH. 216-674-5972

Mohr, Elizabeth, *Administrative Librn & On-Line Search Coordr,* United States Department of Energy, Bartlesville Energy Technology Center, Bartlesville OK. 336-2400 Ext 228

Mohr, Libby, *PIO,* Atlanta Public Library, Atlanta GA. 404-688-4636

Mohr, Margaret, *YA,* Needham Free Public Library, Needham MA. 617-444-0087, 444-0090

Mohr, Marjorie, *Librn,* Gilman Public Library, Alton NH. 603-875-2550

Mohr, Nancy, *Librn,* Kenton County Public Library (Erlanger), Covington KY. 606-341-5115

Mohr, Nelda, *Librn,* Brooklyn Public Library (Pacific), Brooklyn NY. 212-638-5180

Mohrke, Doreen M, *Librn,* Salt Lake City Public Library (Sprague), Salt Lake City UT. 801-363-5733

Mok, Vicky, *Tech Serv,* Fanshawe College of Applied Arts & Technology Library, London ON. 519-452-4350

Mokry, Marilyn, *Ch,* Lebanon Public Library, Lebanon OH. 513-932-4725

Mokry, Nina, *In Charge,* Ukrainian Cultural & Education Centre Library, Winnipeg MB. 204-942-0218

Mokrzycki, Karen, *Acq,* Rand Corp Library, Santa Monica CA. 213-393-0411, Ext 369

Molden, Mrs J B, *In Charge,* Daughters of the Republic of Texas Museum Library, Austin TX. 512-477-1822

Molder, Joy S, *Br Coordr,* Burlingame Public Library, Burlingame CA. 415-344-7107

Molder, Joy S, *Asst Librn,* Burlingame Public Library, Burlingame CA. 415-344-7107

Mole, Deborah, *Per,* Linden Free Public Library, Linden NJ. 201-486-3888

Moles, Jean Ann, *Ser,* University of Arkansas for Medical Sciences Library, Little Rock AR. 501-661-5980

Moles, Ruth, *Librn,* Pickett County Library, Byrdstown TN. 615-864-6281

Molesevich, Christina, *Ad,* Wilmington Memorial Library, Wilmington MA. 617-658-2967

Molesky, Margaret, *Media,* Allentown Public Library, Allentown PA. 215-820-2400

Molesworth, William, *Librn,* York Regional Library (Oromocto Public), Oromocto NB. 506-357-3329, 357-3320

Molholt, Pat A, *Assoc Dir,* Rensselaer Polytechnic Institute, Folsom Library, Troy NY. 518-270-6673

Molin, Karen, *Asst Dir,* Pulaski County Library, Pulaski VA. 703-980-8888, Ext 288

Molinari, Barbara, *Cat,* Merrick Library, Merrick NY. 516-379-3476

Molinaro, Joanne, *Librn,* A W Jones Co Library, New York NY. 212-825-0220

Moline, Sandra, *Librn,* University of Wisconsin-Madison (Physics Library), Madison WI. 608-262-3521

Moll, Marita, *Adminr,* Canadian Teachers' Federation, George G Croskery Memorial Library, Ottawa ON. 613-232-1505

Moll, Mary Ellen, *Librn,* English-Speaking Union, Books-Across-the-Sea Library, New York NY. 212-879-6800, Ext 14 & 20

Mollberg, Amy, *Coordr,* Houston Area Library System, Houston TX. 713-222-4704

Mollberg, Amy, *Coordr, Houston Area Libr Syst,* Houston Public Library, Houston TX. 713-224-5441

Mollema, Jr, Peter C, *Tech Serv,* California State College, Stanislaus Library, Turlock CA. 209-633-2232

Moller, Hans, *Undergraduate,* McGill University Libraries, Montreal PQ. 514-392-4948

Moller, Hans, *Librn,* McGill University Libraries (Undergraduate), Montreal PQ. 514-392-6779

Molleskog, Jean, *Librn,* United States Geological Survey, Public Inquiries Office Library, San Francisco CA. 415-556-5627

Molleson, Marianne, *Dir,* Cudahy Public Library, Cudahy Memorial Library, Cudahy WI. 414-481-4309

Molleur, Rosemary, *Librn,* East Hardwick Library, East Hardwick VT. 802-533-7743

Mollitor, Peggy, *Librn,* Belcher Library, Gaysville VT. 802-234-9794

Molloy, B, *Librn,* University of Southern California (Hoose Philosophy), Los Angeles CA. 213-743-2634

Molod, Samuel E, *Deputy State Librn,* Connecticut State Library, Hartford CT. 203-566-4301

Moloney, Francis X, *Asst Dir Develop,* Boston Public Library, Eastern Massachusetts Library System, Boston MA. 617-536-5400

Moloney, Genevieve A, *Dir,* Abbot Public Library, Marblehead MA. 617-631-1480

Moloney, Louis C, *Dir,* Southwest Texas State University, Learning Resources Center, San Marcos TX. 512-245-2132

Molony, Agnes, *Librn,* Baptist Hospital, Medical & School of Nursing Libraries, New Orleans LA. 504-899-9311, Ext 270

Moloso, III, Phillip J, *Ref,* Glendale Community College, John F Prince Library, Glendale AZ. 602-934-2211, Ext 239, 242

Mols, Francis P, *Cat,* Grand Valley State Colleges, Zumberge Library, Allendale MI. 313-895-6611, Ext 252

Mols, Kathleen B, *Asst Librn,* Saint Mary's Hospital Library, Grand Rapids MI. 616-774-6260

Molsky, Vera, *ILL,* Grove City College, Henry Buhl Library, Grove City PA. 412-458-6600, Ext 270

Molson, Gerda, *Librn,* Niagara on the Lake Public Library, Niagara on the Lake ON. 416-468-2023

Molson, Jean, *Librn,* Registered Nurses Association of British Columbia Library, Vancouver BC. 604-736-7331

Moltke-Hansen, David, *Archivist,* South Carolina Historical Society Library, Charleston SC. 803-723-3225

Moltz, Donna, *Testing Centre,* Lethbridge Community College, Buchanan Resource Centre, Lethbridge AB. 403-327-2141, Ext 350

Moltzan, Jan, *Librn,* Dallas Public Library (Walnut Hill), Dallas TX. 214-357-8434

Molumby, Lawrence E, *Asst Dir,* Public Library of the District of Columbia, Martin Luther King Memorial Library, Washington DC. 202-727-1101

Molyneaux, Gerard, *Media,* West Hartford Public Library, Noah Webster Memorial Library, West Hartford CT. 203-236-6286

Molyneux, Mary L, *Librn,* Bedford Public Library, Bedford VA. 703-586-8911

Molz, Jean Barry, *Assoc Dir,* Baltimore County Public Library, Towson MD. 301-296-8500

Molz, Kathleen, *Prof,* Columbia University in the City of New York, School of Library Service, NY. 212-280-2292

Molzam, Hazel, *Librn,* Ridgewood Public Library (George L Pease Memorial), Ridgewood NJ. 201-445-2136

Molzan, Hazel, *Br Coordr,* Ridgewood Public Library, Ridgewood NJ. 201-652-5200

Moman, Orthella, *Cat,* Jackson State University, Henry Thomas Sampson Library, Jackson MS. 601-968-2123

Momenee, Gary, *Bkmobile Coordr,* Public Library of Johnston County & Smithfield, Smithfield NC. 919-934-8146

Momenee, Karen, *Asst Prof,* University of North Carolina at Chapel Hill, School of Library Science, NC. 919-933-8366

Momosor, Stetson, *Librn,* University of Alaska, Arctic Environmental Information & Data Center Library, Anchorage AK. 907-279-4523

Monacella, Carol, *Libr Asst,* University of Connecticut at Hartford (Undergruate Library), West Hartford CT. 203-523-4841, Ext 317

Monaco, Anthony, *Media,* Edison Community College, Learning Resources Center, Fort Myers FL. 813-481-2121, Ext 219, 220, 360

Monaco, Kathleen, *Ch,* Parkersburg & Wood County Public Library, Wood County Service Center, Parkersburg WV. 304-485-6564

Monaco, Marcia, *Tech Serv,* Charles County Community College, Learning Resource Center, La Plata MD. 301-934-2251, Ext 251

Monaco, Ralph, *Asst Librn & ILL,* Saint John's University Library (Law), Jamaica NY. 212-969-8000, Ext 651, 652 & 653

Monaghan, Helen, *Librn,* Wayne Public Library (Mountain View), Wayne NJ. 201-694-0693

Monahan, Betty, *Tech Serv,* Collier County Free Public Library, Naples FL. 813-262-4130, 261-8208

Moncla, Susie, *Dir,* Moore Memorial Public Library, Texas City TX. 713-948-3111, Ext 160

Mondolfo, Vittoria I, *Asst Dir & Tech Serv,* Hamilton College, Burke Library, Clinton NY. 315-859-4478

Mondowney, Joann G, *Librn,* Enoch Pratt Free Library (Hollins-Payson), Baltimore MD. 301-396-5430, 396-5395

Mondroski, Alli, *Dir,* Mercer Public Library, Mercer WI. 715-476-2368

Monego, Rebecca B, *Librn,* Sherborn Library, Sherborn MA. 617-653-0770

Money, Dave, *Asst Librn,* Oklahoma College of Osteopathic Medicine & Surgery, College Library, Tulsa OK. 918-582-1972, Ext 351

Money, Rebecca, *Librn,* Luverne Public Library, Luverne AL. 205-335-3851

Money, Roslyn, *Personnel,* University of Western Ontario, A B Weldon Library, London ON. 519-679-6191

Monfort, Jay B, *Instr,* Foothill College, Library-Media Technical Assistant Program, CA. 415-948-8590, Ext 390

Mongan, Janet, *Asst Dir Coll Develop,* Cleveland State University Libraries, Cleveland OH. 216-687-2486

Mongan, Mary Ann, *Dir,* Kenton County Public Library, Covington KY. 606-292-2363

Monger, George Anne, *Ref,* Lamar University, Mary & John Gray Library, Beaumont TX. 713-838-8313

Mongrain, Guy, *Prof,* College de Jonquiere, Techniques de la Documentation, PQ. 418-547-2191, Ext 270

Monheit, Albert, *Dir,* Wantagh Public Library, Wantagh NY. 221-1200 & 1201

Monk, Joanne, *Acq,* Fairfax County Public Library, Administrative Offices, Springfield VA. 703-321-9810

Monk, Patricia Rodi, *Chief Librn,* United States Court of Appeals, Eighth Circuit Law Library, Saint Louis MO. 314-622-4930

Monke, Arthur, *Dir,* Bowdoin College Library, Brunswick ME. 207-725-8731, Ext 281

Monkhouse, Valerie, *Chief Librn,* National Museums of Canada Library, Ottawa ON. 998-3923 (gen), 998-4425 (chief librn)

Monnot, Anne, *Librn,* Pro Football Hall of Fame Library, Research Center, Canton OH. 216-456-8207

Monroe, Dolores, *Acq,* Pasadena Public Library, Pasadena TX. 713-477-0276

Monroe, J Hamilton, *Instr,* North Texas State University, School of Library & Information Sciences, TX. 817-788-2445

Monroe, Jean, *Spec Coll,* Wayne State University Libraries (Science Library), Detroit MI. 313-577-4066

Monroe, Judy, *Librn,* Alaska State Film Library, Anchorage AK. 907-274-6625

Monroe, Robert D, *Spec Coll,* University of Washington Libraries, Seattle WA. 206-543-1760

Monroe, Selma, *Dir,* Geneseo Public Library, Geneseo KS. 316-824-6406

Monroe, Shula, *Instr,* Grossmont College, Library Technology Program, CA. 714-465-1700, Ext 319

Monroe, Shula, *Dir,* National City Public Library, National City CA. 714-474-8211

Monsees, Ruth Ann, *Librn,* Boonslick Regional Library (Boonville Branch), Boonville MO. 816-882-5864

Monsell, George, *Librn,* Brooklyn Public Library (Ulmer Park), Brooklyn NY. 212-266-7373

Monsivais, Jean, *In Charge,* Lutheran Medical Center Library, Saint Louis MO. 314-772-1456

Monsma, Marvin E, *Dir,* Calvin College & Seminary Library, Grand Rapids MI. 616-949-4000, Ext 297

Montag, John, *Chmn Advisory Committee,* Northern Lights Library Network, MN. 218-299-4640

Montagna, Dennis, *Ref,* Orange County Community College Library, Middletown NY. 914-343-1121

Montague, Eleanor, *Librn,* University of California, Riverside, University Library, Riverside CA. 714-787-3221

Montague, Louise, *Librn,* Westhampton Memorial Library, Westhampton MA. 413-527-5386

Montalbano, Helena, *Librn,* Shiawassee County Library (Hazelton Township Public), New Lothrop MI. 313-638-5761

Montalbano, Mildred, *In Charge,* New York Aquarium Library, Osborn Laboratories of Marine Science, Brooklyn NY. 212-266-8500, Ext 28

Montalto, Mary, *Librn,* Schroder Capital Corp Library, New York NY. 212-269-6500

Montalvo, Marilyn, *Tech Serv,* Puerto Rico Junior College (Cupey Campus Learning Resources Center), Rio Piedras PR. 809-765-1716

Montana, Patricia, *YA,* Carnegie Library, Rome GA. 404-291-7568

Montana, Jr, Edward J, *Asst to Adminr,* Eastern Massachusetts Regional Library System, Boston MA. 617-536-4010

Montanelli, Dale, *Budget Planning,* University of Illinois Library at Urbana-Champaign, Urbana IL. 217-333-0790

Montavon, Robert, *Asst Dir & Acq,* University of Dayton Libraries, Roesch Library, Dayton OH. 513-229-4221

Monte, Martha, *Dir,* Rathbun Free Memorial Library, East Haddam CT. 203-873-8210

Monte, Robin, *Librn,* Vitramon Inc, Process & Materials Research & Development Laboratory Library, Monroe CT. 203-268-6261

Monte-Griffo, Irene, *ILL,* Maryland Institute College of Art, Decker Library, Baltimore MD. 301-669-9200, Ext 27, 28

Montee, Monty L, *Cat,* Yale University Library (Medical Library), New Haven CT. 203-436-4784, 436-2961

Monteiro, Mary, *Librn,* Sacramento Public Library (E K McClatchy), Sacramento CA. 916-455-8153

Montez, Isabell, *Tech Serv & Acq,* Casa Grande City Library, Casa Grande AZ. 602-836-7242

Montgomery, Ada, *Dir of Instructional Media Ctr,* Jacksonville State University, College of Library Science, Communications & Instructional Media, AL. 205-435-6390

Montgomery, Ada, *Media,* Jacksonville State University Library, Jacksonville AL. 205-435-9820, Ext 213, 214

Montgomery, Aileen, *Asst Librn,* Belle Fourche Public Library, Belle Fourche SD. 605-892-4407

Montgomery, Anne, *Cat,* Palo Alto City Library, Palo Alto CA. 415-329-2436

Montgomery, Colleen, *Tech Serv & Cat,* University of Science & Arts of Oklahoma, Nash Library, Chickasha OK. 405-224-3140, Ext 260

Montgomery, Curtis, *Advancement Serv,* Catawba College, Corriher-Linn-Black Library, Salisbury NC. 704-637-4448, 637-4449

Montgomery, Edith, *Tech Serv,* Cambridge Public Library, Cambridge MA. 617-498-9080

Montgomery, Eleanor, *Librn,* Plaquemines Parish Library (Port Sulphur Branch), Port Sulphur LA. 504-564-3681

Montgomery, Harold, *Ref,* Lorain County Community College Library, Elyria OH. 216-365-4191, Ext 201

Montgomery, James, *Tech Serv,* Victoria College - University of Houston Victoria Campus Library, Victoria TX. 512-575-7436

Montgomery, James W, *Librn,* New York State Office of Mental Health, Psychiatric Institute Research Library, New York NY. 212-568-4000

Montgomery, John E, *Librn,* Northern Illinois University, College Law Library, Glen Ellyn IL. 312-858-7200

Montgomery, K Leon, *Prof,* University of Pittsburgh, School of Library & Information Science, PA. 412-624-5230

Montgomery, Linda, *Dir,* Minnesota Legislative Reference Library, Saint Paul MN. 612-296-3398

Montgomery, Louise, *Bkmobile Coordr,* Okefenokee Regional Library, Waycross GA. 912-283-3126

Montgomery, M E, *Librn,* Eaton Corp, Engineering & Research Library, Southfield MI. 313-354-6979

Montgomery, Marilyn, *Ref & On-Line Servs,* Mankato State University, Memorial Library, Mankato MN. 507-389-6201

Montgomery, Maurice J, *Asst Dir,* Rock County Historical Society, Research Library, Janesville WI. 608-752-4519

Montgomery, Mike, *ILL,* University of Missouri Saint Louis, Thomas Jefferson Library, Saint Louis MO. 314-453-5221

Montgomery, Nancy, *Music,* Oklahoma Baptist University, Mabee Learning Center, Shawnee OK. 405-275-2850, Ext 245

Montgomery, Patricia, *Ref,* Salt Lake County Library System, Whitmore Library, Salt Lake City UT. 801-943-7614

Montgomery, Patricia, *Librn,* Salt Lake County Library System (Whitmore-Hq & Main Libr), Salt Lake City UT. 801-943-7614

Montgomery, Paula, *Branch Chief, Sch Media Servs,* Maryland State Department of Education, Division of Library Development & Services, Baltimore MD. 301-796-8300, Ext 284

Montgomery, Phyllis, *YA,* Weston Public Library, Weston MA. 617-893-3312

Montgomery, Rose, *Per,* Rock Island Public Library, Rock Island IL. 309-788-7627

Montgomery, Sherry, *AV & Media,* Philadelphia College of Pharmacy & Science, Joseph W England Library, Philadelphia PA. 215-386-5800, Ext 296

Montgomery, Susan, *Librn,* Passaic Township Free Public Library, Stirling NJ. 201-647-2088

Montgomery, Susan J, *Mgr,* Continental Illinois National Bank & Trust Co, Information Services Division, Chicago IL. 312-828-8580

Monti, Laura V, *Keeper of Rare Bks & Mss,* Boston Public Library, Eastern Massachusetts Library System, Boston MA. 617-536-5400

Montilli, Vincent J, *Bkmobile Coordr,* Peninsula Public Library, Lawrence NY. 516-239-3262

Montouri, Charles, *Extension Libr,* Rowan Public Library, Salisbury NC. 704-633-5578

Montoya, Cathy, *Librn,* University of Saint Thomas (School of Nursing Library), Houston TX. 713-757-1000, Ext 1838

Montoya, Edward, *Asst Librn,* Northeastern Regional Library, Cimarron NM. 505-376-2474

Moody, Aidan, *Chief Indexer, Newsweek, Inc,* General Library, New York NY. 212-350-2494

Moody, Barbara S, *Coordr, Ch Servs,* Enoch Pratt Free Library, Baltimore MD. 301-396-5430, 396-5395

Moody, Beverly, *Librn,* Dayton & Montgomery County Public Library (Dayton View), Dayton OH. 513-224-1651, Ext 250

Moody, Beverly, *Librn,* Dayton & Montgomery County Public Library (Fort McKinley), Dayton OH. 513-224-1651, Ext 210

Moody, Carol, *Spec Coll,* Saint Louis University (Omer Poos Law Library), Saint Louis MO. 314-658-2755

Moody, Dolores, *Supvr,* Chicago Public Library (Harold Ickes Homes Reading & Study Center), Chicago IL. 312-225-9133

Moody, Eleanor L, *Dir,* Umpqua Community College Library, Roseburg OR. 503-672-5571, Ext 40

Moody, Elizabeth, *Librn,* Windham Free Public Library, Windham CT. 203-423-0636

Moody, Helga, *ILL,* City College of the City University of New York, Morris Raphael Cohen Library, New York NY. 212-690-6612

Moody, Kathran, *Librn,* Niles Memorial Library, Jay ME. 207-645-4681

Moody, Kenneth E, *Dir,* Medical Research Library of Brooklyn, Brooklyn NY. 212-270-1041

Moody, Margaret M, *Planning & Publications Dept Asst Librn,* Harvard University Library (Law School Library), Cambridge MA. 617-495-3170

Moody, Marilyn D, *Dist Coordr,* Free Library of Philadelphia, Philadelphia PA. 215-686-5322

Moody, Myrtle A, *Tech Servs Dept Asst Librn,* Harvard University Library (Law School Library), Cambridge MA. 617-495-3170

Moody, Roland H, *Dean & Dir,* Northeastern University Libraries, Boston MA. 617-437-2350

Moody, Susan H, *Librn,* Muscle Shoals Public Library, Muscle Shoals AL. 205-381-5872

Moody, Velma, *Acq,* Dearborn Department of Libraries, Henry Ford Centennial Library, Dearborn MI. 313-271-1000

Moon, Bernice E, *Chmn of Comt,* First Congregational Church Library, Stamford CT. 203-323-0200

Moon, Edna L T, *Dir,* American Red Cross, National Headquarters Library, Washington DC. 202-857-3491

Moon, Gail, *Head Main Librn,* Middle Georgia Regional Library, Macon GA. 912-745-5813

Moon, Gail, *Librn,* Middle Georgia Regional Library (Washington Memorial), Macon GA. 912-745-5813

Moon, James, *Cat,* University of Pittsburgh, Hillman Library, Pittsburgh PA. 412-624-4400

Moon, Janet, *Asst Librn,* Carnegie Public Library, Upper Sandusky OH. 419-294-1345

Moon, Margaret, *Asst Dir,* Thomas Ford Memorial Library, Western Springs Library, Western Springs IL. 312-246-0520

Moon, Margaret, *Ch,* Memphis-Shelby County Public Library & Information Center, Memphis TN. 901-528-2950

Moon, Margaret, *Librn,* Muskegon Business College Library, Muskegon MI. 616-726-2911

Moon, Paul C, *Librn,* Ottawa County Law Library, Port Clinton OH. 419-734-4125

Mooney, David, *Ref,* Community College of Allegheny County, Allegheny Campus Library, Pittsburgh PA. 412-237-2585

Mooney, James E, *Dir,* Historical Society of Pennsylvania Library, Philadelphia PA. 215-732-6200

Mooney, Judith Ann, *Tech Serv & Cat,* Richmond Public Library, Richmond CA. 415-231-2119

Mooney, Kathleen, *Librn,* RCA Service Co, Keystone Jobs Corps Center Library, Drums PA. 717-788-1164, Ext 323

Mooney, Mrs James, *Librn,* Calhoun County Library (Point Comfort Branch), Point Comfort TX. 512-987-2954

Mooney, Sally, *Librn,* Genesee District Library (Montrose Branch), Montrose MI. 313-639-6388

Mooney, Shirley E, *Librn,* Pacific Press Ltd Library, Vancouver BC. 604-732-2519

Mooney, Jr, Henry J, *Coordr Coll Develop,* Denver Public Library, Denver CO. 303-573-5152, Ext 271

Mooneyham, Dee, *Ch,* Kern County Library, Bakersfield CA. 805-861-2130

Moor, Gloria, *Librn,* Regina Leader-Post Ltd Library, Regina SK. 306-525-8211, Ext 234

Moorachian, Rose, *Librn,* Boston Public Library (Brighton Branch), Brighton MA. 617-782-6032

Moorachian, Rose, *YA,* Boston Public Library, Eastern Massachusetts Library System, Boston MA. 617-536-5400

Moore, Alayne, *Bus Consult, Automation Consult & On-Line Search Coordr,* Kaskaskia Library System, Smithton IL. 618-235-4220

Moore, A Merle, *Dir,* Clarksburg-Harrison Public Library, Clarksburg WV. 304-624-6512, 624-6513

Moore, Alice, *Tech Serv & Acq,* Bristol Public Library, Bristol VA. 703-669-9444

Moore, Alice, *Instruction & Orientation,* Florida State University, Robert Manning Strozier Library, Tallahassee FL. 904-644-5401

Moore, Ann, *Librn,* Jefferson County Public Library (Edgewater Branch), Edgewater CO. 303-237-3395

Moore, Ann, *Librn,* Mid-Continent Public Library (Blue Springs Branch), Blue Springs MO. 816-229-3571

Moore, Anne M, *Asst Prof,* University of Georgia, Dept of Educational Media & Librarianship, GA. 404-542-3810

Moore, Annette, *Personnel & Bus Mgr,* North Olympic Library System, Port Angeles WA. 206-457-4464

Moore, Annie, *Ref,* Chicago State University, Paul & Emily Douglas Library, Chicago IL. 312-995-2254

Moore, Arlene E, *Ref,* Missouri Southern State College, George A Spiva Library, Joplin MO. 417-624-8100, Ext 251

Moore, Augusta, *Librn,* Harris County Public Library (Cypress Creek Branch), Spring TX. 713-376-4610

Moore, Barbara, *Cat,* Mankato State University, Memorial Library, Mankato MN. 507-389-6201

Moore, Becky, *Cat,* Pima Community College, West Campus Learning Resource Center, Tucson AZ. 602-884-6821

Moore, Betsy, *Junior Dept,* Clinton Public Library, Clinton IN. 317-832-8349

Moore, Betty L, *Librn,* Cranbrook Institute of Science Library, Bloomfield Hills MI. 313-645-3238

Moore, Beverly, *Dir,* University of Southern Colorado Library, Pueblo CO. 303-549-2361

Moore, Billie, *Librn,* Anchorage Municipal Libraries (Chugiak-Eagle River), Eagle River AK. 907-694-2500

Moore, Carole A, *Librn,* Veterans Administration, Hospital Library, White City OR. 503-826-2111

Moore, Carolyn, *Librn,* Avon Park Library, Avon Park FL. 813-453-4842

Moore, Carolyn, *Acq,* Clearwater Public Library, Clearwater FL. 813-462-6800

Moore, Carolyn A, *Deputy Librn,* Municipal Reference Library, Chicago IL. 312-744-4992

Moore, Catherine, *Librn,* Lemuel Shattuck Hospital (Medical Library), Jamaica Plain MA. 617-522-8110, Ext 307

Moore, Charles F, *Dir,* Woonsocket Harris Public Library, Woonsocket RI. 401-769-9044

Moore, Cheryl, *Ref,* Hillside Free Public Library, Hillside NJ. 201-923-4413

Moore, Constance, *Librn,* United Air Lines Library, Chicago IL. 312-952-5632

Moore, Curtis P, *Dir,* Lebanon Community Library, H C Grumbine Free Public Library, Lebanon PA. 717-273-7624

Moore, Curtis P, *Dir,* Lebanon County Library System, Lebanon PA. 717-273-7624

Moore, David G, *Librn,* One, Inc, Blanche M Baker Memorial Library, Los Angeles CA. 213-735-5252

Moore, DeAnn, *Librn,* Tacoma Public Library (Charlotte Mottet), Tacoma WA. 206-627-8544

Moore, Donna, *Headquarters Lib,* First Regional Library, DeSoto County Library, Hernando MS. 601-368-4439

Moore, Dorothy, *ILL,* Andover Newton Theological School, Franklin Trask Library, Newton Centre MA. 617-964-1100, Ext 140

Moore, Dorothy, *ILL,* Bucks County Community College Library, Newtown PA. 215-968-5861, Ext 306, 307

Moore, Dorothy W, *Dir,* Pepperdine University Library, Payson Library, Malibu CA. 213-456-4252

Moore, Dorothy W, *Librn,* Pepperdine University, Los Angeles Campus Library, Los Angeles CA. 213-971-7730, Ext 730

Moore, Edith, *Photo Servs,* University of California Los Angeles Library, Los Angeles CA. 213-825-1201

Moore, Edward, *Bkmobile Coordr,* Macon County-Tuskegee Public Library, Tuskegee AL. 205-727-5192

Moore, Edythe, *Mgr Libr Servs,* Aerospace Corp, Charles C Lauritsen Library, El Segundo CA. 213-648-6178

Moore, Elaine, *Ch & YA,* Clarion State College, Rena M Carlson Library, Clarion PA. 814-226-2343

Moore, Eleanor, *Tech Serv,* Southwestern Michigan College, Fred L Mathews Library, Dowagiac MI. 616-782-5113, Ext 27

Moore, Elizabeth, *Librn,* Bartram Trail Regional Library (Taliaferro County), Crawfordville GA. 404-678-7736

Moore, Elizabeth, *Chmn,* Central Georgia Associated Libraries, GA. 912-272-5710

Moore, Elizabeth, *Librn,* Michigan Bell, Corporate Reference Center, Detroit MI. 313-223-8040

Moore, Elizabeth D, *Dir,* Oconee Regional Library, Laurens County Library, Dublin GA. 912-272-5710

Moore, Elma, *Cat,* Hazleton Area Public Library, Hazleton PA. 717-454-2961, 454-0244

Moore, Emily Catherine, *Extension Libr,* Rowan Public Library, Salisbury NC. 704-633-5578

Moore, Emmerine, *Ref & Per,* Muskogee Public Library, Muskogee OK. 918-682-6657

Moore, Erdeal A, *Ser,* University of Alabama in Birmingham (Lister Hill Library of the Health Sciences), Birmingham AL. 205-934-5460

Moore, Ethel, *Librn,* Spearville Library, Spearville KS. 316-385-2501

Moore, Everett L, *Dir,* Woodbury University Library, Los Angeles CA. 482-8491, Ext 25

Moore, Evia Briggs, *Per,* San Joaquin Delta College, Goleman Library, Stockton CA. 209-478-2011, Ext 277

Moore, Faye, *Librn,* Lawrence County Library, Louisa KY. 606-638-4497

Moore, Frances, *Ch,* Brandon Township Public Library, Ortonville MI. 313-627-2804, Ext 44

Moore, Frances, *Ch,* Davidson County Public Library System, Lexington NC. 704-246-2520

Moore, Francis X, *In Charge,* Community Hospital at Glen Cove, Medical Library, Glen Cove NY. 516-676-5000, Ext 609

Moore, Gay, *Cat & Spec Coll,* University of Central Arkansas, Torreyson Library, Conway AR. 501-329-2931, Ext 449

Moore, Glenna, *Media,* Eastern New Mexico University, Roswell Campus Library, Roswell NM. 505-347-5441, Ext 244

Moore, Gloria, *ILL,* Skidmore College, Lucy Scribner Library, Saratoga Springs NY. 518-584-5000, Ext 234

Moore, Grace, *Librn,* Louisiana State Library (Recorder of Documents), Baton Rouge LA. 504-342-4929

Moore, Gwen, *Client Librn,* Terrell State Hospital, Medical & Client Libraries, Terrell TX. 214-563-6452, Ext 302 & 497

Moore, H J, *Br Asst,* Morehouse Parish Library (Bonita Branch), Bonita LA. 318-281-3683

MOORE

Moore, Harriet, *Librn,* Anoka State Hospital Library, Anoka MN. 612-421-3940
Moore, Helen M, *Librn,* North Vancouver City Library, North Vancouver BC. 604-980-0581
Moore, Irene S, *Media,* Mary Riley Styles Public Library, Falls Church VA. 703-241-5030
Moore, Ivy P, *Chief Librn,* Federal Aviation Administration, Alaskan Region Library, Anchorage AK. 907-265-4620
Moore, J, *Ref,* Chatham Public Library, Chatham ON. 519-354-2940
Moore, J Terry, *Tech Serv,* Traverse Des Sioux Library System, Mankato MN. 507-625-6169
Moore, Jacqueline, *Librn,* Tyson Memorial Public Library, Lenoir City Public Library, Lenoir City TN. 615-986-3210
Moore, James E, *Gen Servs Librn,* Albemarle Regional Library, Winton NC. 919-358-7631
Moore, Jane, *Ch,* South Huntington Public Library, Huntington Station NY. 516-549-4411
Moore, Jane R, *Chief Librn,* City University of New York, Library of Graduate School & University Center, New York NY. 212-790-4541
Moore, Janice, *Ref,* Central North Carolina Regional Library, Burlington NC. 919-227-2096
Moore, Jean B, *Ref,* Paramus Public Library, Paramus NJ. 201-265-1800
Moore, Jerrel K, *Dir,* University of Central Arkansas, Torreyson Library, Conway AR. 501-329-2931, Ext 449
Moore, Joan, *Asst Librn,* Corning Public Library, Corning IA. 515-322-3866
Moore, John, *Eng,* Chicago Public Library (Business, Science & Technology Div), Chicago IL. 312-269-2814, 269-2865
Moore, John, *Asst Dir,* Mott Public Library, Mott ND. 701-824-2163
Moore, Joleta, *In Charge,* E-Systems, Inc, Division Library, Greenville TX. 214-455-3450
Moore, Joyce, *Dir & Bibliog Instr,* Houghton College, Willard J Houghton Library, Houghton NY. 716-567-2211, Ext 227
Moore, Joyce, *Librn,* Jefferson Community College, Learning Resources Center, Louisville KY. 502-584-0181, Ext 305
Moore, Katharine E, *Dir,* Balsam Lake Public Library, Balsam Lake WI. 715-485-3215
Moore, Kathryn, *Asst Librn,* Crosby Public Library, Antwerp NY. 315-659-8564
Moore, Kathy, *Librn,* Ruidoso Public Library, Ruidoso NM. 505-257-4335
Moore, Kent, *AV,* Prince George's County Memorial Library System, Hyattsville MD. 301-699-3500
Moore, Kent U, *Librn,* Mark Skinner Library, Manchester VT. 802-362-2607
Moore, L A, *Dir,* Plainfield Free Public Library, Plainfield NJ. 201-757-1111
Moore, Linda, *Librn,* Dunbar Free Library, Grantham NH. 603-863-4743
Moore, Linda, *ILL & Circ,* Hillsdale College, Mossey Learning Resources Center, Hillsdale MI. 517-437-7341, Ext 225
Moore, Linda, *Librn,* Cyrus J Lawrence Inc Library, New York NY. 212-962-2200
Moore, Linda, *Librn,* Millbrook Public Library, Millbrook AL. 205-285-6688
Moore, Lorraine, *Cat,* Brown University (John Carter Brown Library), Providence RI. 401-863-2725
Moore, Marilyn, *Ref, On-Line Servs & Bibliog Instr,* Mississippi Research & Development Center, Information Services Divison, Jackson MS. 601-982-6324
Moore, Marjorie, *Tech Serv,* Bangor Public Library, Bangor ME. 207-947-8336
Moore, Martha C, *Dir,* Gardendale Public Library, Gardendale AL. 205-631-6639
Moore, Mary, *Coordr,* Golden Plains Library Federation, Glasgow MT. 406-228-2731
Moore, Mary, *Librn,* Jackson Metropolitan Library (Triangle Park Library), Mendenhall MS. 601-352-3677
Moore, Mary, *Librn,* Santa Fe Regional Library (Hawthorne Branch), Hawthorne FL. 904-481-3388
Moore, Mary, *YA,* Stanislaus County Free Library, Modesto CA. 209-526-6821
Moore, Mary A, *Librn,* Town of Tonawanda Public Library (Sheridan Parkside), Tonawanda NY. 716-873-2861

Moore, Mary L, *Librn,* Exxon Co USA (General Services Library), Houston TX. 713-656-5915
Moore, Mary Y, *Dir,* Glasgow City County Library, Glasgow MT. 406-228-2731
Moore, Maureen M, *Dir,* United States Department of Justice Library, Washington DC. 202-633-3775
Moore, Maxine, *Ch,* Hattiesburg Public Library System, Hattiesburg MS. 601-582-4461
Moore, Michael, *Media,* Brookhaven College, Learning Resources Center, Farmers Branch TX. 214-746-5250
Moore, Mildred, *Librn,* University of Kentucky (Mathematics), Lexington KY. 606-258-8253
Moore, Millie, *Per,* Tulane University of Louisiana (Matas Medical Library), New Orleans LA. 504-588-5155
Moore, Milton, *Cat,* Southern Illinois University at Edwardsville, Elijah P Lovejoy Library, Edwardsville IL. 618-692-2711
Moore, Mrs B, *Librn,* Burgess Industries, Engineering Library, Dallas TX. 214-631-1410
Moore, Mrs Dwight D, *Dir,* Shenandoah College & Conservatory of Music, Howe Library, Winchester VA. 703-667-8714, Ext 453
Moore, Mrs Gerry, *Librn,* El Paso Museum of Art Library, El Paso TX. 915-543-3800
Moore, Mrs H, *Branch Assistant,* Cumberland Regional Library (Oxford Branch), Amherst NS. 902-447-2440
Moore, Mrs Jacque, *Librn,* Palacios Library Inc, Palacios TX. 512-972-3234
Moore, Mrs Rodney, *Commun Servs,* Okefenokee Regional Library, Waycross GA. 912-283-3126
Moore, Mrs V, *Librn,* Middle Georgia Regional Library (Montezuma Carnegie Branch), Montezuma GA. 912-472-7262
Moore, Myrl, *Librn,* Arley Public Library, Arley AL. 205-387-7537
Moore, Nancy, *ILL & Ad,* North Palm Beach Public Library, North Palm Beach FL. 305-848-0445
Moore, Nancy, *Librn,* Webster Parish Library (Jones Memorial), Minden LA. 318-377-6861
Moore, Nelda P, *Dir,* Nelson County Public Library, Bardstown KY. 502-348-3714
Moore, Olivia, *Librn,* Birmingham Public & Jefferson County Free Library (Pratt City), Pratt City AL. 205-254-2551
Moore, Othelia, *Librn,* Pendleton County Public Library, Falmouth KY. 606-654-8535
Moore, Patricia S, *Dir & Acq,* Emmet O'neal Library, Mountain Brook AL. 205-879-0459
Moore, Paula, *Ch,* Downers Grove Public Library, Downers Grove IL. 312-960-1200
Moore, Pauline, *Librn,* Mount Hope Library, Mount Hope KS. 316-667-2192
Moore, Peggy, *Tech Serv, Circ & Spec Coll,* Shorter College, Livingston Library, Rome GA. 404-291-2121, Ext 43
Moore, Peter, *Circ,* Lincoln Library, Springfield Public Library, Springfield IL. 217-753-4900
Moore, Phyllis, *Librn,* Public Library of Cincinnati & Hamilton County (Clifton), Cincinnati OH. 513-221-6832
Moore, Phyllis C, *Dir & Media,* Alameda Free Library, Alameda CA. 415-522-5413, 522-3578
Moore, R L, *Ser,* University of Maine School of Law, Donald L Garbrecht Library, Portland ME. 207-780-4350
Moore, Ray, *Media,* Olivet Nazarene College, Benner Library & Resource Center, Bourbonnais IL. 815-939-5354
Moore, Rebecca, *Tech Serv,* Graham Public Library, Graham TX. 817-549-0600
Moore, Richard E, *Dir,* Southern Oregon State College Library, Ashland OR. 503-482-6445
Moore, Richard W, *Librn,* Red Bank Public Library, Eisner Memorial Library, Red Bank NJ. 201-842-0690
Moore, Robert E, *Dir,* Bucks County Planning Commission, Staff Library, Doylestown PA. 215-348-2911
Moore, Robert E, *Assoc Exec Dir,* Epilepsy Foundation of America Library, Washington DC. 202-293-2930
Moore, Ross, *Ch,* Burlington Public Library, Burlington ON. 416-639-3611
Moore, Ruby, *Librn,* Darlington County Library (Lamar District Branch), Lamar SC. 803-393-5864
Moore, Russell J, *Dir,* Long Beach Museum of Art Library, Long Beach CA. 213-439-2119

Moore, Russell S, *Cat,* Westfield Athenaeum, Westfield MA. 413-568-7833
Moore, Ruth K, *Tech Serv,* Carroll Public Library, Carroll IA. 712-792-3432
Moore, Sandra, *Coordr,* Clackamas County Cooperative Library Services, OR. 503-655-8543
Moore, Shirley A, *Librn,* J C Wheeler Library, Martin MI. 616-672-7875
Moore, Susan, *Librn,* Ohio Department of Public Welfare Library, Staff Development Multimedia Center, Columbus OH. 614-466-4574
Moore, Susan, *Librn,* United States Navy (Naval Support Activity Library), New Orleans LA. 504-361-2210
Moore, Ted, *ILL,* Georgetown University (John Vinton Dahlgren Memorial Library), Washington DC. 202-625-7577
Moore, Thomas L, *Admin Librn,* Palatine Public Library District, Palatine IL. 312-358-5881
Moore, Travis L, *Librn,* Florence County Library (Timmonsville Public), Timmonsville SC. 803-346-2941
Moore, Treva M, *Dir,* Plant City Public Library, Plant City FL. 813-752-8685, 752-7942
Moore, Victor, *Librn,* North Arkansas Regional Library (Carroll County), Berryville AR. 501-423-2323
Moore, Viola M, *Dir,* Indiana Northern Graduate School of Professional Management Library, Marion IN. 317-674-2900
Moore, Virginia, *Libr Technician,* San Diego County Library (El Cajon Branch), El Cajon CA. 714-579-4454
Moore, Waldo H, *Asst Register for Registration,* Library of Congress (Order Division), Washington DC. 202-287-5000
Moore, William L, *Exec Dir,* Greater Dallas Planning Council Library, Dallas TX. 214-748-2274
Moore, Woodvall R, *Dir & Acq,* Evangel College Library, Springfield MO. 417-865-2811, Ext 267
Moore, Woody S, *Librn,* Marion Military Institute, Baer Memorial Library, Marion AL. 205-683-9593
Moorehead, Joseph H, *Assoc Prof,* State University of New York at Albany, School of Library & Information Science, NY. 518-455-6288
Moorehouse, Mrs D, *Librn,* Lambton County Library (Shetland), Florence ON. 519-692-3213
Moores, Polly, *Libr Adminr,* Wetumpka Public Library, Wetumpka AL. 205-567-8966
Moorhead, Edith H, *Librn,* Jefferson County Law Library, Steubenville OH. 614-283-4111
Moorhead, Roberta, *Librn,* Wayne-Westland Public Library, Wayne MI. 313-721-7832
Moorhead, Wendy, *ILL,* Suburban Library System, Burr Ridge IL. 312-325-6640
Moorhouse, Rubye, *Librn,* Baylor County Free Library, Seymour TX. 817-888-3926
Moorman, John A, *Dir,* Elbert Ivey Memorial Library, Hickory NC. 704-322-2905
Moorman, Patricia, *Librn,* Public Library of Fort Wayne & Allen County (Georgetown), Fort Wayne IN. 219-493-1481
Moorman, Yuki, *Librn,* Juneau Memorial Library (Douglas Public), Douglas AK. 907-364-2378
Moos, Patricia, *Librn,* Smithers Public Library, Smithers BC. 604-847-3043
Moose, Lucinda, *Ch,* Gaston County Public Library, Gastonia NC. 704-866-3756
Morahan, Sister Marie Joseph, *Dir,* Saint Thomas Aquinas College Library, Sparkill NY. 359-9500 Ext 246, 245
Morales, Angelina Claudio De, *Librn,* Inter-American University of Puerto Rico, Arecibo Regional College Library, Arecibo PR. 809-878-2522
Morales, Carla, *Asst Librn,* Clifton-City-Greenlee County Library, Clifton AZ. 602-865-2461
Morales, Luis R Munoz, *Pub Serv,* University of Puerto Rico, Cayey University College Library, Cayey PR. 809-738-2161, Ext 221, 738-5651
Morales, Myra, *Ch,* Adriance Memorial Library, Poughkeepsie NY. 914-485-4790
Morales, Rene, *Hist & Soc Sci,* San Francisco Public Library, San Francisco CA. 415-558-4235
Moran, Barbara, *Coordr,* Parkersburg Community College, Learning Resources Center, Parkersburg WV. 304-424-8260

Moran, David, *Ref*, Northwestern Oklahoma State University Library, Alva OK. 405-327-1700, Ext 219

Moran, Frank, *Soc Sci*, Central Missouri State University, Ward Edwards Library, Warrensburg MO. 816-429-4141

Moran, Gerald D, *Dir & Acq*, Geneva College, McCartney Library, Beaver Falls PA. 412-846-5100, Ext 297

Moran, Hertha H, *Librn*, Garrett Public Library, Garrett IN. 219-357-5485

Moran, James, *Librn*, University of Texas at El Paso Library (Documents & Maps), El Paso TX. 915-747-5685

Moran, Janis, *Asst Librn*, Swarthmore Public Library, Swarthmore PA. 215-543-0436

Moran, John, *Pub Servs*, State University of New York College, Daniel A Reed Library, Fredonia NY. 716-673-3183

Moran, Leila, *Chief, Ref*, National Agricultural Library, Beltsville MD. 301-344-4248

Moran, Marguerite K, *Dir*, M&T Chemicals Inc, Technical & Business Information Center, Rahway NJ. 201-499-2437

Moran, Mary, *Librn*, Oklahoma Historical Society (Newspaper Library), Oklahoma City OK. 405-521-2491

Moran, Michael J, *Dir*, Asnuntuck Community College, Learning Resource Center, Enfield CT. 203-745-1603, Ext 11, 13

Moran, Nancy, *Circ*, Stamford's Public Library, Ferguson Library, Stamford CT. 203-325-4354

Moran, P, *Archivist*, Simcoe County Archives, Minesing ON. 705-726-9300, Ext 287; 726-9305

Moran, Pat, *Archives*, Community College of Allegheny County, Allegheny Campus Library, Pittsburgh PA. 412-237-2585

Moran, Paul F, *Librn*, United States Bureau of Mines, Avondale Research Center Library, Hyattsville MD. 301-436-7552

Moran, Robert F, *Acq*, University of Illinois at Chicago Circle Library, Chicago IL. 312-996-2716

Moran, Robert W, *Librn*, Red Lodge Carnegie Library, Red Lodge MT. 406-446-1905

Moran, Rosemary, *Librn*, Tulsa City-County Library (Woodland View), Tulsa OK. 918-627-7153

Moran, Sally, *Librn*, Nashville Banner Library, Nashville TN. 615-255-5401

Moran, Sylvia J, *Coordr*, Erie Community College-North, Library Resources Center, Buffalo NY. 716-634-0800

Moran, Terry, *Assoc Librn*, Houghton Mifflin Co Library, Boston MA. 617-725-5270

Morash, E, *Librn*, National Film Board of Canada, Reference Library, Montreal PQ. 514-333-3141, 333-3142

Moravec, Georgina, *Librn*, Toronto Planning & Development Dept Library, Toronto ON. 416-367-7182

Morawetz, Gwen, *Librn*, Lakefield College Library, Lakefield ON. 705-652-3324

More, Hazel M, *Tech Librn*, Fairchild Industries, Technical Information Services Library, Germantown MD. 301-428-6000

More, Mrs B, *Br Supvr*, Scarborough Public Library (Woodside Square), Scarborough ON. 416-291-9437

More, Sister M Thomas, *Librn*, Lourdes College, Mother Adelaide Hall & Duns Scotus Library, Sylvania OH. 882-2016 Ext 230

Moreau, Denyse-Helene, *Librn*, Canadian Tobacco Manufacturers Council, Smoking & Health Library, Montreal PQ. 514-937-7428

Moreau, Vivian, *Ref*, Boston College Libraries (School of Social Work Library), Chestnut Hill MA. 617-969-0100, Ext 3233

Moree, Sally, *Ad*, South Mississippi Regional Library, Columbia MS. 601-736-5516

Morehart, Tami, *Ch*, Pickaway County District Public Library, Circleville OH. 614-477-1644

Morehead, Dorothy, *Librn*, Norway Public Library, Norway IA. 319-227-7487

Morehead, Edith, *Ch*, West Georgia Regional Library, Neva Lomason Memorial Library, Carrollton GA. 404-832-1381

Morehouse, Harold G, *Dir*, University of Nevada at Reno, NV. 702-784-6533

Morehouse, Harold G, *Dir*, University of Nevada-Reno, Noble H Getchell Library, Reno NV. 702-784-6533

Morehouse, Helen, *Br Coordr*, Klamath County Library, Klamath Falls OR. 503-882-8894

Morehouse, Val, *Asst Dir*, Plymouth Public Library, Russell Memorial Library, Plymouth MA. 617-746-1927

Morel, Jean, *Health Sci*, Universite Laval Bibliotheque, Quebec PQ. 418-656-3344

Moreland, Bruce, *Ref*, Bibliotheque Municipale Des Sources, Sources Public Library, Roxboro PQ. 514-684-8247, 684-8260

Moreland, Carol, *Asst Dir*, Bismarck Junior College Library, Bismarck ND. 701-223-4500, Ext 50

Moreland, Rachel, *Circ*, Kansas State University, Farrell Library, Manhattan KS. 913-532-6516

Morelli, Bernece, *Librn*, Florence Public Library, Florence CO. 303-784-4649

Morelli, Marcia, *Ref*, New Castle Public Library, New Castle PA. 412-658-6659

Morelock, Genalee, *Librn*, Springfield-Greene County Library (Ash Grove Branch) Ash Grove MO. 417-672-2933

Moren, Harold, *Acq*, Brandeis University, Goldfarb Library, Waltham MA. 617-647-2514

Moreno, E L, *Librn*, Atlantic Richfield Co (Corporate Law Library), Los Angeles CA. 213-486-1560

Moreno, Esperanza A, *Librn*, University of Texas at El Paso Library (Nursing-Medical), El Paso TX. 915-533-6094

Moreno, Pat, *Librn*, Tucson Public Library (Pima County Jail), Tucson AZ. 602-791-4391

Moreno, Ralph, *Ref*, Mill Valley Public Library, Mill Valley CA. 415-388-4245

Moreno, Raphael, *Project Admin*, New York Public Library (South Bronx Project), New York NY. 212-993-5539

Moreo, Stanley D, *Resources, Info & On-Line Search Coordr*, Lewis & Clark Library System, Edwardsville IL. 618-656-3216

Moretti, Frances, *Ref*, Acton Memorial Library, Acton MA. 617-263-2232, 263-9109

Moretti, Patricia C, *Dir*, Eagleville Hospital & Rehabilitation Center, Henry S Louchheim Medical Library, Eagleville PA. 215-539-6000, Ext 304

Moretto, Kathleen J, *Asst Librn*, Yale University Library (Music), New Haven CT. 203-436-8240

Moretto, Shirley M, *Dir*, Westville Public Library, Westville IL. 217-267-3170

Morey, Barbara, *On-Line Servs & Bibliog Instr*, Saint Joseph Hospital, Health Sciences Library, Flint MI. 313-762-8519

Morey, Helen, *Cat*, Central Florida Community College, Library Learning Resources Center, Ocala FL. 904-237-2111, Ext 344

Morey, Thomas J, *Mgr Libr servs*, Xerox Corp, Technical Information Center, Webster NY. 716-422-3505

Morford, Betty S, *Librn & Coordr*, Brevard Community College, Titusville Campus Learning Resource Center, Titusville FL. 305-269-5664

Morgan, Arthur, *Chief Operating Engineer*, Chicago Public Library, Chicago IL. 312-269-2900

Morgan, Candy, *Pub Servs*, Oregon State Library, Salem OR. 503-378-4243

Morgan, Carla, *Activities Coordr & Children's Services*, Austin Memorial Library, Cleveland TX. 713-592-3920

Morgan, Charles, *Media*, University of Southern Mississippi (School of Nursing, Instructional Resource Program), Hattiesburg MS. 601-266-4211

Morgan, Charlotte M, *Librn*, Manteno Mental Health Center, Staff Library, Manteno IL. 815-468-3451

Morgan, Christine G, *Curator*, Rowland E Robinson Memorial Association, Rokeby Museum Special Collections Library, Ferrisburg VT. 802-877-3406

Morgan, Cliff, *Librn*, Memphis-Shelby County Public Library & Information Center (Cossitt-Goodwyn Libr), Memphis TN. 901-528-2994

Morgan, Dana H, *Curator*, Rowland E Robinson Memorial Association, Rokeby Museum Special Collections Library, Ferrisburg VT. 802-877-3406

Morgan, David Forbes, *In Charge*, College of the Rockies Library, Denver CO. 303-832-1547

Morgan, Denise, *Asst Librn*, Paul, Weiss, Rifkind, Wharton & Garrison Library, New York NY. 212-644-8235

Morgan, Dennis, *Dir*, Ohio Legislative Reference Bureau Library, Columbus OH. 614-466-3031

Morgan, Dixie K, *Librn*, Monroe County Traveling Library, Union WV. 304-772-3038

Morgan, Donna, *Librn*, Deere & Co Library (Technical Center Library), Moline IL. 309-757-5363

Morgan, Dorothy, *Librn*, Elliott Public Library, Elliott IA. 712-767-2355

Morgan, Ella, *Cat*, Langston University, G Lamar Harrison Library, Langston OK. 405-466-2231, Ext 231

Morgan, Ella Mae, *Librn*, Prescott Public-Yavapai County Library System (Prescott Valley Public), Prescott Valley AZ. 602-772-8720

Morgan, F Phyllis, *Librn*, United States Air Force (Eglin Air Force Base Library), Eglin AFB FL. 904-882-5088

Morgan, George, *Libr Production Mgr*, Boston State College Library, Boston MA. 617-731-3300

Morgan, Griscom, *Dir*, Community Service Inc Library, Yellow Springs OH. 513-767-2161

Morgan, Harriette, *Ser*, Center for Disease Control Library, Atlanta GA. 404-329-3396

Morgan, Helen, *On-Line Servs & Bibliog Instr*, Leon County Public Library, Leon-Jefferson Library System, Tallahassee FL. 904-487-2665

Morgan, Helen E, *Asst Librn*, Church of the Incarnation, Marmion Library, Dallas TX. 214-521-5101

Morgan, Helen F, *Asst Dir & Ref*, Louisville Public Library, Louisville OH. 216-875-1696

Morgan, James, *Dir*, University of Oregon Health Sciences Center (Health Sciences Library), Portland OR. 503-225-8026

Morgan, Jane Hale, *Dir*, Detroit Public Library, Detroit Associated Libraries, Detroit MI. 313-833-1000

Morgan, Jean M, *Dir*, Ventura College, D R Henry Library, Ventura CA. 805-642-3211, Ext 201

Morgan, Jeanne W, *Dir*, Glenolden Library, Glenolden PA. 215-583-1010

Morgan, Judith, *Librn*, Northern Virginia Community College Libraries (Woodbridge Campus), Woodbridge VA. 703-670-2191, Ext 217

Morgan, June, *ILL & Ref*, Stillwater Public Library, City Library, Stillwater OK. 405-372-3633

Morgan, Kitty, *Tech Serv & Acq*, Loma Linda University Library, Riverside CA. 714-785-5022

Morgan, Linda, *Ch*, East Saint Louis Public Library, East Saint Louis IL. 618-874-7280

Morgan, Lynda, *Librn*, Saint Joseph Hospital, Health Sciences Library, Memphis TN. 901-529-2874

Morgan, Madelyn, *Librn*, West Georgia Regional Library (Villa Rice Public), Villa Rica GA. 404-832-1381

Morgan, Manley, *Actg Dir*, Ellsworth Memorial Association, Oliver Ellsworth Homestead Library, Windsor CT. 203-688-8717

Morgan, Mary Sue, *Librn*, Watauga County Public Library, Boone NC. 704-264-8784

Morgan, Mary T, *Librn*, Lemuel Shattuck Hospital (Patients' Library), Jamaica Plain MA. 617-522-8110, Ext 225

Morgan, Mildred, *Librn*, Trinity Medical Center (Trinity School of Nursing Library), Minot ND. 701-857-5621

Morgan, Mildred W, *Dir*, Lanier Library Association, Inc, Tryon NC. 704-859-9535

Morgan, Miriam, *Ch*, Prospect Heights Public Library District, Prospect Heights IL. 312-259-3500

Morgan, Muriel, *Prof*, Ryerson Polytechnical Institute, Library Arts Dept, ON. 416-595-5285

Morgan, Nancy, *Librn*, Muldrow Public Library, Muldrow OK. 918-427-6703

Morgan, Nancy, *Commun Servs*, Peabody Institute Library, Danvers Public Library, Danvers MA. 617-774-0554, Ext 0557, 0555

Morgan, Olive Elizabeth, *Librn*, Flora Carnegie Library, Flora IL. 618-622-6553

Morgan, Pamela D, *Ser*, University of North Carolina at Greensboro, Walter Clinton Jackson Library, Greensboro NC. 919-379-5880

Morgan, Paula, *Librn*, Princeton University Library (Music), Princeton NJ. 609-452-3180

MORGAN

Morgan, R J, *Archivist,* College of Cape Breton Library (Beaton Institute), Sydney NS. 902-539-5520

Morgan, Rita, *ILL & Media,* Franklin Square Public Library, Franklin Square NY. 516-488-3444

Morgan, Rita, *Librn,* Fuller Public Library, Hillsboro NH. 603-464-3595

Morgan, Shirley, *Humanities,* Northeast Louisiana University, Sandel Library, Monroe LA. 318-342-2195

Morgan, T E, *Gen Coun,* Columbia Gas Systems (Distribution Companies Law Library), Columbus OH. 614-460-2565

Morgan, Thelma, *Librn,* Udall Public Library, Udall KS. 316-782-3327

Morgan, Valarie, *Ch & YA,* Ohio County Public Library, Wheeling WV. 304-232-0244

Morgan, William R, *Librn,* University of Michigan Libraries (Architecture), Ann Arbor MI. 313-764-1303

Morgan, Jr, Mendell D, *Dir & ILL,* Incarnate Word College, Saint Pius X Library, San Antonio TX. 512-828-1261, Ext 215

Morgener, Fred, *Librn,* Cincinnati Enquirer Library, Cincinnati OH. 513-721-2700

Morgenstern, Sali, *History of Medicine & Rare Books,* New York Academy of Medicine Library, New York NY. 212-876-8200

Moriarty, Judith, *Cat & Ser,* University of Wisconsin-Platteville, Elton S Karrmann Library, Platteville WI. 608-342-1688

Moriarty, Paul V, *Asst Dir & Acq,* University of Wisconsin-Platteville, Elton S Karrmann Library, Platteville WI. 608-342-1688

Moriaty, Mary, *Ch,* Oskaloosa Public Library, Oskaloosa IA. 515-673-6214

Morici, Mary D, *Librn,* Birdsboro Community Library, Birdsboro PA. 215-582-2471

Morin, Douglas, *Librn,* G E P Dodge Library, Bennington NH. 603-588-6585

Morin, Ellen I, *Dir,* Fulton Public Library, Fulton NY. 315-592-5159

Morin, Estelle, *Librn,* Chapleau Public Library, Chapleau ON. 705-864-0852

Morin, Mrs Bernard, *Librn,* Bradford M Field Memorial Library, Leverett MA. 413-549-5018

Morin, Mrs Joseph, *Librn,* Charlton Public Library, Charlton MA. 617-248-7876

Morin, Robert, *Cat,* University of New Hampshire, Ezekiel W Dimond Library, Durham NH. 603-862-1540

Morin, Wilfred L, *Dir,* Freeport Memorial Library, Freeport NY. 516-379-3274

Moring, Doug, *Cat,* Cameron University Library, Lawton OK. 405-248-2200, Ext 410

Moringiello, Kathleen B, *Librn,* General Motors Corp (Legal Staff Library), New York NY. 212-486-5090

Morisak, Carol, *Librn,* Friench Simpson Memorial Library, Hallettsville TX. 512-798-3243

Morissette, Yvette, *Librn,* Bibliotheque Municipale, Val d'Or PQ. 819-824-2666

Moritz, Elaine, *Librn,* Kitsap Regional Library (Silverdale Station), Silverdale WA. 206-692-2779

Moritz, William D, *Assoc Dir,* University of Wisconsin-Milwaukee, Golda Meir Library, Milwaukee WI. 414-963-4785

Moriwaki, Frances, *Librn,* Los Angeles Public Library System (Jefferson), Los Angeles CA. 213-734-8573

Morizzo, Nickee, *Librn,* Guilford Memorial Library, Guilford ME. 207-876-4547

Morlan, Joyce, *Librn,* Garrett Memorial Library, Moulton IA. 515-642-3664

Morledge, Grace, *Asst Librn,* Missouri Historical Society Library, Saint Louis MO. 314-361-1424

Morley, Edward F, *Cat,* Bridgewater State College, Clement C Maxwell Library, Bridgewater MA. 617-697-8321, Ext 441, 442

Morner, Claudia, *Dir,* Osterville Free Library, Osterville MA. 617-428-2565

Moro, Barbara, *Libr Pub Info Mgrs: Broadcasting,* Chicago Public Library, Chicago IL. 312-269-2900

Moron, Robert, *Photoduplicating Lab Supvr,* Bureau of Libraries, Museums & Archaeological Services, Saint Thomas VI. 809-774-3407

Morozowsky, Beverly, *Clerk,* John McIntire Public Library Public Library (South Zanesville), South Zanesville OH. 614-454-1511

Morphet, Norman D, *Ch,* Sun Co, Library & Information Service, Marcus Hook PA. 215-447-1723

Morphy, Marjory, *Ref,* Academy of Medicine, William Boyd Library, Toronto ON. 416-964-7088

Morrell, B, *Cat,* Mount Allison University, Ralph Pickard Bell Library, Sackville NB. 506-536-2040, Ext 375

Morrell, Beverly, *Librn,* Westmoreland Hospital Association (Medical Staff Library), Greensburg PA. 412-837-0100, Ext 380

Morrell, Beverly A, *Dir,* Westmoreland Hospital Association (Health Education Center Library), Greensburg PA. 412-837-0100, Ext 380

Morrell, Stephanie R, *Librn,* McKinsey & Co Inc, San Francisco CA. 415-981-0250

Morrill, Juanita H, *Librn,* Eastern State Hospital, Resource Library, Lexington KY. 606-255-1431, Ext 306

Morrill, Richard, *Bus Servs,* Lancaster County Library, Lancaster PA. 717-394-2651

Morrill, Richard, *Educ Ref,* University of Massachusetts at Amherst Library, Amherst MA. 413-545-0284

Morrill, Richard E, *Dir,* Prosser Public Library, Bloomfield CT. 203-243-9721

Morrill, Walter D, *Dir,* Hanover College, Duggan Library, Hanover IN. 812-866-2151, Ext 333

Morris, Ann-Louise, *Dir,* Hyannis Public Library Association, Hyannis MA. 617-775-2280

Morris, Anne L, *Dir,* Southern Lehigh Public Library, Solehi Public Library, Coopersburg PA. 215-965-2364

Morris, Babs, *Asst Librn,* New College of the University of South Florida, Sarasota Campus Library, Sarasota FL. 813-355-7671, Ext 214

Morris, Barbara, *Librn,* Viola Township Library, Viola KS. 316-584-6679

Morris, Brenda, *Bkmobile Coordr,* Danville-Boyle County Public Library, Danville KY. 606-236-8466

Morris, Carol, *Ref,* Nova Scotia Technical College Library, Halifax NS. 902-429-8300, Ext 254

Morris, Caroline, *Librn & Archivist,* Pennsylvania Hospital (Historic Library), Philadelphia PA. 215-829-3998

Morris, Caroline S, *Librn & Archivist,* Pennsylvania Hospital (Medical Library, Packard Reading Room), Philadelphia PA. 215-829-3998

Morris, Carrie, *Librn,* Bureau of Land Management (Colorado State Office Library), Denver CO. 303-837-2402

Morris, Catherine, *Dir,* Brown Deer Public Library, Brown Deer WI. 414-354-3440

Morris, Charlene, *Librn,* E-Systems Inc, Garland Div Technical Libr, Garland TX. 214-272-0515, Ext 4564

Morris, Christine, *Librn,* Clearwater Public Library (Northeast), Clearwater FL. 813-462-6895

Morris, Dilys, *Monographs,* Iowa State University Library, Ames IA. 515-294-1442

Morris, Donna, *Librn,* Metropolitan Library System (Southern Oaks), Oklahoma City OK. 405-235-0571

Morris, Doris O, *Asst Librn,* Smyrna Public Library, Smyrna GA. 404-436-2370

Morris, Dorothy, *Chief Librn,* NASA, Lewis Research Center Library, Cleveland OH. 216-433-4000, Ext 419

Morris, Dorothy G, *Librn,* Fresno County Law Library, Fresno CA. 209-237-2227

Morris, Elizabeth, *Ad,* Melbourne Public Library, Melbourne FL. 305-723-0611

Morris, G, *Librn,* CAE Electronics, Ltd, Engineering Reference Library, Montreal PQ. 514-341-6780, Ext 365

Morris, Georgia, *Tech Serv,* Merritt Island Public Library, Merritt Island FL. 305-452-3834

Morris, Gerald E, *Librn,* Mystic Seaport Museum, G W Blunt White Library, Mystic CT. 203-536-2631, Ext 261

Morris, Grace S, *Circ,* Washington County Library, Saint George UT. 801-673-2562

Morris, Harry, *Librn,* Speech Center Organization Parent Education, Speech & Language Development Center, Buena Park CA. 714-821-3620

Morris, Janie, *Ref,* Morris College, Pinson Memorial Library, Sumter SC. 803-775-9371, Ext 216

Morris, Jeanne, *Librn,* Greenville County Library (Mauldin), Mauldin SC. 803-288-4039

Morris, Jennifer, *ILL & Ref,* Finger Lakes Library System, Ithaca NY. 607-273-4074

Morris, Jo Ann, *Dir,* Stamford Hospital, Health Sciences Library, Stamford CT. 203-327-1234, Ext 527

Morris, Joan, *Ch,* Rosenberg Library, Galveston TX. 713-763-8854

Morris, John H, *Tech Serv,* Wharton County Junior College, J M Hodges Learning Center, Wharton TX. 713-532-4560, Ext 36

Morris, Joyce T, *Dir,* Jamestown Community College, Hultquist Library Learning Center, Jamestown NY. 716-665-5220, Ext 210

Morris, Junius H, *Chief Librn,* Highline Community College Library, Midway WA. 206-878-3710, Ext 230

Morris, L C, *Mgr Info Servs,* General Electric Co (Computer Management Operation Library), Bridgeport CT. 203-382-2682

Morris, Lany, *Circ,* Troy Public Library, Troy NY. 518-274-7071

Morris, Leigh, *Dir,* University of Richmond (T C Williams School of Law), Richmond VA. 804-285-6239

Morris, Leslie R, *Dir,* Xavier University of Louisiana Library, New Orleans LA. 504-486-7411, Ext 317

Morris, Lewise, *Librn,* Charlotte-Glades Library System (Glades County Branch), Moore Haven FL. 813-946-0744

Morris, Lillian, *Film Office,* Providence Public Library, Providence RI. 401-521-7722

Morris, Loree, *Librn,* West Branch Public Library, West Branch MI. 517-345-2235

Morris, Lynne D, *Chief Librn,* Veterans Administration (West Side Hospital Library Service), Chicago IL. 312-666-6500, Ext 381

Morris, Margarete, *Admin Asst,* Richland Parish Library, Rayville LA. 318-728-4806

Morris, Margie F, *Dir,* United Wesleyan College, Etta G Hoffman Library, Allentown PA. 215-439-8709, Ext 32

Morris, Mary, *Acq,* West Hills Community College Library, Coalinga CA. 209-935-0801, Ext 47

Morris, Mary, *Acq,* Western Carolina University (Acquisitions), Cullowhee NC. 704-293-7306

Morris, Mary A, *Station Librn,* United States Navy (Naval Air Station Library), Brunswick ME. 207-921-1110

Morris, Mary E, *Acq,* Western Carolina University, Hunter Memorial Library, Cullowhee NC. 704-293-7306

Morris, Mary Lee, *Cat,* Eastern New Mexico University Library, Portales NM. 505-562-2624

Morris, Miriam, *Librn,* Public Library of Cincinnati & Hamilton County (Madisonville), Cincinnati OH. 513-369-6029

Morris, Nicola, *Acq,* Goddard College, William Shipman Library, Plainfield VT. 802-454-8311, Ext 232

Morris, Pat, *Circ,* Union University, Emma Waters Summar Library, Jackson TN. 901-668-1818, Ext 269

Morris, Paula, *ILL & Ad,* Gadsden-Etowah County Library, Gadsden Public Library, Gadsden AL. 205-547-1611

Morris, Pearl, *Circ,* Addison Public Library, Addison IL. 312-543-3617

Morris, R Philip, *Asst Librn,* High Point Public Library, High Point NC. 919-885-8411

Morris, Rita L, *Cat,* Nassau Community College Library, Garden City NY. 516-222-7400

Morris, Robert, *Dir,* Orange County Community College Library, Middletown NY. 914-343-1121

Morris, Rosa Lee, *Librn,* Public Library of Anniston & Calhoun County (Hobson City Public), Hobson City AL. 205-237-8501, Ext 8503

Morris, Sally, *YA,* Glenview Public Library, Glenview IL. 312-724-5200

Morris, Sandra, *Librn,* United States Army (Huntington District Corps of Engineers Library), Huntington WV. 304-529-5435, 529-5713

Morris, Thelma, *In Charge,* Cleveland Public Library (Social Sciences), Cleveland OH. 216-623-2860

Morris, Thelma, *Librn,* Public Library of Cincinnati & Hamilton County (Avondale), Cincinnati OH. 513-369-6000

Morris, Thelma A, *Asst Dir,* Binghamton Public Library, Binghamton NY. 607-723-6457

Morris, Thom, *Dir,* Trinity College Library, Deerfield IL. 312-945-6700, Ext 217
Morris, Thomas G, *Assoc Prof,* Case Western Reserve University, School of Library Science, OH. 216-368-3500
Morris, Tzvee, *Program Officer,* Metropolitan Library Service Agency, Saint Paul MN. 612-645-5731
Morris, Virginia, *Librn,* Douglas County Library System (Canyonville Public), Canyonville OR. 503-839-4727
Morris, Virginia, *ILL & Media,* Glen Cove Public Library, Glen Cove NY. 516-676-2130
Morris, Waldin, *Bkmobile Coordr,* Tom Green County Library System, San Angelo TX. 915-655-7321
Morris, Jr, Mrs H L, *In Charge,* Edith B Ford Memorial Library, Ovid NY. 607-869-3031
Morriseau, Peter, *Librn,* Fort William Indian Band Library, Thunder Bay ON. 807-623-9543
Morrison, Alan E, *Librn,* University of Pennsylvania Libraries (Fine Arts), Philadelphia PA. 215-243-8325
Morrison, Angus, *On-Line Servs,* Ciba-Geigy Corp Library, Greensboro NC. 919-292-7100, Ext 2860
Morrison, Audrey, *Librn,* Globe Extracts, Inc Library, Farmingdale NY. 516-249-1515
Morrison, Barbara, *Ch & YA,* Pacific Grove Public Library, Pacific Grove CA. 408-373-0603
Morrison, Betty, *Acq,* Morehead State University, Johnson Camden-Julian Carroll Library, Morehead KY. 606-783-2250
Morrison, Carol, *Interlibr Cooperation Consultant,* DuPage Library System, Geneva IL. 312-232-8457
Morrison, Carol, *YA,* Middle Island Public Library, Middle Island NY. 516-924-4160
Morrison, Carol A, *Librn,* Cleveland Metropolitan General Hospital, Harold H Brittingham Memorial Library, Cleveland OH. 216-398-6000, Ext 4313
Morrison, Carol A, *Librn,* Ontario Cancer Institute Library, Toronto ON. 416-924-0671
Morrison, Dorothy, *Librn,* Marshall Public Library, Marshall TX. 214-935-5225
Morrison, Dwon, *Librn,* Downey Public Library, Downey ID. 208-897-5270
Morrison, Frances, *Dir,* Saskatoon Public Library, Saskatoon SK. 306-664-9555
Morrison, Gary R, *Dir,* United States Navy (Submarine Base-Submarine Force Library & Museum), Groton CT. 203-449-3174
Morrison, Helen, *Librn,* Gage Educational Publishing Ltd, Editorial Library, Agincourt ON. 416-293-8141
Morrison, Hilda O, *Media,* Atlanta Public Library, Atlanta GA. 404-688-4636
Morrison, Kathy, *Tech Serv,* Pataskala Public Library, Pataskala OH. 614-927-9986
Morrison, Katy, *Circ,* Cooke County Library, Gainesville TX. 817-665-2401
Morrison, Lillian, *Coordr YA Servs,* New York Public Library (The Branch Libraries), New York NY. 212-790-6262
Morrison, Louise E, *Dir,* Timberland Regional Library, Olympia WA. 206-943-5001
Morrison, M Christine, *Librn,* National Endowment for the Arts Library, Washington DC. 202-634-7640
Morrison, Marcia T, *Chief Librn,* Buffalo Museum of Science, Buffalo Society of Natural Sciences Research Library, Buffalo NY. 716-896-5200, Ext 10
Morrison, Marilyn, *Per,* Burlingame Public Library, Burlingame CA. 415-344-7107
Morrison, Mary, *Br Coordr & Bkmobile Coordr,* Findlay-Hancock County Public Library, Findlay OH. 419-422-1712
Morrison, Mildred, *Ref,* Central Piedmont Community College Library, Charlotte NC. 704-373-6883
Morrison, Mildred W, *President,* Metrolina Library Association, NC. 704-373-6884
Morrison, Naomi, *Librn,* Huntington State Hospital, Medical Library, Huntington WV. 304-525-7801, Ext 325
Morrison, Perry D, *Actg Asst Librn,* University of Oregon Library, Eugene OR. 503-686-3056
Morrison, Rachel E, *In Charge,* E I Du Pont De Nemours & Co, Inc (Pioneering Research Information Center), Wilmington DE. 302-772-3451
Morrison, Ray, *Bibliog Instr,* Pittsburg State University Library, Pittsburg KS. 316-231-7000, Ext 431
Morrison, Rose, *Asst Librn,* Elko County Library (Eureka Library), Eureka NV. 702-237-5307
Morrison, Samuel F, *Asst Dir,* Broward County Division of Libraries, Broward County Library, Pompano Beach FL. 305-972-1100
Morrison, Shawn Casey, *Librn,* Dynamic Sciences Inc Library, Van Nuys CA. 213-782-0829, Ext 64
Morrison, Sherrell R, *Librn,* Shelby County Library District, Shelbyville KY. 502-633-3803
Morrison, Shirley A, *Librn,* Dunlop Research Centre Library, Mississauga ON. 416-822-4711
Morrison, Sibyl, *Assoc Dir,* Texas Tech University Library, Lubbock TX. 806-742-2261
Morrison, Sue, *Asst Dir,* Sidney Public Library, Sidney MT. 406-482-1917
Morrison, V, *Librn,* Precision Cells, Inc Library, Hicksville NY. 516-938-7772
Morrison, Virginia, *Ch,* Dartmouth Public Libraries, Southworth Library, South Dartmouth MA. 617-997-1252
Morriss, Susan, *Ser,* Governors State University, University Library, Park Forest South IL. 312-534-5000, Ext 2231
Morrissett, Elizabeth, *Acq,* Auraria Libraries, Denver CO. 303-629-2805
Morrissey, Eleanor, *Asst Dir Tech Servs & Systs,* Vanderbilt University Library, Nashville TN. 615-322-2834
Morrissey, Jennifer, *Pub Serv,* Fanshawe College of Applied Arts & Technology Library, London ON. 519-452-4350
Morrissey, Kathleen, *Art & Music,* Lansing Public Library, Lansing MI. 517-374-4600
Morrissey, Mrs W L, *Dir,* Bloomington Public Library, Bloomington WI. 608-994-2602
Morrissey, Pat, *Librn,* Mead Public Library, Mead NE. 402-624-6605
Morrone, Kay, *Librn,* Baltimore County Public Library (Essex Area Branch), Essex MD. 301-686-2900
Morrone, Kay, *Librn,* Baltimore County Public Library (Middle River), Baltimore MD. 301-687-0990
Morroni, June, *Ad, YA & Commun Servs,* Centre County Library & Historical Museum, Bellefonte PA. 814-355-3131
Morrow, Alison, *Librn,* Sloan-Kettering Institute for Cancer Research, Donald S Walker Laboratory, C P Rhoads Memorial Library, Rye NY. 914-698-1100, Ext 277
Morrow, Deanna I, *On-Line Servs,* Georgia Pacific Corp Library, Atlanta GA. 404-491-1244
Morrow, Ellen B, *In Charge,* Quaker Chemical Corp, Technical Information Center, Conshohocken PA. 215-828-4250, Ext 378
Morrow, Glenda, *Librn,* Tombigbee Regional Library (Webster County Public), Eupora MS. 601-258-7515
Morrow, Glenn, *ILL,* Northwest Missouri State University, Wells Library, Maryville MO. 816-582-7141, Ext 1192
Morrow, Helene T, *Admin Med Librn,* United States Navy (Naval Regional Medical Center, Medical Library), Philadelphia PA. 215-755-8219
Morrow, Jean M, *Cat,* New England Conservatory of Music, Harriet M Spaulding Library, Boston MA. 617-262-1120
Morrow, Kay, *Librn,* Mccreary County Public Library District, Whitley City KY. 606-376-8738
Morrow, Marjorie S, *Dir,* Bartram Trail Regional Library, Mary Willis Library Headquarters, Washington GA. 404-678-7736
Morrow, Mary, *Ch & YA,* West New York Public Library, Philip A Payne Memorial Library, West New York NJ. 201-854-1028
Morrow, Tanya, *Librn,* South Carolina School for the Deaf & Blind Library, Spartanburg SC. 803-585-7711
Morse, Anita L, *Dir,* Cleveland State University Libraries (Joseph W Bartunek III Law Library), Cleveland OH. 216-687-2250
Morse, Celia, *Librn,* Riverview Public Library, Riverview MI. 313-283-1250
Morse, David, *Tech Serv,* University of Southern California (Norris Medical Library), Los Angeles CA. 213-226-2231
Morse, Elliott H, *Librn,* College of Physicians of Philadelphia Library, Philadelphia PA. 215-561-6050
Morse, Evelyn, *Asst Dir,* Somonauk Public Library, Somonauk IL. 815-498-2440
Morse, Evelyn C, *Librn,* Belmont Public Library, Memorial Library, Belmont NH. 603-267-8166
Morse, Everett, *ILL,* Ithaca College Library, Ithaca NY. 607-274-3182
Morse, Grant W, *Dir,* University of Wisconsin Center-Barron County Library, Rice Lake WI. 715-234-8176, Ext 20
Morse, Grant W, *Dir,* Wisconsin Indianhead Technical Institute, Rice Lake Campus Library, Rice Lake WI. 715-234-7082
Morse, Joan, *Librn,* Santa Clara County Free Library (Alum Rock), San Jose CA. 408-251-1280
Morse, Kenneth T, *Librn,* University of Rhode Island, Graduate School of Oceanography, Pell Marine Science Library, Narragansett RI. 401-792-6161
Morse, Margaret, *Librn,* Preston Public Library, Preston MN. 507-765-4511
Morse, Mark, *Dir,* L E Phillips Memorial Public Library, Eau Claire WI. 715-839-5002
Morse, Martha, *Librn,* Unity Free Library, Unity NH. 603-543-3861
Morse, Nora, *Librn,* Utica Mutual Insurance Co, Reference & Law Library, New Hartford NY. 315-735-3321
Morse, Phyllis, *Tech Serv,* Steele Memorial Library, Chemung-Southern Tier Library System, Elmira NY. 607-733-9173, 733-9174, 733-9175
Morse, Ralph, *Acq,* San Jose State University Library, San Jose CA. 408-277-3377
Morse, Robert G, *Librn,* Florida Department of Transportation, Central Reference Library, Tallahassee FL. 904-488-8572
Morse, Shirley K, *Librn,* GAF Corp, A W Dawes Memorial Library, Rensselaer NY. 518-465-4511
Morse, Yvonne L, *Librn,* Veterans Administration, Medical Center, Fayetteville NC. 919-488-2120, Ext 240
Morset, Ruth, *Circ & Bibliog Instr,* Azusa Pacific College, Marshburn Memorial Library, Azusa CA. 213-969-3434, Ext 198
Mort, Sarah, *Media,* Southwest Missouri State University Library, Springfield MO. 417-836-5104
Morten, Ermel, *Bibliographer,* Ricks College, David O McKay Learning Resources Center, Rexburg ID. 208-356-2351
Mortensen, Geraldine, *Librn,* Tooele Public Library, Tooele UT. 801-882-2182
Mortensen, J, *Head, Pub Servs,* Edmonton Public Library, Edmonton AB. 403-423-2331
Mortensen, Marilyn W, *Coordr,* Department of Public Libraries & Information (Subregional Library for the Blind, Special Services Division), Virginia Beach VA. 804-464-9175
Mortensen, Mary Louise, *Asst Prof,* Georgia College, Education Library Media, GA. 912-453-4047 & 453-5573
Mortensen, Ruth V, *Librn,* Le Boeuf, Lamb, Leiby & MacRae Library, New York NY. 212-269-1100
Mortensen, Vivian, *Reader Serv,* Park Ridge Public Library, Park Ridge IL. 312-825-3123
Mortenson, Kathleen E, *Librn,* Townsend-Greenspan & Co, Inc, New York NY. 212-943-9515
Mortenson, Mary, *ILL,* University of Minnesota, Saint Paul Campus Libraries, Saint Paul MN. 612-373-0904
Mortenson, Phyllis, *Ch,* Yorba Linda Library District, Yorba Linda CA. 714-528-7039
Mortimer, Dorothy, *Librn,* Methodist Medical Center of Illinois (Learning Resource Center-School of Nursing Library & Audio Visual), Peoria IL. 309-672-5570
Mortimer, Lynn B, *Librn,* Welaka Library, Welaka FL. 904-467-2859
Mortimer, Roger, *Rare Bks & Spec Coll,* University of South Carolina, Thomas Cooper Library, Columbia SC. 803-777-3142
Mortimer, Ruth, *Rare Bks,* Smith College Library, Northampton MA. 413-584-2700, Ext 501
Mortimer, William J, *In Charge,* Life Insurance Marketing & Research Association Incorporated Library, Hartford CT. 203-677-0033

Morton, Abigail, *Acq,* Hamilton College, Burke Library, Clinton NY. 315-859-4478
Morton, Barbara G, *Librn,* Inland Steel Co, Industrial Relations Library, Chicago IL. 312-346-0300
Morton, Bruce, *Ref & Bibliog Instr,* Carleton College Library, Northfield MN. 507-645-4431
Morton, Claire J, *Librn,* Technology & Economics Inc Library, Cambridge MA. 617-491-1500
Morton, Courtnay, *Dir,* Black Watch Memorial Library, Ticonderoga NY. 518-585-7380
Morton, Diane, *Librn,* Job Service of Iowa, Des Moines IA. 515-281-5387
Morton, Donald G, *Dir,* Sedalia Public Library, Sedalia MO. 816-826-1314
Morton, Donald J, *Dir,* University of Massachusetts Medical School, Medical Center Library, Worcester MA. 617-856-2511
Morton, Doug, *Civil Eng & Earth Sci,* University of Waterloo Library, Waterloo ON. 519-885-1211
Morton, Joyce, *Libr Officers,* United States Navy (Tactical Library), San Diego CA. 714-225-3273
Morton, Kathleen, *Librn,* Abcor, Inc Library, Wilmington MA. 617-657-4250, Ext 220
Morton, Marjorie B, *Asst Librn,* Post College, Traurig Library, Waterbury CT. 203-755-0121, Ext 252
Morton, Mrs M L, *Dir,* Agriculture Canada (Main Library), Ottawa ON. 613-995-7829
Morton, Natalie G, *Reader Serv,* United States Department of Labor Library, Washington DC. 202-523-6988
Morton, P W, *Manager,* Aluminum Co of America, Information Dept Library, Alcoa Center PA. 412-339-6651, Ext 2283
Morton, Patricia Y, *Cat,* Pennsylvania State University, Milton S Hershey Medical Center, George T Harrell Library, Hershey PA. 717-534-8626
Morton, Robert, *Coordr Planning & Systs,* University of Western Ontario, A B Weldon Library, London ON. 519-679-6191
Morton, Sylvia, *Librn,* Pickens County Library (Sarlin Community), Liberty SC. 803-843-9393
Morton, Walter, *Cat,* Louisiana State University School of Medicine in Shreveport, Medical Library, Shreveport LA. 318-226-3442
Mosby, Helen, *Ch & Media,* Haverhill Public Library, Haverhill MA. 617-373-1586
Mosby, Margaret, *Ref,* Virginia Commonwealth University (Tompkins-McCaw Library), Richmond VA. 804-786-0629
Mosca, Carlo A, *Corp Dir Educ,* Sea World Library, San Diego CA. 714-222-6363, Ext 351
Moscatt, Angeline, *Librn,* New York Public Library (Central Children's Room), New York NY. 212-790-6359
Moscowitz, Beatrice, *Ch,* Bethpage Public Library, Bethpage NY. 516-913-3907
Mosebauer, Geraldine C, *Asst Dir,* State Mutual Life Assurance Co of America Library, Worcester MA. 617-852-1000, Ext 2435
Mosel, Arlene E, *Assoc Prof,* Case Western Reserve University, School of Library Science, OH. 216-368-3500
Moseley, Anne, *ILL & Ref,* Cherokee County Public Library, Gaffney SC. 803-489-4381
Moseley, Barbara A, *Dir,* James H Faulkner State Junior College, Austin R Meadows Library, Bay Minette AL. 205-937-9581, Ext 51
Moseley, Eva, *Curator of Mss,* Radcliffe College, Arthur & Elizabeth Schlesinger Library on the History of Women in America, Cambridge MA. 617-495-8647
Moseley, Gregory, *Pub Servs,* South Georgia Regional Library, Valdosta-Lowndes County Public Library, Valdosta GA. 912-247-3405
Moseley, Judy, *On-Line Servs,* Booz, Allen & Hamilton, Inc Library, New York NY. 212-697-1900, Ext 607
Mosely, Brenda, *Librn,* Kern County Library (Holloway-Gonzales), Bakersfield CA. 805-861-2130
Moser, Beryl, *Ref,* Dawson College Library, Montreal PQ. 514-525-2501, Ext 297
Moser, Darlene, *Ch,* Peoples Library, New Kensington PA. 412-339-1021
Moser, Edward R, *Ser,* California Institute of Technology, Robert A Millikan Memorial Library, Pasadena CA. 213-795-6811

Moser, Helen, *Librn,* Robeson County Public Library (Gilbert Patterson Memorial), Maxton NC. 919-844-3884
Moser, Irene, *Pub Servs,* University of North Carolina at Asheville, D Hiden Ramsey Library, Asheville NC. 704-258-0200
Moser, Margaret, *Tech Proc,* University of Arkansas at Little Rock Library, Little Rock AR. 501-569-3120
Moser, Margaret L, *Dir,* Allegheny College, Lawrence Lee Pelletier Library, Meadville PA. 814-724-3363
Moser, Mary Ann, *Cat,* Bluffton College, Musselman Library, Bluffton OH. 419-358-8015, Ext 114
Moser, Richard, *Libr Aid,* United States Navy (Pearl Harbor Naval Base Library), Honolulu HI. 808-471-8238
Moses, David F, *Asst Dir, Mat Handling & AV,* Purdue University Libraries & Audio-Visual Center, West Lafayette IN. 317-749-2571
Moses, Hanna, *Cat,* Skokie Public Library, Skokie IL. 312-673-7774
Moses, Paula Boyd, *Mgr,* Dow Chemical Co (Technical Information Services), Midland MI. 517-636-0972
Moses, Richard B, *Chief Librn,* Oakville Public Library, Oakville ON. 416-845-3405
Mosgrove, Francis, *Librn,* Port Arthur Public Library (West Side), Port Arthur TX. 713-982-6841
Mosher, Betsy, *Ch,* Goodnow Library, Sudbury MA. 617-443-9112
Mosher, Jeanette, *Librn,* Manatee Memorial Hospital, Wentzel Medical Library Library, Bradenton FL. 813-746-5111, Ext 121
Mosher, Paul H, *Assoc Dir,* Stanford University Libraries, Stanford CA. 415-497-2016
Moshier, Beverly, *Dir,* Chester Public Library, Chester CT. 203-526-5598
Mosier, Camille, *Ch,* Dowagiac Public Library, Dowagiac MI. 616-782-3826, 782-2195 Ext 30
Mosimann, Margaret D, *Dir,* Charleston County Library, Charleston SC. 803-723-1645
Moskal, Fredereike, *Asst Dir, Acq & Cat,* Lewis University Library, Romeoville IL. 815-838-0500, Ext 302
Moskal, Stephen L, *Dir,* La Grange Public Library, La Grange IL. 312-352-0576, Ext 6
Moske, Marjorie L, *Librn,* Parkirew School, Muskogee OK. 918-682-6641
Moskovits, Andrew, *Librn,* Yeshiva University Libraries (Pollack Branch), New York NY. 212-960-5380
Moskwa, Wanda, *Asst Coordr,* Northern Interrelated Library System, Pawtucket RI. 401-723-5350
Moskwa, Wanda J, *Polish Coll,* Pawtucket Public Library & Regional Library Center, Deborah Cook Sayles Memorial Library, Pawtucket RI. 401-725-3714
Mosler, Rona, *Acq,* Warren County Library, Belvidere NJ. 201-475-5361, Ext 114
Mosley, Doris O, *Tech Serv,* United States Army War College Library, Carlisle Barracks PA. 717-245-4319
Mosley, Lee J, *Asst Dir,* University of California Library, San Francisco CA. 415-666-2334
Mosley, Linda, *Admin Asst,* Newberry College, Wessels Library, Newberry SC. 803-276-5010, Ext 300
Mosley, Mary, *Circ,* Alabama Agricultural & Mechanical University, Joseph F Drake Memorial Learning Resources Center, Normal AL. 205-859-7309
Mosley, Mary Mac, *Dir & Cat,* Shorter College, Livingston Library, Rome GA. 404-291-2121, Ext 43
Mosley, Shelley, *Ad,* Velma Teague Library, Glendale Public Library, Glendale AZ. 602-931-5576
Mosley, Sherry, *Cat & Doc,* Dowling College Library, Oakdale NY. 516-589-6100, Ext 218 or 219
Mosnat, Jacalyn E, *Librn,* Norman Municipal Hospital, Health Sciences Library, Norman OK. 405-321-1700, Ext 491
Moss, Alfred G, *Librn,* United Nations Institute for Training & Research, Unitar Library, New York NY. 212-754-8638
Moss, Barbara, *Cat,* Glenview Public Library, Glenview IL. 312-724-5200

Moss, Carol E, *Co Librn,* Los Angeles County Public Library System, South State Cooperative Library System, Los Angeles CA. 213-974-6501
Moss, Carol E, *Admin Coun Chairperson,* South State Cooperative Library System, Los Angeles CA. 213-974-6501
Moss, Effie, *Librn,* Pratt Memorial Library, New Milford PA. 717-465-3098
Moss, Julia, *Cat,* Sul Ross State University, Bryan Wildenthal Memorial Library, Alpine TX. 915-837-3461
Moss, Karen M, *Chief Librn,* United States Court of Appeals, First Circuit Library, Boston MA. 617-223-2891, 223-4346
Moss, Marcia, *Rare Bks & Spec Coll,* Concord Free Public Library, Concord MA. 617-369-5324
Moss, Mary A, *Chief Librn,* Tulsa Metropolitan Area Planning Commission, Tulsa OK. 918-584-7526
Moss, Patricia, *Ad,* Colusa County Free Library, Colusa CA. 916-458-7671
Moss, Paula, *Circ,* Trinity College Library, Deerfield IL. 312-945-6700, Ext 217
Moss, Rebecca, *Readers Adv,* George Amos Memorial Library, Campbell County Library, Gillette WY. 307-682-3223
Moss, Sonja, *ILL,* San Mateo Public Library, San Mateo CA. 415-574-6955
Moss, Stephen, *Media,* Regis College, Dayton Memorial Library, Denver CO. 303-458-4030
Moss, Jr, Roger W, *Librn,* Athenaeum of Philadelphia, Philadelphia PA. 215-925-2688
Mosset, Mrs Euvagh, *Dir,* Linton Public Library, Harry L Petrie Public Library, Linton ND. 701-254-4737
Mossey, Iris, *Librn,* Saint Michael's General Hospital Library, Lethbridge AB. 403-327-1531
Most, Marguerite, *Asst Librn & Ref,* University of San Diego (Marvin Kratter Law Library), San Diego CA. 714-293-4541
Mostecky, Vaclav, *Librn,* University of California, Berkeley (Law Library), Berkeley CA. 415-642-4044
Mosteller, Bette V, *Dir,* Christopher Newport College, Captain John Smith Library, Newport News VA. 804-599-7130
Moster, Mary, *Librn,* Muenster Public Library, Muenster TX. 817-759-4291
Mote, Clara F, *Librn,* Collingsworth County Library, Wellington TX. 806-447-2020
Mothershed, S W, *Dir,* Texas Southern University Library, Houston TX. 713-527-7121
Motley, Drucilla, *Dir,* Trail Blazer Library System, Monroe LA. 318-323-8494
Motley, Frank, *Ref & Bibliog Instr,* Evergreen State College, Daniel J Evans Library, Olympia WA. 206-866-6262
Motley, LaVerne, *Ch,* Ridley Township Public Library, Folsom PA. 215-583-0593
Motley, Sue Jane, *Librn,* Mexico-Audrain County Library (Vandalia Branch), Vandalia MO. 314-594-6600
Moton, Honore, *Ext Servs,* Prince George's County Memorial Library System, Hyattsville MD. 301-699-3500
Mott, Mary Olive, *Asst Dir,* Mesa Public Library, Mesa AZ. 602-834-2207
Mott, Shirley, *Tech Serv,* Troy-Miami County Public Library, Troy OH. 513-339-0502
Mott, William R, *Dir,* Martin College, Warden Memorial Library, Pulaski TN. 615-363-7456, Ext 41
Mott, Jr, Thomas H, *Dean,* Rutgers-The State University of New Jersey, Graduate School of Library & Information Studies, NJ. 201-932-7500
Motta, Camille, *Tech Serv,* State Library of Massachusetts, Boston MA. 617-727-2590
Motte, Hortense, *Pub Servs,* Cosumnes River College, Learning Resources Center, Sacramento CA. 916-421-1000, Ext 266
Motteler, Lee S, *Geographer,* Pacific Scientific Information Center, Honolulu HI. 808-847-3511
Motuzick, Stasia, *Librn,* Theodore A Hungerford Memorial Library, Harwinton CT. 203-482-5113
Motz, Josephine R, *Dir,* Wood River Public Library, Wood River IL. 618-254-4832
Moubayed, Sylvia, *Dir,* Providence Athenaeum, Providence RI. 401-421-6970
Moul, Gail Allan, *Dir,* Baptist Bible Institute, Ida J McMillan Library, Graceville FL. 904-263-3261

Mould, Ralph, *Minister of Educ,* Woods Memorial Presbyterian Church Library, Severna Park MD. 301-647-2550

Moulds, Michael, *Special Services,* Cumberland Trail Library System, Flora IL. 618-662-2679, 622-2741

Moulds, Michael, *In Charge,* Cumberland Trail Library System (Subregional Library for the Blind & Physically Handicapped), Flora IL. 618-662-2676, 662-2741

Moulis, Evelyn, *Librn,* Iberia Parish Public Library (City Park), New Iberia LA. 318-369-3398

Moulton, Catherine, *Cat,* Boston University Libraries (Mugar Memorial Library), Boston MA. 617-353-3710

Moulton, David, *Asst Librn,* Strayer College, Wilkes Library, Washington DC. 202-783-5180, Ext 48

Moulton, Elizabeth C, *Per,* Gordon College, Winn Library, Wenham MA. 617-927-2300, Ext 233

Moulton, Joanne H, *Librn,* Orange Public Library, Orange NH. 603-523-9939

Moulton, Lucille, *Librn,* Saint Johnsbury Community Correctional Center, Saint Johnsbury VT. 802-748-8151

Mounce, Carolyn, *Chmn,* Blue Mountain College, Dept of Library Science, MS. 601-685-5711, Ext 47

Mounce, Carolyn, *Dir,* Blue Mountain College, Guyton Library, Blue Mountain MS. 601-685-5711, Ext 47

Mounce, Clara, *Asst Librn & Commun Servs,* Bryan Public Library, Bryan TX. 713-823-8021

Mounce, Marvin W, *Projects Coordr,* State Library of Florida, Div of Library Services, Dept of State, Tallahassee FL. 904-487-2651

Mounger, Roben, *Cat,* Mississippi College (Law Library), Clinton MS. 601-924-5131, Ext 280

Mount, Albertina F, *Librn,* Presbyterian Hospital (John M Wheeler Library), New York NY. 212-694-2916

Mount, Elaine W, *Librn,* Saint Mary's Dominican College, John XXIII Library, New Orleans LA. 504-865-7761, Ext 225

Mount, Ellis, *Asst Prof,* Columbia University in the City of New York, School of Library Service, NY. 212-280-2292

Mount, Joan, *Ref & Circ,* Laurentian University Library, Bibliotheque de l'Universite Laurentienne, Sudbury ON. 705-675-1151, Ext 251 & 252

Mount, Joe, *Acq,* Colby College, Miller Library, Waterville ME. 207-873-1131, Ext 209

Mountain, Pat E, *Librn,* Chevron USA Inc Library, Denver CO. 303-759-7347

Mountfort, Ruth A, *Media & YA,* Melrose Public Library, Melrose MA. 617-665-2313

Mounts, Charlene, *Librn,* McDowell Public Library (Davy Branch), Davy WV. 304-656-7015

Mounts, Mary, *Librn,* Marion Public Library (Prospect Branch), Prospect OH. 614-494-2684

Moura, Maria, *Cat,* Loyola Marymount University, Charles Von Der Ahe Library, Los Angeles CA. 213-642-2788

Mourre, Edie, *Librn,* Canadian National Institute for the Blind, Manitoba Branch Transcription Library, Winnipeg MB. 204-774-5421

Mourton, Helen, *Librn,* Tulare County Library System (Poplar Branch), Poplar CA. 209-784-3054

Mourton, Helen, *Librn,* Tulare County Library System (Woodville Farm Labor Camp), Porterville CA. 209-781-1836

Mourton, Irene, *Librn,* Tulare County Library System (Tipton Branch), Tipton CA. 209-752-4236

Mouser, Vivian, *Librn,* Randolph Township Library, Heyworth IL. 309-473-2313

Moushey, J, *Bibliog Instr,* Warren Wilson College Library, Swannanoa NC. 704-298-3325, Ext 45

Moushey, Janet, *ILL & Reader Serv,* Warren Wilson College Library, Swannanoa NC. 704-298-3325, Ext 45

Moushey, Suzanne, *Tech Serv,* Mount Union College Library, Alliance OH. 216-821-5320, Ext 260

Moussa, Linda, *Librn,* Los Angeles Public Library System (Police), Los Angeles CA. 213-485-3288

Moussatas, Martha, *Librn,* United States Marine Corps (Recruit Depot Station Library), Parris Island SC. 803-525-2111

Mouton, Jean, *Instr,* University of Southwestern Louisiana, Dept of School Librarianship, LA. 318-264-6713

Moutseous, Margaret, *Dir,* Children's Hospital, Research Foundation Library, Cincinnati OH. 513-559-4300

Mouw, James, *Tech Serv & On-Line Servs,* Gardner-Webb College, Dover Memorial Library, Boiling Springs NC. 704-434-2361

Mow, Sandy, *Cat & Ref,* Hawaii Loa College, Amos Starr & Juliette Montegue Cooke Academic Center, Kaneohe HI. 808-235-3641, Ext 119,136,137

Mowat, V S, *Supvr & Cat,* Hermes Electronics Ltd Library, Dartmouth NS. 902-463-9295

Mowatt, Connie S, *Librn,* North Branch Public Library, North Branch MI. 313-688-2282

Mowell, Barbara, *Librn,* Big Horn County Library (Shell Branch), Shell WY. 307-568-2388

Moweny, Robert, *Bibliog Instr,* Illinois Wesleyan University Library, Bloomington IL. 309-556-3172

Mowery, B, *Dir & Rare Bks,* Wittenberg University, Thomas Library, Springfield OH. 513-327-7016

Mowery, Joy A, *Dir,* Blue Grass Regional Library, Columbia TN. 615-388-9282

Mowery, Loy, *Librn,* Auburn Public Library, Auburn NE. 402-274-4023

Mowrey, Judith M, *Librn,* Rogue Community College Library, Grants Pass OR. 503-479-5541, Ext 235

Mowry, Elizabeth L, *Librn,* New Brighton Public Library, New Brighton PA. 412-846-7991

Mowry, Judy, *Media,* University of Cincinnati Medical Center Libraries (Media Resources Center), Cincinnati OH. 513-872-4173

Moxley, Melody, *Circ,* Rowan Public Library, Salisbury NC. 704-633-5578

Moxness, Mary J, *Ref & Bibliog Instr,* Saint Mary's College, Fitzgerald Library, Winona MN. 507-452-4430, Ext 232

Moxom, Priscilla, *Ch,* Los Angeles Public Library System, Los Angeles CA. 213-626-7555

Moy, Agnes, *Ch,* York Public Library, York ME. 207-363-2818

Moy, Gene P, *Media & Circ,* University of Detroit Library (Law), Detroit MI. 313-961-5444, Ext 239, 240 & 241

Moyer, Anna Jane, *ILL & Ref,* Gettysburg College, Schmucker Memorial Library, Gettysburg PA. 717-334-3131, Ext 366

Moyer, Barbara, *Librn,* Miami-Dade Public Library System (Talking Books), Miami FL. 305-638-6937

Moyer, Dennis, *Ref,* Schwenkfelder Library, Pennsburg PA. 215-679-7175

Moyer, Helen, *Librn,* Fairfax County Public Library (Herndon Fortnightly Branch), Herndon VA. 703-437-8855

Moyer, Jack O, *Dir,* Delaware County Community College Library, Media PA. 215-353-5400

Moyer, Jane S, *Librn,* Northampton County Historical & Genealogical Society, Mary Illick Memorial Library, Easton PA. 215-253-1222

Moyer, Loretta, *ILL,* Whitehall Township Public Library, Whitehall PA. 215-432-4339

Moyer, Orin M, *Librn,* United States Air Force (Edwards Air Force Base Library), Edwards AFB CA. 805-277-1110

Moyers, Carleton, *ILL,* Texas Panhandle Library System, Amarillo TX. 806-378-3043

Moyers, Carlton, *ILL,* Amarillo Public Library, Amarillo TX. 806-378-3000, Ext 2250

Moyers, Joyce C, *Dir,* Rockingham Public Library, Harrisonburg VA. 703-434-4475

Moyle, D, *Librn,* Canada Department of National Defense (Land Technical Library), Ottawa ON. 613-992-9862, 3879

Moyle, Evelyn, *Doc,* Illinois Valley Community College, Jacobs Memorial Library, Oglesby IL. 815-224-2720

Moynihan, Helen, *ILL, Tech Serv & Cat,* Delaware Technical & Community College, Southern Campus Library, Georgetown DE. 302-856-5438

Moynihan, Mary K, *Librn,* Exxon Co USA (Law-Tax Library), New York NY. 212-398-3000

Moysa, Susan, *Librn,* Alberta Department of the Environment Library, Edmonton AB. 403-427-6132, 427-5870

Mozes, George, *Dir,* Michael Reese Medical Center, L W Florsheim Memorial Library, Chicago IL. 312-791-2474

Mozga, John, *AV,* Bur Oak Library System, Shorewood IL. 815-729-3345, 729-3346

Mozorosky, Terry, *Technical Info Specialist,* Loral Electronics Systems, Technical Information Center & Library, Yonkers NY. 914-968-2500, Ext 629

Mraw, Edwina, *Librn,* Atlantic County Library (Ventnor Branch), Ventnor NJ. 609-823-4614

Mros, Linda, *Ch,* Carnegie Library, Rome GA. 404-291-7568

Mrozewski, Andrzej H, *Dir,* Laurentian University Library, Bibliotheque de l'Universite Laurentienne, Sudbury ON. 705-675-1151, Ext 251 & 252

Mubarak, Jill, *Ref,* University of Southern California (Asa V Call Law Library), Los Angeles CA. 213-743-6487

Muchin, John, *Slavic,* University of Manitoba Libraries, Winnipeg MB. 204-474-9881

Muchin, John, *Spec Coll,* University of Manitoba Libraries, Winnipeg MB. 204-474-9881

Muchmore, Linda, *ILL,* Kettering College of Medical Arts Library, Learning Resource Center, Kettering OH. 513-296-7201, Ext 5630

Muchmore, Wendy, *Regional Dir,* Northeast Regional Resource Center, NV. 702-738-3077

Muchmore, Wendy, *Programs Coordr,* Northwest Regional Center, NV. 702-785-4008

Muchmore, Wendy, *Regional Coordr & Media,* Washoe County Library, Reno NV. 702-785-4039

Mucilli, Rosina, *Librn,* Free Public Library of Woodbridge (Avenel Branch), Avenel NJ. 201-634-3238

Muckleroy, Patrick, *ILL, AV & Ref,* University of Maine at Machias, Merrill Library, Machias ME. 207-255-3313, Ext 234

Mudaris, Falih, *Cat,* Cuyahoga Community College (Eastern Campus Library), Warrensville OH. 216-464-1450, Ext 228, 229

Mudaris, Mike, *Cat,* Cuyahoga Community College, District Office, Cleveland OH. 216-241-5966, Ext 220

Mudd, Isabelle, *Librn,* United States Army (Morale Support Activities), Fort Wainwright AK. 907-353-6114

Mudd, Sister Hilda, *Dir,* Brescia College Library, Owensboro KY. 502-685-3131, Ext 213

Mudge, Miriam, *ILL,* Albany Public Library, Albany NY. 518-449-3380

Mudge, Virginia, *Librn,* Kitsap Regional Library (Bainbridge Island Branch), Bainbridge Island WA. 206-842-4162

Mudloff, Cherrie M, *Librn,* Detroit General Hospital, Medical Library, Detroit MI. 313-224-0250

Mudrak, Angela, *Asst Librn,* Youngstown State University Library, William F Maag Library, Youngstown OH. 216-742-3676

Muehlner, Suanne W, *Asst Dir Pub Servs,* Massachusetts Institute of Technology Libraries, Cambridge MA. 617-253-5651

Muellen, Jane, *Historical Consortium,* Santiago Library System, Orange CA. 714-634-7137

Mueller, Beth, *Consult Serv Dir,* Suburban Library System, Burr Ridge IL. 312-325-6640

Mueller, Bonita, *Tech Serv,* United States General Accounting Office Library System (Office of Information Systems & Services), Washington DC. 275-3691 (Br Mgr), 275-5180 (Audit Ref Servs), 275-2585 (Law), 275-2555 (Tech Servs)

Mueller, Dorothy H, *Librn,* Philadelphia Maritime Museum Library, Philadelphia PA. 215-925-5439

Mueller, Elizabeth, *Bkmobile Coordr,* Suburban Library System, Burr Ridge IL. 312-325-6640

Mueller, Elizabeth J, *Cat,* Missouri Southern State College, George A Spiva Library, Joplin MO. 417-624-8100, Ext 251

Mueller, Ethel, *Ref,* Adriance Memorial Library, Poughkeepsie NY. 914-485-4790

Mueller, Friedrich D, *Photog Servs,* Yale University Library (Sterling Memorial Library), New Haven CT. 203-436-8335

Mueller, Gertrude, *In Charge,* Milwaukee Public Library (Capitol Branch), Milwaukee WI. 414-278-3006

Mueller, Heinz Peter, *Assoc Dir,* Brigham Young University (Law Library), Provo UT. 801-378-3593

MUELLER

Mueller, Irene, *Cat,* Cocoa Public Library, Cocoa FL. 305-636-3243, 636-7323
Mueller, J, *Librn,* University of Southern California (Gerontology), Los Angeles CA. 213-743-6060
Mueller, Jane E, *Librn,* Jim Walter Research Corp Library, Saint Petersburg FL. 813-576-4171, Ext 326
Mueller, Jeanne G, *Tech Serv,* Indiana University (School of Medicine Library), Indianapolis IN. 317-264-7182
Mueller, Jenny, *On-Line Servs,* University of Minnesota, Duluth, Duluth MN. 218-726-8100
Mueller, Joan, *YA,* Fond Du Lac City-County Library Service, Fond du Lac WI. 414-921-3670
Mueller, Joan, *Ch & YA,* Mid-Wisconsin Federated Library System, Fond du Lac WI. 414-921-3670
Mueller, Judy, *YA & Circ,* Avon Free Public Library, Avon CT. 203-678-1262
Mueller, Kerstin, *Librn,* Eastern Counties Regional Library, Mulgrave NS. 902-747-2597
Mueller, Leta, *Librn,* Armco, Inc, Technical Information Services, Middletown OH. 513-425-2596
Mueller, Marie M, *Asst Librn,* Grand Rapids Public Library, Grand Rapids MN. 218-326-3081
Mueller, Marion, *Lectr,* University of Wisconsin-Oshkosh, Dept of Library Science, WI. 414-424-2313
Mueller, Martha A, *ILL & Ref,* Alfred University (Scholes Library of Ceramics), Alfred NY. 607-871-2492
Mueller, Rebecca, *Ref,* South Milwaukee Public Library, South Milwaukee WI. 414-762-8692
Mueller, Twyla, *Acq,* Eastern Michigan University, Center of Educational Resources, Ypsilanti MI. 313-487-0020
Muellner, Phillip, *Dir,* Schiller Park Public Library, Schiller Park IL. 312-678-0433
Muench, Evelyn, *Librn,* Red Bud Public Library, Red Bud IL. 618-282-2255
Muenger, Mary, *Cat,* Newburgh Free Library, Newburgh NY. 914-561-1836
Muessle, Barbara A, *Dir,* Chilton Co, Marketing & Advertising Information Center, Radnor PA. 215-687-8200, Exts 2215, 2263
Muetzel, Patricia A, *Librn,* Cuyahoga County Public Library (Solon Branch), Solon OH. 216-248-8777
Muffler, Cathy, *Librn,* Somonauk Public Library, Somonauk IL. 815-498-2440
Mufford, Olive, *Asst Librn,* Kimberley Public Library, Kimberley BC. 604-427-3112
Muffs, Lauren, *Ref,* Bentley College, Solomon R Baker Library, Waltham MA. 617-891-2231
Mugford, John, *ILL & Ref,* Boyden Library, Foxboro MA. 617-543-8882
Muggah, Phyllis, *Ref,* College of Cape Breton Library, Sydney NS. 902-539-5300
Mugnier, Charlotte, *Assoc Prof,* University of Alabama, Graduate School of Library Service, AL. 205-348-4610
Muhich, Robert J, *Dir,* Hibbing Community College, Learning Resources Center, Hibbing MN. 218-262-3877, Ext 53
Muhlberger, Richard, *Dir,* George Walter Vincent Smith Art Museum, Research Library, Springfield MA. 414-733-4214
Muhm, Lolita, *Supvr Tech Proc,* Richardson Public Library, Richardson TX. 214-238-8251
Muir, Clyde H, *Librn,* Wasatch County Library, Heber UT. 801-654-1511
Muir, Linda P, *Ch,* Craven-Pamlico-Carteret Regional Library, New Bern NC. 919-638-2127
Muir, Lucile, *Librn,* Beaufort County Library (Hilton Head Island Branch), Hilton Head Island SC. 803-785-3266
Muir, Marjorie, *Libr Asst,* Hunt Wesson Foods, Information Center, Fullerton CA. 714-871-2100
Muir, R A, *Chief Librn,* Home Oil Co Ltd Library, Calgary AB. 403-232-7207
Muir, Scott, *Pub Serv,* Georgia Power Co Library, Atlanta GA. 522-6060; Ext 2651
Muirhead, Gail, *Librn,* Chicago Public Library (Scottsdale), Chicago IL. 312-581-5545
Mukai, Kyoko, *Asst Librn,* Free Public Library of the Township of Berkeley Heights, Berkeley Heights NJ. 201-464-9333
Mukerji, Jatrindra N, *Dir,* Seton Hall University, School of Law Library, Newark NJ. 201-642-3994

Mukherjee, Betty, *Dir,* Walden Public Library, Lively ON. 705-692-4848
Mukherjee, Y, *Librn,* Imperial Tobacco (Corporate Library), Montreal PQ. 514-932-6161, Ext 356
Mulanax, Martha, *Librn,* El Reno Carnegie Library, El Reno OK. 405-262-2409
Mularchule, Irene, *Dir,* Radio Advertising Bureau, Marketing Information Center, New York NY. 212-599-6666
Mulcahy, Rita, *Librn,* Morris Public Library, Morris MN. 612-589-1634
Mulcahy, Rosemarie, *Ch,* Brooks Free Library, Harwich MA. 617-432-1799
Mulder, Elizabeth C, *Acq,* Tri-County Regional Library, Rome GA. 404-291-9360
Mulder, Marjorie, *Librn,* Gilford Instrument Laboratories Inc Library, Oberlin OH. 216-774-1041, Ext 373
Mulder, Vivian, *Librn,* Kent County Library System (Alto Branch), Alto MI. 616-868-6038
Muldoon, Anne Marie, *Librn,* Carbondale Public Library, Carbondale PA. 717-282-4281
Muldoon, Kathy, *Librn,* Lincoln Public Library, Beamsville ON. 416-563-7014
Muldoon, Norma, *Librn,* Timberlawn Foundation, Inc, Albert F Riedel Memorial Library, Dallas TX. 214-388-0451
Muldoon, Sister Jane, *Asst Dir,* Trocaire College Library, Buffalo NY. 716-826-1200, Ext 239
Mulhern, Ray, *In Charge,* Cadiz Public Library, Cadiz OH. 614-942-2623
Mulhern, Raymond, *Dir,* Greene County District Library, Xenia OH. 513-376-2995
Mulholland, Mike, *Media Production,* Joliet Junior College, Learning Resource Center, Joliet IL. 815-729-9020, Ext 282
Mulica, Virginia, *Librn,* Siskiyou County Public Library (Mount Shasta Branch), Mount Shasta CA. 916-926-2031
Mulkey, Jack C, *Dir,* Jackson Metropolitan Library, Jackson MS. 601-352-3677
Mullally, Lee, *Program Dir,* University of Florida, College of Education, FL. 904-392-0705
Mullaly, Diane L, *Librn,* Arctec Inc, Ice Engineering Laboratories Library, Columbia MD. 301-730-1030
Mullan, Elizabeth, *Librn,* New York Public Library (Riverside), New York NY. 212-877-9186
Mullan, S L, *Librn,* Queen Elizabeth Hospital Library, Montreal PQ. 514-488-2311, Ext 333
Mullane, Ruth, *On-Line Servs & Bibliog Instr,* United States Department of the Army (The Army Library, Pentagon), Washington DC. 202-697-4301, Ext 69-55346
Mullane, William, *Tech Serv,* Northern Arizona University Libraries, Flagstaff AZ. 602-523-9011
Mullaney, M M, *Libr Supvr,* Stackpole Carbon Co, Research Library, Saint Marys PA. 814-781-1234
Mullen, Cleotta, *Librn,* Arkansas Library Commission, Library for the Blind & Physically Handicapped, Little Rock AR. 501-371-1155
Mullen, Cora, *Librn,* Jacksonville Public Library System (Northside), Jacksonville FL. 904-633-4758
Mullen, Donald K, *Librn,* Dover Public Library, Dover NH. 603-742-3513
Mullen, Francis X, *Dir,* Marple Public Library, Broomall PA. 215-356-1510, 356-0550
Mullen, Gail, *Librn,* Bibliotheque Publique De Valley East, Val Caron ON. 705-897-5449
Mullen, Inalea, *Ad,* Tulsa City-County Library, Tulsa OK. 918-581-5221
Mullen, Jan, *AV,* San Joaquin Delta College, Goleman Library, Stockton CA. 209-478-2011, Ext 277
Mullen, Jess, *Humanities,* Tampa-Hillsborough County Public Library System, Tampa FL. 813-223-8947
Mullen, Jocelyn, *Librn,* Richards, Watson, Dreyfuss & Gershon Library, Los Angeles CA. 213-626-8484, Ext 202
Mullen, Kathy, *Librn,* Saint Luke's Hospital, Doctor's Library, Saint Louis MO. 314-361-1212
Mullen, Marion L, *Ref,* Syracuse University Libraries, Ernest S Bird Library, Syracuse NY. 315-423-2575
Mullenbach, Zola, *Librn,* Stacyville Public Library, Stacyville IA. 515-737-2531
Mulleneaux, Marguerite, *Albany Hist,* Albany Public Library, Albany NY. 518-449-3380

Mullenix, Betty, *ILL,* Akron-Summit County Public Library, Akron OH. 216-762-7621
Mullens, Cynthia, *Ref,* West Deptford Public Library, Thorofare NJ. 609-845-5593
Mullens, Diane, *Librn,* Michigan Christian Junior College Library, Rochester MI. 313-651-5800
Mullens, Lyle, *Dept Chmn,* Northern Arizona University, College of Education, AZ. 602-523-2127
Muller, Beverly, *Librn & On-Line Servs,* C F Braun & Co, Reference Library, Alhambra CA. 213-570-2233
Muller, Bill, *Pub Servs,* Eastern Shore Regional Library, Salisbury MD. 301-742-1537
Muller, Charles, *Media,* Ocean County College, Learning Resources Center, Toms River NJ. 201-255-4298
Muller, Claudya B, *Dir,* Worcester County Library, Snow Hill MD. 301-632-2600
Muller, Donald, *Dir,* Ontario County Historical Society Library, Canandaigua NY. 716-394-4975
Muller, Elinor C, *Librn,* Union Carbide Corp (Law Dept Library), New York NY. 212-551-6472
Muller, Ellen R, *Pub Info Officer,* Dutchess County Department of Planning Information Center, Poughkeepsie NY. 914-485-9890
Muller, Frankie, *Tech Serv,* Troy State University Library, Troy AL. 205-566-3000, Ext 263
Muller, Grace, *ILL & Archivist,* Westminster Theological Seminary Library, Glenside PA. 215-887-5511
Muller, Joan, *Librn,* Lambton County Library (Brigden Branch), Brigden ON. 519-864-1142
Muller, Karen L, *Tech Serv,* Art Institute of Chicago (Ryerson & Burnham Libraries), Chicago IL. 312-443-6666
Muller, Mary Benson, *Libr Program Officer (American Republic),* International Communication Agency (Education & Cultural Affairs), Washington DC. 202-632-5346, 632-6752
Muller, Richard, *Union Cat Admin Asst,* New York Public Library (General Reference Service), New York NY. 790-6575; 790-6161 (Tel Ref); 790-6234 (Union Cat)
Muller, Richard L, *Educ Tech Dir,* Hampshire College, Harold F Johnson Library Center, Amherst MA. 413-549-4600
Muller, Robert H, *Dir,* Queens College Library, Flushing NY. 212-520-7616
Mullet, G, *Librn,* Holmes County District Public Library (Berlin Branch), Berlin OH. 216-674-5972
Mullin, B J, *Librn,* Franklin County Library (Youngsville Public), Youngsville NC. 919-496-4942
Mullin, Karen, *Librn,* Wayne Oakland Library Federation (Institutional Services), Wayne MI. 313-326-8910
Mullin, Sister Kathleen, *Dir,* Clarke College Library, Dubuque IA. 319-588-6320
Mullin, Wayne, *Head Loan Dept,* University of Arizona Library, Tucson AZ. 602-626-2101
Mullings, Lyndell, *Br Asst,* Timberland Regional Library (Tenino Branch), Tenino WA. 206-264-2369
Mullins, Charlotte A, *ILL,* Sequoyah Regional Library, R T Jones Memorial Library, Canton GA. 404-479-3090
Mullins, Ethel F, *Chief Librn,* Veterans Administration, Medical Center Library, Lexington KY. 606-233-4511, Ext 323
Mullins, Flora, *Librn,* Letcher County Public Library (Jenkins Branch), Jenkins KY. 606-832-4101
Mullins, James L, *Dir,* Indiana University at South Bend Library, South Bend IN. 219-237-4440
Mullins, Lynn S, *Chief Librn,* Marymount Manhattan College, Thomas J Shanahan Library, New York NY. 212-472-3800, Ext 460, 461
Mullins, Mrs Robert, *Librn,* Rutherford County Library System (Smyrna Public), Smyrna TN. 615-459-4884
Mullins, Mrs Robert, *Librn,* Smyrna Public Library, Smyrna TN. 615-459-4884
Mullins, Tom, *Supvr Ad & YA Servs,* Public Library of Anniston & Calhoun County, Liles Memorial Library, Anniston AL. 205-237-8501, Ext 8503

Mullis, Leonard M, *Dir,* Arapahoe Community College Library, Littleton CO. 303-794-1550, Ext 395

Mullis, Melinda, *Librn,* Brunswick-Glynn County Regional Library (Long County), Kingsland GA. 912-264-7360

Mullis, Mrs Joe, *Librn,* Union County Public Library (Marshville Branch), Marshville NC. 704-624-2828

Mulloney, Paul F, *Librn,* United States Department of the Interior (Bureau of Reclamation Library), Denver CO. 303-234-3019

Mullooly, Elnora E, *Librn,* Fayette County Law Library, Uniontown PA. 412-437-5629

Mulloy, Betty, *Librn,* Lauren Rogers Library & Musuem of Art, Laurel MS. 601-428-4875

Mulloy, C T, *Doc, On-Line Servs & Bibliog Instr,* Addiction Research Foundation Library, Toronto ON. 416-595-6144

Mulready, Alice T, *Dir,* Tufts Library, Public Libraries of Weymouth, Weymouth MA. 617-337-1402

Mulrooney, Terry, *In Charge,* Newfoundland Area Public Library, Newfoundland PA. 717-676-4518

Multer, Ell-Piret, *Tech Serv,* United States Fish & Wildlife Service, National Fisheries Research Laboratory Library, Columbia MO. 314-442-2271, Ext 3201

Multhopp, Jennifer L, *In Charge,* Enoch Pratt Free Library (Fells Point), Baltimore MD. 301-396-5430, 396-5395

Mulvaney, Carol E, *Librn,* Caterpillar Tractor Co (Technical Information Center), Peoria IL. 578-6118 or 578-6119

Mulvey, Dennis V, *Asst Dir,* Warren Public Library, Warren OH. 216-399-8807

Mulvey, Judith, *Juv Cat,* Neenah Public Library, Neenah WI. 414-729-4728

Mumford, Carole, *Acq & Commun Servs,* Petersburg Public Library, Petersburg VA. 804-732-3851

Mumma, Janice E, *Librn,* George Hail Free Library, Warren RI. 401-245-7686

Munch, Janet Butler, *Librn,* Mercy College, Bronx Extension Center, Bronx NY. 212-798-8952

Munch, Leona, *Librn,* Sullivan City Library, Elizabeth Titus Memorial Library, Sullivan IL. 217-728-7221

Munchak, Irene, *Ref,* Marywood College Library, Scranton PA. 717-343-6521, Ext 289

Muncy, Curtis, *ILL & Ref,* Cedar Falls Public Library, Cedar Falls IA. 319-266-2629

Munday, Bessie, *Librn,* Dallas Public Library (Pleasant Grove), Dallas TX. 214-398-6625

Munday, Elaine J, *Dir,* Taylor County Public Library, Campbellsville KY. 502-465-2562

Munday, Jerome, *Pub Servs,* San Jose State University Library, San Jose CA. 408-277-3377

Mundell, Ellen, *Librn,* Merrick Public Library, Brookfield MA. 617-867-6339

Mundell, Yvanna, *Librn,* Associated Press Newsphoto Library, New York NY. 212-262-6061, 262-4086

Munden, Gail, *On-Line Servs,* Mayer, Brown & Platt Law Library, Chicago IL. 312-782-0600

Munder, Carol, *Bkmobile Coordr,* Monroe County Public Library, Key West FL. 305-294-7100

Mundie, Joseph, *Finance,* Prince George's County Memorial Library System, Hyattsville MD. 301-699-3500

Mundkowski, Mrs Ernest, *Librn,* Grandfield Public Library, Grandfield OK. 405-479-5533

Mundo, Ana R, *Asst Librn,* Inter-American University-Fajardo Regional College, Centro de Recursos para el Aprendizaje, Fajardo PR. 809-863-2390

Mundstock, Aileen, *Librn,* Universal Foods Corp, Technical Information Services, Milwaukee WI. 414-271-6755, Ext 66-31

Mundt, Mary, *Learning Resource Technician,* Moraine Park Technical Institute Library, West Bend WI. 414-334-3413

Mundt, Ruth, *Librn,* Manhattan Township Free Public Library, Manhattan IL. 815-478-3987

Mundy, Mary A, *Ad & Tech Serv,* Laurens County Library, Laurens SC. 803-984-0596

Mundy, Sandra, *Librn,* Jesse M Smith Memorial Library, Harrisville RI. 401-568-8244

Munetic, Ann, *Head,* City College of San Francisco, Library Technology Program, CA. 415-239-3586

Munford, Virginia L, *Librn,* Charles H Taylor Memorial Library (Northampton), Hampton VA. 804-838-7036

Munger, Barbara, *Librn,* Essex County Public Library (Harrow Branch), Harrow ON. 519-776-5241

Munger, Freda, *Ref,* Umpqua Community College Library, Roseburg OR. 503-672-5571, Ext 40

Munger, Nancy Terry, *In Charge,* J Walter Thompson Co, Information Center, New York NY. 212-867-1000

Munke, Peggy P, *Librn,* Our Lady of the Lake University Libraries (Worden School), San Antonio TX. 512-434-6711, Ext 218

Munn, David C, *Hist & Exhibits,* New Jersey State Library, Trenton NJ. 609-292-6200

Munn, Ollie M, *Librn,* Florence County Library (Pamplico Public), Pamplico SC. 803-493-5441

Munn, Robert, *Dir,* West Virginia University, University Library, Morgantown WV. 304-293-4040

Munn, Robert F, *Dean,* West Virginia University, Dept of Library Science, WV. 304-293-3540

Munoff, Elsie, *Librn,* Fort Edward Free Library, Fort Edward NY. 518-747-6743

Munoz, Antonio, *Mex-Am Servs,* El Paso Public Library, El Paso TX. 915-543-3804

Munoz, Romeo, *AV,* Olive-Harvey College, City Colleges of Chicago, Olive-Harvey College Library, Chicago IL. 312-568-3700

Munro, Dale, *Librn,* Ontario Science Centre Library, Don Mills ON. 416-429-4100, Ext 194

Munro, June E, *Dir,* Saint Catharines Public Library, Saint Catharines ON. 416-688-6103

Munro, Margaret, *Librn,* Environmental Protection Agency, Region III Field Office Library, Annapolis MD. 301-224-2740

Munro, Marie B, *Asst Librn,* Clapp Memorial Library, Belchertown MA. 413-323-6224

Munro, Mary A, *Asst Dir,* Talbot County Free Library, Easton MD. 301-822-1626

Munro, Robert, *Law,* University of Florida Libraries (Legal Information Center), Gainesville FL. 904-392-0417

Munro, William, *Librn,* Atlanta Public Library (College Park Branch), College Park GA. 404-767-9484

Munson, Kathleen, *Dir,* Canajoharie Library & Art Gallery, Canajoharie NY. 518-673-2314

Munsterman, Marilyn, *Bibliog Instr,* Auraria Libraries, Denver CO. 303-629-2805

Munt, June A, *Librn,* Cummins Engine Co Inc (Business Information Center), Columbus IN. 812-379-8311

Muntz, J Richard, *Librn & Bibliog Instr,* Western Baptist College Library, Salem OR. 503-581-8600, Ext 49

Munzer, Annette E, *Librn,* Phoenix Art Museum Library, Phoenix AZ. 602-257-1222

Muoio, Rose C, *Librn,* Donora Public Library, Donora PA. 412-379-7940

Murata, Louise R, *Librn,* Industrial Indemnity Company Library System, San Francisco CA. 415-986-3535

Murata, M M, *Dir,* Melvindale Public Library, Melvindale MI. 313-381-8677

Murawski, Charlotte, *Librn,* Chicopee Public Library (Aldenville), Chicopee MA. 413-532-4248

Murchie, Betty, *Librn,* Genesee District Library (Burton Memorial), Burton MI. 313-742-0674

Murchie, John, *Dir,* Nova Scotia College of Art & Design Library, Halifax NS. 902-422-7381, Ext 115

Murchio, Christine M, *Projects Coordr,* Free Public Library of Woodbridge, Woodbridge NJ. 201-634-4450

Murden, Frances, *Acq,* Prairie Trails Public Library District, Burbank IL. 312-430-3688

Murdoch, Marion C, *Acq,* University of California, Berkeley (University Library), Berkeley CA. 415-642-3773

Murdoch, Richard, *Rare Bks,* Wake Forest University, Z Smith Reynolds Library, Winston-Salem NC. 919-761-5480

Murdoch, Robert, *Circ,* Utah State University, Merrill Library & Learning Resources Program, Logan UT. 801-750-2637

Murdock, Alice, *Librn,* National Marine Fisheries Service, Biological Lab Library, Fort Crocket TX. 713-763-1211, Ext 506

Murdock, Evelyne K, *Actg Dir,* Consumer Product Safety Commission Library, Bethesda MD. 301-492-6548

Murdock, Mary-Elizabeth, *Dir,* Sophia Smith Collection, Women's History Archive, Smith College, Northampton MA. 413-584-2700, Ext 622

Murdock, Midred, *Branch Asst,* Abbeville-Greenwood Regional Library (Donalds Branch), Donalds SC. 803-223-4515

Murdock, Mrs R, *Librn,* Bancroft Public Library, Bancroft ON. 613-332-3380

Murdock, Robert M, *Dir,* Grand Rapids Art Museum, Art Reference Library, Grand Rapids MI. 616-459-4676

Murdock, S, *Asst Archivist,* Simcoe County Archives, Minesing ON. 705-726-9300, Ext 287; 726-9305

Murdock, Sue, *Librn,* Carnegie Library of Pittsburgh, Library for the Blind & Physically Handicapped, Pittsburgh PA. 412-687-2440

Murdock, Sue O, *Librn Blind & Phys Handicapped,* Carnegie Library of Pittsburgh, Pittsburgh PA. 412-622-3100

Murdock, William J, *Dir,* Pace University, Pleasantville-Briarcliff Library, Pleasantville NY. 914-769-3200, Ext 382

Murgai, Sarla R, *Circ,* University of Tennessee at Chattanooga Library, Chattanooga TN. 615-755-4701

Murley, K A, *Librn,* IBM Corp, Data Systems Division Library, Hopewell Junction NY. 914-897-6219

Murley, Ruth B, *Bkmobile Librn,* Cumberland County Public Library, Burkesville KY. 502-864-2207

Murphey, Barbara A, *Dir,* Largo Library, Largo FL. 813-584-8671, Ext 281, 282

Murphey, Jane, *Asst Librn,* United Automobile Workers Research Library, Detroit MI. 313-926-5388

Murphey, Mrs Wielene, *Personnel,* Chattanooga-Hamilton County Bicentennial Library, Chattanooga TN. 615-757-5320

Murphey, Jr, John A, *Assoc Dir,* South Central Regional Medical Library Program, (TALON), TX. 214-688-2627

Murphree, Janie, *Dir,* Motlow State Community College, Library-Learning Resources Center, Tullahoma TN. 615-455-8511, Ext 225

Murphree, Virginia, *Librn,* Tombigbee Regional Library (Wren Public), Aberdeen MS. 601-256-8604

Murphy, Albina B, *Librn,* Rutland Free Public Library, Rutland MA. 617-886-6266

Murphy, Ann, *Cat,* Princeton University Library, Princeton NJ. 609-452-3180

Murphy, Anne, *Tech Serv,* New England School of Law Library, Boston MA. 617-367-9655, Ext 50

Murphy, Anne M, *Dir of Librs,* Fordham University, Duane Library, Bronx NY. 212-933-2233, Ext 230, 259

Murphy, Barbara G, *Asst Dir,* University of Virginia (Law Library), Charlottesville VA. 804-924-3384

Murphy, Beth, *Librn,* Harper & Row Publishers, School Division Library, New York NY. 212-593-7379

Murphy, C Edwin, *In Charge,* Historical Center of the United Methodist Church Library, Lincoln NE. 466-2371 Ext 304

Murphy, Charles, *Librn,* Pennsylvania State University, Applied Research Laboratory Library, University Park PA. 814-865-6621

Murphy, Colleen, *Media,* University of Maine at Presque Isle Library, Presque Isle ME. 207-764-0311, Ext 223

Murphy, Daniel J, *Mgr,* IBM Corp, Systems Development Div, Laboratory Library, Kingston NY. 914-383-0123

Murphy, David M, *Dir,* Washington Theological Consortium, DC. 202-832-2675

Murphy, Dolores, *Ch,* Garfield Free Public Library, Garfield NJ. 201-478-3800

Murphy, Eleanor, *Dir,* Huntsville-Madison County Public Library, Huntsville AL. 205-536-0021

Murphy, Eleanor E, *Dir,* North Alabama Cooperative Library System, Huntsville AL. 205-534-0735

Murphy, Elizabeth B, *Ch,* Public Library of the District of Columbia, Martin Luther King Memorial Library, Washington DC. 202-727-1101

Murphy, Evelyn, *Tech Serv,* Public Library of Des Moines, Des Moines IA. 515-283-4152

Murphy, Ezevel, *Asst Librn & Ref,* Warren County Library, Monmouth IL. 309-734-6412

Murphy, Florence, *Ad,* South Portland Public Library, South Portland ME. 207-799-2204

Murphy, Franches, *Librn,* Trigg County Public Library, Cadiz KY. 502-522-8517

Murphy, Francis C, *Dir,* Montgomery College-Takoma Park Campus Library, Takoma Park MD. 301-587-4090, Ext 242

Murphy, Gertrude M, *Librn,* Reader's Digest Association, Inc, Editorial Reference Library, Pleasantville NY. 914-769-7000, Ext 2079

Murphy, Helen King, *Dir,* Highland Hospital, Williams Health Sciences Library, Rochester NY. 716-473-2200, Ext 291

Murphy, Henry, *Librn,* Cornell University Libraries (College of Agricultural & Life Sciences & Human Ecology), Ithaca NY. 607-256-5406

Murphy, Henry, *Asst Univ Librn; Statutory Col Librs,* Cornell University Libraries (University Libraries), Ithaca NY. 607-256-4144

Murphy, James D, *Coll Develop,* State University of New York, College of Arts & Science at Oswego, Penfield Library, Oswego NY. 315-341-4232

Murphy, James E, *Dir,* Corfu Free Library, Corfu NY. 716-599-3321

Murphy, Janet, *Pub Servs,* University of San Diego, James S Copley Library, San Diego CA. 714-291-6480, Ext 4312, 4313, 4314

Murphy, Jean, *Pub Servs,* Mesa Public Library, Mesa AZ. 602-834-2207

Murphy, Jeanne B, *Librn,* Dallas Center Public Library, Dallas Center IA. 515-992-3185

Murphy, Joseph P, *Chief, Tech Servs,* AVCO Corp, Lycoming Division Library & Information Center, Stratford CT. 203-378-8211

Murphy, Joseph R, *Instr,* Appalachian State University, Department of Educational Media: Librarianship & Instructional Technology, NC. 704-262-2243

Murphy, Josephine C, *Ad & Ref,* Mary Riley Styles Public Library, Falls Church VA. 703-241-5030

Murphy, Joyce, *Librn,* British Columbia Ministry of Environment, Waste Management Branch Library, Victoria BC. 604-387-5321, Ext 271

Murphy, Joyce, *Asst Librn,* Corydon Public Library, Corydon IN. 812-738-4110

Murphy, Judith, *Tech Serv,* Riverdale Public Library District, Riverdale IL. 312-841-3311

Murphy, Kathleen, *Librn,* Moot, Sprague, Marcy, Landy, Fernbach & Smythe Library, Buffalo NY. 716-845-5200

Murphy, Lawrence Parke, *Keeper of Rare Bks,* New York Public Library (Rare Books), New York NY. 212-790-6296

Murphy, Loretta, *Librn,* Muskegon County Library (Holton), Muskegon MI. 616-724-6248

Murphy, Lynn, *Commun Servs,* Dartmouth Regional Library, Dartmouth NS. 902-466-7623

Murphy, Lynne, *Ch,* Dartmouth Public Libraries, Southworth Library, South Dartmouth MA. 617-997-1252

Murphy, Marcy, *Assoc Prof,* Western Michigan University, School of Librarianship, MI. 616-383-1849

Murphy, Margaret, *Coordr of Libr,* Nova Scotia Government, Dept of the Attorney General Library, Halifax NS. 902-424-7699

Murphy, Margaret M, *Chief,* United States Army (Materials & Mechanics Research Center Library), Watertown MA. 617-923-3460

Murphy, Marilyn, *Librn,* Indiana University-Purdue University at Fort Wayne Library (Fine Arts), Fort Wayne IN. 219-482-5456

Murphy, Marilyn, *Ref & On-Line Servs,* Mount Mercy College, Catherine McAuley Library, Cedar Rapids IA. 319-363-8213, Ext 244

Murphy, Marsha H, *Ref,* Veterans Administration, Hospital Library Service, Loma Linda CA. 714-825-7084, Ext 2391

Murphy, Mary, *Ch,* Kent Memorial Library, Suffield CT. 203-668-2325

Murphy, Mary, *Ref,* Lawrence Public Library, Lawrence KS. 913-843-3833

Murphy, Mary, *Librn,* Saint Patrick's Episcopal Church Library, Washington DC. 202-337-2810

Murphy, Mary J, *Librn,* Barton Library (Norphlet Branch), Norphlet AR. 501-546-2534

Murphy, Michaela, *Librn,* Tacoma Public Library (Fern Hill), Tacoma WA. 206-472-8820

Murphy, Michaela, *Librn,* Tacoma Public Library (Grace R Moore), Tacoma WA. 206-472-2166

Murphy, Mrs L P, *Central Librn,* Steel Company of Canada, Ltd, Corporate Library Services, Hamilton ON. 416-528-2511

Murphy, Nadene, *Librn,* Valemount Public Library, Valemount BC. 604-566-4367

Murphy, P, *Librn,* University of Windsor (Paul Martin Law Library), Windsor ON. 519-253-4232, Ext 878

Murphy, Patricia, *Bibliog Instr,* Kent State University, Stark Campus Learning Resource Center, Canton OH. 216-499-9602

Murphy, Patrick, *Librn,* Medical Research Laboratories, Inc Library, Niles IL. 312-792-2666

Murphy, Paul, *Sci,* Vanderbilt University Library (Central-Science), Nashville TN. 615-322-6603

Murphy, R P, *Librn,* Allied Chemical Corp, Fibers Div, Technical Center Library, Petersburg VA. 804-458-7811, Ext 5617

Murphy, Robert B, *Mgr,* IBM Corp, Data Systems Division Library, Hopewell Junction NY. 914-897-6219

Murphy, Robert L, *Dir,* West Virginia University (Medical Center Library), Morgantown WV. 304-293-2113

Murphy, Rosemonde, *ILL,* Universite De Moncton, Bibliotheque Champlain, Moncton NB. 506-858-4012

Murphy, Rowena, *Librn,* Tri-County Regional Library (Cedartown Branch), Cedartown GA. 404-291-9360

Murphy, Sandy, *Bkmobile Coordr,* Selby Public Library, Sarasota County Federated Library System, Sarasota FL. 814-366-7303

Murphy, Sara L, *Senior Librn,* United States Department of Energy, Grand Junction Office Technical Library, Grand Junction CO. 303-242-8621, Ext 278

Murphy, Suzanne, *Coordr for Developmental Studies,* Oscar Rose Junior College, Learning Resources Center, Midwest City OK. 405-733-7323, 733-7322

Murphy, Terence, *Pub Relations,* New York Public Library, Astor, Lenox & Tilden Foundations Library, New York NY. 212-790-6262

Murphy, Timothy, *ILL & Ref,* Tenafly Public Library, Tenafly NJ. 201-568-8680

Murphy, W, *Librn,* Prince George College Library, Prince George BC. 604-964-4455

Murphy, Walter H, *Dir,* Flint River Regional Library, Griffin GA. 404-227-2756

Murphy, William D, *Librn,* Kirkland & Ellis Law Library, Chicago IL. 312-861-3200

Murphy, Yolanda, *Librn,* Preble County District Library (Camden), Eaton OH. 513-452-3142

Murr, Kenneth, *ILL,* Clemson University, Robert Muldrow Cooper Library, Clemson SC. 803-656-3026

Murra, Virgie Ann, *Dir,* Etta C Ross Memorial Library, Blue Earth Public Library, Blue Earth MN. 507-526-5012

Murrah, David, *Dir,* Texas Tech University Library (Southwest Collection), Lubbock TX. 806-742-3749

Murray, A J, *Dir,* University of the Pacific, McGeorge School of Law Library, Sacramento CA. 916-739-7131

Murray, Alice R, *Librn,* United States Navy (Philadelphia Naval Shipyard Technical Library), Philadelphia PA. 215-755-3657

Murray, Barbara, *Ref,* Santiago Library System, Orange CA. 714-634-7137

Murray, Barbara J, *Supvr,* Libraries of Orange County Network, (LOCNET), CA. 714-834-6225

Murray, Bill, *Dir,* Aurora Public Schools Professional Library, Aurora CO. 303-344-8060, Ext 257

Murray, Carol, *Librn,* Celanese Polymer Specialties Co, Technical Center, Research Library, Jeffersontown KY. 502-585-8053

Murray, Carrie, *Tech Serv,* Hoyt Library, Kingston PA. 717-287-2013

Murray, Cecilia, *Librn,* Mid-Continent Public Library (Gladstone Branch), Kansas City MO. 816-436-4385

Murray, Cheryl, *Ch,* C F Lawrence Memorial Library, Pepperell MA. 617-433-6933

Murray, David, *Dir,* University of Rhode Island, Extension Division Library, Providence RI. 401-277-3818

Murray, Deirdre, *Ref,* Huntingdon Valley Library, Huntingdon Valley PA. 215-947-5138

Murray, Diane, *Tech Serv,* Hope College, Van Zoeren Library, Holland MI. 392-5111, Ext 2130

Murray, Edward, *Librn,* United States Navy (Naval Weapons Center Library), China Lake CA. 714-939-3278, 939-2595

Murray, Elizabeth B, *Librn,* British Columbia Telephone Co, Business Library, Burnaby BC. 604-432-2671

Murray, Gladys, *Spec Coll,* Centre County Library & Historical Museum, Bellefonte PA. 814-355-3131

Murray, Gloria, *ILL,* Peterborough Town Library, Peterborough NH. 603-924-6401

Murray, Grace, *Librn,* Prince Edward Island Provincial Library (Breadalbane Branch), Breadalbane PE. 902-892-3504, Ext 54

Murray, Ida, *Tech Serv & Cat,* Henry Ford Community College, Eshleman Library, Dearborn MI. 313-271-2750, Ext 378

Murray, James, *Librn,* Maryland State Library for the Blind & Physically Handicapped, Baltimore MD. 301-383-3112

Murray, James T, *Librn,* University of Tulsa (Sidney Born Technical Library), Tulsa OK. 918-592-6000, Ext 232

Murray, Jane, *Dir,* Red River County Public Library, Clarksville TX. 214-427-3991

Murray, Joan, *Supvr,* Elgin County Public Library (Belmont Branch), Belmont ON. 519-633-0815

Murray, John D, *Dir,* Westmont College, Roger John Voskuyl Library, Santa Barbara CA. 805-969-5051, Ext 378

Murray, Karen, *In Charge,* Riverside Medical Center, Medical Library, Kankakee IL. 815-933-1671, Ext 4855

Murray, Kathleen, *Cat,* Lamar University, Mary & John Gray Library, Beaumont TX. 713-838-8313

Murray, Kathleen, *Librn & On-Line Servs,* Providence Hospital, Medical Library & Learning Resource Center, Seattle WA. 206-326-5621

Murray, Kay, *Assoc Prof,* University of North Carolina at Chapel Hill, School of Library Science, NC. 919-933-8366

Murray, Laura, *Regional AV Coordr,* Metropolitan Toronto Library Board, Metropolitan Toronto Library, Toronto ON. 416-928-5150

Murray, Loretta S, *Librn,* Hull Public Library, Hull IA. 712-439-1321

Murray, Lorraine, *Librn,* Wainwright Hospital Complex Library, Wainwright AB. 403-842-3324

Murray, Lynn, *Librn,* Marin County Free Library (Point Reyes Branch), Point Reyes CA. 415-663-8375

Murray, Lynn, *Dir,* Northern Hancock County Community Library, Chester WV. 304-387-1010

Murray, Margaret A, *Acq,* Northeast Texas Library System, Dallas TX. 214-651-9266

Murray, Marijean, *Chief Librn,* United States Army (Othon O Valent Learning Resources Center), Fort Bliss TX. 915-568-8176, 8606

Murray, Marilyn, *Librn,* Arthur Andersen & Co Library, Chicago IL. 312-580-0033

Murray, Mary P, *Librn,* Mercy Center for Health Care Services, Medical Library, Aurora IL. 312-859-2222, Ext 2683

Murray, Mavis, *Librn,* Northern Miner Library, Toronto ON. 416-368-3481

Murray, Mrs G, *Asst Dir,* Pinawa Public Library, Pinawa MB. 204-753-2496

Murray, Patrick W, *Bkmobile Coordr,* Public Library of Fort Wayne & Allen County, Fort Wayne IN. 219-424-7241

Murray, Pauline, *Librn,* Fergus Public Library, Fergus ON. 519-843-1180

Murray, Peggy, *YA,* Santa Clara County Free Library, San Jose CA. 408-293-2326

Murray, Raymond, *Asst Dir,* State University of New York, College of Arts & Science at Oswego, Penfield Library, Oswego NY. 315-341-4232

Murray, Richard, *Librn,* Harlan Public Library, Harlan KY. 606-573-5220

Murray, Robert G, *Cat,* Northeastern University Libraries, Boston MA. 617-437-2350

Murray, Robin R B, *Dir & Per,* Alfred University (Scholes Library of Ceramics), Alfred NY. 607-871-2492

Murray, Robinson, *Assoc Libn,* Essex Institute, James Duncan Phillips Library, Salem MA. 617-744-3390

Murray, Rochelle, *Ch,* Davenport Public Library, Davenport IA. 319-326-7832

Murray, Rosalee, *Libn,* Tulare County Library System (Pixley Branch), Pixley CA. 209-757-3880

Murray, Ruth, *Educ, Behav Sci & Sociol,* University of Chicago, Joseph Regenstein Library, Chicago IL. 312-753-2977

Murray, Sabina J, *Libn,* Church of Jesus Christ of Latter-Day Saints, Florida Branch Genealogical Library, Jacksonville FL. 904-398-3487

Murray, Sister Barbara, *Acq,* Pensacola Junior College, Learning Resource Center, Pensacola FL. 904-476-5410

Murray, Sister Jane, *Acq,* Incarnate Word College, Saint Pius X Library, San Antonio TX. 512-828-1261, Ext 215

Murray, Therona, *Tech Serv,* Park Forest Public Library, Park Forest IL. 312-748-3731

Murray, Vivian, *ILL,* Rogers Memorial Library, Southampton NY. 516-283-0774

Murray, Ward, *Bkmobile Coordr,* John McIntire Public Library Public Library, Zanesville OH. 614-453-0391

Murray, Ward, *Bkmobile Coordr,* Washington County Public Library, Marietta OH. 614-373-1057

Murray, Jr, T H, *Supvr Tech Info Servs,* Chevron Overseas Petroleum, Inc, Technical Library, San Francisco CA. 415-894-4332

Murray-O'Hair, Robin, *In Charge,* Charles E Stevens American Atheist Library & Archives, Inc Library, Austin TX. 512-458-3342

Murrell, Susan DeBrecht, *Libn,* Louisville Free Public Library (Talking Book Library), Louisville KY. 502-587-1069, 587-1085

Murren, Mona, *Asst Libn,* Sioux Empire College Library, Hawarden IA. 712-552-9900

Murrey, F Ward, *Dir,* Southeastern Ohio Regional Libraries, OH. 614-732-4817

Murrey, Ward, *Libn,* State Library of Ohio (Regional Library Service Center), Caldwell OH. 614-732-4817

Murrin, Nancy, *Cat,* Butler Public Library, Butler PA. 412-287-5576

Murry, Joyce, *Libn,* First Assembly of God Library, North Little Rock AR. 501-758-8553

Murtinez, C, *On-Line Servs,* University of Colorado at Colorado Springs, Library, Colorado Springs CO. 303-593-3296

Murway, Mark, *Ref & MEDLINE,* Rush-Presbyterian-Saint Luke's Medical Center (Library of Rush University), Chicago IL. 312-942-2271, 942-5950

Muse, Dorothy S, *Dir,* Parkersburg & Wood County Public Library, Wood County Service Center, Parkersburg WV. 304-485-6564

Muse, Frances M, *Ref,* Georgia State University, William Russell Pullen Library, Atlanta GA. 404-658-2185, 658-2172

Muse, Mary M, *Libn,* Barnet Public Library, Barnet VT. 802-633-4436

Muse, Sylvia, *Libn,* Jackson Metropolitan Library (Florence Library), Florence MS. 601-352-3677

Musgrave, Myles T, *Adminr,* Acheson Industries Inc, Corporate Library, Port Huron MI. 313-984-5583, Ext 503

Musgrove, Lola, *Asst Libn,* Grand Prairie Memorial Library, Grand Prairie TX. 214-264-1571

Musgrove, Walter C, *Night Libn,* Pembroke State University, Mary Livermore Library, Pembroke NC. 919-521-4214, Ext 238

Mushrush, Gail Ann, *Libn,* Greenville County Library (West Branch), Greenville SC. 803-269-5210

Muskat, Beatrice T, *Libn,* Temple Israel of Greater Miami Library, Miami FL. 305-573-5900

Musmann, Viki, *Libn,* Glendale Public Library (Crescenta Valley Branch), Montrose CA. 213-956-2030

Musselman, Kathryn A, *Media,* Warren County Library, Belvidere NJ. 201-475-5361, Ext 114

Musser, E Glenn, *Tech Serv,* Worcester Public Library, Worcester MA. 617-752-3751

Musser, Fay, *Per,* Waubonsee Community College, Learning Resources Center, Sugar Grove IL. 312-466-4811, Ext 303

Musser, Marsha, *Bkmobile Coordr,* Taylor County Public Library, Campbellsville KY. 502-465-2562

Musser, Mrs Thomas, *In Charge,* Geographical Society of Philadelphia Library, Philadelphia PA. 215-563-0127

Musser, Necia, *Acq,* Western Michigan University, Dwight B Waldo Library, Kalamazoo MI. 616-383-4961

Musser, Ruth N, *Assoc Libn, Tech Serv & On-Line Servs,* Messiah College, Murray Learning Resources Center, Grantham PA. 717-766-2511, Ext 380

Mustain, Anne, *Cat,* University of Virginia (Law Library), Charlottesville VA. 804-924-3384

Mustain-Wood, Janice R, *Dir,* Fort Lupton Public & School Library, Fort Lupton CO. 303-857-2728

Mustonen, Karlo, *Doc,* Utah State University, Merrill Library & Learning Resources Program, Logan UT. 801-750-2637

Mustonen, Karlo K, *Libn,* Utah State University (Regional Depository Collection of US Government Documents), Logan UT. 801-750-2682

Mutala, Mrs Pat, *Libn,* Portage la Prairie City Library, Portage la Prairie MB. 204-857-4271

Muth, Bell, *Asst Dir,* Bowling Green Public Library, Bowling Green KY. 502-781-4882

Muth, Irene, *Libn,* San Diego Public Library (Logan Heights), San Diego CA. 714-239-6580

Muth, Margaret, *Libn,* Santa Cruz Public Library (La Selva Beach Branch), La Selva Beach CA. 408-722-1958

Muth, Thomas J, *Asst Libn,* Topeka Public Library, Topeka KS. 913-233-2040

Muther, Aimee, *Libn,* Lakeshore General Hospital, Medical Library, Pointe Claire PQ. 514-695-1310, Ext 233

Mutschler, Herbert F, *Dir,* King County Library System, Seattle WA. 206-344-7465

Muzzo, Joseph, *Libn,* Doctors Hospital, Medical Library, Columbus OH. 614-421-4113

Myatt, Barbara, *Asst Prof,* Virginia Commonwealth University, Library Science Program, VA. 804-786-0000

Myatt, Martha, *Libn,* Lost Nation Public Library, Lost Nation IA. 319-678-2235

Myatt, Nina, *Spec Coll,* Antioch College, Olive Kettering Memorial Library, Yellow Springs OH. 513-767-7331, Ext 229

Myco, Donna L, *Ch,* Westfield Athenaeum, Westfield MA. 413-568-7833

Mydland, Karen, *Govt Docs,* Sheridan College, Kooi Library, Instructional Resource Center, Sheridan WY. 307-674-6446, Ext 170

Myer, Nancy E, *Libn,* Veterans Administration, Medical Center Library, Tucson AZ. 602-792-1450, Ext 361

Myers, Agnes M, *Dir,* Loretto Heights College, May Bonfils Stanton Library, Denver CO. 303-936-8441

Myers, Alice, *Dir,* Riverton Free Public Library, Riverton NJ. 609-829-2476

Myers, Anvil, *Libn,* Humeston Public Library, Humeston IA. 515-877-4811

Myers, Barbara, *Cat,* Occidental College, Mary Norton Clapp Library, Los Angeles CA. 213-259-2640

Myers, Barbara L, *Libn,* Fraser Public Library, Fraser MI. 313-293-2055

Myers, Carol B, *Tech Serv,* Public Library of Charlotte & Mecklenburg County, Inc, Charlotte NC. 704-374-2725

Myers, Carolyn, *Per,* James Madison University, Madison Memorial Library, Harrisonburg VA. 703-433-6150

Myers, Claryse D, *Libn,* National Park Service, Great Smoky Mountains National Park Library, Gatlinburg TN. 615-436-5615, Ext 70

Myers, Cynthia, *Cat,* Simpson College, Dunn Library, Indianola IA. 515-961-6251, Ext 663

Myers, Dana, *Bkmobile Libns,* Athens Regional Library, Athens GA. 404-543-0134

Myers, David, *Asst Libn,* Colorado Legislative Council Library, Denver CO. 303-839-3521

Myers, Diana, *Tech Serv,* Ontario College of Art Library, Toronto ON. 416-977-5311, Ext 54 & 55

Myers, Donald, *Chmn & Prof,* Oklahoma State University, Library Science Media-Instructional Media Program, OK. 405-624-6433

Myers, Elissa Matulis, *Dir,* American Society of Association Executives, Information Central, Washington DC. 202-626-2742

Myers, Erma, *Libn,* Storm Lake Public Library, Storm Lake IA. 712-732-2125

Myers, Frances, *Libn,* Free Public Library of the City of Trenton (Cadwalader), Trenton NJ. 609-392-7188

Myers, Fred A, *Dir,* Thomas Gilcrease Institute of American History & Art Library, Tulsa OK. 918-583-3079

Myers, G Richard, *Libn,* General Dynamics Corp, Quincy Shipbuilding Div Library, Quincy MA. 617-471-4200, Ext 3149

Myers, Georgianna, *Bibliog Instr,* University of Wisconsin-Whitewater, Library & Learning Resources, Whitewater WI. 414-472-1000

Myers, Irene L, *Info Mgr,* Procter & Gamble Co (Winton Hill Technical Center Library), Cincinnati OH. 513-562-1100

Myers, James C, *On-Line Servs,* Florida State University, Robert Manning Strozier Library, Tallahassee FL. 904-644-5211

Myers, Jean, *Ch,* Payson Public Library, Payson AZ. 602-474-2585

Myers, Joe I, *Dir,* Stetson University, duPont-Ball Library, De Land FL. 904-734-4121, Ext 220

Myers, John R, *Chief, Info Syst Div,* National Agricultural Library, Beltsville MD. 301-344-4248

Myers, Joseph H, *Pub Libr State Aid,* State Library of Pennsylvania, Harrisburg PA. 717-787-2646

Myers, Judith, *Asst Dir,* New York Medical College, Westchester Medical Center Library, Valhalla NY. 914-347-5237

Myers, Judy, *Doc & Photocopy Serv,* University of Houston (M D Anderson Memorial Library), Houston TX. 713-749-4241

Myers, Karen, *Ref,* Wallingford Public Library, Wallingford CT. 203-265-6754

Myers, Katherine, *Libn,* Dauphin County Library System (Central), Harrisburg PA. 717-234-4961

Myers, Kay, *Ch & YA,* Anchorage Municipal Libraries, Anchorage AK. 907-264-4481

Myers, Laura, *Libn,* Jennings Public Library, Jennings LA. 318-824-4367

Myers, Linda K, *Dir,* Texas State Technical Institute, Waco Library, Waco TX. 817-799-3611, Ext 451

Myers, Lois E, *Asst Libn,* Brazil Public Library, Brazil IN. 812-448-1981

Myers, Lucille, *Circ,* New Albany Floyd County Public Library, New Albany IN. 812-944-8464

Myers, Mae E, *Libn,* Pennsylvania Department of Environmental Resources (Forest Advisory Services Library), Harrisburg PA. 717-787-2105

Myers, Marcia, *Libr Program,* Miami Dade Community College (North Campus Library), Miami FL. 305-685-4436

Myers, Margaret, *Asst Libn,* Heard Museum of Anthropology & Primitive Art Library, Phoenix AZ. 602-252-8848

Myers, Margaret, *Libn,* Indianapolis Bar Association Library, Indianapolis IN. 317-632-8240

Myers, Marilyn, *Coll Develop,* Wichita State University, Library & Media Resources Center, Wichita KS. 316-689-3586

Myers, Martha, *Dir,* Alaska Bible College, Capt Vincent J Joy, Jr Memorial Library, Glennallen AK. 907-822-3201

Myers, Mary, *Libr Asst,* Madera County Library (North Fork Branch), North Fork CA. 209-977-2387

Myers, Mary Ann, *Libn,* Ingham County Library (Mason), Mason MI. 517-676-9088

Myers, Mary Ellen, *Libn,* San Bernardino County Library (Fontana Branch), Fontana CA. 714-822-2321

Myers, Mary H, *Per,* Bridgewater State College, Clement C Maxwell Library, Bridgewater MA. 617-697-8321, Ext 441, 442

Myers, Melinda, *Asst Dir & Commun Servs,* Tri-County Public Library District, Augusta IL. 217-392-2211

Myers, Memory V, *Libn,* Graham Community Library, Ralston AB. 403-544-3670

Myers, Mildred, *Libn,* University of Pittsburgh (Graduate School of Business), Pittsburgh PA. 412-624-6408

Myers, Mindy, *Ref,* Yeshiva University Libraries (Benjamin N Cardozo School of Law Library), New York NY. 212-790-0422

Myers, Nancy, *Ch,* Crystal Lake Public Library, Crystal Lake IL. 815-459-1687
Myers, Nancy, *Acq,* University of South Dakota, I D Weeks Library, Vermillion SD. 605-677-5371
Myers, Paul, *Curator,* New York Public Library (Billy Rose Theatre Collection), New York NY. 212-790-6262
Myers, Pauline, *Librn,* Siskiyou County Public Library (Weed Branch), Weed CA. 916-938-4769
Myers, Peggy, *Librn,* Anchor Hocking Corp, Corporate Library, Lancaster OH. 614-687-2403
Myers, Ramon, *Curator E Asian Coll,* Hoover Institution on War, Revolution & Peace, Stanford CA. 415-497-2058
Myers, Robert J, *Dir,* Atlanta Junior College Library, Atlanta GA. 404-656-6649
Myers, Rose, *Dir,* West Oahu College Library, Aiea HI. 808-487-6402
Myers, Ruby Y, *Librn,* Brunswick-Glynn County Regional Library (Talking Book Center), Brunswick GA. 912-264-7360
Myers, Susan, *Librn,* Denver Public Library (Decker), Denver CO. 303-573-5152, Ext 271
Myers, Susan L, *Public Servs,* Colorado College, Charles Leaming Tutt Library, Colorado Springs CO. 303-473-2233, Ext 415
Myers, W Z, *Actg Librn,* Hammond Inc, Editorial Division Library, Maplewood NJ. 201-763-6000
Myers, Jr, Milner H, *Dir,* University of Southern Mississippi (School of Nursing, Instructional Resource Program), Hattiesburg MS. 601-266-4211
Myerscough, Alice, *Asst Dir,* City of Nanticoke Library Board, Waterford Public Library, Waterford ON. 519-443-7682
Mygrants, Agnes, *Librn,* Lake County Public Library (Merrillville Public), Merrillville IN. 219-769-5291
Myhr, Bessie, *Librn,* Paige Memorial Library, Weare NH. 603-529-2044
Myhre, Mira, *Cat,* New York Academy of Medicine Library, New York NY. 212-876-8200
Mykleby, Elaine, *Librn,* First Lutheran Church Library, Cedar Rapids IA. 319-365-1494
Mylenki, Mary, *Asst Librn,* New York Hospital-Cornell Medical Center Libraries (Psychiatric Clinic Library), New York NY. 212-472-6442
Myles, Colette, *Librn,* University of California, Berkeley (Institute of International Studies Library), Berkeley CA. 415-642-3633
Mymick, Mary Lou, *Librn,* Western Apostolic Bible College Library, Stockton CA. 209-464-3516
Myrick, Carole, *Dir,* Anaheim Memorial Hospital, Medical Library, Anaheim CA. 714-774-1450
Myrick, Lavonia M, *Librn,* Bolivar County Library (Rosedale Public), Rosedale MS. 601-759-6332
Myrick, William J, *Admin Servs,* Brooklyn College Library, Brooklyn NY. 212-780-5342
Myshrall, Dorothy, *Ad,* Wareham Free Library, Wareham MA. 617-295-2343
Mysko, Bohdan W, *Head,* Free Library of Philadelphia (Microforms & Newspapers), Philadelphia PA. 215-686-5322

N

Naab, Michael, *Assoc Dir,* Columbia River Maritime Museum Library, Astoria OR. 503-325-2323
Naar, Anna M, *Librn,* Zelienople Public Library, Zelienople PA. 412-452-9330
Naber, Sister Mary Michelle, *Media,* Spalding College Library, Louisville KY. 502-585-9411
Nabors, Cecile, *ILL,* Information Nevada, NV. 702-885-5150
Nabors, Cecile, *ILL,* Nevada State Library, Carson City NV. 702-885-5130
Nabors, Kenneth L, *Ref,* Washington University Libraries, Saint Louis MO. 314-889-5400
Nabritt, Rose L, *ILL,* National Defense University Library, Washington DC. 202-693-8437
Nacheman, Elinor, *Cat,* Rhode Island School of Design Library, Providence RI. 401-331-3507, Ext 229
Nachreiner, Peter, *Cat,* Lake Michigan College Library, Benton Harbor MI. 616-927-3571, Ext 261

Nacsin, Lorraine, *Librn,* Connecticut Department of Transportation, Technical Library, Wethersfield CT. 203-566-5280
Nadal, Antonio, *Dir,* Commonwealth of Puerto Rico (Department of Justice Library), San Juan PR. 809-722-5219
Nadeau, Claude-Roger, *Dir,* College De L'immaculee Conception, Bibliotheque de Theologie, Montreal PQ. 514-737-1465
Nadeau, Henry, *Rare Bks & Spec Coll,* Saint Michael's College, Durick Library, Colchester VT. 802-655-2000, Ext 2400
Nadeau, M J, *Asst Librn,* Supreme Court of Canada Library, Ottawa ON. 995-6354-55-56
Nadler, Judith, *Cat,* University of Chicago, Joseph Regenstein Library, Chicago IL. 312-753-2977
Nadler, Katherine, *Ch,* Iberville Parish Library, Plaquemine LA. 504-687-2520
Nadler, Myra, *Admin Officer,* Long Beach Public Library System, Long Beach CA. 213-436-9225
Naef, Lisa, *Asst Dir,* Eureka-Humboldt County Library, Eureka CA. 707-445-7284, 445-7513
Naessens, Marie, *Librn,* Merrill District Library, Merrill MI. 517-643-7300
Nagar, Murari, *South Asia,* University of Missouri-Columbia, Elmer Ellis Library, Columbia MO. 314-882-4701
Nagata, K M, *Librn,* Union Carbide Canada Limited, Reference Library, Toronto ON. 416-487-1311, Ext 1160
Nagel, Gail, *Librn,* Columbia Memorial Hospital, School of Nursing Library, Hudson NY. 518-828-7601, Ext 272
Nagel, Jean, *Ch & Br Coordr,* Campbell County Public Library District, Newport KY. 606-261-3114
Nagele, Lynne, *ILL,* Edwin A Bemis Public Library, Littleton Public Library, Littleton CO. 303-795-3826
Nagengast, Caroline, *Ch,* Bloomfield Township Public Library, Bloomfield Hills MI. 313-642-5800
Nager, Pauline, *Spec Coll,* Long Beach Public Library, Long Beach NY. 516-432-7201
Nager, Rae Ann, *Curator of Keats Coll,* Harvard University Library (Houghton Library-Rare Books & Manuscripts), Cambridge MA. 617-495-2441
Nagg, Shirley, *Libr & Bkstore Mgr,* Rochester Business Institute, Betty Cronk Memorial Library, Rochester NY. 716-325-7290
Nagle, Carolyn, *Acq,* University of New Brunswick, Saint John Campus, Ward Chipman Library, Saint John NB. 506-657-7310
Nagle, Sister Helen Mary, *Dir,* Mount Aloysius Junior College Library, Cresson PA. 814-886-4131, Ext 70
Nagy, Louis N, *Dir,* Kean College of New Jersey, Nancy Thompson Library, Union NJ. 201-527-2017
Nagy, Margaret, *Librn,* Essex County Public Library (Saint Clair Beach Libr), St Clair Beach ON. 519-776-5241
Nagy, Marilyn, *Asst Dir & Ref,* Fiske Free Library, Claremont NH. 603-542-4393
Nagy, Mrs K, *Reader Serv & Ref,* Canada Department of Energy, Mines & Resources (Canada Center for Mineral & Energy Technology Library), Ottawa ON. 613-995-4132
Nagy, Paul A, *Librn,* San Francisco Theosophical Society Library, San Francisco CA. 415-781-1677
Nagy, Robert, *Cat, Rare Bks & Spec Coll,* Saint John's University Library (Law), Jamaica NY. 212-969-8000, Ext 651, 652 & 653
Nahorniak, Anne, *Librn,* Derwent Municipal Library, Derwent AB. 403-741-3744
Nahra, Jeanette, *Tech Serv, Acq & Cat,* McGregor Public Library, Highland Park Library, Highland Park MI. 313-252-0288
Nail, K, *Archivist,* NASA, John F Kennedy Space Center Library, Kennedy Space Center FL. 305-867-3600, 3615
Naille, Carol, *Dir,* Grand Canyon Community Library, Grand Canyon AZ. 602-638-2718
Naiman, Sandra, *Ad,* Hillside Public Library, Hillside IL. 312-449-7510
Nair, Vijay, *Librn,* Adirondack Museum Library, Blue Mountain Lake NY. 518-352-7311
Nairn, Charles, *ILL, Ref & Spec Coll,* Lake Superior State College Library, Sault Sainte Marie MI. 906-632-6841, Ext 402

Nairn, Charles E, *Co-chairpersons,* Sault Area International Library Association, MI. 906-632-6841, Ext 402
Nairn, Marjorie, *Librn,* Butler Carnegie Library, Butler IN. 219-868-2351
Naisbitt, J, *Librn,* Saskatchewan Department of Education Library, Regina SK. 306-565-5977
Najdowski, Mary Ann, *Ch & Commun Servs,* Manistee County Library, Manistee MI. 616-723-2519
Najera, Carlos, *Ad Spec,* Houston Public Library, Houston TX. 713-224-5441
Najuch, Elaine, *Librn,* Lawrence Public Library (South Lawrence Branch), South Lawrence MA. 617-682-8561
Nakako, Irene, *Ch,* Rock Springs Public Library, Rock Springs WY. 307-362-6212
Nakamae, Emiko H, *Adminr,* Hawaii State Library System (Hawaii Library District), Hilo HI. 808-935-5407
Naldo, G, *Asst Librn,* Southeastern University, Learning Resource Center, Washington DC. 202-488-8174
Nalizia, Paulette, *Librn,* New York Building & Construction Industry, Board of Urban Affairs Library, New York NY. 212-972-1584
Nall, Annette Cook, *Doc,* West Texas State University, Cornette Library, Canyon TX. 806-656-2761
Namer, Sister Rosella, *Fine Arts,* Viterbo College Library, La Crosse WI. 608-784-0040, Ext 429
Nameth, Nardina L, *Dir,* Henry Ford Hospital, Medical Library, Detroit MI. 313-876-2550
Namie, Martha, *Librn,* Pine Forest Regional Library (Lumberton Public), Lumberton MS. 601-788-6539
Nance, James C, *Pres & Gen Mgr,* Litton Bionetics, Inc Library, Kensington MD. 301-881-5600, Ext 113
Nance, Lena, *Librn,* Cleveland Heights-University Heights Public Library (Noble Neighborhood), Cleveland Heights OH. 216-932-3600
Nance, Marian O, *Chief Librn,* United States Army (United States Army Institute for Military Assistance, Marquat Memorial Library), Fort Bragg NC. 919-396-9383
Nangle, Sister Catharine Maria, *Dir,* Saint Joseph Hospital, Medical Library, Lexington KY. 606-278-3436, Ext 2613
Nania, Tina, *Acq,* University of California, Berkeley (Law Library), Berkeley CA. 415-642-4044
Nankivell, Carolyn, *Librn,* Louisville Free Public Library (Fincastle), Louisville KY. 502-458-4387
Nanney, Scarlett, *Libr Asst,* Hawaii State Library System (Mililani), Wahiawa HI. 808-548-2430
Nansard, Bill, *Dir,* Arkansas State University, Dean B Ellis Library, Jonesboro AR. 501-972-3078, 972-3079
Nanstiel, Barbara, *Librn,* Mercy Hospital, Medical Library, Wilkes-Barre PA. 717-826-3699
Nantais, Robert L, *Librn,* Central Mortgage & Housing Corp (Corporate Library), Ottawa ON. 613-746-4611, Ext 178
Napier, Lucile, *Acq,* United States Air Force (Strughold Aeromedical Library), Brooks AFB TX. 512-536-3321
Napier, Ruth, *Ch,* Kendallville Public Library, Kendallville IN. 219-347-3554
Naples, Lillian, *Acq & Commun Servs,* New Hyde Park Public Library, New Hyde Park NY. 516-354-1413
Napoli, Donald J, *Dir,* South Bend Public Library, South Bend IN. 219-288-4413
Napoli, Gloria, *Chief Librn,* Arnold Bernhard & Co Inc, Research Department Library, New York NY. 212-687-3965, Ext 177
Napper-Mills, Rose, *Librn,* National Graduate University Library, Arlington VA. 703-527-4800, Ext 26
Naqusako, Claudine, *Librn,* Hawaii State Library System (Laupahoehoe Community-School), Laupahoehoe HI. 808-962-6911
Narang, Sat, *Cat,* Eastern Illinois University, Booth Library, Charleston IL. 217-581-2210
Naranjo, Carol, *Acq,* Oklahoma City University (Dulaney-Browne Library), Oklahoma City OK. 405-521-5068
Narbeth, Tom, *Ref & On-Line Servs,* George Washington University Library, Washington DC. 202-676-6455

Narbut, Keltah T, *Librn,* Bancroft-Whitney Co, Editorial Library, San Francisco CA. 415-986-4410

Nardin, Doris, *Libr Asst,* Penn Mutual Life Insurance Co, Law Library, Philadelphia PA. 215-629-0600, Ext 2020 or 3175

Narode, Patricia, *Assocs,* New York State Library, Albany NY. 518-474-5930

Narosny, Judith, *Tech Serv & On-Line Servs,* Emmanuel College, Cardinal Cushing Library, Boston MA. 617-277-9340, Ext 126

Narramore, Bill, *In Charge,* Radio Advertising Bureau (Tape Library of Radio Commercials), New York NY. 212-599-6666

Narris, Jacquelyn, *Librn,* Indianapolis-Marion County Public Library (Shelby), Indianapolis IN. 317-635-5662

Nartker, Raymond H, *Dir,* University of Dayton Libraries, Roesch Library, Dayton OH. 513-229-4221

Narveson, Dolores, *Librn,* McIntosh Public Library, McIntosh MN. 218-563-4555

Nash, Jean L, *Librn,* West Warwick Public Library System, Robert H Champlin Memorial Library, West Warwick RI. 401-828-3750

Nash, June, *Libr Servs Coordr & Tech Serv,* Berkeley Public Library, Berkeley CA. 415-644-6095

Nash, Lorene, *Ref,* Utah State University, Merrill Library & Learning Resources Program, Logan UT. 801-750-2637

Nash, Lorene, *On-Line Servs,* Utah State University, Merrill Library & Learning Resources Program, Logan UT. 801-750-2637

Nash, Martha C, *Librn,* Gulf Oil Corporation (Gulf Companies Law Library), Houston TX. 713-750-3171

Nash, Mary, *Tech Serv,* Bell-Northern Research, Technical Information Center, Ottawa ON. 613-596-2469

Nash, N Frederick, *Rare Bks,* University of Illinois Library at Urbana-Champaign, Urbana IL. 217-333-0790

Nash, N Frederick, *Librn,* University of Illinois Library at Urbana-Champaign (Rare Book Room), Urbana IL. 217-333-3777

Nash, Richard M, *Assoc Librn,* Arizona State University Library (Law Library), Tempe AZ. 602-965-6141

Nashelsky, David, *Librn,* San Jose Public Library (Willow Glen), San Jose CA. 408-998-2022

Nashu, A M, *In Charge,* Upjohn Co, D S Gilmore Research Library, North Haven CT. 203-281-2782

Nason, Fayre L, *Librn,* Worcester County Horticultural Society Library, Worcester MA. 617-752-4274

Nasrallah, Wahib, *Bus Admin,* University of Cincinnati Libraries, Central Library, Cincinnati OH. 513-475-2218

Nasri, William, *Assoc Prof,* University of Pittsburgh, School of Library & Information Science, PA. 412-624-5230

Nass, Gay, *Dir,* Bloomingdale Public Library, Bloomingdale IL. 312-529-3120

Nasser, J, *On-Line Servs,* Amoco Canada Petroleum Co Ltd Library, Calgary AB. 403-233-1451, 233-1867 & 233-1963

Nast, Dorothy L, *Librn,* Chicago Public Library (Roden), Chicago IL. 312-631-4653

Natale, S Fred, *Dir,* Mary H Weir Public Library, Weirton WV. 304-748-7070

Natanson, Leo, *Ref,* Western Michigan University, Dwight B Waldo Library, Kalamazoo MI. 616-383-4961

Natesh, Raji, *Librn,* Materials Research Inc Library, Salt Lake City UT. 801-531-9600

Nath, Herbert T, *Ref,* The Citadel, Daniel Library, Charleston SC. 803-792-5116

Nathan, Cathy, *ILL,* Huntsville-Madison County Public Library, Huntsville AL. 205-536-0021

Nathan, David, *Per,* Congregation B'nai David, Isadore Gruskin Library, Southfield MI. 313-557-8211

Nathan, Joan, *Librn,* Mancos Public Library, Mancos CO. 303-533-7569

Nathanson, David, *Librn,* National Park Service, Harpers Ferry Center Library, Harpers Ferry WV. 304-535-6371, Ext 264

Nathanson, Paul, *Librn,* Vancouver School of Theology Library, Vancouver BC. 604-228-9031, Ext 53

Nation, Irene, *ILL,* Clackamas County Library, Oregon City OR. 503-655-8543

Nation, James R, *Librn,* United States Geological Survey Library, Flagstaff AZ. 602-779-3311, Ext 1386, 1387

Nation, Margaret, *Dir,* Flagstaff City-Coconino County Public Library System, Flagstaff AZ. 602-774-0603

Nations, Rebecca, *Ch,* Lincoln-Lawrence-Franklin Regional Library, Brookhaven MS. 601-833-3369

Natoli, Joseph, *ILL & Ref,* Wake Forest University, Z Smith Reynolds Library, Winston-Salem NC. 919-761-5480

Nauck, Thelma M, *Librn,* Choteau Public Library, Choteau MT. 406-466-2052

Naughton, Dorothy, *Dir,* Waukesha Public Library, Waukesha WI. 414-542-4297

Naughton, Patricia, *Librn,* Aquinas Junior College Library, Milton MA. 617-696-3100

Nault, Mildred, *Librn,* Goodrich Memorial Library, Newport VT. 802-334-7902

Nault, Suzanne M, *ILL, Media & Ref,* Merrimack College, McQuade Library, North Andover MA. 617-683-7111, Ext 210

Naumer, Janet, *Instr,* University of Denver, Graduate School of Librarianship and Information Management, CO. 303-753-2557

Nautiyal, Rakesh, *Syst Coordr,* New York University, Elmer Holmes Bobst Library, New York NY. 212-598-2484

Navari, Leslie N, *Asst Dir, ILL & Cat,* Pacific Grove Public Library, Pacific Grove CA. 408-373-0603

Navarra, Elaine, *Circ,* Rutgers University (Camden Arts & Science Library), Camden NJ. 609-757-6036

Navarrete, Erminia, *ILL,* Tulare County Library System, Visalia CA. 209-733-8440

Nave, Virginia, *Librn,* Mid-Continent Public Library (Platte City Branch), Platte City MO. 816-431-2322

Navratil, Amy R, *Librn,* Norton Simon Museum of Art at Pasadena Library, Pasadena CA. 213-449-6840

Navratil, Joyce, *Librn,* Rudd Public Library, Rudd IA. 515-395-2385

Navy, Jim, *Librn,* Our Lady of the Lake University Libraries (Media Learning Center), San Antonio TX. 512-434-6711, Ext 280

Nawrocki, Robert, *Rec Mgt,* New Jersey State Library, Trenton NJ. 609-292-6200

Nayda, Eileen A, *Dir,* Atikokan Public Library, Atikokan ON. 807-597-4406, 597-4230

Nayer, Alice, *Tech Serv,* Garden City Public Library, Garden City NY. 516-742-8405

Naylor, Alice P, *Chmn & Prof,* Appalachian State University, Department of Educational Media: Librarianship & Instructional Technology, NC. 704-262-2243

Naylor, Barbara, *Librn,* Fairview State Hospital, Staff Library, Costa Mesa CA. 714-957-5394

Naylor, David L, *Ref & On-Line Servs,* Louisiana State University (Law Center Library), Baton Rouge LA. 504-388-8802

Naylor, E R, *Librn,* Barium & Chemicals, Inc Library, Steubenville OH. 614-282-9776

Naylor, Melva L, *Ch,* Four County Library System, Binghamton NY. 607-723-8236

Naylor, Norma, *Librn,* Portsmouth Public Library (Wheelersburg Branch), #Wheelersburg OH. 614-574-6116

Naylor, Patricia A, *Librn,* Holden Arboretum, Warren H Corning Library, Mentor OH. 216-946-4400

Naylor, Richard J, *Librn,* Hopkins County-Madisonville Public Library, Madisonville KY. 502-825-2680

Nazario, Brunilda Perez de, *Per,* Inter-American University of Puerto Rico, Metropolitan Campus Library, Hato Rey PR. 809-754-7215, Ext 246, 245, 256

Naznitsky, Ira, *On-Line Servs,* GAF Corp, Technical Information Services Library, Wayne NJ. 201-628-3320

Nazworth, Patricia M, *Dir,* Satilla Regional Library, Douglas GA. 912-384-4667, 384-1172

Nazzaro, Lorraine T, *Librn,* Avco Everett Research Laboratory Inc Library, Everett MA. 617-389-3000, Ext 618

Neacy, Mary, *Circ,* University of Dayton Libraries, Roesch Library, Dayton OH. 513-229-4221

Neafus, S, *Librn,* ICI America Inc, Darco Experimental Laboratory Library, Marshall TX. 214-938-9211

Neal, Berna E, *Librn,* University of Maryland at College Park (Architecture), College Park MD. 301-454-4316

Neal, Christina W, *Librn,* University of Michigan Libraries (Social Work), Ann Arbor MI. 313-764-5169

Neal, Connie, *Tech Serv,* University of Texas Health Science Center at Houston, School of Public Health Library, Houston TX. 713-792-4350

Neal, Cynthia W, *Ch,* Providence Public Library, Providence RI. 401-521-7722

Neal, James, *Circ,* University of Notre Dame Library, Notre Dame IN. 219-283-7317

Neal, Kathryn B, *Ref & Doc,* Alabama Agricultural & Mechanical University, Joseph F Drake Memorial Learning Resources Center, Normal AL. 205-859-7309

Neal, Myrtle J, *Tech Serv,* Brunswick-Greensville Regional Library, Lawrenceville VA. 804-848-2418

Neal, Robert L, *Dir,* Allegany County Library, Cumberland MD. 301-777-1200

Neal, Rosie, *Acq,* Jackson State University, Henry Thomas Sampson Library, Jackson MS. 601-968-2123

Neal, Susan, *Tech Serv,* Orange Public Library, Orange TX. 713-883-7323

Neal, Sylvia, *Librn,* Amador County Library, Jackson CA. 209-223-0543

Neale, Judy, *Info Specialist,* Johns-Manville Corporation (Corporate Information Center), Denver CO. 979-1000 Ext 3440, 3448

Neale, Marilee, *Exten Servs Coordr,* Rosenberg Library, Galveston TX. 713-763-8854

Neale, Patsy, *Librn,* Teague City Library, Teague TX. 817-739-3311

Neame, Laura, *Pub Servs,* Fraser Valley College, Learning Resource Centres, Abbotsford BC. 604-853-7441

Near, Delia M, *Tech Serv,* Merced County Library, Merced CA. 209-726-7484

Neargardner, Linda, *Librn,* Spohn Hospital Library, Corpus Christi TX. 512-884-2041

Nearhoof, Marilyn H, *Librn,* Tyrone-Snyder Township Public Library, Tyrone PA. 814-684-1133

Nearing, Jane, *Bus & Sci,* Richardson Public Library, Richardson TX. 214-238-8251

Neary, Ann, *Coordr,* Southwestern Connecticut Library Council, CT. 203-367-6439

Neary, Sharon E, *Librn, On-Line Servs & Bibliog Instr,* Saskatchewan Research Council Library, Saskatoon SK. 306-343-8251, Ext 12

Neate, Janette M, *Librn,* Du Bois Public Library, Du Bois PA. 814-371-5930

Neavill, Gordon B, *Asst Prof,* University of Alabama, Graduate School of Library Service, AL. 205-348-4610

Neavill, Helen, *Cat,* College of Saint Teresa, Mary A Molloy Library, Winona MN. 507-454-2930, Ext 210

Neaville, Lillian, *Librn,* Mount Pulaski Township Library, Mount Pulaski IL. 217-792-5919

Neaville, Melva, *Asst Librn,* Mount Pulaski Township Library, Mount Pulaski IL. 217-792-5919

Neblett, Mariann, *Circ,* Western Texas College, Learning Resource Center, Snyder TX. 915-573-8511, Ext 265

Necci, John, *ILL,* Temple University of the Commonwealth System of Higher Education (Law), Philadelphia PA. 215-787-7891

Neds, Nolan, *Deputy Dir,* Milwaukee County Federated Library System, Milwaukee WI. 414-278-3210

Neds, Nolan, *Deputy City Librn & Br Coordr,* Milwaukee Public Library, Milwaukee WI. 414-278-3000

Nedwidek, Sylvia, *Librn,* Trenton Psychiatric Hospital (Annex Library), Trenton NJ. 609-396-8261, Ext 340

Nee, Nancy, *Lit, Philos & Rel,* San Francisco Public Library, San Francisco CA. 415-558-4235

Needham, David M, *Dir,* Massena Public Library, Warren Memorial Library, Massena NY. 315-769-9914

NEEDHAM

Needham, George, *Librn,* Charleston County Library (West Ashley), Charleston SC. 803-766-6635

Needham, Kate, *Librn,* Piedmont Regional Library (Loganville Branch), Loganville GA. 404-867-2762

Needham, Norrine, *Ch,* Weber County Library, Ogden UT. 801-399-8516

Needleman, Frances R L, *Cat,* Massachusetts Institute of Technology Libraries, Cambridge MA. 617-253-5651

Needleman, Harry, *ILL & Acq,* Adrian College, Shipman Library, Adrian MI. 517-265-5161, Ext 220

Needleman, Harry, *Librn,* Yale University Library (Cowles Foundation for Research in Economics), New Haven CT. 203-436-0249

Needler, Dorothy, *Librn,* Converse Jackson Township Public, Converse IN. 317-395-3344

Neel, Virginia D, *Librn,* Western Kentucky University (Science Library), Bowling Green KY. 502-745-3958

Neeley, Sally, *Hist,* University of Cincinnati Libraries, Central Library, Cincinnati OH. 513-475-2218

Neely, Eugene, *Pub Servs,* University of Missouri-Kansas City Libraries, Kansas City MO. 816-276-1531

Neely, Gardner, *Librn,* Public Library of Cincinnati & Hamilton County (Bond Hill), Cincinnati OH. 513-242-0990

Neely, Glenda S, *On-Line Servs,* University of Louisville Library, Louisville KY. 502-588-6745

Neely, Jesse G, *Librn,* Scripps Clinic & Research Foundation, Medical Library, La Jolla CA. 714-455-8705

Neely, Karen, *Bkmobile Coordr,* Daniel Boone Regional Library, Columbia MO. 314-443-3161

Neely, L Ann, *Ref,* Parkland College, Learning Resource Center, Champaign IL. 217-351-2241

Neely, Jr, Mark E, *Dir,* Lincoln National Life Insurance Co (Louis A Warren Lincoln Library & Museum), Fort Wayne IN. 219-424-5421, Ext 7864

Neenan, Peter, *Asst Prof,* Simmons College, Graduate School of Library & Information Science, MA. 617-738-2225

Neeper, Darla S, *Librn,* Rufus Young King Library Public Library, Giddings TX. 713-542-2716

Neeri, Elizabeth P, *Tech Librn,* Xerox Electro-Optical Systems Library, Pasadena CA. 213-351-2351, Ext 2411

Neerman, Sandra, *Librn,* Greensboro Public Librar (Southwest), Greensboro NC. 919-299-1409

Nees, Edith, *Cat,* Warren County Library, Monmouth IL. 309-734-6412

Neese, Gilda, *Librn,* Tyler County Public Library, Middlebourne WV. 304-758-4304

Neese, Janet A, *Tech Serv,* State University of New York College at Geneseo, Milne Library, Geneseo NY. 716-245-5591

Neff, Alice F, *Librn,* Brookings Institution Library, Washington DC. 202-797-6240

Neff, Barbara, *ILL,* Rand Corp Library, Santa Monica CA. 213-393-0411, Ext 369

Neff, Elizabeth, *Librn,* Buckley Public Library, Poteau OK. 918-647-3833

Neff, Elsie, *ILL,* Durango Public Library, Durango CO. 303-247-2492

Neff, Eugene, *ILL & Doc,* Slippery Rock State College Library, Slippery Rock PA. 412-794-2510

Neff, Jerry W, *Dir,* Wagnalls Memorial Library, Lithopolis OH. 614-837-4765

Neff, Mary Jane, *On-Line Servs,* Emporia State University, William Allen White Library, Emporia KS. 316-343-1200, Ext 205

Neff, Mary Jane, *Soc Sci & Educ,* Emporia State University, William Allen White Library, Emporia KS. 316-343-1200, Ext 205

Neff, Nancy S, *Actg Librn,* Montpelier Public Library, Montpelier IN. 317-728-5969

Nefzger, Angelia, *Librn,* Delhi Public Library, Delhi IA. 319-922-2037

Negaard, Chere, *Librn, Acq & Cat,* Northrop University, Alumni Library, Inglewood CA. 213-776-5466

Negin, Arthur W, *Librn,* Richland County Law Library, Mansfield OH. 419-524-9944

Negoro, Karin, *Librn,* International Center for Marine Resource Development Library, Kingston RI. 401-792-2938

Negri, Beverly, *Dist Coordr,* Eastfield College, Learning Resources Center, Mesquite TX. 214-746-3168

Neher, Jack, *Suprv,* Mental Health Materials Center Library, New York NY. 212-889-5760

Neher, Mary, *Librn,* West Hurley Library, West Hurley NY. 914-679-6405

Nehlig, Mary E, *Asst Dir,* West Chester State College, Francis Harvey Green Library, West Chester PA. 215-436-2643

Nehls, Janet, *Circ,* Clackamas County Library, Oregon City OR. 503-655-8543

Neibarger, Joan, *Br Coordr,* Sutter County Free Library, Yuba City CA. 916-673-5773

Neiburg, Lolanda S, *Librn,* Pickens County Library (Clemson Community), Clemson SC. 803-654-4822

Neiger, James I, *ILL,* Hebrew Union College-Jewish Institute of Religion Library, Cincinnati OH. 513-221-1875

Neigh, Pat, *Circ,* Bloomfield College Library, Bloomfield NJ. 201-748-9000, Ext 281

Neighbors, Fred D, *Dir,* Sioux City Public Library, Sioux City IA. 712-279-6179

Neil, Barbara, *Asst Librn,* Mississippi State Law Library, Jackson MS. 601-354-7113

Neil, Mary T, *Dir,* Dwight D Eisenhower Public Library, Totowa NJ. 201-790-3265

Neil, Terri, *Asst Librn,* Ogunquit Memorial Library, Wells ME. 207-646-9024

Neil, Willa, *Asst Dir,* Northland Public Library, Pittsburgh PA. 412-366-8100, 366-8167

Neilands, C E, *Librn,* Northern College, Haileybury School of Mines Library, Haileybury ON. 705-672-3376, Ext 37

Neill, Charlotte, *Spec Projects,* Texas A&m University Libraries (Medical Sciences), College Station TX. 713-845-7427, 845-7428

Neill, D, *Librn,* University of Toronto Libraries (Massey College), Toronto ON. 416-978-2893

Neill, Gretchen H, *Dir,* Dekalb Community College, North Campus, Learning Resources Center, Dunwoody GA. 404-393-3300, Ext 233

Neill, Mildred, *Librn,* Llano County Public Library (Greenwood Exchange Station), Buchanon Dam TX. 915-247-5248

Neill, Priscilla, *ILL,* University of Wisconsin-Madison, Memorial Library, Madison WI. 608-262-3521

Neill, Van Dyke, *Spec Coll,* Greenwood-Leflore Public Library System, Greenwood MS. 601-453-3634

Neilon, Madeline, *Librn,* Middlesex Law Library Association, Lowell MA. 617-452-9301

Neilson, Ann, *Librn,* Gulf Canada Ltd, Research & Development Department Library, Mississauga ON. 416-822-6770

Neilson, Hope B, *Librn,* Rice Public Library, Kittery ME. 207-439-1553

Neiman, Libby, *Tech Serv,* Yeshiva University Libraries (Hedi Steinberg Library), New York NY. 212-481-0570

Neiman, Ruth, *ILL,* Messiah College, Murray Learning Resources Center, Grantham PA. 717-766-2511, Ext 380

Neiman, Sue, *Librn,* Middletown Public Library, Middletown PA. 717-944-6412

Neipert, Marjorie F, *Librn,* Wilton Public Library, Wilton IA. 319-732-2583

Neitz, Cordelia M, *Librn,* Cumberland County Historical Society, Hamilton Library, Carlisle PA. 717-249-7610

Nekomoto, Esther H, *Librn,* United States Army (Medical Library), Honolulu HI. 808-433-6391

Nekritz, Leah K, *Asst Dean,* Prince George's Community College, Learning Resources Center, Largo MD. 301-322-0462

Nelius, Albert, *Circ,* Duke University, William R Perkins Library, Durham NC. 684-2034

Nellis, Leroy W, *Staff & Fiscal Servs,* University of Texas Libraries (General), Austin TX. 512-471-3811

Nellor, Marguerite S, *Librn,* Karlin Memorial Library, Beemer NE. 402-528-3476

Nelms, Dorthy, *Asst Dir,* Tom Green County Library System, San Angelo TX. 915-655-7321

Nelms, Willie E, *Dir,* Bristol Public Library, Bristol VA. 703-669-9444

Nelson, A E, *Dir,* California State College, San Bernardino Library, San Bernardino CA. 714-887-7321

Nelson, Ann, *Librn,* University of British Columbia Library (Animal Resource Ecology), Vancouver BC. 604-228-3324

Nelson, April M, *Tech Serv & Cat,* Rosemont College, Gertrude Kistler Memorial Library, Rosemont PA. 215-527-0200, Ext 226

Nelson, Barbara, *Dir,* Reading Public Library, Reading MA. 617-944-0840

Nelson, Berneil C, *ILL,* University of Minnesota Technical College, Kiehle Library, Crookston MN. 218-281-6510, Ext 252

Nelson, Betty, *Circ,* Hoechst-Roussel Pharmaceuticals, Inc Library, Div of American Hoechst Corp Library, Somerville NJ. 201-685-2394

Nelson, Betty, *Librn,* Modoc County Library (Davis Creek), Davis Creek CA. 916-233-2719

Nelson, Beverly, *Librn,* Hennepin County Library (Rockford Road), Crystal MN. 612-533-5010

Nelson, Brent D, *Librn,* University of Arkansas at Fayetteville, Technology Campus Library, Little Rock AR. 501-370-5178

Nelson, Carol, *Tech Serv & Cat,* New Hampshire College, Shapiro Library, Manchester NH. 603-668-2211, Ext 211

Nelson, Carol, *Circ,* Seward Public Library, Seward NE. 402-643-3318

Nelson, Carolee, *Librn,* Anchorage Municipal Libraries (Girdwood Branch), Girdwood AK. 907-783-2565

Nelson, Carolyn M, *Librn,* Bureau of Land Management Library, Billings MT. 406-657-6671

Nelson, Cecilia, *Librn,* Iowa Department of Environmental Quality Library, Des Moines IA. 515-281-8899

Nelson, Charles, *In Charge,* Arizona Department of Health Services Library, Phoenix AZ. 602-255-1013

Nelson, Charlotte, *Assoc Librn,* Basalt Regional Library, Basalt CO. 303-927-4311

Nelson, Cheryl, *AV & Cat,* Nichols College, Conant Library, Dudley MA. 617-943-1560

Nelson, Christine P, *Dir,* Clewiston Public Library, Clewiston FL. 813-983-9245

Nelson, Clark, *ILL & Ref,* Mayo Foundation (Medical Library), Rochester MN. 507-284-2061

Nelson, Cleo, *Librn,* Quimby Public Library, Quimby IA. 712-445-2882

Nelson, David, *Cat,* Eastern Washington University, John F Kennedy Memorial Library, Cheney WA. 509-359-2261

Nelson, Dee, *Librn,* White Pine Library, Stanton MI. 517-831-4327

Nelson, Donald, *Coordr,* Louisiana Tech University, Teacher Education-Library Science, LA. 318-257-3242

Nelson, Donald E, *Dir,* University of Delaware (Instructional Resources Center, Film Library), Newark DE. 302-738-2685

Nelson, Donna D, *Librn,* Bridgeport Public Library, Bridgeport NE. 308-262-0326

Nelson, Edna, *Circ,* Newport Public Library, Newport RI. 401-847-8720

Nelson, Edna M, *Circ Suprv,* Newport, Middletown, Portsmouth Interlibrary Microform & Periodical Loan Cooperative, RI. 401-847-8720

Nelson, Eleanore J, *Librn,* Dallas County Public Library (Balch Springs Branch), Balch Springs TX. 214-286-8856

Nelson, Elva L, *Tech Serv,* Winchester Public Library, Winchester MA. 617-729-3770

Nelson, Esther, *Bibliog Instr,* Western Illinois University Libraries, Macomb IL. 309-298-2411

Nelson, Evelyn, *Publicity,* Chicago Public Library, Chicago IL. 312-269-2900

Nelson, Eythol, *Librn,* Omaha Public Library (South), Omaha NE. 402-444-4850

Nelson, Florine E, *Librn,* Chili Public Library, Bowen IL. 217-842-5573

Nelson, Frances, *Asst Librn,* Arthur Young & Co Library, New York NY. 212-922-4880

Nelson, Frank L, *Librn,* White City Public Library, White City KS. 913-349-2228

Nelson, Gail, *Ch,* Papillion Public Library, Papillion NE. 402-339-3177

Nelson, Gaye, *Librn,* Otonabee Township Public Library, Keene ON. 705-295-6814

Nelson, Glee, *Ch,* Columbus Public Library, Pawnee Regional Library, Columbus NE. 402-564-7116

Nelson, Gretchen, *Cat,* South Dakota State University, Hilton M Briggs Library, Brookings SD. 605-688-5106
Nelson, Helen, *Librn,* Kern County Library (Boron), Bakersfield CA. 805-861-2130
Nelson, Helen M, *Dir & Acq,* Oceanside Public Library, Oceanside CA. 714-439-7330
Nelson, Herbert, *Librn,* Central Islip State Psychiatric Center (Patient's Library), Central Islip NY. 516-234-6262, Ext 2248
Nelson, I, *Coll Develop,* University of Saskatchewan Library, Saskatoon SK. 306-343-4216
Nelson, Ilene, *ILL, Rare Bks & Spec Coll,* Spartanburg County Public Library, Spartanburg SC. 582-4123 & 585-2441
Nelson, J M, *Assoc Prof,* Saint Cloud State University, Center for Library & Audiovisual Education, MN. 612-255-2022
Nelson, James B, *Dir,* Cabell County Public Library, Western Counties Regional Library System, Huntington WV. 304-523-9451
Nelson, Jane Gray, *Chief Librn,* Fine Arts Museums of San Francisco Library, M H de Young Memorial Museum, San Francisco CA. 415-558-2887
Nelson, Janis, *ILL & Mailorder Delivery,* Pottsville Free Public Library, Pottsville Library District Center, Pottsville PA. 622-8105; 622-8880
Nelson, Jean, *In Charge,* Foothills Art Center Library, Mary S Robinson Art Library, Golden CO. 303-279-3922
Nelson, Jean, *Dir,* Fullerton City Library, Fullerton CA. 714-738-6333, Ext 301
Nelson, Jerold, *Asst Prof,* University of Washington, School of Librarianship, WA. 206-543-1794
Nelson, Jewell M, *Librn,* Oklahoma Publishing Co Library, Oklahoma City OK. 405-231-3387
Nelson, Joann V, *Librn,* First Christian Church of Alexandria Library, Alexandria VA. 703-549-3911
Nelson, John D, *Librn,* University of Nebraska-Lincoln (College of Law Library), Lincoln NE. 402-472-3547
Nelson, Joy, *Acq,* Doane College, Perkins Library, Crete NE. 402-826-2161, Ext 224, 287
Nelson, Karen, *Librn,* San Bernardino County Library (Big Bear Lake Branch), Big Bear Lake CA. 714-886-4190
Nelson, Linda, *Librn,* Museum of Fine Arts Library, Houston TX. 713-526-1361, Ext 25
Nelson, Linda, *Librn,* Rainier City Library, Rainier OR. 503-556-7301
Nelson, Lliane, *Librn,* Agra Public Library, Agra KS. 913-638-2811
Nelson, Loretta, *Librn,* Madison Public Library, Madison NE. 402-454-3500
Nelson, Louise H, *Dir,* Wyckoff Public Library, Wyckoff NJ. 201-891-4866
Nelson, Lydia, *Librn,* Brooklyn Public Library, Brooklyn IA. 515-522-9272
Nelson, Margaret B, *Librn,* Washington Theological Coalition Library, Silver Spring MD. 301-439-0551
Nelson, Margaret B, *Librn,* Wesley United Methodist Church Library, La Crosse WI. 608-782-3018
Nelson, Margaret F, *Dir,* Black Earth Public Library, Black Earth WI. 608-767-2400
Nelson, Marilyn M, *Librn,* Mississippi Laboratories, Pascagoula Facility, Pascagoula MS. 601-762-4591
Nelson, Marjory, *Acq,* Evanston Public Library, Evanston IL. 312-866-0300
Nelson, Mary, *AV,* South Seattle Community College, Instructional Resources Center, Seattle WA. 206-764-5395
Nelson, Mary Jane, *Librn,* Keating of Chicago, Inc, Specialties Appliance Corp Library, Bellwood IL. 312-544-6500
Nelson, Mary Lois, *Ad,* Free Public Library, Council Bluffs IA. 712-323-7553
Nelson, Melanie, *Cat,* University of Arkansas at Little Rock Library (University of Arkansas at Little Rock School of Law & Pulaski County Law Library), Little Rock AR. 501-371-1071
Nelson, Myrtle, *Ch,* Blaine County Library, Chinook MT. 406-357-2932
Nelson, Nancy, *Ref,* Baraboo Public Library, Baraboo WI. 608-356-6166

Nelson, Norman, *Ref,* Albert Einstein College of Medicine, D Samuel Gottesman Library, Bronx NY. 212-430-3108
Nelson, Norman L, *Asst Librn for Admin Servs & On-Line Search Coordr,* Oklahoma State University Library, Stillwater OK. 405-624-6313
Nelson, Pamela, *Ch,* Newark Free Library, Newark DE. 302-731-7550
Nelson, Patricia J, *Librn,* Canadian Air Trans Administration, Trans Canada Regional Library, Edmonton AB. 403-420-3801
Nelson, Paul, *Exten Serv,* Oshkosh Public Library, Oshkosh WI. 414-424-0473
Nelson, Paulette, *Ch,* Minot Public Library, Minot ND. 701-852-1045
Nelson, Priscilla B, *Ch,* North Adams Public Library, North Adams MA. 413-662-2545, 663-3317
Nelson, Rachel W, *Dir,* Cleveland Heights-University Heights Public Library, Cleveland Heights OH. 216-932-7600
Nelson, Randall, *Mobile Servs & Outreach,* Whatcom County Public Library, Bellingham WA. 206-384-3150
Nelson, Richard W, *Dir,* Chippewa Falls Public Library, Chippewa County Library Service, Chippewa Falls WI. 715-723-1147
Nelson, Rosemary, *Circ,* Montreat-Anderson College, L Nelson Bell Library, Montreat NC. 704-669-2382
Nelson, Rosemary, *Central Libr Admin,* Phoenix Public Library, Phoenix AZ. 602-262-6451
Nelson, Rossa, *Librn,* Prescott Public-Yavapai County Library System (Congress Public), Congress AZ. 602-445-8110
Nelson, Ruth L, *Ref,* John Marshall Law School Library, Chicago IL. 312-427-2737, Ext 254
Nelson, Sara L, *Asst Librn,* Texas State Library, Division for the Blind & Physically Handicapped, Austin TX. 512-475-4758
Nelson, Serena S, *Dir,* Southwest Wisconsin Library System, Fennimore WI. 608-822-3393
Nelson, Shirley Jean, *Dir,* Rio Public Library, Rio WI. 414-992-3206
Nelson, Sonja, *Ch,* Chippewa Falls Public Library, Chippewa County Library Service, Chippewa Falls WI. 715-723-1147
Nelson, Stephen, *Ref,* Woodstock Public Library & Art Gallery, Woodstock ON. 519-537-4801
Nelson, Sue, *Librn,* Sussex County Library System (Dennis Memorial-Central District), Newton NJ. 201-383-4810
Nelson, Vance, *Curator,* Nebraska State Historical Society, Fort Robinson Museum Research Library, Crawford NE. 308-665-2852
Nelson, Vernon H, *Archivist,* Moravian Church in America - Northern Province, Moravian Archives, Bethlehem PA. 215-866-3255
Nelson, Wesley, *On-Line Servs,* Ferrum College, Thomas Stanley Library, Ferrum VA. 703-365-2121, Ext 161
Nelson, Wilburta, *Dir & Acq,* Johnsonburg Public Library, Johnsonburg PA. 814-965-4110
Nelson, William N, *Dir,* Mobile College, J L Bedsole Library, Mobile AL. 205-675-5990
Nelson, William N, *Latin Am Studies,* Mobile College, J L Bedsole Library, Mobile AL. 205-675-5990
Nelton, William, *Librn,* Michigan Department of Public Health Library, Lansing MI. 517-373-1343
Nemec, Dolores, *Dir,* University of Wisconsin-Madison (F B Power Pharmaceutical Library), Madison WI. 608-262-2894
Nemeth, Marjorie, *Librn,* Oberlin City Library, Oberlin KS. 913-475-2412
Nemeyer, Carol A, *Nat Progs: Assoc Librn Nat Progs,* Library of Congress, Washington DC. 202-287-5000
Nemiccolo, Harriet J, *Librn,* Boston College Libraries (School of Social Work Library), Chestnut Hill MA. 617-969-0100, Ext 3233
Neptune, Evelyn, *Ch,* Pettigrew Regional Library, Plymouth NC. 919-793-2113
Nepveux, Brabara, *Acq,* San Jacinto College, Lee Davis Library, Pasadena TX. 713-476-1850, 476-1501, Ext 241
Nepveux, Jean B, *Ad,* Lafayette Parish Public Library, Lafayette LA. 318-233-0587
Neri, Rita, *Cat,* Fordham University, School of Law Library, New York NY. 212-841-5223

Neroda, Edward, *Assoc Librn,* New Mexico Highlands University, Donnelly Library, Las Vegas NM. 505-425-7511, Ext 331
Nersinger, Carol, *Ad,* Henrietta Public Library, Rochester NY. 716-334-3401
Nesbit, Jennifer, *Educ,* Chicago Public Library (Social Sciences & History Div), Chicago IL. 312-269-2830
Nesbit, Mrs Thomas, *Librn,* University of Rochester (Memorial Art Gallery), Rochester NY. 716-275-4765
Nesbitt, Ina L, *Librn,* United States Army (Medical Library), Fort Polk LA. 318-537-2073
Nesbitt, Jerry L, *Actg Librn,* Ligonier Public Library, Ligonier IN. 219-894-4511
Nesmith, E Deforest, *Assoc Librn & AV,* Union College Library, Lincoln NE. 402-488-2331, Ext 316
Nesmith, Lorraine, *Syst Consult,* North Central Kansas Libraries System, Manhattan KS. 913-776-4741
Ness, Charles H, *Asst Dean of Librs,* Mid-Atlantic Research Libraries Information Network, (MARLIN), PA. 814-865-7246
Ness, Charles H, *Asst Dean, Ref & Instrnl Servs,* Pennsylvania State University, Fred Lewis Pattee Library, University Park PA. 814-865-0401
Ness, M Judith, *Asst Dir,* Southern Lehigh Public Library, Solehi Public Library, Coopersburg PA. 215-965-2364
Ness, Mary, *Ch,* Akron-Summit County Public Library, Akron OH. 216-762-7621
Ness, Verna, *Librn,* Mountaineers Inc, Mountaineer Library, Seattle WA. 206-623-2314
Nesse, Mark A, *Dir,* Everett Public Library, Everett WA. 206-259-8858
Nesseth, Mrs M M, *Librn,* Mattawa Public Library, John Dixon Public Library, Mattawa ON. 705-744-5550
Nessi, Sister Mary, *Music,* Holy Names College, Paul J Cushing Library, Oakland CA. 415-436-1332
Nestell, Clifford L, *Dir,* Shawnee Mission Medical Center Library, Shawnee Mission KS. 913-676-2102
Nesti, Marguerite, *Asst Librn,* Spring Valley Public Library, Spring Valley IL. 815-663-4741
Nestle, Agnes, *Librn,* Seville Township Public Library, Riverdale MI. 517-833-7776
Nestleroad, Sue, *Librn,* Martinsville Township Library, Martinsville IL. 217-382-4113
Nesvig, Lorraine, *Librn,* Armour & Co & Greyhound Corp, Armour Research Center Library, Scottsdale AZ. 602-991-3000, Ext 420, 422
Neswick, Robert, *In Charge,* Spokesman-Review, Spokane Daily Chronicle, Newspaper Reference Library, Spokane WA. 509-455-6891
Neth, Dorothy, *Ch,* Flint Memorial Library, North Reading MA. 617-664-4942
Neth, John W, *Dir,* Milligan College, P H Welshimer Memorial Library, Milligan College TN. 615-929-0116
Nethercutt, George, *Mat Coordr,* Fort Worth Public Library, Fort Worth TX. 817-870-7700
Nethers, Betty, *Librn,* Owens-Corning Fiberglas Corp, Technical Center Research Library, Granville OH. 614-587-0610
Nett, Diana, *Head Librn,* Cedar Grove Public Library, Cedar Grove WI. 414-668-6834
Nettleman, James, *Doc,* Rutgers University (Camden Arts & Science Library), Camden NJ. 609-757-6036
Nettles, Jess, *Dir,* Oktibbeha County Library System, Starkville MS. 601-323-2766
Netz, David, *Librn,* Western Michigan University (Education Resources Center), Kalamazoo MI. 616-383-1666
Neu, Genevieve, *Ref,* Southern Tier Library System, Corning NY. 607-962-3141
Neu, Helen, *Cat,* Cooke County Library, Gainesville TX. 817-665-2401
Neu, Joel B, *Dir,* United States Department of Commerce, Field Services Library, Greensboro NC. 919-378-5345
Neu, John A, *Hist of Sci,* University of Wisconsin-Madison, Memorial Library, Madison WI. 608-262-3521
Neu, Margaret, *Tech Serv,* Corpus Christi Public Libraries, La Retama Public Library, Corpus Christi TX. 512-882-1937

Neubauer, Adah, *Librn,* Waubonsee Community College, Learning Resources Center, Sugar Grove IL. 312-466-4811, Ext 303
Neubauer, Carol, *Circ,* Bridgewater State College, Clement C Maxwell Library, Bridgewater MA. 617-697-8321, Ext 441, 442
Neubauer, Janice, *Dir,* Duxbury Free Library, Duxbury MA. 617-934-2721, 934-6162
Neubauer, Richard A, *Chairperson,* Bridgewater State College, Library Science Dept, MA. 617-697-8321, Ext 456
Neubauer, Susan, *Cat,* Acton Memorial Library, Acton MA. 617-263-2232, 263-9109
Neucks, Bettye, *Spec Coll,* Evansville Public Library & Vanderburgh County Public Library, Evansville IN. 812-425-2621
Neucomb, Verna, *Librn,* Control Data Corp, Research & Advanced Design Laboratory Library, Arden Hills MN. 612-482-2100
Neuendorf, Klaus, *Librn,* Oregon State Department of Geology & Mineral Industries Library, Portland OR. 312-229-5580
Neuendorffer, Ruth, *Librn,* Historical Society of the Tarrytowns' Reference Library, Tarrytown NY. 914-631-8374
Neufeld, Irving H, *Chief Librn, UTC Libr Serv,* United Technologies Corp Library, East Hartford CT. 203-727-7120
Neufeld, Rachel, *Librn,* Buhler Public Library, Buhler KS. 316-543-2241
Neufeld, Robert, *Spec Coll,* Haverstraw Kings Daughters Public Library, Haverstraw NY. 914-429-3445
Neuhaus, Mrs Robert, *Librn,* Leigh Public Library, Leigh NE. 402-487-2507
Neuhofer, Sister Dorothy, *Dir,* Saint Leo College Library, Saint Leo FL. 904-588-8258
Neujahr, Ludwiga, *ILL,* West Nyack Free Library, West Nyack NY. 914-358-6081
Neuman, Deborah, *Librn,* Arthur Young & Co Library (National EDP Library), New York NY. 212-922-2615
Neuman, Richard J, *Dir,* Salina Public Library, Salina KS. 913-825-4624
Neuman, Susan, *Librn,* University of Pittsburgh (Collection in Regional Economics), Pittsburgh PA. 412-624-4492
Neumann, Alice W, *Librn,* Jewish Hospital (School of Nursing Library), Cincinnati OH. 513-872-3555
Neumann, Lynn, *Adminr,* Library Association of La Jolla, Athenaeum Music & Arts Library, La Jolla CA. 714-454-5872
Neumann, Robert, *Asst Dir Admin & Fiscal Control,* University of Pittsburgh, Hillman Library, Pittsburgh PA. 412-624-4400
Neurohr, Josephine, *Tech Serv,* Martin County Public Library, Stuart FL. 305-287-2257
Neuschafer, Harold, *Area Ref Coordr,* Sussex County Library System, Sussex County Area Reference Library, Newton NJ. 201-948-3660
Nevai, Maria, *Tech Serv,* Thomas M Cooley Law School Library, Lansing MI. 517-371-5140
Neve, Alice, *Ch,* Redwood Falls Public Library, Redwood Falls MN. 507-637-8650
Neves, Donna, *Asst Librn & On-Line Servs,* Kaiser Permanente Medical Center, Health Science Library, Panorama City CA. 213-908-2239
Neves, Phyliss, *Librn,* Odem Public Library, Odem TX. 512-368-2831
Nevett, Micki, *Ch & YA,* Bethlehem Public Library, Delmar NY. 518-439-9314
Neveu, Ruth, *Per,* Lake Superior State College Library, Sault Sainte Marie MI. 906-632-6841, Ext 402
Neveu, Wilma B, *Chief, Libr Serv,* Veterans Administration, Medical Center Library, New Orleans LA. 504-589-5272
Nevil, Leota, *Circ,* Wilkes College, Eugene Shedden Farley Library, Wilkes-Barre PA. 717-824-4651, Ext 331 & 332
Nevill, Ann, *Librn,* Dalhousie University (W K Kellogg Health Sciences Library), Halifax NS. 902-424-2458
Neville, Robert, *ILL & Tech Serv,* University of Connecticut at Stamford Library, Stamford Branch Library, Stamford CT. 203-322-3466
Neville, Sandra, *Asst Dir Interpretive Servs,* University of Georgia Libraries, Athens GA. 404-542-2716
Nevin, Betty, *Asst Dean,* Foothill College, Library-Media Technical Assistant Program, CA. 415-948-8590, Ext 390

Nevin, Betty, *Chief Librn,* Foothill College, Hubert H Semans Library, Los Altos Hills CA. 415-948-8590, Ext 390, 391
Nevin, Susan, *Tech Serv,* Lancaster County Library, Lancaster PA. 717-394-2651
Nevins, Catherine F, *ILL,* Hobart & William Smith Colleges, Warren Hunting Smith Library, Geneva NY. 315-789-5500, Ext 224
Nevins, John P, *Dir,* Marlboro College, Howard & Amy Rice Library, Marlboro VT. 802-257-4333, Ext 51
Nevins, Patrick, *In Charge,* Markham Public Library, Markham IL. 312-331-0130
Nevins, Patrick, *Dir,* Richton Park Public Library District, Richton Park IL. 312-481-5333
New, Bonnie Jean, *Librn,* Mary Sommerville Free Library, Mound City KS. 913-795-2788
New, Doris, *Ser,* University of California Library, Irvine CA. 714-833-5212
New, Lillian, *Head, Thomas Hughes Children's Libr,* Chicago Public Library (Cultural Center), Chicago IL. 312-269-2820
New, Ruth, *Librn,* Gillette Children's Hospital Library, Saint Paul MN. 612-291-2848
New, Susan, *Librn,* Greenville Technical College, Learning Resources Center, Greenville SC. 803-242-3170, Ext 321
Newberry, Barbara, *Dir,* Nederland Public Library, Nederland TX. 713-722-1255
Newberry, Daniel, *Spec Coll,* Portland State University, Branford Price Millar Library, Portland OR. 503-229-4424
Newberry, Lillie, *Librn,* First Baptist Church Library, Miami OK. 918-542-5109
Newberry, Shirley J, *Dir,* Houghton Lake Public Library, Houghton Lake MI. 517-366-9230
Newberry, Vera, *Librn,* Southwest Georgia Regional Library (Miller County), Colquitt GA. 912-246-3887, 3894, 3895
Newborg, Gwen, *Doc,* Portland State University, Branford Price Millar Library, Portland OR. 503-229-4424
Newborn, Dennis E, *Asst Dir for Systs, Res & Analysis,* Howard University Libraries, Founders Library, Washington DC. 202-636-7253
Newburg, Ellen, *On-Line Servs,* Parmly Billings Library, South Central Federation of Libraries, Billings MT. 406-248-7393
Newburg, James, *Ref,* Northern Illinois University, Founders Memorial Library, De Kalb IL. 815-753-1094
Newbury, Roger, *Instr,* Northwestern Connecticut Community College, Library Technology Program, CT. 203-379-8543
Newby, Bob, *Doc,* South Dakota State Library, Pierre SD. 605-773-3131
Newcom, Kirk, *Librn,* Marysville Public Library, Marysville KS. 913-562-2491
Newcomb, Donna, *Ad,* Northeast Regional Library, Corinth MS. 601-287-2441
Newcomb, Donna, *Librn,* Northeast Regional Library (Corinth Library), Corinth MS. 601-287-9678
Newcomb, Dorothy, *Head Pub Servs,* Salisbury State College, Blackwell Library, Salisbury MD. 301-546-3261, Ext 351
Newcomb, Jean A, *Librn,* Atlantic Research Corporation Library, Alexandria VA. 703-642-4178
Newcomb, Mary, *Librn,* Van Buren County Library (Bloomingdale Branch), Bloomingdale MI. 616-521-7601
Newcomb, Nadine J, *Dir,* Glassboro Public Library, Glassboro NJ. 609-881-0001
Newcomb, Ruth, *Tech Serv & Acq,* Macalester College, Weyerhaeuser Library, Saint Paul MN. 612-647-6346
Newcomb, Verna, *Ref,* Control Data Corp, Corporate Library Information Center, Bloomington MN. 612-853-4229, 4375 & 5147
Newcombe, Barbara T, *In Charge,* Chicago Tribune Information Center, Chicago IL. 312-222-4265
Newcombe, Jack, *Head,* Free Library of Philadelphia (West Philadelphia Regional Library), Philadelphia PA. 215-823-8486
Newcomer, Jean, *Librn,* Ida Public Library, Belvidere IL. 815-544-3838
Newcomer, Patricia, *Tech Serv & Cat,* Iowa Wesleyan College, Chadwick Library, Mount Pleasant IA. 319-385-8021, Ext 131
Newell, Alice, *Dir,* Mcdowell County Public Library, Marion NC. 704-652-3858

Newell, Anita, *Mgr,* Westinghouse Electric Corp (Research Library), Pittsburgh PA. 412-256-3463, 256-3464
Newell, Bruce, *Librn,* Baker County Public Library (Haines Branch), Haines OR. 503-523-6414, 523-6419
Newell, Darlene J, *Librn,* Deer Creek District Library, Deer Creek IL. 309-447-6724
Newell, Elizabeth L, *Librn,* Bushnell Public Library, Bushnell IL. 309-772-2060
Newell, Frank E, *Hist, Humanities & Soc Sci,* Wilberforce University, Rembert Stokes Learning Resources Center, Wilberforce OH. 513-376-2911, Exts 226, 227, 228
Newell, Matthias, *Dir,* Wilberforce University, Rembert Stokes Learning Resources Center, Wilberforce OH. 513-376-2911, Exts 226, 227, 228
Newell, Ruth, *Librn,* Randolph Public Library (Ramseur Branch), Ramseur NC. 919-824-2232
Newell, Sue V, *Librn,* Maricopa Medical Society Library, Phoenix AZ. 602-252-8054
Newhall, Suzanne, *Librn,* Haverford College (Stokes (Natural Sciences)), Haverford PA. 215-649-9600, Ext 269
Newhard, Eleanor, *Librn,* Long Beach Public Library System (Bay Shore), Long Beach CA. 213-438-3501
Newhard, Robert H, *Tech Serv,* Torrance Public Library, Torrance CA. 213-328-2251
Newhouse, Anne, *Librn,* Amargosa Valley Community Library, Lathrop Wells NV. 702-372-5340
Newhouse, Frances F, *Librn,* Sebastian County Law Library, Fort Smith AR. 501-783-4730
Newhouse, Gary, *AV,* Skokie Public Library, Skokie IL. 312-673-7774
Newhouse, Jane, *Librn,* Curry Public Library, Gold Beach OR. 503-247-7246
Newhouse, Jeanne, *Per & Doc,* San Diego Mesa College Library, San Diego CA. 714-279-2300, Ext 385
Newhouse, Jill E, *Librn,* Kent County Library System (Library for the Blind & Physically Handicapped), Grand Rapids MI. 616-774-3262
Newhouse, Wade, *Dir,* State University of New York at Buffalo (Charles B Sears Law Library), Buffalo NY. 716-636-2043
Newkumet, Vynola, *Libr Technician,* University of Oklahoma (Music), Norman OK. 405-325-4243
Newland, Elizabeth W, *Cat,* University of North Carolina at Greensboro, Walter Clinton Jackson Library, Greensboro NC. 919-379-5880
Newland, Mary, *Librn,* Carter County Library, Grayson KY. 606-474-5403
Newlands, Sue, *Librn,* Sandy Public Library, Sandy OR. 503-668-5537
Newlands, Theodora B, *Dir,* Hartford College for Women, Bess Graham Library, Hartford CT. 203-236-1215, Ext 8
Newlands-Testa, Sheila, *Librn,* Mount Auburn Hospital, Health Sciences Library, Cambridge MA. 617-492-3500, Ext 1183 & 1187
Newlin, Jeanne T, *Curator of Theater Coll,* Harvard University Library (Houghton Library-Rare Books & Manuscripts), Cambridge MA. 617-495-2441
Newlin, Vera C, *Librn,* Robinson Township Library, Robinson IL. 618-544-2917
Newman, Ann, *AV,* Vigo County Public Library, Terre Haute IN. 812-232-1113
Newman, Anne, *Librn,* Hamlin Memorial Library, Paris Hill Library Association, Paris ME. 207-743-2980
Newman, Bernice E, *ILL,* Dedham Public Library, Dedham MA. 617-326-0583
Newman, Betty, *Comm Info & Referral,* Shelter Rock Public Library, Albertson NY. 516-248-7363
Newman, Charlotte, *Librn,* New Rochelle Public Library (Huguenot Park), New Rochelle NY. 914-632-5757
Newman, Charlotte M, *Br Coordr,* New Rochelle Public Library, New Rochelle NY. 914-632-7878
Newman, Cheryl, *Librn,* Riverview Hospital, Medical Library, Red Bank NJ. 201-741-2700, Ext 275
Newman, D M, *Librn,* De Havilland Aircraft of Canada Ltd, Engineering Library, Downsview ON. 416-633-7310

Newman, David, *On-Line Servs,* Mobil Oil Corp, Secretariat Library, New York NY. 212-883-2454

Newman, Dinah, *Librn,* University of West Los Angeles, Law School Library, Culver City CA. 213-204-0000, Ext 214

Newman, Doris, *Dir & Acq,* Siskiyou County Public Library, Yreka CA. 916-842-5256, 842-3531

Newman, Edward C, *Asst Dir,* Omaha Public Library, W Dale Clark Library, Omaha NE. 402-444-4800

Newman, Ellen J, *Chief Librn,* United States Department of Agriculture, Agricultural Research Service, Eastern Regional Research Center Library, Philadelphia PA. 215-247-5800

Newman, Euthena, *On-Line Servs,* North Carolina Agricultural & Technical State University, F D Bluford Library, Greensboro NC. 919-379-7782, 379-7783

Newman, Euthena, *Info Retrieval,* North Carolina Agricultural & Technical State University, F D Bluford Library, Greensboro NC. 919-379-7782, 379-7783

Newman, Fletcher, *Librn,* University of Texas at El Paso Library (Science), El Paso TX. 915-747-5138

Newman, George Charles, *Dir,* Findlay College, Shafer Library, Findlay OH. 419-422-8313, Ext 327

Newman, Helen, *Librn,* Public Library of Cincinnati & Hamilton County (Price Hill), Cincinnati OH. 513-921-0249

Newman, John, *Spec Coll,* Colorado State University, William E Morgan Library, Fort Collins CO. 303-491-5911

Newman, John, *Biog, Hist & Travel,* Public Library of Columbus & Franklin County, Columbus OH. 614-864-8050

Newman, June, *Actg Librn,* Willow Public Library, Willow AK. 907-495-6424

Newman, Lillian, *Assoc Librn, ILL & Bibliog Instr,* Agnes Scott College, McCain Library, Decatur GA. 404-373-2571, Ext 220

Newman, Lois, *Chief Librn,* Santa Rosa Junior College, Bernard C Plover Library, Santa Rosa CA. 707-527-4391

Newman, Marie, *ILL,* New York City Community College, Namm Hall Library, Brooklyn NY. 212-643-5240

Newman, Michael, *Tech Serv,* Nebraska Library Commission, Lincoln NE. 402-471-2045

Newman, Norma, *Asst Librn,* Gentry County Library, Stanberry MO. 816-782-2335

Newman, Robert G, *Dir,* Berkshire Athenaeum, Pittsfield Public Library, Pittsfield MA. 413-442-1559

Newman, Susan T, *Librn,* Ford Foundation Library, New York NY. 212-573-5155

Newman, Sylvia, *On-Line Servs,* West Virginia College of Graduate Studies Library, Institute WV. 304-768-9711, Ext 262

Newman, William, *Doc,* Capital University Library (Law School Library), Columbus OH. 614-445-8634

Newman, William, *Dir,* Tulane University of Louisiana, Howard-Tilton Memorial Library, New Orleans LA. 504-865-5131

Newman, Jr, Richard, *Dir,* University of Minnesota Libraries-Twin Cities (Library Systems Department), Minneapolis MN. 612-376-7662

Newmann, Evelyn, *Cat,* Flint Public Library, Flint MI. 313-232-7111

Newmeyer, Fritzie, *Cat,* University of Hawaii (University of Hawaii Library), Honolulu HI. 808-948-7205

Newmyer, JoAnn, *ILL,* Eastern Connecticut State College, J Eugene Smith Library, Willimantic CT. 203-456-2231, Ext 374, 422

Newmyer, JoAnn, *Bibliog Instr,* Eastern Connecticut State College, J Eugene Smith Library, Willimantic CT. 203-456-2231, Ext 374, 422

Newnam, Reid G, *Librn,* Greensboro Public Librar (Northeast), Greensboro NC. 919-621-3760

Newport, Dorothea B, *Dir,* Coatesville Area Public Library, Dr Michael Margolies Library, Coatesville PA. 215-384-4115

Newren, Edward F, *Chmn & Prof,* Miami University, Dept of Educational Media, OH. 513-529-3736

Newsom, Harry E, *Dir,* Cariboo Thompson Nicola Library System, Kamloops BC. 604-374-8866

Newsom, Jeanett, *Dir,* Jackson County Public Library, Sylva NC. 704-586-2016

Newsom, Jeanette, *Ch,* Fontana Regional Library, Bryson City NC. 704-488-2382

Newsome, James, *ILL & Ref,* Traverse Des Sioux Library System, Mankato MN. 507-625-6169

Newsome, Margaret, *Bibliog Instr,* University of Idaho Library, Moscow ID. 208-885-6534

Newsome, Margaret W, *Humanities,* University of Idaho Library, Moscow ID. 208-885-6534

Newsom, Keith R, *Open Lit,* United States Air Force (Air Force Weapons Laboratory Technical Library), Kirtland AFB NM. 505-844-7449

Newton, Anne M, *Ch,* Richard H Thornton Library, Oxford NC. 919-693-1121

Newton, Anne W, *Librn,* Arnall, Golden & Gregory, Law Library, Atlanta GA. 404-577-5100

Newton, Bert, *ILL,* Hutchinson Public Library, Hutchinson KS. 316-663-5441

Newton, Beverly, *Librn,* East Owyhee County Library District, Grand View ID. 208-834-2785

Newton, Craig, *Curator,* Columbia County Historical Society Library, Bloomsburg PA. 717-784-5177

Newton, Dorothy E, *Librn,* Massachusetts Correctional Institution Library, Framingham MA. 617-875-5259, Ext 142

Newton, Earle W, *Dir,* College of the Americas, Museum of the Americas Library, Brookfield VT. 802-276-3386

Newton, Elizabeth C, *Librn,* Field Library, Northfield MA. 413-369-4646

Newton, Ethan E, *Dir,* Brownell Library, Essex Junction VT. 802-878-2171

Newton, Frances, *Librn,* Brooklyn Public Library (Rugby), Brooklyn NY. 212-345-9264

Newton, George, *Cat,* Sacramento Public Library, Sacramento CA. 916-440-5926

Newton, Gerald D, *Tech Servs Chief,* California State Library, Sacramento CA. 916-445-2585

Newton, Harriet, *Librn,* Los Angeles Public Library System (Sun Valley Branch), Sun Valley CA. 213-764-7907

Newton, J, *In Charge,* Smith-Corona Laboratory Library, Cortland NY. 607-753-6011, Ext 278

Newton, Lawrence, *Librn,* Dallas County Public Library (Cedar Hill Branch), Cedar Hill TX. 214-291-4216

Newton, Lilian R, *Librn,* Phinehas S Newton Library, Royalston MA. 617-249-3572

Newton, Lyman, *Bkmobile Coordr,* Bur Oak Library System, Shorewood IL. 815-729-3345, 729-3346

Newton, Mildred B, *Asst Librn,* Lewis Egerton Smoot Memorial Library, King George VA. 703-775-7951

Newton, Mrs Bert, *On-Line Servs & Bibliog Instr,* South Central Kansas Library System, Hutchinson KS. 316-663-5441

Newton, Nancy, *Librn,* Brooklyn Public Library (Coney Island), Brooklyn NY. 212-266-1121

Newton, Neoma, *Librn,* Blairstown Public Library, Blairstown IA. 319-454-6497

Newton, Patricia, *Asst Dir & Ad,* Lane Public Library, Hamilton OH. 513-894-7156

Newton, Terra, *Librn,* Logansport State Hospital (Patients' Library), Logansport IN. 219-722-4141, Ext 202

Newton, Terra, *Librn,* Logansport State Hospital (Staff Library), Logansport IN. 219-722-4141, Ext 202

Newton, William R, *Research Servs,* Coca-Cola Co (Business Information Services), Atlanta GA. 404-898-2124

Ney, Neal J, *Librn,* Kankakee Public Library, Kankakee IL. 815-939-4564

Ney, W Roger, *Dir,* National Council on Radiation Protection & Measurements Library, Washington DC. 301-657-2652

Neyland, Cynthia K, *Librn,* United States Department of the Navy (Naval Facilities Engineering Command Technical Library), Alexandria VA. 202-325-8507

Neyman, Sandra B, *ILL & Reader Serv,* Marietta College, Dawes Memorial Library, Marietta OH. 614-373-4643, Ext 215, 216, 285

Ng, H W, *Librn,* Cutter Laboratories Library, Berkeley CA. 415-420-5187

Ng, Marjorie, *Librn,* Association of Bay Area Governments Library, Berkeley CA. 415-841-9730, Ext 220

Ng, Tung King, *Asian Studies,* University of British Columbia Library, Vancouver BC. 604-228-3871

Niblick, Pat, *Librn,* Caylor-Nickel Hospital Library, Bluffton IN. 219-824-3500, Ext 301

Nicely, Claudia K, *Librn,* Clifton Forge Public Library, Clifton Forge VA. 703-862-1334

Nicely, Marilyn, *Acq,* University of Oklahoma (Law Library), Norman OK. 405-325-4311

Nichelson, Suzanne, *Br Coordr,* Beverly Public Library, Beverly MA. 617-922-0310

Nichelson, Suzanne, *Librn,* Beverly Public Library (Beverly Farms), Beverly MA. 617-927-0234

Nichol, C A, *In Charge,* Midland-Ross Corp, Electrical Products Div, Employees Library, Pittsburgh PA. 412-323-5400

Nichol, Della, *Supvr,* Huron County Public Library (Brussells Branch), Brussels ON. 519-887-9235

Nichol, Emma, *Librn,* Beaman Memorial Library, Beaman IA. 515-366-2912

Nichol, Tom, *Coll Develop,* Saint John's University, Alcuin Library, Collegeville MN. 612-363-2119

Nicholaou, Mary, *Asst Dir,* Mohawk Valley Library Association, Schenectady NY. 518-355-2010

Nicholas, Kathryn D, *Librn,* Scott County Public Library, Scottsburg Public Library, Scottsburg IN. 812-752-2751

Nicholas, Katie, *Librn,* Stanislaus County Free Library (Hughson Branch), Hughson CA. 209-883-2293

Nicholas, Martha, *Librn, On-Line Servs & Bibliog Instr,* Southern Baptist College, Felix Goodson Library, Walnut Ridge AR. 501-886-6741, Ext 130

Nicholas, Russ, *ILL & Ref,* De Anza College, Learning Center, Cupertino CA. 408-996-4761

Nicholas, Thomas, *Program Coordr,* Aurora Public Library, Aurora CO. 303-750-5000, Ext 410

Nicholes, Eleanor, *Spec Coll,* Wellesley College, Margaret Clapp Library, Wellesley MA. 617-235-0320, Ext 280

Nicholls, Sheila, *In Charge,* Texas Education Agency (Region XI), Fort Worth TX. 817-625-5311

Nichols, Barbara Best, *Librn, On-Line Servs & Bibliog Instr,* Monsanto Co, Monsanto TPDCI Library, Research Triangle Park NC. 919-549-8111

Nichols, Betty, *Continuing Educ Coordr,* Kansas City Public Library, Kansas City MO. 816-221-2685

Nichols, Connie, *Bibliog Instr,* Northern Kentucky University, W Frank Steely Library, Highland Heights KY. 606-292-5483

Nichols, Darlene C, *Librn,* Karnes County Library System, Kenedy TX. 512-583-3313

Nichols, Diane, *Media,* University of Louisville Library (Kornhauser Health Sciences), Louisville KY. 502-588-5771

Nichols, Dolores D, *Asst Dir,* Upper Cumberland Regional Library, Cookeville TN. 615-526-4016

Nichols, Donna, *Cat,* Nazareth College, David Metzger Library, Nazareth MI. 616-349-7783, Ext 270

Nichols, Doris E, *Asst Dir,* Santa Clara County Free Library, San Jose CA. 408-293-2326

Nichols, Dusty, *Asst Librn,* Harlan Public Library (Rebecca Caudill Branch), Cumberland KY. 606-573-5220

Nichols, Gerald D, *Dir,* Babylon Public Library, Babylon NY. 516-669-1624

Nichols, Isabel B, *Librn,* James A Tuttle Library, Antrim NH. 603-588-6786

Nichols, J Gary, *State Librn,* Maine State Library, Augusta ME. 207-289-3561

Nichols, Jacquelyn, *Librn,* Hewlett-Packard Co, Resource Center, Colorado Springs CO. 303-598-1900, Ext 2708

Nichols, James, *Instr,* University of Denver, Graduate School of Librarianship and Information Management, CO. 303-753-2557

Nichols, Jim, *Historian,* Boynton Beach City Library, Boynton Beach FL. 732-2624 or 732-8111, Ext 223, 224 & 225

Nichols, John, *Dir,* Lewis & Clark Library, Helena MT. 406-442-2380

Nichols, Joyce, *Librn,* Smithtown Library (Nesconset Branch), Nesconset NY. 516-265-3994

Nichols, Joyce, *Br Asst,* Timberland Regional Library (Tumwater Branch), Tumwater WA. 206-943-7790

NICHOLS

Nichols, Judy, *Ad,* Chatham-Effingham-Liberty Regional Library, Savannah Public Library, Savannah GA. 912-234-5127

Nichols, Julia B, *Media,* Medical University of South Carolina Library, Charleston SC. 803-792-2374

Nichols, Kathryn, *Librn,* Sullivan County Public Library (Sullivan County Branch), Blountville TN. 615-323-5301

Nichols, Lee Ann, *Librn,* Elbert County Library (Simla Branch), Simla CO. 303-621-2041

Nichols, Lillian, *Librn,* Cresco Public Library, Cresco IA. 319-547-2540

Nichols, Lyn, *Asst Dir,* Raleigh County Public Library, Beckley WV. 304-255-0511

Nichols, Margaret I, *Instr,* North Texas State University, School of Library & Information Sciences, TX. 817-788-2445

Nichols, Marian, *Exten Servs,* Oakland Public Library, Oakland CA. 415-273-3281

Nichols, Mary, *Asst Librn,* Martin College, Warden Memorial Library, Pulaski TN. 615-363-7456, Ext 41

Nichols, Mary Elizabeth, *Tech Serv,* Goucher College, Julia Rogers Library, Towson MD. 301-825-3300, Ext 360

Nichols, Mrs Nowlan, *Art & Archives,* Louisiana Tech University, Prescott Memorial Library, Ruston LA. 318-257-2577

Nichols, Nancy, *Ch,* Bangor Public Library, Bangor ME. 207-947-8336

Nichols, Nelle, *ILL & Per,* Mary H Weir Public Library, Weirton WV. 304-748-7070

Nichols, R D, *Librn,* Jordan College Library, Cedar Springs MI. 616-696-1180

Nichols, Roger M, *Dir,* Brownwood Public Library, Brownwood TX. 915-646-0155

Nichols, Shirley G, *Librn,* Tennessee Valley Authority, Technical Library, Muscle Shoals AL. 205-383-4631, Ext 2871

Nichols, Stephanie, *Librn,* Morrison-Krudsen Co Inc, Record Center, Boise ID. 208-345-5000, Ext 5936

Nichols, William J, *Librn,* Astor Home for Children, Professional Library, Rhinebeck NY. 914-876-4081, Ext 136

Nicholsen, Margaret, *Chief Librn,* Evanston Historical Society Library, Charles Gates Daves Home Library, Evanston IL. 312-475-3410

Nicholson, Anne, *Tech Serv,* Wake Forest University, Z Smith Reynolds Library, Winston-Salem NC. 919-761-5480

Nicholson, Barbara, *Circ,* Millinocket Memorial Library, Millinocket ME. 207-723-9610

Nicholson, Beth, *Librn,* West Florida Regional Library (Belvedere), Pensacola FL. 904-476-3969

Nicholson, Clifton, *Librn,* Chicago Public Library (Washington Park), Chicago IL. 312-363-1168

Nicholson, Deborah, *Tech Serv, Acq & Cat,* Halifax City Regional Library, Halifax NS. 902-426-6980

Nicholson, James, *Circ,* Wake Forest University, Z Smith Reynolds Library, Winston-Salem NC. 919-761-5480

Nicholson, Janet, *ILL,* San Bernardino Public Library, San Bernardino CA. 714-889-0264

Nicholson, Kathleen, *Librn,* Onondaga County Public Library System (Betts), Syracuse NY. 315-473-3200

Nicholson, Lillian, *Librn,* Shriners Hospital for Crippled Children, Houston Unit Orthopaedic Library, Houston TX. 713-797-1616

Nicholson, Lillian E, *Librn,* Blair County Law Library, Hollidaysburg PA. 814-695-4451, Ext 38

Nicholson, Liza, *Asst Librn,* Morgan, Lewis & Bockius Library, Philadelphia PA. 215-491-9633

Nicholson, Margaret, *Ref,* Holy Names College, Paul J Cushing Library, Oakland CA. 415-436-1332

Nicholson, Marion, *Geneology, Rare Books & Local Hist,* Greenwich Library, Greenwich CT. 203-622-7900

Nicholson, Mary C, *Tech Serv,* Hobart & William Smith Colleges, Warren Hunting Smith Library, Geneva NY. 315-789-5500, Ext 224

Nicholson, Millie, *Librn,* Albert C Martin & Associates, Information Research Center, Los Angeles CA. 213-683-1900

Nicholson, Roland, *Dir,* Virginia Wesleyan College, Henry Clay Hofheimer II Library, Norfolk VA. 804-461-3232

Nicholson, Jr, John B, *Dir & Rare Bks,* University of Baltimore, Langsdale Library, Baltimore MD. 301-727-6350, Ext 444

Nichter, Alan, *Librn,* Tampa-Hillsborough County Public Library System (Lutz Public), Lutz FL. 813-949-5411

Nick, Helen, *Librn,* Caldwell Memorial Hospital Library, Caldwell ID. 208-459-4641, Ext 543

Nickel, Edgar, *Dir,* Northwest Kansas Library System, Norton KS. 913-877-5148

Nickel, Rose Ann, *Dir Instrnl Mat Ctr,* Fort Wayne Bible College, S A Lehman Memorial Library, Fort Wayne IN. 219-456-2111, Ext 223

Nickels, Joseph, *Librn,* Systematics General Corp Library, Falls Church VA. 703-698-8500

Nickelsburg, Marilyn M, *Librn,* University of Iowa Hospitals and Clinics, Patients' Library, Iowa City IA. 319-356-2468

Nickenig, Barbara, *Ref,* Bergen Community College, Learning Resources Center Library, Paramus NJ. 201-447-1500, Ext 405

Nickerson, Don, *Ref,* Roddenbery Memorial Library, Cairo GA. 912-377-3632

Nickerson, Donna L, *Cat,* Manhattanville College Library, Purchase NY. 914-946-9600, Ext 274

Nickerson, Ellen J, *Ch,* Winthrop Public Library, Frost Public Library, Winthrop MA. 617-846-1703

Nickerson, Lovann, *Ref & Spec Coll,* Kern County Library, Bakersfield CA. 805-861-2130

Nickerson, Martha, *Circ,* Framingham Public Library, Framingham MA. 617-879-3570

Nickerson, Mrs J A, *Librn,* Pittsburg - Camp County Library, Pittsburg TX. 214-856-3302

Nickerson, Sarah C, *Dir,* Atkinson Public Library, Atkinson IL. 309-936-7606

Nickerson, Sue, *Librn,* Sacramento Public Library (Sylvan Oaks Community), Citrus Heights CA. 916-961-1752, 726-4484

Nicklas, Linda, *Spec Coll,* Stephen F Austin State University, Ralph W Steen Library, Nacogdoches TX. 713-569-4109

Nickles, I MacArthur, *Dir,* Garfield Free Public Library, Garfield NJ. 201-478-3800

Nickols, Gayle W, *Dir,* Hardin County Public Library, Elizabethtown KY. 502-769-6337

Nickols, Karen, *Doc & Tech Serv,* Sperry Corp, Sperry UNIVAC Div, Information Service Center, Roseville MN. 612-631-5386

Nicks, Hattie Mae, *Br Asst,* Morehouse Parish Library (Dunbar), Bastrop LA. 318-281-1137

Nicks, Pat, *Media & Commun Servs,* Irving Public Library System, Irving TX. 214-253-2639

Nicol, Julie A, *Librn,* Michigan State Library, Blind & Physically Handicapped Library, Lansing MI. 517-373-1590

Nicolai, Pamela J, *Dir,* San Rafael Public Library, San Rafael CA. 415-456-1118, Ext 271

Nicolas, Catherine, *Librn,* Anchorage Municipal Libraries (Sand Lake), Anchorage AK. 907-243-2311

Nicolaus, Jane, *Librn,* Marathon County Public Library (Edgar Branch), Edgar WI. 715-352-2891

Nicolescu, Bonnedene, *Librn,* Baker County Public Library (Richland Branch), Richland OR. 503-523-6414, 523-6419

Nicolescu, S, *Spec Coll,* Medgar Evers College Library, Brooklyn NY. 212-735-1851

Nicolson, Joan, *Librn,* York Regional Library (Perth-Andover Public), Perth-Andover NB. 506-273-2843

Nicosia, Alfonso, *Asst Prof,* Texas Woman's University, School of Library Science, TX. 817-387-2418 & 566-1455

Nicot, Suzanne, *Asst Dir,* Cary Memorial Library, Lexington MA. 617-862-6288

Nicula, Gail, *On-Line Servs,* Old Dominion University Library, Norfolk VA. 804-440-4141

Niebuhr, Gary Warren, *Dir,* Greendale Public Library, Greendale WI. 414-421-2620

Niederer, Jayne, *Dir,* Hamer Public Library, Hamer ID. 208-662-5275

Niederlander, Nicholas, *Insts,* Lewis & Clark Library System, Edwardsville IL. 618-656-3216

Niehaus, Pat, *Ref Asst,* United States Army (Morale Support Activities Division Library), Fort Hood TX. 817-685-6011

Niehaus, Thomas, *Latin Am,* Tulane University of Louisiana, Howard-Tilton Memorial Library, New Orleans LA. 504-865-5131

Nielsen, Betty, *Librn,* Brown Memorial Library, Dumont IA. 515-837-3304

Nielsen, Carol, *Librn,* University of North Carolina at Chapel Hill (Library School), Chapel Hill NC. 919-933-8361

Nielsen, Eva, *Ad,* Swampscott Public Library, Swampscott MA. 617-593-8380

Nielsen, Janet, *Dir,* Kellogg-Hubbard Library, Montpelier VT. 802-223-3338

Nielsen, Kenneth R, *Dir,* Arrowhead Library System, Virginia MN. 218-741-3840

Nielsen, Nancy, *Librn,* Yampa Public Library, Yampa CO. 303-638-4654

Nielsen, Roy J M, *In Charge,* Lawrence Berkeley Laboratory Library, Berkeley CA. 415-486-5621

Nielsen, Royce, *Librn,* Salt Lake County Library System (16MM Film Library), Salt Lake City UT. 801-943-7614

Nielson, Barbara, *Tech Serv,* Saint Bernard's Seminary Library, Rochester NY. 716-254-1020, Ext 25, 26, 27

Nielson, Betty, *Librn,* Salt Lake County Library System (Calvin S Smith Branch), Salt Lake City UT. 801-484-6111

Nielson, June, *Librn,* Shoshone Public Library, Shoshone ID. 208-886-2030

Nielson, Paul, *Instr,* Red River Community College, Library Technician Course, MB. 204-632-2150

Nielson, Ralph, *Cat,* University of Idaho Library, Moscow ID. 208-885-6534

Nielson, William E, *Libr Servs Chief,* Veterans Administration, Hospital Library, Tomah WI. 608-372-3971, Ext 283, 262

Nieman, Barbara, *Head, Coll Develop & ILL,* Chicago Public Library (Illinois Regional Library for the Blind & Physically Handicapped), Chicago IL. 312-738-9210

Niemann, John M, *Dir,* Indiana Vocational Technical College, Learning Resource Center, Gary IN. 219-981-1111, Ext 28

Niemeyer, Dan, *Supvr,* University of Colorado at Boulder (National Center for Audio Tapes), Boulder CO. 303-492-7341

Niemeyer, Herbert, *Media Serv,* Saint Louis Community College (Florissant Valley Campus), Saint Louis MO. 314-595-4494

Niemeyer, Katherine, *Spec Coll,* Pike-Amite-Walthall Library System, McComb Public Library (Headquaters), McComb MS. 601-684-7034

Niemi, Peter G, *Dir,* Kent County Library System, Grand Rapids MI. 616-774-3250

Niemi, Robert, *Tech Serv,* Leominster Public Library, Leominster MA. 617-537-0941

Niemi, Taisto John, *Dir & Acq,* Le Moyne College Library, Syracuse NY. 315-446-2882, Ext 241

Niemira, Margarita, *Info Sup,* El Paso Public Library, El Paso TX. 915-543-3804

Nienaber, Raymond, *Commun Servs,* Kenton County Public Library, Covington KY. 606-292-2363

Niepert, Janice, *Librn,* Grove City Public Library (Prairie), Columbus OH. 614-878-1301

Nier, Paula, *Ref,* Union Service Corp Library, New York NY. 212-432-4002, 432-4003

Nierman, Ruth, *Dir,* Wabeno Public Library, Wabeno WI. 715-473-4333

Nies, Rita A, *ILL & Ref,* Gannon University, Nash Library, Erie PA. 814-871-7352

Niessink, John, *AV,* Portage Public Library, Portage MI. 616-327-6725

Niessner, Mira, *Librn,* Brooklyn Public Library (Homecrest), Brooklyn NY. 212-645-2727

Niewold, Daena, *Librn,* Sycamore Public Library, Sycamore IL. 815-895-2500

Nigh, Mary K, *Asst Dir,* Fort Smith Public Library, Fort Smith AR. 501-783-0229

Nightingale, Bev, *Librn,* British Columbia Law Library Foundation, Kamloops Court House Library, Kamloops BC. 604-374-7415

Nightingale, Margaret A, *Librn,* Pinellas County Law Library, Clearwater Branch, Clearwater FL. 813-448-2411, 448-2412, 448-2413

Nikirk, Robert, *Librn,* Grolier Club of New York Library, New York NY. 212-838-6690

Nikkel, Jane F, *ILL,* Richmond Public Library, Richmond VA. 804-780-4256

Niles, Ann, *Tech Serv,* Carleton College Library, Northfield MN. 507-645-4431

Niles, Judith, *Tech Serv & On-Line Servs,* Laredo Junior College, Harold R Yeary Library, Laredo TX. 512-724-7544, 722-0521

Niles, Judith, *Tech Serv & On-Line Servs,* Laredo State University, Harold R Yeary Library, Laredo TX. 512-722-8001, Ext 42

Nillard, Pamela Anne, *Dir,* Dallas Public Library, Dallas NC. 704-922-3621

Nilon, Mildred, *Public Servs,* University of Colorado at Boulder (University Libraries), Boulder CO. 303-492-7511

Nilsen, Esther, *Tech Serv, Acq & Cat,* King's College Library, Briarcliff Manor NY. 914-941-7200, Ext 243

Nilson, Julieann, *Automated Processing,* Indiana University at Bloomington, University Libraries, Bloomington IN. 812-337-3403

Nilvo, Frank, *Libr Asst,* Los Lunas Hospital & Training School, New Mexico Mental Retardation & Developmental Disabilities Library & Resource Center, Los Lunas NM. 505-865-9611, Ext 298

Nimer, Gilda, *Librn,* American University, Foreign Area Studies Library, Washington DC. 202-686-2740

Nimmer, Ronald J, *Acq,* Ohio State University Libraries (William Oxley Thompson Memorial Library), Columbus OH. 614-422-6151

Nims, Donald F, *Librn,* Standard Register Co, Corporate Library, Dayton OH. 513-223-6181, Ext 412

Nimura, Taku F, *Circ,* California State University, Sacramento Library, Sacramento CA. 916-454-6466

Ninemire, Linda, *Ser,* George Williams College Library, Downers Grove IL. 312-964-3100, Ext 242

Ninham, Jacqueline, *Supvr,* Middlesex County Library (Oneida), RR 2 ON. 519-438-8368

Nini, Eva Mae, *Librn,* Saint Mary Parish Library (Berwick Branch), Berwick LA. 318-385-2943

Nipe, Catherine, *Ref,* Gloucester County College, Library-Media Center, Sewell NJ. 609-468-5000, Ext 294

Nipp, Deanna, *Bibliog Instr,* Mansfield State College Library, Mansfield PA. 717-662-4071

Nipp, Mildred, *Bkmobile Coordr,* Fulton Public Library, Fulton KY. 502-472-3439

Nirella, Vincent K, *Br Coordr,* Middletown Township Public Library, Middletown NJ. 201-671-3700

Nisbett, Gay G, *Dir,* Columbia Christian College Library, Portland OR. 503-255-7060

Nisenoff, Sylvia, *In Charge,* American Personnel & Guidance Association, Professional Library, Falls Church VA. 703-820-4700, Ext 268

Nishimura, Hazel, *Librn,* National Marine Fisheries Service, Southwest Fisheries Center Library, Honolulu HI. 808-946-2181

Nishita, Eleanor, *Librn,* Los Angeles Public Library System (Baldwin Hills), Los Angeles CA. 213-733-1196

Nishizaki, Colette, *Librn,* Reader's Digest Magazines Limited, Editorial Library, Montreal PQ. 514-934-0751, Ext 711

Nissler, Pamela, *Dir,* Edwin A Bemis Public Library, Littleton Public Library, Littleton CO. 303-795-3826

Nist, Joan S, *Asst Prof,* Auburn University, Dept of Educational Media, AL. 205-826-4529

Niswander, Richard E, *Dir,* National Coal Association Library, Washington DC. 202-628-4322, Ext 240

Niswanger, Amy, *Asst Librn,* Eagle County Public Library, Eagle CO. 303-328-7311, Ext 255, 256

Niswanger, Amy, *Librn,* Eagle County Public Library (Minturn Public), Minturn CO. 303-827-4240

Nitecki, A, *Assoc Prof,* University of Alberta, Faculty of Library Science, AB. 403-432-4578

Nitecki, Danuta, *ILL,* University of Illinois Library at Urbana-Champaign, Urbana IL. 217-333-0790

Nitecki, Joseph Z, *Dir,* University of Wisconsin-Oshkosh, Forrest R Polk Library, Oshkosh WI. 414-424-3333

Nitishin, Elizabeth, *Librn,* York Regional Library (Nashwaaksis Public), Fredericton NB. 506-472-4123

Nitsch, Holly, *Asst Librn,* Hastings Public Library, Hastings ON. 705-696-2111

Nitz, Kathryn, *Librn,* Bendix Corporation Instrument & Life Support Div, Bendix Engineering Library, Davenport IA. 319-383-6387

Niven, R Garth, *Librn,* Law Society of Manitoba, Great Library, Winnipeg MB. 204-943-5277

Niverth, Eda, *Librn,* Marianna Community Public Library, Marianna PA. 412-267-3888

Nivison, Patricia, *Dir,* Franklin Township Free Public Library, Somerset NJ. 201-545-8032

Nix, Doris, *Commun Servs,* Milwaukee County Federated Library System, Milwaukee WI. 414-278-3210

Nix, Frances, *Dir,* Arkansas Library Commission, Arkansas State Library, Little Rock AR. 501-371-1524

Nix, Gloria, *Per,* Phillips University, Zollars Memorial Library, Enid OK. 405-237-4433, Ext 251

Nix, Imogene, *Tech Serv,* Northeastern Oklahoma State University, John Vaughan Library-Learning Resource Center, Tahlequah OK. 918-456-5511, Ext 385

Nix, James R, *Rare Bks & Spec Coll,* Loma Linda University Library, Riverside CA. 714-785-2022

Nix, James R, *Rare Bks & Spec Coll,* Loma Linda University, Vernier Radcliffe Memorial Library, Loma Linda CA. 714-796-7311, Ext 2916

Nix, Larry T, *Dir,* Greenville County Library, Greenville SC. 803-242-5000

Nixdorff, John S, *Librn,* Venable, Baetjer & Howard Library, Baltimore MD. 301-752-6780, Ext 353, 346

Nixon, Diane S, *Acq,* Naval Postgraduate School, Dudley Knox Library, Monterey CA. 408-646-2341

Nixon, Esther, *Librn,* Central Arkansas Library System (Jacksonville Branch), Jacksonville AR. 501-982-5533

Nixon, Janet, *Dir,* Lockport Public Library, Lockport NY. 716-433-5935

Nixon, Judith M, *Ref & Bibliog Instr,* University of Wisconsin-Platteville, Elton S Karrmann Library, Platteville WI. 608-342-1688

Nixon, Lynette, *Librn,* Providence Hospital, Medical Library, Moose Jaw SK. 306-692-6471

Nixon, Marjorie, *Dir,* Northlake Public Library District, Northlake IL. 312-562-2301

Nixon, Nadine B, *Tech Serv,* Central Virginia Community College Library, Lynchburg VA. 804-239-0321, Ext 231

Nixon, Nancy, *Librn,* First Presbyterian Church Library, Roseburg OR. 503-673-5559

Nixon, Phyllis J, *Librn,* Delaware Art Museum Library, Wilmington DE. 302-571-9590

Nobari, Nuchine, *Librn,* Davis Polk & Wardwell Library, New York NY. 212-422-3400

Nobbe, Nancy, *Dir,* Parks College Library, Cahokia IL. 618-337-7500, Ext 244, 274

Nobile, Beverly, *Acq,* Mississippi Delta Junior College, Stanny Sanders Library, Moorhead MS. 601-243-8672

Noble, Ann E, *Commun Servs,* Sheppard Memorial Library, Greenville NC. 919-752-4177

Noble, David, *Librn,* Cancer Control Agency of British Columbia Library, Vancouver BC. 604-873-6212

Noble, Dennis L, *Dir,* Delphi Public Library, Delphi IN. 317-564-2929

Noble, Eleanor, *Dir & Rare Bks,* University of Albuquerque, Center for Learning & Information Resources, Albuquerque NM. 505-831-1111, Ext 230

Noble, Geraldine, *Dir,* Lebanon Public Library, Lebanon OH. 513-932-4725

Noble, Hadley, *Ser,* University of Rochester, Rush Rhees Library, Rochester NY. 716-275-4461

Noble, James, *On-Line Servs & Bibliog Instr,* United States Navy (Information & Documentation Technical Library), Panama City FL. 904-234-4321

Noble, Nancy, *Western Regional Librn,* Genesee District Library, Flint MI. 313-732-0110

Noble, Valerie, *In Charge,* Upjohn Company (Business Library), Kalamazoo MI. 616-323-6351

Noble, Wendy, *Dir,* Tarkio College, J A Thompson Library, Tarkio MO. 816-736-4131, Ext 433

Nobles, Nancy D, *Cat,* Chipola Junior College Library, Marianna FL. 904-526-2761, Ext 122

Nobles, Steve, *Doc,* University of Tulsa, McFarlin Library, Tulsa OK. 918-592-6000, Ext 351

Noden, Denys, *Tech Serv,* University of Alberta (University Libraries), Edmonton AB. 403-432-3790

Nodler, Charles E, *Acq & Archivist,* Missouri Southern State College, George A Spiva Library, Joplin MO. 417-624-8100, Ext 251

Noe, Barbara, *Asst Librn,* H B Stamps Memorial Library, Hawkins County Rogersville Public Library, Rogersville TN. 615-272-8710

Noe, Carolyn, *Librn,* Wilson County Public Library (Stantonsburg Branch), Stantonsburg NC. 919-237-3818

Noe, Lillian R, *Librn,* Logan County Public Library, Russellville KY. 502-726-6129

Noe, Sister M, *Tech Serv,* Anna Maria College Library, Paxton MA. 617-757-4586, Ext 56

Noel, Donald, *Media,* Saint Norbert College, Todd Wehr Library, De Pere WI. 414-337-3280

Noel, Evelyn, *Chief Librn,* Canada Department of Indian Affairs & Northern Development, Departmental Library, Ottawa ON. 819-997-0799

Noel, Karen A, *Librn,* Wilson County Technical Institute, Learning Resource Center, Wilson NC. 919-291-1195, Ext 235

Noel, Patricia, *Ad,* Saugus Public Library (Cliftondale), Saugus MA. 617 233 1291

Noel, Sister M, *Librn,* Alvernia College Library, Reading PA. 215-777-5411

Noel, III, Fred J, *Coordr for Prod, Media Servs & Self-Instr Lab,* Southern Illinois University at Edwardsville (Audio Visual Services), Edwardsville IL. 618-692-3050

Noella, Sister M, *Admin,* Saint Joseph Intercommunity Hospital, Medical Staff Library, Cheektowaga NY. 716-896-6300

Noerenberg, Sharon, *Librn,* Winsted Public Library, Winsted MN. 612-485-3909

Noey, Elsie A, *Librn,* General Electric Co, Neutron Devices Department Library, Saint Petersburg FL. 813-544-2511

Noffsinger, Helen, *Dir,* Warren Public Library, Warren IN. 219-375-3450

Nogue, A G, *Librn,* Saskatchewan Department of Co-Operation & Co-Operative Development Library, Regina SK. 306-565-2345

Nohl, Nancy, *Librn,* West Allis Public Library (Lincoln), West Allis WI. 414-321-2250

Nolan, Barbara, *ILL,* Schaumburg Township Public Library, Schaumburg IL. 312-885-3373

Nolan, Edward, *In Charge,* Lane County Museum Library, Eugene OR. 503-687-4239

Nolan, Ethel, *Bkmobile Coordr,* Harlan Public Library, Harlan KY. 606-573-5220

Nolan, Joan, *Librn,* Nassau County Supreme Court, 10th Judicial District, Law Library, Mineola NY. 516-535-3883

Nolan, Joan, *Librn,* Newton Free Library (Newton Highlands Branch), Newton Highlands MA. 617-527-7700, Ext 24

Nolan, Margaret P, *Chief Librn,* Metropolitan Museum of Art (Photograph & Slide Library), New York NY. 212-879-5500, Ext 261

Nolan, Marianne, *Librn,* Empire State College Learning Resources Center, Saratoga Springs NY. 518-587-2100, Ext 205

Nolan, Martha D, *Reader Serv & Ref,* Hartford Public Library, Hartford CT. 203-525-9121

Nolan, Patrick, *Rare Bks & Spec Coll,* Wright State University Library, Dayton OH. 513-873-2380

Noland, Elaine, *Librn,* Greenville Hospital System (Greenville Memorial Hospital Branch Library), Greenville SC. 803-242-7782

Noland, Elaine, *Librn,* Greenville Hospital System (Roger C Peace Rehabilitative Institute Branch Library), Greenville SC. 803-242-7782

Noland, Elaine, *Librn,* Greenville Hospital System (Marshall I Pickens Psychiatric Institute Branch Library), Greenville SC. 803-242-7782

Noland, Jon, *Circ,* Iowa State University Library, Ames IA. 515-294-1442

Nolen, Geraldine, *Cat,* Swisher County Library, Tulia TX. 806-995-3447

Noles, Wilma, *Librn,* Dallas Public Library, Dallas NC. 704-922-3621

Nolf, Marsha, *Instr,* Fairmont State College, Library Science Program, WV. 304-367-4121

Nolf, Richard A, *Dir,* Saint Joseph Museum Library, Saint Joseph MO. 816-232-8471

Nolin, Carolyn, *Asst State Librn,* Maine State Library, Augusta ME. 207-289-3561

Noling, A W, *Dir,* Hurty-Peck, Library of Beverage Literature, Irvine CA. 714-557-1660

Noll, Eleanor, *Acq,* Hamline University (School of Law Library), Saint Paul MN. 612-641-2344

Noll, Mary K, *Librn,* RCA Corp, Lancaster PA. 717-397-7661

Nollar, Judy, *Librn,* California Institute of Technology (Munger Africana Library), Pasadena CA. 213-795-6811, Ext 1468

Noller, D Jean, *In Charge,* General Electric Co, Appliance Components Support Operation Library, Fort Wayne IN. 219-743-7431, Ext 3679

Noller, David C, *Tech Info Specialist & Ref,* Pennwalt Corp, Lucidol Div, Research Library, Buffalo NY. 716-877-1740, Ext 262, 276

Nollner, Katherine A, *Tech Serv,* Peabody Institute Library, Peabody MA. 617-531-0100

Nomer, Genevieve T, *Dir,* Atlantic City Free Public Library, Atlantic City NJ. 609-345-2269

Nomland, John, *Chief Librn,* Los Angeles City College Library, Los Angeles CA. 213-663-9141, Ext 412

Noonan, F Thomas, *Curator of Reading Room,* Harvard University Library (Houghton Library-Rare Books & Manuscripts), Cambridge MA. 617-495-2441

Noonan, Lois C, *Dir,* Bixby Memorial Free Library, Vergennes VT. 802-877-2211

Noonan, Patricia, *Tech Serv,* Knoxville College, Alumni Library, Knoxville TN. 615-524-6554

Noonan, Patricia, *Tech Serv,* Winnipeg Public Library, Winnipeg MB. 204-985-6450

Noonan, Susanne, *Lectr,* Boston University, Dept of Instructional Development-Educational Media, MA. 617-353-3176

Norcross, Judith, *Asst Librn,* Franklin Pierce Law Center Library, Concord NH. 603-228-1541, Ext 50

Nordan, Marilyn, *Librn,* Monroe County Library System (Ida Branch), Ida MI. 313-269-2191

Nordby, Carol, *In Charge,* Golden Valley Health Center, Medical Library, Golden Valley MN. 612-588-2771, Ext 404

Nordby, Gayle, *ILL,* Calaveras County Library, San Andreas CA. 209-754-4266

Nordby, Kenneth E, *Librn,* Our Savior's Lutheran Church Library, Milwaukee WI. 414-342-5252

Nordell, Sr, Warren, *Librn,* Times-Picayune Library, New Orleans LA. 504-586-3777

Norden, Fred R Van, *Asst Librn,* Belmont Public Library, Belmont MA. 617-489-2000

Norden, Margaret, *Ref,* University of Pittsburgh (Maurice & Laura Falk Library of the Health Sciences), Pittsburgh PA. 412-624-2521

Nordene, Diane, *Librn,* Neuropsychiatric Institute, Fargo ND. 701-235-5354, Ext 77

Nordeng, Diane, *Librn,* Neuropsychiatric Institute (Southeast Mental Health & Retardation Center Library), Fargo ND. 701-237-4513

Nordin, Martha, *Librn,* Hay Lakes Municipal Library, Hay Lakes AB. 403-878-3366

Nordine, Ed, *Media,* Western Illinois University Libraries, Macomb IL. 309-298-2411

Nordlund, Cheryl A, *Dir & Librn,* Rolling Meadows Library, Rolling Meadows IL. 312-259-6050

Nordmann, Terrance J, *Assoc Prof,* Alabama Agricultural & Mechanical University, School of Library Media, AL. 205-859-7216 or 859-7238

Nordmeyer, Jean, *Dir & On-Line Servs,* Greene Public Library, Greene IA. 515-823-5642

Nordquist, Dorothy, *Librn,* Northampton Area Public Library (Bath Branch), Bath PA. 215-837-1911

Nordquist, Ellen, *ILL,* Norwood Public Library, Norwood NJ. 201-768-9555

Nordwick, Vivian, *Librn,* Roosevelt County Library (Poplar City Public), Poplar MT. 406-768-3749

Noreau, Patricia, *Per,* University of Lowell Libraries (Alumni-Lydon Library), Lowell MA. 617-452-5000, Ext 378

Norell, Irene, *Assoc Prof,* San Jose State University, Division of Library Science, CA. 408-277-2292

Norelli, Barbara P, *Circ & Per,* Albany Law School Library, Albany NY. 518-445-2311, 445-2340

Norem, Jane, *Circ & Per,* Aurora College, Charles B Phillips Library, Aurora IL. 312-892-6431, Ext 61, 62

Norgard, Norma, *Librn,* Coleraine Public Library, Coleraine MN. 218-245-2315

Noriega, Olivia, *Cat,* United States Navy (Technical Library), China Lake CA. 714-939-2507

Nork, Betty, *Circ,* University of Connecticut at Hartford (Law Library), West Hartford CT. 203-523-4841, Ext 347, 370

Norlin, Sandra K, *Asst Dir,* Brookings Public Library, Brookings SD. 605-692-9407, 692-9408

Norman, Anita, *ILL & Ref,* Kearney State College, Calvin T Ryan Library, Kearney NE. 308-236-4218

Norman, Barbara, *Libr Tech,* United States Army (Corps of Engineers, Fort Worth District Library), Fort Worth TX. 334-2138 or 2139

Norman, Barbara K, *Area Consult,* Northwestern Regional Library, Elkin NC. 919-835-4894

Norman, Carol, *Tech Serv, Acq & Cat,* Beverly Hills Public Library, Beverly Hills CA. 213-550-4711

Norman, Carolyn F, *Head Librn,* Miramar College, Instructional Learning Resource Center, San Diego CA. 714-271-7300

Norman, Cassandra M, *Librn,* Voorhees College, Marian B Wilkinson Library, Denmark SC. 803-793-3346, Ext 261

Norman, Corleen, *Asst Librn,* Conrad Public Library, Conrad MT. 406-278-5751

Norman, Gloria, *Librn,* Montgomery City-County Public Library (Cleveland Avenue Branch), Montgomery AL. 205-264-3324

Norman, Haskell F, *Pres,* Janus Foundation Library, San Francisco CA. 415-563-0344

Norman, Jane L, *Librn,* Crook County Library (Moorcroft Branch), Moorcroft WY. 307-756-3232

Norman, Kim, *Librn,* Stromberg Carlson Library, Longwood FL. 305-339-1600

Norman, Lenora, *Librn,* Sikeston Public Library, Sikeston MO. 314-471-4140

Norman, Mamie S, *Asst Librn,* Springfield College, Babson Library, Springfield MA. 413-787-2340

Norman, Nita, *Librn,* Chicago Public Library (Pilsen), Chicago IL. 312-829-3124

Norman, O Gene, *Ref & On-Line Servs,* Indiana State University, Cunningham Memorial Library, Terre Haute IN. 812-232-6311, Ext 2451

Norman, Ronald V, *Dir,* Kearney Public Library, Kearney NE. 308-237-5133

Norman, Vivian, *Ch,* James Blackstone Memorial Library, Branford CT. 203-488-1441

Norman, Wayne, *Librn,* Parapsychology Foundation, Eileen J Garrett Library, New York NY. 212-751-5940

Normandin, Fern, *Librn,* Wakefield Public Library, Wakefield KS. 913-461-5815

Normandin, Frances, *Ch,* Wakefield Public Library, Wakefield KS. 913-461-5815

Normann, Stephanie L, *Chief Librn,* University of Texas Health Science Center at Houston, School of Public Health Library, Houston TX. 713-792-4350

Normile, E G, *Mgr Personnel Servs,* London Public Libraries & Museums, London ON. 519-432-7166

Normile, Michael R, *ILL,* Siena College, Jerome Dawson Memorial Library, Loudonville NY. 518-783-2522

Normington, Mavis A, *Librn,* Bugbee Memorial Library, Killingly Public Library, Danielson CT. 203-774-9429

Normoyle, Joan, *YA,* Bethpage Public Library, Bethpage NY. 516-913-3907

Noronha, Marilyn S, *Librn,* University of Connecticut at Hartford (Undergratuate Library), West Hartford CT. 203-523-4841, Ext 317

Norr, Janis, *Librn,* Whatcom County Public Library (Lynden Branch), Lynden WA. 206-354-4883

Norris, Catherine, *Ch,* Janesville Public Library, Janesville WI. 608-752-8934, Ext B

Norris, Claudia, *Librn,* Macro Systems, Inc Library, Silver Spring MD. 301-588-5484

Norris, Doris Ann, *Asst Dir & Cat,* Kaubisch Memorial Public Library, Fostoria OH. 419-435-2813

Norris, Edmond J, *Dir,* United States Army (Communications-Electronics Museum), Fort Monmouth NJ. 201-532-2445

Norris, Elizabeth, *Librn,* YWCA National Board Library, New York NY. 212-753-4700

Norris, Gerry, *Lectr,* Simmons College, Graduate School of Library & Information Science, MA. 617-738-2225

Norris, Hellen J, *Asst Librns,* Northeast Mississippi Junior College, Eula Dees Memorial Library, Booneville MS. 601-728-7751, Ext 237

Norris, Jeanne, *Librn,* Detroit Public Library (Chandler Park), Detroit MI. 313-833-9165

Norris, Karalyn, *Tech Serv,* Carbondale Public Library, Carbondale IL. 618-457-0354

Norris, Kevin, *ILL,* University of Scranton, Alumni Memorial Library, Scranton PA. 717-961-7525

Norris, Loretta, *Law Serv Br,* United States Department of Transportation, Library Services Div, Washington DC. 202-426-2565, 426-1792

Norris, Mrs Paul, *Librn,* Washington County Free Library (Boonsboro Free), Boonsboro MD. 301-432-5723

Norris, Peggy, *ILL,* William Paterson College of New Jersey, Sarah Byrd Askew Library, Wayne NJ. 201-595-2113

Norris, Sarah, *Librn,* Tacoma Art Museum Reference Library, Tacoma WA. 206-272-4258

Norris, Shirley, *Chief Librn,* Arcanum Public Library, Arcanum OH. 513-692-8484

Norris, Sue, *Librn,* Wyoming Mineral Corp, Administrative Department Library, Lakewood CO. 303-988-8530

Norris, Susan, *Librn,* Public Library of Columbus & Franklin County (Hilltonia), Columbus OH. 614-222-7106

Norris, Vernal, *Circ,* University of California, Riverside (Physical Sciences), Riverside CA. 714-787-3511

Norrod, Janet, *Media,* Laramie County Library System, Cheyenne WY. 307-634-3561

Norster, Rayna Lee, *Librn,* Analytical Systems Engineering Corp Library, Burlington MA. 617-272-7910

Norten, Melanie, *Cat,* University of Iowa Libraries (Law Library), Iowa City IA. 319-353-5968

North, Clara, *Librn,* Barre Town Public Library, East Barre VT. 802-476-5118

North, Jean, *Doc,* NASA (Technical Library), Moffett Field CA. 415-965-5157

North, John, *Dir,* Ryerson Polytechnical Institute, Donald Mordell Learning Resources Centre, Toronto ON. 416-595-5331

North, LaLee D, *Librn,* United States Air Force (Clinic Medical Library), Randolph AFB TX. 512-652-1110

North, Lois, *ILL & Circ,* Silverton Public Library, Gladys Hoyt Memorial Library, Silverton OR. 503-873-5173

North, Margaret S, *In Charge,* Enoch Pratt Free Library (Saint Paul Street), Baltimore MD. 301-396-5430, 396-5395

North, Patricia, *Ch,* Troy Public Library, Troy NY. 518-274-7071

Northcott, J, *In Charge,* Allied Chemical Corp, Chemicals Company Buffalo Research Library, Buffalo NY. 716-827-6229

Northcutt, Barbara L, *Librn,* United States Army (Saint Louis Area Support Center, Recreational Library), Granite City IL. 618-452-4332

Northcutt, Jane, *Dir,* Ponca City Library, Ponca City OK. 405-762-6311

Northenscold, Doris, *Chief, Cent Libr Servs,* Minneapolis Public Library & Information Center, Minneapolis MN. 612-372-6500

Northern, Bertha, *Film Supvr,* Kansas City Public Library, Kansas City MO. 816-221-2685

Northrop, Alice S, *Asst Librn,* Dean Junior College, E Ross Anderson Library, Franklin MA. 617-528-9100, Ext 261

Northrop, Everett H, *Dir,* United States Merchant Marine Academy, Schuyler Otis Bland Memorial Library, Kings Point NY. 516-482-8200, Ext 500

Northrup, Diana, *Ref,* University of New Mexico General Library (Medical Center Library), Albuquerque NM. 505-277-2311

Northrup, Ingrid, *Librn,* Vermontville Public Library, Vermontville MI. 517-726-1262

Northway, Philip E, *Dir,* Lowell City Library, Subregional Headquarters for Eastern Massachusetts Regional System, Lowell MA. 617-454-8821, Ext 300

Norton, Alice K, *Actg Librn,* Colfax Public Library, Colfax IN. 317-324-2915

Norton, C E, *Librn,* Crowley Ridge Regional Library (Tyronza Branch), Tyronza AR. 501-487-2168

Norton, Carol, *Librn,* United States Army (Fort Myer Post Library), Fort Myer VA. 703-692-9574, 692-9650

Norton, Carol K, *Librn,* United States Army (Fort Lesley J McNair Post Library), Washington DC. 202-693-8622

Norton, Dorothy, *Libr Technician,* San Diego County Library (Fallbrook Branch), Fallbrook CA. 714-728-2373
Norton, Eleanor, *Librn,* Granville Public Library, Granville VT. 802-767-3951
Norton, Frank M, *Lectr,* Baylor University, Dept of Library Science, TX. 817-755-2410
Norton, Frank M, *Chief Librn,* Veterans Administration, Hospital Library Service, Marlin TX. 817-883-3511, Ext 249
Norton, Jimmie S, *Librn,* United States Air Force (Hurlburt Base Library), Eglin AFB FL. 904-884-6504
Norton, Karhryne, *Ad,* Orchard Park Public Library, Orchard Park NY. 716-662-9851
Norton, Linda, *Librn,* Lincoln Ladies Aid Library, Lincoln VT. 802-453-2126
Norton, Linda N, *Librn,* Edgartown Free Public Library, Edgartown MA. 617-627-4221
Norton, M, *Supvr,* Edmonton Public Library (Woodcroft), Edmonton AB. 403-455-4559
Norton, Margaret, *Ad & Acq,* Sturgis Public Library, Sturgis MI. 616-651-7907, 651-2321
Norton, Marguerite, *Spec Coll,* Fort Lewis College Library, Durango CO. 303-247-7738
Norton, Mildred, *Acq,* University of Scranton, Alumni Memorial Library, Scranton PA. 717-961-7525
Norton, Myra, *Chairman,* Hillsborough Community College plant City Center, Learning Resources Center, Plant City FL. 813-223-1761
Norton, Nancy, *Ch,* Logan Library, Logan UT. 801-752-2365
Norton, Pamela, *Ch,* Prince George Public Library, Prince George BC. 604-563-9251
Norton, Patsy G, *Dir,* Wharton County Junior College, J M Hodges Learning Center, Wharton TX. 713-532-4560, Ext 36
Norton, Phoebe, *Librn,* Magrath Municipal Library, Magrath AB. 403-758-3262
Norton, Robert P, *In Charge,* First Federal Savings & Loan Association Library, Fort Wayne IN. 219-423-2377, Ext 284, 285
Norton, Sandra, *AV & Sr Servs,* Ottumwa Public Library, Ottumwa IA. 515-682-7563
Norton, Susan Chapman, *Media,* Lurleen B Wallace State Junior College Library, Andalusia AL. 205-222-6591, Ext 265
Norton, Sylvia, *Librn,* Walker Memorial Hospital, Medical Library, Avon Park FL. 813-453-7511
Norton, Wanda, *Librn,* Pima Public Library, Pima AZ. 602-485-2822
Norum, Daniel C, *Ref,* Ames Public Library, Ames IA. 515-232-4404
Norvell, Belinda, *Tech Serv & Cat,* Hardin-Simmons University, Richardson Library, Abilene TX. 915-677-7281, Ext 236
Norvell, Geneva, *Librn,* Saint John's Hospital, Health Sciences Library, Tulsa OK. 918-744-2345
Norwalk, Nancy, *Librn,* Philip Read Memorial Library, Plainfield NH. 603-675-6866
Norwalk, Sylvia, *Chief Info Consult,* Community Council of Greater New York, Agency Resources Services Library, New York NY. 212-777-5000
Norway, Cynthia, *Asst Librn,* McCome Public Library, McComb OH. 419-293-5425
Norwitch, Linda, *Librn,* Minnesota Pollution Control Agency Library, Roseville MN. 612-296-7373
Norwood, Claudia, *On-Line Servs,* Environmental Protection Agency, Headquarters Library, Washington DC. 202-755-0308
Norwood, Flint, *Dir,* Iredell County Public Library, Statesville NC. 704-872-6512
Norwood, Lorice, *Librn,* Sacred Heart Seminary Library, Washington DC. 202-526-7070
Norwood, Scott M, *ILL & Ref,* Barry-Lawrence Regional Library, Monett MO. 417-235-6646
Noselson, Judith, *Chief Librn,* South Nassau Communities Hospital, Jules Redish Memorial Medical Library, Oceanside NY. 516-764-2600, Ext 258
Noskowitz, Laura, *ILL,* Pratt Institute Library, Brooklyn NY. 212-636-3684
Nosseir, Sawsan, *Asst Dir & Ad,* Ossining Public Library, Ossining NY. 941-2416; 941-9174
Noteboom, Rebecca, *Instr,* Northwestern College, Library Science Program, IA. 712-722-4821
Notheisen, Margaret, *Acq,* University of Illinois at the Medical Center, Library of the Health Sciences, Chicago IL. 312-996-8974

Nothhelfer, Helen, *Librn,* Genesee District Library (McFarland Public Library), Grand Blanc MI. 313-694-5310
Nothum, Lynne M, *Dir,* Lackawanna Public Library, Lackawanna NY. 716-823-0630
Nott, Nancy, *Librn,* Hawaii State Library System (Liliha), Honolulu HI. 808-537-9991
Nottingham, Gloria, *Ch,* Richmond Public Library, Richmond VA. 804-780-4256
Nottingham, Sharon, *Commun Servs,* Onondaga County Public Library System, Syracuse NY. 315-473-2702
Nouza, Helen, *Librn,* Frederick Eugene Lykes Jr Memorial County Library (West Side Branch), Spring Hill FL. 904-683-9000
Novacek, Doreen, *Librn,* Dwight Community Library, Dwight NE. 402-566-2755
Novak, Elaine, *Librn,* Acton Public Library, Old Saybrook CT. 203-388-2037
Novak, Gloria, *Actg Librn,* University of California, Berkeley (Engineering), Berkeley CA. 415-642-3339
Novak, Janice Ryan, *In Charge,* Cleveland Public Library (Public Administration Library), Cleveland OH. 216-623-2919
Novak, Lorrine, *Circ,* Wheaton Public Library, Wheaton IL. 312-668-1374
Novak, Sister Carol Ann, *Dir,* College of Saint Francis Library, Joliet IL. 815-740-3448
Novak, Sister Carol Ann, *Assoc Prof,* College of Saint Francis, Library Science Program, IL. 815-740-3446
Novak, Susan, *Ch,* Stanislaus County Free Library, Modesto CA. 209-526-6821
Novak, Therese, *Asst Librn,* Mahoning Law Library Association, Youngstown OH. 216-747-2000, Ext 260
Novak, Vickie L, *Admin Libr,* Acorn Public Library District, Oak Forest IL. 312-687-3700
Novak, Victor, *Dir,* University of Santa Clara, Michel Orradre Library, Santa Clara CA. 408-984-4411
Novick, Frances, *Med Librn,* Mountainside Hospital (Frank A Assmann Memorial Library), Montclair NJ. 201-746-6000
Novicki, Margaret, *Dir,* African-American Institute Library, New York NY. 212-949-5666
Novotny, Thomas W, *Dep Dir, Cong Res Serv,* Library of Congress, Washington DC. 202-287-5000
Nowack, Beryl, *Tech Serv,* Bethpage Public Library, Bethpage NY. 516-913-3907
Nowack, Mary L, *Librn,* Pfizer, Inc, John L Smith Memorial Research Library, Maywood NJ. 201-845-5665
Nowak, Denise, *Ch,* Mount Horeb Public Library, Mount Horeb WI. 608-437-5021
Nowak, Joyce, *In Charge,* Milwaukee Public Library (Tippecanoe), Milwaukee WI. 414-278-3085
Nowaki, Junko, *Ref,* University of Hawaii at Hilo Libraries, Hilo HI. 808-961-9344
Nowakowski, Jane, *Ref,* Montclair Free Public Library, Montclair NJ. 201-744-0500
Nowell, Glenna, *Dir,* Gardiner Public Library, Gardiner ME. 207-582-3312
Nowell, Mary Ann, *Chief Librn,* Veterans Administration, Medical Center Libraries, Leavenworth KS. 913-682-2000, Ext 223, 224
Nowicki, Leonard, *Ref,* State University College at Buffalo, Edward H Butler Library, Buffalo NY. 716-878-6302
Nowinski, Barbara, *Librn,* Leland Township Public Library, Leland MI. 616-256-9152
Nowland, Rex, *Ref,* Kansas City Kansas Public Library, Kansas City KS. 913-621-3073
Nowlin, Linda, *Librn,* Austin Public Library (North Loop), Austin TX. 512-472-5433
Nowoc, Georgeana, *Pub Servs,* University of Michigan-Flint Library, Flint MI. 313-762-3400
Noyer, William L, *Librn,* Veterans Administration, Medical Center Library, Fresno CA. 209-225-6100, Ext 259
Noyes, Claude, *Acq,* University of Rochester, Rush Rhees Library, Rochester NY. 716-275-4461
Noyes, Gladys, *YA,* Beaman Memorial Public Library, West Boylston MA. 617-835-3711
Noyes, Judith O, *Dir,* Sherrill-Kenwood Free Library, Sherrill NY. 315-363-5980
Noyes, Margaret, *Assoc Dir of Extension,* Waco-McLennan County Library, Waco TX. 817-754-4694

Nuby, Mary, *Cat,* Chicago State University, Paul & Emily Douglas Library, Chicago IL. 312-995-2254
Nuernberg, Donna, *Librn,* Wausau Insurance Companies Library, Wausau WI. 715-847-8504
Nuessle, Selma, *Tech Serv & Cat,* San Antonio Public Library, San Antonio TX. 512-299-7790
Nuessle, Selma, *Librn,* San Antonio Public Library (Technical Services), San Antonio TX. 512-299-7827
Nugent, Betty, *Librn,* Alcor Inc, Library, San Antonio TX. 512-349-3771
Nugent, Eleanor, *Proj Coordr,* University of Wisconsin-Madison (School for Workers Library), Madison WI. 608-262-3521
Nugent, John, *Archivist,* University of Kansas Libraries (University Archives), Lawrence KS. 913-864-4188
Nugent, L M, *Media Coordr,* Omega Engineering, Inc, Technical Library, Stamford CT. 203-359-1660
Nugent, Martha, *Librn,* Price Waterhouse & Co Library, Montreal PQ. 514-879-9050
Nugent, Mrs Robert, *Librn,* Deering Public Library, Deering NH. 603-464-3335
Nugent, Robert S, *Dir,* Jersey City State College, Forrest A Irwin Library, Jersey City NJ. 201-547-3026
Nugent, Roberta F, *Librn,* Givaudan Corp Library, Clifton NJ. 201-546-8563
Null, Coralie, *Librn,* Clover Township Public Library, Woodhull IL. 309-934-2680
Null, David, *Instr,* Miami University-Middletown, Library-Media Technical Assistant Program, OH. 513-424-4444, Ext 221
Null, Wanda S, *Dir,* Acton Memorial Library, Acton MA. 617-263-2232, 263-9109
Nulle, Greg, *Asst Librn, ILL & Ad,* Bound Brook Memorial Library, Bound Brook NJ. 201-356-0043
Numez, Jose M, *Photog Lab,* University of Puerto Rico Library, Jose M Lazaro Memorial Library, Rio Piedras PR. 809-764-0000, Ext 3296
Nunelee, John, *Dir,* Sam Houston State University Library, Huntsville TX. 713-295-6211, Ext 2848
Nunes, Robert, *In Charge,* Sernco, Inc, Metronics Assocs, Inc Library, Santa Clara CA. 408-737-0550
Nunez, Frank, *Dir,* Southwest Virginia Community College Library, Richlands VA. 703-964-2555
Nunn, Anabel, *Librn,* Arlington Public Library (Southeast), Arlington TX. 817-275-3321
Nunn, Betty, *Librn,* Grand County Libraries (Kremmling Branch), Kremmling CO. 303-724-9228
Nunn, Brenda J, *Coordr Libr Servs,* Durham Technical Institute, Learning Resources Center, Durham NC. 919-596-9311, Ext 228
Nunn, Chris, *Librn,* University of Wisconsin-Madison (Agricultural Economics Library), Madison WI. 608-262-3521
Nunn, Helen, *Librn,* Gilbert Public Library, Gilbert AZ. 602-892-3141
Nunn, Victor, *Acq,* McMaster University, Hamilton ON. 416-525-9140
Nunn, Jr, Theodore J, *Media,* Dayton & Montgomery County Public Library, Dayton OH. 513-224-1651
Nunnelee, Janice, *Coordr Pub Servs,* Southeast Missouri State University, Kent Library, Cape Girardeau MO. 314-651-2235
Nurmi, Melinda, *Dir,* Pulaski County Library, Pulaski VA. 703-980-8888, Ext 288
Nurse, Melba, *Librn,* Houston Public Library (Allen Parkway), Houston TX. 713-659-7257
Nurse, Pamela, *ILL,* Saint Patrick's Seminary, McKeon Memorial Library, Menlo Park CA. 415-322-2224
Nurss, Karen T, *Ch,* Nogales City-Santa Cruz County Library, Nogales Public Library, Nogales AZ. 602-287-3343, 287-6310
Nuse, Ron, *Media,* Simmons College, Beatley Library, Boston MA. 617-738-2241
Nuss, Mrs Dwight, *Librn,* Sutton Public Library, Sutton NE. 402-773-5259
Nussbaum, Irwin, *Librn,* Brooklyn Public Library (Kings Highway), Brooklyn NY. 212-375-3037
Nusser, Charlotte, *Librn,* Tucson Citizen Library, Tucson AZ. 602-294-4433, Ext 257, 258, 259
Nutley, Mary, *ILL,* Queensborough Community College Library, Bayside NY. 212-631-6226

Nuttall, D, *Libr Tech,* Queen's University at Kingston (Mathematics), Kingston ON. 613-547-5720

Nuttall, Virginia, *Media,* Provo City Public Library, Provo UT. 801-373-1494

Nutter, Carol, *ILL,* Morehead State University, Johnson Camden-Julian Carroll Library, Morehead KY. 606-783-2250

Nutter, Danice, *Librn,* Louisville Free Public Library (Highland Park), Louisville KY. 502-367-1125

Nutter, Daniel L, *Dir, Ref & Spec Coll,* Southwestern College, Memorial Library, Winfield KS. 316-221-4150, Ext 25

Nutting, Becky, *Govt Docs,* Bangor Public Library, Bangor ME. 207-947-8336

Nutty, David, *Media,* Atlantic County Library, Pleasantville NJ. 609-646-8699, 645-7121, 625-2776

Ny, Pauline, *Librn,* Memorial Hospital of Dupage County, Marguardt Memorial Library, Elmhurst IL. 312-833-1400, Ext 591

Nycum, Peter S, *Dir,* Lewis & Clark College (Paul L Boley Law Library), Portland OR. 503-244-1181, Ext 685

Nycum, Ruth, *Doc,* California State University Fullerton Library, Fullerton CA. 714-773-2714

Nye, Helen, *Librn,* Newbury Public Library, Newbury NH. 603-763-5803

Nye, Helen, *YA,* Tufts Library, Public Libraries of Weymouth, Weymouth MA. 617-337-1402

Nye, James, *Acq & Bibliog Instr,* Gustavus Adolphus College, Folke Bernadotte Memorial Library, Saint Peter MN. 507-931-4300, Ext 2301

Nygaard, Opal L, *Librn,* Wesley Public Library, Wesley IA. 515-679-4214

Nyhan, Catherine A, *Librn,* Anaconda American Brass Co, Research Center Library, Waterbury CT. 203-574-8936

Nyitray, Nancy, *On-Line Servs,* Saint Clair County Community College, Learning Resources Center, Port Huron MI. 313-984-3881, Ext 278

Nyitray, Nancy, *Pub Servs Libr,* Saint Clair County Community College, Learning Resources Center, Port Huron MI. 313-984-3881, Ext 278

Nyland, Anne, *Dir,* Cornwall Public Library, Cornwall ON. 613-932-4796

Nyland, Anne, *Dir,* Seaway Valley Libraries, Simon Fraser Centennial Library, Cornwall ON. 613-932-3699

Nyland, H, *In Charge,* Stormont, Dundas & Glengarry County Library, Cornwall ON. 613-938-9561, 932-3699

Nylin, Miriam S, *Librn,* California State Resources Agency Library, Sacramento CA. 916-445-7752

Nyquist, Bro Paul, *Librn,* Assumption Abbey Library, Richardton ND. 701-974-3315

Nyquist, Corinne, *African,* State University of New York, College at New Paltz, Sojourner Truth Library, New Paltz NY. 914-257-2204

Nyquist, Norma, *Dir,* Santa Monica College Library, Santa Monica CA. 213-450-5150

Nyren, Dorothy, *Chief, Pub Servs,* Brooklyn Public Library, Brooklyn NY. 212-780-7712

Nystrom, Charles W, *Mgr,* R J Reynolds Tobacco Company (Science Information Library), Winston-Salem NC. 919-777-5000

Nystrom, Luella, *Librn,* Scandia City Library, Scandia KS. 913-335-2271

Nytes, Jacqueline, *Ad,* Appleton Public Library, Appleton WI. 414-734-7171

O

O, Taekun, *Librn & On-Line Servs,* Mercy Hospital & Medical Center, Medical Library, Chicago IL. 312-567-2365

O'Bannon, Emma Lou, *Ch,* Brazoria County Library, Angleton TX. 713-849-0591

O'Bannon, Pat, *Librn,* William F Laman Public Library, North Little Rock AR. 501-758-1720

O'Bannon, Paul, *Librn,* California Maritime Academy Library, Vallejo CA. 707-644-5601, Ext 265

O'Bar, Jack, *Dir,* University of Alaska, Anchorage Library, Anchorage AK. 907-263-1825

O'Boyle, Lillian, *Local Hist,* Franklin Park Public Library District, Franklin Park IL. 312-455-6016

O'Brien, Anne, *Circ,* Memorial Hall Library, (Subregional Headquarters for Eastern Massachusetts Regional System), Andover MA. 617-475-6960

O'Brien, Barbara, *Media,* Buena Park Library District, Buena Park CA. 714-826-4100

O'Brien, Betty, *Librn,* Hamilton College (Science), Clinton NY. 315-859-7130

O'Brien, Betty A, *Dir,* Saint Leonard College Library, Dayton OH. 513-433-0480, Ext 325

O'Brien, Bonnie L, *Dir,* Shrewsbury Free Public Library, Shrewsbury MA. 617-842-0081

O'Brien, Daniel E, *Curator,* United States Army (Ordnance Center & School Ordnance Museum Library), Aberdeen Proving Ground MD. 301-278-3602

O'Brien, Dennis, *Ad & Ref,* Middle Island Public Library, Middle Island NY. 516-924-4160

O'Brien, Diane, *Dir,* Florham Park Public Lirbary, Florham Park NJ. 201-377-2694

O'Brien, Elizabeth, *Tech Serv,* Corona Public Library, Corona CA. 714-736-2381

O'Brien, Elizabeth, *Asst Dir, Cat & Acq,* Merrimack College, McQuade Library, North Andover MA. 617-683-7111, Ext 210

O'Brien, Elizabeth A, *Librn,* Erie County Library System (Edinboro Branch), Edinboro PA. 814-734-4497

O'Brien, Elizabeth A, *Head,* Erie County Library System (Southeast), Erie PA. 814-825-2147

O'Brien, Elmer J, *Dir,* United Theological Seminary Library, Dayton OH. 513-278-5817

O'Brien, Esther, *Asst Dir & Acq,* Frederick E Parlin Memorial Library, Everett MA. 617-387-2550

O'Brien, Evelyn M, *Librn,* Eastern Oregon Hospital & Training Center Libraries, Pendleton OR. 503-276-1711

O'Brien, Frances E, *Librn,* Carney Hospital, Medical Library, Dorchester MA. 617-296-4000, Ext 221, 227

O'Brien, Gail, *Librn,* Dover Plains Library, Dover Plains NY. 914-877-6805

O'Brien, Hugh, *Acq,* Shippensburg State College, Ezra Lehman Memorial Library, Shippensburg PA. 717-532-1463

O'Brien, James M, *Librn,* Oak Lawn Public Library, Oak Lawn IL. 312-422-4990

O'Brien, Jean, *Ad,* Public Library of Steubenville & Jefferson County, Steubenville OH. 614-282-9782

O'Brien, Julie M, *Librn,* United States Air Force (Base Library), Pease AFB NH. 603-436-0100

O'Brien, Margaret, *Librn,* Legal Services Society, Legal Resource Centre, Vancouver BC. 604-689-0741

O'Brien, Marie, *Librn,* Howrey & Simon, Law Library, Washington DC. 202-783-0800

O'Brien, Marlys Howe, *Dir & Acq,* Kitchigami Regional Library, Pine River MN. 218-587-2171

O'Brien, Mary Frances, *Librn,* Northern Research & Engineering Corp Library, Woburn MA. 617-935-9050, Ext 232

O'Brien, Mary Jo, *Ref,* Olathe Public Library, Olathe KS. 913-764-2259

O'Brien, Moira, *AV,* Haverstraw Kings Daughters Public Library, Haverstraw NY. 914-429-3445

O'Brien, Patrick M, *Dir,* Cuyahoga County Public Library, Cleveland OH. 216-398-1800

O'Brien, Peggy, *Librn,* Thornton Community College, Learning Resources Center, South Holland IL. 312-596-2000, Ext 240

O'Brien, Phillip M, *Dir,* Whittier College (Bonnie Bell Wardman Library), Whittier CA. 213-693-0771, Ext 223

O'Brien, Robert A, *Dir,* Green Haven Correctional Facility Library, Stormville NY. 914-226-2711, Ext 3443

O'Bryan, Sandy, *Acq & Commun Servs,* Bay County Public Library Association, Northwest Regional Library System, Panama City FL. 904-785-3457

O'Bryant, Alice-Ann, *Ch,* Goshen Public Library, Goshen IN. 219-533-9531

O'Bryant, J Frederick, *Media,* University of Virginia (Claude Moore Health Sciences Library), Charlottesville VA. 804-924-5444

O'Bryant, Mathilda B, *Cat,* University of Notre Dame Library, Notre Dame IN. 219-283-7317

O'Cana, Buddy, *Librn,* Carrie Tingley Hospital Library, Truth or Consequences NM. 505-894-2121

O'Clair, Robert, *Dir,* Manhattanville College Library, Purchase NY. 914-946-9600, Ext 274

O'Connell, Adele, *Circ,* Chester County Library & District Center, Exton PA. 215-363-0884

O'Connell, Edward M, *Librn,* New York County Lawyers' Association Library, New York NY. 212-267-6646

O'Connell, Eileen, *Librn,* John Hay Whitney & Co Library, New York NY. 212-757-0500

O'Connell, Geraldine, *Dir & ILL,* Weston Public Library, Weston CT. 203-227-7679

O'Connell, Helen, *ILL & Acq,* McKinley Memorial Library, Niles OH. 216-652-1704

O'Connell, Linda, *Br Coordr,* Austin Public Library, Austin TX. 512-472-5433

O'Connell, Margie J, *Librn,* Calumet Public-School Library, Calumet MI. 906-337-0811

O'Connell, Michelle D, *Chief Librn,* Veterans Administration, Hospital Library Service, Buffalo NY. 716-834-9200

O'Connell, Sister Marguerite, *Librn,* Saint Francis Hospital, Medical Library, Miami Beach FL. 305-868-5000, Ext 3149

O'Connell, Thomas F, *Univ Librn,* Boston College Libraries, Chestnut Hill MA. 617-969-0100, Ext 3195

O'Conner, Anna, *Librn,* Piedmont Regional Library (Social Circle Branch), Social Circle GA. 404-867-2762

O'Conner, Elaine P, *Asst Librn,* Earl K Long Hospital, Medical Library, Baton Rouge LA. 504-356-3361, Ext 400

O'Conner, Hugh, *ILL,* Wayne State University Libraries, Detroit MI. 313-557-4020

O'Conner, Mike, *On-Line Servs,* Mid-York Library System, Utica NY. 315-735-8328

O'Conner, Patricia, *Collection Development,* North Dakota State University Library, Fargo ND. 701-237-8876

O'Conner, Sister Rose Theresa, *Acq & Ref,* King's College Library, London ON. 519-433-3491, Ext 44

O'Connor, Beth, *Librn,* Northwestern National Life Insurance Co Library, Minneapolis MN. 612-372-5606

O'Connor, Betsy, *Librn,* Burlington County Memorial Hospital, Health-Science Library, Mount Holly NJ. 609-267-0700, Ext 297

O'Connor, Daniel O, *Asst Prof,* Rutgers-The State University of New Jersey, Graduate School of Library & Information Studies, NJ. 201-932-7500

O'Connor, Denis R, *Librn,* Debevoise, Plimpton, Lyons & Gates Law Library, New York NY. 212-752-6400, Ext 278

O'Connor, Dorothy, *Circ,* Montclair State College, Harry A Sprague Library, Upper Montclair NJ. 201-893-4291

O'Connor, Elizabeth, *Rare Bks & Spec Coll,* Manhattanville College Library, Purchase NY. 914-946-9600, Ext 274

O'Connor, Grace T, *Dir,* Clark Public Library, Clark NJ. 201-388-5999

O'Connor, Helen G, *Dir,* Roseville Public Library, Roseville CA. 916-783-7158

O'Connor, John B, *Librn,* Laurel Heights Hospital, Medical Library, Shelton CT. 203-734-2593

O'Connor, Joseph E, *Info Servs,* University of Bridgeport, Magnus Wahlstrom Library, Bridgeport CT. 203-576-4740

O'Connor, Karen, *Commun Servs,* Waterford Township Public Library, Pontiac MI. 313-674-4831

O'Connor, Kathleen, *Librn,* Union Carbide Corp (New York Regional Computer Center Library), Tarrytown NY. 914-345-5091

O'Connor, Kathryn, *Librn,* Niagara Falls Public Library (LaSalle), Niagara Falls NY. 716-283-8309

O'Connor, Linda, *Ch,* Tampa-Hillsborough County Public Library System, Tampa FL. 813-223-8947

O'Connor, Marihelen, *Librn,* Scottsdale Memorial Hospital, Health Sciences Library, Scottsdale AZ. 602-994-9616, Ext 2896

O'Connor, Maryann, *AV,* Bentley College, Solomon R Baker Library, Waltham MA. 617-891-2231

O'Connor, Molly, *Librn,* Dartmouth College (Sherman Art), Hanover NH. 603-646-2305

O'Connor, N, *Librn,* South Woodbury Public Library, South Woodbury VT. 802-452-8951

O'Connor, Patricia, *In Charge,* Bureau of Land Management Library, New Orleans LA. 504-589-6541

O'Connor, Sara B, *Librn,* Scoville Memorial Library, Salisbury CT. 203-435-2838

O'Connor, Thomas, *Ref,* Manhattan College, Cardinal Hayes Library, Bronx NY. 212-548-1400, Ext 366 & 367

O'Connor, Thomas J, *Dir,* Bethesda Hospital, Information Resource Center, Cincinnati OH. 513-961-0966

O'Connor, William J, *Asst to Dir,* Albany Public Library, Albany NY. 518-449-3380

O'Dell, Charles, *Librn,* Ellis Fischel State Cancer Hospital Library, Columbia MO. 314-875-2100, Ext 316, 315

O'Dell, Frances L, *Off Mgr,* International Council for Educational Development, Library & Documentation Center, Centerbrook CT. 203-767-0155

O'Dell, Harold, *Eve Librn,* Marycrest College, Cone Library, Davenport IA. 319-326-9254

O'Dell, Lynn M, *Dir,* Carol Stream Public Library, Carol Stream IL. 312-653-0755

O'Dell, Roberta, *Librn,* North Arkansas Regional Library (Green Forest Public), Green Forest AR. 501-438-6700

O'Dell, Virginia Mae, *Dir,* Paola Free Library, Paola KS. 913-294-3866

O'Doherty, Kathleen, *Asst Dir & Cat,* Bradford College, Madaleine Cooney Hemingway Library, Haverhill MA. 617-372-7161, Ext 386

O'Donnell, Angelina, *Dir,* Washington Star Library, Washington DC. 202-484-4375

O'Donnell, Ellen, *On-Line Servs,* Saint John Hospital, Medical Library, Detroit MI. 313-343-3733

O'Donnell, Jane S, *Librn,* Cranberry Public Library, Mars PA. 412-776-9100

O'Donnell, Joanne, *Ref,* Cecil County Public Library, Elkton MD. 301-398-0914

O'Donnell, Kathleen T, *Acq,* Rohm & Haas Co, Research Div, Information Services Dept, Spring House PA. 215-643-0200

O'Donnell, Linda, *Ch,* Wilbraham Public Library, Wilbraham MA. 413-596-6142

O'Donnell, Marian, *Sci-Tech,* San Francisco Public Library, San Francisco CA. 415-558-4235

O'Donnell, Susan, *Librn,* Mount Pocono Public Library, Mount Pocono PA. 717-839-6031

O'Donnell, William, *Librn,* Thames Valley State Technical College Library, Norwich CT. 203-889-8311

O'Donovan, Phyllis, *Chief Librn,* CTB-McGraw Hill Library, Monterey CA. 408-649-8400

O'Flaherty, Margaret, *Librn,* Ford Aerospace & Communications Corp, Communications Systems Library, Willow Grove PA. 215-659-7700

O'Gorman, Ruth, *Acq,* James Madison University, Madison Memorial Library, Harrisonburg VA. 703-433-6150

O'Grady, R, *In Charge,* University of Toronto Libraries (Dept of Zoology), Toronto ON. 416-978-3492

O'Halloran, Charles, *Dir,* Missouri State Library, Jefferson City MO. 314-751-4214

O'Halloran, Louis R, *Chief Gen Libr Circ & Shelving,* Boston Public Library, Eastern Massachusetts Library System, Boston MA. 617-536-5400

O'Hara, A N, *Bus Mgr,* Great Lakes Historical Society, Clarence S Metcalf Research Library, Vermilion OH. 216-967-3467

O'Hara, Carolyn, *Librn,* Marsh & McLennan, Inc Information Center, New York NY. 212-997-7800

O'Hara, Edward, *Dir,* Sacred Heart University Library, Bridgeport CT. 203-374-9441

O'Hara, Francis C, *Dir,* Holy Apostles College Library, Cromwell CT. 203-635-5311, Ext 20

O'Hara, Frederic J, *Prof,* Long Island University, Palmer Graduate Library School, NY. 516-299-2855 & 299-2856

O'Hara, Kerry, *Librn,* Mercy Hospital (School of Nursing Library), Scranton PA. 717-344-8571, Ext 292, 293

O'Hara, Mary, *Field Consult,* Onondaga County Public Library System, Syracuse NY. 315-473-2702

O'Hara, Mary, *Librn,* Onondaga County Public Library System (Northeast Community Center), Syracuse NY. 315-473-2702

O'Hara, Mary, *Librn,* Onondaga County Public Library System (Southwest Community Center), Syracuse NY. 315-473-2702

O'Hare, Norma, *ILL, Ad & Ref,* Denville Free Public Library, Denville NJ. 201-627-6555

O'Hearn, Konnie J, *Librn,* Columbian Newspaper Library, Vancouver WA. 206-694-3391, Ext 252

O'Keefe, David G, *Video Servs,* Tri-County Regional Library, Rome GA. 404-291-9360

O'Keefe, Fran, *Dir,* Spirit Lake Public Library, Spirit Lake IA. 712-336-2667

O'Keefe, Robert J, *Dir,* State Police Academy Library, Framingham MA. 617-879-5051

O'Keeffe, R L, *Exec Dir,* Houston Area Research Library Consortium, (HARLIC), TX. 713-527-8101, Ext 2642

O'Laughlin, Mary, *Chief Librn,* United States Army (Fort Riley Branch Post Library), Fort Riley KS. 913-239-3630

O'Leary, Anne J, *Librn,* Chicago Public Library (Wrightwood), Chicago IL. 312-471-2696

O'Leary, Barbara, *Librn,* Nippersink District Library, Richmond IL. 815-678-4014

O'Leary, C B, *Librn,* Midland Doherty Limited Library, Toronto ON. 416-361-6063

O'Leary, Francis B, *Dir,* Saint Louis University (Medical Center Library), Saint Louis MO. 314-664-9800

O'Leary, Patrick, *Librn,* Crosby, Heafey, Roach & May, Law Library, Oakland CA. 415-834-4820, Ext 511

O'Leary, Timothy J, *Librn,* Human Relations Area Files, Inc Library, New Haven CT. 203-777-2334

O'Leary, II, Maurice, *Pub Servs,* Frederick Community College, Learning Resource Center, Frederick MD. 301-694-1242

O'Mahoney, Elizabeth, *Librn,* Goldman, Sachs & Co Library, New York NY. 212-676-7400

O'Malley, Ellen, *Per,* Carnegie Library of Pittsburgh, Pittsburgh PA. 412-622-3100

O'Malley, Kenneth, *Dir,* Catholic Theological Union Library, Chicago IL. 312-324-8000, Ext 320

O'Malley, Mary, *Ref,* Waterloo Public Library, Waterloo IA. 319-291-4521

O'Mara, Cindi, *Librn,* Monroe Developmental Center, Lacille Anderson Client Library, Rochester NY. 716-461-2800, Ext 220

O'Meara, John H, *Prof,* Kean College of New Jersey, Library-Media Program, NJ. 201-527-2626, 527-2071

O'Meara, Kathleen, *Asst to Commissioner,* Chicago Public Library, Chicago IL. 312-269-2900

O'Meara, Marie, *Librn,* United States Air Force (School of Health Care Science Academic Library), Sheppard AFB TX. 817-851-2256

O'Neal, Sally, *Educ,* Valdosta State College Library, Valdosta GA. 912-247-3228

O'Neal, Wayne, *Acq,* University of North Alabama, Collier Library, Florence AL. 205-766-4100, Ext 241

O'Neal, Jr, Ellis E, *Dir,* Andover Newton Theological School, Franklin Trask Library, Newton Centre MA. 617-964-1100, Ext 140

O'Neil, B Joseph, *Supv Rd Servs,* Boston Public Library, Eastern Massachusetts Library System, Boston MA. 617-536-5400

O'Neil, Barbara, *Tech Serv & Cat,* Sandwich Public Library, Sandwich MA. 617-888-0625

O'Neil, Eleanor, *Librn,* Brockton Public Library System (East), Brockton MA. 617-584-1263

O'Neil, S, *Librn,* Canada Department of National Defense (Maritime Technical Library), Ottawa ON. 613-996-2477, 2324

O'Neill, B J, *Librn,* Borough of York Public Library (Weston), Toronto ON. 416-241-1111

O'Neill, Carmel, *Librn,* University of Connecticut at Stamford Library, Stamford Branch Library, Stamford CT. 203-322-3466

O'Neill, Dorothy, *Librn,* Castleton Free Library, Castleton VT. 802-468-5574

O'Neill, Edward T, *Dean,* Case Western Reserve University, School of Library Science, OH. 216-368-3500

O'Neill, Edward T, *Assoc Prof,* State University of New York at Buffalo, School of Information & Library Studies, NY. 716-636-2412

O'Neill, Evelyn, *Dir,* Morley Stanwood Community Public Library, Morley MI. 616-856-4298

O'Neill, Frances, *Ref,* Canadian Embassy Library, Washington DC. 202-785-1400, Ext 212 & 366

O'Neill, Isabella, *Librn,* William D Himmelreich Memorial Library, Lewisburg PA. 717-523-8562

O'Neill, James E, *Acting Archivist,* National Archives & Records Service (National Archives), Washington DC. 202-523-3218

O'Neill, James M, *Admin Mgr,* Boston College Libraries, Chestnut Hill MA. 617-969-0100, Ext 3195

O'Neill, James M, *ILL & Ref,* Public Library of the District of Columbia, Martin Luther King Memorial Library, Washington DC. 202-727-1101

O'Neill, Jean, *Librn, On-Line Servs & Bibliog Instr,* Southern Nevada Memorial Hospital, Medical Library, Las Vegas NV. 702-383-2368, 383-2369

O'Neill, Mary, *Librn,* Chase Library, West Harwich MA. 617-432-2610

O'Neill, Mary, *Dir,* Northvale Library Association, Northvale NJ. 201-768-4784

O'Neill, Mary Beth, *Librn,* Syracuse Research Corp Library, Syracuse NY. 315 425 5100, Ext 200

O'Neill, Mary Jo, *Dir,* Riverside County Art & Culture Center Library, Edward-Dean Museum of Decorative Arts, Cherry Valley CA. 714-845-2626

O'Neill, Robert, *Rare Bks & Spec Coll,* Indiana State University, Cunningham Memorial Library, Terre Haute IN. 812-232-6311, Ext 2451

O'Neill, Susan, *Cat,* The Medical College of Wisconsin, Inc, Todd Wehr Library, Milwaukee WI. 414-257-8323

O'Rear, Roberta, *Info Assts,* Colgate-Palmolive Co, Technical Information Center Library, Piscataway NJ. 201-463-1212, Ext 277

O'Regan, M, *Chief Librn,* Township of Uxbridge Public Library, Uxbridge ON. 416-852-5231

O'Reilly, Joan, *Librn,* Ocean Falls Public Library Association, Ocean Falls BC. 604-289-3211

O'Reilly, Lorraine, *Librn,* Kellogg Public Library, Kellogg ID. 208-786-7231

O'Reilly, Mary, *Librn,* University of Minnesota Libraries-Twin Cities (Mines & Metallurgy), Minneapolis MN. 612-373-2313

O'Reilly, Rosella, *Ref,* Wilmette Public Library District, Wilmette IL. 312-256-5025

O'Riordan, Georgeanne, *Librn,* Columbia University (Biological Sciences), New York NY. 212-280-2241

O'Rosky, Sandra M, *Librn,* Austin County Library System, Wallis TX. 713-478-6813

O'Rourke, Jan, *Librn,* Gaston, Snow & Ely Barlett Library, Boston MA. 617-426-4600

O'Rourke, Margaret, *Librn,* Potter-Tioga County Library System, Wellsboro PA. 717-724-4459

O'Rourke, Margaret M, *Librn,* Rees-Stealy Medical Group Library, San Diego CA. 714-234-6261, Ext 398

O'Rourke, Martha L, *Dir,* Stillman College, William H Sheppard Library, Tuscaloosa AL. 205-752-2548, Ext 52

O'Rourke, Mary, *Dir,* Avon Public Library, Avon MA. 617-583-0378

O'Rourke, Mary, *ILL,* Saint Francis Xavier University, Angus L Macdonald Library, Antigonish NS. 902-867-2267

O'Rourke, Penny, *Dir,* Byron Public Library District, Byron IL. 815-234-5107

O'Rourke, Vicki, *Circ,* Elisha D Smith Public Library, Menasha WI. 414-729-5166

O'Shea, Candace, *Media,* Bradford College, Madaleine Cooney Hemingway Library, Haverhill MA. 617-372-7161, Ext 386

O'Shea, H William, *Dir,* Wake County Department of the Public Library, Raleigh NC. 919-755-6077

O'Shea, John M, *Dir,* Suffolk County Community College, Western Campus Library, Brentwood NY. 516-348-4522

O'Shea, Patricia R, *Librn,* Texasgulf Inc, Research Library, Stamford CT. 203-358-5135

O'Shell, Louise, *Librn,* New Florence Community Library, New Florence PA. 412-235-2249

O'Shields, Charles, *AV,* Beaufort Technical College, Learning Resource Center, Beaufort SC. 803-524-3380, Ext 236 & 241

O'Shoughnessy, Molly, *Asst Librn,* Catlin Public Library District, Catlin IL. 217-427-2550

O'Sullivan, Elizabeth, *Asst Librn,* Emo Public Library, Emo ON. 807-482-2575

O'Sullivan, G F, *Cat,* Institute for Advanced Study Libraries, Princeton NJ. 609-924-4400

O'Sullivan, Jane C, *Librn,* United States Navy (Medical Library), Oakland CA. 415-639-2031

O'Sullivan, Mrs George A, *Librn,* Clarence Dillion Public Library, Bedminster NJ. 201-234-2325

Oak, Dorothy M, *Librn,* General Telephone & Electronics, GTE Sylvania, Inc, Lighting Center Engineering Library, Danvers MA. 617-777-1900, Ext 2349

Oakes, Dorothy C, *Librn,* Cragsmoor Free Library, Cragsmoor NY. 914-647-4611

Oakes, Mary Grace, *Librn,* Muncie-Center Township Public Library (Webb Hunt), Muncie IN. 317-284-0390

Oakes, Mrs Billie, *Cat,* Milligan College, P H Welshimer Memorial Library, Milligan College TN. 615-929-0116

Oakes, Susan, *Librn,* Ayerst Research Laboratories Library, Chazy NY. 518-846-7123

Oakley, Carolyn C, *Librn,* Vance-Granville Community College, Learning Resources Center, Henderson NC. 919-492-2061, Ext 251

Oakley, Edna, *Librn,* Bergen County Law Library, Hackensack NJ. 201-342-2200

Oakley, Madeleine, *Ref,* State Library of Massachusetts, Boston MA. 617-727-2590

Oakley, Marion, *Acq,* Piedmont Technical College, Learning Resources Center, Roxboro NC. 919-599-1181, Ext 266

Oakley, Robert L, *Librn,* Boston University Libraries (School of Law), Boston MA. 617-353-3151

Oaks, Claire, *Dir,* Flossmoor Public Library, Flossmoor IL. 312-798-4006

Oaksford, Margaret J, *Librn,* Cornell University Libraries (School of Hotel Administration Library), Ithaca NY. 607-256-3673

Oalmann, Mary, *Librn,* United States Army (National Guard Library), New Orleans LA. 504-271-6262

Oalpoel, Carol, *Librn,* Saint Vincent Hospital, Medical Library, Green Bay WI. 414-432-8621

Oates, Carolyn, *Librn,* Horticultural Society of New York, Inc Library, New York NY. 212-757-0915

Oates, Elaine, *Educ,* Texas Southern University Library, Houston TX. 713-527-7121

Oates, Stanton C, *Prof,* Shippensburg State College, Dept of Library Science, PA. 717-532-1472

Oates, Sue, *Tech Serv,* South Oklahoma City Junior College, Learning Resources Center, Oklahoma City OK. 405-682-7574

Oathout, Melvin C, *Chief Librn,* Camarillo State Hospital, Professional Library, Camarillo CA. 484-3661 Ext 2446

Oatman, Mrs Wilfred, *In Charge,* Oxford County Library (Springford Library), Springford ON. 519-842-3889

Obenauer, Wilma, *Tech Serv,* Rawlins Municipal Library, Pierre SD. 605-224-7421

Obenchain, Lynn, *Bkmobile Coordr,* Monroe County Library System, Monroe MI. 313-241-5277

Obenhaus, Adah May, *Cat,* Southwest Texas State University, Learning Resources Center, San Marcos TX. 512-245-2132

Obenrader, Frances, *Acq,* Clarion State College, Rena M Carlson Library, Clarion PA. 814-226-2343

Ober, Michael, *College Librn,* Flathead County Free Library, Kalispell MT. 406-755-5300, Ext 357

Ober, Michael J, *Librn,* Flathead Valley Community College Library, Kalispell MT. 406-755-5222, Ext 212

Oberembt, Kenneth J, *Librn,* University of Scranton, Alumni Memorial Library, Scranton PA. 717-961-7525

Oberhaus, Harriett, *Librn,* Mohave County Library (Lake Havasu City), Lake Havasu City AZ. 602-885-2140

Oberhausen, Judy, *Curator,* Art Center Library, South Bend IN. 219-284-9102

Oberman-Soroka, Cerise, *Ref,* College of Charleston, Robert Scott Small Library, Charleston SC. 803-792-5530

Obermayer, Jean N, *Librn,* Charlotte-Glades Library System (Punta Gorda Public), Punta Gorda FL. 813-639-2049

Oblak, Harriet, *Ref,* Lorain County Community College Library, Elyria OH. 216-365-4191, Ext 201

Oboler, Eli M, *Librn,* Idaho State University Library, Pocatello ID. 208-236-3202

Obourn, Ann, *Acq,* Western Washington University, Mabel Zoe Wilson Library, Bellingham WA. 206-676-3050

Obrochta, Gerald, *Soc Sci,* Chicago Public Library (Social Sciences & History Div), Chicago IL. 312-269-2830

Obsniok, Rebecca, *Librn,* General Motors Corp (Technical Information Center), Warren MI. 313-575-1112

Obst, Alice M, *Librn,* Dames & Moore Library, Los Angeles CA. 213-879-9700

Ocasek, Mary, *Ad,* Maywood Public Library, Maywood IL. 312-343-1847

Ochal, Bethany J, *Dir,* Orange County Law Library, Santa Ana CA. 714-834-3397

Ocheltree, Colleen, *Asst Librn,* Sutton Public Library, Sutton WV. 304-765-7224

Ochs, Allan, *Librn,* Butte County Library (Paradise Libr), Paradise CA. 916-872-2961, 872-2965

Ochs, Martha, *Librn,* Franklin Township Free Public Library, Malaga NJ. 609-694-2833

Ochs, Michael, *Librn,* Harvard University Library (Eda Kuhn Loeb Music Library), Cambridge MA. 617-495-2794

Ochs, Michael, *Lectr,* Simmons College, Graduate School of Library & Information Science, MA. 617-738-2225

Ochs, Susan H, *Librn,* Starr Library, Rhinebeck NY. 914-876-4030

Ochsner, Sally, *Librn,* Jefferson County Public Library (Daniels), Lakewood CO. 303-233-2131

Ockey, Randl W, *Dir,* Lebanon Public Library, Lebanon OR. 503-258-5844

Oda, Jane, *Tech Serv,* Flesh Public Library, Piqua OH. 513-773-6753

Oda, Kathy J, *Dir,* Edison State Community College Library, Piqua OH. 513-778-8600

Oda, Phyllis, *Librn,* Raychem Corp, Research & Development Library, Menlo Park CA. 415-329-3282

Odabashian, Arax, *Librn,* Needham, Harper & Steers Inc, Research Library, New York NY. 212-758-7600, Ext 354, 376

Oddan, Linda, *Bibliog Instr, Ref & On-Line Servs,* The Medical College of Wisconsin, Inc, Todd Wehr Library, Milwaukee WI. 414-257-8323

Oddie, Rosemary, *Librn,* Regina Public Library (Regent Park), Regina SK. 306-569-7615

Odean, Karen, *Librn Blind,* Northern Illinois Library System, Rockford IL. 815-229-0330

Odell, Glendon, *Sci & Tech,* Princeton University Library, Princeton NJ. 609-452-3180

Odell, Glendon T, *Assoc Librn,* Princeton University Library, Princeton NJ. 609-452-3180

Oden, Gladys, *Asst Librn,* Mitchell County Public Library, Colorado City TX. 915-728-3968

Odenheim, P, *Ch,* William E Dermody Free Public Library, Carlstadt NJ. 201-438-8866

Oderberg, I M, *Acq,* Theosophical University Library, Altadena CA. 213-798-8020, Ext 5

Oderberg, I M, *Religion & Philos,* Theosophical University Library, Altadena CA. 213-798-8020, Ext 5

Oderman, Anita, *Dir Christian Educ,* First United Presbyterian Church Library, Albuquerque NM. 505-247-9593, Ext 24

Odescalchi, Esther, *Ext Servs,* Adriance Memorial Library, Poughkeepsie NY. 914-485-4790

Odette, Philip, *Spec Coll,* Saint Edward's University Library, Austin TX. 512-444-2621

Odofin, Julie, *Librn,* Richmond Public Library (Bayview Branch), Richmond CA. 415-237-3166

Odom, Donn L, *State Librn,* Georgia Department of Law, Georgia State Library, Atlanta GA. 404-658-2172

Odom, Katherine, *Clinical Med,* University of Texas Medical Branch, Moody Medical Library, Galveston TX. 713-765-1971

Odom, Mabel, *Bookmobile Asst,* Carl Elliott Regional Library, Jasper AL. 205-221-2567

Odom, Mary Lucy, *Ref,* Midland County Public Library, Midland TX. 915-683-2708

Odum, Donella, *Ch,* Carbondale Public Library, Carbondale IL. 618-457-0354

Odum, Fredda, *Ch,* Stillwater Public Library, City Library, Stillwater OK. 405-372-3633

Oehler, Eileen L, *Dir,* Hastings Public Library, Hastings MI. 616-945-4263

Oehler, Sarah, *Librn,* Minnesota Valley Regional Library (Mapleton), Mankato MN. 507-524-3513

Oehlerts, Donald E, *Dir,* Miami University, Edgar W King Library, Oxford OH. 513-529-2944

Oehmke, Kirby, *Media,* University of Albuquerque, Center for Learning & Information Resources, Albuquerque NM. 505-831-1111, Ext 230

Oeljen, Vicki, *Librn,* Hennepin County Library (Westonka), Mound MN. 612-472-4105

Oellien, Maxine, *Librn,* Napa County Law Library, Napa CA. 707-253-4481

Oelz, Erling R, *Public Servs,* University of Montana, Maureen & Mike Mansfield Library, Missoula MT. 406-243-6800

Oertli, David L, *Librn,* Chester Mental Health Center (Patient Library), Chester IL. 618-826-4571, Ext 255

Oestreich, Kathleen P, *Mgr Tech Info Serv,* Borg-Warner Corp, Ingersoll Research Center Library, Des Plaines IL. 312-827-3131, Ext 131

Oetting, Frieda R, *Librn,* Chemplex Co Library, Rolling Meadows IL. 312-437-7800, Ext 267

Oettinger, Carolyn, *Ad,* Piedmont Technical College, Learning Resources Center, Roxboro NC. 919-599-1181, Ext 266

Oettinger, David, *Bibliog Instr,* Dutchess Community College Library, Poughkeepsie NY. 914-471-4500, Ext 388

Oey, Giok Po, *Southeast Asia,* Cornell University Libraries (University Libraries), Ithaca NY. 607-256-4144

Offenbeck, J, *On-Line Servs,* Queen's University at Kingston, Douglas Library, Kingston ON. 547-5950 (Admin); 547-6992 (Chief Librn)

Offerle, Sue, *ILL,* Euclid Public Library, Euclid OH. 216-261-5300

Offerman, Glenn W, *Chief Librn,* Concordia College, Buenger Memorial Library, Saint Paul MN. 612-641-8240

Ofiara, David, *AV,* Adirondack Community College Library, Glens Falls NY. 518-793-4491, Ext 60

Ofisa, Tulutulu, *Tech Serv,* American Samoa-Office of Library Services, Pago Pago, Samoa PI. 633-5869

Ofstad, Odessa, *Spec Coll,* Northeast Missouri State University, Pickler Memorial Library, Kirksville MO. 816-665-5121, Ext 7186

Ogan, Betty, *Ad,* Greeley Public Library, Greeley Municipal Library, Greeley CO. 303-353-6123, Ext 392

Ogden, Alan W, *Dir,* University of Tulsa (College of Law Library), Tulsa OK. 918-592-6000, Ext 404

Ogden, Dale T, *Dir,* United States Air Force, Electronic Security Command General Library, San Antonio TX. 512-925-2617

Ogden, Evelyn M, *Libr Tech,* Lewiston City Library (Carnegie), Pioneer Park ID. 308-743-7221

Ogden, Howard, *Dir,* Charles H Taylor Memorial Library, Hampton Public Library, Hampton VA. 804-727-6234

Ogden, Joyce, *Cat,* State University of New York College at Brockport, Drake Memorial Library, Brockport NY. 716-395-2140

Ogden, Marguerite, *Coordr,* Southside Virginia Community College, Christanna Campus Library, Alberta VA. 804-949-7111, Ext 125

Ogden, Mary, *Media,* Linfield College, Northup Library, McMinnville OR. 503-472-4121, Ext 262

Ogden, Nina M, *Dir,* Pierce Free Public Library, Pierce ID. 208-464-2823

Ogden, Raymond P, *Dir,* Southeastern Libraries Cooperating, Rochester MN. 507-288-5513

Ogden, Raymond P, *Exec Dir,* Southeastern Libraries Cooperating, (SELCO), MN. 507-288-5513

Ogden, Susan E, *Ch & YA,* Blue Ridge Regional Library, Martinsville VA. 703-632-7125

Ogeltree, Linda, *ILL,* Tennessee Technological University, Jere Whitson Memorial Library, Cookeville TN. 615-528-3408

Ogg, Harold, *Librn,* Public Library of Cincinnati & Hamilton County (Delhi Hills), Cincinnati OH. 513-369-6019

Ogg, Jean, *Ref,* Worthington Public Library, Worthington OH. 614-885-3185

Ogilvie, Alice E, *Librn,* Merrickville Public Library, Merrickville ON. 613-269-3326

Ogilvie, Lee, *Pub Servs,* Florida Junior College at Jacksonville (Kent Campus Learning Resource Center), Jacksonville FL. 904-387-8222

Ogle, Helen, *Librn,* Ravenna Public Library, Ravenna NE. 308-452-4213

Ogle, Lydia, *Asst Librn,* Oakfield Public Library, Oakfield WI. 414-583-4400

Ogle, Mary, *Asst Librn,* Hancock County Library, Hawesville KY. 502-927-6760

Ogle, Nancy, *Librn,* Augusta Public Library, Augusta KS. 316-775-2681

Oglesby, Judy, *Librn,* Gillette Co, Paper Mate Research Department Library, Santa Monica CA. 213-829-2633

Ogonji, Jewel H, *MLKML Librn,* Public Library of the District of Columbia, Martin Luther King Memorial Library, Washington DC. 202-727-1101

Ogren, Sherryl, *Librn,* McGregor Public Library, McGregor MN. 218-768-3350

Ogura, Irene, *Cat,* University of Colorado Health Sciences Center (Denison Memorial Library), Denver CO. 303-394-5125

Ogurek, Mary A, *Dir,* Thorp Public Library, Thorp WI. 715-669-5953

Oh, Sang Ja, *Dir,* Staten Island Hospital, Medical Staff Library, Staten Island NY. 212-447-6000, Ext 313 & 341

Oh, Soo Young, *Ch,* West Islip Public Library, West Islip NY. 516-661-7080, 661-7082

Ohanian, Phyllis, *Librn,* AMICON Corp, Research & Development Div Library, Lexington MA. 617-861-9600

Ohl, Cynthia, *Librn,* Dow City Public Library, Dow City IA. 712-674-3453

Ohl, Hazel, *Ref,* Reuben McMillan Free Library Free Library Association, Public Library of Youngstown & Mahoning County, Youngstown OH. 216-744-8636

Ohland, Mary Jane, *Librn,* Minnesota Valley Regional Library (Winthrop), Mankato MN. 507-647-5340

Ohlmann, Glenn, *Tech Serv,* Concordia Teachers College, Link Library, Seward NE. 402-643-3651, Ext 258

Ohlson, Mary, *Librn,* Uxbridge Free Public Library, Uxbridge MA. 617-278-3505

Ohm, Elizabeth, *Librn,* Park Forest Public Library, Park Forest IL. 312-748-3731

Ohmer, Linda, *AV,* Chatham-Effingham-Liberty Regional Library, Savannah Public Library, Savannah GA. 912-234-5127

Oi, Gregory, *On-Line Servs,* California State University Dominguez Hills, Educational Resources Center, Carson CA. 213-515-3700

Oistad, Cindy, *Librn,* Genesee District Library (Otisville Branch), Otisville MI. 313-631-6330

Oitzinger, Harvada, *Librn,* Elmbrook Memorial Hospital, Mary Beth Curtis Health Science Library, Brookfield WI. 414-782-2222, Ext 2295

Oiye, Fumiko, *On-Line Servs & Bibliog Instr,* TRW Defense & Space Systems Group, Technical Information Center, Redondo Beach CA. 213-536-2631

Ojala, Marydee, *Librn,* Bank of America (Reference Library), San Francisco CA. 415-622-2068

Okamura, Patricia, *Asst Dir,* University of Hawaii at Hilo Libraries, Hilo HI. 808-961-9344

Okamura, Patricia, *Librn,* University of Hawaii at Hilo Libraries (Hawaii Community College Library), Hilo HI. 808-961-9430

Oke, Elizabeth, *Librn,* Warren Public Library (Maybelle Burnette), Warren MI. 313-758-2115

Okell, Virginia, *Cat,* Rahway Free Public Library, Rahway NJ. 201-388-0761

Oki, Harumi, *ILL,* Sutter County Free Library, Yuba City CA. 916-673-5773

Oki, Laura, *Br Coordr & Bkmobile Coordr,* Elko County Library, Elko NV. 702-738-3066

Okim, Victor, *ILL & Circ,* Catholic University of America, John K Mullen of Denver Memorial Library, Washington DC. 202-635-5055

Okinaka, Masato, *Conservation Assoc,* Drew University, Rose Memorial Library, Madison NJ. 201-377-3000, Ext 469

Okonek, Sharon, *Dir,* Madeline Island Public Library, La Pointe WI. 715-747-3662

Okoniewski, Anne, *Media,* Four County Library System, Binghamton NY. 607-723-8236

Okuda, Robert, *Media,* University of Hawaii at Hilo Libraries, Hilo HI. 808-961-9344

Okuma, Joanne M, *Librn,* United States Air Force (Hickam Base Library), Hickam AFB HI. 808-449-2831

Olberding, Matilda M, *Dir,* Gratton Township Library, O'Neill NE. 402-336-3110

Old, III, Francis E, *Librn,* Baltimore County Public Library (Pikesville Branch), Pikesville MD. 301-484-2131

Old, III, Francis E, *Librn,* Baltimore County Public Library (Wellwood Minilibrary), Towson MD. 301-653-1110

Oldenburg, Adele, *ILL & Ref,* Polk Community College Library, Winter Haven FL. 813-294-7771, Ext 305

Olderr, Steven, *Dir,* Riverside Public Library, Riverside IL. 312-442-6366

Oldfield, Bill, *Cat,* University of Waterloo Library, Waterloo ON. 519-885-1211

Oldham, Earl H, *Dir,* Riverside Regional Library, Jackson MO. 314-243-8141

Oldham, Linda, *Coll Develop,* Fanshawe College of Applied Arts & Technology Library, London ON. 519-452-4350

Oldham, Sister Nancy, *ILL,* Great Bend Public Library, Great Bend KS. 316-792-2409

Oldman, Vera, *Pres,* Grand Encampment Museum, Inc, Encampment WY. 307-327-5310

Olds, Gretchen, *Acq,* Lake Superior State College Library, Sault Sainte Marie MI. 906-632-6841, Ext 402

Olds, Nancy P, *In Charge,* Honeywell Electro-Optics Center, Technical Library, Lexington MA. 617-862-6222, Ext 308, 310

Olechno, Gillian, *Chief Librn,* Los Angeles County-University of Southern California, Medical Center Libraries, Los Angeles CA. 213-226-2622

Olek, Susan, *Circ,* Erie Community College-North, Library Resources Center, Buffalo NY. 716-634-0800

Oleksowicz, Verne D, *Outreach Dir,* Pender County Library, Burgaw NC. 919-259-4521

Olenick, Elmer, *Head, Media Ctr,* Chicago Public Library (Woodson Regional), Chicago IL. 312-881-6900

Olenick, Monte, *Lang, Lit & Fiction,* Brooklyn Public Library (Central Library), Brooklyn NY. 212-780-7712

Oler, Christine, *Ref & On-Line Servs,* Methodist Hospital of Indiana, Inc, Library Department, Indianapolis IN. 317-924-8021

Oles, Louise, *Librn,* Unadilla Public Library, Unadilla NY. 607-369-3421

Olesen, Sine, *Librn,* Iowa Commission for the Blind Library, Des Moines IA. 515-283-2601

Oleson, Douglas D, *Chief Librn,* Davis & Elkins College Library, College Learning Materials Center, Elkins WV. 304-636-1900, Ext 200

Oleson, Fern B, *Dir,* Pocahontas Public Library, Pocahontas IA. 712-335-4471

Oleson, Sherry A, *Dir,* North Memorial Medical Center, Medical Library, Minneapolis MN. 612-588-0616, Ext 431

Olevnik, Peter, *Ref & Bibliog Instr,* State University of New York College at Brockport, Drake Memorial Library, Brockport NY. 716-395-2140

Olian, Irving, *Librn,* Temple Beth El, Rose G Weisman Memorial Library, Plainfield NJ. 201-756-2333

Olin, Ferris, *Librn,* Rutgers University (Art), New Brunswick NJ. 201-932-7739

Olindy, Bernice, *Dir,* Temple Emanuel Library, Willingboro NJ. 609-871-1736

Olinger, Elizabeth B, *Librn,* Greenville Technical College, Learning Resources Center, Greenville SC. 803-242-3170, Ext 321

Oliphant, Anne, *ILL,* Anchorage Municipal Libraries, Anchorage AK. 907-264-4481

Olivares, Barbara, *Circ,* Occidental Research Corp Library, Irvine CA. 714-957-7450

Olivas, Arthur, *In Charge,* Museum of New Mexico (Photographic Archives Library), Santa Fe NM. 505-827-2559

Olivas, Arthur, *Photog Archives,* Museum of New Mexico (Photographic Archives Library), Santa Fe NM. 505-827-2559

Olive, Betsy A, *Librn,* Cornell University Libraries (School of Business & Public Administration Library), Ithaca NY. 607-256-3389

Olive, Evelyn, *Media,* Brewer State Junior College, Main Campus Library, Fayette AL. 205-922-3221, Ext 244

Olive, Karen D, *Dir,* El Reno Junior College, Learning Resources Center, El Reno OK. 405-262-2552, Ext 15

Oliver, Anthony M, *Librn,* Hawaii Department of Planning & Economic Development Library, Honolulu HI. 808-548-3059

Oliver, Bobbie E, *Dir,* Putnam County Library, Cookeville TN. 615-526-2416

Oliver, Elizabeth, *Librn,* South Florida State Hospital (Patient Library), Hollywood FL. 305-983-4321

Oliver, Gwendolyn, *Librn,* Mountain View College, Learning Resources Center, Dallas TX. 214-746-4169

Oliver, Helen, *Librn,* Calais Free Library & Reading Room, Calais ME. 207-454-3223

Oliver, Helen, *ILL,* Holliston Public Library, Holliston MA. 617-429-6070

Oliver, John A, *Dir,* Flint Public Library, Flint MI. 313-232-7111

Oliver, Kent, *YA,* Topeka Public Library, Topeka KS. 913-233-2040

Oliver, Kent D, *Librn,* Agriculture Canada, Research Station Library, Winnipeg MB. 204-269-2100

Oliver, Louise, *Librn,* Weakley County Public Library, Dresden TN. 901-364-2678

Oliver, Louise T, *Librn,* Dadeville Public Library, Dadeville AL. 205-825-9232

Oliver, Mary, *Librn,* University of North Carolina at Chapel Hill (Law Library), Chapel Hill NC. 919-933-1321

Oliver, Richard, *Ref,* Saint John's University, Alcuin Library, Collegeville MN. 612-363-2119

Oliver, Robert S, *Admin Servs Suprv,* Winnipeg Public Library, Winnipeg MB. 204-985-6450

Oliver, Scott, *Media,* University of the South, Jessie Ball duPont Library, Sewanee TN. 615-598-5931, Ext 265, 267

Oliver, Sylvia, *Librn,* Moberly Junior College, Stamper Library, Moberly MO. 816-263-5077

Oliver, Virginia, *Media,* Freed-Hardeman College, Loden-Daniel Library, Henderson TN. 901-989-4611, Ext 133

Oliveras, Lillian, *Librn,* University of Puerto Rico Library (Graduate School of Social Work), Rio Piedras PR. 809-764-0000, Ext 2211

Olivetti, James, *Ref & Bibliog Instr,* George Mason University Libraries, Fairfax VA. 703-323-2616

Olivetti, Trudi, *Tech Serv,* Mount Vernon College Library, Washington DC. 202-331-3475

Olivier, Claudette J, *Asst Librn,* Russell Memorial Library, Acushnet Public Library, Acushnet MA. 617-995-5414

Olivier, Evelyn, *Projects/Planning Librn,* University of Texas Health Science Center at San Antonio Library, San Antonio TX. 512-691-6271

Olivier, Rejean, *Dir,* College de L'Assomption, Bibliotheque Generale, L'Assomption PQ. 514-589-5621, Ext 257

Olivier, Suzanne, *Librn,* Institut Nazareth Et Louis-Braille Bibliotheque, Longueuil PQ. 514-463-1710

Oller, A Kathryn, *Prof,* Drexel University, School of Library & Information Science, PA. 215-895-2474

Ollikkala, George, *Art,* Fresno County Free Library, Fresno CA. 209-488-3191

Olm, Jane G, *Librn,* Texas Tech University Library (School of Law Library), Lubbock TX. 806-742-3794

Olmstead, Anne, *ILL,* J Herman Bosler Memorial Library, Bosler Free Library, Carlisle PA. 717-243-4642

Olmstead, Hugh M, *Head of Slavic Dept,* Harvard University Library (Harvard College Library (Headquarters in Harry Elkins Widener Memorial Library)), Cambridge MA. 617-495-2401

Olney, Arlene, *Librn,* Plattsmouth Public Library, Plattsmouth NE. 402-296-4154

Olsen, Ann Marie, *YA,* Logan Library, Logan UT. 801-752-2365

Olsen, Arthur, *Dir,* Franklin Library, Ray Memorial Library, Franklin MA. 617-528-0371

Olsen, Audun, *Prof,* Shippensburg State College, Dept of Library Science, PA. 717-532-1472

Olsen, David L, *Acq,* Lafayette College, David Bishop Skillman Library, Easton PA. 215-253-6281, Ext 289

Olsen, Don, *Librn,* United States Army (Fort Sam Houston Morale Support Activities, Main Library), Fort Sam Houston TX. 512-221-1211

Olsen, Donald, *Ref,* Southwest State University Library, Marshall MN. 507-537-7021

Olsen, Doris, *Tech Serv & Cat,* Mitchell Public Library, Mitchell SD. 605-996-6693
Olsen, Eleanor, *Asst Librn,* Kendallville Public Library, Kendallville IN. 219-347-3554
Olsen, Emily, *Asst Librn,* Little Wood River Library District, Carey ID. 208-823-4479
Olsen, Harold, *Assoc Prof,* San Jose State University, Division of Library Science, CA. 408-277-2292
Olsen, Ida, *Librn & Cat,* Emo Public Library, Emo ON. 807-482-2575
Olsen, Irving, *Media,* Valparaiso University, Henry F Moellering Memorial Library, Valparaiso IN. 219-464-5364
Olsen, Janet R, *Preparations,* Bloomsburg State College, Harvey A Andruss Library, Bloomsburg PA. 717-389-2716
Olsen, Janus, *Librn,* Mitchell Public Library, Mitchell SD. 605-996-6693
Olsen, Judith, *On-Line Servs,* Cabrini College, Holy Spirit Library, Radnor PA. 215-687-2100, Ext 60
Olsen, Judith M, *Coordr & Media,* Burlington County College Library, Pemberton NJ. 609-894-9311, Ext 222
Olsen, Patricia, *Dir,* Avon Township Public Library, Rochester MI. 313-651-1426
Olsen, Randy J, *Asst Dir, Budget & Admin Serv,* Brigham Young University, Harold B Lee Library, Provo UT. 801-378-2905
Olsen, Richard A, *Dir,* Rhode Island College, James P Adams Library, Providence RI. 401-956-8000
Olsen, Rowena, *Dir,* McPherson College, Miller Library, McPherson KS. 316-241-0731, Ext 67
Olsen, Wallace C, *Chief, Libr Operations Div,* National Agricultural Library, Beltsville MD. 301-344-4248
Olsen, Jr, James L, *Librn,* National Academy of Sciences-National Academy of Engineering Library, Washington DC. 202-389-6272
Olsen, Jr, Robert A, *Librn,* Texas Christian University (Brite Divinity School), Fort Worth TX. 817-921-7106
Olsgaard, Jane, *On-Line Servs & Bibliog Instr,* University of South Dakota, Christian P Lommen Health Sciences Library, Vermillion SD. 605-677-5347
Olsgaard, John, *Govt Docs & Archives,* University of South Dakota, I D Weeks Library, Vermillion SD. 605-677-5371
Olson, Barbara A, *Assoc Prof,* Queens College of the City University of New York, Graduate School of Library & Information Studies, NY. 212-520-7194, 520-7195
Olson, Betty, *Dir,* De Soto Public Library, De Soto MO. 314-586-3858
Olson, Betty, *ILL,* North Tonawanda Public Library, North Tonawanda NY. 716-693-4132
Olson, Carol A, *Acq,* Luther-Northwestern Seminary Library, Saint Paul MN. 612-641-3225
Olson, Connie, *Acq,* Twin Falls Public Library, Twin Falls ID. 208-733-2965
Olson, Darlene E, *In Charge,* Crown Zellerbach Corp, Central Research Library, Camas WA. 206-834-4444
Olson, Dave, *Pub Servs,* University of South Dakota, I D Weeks Library, Vermillion SD. 605-677-5371
Olson, David, *On-Line Servs,* District One Technical Institute Library, Eau Claire WI. 715-836-3971
Olson, David, *Asst Prof,* University of South Dakota, Library Media, SD. 605-677-5371
Olson, Dianne C, *Librn,* Cook County Hospital (Health Sciences Library), Chicago IL. 312-633-7787
Olson, Dianne C, *Librn,* Cook County School of Nursing Library, Chicago IL. 312-633-7787
Olson, Donald, *Asst Librn,* University of North Dakota (Olaf H Thormodsgard Law Library), Grand Forks ND. 701-777-2204
Olson, Dorothy, *Asst Dir,* Driftwood Library of Lincoln City, Lincoln City OR. 503-996-2277
Olson, Dorothy, *Asst Librn,* Northwestern University, Chicago (Joseph Schaffner Library), Chicago IL. 312-649-8422, 649-8423
Olson, Douglas, *Asst Librn,* Eastern Washington State Historical Society Library, Spokane WA. 509-456-3931
Olson, Edith, *Ch,* Madison Public Library, Madison WI. 608-266-6300

Olson, Edwin E, *Prof,* University of Maryland, College of Library & Information Services, MD. 301-454-5441
Olson, Elizabeth, *Librn,* Brown County Library (Howard Village Branch), Howard WI. 414-497-3449
Olson, Eloise, *Asst Dir,* Mamie Doud Eisenhower Public Library, Broomfield Public Library, Broomfield CO. 303-469-1821
Olson, Eric, *Asst Librn,* Reid & Priest Library, New York NY. 212-344-2233
Olson, Evelyn, *Assoc Librn, Tech Serv & Ref,* Sioux Falls College, Norman B Mears Library, Sioux Falls SD. 605-331-5000
Olson, Evelyn N, *Dir,* Roselle Free Public Library, Roselle NJ. 201-245-5809
Olson, Gail, *Dir & Ref,* Inter-American University of Puerto Rico, Guayama Regional College Library, Guayama PR. 809-864-1366
Olson, Gordon, *Archivist,* Grand Rapids Public Library, Grand Rapids MI. 616-456-4400
Olson, Gretchen, *Librn,* Crook County Library, Sundance WY. 307-283-1006
Olson, Helen, *Tech Serv,* Katonah Village Library, Katonah NY. 914-232-3508
Olson, Ivy, *Ref,* Wheaton College Library, Wheaton IL. 312-682-5101
Olson, James, *Media,* Augsburg College, George Sverdrup Library, Minneapolis MN. 612-330-1014
Olson, Joan, *Archives,* Saint Olaf College, Rolvaag Memorial Library, Northfield MN. 507-663-2222
Olson, Joann, *Librn,* Miami University (Art-Architecture Library), Oxford OH. 513-529-3219
Olson, John, *Ref & Bibliog Instr,* Schoolcraft College, Eric J Bradner Library, Livonia MI. 313-591-6400, Ext 412
Olson, Karen, *Libr Specialist,* Eastern Washington University (Music), Cheney WA. 509-359-7843
Olson, Karen, *Librn,* Tioga Community Library, Tioga ND. 701-664-3627
Olson, Leona, *Dir Libr Serv,* Co-operative College of Canada Library, Saskatoon SK. 306-373-0474, Ext 3
Olson, Linda, *Educ Mat Center,* University of Wisconsin-Stout, Pierce Library, Menomonie WI. 715-232-1184
Olson, Lowell E, *Assoc Prof,* University of Minnesota, Library School, MN. 612-373-3100
Olson, Lusetta, *Tech Serv & Cat,* Stickney-Forest View Library District, Stickney IL. 312-749-1050
Olson, Margaret, *Librn,* Minnesota Department of Public Welfare Library, Saint Paul MN. 612-296-6117
Olson, Marie, *Librn,* Berwyn Community Library, Berwyn AB. 403-338-3064
Olson, Marilyn, *Ch,* Johnson Free Public Library, Hackensack NJ. 201-343-4169
Olson, Marjorie, *Ref,* Kewanee Public Library, Kewanee IL. 309-852-4505
Olson, Mary A, *Dir,* Saint Vincent Hospital & Medical Center, Health Sciences Library, Portland OR. 503-297-4411, Ext 2257
Olson, Nancy, *Librn,* Great Lakes Bible College, Louis M Detro Memorial Library, Lansing MI. 517-321-0242, Ext 38
Olson, Nancy, *Ch,* Mendocino County Library, Ukiah CA. 707-468-4491
Olson, Neil B, *Dir & Rare Bks,* Salem State College Library, Salem MA. 617-745-0556, Ext 474, 475
Olson, Neta, *Librn,* Sedgwick Public Library, Sedgwick CO. 303-463-8832
Olson, Ray A, *ILL & Ref,* Luther-Northwestern Seminary Library, Saint Paul MN. 612-641-3225
Olson, Richard D, *Humanities,* Northwestern University Library, Evanston IL. 312-492-7658
Olson, Rue E, *Librn,* Illinois Agricultural Association, IAA & Affiliated Companies Library, Bloomington IL. 309-557-2552
Olson, Ruth, *Archivist,* Santa Fe Trail Center Library, Larned KS. 316-285-2054
Olson, Sally, *Librn,* Green Giant Co Library, Le Sueur MN. 612-665-3515, Ext 4184
Olson, Sharon, *Librn,* Memorial Hospital at Oconomowoc, Health Science Library, Oconomowoc WI. 414-567-0371, Ext 240

Olson, Shirley, *ILL, Rare Bks & Spec Coll,* Whittier College (Bonnie Bell Wardman Library), Whittier CA. 213-693-0771, Ext 223
Olson, Virgil J, *Chief Naturalist,* National Park Service, Death Valley National Monument Library, Death Valley CA. 714-786-2331, Ext 27
Olson, Wayne K, *Dir,* Algona Public Library, Algona IA. 515-295-5476
Olson, Zola, *Librn,* Radcliffe Public Library, Radcliffe IA. 515-899-7914
Olstead, Patricia B, *On-Line Servs,* United States Army (Natick Research & Development Command, Technical Library), Natick MA. 617-653-1000, Ext 2248
Olszewski, Joyce, *Librn,* Chesebrough-Pond's Inc, Research Laboratories Library, Trumbull CT. 203-377-7100
Oltman, Jerilyn, *Bibliog Instr,* Carl Sandburg College, Learning Resources Center, Galesburg IL. 309-344-2518, Ext 247 & 257
Oltmanns, Joanne, *Librn,* Carbon County Public Library (Shirley Basin Branch), Shirley Basin WY. 307-324-4756
OMalley, Dorothy E, *ILL & Ref,* Loyola Marymount University, Charles Von Der Ahe Library, Los Angeles CA. 213-642-2788
Omelchenko, William, *Spec Coll & Rare Bks,* Hunter College of the City University of New York Library, New York NY. 212-570-5511
Omelusik, N E, *Reading Rooms,* University of British Columbia Library, Vancouver BC. 604-228-3871
Omerod, Barbara, *Admin Servs Mgr,* Morgan Stanley & Co, Inc Library, New York NY. 212-974-4369
Omori, Irene, *Librn,* Wood County District Public Library (Northwood-Great Eastern), Bowling Green OH. 419-698-1683
Ondriska, Albert, *Publ Servs,* Illinois Benedictine College, Theodore Lownik Library, Lisle IL. 312-968-7270, Ext 286
Onesto, Serene, *Coordn, Learning Resources,* Chicago State University, Paul & Emily Douglas Library, Chicago IL. 312-995-2254
Oney, Mary Elizabeth, *Librn,* Williamson Public Library, Williamson WV. 304-235-2402
Onieal, Martin, *Ad,* Framingham Public Library, Framingham MA. 617-879-3570
Onley, Betty Q, *Bus Mgr,* South Carolina State Library, Columbia SC. 803-758-3181
Ono, Margaret, *Librn,* United States Air Force (McGuire Base Library), McGuire AFB NJ. 609-724-1100
Onofrio, Kathleen, *Librn,* South Haven Memorial Library, South Haven MI. 616-637-2403
Onorato, Angelina, *Circ,* Elmont Public Library, Elmont NY. 516-354-5280, 354-4091
Onsager, Lawrence W, *Per,* Loma Linda University, Vernier Radcliffe Memorial Library, Loma Linda CA. 714-796-7311, Ext 2916
Onstead, Sheila, *Asst Librn,* Crowley Ridge Regional Library (Library for the Blind & Physically Handicapped), Jonesboro AR. 501-935-5133
Onsted, Kathryn, *Librn,* Lenawee County Library (Onsted Branch), Onsted MI. 517-467-2623
Ontko, Ellen, *Asst Dir,* Stonewall Jackson Regional Library, Buckhannon WV. 304-472-5475, 472-5581
Ontko, Frank, *Dir,* Stonewall Jackson Regional Library, Buckhannon WV. 304-472-5475, 472-5581
Ontko, Michael, *Dir,* Clay County Public Library, Clay WV. 304-587-4254
Onufrock, Jack, *On-Line Servs,* Marquette University Memorial Library, Milwaukee WI. 414-224-7214
Oomens, Astrid, *Tech Serv,* Glenside Public Library District, Glendale Heights IL. 618-858-0840
Ooton, Stephen K, *Librn,* Huron Public Library, Huron SD. 605-352-3778
Opatrny, Judith T, *Librn,* Willkie Farr & Gallagher, Law Library, New York NY. 212-935-8000, Ext 540, 541, 542
Opel, Shirley, *Librn,* Buffalo & Erie County Public Library System (Riverside), Buffalo NY. 716-875-0562
Opello, Olivia, *Ref,* University of Mississippi Library, University MS. 601-232-7091

Operhall, Anthony W, *Eng & Geol,* University of California at Davis, General Library, Davis CA. 916-752-2110

Opgrand, Harold J, *Dir,* University of Minnesota Technical College, Kiehle Library, Crookston MN. 218-281-6510, Ext 252

Oplinger, Phoebe, *Dir,* Central Piedmont Community College Library, Charlotte NC. 704-373-6883

Opocensky, Virginia, *Ch,* Lincoln City Libraries, Lincoln NE. 402-435-2146

Oppenheim, Linda, *On-Line Servs,* Princeton University Library, Princeton NJ. 609-452-3180

Oppenheim, Linda, *Librn,* Princeton University Library (Woodrow Wilson School of Public & International Affairs), Princeton NJ. 609-452-3180

Oppenheim, Vicki, *Acq,* University of San Francisco (School of Law), San Francisco CA. 415-666-6679

Oppenheimer, Gerald J, *Dir,* Pacific Northwest Regional Health Sciences Library, (PNRHSL), WA. 206-543-8262

Oppenheimer, Gerald J, *Asst Dir,* University of Washington Libraries, Seattle WA. 206-543-1760

Oppenheimer, Gerald J, *Dir,* University of Washington Libraries (Health Sciences), Seattle WA. 206-543-5530

Oppenneer, Bernard L, *Dir,* Des Plaines Public Library, Des Plaines IL. 312-827-5551

Opperman, Jacqueline, *Dir,* Kingston Community Public Library, Kingston MI. 517-683-2550

Oppliger, Shirley, *Librn,* Polk City Community Library, Polk City IA. 515-984-6119

Oquita, Paula, *Librn,* Logicon Inc, Training & Tactical Systems Div Library, San Diego CA. 714-455-1330

Oram, E, *Librn,* Victoria General Hospital, Health Sciences Library, Halifax NS. 902-428-2429

Oram, Robert W, *Dir,* Southern Methodist University Libraries (Central University Libraries), Dallas TX. 214-692-2400

Orbesen, Vanessa, *Librn,* Altrurian Public Library, Aztec NM. 505-334-9462

Orbovich, Lynette, *Media,* Marion County Public Library, Fairmont WV. 304-366-4831

Orchard, Margaret, *Asst Librn & Ch,* Stey-Nevant Public Library, Farrell PA. 412-347-7295

Orcutt, Linda, *Intertype Libr Coordr,* Wisconsin Valley Library Service, System Headquarters, Wausau WI. 715-845-7214, Ext 35, 49, 50 & 51

Orcutt, Robert, *Librn,* University of Nevada-Reno (Desert Research Institute), Reno NV. 702-972-1676, Ext 14

Orcutt, Robert, *Librn,* University of Nevada-Reno (Physical Sciences), Reno NV. 702-784-6716

Orcutt, Robert, *Librn,* University of Nevada-Reno (Water Resources Collection), Sparks NV. 702-673-4750, Ext 338

Orcutt, Roberta K, *Librn,* University of Nevada Desert Research Institute, Water Resources Collection, Sparks NV. 702-673-4750, Ext 338

Ord, Mary W, *Librn,* Allegany County Library (Westernport Branch), Westernport MD. 301-359-0455

Ordish, Violet, *Librn,* Grant Public Library, Grant MI. 616-834-5713

Ordogh, Linda, *ILL,* Southern Illinois University School of Medicine Library, Springfield IL. 217-782-2658

Orenczuk, Wolodymir, *Cat,* University of Santa Clara, Michel Orradre Library, Santa Clara CA. 408-984-4415

Orfanos, Minnie, *Librn,* Northwestern University, Chicago (Dental School Library), Chicago IL. 312-649-8332

Orfe, Lynn, *Ref, On-Line Servs & Bibliog Instr,* Shearman & Sterling Library, New York NY. 212-483-1000, Ext 356

Orff, Edward, *Librn,* New York Public Library (Yorkville), New York NY. 212-744-5824

Orgain, Jane M, *Dir,* Brunswick-Greensville Regional Library, Lawrenceville VA. 804-848-2418

Orgain, Marian, *Asst Dir Libr Develop,* University of Houston (M D Anderson Memorial Library), Houston TX. 713-749-4241

Organic, Beila S, *Librn,* Tracor Inc, Applied Sciences Group Library, Rockville MD. 301-279-4388

Orgren, Carl, *Assoc Prof,* University of Iowa, School of Library Science, IA. 319-353-3644

Orlandi, Eugenia, *Ch,* Tenafly Public Library, Tenafly NJ. 201-568-8680

Orlando, Alverda, *Librn,* Santa Cruz Public Library (Branciforte), Santa Cruz CA. 408-426-7054

Orlando, Karen, *Asst Librn,* Bracewell & Patterson, Law Library, Houston TX. 713-223-2900

Orlando, Thomas, *Special Coll Curator & Archivist,* Chicago Public Library (Cultural Center), Chicago IL. 312-269-2820

Orlino, Demetrio, *Ref,* Loyola Marymount University (Loyola Law School Library), Los Angeles CA. 213-642-2934

Orloske, Margaret Q, *Librn,* Timex Corporation, Corporate Library, Waterbury CT. 203-573-5268

Orlov, Vladimir, *Dir,* United Nations, Dag Hammarskjold Library, New York NY. 212-754-7443, 754-7444, 754-7445

Orlowski, Betty, *AV,* Sauk Valley College, Learning Resources Center, Dixon IL. 815-288-5511, Ext 247

Orlowski, Gladys E, *Dir,* West Chester Public Library, West Chester PA. 215-696-1721

Orme, Catherine, *ILL & Circ,* Cornell University Medical College, Samuel J Wood Library, New York NY. 212-472-5300

Orme, Linda S, *Librn,* New York Times Washington Bureau Library, Washington DC. 202-862-0300

Ormon, Deborah, *Librn,* Thomas Crane Public Library (North Quincy), Quincy MA. 617-471-2400

Ormondroyd, Edward, *Tech Serv & Cat,* Finger Lakes Library System, Ithaca NY. 607-273-4074

Ormsby, Eric, *Near East,* Princeton University Library, Princeton NJ. 609-452-3180

Ormsby, Eric, *Curator,* Princeton University Library (Near Eastern Collection), Princeton NJ. 609-452-3180

Orndorff, Louis C, *Dir,* Catonsville Community College, Learning Resources Div, Baltimore MD. 301-455-4586

Ornee, Nell, *Dir,* Texas Wesleyan College, Judge George W Armstrong Library, Fort Worth TX. 817-534-0251, Ext 224

Orosz, Barbara J, *Head Libr,* Union Oil Company of California, Technical Information Ctr, Brea CA. 714-528-7201, Ext 462

Orpwood, Jean, *Deputy Chief Librn,* North York Public Library, Willowdale ON. 416-494-6838

Orr, Cynthia, *Asst to Dir,* Lakewood Public Library, Lakewood OH. 216-226-8275

Orr, E Jean, *Dir,* Miracle Valley Regional Library, City-County Public Library, Moundsville WV. 304-845-6911

Orr, Edith, *Cat,* Free Public Library of the City of Trenton, Trenton NJ. 609-392-7188

Orr, Elizabeth, *Librn,* First Presbyterian Church, Ewing Memorial Library, Houston TX. 713-526-2525

Orr, Iris, *Librn,* Saint Elmo Public Library, Saint Elmo IL. 618-829-5544

Orr, Joella, *Dir,* Emily Fowler Public Library, Denton Public Library, Denton TX. 817-387-7571

Orr, Laurie, *Librn,* Birmingham Public & Jefferson County Free Library (Central Park), Birmingham AL. 205-254-2551

Orr, Margaret, *Order,* Iowa State University Library, Ames IA. 515-294-1442

Orr, Margaret, *Librn,* Whatcom County Public Library (Deming Branch), Deming WA. 206-384-3150

Orr, Maryruth, *Research Librn,* WED Enterprises, Inc (Walt E Disney), Research Library, Glendale CA. 213-956-7263

Orr, Sally, *Asst Librn,* McIver's Grant Public Library, Dyersburg TN. 901-285-5032

Orr, Sister Mary Mark, *Rare Bks & Spec Coll,* Saint Mary College Library, Leavenworth KS. 913-682-5151, Ext 202

Orr, Valerie, *Environ,* University of Calgary Library, Calgary AB. 403-284-5954

Orr, William, *In Charge,* Associated Christian Colleges of Oregon, OR. 503-775-4366

Orr, William M, *Gen Admin,* Warner Pacific College, Otto F Linn Library, Portland OR. 503-775-4366, Ext 18, 19

Orren, Mrs Lynell, *Ref,* Louisiana Tech University, Prescott Memorial Library, Ruston LA. 318-257-2577

Orser, Dorothy, *Tech Serv & Cat,* Ridgewood Public Library, Ridgewood NJ. 201-652-5200

Orser, Lawan, *Cat,* University of Florida Libraries (Agriculture), Gainesville FL. 904-392-1934

Orsini, Lillian K, *Asst Prof,* State University of New York at Albany, School of Library & Information Science, NY. 518-455-6288

Ortega, Edna, *Asst Dir,* Demarest Public Library, Demarest NJ. 201-768-8714

Ortego, Margerite, *Librn,* Avoyelles Parish Library (Plaucheville Branch), Plaucheville LA. 318-253-7559

Orth, Barbara, *Librn,* Farmer Township Community Library, Bushton KS. 316-562-3352

Orth, Kathleen, *Racine Campus Librn,* Gateway Technical Institute, Learning Resources Center, Kenosha WI. 414-656-6924, 656-6923

Orth, William D, *ILL,* Emory University Libraries (General Libraries), Atlanta GA. 404-329-6861

Ortiz, Barbara, *AV,* State Library of Florida, Div of Library Services, Dept of State, Tallahassee FL. 904-487-2651

Ortiz, Cynthia, *Librn,* United States Department of Energy, Nevada Operations Office Technical Library, Las Vegas NV. 702-734-3371

Ortiz, Jose J, *Librn Blind,* University of Puerto Rico Library, Jose M Lazaro Memorial Library, Rio Piedras PR. 809-764-0000, Ext 3296

Ortiz, Luis Roberto, *Media,* Inter-American University of Puerto Rico, Metropolitan Campus Library, Hato Rey PR. 809-754-7215, Ext 246, 245, 256

Ortiz, Miguel Angel, *Dir,* University of Puerto Rico, Mayaguez Campus General Library, Mayaguez PR. 809-832-4044

Ortiz, Oneida R, *Dir,* University of Puerto Rico - Bayamon Regional College, Learning Resources Center, Bayamon PR. 809-786-5225

Ortiz, Pamela, *Librn,* Solano County Library (Rio Vista), Rio Vista CA. 707-374-2664

Ortiz, Roberta, *Tech Serv,* Gail Borden Public Library District, Elgin IL. 312-742-2411

Ortman, Catherine, *Asst Librn,* Blodgett Memorial Library, Fishkill NY. 914-896-9215

Ortman, Elaine C, *Librn,* Two Harbors Public Library, Two Harbors MN. 218-834-3148

Ortutay, Phyllis A, *Librn & On-Line Servs,* United States Army (Van Deusen Post Library), Fort Monmouth NJ. 201-532-9000

Orwig, Gary W, *Asst Prof,* University of Central Florida, Educational Media Programs, FL. 305-275-2426

Osada, T, *Ch,* Carnegie-Stout Public Library, Dubuque Public Library, Dubuque IA. 319-583-9197

Osbaldiston, Diana, *Cat,* University of South Carolina (Coleman Karesh Law Libr), Columbia SC. 803-777-5942

Osborn, Dixie, *Librn,* Nora E Larabee Memorial Library, Stafford KS. 316-234-5762

Osborn, Donna, *Acq,* Madison-Jefferson County Public Library, Madison IN. 812-265-2744

Osborn, Lucie, *Asst Dir,* Laramie County Library System, Cheyenne WY. 307-634-3561

Osborn, Margaret H, *Ref,* Claremont Colleges Libraries (Norman F Sprague Memorial), Claremont CA. 714-621-8000, Ext 3920

Osborn, Raye, *Actg Dir,* Georgia Department of Education (Div of Public Library Services), Atlanta GA. 404-656-2461

Osborn, Raye, *Consult, Ch & YA Servs,* Georgia Department of Education (Div of Public Library Services), Atlanta GA. 404-656-2461

Osborn, Raye, *Actg Dir,* Georgia Library Information Network, (GLIN), GA. 404-656-2461

Osborn, Ruth, *Cat,* Hingham Public Library, Hingham MA. 617-749-0907

Osborn, Walter, *ILL, Tech Serv & Ref,* Moody Bible Institute Library, Chicago IL. 312-329-4138

Osborne, Alice, *Dir,* Breese Public Library, Breese IL. 618-526-7361

Osborne, Diana D, *Dir,* Lewis Egerton Smoot Memorial Library, King George VA. 703-775-7951

Osborne, Donald, *Acq,* State University of New York, Frank Melville Jr Memorial Library, Stony Brook NY. 516-246-5650

Osborne, James W, *Dir,* Northeastern Hospital School of Nursing Library, Philadelphia PA. 215-427-6425

Osborne, Jeanne, *Prof,* University of Iowa, School of Library Science, IA. 319-353-3644

OSBORNE

Osborne, Jo, *Ch,* Worthington Public Library, Worthington OH. 614-885-3185

Osborne, Larry N, *Dir,* Clearfield County Public Library Federation, Curwensville PA. 814-886-2619

Osborne, Nancy, *Pub Servs,* State University of New York College, Memorial Library, Cortland NY. 607-753-2525, 753-2221

Osborne, Reed, *Dir,* Saint Thomas Public Library, Saint Thomas ON. 519-631-6050

Osborne, Robin A, *Librn,* United States Army (Corps of Engineers, Fort Worth District Library), Fort Worth TX. 334-2138 or 2139

Osborne, Ruth, *Ch,* Grand Prairie Memorial Library, Grand Prairie TX. 214-264-1571

Osborne, Ruth, *Bus,* Public Library of Charlotte & Mecklenburg County, Inc, Charlotte NC. 704-374-2725

Osborne, Verniece, *Media,* Wright State University Library (Fordham Library, Cox Heart Institute Library & Fels Research Institute Library), Dayton OH. 513-873-2266

Osborne, Wendy, *Acq,* Bradford Public Library, Bradford ON. 416-775-6482

Osborne, Yost, *Dir,* Mount Union College Library, Alliance OH. 216-821-5320, Ext 260

Osburn, Ann, *Librn,* Jefferson County Public Library (Arvada Regional), Arvada CO. 303-424-5227

Osburn, Charles B, *Coll Mgt,* Northwestern University Library, Evanston IL. 312-492-7658

Osburn, Harriet S, *Chief Librn,* Xerox Education Publications Library, Middletown CT. 203-347-7251

Osburn, Joanne, *Dir,* Weiser Public Library, Weiser ID. 208-549-1243

Osei-Sarfo, Olivia, *Librn,* Norfolk Public Library (Lafayette), Norfolk VA. 804-441-2842

Osenberg, Sharon, *Asst Dir & Tech Serv,* Concordia College, Scheele Memorial Library, Bronxville NY. 914-337-9300, Ext 138

Osgood, Arlene, *Librn,* Thornton Public Library, Thornton NH. 603-726-8981

Osgood, James, *Cat & Asst Librn,* City Colleges of Chicago, Kennedy-King College Library, Chicago IL. 312-962-3262

Osgood, Sara, *ILL,* Kent State University Libraries, Kent OH. 216-672-2962

Osgood, William, *Librn,* Center for Northern Studies Library, Wolcott VT. 802-888-4331

Osheroff, Shiela K, *Cat,* University of Oregon Health Sciences Center (Health Sciences Library), Portland OR. 503-225-8026

Osinalo, Ed, *Bus,* Miami-Dade Public Library System, Miami FL. 305-579-5001

Oslage, Carol, *Librn,* Marathon County Public Library (Rothschild Branch), Rothschild WI. 715-359-6208

Osland, Vera, *Dir,* Northwest Iowa Technical College, NITC Learning Resources Center, Sheldon IA. 712-324-2587, Ext 43

Oslin, Susan, *Ref,* State Library of Massachusetts, Boston MA. 617-727-2590

Osma, Helen, *Tech Serv,* Lawrence Public Library, Lawrence KS. 913-843-3833

Osmanson, Fleur, *Librn,* Hill, Farrer & Burrill Law Library, Los Angeles CA. 213-620-0460

Osmond, Patricia, *Ref,* Wilbraham Public Library, Wilbraham MA. 413-596-6142

Osorio, Nestor, *Sci & Eng,* Florida Atlantic University, S E Wimberly Library, Boca Raton FL. 305-395-5100, Ext 2448

Ossar, Naomi, *Ch,* Manhattan Public Library, Manhattan KS. 913-776-4741

Ossenkop, David, *Ref,* State University of New York College at Potsdam (Crane School of Music, Julia E Crane Memorial Library), Potsdam NY. 315-268-3019

Ostar, Lewis M, *Cat & Acq,* Somerset County College Library, Somerville NJ. 201-526-1200, Ext 224, 304

Ostaszewski, Ted, *Cat,* Lake County Public Library, Merrillville IN. 219-769-3541

Ostendorf, Brother Paul J, *Dir & On-Line Servs,* Saint Mary's College, Fitzgerald Library, Winona MN. 507-452-4430, Ext 232

Ostendorf, Jo Ellen, *Librn,* Mississippi Library Commission, Service for the Handicapped, Jackson MS. 601-354-7208

Oster, Gary, *Librn,* John G Shedd Aquarium Library, Chicago IL. 312-939-2426, Ext 79

Osterbind, Sylvia, *ILL & Ref,* Brock University Library, Saint Catharines ON. 416-684-7201

Osterby, Marian, *Librn,* Timberland Regional Library (Centralia Branch), Centralia WA. 206-736-9966

Ostergaard, Doris, *Librn,* National Film Board of Canada, Calgary District Office Film Library, Calgary AB. 403-231-5414

Ostergren, David, *Ref,* Ledyard Public Libraries, Gales Ferry Library & Bill Library, Ledyard CT. 203-464-9917

Osterheim, Carol M, *Librn,* Westinghouse Oceanic Div Library, Annapolis MD. 301-765-5680

Osterhoudt, Sheila R, *Dir,* Vennard College, Jessop-Bruner Library, University Park IA. 515-673-4104

Osterman, Barbara, *Asst Librn,* Mineral County Public Library, Mira-Luning Community, Hawthorne NV. 702-945-2778

Osterman, Lloyd, *Dir,* Hyconeechee Regional Library, Yanceyville NC. 919-694-6241

Osterman, Lloyd J, *Librn,* Gunn Memorial Public Library, Yanceyville NC. 919-694-6241

Osterreich, Katy, *Ch,* Dwight Foster Public Library, Fort Atkinson WI. 414-563-5124

Osterried, Eunice, *Librn,* Martin Collegiate Institute Library, Regina SK. 306-523-3625

Ostland, Sigrid, *Librn,* Earl Ruble & Associates, Inc Library, Duluth MN. 218-722-3953

Ostler, Larry J, *Dir,* Ricks College, David O McKay Learning Resources Center, Rexburg ID. 208-356-2351

Ostness, Diana, *Asst Librn,* Cumberland Public Library, Cumberland WI. 715-822-2767

Ostrander, Dona, *Media,* Central Connecticut State College, Elihu Burritt Library, New Britain CT. 203-827-7531

Ostrander, Kaveda, *Librn,* Sidney Public Library, Sidney NY. 607-563-1200, 563-8021

Ostrander, Richard E, *Dir,* Yakima Valley Regional Library, Yakima WA. 509-452-8541, Ext 22

Ostrander, Sheila, *Sr Librn,* New York State Library (Genealogy), Albany NY. 518-474-5161

Ostrem, Ardith W, *Librn,* Columbus Junction Public Library, Columbus Junction IA. 319-728-7972

Ostroff, Barbara M, *Ch,* Burton L Wales Public Library, North Abington MA. 617-878-1239

Ostrove, Geraldine, *Dir,* New England Conservatory of Music (Idabelle Firestone Audio Library), Boston MA. 617-262-1120

Ostrove, Geraldine, *Dir,* New England Conservatory of Music, Harriet M Spaulding Library, Boston MA. 617-262-1120

Ostrove, Geraldine, *Lectr,* Simmons College, Graduate School of Library & Information Science, MA. 617-738-2225

Ostrum, Roxane M, *Dir,* Avalon Public Library, Avalon PA. 412-761-2288

Ostwald, Gladys, *Librn,* Whittemore Public Library, Whittemore IA. 515-884-2680

Ostwald, Molly A, *Personnel & Budget,* Syracuse University Libraries, Ernest S Bird Library, Syracuse NY. 315-423-2575

Osuga, William, *ILL,* University of California Los Angeles Library, Los Angeles CA. 213-825-1201

Oswald, Eunice, *Librn,* Springbank Township Library, Allen NE. 402-635-2363

Oswald, Genevieve, *Curator,* New York Public Library (Dance Collections), New York NY. 212-790-6262

Oswald, Leslie, *Librn,* Cherry Valley Village Library, Cherry Valley IL. 815-332-5161

Oswald, Robert M, *Tech Serv & Cat,* Wisconsin Lutheran Seminary Library, Mequon WI. 414-242-2331

Otero, Pilar A, *Cat,* University of Puerto Rico - Bayamon Regional College, Learning Resources Center, Bayamon PR. 809-786-5225

Otis, E, *Librn,* Oakland Public Library (Eastmont), Oakland CA. 415-568-0503

Otis, Esther, *Asst Dir,* Ormond Beach Public Library, Ormond Beach FL. 904-677-0328, Ext 270-243

Otness, Harold, *ILL,* Southern Oregon State College Library, Ashland OR. 503-482-6445

Otsott, Marilyn, *Librn,* Baptist Christian College Library, Shreveport LA. 318-635-4333

Ott, Helen Keating, *Librn,* First United Presbyterian Church Library, Mansfield OH. 419-756-7066

Ott, John Harlow, *Dir,* Shaker Community Inc Library, Pittsfield MA. 413-447-7284

Ott, Katherine, *Librn,* Pike-Amite-Walthall Library System (Osyka Public), Osyka MS. 601-542-5147

Ott, Linda, *Librn,* Portage County District Library (Windham), Hiram OH. 216-326-3145

Ott, Louise, *Ch,* Paoli Public Library, Paoli IN. 812-723-3841

Ott, Retha, *Manager ,* Allergan Pharmaceuticals, Information Services, Irvine CA. 714-752-4500, Ext 4314

Ott, Wendell, *Dir,* Roswell Museum & Art Center Library, Roswell NM. 505-622-4700

Otter, Isabelle, *Librn,* Public Library of Fort Wayne & Allen County (Talking Books Department), Fort Wayne IN. 219-424-7241, Ext 248

Otteraaen, Marion J, *Dir,* Longview Public Library, Longview WA. 206-577-3380

Otterson, Harry, *Lectr,* State University of New York at Buffalo, School of Information & Library Studies, NY. 716-636-2412

Ottewell, W, *Librn,* Okanagan Regional Library District (Revelstoke Branch), Revelstoke BC. 604-837-5095

Otting, Martha F, *Librn,* Pinellas County Law Library, Saint Petersburg Branch, Saint Petersburg FL. 813-893-5875

Otting, Melitta, *Asst Librn,* Cascade Public Library, Cascade IA. 319-852-3011, 852-3222

Ottinger, Richard, *Dir,* Georgia Department of Education (Audio Visual Services), Atlanta GA. 404-656-2421

Ottman, Janet A, *Dir,* Your Home Public Library, Johnson City NY. 607-797-4816

Ottman, Nancy V, *Librn,* Group Health Eastside Hospital, Medical Library, Redmond WA. 206-883-5151

Otto, Betty J, *Curator,* National Park Service, Antietam National Battlefield Library, Sharpsburg MD. 301-432-5124

Otto, Beverly, *Ch,* Ruth Enlow Library of Garrett County, Oakland MD. 301-334-3996

Otto, Cindy, *ILL,* Arcadia Public Library, Arcadia CA. 213-446-7111

Otto, Elisabeth, *Librn,* Hennepin County Library (Eden Prairie Branch), Eden Prairie MN. 612-937-9117

Otto, Evelyn, *Asst Librn,* Newkirk Public Library, Newkirk OK. 405-362-3934

Otto, Gladys, *Spec Coll,* Wabash College, Lilly Library, Crawfordsville IN. 317-362-1400, Ext 215, 216

Otto, Janet, *AV,* Champaign Public Library & Information Center, Champaign IL. 217-356-7243

Otto, Lee, *In Charge,* Saint Bernardine Hospital, Medical Library, San Bernardino CA. 714-883-8711, Ext 2248

Otto, Margaret A, *Librn,* Dartmouth College, Baker Memorial Library, Hanover NH. 603-646-2235

Otto, Sandra, *In Charge,* Annandale Library, Annandale MN. 612-274-8448

Ottum, Rita, *Tech Serv & Acq,* Brazoria County Library, Angleton TX. 713-849-0591

Otwell, Constance, *Librn,* Saint Paul's Episcopal Church Library, Maumee OH. 419-893-3381

Ouderkirk, Jane, *Dir,* West Bridgewater Public Library, West Bridgewater MA. 617-583-2067

Ouellet, Angelo, *Cat,* College Dominicain De Philosophie Et De Theologie, Bibliotheque du College Dominicain, Ottawa ON. 613-233-5696, 233-5697

Ouellet, Jean Marc, *AV & Media,* College De Sainte-Foy, Centre des Medias, Sainte Foy PQ. 418-657-3624

Ouellet, Jocelyne, *Bkmobile Coordr,* Haut-Saint-Jean Regional Library, Bibliotheque Regionale du Haut-Saint-Jean, Edmundston NB. 506-739-7331

Ouimet, Yves, *Dir,* Bibliotheque Municipale De Longueuil, Longueuil PQ. 514-670-1410

Quintana, Diana D, *Asst Librn,* Puerto Rico Department of Education, Biblioteca Publica Central, Santurce PR. 809-723-3739

Ouiros, Angie, *Acq,* University of Houston (William I Dykes Library), Houston TX. 713-749-1991

Ounan, Francis, *Circ,* Saint Charles Borromeo Seminary, Ryan Memorial Library, Philadelphia PA. 215-839-3760, Ext 275

Ounan, Margaret, *Acq,* Saint Charles Borromeo Seminary, Ryan Memorial Library, Philadelphia PA. 215-839-3760, Ext 275

Oupcher, Manya, *Librn,* National Council of Jewish Women, Boys' & Girls' Library, Montreal PQ. 514-738-0755

Ourom, K Julianne, *Librn,* Kitimat Public Library, Kitimat BC. 632-6464 & 632-5656

Ousley, Ann, *Ch,* Amarillo Public Library, Amarillo TX. 806-378-3000, Ext 2250

Outlaw, Carolyn, *Librn,* Evansville Public Library & Vanderburgh County Public Library (East), Evansville IN. 812-425-2621

Outlaw, Pat, *Librn,* Rose Hill Community Memorial Library, Rose Hill NC. 919-289-2490

Outwater, M, *Librn,* Havelock Public Library, Havelock ON. 705-778-2621

Ouyang, Ellen, *Tech Serv & Cat,* University of Utah (Law Library), Salt Lake City UT. 801-581-6438

Ouyang, Joseph, *Ref,* University of Missouri-Kansas City Libraries (Leon E Bloch Law Library), Kansas City MO. 816-276-1659

Ouye, Kathleen, *Youth Servs,* Oakland Public Library, Oakland CA. 415-273-3281

Ouzts, Margaret, *Ref,* Melbourne Public Library, Melbourne FL. 305-723-0611

Ovellet, D, *Tech Serv,* Public Service Commission Library, Ottawa ON. 613-992-4808, 997-3606

Overbay, Kathleen G, *Dir Libr Serv,* Southwestern State Hospital Libraries (Patients' Library), Marion VA. 703-783-3171, Ext 229

Overbay, Kathleen G, *Dir Libr Serv,* Southwestern State Hospital Libraries (Professional Library), Marion VA. 703-783-3171, Ext 161

Overbeck, James, *Dir,* School of Theology at Claremont, Theology Library, Claremont CA. 714-626-3521, Ext 263

Overbey, Alma, *Cat,* Bob Jones University, J S Mack Library, Greenville SC. 803-242-5100, Ext 296

Overbey, Olivia, *Librn,* Robertson County Public Library, Mount Olivet KY. 606-724-5746

Overby, Lalla, *Asst Dir,* Brenau College, Lessie Southgate Simmons Memorial Library, Gainesville GA. 404-534-6113

Overby, Mary, *Spec Coll,* Mercer University, Stetson Memorial Library, Macon GA. 912-745-6811, Ext 284

Overby, Milton S, *Dir,* Haskell Indian Junior College, Learning Resources Center Library, Lawrence KS. 913-841-2000, Ext 258

Overend, W H, *Dir,* Fraser Valley Regional Library, Abbotsford BC. 604-859-7141

Overfield, Joan, *ILL, Ref & Bibliog Instr,* Fairfield University, Gustav & Dagmar Nyselius Library, Fairfield CT. 203-255-5411, Ext 2451

Overfield, Peggy A, *Admin Librn,* State University of New York College at Potsdam, Frederick W Crumb Memorial Library, Potsdam NY. 315-268-2940

Overholt, Maria B, *Dir,* Miami Valley Library Organization, (MILO), OH. 513-224-1686

Overley, Linda, *Ch,* Flesh Public Library, Piqua OH. 513-773-6753

Overman, Dorothy, *Ref & On-Line Servs,* Saint Louis University (Medical Center Library), Saint Louis MO. 314-664-9800

Overmier, Judith, *Head,* University of Minnesota Libraries-Twin Cities (History of Medicine), Minneapolis MN. 612-373-5586

Overmyer, LaVahn M, *Emer Assoc Prof,* Case Western Reserve University, School of Library Science, OH. 216-368-3500

Overton, Elizabeth, *Dir,* Riverhead Free Library, Riverhead NY. 516-727-3228

Overton, Jean, *Librn,* Double Springs Public Library, Double Springs AL. 205-489-2412

Overton, Kay, *ILL,* Oscar Rose Junior College, Learning Resources Center, Midwest City OK. 405-733-7323, 733-7322

Overwein, Martha, *Indust & Sci,* Dayton & Montgomery County Public Library, Dayton OH. 513-224-1651

Ovewiler, Jane, *Cat, On-Line Servs & Bibliog Instr,* Peter White Public Library, Marquette MI. 906-228-9510

Owdom, Thomas, *Librn,* County of Henrico Public Library (Municipal Library), Richmond VA. 804-222-1643

Owen, Alice G, *Librn,* Neighborhood Playhouse School of the Theatre, Irene Lewisohn Library, New York NY. 212-688-3770

Owen, Amy, *Exec Sec,* Utah College Library Council, UT. 801-533-5875

Owen, Amy, *Tech Serv,* Utah State Library, Salt Lake City UT. 801-533-5875

Owen, Arlene, *Librn,* Cumberland County Public Library (East Fayetteville), Fayetteville NC. 919-483-5665

Owen, Berniece, *Tech Serv & Acq,* Gonzaga University, Crosby Library, Spokane WA. 509-328-4220, Ext 3132

Owen, Dolores, *ILL & Ref,* Lee College, Learning Resources Center, Baytown TX. 713-427-5611, Ext 279, 277

Owen, Dorothy, *Librn,* Drake Public Library, Centerville IA. 515-856-6676

Owen, Dorothy, *Librn,* Llano County Public Library (Kingsland Branch), Kingsland TX. 915-388-3170

Owen, Eleanor E, *Dir,* Oberlin Public Library, Oberlin OH. 216-775-8600

Owen, Eleen M, *Librn,* Kansas Technical Institute, Tullis Resource Center, Salina KS. 913-825-0275, Ext 49

Owen, Flavia Reed, *Dir, Acq & Spec Coll,* Randolph-Macon College, Walter Hines Page Library, Ashland VA. 804-798-8372, Ext 256

Owen, Katherine C, *Mgr,* Warner-Lambert Research Institute, Library Services Department, Morris Plains NJ. 201-540-2875

Owen, Kathleen, *Tech Serv,* Fulton County Public Library, Rochester IN. 219-223-2713

Owen, Kenneth E, *Spec Coll,* University of New Orleans, Earl K Long Library, New Orleans LA. 504-283-0353

Owen, Mary Jeanne, *Dir,* Plains & Peaks Regional Library System, Colorado Springs CO. 303-473-3417

Owen, Mildred B, *Librn,* United States Army (MEDDAC Medical Library), Fort Carson CO. 303-579-3209

Owen, Mrs G M, *Archivist,* Old Colony Historical Society Library, Taunton MA. 617-822-1622

Owen, Nell C, *Asst Librn,* Somerville-Fayette County Library, Somerville TN. 901-465-2091

Owen, Patricia, *YA & Ref,* Bronxville Public Library, Bronxville NY. 914-337-7680

Owen, Patricia, *Acq,* Sarah Lawrence College, Esther Raushenbush Library, Bronxville NY. 914-337-0700, Ext 479

Owen, Shirley, *ILL, Ref & On-Line Servs,* Kansas City College of Osteopathic Medicine, Mazzacano Hall Library, Kansas City MO. 816-283-2451, 2454

Owen, W C, *Ch,* Shorter College, Livingston Library, Rome GA. 404-291-2121, Ext 43

Owen, Wiley, *Librn,* Tri-County Regional Library (Carnegie), Rome GA. 404-291-9360

Owen, Wiley C, *Dir & Cat,* Carnegie Library, Rome GA. 404-291-7568

Owen, Jr, R M, *Dir,* Bruce Museum Library, Greenwich CT. 203-869-0376

Owens, Basil T, *Acting Asst Dir for Assignment, Ref & Spec Servs,* Library of Congress, Washington DC. 202-287-5000

Owens, Bette C, *Librn,* Rye Public Library, Rye NH. 603-964-8401

Owens, Billie A, *Librn,* United States Air Force (Sheppard Air Force Base Library), Sheppard AFB TX. 817-851-2687

Owens, Carole, *Librn,* Kern County Library (Kernville Branch), Kernville CA. 805-861-2130

Owens, Dorothy M, *On-Line Servs & Bibliog Instr,* Gulf Oil Corporation (Gulf Refining & Market Co, Library & Information Center), Houston TX. 713-226-1632, 226-1811

Owens, Edward P, *Librn,* Montgomery College, Rockville Campus Library, Rockville MD. 301-762-7400, Ext 204

Owens, Frederick H, *Mgr,* Rohm & Haas Co, Research Div, Information Services Dept, Spring House PA. 215-643-0200

Owens, Geraldine H, *In Charge,* Walker Art Center Staff Reference Library, Minneapolis MN. 612-377-7500

Owens, Irene, *Librn,* Howard University Libraries (Religion Library), Washington DC. 202-636-7277

Owens, Ivy Patterson, *Ch,* West Lafayette Public Library, West Lafayette IN. 317-743-2261

Owens, Jean, *Librn,* Alliston Public Library, Alliston ON. 705-435-5651

Owens, Jean, *Asst Librn,* Polk County Public Library, Columbus NC. 704-894-8721

Owens, Johnnye B Jordan, *Librn,* Mayview State Hospital (Patients Library), Bridgeville PA. 412-221-7500, Ext 610

Owens, June, *Librn,* Livingston Parish Library (Killian), Springfield LA. 504-686-2436

Owens, Kathy, *Librn,* Broward County Division of Libraries (Riverland Branch), Fort Lauderdale FL. 305-791-8900

Owens, Lessie Viola, *Librn,* Public Library of the District of Columbia (Southwest), Washington DC. 202-727-1381

Owens, Margaret, *Dir,* Manchester Community College Library, Manchester CT. 203-646-4900, Ext 295

Owens, Mary Jane, *Spec Coll,* Duluth Public Library, Duluth MN. 218-723-3800

Owens, Nancy, *Librn,* Jones & Laughlin Steel Corp (Commercial Library), Pittsburgh PA. 412-565-4839

Owens, Nell, *Asst Dir,* Paul Sullins Public Library, Crossett Public Library, Crossett AR. 501 364 2230

Owens, Noel, *Soc Sci,* University of Calgary Library, Calgary AB. 403-284-5954

Owens, Pam, *Librn,* West Memphis Public Library, West Memphis AR. 501-735-2720

Owens, Patricia, *President,* Eastern Connecticut Library Association, CT. 203-456-1848

Owens, Richard C, *Librn,* United States Air Force (Columbus Air Force Base Library), Columbus AFB MS. 601-434-7322

Owens, Susie, *YA,* Great Neck Library, Great Neck NY. 516-466-8055

Owens, Sydney, *Lectr,* Simmons College, Graduate School of Library & Information Science, MA. 617-738-2225

Owens, Virginia L, *Head, Okla Resources,* Oklahoma Department of Libraries, Oklahoma City OK. 405-521-2502

Owens, Warren S, *Dir,* University of Idaho Library, Moscow ID. 208-885-6534

Owings, Elise, *Ad,* City of Inglewood Public Library, Inglewood CA. 213-649-7380

Owings, Loren C, *Soc Sci & Hist,* University of California at Davis, General Library, Davis CA. 916-752-2110

Ownbey, Donald C, *Acq,* Lane Community College Library, Eugene OR. 503-747-4501, Ext 2354

Ownby, Margaret, *Librn,* Northern Virginia Training Center for the Mentally Retarded Library, Fairfax VA. 703-323-5000

Owsley, Lucile C, *Chief Librn,* Veterans Administration, Medical Center Library, Salisbury NC. 704-636-2351

Oxley, Anna, *Librn,* Canadian Department of Fisheries & Oceans, Maritimes Regional Library, Halifax NS. 902-426-3972

Oxman, Frieda D, *Librn,* Veterans Administration Center (Medical Research Library), Los Angeles CA. 213-478-3711, Ext 2166

Oyer, Charlotte, *ILL,* California State University, Northridge, Delmar T Oviatt & South Libraries, Northridge CA. 213-885-2271

Oyer, John S, *Dir,* Goshen College (Mennonite Historical Library), Goshen IN. 219-533-3161, Ext 337

Oyer, Ken, *Librn,* Metropolitan Technical Community College (Southwest Campus Instructional Resource Center), Omaha NE. 402-457-5100, Ext 123

Oyler, Beth, *Gen Servs,* University of Utah (Marriott Library), Salt Lake City UT. 801-581-8558

Oyler, David K, *Librn,* Humboldt State University Library, Arcata CA. 707-826-3441

Oyler, Debra J, *Dir,* Alcona County Library, Harrisville MI. 517-724-6796

Oyler, Patricia G, *Assoc Prof,* Simmons College, Graduate School of Library & Information Science, MA. 617-738-2225

Ozburn, Tommy, *Dir,* Tarrant County Junior College System (Northeast Campus Learning Resource Center), Hurst TX. 817-281-7860, Ext 477

Ozeroff, Carole G, *Librn,* Congregation Adath Jeshurun, Gottlieb Memorial Library, Elkins Park PA. 215-635-1337, Ext 25

Ozga, Dawn, *Asst Librn,* Hewitt Associates Library, Lincolnshire IL. 312-295-5000

Ozinga, Connie J, *Ad,* Herrick Public Library, Holland MI. 616-392-3114

Ozment, Judith P, *Librn,* National Sporting Library Inc, Middleburg VA. 703-687-6542
Ozmint, Florine, *Librn,* Anderson County Library (Iva Branch), Iva SC. 803-348-6150
Ozolins, Karl L, *Dir,* Gustavus Adolphus College, Folke Bernadotte Memorial Library, Saint Peter MN. 507-931-4300, Ext 2301
Ozolins, Sulamit, *Tech Serv,* Luther-Northwestern Seminary Library, Saint Paul MN. 612-641-3225

P

Paas, Dorothy V, *Librn,* Ross, Hardies, O'keefe, Babcock & Parsons Library, Chicago IL. 312-467-9300
Pabst, Catherine, *Acq,* Bryn Mawr College, Canaday Library, Bryn Mawr PA. 215-645-5279
Pabst, Kathleen T, *Librn,* Mechanics Institute Library, San Francisco CA. 415-421-1750
Pabst, Margaret, *ILL,* State University of New York College, Daniel A Reed Library, Fredonia NY. 716-673-3183
Paccadolmi, Phyllis, *Circ,* Ridgefield Library & Historical Association, Ridgefield CT. 203-438-2282
Pace, Barbara D, *Librn & On-Line Servs,* Saint Paul Hospital, C B Sacher Library, Dallas TX. 214-688-2390, 688-4573
Pace, Betty M, *Dir,* Alta Public Library, Alta IA. 712-284-1250
Pace, Evelyn, *Librn,* Cherokee Regional Library (Dade County), Trenton GA. 404-638-2992
Pace, Jean, *Ad,* Wheeler Basin Regional Library, Decatur Public Library, Decatur AL. 205-353-2993
Pace, Julian, *Asst Dir,* Southwest Missouri State University Library, Springfield MO. 417-836-5104
Pace, Karen T, *Ch,* Aiken-Bamberg-Barnwell-Edgefield Regional Library, Aiken SC. 803-648-8961
Pace, Miriam M, *Librn,* Alabama Public Library Service, Division for the Blind & Physically Handicapped, Montgomery AL. 205-277-7330
Pace, Trudy, *Br Coordr,* Western Counties Regional Library, Yarmouth NS. 902-742-2486
Pacetti, Esther, *Librn,* PPG Industries Inc (General Office Library), Pittsburgh PA. 412-434-3177
Pacey, Brenda, *Librn,* Paxton Carnegie Library, Paxton IL. 217-379-3431
Pacheco, Gabriel Lopez, *Asst Librn,* Puerto Rico Department of Education, Biblioteca Publica Central, Santurce PR. 809-723-3739
Pacheco, Phyllis, *Acq & Bkmobile Coordr,* Kern County Library, Bakersfield CA. 805-861-2130
Pacheco, Phyllis B, *Librn,* Providence Public Library (Fox Point), Providence RI. 401-421-1436
Pachman, Barbara, *Tech Serv & Cat,* Paterson Free Public Library, Danforth Memorial Library, Paterson NJ. 201-881-3770
Pachman, Frederic C, *Asst Dir,* Township of Washington Public Library, Westwood NJ. 201-664-4586
Pacholik, Louise, *Asst Librn & Cat,* Northwestern University, Chicago (Dental School Library), Chicago IL. 312-649-8332
Pachta, Sister Bernadine, *Dir & Media,* Marymount College of Kansas Library, Salina KS. 913-823-6317, Ext 44
Pachucki, Gail, *Ch,* Waterford Public Library, Waterford WI. 414-534-3988
Pacifico, Fran, *Tech Serv, Cat & Spec Coll,* Elmira College, Gannett-Tripp Learning Ctr, Elmira NY. 607-734-3911, Ext 287
Paciorek, Loretta, *Ref,* Farmingdale Public Library, Farmingdale NY. 516-249-9090
Pack, Annisteen, *Mgt Asst,* Bureau of Land Management, California State Office Library, Sacramento CA. 916-484-4253
Package, John, *Librn,* Veterans Administration, Medical & Regional Office Center Library, White River Junction VT. 802-295-9363
Packard, Agnes K, *Librn,* Huntington Historical Society Library, Huntington NY. 516-427-7045
Packard, George M, *Dir & Tech Serv,* Grahm Junior College Library, Boston MA. 617-536-2050

Packard, Sarah, *Tech Serv & Cat,* George Williams College Library, Downers Grove IL. 312-964-3100, Ext 242
Packard, Tom, *Librn,* Datagraphix, Inc, Engineering Research Library, San Diego CA. 714-291-9960, Ext 1-215
Packer, Diane, *Librn,* Horizons Research Inc Library, Cleveland OH. 216-464-2424, Ext 23
Packer, June, *Rec Mgr,* American Plywood Association, Records Department Library, Tacoma WA. 206-272-2283
Packer, Katherine H, *Dean,* University of Toronto, Faculty of Library Science, ON. 416-978-3234
Packer, Martha L, *Tech Librn,* Institute of Gas Technology Library, Technical Information Center, Chicago IL. 312-567-3650
Packwood, Cyril O, *Chief Librn,* Borough of Manhattan Community College Library, Martin B Dworkis Library, New York NY. 212-262-3530
Paczelt, Anna, *Librn,* Reuben McMillan Free Library Free Library Association (West Branch), Youngstown OH. 612-799-7171
Padden, Barbara K, *Art & Music,* Library Association of Portland, Multnomah County Library, Portland OR. 503-223-7201, Ext 40
Padden, Rita, *Ch & YA,* San Mateo Public Library, San Mateo CA. 415-574-6955
Paden, Joyce M, *Librn,* Martinsburg Community Library, Martinsburg PA. 814-793-3335
Padget, Anne, *Librn,* Tully Free Library, Tully NY. 315-696-8606
Padgett, Dean, *Bus, Sci & Tech,* Orlando Public Library, Orlando FL. 305-425-4694
Padgett, Doris, *Librn,* Dallas County Public Library (Sunnyvale Branch), Sunnyvale TX. 214-285-8296
Padgett, Kay, *Librn,* Columbia Hospital for Women, Medical Library, Washington DC. 293-6500 & 293-6560
Padgett, Lawrence, *ILL,* Morgan State University, Morris A Soper Library, Baltimore MD. 301-444-3488, 444-3489
Padgett, Mary, *In Charge,* McLennan County Law Library, Waco TX. 817-753-7341
Padgett, Ruth, *YA,* Brainerd Public Library, Brainerd MN. 218-829-5574
Padgett, Thomas, *Assoc Prof,* Jacksonville State University, College of Library Science, Communications & Instructional Media, AL. 205-435-6390
Padgitt, Betty, *Librn,* Gnadenhutten Public Library, Gnadenhutten OH. 614-254-9224
Padilla, Dolores, *Dir,* Belen Public Library, Belen NM. 505-864-7522, 864-7797
Padilla, Donald, *Acq,* New Mexico Institute of Mining & Technology, Martin Speare Memorial Library, Socorro NM. 505-835-5614
Padilla, Rosie, *Librn,* Bureau of Land Management (Salt Lake District Office, Records Manager Library), Salt Lake City UT. 801-524-5348
Padno, Milton, *Librn,* Alameda Free Library (West End), Alameda CA. 415-522-4959
Padula, Armand, *Dir,* Mount Alvernia Friary Library, Wappingers Falls NY. 914-297-5706
Padwe, M M, *Librn,* Texaco Inc, Laboratory Library, Austin TX. 512-459-6543
Paeth, Jean, *Br Dist Supvr,* Oakland Public Library, Oakland CA. 415-273-3281
Paeth, Zillah, *Acq,* Oregon College of Education Library, Monmouth OR. 503-838-1220, Ext 240
Paetzold, Marjorie, *Media,* Massapequa Public Library, Massapequa NY. 516-798-4607
Paff, Toby, *Librn,* Boston Public Library (South Boston Branch), South Boston MA. 617-268-0180
Paffhausen, Frederick J, *Librn,* Ecorse Public Library, Ecorse MI. 313-381-6630
Pafford, Catherine, *Librn,* South Georgia Regional Library (Hahira Branch), Hahira GA. 912-794-2330
Pagana, Suzanne, *Tech Serv,* Atlantic Community College, Daniel Leeds Learning Resources Center, Mays Landing NJ. 625-1111 & 646-4950
Page, Ada M, *Librn,* Kingsville Public Library, Kingsville OH. 216-224-0239
Page, Alain, *On-Line Servs,* Universite Du Quebec A Trois-Rivieres Bibliotheque, Trois-Rivieres PQ. 819-376-5706
Page, Angela, *Ch,* Bernardsville Public Library, Bernardsville NJ. 201-766-0118

Page, Benjamin F, *Assoc Prof,* University of Washington, School of Librarianship, WA. 206-543-1794
Page, Bruce, *Park Naturalist,* National Park Service, Glacier Bay National Monument Library, Gustavus AK. 907-697-3242
Page, Cathy, *Asst Librn,* Mount Vernon Public Library, Mount Vernon IL. 618-242-6322
Page, Dennis N, *Dir,* Grand Forks Public City-County Library, Grand Forks ND. 701-772-8116
Page, Dixie, *Library Asst,* Spartanburg County Public Library (Woodruff Branch), Woodruff SC. 803-476-8770
Page, Donna, *Cat,* Loyola-Notre Dame Library, Inc, Baltimore MD. 301-532-8787
Page, E, *Acq,* University of Toronto Libraries (Victoria College), Toronto ON. 416-978-3821
Page, Ella May, *Asst Librn,* Crestline Public Library, Crestline OH. 419-683-3909
Page, James, *Librn,* Los Angeles Public Library System (Junipero Serra), Los Angeles CA. 213-234-1685
Page, Jane, *Librn,* Mississippi State University (Cobb Institute Library), Mississippi State MS. 601-325-3826
Page, Jeanette, *Acq,* Union College Library, Lincoln NE. 402-488-2331, Ext 316
Page, John, *Tech Serv,* University of the District of Columbia, Learning Resources Division, Washington DC. 202-282-7536
Page, Kathryn, *Ref,* The 49-99 Cooperative Library System, Stockton CA. 209-944-8649
Page, Kirk, *Libr Asst,* Western Counties Regional Library (Digby Branch), Digby NS. 902-245-2163
Page, Margaret, *Ad,* Saint Clair County Library System, Port Huron MI. 313-987-7323
Page, Melda W, *Librn,* Veterans Administration, Medical & Regional Office Center Library Service, Augusta ME. 207-623-8411, Ext 275, 504
Page, Mrs Walter, *Librn,* Effingham Community Library, Effingham KS. 913-833-5881
Page, Paul, *Librn,* Control Process Inc Library, Plantsville CT. 203-628-4271
Page, Priscilla, *Bks-by-Mail & Outreach,* State of Vermont Department of Libraries, Montpelier VT. 802-828-3261
Page, Richard, *Art,* Indianhead Federated Library System, Eau Claire WI. 715-839-5082
Page, William, *Sci,* Drexel University Library, Philadelphia PA. 215-895-2750
Pagel, Doris, *Prof,* Mankato State College, Library Media Education, MN. 507-389-1965
Pagel, Helen, *Librn,* Denison Carnegie Library, Denison IA. 712-263-3449
Pagel, Scott B, *Ref,* Thomas M Cooley Law School Library, Lansing MI. 517-371-5140
Pagell, Ruth, *Bus & Admin,* Drexel University Library, Philadelphia PA. 215-895-2750
Pagels, Helen, *Circ,* Dowling College Library, Oakdale NY. 516-589-6100, Ext 218 or 219
Paget, K, *Libr Tech,* Queen's University at Kingston (Mechanical Engineering), Kingston ON. 613-547-2714
Pagliccia, K Priscilla, *Librn,* Malden Public Library (Linden), Malden MA. 617-322-5470
Paglis, Rose, *Librn,* Hammond Public Library (Riley), Munster IN. 219-931-5100
Pahanish, Marjorie, *Bkmobile Coordr,* Lepper Library, Lisbon OH. 216-424-3117
Paice, Evelyn S, *Librn,* Beckley College Library, Beckley WV. 304-253-7351, Ext 33
Paicurich, Gene, *Tech Serv,* El Paso Public Library, El Paso TX. 915-543-3804
Paige, Norma, *Librn,* ASG Industries Inc, Market Research Library, Kingsport TN. 615-245-0211, Ext 258
Paihowshi, Gary F, *Dir,* Grayson County Junior College Library, Denison TX. 214-465-6030, Ext 237
Paine, Barbara, *ILL & Ref,* Decatur Public Library, Decatur IL. 217-428-6617, Ext 33
Paine, F Helen, *Librn,* Manitoba Department of Economic Development & Tourism Library, Winnipeg MB. 204-944-2036
Paine, Patricia M, *Deputy Dir,* Fairfax County Public Library, Administrative Offices, Springfield VA. 703-321-9810
Paine, Roberta M, *Mus Educator,* Metropolitan Museum of Art (Junior Museum Library), New York NY. 212-879-5500, Ext 350

Paine, Ruth, *Librn,* Telegraph Herald Library, Dubuque IA. 319-588-5611
Paine, Thelma, *Ref,* New Bedford Free Public Library, Subregional Headquarters for Eastern Massachusetts Regional Library System, New Bedford MA. 617-999-6291
Painter, Conrad L, *Librn,* Florida Department of Offender Rehabilitation, De Soto Correctional Institution Library, Arcadia FL. 813-494-3727
Painter, Jackie, *Govt Doc,* Norwich University, Henry Prescott Chaplin Memorial Library, Northfield VT. 802-485-5011, Ext 48
Painter, Jane, *In Charge,* Susquehanna River Basin Commission Library, Harrisburg PA. 717-238-0424
Painter, John C, *Dir,* Delaware Technical & Community College, Southern Campus Library, Georgetown DE. 302-856-5438
Painter, Maxine, *Cat,* Upjohn Company (Corporate Technical Library), Kalamazoo MI. 616-385-6114
Painter, Nancy, *Librn,* McDowell Public Library (Keystone Branch), Keystone WV. 304-436-3070
Painter, Patty, *Asst Librn,* Cumston Free Public Library, Monmouth Library, Monmouth ME. 207-933-4788
Painter, Reed, *Cat,* Utah State University, Merrill Library & Learning Resources Program, Logan UT. 801-750-2637
Pajak, June, *ILL & On-Line Servs,* Plattsburgh Public Library, Plattsburgh NY. 518-563-0921
Pajerski, June, *Librn,* California Public Library, California PA. 412-938-2907
Pakala, James C, *Librn & Bibliog Instr,* Biblical Theological Seminary Library, Hatfield PA. 215-368-5000
Pakenham, Barbara, *Librn,* Eastford Public Library, Eastford CT. 203-974-0125
Pakulak, J, *Librn,* Borough of York Public Library (Jane-Dundas), Toronto ON. 416-769-4123
Palacio, John, *Supportive Servs,* Scottsdale Public Library, Scottsdale AZ. 602-994-2471
Palagano, Marie, *Librn,* Middletown Township Public Library (Navesink Branch), Navesink NJ. 201-291-1120
Palais, Elliot, *Soc Sci,* Arizona State University Library, Tempe AZ. 602-965-3417
Palanker, Bonnie, *Media,* Baldwin Public Library, Baldwin NY. 516-223-6228
Palaszynski, Diane, *Ch,* Niagara Falls Public Library, Niagara Falls NY. 716-278-8041
Palay, Judith, *Ref & Bibliog Instr,* Middlesex Community College, Learning Resources Center, Bedford MA. 617-275-8910
Palchak, Jackie, *On-Line Servs,* University of California Library, Irvine CA. 714-833-5212
Palen, Diane, *Bkmobile Coordr,* Fort Worth Public Library, Fort Worth TX. 817-870-7700
Palen, Oloanne Dykeman, *Dir,* Tulare County Library System, Visalia CA. 209-733-8440
Palen, Roberta, *Doc,* Texas A&M University Libraries, College Station TX. 713-845-6111
Palermo, Patricia, *Librn,* Forsyth Dental Center, Percy R Howe Memorial Library, Boston MA. 617-262-5200, Ext 244
Palet, Ruth, *Asst Librn,* Jewish Federation Libraries (Jewish Community Center Library), Nashville TN. 615-297-3588
Paley, Marilyn, *Ref,* Manhasset Public Library, Manhasset NY. 516-627-2300
Paliani, Mary Ann, *Librn,* Rockwell International Corp, Energy Systems Group, Rocky Flats Plant Library, Golden CO. 303-497-2861
Palin, J, *Rare Bks,* Carleton University, Murdoch Maxwell MacOdrum Library, Ottawa ON. 613-231-4357
Palko, Joanne, *Cat,* University of Connecticut Library, Storrs CT. 203-486-2219
Palko, John M, *Librn,* Ludington Public Library, Ludington MI. 616-843-8465
Palling, Barbara R, *Dir,* Buena Vista College, Ballou Library, Storm Lake IA. 712-749-2141
Pallister, Elsie, *ILL,* Eagle County Public Library, Eagle CO. 303-328-7311, Ext 255, 256
Pallone, Susan, *ILL,* Public Library of Fort Wayne & Allen County, Fort Wayne IN. 219-424-7241
Palm, Clara, *Ref,* Michigan City Public Library, Michigan City IN. 219-879-4561
Palm, Ruth, *Librn,* Mount Caesar Union Library, Swanzey NH. 603-352-4574

Palmatier, Susan M, *Librn,* New Hampshire State Library (Keene Branch), Keene NH. 603-271-2392
Palme, Natalie, *Librn,* Harvard Musical Association Library, Boston MA. 617-523-2897
Palmer, Barbara, *Dir,* Earlville Free Library, Earlville NY. 315-691-5931
Palmer, Barbara, *Ref,* NASA, Goddard Institute For Space Studies, New York NY. 212-678-5613
Palmer, Carol, *Librn,* Red Creek Free Library, Red Creek NY. 315-754-8826
Palmer, Dale, *Tech Serv & Cat,* Newmarket Public Library, Newmarket ON. 416-895-5196
Palmer, Daniel J, *Ref,* New Britain Public Library, New Britain CT. 203-224-3155
Palmer, David, *Librn,* Department of Public Libraries & Information (Oceanfront), Virginia Beach VA. 804-428-4113
Palmer, David C, *Asst State Librn,* New Jersey State Library, Trenton NJ. 609-292-6200
Palmer, David W, *Dir,* University of Michigan-Flint Library, Flint MI. 313-762-3400
Palmer, Dawn, *Ch, Media & Commun Servs,* West Orange Free Public Library, West Orange NJ. 201-736-0198
Palmer, Ellen, *Librn,* Public Library of Columbus & Franklin County (Morse Road Branch), Columbus OH. 614-267-7551
Palmer, Eva M, *Librn,* Bowdoinham Public Library, Bowdoinham ME. 207-666-5714
Palmer, Forrest, *Doc,* James Madison University, Madison Memorial Library, Harrisonburg VA. 703-433-6150
Palmer, Gregory, *Bkmobile Coordr,* Susquehanna County Historical Society & Free Library Association, Montrose PA. 717-278-1881
Palmer, Helen, *Librn,* Northwest Regional Library (Hamilton Branch), Hamilton AL. 205-921-2121
Palmer, Helen, *ILL,* Pitkin County Library, Aspen CO. 303-925-7124
Palmer, Jean, *Asst Dir,* Stoneham Public Library, Stoneham MA. 617-438-1324
Palmer, John J, *In Charge,* Sequoia & Kings Canyon National Parks, Ash Mountain Park Library, Three Rivers CA. 209-565-3341
Palmer, Jonathan W, *Circ Dept Head,* Harvard University Library (Baker Library), Boston MA. 617-495-3650
Palmer, Joseph, *Asst Prof,* State University of New York at Buffalo, School of Information & Library Studies, NY. 716-636-2412
Palmer, Lorraine, *Librn,* New York Chiropractic College, Library, Old Westbury NY. 516-686-7657, 686-7658
Palmer, M L, *Ref, Spec Coll & On-Line Servs,* University of Maine School of Law, Donald L Garbrecht Library, Portland ME. 207-780-4350
Palmer, Margaret, *Dir,* Cumberland Public Library, Cumberland WI. 715-822-2767
Palmer, Margaret, *Librn,* Eleanor Daggett Public Library, Chama Valley Library, Chama NM. 505-756-2388
Palmer, Martha, *Dir,* Nantahala Regional Library, Murphy NC. 704-837-2025
Palmer, Mary, *Dir,* Mississippi Gulf Coast Junior College, Jackson County Campus Library, Gautier MS. 601-497-4313, Ext 226, Libr; 497-4313, Ext 255 Media Ctr
Palmer, Mary Alice, *Exec Secy,* Saint Mary's County Historical Society, Leonardtown MD. 301-475-2467
Palmer, Mary Jane, *Commun Servs,* Warren Public Library, Warren MI. 313-264-8720
Palmer, Maxine, *Media,* Northern Nevada Community College, Learning Resources Center, Elko NV. 702-738-8493, Ext 225
Palmer, Nancy, *Ch,* Walla Walla Public Library, Walla Walla WA. 509-525-5353
Palmer, Pamela, *Librn,* Memphis State University Libraries (Engineering), Memphis TN. 901-454-2179
Palmer, Patricia, *In Charge,* Norfolk Public Library (Brambleton), Norfolk VA. 804-441-2843
Palmer, Paul, *Curator,* Columbia University (Columbiana), New York NY. 212-280-2241
Palmer, Ray, *Librn,* General Electric Co, Armament Systems Products Engineering Library, Burlington VT. 802-658-1500
Palmer, Raymond A, *Librn,* Wright State University Library (Fordham Library, Cox Heart Institute Library & Fels Research Institute Library), Dayton OH. 513-873-2266

Palmer, Richard, *Tech Serv,* Public Library of Columbus & Franklin County, Columbus OH. 614-864-8050
Palmer, Richard P, *Assoc Prof,* Simmons College, Graduate School of Library & Information Science, MA. 617-738-2225
Palmer, Robert B, *Dir,* Columbia University (Barnard College), New York NY. 212-280-3846
Palmer, Robert C, *Dir Libr Serv,* Michigan Department of Corrections, State Prison of Southern Michigan Library, Jackson MI. 517-782-0301, Ext 496
Palmer, Shirley, *Librn,* Progressive Grocer Company Research Library, New York NY. 212-490-1000, Ext 212
Palmer, Sister Mary Catherine, *ILL & Ref,* Saint Mary College Library, Leavenworth KS. 913-682-5151, Ext 202
Palmer, Susan, *Librn,* Denver Public Library (Bear Valley), Denver CO. 303-573-5152, Ext 271
Palmer, Susan J, *Asst Dir, Tech Serv & Cat,* William Penn College, Wilcox Library, Oskaloosa IA. 515-673-8311, Ext 291
Palmer, Sylvia C, *ILL,* University of North Carolina at Wilmington, William Madison Randall Library, Wilmington NC. 919-791-4330, Ext 2270
Palmer, III, John M, *In Charge,* Trinity Church Parish Library, New York NY. 212-285-0800, 0807
Palmieri, Lucien E, *Coll Develop,* State University College at Buffalo, Edward H Butler Library, Buffalo NY. 716-878-6302
Palmisano, Kathleen, *On-Line Servs,* Tenneco Chemicals, Inc Library, Piscataway NJ. 201-981-5252
Palmquist, David, *Local Hist,* Bridgeport Public Library, Bridgeport CT. 203-576-7777
Palmquist, Marlene, *Asst Dir & Ref,* James Blackstone Memorial Library, Branford CT. 203-488-1441
Palmquist, Robyn, *Libr Purchasing Agent,* Occidental Exploration & Production Co Library, Bakersfield CA. 805-395-8565
Palmquist, Ruth A, *Dir,* Bellevue College, F Hoyte Freeman Library, Bellevue NE. 291-8100 Ext 64
Palomo, Gerard, *Circ,* University of Texas Health Science Center at San Antonio Library, San Antonio TX. 512-691-6271
Pals, Eunice, *Media,* Simpson College, Dunn Library, Indianola IA. 515-961-6251, Ext 663
Palsson, Gerald, *Asst Dir,* San Diego State University Library, San Diego CA. 714-286-6014
Palsson, Mary Dale, *Pub Servs,* University of Arizona Library, Tucson AZ. 602-626-2101
Paluka, Francis, *Spec Coll,* University of Iowa Libraries, Iowa City IA. 319-353-4450
Palumbo, Richard, *Ref & Bibliog Instr,* Wagner College, Horrmann Library, Staten Island NY. 212-390-3001
Palzer, William, *Cat,* Winona State University, Maxwell Library, Winona MN. 507-457-2040
Pan, Josephine, *Ref,* Milford Public Library, Milford CT. 203-878-7461
Pan, Lois E, *Dir,* Pleasant Valley Free Library, Pleasant Valley NY. 914-635-8460
Pana, Lucy M, *Librn,* Alberta Department of Culture (Alberta Culture Departmental Library), Edmonton AB. 403-427-2571
Panacci, Angela, *AV,* Mary H Weir Public Library, Weirton WV. 304-748-7070
Panaccione, Kate L, *Dir,* Union Beach Memorial Library, Union Beach NJ. 201-264-3792
Panagotopulos, Georgia, *Librn,* Chicopee Public Library (Willimansett), Chicopee MA. 413-532-3364
Panasci, Debbie, *Researcher,* Occidental Exploration & Production Co Library, Bakersfield CA. 805-395-8565
Panasuk, Joanne M, *Librn,* Lake County Public Library (Talking Book Service), Merrillville IN. 219-769-3541, Ext 37
Pancake, Edwina, *Science Tech,* University of Virginia, Alderman Library, Charlottesville VA. 804-924-3026
Pancero, Claire, *Librn,* Athenaeum of Ohio, Saint Gregory Seminary Library, Cincinnati OH. 513-231-2223
Panciera, David J, *Dir,* South County Interrelated Library System, Westerly RI. 401-596-2877

Panciera, David J, *Dir*, Westerly Public Library, Memorial & Library Association of Westerly, Westerly RI. 401-596-2877

Panciuk, Mircea, *Librn*, Concordia College, Arnold Guebert Memorial Library, Edmonton AB. 403-479-8481

Pandell, Karen, *Br Coordr*, Juneau Memorial Library, Juneau AK. 907-586-2429

Pandolfi, Rosemary, *Cat*, School of Visual Arts Library, New York NY. 679-7350 Ext 67, 68

Pandolfo, Steven, *Asst Dir*, Grinnell College, Burling Library, Grinnell IA. 515-236-6181, Ext 598

Pane, Virginia, *Librn*, Alameda County Library (Centerville), Fremont CA. 415-791-4789

Panek, Joan, *Dir*, Dover Town Library, Dover MA. 617-785-0953

Panella, Deborah, *Cat*, Paul, Weiss, Rifkind, Wharton & Garrison Library, New York NY. 212-644-8235

Panella, Nancy, *Librn*, Saint Luke's Hospital Center, Richard Walker Bolling Memorial Medical Library, New York NY. 212-870-1861

Pang, Isabel, *Cat*, Monmouth College, Guggenheim Library, West Long Branch NJ. 201-222-6600, Ext 264

Pangrace, Lynn, *Ch*, Rocky River Public Library, Rocky River OH. 216-333-7610

Panichella, Rosemary, *Librn*, Latrobe Area Hospital, Medical-Nursing Libraries, Latrobe PA. 412-537-1275

Pankey, Marilyn R, *Dir*, Sierra View District Hospital, Medical Library, Porterville CA. 209-784-1110

Pankey, Stephen, *Res Proj Dir*, Vansant Dugdale & Co, Inc Library, Baltimore MD. 301-539-5400

Pankratz, Else, *Librn*, Saint Catharines Public Library (Grantham), Saint Catharines ON. 416-934-7511

Pankratz, Eulalo, *Librn*, Walton Community Library, Walton KS. 316-837-3252

Pannebaker, Patricia R, *Ad*, Middletown Township Public Library, Middletown NJ. 201-671-3700

Pannekoek, Frits, *In Charge*, Alberta Department of Culture (Historic Sites Service Branch), Edmonton AB. 403-427-2022

Pannell, Teena, *Central Divisions: Central Libr Circ*, Dallas Public Library, Dallas TX. 214-748-9071

Panneton, Jacques, *Dir*, Bibliotheque De La Ville De Montreal, Montreal PQ. 514-872-5923

Panoff, Oleg, *Librn*, Hughes Aircraft Co (Information Research), Culver City CA. 213-391-0711, Ext 3474

Pantages, Sandra, *Librn*, Alameda County Library (Fremont Main Branch), Fremont CA. 415-791-4794

Pantano, Richard, *Dir*, New Hampshire College, Shapiro Library, Manchester NH. 603-668-2211, Ext 211

Pantazzi, Sybille, *Librn*, Art Gallery of Ontario, Edward P Taylor Reference Library, Toronto ON. 416-977-0414, Ext 339, 340 & 390

Pantelidis, Veronica S, *Asst Prof*, East Carolina University, Dept of Library Science, NC. 919-757-6621, 757-6627

Pantridge, Barb, *Librn*, Marist College, Learning Resources Center, Poughkeepsie NY. 914-471-3240, Ext 292, 229

Pantridge, Barbara B, *Educ Asst*, Dutchess County Mental Health Library, Poughkeepsie NY. 914-485-9700, Ext 554

Panz, Richard, *Dir*, Finger Lakes Library System, Ithaca NY. 607-273-4074

Pao, Joanne T, *Librn*, Flow Industries, Inc, Kent WA. 206-872-7280

Pao, Miranda, *Assoc Prof*, Case Western Reserve University, School of Library Science, OH. 216-368-3500

Paolicelli, Catherine, *Ch*, Clairton Public Library, Clairton PA. 412-233-7966

Paolini, Christine, *Asst Librn*, College of the Virgin Islands, Saint Croix Campus Library, Saint Croix VI. 809-778-1620

Paonessa, Susan, *Ch & Br Coordr*, Alameda Free Library, Alameda CA. 415-522-5413, 522-3578

Papandrea, Marie, *Asst Librn*, Mutual of New York (Law Department Library), New York NY. 212-586-4000, Ext 400

Paparelli, Marita E, *Librn*, Lackawanna Bar Association Law Library, Scranton PA. 717-342-8089

Papazian, Rosemarie, *Asst Librn*, Marymount Palos Verdes College Library, Rancho Palos Verdes CA. 213-377-5501, Ext 29

Papazian, Rosemary, *Librn*, Commonwealth Club of California Library, San Francisco CA. 415-362-4903

Pape, Marion, *YA*, Saskatoon Public Library, Saskatoon SK. 306-664-9555

Pape, Renee, *Librn*, Glenwood State Hospital-School, Staff Library, Glenwood IA. 712-527-4811

Pape, Ruth P, *Librn*, Saint Elizabeth Hospital Medical Center, Memorial Medical Library, Lafayette IN. 317-423-6125

Papell, Helen, *Librn*, Brooklyn Public Library (Marcy), Brooklyn NY. 212-858-1828

Paper, Randall, *Dir*, Lincoln Library, Springfield Public Library, Springfield IL. 217-753-4900

Papermaster, Cynthia, *Librn*, Orrick, Herrington, Rowley & Sutcliffe, Law Library, San Francisco CA. 415-392-1122

Papillon, Lucien, *Tech Serv*, Universite Laval Bibliotheque, Quebec PQ. 418-656-3344

Paplinski, William E, *Dir*, Troy-Miami County Public Library, Troy OH. 513-339-0502

Pappalardo, Charles, *Chief Librn*, Queensborough Community College Library, Bayside NY. 212-631-6226

Pappas, Florence E, *Bkmobile Coordr*, Wayne Township Library, Morrisson-Reeves Library, Richmond IN. 317-966-8291

Pappas, Florence E, *Librn*, Wayne Township Library (Wayne County Contractual), Richmond IN. 317-966-8291

Pappas, Helen I, *Asst Dir*, Peabody Institute Library, Peabody MA. 617-531-0100

Pappas, Lucia X, *Librn*, Elmwood Park Public Library, Elmwood Park IL. 453-7645 & 453-8236

Paptain, Paige, *Librn*, Houston Public Library (Lakewood), Houston TX. 713-633-3725

Paquette, Barbara J, *Chief Librn*, Park Ridge Public Library, Park Ridge IL. 312-825-3123

Paquette, Claire Marie, *Bus & Mgt*, Ryerson Polytechnical Institute, Donald Mordell Learning Resources Centre, Toronto ON. 416-595-5331

Paquette, Marion, *Librn*, Alice M Ward Memorial Library, Canaan VT. 802-266-3468

Paquette, Rita, *Librn*, University of Montreal Libraries (Mathematics), Montreal PQ. 514-343-6703

Paquin, Marcel, *Librn*, College Lionel-Groulx Bibliotheque, Sainte Theresa-de-Blainville PQ. 514-430-3120

Paquin, Nicole, *Librn*, Regie Des Rentes Du Quebec, Centre de Documentation, Quebec PQ. 418-643-8250

Paradis, Denise, *Acq*, Saint Anselm's College, Geisel Library, Manchester NH. 603-669-1030, Ext 240, 249

Paradis, Gilles, *Philos & Psychol*, Universite Laval Bibliotheque, Quebec PQ. 418-656-3344

Paradis, Jacques, *Coordr*, College Lionel-Groulx, Techniques de la Documentation, PQ. 514-430-3120, Ext 261

Paradis, Olivier, *Cat*, Ecole Polytechnique De Montreal Bibliotheque, Montreal PQ. 514-344-4847

Paras, Lucille P, *Assoc Librn*, Ortho Diagnostics Inc Library, Raritan NJ. 201-524-0400

Parch, Grace D, *Dir*, Plain Dealer Publishing Co Library, Cleveland OH. 216-344-4195

Parchman, June, *Librn*, Lummus Co Library, Houston TX. 713-871-3120

Parchuck, Jill A, *Dir*, Hudson Area Association Library, Hudson NY. 518-828-1792

Pardy, Mary, *Librn*, Essex County Public Library (Stoney Point Branch), Stoney Point ON. 519-776-5241

Pare, Alice, *Dir*, Divernon Township Library, Divernon IL. 217-628-3813

Pare, Gilles, *Librn*, Le Devoir, Centre de Documentation, Montreal PQ. 514-844-4361

Pare, Richard, *Asst Dir*, Assemblee Nationale, Bibliotheque de la legislature, Quebec PQ. 418-643-2121

Paredes, Beverly D, *Librn*, Marymount College of Virginia, Ireton Library, Arlington VA. 703-524-2500

Parent, Anne T, *Asst Dir*, Cranston Public Library, William H Hall Free Library (Administrative & Reference Center), Cranston RI. 401-781-2450, 781-9580

Parent, Helen Marie, *Dir*, Gladstone Public Library, Gladstone OR. 503-656-2411

Parent, Richard, *AV*, Arizona State Library, Dept of Library, Archives & Public Records, Phoenix AZ. 602-255-4035

Paretsky, Mary, *Ch*, Lawrence Public Library, Lawrence KS. 913-843-3833

Parga, Ruth E, *Middle East & Africa*, National Defense University Library, Washington DC. 202-693-8437

Parhad, Bronwyn, *Info Ctr*, Chicago Public Library (General Information Service Div), Chicago IL. 312-269-2800

Parham, Arthur R, *Bibliog Instr*, Chicago State University, Paul & Emily Douglas Library, Chicago IL. 312-995-2254

Parham, Kay, *Ref & Doc*, Southeastern Oklahoma State University Library, Durant OK. 405-924-0121, Ext 245

Parham, Paul, *Dir*, Texas Christian University, Mary Couts Burnett Library, Fort Worth TX. 817-921-7106

Parham, Willibelle S, *Dir*, Olive Warner Memorial Library, Hooker OK. 405-652-2634

Parikh, Kaumudi, *Ref*, Cora J Belden Library, Rocky Hill CT. 203-529-2379

Parikh, Neel, *Librn*, Alameda County Library (Union City Branch), Union City CA. 415-471-6771

Paris, Carolyn, *Bkmobile Coordr*, Crittenden County Library, Marion KY. 502-965-3354

Paris, Dr Janelle A, *Asst Prof*, Sam Houston State University, Library Science Department, TX. 713-295-6211, Ext 1151

Paris, Mrs Jo, *Librn*, Warren County Library (Kirkwood Branch), Kirkwood IL. 309-768-2173

Paris, T, *Ref, On-Line Servs & Bibliog Instr*, Mount Saint Vincent University Library, Halifax NS. 902-443-4450, Ext 120, 121, 125

Parise, Pierina, *Librn*, Hawaii State Library System (Mount View Community-School), Mount View HI. 808-968-6300

Parish, David, *Gov Docs*, State University of New York College at Geneseo, Milne Library, Geneseo NY. 716-245-5591

Parisi, Lawrence, *YA*, Finkelstein Memorial Library, Spring Valley NY. 914-352-5700, Ext 230

Parisky, Helen, *Cat*, California Lutheran College Library, Thousand Oaks CA. 805-492-2411, Ext 205

Park, Choi, *Actg Dean, Tech Serv & Cat*, Maryville College, Lamar Memorial Library, Maryville TN. 615-982-1200

Park, Debra, *Ch*, Schaumburg Township Public Library, Schaumburg IL. 312-885-3373

Park, Hwayang, *Cat*, State University of New York (Health Sciences Center Library), East Setauket NY. 516-246-2512

Park, Janice, *Dir*, Charles A Ransom Public Library, Plainwell MI. 616-685-8024

Park, Leland M, *Dir*, Davidson College, E H Little Library, Davidson NC. 704-892-2000, Ext 331

Park, Mary L, *Dir*, Bethany Public Library, Honesdale PA. 717-253-4349

Park, Mrs A Belva, *Librn*, Regina General Hospital, Medical Library, Regina SK. 306-522-1811, Ext 314

Park, Robert C, *Dir Libr Serv*, Saint Luke's Episcopal Hospital Library, Houston TX. 713-791-3054

Park, Robert C, *Dir Libr Serv*, Texas Chidlren's Hospital, Medical Library, Houston TX. 713-791-3054

Park, Susan, *Cat*, Needham Free Public Library, Needham MA. 617-444-0087, 444-0090

Park, T Peter, *Librn*, Estonian Aid, Inc, Erna Nuth Memorial Library, New York NY. 212-675-0825

Park, T Peter, *ILL*, Lynbrook Public Library, Lynbrook NY. 516-599-8630

Park, Yong H, *Tech Serv*, Tempe Public Library, Tempe AZ. 602-968-8231

Parke, Carol, *Ref*, Virginia Commonwealth University (James Branch Cabell Library), Richmond VA. 804-257-1105

Parker, Anne H, *Librn*, Lilly Pike Sullivan Municipal Library, Enfield Public Library, Enfield NC. 919-445-5203

Parker, Annette, *ILL, State Doc & Serials,* Northwestern Oklahoma State University Library, Alva OK. 405-327-1700, Ext 219
Parker, Annie T, *Librn,* Thomas Hackney Braswell Memorial Library (Harold D Cooley), Nashville NC. 442-1937 & 442-1951
Parker, Barbara, *Dir,* Florala Public Library, Florala AL. 205-858-3525
Parker, Bonnie, *Librn,* Carnegie Public Library, Conneaut Library, Conneaut OH. 216-593-1608
Parker, Candace, *On-Line Servs,* United States Department of the Navy (Naval Air Systems Command, Technical Library), Washington DC. 202-692-9006
Parker, Carolyn, *Media,* Wake Forest University (Bowman Gray School of Medicine Library), Winston-Salem NC. 919-727-4691
Parker, Catherine, *ILL & Ref,* Charles County Community College, Learning Resource Center, La Plata MD. 301-934-2251, Ext 251
Parker, Cheryl, *Tech Serv,* Mount Vernon Public Library, Mount Vernon WA. 206-336-2418
Parker, Collie, *Librn,* Lucy H Patterson Memorial Library, Rockdale TX. 512-446-3410
Parker, Craig, *ILL & Ref,* Catholic University of America (Robert J White Law), Washington DC. 202-635-5155
Parker, D, *Ref,* State University of New York at Buffalo (Lockwood Library), Buffalo NY. 716-636-2816
Parker, Diane, *Learning Res Supvr,* Pasco-Hernando Community College, West Campus Learning Resource Center, New Port Richey FL. 813-842-8478
Parker, Dorris D, *Librn,* Blue Hill Public Library, Blue Hill ME. 207-374-5515
Parker, Elizabeth L, *Librn,* Coastal Ecosystems Management, Inc Library, Fort Worth TX. 817-731-3727
Parker, Elizabeth Penny, *Librn,* Enoch Pratt Free Library (Edmondson Ave), Baltimore MD. 301-396-5430, 396-5395
Parker, Faye, *Actg Librn,* Harnett County Library (Coats Branch), Coats NC. 919-897-5183
Parker, Florence, *Tech Serv,* Cities Service Co, Energy Resources Group Research Library, Tulsa OK. 918-586-2524
Parker, Frances, *Dir,* Jasper Public Library, Jasper IN. 812-482-2712
Parker, Frances M, *Pub Servs,* Colby College, Miller Library, Waterville ME. 207-873-1131, Ext 209
Parker, Frances V, *Dir,* Bay City Public Library, Bay City TX. 713-245-6931
Parker, Grover P, *Librn,* United States Air Force (Wright-Patterson Technical Library), Wright-Patterson AFB OH. 513-255-5511
Parker, Helen, *Order,* Public Library of Cincinnati & Hamilton County, Cincinnati Public Library, Cincinnati OH. 513-369-6000
Parker, J, *Adjunct Assoc Prof,* University of Alberta, Faculty of Library Science, AB. 403-432-4578
Parker, J Carlyle, *Asst Dir & Bibliog Instr,* California State College, Stanislaus Library, Turlock CA. 209-633-2232
Parker, Jeannine, *Dir,* Latter Day Saints Business College Library, Salt Lake City UT. 801-363-2765
Parker, Jennie, *ILL, Ad & Ref,* Wilson County Public Library, Wilson NC. 919-237-3818
Parker, Jo Ann, *Librn,* Crane County Library, Crane TX. 915-558-3142
Parker, John, *Ref,* Norfolk Public Library, Norfolk VA. 804-441-2887
Parker, John, *Curator,* University of Minnesota Libraries-Twin Cities (James Ford Bell Library), Minneapolis MN. 612-373-2888
Parker, John W, *Dir,* Post College, Traurig Library, Waterbury CT. 203-755-0121, Ext 252
Parker, June D, *On-Line Servs,* Sheppard Memorial Library, Greenville NC. 919-752-4177
Parker, Kathy, *Reader Serv,* Western Baptist College Library, Salem OR. 503-581-8600, Ext 49
Parker, Kenneth, *Soc Sci,* Stanford University Libraries, Stanford CA. 415-497-2016
Parker, Kenneth W, *Librn,* Stanford University Libraries (Cubberley Education), Stanford CA. 415-497-2121
Parker, Lanny, *Acq,* Wake County Department of the Public Library, Raleigh NC. 919-755-6077

Parker, Laura B, *Librn,* Sunkist Growers Inc (Research Library), Ontario CA. 714-983-9811, Ext 454
Parker, Leonard, *Mgr Technical Info Servs,* Ciba-Geigy Corp Library, Greensboro NC. 919-292-7100, Ext 2860
Parker, Lillie S, *Dir,* California State University, Fresno Library, Fresno CA. 209-487-2403
Parker, Linda T, *Asst Librn,* Virginia Electric & Power Co Library, Richmond VA. 804-771-3659, 3657
Parker, Loretta, *ILL,* Long Beach Public Library, Long Beach NY. 516-432-7201
Parker, Lydia, *Extension Coordr,* Southeast Alabama Cooperative Library System, Dothan AL. 205-793-9767
Parker, Lydia M, *Dir,* Choctawhatchee Regional Library, Ozark AL. 205-774-5480
Parker, Lynda, *Librn,* West Georgia Regional Library (Warren P Sewell Memorial Library of Bowdon), Bowdon GA. 404-832-1381
Parker, Malcolm G, *Dir,* Louisiana State University in Shreveport Library, Shreveport LA. 318-797-7121, Ext 203
Parker, Marcia, *Librn,* Kent General Hospital, Medical Library, Dover DE. 302-734-4701
Parker, Margaret, *Asst Dir,* Lexington Public Library, Lexington NE. 308-324-2151
Parker, Marian, *Ref,* Duke University (Law School Library), Durham NC. 919-684-2847
Parker, Marian, *Librn,* Wood County District Public Library, Bowling Green OH. 419-352-5104
Parker, Marion, *Ch,* Newburgh Free Library, Newburgh NY. 914-561-1836
Parker, Marjorie, *Ch,* Saugus Public Library (Cliftondale), Saugus MA. 617-233-1291
Parker, Mark, *Librn,* Fresno County Free Library (Leo Politi), Fresno CA. 209-431-6450
Parker, Marsha, *Vol Serv & Personnel Officer,* Saint Charles City County Library, Saint Peters MO. 314-441-2300
Parker, Martha, *Librn,* Lovett Memorial Library, McLean TX. 806-779-2851
Parker, Martha, *Cat & On-Line Servs,* Tennessee State University, Martha M Brown - Lois W Daniel Library, Nashville TN. 615-320-3682, 251-1417
Parker, Mary Ann, *Librn,* San Joaquin College of Law Library, Fresno CA. 209-251-7512
Parker, Mary G, *Librn,* Durham County General Hospital, Medical Library, Durham NC. 919-471-3411, Ext 311
Parker, Mary Lee, *Music & Recreation,* Public Library of the District of Columbia, Martin Luther King Memorial Library, Washington DC. 202-727-1101
Parker, Mason T, *Dir,* Mount Wachusett Community College Library, Gardner MA. 617-632-6600, Ext 126
Parker, Millie M, *Dir,* Paine College, Warren A Candler Memorial Library, Augusta GA. 404-722-4471, Ext 253
Parker, Mrs W R, *Librn,* Memphis Public Library, Memphis TX. 806-259-2062
Parker, Myrtice, *Librn,* Taylor County Public Library, Perry FL. 904-584-4807
Parker, Nancy, *Librn,* Johnson Public Library, Johnson VT. 802-635-7141
Parker, Nancy, *Spec Coll,* William Marsh Rice University, Fondren Library, Houston TX. 713-527-4022
Parker, Nell, *Librn,* Holmes County Library (Goodman Branch), Goodman MS. 601-472-2095
Parker, Pat, *Tech Serv, Acq & Cat,* Westark Community College, Holt Library, Fort Smith AR. 501-785-4241, Ext 308
Parker, Patricia R, *Ch,* Cornwall Public Library, Cornwall-on-Hudson NY. 914-534-8282
Parker, Peter J, *Chief of Mss,* Historical Society of Pennsylvania Library, Philadelphia PA. 215-732-6200
Parker, Philip J, *Assoc Prof,* Manchester College, Educational Media Specialist Program, IN. 219-982-2141, Ext 231
Parker, Richard, *Asst Dir of Pub Serv,* Tulsa City-County Library, Tulsa OK. 918-581-5221
Parker, Richard, *Librn,* Tulsa City-County Library (Central Library), Tulsa OK. 918-581-5222
Parker, Robert L, *Dir Libr Servs,* S D Bishop State Junior College, Library Technical Assistant Program, AL. 205-690-6464, Ext 6464

Parker, Robert L, *Dir,* S D Bishop State Junior College Library, Mobile AL. 205-690-6464
Parker, Rodney, *Circ,* Brigham Young University-Hawaii Campus, Joseph F Smith Library, Laie HI. 808-293-9211, Ext 260, 264
Parker, Rose, *Asst Librn,* Mercedes Memorial Library, Mercedes TX. 512-565-2371
Parker, Sara, *Regional Supvr,* Colorado State Library, Colorado Department of Education, Denver CO. 303-839-3695
Parker, Shirley, *Circ,* Ohio University, Vernon R Alden Library, Athens OH. 614-594-5228
Parker, Sybil, *Supvry Librn,* United States Army (Abrams Library), Fort McClellan AL. 205-238-3715
Parker, Thomas W, *Dir,* Bostonian Society Library, Boston MA. 617-523-7033
Parker, Vera, *Tech & Pub Servs,* Johnson State College, John Dewey Library, Johnson VT. 802-635-2356, Ext 248
Parker, Verle Jean, *Librn,* Aquatic Research Institute Library, Hayward CA. 415-785-2216
Parker, Virginia, *Librn,* Queen's University at Kingston (Bracken Library), Kingston ON. 613-547-5753
Parker, Winifred, *ILL,* Tacoma Public Library, Tacoma WA. 206-572-2000
Parker, Wyman, *Asst Prof,* Southern Connecticut State College, Div of Library Science & Instructional Technology, CT. 203-397-4532
Parker, Jr, Edward D, *Asst Dir Ref & Pub Serv,* Trinity University Library, San Antonio TX. 512-736-8121
Parkes, Darla, *ILL,* Missouri State Library, Jefferson City MO. 314-751-4214
Parkes, Darla, *Ref Librn,* Missouri Statewide Interlibrary Loan Network, MO. 314-751-2696
Parkes, Katherine, *Librn,* National Housing & Economic Development Law Library, Berkeley CA. 415-548-2600, Ext 504
Parkes, Virginia, *Librn,* Kanab City Library, Kanab UT. 801-644-2394
Parkhill, John T, *Libr Bd Dir,* Metropolitan Toronto Library Board, Metropolitan Toronto Library, Toronto ON. 416-928-5150
Parkhill, Rose, *Asst Librn,* Security Public Library, Security CO. 303-392-8912
Parkhurst, Carol, *Systs,* University of Nevada-Reno, Noble H Getchell Library, Reno NV. 702-784-6533
Parkins, Claudia, *Tech Serv,* Spokane County Library, Spokane WA. 509-924-4122
Parkins, Katherine, *Librn,* Los Angeles Public Library System (Vanowen Park), North Hollywood CA. 213-765-0805
Parkinson, George, *Spec Coll,* West Virginia University, University Library, Morgantown WV. 304-293-4040
Parkinson, Greg, *Asst Librn,* Circus World Museum of the State Historical Society of Wisconsin Library, Baraboo WI. 608-356-8341, Ext 31
Parkinson, Linda, *Ref,* Twin Falls Public Library, Twin Falls ID. 208-733-2965
Parkinson, Linda, *Asst Dir,* Twin Falls Public Library, Twin Falls ID. 208-733-2965
Parkinson, Mike, *Philos,* Southern Alberta Institute of Technology, Alberta College of Art Library, Calgary AB. 403-284-8665
Parkinson, Mike, *In Charge,* Southern Alberta Institute of Technology, Alberta College of Art Library, Calgary AB. 403-284-8665
Parkinson, Mike, *Art Col Branch,* Southern Alberta Institute of Technology, Learning Resources Centre, Calgary AB. 284-8647; 284-8648
Parkinson, Robert L, *Chief Librn,* Circus World Museum of the State Historical Society of Wisconsin Library, Baraboo WI. 608-356-8341, Ext 31
Parkison, Anne, *Librn,* Missouri Committee on Legislative Research, Legislative Library, Jefferson City MO. 314-751-4633
Parkison, Nancy, *Media,* Nevada County Library, Nevada City CA. 916-265-2461, Ext 244
Parkman, Ann, *Admin Asst,* Mississippi Library Commission, Jackson MS. 601-354-6369
Parks, Arlene, *Asst Dir,* North Suburban District Library, Loves Park IL. 815-633-4247, 633-4248
Parks, Bernice Z, *Supvr Librn,* United States Army (Military Police School Library), Fort McClellan AL. 205-238-3737

PARKS

Parks, Dennis, *Librn,* Purdue University Libraries & Audio-Visual Center (Aviation Technology), West Lafayette IN. 317-743-9928

Parks, Donna, *Ch,* Washington County Free Library, Hagerstown MD. 301-739-3250

Parks, Dorothy Ruth, *Dir,* Vanderbilt University Library (Divinity), Nashville TN. 615-322-2865

Parks, Eric, *Instr,* California State University-Los Angeles, Library Services Credential Program, CA. 213-224-3765

Parks, Gary D, *Dir,* East Central College, Library Services, Union MO. 314-583-5193, Ext 244

Parks, George R, *Dir,* University of Rhode Island Library, Kingston RI. 401-792-1000

Parks, Gordon E, *Assoc Dean,* University of Wisconsin-Whitewater, Library & Learning Resources, Whitewater WI. 414-472-1000

Parks, Julia, *Librn,* Washburn University of Topeka (Curriculum-Media), Topeka KS. 913-235-5341, Ext 281

Parks, Karl, *Librn,* United States Navy (Naval Security Station General Library), Washington DC. 202-282-0211

Parks, Larry, *Dir,* Wood Dale Library, Wood Dale IL. 312-766-6762

Parks, Lethene, *Spec Servs,* Pierce County Rural Library District, Tacoma WA. 206-572-6760

Parks, Maxine M, *Librn,* Melton Public Library, French Lick IN. 812-936-2177

Parks, May, *Ser,* Kendall Public Library, Kendall WI. 608-463-7103

Parks, Stephen R, *Curator Osborn Coll,* Yale University Library (Beinecke Rare Book & Manuscript), New Haven CT. 203-436-0234

Parks, Jr, James F, *Dir,* Millsaps College, Millsaps-Wilson Library, Jackson MS. 601-354-5201, Ext 324

Parlon, Teresa, *Librn,* Public Library of Nashville & Davidson County (Goodlettsville Branch), Goodlettsville TN. 615-859-0134

Parmenter, Rhoda M, *Ad,* Melrose Public Library, Melrose MA. 617-665-2313

Parmer, Ellen, *Librn,* Ozark Regional Library (Ironton Branch), Ironton MO. 314-546-2615

Parmet, Joseph, *Dir,* Long Beach Jewish Community Center, Stanley S Zack Library, Long Beach CA. 213-426-7601, Ext 52

Parming, Marju, *Asst Mgr,* United States General Accounting Office Library System (Office of Information Systems & Services), Washington DC. 275-3691 (Br Mgr), 275-5180 (Audit Ref Servs), 275-2585 (Law), 275-2555 (Tech Servs)

Parmley, Lane A, *Librn,* United States Air Force (Strategic Air Command Library), Offutt AFB NE. 402-294-7301

Parnell, Patricia, *Librn,* Barclay Public Library of Illini Township, Warrensburg IL. 217-672-3621

Parnes, Daria, *Ch & YA,* Cobb County Public Library System, Marietta GA. 404-427-2462

Parnes, Rosalind, *ILL & Ref,* Bellarmine College Library, Louisville KY. 502-452-8137

Paro, Kathleen, *Bibliog Instr,* Embry-Riddle Aeronautical University, Learning Resource Center, Daytona Beach FL. 904-252-5561, Ext 360

Parody, Edithe, *Ch,* Somers Library, Somers NY. 914-277-3420

Paroff, Claire, *ILL,* Merrick Library, Merrick NY. 516-379-3476

Parot, Joseph, *Hist,* Northern Illinois University, Founders Memorial Library, De Kalb IL. 815-753-1094

Parr, Caroline S, *Ch & YA,* Bridgewater Public Library, Bridgewater MA. 617-697-3331

Parr, Jewel, *ILL,* Irving Public Library System, Irving TX. 214-253-2639

Parr, Mary, *Per,* Hofstra University Library, Hempstead NY. 516-560-3475

Parr, Mary A, *Librn,* Saint Francis Hospital (Medical Library), Peoria IL. 309-672-2210

Parr, Virginia H, *Educ-Psych,* University of Oregon Library, Eugene OR. 503-686-3056

Parratt, Pat, *Librn,* Carnegie Institution of Washington (Carnegie Institution of Washington Library), Washington DC. 202-387-6400

Parratt, Ruth W, *Librn,* David McKee Corp Corp, Information Resource Center, Independence OH. 216-524-9300, Ext 744

Parratto, Henry L, *Librn,* Philadelphia Newspapers, Inc, Inquirer & Daily News Library, Philadelphia PA. 215-854-2823

Parravano, Ellen, *ILL,* Westchester Library System, Hartsdale NY. 914-761-7620

Parrine, Mary Jane, *Romance Lang,* Stanford University Libraries, Stanford CA. 415-497-2016

Parris, Lou, *Librn,* Exxon Co USA (Exxon Production Research Co, Research Library), Houston TX. 713-965-4222, Ext 1620

Parris, Patricia, *Librn,* Kansas State University (Chemistry), Manhattan KS. 913-532-6530

Parrish, Betty, *Librn,* Vidor Public Library, Vidor TX. 713-769-7148

Parrish, Elizabeth, *Ad,* Klamath County Library, Klamath Falls OR. 503-882-8894

Parrish, Frances, *Librn,* Shelby County Regional Library (Helena), Helena AL. 205-669-7851

Parrish, Helen A, *Dir,* University of South Carolina, Union Regional Campus Library, Union SC. 803-427-1654, 427-1627

Parrish, Iris J, *Librn,* Chesapeake Public Library (South Norfolk), Chesapeake VA. 804-545-2436

Parrish, James, *Extramural Prog,* University of Illinois at the Medical Center, Library of the Health Sciences, Chicago IL. 312-996-8974

Parrish, Jenni, *Assoc Dir & Ref,* University of Oklahoma (Law Library), Norman OK. 405-325-4311

Parrish, Judith B, *Librn,* Louisburg College, C W Robbins Library, Louisburg NC. 496-2521 Ext 279, 280, 281

Parrish, Laura, *Ser,* Samford University (Cordell Hull Law), Birmingham AL. 205-870-2714

Parrish, Madlyn, *Cat,* College Misericordia Library, Dallas PA. 717-675-2181, Ext 225

Parrish, Michael, *Librn,* Indiana University at Bloomington (School of Public & Environmental Health), Bloomington IN. 812-337-4584

Parrish, Ramona C, *Librn,* De Paul Hospital, Dr Henry Boone Memorial Library, Norfolk VA. 804-489-5270

Parriss, Jean, *Librn,* Clarkson Gordon & Woods Gordon Library, Toronto ON. 416-864-1234, Ext 2676

Parrott, D, *Librn,* College of Trades & Technology Library (Medical Sciences), Saint John's NF. 709-753-9360, Ext 318

Parrott, Fay A, *Librn,* Buhl Public Library, Buhl ID. 208-543-6500

Parrott, Jim, *Elec Eng & Physics,* University of Waterloo Library, Waterloo ON. 519-885-1211

Parry, David R, *Dir,* Lake County Public Library, Leadville CO. 303-486-0569

Parry, Eleanor, *Ref & Bibliog Instr,* Evangel College Library, Springfield MO. 417-865-2811, Ext 267

Parry, Valerie, *ILL & Ref,* Southampton College Library of Long Island University, Southampton NY. 516-283-4000, Ext 264

Parsch, Janet H, *Librn,* Michigan State University Library (Clinical Center), East Lansing MI. 517-355-2344

Parsley, David, *Tech Serv,* East Tennessee State University, Sherrod Library, Johnson City TN. 615-929-4338

Parsley, Laura, *Librn,* Baca County Public Library, Springfield CO. 303-523-6962

Parsly, Jean, *Br Coordr,* Columbiana Public Library, Columbiana OH. 216-482-2356

Parson, Jessie, *Librn,* Brunswick-Glynn County Regional Library (Wayne County), Jesup GA. 912-427-2500

Parson, Lethiel C, *Assoc Librn,* Atlantic Union College, G Eric Jones Library, South Lancaster MA. 617-365-4561

Parsonage, Dianne, *Dept Librn,* Revenue Canada (Customs & Excise Library), Ottawa ON. 613-995-0007

Parsons, A Lynette, *Tech Serv & Cat,* Charlotte-Glades Library System, Port Charlotte FL. 813-629-1715

Parsons, A Lynette, *Librn,* Charlotte-Glades Library System (Port Charlotte Public), Port Charlotte FL. 813-625-6470

Parsons, Charles, *Govt Docs,* University of Cincinnati Libraries (Robert S Marx Law Library), Cincinnati OH. 513-475-3016

Parsons, Deloris C, *Dir,* Kirtland Public Library, Kirtland OH. 216-256-3747

Parsons, Dolores, *ILL,* Camden County Free Library, Voorhees NJ. 609-772-1636

Parsons, Florine, *ILL & OCLC,* Public Library of Enid & Garfield County, Enid Public Library, Enid OK. 405-234-6313

Parsons, Frances E, *Libr Supvr,* E I Du Pont De Nemours & Co, Inc (Lavoisier Library), Wilmington DE. 302-772-2086

Parsons, Gary, *ILL,* Florida Atlantic University, S E Wimberly Library, Boca Raton FL. 305-395-5100, Ext 2448

Parsons, Jerry L, *Admin,* California State University, Sacramento Library, Sacramento CA. 916-454-6466

Parsons, Joan, *Circ,* Ryerson Polytechnical Institute, Donald Mordell Learning Resources Centre, Toronto ON. 416-595-5331

Parsons, Judith F, *Media,* Wicomico County Free Library, Salisbury MD. 301-749-5171

Parsons, Lucy, *AV,* Broward County Division of Libraries, Broward County Library, Pompano Beach FL. 305-972-1100

Parsons, Marcia, *Librn,* Case Western Reserve University Libraries (Sears), Cleveland OH. 216-368-3506

Parsons, Margaret, *ILL,* Azusa City Library, Azusa CA. 213-334-0338

Parsons, Patricia, *Librn,* Wisconsin State Department of Natural Resources (Department Library), Madison WI. 608-266-2621

Parsons, Patty, *Librn,* Pioneer Multi-County Library (Shawnee Public), Shawnee OK. 405-273-1250

Parsons, Patty J, *Librn,* Shawnee Carnegie Public Library, Shawnee OK. 405-273-1250

Parsons, Robert E, *In Charge,* Indiana State Farm Library, Greencastle IN. 317-653-8441

Parsons, Sara, *ILL,* McMillan Memorial Library, Wisconsin Rapids WI. 715-423-1040

Parsons, Scott, *AV,* Quincy Public Library, Quincy IL. 217-223-1309

Parsons, Thomas, *Librn,* Wildwood Crest Public Library, Wildwood Crest NJ. 609-522-0564

Parsons, Willie Mae, *Librn,* Hutchinson County Library (Stinnett Branch), Stinnett TX. 806-878-2403

Partee, Regina, *Cat,* State Technical Institute at Memphis, George E Freeman Library, Memphis TN. 901-377-4106

Parthasarathy, Kalyani, *Cat,* Austin Public Library, Austin MN. 507-433-2391

Partington, David H, *Asst Librn for Middle Eastern Coll,* Harvard University Library (Harvard College Library (Headquarters in Harry Elkins Widener Memorial Library)), Cambridge MA. 617-495-2401

Partington, Lynn L, *Servs to Older Americans Coordr,* Laurens County Library, Laurens SC. 803-984-0596

Partlow, Richard V, *Dir,* Southern California Interlibrary Loan Network, (SCILL), CA. 213-624-5869

Partridge, Alice, *Librn,* Tampa-Hillsborough County Public Library System (Port Tampa Public), Tampa FL. 813-839-4461

Partridge, Linda, *Media,* Upper Arlington Public Library, Upper Arlington OH. 614-486-9621

Partridge, Phyllis, *Librn,* Berkeley Public Library (West), Berkeley CA. 714-644-6870

Partridge, Shirley, *Librn,* Thompson Free Library, Dover-Foxcroft ME. 207-564-3350

Partridge, William, *Chief Librn,* Huron County Public Library, Goderich ON. 519-524-7751

Pascal, Eleanor, *Librn,* Free Public Library of Woodbridge (Cononia Branch), Colonia NJ. 201-388-3415

Pascarelli, Anne M, *Assoc Librn,* New York Academy of Medicine Library, New York NY. 212-876-8200

Paschal, Mimia L, *Afro-Am,* Benedict College, Benjamin F Payton Learning Resources Ctr, Columbia SC. 803-256-4220

Paschal, Vida, *Librn,* Given Memorial Library, Pinehurst NC. 919-295-6022

Paschall, JoAnne, *Dir,* Atlanta College of Art Library, Atlanta GA. 404-892-3600, Ext 210

Paschall, Katheryn, *Librn,* Chromalloy American Corp, Turbine Support Division Library, San Antonio TX. 512-333-6610

Pascoe, Frank, *Ref,* Missouri State Library, Jefferson City MO. 314-751-4214

Pascucci, Joseph T, *Librn,* New York State Judicial Department, Appellate Division Law Library, Rochester NY. 716-428-5480

Pascucci, Philip J, *Librn,* Don Bosco College Library, Newton NJ. 201-383-3900

Pashkin, Irwin, *Coordr Main Libr,* Free Public Library of Woodbridge, Woodbridge NJ. 201-634-4450

Pashley, Gina, *ILL,* Corning Public Library, Corning NY. 607-936-3713

Paskar, Joanne, *Chief Librn,* Agency for International Development, Development Information Center, Washington DC. 202-632-8571

Pasley, Diana, *Librn,* Lakeside Hospital Library, Kansas City MO. 816-363-6380

Pasley, Sandra S, *Ch,* Ardmore Public Library, Ardmore OK. 405-223-8290

Pason, Edward, *Assoc Dir Pub Servs,* Rutgers University (University Libraries), New Brunswick NJ. 201-932-7505

Pasquarella, Kathie, *Librn,* Ohio Valley Hospital, Health Sciences Library, Steubenville OH. 614-283-7400

Pasquin, M, *Ref,* LaSalle Municipal Library, Bibliotheque Municipale La Salle, La Salle PQ. 514-366-2582

Pass, Donna C, *Dir,* Rainsville Public Library, Rainsville AL. 205-638-3311

Pass, Elizabeth, *Librn,* Royal Alexandra Hospital (School of Nursing Library), Edmonton AB. 403-474-3431, Ext 491

Pass, Gary, *Librn,* Metallurgical Engineers of Atlanta, Inc Library, Atlanta GA. 404-458-9034

Passadin, Maryann, *Librn,* New York Public Library (Record Library), New York NY. 212-790-6262

Passafiume, Maryann, *Ad,* Fairfield Public Library, Fairfield NJ. 201-227-3575

Passage, Mary, *Exten Servs,* Southern Tier Library System, Corning NY. 607-962-3141

Passi, Narendar, *Ref & Bibliog Instr,* McMaster University, Hamilton ON. 416-525-9140

Passidomo, Don, *Dir,* Veterans Administration, Medical Library, Wilmington DE. 302-994-2511, Ext 354, 355

Passmore, David, *Cat,* University of Kansas Libraries, Watson Memorial Library, Lawrence KS. 913-864-3601

Passudetti, Cesare, *Librn,* New York Public Library (Pelham Bay), New York NY. 212-792-6744

Pastan, Barbara P, *Librn,* Faulkner Hospital, Ingersoll Bowditch Library, Jamaica Plain MA. 617-522-5800, Ext 1443

Pastan, Herbert M, *Librn,* United States Army (Institute of Heraldry Library), Alexandria VA. 202-274-6544

Paster, Alma, *ILL,* Avon Lake Public Library, Avon Lake OH. 216-933-8128

Paster, Jane G, *Librn,* Rhode Island State Department of Health Library, Providence RI. 401-277-2506

Pastine, Maureen, *Ref,* University of Illinois Library at Urbana-Champaign, Urbana IL. 217-333-0790

Pastoor, Virginia, *Ch & YA,* Greenville Public Library, Greenville MI. 616-754-6359

Pastor, Harriett, *Departmental Librn,* Nova University Libraries, Fort Lauderdale FL. 305-475-8300, Ext 264, 245

Pastorett, Richard T, *Dir,* Auburn University at Montgomery Library, Montgomery AL. 205-279-9110, Ext 247

Pastre, Laura, *Librn,* Cape May County Library (Avalon Branch), Avalon NJ. 609-967-4010

Pastucha, Joy, *ILL,* Central Michigan University, Charles V Park Library, Mount Pleasant MI. 517-774-3500

Patane, John, *Tech Serv,* Racine Public Library, Racine WI. 414-636-9241

Patarrozi, Pearl, *Asst Dir,* Seneca Public Library, Seneca IL. 815-357-6566

Patch, William, *Coll Maintenance,* University of Wisconsin-Madison, Memorial Library, Madison WI. 608-262-3521

Pate, Gaye, *Librn,* Saint Joseph Public Library (Carnegie), Saint Joseph MO. 816-238-0526

Pate, Jim, *Per,* Birmingham Public & Jefferson County Free Library, Birmingham AL. 205-254-2551

Pate, Michael B, *Librn,* Concord College, J Frank Marsh Library, Athens WV. 304-384-3115, Ext 247

Pate, Mrs C C, *Librn,* Webster Parish Library (Cotton Valley Branch), Cotton Valley LA. 318-832-4290

Pate, Mrs V, *Librn,* Fort Wright College of the Holy Names Library (Music), Spokane WA. 509-328-2970, Ext 21

Pate, Pamela R, *Tech Serv,* Samford University (L R Jordan Library), Birmingham AL. 205-591-2371

Pate, Tannie, *Asst Dir & Acq,* Midland County Public Library, Midland TX. 915-683-2708

Patel, Kailash C, *Librn,* Friendship Junior College Library, Rock Hill SC. 803-327-1186

Paten, Edna, *Personnel,* Prince George's County Memorial Library System, Hyattsville MD. 301-699-3500

Paterakis, Diane, *Tech Serv,* Hellenic College & Holy Cross Greek Orthodox School of Theology, Cotsidas-Tonna Library, Brookline MA. 617-731-3500, Ext 43, 44, 45

Paterman, H Maria, *City Librn,* Sunnyvale Public Library, Sunnyvale CA. 408-738-5585

Paterson, Dora, *Libr Tech,* Conestoga College of Applied Arts & Technology, Waterloo Campus, Educational Resources, Waterloo ON. 519-885-0300, Ext 59

Paterson, Ellen, *ILL,* State University of New York College, Memorial Library, Cortland NY. 607-753-2525, 753-2221

Paterson, Ellen, *Coordr,* State University of New York College, Memorial Library, Cortland NY. 607-753-2525, 753-2221

Paterson, Ellen, *Health & Sci,* State University of New York College, Memorial Library, Cortland NY. 607-753-2525, 753-2221

Paterson, Greta, *Cat,* Old Lyme, Phoebe Griffin Noyes Library, Old Lyme CT. 203-434-1684

Paterson, Mrs J, *Secy,* Creston Public Library, Creston BC. 604-428-4141

Pathe, Ruth, *Soc Sci,* Fairleigh Dickinson University, Friendship Library, Madison NJ. 201-377-4700, Ext 234

Patmon, Marian, *Head Libr Resources,* Oklahoma Department of Libraries, Oklahoma City OK. 405-521-2502

Paton, John, *Librn,* Lantana Correctional Institution Library, Lantana FL. 305-586-6510

Patrias, Karen, *On-Line Servs & Bibliog Instr,* National Institutes of Health (NIH Library), Bethesda MD. 301-496-4000

Patrick, Carol, *Per,* Cleveland State University Libraries, Cleveland OH. 216-687-2486

Patrick, Imogene, *Librn,* Fairview Public Library, Arkville NY. 914-586-3791

Patrick, Lucia, *Consult, Ref, Tech Servs & Ga Libr Info Network,* Georgia Department of Education (Div of Public Library Services), Atlanta GA. 404-656-2461

Patrick, Patricia, *Ch,* Albany Public Library, Albany NY. 518-449-3380

Patrick, Ruth S, *Asst Dir,* Wayne State University Libraries, Detroit MI. 313-557-4020

Patrick, Viola, *Dir,* Craig Public Library, Craig NE. 402-377-2641

Patrick, Wendy, *Librn,* McGill University Libraries (Botany-Genetics), Montreal PQ. 514-392-5829

Patridge, Jr, James C, *Institutional Libr Specialist,* Maryland State Department of Education, Division of Library Development & Services, Baltimore MD. 301-796-8300, Ext 284

Patrino, Lisa, *Bkmobile Coordr,* Raleigh County Public Library, Beckley WV. 304-255-0511

Patrow, Marge, *Tech Serv,* Chippewa Falls Public Library, Chippewa County Library Service, Chippewa Falls WI. 715-723-1147

Patry, Helene, *Coordr,* CEGEP de Victoriaville Centre de Documentation, Victoriaville PQ. 819-758-1571, Ext 232

Patseh, Jean S, *Librn,* Pittsburgh Institute of Mortuary Science Library, Pittsburgh PA. 412-682-0334

Patt, Judith, *Ch,* Tufts Library, Public Libraries of Weymouth, Weymouth MA. 617-337-1402

Pattberg, Eugene P, *Consult Curator,* University of Bridgeport, Magnus Wahlstrom Library, Bridgeport CT. 203-576-4740

Pattela, Rao, *Asst Librn,* Temple University of the Commonwealth System of Higher Education (Law), Philadelphia PA. 215-787-7891

Patten, Charlene, *Ch,* Free Public Library, Rowley MA. 617-948-2850

Patten, David, *Librn,* Oberlin College Library (Clarence Ward Art Library), Oberlin OH. 216-775-8635

Patten, Frederick W, *Cat,* Hughes Aircraft Co (Company Technical Document Center Library), Culver City CA. 213-391-0711, Ext 6187

Patten, Margaret, *Acq, Spec Coll & Archivist,* Onondaga Community College, Sidney B Coulter Library, Syracuse NY. 315-469-7741, Ext 5335-5338

Patterson, Alcha C, *ILL,* Field Library, Peekskill Library, Peekskill NY. 914-737-0010

Patterson, Angela, *Librn,* San Diego Public Library (University Heights), San Diego CA. 714-296-4514

Patterson, Ann, *Librn,* Self Memorial Hospital, Medical Library, Greenwood SC. 803-227-4250

Patterson, Annie MacKay, *Librn,* Salt Lake County Library System (Magna Branch), Magna UT. 801-250-2880

Patterson, Berta F, *Librn,* Mansfield Public Library, Mansfield TX. 817-473-4391

Patterson, Beth, *Dir,* Portage Lake District Library, Houghton MI. 906-482-4570

Patterson, Betty, *Librn,* Sheridan County Fulmer Public Library (Tongue River), Ranchester WY. 307-655-9726

Patterson, Betty H, *Librn,* Monsanto Textiles Co, Technical Center Library, Decatur AL. 205-552-2223

Patterson, Bobbie J, *Librn,* Washington State Department of Public Instruction, Professional Curriculum Library, Olympia WA. 206-753-6731

Patterson, Charles D, *Prof,* Louisiana State University, Graduate School of Library Science, LA. 504-388-3158

Patterson, Constance, *Dir,* DeWitt Community Library, Dewitt NY. 315-446-3578

Patterson, Dewey, *Librn,* Vermont Technical College, Hartness Library, Randolph Center VT. 802-728-3391, Ext 32

Patterson, Elizabeth, *Media,* Mississippi Gulf Coast Junior College, Jackson County Campus Library, Gautier MS. 601-497-4313, Ext 226, Libr; 497-4313, Ext 255 Media Ctr

Patterson, Flora E, *Dir, Pub Serv Br,* National Library of Canada, Ottawa ON. 613-995-9481

Patterson, Gail, *Librn, Cat & Tech Serv,* Jennings County Public Library, North Vernon IN. 812-346-2091

Patterson, Gertrude, *Librn,* Fontanelle Public Library, Fontanelle IA. 515-745-4981

Patterson, Grace, *Media,* Passaic County Community College, Learning Resources Center Library, Paterson NJ. 201-279-5000, Ext 73

Patterson, Grace, *Commun Servs,* Paterson Free Public Library, Danforth Memorial Library, Paterson NJ. 201-881-3770

Patterson, Hazel R, *Librn,* Miles College, Learning Resources Center, Birmingham AL. 205-923-2771, Ext 257

Patterson, Jo, *In Charge,* Coquitlam Public Library (Cottonwood), Coquitlam BC. 604-931-2416

Patterson, Julia A, *Librn,* United States Air Force (Base Library), McClellan AFB CA. 916-643-2111

Patterson, Karen, *ILL, Reader Serv & Bibliog Instr,* Point Park College Library, Helen-Jean Moore Library, Pittsburgh PA. 412-391-4100, Ext 361

Patterson, Kelly S, *ILL,* University of Wyoming, William Robertson Coe Library, Laramie WY. 307-766-3279

Patterson, Kim, *Media,* Ouachita Baptist University, Riley Library, Arkadelphia AR. 501-246-4531, Ext 121

Patterson, L Noel, *Bus Mgr,* Public Library of Annapolis & Anne Arundel County Inc, Annapolis MD. 301-224-7371

Patterson, Laura, *AV & Per,* Lewis University Library, Romeoville IL. 815-838-0500, Ext 302

Patterson, Liselotte, *Librn,* Mountain Regional Library (Union County), Blairsville GA. 404-379-3732

Patterson, Marsha L, *Dir,* W E Walter Memorial Library, Bremen Public Library, Bremen IN. 219-546-2849

Patterson, Martha B, *Librn,* Boston Public Library (West Roxbury Branch), West Roxbury MA. 617-325-3147

Patterson, Maureen L P, *South Asia,* University of Chicago, Joseph Regenstein Library, Chicago IL. 312-753-2977

Patterson, Michael, *Librn,* Anderson County Library (Belton Branch), Belton SC. 803-338-8330

Patterson, Mildred, *Librn,* Farmville Reading Room Library, Farmville VA. 804-392-8662

Patterson, Mrs Jim, *Librn,* Anadarko Public Library, Anadarko OK. 405-247-3087

Patterson, Myron B, *On-Line Servs,* British Columbia Telephone Co, Business Library, Burnaby BC. 604-432-2671

Patterson, P, *Tech Serv, Acq & Cat,* California State College, San Bernardino Library, San Bernardino CA. 714-887-7321

Patterson, Patricia, *AV,* Western Texas College, Learning Resource Center, Snyder TX. 915-573-8511, Ext 265

Patterson, Robert, *Pub Servs,* Michigan Technological University Library, Houghton MI. 906-487-2500

Patterson, Robert H, *Dir,* University of Wyoming, William Robertson Coe Library, Laramie WY. 307-766-3279

Patterson, Roger, *Hist & Travel,* Grand Rapids Public Library, Grand Rapids MI. 616-456-4400

Patterson, Sarah, *Dir,* Tennessee Temple University, Cierpke Memorial Library, Chattanooga TN. 615-698-6021, Ext 250

Patterson, Thomas H, *Ref,* University of Maine at Orono, Raymond H Fogler Library, Orono ME. 207-581-7328

Pattie, Ling-Yuh, *Cat,* Eastern Kentucky University, John Grant Crabbe Library, Richmond KY. 606-622-3606

Pattillo, Aphne, *Librn,* Nixon Public Library, Nixon TX. 512-582-1913

Pattillo, John W, *Dir,* Southern Technical Institute Library, Marietta GA. 404-424-7275

Pattinson, Judy, *Librn,* Rideau Lakes Union Library (Portland Branch), Portland ON. 613-359-5315

Pattishall, C H, *Media,* Kennesaw College Library, Marietta GA. 404-422-8770, Ext 250

Pattison, Helen M, *Librn,* Milford Township Public Library, Milford IL. 815-889-4722

Pattison, Jane, *Librn,* Hooker Chemical Co, Technical Information Center, Grand Island NY. 716-773-8531

Pattison, Joanne, *Ch,* Manatee County Public Library System, Bradenton FL. 813-748-5555

Patton, Alice, *Circ,* Hobbs Public Library, Hobbs NM. 505-397-2451

Patton, Barbara, *Lectr,* Dalhousie University, School of Library Service, NS. 902-424-3656

Patton, David, *Dir & Media,* Rend Lake College, Learning Resource Center, Ina IL. 618-437-5321

Patton, Doris, *Librn,* Oklahoma Children's Memorial Hospital Library, Oklahoma City OK. 405-271-4371

Patton, Glen, *Librn,* Illinois Wesleyan University Library (Music), Bloomington IL. 309-556-3003

Patton, Johnn, *ILL & Ref,* Suffolk Cooperative Library System, Bellport NY. 516-286-1600

Patton, Melba, *Librn,* Southeastern Illinois College, Harrisburg IL. 618-252-6376, Ext 22

Patton, Patricia, *Librn,* Johnson County Public Library, Paintsville KY. 606-789-4355

Patton, Rebecca, *ILL,* Martin Memorial Library, York PA. 717-843-3978

Patton, Theresa, *Tech Serv,* Saint John the Baptist Parish Library, LaPlace LA. 504-652-2144

Patty, Nancy, *Librn,* Memphis-Shelby County Public Library & Information Center (Highland), Memphis TN. 901-452-7341

Patty, Nancy, *Ch,* Otis Library, Norwich CT. 203-889-2365

Patzwald, Gari-Anne, *ILL,* National College of Chiropractic, Sordoni-Burich Library, Lombard IL. 312-629-2000, Ext 50

Paugh, Minnie, *Spec Coll,* Montana State University, Roland R Renne Library, Bozeman MT. 406-994-3119

Paul, A Curtis, *Dir,* Lenoir-Rhyne College, Carl A Rudisill Library, Hickory NC. 704-328-1741, Ext 221

Paul, Alice, *Librn,* Athens Regional Library (Ogelthorpe County), Lexington GA. 404-743-8817

Paul, Alice, *Librn,* Hennepin County Library (Saint Louis Park Branch), St Louis Park MN. 612-929-8108

Paul, Alice I, *Cat,* Forbes Library, Northampton MA. 413-584-8399

Paul, Barbara, *Dir,* Chicago Heights Free Public Library, Chicago Heights IL. 312-754-0323

Paul, Diane C, *Asst Librn,* Camden Public Library, Camden ME. 207-236-3440

Paul, Donald, *Lit & Fine Arts,* Dayton & Montgomery County Public Library, Dayton OH. 513-224-1651

Paul, Donald C, *Librn,* Hughes Aircraft Co, Canoga Park Library, Canoga Park CA. 213-883-2400, Ext 1155

Paul, Gary, *Pub Servs,* Frostburg State College Library, Frostburg MD. 301-689-4396

Paul, George P, *Circ,* University of Virginia (Claude Moore Health Sciences Library), Charlottesville VA. 804-924-5444

Paul, Heather, *Asst Librn,* Ministry of Forests Library, Victoria BC. 604-387-5985

Paul, Huibert, *Ser,* University of Oregon Library, Eugene OR. 503-686-3056

Paul, Jacquelin, *Asst Librn & Tech Serv,* Delaware Law School Library of Widener University, Wilmington DE. 302-478-5280

Paul, Janina, *Asst Dir,* Santa Clara City Library, Santa Clara CA. 408-984-3097

Paul, Jean, *Chief Librn,* Northern Alberta Institute of Technology, McNally Library, Edmonton AB. 403-477-4325

Paul, Lea, *Tech Serv & Acq,* Snow College, Lucy A Phillips Library, Ephraim UT. 801-283-4201, Ext 204

Paul, Patty, *Doc,* State Library of Florida, Div of Library Services, Dept of State, Tallahassee FL. 904-487-2651

Paul, Paula, *Ref,* Orangeburg County Library, Orangeburg SC. 803-534-1429

Paul, Sherri, *Cat,* Sleepy Hollow Restorations Library, Tarrytown NY. 914-631-8200

Paulaitis, Arthur, *Sci & Tech,* Ryerson Polytechnical Institute, Donald Mordell Learning Resources Centre, Toronto ON. 416-595-5331

Paulaskas, Linda, *Pub Servs,* Alpha Park Public Library District, Bartonville IL. 309-697-3822

Paulding, David, *Chief Librn,* Bruce A Garrett Memorial Library & Media Center, San Antonio TX. 512-222-8431, Ext 3507

Paules, JoAnn, *Dir,* New Freedom Library Center, New Freedom PA. 717-235-4313

Pauley, Janet, *Librn,* Osterhout Free Library (Plains Township), Plains PA. 717-824-1862

Pauley, Joy, *Cat,* Southwestern College Library, Oklahoma City OK. 405-947-2331, Ext 214

Pauli, Lowell, *Br Coordr,* Mid-Continent Public Library, Independence MO. 816-836-5200

Paulich, Joan, *Dir,* Library District Number 1, Troy KS. 913-985-2597, Ext 2

Paulk, Betty D, *On-Line Servs,* Valdosta State College Library, Valdosta GA. 912-247-3228

Paulk, Mary, *Ad,* Pike-Amite-Walthall Library System, McComb Public Library (Headquaters), McComb MS. 601-684-7034

Paulos, Joyce, *Circ Coordr,* Eastfield College, Learning Resources Center, Mesquite TX. 214-746-3168

Paulovich, Roseline, *Ch,* Town of Caledon Public Libraries, Bolton ON. 416-857-1400

Pauls, Adonijah, *Dir,* Fresno Pacific College, Hiebert Library, Fresno CA. 209-251-7194, Ext 51

Pauls, Frederick H, *Chief, Govt Div,* Library of Congress, Washington DC. 202-287-5000

Paulsen, Deborah, *Asst Dir,* Southeast Regional Library, Dummerston VT. 802-254-2961

Paulsen, Duane R, *Librn,* Sauk Valley College, Learning Resources Center, Dixon IL. 815-288-5511, Ext 247

Paulsen, Marian, *Assoc Dir & Acq,* Anoka County Library, Blaine MN. 612-784-1100

Paulsen, Philip, *AV,* City College of San Francisco Library, San Francisco CA. 415-239-3404

Paulson, Connie, *Librn,* Harris County Public Library (Tomball Branch), Tomball TX. 713-351-7269

Paulson, Gladys, *Librn,* Dassel Public Library, Dassel MN. 612-275-3756

Paulson, Merle, *Acq,* Wichita State University, Library & Media Resources Center, Wichita KS. 316-689-3586

Paulson, Paula, *Asst Dir,* Berlin Free Town Library, Berlin NY. 518-658-2231

Paulson, Peter J, *Dir,* New York State Interlibrary Loan Network, (NYSILL), NY. 518-474-5129; Data 474-5784 & 474-5786

Paulson, Peter J, *Dir,* New York State Library, Albany NY. 518-474-5930

Paulton, Lucy, *ILL & Tech Serv,* Avon Free Public Library, Avon CT. 203-678-1262

Paulukonis, Joseph T, *Dir,* Dakota State College, Karl E Mundt Library, SD. 605-256-3551, Ext 226

Paulukonis, Joseph T, *Dir,* Dakota State College, Karl E Mundt Library, Madison SD. 605-256-3551, Ext 226

Paulus, David L, *Acq,* Vassar College Library, Poughkeepsie NY. 914-452-7000

Paulus, Linda, *Asst Librn,* Plain Public Library, Plain WI. 608-546-4201

Paulus, Pauline B, *Pub Rels Officer,* Saint Louis Public Library, Saint Louis MO. 314-241-2288

Pauly, Dennis, *Bkmobile Coordr,* Evanston Public Library, Evanston IL. 312-866-0300

Paus, Boma, *Librn,* New Albin Public Library, New Albin IA. 319-544-4260

Paustian, Elva, *Librn,* Barnard Library, La Crosse KS. 913-222-2826

Pautz, Martin R, *Dean,* Greenville Technical College, Learning Resources Center, Greenville SC. 803-242-3170, Ext 321

Pautz, Mary Lynn, *Ref,* Cardinal Stritch College Library, Milwaukee WI. 414-352-5400, Ext 356

Pauwells, Virginia, *Tech Serv,* Amarillo Public Library, Amarillo TX. 806-378-3000, Ext 2250

Pauwels, Colleen K, *Dir,* Indiana University School of Law, Law Library, Bloomington IN. 812-337-9666

Pavars, Mara E, *Tech Serv & Cat,* Nutley Public Library, Nutley NJ. 201-667-0405

Pavelecky, Michael, *ILL,* Tufts University, Medical-Dental Library, Boston MA. 617-956-6707

Pavelka, Marie, *Commun Servs,* Waco-McLennan County Library, Waco TX. 817-754-4694

Pavelko, Charlotte, *Librn,* F D Lanterman State Hospital (Residents' Library & Listening Center), Pomona CA. 714-595-1221

Pavetti, Sally Thomas, *Curator,* Eugene O'neill Member Theater Center Library, Waterford CT. 203-443-5378

Pavitt, Barbara, *Mail Servs,* Alaska State Library, Juneau AK. 907-465-2910

Pavlak, Anne, *Commun Servs,* Hempstead Public Library, Hempstead NY. 516-481-6990

Pavlica, Maxine, *Librn,* Sidney Township Public Library, Batawa ON. 613-398-7344

Pavlich, J, *Asst Librn,* Muskegon Business College Library, Muskegon MI. 616-726-2911

Pavlin, Stefanie A, *Head Libr Servs,* Ontario Ministry of Transportation & Communications Library, Downsview ON. 416-248-3591

Pawelek, Stephanie, *Tech Clerk,* ITT Defense Communications Division, Technical Library, Nutley NJ. 201-284-2096

Pawelkop, Mary, *Ref,* Florida Memorial College Library, Miami FL. 305-625-4141, Ext 148

Pawl, Patricia T, *Dir,* Williams Free Library, Beaver Dam Public Library, Beaver Dam WI. 414-885-4570

Pawle, Martha B, *Dir,* Prince Memorial Library, Cumberland Center ME. 207-829-3180

Pawlek, Cynthia, *Librn,* Dartmouth College (Paddock Music), Hanover NH. 603-646-3234

Pawling, Diane, *Acq,* Wilson College, John Stewart Memorial Library, Chambersburg PA. 717-264-4141, Ext 344

Pawloski, Barbara, *Doc,* Georgetown University (Fred O Dennis Law Library), Washington DC. 202-624-8260

Pawloski, Jean, *Librn,* Cooley Dickinson Hospital (Health Science Library), Northampton MA. 413-584-4090, Ext 2298

Paxton, Frances C, *Librn,* Nitro Public Library, Nitro WV. 304-755-4432

Paxton, Ruby B, *Librn,* Custer County Public Library, Westcliffe CO. 303-783-2423

Payette, Dolores, *Dir,* Palos Heights Public Library, Palos Heights IL. 312-448-4376, 448-1473

Payette, Richard, *Ref,* West Warwick Public Library System, Robert H Champlin Memorial Library, West Warwick RI. 401-828-3750

Paymer, Natalie, *Librn,* Office of the Attorney General, State Law Department Library, Baltimore MD. 301-383-7844

Payne, Charles T, *Systs,* University of Chicago, Joseph Regenstein Library, Chicago IL. 312-753-2977

Payne, Christine, *Librn,* McDowell Public Library (Iager Branch), Iaeger WV. 304-938-9017

Payne, David L, *Dir,* Mississippi University for Women, John Clayton Fant Memorial Library, Columbus MS. 601-328-4808

Payne, Deborah, *ILL,* Walla Walla Public Library, Walla Walla WA. 509-525-5353

Payne, Diane, *Librn,* Wake County Department of the Public Library (Richard B Harrison), Raleigh NC. 919-755-6097

Payne, Donna, *Ad,* Fairfield Public Library, Fairfield NJ. 201-227-3575

Payne, Edward, *Media,* Lakewood Community College Library, White Bear Lake MN. 612-770-1331, Ext 129

Payne, Eleanor R, *Soc & Russian Langs & Lit,* University of California at Davis, General Library, Davis CA. 916-752-2110

Payne, Emily C, *Dir,* Tri-County Regional Library, Rome GA. 404-291-9360

Payne, Florence M, *Librn,* Hugh Embry Library, Dade City FL. 904-567-3576

Payne, Frank, *Librn,* United States Court of Appeals, Sixth Circuit Library, Cincinnati OH. 513-684-2958

Payne, Hollis, *Dir,* Stamford Carnegie Library, Stamford TX. 915-773-2532

Payne, J, *Libr Tech,* Sheridan College of Applied Arts & Technology Library (Visual Arts), Oakville ON. 416-845-9430, Ext 166

Payne, Katherine, *Br Asst,* Timberland Regional Library (South Bend), South Bend WA. 206-875-5532

Payne, Leila, *Cat,* Texas A&M University Libraries, College Station TX. 713-845-6111

Payne, Linda, *Librn,* Auburndale Public Library, Auburndale FL. 813-967-1700

Payne, Maxine, *Consult Pub Libr & Ch Librn,* Rolling Prairie Library System, Decatur IL. 217-429-2586

Payne, Patricia, *Asst Prof,* Clarion State College, School of Library Science, PA. 814-226-2271

Payne, Robert, *Wash Libr Network Dir,* Washington State Library, Olympia WA. 206-753-5592

Payne, Robert D, *Dir,* Washington Library Network, (WLN), WA. 206-753-5595

Payne, Ropha, *Librn,* Overton Community Library, Overton NE. 308-987-2543

Payne, Sally, *Librn,* Papillion Public Library, Papillion NE. 402-339-3177

Payne, Sherry, *Media,* Marshall University, James E Morrow Library, Huntington WV. 304-696-3120

Payne, Shirley, *Ch & YA,* North Kingstown Free Library, North Kingstown RI. 401-294-2521

Payne, Tonia, *Librn,* Clark County Library District (Moapa Valley), Moapa NV. 702-397-2690

Payne, Valerie, *Librn,* North Carolina National Bank Library, Charlotte NC. 704-374-5842

Payne, Walter, *Dir,* University of the Pacific (Stewart Library of Western America), Stockton CA. 209-946-2404

Paynter, David M, *Dir,* Florence County Library, Florence SC. 803-662-8424

Paynter, Eleanor, *Ref,* Bayard Taylor Memorial Library, Kennett Square PA. 215-444-2702

Paynter, John, *ILL & Ref,* Cameron University Library, Lawton OK. 405-248-2200, Ext 410

Payson, Evelyn, *Asst Librn,* Nashotah House Library, Nashotah WI. 414-646-3371, Ext 26

Paysse, James L, *Librn,* Tulane University of Louisiana (Delta Regional Primate Research Center), Covington LA. 504-522-8236, Ext 253

Paysse, James L, *Dir Libr Serv,* Tulane University of Louisiana, Delta Regional Primate Research Center, Science Information Service, Covington LA. 504-892-2040, Ext 223

Paz, Ann, *Ch,* Morris County Free Library, Whippany NJ. 201-285-6101

Pazak, Raffaella, *Librn,* Reuben McMillan Free Library Free Library Association (Boardman), Youngstown OH. 216-758-1414

Pazder, Lorraine, *Asst Ref,* University of Puget Sound, Collins Memorial Library, Tacoma WA. 206-756-3257

Peabody, Sherry, *Librn,* Flagstaff City-Coconino County Public Library System (East Flagstaff), Flagstaff AZ. 602-774-8434

Peace, Helen, *Librn,* Passaic County Historical Society, Paterson NJ. 201-345-6900

Peace, Nance E, *Asst Prof,* Simmons College, Graduate School of Library & Information Science, MA. 617-738-2225

Peace, William K, *Dir,* Lee College, Learning Resources Center, Baytown TX. 713-427-5611, Ext 279, 277

Peach, Jan, *Librn,* Michael J Owens Technical College Library, Perrysburg OH. 419-666-0580, Exts 221 & 251

Peach, Mary, *Talking Bks,* Manatee County Public Library System, Bradenton FL. 813-748-5555

Peach, Phyllis, *Dept Heads: Bibliog Proc,* University of Toronto Libraries (University Library), Toronto ON. 416-978-2294

Peacock, Alma, *Ch,* Mamie Doud Eisenhower Public Library, Broomfield Public Library, Broomfield CO. 303-469-1821

Peacock, Jennie, *Acq,* Tacoma Public Library, Tacoma WA. 206-572-2000

Peacock, Joyce F, *Librn,* AAI Corp Technical Library, Baltimore MD. 301-628-3193

Peake, Ann, *Assoc Dir,* King College, E W King Library, Bristol TN. 615-968-1187, Ext 215

Peake, Carolyn S, *Ch,* Lake Oswego Public Library, Lake Oswego OR. 503-636-7628

Peal, Sara J, *Chief Librn,* Monroe County Library System (Ellis), Monroe MI. 313-241-5277

Pearce, Charles A, *Ref,* Wheeler Basin Regional Library, Decatur Public Library, Decatur AL. 205-353-2993

Pearce, Donald J, *Dir,* University of Minnesota, Duluth, Duluth MN. 218-726-8100

Pearce, Doris, *Tech Serv & Acq,* Bibliotheque Municipale Des Sources, Sources Public Library, Roxboro PQ. 514-684-8247, 684-8260

Pearce, Douglas, *Dir,* Vestal Public Library, Vestal NY. 607-754-4243

Pearce, Edward D, *Librn,* Museum of Science Library, Boston MA. 617-723-2500

Pearce, Helen, *Librn,* Blue Rapids Public Library, Blue Rapids KS. 913-226-7243

Pearce, Hulda, *Dir,* Platteville Public Library, Platteville WI. 608-348-7441

Pearce, Jean K, *Circ,* Stonehill College, Cushing-Martin Library, North Easton MA. 617-238-1081, Ext 328, 329, 313

Pearce, Jeanette, *Librn,* Johns Hopkins University Libraries (Adolf Meyer Library), Baltimore MD. 301-955-5819

Pearce, Judy Gulliver, *Dir,* Pottawatomie-Wabaunsee Regional Library, Saint Marys KS. 913-437-2778

Pearce, Kathy, *Ser,* Brigham Young University (Law Library), Provo UT. 801-378-3593

Pearce, Lillian, *Librn,* Northampton County Memorial Library, Jackson NC. 919-534-3571

Pearce, Margaret T, *Tech Serv,* Washington University Libraries (Freund Law Library), Saint Louis MO. 314-889-6459

Pearce, Mary, *Librn,* Wood County District Public Library (Bradner), Bowling Green OH. 419-352-5104

Pearce, Mona B, *Librn,* Government of Newfoundland & Labrador, Department of Justice Law Library, Saint John's NF. 709-737-2861

Pearce, Mrs A M, *Asst Dir,* Belton City Library, Belton TX. 817-939-1161

Pearce, Robert K, *Dir,* Parsippany-Troy Hills Public Library, Parsippany NJ. 201-335-3442

Pearce, Stanley K, *Librn,* O'Melveny & Myers, Law Library, Los Angeles CA. 213-620-1120

Pearce, Sue, *Dept Head,* Fairleigh Dickinson University, Wayne Campus Library, Wayne NJ. 201-694-4554

Pearce, Jr, John W, *Librn,* Parco Scientific Co, Biological Laboratories Library, Vienna OH. 216-856-2368

Pearcy, Carol, *Librn,* Stone, Marraccini & Patterson Library, San Francisco CA. 415-775-7300

Pearl, Dorothy J, *Tech Serv,* Cochise County Library System, Bisbee AZ. 602-432-5703, Ext 500

Pearl, Katherine J, *Librn,* Sullivan Public Library, Sullivan NH. 603-847-9003

Pearl, Sheila, *Ref,* Nova Scotia Teachers College Library, Truro NS. 902-895-5347, Ext 30

Pearlman, Kay, *Lit,* Ontario Public Library, Ontario CA. 984-2758 Ext 38

Pearlman, Kay, *Tech Serv,* Ontario Public Library, Ontario CA. 984-2758 Ext 38

Pearlman, S, *Managing Editor,* CRC Press Inc Library, Boca Raton FL. 305-994-1375

Pearman, Gayl, *Tech Serv, On-Line Servs & Bibliog Instr,* North Carolina School of the Arts, Semans Library, Winston-Salem NC. 919-784-7170, Ext 2566

Pearsall, John, *Acq,* Monroe County Library System, Rochester NY. 716-428-7345

Pearse, Linda, *Ch,* Dartmouth Regional Library, Dartmouth NS. 902-466-7623

Pearson, Anne, *Ref,* Evansville Public Library & Vanderburgh County Public Library, Evansville IN. 812-425-2621

Pearson, Deb, *Asst Librn,* Southeast Community College-Lincoln Campus, Learning Resource Center, Lincoln NE. 402-471-3333, Ext 249

Pearson, Dorothy, *Asst Librn for Admin Servs,* Princeton University Library, Princeton NJ. 609-452-3180

Pearson, Dorothy E, *Dir,* Camden Public Library, Camden Library Association, Camden NY. 315-245-1980

Pearson, Elizabeth, *Asst Librn,* Montreat-Anderson College, L Nelson Bell Library, Montreat NC. 704-669-2382

Pearson, Elvon, *Prof,* Fullerton College, Library Technician Program, CA. 714-871-8000, Ext 244

Pearson, Evvon, *Ref & Bibliog Instr,* Fullerton College, William T Boyce Library, Fullerton CA. 714-871-8000

Pearson, Frances, *Librn,* California Department of Water Resources, Law Library, Sacramento CA. 916-322-0220

Pearson, Gary, *Photog,* Ricks College, David O McKay Learning Resources Center, Rexburg ID. 208-356-2351

Pearson, Gertrude H, *Bkmobile Coordr,* Wicomico County Free Library, Salisbury MD. 301-749-5171

Pearson, Gladys, *ILL,* Palm Beach County Public Library System, West Palm Beach FL. 305-686-0895

Pearson, Helen, *Asst Librn,* Manson Public Library, Manson IA. 712-469-2237

Pearson, Helen, *YA,* Norfolk Public Library, Norfolk VA. 804-441-2887

Pearson, Irene, *Librn,* Albert City Public Library, Albert City IA. 712-843-2291

Pearson, John, *Media,* Orange County Public Library, Orange CA. 714-634-7841

Pearson, Judy, *Librn Blind,* Columbia-Lafayette-Ouachita-Calhoun Regional Library, Asa C Garrett Memorial Library, Magnolia AR. 501-234-1991

Pearson, Lennart, *Dir,* Presbyterian College, James H Thomason Library, Clinton SC. 803-833-2820, Ext 214

Pearson, Louise, *Tech Serv & Cat,* Dickinson State College, Stoxen Library, Dickinson ND. 701-227-2135

Pearson, Louise, *Cat,* Smith College Library, Northampton MA. 413-584-2700, Ext 501

Pearson, Margery, *Librn,* Taylor Public Library, Taylor TX. 512-352-3434

Pearson, Mary, *Ch,* Smiths Falls Public Library, Smiths Falls ON. 613-283-2911

Pearson, Mary Lou, *Ad & Ref,* Manistee County Library, Manistee MI. 616-723-2519

Pearson, Michael, *Hist,* Metropolitan Toronto Library Board, Metropolitan Toronto Library, Toronto ON. 416-928-5150

Pearson, Mrs Cecil, *In Charge,* Oxford County Library (Kintore Branch), Kintore ON. 519-283-6477

Pearson, Nellie, *Dir,* Northern Virginia Community College Libraries (Manassas Campus), Manassas VA. 703-368-0184, Ext 222

Pearson, Norman, *Tech Serv,* Wright State University Library, Dayton OH. 513-873-2380

Pearson, Patty, *Librn,* Richmond Public Library, Richmond KS. 913-835-3610

Pearson, Penelope, *Librn,* Ohio State University Libraries (Undergraduate Library), Columbus OH. 614-422-8915

Pearson, Roger, *Exec Dir,* South Central Library System, Madison WI. 608-266-4181

Pearson, Sara L, *Dir,* Urbandale Public Library, Urbandale IA. 515-278-3945

Pearson, Waynn, *Ad, Media & Pub Servs,* Ontario Public Library, Ontario CA. 984-2758 Ext 38

Pearsons, Sheila, *Librn,* Bay County Library System (Auburn Branch), Auburn MI. 517-662-2381

PEART

Peart, Sue, *Librn,* Perry County District Library (Shawnee Branch), Shawnee OH. 614-342-1077

Pease, Alice, *Librn,* Berry Memorial Library, Bar Mills ME. 207-929-5484

Pease, Ethel M, *Librn,* Middlefield Public Library, Middlefield MA. 413-623-8903

Pease, Kenneth R, *Dir,* University of Dubuque, Ficke-Laird Library, Dubuque IA. 319-589-3218

Pease, M, *Librn,* Library of the Legal Aid Society of Westchester, White Plains NY. 914-682-0250

Pease, Rebecca, *Librn,* Bonney Memorial Library, Cornish ME. 207-625-3978

Pease, Russell, *Asst Dir Branches & Acting Asst Dir Coll Develop,* University of Georgia Libraries, Athens GA. 404-542-2716

Pease, Sandra, *ILL,* University of Vermont & State Agricultural College, Bailey-Howe Memorial Library, Burlington VT. 802-656-2020

Pease, Susan L, *Asst Librn & ILL,* West Plains Public Library, West Plains MO. 417-256-4775

Pease, Victoria, *Asst Librn,* Warren Public Library, Warren MA. 413-436-7690

Pease, William, *Cat,* San Diego State University Library, San Diego CA. 714-286-6014

Peaslee, Ruth, *Ch,* Oak Park Public Library, Scoville Institute, Oak Park IL. 312-383-8200

Peasley, Darlene, *Librn,* Coudersport Public Library, Coudersport PA. 814-274-9382

Peaster, Max, *Ref,* Raleigh County Public Library, Beckley WV. 304-255-0511

Peatross, Elizabeth, *Acq,* Louisiana State University School of Medicine in Shreveport, Medical Library, Shreveport LA. 318-226-3442

Peattie, Noel R, *Humanities,* University of California at Davis, General Library, Davis CA. 916-752-2110

Peavy, Asa, *Ad,* Nacogdoches Public Library, Nacogdoches TX. 713-569-8282

Peay, Wayne, *Media,* University of Utah (Spencer S Eccles Health Sciences Library), Salt Lake City UT. 801-581-8771

Pechout, Shirley J, *Librn,* Berlin Free Library, Berlin CT. 203-828-3344

Peck, Christine, *Librn,* Timberland Regional Library (Hoquiam Branch), Hoquiam WA. 206-532-1770

Peck, David, *Personnel Officer,* Connecticut State Library, Hartford CT. 203-566-4301

Peck, Elsie, *Librn,* New York Public Library (Dance & Drama), New York NY. 212-790-6262

Peck, Esther, *Librn,* Sequoia & Kings Canyon National Parks, Ash Mountain Park Library, Three Rivers CA. 209-565-3341

Peck, Jane, *Lit & Humanities,* Worcester Public Library, Worcester MA. 617-752-3751

Peck, Jean M, *Cat,* University of California, Berkeley (University Library), Berkeley CA. 415-642-3773

Peck, Leona, *In Charge,* Cochise County Library System (Arizona Sunsites Community Library), Pearce AZ. 602-826-3706

Peck, Marial, *Educ-Fine Arts,* Oregon State University, William Jasper Kerr Library, Corvallis OR. 503-754-3411

Peck, Marian, *Ch,* Montgomery County-Norristown Public Library, Norristown PA. 215-277-3355

Peck, Mary R, *ILL & Ref,* Essex Community College, James A Newpher Library, Baltimore MD. 301-682-6000, Ext 320

Peck, Mrs Horace S, *Chief Librn,* Riverside Church Library, New York NY. 212-749-7000, Ext 340

Peck, Sally, *AV,* Steele Memorial Library, Chemung-Southern Tier Library System, Elmira NY. 607-733-9173, 733-9174, 733-9175

Peck, Jr, John G, *Dir & Media,* Westminster Choir College, Talbott Library, Princeton NJ. 921-3658 (Dir), 921-7826 (Publ Servs), 921-3659 (Choral Libr), 921-7148 (Media Servs)

Peckar, Rissa, *Librn,* Cadwalader, Wickersham & Taft Library, New York NY. 212-785-1711

Peckham, Gloria M, *In Charge,* Canada Department of Energy, Mines & Resources (Canada Center for Mineral & Energy Technology Library), Ottawa ON. 613-995-4132

Peczerski, Juanina, *Librn,* Center for the Environment & Man, Inc, Research Library, Hartford CT. 203-549-4400, Ext 315

Pedbereznak, Florence, *Ad,* Ansonia Library, Ansonia CT. 203-734-6275

Peddle, Heddy M, *Librn,* Newfoundland & Labrador Development Corp Library, Resource Information Center, Saint John's NF. 709-753-3560, Ext 41

Pedersen, Ellinor, *Librn,* Fisher Junior College Library, Boston MA. 617-262-3240

Pedersen, Louise, *Librn,* Kitsap Regional Library (Manchester Station), Manchester WA. 206-871-3921

Pedersen, Naomi, *ILL,* Idaho Falls Public Library, Idaho Falls ID. 208-529-1450

Pedersen, Wayne, *Dir,* Iowa Lutheran Hospital (Levitt Health Sciences Library), Des Moines IA. 515-283-5181

Pedersen-Vogel, Karen, *Ref,* North Dakota State University Library, Fargo ND. 701-237-8876

Pederson, Barbara, *Librn,* Forest Lake Public Library, Forest Lake MN. 612-464-4088

Pederson, Lila, *Actg Dir,* University of North Dakota (Harley French Medical Library), Grand Forks ND. 701-777-3993

Pederson, Marilyn, *Asst Dir & Tech Serv,* Renton Public Library, Renton WA. 206-235-2610

Pederson, Ronald, *Libr Technician,* Canadian Forestry Service, Northern Forest Research Centre Library, Edmonton AB. 403-435-7210

Pedro, Dolores, *Librn,* Pasadena Public Library (La Pintoresca), Pasadena CA. 213-797-1873

Peduzzi, Roberta, *Acq,* Belleville Area College Library, Belleville IL. 618-235-2700, Ext 236

Peek, Norman, *Instr,* Southern Missionary College, Library Science Program, TN. 615-396-4291

Peel, Bruce B, *Dir,* University of Alberta (University Libraries), Edmonton AB. 403-432-3790

Peel, Richard, *Asst Librn,* Arizona State Regional Library for the Blind & Physically Handicapped, Phoenix AZ. 602-255-5578

Peeler, Diane, *Records Clerk,* Bureau of Land Management Library, Fairbanks AK. 907-356-2025

Peelle, Jami, *Circ,* Kenyon College, Gordon Keith Chalmers Memorial Library, Gambier OH. 614-427-2244, Ext 2186

Peelman, Marie, *Librn,* San Diego Gas & Electric Company Library, San Diego CA. 714-232-4252

Peeples, Harvey, *Ref,* Henderson State University, Huie Library, Arkadelphia AR. 501-246-5511, Ext 200

Peeples, Jane, *Librn,* Stanislaus County Free Library (Keyes Branch), Keyes CA. 209-634-2931

Peery, Alice, *ILL,* Public Library of Charlotte & Mecklenburg County, Inc, Charlotte NC. 704-374-2725

Peery, Alice, *Fiction,* Public Library of Charlotte & Mecklenburg County, Inc, Charlotte NC. 704-374-2725

Peetz, John E, *Dir,* Oakland Museum, Art Division Library, Oakland CA. 415-834-2413

Peffers, Marjore, *Tech Serv,* Huntington Beach Library, Information & Cultural Resource Center, Huntington Beach CA. 714-842-4481

Pefley, Lynn, *Librn,* Oxy Metal Industries Corp, Udylite Div Research Library, Warren MI. 313-497-9270

Pegram, Betty, *Librn,* Union County Public Library (Waxhaw Branch), Waxhaw NC. 704-843-3131

Pegram, Donna, *Asst Dir,* Lincoln Public Library, Lincoln IL. 217-732-8878

Pegram, J Wally, *Librn,* University of California Los Angeles Library (Physics), Los Angeles CA. 213-825-4791

Peguese, Charles R, *LSCA, Title I, Pub Libr Servs,* State Library of Pennsylvania, Harrisburg PA. 717-787-2646

Pehler, James, *Instr,* Saint Cloud State University, Center for Library & Audiovisual Education, MN. 612-255-2022

Pehrkon, Anne L, *Librn,* Crete Public Library, Crete IL. 312-672-8017

Peischl, Thomas M, *Dir,* State University of New York College at Potsdam, Frederick W Crumb Memorial Library, Potsdam NY. 315-268-2940

Peitier, Frances, *Librn,* Iberville Parish Library (East Iberville), St Gabriel LA. 504-642-8380

Pekar, Mary Lou, *Ch,* Santa Maria Public Library, Santa Maria CA. 805-925-0994, Ext 261

Pekarski, Mary L, *Asst Univ Librn-Professional School Libs,* Boston College Libraries, Chestnut Hill MA. 617-969-0100, Ext 3195

Pekarski, Mary L, *Librn,* Boston College Libraries (School of Nursing Library), Chestnut Hill MA. 617-969-0100, Ext 3235

Pekich, John, *Media,* Atlantic Community College, Daniel Leeds Learning Resources Center, Mays Landing NJ. 625-1111 & 646-4950

Peladeau, Marius B, *Dir,* William A Farnsworth Library & Art Museum, Rockland ME. 207-596-6457

Pelcyger, Roslyn, *Dir,* Bloomingdale Public Library, Bloomingdale NJ. 201-838-0077

Pelech, Orest, *Slavic,* Princeton University Library, Princeton NJ. 609-452-3180

Pelham, Bobbie M, *Asst Coordr,* Brevard County Library System, Merritt Island FL. 305-453-9509

Pelham, Jo, *Librn,* Ed Rachal Memorial Library, Falfurrias TX. 512-325-2144

Pelissier, Mariette F, *Per,* Bibliotheque Municipale Des Trois-Rivieres, Trois-Rivieres PQ. 819-374-3521, Ext 71

Pelizzari, Mrs G W, *Librn,* La Follette Public Library, La Follette TN. 615-562-5154

Pelkey, Don, *Dir,* Mott Community College, C S Mott Library, Flint MI. 313-762-0400

Pellan, Lawrence, *Librn,* William M Mercer Ltd, Information Centre Library, Toronto ON. 416-868-2909

Pelle, Elizabeth, *ILL,* Jervis Public Library Association, Rome NY. 315-336-4570

Pellegrino, Jane, *Librn,* Saint Francis Hospital & Medical Center (Hospital Library), Hartford CT. 203-548-4746

Pelletier, C, *Librn,* Seminaire De Sherbrooke Bibliotheque, Sherbrooke PQ. 819-563-2050, Ext 31

Pelletier, C H, *Acq,* Universite Laval Bibliotheque, Quebec PQ. 418-656-3344

Pelletier, Claire, *Acq,* Ecole Polytechnique De Montreal Bibliotheque, Montreal PQ. 514-344-4847

Pelletier, Jacqueline, *Librn,* University of Montreal Libraries (Architecture, Town Planning), Montreal PQ. 514-343-6009

Pelletier, Mary Lou, *Librn,* East Carolina University (A J Fletcher Music Center Library), Greenville NC. 919-757-6250

Pelletier, Suzanne I, *Acq,* University of Maine School of Law, Donald L Garbrecht Library, Portland ME. 207-780-4350

Pelletiere, Jean C, *Dir,* Union College, Schaffer Library, Schenectady NY. 518-370-6278

Pelley, Janet, *Tech Serv,* Colchester-East Hants Regional Library, Truro NS. 902-895-4183

Pellington, Mary Ellen, *Personnel,* Tampa-Hillsborough County Public Library System, Tampa FL. 813-223-8947

Pellini, Nancy M, *Mgr,* Stone & Webster Engineering Corporation, Technical Information Center Library, Boston MA. 617-973-2103

Pellor, Barbara, *Asst Librn,* Anselmo Public Library, Anselmo NE. 308-749-2466

Pellowski, Anne, *Dir,* United States Committee for UNICEF, Information Center on Children's Cultures, New York NY. 212-686-5522, Ext 402

Peloquin, Paul, *Asst Prof,* Delta State University, Dept of Media & Library Science, MS. 601-843-8638

Pelowski, Shirley, *Per,* Mayo Foundation (Medical Library), Rochester MN. 507-284-2061

Peltier, Euclid J, *AV,* Boston Public Library, Eastern Massachusetts Library System, Boston MA. 617-536-5400

Peltier, Felecia, *Librn,* Wellesley Free Library (Fells), Wellesley MA. 617-237-0485

Peltier, Jane, *Tech Serv,* Eagleville Hospital & Rehabilitation Center, Henry S Louchheim Medical Library, Eagleville PA. 215-539-6000, Ext 304

Peltier, Marie, *Librn,* Augustana Hospital & Health Care Center, Health Science Library, Chicago IL. 312-975-5109

Pelton, James R, *Dir,* Shreve Memorial Library, Shreveport LA. 318-221-2614

Peluso, Francis E, *Librn,* Monastery of Saint Augustine, Augustinian Recollect Friars, McKenna Memorial Library, Kansas City KS. 913-371-6129

Pelz, Craig L, *In Charge,* United States Army (Corps of Engineers, Fort Worth District Library), Fort Worth TX. 334-2138 or 2139

Pelzmann, Helen L, *Dir,* West Allis Public Library, West Allis WI. 414-476-6550

Pember, Marie, *Librn,* Iosco-Arenac Regional Library (Plainfield Township), Hale MI. 517-728-7781

Pemberton, Anne, *Librn,* Kenilworth Historical Society, Kilner Library, Kenilworth IL. 312-251-2565

Pemberton, J Michael, *Asst Prof,* University of Tennessee, Knoxville, Graduate School of Library & Information Science, TN. 615-974-2148

Pemberton, P N, *Coordr,* Eisenhower Curriculum Cooperative, Palo Heights IL. 312-385-1220

Pen, Emma Fung Chen, *Ch,* American Samoa-Office of Library Services, Pago Pago, Samoa PI. 633-5869

Pena, Euphemia R, *Librn,* Pasadena Public Library (David Coronado Branch), Pasadena TX. 713-472-2364

Pena, Rita, *Librn,* Tulare County Library System (Three Rivers Branch), Three Rivers CA. 209-561-4564

Pence, Cheryl, *Reader Serv,* Lincoln Library, Springfield Public Library, Springfield IL. 217-753-4900

Pence, Doris, *Dir,* Rockville Public Library, Rockville IN. 317-569-5544

Pence, Mrs Herbert, *Librn,* Logan County District Library (Lakeview Branch), Bellefontaine OH. 513-843-2851

Penchansky, Mimi, *Ref,* Queens College Library, Flushing NY. 212-520-7616

Penchansky, Mimi, *On-Line Servs,* Queens College Library, Flushing NY. 212-520-7616

Pender, Gertrude, *ILL,* Lake Worth Public Library, Lake Worth FL. 305-585-9882

Pendergast, Joan C, *Librn,* Grey Advertising, Inc Library, New York NY. 212-751-3500, Ext 258

Pendergraff, Sandra, *Tech Serv,* Longmont Public Library, Longmont CO. 303-776-2236

Pendergraft, Cindy, *Ser,* Davidson College, E H Little Library, Davidson NC. 704-892-2000, Ext 331

Pendergrass, George, *Coordr Media Servs,* Southeast Missouri State University, Kent Library, Cape Girardeau MO. 314-651-2235

Pendleton, Beth, *Librn,* Clancy Memorial Library, Ennis MT. 406-682-7244

Pendleton, Dyette, *Librn,* Hanes Corp, Central Research & Development Dept Library, Winston-Salem NC. 919-744-3217

Pendleton, Eldridge H, *Dir,* Old Gaol Museum Library, York ME. 207-363-3872

Pendleton, Elsa, *Tech Serv, Acq & Cat,* Whittier Public Library, Whittier CA. 213-698-8949

Penfield, Ann, *Librn,* Middlesex Community College Library, Middletown CT. 203-344-3062, 344-3063, 344-3064

Pengelly, Kenneth, *Assoc Prof,* Mankato State College, Library Media Education, MN. 507-389-1965

Pengelly, Margaret, *Librn,* Kent County Library System (Cascade), Grand Rapids MI. 616-949-3130

Penland, Patrick, *Prof,* University of Pittsburgh, School of Library & Information Science, PA. 412-624-5230

Penman, Elizabeth H, *Librn,* Merck & Co, Inc (Law Library), Rahway NJ. 201-574-5805

Penman, Iris, *Librn,* Fort Erie Public Library (Crystal Beach Branch), Crystal Beach ON. 416-894-1783

Penn, Miriam E, *Cat,* Virginia Union University, William J Clarke Library, Richmond VA. 804-359-9331, Ext 256, 257

Penne, Carol, *Asst Dir,* American Bankers Association Library, Washington DC. 202-467-4180

Pennebaker, Fleata, *Librn,* Fish Lake Valley Library, Fish Lake Valley NV. 702-572-3256

Pennell, Lila M, *Librn,* Saxton Community Library, Saxton PA. 814-635-3533

Penner, Erna, *Tech Serv,* Kansas City Kansas Community College Library, Kansas City KS. 913-334-1100, Ext 38

Pennestri, Mary Anne, *Librn,* Southern Railway System, Law Library, Washington DC. 202-383-4000

Penniman, A, *Librn,* Essex Library Association, Inc, Essex CT. 203-767-1560

Pennington, B Blaine, *Dir,* Mohave County Library, Kingman AZ. 602-753-5730

Pennington, Carole, *Tech Serv,* Saint Bernard's Seminary Library, Rochester NY. 716-254-1020, Ext 25, 26, 27

Pennington, Claudia E, *Dean,* Raymer F Maguire Jr Learning Resources Center, Orlando FL. 305-299-5000, Ext 362

Pennington, Helen, *Bkmobile Coordr,* Fleming County Public Library, Flemingsburg KY. 606-845-7851

Pennington, Jasper, *Dir, Rare Bks & Spec Coll,* Saint Bernard's Seminary Library, Rochester NY. 716-254-1020, Ext 25, 26, 27

Pennington, Jerome, *Asst Dir,* Stockton-San Joaquin County Public Library, Stockton Public Libr, Stockton CA. 209-944-8415

Pennington, Jerri, *Media,* Emporia State University, William Allen White Library, Emporia KS. 316-343-1200, Ext 205

Pennington, Michael, *Cat,* Bureau of Land Management (Denver Service Center Library), Denver CO. 303-234-4578

Pennington, Ralph, *Librn,* Atlanta-Jackson Township Public Library (Cicero Branch), Cicero IN. 317-292-2521

Pennington, W W, *Circ & Info Analyst,* University of Alabama in Birmingham, Mervyn H Sterne Library, Birmingham AL. 205-934-6360

Pennino, John, *Painting & Opera,* Long Island University, Brooklyn Center Libraries, Brooklyn NY. 212-834-6060, 834-6064

Pennock, Mary F, *Librn,* Manufacturers Association of Syracuse Library, Syracuse NY. 315-474-4201

Penrose, Anna Mae, *Librn,* Saint Joseph's University Libraries (Campbell Library), Philadelphia PA. 215-879-7489

Penrose, Barbara, *Librn,* Ulysses Philomathic Library, Trumansburg NY. 607-387-5623

Penson, Claudine, *On-Line Servs & Bibliog Instr,* Tuskegee Institute, Hollis Burke Frissell Library, Tuskegee Institute AL. 205-727-8894

Penson, Merryll, *Ser,* Virginia Commonwealth University (James Branch Cabell Library), Richmond VA. 804-257-1105

Pensyl, Mary E, *On-Line Servs,* Massachusetts Institute of Technology Libraries, Cambridge MA. 617-253-5651

Penta, Frances, *Circ,* Beverly Public Library, Beverly MA. 617-922-0310

Pentek, Stephen, *Acq,* Boston University Libraries (School of Theology Library), Boston MA. 617-353-3034

Pentland, Michelle, *Program Coordr,* Health Research and Educational Trust, Learning Center, Princeton NJ. 609-452-9280, Ext 210

Pentoliros, Tina, *ILL,* Newburyport Public Library, Newburyport MA. 617-462-4031

Pepe, Ruth, *Actg Dir,* Riverside Art Center & Museum Library, Riverside CA. 714-684-7111

Pepe, Susan, *Ch,* North Tonawanda Public Library, North Tonawanda NY. 716-693-4132

Pepich, Bruce W, *Actg Dir,* Charles A Wustum Museum of Fine Arts, Racine WI. 414-636-9177

Pepin, Patricia M, *Librn,* United States Army (Biomedical Laboratory, Wood Technical Library), Aberdeen Proving Ground MD. 301-671-4135

Peplowski, Celia, *Ad,* Mobile Public Library, Mobile AL. 205-438-7073

Pepmueller, Calla Ann, *Dept Mgr,* Sandia Laboratories, Technical Libraries, Albuquerque NM. 505-844-2869

Peppard, Dorothy, *Ch & YA,* Southampton Free Library, Southampton PA. 215-322-1415

Peppel, Marjorie, *Br Coordr,* Columbiana Public Library, Columbiana OH. 216-482-2356

Peppel, Martha, *Librn,* Ebasco Services, Inc Library, New York NY. 212-785-5895

Pepper, Alan G, *Dir,* Northwestern Regional Library System, Thunder Bay ON. 807-623-2794

Pepper, Catherine, *Librn,* Canadian Red Cross Society Library, Toronto ON. 416-923-6692

Pepper, David, *Supvr,* Cominco Ltd Library, Vancouver BC. 604-682-0611, Ext 485

Pepper, Janet, *Ch,* Northport Public Library, Northport NY. 516-261-6930

Pepper, Laurence, *AV Coordr,* Rolling Prairie Library System, Decatur IL. 217-429-2586

Pepper, Linda, *Librn,* Dominion Bridge Company Limited Corporate Library, Lachine PQ. 514-634-3551

Pepper, Marie A, *Asst Librn,* Manasquan Public Library, Manasquan NJ. 201-223-1503

Pepper, Sheila, *Librn,* McMaster University (Innis Room (Business Library)), Hamilton ON. 416-525-9140, Ext 2081

Peppler, Christopher, *Dir,* Frontenac County Library, Kingston ON. 613-389-2611

Peppler, M, *On-Line Servs & Bibliog Instr,* Hercules Inc (Fourteenth-T Library), Wilmington DE. 302-575-5401

Perabo, Charlotte, *Supvr Bus Libr,* Monsanto Co, Information Center Library, Saint Louis MO. 694-4736

Peralta, Lydia, *Librn,* Magnavox G & I Electronics Co Engineering Library, Fort Wayne IN. 219-482-4411, Ext 6418

Perch, Theodore, *Dir,* Thompson Public Library, Thompson CT. 203-923-9779

Perchetti, Minnie, *Librn,* Tonopah Public Library, Tonopah NV. 702-482-3374

Percival, Maureen, *Librn,* Frontenac County Library (Sharbot Lake Branch), Sharbot Lake ON. 613-279-2583

Percival, Ruth, *Librn,* Montrose County Regional District Library (Olathe Branch), Olathe CO. 303-323-5775

Percy, Nancy W, *Asst Librn,* California State Library, Sacramento CA. 916-445-2585

Percy, Thelma W, *Dir,* Mill Valley Public Library, Mill Valley CA. 415-388-4245

Percy, Theresa, *Asst Librn,* Old Sturbridge Village, Research Library, Sturbridge MA. 617-347-3362, Ext 132

Perdigone, Helen, *AV,* Sunland Hospital at Orlando, Medical Library, Orlando FL. 305-293-1421, Ext 339

Perdue, Albert, *Soc Sci,* Iowa State University Library, Ames IA. 515-294-1442

Perdue, Charles, *Dir,* Rock Island Public Library, Rock Island IL. 309-788-7627

Perdue, Robert, *On-Line Servs,* University of West Florida, John C Pace Library, Pensacola FL. 904-476-9500, Ext 261

Perduyn, Claire, *Ch,* Concord Free Public Library, Concord MA. 617-369-5324

Pereira, Alberto T, *Community Libr Consult,* Rhode Island Department of State Library Services, Providence RI. 401-277-2726

Pereira, Priscilla, *Educ,* City University of New York, Library of Graduate School & University Center, New York NY. 212-790-4541

Pereira, V A, *Librn,* California Medical Facility, Northern Reception Guidance Center Library, Vacaville CA. 707-448-6841

Perella, Theresa, *ILL,* Goucher College, Julia Rogers Library, Towson MD. 301-825-5300, Ext 360

Perelmuter, Susan, *On-Line Servs,* Arizona Division of Behavioral Health Services, Behavioral Health Library & Information Service, Phoenix AZ. 602-244-1331, Ext 278

Perez, Art, *Dir,* Oklahoma Department of Corrections & the Oklahoma Department of Libraries, State Penitentiary Library, McAlester OK. 918-423-4700

Perez, Daniel, *Circ,* University of Puerto Rico, Cayey University College Library, Cayey PR. 809-738-2161, Ext 221

Perez, Margaret S, *Dir,* El Centro Public Library, El Centro CA. 714-352-0751

Perez, Marta, *Info,* Catholic University of Puerto Rico (Encarnacion Valdes Library), Ponce PR. 809-844-4150, Ext 119

Perez, N, *Dir,* Library of Youngstown, Youngstown NY. 716-745-3555

Perez-Lopez, Rene, *Br Coordr & Exten,* Norfolk Public Library, Norfolk VA. 804-441-2887

Perich, John, *Librn,* Saint Tikhon's Theological Seminary Library, South Canaan PA. 717-937-4411

Perinchief, Elizabeth, *Hq Coordr,* Burlington County Library, Mount Holly NJ. 609-267-9660

Perinchief, Elizabeth, *Geneology & Jerseyana,* Burlington County Library, Mount Holly NJ. 609-267-9660

Perinoff, Kathleen, *Asst Dir,* Palm Beach County Public Library System, West Palm Beach FL. 305-686-0895

Perkins, Arden K, *Librn,* Crystal Lake Public Library, Crystal Lake IL. 815-459-1687

Perkins, Charles F, *Dir,* Massachusetts Bay Community College Library, Wellesley MA. 617-237-1100, Ext 193

PERKINS

Perkins, Dale W, *Dir,* San Luis Obispo City-County Public Library, San Luis Obispo CA. 805-549-5775

Perkins, Dave, *Bibliog,* California State University, Northridge, Delmar T Oviatt & South Libraries, Northridge CA. 213-885-2271

Perkins, Don, *Librn,* Star-Phoenix Library, Saskatoon SK. 306-664-8223

Perkins, Estella B, *Librn,* RCA Engineering Library, Indianapolis IN. 317-267-5925

Perkins, Geneva, *Librn,* Piedmont Regional Library (Statham Branch), Statham GA. 404-867-2762

Perkins, Janet, *In Charge,* Crawford County Federated Library Board, Titusville PA. 814-827-2913

Perkins, Janet H, *Dir,* Benson Memorial Library, Titusville PA. 814-827-2913

Perkins, Jean F, *Asst Librn,* Clark University, Robert Hutchings Goddard Library, Worcester MA. 617-793-7573

Perkins, John W, *Dir & Circ,* City of Inglewood Public Library, Inglewood CA. 213-649-7380

Perkins, Laurie, *Librn,* Needham Free Public Library, Needham MA. 617-444-0087, 444-0090

Perkins, Leanore, *Librn,* Swarthmore Public Library, Swarthmore PA. 215-543-0436

Perkins, Linda, *Ch,* Berkeley Public Library, Berkeley CA. 415-644-6095

Perkins, Linda K, *Ch,* Buffalo & Erie County Public Library System, Buffalo NY. 716-856-7525

Perkins, Marcia, *Pub Libr Consult,* Louisiana State Library, Baton Rouge LA. 504-342-4922

Perkins, Margaret, *Librn,* Louisville Free Public Library (Southwest), Louisville KY. 502-937-6296

Perkins, Marleta S, *Librn,* Tappan-Spaulding Memorial Library, Newark Valley NY. 607-642-9960

Perkins, Mary, *Librn,* Stewart Free Library, Corinna ME. 207-278-2454

Perkins, Milton, *Tech Serv,* Howard County Library, Big Spring TX. 915-267-5295

Perkins, Patricia, *Asst Librn,* Ilsley Library, Middlebury VT. 802-388-2977

Perkins, Steve, *Asst Librn & Ref,* University of Cincinnati Libraries (Robert S Marx Law Library), Cincinnati OH. 513-475-3016

Perkins, Virginia B, *Asst Librn,* Glenwood Public Library, Glenwood IA. 712-527-3286

Perkis, Barbara, *Asst Dir,* Chicago Public Library (Illinois Regional Library for the Blind & Physically Handicapped), Chicago IL. 312-738-9210

Perkofski, Diane, *Dir,* Portage Free Public Library, Zona Gale Breese Memorial, Portage WI. 608-742-4959

Perks, Ruth, *On-Line Servs,* United States Department of Energy, Energy Library, Washington DC. 202-353-4301

Perksy, Gail, *Cat with Copy,* Columbia University (University Libraries), New York NY. 212-280-2241

Perkus, Gerry, *Media,* University of Houston (William I Dykes Library), Houston TX. 713-749-1991

Perlaky, Livia, *Acq,* Topeka Public Library, Topeka KS. 913-233-2040

Perlee, Gail, *Librn,* Phoenix Public Library (Ocotillo), Phoenix AZ. 602-262-6694

Perlin, Janet K, *Librn,* Temple Israel, Leonard M Sandhaus Memorial Library, Sharon MA. 617-784-3986

Perlman, Amy, *Asst Librn,* HJK & A Library, Washington DC. 202-333-0700

Perlman, Michael, *Ref,* Chicago Sun-Times, Editorial Library, Chicago IL. 312-321-2594

Perlman, Stephen, *Librn,* United States Department of Agriculture, Plum Island Animal Disease Center Library, Greenport NY. 516-323-2500, Ext 235

Perlman, V A, *Libr Info Retrieval Systs,* Standard Oil Co (Indiana), Library-Information Center, Chicago IL. 312-856-5961

Perlmutter, Rose, *Tech Serv,* Evergreen Park Public Library, Evergreen Park IL. 312-422-8522

Perona, Gerald, *AV & Ref,* Gateway Technical Institute, Learning Resources Center, Kenosha WI. 414-656-6924, 656-6923

Perras, Ghislaine, *ILL,* University du Quebec: Centre d'Etudes Universitaires Dans L'Ouest Quebecois, Centre de Hull Bibliotheque, Hull PQ. 819-776-8381

Perrault, Arthur, *Librn,* Barreau De Montreal, La Bibliotheque Du Barreau, Montreal PQ. 514-873-3083

Perreault, Jean, *Behav Sci,* University of Alabama in Huntsville Library, Huntsville AL. 205-895-6540

Perreault, Micheline, *Librn,* Bibliotheque Municipale, Pincourt PQ. 514-453-3788

Perreault, Robert, *ILL,* United States Department of Transportation-Transportation Systems Center, Technical Reference Center, Cambridge MA. 617-494-2783

Perreault, Robert B, *Librn,* Institut Canado-Americain, Manchester NH. 603-625-8577

Perrett, M K, *Librn,* United States Navy (Naval Air Station Library), Dallas TX. 214-266-6111

Perri, Denise M, *Tech Serv & Cat,* Cheltenham Township Library System, Glenside PA. 215-885-0457

Perri, Denise M, *Tech Serv,* Glenside Free Library, Glenside PA. 215-885-0455

Perrier, Alain, *Asst Prof,* University of Montreal, Ecole de Biblioteconomie, PQ. 514-343-6044

Perrigan, Laura, *Librn,* Joseph Public Library, Joseph OR. 503-432-3832

Perrin, James, *Acq & Rare Bks,* University of the Pacific, Irving Martin Library, Stockton CA. 209-946-2431

Perrin, June M, *Circ,* Spokane Public Library, Comstock Building Library, Spokane WA. 509-838-3361, Ext 65

Perrin, Nancy, *Asst Dir & Ref,* Corning Public Library, Corning NY. 607-936-3713

Perrin, Richard, *Processing Dept,* Ferris State College Library, Big Rapids MI. 616-796-9494, 796-9971, Ext 323

Perrin, Robert A, *Dir,* University of South Carolina at Spartanburg Library, Spartanburg SC. 803-578-1800, Exts 410

Perrin, Stephanie, *ILL,* Appalachian State University, Carol Grotnes Belk Library, Boone NC. 704-262-2186

Perrine, Helen, *Librn,* Judith Basin County Free Library (Hobson Library Station), Hobson MT. 406-566-2389

Perrine, Lucy, *Librn,* Gooding Public Library, Gooding ID. 208-934-4089

Perrine, Mrs Richard, *Librn,* Hobson Community Library, Hobson MT. 406-423-5378

Perrine, Richard H, *Ref,* William Marsh Rice University, Fondren Library, Houston TX. 713-527-4022

Perrine, Susan, *Librn,* Shea & Gardner, Law Library, Washington DC. 202-737-1255

Perrins, Barbara, *Asst Prof,* Southern Connecticut State College, Div of Library Science & Instructional Technology, CT. 203-397-4532

Perritt, Patsy H, *Assoc Prof,* Louisiana State University, Graduate School of Library Science, LA. 504-388-3158

Perron, Hubert, *Tech Serv,* Bibliotheque Nationale Du Quebec, Montreal PQ. 514-873-4553

Perron, Robert R, *President-Historical Society,* Beverly Historical Society, Charles W Galloupe Memorial Library, Beverly MA. 617-922-1186

Perrone, Charles, *Acq & Spec Coll,* Burlington County College Library, Pemberton NJ. 609-894-9311, Ext 222

Perruso, Mary, *Ch,* Crestwood Public Library District, Crestwood IL. 312-371-4090

Perry, Anna Ruth, *Cat,* James Madison University, Madison Memorial Library, Harrisonburg VA. 703-433-6150

Perry, Betty, *Bkmobile Coordr,* Scott County Public Library, Georgetown KY. 502-863-3566

Perry, Billie Ann, *Librn,* Aerospace Industries Library, Washington DC. 202-347-2315, Ext 274

Perry, Blythe, *Bus Mgr,* Connecticut State Library, Hartford CT. 203-566-4301

Perry, Carmen, *Spec Coll,* University of Texas at San Antonio Library, San Antonio TX. 512-691-4570

Perry, Celia, *ILL,* Mount Saint Alphonsus Seminary Library, Esopus NY. 914-384-6550, Ext 25

Perry, Cynthia, *Asst Librn & Doc,* College of the Virgin Islands, Ralph M Paiewonsky Library, Saint Thomas VI. 809-774-1252, Ext 483

Perry, Doris, *In Charge,* Allen County-Fort Wayne Historical Society Library, Fort Wayne IN. 219-743-5776

Perry, Douglas F, *Librn,* Blue Ridge Regional Library (Patrick County), Stuart VA. 703-694-3352

Perry, Emma, *Circ,* Texas A&m University Libraries, College Station TX. 713-845-6111

Perry, Frances, *Actg Librn,* Tarrant County Law Library, Fort Worth TX. 817-334-1481

Perry, Geraldine, *Ch,* Groton Public Library, Groton MA. 617-448-6761

Perry, Guest, *Librn,* Houghton Mifflin Co Library, Boston MA. 617-725-5270

Perry, Jane M, *Pub Servs,* Lithgow Public Library, Augusta ME. 207-622-6368

Perry, Joyce, *Dir,* Stevens Memorial Library, Attica NY. 716-591-2733

Perry, Karen, *Ch,* High Point Public Library, High Point NC. 919-885-8411

Perry, Laura, *Ref,* Fort Worth Public Library, Fort Worth TX. 817-870-7700

Perry, Louise W, *Br Coordr,* Sheppard Memorial Library, Greenville NC. 919-752-4177

Perry, Margaret, *Reader Serv,* University of Rochester, Rush Rhees Library, Rochester NY. 716-275-4461

Perry, Margaret H, *Librn,* Canton Public Library, Collinsville CT. 203-693-8266

Perry, Mrs Cubian, *Librn,* Ranger Community Library, Ranger TX. 817-647-3549

Perry, Myrna, *Cat,* David Lipscomb College, Crisman Memorial Library, Nashville TN. 615-385-3855, Ext 282, 283

Perry, Pamela, *Tech Serv,* Wareham Free Library, Wareham MA. 617-295-2343

Perry, Pennie E, *Dir,* North Carolina Central University, James E Shepard Memorial Library, Durham NC. 919-683-6475

Perry, Rodney, *Assoc Dir,* Monroe County Library System, Rochester NY. 716-428-7345

Perry, Rodney, *Assoc Dir,* Rochester Public Library, Rochester NY. 716-428-7300

Perry, Sharon, *ILL,* California State University Fullerton Library, Fullerton CA. 714-773-2714

Perry, Yvonne, *Librn,* Pike-Amite-Walthall Library System (Crosby Public), Crosby MS. 601-639-4516

Perryman, Anderson Patrick, *Media,* Minneapolis Community College Library, Minneapolis MN. 612-341-7089, 341-7059

Persak, Susan, *Librn,* Mount Olive Public Library, Budd Lake NJ. 201-691-8686

Persaud, Micheline, *Libr Consultant,* Eastern Ontario Library System, Ottawa ON. 613-238-8457

Persempere, Dominic, *State Agencies & Institutions,* Connecticut State Library, Hartford CT. 203-566-4301

Pershing, Laura M, *Librn,* Idaho Supreme Court, Idaho State Law Library, Boise ID. 208-334-3317

Persicke, Ileen, *Librn,* Anaconda Aluminum Co, Columbia Falls Reduction Div Library, Columbia Falls MT. 406-892-3261, Ext 218

Perslin, Clemence, *Actg Librn,* Howard University Libraries (Engineering Library), Washington DC. 202-636-6620

Person, Dorothy, *Ref,* Public Library of Charlotte & Mecklenburg County, Inc, Charlotte NC. 704-374-2725

Person, Ellen, *Dir,* Lansing Community College Library, Lansing MI. 517-373-9978

Person, Oswell, *Dir,* Mission College, Learning Resource Services, Santa Clara CA. 408-988-2200, Ext 1531

Person, Wilhelmina, *Librn,* Newark Public Library (Clinton), Newark NJ. 201-733-7757

Persons, Billie, *Librn,* Atascosa County Library System, Jourdanton TX. 512-769-2556

Persons, Billie, *Librn,* San Antonio Museum Association, Ellen S Quillin Memorial Library, San Antonio TX. 512-826-0647, Ext 32

Persons, Jerry, *Librn,* Stanford University Libraries (Music), Stanford CA. 415-497-2463

Pertzog, Betsy S, *AV & Circ,* University of Alabama, Health Sciences Library, Tuscaloosa AL. 205-348-4950, Ext 360

Perushek, Diane, *Wason Coll Curator,* Cornell University Libraries (University Libraries), Ithaca NY. 607-256-4144

Peshel, Barbara B, *Acq,* University of Oklahoma Health Sciences Center Library, Oklahoma City OK. 405-271-2285

Peskind, Ira J, *Dir,* Loop College, City Colleges of Chicago, Loop College Library, Chicago IL. 312-269-8015

Pesola, Beverly, *Librn,* American Hoechst Corporation, Research & Development Library, Leominster MA. 617-537-8131

Pesson, Ella, *Librn,* Iberia Parish Public Library (Delcambre Branch), Delcambre LA. 318-685-2388

Pesson, Lou Ella, *Librn,* Vermilion Parish Library (Delcambre Branch), Delcambre LA. 318-685-2388

Peter, Sister Marie Gerard, *Dir,* Cardinal Stritch College Library (Reading Materials Laboratory Library), Milwaukee WI. 414-352-5400, Ext 356

Peterman, Edward, *Dir,* Azusa Pacific College, Marshburn Memorial Library, Azusa CA. 213-969-3434, Ext 198

Peternell, Therese, *Librn,* University of Montreal Libraries (Health Sciences), Montreal PQ. 514-343-7810

Peters, Charlene, *ILL & Ref,* Madison-Jefferson County Public Library, Madison IN. 812-265-2744

Peters, Dorothy, *Ch,* Brookfield Free Public Library, Brookfield IL. 312-485-6917

Peters, E Jean, *Librn,* New Mexico Legislative Council Library, Santa Fe NM. 505-827-3141

Peters, E Warren, *Librn,* Detroit Institute of Arts Research Library, Detroit MI. 313-833-7900

Peters, Eunice, *Librn,* Cleveland Public Library (Glenville), Cleveland OH. 216-681-2040

Peters, Frances E, *Dir,* Pennsylvania College of Podiatric Medicine, Charles E Krausz Library, Philadelphia PA. 215-629-0300, Ext 215

Peters, G A, *President,* Interuniversity Council of the North Texas Area, (IUC), TX. 214-231-7211

Peters, H Virginia, *Dir,* Sinclair Community College, Learning Resources Center, Dayton OH. 513-226-2855

Peters, James, *Asst Dir,* Maurice M Pine Free Public Library, Fair Lawn NJ. 201-796-3400

Peters, Jean, *Librn,* R R Bowker Co, Frederic G Melcher Library, New York NY. 212-764-5126

Peters, Jeff, *Research Librn,* Cargill, Inc, Information Center, Minneapolis MN. 612-475-6498

Peters, John A, *Doc,* State Historical Society of Wisconsin Library, Madison WI. 608-262-3421

Peters, Katherine A, *Librn,* Kauai Community College, Learning Resource Center, Lihue HI. 808-245-8311

Peters, Leanne P, *Chief Librn,* Community Services Administration Library, Washington DC. 202-254-5756

Peters, Margaret, *Librn,* Sabula Public Library, Sabula IA. 319-687-2950

Peters, Marilyn, *Librn,* Evans Products Co, T & E Center Library, Corvallis OR. 503-753-1211

Peters, Marion, *Librn,* University of California Los Angeles Library (Chemistry), Los Angeles CA. 213-825-3254

Peters, Myron, *Asst Librn,* John Brown University Library, Siloam Springs AR. 501-524-3131, Ext 203

Peters, Paul Evan, *Systs Develop,* Columbia University (University Libraries), New York NY. 212-280-2241

Peters, Perian, *Librn,* East Mississippi Regional Library (Waynesboro Memorial), Waynesboro MS. 601-735-2268

Peters, Robert, *Publ & Exhibits,* Milwaukee Public Library, Milwaukee WI. 414-278-3000

Peters, Ronald, *Soc Sci,* University of Calgary Library, Calgary AB. 403-284-5954

Peters, Sister Mary Dennis, *Tech Serv,* Benedictine College (North Campus Library), Atchison KS. 913-367-5340, Ext 290

Peters, Stephen, *Instr,* Northern Michigan University, Dept of Library Science, MI. 906-227-2250

Peters, Stephen, *Cat,* Northern Michigan University, Lydia M Olson Library, Marquette MI. 906-227-2250

Peters, Virginia, *Librn,* Montgomery County Department of Public Libraries (Silver Spring Branch), Silver Spring MD. 301-565-7689

Peters, William, *Acq,* University of Connecticut Library, Storrs CT. 203-486-2219

Peters, William T, *Dir,* Grosse Pointe Public Library, Grosse Pointe MI. 313-343-2074

Petersen, Annette, *Tech Serv,* Tehama County Library, Red Bluff CA. 916-527-0604

Petersen, Carol, *Asst Librn,* De Smet City Library, De Smet SD. 605-854-3842

Petersen, Clark H, *Dir,* Renton Public Library, Renton WA. 206-235-2610

Petersen, Drake, *Cat,* University of King's College Library, Halifax NS. 902-422-1271

Petersen, Eva, *Asst Librn,* West Suburban Hospital, Walter Lawrence Memorial Library, Oak Park IL. 312-383-6200

Petersen, Karla, *Cat,* Center for Research Libraries, Chicago IL. 312-955-4545

Petersen, Keith, *Dir,* Latah County Historical Society, Moscow ID. 208-882-1004

Petersen, Mary, *Librn,* Victoria County Public Library (Woodville Branch), Woodville ON. 705-324-3104

Petersen, Nancy H, *Ad,* Knoxville-Knox County Public Library, Lawson McGhee Library, Knoxville TN. 615-523-0781

Petersen, Phyllis, *Cat,* State University of New York, Agricultural & Technical College at Norrisville Library, Morrisville NY. 315-684-7055

Petersen, Virginia, *Librn,* Rae Hobson Memorial Library, Republic KS. 913-361-2375

Petersiel, Beverly, *Librn,* Arlington County Department of Libraries (Glencarlyn), Arlington VA. 703-671-7121

Peterson, Agnes, *Coordr,* Department of Public Libraries & Information (Wahab Public Law), Virginia Beach VA. 804-427-4419

Peterson, Agnes, *Curator W European Coll,* Hoover Institution on War, Revolution & Peace, Stanford CA. 415-497-2058

Peterson, Amy K, *Doc & Archivist,* University of Wisconsin-Whitewater, Library & Learning Resources, Whitewater WI. 414-472-1000

Peterson, Anita, *Spanish Speaking Servs,* City of Inglewood Public Library, Inglewood CA. 213-649-7380

Peterson, Anna, *Librn,* Friday Reading Club Library, Thayer KS. 316-839-2381

Peterson, Barbara E, *Librn,* American Osteopathic Association, A T Still Memorial Library, Chicago IL. 312-280-5800

Peterson, Barbara J, *Supvr,* 3M (The 201 Technical Library), Saint Paul MN. 612-733-2447

Peterson, Barbara S, *Librn,* Chillicothe & Ross County Public Library (Frankfort Branch), Frankfort OH. 614-998-4083

Peterson, Beth, *Tech Serv,* Western Plains Library System, Montevideo MN. 612-269-5644

Peterson, Betty Jo, *Ch Lit,* California State University, Fresno Library, Fresno CA. 209-487-2403

Peterson, Billie, *Asst Librn,* Lucy H Patterson Memorial Library, Rockdale TX. 512-446-3410

Peterson, Carl O, *Liaison Librn,* Governors State University, Communication Science-Educational Technology, IL. 312-534-5000, Ext 2331

Peterson, Carole, *Ch,* Silvis Public Library, Silvis IL. 309-755-3393

Peterson, Carole A, *Dir,* Signal Hill Public Library, Signal Hill CA. 213-424-5383

Peterson, Carole M, *Dir,* German-Masontown Public Library, Masontown PA. 412-583-7030

Peterson, Caroline R, *Librn,* Ovid Public Library, Ovid CO. 303-463-5524

Peterson, Carolyn, *Ch,* Orlando Public Library, Orlando FL. 305-425-4694

Peterson, Charles, *Media,* North Park College & Theological Seminary (Wallgren Library), Chicago IL. 312-583-2700

Peterson, Christine, *Actg Librn,* Boston Public Library (Parker Hill), Roxbury MA. 617-427-3820

Peterson, Clara J, *Per,* Bethany Nazarene College, R T Williams Memorial Library, Bethany OK. 405-789-6400, Ext 276

Peterson, Clara J., *Per,* Bethany Nazarene College, R T Williams Memorial Library, Bethany OK. 405-789-6400, Ext 276

Peterson, Dennis R, *Pub Servs,* Palmer College of Chiropractic, Davenport IA. 319-324-1611, Ext 242

Peterson, Donald, *Dir & Cat,* Judson College, Benjamin P Browne Library, Elgin IL. 312-695-2500, Ext 550-553

Peterson, Doris, *Librn,* Havelock Public Library, Havelock IA. 712-776-2719

Peterson, Dorothy, *Circ,* University of Minnesota, Saint Paul Campus Libraries, Saint Paul MN. 612-373-0904

Peterson, Dorothy S, *Librn,* Pioneer Memorial City-County Library, Fredericksburg TX. 512-997-4604

Peterson, Ed, *Ref,* Macon Junior College Library, Macon GA. 912-474-2700, Ext 215, 216

Peterson, Elena, *Librn,* Flagstaff City-Coconino County Public Library System (Coconino County Correctional Facility), Flagstaff AZ. 602-774-4523, Ext 26

Peterson, Ellen, *Br Coordr,* Free Public Library of Woodbridge, Woodbridge NJ. 201-634-4450

Peterson, Ellen, *Librn,* Valley of the Tetons Public Library, Victor ID. 208-787-2201

Peterson, Faye V, *In Charge,* Sperry UNIVAC Defense Systems Division, UNIVAC Park Information Service Center, Saint Paul MN. 612-456-2580

Peterson, Florence, *Archivist,* Gustavus Adolphus College, Folke Bernadotte Memorial Library, Saint Peter MN. 507-931-4300, Ext 2301

Peterson, Frances, *Ref,* Shorewood Public Library, Shorewood WI. 414-332-2498

Peterson, Frances M, *Librn,* Rivoli Township Library, New Windsor IL. 309-667-2515

Peterson, Fred M, *Dir,* Catholic University of America, John K Mullen of Denver Memorial Library, Washington DC. 202-635-5055

Peterson, Gail, *Br Coordr,* Palm Beach County Public Library System, West Palm Beach FL. 305-686-0895

Peterson, Gale E, *Dir,* Cincinnati Historical Society Library, Cincinnati OH. 513-241-4622

Peterson, Gerald, *Spec Coll,* University of Northern Iowa Library, Cedar Falls IA. 319-273-2737

Peterson, Harold, *Librn,* Minneapolis Institute of Arts, Art Reference Library, Minneapolis MN. 612-870-3116

Peterson, Janice M, *Dir,* Revere Public Library, Revere MA. 617-284-0102

Peterson, Jean, *Librn,* Cambridge State Hospital, Medical Library, Cambridge MN. 612-689-2121

Peterson, Jeri, *Librn,* Voice of Prophecy Library, Newbury Park CA. 805-499-1911

Peterson, Jo, *Dir,* Rock County Library, Bassett NE. 402-684-3800

Peterson, John, *Librn,* Florida Junior College at Jacksonville (South Campus Learning Resources Center), Jacksonville FL. 904-646-2170

Peterson, John, *Spec Coll,* Lutheran Theological Seminary, Krauth Memorial Library, Philadelphia PA. 215-248-4616

Peterson, Judy, *Asst Librn,* Chrysler Art Museum, Art Reference Library, Norfolk VA. 804-622-1211

Peterson, Judy, *Ch,* Menominee County Library, Stephenson MI. 906-753-6923

Peterson, Julia, *Librn,* Cargill, Inc, Information Center, Minneapolis MN. 612-475-6498

Peterson, June M, *Librn & Ch,* Fremont Public Library District, Mundelein IL. 312-566-8702

Peterson, Karen, *Asst Librn & ILL,* Western Conservative Baptist Seminary, Cline-Tunnell Library, Portland OR. 503-233-8561, Ext 23

Peterson, Kendra, *Ref,* Fairleigh Dickinson University, Weiner Library, Teaneck NJ. 201-836-6300, Ext 265

Peterson, Kenneth G, *Dean,* Southern Illinois University at Carbondale, Delyte W Morris Library, Carbondale IL. 618-453-2522

Peterson, Linda, *Librn,* Ishpeming Public Library, Ishpeming MI. 906-486-4381

Peterson, Lloyd, *Media Coordr,* University of Nebraska-Lincoln (Instructional Media Center), Lincoln NE. 402-472-1910

Peterson, Lois, *ILL,* Swarthmore College, McCabe Library, Swarthmore PA. 215-447-7477, 447-7480

Peterson, Lucille, *Librn,* Harcourt Community Library, Harcourt IA. 515-354-5341

Peterson, Mahlon, *Dir,* Saint Lawrence University, Owen D Young Library, Canton NY. 315-379-5451

Peterson, Marian, *Ref, Rare Bks & Spec Coll,* Palm Springs Public Library, Palm Springs CA. 714-323-8291

Peterson, Marjory, *Actg Asst Dir & Ch,* Kokomo Public Library, Kokomo IN. 317-457-5558

Peterson, Martin, *Per,* Saint John's University Library, Jamaica NY. 212-969-8000, Ext 201

Peterson, Mary E Rinehardt, *Librn,* Harrisburg Hospital Library, Harrisburg PA. 717-782-5510

Peterson, Mary L, *Cat,* Hibbing Community College, Learning Resources Center, Hibbing MN. 218-262-3877, Ext 53

Peterson, Maureen, *Ad,* Cocoa Beach Public Library, Cocoa Beach FL. 305-783-7350

Peterson, Max P, *Assoc Dir,* Utah State University, Merrill Library & Learning Resources Program, Logan UT. 801-750-2637

Peterson, May E, *Librn,* Shaughnessy Hospital, Medical Library, Vancouver BC. 604-876-6767

Peterson, Melva, *Librn,* City College of the City University of New York (Music), New York NY. 212-690-4174

Peterson, Mrs R G, *Asst Librn,* Callender Public Library, Callender IA. 515-548-3803

Peterson, Myra, *Librn,* Pitts-Best Memorial Library, Clifton Public Library, Clifton KS. 913-455-2222

Peterson, Nancy, *Ch,* De Kalb Public Library, Haish Memorial Building, De Kalb IL. 815-756-4431

Peterson, Olive, *Librn,* Strathmore Products, Inc Library, Syracuse NY. 315-488-5401

Peterson, Pat, *Ch,* Bayliss Public Library, Sault Sainte Marie MI. 906-632-9331

Peterson, Pat, *Ch,* Hiawathaland Library Cooperative, Sault Sainte Marie MI. 906-632-9331

Peterson, Pat, *Br & Exten Coordr,* Lincoln City Libraries, Lincoln NE. 402-435-2146

Peterson, Patricia, *Tech Serv,* Saint Lucie County Library Systems, Fort Pierce FL. 305-461-5708

Peterson, Pauline M, *Ref,* Jones Library, Inc, Amherst MA. 413-256-0246

Peterson, Peg, *Librn,* MGIC Investment Corp, Corporate Library, Milwaukee WI. 414-347-6409

Peterson, Pennie, *Coordr,* Wolfner Memorial Library for the Blind & Physically Handicapped, Saint Louis MO. 314-241-4227

Peterson, Randall T, *Dir,* John Marshall Law School Library, Chicago IL. 312-427-2737, Ext 254

Peterson, Richard, *Spec Coll,* Western Washington University, Mabel Zoe Wilson Library, Bellingham WA. 206-676-3050

Peterson, Richard A, *Ref, On-Line Servs & Bibliog Instr,* University of Virginia (Claude Moore Health Sciences Library), Charlottesville VA. 804-924-5444

Peterson, Ruth, *In Charge,* Society for Crippled Children & Adults of Manitoba, Stephen Sparling Library, Winnipeg MB. 204-786-5601, Ext 291

Peterson, Sandra K, *Doc,* College of William & Mary in Virginia, Earl Gregg Swem Library, Williamsburg VA. 804-253-4404

Peterson, Sara, *Librn,* Iowa State University Library (Veterinary Medical Library), Ames IA. 515-294-2225

Peterson, Sara C, *Actg Librn,* Van Buren Public Library, Van Buren IN. 317-934-2171

Peterson, Sharon, *ILL,* North Central Regional Library System, Mason City IA. 515-423-6917

Peterson, Stephen L, *Librn,* Yale University Library (Divinity School), New Haven CT. 203-436-8440

Peterson, Susan, *Ch,* North State Cooperative Library System, Willows CA. 916-934-2173

Peterson, Vivian A, *Dir,* Concordia Teachers College, Link Library, Seward NE. 402-643-3651, Ext 258

Petesch, Dorothy, *Librn,* Fresno County Free Library (Fig Garden), Fresno CA. 209-222-7445

Petesnick, Anne, *Prof,* University of British Columbia, School of Librarianship, BC. 604-228-2404

Petesnick, George, *Prof,* University of British Columbia, School of Librarianship, BC. 604-228-2404

Petgen, Elizabeth, *Info Servs,* Rush-Presbyterian-Saint Luke's Medical Center (Library of Rush University), Chicago IL. 312-942-2271, 942-5950

Peth, Sara Jane, *Ref,* Monroe County Library System, Monroe MI. 313-241-5277

Pethe, Marlyn, *ILL, Ref & On-Line Servs,* University of Tampa, Merl Kelce Library, Tampa FL. 813-253-8861, Ext 385

Pethybridge, Arthur, *Dir & ILL,* Northwestern Connecticut Community College Library, Winsted CT. 203-379-8543, Ext 201

Petinezas, Christina, *Doc,* San Antonio College Library, San Antonio TX. 512-734-7311, Ext 2480

Petit, Mildred, *Rare Bks,* Ashland College Library, Ashland OH. 419-289-4067

Petit, Patrick, *Asst Dir,* Catholic University of America (Robert J White Law), Washington DC. 202-635-5155

Petko, Clayda E, *Librn,* Jackson County Library System (Shady Cove Branch), Shady Cove OR. 503-878-2270

Petrash, Dianne D, *Librn,* Thomson, Rogers, Barristers & Solicitors, Law Library, Toronto ON. 416-868-3100

Petree, Dallas, *Bkmobile Coordr,* Forsyth County Public Library, Winston-Salem NC. 919-727-2556

Petrelli, Evelyn, *Senior Librn,* Jacob Edwards Library, Southbridge MA. 617-764-2544

Petrello, Jo Ann, *Librn,* Cleveland Public Library (Carnegie West), Cleveland OH. 216-961-0998

Petrescu, Adrian, *Dir,* Ministry of Foreign Affairs of Romania, Romanian Library, New York NY. 212-687-0180

Petri, Netti, *Asst Librn,* Devine Public Library, Devine TX. 512-663-2993

Petrie, Claire, *Dir,* Union League Club Library, New York NY. 212-685-3800

Petrie, Ronald, *Dean,* Portland State University, Educational Media-School Librarianship, OR. 503-229-3000

Petring, Patricia, *Rec Adminr,* Occidental Research Corp Library, Irvine CA. 714-957-7450

Petriwsky, Eugene, *Tech Serv,* University of Colorado at Boulder (University Libraries), Boulder CO. 303-492-7511

Petrizzelli, Sophia, *Per,* Mercy College Libraries, Dobbs Ferry NY. 914-693-4500, Ext 260

Petroff, Loumona, *Tech Serv,* Boston University Libraries (School of Theology Library), Boston MA. 617-353-3034

Petron, Kathleen, *Librn,* Anoka County Library (Coon Rapids West Branch), Coon Rapids MN. 612-427-5540

Petrone, Anthony, *On-Line Servs,* De Soto, Inc, Information Center Library, Des Plaines IL. 312-391-9556

Petrone, Patricia, *ILL,* East Detroit Memorial Library, East Detroit MI. 313-775-7221

Petrov, Janet, *Asst Librn,* Kasilof Public Library, Tustumena School Library, Kasilof AK. 906-262-4844

Petrov, Jocelyn, *On-Line Servs & Bibliog Instr,* National Academy of Sciences, Transportation Research Board Library, Washington DC. 202-389-6841

Petrowski, Carol, *Ser,* Loyola Marymount University (Loyola Law School Library), Los Angeles CA. 213-642-2934

Petrucelli, E L, *Librn,* MacDermid, Inc Library, Waterbury CT. 203-754-6161

Petruic, F P, *In Charge,* Saskatchewan Economic Development Corp Library, Regina SK. 306-565-7200

Petrunak, John, *AV,* Cuyahoga Community College (Eastern Campus Library), Warrensville OH. 216-464-1450, Ext 228, 229

Petrusek, Millie, *ILL,* Wharton County Junior College, J M Hodges Learning Center, Wharton TX. 713-532-4560, Ext 36

Petry, Dolores M, *Librn,* Carnegie Institution of Washington (Geophysical Laboratory Library), Washington DC. 202-966-0334

Petschaft, Jane I, *Librn,* Dynatech Corp Library, Cambridge MA. 617-868-8050, Ext 294

Pettas, William, *Ref,* Laney College Library-Learning Resources Center, Oakland CA. 415-763-4791

Pettee, Frederick G, *TV Outreach Coord,* Floyd Junior College Library, Rome GA. 404-295-6318

Pettengill, Richard, *Acq,* Oakland University, Kresge Library, Rochester MI. 313-377-2486, 377-2474

Petterson, Anne H, *Dir,* Stoughton Public Library, Stoughton MA. 617-344-2711

Petterson, Mary, *Asst Dir, Non-Fiction, Spec Coll & Outreach Serv,* Weber County Library, Ogden UT. 801-399-8516

Pettiford, Helen, *Ch,* Albany Dougherty Public Library, Albany GA. 912-435-2104

Pettigrew, Claudie L, *Dir,* Friendswood Public Library, Friendswood TX. 713-482-7135

Pettigrew, Sophie, *Librn,* Houston Public Library (Kendall), Houston TX. 713-497-3590

Pettinger, Joyce, *Bkmobile Coordr,* Lake Agassiz Regional Library, Moorhead MN. 218-233-7594

Pettis, Nancy, *Resident's Librn,* Los Lunas Hospital & Training School, New Mexico Mental Retardation & Developmental Disabilities Library & Resource Center, Los Lunas NM. 505-865-9611, Ext 298

Pettit, Katherine D, *Spec Coll,* Trinity University Library, San Antonio TX. 512-736-8121

Pettit, Mary, *Librn,* Public Library of Columbus & Franklin County (Parsons Branch), Columbus OH. 614-222-7142

Pettit, Mary G, *Librn,* George Coon Memorial Library, Princeton KY. 502-365-2884

Pettit, Rebecca, *Librn,* Preble County District Library (Eldorado), Eaton OH. 513-273-4473

Pettitt, Kenneth, *Calif,* California State Library, Sacramento CA. 916-445-2585

Pettitt, Martha, *Librn,* Du Pont Canada Inc, Maitland Works Library, Maitland ON. 613-348-3611, Ext 301

Pettus, Eloise, *Asst Prof,* Sam Houston State University, Library Science Department, TX. 713-295-6211, Ext 1151

Pettway, Alice, *Ref,* Vicksburg-Warren County Public Library, Vicksburg MS. 601-636-6411

Pettway, Diane, *Librn,* Walter Cecil Rawls Regional Library System (Waverly Library), Waverly VA. 804-834-2192

Pettway, Helen, *Librn,* Kraft, Inc (Research & Development Library), Glenview IL. 312-998-2638

Petty, Donald, *ILL,* City College of the City University of New York, Morris Raphael Cohen Library, New York NY. 212-690-6612

Petty, Hazel G, *Librn,* Aiken-Bamberg-Barnwell-Edgefield Regional Library (New Ellenton Branch), New Ellenton SC. 803-648-8961

Petty, K Michael, *Tech Serv,* Homewood Public Library, Homewood AL. 205-871-7342

Petty, Ruth, *Librn,* Northwest College of the Assemblies of God, Hurst Library, Kirkland WA. 206-822-8266, Ext 255

Pettyjohn, D, *Librn,* Oakland Public Library (Piedmont), Oakland CA. 415-658-3160

Petz, Roberta, *Extension Servs: Chief Northwest District Br,* Chicago Public Library, Chicago IL. 312-269-2900

Peurye, Lloyd Martin, *Dir of Res,* Marquis Who's Who, Inc Library, Research Department Library, Chicago IL. 312-787-2008, Ext 49

Pevey, Jessie, *Librn,* Frontenac County Library (Inverary Branch), Inverary ON. 613-353-2434

Pew, Gordon, *Head, Cat,* University of Lowell Libraries (O'Leary Library), Lowell MA. 617-452-5000, Ext 480

Pew, Michael R, *Asst Register for Automation & Rec,* Library of Congress (Order Division), Washington DC. 202-287-5000

Peyraud, Paula, *Ref,* Chappaqua Central School District Public Library, Chappaqua Library, Chappaqua NY. 914-238-4779

Peyton, Anne, *Ref,* Dartmouth College (Dana Biomedical), Hanover NH. 603-646-2858

Peyton, Gail, *Librn,* Northeastern Illinois University Library (Center for Inner City Studies), Chicago IL. 312-268-7500, Ext 165

Peyton, Gail, *Ctr for Inner City Studies,* Northeastern Illinois University Library, Chicago IL. 312-583-4050, Ext 469, 470, 471, 472

Peyton, Georgina, *Spec Coll,* University of California, San Diego, University Libraries, La Jolla CA. 714-452-3336

Peyton, Ina, *Librn,* Avoca Public Library, Avoca IA. 712-343-6358

Peyton, Janice, *Doc,* Evergreen Valley College Library, San Jose CA. 408-274-7900, Ext 310

Peyton, Madeline A, *Librn,* United States Air Force (Moody Air Force Base Library), Valdosta GA. 912-333-4211, Ext 3539

Peyton, Marguerite S, *Asst Librn,* Mississippi Valley State University, James Herbert White Library, Itta Bena MS. 601-254-9041, Ext 6340

Pezdek, Donna, *Media, Tech Serv & Cat,* Delaware Technical & Community College, Wilmington Campus Learning Resources Center, Wilmington DE. 302-571-2113

Pfaff, Eugene, *Oral Hist,* Greensboro Public Library, Greensboro NC. 373-2474; 373-2471

Pfaff, Larry, *Researcher & Cat,* Art Gallery of Ontario, Edward P Taylor Reference Library, Toronto ON. 416-977-0414, Ext 339, 340 & 390

Pfaff, M, *ILL, Ref & Bibliog Instr,* Northeastern University, Suburban Campus Library, Burlington MA. 617-272-5500, Ext 55

Pfaffenbach, K, *Librn,* Detroit Testing Laboratory Library, Oak Park MI. 313-398-2100, Ext 39

Pfaffenberger, Ann, *Ref,* Texas College of Osteopathic Medicine Library, Fort Worth TX. 817-735-2465

Pfahler, Sandra, *Personnel Librn,* University of Wisconsin-Madison, Memorial Library, Madison WI. 608-262-3521

Pfann, Mary, *Librn,* RCA Corporation (Astro-Electronics Library), Princeton NJ. 609-448-3400, Ext 2247

Pfannenstiel, Brenda, *Ch,* Rapid City Public Library, Rapid City SD. 605-394-4171

Pfannenstiel, Cynthia, *On-Line Search Coordr & Special Servs,* Pittsburg State University Library, Pittsburg KS. 316-231-7000, Ext 431

Pfannkuche, Barbara, *Dir,* Round Lake Area Public Library District, Round Lake IL. 312-546-7060

Pfarrer, Theodore R, *On-Line Servs,* University of Central Florida Library, Orlando FL. 305-275-2564

Pfau, Julia G, *Cat,* University of Alabama in Birmingham (Lister Hill Library of the Health Sciences), Birmingham AL. 205-934-5460

Pfefferle, Richard, *Tech Serv,* Nassau Library System, Uniondale NY. 516-292-8920

Pfeifer, Donald, *Bibliog Instr,* Berkshire Community College, Jonathan Edwards Library, Pittsfield MA. 413-499-4660, Ext 201, 202, 203

Pfeifer, Donald, *Asst Librn & Tech Serv,* Berkshire Community College, Jonathan Edwards Library, Pittsfield MA. 413-499-4660, Ext 201, 202, 203

Pfeifer, Judith, *Librn,* Evans City Public Library, Evans City PA. 412-538-8695

Pfeifer, Lucille, *Circ,* Katonah Village Library, Katonah NY. 914-232-3508

Pfeifer, Mrs Frank, *Librn,* Columbia-Lafayette-Ouachita-Calhoun Regional Library (Chidester Branch), Chidester AR. 501-234-1991

Pfeiffer, Conrad A, *Asst Dir,* Roseville Public Library, Roseville CA. 916-783-7158

Pfeiffer, Katherine, *Nuclear Licensing Librn,* Gulf States Utilities Company Library, Beaumont TX. 713-838-6631, Ext 3541

Pfeiffer, Kathleen M, *Orange Co Librn,* Hyconeechee Regional Library, Yanceyville NC. 919-694-6241

Pfeiffer, Mrs Walter, *Librn,* Hooper Public Library, Hooper NE. 402-654-3833

Pfeiffer, Robert, *Circ,* Milwaukee County Federated Library System, Milwaukee WI. 414-278-3210

Pfeiffer, Robert, *Circ,* Milwaukee Public Library, Milwaukee WI. 414-278-3000

Pfeil, Ruth, *Librn,* West Lawn Community Library, West Lawn PA. 215-678-4888

Pfingsten, C Thomas, *Assoc Dean & Pub Servs,* New York University, Elmer Holmes Bobst Library, New York NY. 212-598-2484

Pfister, Fred, *Assoc Prof,* University of South Florida, Graduate Department of Library, Media & Information Studies, FL. 813-974-2557

Pfister, Michaeleen, *Ch,* Yorkville Public Library, Yorkville IL. 312-553-5513

Pflueger, Kenneth, *Assoc Dir,* Concordia Theological Seminary Library, Fort Wayne IN. 219-482-9611, Ext 226

Pflug, Warner W, *Asst Dir,* Wayne State University Libraries (Walter P Reuther Library of Labor & Urban Affairs), Detroit MI. 313-577-4024

Pfohl, Patricia, *Librn,* Falcon Research & Development Co Library, Buffalo NY. 716-632-4932

Pfrommer, Aloma, *Dir,* Hurley Library Association, Hurley NY. 914-338-2092

Phair, Arden, *Curator,* Saint Catharines Historical Museum, Library & Archives, Saint Catharines ON. 416-227-2962

Phalen, Heather, *Ref,* Upper Arlington Public Library, Upper Arlington OH. 614-486-9621

Phaneuf, Sylvia, *Support Servs,* Genesee District Library, Flint MI. 313-732-0110

Pharis, L J, *Info Tech,* Shell Oil Co, Deer Park Manufacturing Complex Library Services, Deer Park TX. 713-476-6565

Phelan, Jody, *Lectr,* Texas Woman's University, School of Library Science, TX. 817-387-2418 & 566-1455

Phelan, Jody, *Librn,* Texas Woman's University (School of Library Science), Denton TX. 817-387-2418

Phelan, Kathy, *Cat,* Marycrest College, Cone Library, Davenport IA. 319-326-9254

Phelps, Cynthia, *Extension Librn,* Florence County Library, Florence SC. 803-662-8424

Phelps, Doris, *Librn,* Cimarron City Library, Cimarron KS. 316-855-3808

Phelps, Douglas, *Acq,* Vanderbilt University Library, Nashville TN. 615-322-2834

Phelps, Evelyn, *Librn,* Onondaga County Public Library System (Business & Industry), Syracuse NY. 315-473-2702

Phelps, Frances R, *Tech Serv,* Bridgeport Public Library, Bridgeport CT. 203-576-7777

Phelps, Jonathon, *Cat,* University of Massachusetts Medical School, Medical Center Library, Worcester MA. 617-856-2511

Phelps, Laura, *ILL,* Hanover Public Library, Hanover PA. 717-632-5183

Phelps, Miriam E, *Librn,* Publishers Weekly Library, New York NY. 212-764-5161

Phelps, Thomas C, *Ad,* Salt Lake City Public Library, Salt Lake City UT. 801-363-5733

Phene, C J, *Res Leader,* United States Department of Agriculture, Agricultural Research Service, Water Management Research Library, Fresno CA. 209-255-3034

Philbeck, Jo S, *Ref & Bibliog Instr,* Southeastern Baptist Theological Seminary Library, Wake Forest NC. 919-556-3101, Ext 225, 250

Philbin, Edward L, *Dir,* Albany Junior College, Library-Learning Resources Ctr, Albany GA. 912-439-4332

Philbrick, Barbara, *Asst Dir,* Stevens Memorial Library, North Andover MA. 617-682-6260

Philbrick, Douglas R, *Librn,* Bureau of Indian Affairs, Lower Brule Libraries, Lower Brule SD. 605-473-5510

Philbrick, Melanie Hill, *Librn, ILL & YA,* Murrysville Community Library, Murrysville PA. 412-327-1102

Philbrick, Sarah D, *Ch,* Bridgeport Public Library, Bridgeport CT. 203-576-7777

Philibert, Jane V, *Asst Dir,* Tulane University of Louisiana (Norman Mayer Library), New Orleans LA. 504-865-6111

Philip, John, *Supvr Field Opers,* State Library of Ohio, Columbus OH. 614-466-2693

Philip, Mrs J, *Tech Serv,* Stanstead College, John C Colby Memorial Library, Stanstead PQ. 819-876-2702

Philippart, Edyth Anne, *Chief Librn,* Monroe County Library System (Robert A Vivian), Monroe MI. 313-241-1430

Philippi, Tamsen, *Asst Librn,* Howard Bracken Memorial Library, Woodstock CT. 203-928-0046

Philippoff, Martha, *Ch,* Augusta Regional Library, Augusta-Richmond County Public Library, Augusta GA. 404-724-1871

Philippsen, Lola Mae, *ILL & Acq,* Saint Mary's College, Alumnae Centennial Library, Notre Dame IN. 219-284-4242

Philippy, Virginia, *Ch,* Burlington Public Library, Burlington MA. 617-272-2520

Philips, Nadine, *Librn,* Akron Public Library, Akron OH. A. 712-568-2601

Philips, Rosemary, *Librn,* Chester County Historical Society Library, West Chester PA. 215-696-4755

Philips, Sandra, *Librn,* D'Arcy, MacManus & Masius, Information Services Library, New York NY. 212-754-2381, 754-2382

Philips, Sara, *Spec Coll,* Framingham State College, Henry Whittemore Library, Framingham MA. 617-620-1220, Ext 273

Philips, Sarah M, *Cat,* Piedmont Regional Library, Winder GA. 404-867-2762

Phillip, Henrietta, *Reader Serv,* Lane College, J K Daniels Library, Jackson TN. 901-424-4600, Ext 274

Phillip, Sister Marie, *Librn,* Sacred Heart Convent Library, Fargo ND. 701-237-4857

Phillippe, Janie, *Librn,* Fairfax Public Library, Fairfax OK. 918-642-5535

Phillips, Ann, *Cat,* Lambuth College, Luther L Gobbel Library, Jackson TN. 901-427-6743, Ext 14

Phillips, Ann, *Humanities,* Miami University, Edgar W King Library, Oxford OH. 513-529-2944

Phillips, Beverly, *Librn,* University of Wisconsin-Madison (Land Tenure Library), Madison WI. 608-262-3521

Phillips, Blanche, *Librn,* Thomas Hackney Braswell Memorial Library (Wesley Privette Memorial), Bailey NC. 442-1937 & 442-1951

Phillips, Carol, *On-Line Servs,* University of Texas Medical Branch, Moody Medical Library, Galveston TX. 713-765-1971

Phillips, Catherine, *Librn,* Springfield Township Library, Davisburg MI. 313-625-0595

Phillips, Clarence A, *Dir,* Lawrence Institute of Technology Library, Southfield MI. 313-356-0200, Ext 31

Phillips, Clifford, *Tech Serv,* City of Inglewood Public Library, Inglewood CA. 213-649-7380

Phillips, Dennis J, *Pub Servs,* Cedar Crest College, Cressman Library, Allentown PA. 215-437-4471, Ext 264

Phillips, Dennis J, *Pub Servs,* Muhlenberg College, John A W Haas Library, Allentown PA. 215-433-3191, Ext 214

Phillips, Don, *Asst Prof,* Glenville State College, Library Science Program, WV. 304-462-7361, Ext 291, 292

Phillips, Donald, *AV,* Glenville State College, Robert F Kidd Library, Glenville WV. 304-462-7361, Ext 291

Phillips, Donna, *Dir, On-Line Servs & Bibliog Instr,* Marian Health Center, Health Science Library, Sioux City IA. 712-277-7090

Phillips, Donna, *Coordr,* Siouxland Health Science Library Consortium, IA. 712-279-2623

Phillips, Dorothy, *Deputy Librn,* Federal Reserve Bank of Chicago Library, Chicago IL. 312-322-5828

Phillips, Earl, *Coordr,* New Mexico State University, San Juan Campus Library, Farmington NM. 505-325-7556

Phillips, Elizabeth, *Librn,* Sampson-Clinton Public Library (Roseboro Branch), Roseboro NC. 919-525-4121

Phillips, Frank, *Librn,* Western State University, College of Law Library, Fullerton CA. 714-738-1000, Ext 17

Phillips, Freda, *Bkmobile Coordr,* Stone Public Library, Stone KY. 606-353-7386

Phillips, Gary, *Acq,* Saint Charles Parish Library, Luling LA. 504-785-8471

Phillips, Gary, *Librn,* Saint Charles Parish Library (East Bank Regional), Destrehan LA. 504-764-2366

Phillips, Gene H, *Dir Continuing Educ Dept,* Carbarrus Memorial Hospital Library, Concord NC. 704-786-2111, Ext 367

Phillips, Geraldine, *Librn,* Brookline Public Library, Brookline NH. 603-673-3330

Phillips, Ira, *Asst State Librn for Libr Develop,* State Library of Ohio, Columbus OH. 614-466-2693

Phillips, Isobel, *Librn,* Grant County Library, John Day OR. 503-575-1992

Phillips, Jack, *Media,* Kingsborough Community College Library, Brooklyn NY. 212-934-5144

Phillips, James, *Librn,* Asheville-Buncombe Library System (East Asheville), Asheville NC. 704-298-1889

Phillips, James W, *Curator of Print,* Southern Methodist University Libraries (Fikes Hall of Special Collections (incl DeGolyer)), Dallas TX. 214-692-2253

Phillips, Jan, *Bkmobile Coordr,* Taylor County Public Library, Perry FL. 904-584-4807

Phillips, Jan, *Asst Librn, Pub Servs & Projects Coodr,* West Georgia Regional Library, Neva Lomason Memorial Library, Carrollton GA. 404-832-1381

Phillips, Jeanne, *Ch,* Victoria Public Library, Victoria TX. 512-578-6241

Phillips, Jerry C, *Tech Serv,* University of New Mexico General Library (Law Library), Albuquerque NM. 505-277-6236

Phillips, Joan, *Librn,* York Regional Library (McAdam Public), McAdam NB. 506-784-3103

Phillips, John, *Rare Bks & Spec Coll,* Central State University, Hallie Q Brown Memorial Library, Wilberforce OH. 513-376-7212

Phillips, Johnnie, *Ref,* San Diego State University Library, San Diego CA. 714-286-6014

Phillips, Juanita, *Chairperson,* Eastern Kentucky University, Dept of Library Science, KY. 606-622-2481

Phillips, Judith, *Ad,* Louisville Public Library, Louisville OH. 216-875-1696

Phillips, Karen, *YA,* Elisha D Smith Public Library, Menasha WI. 414-729-5166

Phillips, Lillian, *Librn,* Arctic Bible Institute Library, Palmer AK. 907-745-3662

Phillips, Lois, *Ch,* Los Angeles County Public Library System, South State Cooperative Library System, Los Angeles CA. 213-974-6501

Phillips, Loretta, *Asst Librn,* Griggsville Public Library, Griggsville IL. 217-833-2633

Phillips, Lynne, *Librn,* Rollins College (Bush Science), Winter Park FL. 305-646-2000, Ext 2676

Phillips, Mabel G, *Ref,* Ozark Regional Library, Ironton MO. 314-546-2615

Phillips, Marie, *Bus, Sci & Tech,* Rockford Public Library, Rockford IL. 815-965-6731

Phillips, Marion, *Librn,* Negaunee Public Library, Negaunee MI. 906-475-9400

Phillips, Mary Louise, *Local Hist,* Public Library of Charlotte & Mecklenburg County, Inc, Charlotte NC. 704-374-2725

Phillips, Mildred H, *Librn,* Union Carbide Corp, Haynes-Becket Memorial Library, Niagara Falls NY. 716-278-3474, 278-3475

Phillips, Molly, *Libr Asst,* Ohio State University Libraries (Lionel Topaz Memorial Library of Visual Science), Columbus OH. 614-422-1888

Phillips, Mrs Blake, *Librn,* Stone Public Library, Stone KY. 606-353-7386

Phillips, Nancy, *Librn,* Richmond Memorial Hospital, Medical & Nursing Library, Richmond VA. 804-359-6961, Ext 347

Phillips, Norma, *ILL,* Mount Prospect Public Library, Mount Prospect IL. 312-253-5675

Phillips, Patricia, *Cat,* Tennessee Technological University, Jere Whitson Memorial Library, Cookeville TN. 615-528-3408

Phillips, Patricia A, *Librn,* Westinghouse Electric Corp, Engineering Library, Tampa FL. 813-837-7221

Phillips, Patricia L, *Dir of Learning Resources,* Eastern Shore Community College, Learning Resources Center, Melfa VA. 804-787-3972

Phillips, Ray S, *Asst Coordr,* Wolfner Memorial Library for the Blind & Physically Handicapped, Saint Louis MO. 314-241-4227

Phillips, Rita, *Asst Librn, Ad & Ref,* Stickney-Forest View Library District, Stickney IL. 312-749-1050

Phillips, Robert, *Asst Dir & Ref,* Hardin-Simmons University, Richardson Library, Abilene TX. 915-677-7281, Ext 236

Phillips, Robert S, *Dir,* Cameron University Library, Lawton OK. 405-248-2200, Ext 410

Phillips, Roger R, *Rare Bks & Spec Coll,* Wheaton College Library, Wheaton IL. 312-682-5101

Phillips, Rosa, *Librn,* Amos Memorial Public Library (Anna Branch), Anna OH. 513-394-2761

Phillips, Rosemary, *Librn,* Front of Escott Public Library, Mallorytown ON. 613-659-2813

Phillips, Russell, *Lectr,* University of Wisconsin-LaCrosse, Educational Media Dept, WI. 608-784-8134

Phillips, Ruth H, *Dir,* Bexley Public Library, Columbus OH. 614-231-2784

Phillips, Ruth M, *Librn,* Huguenot-Thomas Paine National Historical Association, Hufeland Memorial Library, New Rochelle NY. 914-632-5376

Phillips, Sarah, *Ref,* Lake Lanier Regional Library, Lawrenceville GA. 404-963-5231

Phillips, Scott C, *Librn,* Tufts Library (North), North Weymouth MA. 617-337-1571

Phillips, Sharon A, *Dir,* Oakwood Hospital, McLouth Memorial Health Science Library, Dearborn MI. 313-336-3000, Ext 414

Phillips, Sue, *Librn,* Bemis Memorial Library, Robbinsville NC. 704-479-8796

Phillips, Susan K, *Deputy Asst for Automation & Bibliog Control,* University of Texas Libraries (General), Austin TX. 512-471-3811

Phillips, Ted, *Librn,* Memorial University of Newfoundland Library, Saint John's NF. 709-753-1200

Phillips, Thelma, *Assoc Librn,* Arlington Public Library, Arlington TX. 817-275-2763, 265-3311, Ext 347

Phillips, Thelma, *Librn,* Saint Mary Parish Library (Bunche), Franklin LA. 318-828-5661

Phillips, Varda, *Librn,* Elm Creek Township Library, Wilsey KS. 913-497-2896

Phillips, Vi, *Librn,* Long Beach Independent-Press Telegram Library, Long Beach CA. 213-435-1161, Ext 400

Phillips, Vicki, *Doc,* Oklahoma State University Library, Stillwater OK. 405-624-6313

Phillips, Virginia, *Asst Dir for Branch Servs,* University of Texas Libraries (General), Austin TX. 512-471-3811

Phillips, William F, *Dir Libr Serv,* International Minerals & Chemical Corp, R & D Library, Terre Haute IN. 812-232-0121, Ext 349 & 405

Phillpot, Clive, *Librn,* Museum of Modern Art Library, New York NY. 212-956-7236

Philo, Andrea, *Librn,* Montgomery County-Norristown Public Library (Conshohocken Free Branch), Conshohocken PA. 215-825-1656

Philos, Helen S, *Librn,* American Society of International Law Library, Washington DC. 202-265-4313

Philpot, Mrs Jarvis A, *Librn,* Georgetown Public Library, Georgetown TX. 512-863-3168

Philpott, C E, *Librn,* Canadian Department of Fisheries & Oceans (Newfoundland Forest Research Centre Library), Saint John's NF. 709-737-4672

Philpott, Patricia, *Asst Librn,* Teague City Library, Teague TX. 817-739-3311

Phinazee, Annette L Hoage, *Dean,* North Carolina Central University, School of Library Science, NC. 919-683-6485

Phinney, Chad T, *Museum Asst,* Pueblo Grande Museum, Reference Library, Phoenix AZ. 602-275-3452

Phinney, John A, *Chief of Cat,* Boston Public Library, Eastern Massachusetts Library System, Boston MA. 617-536-5400

Phinney, Jr, Hartley K, *Dir,* Colorado School of Mines, Arthur Lakes Library, Golden CO. 303-279-0300, Ext 2690

Phippen, Mrs Robert, *Librn,* Hull Public Library, Hull MA. 617-925-2295

Phipps, Barbara, *Ref,* Pacific Union College, W E Nelson Memorial Library, Angwin CA. 707-965-6241

Phipps, Bert, *Dir,* University of Maine at Machias, Merrill Library, Machias ME. 207-255-3313, Ext 234

Phipps, Elaine B, *Dir,* Patchogue-Medford Library, Patchogue NY. 516-475-0495

Phipps, Jeanne, *Librn,* Ogden Public Library, Ogden IA. 515-275-4550

Phipps, Julia, *ILL & Ref,* University of Iowa Libraries, Iowa City IA. 319-353-4450

Phipps, M Joann, *Actg Librn,* United States Navy (Naval Weapons Support Center Library), Crane IN. 812-854-1615

Phipps, Michael, *Dir,* Waterloo Public Library, Waterloo IA. 319-291-4521

Phipps, Sheila, *Librn,* Lonesome Pine Regional Library (Lee County Public), Clintwood VA. 703-926-6617

Phipps, Shelley, *Orientation,* University of Arizona Library, Tucson AZ. 602-626-2101

Phoenix, Sister Josetta, *Audio Ctr Servs,* Mundelein College, Learning Resource Center, Chicago IL. 312-262-8100, Ext 301, 302 & 303

Piascik, Ann L, *Dir,* Simon Fairfield Public Library, East Douglas MA. 617-476-2695

Piatt, Fran, *Ch,* Pomona Public Library, Pomona CA. 714-620-2033

Piattelli, Chris, *Ch,* Chappaqua Central School District Public Library, Chappaqua Library, Chappaqua NY. 914-238-4779

Piazza, Clara, *Librn,* Saint Louis Public Library (Baden), Saint Louis MO. 314-388-2400

Piazza, Eileen, *Ref,* Milton Public Library, Milton MA. 617-698-5707

Pibel, Dave, *Coordr,* Long Beach Community College Learning Resources Division (Liberal Arts Campus Library), Long Beach CA. 213-420-4231

Picard, Gilles, *Librn,* University of Montreal Libraries (Sciences), Montreal PQ. 514-343-5965

Picard, Pauline, *On-Line Servs & Bibliog Instr,* Bibliotheque Municipale, Warwick PQ. 819-358-6187

Picca, David, *Acq,* Miami Dade Community College (Niles Trammel Learning Resources), Miami FL. 305-596-1293

Picciafoco, Henry, *Asst Librn,* Carnegie Library of Pittsburgh, Library for the Blind & Physically Handicapped, Pittsburgh PA. 412-687-2440

Picciano, Jacqueline, *Librn,* American Journal of Nursing Co, Sophia F Palmer Memorial Library, New York NY. 212-582-8820

Piccinino, Jr, Rocco, *Ref,* United Engineers & Constructors, Inc Library, Philadelphia PA. 215-422-3374

Picha, Charlotte, *Librn,* Lake County Public Library (Munster Public), Munster IN. 219-836-8450

Picha, Dorothy, *Dir,* Hillsboro Public Library, Hillsboro WI. 608-489-2192

Piche, Judy, *Tech Serv & Cat,* David Thompson University Centre, Nelson BC. 604-352-2241, Ext 29

Pichette, Denis, *ILL,* College De Maisonneuve Bibliotheque, Montreal PQ. 514-254-7131, 254-4035

Pichette, William, *Asst Prof,* Sam Houston State University, Library Science Department, TX. 713-295-6211, Ext 1151

Pick, Paula, *Cat,* British Columbia Institute of Technology Library, Burnaby BC. 604-434-5734, Ext 360

Pickard, Carol K, *Bkmobile Coordr,* Nashua Public Library, Nashua NH. 603-883-4141, 883-4142

Pickard, John C, *Asst Librn,* Biblical Theological Seminary Library, Hatfield PA. 215-368-5000

Pickard, Sue, *Librn,* Good Samaritan Hospital, Medical Library, Downers Grove IL. 312-963-5900, Ext 1070

Pickel, Harriet L, *Librn,* Bucks County Free Library (Pennwood), Langhorne PA. 215-757-2510

Picken, Gilbert, *Dir,* Martin County Library, Fairmont MN. 507-238-4207

Pickenpaugh, Treva, *Librn,* Dayton & Montgomery County Public Library (Huber Heights), Dayton OH. 513-224-1651, Ext 228

Pickens, Dennie, *Ref,* Clarksburg-Harrison Public Library, Clarksburg WV. 304-624-6512, 624-6513

Pickens, Terry, *Ref,* Mesa County Public Library, Grand Junction CO. 303-243-4442

Pickering, Marjorie, *Librn,* Langdon Public Library, Newington NH. 603-436-5154

Picket, Leo, *Instr,* University of the District of Columbia-Mount Vernon Square Campus, Dept of Library Science & Instructional Systems Technology, DC. 202-727-2756, 727-2757 & 727-2758

Pickett, Barbara L, *ILL, Ref & Rare Bks,* Louisville Free Public Library, Louisville KY. 502-584-4154

Pickett, Dorothy, *Dir,* Evansville Association for Retarded Citizens Library, Evansville IN. 812-425-4585

Pickett, Ellen, *Dir,* Liberty Municipal Library, Liberty TX. 713-336-7571

Pickett, Jane, *Tech Serv,* Durham County Library, Durham NC. 919-683-2626

Pickett, Mary Joyce, *Ref & Bibliog Instr,* Augustana College, Denkman Memorial Library, Rock Island IL. 309-794-7266

Pickett, Sharon, *Librn,* Davis, Hockenberg, Wine, Brown & Koehn Library, Des Moines IA. 515-243-2300

Pickle, Mildred, *Librn,* San Diego Public Library (North Park), San Diego CA. 714-283-4535

Picknell, Susan, *Librn,* Bath Public Library, Bath NH. 603-747-2625

Pickron, John, *Asst Librn,* Tulane University of Louisiana (Monte M Lemann Memorial Law Library), New Orleans LA. 504-866-2751

Pickthorn, Barbara, *Acq & Ser,* Cameron University Library, Lawton OK. 405-248-2200, Ext 410

Picot, Leslie, *Librn,* Massillon Public Library (West Side Branch), Massillon OH. 216-833-4217

Picott, John B, *Ref,* Massachusetts College of Pharmacy & Allied Health Sciences, Sheppard Library, Boston MA. 732-2810 (Gen info), 732-2813 (Ref)

Pidala, Veronica C, *Admin,* International Nickel Co, Inc, Technical & Business Library, New York NY. 212-742-4141
Piegay, Marjorie, *Librn,* Buffalo & Erie County Public Library System (East Delavan), Buffalo NY. 716-896-4433
Piehl, Ann L, *Tech Serv,* Carthage College, John Mosheim Ruthrauff Library, Kenosha WI. 414-551-8500, Ext 530
Piel, Mark, *Librn,* New York Society Library, New York NY. 212-288-6900
Piele, Linda J, *Ref,* University of Wisconsin-Parkside Library, Kenosha WI. 414-553-2221
Pielstick, Carol, *Ad,* Pitkin County Library, Aspen CO. 303-925-7124
Pien, Arlene C, *Librn,* Saint Joseph's Hospital, Helene Fuld Learning Resource Center, Elmira NY. 607-733-6541, Ext 375
Pien, Shui-Hsien, *Doc,* Mansfield State College Library, Mansfield PA. 717-662-4071
Pienitz, Eleanor, *Librn,* Harris Corp, PRD Electronics Div, Information Center, Syosset NY. 516-364-0400, Ext 2677
Pientok, Mary, *Dir,* Whitehall Free Library, Whitehall WI. 715-538-4107
Pieper, Imelda, *Librn,* John Rogers Memorial Library, Dodge NE. 402-693-2239
Pieratt, Asa B, *Acq,* University of Delaware, Hugh M Morris Library, Newark DE. 302-738-2231
Pierce, A R, *Planning & Res,* Virginia Polytechnic Institute & State University Library, Blacksburg VA. 703-961-5593
Pierce, Amaretta, *Librn,* Southport-Brunswick County Library (West Brunswick), Shallotte NC. 919-754-6578
Pierce, Ann, *Librn,* Cumberland Bar Association, Cleaves Law Library, Portland ME. 207-773-9712
Pierce, Beverly, *Ref,* Saint Olaf College, Rolvaag Memorial Library, Northfield MN. 507-663-2222
Pierce, C K, *Librn,* Post Public Library, Post TX. 806-495-2149
Pierce, Carleton, *Librn,* Cochise College, Learning Resources Center, Douglas AZ. 602-364-7943, Ext 280
Pierce, Charlotte G, *Librn,* Mississippi State University Agricultural & Forestry Experiment Station, Delta Branch Experiment Station Library, Stoneville MS. 601-686-9311, Ext 261
Pierce, Daniel, *Cat,* Saint John's University Library, Jamaica NY. 212-969-8000, Ext 201
Pierce, Donna, *Ch,* Ketchikan Public Library, Ketchikan AK. 907-225-2748
Pierce, Elizabeth, *Cat,* New Hanover County Public Library, Wilmington NC. 919-763-3303
Pierce, Faye, *Librn,* Erie City Public Library, Erie KS. 316-244-5119
Pierce, Frances B, *ILL, Per & On-Line Servs,* Grossmont College, Lewis F Smith Learning Resource Center Library, El Cajon CA. 714-465-1700, Ext 333, 334
Pierce, Gayle, *Tech Serv & Cat,* Meridian Junior College Library, Meridian MS. 601-483-8241, Ext 240
Pierce, Jo Anne, *Dir,* Simsbury Public Library, Simsbury CT. 203-658-5382
Pierce, Kathy, *Ch,* Antioch Township Library, Antioch IL. 312-395-0874
Pierce, Kellie, *Asst Librn,* Bullard-Sanford Memorial Library, Vassar MI. 517-823-2171
Pierce, Lois, *Ch,* Cocoa Public Library, Cocoa FL. 305-636-3243, 636-7323
Pierce, Louise, *Tech Serv,* Davidson County Community College, Grady E Love Learning Resources Center, Lexington NC. 704-249-8186, Ext 270
Pierce, M Edith, *Librn,* United States Air Force (Cannon Air Force Base Library), Cannon AFB NM. 505-784-3311
Pierce, Marjorie MacLeod, *Dir,* Curry College, Louis R Levin Memorial Library, Milton MA. 617-333-0500, Ext 177
Pierce, Ranae, *Br Coordr & Bkmobile Coordr,* Salt Lake City Public Library, Salt Lake City UT. 801-363-5733
Pierce, Renee, *Librn,* Miami-Dade Public Library System (Homestead Branch), Homestead FL. 305-245-6444
Pierce, William R, *Dir,* Sierra Joint Junior College District, William M Winstead Memorial Library, Rocklin CA. 916-624-3333, Ext 257

Piercy, Billie J, *Librn,* Buckeye Public Library, Buckeye AZ. 602-386-2778
Piercy, Nancy Anne, *Librn,* American United Life Insurance Co Library, Indianapolis IN. 317-927-1709
Pierre, Frank Saint, *Ref,* Rhode Island Junior College, William F Flanagan Campus Library, Lincoln RI. 401-333-7053
Pierre, Margaret, *Librn,* Alberta Hospital Library, Edmonton AB. 403-973-2268, 973-2361
Piersall, Glenna J, *Chief Librn,* United States Army (R F Sink Memorial Library), Fort Campbell KY. 502-798-5729
Piersma, Mrs August, *Asst Dir,* Inwood Public Library, Inwood IA. 515-753-4427
Piersol, Charlotte A, *Librn,* E I Du Pont De Nemours & Co, Inc, Washington Laboratory Library, Parkersburg WV. 304-863-4528
Pierson, Betty, *Asst Librn,* Southern Publishing Association of Seventh-Day Adventists, Editorial Library, Nashville TN. 615-889-8000
Pierson, Diana, *Asst Dir,* Loutit Library, Grand Haven MI. 616-842-5560
Pierson, Elizabeth A, *Asst Prof,* Our Lady of the Lake University of San Antonio, Learning Resources Certification, TX. 512-434-6711, Ext 245
Pierson, Robert M, *Spec Coll,* University of Maryland at College Park (University Libraries), College Park MD. 301-454-3011
Pierson, Roscoe, *Dir,* Lexington Theological Seminary, Bosworth Memorial Library, Lexington KY. 606-252-0361, Ext 21
Pierson, Roscoe M, *Librn,* Lancaster Theological Seminary, Philip Schaff Library, Lancaster PA. 606-252-0361
Pieschel, Terri, *Librn,* Standard Oil Co of California, Chevron Standard Ltd Library, Calgary AB. 403-267-5910, Ext 536
Pieters, Donald L, *Reader Serv & Archivist,* Saint Norbert College, Todd Wehr Library, De Pere WI. 414-337-3280
Pietris, Mary K D, *Chief, Subj Cat Div,* Library of Congress, Washington DC. 202-287-5000
Pietro, Carole, *Supvr,* Montreal Board of Trade Information Center, Montreal PQ. 514-878-4651
Pietropaoli, Frank A, *Librn,* Smithsonian Institution Libraries (National Museum of History & Technology Bureau Library), Washington DC. 202-381-5684
Piety, John, *Acq,* Pan American University, Learning Resource Center, Edinburg TX. 512-381-2751
Pifalo, Victoria G, *Asst Librn,* Elmira Psychiatric Center Professional Library, Elmira NY. 607-737-4769
Pifer, Richard, *Area Res Ctr & Archives,* University of Wisconsin-Eau Claire, William D McIntyre Library, Eau Claire WI. 715-836-3715
Piggford, Carole M, *Tech Serv,* Weston Public Library, Weston MA. 617-893-3312
Piggford, Roland, *Head Libr Info Servs,* Massachusetts Board of Library Commissioners, Office for the Development of Library Services, Boston MA. 617-267-9400
Piggie, Joyce, *Media,* Livingstone College, Andrew Carnegie Library, Salisbury NC. 704-633-7960, Ext 61 & 62
Pignatello, Leonard J, *Bus&Sci,* Minneapolis Public Library & Information Center, Minneapolis MN. 612-372-6500
Pigno, Antonia, *Minorities,* Kansas State University, Farrell Library, Manhattan KS. 913-532-6516
Pigot, Charles, *Pres,* Pacific Car & Foundry, Military Engineering Library, Renton WA. 206-235-3030
Pigot, F, *Spec Coll,* University of Prince Edward Island, Robertson Library, Charlottetown PE. 902-892-1243
Pigott, Louis I, *Librn,* International Engineering Co Inc Library, San Francisco CA. 415-442-7300
PiHari, S, *Coll Dev,* Library of the Legal Aid Society of Westchester, White Plains NY. 914-682-0250
Pikaart, Philip, *Acq,* Grand Rapids Junior College, Arthur Andrews Memorial Library, Grand Rapids MI. 616-456-4841
Pike, Alice, *Tech Serv,* Lepper Library, Lisbon OH. 216-424-3117

Pike, Crawford, *Librn,* Chattahoochee Valley Regional Library (Talking Book Center), Columbus GA. 404-327-0211
Pike, Dorothy, *Librn,* Harriston Public Library, Harriston ON. 519-338-2396
Pike, Jeanne, *Librn,* Bureau of Land Management, Oregon State Office Library, Portland OR. 503-231-6251
Pike, Jeanne, *Media,* Thomas More College, Learning Resources Center, Fort Mitchell KY. 606-341-5800, Ext 61
Pike, Kermit, *Adjunct Prof,* Case Western Reserve University, School of Library Science, OH. 216-368-3500
Pike, Kermit J, *Dir,* Western Reserve Historical Society, History Library, Cleveland OH. 216-721-5722
Pike, Lorraine, *Librn,* Ascension Lutheran Church Library, Milwaukee WI. 414-645-2933
Pike, Mary L, *Dir,* National Association of Housing & Redevelopment Officials Library, Washington DC. 202-333-2020
Pike, Susan, *ILL & Ad,* Aberdeen-Matawan Public Library, Matawan NJ. 201-583-9100
Pike, Zan, *Librn,* Bureau of Land Management, Lakeview District Office Library, Lakeview OR. 503-947-2177
Pikes, Lee, *Librn,* Jefferson County Public Library (Evergreen Regional), Evergreen CO. 303-674-3389
Pikoff, H, *Psychol,* State University of New York at Buffalo, University Libraries, Buffalo NY. 716-636-2965
Pilachowski, David, *On-Line Servs,* University of Vermont & State Agricultural College, Bailey-Howe Memorial Library, Burlington VT. 802-656-2020
Pilarski, Esther, *Librn,* Jewish Congregation of Pacific Palisades, Berrie Library, Pacific Palisades CA. 213-459-2328
Pilcher, Ned, *Dir Instrnl Dev,* Odessa College, Murry H Fly Learning Resources Center, Odessa TX. 915-337-5381, Ext 299
Pilibosian, Diane, *Librn,* Oshkosh Public Library (South Side), Oshkosh WI. 414-424-0477
Pilkington, James P, *Adminr,* Vanderbilt University Library (Vanderbilt Television News Archive), Nashville TN. 615-322-2927
Pillack, Norma, *Ch,* Hampton Public Library, Hampton IA. 515-456-4451
Pillau, Estra R, *Librn,* Broward County Law Library, Fort Lauderdale FL. 305-765-4096
Pillen, Mrs H B, *In Charge,* Oxford County Library (Plattsville Branch), Plattsville ON. 519-684-7474
Pillepich, Mary, *Librn,* University of Illinois Library at Urbana-Champaign (Library Science), Urbana IL. 217-333-3804
Piller, Raymond, *Dir,* Southeastern Oklahoma State University Library, Durant OK. 405-924-0121, Ext 245
Pillette, Mrs Marden, *Librn,* Guam Community College Library, Mangilao PI. 734-2169
Pillifant, Janet, *Dir,* Aurora Public Library, Aurora IL. 312-896-9761
Pilling, Emily, *Librn,* Dighton Public Library, Dighton MA. 617-669-6421
Pillion, George L, *Dir & Cat,* Winthrop Public Library, Frost Public Library, Winthrop MA. 617-846-1703
Pillon, Nancy B, *Prof,* Indiana State University, Dept of Library Science, IN. 812-232-6311, Ext 2834
Pillsbury, Mary Jane, *Asst Dir,* Wareham Free Library, Wareham MA. 617-295-2343
Pillsbury, Penelope, *Bibliog Instr,* University of Vermont & State Agricultural College, Bailey-Howe Memorial Library, Burlington VT. 802-656-2020
Pilmes, Irmine, *Librn,* Toms River Chemical Corp, Dyes Research & Development Laboratory Library, Toms River NJ. 201-349-5200
Pilon, Marie, *Librn,* Bibliotheque De La Ville De Montreal (Ahuntsic Adult), Montreal PQ. 514-872-4603
Pilon, Nicole B, *Librn,* American Homes Corp, Ayerst Laboratories Research Library, Montreal PQ. 514-744-6771, Ext 353
Piltch, Aidee L, *Librn,* Har Zion Temple, Frankel Library, Narberth PA. 215-439-1250
Piltingsrud, Evelyn, *Librn,* Callender Public Library, Callender IA. 515-548-3803

Pim, Cornelia, *Librn,* Fort Worth Public Library (East Branch), Fort Worth TX. 817-451-0916
Pina, Janet, *ILL & Ref,* Downey City Library, Downey CA. 213-923-3256
Pinaire, Pat, *Asst Librn,* Mid Michigan Community College, Charles A Amble Library, Harrison MI. 517-386-7792, Ext 258
Pinckard, Mary Margaret, *On-Line Servs,* University of Texas at San Antonio Library, San Antonio TX. 512-691-4570
Pinckard, Susan H, *Cat,* University of Tennessee at Chattanooga Library, Chattanooga TN. 615-755-4701
Pinckney, Cathy L, *Librn,* Saint John's Hospital & Health Center, Medical Library, Santa Monica CA. 213-829-8494
Pincus, Lena, *Librn,* Southern California Psychoanalytic Institute, Franz Alexander Library, Beverly Hills CA. 213-276-2455
Pinder, Armelia K, *Acq,* Riviera Beach Public Library, Riviera Beach FL. 305-845-4194, 845-4195, 845-4196
Pine, Betty, *Commun Servs,* Jacksonville Public Library, Jacksonville IL. 217-243-5435
Pine, Carole, *Curator of Archives & Mss,* Harvard University Library (Francis A Countway Library of Medicine), Boston MA. 617-732-2142
Pine, Connie, *Assoc Dir,* Nova University Libraries (Law Center Library), Fort Lauderdale FL. 522-2300 Ext 113
Pine, Kathie, *Ch,* County of Strathcona Municipal Library, Sherwood Park AB. 403-467-3513
Pine, Maureen, *Ref,* Young & Rubicam, Inc Library, New York NY. 212-953-3075
Pine, Patricia E, *Librn,* Dayton & Montgomery County Public Library (Northmont), Englewood OH. 513-836-1610
Pine, Ruby C, *Ch,* Seymour Library, Auburn NY. 315-252-2571
Pineda, Lolly, *Librn,* Mobil Land Development Corporation Library, San Francisco CA. 415-764-1516
Pinero, Belsie C, *Ref,* University of Puerto Rico Library, Jose M Lazaro Memorial Library, Rio Piedras PR. 809-764-0000, Ext 3296
Pinero, Belsie Cappas, *ILL,* University of Puerto Rico Library, Jose M Lazaro Memorial Library, Rio Piedras PR. 809-764-0000, Ext 3296
Pines, Philip A, *Dir,* Hall of Fame of the Trotter Library, Goshen NY. 914-294-6330
Pinet, Gina, *Ref,* College de Rimouski (CEGEP) Bibliotheque, Rimouski PQ. 418-723-1880
Pingitore, Connie, *Librn,* Mary E Seymour Memorial Free Library, Stockton NY. 716-595-3323
Pings, Vern M, *Dir,* Wayne State University Libraries, Detroit MI. 313-557-4020
Pings, Vern M, *Dir,* Wayne State University, Southfield Extension Center Library, Southfield MI. 313-358-2104
Pinkerton, Frank R, *Dir,* Chaffey College Library, Alta Loma CA. 714-987-1737, Ext 303
Pinkerton, Harriett, *Librn,* Hammond Public Library (Howard), Hammond IN. 219-931-5100
Pinkerton, J Wesley, *Cat,* Wilmington College, Sheppard Arthur Watson Library, Wilmington OH. 513-382-6661, Ext 206
Pinkerton, Marjorie, *Media,* William Woods College, Dulany Memorial Library, Fulton MO. 314-642-3269
Pinkham, Eleanor H, *Dir,* Kalamazoo College, Upjohn Library, Kalamazoo MI. 616-383-8481
Pinkney, Elaine, *Librn,* Johns Hopkins University Libraries (Radiology Library), Baltimore MD. 301-955-6029
Pinkney, Helen L, *Dir,* Dayton Art Institute Library, Dayton OH. 513-223-5277
Pinkston, Helen, *Librn,* United States Navy (Naval Communications Area Master Station Eastern Pacific), Wahiawa HI. 808-653-5577
Pinkston, Jane, *Readers Assistance,* Champaign Public Library & Information Center, Champaign IL. 217-356-7243
Pinkus, Deborah, *YA,* West Orange Free Public Library, West Orange NJ. 201-736-0198
Pinkwas, David, *Dir,* Bethpage Public Library, Bethpage NY. 516-913-3907
Pinnell, June, *Librn,* Bellingham Public Library, Bellingham WA. 206-676-6860
Pinnell, Richard, *Librn,* University of Waterloo Library (University Map Library), Waterloo ON. 519-885-1211, Ext 2795

Pinnix, Edna, *Asst Librn,* Surry County-Dobson Library, Dobson NC. 919-386-8208
Pins, Therese, *Tech Serv & Ref,* Divine Word College, Mat Jacoby Library, Epworth IA. 319-876-3354
Pinske, Judith, *Librn,* Minnesota Valley Regional Library (Gaylord), Mankato MN. 612-237-2280
Pinson, Leo A, *Librn,* Providence Public Library (Knight Memorial), Providence RI. 401-461-7348
Pinto, Rosalina, *ILL,* Northrop University, Alumni Library, Inglewood CA. 213-776-5466
Pinzelik, Barbara, *Gen Servs,* Purdue University Libraries & Audio-Visual Center (General), West Lafayette IN. 317-749-2577, 494-8516
Pinzelik, John, *Librn,* Purdue University Libraries & Audio-Visual Center (M G Mellon Library of Chemistry), West Lafayette IN. 317-494-8736
Pinzon, Amalia, *Circ,* Imperial Valley College, Spencer Library Media Center, Imperial CA. 714-352-8320, Ext 270
Piontek, Frank, *Ref,* Beverly Hills Public Library, Beverly Hills CA. 213-550-4711
Piorkowska, Janina, *Cat & Ref,* Alliance College Library, Cambridge Springs PA. 814-398-4611, Ext 283
Piotrowski, Thaddeus, *Learning Resources Ctr,* Bloomsburg State College, Harvey A Andruss Library, Bloomsburg PA. 717-389-2716
Piper, David, *Media,* Albany Dougherty Public Library, Albany GA. 912-435-2104
Piper, Jean M, *Librn,* Woolworth Community Library, Jal NM. 505-395-3268
Piper, Larry W, *Librn,* Stoel, Rives, Boley, Fraser & Wyse, Law Library, Portland OR. 503-224-3380
Piper, Mary, *Acq,* Case Western Reserve University & Cleveland Medical Library Association, Cleveland Health Sciences Library, Cleveland OH. 216-368-3426
Piper, Mary C, *Mgr Libr Serv,* Quaker Oats Co, John Stuart Research Laboratories-Research Library, Barrington IL. 312-381-1980
Piper, Michael, *Ext-Outreach,* Roxanne Whipple Memorial-Navajo County Library, Winslow City-Navajo County Library, Winslow AZ. 602-289-4982
Piper, Muriel, *In Charge,* Oxford County Library (Salford Library), Salford IN. 519-537-3322
Piper, Nelson A, *Asst Univ Librn Colls,* University of California at Davis, General Library, Davis CA. 916-752-2110
Piper, Patricia L, *Asst Librn Tech Servs,* University of California at Davis (Law Library), Davis CA. 916-752-3322
Piper, Rosemary, *Dir,* Swayzee Public Library, Swayzee IN. 317-922-7526
Piper, Wayne, *Librn,* Toledo-Lucas County Public Library (Locke), Toledo OH. 419-255-7055
Pipes, Alice, *Librn,* Kaiser Permanente Medical Center Library, Hayward CA. 415-784-5298
Pipes, Charles D, *Dir,* Northwestern Regional Library, Elkin NC. 919-835-4894
Pipkin, Joyce, *Processing,* Black Gold Cooperative Library System, Ventura CA. 805-654-2643
Pippen, Esther W, *Dir,* Tombigbee Regional Library, Bryan Public Library, West Point MS. 601-494-4872
Pippen, Esther W, *Dir,* Tombigbee Regional Library (Tombigbee Regional), West Point MS. 601-494-4872
Pippen, Lois, *Tech Serv,* East Albemarle Regional Library, Elizabeth City NC. 919-335-2511
Pippenger, Cinda G, *Ch,* Urbana Free Library, Urbana IL. 217-367-4057
Pippin, Helen, *Librn,* Bay Memorial Medical Center, Medical Library, Panama City FL. 904-769-1511, Ext 463
Pippins, Jesse, *Librn,* Public Library of Columbus & Franklin County (Martin Luther King), Columbus OH. 614-222-7122
Pippins, M, *Librn,* University of Southern California (Hancock Biology & Oceanography Library), Los Angeles CA. 213-743-6005
Pirino, Karen, *Librn,* Saint John's Mercy Medical Center, John Young Brown Memorial Library, Saint Louis MO. 314-569-6000
Piro, Cora, *Librn,* Cape May County Library (Sea Isle City Branch), Sea Isle City NJ. 609-263-8485
Piro, Cora M, *Dir,* Sea Isle City Public Library, Sea Isle City NJ. 609-263-8485
Piro, Jean V, *Ad,* Nutley Public Library, Nutley NJ. 201-667-0405

Pirtle, Dorothea M, *ILL,* Yuma City-County Library, Yuma AZ. 602-782-1871
Pirtle, June, *Librn,* Eula and David Winterman Library, Eagle Lake TX. 713-234-5411
Pisani, Assunta, *Bk Selection Specialists,* Harvard University Library (Harvard College Library (Headquarters in Harry Elkins Widener Memorial Library)), Cambridge MA. 617-495-2401
Pisano, Ronald G, *Dir,* Parrish Art Museum Library, Southampton NY. 516-283-2118
Piscadlo, Bruce, *On-Line Servs,* Temple University of the Commonwealth System of Higher Education (Law), Philadelphia PA. 215-787-7891
Piskorik, Elizabeth, *Circ,* Linden Free Public Library, Linden NJ. 201-486-3888
Pistorius, Marie, *Cat,* Williams College, Sawyer Library, Williamstown MA. 413-597-2501
Pita, Lorene S, *Librn,* Provident Hospital, Library Services, Baltimore MD. 301-225-2351, 225-2352
Pitchen, John, *Ser,* University of Arizona Library, Tucson AZ. 602-626-2101
Pitkin, Patricia, *Tech Serv,* Rochester Institute of Technology, Wallace Memorial Library, Rochester NY. 716-475-2566
Pitluck, Donna Mae, *Reader Serv & Ref,* Los Angeles Mission College, Learning Resources Center, San Fernando CA. 213-365-8271, Ext 283
Pitney, Mrs James, *In Charge,* Morris Museum of Arts & Sciences Reference Library, Morristown NJ. 201-538-0454
Pitsenberger, Margaret A, *Ch, Commun Servs & Spec Coll,* Providence Public Library, Providence RI. 401-521-7722
Pittet, Marcel, *Librn,* University of Maine at Fort Kent, Blake Library, Fort Kent ME. 207-834-3165, Ext 215
Pittman, Alex, *Dir,* Wright State University, Western Ohio Branch Campus Library, Celina OH. 419-586-2365, Ext 33
Pittman, Donna, *Dir,* Ohio Valley College, Learning Resources Center, Parkersburg WV. 304-485-7384, Ext 26
Pittman, Dorothy, *Librn,* Seminole County Public Library System (Sanford Public Library), Sanford FL. 305-322-2182
Pittman, Edna, *Librn,* Wilson County Public Library (Five Points), Wilson NC. 919-237-3818
Pittman, Louise, *Dir,* Troy Public Library, Troy NY. 518-274-7071
Pittman, Mary, *Librn,* Scott Sebastian Regional Library (Hackett Library), Hackett AR. 501-996-2856
Pittman, Mary V, *Librn,* Bucks County Free Library (Samuel Pierce), Perkasie PA. 215-257-2821
Pitts, Ben, *Assoc Prof,* Delta State University, Dept of Media & Library Science, MS. 601-843-8638
Pitts, Cynthia, *Dir, Info Resources,* Arkansas Library Commission, Arkansas State Library, Little Rock AR. 501-371-1524
Pitts, Mary P, *Reader Serv,* United States Air Force, Air University Library, Maxwell AFB AL. 205-293-2888
Pitts, Patricia, *Librn,* Cape May County Library (Stone Harbor Branch), Stone Harbor NJ. 609-368-5102
Pitts, Terence R, *Librn,* University of Arizona Library (Center for Creative Photography), Tucson AZ. 602-626-4636
Pitzer, John D, *Asst Dir,* Furman University Library, Greenville SC. 803-294-2191
Pitzer, Laura F, *Librn,* Greenville Mental Health Center Library, Greenville SC. 803-242-8058
Pivarnik, Janis, *Govt publications,* University of Kentucky, Margaret I King Library, Lexington KY. 606-257-3801
Pivawer, Barbara, *In Charge,* Temple Emanuel Library, Orange CT. 203-397-3000
Pivonka, Sister Simeon, *Instr,* Saint Mary of the Plains College, Library Science Program, KS. 316-225-4171, Ext 68
Pizarro, Armando, *Media,* Inter-American University of Puerto Rico, Ponce Regional College Library, Ponce PR. 809-843-3480
Pizer, Irwin H, *Regional Med Libr Dir,* Midwest Health Science Library Network, (MHSLN), IL. 312-996-2464

Pizer, Irwin H, *Librn,* University of Illinois at the Medical Center, Library of the Health Sciences, Chicago IL. 312-996-8974

Pizzey, Mrs N, *Tech Serv,* King's College Library, London ON. 519-433-3491, Ext 44

Pizzi, Cecelia, *YA & Media,* Free Public Library of the Township of Berkeley Heights, Berkeley Heights NJ. 201-464-9333

Pizzimenti, Benette, *Dir,* Concord Public Library, Concord NH. 603-225-2743

Pizzuto, Carol T, *AV Coordr,* Diocese of Pittsburgh, Learning Media Center, Pittsburgh PA. 412-456-3120

Pla, Steven A, *Librn,* American Philatelic Research Library, State College PA. 814-237-3803

Place, Janet, *Coordr Ch,* West Warwick Public Library System, Robert H Champlin Memorial Library, West Warwick RI. 401-828-3750

Place, Melinda J, *Librn,* Framingham Public Library (Framingham Centre), Framingham MA. 617-872-4383

Place, Pat, *Librn,* University Research Corporation Library, Chevy Chase MD. 301-654-8338

Place, Philip A, *Dir,* Manatee County Public Library System, Bradenton FL. 813-748-5555

Place, Philip A, *Librn,* Manatee County Public Library System (Manatee County Central), Bradenton FL. 813-748-5555

Plachta, Helen, *Ser & Acq,* New York Academy of Medicine Library, New York NY. 212-876-8200

Placke, Mabel C, *Librn,* Madison Parish Library, Tallulah LA. 318-574-4308

Placzek, Adolf, *Librn,* Columbia University (Avery Architectural, Fine Arts Library), New York NY. 212-280-2241

Plair, Norman V, *Commun Servs,* Dayton & Montgomery County Public Library, Dayton OH. 513-224-1651

Plaisted, Dena K, *Librn,* University of Arkansas for Medical Sciences, Area Health Education Center-Southwest, Texarkana AR. 501-772-0034

Plaisted, Glen, *Dir,* Northeast Kansas Library System, Shawnee Mission KS. 913-831-4993

Plamann, Paul E, *Historian,* National Park Service, Fort McHenry National Monument Library, Baltimore MD. 301-962-4290

Plamondon, Yolande, *Asst Librn,* Centre Hospitalier Robert-Gifford, Quebec PQ. 418-663-5321, 663-5300

Plane, Daphne, *Librn,* California Institute of Technology (Geology & Planetary Science Library), Pasadena CA. 213-795-6811, Ext 2118

Plank, Barbara, *Librn,* Gothenburg Public Library, Gothenburg NE. 308-537-2591

Plant, Hazel, *Librn,* Suwannee River Regional Library, Seven-County Region (Madison (Madison County)), Live Oak FL. 904-362-5779

Planton, Barbara, *Ch,* Boyden Library, Foxboro MA. 617-543-8882

Planton, Stanley, *Dir,* Ohio University, Chillicothe Library, Chillicothe OH. 775-9500 Ext 215, 260

Plaso, Kathy, *Librn (Circuit),* Somerset County Medical Library Consortium, PA. 814-455-6501, Ext 216

Plater, Grace, *Librn,* Trenton State Prison Library, Trenton NJ. 609-292-9700

Platnick, Phyllis, *Librn,* York University, Glendon Campus, Leslie Frost Library, Toronto ON. 416-487-6139

Platou, Mary Jane, *Bibliog Instr,* State University of New York Agricultural & Technical College at Delhi, Delhi College Library, Delhi NY. 607-746-4107

Platt, Dee, *Dir,* Saint Thomas Hospital, Health Sciences Library, Nashville TN. 615-320-2658

Platt, Frances, *Librn,* Ashland Town Library, Ashland NH. 603-968-7928

Platt, Glenn E, *Dir & ILL,* Flagler College, Louise Wise Lewis Library, Saint Augustine FL. 904-829-6481, Ext 205 & 206

Platt, John H, *Librn,* Historical Society of Pennsylvania Library, Philadelphia PA. 215-732-6200

Platt, Mary, *Ref,* Chappaqua Central School District Public Library, Chappaqua NY. 914-238-4779

Platt, Mary E, *Librn,* Elbridge Free Library, Elbridge NY. 315-689-7111

Platt, Mrs Noel A, *Librn,* Dalton Community Library, Dalton PA. 717-563-2014

Platt-Brown, Jane, *Librn,* National Economic Research Associates Inc Library, Washington DC. 202-466-3510, Ext 274

Plattenburg, Roberta, *Librn,* Martelle Community Library, Martelle IA. 319-482-4121

Platter, Virginia, *Dir & Ad,* Huntington Woods Public Library, Huntington Woods MI. 313-543-3073

Platteter, Leo, *Librn,* Buffalo Bill Museum, Buffalo Bill & W R Coe Library, Cody WY. 307-587-4771

Platthy, Jeno, *Librn,* Harvard University Library (Center for Hellenic Studies Library), Washington DC. 202-234-3738

Platts, Daphne, *Asst Dir,* Sublette County Library, Pinedale WY. 307-367-2240

Playfoot, Marion, *Ser,* University of Nebraska at Omaha, University Library, Omaha NE. 402-554-2361

Pleak, Ruth, *In Charge,* Cobb County Public Library System (East Marietta Branch), Marietta GA. 404-973-6078

Pleasant, Thella Winters, *Chief Librn,* Sonoma State Hospital (Professional Library), Eldridge CA. 707-938-6000

Pleasants, Audrey K, *Acq,* Southeastern Baptist Theological Seminary Library, Wake Forest NC. 919-556-3101, Ext 225, 250

Pleasants, Loyce, *Dir of Cent Libr,* Los Angeles Public Library System, Los Angeles CA. 213-626-7555

Pless, Jean, *Librn,* Cherokee Regional Library (Chattooga County), Summerville GA. 404-857-2553

Plessner, Joan, *Pub Info Librn,* New Mexico State Library, Santa Fe NM. 505-827-2033

Plesums, Rita, *Librn,* Montgomery County Department of Public Libraries (Davis), Bethesda MD. 301-530-4411

Pletcher, Kathy, *Gov Pubs,* University of Wisconsin-Green Bay, Library Learning Center, Green Bay WI. 414-465-2382

Pletkovich, Jane A, *Librn,* Neponset Public Library, Neponset IL. 309-594-2204

Pletz, James, *Sr Citizens,* Chicago Public Library, Chicago IL. 312-269-2900

Plewa, Michele, *Admin Asst to Dir,* Marquette University Memorial Library, Milwaukee WI. 414-224-7214

Plimpton, Marcine, *Tech Serv,* Melbourne Public Library, Melbourne FL. 305-723-0611

Pliszkar, Maria, *Dir,* North Arlington Free Public Library, North Arlington NJ. 201-991-9335

Plitt, Jeanne G, *Dir,* Alexandria Library, Alexandria VA. 703-750-6351

Ploch, C S, *On-Line Servs,* Good Samaritan Hospital, Richard S Beinecke Medical Library, West Palm Beach FL. 305-655-5511, Ext 4315

Plockelman, Cynthia H, *Ref,* South Florida Water Management District, Reference Center Library, West Palm Beach FL. 305-686-8800, Ext 237

Ploger, Mary, *Librn,* Garden City Public Library, Garden City KS. 316-276-3941

Plomondon, Teresa, *ILL,* College of Saint Thomas, O'Shaughnessy Library, Saint Paul MN. 612-647-5720

Ploof, Charmaine, *Librn,* Iosco-Arenac Regional Library (Standish Library), Standish MI. 517-362-2651

Ploshnick, Mary, *Ch,* Detroit Public Library, Detroit Associated Libraries, Detroit MI. 313-833-1000

Plosia, Kathryn, *Librn,* East Rutherford Memorial Library, East Rutherford NJ. 201-939-3930

Plosz, W J, *Librn,* Unifarm Association Library, Edmonton AB. 403-423-1684

Ploszaj, Stanley, *Tech Serv,* Rutgers University, the State University of New Jersey, John Cotton Dana Library, Newark NJ. 201-648-5222

Plotkin, Nathan, *Reader Serv,* California Maritime Academy Library, Vallejo CA. 707-644-5601, Ext 265

Plotkin, Susan Lannon, *Info Systs Specialist & Librn,* Honeywell Inc, Process Controls Div, Information Center, Fort Washington PA. 215-641-3982

Plotnick, Robert N, *Librn,* Connecticut State Library (Bridgeport Branch), Bridgeport CT. 203-576-8401

Plotzke, Robert F, *Dir,* Rolling Prairie Library System, Decatur IL. 217-429-2586

Plowden, Christel, *Cat,* Polk Community College Library, Winter Haven FL. 813-294-7771, Ext 305

Plucinski, Veronica, *Librn,* Pfizer Inc, Pharmaceuticals Library, New York NY. 212-573-2323

Plucinsky, Marie E, *Dir,* John F Kennedy Memorial Library, Wallington NJ. 201-471-1692

Pluckhahn, Bruce, *Dir,* National Bowling Museum & Hall of Fame Library, Greendale WI. 414-421-6400

Plue, Blanche, *Ch,* Lexington Public Library, Lexington IL. 309-365-7801

Pluene, Joyce, *Asst Dir,* Kent County Library System, Grand Rapids MI. 616-774-3250

Plum, Dorothy A, *Librn,* Essex County Historical Society Library, Elizabethtown NY. 518-873-6466

Plumanis, Guna, *On-Line Servs & Bibliog Instr,* Ontario Ministry of Transportation & Communications Library, Downsview ON. 416-248-3591

Plumley, Boyd, *Tech Serv & Acq,* Lorain Public Library, Lorain OH. 216-244-1192

Plumley, Boyd F, *Librn,* Naval Training Center Library, Great Lakes IL. 312-688-5500

Plumley, Mrs Donald, *Librn,* Wales Public Library, Wales MA. 413-245-9072

Plummer, Bruce, *Asst Dir,* Worcester State College, Learning Resources Center, Worcester MA. 617-752-7700, Ext 132, 135

Plummer, Edward, *Bus,* Fresno County Free Library, Fresno CA. 209-488-3191

Plummer, Eleanor, *Librn,* Raymond Village Library, Raymond ME. 207-655-4836

Plummer, Mary, *Ch,* Auburn Public Library, Auburn MA. 617-832-2081

Plummer, Mary, *Skills Advancement,* Indiana Vocational Technical College, Region 4, Lafayette, Learning Resources Center, Lafayette IN. 317-477-7401

Plummer, Ruth, *Librn,* Nute Public Library, Milton NH. 603-652-4591

Plummer, III, Bill, *Communications Coordr,* Amateur Softball Association Research Center & Library, Oklahoma City OK. 405-424-5266

Plunges, Gregory J, *Librn,* Monmouth County Historical Association Library, Freehold NJ. 201-462-1466

Plungis, Joan, *Mss Curator,* Cincinnati Historical Society Library, Cincinnati OH. 513-241-4622

Plunket, Joy, *Librn,* Choate, Hall & Stewart Library, Boston MA. 617-227-5020, Ext 414, 415

Plunkett, Charlene M, *ILL,* Mary Baldwin College, Martha S Grafton Library, Staunton VA. 703-885-0811, Ext 382

Plunkett, Joan, *Tech Serv,* Nevada County Library, Nevada City CA. 916-265-2461, Ext 244

Plyler, Francis G, *Librn,* United States Bureau of Reclamation, Technical Library, Boulder City NV. 702-293-8570

Plymesser, Bette J, *Actg Librn,* Union Township Public Library, Ripley OH. 513-392-4871

Plympton, Eva G, *Asst Librn,* Steep Falls Library, Steep Falls ME. 207-675-3132

Poarch, Elizabeth, *Tech Serv,* Village Library of Wrightstown, Wrightstown PA. 215-598-3322

Poarch, Margaret E, *Lectr,* State University of New York, College of Arts & Science, School of Library & Information Science, NY. 716-245-5322

Pober, Susan J, *Librn,* Brooklyn Children's Museum Library (Children's Resource Library), Brooklyn NY. 212-735-4400

Poburko, Mary Jo Mahler, *Librn,* Nova Scotia Barristers' Society Library, Halifax NS. 902-422-1491

Pobutsky, Olga, *Librn,* Detroit Public Library (Edison), Detroit MI. 313-833-9760

Pochciol, Judith R, *Librn,* Saint Agnes Hospital, Lewis P Gundry Health Sciences Library, Baltimore MD. 301-368-7565

Podboy, Jr, Alvin M, *Librn,* Baker & Hostetler Library, Cleveland OH. 216-621-0200

Podesva, Ruth D, *Cat,* Rider College, Franklin F Moore Library, Lawrenceville NJ. 609-896-5111

Podlasek, Jean, *Librn,* Orwigsburg Area Free Public Library, Orwigsburg PA. 717-366-1638

Podlesnik, Cheryl, *On-Line Servs,* United States Gypsum Co, Research Center Library, Des Plaines IL. 312-299-3381, Ext 210

Podruzny, Olga, *Librn,* Wanham Community Library, Wanham AB. 403-694-3828

Poe, Charlotte V, *Librn,* University of Arkansas, Area Health Education Center Library, Jonesboro AR. 501-972-2054
Poe, Debbie, *Librn,* Balmorhea Public Library, Balmorhea TX. 915-375-2572
Poe, Hazel, *Librn,* Conran Memorial Library, Hayti MO. 314-359-0599
Poe, Martha K, *Dir,* Maricopa County Library System, Phoenix AZ. 602-269-2535
Poe, Miriam, *Bkmobile Coordr,* Shelbyville-Shelby County Public Library, Shelbyville IN. 317-398-7121
Poechmann, Nancy, *Commun Servs,* Ramsey County Public Library, Roseville MN. 612-631-0494
Poehlman, Dorothy, *10A Serv Br,* United States Department of Transportation, Library Services Div, Washington DC. 202-426-2565, 426-1792
Poehlman, Ruth, *Circ & Per,* Evergreen Valley College Library, San Jose CA. 408-274-7900, Ext 310
Poel, Elizabeth, *Audit Ref Servs,* United States General Accounting Office Library System (Office of Information Systems & Services), Washington DC. 275-3691 (Br Mgr), 275-5180 (Audit Ref Servs), 275-2585 (Law), 275-2555 (Tech Servs)
Poellot, Capitola, *Ad,* Bridgeville Public Library, Bridgeville PA. 412-221-3737
Poertner, Marilyn, *Asst Dir,* Boise Public Library & Information Center, Boise ID. 208-384-4466
Poeschl, Lois, *Cat,* Elisha D Smith Public Library, Menasha WI. 414-729-5166
Poff, Barbara, *YA,* Orange Public Library, Orange CA. 714-532-0391
Poff, G, *Dir,* Canadore College of Applied Arts & Technology Library, North Bay ON. 705-474-7600
Pogany, Ann, *Cat,* Oakland University, Kresge Library, Rochester MI. 313-377-2486, 377-2474
Pogue, Lisa, *Commun Servs,* Central Arkansas Library System, Little Rock AR. 501-374-7546
Pohl, Gunther E, *Chief,* New York Public Library (Local History & Genealogy), New York NY. 212-790-6201
Pohl, Mary Ann, *Bus Office,* Lincoln Library, Springfield Public Library, Springfield IL. 217-753-4900
Pohnl, Donald R, *Dir,* Park Falls Public Library, Park Falls WI. 715-762-3121
Pointer, Beth, *Ad,* Homewood Public Library, Homewood AL. 205-871-7342
Pointer, Dorothy, *Cat,* Iosco-Arenac Regional Library, Tawas City MI. 517-362-2651
Pointer, James E, *Dir,* Kittrell College, B N Duke Library, Kittrell NC. 919-492-1070
Points, Larry G, *Chief of Interpretation,* United States Department of the Interior, Assateague Island National Seashore, Berlin MD. 301-641-1441
Poirier, Faith A, *Librn,* Northern College of Applied Arts & Technology Library, South Porcupine ON. 705-235-3211
Poirier, Maria, *Asst Dir & Commun Servs,* Cheshire Public Library, Cheshire CT. 203-272-2245
Poisson, Beth G, *Librn,* Pondville Hospital, Medical Library, Walpole MA. 617-668-0385, Ext 365
Poisson, Philippe L, *Dir & Acq,* Assumption College Library, Worcester MA. 617-752-5615, Ext 272
Polach, Frank, *Asst Librn,* Rutgers University (Library of Science & Medicine), Piscataway NJ. 201-932-3850
Polacheck, Janet E, *YA & Br Coordr,* Stark County District Library, Canton OH. 216-452-0665, Ext 31
Polacsek, Richard A, *Dir,* Johns Hopkins University Libraries (William H Welch Medical Library), Baltimore MD. 301-955-3411
Polak, Renata, *On-Line Servs,* Atomic Energy of Canada Ltd, Engineering Company Library, Mississauga ON. 416-823-9040, Ext 2247
Polak, Virginia, *Dir,* University of California Extension, Continuing Education of the Bar Library, Berkeley CA. 415-642-5343
Polan, Morris, *Dir,* California State University, John F Kennedy Memorial Library, Los Angeles CA. 213-224-2201
Poland, Ursula H, *Dir,* Albany Medical Center College of Union University, Schaffer Library of Health Sciences, Albany NY. 518-445-5534

Poland, Ursula H, *Archivist,* Albany Medical Center College of Union University (Capital District Psychiatric Center Library), Albany NY. 518-445-6609
Polanda, David, *Tech Serv,* La Crosse Public Library, La Crosse WI. 608-784-8623
Polando, Jean M, *Asst Librn,* Fayette County Law Library, Uniontown PA. 412-437-5629
Polardino, Linda S, *Chief Librn,* Veterans Administration, Medical Center Library, Montrose NY. 914-737-4400, Ext 578
Polcari, Linda, *On-Line Servs,* University of Connecticut Library, Storrs CT. 203-486-2219
Polczynski, Amy, *Dir,* Elm Grove Public Library, Elm Grove WI. 414-782-6717
Polep, Janet, *Ad,* Crystal Lake Public Library, Crystal Lake IL. 815-459-1687
Polesak, Fred, *Instr,* Saint Cloud State University, Center for Library & Audiovisual Education, MN. 612-255-2022
Polhamus, Donna, *Ch,* Cary Memorial Library, Lexington MA. 617-862-6288
Polikoff, Susan J, *Dir,* Hyde Park Free Library, Hyde Park NY. 914-229-7791
Poling, Christine, *ILL, Ref & Cat,* Allerton Public Library, Monticello IL. 217-762-4676
Poling, John William, *In Charge,* Anderson Fine Arts Center Library, Anderson IN. 317-649-1248
Polinsky, Arlene, *Acq,* University of Chicago (Law Library), Chicago IL. 312-753-3425
Polishook, Louis, *Asst Supv of Rd Servs,* Boston Public Library, Eastern Massachusetts Library System, Boston MA. 617-536-5400
Politi, Dorothy, *Ch,* Public Library of Steubenville & Jefferson County, Steubenville OH. 614-282-9782
Politis, Mary, *Asst Librn,* Oxford Public Library, Oxford CT. 203-888-6944
Polito, Ruth, *Librn,* La Salle Steel Co, Research & Develop Library, Hammond IN. 219-853-6000
Polivka, Emily, *Librn,* Berwyn Public Library, Berwyn IL. 312-484-6654
Polizzi, Barbara, *Dir,* Mineral Point Public Library, Mineral Point WI. 608-987-2447
Polk, Dave, *Video,* Greenville Technical College, Learning Resources Center, Greenville SC. 803-242-3170, Ext 321
Polk, Diana, *Ref,* Deere & Co Library, Moline IL. 309-752-4442
Polk, Diane, *Dir & Cat,* Ritter Memorial Library, Lunenburg MA. 617-582-7817
Polk, Johnnie M, *Cat,* Pearl River County Library System, Margaret Reed Crosby Memorial Library, Picayune MS. 601-798-5081
Polk, Lorraine A, *Librn,* 3M Canada Ltd, Technical Information Centre, London ON. 519-451-2500, Ext 2486
Polk, Ruth, *ILL & Ref,* University of Maryland-Eastern Shore, Frederick Douglass Library, Princess Anne MD. 301-651-2200, Ext 229
Pollack, Carol, *Librn,* Detroit Bank & Trust Library, Detroit MI. 313-222-3300
Pollack, Robert, *Librn,* Genesee District Library (Flushing Branch), Flushing MI. 313-659-9755
Pollak, Sally, *Pub Servs,* University of Texas Health Science Center at San Antonio Library, San Antonio TX. 512-691-6271
Pollard, Carol, *AV,* Christian Brothers College Library, Memphis TN. 901-278-0100, Ext 220
Pollard, Dolly, *Genealogy,* West Florida Regional Library, Pensacola Public Library, Pensacola FL. 904-438-5479
Pollard, Elizabeth, *Fine Arts & Lit,* University of Alabama in Huntsville Library, Huntsville AL. 205-895-6540
Pollard, Elizabeth G, *Librn,* Shiloh Baptist Church, Susie E Miles Library, Washington DC. 202-234-6667, 232-4041
Pollard, Larry, *Ref,* Radford University, John Preston McConnell Library, Radford VA. 703-731-5471, 5472
Pollard, Louise, *Librn,* Kennecott Minerals Company Library, Salt Lake City UT. 801-534-8111
Pollard, Opal M, *Dir,* Palo Verde Community College Library, Blythe CA. 714-922-6168, 922-6169
Pollard, Patricia N, *Assoc Librn,* Petawawa Village & Township Union Public Library, Petawawa ON. 613-687-2227

Pollard, Rhonda, *Librn,* Stanly County Public Library (Norwood), Norwood NC. 704-474-3625
Pollard, Rhonda H, *Librn,* Norwood Library, Norwood NC. 704-474-3625
Pollard, Richard, *Tech Serv,* University of Tennessee, Knoxville, James D Hoskins Library, Knoxville TN. 615-974-0111
Pollard, Stewart M L, *In Charge,* Library of the Masonic Service Association, Silver Spring MD. 301-588-4010
Pollard, Suzanne, *Ref,* Columbia-Greene Community College Library, Hudson NY. 518-828-4181
Pollard, W Robert, *Ref,* North Carolina State University, D H Hill Library, Raleigh NC. 919-737-2843, 2595
Pollard, William C, *Librn,* Mary Baldwin College, Martha S Grafton Library, Staunton VA. 703-885-0811, Ext 382
Pollard, Jr, Marvin E, *Dir,* Navajo Community College, Naaltsoos Ba'Hooghan Library, Tsaile AZ. 602-724-6132
Pollari, Catherine, *ILL & Ref,* Campbell University, Carrie Rich Memorial Library, Buies Creek NC. 919-893-4111, Ext 238
Pollet, Dorothy, *Educ Liaison Officer,* Library of Congress, Washington DC. 202-287-5000
Polley, Brian S, *Librn,* Florida Supreme Court Library, Tallahassee FL. 904-488-8919
Polley, Deborah, *ILL,* Wabash College, Lilly Library, Crawfordsville IN. 317-362-1400, Ext 215, 216
Pollis, Angela R, *In Charge,* United States Steel Corp, Research Laboratory Technical Information Center, Monroeville PA. 412-372-1212, Ext 2344
Pollock, Anne, *In Charge,* East Chicago Public Library (Roxana), East Chicago IN. 219-397-2453
Pollock, Carol, *Librn,* Hildreth Public Library, Hildreth Township Library, Hildreth NE. 308-938-4215
Pollock, Carol J, *Dir,* Danville Community College Library, Danville VA. 804-797-3553, Ext 204, 205
Pollock, Constance, *Media,* Schenectady County Community College Library, Library Resources Center, Schenectady NY. 518-346-6211, Ext 240, 241
Pollock, Ida C, *Librn,* Temple Beth El, Ziskind Memorial Library, Fall River MA. 617-674-3529
Pollock, Irene, *Media,* Woodstock Public Library & Art Gallery, Woodstock ON. 519-537-4801
Pollock, James, *Near East Studies,* Indiana University at Bloomington, University Libraries, Bloomington IN. 812-337-3403
Pollock, James A, *Ref,* Central Virginia Community College Library, Lynchburg VA. 804-239-0321, Ext 231
Pollock, Jean, *Librn,* Mount Sterling Public Library, Mount Sterling OH. 614-869-2430
Pollock, Joseph M, *Librn,* Highland Park Public Library, Highland Park IL. 312-432-0216
Pollock, Luella R, *Dir,* Reed College, E V Hauser Memorial Library, Portland OR. 503-771-1112, Ext 260
Pollock, Pamela A Avis, *Librn,* Ontario Medical Association Library, Toronto ON. 416-925-3264, Ext 230
Pollock, Ruth, *Librn,* Highland Township Library, Highland MI. 313-887-2218
Polly, Margaret A, *Librn,* Whiting Public Library, Whiting IA. 712-458-2532
Polonsky, Aaron, *Acq,* Bloomsburg State College, Harvey A Andruss Library, Bloomsburg PA. 717-389-2716
Polonsky, Kathy, *Tech Serv, Acq & Cat,* East Brunswick Public Library, East Brunswick NJ. 201-254-1220
Polovitch, Sylvia, *Redistribution Ctr,* Chicago Public Library, Chicago IL. 312-269-2900
Polowniak, Henry J, *Dir,* Saint Mary's College, Alumni Memorial Library, Orchard Lake MI. 313-682-1885
Polowy, Barbara C, *Librn,* Everson Museum of Art Library, Syracuse NY. 315-474-6064
Pols, Wendell B, *Ref, Spec Coll & Bibliog Instr,* Roger Williams College Library, Bristol RI. 401-255-2361

Polsinelli, Antonia, *Librn,* Schenectady County Public Library (Pleasant Valley), Schenectady NY. 518-382-3505
Polson, Joseph, *Librn,* American Standards Testing Bureau, Inc, Sam Tour Memorial Library, New York NY. 212-943-3156
Polster, Joanne, *Librn,* American Craft Council Library, New York NY. 212-397-0638
Polston, Beatrice, *Librn,* Lockwood Public Library, Lockwood MO. 417-232-4221
Polucha, Joyce, *Ch,* Woonsocket Harris Public Library, Woonsocket RI. 401-769-9044
Pomerance, Deborah S, *Librn,* Data Use & Access Laboratories Library, Arlington VA. 703-525-1480
Pomerance, H S, *On-Line Servs,* Oak Ridge National Laboratory Library, Oak Ridge TN. 615-574-6722
Pomerantz, Barbara, *Acq,* Hebrew Union College-Jewish Institute of Religion Library, Cincinnati OH. 513-221-1875
Pomerantz, Gloria, *Programming,* Peninsula Public Library, Lawrence NY. 516-239-3262
Pomerantz, Julius M, *Librn,* Carter, Ledyard & Milburn, Law Library, New York NY. 212-732-3200, Ext 274
Pomerantz, Sandra, *Librn,* Beth Zion-Beth Israel Library, Philadelphia PA. 215-735-5148
Pomerhn, Janice, *Tech Serv,* Flathead County Free Library, Kalispell MT. 406-755-5300, Ext 357
Pomerleau, Suzanne, *ILL, YA & Ref,* Carnegie Free Library, Beaver Falls PA. 412-846-4340
Pomeroy, Cornelia, *Circ,* Worcester Polytechnic Institute, George C Gordon Library, Worcester MA. 617-753-1411, Ext 410
Pomirko, Kalyna, *Librn,* Mayor's Office for Senior Citizens Library, Chicago IL. 312-744-4016
Pommer, Michelle A, *Librn,* Hawaiian Telephone Co Library, Honolulu HI. 808-546-2600
Pompa, Dorothea, *Dir,* Chili Public Library, Rochester NY. 716-889-2200
Pona, Maureen, *YA,* Steele Memorial Library, Chemung-Southern Tier Library System, Elmira NY. 607-733-9173, 733-9174, 733-9175
Ponce, Barbara, *Ref,* Pinellas Park Public Library, Pinellas Park FL. 813-544-4868
Poncek, Elaine, *AV,* Lackawanna Junior College, Seeley Memorial Library, Scranton PA. 717-961-7831
Pond, Patricia, *Instr,* University of Pittsburgh, School of Library & Information Science, PA. 412-624-5230
Pond, William, *Ref, Per & On-Line Servs,* University of Winnipeg Library, Winnipeg MB. 204-786-7811, Ext 520
Ponder, Ann, *Librn,* Louisville Free Public Library (Outer Highlands), Louisville KY. 502-584-4154
Pons, Isabel W, *Dir,* Annie Halenbake Ross Library, Lock Haven PA. 717-748-3321
Ponsell, Mary Louise, *Dir,* Wilmington College Library, New Castle DE. 302-328-9401
Pontius, Jack, *Microforms,* Pennsylvania State University, Fred Lewis Pattee Library, University Park PA. 814-865-0401
Pontius, Marjorie, *Librn,* Carnegie Library, Deadwood SD. 605-578-2821
Ponton, Melbourne, *AV,* Pikeville College, O'Rear-Robinson Library, Pikeville KY. 606-432-9372
Ponzo, Sharon M, *Librn,* Palm Beach County Public Library System (Talking Book Library), West Palm Beach FL. 305-686-0895
Pool, Kathryn, *Librn,* Saint Louis County Library (Tesson Ferry), St Louis MO. 314-843-0560
Pool, Mary B, *Asst Dir,* Piedmont Regional Library, Winder GA. 404-867-2762
Pool, Pat, *Dir,* Archuleta County Public Library, Pagosa Springs CO. 303-264-5698
Pool, Robert, *Doc,* University of Baltimore, Langsdale Library, Baltimore MD. 301-727-6350, Ext 444
Poole, Betty, *Librn,* Dalton Public Library, Inc (Calhoun-Gardon County), Calhoun GA. 404-629-3405
Poole, Carolyn, *YA,* Chatham Public Library, Chatham ON. 519-354-2940
Poole, D W, *Mgr,* Lethbridge Community College, Buchanan Resource Centre, Lethbridge AB. 403-327-2141, Ext 350
Poole, David, *Chmn Learning Resources Ctr,* Olds College Library, Olds AB. 403-556-8243
Poole, Herbert, *Dir,* Guilford College Library, Greensboro NC. 919-292-5511, Ext 250

Poole, Kathleen, *Librn,* Prince Edward Island Provincial Library (Souris Branch), Souris PE. 902-892-3504, Ext 54
Poole, Martha, *Media,* Palm Beach County Public Library System, West Palm Beach FL. 305-686-0895
Poole, Sandra, *Pub Servs,* Wicomico County Free Library, Salisbury MD. 301-749-5171
Poole, William R, *Dir,* Redondo Beach Public Library, Redondo Beach CA. 213-376-8723
Pooler, Marlene, *Librn,* Fort Kent Public Library, Fort Kent ME. 207-834-3048
Pooley, Beverley J, *Dir,* University of Michigan (Law Library), Ann Arbor MI. 313-764-9322
Pooley, Mary, *Librn,* Okanagan Regional Library District (Kelowna (Regional Resource Ctr)), Kelowna BC. 604-762-2800
Poor, Elizabeth Booth, *Circ,* Bartholomew County Library, Cleo Rogers Memorial Library, Columbus IN. 812-379-1255
Poor, Sara H, *Librn,* Sequoyah Regional Library (Woodstock Public), Woodstock GA. 404-926-5859
Poor, W E, *Librn,* Cummins Engine Co Inc, Technical Information Center, Columbus IN. 812-372-7211
Popa, Peggy, *Tech Serv,* Continental Illinois National Bank & Trust Co, Information Services Division, Chicago IL. 312-828-8580
Pope, A, *Librn,* University of New Brunswick (Education Resource Ctr), Fredericton NB. 506-453-3516
Pope, Elizabeth, *Cat,* Illinois State University, Milner Library, Normal IL. 309-438-3675
Pope, Kitty, *Ch,* Owen Sound Public Library, Owen Sound ON. 519-376-6623
Pope, Mary L, *Chief, Tech Servs Br,* United States Department of the Treasury Library, Washington DC. 202-566-2777, 566-3279
Pope, Maurice A, *Asst Dir & Cat,* University of Arkansas Libraries (Law), Fayetteville AR. 501-575-5604
Pope, Michael, *Dir & Acq,* Dutchess Community College Library, Poughkeepsie NY. 914-471-4500, Ext 388
Pope, Mrs Neater, *Librn,* Kinston-Lenoir County Public Library (East Branch), Kinston NC. 919-523-3947
Pope, Nanette, *President,* Interlibrary Users Association, MD. 301-953-7100, Ext 604
Pope, Nannette M, *Chief Librn,* Armed Forces Radiobiology Research Institute, Bethesda MD. 301-295-0428
Pope, Royal V, *Dir,* University of Arkansas Libraries, Fayetteville AR. 501-575-4101
Pope, Ruth, *Librn,* Chatham-Effingham-Liberty Regional Library (Ogeechee), Savannah GA. 912-232-1339
Pope, Ruth Nello, *Dir,* Llano County Public Library, Llano TX. 915-247-5248
Popecki, Jeanne M, *Dir,* Champlain College Library, Burlington VT. 802-658-0800, Ext 374
Popecki, Joseph T, *Dir,* Saint Michael's College, Durick Library, Colchester VT. 802-655-2000, Ext 2400
Popenoe, John, *Dir,* Fairchild Tropical Garden, Montgomery Library, Miami FL. 305-667-1651
Popenoe, Paul, *Ch,* American Institute of Family Relations, Roswell H Johnson Reference Library, Los Angeles CA. 213-465-5131
Popescu, Constantin C, *Resource Develop,* Milwaukee School of Engineering, Walter Schroeder Library, Milwaukee WI. 414-272-8720, Ext 388
Popik, Judith B, *Asst Librn,* Winthrop, Stimson, Putnam & Roberts Library, New York NY. 212-943-0700
Popik, Marilyn L, *Librn,* Braddock General Hospital, Medical Library, Braddock PA. 412-351-3800, Ext 322
Popkave, Dixie, *Tech Serv,* West Nyack Free Library, West Nyack NY. 914-358-6081
Popko, Denise L, *Coordr,* Massachusetts Film & Media Cooperative, MA. 617-345-0166
Poplawski, Andrew, *Bkmobile Coordr,* Halifax County Regional Library, Halifax NS. 902-477-6265
Poplin, Jacquie, *Media,* Phillips University, Zollars Memorial Library, Enid OK. 405-237-4433, Ext 251
Popoff, Annis T, *Dir,* Glen Ridge Free Public Library, Glen Ridge NJ. 201-748-5482

Popovich, C, *Econ & Mgt,* State University of New York at Buffalo, University Libraries, Buffalo NY. 716-636-2965
Popovich, Marjorie L, *Head Info Servs,* Kennecott Copper Corp, Corporate Planning & Development Group Library, Niagara Falls NY. 716-278-2484
Popowich, Fred, *Asst Dir & Bkmobile Coordr,* Pictou Antigonish Regional Library, New Glasgow NS. 902-752-6217
Popowich, Sharon, *Librn,* Winnipeg Public Library (Saint John's), Winnipeg MB. 204-582-6431
Popp, Linda, *Spec Coll,* Azusa Pacific College, Marshburn Memorial Library, Azusa CA. 213-969-3434, Ext 198
Popp, Mary, *Actg Librn,* Indiana University at Bloomington (Halls of Residence), Bloomington IN. 812-337-7711
Popp, Mary, *Actg Halls of Residence,* Indiana University at Bloomington, University Libraries, Bloomington IN. 812-337-3403
Popp, Richard H, *Librn,* Western Publishing Co, Inc, Corporate Training Center Library, Racine WI. 414-633-2431, Ext 369
Popper, Doris, *Librn,* Wentworth Library (Glanford), Mount Hope ON. 416-526-4126
Popper, Irene, *Ser,* John C Hart Memorial Library, Shrub Oak NY. 914-245-5262
Popple, Ken, *In Charge,* Mental Health Center Penetanguishene, Penetanguishene ON. 705-549-7431
Porath, Patricia, *Librn,* Calaveras County Library, San Andreas CA. 209-754-4266
Porcella, Brewster, *Librn,* Trinity Evangelical Divinity School, Rolfing Memorial Library, Deerfield IL. 312-945-6700, Ext 317
Porcelli, Elizabeth, *Librn,* Essex County College (Allied Health Learning Resources Center), Newark NJ. 201-877-3473
Porcher, Gwen, *Asst Librn,* Catharine Young Library, Margate FL. 972-1188 & 972-1196
Porras, Susan, *Ad,* Yuma City-County Library, Yuma AZ. 602-782-1871
Port, Adelle, *Actg Dir,* California State University, Northridge, Delmar T Oviatt & South Libraries, Northridge CA. 213-885-2271
Port, Jane S, *Dir,* Mount Sinai School of Medicine of City University of New York, Gustave L & Janet W Levy Library, New York NY. 212-650-6671
Port, Toby G, *Admin Librn,* Saint Elizabeth's Hospital (Health Sciences Library), Washington DC. 202-574-7274
Portal, Doreen, *Ref,* Oregon College of Education Library, Monmouth OR. 503-838-1220, Ext 240
Portal, Doreen, *On-Line Servs & Bibliog Instr,* Oregon College of Education Library, Monmouth OR. 503-838-1220, Ext 240
Porte, Barbara, *Ch,* Nassau Library System, Uniondale NY. 516-292-8920
Porte, Masha R, *Motion Picture Spec,* Dallas Public Library, Dallas TX. 214-748-9071
Porter, B B, *Librn,* Peterborough Public Library, Peterborough ON. 705-745-5382
Porter, Barry, *Dir,* Iowa Library Information Teletype Exchange, (I-LITE), IA. 515-281-4406
Porter, Barry L, *State Librn,* State Library Commission of Iowa, Des Moines IA. 515-281-4102
Porter, Bess S, *Librn,* Kent County Rural Library, Jayton TX. 806-237-9440
Porter, Charles R, *Media,* Utica Junior College, William H Holtzclaw Library, Utica MS. 601-885-6062, Ext 48
Porter, Cynthia, *Dir,* Bank Marketing Association, Information Center, Chicago IL. 312-782-1442
Porter, Dorothy, *Librn,* West Woodstock Library, Woodstock Valley CT. 203-974-0376
Porter, Eva, *Tech Serv,* Township of Hamilton Free Public Library, Trenton NJ. 609-890-3460
Porter, Gaynelle, *Bkmobile Coordr,* Butler County Library, Morgantown KY. 502-526-4722
Porter, Hazel, *Dir,* Oklahoma City Southwestern College, Irvin Learning Center, Oklahoma City OK. 405-947-2331, Ext 355
Porter, Helen, *Librn,* Muskingum County Law Library, Zanesville OH. 614-452-9143
Porter, Helen I, *Librn,* Osawatomie State Hospital, Rapaport Professional Library, Osawatomie KS. 913-755-3151, Ext 364
Porter, Kathryn, *Bkmobile Coordr,* Allegany County Library, Cumberland MD. 301-777-1200

PORTER

Porter, Kathryn, *Librn,* Bethel Public Library, Bethel CT. 203-744-0170

Porter, Larry, *Acq,* Wright State University Library, Dayton OH. 513-873-2380

Porter, Lee W, *Librn,* United States Army (Carlisle Barracks Post Library), Carlisle Barracks PA. 717-245-3718

Porter, Lee W, *Chief Librn,* United States Army (Fort McPherson Library System), Fort McPherson GA. 404-752-2528, 752-3045

Porter, Lisbeth, *Bibliog Instr,* Virginia Wesleyan College, Henry Clay Hofheimer II Library, Norfolk VA. 804-461-3232

Porter, Margaret L, *Librn,* Chatham College, Jennie King Mellon Library, Pittsburgh PA. 412-441-8200, Ext 220 & 221

Porter, Maria, *Librn,* South Bend Public Library (Roger B Francis), South Bend IN. 219-277-3117

Porter, Marion, *Circ,* Palo Alto City Library, Palo Alto CA. 415-329-2436

Porter, Miriam F, *Dir,* Ardsley Public Library, Ardsley NY. 914-693-6636

Porter, Mrs D E, *Librn,* Gore Bay Union Public Library, Gore Bay ON. 705-282-2221

Porter, Mrs I, *Librn,* Shelburne Public Library, Shelburne OH. 519-925-2168

Porter, Mrs J J, *Librn,* Cisco Public Library, Cisco TX. 817-442-2111

Porter, Pat, *Tech Serv,* Chickasaw Library System, Ardmore OK. 405-223-3164

Porter, Pat, *Media,* Findlay-Hancock County Public Library, Findlay OH. 419-422-1712

Porter, Pat, *Librn,* Sibley Public Library, Sibley IA. 712-754-2888

Porter, Peggy, *Librn,* United States Navy (United States Marine Corps Technical Library), Camp Pendleton CA. 714-725-2875

Porter, Rebecca, *Ch & YA,* Mayne Williams Public Library, Johnson City TN. 615-928-3116

Porter, Shannon, *Librn,* Foresta Institute for Ocean & Mountain Studies Library, Carson City NV. 702-882-6361

Porter, Sheila C, *Librn,* Dallas County Law Library, Dallas TX. 214-749-8481

Porter, Shlomo, *Librn,* Ner Israel Rabbinical College Library, Baltimore MD. 301-484-7200

Porter, Susan, *Assoc Prof,* McNeese State University, School of Education, LA. 318-477-2520, Ext 452

Porter, William, *Media,* Community College of Baltimore (Harbor Campus), Baltimore MD. 301-396-1860

Porter, Jr, Stuart T, *Dir,* Russell Public Library, Middletown CT. 203-347-2528

Porterfield, Paul C, *Media,* Queens College, Everett Library, Charlotte NC. 704-332-7121, Ext 278

Porth, Rosemary, *Media,* Northern Arizona University Libraries, Flagstaff AZ. 602-523-9011

Portillo, Jessica, *Librn,* Fresno City Planning Department Library, Fresno CA. 209-488-1567

Portis, Juanita W, *Deputy Dir,* Howard University Libraries, Founders Library, Washington DC. 202-636-7253

Portis, Juanita W, *Deputy Dir,* Howard University Libraries (Pharmacy Library), Washington DC. 202-636-7253

Portlock, Lucille, *Rare Bks & Spec Coll,* Norfolk Public Library, Norfolk VA. 804-441-2887

Portluck, Lucille, *Genealogy & Local History,* Norfolk Public Library, Norfolk VA. 804-441-2887

Portman, Jeff, *Librn,* Congregation Agudas Achim Library, Iowa City IA. 319-337-3813

Portmann, Billie K, *Librn,* United States Army (Post Library), Watertown NY. 315-782-6900, Ext 2929

Portmann, Douglas A, *Librn,* Mobay Chemical Corp, Research Library, New Martinsville WV. 304-455-4400

Portolese, Margaret, *AV,* Public Library of Fort Wayne & Allen County, Fort Wayne IN. 219-424-7241

Portsch, Joanne, *Librn,* Raytheon Co, Technical Information Center, Wayland MA. 617-358-2721, Ext 349

Portschy, Arthur D, *Main Libr Head,* Omaha Public Library, W Dale Clark Library, Omaha NE. 402-444-4800

Portugal, Rhonda, *Dir,* Lyndhurst Free Public Library, Lyndhurst NJ. 201-939-6548

Posel, Nancy R, *Dir,* Abington Free Library, Abington PA. 215-885-5180

Posey, Betty, *Ser,* University of Southern Mississippi, Cook Memorial Library, Hattiesburg MS. 601-266-7301

Posey, Edwin, *Librn,* Purdue University Libraries & Audio-Visual Center (Engineering), West Lafayette IN. 317-749-2912

Posey, Jasmine, *Ch,* Greenwich Library, Greenwich CT. 203-622-7900

Posey, Jean, *Tech Serv,* Penn Valley Community College Library, Kansas City MO. 816-756-2800, Ext 428

Posey, Susann, *Librn,* Blue Ridge Summit Free Library, Blue Ridge Summit PA. 717-794-2240

Poska, Valentine, *Per,* San Antonio College Library, San Antonio TX. 512-734-7311, Ext 2480

Posner, Adolph, *Librn,* Institute for Glaucoma Research, Inc, Carl C Swisher Library, New York NY. 212-838-7540

Posner, Geraldine, *AV,* Brainerd Public Library, Brainerd MN. 218-829-5574

Posner, Lee, *Tech Serv, Acq & Cat,* Harrison Public Library, Harrison NY. 914-835-0324

Posner, Shirley, *Librn,* A M Kinney, Inc Library, Cincinnati OH. 513-281-2900

Posner, Shirley, *Acq,* State University College at Buffalo, Edward H Butler Library, Buffalo NY. 716-878-6302

Posniak, John R, *Asst Librn,* Export-Import Bank of the United States, Eximbank Library, Washington DC. 202-566-8320, 566-8897

Possner, Susan, *Media,* Long Beach Public Library System, Long Beach CA. 213-436-9225

Post, Ann S, *Librn,* Hudson River Psychiatric Center, Poughkeepsie NY. 914-452-8000

Post, Doris, *Dir,* Godfrey Memorial Library, Middletown CT. 203-346-4375

Post, Earlene, *Librn,* Stanislaus County Free Library (Denair Branch), Denair CA. 209-634-1283

Post, G L, *Dir,* Point Loma College, Ryan Library, San Diego CA. 714-222-6474, Ext 355, 338

Post, Helen, *Librn,* Veterans Administration, Medical Library, Wilmington DE. 302-994-2511, Ext 354, 355

Post, J B, *In Charge,* Free Library of Philadelphia (Map Collection), Philadelphia PA. 215-686-5322

Post, James, *Chief Librn,* Indianapolis Newspapers, Inc Library, Indianapolis IN. 317-633-9293

Post, Margaret, *Librn,* Newport Beach Public Library (Balboa Branch), Balboa CA. 714-640-2241

Post, Mary M, *Librn,* Cook Christian Training School, Mary M McCarthy Library, Tempe AZ. 602-968-9354

Postal, Justin, *Doc,* Palm Beach County Public Library System, West Palm Beach FL. 305-686-0895

Postell, Jr, W D, *Dir,* Tulane University of Louisiana (Matas Medical Library), New Orleans LA. 504-588-5155

Postich, K, *Media,* John McIntire Public Library Public Library, Zanesville OH. 614-453-0391

Poston, Lura H, *Librn,* Florence County Library (Johnsonville Public), Johnsonville SC. 803-386-2052

Potash, Loree, *Ref,* Case Western Reserve University Libraries (School of Law Library), Cleveland OH. 216-368-2792

Pote, Anne H, *Dir,* Chicago Ridge Public Library, Chicago Ridge IL. 312-423-7753

Poteat, James B, *Librn,* Television Information Office Library, New York NY. 212-759-6800

Poteet, Susan, *Cat,* Southern Illinois University at Carbondale, Delyte W Morris Library, Carbondale IL. 618-453-2522

Potenza, Harriett, *Ref,* Thomas Ford Memorial Library, Western Springs Library, Western Springs IL. 312-246-0520

Pothaar, William, *Media,* Centennial College of Applied Arts & Technology, Resource Centre, Scarborough ON. 416-439-7180

Potter, Corinne, *Dir,* Saint Ambrose College, Learning Resource Center, Davenport IA. 319-324-1681, Ext 241

Potter, Donald C, *Sr Assoc Dir,* Carnegie Library of Pittsburgh, Pittsburgh PA. 412-622-3100

Potter, Dorothy, *Librn,* Jellico Public Library, Jellico TN. 615-424-7488

Potter, Edward R, *Dir,* Real Estate Board of New York Library, New York NY. 212-532-3100

Potter, Emily, *Librn,* Kinney Memorial Library, Hartwick NY. 607-293-6600

Potter, Evelyn, *Librn,* Norfolk Public Library (Larchmont), Norfolk VA. 804-441-2854

Potter, Frances F, *Dir,* West Springfield Public Library, West Springfield MA. 413-736-4561

Potter, George E, *Ref,* Harvard University Library (Harvard-Yenching Library), Cambridge MA. 617-495-3327

Potter, Gregory, *Asst Dir,* Glassboro State College, Savitz Learning Resource Center, Glassboro NJ. 609-445-6101

Potter, Janet, *Asst Librn,* Digital Equipment Corp, Tewksbury Library, Tewksbury MA. 617-851-5071, Ext 2643

Potter, Janet, *Bkmobile Coordr,* Ocean County Library, Toms River NJ. 201-349-6200

Potter, Jo, *Ch,* Alpha Park Public Library District, Bartonville IL. 309-697-3822

Potter, Joyce A, *Librn,* Federal Home Loan Bank Board (Law Library), Washington DC. 202-377-6470

Potter, June, *On-Line Servs,* Zion-Benton Public Library District, Zion IL. 312-872-4680

Potter, L Ernestine, *Cat,* University of Texas Libraries (General), Austin TX. 512-471-3811

Potter, Marjorie P, *Librn,* Supreme Court Library, Lake George NY. 518-792-9951

Potter, Maxine E, *Librn,* Wayne Township Library (Richardson), Richmond IN. 317-966-8291

Potter, Pamela A, *Media,* Maryland Institute College of Art, Decker Library, Baltimore MD. 301-669-9200, Ext 27, 28

Potter, Paula, *Instrl Mat Ctr,* Medford Public Library, Medford MA. 617-395-7950

Potter, Pauline A, *Asst Dir,* Morristown-Hamblen Library, Morristown TN. 615-586-6410

Potter, Robert, *Ref,* Bellevue Public Library System, Bellevue NE. 402-291-8000

Potter, Sally N, *Tech Serv & Cat,* Onondaga Community College, Sidney B Coulter Library, Syracuse NY. 315-469-7741, Ext 5335-5338

Potter, Sue, *Math,* Wayne Community College, Learning Resource Center, Goldsboro NC. 919-735-5151, Ext 64

Potter, Susan L, *Asst Librn,* Plymouth Public Library, Plymouth WI. 414-892-4416

Potter, Virginia, *Ref,* Wisconsin Department of Public Instruction (Reference & Loan Library), Madison WI. 608-266-1053

Potter, Wanda, *Dir,* Muhlenberg County Libraries, Greenville KY. 502-338-4760

Potter, Jr, Rockwell H, *Pub Rec Adminr,* Connecticut State Library, Hartford CT. 203-566-4301

Potter, Jr, Rockwell H, *Geneology & Hist,* Connecticut State Library, Hartford CT. 203-566-4301

Pottharst, Kris, *Librn,* New Orleans Public Library (Napolean), New Orleans LA. 504-891-9411

Potthast, Cheryl D, *Librn,* Veterans Administration (Lakeside Medical Center Medical Library), Chicago IL. 312-943-6600, Ext 259

Potthoff, Renita, *Librn,* Monterey-Tippecanoe Township Public Library, Monterey Public Library, Monterey IN. 219-542-2171

Pottle, N, *Librn,* Calgary Public Library (Louise Riley), Calgary AB. 403-289-8535

Potts, Don, *Data Processing,* Medical Library Center of New York, New York NY. 212-427-1630

Potts, Dorothy, *Librn,* Grundy Center Public Library, Grundy Center IA. 319-824-3607

Potts, Ethelda O, *Librn,* Aliceville Public Library, Aliceville AL. 205-373-6691

Potts, Jean, *Librn,* Lake Lanier Regional Library (Forsyth County), Cumming GA. 404-887-3931

Potts, Judy, *Librn,* George S Houston Memorial Library (Rossie Purcell), Columbia AL. 205-696-3345

Potts, June, *ILL & Cat,* North Bay Public Library, North Bay ON. 705-474-4830

Potts, Mrs L, *Librn,* Lincoln Public Library (Rittenhouse), Vineland Station ON. 416-562-5711

Potts, Nancy L, *Tech Serv,* National Park Service, Harpers Ferry Center Library, Harpers Ferry WV. 304-535-6371, Ext 264

Potts, Shirley E, *Librn,* Town of Tonawanda Public Library (Brighton), Tonawanda NY. 716-873-2861

Potts, William M, *Dir,* Bryan Public Library, Bryan OH. 419-636-2937

Potvin, Claude, *Dir,* Albert-Westmorland-Kent Regional Library, Moncton NB. 506-389-2631

Poucher, Lucy A, *Cat,* Southern Oregon State College Library, Ashland OR. 503-482-6445

Poulin, Gloria, *Cat,* Lawrence Public Library, Fairfield ME. 207-453-6867

Pouliott, Marianne, *Librn,* General Electric Co, Silicone Products Division Library, Waterford NY. 237-3330 Ext 2264

Poulos, Angela, *Coll Dev,* Bowling Green State University Library, Bowling Green OH. 419-372-2856

Poulos, George, *Sci,* Bowling Green State University Library, Bowling Green OH. 419-372-2856

Poulson, Patricia, *Tech Serv & Acq,* Camden Free Public Library, Camden NJ. 609-963-4807

Poulter, Beulah, *Librn,* Wisconsin Taxpayers Alliance Library, Madison WI. 608-255-4581

Poulton, Kathryn, *Librn,* Public Library of Columbus & Franklin County (Linden), Columbus OH. 614-262-4113

Pouncil, Jean, *Librn,* Wichita Public Library (Evergreen), Wichita KS. 316-262-0611

Pouncy, Mitchell, *Tech Serv & Cat,* Southern University Library, Baton Rouge LA. 504-771-4990, 771-4991, 771-4992

Pound, Marilyn M, *Music,* William Carey College, I E Rouse Library, Hattiesburg MS. 601-582-5051, Ext 245 & 246

Pound, Marilyn M, *Asst Dir, Per & Bibliog Instr,* William Carey College, I E Rouse Library, Hattiesburg MS. 601-582-5051, Ext 245 & 246

Pound, Mary E, *Publications Coordr,* University of Texas Libraries (General), Austin TX. 512-471-3811

Pounds, Beth, *Dir,* Palatka Public Library, Palatka FL. 904-328-2385

Poundstone, Kathie, *ILL,* Porterville Public Library, Porterville CA. 209-784-0177, 784-1400, Ext 523

Poundstone, Sally, *Dir,* Mamaroneck Free Library, Mamaroneck NY. 914-698-1250

Pounian, Barbara, *Librn,* Trans-Union Corporation Library, Lincolnshire IL. 312-295-4200

Pourciau, Jr, Lester J, *Dir,* Memphis State University Libraries, Memphis TN. 901-454-2201

Pourron, Eleanor, *YA,* Arlington County Department of Libraries, Arlington Public Library, Arlington VA. 703-527-4777

Poush, Virginia, *Bkmobile Coordr,* Hastings - Adams County Library, Hastings NE. 402-463-9855

Pousson, Marie, *Librn,* Acadia Parish Library (Iota Branch), Iota LA. 318-788-1880

Povey, Cherry M, *Chief Librn,* Veterans Administration, Medical Center Library, Reno NV. 702-786-7200, Ext 470

Povilaitis, Leanna, *ILL & Ad,* Madison Public Library, Madison NJ. 201-377-0722

Povilonis, Louise E, *Tech Processes,* Hartford Public Library, Hartford CT. 203-525-9121

Povsic, Frances, *Curriculum,* Bowling Green State University Library, Bowling Green OH. 419-372-2856

Powden, Doreen, *Librn,* Minot-Sleeper Library, Bristol NH. 603-744-3352

Powell, Anice, *Dir,* Sunflower County Library System, Indianola MS. 601-887-2153, 887-2298

Powell, Antoinette, *Librn,* University of Kentucky (Agriculture), Lexington KY. 606-258-2758

Powell, Barbara, *ILL & Ref,* Concord Free Public Library, Concord MA. 617-369-5324

Powell, Bettie, *Acq,* Fort Hays State University, Forsyth Library, Hays KS. 913-628-4431

Powell, Betty J, *Asst Librn,* United States Navy (Marine Corps Air Station Library), Santa Ana CA. 714-559-2569, 3474

Powell, Bobby H, *Librn,* Carraway Methodist Medical Center, Medical Library, Birmingham AL. 205-254-6265

Powell, Camille, *Librn,* Fluor Engineers & Constructors, Fluor Houston Library, Houston TX. 713-662-3959

Powell, Carolyn, *Librn,* Department of Public Libraries & Information (Windsor Wood), Virginia Beach VA. 804-340-1043

Powell, Carrie L, *Bkmobile Coordr,* Pendleton County Public Library, Falmouth KY. 606-654-8535

Powell, Charlene, *Librn,* Cherokee Regional Library (Menlo Branch), Menlo GA. 404-638-2992

Powell, Donald, *Res Bibliog,* Tucson Museum of Art Library, Tucson AZ. 602-623-4881

Powell, Elaine J, *Librn,* Todd County Public Library, Elkton KY. 502-265-9071

Powell, Elizabeth, *Rare Bks & Spec Coll,* Ector County Library, Odessa TX. 915-332-0633

Powell, Janice, *Ref,* University of Maryland at College Park (Theodore R McKeldin Library), College Park MD. 301-454-2853, 454-5977

Powell, Karen, *Asst Librn,* Emmanuel College Library, Franklin Springs GA. 404-245-7226, Ext 32

Powell, Kathleen A, *Ch,* Brunswick-Glynn County Regional Library, Brunswick GA. 912-264-7360

Powell, Kelley, *Pub Servs,* Santa Ana College, Nealley Library, Santa Ana CA. 714-835-3000, Ext 357

Powell, Lawrence Clark, *Emer Prof,* University of Arizona, Graduate Library School, AZ. 602-626-3565

Powell, Lois C, *Asst Dir & Tech Serv,* Macon Junior College Library, Macon GA. 912-474-2700, Ext 215, 216

Powell, Marjorie, *Cat,* Volusia County Public Libraries, Daytona Beach FL. 904-252-8374

Powell, Martha, *Librn,* Southern Baptist Theological Seminary (School of Church Music), Louisville KY. 502-897-4712

Powell, Maxine B, *Librn,* Procter & Gamble Co (Ivorydale Technical Center Library), Cincinnati OH. 513-562-1100

Powell, Michael E, *Dir,* Washington University Libraries (GWB School of Social Work), Saint Louis MO. 314-889-6616

Powell, Mrs Victor, *Ch & YA,* Crawfordsville District Public Library, Crawfordsville IN. 317-362-2242

Powell, Murella, *Genealogist,* Biloxi Public Library, Biloxi MS. 601-374-0330

Powell, N L, *Librn,* Catholic University of America (Nursing), Washington DC. 202-635-5411

Powell, Nancy, *Ad,* Renton Public Library, Renton WA. 206-235-2610

Powell, Nellie Lee, *Librn,* Catholic University of America (Biology, Chemistry & Physics), Washington DC. 202-635-5411

Powell, Netha Lea, *Asst,* Sabine Parish Library (Florein Branch), Florien LA. 318-256-2212

Powell, Patricia, *Librn,* West Virginia University Medical Center-Charleston Division, Learning Resources Center, Charleston WV. 304-347-1285

Powell, Patricia J, *Dir,* Fayetteville Area Health Education Center Library, Fayetteville NC. 919-323-1152

Powell, Paul R, *Dir,* Georgetown College, Cooke Memorial Library, Georgetown KY. 502-863-8011

Powell, Richard K, *Assoc Prof,* Andrews University, Library Science Dept, MI. 616-471-3549

Powell, Ronald, *Bibliog Instr,* Prince George's Community College, Learning Resources Center, Largo MD. 301-322-0462

Powell, Ronald R, *Asst Prof,* University of Michigan, School of Library Science, MI. 313-764-9376

Powell, Ruby, *Eng Lab-Tech,* State Technical Institute at Memphis, George E Freeman Library, Memphis TN. 901-377-4106

Powell, Russell, *Librn,* University of Kentucky (Engineering), Lexington KY. 606-258-2965

Powell, Ruth Ann, *Tech Serv,* Fairmont State College Library, Fairmont WV. 304-367-4121

Powell, Salley, *Circ,* Bethany Nazarene College, R T Williams Memorial Library, Bethany OK. 405-789-6400, Ext 276

Powell, Ted F, *Dir,* Church of Jesus Christ of Latter-Day Saints (Genealogical Society of Utah), Salt Lake City UT. 801-531-2323

Powell, Theresa, *Circ,* Rutgers University, the State University of New Jersey, John Cotton Dana Library, Newark NJ. 201-648-5222

Powell, Virginia, *AV, Music & Curriculum,* Wheaton College Library, Wheaton IL. 312-682-5101

Powell, Wayne B, *Sci & Eng Librn,* Tufts University (Richard H Lufkin Engineering), Medford MA. 617-628-5000, Ext 235

Power, Anna, *Circ,* Fall River Public Library, Fall River MA. 617-676-8541

Power, Catherine, *Spec Coll,* Newfoundland Public Library Services (Provincial Reference Dept), Saint John's NF. 709-737-3964

Power, Hattie, *Dir,* Chicago Public Library (Woodson Regional), Chicago IL. 312-881-6900

Power, Loease, *Asst Librn,* Jasonville Public Library, Jasonville IN. 812-665-3366

Power, Margaret, *ILL & Ref,* De Paul University Libraries (Lincoln Park Campus Library), Chicago IL. 312-321-7934

Power, Mary F, *Ref,* National Gerontology Resource Center, National Retired Teachers Asn-American Asn of Retired Persons, Washington DC. 202-872-4844

Power, Pauline V, *Tech Serv,* University of Texas Medical Branch, Moody Medical Library, Galveston TX. 713-765-1971

Power, Terri, *Ch,* Baldwin Public Library, Baldwin WI. 715-684-3813

Powers, Anna Laura, *Librn,* Galva Public Library, Galva IL. 309-932-2180

Powers, Anne, *Ref,* Santa Monica College Library, Santa Monica CA. 213-450-5150

Powers, Barbara S, *Librn,* Sanbornton Public Library, Sanbornton NH. 603-286-8288

Powers, Beatrice, *ILL, Ref & Govt Ref Librn,* San Diego County Library, San Diego CA. 714-565-5100

Powers, Beverly A, *Dir,* Butler Public Library, Butler PA. 412-287-5576

Powers, Carol, *Ref,* University of Central Arkansas, Torreyson Library, Conway AR. 501-329-2931, Ext 449

Powers, Charles, *AV,* University of Massachusetts at Amherst Library, Amherst MA. 413-545-0284

Powers, Charles V, *Dir,* Queen Anne's County Free Library, Centreville MD. 301-758-0980

Powers, Christine, *Media & Ref,* Windsor Public Library, Windsor CT. 203-688-6433

Powers, Cleo, *Media,* University of Wisconsin-Eau Claire, William D McIntyre Library, Eau Claire WI. 715-836-3715

Powers, Denise, *Circ,* Northland Public Library, Pittsburgh PA. 412-366-8100, 366-8167

Powers, Geraldine, *Librn,* Beth Am Congregation Community Temple, Dorothy Feldman Library, Cleveland OH. 216-321-1000

Powers, James C, *Ad,* Ashland Public Library, Ashland KY. 606-324-4195

Powers, Jane, *Librn,* East Ridge Library, Hankins NY. 914-887-5499

Powers, Jane B, *Dir,* Township of Hamilton Free Public Library, Trenton NJ. 609-890-3460

Powers, Jewett, *Librn,* Ames Laboratory Document Library, Technical Information Department, Ames IA. 515-294-1856

Powers, Kathleen A, *Circ,* Loyola University of Chicago Libraries (Law School Library), Chicago IL. 312-670-2952

Powers, Kathleen A, *ILL,* Massachusetts Institute of Technology Libraries, Cambridge MA. 617-253-5651

Powers, Lois, *Librn,* Wilburton Public Library, Wilburton OK. 918-465-3751

Powers, Mary A, *ILL & Ref,* Clark University, Robert Hutchings Goddard Library, Worcester MA. 617-793-7573

Powers, Mary Carol, *Librn,* Watertown Free Public Library, Watertown WI. 414-261-5757

Powers, Mary Jo, *Dir & Head Librn,* Albany Public Library, Albany WI. 608-862-3491

Powers, Nancy, *Acq,* Atlanta Public Library, Atlanta GA. 404-688-4636

Powers, Patricia, *Ad,* Prince Memorial Library, Cumberland Center ME. 207-829-3180

Powers, Ruth, *Librn,* Meigs Local School District Public Library (Middleport Branch), Middleport OH. 614-992-5713

Powers, Sister D, *ILL & Ref,* Marianopolis College Library, Montreal PQ. 514-931-8792

Powers, Jr, William, *Librn,* Cook County Law Library, Chicago IL. 312-443-5423

Poyer, Helen, *Ad,* Glenside Public Library District, Glendale Heights IL. 618-858-0840

Poyer, Robert K, *Pub Servs & Bibliog Instr,* Medical University of South Carolina Library, Charleston SC. 803-792-2374

Pozezanac, Bess, *Librn,* Lake County Public Library (Cedar Lake Public), Cedar Lake IN. 219-374-7121

Pracejus, W Glenn, *Dir,* Electrical Testing Laboratories, Inc Library, Cortland NY. 607-288-2600
Pradd, Louise La, *Bkmobile Coordr,* Grant County Public Library, Williamstown KY. 606-824-4723
Praeter, Jacqueline K, *Librn,* Mary L Cook Public Library, Waynesville OH. 513-897-4826
Prager, Herta, *Librn,* United States Court of Appeals, Second Circuit Court Library, New York NY. 212-791-1052
Pragnell, Ruth, *Librn,* General Theological Library, Boston MA. 617-227-4557
Prahl, Jeanne, *Cat,* Morley Library, Painesville OH. 216-352-3383
Prakash, Carla, *Ref,* Washington County Library, Lake Elmo MN. 612-777-8143
Prakash, Carla, *Librn,* Washington County Library (Park-Grove), Cottage Grove MN. 612-459-2040
Pralle, Marilee, *Per,* Phillips University (John Rogers Graduate Seminary Library), Enid OK. 405-237-4433, Ext 227
Pralle, Ruth, *ILL,* Alma College Library, Alma MI. 517-463-2141, Ext 332
Prancl, Charles, *Media,* Queensborough Community College Library, Bayside NY. 212-631-6226
Prange, Roberta L, *Dir,* Eagle River Public Library, Eagle River WI. 715-479-8070
Prangley, Adelaide, *Librn,* Haskell Free Library, Derby Line VT. 819-876-2471
Prangley, Adelaide, *Librn,* Haskell Free Library, Inc, Rock Island PQ. 819-876-2471
Pranulis, Trudy, *Librn,* Marissa Public Library, Marissa IL. 618-295-2825
Prater, Darlene, *Librn,* Logan County District Library (DeGraff Branch), Bellefontaine OH. 513-585-5000
Prater, Faye, *Librn,* Bolivar County Library (Gunnison Public), Gunnison MS. 601-747-2213
Prather, Kathryn, *Dir,* Post Falls Public Library, Post Falls ID. 208-773-3511
Prator, Georgena, *Cat,* Houston Baptist University, Moody Memorial Library, Houston TX. 713-774-7661, Ext 303
Pratt, Angie M, *Circ,* Washington County Library, Saint George UT. 801-673-2562
Pratt, Barbara, *Librn,* Dickinson County Library (Norway Branch), Norway MI. 906-563-8617
Pratt, Bob, *Bkmobile Coordr,* North Arkansas Regional Library, Harrison AR. 501-741-3665
Pratt, Carolyn A, *Dir,* Audubon Regional Library, Clinton LA. 504-683-8753
Pratt, Dana, *Dir, Publ Off,* Library of Congress, Washington DC. 202-287-5000
Pratt, David, *Librn,* Piedmont College, E Louise Patten Library, Demorest GA. 404-778-4196
Pratt, Doris, *Librn,* Melrose Public Library (Highlands), Melrose MA. 617-665-7493
Pratt, Doris, *Libr Assts,* Surry Community College, Learning Resources Center, Dobson NC. 919-386-8121, Ext 52
Pratt, Florine, *Librn,* Chicago Public Library (Hall), Chicago IL. 312-536-2275
Pratt, Hal, *Dir,* Township Library of Lower Southampton, Feasterville PA. 215-355-1183
Pratt, Laura C, *Librn,* Maryland College of Art & Design Library, Silver Spring MD. 301-649-4454
Pratt, Leoma, *Librn,* Tyler Courier-Times-Telegraph Library, Tyler TX. 214-597-8111
Pratt, Lucille, *ILL,* North Arkansas Regional Library, Harrison AR. 501-741-3665
Pratt, Molly, *Asst Librn,* Bozeman Public Library, Bozeman MT. 406-586-2148
Pratt, Mrs E, *Librn,* Windsor Public Library (South Walkerville), Windsor ON. 519-253-3600
Pratt, Pamela, *Ref,* University of Charleston, Andrew S Thomas Memorial Library, Charleston WV. 304-346-1400
Pratt, Patricia, *Media,* Southern Adirondack Library System, Saratoga Springs NY. 518-584-7300, 792-3343, 885-1073
Pratt, Patty, *Librn,* Community Methodist Hospital, Doctors' Memorial Library, Paragould AR. 501-236-7733, Ext 112
Pratt, R L, *Librn,* Illinois College, Schewe Library, Jacksonville IL. 217-245-7126, Ext 227
Pratt, Ruth, *Librn,* Gilford Public Library, Gilford NH. 603-524-6042
Pratt, V Lorraine, *Dir,* S R I International Library, Research Information Services, Menlo Park CA. 415-326-6200, Ext 2634

Pratt, Virginia, *Librn,* University of California, Berkeley (Library School), Berkeley CA. 415-642-2253
Praver, Robin, *Cat,* Mobil Oil Corp, Secretariat Library, New York NY. 212-883-2454
Pray, Wilma, *Tech Serv,* Hanover College, Duggan Library, Hanover IN. 812-866-2151, Ext 333
Preast, Christine, *In Charge,* Cobb County Public Library System (Kennesaw Branch), Kennesaw GA. 404-422-2140
Precoda, Robert, *Librn,* Northwest Regional Library, Georgia VT. 802-524-3429
Preece, Bonnie M, *Librn,* Blake, Cassels & Graydon, Law Library, Toronto ON. 416-863-2650
Preece-Canfield, Rebecca, *Librn,* National Oceanic & Atmospheric Administration, Geophysical Fluid Dynamics Laboratory Library, Princeton NJ. 609-452-6550
Preibish, Andre, *Dir, Coll Develop Br,* National Library of Canada, Ottawa ON. 613-995-9481
Preiser, Sharon, *ILL,* Indiana University at Kokomo, Learning Resource Center, Kokomo IN. 317-453-2000, Ext 237
Preisler, Mary Ann, *Librn,* Standard Oil Co (Ohio) (Vistron Information Services), Cleveland OH. 216-575-4141
Preisler, Rene, *Pub Servs Librn,* Los Angeles County-University of Southern California (General Hospital Library), Los Angeles CA. 213-226-2622
Preiss, Margaret, *Commun Res,* Saint Charles City County Library, Saint Peters MO. 314-441-2300
Prelec, Antonija, *Coordr Tech Servs,* State University of New York (Health Sciences Center Library), East Setauket NY. 516-246-2512
Preminger, Alexander, *Coll Develop,* Hofstra University Library, Hempstead NY. 516-560-3475
Premont, M Jacques, *Dir,* Assemblee Nationale, Bibliotheque de la Legislature, Quebec PQ. 418-643-2121
Prendergast, Sharon, *ILL,* Gonzaga University, Crosby Library, Spokane WA. 509-328-4220, Ext 3132
Prendes, Ena, *Fed Doc,* University of Florida Libraries (Agriculture), Gainesville FL. 904-392-1934
Prentice, Ann E, *Dir,* University of Tennessee, Knoxville, Graduate School of Library & Information Science, TN. 615-974-2148
Prentice, B, *Acq,* Shoreham-Wading River Public Library, Shoreham NY. 516-929-4488
Prentice, Barbara, *Ser,* Williams College, Sawyer Library, Williamstown MA. 413-597-2501
Prentice, Drene, *Ed Canadiana,* National Library of Canada, Ottawa ON. 613-995-9481
Prentice, Ruth, *ILL,* Wascana Institute of Applied Arts & Sciences, Resource & Information Center, Regina SK. 306-565-4321
Presberry, Rosa, *Sch Libr Media Specialists,* Maryland State Department of Education, Division of Library Development & Services, Baltimore MD. 301-796-8300, Ext 284
Presby, Richard, *Librn,* JHK & Associates Technical Library, Emeryville CA. 415-428-2550
Prescott, Barbara W, *Dir,* Jefferson County Library, Louisville GA. 912-625-3751
Prescott, Helen W, *Dir,* Imperial Public Library, Imperial CA. 714-355-1332
Prescott, Myrtle G, *Librn,* Adat Shalom Synagogue Library, Farmington MI. 313-851-5100
Prescott, Ruth A, *Tech Serv,* Kinchafoonee Regional Library, Dawson GA. 912-995-2902
Prescott, Sandra, *Librn,* Sheffield Public Library, Sheffield IA. 515-892-4717
Preshiren, Rosemary, *Ref & ILL,* Sioux Falls Public Library, Sioux Falls SD. 605-339-7081
President, Pat, *Archivist,* College of Medicine & Dentistry of New Jersey, George F Smith Library of the Health Sciences, Newark NJ. 201-456-4500
Preslan, Kristina, *Librn,* San Bernardino County Library (Rancho Cucamonga), Cucamonga CA. 714-987-3107
Preslar, M Gail, *Asst Res Librn,* Tennessee Eastman Co (Research Library), Kingsport TN. 615-246-2111, Ext 2541, 3870
Presley, June, *Media,* Kingsport Public Library, J Fred Johnson Memorial Library, Kingsport TN. 615-245-3141

Presley, Marion, *ILL,* Monmouth College, Guggenheim Library, West Long Branch NJ. 201-222-6600, Ext 264
Presnell, Ruth F, *Ad,* Haywood County Public Library, Waynesville NC. 704-452-5169
Press, Nancy Boyle, *AV,* Baltimore Museum of Art Library, Baltimore MD. 301-396-6317
Presseau, Jane T, *On-Line Servs & Bibliog Instr,* Presbyterian College, James H Thomason Library, Clinton SC. 803-833-2820, Ext 214
Pressen, Ruth, *Librn,* Scott Sebastian Regional Library (Huntington Library), Huntington AR. 501-996-2856
Presser, Carolynne, *Asst Librn for EMS Libr,* University of Waterloo Library, Waterloo ON. 519-885-1211
Presser, Richard, *Ref,* Manhattan School of Music, Frances Hall Ballard Library, New York NY. 212-749-2802, Ext 507, 510, 511, 512
Pressey, Patricia B, *Assoc Dir,* Iliff School of Theology, Ira J Taylor Library, Denver CO. 303-744-1287, Ext 30
Pressing, Kirk, *Supvr, Cent Libr Servs,* Milwaukee Public Library, Milwaukee WI. 414-278-3000
Pressler, Wayne N, *Ref,* Southwestern College Library, Chula Vista CA. 714-421-6700, Ext 237
Pressley, William, *Admin,* Atlanta Historical Society Library, Atlanta GA. 404-261-1837
Pressman, Sylvia, *ILL,* Henry Ford Community College, Eshleman Library, Dearborn MI. 313-271-2750, Ext 378
Presson, Peggy F, *Librn,* National Distillers & Chemical Corp, United States Industrial Chemicals Co Division Library, New York NY. 212-949-5299
Prestage, Margaret, *Librn,* Jackson Metropolitan Library (Pelahatchie Library), Pelahatchie MS. 601-352-3677
Preston, Ann, *Spec Coll,* Drexel University Library, Philadelphia PA. 215-895-2750
Preston, Bonita, *ILL & Ref,* Catonsville Community College, Learning Resources Div, Baltimore MD. 301-455-4586
Preston, Carol, *Librn,* Hudson's Bay Co Library, Winnipeg MB. 204-943-0881, Ext 269
Preston, Catherine M, *Librn,* Tobacco Merchants Association of the United States, Howard S Cullman Library, New York NY. 212-239-4435
Preston, Gregor A, *Cat,* University of California at Davis, General Library, Davis CA. 916-752-2110
Preston, James, *Commun Servs,* Veterans Memorial Public Library, Bismarck ND. 701-222-6410
Preston, Jean, *Mss,* Princeton University Library, Princeton NJ. 609-452-3180
Preston, Laura, *Librn,* Bureau of Land Management, Idaho State Office Library, Boise ID. 208-334-1436
Preston, Leona, *Librn,* Whiteriver Public Library, Whiteriver AZ. 602-338-4884
Preston, Linda D, *Librn,* National Oceanic & Atmospheric Administration, National Climatic Center Library, Asheville NC. 704-258-2850, Ext 677
Preston, Lucille, *Librn,* De Leon Public Library, De Leon TX. 817-893-2530
Preston, Lynn, *Librn,* Hastings Public Library, Hastings ON. 705-696-2111
Preston, Marcia, *Bibliog Instr,* University of Michigan-Dearborn Library, Dearborn MI. 313-593-5400
Preston, Nadine, *Librn,* Magoffin County Library, Salyersville KY. 606-349-2411
Preston, Rita, *Tech Serv,* Saint John's Seminary, Edward Laurence Doheny Memorial Library, Camarillo CA. 805-482-4697
Preston, Steven L, *Dir,* College of Southern Idaho Library, Twin Falls ID. 208-733-9554, Ext 236
Preston, Steven L, *Head,* College of Southern Idaho, Library Technology Curriculum, ID. 208-733-9554, Ext 236
Preston, Virginia, *Tech Serv Supvr,* Saint Louis Public Library, Saint Louis MO. 314-241-2288
Preston, William J, *Chief Libr Servs,* Veterans Administration, Medical Center Library, West Haven CT. 203-932-5711
Prestridge, Mrs Clyde, *Librn,* Exxon Chemical Co USA (B R Chemical Plant Laboratory Library), Baton Rouge LA. 504-359-5211
Pretorius, Jean, *Coordr,* Kern County Library (Beale Memorial), Bakersfield CA. 805-861-2130

Pretorius, Jean N, *Asst Dir,* Kern County Library, Bakersfield CA. 805-861-2130
Preuit, Ruby, *Librn, Acq & Spec Coll,* Platte County Public Library, Wheatland WY. 307-322-2689
Preuss, Florence L, *Dir,* Pinckney Community Public Library, Pinckney MI. 313-878-3888
Prevedel, Vivian, *Tech Serv,* Alhambra Public Library, Alhambra CA. 213-570-5008
Prever, Phil, *Dir,* New Hampshire Vocational-Technical Library, Claremont NH. 603-542-7744
Prevett, Marie, *Tech Serv,* Mount Ida Junior College, Hallden Library, Newton Centre MA. 617-969-7000, Ext 152
Previti, Andrea, *Ch,* Meriden Public Library, Meriden CT. 203-238-2344
Prevost, K A, *Librn,* Presbyterian College Library, Montreal PQ. 514-288-5256
Prewitt, Barbara G, *Librn,* Rohm & Haas Co (Bristol Research Laboratories), Spring House PA. 215-785-8055
Prewitt, Eileen, *Librn,* Henry County Library, Eminence KY. 502-845-5682
Prewitt, Laura, *Dir,* North Richland Hills Public Library, Fort Worth TX. 817-281-8416
Prezel, Linda, *Asst Children's Servs,* Bethel Park Public Library, Bethel Park PA. 412-835-2207
Pribram, Helen, *Ref,* Russell Public Library, Middletown CT. 203-347-2528
Pribramska, Milena, *Media,* Maplewood Memorial Library, Maplewood NJ. 201-762-1622
Pricco, Laviala, *Librn,* Bessemer Public Library, Bessemer MI. 906-667-0404
Price, Adrienne, *Librn,* Bradford Public Library, Bradford ON. 416-775-6482
Price, Anna, *Ser,* Montana State University, Roland R Renne Library, Bozeman MT. 406-994-3119
Price, Bernice H, *Librn,* Professional Golfers Association of America Library, Lake Park FL. 305-844-5000
Price, Carol, *Cat,* Floral Park Public Library, Floral Park NY. 516-354-0666
Price, Carolyn, *Librn,* Dayton & Montgomery County Public Library (Vandalia Branch), Vandalia OH. 513-898-6541
Price, Cheryl, *Polit Sci & Law,* Northern Illinois University, Founders Memorial Library, De Kalb IL. 815-753-1094
Price, David M, *Dir,* Aurora Public Library, Aurora CO. 303-750-5000, Ext 410
Price, G, *Librn,* London Public Libraries & Museums (R E Crouch Branch), London ON. 519-673-0111
Price, Genevieve R, *Ch,* Omaha Public Library, W Dale Clark Library, Omaha NE. 402-444-4800
Price, George W, *Media,* Slippery Rock State College Library, Slippery Rock PA. 412-794-2510
Price, Gloria, *Librn,* Sno-Isle Regional Library (Mountlake Terrace Branch), Mountlake Terrace WA. 206-776-8722
Price, Harry, *Coordr,* Lehigh Valley Association of Independent Colleges, Inc, PA. 215-691-6131
Price, Hazel, *Librn,* Burlington Public Library (Kilbridge), Burlington ON. 416-335-6394
Price, Helen D, *Dir,* Oneida County Free Library, Malad City ID. 208-766-2229
Price, Janet, *State Aid & Cert Consult,* Massachusetts Board of Library Commissioners, Office for the Development of Library Services, Boston MA. 617-267-9400
Price, John F, *Chief, Sci & Tech Div,* Library of Congress, Washington DC. 202-287-5000
Price, John J, *Chief, Libr Serv,* Veterans Administration, Hospital Library, Brooklyn NY. 212-838-6600, Ext 278
Price, Judy, *Circ,* Umatilla County Library, Pendleton OR. 503-276-1881
Price, Kathleen, *Dir,* Duke University (Law School Library), Durham NC. 919-684-2847
Price, Kathleen, *Dir,* University of Minnesota Libraries-Twin Cities (Law Library), Minneapolis MN. 612-373-2737
Price, Lane, *Unifour Circuit Libn,* Wake Forest University (Bowman Gray School of Medicine Library), Winston-Salem NC. 919-727-4691
Price, Larry C, *Asst Dir,* Berkshire Athenaeum, Pittsfield Public Library, Pittsfield MA. 413-442-1559
Price, Leslie, *Ch,* Framingham Public Library, Framingham MA. 617-879-3570

Price, Mary, *Chairman,* Crowsnest Municipal Library, Coleman AB. 403-562-8393
Price, May E, *Cat,* University of California at Davis (Health Sciences Library), Davis CA. 916-752-1214
Price, Millicent, *Ref,* Plano Public Library System, Plano TX. 214-423-6502, 867-1002
Price, Nancy P, *Librn,* Oaklawn Psychiatric Center, Staff Library, Elkhart IN. 219-294-3551
Price, Neil V, *Chmn,* University of North Dakota, Dept of Library Science & Audiovisual Instruction, ND. 701-777-3003
Price, Norma, *YA,* Bloomfield Public Library, Northwest Essex Area Library, Bloomfield NJ. 201-429-9292
Price, Paulette, *ILL,* Schools of Theology in Dubuque Library, Dubuque IA. 319-589-3100, 556-8151
Price, Phyllis D, *Cat,* Clinch Valley College of the University of Virginia, John Cook Wyllie Library, Wise VA. 703 328 2431, Ext 255
Price, R, *Media,* Methodist Medical Center of Illinois (Learning Resource Center-School of Nursing Library & Audio Visual), Peoria IL. 309-672-5570
Price, Richard Lee, *In Charge,* Civil Court of the City of New York Library, New York NY. 212-374-8043
Price, Robert, *Dir,* Gloucester Public Library, Bibliotheque Publique de Gloucester, Ottawa ON. 613-824-8366
Price, Robert V, *Asst Prof,* Baylor University, Dept of Library Science, TX. 817-755-2410
Price, Rose M, *Librn,* Brakeley, John Price Jones Inc Library, New York NY. 212-697-7120
Price, Stephanie, *Librn,* Beech-Nut Foods Corp Library, Canajoharie NY. 518-673-3251
Price, Thelma, *Librn,* Saint Louis Public Library (Walnut Park), Saint Louis MO. 314-383-1210
Price, Verna W, *Dir,* Lake County Library, Lakeview OR. 503-947-2321
Price, William P, *Chief Librn,* Veterans Administration, Hospital Health Science Library, Kerrville TX. 512-896-2020
Price, Jr, James H, *Dir,* Stanly Technical Institute, Learning Resources Center, Albemarle NC. 704-982-0121
Prichard, Bro Leo, *ILL, Ref & Tech Serv,* Conception Abbey & Conception Seminary College Library, Conception MO. 816-944-2211
Prichard, Donald, *Acq,* Erie Community College-North, Library Resources Center, Buffalo NY. 716-634-0800
Prichard, Hazel W, *Dir,* Southwest Arkansas Regional Library, Hope AR. 501-777-4564
Pricone, Rosellyn R, *Librn,* Wilson, Haight & Welch Business Library, Hartford CT. 203-278-1500, Ext 280
Pride, Richard, *Assoc Dir,* Midcontinental Regional Medical Library Program, NE. 402-541-4646, 541-4006
Pride, Richard B, *Midcontinental Regional Med Libr Program,* University of Nebraska Medical Center, Library of Medicine, Omaha NE. 402-541-4006
Prideaux, Jerome, *Administrative Service,* Contra Costa County Library, Pleasant Hill CA. 415-944-3423
Pridham, Sherman, *Dir,* Portsmouth Public Library, Portsmouth NH. 603-431-2000, Ext 252
Pridmore, Kathy, *Librn,* Peoria Journal Star Library, Peoria IL. 309-686-3021
Priebe, Betty, *Librn,* DePaul Rehabilitation Hospital, Staff Library, Milwaukee WI. 414-281-4400, Ext 424, 425
Priest, Betty, *Bkmobile Coordr,* Bladen County Public Library, Elizabethtown NC. 919-862-8171
Priest, Cheryl D, *Dir,* William H & Edgar Magness Community House & Library, McMinnville TN. 615-473-2428
Priest, Margaret, *Librn,* Jaffrey Public Library, Jaffrey NH. 603-532-7301
Priest, Susan, *Acq, Cat & Ref,* Citizens Library, Washington PA. 412-222-2400
Priest, Susan, *Genealogy & Local Hist,* Citizens Library, Washington PA. 412-222-2400
Priestly, D, *Librn,* University of Victoria (Law), Victoria BC. 604-477-6911
Prieto, Mary Lou, *Dir,* Oradell Free Public Library, Oradell NJ. 201-262-2613

Prieto, Mrs Pura, *Librn,* Miami-Dade Public Library System (Grapeland Heights), Miami FL. 305-638-6345
Priller, Jane, *Cat,* Normal Public Library, Normal IL. 309-452-1757
Prilop, Iona, *Librn,* Blue Cross & Blue Shield of Greater New York, Reference Library, New York NY. 212-481-2386
Prim, Philip L, *ILL & Ref,* Temple Public Library, Temple TX. 817-778-5555
Prince, Barbara, *Ref,* Dartmouth Regional Library, Dartmouth NS. 902-466-7613
Prince, Katrina, *Libr Techn,* University of Oklahoma (Drama), Norman OK. 405-325-4201
Prince, Mary R, *Reader's Adviser,* Mississippi Valley State University, James Herbert White Library, Itta Bena MS. 601-254-9041, Ext 6340
Prince, Mrs R T, *Librn,* Jackson Metropolitan Library (Mize Library), Mize MS. 601-352-3677
Prince, Phyllis E, *Librn,* Champion International Corp, Corporate Library, Stamford CT. 203 358-7000
Prince, Roger O, *Dir,* Wooster Community Art Center Library, Danbury CT. 203-744-4825
Prince, Runcie, *Librn,* Public Library of Nashville & Davidson County (Edgehill), Nashville TN. 615-298-3173
Prince, Ruth E, *Librn,* Saskatchewan Department of the Attorney General (Queen's Bench & District Court Library), Regina SK. 306-565-5391
Prince, W, *Undergrad,* State University of New York at Buffalo, University Libraries, Buffalo NY. 716-636-2965
Prince, William, *Librn,* State University of New York at Buffalo (Undergraduate), Buffalo NY. 716-636-2943
Prince, Wynona, *Circ & Ref,* Letourneau College, Margaret Estes Library, Longview TX. 214-753-0231, Ext 230
Princz, Joseph, *Assoc Dir,* Concordia University Library, Montreal PQ. 514-879-2820
Prine, Cynthia, *Librn,* Volusia County Public Libraries (S Cornelia Young Memorial), Daytona Beach FL. 904-252-8374
Prine, Jr, S Stephen, *Dir,* South Carolina State Library, Division for the Blind & Physically Handicapped, Cayce SC. 803-758-2726
Pringle, Daphne S, *Librn,* New York University Medical Center (Patients' & Staff Library), New York NY. 212-679-3200, Ext 3404
Pringle, J Howard, *ILL,* Waukesha Public Library, Waukesha WI. 414-542-4297
Pringle, Linda D, *Librn,* Bryan Public Library, Bryan TX. 713-823-8021
Pringle, Terry, *Librn,* San Bernardino County Library (Loma Linda Branch), Loma Linda CA. 714-796-8621
Prinstert, Inez Dillion, *Asst Archivist,* Museum of Western Colorado, Museum Archives, Grand Junction CO. 303-242-0971
Pritchard, C J, *Acq,* University of Regina Library, Regina SK. 306-584-4132
Pritchard, Dolores, *ILL & Ref,* Corvallis Public Library, Corvallis-Benton County Library, Corvallis OR. 503-757-6928
Pritchard, Doris, *Librn,* University of Manitoba Libraries (Dental), Winnipeg MB. 204-786-3635
Pritchard, Eileen, *Sci,* California Polytechnic State University Library, San Luis Obispo CA. 805-546-2345
Pritchard, Hugh, *Ref & Bibliog Instr,* University of New Hampshire, Ezekiel W Dimond Library, Durham NH. 603-862-1540
Pritchard, John A, *Dir,* Catawba County Library, Newton NC. 704-464-2421
Pritchard, Joseph, *Media,* University of Wisconsin-Superior, Jim Dan Hill Library, Superior WI. 715-392-8101, Ext 346
Pritchard, Joseph W, *Instr,* University of Wisconsin-Superior, Library Science Program, WI. 715-392-8101, Ext 346, 347
Pritchard, Mary, *Librn,* Bangor Public Library, Bangor PA. 215-588-4136
Pritchard, Mary, *Asst Librn,* United States Army (Corps of Engineers, Seattle District Library), Seattle WA. 206-764-3728
Pritchard, Patricia, *Ch,* Fondulac Public Library District, East Peoria IL. 309-699-3917
Pritchard, Russ, *Dir,* Military Order of the Loyal Legion of the United States, War Library & Museum, Philadelphia PA. 215-735-8196

PRITCHETT

Pritchett, D Wayne, *Dir Educ,* King's College Library, Charlotte NC. 704-372-0266

Pritchett, Emma Lou, *Librn,* Louisville Free Public Library (Jeffersontown), Louisville KY. 502-267-5713

Pritchett, John, *Instr,* Appalachian State University, Department of Educational Media: Librarianship & Instructional Technology, NC. 704-262-2243

Pritchett, Mona, *Acq & Ref,* Meridian Junior College Library, Meridian MS. 601-483-8241, Ext 240

Pritchett, Morgan H, *Md,* Enoch Pratt Free Library, Baltimore MD. 301-396-5430, 396-5395

Pritchett, Myra S, *Librn,* Veterans Administration, Hospital Library, Manchester NH. 603-624-4366

Pritchett, Pauline, *Librn,* Ozark Regional Library (Fredericktown Branch), Fredericktown MO. 314-783-2120

Pritkin, Joel M, *Curator,* Music Center Operating Company Archives, Los Angeles CA. 213-972-7499

Pritsky, Gretchen, *Outreach,* Way Public Library, Perrysburg OH. 419-874-3135

Pritting, Mary, *AV & YA,* Rahway Free Public Library, Rahway NJ. 201-388-0761

Prival, Herbert, *ILL,* Yeshiva University Libraries (Landowne-Bloom Library), New York NY. 212-790-0238

Privat, Jeannette M, *Librn,* Seattle-First National Bank Library, Seattle WA. 206-583-4056

Probst, Christina, *Educational Asst,* Tanner Memorial Hospital, Allied Health Science Library, Carrollton GA. 404-834-8811, Ext 543

Probst, Helena, *Circ,* Spring Arbor College, Hugh A White Library, Spring Arbor MI. 517-750-1200, Ext 234

Probst, Virginia, *Librn,* Holbrook Public Library, Holbrook AZ. 602-524-3732

Probsting, Lenore, *Ch,* Riverton Free Public Library, Riverton NJ. 609-829-2476

Prochovnick, Ammiel, *Res Servs,* John Crerar Library, Chicago IL. 312-225-2526

Procopio, Concetta E, *Librn,* Liberty Mutual Insurance Co (Law Library), Boston MA. 617-357-9500, Ext 3359

Procopio, Lou, *Media,* North Shore Community College, Learning Resource Center, Beverly MA. 617-927-4850, Ext 195, 199, 237

Procter, Elizabeth, *Supvr,* Huron County Public Library (Belgrave Branch), Belgrave ON. 519-887-9478

Procter, Letitia B, *Librn,* Brooks Memorial Art Gallery Library, Memphis TN. 901-726-5266

Proctor, Anne, *Librn,* Contra Costa County Library (Oakley Branch), Oakley CA. 415-625-2400

Proctor, Barbara, *Tech Serv,* Eastern Oklahoma District Library System, Muskogee OK. 918-683-2846

Proctor, Betty, *Secretary,* Morris-Union Federation, New Providence NJ. 201-665-0311

Proctor, Betty C, *Dir,* New Providence Memorial Library, New Providence NJ. 201-665-0311

Proctor, David, *Ref & On-Line Servs,* Theodore F Jenkins Memorial Law Library, Philadelphia PA. 215-686-5692

Proctor, E, *Librn,* Madison Public Library (Lakeview), Madison WI. 608-266-6360

Proctor, Elizabeth, *Librn,* Middle Georgia Regional Library (Gordon Public), Gordon GA. 912-628-5352

Proctor, Elizabeth, *Librn,* Ministry of Consumer and Commercial Relations, Consumer Information Centre, Toronto ON. 416-963-0200

Proctor, Gregg, *ILL,* Sacramento Public Library, Sacramento CA. 916-440-5926

Proctor, Gwen, *Librn,* Kellogg Corp Library, Littleton CO. 303-794-1818

Proctor, Gwen M, *Librn,* Harman, O'Donnell & Henninger Library, Denver CO. 303-399-7602

Proctor, Judy C, *Dir,* Brazil Public Library, Brazil IN. 812-448-1981

Proctor, Linda, *Ser,* Jackson-George Regional Library System, Pascagoula MS. 601-762-3406

Proctor, Linda, *Librn,* Julia Adams Morse Memorial Library, Greene ME. 207-946-5544

Proctor, Margaret, *Cat,* Leominster Public Library, Leominster MA. 617-537-0941

Proctor, Martha Jane, *Statistics, Pub Rel & Publications,* State Library of Florida, Div of Library Services, Dept of State, Tallahassee FL. 904-487-2651

Proctor, Myrna, *Tech Serv,* Saint John Hospital, Medical Library, Detroit MI. 313-343-3733

Proctor, Patricia, *Bkmobile Services,* Spokane County Library, Spokane WA. 509-924-4122

Proctor, Tilley, *Librn,* Wake County Department of the Public Library (Fuguay-Varina Public), Fuquay-Varina NC. 919-552-5760

Proehl, Karl, *Maps & Atlases,* Pennsylvania State University, Fred Lewis Pattee Library, University Park PA. 814-865-0401

Proehl, Mercedes, *Librn,* Vernonia Public Library, Vernonia OR. 503-429-5291

Proeschel, Diana C, *Field Servs Librn,* United States Department of the Army (Office of the Adjutant General, Morale Support Directorate, Library Activities Division), Washington DC. 202-325-9700

Progar, Dorothy, *Dir,* Waco-McLennan County Library, Waco TX. 817-754-4694

Progar, Jim, *Dir,* Meridian Public Library, Meridian MS. 601-693-6771, 693-4913

Projansky, Matthew, *Media,* Goddard College, William Shipman Library, Plainfield VT. 802-454-8311, Ext 232

Prokop, Emma, *Librn,* Three Forks Community Library, Three Forks MT. 406-285-3747

Prokosch, Wendy, *Librn,* Mora Public Library, Mora MN. 612-679-2642

Promen, Peter J, *Dir & Acq,* Johns Hopkins University School of Advanced International Studies, Sydney R & Elsa W Mason Library, Washington DC. 202-785-6296

Promisel, Judy, *Librn,* Dataflow Systems, Inc Library, Bethesda MD. 301-654-9133

Pronovost, Muriel, *Assoc Prof,* Southern Connecticut State College, Div of Library Science & Instructional Technology, CT. 203-397-4532

Pront, Marsha, *Librn,* Proskauer Rose Goetz & Mendelsohn Library, New York NY. 212-593-9400

Prop, Dale, *Govt Publications,* Texas State Library, Austin TX. 512-475-2166

Proper, David R, *Librn,* Memorial Libraries, Henry N Flynt Library of Historic Deerfield & Pocumtuck Valley Memorial Asn Library, Deerfield MA. 413-772-0882

Proper, Dorothy, *Librn,* Atchison County Library, Rock Port MO. 816-744-5404

Proper, Fanna, *Librn,* Bradford-Wyoming County Libraries, Troy PA. 717-297-2436

Propes, Terry, *Librn,* Houston Public Library (Park Place), Houston TX. 713-645-4183

Propst, Mary Frances, *Dir,* Southside Regional Library, Boydton VA. 804-738-6580

Proscino, Patricia, *Acq & Ref,* Balch Institute for Ethnic Studies Library, Philadelphia PA. 215-925-8090

Pross, Cynthia, *Asst Librn,* Mutual of New York (Library Information Service), New York NY. 212-586-4000, Ext 703

Prosser, Esther, *Cat,* Norwich University, Henry Prescott Chaplin Memorial Library, Northfield VT. 802-485-5011, Ext 48

Prosser, Judith, *Tech Serv,* West Virginia Library Commission, Science & Cultural Center, Charleston WV. 304-348-2041

Prosser, Layton, *Ref,* North Dakota State School of Science, Mildred Johnson Library, Wahpeton ND. 701-671-2298

Prosser, Marilyn, *Librn,* Christian County Library, Ozark MO. 417-485-2432

Prosser, Ronald, *Circ,* Iowa City Public Library, Iowa City IA. 319-354-1265

Prostano, Emanuel T, *Dir,* Southern Connecticut State College, Div of Library Science & Instructional Technology, CT. 203-397-4532

Prothero, Kathy, *On-Line Servs,* Vigo County Public Library, Terre Haute IN. 812-232-1113

Prott, M Carl, *Assoc Prof,* Drexel University, School of Library & Information Science, PA. 215-895-2474

Prottsman, Mary Fran, *Chief Librn,* Veterans Administration, Medical Center Library, Fayetteville AR. 501-443-4301

Protzman, Lois A, *Librn,* Fort Hamilton-Hughes Memorial Hospital Center, Sohn Memorial Health Services Library, Hamilton OH. 513-867-2260

Protzman, Margaret, *Librn,* Sarah Lawrence College (Music), Bronxville NY. 914-337-0700, Ext 375

Proudfit, Elisabeth R, *In Charge,* Advertising Research Foundation Library, New York NY. 212-751-5656

Proulx, Gilles, *Librn,* Seminaire De Nicolet Library, Nicolet PQ. 819-293-4838

Proulx, Steven D, *Chief Librn,* Ottawa Citizen Library, Ottawa ON. 613-829-9100, Ext 317

Proust, Joycelyn, *ILL & Non-print Cat,* Long Beach Community College Learning Resources Division (Liberal Arts Campus Library), Long Beach CA. 213-420-4231

Prout, Edith, *ILL,* Jenkintown Library, Abington Library Society, Jenkintown PA. 215-884-0593

Provah, Gladys, *Ad,* Fairfield Public Library, Fairfield NJ. 201-227-3575

Provenzano, Laura, *ILL,* Suffolk County Community College (Selden Campus Library), Selden NY. 516-233-5181

Provost, Virginia, *Librn,* Township of Hamilton Free Public Library (Hamilton Square), Trenton NJ. 609-890-3786

Prowler, Joan, *Dir,* Uniondale Public Library, Uniondale NY. 516-489-2220

Prucha, Isabel, *Instr Libr Res,* West Valley College, Learning Resource Center, Saratoga CA. 408-867-2200, Ext 284

Prue, Holly, *Asst Librn,* Centennial College of Applied Arts & Technology (Warden Woods Resource Centre), Scarborough ON. 416-694-3241

Pruelz, Sadie, *Dir,* Morley Stanwood Community Public Library, Morley MI. 616-856-4298

Prueter, Sarah, *Circ & Historian,* Sturgis Public Library, Sturgis MI. 616-651-7907, 651-2321

Pruett, Mary B, *Librn,* Hickman County Public Library, Centerville TN. 615-729-5130

Pruett, Nancy, *Librn,* University of California Los Angeles Library (Geology-Geophysics), Los Angeles CA. 213-825-1055

Pruett, Vicki C, *Librn,* Maquon Township Library, Maquon IL. 309-875-3573

Pruitt, Rane, *Rare Bks,* Huntsville-Madison County Public Library, Huntsville AL. 205-536-0021

Pruksarnukul, Josefina, *Librn,* Scher Brothers, Inc Library, Clifton NJ. 201-471-1300

Prybis, Raymond, *In Charge,* Cluster of Independent Theological Schools, DC. 202-529-5244

Prybis, Raymond A, *Librn,* Oblate College Library, Washington DC. 202-529-5244

Pryde, Ann, *Tech Serv,* Sheridan County Fulmer Public Library, Sheridan WY. 307-674-8585, 674-9898

Pryjma, Marta, *Foreign Law,* Northwestern University, Chicago (School of Law Library), Chicago IL. 312-649-8450

Pryor, Carolyn P, *Asst Dir & Area Coordr,* Linden Free Public Library, Linden NJ. 201-486-3888

Pryor, Florence, *ILL,* John McIntire Public Library Public Library, Zanesville OH. 614-453-0391

Pryor, Nancy, *Head NW Section of Wash,* Washington State Library, Olympia WA. 206-753-5592

Pryse, Doris, *Librn,* Tulare County Library System (Alpaugh Branch), Alpaugh CA. 209-949-8355

Przybylski, Edmund S, *Dir,* Mundelein College, Learning Resource Center, Chicago IL. 312-262-8100, Ext 301, 302 & 303

Ptacek, William, *Adminr,* Eastern Idaho Regional Library System, Idaho Falls ID. 208-529-1450

Ptacek, William H, *Dir,* Idaho Falls Public Library, Idaho Falls ID. 208-529-1450

Ptasinski, Margaret, *Ch,* Long Beach Public Library, Long Beach NY. 516-432-7201

Puckett, C Doran, *Librn,* Worcester County Library (Berlin Branch), Berlin MD. 301-641-0650

Puckett, Josephine W, *Chief Librn,* Time-Life Books Inc, Reference Library, Alexandria VA. 703-960-5353

Puckett, Marianne, *Circ,* Louisiana State University School of Medicine in Shreveport, Medical Library, Shreveport LA. 318-226-3442

Puckett, Ranye, *Bks By Mail,* Meridian Public Library, Meridian MS. 601-693-6771, 693-4913

Puckett, Wilma, *Librn,* Wakeeney City Library, Wakeeney KS. 913-743-2960

Puddicombe, Lu, *Tech Serv,* Joliet Junior College, Learning Resource Center, Joliet IL. 815-729-9020, Ext 282

Pueschel, Judy, *Acq,* Skokie Public Library, Skokie IL. 312-673-7774

Puff, Anita, *Ch & YA,* Buena Park Library District, Buena Park CA. 714-826-4100
Puffenberger, Gelia K, *Librn,* Allegany County Library (South Cumberland), Cumberland MD. 301-724-1607
Puffer, David B, *Dir,* Johnson & Wales College Library, Providence RI. 401-456-1098, 456-1076
Puffer, Karen J, *Librn,* NASA, Dryden Flight Research Center Library, Edwards AFB CA. 805-258-3311, Ext 334
Puffer, Kathleen M, *Chief Librn,* Veterans Administration, Hospital Library Service, Loma Linda CA. 714-825-7084, Ext 2391
Puffer, Nathaniel H, *Asst Dir,* University of Delaware, Hugh M Morris Library, Newark DE. 302-738-2231
Puffer, Yvonne L, *Dir,* Newark Free Library, Newark DE. 302-731-7550
Puggle, Sister Teresa, *Librn,* Mount Saint Clare College Library, Clinton IA. 319-242-4023
Pugh, Constance, *Librn,* Schuylkill County Law Library, Pottsville PA. 717 622 5570, Ext 251
Pugh, Elizabeth, *Admin Asst,* ERIC Processing & Reference Facility, MD. 301-656-9723
Pugh, Eva, *Br Coordr,* Raleigh County Public Library, Beckley WV. 304-255-0511
Pugh, Eva, *Librn,* Raleigh County Public Library (Sophia Branch), Sophia WV. 304-255-0511
Pugh, Mary, *Librn,* Birmingham Public & Jefferson County Free Library (Southside), Birmingham AL. 205-254-2551
Pugliese, Paul, *Dir,* Duquesne University Library, Pittsburgh PA. 412-434-6130
Puglisi, Deedee Andrea, *Librn,* Brockton Art Center Library, Brockton MA. 617-588-6000
Pugsley, Sharon, *Archivist,* University of California Library, Irvine CA. 714-833-5212
Puhek, Esther L, *Librn,* Kenosha Memorial Hospital, Health Sciences Library, Kenosha WI. 414-656-2120
Puissegur, Joyce, *Librn,* Plantation Library, Plantation FL. 305-475-2140
Pujat, Duressa, *Librn,* Hackensack Hospital, Medical Library, Hackensack NJ. 201-487-4000
Pula, Cheryl, *ILL,* Mid-York Library System, Utica NY. 315-735-8328
Pulham, Brian, *Media,* Fraser Valley College, Learning Resource Centres, Abbotsford BC. 604-853-7441
Pulikonda, Ellie, *Extension,* Kokomo Public Library, Kokomo IN. 317-457-5558
Pulis, Jane, *Germanic,* University of California, Berkeley (University Library), Berkeley CA. 415-642-3773
Pullen, Ann, *Librn,* Norlina Public Library, Norlina NC. 919-456-2342
Pullen, Caralene, *Librn,* Roanoke City Public Library System (Gainsboro), Roanoke VA. 703-981-2540
Pullen, Geneva, *Bkmobile Coordr,* Lexington Public Library, Lexington KY. 606-252-8871
Pullen, Geneva B, *Librn,* Lexington Public Library (Southland), Lexington KY. 606-277-5719
Pullen, Mary, *Exten Coordr,* Reuben McMillan Free Library Free Library Association, Public Library of Youngstown & Mahoning County, Youngstown OH. 216-744-8636
Pullen, Mary L, *Libr Mgr,* Southern Research Institute, Thomas W Martin Memorial Library, Birmingham AL. 205-323-6592
Pulles, Patrice, *Librn,* Chicago Public Library (Gads Hill), Chicago IL. 312-829-2033
Pulles, Patrice, *Librn,* Valparaiso-Porter County Public Library System & Administrative Headquarters (Portgage Public), Portage IN. 219-762-2309
Pulley, T E, *Dir,* Houston Museum of Natural Science Library, Houston TX. 713-526-4273
Pulley, Virginia, *ILL,* Pensacola Junior College, Learning Resource Center, Pensacola FL. 904-476-5410
Pullin, Mary, *Librn,* Reuben McMillan Free Library Free Library Association (Lowellville Branch), Lowellville OH. 216-536-6216
Pullin, Mary, *Librn,* Reuben McMillan Free Library Free Library Association (Sebring Branch), Sebring OH. 216-938-6119
Pullin, Mary, *Librn,* Reuben McMillan Free Library Free Library Association (Fosterville), Youngstown OH. 216-782-8720
Pullin, Mary, *Librn,* Reuben McMillan Free Library Free Library Association (East Branch), Youngstown OH. 216-744-2790
Pullin, Mary, *Librn,* Reuben McMillan Free Library Free Library Association (McGuffey Mall), Youngstown OH. 216-743-1721
Puls, Elaine A, *Dir,* Loveland Public Library, Loveland CO. 303-667-4040
Pulsifer, Eileen B, *Librn,* Providence Public Library (Wanskuck), Providence RI. 401-331-4887
Pulsifer, Laura, *Librn,* Campton Grange Town Library, Campton NH. 603-536-1095
Pummell, Gary, *Adminr Northern Ohio Regional Film Circuit,* Elyria Public Library, Elyria OH. 216-323-5747
Pummell, Gary, *Adminr,* Northern Ohio Film Circuit, OH. 216-323-5747
Pumpelly, C T, *Dir,* Dow Chemical Co, Dowell Div Research & Develop Library, Tulsa OK. 918-582-0101
Pumplin, Paula L, *Ref,* Frick Art Reference Library, New York NY. 212-288-8700
Punch, K, *Ad,* Sault Sainte Marie Public Library, Sault Sainte Marie ON. 705-949-2152
Pung, Patricia, *Cat,* University of California, Santa Barbara Library, Santa Barbara CA. 805-961-2741
Pungartnik, Erentraut, *In Charge,* CIBA-GEIGY Canada Limited, Pharmaceutical Library, Dorval PQ. 514-631-4841, Ext 192,193
Punsalan, Victoria J, *Spec Coll,* Morgan State University, Morris A Soper Library, Baltimore MD. 301-444-3488, 444-3489
Punshon, Bette, *Asst Dir,* Wayne Public Library, Wayne NJ. 201-694-4272
Pupius, Nijole K, *Librn,* Union Carbide Corp (Films Packaging Div, Technical Library), Chicago IL. 312-496-4286
Purcell, Donald, *Librn,* Nova Scotia Department of Development Library, Halifax NS. 902-424-5807
Purcell, Doreen Y, *Admin Officer,* North Central Regional Library, Wenatchee WA. 509-663-1117
Purcell, Eileen, *Ch,* Cohoes Public Library, Cohoes NY. 518-235-2570, 235-0503
Purcell, Eleanor M, *Librn,* Mountainside Hospital (Louise A Mershon Library), Montclair NJ. 201-764-6000
Purcell, Gary R, *Prof,* University of Tennessee, Knoxville, Graduate School of Library & Information Science, TN. 615-974-2148
Purcell, Helen, *Tech Serv,* Utica Public Library, Utica NY. 315-735-2279
Purcell, Jane, *Librn,* Litchfield Park Public Library, Litchfield Park AZ. 602-935-4118
Purcell, John, *Ref,* Southern Oregon State College Library, Ashland OR. 503-482-6445
Purcell, Judith, *Acq,* Duke University (Law School Library), Durham NC. 919-684-2847
Purcell, Kathleen, *Librn,* Public Library of Annapolis & Anne Arundel County Inc (South County), Deale MD. 301-867-4164
Purcell, Mary Alice, *Ad,* Pottsville Free Public Library, Pottsville Library District Center, Pottsville PA. 622-8105; 622-8880
Purcell, V Nadine, *Cat,* Jackson County Library System, Medford OR. 503-776-7281
Purcell, William L, *Librn,* Wistar Institute Library, Philadelphia PA. 215-243-3805
Purdie, Celia, *Br Coordr,* Cumberland County Public Library, Anderson Street Library, Frances Brooks Stein Memorial Library, Fayetteville NC. 919-483-1580
Purdie, Hazel, *Per,* Georgia Department of Education (Div of Public Library Services), Atlanta GA. 404-656-2461
Purdie, Mrs K, *Librn,* Burk's Falls & District Public Library, Union Library, Burk's Falls ON. 705-382-3327
Purdom, Iva, *Librn,* Business Men's Assurance Co of America Library, Kansas City MO. 816-753-8000, Ext 350
Purdum, Clarence, *Librn,* Standard Oil Co (Ohio) (Research Dept Div Library), Cleveland OH. 216-581-5600
Purdy, Dorothy M, *Info Rep,* Oklahoma Department of Human Services, Employees Library, Oklahoma City OK. 405-521-3518
Purdy, Helen, *Archivist & Spec Coll,* University of Miami, Otto G Richter Library, Coral Gables FL. 305-284-3551
Purdy, Joan, *Supvr,* Middlesex County Library (Wardsville Branch), Wardsville ON. 519-438-8368
Purdy, John, *Per,* Central State University Library, Edmond OK. 405-341-2980, Ext 494, 495 & 496
Purdy, John, *Micro,* Central State University Library, Edmond OK. 405-341-2980, Ext 494, 495 & 496
Purdy, L, *ILL,* Halton Hills Public Libraries, Georgetown ON. 416-877-2631
Purdy, Martha, *ILL & Ref,* DuPage Library System, Geneva IL. 312-232-8457
Purdy, Martha, *ILL,* Wheaton Public Library, Wheaton IL. 312-668-1374
Purdy, Victor W, *Asst Prof,* Brigham Young University, School of Library & Information Sciences, UT. 801-378-2976
Purins, Sandra, *Asst Dir & Ch,* Lindenhurst Memorial Library, Lindenhurst NY. 516-888-7575
Purnell, Jacquelyn, *Librn,* Enoch Pratt Free Library (Pimlico), Baltimore MD. 301-396-5430, 396-5395
Purnell, James, *Librn,* University of Connecticut Library (Pharmacy), Storrs CT. 203-486-2218
Purnell, Kathleen, *Order & Cat,* Catholic University of America, John K Mullen of Denver Memorial Library, Washington DC. 202-635-5055
Pursell, Pauline, *Librn,* Atchison County Library (Tarkio Branch), Tarkio MO. 816-736-5832
Purser, Pat, *Mgr Tech Servs,* Cubic Corp, Research Technical Library, San Diego CA. 714-277-6780, Ext 392
Pursley, Jim, *Ext Serv,* Washoe County Library, Reno NV. 702-785-4039
Pursley, Jim, *Librn,* Washoe County Library (Stead Branch), Stead NV. 702-785-4039
Pursley, Nadene, *Libr Technician,* San Diego County Library (Ramona Branch), Ramona CA. 714-789-0430
Purtill, Diane, *Head, Pop Libr,* Chicago Public Library (Cultural Center), Chicago IL. 312-269-2820
Purvis, Brenda S, *Librn,* Gainesville Junior College, John Harrison Hosch Library, Gainesville GA. 404-536-5226, Ext 254
Purvis, Eleana, *Librn,* Brooklyn Public Library (Fort Hamilton), Brooklyn NY. 212-745-5502
Purvis, Louise, *Dir,* Stephenville Public Library, Stephenville TX. 817-965-5665
Purvis, Marjorie A, *Communications Res Supvr,* Metropolitan Life Insurance Company, Ottawa ON. 613-231-3531
Puryear, Cynthia L, *Asst Librn,* Louisburg College, C W Robbins Library, Louisburg NC. 496-2521 Ext 279, 280, 281
Puryear, Mary Claire, *Asst Dir,* Northwest Mississippi Junior College, R C Pugh Library, Senatobia MS. 601-562-5262, Ext 246
Pusch, Joachim, *AV,* North Hennepin Community College Library, Brooklyn Park MN. 612-425-4541
Pusztai, Andrew, *Dir,* Free Public Library of Oakland, Oakland NJ. 201-337-3742
Putman, Linda, *Asst Librn,* White County Public Library, Searcy AR. 501-268-2449
Putnam, Jane, *Tech Serv,* Clackamas County Library, Oregon City OR. 503-655-8543
Putnam, Margaret A, *Section Head Reports,* United States Air Force (Air Force Weapons Laboratory Technical Library), Kirtland AFB NM. 505-844-7449
Putnam, Rebecca, *Librn,* Mount Holly Public Library, Mount Holly NC. 704-827-3581
Putnam, Virginia, *Librn,* Bridge Memorial Library, Walpole NH. 603-756-9806
Putney, Marie, *Librn,* Charleston County Library (James Island), Charleston SC. 803-795-6679
Putney, Taylor, *Pub Servs,* Wright State University Library (Fordham Library, Cox Heart Institute Library & Fels Research Institute Library), Dayton OH. 513-873-2266
Putz, John, *Media,* Elgin Community College, Renner Learning Resources Center, Elgin IL. 312-697-1000, Ext 258
Putzey, Lloyd J, *Librn,* Coker College, James Lide Coker III Memorial Library, Hartsville SC. 803-332-1381
Puyot, Alice, *ILL,* Dekalb Library System, Maud M Burrus Library, Decatur GA. 404-378-7569
Puz, Marshea, *Librn,* Kern County Library (Ridgecrest Branch), Ridgecrest CA. 805-861-2130

Pyburn, Janet, *Ref & Bibliog Instr,* Shelby State Community College Library, Memphis TN. 901-528-6743
Pye, Frances, *Dir,* Brazosport College Library, Lake Jackson TX. 713-265-6131, Ext 62
Pye, Frances, *Chief Librn,* San Jacinto Junior College (North Campus Library), Houston TX. 713-458-4050
Pye, Gordon L, *In Charge,* NASA, Goddard Institute For Space Studies, New York NY. 212-678-5613
Pyka, Myrna, *Tech Serv & Cat,* Fort Bend County Library, Richmond TX. 713-342-4455
Pyke, Carol J, *Dir,* Urban Institute Library, Washington DC. 202-223-1950, Ext 362
Pyle, Claire, *Head, Br Servs,* Carnegie Library of Pittsburgh, Pittsburgh PA. 412-622-3100
Pyle, Connie, *ILL & Ref,* Mills College Library, Oakland CA. 415-632-2700, Ext 260, 261, 262
Pyle, Janie, *Librn,* Public Library of Cincinnati & Hamilton County (Madeira Branch), Madeira OH. 513-369-6028
Pyle, Joyce, *Tech Serv,* California State University, Hayward Library, Hayward CA. 415-881-3664
Pyle, Lola Ann, *Instr,* University of Arkansas, Instructional Resources Education, AR. 501-575-5444
Pyle, Nan, *Librn,* Payson Public Library, Payson AZ. 602-474-2585
Pyle, Robert R, *Librn,* Northeast Harbor Library, Northeast Harbor ME. 207-276-3251
Pyle, Susan, *Cat,* Capital University Library (Law School Library), Columbus OH. 614-445-8634
Pyles, David, *Librn,* Hammer, Siler, George Associates Library, Washington DC. 202-223-1100
Pyne, Henry J, *Librn,* Milford Town Library, Milford MA. 617-473-2145
Pyonteck, William P, *Dir,* Hunterdon County Library, Flemington NJ. 201-788-1444
Pyper, Virginia, *Asst Librn,* Elko County Library (Wells Library), Wells NV. 702-752-3355

Q

Quackenbush, Audrey, *Dir,* Goulbourn Township Public Library, Stittsville ON. 613-836-4600
Quade, Robert, *AV,* Waukegan Public Library, Waukegan IL. 312-623-2041
Quain, Julie R, *Chief Librn,* Lutheran Hospital of Maryland, Charles G Reigner Medical Library, Baltimore MD. 301-945-1600, Ext 2239
Quain, Mildred, *YA,* Peninsula Public Library, Lawrence NY. 516-239-3262
Quale, Helen C, *Ch,* Corvallis Public Library, Corvallis-Benton County Library, Corvallis OR. 503-757-6928
Qualls, Kay, *Librn,* Stanislaus County Free Library (Empire Branch), Empire CA. 209-524-5505
Qualters, Roger, *Librn,* Arlington County Department of Libraries (Aurora Hills), Arlington VA. 703-521-3066
Quam, Eileen, *Tech Serv,* College of Saint Thomas, O'Shaughnessy Library, Saint Paul MN. 612-647-5720
Quam, Kirsten, *Tech Serv,* William N Wishard Memorial Hospital, Library & Media Services, Indianapolis IN. 317-630-7028
Quam, Lola, *Librn,* Lisbon Public Library, Lisbon ND. 701-683-5174
Quam, Mary, *Dir,* Marshalltown Public Library, Marshalltown IA. 515-754-5738
Quanbeck, Clenora E, *Dir,* Mayville State College Library, Mayville ND. 701-786-2301, Ext 263
Quandt, Ellen, *Librn,* Heiserman Memorial Library, West Union IA. 319-422-3103
Quartarone, John, *Ch,* Sharon Public Library, Sharon MA. 617-784-5974
Quarterman, Patricia, *Asst Dir, Tech Servs & Cat,* Huston-Tillotson College, Downs-Jones Library, Austin TX. 512-476-7421, Ext 300
Quattlebaun, Janet, *Librn Blind,* George S Houston Memorial Library, Dothan AL. 205-793-9767
Quay, Caren K, *Coordr,* Kaiser-Permanente Medical Center, Health Library, Oakland CA. 415-645-6569
Quealey, Mrs M, *Librn,* Ontario Ministry of Culture & Recreation, Huronia Historical Resource Center, Midland ON. 705-526-7838, Ext 22

Queen, Margaret, *Sci & Indust,* San Diego Public Library, San Diego CA. 714-236-5800
Queener, Frank, *LINK,* Grand Rapids Public Library, Grand Rapids MI. 616-456-4400
Quelland, Nancy, *Bkmobile Coordr,* Nelson County Public Library, Bardstown KY. 502-348-3714
Quelle, Catharina, *Asst Librn,* Gas City-Mill Township Public Library, Gas City IN. 317-674-4718
Quesenberry, Geneva, *Librn,* Adairville Library, Adairville KY. 502-539-6051
Quessy, Ginette, *Tech Serv,* Bibliotheque Municipale Des Trois-Rivieres, Trois-Rivieres PQ. 819-374-3521, Ext 71
Quick, June, *ILL,* Malheur County Library, Ontario Public Library, Ontario OR. 503-889-6371
Quick, Mrs Young Hi, *Librn,* Western Electric Co, Inc (Public Relations Library), New York NY. 212-571-5115
Quick, Richard C, *Dir,* State University of New York College at Geneseo, Milne Library, Geneseo NY. 716-245-5591
Quicker, Sharon, *Asst Librn,* University of Wisconsin Center-Sheboygan, Battig Memorial Library, Sheboygan WI. 414-459-3725
Quiel, Kathleen, *YA,* Grand Rapids Public Library, Grand Rapids MN. 218-326-3081
Quigley, Beatrice D, *Librn,* Veterans Administration, Hospital Library, Clarksburg WV. 304-623-3461, Ext 235
Quigley, Elizabeth-Anne, *Dir,* University of San Francisco (School of Law), San Francisco CA. 415-666-6679
Quigley, Iris, *Acq,* Long Beach Public Library, Long Beach NY. 516-432-7201
Quigley, Mary Pat, *Br Coordr,* John C Hart Memorial Library, Shrub Oak NY. 914-245-5262
Quigley, Mary Pat, *Librn,* John C Hart Memorial Library (Yorktown Heights Branch), Yorktown Heights NY. 914-962-2818
Quillen, Dorothy, *Librn,* Selbyville Public Library, John G Townsend Jr Memorial Library, Selbyville DE. 302-436-8195
Quillen, Novella I, *Dir,* Watauga Regional Library Center, Johnson City TN. 615-282-1031
Quimby, Dorothy W, *Chief Librn,* Unity College Library, Unity ME. 207-948-3131, Ext 234
Quimby, Harriet, *Assoc Prof,* Saint John's University, Div of Library & Information Science, NY. 212-969-8000, Ext 200
Quimper, Yvette, *Libr Clerk,* Haut-Saint-Jean Regional Library (Saint Quentin Public), Saint Quentin NB. 506-235-2513
Quina, Catherine, *Circ,* Homewood Public Library, Homewood AL. 205-871-7342
Quinlan, Barbara M, *Librn,* Cades, Schutte, Fleming & Wright, Law Library, Honolulu HI. 808-521-9218
Quinlan, Kathleen A, *Assoc Librn,* Boston University Libraries (School of Law), Boston MA. 617-353-3151
Quinn, Alicia, *Librn,* Houston Lighting & Power Co Library, Houston TX. 713-228-9211, Ext 2060
Quinn, Ann, *Coordr Educ Servs,* San Bernardino County Museum Library, Redlands CA. 714-792-1334
Quinn, Carol, *ILL & Ref,* Western Maryland College, Hoover Library, Westminster MD. 301-848-7000, Ext 281
Quinn, Cynthia S, *Ref,* Alaska Court Libraries, Anchorage AK. 907-274-8611, Ext 580
Quinn, David, *AV,* Suffolk County Community College, Western Campus Library, Brentwood NY. 516-348-4522
Quinn, Dolores, *Librn,* Oak Forest Hospital (Medical Library), Oak Forest IL. 312-928-4200
Quinn, Elizabeth, *Asst Librn,* General Dynamics Corp, Public Affairs Library, Saint Louis MO. 314-862-2440
Quinn, Elizabeth, *Dir,* Alexander Mitchell Library, Aberdeen Public Library, Aberdeen SD. 605-225-4186
Quinn, Frances M, *Librn,* United States Air Force (Technical Library), Eglin AFB FL. 904-882-3212
Quinn, Gertrude, *Br Coordr & Spec Servs,* Public Library of Cincinnati & Hamilton County, Cincinnati Public Library, Cincinnati OH. 513-369-6000

Quinn, James, *Librn,* Public Library of the District of Columbia (Langston), Washington DC. 202-727-1357
Quinn, Jane Taggart, *Librn,* Delaware County Planning Commission, Research & Mapping Library, Media PA. 215-891-2381
Quinn, Karen, *Lectr,* San Jose State University, Division of Library Science, CA. 408-277-2292
Quinn, Karen Takle, *Librn,* International Business Machines Corp (Santa Teresa Laboratory Library & Learning Center), San Jose CA. 408-463-4050
Quinn, Louis, *Ad,* Greenwood-Leflore Public Library System, Greenwood MS. 601-453-3634
Quinn, Lucy, *Librn,* Jackson Metropolitan Library (Livingston Park), Jackson MS. 601-352-3677
Quinn, Madeline, *Cat,* Stetson University, duPont-Ball Library, De Land FL. 904-734-4121, Ext 220
Quinn, Madeline, *Chief Librn,* West Jefferson Public Library, West Jefferson OH. 614-879-8448
Quinn, Martha, *Asst Prof,* University of Guam, Library Science Program, GU. 734-2921
Quinn, Mary, *Librn,* Louisville Free Public Library (Eline Memorial), Louisville KY. 502-895-8134
Quinn, Mary A, *Librn,* Somerville Hospital, Carr Health Sciences Library, Somerville MA. 617-666-4400, Ext 301
Quinn, Natalie, *ILL,* Crow River Regional Library, Willmar MN. 612-235-3162
Quinn, Patrick M, *Univ Archives,* Northwestern University Library, Evanston IL. 312-492-7658
Quinn, Penelope, *Ch,* Woodstock Public Library & Art Gallery, Woodstock ON. 519-537-4801
Quinn, Sally, *Librn,* Southwest Arkansas Regional Library (Horatio Branch), Horatio AR. 501-777-4564
Quinn, Thomas, *Ser,* Henry Ford Community College, Eshleman Library, Dearborn MI. 313-271-2750, Ext 378
Quinn, William P, *Assoc Dir & Tech Serv,* University of Massachusetts at Boston Library, Boston MA. 617-287-1900, Ext 2224
Quinnell, Edwin, *Media,* Chabot College, Learning Resource Center, Hayward CA. 415-786-6762
Quint, Barbara, *Ref,* Rand Corp Library, Santa Monica CA. 213-393-0411, Ext 369
Quint, Mary, *Dir,* Illinois State Library, Springfield IL. 217-782-2994
Quint, Sharon, *Ch,* Brockton Public Library System, Brockton MA. 617-587-2515
Quint, Sharon, *Ch,* Holyoke Public Library, Holyoke MA. 413-534-3357
Quintal, Cecile C, *Assoc Dir,* University of New Mexico General Library (Medical Center Library), Albuquerque NM. 505-277-2311
Quintanilla, Helen, *Ref,* Dallas County Public Library, Dallas TX. 214-749-8566, 749-8886
Quinters, Robert A, *Mgr,* Synthane-Taylor Corp, Technical Division Library, Valley Forge PA. 215-666-0300
Quintiliano, Barbara, *Doc,* Saint Joseph's University Libraries (Drexel Library), Philadelphia PA. 215-879-7559
Quiring, Virginia M, *Assoc Dir for Pub Servs,* Kansas State University, Farrell Library, Manhattan KS. 913-532-6516
Quirk, S, *Librn,* Okanagan Regional Library District (Coldstream Branch), Coldstream BC. 604-545-5897
Quirk, Thomas, *Librn,* Detroit Public Library (Butzel), Detroit MI. 313-833-9173
Quist, Edwin A, *Librn,* Peabody Conservatory of Music Library, Baltimore MD. 301-837-0600, Ext 53
Quist, John R, *Dir,* Mount Laurel Free Public Library, Mount Laurel NJ. 609-234-7319
Quist, Pat, *Tech Serv & Cat,* Bennington Free Library, Bennington VT. 802-442-9051
Qureski, M Jamil, *Dir & Acq,* Pikes Peak Community College, Learning Materials Center, Colorado Springs CO. 303-576-7711, Ext 536

R

Raab, Kathleen, *Bkmobile Coordr,* Milwaukee Public Library, Milwaukee WI. 414-278-3000
Raab-Cook, Nancy, *Librn,* Smyth-Bland Regional Library, Marion VA. 703-783-2323

Raadt, Becky, *Librn,* Owatonna Free Public Library (Blooming Prairie Branch), Blooming Prairie MN. 507-583-7750

Raap, Christine, *Cat,* Evergreen Park Public Library, Evergreen Park IL. 312-422-8522

Raasch, Mildred, *ILL & Ref,* Merced College, Lesher Library, Merced CA. 209-723-4321, Ext 274

Raats, Josephine, *Assoc Librn,* Kenai Community Library, Kenai AK. 907-283-4378

Raaum, Gordon, *Librn,* West Plains Rural Library, Williston ND. 701-572-2811

Rabalais, Mrs Calvin, *Librn,* Avoyelles Parish Library (Simmesport Branch), Simmesport LA. 318-253-7559

Rabalais, Sadie, *Librn,* East Baton Rouge Parish Library (Pride Branch), Pride LA. 504-654-8811

Rabasca, Iris, *Reader Serv,* Suffolk County Community College, Western Campus Library, Brentwood NY. 516-348-4522

Rabatin, Toni, *Librn,* Chamber of Commerce of Greater Pittsburgh, Research Library, Pittsburgh PA. 412-391-3400

Rabb, Mary, *Librn,* Chicago Zoological Park Library, Brookfield IL. 312-485-0263

Rabbe, Janet, *Ch,* Wareham Free Library, Wareham MA. 617-295-2343

Rabe, Dorothy B, *Librn,* Winter Haven Hospital, Medical Library, Winter Haven FL. 813-293-1121

Rabenberg, Mary, *Dir,* York Public Library, York NE. 402-362-3039

Rabenstein, Bernard, *Cat,* Hebrew Union College-Jewish Institute of Religion Library, Cincinnati OH. 513-221-1875

Raber, Alice, *Librn,* Edna Bentley Memorial Library, Perry MI. 517-625-3166

Raber, Douglas, *Dir,* Delos F Diggins Public Library, Harvard Public Library, Harvard IL. 815-943-4671

Raber, Nevin, *Librn,* Indiana University at Bloomington (Business), Bloomington IN. 812-337-1957

Rabinoff, Miriam, *Librn,* New York Public Library (Fifty-Eighth Street), New York NY. 212-759-7358

Rabinowitz, Morris, *Ad,* Dedham Public Library, Dedham MA. 617-326-0583

Rabinowitz, Susan, *Librn,* Temple Sinai Library, Brookline MA. 617-277-5888

Rabjohns, Albert, *Asst Dir,* Dearborn Department of Libraries, Henry Ford Centennial Library, Dearborn MI. 313-271-1000

Rabjohns, Ann, *Lang & Lit,* Detroit Public Library, Detroit Associated Libraries, Detroit MI. 313-833-1000

Rabkin, Sara, *Librn,* Symmes Hospital Library, Arlington MA. 617-646-1500

Raborn, Garvis, *Librn,* Montgomery County Library (East), New Caney TX. 713-354-6152

Raby, Eva, *Librn,* McGill University Libraries (Social Work), Montreal PQ. 514-392-5054

Raby, Pat, *Librn,* Jackson District Library (Napoleon Branch), Napoleon MI. 517-536-4266

Race, Carol, *Librn,* Juneau Memorial Library (Douglas Public), Douglas AK. 907-364-2378

Race, Carol, *AV,* Northeast Missouri State University, Pickler Memorial Library, Kirksville MO. 816-665-5121, Ext 7186

Rachal, Mrs Charlie S, *Librn,* Atlantic Richfield Co, Arco Chemical Co, Lyondell Plant Library, Channelview TX. 713-452-8147

Rachel, Catherine S, *Dir,* Harris County Public Library, Houston TX. 713-221-5350

Rachfalski, Sister Marie, *Dir, Tech Serv & Acq,* Our Lady of Angels College Library, Aston PA. 215-449-0905, Ext 10

Rachow, Louis A, *Librn,* Players, Walter Hampden-Edwin Booth Theatre Collection & Library, New York NY. 212-228-7610

Rachter, Carol, *Cat,* McMaster University, Hamilton ON. 416-525-9140

Rachuig, Florence, *Tech Serv & Cat,* Benton Harbor Public Library (Filmco-Cooperative Service Center for Southwest Michigan Library Cooperative), Benton Harbor MI. 616-926-6741

Racine, Andre Paul, *Librn,* Hopital du Sacre Coeur, Bibliotheque Medicale, Hull PQ. 819-776-1581

Racine, Rose, *Librn,* Chamber of Commerce of the United States Library, Washington DC. 202-659-6053

Racioppo, Marie, *Acq,* Pace University, School of Law Library, White Plains NY. 914-682-7272

Rack, Marita, *Librn,* Pawling Free Library, Pawling NY. 914-855-3444

Rackashi, Florence, *Dir,* Linwood Public Library, Linwood NJ. 609-927-6756

Racklyeft, Mary J, *Librn,* Butzel, Long, Gust, Klein & Van Zile Library, Detroit MI. 313-963-8142

Racknor, Mrs Ralph, *Supvr,* Oxford County Library (Drumbo Branch), Drumbo ON. 519-463-5282

Radcliff, Ann, *Librn,* Amherst Public Library, Amherst OH. 216-988-4280

Radcliff, Barbara, *Ch,* Chester County Library & District Center, Exton PA. 215-363-0884

Raddant, Eugene R, *Asst Prof,* Miami University-Middletown, Library-Media Technical Assistant Program, OH. 513-424-4444, Ext 221

Radde, Laurie, *Ad,* Charles M White Memorial Public Library, Stevens Point WI. 715-346-2841

Radel, Susan, *Librn,* Fairfield Public Library (Fairfield Woods), Fairfield CT. 203-374-9485

Radell, Sheila, *Ch,* Topeka Public Library, Topeka KS. 913-233-2040

Rademacher, Matt, *Spec Coll,* Lansing Community College Library, Lansing MI. 517-373-9978

Rademacher, Richard J, *Dir,* Wichita Public Library, Wichita KS. 316-262-0611

Radenbaugh, Mary, *Librn,* Milan Public Library, Milan MI. 313-439-1240

Rader, Beatrice, *Supvr,* Huron County Public Library (Zurich Branch), Zurich ON. 519-236-4965

Rader, Cecelia, *Ser,* Laramie County Community College Library, Cheyenne WY. 307-634-5853

Rader, Hannelore, *Educ Psychol,* Eastern Michigan University, Center of Educational Resources, Ypsilanti MI. 313-487-0020

Rader, Isobel, *Supvr,* Huron County Public Library (Dashwood Branch), Dashwood ON. 519-237-3244

Rader, Jennette S, *Librn,* University of Chicago, Human Resources Center, A G Bush Library, Chicago IL. 312-753-2024

Rader, Margaret M, *Asst Librn,* Oregon State Library Services for the Blind & Physically Handicapped, Salem OR. 503-378-3849

Rader, Miriam, *Librn,* McCome Public Library, McComb OH. 419-293-5425

Radley, Peter, *Bibliog Instr,* Rome Historical Society, William E & Elaine Scripture Memorial Library, Rome NY. 315-336-5870

Radmacher, Camille J, *Dir,* Warren County Library, Monmouth IL. 309-734-6412

Radmacher, Camille J, *Exec Dir,* Western Illinois Library System, Monmouth IL. 309-734-7141

Radmcher, Mary, *Chief Librn,* Skokie Public Library, Skokie IL. 312-673-7774

Radoff, Len, *Chief, Br Servs,* Houston Public Library, Houston TX. 713-224-5441

Radosh, Sondra M, *Asst Dir & Ch,* Jones Library, Inc, Amherst MA. 413-256-0246

Radosh, Stanley, *Slavic & E European Studies,* University of Massachusetts at Amherst Library, Amherst MA. 413-545-0284

Radovich, Rena, *ILL,* USV Pharmaceutical Corp, Information Services Department, Tuckahoe NY. 914-779-6300, Ext 2592

Radtke, Gene, *ILL & Ref,* Kalamazoo Valley Community College, Learning Resources Center, Kalamazoo MI. 616-372-5000, Ext 328

Radtke, Lenore, *Cat,* Sonoma State University, Ruben Salazar Library, Rohnert Park CA. 707-664-2397

Radwan, Eleanor, *Librn,* New York Public Library (General Reference Service), New York NY. 790-6575; 790-6161 (Tel Ref); 790-6234 (Union Cat)

Radway, G, *On-Line Servs,* General Electric Co, Electronics Park Library, Syracuse NY. 315-456-2023

Radway, Mrs R F, *Math Librn,* Institute for Advanced Study Libraries, Princeton NJ. 609-924-4400

Radziejowski, Anna, *Tech Serv,* Borough of Manhattan Community College Library, Martin B Dworkis Library, New York NY. 212-262-3530

Rae, A, *Tech Serv,* University of Victoria (Law), Victoria BC. 604-477-6911

Rae, Jane, *Librn,* Wentworth Library (Ancaster), Hamilton ON. 416-526-4126

Rae, Linda M, *Librn,* Hastings - Adams County Library, Hastings NE. 402-463-9855

Rae, Ruth, *Film officer,* Hampshire College, Harold F Johnson Library Center, Amherst MA. 413-549-4600

Raeder, Aggi, *Librn,* Peat, Marwick, Mitchell & Co Library, Los Angeles CA. 213-972-4000, Ext 405

Rael, Constance, *Ref,* El Dorado County Library, Placerville CA. 916-626-2561

Raene, Bert A, *Dir,* Habitat Inc, Institute for the Environment Library, Belmont MA. 617-489-3850

Rafael, Ruth, *Archivist,* Judah L Magnes Memorial Museum (Western Jewish History Center), Berkeley CA. 415-849-2710, Ext D & E

Rafal, Marian, *Ch,* Royal Oak Public Library, Royal Oak MI. 313-541-1470

Rafferty, Josephine, *Librn,* United States Navy (Portsmouth Naval Shipyard Library), Portsmouth NH. 207-439-1000, Ext 2769

Raffile, John, *Librn,* California State Department of Corrections, Correctional Training Facility Library, Soledad CA. 408-678-2616

Raftery, Gerald, *Dir,* Martha Canfield Memorial Free Library, Arlington Library, Arlington VT. 802-375-6153

Ragin, Elizabeth, *Asst Dir,* Calhoun County Library, Port Lavaca TX. 512-552-2661

Raglan, John, *Actg Dir,* Western Connecticut State College, Ruth A Haas Library, Danbury CT. 203-797-4053

Ragland, Mrs Mervyn, *Dir,* Forrest City Public Library, Forrest City AR. 501-633-5646

Rago, J, *Tech Serv,* Atlantic Christian College, Hackney Library, Wilson NC. 919-237-3161, Ext 330

Ragosin, David R, *Exec Dir,* East Central College Consortium, OH. 216-821-5320

Ragsdale, Betty M, *Dir,* Blue Ridge Regional Library, Martinsville VA. 703-632-7125

Ragsdale, Clementine, *Tech Serv,* Veterans Administration, Medical Center Library, Decatur GA. 404-321-6111, Ext 254

Ragsdale, R, *Sci & Sociol,* Oakland Public Library, Oakland CA. 415-273-3281

Ragsdale, Robert, *Dir,* Covina Public Library, Covina CA. 213-967-3935

Ragsdale, Winifred, *Dir,* Educational Resource & Information Center & George G Stone Center for Childrens Books, Claremont CA. 714-621-8000, Ext 3670

Rahal, Patricia, *Dir,* College of Trades & Technology Library, Saint John's NF. 709-753-9360, Ext 318

Rahill, Georgette, *Librn,* Bibliotheque Municipale, Farnham PQ. 514-293-3375

Rahill, Michael, *Librn,* United States Department of Justice Library (Antitrust Division), Washington DC. 202-739-2457

Rahilly, Maurice F, *Div Libr,* Northeastern University Libraries, Boston MA. 617-437-2350

Rahilly, Maurice F, *Librn,* Northeastern University Libraries (Chemistry Graduate Research (Chemistry, Chemical Engineering, Biology, Pharmacy, Nursing, Health Sciences, Forensic Chemistry)), Boston MA. 617-437-2821

Raible, Patricia, *Librn,* Northborough Free Library, Northborough MA. 617-393-2401

Raichman, Sherwin, *In Charge,* Saint Lawrence College of Applied Arts & Technology Library Services, Kingston ON. 613-544-5400, Ext 163

Raidt, Mrs Jack, *Dir,* North Park Baptist Church Library, Sherman TX. 214-892-8429

Raikes, Deborah, *Docs & Micro,* Princeton University Library, Princeton NJ. 609-452-3180

Railo, Barbara, *Dir,* Mannes College of Music, Harry Scherman Library, New York NY. 212-737-0700, Ext 9

Railsback, Florence, *Dir,* Carleton A Friday Memorial Library, New Richmond Public Library, New Richmond WI. 715-246-2364

Raimondo, Paula, *Librn,* Helene Fuld Medical Center, Medical Library, Trenton NJ. 609-396-6575, Ext 2112

Rainbow, Bernice, *Ref,* Shaw University, Learning Resources Center, Raleigh NC. 919-755-4930

Raine, Marjorie, *Sr Libr Asst,* Northrop Corp, Ventura Div, Technical Information Center, Newbury Park CA. 805-498-3131, Ext 1050

Raine, Melinda, *Librn,* Public Library of Des Moines (East Side), Des Moines IA. 515-283-4942

Raine, Susan, *Librn,* Victoria County Public Library (Oakwood Branch), Oakwood ON. 705-324-3104
Rainer, Cathy, *Mat Coordr,* Lake Lanier Regional Library, Lawrenceville GA. 404-963-5231
Raines, Addie, *Acq,* Simpson College, Start-Kilgour Memorial Library, San Francisco CA. 415-334-7400, Ext 17
Raines, Elaine Y, *Librn,* Arizona Daily Star Library, Tucson AZ. 602-294-4433, Ext 345
Raines, LaCona C, *Librn,* Polk County Historical & Genealogical Library, Bartow FL. 813-533-5146
Raines, M Diane, *Asst Librn,* Walsh College Library, Canton OH. 216-499-7090, Ext 40
Raines, Margaret F, *Dir,* Fort Scott Community College Library, Fort Scott KS. 316-223-2700, Ext 36
Raines, Mary P, *Cat,* Queens College, Everett Library, Charlotte NC. 704-332-7121, Ext 278
Raines, Sally, *Librn,* United States Department of the Interior (Office of Regional Solicitor Library), Denver CO. 303-234-3175
Raines, Tom, *Librn,* Memphis-Shelby County Public Library & Information Center (Literature, Philosophy, Religion), Memphis TN. 901-528-2950
Rainey, Frances M, *Curator,* Dawgwood Library, Refugio TX. 512-526-2451
Rainey, Joan, *Acq,* Mohawk Valley Library Association, Schenectady NY. 518-355-2010
Rainey, Laura J, *Dir,* Rockwell International Corp, Rocketdyne Division Technical Information Center, Canoga Park CA. 213-884-2575
Rainey, Rose L, *Tech Serv,* William Carey College, I E Rouse Library, Hattiesburg MS. 601-582-5051, Ext 245 & 246
Rains, Gertrude, *Br Asst,* Morehouse Parish Library (Mer Rouge Branch), Mer Rouge LA. 318-281-3683
Rains, Louis, *Librn,* Office of Naval Research, Boston Branch Library, Boston MA. 617-542-6000
Rains, Marion E, *Dir, Acq & Ref,* William Penn College, Wilcox Library, Oskaloosa IA. 515-673-8311, Ext 291
Rains, Ruth, *Exec Dir,* Consortium of University Film Centers, IL. 217-333-7614
Rains, Suzanne, *Librn,* Santa Cruz Public Library (Capitola Branch), Capitola CA. 408-475-6547
Rains, Virginia, *Asst Librn,* Sharon Springs Public Library, Sharon Springs KS. 913-852-4527
Rainwater, Barbara, *Librn,* El Paso County Law Library, Colorado Springs CO. 303-471-5419
Raisig, L Miles, *Dir,* Pembroke State University, Mary Livermore Library, Pembroke NC. 919-521-4214, Ext 238
Raisor, Douglas, *Dir,* Kentucky State Department for Human Resources Library, Frankfort KY. 502-564-4530
Raith, Edel, *ILL & Ref,* San Francisco Public Library, San Francisco CA. 415-558-4235
Raithel, Frederick J, *Coordr,* Mid-Missouri Library Network, MO. 314-443-3161, Ext 216 & 217
Rajaneimi, Joyce, *Librn,* Boynton Public Library (Baldwinville), Templeton MA. 617-939-5582
Rajec, Elizabeth, *Acq,* City College of the City University of New York, Morris Raphael Cohen Library, New York NY. 212-690-6612
Rajguru, Nalini A, *Librn,* Sutherland, Asbill & Brennan Library, Washington DC. 202-872-7895, 7896
Rake, Patricia T, *Librn,* United States Navy (Naval Construction Battalion Center Base Library), Gulfport MS. 601-865-2409
Rakert, Mrs Merl, *Asst Librn,* Vicksburg Community Library, Vicksburg PA. 717-
Rakestraw, Jane, *Cat,* Detroit Public Library, Detroit Associated Libraries, Detroit MI. 313-833-1000
Rakow, Mary Lou, *Ch & Media,* Wilson County Public Library, Wilson NC. 919-237-3818
Rakus, Mildred W, *Librn,* Washington Crossing Library of the American Revolution, Washington Crossing PA. 215-493-5532
Raleigh, Marilyn, *Cat,* West Bridgewater Public Library, West Bridgewater MA. 617-583-2067
Rallis, George J, *Librn,* Rumford Public Library, Rumford ME. 207-364-3661
Ralph, Corrine, *AV,* Mundelein College, Learning Resource Center, Chicago IL. 312-262-8100, Ext 301, 302 & 303

Ralph, I, *Librn,* Okanagan Regional Library District (Oyama Branch), Oyama BC. 604-548-3580
Ralph, J H, *Pub Servs,* California State College, San Bernardino Library, San Bernardino CA. 714-887-7321
Ralph, Lucile, *Librn,* Carson City Public Library, Carson City MI. 517-584-3680
Ralph, Ruth, *Dir,* Divide County Public Library, Crosby ND. 701-965-6305
Ralphs, Willa, *Librn,* Saint Helens Public Library, Saint Helens OR. 503-397-4544
Ralston, Barbara, *Librn,* Defense Logistics Agency, Headquarters Library, Alexandria VA. 703-274-6055
Ralston, Carol, *Dir,* Plainville Public Library, Plainville CT. 203-793-0221
Ralston, Charles, *Tech Serv,* United States Military Academy Library, West Point NY. 914-938-2230
Ralston, Jack L, *Librn,* University of Missouri-Kansas City Libraries (Music), Kansas City MO. 816-363-4300
Ralston, Thelma, *Librn,* Clementon Memorial Library, Clementon NJ. 609-783-3233
Ramaccia, Helen, *Ch,* Lucy Robbins Welles Library, Newington CT. 203-666-9350
Ramage, Patricia, *Ser,* University of South Alabama (Biomedical Library), Mobile AL. 205-460-7043
Ramagos, Anne Michelle, *Dir,* Loyola University Library (Media Center), New Orleans LA. 504-865-2549
Ramberg, Anne P, *Ad & Ref,* San Bruno Public Library, San Bruno CA. 415-877-8878
Rambo, Pearl, *Dir,* Walla Walla Community College Library, Walla Walla WA. 509-527-4273, 527-4274
Rambow, Elizabeth, *ILL,* Simpson College, Dunn Library, Indianola IA. 515-961-6251, Ext 663
Rambow, James, *Soc Sci,* University of Missouri-Columbia, Elmer Ellis Library, Columbia MO. 314-882-4701
Ramer, James D, *Dean,* University of Alabama, Graduate School of Library Service, AL. 205-348-4610
Ramey, D, *Tech Serv,* Los Angeles Trade Technical College Library, Los Angeles CA. 213-746-0800, Ext 217
Ramey, Mary Ann, *Bibliog Instr,* Georgia State University, William Russell Pullen Library, Atlanta GA. 404-658-2185, 658-2172
Ramey, Mary Margaret, *Librn,* Kitsap Regional Library (Bremerton Branch), Bremerton WA. 206-377-3955
Ramirez, Connie, *Circ,* Howard County Library, Big Spring TX. 915-267-5295
Ramirez, Kathleen, *Circ,* University of Santa Clara (Heafey Law Library), Santa Clara CA. 408-984-4451
Ramirez, Manuel E Velez, *Librn,* Commonwealth of Puerto Rico (Legislative Library), San Juan PR. 809-724-7171
Ramirez, William, *Ch,* San Francisco Public Library, San Francisco CA. 415-558-4235
Ramois, Sandra, *Acq,* Holy Names College, Paul J Cushing Library, Oakland CA. 415-436-1332
Ramos, Donna, *Cat,* University of Scranton, Alumni Memorial Library, Scranton PA. 717-961-7525
Ramos, Karen, *Librn,* Stockton-San Joaquin County Public Library (Southeast Neighborhood Branch), Stockton CA. 209-944-8415
Ramoth, Sue, *Librn,* New Jersey Department of Education, Center for Occupational Education, Experimentation & Demonstration Library, Newark NJ. 201-648-4282
Ramp, Marlene, *Librn,* Falmouth Public Library (North Falmouth), Falmouth MA. 617-563-2922
Rampenthal, Ruth, *Librn,* General Electric Co, Ground Systems Dept, AS Library, Daytona Beach FL. 904-258-2621
Ramquist, Raymond C, *Dept Head,* James Madison University, Department of Library Science & Educational Media, VA. 703-433-6302
Ramsay, Jane H, *Librn,* Hebron Public Library, Hebron NH. 603-744-5095
Ramsay, John E, *Dir,* Auburn Public Library, Auburn MA. 617-832-2081
Ramseur, Vanessa, *Librn,* Public Library of Charlotte & Mecklenburg County, Inc (North), Charlotte NC. 704-374-2882
Ramsey, Elaine, *Librn,* Newport-Vermillion County Library, Newport IN. 317-492-3555

Ramsey, Jack, *Dir,* Glendale Public Library, Glendale CA. 213-956-2030
Ramsey, Marilyn, *Acq,* University of San Diego, James S Copley Library, San Diego CA. 714-291-6480, Ext 4312, 4313, 4314
Ramsey, Mildred, *Asst Dir,* East Baton Rouge Parish Library, Baton Rouge LA. 504-389-3360
Ramsey, Ruth, *Librn,* Brooklyn Public Library (Kensington), Brooklyn NY. 212-436-0525
Ramsey, Shirley, *Librn,* White County Public Library (Pangburn), Searcy AR. 501-728-4612
Ranadive, Ujwal, *Librn,* Burns & Roe Inc, Technical Library, Oradell NJ. 201-265-2000
Rancans, Tereze, *Cat,* State University of New York Maritime College, Stephen B Luce Library, Bronx NY. 212-892-3004, Ext 235
Rand, Duncan, *Dir,* Lethbridge Public Library, Lethbridge AB. 403-329-3233
Rand, Jane, *Librn,* Brattleboro Retreat, Patient's Library, Brattleboro VT. 257-7785 Ext 352
Rand, Robin, *Chief Librn,* Saginaw Health Sciences Library, Saginaw MI. 517-771-6846
Randall, Ann K, *Asst Univ Librn-Ref & Coll Develop,* Brown University (University Library), Providence RI. 401-863-2167
Randall, Anne, *Asst Librn,* Peacham Library, Peacham VT. 802-592-3216
Randall, Cynthia, *Ref & Doc,* Nassau Library System, Uniondale NY. 516-292-8920
Randall, Dolly, *Dir,* Jonathan Trumbull Library, Lebanon CT. 203-642-7763
Randall, Doris, *Doc,* Tulare County Library System, Visalia CA. 209-733-8440
Randall, Frances B, *Librn,* Peacham Library, Peacham VT. 802-592-3216
Randall, Jane, *Dir,* Greenville Public Library, Greenville NY. 518-966-8205
Randall, Laurel, *Librn,* Westlock Municipal Library, Westlock AB. 403-349-3060
Randall, Lenore L, *Cat,* Ashtabula County District Library, Ashtabula OH. 216-997-9341
Randall, Lynn E, *Dir,* Northeastern Bible College, Lincoln Memorial Library, Essex Fells NJ. 201-226-1074, Ext 29, 50
Randall, Margaret, *Dir,* Harnett County Library, Lillington NC. 919-893-3446
Randall, Mary, *Media,* Arlington Public Library, Arlington TX. 817-275-2763, 265-3311, Ext 347
Randall, Ruth, *Supvr,* New Jersey Correctional Institution for Women, Edna Mahan Hall Library, Clinton NJ. 201-735-7111, Ext 237
Randall, Virginia, *Librn,* New England Deaconess Hospital (School of Nursing Library), Boston MA. 617-732-8382
Randazzo, Marguerite D, *Cat,* Saint Martin Parish Library, Saint Martinville LA. 318-394-4086
Randel, Janet, *ILL,* Newport Beach Public Library, Newport Beach CA. 714-640-2141
Randell, Barbara, *On-Line Servs,* Sperry Corp, Sperry UNIVAC Div, Information Service Center, Roseville MN. 612-631-5386
Randich, Karla, *Ref,* California Western School of Law, San Diego CA. 714-239-0391, Ext 36
Randle, Jeanne, *Lectr,* Concordia University, Library Studies Program, PQ. 514-482-0320, Ext 324
Randle, Rasheeda, *ILL & Circ,* Indianapolis-Marion County Public Library, Indianapolis IN. 317-635-5662
Randleman, Lillian, *Librn,* Paragould Public Library (Rector Public), Rector AR. 501-595-2410
Randolfe, Anita, *Librn,* New York Chamber of Commerce & Industry Library, New York NY. 212-760-1300
Randolph, Elise, *Librn,* Bancroft Memorial Library, Hopedale MA. 617-473-7692
Randolph, Elise P, *Dir,* Patten Free Library, Bath ME. 207-443-5141
Randolph, Eva, *Circ & Ref,* Lurleen B Wallace State Junior College Library, Andalusia AL. 205-222-6591, Ext 265
Randolph, Jane, *Librn,* Kern County Library (Delano Branch), Delano CA. 805-861-2130
Randolph, Lois M, *Librn,* William H Aitken Memorial Library, Croswell MI. 313-679-3627
Randolph, Virginia, *Spec Coll & Bibliog Instr,* Pepperdine University Library, Payson Library, Malibu CA. 213-456-4252
Randorf, Patricia, *Acq,* North Country Community College, Learning Resource Center, Saranac Lake NY. 518-891-2915, Ext 222
Raney, Carolyn, *Tech Serv,* Hendrix College, Olin C Bailey Library, Conway AR. 501-329-9323

Raney, Elizabeth, *Librn,* Tallahatchie County Library, Charleston MS. 601-647-2638
Raney, Leon, *Dean,* South Dakota State University, Hilton M Briggs Library, Brookings SD. 605-688-5106
Ranger, Lydia S, *Librn,* Hawaii State Library System, Library for the Blind & Physically Handicapped, Honolulu HI. 808-732-7767
Ranger, Paquerette, *Librn,* University of Montreal Libraries (Law), Montreal PQ. 514-343-7028
Ranger, William R, *Librn,* Federal Aviation Administration, Pacific-Asia Region Library, Honolulu HI. 808-546-7544
Rankeillor, Robert K, *Librn,* Santa Fe Community College Library (South Campus Medical Library), Gainesville FL. 904-375-4200, Ext 200
Rankey, Brother Edward, *Librn,* Atonement Seminary Library, Washington DC. 202-529-1114, Ext 21
Rankie, Mary, *Librn,* Thorold Public Library (Port Robinson Deposit Branch), Port Robinson ON. 416-384-9020
Rankin, John L, *Librn,* Masonic Grand Lodge Library, A F & A M Masonic Library, Winnipeg MB. 204-284-2423
Rankin, Joseph T, *Curator,* New York Public Library (Special Collections (Cent Bldg) Arents Collections), New York NY. 212-790-6110
Rankin, Joseph T, *Curator,* New York Public Library (Spencer Collection), New York NY. 212-790-6110
Rankin, Lynne, *Librn,* San Diego Public Library (North Claremont), San Diego CA. 714-274-4610
Rankin, Mrs G B, *Librn,* Truro Public Library, Truro IA. 515-765-4220
Rannit, Aleksis, *Curator Slavic & E European Coll,* Yale University Library (Sterling Memorial Library), New Haven CT. 203-436-8335
Ranschenberg, Bradford L, *In Charge,* Museum of Early Southern Decorative Arts Library, Winston-Salem NC. 919-722-6148
Ransley, Virginia, *Acq,* Greensboro College, James Addison Jones Library, Greensboro NC. 919-272-7102, Ext 234
Ransom, Charles, *Librn,* Indianapolis-Marion County Public Library (Emerson), Indianapolis IN. 317-635-5662
Ransom, Doris, *Librn,* Schenectady County Public Library (Wingate), Schenectady NY. 518-382-3507
Ransom, Hariette, *Librn,* Corvallis Public Library (Alsea Branch), Alsea OR. 503-487-5061
Ransom, Helen, *Librn,* Columbia Scientific Industries Library, Austin TX. 512-258-5191
Ransom, Mary Louise, *Librn,* Civil Aeronautics Board Library, Washington DC. 202-673-5101
Ransom, Stanley A, *Dir,* Clinton-Essex-Franklin Library System, Plattsburgh NY. 518-563-5190
Ranson, Brian, *ILL,* Dartmouth Regional Library, Dartmouth NS. 902-466-7623
Rantala, Donald, *Librn,* Wisconsin-Indianhead Technical Institute Library, Superior WI. 715-394-6677
Rantanen, Mary, *Asst Librn,* Maclure Library, Pittsford VT. 802-483-2972
Ranville, Judy, *Dir,* Mackinaw Area Public Library, Mackinaw City MI. 616-436-5451
Ranz, James, *Dean,* University of Kansas Libraries, Watson Memorial Library, Lawrence KS. 913-864-3601
Rao, Angelo, *AV,* Ontario College of Art Library, Toronto ON. 416-977-5311, Ext 54 & 55
Rao, Paladugu V, *Media,* Eastern Illinois University, Booth Library, Charleston IL. 217-581-2210
Rao, Rama K, *Cat,* Carlow College, Grace Library, Pittsburgh PA. 412-578-6137
Rapacki, Florence, *Librn,* Free Public Library of Woodbridge (Iselin Branch), Iselin NJ. 201-283-1200
Rapard, Carol, *Librn,* Burlingame Community Library, Burlingame KS. 913-654-3922
Raper, Francine, *Circ,* Arlington Public Library, Arlington TX. 817-275-2763, 265-3311, Ext 347
Raper, Jr, James E, *Tech Serv,* Medical Library Center of New York, New York NY. 212-427-1630
Rapetti, Vincent, *Dir,* NASA, John F Kennedy Space Center Library, Kennedy Space Center FL. 305-867-3600, 3615

Raphael, Mary E, *Philos, Psychol & Relig,* Public Library of the District of Columbia, Martin Luther King Memorial Library, Washington DC. 202-727-1101
Rapking, Hortenzia, *Librn,* Kanawha County Public Library (Library for the Blind & Physically Handicapped), Charleston WV. 304-343-4061, 348-4062
Rapking, Hortenzia, *Librn Blind,* West Virginia Library Commission, Science & Cultural Center, Charleston WV. 304-348-2041
Rapking, Hortenzia, *Librn,* West Virginia Regional Library, Services for the Blind & Physically Handicapped, Charleston WV. 304-348-4061
Rapp, Derinda D, *In Charge,* Bureau of Land Management Library, Shoshone District, Shoshone ID. 208-886-2208, Ext 35
Rapp, Gloria P, *Dir,* Monroe Free Library, Monroe NY. 914-783-4411
Rapp, Joan, *Librn,* Temple University of the Commonwealth System of Higher Education (Center City), Philadelphia PA. 215-787-6950
Rapp, Kenneth, *Acting Archivist,* United States Military Academy Library, West Point NY. 914-938-2230
Rapp, Marilyn A, *Librn,* Chicago Public Library (Jefferson Park), Chicago IL. 312-736-9075
Rappaport, Gersten, *Asst Dir,* Fordham University, School of Law Library, New York NY. 212-841-5223
Rapping, Ethel, *Librn,* Chicago Public Library (Austin-Irving), Chicago IL. 312-286-6222
Rapske, A, *Librn,* North American Baptist College Library, Edmonton AB. 403-437-1960
Raring, Ellen, *Ref,* Pottsville Free Public Library, Pottsville Library District Center, Pottsville PA. 622-8105; 622-8880
Rasch, Kathryn M, *Asst Librn, YA & Ch,* North Suburban District Library, Loves Park IL. 815-633-4247, 633-4248
Rasche, Richard R, *Curator,* University of Texas Medical Branch, Moody Medical Library, Galveston TX. 713-765-1971
Raschiatore, Amelia, *Ch,* Greece Public Library, Rochester NY. 716-225-8930, 225-8951
Raschke, V, *ILL,* Boreal Institute for Northern Studies Library, Edmonton AB. 403-432-4409
Raschkow, Elenka, *Circ,* Lansing Community College Library, Lansing MI. 517-373-9978
Rasco, Estela, *Librn,* Hialeah John F Kennedy Library (Lua A Curtis), Hialeah FL. 305-888-1652
Rasco, Nancy, *Librn,* Coke County Library, Robert Lee TX. 915-453-2495
Rashap, Harriett, *Acq,* Edison Free Public Library, Edison NJ. 201-287-2298
Rask, Stephen, *Librn,* Carnegie Library, Rockport MA. 617-546-6934
Raski, Charlotte, *Librn,* Public Library of Charlotte & Mecklenburg County, Inc (Huntersville Branch), Huntersville NC. 704-875-2412
Rasmus, Evelyn, *Librn,* West Point Public Library, West Point NE. 402-372-3831
Rasmussen, Dorothy, *Ad,* Skokie Public Library, Skokie IL. 312-673-7774
Rasmussen, Gary C, *Cat,* University of Texas Medical Branch, Moody Medical Library, Galveston TX. 713-765-1971
Rasmussen, Gordon, *Circ,* Northern Illinois University, Founders Memorial Library, De Kalb IL. 815-753-1094
Rasmussen, Helga, *Librn,* Tyler Public Library, Tyler MN. 507-247-5175
Rasmussen, Jane, *Librn,* Chemical Manufacturers Association Library, Washington DC. 202-328-4229
Rasmussen, Joy, *Librn,* Fresno County Free Library (Cedar-Clinton), Fresno CA. 209-442-1770
Rasmussen, Marie, *ILL,* McCook Community College, Learning Resource Center, McCook NE. 308-345-6303, Exts 40&41
Rasmussen, Marsha, *ILL & Ref,* Southwestern Adventist College, Findley Memorial Library, Keene TX. 817-645-3921, Ext 242
Rasmussen, Rosemary, *Ch,* Union City Free Public Library, Union City NJ. 201-866-7500
Rasmussen, Ruth, *Ref,* Dana College, C A Dana-Life Library, Blair NE. 402-426-4101, Ext 119
Rasmussen, Shirley, *Librn,* Sidney Public Library, Sidney IA. 712-374-2223

Rasmusson, Alyce, *Dir,* Heart of America Library, Rugby Public Library, Rugby ND. 701-776-6223
Rasnick, Phyllis, *Librn,* Johns Hopkins University Libraries (Oncology Center Library), Baltimore MD. 301-955-8850
Rasor, John, *Ref,* McLennan Community College Library, Waco TX. 817-756-6551, Ext 264
Rassmussen, Barbara, *ILL,* Grand Rapids Public Library, Grand Rapids MN. 218-326-3081
Ratchford, Esther, *Librn,* Scenic Regional Library of Franklin, Gasconade & Warren Counties (Herman Service Center), Hermann MO. 314-486-2024
Ratcliff, Elnora, *Dir,* God's Bible School & College Library, Cincinnati OH. 513-721-7944, Ext 58
Ratcliff, Linda, *Bkmobile Coordr,* Butte County Library, Oroville CA. 916-534-4525
Ratcliff, Marcia G, *Dir,* C B S Inc, CBS News Reference Library, New York NY. 212-975-2877
Rathbone, Marjorie, *Asst Dir & Acq,* Saint Joseph's University Libraries (Drexel Library), Philadelphia PA. 215-879-7559
Rathclement, Charles, *Music,* Thomas Crane Public Library, Subregional Headquarters for Eastern Massachusetts Regional Library System, Quincy MA. 617-471-2400
Rathe, Celine, *Circ,* College De Sainte-Foy, Centre des Medias, Sainte Foy PQ. 418-657-3624
Rather, Lucia J, *Dir, Cataloging,* Library of Congress, Washington DC. 202-287-5000
Rathgeb, Eileen, *Librn,* Adams Memorial Library, Latrobe PA. 412-537-2821
Ratliff, Neal, *Music,* University of Maryland at College Park (Theodore R McKeldin Library), College Park MD. 301-454-2853, 454-5977
Ratliff, Priscilla, *Supvr,* Ashland Oil Inc, Ashland Chemical Co Research Library, Dublin OH. 614-889-3281
Ratner, Rhoda, *Librn,* Smithsonian Institution Libraries (Museum Reference Center), Washington DC. 202-381-6551
Ratte, Michele Bazin, *Librn,* Government of the Province of Quebec, Documentation Center of the Dept of Municipal Affairs, Quebec PQ. 418-643-6570
Ratzenberger, Katherine M, *Ref,* Smithsonian Institution Libraries (Library of the National Collection of Fine Arts & the National Portrait Gallery), Washington DC. 202-357-1886
Ratzlaff, Nina, *Dir,* Warner Southern College, Learning Resource Center, Lake Wales FL. 813-638-1426, Ext 28
Rau, Charlotte, *ILL,* Valparaiso-Porter County Public Library System & Administrative Headquarters, Valparaiso IN. 219-462-0524
Rau, Susan L, *Librn,* 3M (The 230 Technical Library), Saint Paul MN. 612-733-5017
Rau, Wendy F, *Asst Librn,* Androscoggin County Law Library, Auburn ME. 207-782-3121
Rauch, Ann B, *Librn,* General Electric Co (Ordnance Systems, Engineering Library), Pittsfield MA. 413-494-4207
Rauch, Ellen, *Circ,* Public Library of the City of Somerville, Somerville MA. 617-623-5000
Rauch, Ellen, *Librn,* Public Library of the City of Somerville (West), Somerville MA. 617-625-1985
Rauch, Jerome, *Librn,* University of Pennsylvania Libraries (Medical, Nursing & Biological Sciences Library), Philadelphia PA. 215-243-5815
Rauch, Marian, *Librn,* Globe-Union, Inc, Technical Library, Milwaukee WI. 414-228-2382
Raucher, Marlene, *Bibliog Instr,* Vernon Area Public Library, Prairie View IL. 312-634-3650
Rauco, Louis F, *Newspaper Section,* State Library of Pennsylvania, Harrisburg PA. 717-787-2646
Raudzens, Jadwiga, *Cat Rec,* University of Toronto Libraries (University Library), Toronto ON. 416-978-2294
Raue, Philip, *Cat,* University of Texas at El Paso Library, El Paso TX. 747-5683; 747-5684
Rauff, Edward A, *Dir,* Lutheran Council in the Usa, Research & Information Center, New York NY. 212-532-6350
Rauh, Ed, *Dir,* Jackson County Public Library, Ripley WV. 304-372-2831
Raum, Hans, *Assoc Dir,* Middlebury College, Egbert Starr Library, Middlebury VT. 802-388-7621

Rausch, Carol-Ann, *In Charge,* Pawtucket Memorial Hospital, Health Sciences Library, Pawtucket RI. 401-722-6000
Rausch, Ervin J, *Dir,* Crosier House of Studies Library, Fort Wayne IN. 219-489-3521
Rausch, G Jay, *Dean,* Kansas State University, Farrell Library, Manhattan KS. 913-532-6516
Rausch, Lynn, *Tech Serv,* Loras College, Wahlert Memorial Library, Dubuque IA. 319-588-7125
Rauschenberger, Douglas, *Ref,* Haddonfield Public Library, Haddonfield NJ. 609-429-1304
Rauscher, Margaret A, *Librn,* Berlin Public Library, Berlin MA. 617-838-2812
Rauth, Eileen, *Media,* Burlington County Library, Mount Holly NJ. 609-267-9660
Rauth, Irene, *Ch,* Avon Township Public Library, Rochester MI. 313-651-1426
Rauzi, Ellen M, *Asst Librn,* Eveleth Public Library, Eveleth MN. 218-741-4913
Raveling, Betty L, *Librn,* Melvin Public Library, Melvin IA. 712-736-2107
Raven, Donald, *Librn,* Hawaii State Library System (Hawaii-Kait), Honolulu HI. 808-395-2310
Raven, Leila, *Asst Dir,* Spencer Public Library, Spencer IA. 712-262-2960
Ravina, Doris M, *Librn,* New York Supreme Court, Fifth Judicial District Law Library, Utica NY. 315-798-5703
Ravvin, Linda, *Ref,* Dawson College Library, Montreal PQ. 514-525-2501, Ext 297
Rawhouser, Donna, *Ch,* Anacortes Public Library, Anacortes WA. 206-293-2700
Rawles, Carolyn, *Dir,* Clinton Public Library, Clinton IN. 317-832-8349
Rawles, Jr, Henry A, *Librn,* Battelle Columbus Laboratories Library, Columbus OH. 614-424-6306
Rawley, III, Wayne, *Reader Serv,* University of Iowa Libraries, Iowa City IA. 319-353-4450
Rawlings, Lattie, *Acq,* Leavenworth Public Library, Leavenworth KS. 913-682-5666
Rawlings, Margaret L, *Librn,* Barry Public Library, Barry IL. 217-335-2149
Rawlins, Eric, *Librn,* Broward County Division of Libraries (Dania Branch), Dania FL. 305-925-1508
Rawlins, Gordon W, *Asst Dean, Bibliog Resources & Servs,* Pennsylvania State University, Fred Lewis Pattee Library, University Park PA. 814-865-0401
Rawlins, Susan, *ILL,* University of Evansville, Clifford Memorial Library & Learning Resources, Evansville IN. 812-479-2462
Rawlinson, Jo Ann, *Librn,* Coconino County Law Library, Flagstaff AZ. 602-774-5011, Ext 56
Rawls, Andrew, *Media,* Southern Baptist Theological Seminary, James P Boyce Centennial Library, Louisville KY. 502-897-4807
Rawls, D E, *Libr Supv,* Newport News Shipbuilding & Dry Dock Co, Library Services Department, Newport News VA. 804-380-2610
Rawls, Karen, *Librn,* Georgia Department of Offender Rehabilitation, Reference-Resource Center, Atlanta GA. 404-894-5383
Rawls, Linda, *Librn,* Yuma City-County Library (Wenden), Wenden AZ. 602-782-1871
Rawls, M, *Reader Serv & Ref,* NASA, John F Kennedy Space Center Library, Kennedy Space Center FL. 305-867-3600, 3615
Rawls, Molly G, *Mgr,* R J Reynolds Tobacco Company (Management Information Library), Winston-Salem NC. 919-777-5000
Rawnsley, Jill, *On-Line Servs,* University of North Dakota, Chester Fritz Library, Grand Forks ND. 701-777-2617
Rawoof, Jane, *Tech Serv & Acq,* Broome Community College, Cecil C Tyrrell Learning Resources Center, Binghamton NY. 607-772-5020
Rawson, Barbara K, *Librn,* Richmond Free Public Library, Richmond MA. 413-698-3834
Rawson, Craig, *Media,* Loma Linda University Library, Riverside CA. 714-785-2022
Rawson, Marion, *Librn,* South Londonderry Free Library, South Londonderry VT. 802-824-4371
Rawson, Nancy, *YA,* Wellesley Free Library, Subregional Headquarters for Eastern Massachusetts Regional Library System, Wellesley MA. 617-235-1610
Rawstron, Helen, *Librn,* New York Public Library (Muhlenberg), New York NY. 212-924-1585

Ray, Audrey, *Librn,* Dallas County Public Library (Maxine Gilliam Memorial Branch), Wilmer TX. 214-225-6620
Ray, Betty, *Circ,* Gardendale Public Library, Gardendale AL. 205-631-6639
Ray, Betty, *Librn,* Lake County Public Library (Hobart Public), Hobart IN. 219-942-2243
Ray, Carol, *Med Ref & Search Analyst,* Indiana University (School of Medicine Library), Indianapolis IN. 317-264-7182
Ray, Debbie, *Actg Librn,* Harnett County Library (Angier Branch), Angier NC. 919-639-4413
Ray, Dee Ann, *Dir,* Western Plains Library System, Clinton OK. 405-323-0974
Ray, Dorothea, *Asst Dir,* Central State University Library, Edmond OK. 405-341-2980, Ext 494, 495 & 496
Ray, Edwin, *On-Line Servs,* Mississippi State University, Mitchell Memorial Library, Mississippi State MS. 601-325-4225
Ray, Frances W, *Cat,* Maud Preston Palenske Memorial Library, Saint Joseph Public Library, Saint Joseph MI. 616-983-7106
Ray, Gordon, *Ad,* Saskatoon Public Library, Saskatoon SK. 306-664-9555
Ray, H Annette, *Librn,* United States Army (Fort Polk Recreation Services Div Library), Fort Polk LA. 318-537-2911
Ray, Helen, *Ref & Rare Bks,* Franklin Library Association, Franklin PA. 814-432-5062
Ray, Jean M, *Maps,* Southern Illinois University at Carbondale, Delyte W Morris Library, Carbondale IL. 618-453-2522
Ray, John G, *Asst Dir,* Loyola-Notre Dame Library, Inc, Baltimore MD. 301-532-8787
Ray, Joyce, *Spec Coll,* University of Texas Health Science Center at San Antonio Library, San Antonio TX. 512-691-6271
Ray, Kathryn, *Acq & Per,* Brookings Institution Library, Washington DC. 202-797-6240
Ray, Lillian, *Media,* Fairfield Public Library, Fairfield CT. 203-259-8303
Ray, Margaret L, *Librn,* Stephentown Memorial Library, Stephentown NY. 518-733-5750
Ray, Mary Frances, *Acq,* Henry Ford Community College, Eshleman Library, Dearborn MI. 313-271-2750, Ext 378
Ray, Mel, *Librn,* United States Navy (Underwater Sound Reference DET Technical Library), Orlando FL. 305-859-5120
Ray, Nancy, *Librn,* Public Library of Charlotte & Mecklenburg County, Inc (West), Charlotte NC. 704-374-2721
Ray, Patricia, *Tech Serv,* Geauga County Public Library, Chardon OH. 216-285-7601
Ray, Sherry, *Librn,* Houston Chronicle Editorial Library, Houston TX. 713-220-7313
Rayas, Tomas, *Clerk III,* San Antonio Public Library (Circulation), San Antonio TX. 512-299-7807
Raybon, Elaine, *Cat,* Henderson State University, Huie Library, Arkadelphia AR. 501-246-5511, Ext 200
Raybon, Jean, *Asst Librn, Tech Serv & Cat,* Ouachita Baptist University, Riley Library, Arkadelphia AR. 501-246-4531, Ext 121
Rayburn, Ella Sue, *Asst Hist,* United States Department of the Interior, Petersburg National Battlefield Library, Petersburg VA. 804-732-3531
Rayburn, Helen, *Bkmobile Librn,* Buffalo Trace Regional Library, Flemingsburg KY. 606-845-9571
Rayburn, Helen H, *Librn,* Lewis County Public Library, Vanceburg KY. 606-796-2532
Rayburn, June, *Librn,* Methodist Hospital, School of Nursing Library, Lubbock TX. 806-792-1011, Ext 442
Raych, A Morton, *Dir,* Hyde Collection Library, Glens Falls NY. 518-792-1761
Rayman, Ron, *ILL,* Western Illinois University Libraries, Macomb IL. 309-298-2411
Rayment, Peter, *Circ,* Salem Public Library, Salem OR. 503-588-6071
Raymond, Betty, *Circ,* Iowa Wesleyan College, Chadwick Library, Mount Pleasant IA. 319-385-8021, Ext 131
Raymond, Chadwick, *Dir,* Lincoln Township Public Library, Stevensville MI. 616-429-9575
Raymond, Estelle, *Librn,* North Country Hospital & Health Center, Inc, Newport VT. 802-334-8559

Raymond, J H, *In Charge,* Investart Publishers, Research Library, New York NY. 212-780-0053
Raymond, Jean, *Librn,* Staten Island Institute of Arts & Sciences Library & Archives (High Rock Park Conservation Center), Staten Island NY. 212-987-6233
Raymond, Joan Bieri, *Asst Dir,* Mount Lebanon Public Library, Pittsburgh PA. 412-531-1912
Raymond, Judith, *Librn,* Twinsburg Public Library, Twinsburg OH. 216-425-4268
Raymond, Leitha, *Librn,* Ingham County Library (Leslie Branch), Leslie MI. 517-589-9400
Raymond, Lorraine M, *Pub Servs,* University of Washington Libraries (Health Sciences), Seattle WA. 206-543-5530
Raymond, M, *Bio-Sci,* Mount San Antonio College, Learning Resources Center, Walnut CA. 714-594-5611, Ext 260
Raymond, Marilyn, *Librn,* Bridgewater Public Library, Plymouth NH. 603-536-2616
Raymond, Miriam, *Ref,* Fremont Public Library District, Mundelein IL. 312-566-8702
Raymond, Ruth S, *Librn,* Barrett Friendly Library, Mountainhome PA. 717-595-7171
Raymond, Sister M, *Ref,* Madonna College Library, Livonia MI. 313-591-1200
Raynard, Shirley M, *Librn,* Flint Public Library, Middleton MA. 617-774-8132
Rayner, Shirley, *Librn,* New Haven Free Public Library (Fair Haven), New Haven CT. 203-787-8115
Raynock, Jean, *Librn,* Midland-Ross Corp, Thermal Systems Technical Center Library, Toledo OH. 419-537-6449
Raynor, Georgia E, *Cat,* Lehigh University Libraries, Bethlehem PA. 861-3026 (Dir), 861-3050 (Ref), 861-3030 (Circ), 861-3055 (ILL)
Raynsford, Barbara, *On-Line Servs,* Maricopa County Library System, Phoenix AZ. 602-269-2535
Rayward, W Boyd, *Dean,* University of Chicago, Graduate Library School, IL. 312-753-3482
Raz, Robert E, *Dir,* Grand Rapids Public Library, Grand Rapids MI. 616-456-4400
Raz-Smith, Mary E, *Asst Dir,* Hayner Public Library District, Alton IL. 618-462-0651
Razer, Bob, *Tech Serv,* Central Arkansas Library System, Little Rock AR. 501-374-7546
Rea, Jay, *Rare Bks, Archives & Spec Coll,* Eastern Washington University, John F Kennedy Memorial Library, Cheney WA. 509-359-2261
Rea, Louise, *Circ,* East Saint Louis Public Library, East Saint Louis IL. 618-874-7280
Read, Don, *Hist,* California State University, Northridge, Delmar T Oviatt & South Libraries, Northridge CA. 213-885-2271
Read, Glenn, *Latin Am Studies,* Indiana University at Bloomington, University Libraries, Bloomington IN. 812-337-3403
Read, Lucille, *Ch,* Keene Public Library, Keene NH. 603-352-0157
Read, Lynn L, *Librn,* Basf Wyandotte Corporation, Pigments Div Library, Holland MI. 616-392-2391
Read, Marilyn, *Librn,* City of Brampton Public Library & Art Gallery (Four Corners), Brampton ON. 416-453-2444
Reade, Rita D, *Librn,* Life Savers, Inc, Research & Development Library, Port Chester NY. 914-937-3200
Reading, Kenneth, *Dir,* Public Library of Johnston County & Smithfield, Smithfield NC. 919-934-8146
Ready, Michael J, *Head Librn,* Peat, Marwick, Mitchell & Co (Accounting & Auditing Library), New York NY. 212-758-9700
Reagan, Chris E, *In Charge,* Westinghouse Electric Corp, Technical Library, Philadelphia PA. 215-595-4203
Reagan, Fannie, *Librn,* Lake Lanier Regional Library (Dawson County), Dawsonville GA. 404-265-3221
Reagan, Lola, *Librn,* Summit County Library (Breckenridge Branch), Breckenridge CO. 303-453-6098
Reagan, Michael, *Librn,* Glendale Public Library (Grandview), Glendale CA. 213-956-2030
Realmuto, Ann, *Librn,* Paterson Free Public Library (Totowa), Paterson NJ. 201-881-3784
Ream, Diane, *Librn & On-Line Servs,* Baptist Hospital, Health Sciences Library, Miami FL. 305-596-1960, Ext 6139

Ream, Judith, *Head Librn,* Kendall College Library, Evanston IL. 312-869-5240, Ext 247, 248

Ream, Karen, *Bibliog Instr,* Indiana Central University Library, Krannert Memorial Library, Indianapolis IN. 317-788-3268

Ream, Sally, *Dir,* Miami Dade Community College (Medical Center Campus Library), Miami FL. 305-547-1256

Reaman, Elaine, *Circ,* University of Waterloo Library, Waterloo ON. 519-885-1211

Reames, J Mitchell, *Dir,* Francis Marion College, James A Rogers Library, Florence SC. 803-669-4121, Ext 321

Reames, Mary Alice, *Circ,* South Georgia Regional Library, Valdosta-Lowndes County Public Library, Valdosta GA. 912-247-3405

Reams, Pearl, *Libr Assts,* Cumberland Valley Regional Library, Subheadquarters, London KY. 606-864-9346

Reams, Jr, Bernard D, *Dir,* Washington University Libraries (Freund Law Library), Saint Louis MO. 314-889-6459

Reandeau, Walter E, *Dir,* Sun Prairie Public Library, Sun Prairie WI. 608-837-5644

Reasoner, Emmalou, *Librn,* Osburn Public Library, Osburn ID. 208-752-0001

Reasoner, Lynne, *Govt Pub & Spec Coll,* University of Redlands, George & Verda Armacost Library, Redlands CA. 714-793-2121, Ext 472

Reasoner, Mary Beth, *Asst Dir,* Tecumseh Public Library, Tecumseh MI. 517-423-2238

Reasor, Daniel W, *Librn,* McDowell Public Library, Welch WV. 304-436-3070

Reaves, Alice C, *Asst Librn,* North Carolina Supreme Court Library, Raleigh NC. 919-733-3425

Reaves, Deleath, *Prof,* Jacksonville State University, College of Library Science, Communications & Instructional Media, AL. 205-435-6390

Reaves, George A, *In Charge,* National Park Service, Shiloh National Military Park Service Library, Shiloh TN. 901-689-5275

Reaves, Gloria, *Instr,* Jacksonville State University, College of Library Science, Communications & Instructional Media, AL. 205-435-6390

Reavis, Raymond, *Librn,* Penitentiary of New Mexico, La Biblioteca Central, Santa Fe NM. 505-827-2485

Reback, Ruth, *Librn,* Syracuse Police Department Library, Syracuse NY. 315-425-6101

Rebar, Diane, *Ad,* Hoyt Library, Kingston PA. 717-287-2013

Rebeck, Robbyn, *Ref,* Blue Island Public Library, Blue Island IL. 312-388-1078

Rebenack, John H, *Dir,* Akron-Summit County Public Library, Akron OH. 216-762-7621

Rebenstock, Anne, *Librn,* Morton County Library, Mandan ND. 701-663-6133

Reber, Patricia, *Cat,* Brescia College Library, Owensboro KY. 502-685-3131, Ext 213

Rebischke, Anne F, *Librn,* Carnegie City Library, Little Falls MN. 612-632-9676

Reboks, Aija, *Asst Librn,* Ignace Public Library, Ignace ON. 807-934-2548

Rebuldela, Harriet, *Acq,* University of Colorado at Boulder (University Libraries), Boulder CO. 303-492-7511

Rechkemer, Elaine C, *Librn,* Mokena Community Public Library District, Mokena IL. 312-479-9663

Recker, Linda, *YA & Circ,* New Milford Public Library, New Milford NJ. 201-262-1221

Reckner, Joyce, *Cat,* Kenton County Public Library, Covington KY. 606-292-2363

Reckoff, Lola, *Librn,* Canby Public Library, Canby MN. 507-223-5738

Record, Kay, *Librn,* Indianapolis-Marion County Public Library (Marwood), Indianapolis IN. 317-635-5662

Record, William J, *Librn,* Misericordia Hospital (Medical Library), Bronx NY. 212-920-9869

Record, Winifred, *Librn,* Osmond Public Library, Osmond NE. 402-748-3382

Rector, Mrs A, *Librn,* British Columbia Department of the Attorney General, Judges Library, Vancouver BC. 604-668-2799

Rector, Patricia, *ILL,* Thomas Hackney Braswell Memorial Library, Rocky Mount NC. 442-1937 & 442-1951

Rector, Peggy, *Bkmobile Coordr,* Mccreary County Public Library District, Whitley City KY. 606-376-8738

Rector, Warren, *Dir,* Franciscan Friars, Education Center Library, Lake Geneva WI. 414-248-6203

Red, Lynn, *Librn,* Washington State Library (Rainier School Resident Library), Buckley WA. 206-829-1111, Ext 367

Redd, Brenda, *ILL & Circ,* Jeffersonville Township Public Library, Jeffersonville IN. 812-282-7765

Redd, Gwendolyn L, *Supvry Librn,* United States Army (Morale Support Activities Libraries), Fort Benning GA. 404-545-1769

Redd, Jan, *Acq,* De Anza College, Learning Center, Cupertino CA. 408-996-4761

Redd, Kathy, *Librn,* Montrose County Regional District Library (Paradox Branch), Paradox CO. 303-859-7346

Redd, Lisa, *Asst Librn,* Oklahoma State University, Oklahoma City Branch, Technical Institute Library, Oklahoma City OK. 405-947-4421, Ext 251

Redd, Norma, *Librn,* Marion Public Library (Henkle-Holliday Memorial), La Rue OH. 614-499-3066

Redden, Camille, *Ref,* Southern University, Shreveport-Bossier City Campus Library, Shreveport LA. 318-424-6552, Ext 238

Reddick, Haul M, *Dir,* Arizona Resources Consortium, AZ. 602-757-4331, Ext 59

Reddick, Haul M, *Dir,* Mohave Community College, Resource Center, Kingman AZ. 602-757-4331, Ext 19

Reddick, Jean, *AV,* Coshocton Public Library, Coshocton OH. 614-622-0956

Reddick, Mary L, *Librn,* Lake Worth Public Library, Lake Worth TX. 817-237-9681

Reddick, Mrs E M, *Librn,* Burleigh, Anstruther & Chandos Union Public Library, Apsley ON. 705-656-4333

Redding, Claire P, *Asst Librn,* T O H P Burnham Public Library, Essex MA. 617-768-7410

Redding, Heather, *Ref,* EG&G Idaho, Inc, INEL Technical Library, Idaho Falls ID. 208-526-1185

Redding, John, *Librn,* National Baseball Hall of Fame & Museum Inc, National Baseball Library, Cooperstown NY. 607-547-9988

Reddy, Alla R, *Actg Dir,* Cheyney State College, Leslie Pinckney Hill Library, Cheyney PA. 215-758-2000, Ext 2203, 2208, 2245

Reddy, Ida, *Ref,* Hamilton Public Library, Hamilton ON. 416-529-8111

Reddy, Sigrid R, *Dir,* Watertown Free Public Library, Watertown MA. 617-924-5390

Redfern, Sheila, *Librn,* Dranetz Engineering Laboratories Library, South Plainfield NJ. 201-755-7080

Rediess, Patricia, *Ref,* Waukesha Public Library, Waukesha WI. 414-542-4297

Redifer, Cynthia, *Librn,* Jefferson County Public Library (Wheatridge Branch), Wheatridge CO. 303-424-8949

Rediger, Mrs Jack, *Librn,* Webermeier Memorial Library, Milford NE. 402-761-2937

Reding, Helena, *Librn,* Rossville Community Library, Rossville KS. 913-584-6454

Redlin, Dorothy, *Librn,* Photographic-Art Library, Regina SK. 306-565-6298

Redman, Edith, *Tech Serv,* Houghton College, Willard J Houghton Library, Houghton NY. 716-567-2211, Ext 227

Redman, Frances, *Asst Dir,* A K Smiley Public Library, Redlands CA. 714-793-2201

Redmon, Mary, *Cat,* William Jewell College, Curry Library, Liberty MO. 816-781-3806

Redmon, Sandra, *Bkmobile Coordr,* Shelby County Library District, Shelbyville KY. 502-633-3803

Redmond, D A, *Geology & Maps,* Queen's University at Kingston, Douglas Library, Kingston ON. 547-5950 (Admin); 547-6992 (Chief Librn)

Redmond, Elizabeth, *Librn & On-Line Servs,* Leo Burnett Co, Inc, Research Department Library, Chicago IL. 312-565-5959

Redmond, Jennie M, *Librn,* Calhoun County Public Library, Saint Matthews SC. 803-874-3389

Redmond, Joan, *Librn,* Brantford General Nursing Library, Brantford ON. 519-759-2770

Redmond, Judy, *Ch,* Fairbanks North Star Borough Public Library & Regional Center, Fairbanks AK. 907-452-5177

Redmond, Mary, *Ref,* Illinois State Library, Springfield IL. 217-782-2994

Redmond, Ruth, *In Charge,* Enoch Pratt Free Library (Keyworth Avenue), Baltimore MD. 301-396-5430, 396-5395

Redshaw, Mrs M L, *Librn,* Atlas Steel Library, Welland ON. 416-735-5661, Ext 501

Redslob, Monette E, *Dir,* Aiken Technical College, Learning Resources Division, Aiken SC. 803-593-9231, Ext 305

Reece, Janice A, *Librn,* Azle Public Library, Azle TX. 817-444-3213

Reece, Lori, *Librn,* Bonnyville Municipal Library, Bonnyville AB. 403-826-3071

Reece, Samuel W, *Media,* Baptist Sunday School Board of the Southern Baptist Convention, Dargan-Carver Library, Nashville TN. 615-251-2133

Reech, Coletta, *Asst Librn,* Crystal City Public Library, Crystal City MO. 314-937-7166

Reed, Betsy, *Ch,* Fairport Public Library, Fairport Harbor OH. 216-354-8191

Reed, Blake, *AV,* Thornton Community College, Learning Resources Center, South Holland IL. 312-596-2000, Ext 240

Reed, Bonnie, *Bkmobile Coordr,* Powell County Public Library, Stanton KY. 606-663-4511

Reed, Carol Lee, *Librn,* Canton Carnegie Township Library, Canton KS. 316-628-4305

Reed, Carolyn A, *Coordr,* University of Southern Mississippi (School of Nursing, Instructional Resource Program), Hattiesburg MS. 601-266-4211

Reed, Cecil, *Clerk,* Western States College of Engineering Library, Inglewood CA. 213-641-5888

Reed, David F, *Pub Servs,* North Dakota State University Library, Fargo ND. 701-237-8876

Reed, Dick, *Acq,* Miami-Dade Public Library System, Miami FL. 305-579-5001

Reed, Duane, *Spec Coll,* United States Air Force Academy Library, United States Air Force Academy CO. 303-472-2590

Reed, Evelyn, *Librn,* Coldwater District Library, Coldwater KS. 316-582-9869

Reed, Geneva, *Asst Librn,* Julia Adams Morse Memorial Library, Greene ME. 207-946-5544

Reed, George, *Methods Analyst,* Denver Public Library, Denver CO. 303-573-5152, Ext 271

Reed, Gerry, *Ref,* Calloway County Public Library, Murray KY. 502-753-2288

Reed, Gertrude, *Ref & On-Line Servs,* Bryn Mawr College, Canaday Library, Bryn Mawr PA. 215-645-5279

Reed, Ida, *Music & Art,* Carnegie Library of Pittsburgh, Pittsburgh PA. 412-622-3100

Reed, Irene, *ILL,* Marion Public Library, Marion IN. 317-664-7363

Reed, James R, *In Charge,* Missouri Botanical Garden Library, Saint Louis MO. 314-772-7600

Reed, Jane, *Asst Librn,* Sleepy Hollow Restorations Library, Tarrytown NY. 914-631-8200

Reed, Jane, *Librn,* Morrison-Mary Wiley Library District, Elmwood IL. 309-742-2431

Reed, Janet S, *Asst Mgr,* Continental Illinois National Bank & Trust Co, Information Services Division, Chicago IL. 312-828-8580

Reed, Jean K, *Actg Librn,* Belle Vernon Public Library, Belle Vernon PA. 412-929-6642

Reed, John, *Spec Coll,* Ohio Wesleyan University, L A Beeghly Library, Delaware OH. 614-369-4431, Ext 509

Reed, Judy D, *Librn,* Swaney Memorial Library Court, New Cumberland WV. 304-563-3471

Reed, Jutta R, *Coll Develop,* Massachusetts Institute of Technology Libraries, Cambridge MA. 617-253-5651

Reed, L L, *Bibliog Instr,* Moorhead State University, Livingston Lord Library, Moorhead MN. 218-236-2922

Reed, L L, *On-Line Servs,* Moorhead State University, Livingston Lord Library, Moorhead MN. 218-236-2922

Reed, Lola N, *Dir,* West Orange Free Public Library, West Orange NJ. 201-736-0198

Reed, Loyce L, *Librn,* Dexter Public Library, Dexter MO. 314-624-3764

Reed, Mac, *Govt Doc,* Fort Hays State University, Forsyth Library, Hays KS. 913-628-4431

Reed, Marge, *Tech Serv,* Carl Sandburg College, Learning Resources Center, Galesburg IL. 309-344-2518, Ext 247 & 257

Reed, Marie, *Acq,* Mesa College, Learning Resource Services, Lowell Heiny Library, Grand Junction CO. 303-248-1436
Reed, Marieta, *Librn,* Colon Township Library, Colon MI. 616-432-3958
Reed, Mary, *Cat,* Howell Carnegie Library, Howell MI. 517-546-0720
Reed, Mary Jane, *Res & Planning,* Washington State Library, Olympia WA. 206-753-5592
Reed, Mary T, *Asst Librn,* Gorham-MacBane Public Library, Springfield TN. 615-384-5123
Reed, Maryruth, *Dir,* Mitchell Public Library, Mitchell NE. 308-623-2222
Reed, Melvin G, *Chief Librn,* New York State Office of Mental Health Library, Albany NY. 518-474-7165
Reed, Minerva, *Librn,* Whitingham Free Public Library, Jacksonville VT. 802-368-2877
Reed, Mrs Hobart, *Librn,* Cherokee County Public Library, Centre AL. 205-927-5838
Reed, Ophelia S, *Dir,* Portville Free Library, Portville NY. 716-933-8441
Reed, Paulette, *Bkmobile Coordr,* Magoffin County Library, Salyersville KY. 606-349-2411
Reed, Pearl, *Circ,* Princeton Public Library, Mercer Memorial Library, Princeton WV. 304-425-3324
Reed, Richard S, *Dir,* Fruitlands Museums Library, Harvard MA. 617-456-3924
Reed, Robert C, *Acq,* University of New Hampshire, Ezekiel W Dimond Library, Durham NH. 603-862-1540
Reed, Ronald, *Librn,* Marion Carnegie Library, Marion IL. 618-993-5935
Reed, Rosalie E, *Asst Librn,* Riverside General Hospital, University Medical Center, Medical Library, Riverside CA. 714-785-7066
Reed, Rowland, *Media,* Trinidad State Junior College, Samuel Freudenthal Memorial Library, Trinidad CO. 303-846-5593
Reed, Sandra, *Ch,* Ashtabula County District Library, Ashtabula OH. 216-997-9341
Reed, Shelia, *Asst Librn & Ch,* Haines City Public Library, Haines City FL. 813-422-1749
Reed, Shirley A, *Dir,* Spoon River College, Learning Resources Center, Canton IL. 309-647-4645, Ext 222 & 313
Reed, Sidney W, *Librn,* Beulah Heights Bible College, Barth Memorial Library, Atlanta GA. 404-627-2681
Reed, Sue, *Librn,* Scenic Regional Library of Franklin, Gasconade & Warren Counties (Pacific Service Center), Pacific MO. 314-257-2712
Reed, Susanne, *AV,* Hanover Public Library, Hanover PA. 717-632-5183
Reed, Susanne, *Lit Searcher,* Lockheed Corporation (Lockheed-California Company Central Library), Burbank CA. 213-847-5646
Reed, Virginia, *Doc,* Lewis University Library, Romeoville IL. 815-838-0500, Ext 302
Reed, Virginia, *Ser,* Northeastern Illinois University Library, Chicago IL. 312-583-4050, Ext 469, 470, 471, 472
Reed, Virginia H, *Librn,* Mercy Hospital & Medical Center, Medical Library, San Diego CA. 714-294-8024
Reed, Vivian, *Asst Librn,* Saint Thomas Seminary Library, Denver CO. 303-722-4687, Ext 50
Reed, Jr, Edward V, *Dir,* Kelley Library, Salem Public Library, Salem NH. 603-898-7064
Reed-Ehm, Elaine, *Ch,* Klamath County Library, Klamath Falls OR. 503-882-8894
Reeder, Carol, *Tech Serv,* Pocatello Public Library, Information and Video Center, Pocatello ID. 208-232-1263
Reeder, June, *Librn,* California Baptist College, Annie Gabriel Library, Riverside CA. 714-689-5771
Reeder, Norman, *Librn,* Torrance Public Library (El Retiro), Torrance CA. 213-375-0922
Reeder, Ray, *Music,* California State University, Hayward CA. 415-881-3664
Reeder, W G, *Dir,* Texas Memorial Museum Library, Austin TX. 512-471-1604
Reedy, Conrad, *Circ,* University of Wisconsin-Green Bay, Library Learning Center, Green Bay WI. 414-465-2382
Reedy, Dianne, *Librn,* Houston Public Library (Jungman), Houston TX. 713-789-7211
Reedy, Judith El, *Librn,* Champlain Valley Physicians Hospital Medical Center, Medical Library, Plattsburgh NY. 518-561-2000, Ext 248

Reedy, Ruth C, *Dir,* McNeese State University, Lether E Frazar Memorial Library, Lake Charles LA. 318-477-2520, Ext 271
Reedy, Sid, *Assoc Prof,* Saint Louis Community College at Florissant Valley, Library Technical Assistant Program, MO. 314-595-4494
Reekes, Pamela, *Lectr,* Simmons College, Graduate School of Library & Information Science, MA. 617-738-2225
Reeling, Patricia G, *Assoc Prof,* Rutgers-The State University of New Jersey, Graduate School of Library & Information Studies, NJ. 201-932-7500
Reen, Ellen, *Librn,* Acres American Engineering Library, Buffalo NY. 853-7525 Ext 290
Reens, Jane, *Librn,* Chicago Public Library (West Town), Chicago IL. 312-486-5612
Reenstjerna, Fred, *Librn,* Roanoke County Public Library (Hollins Branch), Hollins VA. 703-366-8817
Reep, Allene, *Librn,* Darlington County Library (Hartsville Memorial), Hartsville SC. 803-393-5864
Rees, Alan M, *Prof,* Case Western Reserve University, School of Library Science, OH. 216-368-3500
Rees, Larry, *Adminr,* Central Iowa Regional Library, Des Moines IA. 515-280-9092
Rees, Marnie, *Assoc Dir,* Scranton Public Library, Albright Memorial Library, Scranton PA. 717-961-2451
Rees, Merril, *Librn,* Des Moines Area Community College Library, Ankeny IA. 515-964-6360, Ext 360
Rees, Pamela Clark, *Med Dir,* State Library Commission of Iowa (Medical Library), Des Moines IA. 515-281-5772
Rees, Philip, *Librn,* University of North Carolina at Chapel Hill (Art), Chapel Hill NC. 919-933-3397
Reese, Anne O, *Librn,* Toledo Museum of Art, Reference Library, Toledo OH. 419-255-8000, Ext 37
Reese, Carol, *Spec Coll,* Brookdale Community College, Learning Resources Center, Lincroft NJ. 201-842-1900, Ext 392
Reese, D Andrews, *Acq,* Salisbury State College, Blackwell Library, Salisbury MD. 301-546-3261, Ext 351
Reese, Elizabeth, *Librn,* Cabell County Public Library (Milton Branch), Milton WV. 304-743-6711
Reese, Flora G, *ILL, Cat & Ref,* Huntingdon College, Houghton Memorial Library, Montgomery AL. 205-265-0511, Ext 221
Reese, Gary Fuller, *Spec Coll,* Tacoma Public Library, Tacoma WA. 206-572-2000
Reese, Greg, *Librn,* Cuyahoga County Public Library (Warrensville Branch), Warrensville Heights OH. 216-464-5280
Reese, Gwynne H, *Per,* East Stroudsburg State College, Kemp Library, East Stroudsburg PA. 717-424-3467
Reese, Judith R, *Cat,* Skidmore College, Lucy Scribner Library, Saratoga Springs NY. 518-584-5000, Ext 234
Reese, Mrs Odeniah, *Librn,* Pack Memorial Library, Mountain View MO. 417-934-6154
Reese, Ray D, *Librn,* United States Bureau of Indian Affairs, National Indian Training Center Professional Library, Brigham City UT. 801-723-8591, Ext 346
Reese, Rebecca, *Ch,* Millville Public Library, Millville NJ. 609-825-7087
Reeser, Gale, *Acq,* Ricks College, David O McKay Learning Resources Center, Rexburg ID. 208-356-2351
Reeve, Elizabeth, *Librn,* United States Army (Special Services Division Library), Lathrop CA. 209-982-2404
Reeve, Russell J, *Dir,* Stevens Memorial Library, North Andover MA. 617-682-6260
Reeves, Helen C, *Actg Librn,* Union Parish Library, Farmerville LA. 318-368-9226
Reeves, Jean K, *Asst Librn,* Windham Public Library, Windham ME. 207-892-8086
Reeves, Mariette, *Librn,* Oratoire Saint-Joseph, Bibliotheque et Centre de Documentation, Montreal PQ. 514-733-8211
Reeves, Mrs Herbert, *Tech Serv & Cat,* Okefenokee Regional Library, Waycross GA. 912-283-3126

Reeves, Pamela, *Assoc Librn,* Eastern Michigan University, Center of Educational Resources, Ypsilanti MI. 313-487-0020
Reeves, Patricia Ann, *Chief Librn,* United States Army (Post Library), Fort Sheridan IL. 312-926-3188
Reeves, Richard, *Spec Coll,* Free Public Library of the City of Trenton, Trenton NJ. 609-392-7188
Reeves, Robert, *In Charge,* Texas Education Agency (Region I), Edinburg TX. 512-383-5611
Reeves, S, *Librn,* Oakland Public Library (Rockridge), Oakland CA. 415-652-1065
Reeves, Sharon Stewart, *Librn,* Union-Tribune Publishing Co Library, San Diego CA. 714-299-3131, Ext 1411
Reeves, Steve, *Media,* Oscar Rose Junior College, Learning Resources Center, Midwest City OK. 405-733-7323, 733-7322
Rega, Christina V, *Librn,* Farm Journal Marketing Research Library, Philadelphia PA. 215-574-1360, 574-1359
Regan, Eda, *Asst Librn,* Mills College Library, Oakland CA. 415-632-2700, Ext 260, 261, 262
Regan, Helen, *Librn,* Pepsico Inc, Technical Information Center, Valhalla NY. 914-683-0500
Regan, Lee, *Per,* George Mason University Libraries, Fairfax VA. 703-323-2616
Regan, Marguerite, *Spec Coll,* Hofstra University Library, Hempstead NY. 516-560-3475
Regan, Muriel, *Librn,* Rockefeller Foundation Library, New York NY. 212-869-8500, Ext 315
Reger, Norma, *ILL,* West Texas State University, Cornette Library, Canyon TX. 806-656-2761
Regier, Don, *Media,* Dallas Theological Seminary, Mosher Library, Dallas TX. 214-824-3094, Ext 285
Regina, Mary, *Prov Superior,* Mother of Sorrows Convent, Mater Dolorosa College Library, Milwaukee WI. 414-352-1340
Regis, Bill, *Circ,* Santa Barbara City College Library, Santa Barbara CA. 805-965-0581, Ext 242
Regis, June, *Librn,* New Berlin Memorial Hospital Library, New Berlin WI. 414-782-2700, Ext 284, 286
Regner, Mrs Jim, *Asst Librn,* Ashland Public Library, Ashland NE. 402-944-7430
Reh, Lisa, *Clerical Assts,* Pacific Scientific Information Center, Honolulu HI. 808-847-3511
Rehard, Karen, *Librn,* City-County Library of Missoula (Bonner Branch), Bonner MT. 406-728-5900
Rehill, Marie, *ILL,* Bethpage Public Library, Bethpage NY. 516-913-3907
Rehlander, Marilyn, *Librn,* La Porte County Library (Fish Lake), Walkerton IN. 219-369-1337
Rehm, Nettie, *ILL,* Leavenworth Public Library, Leavenworth KS. 913-682-5666
Rehmar, Marie, *Reader Serv,* Cleveland State University Libraries (Joseph W Bartunek III Law Library), Cleveland OH. 216-687-2250
Rehms, Jane, *Media,* Spokane Community College, East Mission Campus Library, Spokane WA. 509-455-7699
Rehnberg, Marilyn, *Sp Serv,* Rockford Public Library, Rockford IL. 815-965-6731
Rehnberg, Marilyn, *Br Coordr,* Rockford Public Library (Montague), Rockford IL. 815-965-1912
Rehnberg, Marilyn, *Librn,* Rockford Public Library (Rock River), Rockford IL. 815-398-7514
Rehrauer, George P, *Prof,* Rutgers-The State University of New Jersey, Graduate School of Library & Information Studies, NJ. 201-932-7500
Reibel, Daniel B, *In Charge,* Pennsylvania Historical & Museum Commission, Old Economy Village Library, Ambridge PA. 412-266-4500
Reibman, Jean, *Cat,* Cornell University Medical College, Samuel J Wood Library, New York NY. 212-472-5300
Reich, David L, *Dir,* Massachusetts Board of Library Commissioners, Office for the Development of Library Services, Boston MA. 617-267-9400
Reich, Marcia, *Bkmobile Coordr,* Worcester Public Library, Worcester MA. 617-752-3751
Reich, Phyllis, *Ref & On-Line Servs,* University of Minnesota, Saint Paul Campus Libraries, Saint Paul MN. 612-373-0904

Reich, Raymond E, *Librn,* Grace Bible College, Bultema Memorial Library, Grand Rapids MI. 616-538-2332

Reich, Richard B, *Librn,* Indiana University Northwest Library, Gary IN. 219-980-6580

Reichart, Bruce, *Librn,* Boise Basin Library District, Idaho City ID. 208-392-4558

Reiche, Mrs R B, *Libr Clerk,* Canadian Forestry Service, Chalk River-Petawawa National Forestry Institute Library, Chalk River ON. 613-589-2880

Reichel, Jill, *Dir,* North Syracuse Free Library, North Syracuse NY. 315-458-6184

Reichelt, Anne, *Dir User Serv,* Kearney State College, Calvin T Ryan Library, Kearney NE. 308-236-4218

Reicher, Daniel, *Dir,* University of Montreal, Ecole de Bibliotheconomie, PQ. 514-343-6044

Reichert, Leslie L, *Regional Librn,* United States Department of Housing & Urban Development, Region IX Library, San Francisco CA. 415-556-5900

Reicherter, Joan, *Chief Librn,* Earl Newsom & Company, Inc Library, New York NY. 212-755-4664

Reichhardt, Carol, *Commun Servs,* Weld County Library, Greeley CO. 303-330-7691

Reichlin, Bro Casimir, *Dir,* Saint Mary's College of California, Saint Albert Hall Library, Moraga CA. 415-376-4411, Ext 229, 230

Reichlin, Ellie, *Librn,* Library of the Society for the Preservation of New England Antiquities, Boston MA. 617-227-3956

Reichner, Carol, *On-Line Servs,* ESL Inc, Research Library, Sunnyvale CA. 408-734-2244, Ext 6796

Reicker, E, *On-Line Servs,* Parliament of Canada, Library of Parliament, Ottawa ON. 613-995-7113

Reid, Annis Rae, *Br Coordr,* New Orleans Public Library, Simon Heinsheim & Fisk Libraries, New Orleans LA. 504-586-4905

Reid, Camilla Brown, *In Charge,* West Central Georgia Regional Hospital Library, Columbus GA. 404-568-5236

Reid, Carol, *Librn,* Mercy Hospital, Medical & Nursing Library, Rockville Centre NY. 516-255-2255

Reid, Carolyn, *On-Line Servs,* University of Missouri-Kansas City Libraries (Medical Library), Kansas City MO. 816-474-4100, Ext 280

Reid, Donna G, *Asst Dir,* Plant City Public Library, Plant City FL. 813-752-8685, 752-7942

Reid, Douglas G, *Librn,* Bridgeport Public Library, Bridgeport CT. 203-576-7777

Reid, Grace, *Asst Dir & Ch,* Vestavia Hills Library, Vestavia Hills AL. 205-823-0520, 823-0521

Reid, Helen W, *Librn,* Utah International Incorporated Library, San Francisco CA. 415-981-1515

Reid, Hope B, *Chief Librn,* Belhaven College, Warren Hood Library, Jackson MS. 601-353-0012

Reid, Jo, *Librn,* Newell Public Library, Newell SD. 605-456-2179

Reid, John C, *Dir,* West Bend Community Memorial Library, West Bend WI. 414-334-4041

Reid, Joyce, *Ch & YA,* Lewis & Clark Library System, Edwardsville IL. 618-656-3216

Reid, Joyce, *Circ,* Windsor Public Library, Windsor CT. 203-688-6433

Reid, Laurel, *Librn,* Dabney S Lancaster Community College Library, Clifton Forge VA. 703-862-4246

Reid, Lucielle, *Mgr Info Serv,* CPC International, Inc, Moffett Technical Library, Summit IL. 312-458-2000

Reid, M, *Ad,* Topsfield Town Library, Topsfield MA. 617-887-2914

Reid, M H, *Dir,* Hockey Hall of Fame Library, Toronto ON. 416-595-1345

Reid, Margaret, *Chief Southwest District Br,* Chicago Public Library, Chicago IL. 312-269-2900

Reid, Margaret B, *Ch,* Lynchburg Public Library, Lynchburg VA. 804-847-1565

Reid, Marion T, *Tech Serv,* Louisiana State University (Troy H Middleton Library), Baton Rouge LA. 504-388-2217

Reid, Martha, *Ch,* Pamunkey Regional Library, Hanover VA. 804-798-6081, Ext 285, 287

Reid, Mary, *Libr Servs Coordr,* Tulsa Junior College, Learning Resource Center, Tulsa OK. 918-587-6561, Ext 363

Reid, Mary E, *Tech Serv & Cat,* Southwest Missouri State University Library, Springfield MO. 417-836-5104

Reid, Maynard, *Actg Librn,* La Grange College (Curriculum), La Grange GA. 404-882-2911, Ext 76

Reid, Nelda M, *Dir,* Southwestern Technical Institute Library, Sylva NC. 704-586-4091, Ext 228

Reid, Robert W, *Chief Librn,* Southern Arkansas University, Magale Library, Magnolia AR. 501-234-5120, Ext 260, 262, 263

Reid, Ronald H, *Media,* University of Wisconsin-Oshkosh, Forrest R Polk Library, Oshkosh WI. 414-424-3333

Reid, Ruth Salisbury, *Archivist,* Historical Society of Western Pennsylvania Library, Pittsburgh PA. 412-681-5533

Reid, Thelma E, *Dir,* Upsala College Library, East Orange NJ. 201-266-7295

Reid, Velva, *Librn,* Scottdale Free Public Library, Scottdale PA. 412-887-6140

Reid, William K, *Librn,* Crawford County Bar Association, Law Library, Meadville PA. 814-336-1151

Reid, Jr, Cecil, *Librn,* County of Henrico Public Library (Fairfield), Richmond VA. 804-222-1531

Reider, Alan, *Outreach Serv,* Montgomery County-Norristown Public Library, Norristown PA. 215-277-3355

Reidner, Nancy, *Ch,* City & County Library, Ladysmith Public Library, Ladysmith WI. 715-532-6275

Reidy, Gerald P, *Indust Rel Off,* Boston Public Library, Eastern Massachusetts Library System, Boston MA. 617-536-5400

Reidy, Robin E, *Librn,* Sacramento Union Library, Sacramento CA. 916-442-7811, Ext 218

Reiersen, Jean, *Tech Serv, Cat & On-Line Servs,* Anchorage Municipal Libraries, Anchorage AK. 907-264-4481

Reif, Corinne, *Librn,* Saint Louis County Library (Mid-County), St Louis MO. 314-721-3008

Reif, Kathleen, *Librn,* Harford County Library (Joppa Branch), Joppa MD. 301-679-7520

Reif, Marcia, *Librn,* Osborne Public Library, Osborne KS. 913-346-5486

Reifers, Annie Mae, *Librn,* Dixie Regional Library (Okolona Carnegie), Okolona MS. 601-489-3522

Reiff, Harry B, *NW Area Adminr,* Free Library of Philadelphia, Philadelphia PA. 215-686-5322

Reiff, Mary Sue, *Asst Dir,* North Manchester Public Library, North Manchester IN. 219-982-4773

Reifsteck, II, William, *Dir,* Wayne County, Indiana, Historical Museum Library, Richmond IN. 317-962-5756

Reihl, Richard E, *Dir,* Lakeshore Technical Institute, Educational Resources Center, Cleveland WI. 414-693-8211, 684-4408, Ext 150

Reilein, Dean A, *On-Line Servs,* Eastern Connecticut State College, J Eugene Smith Library, Willimantic CT. 203-456-2231, Ext 374, 422

Reilein, Dean A, *Tech Serv & Cat,* Eastern Connecticut State College, J Eugene Smith Library, Willimantic CT. 203-456-2231, Ext 374, 422

Reilley, Elizabeth K, *Librn,* Planting Fields Arboretum Horticultural Library, Oyster Bay NY. 516-922-1130

Reilley, Jeanne M, *Librn,* Veterans Administration (Patients' Library), Pittsburgh PA. 412-363-4900

Reilly, Carol, *Info & Referral Specialist, Wake Info Ctr,* Wake County Department of the Public Library, Raleigh NC. 919-755-6077

Reilly, Catherine, *Asst Dir & Ch,* Massapequa Public Library, Massapequa NY. 516-798-4607

Reilly, Catherine, *Librn,* Massapequa Public Library (Bar Harbour), Massapequa Park NY. 516-799-0770

Reilly, Catherine R, *Asst Treasurer,* Chase Manhattan Bank (Business Research Library), New York NY. 212-552-6869

Reilly, Cathy, *Librn,* Saint Louis Police Library, Saint Louis MO. 314-444-5581

Reilly, Daniel, *Librn,* New Ulm Public Library, New Ulm MN. 507-354-2151

Reilly, Dayle, *Dir,* East Longmeadow Public Library, East Longmeadow MA. 413-525-7813

Reilly, Jane A, *Asst Prof,* Sam Houston State University, Library Science Department, TX. 713-295-6211, Ext 1151

Reilly, Lois, *Performing Arts,* Oakland University, Kresge Library, Rochester MI. 313-377-2486, 377-2474

Reilly, Mary, *Librn,* Van Horne Public Library, Van Horne IA. 319-228-8238

Reilly, Maureen, *Librn,* Bache Halsey Stuart Shields Inc, Research Library, New York NY. 212-791-4819

Reilly, Michael M, *Dir,* Reilly Translations Library, Fullerton CA. 714-738-3683

Reilly, Pamela, *Pub Servs,* Bryn Mawr College, Canaday Library, Bryn Mawr PA. 215-645-5279

Reilly, S Kathleen, *Librn,* Capital Research Co, Research Library, Los Angeles CA. 213-486-9261

Reilly, Violet, *Tech Serv & Cat,* Lakewood Public Library, Lakewood OH. 216-226-8275

Reily, Mrs M G, *Dir,* Corrigan Public Library, Corrigan TX. 713-398-4156

Reiman, Donald H, *Ed, Shelley & His Circle,* Carl and Lily Pforzheimer Foundation, Inc, Carl H Pforzheimer Library, New York NY. 212-697-7217

Reiman, Eva, *ILL,* Pace University, Pleasantville-Briarcliff Library, Pleasantville NY. 914-769-3200, Ext 382

Reimer, Louise, *Exten Coordr,* Howard County Library, Columbia MD. 301-997-8000

Reimer, Mary, *Librn,* Wesleyan University (Music), Middletown CT. 203-347-9411, Ext 678

Reimers, Irene, *Asst Dir,* Cumberland Regional Library, Amherst NS. 902-667-2135

Reimers, Irene, *Librn,* Cumberland Regional Library (Amherst), Amherst NS. 902-667-2549

Rein, Joanne, *Ser & Doc,* State University of New York, College at New Paltz, Sojourner Truth Library, New Paltz NY. 914-257-2204

Reinat, Monserate Yuljo, *Asst Dir,* Inter-American University of Puerto Rico, Aguadilla Regional College Library, Aguadilla PR. 809-891-0998

Reinbergs, Gloria, *Librn,* Saint Lawrence College of Applied Arts & Technology Library, Brockville ON. 613-345-0660

Reiner, M Aloyne, *Asst Cat,* Cardinal Ritter Library, Saint Louis MO. 314-544-0455, Ext 56

Reiners, Margaret, *Media & Ser,* New England School of Law Library, Boston MA. 617-267-9655, Ext 50

Reinert, Ann, *Librn,* Nebraska State Historical Society Library, Lincoln NE. 402-432-2793

Reinertsen, Gail, *Asst Librn,* Gaston, Snow & Ely Barlett Library, Boston MA. 617-426-4600

Reingoldas, Elena, *Asst Dir,* Boston University Libraries (School of Education), Boston MA. 617-353-3272

Reinhard, Mary V, *Acq,* University of New Orleans, Earl K Long Library, New Orleans LA. 504-283-0353

Reinhardt, Alice, *Librn,* Los Angeles County-University of Southern California (Nursing Library), Los Angeles CA. 213-226-2622

Reinhardt, Darlene, *Librn,* Jesup Public Library, Jesup IA. 319-827-1533

Reinhardt, Patricia, *Headquarters Coordr,* Caroline County Public Library, Denton MD. 301-479-1343

Reinhart, B J, *Sci & Tech,* Cleveland State University Libraries, Cleveland OH. 216-687-2486

Reinhold, Dorothy Anne, *Dir,* Waynesboro Public Library, Waynesboro VA. 703-942-6173

Reinhold, Edna J, *Humanities & Soc Sci,* Saint Louis Public Library, Saint Louis MO. 314-241-2288

Reinholt, Susie, *Cat,* Plymouth Public Library, Plymouth IN. 219-936-2324

Reinke, Bernett, *Dir & Ref,* Dickinson State College, Stoxen Library, Dickinson ND. 701-227-2135

Reinke, Carol, *Librn,* Saginaw Public Libraries (Zauel), Saginaw MI. 517-799-2771

Reinke, Jean, *Cat,* Ashland Public Library, Ashland NE. 402-944-7430

Reinke, Luella, *Librn,* Hartley Public Library, Hartley IA. 712-728-2080

Reinmann, Alyce, *Board President,* Bond Library, Wenona IL. 815-853-4665
Reinmiller, Elinor, *Coll Develop,* University of Texas Health Science Center at Dallas Library, Dallas TX. 214-688-3368
Reinmiller, Jim, *Dir,* Hazleton Area Public Library, Hazleton PA. 717-454-2961, 454-0244
Reis, Kathleen, *Asst Librn,* Elizabeth Taber Library, Marion MA. 617-748-1252
Reis, Nola, *Br & Exten,* Troy Public Library, Troy NY. 518-274-7071
Reis, Steve, *Librn,* Indiana University-Purdue University at Indianapolis (School of Physical Education), Indianapolis IN. 317-264-3764
Reise, Elaine, *ILL, Ad & Ref,* South Brunswick Public Library, Monmouth Junction NJ. 201-821-8224, 821-8225
Reisinger, Landon Chas, *Librn,* Historical Society of York County Library-Archives, York PA. 717-848-1587, Ext 25
Reisner, Genevieve, *Group Servs,* Vigo County Public Library, Terre Haute IN. 812-232-1113
Reiss, Anna, *Librn,* Uncas-On-Thames Hospital, Mary Lerou Memorial Medical Library, Norwich CT. 203-889-1321, Ext 296
Reiss, Laurel M, *Dir,* Erie Public Library District, Erie IL. 309-659-2707
Reissig, Ruth Lee, *Librn,* Bureau of Land Management, Montrose District Office Library, Montrose CO. 303-249-7791
Reister, Helen, *Acting Ref,* University of California Library, Irvine CA. 714-833-5212
Reister, John F, *Circ,* California State University, Chico Library, Chico CA. 916-895-6212
Reister, Willa, *Librn,* Clinton Public Library, Clinton TN. 615-457-0519
Reister, Willa, *ILL,* Knoxville-Knox County Public Library, Lawson McGhee Library, Knoxville TN. 615-523-0781
Reiter, Berle G, *Librn,* Michigan State University Library (Mathematics), East Lansing MI. 517-355-2344
Reiter, Richard, *ILL,* Trinity College Library, Deerfield IL. 312-945-6700, Ext 217
Reiterman, Edna, *Asst Librn,* Mount Pulaski Township Library, Mount Pulaski IL. 217-792-5919
Reiterman, Sue, *AV,* Burlingame Public Library, Burlingame CA. 415-344-7107
Reith, Anita, *Pub Servs,* Concordia Teachers College, Link Library, Seward NE. 402-643-3651, Ext 258
Reith, Louis J, *Franciscana,* Saint Bonaventure University, Friedsam Memorial Library & Resource Center, Saint Bonaventure NY. 716-375-2323
Reith, Mariana, *Dir of Tech Servs,* Los Angeles Public Library System, Los Angeles CA. 213-626-7555
Reith, Marjorie, *Hq Librn,* Forsyth County Public Library, Winston-Salem NC. 919-727-2556
Reitman, Jo, *Librn,* Newspapers, Inc, Editorial Library, Milwaukee WI. 414-224-2000, 224-2376
Reitz, C Barbara, *Librn,* Summerville Public Library, Summerville PA. 814-856-2384
Reitz, C H, *Tech Serv,* University of Windsor, Leddy Library, Windsor ON. 519-253-4232, Ext 198
Reitz, Thomas L, *Dir & Acq,* Seminole Community College Library, Sanford FL. 305-323-1450, Ext 450
Reitzel, Hilda M, *Librn,* Mine Safety Appliances Co Library, Pittsburgh PA. 412-273-5131
Rekey, Tibor, *Cat,* Dartmouth College, Baker Memorial Library, Hanover NH. 603-646-2235
Reld, Elizabeth A, *Librn,* Toronto Western Hospital, Health Sciences Library, Toronto ON. 416-369-5750
Relph, Martha H, *Cat,* United States Army (Morris Swett Library), Fort Sill OK. 405-351-4525, 351-4477
Relyea, Mary, *Librn,* Clark Memorial Library, Bethany CT. 203-393-2103
Relyes, Donald P, *Librn,* Hoffrel Instruments, Inc Library, Norwalk CT. 203-866-9205
Remaly, Helen, *Ch,* McMillan Memorial Library, Wisconsin Rapids WI. 715-423-1040
Rembold, Mrs Harold, *Librn,* Blair Public Library, Blair NE. 402-426-3617
Remele, Larry, *Dir,* North Dakota Historical Society, Research & Reference Div Library, Bismarck ND. 701-224-2668

Remelts, Glen, *ILL & Ref,* Beloit College, Col Robert H Morse Library, Beloit WI. 608-365-3391, Ext 230
Remer, Jeanette, *Cat,* Jacksonville State University Library, Jacksonville AL. 205-435-9820, Ext 213, 214
Remillard, Juliette, *Librn,* Institut D'histoire De L'amerique Francaise, Fondation Lionel-Groulx, Centre de recherche Lionel-Groulx, Montreal PQ. 514-271-8264
Remillard, Sister E, *Librn,* Institut Familial Saint-Joseph, Bibliotheque, Saint Hyacinthe PQ. 514-774-7087
Remling, Mary Lou, *Asst Librn,* Carlinville Public Library, Carlinville IL. 217-854-3505
Rempel, B, *Ch & YA,* Saint Catharines Public Library, Saint Catharines ON. 416-688-6103
Rempel, Betty, *Cat,* Logan-Hocking County District Library, Logan OH. 614-385-2348
Rempel, Patricia, *Librn,* University of Alberta (Weir Memorial Law Library), Edmonton AB. 403-432-5560
Remsen, Carol, *Commun Servs,* Sandpoint-East Bonner County Free Public Library District, Sandpoint ID. 208-263-6930
Remy, Helga, *Ch,* San Diego County Library, San Diego CA. 714-565-5100
Rendell, Douglas W, *Dir & Ad,* Bellingham Public Library, Bellingham MA. 617-966-1660
Rendell, M, *Head, Br Servs,* Edmonton Public Library, Edmonton AB. 403-423-2331
Rendle, Judith, *Librn,* Charles Camsell Hospital, Peter Wilcock Library, Edmonton AB. 403-452-8770, Ext 271
Rendler, Richard E, *Personnel & Support Serv Deputy,* San Jose Public Library, San Jose CA. 408-277-4822
Rendon, Noelia, *Dir,* Inter-American University of Puerto Rico, Fort Buchanan Campus Library, Fort Buchanan PR. 809-783-2424, Ext 5192
Rendon, Ruben, *Librn,* San Benito Public Library, San Benito TX. 512-399-2311
Renfrow, Florinette, *Librn,* Dillon County Library (Lake View Branch), Lake View SC. 803-759-2692
Renick, Paul R, *Asst Prof,* University of North Dakota, Dept of Library Science & Audiovisual Instruction, ND. 701-777-3003
Renkes, Marcia G, *Librn,* Odell Public Library, Morrison IL. 815-772-4089
Renkiewicz, Nancy, *Assoc Dean,* Sacramento City College Library, Sacramento CA. 916-449-7373
Renlault, Jacque, *Field Worker (French Lang),* Northeastern Regional Library System, Kirkland Lake ON. 705-567-7043
Renne, Mildred, *Librn,* Newberg Library Association, Newberg OR. 503-538-4389
Rennebohm, Carolyn, *Ref,* New Berlin Public Library, New Berlin WI. 414-786-2990
Renner, Charlene, *Automated Recs,* University of Illinois Library at Urbana-Champaign, Urbana IL. 217-333-0790
Renner, D S, *Librn & On-Line Servs,* Geotronic Laboratories Library, Dallas TX. 214-946-7573
Renner, Helen, *Librn,* Solomon Wright Library, Pownal VT. 802-823-7350, 823-7922
Renner, Iris, *Dir,* Capitol Area Health Consortium Libraries, CT. 203-666-6951, Ext 302
Renner, Iris A, *Librn & On-Line Servs,* Veterans Administration, Hospital Library, Newington CT. 203-666-6951, Ext 302
Renner, Melinda, *Libr Training Officer,* International Communication Agency (Education & Cultural Affairs), Washington DC. 202-632-5346, 632-6752
Reno, Margaret M, *Librn,* Sharon Hill Public Library, Sharon Hill PA. 215-586-3993
Rensel, Jeanne, *Librn,* Washington State Library (Department of Ecology Library), Olympia WA. 206-753-2959
Renshaw, Dorothy, *Librn,* Tampa-Hillsborough County Public Library System (Ruskin Public), Ruskin FL. 813-645-3721
Renshaw, Dorothy, *Librn,* Tampa-Hillsborough County Public Library System (Sun City Library Station), Sun City FL. 813-634-1315
Renshawe, Michael, *Law,* McGill University Libraries, Montreal PQ. 514-392-4948
Renshawe, Michael, *Librn,* McGill University Libraries (Law), Montreal PQ. 514-392-5060
Renter, Lois, *Librn & On-Line Servs,* American College Testing Program Library, Iowa City IA. 319-337-1165

Renteria, Charleen M, *Ad,* Merced County Library, Merced CA. 209-726-7484
Renthal, Helen, *Emer Assoc Prof,* University of Arizona, Graduate Library School, AZ. 602-626-3565
Rentner, Erlene, *ILL,* Mercer County Library, Trenton NJ. 609-989-6917
Rentof, Beryl, *Ref,* Fashion Institute of Technology, Library-Media Services Dept, New York NY. 212-760-7695
Rentz, B, *Bibliog Instr,* Cabrillo College, Robert E Swenson Library, Aptos CA. 408-425-6473, 688-6458
Rentz, Betty, *Asst Librn,* Cabrillo College, Robert E Swenson Library, Aptos CA. 408-425-6473, 688-6458
Rentz, Marie, *Instr,* Illinois Valley Community College, Library Technical Assistant Program, IL. 815-224-2720
Renwick, Mrs E, *Supvr,* Huron County Public Library (Belmore), Clifford ON. 519-367-2524
Renz, James H, *Assoc Dir Tech Serv,* University of Florida Libraries, Gainesville FL. 904-392-0341
Renz, Janet, *Asst Librn,* Barnard Library, La Crosse KS. 913-222-2826
Renz, Marion C, *Librn,* White Plains Hospital, Bertin Lattin Memorial Library, White Plains NY. 914-949-4500, Ext 2198
Renz, Walter A, *Pres,* American Railway Car Institute Library, New York NY. 212-867-6577
Renzema, Judy, *Librn,* Sacramento Public Library (Belle Cooledge), Sacramento CA. 916-421-1222
Renzetti, V, *Librn,* British Columbia Telephone, Microtel Pacific Research Limited Library, Burnaby BC. 604-420-1333, Ext 452
Repetto, Ann, *Asst Librn,* Saint Louis Society for Medical & Scientific Education Library, Saint Louis MO. 314-371-5225
Repp, Joan, *Cat,* Bowling Green State University Library, Bowling Green OH. 419-372-2856
Repp, III, Robert W, *Ref,* Carnegie Library of Pittsburgh, Pittsburgh PA. 412-622-3100
Reppenhagen, Eleanor, *Dir,* Fulton-Montgomery Community College Library, Johnstown NY. 518-762-4651, Ext 396
ReQua, Eloise G, *Librn,* Library of International Relations, Chicago IL. 312-787-7928
Requa, L K, *AV,* Central Texas College, Oveta Culp Hobby Memorial Library, Killeen TX. 817-526-1237
Requena, Linda, *Librn,* Naval Aerospace Regional & Medical Center, Medical & General Libraries, Pensacola FL. 904-452-6635
Rescigna, Mary Ellen, *Media Specialist,* Pasco-Hernando Community College, West Campus Learning Resource Center, New Port Richey FL. 813-842-8478
Resh, Alta, *Librn,* Graettinger Public Library, Graettinger IA. 712-859-3592
Reside, Karin, *On-Line Servs,* Fayetteville Area Health Education Center Library, Fayetteville NC. 919-323-1152
Resnick, Mary, *Librn,* Foundation Center Library, Washington DC. 202-331-1400
Resnick, N Janeen, *Asst Dir,* Western Regional Public Library System, Springfield MA. 413-732-3115
Respass, Marie, *Ref & On-Line Servs,* Georgian Court College, Farley Memorial Library, Lakewood NJ. 201-364-2200, Ext 19
Rest, Ruth Ann, *Librn,* Chicago Public Library (Archer), Chicago IL. 312-582-9241
Retfalvi, A, *Librn,* University of Toronto Libraries (Dept of Fine Arts), Toronto ON. 416-978-3290
Rettie, Jean E, *Circ,* Schenectady County Public Library, Schenectady NY. 518-382-3500
Rettig, Ernestine, *Dir,* Texas College, D R Glass Library, Tyler TX. 214-593-8311, Ext 37
Rettino, Janice, *Mgr Libr Develop,* College of Medicine & Dentistry of New Jersey, George F Smith Library of the Health Sciences, Newark NJ. 201-456-4580
Rettkowski, Jean P, *Librn,* Hesseltine Public Library, Wilbur WA. 509-647-5337
Retzel, Maureen K, *In Charge,* Spokane Public Library (Hillyard), Spokane WA. 509-487-1774
Reucker, Elaine, *Librn,* Saskatchewan Government Insurance Office Library, Regina SK. 306-565-1200
Reusch, Rita, *Reader Serv & Ref,* University of Idaho Library (College of Law), Moscow ID. 208-885-6521

Reuter, Ann, *Dir,* Cazenovia College, Daniel W Terry Library, Cazenovia NY. 315-655-3466, Ext 240

Reuter, J Robert, *Librn,* Morgan Guaranty Trust Co of New York Library, New York NY. 212-483-2180

Reuter, Ruth, *Librn,* Warsaw Free Public Library, Warsaw IL. 217-256-3417

Reuter, Shirley, *Acq,* Bowdoin College Library, Brunswick ME. 207-725-8731, Ext 281

Reveal, Arlene H, *Dir,* Mono County Free Library, Bridgeport CA. 714-932-7482

Revelle, Keith, *Dir,* Anchorage Municipal Libraries, Anchorage AK. 907-264-4481

Revill, Lynne, *Asst Librn,* Wetaskiwin Public Library, Wetaskiwin AB. 403-352-4055

Rex, Karen Haley, *Ch & Commun Servs,* Graham Public Library, Graham TX. 817-549-0600

Rex, Olga, *Librn,* Anderson Oil & Chemical Co, Inc Library, Portland CT. 203-342-0660

Rey, Joyce M, *Librn,* Smithsonian Institution, Astrophysical Observatory Library, Cambridge MA. 617-495-7264, 7289

Rey, Marguerite A, *Cat,* Loyola University Library (School of Law), New Orleans LA. 504-865-3426, 865-3427, 865-3136

Reyburn, Patricia, *Librn,* Galesburg Cottage Hospital, Health Services Library, Galesburg IL. 309-343-8131, Ext 237

Reyburn, Patricia, *Librn,* Saint Mary's Hospital Library, Medical Library, Galesburg IL. 309-344-3161, Ext 262

Reyes, Laura H, *Librn,* Boston Public Library (Multilingual Library), Boston MA. 617-426-0963

Reyes, Laura H, *Librn,* Boston Public Library (South End), Boston MA. 617-536-8241

Reyff, Richard, *Librn,* Thornapple-Kellogg School & Community Library, Middleville MI. 616-795-3394

Reyling, August, *Rare Bks,* Quincy College Library, Quincy IL. 217-222-8020, Ext 225

Reynen, Richard G, *Librn,* Deloitte, Haskins & Sells, Minneapolis MN. 612-339-9744

Reynolds, Allen H, *Medical,* United States Department of Labor, National Mine Health & Safety Academy Learning Resource Center, Beckley WV. 304-255-0451, Ext 266

Reynolds, Anne, *Cat,* Wellesley Free Library, Subregional Headquarters for Eastern Massachusetts Regional Library System, Wellesley MA. 617-235-1610

Reynolds, Arthur, *Dir,* Kentucky State Department of Corrections, Division of Education & Special Services Library, Frankfort KY. 502-564-4726

Reynolds, Beatrice, *Librn,* Washington County Library System (Leland Library), Leland MS. 601-686-7353

Reynolds, Betty, *Chief Cat,* University of Missouri-Kansas City Libraries, Kansas City MO. 816-276-1531

Reynolds, Cathrine, *Govt Publ,* University of Colorado at Boulder (University Libraries), Boulder CO. 303-492-7511

Reynolds, Christine, *Asst Librn,* Aetna Life & Casualty (Engineering Research & Development Library), Hartford CT. 203-273-2406

Reynolds, David, *On-Line Servs,* University of Rochester, Rush Rhees Library, Rochester NY. 716-275-4461

Reynolds, Doris, *ILL,* Haltom City Public Library, Haltom City TX. 817-834-7341

Reynolds, Doris, *Ad & Ch,* Milford Memorial Library, Milford IA. 712-338-4643

Reynolds, Dorsey, *Dir,* Valley Forge Christian College Library, Phoenixville PA. 215-935-0450, Ext 40

Reynolds, Elinor, *Dir,* Monroe Community Hospital, Medical Nursing Library, Rochester NY. 716-473-4080, Ext 203

Reynolds, Ellen J, *Librn,* Ontario Public Library, Ontario NY. 315-524-8381

Reynolds, Estella, *Supvr,* Middlesex County Library (Dorchester Branch), Dorchester ON. 519-268-3451

Reynolds, Jeanne, *Doc & Genealogy,* El Paso Public Library, El Paso TX. 915-543-3804

Reynolds, Joyce, *Info,* Canadian Restaurant & Food Services Association, Resource Centre, Toronto ON. 416-923-8416, Ext 20

Reynolds, Judith, *Bibliog Instr,* San Jose State University Library, San Jose CA. 408-277-3377

Reynolds, Julia, *Librn,* Maclure Library, Pittsford VT. 802-483-2972

Reynolds, Karen Moore, *Librn,* Fresno County Free Library (Gillis), Fresno CA. 209-225-0140

Reynolds, Kathlyn, *Librn,* Ocean County Library (Lacey Township), Forked River NJ. 201-693-8566

Reynolds, Kay, *Librn,* Woodruff County Library (I N Arnof), McCrory AR. 501-347-5331

Reynolds, Lynn A, *Dir,* Bentonville Public Library, Bentonville AR. 501-273-3535

Reynolds, Margaret, *On-Line Servs,* Weld County Library, Greeley CO. 303-330-7691

Reynolds, Marilyn, *Tech Serv,* Bradford Public Library, Bradford ON. 416-775-6482

Reynolds, Martha L, *Dir,* Frederick County Public Library, Frederick MD. 301-694-1613

Reynolds, Mary, *Br Coordr & Bkmobile Coordr,* Racine Public Library, Racine WI. 414-636-9241

Reynolds, Michael M, *Prof,* University of Maryland, College of Library & Information Services, MD. 301-454-5441

Reynolds, Mrs D, *Librn,* Canada Department of National Defence (Base Borden Public & Military Library), Borden ON. 705-424-1200, Ext 2273

Reynolds, Norman, *Media Supvrs,* Kent State University Libraries (Audio-Visual Services), Kent OH. 216-672-3456

Reynolds, Richard C, *Librn,* Saint Petersburg Junior College, Tarpon Springs Learning Resources Center, Tarpon Springs FL. 813-546-0011, Ext 463

Reynolds, Ruth M, *Asst Librn,* New York Psychoanalytic Institute, Abraham A Brill Library, New York NY. 212-879-6900

Reynolds, Sally Jo, *Cat,* American University, Jack I & Dorothy G Bender Library & Learning Resources Center, Washington DC. 202-686-2323

Reynolds, Stanley G, *Curator,* Reynolds Museum Library, Wetaskiwin AB. 403-352-5201

Reynolds, Stephen M, *Librn,* Faith Theological Seminary Library, Elkins Park PA. 215-635-3300

Reynolds, T, *Govt Pub,* University of Rhode Island Library, Kingston RI. 401-792-1000

Reynolds, Thomas H, *Asst Librn,* University of California, Berkeley (Law Library), Berkeley CA. 415-642-4044

Reynolds, Wanetca, *Librn,* J M Huber Corp, Research Library, Borger TX. 806-274-6331, Ext 331

Rezab, Gordana, *Rare Bks & Spec Coll,* Western Illinois University Libraries, Macomb IL. 309-298-2411

Rezak, Shelia A, *ILL,* Purdue University Calumet Library, Hammond IN. 219-844-0520, Ext 249

Rezash, Anita, *Asst Librn,* Coshocton Public Library, Coshocton OH. 614-622-0956

Rezazadeh, Gloria I, *Instructional Mat Librn,* University of Wisconsin-Platteville, Elton S Karrmann Library, Platteville WI. 608-342-1688

Reznack, Lauren, *Librn,* Higgs, Fletcher & Mack, Law Library, San Diego CA. 714-236-1551

Rheay, Mary Louise, *Dir,* Cobb County Public Library System, Marietta GA. 404-427-2462

Rhee, Sue, *Cat,* Northwest Christian College, Learning Resource Center, Eugene OR. 503-343-1641, Ext 35

Rhee, Susan, *Cat,* University of California, San Diego, University Libraries, La Jolla CA. 714-452-3336

Rhee, Yang Hoon, *On-Line Servs,* John Deere Product Engineering Center Library, Waterloo IA. 319-235-4668

Rhein, Jean F, *Librn,* Seminole County Public Library System, Sanford FL. 305-323-4330, Ext 362

Rhein, Robert, *Media,* Drexel University Library, Philadelphia PA. 215-895-2750

Rheineck, Mary, *Librn,* West Allis Memorial Hospital, Medical Library, West Allis WI. 414-321-2200, Ext 3060

Rheingans, Martha, *Librn,* De Witt Public Library, De Witt IA. 319-659-5523

Rhem, Margaret W, *Librn,* Crittenden County Library, Marion KY. 502-965-3354

Rhew, David, *Dir,* Grand Canyon College, Fleming Library, Phoenix AZ. 602-249-3300, Ext 207

Rhinberger, Evelyn, *Librn,* Camp Point Free Public Library, Camp Point IL. 217-593-7021

Rhine, Leonard, *Tech Serv,* University of Florida Libraries (J Hillis Miller Health Center), Gainesville FL. 904-392-4011

Rhinehart, Ruth, *Genealogy,* Morley Library, Painesville OH. 216-352-3383

Rhinehart, William, *Tech Serv & Cat,* Saint Ambrose College, Learning Resource Center, Davenport IA. 319-324-1681, Ext 241

Rhinewalt, Mrs Ozell, *Librn,* Jackson Metropolitan Library (Cash Library), Lena MS. 601-352-3677

Rhoades, David, *Media,* Geneva College, McCartney Library, Beaver Falls PA. 412-846-5100, Ext 297

Rhoades, Marjorie, *Eng Sci,* Colorado State University, William E Morgan Library, Fort Collins CO. 303-491-5911

Rhoads, Lynne A, *Publications,* University of Washington Libraries, Seattle WA. 206-543-1760

Rhode, Mrs Reinold, *Dir,* Howells Public Library, Howells NE. 402-986-1544

Rhodehamel, John H, *Archivist,* Mount Vernon Ladies' Association of the Union, Research & Reference Library, Mount Vernon VA. 703-780-2000

Rhoden, Hazel T, *Librn,* Northeast Florida State Hospital Library, Macclenny FL. 904-259-6211, Ext 283

Rhodes, Barbara, *Ch,* Waco-McLennan County Library, Waco TX. 817-754-4694

Rhodes, Clayton E, *Librn,* Enoch Pratt Free Library (Waverly), Baltimore MD. 301-396-5430, 396-5395

Rhodes, Dolores, *Asst Dir,* Uniontown Public Library, Uniontown PA. 412-437-1165

Rhodes, Evelyn, *Cat,* Catawba County Library, Newton NC. 704-464-2421

Rhodes, Gladys J, *Coordr,* Texas Information Exchange, (TIE), TX. 713-528-3553

Rhodes, Glenda, *AV,* Salt Lake City Public Library, Salt Lake City UT. 801-363-5733

Rhodes, James, *Ad,* Topeka Public Library, Topeka KS. 913-233-2040

Rhodes, Janet, *Librn,* Sarah Hull Hallock Free Library, Milton NY. 914-795-2200

Rhodes, Jo Ella, *Ch,* Northeast Regional Library, Corinth MS. 601-287-2441

Rhodes, Lace, *Librn,* Copiah-Jefferson Regional Library, George W Covington Memorial Library, Hazlehurst MS. 601-894-1681

Rhodes, Lace, *Librn,* Copiah-Jefferson Regional Library (Hazlehurst Branch (Headquarters)), Hazlehurst MS. 601-894-1681

Rhodes, Lelia G, *Dir,* Jackson State University, Henry Thomas Sampson Library, Jackson MS. 601-968-2123

Rhodes, Leola, *Bibliog Instr,* Morris College, Pinson Memorial Library, Sumter SC. 803-775-9371, Ext 216

Rhodes, Lorna F, *Librn,* Taft Public Library, Mendon MA. 617-473-3259

Rhodes, Maxine, *Media,* Altoona Area Public Library, Altoona PA. 814-946-0417

Rhodes, Maxine, *Librn,* Altoona Area Public Library (Media Center), Altoona PA. 814-946-1224

Rhodes, Mrs Cornell, *Librn,* Tiptonville Public Library, Tiptonville TN. 901-253-7391

Rhodes, Myrtle J, *Librn,* United States Navy (Information & Documentation Technical Library), Panama City FL. 904-234-4321

Rhodes, Naomi, *Librn,* Tonawanda City Public Library, Tonawanda NY. 716-693-5043

Rhodes, Robert H, *Dir,* Rockingham Free Public Library, Bellows Falls VT. 802-463-4270

Rhodes, Roberta M, *Librn,* Merriam-Gilbert Public Library, West Brookfield MA. 617-867-8784

Rhodes, Suzan, *Exten,* Bartram Trail Regional Library, Mary Willis Library Headquarters, Washington GA. 404-678-7736

Rhodes, Verna, *Librn,* Clark County Library District (Searchlight Branch), Searchlight NV. 702-297-1442

Rhodes, Yvonne M, *Librn,* United States Army (Fitzsimons Army Medical Center, Medical-Technical Library), Aurora CO. 303-341-8918

Rhone, Virginia S, *Dir,* George T Boyd Memorial Library, Port Neches Public Library, Port Neches TX. 713-722-4554

Rhu, Sue, *Sr Libr Asst,* Madera County Library (Oakhurst Branch), Oakhurst CA. 209-683-4838

Rhydwen, D, *Librn,* Globe & Mail Library, Toronto ON. 416-361-5000

Rhyne, Julia A, *Dir,* Madison General Hospital (Maude Webster Middleton School of Nursing Library), Madison WI. 608-267-6250, Ext 19

Rials, Mattie J, *Ch,* Pike-Amite-Walthall Library System, McComb Public Library (Headquaters), McComb MS. 601-684-7034

Riba, Betty, *Libr Technician,* San Diego County Library (Castle Park), Chula Vista CA. 714-427-1151

Ribaud, Ruth, *YA,* Katonah Village Library, Katonah NY. 914-232-3508

Ribback, Edgar G, *Dir,* Port of Seattle Library, Seattle WA. 206-382-3253

Ribbens, Dennis, *Dir,* Lawrence University, Seeley G Mudd Library, Appleton WI. 414-739-3681, Ext 264

Ribiere, Michelle, *Cat,* College De Sainte-Foy, Centre des Medias, Sainte Foy PQ. 418-657-3624

Ribner, Andrew, *Chief Librn,* Veterans Administration, Hospital Library, Boise ID. 208-336-5100, Ext 228

Riccardi, Ann, *Librn,* Brockton Public Library System (Campello), Brockton MA. 617-583-5519

Riccardo-Markot, Vicki, *Assoc Mgr,* Prudential Insurance Co of America (Law Library), Newark NJ. 201-877-6804

Ricci, Frances, *Pub Servs,* Johnson County Library, Shawnee Mission KS. 913-831-1550

Ricci, Patricia, *On-Line Servs & Bibliog Instr,* James Jerome Hill Reference Library, Saint Paul MN. 612-227-9531

Ricciardi, Ann, *Circ,* IBM Corp System Products Division Library, Endicott NY. 607-755-3223

Ricciardi, Dana D, *Librn,* Museum of the American China Trade, Archives, Milton MA. 617-696-1815

Rice, Agnes G, *Librn,* Allen-Bradley Co, Coporate Library, Milwaukee WI. 414-671-2000, Ext 2079

Rice, Barbara, *Librn,* Augusta County Library, Fishersville VA. 703-885-3961

Rice, Bette M, *Asst Dir,* Mississippi State University, Mitchell Memorial Library, Mississippi State MS. 601-325-4225

Rice, Brenda, *Dir,* University of Chicago (Chemistry), Chicago IL. 312-753-3443

Rice, Carla, *Librn,* Daingerfield Public Library, Daingerfield TX. 214-645-2823

Rice, Carol, *Pre-Automation,* Howard County Library, Columbia MD. 301-997-8000

Rice, Carol, *Asst Librn,* United States Geological Survey, EROS Applications Assistance Facility Library, Bay Saint Louis MS. 601-688-3541

Rice, Cecelia E, *Pub Servs,* Xerox Corp, Technical Information Center, Webster NY. 716-422-3505

Rice, Chuck, *Dir Libr Serv,* National Rural Electric Cooperative Association, Norris Memorial Library, Washington DC. 202-857-9788

Rice, Corliss, *ILL & Ad,* Saint Joseph Public Library, Saint Joseph MO. 816-232-7729, 232-7720

Rice, D A, *Librn,* Borg-Warner Corp, Weston Hydraulics Div Library, Van Nuys CA. 213-781-4000

Rice, Doris, *In Charge,* Presbyterian Church Library, Westfield NJ. 201-232-7123

Rice, Dorothy, *Admin Serv,* University of Nevada-Reno, Noble H Getchell Library, Reno NV. 702-784-6533

Rice, Dorothy M, *Librn,* Bendix Corp, Engineering Reference Library, Teterboro NJ. 201-288-2000, Ext 5846

Rice, Eleanor M, *Librn,* Raytheon Co, Badger Co Inc Library, Cambridge MA. 617-492-7000

Rice, Ethel, *Tech Serv,* Western State College of Colorado, Leslie J Savage Library, Gunnison CO. 303-943-2053

Rice, G Sean, *In Charge,* United States Navy (Atlantic Fleet Headquarters Support Activity), Norfolk VA. 804-444-1521

Rice, Gail, *Asst Librn,* Mark Skinner Library, Manchester VT. 802-362-2607

Rice, Gloria M, *Librn,* Public Library of the District of Columbia (Trinidad), Washington DC. 202-727-1351

Rice, Gwen, *Ref & ILL,* Wyoming State Library, Cheyenne WY. 307-777-7281

Rice, Harvey F, *Dir,* Oregon Institute of Technology Library, Klamath Falls OR. 503-882-6321, Ext 187

Rice, Helen, *Librn,* Kirbyville Public Library, Kirbyville TX. 713-423-4653

Rice, James, *Asst Prof,* Western Michigan University, School of Librarianship, MI. 616-383-1849

Rice, Jean, *Librn,* Springfield Public Library, Springfield NE. 402-253-2204

Rice, Jeanette, *Librn,* Monmouth County Library (Hazlet Branch), Hazlet NJ. 201-264-7164

Rice, Jeanne, *Acq, Cat & Ref,* Booth & Dimock Memorial Library, Coventry CT. 203-742-7606

Rice, Larry, *AV,* Saint Petersburg Junior College, Michael M Bennett Library, Clearwater FL. 813-441-0681, Ext 2616

Rice, Linda, *Librn,* Cabell County Public Library (Guyandotte), Huntington WV. 304-522-8161

Rice, Margot, *ILL,* Lake Forest College, Donnelley Library, Lake Forest IL. 312-234-3100, Ext 405

Rice, Marjory, *Asst,* Grant County Library, Hyannis NE. 308-458-2218

Rice, Mary, *Asst Librn,* Hildebrand Memorial Library, Boscobel WI. 608-375-5723

Rice, Maude S, *Librn,* Aiken-Bamberg-Barnwell-Edgefield Regional Library (Bamberg County Public), Bamberg SC. 803-245-4280

Rice, Nancy, *Acq,* Vermont Technical College, Hartness Library, Randolph Center VT. 802-728-3391, Ext 32

Rice, Patricia, *Acq,* Winthrop College, Ida Jane Dacus Library, Rock Hill SC. 803-323-2131

Rice, Robert L, *Dir,* Levi Heywood Memorial Library, Gardner MA. 617-632-5298

Rice, Ruth, *Ch,* Utah State University, Merrill Library & Learning Resources Program, Logan UT. 801-750-2637

Rice, Ruth, *Librn,* Utah State University (Ann Carroll Moore Children's Library), Logan UT. 801-750-3091

Rice, Sally E, *Ad,* East Orange Public Library, East Orange NJ. 201-266-5600

Rice, Sher, *Librn,* Congregation B'nai David, Isadore Gruskin Library, Southfield MI. 313-557-8211

Rice, Sister Mercia, *Ref,* Ohio Dominican College Library, Columbus OH. 614-253-2741, Ext 258, 210

Rice-Billings, Rose, *Ref & Bibliog Instr,* Saginaw Valley State College Library & Learning Resources Center, University Center MI. 517-790-4237

Rich, Beth, *Asst Dir,* Needham Free Public Library, Needham MA. 617-444-0087, 444-0090

Rich, Betty, *Bkmobile Coordr,* Webster County Public Library, Dixon KY. 502-639-9171

Rich, Carol, *Ch,* Nichols Memorial Library, Kingston NH. 603-642-3521

Rich, Dixie, *Br Coordr,* Bear Lake County Free Library, Montpelier ID. 208-847-1664

Rich, Hester, *Asst Librn,* Maryland Historical Society Library, Baltimore MD. 301-685-3750

Rich, Jessica, *Chief Librn,* United States Air Force (Technical Library, Western Space & Missile Center), Vandenberg AFB CA. 805-866-9745

Rich, Margaret, *Govt Doc,* State University of New York College at Brockport, Drake Memorial Library, Brockport NY. 716-395-2140

Rich, Margie, *Librn,* Waynesville Public Library, Waynesville IL. 217-949-5111

Rich, Pat Underwood, *Ref,* Time, Inc (Main Library), New York NY. 212-841-3745

Rich, Tom, *ILL,* Zion-Benton Public Library District, Zion IL. 312-872-4680

Richard, Alice, *Librn,* Adath Israel Synagogue, Leshner Memorial Library, Cincinnati OH. 513-793-1800

Richard, Carol, *Librn,* Pennsylvania Department of Environmental Resources (Law Library, Office of Chief Counsel), Harrisburg PA. 717-787-4460

Richard, George M, *Librn,* Charles A Wustum Museum of Fine Arts, Racine WI. 414-636-9177

Richard, Glenda G, *Dir,* LaFourche Parish Library, Thibodaux LA. 504-446-1163

Richard, Harris M, *Dir,* College of Ganado Library, Ganado AZ. 602-755-3442

Richard, John B, *Dir,* East Baton Rouge Parish Library, Baton Rouge LA. 504-389-3360

Richard, Marcelle, *Librn,* Bibliotheque Municipale, Montmorency PQ. 418-661-5626

Richard, Robert, *Southern Regional Librn,* Orange County Public Library, Orange CA. 714-634-7841

Richard, Simone, *Librn,* Chaleur Regional Library (Atholville Public), Atholville NB. 506-753-5691

Richards, Alice, *Librn,* Lamont Municipal Library, Lamont AB. 403-895-2138

Richards, Annegret, *Acq,* State University of New York at Buffalo (Charles B Sears Law Library), Buffalo NY. 716-636-2043

Richards, Barbara, *Asst Librn,* Carnegie-Mellon University (Mellon Institute Library), Pittsburgh PA. 412-578-3172

Richards, Benjamin, *Dir,* Western New York Library Resources Council, NY. 716-852-3844

Richards, Berry G, *Dir,* Lehigh University Libraries, Bethlehem PA. 861-3026 (Dir), 861-3050 (Ref), 861-3030 (Circ), 861-3055 (ILL)

Richards, Carol, *Bibliog Instr,* State University College at Buffalo, Edward H Butler Library, Buffalo NY. 716-878-6302

Richards, Catherine, *Librn,* Houston Public Library (Books by Mail), Houston TX. 713-869-0318

Richards, Dana, *AV,* University of Pittsburgh at Bradford Library, Bradford PA. 814-362-3801, Ext 126

Richards, Dargan, *Librn,* Columbia Newspapers Inc Library, Columbia SC. 803-771-8340

Richards, Darlene, *Ref,* McHenry County College, Learning Resource Center System, Crystal Lake IL. 815-455-3700, Ext 276

Richards, Dawn, *Librn,* North Versailles Public Library, North Versailles PA. 412-672-9817

Richards, Deborah, *Coordr Print Serv,* Brigham Young University-Hawaii Campus, Joseph F Smith Library, Laie HI. 808-293-9211, Ext 260, 264

Richards, Diana Mae, *Chief, Libr Program Staff,* International Communication Agency (Education & Cultural Affairs), Washington DC. 202-632-5346, 632-6752

Richards, Elaine, *Media,* Blue Mountain Community College Library, Pendleton OR. 503-276-1260, Ext 234

Richards, Eleanor, *Librn,* Harris-Elmore Public Library (Genoa), Elmore OH. 419-855-3380

Richards, Emma S, *Asst Dir, ILL & Ad,* Wicomico County Free Library, Salisbury MD. 301-749-5171

Richards, Helen M, *Dir,* Cleary College Library, Ypsilanti MI. 313-483-4400

Richards, Jane, *Librn,* Cary Memorial Library, Wayne ME. 207-685-3612

Richards, Jane, *Supvr Learning Skills Ctr,* Friends University, Edmund Stanley Library, Wichita KS. 316-263-9131, Ext 220

Richards, Katherine, *Librn,* Cooper Medical Center, Reuben L Sharp Health Science Library, Camden NJ. 609-963-7230

Richards, Lee, *Dir,* Iowa Central Community College, Eagle Grove Center Library, Eagle Grove IA. 515-448-4723

Richards, Lee, *Dir,* Iowa Central Community College, Webster City Center Library, Webster City IA. 515-832-1632, Ext 8

Richards, Louise, *Teaching Materials,* Indiana State University, Cunningham Memorial Library, Terre Haute IN. 812-232-6311, Ext 2451

Richards, Louise, *Cat & Rare Bks,* Randolph-Macon College, Walter Hines Page Library, Ashland VA. 804-798-8372, Ext 256

Richards, Marcia, *Mgr,* Burbank Public Library, Burbank CA. 213-847-9744

Richards, Melva, *Acq,* Illinois Valley Community College, Jacobs Memorial Library, Oglesby IL. 815-224-2720

Richards, Nancy, *ILL,* Memorial Hall Library, (Subregional Headquarters for Eastern Massachusetts Regional System), Andover MA. 617-475-6960

Richards, Pamela S, *Asst Prof,* Rutgers-The State University of New Jersey, Graduate School of Library & Information Studies, NJ. 201-932-7500

Richards, Paul, *ILL & Ad,* Mesquite Public Library, Mesquite TX. 214-285-6369

Richards, Pauline, *Librn,* William Adams Bachelder Library, East Andover NH. 603-735-5333

Richards, R F, *Librn,* Kaplan, Livingston, Goodwin, Berkowity & Selvin Library, Beverly Hills CA. 213-274-8011

Richards, Robert, *Regional Librn,* Chaleur Regional Library, Campbellton NB. 506-753-4500

Richards, Rosemary, *In Charge,* Texas Education Agency (Region XII), Waco TX. 817-756-7494

Richards, Ruth, *Ad,* Carnegie Free Library, McKeesport PA. 412-672-0625

Richards, Sharon, *Ch,* Security Public Library, Security CO. 303-392-8912

Richards, Vincent, *Dir,* Edmonton Public Library, Edmonton AB. 403-423-2331

Richards, Jr, James H, *Dir,* Gettysburg College, Schmucker Memorial Library, Gettysburg PA. 717-334-3131, Ext 366

Richardson, Beverly, *Librn,* Montgomery County Public Library, Troy NC. 919-572-1311

Richardson, Beverly, *Pub Servs,* Sandhill Regional Library System, Rockingham NC. 919-997-3388

Richardson, Brenda, *Librn,* Columbia Hospital (School of Nursing Library), Milwaukee WI. 414-961-3533

Richardson, Christine, *Librn,* German Society of Pennsylvania, Joseph Horner Memorial Library, Philadelphia PA. 215-627-4365

Richardson, Cynthia, *Orig Cat,* Western Washington University, Mabel Zoe Wilson Library, Bellingham WA. 206-676-3050

Richardson, Denise, *Supervisor,* Chicago Public Library (Cabrini-Green Homes Reading & Study Center), Chicago IL. 312-649-6683

Richardson, Donald, *Tech Reports,* Worcester Polytechnic Institute, George C Gordon Library, Worcester MA. 617-753-1411, Ext 410

Richardson, Donald S, *Librn,* Seminole Public Library, Seminole OK. 405-382-4221

Richardson, Doris, *Circ,* Central State University, Hallie Q Brown Memorial Library, Wilberforce OH. 513-376-7212

Richardson, Edna, *Libr Technician,* Universite De Moncton (Centre de Documentation Scolaire et Professionnelle), Moncton NB. 506-858-4164

Richardson, Evelyn, *Librn,* Barren River Regional Library, Russellville KY. 502-726-9889

Richardson, Gail, *Librn,* La Jolla Museum of Contemporary Art, Helen Palmer Geisel Library, La Jolla CA. 714-454-3541

Richardson, Heidi, *Librn,* Harford County Library (Whiteford Branch), Whiteford MD. 301-838-7484

Richardson, Hugh, *Librn,* Butler County Community Junior College, L W Nixon Library, El Dorado KS. 316-321-5083, Ext 168

Richardson, Jeanne, *RI Coll,* Providence Public Library, Providence RI. 401-521-7722

Richardson, Jeanne, *Librn,* University of Kansas Libraries (Science), Lawrence KS. 913-864-3465

Richardson, Jessie, *Head,* University of Minnesota Libraries-Twin Cities (Reference & Bibliographic Services), Minneapolis MN. 612-373-5584

Richardson, Joseph A, *Asst Dir & Acq,* Winona State University, Maxwell Library, Winona MN. 507-457-2040

Richardson, Joy, *Tech Serv & Cat,* Paul D Camp Community College Library, Franklin VA. 804-562-2171, Ext 234

Richardson, Judy, *Nat & Soc Sci,* Arlington Public Library, Arlington TX. 817-275-2763, 265-3311, Ext 347

Richardson, Kathy, *Librn,* Whatcom County Public Library (Blaine Community), Blaine WA. 206-332-8146

Richardson, Kathy E, *Ch,* Nashua Public Library, Nashua NH. 603-883-4141, 883-4142

Richardson, Larry, *ILL, Ref & On-Line Servs,* Linfield College, Northup Library, McMinnville OR. 503-472-4121, Ext 262

Richardson, Margaret B, *Ref,* Palm Beach Junior College, Library Learning Resources Center, Lake Worth FL. 305-965-8000, Ext 213

Richardson, Margie, *Librn,* Richland County Public Library (Saint Andrews), Columbia SC. 803-772-6675

Richardson, Martha, *Dir, Ad & Acq,* Franklin Library Association, Franklin PA. 814-432-5062

Richardson, Martha, *ILL,* Iowa State University Library, Ames IA. 515-294-1442

Richardson, Mary, *Ch,* Sausalito Public Library, Sausalito CA. 415-332-2325

Richardson, Miriam, *Asst Librn,* Eldorado Memorial Library, Eldorado IL. 618-273-7922

Richardson, Molly, *Asst Dir,* Santa Monica Public Library, Santa Monica CA. 213-451-5751

Richardson, Robert, *Asst Dir,* Chattahoochee Valley Regional Library, W C Bradley Memorial Library, Headquarters, Columbus GA. 404-327-0211

Richardson, Robert, *Media,* Montclair State College, Harry A Sprague Library, Upper Montclair NJ. 201-893-4291

Richardson, Robert W, *Dir,* Colorado Railroad Historical Foundation, Inc, Colorado Railroad Museum Library, Golden CO. 303-279-4591

Richardson, Ruth, *Asst Dir,* Cedar Rapids Public Library, Cedar Rapids IA. 319-398-5123

Richardson, Samuel E, *Chief Librn,* Morristown College, Myriam Parlian Library, Morristown TN. 615-586-5262

Richardson, Sara, *Acq,* United Engineers & Constructors, Inc Library, Philadelphia PA. 215-422-3374

Richardson, Selma, *Assoc Prof,* University of Illinois, Graduate School of Library Science, IL. 217-333-3280

Richardson, Shirley, *Ser,* University of Texas at El Paso Library, El Paso TX. 747-5683; 747-5684

Richardson, Thelma, *ILL, Reader Serv & Ref,* Grambling State University, A C Lewis Memorial Library, Grambling LA. 318-247-6941, Ext 220

Richardson, Virginia, *Librn,* Pascoag Public Library, Pascoag RI. 401-568-6226

Richardson, Virginia J, *Tech Reports,* Morgan State University, Morris A Soper Library, Baltimore MD. 301-444-3488, 444-3489

Richardson, William, *Ref,* Santa Barbara Public Library, Santa Barbara CA. 805-962-7653

Richardson, William H, *Librn,* General Motors Corp, Detroit Diesel Allison Div Library, Indianapolis IN. 317-243-5651

Richer, Rene, *Asst Dir,* Chateauguay Municipal Library, Chateauguay PQ. 514-691-1934

Richer, Suzanne, *Dir,* Secretary of State, Documentation Directorate, Translation Bureau, Hull PQ. 819-997-3857

Richer, Yvon, *Dir,* University of Ottawa Libraries (Morisset Library (Humanities & Social Sciences)), Ottawa ON. 613-231-6892

Richerson, Mary, *Librn,* Rockbridge Regional Library (Highland), Monterey VA. 703-468-2373

Richert, Linda, *Circ,* Yeshiva University Libraries (Benjamin N Cardozo School of Law Library), New York NY. 212-790-0422

Richert, Paul, *Librn,* University of Akron (McDowell Library), Akron OH. 216-375-7330

Richeson, Marian E, *Mgr, Instructional Services,* Justice Institute of British Columbia, Resource Centre, Vancouver BC. 604-224-2311

Richey, Alice, *Instr,* Phillips University, Education & Library Science Study Area, OK. 405-237-4433, Ext 417

Richey, Alice L, *Asst Dir,* Phillips University, Zollars Memorial Library, Enid OK. 405-237-4433, Ext 251

Richey, Ann, *Tech Serv,* Rocky River Public Library, Rocky River OH. 216-333-7610

Richey, Cynthia K, *Ch,* Pleasant Hills Public Library, Pleasant Hills PA. 412-655-2424

Richey, James I, *Librn, Ref & Bibliog Instr,* Cuyahoga Community College (Eastern Campus Library), Warrensville OH. 216-464-1450, Ext 228, 229

Richey, James L, *Librn,* Cuyahoga Community College-Eastern Campus, District Technical Services Library, Warrensville Township OH. 216-464-1450

Richie, Mary L, *Librn,* Beaver Falls Library, Beaver Falls NY. 315-346-6216

Richman, Ethel, *Ch,* Cattermole Memorial Library, Fort Madison IA. 319-372-5721

Richman, Gratia, *Librn,* Eastminster Presbyterian Church Library, Indialantic FL. 305-723-8371

Richman, Linda, *On-Line Servs,* Westinghouse Electric Corp (Nuclear Energy Systems, Information Resources), Pittsburgh PA. 412-373-4200

Richmond, Alice, *Asst Prof,* North Carolina Central University, School of Library Science, NC. 919-683-6185

Richmond, Alice S, *Librn,* North Carolina Central University (School of Library Science), Durham NC. 919-683-6400

Richmond, John, *Serv Ctr Mgr,* North Bay Cooperative Library System, Santa Rosa CA. 707-545-0831

Richmond, June E, *Librn,* Normandeau Associates, Inc Library, Bedford NH. 603-472-5191

Richmond, Lloyd N, *Librn,* Ohio University, Ironton Campus Library, Ironton OH. 614-532-9021

Richmond, Lynne, *Acq,* Massachusetts Maritime Academy, Captain Charles H Hurley Library, Buzzards Bay MA. 617-759-5761, Ext 281

Richmond, Phyllis A, *Prof,* Case Western Reserve University, School of Library Science, OH. 216-368-3500

Richmond, Rick, *Syst Off,* Pikes Peak Regional Library District, Penrose Public Library, Colorado Springs CO. 303-473-2080

Richmond, Roberta J, *Librn,* Pigeon District Library, Pigeon MI. 517-453-2341

Richter, Bernice, *Librn,* Museum of Science & Industry Library, Chicago IL. 312-684-1414, Ext 373

Richter, Donald, *Sci,* Stephen F Austin State University, Ralph W Steen Library, Nacogdoches TX. 713-569-4109

Richter, Edward, *Ref,* Eastern New Mexico University Library, Portales NM. 505-562-2624

Richter, Genevieve, *Asst Librn,* North Haledon Free Public Library, North Haledon NJ. 201-427-6213

Richter, Heddy, *Am Lit,* University of Southern California, Edward L Doheny Memorial Library, Los Angeles CA. 213-743-6050

Richter, Joyce A, *Librn,* Ralph Stone & Co, Inc Library, Los Angeles CA. 213-478-1501

Richter, R G, *Media,* Concordia College, Klinck Memorial Library, River Forest IL. 312-771-8300, Ext 450

Richter, Regina, *Ref,* Saint Mary's University (Academic Library), San Antonio TX. 512-436-3441

Richwine, Eleanor, *Tech Serv & Cat,* Western Maryland College, Hoover Library, Westminster MD. 301-848-7000, Ext 281

Rick, Thomas, *Cat,* Christ Seminary-Seminex Library, Saint Louis MO. 314-534-7535

Rickard, Kay, *Dir,* Benton County Public Library, Fowler IN. 317-884-1720

Rickards, Doris J, *Librn,* Paoli Memorial Hospital, Robert M White Memorial Library, Paoli PA. 215-648-1218

Rickerby, Gregory, *Commun Servs,* Bishop's University & Champlain Regional College, John Bassett Memorial Library, Lennoxville PQ. 819-569-9551, Ext 341

Rickerson, Connie, *Librn,* Holmes & Narver, Inc, Resources Sciences, Technical Library, Orange CA. 714-973-1100

Rickerson, George, *Tech Serv,* Evergreen State College, Daniel J Evans Library, Olympia WA. 206-866-6262

Rickerson, Judy, *Ch,* Autauga-Prattville Public Library, Prattville AL. 205-365-3396

Rickerson, Judy, *Ch,* Autauga-Prattville Public Library System, Prattville AL. 205-365-3396

Rickert, Carol, *Bkmobile Coordr,* Arlington Heights Memorial Library, Arlington Heights IL. 312-392-0100

Ricketts, Arthur S, *Tech Serv,* Flint Public Library, Flint MI. 313-232-7111

Ricketts, Lynne, *Librn,* Bexar County Medical Library Association, San Antonio TX. 512-734-6691

Ricketts, Mattie, *Librn,* Lebanon-Wilson County Library (Watertown Branch), Watertown TN. 615-444-0632

Ricketts, Nancy, *ILL,* Sheldon Jackson College, Stratton Library, Sitka AK. 907-747-5235, 747-5259

Ricketts, Shannon, *Librn,* Vancouver Museums & Planetarium Association, Resource Centre, Vancouver BC. 604-736-4431, Ext 239

Ricketts, Tym, *Asst Librn,* Henry County Library, Eminence KY. 502-845-5682

Rickey, Doris, *Librn,* Roseville Public Library (Coloma Way), Roseville CA. 916-782-4090

Rickles, Suzanne, *Librn,* New Haven Free Public Library (Chapel), New Haven CT. 203-787-8120

Rickling, Iraida B, *Librn,* Florida Solar Energy Center Library, Cape Canaveral FL. 305-783-0300, Exts 120, 121 & 113

Rickman, Edna, *Librn,* Barry-Lawrence Regional Library (Cassville Branch), Cassville MO. 417-847-2121

Ricks, Bonnie, *Librn,* United States Army (Fort Greely Post Library), Fort Greely AK. 907-873-3217, 873-4117

Ricks, Frances, *Librn,* Brooklyn Public Library (New Utrecht), Brooklyn NY. 212-236-4086
Ricks, Johnnie, *Dir,* Lawson State Community College Library, Birmingham AL. 205-925-1666
Ricks, Johnnie Copeland, *Dir,* Theodore A Lawson State Community College Library, Birmingham AL. 205-925-1666
Ricks, Miriam G, *Asst Prof,* North Carolina Central University, School of Library Science, NC. 919-683-6485
Rickus, Mary, *Rare Bks & Spec Coll,* Clarksburg-Harrison Public Library, Clarksburg WV. 304-624-6512, 624-6513
Riddick, John, *Ser,* Central Michigan University, Charles V Park Library, Mount Pleasant MI. 517-774-3500
Riddle, Donna, *Asst Librn,* W A Rankin Memorial Library, Neodesha KS. 316-325-3275
Riddle, Jane, *On-Line Servs & Bibliog Instr,* NASA, Goddard Space Flight Center Library, Greenbelt MD. 301-344-6244
Riddle, Mary Ellen, *ILL,* University of Missouri-Kansas City Libraries (Medical Library), Kansas City MO. 816-474-4100, Ext 280
Riddle, Peggy, *Research,* Dallas Historical Society Research Center, Dallas TX. 214-421-5136
Riddle, Raymond E, *Dir,* Cass County Public Library, Harrisonville MO. 816-884-3483
Riddle, Tena, *Librn,* Stark County District Library (Perry Heights), Massillon OH. 216-477-8482
Riddleberger, Sharon, *Librn,* Magic Valley Memorial Hospital Library, Twin Falls ID. 733-1511 & 737-2000
Ridenhour, Erlyne Fern, *Librn,* Thomas Jefferson Library (Maries County Library Service Center), Belle MO. 314-859-6285
Ridenour, Alice, *Assoc Dir & Tech Serv,* Montana State University, Roland R Renne Library, Bozeman MT. 406-994-3119
Ridenour, Sandra S, *Ch,* Speedway Public Library, Speedway IN. 317-243-8959
Rider, William, *Circ,* Herbert H Lehman College Library, Bronx NY. 212-960-8577, 960-8582
Ridge, Davy-Jo, *Assoc Dir,* University of South Carolina, Thomas Cooper Library, Columbia SC. 803-777-3142
Ridge, Frank P, *ILL & Circ,* Tampa-Hillsborough County Public Library System, Tampa FL. 813-223-8947
Ridge, Hope S, *Librn,* Randolph Circuit Court, Law Library, Winchester IN. 317-584-7231
Ridge, Hope S, *Librn,* Rawle & Henderson, Law Library, Philadelphia PA. 215-569-2500, Ext 260
Ridge, Michele M, *Actg Dir,* Erie County Library System, Erie PA. 814-452-2333
Ridge, Ruth, *Librn,* Carnegie Free Public Library, Rockwell City IA. 712-297-8422
Ridgell, Gary, *ILL & Ref,* Charles County Community College, Learning Resource Center, La Plata MD. 301-934-2251, Ext 251
Ridgeway, Isabelle, *Librn & On-Line Servs,* Ontario Paper Co Ltd Library, Thorold ON. 416-227-1121, Ext 306
Ridgeway, Jan, *Librn,* Anchorage Municipal Libraries (Z J Loussac Public Library), Anchorage AK. 907-264-4481
Ridgeway, Janice, *Asst Dir,* Anchorage Municipal Libraries, Anchorage AK. 907-264-4481
Ridgeway, Michael, *AV & On-Line Servs,* United States Military Academy Library, West Point NY. 914-938-2230
Ridgeway, Patricia M, *Ref,* Winthrop College, Ida Jane Dacus Library, Rock Hill SC. 803-323-2131
Ridgway, Elna, *Librn,* Atwood Public Library, Atwood KS. 913-626-3805
Ridings, Elisabeth, *Librn,* Public Library of Cincinnati & Hamilton County (Hyde Park), Cincinnati OH. 513-321-6308
Ridings, Lois, *Librn,* Dunklin County Library (Arbyrd Branch), Arbyrd MO. 314-654-2385
Ridley, Saundra, *Prof Libr Tech Servs,* Massachusetts Board of Library Commissioners, Office for the Development of Library Services, Boston MA. 617-267-9400
Riebe, Eileen, *Librn,* Girard Public Library, Girard KS. 316-724-4317
Riebel, Ellis, *Media,* East Stroudsburg State College, Kemp Library, East Stroudsburg PA. 717-424-3467

Riecks, Donald, *Media,* Highline Community College Library, Midway WA. 206-878-3710, Ext 230
Riedel, Betty, *Tech Serv,* Indiana Vocational Technical College Northcentral, Learning Resources Center, South Bend IN. 219-289-7001, Ext 76
Riedesel, Laureen, *Dir,* Beatrice Public Library, Beatrice NE. 402-223-3584
Riedlinger, Barbara, *Librn,* Plymouth Public Library, Plymouth PA. 717-779-4775
Riedlinger, Charles, *Dir,* College Misericordia Library, Dallas PA. 717-675-2181, Ext 225
Rieffel, Barbara, *Librn,* Chicago Public Library (West Addison), Chicago IL. 312-625-6056
Rieffel, Robert d'O, *Librn,* Enoch Pratt Free Library (Bookmobile Headquarters), Baltimore MD. 301-396-5430, 396-5395
Riegel, Betty Jo, *ILL,* Glasgow City County Library, Glasgow MT. 406-228-2731
Riegel, Betty Jo, *On-Line Servs,* Golden Plains Library Federation, Glasgow MT. 406-228-2731
Riegel, Jo, *Librn,* Wagnalls Memorial Library, Lithopolis OH. 614-837-4765
Riegger, Sachiko, *Cat,* University of New Brunswick, Saint John Campus, Ward Chipman Library, Saint John NB. 506-657-7310
Riegle, Karen, *Learning Skills Ctr Dir,* Alpena Community College Library, Alpena MI. 517-356-9021, Ext 249
Riehl, Sallie K, *County Librn,* Madera County Library, Madera CA. 209-674-4641, Ext 263
Riehle, Hal F, *Dir,* University of Wisconsin-Extension (Bureau of Audio-Visual Instruction), Madison WI. 608-262-1644
Riehm, Sue, *Asst Librn,* Kendallville Public Library, Kendallville IN. 219-347-3554
Rieke, Kenneth, *Dir,* Connecticut State Library (State Records Center), Rocky Hill CT. 203-529-5662
Riekels, Claudette, *Bkmobile Coordr,* Benton Harbor Public Library, Benton Harbor MI. 616-926-6139
Riekena, Elizabeth, *Asst Librn,* Valdez Public Library, Valdez AK. 907-835-4632
Riemann, Frederick A, *Doc,* Texas State Law Library, Austin TX. 512-475-3807
Riepma, Helen, *Cat,* West Texas State University, Cornette Library, Canyon TX. 806-656-2761
Ries, LaVonne, *Librn,* Gilmore City Public Library, Gilmore City IA. 515-373-6562
Riese, Pat, *Asst Librn,* Raltech Scientific Services, Inc Library, Madison WI. 608-241-4471, Ext 397
Riesenman, Patricia, *Computer Assisted Ref Servs,* Indiana University at Bloomington, University Libraries, Bloomington IN. 812-337-3403
Riesgraf, Nancy, *Actg Dir & Ad,* Hibbing Public Library, Hibbing MN. 218-262-1038
Riess, Marion, *Circ,* Long Island University, Brooklyn Center Libraries, Brooklyn NY. 212-834-6060, 834-6064
Riess, Pamela, *Librn,* Fort Vancouver Regional Library (White Salmon Community), White Salmon WA. 509-493-1132
Rife, Mary, *Ch,* Kalamazoo Public Library, Kalamazoo MI. 616-342-9837
Rife, Wilma, *ILL,* Washburn University of Topeka, Mabee Library, Topeka KS. 913-295-6479
Rifenburg, Nancy, *Acq,* Otis Library, Norwich CT. 203-889-2365
Riffle, Brenda, *Librn,* Hampshire County Public Library, Romney WV. 304-822-3185
Rifkind, Eugene, *Tech Serv & Cat,* Willingboro Public Library, Willingboro NJ. 609-877-6668
Rigal, Edna E, *Dir,* Liberty Center Public Library, Liberty Center OH. 419-533-5721
Rigby, Becky, *Librn,* Madison County-Canton Public Library (Madison Public), Madison MS. 601-856-2749
Rigby, Paul, *Dir,* W Leslie Rogers Library, Pennsauken Public Library, Pennsauken NJ. 609-665-5959
Rigelman, Delma, *Librn,* First Lutheran Church, Schendel Memorial Library, Red Wing MN. 612-388-9311
Riger, Robert, *ILL & Ref,* Fordham University, School of Law Library, New York NY. 212-841-5223
Rigg, Cynthia, *Librn,* Wall Street Journal Library, New York NY. 212-285-5075
Rigg, Cynthia Walter, *Librn,* Dow Jones & Co, Inc Library, New York NY. 212-285-5000

Rigg, Sarah L, *Pub Servs,* West Georgia College Library, Carrollton GA. 404-834-1370
Riggall, Alan G, *Dir,* Pinebrook Junior College Library, Coopersburg PA. 215-282-4000, 282-4521
Riggen, Jennie, *Tech Serv,* Alaska State Library, Juneau AK. 907-465-2910
Riggenbach, Richard W, *Librn,* Van Wert County Law Library, Van Wert OH. 419-238-6935
Riggins, Bonnie Beth, *Dir,* Carnegie Public Library, Washington IN. 812-254-4586
Riggs, Arlie, *Dir,* Custer County Public Library, Westcliffe CO. 303-783-2423
Riggs, Dean, *Acq,* University of Toledo, William S Carlson Library, Toledo OH. 419-537-2324
Riggs, Donald E, *Librn,* Arizona State University Library, Tempe AZ. 602-965-3417
Riggs, Gladys B, *Librn,* Bureau of Land Management, Kanab District Office Library, Kanab UT. 801-644-2672
Riggs, Jimmie, *Ref,* Humboldt County Library, Winnemucca NV. 702-623-5081, Ext 315 & 316
Riggs, Mary Jane, *ILL & Acq,* Charlotte-Glades Library System, Port Charlotte FL. 813-629-1715
Riggs, Mrs Leroy, *Librn,* Marion Public Library, Marion KS. 316-382-2442
Riggs, Ruth E, *Dir,* Schenectady County Community College Library, Library Resources Center, Schenectady NY. 518-346-6211, Ext 240, 241
Righter, Loretta, *Ref,* Montgomery County-Norristown Public Library, Norristown PA. 215-277-3355
Rightmyer, Sandra P, *Dir,* Saugerties Public Library, Saugerties NY. 914-246-4317
Rights, Edith A, *Librn,* Montclair Art Museum, LeBrun Library, Montclair NJ. 201-746-5555
Rigia, Violet, *Dir,* Bridgeport Hospital, Reeves Memorial Library, Bridgeport CT. 203-384-3254
Rigney, Janet M, *Librn,* Council on Foreign Relations Library, New York NY. 212-734-0400
Rigo, Tibor, *Cat,* Southampton College Library of Long Island University, Southampton NY. 516-283-4000, Ext 264
Rigoulot, Lois, *Librn,* Millbrook Library, Millbrook NY. 914-677-3611
Rigsby, Texas Marie, *Librn,* Livingston Parish Library (Livingston Branch), Livingston LA. 504-686-2436
Riisness, Catherine, *Dir,* Mentor Public Library, Mentor OH. 216-255-8811
Rike, Galen E, *Assoc Prof,* Ball State University, Dept of Library Science, IN. 317-285-7180, 285-7189
Riley, Barbara, *Librn,* Union County Technical Institute, Scotch Plains NJ. 201-889-2000, Ext 280
Riley, Beatrice, *Librn,* Jamesburg Public Library, Jamesburg NJ. 201-521-0440
Riley, Bethany, *Librn,* Chatham-Effingham-Liberty Regional Library (Hitch), Savannah GA. 912-234-2463
Riley, Bethany, *Librn,* Chatham-Effingham-Liberty Regional Library (Kayton Homes), Savannah GA. 912-236-3790
Riley, Edith M, *Librn,* Maine Charitable Mechanic Association Library, Portland ME. 207-773-8396
Riley, Elizabeth, *Per,* Saint Mary's University (Academic Library), San Antonio TX. 512-436-3441
Riley, Emma Jean, *Librn,* Garnett Public Library, Garnett KS. 913-448-3388
Riley, Esta Lou, *Tech Serv,* Fort Hays State University, Forsyth Library, Hays KS. 913-628-4431
Riley, Francess, *Librn,* Atlantic City Free Public Library (New Jersey Ave Branch), Atlantic City NJ. 609-345-8284
Riley, James P, *Exec Dir,* Federal Library Committee, (FLC), DC. 202-287-6055
Riley, James P, *Network Dir,* FEDLINK, DC. 202-287-6454
Riley, James P, *Exec Dir, Fed Libr Comt,* Library of Congress, Washington DC. 202-287-5000
Riley, Jeanne, *Circ,* Glasgow City County Library, Glasgow MT. 406-228-2731
Riley, Loralee, *In Charge,* Coquitlam Public Library (Ridgeway), Coquitlam BC. 604-931-2416

Riley, Lyman, *Spec Coll,* University of Pennsylvania Libraries, Van Pelt Library, Philadelphia PA. 215-243-7091

Riley, Margaret C, *Librn,* Western State Hospital, Professional Library, Hopkinsville KY. 502-886-4431

Riley, Mary, *Spec Coll,* Bates College, George and Helen Ladd Library, Lewiston ME. 207-784-2949

Riley, Mary E, *Pub Servs,* Lehigh University Libraries, Bethlehem PA. 861-3026 (Dir), 861-3050 (Ref), 861-3030 (Circ), 861-3055 (ILL)

Riley, Mary F, *Ref,* Fordham University, Duane Library, Bronx NY. 212-933-2233, Ext 230, 259

Riley, Maureen, *Bibliog Instr,* William Paterson College of New Jersey, Sarah Byrd Askew Library, Wayne NJ. 201-595-2113

Riley, Pat, *Ref,* University of Texas Health Science Center at San Antonio Library, San Antonio TX. 512-691-6271

Riley, Pat, *Ref,* University of Texas Health Science Center at San Antonio Library, San Antonio TX. 512-691-6271

Riley, Patrick, *Circ,* University of Chicago (Law Library), Chicago IL. 312-753-3425

Riley, Richard K, *Librn,* Trenton Junior College Library, Trenton MO. 816-359-3948

Riley, Ruby, *Bkmobile Librns,* Reelfoot Regional Library Center, Martin TN. 901-587-2347

Riley, S, *Librn,* University of Southern California (Human Relations Area Files), Los Angeles CA. 213-743-6168

Riley, Sally A, *Technician,* McCormick & Co, Inc, Research & Development Laboratories Technical Information Center, Hunt Valley MD. 301-667-7485

Riley, Sharon, *Libr Asst,* Flenniken Memorial Public Library, Carmichaels PA. 412-966-5263

Riley, Viola, *Asst Librn,* Evangelical School of Nursing, Wojniak Memorial Library, Oak Lawn IL. 312-425-8000, Ext 5515

Rimbach, Cynthia, *Program Librn,* Litton Industries, Mellonics Development Division Software Library, Sunnyvale CA. 408-245-0795, Ext 251

Rimbeck, Marcella, *Librn,* Douglas County Library System (Giles Hunt Memorial Library), Sutherlin OR. 503-459-9161

Rimmele, Leo, *Dir,* Mount Angel Abbey Library, Saint Benedict OR. 503-845-3030

Rinaldi, David P, *Librn,* Middletown Psychiatric Center, Bolles Memorial Library, Middletown NY. 914-342-5511

Rinaldo, Doris Lewis, *Dir,* Brentwood Public Library, Brentwood NY. 516-273-7883

Rinaldo, Dorothy, *Per,* Sarah Lawrence College, Esther Raushenbush Library, Bronxville NY. 914-337-0700, Ext 479

Rincker, Cinda, *Ch,* Helen Matthes Library, Effingham IL. 217-342-2464

Rinden, Constance T, *Librn,* New Hampshire State Library (Law Division), Concord NH. 603-271-3777

Rindone, John, *Dir,* Carteret Public Library, Carteret NJ. 201-541-5737

Rine, Joseph, *Librn,* Minneapolis Community College Library, Minneapolis MN. 612-341-7089, 341-7059

Rine, Marie, *Librn,* McFarland Mental Health Center Library, Springfield IL. 217-786-6900

Rine, Patricia, *Cat,* University of Cincinnati Libraries, Central Library, Cincinnati OH. 513-475-2218

Rinegar, MarJean, *Librn,* Weston County Public Library (Upton), Upton WY. 307-746-2206

Rinehart, Carol, *Librn,* Homer Community Library, Homer IL. 217-869-2521

Rinehart, Constance, *Prof,* University of Michigan, School of Library Science, MI. 313-764-9376

Rinehart, Jeanne, *Ch,* Stamford's Public Library, Ferguson Library, Stamford CT. 203-325-4354

Rinehart, Michael, *Librn,* Sterling and Francine Clark Art Institute Library, Williamstown MA. 413-458-8109

Rinehart, Mitzi M, *Asst Dir,* Maricopa County Library System, Phoenix AZ. 602-269-2535

Rinehart, Sarah, *Cat,* University of Oklahoma (Law Library), Norman OK. 405-325-4311

Rinehart, Vicki, *Librn,* Beardstown Public Library, Beardstown IL. 217-323-4204

Rinella, Kristine, *Ad,* Bedford Public Library, Bedford IN. 812-275-4471

Ring, Angeline, *Librn,* Fairfield County District Library (Griley Memorial), Baltimore OH. 614-862-8505

Ring, Daniel, *Archivist,* Oakland University, Kresge Library, Rochester MI. 313-377-2486, 377-2474

Ring, Judith, *Head,* Erie County Library System (Millcreek Branch), Millcreek PA. 814-868-5205

Ring, Laurene, *Media,* Maryville College, Father Edward Dowling Memorial Library, Saint Louis MO. 314-434-4100, Ext 241

Ring, Melanie, *Asst Librn,* Fryeburg Public Library, Fryeburg ME. 207-935-2731

Ring, Patricia M, *Tech Serv,* Cleveland State University Libraries (Joseph W Bartunek III Law Library), Cleveland OH. 216-687-2250

Ringe, Vicki, *Ref,* North Vancouver District Public Library, North Vancouver BC. 604-984-0286

Ringelstein, Eunice, *Dir,* Demarest Public Library, Demarest NJ. 201-768-8714

Ringland, Inez, *ILL & Ref,* De Paul University Libraries (Frank J Lewis Center Library), Chicago IL. 312-321-7619

Ringle, Marie M, *Librn,* Fairfax County Public Library (Centerville Branch), Centreville VA. 703-830-2223

Ringo, Joyce, *Actg Librn,* Canton Free Library, Canton NY. 315-386-3712

Ringwood, Joan, *Per,* Cayuga County Community College, Norman F Bourke Memorial Library Learning Resources Center, Auburn NY. 315-255-1743, Ext 296 & 298

Rink, Bernard C, *Dir,* Northwestern Michigan College, Mark Osterlin Library, Traverse City MI. 616-946-5650, Ext 541

Rink, Evak, *Bibliog Instr,* Eleutherian Mills-Hagley Foundation, Eleutherian Mills Historical Library, Greenville DE. 302-658-2400

Rinkel, Gene, *Circ,* University of Illinois Library at Urbana-Champaign, Urbana IL. 217-333-0790

Rinkes, Irene, *Librn,* Martins Ferry Public Library (Flushing Public), Flushing OH. 614-633-0314

Rinquet, Gemma, *Acq,* Bibliotheque De La Ville De Montreal, Montreal PQ. 514-872-5923

Rintelman, Joan K, *Dir,* Watertown Library Association, Watertown CT. 203-274-6729

Rinz, Ethel, *ILL,* Township of Hamilton Free Public Library, Trenton NJ. 609-890-3460

Rio, Betty, *Librn,* Lyon County Library (Fernley Branch), Fernley NV. 702-463-3717

Riolo, Margaret, *Bkmobile Coordr,* Grand Rapids Public Library, Grand Rapids MI. 616-456-4400

Riordan, Claudia, *Researcher,* Northeastern Nevada Historical Society, Museum Research Library, Elko NV. 702-738-3418

Riordan, Marianna, *In Charge,* United States Air Force (Grissom Air Force Base Library), Grissom AFB IN. 317-689-2056

Rioth, J Marion, *Dir, Media & Spec Coll,* Ottawa University, Myers Library, Ottawa KS. 913-242-5200, Ext 317

Rioux, Gaston, *Dir,* Saint Paul University Library, Ottawa ON. 613-235-1421, Ext 54

Rioux, Muriette Chretien, *Actg Dir,* University of Ottawa Libraries (Law Library (Common & Civil Law)), Ottawa ON. 613-231-4943

Ripin, Laura, *Chief Librn,* Drexel Burnham Lambert Inc (Research Library), New York NY. 212-480-6475, 480-6476

Ripley, Hugh, *Ref,* Barry College, Monsignor William Barry Memorial Library, Miami Shores FL. 305-758-3392, Ext 263

Ripley, Hugh, *Hist,* Barry College, Monsignor William Barry Memorial Library, Miami Shores FL. 305-758-3392, Ext 263

Ripley, Ruby, *Librn,* Pawnee Public Library, Pawnee OK. 918-762-2138

Ripley, Victoria, *Chief Librn,* Huron College, Silcox Memorial Library, London ON. 519-438-7224, Ext 13

Rippe, Peter, *Exec Dir,* Roanoke Museum of Fine Arts Library, Roanoke VA. 703-342-8945

Rippel, Jeffrey A, *Deputy Dir,* Greenville County Library, Greenville SC. 803-242-5000

Rippeon, Janet D, *Law Libr,* Frederick County Law Library, Frederick MD. 301-694-2018

Ripple, Ruth, *Circ,* Cambria County Library System, Johnstown PA. 814-536-5131

Ripplinger, Marlene, *Librn,* Harvey Public Library, Harvey ND. 701-324-2156

Riquier, Myrna D, *Librn,* Rogers Corp, Lurie Library, Rogers CT. 203-774-9605, Ext 319

Ririe, Dawn, *Librn,* Challis Public Library, Challis ID. 208-879-4267

Risan, Mrs John, *Dir,* Parshall Public Library, Parshall ND. 701-862-3466

Risch, Joan, *Ref,* College of Marin Library, Kentfield CA. 415-485-9470

Risch, Linda A, *Tech Librn,* Mohasco Corp, Corporate Planning Library, Amsterdam NY. 518-841-2211

Risdon, Mabelle, *Supvr,* Middlesex County Library (West Nissouri), Thorndale ON. 519-461-1150

Risi, Marcel, *Dir,* Centre De Recherche Industrielle Du Quebec Library, Sainte Foy PQ. 418-659-1550, Ext 320

Risinger, C Frederick, *Coordr,* Indiana University Social Studies Development Center, Curriculum Resource Center, Bloomington IN. 812-337-3584

Risinger, Mrs Warren, *Asst Librn,* Orchard Public Library, Orchard NE. 402-893-4606

Riske, Joy, *Ref,* Laramie County Community College Library, Cheyenne WY. 307-634-3833

Risko, Terence W, *Dir,* Saginaw Public Libraries, Hoyt Public Library, Saginaw MI. 517-755-0904

Riss, Jane, *Ref,* Golden West College Library, Huntington Beach CA. 714-892-7711, Ext 541

Rissberger, Mrs Arthur, *Dir & Ad,* Webster Public Library, Webster NY. 872-3251 & 872-0240

Risseeuw, Linda, *Cat,* Vermillion Public Library, Vermillion SD. 605-624-2741

Ristau, Shirley, *Asst Librn,* Rivoli Township Library, New Windsor IL. 309-667-2515

Risto, Thomas, *Dir,* Wayne Community College Library, Detroit MI. 313-496-2759

Ritchey, Doug, *Ref,* Morton Arboretum, Sterling Morton Library, Lisle IL. 312-968-0074

Ritchey, Frances, *In Charge,* Free Library of Philadelphia (Regional Foundation Center), Philadelphia PA. 215-686-5322

Ritchie, Dave, *Media,* Mesa College, Learning Resource Services, Lowell Heiny Library, Grand Junction CO. 303-248-1436

Ritchie, Dave, *Ref,* State University of New York College, Memorial Library, Cortland NY. 607-753-2525, 753-2221

Ritchie, Florence, *Librn,* First Congregational Church Library, Saint Joseph MI. 616-983-5519

Ritchie, Gaylan, *Regional Marine Librn,* Transport Canada, Marine Library, Dartmouth NS. 902-426-5182

Ritchie, Sondra R, *Librn,* Allegany County Library (LaVale Branch), LaVale MD. 301-729-0855

Ritchie, Stella, *ILL,* Palm Springs Public Library, Palm Springs CA. 714-323-8291

Ritchie, Verna, *Art & Music,* University of Northern Iowa Library, Cedar Falls IA. 319-273-2737

Ritecz, Lanis J, *Dir,* Denio Memorial Library, Akron Library, Akron NY. 716-542-2327

Ritenour, Sharon R, *Actg Librn,* George C Marshall Research Foundation Library, Lexington VA. 703-463-7103

Riter, Marilyn, *Librn,* Monroe County Library System (Dundee Branch), Dundee MI. 313-529-3310

Rittenhouse, Bob, *In Charge,* Gould, Inc (Ocean Systems Information Center), Cleveland OH. 216-851-5500

Rittenhouse, Harriet, *Acq,* Miracle Valley Regional Library, City-County Public Library, Moundsville WV. 304-845-6911

Rittenhouse, Shirley, *Cat & Doc,* Maryland State Law Library, Annapolis MD. 301-269-3395

Ritter, Ann, *Tech Serv,* College of Saint Benedict Library, Saint Joseph MN. 612-363-5011

Ritter, Audrey, *Librn,* Rochester Institute of Technology (National Technical Institute for the Deaf, Staff Resource Center), Rochester NY. 716-475-6823

Ritter, Marian, *Librn,* Western Washington University (Music), Bellingham WA. 206-676-3716

Ritter, Philip W, *Dir,* Central North Carolina Regional Library, Burlington NC. 919-227-2096

Ritter, Ronald F, *Tech Serv,* Davidson County Public Library System, Lexington NC. 704-246-2520

Ritter, Victoria, *Asst Dir,* Rock Creek Public Library, Rock Creek OH. 216-563-3340

Ritter, Wilma, *Librn,* Isabelle Hunt Memorial Public Library, Pine AZ. 602-476-3678

Ritts, Sue, *Librn,* Washta Library, Washta IA. 712-447-6216, 447-6186

Ritz, Margaret E, *Librn Blind,* Willard Library, Battle Creek MI. 616-968-8166
Ritzie, Loretta, *Head Librn,* Pennsylvania State University, Wilkes-Barre Campus Library, Wilkes-Barre PA. 717-675-2171
Ritzke, Nancy, *Librn,* New Rockford Public Library, New Rockford ND. 701-947-5540
Ritzman, Dean F, *Dir,* Edison Community College, Learning Resources Center, Fort Myers FL. 813-481-2121, Ext 219, 220, 360
Ritzmann, Sheila, *Public Serv,* Miracle Valley Regional Library, City-County Public Library, Moundsville WV. 304-845-6911
Rivard, Mary, *ILL, Ref & Bibliog Instr,* Saint Michael's College, Durick Library, Colchester VT. 802-655-2000, Ext 2400
Rivard, Monique, *Media,* College De Maisonneuve Bibliotheque, Montreal PQ. 514-254-7131, 254-4035
Rivard, Paul E, *Dir,* Maine State Museum Library, Augusta ME. 207-289-2301
Rivas, Yolanda, *Librn,* Boston Public Library (Connolly), Jamaica Plain MA. 617-522-1960
Rivas, Yolanda, *Librn,* Boston Public Library (Jamaica Plain Branch), Jamaica Plain MA. 617-524-2053
Rivenburgh, Edwin F, *Dir,* Community College of the Finger Lakes Library, Canandaigua NY. 315-394-3500, Ext 127
Rivera, Adelaida, *ILL,* University of Puerto Rico Library, Jose M Lazaro Memorial Library, Rio Piedras PR. 809-764-0000, Ext 3296
Rivera, Adelaida, *Circ,* University of Puerto Rico Library, Jose M Lazaro Memorial Library, Rio Piedras PR. 809-764-0000, Ext 3296
Rivera, Flor P, *Selection,* University of Puerto Rico Library, Jose M Lazaro Memorial Library, Rio Piedras PR. 809-764-0000; Ext 3296
Rivera, Vilma, *Librn,* University of Puerto Rico Library (Graduate School of Library Sciences), Rio Piedras PR. 809-764-0000, Ext 3482
Rivera, William, *Asst Librn,* Inter-American University-Fajardo Regional College, Centro de Recursos para el Aprendizaje, Fajardo PR. 809-863-2390
Rivera-Davis, Carlos, *Dir,* Inter-American University of Puerto Rico, School of Law Library, Santurce PR. 809-754-7215
Rivero, A Pualani, *Librn,* Hawaii State Library System (Kaimuki Regional), Honolulu HI. 808-732-0727
Rives, Gladys, *Librn,* First Regional Library (M R Dye Public), Horn Lake MS. 601-393-5654
Rivest, John, *Music,* Shorter College, Livingston Library, Rome GA. 404-291-2121, Ext 43
Rivet, Paula A, *Asst Librn,* Blackstone Public Library, Blackstone MA. 617-883-1931
Rivoire, Helena G, *Tech Serv,* Bucknell University, Ellen Clarke Bertrand Library, Lewisburg PA. 717-524-3056
Rivolta, Agostino C, *Circ,* Clark University, Robert Hutchings Goddard Library, Worcester MA. 617-793-7573
Rizer, Hazel, *Librn,* Edgewood Public Library, Edgewood IA. 319-928-6829
Rizer, Sally, *Librn,* Warder Public Library (Southern Village), Springfield OH. 513-322-2761
Rizzo, Daniel C, *Chairman,* Onondaga Community College, Sidney B Coulter Library, Syracuse NY. 315-469-7741, Ext 5335-5338
Rizzo, Lawrence, *Asst Librn,* Langley Porter Psychiatric Institute Library, University of California at San Francisco, San Francisco CA. 415-681-8080, Ext 380
Rizzuto, Ann, *Librn,* Mifflin County Library (Kishacoquillas), Belleville PA. 717-935-2880
Roach, Andrea, *Circ,* West Warwick Public Library System, Robert H Champlin Memorial Library, West Warwick RI. 401-828-3750
Roach, Beverly, *Librn,* Andover Public Library, Andover OH. 216-293-6792
Roach, David M, *Bkmobile Coordr,* Dayton & Montgomery County Public Library, Dayton OH. 513-224-1651
Roach, Jeannetta C, *Dir & Cat,* Tougaloo College, L Zenobia Coleman Library, Tougaloo MS. 601-956-4941, Ext 271
Roach, Kenneth, *Dir,* Abilene Christian University, Margarett & Herman Brown Library, Abilene TX. 915-677-1911, Ext 2344

Roach, Lenore J, *Librn,* Kingsboro Psychiatric Center, Medical Library, Brooklyn NY. 212-735-1273
Roach, Linda, *Librn,* Morgan, Lewis & Bockius Library, Philadelphia PA. 215-491-9633
Roach, Margaret, *Sci & Eng,* Wright State University Library, Dayton OH. 513-873-2380
Roach, Margaret, *On-Line Servs,* Wright State University Library, Dayton OH. 513-873-2380
Roach, Mary, *On-Line Servs,* University of Kansas Libraries, Watson Memorial Library, Lawrence KS. 913-864-3601
Roach, Sue, *Asst Librn,* United States Department of the Navy, Alexandria VA. 202-694-3299
Road, Rachel, *Curator of Photog,* Tippecanoe County Historical Association, Alameda McCollough Library, Lafayette IN. 317-742-8411
Roake, Jo Anne, *Ref,* Palomar Community College, Phil H Putnam Memorial Library, San Marcos CA. 714-744-1150, Ext 275, 276 & 473
Roane, Mattie, *Cat & On-Line Servs,* Norfolk State University, Lyman Beecher Brooks Library, Norfolk VA. 804-623-8873
Roark, Denis D, *Dir,* Eastern New Mexico University, Roswell Campus Library, Roswell NM. 505-347-5441, Ext 244
Roark, Derrie, *Tech Serv,* Pensacola Junior College, Learning Resource Center, Pensacola FL. 904-476-5410
Robak, Patricia, *ILL, Ref & On-Line Servs,* Keuka College, Lightner Library, Keuka Park NY. 315-536-4411, Ext 224, 248 & 338
Robb, Darel, *Cat,* Southern Illinois University School of Medicine Library, Springfield IL. 217-782-2658
Robb, Deborah, *Asst Dir,* Kentucky State Department for Human Resources Library, Frankfort KY. 502-564-4530
Robb, Dorothy V, *Librn,* Captiva Memorial Library, Captiva FL. 813-472-2133
Robb, James A, *Tech Serv,* Marion Carnegie Library, Marion IL. 618-993-5935
Robb, James R, *Admin Deputy,* Los Angeles County Public Library System, South State Cooperative Library System, Los Angeles CA. 213-974-6501
Robb, Pat, *Tech Serv,* Boise Public Library & Information Center, Boise ID. 208-384-4466
Robb, Randal, *Ref,* Orange Public Library, Orange CA. 714-532-0391
Robb, S R, *Asst Librn,* G D Searle & Co, Research Library, Skokie IL. 312-982-7884
Robba, Diana M, *In Charge,* Hewlett-Packard Co, Santa Clara Division Library, Santa Clara CA. 408-246-4300
Robben, Dorothy D, *Supvr Libr & Records,* American Tobacco Co, Dept of Research & Development Library, Chester VA. 804-748-4561, Ext 232, 233
Robbers, Sandra, *Asst Dir, ILL & Ref,* Southwest Wisconsin Library System, Fennimore WI. 608-822-3393
Robbert, Maxine, *Tech Serv,* Herrick Public Library, Holland MI. 616-392-3114
Robbins, Allan, *Librn,* Alexandria Library (Lloyd House Collection), Alexandria VA. 703-750-6645
Robbins, Ann, *Librn,* Bay County Public Library Association (Springfield Library), Panama City FL. 904-785-1181
Robbins, Emma B, *Tech Serv & Cat,* Saint Paul Public Library, Saint Paul MN. 612-292-6311
Robbins, Irene, *Librn,* Athabasca Municipal Public Library, Athabasca AB. 403-675-2735
Robbins, James H, *Librn,* United States Navy (Marine Corps Air Ground Combat Center), Twentynine Palms CA. 714-368-6875
Robbins, Laura, *Circ,* Guilford College Library, Greensboro NC. 919-292-5511, Ext 250
Robbins, Nora, *Humanities,* University of Calgary Library, Calgary AB. 403-284-5954
Robbins, Ortha, *Circ,* Saint Paul Public Library, Saint Paul MN. 612-292-6311
Robbins, Pamela L, *Ch,* Coyle Free Library, Chambersburg PA. 717-263-8409
Robbins, Patricia, *Ser,* Louisiana State University in Shreveport Library, Shreveport LA. 318-797-7121, Ext 203
Robbins, Patricia V, *Dir Ref & Libr,* Wisconsin Legislative Reference Bureau Library, Madison WI. 608-266-0341

Robbins, Ray, *Circ,* Peninsula Public Library, Lawrence NY. 516-239-3262
Robbins, Richard W, *Dir,* Warwick Public Library and Regional Center, Warwick RI. 401-739-5440
Robbins, Richard W, *Dir,* Western Interrelated Library System, Warwick RI. 401-739-1919
Robbins, Ronald E, *Ref,* Lafayette College, David Bishop Skillman Library, Easton PA. 215-253-6281, Ext 289
Robbins, Sara, *Tech Serv,* Yeshiva University Libraries (Benjamin N Cardozo School of Law Library), New York NY. 212-790-0422
Robbins, Sid, *On-Line Servs,* Tennessee Technological University, Jere Whitson Memorial Library, Cookeville TN. 615-528-3408
Robbins, Stephen, *Asst Librn,* Maine State Department of Human Services Library, Augusta ME. 207-289-3055
Robbins, Terri, *Res Dir,* Education Today Co, Inc, Learning Magazine Research Dept Library, Palo Alto CA. 415-321-1770
Robbins, William R, *Dir,* Brant Historical Society, Brant County Museum Library, Brantford ON. 519-752-2483
Robboy, Stanley J, *Librn,* Massachusetts General Hospital (Tracy Burr Mallory Memorial Library), Boston MA. 617-726-2967
Robbs, Sybil, *Librn,* Venice Public Library, Venice IL. 618-877-1330
Robel, Betty, *Per,* University of Pittsburgh, Johnstown Campus Library, Johnstown PA. 814-266-9661, Ext 314
Robenalt, Marc, *Asst Dir,* Fairleigh Dickinson University, Weiner Library, Teaneck NJ. 201-836-6300, Ext 265
Robens, Janet, *Librn,* Rockbridge Regional Library (Glasgow Branch), Glasgow VA. 703-258-2509
Roberds, Louise, *Assoc Prof,* Phillips University, Education & Library Science Study Area, OK. 405-237-4433, Ext 417
Roberge, Monique, *AV & Spec Coll,* Trois-Rivieres College Library, Trois-Rivieres PQ. 819-376-1721, Ext 286
Roberge, Terressa T, *Media,* Louisburg College, C W Robbins Library, Louisburg NC. 496-2521 Ext 279, 280, 281
Roberson, A, *Librn,* Oakland Public Library (Lakeview), Oakland CA. 415-451-1610
Roberson, Arthur, *Ref,* Dillard University, Will W Alexander Library, New Orleans LA. 504-949-2123, Ext 256, 257
Roberson, Bernadine C, *Info Asst,* United States Department of Commerce Library, Chicago District Office, Chicago IL. 312-353-4450
Roberson, Iris, *Librn,* Three Oaks Township Library, Three Oaks MI. 616-756-5621
Roberson, Janis, *Librn,* Grapevine Public Library, Grapevine TX. 817-488-0413
Roberson, Marilyn, *Librn,* Wichita General Four, Medical Library, Wichita Falls TX. 817-723-1461, Ext 309
Roberson, William, *Ref,* Southampton College Library of Long Island University, Southampton NY. 516-283-4000, Ext 264
Robert, Constance, *Ref & Reader Serv,* College of the Virgin Islands, Saint Croix Campus Library, Saint Croix VI. 809-778-1620
Robert, Michel, *Dir,* Saint Jean-Sur-Richelieu College Bibliotheque, Saint Jean PQ. 514-347-5301, Ext 333
Roberts, A V, *Per & Curric,* Concordia College, Klinck Memorial Library, River Forest IL. 312-771-8300, Ext 450
Roberts, Alice, *Ref,* Wayne County Public Library, Wooster OH. 216-262-0916
Roberts, Alice L, *Librn,* Boston Public Library (Lower Mills), Dorchester MA. 617-298-7841
Roberts, Ammarette, *Mgr,* Mobil Research & Development Corp, Field Research Laboratory, Technical Information Services Library, Dallas TX. 214-333-6531
Roberts, Ann, *Admin Asst,* Flagstaff City-Coconino County Public Library System, Flagstaff AZ. 602-774-0603
Roberts, Ann, *Librn,* McKinsey & Co, Inc Library, Washington DC. 202-393-6820
Roberts, Ann Burnette, *Librn,* McGuire, Woods & Battle, Law Library, Richmond VA. 804-644-4131, Ext 160

Roberts, Anna Ray, *Coordr,* Wytheville Community College Library, Wytheville VA. 703-228-5541, Ext 227

Roberts, Avon, *Assoc Librn,* Arcanum Public Library, Arcanum OH. 513-692-8484

Roberts, Barbara, *Archivist,* Urbana Free Library, Urbana IL. 217-367-4057

Roberts, Benjamin S, *Asst Librn,* Palm Beach Junior College, Library Learning Resources Center, Lake Worth FL. 305-965-8000, Ext 213

Roberts, Bertha, *Ch,* Rodman Public Library, Alliance OH. 216-821-1410

Roberts, Bob, *Librn,* Pikes Peak Regional Library District (Eastern Plains Community), Colorado Springs CO. 303-347-2223

Roberts, Bobby, *Archivist,* University of Arkansas at Little Rock Library, Little Rock AR. 501-569-3120

Roberts, Bryan, *Coordr, Programs & Servs,* Queens Borough Public Library, Jamaica NY. 212-990-0700

Roberts, Carol, *Media & Spec Coll,* Maryville College, Lamar Memorial Library, Maryville TN. 615-982-1200

Roberts, Carole, *Asst Librn,* Patrick Henry State Junior College, John Dennis Forte Library, Monroeville AL. 205-575-3156, Ext 27

Roberts, Carolyn A, *Librn,* Library Association of Portland (Capitol Hill), Portland OR. 503-244-9620

Roberts, Celia, *Ref,* Simsbury Public Library, Simsbury CT. 203-658-5382

Roberts, Charlotte, *Librn,* Ravena Free Library, Ravena NY. 518-756-2053

Roberts, Constance, *Hq Librn,* Wheeler Basin Regional Library, Decatur Public Library, Decatur AL. 205-353-2993

Roberts, Cynthia, *Slide Curator,* School of Visual Arts Library, New York NY. 679-7350 Ext 67, 68

Roberts, David J, *Dir,* Lower Merion Library Association, Bryn Mawr PA. 215-527-3889

Roberts, Delno W, *ILL & Ref,* Abilene Christian University, Margarett & Herman Brown Library, Abilene TX. 915-677-1911, Ext 2344

Roberts, Don L, *Librn,* Northwestern University Library (Music), Evanston IL. 312-492-3434

Roberts, Doris E, *Dir,* Richland City Library, Richland WA. 509-943-9117

Roberts, Dorthea, *Librn,* Raymond Municipal Library, Raymond AB. 403-752-3236

Roberts, E G, *Dir,* Georgia Institute of Technology, Price Gilbert Memorial Library, Atlanta GA. 404-894-4510

Roberts, E Joe, *Dir,* Louisiana State Penitentiary Library, Angola LA. 504-655-4411

Roberts, Edith, *Librn,* Bellevue Public Library, Bellevue IA. 319-872-4354

Roberts, Edith, *Cat,* United States Army (Morris Swett Library), Fort Sill OK. 405-351-4525, 351-4477

Roberts, Edward A, *Mgr,* IBM Corp, Library Center, Poughkeepsie NY. 914-463-1630

Roberts, Elizabeth, *Librn,* Beene-Pearson Public Library, South Pittsburg TN. 615-837-6513

Roberts, Elizabeth, *Librn,* Washington State University Library (Science & Engineering), Pullman WA. 509-335-2671

Roberts, Ellin K, *Librn,* Woodstock Library, Woodstock NY. 914-679-2213

Roberts, Erna Bennett, *Librn,* City Library (Pine Point), Springfield MA. 413-782-2335

Roberts, Everdean, *Ser,* Alabama Public Library Service, Montgomery AL. 205-832-5743

Roberts, Frances, *Asst Librn,* Grant County Library, Ulysses KS. 316-356-1433

Roberts, Frances, *Librn,* Southwest Regional Library, Bolivar MO. 417-326-4531

Roberts, Gary K, *Actg Dir,* Nevada Historical Society, Museum-Research Library, Reno NV. 702-784-6397, 784-6398

Roberts, Gerald, *Spec Coll,* Berea College, Hutchins Library, Berea KY. 606-986-9341, Ext 289

Roberts, Gerrard, *Librn,* Cleveland Electric Illuminating Co Library, Cleveland OH. 216-622-9800, Ext 2046

Roberts, Gloria A, *Head Librn & Bibliog Instr,* Planned Parenthood Federation of America, Inc, Katharine Dexter McCormick Library, New York NY. 212-541-7800, Ext 285

Roberts, Gretchen, *Media,* Crouse-Irving Memorial Hospital Library, Syracuse NY. 315-424-6380

Roberts, Harry, *Per,* Florida Southern College, Roux Library, Lakeland FL. 813-683-5521, Ext 211

Roberts, Hazel, *Tech Serv,* Snead State Junior College, Virgil B McCain Learning Resource Center, Boaz AL. 205-593-5120, Ext 274

Roberts, Hazel J, *Chief Librn,* Association of Universities & Colleges of Canada Library, Ottawa ON. 613-563-3670

Roberts, Helen V, *Librn,* Jackson County Library System (Jacksonville Branch), Jacksonville OR. 503-899-1665

Roberts, Jackie, *Librn,* Colquitt-Thomas Regional Library (Berlin Community Branch), Berlin GA. 912-324-2425

Roberts, Jane, *Librn,* Flint River Regional Library (Carnegie), Barnesville GA. 404-358-3270

Roberts, Janice, *Asst Dir, ILL & Ref,* Ottawa University, Myers Library, Ottawa KS. 913-242-5200, Ext 317

Roberts, Jean Ellen, *Ch,* Nutley Public Library, Nutley NJ. 201-667-0405

Roberts, Jessica, *Librn,* Broward County Division of Libraries (Hallandale Branch), Hallandale FL. 305-454-5353

Roberts, Jessica, *Librn,* Hallandale Public Library, Hallandale FL. 305-454-5353

Roberts, Joan, *ILL,* Northport Public Library, Northport NY. 516-261-6930

Roberts, Joetta, *Librn,* Mansfield-Richland County Public Library (Bellville Branch), Bellville OH. 419-886-3811

Roberts, John P, *In Charge,* National Museum of Transport, Reference Library, Saint Louis MO. 314-965-6885

Roberts, Joseph G, *Commun Servs,* Ann Arbor Public Library, Ann Arbor MI. 313-994-2333

Roberts, Joseph W, *In Charge,* Yale Club Library, New York NY. 212-661-2070

Roberts, Juanita, *Librn,* Dartnell Corp, Editorial Research Library, Chicago IL. 312-561-4000, Ext 248

Roberts, Juanita, *Media,* Tuskegee Institute, Hollis Burke Frissell Library, Tuskegee Institute AL. 205-727-8894

Roberts, Justine, *Libr Syst Off,* University of California Library, San Francisco CA. 415-666-2334

Roberts, Kenneth, *Ch,* Lethbridge Public Library, Lethbridge AB. 403-329-3233

Roberts, Leila-Jane, *Dir,* Winchester Public Library, Winchester MA. 617-729-3770

Roberts, Lesslie H, *Librn,* Guthrie Public Library, Guthrie OK. 405-282-3137

Roberts, Linda, *Librn,* Oklahoma College of Osteopathic Medicine & Surgery, College Library, Tulsa OK. 918-582-1972, Ext 351

Roberts, Linda L, *Librn,* Public Library of Des Moines (Mid City), Des Moines IA. 515-283-4593

Roberts, Linda L, *Librn,* Public Library of Des Moines (North Side), Des Moines IA. 515-283-4941

Roberts, Linda R, *On-Line Servs & Bibliog Instr,* Rockwell International, Science Center Library, Thousand Oaks CA. 805-498-4545, Ext 414

Roberts, Liz, *Dir,* Hillsboro City Library, Hillsboro TX. 817-582-8166

Roberts, Lucile, *Dir,* Madison County Public Library, Marshall NC. 704-649-3741

Roberts, Lucille, *Librn,* Richard H Thornton Library (Butner Branch), Butner NC. 919-575-4626

Roberts, Lucille, *Librn,* Richard H Thornton Library (Creedmoor Branch), Creedmoor NC. 919-528-1752

Roberts, Marceline, *In Charge,* Milwaukee Public Library (North Milwaukee), Milwaukee WI. 414-278-3079

Roberts, Margie, *Librn,* Palco Public Library, Palco KS. 913-737-4285

Roberts, Marie, *Librn,* Gerrish-Higgins School District Public Library (Gerrish-Higgins School District Public Library Branch), Higgins Lake MI. 517-821-9111

Roberts, Marion, *Pub Servs,* Tennessee State University, Martha M Brown - Lois W Daniel Library, Nashville TN. 615-320-3682, 251-1417

Roberts, Martha, *Librn,* Santa Fe Regional Library (High Springs Branch), High Springs FL. 904-454-2515

Roberts, Mary, *Cat,* Broward Community College, Learning Resources Center, Fort Lauderdale FL. 305-475-6500

Roberts, Mary K, *Librn,* Hueytown Public Library, Hueytown AL. 205-491-1443

Roberts, Mary Lou, *Librn,* Hillcrest Medical Center Library, Tulsa OK. 918-584-1351, Ext 7816

Roberts, Marylyn M, *Librn,* Intelcom Industries, Inc, Radiation Technology Library, San Diego CA. 714-565-7171, Ext 223

Roberts, Marylyn M, *Librn,* National University Library, San Diego CA. 714-563-7181

Roberts, Opal, *Asst Librn,* Yoakum County Library, Denver City TX. 806-592-2754

Roberts, Patricia A B, *Res Specialist,* Montana Department of Community Affairs Resource Center, Helena MT. 406-449-2896

Roberts, Patricia S, *Exec Libr,* Reorganized Church of Jesus Christ of Latter Day Saints, Independence MO. 816-833-1000, Ext 400

Roberts, Paul, *Ref & Bibliog Instr,* Loras College, Wahlert Memorial Library, Dubuque IA. 319-588-7125

Roberts, Phyllis, *ILL,* Mankato State University, Memorial Library, Mankato MN. 507-389-6201

Roberts, R L, *Per,* Abilene Christian University, Margarett & Herman Brown Library, Abilene TX. 915-677-1911, Ext 2344

Roberts, Randall, *Soc Sci,* University of Cincinnati Libraries, Central Library, Cincinnati OH. 513-475-2218

Roberts, Rubie, *Librn,* Field Memorial Library, Conway MA. 413-369-4646

Roberts, Ruth, *Librn,* Hay River Library, Hay River NT. 403-874-6531

Roberts, Ruth L, *Librn,* Galien Township Public Library, Galien MI. 616-545-8281

Roberts, Ruth V, *Librn,* Brunswick Corp (Management Library), Skokie IL. 312-470-4880

Roberts, Sallie H, *Instr,* Ohio University, Educational Media Program, OH. 614-594-5404

Roberts, Sally B, *Exec Dir,* New England Library Board, (NELB), CT. 203-525-2681

Roberts, Sandra, *Br Asst,* Allen Parish Library (Kinder Branch), Kinder LA. 318-738-2126

Roberts, Sandra, *Librn,* Minnesota Valley Regional Library (Lake Crystal), Mankato MN. 507-726-2726

Roberts, Sandra, *Librn,* Tennessean Library, Nashville TN. 615-255-1221, Ext 327

Roberts, Sharon, *Asst Dir,* Logan-Helm Woodford County Public Library, Versailles KY. 606-873-5191, 873-9703

Roberts, Simmie, *Construction Consult,* Mississippi Library Commission, Jackson MS. 601-354-6369

Roberts, Sister Jean B, *Librn,* Saint Vincent Infirmary Medical Library, Little Rock AR. 501-661-3991

Roberts, Susan, *Asst Librn,* Waycross Junior College Library, Waycross GA. 912-285-6136

Roberts, Susan I, *Asst Librn, Pub Servs & On-Line Servs,* University of South Carolina at Aiken, Gregg-Graniteville Library, Aiken SC. 803-648-6851, Ext 165

Roberts, Sywnette, *Commun Servs,* Marion County Library, Marion SC. 803-423-2244

Roberts, T W, *Dir,* Wayne State University Libraries (Instructional Materials Library), Detroit MI. 313-577-1980

Roberts, Ted E, *Dir,* Piedmont Regional Library, Winder GA. 404-867-2762

Roberts, Tena, *Librn,* Wesleyan College, Willet Memorial Library, Macon GA. 912-477-1110, Ext 200

Roberts, Vann, *Librn,* Atlanta Public Library (Stewart Lakewood), Atlanta GA. 404-767-8671

Roberts, Victoria Mosty, *Librn,* Federal Reserve Bank of Dallas Library, Dallas TX. 214-651-6392

Roberts, Virginia, *Circ,* Central State University Library, Edmond OK. 405-341-2980, Ext 494, 495 & 496

Roberts, Yvonne E, *Librn,* Lakeland Public Library (Northwest Reading Room), Lakeland FL. 813-688-8446

Roberts, III, William H, *Dir,* Forsyth County Public Library, Winston-Salem NC. 919-727-2556

Robertson, Ann, *Sci & Eng Ref & Resources,* University of Houston (M D Anderson Memorial Library), Houston TX. 713-749-4241

Robertson, Anne, *Admin Asst,* Monroe County Public Library, Stroudsburg PA. 717-421-0800
Robertson, Augusta M, *Asst Dir,* Franklin County Library, Rocky Mount VA. 703-483-5163, 5164
Robertson, Barbara, *ILL,* Xavier University, McDonald Memorial Library, Cincinnati OH. 513-745-3881
Robertson, Betty J, *Librn,* Moore County Public Library, Lynchburg TN. 615-759-7285
Robertson, Bonnie, *Instr,* University of Wyoming, Library Media Program, WY. 307-766-2349
Robertson, Caroline M, *Asst Dir,* Chesterfield County Central Library, Chesterfield VA. 804-748-1601
Robertson, Carolyn, *Librn,* National Cotton Council of America Library, Memphis TN. 901-274-9030
Robertson, D F, *Dir,* Kelsey Institute of Applied Arts & Sciences, Learning Resources Center, Saskatoon SK. 306-664-6417
Robertson, David S, *Librn,* Passaic Public Library (Reid Mem), Passaic NJ. 201-777-6044
Robertson, Dulcina, *Librn,* Baker County Public Library (Halfway Branch), Halfway OR. 503-523-6414, 523-6419
Robertson, Elizabeth, *Br Coordr,* Memphis-Shelby County Public Library & Information Center, Memphis TN. 901-528-2950
Robertson, Ellen, *On-Line Servs,* University of New Mexico General Library, Albuquerque NM. 505-277-4241
Robertson, Evelyn, *Ref,* Glendale Public Library, Glendale CA. 213-956-2030
Robertson, Francis, *Tech Serv,* Elwood Public Library, Elwood IN. 317-552-5001
Robertson, Helen, *Asst Librn,* Devine Public Library, Devine TX. 512-663-2993
Robertson, Jack, *Ref,* Hutchinson Public Library, Hutchinson KS. 316-663-5441
Robertson, Jean, *In Charge,* National Society of Professional Engineers, Information Center Library, Washington DC. 331-7020 & 337-0420
Robertson, John, *Art,* Vanderbilt University Library (Central-Science), Nashville TN. 615-322-6603
Robertson, Joyce, *Libr Asst,* Saint Alphonsus Hospital, Health Sciences Library, Boise ID. 208-376-1211, Ext 271
Robertson, Juanita P, *Librn,* Rutherford County Library (Spindale Public), Spindale NC. 704-631-3879
Robertson, Lavonne D, *Librn,* Salvation Army School for Officer's Training, Elftman Memorial Library, Rancho Palos Verdes CA. 213-377-0481
Robertson, Linda, *Librn,* Alaska Department of Highways, Department of Transportation & Public Facilities Library, Juneau AK. 907-465-3900
Robertson, Linda, *Dir,* Wabash Carnegie Public Library, Wabash IN. 219-563-2972
Robertson, Lynn, *Librn,* Douglas County Public Library (Louviers Branch), Louviers CO. 303-794-5365
Robertson, M, *Librn,* New Brunswick Museum, Ganong & Webster Libraries, Saint John NB. 506-693-1196
Robertson, Mary, *Asst Dir, ILL & Ref,* Cherokee Regional Library, LaFayette-Walker County Library, LaFayette GA. 404-638-2992
Robertson, Mary, *Acq,* Huron College, Silcox Memorial Library, London ON. 519-438-7224, Ext 13
Robertson, Mary, *Media,* John Packard Library of Yuba County, Marysville CA. 916-674-6241
Robertson, Russell R, *Phys Sci,* Brigham Young University, Harold B Lee Library, Provo UT. 801-378-2905
Robertson, S Donald, *Librn,* Scott, Foresman & Co, Editorial Library, Glenview IL. 312-729-3000, Ext 433
Robertson, Sandra, *Asst Librn,* Pearisburg Public Library, Pearisburg VA. 703-921-2556
Robertson, Sandra D, *Librn,* Prestonsburg Community College Library, Prestonsburg KY. 606-886-3863
Robertson, Sue, *Librn,* Bay Head Public Library, Bay Head NJ. 201-892-0662
Robertson, Velma, *Librn,* Russell County Public Library, Jamestown KY. 502-343-3545
Robertson, W Davenport, *Head,* National Institute of Environmental Health Sciences Library, Research Triangle Park NC. 919-541-3426

Robichally, Catherine, *Librn,* Houston Lighting & Power Co Library, Houston TX. 713-228-9211, Ext 2060
Robichaud, Denis, *Librn,* Gouvernement Du Quebec Ministere De L'immigration, Centre de Documentation, Montreal PQ. 514-873-3255
Robichaud, Diane, *Libr Asst I,* Chaleur Regional Library (Tracadie Municipal), Tracadie NB. 506-395-5387
Robicheaux, Betty, *Br Asst,* Jefferson Davis Parish Library (McBurney Memorial), Welsh LA. 318-734-3262
Robie, Cynthia, *Asst Librn,* Hill Public Library, Hill NH. 603-934-4015
Robillard, Grace, *Circ,* Milford Public Library, Milford CT. 203-878-7461
Robillard, Gretchen, *In Charge,* Milwaukee Public Library (Llewellyn), Milwaukee WI. 414-278-3019
Robillard, Jean-Jacques, *Librn,* College Dominicain De Philosophie Et De Theologie, Bibliotheque du College Dominicain, Ottawa ON. 613-233-5696, 233-5697
Robin, Florence, *Tech Serv & Cat,* Los Angeles Pierce College Library, Woodland Hills CA. 213-347-0551, Ext 267
Robin, Madeleine, *Art & Archit,* Universite Laval Bibliotheque, Quebec PQ. 418-656-3344
Robinow, Beatrix H, *Librn,* McMaster University (Health Sciences), Hamilton ON. 416-525-9140, Ext 2320
Robins, Barbara, *Humanities,* Emporia State University, William Allen White Library, Emporia KS. 316-343-1200, Ext 205
Robins, Barbara, *Bibliog Instr,* Emporia State University, William Allen White Library, Emporia KS. 316-343-1200, Ext 205
Robins, Henriann, *Dir,* Milltown Public Library, Milltown NJ. 201-247-2270
Robins, Margaret, *Librn,* Women's College Hospital, Medical Library, Toronto ON. 416-966-7468
Robinson, Alice B, *Black Studies,* Public Library of the District of Columbia, Martin Luther King Memorial Library, Washington DC. 202-727-1101
Robinson, Amanda, *Librn,* Wood Gundy Limited, Research Library, Toronto ON. 416-362-4433, Ext 239, 426
Robinson, Barbara, *Chief,* Metropolitan Washington Library Council, DC. 202-223-6800
Robinson, Barbara, *Soc Sci,* University of California, Riverside, University Library, Riverside CA. 714-787-3221
Robinson, Barrie J, *Dir,* Lake Ontario Regional Library System, Kingston ON. 613-546-9400
Robinson, Becky, *Librn,* Annawan-Alba Township Library, Annawan IL. 309-935-6483
Robinson, Billie, *Dir,* Spotswood Public Library, Spotswood NJ. 201-251-1515
Robinson, Bonnie, *Cat,* Quincy Public Library, Quincy IL. 217-223-1309
Robinson, Catherine, *Librn,* United States Army (Fort George G Meade Recreation Services Library), Fort George G Meade MD. 301-667-4509
Robinson, Celia, *On-Line Servs,* Henderson State University, Huie Library, Arkadelphia AR. 501-246-5511, Ext 200
Robinson, Charles W, *Dir,* Baltimore County Public Library, Towson MD. 301-296-8500
Robinson, Cindy, *Ch,* Jacob Edwards Library, Southbridge MA. 617-764-2544
Robinson, Dan, *Librn,* Russell Public Library, Russell KS. 913-483-2742
Robinson, David J S, *Librn,* Canadian Forestry Service, Northern Forest Research Centre Library, Edmonton AB. 403-435-7210
Robinson, Dean, *Cat,* Chattanooga State Technical Community College, Augusta R Kolwyck Instructional Materials Center, Chattanooga TN. 615-622-6262
Robinson, Douglas, *Librn,* Public Library of Cincinnati & Hamilton County (Sycamore), Cincinnati OH. 513-369-6051
Robinson, Dwight, *Instr,* Highline Community College Library, Library Technician Program, WA. 206-878-3710, Ext 233
Robinson, Dwight W, *Dir & On-Line Servs,* Ashland College Library, Ashland OH. 419-289-4067

Robinson, E, *Librn,* Coney Island Hospital, Harold Fink Memorial Library, Brooklyn NY. 212-743-4100, Ext 429, 225
Robinson, Elizabeth A, *Librn,* Good Samaritan Hospital & Health Center, Shank Memorial Library, Dayton OH. 513-278-2612, Ext 3091
Robinson, Elizabeth S, *Librn,* Weld Memorial Library, Weld ME. 207-585-2512
Robinson, Ethel, *Head Main Libr,* Cleveland Public Library, Cleveland OH. 216-623-2800
Robinson, Geneva J, *Materials Management,* Baltimore County Public Library, Towson MD. 301-296-8500
Robinson, George, *Ref,* University of Western Ontario, A B Weldon Library, London ON. 519-679-6191
Robinson, George H, *Coordr,* Winthrop College, School Librarianship Program, SC. 803-323-2136
Robinson, Giesela B, *Librn,* Union Texas Petroleum Library, Division of Allied Chemical, Houston TX. 713-960-7500
Robinson, Halcyon S, *Librn,* United States Air Force (Charleston Air Force Base Library), Charleston AFB SC. 803-554-0230
Robinson, Hank, *On-Line Servs,* Mitre Corp (Technical Report Center), Bedford MA. 617-271-2351
Robinson, Harriet, *In Charge,* Albert-Westmorland-Kent Regional Library (Dorchester Public), Dorchester NB. 506-389-2631
Robinson, Helen, *Libr Tech,* Hawaii State Library System (Hanapepe Branch), Hanapepe HI. 808-335-5811
Robinson, Helen H, *Librn,* Baker Free Library, Bow NH. 603-224-7113
Robinson, Hilda, *Asst Librn,* Concordia College, Arnold Guebert Memorial Library, Edmonton AB. 403-479-8481
Robinson, Joel, *Bldg Project Coordr,* Broward County Division of Libraries, Broward County Library, Pompano Beach FL. 305-972-1100
Robinson, Joyce, *Tech Serv,* Alexander City State Junior College, Thomas D Russell Library, Alexander City AL. 205-234-6346, Ext 290
Robinson, Judith, *Librn,* Rockland School Community Library, Rockland ID. 208-548-2222
Robinson, Judy, *Librn,* San Antonio Express & San Antonio News Library, San Antonio TX. 512-225-7411
Robinson, Judy B, *Librn,* Springs Mills, Inc, Computer Information Services, Data Processing Technical Library, Lancaster SC. 803-285-4343
Robinson, Julia, *Librn,* Center for Research on the Acts of Man Library, Philadelphia PA. 215-387-4081
Robinson, Julie L, *Tech Serv,* Francis Bacon Library, Francis Bacon Foundation Inc, Claremont CA. 714-624-6305
Robinson, Juliet, *Librn,* Walter C McCrone Associates Library Associates Library, Chicago IL. 312-842-7100, Ext 59
Robinson, Kathryn, *Librn,* Laughlin Memorial Free Library, Ambridge PA. 412-266-3857
Robinson, L, *Librn,* Madison Public Library (Meadowridge), Madison WI. 608-266-6377
Robinson, Leatrice, *Ref,* Sharon Public Library, Sharon MA. 617-784-5974
Robinson, Linda, *ILL,* Adams Library, Chelmsford MA. 617-256-5521
Robinson, Linda, *Admin Asst,* Brookdale Community College, Learning Resources Center, Lincroft NJ. 201-842-1900, Ext 392
Robinson, Louisa S, *Dir,* Claflin College, H V Manning Library, Orangeburg SC. 803-534-2710, Ext 56
Robinson, Lowell, *Chief Librn,* United States Army (Stimson Library), Fort Sam Houston TX. 512-221-1211
Robinson, Lynn, *Ch,* Community Library, Ketchum ID. 208-726-3493
Robinson, Lynn H, *Librn,* Wentworth Institute of Technology Library, Boston MA. 617-442-9010, Ext 344
Robinson, Marjorie, *Librn,* Canadian Tax Foundation Library, Toronto ON. 416-368-4657
Robinson, Mary, *Cat,* Medical College of Pennsylvania, Florence A Moore Library of Medicine, Philadelphia PA. 215-842-6910
Robinson, Mary, *Ad,* Park Ridge Public Library, Park Ridge IL. 312-825-3123

Robinson, Mary, *Librn,* Tucson Public Library (Himmel Park), Tucson AZ. 602-791-4397
Robinson, Mary B, *Librn,* Lowe Public Library, Shinnston WV. 304-592-1700
Robinson, Mary L, *Dir,* North Chicago Public Library, North Chicago IL. 312-689-0125
Robinson, Maryann, *ILL,* United States Air Force Academy Library, United States Air Force Academy CO. 303-472-2590
Robinson, Mavis, *ILL,* Scarborough Public Library, Scarborough ON. 416-291-1991
Robinson, Mayme, *Dir,* Granum Public Library, Granum AB. 403-687-3884
Robinson, Melinda, *Librn,* Reading Hospital & Medical Center (Medical Library), Reading PA. 215-378-6418
Robinson, Michaele M, *Librn,* Zoological Society of San Diego, Ernst Schwarz Library, San Diego CA. 714-231-1515
Robinson, Mildred, *Librn,* Paragould Public Library (Piggott Branch), Piggott AR. 501-598-3666
Robinson, Mrs J R, *In Charge,* Peachtree Presbyterian Church, Pattillo Library, Atlanta GA. 404-261-2592
Robinson, Nancy, *Cat,* Southern Baptist Theological Seminary, James P Boyce Centennial Library, Louisville KY. 502-897-4807
Robinson, Olga, *Cat,* Mary Lou Johnson-Hardin County District Library, Kenton OH. 419-673-2278
Robinson, Orvetta M, *Librn,* Illinois State Museum Library, Springfield IL. 217-782-6623
Robinson, Pearl O, *Librn,* United States Navy (Naval Ship Systems Engineering Station Library), Philadelphia PA. 215-755-3922, Ext 230
Robinson, Perry, *Media,* Ludington Public Library, Bryn Mawr PA. 215-527-1550, 525-1776
Robinson, Phil, *Tech Serv, Acq & Cat,* Ambassador College Library, Pasadena CA. 213-577-5540
Robinson, Rosalind Forebaugh, *Dir,* Islip Public Library, Islip NY. 516-581-5933
Robinson, Rosemary, *Circ,* Flagstaff City-Coconino County Public Library System, Flagstaff AZ. 602-774-0603
Robinson, Ruth, *Librn,* Frank W Horner Ltd, Research Library, Montreal PQ. 514-731-3931, Ext 216
Robinson, Sheila, *Circ,* State Technical Institute at Memphis, George E Freeman Library, Memphis TN. 901-377-4106
Robinson, Sheilah R, *ILL,* Yale University Library (Divinity School), New Haven CT. 203-436-8440
Robinson, Shirley, *Librn,* Oceanic Institute Library, Waimanalo HI. 808-259-7951, Ext 16
Robinson, Smith Garrett, *Science,* Hunter College of the City University of New York Library, New York NY. 212-570-5511
Robinson, T J, *Librn,* University of Windsor (Faculty of Education Library), Windsor ON. 519-969-0520
Robinson, Velma, *Supvr,* Huron County Public Library (Hensall Branch), Hensall ON. 519-262-2445
Robinson, Vera L, *Cat,* Bethany & Northern Baptist Theological Seminaries Library, Oak Brook IL. 312-620-2214
Robinson, Verdi, *Librn,* Robertson County Library, Franklin TX. 713-828-4331
Robinson, William C, *Assoc Prof,* University of Tennessee, Knoxville, Graduate School of Library & Information Science, TN. 615-974-2148
Robinson, Jr, George, *Circ, Per & Doc,* Haverhill Public Library, Haverhill MA. 617-373-1586
Robinson, Jr, Harry, *Dir,* Bishop College, Zale Library, Dallas TX. 214-372-8134
Robinson, Sr, Mrs Aubrey, *Librn,* Webster Parish Library (Crichton Hill), Minden LA. 318-377-1411
Robison, Carolyn L, *Assoc Dir,* Georgia State University, William Russell Pullen Library, Atlanta GA. 404-658-2185, 658-2172
Robison, Dennis E, *Dir,* University of Richmond, Boatwright Memorial Library, Richmond VA. 804-285-6452
Robison, Jane R, *Dir,* Cultural Heritage & Arts Center Library, Kansas Heritage Center, Dodge City KS. 316-227-2823
Robison, Joan Settle, *Librn,* Baltimore Museum of Art Library, Baltimore MD. 301-396-6317

Robison, Juanita, *Tech Serv,* Phoenix Public Library, Phoenix AZ. 602-262-6451
Robison, Richard, *Finance Mgr,* Altadena Library District, Altadena CA. 213-798-0833
Robison, Sister Mary Verena, *Librn,* Ancilla College, Ancilla Domini Library, Donaldson IN. 219-936-8898, Ext 123
Robitaille, Louise, *Cat,* Ecole Des Hautes Etudes Commerciales De Montreal Bibliotheque, Montreal PQ. 514-343-4481
Robles, Concepcion, *Per,* Puerto Rico Junior College (Cupey Campus Learning Resources Center), Rio Piedras PR. 809-765-1716
Robles, Daniel O, *Dir,* Santa Paula Union High School Public Library District, Blanchard Community Library, Santa Paula CA. 805-525-3615
Robnett, Harris H, *Dept Head,* Community College of Denver, Information Media Technology Program, CO. 303-629-2467
Robotham, John, *Librn,* New York Public Library (Francis Martin Branch), New York NY. 212-295-5287
Robson, Betty J, *Librn,* United States Borax Research Corp, Research Library, Anaheim CA. 714-744-2670
Robson, Ed, *Media,* Sir Sandford Fleming College of Applied Arts & Technology Library, Peterborough ON. 705-743-5610, Ext 268
Robson, John M, *Dir,* Southwest State University Library, Marshall MN. 507-537-7021
Robson, Nadine, *Librn,* Herbert Wescoat Memorial Library, McArthur OH. 614-596-5691
Robuck, Wendy K, *Dir & Ad,* Winter Park Public Library, Winter Park FL. 305-647-1638
Roby, Bruce E, *Dir,* Jasper County Public Library, Rensselaer Public Library (Hq), Rensselaer IN. 219-866-5881
Rocafort, Maria de los A, *Assoc Dean,* Puerto Rico Junior College (Cupey Campus Learning Resources Center), Rio Piedras PR. 809-765-1716
Roch, Margaret, *Asst Dir,* Shelby State Community College Library, Memphis TN. 901-528-6743
Roche, Sally, *ILL,* University of Rochester, Rush Rhees Library, Rochester NY. 716-275-4461
Rochell, Carlton C, *Dean of Librs,* New York University, Elmer Holmes Bobst Library, New York NY. 212-598-2484
Rock, Clara, *Archivist,* Oakwood College, Eva B Dykes Library, Huntsville AL. 205-837-1630, Ext 275
Rock, Dorothy, *Librn,* Sterling Public Library, Sterling IL. 815-625-1370
Rock, Les, *Mari Sandoz Network Coordr,* Nebraska Library Commission, Lincoln NE. 402-471-2045
Rock, Luanne, *Circ,* Garfield County Public Library, New Castle CO. 303-984-2346
Rock, Sue, *Asst Dir,* Princeton Public Library, Princeton NJ. 609-924-9529
Rocke, Ellryn, *Chmn,* Palos Community Hospital, Medical Library, Palos Heights IL. 312-361-4500
Rocke, Hans J, *Zoology,* University of California at Davis, General Library, Davis CA. 916-752-2110
Rocke, Hans J, *On-Line Servs,* University of California at Davis, General Library, Davis CA. 916-752-2110
Rockey, Steven, *Librn,* Cornell University Libraries (Mathematics), Ithaca NY. 607-256-5076
Rockman, Connie, *Ch,* Northland Public Library, Pittsburgh PA. 412-366-8100, 366-8167
Rockmuller, Ellen, *Dir,* East Rockaway Public Library, East Rockaway NY. 516-599-1664
Rockstad, Shirley, *Librn,* Ada Public Library, Ada MN. 218-784-4480
Rockwell, Jill, *Ref,* Yakima Valley Regional Library, Yakima WA. 509-452-8541, Ext 22
Rockwell, Robert, *Circ,* Merrimack College, McQuade Library, North Andover MA. 617-683-7111, Ext 210
Rockwell, Jr, Ralph E, *Dir,* Otero Junior College, Wheeler Library, La Junta CO. 303-384-8721, Ext 296
Rockwood, Arlene R, *Librn,* Butler Public Library, Butler MO. 816-679-4321
Rockwood, Derek, *Librn,* Waterford Hospital, Health Services Library, Saint John's NF. 709-368-6061, Ext 269

Rockwood, Ruth L, *Dir & Rare Bks,* Free Public Library of Livingston, Livingston NJ. 201-992-4600
Rockwood, Steven, *Per & Doc,* Albion College, Stockwell Memorial Library, Albion MI. 517-629-5511, Ext 285
Rocky, Helen K, *Dir,* International Academy at Santa Barbara, Environmental Studies Institute Library, Santa Barbara CA. 805-965-5010
Rocque, Helen, *Librn,* Redwater Municipal Library, Redwater AB. 403-735-3464
Rod, Donald O, *Dir,* University of Northern Iowa Library, Cedar Falls IA. 319-273-2737
Rodak, Valerie, *Librn,* Nevada County Library (Grass Valley Branch), Grass Valley CA. 916-273-4117
Rodda, Catherine, *ILL,* Sudbury Public Library, La Bibliotheque Publique de Sudbury, Sudbury ON. 705-673-1155
Rodden, Dwight, *Ref,* Boca Raton Public Library, Boca Raton FL. 395-2980 & 395-1110, Ext 285, 286, 336
Roddy, Philip, *Asst Dir,* Pikeville College, O'Rear-Robinson Library, Pikeville KY. 606-432-9372
Rodeffer, Georgia H, *Librn,* North Carolina State University (Burlington Textiles), Raleigh NC. 919-737-3231
Rodel, Judith A, *Librn,* Woodville Community Library, Woodville WI. 715-698-2430
Roden, Jean, *Acq & Ref,* Shoreline Community College, Library/Media Center, Seattle WA. 206-546-4663
Roden, Ruth, *Cat,* University of California Library, Irvine CA. 714-833-5212
Rodenhaver, Dale Ann, *Mgr,* Budd Co, Technical Center Library, Fort Washington PA. 215-643-2950, Ext 257
Roderick, Bette, *Asst Librn,* Shelbyville Free Public Library, Shelbyville IL. 217-774-4432
Roderick, Pat, *Bkmobile Coordr,* El Paso Public Library, El Paso TX. 915-543-3804
Roderick, Ruth C, *Dir,* Free Public Library of Stratford, Stratford NJ. 609-783-0602
Rodes, Barbara K, *Librn,* Environmental Law Institute Library, Washington DC. 202-452-9600, Ext 206
Rodes, Lynn, *Ref,* Old Bridge Public Library, Old Bridge NJ. 201-679-5622
Rodger, Ramona, *Media,* Escondido Public Library, Escondido CA. 714-741-4683
Rodgers, Althea, *Tech Serv,* Riviera Beach Public Library, Riviera Beach FL. 305-845-4194, 845-4195, 845-4196
Rodgers, Betty, *Dir,* Indian River County Library, Vero Beach FL. 305-567-4111
Rodgers, Charles R, *L R C Supvrs,* Pasco-Hernando Community College Library, Dade City FL. 904-567-6701
Rodgers, Elmer E, *Dir,* Missouri Southern State College, George A Spiva Library, Joplin MO. 417-624-8100, Ext 251
Rodgers, Frank, *Dir,* University of Miami, Otto G Richter Library, Coral Gables FL. 305-284-3551
Rodgers, Gertrude R, *Personnel,* Enoch Pratt Free Library, Baltimore MD. 301-396-5430, 396-5395
Rodgers, Helen E, *Dir Libr Serv,* El Camino College Library, Torrance CA. 213-532-3670, Ext 552, 553, 554
Rodgers, Jane C, *Libr Supvr,* Shell Oil Co, Information & Library Services, Houston TX. 713-241-5433
Rodgers, Martha Jo, *Librn,* San Diego Public Library (College Heights), San Diego CA. 714-583-6810
Rodgers, Mrs Jackson, *ILL,* Glen Rock Public Library, Glen Rock NJ. 201-445-4222, 445-4223
Rodgers, Pamela Q, *Br Coordr,* Jackson County Public Library, Ripley WV. 304-372-2831
Rodgers, Pamela Q, *Librn,* Jackson County Public Library (Ravenswood Public), Ravenswood WV. 304-273-4241
Rodgers, Patricia, *Coordr Tech Servs,* University of South Alabama (Biomedical Library), Mobile AL. 205-460-7043
Rodgers, Rose, *Librn,* British Columbia Provincial Museum Library, Victoria BC. 604-387-5533
Rodgers, Warren D, *Dir,* Stuhr Museum of the Prairie Pioneer, Research Library, Grand Island NE. 308-384-1380

Rodich, Lorraine, *Ref,* University of Santa Clara (Heafey Law Library), Santa Clara CA. 408-984-4451

Rodich, Nancy, *Tech Serv & Cat,* Mid-Mississippi Regional Library System, Kosciusko MS. 601-289-5141, 289-5146

Rodiman, Jackie, *Librn,* Woodsville Free Public Library, Haverhill NH. 603-747-3483

Rodin, Irwin, *Chem Eng,* University of Waterloo Library, Waterloo ON. 519-885-1211

Rodino, Linda, *Librn,* Argus Research Co Library, New York NY. 212-425-7500

Rodman, Janis, *ILL,* Darien Library, Inc, Darien CT. 203-655-2568

Rodman, Mary Ann, *ILL & Br Coordr,* Northeast Regional Library, Corinth MS. 601-287-2441

Rodney, H M, *Ref,* University of Victoria, McPherson Library, Victoria BC. 604-477-6911, Ext 4466

Rodolff, Jeanenne, *Circ,* California State University Dominguez Hills, Educational Resources Center, Carson CA. 213-515-3700

Rodrigues, Mario, *Asst Librn,* Weil, Gotshal & Manges Library, New York NY. 212-758-7800, Ext 212

Rodrigues, R, *Librn,* Oakland Public Library (Martin Luther King), Oakland CA. 415-632-4861

Rodriguez, Awilda, *Ref,* University of Puerto Rico - Bayamon Regional College, Learning Resources Center, Bayamon PR. 809-786-5225

Rodriguez, Carmen, *Outreach Aide,* Howland Circulating Library Company, Beacon NY. 914-831-1134

Rodriguez, Carmen, *Per,* University of Puerto Rico, Cayey University College Library, Cayey PR. 809-738-2161, Ext 221

Rodriguez, Gracie, *Asst Librn,* Austin Memorial Library, Cleveland TX. 713-592-3920

Rodriguez, Hortensia, *Doc,* Florida International University, Tamiami Campus, Athenaeum, Miami FL. 305-552-2461

Rodriguez, Jorge, *Media,* Inter-American University of Puerto Rico, Library-Metropolitan Campus Bayamon Unit, Bayamon PR. 809-780-4040, Ext 16

Rodriguez, Louise, *Per,* University of Calgary Library (Faculty of Medicine Medical Library), Calgary AB. 403-284-6858

Rodriguez, Marge, *Librn,* Copper Queen Library, Bisbee City Library, Bisbee AZ. 602-432-4232

Rodriguez, Norma, *Librn,* Miami-Dade Public Library System (Shenandoah), Miami FL. 305-931-5512

Rodriguez, Reinaldo E, *Librn,* Puerto Rico Department of Education, Biblioteca Publica Central, Santurce PR. 809-723-3739

Rodriguez, Robert, *Cat,* College of the Mainland, Learning Resources Center, Texas City TX. 713-938-1211, Ext 447

Rodriguez, Robert, *Acq,* Robert J Kleberg Public Library, Kingsville TX. 512-592-6381

Rodriguez-Cairo, Carmen, *Acq & Per,* Miami Dade Community College (New World Center Campus), Miami FL. 305-577-6890

Rodriquez, Ana Milagros, *Librn,* Commonwealth of Puerto Rico (Office of Criminal Justice Library), San Juan PR. 809-723-3863

Rodstein, Frances M, *Ad,* Manatee County Public Library System, Bradenton FL. 813-748-5555

Roe, Connie, *Asst Librn,* Tyler Free Library, Foster RI. 401-397-7930

Roe, Donna M, *Cat,* Siena Heights College Library, Adrian MI. 517-263-0731, Ext 242

Roe, Keith, *Agr & Biol Sci,* Pennsylvania State University, Fred Lewis Pattee Library, University Park PA. 814-865-0401

Roe, Margaret, *Southeastern Network Coordr,* Nebraska Library Commission, Lincoln NE. 402-471-2045

Roe, Maureen M, *Librn,* Kilborn Limited Library, Toronto ON. 416-252-5311, Ext 291

Roe, Ruth E, *Librn,* Newport Harbor Art Museum Library, Newport Beach CA. 714-759-1122

Roebuck, Agnes, *ILL,* Albany Public Library, Albany NY. 503-967-4304

Roebuck, Edith V, *Librn,* United States Air Force (Dyess Air Force Base Library), Dyess AFB TX. 915-696-2618

Roebuck, Evelyn, *Librn,* Maplesville Public Library, Maplesville AL. 205-366-4211

Roeckel, Alan, *Ad,* Garden City Public Library, Garden City NY. 516-742-8405

Roedel, Mary K, *Librn,* Public Library of Cincinnati & Hamilton County (Oakley), Cincinnati OH. 513-369-6038

Roedell, Ray F, *Dir,* Norristown State Hospital, Professional & Staff Library System, Norristown PA. 215-631-2879, 631-2948

Roeder, Catherine, *On-Line Servs,* Southeast Missouri State University, Kent Library, Cape Girardeau MO. 314-651-2235

Roeder, Christine, *Asst Librn,* Youngstown Hospital Association, Health Sciences Library, Youngstown OH. 216-747-0751

Roeder, Joan, *Dir,* Nesbitt Memorial Library, Columbus TX. 713-732-3392

Roeder, Mrs Edwin, *Librn,* Hankinson Public Library, Hankinson ND. 701-242-7929

Roeder, Randall, *Ref,* Coe College, Stewart Memorial Library, Cedar Rapids IA. 319-399-8585, 399-8586

Roeder, Walter H, *Ref,* California State Polytechnic University Library, Pomona CA. 714-598-4671

Roegge, Eleanor, *Librn,* Little Dixie Regional Libraries (Paris Dulany Branch), Paris MO. 816-327-4707

Roehling, Steven, *Asst Dir,* Emory & Henry College, Frederick T Kelly Library, Emory VA. 703-944-3121, Ext 56

Roehr, Robert W, *Dir,* Pueblo Library District, Pueblo CO. 303-544-1940

Roehrenbeck, Carol, *Dir,* Nova University Libraries (Law Center Library), Fort Lauderdale FL. 522-2300 Ext 113

Roelf, Pauline, *Asst Librn,* Allison Public Library, Allison IA. 319-267-2562

Roellig, Margaret, *Dir,* Tolono Township Library, Tolono IL. 217-485-5558

Roellinger, Mary, *Admin Asst & Tech Serv,* Bethel Park Public Library, Bethel Park PA. 412-835-2207

Roembach, Mary, *Librn,* Cheney Public Library, Cheney KS. 316-542-3331

Roemen, Bertha, *Librn,* Larchwood Public Library, Larchwood IA. 712-477-2583

Roepka, Evelyn L, *Librn,* Nickerson City Library, Nickerson KS. 316-422-3361

Roesch, Gay Ellen, *Librn,* Colorado National Building Law Library, Denver CO. 303-892-4306

Roesch, Gay Ellen, *Librn,* Davis, Graham & Stubbs Law Library, Denver CO. 303-892-9400, Exts 500, 501

Roesller, Patricia, *Librn,* Dodge County Library Service (Hustisford Public), Hustisford WI. 414-885-4571, 885-5134

Roess, Anne C, *Senior Librn,* Institute of Gas Technology Library, Technical Information Center, Chicago IL. 312-567-3650

Roessiger, Lucybell K, *Librn,* Tuftonboro Free Library, Tuftonboro NH. 603-569-4256

Rofen, Robert R, *Dir,* Aquatic Research Institute Library, Hayward CA. 415-785-2216

Rogal, Margi, *ILL,* Oberlin College Library, Oberlin OH. 216-775-8285

Rogalski, Leonore, *In Charge,* UOP, Inc (Research Library), Des Plaines IL. 312-391-3361

Rogalski, Mary E, *Ad,* Peabody Institute Library, Peabody MA. 617-531-0100

Roger, Lila L, *Actg Librn,* La Mesa United Presbyterian Church Library, Albuquerque NM. 505-255-8095

Rogero, Kathryn, *Tech Serv,* Saint Johns River Community College, B C Pearce Learning Resources Center, Palatka FL. 904-328-1571, Ext 216

Rogero, Thomas T, *Librn,* University of Miami (Engineering & Architecture), Coral Gables FL. 305-284-4126

Rogero, Thomas T, *Sci,* University of Miami, Otto G Richter Library, Coral Gables FL. 305-284-3551

Rogero, Thomas T, *Librn & Bibliog Instr,* University of Miami, Rosentiel School of Marine & Atmospheric Sciences, Miami FL. 305-350-7207

Rogers, A Robert, *Dean,* Kent State University, School of Library Science, OH. 216-672-2782, 672-7988

Rogers, Anita C, *Librn,* Paris Public Library, South Paris ME. 207-743-6994

Rogers, Anne M, *Dir,* Paris-Bourbon County Library, Paris KY. 606-987-4419

Rogers, B J, *Dir,* Lee Pharmaceuticals Library, South El Monte CA. 213-442-3141

Rogers, Barbara, *Librn,* Occidental Exploration & Production Co Library, Bakersfield CA. 805-395-8565

Rogers, Barbara, *Bkmobile Coordr,* Pineville-Bell County Public Library, Pineville KY. 606-337-3422

Rogers, Barbara, *In Charge,* Saint Paul Public Library (Sun Ray), Saint Paul MN. 612-292-6640

Rogers, Beverly, *Circ,* Fargo Public Library, Fargo ND. 701-241-1490

Rogers, Bonnie L, *Dean,* Palomar Community College, Library Technology Certificate Program, CA. 714-744-1150, Ext 473 & 480

Rogers, Bonnie L, *Dean,* Palomar Community College, Phil H Putnam Memorial Library, San Marcos CA. 714-744-1150, Ext 275, 276 & 473

Rogers, Brian, *Dir,* Connecticut College Library, New London CT. 203-442-1630

Rogers, Carole, *Libr Supvr,* United Grain Growers Library, Winnipeg MB. 204-944-5572

Rogers, D, *Cat,* Carleton University, Murdoch Maxwell MacOdrum Library, Ottawa ON. 613-231-4357

Rogers, Dean, *ILL,* Rappahannock Community College, South Campus Library, Glenns VA. 804-758-5324, Ext 208

Rogers, Dee, *Librn,* American Cyanamid Co, Fiber Division Library, Milton FL. 904-994-5311, Ext 220

Rogers, Doris, *Librn,* Jackson Metropolitan Library (White Rock Library), Jackson MS. 601-352-3677

Rogers, Dorothy, *Tech Serv,* Eugene Public Library, Eugene OR. 503-687-5450

Rogers, Elaine, *Librn,* General Motors Corp (Tax Section Library), Detroit MI. 313-556-1567

Rogers, Emma, *Circ,* University of Mississippi Library, University MS. 601-232-7091

Rogers, Ethel M, *Asst Dir,* Gordon-Nash Library, New Hampton NH. 603-744-8061

Rogers, Glenn E, *Librn,* John Brown University Library, Siloam Springs AR. 501-524-3131, Ext 203

Rogers, Helen, *Chief, Computer-Based Ref Serv,* National Library of Canada, Ottawa ON. 613-995-9481

Rogers, Irene, *Asst Dir,* Yonkers Public Library, Yonkers NY. 914-337-1500

Rogers, James, *Dir,* East Cleveland Public Library, East Cleveland OH. 216-541-4128

Rogers, James E, *Adjunct Prof,* Case Western Reserve University, School of Library Science, OH. 216-368-3500

Rogers, Janet E, *Dir,* Chester Public Library, Chester NY. 914-469-4252

Rogers, Jeanne E, *Librn,* Beaumont Enterprise & Journal Library, Beaumont TX. 713-833-3311

Rogers, Jo Ann V, *Asst Prof,* University of Kentucky, College of Library Science, KY. 606-258-8876

Rogers, John, *Dir,* Kimball Public Library, Kimball NE. 308-235-4523

Rogers, Judith, *Librn,* Greenwich Free Library, Greenwich NY. 518-692-7157

Rogers, Kathleen, *Librn,* Newton Free Library (Newton Lower Falls Branch), Newton Lower Falls MA. 617-527-7700, Ext 24

Rogers, Kathleen C, *Asst Librn & Ref,* Saint John the Baptist Parish Library, LaPlace LA. 504-652-2144

Rogers, Ken E, *In Charge,* Texas Forest Service, Texas Forest Products Laboratory Library, Lufkin TX. 713-634-7709

Rogers, Laura, *Librn,* Springerville Public Library, Springerville AZ. 602-333-4694

Rogers, Margaret N, *Dir,* Northwest Mississippi Junior College, R C Pugh Library, Senatobia MS. 601-562-5262, Ext 246

Rogers, Marilyn, *Tech Serv,* Louisiana State University School of Medicine in Shreveport, Medical Library, Shreveport LA. 318-226-3442

Rogers, Marlin, *Info Sci,* Alcon Laboratories, Inc, Technical Library, Fort Worth TX. 817-293-0450, Ext 2263

Rogers, Marsha, *Archivist,* University of Virginia (Law Library), Charlottesville VA. 804-924-3384

Rogers, Martha S, *Librn,* Leeds Public Library, Leeds AL. 205-699-5962

Rogers, Mary, *Tech Serv,* Seminole Community College Library, Sanford FL. 305-323-1450, Ext 450

Rogers, Mary R, *Br Coordr,* Aiken-Bamberg-Barnwell-Edgefield Regional Library, Aiken SC. 803-648-8961

Rogers, Maxine W, *Librn,* Richmond Public Library (Westover Hills), Richmond VA. 804-780-6140

Rogers, Myrtle, *Librn,* Farnam Public Library, Farnam NE. 308-569-2339

Rogers, Nancy, *Librn,* Bechtel, Inc, Houston Central Library, Houston TX. 713-877-4707

Rogers, Nancy Ann, *Librn,* Lynn Daily Evening Item Library, Lynn MA. 617-593-7700

Rogers, Nellie E, *Librn,* Randolph Free Library, Randolph NY. 716-358-3712

Rogers, Pamela, *Museum Coordr,* Pejepscot Historical Society, Curtis Memorial Library, Brunswick ME. 207-729-4622

Rogers, Rebecca W, *ILL,* Eastern Shore Public Library, Accomac VA. 804-787-3400

Rogers, Richard H, *Cat,* Union University, Emma Waters Summar Library, Jackson TN. 901-668-1818, Ext 269

Rogers, Rosalyn, *Librn,* Lowell Public Library, Lowell NC. 704-824-1266

Rogers, Ruth R, *Librn,* East Mississippi Junior College Library, Scooba MS. 601-476-5671

Rogers, Ruth T, *Admin Librn,* United States Navy (Naval Aerospace Medical Institute Library), Pensacola FL. 904-452-2256

Rogers, Rutherford D, *Univ Librn,* Yale University Library (University Library), New Haven CT. 203-436-8335

Rogers, Sally, *Dir,* Minoa Library, Minoa NY. 315-656-7401

Rogers, Sharon, *Soc Sci,* University of Toledo, William S Carlson Library, Toledo OH. 419-537-2324

Rogers, Sheila, *Librn,* Saint Joseph's Hospital, Medical Library, Hamilton ON. 416-522-4941, Ext 410

Rogers, Stephanie, *On-Line Servs,* San Jose State University Library, San Jose CA. 408-277-3377

Rogers, Steven E, *AV,* University of Tennessee at Martin, Paul Meek Library, Martin TN. 901-587-7060

Rogers, Susan, *Asst Librn,* Manitoba Department of Health Library, Winnipeg MB. 204-786-5867, 786-5868

Rogers, Vicky L, *Librn,* Public Library of the District of Columbia (Northeast), Washington DC. 202-727-1365

Rogers, William F, *Asst Dir,* Ohio University, Vernon R Alden Library, Athens OH. 614-594-5228

Rogerson, Gay, *Asst Librn,* Springdale Free Public Library, Springdale PA. 412-274-9717

Rogerson, Mary F, *Ref,* United States Army (Morale Support Activities Division Library), Fort Hood TX. 817-685-6011

Rogets, Susan, *Cat,* Reelfoot Regional Library Center, Martin TN. 901-587-2347

Rogge, Rena, *Ref,* Kean College of New Jersey, Nancy Thompson Library, Union NJ. 201-527-2017

Rogge, Stephen, *Dir,* Mason City Public Library, Mason City IA. 515-423-7552

Rogier, June, *Librn,* University of Minnesota Landscape Arboretum, Andersen Horticultural Library, Chaska MN. 612-443-2460

Rogne, Deborah, *Asst Librn,* Stewartville Public Library, Stewartville MN. 507-533-4902

Rogstad, Betty, *Librn,* Minot Daily News Library, Minot ND. 701-852-3341, Ext 241

Rohde, Gladys, *Asst Librn,* California State University Fullerton Library, Fullerton CA. 714-773-2714

Rohde, Nancy J, *Asst Prof,* University of Minnesota, Library School, MN. 612-373-3100

Rohdy, Margaret, *Tech Serv,* Saint Lawrence University, Owen D Young Library, Canton NY. 315-379-5451

Rohlf, Mark A, *Librn,* COMSAT Central Library, (Communications Satellite Corp), Washington DC. 202-554-6658

Rohlf, Robert H, *Dir,* Hennepin County Library, Edina MN. 612-830-4944

Rohlfing, Waunita, *Librn,* Lewellen Public Library, Lewellen NE. 308-778-5511

Rohmiller, Ellen Lukas, *Acq,* Sinclair Community College, Learning Resources Center, Dayton OH. 513-226-2855

Rohmiller, Thomas, *Bibliog Instr,* University of Dayton Libraries, Roesch Library, Dayton OH. 513-229-4221

Rohovec, Lee, *Media,* New Mexico State University at Alamogordo Library, Learning Resource Center, Alamogordo NM. 505-437-6864

Rohowetz, Paul, *Media,* Saint Mary's College, Fitzgerald Library, Winona MN. 507-452-4430, Ext 232

Rohr, Judy, *Media,* Fullerton City Library, Fullerton CA. 714-738-6333, Ext 301

Rohr, Ted, *Assoc Dean,* Saint Louis Community College (Forest Park Campus), Saint Louis MO. 314-644-9209

Rohrbach, Kenneth J, *Asst Dir,* Scenic Regional Library of Franklin, Gasconade & Warren Counties, Union MO. 314-583-3224

Rohrbach, Marion G, *Dir,* Sea Cliff Public Library, Sea Cliff NY. 516-671-4290

Rohrbacher, Elizabeth, *Ch,* Hunterdon County Library, Flemington NJ. 201-788-1444

Rohrbaugh, Ann, *Admin Asst,* Kalamazoo Public Library, Kalamazoo MI. 616-342-9837

Rohrbaugh, Valerie, *On-Line Servs,* University of Nebraska at Omaha, University Library, Omaha NE. 402-554-2361

Rohrer, Maryanne, *Asst Librn,* Rapid City Regional Hospital, Health Science Library, Rapid City SD. 605-341-7108

Rohrer, Richard, *Dir,* University of Minnesota, Saint Paul Campus Libraries, Saint Paul MN. 612-373-0904

Rohrs, Elaine, *Circ,* Pomona Public Library, Pomona CA. 714-620-2033

Rohrs, Lucinda Eggleston, *Dir,* Kemper Military School & College Library, Boonville MO. 816-882-5623

Roinestad, Lisa, *Ch,* Etta C Ross Memorial Library, Blue Earth Public Library, Blue Earth MN. 507-526-5012

Roizman, Betty, *Librn,* Chadwell, Kayser, Ruggles, McGee, Hastings & McKinney Law Library, Chicago IL. 312-876-2209

Roland, Barbara, *Chief, Automation Planning & Liaison Off,* Library of Congress, Washington DC. 202-287-5000

Roland, Elizabeth, *ILL & Ref,* Gloucester Lyceum & Sawyer Free Library, Gloucester MA. 617-283-0376

Roland, John E, *Librn,* Northwest Community College Library, Powell WY. 307-754-6207

Rolbiecki, Verne, *Dir,* New Holstein Public Library, New Holstein WI. 414-898-5165

Rolfs, R, *Librn,* University of Southern California (Music), Los Angeles CA. 213-743-2525

Rolich, Alexander J, *Slavic,* University of Wisconsin-Madison, Memorial Library, Madison WI. 608-262-3521

Rolland, Hazel, *Librn,* Canada Department of National Defense (Dept of National Defence-Chief Computer Services Library), Ottawa ON. 613-996-6296

Rolland-Thomas, Paule, *Assoc Prof,* University of Montreal, Ecole de Bibliotheconomie, PQ. 514-343-6044

Roller, Duane H D, *Hist of Sci Coll,* University of Oklahoma MUniversity Libraries, Norman OK. 405-325-2611

Roller, Mary Jane, *Librn,* Pulaski County Public Library (Medaryville), Medaryville IN. 219-843-4141

Roller, Sharon, *ILL,* Northeast Georgia Regional Library System, Clarkesville GA. 404-754-4413

Rollin, Marian, *AV,* University of Connecticut Library, Storrs CT. 203-486-2219

Rollins, Alden, *Doc,* University of Alaska, Anchorage Library, Anchorage AK. 907-263-1825

Rollins, Arline, *Librn,* Ohio State University Libraries (West Campus Learning Resources Center), Columbus OH. 614-422-0183

Rollins, Doris, *Librn,* New Durham Free Public Library, New Durham NH. 603-859-2201

Rollins, Eleanor, *On-Line Servs,* University of Miami (Louis Calder Memorial Library), Miami FL. 305-547-6441

Rollins, James, *Librn,* Saint Louis University (School of Social Service), Saint Louis MO. 314-658-2718

Rollins, Jane G, *Assocs,* New York State Library, Albany NY. 518-474-5930

Rollins, Janet J, *Chief Librn,* Brawley Public Library, Brawley CA. 714-344-1891

Rollins, Ottilie H, *Head Librn,* Clarkson College of Technology, Harriet Call Burnap Memorial Library, Potsdam NY. 315-268-6645

Rollins, S, *Circ,* University of Rhode Island Library, Kingston RI. 401-792-1000

Rollins, Wendell, *Dir,* Iowa Central Community College, Fort Dodge Center Library, Fort Dodge IA. 515-576-3103

Rollins, William L, *Pub Info Officer,* New Hampshire Department Public Works & Highways, Public Information Library, Concord NH. 603-271-2515

Rollinson, M Elizabeth, *Clerk,* Pomfret Free Public Library, Pomfret CT. 203-928-3475

Rollock, Barbara, *Coordr Ch Servs,* New York Public Library (The Branch Libraries), New York NY. 212-790-6262

Rullow, Jean, *Librn,* Garvin County Library, Pauls Valley OK. 405-238-5188

Rolls, Erlinda, *On-Line Servs,* Western Michigan University, Dwight B Waldo Library, Kalamazoo MI. 616-383-4961

Rolnick, Nancy, *YA,* Croton Free Library, Croton-on-Hudson NY. 914-271-4098

Roloff, Daphne C, *Dir,* Art Institute of Chicago (Ryerson & Burnham Libraries), Chicago IL. 312-443-6666

Rolston, Judy, *Acq & Cat,* Grand Rapids Baptist College & Seminary, Ketcham Library, Grand Rapids MI. 616-949-5300, Ext 228

Romalis, Carl, *Librn,* Electric Railroaders' Association, Inc, Sprague Library, New York NY. 212-986-4482

Romalis, Carl, *Librn,* New York State Department of Correctional Services Library, Long Island City NY. 212-361-8920, Ext 261

Roman, Mary Ann, *Librn,* Barnes, Hickam, Pantzer & Boyd Library, Indianapolis IN. 317-638-1313

Roman, Susan, *Ch,* Northbrook Public Library, Northbrook IL. 312-272-6224

Romanelli, Catherine, *Dir,* Farmingdale Public Library, Farmingdale NY. 516-249-9090

Romani, Dorothy, *Serv to Shut-Ins & Retirees,* Detroit Public Library, Detroit Associated Libraries, Detroit MI. 313-833-1000

Romano, Kathy, *Ref,* Rolling Prairie Library System, Decatur IL. 217-429-2586

Romano, Madeline, *Librn,* Cheektowaga Public Library (South), Cheektowaga NY. 716-896-1272

Romano, Rosemarie, *Librn,* Auburn Memorial Hospital, Library-Resource Center, Auburn NY. 315-255-7231

Romans, Anne F, *Ch,* Plattsburgh Public Library, Plattsburgh NY. 518-563-0921

Romans, Judy, *Librn,* Bandon Public Library, Bandon OR. 503-347-3221

Romans, Mary, *Librn,* Akron-Summit County Public Library (West Hill), Akron OH. 216-376-2927

Romans, Vivian, *Librn,* Jackson Metropolitan Library (Northside), Jackson MS. 601-352-3677

Rome, D, *Archivist,* Canadian Jewish Congress, National Archives & Library, Montreal PQ. 514-937-7531

Rome, Linda L, *Media Dir & Librn,* Huston-Tillotson College, Downs-Jones Library, Austin TX. 512-476-7421, Ext 300

Romelczyk, Gerald, *Tech Serv, On-Line Servs & Bibliog Instr,* Haverhill Public Library, Haverhill MA. 617-373-1586

Romero, Dorothy, *Librn,* Our Lady of the Lake Medical Center Library, Baton Rouge LA. 504-769-3100, Ext 8140

Romero, Jennie, *Acq,* Albuquerque Public Library, Albuquerque NM. 505-766-7882

Romero, Nancy, *Original Cat,* University of Illinois Library at Urbana-Champaign, Urbana IL. 217-333-0790

Romero, Orlando, *Spec Coll,* New Mexico State Library, Santa Fe NM. 505-827-2033

Romero, Ray, *Librn,* Bernalillo County Second Judicial District, Law Library, Albuquerque NM. 505-242-2961

Romero, Yvonne, *Librn,* Controls for Environmental Pollution, Inc Library, Santa Fe NM. 505-982-9841

Romich, Nancy, *Ch & Cat,* Whitehall Township Public Library, Whitehall PA. 215-432-4339

Romig, Lee, *Librn,* Morton County Library, Elkhart KS. 316-697-4591

Rommel, Jeanne, *Coll Develop,* Kenosha Public Library, Kenosha WI. 414-656-6034

Romnes, James B, *Libr Asst,* Lutheran Bible Institute Library, Issaquah WA. 206-392-0400

Romo, Rochelle, *Librn,* Roosevelt County Library (Bainville Public), Bainville MT. 406-653-2411

Romo, Rolando, *Librn,* Austin Public Library (Terrazas), Austin TX. 512-472-5433

Romportl, Amelia Francis, *Circ, Ref & Per,* Saint Paul Seminary, John Ireland Memorial Library, Saint Paul MN. 612-690-4355

Ronan-Clarke, Mary, *In Charge,* TRW Defense & Space Systems Group Technical Library, McLean VA. 703-734-6243

Rondeau, Elaine, *Librn,* Saint Anne's Hospital, Sullivan Medical Library, Fall River MA. 617-674-5741, Ext 282

Rondelli, Marilyn, *Mgr,* Ortho Diagnostics Inc Library, Raritan NJ. 201-524-0400

Roney, Raymond E, *Deputy Dir,* University of the District of Columbia, Learning Resources Division, Washington DC. 202-282-7536

Rongione, L A, *Dir,* Villanova University, Falvey Memorial Library, Villanova PA. 215-527-2100, Ext 350, 351 & 352

Rongione, Louis A, *Prof,* Villanova University, Graduate Dept of Library Science, PA. 215-527-2100, Ext 354, 355

Ronk, Mary S, *Asst Librn,* Sanibel Island Public Library, Sanibel Island FL. 813-472-2483

Ronnenberg, Loraine, *Librn,* Somerset Public Library, Somerset WI. 715-247-5228

Ronningen, Elayne, *Bkmobile Coordr,* Griggs County Library, Cooperstown ND. 701-797-2214

Roochvarg, Joan, *Acq,* Massapequa Public Library, Massapequa NY. 516-798-4607

Rood, Debra, *On-Line Servs,* Upper Hudson Library Federation, Albany NY. 518-449-3387, 449-3380

Rood, Negina, *Alliance Liason,* Donaldson, Lufkin & Jenrette Securities Corp, Corporate Library, New York NY. 212-943-0300, Ext 1356-9

Rood, Sophia, *In Charge,* Irvington Public Library (Union Avenue), Irvington NJ. 201-372-6402

Rook, Lois, *Librn,* Frederick County Public Library (Middletown), Frederick MD. 301-694-1613

Rook, Velma, *In Charge,* Calhoun County Historical Library, Rockwell City IA. 712-297-8307

Rooker, Joyce, *In Charge,* Jacobs Engineering Group, Technical Information Services, Houston TX. 713-626-2020, Ext 433

Rooney, Anita, *Ref,* East Providence Public Library, Weaver Memorial Library, East Providence RI. 401-434-2453

Rooney, Elizabeth B, *Librn,* Hampstead Public Library, Hampstead NH. 603-329-6411

Rooney, Maureen, *Ref,* Newport Public Library, Newport RI. 401-847-8720

Rooney, Paul M, *Dir,* Buffalo & Erie County Public Library System, Buffalo NY. 716-856-7525

Rooney, Sieglinde, *Acq,* University of Alberta (University Libraries), Edmonton AB. 403-432-3790

Roop, Madeline, *Circ,* Millinocket Memorial Library, Millinocket ME. 207-723-9610

Roos, Marcia, *Asst Librn,* Temple University, Ambler Campus Library, Ambler PA. 215-643-1200, Ext 250

Roos, Philip, *Dir,* National Association for Retarded Citizens Library, Arlington TX. 817-261-4961

Roos, Shirley, *Librn,* Holly Township Library, Holly MI. 313-634-7331

Roos, Tedine, *In Charge,* Milwaukee Public Library (Mill Road), Milwaukee WI. 414-278-3088

Roose, Tina, *Ref,* North Suburban Library System, Wheeling IL. 312-459-1300

Roossien, Arlene, *Librn,* Kent County Library System (Byron Township), Byron Center MI. 616-878-1665

Root, Christine, *Acq,* Hudson Valley Community College Learning Resources Center, Dwight Marvin Library, Troy NY. 518-283-1100, Ext 629

Root, Clyde R, *Dir,* Northwest Bible College Library, Minot ND. 701-852-3781, Ext 41

Root, Joyce, *Asst Librn,* Lakeland College, Community Memorial Library, Sheboygan WI. 414-565-1238

Root, Mary, *ILL,* River Bend Library System, Coal Valley IL. 309-799-3131

Root, Nina J, *Chief Librn,* American Museum of Natural History Library, New York NY. 212-873-1300, Ext 494

Root, Ron, *Ref,* Tulsa Junior College (Northeast Campus), Tulsa OK. 918-932-5071, Ext 58

Roper, Fred, *Assoc Prof,* University of North Carolina at Chapel Hill, School of Library Science, NC. 919-933-8366

Roper, Grace T, *Dir,* Belmar Public Library, Belmar NJ. 201-681-0775

Roper, Robert J, *Chief Librn,* CBS Technology Center Library, Stamford CT. 203-327-2000

Ropp, Mary, *Dir,* Worthington Jefferson Township Public Library, Worthington IN. 812-875-3815

Rores, Katherine C, *Colls Coordr,* Buffalo & Erie County Public Library System, Buffalo NY. 716-856-7525

Rorick, Janice, *Librn,* Sacramento Public Library (Southgate Community), Sacramento CA. 916-421-6327

Rorie, William E, *Asst Dir,* H Leslie Perry Memorial Library, Henderson NC. 919-438-3316

Rorie, William E, *Librn,* H Leslie Perry Memorial Library (Chestnut Street Branch), Henderson NC. 919-492-6727

Rork, Susan S, *Librn,* Bucks County Free Library (Yardley-Makefield Branch), Yardley PA. 215-493-4658

Rosa, Clarice, *Librn,* Michigan State University Library (Undergraduate), East Lansing MI. 517-355-2344

Rosa, Hazel M, *Librn,* South Ryegate Public Library, Inc, South Ryegate VT. 802-584-3655

Rosa, Joan, *Circ,* Harrison Public Library, Harrison NY. 914-835-0324

Rosa, Paul J, *Librn,* Connecticut Correctional Institution, Somers Library, Somers CT. 203-749-8391

Rosar, Luella M, *Chief Librn,* Doyle Dane Bernbach, Inc, Research Library, New York NY. 212-826-2000

Rosaschi, Jim, *Dir,* Nampa Public Library, Nampa ID. 208-466-6121

Rosasco, Joan, *Chief Librn,* Bechtel Central Library, San Francisco CA. 415-768-5306

Rosati, Ruth, *Librn,* Contra Costa County Library (Crockett Branch), Crockett CA. 415-787-2345

Rosche, Marie, *Librn,* Montgomery County Department of Public Libraries (Kensington Park Branch), Kensington MD. 301-949-4100

Roscoe, Donna, *Librn,* Sanders Associates, Inc, Technical Library, Nashua NH. 603-885-4321

Rose, Adelaide, *In Charge,* Tulare County Mental Health Services Library, Visalia CA. 209-734-1916

Rose, Avanelle C, *Librn,* Crouse-Hinds Co Library, Syracuse NY. 315-477-7000

Rose, Carole, *Braille Librn,* Indiana State Library, Division for the Blind & Physically Handicapped, Indianapolis IN. 317-232-3684

Rose, David P, *Librn,* United Nations Fund for Population Activities, Library for Technical Services, New York NY. 212-754-8194

Rose, Diana, *Librn,* Newfoundland Public Library Services (Technical Services Dept), Saint John's NF. 709-737-3964

Rose, Donald, *Cat,* University of Texas Health Science Center at San Antonio Library, San Antonio TX. 512-691-6271

Rose, Dorothy H, *Librn,* Erie Community College-North (City Campus Library Resource Center), Buffalo NY. 716-881-4200, Ext 320

Rose, Elizabeth, *Media,* Boston College Libraries (Bapst (Central Library)), Chestnut Hill MA. 617-969-0100, Ext 3205

Rose, F, *Doc,* University of Victoria, McPherson Library, Victoria BC. 604-477-6911, Ext 4466

Rose, Inez V, *Libr Technician,* Crosby Public Library, Antwerp NY. 315-659-8564

Rose, Isabel, *Music,* Metropolitan Toronto Library Board, Metropolitan Toronto Library, Toronto ON. 416-928-5150

Rose, Janet, *Ch,* Saint Clair County Library System, Port Huron MI. 313-987-7323

Rose, Josephine, *Librn,* Yolo County Library (Clarksburg Branch), Clarksburg CA. 916-744-1755

Rose, Julia, *Librn,* Sue Bennett College, Minerva McDaniel Library, London KY. 606-864-6770

Rose, Lee, *Librn,* Hartington Public Library, Hartington NE. 402-254-6245

Rose, Margaret, *Local Hist,* Corpus Christi Public Libraries, La Retama Public Library, Corpus Christi TX. 512-882-1937

Rose, Margaret, *Reserves,* New School for Social Research, Raymond Fogelman Library, New York NY. 212-741-7906

Rose, Marion, *Librn,* West Warwick Public Library System (Crompton Free Library), West Warwick RI. 401-828-2914

Rose, Martin, *Tech Serv,* Cumberland Regional Library, Amherst NS. 902-667-2135

Rose, Mary, *Librn,* Stilwell Public Library, Stilwell OK. 918-774-7512

Rose, Melissa, *Pub Servs,* California State University, Hayward Library, Hayward CA. 415-881-3664

Rose, Mrs C, *Librn,* Building Products of Canada Ltd, Library, Lachine PQ. 514-636-6810

Rose, Patricia, *Librn,* West Florida Regional Library (Gulf Breeze Branch), Gulf Breeze FL. 904-932-5166

Rose, Philip, *ILL,* Aurora Public Library, Aurora CO. 303-750-5000, Ext 410

Rose, Robert F, *On-Line Servs,* California State University Fullerton Library, Fullerton CA. 714-773-2714

Rose, Susan, *Librn,* Fayetteville Technical Institute, Paul H Thompson Library, Fayetteville NC. 919-323-1961

Rose, Timothy G, *Dir,* Springville Museum of Art Library, Springville UT. 801-489-9434

Rose, Wilma, *Librn,* Pataskala Public Library, Pataskala OH. 614-927-9986

Rose, Jr, W Russell, *Dir & Acq,* Lassen College, Media Center, Susanville CA. 916-257-6181, Ext 261

Roselle, William C, *Dir,* University of Wisconsin-Milwaukee, Golda Meir Library, Milwaukee WI. 414-963-4785

Roselli, Florence, *Librn,* Italian Cultural Center Library, Melrose Park IL. 312-345-3842

Rosen, Frances, *Acq & Cat,* Huntington Public Library, Huntington NY. 516-427-5165

Rosen, Gloria K, *Librn,* Montefiore Hospital, Medical Library, Pittsburgh PA. 412-683-1100

Rosen, Jocelyn, *In Charge,* ITT Continental Baking Co, Research Library, Rye NY. 914-899-0380

Rosen, Kenneth E, *Librn,* Branford Electric Railway Association, Inc, Trolley Museum, East Haven CT. 203-467-6927

Rosen, Martha A, *AV & Doc,* Louisiana State University, LeDoux Library, Eunice LA. 318-457-7311, Ext 38

Rosenbaum, Don, *Librn,* Hebrew Theological College, Saul Silber Memorial Library, Skokie IL. 312-267-9800

Rosenbaum, Ferne, *Librn,* Brown County Library (North), Green Bay WI. 414-497-3445

Rosenberg, Gail, *Exten Servs,* Hunterdon County Library, Flemington NJ. 201-788-1444

Rosenberg, Gayle, *Ch,* Avon Township Public Library, Rochester MI. 313-651-1426

Rosenberg, Goldie, *In Charge,* Hoffmann-La Roche Inc (Business Information Center), Nutley NJ. 201-235-3901

Rosenberg, Hanna, *Ch,* International Falls Public Library, International Falls MN. 218-283-8051

Rosenberg, Joan, *Librn,* Polorad Electronics Inc Library, Lake Success NY. 516-328-1100

Rosenberg, John E, *Librn,* Harry Diamond Laboratories, Scientific & Technical Information Office Library, Adelphi MD. 301-394-1010

Rosenberg, Kenyon, *Pub Servs,* Kent State University Libraries, Kent OH. 216-672-2962

Rosenberg, Marc, *Asst Prof,* Southern Illinois University at Carbondale, Educational Media Program, IL. 618-453-5764

Rosenberg, Mel, *YA,* Los Angeles Public Library System, Los Angeles CA. 213-626-7555

Rosenberg, Nancy, *Librn,* Montgomery, McCracken, Walker & Rhoads Library, Philadelphia PA. 215-563-0650, ext 211 & 241

Rosenberg, Paul M, *Librn,* Beth El Hebrew Congregation Library, Alexandria VA. 703-370-9400

Rosenberg, Phyllis, *Dir,* Branch County Library, Coldwater MI. 517-278-2341

Rosenberg, Victor, *Assoc Prof,* University of Michigan, School of Library Science, MI. 313-764-9376
Rosenberger, Alice M, *Librn,* Palo Verde Valley District Library, Blythe CA. 714-922-5371
Rosenberger, Lois, *Dir,* Switzerland County Public Library, Vevay IN. 812-427-3363
Rosenberger, Norma, *Chief Librn & Acq,* Spokane Falls Community College, Library Media Services, Spokane WA. 509-456-2860
Rosenberger, Sister Marielda, *Cat,* Assumption College for Sisters Library, Mendham NJ. 201-543-6528
Rosenberry, Margaret, *Chief Librn,* De Forest Area Public Library, De Forest WI. 608-846-5482
Rosenblum, Richard S, *Dir,* West New York Public Library, Philip A Payne Memorial Library, West New York NJ. 201-854-1028
Rosenbluth, Linda, *ILL,* Mount Pleasant Public Library, Pleasantville NY. 914-769-0548
Rosencrantz, Barbara, *Asst Librn,* Dorset Village Public Library Association, Inc, Dorset VT. 802-867-5774
Rosencranz, Tricia, *Ref,* Irving Public Library System, Irving TX. 214-253-2639
Rosendall, Glynis, *Librn,* Evansville Public Library & Vanderburgh County Public Library (Meadow Park), Evansville IN. 812-425-2621
Rosenfeld, Edward, *Acq,* Boston College Libraries (Bapst (Central Library)), Chestnut Hill MA. 617-969-0100, Ext 3205
Rosenfeld, Joel C, *Dir,* Rockford Public Library, Rockford IL. 815-965-6731
Rosenfield, Kate, *Manager,* Church of the Incarnation, Marmion Library, Dallas TX. 214-521-5101
Rosenkranz, Sylvia, *Librn,* Brownsville Public Library, Brownsville WI. 414-583-4325
Rosenplat, D W, *Research Librn,* Steel Company of Canada, Ltd, Corporate Library Services, Hamilton ON. 416-528-2511
Rosenstein, Philip, *Dir,* College of Medicine & Dentistry of New Jersey, George F Smith Library of the Health Sciences, Newark NJ. 201-456-4580
Rosenstock, Michael, *Bk Selection,* University of Toronto Libraries (University Library), Toronto ON. 416-978-2294
Rosenstock, Morton, *Dir,* Bronx Community College Library, Bronx NY. 212-367-7300, Ext 315
Rosenstock, Sandra, *Ref & Bibliog Instr,* Goddard College, William Shipman Library, Plainfield VT. 802-454-8311, Ext 232
Rosensweig, Ruth, *Dir Libr Servs,* Saint Joseph's Hospital & Medical Center, Health Sciences Library, Paterson NJ. 201-977-2104
Rosenthal, Avram, *Dir,* Henry Ford Community College, Eshleman Library, Dearborn MI. 313-271-2750, Ext 378
Rosenthal, Barbara, *Librn,* Saint Elizabeth Hospital (Medical Library), Youngstown OH. 216-746-7211
Rosenthal, Carole, *Asst Dir,* Cordova Public Library, Cordova AK. 907-424-7444
Rosenthal, Franz, *In Charge,* Yale University Library (Semitic Reference), New Haven CT. 203-436-4641
Rosenthal, Grace, *Cat,* Hanover College, Duggan Library, Hanover IN. 812-866-2151, Ext 333
Rosenthal, Joseph A, *Dir,* University of California, Berkeley (University Library), Berkeley CA. 415-642-3773
Rosenthal, Lenore, *Librn,* Brooklyn Public Library (Canarsie), Brooklyn NY. 212-257-2180
Rosenthal, Patricia, *North Carolina Hist & Genealogy,* Rowan Public Library, Salisbury NC. 704-633-5578
Rosenthal, Phyllis, *Ch,* Cliffside Park Free Public Library, Cliffside Park NJ. 201-945-2867
Rosenthal, Richard, *Librn,* Lincolnton-Lincoln County Public Library, Lincolnton NC. 704-735-8044
Rosenthal, Robert, *Spec Coll,* University of Chicago, Joseph Regenstein Library, Chicago IL. 312-753-2977
Rosenthal, Susan, *Tech Serv,* Oakland Park City Library, Oakland Park FL. 305-561-6287
Rosenwald, Peter Joseph, *Chief Librn,* Los Lunas Hospital & Training School, New Mexico Mental Retardation & Developmental Disabilities Library & Resource Center, Los Lunas NM. 505-865-9611, Ext 298

Rosenwinkel, Deborah, *Tech Serv,* Itasca Community Library, Itasca IL. 312-773-1699
Rosenwinkel, Heather, *Acq,* University of Oregon Health Sciences Center (Health Sciences Library), Portland OR. 503-225-8026
Rosenzweig, Bernard, *Dir,* Little Falls Free Public Library, Little Falls NJ. 201-256-2784
Rosetta, Judith, *Librn,* Northland Community College Library, Thief River Falls MN. 218-681-2181
Roshee, Jo Anne, *Commun Servs,* Andalusia Public Library, Andalusia AL. 205-222-6612
Roshon, Samuel, *Spec Coll,* Public Library of Columbus & Franklin County, Columbus OH. 614-864-8050
Rosichan, Richard H, *Dir,* Heed University Library, Hollywood FL. 305-925-1600
Rosicky, Henry, *Mgr,* United States Patent and Trademark Office, Science Library, Arlington VA. 703-557-2957
Rosier, Kathleen, *ILL,* Alaska State Library, Juneau AK. 907-465-2910
Rosignolo, Beverly, *Cat,* College of Insurance Library, New York NY. 212-962-4111, Ext 277
Rosiles, Marianne, *Librn,* La Salle Steel Co, Research & Develop Library, Hammond IN. 219-853-6000
Rosine, Betty, *Outreach & Circ,* Palm Springs Public Library, Palm Springs CA. 714-323-8291
Rosinski, Richard, *Assoc Prof,* University of Pittsburgh, School of Library & Information Science, PA. 412-624-5230
Roskey, Rita, *Circ Control,* Enoch Pratt Free Library, Baltimore MD. 301-396-5430, 396-5395
Rosnagle, Barbara M, *Dir,* Lyme Public Library, Lyme CT. 203-434-2272
Rosner, George W, *Asst Dir Archives,* University of Miami, Otto G Richter Library, Coral Gables FL. 305-284-3551
Rosonke, Richard, *Dir,* Joliet Junior College, Learning Resource Center, Joliet IL. 815-729-9020, Ext 282
Rosow, Stella M, *Librn,* Carlson Companies Library, Minneapolis MN. 612-540-5236
Ross, Alex, *Art,* Stanford University Libraries, Stanford CA. 415-497-2016
Ross, Alex, *Librn,* Stanford University Libraries (Art), Stanford CA. 415-497-3408
Ross, Alice, *Librn,* Odebolt Public Library, Odebolt IA. 712-668-4321
Ross, Anne, *Cat,* Kitsap Regional Library, Bremerton WA. 206-377-7601
Ross, Anne R, *Social, Educ & Govt,* Public Library of the District of Columbia, Martin Luther King Memorial Library, Washington DC. 202-727-1101
Ross, Bessie, *Librn,* Norwich Public Library, Norwich KS. 316-478-2569
Ross, Beth, *Ad,* Oxford County Library, Woodstock ON. 519-537-3322
Ross, Betty Ruth, *Librn,* Southeast Arkansas Regional Library (Grady Public), Grady AR. 501-367-3336
Ross, Edgar L, *Librn,* New York State Supreme Court (First Judicial District Criminal Law Library), New York NY. 212-374-8524
Ross, Ethel, *Librn,* Sleeper Public Library, Ubly MI. 517-658-2141
Ross, Hazel, *Libr Asst,* Pictou Antigonish Regional Library (New Glasgow Branch), New Glasgow NS. 902-752-0022
Ross, I C, *Systs Program Supvr,* Bell Telephone Laboratories (Bell Telephone Laboratories Technical Library), Murray Hill NJ. 582-4612 (Supvr); 582-3740 (Circ); 582-3604 (Info Alerting Servs); 582-3901 (Systs Design Program); 582-3453 (Computing Info Serv); 582-7330 (Computing)
Ross, Jacqueline, *Ch,* Mount Vernon Public Library, Mount Vernon IL. 618-242-6322
Ross, Jean, *Ch,* Prince William Public Library, Manassas VA. 703-361-8211
Ross, Jean Carol, *Librn,* Ingalls Memorial Hospital, Medical Library, Harvey IL. 312-333-2300, Ext 5155
Ross, Johanna, *On-Line Servs,* University of California at Davis (Physical Sciences Library), Davis CA. 916-752-0459
Ross, Johanna C, *Phys Sci,* University of California at Davis, General Library, Davis CA. 916-752-2110

Ross, Johanna C, *Math & Chem,* University of California at Davis, General Library, Davis CA. 916-752-2110
Ross, Joseph E, *Chief, Am Law Div,* Library of Congress, Washington DC. 202-287-5000
Ross, Juanita, *Librn,* Macon County-Tuskegee Public Library (Westbrook Public), Tuskegee AL. 205-727-5489
Ross, Judi, *Spec Servs,* Wisconsin Department of Public Instruction (Public & Cooperative Library Service), Madison WI. 608-266-7270
Ross, Karol, *Librn,* Molalla Public Library, Molalla OR. 503-829-2593
Ross, Kent, *Cat,* Arcadia Public Library, Arcadia CA. 213-446-7111
Ross, Lillian, *Librn,* Central Agency for Jewish Education, Educational Resource Center, Miami FL. 305-573-5720
Ross, Lynora, *Asst Librn,* Lee County Public Library, Woodward Memorial Library, Bishopville SC. 803-484-5921
Ross, Margaret, *Tech Serv,* Maywood Public Library, Maywood IL. 312-343-1847
Ross, Margaret J, *Librn,* Oakland Public Library, Oakland MS. 601-623-8788
Ross, Margery, *Librn,* Randolph Public Library (Asheboro), Asheboro NC. 919-629-2131
Ross, Marguerite S, *Instr,* Andrews University, Library Science Dept, MI. 616-471-3549
Ross, Martha, *ILL,* Miracle Valley Regional Library, City-County Public Library, Moundsville WV. 304-845-6911
Ross, Mary Ann, *Librn,* Chicago Board of Education Library, Chicago IL. 312-641-4105
Ross, Mrs N, *Librn,* Canada Institute for Scientific & Technical Information (Chemistry), Ottawa ON. 613-993-1600
Ross, Nancy, *Ad & Ref,* Bryan Public Library, Bryan TX. 713-823-8021
Ross, Nancy, *Genealogy,* Bryan Public Library, Bryan TX. 713-823-8021
Ross, Novelene, *Curator,* Wichita Art Museum Library, Wichita KS. 316-268-4621
Ross, Pamela, *Circ,* Boston College Libraries (Bapst (Central Library)), Chestnut Hil MA. 617-969-0100, Ext 3205
Ross, Patsy, *Ser,* University of Alabama, Amelia Gayle Gorgas Library, University AL. 205-348-5298
Ross, Philip R, *Asst Dir,* West Liberty State College, Paul N Elbin Library, West Liberty WV. 304-336-8035
Ross, Richard S, *Dir,* Northeastern University, Suburban Campus Library, Burlington MA. 617-272-5500, Ext 55
Ross, Robert D, *Dir,* Ridgewood Public Library, Ridgewood NJ. 201-652-5200
Ross, Robert O, *Dir,* Tompkins-Cortland Community College, Gerald A Barry Memorial Library, Instructional & Learning Resource Div, Dryden NY. 607-844-8211, Ext 354
Ross, Rosalinda, *On-Line Servs,* Thomas Jefferson University (Scott Memorial Library), Philadelphia PA. 215-928-8848
Ross, Ruth, *ILL & Ref,* Olympic College, Learning Resources Center, Bremerton WA. 206-478-4609
Ross, Ryburn M, *Asst Univ Librn, Tech & Automated Servs,* Cornell University Libraries (University Libraries), Ithaca NY. 607-256-4144
Ross, Scotty, *ILL & Per,* Harrison Public Library, Harrison NY. 914-835-0324
Ross, Sheila, *On-Line Servs,* University of Texas (M D Anderson Hospital & Tumor Institute), Houston TX. 713-792-2282
Ross, Sidnie, *Asst Librn,* Cargill, Inc, Information Center, Minneapolis MN. 612-475-6498
Ross, Stephen, *Ref,* Muhlenberg College, John A W Haas Library, Allentown PA. 215-433-3191, Ext 214
Ross, Steven, *Librn,* Southeastern University, Learning Resource Center, Washington DC. 202-488-8174
Ross, Theobel, *Librn,* Marlette Public Library, Marlette MI. 517-635-2838
Ross, Tina B, *Supvr,* Gulf Oil Corp (Gulf Research & Development Co, Technical Information Service), Pittsburgh PA. 412-263-5000
Ross, Tina B, *Dir Tech Info Servs,* Gulf Oil Corp (Gulf Science & Technology Co Library), Pittsburgh PA. 412-665-5576

Ross, Victoria, *Media,* Public Library of Nashville & Davidson County, Nashville TN. 615-244-4700

Ross, Virginia, *Librn,* Kings County Library (Avenal Branch), Avenal CA. 209-386-5741

Rosse, Rosanna H, *Reader Serv,* Clarkson College of Technology, Harriet Call Burnap Memorial Library, Potsdam NY. 315-268-6645

Rossell, Glenora E, *Dir,* University of Pittsburgh, Hillman Library, Pittsburgh PA. 412-624-4400

Rosser, Barbara L, *Dir,* Gatesville Public Library, Gatesville TX. 817-865-5367

Rosser, Helen, *Librn,* Burlington County Times Library, Willingboro NJ. 609-877-1600, Ext 343

Rosser, J Marcus, *Librn,* Choctawhatchee Regional Library (Newton Public), Newton AL. 205-299-3361

Rosser, Mildred W, *Librn,* Hansell, Post Brandon & Dorsey, Law Library, Atlanta GA. 404-581-8000

Rosser, Virginia, *Media,* Kalamazoo Public Library, Kalamazoo MI. 616-342-9837

Rossetti, Jane K, *Asst Librn,* Foley, Hoag & Eliot Library, Boston MA. 617-482-1390

Rossetto, Mrs M, *Coordr Central Libr Servs,* Saint Catharines Public Library, Saint Catharines ON. 416-688-6103

Rossi, Joan B, *Ch,* Russell Public Library, Middletown CT. 203-347-2528

Rossi, Joanne, *Media,* West Haven Public Library, West Haven CT. 203-932-2221

Rossi, Peter C, *Cat,* University of Central Florida Library, Orlando FL. 305-275-2564

Rossiter, Phyllis, *Librn,* Trails Regional Library (Odessa Branch), Odessa MO. 816-633-4089

Rossman, Renee, *Ad,* Portage Public Library, Portage MI. 616-327-6725

Rossmann, Louise, *ILL & Ref,* Wells College, Louis Jefferson Long Library, Aurora NY. 315-364-3351

Rossoff, Judith, *Media,* Liverpool Public Library, Liverpool NY. 315-457-0310

Rossom, Beva, *Librn,* Eleanor Daggett Public Library, Chama Valley Library, Chama NM. 505-756-2388

Rosswurn, Kevin, *Philos, Religion Education,* Akron-Summit County Public Library, Akron OH. 216-762-7621

Rost, Betty, *Cat,* Alberta Department of the Environment Library, Edmonton AB. 403-427-6132, 427-5870

Rostad, Barbara, *On-Line Servs,* Pillsbury Company (Main Office Library), Minneapolis MN. 612-330-4047

Rotan, Katy V, *Librn,* Southeastern Regional Library, Lovington NM. 505-396-4313

Rotella, Nancy A, *Dir,* Westwood Free Public Library, Westwood NJ. 201-664-0583

Roten, Margot, *Circ,* Quinnipiac College Library, Hamden CT. 203-288-5251, Ext 271

Roten, Paul, *Dir,* Associated Mennonite Biblical Seminaries Library, Elkhart IN. 219-295-3726, Ext 34, 37

Rotenberg, Goldie, *Librn,* Baker & McKenzie Library, New York NY. 212-751-5700

Rotgin, Rheba, *Librn,* Temple Emanu-El Library, Long Beach NY. 516-431-4060

Roth, Beth, *Per,* Veterans Administration (Library Division), Washington DC. 202-389-2781

Roth, Britain G, *Medical Librn,* Veterans Administration (Medical Library), Miami FL. 305-344-4455, Ext 3461 or 3462

Roth, Charles P, *Tech Serv,* Philadelphia College of Pharmacy & Science, Joseph W England Library, Philadelphia PA. 215-386-5800, Ext 296

Roth, Claire J, *Dir,* Mercantile Library Association, New York NY. 212-755-6710

Roth, Dana L, *Librn,* California Institute of Technology (Biology Library), Pasadena CA. 213-795-6811, Ext 2424

Roth, Dana L, *Librn,* California Institute of Technology (Chemistry Library), Pasadena CA. 213-795-6811, Ext 2423

Roth, Dana L, *Sci,* California Institute of Technology, Robert A Millikan Memorial Library, Pasadena CA. 213-795-6811

Roth, Doris R, *Asst Librn,* Hockessin Public Library, Hockessin DE. 302-239-5160

Roth, Edna, *Asst Librn,* Sherborn Library, Sherborn MA. 617-653-0770

Roth, Elizabeth E, *Keeper of Prints,* New York Public Library (Prints), New York NY. 212-790-6207

Roth, Frank, *Librn,* Kansas State Department of Social & Rehabilitation Services, Staff Development Library, Topeka KS. 913-295-9521

Roth, Gail, *ILL,* West Florida Regional Library, Pensacola Public Library, Pensacola FL. 904-438-5479

Roth, Harold L, *Dir,* Bryant Library, Roslyn NY. 516-621-2240

Roth, Karla M, *Bibliog Instr,* New Hampshire State Library, Concord NH. 603-271-2392

Roth, Marilyn, *Dir,* Bridgman Public Library, Bridgman MI. 616-465-3663

Roth, Norman, *Instr,* Foothill College, Library-Media Technical Assistant Program, CA. 415-948-8590, Ext 390

Roth, Reba B, *Librn,* El Paso Public Library, El Paso IL. 309-527-4360

Roth, Rita R, *Librn,* East Dubuque Public Library, East Dubuque IL. 815-742-3052

Roth, Ruth C, *Librn,* Eureka Public Library, Eureka IL. 309-467-2922

Roth, Susan Harned, *Ch,* Highland Park Public Library, Highland Park NJ. 201-572-2750

Roth, Terri M, *Librn,* Regional Comprehensive Rehabilitation Center, Home for Crippled Children Library, Pittsburgh PA. 412-521-9000, Ext 247

Rothacker, J Michael, *Assoc Prof,* George Peabody College for Teachers, Department of Library Science, TN. 615-327-8037

Rothberg, Ryna, *Ch & YA,* Newport Beach Public Library, Newport Beach CA. 714-640-2141

Rothe, Eckhard, *Ref,* Bishop's University & Champlain Regional College, John Bassett Memorial Library, Lennoxville PQ. 819-569-9551, Ext 341

Rothe, Kurt, *Dir,* University of Wisconsin-Green Bay, Library Learning Center, Green Bay WI. 414-465-2382

Rothebart, Bonnie, *Mgr,* Metro-Goldwyn-Mayer Inc, Research Library, Culver City CA. 213-870-3311

Rothenberger, Charlene, *AV,* New Albany Floyd County Public Library, New Albany IN. 812-944-8464

Rothenberger, James, *Govt Publications,* University of California, Riverside, University Library, Riverside CA. 714-787-3221

Rothers, Karen, *Librn,* Western Plains Library System (Clara City Branch), Clara City MN. 612-269-5644

Rothgeb, Jeanne Hickling, *Dir,* Indiana Institute of Technology, McMillen Library, Fort Wayne IN. 219-422-5561, Ext 215

Rothlisberg, Allen, *Dir,* Northland Pioneer College (District Learning Resources Center), Holbrook AZ. 602-524-6111, Ext 234 & 243

Rothlisberg, Allen, *Dir,* Northland Pioneer College (Holbrook Center Library), Holbrook AZ. 602-524-6111, Ext 243 & 234

Rothlisberg, Allen, *Dir,* Northland Pioneer College, Oraibi Center, Oraibi AZ. 602-734-2451

Rothlisberg, Allen, *Dir,* Northland Pioneer College, Show Low Center Library, Show Low AZ. 602-537-2976

Rothlisberg, Allen, *Librn,* Northland Pioneer College, Snowflake Center Library, Snowflake AZ. 602-536-7871

Rothlisberg, Allen, *Librn,* Northland Pioneer College, White River Learning Resources Center, White River AZ. 602-338-4662

Rothlisberg, Allen, *Librn,* Northland Pioneer College, Winslow Center Library, Winslow AZ. 602-289-5082

Rothlisberg, Allen P, *Librn,* Holbrook Hospital, Professional Library, Holbrook AZ. 602-524-3913

Rothlisberg, Allen P, *Coordr,* Northland Pioneer College, Dept of Library Science, AZ. 602-524-6111, Ext 234 or 243

Rothlisberg, Allen P, *Librn,* Saint George's Episcopal Mission Library, Holbrook AZ. 602-524-2361

Rothman, Mrs E, *Librn,* Stone & Webster Engineering Library, New York NY. 212-760-2000

Rothrock, Ilse S, *Librn,* Kimbell Art Museum Library, Fort Worth TX. 817-332-8451

Rothschild, Evelyn, *YA,* Garden City Public Library, Garden City NY. 516-742-8405

Rothschild, Nelsie, *Cat,* Guilford College Library, Greensboro NC. 919-292-5511, Ext 250

Rothschild, Sieglinde H, *Chief Librn,* New York Law Institute, New York NY. 212-732-8720

Rothsvein, Jannice, *Prof,* University of British Columbia, School of Librarianship, BC. 604-228-2404

Rothwell, A, *Chairman,* Grace Hospital Library, Calgary AB. 403-284-1141

Rotkowicz, Renata, *Dir of Libr Pub Servs & Coll Develop,* Washington University Libraries, Saint Louis MO. 314-889-5400

Rotman, Elaine C, *Librn,* Hospital Association of New York State, Lillian R Hayt Memorial Library, Albany NY. 518-458-7940, Ext 560

Rotman, Laurie, *Asst Librn,* Charles Stark Draper Laboratory Inc, Technical Information Center, Cambridge MA. 617-258-3555

Rotolo, Mary, *Dir Libr Serv,* Saint Charles Hospital Library, Port Jefferson NY. 516-473-2800, Ext 147

Rotondi, Linda, *Librn,* Lahey Clinic Foundation, Medical Library, Boston MA. 617-262-4900, Ext 322

Rott, Carol Ann, *Ref Coord,* Tucson Public Library, Tucson AZ. 602-791-4391

Rotter, Harriet, *Librn,* District of Columbia Superior Court Judges Library, Washington DC. 202-727-1435

Rotto, Luther, *AV,* Great River Regional Library, Saint Cloud MN. 612-251-7282

Rottsolk, Katherine, *ILL,* Saint Olaf College, Rolvaag Memorial Library, Northfield MN. 507-663-2222

Rottsolk, Sue, *Librn,* First National Bank of Oregon Library, Portland OR. 503-225-3725

Rotz, Barbara, *Cat,* Wilson College, John Stewart Memorial Library, Chambersburg PA. 717-264-4141, Ext 344

Rouch, Marjory, *Librn,* Logansport-Cass County Public Library (Twelve-Mile Librn), Galveston IN. 219-699-6170

Rough, Allan, *Media,* Adelphi University Library, Garden City NY. 516-294-8700

Roullard, June, *Med Librn & AV,* Veterans Administration, Medical & Regional Office Center Library Service, Augusta ME. 207-623-8411, Ext 275, 504

Roulston, Mrs P, *Librn,* Norman MacKenzie Art Gallery Library, Regina SK. 306-352-5801

Roulston, W, *Librn,* University of Toronto Libraries (Industrial Relations Centre for Jean & Dorothy Newman), Toronto ON. 416-978-2928

Roumfort, Susan B, *Law & Ref Bur Head,* New Jersey State Library, Trenton NJ. 609-292-6200

Roundtree, Elizabeth, *Tech Servs & Processing Ctr,* Louisiana State Library, Baton Rouge LA. 504-342-4922

Roundtree, Nell, *Librn,* Hugo - Choctaw County Library, Hugo OK. 405-326-5591

Rountree, Elizabeth, *Asst Dir,* New Orleans Public Library, Simon Heinsheim & Fisk Libraries, New Orleans LA. 504-586-4905

Rountree, Louise M, *Librn, Rare Bks & Spec Coll,* Livingstone College, Andrew Carnegie Library, Salisbury NC. 704-633-7960, Ext 61 & 62

Rountree, Martha E, *Chief Librn,* McNeil Laboratories, Inc Library, Fort Washington PA. 215-628-5000

Rourke, Cindy, *Ext Librn for Educ & Consult,* Mid-Eastern Regional Medical Library Service, PA. 215-561-6050

Rourke, Doris Ann, *Tech Serv,* Western Connecticut State College, Ruth A Haas Library, Danbury CT. 203-797-4053

Rouse, David, *Bus,* Chicago Public Library (Business, Science & Technology Div), Chicago IL. 312-269-2814, 269-2865

Rouse, Hazel, *Tech Serv,* Corning Public Library, Corning NY. 607-936-3713

Rouse, Jean, *Media & Cat,* Louisiana State University Medical Center Library, New Orleans LA. 504-568-6100

Rouse, Jeffrey P, *Librn,* Westmoreland County Museum of Art, Reference Library, Greensburg PA. 412-837-1500

Rouse, Joan, *Librn,* Birmingham News, Reference Library, Birmingham AL. 205-325-2408

Rouse, John, *Librn,* Wichita Art Association, Inc, Maude Gowan Schollenberger Memorial Library, Wichita KS. 316-686-6687

Rouse, Kendall, *Librn,* University of Wisconsin-Madison (Chemistry Library), Madison WI. 608-262-3521

Rouse, Madge, *Librn,* Coastal Plain Regional Library (Victoria Evans Memorial), Ashburn GA. 912-567-4027

Rouse, Margaret, *Ref,* Gadsden-Etowah County Library, Gadsden Public Library, Gadsden AL. 205-547-1611

Rouse, Michael, *Tech Serv, Cat & On-Line Servs,* Southwest Wisconsin Library System, Fennimore WI. 608-822-3393

Rouse, Roscoe, *Dir,* Oklahoma State University Library, Stillwater OK. 405-624-6313

Rouse, W F, *Superintendent,* Florida Department of Corrections, Lake Correctional Institution Library, Clermont FL. 904-394-6146, Ext 54

Rousek, Sister Marie, *Dir,* College of Saint Elizabeth, Mahoney Library, Convent Station NJ. 201-539-1600, Ext 365

Roush, Arlene, *Librn,* Colony City Library, Colony KS. 316-832-3330

Roush, Dona, *Assoc Dir,* Texas Tech University Regional Academic Health Center Library, El Paso TX. 915-533-3020

Roush, Hettie A, *Librn,* Hamlin-Lincoln County Public Library, Hamlin WV. 304-824-5481

Roush, Russell J, *Libr Consult,* Pataskala Public Library, Pataskala OH. 614-927-9986

Rousseau, Angeline M, *Librn,* Livonia Public Library (Alfred Noble Branch), Livonia MI. 313-421-6600

Routhier, Josephine R, *Admin Libr,* United States Navy (Naval Air Station Library, North Island), San Diego CA. 714-437-7041

Routt, Beverly, *Librn,* Filer Public Library, Filer ID. 208-326-4143

Roux, Helen, *Dir,* Tri-County Library Consortium, PA. 412-658-6659

Roux, Helen M, *Dir,* New Castle Public Library, New Castle PA. 412-658-6659

Roux, Monique, *Librn,* Bibliotheque Municipale, Cap-de-la-Madeleine PQ. 819-375-1666

Roux, Yvonne, *Ch,* Franklin Lakes Free Public Library, Franklin Lakes NJ. 201-891-2224

Rouzie, Katherine W, *Librn,* Emanuel Hospital Library, Portland OR. 503-280-3558

Rovenger, Judith, *Ch,* Englewood Library, Englewood NJ. 201-568-2215

Rovira, Anna, *Dir,* LaSalle Municipal Library, Bibliotheque Municipale La Salle, La Salle PQ. 514-366-2582

Rowan, Christine, *Librn,* Wellesley Free Library (Wellesley Hills Branch), Wellesley Hills MA. 617-237-0381

Rowan, M, *Mag & Newsp,* Oakland Public Library, Oakland CA. 415-273-3281

Rowan, Mavis, *Librn,* Osceola Public Library, Osceola NE. 402-747-4301

Rowden, Virginia, *Librn,* Gladbrook Library, Gladbrook IA. 515-473-2582

Rowe, Allen, *Adminr,* Edmonton Public Library, Edmonton AB. 403-423-2331

Rowe, Barbara, *YA,* Burlingame Public Library, Burlingame CA. 415-344-7107

Rowe, Bettie, *Librn,* Cheaha Regional Library, Anniston AL. 205-238-1581

Rowe, Beverly, *Librn,* Mesa County Public Library (DeBeque Branch), DeBeque CO. 303-243-4442

Rowe, Dorothy, *Librn,* Hammond Public Library (Harrison Park), Hammond IN. 219-931-5100

Rowe, Dorothy B, *Librn,* Central DuPage Hospital, Medical Library, Winfield IL. 312-682-1600, Ext 535

Rowe, H Edward, *Admin Dir,* American Security Council Education Foundation, Boston VA. 703-825-7177

Rowe, Harold E, *Librn,* San Francisco Law Library, San Francisco CA. 415-558-4627

Rowe, Helen, *Cat,* University of Denver, Penrose Library, Denver CO. 303-753-2007

Rowe, J E, *Librn,* Canada Department of Justice Library, Ottawa ON. 613-995-0144

Rowe, Kathleen M, *Librn,* Gray & Rogers, Inc, Advertising Research Library, Philadelphia PA. 215-864-6800

Rowe, Kenneth, *Methodist Librn,* Drew University, Rose Memorial Library, Madison NJ. 201-377-3000, Ext 469

Rowe, Linda, *Asst Librn,* Saint John's Hospital & Health Center, Medical Library, Santa Monica CA. 213-829-8494

Rowe, Linda J, *Librn,* Saint Anthony's Hospital, Inc Library, Saint Petersburg FL. 813-823-5111

Rowe, Marianna H, *Ch,* Portland Public Library, Baxter Library, Portland ME. 207-773-4761

Rowe, Mary, *Head Tech Processing & Exten Serv,* Central Florida Regional Library, Ocala Public Library, Ocala FL. 904-629-8551

Rowe, Mary Lou, *Librn,* Marin County Free Library, San Rafael CA. 415-479-1100, Ext 2577

Rowe, Terry, *Librn,* Flint River Regional Library (George C Alexander Public), McDonough GA. 404-957-5656

Rowe, Violet, *Dir,* Glenshaw Public Library, Glenshaw PA. 412-487-2121

Rowell, Jo Ann, *Soc Sci,* Austin Public Library, Austin TX. 512-472-5433

Rowell, John A, *Prof,* Case Western Reserve University, School of Library Science, OH. 216-368-3500

Rowell, Kathryn H, *Asst Dir,* Jefferson County Library, Louisville KY. 912-625-3751

Rowell, Regina A, *On-Line Servs & Bibliog Instr,* Veterans Administration, Audie L Murphy Veterans Administration Hospital, San Antonio TX. 512-696-9660, Ext 511

Rowell, William, *Librn,* Resident Alcohol Treatment Facility Library, Windsor VT. 802-674-6717

Rowland, A Ray, *Librn,* Augusta College, Reese Library, Augusta GA. 404-828-4566, 828-4066

Rowland, A Ray, *Curator,* Richmond County Historical Society Library, Augusta GA. 404-828-4566, 828-4801

Rowland, Clarissa, *ILL & Ref,* Randolph-Macon Woman's College, Lipscomb Library, Lynchburg VA. 804-846-7392, Ext 242

Rowland, Donald C, *Dir,* Black Hawk College, Learning Resource Center, Moline IL. 309-796-1311, Ext 344

Rowland, Eileen, *Chief Librn,* John Jay College of Criminal Justice Library, New York NY. 212-489-5169

Rowland, Elizabeth, *Chief Librn,* Richmond Hill Public Library, Richmond Hill ON. 416-884-9288

Rowland, Gerry, *Dir,* Shenandoah Public Library, Shenandoah IA. 712-246-2315

Rowland, Helen M, *In Charge,* Association of American Railroads, Economics & Finance Dept Library, Washington DC. 202-293-4068

Rowland, Marie, *ILL,* New Britain Public Library, New Britain CT. 203-224-3155

Rowland, Ruth, *Librn,* Northwest Regional Library (Vernon Branch), Vernon AL. 205-695-7718

Rowland, Virginia, *Asst Dir,* Clearwater Memorial Public Library, Orofino Library, Orofino ID. 208-476-3411

Rowland, Virginia, *Librn,* Filger Library, Minonk IL. 309-432-2929

Rowlett, Bethenia, *Ch,* Jackson-Madison County Library, Jackson TN. 901-423-0225

Rowlett, Brenda, *Dir,* Purchase Regional Library, Murray KY. 502-753-6461

Rowley, Ed, *Asst Librn,* New Bern-Craven County Public Library, New Bern NC. 919-638-2127

Rowley, Gordon, *Librn,* Northern Illinois University (Audio-Score), De Kalb IL. 815-753-1426

Rowley, Gordon, *Art & Music,* Northern Illinois University, Founders Memorial Library, De Kalb IL. 815-753-1094

Rowley, H Jean, *Cat,* University of Wisconsin-Madison, Memorial Library, Madison WI. 608-262-3521

Rowley, Judy, *Librn,* Wayland Free Library, Gunlocke Memorial Library, Wayland NY. 716-728-5380

Rowley, Lovina, *Librn,* United States Army (Recreation Services Library), El Paso TX. 915-569-2379

Rowley, Norma P, *Circ,* Nashua Public Library, Nashua NH. 603-883-4141, 883-4142

Rowley, Sally, *Info Servs Coordr,* University of Pittsburgh, Hillman Library, Pittsburgh PA. 412-624-4400

Rowley, Virginia L, *Dir,* Santa Barbara City College Library, Santa Barbara CA. 805-965-0581, Ext 242

Rowling, James, *Tech Serv,* Kearney State College, Calvin T Ryan Library, Kearney NE. 308-236-4218

Rowswell, Ron, *Tech Serv & Systs Develop,* Grant MacEwan Community College, Learning Resource Centres, Edmonton AB. 403-484-7791

Rowton, Leah, *Librn,* Chicago Public Library (Hild Regional), Chicago IL. 312-728-8652

Roy, Barbara, *Librn,* Broward County Division of Libraries (Fort Lauderdale Branch), Fort Lauderdale FL. 305-765-4263

Roy, Camille, *On-Line Servs & Bibliog Instr,* Seminaire Saint-Augustin Bibliotheque, Cap-Rouge PQ. 418-872-0954

Roy, Donald E, *Dir,* New York Medical College, Westchester Medical Center Library, Valhalla NY. 914-347-5237

Roy, E Irene, *Librn,* Law Reform Commission of Canada Library, Ottawa ON. 613-995-8648

Roy, Irene, *Ref,* Waterville Public Library, Waterville ME. 207-872-5433

Roy, Jacques, *Prof,* College de Jonquiere, Techniques de la Documentation, PQ. 418-547-2191, Ext 270

Roy, Janet, *Librn,* Douglas County Library System (Myrtle Creek Public), Myrtle Creek OR. 503-863-5945

Roy, Jean-Luc, *Librn,* Centre D'animation De Development Et De Recherche En Education Bibliotheque, Montreal PQ. 514-381-8891

Roy, Lise, *Coordr,* CEGEP Francois-Xavier Garneau, Techniques de la documentation, PQ. 418-688-8310, Ext 290

Roy, Lise, *Librn,* Quebec Ministere De L'agriculture, Bibliotheque Agricole, Quebec PQ. 418-643-2428

Roy, Mary L, *Librn,* Northwestern University Library (Transportation), Evanston IL. 312-492-5273

Roy, R, *Tech Serv,* British Columbia Institute of Technology Library, Burnaby BC. 604-434-5734, Ext 360

Roy, Saktidas, *Dir,* State University of New York at Buffalo, University Libraries, Buffalo NY. 716-636-2965

Roy, Shannon, *Coordr,* Southwest Missouri Library Network, MO. 417-869-4621

Roy, Sister Bibiane, *Coordr,* Diocese of Tucson Resource Center, Regina Cleri Library, Tucson AZ. 602-886-5201

Roy, Sister Mary, *Librn,* Annhurst College Library, South Woodstock CT. 203-928-7773

Royal, Henrietta, *Genealogy,* Statesboro Regional Library, Statesboro GA. 912-764-7573

Royal, Henrietta, *Ad & Circ,* Statesboro Regional Library, Statesboro GA. 912-764-7573

Royal, Lizzie, *Br Coordr,* High Point Public Library, High Point NC. 919-885-8411

Royal, Selvin W, *Dept Chmn,* University of Central Arkansas, Dept of Educational Media & Library Science, AR. 501-329-2931, Ext 255

Royce, Diana, *Librn,* Stowe-Day Library, Hartford CT. 203-522-9258

Royce, Robert H, *Librn,* World University Library, Hato PR. 809-765-4646, Ext 224

Roye, Josephine S, *Ref,* York College of Pennsylvania Library, York PA. 717-846-7788, Ext 353

Royer, Robert, *Asst Librn,* Tunxis Community College Library, Farmington CT. 203-677-7701, Ext 44

Royer, Susan B, *Coordr,* North Alabama Cooperative Library System, Huntsville AL. 205-534-0735

Roylance, Dale, *Curator,* Princeton University Library (Graphic Arts Collection), Princeton NJ. 609-452-3180

Royle, Mary Anne, *Librn,* Washoe County Law Library, Reno NV. 702-785-4188

Roysdon, Christina L, *Ref,* Lehigh University Libraries, Bethlehem PA. 861-3026 (Dir), 861-3050 (Ref), 861-3030 (Circ), 861-3055 (ILL)

Royster, Judith, *Coordr,* Madison Area Library Council, (MALC), WI. 608-221-9231

Rozenberg, Sandra, *YA,* Bryant Library, Roslyn NY. 516-621-2240

Rozie, Betty, *Ch,* Beaver Area Memorial Library, Beaver PA. 412-775-1132

Roziewski, Walter, *Borough Coordr Manhattan,* New York Public Library (The Branch Libraries), New York NY. 212-790-6262

Rozman, Ruth, *AV,* George Amos Memorial Library, Campbell County Library, Gillette WY. 307-682-3223

Rozmyslowska, Eva, *Cat,* Kaye, Scholer, Fierman, Hays & Handler Law Library, New York NY. 212-759-8400, Ext 312
Rozniatowski, David W, *Librn,* Clara Lander Library, Winnipeg MB. 204-338-2028
Ruan, Mrs J S, *Dir,* City of Brampton Public Library & Art Gallery, Brampton ON. 416-453-2444
Ruane, Sister Claire Imelda, *Tech Serv,* Saint Joseph's College (Suffolk Campus), Patchogue NY. 516-231-3054
Rubaloff, Marijoy, *Librn,* Eugene Register-Guard Library, Eugene OR. 503-485-1234, Ext 339
Rubenfeld, Majory, *Ch,* Alhambra Public Library, Alhambra CA. 213-570-5008
Rubens, Jane C, *Librn,* Coudert Brothers Library, New York NY. 212-880-4796
Rubenstein, Nancy, *ILL & Ref,* Heidelberg College, Beeghly Library, Tiffin OH. 419-448-2104
Rubercheck, Alice, *Tech Serv,* Veterans Administration, Medical Library, Wilmington DE. 302-994-2511, Ext 354, 355
Ruberson, Melissa, *Asst Librn,* Independence Community Junior College Library, Independence KS. 316-331-4100, Ext 55
Rubery, Mrs Paul T, *Dir,* Palmyra King's Daughters' Free Library Inc, Palmyra NY. 315-597-5276
Rubin, Alice, *Librn,* Jewish Community Center of Greater Rochester, Feinbloom Library, Rochester NY. 716-461-2000
Rubin, Audrey, *Asst Dir, On-Line Servs & Bibliog Instr,* Fairleigh Dickinson University, Weiner Library, Teaneck NJ. 201-836-6300, Ext 265
Rubin, Dorothy, *Librn,* Temple Emanu El Library (Budner Young People's Books), Dallas TX. 214-368-3613, Ext 411
Rubin, Elizabeth, *Ad,* Newton Free Library, Newton MA. 617-527-7700, Ext 24
Rubin, George, *Research Mgr,* Welch Foods, Inc, Science & Technology Library, Westfield NY. 716-326-3131
Rubin, Helen, *Ref,* Fashion Institute of Technology, Library-Media Services Dept, New York NY. 212-760-7695
Rubin, Judith, *Chief Librn,* Canada Labour Relations Board Library, Ottawa ON. 613-995-0895
Rubin, June, *Media,* Bureau of Jewish Education, Jewish Community Library, San Francisco CA. 415-751-6983, Ext 12
Rubin, Maida, *Tech Serv & Cat,* Public Library of the City of Somerville, Somerville MA. 617-623-5000
Rubin, Nan, *Librn,* Temple Sinai Library, Rochester NY. 716-381-6890
Rubin, Stephanie, *Ch,* Sayville Library, Sayville NY. 516-589-4440
Rubin, Susan, *Librn,* Broward County Division of Libraries (Pembroke Pines Branch), Pembroke Pines FL. 305-989-8935
Rubin-Cohen, Ira M, *Ref,* Hebrew Union College-Jewish Institute of Religion, The Klau Library, New York NY. 212-674-5300
Rubinstein, Edith, *Dir,* Peninsula Hospital Center, Medical Library, Far Rockaway NY. 212-945-7100
Rubinstein, Judah, *Librn,* Jewish Community Federation Library, Cleveland OH. 216-566-9200, Ext 218
Rubinton, Phyllis, *Librn,* New York Hospital-Cornell Medical Center Libraries (Psychiatric Clinic Library), New York NY. 212-472-6442
Rubis, James, *Dir,* Fairfield Public Library, Fairfield IA. 515-472-6551
Rubis, Mrs E, *Shuttle Librn,* NASA, John F Kennedy Space Center Library, Kennedy Space Center FL. 305-867-3600, 3615
Ruble, Dorothy A, *Librn,* Greene Township Library, Viola IL. 309-596-2620
Ruble, Myrtle, *Per,* Lake Erie College, James F Lincoln Learning Resource Center, Painesville OH. 216-352-3361, Ext 280
Rubush, Sarah, *Librn,* Roanoke City Public Library System (Williamson Road), Roanoke VA. 703-981-2340
Ruby, Denise, *Circ,* Nathaniel Hawthorne College, Silver Library, Antrim NH. 603-588-6341, Ext 235
Ruby, Florence V, *Librn,* Sacred Heart Hospital, Medical Library, Pensacola FL. 904-476-7851, Ext 4222

Ruccio, Nancy, *Coordr,* Westmoreland County Library Board, Greensburg PA. 412-836-3414
Ruchti, G Deanne, *In Charge,* Union Carbide Corp, Crystal Products Dept, Electronics Library, San Diego CA. 714-279-4500, Ext 51
Rucker, Jessie, *Asst Librn,* Rolla Free Public Library, Rolla MO. 314-364-2604
Rucker, Laura A, *Pub Servs,* University of Oklahoma Health Sciences Center Library, Oklahoma City OK. 405-271-2285
Rucker, Mildred, *Tech Serv & Cat,* Dayton & Montgomery County Public Library, Dayton OH. 513-224-1651
Rucker, Ronald, *Dir,* Middlebury College, Egbert Starr Library, Middlebury VT. 802-388-7621
Ruckert, Ilse Maria, *Librn,* IBM Corp (Legal Library), Armonk NY. 914-765-4862
Ruckman, Stanley N, *Dir & Ref,* Linn-Benton Community College, Learning Resource Center, Albany OR. 503-928-2361, Ext 330
Rudberg, Peggy, *Slide Librn,* Minneapolis College of Art & Design Library, Minneapolis MN. 612-870-3291
Rudd, Amanda S, *Deputy Commissioner for The Chicago Libr Syst,* Chicago Public Library, Chicago IL. 312-269-2900
Rudd, Nancy, *Tech Serv,* Hyconeechee Regional Library, Yanceyville NC. 919-694-6241
Rudder, Jane, *Librn,* Wymore Public Library, Wymore NE. 402-645-3787
Ruddick, Brian P, *Asst Dir Tech Serv,* Cleveland State University Libraries, Cleveland OH. 216-687-2486
Ruddick, Patsy, *Dir,* Garden City Community College Library, Garden City KS. 316-276-7611, Ext 55
Ruddy, JoAnne, *Librn,* United States Army (Tobyhanna Army Depot Post Library), Tobyhanna PA. 717-894-8301
Ruddy, Mary Karen, *Acq,* Amarillo College, Learning Resource Center, Amarillo TX. 806-376-5111, Ext 2420
Ruddy, Sister Margaret, *Per,* Cardinal Stritch College Library, Milwaukee WI. 414-352-5400, Ext 356
Ruddy, Thomas, *Circ,* King's College, D Leonard Corgan Library, Wilkes-Barre PA. 717-824-9931, Ext 245
Rude, Alice, *Librn,* Muncie-Center Township Public Library (John F Kennedy), Muncie IN. 317-289-3444
Rude, Nancy, *Supvr,* Syracuse University Libraries (Mathematics), Syracuse NY. 315-423-2092
Rudeen, Jacqueline, *Chief, Tech Servs,* Washington State Library, Olympia WA. 206-753-5592
Rudin, P, *Librn,* Methodist Hospital, Medical Library, Saint Louis Park MN. 932-5451 Ext 316
Rudio, Barbara, *Br Coordr, Bkmobile Coordr & Bibliog Instr,* City-County Library of Missoula, Missoula MT. 406-728-5900
Rudio, Barbara, *Librn, On-Line Servs & Bibliog Instr,* Tamarack Federation of Libraries, Missoula MT. 406-728-5900
Rudisill, Richard, *Photog History,* Museum of New Mexico (Photographic Archives Library), Santa Fe NM. 505-827-2559
Rudisill, Theresa, *Asst Librn,* Woden Public Library, Woden IA. 515-926-5716
Rudman, Frances, *ILL,* University of California, San Diego, University Libraries, La Jolla CA. 714-452-3336
Rudner, Charlotte P, *Librn,* Chadbourne, Parke, Whiteside & Wolff Library, New York NY. 212-344-8900
Rudnik, Sister Mary Chrysantha, *Chmn,* Felician College, Dept of Library Science, IL. 312-539-2328
Rudnik, Sister Mary Chrysantha, *Chief Librn & On-Line Servs,* Felician College Library, Chicago IL. 312-539-2328
Rudolph, Gerald A, *Dean,* University of Nebraska-Lincoln, University Libraries, Lincoln NE. 402-472-2526
Rudolph, Mary Jane, *Acq,* City Colleges of Chicago, Kennedy-King College Library, Chicago IL. 312-962-3262
Rudser, Ronald J, *Dept Head,* Minot State College, Library Science Program, ND. 701-857-3200
Rudser, Ronald J, *AV & Media,* Minot State College, Memorial Library, Minot ND. 701-857-3200

Rudy, Christine R, *Librn,* Peavey Company, Corporate Information Center, Minneapolis MN. 612-370-7506
Rudy, Wilfrid, *Dir,* Thorold Public Library, Thorold ON. 416-227-2581
Rudzik, Rita, *Librn,* Taylor Alexander Papp Public Library, Taylor MI. 313-291-1171
Rue, Fay, *Asst Librn,* Aultman Hospital, School of Nursing Library, Canton OH. 216-452-9911, Ext 344
Rue, Nancy, *Per,* Ohio University, Vernon R Alden Library, Athens OH. 614-594-5228
Rueber, Mrs Ted, *Librn,* Westgate Public Library, Westgate IA. 515-226-5351
Rueby, Cheryl, *Cat & Ser,* Wright State University Library (Fordham Library, Cox Heart Institute Library & Fels Research Institute Library), Dayton OH. 513-873-2266
Ruef, Joseph A, *Dir,* Windsor Public Library, Windsor CT. 203-688-6433
Ruege, Ruth, *Exten Servs,* Milwaukee Public Library, Milwaukee WI. 414-278-3000
Ruehl, Jane Anneken, *Asst Ed,* Nutrition Today, Inc Library, Annapolis MD. 301-267-8616
Rueter, Sarah L, *Ch,* Wilmington Memorial Library, Wilmington MA. 617-658-2967
Rufe, Charles P, *Asst Librn,* Waynesboro Public Library, Waynesboro VA. 703-942-6173
Ruff, Gloria, *ILL,* University of Maryland at Baltimore (Health Sciences Library), Baltimore MD. 301-528-7545
Ruff, Margaret, *In Charge,* Eureka-Humboldt County Library (Blue Lake), Blue Lake CA. 707-445-7284, 445-7513
Ruffin, Elizabeth, *ILL,* Enoch Pratt Free Library, Baltimore MD. 301-396-5430, 396-5395
Ruffin, Elizabeth, *Head,* Enoch Pratt Free Library (Maryland Interlibrary Loan Organization (MILO)), Baltimore MD. 301-396-5430, 396-5395
Ruffin, Margaret, *Librn,* United States Navy (Atlantic General Library), Albany GA. 912-439-5242
Ruffner, Jim, *Tech Serv,* Wayne State University Libraries (Science Library), Detroit MI. 313-577-4066
Rufts, Leslie, *Ad & Ref,* Bossier Parish Public Library, Benton LA. 318-965-2751
Rufty, Geraleen, *Librn,* Public Library of Charlotte & Mecklenburg County, Inc (Davidson Branch), Davidson NC. 704-892-8557
Rugelis, Rasma, *Asst Dir Tech Servs,* York University, Scott Library, Downsview ON. 416-667-2235
Rugen, Frances J, *Dir,* United States Navy (Civil Engineering Laboratory), Port Hueneme CA. 805-982-4252, 982-4788
Rugen, Paul, *Keeper of Mss,* New York Public Library (Manuscripts & Archives), New York NY. 212-790-6338
Rugeoni, Carla, *Librn,* Brown & Caldwell Library, Walnut Creek CA. 415-937-9010
Rugg, Betty, *Librn,* Umatilla County Library (Pilot Rock Branch), Pilot Rock OR. 503-276-1881
Rugg, Jennifer, *Ref,* University of Pittsburgh (Western Psychiatric Institute & Clinic Library), Pittsburgh PA. 412-624-2378
Rugg, John D, *In Charge,* Licking County Genealogical Society Library, Newark OH. 614-345-3571
Rugg, John D, *In Charge,* Ohio Genealogical Society Library, Mansfield OH. 419-522-9077
Rugg, Patricia S, *Ref,* Knoxville-Knox County Public Library, Lawson McGhee Library, Knoxville TN. 615-523-0781
Ruggeri, Cynthia, *Librn,* Saint Louis Public Library (Carondelet), Saint Louis MO. 314-752-9224
Ruggers, Christine, *Hist Coll & Rare Books,* College of Physicians of Philadelphia Library, Philadelphia PA. 215-561-6050
Ruggles, Florence, *Librn,* Annapolis Valley Regional Library Headquarters (Bridgetown Branch), Bridgetown NS. 902-665-2758
Rughe, Colleen, *ILL & Ref,* Adams State College Library, Alamosa CO. 303-589-7781
Ruhl, Taylor, *Circ,* Pacific Union College, W E Nelson Memorial Library, Angwin CA. 707-965-6241
Ruhland, Helen, *Librn,* Jeannette Public Library Association, Jeannette PA. 412-523-5702

Ruhling, Carmel, *Acq,* Brevard Community College, Melbourne Campus Learning Resources Center, Melbourne FL. 305-254-0305, Ext 227, 228

Ruiz, D, *Librn,* Oakland Public Library (Latin American), Oakland CA. 532-7882 & 532-7883

Ruiz, Irene, *Mex-Am Archives,* Kansas City Public Library, Kansas City MO. 816-221-2685

Ruiz, Irene, *Librn,* Kansas City Public Library (West), Kansas City MO. 816-471-1591

Ruiz, Karleen M, *Librn,* Kutztown Public Library, Kutztown PA. 215-683-3460

Ruiz, Oralia, *Asst Librn,* Southwest Research Institute, Thomas Baker Slick Memorial Library, San Antonio TX. 512-684-5111, Ext 2125

RuizdeNieves, Angela M, *Tech Serv & Cat,* University of Puerto Rico, Humacao University College Library, Humacao PR. 809-852-2525, Ext 200

Rukavina, Helen M, *Librn,* South Holland Public Library, South Holland IL. 312-331-5262

Rukuts, Velga B, *Librn,* ICI Americas Inc, Atlas Library, Wilmington DE. 302-575-8232

Rule, Judy K, *Asst Dir & Bkmobile Coordr,* Cabell County Public Library, Western Counties Regional Library System, Huntington WV. 304-523-9451

Rule, Margaret, *Regional Servs Coordr,* Lake Erie Regional Library System, London ON. 519-453-9100

Rule, Virginia, *Dir,* Ormsby Public Library, Carson City NV. 702-882-5665

Rule, II, J Robert, *Dir,* Morristown-Hamblen Library, Morristown TN. 615-586-6410

Rulkowski, Carolyn, *Librn,* Valley New Dispatch, George D Stuart Research Library, Tarentum PA. 412-224-4321

Rulli, Linda, *YA & Circ,* Albany County Public Library, Laramie WY. 307-745-3365

Rumack, Shirley, *Librn,* Congregation Emanuel B'Ne Jeshurun, Rabbi Dudley Weinburg Library, Milwaukee WI. 414-964-4100

Rumbaugh, Maxine, *Librn,* Eccles-Lesher Memorial Library, Rimersburg PA. 814-473-3800

Rumbaugh, Zona, *Admin Serv,* Jefferson County Public Library, Lakewood CO. 303-238-8411

Rumery, Helen, *Librn,* Los Angeles Public Library System (San Pedro Branch), San Pedro CA. 213-548-7521

Rumfield, Sally, *Librn,* Sunfield District Library, Sunfield MI. 517-566-8065

Rumics, Elizabeth, *ILL & Ref,* Upsala College Library, East Orange NJ. 201-266-7295

Rummel, Georganne, *Acq,* Tennessee Technological University, Jere Whitson Memorial Library, Cookeville TN. 615-528-3408

Rummel, Rosa M, *Librn,* Rosemount Inc, Technical Library, Eden Prairie MN. 612-941-5560, Ext 337

Rump, Marje, *Spec Asst to County Librn,* Kern County Library, Bakersfield CA. 805-861-2130

Rumpf, Barbara, *Ref,* Renton Public Library, Renton WA. 206-235-2610

Rumrill, Alan, *Librn,* Davis Memorial Library, Stoddard NH. 603-847-3403

Rumsa, Phyllis, *Ch,* Algonquin Area Public Library District, Algonquin IL. 312-658-4343

Rumsby, K, *Media,* Malaspina College, Learning Resources Center, Nanaimo BC. 604-753-3245

Rumsey, Gary L, *Dir,* United States Fish & Wildlife Service, Tunison Laboratory of Fish Nutrition Library, Cortland NY. 607-753-9391

Runblad, Christine, *Ch,* New Berlin Public Library, New Berlin WI. 414-786-2990

Runft, Dorothy, *Librn,* Sheffield Public Library, Sheffield IL. 815-454-2628

Runge, DeLyle P, *Dir,* Saint Petersburg Public Library, Saint Petersburg FL. 813-893-7724

Runge, Kay K, *Dir,* Scott County Library, Eldridge IA. 319-285-4794

Runion, Ruth, *ILL,* Pennsylvania State University, Capitol Campus Heindel Library, Middletown PA. 717-787-7771

Runkel, Karen, *Ch,* North Manchester Public Library, North Manchester IN. 219-982-4773

Runkle, Ellen J, *Librn,* Armstrong Cork Company (Product Styling & Design Library), Lancaster PA. 717-397-0611

Runkle, Martin, *Tech Serv,* University of Chicago, Joseph Regenstein Library, Chicago IL. 312-753-2977

Runnells, Ruth, *Librn,* People's Bible College Library, Colorado Springs CO. 303-632-0201

Runser, Robert E, *Bibliogr,* Michigan State University Library, East Lansing MI. 517-355-2344

Runton, Gloria, *Acq,* University of Tampa, Merl Kelce Library, Tampa FL. 813-253-8861, Ext 385

Runyan, Marjorie, *Dir,* Aurora Public Library, Aurora IN. 812-926-0646

Runyon, Cynthia, *Librn,* Glenn Memorial Church Library, Atlanta GA. 404-634-4375

Runyon, Robert S, *Dir,* University of Nebraska at Omaha, University Library, Omaha NE. 402-554-2361

Ruocco, Patricia, *Ref,* Westmont Public Library, Westmont IL. 312-969-5625

Ruotsala, Georgianna, *Librn,* United States Air Force (K I Sawyer Air Force Base Library), K I Sawyer AFB MI. 906-346-2864

Rupe, Donnie, *Tech Serv,* Wichita Public Library, Wichita KS. 316-262-0611

Rupert, Elizabeth A, *Dean,* Clarion State College, School of Library Science, PA. 814-226-2271

Rupert, Mary Ann, *ILL & Ref,* Howe Library, Hanover NH. 603-643-4120

Rupp, Patricia A, *Librn,* Hudson Public Library, Hudson MI. 517-448-3801

Ruppert, Ann, *Circ,* Point Loma College, Ryan Library, San Diego CA. 714-222-6474, Ext 355, 338

Ruppert, Gerda, *Ch,* Nampa Public Library, Nampa ID. 208-466-6121

Ruppert, Mary, *Admin Assts,* Southeast Kansas Library System, Iola KS. 316-365-3833

Rupprecht, Leslie P, *Librn,* Newark Business Library, Newark NJ. 201-733-7849

Rupprecht, T A, *Supvr,* Bendix Corp, Engineering Development Center Library, Southfield MI. 313-827-5620

Rups, Anna W, *Falls Church Coll,* Mary Riley Styles Public Library, Falls Church VA. 703-241-5030

Rusche, Linda, *Bkmobile Coordr,* Madison Public Library, Madison WI. 608-266-6300

Ruschin, Siegfried, *Coll Development,* Linda Hall Library, Kansas City MO. 816-363-4600

Ruschival, Adam, *Dir,* Kentucky Regional Library for the Blind & Physically Handicapped, Frankfort KY. 502-564-5532

Rusczek, Linda, *Ad,* Russell Public Library, Middletown CT. 203-347-2528

Ruse, Mrs Leroy, *Asst Librn,* Mary Cotton Public Library, Sabetha KS. 913-284-3160

Rush, Betsy, *Ch,* Ossining Public Library, Ossining NY. 941-2416; 941-9174

Rush, Brother J Richard, *Librn,* Saint Charles Borromeo Seminary Library, Romeoville IL. 815-838-8100

Rush, David E, *Assoc Librn,* Massachusetts College of Pharmacy & Allied Health Sciences, Sheppard Library, Boston MA. 732-2810 (Gen info), 732-2813 (Ref)

Rush, Diana, *Dir,* Millinocket Memorial Library, Millinocket ME. 207-723-9610

Rush, Elizabeth, *Librn,* Summit County Library, Frisco CO. 303-668-5555

Rush, Gearlene, *Asst Dir,* Hockley County Memorial Library, Levelland TX. 806-894-6750

Rush, Janis, *Tech Serv,* Sherman Public Library, Sherman TX. 214-892-4545, Ext 242

Rush, John, *Tech Serv,* Bob Jones University, J S Mack Library, Greenville SC. 803-242-5100, Ext 296

Rush, Mary, *ILL,* Warren County Library, Belvidere NJ. 201-475-5361, Ext 114

Rush, Pamela K, *Asst Librn,* Somerset Community College Library, Somerset KY. 606-678-8174, Ext 238

Rush, Stephan, *Librn,* Canadian Department of Industry, Trade & Commerce Library, Ottawa ON. 613-995-5771

Rushing, Billie, *Librn,* Greenwood-Leflore Public Library System (Itta Bena Branch), Itta Bena MS. 601-254-7790

Rushing, Darla, *Tech Serv & Cat,* Loyola University Library, Main Library, New Orleans LA. 504-865-3346

Rushing, Mabel, *Librn,* Lincoln County Library, Chandler OK. 405-258-1321

Rushing, Paula, *Librn,* Ferris Public Library, Ferris TX. 214-544-3696

Rusis, Inita, *Librn,* Bucks County Free Library (Lower County Center), Levittown PA. 215-949-2323

Rusk, David, *Librn,* Tulare County Library System (Orosi Branch), Orosi CA. 209-528-4981

Rusk, Mike, *Librn,* Tulsa City-County Library (Nathan Hale), Tulsa OK. 918-836-3578

Rusk, Paul C, *Asst Prof,* Our Lady of the Lake University of San Antonio, Learning Resources Certification, TX. 512-434-6711, Ext 245

Ruske, Martha, *Tech Serv & Cat,* Wells Fargo Bank (Corporate Library), San Francisco CA. 396-3744 or 3745

Ruskell, Jan, *Bibliog Instr,* West Georgia College Library, Carrollton GA. 404-834-1370

Ruskin, Eugene D, *Librn,* Illinois Department of Mental Health & Development Disabilities (Professional Library), Decatur IL. 217-877-3410, Ext 220, 221

Russ, Jon, *Chmn Libr Comt,* Portsmouth Athenaeum, Inc Library, Portsmouth NH. 603-964-8284, 436-5723

Russ, Narine, *Librn,* Southport-Brunswick County Library (Leland Branch), Leland NC. 919-371-2978

Russel, Ruth, *Librn,* Contra Costa County Library (Central Library), Pleasant Hill CA. 415-935-6420

Russell, A, *Librn,* Wollaston & Limerick Public Library, Coe Hill ON. 613-337-5731

Russell, Barbara, *Cat,* Southwestern Baptist Theological Seminary, Fleming Library, Fort Worth TX. 817-923-1921, Ext 277

Russell, Beatrice, *Librn,* Havana Study Club Library, Havana KS. 316-673-4958

Russell, Bernard C, *Spec Coll,* Pfeiffer College, Gustavus Adolphus Pfeiffer Library, Misenheimer NC. 704-463-7343, Ext 278

Russell, Beverly, *Librn,* Seattle Times Library, Seattle WA. 206-464-2111

Russell, Brenda, *Dir,* T L L Temple Memorial Library, Diboll TX. 713-829-5497

Russell, Carol N, *Librn,* State Law Library in Kent County, Dover DE. 302-736-5467

Russell, Charlotte, *Librn,* Texas Forest Service, Texas Forest Products Laboratory Library, Lufkin TX. 713-634-7709

Russell, Christina, *Dir, On-Line Servs & Bibliog Instr,* Community College of Allegheny County, Allegheny Campus Library, Pittsburgh PA. 412-237-2585

Russell, David L, *Assoc Exec Dir,* Capitol Region Library Council, CT. 203-549-0404

Russell, E C, *Asst Dir & Cat,* King's College Library, London ON. 519-433-3491, Ext 44

Russell, Gretchen, *Tech Serv,* Dunedin Public Library, Dunedin FL. 813-733-4115

Russell, Ida, *Libr Tech,* United States Navy (Naval Air Station Library), Beeville TX. 512-354-2706

Russell, J Thomas, *Librn,* National Defense University Library, Washington DC. 202-693-8437

Russell, James, *Assoc Prof,* Purdue University, Dept of Education, Library Media & Instructional Development, IN. 317-749-2902

Russell, James M, *Ad,* Lompoc Public Library, Lompoc CA. 805-736-3477

Russell, Jane, *ILL,* University of New Hampshire, Ezekiel W Dimond Library, Durham NH. 603-862-1540

Russell, Janet, *Libr Sci,* Chicago Public Library (Literature & Philosophy Div), Chicago IL. 312-269-2880

Russell, John, *AV,* Johnson County Community College Library, Overland Park KS. 913-888-8500, Ext 532

Russell, John, *Design Develop Spec,* Mission College, Learning Resource Services, Santa Clara CA. 408-988-2200, Ext 1531

Russell, John S, *City Librn,* Winnipeg Public Library, Winnipeg MB. 204-985-6450

Russell, Judy, *Tech Serv,* Parkersburg Community College, Learning Resources Center, Parkersburg WV. 304-424-8260

Russell, Julia, *YA,* Nassau Library System, Uniondale NY. 516-292-8920

Russell, Julia G, *Librn,* Nassau Library System (Subregional Library for the Blind & Physically Handicapped), Uniondale NY. 516-292-8920, Ext 222

Russell, Keith, *Head Sci & Eng,* University of Arizona Library, Tucson AZ. 602-626-2101

RUSSELL

Russell, Keith W, *Librn,* University of Arizona Library (Science - Engineering), Tucson AZ. 602-626-3706

Russell, Lee G, *Librn,* AVCO Corp, Lycoming Division Library & Information Center, Stratford CT. 203-378-8211

Russell, Leland E, *Dir,* Miracosta College Learning Resource Center, Oceanside CA. 714-757-2121, Ext 250

Russell, Lois B, *Librn,* Norfolk County Law Library, Dedham MA. 617-326-1600, Ext 211

Russell, Lucile, *Outreach,* Albany County Public Library, Laramie WY. 307-745-3365

Russell, Marjorie, *Ch,* Scottsbluff Public Library, Scottsbluff NE. 308-632-4424

Russell, Mary, *Librn,* Timberland Regional Library (Lacey Branch), Lacey WA. 206-491-3860

Russell, Mary Katherine, *Dir,* Washington County Public Library, Abingdon VA. 703-628-2971

Russell, Mary Nelle, *Commun Servs, Br Coordr & Bkmobile Coordr,* Public Library of Anniston & Calhoun County, Liles Memorial Library, Anniston AL. 205-237-8501, Ext 8503

Russell, Mattie, *Mss,* Duke University, William R Perkins Library, Durham NC. 684-2034 (Main).

Russell, Maurice T, *Assoc Prof,* University of North Dakota, Dept of Library Science & Audiovisual Instruction, ND. 701-777-3003

Russell, May Hill, *Commun Servs,* Monroe County Public Library, Key West FL. 305-294-7100

Russell, Mrs Harold, *Librn,* Chesterfield Public Library, Chesterfield MA. 413-296-4735

Russell, Myrtle L, *Librn,* Electra Public Library, Electra TX. 817-495-2208

Russell, Nancy, *Bibliog Instr,* Western Kentucky University, Helm-Cravens Library, Bowling Green KY. 502-745-4875

Russell, Nancy P, *Instr,* Western Kentucky University, Dept of Library Science & Instructional Media, KY. 502-745-3446

Russell, Noel, *Bkmobile Coordr,* Carnegie Public Library, Clarksdale MS. 601-624-4461

Russell, O Dean, *Per,* Ector County Library, Odessa TX. 915-332-0633

Russell, Pat, *On-Line Servs & Bibliog Instr,* Spoon River College, Learning Resources Center, Canton IL. 309-647-4645, Ext 222 & 313

Russell, Phyllis J, *Librn,* University of Alberta (Health Sciences Library), Edmonton AB. 403-432-3791

Russell, Ralph E, *Dir,* Georgia State University, William Russell Pullen Library, Atlanta GA. 404-658-2185, 658-2172

Russell, Reba, *Curator,* Dixon Gallery & Gardens Library, Memphis TN. 901-761-5250

Russell, Richard, *Librn,* Bro-Dart Inc Reference Library, Williamsport PA. 717-326-2461, Ext 383

Russell, Richard, *Popular Libr & Music,* Saint Louis Public Library, Saint Louis MO. 314-241-2288

Russell, Robert, *Dir,* Southport-Brunswick County Library, Southport NC. 919-457-6237

Russell, Robert, *Bkmobile Coordr,* Wythe-Grayson Regional Library, Independence VA. 703-773-2761

Russell, Roberta, *Librn,* Patrick Henry School District Public Library (Malinta), Malinta OH. 419-256-7223

Russell, Sharon, *Librn,* Stayton Public Library, Stayton OR. 503-769-3313

Russell, Stephen, *Ch,* James Prendergast Library Association, Jamestown NY. 716-484-7135

Russell, Susan, *Librn,* San Jose Health Center, Health Science Library, San Jose CA. 408-998-3212, Ext 304

Russell, Teresa, *Librn,* San Diego Public Library (San Ysidro Branch), San Ysidro CA. 714-236-5800

Russell, Violet, *Librn,* Aultman Hospital, School of Nursing Library, Canton OH. 216-452-9911, Ext 344

Russell, Volante, *Dir,* Graceland College, Frederick Madison Smith Library, Lamoni IA. 515-784-3311, Ext 144

Russell, Winnie, *Asst,* Sabine Parish Library (Fisher Branch), Fisher LA. 318-256-2212

Russo, Barbara, *Librn,* Washington State Library (Department of Transportation Library), Olympia WA. 206-753-2107

Russo, Edward, *Local Hist,* Lincoln Library, Springfield Public Library, Springfield IL. 217-753-4900

Russo, Marcia, *Asst Librn,* Travelers Insurance Co Library, Hartford CT. 203-277-5048

Russo, Mary, *Ch,* Paramus Public Library (Midland Ave), Paramus NJ. 201-444-4911

Russo, Miriam, *Ad & YA,* West Islip Public Library, West Islip NY. 516-661-7080, 661-7082

Russo, Philomena, *Ad,* Clairton Public Library, Clairton PA. 412-233-7966

Russo, Robin, *Librn,* Newark Public Library, Newark VT. 802-467-3336

Rust, Alice, *Ch,* Greensburg Public Library, Greensburg IN. 812-663-2826

Rust, Beverly, *Asst Dir,* Watonwan County Library, Saint James MN. 507-375-3791

Rust, Linda, *Librn,* Webb Town Library, Webb IA. 712-838-7719

Rust, Phyllis A, *Dir,* Milford Public Library, Milford DE. 302-422-8996

Rust, Rebecca, *YA,* Grandview Heights School District Public Library, Columbus OH. 614-486-2951

Rusterholtz, Beverly, *Librn,* Willcox Library, Girard PA. 814-774-4982

Ruter, Thelma, *Librn,* Wellsburg Public Library, Wellsburg IA. 515-869-5234

Ruth, Sister Mary, *Librn,* Saint John's Seminary (Carrie Estelle Doheny Memorial Library), Camarillo CA. 805-482-4697, Ext 283

Ruthenberg, Dee, *ILL & Circ,* Southwestern College, Memorial Library, Winfield KS. 316-221-4150, Ext 25

Rutherford, Doris P, *Dir,* Jarvis Christian College, Ohlin Library & Communication Center, Hawkins TX. 214-769-2174, Ext 154

Rutherford, Fred, *Media,* Kalamazoo Valley Community College, Learning Resources Center, Kalamazoo MI. 616-372-5000, Ext 328

Rutherford, Ginger, *Chmn,* Atlanta Health Science Libraries Consortium, GA. 404-378-4311, Ext 42

Rutherford, Ginger, *Librn,* Dekalb County Board of Education, Fernbank Science Center Library, Atlanta GA. 404-378-4311, Ext 42

Rutherford, Irmgard, *Librn,* University of Washington Libraries (Chemistry-Pharmacy), Seattle WA. 206-543-1603

Rutherford, Mrs F W, *Asst Librn,* Kurth Memorial Library, Lufkin TX. 713-634-7923

Ruthven, Patricia, *ILL & Ref,* University of New Brunswick, Harriet Irving Library, Fredericton NB. 506-453-4740

Rutkovskis, Gunars, *Asst Dir Resources & Proc Servs,* Boston Public Library, Eastern Massachusetts Library System, Boston MA. 617-536-5400

Rutkowski, Holly, *On-Line Servs,* Franklin Mint Corp, Information Research Services, Franklin Center PA. 215-459-6374

Rutkowski, Patricia O, *YA,* New Britain Public Library, New Britain CT. 203-224-3155

Rutledge, Debbie, *Librn,* Albany Dougherty Public Library (Albany Talking Books Center), Albany GA. 912-439-4321

Rutledge, Diana M, *Librn,* Parma Public Library, Parma ID. 208-722-5138

Rutledge, Margaret, *In Charge,* Texas Education Agency (Region XIV), Abilene TX. 915-677-2911

Rutledge, Patricia P, *Librn,* Cincinnati Art Museum Library, Cincinnati OH. 513-721-5204, Ext 51 & 52

Rutledge, Shirley, *Librn,* David Winton Bell Memorial Library, Delta Waterfowl Research Station Library, Portage la Prairie MB. 204-857-9125

Rutledge, William, *Asst Dir,* Kinchafoonee Regional Library, Dawson GA. 912-995-2902

Rutsis, Peggy, *Librn,* Beecham Inc, Beecham Laboratories, Bristol TN. 615-764-5141, Ext 256

Ruttenber, Susan J, *Dir,* Montvale Free Public Library, Montvale NJ. 201-391-5090

Rutter, Deborah, *Ch,* Guilford Free Library, Guilford CT. 203-453-6561

Ruud, M, *Librn,* London Public Libraries & Museums (Broughdale), London ON. 519-432-7166

Ruus, Laine, *Librn,* University of British Columbia Library (Data Library), Vancouver BC. 604-228-5587

Ruxin, Olyn, *Cat,* Case Western Reserve University & Cleveland Medical Library Association, Cleveland Health Sciences Library, Cleveland OH. 216-368-3426

Ruys, Sister Alberta Anne, *Dir,* Fontbonne College Library, Saint Louis MO. 314-862-3456, Ext 352

Ruzicka, Aimee, *State Law Librn,* Alaska Court Libraries, Anchorage AK. 907-274-8611, Ext 580

Ruzin, Jane, *In Charge,* Saint Paul Public Library (Rice Street), Saint Paul MN. 612-292-6630

Ryan, Ann, *Librn,* Valley Presbyterian Hospital, Library for Medical & Health Sciences, Van Nuys CA. 213-782-6600, Ext 216

Ryan, Ann H, *Librn,* United States Army (Corps of Engineers, Technical Library), New Orleans LA. 504-838-2560

Ryan, Anne C, *Dir,* Bernards Township Library, Basking Ridge NJ. 201-766-0356

Ryan, Bobby, *Chief Librn,* Airways Engineering Corp, James C Buckley Library, Arlington VA. 703-522-4050

Ryan, Carol, *Coordr,* North East Wisconsin Intertype Libraries, Inc, (NEWIL), WI. 414-465-2798

Ryan, Christine, *Librn,* Center for Governmental Research, Inc Library, Rochester NY. 716-325-6360, Ext 38

Ryan, Clare E, *Tech Serv,* New Hampshire State Library, Concord NH. 603-271-2392

Ryan, Constance, *Tech Serv,* State University of New York, College of Arts & Science at Oswego, Penfield Library, Oswego NY. 315-341-4232

Ryan, David, *Dir,* Fort Worth Art Museum Library, Fort Worth TX. 817-738-9215

Ryan, Dell, *Librn,* Shreve Memorial Library (North Caddo), Vivian LA. 318-375-3975

Ryan, Donald, *Librn,* Russell Sage College, Junior College of Albany Library, Albany NY. 518-445-1727

Ryan, Donald L, *Dir,* Russell Sage College, James Wheelock Clark Library, Troy NY. 518-270-2249

Ryan, Dorothy, *ILL,* Oil City Library, Oil City PA. 814-646-8771

Ryan, Ermine, *Librn,* Tulsa City-County Library (North Harvard), Tulsa OK. 918-939-3013

Ryan, Frederick W, *Tech Serv,* California State University, Chico Library, Chico CA. 916-895-6212

Ryan, J, *Actg Librn,* Canadian Department of Regional Economic Expansion, Prairie Farm Rehabilitation Administration Library, Regina SK. 306-569-5100

Ryan, J Elaine, *Dir,* Charles County Community College, Learning Resource Center, La Plata MD. 301-934-2251, Ext 251

Ryan, Joan I, *Dir,* Victoria Union Hospital, Medical Library, Prince Albert SK. 306-764-1551, Ext 332

Ryan, Joyce, *Librn,* LaFayette Public Library, LaFayette NY. 315-677-3782

Ryan, Juanita, *Librn,* Newfoundland Department of Mines & Energy, Mineral Development Div Library, Saint John's NF. 709-737-3159

Ryan, Judith, *Rec & Bus,* Royal Oak Public Library, Royal Oak MI. 313-541-1470

Ryan, Lois, *Dir, Acq & Ref,* River Grove Public Library, River Grove IL. 312-453-4484

Ryan, Lois A, *Ref,* Dolton Public Library District, Dolton IL. 312-849-2385

Ryan, Madeline, *Librn,* C-I-L Inc (Patent & Law Library), Montreal PQ. 514-874-3373

Ryan, Maggie, *Librn,* Kaysville City Library, Kaysville UT. 801-376-2826

Ryan, Marianne E, *Director,* Maricopa County Community College District, Library Technical Services, AZ. 602-275-3301, 275-0474

Ryan, Marie, *Librn,* Saskatchewan Department of the Attorney General (Court of Appeal Library), Regina SK. 306-565-2345

Ryan, Mary, *Cat,* North Dakota State Library, Bismarck ND. 701-224-2490

Ryan, Mary, *Tech Serv,* University of Arkansas for Medical Sciences Library, Little Rock AR. 501-661-5980

Ryan, Mary, *Humanities,* University of California Los Angeles Library, Los Angeles CA. 213-825-1201

Ryan, Mary, *Ref,* University of Missouri-Columbia, Elmer Ellis Library, Columbia MO. 314-882-4701
Ryan, Mary Ellen, *ILL, Ref & On-Line Servs,* Northern Kentucky University, W Frank Steely Library, Highland Heights KY. 606-292-5483
Ryan, Michael T, *Tech Serv & Cat,* Mesa Public Library, Mesa AZ. 602-834-2207
Ryan, Mrs Jeri A, *Librn,* American College of Surgeons Library, Chicago IL. 312-664-4050
Ryan, Nancy, *Building & Planning,* Monroe County Library System, Rochester NY. 716-428-7345
Ryan, Noel, *Chief Librn,* Mississauga Public Library, Mississauga ON. 416-625-8681
Ryan, Patricia M, *Dir & Ch,* Ridley Township Public Library, Folsom PA. 215-583-0593
Ryan, Roberta, *Dir & Acq,* Rochester Public Library, Rochester NH. 603-332-1428
Ryan, Ruth, *Librn,* Milton Public Library, Milton VT. 802-893-4644
Ryan, Terry, *Acq,* Houston Academy of Medicine, Texas Medical Center Library, Houston TX. 713-797-1230
Ryan, William L, *Media,* Lamar University, Mary & John Gray Library, Beaumont TX. 713-838-8313
Ryan, William V, *Dir,* Bloomsburg State College, Harvey A Andruss Library, Bloomsburg PA. 717-389-2716
Ryberg, Susan, *Ch,* Oswego City Library, Oswego NY. 315-341-5867
Rybezyk, Fran, *OCLC, Inc Dirs,* University of Connecticut at Hartford (Law Library), West Hartford CT. 203-523-4841, Ext 347, 370
Rybicki, Steve, *Ref,* Macomb County Community College, Center Campus Library, Mount Clemens MI. 313-286-2104
Rycharski, Barbara L, *Actg Dir,* Howland Circulating Library Company, Beacon NY. 914-831-1134
Ryckman, Patricia, *Librn,* Chester County Free Public Library, Chester SC. 377-8145 & 377-8146
Ryd, Beverly J, *Librn,* First Boston Corp Library, New York NY. 212-825-7781
Rydberg, David, *Prof,* Saint Cloud State University, Center for Library & Audiovisual Education, MN. 612-255-2022
Ryder, Kenneth A, *Librn,* Rensselaer Public Library, Rensselaer NY. 518-462-1193
Ryder, Leah, *Acq,* University of Hartford, Mortensen Library, West Hartford CT. 203-243-4265
Rydesky, Mary, *Media,* University of Texas Health Science Center at Dallas Library, Dallas TX. 214-688-3368
Rye, Mrs Tommy G, *Librn,* Tombigbee Regional Library (Evans Memorial), Aberdeen MS. 601-369-4601
Rygh, Jacquelyn, *Librn,* Iowa Public Service Co Library, Sioux City IA. 712-277-7500
Ryken, Jorena, *Asst Dir & Bibliog Instr,* Wheaton College Library, Wheaton IL. 312-682-5101
Ryken, Peggy, *Librn,* Stanford University Libraries (Swain Chemistry), Stanford CA. 415-497-2511
Rylance, Dan, *Spec Coll,* University of North Dakota, Chester Fritz Library, Grand Forks ND. 701-777-2617
Ryland, John, *Dir,* Hampden Sydney College, Eggleston Library, Hampden Sydney VA. 804-223-4381, Ext 190
Rylander, Beth, *Dir,* Barron Public Library, Barron WI. 715-537-3881
Rylander, Carolyn, *Curric Mat,* Central State University Library, Edmond OK. 405-341-2980, Ext 494, 495 & 496
Rymshaw, Eleanor, *Dir, Acq & Cat,* Norwood Public Library, Norwood NJ. 201-768-9555
Rynders, Kathryn, *On-Line Servs & Bibliog Instr,* University of Minnesota, Waseca, Learning Resource Center, Waseca MN. 507-835-1000
Rynex, Betty, *Acq,* Loudoun County Public Library, Leesburg VA. 703-777-0368
Rynkiewicz, Robert, *Media,* Atlantic City Free Public Library, Atlantic City NJ. 609-345-2269
Rynne, Diane, *Ad,* Santa Clara City Library, Santa Clara CA. 408-984-3097
Ryskamp, Charles A, *Dir,* Pierpont Morgan Library, New York NY. 212-685-0008
Rystrom, Barbara, *ILL,* University of Georgia Libraries, Athens GA. 404-542-2716

Ryte, Carla, *On-Line Servs,* Control Data Corp, Corporate Library Information Center, Bloomington MN. 612-853-4229, 4375 & 5147
Ryther, Jane, *Dir,* Village Library of Morris, Morris NY. 607-263-5400
Ryther, Sherry, *Ch,* Ilsley Library, Middlebury VT. 802-388-2977
Ryun, Rita, *Ref & On-line Data Bank,* University of Wisconsin-Stout, Pierce Library, Menomonie WI. 715-232-1184
Ryynanen, Ellen, *Librn,* Suomi College Library (Finnish-American Archives), Hancock MI. 906-482-5300, Ext 252
Rzepecki, Arnold, *Librn,* Sacred Heart Seminary, Ward Memorial Library, Detroit MI. 313-868-2700

S

Saar, Amanda, *Circ,* University of Arkansas for Medical Sciences Library, Little Rock AR. 501-661-5980
Saathoff, Keith, *Dir,* Mid-Plains Community College, Learning Resource Center, North Platte NE. 308-532-8740
Sabatini, Joseph, *Actg Librn,* Albuquerque Public Library (Main Library), Albuquerque NM. 505-766-7720
Sabbe, Nancy, *Dir,* Madison Public Library, Madison SD. 605-256-3006
Sabin, Gertrude, *Circ,* Villa Park Public Library, Villa Park IL. 312-834-1164
Sabin, Robert G, *Sci,* Juniata College, L A Beeghly & O R Myers Science Library, Huntingdon PA. 814-643-4310, Ext 57
Sable, Martin H, *Prof,* University of Wisconsin-Milwaukee, School of Library Science, WI. 414-963-4707
Sabnis, Vasu, *Asst Dir & Ref,* West Haven Public Library, West Haven CT. 203-932-2221
Sabol, Cathy, *Librn,* Northern Virginia Community College Libraries (Manassas Campus), Manassas VA. 703-368-0184, Ext 222
Sabol, Elizabeth, *Asst Dir,* New Mexico Institute of Mining & Technology, Martin Speare Memorial Library, Socorro NM. 505-835-5614
Sabowitz, Norman, *Systs Librn,* Canada Department Fisheries & Oceans, Bedford Institute of Oceanography Library, Dartmouth NS. 902-426-3675
Sabre, Christine, *Info Specialists,* Occidental Research Corp Library, Irvine CA. 714-957-7450
Sabsay, David, *Dir & Fiscal Officer,* North Bay Cooperative Library System, Santa Rosa CA. 707-545-0831
Sabsay, David, *Dir,* Sonoma County Library, Santa Rosa CA. 707-545-0831
Sacco, Concetta N, *Dir,* West Haven Public Library, West Haven CT. 203-932-2221
Saccoccia, Cynthia, *Tech Serv,* Providence Athenaeum, Providence RI. 401-421-6970
Sachdeva, Dewan, *Librn,* New Brunswick Community College, Saint John Campus Library, Saint John NB. 506-696-1860, Exts 55, 56
Sacherek, Lynetta S, *Asst Librn,* Seattle-First National Bank Library, Seattle WA. 206-583-4056
Sachs, Alma, *ILL,* Whittier Public Library, Whittier CA. 213-698-8949
Sachs, Betty K, *Tech Serv,* Baltimore Hebrew College, Joseph M Meyerhoff Library, Baltimore MD. 301-466-7900, Ext 307
Sachs, Iris, *Librn,* Weiss Memorial Hospital, L Lewis Cohen Memorial Library, Chicago IL. 312-878-8700
Sachse, Gladys, *Educ,* University of Central Arkansas, Torreyson Library, Conway AR. 501-329-2931, Ext 449
Sachse, Renate, *Cat,* Franklin & Marshall College Library, Lancaster PA. 717-291-4223
Sachtleben, Carl H, *Chmn,* Kalamazoo (et al) Library Consortium, (KETAL), MI. 616-383-4960
Sachtleben, Carl H, *Dir,* Western Michigan University, Dwight B Waldo Library, Kalamazoo MI. 616-383-4961
Sacier, Louise, *Chief Librn,* Centre Hospitalier Hotel-Dieu, Bibliotheque Medicale, Sherbrooke PQ. 819-569-2551, Ext 226

Sackarnoski, Vivian, *Actg Librn,* Annie Halenbake Ross Library (Renovo Area Branch), Renovo PA. 717-923-0390
Sackett, Judy, *Microtext,* University of Kentucky, Margaret I King Library, Lexington KY. 606-257-3801
Sackett, Rossi C, *Librn,* Leamington Public Library, Leamington ON. 519-326-3441
Sackreiter, Betty, *Librn,* Sacramento Public Library (Rio Linda Branch), Rio Linda CA. 916-991-4515
Sacks, Lorraine, *Librn,* Salvation Army School for Officer's Training, Brengle Memorial Library, Suffern NY. 914-357-3500, Ext 38
Sacks, Patricia Ann, *Dir,* Cedar Crest College, Cressman Library, Allentown PA. 215-437-4471, Ext 264
Sacks, Patricia Ann, *Dir,* Muhlenberg College, John A W Haas Library, Allentown PA. 215-433-3191, Ext 214
Saczawa, Rosemary, *Tech Serv,* Anderson City-Anderson & Stony Creek Township Public Library, Anderson Public Library, Anderson IN. 317-644-0938
Saddington, Mirian, *Librn,* Abington Free Library (Roslyn Branch), Roslyn PA. 215-886-9818
Saddlemire, Frieda, *Asst Librn,* Town of Berne Free Library, Berne NY. 518-872-1246
Saddler, Nancy, *Pub Rel,* Pioneer Memorial Library, Colby KS. 913-462-3881
Saddler, Virginia B, *Asst Dir,* Union College, Abigail E Weeks Memorial Library, Barbourville KY. 606-546-4151, Ext 137
Saddler, Yvonne M, *Dir,* Douglas County Public Library, Minden NV. 702-782-3023
Saddoris, Eleanor, *Film,* Mesa College, Learning Resource Services, Lowell Heiny Library, Grand Junction CO. 303-248-1436
Sadecki, Winifred A, *Librn,* Household Finance Corp, Corporate Library, Prospect Heights IL. 312-564-5000
Sadler, Catherine E, *Librn,* Charleston Library Society, Charleston SC. 803-723-9912
Sadler, Cynthia, *Librn,* Texas State Technical Institute, Mid-Continent Campus Library, Amarillo TX. 806-335-2316, Ext 273
Sadler, Graham H, *Dir,* County of Henrico Public Library, Richmond VA. 804-222-1643
Sadler, Judith D, *Assoc Prof,* East Carolina University, Dept of Library Science, NC. 919-757-6621, 757-6627
Sadler, Philip, *Asst Prof,* Central Missouri State University, Dept of Library Science and Instructional Technology, MO. 816-429-4835
Sadler, Rowena S, *Chief Librn,* Social Security Administration Library, Baltimore MD. 301-594-1650
Sadler, Sandra Lee, *Libr Asst,* Texas A & I University Citrus Center Library, Weslaco TX. 512-968-2132, Ext 27
Sadlier, Mary Ann, *Adminr,* Western Ohio Film Circuit, OH. 419-228-5113
Sadlker, Mary Ann, *Librn,* Lima Public Library, Lima OH. 419-228-5113
Sadow, Sandra, *Ref & Doc,* Delaware Law School Library of Widener University, Wilmington DE. 302-478-5280
Sadowitz, Daniel, *Instr,* University of Guam, Library Science Program, GU. 734-2921
Sadvig, Janice, *Librn,* Ellsworth Public Library, Ellsworth IA. 515-836-4852
Saemisch, Delores, *Dir,* Graham Public Library, Union Grove WI. 414-878-2910
Saenger, Paul H, *Hist Studies & Soc Sci,* Northwestern University Library, Evanston IL. 312-492-7658
Saenz, Mercedes, *Spec Coll,* University of Puerto Rico Library, Jose M Lazaro Memorial Library, Rio Piedras PR. 809-764-0000, Ext 3296
Saferin, Ethel I, *Librn,* Park Synagogue, Kravitz Memorial Library, Cleveland OH. 216-371-2244
Saferite, Linda, *Dir,* Scottsdale Public Library, Scottsdale AZ. 602-994-2471
Saffer, Melinda, *Dir & On-Line Servs,* Worcester Foundation for Experimental Biology, George F Fuller Research Library, Shrewsbury MA. 617-842-8921, Ext 302
Safford, Eunice, *Rare Bks,* Peterborough Town Library, Peterborough NH. 603-924-6401
Saffren, Arlene, *Librn,* Interpace Corp Library, Los Angeles CA. 213-663-3361
Safley, Mrs Harlan, *Asst Librn,* Blair Public Library, Blair NE. 402-426-3617

Safran, Jill D, *ILL & Ref,* Niagara University Library, Niagara University NY. 716-285-1212, Ext 376

Safran, Jill D, *On-Line Servs,* Niagara University Library, Niagara University NY. 716-285-1212, Ext 376

Sagal, Kenneth P, *Librn,* Saskatchewan Technical Institute Library, Moose Jaw SK. 306-693-8236

Sagar, Alfred V, *Dir & Asst Dean,* Kalamazoo Valley Community College, Learning Resources Center, Kalamazoo MI. 616-372-5000, Ext 328

Sage, Gail M, *Ch,* Sonoma County Library, Santa Rosa CA. 707-545-0831

Sage, Maria J, *Dir,* Fort Fairfield Public Library, Fort Fairfield ME. 207-476-8161

Sage, Mary A, *Dir,* Sapulpa Public Library, Sapulpa OK. 918-224-5624

Sage, Norman, *Ref,* College of Lake County, Learning Resource Center, Grayslake IL. 312-223-6601, Ext 392

Sagebiel, Kathy, *ILL,* Southwest Texas State University, Learning Resources Center, San Marcos TX. 512-245-2132

Sagebiel, Shirley, *Circ & Ref,* Wharton County Junior College, J M Hodges Learning Center, Wharton TX. 713-532-4560, Ext 36

Sager, Donald J, *Commissioner,* Chicago Public Library, Chicago IL. 312-269-2900

Sager, Estella, *Librn,* Round Rock Public Library, Round Rock TX. 512-255-3939

Sager, Linda, *Ad & Ref,* Carleton A Friday Memorial Library, New Richmond Public Library, New Richmond WI. 715-246-2364

Sager, Rochell, *Reader Serv,* University of Alaska, Juneau Library, Juneau AK. 907-789-2101, Ext 126, 127 & 128

Sagi, Raya, *Ad,* Corona Public Library, Corona CA. 714-736-2381

Sahak, Judy Harvey, *Asst Dir & Librn Denison Libr,* Claremont Colleges Libraries, Claremont CA. 714-621-8000, Ext 3721

Sahak, Judy Harvey, *Librn,* Claremont Colleges Libraries (Ella Strong Denison Library), Claremont CA. 714-621-8000, Ext 3941

Sahaweh, Mrs L, *Librn,* Ben Taub General Hospital Library, Houston TX. 713-791-7441

Sahlem, James, *Librn,* Buffalo & Erie County Public Library System (Crane), Buffalo NY. 716-883-6651

Sahli, Sue, *Asst Prof,* Northern Illinois University, Dept of Library Science, IL. 815-753-1735

Sahm, Charlotte, *Librn,* Indianola Public Library, Indianola NE. 308-364-9259

Sahraie, Arlene, *Dir,* Fairview Free Public Library, Fairview NJ. 201-943-6244

Sahs, Belva, *Tech Serv,* Bellevue Public Library System, Bellevue NE. 402-291-8000

Sahu, Mrs Krishna, *Dir,* College of Osteopathic Medicine & Surgery Library, Des Moines IA. 515-274-4861, Ext 118

Said, Josephine, *Librn,* Iowa Department of Transportation Library, Ames IA. 515-296-1200

Saiet, Ronald, *Assoc Dir Learning Servs,* Northeastern Illinois University Library, Chicago IL. 312-583-4050, Ext 469, 470, 471, 472

Saiki, Anne H, *Librn,* Belt, Collins-Lyon Associates, Information Services, Honolulu HI. 808-521-5361

Sails, Mary, *Librn,* Jemison Public Library, Jemison AL. 205-688-4525

Saint-Clair, Albert W, *Librn,* Wyoming State Law Library, Cheyenne WY. 307-777-7509

Saint-Clair, Guy, *Asst Dir,* University Club Library, New York NY. 212-572-3418

Saint-Clair, Helen, *Librn,* Wilmington Medical Center, Medical Library, Wilmington DE. 302-428-2201

Saint-Clair, Jeffrey, *Librn,* Saint Mary's Hospital & Health Center, Ralph Henry Fuller Medical Library, Tucson AZ. 602-622-5833, Ext 1076

Saint-Clair, Norbert, *Spec Coll,* University of Central Florida Library, Orlando FL. 305-275-2564

Saint-Hilaire, Sharon E, *Librn,* Seekonk Public Libraries, Seekonk MA. 617-761-6424

Saint-Ivanyi, Alexander, *Librn,* American Hungarian Library & Historical Society, New York NY. 212-744-5298

Saint-John, Louise, *Librn,* United States Air Force (Bergstrom Air Force Base Library), Bergstrom AFB TX. 512-385-4100, Ext 3740

Saint-Leger, John B, *Dir,* Central Virginia Community College Library, Lynchburg VA. 804-239-0321, Ext 231

Saint-Martin, Lucienne, *Biomed,* Hospital Sainte-Justine, Centre d'Information Sur La Sante de L'Enfant, Montreal PQ. 514-731-4931, Ext 339

Saint-Peters, Mrs F, *Librn,* Beeton Public Library, Beeton ON. 416-729-7726

Sainte-Maria, Ofelia, *Cat,* West Virginia Institute of Technology, Vining Library, Montgomery WV. 304-442-3141

Saito, Deborah, *Media,* Sheldon Jackson College, Stratton Library, Sitka AK. 907-747-5235, 747-5259

Saiz, John T, *Librn & Acq,* Saint John's University Library (Law), Jamaica NY. 212-969-8000, Ext 651, 652 & 653

Sakai, Charlotte, *Librn,* San Jose Public Library (Pearl Avenue), San Jose CA. 408-265-7833

Sakai, Diane H, *Asst Librn, Tech Serv & Cat,* Honolulu Community College Library, Honolulu HI. 808-845-9220

Sakai, Kay, *Per,* Los Angeles Harbor College Library, Wilmington CA. 213-518-1000, Ext 292 & 293

Sakamoto, Louise Y, *Librn,* Purex Corp, Technical Library, Carson CA. 213-775-2111, Ext 596

Sakey, Joseph G, *Dir,* Cambridge Public Library, Cambridge MA. 617-498-9080

Saklad, Joan, *Cat,* Burlington Public Library, Burlington MA. 617-272-2520

Sakmar, M, *Dir,* Southeastern University, Learning Resource Center, Washington DC. 202-488-8174

Sakoian, Mary A, *Librn,* Bituminous Coal Research Inc Library, Monroeville PA. 412-327-1600

Sakyoun, Naim K, *Librn,* Pontiac General Hospital, Medical Library, Pontiac MI. 313-857-7412

Salam, Abdus, *Soc Sci,* Metropolitan Toronto Library Board, Metropolitan Toronto Library, Toronto ON. 416-928-5150

Salaman, David J, *Librn,* Beth Sholom Congregation, Joseph & Elizabeth Schwartz Library, Elkins Park PA. 924-2223 & 887-1342, Ext 22

Salamona, Barbara, *Commun Servs,* San Jose Public Library, San Jose CA. 408-277-4822

Salandy, Pat, *Librn,* F Eberstadt & Co Inc Library, New York NY. 212-480-0807

Salas, K, *Ref,* John McIntire Public Library Public Library, Zanesville OH. 614-453-0391

Salas, Patricia W, *Asst Librn,* Staunton Public Library, Fannie Bayly King Library, Staunton VA. 703-886-7231

Salassi, Odelia M, *Librn,* Livingston Parish Library, Livingston LA. 504-686-2436

Salazar, David R, *Actg Exec Dir,* Michigan Library Consortium, (MLC), MI. 313-577-4061

Salazar, Ramiro S, *Librn,* Eagle Pass Public Library, Eagle Pass TX. 512-773-2516

Salber, Peter, *Asst Dir,* Newsweek, Inc, General Library, New York NY. 212-350-2494

Salberg, Anne, *Dir,* Glenn A Jones Md Memorial Library, Johnstown Public Library, Johnstown CO. 303-587-2459

Saldana, Lupe, *Ad,* Loveland Public Library, Loveland CO. 303-667-4040

Saldinger, Jeffrey P, *Librn,* Exxon Co USA, Information Center Library, Florham Park NJ. 201-765-6704

Sale, E T, *Exec Dir,* Social Planning Council of Winnipeg Library, Winnipeg MB. 204-943-2561

Sale, Melanie Laura, *Ser,* College of William & Mary in Virginia (Marshall-Wythe Law Library), Williamsburg VA. 804-253-4680

Salen, George P, *Chmn & Prof,* Purdue University, Dept of Education, Library Media & Instructional Development, IN. 317-749-2902

Salerno, Haraldgan, *Media,* Barry College, Monsignor William Barry Memorial Library, Miami Shores FL. 305-758-3392, Ext 263

Sales, Carole, *Librn,* Rock Island Public Library (Southwest), Rock Island IL. 309-787-6038

Saley, Al, *Dir,* Manville Public Library, Manville NJ. 201-722-9722

Saley, Stacey, *Librn,* City Hospital Center at Elmhurst, Medical Library, Elmhurst NY. 212-830-1538

Salgat, Anne-Marie, *Dir,* General Theological Seminary, Saint Mark's Library, New York NY. 212-243-5150, Ext 222

Salik, Felicia, *Soc Sci & Hist,* Enoch Pratt Free Library, Baltimore MD. 301-396-5430, 396-5395

Salinas, Alicias, *Librn,* Alice Public Library, Alice TX. 512-664-9506

Salinger, Florence, *Tech Serv,* Pennsylvania State University, Capitol Campus Heindel Library, Middletown PA. 717-787-7771

Salisbury, Anne, *ILL,* North Kingstown Free Library, North Kingstown RI. 401-294-2521

Salisbury, Mary, *Asst Dir,* Trenton Memorial Public Library, Trenton ON. 613-394-3381

Salita, Christine, *ILL & Ref,* South Huntington Public Library, Huntington Station NY. 516-549-4411

Sall, Janice, *Librn,* Allendale Township Library, Allendale MI. 616-895-4178

Salle, Irene E La, *Librn,* Stamford Village Library, Stamford NY. 607-652-5001

Sallee, Brenda, *Bkmobile Coordr,* Hardin County Public Library, Elizabethtown KY. 502-769-6337

Salley, Coleen, *Assoc Prof,* University of New Orleans, College of Education, LA. 504-282-0607

Salley, Sarah, *Tech Serv & Coll Develop,* Rush-Presbyterian-Saint Luke's Medical Center (Library of Rush University), Chicago IL. 312-942-2271, 942-5950

Sallitt, Emily F Hosey, *Lectr,* Marywood College, Dept of Librarianship, PA. 717-342-6521

Sally, Dana, *Librn,* University of North Carolina at Chapel Hill (Math-Physics), Chapel Hill NC. 919-933-2323

Salmon, Elvena, *Librn,* Horse Cave Free Public Library, Horse Cave KY. 502-786-1130

Salmon, Eugene N, *Humanities,* California State University, Sacramento Library, Sacramento CA. 916-454-6466

Salmon, Hazel, *Librn,* Public Library of Johnston County & Smithfield (Selma Public), Selma NC. 919-965-8613

Salmon, Kay H, *Dir,* Corvallis Public Library, Corvallis-Benton County Library, Corvallis OR. 503-757-6928

Salo, Anna B, *Librn,* Manchester Memorial Hospital, Medical Library, Manchester CT. 203-646-1222, Ext 325

Salo, Annette, *Media,* Saint Paul Public Library, Saint Paul MN. 612-292-6311

Salois, Jan, *Librn,* Bay County Library System (Linwood Branch), Linwood MI. 517-697-5191

Salomon, Julius L, *Librn,* Sciaky Brothers Inc Library, Chicago IL. 312-767-5600

Salovaard, Mary K, *Asst Librn,* Kirkland & Ellis Law Library, Chicago IL. 312-861-3200

Saltalamachia, Joyce, *Pub Servs,* Golden Gate University (School of Law Library), San Francisco CA. 415-442-7260

Salter, Billie I, *Dir,* Yale University Library (Social Science & Economic Growth Center), New Haven CT. 203-436-3412

Salter, Jeffrey L, *Librn,* Catahoula Parish Library, Harrisonburg LA. 318-744-5271

Saltus, Elinor C, *Emer Prof,* University of Arizona, Graduate Library School, AZ. 602-626-3565

Saltzman, Alice, *Cat,* Nicholls State University, Allen J Ellender Memorial Library, Thibodaux LA. 504-446-8111, Ext 401, 402

Saltzman, E Jane, *Coordr,* Evansville Area Health Science Library Consortium, IN. 812-479-4151

Saltzman, E Jane, *Dir,* Saint Mary Medical Center Inc Library, Evansville IN. 812-479-4000

Saltzman, Sylvia, *Asst Dir, Ad & Commun Servs,* Field Library, Peekskill Library, Peekskill NY. 914-737-0010

Salvador, Carman L, *Librn,* United States Army Medical Center (Medical Library), Washington DC. 202-576-1238

Salvadore, Maria, *Ch,* Cambridge Public Library, Cambridge MA. 617-498-9080

Salvail, Martha Dumont, *Chief Librn,* Professional Corporation of Physicians of Quebec, Documentation Centre, Montreal PQ. 514-878-4441

Salvati, Janet S, *Ref,* Fairmont State College Library, Fairmont WV. 304-367-4121

Salvatore, Lucy, *Assoc Prof,* University of Rhode Island, Graduate Library School, RI. 401-792-2878 or 792-2947

Salvayon, Connie, *Librn,* Indiana Free Library Inc, Indiana PA. 412-465-8841

Salvidore, Maria, *Lectr,* Simmons College, Graduate School of Library & Information Science, MA. 617-738-2225
Salyers, Connie, *Dir,* Urbana College, Swedenborg Memorial Library, Urbana OH. 513-652-1301
Salzburger, Sheree, *Librn,* Gulfport-Harrison County Library (D'Iberville), N Biloxi MS. 601-392-2279
Salzer, Ann, *YA & Ref,* Auburn Public Library, Auburn WA. 206-931-3018
Salzer, Anne, *ILL,* Yorba Linda Library District, Yorba Linda CA. 714-528-7039
Salzer, Elizabeth, *Librn,* Stanford University Libraries (J Henry Meyer Memorial), Stanford CA. 415-497-4983
Salzman, Beverly, *Librn,* Indianapolis-Marion County Public Library (East Washington), Indianapolis IN. 317-635-5662
Salzman, Edith, *Librn,* Northwest Community Hospital, Medical Staff Library, Arlington Heights IL. 312-259-1000, Ext 228
Salzman, Kristin M, *Librn,* Forrest Township Public Library, Forrest IL. 815-657-8805
Samard, Emiko, *Chief Librn,* Orange County Medical Center, Medical Library, Orange CA. 714-633-9393
Samb, LaVerne, *Librn,* La Crosse Lutheran Hospital, Health Science Library, La Crosse WI. 608-785-0530
Samb, LaVerne, *Librn,* Western Wisconsin Hospital Library Consortium, WI. 608-785-0530, Ext 3442
Samek, Lois J, *Librn,* Mental Health Institute, Medical Library, Independence IA. 319-334-2583
Samer, Marcia G, *On-Line Servs & Bibliog Instr,* Norwich-Eaton Pharmaceuticals, Research Library, Norwich NY. 607-335-2539
Sameth, Marian, *Assoc Dir,* Citizens' Housing & Planning Council of New York, Inc Library, New York NY. 212-391-9030
Samkoff, Julie, *In Charge,* Hawaii Planned Parenthood, Inc, Family Planning Information Center Library, Honolulu HI. 808-521-6991
Sammons, Christa A, *Librn German Lit Coll,* Yale University Library (Beinecke Rare Book & Manuscript), New Haven CT. 203-436-0234
Sammons, Eleanor, *Bkmobile Coordr,* Satilla Regional Library, Douglas GA. 912-384-4667, 384-1172
Sammons, Pam, *Librn,* Fluor Engineers & Constructors, Design Engineering Library, Irvine CA. 714-975-3238
Sammons, Sandra, *Circ,* Muhlenberg College, John A W Haas Library, Allentown PA. 215-433-3191, Ext 214
Samore, Theodore, *Prof,* University of Wisconsin-Milwaukee, School of Library Science, WI. 414-963-4707
Sampedro, Delores, *Tech Serv & Cat,* Forsyth County Public Library, Winston-Salem NC. 919-727-2556
Sample, Judith A, *Pub Serv,* Abilene Public Library, Abilene TX. 915-677-2474
Sampler, Theda, *Librn,* Dalton Public Library, Inc (Murray County), Chatsworth GA. 404-695-4200
Samples, Gordon, *Rare Bks,* San Diego State University Library, San Diego CA. 714-286-6014
Samples, Judy, *Cat,* Grove City Public Library, Grove City OH. 614-875-6716
Sampley, Mrs C W, *Librn,* Monteagle Public Library, Monteagle TN. 615-924-2638
Sampson, Anne, *Cat,* Chelsea Public Library, Chelsea MA. 617-884-2335
Sampson, Arlene, *Librn,* Jackson County Library (Interior Branch), Interior SD. 605-837-2689
Sampson, Dennis, *Instr,* Manchester College, Educational Media Specialist Program, IN. 219-982-2141, Ext 231
Sampson, Dennis, *Ref & Bibliog Instr,* Manchester College, Funderburg Library, North Manchester IN. 219-982-2141, Ext 231
Sampson, Elaine, *Acq,* Gulfport Public Library, Gulfport FL. 813-347-0218
Sampson, Ellanie, *Dir,* Northeast Missouri Library Service, Kahoka MO. 816-727-2327
Sampson, Ellanie, *Librn,* Truth or Consequences Public Library, Truth or Consequences NM. 505-894-3027
Sampson, Frances, *Ad,* Marysville Public Library, Marysville OH. 513-642-1876

Sampson, Karen L, *Asst Dir,* University of Nebraska at Omaha, University Library, Omaha NE. 402-554-2361
Sampson, Katherine, *Ref,* Creighton University, Alumni Memorial Library, Omaha NE. 402-449-2705
Sampson, Lynda, *Librn,* Mount Saint Mary's College (Dohney Campus Library), Los Angeles CA. 213-746-0450, Exts 40 & 41
Sampson, Robert E, *Librn,* East Liberty Presbyterian Church Library, Pittsburgh PA. 412-441-3800
Sams, Jan, *Librn,* Georgia-Pacific Corp, Bellingham Div Library, Bellingham WA. 206-733-4410
Sams, Margaret E, *Librn,* Petersburg Public Library, Petersburg IL. 217-632-2807
Sams, Merolyn, *Asst Librn,* Buffalo Trace Regional Library, Flemingsburg KY. 606-845-9571
Sams, Norman, *Dir,* Dallas Public Library, Dallas OR. 503-623-2633
Samson, Carole, *Studio Dir,* La Magnetotheque, Montreal PQ. 514-524-6831
Samuel, Evelyn, *Dir,* New York University (Stephen Chen Library of Fine Arts), New York NY. 212-988-5550
Samuel, Harold E, *Librn,* Yale University Library (Music), New Haven CT. 203-436-8240
Samuel, Peter, *YA,* Greece Public Library, Rochester NY. 716-225-8930, 225-8951
Samuel, Peter, *Librn,* Greece Public Library (Lowden Point Branch), Lowden Point NY. 716-225-8930, 225-8951
Samuels, Alan R, *Asst Prof,* University of North Carolina at Greensboro, Library Science-Educational Technology Div, NC. 919-379-5710
Samuels, Christopher J, *Librn,* Information for Business Decisions Library, New York NY. 212-840-1220
Samuels, Joel L, *Dir Libr Servs,* Newberry Library, Chicago IL. 312-943-9090
Samuels, Linda, *Librn, On-Line Servs & Bibliog Instr,* Getty Oil Co, Technical Library, Houston TX. 713-972-1749
Samuels, Martha, *Dir,* Greensburg Public Library, Greensburg IN. 812-663-2826
Samuelson, Eileen L, *Dir,* Gratz College Library (Elsie and William Chomsky Educational Resource Center), Philadelphia PA. 215-329-3363
Samuelson, Howard K, *Dir,* Santa Ana Public Library, Santa Ana CA. 714-834-4021
Samuelson, Richard T, *Dir,* Colonie Town Library, Loudonville NY. 518-458-9274
Samuelson, Sara, *Bkmobile Coordr,* Miles City Public Library, Sagebrush Federation of Libraries, Miles City MT. 406-232-1496
Sanak, Francine, *On-Line Servs,* Madonna College Library, Livonia MI. 313-591-1200
Sanborn, Ann, *Per,* Gloucester Lyceum & Sawyer Free Library, Gloucester MA. 617-283-0376
Sanborn, Bill, *Dir,* Emanuel Medical Center Library, Turlock CA. 209-634-9151, Ext 330
Sanborn, Dorothy C, *Dir,* Auburn-Placer County Library, Auburn CA. 916-823-4391
Sanborn, Helen, *Librn,* Consolidated Papers, Inc, Research & Development Library, Wisconsin Rapids WI. 715-422-3768
Sanborn, Marie, *Librn,* Leach Library, Londonderry NH. 603-434-4791
Sanborn, Rachel B, *Librn,* New Hampshire State Library (Exeter Branch), Exeter NH. 603-271-2392
Sanborn, Richard, *Librn,* California School of Professional Psychology Library, San Diego CA. 714-452-1664
Sanchez, Bertha, *Bkmobile Coordr,* Thomas Branigan Memorial Library, Las Cruces Public Library, Las Cruces NM. 505-526-0347
Sanchez, Carmen, *Librn,* Albany County Public Library (Centennial Valley Branch), Centennial WY. 307-745-3365
Sanchez, Millie, *Librn,* East Baton Rouge Parish Library (Central), Baton Rouge LA. 504-261-3787
Sand, Janice, *Dir,* Roosevelt County Library, Wolf Point MT. 406-653-2411
Sand, Mary, *Librn,* Audubon Public Library, Audubon IA. 712-563-3301
Sand, Peter, *In Charge,* Assumption Church, Parish Library, Seattle WA. 206-523-2636
Sandahl, Frona, *Librn,* Belleview College Library, Westminster CO. 303-427-5461

Sandberg, Jane, *Librn,* Bloomfield Carnegie Public Library, Bloomfield IN. 812-384-4125
Sandberg, Joy, *Info Ctr Mgr,* Mountain States Employers Council-Information Center, Denver CO. 303-839-5177
Sandberg, Wanda H, *Asst Librn,* Worcester County Horticultural Society Library, Worcester MA. 617-752-4274
Sande, Betty, *Supvr,* Mayo Foundation (Mayo Clinic Hospital Library for Patients), Rochester MN. 507-284-3240
Sandel, Jean, *Librn,* Deutsch, Kerrigan & Stiles Law Library, New Orleans LA. 504-581-5141, Ext 217
Sandell, Mrs M E, *Librn,* Collingwood Municipal Public Library, Collingwood ON. 705-445-1571
Sandercox, Nancy, *Tech Serv,* Bethany College, T L Phillips Memorial Library, Bethany WV. 304-829-7000
Sanderlin, John C, *Syst Coordr,* University of Central Florida Library, Orlando FL. 305-275-2564
Sanderlin, Rebecca, *Juvenile Servs Coordr,* Phoenix Public Library, Phoenix AZ. 602-262-6451
Sanders, Anne D, *Dir,* East Albemarle Regional Library, Elizabeth City NC. 919-335-2511
Sanders, Ara B, *Dept Head,* Snead State Junior College, Library Technology, AL. 205-593-5120, Ext 275
Sanders, Ara B, *Dir,* Snead State Junior College, Virgil B McCain Learning Resource Center, Boaz AL. 205-593-5120, Ext 274
Sanders, Arthur H, *Curator,* Musical Museum Library, Deansboro NY. 315-841-8774
Sanders, Beverly, *Spec Servs Consult,* Kaskaskia Library System, Smithton IL. 618-235-4220
Sanders, Beverly J, *Librn,* Kaskaskia Library System (Subregional Library for the Blind & Physically Handicapped), Smithton IL. 618-235-4220
Sanders, Carla, *Librn,* Genesee District Library (Clio Branch), Clio MI. 313-686-7130
Sanders, Carol J, *Librn,* Henryetta Public Library, Henryetta OK. 918-652-7377
Sanders, Charlene, *Ref,* Alsip-Merrionette Park Library, Alsip IL. 312-371-5666
Sanders, Don, *Cat &,* University of Calgary Library (Law), Calgary AB. 403-284-5090
Sanders, Eleanor, *Cat,* Kansas City College of Osteopathic Medicine, Mazzacano Hall Library, Kansas City MO. 816-283-2451, 2454
Sanders, Ethel, *Assoc Dir,* Troy State University Library, Troy AL. 205-566-3000, Ext 263
Sanders, Eugene R, *Librn,* Jefferson County Library System, Punxsutawney PA. 814-938-5020
Sanders, Eugene R, *Librn,* Punxsutawney Memorial Library, Punxsutawney PA. 814-938-5020
Sanders, George, *Media,* Hutchinson Community Junior College, John F Kennedy Library & Learning Resources Center, Hutchinson KS. 316-663-5781, Ext 125
Sanders, Irene F, *Librn,* Cape Canaveral Public Library, Cape Canaveral FL. 305-783-5140
Sanders, J Walter, *Librn,* Clark-Schwebel Fiberglass Corp, Research & Development Division Library, Anderson SC. 803-224-3506
Sanders, James R, *In Charge,* Legislative Reference Library, Austin TX. 512-475-4626
Sanders, Louise, *Media Servs,* Tri-County Technical College, Learning Resource Center, Pendleton SC. 803-646-3227
Sanders, Lucy, *Res Librn,* Tracy-Locke Advertising & Public Relations, Inc Library, Dallas TX. 214-742-3131, Ext 422
Sanders, Lylah, *Br Coordr,* Santa Barbara Public Library, Santa Barbara CA. 805-962-7653
Sanders, Martha, *Librn,* Muncie-Center Township Public Library (Grace Maring), Muncie IN. 317-282-2661
Sanders, Mary K, *Librn,* California Department of Justice Library, San Francisco CA. 415-557-2177
Sanders, Melodie, *ILL & AV,* Eastern Oklahoma District Library System, Muskogee OK. 918-683-2846
Sanders, Nelle, *In Charge,* Cobb County Public Library System (Sweetwater Valley), Austell GA. 404-948-2132
Sanders, Ola, *Librn,* Wichita Public Library (Northeast), Wichita KS. 316-262-0611

Sanders, Patricia, *Ref,* Montclair State College, Harry A Sprague Library, Upper Montclair NJ. 201-893-4291

Sanders, Peggy, *Dir,* Sarah Vaughan Public Library, Sioux Lookout Public Library, Sioux Lookout ON. 807-737-3660

Sanders, Phyllis J, *Librn,* Hebron Public Library, Hebron IN. 219-996-3684

Sanders, Rosann M, *Librn,* Brainerd Public Library, Brainerd MN. 218-829-5574

Sanders, Ruth, *Acq,* Hutchinson Public Library, Hutchinson KS. 316-663-5441

Sanders, Shirley, *ILL,* Peninsula Public Library, Lawrence NY. 516-239-3262

Sanders, Sue, *Asst Dir,* Tarrant County Junior College System (South Campus Learning Resource Center), Fort Worth TX. 817-534-4861, Ext 223

Sanders, Virginia, *Tech Serv,* Public Library of Johnston County & Smithfield, Smithfield NC. 919-934-8146

Sanders, Vonda, *Commun Servs,* Dodge City Public Library, Dodge City KS. 316-225-0248

Sanderson, Barbara L, *Librn,* Workers' Compensation Board of British Columbia Library, Vancouver BC. 604-266-0211, Ext 290, 529

Sanderson, Harlan, *Media,* Luther College, Preus Library, Decorah IA. 319-387-1163

Sanderson, Judith, *ILL,* Taunton Public Library, Subregional Headquarters for Eastern Massachusetts Regional Library System, Taunton MA. 617-823-3570

Sanderson, Mrs Owen, *Asst Librn,* Marshall Community Library, Marshall WI. 414-655-3123

Sandford, Mary L, *Dir,* Frothingham Free Library, Fonda NY. 518-853-3016

Sandfort, Josef, *Circ,* Ledding Library of Milwaukie, Milwaukie Public Library, Milwaukie OR. 503-659-3911

Sandifer, Joy, *ILL & Ref,* Gardner-Webb College, Dover Memorial Library, Boiling Springs NC. 704-434-2361

Sandifer, Joy, *Bibliog Instr,* Gardner-Webb College, Dover Memorial Library, Boiling Springs NC. 704-434-2361

Sandilands, Joan, *Info, Orientation & On-Line Servs,* University of British Columbia Library, Vancouver BC. 604-228-3871

Sandine, Edna, *Librn,* United States Navy (Station Library), Keyport WA. 206-396-2710, 396-2711

Sandine, Margaret, *Tech Serv & Cat,* South Dakota School of Mines & Technology, Devereaux Library, Rapid City SD. 605-394-2418

Sandique, Amelia A, *Cat,* American University (Washington College of Law Library), Washington DC. 202-686-2625

Sandler, Arlene, *Librn,* Saint Louis Public Library (Des Peres), Saint Louis MO. 314-726-2653

Sandler, Rhoda F, *Media,* Montgomery County Community College, Learning Resources Center, Blue Bell PA. 215-643-6000, Ext 340

Sandlin, Minnie Ola, *Dir,* Harlingen Public Library, Lon C Hill Memorial Library, Harlingen TX. 423-3580; 423-3563

Sandlin, Tootie, *Librn,* Tulsa City-County Library (Bixby Branch), Bixby OK. 918-366-3397

Sandmeyer, Ulrich, *Librn,* Chicago Public Library (Galewood-Mont Clare), Chicago IL. 312-745-0565

Sandner, Fred, *AV & Ref,* Asnuntuck Community College, Learning Resource Center, Enfield CT. 203-745-1603, Ext 11, 13

Sandness, Susan Stow, *Dir,* Minnehaha County Library, Hartford SD. 605-528-3532

Sandoval, Hugo F, *Assoc Prof,* George Peabody College for Teachers, Department of Library Science, TN. 615-327-8037

Sandridge, Polly, *Librn,* Fluvanna County Library, Palmyra VA. 804-589-8117

Sands, Jean, *Dir,* Lexington Public Library, Lexington NE. 308-324-2151

Sands, Kathleen M, *Chief Librn,* Malta Township Public Library, Malta IL. 815-825-2525

Sands, Lu, *Dir,* North Florida Junior College Library, Madison FL. 904-973-2288, Ext 52

Sands, Nathan J, *Mgr,* Singer Co, Librascope Div, Technical Information Center, Glendale CA. 213-244-6541, Ext 1751

Sands, Jr, George A, *Dir,* Caroline County Public Library, Denton MD. 301-479-1343

Sandstedt, Carl, *Dir,* Saint Charles City County Library, Saint Peters MO. 314-441-2300

Sandstedt, Russann, *Librn,* United States Court of Appeals, Eighth Circuit Law Library, Saint Louis MO. 314-622-4930

Sandstrom, Judith J, *Chief, Readers Servs Br,* United States Department of the Treasury Library, Washington DC. 202-566-2777, 566-3279

Sandstrom, Rita, *Librn,* Kern County Library (California City), Bakersfield CA. 805-861-2130

Sanduleak, Barbara, *Chief Librn,* Gould, Inc, Information Center, Cleveland OH. 216-851-5500

Sandvik, Karin, *Acq,* University of Wisconsin-La Crosse, Murphy Library, La Crosse WI. 608-785-8505

Sandy, Gerald, *Dir,* Armstrong State College, Lane Memorial Library, Savannah GA. 912-927-5332

Sandy, John, *Librn,* University of Texas Libraries (Physics-Math-Astronomy), Austin TX. 512-471-7539

Sandys, Mabel, *Librn,* Temple City Nazarene Church, Carl W Mischke Memorial Library, Temple City CA. 213-287-1136

Sanfilipo, Jon W, *Clerk of Courts,* Washington County Law Library, West Bend WI. 414-284-9411

Sanfilippo, Jane V, *Librn,* United States Navy (Curriculum Support Library), Newport RI. 401-841-3518

Sanfilippo, Jane V, *Br Coordr,* United States Navy (Naval Education & Training Center), Newport RI. 401-841-3044, 841-4352

Sanford, Ethel, *Ch,* Rogers Memorial Library, Southampton NY. 516-283-0774

Sanford, Gary, *AV,* Onondaga County Public Library System, Syracuse NY. 315-473-2702

Sanford, Moody, *Media,* Tompkins-Cortland Community College, Gerald A Barry Memorial Library, Instructional & Learning Resource Div, Dryden NY. 607-844-8211, Ext 354

Sanftleben, Sharon, *Librn,* Caseyville Public Library, Caseyville IL. 618-345-5848

Sanger, Carol, *Lang & Lit,* Queensborough Community College Library, Bayside NY. 212-631-6226

Sanger, Helen, *Librn,* Frick Art Reference Library, New York NY. 212-288-8700

Sangiamo, Irma, *Asst Dir,* Maryland Institute College of Art, Decker Library, Baltimore MD. 301-669-9200, Ext 27, 28

Sangster, Collette, *Dir,* Saint Mary's School for the Deaf, Information Center, Buffalo NY. 716-834-3810, Ext 152

Sangster, Margaret, *Assoc Prof,* University of North Carolina at Greensboro, Library Science-Educational Technology Div, NC. 919-379-5710

Sanguino, Evelyn, *Librn,* Miami-Dade Public Library System (West Flagler), Miami FL. 305-442-8710

Sanito, Thelma, *Dir,* Phoebe Apperson Hearst Free Library, Lead SD. 605-584-2013

Sanker, Paul, *Public Relations Consult,* Mid-Hudson Library System, Poughkeepsie NY. 914-471-6060

Sankey, Virginia, *Ch,* Altoona Area Public Library, Altoona PA. 814-946-0417

Sannwald, Susan, *Librn,* Superior Public Library (Billings Park Station), Superior WI. 715-394-0246

Sannwald, William, *Dir,* San Diego Public Library, San Diego CA. 714-236-5800

Sansbury, Edwin F, *AV,* Southeastern Baptist Theological Seminary Library, Wake Forest NC. 919-556-3101, Ext 225, 250

Sansbury, Michele M, *Assoc Librn,* Frederick Cancer Research Center, Scientific Library, Frederick MD. 301-663-7261

Sansfacon, Jacques, *Prof,* College Lionel-Groulx, Techniques de la Documentation, PQ. 514-430-3120, Ext 261

Sansoucy, Leo, *Librn,* Seminaire De Saint-Hyacinthe Bibliotheque, Saint Hyacinthe PQ. 514-774-4232

SantaVicca, Edmund F, *Asst Prof,* George Peabody College for Teachers, Department of Library Science, TN. 615-327-8037

Santerre, Louis A, *Dir & Ad,* Bibliotheque Municipale, Sept-Iles PQ. 418-968-6722

Santi, Ella, *Librn,* Bureau of Land Management, Price District Office Library, Price UT. 801-637-4584

Santiago, Gladys, *Librn,* Commonwealth of Puerto Rico (Bureau of the Budett Library), San Juan PR. 809-724-6260

Santiago, Luisa, *Librn,* University of Puerto Rico Library (Social Sciences Reserve Room), Rio Piedras PR. 809-764-0000, Ext 2483

Santiago, Maria, *Tech Serv,* World University Library, Hato Rey PR. 809-765-4646, Ext 224

Santiago, Raymond, *Media,* World University Library, Hato Rey PR. 809-765-4646, Ext 224

Santini, Deborah, *On-Line Servs & Bibliog Instr,* Scranton Public Library, Albright Memorial Library, Scranton PA. 717-961-2451

Santini, Virginia, *Coordr,* Yakima Valley Community College, Raymond Library Media Ctr, Yakima WA. 509-575-2374

Santolla, Annette, *Commun Servs & Bkmobile Coordr,* New Castle Public Library, New Castle PA. 412-658-6659

Santonastaso, Adelaide, *Librn,* Editor & Publisher Library, New York NY. 212-752-7050

Santoro, Arlene, *Dir,* Frankfort Public Library District, Frankfort IL. 815-469-2423

Santoro, Helen C, *Coordr,* First Presbyterian Church Library, Perth Amboy NJ. 826-2138 & 2132

Santoro, Tesse, *Bibliog Instr,* Brooklyn College Library, Brooklyn NY. 212-780-5342

Santos, Bob, *Acq,* California State College, Stanislaus Library, Turlock CA. 209-633-2232

Santos, Emerenciana S, *Librn,* Burns & Roe, Inc, James B MacLean Technical Library, Woodbury NY. 516-677-4000

Santos, Josephine, *Librn,* Guam Public Library (Agat), Agana, Guam PI. 565-2661

Santos, Vera, *Librn,* Ak-Chin Community Library, Maricopa AZ. 602-568-2305

Sanz, Timothy L, *Dir,* Midway College, Marrs Library, Midway KY. 606-846-4421, Ext 38

Saperstein, Mrs Harry, *Pres,* Bridgeville Public Library, Bridgeville PA. 412-221-3737

Sapienza, Diane G, *Librn,* Kadison Pfaelzer Woodard Quinn & Rossi Library, Los Angeles CA. 213-688-9000

Sapienza, Vicky, *Librn,* Our Lady Queen of Martyrs Church, Saint Lucian Library, Birmingham MI. 313-644-8620

Saporito, Donald L, *Dir,* University of Southwestern Louisiana, Dupre Library, Lafayette LA. 318-264-6396

Sapp, Jane, *Circ,* West Georgia College Library, Carrollton GA. 404-834-1370

Sapp, Myrl, *Librn,* Choctawhatchee Regional Library (Daleville Community Reading Room), Daleville AL. 205-598-3111

Sapp, V J, *Librn,* Ohio Agricultural Research & Development Center Library, Wooster OH. 216-264-1021, Ext 265

Sappington, Melvin J, *Dir,* Pinal County Library System, Florence AZ. 602-868-5801, Ext 456

Sappington, Sue, *Librn,* Lubbock City-County Library (Slaton Branch), Slaton TX. 806-762-6411, Ext 2828

Saquet, Janette K, *Librn,* Smithsonian Institution Libraries (Anthropology), Washington DC. 202-381-5048

Saracevic, Tefko, *Prof,* Case Western Reserve University, School of Library Science, OH. 216-368-3500

Saracino, Stephanie, *ILL,* Ambassador College Library, Pasadena CA. 213-577-5540

Saraidaridis, Susan, *Librn,* Hewlett-Packard Medical Products Group Library, Waltham MA. 617-890-6300, Ext 337, 311

Sarangapane, Chet, *On-Line Servs,* University of the District of Columbia, Learning Resources Division, Washington DC. 202-282-7536

Sarault, Denyse, *Media,* College de Rimouski (CEGEP) Bibliotheque, Rimouski PQ. 418-723-1880

Sarazin, Molly, *Librn,* Blind River Public Library, Blind River ON. 705-356-7616

Sarber, Mary A, *Pub Servs,* El Paso Public Library, El Paso TX. 915-543-3804

Sardiello, Lucille, *Cat,* Rockville Centre Public Library, Rockville Centre NY. 516-766-6258

Sarenius, Ann, *Ch,* Comstock Township Library, Comstock MI. 616-345-0136

Sarette, Catherine, *Ch & Pub Servs,* Whatcom County Public Library, Bellingham WA. 206-384-3150

Sargent, Dency, *Exec Dir,* Capitol Region Library Council, CT. 203-549-0404

Sargent, Mary, *ILL,* University of Maine at Augusta, Learning Resources Center, Augusta ME. 207-622-7131
Sargent, Phyllis M, *Librn,* Mobay Chemical Corp, Agricultural Chemicals Division Library, Kansas City MO. 816-242-2236
Sargent, Seymour, *Asst Prof,* University of Wisconsin-Oshkosh, Dept of Library Science, WI. 414-424-2313
Sarich, Diane, *Asst Librn,* Saskatoon Public Library (Mayfair), Saskatoon SK. 306-664-9591
Sariego, Mary A, *Dir,* Robertsdale Public Library, Robertsdale AL. 205-947-5720
Sarle, Rodney, *Chief, Overseas Opers Div,* Library of Congress, Washington DC. 202-287-5000
Sarli, Frances, *Cat & Ref,* Field Library, Peekskill Library, Peekskill NY. 914-737-0010
Sarna, Helen, *Asst Dir,* Hebrew College, Jacob & Rose Grossman Library, Brookline MA. 617-232-8710, 232-8711
Saron, Phyllis, *YA,* Eager Free Public Library, Evansville WI. 608-882-4230
Sarraga, Raquel, *Spec Coll,* University of Puerto Rico Library, Jose M Lazaro Memorial Library, Rio Piedras PR. 809-764-0000, Ext 3296
Sarrasin, Louis, *Librn,* University of Montreal Libraries (Computer Science), Montreal PQ. 514-343-6819
Sartorius, Richard C, *Librn,* Gulf Oil Corporation (Gulf Oil Chemicals Co, Houston Research Labs Library), Houston TX. 713-493-0100, Ext 215
Sarver, Joyce, *Asst Librn,* Acadia Parish Library (Crowley Branch), Crowley LA. 318-788-1880
Sarver, Mary Ann, *Ch,* Rockford Public Library, Rockford IL. 815-965-6731
Sarwat, Catherine Picory, *Ref,* Chateauguay Municipal Library, Chateauguay PQ. 514-691-1934
Sass, Herman, *Librn,* Buffalo & Erie County Historical Society Library, Buffalo NY. 716-873-9644
Sass, Patricia, *Librn,* Saint Clair County Library System (Clay Township), Algonac MI. 313-794-4471
Sasse, Margo, *Media,* San Diego Mesa College Library, San Diego CA. 714-279-2300, Ext 385
Sasseen, Elizabeth, *Librn,* General Foods Corp (Marketing Information Center), White Plains NY. 914-683-3911
Sasser, Bessie, *Librn,* Tuscaloosa Public Library, Tuscaloosa AL. 205-345-5820
Sasser, Caroline A, *Librn,* W R Grace & Co, Washington Research Center Library, Columbia MD. 301-531-4000
Sasso, Theresa, *Actg Dir,* Hoboken Public Library, Hoboken NJ. 201-420-2346
Sassoon, Joseph, *Asst Librn,* Civil Court of the City of New York Library, New York NY. 212-374-8043
Satagaj, Sallie Ann, *Librn,* Austin Public Library (Twin Oaks), Austin TX. 512-472-5433
Satchell, Mary Alice, *Librn,* Hillsborough Community College Library, Tampa FL. 813-247-6641, Ext 261
Satcher, Constance Ann, *Librn,* Laurens County Library (Joanna Memorial Branch), Joanna SC. 803-697-5291
Sathrum, Bob, *On-Line Servs,* Humboldt State University Library, Arcata CA. 707-826-3441
Satlerwhite, Robert, *Area Ref,* Florence County Library, Florence SC. 803-662-8424
Sato, Fumi, *Librn,* International Pacific Salmon Fisheries Commission Library, New Westminster BC. 604-521-3771
Sato, Miriam H, *Librn,* Hawaii Institute of Geophysics Library, Honolulu HI. 808-948-7040
Satory, Ione, *Ch,* LeMars Public Library, Le Mars IA. 712-546-5004
Satterfield, Helen C, *Dir,* Highland County District, Hillsboro Public Library, Hillsboro OH. 513-393-3114
Satterwhite, Mary H, *Asst Librn,* Temple Terrace Public Library, Temple Terrace FL. 813-988-4731
Sattley, Enid, *Librn,* Illiopolis Public Library, Illiopolis IL. 217-486-5561
Saucier, Claire L, *Librn,* Dayton Memorial Library, Dayton WA. 509-382-4131
Saucier, Cynthia, *Ad,* Pasadena Public Library, Pasadena TX. 713-477-0276

Saucier, Diane, *On-Line Servs & Bibliog Instr,* East Texas State University, James Gilliam Gee Library, Commerce TX. 214-886-5717
Saucier, Marion, *Acq,* Leominster Public Library, Leominster MA. 617-537-0941
Sauder, Joseph B, *TV,* County College of Morris, Sherman H Masten Learning Resource Center, Randolph Township NJ. 201-361-5000, Ext 470
Sauder, Judy, *Circ & AV,* Florida Institute of Technology Library, Melbourne FL. 305-723-3701, Ext 270
Sauder, Phil, *Dir,* Kenosha County Historical Museum Library, Kenosha WI. 414-654-5770
Sauer, Charlotte E, *Librn,* American Patent Law Association Library, Patent Law Library, Arlington VA. 703-521-1680
Sauer, Dora, *Purchasing,* Detroit Public Library, Detroit Associated Libraries, Detroit MI. 313-833-1000
Sauer, Eloise A, *Librn,* United States Army (Corps of Engineers, South Pacific Div Library), San Francisco CA. 415-556-0914
Sauer, James L, *Assoc Librn & Ref,* Eastern College, Frank Warner Memorial Library, Saint Davids PA. 215-688-3300, Ext 210
Sauer, Jean, *Acq,* State University of New York, College at New Paltz, Sojourner Truth Library, New Paltz NY. 914-257-2204
Sauer, Jeff, *Circ,* Western Carolina University, Hunter Memorial Library, Cullowhee NC. 704-293-7306
Sauer, Kathryn, *Admin,* West Chicago Public Library, West Chicago IL. 312-231-1552
Sauer, Luana, *Asst Librn,* Hill County Rural Free Library, Havre MT. 406-265-5481, Ext 49
Sauer, Mary, *Chief, Serial Record Div,* Library of Congress, Washington DC. 202-287-5000
Sauerbier, Yvonne, *Librn,* Chicago Public Library (Marshall Square), Chicago IL. 312-523-0061
Sauke, Nora H, *Acq,* Baldwin-Wallace College, Ritter Library, Berea OH. 216-826-2204, 2205, Ext 2455
Saul, Beth, *Librn,* Library Association of Portland (Belmont), Portland OR. 503-232-3581
Saul, Frederick, *Bkmobile Coordr,* Park County Public Library, Bailey CO. 303-838-5539
Saul, Patricia, *Cat,* County of Henrico Public Library, Richmond VA. 804-222-1643
Saulen, Patricia A, *Dir,* Huntingdon County Library, Huntingdon PA. 814-643-0200
Saulitis, John P, *Dir,* State University of New York College, Daniel A Reed Library, Fredonia NY. 716-673-3183
Sauls, Rachel, *Librn,* Allendale-Hampton-Jasper Regional Library (Estill), Allendale SC. 803-584-3513
Saunders, Calvin, *In Charge,* Halliburton Services, Research Center Library, Duncan OK. 405-251-3080
Saunders, Charlotte, *Librn,* UTHE Technology, Inc, Library, Sunnyvale CA. 408-738-3301
Saunders, Edwina, *Librn,* Tampa Bay Regional Planning Council, Research & Information Library, Saint Petersburg FL. 813-577-5151
Saunders, Eleanor, *Institution & Homebound,* Bedford Public Library, Bedford VA. 703-586-8911
Saunders, Esther, *Cat,* Geauga County Public Library, Chardon OH. 216-285-7601
Saunders, Frances P, *Tech Serv & Cat,* Baldwin-Wallace College, Ritter Library, Berea OH. 216-826-2204, 2205, Ext 2455
Saunders, Isabelle M, *Librn,* Leechburg Public Library, Leechburg PA. 412-845-1911
Saunders, Janice, *Librn,* Deer Lodge Hospital, Medical Reference Library, Winnipeg MB. 204-837-1301
Saunders, Joan D, *Acq,* Eisenhower College of the Rochester Institute of Technology, Ellis Slater Library, Seneca Falls NY. 315-568-7171
Saunders, Joleen, *ILL & On-Line Servs,* Southwest Kansas Library System, Dodge City KS. 316-225-1231
Saunders, Juliet, *Asst Librn,* Providence Athenaeum, Providence RI. 401-421-6970
Saunders, June, *Librn,* Estacada Public Library, Estacada OR. 503-630-3224
Saunders, Karen, *Tech Serv,* Santa Clara City Library, Santa Clara CA. 408-984-3097
Saunders, Larry N, *Media,* Alabama Agricultural & Mechanical University, Joseph F Drake Memorial Learning Resources Center, Normal AL. 205-859-7309

Saunders, Laurel B, *Ch,* United States Army (Legal Library), White Sands Missile Range NM. 505-678-1317
Saunders, Laurel B, *Librn,* United States Army (Technical Library), White Sands Missile Range NM. 505-678-1317
Saunders, Laverna M, *Media,* Union College, Abigail E Weeks Memorial Library, Barbourville KY. 606-546-4151, Ext 137
Saunders, Lelia B, *Dir,* Arlington County Department of Libraries, Arlington Public Library, Arlington VA. 703-527-4777
Saunders, Marilyn, *Flm,* Russell Public Library, Middletown CT. 203-347-2528
Saunders, Marjorie, *Assoc Librn,* Case Western Reserve University & Cleveland Medical Library Association, Cleveland Health Sciences Library, Cleveland OH. 216-368-3426
Saunders, Marjorie, *Adjunct Prof,* Case Western Reserve University, School of Library Science, OH. 216-368-3500
Saunders, Michael C, *AV,* Floyd Junior College Library, Rome GA. 404-295-6318
Saunders, Patricia, *Librn,* Cleveland Public Library (Rockport), Cleveland OH. 216-251-4466
Saunders, William B, *Dir,* Antioch University Library, Philadelphia Center Library, Philadelphia PA. 215-849-3505, Ext 47
Saunders, Wilma B, *Librn,* Putnam County Library (Hurricane Branch), Hurricane WV. 304-562-6711
Saunter, Robert E, *Dir,* Warder Public Library, Springfield OH. 323-8616 & 323-9751
Saur, Jean, *Librn,* Sparta Township Library, Sparta MI. 616-887-9937
Sauro, Nancy, *Head,* University of Minnesota Libraries-Twin Cities (Learning Center), Minneapolis MN. 612-376-7005
Sauro, Ricardo H, *Librn,* Corning Public Library, Corning IA. 515-322-3866
Sausedo, Ann E, *Dir,* Los Angeles Herald-Examiner Library, Los Angeles CA. 213-748-1212
Saut, Mary Ann, *ILL & Ref,* American University (Washington College of Law Library), Washington DC. 202-686-2625
Sauter, Dortha, *Ch,* Boulder City Library, Boulder City NV. 702-293-1281
Sauter, Hubert E, *Admin,* Defense Technical Information Center, VA. 703-274-6881
Sautter, Mrs Dan, *Dir,* Scotia Public Library, Scotia NE. 308-245-3431
Sauvageau, Philippe, *Dir,* Bibliotheque De Quebec, Quebec PQ. 418-694-6356
Sauve, Hannah, *Librn,* Township of the North Shore Public Library, Spanish ON. 705-844-2555
Savage, Carl, *Prof,* Saint Cloud State University, Center for Library & Audiovisual Education, MN. 612-255-2022
Savage, Elizabeth, *Librn,* Pasadena Public Library (Hill Ave), Pasadena CA. 213-794-1219
Savage, Gail, *Asst Librn,* Baltimore Museum of Art Library, Baltimore MD. 301-396-6317
Savage, Jan, *Spec Coll,* Ouachita Baptist University, Riley Library, Arkadelphia AR. 501-246-4531, Ext 121
Savage, John, *Librn,* North Babylon Public Library, North Babylon NY. 516-669-4020
Savage, Linda, *Circ,* Massachusetts College of Art Library, Boston MA. 617-731-2340, Ext 26
Savage, N, *Ch,* Kennebunk Free Library, Kennebunk ME. 207-985-2173
Savage, Pearl J, *Librn,* United States Air Force (Mountain Home Air Force Base Library), Mountain Home AFB ID. 208-828-2544
Savage, Rosalind, *Curator Black Heritage Ctr,* Langston University, G Lamar Harrison Library, Langston OK. 405-466-2231, Ext 231
Savage, Vandolyn, *Asst Dir Tech Servs,* University of Houston (M D Anderson Memorial Library), Houston TX. 713-749-4241
Savalli, Antonette E, *Coll Develop,* Spokane Public Library, Comstock Building Library, Spokane WA. 509-838-3361, Ext 65
Savard, Louise, *Prof,* CEGEP Francois-Xavier Garneau, Techniques de la Documentation, PQ. 418-688-8310, Ext 290
Savaro, Josephine, *Dir,* Saint Joseph's University Libraries (Drexel Library), Philadelphia PA. 215-879-7559

Savedra, Catherine, *AV,* West Los Angeles College Library, Culver City CA. 213-836-7110, Ext 301
Savell, Sue, *Librn,* First Baptist Church, Mattie D Hall Memorial Library, Rosedale MS. 601-759-6378
Saviers, Dorothy, *Cat,* Taylor Memorial Public Library, Cuyahoga Falls Public Library, Cuyahoga Falls OH. 216-928-2117
Saville, Jr, James, *Media,* Albany Junior College, Library-Learning Resources Ctr, Albany GA. 912-439-4332
Saviteer, Loretta, *Asst Librn,* Meriden-Wallingford Hospital, Health Sciences Library, Meriden CT. 203-238-0771, Ext 342
Savoie, Edmond A, *Dir,* North Bergen Free Public Library, North Bergen NJ. 201-869-4715
Savoie, Terttu, *Cat,* Eastern Nazarene College, Nease Library, Wollaston MA. 617-773-6350, Ext 251
Sawa, Maureen, *Commun Servs,* Kitchener Public Library, Kitchener ON. 519-743-0271
Sawaryn, Radomira M, *Librn,* Western Electric Co, Inc, Technical Library, Baltimore MD. 301-563-6373
Sawczuk, Marta, *Acq,* Jersey City State College, Forrest A Irwin Library, Jersey City NJ. 201-547-3026
Sawdey, Erla, *Librn,* Lenawee County Library (Clayton Branch), Clayton MI. 517-263-1011
Sawhill, Mrs John, *Librn,* New Canaan Nature Center Library, New Canaan CT. 203-966-9577
Sawin, Philip, *Coll Devel,* University of Wisconsin-Stout, Pierce Library, Menomonie WI. 715-232-1184
Sawyer, Ardis, *Dir,* Minnesota Bible College Library, Rochester MN. 507-288-4563, Ext 30
Sawyer, Elsie R, *Asst Librn,* Tyrrell County Public Library, Columbia NC. 919-796-3771
Sawyer, Jean, *Librn,* Canada Department of Agriculture, Research Station Library, Kentville NS. 902-678-2171, Ext 213
Sawyer, Joanne, *Rare Bks & Spec Coll,* Hiram College, Teachout-Price Memorial Library, Hiram OH. 216-569-3211, Ext 220
Sawyer, Karol, *Librn,* New Gloucester Public Library, New Gloucester ME. 207-926-4840
Sawyer, Larry, *Media & Tech Serv,* Kearney State College, Calvin T Ryan Library, Kearney NE. 308-236-4218
Sawyer, Lola, *Librn,* Prince George's County Memorial Library System (Marlboro Branch), Marlboro MD. 301-627-3237
Sawyer, Mary, *Ref,* Oakland Public Library, Oakland CA. 415-273-3281
Sawyer, Michael, *Librn,* Southern Ohio Correctional Facility Library, Lucasville OH. 614-259-5544, Ext 28
Sawyer, Miriam, *Dir,* William E Dermody Free Public Library, Carlstadt NJ. 201-438-8866
Sawyer, Pearl, *Librn,* Newport News Public Library System (Newport News Public Law), Newport News VA. 804-247-8678
Sawyer, Ruth, *Librn,* University of Texas Libraries (Library School), Austin TX. 512-471-7598
Sawyer, Stan, *Commun Servs,* Colquitt-Thomas Regional Library, Moultrie-Colquitt County Library, Moultrie GA. 912-985-6540
Sawyer, Stan, *Ad,* Roddenbery Memorial Library, Cairo GA. 912-377-3632
Sawyer, Warren A, *Dir,* Medical University of South Carolina Library, Charleston SC. 803-792-2374
Sawyers, Beryl, *Librn,* Gary Public Library (Tolleston), Gary IN. 219-944-2795
Sawyers, Elizabeth J, *Dir,* Ohio State University Libraries (Health Sciences Library), Columbus OH. 614-422-9810
Sax, J, *In Charge,* University of Toronto Libraries (Physiology), Toronto ON. 416-978-2588
Saxe, Charles, *Sr Librns,* New York State Library (Serials Processing), Albany NY. 518-474-6280, 474-7868
Saxe, Minna, *Ser,* City University of New York, Library of Graduate School & University Center, New York NY. 212-790-4541
Saxine, Anita C, *Spec Coll,* Saint Mary's University (Academic Library), San Antonio TX. 512-436-3441
Saxon, Jo Ann, *Dir,* Worthington Community College, Learning Resource Center, Worthington MN. 507-372-2107, Ext 50

Saxon, Virginia, *Bkmobile Coordr,* Joliet Public Library, Joliet IL. 815-727-4726
Saxton, Evelyn, *Cat,* Yuma Public Library, Yuma CO. 303-848-2368
Sayah, Pauline, *Librn,* Waterbury Town Library, Waterbury Center VT. 802-244-7079
Sayce, Bonnie, *Br Asst,* Timberland Regional Library (Ocean Park Branch), Ocean Park WA. 206-665-4184
Saye, Jerry, *Asst Prof,* Drexel University, School of Library & Information Science, PA. 215-895-2474
Saye, Sharon R, *Dir,* Benedum Civic Center Library, Bridgeport WV. 304-842-6201, Ext 33
Sayen, Dorothy, *Circ,* Bala Cynwyd Library, Bala-Cynwyd PA. 215-664-1196
Sayen, Louise Dodd, *Dir,* Vermillion Public Library, Vermillion SD. 605-624-2741
Sayer, Edith, *Dir,* North Greenville College, Averyt Learning Center Library, Tigerville SC. 803-895-1410
Sayer, Karen, *Acq,* University of Michigan Libraries (Ford L Lemler Educational Film Library), Ann Arbor MI. 313-764-5360
Sayers, John E, *Dir,* Vandercook College of Music, Harry Ruppel Memorial Library, Chicago IL. 312-326-4284
Sayers, R B, *Librn,* Veterans Administration, Medical Center Library Service, Knoxville IA. 515-842-3101, Ext 342, 242
Sayers, Winifred F, *In Charge,* GPU Service Corp Library, Reading PA. 215-376-5628
Sayers, Winifred F, *Librn,* GPU Service Corporation, Corporate Library, Parsippany NJ. 201-263-6184
Sayles, Adele, *Librn,* Temple Israel Library of Judaica, West Palm Beach FL. 305-833-8421
Sayles, Eleanor G, *Librn,* EduCom, Interuniversity Community Council, Inc Library, Princeton NJ. 609-921-7575
Sayles, Jeremy, *Instr,* Georgia College, Education Library Media, GA. 912-453-4047 & 453-5573
Sayles, Jeremy, *Reader Serv,* Georgia College, Ina Dillard Russell Library, Milledgeville GA. 912-453-4047, 453-5573
Saylor, L, *Librn,* Stauffer Chemical Co, de Guigne Technical Center Research Library, Richmond CA. 415-231-1020
Saylor, Lorna, *ILL,* Lebanon County Library System, Lebanon PA. 717-273-7624
Sayre, Edward C, *Dir,* Mesa Public Library, Los Alamos NM. 662-3209; 662-2997
Sayre, Elissa, *Librn,* Weston State Hospital, Patients' Library, Weston WV. 304-269-1210, Ext 399
Sayre, John L, *Dir,* Phillips University, Education & Library Science Study Area, OK. 405-237-4433, Ext 417
Sayre, John L, *Dir,* Phillips University (John Rogers Graduate Seminary Library), Enid OK. 405-237-4433, Ext 227
Sayre, John L, *Dir,* Phillips University, Zollars Memorial Library, Enid OK. 405-237-4433, Ext 251
Sayre, Sam, *Asst Ref & On-Line Servs,* Idaho State University Library, Pocatello ID. 208-236-3202
Sayrs, Judith, *Ref,* Credit Union National Association, Inc, Information Resource Center, Madison WI. 608-231-4170
Sazarin, Shirley, *Librn,* Golden Lake Public Library, Golden Lake ON. 613-625-2180
Sazima, Sue, *Librn,* Veterans Memorial Library (Coe Township), Shepherd MI. 517-828-5163
Sbacchi, Margareta E G, *Cat,* Atlantic Union College, G Eric Jones Library, South Lancaster MA. 617-365-4561
Scaini, Lea, *Documentarian,* Beauchemin-Beaton-LaPointe, Inc, BBL Library, Montreal PQ. 514-871-9555, Ext 204
Scally, William, *Librn,* Allendale-Hampton-Jasper Regional Library (Hardeeville), Allendale SC. 803-584-3513
Scalzi, Francis J, *Librn,* Veterans Administration, Hospital Medical Library, Erie PA. 814-868-8661
Scalzo, Geraldine, *Librn,* University of California, Berkeley (Social Sciences), Berkeley CA. 415-642-0370
Scammahorn, Muriel E, *Dir,* Roxana Public Library, Roxana IL. 618-254-6713
Scammell, Harry D, *Librn,* Yale University Library (Geology), New Haven CT. 203-436-2480

Scanderva, J S, *Dir,* Rushmore Memorial Public Library, Highland Mills NY. 914-928-6162
Scanga, Mary, *Cat,* Abington Free Library, Abington PA. 215-885-5180
Scanlan, C Patrick, *Libr Security & Safety,* Chicago Public Library, Chicago IL. 312-269-2900
Scanlan, Jean M, *Dir,* Price Waterhouse Information Center, Boston MA. 617-423-7330, Ext 219
Scanlan, Jeffrey, *Ref,* Greenwich Library, Greenwich CT. 203-622-7900
Scanlon, Betty, *Librn,* Lockheed Corporation (International Marketing Library), Burbank CA. 213-847-6527
Scanlon, Joan, *Cat,* University of Winnipeg Library, Winnipeg MB. 204-786-7811, Ext 520
Scanlon, Mary E, *ILL & Ref,* West Islip Public Library, West Islip NY. 516-661-7080, 661-7082
Scanlon, Mary R, *Dir,* Middlesex General Hospital, Medical Library, New Brunswick NJ. 201-828-3000, Ext 594
Scanlon, Patrick J, *Dir,* Baldwin-Wallace College, Ritter Library, Berea OH. 216-826-2204, 2205, Ext 2455
Scanlon, Regina, *Cat,* Connetquot Public Library, Bohemia NY. 516-567-5115
Scanlon, Virginia, *Librn,* Connecticut State Library (Middletown Branch), Middletown CT. 203-566-4301
Scanlon, Virginia, *Librn,* Connecticut State Library (Rockville Branch), Rockville CT. 203-566-4301
Scannell, Elizabeth F, *Librn,* Boston School Committee, Administration Library, Boston MA. 617-726-6449
Scannell, Francis X, *State Librn,* Michigan State Library, Lansing MI. 517-373-1580
Scannell, Karen, *Ch,* San Francisco Public Library, San Francisco CA. 415-558-4235
Scannell, Mary R, *Dir,* Grand Ledge Public Library, Grand Ledge MI. 517-627-7014
Scantland, Jean-M, *Media,* Universite Laval Bibliotheque, Quebec PQ. 418-656-3344
Scarberry, Glenna, *Asst Librn,* McDowell Public Library, Welch WV. 304-436-3070
Scarberry, Helen, *Cat,* Cabell County Public Library, Western Counties Regional Library System, Huntington WV. 304-523-9451
Scarborough, John, *Librn,* Arkansas Baptist College Library, Little Rock AR. 501-374-4923
Scarborough, Mayra, *On-Line Servs & Bibliog Instr,* Hoffmann-La Roche Inc (Business Information Center), Nutley NJ. 201-235-3901
Scarborough, Ruth Ellen, *Dir,* Centenary College, Taylor Memorial Learning Resource Center, Hackettstown NJ. 201-852-1400, Ext 244
Scardaville, Michael C, *Librn,* Saint Augustine Historical Society Library, Saint Augustine FL. 904-829-5514
Scardenski, Irene, *Librn,* General Electric Co (Direct Current Motor & Generator Products Dept Library), Erie PA. 814-455-5466
Scaritt, Valerie, *Librn,* Tuscaloosa Public Library (Northport Branch), Northport AL. 205-345-5820
Scarlet, Robert, *Librn,* Memphis Academy of Arts, G Pillow Lewis Memorial Library, Memphis TN. 901-726-4085
Scarpato, Loann, *Ref,* Eastern Pennsylvania Psychiatric Institute Library, Philadelphia PA. 215-842-4508, 842-4509 & 842-4510
Scarry, Patricia, *Dir,* Sussex County Department of Libraries, Georgetown DE. 302-856-7701, Ext 292
Scarseth, Sonja, *Tech Serv, Cat & On-Line Servs,* Aurora College, Charles B Phillips Library, Aurora IL. 312-892-6431, Ext 61, 62
Scaruff, Ellen, *Bibliog Prep,* Loyola University of Chicago Libraries, Chicago IL. 312-274-3000, Ext 771
Scavone, Patricia, *Ad,* Westmont Public Library, Westmont IL. 312-969-5625
Scepanski, Jordan M, *Dir,* Vanderbilt University Library (Central-Science), Nashville TN. 615-322-6603
Schaad, Mrs Leroy, *Librn,* Callaway Township Library, Callaway NE. 308-836-2610
Schaaf, Kathy, *Ch,* George W Norris Regional Library, McCook Public Library, McCook NE. 308-345-1906
Schaaf, Willa, *Dir,* La Veta Public Library, La Veta CO. 303-742-3572

Schaafsma, Carol, *Acq & Ser,* University of Hawaii (University of Hawaii Library), Honolulu HI. 808-948-7205
Schabel, Donald, *Tech Serv,* Chicago Public Library, Chicago IL. 312-269-2900
Schacher, Betty, *Ch,* Ridgefield Public Library, Ridgefield NJ. 201-941-0192
Schacht, Charles, *Ch & YA,* Southwest Wisconsin Library System, Fennimore WI. 608-822-3393
Schacht, David, *Geol-Earth Sci,* Oregon State University, William Jasper Kerr Library, Corvallis OR. 503-754-3411
Schachter, Bert, *Librn,* Ted Bates & Co, Inc Library, New York NY. 212-869-3131, Ext 7810
Schad, Evelyn B, *Librn,* Royersford Free Public Library, Royersford PA. 215-948-7277
Schad, Jasper G, *Dean,* Wichita State University, Library & Media Resources Center, Wichita KS. 316-689-3586
Schade, Barbara, *Dir,* Crowder College, Learning Resources Center, Neosho MO. 417-451-3223, Ext 9
Schade, Donald, *Librn,* Brooklyn Public Library (Borough Park), Brooklyn NY. 212-435-3375
Schade, Rudolf, *Archives,* Elmhurst College, A C Buehler Library, Elmhurst IL. 312-279-4100, Ext 255
Schade, Susan, *Ref,* Old Lyme, Phoebe Griffin Noyes Library, Old Lyme CT. 203-434-1684
Schadel, Ann, *Libr Aid,* Environmental Protection Agency (Office of Air Quality Planning & Standards Library), Research Triangle Park NC. 919-541-5255
Schader, Sondra E, *Librn,* Detrex Chemical Industries Inc Library, Southfield MI. 313-358-5800
Schadlich, Thomas, *Tech Serv & Cat,* Prosser Public Library, Bloomfield CT. 203-243-9721
Schaeder, Caryl, *Ch,* Bergenfield Free Public Library, Bergenfield NJ. 201-384-2765
Schaeder, Patricia, *Ch & YA,* Bala Cynwyd Library, Bala-Cynwyd PA. 215-664-1196
Schaefer, Lyle L, *In Charge,* Lutheran Church Missouri Synod, Archives Colorado District Library, Aurora CO. 303-364-9148
Schaefer, Patricia, *Librn,* Muncie-Center Township Public Library (Audio-Visual Center), Muncie IN. 317-288-1411
Schaefer, Patricia, *Librn,* Pasadena Public Library (Linda Vista), Pasadena CA. 213-793-1808
Schaefer, Renate, *Dir,* Ridgefield Public Library, Ridgefield NJ. 201-941-0192
Schaefer, Rose Mary, *Librn,* University of Minnesota Libraries-Twin Cities (Natural History), Minneapolis MN. 612-373-7771
Schaefer, Steve, *Public Servs,* Ohoopee Regional Library, Vidalia-Toombs County Library Headquarters, Vidalia GA. 912-537-9283
Schaeffer, Lorraine D, *Asst Dir,* State Library of Florida, Div of Library Services, Dept of State, Tallahassee FL. 904-487-2651
Schaeffer, Rex, *Librn,* Gannett Rochester Newspapers Library, Rochester NY. 716-232-7100
Schaeffer, Sister M Josepha, *In Charge,* Saint Mary's Hospital Medical Center (Nurses Library), Green Bay WI. 414-494-3474, Ext 262
Schael, Donna, *Librn,* Lawler Public Library, Lawler IA. 515-238-3672
Schaer, Martha, *Dir,* Yankton Community Library, Yankton SD. 605-665-4501, Ext 34
Schaerrer, Maggie, *Tech Serv, Commun Servs & Spec Coll,* Provo City Public Library, Provo UT. 801-373-1494
Schafer, Allene, *Acq,* New Brunswick Theological Seminary, Gardner A Sage Library, New Brunswick NJ. 201-247-5241, Ext 6
Schafer, James E, *Librn,* Lincoln Park Public Library, Lincoln Park MI. 313-381-0374
Schafer, Jane E, *Dir,* Northwest Regional Library, Belle Fourche SD. 605-892-4420
Schafer, Jay, *Librn,* Denver Public Library (Hadley), Denver CO. 303-573-5152, Ext 271
Schafer, Jean, *Asst Librn,* Kings County Library, Hanford CA. 209-582-0261
Schafer, Jean, *Librn,* Kings County Library (Hanford), Hanford CA. 209-582-0261
Schafer, Quynh, *Ref,* Saint Mary's Dominican College, John XXIII Library, New Orleans LA. 504-865-7761, Ext 225
Schafer, Sherry, *Librn,* Ernst & Whinney Library, Los Angeles CA. 213-977-4401

Schaff, Cynthia, *Librn,* James Memorial Library, Williston ND. 701-572-9751
Schaffer, Carol, *Tech Serv,* Lakeshore Technical Institute, Educational Resources Center, Cleveland WI. 414-693-8211, 684-4408, Ext 150
Schaffer, Evelyn J, *Dir Libr Serv,* Veterans Administration, Medical Center, Huntington WV. 304-429-6741, Ext 328, 370
Schaffer, Jo, *Curator,* State University of New York College (Art Slide), Cortland NY. 607-753-4316
Schaffner, Dorothy, *Librn,* Shaker Heights Public Library (Bertram Woods Branch), Shaker Heights OH. 216-991-2421
Schaffner, Richard, *Librn,* Stark County District Library (DeHoff), Canton OH. 216-452-9014
Schaible, Helen, *Dir,* Mott Public Library, Mott ND. 701-824-2163
Schaich, Barbara, *Program Servs,* Detroit Public Library, Detroit Associated Libraries, Detroit MI. 313-833-1000
Schaich, Barbara Eierman, *Tech Serv,* Shawnee State College Library, Portsmouth OH. 614-354-3205, Ext 29
Schaiewitz, Regina, *Tech Serv,* Mount Vernon Public Library, Mount Vernon NY. 914-668-1840
Schaitberger, Ann, *Br Coordr,* Johnson Free Public Library, Hackensack NJ. 201-343-4169
Schaitberger, Ann, *Librn,* Johnson Free Public Library (Washington Institute), Hackensack NJ. 201-343-4155
Schalau, Sr, Robert D, *Dir,* Chesapeake Public Library, Chesapeake VA. 804-547-6579, 547-6592
Schalk, Katherine, *Asst Dir,* South Jersey Regional Film Library, Inc, Voorhees NJ. 609-772-1642
Schall, Marguerite, *Librn,* Cragin Memorial Library, Colchester CT. 203-537-5752
Schaller, Barbara J, *Dir & Acq,* Lynn Public Library, Lynn MA. 617-595-0567
Schallert, Ruth E, *Librn,* Smithsonian Institution Libraries (Botany), Washington DC. 202-381-5996
Schalow, Gertrude E, *Asst Librn,* United States Department of the Interior (Bureau of Reclamation Library), Denver CO. 303-234-3019
Schalow, John, *Tech Serv,* Cary Memorial Library, Lexington MA. 617-862-6288
Schalow, Mary J, *Librn,* Salt River Project Library, Tempe AZ. 602-273-5304
Schambow, Karen H, *Ch & Ref,* Burlington Public Library, Burlington WI. 414-763-7623
Schanck, Peter C, *Dir,* University of Detroit Library (Law), Detroit MI. 313-961-5444, Ext 239, 240 & 241
Schandorff, Esther, *Chief Librn,* Point Loma College, Ryan Library, San Diego CA. 714-222-6474, Ext 355, 338
Schapiro, Sue H, *Ref & Ser,* State University Agricultural & Technical College at Farmingdale, Thomas D Greenley Library, Farmingdale NY. 516-420-2011, 420-2012
Schappler, Norbert, *Dir,* Conception Abbey & Conception Seminary College Library, Conception MO. 816-944-2211
Schara, Rita M, *Dir,* Norwalk State Technical College Library, Norwalk CT. 203-838-0601
Scharf, Charlotte, *Per,* State University Agricultural & Technical College at Farmingdale, Thomas D Greenley Library, Farmingdale NY. 516-420-2011, 420-2012
Scharf, Mary, *Librn,* Fond Du Lac Circuit Court, Law Library, Fond Du Lac WI. 414-921-5600
Scharff, Chris, *Librn,* Langston Laboratories, Inc Library, Leawood KS. 913-341-7800
Scharlock, Nidia T, *Ref & On-Line Servs,* University of Rochester (Edward G Miner Library, School of Medicine & Dentistry), Rochester NY. 716-275-3364
Scharmer, Roger C J, *Librn,* United States Forest Service, Forest Products Laboratory Library, Madison WI. 608-264-5713
Schatz, Natalie, *Chief, Doc,* Harvard University Library (Harvard College Library (Headquarters in Harry Elkins Widener Memorial Library)), Cambridge MA. 617-495-2401
Schatz, Scherelene, *ILL,* Cedar Crest College, Cressman Library, Allentown PA. 215-437-4471, Ext 264

Schatz, Scherelene, *ILL,* Muhlenberg College, John A W Haas Library, Allentown PA. 215-433-3191, Ext 214
Schatzman, Erna, *Data Serv,* University of Wisconsin-Milwaukee, Golda Meir Library, Milwaukee WI. 414-963-4785
Schaub, Lynda, *Librn,* Lennox & Addington County Public Library (Bath Branch), Bath ON. 613-354-2585
Schaub, Theresa, *Ch,* Traverse City Public Library, Traverse City MI. 616-941-2311
Schauble, Leona, *Dir,* Ramsey Free Public Library, Ramsey NJ. 201-327-1445
Schauer, Lucille, *Dir,* Spalding College Library, Louisville KY. 502-585-9411
Schauman, Claudia, *Librn,* Public Library of Nashville & Davidson County (Thompson Lane), Nashville TN. 615-833-4270
Schaumburg, William B, *Tech Serv,* Rock Island Public Library, Rock Island IL. 309-788-7627
Schaut, E L, *Mgr,* S C Johnson & Son Inc, Technical & Business Information Center, Racine WI. 414-554-2372
Schaver, Diane, *Circ,* Beaverton City Library, Beaverton OR. 503-644-2197
Schear, Thomas W, *Dir,* Passaic Public Library, Julius Forstmann Library, Passaic NJ. 201-779-0474
Schechter, Fred, *Central Libr,* San Diego Public Library, San Diego CA. 714-236-5800
Schechtman, Joan, *In Charge,* Union Carbide Corp (Library & Technical Information Serv), Tarrytown NY. 914-789-3700
Scheck, George, *ILL,* State University of New York, College of Arts & Science at Oswego, Penfield Library, Oswego NY. 315-341-4232
Scheckter, June R, *Tech Serv,* Burlington County Library, Mount Holly NJ. 609-267-9660
Scheckter, Stella J, *ILL & Ref,* New Hampshire State Library, Concord NH. 603-271-2392
Schedley, Esther, *Librn,* Milan-Berlin Township Public Library (Berlin Township Public), Berlin Heights OH. 419-588-2250
Scheel, Flora, *YA,* Morton Grove Public Library, Morton Grove IL. 312-965-4220
Scheel, Grace, *Librn,* Mississauga Public Library (Lakeview), Mississauga ON. 416-274-5027
Scheele, Barbara, *On-Line Servs,* Brooklyn College Library, Brooklyn NY. 212-780-5342
Scheele, William E, *Dir,* Columbus Museum of Arts & Sciences, Research Library, Columbus GA. 404-323-3617
Scheer, Anne B, *Librn,* Internal Revenue Service Library, Washington DC. 202-566-6342
Scheer, Carolyn, *Ref,* Scenic Regional Library of Franklin, Gasconade & Warren Counties, Union MO. 314-583-3224
Scheer, Gladys E, *Asst Librn,* Lexington Theological Seminary, Bosworth Memorial Library, Lexington KY. 606-252-0361, Ext 21
Scheer, Jon, *Librn,* Jackson Metropolitan Library (South Hills), Jackson MS. 601-352-3677
Scheer, Wm K, *Librn,* Adams County Public Library (Perl Mack), North Glenn CO. 303-428-3576
Scheetz, Stanley, *Librn,* Medina County Law Library Association, Medina OH. 216-723-3641, Ext 2877
Scheffler, Diana, *Tech Serv & Acq,* San Diego County Library, San Diego CA. 714-565-5100
Scheffler, Hannah N, *Librn,* New York Public Library (Early Childhood Resource & Information Center), New York NY. 212-929-0815
Scheffler, Margaret, *Acq,* Kirkwood Public Library, Kirkwood MO. 314-821-5770
Scheffler, Patricia, *Librn,* Interlochen Arts Academy Library, Interlochen MI. 616-276-9221, Ext 320
Schefter, J, *Dir,* Modesto Junior College Library, Modesto CA. 209-526-2000, Ext 569
Scheibal, Doris, *Ref,* Grand Prairie Memorial Library, Grand Prairie TX. 214-264-1571
Scheibe, Robert, *Bus Asst,* Kansas City Public Library, Kansas City MO. 816-221-2685
Scheid, Ann, *Librn,* Gay-Kimball Library, Troy NH. 603-242-7743
Scheid, Annette, *Librn,* Idaho Springs Public Library, Idaho Springs CO. 303-567-2020
Scheide, Benton F, *Dir,* California State College, Bakersfield Library, Bakersfield CA. 805-833-2151

SCHEIDEMANT

Scheidemant, Jack L, *Av Dir,* Manchester Community College Library, Manchester CT. 203-646-4900, Ext 295

Scheiman, Royal, *Chief Librn,* Grumman Aerospace Corp, Technical Information Center, Bethpage NY. 516-575-3912

Schein, Helen R, *Librn,* Beth Tfiloh Congregation, Alfred L Tuvin Memorial Library, Baltimore MD. 301-486-1900

Schein, Lorraine, *Librn,* Polytechnic Institute of New York, Long Island Center Library, Farmingdale NY. 516-

Scheinholtz, Joan, *Librn,* Pensacola Junior College (Warrington Campus), Pensacola FL. 904-476-5410

Scheirer, Susan L, *Librn,* Anson Technical College, Learning Resource Center, Ansonville NC. 704-826-8333, Ext 26

Schelin, Carol, *Cat,* West Nyack Free Library, West Nyack NY. 914-358-6081

Schelin, Janice, *Librn,* East Baton Rouge Parish Library (Baker Branch), Baker LA. 504-775-3125

Schell, Carolyn, *Librn,* Library Association of Portland (Saint Johns), Portland OR. 503-286-0562

Schell, Deborah A, *Dir,* Chesaning Public Library, Chesaning MI. 517-845-3211

Schell, Dorothy, *Librn,* Schenectady County Public Library (Scotia Branch), Scotia NY. 518-382-3506

Schell, Edwin, *Exec Secy,* United Methodist Historical Society, Lovely Lane Museum Library, Baltimore MD. 301-889-4458

Schell, Fran, *Ref,* Tennessee State Library & Archives, Nashville TN. 615-741-2764

Schell, Hal B, *Vice Provost for Univ Librs,* University of Cincinnati Libraries, Central Library, Cincinnati OH. 513-475-2218

Schell, Irene I, *Dir,* Gloucester City Library, Gloucester City NJ. 609-456-4181

Schell, Mary E, *Chief Librn,* California State Library (Government Publications Section), Sacramento CA. 916-322-4572

Schell, Maxine, *Vol Coordr,* Kansas City Public Library, Kansas City MO. 816-221-2685

Schell, Nancy Sue, *Ch, YA & Tech Serv,* Cumberland Trail Library System, Flora IL. 618-662-2679, 622-2741

Schell, Rosalie, *Reader Serv,* Central Missouri State University, Ward Edwards Library, Warrensburg MO. 816-429-4141

Schell, William H, *Dir,* Bensenville Community Public Library, Bensenville IL. 312-766-4642

Schellenberg, D, *Asst Dir Financial,* Calgary Public Library, Calgary AB. 403-268-2880

Scheller, Sally, *ILL & Ref,* League City Public Library, League City TX. 713-554-6612

Schellhase, Kay, *Librn,* Pacific School of Religion (Palestine Institute Library), Berkeley CA. 415-848-0528

Schellhorn, Mary, *Cat,* Governors State University, University Library, Park Forest South IL. 312-534-5000, Ext 2231

Schellings, Adrienne, *Acq,* Old Dominion University Library, Norfolk VA. 804-440-4141

Schellpfeffer, Everett, *On-Line Servs,* Illinois Institute of Technology, James S Kemper Library, Chicago IL. 312-567-3355

Schelter, Sue F, *Adminr,* Pasadena Historical Society & Museum Library, Pasadena CA. 213-577-1660

Schemm, Louise, *Librn,* Bay County Library System (Sage), Bay City MI. 517-892-8555

Schemm, Vera, *Librn,* Clairol Research Library, Stamford CT. 203-357-5001

Schenck, Mary L, *Librn,* Hooker County Library, Mullen NE. 308-546-2240

Schenck, William, *Acq,* University of North Carolina at Chapel Hill, Louis Round Wilson Academic Affairs Library, Chapel Hill NC. 919-933-1301

Schendel, Elizabeth, *Librn,* Hopkins, Sutter, Mulroy, Davis & Cromartie, Law Library, Chicago IL. 312-558-6732

Schenewerk, Colette, *Acq,* Oklahoma Department of Libraries, Oklahoma City OK. 405-521-2502

Schenk, Harlen, *Librn,* Houston Public Library (Bibliographic & Information Center), Houston TX. 713-224-5441

Schenk, Kathryn L, *Cat,* Canisius College, Andrew L Bouwhuis Library, Buffalo NY. 716-883-7000, Ext 253, 254, 290

Schenk, Margot, *On-Line Servs,* Saint Mary's University, Patrick Power Library, Halifax NS. 902-422-7361

Scheper, Agnes, *On-Line Servs,* MTS Systems Corp, Information Services, Minneapolis MN. 612-944-4000

Schepis, Frank J, *Asst Dir,* Springfield-Greene County Library, Springfield MO. 417-869-4621

Schepis, Sandra, *Librn,* March of Dimes Birth Defects Foundation, Reference Room, White Plains NY. 914-428-7100, Ext 418

Scheppke, Jim, *Ad,* Lubbock City-County Library, Lubbock TX. 806-762-6411, Ext 2828

Scheps, Susan, *Librn,* Fairmount Temple, Sam & Emma Miller Library, Cleveland OH. 216-464-1330, Ext 37

Scher, Rita, *Pub Servs,* East Tennessee State University, Sherrod Library, Johnson City TN. 615-929-4338

Scherba, Sandra, *Dir,* Cromaine Library, Hartland MI. 313-632-5200

Scherbinske-Tysdal, Wynne, *Librn,* United States Air Force (Grand Forks Air Force Base Library), Grand Forks AFB ND. 701-594-6725

Scherdin, Mary Jane, *Learning Mat Ctr,* University of Wisconsin-Whitewater, Library & Learning Resources, Whitewater WI. 414-472-1000

Scherer, Betty, *Ch,* Lake Worth Public Library, Lake Worth FL. 305-585-9882

Scherer, Carol M, *Librn,* Delta Public Library, Delta OH. 419-822-3110

Scherer, Herbert, *Librn,* University of Minnesota Libraries-Twin Cities (Art), Minneapolis MN. 612-373-2875

Scherer, Leslie, *Dir,* Wallingford Public Library, Wallingford CT. 203-265-6754

Scherma, George W, *Dir,* Rocky River Public Library, Rocky River OH. 216-333-7610

Scherr, Elizabeth B, *Asst Dir & Acq,* Williams College, Sawyer Library, Williamstown MA. 413-597-2501

Scherr, Jean, *Cat,* State Library of Ohio, Columbus OH. 614-466-2693

Schertz, Morris, *Dir,* University of Denver, Penrose Library, Denver CO. 303-753-2007

Scherzinger, Bettie Alice, *Ch,* Mishawaka-Penn Public Library, Mishawaka IN. 219-259-5277

Schett, Karen, *Asst Librn,* Ortonville Public Library, Ortonville MN. 612-839-2494

Scheuer, Caryl L, *Dir,* Hutzel Hospital, Medical Library, Detroit MI. 313-494-7179

Scheuer, Caryl L, *Coordr,* Pontiac-Allen Park-Detroit Consortium, (PAD), MI. 313-494-7179

Scheuerer, Elaine, *In Charge,* Trenton Psychiatric Hospital (Medical Library), Trenton NJ. 609-396-8261, Ext 264

Scheuermann, Joan M, *Dir,* Kenilworth Free Public Library, Kenilworth NJ. 201-276-2451

Scheule, Marjorie F, *Dir,* Woodstown-Pilesgrove Public Library, Woodstown NJ. 609-769-0098

Scheven, Yvette, *Africa,* University of Illinois Library at Urbana-Champaign, Urbana IL. 217-333-0790

Scheverman, Clara, *Librn,* Western Reserve Psychiatric Habilitation Center, Patients & Medical Library, Northfield OH. 216-467-7131

Schewe, Donald, *Asst Dir,* General Services Administration - National Archives & Records Service, Franklin D Roosevelt Library, Hyde Park NY. 914-229-8114

Schiavina, L M, *Librn,* William M Mercer Inc, Library Information Center, New York NY. 212-997-7027

Schiavo, Joseph Lo, *ILL,* Fordham University, Duane Library, Bronx NY. 212-933-2233, Ext 230, 259

Schibbelhut, Johanna, *Librn,* Kearny County Library, Lakin KS. 316-355-6674

Schick, Dorothy, *Asst Dir,* Curtis Public Library, Curtis NE. 308-367-4148

Schick, Wendy, *Actg Deputy Chief & Tech Serv,* Burlington Public Library, Burlington ON. 416-639-3611

Schickler, Shirley, *Chief, Br Admin,* Brooklyn Public Library, Brooklyn NY. 212-780-7712

Schiechl, Anne, *Asst Librn,* Elko County Library (Austin Library), Austin NV. 702-964-2428

Schieding, Marjorie, *Librn,* Graves Memorial Library, Sunderland MA. 413-665-2642

Schiefebbein, Margaret, *Librn,* Philippi Public Library, Philippi WV. 304-457-3700

Schiefelbein, Mrs Gene, *Librn,* Nemours Foundation, Alfred I Du Pont Institute Library, Wilmington DE. 302-573-3259

Schieferstein, Grace, *Ad,* Reading Public Library, Reading Public Library District, Reading PA. 215-374-4548

Schiermeier, Cheryl J, *Librn,* H F Tyler Memorial Library, Dewey OK. 918-534-2106

Schietinger, E F, *Dir of Res,* Southern Regional Education Board Library, Atlanta GA. 404-875-9211

Schifano, Ann M, *On-Line Servs & Bibliog Instr,* Institute for Cancer Research Library, Talbot Research Library, Philadelphia PA. 215-728-2710, 728-2711

Schiff, Dorothy, *Dir,* Saint Margaret Memorial Hospital (Louise Suydam McClintic School of Nursing Library), Pittsburgh PA. 412-622-7090

Schiff, Ruth, *Talking Bk Librn,* Evansville Public Library & Vanderburgh County Public Library, Evansville IN. 812-425-2621

Schiffenbauer, Zelda, *Exec Dir,* Illinois Regional Library Council, IL. 312-828-0928

Schifferli, Mary, *Ad,* Mid-York Library System, Utica NY. 315-735-8328

Schifrin, Nancy C, *YA,* Fairfax County Public Library, Administrative Offices, Springfield VA. 703-321-9810

Schifter, Patti, *Dir,* California School of Professional Psychology, Los Angeles Campus Library, Los Angeles CA. 213-665-4201, Ext 36

Schild, Laura, *Librn,* Wheaton Public Library, Wheaton MN. 612-563-8487

Schilder, Jean E, *Librn,* Cleveland Public Library (Walz), Cleveland OH. 216-651-0051

Schiller, Timothy, *Bus Admin,* Rutgers University (Camden Arts & Science Library), Camden NJ. 609-757-6036

Schilling, Barbara, *Librn,* First United Methodist Church Library, Green Bay WI. 414-437-9252

Schilling, Deborah, *Cat,* Falmouth Public Library, Subregional Headquarters for Eastern Massachusetts Regional System, Falmouth MA. 617-548-0280

Schilling, Floy, *Librn,* Pike-Amite-Walthall Library System (Progress Public), McComb MS. 601-684-7034

Schilling, Gredel, *Librn,* Sno-Isle Regional Library (Lake Stevens Branch), Lake Stevens WA. 206-334-1900

Schilling, Irene, *Tech Serv,* Augsburg College, George Sverdrup Library, Minneapolis MN. 612-330-1014

Schilling, Meryl E, *Librn,* Tinley Park Public Library, Tinley Park IL. 312-532-0160

Schilling, Myrtle, *Spec Proj,* Amarillo Art Center Library, Amarillo TX. 806-372-8356

Schilling, Roberta, *ILL,* Fort Lewis College Library, Durango CO. 303-247-7738

Schillinglaw, Mrs C M, *Librn,* Forestburg Community Library, Forestburg AB. 403-582-3513

Schiltz, Irene, *ILL,* Blauvelt Free Library, Blauvelt NY. 914-359-2811

Schimke, Ruth, *Asst Dir,* Holy Redeemer College Library, Waterford WI. 414-534-3191, Ext 51

Schimmelbusch, Johannes S, *Librn,* United States Department of Energy, Bonneville Power Administration Library, Portland OR. 503-234-3361, Ext 4445

Schimmelpfeng, Richard, *Spec Coll,* University of Connecticut Library, Storrs CT. 203-486-2219

Schimps, Erich, *Spec Coll,* Humboldt State University Library, Arcata CA. 707-826-3441

Schindler, Ferdinand A, *Librn,* Indiana State Prison, Michael S Thomas Memorial Library, Michigan City IN. 219-874-7256, Ext 380

Schindler, Merril, *AV,* Mount Sinai School of Medicine of City University of New York, Gustave L & Janet W Levy Library, New York NY. 212-650-6671

Schinina, Alice, *Librn,* Volusia County Public Libraries (Deltona Branch), Deltona FL. 904-252-8374

Schinlever, Ann Macauley, *Librn,* Varian Associates, Eimac Technical Library, San Carlos CA. 415-592-1221, Ext 461

Schinzel, Adelaide F, *Librn,* Plymouth Library Association, Plymouth CT. 203-283-5977

Schippers, Donald, *Acq,* University of California, Santa Barbara Library, Santa Barbara CA. 805-961-2741

Schippleck, Suzanne, *Tech Serv,* Azusa City Library, Azusa CA. 213-334-0338
Schirch, Liese, *Acq & Ref,* Lake Erie College, James F Lincoln Learning Resource Center, Painesville OH. 216-352-3361, Ext 280
Schirm, Sara, *Librn,* Belmont Hills Public Library, Bala-Cynwyd PA. 215-664-8427
Schiro, Frank, *Mgr,* Riverside Press Library, Dallas TX. 214-631-1150
Schisler, Myrtle, *Librn,* Richfield Library District, Richfield ID. 208-487-2340
Schissel, Robert, *Chmn,* University of Wisconsin-Whitewater, Dept of Educational Foundations & Counselor Education, WI. 414-472-1380
Schlachter, Gail A, *Asst Univ Librn Pub Servs,* University of California at Davis, General Library, Davis CA. 916-752-2110
Schlackman, Deborah R, *Instr,* University of North Florida, Library Science Program, FL. 904-646-2553
Schlaeger, Susan, *Cat,* Carleton College Library, Northfield MN. 507-645-4431
Schlaegle, Irene J, *Librn,* Instrument Society of America, Albert F Sperry Library, Pittsburgh PA. 412-281-3171
Schlaerth, Sally G, *Librn,* Buffalo Evening News Library, Buffalo NY. 716-849-4444
Schlaf, Suzanne, *Ref,* Poplar Creek Public Library District, Streamwood IL. 312-837-6800
Schlansky, Marilyn, *Librn,* Patterson Library Association, Patterson NY. 914-878-6121
Schlanz, Joseph, *Librn,* Belmont County Law Library, Saint Clairsville OH. 614-695-2121
Schlappi, Jean, *Librn,* Seaside Public Library, Seaside OR. 503-738-6742
Schleck, Sister Mariel, *Per,* Saint Mary's Junior College Library, Minneapolis MN. 612-332-5521
Schlee, Marilyn J, *Librn,* Northwest Bancorporation Library, Minneapolis MN. 612-372-8263
Schleef, Vonda, *Br Coordr,* Marshalltown Public Library, Marshalltown IA. 515-754-5738
Schlegel, Alton G, *Dir,* Parker Pen Co, Corporate Technical Center Libr, Janesville WI. 608-755-7203
Schlegel, Yolanda, *ILL,* Fullerton City Library, Fullerton CA. 714-738-6333, Ext 301
Schleicher, Jane K, *Librn,* Coyle Free Library, Chambersburg PA. 717-263-8409
Schleicher, Linda, *Circ,* Laramie County Community College Library, Cheyenne WY. 307-634-5853
Schleicher, Patricia F, *Dir,* Bess Tilson Sprinkle Memorial Library, Weaverville NC. 704-645-3592
Schleicher, Patti, *Librn,* Asheville-Buncombe Library System (Weaverville Branch), Weaverville NC. 704-645-3592
Schleicher, Shirley, *Tech Serv,* Cheshire Public Library, Cheshire CT. 203-272-2245
Schleifer, Harold B, *Asst Dir Tech Servs,* State University of New York, Frank Melville Jr Memorial Library, Stony Brook NY. 516-246-5650
Schlemmer, Helen L, *Librn,* Akron General Medical Center, J D Smith Memorial Library, Akron OH. 216-384-6242
Schlenk, Pam, *Rec Libr,* Cleveland Institute of Music Library, Cleveland OH. 216-791-5165
Schlesinger, Deborah, *Librn,* South Park Township Community Library, Library PA. 412-833-5585
Schlesinger, Max, *Media,* Missouri Western State College, Hearnes Learning Resources Center, Saint Joseph MO. 816-271-4368
Schlessinger, Bernard, *Dean,* University of Rhode Island, Graduate Library School, RI. 401-792-2878 or 792-2947
Schlichting, Catherine, *ILL, Ref & Bibliog Instr,* Ohio Wesleyan University, L A Beeghly Library, Delaware OH. 614-369-4431, Ext 509
Schlimgen, Joan, *Librn,* National Economic Research Associates Inc Library, Los Angeles CA. 213-628-0131
Schlimm, Chrysodith V, *Asst Cat,* Saint Vincent College & Archabbey Libraries, Latrobe PA. 412-539-9761, Ext 378
Schling, Dorothy T, *Dir,* Danbury Scott-Fanton Museum & Historical Society Research Library, Danbury CT. 203-743-5200
Schlipf, Frederick A, *Exec Dir,* Urbana Free Library, Urbana IL. 217-367-4057

Schlitz, Katherine, *Librn,* Timberland Regional Library (Raymond Branch), Raymond WA. 206-942-2408
Schlobohm, Holly W, *Librn,* New York University Medical Center (Institute of Rehabilitation Medicine Auxiliary Library), New York NY. 212-679-3200, Ext 2291
Schloeder, Mary C, *Librn,* United States Department of State, Foreign Service Institute, Arlington VA. 703-235-8717
Schlosser, Anne G, *Librn,* American Film Institute, Charles K Feldman Library, Beverly Hills CA. 213-278-8777, Ext 315
Schlosser, Mary C, *In Charge,* Guild of Book Workers Library, New York NY. 212-757-6454
Schlosser, Priscilla, *Asst Librn,* Vermont State Hospital (Agency Of Human Services Library), Waterbury VT. 802-241-2248
Schlosser, Sue, *Instr,* Saint Louis Community College at Florissant Valley, Library Technical Assistant Program, MO. 314-595-4494
Schlosser, Sue Ann, *Dir,* Ferguson Municipal Public Library, Ferguson MO. 314-521-4820
Schlueter, Ray, *In Charge,* Allis-Chalmers Corp, Advanced Technology Center Library, Milwaukee WI. 414-475-2102
Schluge, Vickie, *Ref,* Francis D Murphy Medical Library, Milwaukee WI. 414-257-5897
Schluter, Eulala, *Librn,* Weldon Public Library, Weldon IL. 217-736-2215
Schluter, Helmtrud, *Librn,* Goethe-Institute Library, San Francisco CA. 415-391-0370
Schmachtenberger, Margaret, *Chief Librn,* Johns-Manville Corporation (Research Information Center), Denver CO. 303-979-1000, Ext 4471, 4374
Schmalz, Rochelle, *Librn,* Kaiser-Permanente Medical Center, Health Library, Oakland CA. 415-645-6569
Schmelefske, Mike, *Acq & Doc,* College of Cape Breton Library, Sydney NS. 902-539-5300
Schmelzer, Ingrid, *Librn,* Lake County Public Library (New Chicago Public), Hobart IN. 219-962-2421
Schmelzer, Menahem, *Dir,* Jewish Theological Seminary of America Library, New York NY. 212-749-8000
Schmelzle, Joan, *Doc,* University of Texas at San Antonio Library, San Antonio TX. 512-691-4570
Schmezer, Helene, *Ch,* Morgantown Public Library, Morgantown Service Center, Morgantown WV. 304-296-4425
Schmezer, Mary S, *Media,* Morgantown Public Library, Morgantown Service Center, Morgantown WV. 304-296-4425
Schmidt, Andrew, *Dir,* Sunrise Public Library, Sunrise FL. 305-742-8585
Schmidt, Anne Marie, *Librn,* General Foods Corp, Maxwell House Div, Research Dept Library, Hoboken NJ. 201-420-3309
Schmidt, Barbara, *ILL,* Ohio State University Libraries (Health Sciences Library), Columbus OH. 614-422-9810
Schmidt, Barbara E, *Librn,* Doherty, Rumble & Butler, Law Firm Library, Saint Paul MN. 612-291-9257
Schmidt, Betty, *Librn,* Pincher Creek Municipal Library, Pincher Creek AB. 403-627-3813
Schmidt, Betty, *Circ,* Veterans Memorial Public Library, Bismarck ND. 701-222-6410
Schmidt, Bruce K, *Dir,* Southfield Public Library, David Stewart Memorial Library, Southfield MI. 313-354-9100
Schmidt, C James, *Univ Librn,* Brown University (University Library), Providence RI. 401-863-2167
Schmidt, Carol, *ILL,* Royal Oak Public Library, Royal Oak MI. 313-541-1470
Schmidt, Charles J, *Dir,* Middle Georgia Regional Library, Macon GA. 912-745-5813
Schmidt, Connie, *In Charge,* Santa Barbara Public Library (Montecito), Santa Barbara CA. 805-969-0922
Schmidt, Dean, *Librn,* University of Missouri-Columbia (Medical), Columbia MO. 314-882-8086
Schmidt, Donald T, *Dir,* Church of Jesus Christ of Latter-Day Saints (Library-Archives, Historical Department), Salt Lake City UT. 801-531-2787
Schmidt, Dorothy, *Acq,* Kraft, Inc (Corporate Library), Glenview IL. 312-998-2465

Schmidt, Dorothy, *Asst Librn & Tech Serv,* Temple Public Library, Temple TX. 817-778-5555
Schmidt, Ellen, *Librn,* Manatee County Public Library System (South Manatee County), Bradenton FL. 813-755-3892
Schmidt, Erika, *Librn,* Butler Hospital, Issac Ray Medical Library, Providence RI. 401-456-3869
Schmidt, Frances, *Asst Librn,* Lake View Public Library, Lake View IA. 712-657-2310
Schmidt, Fritzi S, *Librn,* Farnsworth Public Library, Oconto WI. 414-834-3488
Schmidt, Grace, *Asst Dir & Br Coordr,* Kitchener Public Library, Kitchener ON. 519-743-0271
Schmidt, H K, *ILL & Ref,* American University, Jack I & Dorothy G Bender Library & Learning Resources Center, Washington DC. 202-686-2323
Schmidt, Jean, *Librn,* Kings County Law Library, Hanford CA. 209-582-3211, Ext 146
Schmidt, Jean, *Archives,* Montana State University, Roland R Renne Library, Bozeman MT. 406-994-3119
Schmidt, Jeaneth Stevens, *Librn,* New Hartford Public Library, New Hartford IA. 319-983-2533
Schmidt, John Francis, *Circ & Ref,* Cardinal Ritter Library, Saint Louis MO. 314-544-0455, Ext 56
Schmidt, Joyce E, *Librn,* Jefferson Borough Public Library, Clairton PA. 412-384-7131
Schmidt, Judith, *Ch,* Marion Public Library, Marion OH. 614-387-0992
Schmidt, Julia, *Librn,* Marin General Hospital, Medical Library, Greenbrae CA. 415-461-0100, Ext 280
Schmidt, Karl, *Librn,* Approved Engineering Test Laboratories Library, Encino CA. 213-783-5985
Schmidt, Lillian, *Asst Librn & Cat,* Millicent Library, Fairhaven MA. 617-992-5342
Schmidt, Marilyn, *Ad,* Newton Public Library, Newton KS. 316-283-2890
Schmidt, Martin F, *Librn,* Filson Club Library, Louisville KY. 502-582-3727
Schmidt, Mary, *Librn,* Coplay Library, Coplay PA. 215-262-7351
Schmidt, Mary, *Librn,* Princeton University Library (Art & Archaeology), Princeton NJ. 609-452-3180
Schmidt, Mary Ann, *Info Serv,* Milwaukee School of Engineering, Walter Schroeder Library, Milwaukee WI. 414-272-8720, Ext 388
Schmidt, Mary Ellen, *Dir,* Danville Public Library, Danville IN. 317-745-2604
Schmidt, MaryJane, *Librn,* Wilton Manors Public Library, Wilton Manors FL. 305-566-7915
Schmidt, Maryls, *Dir,* Moose Lake Public Library, Moose Lake MN. 218-485-4010
Schmidt, Meribeth, *Dir, Continuing Educ Servs,* Newton Public Library, Newton KS. 316-283-2890
Schmidt, Myra, *Librn,* City-County Library of Missoula (Lolo Branch), Lolo MT. 406-273-6348
Schmidt, Nancy J, *Librn,* Harvard University Library (Tozzer Library), Cambridge MA. 617-495-2253
Schmidt, Naomi, *Asst Dir,* Ethel Briggs Memorial Library, Barnsdall OK. 918-847-2980, Ext 2980
Schmidt, Oscar R, *Librn,* Atlantic Union College, G Eric Jones Library, South Lancaster MA. 617-365-4561
Schmidt, Oscar R, *Dept Head,* Atlantic Union College, School Librarianship Program, MA. 617-365-4561, Ext 276
Schmidt, Patricia, *Cat,* Hamilton County Library, Syracuse KS. 316-384-5622
Schmidt, Paula O, *Librn,* Baker & Daniels Library, Indianapolis IN. 317-636-4535
Schmidt, Scott, *Acq,* Grinnell College, Burling Library, Grinnell IA. 515-236-6181, Ext 598
Schmidt, Sherrie, *Asst Dir,* Callier Center for Communication Disorders, Materials Resource Center Library, Dallas TX. 214-783-3143
Schmidt, Sherrie, *Asst Dir,* University of Texas at Dallas, University Library, Richardson TX. 214-690-2950
Schmidt, Stan, *Librn,* Public Library of Cincinnati & Hamilton County (Walnut Hills), Cincinnati OH. 513-369-6053
Schmidt, Stan, *Librn,* Public Library of Cincinnati & Hamilton County (North Cincinnati), Cincinnati OH. 513-369-6034
Schmidt, Stanley, *Lectr,* Concordia University, Library Studies Program, PQ. 514-482-0320, Ext 324

SCHMIDT

Schmidt, Stanley, *Librn,* Public Library of Cincinnati & Hamilton County (Lincoln Park), Cincinnati OH. 513-369-6026

Schmidt, Ted, *Asst Dir,* Loveland Public Library, Loveland CO. 303-667-4040

Schmidt, Valentine L, *Librn,* Ringling Museum of Art, Art Research Library, Sarasota FL. 813-355-5101, Ext 231

Schmidt, Valerie, *Media,* Newport Beach Public Library, Newport Beach CA. 714-640-2141

Schmidt, Vincent, *Bkmobile Coordr & Interlibr Coop Consult,* Cumberland Trail Library System, Flora IL. 618-662-2679, 622-2741

Schmidt, Virginia, *Dir,* Forest City Public Library, Forest City IA. 515-582-4542

Schmidtendorff, Mamie, *Tech Serv,* Cass County Library, Cassopolis MI. 616-445-8651

Schmieding, Virginia, *ILL,* Eastern New Mexico University Library, Portales NM. 505-562-2624

Schmitt, Bonnie C, *Librn,* Eagle Grove Public Library, Eagle Grove IA. 515-448-4115

Schmitt, Calvin H, *Librn,* McCormick Theological Seminary, McGaw Memorial Library, Chicago IL. 312-549-3700

Schmitt, Carol, *Librn,* Allegheny County Health Department Library, Pittsburgh PA. 412-578-8028

Schmitt, Laurence A, *Librn,* Saint Joseph's Seminary Library, Washington DC. 202-526-4231

Schmitt, Margaret S, *Dir,* Alsip-Merrionette Park Library, Alsip IL. 312-371-5666

Schmitt, Martha, *Cat,* Springfield Public Library, Springfield OR. 503-726-3765

Schmitt, Shirley, *Librn,* Brown County Library (Wrightstown Branch), Wrightstown WI. 414-432-4011

Schmitt, Sister Fleurette, *Ref & Per,* Divine Word College, Mat Jacoby Library, Epworth IA. 319-876-3354

Schmitz, Ann, *Dir,* Algoma Public Library, Algoma WI. 414-487-2295

Schmitz, Eugenia, *Prof,* University of Wisconsin-Oshkosh, Dept of Library Science, WI. 414-424-2313

Schmock, Hilarion, *Librn,* Gethsemani, Abbey Library, Trappist KY. 502-549-3117

Schmoll, Donavon, *Dir,* Wartburg College, Engelbrecht Library, Waverly IA. 319-352-1200, Ext 244

Schmuch, Joseph J, *Librn,* Belmont Public Library, Belmont MA. 617-489-2000

Schmuck, John, *Librn,* Los Gatos Memorial Library, Los Gatos CA. 408-354-6891

Schmucker, Doris, *AV,* Stark County District Library, Canton OH. 216-452-0665, Ext 31

Schnabel, Cathrine M, *Librn,* Rogers & Wells Library, New York NY. 212-972-7000, Ext 5432

Schnaitter, Allene, *Dir,* Washington State University Library, Pullman WA. 509-335-4557

Schnakenberg, Virginia, *Librn,* Trails Regional Library (Concordia Branch), Concordia MO. 816-463-2277

Schnall, Janet, *Librn,* Waldo General Hospital Library, Seattle WA. 206-364-2050

Schnall, Janice, *Business,* Youngstown State University Library, William F Maag Library, Youngstown OH. 216-742-3676

Schnare, Mary Kay W, *Librn,* University of Connecticut, School of Business Administration Library, Hartford CT. 203-527-2149

Schnare, Robert E, *Spec Coll,* United States Military Academy Library, West Point NY. 914-938-2230

Schnatzmeyer, Hazel, *Libr Tech,* United States Army (Corps of Engineers, District Library Saint Louis), Saint Louis MO. 314-263-5675

Schneberg, Ben, *Librn,* Berlack-Israels & Liberman Library, New York NY. 212-248-6900, Ext 50

Schneberger, Lois, *Cat,* Arizona State University Library, Tempe AZ. 602-965-3417

Schneberger, Patricia, *Asst Dir,* Elmwood Park Public Library, Elmwood Park NJ. 201-796-8888

Schneck, Mildred, *Librn,* Hudson Institute Library, Croton-On-Hudson NY. 914-762-0700

Schneeberger, Brother Paul, *Tech Serv,* Sacred Heart School of Theology, Leo Dehon Library, Hales Corners WI. 425-8300 & 425-8301, Ext 27

Schneider, A Kay, *Exten Servs,* Anderson City-Anderson & Stony Creek Township Public Library, Anderson Public Library, Anderson IN. 317-644-0938

Schneider, A R, *Dir,* Dwyer-Mercer County District Library, Celina OH. 419-586-2314

Schneider, Adele, *Tech Serv & Cat,* Kingsborough Community College Library, Brooklyn NY. 212-934-5144

Schneider, Beverly, *Librn,* Campbell County Public Library District, Newport KY. 606-261-3114

Schneider, Carol, *Librn,* Swedish Hospital Medical Center, N A Johanson Memorial Library, Seattle WA. 206-292-2121

Schneider, D W, *Assoc Dir,* Louisiana State University (Troy H Middleton Library), Baton Rouge LA. 504-388-2217

Schneider, Debra, *Inst Libr Program Technician,* Wyoming State Hospital Library, Evanston WY. 307-789-3464, Ext 279

Schneider, E Ruth, *Asst Prof,* Bowling Green State University, Dept of Library & Educational Media, OH. 419-372-2461

Schneider, Elizabeth, *Librn,* Grant County Public Library, Williamstown KY. 606-824-4723

Schneider, Frank A, *Dean,* Central Washington University Library, Ellensburg WA. 509-963-1901

Schneider, Gail K, *Librn,* Staten Island Institute of Arts & Sciences Library & Archives, Staten Island NY. 212-727-1135, Ext 12

Schneider, Helen, *Dir,* Whippanong Library, Whippany NJ. 201-887-3394

Schneider, J Kaye, *Dir,* Western Ohio Regional Library Development System, (WORLDS), OH. 419-227-9370

Schneider, Janet, *Librn,* United States Air Force (Air Force Communications Command Library), Scott AFB IL. 618-256-4437

Schneider, Jeanne, *Dir, ILL & Acq,* Redwood Falls Public Library, Redwood Falls MN. 507-637-8650

Schneider, Judy, *Librn,* George Public Library, George IA. 712-475-3341

Schneider, Julia, *Tech Serv,* Missouri Western State College, Hearnes Learning Resources Center, Saint Joseph MO. 816-271-4368

Schneider, Karen, *Ch,* Lincolnwood Public Library, Lincolnwood IL. 312-677-5277

Schneider, Kathryn, *Doc,* Wisconsin Department of Public Instruction (Reference & Loan Library), Madison WI. 608-266-1053

Schneider, Kiki, *On-Line Servs & Bibliog Instr,* Emerson College, Abbot Memorial Library, Boston MA. 617-262-2010, Ext 281

Schneider, Laura-Lee, *Librn,* Reynolds, Smith & Hills, Architects, Engineers & Planners Library, Jacksonville FL. 904-396-2011

Schneider, Lynette, *Librn,* American Telephone & Telegraph Co, Corporate Library, Basking Ridge NJ. 201-221-4141

Schneider, Marcella, *Librn,* Illinois Prairie District Public Library (Germantown-Hills Branch), Germantown-Hills IL. 309-383-2263

Schneider, Mary Lu, *In Charge,* Cold Spring Library, Cold Spring MN. 612-685-8281

Schneider, Mellicent M, *Dir,* Huntington Memorial Library, Oneonta NY. 607-432-1980

Schneider, Monique, *Tech Serv,* Hinsdale Public Library, Hinsdale IL. 312-986-1976

Schneider, Mrs Robert, *Ch,* East Lyme Public Library, Inc, Niantic CT. 203-739-6926

Schneider, Paul, *Librn,* Memphis-Shelby County Public Library & Information Center (Randolph Libr), Memphis TN. 901-452-1068

Schneider, Phyllis, *Ch,* Marshfield Free Library, Marshfield WI. 715-384-2929, 387-1302

Schneider, Priscilla T, *Librn, Acq & Spec Coll,* Endicott College, Fitz Memorial Library, Beverly MA. 617-927-0585, Ext 280

Schneider, Ralph, *Hist,* Chicago Public Library (Social Sciences & History Div), Chicago IL. 312-269-2830

Schneider, Richard, *Asst Librn,* Maharishi International University Library, Fairfield IA. 515-472-5031, Ext 152, 232

Schneider, Richard, *Librn, On-Line Servs & Bibliog Instr,* United States Army (Corps of Engineers, North Central Division Library), Chicago IL. 312-353-5038

Schneider, Robert A, *Actg Dir,* Northern Kentucky University, W Frank Steely Library, Highland Heights KY. 606-292-5483

Schneider, Ruth, *Librn,* New York Public Library (Parkchester), New York NY. 212-829-7830

Schneider, Ruth, *Tech Serv,* Warren Public Library, Warren OH. 216-399-8807

Schneider, Stewart, *Assoc Prof,* University of Rhode Island, Graduate Library School, RI. 401-792-2878 or 792-2947

Schnek, M, *Eng,* State University of New York at Buffalo, University Libraries, Buffalo NY. 716-636-2965

Schnell, Roger, *Assoc Prof,* Saint Louis Community College at Florissant Valley, Library Technical Assistant Program, MO. 314-595-4494

Schnelle, Margaret, *Librn,* Hamden Library (Whitneyville), Hamden CT. 203-248-6715

Schneyer, Rosemary, *Librn,* Stockbridge Library Association, Stockbridge MA. 413-298-5501

Schnick, Rosalie A, *Librn,* United States Fish & Wildlife Service, National Fishery Research Laboratory Library, La Crosse WI. 608-784-9666

Schnidler, Denise, *Asst Librn,* Judith Basin County Free Library, Stanford MT. 406-566-2389

Schnippel, Catherine, *Librn,* Amos Memorial Public Library (Botkins Branch), Botkins OH. 513-693-6671

Schnitz, Noel H, *Dir,* Central Texas College, Oveta Culp Hobby Memorial Library, Killeen TX. 817-526-1237

Schnitzer, Gloria, *Librn,* Malden Public Library (Faulkner), Malden MA. 617-324-3446

Schnoor, Harriet, *Librn,* University of Chicago (Eckhart Library), Chicago IL. 312-753-3454

Schnur, Dorothy M, *Libr Asst,* Beloit Corp (Technical Library), Beloit WI. 608-365-3311, ext 8-211

Schnure, M Jane, *Acq,* Susquehanna University, Roger M Blough Learning Ctr, Selinsgrove PA. 717-374-0101, Ext 329

Schnurmann, Erika, *Dir,* Kearny Public Library, Kearny NJ. 201-998-2666

Schnurr, Daniel, *On-Line Servs,* Hampshire College, Harold F Johnson Library Center, Amherst MA. 413-549-4600

Schnuttgen, Hildegard, *ILL & Ref,* Youngstown State University Library, William F Maag Library, Youngstown OH. 216-742-3676

Schoch, Marjorie, *Asst Dir,* Indiana Central University Library, Krannert Memorial Library, Indianapolis IN. 317-788-3268

Schochet, Lois, *Librn,* Middlesex County Planning Board Library, New Brunswick NJ. 201-745-2890

Schock, Richard, *Dir & Acq,* Moody Bible Institute Library, Chicago IL. 312-329-4138

Schock, Shirley L, *Librn,* Camden-Jackson Township Public Library, Camden IN. 219-686-2120

Schockmel, Richard, *Materials Selection,* Utah State University, Merrill Library & Learning Resources Program, Logan UT. 801-750-2637

Schoel, Rebecca, *Asst Librn,* Ruby Pickens Tartt Public Library, Livingston Public Library, Livingston AL. 205-652-2349

Schoeler, Diane, *Acq,* University of Texas at El Paso Library, El Paso TX. 747-5683; 747-5684

Schoeler, Mary-Jane, *Librn,* Wilmot Center Public Library, Wilmot NH. 603-526-4683

Schoelkopf, R Gerald, *Rare Bks & Spec Coll,* West Chester State College, Francis Harvey Green Library, West Chester PA. 215-436-2643

Schoellkopf, Catharine, *Librn,* Fidelity Management & Research Co Library, Boston MA. 617-726-0293

Schoen, Charlotte, *Librn,* Association for Research & Enlightenment, Edgar Cayce Memorial Library, Virginia Beach VA. 804-428-3588, Ext 178

Schoen, Evelyn, *Librn,* Warner Municipal Library, Warner AB. 403-642-3648

Schoen, Marilyn, *Admin Asst,* Rand Corp Library, Santa Monica CA. 213-393-0411, Ext 369

Schoen, Molly, *Br Coordr,* Huntington Public Library, Huntington NY. 516-427-5165

Schoen, Molly, *Librn,* Huntington Public Library (Huntington Station), Huntington Station NY. 516-421-5053

Schoen, Myron E, *Dir,* Union of American Hebrew Congregations, Synagogue Art & Architectural Library, New York NY. 212-249-0100

Schoenberg, Evelyn, *Ch,* Maurice M Pine Free Public Library, Fair Lawn NJ. 201-796-3400

Schoenberg, Irene, *Librn*, Saint Clair County Library System (Capac Public), Capac MI. 313-395-7000

Schoenberger, Joan, *Librn*, Carnegie Public Library, Upper Sandusky OH. 419-294-1345

Schoenfeld, Madalynne J, *Ch & Commun Servs*, Yonkers Public Library, Yonkers NY. 914-337-1500

Schoenfeld, Mrs Melvin, *Librn*, Deshler Public Library, Deshler NE. 402-365-4107

Schoenfelder, Elizabeth, *Ad*, Cedar Rapids Public Library, Cedar Rapids IA. 319-398-5123

Schoenly, Steven B, *Asst Prof*, University of Mississippi, Graduate School of Library & Information Science, MS. 601-232-7440

Schoenmann, Catherine, *Dir*, Sioux Falls Public Library, Sioux Falls SD. 605-339-7081

Schoenrock, Mae L, *Dir*, Sno-Isle Regional Library, Marysville WA. 206-659-8447

Schoenthaker, Jean, *Tech Serv*, Drew University, Rose Memorial Library, Madison NJ. 201-377-3000, Ext 469

Schoenung, James G, *Exec Dir*, PALINET & Union Library Catalogue of Pennsylvania, PA. 215-382-7031

Schoer, Marilyn, *Ch & YA*, City-County Library of Missoula, Missoula MT. 406-728-5900

Schoessling, Ray, *Gen Sec-Treasurer*, International Brotherhood of Teamsters Library, Washington DC. 202-624-6978

Schofield, Pamela, *Librn*, Watertown Free Public Library (North), Watertown MA. 617-924-6224

Schofield, Susan R S, *Res Analyst*, Ally & Gargano Inc Advertising, Information Center, New York NY. 212-688-5300, Ext 497

Scholand, Julia, *On-Line Servs*, City College of San Francisco Library, San Francisco CA. 415-239-3404

Scholberg, Henry, *Librn*, University of Minnesota Libraries-Twin Cities (Ames Library of South Asia), Minneapolis MN. 612-373-2890

Scholding, Marie, *Ref & Pub Servs*, James H Johnson Memorial Library, Deptford NJ. 609-227-4424

Scholl, Marlene, *Librn*, Elgin Public Library, Elgin NE. 402-843-2460

Scholten, Frances, *Librn*, American Cyanamid Co (Environmental Services Library), Wayne NJ. 201-831-3027

Scholtes, Dorothy, *Acq*, Fordham University, School of Law Library, New York NY. 212-841-5223

Scholtes, Flora, *Ad*, Jackson-George Regional Library System (Pascagoula City Branch), Pascagoula MS. 601-762-3406

Scholtz, Margaret E, *Dir*, Lena Community District Library, Lena IL. 815-369-4211

Scholtz, Matthew, *Dir*, Tillsonburg Public Library, Tillsonburg ON. 519-842-5571

Scholz, Jane, *Ch*, Peru Public Library, Peru IN. 317-473-3069

Schon, Barbara, *Chief Librn*, Newcastle Public Library, Bowmanville ON. 416-623-7322

Schonbrun, Rena, *Librn*, United States Department of Agriculture, Science & Education Administration Western Regional Research Center Library, Albany CA. 415-486-3351

Schondelmeier, Ruth B, *Librn*, North Hampton Public Library, North Hampton NH. 603-964-6326

Schonfeld, Eleanore, *Dir*, Bibliotheque Municipale De Dorval, Dorval PQ. 514-631-3575

Schonske, George, *Fire Tech*, Indiana Vocational Technical College, Learning Resource Center, Gary IN. 219-981-1111, Ext 28

Schoon, Margaret S, *Cat*, Purdue University Calumet Library, Hammond IN. 219-844-0520, Ext 249

Schoonen, Helen, *Circ*, Idaho Falls Public Library, Idaho Falls ID. 208-529-1450

Schoonhoven, Calvin R, *Dir*, Fuller Theological Seminary, McAlister Library, Pasadena CA. 213-449-1745

Schoonover, Phyllis, *Librn*, Butler University (Jordon College of Fine Arts), Indianapolis IN. 317-283-9243

Schorgl, Thomas B, *Dir*, Art Center Library, South Bend IN. 219-284-9102

Schorr, Alan Edward, *Dir*, University of Alaska, Juneau Library, Juneau AK. 907-789-2101, Ext 126, 127 & 128

Schorrig, Claudia, *Asst Dir*, Florida Atlantic University, S E Wimberly Library, Boca Raton FL. 305-395-5100, Ext 2448

Schott, Michael J, *Dir*, Southbury Public Library, Southbury CT. 203-264-0606, Ext 239

Schott, Pamela R, *Reader Serv*, Harford Community College Learning Resources Center, Bel Air MD. 301-838-1000, Ext 268

Schott, Sandra, *Librn*, Castroville Public Library, Castroville TX. 512-538-2656

Schott, Susan, *Ref*, New Milford Public Library, New Milford CT. 203-355-1191

Schow, Lenore, *Tech Serv*, Murray Public Library, Murray UT. 801-266-1137

Schow, Linda, *Librn*, Plummer Public Library, Plummer ID. 208-686-1671

Schoyer, George P, *Librn*, Ohio State University Libraries (History, Political Science, Philosophy Graduate Library), Columbus OH. 614-422-2393

Schrader, Don, *Media*, Southeast Community College-Lincoln Campus, Learning Resource Center, Lincoln NE. 402-471-3333, Ext 249

Schrader, Dorothy M, *Copyright Gen Counsel*, Library of Congress (Order Division), Washington DC. 202-287-5000

Schrader, Jan, *Librn*, Jonesboro Public Library, Jonesboro IN. 317-674-8716

Schrader, Jane Marie, *Librn*, Silver Burdett Co, Editorial Library, Morristown NJ. 201-285-7700

Schrader, Mary, *Librn*, Colfax Public Library, Colfax IA. 515-674-3625

Schrader, Vera, *Ch*, Thomas Branigan Memorial Library, Las Cruces Public Library, Las Cruces NM. 505-526-0347

Schrag, Dale, *Spec Coll*, Wichita State University, Library & Media Resources Center, Wichita KS. 316-689-3586

Schrag, Ruth, *Librn*, Saint Stephen's College for Continuing Education Library, Edmonton AB. 403-439-7311

Schramm, Jeanne, *Ref*, West Liberty State College, Paul N Elbin Library, West Liberty WV. 304-336-8035

Schramm, Mary T, *Librn*, PCR Consoer, Townsend, Inc, Library & Information Center, Chicago IL. 312-337-6900, Ext 271

Schreder, Betsy S, *Chief Librn*, Veterans Administration, Hospital Library, Wilkes-Barre PA. 717-824-3521

Schreiber, Linda, *Ad*, Concord Free Public Library, Concord MA. 617-369-5324

Schreiber, Margaret, *Librn*, Modoc County Library (M Howard Milligan Memorial), Cedarville CA. 916-233-2719

Schreiber, Marilyn, *Librn*, Winnetka Public Library District (Northfield), Winnetka IL. 312-446-5990

Schreiber, Michael, *Dir*, Indiana Vocational Technical College Northcentral, Learning Resources Center, South Bend IN. 219-289-7001, Ext 76

Schreiber, Mrs T O, *Librn*, Downs Carnegie Library, Downs KS. 913-454-3821

Schreiber, Reta, *Circ*, Bangor Public Library, Bangor ME. 207-947-8336

Schreiber, Susan L, *Asst Dir*, Frederick County Public Library, Frederick MD. 301-694-1613

Schreibstein, Florence, *Per*, Albert Einstein College of Medicine, D Samuel Gottesman Library, Bronx NY. 212-430-3108

Schreiner, Gene H, *Librn*, United States Air Force (Plattsburgh Air Force Base Library), Plattsburgh AFB NY. 518-565-7046

Schreiner, Gwen R, *Librn*, United States Department of Energy, National Atomic Museum Library, Kirtland AFB NM. 505-844-8443

Schreiner, Katherine J, *Tech Serv*, Agnes Scott College, McCain Library, Decatur GA. 404-373-2571, Ext 220

Schrempp, Georgia, *Librn*, Chewelah Public Library, Chewelah WA. 509-935-6805

Schremser, Bob, *Network & Institutions*, Alabama Public Library Service, Montgomery AL. 205-832-5743

Schreyack, Marian, *YA*, Berkshire Athenaeum, Pittsfield Public Library, Pittsfield MA. 413-442-1559

Schricker, George, *AV*, Plymouth Public Library, Plymouth IN. 219-936-2324

Schrieber, T O, *Dir*, Downs Carnegie Library, Downs KS. 913-454-3821

Schriefer, Kent, *Tech Serv*, University of California, Berkeley (Law Library), Berkeley CA. 415-642-4044

Schroader, Joann, *Tech Serv*, Purchase Regional Library, Murray KY. 502-753-6461

Schroader, Vanessa R L, *Info Spec*, EG&G Inc, Washington Analytical Services Center, Rockville MD. 301-840-3242

Schroeck, Bernard, *Spec Coll*, Gannon University, Nash Library, Erie PA. 814-871-7352

Schroeder, Adelaide, *ILL*, Canisius College, Andrew L Bouwhuis Library, Buffalo NY. 716-883-7000, Ext 253, 254, 290

Schroeder, Alvin H, *Dir*, C C Mellor Memorial Library, Pittsburgh PA. 412-731-0909

Schroeder, Betty, *Librn*, Anderson-Lee Library, Silver Creek NY. 716-934-3468

Schroeder, Carol, *On-Line Servs*, Adelphi University Library, Garden City NY. 516-294-8700

Schroeder, Carol, *Librn*, Oxford Public Library, Oxford NE. 308-824-3381

Schroeder, Edwin M, *Dir*, Florida State University (Law Library), Tallahassee FL. 904-644-1004

Schroeder, Erwin M, *Librn*, Northwestern College Library, Watertown WI. 414-261-5343

Schroeder, Eva I A, *Dir*, Monterey Institute of International Studies, William Tell Coleman Library, Monterey CA. 408-649-3113, Ext 50&52

Schroeder, Jan, *Dir*, Duluth Public Library, Duluth MN. 218-723-3800

Schroeder, Jean, *Acq*, Occidental College, Mary Norton Clapp Library, Los Angeles CA. 213-259-2640

Schroeder, Joanne, *Ch*, Friendswood Public Library, Friendswood TX. 713-482-7135

Schroeder, Joseph P, *AV*, University of Houston (M D Anderson Memorial Library), Houston TX. 713-749-4241

Schroeder, Judy, *Librn*, Putnam County District Library (Columbus Grove Branch), Columbus Grove OH. 419-659-2355

Schroeder, Julia, *Librn*, Caledonia Public Library, Caledonia MN. 507-724-2671

Schroeder, June, *Cat*, Bacon Memorial Public Library, Wyandotte MI. 313-282-7660

Schroeder, Madeline, *Dir*, New Lisbon Memorial Library, New Lisbon WI. 608-562-3213

Schroeder, Mary, *Librn*, Howard County Library (Miller Library), Ellicott City MD. 301-465-8980

Schroeder, Mrs E, *Supvr*, Huron County Public Library (Exeter Branch), Exeter ON. 519-235-1890, 235-0576

Schroeder, W R Bill, *Managing Dir*, Citizens Savings Athletic Foundation Library, Los Angeles CA. 213-642-0200

Schroer, Carol, *Librn*, Grand County Libraries (Hot Sulphur Springs Branch), Hot Sulphur Springs CO. 303-725-3323

Schroeter, Kay, *Asst Dir*, Norfolk Public Library, Lewis & Clark Regional Library, Norfolk NE. 402-371-4590

Schroether, Marian, *Ch*, Waukegan Public Library, Waukegan IL. 312-623-2041

Schroff, Rebecca L T, *Asst Librn*, Kirkland & Ellis Law Library, Chicago IL. 312-861-3200

Schroll, Jessie, *Asst Dir*, Hamilton County Library, Syracuse KS. 316-384-5622

Schrum, Mary, *Med Records Librn*, Sheridan Park Hospital Library, Tonawanda NY. 716-877-8300

Schu, Anne, *Tech Serv*, Southampton Free Library, Southampton PA. 215-322-1415

Schual, Nora, *Ref*, Lindenhurst Memorial Library, Lindenhurst NY. 516-888-7575

Schuback, Judy, *Librn*, John F Kennedy Memorial Hospital, Dr Jerrold S Schwartz Memorial Library, Stratford NJ. 609-784-4000

Schuberg, Delphie, *Librn*, Oregon School for the Blind Library, Salem OR. 503-378-3820

Schubert, Ann, *Librn*, Greendale Public Library, Greendale WI. 414-421-2620

Schubert, Eileen, *Asst Librn*, Haltom City Public Library, Haltom City TX. 817-834-7341

Schubert, James M, *Supvr Libr for the Blind & Physically Handicapped*, Colorado State Library, Colorado Department of Education, Denver CO. 303-839-3695

Schubert, Jim, *Supvr*, Colorado State Library - Services for the Blind & Physically Handicapped, Denver CO. 303-839-2081

Schubert, Ruth, *Ref,* Hingham Public Library, Hingham MA. 617-749-0907

Schuchman, Eileen, *Info Serv,* Fenton Free Library, Moody Memorial Library Building, Binghamton NY. 607-724-8649

Schuckel, Sally, *Ref,* Kellogg Community College, Emory W Morris Learning Resource Center, Battle Creek MI. 616-965-3931, Ext 333

Schuerman, Sylvia, *Extension & Bkmobile Coordr,* Saint Charles City County Library, Saint Peters MO. 314-441-2300

Schuermann, Sylvia, *Librn,* Saint Charles City County Library (Extention Services Div), St Charles MO. 314-723-3421

Schuette, Mrs Don, *Asst Dir,* Cedarburg Public Library, Cedarburg WI. 414-377-1730

Schuetz, Sharon, *Librn,* Grainfield Public Library, Grainfield KS. 913-673-4770

Schug, Janet J, *Librn,* Franklin County Law Library, Chambersburg PA. 717-263-4809

Schuhl, Edith S, *Dir,* Booth & Dimock Memorial Library, Coventry CT. 203-742-7606

Schuhle, Jacob, *Librn,* State University of New York College (Institute for Experimentation in Teacher Education), Cortland NY. 607-753-4706

Schuiteman, Robert, *Instr,* Northwestern College, Library Science Program, IA. 712-722-4821

Schuler, Betty K, *Librn,* Wayne County Law Library Association, Wooster OH. 216-262-5561

Schuler, Bob, *Media,* Tacoma Public Library, Tacoma WA. 206-572-2000

Schulert, Mary Lee, *Br Coordr,* Cuyahoga County Public Library, Cleveland OH. 216-398-1800

Schuller, Carla N Vasquez, *Adminr,* Lewiston City Library, Lewiston ID. 208-743-6519

Schuller, Michael, *AV,* Olympic College, Learning Resources Center, Bremerton WA. 206-478-4609

Schulman, Elias, *Dir,* Jewish Education Committee of New York Library, New York NY. 212-254-8200

Schulman, Frank J, *East Asia,* University of Maryland at College Park (Theodore R McKeldin Library), College Park MD. 301-454-2853, 454-5977

Schulman, Jacque-Lynne, *On-Line Servs & Bibliog Instr,* George Washington University Library (Paul Himmelfarb Health Sciences Library), Washington DC. 202-676-2850

Schulman, Rebecca, *Acq,* Loyola Marymount University (Loyola Law School Library), Los Angeles CA. 213-642-2934

Schulmeister, Ann Marie, *Libr Tech,* Hawaii State Library System (Kailua-Kona Branch), Kailua-Kona HI. 808-329-2196

Schult, Ruth, *Spec Coll,* Scottsdale Public Library, Scottsdale AZ. 602-994-2471

Schulte, Deborah, *Librn,* New Castle Public Library, New Castle NH. 603-431-6773

Schulte, Linda A, *Pub Servs,* Southwestern University, School of Law Library, Los Angeles CA. 213-738-6723

Schulte, Lorraine, *In Charge,* Upjohn Company (Corporate Technical Library), Kalamazoo MI. 616-385-6414

Schulte, Marie K, *Librn,* Saint Vincent Charity Hospital, Medical Library, Cleveland OH. 216-861-6200

Schulte, Stephanie, *Librn,* Mercy Hospital, Health Services Library, Cedar Rapids IA. 319-398-6165

Schulteiss, L A, *Asst Librn, Budget & Planning,* University of Illinois at Chicago Circle Library, Chicago IL. 312-996-2716

Schultes, Mary, *Librn,* Dalton Public Library, Inc (Catoosa County Library-Fort Oglethorpe), Fort Oglethorpe GA. 404-866-8355

Schultis, Ann, *ILL,* University of Texas at El Paso Library, El Paso TX. 747-5683; 747-5684

Schultz, Abigail, *Ch,* Sun Prairie Public Library, Sun Prairie WI. 608-837-5644

Schultz, Barbara A, *Chief, Libr Serv,* Veterans Administration, Library Service, Chillicothe OH. 614-773-1141, Ext 281

Schultz, Charles R, *Archives,* Texas A&m University Libraries, College Station TX. 713-845-6111

Schultz, Claire K, *Dir,* Medical College of Pennsylvania, Florence A Moore Library of Medicine, Philadelphia PA. 215-842-6910

Schultz, Deborah M, *Cat,* University of Minnesota, Duluth (Health Science Library), Duluth MN. 218-726-8585

Schultz, Dorothy, *Librn,* University of Wisconsin-Madison (College (Undergraduate) Library), Madison WI. 608-263-2009

Schultz, Edward M, *Dir,* Dover Free Public Library, Dover NJ. 201-366-0172

Schultz, Elaine V, *Asst Librn,* Bank of Hawaii, Information Center, Honolulu HI. 808-537-8375

Schultz, Erich R W, *Dir,* Wilfrid Laurier University Library, Waterloo ON. 519-884-1970

Schultz, Gary, *ILL,* Quincy Public Library, Quincy IL. 217-223-1309

Schultz, Glenda, *Librn,* Conrad Public Library, Conrad MT. 406-278-5751

Schultz, Henrietta, *Librn,* Chicago Sinai Congregation, Emil G Hirsch Library, Chicago IL. 312-288-1600

Schultz, Henrietta, *Librn,* Congregation Rodfei Zedek, J S Hoffman Memorial Library, Chicago IL. 312-752-4489

Schultz, Irene, *Outreach Van Serv,* McMillan Memorial Library, Wisconsin Rapids WI. 715-423-1040

Schultz, Jon, *Dir,* University of Houston (Law Library), Houston TX. 713-749-3119

Schultz, Lois, *Lectr,* Northern Illinois University, Dept of Library Science, IL. 815-753-1735

Schultz, Lois, *Cat,* Northern Kentucky University, W Frank Steely Library, Highland Heights KY. 606-292-5483

Schultz, Lorane, *Librn,* Lakota Public Library, Lakota IA. 515-886-2312

Schultz, Marion, *Tech Serv,* Salem Free Public Library, Salem NJ. 609-935-0526

Schultz, Mary Lou, *Mail Box Librn,* Dodge County Library Service, Beaver Dam WI. 414-885-4571, 885-5134

Schultz, Maxine, *Ref,* Stoneham Public Library, Stoneham MA. 617-438-1324

Schultz, Nancy, *Acq,* Andover Newton Theological School, Franklin Trask Library, Newton Centre MA. 617-964-1100, Ext 140

Schultz, Ronald, *Br Coordr,* Tulare County Library System, Visalia CA. 209-733-8440

Schultz, Ruth, *On-Line Servs & Bibliog Instr,* American Dental Association, Bureau of Library Services, Chicago IL. 312-440-2653

Schultz, Shirley, *Librn,* Stanislaus County Free Library (Nora Ballard), Waterford CA. 209-874-2191

Schultz, Susan W, *Ref,* Woburn Public Library, Woburn MA. 617-933-0148

Schultz, Virginia, *Librn,* Brown County Library (Denmark Branch), Denmark WI. 414-863-6613

Schultz, Zora C, *Librn,* Waelder Public Library, Waelder TX. 512-665-3131

Schulz, Gail L, *Librn,* United States Department of Defense, Defense Supply Agency, Defense Administration Services District Library, Milwaukee WI. 414-272-8180, Ext 212

Schulz, Justine, *Ref,* National Maritime Museum, J Porter Shaw Library, San Francisco CA. 415-556-8177

Schulz, Phyllis, *Librn,* Dodge County Library Service (Reeseville Public), Reeseville WI. 414-927-5799

Schulz, Stan, *Asst Dir,* Keene Memorial Library, Fremont Public Library, Fremont NE. 402-721-5084

Schulze, Jeannie, *Asst Librn,* Friench Simpson Memorial Library, Hallettsville TX. 512-798-3243

Schulze, Kathryn, *Librn,* North Wales Memorial Free Library, North Wales PA. 215-699-5410

Schulzetenberg, Anthony, *Prof,* Saint Cloud State University, Center for Library & Audiovisual Education, MN. 612-255-2022

Schumacher, Hazen, *Librn,* University of Michigan Libraries (Ford L Lemler Educational Film Library), Ann Arbor MI. 313-764-5360

Schumacher, Herbert, *Media,* Ohio University-Lancaster Library, Lancaster OH. 614-654-6711, Ext 221

Schumacher, Herbert, *Instr,* Ohio University-Lancaster, Library Media Technology, OH. 614-654-6711

Schumacher, Wanda Lee, *Librn,* Crestwood Public Library District, Crestwood IL. 312-371-4090

Schumaker, Ann, *Librn,* Trails Regional Library (Corder Branch), Corder MO. 816-394-2565

Schumaker, Marvin, *Ref,* Joliet Junior College, Learning Resource Center, Joliet IL. 815-729-9020, Ext 282

Schumers, Dorothy M, *Librn,* Onarga Public Library, Onarga IL. 815-268-7626

Schumm, Daniel, *Librn,* Massachusetts Correctional Institution-Concord Library, Concord MA. 617-369-3220

Schupp, Maria, *Librn,* Tuscarawas County Public Library (Tuscarawas Branch), Tuscarawas OH. 614-922-4189

Schurb, Sister Avila, *ILL & Ref,* College of Saint Teresa, Mary A Molloy Library, Winona MN. 507-454-2930, Ext 210

Schurk, William, *Spec Mats,* Bowling Green State University Library, Bowling Green OH. 419-372-2856

Schurr, Arlene, *Cat,* Norfolk Public Library, Lewis & Clark Regional Library, Norfolk NE. 402-371-4590

Schurwan, Mrs Bobbie, *Librn,* Mercantile Trust Company National Association Library, Saint Louis MO. 314-231-3500

Schuster, Adeline, *Librn,* Harrington Institute of Interior Design Library, Chicago IL. 312-939-4975

Schuster, Adeline, *Librn,* ISD Inc, Resource Library, Chicago IL. 312-427-3834

Schuster, Elizabeth, *Tech Serv & Cat,* Dearborn Department of Libraries, Henry Ford Centennial Library, Dearborn MI. 313-271-1000

Schuster, Richard L, *Dir,* Mount Vernon Nazarene College Library, Mount Vernon OH. 614-397-1244

Schuter, George, *YA,* Binghamton Public Library, Binghamton NY. 607-723-6457

Schutt, Elizabeth, *Cat,* University of Lowell Libraries (O'Leary Library), Lowell MA. 617-452-5000, Ext 480

Schutt, Ruth, *ILL,* Rush-Presbyterian-Saint Luke's Medical Center (Library of Rush University), Chicago IL. 312-942-2271, 942-5950

Schutte, Darlene, *Dir,* Postville Public Library, Postville IA. 319-864-7600

Schutten, Peggy A, *Ref,* Kraft, Inc (Research & Development Library), Glenview IL. 312-998-2638

Schutz, Bobbie, *Librn,* Kilgore Public Library, Kilgore TX. 214-984-1529

Schutz, Gertrude, *Librn,* Lake County Public Library (Saint John Public), Saint John IN. 219-365-5379

Schutz, Susan, *Librn,* Insurance Institute of Province of Quebec Library, Montreal PQ. 514-845-2238

Schutzman, Janet E, *Bkmobile Coordr,* Harford County Library, Bel Air MD. 301-838-7484

Schuurman, Guy, *Dir,* Salt Lake County Library System, Whitmore Library, Salt Lake City UT. 801-943-7614

Schuyler, Michael, *Ad,* Kitsap Regional Library, Bremerton WA. 206-377-7601

Schwab, Bernard, *Dir,* Madison Public Library, Madison WI. 608-266-6300

Schwab, Jean, *Dir,* Coralville Public Library, Coralville IA. 319-351-2163

Schwab, Linda, *YA,* River Forest Public Library, River Forest IL. 312-366-5205

Schwab, Ruth, *Ref,* Ossining Public Library, Ossining NY. 941-2416; 941-9174

Schwabe, J M, *Librn,* Spectra Research Systems Library, Irvine CA. 714-833-9088

Schwabel, Lexie, *Librn,* Sussex County Library System (Sussex-Wantage-Northern District), Sussex NJ. 201-875-8940

Schwacha, Ruth, *Asst Dir,* East Hanover Township Free Public Library, East Hanover NJ. 201-887-6215

Schwager, Emanuel, *Tech Serv & Acq,* Montgomery County Community College, Learning Resources Center, Blue Bell PA. 215-643-6000, Ext 340

Schwager, Sister Donna, *Tech Serv & Cat,* Viterbo College Library, La Crosse WI. 608-784-0040, Ext 429

Schwalbach, Barbara, *Librn,* Akron-Summit County Public Library (Coventry), Akron OH. 216-644-6932

Schwaller, Janet, *ILL & Ref,* Lincoln University, Inman E Page Library, Jefferson City MO. 314-751-2325, Ext 326

Schwalm, Helen, *Librn,* Pottawatomie-Wabaunsee Regional Library (Alma Branch), Alma KS. 913-765-3647

Schwank, Jean, *Librn,* Community Hospital Library, Indianapolis IN. 317-353-5591

Schwanz, Bonnie, *Tech Serv,* Broadview Public Library, Broadview IL. 312-345-1325

Schwappach, Pat, *Dir,* Anoka County Historical-Genealogical Resource Library, Anoka MN. 612-421-0600

Schwark, Bryan L, *ILL, Per & On-Line Servs,* University of Wisconsin-Platteville, Elton S Karrmann Library, Platteville WI. 608-342-1688

Schwark, Sabine, *ILL & Ref,* De Paul University Libraries (Law Library), Chicago IL. 312-321-7710

Schwartz, Amelia, *Dir Libr Serv,* Ziff-Davis Publishing Co, Travel Div Library, New York NY. 212-725-3600, Ext 3712, 3713

Schwartz, Anne B, *Librn,* Passaic County Law Library, Paterson NJ. 201-881-4130

Schwartz, Arlene, *Mgr ILL & Data Base Services,* Illinois State Library, Springfield IL. 217-782-2994

Schwartz, Barbara, *Undergrad Bibliog Instr,* University of Texas Libraries (General), Austin TX. 512-471-3811

Schwartz, Barbara, *Bibliog Instr,* University of Texas Libraries (Undergraduate), Austin TX. 512-471-5222

Schwartz, Berthe, *Dir,* Belgian Consulate General Library, New York NY. 212-586-5110

Schwartz, Carol, *Librn,* International Longshoremen's & Warehousemen's Union, Anne Rand Research Library, San Francisco CA. 415-775-0533

Schwartz, Carol, *Librn,* TRW Semiconductors, Research & Development Library, Lawndale CA. 213-679-4561

Schwartz, Caroline, *Ch & YA,* McKinley Memorial Library, Niles OH. 216-652-1704

Schwartz, Carolyn, *Dir,* Caldwell Public Library, Caldwell NJ. 201-226-2837

Schwartz, Carolyn, *Asst Prof,* Simmons College, Graduate School of Library & Information Science, MA. 617-738-2225

Schwartz, David Louis, *Dir,* Saratoga Springs Public Library, Saratoga Springs NY. 518-584-7860

Schwartz, Diane, *On-Line Servs,* Squire, Sanders & Dempsey, Law Library, Cleveland OH. 216-696-9200

Schwartz, Diane G, *Bibliog Instr,* University of Michigan Libraries (Medical Center), Ann Arbor MI. 313-764-1210

Schwartz, Elaine, *Dir,* Jetmore Municipal Library, Jetmore KS. 316-357-8336

Schwartz, Eleanor E, *Coordr,* Kean College of New Jersey, Library-Media Program, NJ. 201-527-2626, 527-2071

Schwartz, Ellen, *In Charge,* Crocker Art Museum Library, Sacramento CA. 916-446-4677, 449-5423

Schwartz, Georgia, *Librn,* Walnut Public Library, Walnut KS. 316-354-6593

Schwartz, Herb, *Systs,* Wilfrid Laurier University Library, Waterloo ON. 519-884-1970

Schwartz, Jay, *Media & Spec Coll,* Suffolk County Community College (Selden Campus Library), Selden NY. 516-233-5181

Schwartz, Julie, *Librn,* Square D Co Library, Milwaukee WI. 414-332-2000

Schwartz, Lillian, *Librn,* Temple Emanu-El Library, Providence RI. 401-331-1616

Schwartz, Marcia, *Asst Dir,* Mount Vernon Public Library, Mount Vernon NY. 914-668-1840

Schwartz, Marilyn, *Librn,* United States Navy (Thompson Medical Library), San Diego CA. 714-233-2367

Schwartz, Mortimer D, *Librn,* University of California at Davis (Law Library), Davis CA. 916-752-3322

Schwartz, Mrs Charles, *Librn,* Temple Judah Library, Cedar Rapids IA. 319-362-1261

Schwartz, Roberta B, *Cat,* Regis College Library, Weston MA. 617-893-1820, Ext 252

Schwartz, Ruth, *Actg Librn,* Fairleigh Dickinson University (School of Dentistry), Hackensack NJ. 201-836-6300, Ext 578

Schwartz, Ruth, *Per,* Fairleigh Dickinson University, Weiner Library, Teaneck NJ. 201-836-6300, Ext 265

Schwartz, Sandra, *Cat,* Williamsport Area Community College Library, Williamsport PA. 717-326-3761, Ext 211

Schwartz, Stephen H, *Dir,* Kenosha Public Museum Library, Kenosha WI. 414-656-6026

Schwartzbauer, Eileen, *Sociol, Relig & Sports,* Minneapolis Public Library & Information Center, Minneapolis MN. 612-372-6500

Schwartzburg, Betty P, *Dir,* Town Hall Library, North Lake WI. 414-966-2933

Schwartzentruber, Mrs H, *In Charge,* Oxford County Library (Tavistock Library), Tavistock ON. 519-655-2920

Schwarz, Barbara A, *Media & YA,* Port Jefferson Free Library Association, Port Jefferson NY. 516-473-0022

Schwarz, Betty P, *Librn,* Aluminum Co of America, Information Dept Library, Alcoa Center PA. 412-339-6651, Ext 2283

Schwarz, Jeanne, *Asst Librn & Tech Serv,* Sarah Lawrence College, Esther Raushenbush Library, Bronxville NY. 914-337-0700, Ext 479

Schwarz, Karen, *ILL,* Saint Xavier College, Byrne Memorial Library, Chicago IL. 312-779-3300, Ext 217

Schwarz, Marta O, *Media & Tech Serv,* Yonkers Public Library, Yonkers NY. 914-337-1500

Schwarz, Philip, *Automation & Micrographics,* University of Wisconsin-Stout, Pierce Library, Menomonie WI. 715-232-1184

Schwarz, Sara, *Archives,* Northeastern Illinois University Library, Chicago IL. 312-583-4050, Ext 469

Schwarzbauer, Ann, *Librn,* Pine River Library, Pine River MN. 218-587-2171

Schwarzkopf, Leroy, *Doc,* University of Maryland at College Park (Theodore R McKeldin Library), College Park MD. 301-454-2853, 454-5977

Schwarzmann, Diane, *Asst Dir, Ref & Spec Coll,* Yorba Linda Library District, Yorba Linda CA. 714-528-7039

Schwass, Earl R, *Chmn,* Consortium of Rhode Island Academic & Research Libraries, RI. 401-841-2641

Schwass, Earl R, *Dir,* United States Naval War College Library, Newport RI. 401-841-2641

Schwebke, Ruth, *Libr Instr,* Southern Illinois University at Edwardsville, Elijah P Lovejoy Library, Edwardsville IL. 618-692-2711

Schweda, Joyce, *ILL & Cat,* Rolling Meadows Library, Rolling Meadows IL. 312-259-6050

Schweder, Joan T, *Dir,* Markesan Public Library, Markesan WI. 414-398-3434

Schween, Roger E, *Dir,* University of Wisconsin-Extension (Extension Library Services), Madison WI. 608-262-3340

Schweibish, Gertrude F, *Dir & Acq,* East Islip Public Library, East Islip NY. 516-581-9200, 581-9228

Schweiger, Ethel, *Librn,* Saint Petersburg Public Library (Tyrone), Saint Petersburg FL. 813-893-7434

Schweik, Joanne, *Spec Coll,* State University of New York College, Daniel A Reed Library, Fredonia NY. 716-673-3183

Schweinfurth, Pat, *Br Coordr,* Troup Harris Coweta Regional Library, La Grange Memorial Library, La Grange GA. 404-882-7784

Schweiss, Helen, *Art & Music,* Sacramento Public Library, Sacramento CA. 916-440-5926

Schweitzer, Fay C, *Ref,* Lewis & Clark Community College, Reid Memorial Library, Godfrey IL. 618-466-3411, Ext 350

Schweitzer, Lynn, *Acting Curator,* University of Minnesota Libraries-Twin Cities (Immigration History Research Center), Minneapolis MN. 612-373-5581

Schweizer, Susanna, *Asst Prof,* Simmons College, Graduate School of Library & Information Science, MA. 617-738-2225

Schwellenbauch, Susan, *Asst Librn,* Rocky Mountain News Library, Denver CO. 303-892-5416

Schwenger, Frances, *Br Coordr,* Hamilton Public Library, Hamilton ON. 416-529-8111

Schwenke, Esther, *Media,* York Regional Library, Fredericton NB. 506-454-4481

Schwenn, Janet, *Ref,* Edison Community College, Learning Resources Center, Fort Myers FL. 813-481-2121, Ext 219, 220, 360

Schweppe, Dolores, *Circ,* Villa Park Public Library, Villa Park IL. 312-834-1164

Schwerner, Nancy, *Ref,* Clark Technical College, Learning Resource Center, Springfield OH. 513-325-0691, Ext 66

Schwerzel, Sharon, *Librn,* Ohio State University Libraries (Biological Sciences Library), Columbus OH. 614-422-1744

Schwind, Penny, *Cat,* Bryn Mawr College, Canaday Library, Bryn Mawr PA. 215-645-5279

Schwob, Mrs B, *Librn,* University of Alberta (Undergraduate Library), Edmonton AB. 403-432-5544

Schwoch, Arlie J, *Dir,* Osseo Public Library, Osseo WI. 715-597-2207

Schwoerer, Jane, *Librn,* Wisconsin State Department of Transportation Libraries (Aeronautics Bureau Library), Madison WI. 608-266-1797

Sciacca, Joseph, *Librn,* El Paso Public Library (Cielo Vista), El Paso TX. 915-543-3822

Sciacca, Theresa, *Asst Dir,* Dwight D Eisenhower Public Library, Totowa NJ. 201-790-3265

Sciascia, Donna, *Cat,* Bowdoin College Library, Brunswick ME. 207-725-8731, Ext 281

Scilken, Marvin H, *Dir,* Free Public Library of the City of Orange, Orange NJ. 201-673-0153

Sciotti, Angela M, *Dir,* Swain School of Design Library, New Bedford MA. 617-997-7831, Ext 22

Scism, Nancy F, *Asst Dir,* Sandhills Community College Library, Carthage NC. 919-692-6185, Ext 221, 223

Scoble, William F, *Librn,* Lake Tahoe Community College, Learning Resources Center, South Lake Tahoe CA. 916-541-4600, Ext 33

Scofield, Geraldine A, *Head Librn,* Michael Reese Medical Center (Michael Reese Hospital School of Nursing), Chicago IL. 312-791-3459

Scofield, James S, *Chief Librn,* Times Publishing Co, Saint Petersburg Times & Evening Independent Library, Saint Petersburg FL. 813-893-8111

Scoggins, Lillian, *Tech Serv,* Lutheran Theological Seminary, Krauth Memorial Library, Philadelphia PA. 215-248-4616

Scoles, Clyde S, *Asst Dir,* Toledo-Lucas County Public Library, Toledo OH. 419-255-7055

Scoles, Muriel H, *Spec Coll,* Long Branch Public Library, Long Branch NJ. 201-222-3900

Scott, Alice H, *Directors: Commun Relations & Spec Programs of Serv,* Chicago Public Library, Chicago IL. 312-269-2900

Scott, Amelia, *In Charge,* Cochise County Library System (Cochise Public Library), Cochise AZ. 602-432-5703, Ext 500

Scott, Andreal, *Bkmobile Coordr,* Lewis County Public Library, Vanceburg KY. 606-796-2532

Scott, Anita, *Librn,* Houston Public Library (Smith), Houston TX. 713-741-6220

Scott, Ann, *Educ,* Kansas State University, Farrell Library, Manhattan KS. 913-532-6516

Scott, Ann, *On-Line Servs,* Kansas State University, Farrell Library, Manhattan KS. 913-532-6516

Scott, Anna, *On-Line Servs & Bibliog Instr,* San Mateo County Library, Belmont CA. 415-573-2056

Scott, Arnita, *Acq,* Texas College, D R Glass Library, Tyler TX. 214-593-8311, Ext 37

Scott, Barbara, *Librn,* Burrton Public Library, Burrton KS. 316-463-7902

Scott, Barbara G, *Dir,* Birmingham-Southern College, Charles Andrew Rush Learning Center, Birmingham AL. 205-328-5250

Scott, Betty Ann, *Ad,* State Library of Florida, Div of Library Services, Dept of State, Tallahassee FL. 904-487-2651

Scott, Beulah, *Librn,* Gretna Public Library, Gretna NE. 402-332-4480

Scott, Brenda, *Dir,* Georgia Mental Health Institute, Addison M Duval Library, Atlanta GA. 404-894-5663

Scott, Carolyn, *Librn,* Faegre & Benson, Law Library, Minneapolis MN. 612-371-5300

Scott, Carolynne, *Area Head,* Winnipeg Public Library (Saint Vital Branch), Winnipeg MB. 204-257-0011

Scott, Catherine D, *Librn,* Smithsonian Institution Libraries (National Air & Space Museum Bureau Library), Washington DC. 202-381-6591, 381-6592, 381-6593

SCOTT

Scott, Consuela, *Ref,* West Los Angeles College Library, Culver City CA. 213-836-7110, Ext 301

Scott, Dale J, *Media,* Delaware Valley College of Science and Agriculture, Krauskopf Memorial Library, Doylestown PA. 215-345-1500, Ext 255

Scott, Deborah, *In Charge,* Oakville Public Library (Woodside), Oakville ON. 416-827-3321

Scott, Dixie, *Per,* Fullerton College, William T Boyce Library, Fullerton CA. 714-871-8000

Scott, Dixie, *Prof,* Fullerton College, Library Technician Program, CA. 714-871-8000, Ext 244

Scott, Donald, *Dir,* Prince Edward Island Provincial Library, Charlottetown PE. 902-892-3504, Ext 54

Scott, Dorothy, *In Charge,* Canadian Hearing Society Library, Toronto ON. 416-964-9595

Scott, Duscha, *Archivist,* Jackson Homestead Archives, Newton MA. 617-552-7238

Scott, Edith, *Chief Instr, Cat Instr Off,* Library of Congress, Washington DC. 202-287-5000

Scott, Edward Alderman, *Dir,* Castleton State College, Calvin Coolidge Library, Castleton VT. 802-468-5611, Ext 255

Scott, Elaine, *Librn,* Robert J Kleberg Public Library, Kingsville TX. 512-592-6381

Scott, Elizabeth, *Asst Librn,* Kilpatrick & Cody, Law Library, Atlanta GA. 404-572-6397

Scott, Elizabeth, *Tech Serv & Acq,* Long Branch Public Library, Long Branch NJ. 201-222-3900

Scott, Evelyn, *Acq,* University of Dallas, William A Blakley Library, Irving TX. 214-438-1123, Ext 328

Scott, Faith, *Librn,* Springboro Public Library, Springboro PA. 814-587-2700

Scott, Freda, *Librn,* Boonslick Regional Library (Warsaw Branch), Warsaw MO. 816-438-5211

Scott, Harry, *Bkmobile Coordr,* Lee County Library System Administrative Office, Fort Myers FL. 813-334-3221

Scott, Helen, *Librn,* East York Public Library (Thorncliffe), Toronto ON. 416-421-4791

Scott, Jack W, *Tech Serv,* Kent State University Libraries, Kent OH. 216-672-2962

Scott, James F, *Dir,* Multnomah School of the Bible, John & Mary Mitchell Library, Portland OR. 503-255-0332, Ext 362

Scott, Janice, *Librn,* Los Angeles Public Library System (J C Fremont), Los Angeles CA. 213-465-9593

Scott, Joan, *Librn,* Highland Free Library, Highland NY. 914-691-2275

Scott, Joan S, *Dir,* Josephine-Louise Public Library, Walden NY. 914-778-7621

Scott, John E, *Dir,* West Virginia State College, Drain-Jordan Library, Institute WV. 304-766-3116

Scott, Kenneth J, *Chief Librn,* Louis B Goodall Memorial Library, Sanford Public Library, Sanford ME. 207-324-4714

Scott, Laura L, *Librn,* Bradford Public Library, Bradford IL. 309-897-2071

Scott, Linda, *Librn,* Misericordia Hospital, Weinlos Library, Edmonton AB. 403-484-8811

Scott, Lucile, *Librn,* Youngtown Public Library, Youngtown AZ. 602-977-3438

Scott, Maria, *Asst Librn,* Patterson, Belknap, Webb & Tyler Library, New York NY. 212-541-4000

Scott, Marianne, *Dir,* McGill University Libraries, Montreal PQ. 514-392-4948

Scott, Mark, *Media,* Anoka County Library, Blaine MN. 612-784-1100

Scott, Mary, *Circ,* Sturgis Library, Barnstable MA. 617-362-6636

Scott, Mary Ellen, *Cat,* Pittsburgh Theological Seminary, Clifford E Barbour Library, Pittsburgh PA. 412-362-5610, Ext 280

Scott, Mrs Siebert, *Librn,* Judith Basin County Free Library (Moccasin Library Station), Moccasin MT. 406-566-2389

Scott, Mrs W, *Supvr,* Huron County Public Library (Brucefield Branch), Brucefield ON. 519-482-7135

Scott, Nancey, *Librn,* Jackson Metropolitan Library (Vicksburg Library), Vicksburg MS. 601-352-3677

Scott, Nancy, *Librn,* Vicksburg-Warren County Public Library, Vicksburg MS. 601-636-6411

Scott, Neil, *Circ, Ref & ILL,* William Carey College, I E Rouse Library, Hattiesburg MS. 601-582-5051, Ext 245 & 246

Scott, Pamela, *Librn,* Lonesome Pine Regional Library (Rose Hill Public), Rose Hill VA. 703-445-5329

Scott, Philip, *Dir,* Oak Creek Public Library, Oak Creek WI. 414-764-4400

Scott, Ralph, *On-Line Servs,* East Carolina University, J Y Joyner Library, Greenville NC. 919-757-6514

Scott, Ramona, *Spec Coll,* Indian River Community College, Charles S Miley Learning Resources Center, Fort Pierce FL. 305-464-2000, Ext 347

Scott, Richard, *On-Line Servs & Bibliog Instr,* National Science Foundation Library, Washington DC. 202-632-4070

Scott, Rita Loftus, *Dir,* Citrus College, Library Technology Program, CA. 213-335-0521, Ext 290 & 291

Scott, Robert, *Librn,* Blair Memorial Library, Clawson MI. 313-588-5500

Scott, Rose, *Librn,* Osceola Public Library, Osceola IA. 515-342-2237

Scott, Ruth F, *Dir,* Brush Carnegie Library, Brush CO. 303-842-4596

Scott, Sherry, *Exten Librn,* York County Library, Headquarters Rock Hill Public Library, Rock Hill SC. 803-328-8402

Scott, Susan, *Asst Librn & On-Line Servs,* Algoma University College Library, Sault Sainte Marie ON. 705-949-2301

Scott, Thelma J, *Cat & On-Line Servs,* Waynesburg College Library, Waynesburg PA. 412-627-8191, Ext 278

Scott, Thomas L, *Dir,* Plum Creek Library System, Worthington MN. 507-376-5803

Scott, Valerie, *Librn,* Cobourg Public Library, Cobourg ON. 416-372-9271

Scott, Virginia, *Sci & Tech,* Birmingham Public & Jefferson County Free Library, Birmingham AL. 205-254-2551

Scott, Wendy, *Librn,* Centennial College of Applied Arts & Technology (Ashtonbee Resource Centre), Scarborough ON. 416-694-3241, Ext 606

Scott, Wendy, *Librn,* National Museums of Canada Library (National Museum of Science & Technology Branch Library), Ottawa ON. 613-998-9520

Scott, William E, *Media,* Meridian Junior College Library, Meridian MS. 601-483-8241, Ext 240

Scott, William H O, *Doc,* Western Washington University, Mabel Zoe Wilson Library, Bellingham WA. 206-676-3050

Scott, Yvonne, *Head MEDLARS Mgt Section,* National Library of Medicine, Bethesda MD. 301-496-6308

Scott, Yvonne, *In Charge,* National Library of Medicine, MEDLINE, MD. 301-496-6193

Scougall, Jean, *Dir,* Baystate Medical Center, Health Sciences Library, Springfield MA. 413-787-4293, 787-4294

Scoville, M A, *Asst Librn,* Hittman Associates, Inc, Technical Information Dept-Library, Columbia MD. 301-730-7800, Ext 358

Scowcroft, Mrs P, *Asst Dir & Acq,* Vaughan Public Libraries, Maple ON. 416-832-1432

Scoyoc, Lucille Van, *Dir,* Patrick Henry School District Public Library, Edwin Wood Memorial Library, Deshler OH. 419-278-3616

Scribner, Mary L, *Librn,* Institute of Paper Chemistry Library, Appleton WI. 414-734-9251

Scribner, Myrtle T, *Asst Dir,* Athol Public Library, Athol MA. 617-249-9515

Scribner, Sara, *YA,* San Jose Public Library, San Jose CA. 408-277-4822

Scrimgeour, Andrew D, *Dir,* Boston Theological Institute Library Development Program, MA. 617-495-5780

Scripter, Kathleen, *Ref,* Capital Library Cooperative, Mason MI. 517-676-9511

Scripter, Kathleen, *ILL,* Ingham County Library, Library Service Center, Mason MI. 517-676-9088

Scroggs, Joyce F, *Dir,* Plumas County Library, Quincy CA. 916-283-0780

Scroggs, W B, *Librn,* Arbrook, Inc, Research Library, Arlington TX. 817-465-3141

Scruggs, Lois, *Librn,* Chattanooga-Hamilton County Bicentennial Library (South Chattanooga), Chattanooga TN. 615-267-7535

Scruggs, May, *Librn,* Fruitland Park Library, Fruitland Park FL. 904-728-3387

Scrutchins, Glenda, *Currie Mat,* Oklahoma Baptist University, Mabee Learning Center, Shawnee OK. 405-275-2850, Ext 245

Scudamore, Joy, *Coordr,* Greater Vancouver Library Federation, Vancouver BC. 604-251-1147

Scudder, Joanne, *Ch,* Columbia Heights Public Library, Columbia Heights MN. 612-788-3924

Scudder, Mary C, *Dir,* Lynchburg College, Knight Memorial & Capron Libraries, Lynchburg VA. 804-845-9071, Ext 271

Scudder, S A, *Librn,* Insurance Institute of Northern Alberta Library, Edmonton AB. 403-424-1268

Scullock, Sheila, *Ref & Bibliog Instr,* Shelby State Community College Library, Memphis TN. 901-528-6743

Scully, Mariwayne, *Librn,* Southeast Metropolitan Board of Cooperative Services, Professional Information Center, Denver CO. 303-757-6201

Scully, Mary, *Librn,* Dalton Public Library, Inc (Cohutta Town), Cohutta GA. 404-694-3330

Scully, Thomas F, *Dir,* Peabody Institute Library, Peabody MA. 617-531-0100

Sculthorp, Mrs J, *Ch & YA,* Vaughan Public Libraries, Maple ON. 416-832-1432

Sczesniak, Bob, *Instr,* Saint Louis Community College at Florissant Valley, Library Technical Assistant Program, MO. 314-595-4494

Seab, Myra, *YA,* East Baton Rouge Parish Library, Baton Rouge LA. 504-389-3360

Seaberry, Ivy, *Librn,* United States Navy (Naval Supply Center, Technical Library), San Diego CA. 714-235-3237

Seaberry, Nettie, *Librn,* Reader's Digest Association (Editorial Research Dept Library), New York NY. 212-972-8452

Seabold, Yvonne, *Supvry Librn,* Ventura County Library Services Agency (E P Foster), Ventura CA. 805-648-2715

Seabold, Yvonne, *Supvry Librn,* Ventura County Library Services Agency (H P Wright), Ventura CA. 805-642-0336

Seabright, Alice, *On-Line Servs & Bibliog Instr,* Lord Fairfax Community College, Learning Resource Center, Middletown VA. 703-869-1120

Seabron, Patricia, *Librn,* Newport News Public Library System (Wickham Avenue), Newport News VA. 804-247-8677

Seabrooks, Nettie H, *Mgr,* General Motors Corp (Public Relations Staff Library), Detroit MI. 313-556-2051

Seafert, Edward C, *Librn,* Lindsey Wilson College, Katie Murrell Library, Columbia KY. 502-384-2126

Seager, Donald E, *Prof,* University of Northern Colorado, Department of Educational Media, CO. 303-351-2807

Seager, George W, *Dir,* New York State Supreme Court Library, Syracuse NY. 315-425-2063

Seager, Phillip, *Instr,* University of Northern Colorado, Department of Educational Media, CO. 303-351-2807

Seagle, Cam, *Ch,* Elbert Ivey Memorial Library, Hickory NC. 704-322-2905

Seagle, Janet, *Librn,* United States Golf Association Library, Far Hills NJ. 201-234-2300

Seagle, Sara G, *Asst Librn,* Saint Mary's College, Sarah Graham Kenan Library, Raleigh NC. 919-828-2521, Ext 313, 314

Seagly, Richard, *Ad,* Public Library of Fort Wayne & Allen County, Fort Wayne IN. 219-424-7241

Seal, AnnaMae, *Librn,* Hancock County Public Library, Sneedville TN. 615-733-2254

Seal, Robert, *Admin Servs,* University of Virginia, Alderman Library, Charlottesville VA. 804-924-3026

Seale, Emily Jane, *Librn,* Montgomery County Law Library, Montgomery AL. 205-269-1261, Ext 58

Seale, Mary, *Librn,* Holmes County Library (Tchula Branch), Tchula MS. 601-235-5111

Seale, Mary, *Librn,* Mid-Mississippi Regional Library System (Tchula Public), Tchula MS. 601-235-4056

Sealock, Richard B, *Interim Dir,* College of Wooster, Andrews Library, Wooster OH. 216-264-1234, Ext 483

Sealy, Bertha Mae, *Librn,* Brownsville Free Public Library, Brownsville PA. 412-785-7272

Seaman, Anne T, *Librn,* Honolulu Academy of Arts, Robert C Allerton Library, Honolulu HI. 808-538-3693, Ext 235
Seaman, Barbara, *Commun Servs,* Crown Point-Center Public Library, Crown Point IN. 219-663-0270
Seaman, Catherine C, *Libr Tech,* Cape Hatteras National Seashore Group Reference Library, Manteo NC. 919-473-2116
Seaman, Cyril, *Asst Librn,* Siena College, Jerome Dawson Memorial Library, Loudonville NY. 518-783-2522
Seaman, Jackie, *Librn,* Williams Public Library, Williams AZ. 602-635-2263
Seaman, Martha, *Tech Serv, On-Line Servs & Bibliog Instr,* Grand Rapids Public Library, Grand Rapids MI. 616-456-4400
Seaman, Maureen G, *Dir,* Oregon Graduate Center for Study & Research Library, Beaverton OR. 503-645-1121, Ext 215
Seaman, Sheila, *Pub Serv,* University of the South, Jessie Ball duPont Library, Sewanee TN. 615-598-5931, Ext 265, 267
Seamans, Nancy H, *Librn,* Hayes, Seay, Mattern & Mattern Library, Roanoke VA. 703-343-6971, Ext 160
Seamans, Warren A, *Dir,* Massachusetts Institute of Technology Libraries (Historical Collections), Cambridge MA. 617-253-4444
Seamons, Cynthia, *Tech Serv,* Lawton Public Library, Lawton OK. 405-248-6287
Searcy, David, *Librn,* Atlanta Public Library (Anne Wallace), Atlanta GA. 404-881-6872
Searcy, Herbert, *Cat,* University of Wisconsin-La Crosse, Murphy Library, La Crosse WI. 608-785-8505
Searcy, Linda, *ILL & Ref,* Buena Vista College, Ballou Library, Storm Lake IA. 712-749-2141
Searle, Faith Ann, *Music,* Fresno County Free Library, Fresno CA. 209-488-3191
Searle, JoAnne M, *Librn,* Morristown Memorial Hospital, Lathrope Health Sciences Library, Morristown NJ. 201-540-5657
Searles, Ellen, *Librn,* Lincoln Carnegie Library, Lincoln KS. 913-524-4034
Searls, Eileen H, *Librn,* Saint Louis University (Omer Poos Law Library), Saint Louis MO. 314-658-2755
Searn, James, *Media,* Grand Rapids Public Library, Grand Rapids MI. 616-456-4400
Sears, Calantha, *Ch,* Nahant Public Library, Nahant MA. 617-581-0306
Sears, Carlton, *Ad,* Asheville-Buncombe Library System, Asheville NC. 704-252-8701
Sears, Cindy, *Librn,* Granite Falls Public Library, Granite Falls NC. 704-396-7703
Sears, Jean, *Doc,* Miami University, Edgar W King Library, Oxford OH. 513-529-2944
Sears, Jewell, *Librn,* Crawford County Public Library, English Public Library, English IN. 812-338-2606
Sears, Julienne, *Ref,* El Paso Public Library, El Paso TX. 915-543-3804
Sears, Linda, *Dir,* Hamburg Public Library, Hamburg IA. 712-382-1395
Sears, Linda, *Librn,* Mishawaka-Penn Public Library (Osceola Branch), Osceola IN. 219-674-8114
Sears, Mrs D, *Branch Assistant,* Cumberland Regional Library (Springhill Branch), Springhill NS. 902-597-2211
Sears, Phyllis J, *Supvr,* Chrysler Corp, Engineering Library, Highland Park MI. 313-956-4881
Sears, Ryssell L, *Acq,* American Graduate School of International Management, Barton Kyle Yount Memorial Library, Glendale AZ. 602-978-7232
Sears, Sarah, *Music,* Glen Ellyn Public Library, Glen Ellyn IL. 312-469-0879
Sears, Sarah, *Commun Servs,* Glen Ellyn Public Library, Glen Ellyn IL. 312-469-0879
Sears, Velma, *ILL,* City of Inglewood Public Library, Inglewood CA. 213-649-7380
Seaton, Elaine, *Dir,* Manhasset Public Library, Manhasset NY. 516-627-2300
Seaver, C Ernest, *Librn,* Hughes, Hubbard & Reed Library, New York NY. 212-943-6500
Seavey, Helen, *Librn,* Fremont Public Library, Fremont NH. 603-895-2750
Seavey, Pamela G, *Librn,* Baxter Memorial Library, Gorham ME. 207-839-4653
Seavy, Dorothy, *Librn,* Newton Free Library (Auburndale Branch), Auburndale MA. 617-527-7700, Ext 24
Seawell, Karen, *Librn,* Moore County Library, Carthage NC. 919-947-5335
Seawell, Karen, *Pub Servs,* Sandhill Regional Library System, Rockingham NC. 919-997-3388
Seay, Robert T, *Circ,* University of Wisconsin-Milwaukee, Golda Meir Library, Milwaukee WI. 414-963-4785
Sebastian, Diane S, *Ser,* King's College Library, Briarcliff Manor NY. 914-941-7200, Ext 243
Sebastian, Fern, *Asst Librn & Ref,* Portage County District Library, Hiram OH. 216-569-7666
Sebold, Cheryl, *Asst Adminr,* Gateway Regional Library System, Pocatello ID. 208-237-2192
Sebright, Terence, *In Charge,* Indiana University East, Learning Resources Center, Richmond IN. 317-966-8261
Sebring, Leila L, *Dir,* South Florida Junior College Library, Avon Park FL. 813-453-6661, Ext 191
Secard, Ella H, *Dir,* Sturm Public Library, Manawa Public Library, Manawa WI. 414-596-2252
Sechler, Martha, *Ch,* Bartholomew County Library, Cleo Rogers Memorial Library, Columbus IN. 812-379-1255
Sechrest, Sandra, *Doc,* University of Wisconsin-La Crosse, Murphy Library, La Crosse WI. 608-785-8505
Sechrist, Patricia, *Librn,* Aetna Life & Casualty (Law Library), Hartford CT. 203-273-8183
Seckelson-Simpson, Linda, *Art & Music,* Evanston Public Library, Evanston IL. 312-866-0300
Seckler, Janet F, *Librn,* Getty Refining & Marketing Co, Law Library, Tulsa OK. 918-560-6000
Secor, Bea, *Librn,* Colville Public Library, Colville WA. 509-684-6620
Secord, Ralph W, *Dir,* Mid-Peninsula Library Cooperative, Iron Mountain MI. 906-774-1218
Secrest, Christina, *Librn,* Leetonia Community Public Library, Leetonia OH. 216-427-6635
Secunda, Jeannette L, *Librn,* Home Life Insurance Co Library, New York NY. 212-233-6400
Sedberry, Lisa, *Librn,* Montgomery County Public Library (Biscoe Branch), Biscoe NC. 919-428-2551
Seder, Devra A, *Librn,* United States Courts, William J Campbell Library, Chicago IL. 312-435-5660
Sedgwick, Dorothy, *Librn,* Price Waterhouse & Co, Accounting & Auditing Research Library, Toronto ON. 416-863-1133
Sedgwick, Frederica M, *Dir,* Loyola Marymount University (Loyola Law School Library), Los Angeles CA. 213-642-2934
Sedgwick, Gregory, *In Charge,* Leeds, Hill & Jewett, Inc Library, San Francisco CA. 415-626-2070
Sedgwick, Margaret, *Dir,* Fort Frances Public Library, Fort Frances ON. 807-274-9879
Sedgwick, Mary, *Tech Serv,* Mount Saint Mary's College, Charles Willard Coe Memorial Library, Los Angeles CA. 213-476-2237, Ext 233
Sedlacek, Lorene, *Librn,* Kingsley Public Library, Kingsley MI. 616-263-5484
Sedlack, Ellen M, *Dir,* Greencastle-Putnam County Library, Greencastle IN. 317-653-6216
Sedlmayr, Linda, *Printing & Publicity,* Mid-Wisconsin Federated Library System, Fond du Lac WI. 414-921-3670
Sedney, Frances V, *Ch,* Harford County Library, Bel Air MD. 301-838-7484
See, Donna, *Asst Librn,* West Virginia School for the Blind Library, Romney WV. 304-822-3521
See, Larry E, *Librn,* Robert F Kennedy Youth Center Library, Morgantown WV. 304-296-4416, Ext 37
See, Patricia, *Circ,* Elkhart Public Library, Elkhart IN. 219-294-5463
Seeber, Frances, *Archivist,* General Services Administration - National Archives & Records Service, Franklin D Roosevelt Library, Hyde Park NY. 914-229-8114
Seeburger, C L, *Librn,* American Swedish Historical Museum, Philadelphia PA. 215-389-1776
Seed, Speth, *Tech Serv,* County of Strathcona Municipal Library, Sherwood Park AB. 403-467-3513
Seeds, Robert, *Heath Sci,* Pennsylvania State University, Fred Lewis Pattee Library, University Park PA. 814-865-0401
Seefeldt, Geraldine, *Librn,* Barnesville Public Library, Barnesville MN. 218-354-2301
Seeger, Lucille, *Librn,* Morley Public Library, Morley IA. 319-489-2362
Seeger, Marjorie J, *Librn,* McKay-Dee Hospital Center Library, Ogden UT. 801-399-4141, Ext 2152 & 627-2800
Seeger, William H, *Dir,* Schoharie County Historical Society Reference Library, Schoharie NY. 518-295-7192
Seegraber, Frank J, *Rare Bks & Spec Coll,* Boston College Libraries (Bapst (Central Library)), Chestnut Hill MA. 617-969-0100, Ext 3205
Seegraber, Rita, *Circ,* Thomas Crane Public Library, Subregional Headquarters for Eastern Massachusetts Regional Library System, Quincy MA. 617-471-2400
Seekatz, Kathleen, *Librn,* Honeywell Training & Control Systems Center, Technical Library, West Covina CA. 213-331-0011, Ext 2264
Seelen, Cheryl, *Ch,* Carnegie City Library, Little Falls MN. 612-632-9676
Seeley, Elizabeth, *Librn,* Hackley Hospital, Medical Library, Muskegon MI. 616-726-3511
Seeley, Nancy, *AV & Circ,* Reformed Theological Seminary Library, Jackson MS. 601-922-4988, Ext 52
Seely, Alice, *Asst Dir,* Butte County Library, Oroville CA. 916-534-4525
Seely, Doris J, *Cat,* Monterey Institute of International Studies, William Tell Coleman Library, Monterey CA. 408-649-3113, Ext 50&52
Seely, Edward, *Tech Serv,* Cleveland Public Library, Cleveland OH. 216-623-2800
Seely, Ella, *Media,* Library Association of Portland, Multnomah County Library, Portland OR. 503-223-7201, Ext 40
Seeman, Janis, *Cat,* Richmond Public Library, Richmond VA. 804-780-4256
Seens, Paul D, *Dir,* College of New Caledonia Library, Prince George BC. 604-562-2131, Ext 296,271
Seer, Gitelle, *Librn,* Dewey, Ballantine, Bushby, Palmer & Wood Library, New York NY. 212-344-8000
Seery, John, *Asst Dir,* Asbury Theological Seminary, B L Fisher Library, Wilmore KY. 606-858-3581, Ext 246
Seese, Pauline E, *Librn,* Stark County District Library (Hartville Branch), Hartville OH. 216-877-9975
Sefcik, Rosalie, *Librn,* Linden Free Public Library (Grier), Linden NJ. 201-486-3999
Sefcik, Rosalie, *Librn,* Linden Free Public Library (South Wood), Linden NJ. 201-862-8113
Sefranek, Barbara, *ILL & Acq,* Allentown Public Library, Allentown PA. 215-820-2400
Sefton, Amelia K, *Librn,* United States Army (Fort Hamilton Morale Support Activities Post Library), Brooklyn NY. 212-836-4100, Ext 5275
Segal, Joan S, *Dir Resource Sharing Div,* Bibliographical Center for Research, Rocky Mountain Region, Inc, Denver CO. 303-388-9261
Segal, Joan S, *Asst Exec Dir,* Bibliographical Center for Research, Rocky Mountain Region, Inc (Resource Sharing Division), CO. 303-388-9261
Segal, Molly E, *Librn,* City Library (Brightwood Library), Springfield MA. 413-737-4765
Segal, N, *Educ & Ch Lit,* State University of New York at Buffalo, University Libraries, Buffalo NY. 716-636-2965
Segal, Naomi, *Librn,* Brunswick Corp (Technical Library), Skokie IL. 312-470-4775
Segal, Sheryl A, *Dir,* Federal Communications Commission Library, Washington DC. 202-632-7100
Segalini, Julice, *Librn,* Lebanon Public Library (West Lebanon Branch), West Lebanon NH. 603-298-8544
Segall, Andrea, *Librn,* Lincoln University, Law School Library, San Francisco CA. 415-221-1212, Ext 24
Segall, Rise, *Librn,* Reader's Digest Magazines Limited (Readers Digest Association-Canada-Ltd, Book Department Library), Montreal PQ. 514-934-0751, Ext 496
Segar, Gladys, *Librn,* Langworthy Public Library, Hope Valley RI. 401-539-2851

Segarra, Roberto, *Dir,* Inter-American University-Fajardo Regional College, Centro de Recursos para el Aprendizaje, Fajardo PR. 809-863-2390

Segdwick, Shirley, *Acq,* Wyoming State Library, Cheyenne WY. 307-777-7281

Segel, Judith, *Dir,* Loudoun County Public Library, Leesburg VA. 703-777-0368

Seger, Robert M, *Dir,* Clinton Public Library, Clinton IA. 319-242-8441

Seger, Susan I, *Librn,* University of Michigan Libraries (Dentistry), Ann Arbor MI. 313-764-1526

Segina, Beverly, *Acq,* Harrisburg Area Community College, McCormick Library, Harrisburg PA. 717-236-9533, Ext 257

Segleau, Patricia M, *Dir,* Saint Bernard Parish Library, Chalmette LA. 504-279-0448

Seglin, Adelia Zdanowski, *Dir,* Saint Johns Hickey Memorial Hospital, Health Science Library, Anderson IN. 317-646-8292

Segraves, Mary, *Doc,* Montana College of Mineral Science and Technology Library, Butte MT. 406-792-8321, Ext 371

Segraves, Nell J, *Librn,* Creation-Science Research Center Library, San Diego CA. 714-277-3807

Segre, Rose, *Acq,* Adelphi University Library, Garden City NY. 516-294-8700

Seheult, Anne, *Acq,* University of Western Ontario (Health Sciences Library), London ON. 519-679-6175

Sehm, Carol A, *Dir,* Rose Free Library, Rose NY. 315-587-2335

Sehnert, Carol, *Media,* Findlay College, Shafer Library, Findlay OH. 419-422-8313, Ext 327

Sehr, Evelyn, *Dir,* Midland Park Memorial Library, Midland Park NJ. 201-444-2390, 444-2419

Sei, Arline, *Librn,* Colorado State Department of Natural Resources (Div of Wildlife Library), Denver CO. 303-825-1192, Ext 319

Seibel, Elaine, *Librn,* Hill Public Library, Hill NH. 603-934-4015

Seibel, Lois, *Ref,* Norwood Public Library, Norwood NJ. 201-768-9555

Seibel, Mrs Sidney, *Librn,* Big Horn County Library (Cowley Branch), Cowley WY. 307-568-2388

Seiber, T David, *Media,* Austin Peay State University, Felix G Woodward Library, Clarksville TN. 615-648-7346

Seibert, Donald, *Fine Arts,* Syracuse University Libraries, Ernest S Bird Library, Syracuse NY. 315-423-2575

Seibert, Karen S, *Ref,* University of Illinois at Chicago Circle Library, Chicago IL. 312-996-2716

Seibert, Lillian, *Librn,* Cullman County Public Library (Garden City Branch), Garden City AL. 205-352-4479

Seidel, Diana, *Dir,* Logan-Helm Woodford County Public Library, Versailles KY. 606-873-5191, 873-9703

Seidel, Irene, *Librn,* Alice Public Library (Orange Grove School & Public Library), Orange Grove TX. 512-384-2461

Seidel, Leslie R, *Librn,* United States Army (Cutler Army Hospital Library), Fort Devens MA. 617-796-2031

Seidel, Richard R, *Asst Libr Tech Servs,* Newberry Library, Chicago IL. 312-943-9090

Seider, Marjorie, *Librn,* Gruver City Library, Gruver TX. 806-733-2191

Seidler, Louise M, *Librn,* Standard Oil Co (Indiana), Amoco Production Co, Central Library, New Orleans LA. 504-586-6572

Seidman, Ann M, *Librn,* A E Staley Manufacturing Co, Research Library, Decatur IL. 217-423-4411, Ext 543

Seidman, Roslyn, *Ch,* Jericho Public Library, Jericho NY. 516-935-6790

Seidman, Ruth K, *Librn,* Environmental Protection Agency, Region I Library, Boston MA. 617-223-5791

Seifert, Betty, *Librn,* Grosse Pointe Public Library (Woods), Grosse Pointe Woods MI. 313-343-2072

Seifert, Jan E, *Assoc Dir of Pub Serv,* University of Oklahoma MUniversity Libraries, Norman OK. 405-325-2611

Seigal, Arlene, *Librn,* Newton Free Library (West Newton Branch), West Newton MA. 617-527-7700, Ext 24

Seigle, Jeanne C, *Mgr, Marketing Info Ctr,* Sales & Marketing Executives International, Marketing Information Center Library, New York NY. 212-986-9300

Seigler, Michael E, *Librn,* Atlanta Law School Library, Atlanta GA. 404-521-0086

Seiler, Charlotte, *Librn,* United States Air Force (Randolph Air Force Base Library), Randolph AFB TX. 512-652-2617

Seiler, Sigrid, *Ch,* Long Beach Public Library, Long Beach MS. 601-863-0711

Seilhamer, Larry, *Cat,* Lord Fairfax Community College, Learning Resource Center, Middletown VA. 703-869-1120

Seim, Joan E, *Exten Serv,* Sonoma County Library, Santa Rosa CA. 707-545-0831

Seinfeld, Evelyn, *Librn,* American Federation of State, County, Municipal Employees, AFL-CIO Dept of Research & Negotiations Library, New York NY. 212-766-1032

Seiple, Stanley, *Acq,* Saint Michael's College, Durick Library, Colchester VT. 802-655-2000, Ext 2400

Seitz, Hedy, *ILL,* Rutgers University (Archibald Stevens Alexander Library), New Brunswick NJ. 201-932-7129

Sekaly, Simone, *Cat,* Eastern Ontario Library System, Ottawa ON. 613-238-8457

Sekerak, John M, *Animal Sci,* University of California at Davis, General Library, Davis CA. 916-752-2110

Sekine, Gail, *ILL,* Mohawk College of Applied Arts & Technology, Library Resource Centre, Hamilton ON. 416-389-5665

Sekula, Linda, *Acq,* Delaware Valley College of Science and Agriculture, Krauskopf Memorial Library, Doylestown PA. 215-345-1500, Ext 255

Sekula, Linda, *Ref,* Temple University of the Commonwealth System of Higher Education (Zahn Instructional Materials Center), Philadelphia PA. 215-787-7898

Selakoff, Judith, *Librn,* Research Institute for the Study of Man Library, New York NY. 212-535-8448

Selby, Eula, *Circ,* North Park Baptist Church Library, Sherman TX. 214-892-8429

Selby, Lori L, *Librn,* Eastman Kodak Co, Colorado Div Engineering Library, Windsor CO. 303-686-7611, Ext 2079

Selby, Vickie, *Librn,* Missouri Court of Appeals Library, Western District, Kansas City MO. 816-881-3293

Selden, Catherine, *Librn,* Business & Professional Women's Foundation Library, Washington DC. 202-293-1200

Seldes, Norman M, *Dir,* East Meadow Public Library, East Meadow NY. 516-794-2570

Seldin, Daniel, *Librn,* Indiana University at Bloomington (Geography & Map), Bloomington IN. 812-337-8651

Selesky, Helen M, *Financial Serv,* Columbia University (University Libraries), New York NY. 212-280-2241

Self, David, *Librn,* University of Illinois Library at Urbana-Champaign (Veterinary Medicine), Urbana IL. 217-333-2193

Self, James, *Undergrad Librn,* Indiana University at Bloomington, University Libraries, Bloomington IN. 812-337-3403

Self, Phyllis, *Librn,* University of Illinois Library at Urbana-Champaign (Health Sciences), Urbana IL. 217-333-4893

Self, Phyllis, *Librn,* University of Illinois, Library of the Health Sciences, Urbana IL. 217-333-4893

Self, Sharon, *Ref & Bibliog Instr,* Columbus College, Simon Schwob Memorial Library, Columbus GA. 404-568-2042

Selfridge, Anna B, *ILL & Ref,* Greenville Public Library, Carnegie Library, Greenville OH. 513-548-3915

Selgestad, Marcel, *Tech Serv,* Dakota State College, Karl E Mundt Library, Madison SD. 605-256-3551, Ext 226

Selig, Edith, *Supv,* National Conference of Christians & Jews Inc, Paula K Lazrus Library of Intergroup Relations, New York NY. 212-688-7530

Selig, Pat, *Spec Coll,* Madison-Jefferson County Public Library, Madison IN. 812-265-2744

Selig, Susan, *Librn,* University of Tennessee Center for the Health Sciences Library (City of Memphis Hospitals), Memphis TN. 901-528-7975

Seligman, Joan C, *Acq,* New York Public Library (Preparation Services), New York NY. 212-790-6262

Selix, Harold, *Asst Dir,* Eagleville Hospital & Rehabilitation Center, Henry S Louchheim Medical Library, Eagleville PA. 215-539-6000, Ext 304

Selk, Loraine H, *Librn,* Ayer Public Library, Delavan IL. 309-244-8236

Selke, Elaine, *Librn,* Connaught Laboratories Ltd Library, Balmer Neilly Library, Willowdale ON. 416-667-2921, 667-2922

Sell, Betty, *Dir,* Catawba College, Corriher-Linn-Black Library, Salisbury NC. 704-637-4448, 637-4449

Sell, Mary Alice, *Ch,* Washington County Library, Lake Elmo MN. 612-777-8143

Sell, Mary Alice, *Librn,* Washington County Library (Woodbury Branch), Woodbury MN. 612-735-8153

Sella, Gladys, *Librn,* Scudder, Stevens & Clark Library, New York NY. 212-350-8370

Sellar, Pat, *Asst Librn,* Washakie County Library, Worland WY. 307-347-2231

Sellars, Judith S, *Librn,* Museum of New Mexico (Museum of International Folk Art Library), Santa Fe NM. 505-827-2544

Selle, Donna M, *Coordr,* Washington County Cooperative Library Services, OR. 503-645-7402

Selle, Donna M, *Coordr,* Washington County Cooperative Library Services, Portland OR. 503-645-5112

Selleck, Roberta, *Bk Selection Specialists,* Harvard University Library (Harvard College Library (Headquarters in Harry Elkins Widener Memorial Library)), Cambridge MA. 617-495-2401

Sellen, Betty-Carol, *Ref & Coll Development,* Brooklyn College Library, Brooklyn NY. 212-780-5342

Sellers, Brenda A, *ILL, Ref & Spec Coll,* Abraham Baldwin Agricultural College, Baldwin Library, Tifton GA. 912-386-3223

Sellers, Dale, *Media,* Mississippi Gulf Coast Junior College, Perkinston Campus Learning Resource Center, Perkinston MS. 601-928-5211, Ext 286

Sellers, H H, *Librn,* Thiokol Chemical Corp, Hunstville Division Technical Library, Huntsville AL. 205-882-8000

Sellers, Helen, *Asst Librn,* Winterset Public Library, Winterset IA. 515-462-1731

Sellers, Lee, *Dir,* University of Connecticut at Hartford (Harleigh B Trecker Library), West Hartford CT. 203-523-4841

Sellers, Linda, *Pub Servs,* Southern Methodist University Libraries (Fondren Humanities & Social Sciences), Dallas TX. 214-692-2323

Sellers, Marjorie, *ILL,* Park College Library, Parkville MO. 816-741-2000, Ext 254

Sellers, Martha M, *Tech Librn,* Olin Corp, Ecusta-Film Technical Library, Pisgah Forest NC. 704-877-2339

Sellers, Norma, *Ser & Doc,* United States Air Force (Strughold Aeromedical Library), Brooks AFB TX. 512-536-3321

Sells, Deborah Jane, *Bkmobile Librn,* Clinton County Public Library, Albany KY. 606-387-5989

Sells, Jenet, *Librn,* Muncie-Center Township Public Library (Centennial Branch), Muncie IN. 317-288-1597

Selmer, Marsha L, *Maps,* University of Illinois at Chicago Circle Library, Chicago IL. 312-996-2716

Selth, Geoffrey, *Humanities & Arts,* University of California, Riverside, University Library, Riverside CA. 714-787-3221

Selvar, Jane Cumming, *Dir,* Bronxville Public Library, Bronxville NY. 914-337-7680

Selvera, Frank, *Ref,* Cerro Coso Community College, Learning Resources Center, Ridgecrest CA. 714-375-5001, Ext 47

Selzer, Nancy S, *Librn,* E I Du Pont De Nemours & Co, Inc (Haskell Laboratory for Toxicology & Industrial Medicine Library), Newark DE. 302-366-5225

Selzer, Olga J, *Librn,* Pierce County Law Library, Tacoma WA. 206-593-4346

Semanchik, Josephine, *Librn,* Portage Public Library, Portage PA. 814-736-4340

Semanco, Judith A, *Librn,* National Business College Library, Roanoke VA. 703-982-6822

Semaskvich, Helen, *Circ,* Silas Bronson Library, Waterbury CT. 203-574-8200

Semick, G, *Project Dir,* United States Department of Justice, National Criminal Justice Reference Service, MD. 202-862-2900

Seminara, Eleanor, *Dir,* Niagara County Community College, Library Learning Center, Sanborn NY. 716-731-3271, Ext 145

Semkoco, Julie, *AV,* Westchester Library System, Hartsdale NY. 914-761-7620

Semlak, William D, *Dept Head,* Illinois State University, Department of Information Sciences, IL. 309-438-3671

Semoneit, Joyce, *Media,* Brookdale Community College, Learning Resources Center, Lincroft NJ. 201-842-1900, Ext 392

Semonoff, Hinda P, *Co Dir,* Miriam Hospital (Patients' Library), Providence RI. 401-274-3700, Ext 279

Semowich, Charles, *Librn,* Unitarian Universalist Church, Margaret Jackson Memorial Library, Binghamton NY. 607-729-1641

Semple, Rosella, *Librn,* Boyne Regional Library, Carman MB. 204-745-3504

Semrau, Jeannie, *YA,* Fresno County Free Library, Fresno CA. 209-488-3191

Send, Betty S, *Coordr,* United States Army (Van Deusen Post Library), Fort Monmouth NJ. 201-532-9000

Seneca, Kristen, *Circ,* Linfield College, Northup Library, McMinnville OR. 503-472-4121, Ext 262

Senechal, Richard, *Info Retrieval Officer,* Sidbec-Dosco Corp, Service de Documentation, Montreal PQ. 514-875-7070

Seng, Mary, *On-Line Search Coordr & Grad Bibliog Instr,* University of Texas Libraries (General), Austin TX. 512-471-3811

Seng, Ruth, *Tech Serv,* Marple Public Library, Broomall PA. 215-356-1510, 356-0550

Senior, Sarah, *Librn,* Clear Lake Public Library, Clear Lake IA. 515-357-6133

Senko, Barbara, *Librn,* Wiggin Memorial Library, Stratham NH. 603-772-4346

Senko, Joan, *Librn,* Braidwood Public Library, Braidwood IL. 815-458-2236

Senkus, Linda, *Ser,* University of New Haven, Marvin K Peterson Library, West Haven CT. 203-934-6321

Senkyr, Kathryn, *Asst Librn,* Kirtland Public Library, Kirtland OH. 216-256-3747

Senn, Teresa, *Asst Librn,* Jacksonville College Library, Jacksonville TX. 214-586-2518, Ext 27

Senner, Kathryn, *Asst Librn & Cat,* Morningside College, Wilhemina Petersmeyer Library, Sioux City IA. 712-277-5195

Sentner, Sylvia, *Per,* Cornell University Medical College, Samuel J Wood Library, New York NY. 212-472-5300

Senuk, Agnes, *Actg Librn,* Calvary Hospital (Medical Library), Bronx NY. 212-430-4600

Senyk, Genevieve, *Librn,* Henry Stephen Memorial Library, Almont Library, Almont MI. 313-798-3100

Seo, Shirley H, *Br Librn,* Ledyard Public Libraries, Gales Ferry Library & Bill Library, Ledyard CT. 203-464-9917

Sepanik, Mary, *Pub Servs,* University of South Florida (University Library), Tampa FL. 813-974-2721

Sepehri, Abazar, *Librn,* University of Texas Libraries (Middle East Collection), Austin TX. 512-471-4675

Sepin, Arline, *Asst Librn,* Dodge Center Public Library, Dodge Center MN. 507-374-2275

Sepul, Paulette, *Librn,* Rhode Island Hospital, Peters Memorial Library, Providence RI. 401-277-4671

Sepulveda, Mary, *Acq,* Seattle University, A A Lemieux Library, Seattle WA. 206-626-6859

Sepulveda-Vasquez, Gloria, *Ref,* Lansing Community College Library, Lansing MI. 517-373-9978

Seputis, Sophie, *Dir,* Worth Public Library District, Worth IL. 312-448-2855

Sequeira, Helen, *Dir,* Haverstraw Kings Daughters Public Library, Haverstraw NY. 914-429-3445

Serban, William, *Doc & On-Line Servs,* Louisiana Tech University, Prescott Memorial Library, Ruston LA. 318-257-2577

Serbe, Mary Jane, *Dir,* Chester Free Public Library, Chester NJ. 201-879-7612

Sercl, Jo Ann, *Librn,* Valparaiso Public Library, Valparaiso NE. 402-784-6141

Sereiko, George E, *Dir & Pub Servs,* University of Notre Dame Library, Notre Dame IN. 219-283-7317

Serena, Richard M, *Librn,* Golden Valley Lutheran College Library, Minneapolis MN. 612-542-1210

Sereno, Madalene, *ILL,* Long Branch Public Library, Long Branch NJ. 201-222-3900

Sergeson, Helen, *Asst Librn & Cat,* Lake-Sumter Community College, Learning Resources Center, Leesburg FL. 904-787-3747, Ext 33

Serha, Liza, *Librn,* National Institutes of Health, Rocky Mountain Laboratory Library, Hamilton MT. 406-363-3211, Ext 52

Serich, Genevieve, *Librn,* Calumet Public Library, Calumet MN. 218-247-7542

Serico, Susan, *Librn,* North Haledon Free Public Library, North Haledon NJ. 201-427-6213

Serignet, Estelle, *Librn,* Plaquemines Parish Library (Pointe-a-la-Hache Branch), Pointe-a-la-Hache LA. 504-333-4239

Serio, Nora, *Librn,* Pointe Coupee Parish Library (Morganza Libr), Morganza LA. 504-638-7593

Sern, M, *Librn,* Falkirk Hospital Library, Central Valley NY. 914-928-2256

Serode, Delores, *ILL,* New Bedford Free Public Library, Subregional Headquarters for Eastern Massachusetts Regional Library System, New Bedford MA. 617-999-6291

Serota, Barbara Jo, *Assoc Librn,* Texas State Law Library, Austin TX. 512-475-3807

Serpas, Virginia, *Librn,* Saint Bernard Parish Library (Ducros Museum), Chalmette LA. 504-682-2713

Serra, Mrs D W, *Librn,* Bunker-Ramo Corp, Engineering Library, Trumbull CT. 203-377-4141

Serra, Virginia S, *Librn,* Luce, Forward, Hamilton & Scripps, Law Library, San Diego CA. 714-236-1414

Serroao, Consuelo, *Librn,* State Psychiatric Hospital, Library of Mental Health Program, Rio Piedras PR. 809-765-9965

Sertic, Kenneth J, *Dir,* Fort Morgan Public Library, Fort Morgan CO. 303-867-7116

Servies, James A, *Dir,* University of West Florida, John C Pace Library, Pensacola FL. 904-476-9500, Ext 261

Serynek, William P, *Dir,* Peninsula Public Library, Lawrence NY. 516-239-3262

Serzan, Sharon, *Per,* Pennsylvania State University, Capitol Campus Heindel Library, Middletown PA. 717-787-7771

Sessions, Judith A, *Dir,* Mount Vernon College Library, Washington DC. 202-331-3475

Sessions, Robert, *Ref,* Cornell College, Russell D Cole Library, Mount Vernon IA. 319-895-8811, Ext 117

Sessions, Vivian S, *Dir & Prof,* McGill University, Graduate School of Library Science, PQ. 514-392-5947

Seter, Connie, *Ch & YA,* Norwood Public Library, Norwood NJ. 201-768-9555

Seto, Gail, *Dir of Acq & Ref,* Pioneer Multi-County Library, Norman OK. 405-321-1481

Seton, Sister Mary, *Librn,* Catholic Center Library at New York University, New York NY. 212-674-7236, Ext 22

Setter, Margaret K, *Librn,* Cattaraugus Free Library, Cattaraugus NY. 716-257-9500

Settle, Elizabeth, *Ref & Bibliog Instr,* California State University Dominguez Hills, Educational Resources Center, Carson CA. 213-515-3700

Settle, Patricia, *Ad,* Medicine Hat Public Library, Medicine Hat AB. 403-527-5551

Settlemeyer, Louise, *Librn,* Cannon Memorial Ymca Public Library, Kannapolis NC. 704-933-2636

Setton, Sarah, *Librn,* Sugar Association, Inc Washington DC. 202-628-0189

Settoon, Geraldine, *Librn,* Iberville Parish Library (Bayou Pigeon), Plaquemine LA. 504-545-8567

Setzer, Patricia, *Asst Dir & Br Coordr,* Wayne County Public Library, Inc, Goldsboro NC. 919-735-1824

Seugling, Alta, *Br Coordr,* Pequannock Township Public Library, Pompton Plains NJ. 201-835-7460

Seugling, Alta, *Librn,* Pequannock Township Public Library (Branch Library), Pequannock NJ. 201-835-7460

Seumptewa, Owen, *Librn,* Northland Pioneer College, Oraibi Center, Oraibi AZ. 602-734-2451

Seuss, Herbert J, *Librn,* Eaton Corp, Cutler-Hammer Library, Milwaukee WI. 414-442-7800, Ext 3679

Seuss, Jacqueline, *Librn,* Boston College Libraries (Resource Center), Chestnut Hill MA. 617-969-0100, Ext 4412

Sevart, Sister Denise, *Asst Dir,* Saint Mary of the Plains College, Michael Hornung Library, Dodge City KS. 316-225-4171, Ext 68

Sevart, Sister Denise, *Instr,* Saint Mary of the Plains College, Library Science Program, KS. 316-225-4171, Ext 68

Sever, Eileen, *Librn,* Los Angeles Public Library System (Palms-Rancho Park), Los Angeles CA. 213-838-2157

Severance, C, *Curator Hist Museums,* London Public Libraries & Museums, London ON. 519-432-7166

Severson, Mary, *Ch,* Everett Public Library, Everett WA. 206-259-8858

Severson, Ruth, *Librn,* Kenyon Public Library, Kenyon MN. 507-789-6821

Sevier, Jeffrey A, *Tech Serv,* Hughes Aircraft Co (Company Technical Document Center Library), Culver City CA. 213-391-0711, Ext 6187

SeVigniy, Emily, *Librn,* Plamondon Community Library, Plamondon AB. 403-798-3840

Seville, Ann, *Librn,* Enoch Pratt Free Library (Herring Run), Baltimore MD. 301-396-5430, 396-5395

Sevy, Barbara, *Librn,* Philadelphia Museum of Art, Marian Angell Boyer Library, Philadelphia PA. 215-763-8100, Ext 229

Sewak, Sophia, *Librn,* Frenchtown Public Library, Frenchtown NJ. 201-996-4788

Sewald, Beatrice R, *Asst Librn,* Nassau County Department of Health, Div of Laboratories & Research Medical Library, Hempstead NY. 516-483-9158

Seward, Jean, *Ch,* Lincoln Library, Springfield Public Library, Springfield IL. 217-753-4900

Seward, Lillie, *Pub Libr Specialists,* Maryland State Department of Education, Division of Library Development & Services, Baltimore MD. 301-796-8300, Ext 284

Seward, Ruby F, *Actg Librn,* Fairmount Public Library, Fairmount IN. 317-948-3177

Sewell, Eleanor, *Librn,* Harris County Public Library (Fairbanks), Houston TX. 713-466-4438

Sewell, Jean R, *Dir,* Ohio State University, Lima Regional Campus Library, Lima OH. 419-228-2641, Ext 310

Sewell, Lillian, *Librn,* Murphy Memorial Library, Livingston TX. 713-327-4252

Sewell, Martha, *Tech Serv & Cat,* Baldwin Public Library, Birmingham MI. 313-647-1700

Sewell, Mary M, *Librn,* Athens Regional Library (Carnesville Public), Carnesville GA. 404-543-0134

Sewell, Rusty, *Librn,* Helena Laboratories Library, Beaumont TX. 713-842-3714

Sewell, Winifred, *Lectr,* University of Maryland, College of Library & Information Services, MD. 301-454-5441

Sexton, Carol, *Tech Serv, Acq & Doc,* Chowan College, Whitaker Library, Murfreesboro NC. 919-398-4101, Ext 241

Sexton, Frances, *Librn,* Tyrrell County Public Library, Columbia NC. 919-796-3771

Sexton, Irwin, *Dir,* San Antonio Public Library, San Antonio TX. 512-299-7790

Sexton, Julie, *Librn,* Bremerton Sun Newspaper Library, Bremerton WA. 206-377-3711

Sexton, Kathryn, *Librn,* Titonka Public Library, Titonka IA. 515-928-2509

Sexton, M E, *Libr Supvr,* Bell Telephone Laboratories (Western Electric Technical Library), North Andover MA. 617-681-6752

Sexton, Melinda, *Librn,* Lonesome Pine Regional Library (C Bascom Slemp Memorial, Subregional Library for the Blind & Physically Handicapped), Big Stone Gap VA. 703-523-1334

Seybold, Marilyn R, *Librn,* Charles H Taylor Memorial Library (Willow Oaks), Hampton VA. 804-727-6279

Seydoux, Aline, *Pub Servs,* Loyola Marymount University, Charles Von Der Ahe Library, Los Angeles CA. 213-642-2788

Seymour, Amy, *Tech Serv,* Annie Halenbake Ross Library, Lock Haven PA. 717-748-3321

Seymour, Bonnie, *Librn,* Lincoln Trail Regional Library, Elizabethtown KY. 502-769-1597

Seymour, Celine, *Librn,* Conservation Foundation Library, Washington DC. 202-797-4300, Ext 75

Seymour, Diana, *Order-Receipt,* Dartmouth College, Baker Memorial Library, Hanover NH. 603-646-2235

Seymour, Jill, *Asst Librn,* Graceland College, Frederick Madison Smith Library, Lamoni IA. 515-784-3311, Ext 144

Seymour, Margaret A, *Librn,* Cuyahoga County Public Library (Gates Mills Branch), Gates Mills OH. 216-423-4808

Seymour, Marilyn, *Ref,* Maitland Public Library, Maitland FL. 305-647-7700

Seymour, Patricia, *Ch,* Morley Library, Painesville OH. 216-352-3383

Sgro, Larry, *Dir,* Nicolet College & Technical Institute, Learning Resources Center, Rhinelander WI. 715-369-4429

Sha, Marjorie Y, *Tech Serv,* New Rochelle Public Library, New Rochelle NY. 914-632-7878

Shabowich, Stanley A, *Acq,* Purdue University Calumet Library, Hammond IN. 219-844-0520, Ext 249

Shackelford, Eileen, *Acq,* Yuma City-County Library, Yuma AZ. 602-782-1871

Shackelford, Margaret G, *Librn,* Tenneco Inc, Deepsea Ventures Inc Library, Gloucester Point VA. 804-642-6843

Shackelford, Marilyn, *Regional Librn,* Tulsa City-County Library, Tulsa OK. 918-581-5221

Shackelford, Mary Leslie, *Dir,* Vaughan Memorial Library, Galax Public Library, Galax VA. 703-236-2351

Shackleford, Marilyn, *Regional Librn,* Tulsa City-County Library (Martin East Regional), Tulsa OK. 918-581-5221

Shackleford, Mrs Jerry, *Librn,* Meigs County Public Library, Decatur TN. 615-334-3332

Shackleford, Ruby, *Librn,* Urbanna Public Library, Urbanna VA. 804-758-5717

Shackley, Betty, *Libr Technician,* San Diego County Library (Casa de Oro), Spring Valley CA. 714-463-3236

Shaddox, Nina, *YA,* Leominster Public Library, Leominster MA. 617-537-0941

Shade, Diana, *ILL,* Meadville Library Art & Historical Association, Meadville PA. 814-336-1773

Shade, Linnet, *Librn,* Smithville Public Library, Smithville TX. 512-237-2707

Shady, Kathy, *Asst Librn,* Chester County Historical Society Library, West Chester PA. 215-696-4755

Shaeffer, Suzanne, *Ch,* Volusia County Public Libraries, Daytona Beach FL. 904-252-8374

Shafer, Linda, *Tech Serv,* Coffeyville Public Library, Coffeyville KS. 316-251-1370

Shafer, Marcia, *Ch,* Ann Arbor Public Library, Ann Arbor MI. 313-994-2333

Shafer, Suzanne, *Tech Serv,* Lake-Sumter Community College, Learning Resources Center, Leesburg FL. 904-787-3747, Ext 33

Shaff, Jimmie Lee, *Acq & Cat,* San Diego City College Library, San Diego CA. 714-238-1181, Ext 250

Shaffer, Dale E, *Dir,* Jennings Library, Salem OH. 216-337-3348

Shaffer, Dallas, *Info Officer,* Prince George's County Memorial Library System, Hyattsville MD. 301-699-3500

Shaffer, Ellen, *Curator,* Silverado Museum Library, Saint Helena CA. 707-963-3757

Shaffer, Frank K, *Dir,* Monessen Public Library, Monessen PA. 412-684-4750

Shaffer, Georgia, *Librn,* Gilliam County Library, Condon OR. 503-384-6052

Shaffer, Harold A, *Tech Serv,* Indiana University (School of Dentistry Library), Indianapolis IN. 317-264-7204

Shaffer, Jack, *Librn,* Saint Vincent Hospital & Medical Center, Health Science Library, Toledo OH. 419-259-4324

Shaffer, Jane, *Ref,* Cocoa Beach Public Library, Cocoa Beach FL. 305-783-7350

Shaffer, Judith, *Acq,* Central Piedmont Community College Library, Charlotte NC. 704-373-6883

Shaffer, Kathryn, *Librn,* Sacramento Public Library (Walnut Grove Branch), Walnut Grove CA. 916-776-1412

Shaffer, Lila, *Asst Dir,* Cambridge Springs Public Library, Cambridge Springs PA. 814-398-2123

Shaffer, Margaret M, *Dir,* Terrebonne Parish Library, Houma LA. 504-876-5861

Shaffer, Mary Ann, *Librn,* Timberland Regional Library (W H Abel Memorial), Montesano WA. 206-249-4211

Shaffer, Mary L, *Dir,* United States Department of the Army (The Army Library, Pentagon), Washington DC. 202-697-4301, Ext 69-55346

Shaffer, Mrs Shelby J, *Librn,* Chillicothe & Ross County Public Library (Kingston Branch), Kingston OH. 614-642-2099

Shaffer, Nancy R, *Librn,* Hillside Public Library, Hillside IL. 312-449-7510

Shaffer, Norman, *Chief, Photoduplication Serv,* Library of Congress, Washington DC. 202-287-5000

Shaffer, Sylvia W, *Spec Asst for Prof Publications & Tech Info,* United States Bureau of Medicine & Surgery, Surgeon General's Library, Washington DC. 202-655-4000

Shaffer, Jr, Kenneth M, *Acq,* Bethany & Northern Baptist Theological Seminaries Library, Oak Brook IL. 312-620-2214

Shagg, Jeanne R, *Dir,* Hopewell Valley Free Public Library, Pennington NJ. 609-737-0404

Shah, Chandra, *Circ,* Francis D Murphy Medical Library, Milwaukee WI. 414-257-5897

Shah, Chandra, *Circ,* The Medical College of Wisconsin, Inc, Todd Wehr Library, Milwaukee WI. 414-257-8323

Shah, Neeta N, *Chief Med Librn,* William S Hall Psychiatric Institute, Professional Library, Columbia SC. 803-758-7448

Shahoff, D, *Reader Serv,* Barrie Public Library, Barrie ON. 705-728-1010

Shahriary, Carol, *On-Line Servs,* Saint Louis Community College (Forest Park Campus), Saint Louis MO. 314-644-9209

Shaines, Karen, *Asst Librn,* Frederick Cancer Research Center, Scientific Library, Frederick MD. 301-663-7261

Shaker, Kathy, *Ch,* Reedsburg Public Library, Reedsburg WI. 608-524-3316

Shaker, Lila, *Librn,* Barden Corp, Technical Library, Danbury CT. 203-744-2211, Ext 305

Shaklee, Robert, *In Charge,* Denver Public Library (Documents), Denver CO. 303-573-5152, Ext 271

Shakleton, Mary, *Ref, Circ, ILL & On-Line Servs,* Gordon College, Winn Library, Wenham MA. 617-927-2300, Ext 233

Shalabi, Mahmound, *Ref,* Olive-Harvey College, City Colleges of Chicago, Olive-Harvey College Library, Chicago IL. 312-568-3700

Shalala, Karen, *Asst Librn,* University of New Brunswick (Law), Fredericton NB. 506-453-4669

Shamalla, Michael, *Dir,* Willard Library, Battle Creek MI. 616-968-8166

Shamble, Mary R, *Librn,* Ebensburg Free Public Library, Ebensburg PA. 814-472-7957

Shamblin, Betty Ann, *Librn,* United States Air Force (Williams Air Force Base Library), Williams AFB AZ. 602-988-2611

Shambrook, Betty H, *Dir,* Big Bend Community College Library, Moses Lake WA. 509-762-5351

Shames, Pat, *Librn,* Orange County Department of Education, Education Library, Santa Ana CA. 714-834-3980

Shames, Susan P, *Librn,* Colonial Williamsburg (Department of Collections Library), Williamsburg VA. 804-229-1000, Ext 2415

Shamleffer, Doris, *Dir,* New York Friends Group, Inc, Center for Global Perspectives Library, New York NY. 212-475-0850

Shampine, Gayle A, *Dir,* Park Forest South Public Library District, Park Forest South IL. 312-534-2580

Shanaberger, W, *Rec Technician,* Maryland-National Capital Park & Planning Commission Library (Records Management), Silver Spring MD. 301-565-7404, 565-7405 & 565-7429

Shandrick, Maureen F, *Dir,* Southside Virginia Community College, John H Daniel Campus Library, Keysville VA. 804-736-8484

Shands, Alice, *Librn,* Central Arkansas Library System (Southwest), Little Rock AR. 501-568-7494

Shane, Charlotte, *Ref,* School of the Ozarks, Lyons Memorial Library, Point Lookout MO. 417-334-6411, Ext 460

Shane, Dorothy, *Librn,* Sparks Memorial Library, Berrien Springs MI. 616-471-7074

Shank, Beverly, *Commun Servs,* Medford Public Library, Medford MA. 617-395-7950

Shank, Diane, *Cat & On-Line Servs,* Oklahoma Baptist University, Mabee Learning Center, Shawnee OK. 405-275-2850, Ext 245

Shank, Russell, *Univ Librn,* University of California Los Angeles Library, Los Angeles CA. 213-825-1201

Shank, Susan A, *Dir,* Abbott Memorial Library, Dexter ME. 207-924-7292

Shank, William, *Music,* City University of New York, Library of Graduate School & University Center, New York NY. 212-790-4541

Shankin, Mrs Leonard, *Dir,* Audubon Public Library, Audubon NJ. 609-547-8686

Shankle, Betty, *ILL,* Greenville County Library, Greenville SC. 803-242-5000

Shanklin, Mel, *Librn,* Gorham Free Library, Gorham NY. 315-526-6655

Shanks, Betty M, *Librn,* Saint Mary's Medical Center Library, Knoxville TN. 615-971-6749

Shanks, Beulah, *Librn,* Warren County Library (Alexis Branch), Alexis IL. 309-482-6109

Shanks, Doreen, *Librn,* University of Manitoba Libraries (Education), Winnipeg MB. 204-474-9976

Shanks, Jean, *Govt Doc,* Birmingham Public & Jefferson County Free Library, Birmingham AL. 205-254-2551

Shanks, Polly, *Tech Serv,* Mississippi Research & Development Center, Information Services Divison, Jackson MS. 601-982-6324

Shanley, Brian, *Librn,* Montgomery Technical Institute Library, Troy NC. 919-572-3691

Shanley, Catherine, *Ref,* Manhattan College, Cardinal Hayes Library, Bronx NY. 212-548-1400, Ext 366 & 367

Shanley, Dennis M, *Dir,* Anoka Public Library, Anoka MN. 612-421-5800

Shanley, Elaine, *Cat,* Providence College, Phillips Memorial Library, Providence RI. 401-865-2242

Shanley, Eleanor, *Asst Prof,* Augustana College, Library Science Program, SD. 605-336-4921

Shanley, Eleanor, *Tech Serv, On-Line Servs & Bibliog Instr,* Augustana College, Mikkelsen Library & Learning Resources Center, Sioux Falls SD. 605-336-4921

Shanley, Evelyn, *Librn,* Morristown Centennial Library, Morrisville VT. 802-888-3853

Shannon, Charlotte, *Librn,* Monaca Library, Monaca PA. 412-774-4234

Shannon, Donn, *Librn,* Press Club of San Francisco, Will Aubrey Memorial Library, San Francisco CA. 415-775-7800

Shannon, Dwight W, *Librn,* California State University, Chico Library, Chico CA. 916-895-6212

Shannon, Elaine, *Asst Dir, ILL & Ref,* Alexander Mitchell Library, Aberdeen Public Library, Aberdeen SD. 605-225-4186

Shannon, Inez, *Librn,* Jackson Metropolitan Library (Mims Memorial), Magee MS. 601-352-3677

Shannon, Jean, *Librn,* Knoxville-Knox County Public Library (Karns), Knoxville TN. 615-690-0363

Shannon, Joyce, *Libr Asst,* Haut-Saint-Jean Regional Library (Grand Falls Public), Grand Falls NB. 506-473-1248

Shannon, Marcia, *Librn,* Almonte Public Library, Almonte ON. 613-256-1037

Shannon, Michael, *Doc,* Herbert H Lehman College Library, Bronx NY. 212-960-8577, 960-8582

Shannon, Michele, *Librn,* Pennsylvania Board of Probation & Parole Library, Harrisburg PA. 717-787-7037

Shannon, Zella, *Assoc Dir,* Minneapolis Public Library & Information Center, Minneapolis MN. 612-372-6500

Shantz, Mary, *Librn,* Sudbury Public Library (Information and Reference Services), Sudbury ON. 705-673-1155, Ext 41 & 42

Shantz, Mary, *Ref,* Sudbury Public Library, La Bibliotheque Publique de Sudbury, Sudbury ON. 705-673-1155
Shantz, Mary, *Local Hist,* Sudbury Public Library, La Bibliotheque Publique de Sudbury, Sudbury ON. 705-673-1155
Shanyfelt, Tom, *Dir,* Wyoming State Penitentiary Library, Rawlins WY. 307-324-6661
Shapiola, Michael, *Ch,* Wanaque Public Library, Wanaque NJ. 201-839-4434
Shapiro, Barbara G, *Dir,* Margate City Public Library, Margate City NJ. 609-822-4700
Shapiro, Beth, *Soc Sci,* Michigan State University Library, East Lansing MI. 517-355-2344
Shapiro, Beth J, *Librn,* Michigan State University Library (Urban Policy & Planning), East Lansing MI. 517-355-2344
Shapiro, Ethan D, *AV,* County College of Morris, Sherman H Masten Learning Resource Center, Randolph Township NJ. 201-361-5000, Ext 470
Shapiro, Gertrude, *Ad & Ref,* Downers Grove Public Library, Downers Grove IL. 312-960-1200
Shapiro, June, *Dir Libr Develop,* Connecticut State Library, Hartford CT. 203-566-4301
Shapiro, Karen, *Ch,* Pasadena Public Library, Pasadena TX. 713-477-0276
Shapiro, Leonard P, *Dir & On-Line Servs,* California College of Podiatric Medicine, Schmidt Medical Library, San Francisco CA. 415-563-3444, Ext 246
Shapiro, Marsha, *Asst Librn,* Manulife, Business Library, Toronto ON. 416-928-4104
Shapiro, Milton D, *Dir,* Helen Kate Furness Free Library, Wallingford PA. 215-566-9331
Shapiro, Peggy, *Reader Serv,* Wisconsin Supreme Court, Wisconsin State Law Library, Madison WI. 608-266-1424, 266-1600
Shapiro, Sandra, *Librn,* Brooklyn Public Library (Clarendon), Brooklyn NY. 212-434-3620
Shapiro, Susan Simon, *Ch,* Huntingdon Valley Library, Huntingdon Valley PA. 215-947-5138
Shapland, Elaine, *Librn,* Lane County Library, Dighton KS. 316-397-5829
Shappe, Ellen, *Mgr Libr Serv,* National Association of Accountants Library, New York NY. 212-754-9736, 754-9737
Shaps-Eidelson, Elizabeth, *Librn,* Ludington Public Library, Bryn Mawr PA. 215-527-1550, 525-1776
Shapton, Eleanor, *Tech Serv,* Covina Public Library, Covina CA. 213-967-3935
Shapton, Gregory, *Ref,* Pomona Public Library, Pomona CA. 714-620-2033
Shar, H K, *Librn,* Regina Mundi College Library, London ON. 519-685-2133
Sharbaugh, Mary L, *Librn,* Carrolltown Public Library, Carrolltown PA. 814-344-6300
Sharbaugh, Thomas L, *Dir,* Salamanca Public Library, Salamanca NY. 716-945-1890
Share, Carol, *Librn,* Memphis-Shelby County Public Library & Information Center (Poplar-White Station), Memphis TN. 901-682-1616
Sharify, Nasser, *Dean,* Pratt Institute, Graduate School of Library & Information Science, NY. 212-636-3702
Sharma, Katherine, *Librn,* Cross Cancer Institute, Edmonton AB. 403-432-8593
Sharma, Prabha, *Hist & Political Sci,* University of Alabama in Huntsville Library, Huntsville AL. 205-895-6540
Sharma, Ramesh, *Tech Serv,* Pittsburg State University Library, Pittsburg KS. 316-231-7000, Ext 431
Sharma, Ravindra, *ILL,* Colgate University, Everett Needham Case Library, Hamilton NY. 315-824-1000
Sharma, Savita, *Asst Librn,* W J Levy Consultants Corp Library, New York NY. 212-586-5263
Sharon, Dan, *Cat,* Spertus College of Judaica, Norman & Helen Asher Library, Chicago IL. 312-922-9012, Ext 50
Sharp, Avery, *Ch,* Waco-McLennan County Library (East Side), Waco TX. 817-753-6044
Sharp, D, *Tech Serv & Cat,* Lakehead University Library, Thunder Bay ON. 807-345-2121
Sharp, Florence R, *Librn,* National Lead Industries Inc, National Lead Co of Ohio Library, Cincinnati OH. 513-738-1151, Ext 509
Sharp, Helen, *Librn,* Kirwin City Library, Kirwin KS. 913-646-2752

Sharp, Janis, *Personnel,* Houston Academy of Medicine, Texas Medical Center Library, Houston TX. 713-797-1230
Sharp, Jeanne, *Local hist & Genealogy,* Newburgh Free Library, Newburgh NY. 914-561-1836
Sharp, Kathleen, *Dir,* Paragould Public Library, Greene County Library, Paragould AR. 501-236-8711
Sharp, Mary Jane, *Ser,* University of Tennessee, Knoxville, James D Hoskins Library, Knoxville TN. 615-974-0111
Sharp, Mary Jane, *Head,* University of Tennessee, Knoxville (Serials), Knoxville TN. 615-974-4236
Sharp, Patricia A, *Asst Prof,* Baylor University, Dept of Library Science, TX. 817-755-2410
Sharp, Susan, *Dir,* Pine City Public Library, Pine City MN. 612-629-6403
Sharp, Thomas, *Circ,* University of California, San Diego, University Libraries, La Jolla CA. 714-452-3336
Sharp, Valetta, *Librn,* United States Army (Corps of Engineers, Missouri River Division Library), Omaha NE. 402-221-3020
Sharpe, David, *Asst Prof,* San Diego State University, Dept of Educational Technology & Librarianship, CA. 714-265-6718
Sharpe, Jean H, *Librn,* American Enka Co, Business & Technical Library, Enka NC. 704-667-6936
Sharpe, Jodee, *Acq,* Wayne State University Libraries (Arthur Neef Law Library), Detroit MI. 313-577-3925
Sharpe, John, *Rare Bks,* Duke University, William R Perkins Library, Durham NC. 684-2034 (Main).
Sharpe, Karen, *Media,* San Diego City College Library, San Diego CA. 714-238-1181, Ext 250
Sharpe, Ruth, *Librn,* Memorial Hall Library (Ballardvale), Andover MA. 617-475-0521
Sharpell, Marguerite, *Acq,* Pequannock Township Public Library, Pompton Plains NJ. 201-835-7460
Sharples, David, *Librn,* National Film Board Library, Regina SK. 306-569-5012
Sharpley, Mary E, *Librn,* Sharpley Laboratories Inc Library, Fredericksburg VA. 703-373-7336
Sharpsteen, Mickey, *Pub Servs,* Citrus College, Hayden Memorial Library, Azusa CA. 213-335-0521, Ext 290, 291
Sharrett, R, *Librn,* Agriculture Canada (Entomology Research Library), Ottawa ON. 613-995-4502
Sharring, Marjorie, *Ad,* Glen Ellyn Public Library, Glen Ellyn IL. 312-469-0879
Sharrow, M J, *Dir,* University of Manitoba Libraries, Winnipeg MB. 204-474-9881
Sharrow, Marilyn, *Asst Librn,* Boone-Madison Public Library, Madison WV. 304-369-4675
Shasky, Florian, *Spec Coll,* Stanford University Libraries, Stanford CA. 415-497-2016
Shasteen, Agnes R, *Librn,* Chillicothe & Ross County Public Library (Paxton), Bainbridge OH. 614-634-3524
Shatkin, Leon, *Dir,* Connecticut State Library (Interlibrary Loan Center), Hartford CT. 203-566-3024
Shatto, Ruth, *Ad,* Lancaster County Library, Lancaster PA. 717-394-2651
Shattuck, Beverly, *Pub Servs, On-Line Servs & Bibliog Instr,* University of Massachusetts Medical School, Medical Center Library, Worcester MA. 617-856-2511
Shattuck, Kathleen G, *Dir,* Highland Community Junior College Library, Highland KS. 913-442-3238, Ext 54
Shattuck, Marian L, *Dir,* Kinnelon Public Library, Kinnelon NJ. 201-838-1321
Shaughnessy, Jean, *Ch,* Euclid Public Library, Euclid OH. 216-261-5300
Shaughnessy, Thomas W, *Asst Dir of Pub Servs,* University of Houston (M D Anderson Memorial Library), Houston TX. 713-749-4241
Shaup, Phyllis, *Ch,* Hazleton Area Public Library, Hazleton PA. 717-454-2961, 454-0244
Shaver, Donna, *On-Line Servs,* Northwest Regional Education Laboratory, Information Center Library, Portland OR. 503-248-6922
Shaver, Dorothy M, *Librn,* Beaverton City Library, Beaverton OR. 503-644-2197
Shaver, Helen, *Cat,* Merritt Island Public Library, Merritt Island FL. 305-452-3834

Shaver, Helen, *Tech Serv & Cat,* Mohawk College of Applied Arts & Technology, Library Resource Centre, Hamilton ON. 416-389-5665
Shaver, Helen B, *Cat,* Cocoa Beach Public Library, Cocoa Beach FL. 305-783-7350
Shaver, Marlene, *Librn,* Altoona Public Library, Altoona IA. 515-967-3881
Shaver, Mrs Lolly, *Librn,* Cross County Library, Wynne AR. 501-238-3850
Shavitz, Evelyn, *Librn,* Temple Judea Mizpah Library, Skokie IL. 312-676-1566
Shaw, Agnes, *Librn,* Abbey of Regina Laudis Library, Bethlehem CT. 203-266-7727
Shaw, Anne P, *Spec Admin,* Maryland Interlibrary Organization, (MILO), MD. 301-396-5498
Shaw, Anne P, *Chief, State Network Servs,* Enoch Pratt Free Library, Baltimore MD. 301-396-5430, 396-5395
Shaw, Barbara W, *Dir,* Gordon-Nash Library, New Hampton NH. 603-744-8061
Shaw, Betty, *Ref,* Indiana University Northwest Library, Gary IN. 219-980-6580
Shaw, Carl, *Media,* Nova Scotia Teachers College Library, Truro NS. 902-895-5347, Ext 30
Shaw, Carole L, *Librn,* Albion Public Library, Albion IL. 618-445-3314
Shaw, Claire J, *Dir,* Marshall County Library, Holly Springs MS. 601-252-3823
Shaw, Courtney, *Librn,* University of Maryland at College Park (Art), College Park MD. 301-454-2065
Shaw, Diane, *Dir,* Paoli Library, Paoli PA. 215-296-7996
Shaw, Diane E, *Art,* Melrose Public Library, Melrose MA. 617-665-2313
Shaw, Dorothy, *Librn,* Hancock Community Library, Hancock MN. 612-392-5285
Shaw, Edna M, *Cat,* Reading Public Library, Reading MA. 617-944-0840
Shaw, Edward, *President,* Research Libraries Group, Inc, (RLG), CA. 415-497-0657
Shaw, Elizabeth, *Asst Dir,* Dalton Public Library, Inc, Dalton Regional Library, Dalton GA. 404-278-4507, 278-9247, 226-2039
Shaw, Evelyn, *Librn,* Akron-Summit County Public Library (Mogadore Branch), Mogadore OH. 216-628-9228
Shaw, Evelyn, *Asst Dir, Ref & Br Coordr,* Okefenokee Regional Library, Waycross GA. 912-283-3126
Shaw, Evelyn, *Librn,* Portage County District Library (Mogadore), Hiram OH. 216-628-9228
Shaw, Helen, *Asst Librn,* Skowhegan Free Public Library, Skowhegan ME. 207-474-9072
Shaw, J, *Dir,* Lisle Library District, Lisle IL. 312-971-1675
Shaw, J T, *Libr Supvr,* Bell Telephone Laboratories (Western Electric Technical Library), Norcross GA. 404-447-2803
Shaw, Kay, *Librn,* Tangipahoa Parish Library (Hammond Branch), Hammond LA. 504-345-0937
Shaw, Kerrie, *Ref,* Eastern Virginia Medical School, Moorman Memorial Library, Norfolk VA. 804-446-5840
Shaw, Lois C, *Librn,* Louise Adelia Read Memorial Library, Hancock NY. 607-637-2519
Shaw, Louis, *Cat,* Carrier Mills Public Library, Carrier Mills IL. 618-994-2011
Shaw, Mabel, *ILL & Ref,* Tallahassee Community College Library, Tallahassee FL. 904-576-5181
Shaw, Mary, *Asst Librn,* Papillion Public Library, Papillion NE. 402-339-3177
Shaw, Mary D, *Librn,* Onondaga County Public Library System (Beauchamp), Syracuse NY. 315-473-4395
Shaw, Mary L, *Librn,* Michigan State University W K Kellogg Biological Station, Walter F Morofsky Memorial Library, Hickory Corners MI. 517-671-5142
Shaw, Mary M, *Dir,* Johnson-Humrickhouse Memorial Museum Library, Coshocton OH. 614-622-3155
Shaw, Michael, *Librn,* Highway Traffic Board Library, Regina SK. 306-565-2345
Shaw, Minnie L, *Coordr,* Los Angeles Southwest College, Learning Resources Center, Los Angeles CA. 213-777-2225, Ext 235
Shaw, P, *Commun Servs,* Jacob Edwards Library, Southbridge MA. 617-764-2544

Shaw, Priscilla B, *Librn,* American Baptist Churches in the United States of America (Library & Central Files), Valley Forge PA. 215-768-2365

Shaw, Robert B, *Librn,* California Department of Justice Library, San Diego CA. 714-237-7642

Shaw, Shauna, *Ref,* Lethbridge Community College, Buchanan Resource Centre, Lethbridge AB. 403-327-2141, Ext 350

Shaw, Sister Rose Maurice, *Ref & Bibliog Instr,* College of Saint Elizabeth, Mahoney Library, Convent Station NJ. 201-539-1600, Ext 365

Shaw, Spencer, *Prof,* University of Washington, School of Librarianship, WA. 206-543-1794

Shaw, Teri, *Chief Librn,* Bibliotheque Publique, Beaconsfield Public Library, Beaconsfield PQ. 514-697-4662

Shaw, Thomas, *Acq,* University of Northern Iowa Library, Cedar Falls IA. 319-273-2737

Shaw, Vivian, *Librn,* Bar Library Association of Kansas City, Kansas City MO. 816-474-4322

Shaw, William, *Media,* Orange Public Library, Orange CA. 714-532-0391

Shaw, William M, *Asst Prof,* Case Western Reserve University, School of Library Science, OH. 216-368-3500

Shaw, Jr, Clyde A, *Bus Mgr,* Dallas Public Library, Dallas TX. 214-748-9071

Shawkey, Dallas, *Cat,* Brooklyn Public Library, Brooklyn NY. 212-780-7712

Shawl, Janice H, *Dir & Bibliog Instr,* Chapman College, Thurmond Clarke Memorial Library, Orange CA. 714-997-6806

Shawley, Pam, *Librn,* United States Navy (Station Library), Bremerton WA. 206-478-3178

Shay, Anthony, *Librn,* Los Angeles Public Library System (Los Feliz), Los Angeles CA. 213-664-2903

Shay, Jane, *Bkmobile Coordr,* Northeast Missouri Library Service, Kahoka MO. 816-727-2327

Shea, Eleanor C, *Circ,* Forbes Library, Northampton MA. 413-584-8399

Shea, John D, *Librn,* Union Bank Library, Los Angeles CA. 213-687-5259

Shea, Kevin G, *In Charge,* Bureau of Prisons, Federal Correctional Institution Library, Englewood CO. 303-985-1566, Ext 254

Shea, Margaret, *Ad,* Rhode Island Department of State Library Services, Providence RI. 401-277-2726

Shea, Marsha, *Libr Technician,* San Diego County Library (Descanso Branch), Descanso CA. 714-445-5279

Shea, Martha, *Ch,* Jonathan Trumbull Library, Lebanon CT. 203-642-7763

Shea, Mary M, *Librn,* Morse School of Business Library, Hartford CT. 203-522-2261

Shea, Maureen, *Ch,* Judge George W Armstrong Library, Homochitto Valley Regional Library, Natchez MS. 601-445-8862

Sheaffer, Patricia S, *Ch,* Hanover Public Library, Hanover PA. 717-632-5183

Sheahan, Eileen, *Ref,* Vanderbilt University Library (Central-Science), Nashville TN. 615-322-6603

Shealy, Carrie M, *Librn,* Kemper-Newton Regional Library (Decatur Public), Decatur MS. 601-635-2777

Shealy, G Barry, *Cat,* Newberry College, Wessels Library, Newberry SC. 803-276-5010, Ext 300

Shealy, Myrtis, *Librn,* Lexington County Circulating Library (Chapin Branch), Chapin SC. 803-532-9223

Sheard, Delores, *Librn,* Umatilla County Library (Athena Branch), Athena OR. 503-276-1881

Shearer, Barabara S, *Dir,* Elizabethton Public Library, Elizabethton TN. 615-542-4841

Shearer, Benjamin, *Gov Docs & Law,* East Tennessee State University, Sherrod Library, Johnson City TN. 615-929-4338

Shearer, Darlene, *Librn,* Bureau of Land Management, Lake States Office Library, Duluth MN. 218-727-6692, Ext 219

Shearer, Gary W, *ILL & Ref,* Loma Linda University Library, Riverside CA. 714-785-2022

Shearer, Kenneth, *Prof,* North Carolina Central University, School of Library Science, NC. 919-683-6485

Shearer, Susan, *Libr Servs Coordr,* National Trust for Historic Preservation Library, Washington DC. 202-673-4038

Shearin, Malcolm, *Media,* Wayne Community College, Learning Resource Center, Goldsboro NC. 919-735-5151, Ext 64

Shearouse, Jr, Henry G, *Librn,* Denver Public Library, Denver CO. 303-573-5152, Ext 271

Sheary, Edward J, *Area Consult,* Thelma Dingus Bryant Library, Wallace NC. 919-285-3796

Sheary, Edward J, *Area Consult,* Northwestern Regional Library, Elkin NC. 919-835-4894

Sheaves, Miriam, *Librn,* University of North Carolina at Chapel Hill (Geology), Chapel Hill NC. 919-933-2386

Shechtman, Dorothy, *Dir,* Orangeburg Public Library, Orangeburg NY. 914-359-2244

Shedd, Virgia Brocks, *Spec Coll,* Tougaloo College, L Zenobia Coleman Library, Tougaloo MS. 601-956-4941, Ext 271

Shedlarz, Ellen, *Ref,* McKinsey & Co, Inc Library, New York NY. 212-692-6000

Shedlock, James, *ILL,* Wayne State University Libraries (Vera P Shiffman Medical Library), Detroit MI. 313-577-1088

Sheedy, Catherine T, *Dir,* Shelton Public Library, Shelton WA. 206-426-3512

Sheehan, C, *Ref,* Memorial University of Newfoundland Library (Health Sciences Library), Saint John's NF. 709-737-6670

Sheehan, David T, *Assoc Librn,* Worcester Public Library, Worcester MA. 617-752-3751

Sheehan, Elizabeth, *Dir,* Holyoke Community College Library, Holyoke MA. 413-538-7000, Ext 261

Sheehan, Judith F, *Bookmobile Librn,* Piedmont Regional Library, Winder GA. 404-867-2762

Sheehan, Karen, *Asst to Coordr,* Houston Area Library System, Houston TX. 713-222-4704

Sheehan, Kathleen, *Ch,* Suffolk Cooperative Library System, Bellport NY. 516-286-1600

Sheehan, Kathryn, *Librn,* A T Kearney Inc, Information Center, Chicago IL. 312-782-2868

Sheehan, Marie-Louise, *Dir,* Chillicothe & Ross County Public Library, Chillicothe OH. 614-773-4145

Sheehan, Mary, *Librn,* Monsanto Co, Springfield Laboratory Research Library, Indian Orchard MA. 413-788-6911, Ext 348

Sheehan, Maryann, *Ch,* Free Public Library of Mountainside, Mountainside NJ. 201-233-0115

Sheehan, Olive A, *Librn,* Frank D Campbell Memorial Library, Bessemer PA. 412-667-7939

Sheehan, Pamela, *Librn,* Elrick & Lavidge, Inc Library, Chicago IL. 312-726-0666, Ext 75

Sheehan, Robert, *Librn,* New York Public Library (History & Social Science Dept), New York NY. 212-790-6591

Sheehan, Sarah, *Local & CA Hist,* Redwood City Public Library, Redwood City CA. 415-369-6251, Ext 288

Sheehan, Shirley, *Librn,* Mobile Public Library (Parkway), Mobile AL. 205-479-7472

Sheehy, Eugene, *Ref,* Columbia University (University Libraries), New York NY. 212-280-2241

Sheehy, Louis G, *Asst Dir,* Ansonia Library, Ansonia CT. 203-734-6275

Sheel, Frieda, *Ref,* Rosenberg Library, Galveston TX. 713-763-8854

Sheeley, Larry, *Acq,* Ohio State University Libraries (Vocational Education Research Library), Columbus OH. 614-486-3655, Ext 221

Sheerr, Lucy, *ILL, Ref & Bibliog Instr,* Colby-Sawyer College, Fernald Library, New London NH. 603-526-2010, Ext 245

Sheets, Gary, *Media,* Cerro Coso Community College, Learning Resources Center, Ridgecrest CA. 714-375-5001, Ext 47

Sheets, Grace, *Tech Serv, Acq & Cat,* Newton Public Library, Newton KS. 316-283-2890

Sheets, Shirley, *Asst Dir,* University of Texas at Arlington Library, Arlington TX. 817-273-3391

Sheetz, Jenny, *Commun Servs,* Altoona Area Public Library, Altoona PA. 814-946-0417

Sheffield, Betty, *Librn,* Jacksonville Public Library, Jacksonville TX. 214-586-4152

Shehi, Billie, *Librn,* Tulsa City-County Library (Skiatook Branch), Skiatook OK. 918-396-2408

Sheible, Doris, *Asst Librn,* United States Army (Fort Carson Recreation Div Libraries), Fort Carson CO. 303-579-2350, 579-2842

Sheil, Sister Joan, *Chmn,* Bi-State Academic Libraries, (BI-SAL), IA. 319-326-9254

Sheil, Sister Joan, *Dir,* Marycrest College, Cone Library, Davenport IA. 319-326-9254

Sheiman, Nettie, *Asst Librn,* Temple B'rith Kodesh Library, Rochester NY. 716-244-7060

Sheinbaum, Ken, *Tech Serv, Acq & Cat,* Monmouth County Library, Freehold NJ. 201-431-7220

Shekmar, Llewellyn, *Acq,* Broward Community College, Learning Resources Center, Fort Lauderdale FL. 305-475-6500

Shelander, Anne, *Curator,* Coastal Georgia Historical Society Archives, Saint Simons Island GA. 912-638-4666

Shelato, Lanone, *Assoc Librn,* Georgetown Public Library, Georgetown IL. 217-662-2164

Shelby, Jill, *ILL,* University of Tennessee, Knoxville, James D Hoskins Library, Knoxville TN. 615-974-0111

Shelby, Marjorie E, *Dir,* Panhandle Regional Library System, Coeur d'Alene ID. 208-772-7456

Sheldon, Anne L, *Lectr,* University of Maryland, College of Library & Information Services, MD. 301-454-5441

Sheldon, Brooke E, *Dir,* Texas Woman's University, School of Library Science, TX. 817-387-2418 & 566-1455

Sheldon, Cathy, *Teaching Resources Librn,* Lesley College Library, Cambridge MA. 617-868-9600, Ext 170, 171

Sheldon, Jim, *Tech Serv & Cat,* Bethel College, Learning Resource Center, Saint Paul MN. 612-641-6222

Sheldon, La Duska, *Dir,* Putnam Public Library, Nashville MI. 517-852-9723

Sheldon, Lita, *Asst Librn,* Navajo Community College, Naaltsoos Ba'Hooghan Library, Tsaile AZ. 602-724-6132

Sheldon, Patsy, *Librn,* Bureau of Land Management, Battle Mountain District Office Library, Battle Mountain NV. 702-635-5181

Sheldon, Paul, *Cat,* University of Colorado at Boulder (University Libraries), Boulder CO. 303-492-7511

Sheley, JoAnn, *Dir,* Goshen Public Library, Goshen IN. 219-533-9531

Sheley, Kathlyn, *Dir,* Chambers County Library, Anahuac TX. 713-267-3372

Shelhart, Kitty, *Librn,* War Memorial Public Library (Brentwood Public Library), Brentwood TN. 615-373-2427

Shelhorse, Carolyn, *Ch,* Danville Public Library, Danville VA. 804-799-5195

Shelkrot, Elliot L, *State Librn,* State Library of Pennsylvania, Harrisburg PA. 717-787-2646

Shell, Elton E, *Dir,* San Bernardino Valley College, Samuel E Andrews Memorial Library, San Bernardino CA. 714-888-6511, Ext 237

Sheller, Bess, *Librn,* Carbon County Public Library, Rawlins WY. 307-324-4756

Shelley, Geraldine, *Dir,* Central Association of Libraries, (CAL), CA. 209-944-8649

Shelley, Geraldine C, *Dir,* The 49-99 Cooperative Library System, Stockton CA. 209-944-8649

Shelley, Harry S, *Hist of Med,* Vanderbilt University Medical Center Library, Nashville TN. 615-322-2292

Shelley, Laura, *Dir,* Northland Public Library, Pittsburgh PA. 412-366-8100, 366-8167

Shelley, Leo, *On-Line Servs,* Millersville State College, Helen A Ganser Library, Millersville PA. 717-872-5411, Ext 341

Shelley, Michael H, *Chief, MARC Editorial Div,* Library of Congress, Washington DC. 202-287-5000

Shelley, Nancy, *Librn,* Denver Public Library (Byers), Denver CO. 303-573-5152, Ext 271

Shelley, Thelma, *Dir,* Fairhope Public Library, Fairhope AL. 205-928-7483

Shelly, Jean, *Librn,* North Canton Public Library (Greentown Library), Greentown OH. 216-499-3971

Shelly, Patricia A, *Librn,* Jewish Hospital (Medical Library), Cincinnati OH. 513-872-3136

Shelstad, Kirsten R, *Librn,* University of Wisconsin Center, Medford Library, Medford WI. 715-748-3600, Ext 7

Shelton, Barbara, *Librn,* Wiscasset Public Library, Wiscasset ME. 207-882-7161

Shelton, Clara, *Ser,* South Dakota State University, Hilton M Briggs Library, Brookings SD. 605-688-5106

Shelton, Diane, *Librn,* Little Rock Township Public Library, Plano IL. 312-552-3310

Shelton, Flo, *Librn,* Tri-City Herald Library, Pasco WA. 509-547-3366

Shelton, Hildred C, *Librn,* Pittsylvania County Public Library, Chatham VA. 804-432-3271

Shelton, J Walter, *Tech Serv,* John Crerar Library, Chicago IL. 312-225-2526

Shelton, Jack, *In Charge,* Texas Education Agency (Region XVI), Amarillo TX. 806-376-5521

Shelton, John, *Dir,* Lake Lanier Regional Library, Lawrenceville GA. 404-963-5231

Shelton, Julie, *Ch & YA,* Palm Beach County Public Library System, West Palm Beach FL. 305-686-0895

Shelton, Kathryn H, *In Charge,* Alaska Legislative Affairs Agency, Reference Library, Juneau AK. 907-465-3808

Shelton, Larry, *Librn,* Litton Industries, Inc, Chemical & Metallurgical Laboratory Library, Springfield MO. 417-862-0751

Shelton, Pamela, *Cat,* United States Army (Morale Support Activities Division Library), Fort Hood TX. 817-685-6011

Shelton, Shirley, *Librn,* North Arkansas Regional Library (Newton County), Jasper AR. 501-446-2983

Shelton, Tina, *AV,* Wheeler Basin Regional Library, Decatur Public Library, Decatur AL. 205-353-2993

Shelver, Elizabeth, *Personnel Librn,* Minneapolis Public Library & Information Center, Minneapolis MN. 612-372-6500

Shemanski, Thomas, *Media,* Queensborough Community College Library, Bayside NY. 212-631-6226

Shemin, Charlotte, *Librn,* Northwestern University Library (Mathematics), Evanston IL. 312-492-7627

Shemwell, Judy, *ILL,* Detroit Public Library, Detroit Associated Libraries, Detroit MI. 313-833-1000

Shen, Justin, *Chief Librn,* Transportation Institute Library, Washington DC. 202-347-2590, Ext 12

Shen, Raphael, *Reader Serv,* Saint Paul's College, Russell Memorial Library, Lawrenceville VA. 804-848-3111, Ext 221

Shen, Shirley, *Librn,* University of Wisconsin-Madison (Mathematics Library), Madison WI. 608-262-3521

Shen, Stella, *Cat,* Robbins Library, Arlington MA. 617-643-0026

Shen, Tseng-wen, *Tech Serv,* Memorial Hall Library, (Subregional Headquarters for Eastern Massachusetts Regional System), Andover MA. 617-475-6960

Sheng, Jack T, *Chief Librn,* Duval County Law Library, Jacksonville FL. 904-633-4756

Shenholm, Daisy E, *Dir,* Rutgers University (Douglas College-Cook College), New Brunswick NJ. 201-932-9346

Shenk, Margaret M, *Cat,* Eastern Mennonite College & Seminary Library, Harrisonburg VA. 703-433-2771, Ext 171

Shenk, Marjorie, *Librn,* Lima Public Library (Elida Branch), Elida OH. 419-228-5113

Shenouda, Wagih, *Ref & Bibliog Instr,* State University of New York, College at Old Westbury Library, Old Westbury NY. 516-876-3156, 876-3152

Shepard, Caroline, *Ch,* Nantahala Regional Library, Murphy NC. 704-837-2025

Shepard, Elizabeth, *Cat,* Warren Wilson College Library, Swannanoa NC. 704-298-3325, Ext 45

Shepard, Florence C, *Ad,* Nashua Public Library, Nashua NH. 603-883-4141, 883-4142

Shepard, Joan, *Ch,* Somerville Free Public Library, Somerville NJ. 201-725-1336

Shepard, Josephine, *Tech Serv,* Denver Public Library, Denver CO. 303-573-5152, Ext 271

Shepard, Judy, *ILL,* Alabama Public Library Service, Montgomery AL. 205-832-5743

Shepard, Martha L, *Librn,* United States Department of the Interior, Alaska Resources Library, Anchorage AK. 907-271-5025

Shepard, Nancy, *Librn,* United States Navy (Naval Ammunition Disposal Library), Colts Neck NJ. 201-462-9500

Shepard, Nora, *Librn,* Margaret Welch Memorial Library, Longville MN. 218-363-2710

Shepard, Patricia A, *Librn,* Control Data Corp, Technical Library, La Jolla CA. 714-452-6000

Shepard, Stanley A, *Assoc Dir & Tech Serv,* University of Idaho Library, Moscow ID. 208-885-6534

Shepard, Violet, *ILL & Ref,* Harrisburg Area Community College, McCormick Library, Harrisburg PA. 717-236-9533, Ext 257

Sheparovych, Zenon B, *Assoc Dean,* Essex County College, Learning Resources Center, Newark NJ. 201-877-3233

Shepherd, G Frederick, *Dir,* Geological Information Library of Dallas, Dallas TX. 214-363-1078

Shepherd, Julia, *Dir,* George Corley Wallace State Community College Library, Selma AL. 205-875-2634, Ext 55

Shepherd, Mrs Ronald, *Tech Serv,* Frankfort Community Public Library, Frankfort IN. 317-654-8746

Shepherd, Murray C, *Univ Librn,* University of Waterloo Library, Waterloo ON. 519-885-1211

Shepherd, Odette, *Ser,* Indiana University at Bloomington, University Libraries, Bloomington IN. 812-337-3403

Shepherd, Rae, *Cat,* State University of New York College, Memorial Library, Cortland NY. 607-753-2525, 753-2221

Shepler, Eva Ellen, *Ad,* Edwin A Bemis Public Library, Littleton Public Library, Littleton CO. 303-795-3826

Shepler, Gayle, *Librn,* Ingham County Library (Webberville Branch), Webberville MI. 517-521-3643

Shepley, Joan, *ILL,* Oxford County Library, Woodstock ON. 519-537-3322

Shepp, Lawrence R, *Librn,* Fitzgerald, Abbott & Beardsley, Law Library, Oakland CA. 415-451-3300

Sheppard, George K, *Assoc Prof,* Idaho State University, Dept of Education-Library Science, ID. 208-236-2310

Sheppard, Jan, *Dir,* University of South Carolina, Medford Library, Lancaster SC. 803-285-7471, Ext 13 & 19

Sheppard, Sandra, *Acq,* Lincoln Land Community College, Learning Resources Center, Springfield IL. 217-786-2354

Shepperson, Sandy, *Info Asst,* George Amos Memorial Library, Campbell County Library, Gillette WY. 307-682-3223

Shera, Jesse Hauk, *Emer Prof,* Case Western Reserve University, School of Library Science, OH. 216-368-3500

Sherard, Mary, *AV,* Vicksburg-Warren County Public Library, Vicksburg MS. 601-636-6411

Sherer, Elaine, *Ref,* Massachusetts Bay Community College Library, Wellesley MA. 617-237-1100, Ext 193

Sherer, Joan, *Ad,* Monroe County Public Library, Stroudsburg PA. 717-421-0800

Sheridan, Alice J, *Librn,* Fairfax Hospital, Jacob D Zylman Memorial Library, Falls Church VA. 703-698-3234

Sheridan, Clare, *Librn,* University of Massachusetts at Boston Library (College of Public & Community Service), Boston MA. 617-287-1900, Ext 255

Sheridan, Connie, *Tech Processes,* Los Alamos Scientific Laboratory Libraries, Library Services Group, Los Alamos NM. 505-667-4448

Sheridan, Diana, *Reader Serv,* Highline Community College Library, Midway WA. 206-878-3710, Ext 230

Sheridan, F P, *AV,* Saint Leo College Library, Saint Leo FL. 904-588-8258

Sheridan, Helen, *Chief Librn,* Kalamazoo Institute of Arts Library, Kalamazoo MI. 616-349-7775, Ext 5

Sheridan, John, *Chief Librn,* Transylvania University, Frances Carrick Thomas Library, Lexington KY. 606-233-8225

Sheridan, Leslie W, *Dir,* University of Toledo, William S Carlson Library, Toledo OH. 419-537-2324

Sheridan, Mrs Robert, *Ch,* Irvington Public Library, Guiteau Foundation, Irvington NY. 914-591-7840

Sheridan, Ney, *Dir,* Arthur Temple Sr Memorial Library, Pineland TX. 713-584-2546

Sheridan, Robert N, *Dir,* Suffolk Cooperative Library System, Bellport NY. 516-286-1600

Sherif, Joan, *YA,* Gaston-Lincoln Regional Library, Gastonia NC. 704-866-3756

Sherif, Sue, *Ch,* Fontana Regional Library, Bryson City NC. 704-488-2382

Sheriff, Elsie, *ILL,* Bethel College Library, North Newton KS. 316-283-2500, Ext 377

Sheriff, Lillian, *Librn,* Minersville Free Public Library, Minersville PA. 717-544-5196

Sherk, Dennis, *Dir,* University of Toledo (University Television Services), Toledo OH. 419-537-3386

Sherlock, Valerie, *Pub Info Officer,* Houston Public Library, Houston TX. 713-224-5441

Sherman, Andrea, *Media Consortium Coordr,* Cornell University Medical College, Samuel J Wood Library, New York NY. 212-472-5300

Sherman, Barbara, *Circ,* De Paul University Libraries (Frank J Lewis Center Library), Chicago IL. 312-321-7619

Sherman, Barbara, *Circ,* De Paul University Libraries (Lincoln Park Campus Library), Chicago IL. 312-321-7934

Sherman, Bob, *Librn & On-Line Servs,* Bayfront Medical Center, Inc Library, Health Sciences Library, Saint Petersburg FL. 813-823-1234, Ext 2136

Sherman, C Neil, *Dir, Div of Libr Servs,* United States Department of Energy, Energy Library, Washington DC. 202-353-4301

Sherman, Dorothy N, *Librn,* Philadelphia Electric Co Library, Philadelphia PA. 215-841-4357

Sherman, Dottie, *Dir,* American Nuclear Insurers Library, Farmington CT. 203-677-7305

Sherman, Edith, *Bkmobile Coordr,* Pender County Library, Burgaw NC. 919-259-4521

Sherman, Frances, *ILL & Per,* Oceanside Public Library, Oceanside CA. 714-439-7330

Sherman, Jackie, *Librn,* New Orleans Public Library (Navra), New Orleans LA. 504-947-6822

Sherman, Jacob R, *Cat,* Rutland Free Library, Rutland VT. 802-773-6880

Sherman, Janice, *Dir,* Morton Public Library, Morton IL. 309-264-6401

Sherman, John, *Assoc Prof,* Queens College of the City University of New York, Graduate School of Library & Information Studies, NY. 212-520-7194, 520-7195

Sherman, Kathy, *Circ,* Kansas City Kansas Public Library, Kansas City KS. 913-621-3073

Sherman, Lucy A, *Librn,* New Bedford Free Public Library (Buttonwood Community), New Bedford MA. 617-992-5702

Sherman, Margaret, *Librn,* Carnegie Library of Pittsburgh (Bookmobile Center & Warehouse), Pittsburgh PA. 412-622-3100

Sherman, Marion, *Librn,* Saint Louis Conservatory & Schools for the Arts, Saint Louis Conservatory of Music Library, Saint Louis MO. 314-863-3033

Sherman, Mary, *Asst Dir,* Pioneer Multi-County Library, Norman OK. 405-321-1481

Sherman, Mary, *Br Coordr,* Pioneer Multi-County Library, Norman OK. 405-321-1481

Sherman, Paul T, *Adm Serv,* New York City Community College, Namm Hall Library, Brooklyn NY. 212-643-5240

Sherman, Sandra, *Commun Servs,* Wheeler Basin Regional Library, Decatur Public Library, Decatur AL. 205-353-2993

Sherman, Virginia, *Bus,* California State University, Northridge, Delmar T Oviatt & South Libraries, Northridge CA. 213-885-2271

Sherosky, Pat, *Asst Librn,* Springdale Free Public Library, Springdale PA. 412-274-9717

Sherr, Janet M, *Librn,* Biosciences Information Service Library, Philadelphia PA. 215-568-4016, Ext 220

Sherr, Merrill F, *Librn,* New York Post Library, New York NY. 212-349-5000, Ext 389

Sherr, Mrs R, *Soc Sci Librn,* Institute for Advanced Study Libraries, Princeton NJ. 609-924-4400

Sherrard, McCluer, *Tech Serv & Cat,* Blue Ridge Regional Library, Martinsville VA. 703-632-7125

Sherrer, Johannah, *On-Line Servs,* University of Northern Colorado, James A Michener Library, Greeley CO. 303-351-2601

Sherrick, Lena, *Librn,* Greenup Township Carnegie Library, Greenup IL. 217-923-3616

Sherrill, Adena S, *Asst Dir, ILL & Ref,* Alpha Regional Library, Spencer WV. 304-927-1770

Sherrill, Inez, *Librn,* Klamath County Library (Merrill Branch), Merrill OR. 503-882-8894

Sherrill, Rebecca, *Librn,* Middle Georgia Regional Library (Shurling), Macon GA. 912-745-5813

Sherrill, Richard M, *In Charge,* Monroe County Public Library (Islamorada Branch), Islamorada FL. 305-664-4645

Sherrod, John, *Instr,* United States Department of Agriculture Graduate School, Certificate Program for Library Technicians, DC. 202-447-5885

Sherry, Barbara, *Asst Librn,* Lower Columbia College, Learning Resource Center, Longview WA. 206-577-2310

Sherry, Tali, *Librn,* Israel Embassy Reference Library, Washington DC. 202-483-4100

Sherson, Elizabeth B, *Librn,* Hospital of the Good Samaritan, Medical Library, Los Angeles CA. 213-488-8911

Shertz, Barbara, *Ch,* Wolfsohn Memorial Library, King of Prussia PA. 215-265-5151

Sherwin, Margaret, *Cat Adjustments,* Southern Illinois University at Edwardsville, Elijah P Lovejoy Library, Edwardsville IL. 618-692-2711

Sherwin, Nancy, *Coordr Info Serv,* Cleveland Heights-University Heights Public Library, Cleveland Heights OH. 216-932-3600

Sherwood, Betty, *Librn,* Butterworth Hospital (School of Nursing Library), Grand Rapids MI. 616-774-1779

Sherwood, Betty, *ILL,* NASA (Technical Library), Moffett Field CA. 415-965-5157

Sherwood, C, *Librn,* Calgary Public Library (Varsity), Calgary AB. 403-288-1540

Sherwood, Joan, *Tech Serv, Cat & Bibliog Instr,* Columbia Basin College, Library Media Center, Pasco WA. 509-547-0511, Ext 287, 289, 290 & 294

Sherwood, Judith, *Librn,* San Diego Public Library (Skyline Hills), San Diego CA. 714-479-5835

Sherwood, Lawrence H, *Instrnl Servs,* Grossmont College, Lewis F Smith Learning Resource Center Library, El Cajon CA. 714-465-1700, Ext 333, 334

Sherwood, Lillian, *Ref,* Plymouth Public Library, Plymouth IN. 219-936-2324

Sherwood, Linda, *Librn,* La Crosse Public Library (North), La Crosse WI. 608-784-8623

Sherwood, Linda, *Librn,* La Crosse Public Library (South), La Crosse WI. 608-784-8623

Sherwood, Robert, *Asst Dir,* Herrick Public Library, Holland MI. 616-392-3114

Sherwood, William F, *Computer Librn,* University of Texas Medical Branch, Moody Medical Library, Galveston TX. 713-765-1971

Shetson, Stephen G, *Coordr,* Michigan Technological University, Ford Forestry Center Library, L'Anse MI. 906-524-6181

Sheufelt, Janet, *Ad,* Roseville Public Library, Roseville MI. 313-777-6012

Sheuman, Dick, *Sci & Nursing,* Loyola University of Chicago Libraries (Elizabeth M Cudahy Memorial Library), Chicago IL. 312-274-3000, Ext 771

Shevack, H N, *Logistics & Data Manager,* General Instrument Corp, Engineering Library, Hicksville NY. 516-733-3000, Ext 3443, 3514

Shevory, Joan P, *ILL & Ref,* Jamestown Community College, Hultquist Library Learning Center, Jamestown NY. 716-665-5220, Ext 210

Shew, Anita K, *Librn,* Butler County Law Library Association, Hamilton OH. 513-867-5714

Shew, Anne L, *Librn,* Ralph K Davies Medical Center, Franklin Hospital Medical Library, San Francisco CA. 415-555-6352

Shew, Virginia, *Tech Serv,* Ann Arbor Public Library, Ann Arbor MI. 313-994-2333

Shewan, Elizabeth, *Librn,* Canadian Press Library, Toronto ON. 416-364-0321

Shewbridge, Anna M, *Librn,* Charles Town Library, Charles Town WV. 304-725-2208

Shewfelt, Betty, *Librn,* Essex Agricultural & Technical Institute Library, Danvers MA. 617-

Sheynin, Hayim Y, *Dir,* Dropsie University Library, Philadelphia PA. 215-229-0110

Shibla, Julia, *Librn,* Dean Witter & Co, Inc, Research Library, New York NY. 212-437-3000

Shieh, Vivien, *Cat,* Bronxville Public Library, Bronxville NY. 914-337-7680

Shields, Burndine, *Librn,* Wellsville City Library, Wellsville KS. 913-883-2870

Shields, Dorothy M, *Asst Prof,* Brigham Young University, School of Library & Information Sciences, UT. 801-378-2976

Shields, Gerald, *Assoc Prof,* State University of New York at Buffalo, School of Information & Library Studies, NY. 716-636-2412

Shields, Joyce F, *Dir,* Niagara Falls Public Library, Niagara Falls NY. 716-278-8041

Shields, Maxine, *Librn,* Eldon Carnegie Library, Eldon IA. 515-652-7517

Shields, Robert M, *Dir,* Central Methodist College, George M Smiley Memorial Library, Fayette MO. 816-248-3391, Ext 261

Shields, Sister Jean E, *Librn,* Don Bosco Technical Institute, Lee Memorial Library, Rosemead CA. 213-280-0451

Shiery, Floyd, *Cat,* Louisiana Tech University, Prescott Memorial Library, Ruston LA. 318-257-2577

Shiffler, Dorothy, *Cat,* Hastings - Adams County Library, Hastings NE. 402-463-9855

Shiffler, Mrs Hal, *Librn,* First Presbyterian Church Library, Hastings NE. 402-462-5147

Shiflett, Debra, *Photodup,* Rappahannock Community College, South Campus Library, Glenns VA. 804-758-5324, Ext 208

Shiflett, Gertrude, *Asst Dir & Cat,* Amos Memorial Public Library, Sidney Public Library, Sidney OH. 513-492-8354

Shiflett, Lee, *Asst Prof,* Louisiana State University, Graduate School of Library Science, LA. 504-388-3158

Shigematsu, Mieko, *Libr Tech,* Hawaii State Library System (Honokaa Branch), Honokaa HI. 808-775-7497

Shigley, Lavon, *Tech Serv & On-Line Servs,* Taylor University, Ayres Alumni Memorial Library, Upland IN. 317-998-2751, Ext 241

Shih, Jenny, *Actg Librn,* Quinsigamond Community College Library, Worcester MA. 617-853-2300

Shih, Philip C, *Dir,* Logansport-Cass County Public Library, Logansport Public Library, Logansport IN. 219-753-6383

Shih, Una, *ILL,* Westchester Community College Library, Valhalla NY. 914-347-6939

Shih, Walter, *Asst Dir Datamation,* Prince George's County Memorial Library System, Hyattsville MD. 301-699-3500

Shikada, Betty, *Libr Tech,* Hawaii State Library System (Kealakekua Branch), Kealakekua HI. 808-323-3653

Shiland, Sally, *Librn,* Public Library of Columbus & Franklin County (Beechwold), Columbus OH. 614-262-2121

Shill, Harold B, *Asst Prof,* West Virginia University, Dept of Library Science, WV. 304-293-3540

Shilling, Lisa, *Librn,* Hammermill Paper Co, Technical Library, Erie PA. 814-456-8811

Shilling, Mrs Floyd, *Dir,* Allens Hill Library, Holcomb NY. 716-229-5636

Shillington, Betty, *Librn,* Rideau Lakes Union Library (Newboro Branch), Newboro ON. 613-359-5315

Shilson, Marie, *Librn,* Lambton County Library (Inwood Branch), Inwood ON. 519-844-2491

Shilstone, Marian, *Ser,* Connecticut College Library, New London CT. 203-442-1630

Shilts, Dorothy, *Librn,* Wichita Scouting Co-op Inc, Oil Information Library, Wichita Falls TX. 817-322-4241

Shimabukuro, Katherine T, *Head, Acq Branch,* International Communication Agency (Agency Library), Washington DC. 202-724-9214

Shimada, Bruce, *Librn,* Hawaii State Library System (Kahuku Community-School), Kahuku HI. 808-293-9275

Shimane, Robert, *Media,* University of Southern California (Asa V Call Law Library), Los Angeles CA. 213-743-6487

Shimko, Florence, *Dir,* North Brunswick Free Public Library, North Brunswick NJ. 201-246-3545

Shinder, James N, *Dir,* City County Clinic in Johnstown, Inc, Johnstown PA. 814-535-8531

Shindo, Frank, *Circ,* Southwest State University Library, Marshall MN. 507-537-7021

Shine, John D, *Dir,* Johnson Free Public Library, Hackensack NJ. 201-343-4169

Shiner, Marcia, *Librn,* Gottlieb Memorial Hospital, Medical Library, Melrose Park IL. 312-681-3200, Ext 1173

Shinn, Barbara, *Librn,* Kuna School Community Library, Kuna ID. 208-922-5611

Shinn, Betty M, *Librn,* Lake Alfred Public Library, Lake Alfred FL. 813-956-3434

Shinn, Sydniciel, *Dir,* Dunedin Public Library, Dunedin FL. 813-733-4115

Shinnick, Joseph, *Video,* Brunswick-Glynn County Regional Library, Brunswick GA. 912-264-7360

Shiozawa, May, *Librn,* Saint Anthony Community Hospital Library, Pocatello ID. 208-232-2733, Ext 275

Shipe, Belle B, *Librn,* Barnes Engineering Co Library, Stamford CT. 203-348-5381, Ext 240

Shipman, George W, *Librn,* University of Oregon Library, Eugene OR. 503-686-3056

Shipman, L Wade, *Librn,* Spartanburg County Technical Education Center Library, Spartanburg SC. 803-576-5770, Ext 168

Shipman, Patricia E, *Chief Librn,* Carolina Population Center Library, Chapel Hill NC. 919-933-3081

Shipp, Ann, *Per,* Utah State University, Merrill Library & Learning Resources Program, Logan UT. 801-750-2637

Shipp, Dixie Black, *Librn,* Mount Zion Hospital & Medical Center, Sinai Memorial Medical Library, San Francisco CA. 415-567-6600, Ext 2339

Shipp, Leola, *Librn,* Saint Louis County Library (Kinloch), St Louis MO. 314-524-7600

Shipp, Pamela, *On-Line Servs,* University of South Florida (University Library), Tampa FL. 813-974-2721

Shipp, Ruth, *Tech Serv,* Seattle Public Library, Seattle WA. 206-625-2665

Shippen, Darlene, *Librn,* Gilbert Memorial Library, Friend NE. 402-947-5081

Shippey, Orrline E, *Dir & ILL,* Nicholson Memorial Public Library, Longview TX. 214-758-4252

Shippey, Peggy, *Librn,* Kinchafoonee Regional Library (Calhoun County), Arlington GA. 912-995-2902

Shippey, Peggy, *Librn,* Kinchafoonee Regional Library (Calhoun County), Edison GA. 912-995-2902

Shipps, Anthony, *English, Theatre & Drama,* Indiana University at Bloomington, University Libraries, Bloomington IN. 812-337-3403

Shipps, Jr, Harrold S, *Ref,* Fort Lewis College Library, Durango CO. 303-247-7738

Shires, Leslyn, *Dir,* Wauwatosa Public Library, Wauwatosa WI. 414-258-5700

Shirk, Gary, *Head,* University of Minnesota Libraries-Twin Cities (Book Acquisitions), Minneapolis MN. 612-373-7807

Shirk, John, *Librn,* Houston Public Library (Library Resources Center), Houston TX. 713-869-5161

Shirk, Virginia B, *Librn,* Minnesota Gas Co Library, Minneapolis MN. 612-372-4824

Shirky, Doris, *Librn,* Pahrump Community Library, Pahrump NV. 702-727-5930

Shirley, Andrea, *Cat,* Newton Free Library, Newton MA. 617-527-7700, Ext 24

Shirley, David, *Doc,* Central Michigan University, Charles V Park Library, Mount Pleasant MI. 517-774-3500

Shirley, Iris, *Librn,* Lexington County Circulating Library (R H Smith), Cayce SC. 803-532-9223

Shirley, Linda, *Tech Serv,* Rowan Technical College, Learning Resource Center, Salisbury NC. 704-637-0760, Ext 69

Shirley, Marilyn, *Ch,* Westmont Public Library, Westmont IL. 312-969-5625

Shirley, Mary Katherine, *Asst Librn,* Orena Humphrey Public Library, Whitwell TN. 901-658-6134

Shirley, Sandra, *Cat,* University of San Diego (Marvin Kratter Law Library), San Diego CA. 714-293-4541

Shirley, Sherrilynne, *Assoc Dir,* University of Southern California (Norris Medical Library), Los Angeles CA. 213-226-2231

Shirmer, Robert, *Pub Servs,* Findlay College, Shafer Library, Findlay OH. 419-422-8313, Ext 327

Shirokey, Jean, *Librn,* Centre County Library & Historical Museum (Philipsburg Branch), Philipsburg PA. 814-342-1987

Shisler, Shirley, *Ref & ILL,* Public Library of Des Moines, Des Moines IA. 515-283-4152

Shively, Daniel C, *Cat,* Indiana University of Pennsylvania, Rhodes R Stabley Library, Indiana PA. 412-357-2340

Shively, Helen, *Ref & Bibliog Instr,* Ashland College Library, Ashland OH. 419-289-4067

Shiverick, Ethel J, *Librn,* Frederic C Adams Public Library, Kingston MA. 617-585-2557

Shivery, Gladys, *Librn,* Appoquinimink Public Library, Middletown DE. 302-378-9133

Shivley, Robert, *Librn,* Garfield County Public Library (Gordon Cooper), Carbondale CO. 303-963-2889

Shlapak, Irene, *Chief Librn,* Ontario Ministry of Community & Social Services Library, Toronto ON. 416-965-5980

Shnay, Zipporah, *Chief Librn,* Bibliotheque Municipale Des Sources, Sources Public Library, Roxboro PQ. 514-684-8247, 684-8260

Shnyder, Dorothy, *Librn,* Belvidere Free Public Library, Belvidere NJ. 201-475-3565

Shock, Mrs J, *Librn,* Mannville Community Library, Mannville AB. 403-763-3660

Shocket, Eileen, *ILL & Ref,* Saint Edward's University Library, Austin TX. 512-444-2621

Shocklee, David, *ILL,* Saint Louis University, Pius XII Memorial Library, Saint Louis MO. 314-658-3100

Shockley, Ann A, *Assoc Librn Pub Servs,* Fisk University Library & Media Center, Nashville TN. 615-329-8730

Shockley, Charlotte L, *Librn,* Stockton, West, Burkhart, Inc Library, Cincinnati OH. 513-381-5600

Shoemake, Mrs James, *Librn,* Pine Forest Regional Library (Conway Hall Public), Hattiesburg MS. 601-788-6539

Shoemaker, Betty, *Lang & Biography,* Grand Rapids Public Library, Grand Rapids MI. 616-456-4400

Shoemaker, Betty G, *Librn,* First Christian Reformed Church Library, Zeeland MI. 616-772-2620

Shoemaker, James, *Librn,* Harris County Public Library (Channelview Branch), Channelview TX. 713-452-0181

Shoemaker, Joy, *ILL,* Northland Library Cooperative, Alpena MI. 517-356-4444

Shoemaker, Kathryn G, *Librn,* Vicksburg Community Library, Vicksburg PA. 717-

Shoemaker, Marie S, *Asst Dir,* John Graham Newville Public Library, Newville PA. 717-776-5900

Shoemaker, Ruth G, *Librn,* Springborn Laboratories, Inc, Technical Information Center Library, Enfield CT. 203-749-8371

Shoenhair, Janet, *Librn,* Bancroft Public Library, Bancroft IA. 515-885-2753

Shoffit, Judy M, *Cat,* Texas Woman's University, Bralley Memorial Library, Denton TX. 817-566-6415

Shofner, Nancy C, *Asst Dir, Tech Serv & Cat,* Southern Technical Institute Library, Marietta GA. 404-424-7275

Sholar, Thomas P, *Assoc Prof,* Murray State University, Dept of Library Science, KY. 502-762-2291

Shold, Rosemary, *Supvr Bibliog Maintenance,* Washington State Library, Olympia WA. 206-753-5592

Sholler, Herbert C, *Libr Syst Coordr,* University of Toronto Libraries (University Library), Toronto ON. 416-978-2294

Sholund, N, *On-Line Servs & Bibliog Instr,* Port Moody Public Library, Port Moody BC. 604-939-1588

Shong, Joy, *Coordr,* Saint Francis Hospital, Health Science Learning Center, Milwaukee WI. 414-647-5156

Shong, Joy, *Coordr,* Southeastern Wisconsin Health Science Library Consortium, WI. 414-647-5156

Shoniker, Fintan R, *Dir,* Saint Vincent College & Archabbey Libraries, Latrobe PA. 412-539-9761, Ext 378

Shonkwiler, Paula, *Librn,* Rocky Mountain News Library, Denver CO. 303-892-5416

Shonn, Eleanor, *Librn & On-Line Servs,* Ohio Valley Medical Center, Inc, Hupp Medical Library, Wheeling WV. 304-243-0123

Shonrock, Dorothy, *Librn,* Marcus P Beebe Memorial Library, Ipswich SD. 605-426-6707

Shook, Constanee, *Dir,* Delaware Valley College of Science and Agriculture, Krauskopf Memorial Library, Doylestown PA. 215-345-1500, Ext 255

Shook, Gary, *Dir,* Canon City Public Library, Canon City CO. 303-275-3669

Shook, Lillian, *Br Coordr,* Martins Ferry Public Library, Martins Ferry OH. 614-633-0314

Shook, Margie, *Librn,* Knoxville-Knox County Public Library (Powell Branch), Powell TN. 615-947-6210

Shoop, Jane, *Librn,* Roanoke County Public Library (Glenvar Branch), Salem VA. 703-387-6163

Shopa, Mary A, *Chief Librn,* Veterans Administration, Hospital Library, Northport NY. 516-261-4400

Shore, Jenafred J, *Librn,* National Wildlife Federation, Frazier Memorial Library, Washington DC. 202-797-6829

Shore, Philip D, *Asst Dir, Tech Serv & Cat,* Earlham College, Lilly Library, Richmond IN. 317-962-6561, Ext 360

Shore, Sunny H, *Ch,* Cedar Grove Public Library, Cedar Grove NJ. 609-239-1447

Shores, C, *Acq,* University of Rhode Island Library, Kingston RI. 401-792-1000

Shores, Winifred, *Ch,* Woodward Memorial Library, LeRoy NY. 716-768-8300

Shorey, Christine, *Librn,* Veterans Memorial Library, Patten ME. 207-528-2164

Short, Elizabeth D, *Acq, Cat & Books By Mail,* Alpha Regional Library, Spencer WV. 304-927-1770

Short, Eunice, *Archivist,* Oklahoma Baptist University, Mabee Learning Center, Shawnee OK. 405-275-2850, Ext 245

Short, Jerri, *Librn,* Salem Township Public Library, Morrow OH. 513-899-2588

Short, Joyce, *Media,* Southwestern Michigan College, Fred L Mathews Library, Dowagiac MI. 616-782-5113, Ext 27

Short, Peggy, *Acq,* Louisiana Tech University, Prescott Memorial Library, Ruston LA. 318-257-2577

Short, Priscilla, *Librn,* Jenkins Public Library, Jenkins KY. 606-832-4101

Short, Priscilla, *Bkmobile Coordr,* Letcher County Public Library (Jenkins Branch), Jenkins KY. 606-832-4101

Short, Sylvia, *State Librn,* Delaware Division of Libraries, Dept of Community Affairs & Economic Development, Dover DE. 302-678-4748

Short, Virginia, *Dir,* Mountain-Valley Library System, Sacramento CA. 916-444-0926

Short, William, *ILL, Ref & Bibliog Instr,* Southwestern at Memphis, Burrow Library, Memphis TN. 901-274-1800, Ext 365, 366

Shorter, Willie Jean, *Librn,* Jackson Metropolitan Library (Harrisville Branch), Harrisville MS. 601-352-3677

Shorthill, Rachel, *Ref & Bibliog Instr,* Washburn University of Topeka, Mabee Library, Topeka KS. 913-295-6479

Shorthill, Rachel, *Spec Coll,* William Jewell College, Curry Library, Liberty MO. 816-781-3806

Shorthouse, Tom, *Librn,* University of British Columbia Library (Law), Vancouver BC. 604-228-2275

Shortreed, Vivian H, *Dir,* Quinebaug Valley Community College Library, Danielson CT. 203-774-4246

Shortt, M, *Librn,* University of Toronto Libraries (Faculty of Education), Toronto ON. 416-978-2908

Shortt, Mrs Vincent, *Librn,* La Porte County Library (Rolling Prairie Branch), Rolling Prairie IN. 219-778-2390

Shotela, Joan, *Ref,* Bellwood Public Library, Bellwood IL. 312-547-7393

Shotwell, Jan, *Dir,* Dryden Township Library, Dryden MI. 313-796-3586

Shotwell, Janice, *Librn,* South Portland Public Library (South Portland Branch), South Portland ME. 207-775-1835

Shou, Stephens, *Polit Sci-Law,* Oregon State University, William Jasper Kerr Library, Corvallis OR. 503-754-3411

Shoults, Mary Lee, *Librn,* Douglas County Library System (Winston Public), Winston OR. 503-679-5501

Shoultz, Cathy, *Librn,* Florida Department of Corrections, Bureau of Planning, Research, & Statistics Library, Tallahassee FL. 904-488-2335, 1801

Shoultz, Katie, *Asst Librn,* Mayo Foundation (Medical Library), Rochester MN. 507-284-2061

Shoup, Agnes, *Asst Librn,* University of Detroit Library (Dental School), Detroit MI. 313-259-6622, Ext 298

Shoup, Jan, *Ch,* Franklin Park Public Library District, Franklin Park IL. 312-455-6016

Shoup, Jane, *Cat,* Putnam Public Library, Nashville MI. 517-852-9723

Shoupe, Louisa M, *Librn,* Pacific Gas & Electric Co (James Hugh Wise Library), San Francisco CA. 415-781-4211, Ext 2573

Shouse, Betty, *Pub Servs,* Kansas City Public Library, Kansas City MO. 816-221-2685

Shouse, Jeanette, *Librn,* Breathitt County Library, Jackson KY. 606-666-5541

Shouse, Robert, *Ref,* Towson State University, Albert S Cook Library, Towson MD. 301-321-2450

Shovar, Mary W, *Librn,* Andalusia Township Library, Andalusia IL. 309-798-2542

Shovp, Gloria, *Librn,* Peoria Public Library (McClure), Peoria IL. 309-672-8839

Showalter, Grace I, *Rare Bks & Spec Coll,* Eastern Mennonite College & Seminary Library, Harrisonburg VA. 703-433-2771, Ext 171

Showers, Arlene, *Asst Librn,* Maryville Public Library, Maryville MO. 816-582-5281

Showman, Frances, *Acq,* Oregon State Library, Salem OR. 503-378-4243

Shreeves, C Edward, *Ser & Doc,* Berry College, Memorial Library, Mount Berry GA. 404-232-5374, Ext 221, 388

Shrene, Lillian S, *Librn,* Fort Myers-Lee County Library, Fort Myers FL. 813-334-3992

Shreve, Joan, *Librn,* University of Pittsburgh (Buhl Library of Social Work), Pittsburgh PA. 412-624-4456

Shrewsbury, Judy, *Librn,* Free Will Baptist Bible College, Welch Library, Nashville TN. 615-297-4676

Shrier, Helene, *Asst Librn,* Saint Joseph's Hospital Health Center, School of Nursing & Medical Library, Syracuse NY. 315-424-5053

Shriner, Meta, *Librn,* Barry-Lawrence Regional Library (Purdy), Monett MO. 417-442-7314

Shriner, R D, *Dir,* Indiana University, Aerospace Research Application Center Library, Bloomington IN. 812-332-0211

Shriver, Wilma, *Librn,* Carroll County Bar Association Library, Westminster MD. 301-848-7500

Shroder, Emelie J, *Chief,* Chicago Public Library (Business, Science & Technology Div), Chicago IL. 312-269-2814, 269-2865

Shropshire, Helen, *Ch,* Charles A Cannon Memorial Library, Concord NC. 704-788-3167

Shropshire, Kathy, *Handicapped,* Greensboro Public Library, Greensboro NC. 373-2474; 373-2471

Shroyer, Esther, *Librn,* Mercer County Library, Princeton MO. 816-748-3725

Shroyer, Verna M, *Librn,* United States Air Force (Keesler Air Force Academic Library), Keesler AFB MS. 601-377-4295

Shub, Bertha J, *Librn,* North Charles General Hospital, Medical Staff Library, Baltimore MD. 301-338-2000

Shub, Louis, *Dir,* University of Judaism Library, Los Angeles CA. 213-476-9777, 879-4110

Shubeck, Betty, *ILL & Ref,* Addison Public Library, Addison IL. 312-543-3617

Shubel, Ethel, *Librn,* Port Austin Township Library, Port Austin MI. 517-738-7637

Shubert, Joseph, *State Librn,* New York State Library, Albany NY. 518-474-5930

Shubert, Joseph F, *State Librn,* New York State Interlibrary Loan Network, (NYSILL), NY. 518-474-5129; Data 474-5784 & 474-5786

Shubert, Marcia B, *ILL & Ad,* Beaman Memorial Public Library, West Boylston MA. 617-835-3711

Shueller, Malanea M, *Librn,* Wabasso Public Library, Wabasso MN. 507-342-5279

Shuey, Lee, *Librn,* Dallas Public Library (Lakewood), Dallas TX. 214-821-5128

Shufeldt, Patricia, *Acq,* Greenville County Library, Greenville SC. 803-242-5000

Shuff, Jim, *Media,* Henderson State University, Huie Library, Arkadelphia AR. 501-246-5511, Ext 200

Shuff, Lucretia, *AV,* Tiffin-Seneca Public Library, Tiffin OH. 419-447-3751

Shuffelton, David B, *Librn,* Shelby County Law Library, Sidney OH. 513-492-6925

Shuford, C L, *Librn,* Liggett Group, Inc (Liggett & Myers Tobacco Co, Research Center Information Services), Durham NC. 919-683-5521, Ext 492

Shular, James W, *Librn,* Arnold & Porter Library, Washington DC. 202-872-6870

Shuler, Jane, *Circ & Ad,* Elbert Ivey Memorial Library, Hickory NC. 704-322-2905

Shuler, Virginia, *Ch,* Richland County Public Library, Columbia SC. 803-799-9084

Shull, Doris, *Librn,* Lindenwold Public Library, Lindenwold NJ. 609-784-5602

Shultes, Dorothea, *Librn,* Crouse-Irving Memorial Hospital Library, Syracuse NY. 315-424-6380

Shults, James, *Ch,* Liverpool Public Library, Liverpool NY. 315-457-0310

Shults, John, *Librn,* Houston Public Library (Ring), Houston TX. 713-468-2643

Shults, Linda S, *On-Line Servs & Bibliog Instr,* Tenneco, Inc, Corporation Library, Houston TX. 713-757-2788

Shultz, Jane, *Media,* Tennessee Wesleyan College, Merner-Pfeiffer Library, Athens TN. 615-745-2363

Shultz, Linda J, *Librn,* Noble County Public Library, Albion IN. 219-636-7197

Shultz, Suzanne M, *Librn,* Polyclinic Medical Center, Medical Staff Library, Harrisburg PA. 717-782-4292

Shumaker, Lois, *Tech Serv,* Sacramento Public Library, Sacramento CA. 916-440-5926

Shumaker, Mollie, *Librn,* Bay County Public Library Association (Washington County Branch), Chipley FL. 904-638-1314

Shumaker, William N, *Librn,* Episcopal Diocese of Rhode Island Library, Providence RI. 401-274-4500

Shuman, Bruce A, *Assoc Prof,* Queens College of the City University of New York, Graduate School of Library & Information Studies, NY. 212-520-7194, 520-7195

Shumer, Barbara, *Sr Citizen Serv,* Farmington Community Library, Farmington Hills MI. 313-553-0300

Shumer, Barbara, *Librn,* Farmington Community Library (Oakland County Library for Blind & Physically Handicapped), Farmington Hills MI. 313-553-0300, Ext 39

Shumofsky, Claire, *Librn,* Congregation B'nai Israel Library, Bridgeport CT. 203-336-1858

Shumpert, Charlene, *YA,* Free Public Library of the City of Orange, Orange NJ. 201-673-0153

Shupe, Barbara, *Map Libr,* State University of New York, Frank Melville Jr Memorial Library, Stony Brook NY. 516-246-5650

Shurgot, Gail, *Cat,* El Paso Public Library, El Paso TX. 915-543-3804

Shurman, Richard, *Libr Automation Coordr,* DuPage Library System, Geneva IL. 312-232-8457

Shurtleff, Carl, *ILL & Circ,* Augusta College, Reese Library, Augusta GA. 404-828-4566, 828-4066

Shurtleff, Thalia, *Ref,* Medford Public Library, Medford MA. 617-395-7950

Shuster, Helen, *Tech Serv,* Clark University, Robert Hutchings Goddard Library, Worcester MA. 617-793-7573

Shuster, Helen, *Tech Serv,* Worcester Polytechnic Institute, George C Gordon Library, Worcester MA. 617-753-1411, Ext 410

Shuster, Susanna, *On-Line Servs,* Los Angeles Times Editorial Library, Los Angeles CA. 213-972-7184

Shute, D J, *Asst Librn,* Presbyterian College Library, Montreal PQ. 514-288-5256

Shutt, Thelma, *Chief Librn,* United States Navy (Avionic Center Technical Library), Indianapolis IN. 317-353-3232

Shwarz, Marta O, *Fine Arts,* Yonkers Public Library, Yonkers NY. 914-337-1500

Siao, Cheng, *Ser,* University of Scranton, Alumni Memorial Library, Scranton PA. 717-961-7525

Siao, Cheng H, *Dir,* Saint Pius X Seminary Library, Dalton PA. 717-563-1131

Siarny, Jr, William D, *Coordr,* Illinois Health Libraries Consortium, IL. 312-467-5520, Ext 33

Siarny, Jr, William D, *Librn,* National Live Stock & Meat Board, Meat Industry Information Center, Chicago IL. 312-467-5520, Ext 33

Sibbett, Diane, *Librn,* Canadian Education Association Library, Toronto ON. 416-924-7721

Sibbitt, Marian, *Librn,* Rinard Public Library, Rinard IA. 712-467-5667

Sibert, Martha, *Ch,* Roanoke County Public Library, Roanoke VA. 703-774-1681

Sibia, Tejinder S, *Biol & Agr,* University of California at Davis, General Library, Davis CA. 916-752-2110

Sibley, Ann R, *Librn,* Malden Public Library (West), Malden MA. 617-324-1055

Sibley, Anna Margaret, *Librn,* Yuma County Law Library, Yuma AZ. 602-782-4534

Sibley, Jennings G, *Librn,* United States Air Force (Base Library), Jacksonville AR. 501-988-3131

Sibley, Marjorie, *Ref,* Augsburg College, George Sverdrup Library, Minneapolis MN. 612-330-1014

Sibley, Jr, Richard P, *Librn,* Waterville Public Library, Waterville ME. 207-872-5433

Sica, Theresa, *Tech Serv,* Dominican College Library, Blauvelt NY. 914-359-8188

Sichel, Beatrice, *Librn,* Western Michigan University (Physical Sciences), Kalamazoo MI. 616-383-4943

Siciliano, Anthony, *Circ,* Skokie Public Library, Skokie IL. 312-673-7774

Sickels, Steven M, *Tech Serv,* Buena Vista College, Ballou Library, Storm Lake IA. 712-749-2141

Sickendick, Imogene, *Librn,* Kellwood Co, Research Center Library, New Haven MO. 314-237-4235

Sickles, Linda, *Ad,* Avon Township Public Library, Rochester MI. 313-651-1426

Sickles, Robert, *Biol Sci & Agr,* Iowa State University Library, Ames IA. 515-294-1442

Sickmund, Constance, *Ref,* Salisbury State College, Blackwell Library, Salisbury MD. 301-546-3261, Ext 351

Siddiqui, Amira, *Cat,* Bloomfield College Library, Bloomfield NJ. 201-748-9000, Ext 281

Siddiqui, Ghulam Y, *Asst Dir Acq,* University of Maryland-Eastern Shore, Frederick Douglass Library, Princess Anne MD. 301-651-2200, Ext 229

Siddon, Una D, *Librn,* Holmes County Library (West Branch), West MS. 601-967-2510

Sidebottom, Helen, *Librn,* Martins Ferry Public Library (Bethesda Public), Bethesda OH. 614-633-0314

Sidel, Victor W, *Dir,* Montefiore Hospital & Medical Center (Karl Cherkasky Social Medicine Library), Bronx NY. 212-920-5508

Sides, Virginia N, *Ch,* Abbeville-Greenwood Regional Library, Greenwood SC. 803-223-4515

Sidey, Margaret M, *Librn,* Providence Medical Center, Medical Library, Portland OR. 503-234-8211

Sidhu, Bhagwant K, *Coordr,* College of DuPage, Library Technical Assistant Program, IL. 312-858-2800, Ext 2065 or 2407

Sidlek, Laura, *Ref,* Macomb County Community College, Center Campus Library, Mount Clemens MI. 313-286-2104

Sidlo, Melinda, *Asst Librn,* Edmonton Art Gallery Library, Edmonton AB. 403-429-6781

Sidrow, Siegfried, *Librn,* Jacques Marchais Center & Tibetan Art Library, Staten Island NY. 212-987-3478

Siebe, Mary Jane, *Librn,* Mascoutah Public Library, Mascoutah IL. 618-566-2562

Siebecker, Dorothy, *Head Cat,* Tucson Museum of Art Library, Tucson AZ. 602-623-4881

Sieben, Gloria, *Librn,* Saint Mary of the Lake Seminary, Feehan Memorial Library, Mundelein IL. 312-566-6401, Ext 50

Sieben, William R, *Dir,* Niles College of Loyola University Library, Chicago IL. 312-631-1017

Siebenheller, Norma, *Librn,* Staten Island Historical Society Library, Staten Island NY. 212-351-1611

Siebenlist, Beverly, *Librn,* Shattuck Public Library, Shattuck OK. 405-938-5104

Sieber, Robert N, *Dir,* Pennsylvania Farm Museum of Landis Valley, Reference Library, Lancaster PA. 717-569-0401

Sieber, Sister Georgine, *Dir,* La Roche College, John J Wright Library, Pittsburgh PA. 412-931-9333, Ext 175

Siebersma, Dan, *Tech Serv &* , George Amos Memorial Library, Campbell County Library, Gillette WY. 307-682-3223

Siebersma, Lois, *Dir,* Sioux Center Public Library, Sioux Center IA. 712-722-2138

Siebert, Evelyn M, *Dir,* Ritter Public Library, Vermilion OH. 216-967-3798

Siebert, John, *Media,* Central Missouri State University, Ward Edwards Library, Warrensburg MO. 816-429-4141

Siebert, Mary D, *Librn,* Saint Francis Hospital (School of Nursing Library), Peoria IL. 309-672-2210

Siecker, Mrs John, *Supvr,* Huron County Public Library (Saint Helen's), Lucknow ON. 519-528-5850

Siedenberg, Jeffrey, *Res Assoc,* Joint Council on Economic Education Library, New York NY. 212-582-5150

Siedle, Veronica, *Librn,* United States Fish & Wildlife Service, Science Reference Library, Twin Cities MN. 612-725-3576

Siedschlaw, Betty, *Inst Servs,* South Dakota State Library, Pierre SD. 605-773-3131

Siefer, Marjorie, *YA,* Oil City Library, Oil City PA. 814-646-8771

Siefker, Donald L, *Ref,* Ball State University, Alexander M Bracken Library, Muncie IN. 317-285-6261

Siege, Selma, *YA,* Rockville Centre Public Library, Rockville Centre NY. 516-766-6258

Siegel, Allan, *Librn,* Tehama County Library, Red Bluff CA. 916-527-0604

Siegel, Blanche, *Ref,* Family Service Association of America Library, New York NY. 212-674-6100, Ext 49, 50

Siegel, Ernest, *Dir,* Enoch Pratt Free Library, Baltimore MD. 301-396-5430, 396-5395

Siegel, Ernest, *Prof,* William Paterson College, Library-Media Services, NJ. 201-595-2345, 595-2619

Siegel, Gladys E, *Librn,* American Petroleum Institute Library, Washington DC. 202-457-7269

Siegel, J, *Ad & Ref,* Saint Thomas Public Library, Saint Thomas ON. 519-631-6050

Siegel, Lenny, *Dir,* Pacific Studies Center, Mountain View CA. 415-969-1545

Siegel, Lorraine J, *Ref,* American Arbitration Association, Eastman Arbitration Library, New York NY. 212-484-4127

Siegel, Margot, *Ref,* Hunterdon County Library, Flemington NJ. 201-788-1444

Siegel, Mark, *Instr,* University of the District of Columbia-Mount Vernon Square Campus, Dept of Library Science & Instructional Systems Technology, DC. 202-727-2756, 727-2757 & 727-2758

Siegel, Mrs A, *Supvr,* Edmonton Public Library (Southgate), Edmonton AB. 403-435-3214

Siegel, Shalva, *Spec Coll,* Hebrew College, Jacob & Rose Grossman Library, Brookline MA. 617-232-8710, 232-8711

Siegel, Suzanne, *Acq,* Hunter College of the City University of New York Library, New York NY. 212-570-5511

Siegel, Sylvia, *Asst Librn,* Weil, Gotshal & Manges Library, New York NY. 212-758-7800, Ext 212

Siegelman, Lynn, *Ref,* Georgetown University (John Vinton Dahlgren Memorial Library), Washington DC. 202-625-7577

Siegeltuch, Marian, *Asst Dir Pub Serv,* Montclair State College, Harry A Sprague Library, Upper Montclair NJ. 201-893-4291

Siegenthaler, David, *Spec Coll,* Episcopal Divinity School, Sherrill Hall Library, Cambridge MA. 617-868-3450, Ext 31

Siegenthaler, Myra, *Circ,* Tufts University, Nils Yngve Wessell Library, Medford MA. 617-628-5000, Ext 235

Sieger, Britt, *Librn,* Kennecott Exploration Inc Library, San Diego CA. 714-453-3751

Siegfried, Diana, *ILL,* Anacortes Public Library, Anacortes WA. 206-293-2700

Siegler, Sharon L, *Pub Servs,* Lehigh University Libraries (Mart Engineering), Bethlehem PA. 861-3026 (Dir), 861-3050 (Ref), 861-3030 (Circ), 861-3055 (ILL)

Siegrist, Edith, *Learning Resources,* University of South Dakota, I D Weeks Library, Vermillion SD. 605-677-5371

Sieh, Barbara, *Cat,* University of Wisconsin-Stout, Pierce Library, Menomonie WI. 715-232-1184

Siehl, Judy, *Cat & On-Line Servs,* Butler University, Irwin Library, Indianapolis IN. 317-283-9225

Siehl, Lois J, *Dir,* Highland Community Library, Johnstown PA. 814-266-5610

Siekevitz, Rebecca, *Librn,* New York Public Library (Art Library), New York NY. 212-790-6486
Siemans, Rosanne, *Ch,* Newton Public Library, Newton KS. 316-283-2890
Siemens, William, *Ref,* University of Alaska, Anchorage Library, Anchorage AK. 907-263-1825
Siemer, Rose Ann, *ILL,* Notre Dame College, Clara Fritzsche Library, Cleveland OH. 216-381-1680, Ext 59
Siemers, L, *Librn,* Minnesota Department of Health, Robert N Barr Public Health Library, Minneapolis MN. 612-296-5240
Siemion, Margaret, *Ch,* Brookfield Public Library, Brookfield WI. 414-782-4140
Siemsen, David P, *Dir,* Williamsport Area Community College Library, Williamsport PA. 717-326-3761, Ext 211
Siena, Sister Mary, *Librn,* Catholic Diocese of Providence, Office of Religious Education Library, Providence RI. 401-278-4646
Sienda, Madeline, *Librn,* Sundstrand Data Control, Inc Library, Redmond WA. 206-885-8420
Sienkiewicz, Evelyn, *Asst Librn,* Faulkner Hospital, Ingersoll Bowditch Library, Jamaica Plain MA. 617-522-5800, Ext 1443
Sienus, Lynne, *Librn,* Hennepin County Medical Center, Thomas Lowry Library, Minneapolis MN. 612-347-2710
Sierra, Angel, *Librn,* University of Puerto Rico Library (Commerce Reserve Room), Rio Piedras PR. 809-764-0000, Ext 3322
Sierra, Damaris Fernandez, *Dir,* Frederick Sargent Huntington Memorial Library, Worthington Library Corp, Worthington MA. 413-238-5565
Siever, Robert, *Acq,* Franklin & Marshall College Library, Lancaster PA. 717-291-4223
Sievers, Tom, *ILL & Ref,* Ela Area Public Library District, Lake Zurich IL. 312-438-3433
Sievert, Irene, *In Charge,* Myrtle Mabee Library, Belgrade MN. 612-254-8842
Sievert, Mary Ellen, *Instr,* University of Missouri-Columbia, School of Library & Informational Science, MO. 314-882-4546
Siewers, Iris J, *Info Sci,* Union Carbide Corp (Library & Technical Information Serv), Tarrytown NY. 914-789-3700
Siewert, Susan, *Librn,* Kenosha Public Library (Gilbert M Simmons), Kenosha WI. 414-656-6034
Sifferman, Cornelia, *Dir,* Pryor Public Library, Pryor OK. 918-825-0777
Sifford, Harlan L, *Librn,* University of Iowa Libraries (Art), Iowa City IA. 319-353-4440
Sifleet, Inez, *Librn,* Weatherhead Co, Research & Development Library, Cleveland OH. 216-451-5200
Sifton, Pat, *Instr,* Fanshawe College of Applied Arts & Technology, Library Technician Programme, ON. 519-452-4369
Sifuentes, U A, *Ref & Bibliog Instr,* Ventura College, D R Henry Library, Ventura CA. 805-642-3211, Ext 201
Sigerson, Mrs David, *Librn,* Museum of Arts & Sciences Library, Daytona Beach FL. 904-255-0285
Siggins, Jack A, *Assoc Dir, Pub Servs,* University of Maryland at College Park (University Libraries), College Park MD. 301-454-3011
Sigler, Judy, *ILL,* Mobile Public Library, Mobile AL. 205-438-7073
Sigler, Lois, *Cat,* Florida Institute of Technology Library, Melbourne FL. 305-723-3701, Ext 270
Sigler, Ronald F, *Asst Prof,* University of Wisconsin-Milwaukee, School of Library Science, WI. 414-963-4707
Sigley, Judith, *Ch,* Cranford Public Library, Cranford NJ. 201-276-1826
Sigmon, Dolores, *Tech Serv,* Imperial Valley College, Spencer Library Media Center, Imperial CA. 714-352-8320, Ext 270
Signon, Teresa, *Tech Serv,* Caldwell County Public Library, Lenoir NC. 704-758-8451
Siiro, John, *Ref,* University of Denver (Westminster Law Library), Denver CO. 303-753-3405
Sikes, Cindy, *Librn,* Chatham-Effingham-Liberty Regional Library (Port Wentworth Branch), Port Wentworth GA. 912-964-8097
Sikes, Evelyn, *Asst Librn,* Kitchell Memorial Library, Morrisonville IL. 217-526-4553

Sikes, Mrs Wickly, *Librn,* Burke County Library (Midville Branch), Midville GA. 912-589-7825
Sikes, Myrtice, *Librn,* Brazoria County Library (Sweeny Branch), Sweeny TX. 713-548-2567
Sikora, Judith A, *ILL, Ref & On-Line Servs,* Genesee Community College, Alfred C O'Connell Library, Batavia NY. 716-343-0055, Ext 350
Sikorski, Leona, *In Charge,* Allegheny Ludlum Industries, Inc, Research Center Library, Brackenridge PA. 412-226-2000
Silas, David E, *Bk Selection Specialists,* Harvard University Library (Harvard College Library (Headquarters in Harry Elkins Widener Memorial Library)), Cambridge MA. 617-495-2401
Silber, Rivka N, *Res Librn,* Whitney Communications Corporation, Research Library, New York NY. 212-582-2300, Ext 48, 49
Silberstein, Barbara, *Ref,* W Leslie Rogers Library, Pennsauken Public Library, Pennsauken NJ. 609-665-5959
Silberstein, Joel, *Librn,* Brooklyn Public Library (Williamsburgh), Brooklyn NY. 212-782-4600
Silchuk, Barbara, *Librn,* Wayne County Public Library (Rittman Branch), Rittman OH. 216-925-2761
Siles, Dorothy, *Cat,* Ithaca College Library, Ithaca NY. 607-274-3182
Silk, Diane, *Libr Mgr,* Northrop Corp, Research & Technology Center, Palos Verde Peninsula CA. 213-377-4811, Ext 408
Sill, Mrs Elmer, *Asst Librn,* Waupaca Free Public Library, Waupaca WI. 715-258-3393
Sillers, Dan, *Instr,* University of the District of Columbia-Mount Vernon Square Campus, Dept of Library Science & Instructional Systems Technology, DC. 202-727-2756, 727-2757 & 727-2758
Sillito, John, *Archives,* Weber State College Library, Stewart Library, Ogden UT. 801-626-6403
Sillius, Irene, *In Charge,* Mallory Battery Co of Canada Ltd, Research Library, Mississauga ON. 416-823-4410
Silva, Carolyn, *Acq,* Taunton Public Library, Subregional Headquarters for Eastern Massachusetts Regional Library System, Taunton MA. 617-823-3570
Silva, Jerry, *Librn,* Golden Correctional Center, Camp George West Library, Golden CO. 303-279-4090
Silva, Joan, *Ch,* Colonie Town Library, Loudonville NY. 518-458-9274
Silva, R, *Health Educ,* State University of New York at Buffalo (Health Sciences), Buffalo NY. 716-831-5465
Silva, R, *Health Educ,* State University of New York at Buffalo, University Libraries, Buffalo NY. 716-636-2965
Silva, Remedios, *Cat,* State University of New York at Buffalo (Health Sciences), Buffalo NY. 716-831-5465
Silver, Cheryl, *Analysts,* Cornell University Medical College, Samuel J Wood Library, New York NY. 212-472-5300
Silver, Constance, *Ad,* Avon Township Public Library, Rochester MI. 313-651-1426
Silver, Cy H, *Libr Develop Servs Chief,* California State Library, Sacramento CA. 916-445-2585
Silver, Dale, *Librn,* County of Henrico Public Library (Tuckahoe), Richmond VA. 804-270-4105
Silver, David, *Dir,* Prentice-Hall, New York Institute of Finance Library, New York NY. 212-952-0822
Silver, Dorcus L, *Librn,* Stanly Technical Institute, Learning Resources Center, Albemarle NC. 704-982-0121
Silver, Helene, *Lit & Hist,* Long Beach Public Library System, Long Beach CA. 213-436-9225
Silver, Janet W, *Talking Bks Ctr Librn,* Athens Regional Library, Athens GA. 404-543-0134
Silver, Kate, *Librn,* Joslin Memorial Library, Waitsfield VT. 802-496-4205
Silver, Lenoa, *Tech Serv & Cat,* Olympic College, Learning Resources Center, Bremerton WA. 206-478-4609
Silver, Linda, *Ch,* Cuyahoga County Public Library, Cleveland OH. 216-398-1800
Silver, Lynn A, *Dir,* Bauder Fashion College Library, Arlington TX. 817-277-6666

Silver, Martin, *Music,* University of California, Santa Barbara Library, Santa Barbara CA. 805-961-2741
Silverberg, Mary E, *Librn,* Boylston Public Library, Boylston MA. 617-869-2371
Silverberg, Mrs C, *Br Supvr,* Scarborough Public Library (Bridlewood), Scarborough ON. 416-499-4284
Silverman, Brad, *Bus,* Bryant Library, Roslyn NY. 516-621-2240
Silverman, Eileen, *Ref,* Tenafly Public Library, Tenafly NJ. 201-568-8680
Silverman, Evie, *Coordr,* Jewish Community Center of Greater Minneapolis Library, Minneapolis MN. 612-377-8330
Silverman, Helen F, *Librn,* Saint Louis College of Pharmacy, O J Cloughly Alumni Library, Saint Louis MO. 314-367-8700, Ext 30
Silverman, Howard, *Media,* Gloucester County College, Library-Media Center, Sewell NJ. 609-468-5000, Ext 294
Silverman, Judith, *Asst Dir,* Baldwin Public Library, Baldwin NY. 516-223-6228
Silverman, Marion H, *Librn,* Albert Einstein Medical Center (Alexander & Herbert Luria Memorial Library), Philadelphia PA. 215-329-0700, Ext 276
Silverman, Sanford L, *Dir,* Hadley-Luzerne Public Library, Lake Luzerne NY. 518-696-3423
Silvernail, Jean M, *Instrnl Design,* Robert Morris College Library, Coraopolis PA. 412-264-9300
Silvers, Harriet, *Libr Tech,* San Diego County Library (Julian Branch), Julian CA. 714-765-0370
Silversteen, Sophy, *Ser,* William Marsh Rice University, Fondren Library, Houston TX. 713-527-4022
Silverstein, Ida, *Ch,* Miami Beach Public Library, Miami Beach FL. 305-673-7535
Silvester, Myrtle B, *Asst Dir & Tech Serv,* Beaman Memorial Public Library, West Boylston MA. 617-835-3711
Silvestro, Clement M, *Dir,* Museum of Our National Heritage, Scottish Rite Masonic Museum & Library, Lexington MA. 617-861-6559
Silvestro, Josephine, *Librn,* GCA Corp, Technology Division Library, Bedford MA. 617-275-5444, Ext 4134
Silvin, John, *Dir,* Bristol Myers Co, Bristol Laboratories Library & Information Service, Syracuse NY. 315-432-2232
Silvis, Rosalie, *Ch,* Grand Rapids Public Library, Grand Rapids MN. 218-326-3081
Silvius, Wendell C, *Circ,* West Virginia Institute of Technology, Vining Library, Montgomery WV. 304-442-3141
Sim, Derek, *Librn,* Sherritt Gordon Mines Ltd, Research Center Library, Fort Saskatchewan AB. 403-998-6911
Sim, Patrick, *Librn,* American Society of Anesthesiologists, Wood Library-Museum of Anesthesiology, Park Ridge IL. 312-825-5586
Sim, Yong Sup, *Ref, Circ & On-Line Servs,* Mercer County Community College Library, Trenton NJ. 609-586-4800, Ext 358
Sim, Yong Sup, *Asst Prof,* Mercer County Community College, Library-Media Center Technical Assistant Program, NJ. 609-586-4800, Ext 360
Simak, Andrew, *Librn,* New York Law School Library, New York NY. 212-966-3500
Simchovitch, Samuel, *Librn,* Beth Tzedec Congregation Library, Toronto ON. 416-781-3511, 781-5658, Ext 30
Simenson, Joyce, *Asst Dir,* Newport Public Library, Newport OR. 503-265-2153
Simenz, Sue, *Librn,* Brown County Library (Ashwaubenon), Green Bay WI. 414-497-3448
Siminski, Richard, *YA,* City of Inglewood Public Library, Inglewood CA. 213-649-7380
Simkin, Faye, *Exec Officer,* New York Public Library (The Research Libraries), New York NY. 212-790-6262
Simmon, Katherine, *Circ,* Fall River Public Library, Fall River MA. 617-676-8541
Simmonds, A J, *Spec Coll & Rare Bks,* Utah State University, Merrill Library & Learning Resources Program, Logan UT. 801-750-2637
Simmons, Alma, *Curriculum Mat Ctr Librn,* Fort Valley State College, Henry Alexander Hunt Memorial Library, Fort Valley GA. 912-825-6342

Simmons, Arline, *Librn,* United States Navy (Portsmouth Naval Shipyard Hospital Library), Portsmouth NH. 207-439-1000, Ext 1807
Simmons, Barbara, *Librn,* Synectics Corp Library, Fairfax VA. 703-385-0190
Simmons, Caroline, *Asst Dir,* Lexington Public Library, Lexington KY. 606-252-8871
Simmons, Charlotte, *Librn,* Howe Memorial Library, Breckenridge MI. 517-842-3202.
Simmons, Collene, *In Charge,* Texas Education Agency (Region V), Beaumont TX. 713-892-9562
Simmons, Daniel, *Tech Serv,* Elyria Public Library, Elyria OH. 216-323-5747
Simmons, Essie, *Librn,* Coastal Plain Regional Library (Lenox Satelite Branch), Lenox GA. 912-546-4252
Simmons, Faye, *Librn,* New York Public Library (Kips Bay), New York NY. 212-683-2520
Simmons, Georjane, *Librn,* Panhandle Eastern Pipe Line Co Library, Kansas City MO. 816-753-5600, Ext 2849
Simmons, Henry, *Asst Curator for Mississippiana,* University of Southern Mississippi (William David McCain Library), Hattiesburg MS. 601-266-4172
Simmons, Jimmie Sue, *Coordr,* Texarkana Community College, Palmer Memorial Library, Texarkana TX. 214-838-4541, Ext 215, 231
Simmons, Joseph M, *Librn,* Towers Perrin Forster & Crosby, Inc, Research Department Library, New York NY. 212-661-5080, Ext 366
Simmons, Joyce, *Librn,* Greenacres City Public Library, Greenacres City FL. 305-965-0388
Simmons, Karen, *Librn,* Glenwood Public Library, Glenwood MN. 612-634-3375
Simmons, Karen Hegge, *Chief Librn,* American Institute of Certified Public Accountants Library, New York NY. 212-575-6322
Simmons, Kathy, *Librn,* Kansas City Public Library (Northeast), Kansas City MO. 816-231-6313
Simmons, Leslie Jean, *Asst Librn,* Reader's Digest Association, General Books Division Library, New York NY. 212-972-8452
Simmons, Linda C, *Assoc Curator,* Corcoran Gallery of Art, Curatorial Library, Washington DC. 202-638-3211, Ext 34, 35
Simmons, Mattie Lou, *Librn,* Sunflower County Library System (Drew Public), Drew MS. 601-745-2237
Simmons, Maxine, *Librn,* George Library, Fairfield NC. 919-926-8841
Simmons, Melnee, *Librn,* Chicago Public Library (Pullman), Chicago IL. 312-995-0110
Simmons, Nadyne, *Libr Techn,* Oklahoma Department of Human Services, Employees Library, Oklahoma City OK. 405-521-3518
Simmons, Paul, *Acq,* Claremont Colleges Libraries, Claremont CA. 714-621-8000, Ext 3721
Simmons, Paul, *Media,* Wright State University Library, Dayton OH. 513-873-2380
Simmons, Peter, *Assoc Prof,* University of British Columbia, School of Librarianship, BC. 604-228-2404
Simmons, Phyllis, *Librn,* Genesee District Library (Flint Township), Flint MI. 313-732-9150
Simmons, Randall, *ILL & Ref,* Olivet Nazarene College, Benner Library & Resource Center, Bourbonnais IL. 815-939-5354
Simmons, Robert, *Ad,* Mid-Hudson Library System, Poughkeepsie NY. 914-471-6060
Simmons, Robert H, *Dir,* Austin Peay State University, Felix G Woodward Library, Clarksville TN. 615-648-7346
Simmons, Robert M, *Curriculum,* Bridgewater State College, Clement C Maxwell Library, Bridgewater MA. 617-697-8321, Ext 441, 442
Simmons, Rosetta, *Dir & Bibliog Instr,* Mineral Area College, Instructional Resources Center, Flat River MO. 314-431-4593, Ext 38
Simmons, Ruth, *Librn,* Lowman United Methodist Church Library, Topeka KS. 913-272-8921
Simmons, Sheila, *ILL,* Rochester Institute of Technology, Wallace Memorial Library, Rochester NY. 716-475-2566
Simmons, Simmona, *Ser,* University of Maryland Baltimore County Library, Baltimore MD. 301-455-2457
Simmons, Susan, *Librn,* Aetna Life & Casualty (Corporate Data Processing Reference & Learning Center), Hartford CT. 203-273-2443

Simmons, Walter T, *Clerk,* Illinois Appellate Court, Fifth District, Law Library, Mount Vernon IL. 618-242-3120
Simmons, William B, *Librn,* Holy Cross Junior College Library, Notre Dame IN. 219-233-6813, Ext 25
Simms, Betty B, *Librn,* United Catalysts Inc, Technical Library, Louisville KY. 502-637-9751, Ext 256
Simms, Carol J, *Librn & ILL,* Gunn Memorial Library, Washington CT. 203-868-7586, 868-2310
Simms, Georgia, *Librn,* Lane Public Library (Community Ctr), Hamilton OH. 513-893-4086
Simon, Anabel, *Chief Librn,* Baptist Hospital, Medical Library, Pensacola FL. 904-434-4877
Simon, Andrew, *Cat,* Saint Mary's College of California, Saint Albert Hall Library, Moraga CA. 415-376-4411, Ext 229, 230
Simon, Anne, *Ch,* Ramapo Catskill Library System, Middletown NY. 914-343-1131, 352-4825, 565-3030
Simon, Bradley A, *Librn,* Chula Vista Public Library, Chula Vista CA. 714-427-1151
Simon, Carolyn, *ILL,* Austin Public Library, Austin TX. 512-472-5433
Simon, Doris, *Ref,* Paducah Public Library, Paducah KY. 502-442-2510, 443-2664
Simon, Dorothy B, *Libr Instr,* New York City Community College, Namm Hall Library, Brooklyn NY. 212-643-5240
Simon, Dorothy W, *Librn,* United States Department of Energy, Morgantown Energy Technology Center, Morgantown WV. 304-599-7183
Simon, Edward, *Librn,* Sheguiandah Band Public Library, Sheguiandah ON. 705-368-2781
Simon, Genivieve, *Librn,* Acadia Parish Library (Estherwood Branch), Esterwood LA. 318-788-1880
Simon, James, *Librn,* Indianapolis-Marion County Public Library (Wanamaker), Indianapolis IN. 317-635-5662
Simon, John V, *Ulysses S Grant,* Southern Illinois University at Carbondale, Delyte W Morris Library, Carbondale IL. 618-453-2522
Simon, Lorraine, *Admin Asst & AV,* East Chicago Public Library, East Chicago IN. 219-397-2453
Simon, Luella, *Dir,* Saint Mary's Junior College Library, Minneapolis MN. 612-332-5521
Simon, Luella A, *Librn,* Milan-Berlin Township Public Library, Milan OH. 419-499-4117
Simon, Marie-Louise, *Librn,* Saint-Laurent Municipal Library, Saint Laurent PQ. 514-744-6411, Ext 220
Simon, Matthew, *Librn,* Columbia University (Lehman Library (International Affairs)), New York NY. 212-280-2241
Simon, Myrtle H, *Dir,* Harlem Hospital Medical Center (Patients' Library), New York NY. 212-694-1201, 694-1202
Simon, Nancy, *Librn,* Rose Medical Center, Medical Library, Denver CO. 303-320-2160
Simon, Patricia, *Ad,* New City Free Library, New City NY. 914-634-4997
Simon, Ralph C, *Dir,* Michael J Owens Technical College Library, Perrysburg OH. 419-666-0580, Exts 221 & 251
Simon, Ralph R, *Librn,* Temple Emanu El Library, Cleveland OH. 216-381-6600
Simon, Rose, *Ref,* Guilford College Library, Greensboro NC. 919-292-5511, Ext 250
Simon, Rose Anne, *Dir,* Salem College, Dale H Gramley Library, Winston-Salem NC. 919-721-2649
Simon, Samuel L, *Dir,* Finkelstein Memorial Library, Spring Valley NY. 914-352-5700, Ext 230
Simon, Vaughn, *Proc,* Enoch Pratt Free Library, Baltimore MD. 301-396-5430, 396-5395
Simonds, Lorraine, *YA,* East Islip Public Library, East Islip NY. 516-581-9200, 581-9228
Simonds, Patricia, *ILL & Ref,* Florida State University (Law Library), Tallahassee FL. 904-644-1004
Simone, Debby L, *ILL, Ad & Ref,* Santa Fe Regional Library, Gainesville Public Library Headquarters, Gainesville FL. 904-374-2091
Simone, Janet, *Assoc Prof,* Kutztown State College, Dept of Library Science, PA. 215-683-4300, 683-4301

Simonetti, Madeline, *Tech Serv,* Saint John Hospital, Medical Library, Detroit MI. 313-343-3733
Simonis, James J, *Dir,* Mansfield State College Library, Mansfield PA. 717-662-4071
Simons, Barbara A, *Reader Serv & Bibliog Instr,* Goucher College, Julia Rogers Library, Towson MD. 301-825-3300, Ext 360
Simons, Eleanor B, *Librn,* Northeastern Vermont Regional Hospital, Information Center, Saint Johnsbury VT. 802-748-8141, Ext 242
Simons, Gordon N, *Curator,* Pensacola Historical Society, Lelia Abercrombie Historical Library, Pensacola FL. 904-433-1559
Simons, Marilyn, *Ch,* Mill Valley Public Library, Mill Valley CA. 415-388-4245
Simons, Marjorie, *Dir,* Ridgefield Park Free Public Library, Ridgefield Park NJ. 201-641-0689
Simons, Maurice, *Ref & Bibliog Instr,* Roseville Public Library, Roseville CA. 916-783-7158
Simons, Michael, *Instr,* Saint Cloud State University, Center for Library & Audiovisual Education, MN. 612-255-2022
Simons, Samuel, *Per,* Memorial Hall Library, (Subregional Headquarters for Eastern Massachusetts Regional System), Andover MA. 617-475-6960
Simons, Tanya, *Librn,* Broward County Division of Libraries (Von D Mizell), Fort Lauderdale FL. 305-765-4269
Simons, Ute, *Librn,* Hoag Presbyterian Memorial Hospital, Robert & Winifred Bacon Memorial Medical Library, Newport Beach CA. 714-645-8600, Ext 2438
Simons, Wendell, *Dir,* Judson Baptist College Library, The-Dalles OR. 503-298-4455
Simonsen, Lynette E, *Librn,* South Dakota Human Service Center (Patient's Library), Yankton SD. 605-665-3671
Simonsen, Wilma, *Ad,* Eugene Public Library, Eugene OR. 503-687-5450
Simonsmeier, Irene E, *Librn,* Swea City Public Library, Swea City IA. 515-272-4216
Simonson, Inez, *Asst Librn,* Stratford Public Library, Stratford IA. 515-838-2131
Simonson, Joyce, *Asst Librn,* Walter A Woodward Memorial Library, Cottage Grove OR. 503-942-3828
Simonton, Wesley, *Dir,* University of Minnesota, Library School, MN. 612-373-3100
Simoons, Elizabeth, *Asst Dir,* Yolo County Library, Woodland CA. 916-666-8323
Simoons, Elizabeth, *Librn,* Yolo County Library (Davis Branch), Davis CA. 916-756-2332
Simor, George, *Acq,* City University of New York, Library of Graduate School & University Center, New York NY. 212-790-4541
Simor, Suzanna, *Art,* Queens College Library, Flushing NY. 212-520-7616
Simosko, Vladimir, *Librn,* University of Manitoba Libraries (Science), Winnipeg MB. 204-474-8171
Simpkins, Alice G, *Ref,* Mary Baldwin College, Martha S Grafton Library, Staunton VA. 703-885-0811, Ext 382
Simpkins, Irwin F, *Dir,* Dekalb Community College, South Campus, Learning Resources Center, Decatur GA. 404-243-3860, Ext 12
Simplot, Dolly, *In Charge,* Bellingham Public Library (Fairhaven Branch), Bellingham WA. 206-676-6877
Simpson, Alice A, *In Charge,* Library Services Branch, Lower Mainland Office, Burnaby BC. 604-298-0422
Simpson, Arlene B, *Asst Dir, Tech Serv & Cat,* Mary Riley Styles Public Library, Falls Church VA. 703-241-5030
Simpson, Barbara, *Librn,* Cuyahoga Community College, Metropolitan Campus Learning Resources Center, Cleveland OH. 216-241-5966
Simpson, Barbara, *YA,* Massapequa Public Library, Massapequa NY. 516-798-4607
Simpson, Carol, *Librn,* Grand Rapids Public Museum Library, Grand Rapids MI. 616-456-3977
Simpson, Christine, *Doc,* San Jose State University Library, San Jose CA. 408-277-3377
Simpson, Donald B, *Dir,* Center for Research Libraries, Chicago IL. 312-955-4545

Simpson, Donald B, *Dir,* Center for Research Libraries, IL. 312-955-4545
Simpson, Evelyn, *Librn,* Santa Ana-Tustin Community Hospital, Medical Library, Santa Ana CA. 714-835-3555, Ext 1381
Simpson, Harold B, *Civil War Research,* Hill Junior College Library, Hillsboro TX. 817-582-2555, Ext 40
Simpson, Helen, *Local Hist & Genealogy,* Oshkosh Public Library, Oshkosh WI. 414-424-0473
Simpson, Helen J, *Librn,* Newfields Free Public Library, Newfields NH. 603-772-4908
Simpson, Imogene, *Prof,* Western Kentucky University, Dept of Library Science & Instructional Media, KY. 502-745-3446
Simpson, Jay, *Media,* Dutchess Community College Library, Poughkeepsie NY. 914-471-4500, Ext 388
Simpson, Joseph H, *Tech Serv & Cat,* California Western School of Law, San Diego CA. 714-239-0391, Ext 36
Simpson, Juanita, *Circ,* Duncan Public Library, Duncan OK. 405-255-0636
Simpson, Lois, *Librn,* Nelsonville Public Library (Chauncey Branch), Chauncey OH. 614-797-2512
Simpson, M A, *Area Superintendent,* Canada Department of Indian Affairs & Northern Development, Battleford National Historic Park, Campbell Innes Memorial Library, Battleford SK. 306-937-2621
Simpson, Mary, *Tech Serv & Cat,* Casper College, Goodstein Foundation Library, Casper WY. 307-268-2269
Simpson, Mary Ellen, *Librn,* Mississippi Department of Public Welfare, Jackson MS. 601-981-7080, Ext 6555
Simpson, Michael, *Media,* University of Cincinnati Libraries (Raymond Walters General & Technical College Library), Blue Ash OH. 513-745-4313
Simpson, Minnie, *Librn,* Carteret County Public Library, Beaufort NC. 919-728-2050
Simpson, Mrs Howard E, *Librn,* Winslow Public Library, Winslow ME. 207-872-2209
Simpson, Sharon, *Asst Librn,* McIver's Grant Public Library, Dyersburg TN. 901-285-5032
Simpson, Stephen R, *Asst Librn,* Hawaii Pacific College, Meader Library, Honolulu HI. 808-521-3881
Simpson, Su-Lynda, *ILL,* Fondulac Public Library District, East Peoria IL. 309-699-3917
Simpson, William, *Lit & Hist,* Richmond Public Library, Richmond VA. 804-780-4256
Sims, Ann M, *Ad,* Fort Smith Public Library, Fort Smith AR. 501-783-0229
Sims, Carolyn, *Asst Librn,* Lyon County Public Library, Eddyville KY. 502-388-7720
Sims, Chester, *Media,* Greenville Technical College, Learning Resources Center, Greenville SC. 803-242-3170, Ext 321
Sims, Edith M, *On-Line Servs,* Louisiana State University (Troy H Middleton Library), Baton Rouge LA. 504-388-2217
Sims, Elizabeth, *Circ,* Transylvania County Library, Inc, Brevard NC. 704-883-9880
Sims, Jacquelyn, *Ill & Info Serv,* Catawba College, Corriher-Linn-Black Library, Salisbury NC. 704-637-4448, 637-4449
Sims, Janice, *Asst Librn,* Environmental Protection Agency, Environmental Research Laboratory Library, Athens GA. 404-546-3103
Sims, Jerome, *ILL & Ref,* Port Arthur Public Library, Port Arthur TX. 713-982-6491
Sims, Larry, *Media,* Jefferson State Junior College, James B Allen Library, Birmingham AL. 205-853-1200, Ext 280
Sims, Marcy J, *Dir,* Department of Public Libraries & Information, Virginia Beach VA. 804-427-4321
Sims, Moyna, *Bkmobile Coordr,* Todd County Public Library, Elkton KY. 502-265-9071
Sims, Nita, *Tech Serv,* Brewer State Junior College, Main Campus Library, Fayette AL. 205-922-3221, Ext 244
Sims, Oscar, *Soc Sci,* University of California Los Angeles Library, Los Angeles CA. 213-825-1201
Sims, Patricia, *In Charge,* Albert-Westmorland-Kent Regional Library (Sackville Public), Sackville NB. 506-389-2631

Sims, Phil, *Church Music,* Southwestern Baptist Theological Seminary, Fleming Library, Fort Worth TX. 817-923-1921, Ext 277
Sims, Philip, *Librn,* Southwestern Baptist Theological Seminary (Music), Fort Worth TX. 817-923-1921, Ext 277
Sims, Ronald, *Tech Serv,* Garrett-Evangelical Theological Seminary Library, Evanston IL. 312-866-3911
Sims, Ruth, *Circ,* Randolph-Macon Woman's College, Lipscomb Library, Lynchburg VA. 804-846-7392, Ext 242
Sims, Ruth, *Librn,* South Valley Bernalillo County Library, Albuquerque NM. 505-766-4424
Sims, Sharon, *Asst Librn,* Wilberforce University, Rembert Stokes Learning Resources Center, Wilberforce OH. 513-376-2911, Exts 226, 227, 228
Sims, Virginia Y, *Librn,* East Mississippi Regional Library (Bay Springs Municipal), Bay Springs MS. 601-764-2291
Sims, W S, *Librn,* Searcy Hospital Library, Mount Vernon AL. 205-829-2811
Sina, Fran, *Circ & Ref,* Hahnemann Medical College & Hospital of Philadelphia, Warren H Fake Library, Philadelphia PA. 215-448-7186
Sinanan, C, *Bibliog Instr,* Mount Royal College Library, Calgary AB. 403-246-6111
Sinate, Rasma, *Ch,* Ferndale Public Library, Ferndale MI. 313-548-5959
Sincavage, Marcia, *Tech Serv,* Hazleton Area Public Library, Hazleton PA. 717-454-2961, 454-0244
Sinclair, A I S, *Librn,* Public Works Canada, Departmental Library, Ottawa ON. 613-998-4705, 996-8211
Sinclair, Dianne, *Librn,* Singletary Memorial Library, Rusk TX. 214-683-5916
Sinclair, Donald, *Rare Bks & Spec Coll,* Rutgers University (Archibald Stevens Alexander Library), New Brunswick NJ. 201-932-7129
Sinclair, Dorothy M, *Prof,* Case Western Reserve University, School of Library Science, OH. 216-368-3500
Sinclair, Eleanor, *Humanities,* West Chester State College, Francis Harvey Green Library, West Chester PA. 215-436-2643
Sinclair, Jeanne, *Asst Librn,* Fernie Centennial Library, Fernie BC. 604-423-7017
Sinclair, Julia M, *Librn,* Mary Wilcox Memorial Library, Whitney Point NY. 607-692-3159
Sinclair, Michael P, *Chief Librn,* Nepean Public Library, Ottawa ON. 613-224-4338
Sinclair, R Frank, *Asst Librn & ILL,* Vance-Granville Community College, Learning Resources Center, Henderson NC. 919-492-2061, Ext 251
Sinclair, Sabina, *Librn,* Indiana University at Bloomington (Biology), Bloomington IN. 812-337-9791
Sindall, Barbara J, *Librn,* Varnum Memorial Library, Jeffersonville VT. 802-644-2986
Sindberg, James H, *Video Librn,* Defense Language Institute, Learning Resources Center, Presidio of Monterey CA. 408-242-8206
Sindlinger, Pat, *ILL,* Ohio State University, Agricultural Technical Institute Learning Resources Center, Wooster OH. 264-3911 Ext 224
Sineath, Timothy W, *Dean,* University of Kentucky, College of Library Science, KY. 606-258-8876
Sines, Jessie, *Librn,* Ruth Enlow Library of Garrett County (Friendsville Community Ctr), Friendsville MD. 301-746-5663
Sing, Vivian Saint, *Librn,* Public Library of Charlotte & Mecklenburg County, Inc (Matthews Branch), Matthews NC. 704-847-6691
Singer, Barry L, *Ad,* Superior Public Library, Superior WI. 715-394-0248
Singer, Diane, *Librn,* New Orleans Public Library (Smith), New Orleans LA. 504-488-6609
Singer, Dona, *Pub Serv,* Bergen Community College, Learning Resources Center Library, Paramus NJ. 201-447-1500, Ext 405
Singer, Gayle, *Ch,* Ridgewood Public Library, Ridgewood NJ. 201-652-5200
Singer, Jean H, *Dir,* Governors State University, University Library, Park Forest South IL. 312-534-5000, Ext 2231
Singer, Phyllis, *Librn,* Laceyville Public Library, Laceyville PA. 717-869-1958

Singerman, Robert, *Librn,* University of Florida Libraries (Isser & Rae Price Library of Judaica), Gainesville FL. 904-392-0308
Singh, Betty, *Linguistics,* Southern University Library, Baton Rouge LA. 504-771-4990, 771-4991, 771-4992
Singh, Gurnek, *Area Studies,* Syracuse University Libraries, Ernest S Bird Library, Syracuse NY. 315-423-2575
Singh, I, *Librn,* Wascana Institute of Applied Arts & Sciences, Resource & Information Center, Regina SK. 306-565-4321
Singh, Jennifer, *Circ,* Seneca College of Applied Arts & Technology, Finch Campus Learning Resource Centre, Willowdale ON. 416-491-5050, Ext 381
Singh, Mrs K, *Librn,* Ear Falls Public Library, Ear Falls ON. 807-222-3209
Singh, Rosemary, *Ad,* Manitowoc Public Library, Manitowoc WI. 414-682-6861
Singler, Mildred R, *Chief Librn,* Wood, Struthers & Winthrop, Inc Library, New York NY. 212-285-0010
Singletary, Jeannette, *Librn,* Colquitt-Thomas Regional Library (Thomasville Branch), Thomasville GA. 912-226-3853
Singletary, Maxine, *Circ,* Brunswick Junior College, Clara Wood Gould Memorial Library, Brunswick GA. 912-264-7270
Singletary, Myrtle, *Librn,* Suwannee River Regional Library, Seven-County Region (Mayo (Lafayette County)), Live Oak FL. 904-947-8100
Singletary, Pauline, *Librn,* New York Public Library (Macomb's Bridge), New York NY. 212-281-4900
Singletary, Pauline, *Librn,* New York Public Library (One Hundred & Fifteenth Street), New York NY. 212-666-9393
Singletary, Virginia, *Dir,* Stella Hill Memorial Library, Alto City Library, Alto TX. 713-858-7411
Singleton, Christine M, *Librn,* New York University Medical Center, Institute of Environmental Medicine Library, Sterling Forest NY. 351-4232 & 679-3200, Ext 5213 & 5214
Singleton, Del, *Librn,* Independence Community Junior College Library, Independence KS. 316-331-4100, Ext 55
Singleton, Doris, *Dir,* Boaz Public Library, Boaz AL. 205-593-8056
Singleton, Edith H, *NJ Hist,* Johnson Free Public Library, Hackensack NJ. 201-343-4169
Singleton, Edith H, *Spec Coll,* Johnson Free Public Library, Hackensack NJ. 201-343-4169
Singleton, Jean, *Indiana,* Indiana State Library, Indianapolis IN. 317-232-3675
Singleton, Julia, *Circ & Per,* Rockhurst College, Greenlease Library, Kansas City MO. 816-363-4010, Ext 253
Singleton, Lucille, *Librn,* Dora Public Library, Dora AL. 205-648-3211
Singleton, Nancy L, *Dir,* Madison Public Library, Madison NJ. 201-377-0722
Singleton, Patricia M, *Ref,* Alabama State University, Library & Learning Resources, Montgomery AL. 205-832-6072
Singleton, Patricia M, *Instr,* Alabama State University, Library Educational Media Program, AL. 205-832-6072, Ext 502
Singleton, Susan, *Ref,* University of Missouri-Rolla Library, Rolla MO. 314-341-4227
Singley, Elijah, *Ref & On-Line Servs,* Lincoln Land Community College, Learning Resources Center, Springfield IL. 217-786-2354
Singley, Elsie, *Librn,* Choctaw County Public Library (Silas Branch), Silas AL. 205-459-2542
Singley, Muriel, *Librn,* Central Florida Regional Library (Hernando), Ocala FL. 904-629-8551
Sink, Darryl, *Instr Develop,* West Valley College, Learning Resource Center, Saratoga CA. 408-867-2200, Ext 284
Sink, Mattie, *Acq,* Public Library of Charlotte & Mecklenburg County, Inc, Charlotte NC. 704-374-2725
Sinkankas, George M, *Asst Prof,* University of Tennessee, Knoxville, Graduate School of Library & Information Science, TN. 615-974-2148
Sinkey, Margaret, *Environ-Sci-Tech Libr,* University of Calgary Library, Calgary AB. 403-284-5954

Sinkfield, Pauline, *Bkmobile Coordr,* Pine Mountain Regional Library, Manchester GA. 404-846-2186

Sinkin, Benita, *Librn, Lum,* Biunno & Tompkins Law Library, Newark NJ. 201-622-2300

Sinko, Peggy T, *Supvr, Local & Family Hist Reading Room,* Newberry Library, Chicago IL. 312-943-9090

Sinnott, Jean, *ILL,* Utah State Library, Salt Lake City UT. 801-533-5875

Sinsheimer, Florence, *YA,* Scarsdale Public Library, Scarsdale NY. 914-723-2005

Sintz, Edward F, *Dir,* Miami-Dade Public Library System, Miami FL. 305-579-5001

Siock, Hedy A, *Librn,* Lackawanna Public Library, Lackawanna NY. 716-823-0630

Sipe, L, *Librn,* University of Southern California (VonKleinSmid World Affairs), Los Angeles CA. 213-743-7347

Sipes, Lottie, *Asst Librn,* Odem Public Library, Odem TX. 512-368-2831

Sippie, Velma L, *Librn,* Frackville Free Public Library, Frackville PA. 717-874-3382

Sipple, Alice, *Dir,* Floyd County Public Library, Prestonsburg KY. 606-886-2981

Sippola, Shirley J, *Dir,* Warren Public Library, Warren OH. 216-399-8807

Sipsma, Mary, *Libr Mgr,* Saint Catherine's Hospital, Medical Staff Library, Kenosha WI. 414-656-3230

Siqueira, J, *Dir,* Richmond Public Library, Richmond BC. 604-273-6606

Sirls, Barbara, *Dir,* Marshall County Public Library, Benton KY. 502-527-9969

Sirman, Margaret, *Librn,* Gulf Oil Corporation (Gulf Science & Technology Co, Engineering Library), Houston TX. 713-750-3624

Sirmans, Barbara, *Librn,* Birmingham Public & Jefferson County Free Library (Smithfield), Birmingham AL. 205-254-2551

Sirois, Dorothy, *Librn,* Montreal Children's Hospital, Medical Library, Montreal PQ. 514-937-8511, Ext 374

Sirois, Julie J, *Librn,* Saint Francis Hospital, Medical Library, Honolulu HI. 808-547-6481

Sirois, Nicole, *Librn,* Bibliotheque Municipale, Trois-Pistoles PQ. 418-851-2374

Sirois, Virginia, *Librn,* Southern Tier Library System (Cohocton Reading Center), Cohocton NY. 607-962-3141

Siron, Catherine, *Dir,* Saint Joseph Hospital, Health Science Library, Joliet IL. 815-725-7133, Ext 791, 792

Siroonian, Harold, *Sci & Eng,* McMaster University, Hamilton ON. 416-525-9140

Siroonian, Harold, *Assoc Librn,* McMaster University, Hamilton ON. 416-525-9140

Siroonian, Harold, *Librn,* McMaster University (H G Thode Library of Science & Engineering), Hamilton ON. 416-525-9140, Ext 4252

Sirrine, Marge, *Asst Librn,* Pomfret Free Public Library, Pomfret CT. 203-928-3475

Sirrocco, Angela L, *Chief,* National Institute of Mental Health Library, Communication Center, Rockville MD. 301-443-4278, 443-4279

Sirskyj, Wasyl, *Tech Serv & Cat,* Wilfrid Laurier University Library, Waterloo ON. 519-884-1970

Sisamis, Paul, *Media Supvrs,* Kent State University Libraries (Audio-Visual Services), Kent OH. 216-672-3456

Sisco, Ellen, *Asst Dir,* Lincoln Public Library, Lincoln MA. 617-259-8465

Sisco, Marilyn, *Librn,* San Diego Public Library (Paradise Hills), San Diego CA. 916-479-3538

Sisk, Virginia L, *Librn,* Jones College, James V Forrestal Library, Jacksonville FL. 904-743-1122, Ext 101

Sisson, Helen, *Main Librn,* Detroit Public Library, Detroit Associated Libraries, Detroit MI. 313-833-1000

Sisson, Laurel, *YA,* Riverhead Free Library, Riverhead NY. 516-727-3228

Sistrunk, Carol, *Chief Librn,* Veterans Administration, Medical Library, Jackson MS. 601-362-4471, Ext 322

Sistrunk, Helen Anna, *Asst Dir, Tech Serv & Rare Bks,* Campbell University, Carrie Rich Memorial Library, Buies Creek NC. 919-893-4111, Ext 238

Sistrunk, James D, *Dir,* Campbell University, Carrie Rich Memorial Library, Buies Creek NC. 919-893-4111, Ext 238

Sites, Katherine P, *Librn,* United States Army (Fort Monroe Post Library), Fort Monroe VA. 804-727-2111

Sites, Margaret E, *ILL & Ref,* Columbia College, J Drake Edens Library, Columbia SC. 803-786-3878

Sitler, Bryon, *AV,* Northern Illinois Library System, Rockford IL. 815-229-0330

Sitterding, Linda, *Ch,* Madera County Library, Madera CA. 209-674-4641, Ext 263

Sitz, Peggy, *Librn,* Harney County Library, Burns OR. 503-573-6670

Sitzer, Evelyn B, *Dir of Research,* George S Armstrong & Co Inc Library, New York NY. 212-889-2280

Sivertsen, Gary L, *Assoc Dean,* Fort Steilacoom Community College, Learning Resources Center, Tacoma WA. 206-964-6549

Sivertsen, Ruth, *Librn,* New Bethlehem Area Free Public Library, New Bethlehem PA. 814-275-2870

Sivwright, Charleen, *Librn,* Rockwell Public Library, Rockwell IA. 515-822-3268

Six, Ruth, *Librn,* Gassaway Public Library, Gassaway WV. 304-364-8292

Sixton, Sally, *Ref,* Miami Valley Hospital, Memorial Medical Library, Dayton OH. 513-223-6192

Size, Bette, *Librn,* Iron Bridge Public Library, Iron Bridge ON. 705-843-2192

Sizemore, Earline, *Librn,* Appalachian Regional Hospital, Medical Library, Beckley WV. 304-255-3000

Sizemore, Ellen, *Librn,* Prescott City Public Library, Prescott KS. 913-471-2431

Sizemore, Jean, *Dir,* Portage County District Library, Hiram OH. 216-569-7666

Sizer, Samuel, *Spec Coll,* University of Arkansas Libraries, Fayetteville AR. 501-575-4101

Sjoblom, Jorma J, *Acq,* University of Baltimore, Langsdale Library, Baltimore MD. 301-727-6350, Ext 444

Sjostrom, Joan, *Dir,* Norwalk Hospital (R Glen Wiggans Memorial Library), Norwalk CT. 203-852-2793

Skaggs, Betty A, *Librn,* Oklahoma County Law Library, Oklahoma City OK. 405-236-2727, Ext 291

Skaggs, Gwinn, *Media,* Campbellsville College Library, Campbellsville KY. 502-465-8158, Ext 272

Skaggs, Susan, *Ch,* Fairfield Public Library, Fairfield IA. 515-472-6551

Skallerud, Carol, *Circ,* University of South Dakota, Christian P Lommen Health Sciences Library, Vermillion SD. 605-677-5347

Skallerup, Harry R, *Dir,* Florida Atlantic University, S E Wimberly Library, Boca Raton FL. 305-395-5100, Ext 2448

Skarbek, Valeria, *Librn,* Public Library of Annapolis & Anne Arundel County Inc (Riviera Beach), Pasadena MD. 301-255-7600

Skaredoff, Georgiana, *Tech Serv,* Daemen College, Marian Library, Amherst NY. 716-839-3600, Ext 243

Skarr, Robert J, *Librn,* Jack Faucett Associates Library, Chevy Chase MD. 301-657-8223, Ext 47, 48

Skau, Dorothy B, *Librn,* United States Department of Agriculture, Southern Regional Research Center, New Orleans LA. 504-589-7072

Skeen, Douglas, *Librn,* Baltimore County Circuit Court, Law Library, Towson MD. 301-494-3086

Skelley, Grant T, *Assoc Prof,* University of Washington, School of Librarianship, WA. 206-543-1794

Skelton, Dortha H, *Ref,* College of William & Mary in Virginia, Earl Gregg Swem Library, Williamsburg VA. 804-253-4404

Skelton, Juanita, *Assoc Prof,* University of Georgia, Dept of Educational Media & Librarianship, GA. 404-542-3810

Skelton, L Wayne, *Dir,* Greenwood-Leflore Public Library System, Greenwood MS. 601-453-3634

Skelton, Victoria, *Instr,* Cambrian College of Applied Arts & Technology, Library Techniques Program-Programme en Bibliotheques, ON. 705-566-8101

Skelton, William, *Assoc Dir Mgt Servs,* Fort Vancouver Regional Library, Vancouver WA. 206-695-1561

Skemer, Margaret, *Cat,* Mannes College of Music, Harry Scherman Library, New York NY. 212-737-0700, Ext 9

Skenadore, Lynne, *Dir,* Menominee County Library, Keshena WI. 715-799-3920

Skerrett, Claire, *Ch & YA,* Lower Merion Library Association, Bryn Mawr PA. 215-527-3889

Skerrett, Claire, *Ch,* Ludington Public Library, Bryn Mawr PA. 215-527-1550, 525-1776

Skerritt, Elizabeth, *Librn,* International Paper Co, Corporate Information Center, New York NY. 212-490-5952

Skertic, Stephen, *Ref,* Lorain County Community College Library, Elyria OH. 216-365-4191, Ext 201

Skibo, Polly J, *Librn,* Joy Manufacturing Co Library, Michigan City IN. 219-872-7221

Skica, Janice, *AV & Per,* Hahnemann Medical College & Hospital of Philadelphia, Warren H Fake Library, Philadelphia PA. 215-448-7186

Skidmore, Carolyn, *Dir,* West Virginia Department of Education, Education Media Center, Charleston WV. 304-348-3925

Skidmore, Mary, *Librn,* Arlington County Department of Libraries (Shirlington), Arlington VA. 703-578-4911

Skidmore, Stephen C, *Per,* Roosevelt University, Murray-Green Library, Chicago IL. 312-341-3639

Skidmore, Warren, *Lang, Lit, Hist,* Akron-Summit County Public Library, Akron OH. 216-762-7621

Skifstad, Carmen, *Ad & Ref,* Carleton A Friday Memorial Library, New Richmond Public Library, New Richmond WI. 715-246-2364

Skiles, Jo, *Librn,* State Board of Vocational Education, Division of Vocational Rehabilitation, State Development Library, Institute WV. 304-768-8861, Ext 289

Skiles, William, *Per,* Southwestern at Memphis, Burrow Library, Memphis TN. 901-274-1800, Ext 365, 366

Skillern, Elizabeth, *Cat,* Jefferson County Public Library, Lakewood CO. 303-238-8411

Skillman, Gaynia S, *Librn,* Fish Memorial Hospital, Medical Library, De Land FL. 904-734-2323

Skinkle, John, *Cat & Ref,* Northeast Georgia Regional Library System, Clarkesville GA. 404-754-4413

Skinner, Aubrey E, *Librn,* University of Texas Libraries (Chemistry), Austin TX. 512-471-1303

Skinner, Barbara, *Librn,* Whatcom County Public Library (Everson Community), Everson WA. 206-966-5100

Skinner, Debra, *Commun Servs,* Chatham-Effingham-Liberty Regional Library, Savannah Public Library, Savannah GA. 912-234-5127

Skinner, Diana, *Tech Serv,* Spring Arbor College, Hugh A White Library, Spring Arbor MI. 517-750-1200, Ext 234

Skinner, Elizabeth, *Acq,* Public Library of Columbus & Franklin County, Columbus OH. 614-864-8050

Skinner, George E, *Dir,* University of Arkansas Libraries (Law), Fayetteville AR. 501-575-5604

Skinner, Gisele, *ILL & Bibliog Instr,* Utica College of Syracuse University, Frank E Gannett Memorial Library, Utica NY. 315-792-3041

Skinner, Irene V, *Librn,* Coulterville Public Library, Coulterville IL. 618-758-3013

Skinner, Jane, *On-Line Servs,* Indiana University-Purdue University at Fort Wayne Library, Walter E Helmke Library, Fort Wayne IN. 219-482-5456

Skinner, Linde J, *Learning Resources Librn,* Indiana State University, Evansville Library, Evansville IN. 812-464-1824

Skinner, Lois M, *Librn,* Ethyl Corp, Chemical Research Development Library, Baton Rouge LA. 504-359-2011

Skinner, Robert, *Librn,* Southern Methodist University Libraries (Music), Dallas TX. 214-692-2894

Skinner, Ted R, *Ref,* Mountain View College, Learning Resources Center, Dallas TX. 214-746-4169

Skinner, Tom, *Tech Serv,* Southern Alberta Institute of Technology, Learning Resources Centre, Calgary AB. 284-8647; 284-8648

Skinner, Vicki, *Popular Libr,* Austin Public Library, Austin TX. 512-472-5433

Skipper, Marie, *Tech Serv,* Mobile Public Library, Mobile AL. 205-438-7073

Skipper, Peggy, *Librn,* Uncle Remus Regional Library (Jasper County), Monticello GA. 404-468-6966
Skipsna, Alvin, *Dir,* Skidmore College, Lucy Scribner Library, Saratoga Springs NY. 518-584-5000, Ext 234
Skirrow, Helen, *Head Libr Servs Unit,* Alberta Education Library, Edmonton AB. 403-427-2985
Skirvin, Shirley, *Librn,* Auburn Theological Seminary, Auburn-Union Lending Library, New York NY. 212-662-4315
Skjellum, Hazel, *Tech Serv,* Orlando Public Library, Orlando FL. 305-425-4694
Skladanowski, Larry, *On-Line Servs & Bibliog Instr,*Lorillard Research Center Library, Greensboro NC. 919-373-6895
Skokan, Anne, *ILL,* New Hyde Park Public Library, New Hyde Park NY. 516-354-1413
Skold, Marlene, *Librn,* Our Redeemers Lutheran Church Library, Benson MN. 612-843-3151
Skonezny, Nancle, *Librn,* Brush Wellman, Inc, Technical Library, Cleveland OH. 216-486-4200
Skoog, Anne, *Rare Bks,* Carnegie-Mellon University, Hunt Library, Pittsburgh PA. 412-578-2446, 578-2447
Skowronska, Helen, *Librn,* Sherwin Williams Chemicals (Technical Library), Cleveland OH. 216-566-2858
Skowronski, Nancy, *Coordr Tech Serv,* University of Detroit Library, Detroit MI. 313-927-1090
Skrdle, Lacreta, *Circ,* Cameron University Library, Lawton OK. 405-248-2200, Ext 410
Skrede, Mary L, *Dir,* McIntosh Memorial Library, Viroqua WI. 608-637-7151
Skriver, Marianne, *Music & Fine Arts,* Morris County Free Library, Whippany NJ. 201-285-6101
Skrobela, Katherine, *Librn,* Middlebury College (Music), Middlebury VT. 802-388-4256
Skrzeszewski, Stan, *Dir,* Parkland Regional Library, Yorkton SK. 306-783-2876
Skubish, Karen, *Supvr, Main Reading Room,* Newberry Library, Chicago IL. 312-943-9090
Skuja, Lucija, *Music & Art,* Grand Rapids Public Library, Grand Rapids MI. 616-456-4400
Skuja, V Peter, *Librn,* Blodgett Memorial Medical Center, Richard R Smith Medical Library, Grand Rapids MI. 616-774-7624
Skurdenis, Julian, *Tech Serv,* Bronx Community College Library, Bronx NY. 212-367-7300, Ext 315
Skymba, Joseph, *Media,* Carlsbad City Library, Carlsbad CA. 714-438-5614
Skynner, H J, *Assoc Dir Tech Servs,* University of Manitoba Libraries, Winnipeg MB. 204-474-9881
Skyrm, Sally, *Assoc Librn,* State University of New York College at Potsdam (Crane School of Music, Julia E Crane Memorial Library), Potsdam NY. 315-268-3019
Slack, Kenneth T, *Dir,* Marshall University, James E Morrow Library, Huntington WV. 304-696-3120
Slack, Lois, *Librn,* Webster Parish Library (Sarepta Branch), Sarepta LA. 318-377-1411
Slack, Lucille, *Librn,* Datacrown Library, Willowdale ON. 416-499-1012, Ext 502
Slack, Marion, *ILL & Ref,* Framingham State College, Henry Whittemore Library, Framingham MA. 617-620-1220, Ext 273
Slade, Alexander, *ILL,* University of Waterloo Library, Waterloo ON. 519-885-1211
Slade, Alexander, *Psychol & Sociol,* University of Waterloo Library, Waterloo ON. 519-885-1211
Slade, Cynthia, *Librn,* Murray State University (Science), Murray KY. 502-762-2291
Slade, Joseph, *Spec Coll,* Wagner College, Horrmann Library, Staten Island NY. 212-390-3001
Slade, Louise, *Librn,* Colorado State Department of Natural Resources (Colorado Geological Survey Library), Denver CO. 303-839-2611
Slade, Marylin, *Bkmobile Coordr,* Maurice M Pine Free Public Library, Fair Lawn NJ. 201-796-3400
Slade, Rodney, *On-Line Servs,* University of Oregon Library, Eugene OR. 503-686-3056
Sladky, Marie, *Cat,* University of Minnesota, Duluth, Duluth MN. 218-726-8100
Slager, Colleen, *Acq,* Western Theological Seminary, Beardslee Library, Holland MI. 616-392-8555, Ext 37 & 38

Slagle, Anna, *Bus Officer,* King College, E W King Library, Bristol TN. 615-968-1187, Ext 215
Slagle, Frances, *Dir,* Edwards Public Library, Henrietta TX. 817-538-4791
Slagle, June, *Librn,* Hart Public Library, Hart MI. 616-873-4476
Slagle, Roberta J, *Librn,* Sullivan County Public Library, Blountville TN. 615-323-5301
Slaight, Wilma, *Archives,* Wellesley College, Margaret Clapp Library, Wellesley MA. 617-235-0320, Ext 280
Slain, Marion, *Info Specialist,* McCaffrey & McCall Inc Library, New York NY. 212-421-7500, Ext 274
Slama, Betty, *Supvry Librn,* Ventura County Library Services Agency (Simi Valley Branch), Simi Valley CA. 805-526-1735
Slama, Michael M, *Dir,* Moorpark College Library, Moorpark CA. 805-529-2321, Ext 270
Slamin, Mary B, *Librn,* Framingham Public Library (Sturtevant), Framingham MA. 617-873-8114
Slamkowski, Donna, *Librn,* Minnesota Energy Agency Library, Saint Paul MN. 612-296-8902
Slane, Colette, *Tech Serv,* Dunlap Public Library District, Dunlap IL. 309-243-5716
Slaney, Robert, *Dir Libr Serv,* College of the Mainland, Learning Resources Center, Texas City TX. 713-938-1211, Ext 447
Slate, Ted, *Dir,* Newsweek, Inc, General Library, New York NY. 212-350-2494
Slater, Evelyn, *Tech Serv,* Western Texas College, Learning Resource Center, Snyder TX. 915-573-8511, Ext 265
Slater, Francis L, *Libr Systs Develop,* University of Pittsburgh, Hillman Library, Pittsburgh PA. 412-624-4400
Slater, Jack, *Assoc Dir,* Drexel University Library, Philadelphia PA. 215-895-2750
Slater, James R, *Librn,* Free Public Library of Woodbridge (Henry Inman), Colonia NJ. 201-382-5090
Slater, John, *Field Worker (English Lang),* Northeastern Regional Library System, Kirkland Lake ON. 705-567-7043
Slater, June, *Asst Librn,* Potwin Public Library, Potwin KS. 316-752-3253
Slater, Mrs N, *ILL,* Ajax Public Library, Ajax ON. 416-683-6911
Slater, Nancy, *Ad & YA,* Free Public Library of Woodbridge, Woodbridge NJ. 201-634-4450
Slater, Robert O, *Librn,* Center for New Schools Inc Library, Resource Center, Chicago IL. 312-939-7025
Slater, Ron, *Cat,* Laurentian University Library, Bibliotheque de l'Universite Laurentienne, Sudbury ON. 705-675-1151, Ext 251 & 252
Slatoff, Saul H, *Dir,* Kapiolani Community College Library, Honolulu HI. 808-531-4654, Ext 154
Slaton, Gwendolyn, *Media,* Essex County College, Learning Resources Center, Newark NJ. 201-877-3233
Slattery, James J, *Dir,* Lesley College Library, Cambridge MA. 617-868-9600, Ext 170, 171
Slattery, William J, *Mgr,* National Bureau of Standards (Standards Information Service), Washington DC. 301-921-2587
Slatton, Ludene, *Doc,* Abilene Christian University, Margarett & Herman Brown Library, Abilene TX. 915-677-1911, Ext 2344
Slaughter, Catherine, *Librn,* Newberry-Saluda Regional Library, Newberry SC. 803-276-0854
Slaughter, Dorothy L, *Librn,* Van Zandt County Library, Canton TX. 214-567-4276
Slaughter, Ellen, *Asst Dir,* East Point Public Library, East Point GA. 404-761-1222
Slaughter, Helen H, *Acq,* Georgia Southwestern College, James Earl Carter Library, Americus GA. 912-928-1352
Slaughter, Sara B, *Librn,* District of Columbia General Hospital, Medical Library, Washington DC. 202-675-5000
Slaughter, William J, *Assoc Dir, Mgt Servs,* Dallas Public Library, Dallas TX. 214-748-9071
Slaughter, Zella, *Dir,* Hockley County Memorial Library, Levelland TX. 806-894-6750
Slavens, Thomas P, *Prof,* University of Michigan, School of Library Science, MI. 313-764-9376
Slavik, Evelyn, *Dir,* Bethel College Library, Mishawaka IN. 219-259-8511, Ext 54
Slavin, Vicky, *ILL & Ref,* Bedford Free Public Library, Bedford MA. 617-275-9440
Slavinsky, Nancy B, *YA,* Belmont Public Library, Belmont MA. 617-489-2000

Slayton, Gale, *Asst Dir,* Banning Public Library, Banning CA. 714-849-3192
Slayton, Robert, *Dir,* Vincennes University Junior College, Shake Learning Resources Library, Vincennes IN. 812-885-4423
Slebodnik, Patricia, *Ref,* Tehama County Library, Red Bluff CA. 916-527-0604
Sledge, Ina, *Librn,* Southern Illinois University, East Saint Louis Center Library, East Saint Louis IL. 618-271-1937
Sledge, Mrs Terry, *Librn,* Helen Keller Public Library, Tuscumbia AL. 205-383-7065
Sleep, Esther, *Ser,* Brock University Library, Saint Catharines ON. 416-684-7201
Sleeter, Thomas, *Asst Librn,* Elko County Library (Beowawe Library), Beowawe NV. 702-738-3066
Sleeth, James G, *Asst Dir,* Lincoln Library, Springfield Public Library, Springfield IL. 217-753-4900
Sleight, Dorothy M, *Librn,* Century Research Corp Library, Arlington VA. 703-527-5373
Sleight, Frederick W, *Librn,* Palm Springs Desert Museum Library, Palm Springs CA. 714-325-7186
Sleight, Wicky, *Chief Librn,* Texas Department of Water Resources Library, Austin TX. 512-475-3781
Slemmer, William C, *Dir,* Douglas County Library System, Roseburg OR. 503-673-1111, Ext 310
Slenker, Marilyn K, *Asst Dir,* Covenant College, Anna Emma Kresge Memorial Library, Lookout Mountain TN. 615-820-1560, Ext 216
Sletwick, Clarence R, *Chmn,* Pacific Union College, Library Science Dept, CA. 707-965-6241
Sletwick, Clarence R, *Dir,* Pacific Union College, W E Nelson Memorial Library, Angwin CA. 707-965-6241
Sletwick, Marion, *Acq,* Pacific Union College, W E Nelson Memorial Library, Angwin CA. 707-965-6241
Slevinsky, Patricia, *OCLC, Inc Dirs,* University of Connecticut at Hartford (Law Library), West Hartford CT. 203-523-4841, Ext 347, 370
Sliekers, Hendrik, *Dir,* Trinity Christian College Library, Palos Heights IL. 312-597-3000, Ext 55
Sliepcevich, Natalie, *Dir & Cat,* Hearst Free Library, Anaconda MT. 406-563-9990
Sligh, Roberta, *Librn,* Samuel Merritt Hospital, Medical Library, Oakland CA. 415-655-4000, Ext 10
Slight, Judith, *Media,* Forbes Library, Northampton MA. 413-584-8399
Slimp, Fred A, *Humanities & Social Sci,* University of California at Davis, General Library, Davis CA. 916-752-2110
Slinde, Lois, *Dir,* Walworth Memorial Library, Walworth WI. 414-275-6322
Slingerland, Charmaine, *Ser,* Miami University, Edgar W King Library, Oxford OH. 513-529-2944
Slingluff, Deborah H, *Librn,* Enoch Pratt Free Library (Patterson Park), Baltimore MD. 301-396-5430, 396-5395
Slinn, Janet R, *Librn & On-Line Servs,* Digital Equipment Corp, Tewksbury Library, Tewksbury MA. 617-851-5071, Ext 2643
Slinn, Janet R, *Librn,* New England Board of Higher Education Library, Wenham MA. 617-235-8071
Slinn, John D J, *Asst Univ Librn-Central Servs,* Boston College Libraries, Chestnut Hill MA. 617-969-0100, Ext 3195
Slinn, John D J, *Librn,* Boston College Libraries (Bapst (Central Library)), Chestnut Hill MA. 617-969-0100, Ext 3205
Sliver, Betty, *Ch,* Martin Memorial Library, York PA. 717-843-3978
Slivka, Enid M, *Librn,* R W Beck & Associates Library, Seattle WA. 206-622-5000
Slivka, Jacqueline W, *Librn,* United States Navy (Naval Weapons Station Library), Yorktown VA. 804-887-4726, 4720
Slivka, Regina, *YA,* Saint Clair Shores Public Library, Saint Clair Shores MI. 313-771-9020
Sloan, Barbara, *Info Specialist,* European Community Information Service Library, Commission of the European Communities, Washington DC. 202-862-9500
Sloan, Brenda, *Spec Coll,* Virginia State College, Johnston Memorial Library, Petersburg VA. 804-520-6171

Sloan, Charlotte, *Life & Phys Sci,* University of Alabama in Huntsville Library, Huntsville AL. 205-895-6540

Sloan, George W, *Dean,* De Anza College, Learning Center, Cupertino CA. 408-996-4761

Sloan, Steve, *Bkmobile Coordr,* Fort McMurray Public Library, Fort McMurray AB. 403-743-2121

Sloan, Thelma, *Librn,* Overbrook Public Library, Overbrook KS. 913-665-7266

Sloan, Virgene, *Librn,* Woodmen Accident and Life Co Library, Lincoln NE. 402-476-6500, Ext 318

Sloan, William, *Librn,* New York Public Library (Film Library), New York NY. 212-790-6418

Sloan, Jr, Andrew J, *Librn,* Warsaw Public Library, Warsaw IN. 219-267-6011

Sloan, Jr, Royal Daniel, *Dir Govt Serv,* University of Colorado at Boulder (Bureau of Government Research & Service Library), Boulder CO. 303-492-8586

Sloane, Elaine, *Assoc Dir Pub Servs,* University of California, Berkeley (University Library), Berkeley CA. 415-642-3773

Sloane, Grace P, *Librn,* Knott County Public Library, Hindman KY. 606-785-5412

Sloane, Margaret N, *Dir,* City of Cerritos Public Library, Cerritos CA. 213-924-5775

Sloane, Richard, *Librn,* University of Pennsylvania Libraries (Biddle Law Library), Philadelphia PA. 215-243-7488

Sloat, Mrs John, *Librn,* Northminster United Presbyterian Church Library, New Castle PA. 412-658-9051

Slobodchikoff, Nicholas A, *Dir,* Museum of Russian Culture, Inc Library, San Francisco CA. 415-921-4082

Sloboelian, Carol Ann, *Librn,* Reuben & Proctor Library, Chicago IL. 312-558-5500

Slocomb, Mary Ann, *Librn,* Rhode Island Hospital, Peters Memorial Library, Providence RI. 401-277-4671

Slocombe, Patty S, *Librn,* Maritz Inc, Motivation Library, Fenton MO. 314-225-4000, Ext 226

Slocum, Alice, *Librn,* Lenawee County Library (Addison Branch), Addison MI. 517-547-3414

Slocum, Christine, *Librn,* Southworth Library Association, Dryden NY. 607-844-4782

Slocum, Grace P, *Dir,* Cecil County Public Library, Elkton MD. 301-398-0914

Slocumb, J Richard, *Media,* Ocmulgee Regional Library, Eastman GA. 912-374-4711

Sloggy, William E, *Dir,* Vaughn Public Library, Ashland WI. 715-682-3883

Slonski, Frances A, *Librn,* Lake City Library, Lake City PA. 814-774-2116

Sloss, Peggy, *Librn,* Henderson County, Clint W Murchison Memorial Library, Athens TX. 214-675-1717

Slotkin, Helen W, *Rare Bks & Spec Coll,* Massachusetts Institute of Technology Libraries, Cambridge MA. 617-253-5651

Slotkin, Helen W, *Institute Archivist,* Massachusetts Institute of Technology Libraries (Institute Archives & Special Collections), Cambridge MA. 617-253-5688

Slott, Rita Loftus, *Librn,* Citrus College, Hayden Memorial Library, Azusa CA. 213-335-0521, Ext 290, 291

Slotten, Martha, *Spec Coll,* Dickinson College, Boyd Lee Spahr Library, Carlisle PA. 717-245-1396

Slovasky, Stephen, *Cat,* Middlebury College, Egbert Starr Library, Middlebury VT. 802-388-7621

Slovasky, Stephen, *Cat,* Xavier University, McDonald Memorial Library, Cincinnati OH. 513-745-3881

Slowinski, Rose, *Librn,* Evanston Hospital, Webster Medical Library, Evanston IL. 312-492-4585

Sluiter, Barbara, *Cat,* Calvin College & Seminary Library, Grand Rapids MI. 616-949-4000, Ext 297

Slump, Beverly, *Coordr,* Estherville Public Library, Estherville IA. 712-362-3869

Slusarchuk, Alexander R, *Dir,* Westville Historic Handicrafts, Inc Library, Lumpkin GA. 912-838-6310

Slusher, Donna C, *Dir,* Murray Public Library, Murray UT. 801-266-1137

Sly, Dale W, *President,* San Francisco College of Mortuary Science Library, San Francisco CA. 415-567-0674

Smaalders, Oscar W J, *Dir,* Stanislaus County Free Library, Modesto CA. 209-526-6821

Smalko, Claire, *Asst Librn,* Leamington Public Library, Leamington ON. 519-326-3441

Small, Anne, *Librn,* Hamden Library (Mt Carmel), Hamden CT. 203-248-6152

Small, Barbara, *Circ,* West Coast Bible College, McBrayer Library, Fresno CA. 209-299-7205

Small, Constance, *Librn,* New Braintree Public Library, New Braintree MA. 617-867-2350

Small, Doris, *Cat,* Rand Corp Library, Santa Monica CA. 213-393-0411, Ext 369

Small, Edward, *Librn,* Newark Public Library (Vailsburg), Newark NJ. 201-733-7755

Small, Jane, *Librn,* Defiance Public Library, Defiance OH. 419-782-1456

Small, Margaret, *Dir,* Bellport Memorial Library, Bellport NY. 516-286-0818

Small, Marion S, *Asst Curator,* Maine Maritime Museum Library Archives, Bath ME. 207-443-6311

Small, Sally S, *Head Librn,* Pennsylvania State University, Berks Campus Library, Reading PA. 215-375-4211, Ext 22, 23 & 43

Small, Sandra, *Media,* Cary Memorial Library, Lexington MA. 617-862-6288

Small, Jr, Wendell G, *Librn,* State Mutual Life Assurance Co of America Library, Worcester MA. 617-852-1000, Ext 2435

Smalley, Barbara, *Librn,* Nute Public Library (Milton Mills Public), Milton NH. 603-652-4591

Smallman, Mary H, *County Historian,* Saint Lawrence County Research Center Library, Canton NY. 315-386-8118

Smalloy, Topsy N, *Asst Dir,* Clinton Community College, LeRoy M Douglas Memorial Library, Plattsburgh NY. 518-561-6650, Ext 360

Smallwood, Lona, *Acq,* Midwestern State University, George Moffett Library, Wichita Falls TX. 817-692-6611, Ext 204

Smallwood, Wilma, *Spec Coll,* Arizona State Library, Dept of Library, Archives & Public Records, Phoenix AZ. 602-255-4035

Smardo, Toni, *Librn for Serv to Pre-School Ch,* Dallas Public Library, Dallas TX. 214-748-9071

Smarjesse, Myrtle, *Librn,* Memorial Medical Center, Kenneth H Schnepp Medical Library, Springfield IL. 217-788-3336

Smart, Beatrice, *Librn,* Ossipee Public Library, Ossipee NH. 603-539-6390

Smart, Elsie, *Librn,* Pioneer Public Library (Pioneer), Montpelier OH. 419-737-2833

Smart, M, *Ch,* Teck Centennial Library, Kirkland Lake ON. 705-567-7966

Smart, Margaret, *Doc,* Colorado School of Mines, Arthur Lakes Library, Golden CO. 303-279-0300, Ext 2690

Smart, Marriott W, *Librn,* Gulf Mineral Resources Co, Exploration Library, Denver CO. 303-758-1700

Smart, Mrs P, *Librn,* Bryan Public Library (Pioneer Public), Pioneer OH. 419-737-2833

Smedlund, Ruth, *Librn,* International Minerals & Chemical Corp Library, Mundelein IL. 312-566-2600

Smeijers, Rachel, *Tech Serv,* Huron College, Silcox Memorial Library, London ON. 519-438-7224, Ext 13

Smelcer, Josephine, *Librn,* Modoc County Library (Adin), Adin CA. 916-233-2719

Smelkinson, Tenna, *Supvr,* Computer Sciences Corp, Systems Sciences Div, Technical Information Center, Silver Spring MD. 301-589-1545, Ext 517

Smellie, Don C, *Dept Head,* Utah State University, Dept of Instructional Media, UT. 801-750-2694

Smelser, Lawrence, *Prof,* Saint Cloud State University, Center for Library & Audiovisual Education, MN. 612-255-2022

Smeltzer, Dennis K, *Dept Head,* Purdue University-Calumet Campus, Media Sciences Program, IN. 219-844-0520, Ext 335

Smethers, Phyllis, *Acq,* Wharton County Junior College, J M Hodges Learning Center, Wharton TX. 713-532-4560, Ext 36

Smid, Marcelyn J, *Librn,* Saint Paul Bible College, Peter Watne Memorial Library, Saint Bonifacius MN. 612-446-1411, Ext 243

Smigurowski, Mary, *Librn,* Saskatchewan Health Library, Regina SK. 306-565-3090

Smiley, Lucille, *Librn,* Howard University Libraries (Business & Public Administration Library), Washington DC. 202-636-7838

Smiley, Virginia E, *Librn,* Ohio State University Libraries (Commerce Library), Columbus OH. 614-422-2136

Smillie, James B, *Dir,* Susquehanna University, Roger M Blough Learning Ctr, Selinsgrove PA. 717-374-0101, Ext 329

Smillie, Judith R, *Librn,* Ventura Public Library, Ventura IA. 515-829-4410

Smillie, Sella, *Librn,* Irving Public Library System (Northwest), Irving TX. 214-253-2691

Smilnak, Mary Ann, *Exten & Cir,* Four County Library System, Binghamton NY. 607-723-8236

Smink, Esther, *Cat,* Wilkes Community College, Learning Resources Library, Wilkesboro NC. 919-667-7136, Ext 26

Smink, June E, *Librn,* Virginia National Bank Library, Norfolk VA. 804-441-4419

Smink, Nancy, *Distr Consultant,* Pottsville Free Public Library, Pottsville Library District Center, Pottsville PA. 622-8105; 622-8880

Smith, A R, *Interdisciplinary,* Cleveland State University Libraries, Cleveland OH. 216-687-2486

Smith, Agnes, *Tech Serv & ILL,* Liberal Memorial Library, Liberal KS. 316-624-0148

Smith, Al, *Librn,* Georgia Forestry Commission Library, Macon GA. 912-744-3211

Smith, Alice, *Ref,* Cleveland State University Libraries, Cleveland OH. 216-687-2486

Smith, Alice, *Circ & Ref,* Culver-Stockton College, Carl Johann Memorial Library, Canton MO. 314-288-5221, Ext 21

Smith, Alice, *Prof,* University of South Florida, Graduate Department of Library, Media & Information Studies, FL. 813-974-2557

Smith, Alice B, *Asst Librn,* Swedish Medical Center Library, Englewood CO. 303-789-6616

Smith, Alice L, *Librn,* Tekonsha Public Library, Tekonsha MI. 517-767-4769

Smith, Allen, *Asst Prof,* Simmons College, Graduate School of Library & Information Science, MA. 617-738-2225

Smith, Ann, *Media,* Minnesota Valley Regional Library, Mankato MN. 507-387-1856

Smith, Ann M, *Librn,* Enoch Pratt Free Library (Gardenville), Baltimore MD. 301-396-5430, 396-5395

Smith, Ann Montgomery, *Servs to the Blind & Physically Handicapped Consult,* Massachusetts Board of Library Commissioners, Office for the Development of Library Services, Boston MA. 617-267-9400

Smith, Ann S, *ILL,* North Carolina State University, D H Hill Library, Raleigh NC. 919-737-2843, 2595

Smith, Ann Y, *Dir,* Mattatuck Historical Society Library, Waterbury CT. 203-754-5500

Smith, Anne, *Librn,* Harrison Community Library, Harrison MI. 517-539-6711

Smith, Annette, *Librn,* Adams Memorial Library, Woodbury TN. 615-563-5861

Smith, Arlene, *Librn,* Detroit Osteopathic Hospital Corp, Medical Library, Detroit MI. 313-869-1200, Ext 380

Smith, Audrey J, *In Charge,* New York State Library for the Blind & Visually Handicapped, Albany NY. 518-474-5935

Smith, Augustine, *Indian Pamphlet File,* Navajo Community College, Naaltsoos Ba'Hooghan Library, Tsaile AZ. 602-724-6132

Smith, Ava, *Librn,* Kentucky Mountain Bible Institute, Gibson Library, Vancleve KY. 606-666-5000

Smith, Barbara, *Librn,* Austin Memorial Library, Cleveland TX. 713-592-3920

Smith, Barbara, *Librn,* Contra Costa County Library (Lafayette Branch), Lafayette CA. 415-283-3872

Smith, Barbara, *Coordr, Commonwealth Campuses,* Pennsylvania State University, Fred Lewis Pattee Library, University Park PA. 814-865-0401

Smith, Barbara, *Librn,* H L Snyder Memorial Research Foundation, Cecil Snyder Laboratory Library, Winfield KS. 316-221-4080, Ext 6

Smith, Barbara D, *Asst Dir,* Portland Public Library, Baxter Library, Portland ME. 207-773-4761

Smith, Barbara E, *Govt Doc,* Skidmore College, Lucy Scribner Library, Saratoga Springs NY. 518-584-5000, Ext 234

Smith, Barbara E, *Asst Librn,* Webster Parish Library, Minden LA. 318-377-1411

Smith, Barbara I, *Librn,* Virginia Chemicals Inc Library, Portsmouth VA. 804-484-5000, Ext 213

Smith, Barbara J, *Coordr & Media,* Peel Board of Education, J A Turner Professional Library, Mississauga ON. 416-279-6010

Smith, Barbara M, *Prog Dir,* Georgia Conservancy Library, Atlanta GA. 404-262-1967

Smith, Barrett G, *Librn,* Southern California Institute of Architecture, Science-Architecture Library, Santa Monica CA. 213-829-3482

Smith, Bernadine, *Commun Servs,* Monroe County Library System, Monroe MI. 313-241-5277

Smith, Bernice, *ILL & Ref,* Tougaloo College, L Zenobia Coleman Library, Tougaloo MS. 601-956-4941, Ext 271

Smith, Bessie, *Librn,* Baylor University (Music), Waco TX. 817-755-1366

Smith, Betty, *Librn,* Burlington Public Library (Tyandaga), Burlington ON. 416-639-3611, Ext 57

Smith, Betty, *Librn,* Kerrville State Hospital, Professional Library, Kerrville TX. 512-896-2211, Ext 283

Smith, Betty, *Librn,* Lansing Public Library (Jolly Cedar), Lansing MI. 517-374-4260

Smith, Betty, *Cat & Ref,* Walters State Community College, Learning Resource Center, Morristown TN. 615-581-2121, Ext 212

Smith, Betty Anne, *Cat,* Southeastern Baptist Theological Seminary Library, Wake Forest NC. 919-556-3101, Ext 225, 250

Smith, Betty C, *Librn,* Lake City Public Library, Lake City FL. 612-345-4013

Smith, Betty W, *Ch & YA,* Hopkinsville-Christian County Public Library, Hopkinsville KY. 502-886-2341

Smith, Beverly, *Librn,* Wilson County Library, Floresville TX. 512-393-2886

Smith, Bobye Faye, *ILL,* Ocmulgee Regional Library, Eastman GA. 912-374-4711

Smith, Brian C, *Librn,* American Library of Railway and Traction History, Burbank CA. 213-846-6098

Smith, Bruce, *Media,* Greenville Technical College, Learning Resources Center, Greenville SC. 803-242-3170, Ext 321

Smith, C F, *Librn,* Santa Barbara Museum of Natural History Library, Santa Barbara CA. 805-682-4711

Smith, C Richard, *Asst Dir,* Stanford University Libraries, Stanford CA. 415-497-2016

Smith, Carol, *Film,* Jacksonville Public Library System, Haydon Burns Library, Jacksonville FL. 904-633-6870

Smith, Carol, *Spec Coll,* Morgantown Public Library, Morgantown Service Center, Morgantown WV. 304-296-4425

Smith, Carol A, *On-Line Servs,* Arkansas Valley Regional Library Service System, Pueblo CO. 303-542-2156

Smith, Carol T, *Life Sci,* Brigham Young University, Harold B Lee Library, Provo UT. 801-378-2905

Smith, Carole, *Media,* Altadena Library District, Altadena CA. 213-798-0833

Smith, Carolyn, *Cat,* Rockhurst College, Greenlease Library, Kansas City MO. 816-363-4010, Ext 253

Smith, Carolyn L, *Dir & Ad,* Penfield Public Library, Penfield NY. 716-586-4460

Smith, Catherine, *Librn,* Cuyahoga County Public Library (Olmsted Falls Branch), Olmsted Falls OH. 216-235-1150

Smith, Catherine, *Librn,* Saint Luke's Hospital, Health Sciences Library, Denver CO. 303-839-1000, Ext 2460

Smith, Catherine J, *Circ,* Swarthmore College, McCabe Library, Swarthmore PA. 215-447-7477, 447-7480

Smith, Celia, *Br Coordr,* Pemberville Public Library, Pemberville OH. 419-287-4012

Smith, Celia, *Librn,* Pemberville Public Library (Stony Ridge Branch), Stony Ridge OH. 419-837-5948

Smith, Charles, *Tech Serv,* Contra Costa College Library, San Pablo CA. 415-235-7800, Ext 213

Smith, Charlet, *Ad,* Peru Public Library, Peru IN. 317-473-3069

Smith, Christine, *Librn,* Mobil Oil Corp, E & P Division Library, Denver CO. 303-572-2287

Smith, Clarence F, *Chief Librn,* United States Department of Health & Human Services (Food & Drug Administration, Bureau of Radiological Health Library), Rockville MD. 301-443-1039

Smith, Clifford, *Exten,* Salem Public Library, Salem OR. 503-588-6071

Smith, Connie, *Actg Head, Sub-Div of Spec Servs,* North Carolina Agricultural & Technical State University, F D Bluford Library, Greensboro NC. 919-379-7782, 379-7783

Smith, Constance, *Tech Serv & Cat,* Peninsula Public Library, Lawrence NY. 516-239-3262

Smith, Constance, *Acq,* Saint Louis University, Pius XII Memorial Library, Saint Louis MO. 314-658-3100

Smith, Craig, *Ref,* Oregon State Library, Salem OR. 503-378-4243

Smith, Cynthia, *Librn,* Dekalb Library System (Lithonia Branch), Lithonia GA. 404-482-8302

Smith, Cynthia, *Librn, On-Line Servs & Bibliog Instr,* International Nickel Co of Canada Ltd, Technical Library, Toronto ON. 416-361-7641

Smith, Cynthia, *Librn,* New York Public Library (Inwood), New York NY. 212-942-2445

Smith, D Lynne, *Dir,* University of South Carolina, Coastal Carolina College Kimbel Library, Conway SC. 803-347-3161, Ext 242

Smith, Dana R, *Cat,* Shreve Memorial Library, Shreveport LA. 318-221-2614

Smith, Daniel L, *Asst Dir,* Depauw University, Roy O West Library, Greencastle IN. 317-653-9721, Ext 250

Smith, Daniel T, *Librn,* Bradford County Public Library, Starke FL. 904-964-6400

Smith, Darlene, *Librn,* Tucson Electric Power Co, Records Management Library, Tucson AZ. 602-884-3826

Smith, David, *Cat,* Auburn University, Ralph Brown Draughton Library, Auburn AL. 205-826-4500

Smith, David, *Spec Programs of Serv Supvr: Correctional Servs Libr Program,* Chicago Public Library, Chicago IL. 312-269-2900

Smith, David, *Bibliog Projects,* University of Washington Libraries, Seattle WA. 206-543-1760

Smith, David A L, *Librn,* United States Air Force (Langley Air Force Base Library), Langley AFB VA. 804-764-3319, 764-3078

Smith, David R, *Assoc Dir,* Hennepin County Library, Edina MN. 612-830-4944

Smith, David S, *Bibliog Records,* University of Washington Libraries, Seattle WA. 206-543-1760

Smith, Deanna, *Librn,* Delaware County Library, Jay OK. 918-253-8521

Smith, Deatra, *Tech Serv,* Crawfordsville District Public Library, Crawfordsville IN. 317-362-2242

Smith, Diana, *Ch & Tech Serv,* Jennings County Public Library, North Vernon IN. 812-346-2091

Smith, Diane, *Asst Librn,* Pennhurst Center, Staff Library & Pennhurst Clients' Library, Spring City PA. 215-948-3500, Ext 209, 270

Smith, Diane Green, *Asst Prof,* Northeast Louisiana University, Library Science Program, LA. 318-342-4175 & 342-4177

Smith, Donald, *Educ,* Southern Illinois University at Edwardsville, Elijah P Lovejoy Library, Edwardsville IL. 618-692-2711

Smith, Donald A, *Personnel,* University of Toronto Libraries (University Library), Toronto ON. 416-978-2294

Smith, Donald R, *Librn,* Saint Elizabeth Medical Center, Medical Library, Covington KY. 606-292-4048

Smith, Donna, *Librn,* Southern Prairie Library System, Altus OK. 405-477-1930

Smith, Donna Pigg, *Librn,* Altus Library, Altus OK. 405-482-0515

Smith, Dorabeth, *Br Coordr,* Joliet Public Library, Joliet IL. 815-727-4726

Smith, Dorabeth, *Librn,* Joliet Public Library (Joliet Pub), Joliet IL. 815-726-4360

Smith, Doris N, *Librn,* Oregonian Publishing Co Library, Portland OR. 503-221-8131

Smith, Dorman, *Coll Develop,* University of Wisconsin-Parkside Library, Kenosha WI. 414-553-2221

Smith, Dorothy, *Librn,* Batavia Public Library, Batavia IA. 515-662-2317

Smith, Dorothy, *Ad,* Burlington Public Library, Burlington ON. 416-639-3611

Smith, Dorothy, *Doc,* Doane College, Perkins Library, Crete NE. 402-826-2161, Ext 224, 287

Smith, Dorothy, *Librn,* Durham Public Library, Durham ON. 519-369-2107

Smith, Dorothy C, *Assocs,* New York State Library, Albany NY. 518-474-5930

Smith, Dorothy J, *Ref,* Allegheny College, Lawrence Lee Pelletier Library, Meadville PA. 814-724-3363

Smith, Dorothy J, *Librn,* Barnesville Public Library, Barnesville OH. 614-425-1651

Smith, Dorothy K, *Librn,* Levi E Coe Library, Middlefield CT. 203-349-3857

Smith, Dot, *Tech Serv, Cat & Acq,* Rappahannock Community College, North Campus Learning Resource Center, Warsaw VA. 804-333-4024, Ext 208, 209

Smith, Dot, *Tech Serv,* Rappahannock Community College, South Campus Library, Glenns VA. 804-758-5324, Ext 208

Smith, Douglas C, *ILL & Circ,* Orange Coast College Library, Costa Mesa CA. 714-556-5885

Smith, Drucilla L, *Librn,* Pleasant Grove City Library, Pleasant Grove UT. 801-785-3950

Smith, E Jean, *Arts & Archit,* Pennsylvania State University, Fred Lewis Pattee Library, University Park PA. 814-865-0401

Smith, E V, *Dir,* Canada Institute for Scientific & Technical Information, Ottawa ON. 613-993-1600

Smith, Earl, *Media,* J Sargeant Reynolds Community College (Parham Campus Learning Resources Center), Richmond VA. 804-264-3220

Smith, Earl P, *Assoc Prof,* Auburn University, Dept of Educational Media, AL. 205-826-4529

Smith, Ed, *Media,* Illinois Central College, Learning Resources Center, East Peoria IL. 309-694-5461

Smith, Eda B, *In Charge,* Religious Society of Friends, Monthy Meeting Library, New York NY. 212-777-8866

Smith, Edith, *Librn,* King Public Library, King NC. 919-983-3868

Smith, Elaine, *Dir,* Verdigre Public Library, Verdigre NE. 402-668-2677

Smith, Elaine Quintana, *Librn,* Carle Foundation Hospital, Medical Library, Urbana IL. 217-337-3011

Smith, Eldred, *Dir,* University of Minnesota Libraries-Twin Cities, Minneapolis MN. 612-373-3097

Smith, Eleanor, *Librn,* Congregation Beth Shalom, Rabbi Mordecai S Halpern Memorial Library, Oak Park MI. 313-547-7970

Smith, Eleanor E, *Librn,* Edwardsburg Township Public Library, Spencerville ON. 613-658-5575

Smith, Eleanor M, *Librn,* Joseph F Egan Memorial Supreme Court Library, Schenectady NY. 518-382-3310

Smith, Elinore, *Supvr,* Middlesex County Library (Glanworth Branch), Glanworth ON. 519-438-8368

Smith, Elizabeth, *Cat,* East Carolina University, J Y Joyner Library, Greenville NC. 919-757-6514

Smith, Elizabeth, *Doc & Bibliog Instr,* Grand Valley State Colleges, Zumberge Library, Allendale MI. 313-895-6611, Ext 252

Smith, Elizabeth, *Tech Serv & Cat,* Jackson-George Regional Library System, Pascagoula MS. 601-762-3406

Smith, Elizabeth K, *Br Coordr & Br Librn,* Fort Bend County Library, Richmond TX. 713-342-4455

Smith, Elizabeth L, *Mgr,* Campbell-Ewald Co, Reference Center, Warren MI. 313-574-3400, Ext 6102

Smith, Elizabeth Martinez, *County Librn,* Orange County Public Library, Orange CA. 714-634-7841

Smith, Ellen H, *Dir,* D'Youville College, Library Resources Center, Buffalo NY. 716-886-8100, Ext 304

Smith, Elsie, *Circ,* Judson College, Benjamin P Browne Library, Elgin IL. 312-695-2500, Ext 550-553

Smith, Emilie V, *Cat,* University of Kentucky, Margaret I King Library, Lexington KY. 606-257-3801

Smith, Eric, *Librn,* Duke University (Chemistry), Durham NC. 919-684-3004

SMITH

Smith, Esther, *Coll Develop,* Center for Research Libraries, Chicago IL. 312-955-4545
Smith, Ethanne, *Librn,* Perkins School for the Blind (School Libraries), Watertown MA. 617-924-3434, Ext 240
Smith, Eugene, *Law Cat,* State Library of Pennsylvania, Harrisburg PA. 717-787-2646
Smith, Eugene J, *Law, Ref Cat,* State Library of Pennsylvania, Harrisburg PA. 717-787-2646
Smith, Eugenie, *Librn,* Bracebridge Public Library, Bracebridge ON. 705-645-4171
Smith, Eurydice W, *Asst Prof,* North Carolina Central University, School of Library Science, NC. 919-683-6485
Smith, Evelina, *Librn,* Kent State University, Trumbull County Campus Library, Warren OH. 216-847-0571
Smith, Evelyn, *Librn,* Lost River Community Library, Arco ID. 208-527-8511
Smith, Evelyn, *Cat,* University of Michigan (Law Library), Ann Arbor MI. 313-764-9322
Smith, Faith, *Librn,* Wahoo Public Library, Wahoo NE. 402-443-3871
Smith, Floda V, *Librn,* Union College Library, Lincoln NE. 402-488-2331, Ext 316
Smith, Flora, *Librn,* Allendale-Hampton-Jasper Regional Library (Hampton), Allendale SC. 803-584-3513
Smith, Frances, *Librn,* Nicholson Memorial Public Library (Greggton), Longview TX. 214-759-4331
Smith, Frances, *Librn & On-Line Servs,* Straub Clinic & Hospital, Inc, Arnold Library, Honolulu HI. 808-544-0317, Ext 317
Smith, Frances, *Asst Librn,* United States Court of Appeals, Fifth Circuit Library, New Orleans LA. 504-589-6510
Smith, Frances E, *Librn,* United States Navy (Naval Air Station Library), Millington TN. 901-872-5683
Smith, Franklin L, *Librn,* Oregon State Correctional Institution Library, Salem OR. 503-378-4780
Smith, Fred, *Per,* College of New Rochelle, Gill Library, New Rochelle NY. 914-632-5300, Ext 347
Smith, Fred, *Bibliog Instr,* Shippensburg State College, Ezra Lehman Memorial Library, Shippensburg PA. 717-532-1463
Smith, Frederick, *Per,* Columbus College, Simon Schwob Memorial Library, Columbus GA. 404-568-2042
Smith, Frederick E, *Librn,* University of California Los Angeles Library (Law), Los Angeles CA. 213-825-7826
Smith, Frederick E, *Dir,* Westminster College, McGill Library, New Wilmington PA. 412-946-8761, Ext 342
Smith, Gail, *Asst Librn,* Ayerst Labs Inc Library, Science Library, Rouses Point NY. 518-297-6611, Ext 293
Smith, Gene, *Pres,* Theosophical Book Association for the Blind, Baker Memorial Library, Ojai CA. 805-646-2121
Smith, Geneva, *Librn,* Knoxville-Knox County Public Library (Halls), Knoxville TN. 615-922-2552
Smith, George F, *Dir,* International College of Surgeons, Hall of Fame Library, Chicago IL. 312-642-3555
Smith, Georgeianna, *ILL,* Westwood Public Library, Westwood MA. 617-326-7562
Smith, Gerald A, *Dir,* San Bernardino County Museum Library, Redlands CA. 714-792-1334
Smith, Geraldine, *Dir,* McCord Memorial Library, North East PA. 814-725-4057
Smith, Geraldine D, *Hosp Librn,* Berkshire Athenaeum, Pittsfield Public Library, Pittsfield MA. 413-442-1559
Smith, Grace E, *Therapist Technician,* Wichita Falls State Hospital, Medical & Patient's Library, Wichita Falls TX. 817-692-1220, Ext 307, 309
Smith, H, *Librn,* University of Toronto Libraries (Erindale College), Mississauga ON. 416-828-5235
Smith, Hardin E, *Dir,* Jackson County Library System, Medford OR. 503-776-7281
Smith, Harold F, *Dir,* Park College Library, Parkville MO. 816-741-2000, Ext 254
Smith, Harriet, *Ch,* Georgia Southern College Library, Statesboro GA. 912-681-5115
Smith, Harriet, *Instr,* Georgia Southern College, Library - Media, GA. 912-681-5204
Smith, Harriet E, *Librn,* Supreme Court Library, White Plains NY. 914-682-2574
Smith, Hazel, *Librn,* University of Florida, Agricultural Research & Education Center Library, Bradenton FL. 813-755-1568
Smith, Heidi Jaeger, *Librn,* Santa Cruz Public Library (Aptos Branch), Aptos CA. 408-688-5688
Smith, Helen, *Librn,* Public Library of Cincinnati & Hamilton County (Loveland), Cincinnati OH. 513-683-3322
Smith, Helen, *Spec Coll,* Worcester State College, Learning Resources Center, Worcester MA. 617-752-7700, Ext 132, 135
Smith, Helen G, *Librn,* Sodus Free Library, Sodus NY. 315-483-9292
Smith, Helen L, *Librn,* Thomas County Historical Library, Colby KS. 913-462-6972
Smith, Helen M, *Librn,* Aiken-Bamberg-Barnwell-Edgefield Regional Library (Blackville Branch), Blackville SC. 803-648-8961
Smith, Helen M, *Dir,* Greece Public Library, Rochester NY. 716-225-8930, 225-8951
Smith, Helena D, *Supvr,* Middlesex County Library (Harrietsville Branch), Harrietsville ON. 519-438-8368
Smith, Henry M, *Dir,* United Way of America, Information Center Library, Alexandria VA. 703-836-7100, Ext 384
Smith, Hope, *Librn,* American Bibliographical Center of ABC-CLIO, Inc, Inge Boehm Library, Santa Barbara CA. 805-963-4221
Smith, Howard M, *Librn,* Richmond Public Library, Richmond VA. 804-780-4256
Smith, Hugh L, *Assts To Chief Librarian,* University of Toronto Libraries (University Library), Toronto ON. 416-978-2294
Smith, Ilene N, *Librn,* Rockingham Memorial Hospital, Health Sciences Library, Harrisonburg VA. 703-433-8311, Ext 442
Smith, Irma, *Asst Librn,* Chatham College, Jennie King Mellon Library, Pittsburgh PA. 412-441-8200, Ext 220 & 221
Smith, J, *Asst Librn,* Santa Fe Springs City Library, Santa Fe Springs CA. 213-868-7738
Smith, J B, *Tech Serv,* Union Pacific Railroad Library, Omaha NE. 402-271-4785
Smith, J Edward, *Dir,* Capital Library Cooperative, Mason MI. 517-676-9511
Smith, J Edward, *Dir,* Ingham County Library, Library Service Center, Mason MI. 517-676-9088
Smith, Jacqueline V, *Librn,* Jackson Metropolitan Library (Albemarie), Jackson MS. 601-352-3677
Smith, James, *Librn,* Merrimack Valley College Library, Manchester NH. 603-668-0700
Smith, James E, *Librn,* Chicago Public Library (Toman), Chicago IL. 312-521-8114
Smith, James H, *Dir,* Thomas Public Library, Peach Public Libraries, Fort Valley GA. 912-825-8540
Smith, James L, *Sch Libr Media Specialists,* Maryland State Department of Education, Division of Library Development & Services, Baltimore MD. 301-796-8300, Ext 284
Smith, James O, *Librn,* W R Grace & Co, Law Library, New York NY. 212-764-5960
Smith, Jan, *Librn,* James V Brown Library of Williamsport & Lycoming County (Newberry), Williamsport PA. 717-322-3551
Smith, Jane, *Per,* Jacksonville State University Library, Jacksonville AL. 205-435-9820, Ext 213, 214
Smith, Jane, *Gen Consult,* Mississippi Library Commission, Jackson MS. 601-354-6369
Smith, Jane E, *Media,* Urbandale Public Library, Urbandale IA. 515-278-3945
Smith, Jane F, *Dir,* Boone County Public Library, Florence KY. 606-371-6222
Smith, Jane Fulton, *Exec Dir,* Southeastern New York Library Resources Council, NY. 914-471-0625
Smith, Janelle, *Acq,* Sul Ross State University, Bryan Wildenthal Memorial Library, Alpine TX. 915-837-3461
Smith, Janet, *Programs & Exhibits Coordr,* Chicago Public Library (Cultural Center), Chicago IL. 312-269-2820
Smith, Janet, *Asst Librn,* Goodnow Library, Sudbury MA. 617-443-9112
Smith, Janet, *Librn,* Highland Rim Regional Library Center, Murfreesboro TN. 615-893-3380
Smith, Janet, *Librn,* Jackson-George Regional Library System (George County), Lucedale MS. 601-947-2123
Smith, Janet, *Tech Serv, Acq & Cat,* Northeast Missouri Library Service, Kahoka MO. 816-727-2327
Smith, Janet, *Librn,* Saint Joseph Hospital, Health Sciences Library, Flint MI. 313-762-8519
Smith, Janet, *Ch,* Willingboro Public Library, Willingboro NJ. 609-877-6668
Smith, Janet B, *Librn,* Federal Home Loan Bank Board (Research Library), Washington DC. 202-377-6296
Smith, Jean, *Librn,* Hennepin County Library (Saint Anthony), St Anthony MN. 612-781-1900
Smith, Jean, *President,* Southern Oregon Library Federation, OR. 503-776-7285
Smith, Jean M, *Media,* School of the Ozarks, Lyons Memorial Library, Point Lookout MO. 417-334-6411, Ext 460
Smith, Jeanette, *Librn,* Jesse F Hallett Crosby Memorial Library, Crosby MN. 218-546-8005
Smith, Jeanette, *Librn,* Duluth Public Library (Lincoln), Duluth MN. 218-722-7232
Smith, Jeanette, *Librn,* Saint Louis Public Library (Julia Davis), Saint Louis MO. 314-383-3021
Smith, Jessie C, *Dir,* University of Maryland-Eastern Shore, Frederick Douglass Library, Princess Anne MD. 301-651-2200, Ext 229
Smith, Jessie Carney, *Librn,* Fisk University, Faculty of Education, TN. 615-329-9111, Ext 208
Smith, Jessie Carney, *Dir,* Fisk University Library & Media Center, Nashville TN. 615-329-8730
Smith, Jewell, *Supvr,* Southwest Missouri Library Network, MO. 417-869-4621
Smith, Jewell, *Dir,* Springfield-Greene County Library, Springfield MO. 417-869-4621
Smith, Jewell, *Librn,* Tulare County Library System (Lindsay Branch), Lindsay CA. 209-562-3021
Smith, Jill, *Librn,* Woodbury Library, Woodbury CT. 203-263-3502
Smith, Jimmie, *Asst Librn,* Hobbs Public Library, Hobbs NM. 505-397-2451
Smith, Jo Ann, *Dir,* Saint Louis Christian College Library, Florissant MO. 314-837-6777
Smith, Jo Therese, *Librn & Bibliog Instr,* Witco Chemical Corp, Corporate Technical Center Library, Oakland NJ. 201-337-5812, Ext 315
Smith, Joan A, *Dir,* York Public Library, York ME. 207-363-2818
Smith, Joan M B, *Librn,* William Beaumont Hospital, Medical Library, Royal Oak MI. 313-288-8340
Smith, Joan N, *ILL & Ref,* Huntingdon County Library, Huntingdon PA. 814-643-0200
Smith, JoAnne, *Librn,* Lebanon Public Library, Lebanon IL. 618-537-4504
Smith, Jodi, *Govt Docs,* Jacksonville Public Library System, Haydon Burns Library, Jacksonville FL. 904-633-6870
Smith, John Brewster, *Dir,* State University of New York, Frank Melville Jr Memorial Library, Stony Brook NY. 516-246-5650
Smith, John M, *Tech Serv,* University of Texas Medical Branch, Moody Medical Library, Galveston TX. 713-765-1971
Smith, Josten W, *Assoc Dir,* Buffalo & Erie County Historical Society Library, Buffalo NY. 716-873-9644
Smith, Joyce, *Huntsville Subregional Libr for the Blind & Physically Handicapped,* Huntsville-Madison County Public Library, Huntsville AL. 205-536-0021
Smith, Juanita, *Rare Bks & Spec Coll,* Ball State University, Alexander M Bracken Library, Muncie IN. 317-285-6261
Smith, Juanita, *Asst Librn,* Duncan Memorial Library, Casey Public Library, Casey IA. 515-746-2670
Smith, Judith A, *Dir,* Anson Technical College, Learning Resource Center, Ansonville NC. 704-826-8333, Ext 26
Smith, Judy, *Dir,* Unger Memorial Library, Plainview TX. 806-293-4178
Smith, Julia, *Librn,* Public Library of Nashville & Davidson County (Donelson), Nashville TN. 615-883-7996

Smith, Julie, *Librn,* Montgomery County Department of Public Libraries (Potomac), Rockville MD. 301-365-0662

Smith, Julie L, *Librn & Bibliog Instr,* Saint Joseph Hospital & Childrens Hospital of Orange County, Burlew Medical Library, Orange CA. 714-633-9111, Ext 7291, 7292

Smith, Juliette S, *Dir,* Talladega College, Savery Library, Talladega AL. 205-362-2046

Smith, Karen, *Tech Serv,* Ottawa Public Library, Ottawa ON. 613-236-0301

Smith, Karen, *Doc,* State University of New York at Buffalo (Charles B Sears Law Library), Buffalo NY. 716-636-2043

Smith, Karen, *Bkmobile Coordr,* Walker Memorial Library, Westbrook ME. 207-854-2391

Smith, Karen A, *Coll Develop Consult,* Central Texas Library System, Austin TX. 512-474-5355

Smith, Kate, *Librn,* North Arkansas Regional Library (Eureka Springs Carnegie Public), Eureka Springs AR. 501-253-8754

Smith, Katherine, *Sci,* University of Richmond, Boatwright Memorial Library, Richmond VA. 804-285-6452

Smith, Katherine M, *Pub Servs,* Virginia State Library, Richmond VA. 804-786-8929

Smith, Katherine R, *Librn & On-Line Servs,* University of Richmond-Virginia Institute for Scientific Research, Science Library, Richmond VA. 804-285-6309

Smith, Kathleen W, *Librn,* Coal City Public Library, Coal City IL. 815-634-4552

Smith, Kathryn L, *Librn,* Winter Haven Public Library, Winter Haven FL. 813-294-5964

Smith, Kristi, *Circ,* Kaubisch Memorial Public Library, Fostoria OH. 419-435-2813

Smith, L, *Librn,* Saskatoon Public Library (Carlyle King), Saskatoon SK. 306-664-9592

Smith, L C, *Librn,* Northeast Instrument Co Library, Staten Island NY. 212-448-0933

Smith, Laura, *Soc Sci,* Dayton & Montgomery County Public Library, Dayton OH. 513-224-1651

Smith, LaVerne, *Flm Librn,* Chickasaw Library System, Ardmore OK. 405-223-3164

Smith, LaVerne, *Bkmobile Coordr,* Chickasaw Library System, Ardmore OK. 405-223-3164

Smith, LaVina, *Dir,* Richfield Township Public Library, Saint Helen MI. 517-389-7630

Smith, LaVonna, *Cat,* Ottumwa Public Library, Ottumwa IA. 515-682-7563

Smith, Leigh Ann, *ILL & Ref,* Cumberland Trail Library System, Flora IL. 618-662-2679, 622-2741

Smith, Len, *Math Lab Tech,* State Technical Institute at Memphis, George E Freeman Library, Memphis TN. 901-377-4106

Smith, Len, *Sci,* University of California, University Library, Santa Cruz CA. 408-429-2076

Smith, LePoint C, *Dir,* Bolivar County Library, Robinson-Carpenter Memorial Library, Cleveland MS. 601-843-2774

Smith, Leslie, *Librn,* Northeast Regional Library, Saint Johnsbury VT. 802-748-3428

Smith, Lesly M, *Librn,* Arkansas City Public Library, Arkansas City KS. 316-442-1280

Smith, Lester K, *Assoc Dir,* Northern Illinois University, Founders Memorial Library, De Kalb IL. 815-753-1094

Smith, Letha M, *Librn,* Minneola City Library, Minneola KS. 316-885-4749

Smith, Libby, *Librn,* Environmental Protection Agency (Library Services), Research Triangle Park NC. 919-541-2111

Smith, Linda, *Asst Prof,* University of Illinois, Graduate School of Library Science, IL. 217-333-3280

Smith, Linda L, *Cat,* University of North Florida Library, Jacksonville FL. 904-646-2553

Smith, Linda-Jean, *Librn,* Stradley, Ronon, Stevens & Young Library, Philadelphia PA. 215-569-3800, Ext 294, 321

Smith, Lois, *Dir,* Stanton County Library & Museum, Stanton County Library, Johnson KS. 316-492-2302

Smith, Lois E, *Librn,* South Side Hospital, Medical Library, Pittsburgh PA. 412-481-3300, Ext 324

Smith, Lois H, *Coordr Libr Serv,* Northern Virginia Community College Libraries (Annandale Campus), Annandale VA. 703-323-3128

Smith, Lois W, *Librn,* South Carolina Baptist Hospital, Amelia White Pitts Memorial Library, Columbia SC. 803-771-5281

Smith, Lora E, *Librn,* Anthony Public Library, Anthony KS. 316-842-5344

Smith, Lorene, *Ofc Mgr,* Blount County Library, Maryville TN. 615-982-0981

Smith, Lori, *Librn,* Milford-Whitinsville Hospital Library, Milford MA. 617-473-1190

Smith, Lorre, *Librn,* Madisonville Community College Media Center, Madisonville KY. 502-821-2250, Ext 66

Smith, Lotsee P, *Asst Prof,* Texas Woman's University, School of Library Science, TX. 817-387-2418 & 566-1455

Smith, Louise, *Asst Dir,* Burlington County Lyceum of History & Natural Sciences, Mount Holly Library, Mount Holly NJ. 609-267-7111

Smith, Louise, *Ref,* Victoria Public Library, Victoria TX. 512-578-6241

Smith, Lucille, *Cat,* University of Dallas, William A Blakley Library, Irving TX. 214-438-1123, Ext 328

Smith, Luetta, *Librn,* Palos Park Public Library, Palos Park IL. 312-448-1530

Smith, Lynn, *Ser,* Indiana University (School of Medicine Library), Indianapolis IN. 317-264-7182

Smith, M E, *Librn,* Imperial Oil Ltd, Technical Library, Dartmouth NS. 902-424-7292

Smith, M Jane, *Dir,* Ricks Memorial Library, Yazoo-Sharkey-Issaquena Library System, Yazoo City MS. 601-746-5557

Smith, Mabel, *Librn,* Knox County Public Library, Barbourville KY. 606-546-5339

Smith, Madge, *Ref,* Carbondale Public Library, Carbondale IL. 618-457-0354

Smith, Mara, *Acq,* University of Minnesota, Duluth MN. 218-726-8100

Smith, Margaret, *Br Coordr,* Cape May County Library, Cape May Court House NJ. 609-465-7837

Smith, Margaret, *Librn,* Cherryville Public Library, Cherryville NC. 704-435-6767

Smith, Margaret, *Commun Servs & Br Coordr,* Dakota County Library System, Burnsville MN. 612-435-8111

Smith, Margaret, *Dir,* First Presbyterian Church Library, Gadsden AL. 205-547-5747

Smith, Margaret, *Librn,* Jacksonville Public Library System (Charles D Webb Wesconnett), Jacksonville FL. 904-778-7305

Smith, Margaret, *Ref,* Pennsylvania State University, Behrend College Library, Erie PA. 814-898-1511, Ext 273, 259

Smith, Margaretta W, *Dir,* New York Institute of Technology Library, Old Westbury NY. 516-686-7657, 686-7658

Smith, Marge, *Librn,* Marengo Public Library, Marengo IL. 815-568-8236

Smith, Margery, *Tech Serv & Cat,* Edwin A Bemis Public Library, Littleton Public Library, Littleton CO. 303-795-3826

Smith, Margie, *Librn,* Ruby Pickens Tartt Public Library, Livingston Public Library, Livingston AL. 205-652-2349

Smith, Marian, *On-Line Servs,* General Electric Co (Main Library), Schenectady NY. 518-385-2117

Smith, Marie G, *Cat,* Satilla Regional Library, Douglas GA. 912-384-4667, 384-1172

Smith, Marilyn, *Br Asst,* Timberland Regional Library (White Pass), Packwood WA. 206-494-5111

Smith, Marilyn L, *Librn,* London Public Library, London OH. 614-852-9543

Smith, Marilynn K, *Commun Servs,* United States Military Academy Library, West Point NY. 914-938-2230

Smith, Marion, *Tech Serv,* Kenton County Public Library, Covington KY. 606-292-2363

Smith, Marion, *Cat,* Zion-Benton Public Library District, Zion IL. 312-872-4680

Smith, Marjorie, *Circ,* University of Hawaii (University of Hawaii Library), Honolulu HI. 808-948-7205

Smith, Marjorie I, *Asst Dir,* Wissahickon Valley Public Library, Ambler PA. 215-646-1072

Smith, Martha F, *ILL, Ref & Bibliog Instr,* Claremont Colleges Libraries, Claremont CA. 714-621-8000, Ext 3721

Smith, Martha M, *Librn,* Burbank Hospital School of Nursing, Grace Gummo Library, Fitchburg MA. 617-345-4311, Ext 272

Smith, Martin, *Librn,* University of Texas Libraries (Geology), Austin TX. 512-471-1257

Smith, Marvin E, *Dir,* Fairbanks North Star Borough Public Library & Regional Center, Fairbanks AK. 907-452-5177

Smith, Mary, *Librn,* Concord Free Public Library (Fowler Memorial), Concord MA. 617-369-3110

Smith, Mary, *Asst Librn,* Greene Public Library, Greene IA. 515-823-5642

Smith, Mary, *Librn,* Saint Vincent's Hospital Library, Billings MT. 406-657-7004

Smith, Mary Ann, *Librn,* Kings County Library (Lemoore Branch), Lemoore CA. 209-924-2188

Smith, Mary Ann, *ILL & Circ,* Southwest Foundation for Research & Education, Preston G Northrup Memorial Library, San Antonio TX. 512-674-1410, Ext 226

Smith, Mary Ann C, *Dir,* William B Ogden Free Library, Walton NY. 607-865-5929

Smith, Mary C, *Librn,* Ketchikan Public Library, Ketchikan AK. 907-225-2748

Smith, Mary E, *Librn,* Smith, Kline & French (Canada) Ltd Library, Mississauga ON. 416-821-2200

Smith, Mary Jane, *Librn,* Amherst Public Library (Eggertsville-Snyder), Amherst NY. 716-839-0700

Smith, Mary Kay, *ILL, Instruc Servs & Online Search Coordr,* Bemidji State University, A C Clark Library, Bemidji MN. 218-755-2955

Smith, Mary Kay, *Instr,* Bemidji State University, Library Science Program, MN. 218-755-2955

Smith, Mary Kay, *Librn,* Johnson County Library (Antioch Branch), Merriam KS. 913-831-1550

Smith, Mary L, *Spec Coll & Doc,* Colby Community College, H F Davis Memorial Library, Colby KS. 913-462-3984, Ext 265

Smith, Mary Louise, *Assoc Librn,* Academy of Medicine, William Boyd Library, Toronto ON. 416-964-7088

Smith, Matthew J, *Archivist,* Providence College, Phillips Memorial Library, Providence RI. 401-865-2242

Smith, Maureen, *Cat,* Temple University of the Commonwealth System of Higher Education (Health Science Center), Philadelphia PA. 215-221-4032

Smith, Maureen, *ILL,* Wake County Department of the Public Library, Raleigh NC. 919-755-6077

Smith, Mavis L, *Librn,* Lake County Law Library, Lakeport CA. 707-263-2291

Smith, Maxine, *Dir,* Chautauqua County Historical Society Library, Westfield NY. 716-326-2977

Smith, Maxine, *Lit Searcher,* Environmental Protection Agency, Environmental Research Center Library, Cincinnati OH. 513-684-7701

Smith, Maxine C, *Librn,* United States Army (Southwestern Div Corps of Engineers Library), Dallas TX. 214-767-2325

Smith, Melva, *Asst Librn,* Corunna Public Library, Corunna MI. 517-743-4800

Smith, Merlanne V, *Tech Serv & Cat,* City of Cerritos Public Library, Cerritos CA. 213-924-5775

Smith, Merrill, *Librn,* Massachusetts Institute of Technology Libraries (Rotch Library (Visual Collections)), Cambridge MA. 617-253-7098

Smith, Merrill, *Dir,* Randolph Technical Institute, Learning Resources Center, Asheboro NC. 919-629-1471, Ext 27

Smith, Michael R, *Dir,* Forest Grove City Library, Forest Grove OR. 503-357-3023

Smith, Mickie, *Br Asst,* Catahoula Parish Library (Sicily Island Branch), Sicily Island LA. 318-744-5271

Smith, Mildred, *Librn,* United States Geological Survey, Public Inquiries Office Library, Dallas TX. 214-749-3230

Smith, Mildred W, *Librn,* United States Navy (Operational Test & Evaluation Force Technical Library), Norfolk VA. 804-444-5619

Smith, Moise, *Reader Serv & Circ,* Greenville County Library, Greenville SC. 803-242-5000

Smith, Mrs A, *Supvr,* Edmonton Public Library (Idylwylde), Edmonton AB. 403-469-2743

Smith, Mrs Carl, *Dir,* Park Place Church of God, Carl Kardatzke Memorial Library, Anderson IN. 317-642-0216

Smith, Mrs D, *Librn,* Tottenham Public Library, Tottenham ON. 416-936-2291

Smith, Mrs E W, *Librn,* Thomas County Library (Seneca Branch), Seneca NE. 308-645-2237

Smith, Mrs Floyd, *Curator,* Historical Society of the Tarrytowns' Reference Library, Tarrytown NY. 914-631-8374

SMITH

Smith, Mrs Frankie, *Dir,* Macon County Library, Lafayette TN. 615-666-4340

Smith, Mrs J M, *Librn,* Claiborne County Public Library, Tazewell TN. 615-626-5414

Smith, Mrs J W, *Librn,* Middle Georgia Regional Library (Marshallville Public), Marshallville GA. 912-967-2413

Smith, Mrs John, *Librn,* Johnson County Public Library, Mountain City TN. 615-727-6544

Smith, Mrs L R, *Librn,* Coronation Community Library, Coronation AB. 403-578-3751

Smith, Mrs N R, *Dir,* Fayetteville State University, Charles W Chesnutt Library, Fayetteville NC. 919-486-1232

Smith, Mrs Royal E, *Librn,* Abington Social Library, Abington CT. 203-974-0415

Smith, Mrs Russell D, *Dir,* Bolton Free Library, Bolton Landing NY. 518-644-2233

Smith, Murphy D, *Assoc Librn,* American Philosophical Society Library, Philadelphia PA. 215-627-0706

Smith, Myrtis Y, *Librn,* Aiken-Bamberg-Barnwell-Edgefield Regional Library (Trenton Branch), Trenton SC. 803-648-8961

Smith, Myrtle, *Librn,* Lilbourn Memorial Library, Lilbourn MO. 314-688-2622

Smith, Nadine, *AV,* Wabash Valley College, Bauer Media Center, Mount Carmel IL. 618-262-8641, Ext 225, 226

Smith, Nan, *Acq,* Washington & Lee University (Wilbur C Hall Library), Lexington VA. 703-463-3157

Smith, Nancy, *Dir,* Mesquite Public Library, Mesquite TX. 214-285-6369

Smith, Nancy, *Dep Dir,* West Bloomfield Township Public Library, West Bloomfield MI. 313-682-2120

Smith, Nancy A, *Tech Serv,* Oklahoma City University (Law Library), Oklahoma City OK. 405-521-5271

Smith, Nancy J, *Librn & On-Line Servs,* McLeod Regional Medical Center, Pee Dee Area Health Education Center Library, Florence SC. 803-667-2275, 667-2274

Smith, Nancy K, *Librn,* University of Pennsylvania Libraries (Fels Center of Government), Philadelphia PA. 215-594-8217

Smith, Nancy L, *Librn,* Mount Morris Public Library, Mount Morris IL. 815-734-4927

Smith, Nancy Lee, *Librn,* Clay County Library, Manchester KY. 606-598-2617

Smith, Nathan M, *Assoc Prof,* Brigham Young University, School of Library & Information Sciences, UT. 801-378-2976

Smith, Nellie E, *Librn,* Aiken-Bamberg-Barnwell-Edgefield Regional Library (Aiken County Public), Aiken SC. 803-649-2352

Smith, Nellie Ford, *Asst Librn,* Mississippi College, Leland Speed Library, Clinton MS. 601-924-5131, Ext 232, 307

Smith, Nicholas N, *Dir,* Ogdensburg Public Library, Ogdensburg NY. 315-393-4325

Smith, Norma, *Bkmobile Coordr,* Monroe County Library System, Monroe MI. 313-241-5277

Smith, Norma J, *Dir,* Fondulac Public Library District, East Peoria IL. 309-699-3917

Smith, Norma M, *Librn,* Autaugaville Public Library, Autaugaville AL. 205-365-8261

Smith, P B, *Dir & Bibliog Instr,* Doane College, Perkins Library, Crete NE. 402-826-2161, Ext 224, 287

Smith, Pamela, *Librn,* Brazoria County Library (West Columbia Branch), West Columbia TX. 713-345-3394

Smith, Patricia, *Acq,* Colorado State University, William E Morgan Library, Fort Collins CO. 303-491-5911

Smith, Patricia, *Tech Serv,* Columbia College Library, Chicago IL. 312-663-1600, Ext 465

Smith, Patricia, *Librn,* Kansas City Public Library (Southwest), Kansas City MO. 816-444-7500

Smith, Patricia, *Librn,* New York Public Library (Riverdale), New York NY. 212-549-1212

Smith, Patricia, *Librn,* Virginia College, Mary Jane Cachelin Library, Lynchburg VA. 804-845-0941

Smith, Patricia E, *Tech Servs Admin,* Norton Co Coated Abrasive Div, Technical Library, Watervliet NY. 518-273-0100, Ext 442

Smith, Patricia L, *Dir,* Public Library Services of the Northwest Territories, Hay River NT. 403-874-6531

Smith, Pattisue, *ILL & Ref,* Oklahoma Baptist University, Mabee Learning Center, Shawnee OK. 405-275-2850, Ext 245

Smith, Paula V, *Dir,* Musser Public Library, Muscatine IA. 319-263-3065

Smith, Pauline T, *Lit,* Buffalo & Erie County Public Library System, Buffalo NY. 716-856-7525

Smith, Peggy, *Dir,* Maricopa Technical Community College, Library Resource Center, Phoenix AZ. 602-258-7251, Ext 313

Smith, Philip, *Spec Coll,* Academy of Aeronautics Library, East Elmhurst NY. 212-429-6600

Smith, Phyllis M, *ILL,* Chaffey College Library, Alta Loma CA. 714-987-1737, Ext 303

Smith, Priscilla P, *Librn,* Smithsonian Institution Libraries (Freer Gallery of Art Library), Washington DC. 202-381-5332

Smith, R, *Librn,* Okanagan Regional Library District (Okanagan Falls Branch), Okanagan Falls BC. 604-497-5886

Smith, R A, *Dir,* Algonquin Regional Library System, Parry Sound ON. 705-746-9161

Smith, R B, *Info Spec,* Air Products & Chemicals, Inc (Corporate Library), Allentown PA. 215-398-7288

Smith, R J, *Dept Head,* University of Toronto, Faculty of Education, ON. 416-978-3242

Smith, Rachel, *Cat,* Mississippi College, Leland Speed Library, Clinton MS. 601-924-5131, Ext 232, 307

Smith, Rachel C, *Librn,* Portland Public Library (Jane L Burbank), Portland ME. 207-772-3389

Smith, Raymond W, *Dir,* Four County Library System, Binghamton NY. 607-723-8236

Smith, Rebecca, *Librn,* Argonne National Laboratory (Biology & Medicine), Argonne IL. 312-972-3876

Smith, Rebecca, *Bkmobile Coordr,* H Grady Bradshaw Chambers County Library and Cobb Memorial Archives, Shawmut AL. 205-768-3150

Smith, Rebecca A, *Librn & Ref,* Historical Association of Southern Florida, Charlton W Tebeau Library of Florida History, Miami FL. 305-854-3289

Smith, Regina A, *Circ & Ref,* Villanova University (Pulling Law Library), Villanova PA. 215-527-2100, Ext 702, 703, 704

Smith, Reginald, *Assoc Dir,* College of Medicine & Dentistry of New Jersey, George F Smith Library of the Health Sciences, Newark NJ. 201-456-4580

Smith, Richard, *Bkmobile Coordr,* Public Library of Nashville & Davidson County, Nashville TN. 615-244-4700

Smith, Richard, *Media,* State Library of Ohio, Columbus OH. 614-466-2693

Smith, Rita, *Librn,* Airco Speer Carbon-Graphite, Research Library, Niagara Falls NY. 716-285-6971

Smith, Rita, *Chmn,* Gulf Coast Biomedical Library Consortium, MS. 601-377-2042

Smith, Rita, *Ch,* McAllen Memorial Library, McAllen TX. 512-682-4531

Smith, Rita, *Librn,* United States Air Force (Medical Center Library), Keesler AFB MS. 601-377-2042

Smith, Rita F, *Librn,* United States Air Force (Griffiss Air Force Base Library), Griffiss AFB NY. 315-377-2042

Smith, Rita M, *Automated Cat,* University of Texas Libraries (General), Austin TX. 512-471-3811

Smith, Robert, *Asst Librn,* Fort Hays State University, Forsyth Library, Hays KS. 913-628-4431

Smith, Robert, *Cat,* Vassar College Library, Poughkeepsie NY. 914-452-7000

Smith, Robert C, *Assoc Prof,* Western Kentucky University, Dept of Library Science & Instructional Media, KY. 502-745-3446

Smith, Robert F, *Chief Librn,* Memphis-Shelby County Public Library & Information Center, Memphis TN. 901-528-2950

Smith, Robert J, *Rare Bks,* University Club Library, New York NY. 212-572-3418

Smith, Robert S, *Cat,* Cuyahoga County Public Library (Garfield Heights Branch), Garfield Heights OH. 216-475-8178

Smith, Robin E, *Legis Historian,* Kirkland & Ellis Library, Washington DC. 202-857-5000

Smith, Rodger, *Librn,* South Bend Public Library (Virginia M Tutt), South Bend IN. 219-289-1421

Smith, Rose B, *Librn,* Bay Minette Public Library, Hampton D Ewing Library, Bay Minette AL. 205-937-7947

Smith, Ruby H, *Librn,* Wythe-Grayson Regional Library (Wythe County Public Library), Wytheville VA. 703-228-4951

Smith, Ruby J, *Librn,* Amos Memorial Public Library (Jackson Center Memorial), Jackson Center OH. 513-596-6612

Smith, Ruby Nell, *Br Asst,* Catahoula Parish Library (Jonesville Branch), Jonesville LA. 318-744-5271

Smith, Russell, *Cat,* New Mexico Highlands University, Donnelly Library, Las Vegas NM. 505-425-7511, Ext 331

Smith, Ruth, *Librn,* Cabell County Public Library (Salt Rock Public), Salt Rock WV. 304-523-9451

Smith, Ruth, *Librn,* Grafton Public Library, Grafton IA. 515-748-2735

Smith, Ruth A, *Librn,* Hepler City Library, Hepler KS. 316-368-4379

Smith, Ruth Camp, *Chief Librn,* National Institutes of Health (NIH Library), Bethesda MD. 301-496-4000

Smith, Ruth M, *Librn,* Winnebago County Law Library, Oshkosh WI. 414-235-2500

Smith, Ruth P, *Librn,* Toronto Dominion Bank, Department of Economic Research Library, Toronto ON. 416-866-8068

Smith, Ruth S, *Asst Dir & Ch,* Cynthiana Public Library, Harrison County Library District, Cynthiana KY. 606-234-4881

Smith, Ruth S, *In Charge,* Institute for Defense Analyses, Technical Information Services, Arlington VA. 703-558-1456

Smith, Sadie, *AV, Doc & Spec Coll,* North Carolina Agricultural & Technical State University, F D Bluford Library, Greensboro NC. 919-379-7782, 379-7783

Smith, Sadie, *Archives & Chemistry,* North Carolina Agricultural & Technical State University, F D Bluford Library, Greensboro NC. 919-379-7782, 379-7783

Smith, Sallie, *Librn,* Saint Joe Minerals Corp, Research Dept Library, Monaca PA. 412-774-1020, Ext 481

Smith, Sally, *Asst Librn,* Carrollton Public Library, Carrollton IL. 217-942-6715

Smith, Sallye, *On-Line Servs,* University of Denver, Penrose Library, Denver CO. 303-753-2007

Smith, Sandy, *Clerk,* John McIntire Public Library Public Library (East Fultonham Branch), East Fultonham OH. 614-849-2274

Smith, Saundra, *Reading,* Wayne Community College, Learning Resource Center, Goldsboro NC. 919-735-5151, Ext 64

Smith, Scott, *Per & On-Line Servs,* Nazareth College of Rochester Library, Lorette Wilmot Library, Rochester NY. 716-586-2525, Ext 232

Smith, Sharman, *Info Serv,* Mississippi Library Commission, Jackson MS. 601-354-6369

Smith, Sharon, *Librn,* Mcdowell Technical College Library, Marion NC. 704-652-6021

Smith, Sharon M, *Librn,* Third District Appellate Court Library, Ottawa IL. 815-434-5050

Smith, Sharron, *Tech Serv, Cat & On-Line Servs,* Avon Lake Public Library, Avon Lake OH. 216-933-8128

Smith, Shaughn, *Ch,* Carthage Free Library, Carthage NY. 315-493-2620

Smith, Sheron L, *Cat,* Santa Fe Community College Library, Gainesville FL. 904-377-5161, Ext 315

Smith, Sherrill, *Media & YA,* Saginaw Public Libraries, Hoyt Public Library, Saginaw MI. 517-755-0904

Smith, Sherry, *Br Coordr,* Warren County Library, Monmouth IL. 309-734-6412

Smith, Sherwood, *ILL & Ref,* Borough of Manhattan Community College Library, Martin B Dworkis Library, New York NY. 212-262-3530

Smith, Shirley, *Librn,* Canadian National Railways, Canadian National Telecommunications, Great Lakes Regional Library, Toronto ON. 416-365-3027

Smith, Shirley, *Assoc Dir,* University of Michigan-Dearborn Library, Dearborn MI. 313-593-5400

Smith, Shirley, *State Inst,* West Virginia Library Commission, Science & Cultural Center, Charleston WV. 304-348-2041

Smith, Shirley J, *Dir,* Tulsa Junior College, Learning Resource Center, Tulsa OK. 918-587-6561, Ext 363

Smith, Sibbald, *Superintendent,* National Park Service, Ocmulgee National Monument Resource Center, Macon GA. 912-742-0447

Smith, Sirleine, *Dir,* Eckhart Public Library, Auburn IN. 219-925-2414

Smith, Sister M Elfreda, *Per,* Rosemont College, Gertrude Kistler Memorial Library, Rosemont PA. 215-527-0200, Ext 226

Smith, Sister Pauline, *ILL & AV,* Cardinal Stritch College Library, Milwaukee WI. 414-352-5400, Ext 356

Smith, Sister R Patricia, *Ref & Per,* D'Youville College, Library Resources Center, Buffalo NY. 716-886-8100, Ext 304

Smith, Sister Rita, *Media,* Benedictine College (North Campus Library), Atchison KS. 913-367-5340, Ext 290

Smith, Sister Suzanne, *Librn,* Saint Mary's Health Center Library, Saint Louis MO. 314-644-3000

Smith, Stan, *Dir,* Prince George Public Library, Prince George BC. 604-563-9251

Smith, Stephanie, *Bkmobile Coordr,* Zion-Benton Public Library District, Zion IL. 312-872-4680

Smith, Stephen C, *Librn,* United States Navy (Naval Regional Medical Center Hospital, Memphis), Millington TN. 901-872-5846

Smith, Steve, *AV,* Community College of the Finger Lakes Library, Canandaigua NY. 315-394-3500, Ext 127

Smith, Sue, *Cat,* University of Mississippi Library, University MS. 601-232-7091

Smith, Susan, *Ch,* Beaufort, Hyde, Martin Regional Library, Washington NC. 919-946-6401

Smith, Susan, *Media,* Evergreen State College, Daniel J Evans Library, Olympia WA. 206-866-6262

Smith, Susan, *Ch,* Vineyard Haven Public Library, Vineyard Haven MA. 617-693-9721

Smith, Susan, *Ser & On-Line Servs,* West Georgia College Library, Carrollton GA. 404-834-1370

Smith, Susan, *Librn,* Whitesboro Public Library, Whitesboro TX. 214-564-5432

Smith, Susan A, *Law Librn,* John F Kennedy University Library, Orinda CA. 415-254-0200, Ext 36

Smith, Susan Christine, *Dir,* Harper Grace Hospitals (Grace Hospital School of Nursing Library), Detroit MI. 313-494-6028

Smith, Susan L, *Admin Librn,* United States Navy (Naval Air Station Library), Oak Harbor WA. 206-257-2702

Smith, Sweetman, *ILL & Bus ref,* Fashion Institute of Technology, Library-Media Services Dept, New York NY. 212-760-7695

Smith, Sylvia, *Circ,* Central Florida Regional Library, Ocala Public Library, Ocala FL. 904-629-8551

Smith, Sylvia, *Asst Librn & On-Line Servs,* Texas Department of Water Resources Library, Austin TX. 512-475-3781

Smith, Terry, *Coordr Cent Libr Servs,* London Public Libraries & Museums, London ON. 519-432-7166

Smith, Thedus, *Govt Publ,* Ball State University, Alexander M Bracken Library, Muncie IN. 317-285-6261

Smith, Thelma, *Librn,* Dummer Public Library, Dummer NH. 603-449-6653

Smith, Thomas, *Acq & Ref,* Los Angeles Pierce College Library, Woodland Hills CA. 213-347-0551, Ext 267

Smith, Thomas A, *Mss Librn,* Rutherford B Hayes Library, Fremont OH. 419-332-2081

Smith, Thomas O C, *Librn,* National Park Service, Morristown National Historical Park Library, Morristown NJ. 201-539-2016, 539-2017

Smith, Timothy D, *Asst Librn,* Wytheville Community College Library, Wytheville VA. 703-228-5541, Ext 227

Smith, Toms E, *Librn,* Utica Psychiatric Center, Library Services-Medical (Utica Campus), Utica NY. 315-797-6800, Ext 415

Smith, Valerie, *Ch,* Lorain Public Library, Lorain OH. 216-244-1192

Smith, Vaughn, *Librn,* Brooklyn Public Library (Cypress Hills), Brooklyn NY. 212-277-8257

Smith, Velma, *Librn,* Copiah-Jefferson Regional Library (Jefferson County), Fayette MS. 601-786-3982

Smith, Vera, *Dir,* Stickney-Forest View Library District, Stickney IL. 312-749-1050

Smith, Vicky, *Actg Dir,* Mexico-Audrain County Library, Mexico MO. 314-581-4939, Ext 4940

Smith, Vicky, *Assoc Dean,* Moraine Valley Community College, Learning Resources Center, Palos Hills IL. 312-974-4300, Ext 222

Smith, Victoria, *Acq,* Cumberland County Public Library, Anderson Street Library, Frances Brooks Stein Memorial Library, Fayetteville NC. 919-483-1580

Smith, Virgie B, *Cat,* Washburn University of Topeka (School of Law Library), Topeka KS. 913-295-6688

Smith, Virginia, *ILL,* Louisiana State University Medical Center Library, New Orleans LA. 504-568-6100

Smith, Virginia, *Librn,* Mobile Public Library (Toulminville), Mobile AL. 205-457-1396

Smith, Vivian, *Librn,* Genesee District Library (Davison Area Library), Davison MI. 313-653-2022

Smith, Vivienne, *Librn,* Canada Department of Agriculture, Summerland Research Station Library, Summerland BC. 604-494-7711

Smith, W G, *Film Serv Supvr,* Stamford's Public Library, Ferguson Library, Stamford CT. 203-325-4354

Smith, Wanda B, *Librn,* Green County Law Library, Waynesburg PA. 412-852-1171, Ext 237

Smith, Wayne, *Librn,* Communications Satellite Corp Laboratories, Technical Library, Clarksburg MD. 301-428-4512

Smith, Willamette, *Bkmobile Coordr,* Iberia Parish Public Library, New Iberia LA. 318-369-6321

Smith, William, *Cat,* State Library of Florida, Div of Library Services, Dept of State, Tallahassee FL. 904-487-2651

Smith, William, *Asst Prof,* Western Michigan University, School of Librarianship, MI. 616-383-1849

Smith, Winifred W, *Asst Librn,* South Georgia College, William S Smith Library, Douglas GA. 912-384-1100, Ext 233, 290

Smith, Winona, *Asst Librn,* Hamlin-Lincoln County Public Library, Hamlin WV. 304-824-5481

Smith, Winston H, *Asst Librn,* Presbyterian Hospital (John M Wheeler Library), New York NY. 212-694-2916

Smith, Yvonne B, *Info Spec,* International Flavors & Fragrances, Inc, IFF Research & Development Laboratory, Technical Information Center, Union Beach NJ. 201-264-4500, Ext 521

Smith, III, Newland F, *Dir,* Seabury-Western Theological Seminary Library, Evanston IL. 312-328-9300

Smith, Jr, Jack T, *Acq,* University of Alabama in Birmingham (Lister Hill Library of the Health Sciences), Birmingham AL. 205-934-5460

Smith, Jr, Myron J, *Dir,* Salem College, Benedum Learning Resources Center, Salem WV. 304-782-5238

Smith, Jr, Phillip C, *Reader Serv, On-Line Servs & Bibliog Instr,* University of North Carolina at Wilmington, William Madison Randall Library, Wilmington NC. 919-791-4330, Ext 2270

Smith, Jr, Vincent J, *Cat,* California State University, Fresno Library, Fresno CA. 209-487-2403

Smith-Epps, Paulette, *Librn,* Atlanta Public Library (Peachtree), Atlanta GA. 404-892-3321

Smithbauer, Bette, *Librn,* Ocean County Library (Beachwood Branch), Beachwood NJ. 201-244-4573

Smitherman, Marion, *ILL & Ref,* Burlington County College Library, Pemberton NJ. 609-894-9311, Ext 222

Smithey, Mary, *Librn,* Webster Parish Library (Minden Branch), Minden LA. 318-177-1411

Smithson, Dolores, *Librn,* Tarrant City Public Library, Tarrant AL. 205-841-3292

Smithson, Paul G, *Tech Serv,* Kalamazoo College, Upjohn Library, Kalamazoo MI. 616-383-8481

Smithyman, Ann, *Ad & Ch,* Bayard Taylor Memorial Library, Kennett Square PA. 215-444-2702

Smoak, Deborah, *Librn,* Gates County Library, Gatesville NC. 919-357-0110

Smoak, Lila W, *Librn,* Colleton County Memorial Library, Walterboro SC. 803-549-5621

Smock, Mildred K, *Dir,* Free Public Library, Council Bluffs IA. 712-323-7553

Smock, Stella, *Cat,* Vanderbilt University Library, Nashville TN. 615-322-2834

Smock, William H, *Exec Dir,* Greater New York Safety Council Inc, Accident Prevention Reference Library, New York NY. 212-594-6020

Smolek, J M, *Actg Dir,* Harry Lundeberg School of Seamanship Library, Piney Point MD. 301-994-0010, Ext 248

Smolen, Roberta S, *Librn,* New York Hospital-Cornell Medical Center Libraries (Helen Mitchell Graves Patients' Memorial Library), New York NY. 212-472-6684

Smolenski, Lottie, *Dir,* Hillside Free Public Library, Hillside NJ. 201-923-4413

Smoot, Samille, *Circ,* Medical College of Georgia Library, Augusta GA. 404-828-3441

Smoots, Greg, *Librn,* Cedar Mill Community Library, Portland OR. 503-644-0043

Smorch, Thomas, *Southern Regional Librn,* Genesee District Library, Flint MI. 313-732-0110

Smorjesse, Myrtle, *Coordr,* Capital Area Consortium, IL. 217-788-3336

Smothers, Joyce, *Ch & YA,* Monmouth County Library, Freehold NJ. 201-431-7220

Smothers, Ruby, *Librn,* Shelby County Regional Library (Vincent Branch), Vincent AL. 205-669-7851

Smrekar, Marian N, *Librn,* Kern County Law Library, Bakersfield CA. 805-861-2379

Smuck, Jane, *Librn,* Public Library of Steubenville & Jefferson County (Hilltop), Steubenville OH. 614-282-4031

Smuck, Norman, *Dir,* Northwood Institute Library, West Baden IN. 812-936-9971, Ext 42

Smutny, Paula S, *Librn,* Harmony Public Library, Harmony MN. 507-886-8133

Smyczek, Janet, *Ref,* Spotswood Public Library, Spotswood NJ. 201-251-1515

Smyth, Alice, *Libr Asst,* Harvard University Library (Social Relations Library), Cambridge MA. 617-495-3838

Smyth, Ann, *Librn,* Smith Kline & French Laboratories (Marketing Research Library), Philadelphia PA. 215-854-5328

Smyth, Gary R, *Dir, Learning Systs,* Robert Morris College Library, Coraopolis PA. 412-264-9300

Smyth, Gary R, *Dir, Learning Systs,* Robert Morris College Library, Pittsburgh PA. 412-227-6839

Smyth, Mary Frances, *Librn,* Sullivan Free Library, Chittenango Library, Chittenango NY. 315-687-6331

Smyth, Robert O, *Sr Planner,* New Jersey Department of Community Affairs, Div of State & Regional Planning Library, Trenton NJ. 609-292-6392

Smyth, Sheila A, *Assoc Dir & Tech Serv,* Nazareth College of Rochester Library, Lorette Wilmot Library, Rochester NY. 716-586-2525, Ext 232

Smyth, Verna, *Supvr,* Elgin County Public Library (Vienna Branch), Vienna ON. 519-633-0815

Smythe, Alvetta D, *Librn,* United States Navy (Naval Ship Research & Development Laboratory Technical Library), Annapolis MD. 301-267-6100

Smythe, Andrea, *Librn,* Lambton County Library (Courtright Branch), Courtright ON. 519-867-2712

Snapp, Elizabeth, *Actg Librn,* Texas Woman's University, Bralley Memorial Library, Denton TX. 817-566-6415

Snapp, Suellen, *Librn,* Kane Public & School Libraries, Kane PA. 814-837-9640

Snead, Barbara, *Dir,* Hiram College, Teachout-Price Memorial Library, Hiram OH. 216-569-3211, Ext 220

Snead, George, *Cat,* Portage County District Library, Hiram OH. 216-569-7666

Snead, Karen, *Acq,* Missouri Baptist College Library, Saint Louis MO. 314-434-1115, Ext 73

Snead, Marie E, *Acq,* Indiana University of Pennsylvania, Rhodes R Stabley Library, Indiana PA. 412-357-2340

Snedaker, Dorothy, *Dir, Acq & Cat,* Grafton Public Library, Grafton OH. 216-926-3317

Snedeker, Harold, *Spec Coll,* East Brunswick Public Library, East Brunswick NJ. 201-254-1220

Snediker, Helen L, *Young People,* Spokane Public Library, Comstock Building Library, Spokane WA. 509-838-3361, Ext 65

Sneed, John, *AV,* Catonsville Community College, Learning Resources Div, Baltimore MD. 301-455-4586

Sneed, Marilynn, *In Charge,* Northrop Corp, Electro-Mechanical Division, Technical Information Center Library, Anaheim CA. 714-871-5000

Sneid, Madeline, *Librn,* Congoleum Corporation, Inc, Technical Research Library, Trenton NJ. 609-587-1000, Ext 339

Snell, J, *Librn,* London Public Libraries & Museums (Westminster Branch), London ON. 519-685-1333

Snell, Katherine H, *Librn,* Hubbard Free Library, Hallowell ME. 207-622-6582

Snell, Mary Kay, *Asst Dir & Br Coordr,* Amarillo Public Library, Amarillo TX. 806-378-3000, Ext 2250

Snell, Sherry, *Asst Librn,* Grant Hospital of Chicago, Medical Library, Chicago IL. 312-883-2230

Snelling, Kathleen, *Librn,* Tripoli Public Library, Tripoli IA. 319-882-4807

Snelson, Pamela, *On-Line Servs,* Drew University, Rose Memorial Library, Madison NJ. 201-377-3000, Ext 469

Sneyd, Elizabeth, *Librn,* Oxford-On-Rideau Township Public Library, Burritt's Rapids ON. 613-269-3636

Snezek, Paul, *Dir,* Wheaton College Library, Wheaton IL. 312-682-5101

Snider, Daniel D, *Librn,* Lovett Memorial Library, Pampa TX. 806-665-3981

Snider, David P, *Dir,* Casa Grande City Library, Casa Grande AZ. 602-836-7242

Snider, Helen, *Dir,* Madisonville Community College Media Center, Madisonville KY. 502-821-2250, Ext 66

Snider, Jack E, *In Charge,* Mid-Appalachia College Council, Inc, TN. 615-968-4433

Snider, Larry, *Support Servs & ILL,* California State University, Long Beach, University Library, Long Beach CA. 213-498-4047

Snider, Neil, *Dir & Acq,* Livingston University, Julia Tutwiler Library, Livingston AL. 205-652-9661, Ext 238

Snider, Rose, *Acq,* Los Angeles Harbor College Library, Wilmington CA. 213-518-1000, Ext 292 & 293

Snider, Sondra, *Ad & Acq,* Upper Arlington Public Library, Upper Arlington OH. 614-486-9621

Sniderman, Gloria, *Ref,* Wayne State University Libraries (Kresge Library), Detroit MI. 313-577-4035

Snodgrass, Connie, *Librn,* Sistersville Public Library, Sistersville WV. 304-652-6701

Snodgrass, Edith, *Librn,* Allerton Public Library, Allerton IA. 515-873-4726

Snodgrass, Mrs Jim, *Asst Librn,* Fairmont Public Library, Fairmont NE. 402-268-6081

Snodgrass, Mrs Russell, *Librn,* Fairmont Public Library, Fairmont NE. 402-268-6081

Snodgrass, Wilson D, *Assoc Dir,* Southern Methodist University Libraries (Central University Libraries), Dallas TX. 214-692-2400

Snodgrass-Pilla, Lynn, *Tech Serv, Acq & Cat,* Montgomery County-Norristown Public Library, Norristown PA. 215-277-3355

Snoke, Helen Lloyd, *Prof,* University of Michigan, School of Library Science, MI. 313-764-9376

Snow, Barbara, *ILL,* University of Michigan (Law Library), Ann Arbor MI. 313-764-9322

Snow, Bonnie, *Ref & Bibliog Instr,* Philadelphia College of Pharmacy & Science, Joseph W England Library, Philadelphia PA. 215-386-5800, Ext 296

Snow, Bonnie, *Naval Regional Librn,* United States Navy (Naval Education & Training Support Center, Pacific), San Francisco CA. 415-765-6300

Snow, C Richard, *Asst Dir,* Clarion State College, Venango Campus Library, Oil City PA. 814-676-6591, Ext 42

Snow, David E, *Dir,* Placentia Library District of Orange County, Placentia CA. 714-528-1906

Snow, Ellen, *ILL,* Nebraska Library Commission, Lincoln NE. 402-471-2045

Snow, Helen, *Librn,* Charles H Stone Memorial Library, Pilot Mountain NC. 919-368-2370

Snow, J Richard, *Doc,* Loyola University Library (School of Law), New Orleans LA. 504-865-3426, 865-3427, 865-3136

Snow, Jane E, *Ch,* William Jeanes Memorial Library, Lafayette Hill PA. 215-828-0441

Snow, Sharon, *Librn,* Umatilla County Library (Milton-Freewater Branch), Milton-Freewater OR. 503-938-3034

Snow, Timothy, *Circ,* University of Central Arkansas, Torreyson Library, Conway AR. 501-329-2931, Ext 449

Snow, Vida, *Acq,* Long Beach Community College Learning Resources Division (Liberal Arts Campus Library), Long Beach CA. 213-420-4231

Snowball, George J, *Lectr,* Concordia University, Library Studies Program, PQ. 514-482-0320, Ext 324

Snowden, Deanna, *Asst Dir,* Mississippi County Library System, Blytheville AR. 501-762-2431

Snowdon, Jewell, *Chief Librn,* Lakeland Regional Library, Killarney MB. 204-523-4949

Snowhite, Morton, *Librn,* New Jersey Institute of Technology, Robert W Van Houten Library, Newark NJ. 201-645-5306

Snyder, Ann B, *Librn,* Peter Bent Brigham Hospital, School of Nursing Library, Boston MA. 617-732-5922, 732-5923

Snyder, Carolyn A, *Asst Dir Pub Servs,* Indiana University at Bloomington, University Libraries, Bloomington IN. 812-337-3403

Snyder, Charles J, *Librn,* Harvard University Library (Lucien Howe Library of Ophthalmology), Boston MA. 617-523-7900, Ext 575

Snyder, Charlotte R, *ILL,* United States Military Academy Library, West Point NY. 914-938-2230

Snyder, Cynthia L, *Dir,* Council for Advancement & Support of Education, Case Reference Center, Washington DC. 202-328-5900

Snyder, David, *On-Line Servs,* Boston University Libraries (Mugar Memorial Library), Boston MA. 617-353-3710

Snyder, Donna, *ILL,* Western Wyoming Community College, Library Learning Resources Center, Rock Springs WY. 307-382-2121, Ext 154

Snyder, Doris, *Supvr,* Middlesex County Library (Glencoe Branch), Glencoe ON. 519-287-2735

Snyder, Duke W, *In Charge,* Founding Church of Scientology, Library of Dianetics & Scientology, Washington DC. 202-797-3700

Snyder, Eileen, *Librn,* Syracuse University Libraries (Chemistry), Syracuse NY. 315-423-2212

Snyder, Eileen, *Librn,* Syracuse University Libraries (Geology), Syracuse NY. 315-423-3337

Snyder, Eileen, *Librn,* Syracuse University Libraries (Physics), Syracuse NY. 315-423-2692

Snyder, Elizabeth, *Asst Librn,* Oak Brook Free Public Library, Oak Brook IL. 312-654-2222

Snyder, Esther, *Librn, Interlibr Loan & Ref,* Colorado State Library, Colorado Department of Education, Denver CO. 303-839-3695

Snyder, Evelyn G, *Librn,* Fort Recovery Public Library, Fort Recovery OH. 419-375-2869

Snyder, Fifi, *Librn,* Sterling Public Library, Sterling CO. 303-522-2023

Snyder, George, *Rare Bks & Spec Coll,* University of Denver, Penrose Library, Denver CO. 303-753-2007

Snyder, Jack, *In Charge,* Philadelphia College of Art Library (Film Library), Philadelphia PA. 215-893-3126

Snyder, Jane, *Librn,* Duke University (Undergraduate Library), Durham NC. 919-684-2326

Snyder, Jane, *Slide,* Indiana University-Purdue University at Indianapolis (Herron School of Art), Indianapolis IN. 317-923-3651

Snyder, Jessie, *Librn,* Putnam County Public Library, Unionville MO. 816-947-3192

Snyder, Linda H, *Dir,* Washington Township Public Library, Turnersville NJ. 609-589-3334

Snyder, Louise C, *Dir,* Sterling College, Kelsey Library, Sterling KS. 316-278-2173, Ext 234

Snyder, Lulu, *Dir,* First Christian Church, Winona Roehl Library, Knoxville TN. 615-522-0545

Snyder, Madge, *Librn,* American Management Associations Inc, Donald W Mitchell Memorial Library, Hamilton NY. 315-824-2000, Ext 207

Snyder, Marjorie, *Tech Serv,* W E Walter Memorial Library, Bremen Public Library, Bremen IN. 219-546-2849

Snyder, Marjorie R, *Cat,* Lincoln Public Library, Lincoln MA. 617-259-8465

Snyder, Michael S, *Asst Dir,* Great River Regional Library, Saint Cloud MN. 612-251-7282

Snyder, Nancy, *Br Asst,* Timberland Regional Library (Yelm Branch), Yelm WA. 206-943-5001

Snyder, Nathan, *Cat,* Spertus College of Judaica, Norman & Helen Asher Library, Chicago IL. 312-922-9012, Ext 50

Snyder, Patt, *Librn,* Shell Development Co, Biological Sciences Research Center Library, Modesto CA. 209-545-0761

Snyder, Paul, *Media,* Linn-Benton Community College, Learning Resource Center, Albany OR. 503-928-2361, Ext 330

Snyder, Richard E, *Dir,* Anderson College (Charles E Wilson Library), Anderson IN. 317-649-9071

Snyder, Richard L, *Dir,* Drexel University Library, Philadelphia PA. 215-895-2750

Snyder, Ross C, *Media,* Missouri Southern State College, George A Spiva Library, Joplin MO. 417-624-8100, Ext 251

Snyder, Ruth, *Curric Mat,* Jersey City State College, Forrest A Irwin Library, Jersey City NJ. 201-547-3026

Snyder, Sharron, *Acq,* William Marsh Rice University, Fondren Library, Houston TX. 713-527-4022

Snyder, Sheryl, *Librn,* Carnegie Public Library, Charleston Public Library, Charleston IL. 217-345-4913

Snyder, Shirley Ann, *Head Librn,* Pennsylvania State University, Shenango Valley Campus Library, Sharon PA. 412-981-1640

Snyder, Susan, *Librn,* Monsanto Co, Fabricated Products Division Library, Bloomfield CT. 203-242-6221

Snyder, Virginia J, *Base Librn,* United States Air Force (Andrews Air Force Base Library), Andrews AFB MD. 202-981-6454

Snyder, Wayne A, *Librn,* Battelle Memorial Institute, Pacific Northwest Division Technical Library, Richland WA. 509-946-2121

Snyder, William, *Dir,* Ohio State University, Newark Campus & Central Ohio Technical College, Newark Regional Campus Library, Newark OH. 614-366-3321, Ext 306, 307, 308

Snyder, William E, *Dir,* Sampson-Clinton Public Library, Clinton NC. 919-592-4153

Snyder, William H, *Dir & Acq,* City-County Library of Missoula, Missoula MT. 406-728-5900

Snyder, William H, *Coordr,* Tamarack Federation of Libraries, Missoula MT. 406-728-5900

Snyders, Robert, *Pub Servs,* Kaskaskia Library System, Smithton IL. 618-235-4220

Snyderwine, L Thomas, *Asst Dir & On-Line Servs,* Gannon University, Nash Library, Erie PA. 814-871-7352

Sobel, Bessie, *Ch, YA & Tech Serv,* Blauvelt Free Library, Blauvelt NY. 914-359-2811

Sobel, Richard, *Dir,* Bristol Community College, Learning Resources Center, Fall River MA. 617-678-2811

Sobel, Richard, *Program Dir,* Bristol Community College, Library Science-Audiovisual Program, MA. 617-678-2811, Ext 110

Sobel, Sharon G S, *Librn,* Owens-Corning Fiberglas Corp (Law Dept Library), Toledo OH. 419-248-7787

Sobers, Ellen, *Tech Serv, Cat & On-Line Servs,* Lane Public Library, Hamilton OH. 513-894-7156

Sobicinski, Brother Anthony, *Cat,* Saint Mary's University (Academic Library), San Antonio TX. 512-436-3441

Sobin, M, *Librn,* Engelhard Minerals & Chemicals Corp, Technical Information Center, Edison NJ. 201-321-5271

Sobol, Nick, *Per,* College of Cape Breton Library, Sydney NS. 902-539-5300

Sobon, Juliette L, *Asst Curator,* Hispanic Society of America Library, New York NY. 212-926-2234

Sobotka, John, *Archivist,* University of Mississippi, Law Library, University MS. 601-232-7361

Sobottka, Pat, *Tech Serv,* Pacific University, Harvey W Scott Memorial Library, Forest Grove OR. 503-357-6151, Ext 301

Sockbeson, Deidre, *ILL & Ref,* Eureka-Humboldt County Library, Eureka CA. 707-445-7284, 445-7513

Sockyma, Debra, *Librn,* Kykotsmovi Community Library, Oraibi AZ. 602-734-2474

Soderberg, Dorothy, *Librn,* Asbury School of Nursing Library, Salina KS. 913-827-4411

Soderberg, Jean, *Ch,* Fanwood Memorial Library, Fanwood NJ. 201-322-6400

Soderland, Kenneth W, *Ad,* University of Chicago, Joseph Regenstein Library, Chicago IL. 312-753-2977

Soderquist, Sharon, *Br Coordr & Bkmobile Coordr,* San Antonio Public Library, San Antonio TX. 512-299-7790

Sodhi, B S, *Dir,* Nova Scotia Agricultural College Library, Truro NS. 902-895-1571, Ext 231, 228 & 291

Sodt, James D, *Asst Prof,* University of Kentucky, College of Library Science, KY. 606-258-8876

Soenksen, Shirley, *Ref,* Greeley Public Library, Greeley Municipal Library, Greeley CO. 303-353-6123, Ext 392

Soergel, Dagobert, *Prof,* University of Maryland, College of Library & Information Services, MD. 301-454-5441

Soester, James, *ILL & Circ,* Chadron State College Library, Chadron NE. 308-432-4451, Ext 271

Soete, George, *Ref,* University of California, San Diego, University Libraries, La Jolla CA. 714-452-3336

Sofield, Jean C, *Trustee,* Roger Clark Memorial Library, Pittsfield VT. 802-746-5641

Soft, Clara, *Librn,* Glendive Public Library (Richey Public Library), Glendive MT. 406-773-2656

Sohl, Marjorie, *Ad,* Hammond Public Library, Hammond IN. 219-931-5100

Sohn, Jeanne, *Coll Develop Chief,* Temple University of the Commonwealth System of Higher Education, Samuel Paley Library, Philadelphia PA. 215-787-8231

Sokalzuk, Pauline M, *Librn,* Northumberland County Law Library, Sunbury PA. 717-286-7721, Ext 45

Sokan, Robert, *Rare Bks,* Illinois State University, Milner Library, Normal IL. 309-438-3675

Sokol, Christine, *Dir & Ref,* Franklin Public Library, Franklin NH. 603-934-2911

Sokol, Karol M, *Librn,* Cleary, Gottlieb, Steen & Hamilton Library, New York NY. 212-344-0600, Ext 364

Sokolnicki, Marcia, *Ref & ILL,* Southington Public Library, Southington CT. 203-628-0947

Sokolov, Barbara, *Librn,* University of Alaska, Arctic Environmental Information & Data Center Library, Anchorage AK. 907-279-4523

Sokolow, Alan V, *Eastern Regional Dir,* Council of State Governments Library, New York NY. 212-221-3630

Sokolow, Joyce, *Chief Librn,* Sperry & Hutchinson Co, Marketing Research Library, New York NY. 212-983-2000

Sokolowski, Denise, *ILL, YA & Acq,* La Porte Public Library, La Porte IN. 219-362-6156

Sol, Ellen, *Dir,* System Development Corp, Information Retrieval Center, Santa Monica CA. 213-829-7511, Ext 3433

Solano, Deborah, *Acq,* Albany Law School Library, Albany NY. 518-445-2311, 445-2340

Solberg, Mrs Orlin, *Librn,* Ringsted Public Library, Ringsted IA. 712-866-0878

Solbrig, Dorothy J, *Librn,* Harvard University Library (Biological Laboratories), Cambridge MA. 617-495-2332

Soldner, Dean, *Humanities,* Mobile Public Library, Mobile AL. 205-438-7073

Soldwisch, Marilyn, *Libr Tech,* United States Navy (Technical Library (US Navy FCDSSASD)), San Diego CA. 714-225-2697

Sole, Thelma, *ILL,* Hastings - Adams County Library, Hastings NE. 402-463-9855

Soler, Eleanor, *Dir,* New York Theological Seminary Library, New York NY. 212-532-4012, Ext 216

Solis, Neomi, *Librn,* Houston Public Library (Melcher), Houston TX. 713-641-5611

Solley, Anna, *Learning Assistance Ctr,* Glendale Community College, John F Prince Library, Glendale AZ. 602-934-2211, Ext 239, 242

Soloman, Eric, *Actg Dir,* San Francisco State University, J Paul Leonard Library, San Francisco CA. 415-469-1681

Soloman, Genevieve, *Librn,* Prince Edward Island Provincial Library (Georgetown Branch), Georgetown PE. 902-892-3504, Ext 54

Soloman, Marvin, *Social Sci,* Southern Illinois University at Edwardsville, Elijah P Lovejoy Library, Edwardsville IL. 618-692-2711

Soloman, Meredith, *Circ,* Southwestern Oklahoma State University, Al Harris Library, Weatherford OK. 405-772-6611, Ext 5311

Solomon, Brad, *Asst Dir (SRS),* Eastfield College, Learning Resources Center, Mesquite TX. 214-746-3168

Solomon, Diane, *Librn,* Chatham-Effingham-Liberty Regional Library (Tybee Branch), Tybee Island GA. 912-786-4573

Solomon, Fern, *ILL & Ref,* Montgomery County Department of Public Libraries, Rockville MD. 301-279-1401

Solomon, Judy A, *Librn,* Hartford Public Library (Campfield), Hartford CT. 203-527-2209

Solomon, Laurence H, *Dir,* New Bedford Free Public Library, Subregional Headquarters for Eastern Massachusetts Regional Library System, New Bedford MA. 617-999-6291

Solomon, Lillian M, *Librn,* Kent State University, East Liverpool Campus Library, East Liverpool OH. 216-385-3805

Solomon, Linda, *Librn,* Canadian Hospital Association, Blackader Library, Ottawa ON. 613-238-8005, Ext 58 & 38

Solomon, Linda, *Librn,* Centraide Montreal Library, Montreal PQ. 514-288-1261, Ext 220

Solomon, Seena, *Media,* Johnson Free Public Library, Hackensack NJ. 201-343-4169

Solomonoff, Sonja, *Cat,* Case Western Reserve University Libraries (School of Law Library), Cleveland OH. 216-368-2792

Solow, Linda I, *Librn,* Massachusetts Institute of Technology Libraries (Music), Cambridge MA. 617-253-5689

Solt, George, *Chief Prov Law Librn,* Alberta Attorney General & Law Society of Alberta, Law Library, Edmonton AB. 403-423-7601, 423-7602

Soltis, Laura W, *ILL, Ad & Ref,* Haywood County Public Library, Waynesville NC. 704-452-5169

Soltis-Stolz, Ann, *Librn,* Pikes Peak Regional Library District (Old Colorado City), Colorado Springs CO. 303-634-1698

Soltow, Martha Jane, *Librn,* Michigan State University Library (Labor & Industrial Relations), East Lansing MI. 517-355-2344

Soltys, Amy, *Librn,* Grande Prairie Public Library, Grande Prairie AB. 403-532-3580

Solum, Treva, *Dir,* Rice Lake Public Library, Rice Lake WI. 715-234-4861

Solvick, Shirley, *Fine Arts,* Detroit Public Library, Detroit Associated Libraries, Detroit MI. 313-833-1000

Solyma, Alice, *Librn,* Canada Department of the Environment, Pacific Forest Research Center Library, Victoria BC. 604-388-3811, Ext 146

Sombs, April, *Librn,* Tulare County Library System (Badger Branch), Badger CA. 209-337-2514

Somerman, Nelly, *Librn,* A B Dick Co Library, Chicago IL. 312-647-8800, Ext 2280

Somers, Gerald A, *Dir,* Brown County Library, Green Bay WI. 414-497-3450

Somers, Janet, *Music,* Juilliard School, Lila Acheson Wallace Library, New York NY. 212-799-5000, Ext 265

Somers, Janet, *Tech Serv, Cat & Ref,* Juilliard School, Lila Acheson Wallace Library, New York NY. 212-799-5000, Ext 265

Somers, Jeanne, *Cat,* Kent State University Libraries, Kent OH. 216-672-2962

Somers, Lucretia M, *Dir,* Homewood Public Library, Homewood AL. 205-871-7342

Somers, Robert B, *Dir & Acq,* University of Montevallo, Oliver Cromwell Carmichael Library, Montevallo AL. 205-665-2521, Ext 498

Somers, Sally, *Acq,* University of Georgia Libraries, Athens GA. 404-542-2716

Somerville, Arleen, *Librn,* University of Rochester (Dept of Science & Engineering), Rochester NY. 716-275-4488

Somerville, Emily, *Librn,* Essex County Public Library (Cottam Branch), Cottam ON. 519-776-5241

Somerville, Joan, *ILL,* Grace A Dow Memorial Library, Midland Public Library, Midland MI. 517-835-7151

Somerville, Mary, *Ch,* Louisville Free Public Library, Louisville KY. 502-584-4154

Somerville, Romaine S, *Dir,* Maryland Historical Society Library, Baltimore MD. 301-685-3750

Sommer, Frank H, *Head of Libr,* Henry Francis Du Pont Winterthur Museum Library, Winterthur DE. 302-656-8591, Ext 281

Sommer, Hulda E, *Librn,* Jackson County Library System (Talent Branch), Talent OR. 503-535-4163

Sommer, June, *Asst Librn,* Saint Louis County Library (Daniel Boone), Ellisville MO. 314-227-9630

Sommer, Ronald, *ILL & Reader Serv,* University of Tennessee Center for the Health Sciences Library, Memphis TN. 901-528-5638

Sommer, Ursula, *Media,* Fairleigh Dickinson University, Friendship Library, Madison NJ. 201-377-4700, Ext 234

Sommerfeld, V, *In Charge,* McKinnon, Allen & Associates (Western) Ltd Library, Calgary AB. 403-243-4345

Sommers, Brother James, *Librn,* Holy Cross Abbey Library, Berryville VA. 703-955-1425

Sommers, Diane, *YA,* Bettendorf Public Library & Information Center, Bettendorf IA. 319-359-4427

Sommerville, Betty, *YA & Ref,* Bound Brook Memorial Library, Bound Brook NJ. 201-356-0043

Sommerville, James, *Librn,* Iowa Department of Social Services, Mental Health Institute Library, Mount Pleasant IA. 319-385-7231, Ext 481

Sommerville, James, *Ref,* Somerville Free Public Library, Somerville NJ. 201-725-1336

Sommerville, Sylvia, *Librn,* New York City Board of Education, Curriculum Development Library, Brooklyn NY. 212-596-4903

Somosheghyi-Szokol, Gaston, *Ibero-American,* University of California, Berkeley (University Library), Berkeley CA. 415-642-3773

Soncksen, Donna, *Librn,* Arapahoe Public Library, Arapahoe NE. 308-962-7806

Sondag, Pauline A, *Librn,* Michigan State University Library (Agricultural Economics), East Lansing MI. 517-355-2344

Sondrol, Robert O, *Dir,* Chester County Library & District Center, Exton PA. 215-363-0884

Sonet, Louise, *Ch,* New Rochelle Public Library, New Rochelle NY. 914-632-7878

Sonevysky, Natalie, *Ref & Bibliog Instr,* Columbia University (Barnard College), New York NY. 212-280-3846

Song, Agnes, *ILL,* Beverly Hills Public Library, Beverly Hills CA. 213-550-4711

Song, Seungja Y, *Librn,* United States Public Health Service Hospital, Medical Service Library, Seattle WA. 206-324-7650, Ext 227

Song, Thomas, *Assoc Dir,* Bryn Mawr College, Canaday Library, Bryn Mawr PA. 215-645-5279

Songer, Elverda, *Librn,* Alexandria Public Library, Alexandria IN. 317-724-2196

Sonin, Hille, *Acq,* University of San Francisco, Richard A Gleeson Library, San Francisco CA. 415-666-6167

Sonnelitter, Jane, *Librn,* Amherst Public Library (Williamsville), Williamsville NY. 716-632-6176

Sonnenberg, Barbara, *ILL,* Public Library of Cincinnati & Hamilton County, Cincinnati Public Library, Cincinnati OH. 513-369-6000

Sonnier, Clytie, *Librn,* Harris County Law Library, Houston TX. 713-221-5183

Sonntag, Edith, *Soc Work,* Indiana University-Purdue University at Indianapolis, University Library, Indianapolis IN. 317-264-4101

Soo, Sze, *Tech Serv,* Hartnell College, Learning Resources Center, Salinas CA. 408-758-8211, Ext 400

Sook, Lois, *Librn,* Beekman Downtown Hospital, Elisha Walker Staff Library, New York NY. 212-233-5300, Ext 341

Soong, Mrs S, *Librn,* Windsor Public Library (Ambassador), Windsor ON. 519-253-7340

Soos, Maria, *Tech Serv,* Wagner College, Horrmann Library, Staten Island NY. 212-390-3001

Sopalsky, Donna, *Ch,* Orangeburg Public Library, Orangeburg NY. 914-359-2244

Soper, Betty, *Librn,* Roseville Public Library (Carnegie Branch), Roseville CA. 916-782-7909

Soper, Marley H, *Chmn,* Andrews University, Library Science Dept, MI. 616-471-3549

Soper, Mary Ellen, *Asst Prof,* University of Washington, School of Librarianship, WA. 206-543-1794

Sorem, Janet H, *Librn,* Ernst & Whinney, Audit Management Services, International, Tax & Data Systems Technical Library, New York NY. 212-888-9100

Sorensen, Joan, *Libr Servs,* Greenville County Library, Greenville SC. 803-242-5000

Sorensen, Joanne R, *Librn,* Converse Ward Davis Dixon Library, Caldwell NJ. 201-226-9191, 212-964-0405, Ext 455

Sorensen, John Mark, *Ref,* Utah State University, Merrill Library & Learning Resources Program, Logan UT. 801-750-2637

Sorensen, Lynn, *Librn,* Detroit-Macomb Hospitals Association, Detroit Memorial Hospital Library, Detroit MI. 313-225-5185

Sorensen, Lynn, *Librn,* Detroit-Macomb Hospitals Association, South Macomb Hospital Library, Warren MI. 313-573-5117

Sorensen, Stanford, *Tech Serv,* College of Notre Dame Library, Belmont CA. 415-593-1601, Ext 57

Sorensen, Virginia, *Instr,* Saint Cloud State University, Center for Library & Audiovisual Education, MN. 612-255-2022

Sorenson, C, *Librn,* Oakland Public Library (Laurel), Oakland CA. 415-530-1021

Sorenson, Deanna, *Asst Librn,* Pinehurst-Kingston Free Library District, Pinehurst ID. 208-682-3483

Sorenson, Doris, *Dir,* Bayville Free Library, Bayville NY. 516-628-2765

Sorenson, John W, *Coordr,* Southwestern Community College, Learning Resource Center, Creston IA. 515-782-7081, Ext 224

Sorenson, Mary, *Cat,* North Idaho College Library, Coeur d'Alene ID. 208-667-7422, Ext 220

Sorenson, Richard, *Supvr Instrnl Media Programs,* Wisconsin Department of Public Instruction (Bureau of Instructional Media Program), Madison WI. 608-266-1965

Sorenson, Verla, *Librn,* Big Horn County Library (Deaver Branch), Deaver WY. 307-568-2388

Sorg, Elizabeth A, *Librn,* Eastern State School & Hospital Professional Library, Trevose PA. 215-671-3129, 671-3389

Sorg, Hannelore, *Ch,* Dunedin Public Library, Dunedin FL. 813-733-4115

Sorgen, Herbert J, *Dir & Acq,* State University of New York Agricultural & Technical College at Delhi, Delhi College Library, Delhi NY. 607-746-4107

Sorger, Joan, *In Charge,* Cleveland Public Library (General Reference), Cleveland OH. 216-623-2856

Soriano, Alyce, *Tech Serv & Acq,* Cypress College Library, Cypress CA. 714-826-2220, Ext 124, 125

Soriano, Doris, *Librn,* Long Beach Public Library System (Brewitt), Long Beach CA. 213-438-9200

Sorkin, Gary, *Asst to Dir,* Massachusetts Board of Library Commissioners, Office for the Development of Library Services, Boston MA. 617-267-9400

Sorley, Geraldine, *Librn,* Grand Centre & District Public Library, Grand Centre AB. 403-594-5101

Sorrel, Helen, *Dir,* Grant Parish Library, Colfax LA. 318-627-9920

Sorrel, Patricia S, *Dir,* Wharton County Library, Wharton TX. 713-532-4822

Sorrell, Jodie, *Librn,* Waverly Memorial Library, Waverly PA. 717-563-1491

Sorrells, Dillman B, *In Charge,* Clemson University (College of Architecture Library), Clemson SC. 803-656-3026

Sorrels, Harlene, *Librn,* Fremont County Library (Fort Washakie Branch), Fort Washakie WY. 307-255-8387

Sorrentino, Sherrill, *Librn,* Rancho Los Amigos Hospital, Medical Library, Downey CA. 213-922-7696

Sorrier, Isabel, *Dir,* Statesboro Regional Library, Statesboro GA. 912-764-7573

Sosa, James, *Librn,* San Antonio Public Library (Business, Science & Technology), San Antonio TX. 512-299-7800, 299-7801

Sosh, Gertrude, *Librn,* Delaware Valley Regional Planning Commission Library, Philadelphia PA. 215-567-3000, Ext 160

Sossa, Magda, *Librn,* Atlanta Public Library (Inman Park), Atlanta GA. 404-525-2066

Sotendahl, Audrey B, *ILL & Ref,* Mohawk Valley Community College Library, Utica NY. 315-792-5337

Sotile, Michael P, *Spec Areas,* Louisiana State University (Troy H Middleton Library), Baton Rouge LA. 504-388-2217

Sotirin, Paul G, *Dir,* New Berlin Public Library, New Berlin WI. 414-786-2990

Soto, Alicia, *ILL,* Calexico Public Library, Calexico CA. 714-357-2605

Soto, Donna, *Asst Dir,* Fairhope Public Library, Fairhope AL. 205-928-7483

Sottosanti, Mary Louise, *Asst Dir,* Englewood Library, Englewood NJ. 201-568-2215

Soucie, Yan, *ILL,* Humboldt State University Library, Arcata CA. 707-826-3441

Soucy, Gloria, *Tech Serv,* University of Maine at Fort Kent, Blake Library, Fort Kent ME. 207-834-3165, Ext 215

Soudek, Miluse, *Psychol, Philos & Relig,* Northern Illinois University, Founders Memorial Library, De Kalb IL. 815-753-1094

Souders, Marilyn, *Acq & Cat,* Newsweek, Inc, General Library, New York NY. 212-350-2494

Souffront, Blanche L, *Asst Dir & Br Coordr,* Bureau of Libraries, Museums & Archaeological Services, Saint Thomas VI. 809-774-3407

Soulard, Claude, *Librn,* University of Montreal Libraries (Music), Montreal PQ. 514-343-6432

Soule, Gardner, *Librn,* Pike County Public Library, Milford PA. 717-296-8211

Soule, Harvey, *On-Line Servs,* Kent State University Libraries, Kent OH. 216-672-2962

Soulen, Marillyn, *Govt Docs,* Hamline University (School of Law Library), Saint Paul MN. 612-641-2344

Soules, A, *Cat,* University of Windsor, Leddy Library, Windsor ON. 519-253-4232, Ext 198

Soult, John, *Bkmobile Coordr,* Martins Ferry Public Library, Martins Ferry OH. 614-633-0314

Sourd, Odette Le, *In Charge,* Centre De Documentation Du Conservatoire De Musique De Montreal (Bibliotheque Du Conservatoire D'Art Dramatique), Montreal PQ. 514-873-4031

Sours, Kay, *Br Coordr,* Broward County Division of Libraries, Broward County Library, Pompano Beach FL. 305-972-1100

Souter, T A, *Assoc Dir,* Virginia Polytechnic Institute & State University Library, Blacksburg VA. 703-961-5593

South, Onetha, *Tech Serv,* Washington County Public Library, Abingdon VA. 703-628-2971

Southall, Genevia E, *Librn,* Tuscaloosa Public Library (Weaver), Tuscaloosa AL. 205-345-5820

Southerland, Willouise, *Cat,* Coastal Plain Regional Library, Tifton GA. 912-386-3400

Southern, Verona, *Librn,* Spokane Community College, East Mission Campus Library, Spokane WA. 509-455-7699

Southern, Walter A, *In Charge,* Abbott Laboratories, Information Service, North Chicago IL. 312-937-4513

Southward, Lonette, *Librn,* Northeast Regional Library (Tishomingo Library), Tishomingo MS. 601-438-6302

Southwell, Mary, *Acq,* Utah State Library, Salt Lake City UT. 801-533-5875

Southwick, Peggy, *Asst Librn,* Slayton Public Library, Slayton MN. 507-836-8778

Southworth, Bud, *Dir,* Mount Vernon Public Library, Mount Vernon WA. 206-336-2418

Southworth, Marvin, *Dir,* Grady C Hogue Library, Learning Resource Center, Beeville TX. 512-358-7032

Southworth, Mrs V C, *Dir,* English-Speaking Union Library, Washington DC. 202-234-4602

Southworth, Susan, *Law & Legislative Ref,* Connecticut State Library, Hartford CT. 203-566-4301

Souza, Katherine P, *Librn,* Gloucester Lyceum & Sawyer Free Library (Lincoln Park), Gloucester MA. 617-283-7523

Souza, Sandra J, *Librn,* Massachusetts Department of Correction, State Hospital Library, Bridgewater MA. 617-697-6941, Ext 329

Sowchek, Ellen, *Archivist,* Young Men's Christian Association, Bowne Historical Library, New York NY. 212-374-2042

Sowder, Judy, *Media Spec,* Carl Albert Junior College, Learning Resource Center, Poteau OK. 918-647-2124, Ext 218

Sowell, Joyce, *Blind & Physically Handicapped,* Mobile Public Library, Mobile AL. 205-438-7073

Sowell, Steven L, *Pub Servs,* Texas College of Osteopathic Medicine Library, Fort Worth TX. 817-735-2465

Sower, Marjorie J, *Librn,* Price City Library, Price UT. 801-637-0744

Sowers, Bill, *Ad & Spec Coll,* Dodge City Public Library, Dodge City KS. 316-225-0248

Sowers, Conant, *Bibliog Instr,* Rapid City Public Library, Rapid City SD. 605-394-4171

Sowers, Naomi, *ILL,* Sturgis Public Library, Sturgis MI. 616-651-7907, 651-2321

Spadaccini, Normae, *Ad,* Norwood Public Library, Norwood NJ. 201-768-9555

Spadafore, Frances, *Ref & Spec Coll,* Bemidji State University, A C Clark Library, Bemidji MN. 218-755-2955

Spade, Eleanor, *Librn,* Constantine Township Library, Constantine MI. 616-435-7957

Spader, Eunice W, *Dir,* Penn Yan Public Library, Penn Yan NY. 315-536-6114

Spaeth, Janet, *Circ,* Grand Forks Public City-County Library, Grand Forks ND. 701-772-8116

Spahn, Kathy, *Asst Dir,* Waunakee Public Library, Waunakee WI. 608-849-4217

Spain, Victoria J, *Librn,* University of Missouri-Kansas City Libraries (Instructional Materials Ctr), Kansas City MO. 816-276-2744

Spaite, Joan, *Bibliog Instr,* University of Wisconsin-Green Bay, Library Learning Center, Green Bay WI. 414-465-2382

Spak, Karen, *Ch Coordr,* Cambria County Library System, Johnstown PA. 814-536-5131

Spak, Susan, *Tech Serv,* Amherst College, Robert Frost Library, Amherst MA. 413-542-2212

Spalding, Helen, *Tech Serv,* University of Missouri-Kansas City Libraries, Kansas City MO. 816-276-1531

Spangelo, L P S, *Dir,* Agriculture Canada, Research Station Library, Beaverlodge AB. 403-354-2212

Spangler, Charline, *Asst Librn,* Carrollton Public Library, Carrollton MO. 816-542-0183

Spangler, Macon, *ILL,* Bellaire City Library, Bellaire TX. 713-664-4098

Spangler, Margaret, *Ch,* McPherson Public Library, McPherson KS. 316-241-6530

Spangler, Romaine, *Circ,* Martin Memorial Library, York PA. 717-843-3978

Spangler, Rose, *Librn,* Morgan Public Library, Morgan MN. 507-249-3153

Spangler, William, *Film Dept,* Free Public Library of Woodbridge, Woodbridge NJ. 201-634-4450

Spangler, William T, *Dir,* Atlantic Community College, Daniel Leeds Learning Resources Center, Mays Landing NJ. 625-1111 & 646-4950

Spanier, Gina, *Ch,* Cote Saint-Luc Public Library, Cote Saint-Luc PQ. 514-481-5676

Spann, Grace H, *Ref,* Kinchafoonee Regional Library, Dawson GA. 912-995-2902

Spann, Idell, *Librn,* Justin Potter Public Library, Smithville TN. 615-597-4359

Spann, Kutrichia, *Librn,* Public Library of Charlotte & Mecklenburg County, Inc (Belmont Center), Charlotte NC. 704-374-2470

Spann, Melvin L, *In-Charge,* National Library of Medicine (TOXLINE), Bethesda MD. 301-496-1131

Sparkman, Frances, *Bkmobile Coordr,* Marlboro County Library, Bennettsville SC. 803-479-6201

Sparkman, Yvonne L, *Info Ctr Administrator,* Dart Industries, Inc, Chemical Group, Research & Development Center, Paramus NJ. 201-262-6700

Sparks, Barbara, *Asst Librn,* Barnes-Hind Pharmaceuticals Inc, Technical Library, Sunnyvale CA. 408-736-5462

Sparks, Barbara, *Librn,* Carson County Public Library, Panhandle TX. 806-537-3742

Sparks, C G, *Dean,* University of Texas at Austin, Graduate School of Library Science, TX. 512-471-3821

Sparks, Eva, *Chief Librn,* Northwest Alabama State Junior College Library, Phil Campbell AL. 205-993-5331

Sparks, Freda, *Bookmobile Librn,* Nicholas County Public Library, Carlisle KY. 606-289-5595
Sparks, Lillian, *Libmn,* Jefferson-Madison Regional Library (Louisa County Branch), Louisa VA. 804-967-1103
Sparks, M M, *Asst Dir,* Whitman College, Penrose Memorial Library, Walla Walla WA. 509-527-5191
Sparks, Marie C, *Ser,* University of Oklahoma Health Sciences Center Library, Oklahoma City OK. 405-271-2285
Sparks, Raymond E, *Libmn,* General Motors Corp, Delco Electronics Division Technical Library, Kokomo IN. 317-459-7262
Sparks, William S, *Dir,* Saint Paul School of Theology, Dana Dawson Library, Kansas City MO. 816-483-9600
Sparrow, Mary N, *Dir,* Guy Gannett Publishing Co Library, Portland ME. 207-775-5811, Ext 312
Sparvier, David L, *Coordr,* Federation of Saskatchewan Indians, Saskatchewan Indian Cultural College Library, Saskatoon SK. 306-244-1146, Ext 41
Spatorico, Carmelina C, *Libmn,* NL Industries, TAM Division Library, Niagara Falls NY. 716-285-3333
Spaude, Karen, *Libmn,* Minnesota Valley Regional Library (Gibbon), Mankato MN. 507-834-6551
Spaude, Milton P, *Dir,* Michigan Lutheran Seminary Library, Saginaw MI. 517-793-1041
Spaulding, Blanche, *Libmn,* Western District of the General Conference Mennonite Church, Loan Library, North Newton KS. 316-283-2500
Spaulding, Dorothy, *Libmn,* Saint Paul's Episcopal Church, Parish Library, Washington DC. 202-337-2020
Spaulding, F H, *Head Libr Operations Dept,* Bell Telephone Laboratories, Libraries & Information Systems Center, Murray Hill NJ. 582-2854 (General); 582-4466 (Info Systs Dept); 582-6880 (Info Servs Dept); 949-3456 (Libr Operations Dept)
Spaulding, Marilyn J, *Libmn,* Langley-Adams Library, Groveland MA. 617-372-1732
Spaulding, Patricia E, *Libmn,* Pinellas County Law Library, Clearwater Branch, Clearwater FL. 813-448-2411, 448-2412, 448-2413
Spaziani, Carol, *Commun Servs,* Iowa City Public Library, Iowa City IA. 319-354-1265
Speakman, Carol, *Libmn,* South Metropolitan Association Library, Dolton IL. 312-841-7800
Speaks, Frances, *Reader Serv,* Lexington County Circulating Library, Batesburg SC. 803-532-9223
Speaks, Norita, *ILL,* Greensboro Public Library, Greensboro NC. 373-2474; 373-2471
Spear, Jack B, *Assocs,* New York State Library, Albany NY. 518-474-5930
Spear, Laura, *Per,* Wake Forest University, Z Smith Reynolds Library, Winston-Salem NC. 919-761-5480
Spear, Marion, *Acq,* Jefferson County Public Library, Lakewood CO. 303-238-8411
Spear, Patricia, *Consultant,* North Texas Library System, Fort Worth TX. 817-335-6073
Speare, Anne, *Asst Libmn,* Communications Satellite Corp Laboratories, Technical Library, Clarksburg MD. 301-428-4512
Spearman, Betty R, *Libmn,* Anson Technical College, Learning Resource Center, Ansonville NC. 704-826-8333, Ext 26
Spearman, Nelle, *Branch Asst,* Abbeville-Greenwood Regional Library (Ninety Six Branch), Ninety Six SC. 803-223-4515
Spearman, Wessie, *Commun Servs,* Camden Free Public Library, Camden NJ. 609-963-4807
Spears, Janice, *Libmn,* Siouxland Mental Health Center, Health Sciences Library, Sioux City IA. 712-252-3871
Spears, Jo E, *Libmn,* Prague Public Library, Prague OK. 405-567-4013
Spears, Norman L, *Asst Libmn,* Angelo State University, Porter Henderson Library, San Angelo TX. 915-942-2222
Spears, Zella C, *Libmn,* McDonald County Library, Pineville MO. 417-223-4489
Specht, Joe W, *Dir,* McMurry College, Jay-Rollins Library, Abilene TX. 915-692-4130, Ext 291
Specht, Rita, *ILL,* Davenport Public Library, Davenport IA. 319-326-7832
Speck, Louise, *Libmn,* Williamsburg Public Library, Williamsburg PA. 814-832-3367

Spector, Beverly, *Libmn,* Congregation Shalom, Sherman Pastor Memorial Library, Milwaukee WI. 414-352-9288
Speed, Bert L, *Chief Park Interpreter,* National Park Service, Travertine Nature Center Library, Sulphur OK. 405-622-3165
Speed, William, *AV,* Los Angeles Public Library System, Los Angeles CA. 213-626-7555
Speenburgh, Susan, *Libmn,* Morton Memorial Library, Rhinecliff NY. 914-876-2903
Speer, Carol J, *Libmn,* Santa Barbara General Hospital Library, Santa Barbara CA. 805-967-2311
Speer, Effie, *Libmn,* Kilgore Public Library (Liberty City Branch Library), Gladewater TX. 214-984-4732
Speer, Rick, *Dir,* Oil City Library, Oil City PA. 814-646-8771
Speers, Gordon, *Dir,* Odell Public Library, Odell IL. 815-998-2012
Speiden, Virginia M, *Tech Serv,* Washington College, Clifton M Miller Library, Chestertown MD. 301-778-2800, Ext 242
Speirs, Charles H, *Acq,* Monroe Community College, LeRoy V Good Library, Rochester NY. 716-442-9950, Ext 2310
Speirs, Gilman, *Commun Libr Servs,* Marywood College Library, Scranton PA. 717-343-6521, Ext 289
Spelker, Paulette, *Tech Serv,* Bay County Library System, Bay City MI. 517-894-2837
Spell, Margaret, *Dir,* Village Library of Wrightstown, Wrightstown PA. 215-598-3322
Speller, Benjamin F, *Prof,* North Carolina Central University, School of Library Science, NC. 919-683-6485
Spellissy, Pamela C, *Libmn,* Government Research Corp, National Journal Library, Washington DC. 202-857-1400, Ext 413
Spellman, Dennis, *Bus Mgr,* Saint Louis Public Library, Saint Louis MO. 314-241-2288
Spellman, Jane S, *Dir,* Herkimer County Historical Society Library, Herkimer NY. 315-866-6413
Spellman, Lawrence, *Curator,* Princeton University Library (Richard Halliburton Map Collection), Princeton NJ. 609-452-3180
Spellman, Rosalie, *Libmn,* Timberland Regional Library (Aberdeen Branch), Aberdeen WA. 206-533-2360
Spellmire, Mary, *Cat,* Lebanon Public Library, Lebanon OH. 513-932-4725
Spence, Aurelia S, *Dir,* Central State Hospital, Medical, Mental Health & Resident's Libraries, Milledgeville GA. 912-453-4153
Spence, Charlotte, *Indo-Pacific,* University of California Los Angeles Library, Los Angeles CA. 213-825-1201
Spence, Elizabeth, *Tech Serv,* Pierce County Rural Library District, Tacoma WA. 206-572-6760
Spence, Jane, *Dir,* Wolbach Public Library, Wolbach NE. 308-246-3201
Spence, Linda, *On-Line Servs,* Westinghouse Electric Corp (Nuclear Energy Systems, Information Resources), Pittsburgh PA. 412-373-4200
Spence, Marcia, *ILL,* Monroe County Library System, Monroe MI. 313-241-5277
Spence, Melville, *Doc,* Bowling Green State University Library, Bowling Green OH. 419-372-2856
Spence, Mrs Cleo, *Libmn,* Gaines County Library (Seagraves), Seminole TX. 806-546-2480
Spence, Paul H, *Dir,* University of Alabama in Birmingham, Mervyn H Sterne Library, Birmingham AL. 205-934-6360
Spence, Ruth, *Map Curator,* Birmingham Public & Jefferson County Free Library, Birmingham AL. 205-254-2551
Spence, Tavila, *Per,* McMaster University, Hamilton ON. 416-525-9140
Spence, Theresa S, *Archivist,* Michigan Technological University Library, Houghton MI. 906-487-2500
Spencer, Bette, *Chief Law Br,* United States Department of the Interior, Natural Resources Library, Washington DC. 202-343-5821
Spencer, Cathy J, *ILL & Talking Bks Libmn,* Waterville Public Library, Waterville ME. 207-872-5433
Spencer, Eloise C, *Libmn,* Nephi City Library, Nephi UT. 801-623-0822
Spencer, Gladys S, *Libmn,* Denton Public Library, Denton NC. 704-869-2215

Spencer, Helen, *Tech Serv,* Topeka Public Library, Topeka KS. 913-233-2040
Spencer, Helen, *Dir,* Valley Cottage Free Library, Valley Cottage NY. 268-7700 & 7760
Spencer, Janice, *Libmn,* Biloxi Public Library (Division Street), Biloxi MS. 601-435-2435
Spencer, Jeannie F, *Libmn,* First Presbyterian Church Library, El Paso TX. 915-533-7551
Spencer, Jo Ann, *Dir,* Bio-Dynamics-BMC Library, Technical Information Center, Indianapolis IN. 317-849-6635
Spencer, Joan, *YA,* Wake County Department of the Public Library, Raleigh NC. 919-755-6077
Spencer, Joan M, *Ch,* Joliet Public Library, Joliet IL. 815-727-4726
Spencer, Leon P, *Archivist,* Talladega College, Savery Library, Talladega AL. 205-362-2046
Spencer, Linda G, *Acq & Cat,* Santa Fe Regional Library, Gainesville Public Library Headquarters, Gainesville FL. 904-374-2091
Spencer, Lois, *Biblig Instr,* York University, Scott Library, Downsview ON. 416-667-2235
Spencer, Mae, *Libmn,* Nottoway County Library (Crewe Branch), Crewe VA. 804-645-9453
Spencer, Marian, *Coordr,* Wilson Memorial Hospital, Learning Center Library, Wilson NC. 919-399-8253
Spencer, Marjorie, *Libmn,* Middletown Free Library, Lima PA. 215-566-7828
Spencer, Martha, *AV,* Montgomery County Department of Public Libraries, Rockville MD. 301-279-1401
Spencer, Mary Ann, *In Charge,* Illinois Prairie District Public Library (Metamora), Metamora IL. 309-367-4594
Spencer, Meredith, *Circ,* Lowndes County Library System, Columbus Public Library, Columbus MS. 601-328-1056
Spencer, Michael, *Ref & Exchange,* Saint Bonaventure University, Friedsam Memorial Library & Resource Center, Saint Bonaventure NY. 716-375-2323
Spencer, Patricia, *Archivist,* Saint Joseph Hospital, Medical Library, Chicago IL. 312-975-3038
Spencer, Rosiland A, *Libmn,* Steed College Library, Johnson City TN. 615-928-7332
Spencer, Ruth, *Per & Micro,* California Polytechnic State University Library, San Luis Obispo CA. 805-546-2345
Spencer, Samuel E, *Dir,* Lillie M Evans Memorial Library, Princeville IL. 309-385-4540
Spencer, Sherman, *Libmn,* University of the Pacific (Music Library), Stockton CA. 209-946-2188
Spencer, Valerie Taylor, *Libmn,* Jackson Memorial Hospital, School of Nursing Library, Miami FL. 305-325-6833
Spengler, Diane, *Libmn,* Ocheyedan Public Library, Ocheyedan IA. 712-758-3352
Spenik, Frances, *ILL,* Morgantown Public Library, Morgantown Service Center, Morgantown WV. 304-296-4425
Spenner, Judy, *ILL,* South Dakota State University, Hilton M Briggs Library, Brookings SD. 605-688-5106
Sperauskas, Maija, *Tech Serv,* Glen Cove Public Library, Glen Cove NY. 516-676-2130
Sperauskas, Milda, *Dir,* Mahwah Free Public Library, Mahwah NJ. 201-529-2183
Sperber, G Matthew, *Dir,* Bridgewater Public Library, Bridgewater MA. 617-697-3331
Spergel, Rosalyn, *Ref,* County College of Morris, Sherman H Masten Learning Resource Center, Randolph Township NJ. 201-361-5000, Ext 470
Sperhoga, Victoria, *Ref,* Ohio State University Libraries (Health Sciences Library), Columbus OH. 614-422-9810
Sperl, Virginia R, *ILL,* Dowling College Library, Oakdale NY. 516-589-6100, Ext 218 or 219
Sperlbaum, Andrea, *Ser,* Wayne State University Libraries (Vera P Shiffman Medical Library), Detroit MI. 313-577-1088
Sperlongano, JoAnne, *Libmn,* Cranston Public Library (Arlington), Cranston RI. 401-944-1662
Sperry, John A, *Egyptology, Archaeol & Ancient Hist,* Culver-Stockton College, Carl Johann Memorial Library, Canton MO. 314-288-5221, Ext 21
Sperry, Jr, John, *Rare Bks,* Culver-Stockton College, Carl Johann Memorial Library, Canton MO. 314-288-5221, Ext 21
Spesard, Marjorie, *Libmn,* Elwood Township Carnegie Library, Ridge Farm IL. 217-247-2820

Speser, Carol, *YA & Ch,* Lancaster Public Library, Lancaster NY. 716-683-1120
Spessard, Bebe, *Librn,* Tulsa City-County Library (Sheridan), Tulsa OK. 918-836-1886
Spessard, Ronnie, *Infor Ser,* Cameron University Library, Lawton OK. 405-248-2200, Ext 410
Speziale, N Paul, *In Charge,* South Bergen Library Group, Lodi Memorial Library, Lodi NJ. 201-777-9195
Speziale, Paul, *Dir,* Lodi Memorial Library, Lodi NJ. 201-777-9195
Spguenza, Jr, Peter, *Librn,* California State Court of Appeal Law Library, Sacramento CA. 916-445-4677
Sphar, Carol, *Tech Serv & Cat,* Brevard Community College, Learning Resources Center, Cocoa FL. 305-632-1111, Ext 295, 298
Spicer, Carol, *Bkmobile Coordr,* Winchester-Clark County Public Library, Winchester KY. 606-744-5661
Spicer, Caroline, *Ref,* Cornell University Libraries (University Libraries), Ithaca NY. 607-256-4144
Spicer, Erik J, *Librn,* Parliament of Canada, Library of Parliament, Ottawa ON. 613-995-7113
Spicer, Judith, *On-Line Servs,* Wayne Township Library, Morrisson-Reeves Library, Richmond IN. 317-966-8291
Spicer, Susanne J, *Librn,* Paris Carnegie Public Library, Paris IL. 217-463-3950
Spicher, Norma, *Reader Serv,* Greenfield Community College, Library-Learning Resources Center, Greenfield MA. 413-774-3131, Ext 285
Spidell, Dorothy K, *Per,* Saddleback Community College Library, Mission Viejo CA. 714-831-4515
Spielman, Enid, *Asst Librn,* Whipple Free Library, New Boston NH. 603-487-3391
Spielman, Rozelin, *Librn,* John Curtis Free Library, Hanover MA. 617-826-2972
Spiers, Mrs Dudley, *Librn,* Screven-Jenkins Regional Library (Jenkins County Memorial), Millen GA. 912-982-4244
Spiess, Johanna, *Librn,* Brooklyn Public Library (Sheepshead Bay), Brooklyn NY. 212-743-0663
Spiess, M Lucille, *In Charge,* American University (Periodicals), Washington DC. 202-686-2322
Spieth, Lucile A, *Librn,* Cuyahoga County Public Library (Strongsville Branch), Strongsville OH. 216-238-5330
Spiker, Carlyn, *Tech Serv,* Spokane Community College, East Mission Campus Library, Spokane WA. 509-455-7699
Spilchuk, Christine, *ILL & Acq,* Atikokan Public Library, Atikokan ON. 807-597-4406, 597-4230
Spilka, Ellen P, *Coordinator,* Northern Interrelated Library System, Pawtucket RI. 401-723-5350
Spilka, Ellen P, *ILL,* Pawtucket Public Library & Regional Library Center, Deborah Cook Sayles Memorial Library, Pawtucket RI. 401-725-3714
Spiller, Deborah, *Coll & Program Develop,* Chicago Public Library, Chicago IL. 312-269-2900
Spiller, Henrietta, *Librn,* Detroit Public Library (Parkman), Detroit MI. 313-833-9770
Spiller, Pat, *Media,* Ector County Library, Odessa TX. 915-332-0633
Spillers, Roger E, *Project Dir,* Central Ohio Interlibrary Network, (COIN), OH. 419-526-1337
Spillman, Pamela, *Librn,* United States Air Force (Medical Center Library), Wright-Patterson AFB OH. 513-257-4506
Spindler, Ruth, *Librn,* Sherwin Williams Chemicals (Commercial Intelligence Library), Cleveland OH. 216-566-2245
Spinelli, Frances B, *Acq,* State of Vermont Department of Libraries, Montpelier VT. 802-828-3261
Spinks, Paul, *Dir,* Naval Postgraduate School, Dudley Knox Library, Monterey CA. 408-646-2341
Spinnegan, Martha, *Dir,* Richmond Memorial Library, Batavia NY. 716-343-9550
Spinney, Molly P, *Ref,* Westminster College, McGill Library, New Wilmington PA. 412-946-8761, Ext 342
Spire, Ellen, *Pub Relations,* San Jacinto Junior College (North Campus Library), Houston TX. 713-458-4050

Spirito, Mrs S, *Group Leader,* George Brown College of Applied Arts & Technology Library (Kensington Campus), Toronto ON. 416-967-1212
Spiro, Elizabeth, *Dir, Tech Serv & Acq,* Carnegie Free Library, Beaver Falls PA. 412-846-4340
Spiro, Louise, *Librn,* Cleveland Public Library (Arlington), Cleveland OH. 216-451-0306
Spirt, Diana L, *Prof,* Long Island University, Palmer Graduate Library School, NY. 516-299-2855 & 299-2856
Spitler, Dian, *Ref,* Atlantic City Free Public Library, Atlantic City NJ. 609-345-2269
Spitz, Herman H, *Dir,* E R Johnstone Training & Research Center, Johnstone Professional Library, Bordentown NJ. 609-298-2500, Ext 382
Spitzer, Ann, *Cat,* College of Alameda Library & Resources Center, Alameda CA. 415-522-7221, Ext 365
Spitzer, Paul G, *Boeing Historian,* Boeing Co (Boeing Historical Library), Seattle WA. 206-655-4756
Spitzer, Roberta, *Media,* Elyria Public Library, Elyria OH. 216-323-5747
Spitzform, Danna, *Cat,* Dickinson School of Law, Sheely-Lee Law Library, Carlisle PA. 717-243-4611, Ext 9
Spitzmiller, Christina, *Bkmobile Coordr,* Edison Free Public Library, Edison NJ. 201-287-2298
Spivey, Donna, *Ad,* Pasquotank-Camden Library, Elizabeth City NC. 919-335-2473
Spivey, J Allen, *Dir,* Brunswick Junior College, Clara Wood Gould Memorial Library, Brunswick GA. 912-264-7270
Spivey, Marie, *Chief Librn,* United States Army Engineer Waterways Experiment Station, Technical Information Center Library Branch, Vicksburg MS. 601-636-3111, Ext 2542, 2543, 2544, 2545
Spivey, Noreen, *Librn,* Kinchafoonee Regional Library (Webster County), Preston GA. 912-995-2902
Spivey, Ruth, *Librn,* Woods Hole Oceanographic Institution (Document Library), Woods Hole MA. 617-548-1400, Ext 2269
Spivey, Suzanne, *Librn,* Pamunkey Regional Library (West Point Branch), West Point VA. 804-843-3244
Splichal, LaMoyne, *In Charge,* North Dakota State Highway Department Technical Library, Bismarck ND. 701-224-2560
Spoede, Mary H, *Librn,* Scott & White Memorial Hospital, Medical Library, Temple TX. 817-774-2228
Spohn, Richard, *Head,* University of Cincinnati Libraries (Geology), Cincinnati OH. 513-475-4332
Spolarich, Eleanor, *Librn,* General Motors Corp, Electro-Motive Division Engineering Library, La Grange IL. 312-387-6706
Spolsky, Myron J, *In Charge,* Ukrainian Cultural & Education Centre Library, Winnipeg MB. 204-942-0218
Spoo, Margaret G, *Librn,* Rochester State Hospital Libraries, Rochester MN. 507-285-7114, 285-7058
Spooner, Gloria, *Institutional Libr Consult,* Louisiana State Library, Baton Rouge LA. 504-342-4922
Spooner, Therese, *ILL,* Pembroke Public Library, Pembroke ON. 613-732-8844
Spoor, Jean, *Asst Librn,* Monterey-Tippecanoe Township Public Library, Monterey Public Library, Monterey IN. 219-542-2171
Spoor, Richard D, *Librn,* Union Theological Seminary Library, New York NY. 212-662-7100, Ext 274
Spore-Alhadef, Mary, *Media,* Redwood City Public Library, Redwood City CA. 415-369-6251, Ext 288
Sporring, Reta, *Librn,* Madoc Public Library, Madoc ON. 613-473-4456
Spotts, Mrs H B, *Librn,* Cochran County Library, Morton TX. 806-266-5051
Spradley, Albert, *Media,* Tallahassee Community College Library, Tallahassee FL. 904-576-5181
Spradlin, Emily, *Ser,* University of Louisville Library, Louisville KY. 502-588-6745
Spradlin, Frances R, *ILL,* University of Oregon Health Sciences Center (Health Sciences Library), Portland OR. 503-225-8026

Sprague, Mildred, *Tech Serv,* Mid-Continent Public Library, Independence MO. 816-836-5200
Sprang, Rea Dot, *Librn,* Wayne General & Technical College Library, Orrville OH. 216-683-2010
Sprankle, Anita, *Non-print,* Kutztown State College, Rohrbach Library, Kutztown PA. 215-683-4480
Spratt, Albert, *Ref & Rare Bks,* Mississauga Public Library, Mississauga ON. 416-625-8681
Sprehe, Beverly, *Cat,* Metropolitan Library System, Oklahoma City OK. 405-235-0571
Spreitzer, F, *Librn,* University of Southern California (Microtext Reading Room), Los Angeles CA. 213-743-6077
Spreitzer, Mary Margaret, *Asst Dir & Ad,* Joliet Public Library, Joliet IL. 815-727-4726
Sprengel, Julia, *Tech Serv,* Union College Library, Lincoln NE. 402-488-2331, Ext 316
Spriestersbach, Jannean, *Librn,* Pasadena Public Library (Lamanda Park), Pasadena CA. 213-793-5672
Sprietsma, R, *Ch,* Lisle Library District, Lisle IL. 312-971-1675
Spriggs, Betty, *Librn Blind,* Wichita Public Library, Wichita KS. 316-262-0611
Springenberg, V, *Librn,* Central States Institute of Addiction Library, Chicago IL. 312-266-6100, Ext 340
Springer, Daidee, *Librn,* Ferndale Public Library, Ferndale MI. 313-548-5959
Springer, Jean M, *Dir,* Young Men's Mercantile Library Association, Cincinnati OH. 513-621-0717
Springer, John J, *Librn,* Kansas City Star Library, Kansas City MO. 816-234-4406
Springer, Judy, *Librn,* Hanover Public Library, Hanover KS. 913-337-2485
Springer, Lawrence K, *Media,* Western Maryland Public Libraries, Hagerstown MD. 301-739-3250
Springer, Linda, *Ad,* Springfield-Greene County Library, Springfield MO. 417-869-4621
Springer, Marcia, *Asst Librn,* Ebensburg Free Public Library, Ebensburg PA. 814-472-7957
Springer, Nelson P, *Actg Dir & On-Line Servs,* Goshen College (Mennonite Historical Library), Goshen IN. 219-533-3161, Ext 337
Springstead, Ruth, *Exten Serv,* Tucson Public Library, Tucson AZ. 602-791-4391
Sprinkle, Michael D, *Dir,* Wake Forest University (Bowman Gray School of Medicine Library), Winston-Salem NC. 919-727-4691
Sprinkle, Sylvia, *Ch & Outreach,* Forsyth County Public Library, Winston-Salem NC. 919-727-2556
Spritzer, Donald, *Doc & Spec Coll,* City-County Library of Missoula, Missoula MT. 406-728-5900
Sprott, Elizabeth A, *Librn,* South Carolina Supreme Court Library, Columbia SC. 803-758-3741
Sproul, Allison, *ILL,* University of Winnipeg Library, Winnipeg MB. 204-786-7811, Ext 520
Sproul, Olive, *Supvr,* Huron County Public Library (Ethel Branch), Ethel ON. 519-887-9587
Sprudzs, Adolf, *Foreign Law,* University of Chicago (Law Library), Chicago IL. 312-753-3425
Sprug, Joseph, *Dir,* Saint Edward's University Library, Austin TX. 512-444-2621
Sprung, George, *Ref,* College of Medicine & Dentistry of New Jersey, George F Smith Library of the Health Sciences, Newark NJ. 201-456-4580
Sprunger, Ann, *Media,* University of Michigan Libraries (Ford L Lemler Educational Film Library), Ann Arbor MI. 313-764-5360
Sprunt, James, *Chmn,* Woodrow Wilson Birthplace Foundation, Inc, Research Library, Staunton VA. 703-885-0897
Sprynczynatyk, Betty, *Ref,* North Dakota State Library, Bismarck ND. 701-224-2490
Spuler, Andrew E, *Tech Serv & Acq,* Williamsport Area Community College Library, Williamsport PA. 717-326-3761, Ext 211
Spurgeon, Katherine, *Dir & Acq,* Greenwood Public Library, Greenwood IN. 317-881-1953
Spurling, Norman, *Librn,* Chevy Chase Baptist Church, Sebring Memorial Library, Washington DC. 202-966-9496
Spurlock, Lucretia, *Librn,* Sun City Library (Fairway), Sun City AZ. 602-933-7433

Spurlock, Paula, *Ref*, Missouri Western State College, Hearnes Learning Resources Center, Saint Joseph MO. 816-271-4368

Spurlock, Sandra, *Dir & On-Line Servs*, Long Island Jewish-Hillside Medical Center, Sylvia Harris Health Sciences Library, New Hyde Park NY. 516-470-2673

Spurrier, Suzanne, *Circ & On-Line Servs*, Harding University, Beaumont Memorial Library, Searcy AR. 501-268-6161, Ext 354

Spyers-Duran, Peter, *Dir*, California State University, Long Beach, University Library, Long Beach CA. 213-498-4047

Spyra, Rosemarie, *Cat*, D'Youville College, Library Resources Center, Buffalo NY. 716-886-8100, Ext 304

Squint, Charlene, *Librn*, Cass County Library (Howard Community), Niles MI. 616-445-8651

Squire, Jeannette W, *Librn*, Plymouth Congregational Church, Vida B Varey Library, Seattle WA. 206-622-4865

Squire, Stephen E, *Librn*, Virginia Division of Justice & Crime Prevention Library, Richmond VA. 804-281-9276, Ext 244

Squires, Helene, *Acq*, Lyndon State College, Samuel Read Hall Library, Lyndonville VT. 802-626-3555

Squires, Lillian, *Med Librn*, Terrell State Hospital, Medical & Client Libraries, Terrell TX. 214-563-6452, Ext 302 & 497

Squires, Roger, *ILL*, Klamath County Library, Klamath Falls OR. 503-882-8894

Squires, Stan, *Ch*, Oakville Public Library, Oakville ON. 416-845-3405

Squyres, Barbara, *Librn*, Hughes Aircraft Co, Research & Development Library, Newport Beach CA. 714-759-2492

Sroat, Ena M, *Dir, ILL & Acq*, Trinidad State Junior College, Samuel Freudenthal Memorial Library, Trinidad CO. 303-846-5593

Sroka, Mrs K, *Librn*, John McKay-Clements Library Library, Haileybury Public Library, Haileybury ON. 705-672-3707

Sroufe, P Gordon, *Media*, Siena Heights College Library, Adrian MI. 517-263-0731, Ext 242

Srygley, Ted F, *Dir*, University of Florida Libraries (J Hillis Miller Health Center), Gainesville FL. 904-392-4011

St-Clair, Ann, *Cat*, Mobile Public Library, Mobile AL. 205-438-7073

St-John, Joanne, *On-Line Servs*, International Academy at Santa Barbara, Environmental Studies Institute Library, Santa Barbara CA. 805-965-5010

St-Onge, Sylvie, *In Charge*, Albert-Westmorland-Kent Regional Library (Dieppe Public), Dieppe NB. 506-389-2631

St-Pierre, Michel, *Prof*, College de Maisonneuve, Techniques de la Documentation, PQ. 514-254-7131

St-Pierre, Normand, *Chief Librn*, Public Archives of Canada Library, Ottawa ON. 613-992-2669

Staab, Kathryn, *School Servs*, Imperial County Free Library, Imperial CA. 714-355-2260

Staack, Katharine, *Cat*, Tufts University, Nils Yngve Wessell Library, Medford MA. 617-628-5000, Ext 235

Staar, Richard F, *Assoc Dir*, Hoover Institution on War, Revolution & Peace, Stanford CA. 415-497-2058

Staar, Richard F, *Dir*, Stanford University Libraries (Hoover Institution), Stanford CA. 415-497-2062

Staats, Jean L, *Librn*, Fall River Public Library (East End), Fall River MA. 617-672-4545

Staats, Joan, *Librn*, Jackson Laboratory, Research Library, Bar Harbor ME. 207-288-3373, Ext 208

Staatz, Evelyn, *Ref*, Penn Valley Community College Library, Kansas City MO. 816-756-2800, Ext 428

Stabe, Daniel, *ILL*, Case Western Reserve University Libraries (Freiberger), Cleveland OH. 216-368-3506

Stabile, Brenda, *Cat*, Carnegie Library of Pittsburgh, Pittsburgh PA. 412-622-3100

Stacey, G, *Forestry*, Lakehead University Library, Thunder Bay ON. 807-345-2121

Stacey, George, *Librn*, Banff Library, Banff AB. 403-762-2661

Stacey, Muriel I, *Dir*, Milford Township Library, Milford MI. 313-684-0845

Stacey, Ovaline, *Librn*, Essex County Public Library (Comber Branch), Comber ON. 519-776-5241

Stachacz, John, *Ser*, Washburn University of Topeka, Mabee Library, Topeka KS. 913-295-6479

Stachowiak, Kathleen, *Asst Dir*, Saint Paul Public Library, Saint Paul MN. 612-292-6311

Stachura, Leonard, *Dir*, Saint John Vianney College, Seminary Library, Miami FL. 305-223-4561

Stack, Elizabeth, *Librn*, Marion County Library (Nicholas Branch), Nichols SC. 803-526-2641

Stack, Rita B, *Librn*, Eastman Kodak Co (Health, Safety & Human Factors Laboratory Library), Rochester NY. 716-458-1000, Ext 83619

Stack, Robert, *Cat*, Florida International University, North Miami Campus Library, North Miami FL. 305-940-5730

Stack, Robert J, *Dir*, Granite City Public Library, Granite City IL. 618-876-0550

Stacy, Betty A, *Librn*, Virginia Museum of Fine Arts Library, Richmond VA. 804-257-0827

Stadelbacher, Harold, *Publ Libr Consult*, Shawnee Library System, Carterville IL. 618-985-3711

Stadelman, Margaret, *Librn*, Lang Memorial Library, Wilson KS. 913-658-7660

Staehlin, Robert H, *Dir*, Yuba Community College, Library Learning Center, Marysville CA. 916-742-7351, Ext 242

Staff, Linda, *Librn*, Boston State Hospital, Medical Library, Dorchester MA. 617-436-6000, Ext 221

Stafford, Beverly B, *Librn*, Oregon School of Arts & Crafts Library, Portland OR. 503-297-5544

Stafford, Edna, *Librn*, Tangipahoa Parish Library (Amite Branch), Amite LA. 504-748-9387

Stafford, Irene, *Librn*, Bethel Public Library, Bethel VT. 802-234-9107

Stafford, M, *Acq*, Saint Thomas Public Library, Saint Thomas ON. 519-631-6050

Stafford, Robert M, *Dir*, John McIntire Public Library Public Library, Zanesville OH. 614-453-0391

Stafiej, Eileen, *Ref*, Fall River Public Library, Fall River MA. 617-676-8541

Stager, David, *Librn*, Princeton University Library (Geology), Princeton NJ. 609-452-3180

Stagg, Deborah, *Cat & Tech Serv*, Philadelphia College of Art Library, Philadelphia PA. 215-893-3126

Stagg, Kathleen, *Asst Librn*, Calcasieu Parish Public Library System, Lake Charles LA. 318-433-1045

Staggs, Edwin A, *Chief Librn*, 3M Co, Riker Laboratories, Incorporated, Northridge Library, Northridge CA. 213-341-1300, Ext 441

Staggs, Esther P, *Librn*, Hennessey Public Library, Hennessey OK. 405-853-2073

Staggs, Marge, *Librn*, Washington State Library (Echo Glen Children's Center), Snoqualmie WA. 206-222-5152

Stagner, Adalene, *Librn*, Burns & McDonnell Engineering Co Library, Kansas City MO. 816-333-4375

Stagner, Dorothy, *Circ*, Bradford Memorial Library, El Dorado KS. 316-321-3363

Stagnolia, Martha, *ILL & Acq*, Southeast Community College, Learning Resources Center, Cumberland KY. 606-589-2145, Ext 25

Stahl, Barry, *ILL & Ref*, Western Regional Public Library System, Springfield MA. 413-732-3115

Stahl, Dorothy, *Ad*, Bethpage Public Library, Bethpage NY. 516-913-3907

Stahl, Freda D, *Dir*, Algonquin Area Public Library District, Algonquin IL. 312-658-4343

Stahl, Hella, *Inf Retrieval Specialist*, Pulp & Paper Research Institute of Canada Library, Pointe-Claire PQ. 514-697-4110, Ext 226

Stahl, Joan, *Fine Arts*, Enoch Pratt Free Library, Baltimore MD. 301-396-5430, 396-5395

Stahl, Lois, *Tech Serv & Cat*, Public Library of Anniston & Calhoun County, Liles Memorial Library, Anniston AL. 205-237-8501, Ext 8503

Stahl, Mildred, *Librn*, Salisbury Free Library, Salisbury NH. 603-648-2473

Stahl, Milo D, *Media*, Eastern Mennonite College & Seminary Library, Harrisonburg VA. 703-433-2771, Ext 171

Stahl, Natalia, *Acq & Ser*, Clarkson College of Technology, Harriet Call Burnap Memorial Library, Potsdam NY. 315-268-6645

Stahl, Robert J, *Librn*, Notre Dame Seminary Library, New Orleans LA. 504-866-7426

Stahl, Wilson M, *Assoc Dir, Pub Servs & On-Line Servs*, Stockton State College Library, Pomona NJ. 609-652-1776, Ext 343

Stahlhut, Dale S, *Superintendent*, University of Texas, Balcones Research Center, Austin TX. 512-836-0440, Ext 278

Stahlschmidt, Agnes, *Instr*, University of Iowa, School of Library Science, IA. 319-353-3644

Stahr, Martha, *Librn*, United States Army (Educational Development), Fort Knox KY. 502-624-5344

Staiger, Lillian, *ILL*, Schools of Theology in Dubuque Library, Dubuque IA. 319-589-3100, 556-8151

Staiger, Margaret, *Acq, Ref & On-Line Servs*, Ursinus College, Myrin Library, Collegeville PA. 215-489-4111, Ext 290

Stailey, Wilford, *Dir LRC*, Eastern Arizona College, Learning Resources Center, Thatcher AZ. 602-428-1133, Ext 305, 306, 307

Stainaker, Enolia L, *Chief Librn*, Veterans Administration, Library Service, Amarillo TX. 806-355-9703, Ext 263

Stainbrook, Lynn, *YA*, Janesville Public Library, Janesville WI. 608-752-8934, Ext B

Stainbrook, Patricia, *Librn*, Library Association of Portland (Woodstock), Portland OR. 503-771-3538

Stair, Angela, *Librn*, Van Buren County Library (Mattawan Branch), Mattawan MI. 616-423-4771

Stair, Fred, *ILL*, Colorado School of Mines, Arthur Lakes Library, Golden CO. 303-279-0300, Ext 2690

Stajniak, Elizabeth T, *Librn*, Detroit Bar Association Foundation Library, Detroit MI. 313-961-3507

Stakus, Margaret, *Librn*, Taunton Public Library (Bay St), Taunton MA. 617-823-3570

Stalcup, Patricia S, *Acq*, Hayner Public Library District, Alton IL. 618-462-0651

Staley, Barbara A, *Librn*, Human Sciences Research Inc Library, McLean VA. 703-893-5200

Staley, Mary, *Librn*, Wornstaff Memorial Public Library, Ashley OH. 614-747-2085

Stalker, Gene R, *Librn*, G Pierce Wood Memorial Hospital, Patients' Library, Arcadia FL. 813-494-3323, Ext 414

Stalker, John, *Pub Servs & On-Line Servs*, Atlanta University, Trevor Arnett Library, Atlanta GA. 404-681-0251, Ext 225

Stallings, Larry, *Dir*, Florida Southern College, Roux Library, Lakeland FL. 813-683-5521, Ext 211

Stallings, Oma, *Tech Serv*, Eastern New Mexico University, Roswell Campus Library, Roswell NM. 505-347-5441, Ext 244

Stallings, Tom, *Media Design & TV Production*, Lake City Community College, G T Melton Learning Resources Center, Lake City FL. 904-752-1822, Ext 260

Stallion, Vera, *Librn*, Knoxville-Knox County Public Library (Southgate), Knoxville TN. 615-573-2311

Stalsitz, Emma, *Asst Librn*, Sacred Heart Hospital, Health Service Library, Allentown PA. 215-821-3280

Stalzer, Sister Rita, *Philos & Theology*, Loyola University of Chicago Libraries (Elizabeth M Cudahy Memorial Library), Chicago IL. 312-274-3000, Ext 771

Stam, David, *Andrew W Mellon Dir*, New York Public Library (The Research Libraries), New York NY. 212-790-6262

Stam, Juanita, *Tech Serv*, Bradford Public Library, Bradford ON. 416-775-6482

Stambaugh, Catherine T, *Librn*, Pennsylvania Department of Justice Law Library, Harrisburg PA. 717-787-3176

Stamey, Roy, *Librn*, Saint Herman's Theological Seminary Library, Kodiak AK. 907-486-3524

Stamm, Barbara, *AV & Cat*, Boyden Library, Foxboro MA. 617-543-8882

Stamm, Jean, *Asst Librn*, New Milford Public Library, New Milford CT. 203-355-1191

Stamm, Jean, *ILL*, Saratoga Springs Public Library, Saratoga Springs NY. 518-584-7860

Stammers, Gina, *Circ*, Town of Caledon Public Libraries, Bolton ON. 416-857-1400

Stammes, Pamela, *Commun Servs,* Burlingame Public Library, Burlingame CA. 415-344-7107
Stamoolis, Peter, *Libm,* Consolidation Coal Co, Exploration Services Library, Pittsburgh PA. 412-831-4513
Stampfl, Barbara, *ILL,* Rosenberg Library, Galveston TX. 713-763-8854
Stan, David, *General Administrative Officers: Dir Res Libr,* New York Public Library, Astor, Lenox & Tilden Foundations Library, New York NY. 212-790-6262
Stanaitis, Dorothy M, *Ch,* Gloucester City Library, Gloucester City NJ. 609-456-4181
Stanbery, G W, *Dir,* Findlay-Hancock County Public Library, Findlay OH. 419-422-1712
Stanbery, Judy, *Tech Serv, Acq & Cat,* John McIntire Public Library Public Library, Zanesville OH. 614-453-0391
Stanbury, Robert, *ILL & Ref,* Essex County College, Learning Resources Center, Newark NJ. 201-877-3233
Stancill, Linda M, *Tech Serv & Cat,* Sheppard Memorial Library, Greenville NC. 919-752-4177
Stanczak, Mark M, *Libm,* Cleveland Public Library (Fleet), Cleveland OH. 216-641-5666
Standera, Oldrich, *Info Systs,* University of Calgary Library, Calgary AB. 403-284-5954
Standford, Linda, *Libm,* Bossier Parish Public Library (Plain Dealing Branch), Plain Dealing LA. 318-326-4233
Standiford, Ann, *Ref,* New Martinsville Public Library, New Martinsville WV. 304-455-4545
Standing, Doris A, *Libm,* Ontario Ministry of Health, Public Health Laboratories Library, Toronto ON. 416-248-3165
Standish, Beulah I, *Libm,* Consumers Power Co, Legal Library, Jackson MI. 517-788-1087
Standley, Emily, *Libm,* Seattle Weaver's Guild Library, Seattle WA. 206-324-1125
Stanek, E, *Libm,* University of Saskatchewan Library (Law), Saskatoon SK. 306-343-4273
Stanfield, Barrie, *Libm,* Canada Department of Agriculture, Research Station Library, Charlottetown PE. 902-892-5461, Ext 113
Stanfield, Linda, *Ch,* North Vancouver District Public Library, North Vancouver BC. 604-984-0286
Stang, Karen, *Ch,* Bedford Park Public Library District, Argo IL. 312-458-6826
Stangeland, Blanche, *Libm,* Carrington City Library, Carrington ND. 701-652-3921
Stanger, Carole, *Dir, Acq & Ref,* Matilda J Gibson Memorial Library, Creston IA. 515-782-2277
Stanger, Cary David, *Libm,* International Ladies' Garment Workers' Union, Research Dept Library, New York NY. 212-265-7000
Stanger, Keith, *Bibliog Instr,* Eastern Michigan University, Center of Educational Resources, Ypsilanti MI. 313-487-0020
Stangl, Peter, *Dir,* Stanford University Libraries (Lane Medical), Stanford CA. 415-497-6831
Stangl, Teresa, *On-Line Servs & Bibliog Instr,* Nobles County Library & Information Center, Worthington MN. 507-372-2981
Stangs, Loretta F, *Mgr, Libr Servs,* Hoechst-Roussel Pharmaceuticals, Inc Library, Div of American Hoechst Corp Library, Somerville NJ. 201-685-2394
Stanhope, Sara, *Ad,* Westwood Public Library, Westwood MA. 617-326-7562
Staniszewski, Victoria, *Asst Libm,* Detroit-Macomb Hospitals Association, South Macomb Hospital Library, Warren MI. 313-573-5117
Staniszewski, Victoria, *In Charge,* South Macomb Hospital, Hospital Library, Warren MI. 313-573-5117
Stanka, Sister Marguerite, *Dir,* Dominican College of San Rafael, Archbishop Alemany Library, San Rafael CA. 415-457-4440, Ext 251
Stankevich, Mary, *Libm,* Metropolitan Jewish Geriatric Center, Max B & Luisa Spiero Marks Memorial Medical Library, Brooklyn NY. 212-853-2800
Stankewicz, Mary C, *Libm,* Free Public Library of Woodbridge (Hopelawn Branch), Hopelawn NJ. 201-826-3097
Stanko, Emily, *Libm,* Detroit Public Library (Conely), Detroit MI. 313-833-9750
Stankus, Anthony V, *Libm,* College of the Holy Cross (O'Callahan Science Library), Worcester MA. 617-793-2501

Stanley, Elsie, *Libm,* Norridgewock Free Public Library, Norridgewock ME. 207-634-2828
Stanley, Emma, *Prog Planner,* Atlanta Public Library, Atlanta GA. 404-688-4636
Stanley, Esta, *Libm,* Columbus County Public Library (Tabor City Public), Tabor City NC. 919-653-3774
Stanley, Janet L, *Bureau Libm,* Smithsonian Institution Libraries (Museum of African Art Library), Washington DC. 202-547-6222
Stanley, John R, *Libm,* Dallas Bible College, Gould Memorial Library, Dallas TX. 214-328-7171
Stanley, Laurel, *Media,* Lyndon State College, Samuel Read Hall Library, Lyndonville VT. 802-626-3555
Stanley, Lee, *Asst Libm,* Congregation Rodeph Shalom Library, Philadelphia PA. 215-627-6747
Stanley, Louise M, *Curric Mats,* Alabama State University, Library & Learning Resources, Montgomery AL. 205-832-6072
Stanley, Luana, *Cat,* Indianapolis-Marion County Public Library, Indianapolis IN. 317-635-5662
Stanley, Marie, *Readers Adv,* Fresno County Free Library, Fresno CA. 209-488-3191
Stanley, Mildred, *Circ,* Morehead State University, Johnson Camden-Julian Carroll Library, Morehead KY. 606-783-2250
Stanley, Mrs Tempie, *Libm,* Oconee Regional Library (Katherine W Gray), Dublin GA. 912-272-0524
Stanley, Nancy Nell, *In Charge,* Southern Baptist Convention Foreign Mission Board, Jenkins Memorial Library & Archives Center, Richmond VA. 804-353-0151, Ext 311
Stanley, Ralph, *Pres,* Mount Desert Island Historical Society Library, Mount Desert ME. 207-244-3673
Stanley, Richard, *Fiscal Affairs,* New York University, Elmer Holmes Bobst Library, New York NY. 212-598-2484
Stanley, Sue, *Ref,* Hilbert College, McGrath Library, Hamburg NY. 716-649-7900, Ext 237
Stanley, William, *Coordr,* Skyline College Library, San Bruno CA. 415-355-7000, Ext 311
Stannard, Emma, *Libm,* Dorset Village Public Library Association, Inc, Dorset VT. 802-867-5774
Stansbery, Kay, *Tech Serv,* Tarrant County Junior College System, Fort Worth TX. 817-281-7860, Ext 485
Stansfield, George J, *Spec Coll,* National Defense University Library, Washington DC. 202-693-8437
Stansfield, Marilyn, *Libm,* Humboldt County Library (McDermitt Branch), Winnemucca NV. 702-623-5081, Ext 315 & 316
Stanton, Mae, *Libm,* Avon Public Library, Avon-By-The-Sea NJ. 201-775-6998
Stanton, Mrs James H, *Libm,* Cambridge Hospital, Medical Library, Cambridge MA. 617-498-1439
Stanton, R O, *Head Info Syst Dept,* Bell Telephone Laboratories, Libraries & Information Systems Center, Murray Hill NJ. 582-2854 (General); 582-4466 (Info Systs Dept); 582-6880 (Info Servs Dept); 949-3456 (Libr Operations Dept)
Stanton, Vida C, *Asst Prof,* University of Wisconsin-Milwaukee, School of Library Science, WI. 414-963-4707
Stanton, Virginia B, *Dir,* Garden City Public Library, Garden City NY. 516-742-8405
Stanwood, Cheryl, *Libm,* Court of Appeal, Second Appellate District Library, Los Angeles CA. 213-736-2661
Staples, Elna, *Libm,* Southern Wisconsin Center for the Developmentally Disabled, Union Grove WI. 414-878-2411, Ext 230
Staples, Lena, *Libm,* Lakeville Public Library, Lakeville MA. 617-947-9028
Staples, Martha, *Libm,* Orlando Public Library (Fort Gatlin), Orlando FL. 305-859-0110
Staples, Robert H, *Dir,* Princeton Public Library, Princeton NJ. 609-924-9529
Stapleton, Dorie, *Doc,* Morehead State University, Johnson Camden-Julian Carroll Library, Morehead KY. 606-783-2250
Stapleton, Dorthy, *Libm,* Tom Green County Library System (Angelo West), San Angelo TX. 915-944-1350
Stapleton, Joseph J, *Libm,* Fairchild Camera & Instrument Corp, Fairchild Space & Defense System Library, Syosset NY. 516-931-4500, Ext 445

Stapleton, Lorraine, *Libm,* Denton Public Library, Denton MT. 406-567-2571
Stapleton, Scott, *Art,* University of Chicago, Joseph Regenstein Library, Chicago IL. 312-753-2977
Stapleton, Sister Mauricita, *Libm,* Salve Regina College Library, Newport RI. 401-847-6650, Ext 272
Stapp, Delores, *Tech Serv,* Northwest Kansas Library System, Norton KS. 913-877-5148
Stapper, Antoinette, *Libm,* National Association of Mutual Savings Banks, Library Central Files, New York NY. 212-973-5432
Starbird, Hilda, *AV & Per,* Westborough Public Library, Westborough MA. 617-366-2812
Starck, Martha, *Libr Tech,* Milwaukee Area Technical College, West Region Campus Library, West Allis WI. 414-278-6205
Starin, Mary E, *Spec Coll,* Talbot County Free Library, Easton MD. 301-822-1626
Stark, A, *Libm,* Algonquin College of Applied Arts & Technology (Rideau Campus), Ottawa ON. 613-237-3120
Stark, Caroline, *Br Coordr,* Public Library of Nashville & Davidson County, Nashville TN. 615-244-4700
Stark, Delia, *Cat,* University of Maryland at Baltimore (School of Law Library), Baltimore MD. 301-528-7270
Stark, Freda A, *Libm,* Valley Falls Free Library, Valley Falls NY. 518-753-4230
Stark, Harold E, *Head Libm,* Harford Community College Learning Resources Center, Bel Air MD. 301-838-1000, Ext 268
Stark, Linda, *Cat,* Shelbyville-Shelby County Public Library, Shelbyville IN. 317-398-7121
Stark, Lucile, *Dir,* University of Pittsburgh (Western Psychiatric Institute & Clinic Library), Pittsburgh PA. 412-624-2378
Stark, Marilyn, *Libm,* Beauregard Parish Public Library (Merryville Branch), Merryville LA. 318-825-3371
Stark, Marilyn, *Libm,* Dames & Moore Library, Denver CO. 303-232-6262
Stark, Mary E, *Libm,* United States Army (Morale Support Activity), West Point NY. 914-938-4819
Stark, Mrs Virgil, *ILL,* Girard Free Public Library, Girard OH. 216-545-2508
Starke, Hugh, *Tech Serv,* Clinton-Essex-Franklin Library System, Plattsburgh NY. 518-563-5190
Starke, Ray, *Libm,* Veterans Administration (Medical Library), Temple TX. 817-778-4811, Ext 526, 527, 528
Starkey, Edward, *Ref,* University of Dayton Libraries, Roesch Library, Dayton OH. 513-229-4221
Starkey, Isabelle, *Asst Libm,* Curry Public Library, Gold Beach OR. 503-247-7246
Starkey, Richard E, *Dir,* Wilbraham Public Library, Wilbraham MA. 413-596-6142
Starkey, Robin, *Ref,* East Orange Public Library, East Orange NJ. 201-266-5600
Starks, Edna, *Libm,* New Haven Free Public Library (Stetson), New Haven CT. 203-787-8119
Starks, Myra, *Cat,* Bedford Public Library, Bedford TX. 817-283-2751
Starks, Rosalie, *Libm,* Metropolitan Library System (Village), Oklahoma City OK. 405-235-0571
Starks, Verna, *Libm,* Human Factors Research, Inc Library, Goleta CA. 805-964-0591
Starling, Judy, *In Charge,* Riverside Presbyterian Church, Jean Miller Memorial Library, Jacksonville FL. 904-355-4585
Starling, Leonard W, *Libm,* Mount Vernon Public Library, Mount Vernon IL. 618-242-6322
Starman, Ada, *Ref,* Rock Springs Public Library, Rock Springs WY. 307-362-6212
Starr, Barbara, *Libm,* Fairfax County Public Library (Sherwood Regional), Alexandria VA. 703-765-3645
Starr, Carol, *YA,* Alameda County Library, Hayward CA. 415-881-6337
Starr, Daniel, *Cat,* Museum of Modern Art Library, New York NY. 212-956-7236
Starr, Gail, *Libm,* University of Calgary Library (Law), Calgary AB. 403-284-5090
Starr, Georgia, *Libm,* Iowa School for the Deaf Library, Council Bluffs IA. 712-366-0571
Starr, Lee, *Dir,* Hayden Lake Area Free District Library, Hayden Lake ID. 208-772-5612
Starr, Lee, *YA,* Santa Clara City Library, Santa Clara CA. 408-984-3097

Starr, Margaret, *Librn,* Chicago Public Library (Back of the Yards), Chicago IL. 312-247-8367

Starr, Marilyn, *Ref,* Point Loma College, Ryan Library, San Diego CA. 714-222-6474, Ext 355, 338

Starr, Marsha, *Asst Librn,* Pine Manor College, Alumnae Library, Chestnut Hill MA. 617-731-7081, 731-7083

Starr, Mary M, *Ch,* Barnesville Public Library, Barnesville OH. 614-425-1651

Starr, Paul D, *Dir & ILL,* Carroll College, Carrier Memorial Library, Waukesha WI. 414-547-1212

Starr, Ruby, *Publicity Coordr,* Harford County Library, Bel Air MD. 301-838-7484

Starr, Susan S, *Asst Librn,* University of California at Davis (Medical Library), Sacramento CA. 916-453-3529

Starring, Robert J, *Asst to Assoc Dir for Pub Servs,* University of Michigan Libraries (University Library), Ann Arbor MI. 313-764-9356

Starr, Robert L, *Librn,* Marquette University Memorial Library (Legal Research Center), Milwaukee WI. 414-224-7031

Stasek, Mary Ellen, *ILL,* Lakewood Public Library, Lakewood OH. 216-226-8275

Stasko, Joseph, *Head,* New York Public Library (Periodicals Section), New York NY. 212-790-6315

Staten, Jean, *Dir & Media,* Glendale Community College, John F Prince Library, Glendale AZ. 602-934-2211, Ext 239, 242

Statezny, Elaine, *Dir,* Crandon Public Library, Crandon WI. 715-478-3784

Statham, Elizabeth, *Assoc Librn,* United States Court of Appeals, Fifth Circuit Library, New Orleans LA. 504-589-6510

Statsky, William P, *Librn,* Antioch School of Law Library, Washington DC. 202-265-9500, Ext 301, 298

Stauber, Barbara, *Tech Serv & Ref,* New Hyde Park Public Library, New Hyde Park NY. 516-354-1413

Staubs, Steve, *In Charge,* American Orthotics & Prosthetics Association Headquarters Library, Washington DC. 202-234-8400

Staudenmeier, Mary, *Librn,* Ashland Public Library, Ashland PA. 717-875-3175

Stauder, Wanda, *Ad,* Three Rivers Public Library, Three Rivers MI. 616-279-2245

Staudt, Cecilia, *Actg Librn,* Lindenwood Colleges, Margaret L Butler Library, Saint Charles MO. 314-946-6912

Stauffer, Cecilia, *Asst Dir,* Kittanning Free Library, Kittanning PA. 412-543-1383

Stauffer, Jessie, *Librn,* Public Library of Fort Wayne & Allen County (Woodburn Branch), Woodburn IN. 219-632-4712

Stauffer, Lillian R, *Br Coordr,* Merced County Library, Merced CA. 209-726-7484

Stauffer, Sharon, *Ad & Ref,* South Pasadena Public Library, South Pasadena CA. 213-799-9108

Stave, Louise, *Librn,* Library Association of Portland (Southwest Hills), Portland OR. 503-246-2944

Stave, Thomas A, *Doc,* University of Oregon Library, Eugene OR. 503-686-3056

Stavinoha, Lillian, *Dir,* Fort Bend County Library, Richmond TX. 713-342-4455

Stavrides, Dorothy S, *Librn,* Phoenixville Public Library, Phoenixville PA. 215-933-3013

Stayner, M, *Librn,* Saskatoon Public Library (J S Wood), Saskatoon SK. 306-664-9590

StClair, Josephine, *In Charge,* Oxford County Library (Embro Branch), Embro ON. 519-475-4135

StClair, Katherine, *AV,* Mount Holyoke College, Williston Memorial Library, South Hadley MA. 413-538-2226

StCroix, Walter, *Cat,* Free Public Library of the City of Orange, Orange NJ. 201-673-0153

Steading, Alma D, *Cat,* Furman University Library, Greenville SC. 803-294-2191

Steadly, Evelyn, *Doc,* Stamford's Public Library, Ferguson Library, Stamford CT. 203-325-4354

Steadman, Vincent J, *Librn,* Enoch Pratt Free Library (Walbrook), Baltimore MD. 301-396-5430, 396-5395

Steagald, Sadie, *Ref,* Baptist Sunday School Board of the Southern Baptist Convention, Dargan-Carver Library, Nashville TN. 615-251-2133

Stearn, Helen, *ILL,* Upper Saddle River Public Library, Upper Saddle River NJ. 201-326-2583

Stearns, Charlene, *Dir,* Park County Library, Cody WY. 307-587-6204

Stears, Thelma A, *Dir,* Carnegie Public Library District, Fortville IN. 317-485-5432

Stebbing, William, *Asst Dir,* Church of Jesus Christ of Latter Day Saints, Arizona Branch Genealogical Library, Mesa AZ. 602-964-1200

Stebbins, Dorothy, *ILL,* Harrison County Library System, Gulfport MS. 601-868-1383

Stebbins, Kay, *Librn,* Transcontinental Oil Corporation Library, Shreveport LA. 318-222-9511

Stecher, Bonnie, *Sec-Treas,* Essex County Cooperating Libraries, MA. 617-774-5000, Ext 146

Steck, Beatrice, *Ch,* Owosso Public Library, Owosso MI. 517-725-5134

Steckel, Barbara, *Ref,* Bexley Public Library, Columbus OH. 614-231-2784

Steckel, Christine M, *Librn,* Mary Meuser Memorial Library, Easton PA. 215-258-3040

Steckley, Mrs M, *Supvr,* Huron County Public Library (Bluevale Branch), Bluevale ON. 519-357-2546

Steckman, Elizabeth, *ILL,* New Jersey State Library, Trenton NJ. 609-292-6200

Stedl, Karen, *Asst Librn,* Winnebago Mental Health Institute (Instructional Materials Center Library), Winnebago WI. 414-235-4910, Ext 473

Stedman, Audrey, *Ad,* Bettendorf Public Library & Information Center, Bettendorf IA. 319-359-4427

Stedman, Waunda, *Mgr,* Texas Education Agency, CITE Resource Center, Austin TX. 512-476-6861, Ext 256

Stedronsky, Louise S, *Librn,* Norfolk Library, Norfolk CT. 203-542-5075

Steeby, Sue, *Ch,* Willard Library, Battle Creek MI. 616-968-8166

Steedman, Isobel M, *Librn,* Manitoba Cancer Treatment & Research Foundation Library, Winnipeg MB. 787-2136 & 787-2197

Steege, Barbara, *Dir,* Concordia Theological Seminary Library, Fort Wayne IN. 219-482-9611, Ext 226

Steel, Dell, *Librn,* Dallam County Library, Dalhart TX. 806-249-2761

Steel, Gloria, *Tech Serv,* Indiana Vocational Technical College, Region 4, Lafayette, Learning Resources Center, Lafayette IN. 317-477-7401

Steel, Joan, *Librn,* Saskatoon Gallery & Conservatory Corporation Library, Saskatoon SK. 306-652-8355

Steele, Anita, *Dir,* University of Puget Sound (Law Library), Tacoma WA. 206-756-3322

Steele, Anitra, *Ch,* Mid-Continent Public Library, Independence MO. 816-836-5200

Steele, Apollonia, *Spec Coll,* University of Calgary Library, Calgary AB. 403-284-5954

Steele, Carl L, *Dir,* Rock Valley College Educational Resources Center, Rockford IL. 815-226-3762

Steele, Carl L, *Dir Educ Resources Ctr,* Rock Valley College, Library-Media Technical Assistant Program, IL. 815-226-3762

Steele, Charles, *Sci,* Ohio Northern University, Heterick Memorial Library, Ada OH. 419-634-9921, Ext 370, 490

Steele, Charles, *On-Line Servs,* Ohio Northern University, Heterick Memorial Library, Ada OH. 419-634-9921, Ext 370, 490

Steele, Doris, *Asst Librn,* Marissa Public Library, Marissa IL. 618-295-2825

Steele, Elizabeth B, *State Chmn,* John Fox Jr Memorial Library, Paris KY. 606-987-1788

Steele, Eric, *Librn,* New York Public Library (Literature & Language Dept), New York NY. 212-790-6504

Steele, Frances E, *Tech Serv,* J T Baker Chemical Co, Research Library, Phillipsburg NJ. 201-859-2151, Ext 662

Steele, H F, *Librn,* Ontario Ministry of Correctional Services, Guelph Correctional Center Library, Guelph ON. 519-822-0020, Ext 313

Steele, Helen T, *Dir,* Park City Hospital, Carlson Memorial Health & Science Library, Bridgeport CT. 203-579-5097

Steele, Lee, *Ref,* Delaware Division of Libraries, Dept of Community Affairs & Economic Development, Dover DE. 302-678-4748

Steele, M, *Cat,* Wetaskiwin Public Library, Wetaskiwin AB. 403-352-4055

Steele, Martha, *Ref,* Public Library of Nashville & Davidson County, Nashville TN. 615-244-4700

Steele, Nancy, *Asst Librn,* Etta C Ross Memorial Library, Blue Earth Public Library, Blue Earth MN. 507-526-5012

Steele, Nancy, *ILL & Ref,* State University of New York College of Technology, Utica-Rome Library, Utica NY. 315-792-3420

Steele, Noreen O, *Librn,* Saxton B Little Free Library, Inc, Columbia CT. 203-228-0350

Steele, Patricia, *Head,* Indiana University at Bloomington (Health, Physical Education & Recreation), Bloomington IN. 812-337-4420

Steele, Rita E, *Dir,* Millicent Library, Fairhaven MA. 617-992-5342

Steele, Susan, *Librn,* Mercer County Library (West Windsor), Princeton Junction NJ. 609-799-0462

Steele, Thomas M, *Librn,* Franklin Pierce Law Center Library, Concord NH. 603-228-1541, Ext 50

Steele, Virginia, *Dir,* Alexandrian Free Public Library, Mount Vernon IN. 812-838-3286

Steelman, Raylene, *Reader Serv,* University of Arkansas-Monticello Library, Monticello AR. 501-367-6811, Ext 80,81

Steely, Jessie, *Dir,* Madison County Library, Inc, Madison VA. 703-948-4720

Steen, David L, *Dir,* Manitoba Department of Cultural Affairs & Historical Resources, Public Library Services Branch, Winnipeg MB. 204-453-7549

Steenberg, Gerald W, *Dir,* Saint Paul Public Library, Saint Paul MN. 612-292-6311

Steenbergen, Jame, *Asst Librn & Ad,* Riverdale Public Library District, Riverdale IL. 312-841-3311

Steenblock, Maureen, *Ch,* Austin Public Library, Austin MN. 507-433-2391

Steensland, Ronald, *Dir,* Lexington Public Library, Lexington KY. 606-252-8871

Steeper, Joan, *Supvr,* Middlesex County Library (Parkhill Branch), Parkhill ON. 519-294-6583

Steer, Charity, *Librn,* Jackson District Library (Grass Lake Branch), Grass Lake MI. 517-522-8211

Steer, Inge, *Librn,* Lockwood House Museum, Norwalk Historical Reference Library, Norwalk CT. 203-866-0202

Steere, Shirley, *Asst Librn,* Greenville Public Library, Greenville RI. 401-949-3630

Steever, Jean, *Tech Serv,* Camden County Free Library, Voorhees NJ. 609-772-1636

Steeves, H A, *Librn,* Sperry Rand Corp, Sperry Research Center Library, Sudbury MA. 617-369-4000

Steeves, Judith, *Circ,* Florence-Lauderdale Public Library, Florence AL. 205-764-6563

Steeves, Lillian, *Dir, Acq & Cat,* South Plainfield Free Public Library, South Plainfield NJ. 201-754-7885

Stefancic, Emil, *Assoc Dir,* Cleveland State University Libraries, Cleveland OH. 216-687-2486

Stefanek, Margaret, *Chief Librn,* Grande Prairie Public Library District, Hazel Crest IL. 312-798-5563

Stefanski, Gail, *Head,* Free Library of Philadelphia (Northeast Regional Libr), Philadelphia PA. 215-686-3930

Stefanski, Helena, *In Charge,* Denver Public Library (Sociology & Business), Denver CO. 303-573-5152, Ext 271

Steffa, Dorothy B, *Acq,* Omaha Public Library, W Dale Clark Library, Omaha NE. 402-444-4800

Steffans, Maud, *ILL,* Calcasieu Parish Public Library System, Lake Charles LA. 318-433-1045

Steffen, Faith, *Librn,* Oregon Department of Transportation Library, Salem OR. 503-378-6268

Steffen, Linda R, *Dir,* Patterson Memorial Library, Wild Rose WI. 414-622-3835

Steffen, Nancy, *Ad,* Oak Lawn Public Library, Oak Lawn IL. 312-422-4990

Steffen, Susan Swords, *Humanities,* Saint Xavier College, Byrne Memorial Library, Chicago IL. 312-779-3300, Ext 217

Steffens, Esther L, *Cat,* Georgian Court College, Farley Memorial Library, Lakewood NJ. 201-364-2200, Ext 19

Steffens, Mary, *Librn,* La Porte City Public Library, La Porte City IA. 319-342-3025

Steffensen, Jean, *Librn,* Contra Costa County Law Library, Martinez CA. 415-372-2783

Steffenson, Martin, *Ref,* South Dakota State University, Hilton M Briggs Library, Brookings SD. 605-688-5106

Steffes, Leslie, *Acq,* Madison Public Library, Madison WI. 608-266-6300

Steffey, Jane, *Dir,* American Horticultural Society, Harold B Tukey Memorial Library, Mount Vernon VA. 703-768-5700

Stege, Jerry, *Media & Tech Serv,* Manistee County Library, Manistee MI. 616-723-2519

Stegeman, Helen, *Per,* Cincinnati Historical Society Library, Cincinnati OH. 513-241-4622

Stegeman, Olga, *Librn,* Van Buren County Library (Covert Branch), Covert MI. 616-764-1298

Stegh, Les, *Archivist,* Deere & Co Library, Moline IL. 309-752-4442

Stegman, Betty, *Ch,* Thomas Ford Memorial Library, Western Springs Library, Western Springs IL. 312-246-0520

Stegman, Richard, *Librn,* Southern Nevada Regional Services, NV. 702-733-7810

Stegner, Harriet M, *Assoc Dir,* Irving Public Library System, Irving TX. 214-253-2639

Stehlik, Jane, *Dir,* McHenry County College, Learning Resource Center System, Crystal Lake IL. 815-455-3700, Ext 276

Stehman, Angie, *Librn,* Minnesota Zoological Garden Library, Apple Valley MN. 612-432-9010, Ext 230

Steichen, Agnes, *Ch,* Waunakee Public Library, Waunakee WI. 608-849-4217

Steidel, Hermann, *Acq,* University of Puerto Rico, Cayey University College Library, Cayey PR. 809-738-2161, Ext 221

Steigerwald, Karen, *Ch,* Geauga County Public Library, Chardon OH. 216-285-7601

Stein, Arlene, *Circ,* College of New Rochelle, Gill Library, New Rochelle NY. 914-632-5300, Ext 347

Stein, Benjamin, *Cat,* Saint John's University, Alcuin Library, Collegeville MN. 612-363-2119

Stein, Bessie A, *Dir,* Francis D Murphy Medical Library, Milwaukee WI. 414-257-5897

Stein, Bessie A, *Dir,* The Medical College of Wisconsin, Inc, Todd Wehr Library, Milwaukee WI. 414-257-8323

Stein, Denise E, *Actg Dir,* Palm Beach Atlantic College, E C Blomeyer Library, West Palm Beach FL. 305-833-8592, Ext 210

Stein, Douglas L, *Mss,* Mystic Seaport Museum, G W Blunt White Library, Mystic CT. 203-536-2631, Ext 261

Stein, Hadassah, *Librn,* Roger Williams General Hospital, Health Sciences Library, Providence RI. 401-456-2036

Stein, Hilda, *Actg Librn,* Edison Free Public Library, Edison NJ. 201-287-2298

Stein, Irma, *Librn,* Presque Isle Library, Presque Isle WI. 715-686-2473

Stein, Irwin S, *Dir,* Corning Community College, Arthur A Houghton, Jr Library, Corning NY. 607-962-9251

Stein, Marcia, *Ch,* Easton Area Public Library, Easton PA. 215-258-2917

Stein, Marvin, *Dir,* Mount Sinai Hospital, Harry S Dale Memorial Library, New York NY. 212-650-7793

Stein, Mary C, *Acq,* Enoch Pratt Free Library, Baltimore MD. 301-396-5430, 396-5395

Stein, Mary Lou, *AV & Doc,* Franklin Public Library, Franklin NH. 603-934-2911

Stein, Rose, *Asst Librn,* De Pue Public Library, De Pue IL. 815-447-2660

Stein, Sheila, *Ad & Ref,* Syosset Public Library, Syosset NY. 516-921-7161

Steinbach, AnnaBelle, *Librn,* United States Public Health Service Hospital, Medical Library, Carville LA. 504-642-7771

Steinberg, Celia, *Ref,* University of Miami (Louis Calder Memorial Library), Miami FL. 305-547-6441

Steinberg, Marilyn, *In Charge,* Miami Beach Public Library (North Shore), Miami Beach FL. 305-673-7539

Steinberg, Toby, *Info Servs,* University of Colorado Health Sciences Center (Denison Memorial Library), Denver CO. 303-394-5125

Steinbrenner, Julie, *Dir,* Sandusky Library Association, Sandusky OH. 419-625-3834

Steiner, Ann, *Librn,* Prescott Public Library, Prescott ON. 613-925-4340

Steiner, Bernadette, *Librn,* Sadtler Research Laboratories Library, Division of Bio-Rad Laboratories, Inc, Philadelphia PA. 215-382-7800, Ext 46

Steiner, Janet, *Dir,* Elk Grove Village Public Library, Elk Grove Village IL. 312-439-0447

Steiner, Karl, *On-Line Servs,* Mid-Michigan Library League, Cadillac MI. 616-775-6541

Steiner, Mary Lou, *Cat,* Macalester College, Weyerhaeuser Library, Saint Paul MN. 612-647-6346

Steiner, Maude, *Asst Librn,* Milford Public Library, Milford CT. 203-878-7461

Steiner, Ronald A, *Assoc Dir,* Indiana University of Pennsylvania, Rhodes R Stabley Library, Indiana PA. 412-357-2340

Steiner, Stephen, *Media Production,* Bureau of Jewish Education, Jewish Community Library, San Francisco CA. 415-751-6983, Ext 12

Steinfeld, Michael, *Dir,* Mount Kisco Public Library, Mount Kisco NY. 914-666-8041

Steinfirst, Susan, *Asst Prof,* University of North Carolina at Chapel Hill, School of Library Science, NC. 919-933-8366

Steinhardt, Beth E, *Tech Serv,* Crawford & Russell, Inc Technical Library, Stamford CT. 203-327-1450, Ext 393 & 390

Steinhauer, Dale, *Ref,* University of Maine at Presque Isle Library, Presque Isle ME. 207-764-0311, Ext 223

Steinhoff, Cynthia, *Asst Librn,* Ridgway Public Library, Ridgway PA. 814-773-7573

Steininger, Ellen, *Librn,* Marsteller Inc Library, Chicago IL. 312-329-1100, Ext 450

Steinke, Cynthia, *Sci, Eng & Math,* University of Illinois at Chicago Circle Library, Chicago IL. 312-996-2716

Steinke, Cynthia, *Librn,* University of Illinois at Chicago Circle Library (Science), Chicago IL. 312-996-5396

Steinke, Paul K, *Tech Dir,* Pfizer Inc, Milwaukee Operations Library, Milwaukee WI. 414-332-3545

Steinke, Ralph G, *Librn,* Olney Central College, Anderson Library, Olney IL. 618-395-4351, Ext 47

Steiskal, Lois, *Ch,* Blackfoot Public Library, Edna Gillespie Memorial Library, Blackfoot ID. 208-785-1251

Stell, Ann, *Ch,* Smithtown Library, Smithtown NY. 516-265-2072

Stell, Melvina W, *Librn,* Good Samaritan Hospital & Medical Center, Good Samaritan Health Sciences Library, Portland OR. 503-229-7336

Stella, Colleen, *ILL & Ref,* State University of New York, Agricultural & Technical College at Norrisville Library, Morrisville NY. 315-684-7055

Stella, David, *Librn,* San Bernardino County Library (Adelanto Branch), Adelanto CA. 714-246-5661

Stella, Florence, *Librn,* Mount Sinai Hospital Medical Center (Lewisohn Memorial Library), Chicago IL. 312-542-2000

Stella, JoAnn, *Per,* Midland College, Learning Resources Center, Midland TX. 915-684-7851, Ext 214

Stelle, Janet M, *Librn,* Applied Science Laboratories, Inc Library, State College PA. 814-238-2406

Stellhorn, Cheryl A, *Librn,* International Harvester Co, Solar Turbines International Libr, San Diego CA. 714-238-5500

Stelling, Valerie, *Asst Dir,* Gleason Public Library, Carlisle MA. 617-369-4898

Stelzig, Virginia, *Ref & Br Coordr,* Morgantown Public Library, Morgantown Service Center, Morgantown WV. 304-296-4425

Stembal, Mary Ellen, *Tech Serv,* Cook Memorial Public Library District, Libertyville IL. 312-362-2330

Stembridge, Mrs Billie, *Librn,* Northwest Regional Library (Kennedy Branch), Kennedy AL. 205-596-3530

Stenberg, Beth, *Librn,* San Antonio State Hospital Library, Professional Library, San Antonio TX. 512-532-8811

Stenberg, Beth M, *Librn,* Physicians & Surgeons Hospital Medical Library, Corpus Christi TX. 512-854-2031

Stenberg, Debora K, *Librn,* New Britain General Hospital, Health Science Library, New Britain CT. 203-224-5122

Stendal, Dolores, *Librn,* Sedro Woolley Public Library, Sedro Woolley WA. 206-855-1166

Stenesh, Mabel, *Ref & ILL,* Kalamazoo Public Library, Kalamazoo MI. 616-342-9837

Stengel, Gary J, *Tech Serv & Cat,* Jeffersonville Township Public Library, Jeffersonville IN. 812-282-7765

Stengel, Olive G, *Circ,* Lehigh University Libraries, Bethlehem PA. 861-3026 (Dir), 861-3050 (Ref), 861-3030 (Circ), 861-3055 (ILL)

Stenner, Alice P, *Librn,* First Presbyterian Church of San Diego Library, San Diego CA. 714-232-7513

Stensrud, Barbara, *Librn,* Wells Public Library, Wells MN. 507-553-3702

Stenstrom, Ralph H, *Dir,* Hamilton College, Burke Library, Clinton NY. 315-859-4478

Stensvold, Lilly, *Dir,* Spooner Memorial Library, Spooner WI. 715-635-2792

Stenten, Kay, *Cur Nebr Auth Coll,* Lincoln City Libraries, Lincoln NE. 402-435-2146

Stenzel, Eleanor, *Librn,* Burt Public Library, Burt IA. 515-924-3257

Stepan, Jan, *Foreign & Int Law Librn,* Harvard University Library (Law School Library), Cambridge MA. 617-495-3170

Stepanek, Robert H, *In Charge,* Connecticut Aeronautical Historical Association, Inc, Bradley Air Museum Library, Windsor Locks CT. 203-623-8803

Stepek, Susan, *Asst Mgr,* Campbell-Ewald Co, Reference Center, Warren MI. 313-574-3400, Ext 6102

Stephan, Aurelia, *Per,* Nassau Community College Library, Garden City NY. 516-222-7400

Stephan, Evelyn B, *Chief Librn,* United States Army (Fort Bragg Recreation Service Library System), Fort Bragg NC. 919-396-0011

Stephan, Jere, *Ch,* Tucson Public Library, Tucson AZ. 602-791-4391

Stephan, Paul D, *Instr,* Case Western Reserve University, School of Library Science, OH. 216-368-3500

Stephan, Sharon L, *Librn,* Wheeling-Pittsburgh Steel Corp, Corporation Library, Wheeling WV. 304-232-2538

Stephan, Susan, *Librn,* Florida Department of Health & Rehabilitative Services, Sunland Training Center Library, Gainesville FL. 904-376-5381, Ext 292

Stephanian, Charles, *Media,* San Francisco Art Institute, Anne Bremer Memorial Library, San Francisco CA. 415-771-7020, Ext 59

Stephanoff, Kathryn, *Dir,* Allentown Public Library, Allentown PA. 215-820-2400

Stephanoff, Kathryn, *Adjunct Prof,* Northampton County Area Community College, Library Technical Assistant Program, PA. 215-865-5351, Ext 221

Stephen, Lorraine, *Asst Librn,* Law Society of Manitoba, Great Library, Winnipeg MB. 204-943-5277

Stephen, Marguerite, *Librn,* Humboldt County Library (Denio Branch), Winnemucca NV. 702-623-5081, Ext 315 & 316

Stephen, Ross G, *Tech Serv,* University of Wisconsin-Oshkosh, Forrest R Polk Library, Oshkosh WI. 414-424-3333

Stephen, Sandra, *Pub Libr Specialists,* Maryland State Department of Education, Division of Library Development & Services, Baltimore MD. 301-796-8300, Ext 284

Stephens, Alice G, *Actg Head of Libr Operations,* Alabama Public Library Service, Montgomery AL. 205-832-5743

Stephens, Alphia H, *Librn,* Florida Department of Insurance Library, Tallahassee FL. 904-488-3243

Stephens, Ann, *Ref,* Birmingham Public & Jefferson County Free Library, Birmingham AL. 205-254-2551

Stephens, Arial A, *Dir,* Public Library of Charlotte & Mecklenburg County, Inc, Charlotte NC. 704-374-2725

Stephens, Bobbie, *Asst Librn,* Wakulla County Public Library, Crawfordville FL. 904-926-7415

Stephens, Dennis, *Acq,* University of Alaska, Fairbanks, Elmer E Rasmuson Library, Fairbanks AK. 907-479-7224

Stephens, Denny, *Asst Dir,* Oklahoma Department of Libraries, Oklahoma City OK. 405-521-2502

Stephens, Doris G, *Dir,* Amos Memorial Public Library, Sidney Public Library, Sidney OH. 513-492-8354

Stephens, Eunice, *Librn,* Memorial Hospital, Medical Library, Lufkin TX. 713-634-8111

Stephens, Glenda, *Ad,* Scott County Public Library, Georgetown KY. 502-863-3566

Stephens, Gretchen, *Librn,* Purdue University Libraries & Audio-Visual Center (Veterinary Medicine), West Lafayette IN. 317-749-2249

Stephens, J M, *In Charge,* Association of Consulting Management Engineers Inc Library, New York NY. 212-697-9693

Stephens, Jerry W, *Admin Asst,* University of Alabama in Birmingham, Mervyn H Sterne Library, Birmingham AL. 205-934-6360

Stephens, John, *Bkmobile Coordr,* Oceanside Public Library, Oceanside CA. 714-439-7330

Stephens, Joycelyn G, *Mgr Info Ctr,* De Soto, Inc, Information Center Library, Des Plaines IL. 312-391-9556

Stephens, Kent, *ILL,* California State University, Chico Library, Chico CA. 916-895-6212

Stephens, L G, *Librn,* Florida Department of Corrections, Lake Correctional Institution Library, Clermont FL. 904-394-6146, Ext 54

Stephens, Lois, *Spec Coll,* Warren Public Library, Warren OH. 216-399-8807

Stephens, Louise, *Ad,* Velma Teague Library, Glendale Public Library, Glendale AZ. 602-931-5576

Stephens, Marcia, *Librn,* Saint Luke's Hospitals Learning Resources System, Fargo ND. 701-280-5571

Stephens, Margaret, *Librn,* Jackson District Library (Clarklake Branch), Clarklake MI. 517-529-9600

Stephens, Marian, *Doc,* Montana State University, Roland R Renne Library, Bozeman MT. 406-994-3119

Stephens, Marian, *Librn,* Southern Tier Library System (Camp Monterey Reading Center), Beaver Dams NY. 607-962-3141

Stephens, Mary L, *Dir,* Yolo County Library, Woodland CA. 916-666-8323

Stephens, Nancy, *Librn,* Harris County Public Library (Crosby Branch), Crosby TX. 713-328-1313

Stephens, Nina, *Asst,* Sabine Parish Library (Pleasant Hill Branch), Pleasant Hill LA. 318-256-2212

Stephens, Norris, *Librn,* University of Pittsburgh (Music), Pittsburgh PA. 412-624-4130

Stephens, Peggy, *Librn,* Clark County Library District (Goodsprings Branch), Goodsprings NV. 702-874-1366

Stephens, Roselyn, *Dir,* Salem Public Library, Salem OH. 216-332-0042

Stephens, Ruth, *Librn,* Hennepin County Library (Champlin Branch), Champlin MN. 612-427-1010

Stephens, Saundra, *Tech Serv,* Maryville College, Lamar Memorial Library, Maryville TN. 615-982-1200

Stephens, Winnifred, *Libr Asst,* Western Counties Regional Library (Lockeport Branch), Lockeport NS. 902-656-2817

Stephenson, Anna, *Dir,* Lenora Public Library, Lenora KS. 913-567-4760

Stephenson, Dawn, *Archivist,* Clarke Institute of Psychiatry, Farrar Library, Toronto ON. 416-979-2221, Ext 467

Stephenson, Doris, *Cat & On-Line Servs,* Manchester College, Funderburg Library, North Manchester IN. 219-982-2141, Ext 231

Stephenson, Doris, *Dir,* Tomlinson College Library, Cleveland TN. 615-476-3271, Ext 54

Stephenson, Elizabeth, *Librn,* Case Western Reserve University Libraries (Astronomy), Cleveland OH. 216-368-3506

Stephenson, Grant D, *Assoc Prof,* Lakehead University, School of Library Technology, ON. 807-345-2121, Ext 240

Stephenson, Ida Kathleen, *Librn,* North Arkansas Regional Library (Searcy County), Marshall AR. 501-448-2420

Stephenson, Lynette, *Asst Dir,* Carl Elliott Regional Library, Jasper AL. 205-221-2567

Stephenson, Marion, *Librn,* Victoria County Public Library (Omemee Branch), Omemee ON. 705-324-3104

Stephenson, Martin W, *Asst Dir,* Corvallis Public Library, Corvallis-Benton County Library, Corvallis OR. 503-757-6928

Stephenson, Robert E, *Librn,* Virginia Polytechnic Institute & State University Library (Architecture), Blacksburg VA. 703-961-6182

Stephenson, Ruth J, *Asst Dir & Ref,* Spring Arbor College, Hugh A White Library, Spring Arbor MI. 517-750-1200, Ext 234

Stephenson, Shirley, *Librn,* Aerojet Ordnance Co, Technical Library, Downey CA. 213-923-7511, Ext 247

Stephonson, Hester, *Ch,* North Brunswick Free Public Library, North Brunswick NJ. 201-246-3545

Stepko, Dorothy, *Librn,* Samuel A Weiss Community Library, Glassport PA. 412-672-6368

Stepney, Anne W, *In Charge,* Enoch Pratt Free Library (Cherry Hill), Baltimore MD. 301-396-5430, 396-5395

Stepney, Rebecca M, *Librn,* Charleston County Library (John L Dart), Charleston SC. 803-722-7105

Stepp, Robert, *Proj Dir Media Develop for Hearing Impaired,* University of Nebraska-Lincoln, School Media Specialist Program, NE. 402-472-3726

Stepp, T Kathleen, *Dir,* Ford City Public Library, Ford City PA. 412-762-3091

Sterganos, Deena J, *Ref,* Pennsylvania State University, Berks Campus Library, Reading PA. 215-375-4211, Ext 22, 23 & 43

Sterlin, Annette S, *Cat,* Hughes Aircraft Co (Technical Library), Culver City CA. 213-391-0711, Ext 2615

Sterling, Cynthia R, *Chief, Libr Serv,* Veterans Administration, Hospital Library, Cincinnati OH. 513-861-3100

Sterling, Helen E, *Librn,* Nancy Fawcett Memorial Library, Lodgepole NE. 308-483-5714

Sterling, Lucile F, *Librn,* Savanna Township Public Library, Savanna IL. 815-273-3714

Sterling, Lucille, *Librn,* Public Library of Nashville & Davidson County (Richland Park), Nashville TN. 615-292-2426

Sterling, Sandra, *Librn,* Southwestern Manitoba Regional Library (Pierson), Melita MB. 204-634-2215

Sterling, Sheila, *Librn,* E F Hutton & Co, Inc, Research Library, New York NY. 212-742-6563

Stern, Deborah, *Librn,* Temple Beth Torah Library, Upper Nyack NY. 914-358-2248

Stern, Janice R, *Dir,* Milgo Electronic Corp, Technical Information Center, Miami FL. 305-592-8600

Stern, Joan, *Ref,* Los Angeles Times Editorial Library, Los Angeles CA. 213-972-7184

Stern, Joanne, *Asst Librn,* Martinsburg Community Library, Martinsburg PA. 814-793-3335

Stern, Joel, *Asst Dir,* Kanawha County Public Library, Kanawha County Service Center, Charleston WV. 304-343-4646

Stern, Lotta R, *ILL, Ad & Ref,* Glencoe Public Library, Glencoe IL. 312-835-5056

Stern, M, *Coll Develop,* State University of New York at Buffalo (Lockwood Library), Buffalo NY. 716-636-2816

Stern, M, *French, Classics, Slavic,* State University of New York at Buffalo, University Libraries, Buffalo NY. 716-636-2965

Stern, Shirley, *Librn,* Blackduck Library, Blackduck MN. 218-835-6600

Sternberg, Marilyn, *Educ,* Adelphi University Library, Garden City NY. 516-294-8700

Sternberg, Marilyn, *Bibliog Instr,* Adelphi University Library, Garden City NY. 516-294-8700

Sterne, Bernice, *Librn,* Los Angeles Public Library System (Sylmar Branch), Sylmar CA. 213-367-6102

Sterne, Loretta, *Librn,* Louisiana Public Library, Louisiana MO. 314-754-4491

Sternecker, Carol Greb, *Librn,* Children's Museum of Indianapolis, Rauh Memorial Library, Indianapolis IN. 317-924-5431

Sterner, Christine N-R, *Ad & Outreach,* Oberlin Public Library, Oberlin OH. 216-775-8600

Sterner, Sue, *Cat,* Denver Public Library, Denver CO. 303-573-5152, Ext 271

Sternik, Marsha, *Librn,* United States Department of Energy, Bartlesville Energy Technology Center, Bartlesville OK. 336-2400 Ext 228

Sterns, Laura, *ILL,* University of Miami, Rosentiel School of Marine & Atmospheric Sciences, Miami FL. 305-350-7207

Sterns, Z, *Librn,* University of Toronto Libraries (Astronomy), Toronto ON. 416-884-2112

Sterrett, N, *Bkmobile Coordr,* Napa City - County Library, Napa CA. 707-253-4241

Stetson, Anna M, *Librn,* Case Memorial Library, Kenduskeag ME. 207-884-7364

Stetson, Catherine, *Asst Dir & Ch,* Canton Public Library, Canton MA. 617-828-0177

Stetter, Ruth, *Librn,* Berlin Public Library, Berlin WI. 414-361-2650

Stetz, Elizabeth A, *Dir,* Waterloo Library & Historical Society, Waterloo NY. 315-539-3313

Stetzel, Maxine, *Librn,* Duncan Memorial Library, Casey Public Library, Casey IA. 515-746-2670

Steuben, Larry R, *Dir,* Columbia College Library, Columbia CA. 209-532-3141, Ext 228

Steuck, Adele, *Librn,* Bloomfield Public Library, Bloomfield NE. 402-373-4589

Steudel, Connie H, *Librn,* Springfield College in Illinois, Charles E Becker Library, Springfield IL. 217-525-1420, Ext 13

Steuernagel, Harriet, *Dir & Media,* Washington University Libraries (School of Dental Medicine Library), Saint Louis MO. 314-454-0385

Stevanovic, Bosiljka, *Librn,* New York Public Library (Foreign Language Library), New York NY. 212-790-6406

Stevanus, Georgia, *Librn,* Pleasanton-Lincoln Library, Pleasanton KS. 913-352-8257

Steven, Dorothy, *Dir,* Monterey Public Library, Monterey CA. 408-646-3930

Stevens, Alida, *Ch,* Bexley Public Library, Columbus OH. 614-231-2784

Stevens, Ann, *Librn,* Staatsburg Library Society, Staatsburg NY. 914-889-4683

Stevens, Barbara E, *Librn,* United States Army, Concepts Analysis Agency, Information Center, Bethesda MD. 301-295-1530

Stevens, Bill, *Librn,* Warren County Library (Little York Branch), Little York IL. 309-729-3791

Stevens, Billie, *Librn,* Bossier Parish Public Library (Benton Branch), Benton LA. 318-965-2751

Stevens, Christine L, *Ref,* Indiana University (School of Law Library), Indianapolis IN. 317-264-4028

Stevens, Curtis L, *Instr,* Grossmont College, Library Technology Program, CA. 714-465-1700, Ext 319

Stevens, Curtis L, *Cat,* Grossmont College, Lewis F Smith Learning Resource Center Library, El Cajon CA. 714-465-1700, Ext 333, 334

Stevens, Don, *Media,* Red Deer College, Learning Resources Center, Red Deer AB. 403-346-6450

Stevens, Dorothy N, *Librn,* Rowe Town Library, Rowe MA. 413-339-4761

Stevens, Eugene A, *Librn,* Veterans Administration, Medical Center Library, Fort Lyon CO. 303-456-1260, Ext 256

Stevens, Florence, *Bkmobile Coordr,* Framingham Public Library, Framingham MA. 617-879-3570

Stevens, Florence, *Ch,* John C Hart Memorial Library, Shrub Oak NY. 914-245-5262

Stevens, Helen, *Librn,* Contra Costa County Library (Pacheco Branch), Pacheco CA. 415-689-7226

Stevens, Irene, *Media,* Phoenix Public Library, Phoenix AZ. 602-262-6451

Stevens, Jane, *Assoc Prof,* Columbia University in the City of New York, School of Library Service, NY. 212-280-2292

Stevens, Jane, *Cat,* Tulane University of Louisiana, Howard-Tilton Memorial Library, New Orleans LA. 504-865-5131

Stevens, Janet A, *Librn,* Mason Public Library, Mason NH. 603-878-2169

Stevens, Jean, *Acq,* Franklin Square Public Library, Franklin Square NY. 516-488-3444

Stevens, Jean, *Librn,* University of Texas at El Paso Library (Education), El Paso TX. 915-747-5417

Stevens, Jeanine, *Librn,* Santa Cruz Public Library (Ben Lomond Branch), Ben Lomond CA. 408-336-5639

Stevens, Julia, *Librn,* Saint Paul Public Library, Saint Paul NE. 308-754-5223

Stevens, June R, *Mgt Asst I,* Nevada State County Municipal Archives Reference Library, Carson City NV. 702-885-5210

Stevens, Lee, *Librn,* Canby Public Library, Canby OR. 503-266-3394

Stevens, Linda, *ILL & Ref,* Hoyt Library, Kingston PA. 717-287-2013

Stevens, Linda, *Librn,* Kingston Hospital Library, Kingston NY. 914-331-3131, Ext 286

Stevens, Marjorie, *Acq,* Olivet College Burrage Library, Olivet MI. 616-749-7608

Stevens, Marjorie, *Dir,* Parkland Community Library, Guthsville PA. 215-398-1361

Stevens, Mary, *Systs Librn,* York University, Scott Library, Downsview ON. 416-667-2235

Stevens, Mary F, *Asst Librn,* Fall River Public Library, Fall River MA. 617-676-8541

Stevens, Mary P, *Librn,* Mississippi Museum of Natural Science Library, Jackson MS. 601-354-7303

Stevens, Michael L, *Asst Dir,* Victoria Public Library, Victoria TX. 512-578-6241

Stevens, Norman D, *Univ Librn,* University of Connecticut Library, Storrs CT. 203-486-2219

Stevens, Pam, *Librn,* Great Western Sugar Co, Manufacturing Process & Development Laboratory Library, Loveland CO. 303-667-1125

Stevens, Pamela, *Librn,* Great Western Sugar Co, Research Library, Denver CO. 303-893-4600, Ext 230

Stevens, Patricia, *Dir,* Principia College, Marshall Brooks Library, Elsah IL. 618-374-2131, Ext 325

Stevens, Peter, *Acq,* University of Washington Libraries, Seattle WA. 206-543-1760

Stevens, Peter, *Head, Acq,* University of Washington Libraries (Book Order Section, Acquisitions Division), Seattle WA. 206-543-1760

Stevens, Peter, *Head, Acq,* University of Washington Libraries (Gifts & Exchanges Section, Acquisitions Division), Seattle WA. 206-543-1760

Stevens, Richard, *Ref,* Colorado State University, William E Morgan Library, Fort Collins CO. 303-491-5911

Stevens, Richard, *Librn,* Somerset County Library (North Plainfield Memorial Library), North Plainfield NJ. 201-755-7909

Stevens, Rita, *Librn,* Thompson Public Library (North Grosvenordale Branch), North Grosvenordale CT. 203-923-2142

Stevens, Robert, *Rare Bks,* Rosenberg Library, Galveston TX. 713-763-8854

Stevens, Robert, *Dir,* Vincennes University Junior College (Byron R Lewis Historical Collections Library), Vincennes IN. 812-885-4330

Stevens, Roberta, *Acting Dir Tech Operations,* Fairfax County Public Library, Administrative Offices, Springfield VA. 703-321-9810

Stevens, Rolland, *Prof,* University of Illinois, Graduate School of Library Science, IL. 217-333-3280

Stevens, Safarona, *Librn,* Kern County Library (McFarland Branch), McFarland CA. 805-861-2130

Stevens, Stan, *Maps,* University of California, University Library, Santa Cruz CA. 408-429-2076

Stevens, Vaun, *Ref & On-Line Servs,* City-County Library of Missoula, Missoula MT. 406-728-5900

Stevens, W, *Librn,* Okanagan Regional Library District (Vernon Branch), Vernon BC. 604-542-7610

Stevens, Walter, *Law Circ,* State Library of Pennsylvania, Harrisburg PA. 717-787-2646

Stevens, Willie, *Librn,* Northeastern Regional Library System (Kashechewan Bend Branch), Kashechewan ON. 705-567-7043

Stevens-Becksvoort, Margaret A, *Ch,* Prince Memorial Library, Cumberland Center ME. 207-829-3180

Stevenson, B, *Librn,* Dakota County Library System (Burnsville Branch), Burnsville MN. 612-435-7177

Stevenson, Carol E, *In Charge,* E I Du Pont De Nemours & Co, Inc, Pigments Dept Research Library, Newport DE. 302-774-1000

Stevenson, Charles, *Resources & Tech Servs,* Greenville County Library, Greenville SC. 803-242-5000

Stevenson, Elizabeth, *Librn,* Union Carbide Corp, Chemicals Div, Plant Library, Texas City TX. 713-945-7411, Ext 526

Stevenson, Elizabeth A, *Media,* Finger Lakes Library System, Ithaca NY. 607-273-4074

Stevenson, Emma Lou, *Asst Librn,* Price City Library, Price UT. 801-637-0744

Stevenson, Fern, *Librn,* Gresham Public Library, Gresham NE. 402-735-7376

Stevenson, Gordon, *Assoc Prof,* State University of New York at Albany, School of Library & Information Science, NY. 518-455-6288

Stevenson, Helen, *Acq,* Belmont Abbey College, Abbot Vincent Taylor Library, Belmont NC. 704-825-3711, Ext 342

Stevenson, Iris C, *Chief Librn,* United States Court of Appeals, Fourth Circuit Library, Richmond VA. 703-782-2291

Stevenson, Isabel, *Cat,* John Carroll University, Grasselli Library, University Heights OH. 491-4233 & 491-4231

Stevenson, Isabel, *Tech Serv,* John Carroll University, Grasselli Library, University Heights OH. 491-4233 & 491-4231

Stevenson, James, *Cat,* Tulsa City-County Library, Tulsa OK. 918-581-5221

Stevenson, James W, *Dir,* Newburgh Free Library, Newburgh NY. 914-561-1836

Stevenson, Jean, *Libr Tech,* Queen's University at Kingston (Biology), Kingston ON. 613-547-2896

Stevenson, Joan, *Bkmobile Coordr,* Yonkers Public Library, Yonkers NY. 914-337-1500

Stevenson, Margaret, *Librn,* Farmers' Library Co of the Town of Ogden, Spencerport NY. 716-352-5611

Stevenson, Marjorie, *Registrar,* Bridgeport Engineering Institute Library, Bridgeport CT. 203-372-4395

Stevenson, Marjorie, *Librn,* Tracy Memorial Library, New London NH. 603-526-4656

Stevenson, Marsha, *Ref,* Ohio State University, Newark Campus & Central Ohio Technical College, Newark Regional Campus Library, Newark OH. 614-366-3321, Ext 306, 307, 308

Stevenson, Mary Jane, *YA,* Nicholson Memorial Library, Garland TX. 214-494-7187

Stevenson, Michele, *Ad,* Erie County Library System, Erie PA. 814-452-2333

Stevenson, Mona L D, *Asst Dir, Cat & Ref,* McKinley Memorial Library, Niles OH. 216-652-1704

Stevenson, Octave S, *Lang & Lit,* Public Library of the District of Columbia, Martin Luther King Memorial Library, Washington DC. 202-727-1101

Stevenson, Roberta B, *Ser,* University of California at Davis, General Library, Davis CA. 916-752-2110

Stevenson, Ruth B, *Librn,* City & County of San Francisco, City Attorney's Office Library, San Francisco CA. 415-558-4993

Stevenson, Sheila, *Ad,* Oak Park Public Library, Scoville Institute, Oak Park IL. 312-383-8200

Stever, Louise, *Librn,* Tulare County Library System (Exeter Branch), Exeter CA. 209-592-5361

Steward, Auburn, *Librn,* Baptist Medical Center System (Medical Center Library), Little Rock AR. 501-227-2671

Steward, C, *Librn,* General Electric Co, Electronics Park Library, Syracuse NY. 315-456-2023

Steward, Katherine, *Librn,* Hennepin County Library (Maple Plain Branch), Maple Plain MN. 612-479-2237

Stewart, Agnes, *In Charge,* Eastern Counties Regional Library (Mulgrave Branch), Mulgrave NS. 902-747-2597

Stewart, Alva W, *Ref,* Memphis State University Libraries, Memphis TN. 901-454-2201

Stewart, Ann, *Librn,* Comfort Public Library, Comfort TX. 512-995-2398

Stewart, Anne B, *Head Pub Serv,* Vanderbilt University Library (Education), Nashville TN. 615-327-8184

Stewart, Barbara, *Librn,* Saint Louis Public Library (Wellston), Saint Louis MO. 314-385-4042

Stewart, Barbara Rose, *Librn,* Reed, Smith, Shaw & McClay, Law Library, Pittsburgh PA. 412-288-3340

Stewart, Beverly J, *Librn,* Parlin Public Library, Canton IL. 309-647-0064

Stewart, Carolyn, *Librn,* Jasper Public Library, Jasper TN. 615-942-3369

Stewart, Charlotte, *Res Coll,* McMaster University, Hamilton ON. 416-525-9140

Stewart, Cobb, *Ref,* John C Hart Memorial Library, Shrub Oak NY. 914-245-5262

Stewart, Coy E, *Librn,* Westinghouse Electric Corp, NRF Library, Idaho Falls ID. 208-526-0111

Stewart, Darlene, *Circ,* Juneau Memorial Library, Juneau AK. 907-586-2429

Stewart, David Marshall, *Dir,* Public Library of Nashville & Davidson County, Nashville TN. 615-244-4700

Stewart, Deborah, *Ch,* Cass County Public Library (Harrisonville Branch), Harrisonville MO. 816-884-3483

Stewart, Dr Glen C, *Ref & Per,* North Central College Library, Naperville IL. 312-355-0597, 420-3425

Stewart, Elisabeth N, *Dir,* Carnegie Public Library, Angola Public Library, Angola IN. 219-665-3362

Stewart, Elizabeth, *Dir,* Tuxedo Park Library, Tuxedo Park NY. 914-351-2207

Stewart, Ethel, *In Charge,* University of Kansas Libraries (Journalism), Lawrence KS. 913-864-3680

Stewart, Evelyn, *Librn,* Chicago Public Library (Altgeld), Chicago IL. 312-264-5952

Stewart, Frances, *Media,* West Liberty State College, Paul N Elbin Library, West Liberty WV. 304-336-8035

Stewart, Frances S, *Bibliog Instr,* Alabama Agricultural & Mechanical University, Joseph F Drake Memorial Learning Resources Center, Normal AL. 205-859-7309

Stewart, George, *Media,* Amarillo Public Library, Amarillo TX. 806-378-3000, Ext 2250

Stewart, George, *Ref,* Oglethorpe University Library, Atlanta GA. 404-261-1441, Ext 24

Stewart, George R, *Dir,* Birmingham Public & Jefferson County Free Library, Birmingham AL. 205-254-2551

Stewart, Gig, *Dir,* North Central Michigan College Library, Petoskey MI. 616-347-3973, Ext 240

Stewart, Harriet, *Librn,* First Presbyterian Church Library, Charlotte NC. 704-332-5123

Stewart, Helen, *Ref,* Fulton County Public Library, Rochester IN. 219-223-2713

Stewart, Henry, *Pub Servs,* Old Dominion University Library, Norfolk VA. 804-440-4141

Stewart, Imogene, *Commun Servs,* Andalusia Public Library, Andalusia AL. 205-222-6612

Stewart, Inez, *Librn,* Livingston Parish Library (Albany Branch), Albany LA. 504-686-2436

Stewart, Irene, *Librn,* North Bridgton Public Library, Bridgton ME. 207-647-3961

Stewart, James B, *Dir,* Victoria Public Library, Victoria TX. 512-578-6241

Stewart, Jane, *Librn,* Perkins, Coie, Stone, Olsen & Williams Library, Seattle WA. 206-682-8770, Ext 444

Stewart, Janet, *Librn,* University of Massachusetts at Boston Library (Science), Boston MA. 617-287-1900, Ext 2441

Stewart, Janet, *Ref & Bibliog Instr,* University of Massachusetts at Boston Library, Boston MA. 617-287-1900, Ext 2224

Stewart, Janice, *Librn,* Absecon Public Library, Absecon NJ. 609-646-2228

Stewart, Jean, *Librn,* Duluth Public Library (West Duluth Branch), Duluth MN. 218-624-1622

Stewart, Jerald K, *Dir,* North Dakota State School of Science, Mildred Johnson Library, Wahpeton ND. 701-671-2298

Stewart, Joan, *Librn,* Vienna Public Library, Vienna IL. 618-658-5051

Stewart, Joan, *Ref,* Waterford Township Public Library, Pontiac MI. 313-674-4831

Stewart, Joan G, *Dir,* Morton Grove Public Library, Morton Grove IL. 312-965-4220

Stewart, Judith E, *Librn,* Motorola, Inc, Government Electronics Div, Technical Library, Scottsdale AZ. 602-949-3471

Stewart, Karen L, *Librn,* Cincinnati Milacron Chemicals, Research Library, Cincinnati OH. 513-554-1554, Ext 171

Stewart, Kathryn A, *Coordr,* Brevard County Library System, Merritt Island FL. 305-453-9509

Stewart, Kathryn A, *Librn,* Carnation, Van Nuys CA. 213-787-7820, Ext 253

Stewart, Kristine, *Bkmobile Coordr,* Marshall-Lyon County Library, Marshall MN. 532-2646; 532-2849

Stewart, Lilly F, *Dir,* Beauregard Parish Public Library, De Ridder LA. 318-463-6217

Stewart, Linda, *Libr Asst,* San Bernardino County Library (Bloomington Branch), Bloomington CA. 714-877-1453

Stewart, Louann, *Librn,* Samaritan Health Center, Deaconess Hospital Unit Medical Library, Detroit MI. 313-259-2200, Ext 285

Stewart, M E, *Asst Dir, ILL & Ref,* Florida Institute of Technology, Jensen Beach Library, Jensen Beach FL. 305-334-4200, Ext 60, 61

Stewart, Mae L, *Ser,* Illinois Benedictine College, Theodore Lownik Library, Lisle IL. 312-968-7270, Ext 286

Stewart, Marcia, *Media,* Corning Public Library, Corning NY. 607-936-3713

Stewart, Margaret, *Film Servs,* Maine State Library, Augusta ME. 207-289-3561

Stewart, Margaret A, *Asst Dir Pub Servs,* Christopher Newport College, Captain John Smith Library, Newport News VA. 804-599-7130

Stewart, Marilyn, *Media,* Saint Charles Public Library District, Saint Charles IL. 312-584-0076

Stewart, Marjory, *Coordr,* Massachusetts Bay Community College Library, Wellesley MA. 617-237-1100, Ext 193

Stewart, Marlene, *Ad,* Ponca City Library, Ponca City OK. 405-762-6311

Stewart, Mary A, *Asst Dir, Ad & Bkmobile Coordr,* Southern Adirondack Library System, Saratoga Springs NY. 518-584-7300, 792-3343, 885-1073

Stewart, Mary Anne, *Ad,* River Bend Library System, Coal Valley IL. 309-799-3131

Stewart, Mary G, *Asst Prof,* Jacksonville State University, College of Library Science, Communications & Instructional Media, AL. 205-435-6390

Stewart, Mary Nell, *Librn,* Sullivan County Public Library (Bluff City Branch), Bluff City TN. 615-538-4241

Stewart, Mrs C, *Librn,* Borough of Etobicoke Public Library (Albion), Rexdale ON. 416-248-5681

Stewart, Nancy, *Librn,* Ball Corp, Research Library, Muncie IN. 317-747-6707

Stewart, Nancy S, *Librn,* South Yarmouth Library Association, South Yarmouth MA. 617-398-6626

Stewart, Ora Marie, *Dir,* Carnegie Bookmobile Library, Grafton ND. 701-352-2754

Stewart, Pearl, *Librn,* Imperial Life Assurance Co of Canada Library, Toronto ON. 416-923-6661

Stewart, Polly, *Librn,* Research & Review of America, Inc Library, Indianapolis IN. 317-297-4360

Stewart, Robert W, *Dir,* Asbury Park Free Public Library, Asbury Park NJ. 201-774-4221

Stewart, Sister M Ian, *Dir,* Loyola-Notre Dame Library, Inc, Baltimore MD. 301-532-8787

Stewart, Susan K, *Librn,* Irving Trust Co, General Business Library, New York NY. 212-487-6431

Stewart, Verna, *Librn,* San Diego Public Library (Normal Heights-Kensington), San Diego CA. 415-283-3733

Stewart, W James, *AV,* Oakton Community College, Learning Resource Center, Morton Grove IL. 312-967-5120, Ext 331

Stewart, William, *Dir,* Lubbock City-County Library, Lubbock TX. 806-762-6411, Ext 2828

Stewart, William, *Dir,* West Texas Library System, Lubbock TX. 806-762-5442

Stewart, William L, *Tech Serv,* University of Texas at San Antonio Library, San Antonio TX. 512-691-4570

Stibolt, Marcie, *Librn,* Northwestern University, Chicago (Joseph Schaffner Library), Chicago IL. 312-649-8422, 649-8423

Stickle, Cheryl R, *Librn,* Scott Paper Co (Research Library & Technical Information Service), Philadelphia PA. 215-521-5000, Ext 2416

Stickle, Gertrude, *Librn,* Candor Free Library, Candor NY. 607-659-7258

Stickler, Dianalee, *Librn,* Human Resources Research Organization, HumRRO Western Div Library, Carmel CA. 408-625-1347

Stickney, Edith P, *Librn,* Trinity Church Library, Santa Barbara CA. 805-965-7419

Stickney, Eleanor H, *In Charge,* Yale University Library (Ornithological), New Haven CT. 203-436-8547

Stidd, Dorothy, *Librn,* Martins Ferry Public Library (Bridgeport Public), Bridgeport OH. 614-635-2563

Stiefel, Lucy, *Dir,* Port Arthur Public Library, Port Arthur TX. 713-982-6491

Stieg, Gilbert, *Dir,* Racine County Historical Museum, Inc, Museum Reference Library of Genealogy & Local History, Racine WI. 414-637-8585

Stieg, Margaret, *Asst Prof,* Columbia University in the City of New York, School of Library Service, NY. 212-280-2292

Stiegelbauer, Alyce, *Cat,* York College Library, Jamaica NY. 212-969-4026

Stieger, Elaine, *Cat,* University of Southern California (Asa V Call Law Library), Los Angeles CA. 213-743-6487

Stiel, Beth, *Acq,* California State University Fullerton Library, Fullerton CA. 714-773-2714

Stierwalt, Ralph E, *Dir,* Ontario Universities' Library Cooperative System, (OULCS), ON. 416-979-2165

Stierwalt, Ralph E, *Dir,* UNICAT-TELECAT, (Union Catalogue-Telecataloguage), ON. 416-979-2165

Stiff, Dave, *Librn,* Billy Graham Evangelistic Association Library, Minneapolis MN. 612-338-0500

Stifflear, Allan, *Dir,* Episcopal Divinity School, Sherrill Hall Library, Cambridge MA. 617-868-3450, Ext 31

Stifflear, Allan J, *Dir,* Weston School of Theology Library, Cambridge MA. 617-868-3450, Ext 31

Stiffler, Stuart A, *Dir Libr Serv,* Cornell College, Russell D Cole Library, Mount Vernon IA. 319-895-8811, Ext 117

Stile, Fern, *Librn,* Milan Public Library, Milan NH. 603-449-6676

Stiles, Jane A, *Asst Dir,* Kingwood Public Library, Kingwood WV. 304-329-1499

Stiles, Lauren, *Ref,* State University of New York College, Memorial Library, Cortland NY. 607-753-2525, 753-2221

Stiles, Lauren, *Humanities,* State University of New York College, Memorial Library, Cortland NY. 607-753-2525, 753-2221

Stiles, Lauren, *Bibliog Instr,* State University of New York College, Memorial Library, Cortland NY. 607-753-2525, 753-2221

Stiles, Lois K, *Art,* Public Library of the District of Columbia, Martin Luther King Memorial Library, Washington DC. 202-727-1101

Stiles, May, *Bkmobile Coordr,* West Haven Public Library, West Haven CT. 203-932-2221

Stiles, Muriel H, *Dir, Acq & Commun Servs,* Beaman Memorial Public Library, West Boylston MA. 617-835-3711

Stiles, W G, *Info Dissemination Div,* Parliament of Canada, Library of Parliament, Ottawa ON. 613-995-7113

Still, Bayrd, *Dir,* New York University (New York University Archives), New York NY. 212-598-2484

Stiller, Jane R, *Librn,* Wolcott Public Library, Wolcott IN. 219-279-2695

Stilley, Bettye, *Librn,* United States Navy (Crew's Library), Jacksonville FL. 904-772-2201

Stilley, Bettye W, *Librn,* Jacksonville Health Educational Program, James L Borland Medical Library, Jacksonville FL. 904-353-9696

Stilley, Bettye W, *Librn,* United States Navy (Naval Regional Medical Center Library), Jacksonville FL. 904-772-3415

Stilley, Cynthia, *Librn,* Toledo-Lucas County Public Library (Mott), Toledo OH. 419-255-7055

Stilley, Judith, *Asst Librn,* Whiting Public Library, Whiting IN. 219-659-0269, 659-0320

Stillings, Craig, *Per & Spec Coll,* University of North Alabama, Collier Library, Florence AL. 205-766-4100, Ext 241

Stillisano, Gail, *Librn,* Collier County Free Public Library (Golden Gate), Naples FL. 813-262-4130, 261-8208

Stillman, Charles, *Librn,* Kennebec Bar Association, Law Library, Augusta ME. 207-623-9293

Stillman, June S, *Ref,* University of Central Florida Library, Orlando FL. 305-275-2564

Stillman, Mary E, *Dir,* Albright College Library, Reading PA. 215-921-2381, Ext 224

Stillwagon, Joyce, *Dir,* Eatontown Public Library, Eatontown NJ. 201-542-2341

Stillwater, Susan, *Ser,* Northern Michigan University, Lydia M Olson Library, Marquette MI. 906-227-2250

Stillwell, Kamala, *Tech Serv,* Palm Springs Public Library, Palm Springs CA. 714-323-8291

Stillwell, Oliver D, *Dir & Acq,* Cisco Junior College, Maner Learning Resources Center, Cisco TX. 817-442-2567

Stillwell, Sharon, *Asst Dir,* Toledo Public Library, Toledo OR. 503-336-3132

Stilson, Janet A, *Librn,* Northern Illinois University (Curriculum & Instruction-Outdoor Teacher Education), Oregon IL. 815-732-2111, Ext 63

Stilson, Janet A, *Librn,* Northern Illinois University, Taft Instructional Materials Center, Oregon IL. 815-732-2111, Ext 63

Stilson, Malcolm, *Per & Doc,* Evergreen State College, Daniel J Evans Library, Olympia WA. 206-866-6262

Stilwell, Arlene, *Librn,* New Sharon Public Library, New Sharon IA. 515-637-4049

Stilwell, Ruth, *Asst Dir,* Mountain View Public Library, Mountain View CA. 415-968-6595

Stimpson, Anne D, *Librn,* Mark & Emily Turner Memorial Library, Presque Isle ME. 207-768-5081

Stimpson, Eleanor, *Tech Serv, Cat & Spec Coll,* Porterville Public Library, Porterville CA. 209-784-0177, 784-1400, Ext 523

Stimson, Andrew W, *Librn,* Shimer College Library, Waukegan IL. 815-244-2811

Stimson, Andrew W, *Dir,* Waukegan Public Library, Waukegan IL. 312-623-2041

Stimson, Sheila, *Friends of Lovejoy Libr,* Southern Illinois University at Edwardsville, Elijah P Lovejoy Library, Edwardsville IL. 618-692-2711

Stine, Fern, *Tech Serv,* Denison Public Library, Denison TX. 214-465-1797

Stine, Immogene, *Librn,* Edna Public Library, Edna KS. 316-922-3453

Stine, Jane, *Librn,* Adel Public Library, Adel IA. 515-993-3512

Stine, Kay, *Ch,* Huntington City Township Public Library, Huntington IN. 219-356-0824

Stiner, Margaret, *Ad,* Elwood Public Library, Elwood IN. 317-552-5001

Stines, Joe R, *Ch,* Sheppard Memorial Library, Greenville NC. 919-752-4177

Stinger, June, *Librn,* Weyerhauser Co, Technical Center Library, Longview WA. 206-425-2150, Ext 467

Stingo, Salvatore L, *Dir,* Clifton Public Library, Clifton NJ. 201-772-5500

Stinnette, Myrna, *Tech Serv,* Wheaton Public Library, Wheaton IL. 312-668-1374

Stinson, Dorothy A, *Librn,* Cuyahoga County Public Library (Chagrin Falls), Chagrin Falls OH. 216-247-3556

Stinson, Gay, *Asst Librn,* Northland Pioneer College, Winslow Center Library, Winslow AZ. 602-289-5082

Stinson, Helen, *Supvr,* Elgin County Public Library (Rodney Branch), Rodney ON. 519-633-0815

Stinson, Janet, *Asst Dir,* Bossier Parish Public Library, Benton LA. 318-965-2751

Stinson, Janet, *Librn,* Bossier Parish Public Library (Bossier City Branch), Bossier City LA. 318-746-1693

Stinson, Judy, *Ref & Doc,* Washington & Lee University (Wilbur C Hall Library), Lexington VA. 703-463-3157

Stinson, Pat, *ILL,* East Texas State University, James Gilliam Gee Library, Commerce TX. 214-886-5717

Stirling, Joyce, *Coordr,* McKim Advertising Ltd, Research Services Library, Toronto ON. 416-863-5471

Stirling, Keith H, *Assoc Prof,* Brigham Young University, School of Library & Information Sciences, UT. 801-378-2976

Stirneman, Grace, *Ref,* Bridgeton Free Public Library, Bridgeton NJ. 609-451-2620

Stirrat, Agnes, *Tech Serv & Cat,* Webster College, Eden Theological Seminary, Eden-Webster Libraries, Saint Louis MO. 314-968-0500, Ext 235

Stitely, C, *Cat,* University of Rhode Island Library, Kingston RI. 401-792-1000

Stith, Janet B, *Asst Dir,* University of Kentucky (Medical Center Library), Lexington KY. 606-233-5300

Stith, Linda, *AV,* Kentucky Department of Library & Archives, Frankfort KY. 502-564-7910

Stith, Nancy, *Actg Librn,* American Numismatic Association Library, Colorado Springs CO. 303-473-9142

Stitsworth, Karen, *Ref,* University of Arkansas at Little Rock Library (University of Arkansas at Little Rock School of Law & Pulaski County Law Library), Little Rock AR. 501-371-1071

Stitt, Eleanor, *Sci,* Rutgers University (Camden Arts & Science Library), Camden NJ. 609-757-6036

Stitt, III, Walter, *Dir,* Attleboro Public Library, Joseph L Sweet Memorial, Attleboro MA. 617-222-0157

Stivers, Lloyd E, *Librn,* South Dakota State Penitentiary, Donald M Cole Library, Sioux Falls SD. 605-339-6760, 339-6769

Stivers, Robert, *Planning,* Seattle Public Library, Seattle WA. 206-625-2665

Stjernolm, Kirstine, *Commun Servs,* University of Southern Colorado Library, Pueblo CO. 303-549-2361

Stjernquist, Alice, *Dir,* El Dorado County Library, Placerville CA. 916-626-2561

StJohn, M L, *Librn,* Trans-Tech Inc, Ceramic Research & Development Laboratory Library, Gaithersburg MD. 301-948-3800

StLaurent, Flo, *Ch,* Swansea Free Public Library, Swansea MA. 617-674-9609

StLaurent, Laurie, *ILL,* Transylvania University, Frances Carrick Thomas Library, Lexington KY. 606-233-8225

Stoan, Stephen, *Soc Sci,* Wichita State University, Library & Media Resources Center, Wichita KS. 316-689-3586

Stobbe, Anne, *Dir,* Maud Preston Palenske Memorial Library, Saint Joseph Public Library, Saint Joseph MI. 616-983-7106

Stobbe, Patricia, *Librn,* Detroit Public Library (Redford), Detroit MI. 313-833-9823

Stoch, Ronald V, *Dir,* Eisenhower Public Library District, Harwood Heights IL. 312-867-7828, 452-8989

Stock, Alice, *Librn,* Baldwin Township Library, Pittsburgh PA. 412-344-5585

Stock, Jonathan, *Librn,* Connecticut State Library (Stamford Branch), Stamford CT. 203-566-4301

Stock, Juanita, *Per,* Warren Wilson College Library, Swannanoa NC. 704-298-3325, Ext 45

Stock, Norman, *Spec Coll,* Montclair State College, Harry A Sprague Library, Upper Montclair NJ. 201-893-4291

Stockard, Joan, *ILL & Ref,* Wellesley College, Margaret Clapp Library, Wellesley MA. 617-235-0320, Ext 280

Stockdale, Carolyn, *Media,* Saint John Fisher College, Lavery Library, Pittsford NY. 716-586-4140, Ext 222

Stockdale, Jose, *Acq,* British Columbia Institute of Technology Library, Burnaby BC. 604-434-5734, Ext 360

Stockey, Bill, *Dir,* John Wood Community College Library, Quincy IL. 217-224-6500, Ext 20

Stocking, Carolyn, *Govt Publications,* University of Connecticut Library, Storrs CT. 203-486-2219

Stockley, Ruth G, *Librn,* Quemado Public Library, Quemado TX. 512-757-1270

Stockly, Elizabeth, *Asst Librn,* Art Center College of Design, Fogg Memorial Library, Pasadena CA. 213-577-1700, Ext 265

Stockman, Herbert E, *Dir,* Evansville State Hospital, Medical Library, Evansville IN. 812-473-2261

Stockton, Gloria, *Circ,* Stanford University Libraries, Stanford CA. 415-497-2016

Stockton, Harlan, *Media,* Motlow State Community College, Library-Learning Resources Center, Tullahoma TN. 615-455-8511, Ext 225

Stockton, Mary Ann, *Librn,* Johnson-Saint Public Library, Saint Paris OH. 513-663-4349

Stockwell, Dorothy, *Librn,* Bureau of Indian Affairs, Bethel Regional Library, Bethel AK. 907-543-2749

Stockwell, Zizi, *ILL,* University of Western Ontario, A B Weldon Library, London ON. 519-679-6191

Stoddard, Nancy Williams, *Librn,* Pulitzer Publishing Co, Saint Louis Post Dispatch Reference Library, Saint Louis MO. 314-621-1111, Ext 535

Stoddard, Roger E, *Assoc Librn,* Harvard University Library (Houghton Library-Rare Books & Manuscripts), Cambridge MA. 617-495-2441

Stoddard, Ruth, *Tech Serv & Acq,* Cobb County Public Library System, Marietta GA. 404-427-2462

Stoddard, William S, *Librn,* Michigan State University Library (Business), East Lansing MI. 517-355-2344

Stoeker, Joan S, *Dir & Cat,* Garfield Memorial Library, Clare Public Library, Clare MI. 517-386-7576

Stoekl, Mary E, *Librn,* Chesapeake Public Library (Russell Memorial), Chesapeake VA. 804-488-9270

Stoel, Roger, *Acq & Ref,* Muskegon Community College, Allen G Umbreit Library, Muskegon MI. 616-773-9131, Ext 260

Stoffel, Edna M, *Librn,* G N Wilcox Memorial Hospital & Health Center, Medical Library, Lihue HI. 808-245-4811, Ext 439

Stoffel, Lester, *Dir,* Suburban Library System, Burr Ridge IL. 312-325-6640

Stoia, Joseph P, *Librn,* Kettering College of Medical Arts Library (Kettering Memorial Hospital Library), Kettering OH. 513-298-4331, Ext 5561

Stoicovy, Monica R, *Librn,* Brentwood Library, Pittsburgh PA. 412-882-5694

Stoker, Joyce, *Circ & On-Line Servs,* Coe College, Stewart Memorial Library, Cedar Rapids IA. 319-399-8585, 399-8586

Stoker, Ruth, *Librn,* General Electric Co, Laminated Products Engineering Library, Coshocton OH. 614-622-5310

Stokes, Esther M, *Adjunct Asst Prof,* Emory University, Div of Librarianship, GA. 404-329-6840

Stokes, J Parker, *Dir,* Macon Public Library, Macon MO. 816-385-3314

Stokes, Jean, *Librn,* Peoria Public Library (Lincoln), Peoria IL. 309-672-8839

Stokes, Kathryne, *Pub Servs,* University of Miami (Law), Coral Gables FL. 305-284-2250

Stokes, Pamela, *Ch,* Butler Public Library, Butler PA. 412-287-5576

Stokes, Roy B, *Dir,* University of British Columbia, School of Librarianship, BC. 604-228-2404

Stokes, Thomas E, *Dir,* Emmanuel School of Religion Library, Johnson City TN. 615-926-1186, Ext 49

Stokes, William, *Instr,* University of Denver, Graduate School of Librarianship and Information Management, CO. 303-753-2557

Stokesberry, Ruth, *Commun Servs,* Public Library of Des Moines, Des Moines IA. 515-283-4152

Stoksik, Pamela, *Tech Serv,* Ontario Legislative Library, Research & Information Services, Toronto ON. 416-965-4545

Stolinas, Mary Ann, *Librn,* Historical Society of Berks County Library, Reading PA. 215-375-4375

Stoll, Brenda, *Circ,* Hurst Public Library, Hurst TX. 817-485-5320

Stoll, Karen, *Rare Bks & Spec Coll,* Monroe County Library System, Monroe MI. 313-241-5277

Stoll, Karen S, *Deputy Head Librn,* Los Alamos Scientific Laboratory Libraries, Library Services Group, Los Alamos NM. 505-667-4448

Stoller, Irene, *Asst Dir,* Madison Public Library, Madison WI. 608-266-6300

Stoller, Janet, *Librn,* Mutual of New York (Law Department Library), New York NY. 212-586-4000, Ext 400

Stoller, Janet, *Librn,* Mutual of New York (Library Information Service), New York NY. 212-586-4000, Ext 703

Stolliday, Catherine G, *Dir,* Puyallup Public Library, Puyallup WA. 206-845-6353

Stolnitz, Dia, *Coordr,* Museum of American Folk Art, Research Library, New York NY. 212-581-2474

Stolp, James, *Bkmobile Coordr,* San Jose Public Library, San Jose CA. 408-277-4822

Stolper, Gertrude, *Librn,* University of Michigan Libraries (Bureau of Government), Ann Arbor MI. 313-763-3185

Stolt, Wilbur, *Archivist,* University of Wisconsin-Milwaukee, Golda Meir Library, Milwaukee WI. 414-963-4785

Stoltenberg, Marianne, *Acq,* Ocean County College, Learning Resources Center, Toms River NJ. 201-255-4298

Stoltz, James R, *Dir & Acq,* Clatsop Community College Library, Astoria OR. 503-324-0910

Stolz, Marty, *Librn,* Saint Alphonsus Hospital, Health Sciences Library, Boise ID. 208-376-1211, Ext 271

Stolz, Ruth, *Deputy Dir Main Libr Serv,* Rochester Public Library, Olmsted County Library System, Rochester MN. 507-285-8000

Stomz, Lera Patricia, *Librn,* Upham Memorial Library, Fredericksburg IA. 515-237-6498

Stone, Ann, *Personnel,* Duke University, William R Perkins Library, Durham NC. 684-2034 (Main).

Stone, Barbara, *Reading,* Wilkes Community College, Learning Resources Library, Wilkesboro NC. 919-667-7136, Ext 26

Stone, Bernice N, *Librn,* Fort Logan Mental Health Center, Medical Library, Denver CO. 303-761-0220, Ext 517

Stone, Carl, *Dir,* Anderson County Library, Anderson SC. 803-225-1429

Stone, Carol, *Ser,* Miami-Dade Public Library System, Miami FL. 305-579-5001

Stone, Dennis J, *Law,* Gonzaga University (Law Library), Spokane WA. 509-328-4220, Ext 3781

Stone, Dennis J, *Librn,* Gonzaga University (Law Library), Spokane WA. 509-328-4220, Ext 3781

Stone, Earl E, *Dir,* Allen Knight Maritime Museum Library, Monterey CA. 408-375-2553

Stone, Elizabeth W, *Chmn,* Catholic University of America, Graduate Dept of Library & Information Sciences, DC. 202-635-5085

Stone, Gary, *AV,* Lewis & Clark Library System, Edwardsville IL. 618-656-3216

Stone, Gordon, *Librn,* Metropolitan Museum of Art (Irene Lewisohn Costume Reference Library), New York NY. 212-879-5500, Ext 628

Stone, Jean, *ILL & Cat,* Brooks Free Library, Harwich MA. 617-432-1799

Stone, Jean, *Dir,* Roxbury Public Library, Roxbury NY. 607-326-7901

Stone, Leona P, *Circ & ILL,* Columbia Union College, Theofield G Weis Library, Takoma Park MD. 301-270-4999

Stone, Margaret, *Educ,* Florida Atlantic University, S E Wimberly Library, Boca Raton FL. 305-395-5100, Ext 2448

Stone, Margaret, *Soc Sci,* Morehead State University, Johnson Camden-Julian Carroll Library, Morehead KY. 606-783-2250

Stone, Martha B, *Chief Librn,* Canada Department of National Health & Welfare, Departmental Library Services, Ottawa ON. 613-996-4950

Stone, Marvin H, *Librn for Fine Coll,* Dallas Public Library, Dallas TX. 214-748-9071

Stone, Maude M, *Librn,* Fobes Memorial Library, Oakham MA. 617-882-3372

Stone, Norma, *Librn,* Gibbonsville Library Station, Gibbonsville ID. 208-865-2262

Stone, Orlando L, *Tech Serv,* Tidewater Community College, Frederick Campus Library, Portsmouth VA. 804-484-2121, Ext 226

Stone, Pat, *Chief Librn,* United States Department of the Navy (Naval Air Systems Command, Technical Library), Washington DC. 202-692-9006

Stone, Patricia, *ILL & Media,* Mount Union College Library, Alliance OH. 216-821-5320, Ext 260

Stone, Rosalie, *Tech Serv,* New York Medical College, Westchester Medical Center Library, Valhalla NY. 914-347-5237

Stone, Sharon, *Librn,* Council Grove Public Library, Council Grove KS. 316-767-5716

Stone, Sharon M, *Librn,* Ceredo-Kenova Public Library, Kenova WV. 304-453-2462

Stone, Thelma, *Librn,* Abington Public Library, Abington MA. 617-878-0449

Stone, Thelma, *Librn,* Fort Worth Public Library (South Branch), Fort Worth TX. 817-926-0215
Stoneberg, John, *Ref,* L E Phillips Memorial Public Library, Eau Claire WI. 715-839-5002
Stonebrook, Margaret A, *Ch,* Eau Gallie Public Library, Melbourne FL. 305-254-1739
Stoneburg, Mary Jane, *Per,* Bucknell University, Ellen Clarke Bertrand Library, Lewisburg PA. 717-524-3056
Stoneburg, Mary Jane, *Spec Coll,* Bucknell University, Ellen Clarke Bertrand Library, Lewisburg PA. 717-524-3056
Stoneburner, CW, *Eng,* University of Texas at Arlington Library, Arlington TX. 817-273-3391
Stoneham, John, *Dir,* Maryland Institute College of Art, Decker Library, Baltimore MD. 301-669-9200, Ext 27, 28
Stoneham, Olwen, *Libr Asst,* S E D Systems Ltd Library, Saskatoon SK. 306-244-0976
Stonehill, Helen, *Chief Librn,* ICD Rehabilitation & Research Center Library, New York NY. 212-679-0100, Ext 253, 254
Stonehouse, Marie Louise, *Coordr,* Merck & Co, Calgon Corp Information Center, Pittsburgh PA. 412-777-8203
Stoneman, Joan, *Librn,* Pamunkey Regional Library (Goochland Branch), Goochland VA. 804-556-4774
Stoner, Carol, *ILL,* Rappahannock Community College, North Campus Learning Resource Center, Warsaw VA. 804-333-4024, Ext 208, 209
Stoner, Nellie A, *Librn,* E F Houghton Technical Center Library, Norristown PA. 215-666-7756
Stonestreet, R D, *Clerk-Treas,* Public Library of Cincinnati & Hamilton County, Cincinnati Public Library, Cincinnati OH. 513-369-6000
Stonis, John, *Cat,* Edinboro State College, Baron-Forness Library, Edinboro PA. 814-732-2780
Stonner, Margaret, *Librn,* North Chatham Free Library, North Chatham NY. 518-766-3211
Stookey, Roberta, *Ch,* Hammond Public Library, Hammond IN. 219-931-5100
Stoops, Louise, *Chief Librn,* Lehman Bros Kuhn Loeb, Inc Library, New York NY. 212-558-2134
Stopher, Mary K, *Librn,* Centerburg Public Library, Centerburg OH. 614-625-6538
Stoppel, Gordon E, *Asst Dir, Tech Serv & Cat,* Pinal County Library System, Florence AZ. 602-868-5801, Ext 456
Stoppel, Kaye, *Ser,* Drake University (Drake Law Library), Des Moines IA. 515-271-2141
Stoppel, William A, *Dir,* Drake University, Cowles Library, Des Moines IA. 515-271-3993
Stopper, Sister Antonette, *Ref,* Assumption College for Sisters Library, Mendham NJ. 201-543-6528
Storch, Alison, *Librn,* ITT Research Institute, Technical Information Services Library, Annapolis MD. 301-267-2251
Storck, Bernadette, *Head, Cent Libr,* Tampa-Hillsborough County Public Library System, Tampa FL. 813-223-8947
Storck, John N, *Dir,* Lima Public Library, Lima OH. 419-228-5113
Storck, John W P, *Librn,* Martins Ferry Public Library, Martins Ferry OH. 614-633-0314
Stordy, Olga, *Librn,* Prince Edward Island Provincial Library (Crapaud Branch), Crapaud PE. 902-892-3504, Ext 54
Stores, Daphne G, *Media,* North Olympic Library System, Port Angeles WA. 206-457-4464
Storey, Janus, *YA & Cat,* Bayliss Public Library, Sault Sainte Marie MI. 906-632-9331
Storey, Janus, *Cat,* Hiawathaland Library Cooperative, Sault Sainte Marie MI. 906-632-9331
Storey, Jill, *Info & Referral Coord,* Womens Action Alliance Library, New York NY. 212-532-8330
Storey, Joe L, *Tech Serv & On-Line Servs,* Saint Mary's College of Maryland Library, Saint Mary's City MD. 301-994-1600, Ext 216
Storey, Lillian, *Ad,* Adams Library, Chelmsford MA. 617-256-5521
Storey, Susan, *ILL,* Great Falls Public Library, Pathfinder Federation of Libraries Headquarters, Great Falls MT. 406-453-0349
Storey, Theo H, *Interim Librn,* Baptist Medical Center System (Sheppard Professional Library), Little Rock AR. 501-227-3235

Storey, Virginia, *ILL & Ref,* Chattahoochee Valley Regional Library, W C Bradley Memorial Library, Headquarters, Columbus GA. 404-327-0211
Storey, Gayla, *Librn,* Langlois Public Libraries, Langlois OR. 503-348-2278
Storm, Herman R, *On-Line Servs,* University of Wisconsin-River Falls, Chalmer Davee Library, River Falls WI. 715-425-3321
Storm, Joyce, *ILL,* University of Delaware, Hugh M Morris Library, Newark DE. 302-738-2231
Storm, Sarah, *Librn,* Arthur Public Library, Arthur IL. 217-543-2037
Storms, Dale, *Genealogy & Local Hist,* Guernsey Memorial Library, Norwich NY. 607-334-4034
Stortz, Gene, *Consult Info Retrieval,* Colorado State Library, Colorado Department of Education, Denver CO. 303-839-3695
Story, Allen C, *Librn,* Pension Benefit Guaranty Corp Library, Washington DC. 202-254-4889
Story, Loraine, *Librn,* W Walworth Harrison Public Library, Greenville TX. 214-455-2205
Storz, Ethel, *Curric,* Pacific Union College, W E Nelson Memorial Library, Angwin CA. 707-965-6241
Stott, Ethelyn, *Ser,* Louisiana State University (Troy H Middleton Library), Baton Rouge LA. 504-388-2217
Stottman, Dorothea, *Dir,* Ridgway Memorial Library, Bullitt County Library, Shepherdsville KY. 502-543-7675
Stotts, Ruth, *Librn,* Bement Township Public Library, Bement IL. 217-678-7101
Stouder, Vicki, *Librn, On-Line Servs & Bibliog Instr,* NCR Corp, Technical Library, Dayton OH. 513-449-2637
Stoudimire, Mrs Sam, *Librn,* Shelby County Regional Library (Wilsonville Branch), Wilsonville AL. 205-669-7851
Stough, Mary L, *Asst Dir for Pub Servs,* Timberland Regional Library, Olympia WA. 206-943-5001
Stout, Barbara, *Acq,* Danbury Public Library, Danbury CT. 203-797-4505
Stout, C B, *Dir,* McKinley Memorial Library, Niles OH. 216-652-1704
Stout, Cathy A, *Librn,* New Jersey State Department of Health Library, Trenton NJ. 609-292-5693
Stout, Joan, *Librn,* Clark College Library, Vancouver WA. 206-699-0251
Stout, Judy, *Librn,* Marine Environmental Sciences Consortium, AL. 205-861-2141
Stout, Larella, *Dir,* Louisville Public Library, Louisville OH. 303-666-6037
Stout, Leon, *Penn State Room,* Pennsylvania State University, Fred Lewis Pattee Library, University Park PA. 814-865-0401
Stout, Lt, *Libr Officers,* United States Navy (Tactical Library), San Diego CA. 714-225-3273
Stout, Paul W, *Maps,* Ball State University, Alexander M Bracken Library, Muncie IN. 317-285-6261
Stout, Robert, *Chief Librn,* Ohio State University Libraries (Children's Hospital Library), Columbus OH. 614-461-2375
Stout, Robert J, *Coordr,* Catawba-Wateree Area Health Education Center, Learning Resources Center, Rock Hill SC. 803-382-2419
Stoutenburg, Brian H, *Dir,* Dunkirk Free Library, Dunkirk NY. 716-366-2511
Stoutt, E E, *Eng Admin Coordr,* Mack Trucks, Inc, Engineering Div Technical Information Center, Hagerstown MD. 301-733-8308
Stovall, Ida S, *Librn,* Richard H Thornton Library (Stovall Branch), Stovall NC. 919-693-5722
Stovall, Lois, *Librn,* Saint Louis Public Library (Cabanne), Saint Louis MO. 314-367-0717
Stovall, Martha W, *Librn,* Veterans Administration, Hospital Medical Library, Sepulveda CA. 213-894-8271, Ext 418
Stover, Celeste, *Br Coordr,* Bartram Trail Regional Library, Mary Willis Library Headquarters, Washington GA. 404-678-7736
Stover, Glenn S, *Chief Librn,* United States Army (Yuma Proving Ground Post Library), Yuma AZ. 602-328-2151
Stover, Irene, *Librn,* Conrad Public Library, Conrad IA. 515-366-2583
Stover, Jean, *Ref,* Free Public Library of the City of Orange, Orange NJ. 201-673-0153
Stover, Lorna, *Librn,* Valley Center Public Library, Valley Center KS. 316-755-1507

Stowe, Erick D, *In Charge,* American National Bank Building Law Library, Denver CO. 303-572-1776
Stowe, Stephanie H, *Librn,* Denver Museum of Natural History Library, Denver CO. 303-575-3610
Stowers, Anne F, *Librn,* Obion County Public Library, Union City TN. 901-885-9411
Stowers, Joel A, *Dir,* University of Tennessee at Martin, Paul Meek Library, Martin TN. 901-587-7060
Stowers, Joyce, *Librn,* Kern County Library (Tehachapi Branch), Tehachapi CA. 805-861-2130
StPierre, Dick, *LRC Coordr,* North Shore Community College, Learning Resource Center, Beverly MA. 617-927-4850, Ext 195, 199, 237
Strable, Edward G, *In Charge,* J Walter Thompson Co, Information Center, Chicago IL. 312-664-6700, Ext 6151
Strable, Jane, *Cat,* University of Chicago (Law Library), Chicago IL. 312-753-3425
Strachan, Ann, *Ch,* Indianapolis-Marion County Public Library, Indianapolis IN. 317-635-5662
Strachan, Donna D, *Librn,* Porter Memorial Library, Machias ME. 207-255-3933
Strachan, Nancy, *Asst Librn,* Bedford Public Library, Bedford VA. 703-586-8911
Stracke, David, *Ref & Bus,* Grand Rapids Public Library, Grand Rapids MI. 616-456-4400
Strader, Beverly, *AV,* South Dakota State Library, Pierre SD. 605-773-3131
Strader, Helen, *Outreach Servs,* Manatee County Public Library System, Bradenton FL. 813-748-5555
Strader, Thomas E, *Dir,* Towson State University, Albert S Cook Library, Towson MD. 301-321-2450
Strah, Gerda, *Librn,* McKinley Public Library, McKinley MN. 218-749-5313
Strahan, Jean D, *Librn,* National Genealogical Society Library, Washington DC. 202-785-2123
Straight, Elsie H, *Chief Librn & Bibliog Instr,* Ringling School of Art Library, Sarasota FL. 813-355-1232
Straight, Nilta J, *Librn,* Grant County Library, Sheridan AR. 501-942-4436
Strain, Laura M, *Librn,* Latham & Watkins, Law Library, Los Angeles CA. 213-485-1234
Strain, Paula M, *In Charge,* Mitre Corp Library, McLean VA. 703-827-6481
Strait, George A, *Dir,* University of Iowa Libraries (Law Library), Iowa City IA. 319-353-5968
Straits, David, *Media,* Ashland College Library, Ashland OH. 419-289-4067
Straker, Patricia, *Librn,* Lane Public Library (Oxford Branch), Oxford OH. 513-523-2366
Stramiello, Angela, *Librn,* Mershon, Sawyer, Johnston, Dunwody & Cole Library, Miami FL. 305-358-5100
Strampe, Clara, *Commun Servs,* Washakie County Library, Worland WY. 307-347-2231
Stranairi, Paul, *AV & Media,* University of Massachusetts Medical School, Medical Center Library, Worcester MA. 617-856-2511
Stranberry, Patsy, *ILL & Circ,* East Tennessee State University (Medical Library), Johnson City TN. 615-928-6426, Ext 252
Strand, Elaine L, *Ad & Ref,* Grand Forks Public City-County Library, Grand Forks ND. 701-772-8116
Strand, Kathryn, *Librn,* National Center for Atmospheric Research (High Altitude Observatory Library), Boulder CO. 303-494-5151
Strang, Eleanor, *Ref,* Kelley Library, Salem Public Library, Salem NH. 603-898-7064
Strang, Joan, *Asst Dir,* Leominster Public Library, Leominster MA. 617-537-0941
Strang, Melva, *Ref,* University of Alabama in Huntsville Library, Huntsville AL. 205-895-6540
Strange, Allan, *Asst Librn,* Crystal City Public Library, Crystal City MO. 314-937-7166
Strange, Beth, *Coordr,* Itawamba Junior College Vocational-Technical Center, Itawamba Junior College-Tupelo Branch, Learning Resources Ctr, Tupelo MS. 601-842-5621, Ext 25
Strange, Cheryl L, *Asst Librn,* FMC Corp, CEL Library, Santa Clara CA. 408-289-2529
Strange, Marjorie, *Bkmobile Coordr,* Jefferson-Madison Regional Library, McIntire Public Library, Charlottesville VA. 804-296-6157

Strange, Rita, *Librn,* Public Library of the District of Columbia (Parklands), Washington DC. 202-767-7199
Strange, Thomas R, *Dir,* Benton Harbor Public Library, Benton Harbor MI. 616-926-6139
Strange, William J, *Dir,* Glendale Community College Library, Glendale CA. 213-240-1000, Ext 271
Strapp, Elizabeth, *Network Ref Supvr,* New Jersey State Library, Trenton NJ. 609-292-6200
Strasner, Edna B, *Librn,* Soutar Memorial Library, Boise City OK. 405-544-2715
Strasshofer, Rae, *Media,* Shaker Heights Public Library, Shaker Heights OH. 216-991-2030
Strassler, Ruth Ellen, *Dir,* Neligh Public Library, Neligh NE. 402-887-5140
Stratelak, Ernest, *Media,* Grosse Pointe Public Library, Grosse Pointe MI. 313-343-2074
Strater, Joann G, *Librn,* Runnemede Public Library, Runnemede NJ. 609-939-4688
Stratford, Sandra, *Circ,* Columbus College, Simon Schwob Memorial Library, Columbus GA. 404-568-2042
Stratford, Vaughn, *Librn,* Solano County Library (Vacaville Public), Fairfield CA. 707-448-4900
Strathern, G, *Assoc Prof,* University of Alberta, Faculty of Library Science, AB. 403-432-4578
Stratton, Barbara, *Ref & Per,* Imperial Valley College, Spencer Library Media Center, Imperial CA. 714-352-8320, Ext 270
Stratton, Doris, *Asst Librn,* Nichols Memorial Library, Kingston NH. 603-642-3521
Stratton, George W, *Asst Dir,* South Bend Public Library, South Bend IN. 219-288-4413
Stratton, Jan, *Librn,* Stockbridge Free Public Library, Stockbridge VT. 802-234-5047
Stratton, Joyce, *Librn,* Beaver City Public Library, Beaver City NE. 308-268-4115
Stratton, Julia, *Librn,* Solano County Library (Springstowne), Vallejo CA. 707-553-5546
Stratton, Lucile, *Librn,* Bendix Corp, Technical Information Center Library, Kansas City MO. 816-997-2694
Straub, Lois, *Librn,* Scott Environmental Technology, Inc, Scott Technical Information Center Library, Plumsteadville PA. 215-766-8861
Strauch, Susan, *Librn,* Lake County Law Library, Waukegan IL. 312-689-6654
Straughn, Arlene M, *Dir,* Huntington Public Library, Huntington NY. 516-427-5165
Strausbaugh, Jennifer, *Librn,* Borden Inc Library, Columbus OH. 614-225-4000
Strauss, Carol D, *Librn,* Westlake Community Hospital Library, Melrose Park IL. 312-681-3000, Ext 215
Strauss, Diane, *Ref, Bus & Social Sci,* University of North Carolina at Chapel Hill, Louis Round Wilson Academic Affairs Library, Chapel Hill NC. 919-933-1301
Strauss, Laura C, *Asst Dir,* Lapeer County Library, Lapeer MI. 313-664-9521
Strauss, Maxine, *Ch,* Aberdeen-Matawan Public Library, Matawan NJ. 201-583-9100
Strauss, Richard, *Actg Dir,* Montgomery County-Norristown Public Library, Norristown PA. 215-277-3355
Strauss, Stanley, *Ch,* Ontario Public Library, Ontario OR. 984-2758 Ext 38
Straw, Deah F, *Dir,* Southern Pines Public Library, Southern Pines NC. 919-692-7692
Strawbridge, Frederic, *ILL,* Temple University, Ambler Campus Library, Ambler PA. 215-643-1200, Ext 250
Strawder, Maxine, *Librn,* Memphis-Shelby County Public Library & Information Center (Gaston Park), Memphis TN. 901-942-0836
Strawn, M B, *Chief Librn,* Vandergrift Public Library Association, Vandergrift PA. 412-568-2212
Strawn, Mrs Richard, *Media,* Crawfordsville District Public Library, Crawfordsville IN. 317-362-2242
Strawn, Richard R, *Dir,* Wabash College, Lilly Library, Crawfordsville IN. 317-362-1400, Ext 215, 216
Strawser, Dorothy, *Librn,* Logan County District Library (Rushsylvania Branch), Bellefontaine OH. 513-599-4189
Strayer, Jean-Jacques L, *Ref,* Darien Library, Inc, Darien CT. 203-655-2568

Strazdon, Maureen E, *Librn,* American College, Vane B Lucas Memorial Library, Bryn Mawr PA. 215-896-4507, 896-4508
Streamer, Jr, William A, *Libr Info & Reports Specialist,* Maryland State Department of Education, Division of Library Development & Services, Baltimore MD. 301-796-8300, Ext 284
Strebig, Judy P, *Dir,* University of Wisconsin Center-Marathon County Library, Wausau WI. 715-845-9602, Ext 220
Strecker, Lois, *Asst Librn & ILL,* Mount Laurel Free Public Library, Mount Laurel NJ. 609-234-7319
Streeb, Elsie, *Librn,* Windsor Public Library, Windsor CO. 303-686-2055
Streeper, Mary Sue, *Automation, Bibliog Servs & On-Line Servs,* Wyoming State Library, Cheyenne WY. 307-777-7281
Street, Geraldine, *Coordr of Admin Servs,* Everett Public Library, Everett WA. 206-259-8858
Street, Geraldine, *On-Line Servs & Bibliog Instr,* Everett Public Library, Everett WA. 206-259-8858
Street, Jean, *Cat,* Meridian Public Library, Meridian MS. 601-693-6771, 693-4913
Street, Shirley, *Librn,* Williamsburg County Library, Kingstree SC. 803-354-9486
Streeter, David, *Spec Coll,* Pomona Public Library, Pomona CA. 714-620-2033
Streetman, III, John W, *Dir,* Evansville Museum of Arts & Science Library, Evansville IN. 812-425-2406
Streff, Sister Marie, *Cat & Ref,* Marylhurst Education Center, Shoen Library, Marylhurst OR. 503-636-8141, Ext 56 & 61
Strege, Karen, *Asst Dir & YA,* Moscow-Latah County Library System, Moscow ID. 208-882-3925
Streiff, Ann W, *Dir,* Bethlehem Steel Corp (Charles M Schwab Memorial Library), Bethlehem PA. 215-694-3325
Streiff, Kwang Hee, *Chief Librn,* Veterans Administration, Medical Center, Poplar Bluff MO. 314-686-4151
Strein, Barbara, *YA,* Harford County Library, Del Air MD. 301-838-7484
Streit, Samuel A, *Asst Univ Librn-Spec Colls,* Brown University (University Library), Providence RI. 401-863-2167
Strelecky, Katherine A, *Librn,* Upper Perkiomen Valley Library, Red Hill PA. 215-679-2020
Strelecky, Kay, *Librn,* Montgomery County-Norristown Public Library (Upper Perkiomen Valley), Red Hill PA. 215-679-2020
Streler, Terry, *ILL,* Somers Library, Somers NY. 914-277-3420
Strempek, Carol, *Cat & Ser,* Curry College, Louis R Levin Memorial Library, Milton MA. 617-333-0500, Ext 177
Strezloff, Claire, *Librn,* Saint Anne's Hospital, Medical Staff Library, Chicago IL. 312-378-7100
Stribling, Inez, *Librn,* Uncle Remus Regional Library (Eatonton Public), Eatonton GA. 404-485-6768
Stribling, Matrel, *Circ,* Union Carnegie Library, Union SC. 803-427-7140
Strickland, Albert C, *Librn,* University of Florida Libraries (Agriculture), Gainesville FL. 904-392-1934
Strickland, Bonnie, *Librn,* Tacoma Public Library (George O Swasey), Tacoma WA. 206-564-1599
Strickland, Carmen, *Bibliotherapist,* New England Baptist Hospital (Patients' Library), Boston MA. 617-738-5800, Ext 108
Strickland, Enide, *Librn,* Athens Regional Library (Royston Branch), Royston GA. 404-245-6748
Strickland, Helen, *Librn,* Cumberland County Public Library (Stedman Branch), Stedman NC. 919-323-1857
Strickland, Janice, *Dir,* Heidelberg College, Beeghly Library, Tiffin OH. 419-448-2104
Strickland, June M, *Librn,* Pennsylvania Hospital (Institute of Pennsylvania Hospital Medical Library), Philadelphia PA. 215-829-2765
Strickland, June M, *Librn,* Philadelphia Association for Psychoanalysis, Daniel Silverman Memorial Library, Bala-Cynwyd PA. 215-839-3966, 839-3967
Strickland, Leslie H, *Librn,* Delray Beach Public Library Association, Inc, Delray Beach FL. 305-276-6482

Strickland, Leslie H, *Librn & Ad,* Monroe County Public Library, Key West FL. 305-294-7100
Strickland, Maryll, *Commun Servs,* Larchmont Public Library, Larchmont NY. 914-834-1960
Strickland, Mrs C L, *Librn,* Earl A Rainwater Memorial Library, Childersburg AL. 205-378-7239
Strickland, Nellie, *Dir,* United States Department of the Army (Office of the Adjutant General, Morale Support Directorate, Library Activities Division), Washington DC. 202-325-9700
Strickland, Norma, *Ad & Ref,* Grant County Library, Ulysses KS. 316-356-1433
Strickland, Normalie, *Dir,* Helen Matthes Library, Effingham IL. 217-342-2464
Strickland, Patricia, *Librn,* Marlow Town Library, Marlow NH. 603-876-4479
Strickland, Pauline, *Asst,* Sabine Parish Library (Oak Grove), Converse LA. 318-428-2697
Strickland, Susan M, *Media,* Statesboro Regional Library, Statesboro GA. 912-764-7573
Strickler, Charles O, *Sr Librn,* Baltimore Department of Legislative Reference Library, Baltimore MD. 301-396-4730
Strickler, Kenneth, *Cat,* Parkland College, Learning Resource Center, Champaign IL. 217-351-2241
Strickler, Margaret, *Ch,* Howe Library, Hanover NH. 603-643-4120
Stricklin, David, *Librn for Oral Hist,* Dallas Public Library, Dallas TX. 214-748-9071
Striedel, Lula, *Librn,* Bee County Public Library, Beeville TX. 512-358-5541
Striedieck, Suzanne, *Ser,* Pennsylvania State University, Fred Lewis Pattee Library, University Park PA. 814-865-0401
Striegel, Mary Jane, *Cat & Ref,* Southwest State University Library, Marshall MN. 507-537-7021
Striemer, Pauline, *Bkmobile Coordr,* Sioux Falls Public Library, Sioux Falls SD. 605-339-7081
Strife, Janina, *Asst Librn,* Utica Psychiatric Center (Professional Library), Utica NY. 315-736-3301, Ext 261
Striman, Brian, *Cat,* Creighton University (Klutznick Law Library), Omaha NE. 402-449-2875
String, Alfred C, *Librn,* NASA, Headquarters Library, Washington DC. 202-755-2210
Stringer, Ann, *YA & Br Coordr,* Moline Public Library, Moline IL. 309-762-6883
Stringer, Ann, *Librn,* Moline Public Library (Southeast), Moline IL. 309-797-4141
Stringer, Frances M, *Asst Librn,* Orange Public Library, Orange CT. 203-795-0288
Stringfellow, Noreen I, *Genealogy Coll,* Pueblo Library District, Pueblo CO. 303-544-1940
Stringfellow, Shirley, *Acq,* Craft Memorial Library, Mercer County Service Center, Bluefield WV. 304-325-3943
Striplin, Lanelle, *Ch & YA,* Public Library of Anniston & Calhoun County, Liles Memorial Library, Anniston AL. 205-237-8501, Ext 8503
Stritz, Linda, *Librn,* Van Meter Public Library, Van Meter IA. 515-996-2827
Strock, G M, *Actg Librn,* National Park Service, Southeast Regional Office Library, Atlanta GA. 404-221-4916
Stroede, Mary, *Asst Librn,* University of Wisconsin Center, Baraboo-Sauk County Library, Baraboo WI. 608-356-8351, Ext 49
Stroemgren, C, *Librn,* Qit-Fer Et Titane Inc, La Bibliotheque, Sorel PQ. 514-742-6671
Stroetker, Velma Jones, *Librn,* Washington Public Library, Washington MO. 314-239-4724
Strogi, Jessica, *Librn,* Camden-Clark Memorial Hospital Library (Medical Library), Parkersburg WV. 304-424-2111, 424-2237
Strohecker, Edwin C, *Chmn,* Murray State University, Dept of Library Science, KY. 502-762-2291
Strohecker, Edwin C, *Dean,* Murray State University, Harry Lee Waterfield Library, Murray KY. 502-762-2291
Strohl, LeRoy S, *Dir,* Emory & Henry College, Frederick T Kelly Library, Emory VA. 703-944-3121, Ext 56
Strohl, Woody, *Media,* Ohio State University-Mansfield Campus, Louis Bromfield Learning Resources Center, Mansfield OH. 419-755-4321
Strohm, Paul M, *Librn,* Brazoria County Library (Central Headquarters), Angleton TX. 713-849-5711, Ext 451

Strohofer, Jean A, *Librn,* Cravath, Swaine & Moore, Law Library, New York NY. 212-422-3000

Strolle, H S, *Mgr,* E I Du Pont De Nemours & Co, Inc (Technical Library), Wilmington DE. 302-774-7232

Strom, Jackie T, *Librn,* Maxwell Public Library, Maxwell IA. 515-387-3355

Strom, Joan, *Librn,* Bow Island Municipal Library, Bow Island AB. 403-545-2828

Stroman, Josh, *Assoc Dir & Acq,* University of Tulsa, McFarlin Library, Tulsa OK. 918-592-6000, Ext 351

Stromborn, Peggy, *ILL,* Ocean County Library, Toms River NJ. 201-349-6200

Stromei, Susan, *Asst Librn,* Colonial Williamsburg (Research Center Library), Williamsburg VA. 804-229-1000, Ext 2275

Stromer, Richard S, *Ref,* Peabody Institute Library, Peabody MA. 617-531-0100

Stromme, Gary L, *Librn & On-Line Servs,* Pacific Gas & Electric Co (Law Library), San Francisco CA. 415-781-4211

Strommen, Lois, *Librn,* Climax Public Library, Climax MN. 218-857-2455

Stromp, Agnes, *Librn,* Spalding Public Library, Spalding NE. 308-497-2578

Strong, Brenda, *Cat,* Duncan Public Library, Duncan OK. 405-255-0636

Strong, Donald R, *Dir,* West Liberty State College, Paul N Elbin Library, West Liberty WV. 304-336-8035

Strong, Gary E, *Deputy State Librn,* Washington State Library, Olympia WA. 206-753-5592

Strong, Jean E, *Dir,* Hardy Associates Ltd Library, Edmonton AB. 403-436-2152, Ext 228

Strong, Jean M, *Librn,* Star Gazette Library, Elmira NY. 607-734-5151, Ext 272

Strong, Judith, *Tech Serv & Cat,* Great Falls Public Library, Pathfinder Federation of Libraries Headquarters, Great Falls MT. 406-453-0349

Strong, Loretta, *Librn,* Mackinaw Area Public Library (Pellston Public Library), Pellston MI. 616-436-5451

Strong, M A, *Librn,* Saint Michael Medical Center, Aquinas Medical Library, Newark NJ. 201-623-8200, Ext 350

Strong, Moira O, *Librn,* New Jersey State Department of Law & Public Safety, Attorney General's Library, Trenton NJ. 609-292-4958

Strong, Mrs P J, *Librn,* Sun Oil Co Ltd, Calgary Region Library, Calgary AB. 403-269-8128

Strong, Robert, *Asst Dir,* Wayland Baptist College, Van Howeling Memorial Library, Plainview TX. 806-296-5521, Ext 29

Strong, Susan S, *AV & Spec Coll,* Alfred University (Scholes Library of Ceramics), Alfred NY. 607-871-2492

Strong, Susan S, *Ceramic Art Design,* Alfred University (Scholes Library of Ceramics), Alfred NY. 607-871-2492

Strong, Tressa, *Librn,* Timmins Public Library (Schumacher Memorial), Schumacher ON. 705-264-3545

Strother, Garland, *Asst Librn,* Saint Charles Parish Library, Luling LA. 504-785-8471

Strother, Nina, *Librn,* Franklin County Library (Franklinton Public), Franklinton NC. 919-496-4942

Strother, Phoebe, *Ch,* Killgore Memorial Library, Moore County Library, Dumas TX. 806-935-4941

Strother, Seldon D, *Dept Head,* Ohio University, Educational Media Program, OH. 614-594-5404

Strothers, Oscar E, *Chief Librn,* United States Department of Energy (Law Library), Washington DC. 202-666-8922

Strothmann, Willa, *Dir,* Carterville Public Library, Carterville IL. 618-985-3298

Stroud, Janet, *Asst Prof,* Purdue University, Dept of Education, Library Media & Instructional Development, IN. 317-749-2902

Stroud, Robert F, *Chief, Learning Resources Div,* National Naval Dental Center, William L Darnall Library, Bethesda MD. 301-652-6318

Stroud, Ronald D, *Assoc Librn,* Gonzaga University (Law Library), Spokane WA. 509-328-4220, Ext 3781

Stroup, Betty Anne, *Dir,* Mount Lebanon Public Library, Pittsburgh PA. 412-531-1912

Stroup, Elizabeth F, *Dir, Gen Ref,* Library of Congress, Washington DC. 202-287-5000

Stroup, M Jane, *Librn,* Nantucket Maria Mitchell Association, Maria Mitchell Science Library, Nantucket MA. 617-228-9198

Stroup, Vera Kay, *Secy,* Oregon State Department of Revenue, Dept of Revenue Tax Library, Salem OR. 503-378-3727

Stroupe, Elizabeth B, *Tech Serv,* Tri-County Regional Library, Rome GA. 404-291-9360

Strowd, Elvin, *Pub Servs,* Duke University, William R Perkins Library, Durham NC. 684-2034

Stroyan, Susan E, *Instr,* Illinois State University, Department of Information Sciences, IL. 309-438-3671

Strub, Jeane E, *Librn & On-Line Servs,* Lovelace Medical Center, Lassetter Foster Memorial Library, Albuquerque NM. 505-842-7158

Strubbe, Patricia A, *Ch,* Herrick Memorial Library, Wellington Public Library, Wellington OH. 216-647-2120

Struble, Jewell, *Librn,* American Synthetic Rubber Corp, Research Library, Louisville KY. 502-448-2761

Struble, Sister Hildegarde, *Dir,* Saint Mary of the Plains College, Michael Hornung Library, Dodge City KS. 316-225-4171, Ext 68

Struble, Sister M Hildegarde, *Librn,* Saint Mary of the Plains College, Library Science Program, KS. 316-225-4171, Ext 68

Struck, Christine, *Librn,* Dexter Public Library, Dexter IA. 515-789-4490

Struckhoff, Sonia, *Librn,* Saint Charles City County Library (South County), Augusta MO. 314-228-4855

Struckmeyer, Mary, *ILL,* Wisconsin Department of Public Instruction (Reference & Loan Library), Madison WI. 608-266-1053

Strugats, Selma, *Librn,* KLD Associates, Inc Library, Huntington Station NY. 516-549-9803

Strum, Fred, *Ref,* Lindenhurst Memorial Library, Lindenhurst NY. 516-888-7575

Strunk, Mrs Ray, *Librn,* Cheatham County Public Library, Ashland City TN. 615-792-4828

Strunk, Robert K, *Librn,* Jane I & Annetta M Herr Memorial Library, Mifflinburg PA. 717-966-0831

Strunk, Sister Dolores, *Assoc Prof,* Kansas Newman College, Library Science Program, KS. 316-942-4291

Strunk, Sister Mary Dolores, *Cat,* Friends University, Edmund Stanley Library, Wichita KS. 316-263-9131, Ext 220

Strunk, Sister Mary Dolores, *Cat,* Kansas Newman College, Ryan Library, Wichita KS. 316-942-4291, Ext 40

Struthers, Donna, *Cat,* University of Arkansas, Pine Bluff, Watson Memorial Library, Pine Bluff AR. 501-541-6825

Struthers, Helen, *AV,* Orlando Public Library, Orlando FL. 305-425-4694

Stryck, B Camille, *Librn,* Standard Oil Co (Indiana), Research Information Center, Naperville IL. 312-420-5545

Stryker, Maxine G, *Reader Serv,* Onondaga Community College, Sidney B Coulter Library, Syracuse NY. 315-469-7741, Ext 5335-5338

Stuart, Donna, *Media,* Public Library of Steubenville & Jefferson County, Steubenville OH. 614-282-9782

Stuart, Edna S, *Librn,* Choctawhatchee Regional Library (Union Springs Public), Union Springs AL. 205-738-2760

Stuart, Frances, *Dir,* Midlands Technical College (Airport Campus), Columbia SC. 803-782-5471, Ext 265

Stuart, Frances C, *Dir,* Midlands Technical College, Beltline Campus Library, Columbia SC. 803-782-5471, Ext 265

Stuart, Jane, *Tech Serv,* Glasgow City County Library, Glasgow MT. 406-228-2731

Stuart, Joyce, *Acq,* Assemblies of God Graduate School Library, Cordas C Burnett Library, Springfield MO. 417-862-2781, Ext 5505

Stuart, June, *Dir & Acq,* McHenry Public Library, McHenry IL. 815-385-0036

Stuart, Kathleen, *Asst Dir,* Will Rogers Library, Claremore OK. 918-341-1564

Stuart, Kim, *Tech Serv,* Thomas Branigan Memorial Library, Las Cruces Public Library, Las Cruces NM. 505-526-0347

Stuart, Louise, *Dir,* Citizens Library, Washington PA. 412-222-2400

Stuart, Sandra, *Librn,* Houston Public Library (Pleasantville), Houston TX. 713-676-0693

Stuart, Virginia, *Librn,* Herington Public Library, Herington KS. 913-258-2011

Stuart-Stubbs, Basil, *Librn,* University of British Columbia Library, Vancouver BC. 604-228-3871

Stubblefield, Carolyn, *Cat & On-Line Servs,* McNeese State University, Lether E Frazar Memorial Library, Lake Charles LA. 318-477-2520, Ext 271

Stubbs, Kendon, *Assoc Dir,* University of Virginia, Alderman Library, Charlottesville VA. 804-924-3026

Stubbs, Mary, *Actg Dir,* Westmoreland County Community College Library, Youngwood PA. 412-925-4101

Stuchlik, Pauline R, *Librn,* Milton Public Library, Milton DE. 302-684-8284

Stuck, Debbie, *AV,* Virginia Intermont College, J F Hicks Memorial Library, Bristol VA. 703-669-6101, Ext 26

Stuckert, Jewell, *Ref,* Katonah Village Library, Katonah NY. 914-232-3508

Stuckey, Kenneth A, *Librn,* Perkins School for the Blind (Samuel P Hayes Research Library), Watertown MA. 617-924-3434, Ext 240

Stucki, Curtis W, *Cat,* University of Washington Libraries, Seattle WA. 206-543-1760

Stucki, Loretta, *Coordr,* PHILSOM Network, (Periodical Holdings in Libraries of Schools of Medicine), MO. 314-454-3711

Stuckman, Susan, *Dir,* Bucyrus Public Library, Bucyrus OH. 419-562-7327

Stucky, Martha, *Librn,* Bethel College Library, North Newton KS. 316-283-2500, Ext 377

Stucky, Mrs Henry, *Dir,* Freeman Public Library, Freeman SD. 605-925-7127

Stucky, Zenas, *Acq,* Oscar Rose Junior College, Learning Resources Center, Midwest City OK. 405-733-7323, 733-7322

Studer, Linnea, *Ch,* Delaware County District Library, Delaware OH. 614-362-3861

Studer, Paul A, *Assoc Prof,* State University of New York, College of Arts & Science, School of Library & Information Science, NY. 716-245-5322

Studer, William J, *Dir,* Ohio State University Libraries (William Oxley Thompson Memorial Library), Columbus OH. 614-422-6151

Studt, Shirlee, *Humanities,* Michigan State University Library, East Lansing MI. 517-355-2344

Studt, Shirlee A, *Librn,* Michigan State University Library (Art & Maps), East Lansing MI. 517-355-2344

Studwell, William, *Cat,* Northern Illinois University, Founders Memorial Library, De Kalb IL. 815-753-1094

Stueart, Robert D, *Dean,* Simmons College, Graduate School of Library & Information Science, MA. 617-738-2225

Stuebing, Teresa, *Librn,* Marie Fleche Memorial Library, Berlin NJ. 609-767-2448

Stugart, Betty, *Librn,* Muncy Public Library, Muncy PA. 717-546-5014

Stuhl, Anna N, *Asst Dir,* Monmouth County Library, Freehold NJ. 201-431-7220

Stuhldreher, Janet, *Circ,* Greenville Public Library, Greenville MI. 616-754-6359

Stuhlreyer, Margaret, *Librn,* Public Library of Cincinnati & Hamilton County (Deer Park), Cincinnati OH. 513-984-8324

Stukenberg, Sandra, *Librn,* Forreston Public Library, Forreston IL. 815-938-2624

Stukes, Patricia, *Asst Librn,* Sumter Technical College Library, Sumter SC. 803-773-3971

Stull, Judith E, *Librn,* Ocean Shores Public Library, Ocean Shores WA. 206-289-3919

Stull, Leona, *Librn,* Hemingford Public Library, Hemingford NE. 308-487-3454

Stuller, Lola, *Instr,* Alverno College, Dept of Library Science, WI. 414-671-5400, Ext 213

Stultz, Darlene, *Circ,* Minot Public Library, Minot ND. 701-852-1045

Stultz, George B, *Libr Supvr,* EG&G Idaho, Inc, INEL Technical Library, Idaho Falls ID. 208-526-1185

Stultz, Sue Ellen, *Dir,* Jeffersonville Township Public Library, Jeffersonville IN. 812-282-7765

Stumberg, Mary Sue, *Librn,* Patton State Hospital, Staff Library, Patton CA. 714-862-8121, Ext 484

STUMP

Stump, Bonnie, *Acq,* Lockheed Corporation (Lockheed-California Company Central Library), Burbank CA. 213-847-5646

Stump, Michael, *Dir,* First Baptist Church of Van Nuys Library, Van Nuys CA. 213-787-4450, Ext 205

Stumpf, Dorothy, *Circ,* State Library of Pennsylvania, Harrisburg PA. 717-787-2646

Stunard, E Arthur, *Program Dir,* National College of Education, Graduate Program in Library Science & Instructional Media, IL. 312-256-5150, Ext 278

Stunard, E Arthur, *Dir,* National College of Education, Learning Resources Center, Evanston IL. 312-256-5150, Ext 273

Stunkel, Pamela, *Acting Archivist,* Indiana State University, Evansville Library, Evansville IN. 812-464-1824

Stupar, Kathleen, *Libr Clerk,* United States Steel Corporation (Law Library), Pittsburgh PA. 412-433-1121

Sturahan, H, *Librn,* Northwest Baptist Theological College & Seminary Library, Vancouver BC. 604-433-2475

Sturcken, Frank, *Media,* Southwest State University Library, Marshall MN. 507-537-7021

Sturdevant, Mabel, *Dir,* Union City Public Library, Union City PA. 814-438-3209

Sturdivant, Nan, *Ch,* Tulsa City-County Library, Tulsa OK. 918-581-5221

Sturdy, Dorothy, *Librn,* Central Arkansas Library System (Sherwood Branch), Sherwood AR. 501-835-7756

Sturgeon, Susan, *Tech Serv,* Lesley College Library, Cambridge MA. 617-868-9600, Ext 170, 171

Sturges, Mrs W E, *Librn,* Christ Lutheran Church Library, Bethesda MD. 301-652-5160

Sturgis, Cynthia, *Ch,* Ledding Library of Milwaukie, Milwaukie Public Library, Milwaukie OR. 503-659-3911

Sturko, Trudy, *Librn,* Calmer Library, Calmer AB. 403-985-3472

Sturm, Sally D, *Actg Librn,* Mars Area Public Library, Mars PA. 412-625-9048

Sturm, W, *Local Hist,* Oakland Public Library, Oakland CA. 415-273-3281

Sturrock, Catherine, *Acq & Per,* West Valley College, Learning Resource Center, Saratoga CA. 408-867-2200, Ext 284

Sturtevant, John G, *Librn,* West Hartford Public Library (Bishop's Corner), West Hartford CT. 203-236-5446

Sturts, Keith, *Dir,* North Idaho College Library, Coeur d'Alene ID. 208-667-7422, Ext 220

Sturtz, Arlene, *Dir,* Vinton Public Library, Vinton IA. 319-472-4208

Sturtz, Richard S, *Librn,* Wadhams Hall Seminary-College Library, Ogdensburg NY. 315-393-4231, Ext 20

Stutts, Corinne, *Tech Serv,* New Hampshire Technical Institute, Farnum Library, Concord NH. 603-271-2584

Stutz, Mary, *Librn,* Brockway Glass Company, Inc, Engineering & Research Center Library, Brockway PA. 814-261-5442

Stutz, Pearl H, *Dir,* Irondequoit Public Library, West Branch, Rochester NY. 716-266-0514

Stutzman, Jeanette, *Librn,* Hanover Township Library, Hanover IL. 815-591-3517

Stuve, William E, *Doc,* California State University, Chico Library, Chico CA. 916-895-6212

Stuyvenberg, Nori, *ILL,* Cypress College Library, Cypress CA. 714-826-2220, Ext 124, 125

Styer, Marion, *ILL,* Montgomery County-Norristown Public Library, Norristown PA. 215-277-3355

Stypula, Carolyn, *Ch,* Cambria County Library System, Johnstown PA. 814-536-5131

Su, S T, *Cat,* University of Florida Libraries (Agriculture), Gainesville FL. 904-392-1934

Suarez, Celia C, *Dir,* Miami Dade Community College (North Campus Library), Miami FL. 305-685-4436

Suarez, Diana W, *Curator,* Hunter Museum of Art Reference Library, Chattanooga TN. 615-267-0968

Suarez, John L, *Librn,* Conboy, Hewitt, O'Brien & Boardman, Law Library, New York NY. 212-344-3131

Suayne, Elizabeth, *ILL, Ref, On-Line Servs & Bibliog Instr,* Boston University Libraries (School of Theology Library), Boston MA. 617-353-3034

Subber, Barbara, *ILL,* Bethlehem Public Library, Bethlehem PA. 215-867-3761

Suber, Doris, *Librn,* Mid-Mississippi Regional Library System (Winston County), Louisville MS. 601-773-3212

Suber, E M, *Librn,* Hay Memorial Library, Sackets Harbor NY. 315-646-2228

Subin, Nancy Ellen, *Ch,* Waldwick Public Library, Waldwick NJ. 201-652-5104

Sublett, Dorothy, *Librn,* Bureau of Land Management Library, Grand Junction CO. 303-243-6552

Sublette, Doris, *Librn,* University of Illinois Library at Urbana-Champaign (Natural History Survey-State), Urbana IL. 217-333-6892

Subramanyam, Krishnappa, *Assoc Prof,* Drexel University, School of Library & Information Science, PA. 215-895-2474

Substalae, Dana, *Asst Librn,* Catalytic Inc, Engineering Library, Philadelphia PA. 215-864-8559

Suckow, Stephen W, *Dir,* Bartholomew County Library, Cleo Rogers Memorial Library, Columbus IN. 812-379-1255

Sucoe, Virginia, *ILL,* Great River Library System, Quincy IL. 217-223-2560

Sudall, Arthur D, *Dir,* Rahway Free Public Library, Rahway NJ. 201-388-0761

Sudano, Barbara, *Curriculum Specialist,* Florida International University, North Miami Campus Library, North Miami FL. 305-940-5730

Sudar, D D, *Dir,* Lake Erie Regional Library System, London ON. 519-453-9100

Suddeth, Betty, *Circ,* Fairhope Public Library, Fairhope AL. 205-928-7483

Suddeth, Paula F, *Dir,* Elbert County Library, Elberton GA. 404-283-5375

Suddon, Alan, *Fine Art,* Metropolitan Toronto Library Board, Metropolitan Toronto Library, Toronto ON. 416-928-5150

Sudduth, Jo Ann, *Cat,* Temple Public Library, Temple TX. 817-778-5555

Suderman, Robert C, *Dir,* Bethel College, Learning Resource Center, Saint Paul MN. 612-641-6222

Suderow, Edwin, *Lit,* Chicago Public Library (Literature & Philosophy Div), Chicago IL. 312-269-2880

Sudlow, Roy, *Bus, Finance & Music,* Massapequa Public Library, Massapequa NY. 516-798-4607

Sudol, Georgia, *Coordr,* Terra Tek, Research Library, Salt Lake City UT. 801-582-2220, Ext 167

Suedkamp, Michael, *Librn,* Public Library of Cincinnati & Hamilton County (Valley), Reading OH. 513-821-2795

Suehl, Mrs Harry F, *Librn,* Winside Public Library, Winside NE. 402-286-4285

Suelflow, August R, *Dir,* Lutheran Church-Missouri Synod, Concordia Historical Institute Library, Saint Louis MO. 314-721-5934, Ext 320, 321

Suell, Vernisa, *ILL & Media,* Texas College, D R Glass Library, Tyler TX. 214-593-8311, Ext 37

Suellentrop, Helen, *Asst Librn,* Central Kansas Library System, Great Bend KS. 316-792-4865

Suen, Marilyn, *Cat,* Stamford's Public Library, Ferguson Library, Stamford CT. 203-325-4354

Suessmuth, Charles, *Librn,* Tenneco, Inc, Corporation Library, Houston TX. 713-757-2788

Sugarman, Ruth, *Librn,* Tymshare Technical Library, Cupertino CA. 408-446-6229

Sugden, Barbara L, *Librn,* Barrington Public Library District, Barrington IL. 312-382-1300

Sugden, Martin, *Ref,* Jacksonville University, Carl S Swisher Library, Jacksonville FL. 904-744-3950, Ext 266, 267

Sugg, Cynthia, *Media,* J Sargeant Reynolds Community College (Downtown Campus-Learning Resources Center), Richmond VA. 804-786-6249

Suggs, Pamela D, *Bkmobile Coordr,* Claiborne Parish Library, Homer LA. 318-927-3845

Suggs, Sharon A, *Regional Librn,* Public Library of the District of Columbia (Fort Davis (Regional)), Washington DC. 202-727-1349

Suggs, Wayne L, *Dir,* Albany Public Library, Albany OR. 503-967-4304

Sughroe, Patricia, *ILL & Ref,* George Williams College Library, Downers Grove IL. 312-964-3100, Ext 242

Sugimura, Sue S, *Circ,* Hawaii State Library System, Library for the Blind & Physically Handicapped, Honolulu HI. 808-732-7767

Suhfras, Martha, *Admin Asst,* New Berlin Public Library, New Berlin WI. 414-786-2990

Suhler, Sam, *Spec Coll,* Fresno County Free Library, Fresno CA. 209-488-3191

Suhr, Paul A, *Dir,* Pender County Library, Burgaw NC. 919-259-4521

Suits, Ruby, *Acq,* Indianapolis-Marion County Public Library, Indianapolis IN. 317-635-5662

Suitt, S Bonita, *Ref & Circ,* Somerset County College Library, Somerville NJ. 201-526-1200, Ext 224, 304

Sukovich, John, *Dir,* South Carolina Foundation of Independent Colleges, SC. 803-276-5010, Ext 300

Sukovich, John E, *Dir,* Newberry College, Wessels Library, Newberry SC. 803-276-5010, Ext 300

Sukovich, Mary L, *Librn,* Hoyt Lakes Public Library, Hoyt Lakes MN. 218-225-2412

Sukut, Joyce, *Librn,* Central Florida Regional Library (Inverness), Ocala FL. 904-726-2357

Suleiman, Jo-Ann D, *Librn,* United States Air Force (Medical Center Library), Wright-Patterson AFB OH. 513-257-4506

Sulen, Marsha, *Librn,* Mixing Equipment Co, Inc Library, Rochester NY. 716-436-5550

Sulerud, Grace, *Acq,* Augsburg College, George Sverdrup Library, Minneapolis MN. 612-330-1014

Suley, Sherrie, *Asst Librn,* Catskill Public Library, Catskill NY. 518-943-4230

Suljak, Nedjelko D, *Librn,* University of California at Davis (Institute of Government Affairs Library), Davis CA. 916-752-2045

Sulkowski, Elizabeth, *YA,* Roseville Public Library, Roseville MI. 313-777-6012

Sullenger, Lee, *Assoc Dir Pub Serv,* Stephen F Austin State University, Ralph W Steen Library, Nacogdoches TX. 713-569-4109

Sullivan, Ann H, *Ref,* Lasell Junior College, Jessie Shepherd Brennan Library, Auburndale MA. 617-243-2242

Sullivan, Barbara, *Librn,* Brown Public Library, Northfield VT. 802-485-5411

Sullivan, Bettie, *Ch,* Wicomico County Free Library, Salisbury MD. 301-749-5171

Sullivan, Bev, *Librn Blind,* Hutchinson Public Library, Hutchinson KS. 316-663-5441

Sullivan, Beverly, *Ref,* New York Public Library (The Branch Libraries), New York NY. 212-790-6262

Sullivan, Beverly, *Librn,* South Central Kansas Library System (Subregional Talking Book Library), Hutchinson KS. 316-663-5441, Ext 6

Sullivan, Bonnie, *Asst Librn,* Nelson Municipal Library, Nelson BC. 604-352-6333

Sullivan, Calista S, *Tech Serv, On-Line Servs & Cat,* Carlsbad City Library, Carlsbad CA. 714-438-5614

Sullivan, Callie M, *Librn,* University of Florida, Agricultural Research & Education Center, Institute of Food & Agricultural Sciences Library, Homestead FL. 305-247-4624

Sullivan, Catherine, *Librn,* Tucson Public Library (Ajo Branch), Ajo AZ. 602-387-6075

Sullivan, Dan, *Cat,* University of Southern Colorado Library, Pueblo CO. 303-549-2361

Sullivan, Dorothy, *Asst Librn,* Saint Joseph Health Science Library, Denver CO. 303-837-7188

Sullivan, Elaine, *Librn,* Douglas Hospital, Medical Library, Montreal PQ. 514-761-6131

Sullivan, Eleanor, *Ref,* Burlington Public Library, Burlington ON. 416-639-3611

Sullivan, Ella, *Librn,* Brooklyn Public Library (Mill Basin), Brooklyn NY. 212-763-8700

Sullivan, Ellen, *Librn,* Boonville-Warrick County Public Library, Boonville IN. 812-897-1500

Sullivan, Ellen, *Librn,* Pike-Amite-Walthall Library System (Walthall Public), Tylertown MS. 601-876-4348

Sullivan, Eugene V, *Acq,* University of South Alabama (University Library), Mobile AL. 205-460-7021

Sullivan, Helen, *Librn,* Greeley Public Library, Greeley NE. 308-428-2545

Sullivan, Helen A, *In Charge,* Spokane Public Library (Mobile Services Headquarters & Heath Branch), Spokane WA. 509-487-1241

Sullivan, James, *Dir,* Northern Indiana Historical Museum Library, South Bend IN. 219-284-9664

Sullivan, James E, *Dir,* Barre Town Library, Woods Memorial, Barre MA. 617-355-2533

Sullivan, Jan, *Asst Librn,* Capital Times Library, Madison WI. 608-252-6412

Sullivan, Jane F, *Librn,* United States Navy (Naval Station Library), Norfolk VA. 804-444-2888

Sullivan, Jeanette, *Librn,* Southwest State University Library (Community Development Information Center), Marshall MN. 507-537-7337

Sullivan, Joan, *Mgr,* Hattiesburg Public Library System (Petal), Petal MS. 601-584-7610

Sullivan, John, *Asst Librn,* Daly City Public Library, Daly City CA. 415-992-4500, Ext 220

Sullivan, Kathryn, *Per,* Winona State University, Maxwell Library, Winona MN. 507-457-2040

Sullivan, Larry E, *Librn,* Maryland Historical Society Library, Baltimore MD. 301-685-3750

Sullivan, Marguerite, *Librn,* Sacramento Public Library (Rancho Cordova Community), Sacramento CA. 916-362-0641

Sullivan, Marie M, *Librn,* Snohomish County Law Library, Everett WA. 206-259-5326

Sullivan, Marilyn B, *Asst Librn,* The Medical College of Wisconsin, Inc, Todd Wehr Library, Milwaukee WI. 414-257-8323

Sullivan, Marina, *Ch,* Lynbrook Public Library, Lynbrook NY. 516-599-8630

Sullivan, Marion L, *Librn,* Richardson Memorial Library, Sugar Hill NH. 603-823-8126

Sullivan, Marjorie E, *Chief Librn,* Veterans Administration, Hospital Library, Northampton MA. 413-584-4040

Sullivan, Martha, *Librn,* Connecticut State Library (New Haven Branch), New Haven CT. 203-566-4301

Sullivan, Mary L, *Librn,* Fall River Law Library, Fall River MA. 617-676-8541

Sullivan, Maureen P, *Asst Prof,* Duquesne University, School of Education, Library Science Program, PA. 412-434-6100

Sullivan, Michael, *Librn,* Stanford University Libraries (Falconer Biology), Stanford CA. 415-497-1528

Sullivan, Mrs Quaidie, *Librn,* Allan Shivers Library, Woodville TX. 713-283-3709

Sullivan, Nancy, *Librn,* Warner-Eddison Associates, Inc Library, Cambridge MA. 617-661-8124

Sullivan, Patricia, *Tech Serv, Acq & Cat,* Anaheim Public Library, Anaheim CA. 714-533-5221

Sullivan, Patricia E, *Ser,* California State University, Chico Library, Chico CA. 916-895-6212

Sullivan, Patrick J, *Spec Coll,* International University Library, Kansas City MO. 816-931-6374

Sullivan, Patsy, *Librn,* Texas Alkyls, Inc, Technical Center Library, Deer Park TX. 713-479-8411

Sullivan, Peggy A, *Asst Commissioner for Extension Servs,* Chicago Public Library, Chicago IL. 312-269-2900

Sullivan, Peter, *Assoc Dir,* Great Bend Public Library, Great Bend KS. 316-792-2409

Sullivan, Rita, *YA,* Taunton Public Library, Subregional Headquarters for Eastern Massachusetts Regional Library System, Taunton MA. 617-823-3570

Sullivan, Robert C, *Chief,* Library of Congress (Order Division), Washington DC. 202-287-5000

Sullivan, Roll A, *Dir,* Chesapeake College Library, Learning Resources Center, Wye Mills MD. 301-758-1537, 822-5400, Ext 56, 57

Sullivan, Rubye, *Per & Doc,* Jackson State University, Henry Thomas Sampson Library, Jackson MS. 601-968-2123

Sullivan, Ruth M, *Librn,* New England Deaconess Hospital (Gilbert Horrax Memorial Library), Boston MA. 617-734-7000

Sullivan, Sarabeth, *Bus & Tech,* Dallas Public Library, Dallas TX. 214-748-9071

Sullivan, Sean, *Dir,* Waterford Public Library, Waterford NY. 518-237-0891

Sullivan, Sister Marian M, *Dir,* Elizabeth Seton College Library, Yonkers NY. 914-969-4000, Ext 261

Sullivan, Sophia E, *Cat,* Clemson University, Robert Muldrow Cooper Library, Clemson SC. 803-656-3026

Sullivan, Susanne S, *Ch,* Stoneham Public Library, Stoneham MA. 617-438-1324

Sullivan, Suzanne, *ILL & Ref,* Broome Community College, Cecil C Tyrrell Learning Resources Center, Binghamton NY. 607-772-5020

Sullivan, Suzanne, *Curric & Libr Instr,* California State University, John F Kennedy Memorial Library, Los Angeles CA. 213-224-2201

Sullivan, Timothy, *Librn,* Ottawa Library, Ottawa KS. 913-242-3080

Sullivan, Timothy F, *Dir,* Olympic Savings & Loan Association Library, Berwyn IL. 312-795-8700

Sullivan, Vicki, *Librn,* Oklahoma Historical Society (Division of Library Resources), Oklahoma City OK. 405-521-2491

Sult, Velma, *Librn,* Gilman Public Library, Gilman IA. 515-498-2120

Sultan, Phyllis, *Librn,* Asheville-Buncombe Library System (South Asheville), Asheville NC. 704-274-1007

Sultana, Pierre, *Librn,* University of Montreal Libraries (Library Science), Montreal PQ. 514-343-6047

Sulzbach, Deborah, *Cat,* Northeast Louisiana University, Sandel Library, Monroe LA. 318-342-2195

Sulzbach, James, *Media,* Minneapolis Community College Library, Minneapolis MN. 612-341-7089, 341-7059

Sumara, B Michele, *Pub Servs,* Indiana University School of Law, Law Library, Bloomington IN. 812-337-9666

Sumblin, Susan, *Dir,* Enterprise State Junior College, Learning Resource Center, Enterprise AL. 205-347-2623, Ext 281

Sumerlin, Katherine, *ILL,* Ouachita Baptist University, Riley Library, Arkadelphia AR. 501-246-4531, Ext 121

Sumfleth, Henry, *Librn,* New York Public Library (Tottenville), New York NY. 212-984-0945

Sumler, Claudia, *Dir,* Kent County Public Library, Chestertown MD. 301-778-3636

Summer, Jeanette, *Librn,* Henderson County Junior College Library, Athens TX. 214-675-6211

Summer, John, *Circ,* Newberry College, Wessels Library, Newberry SC. 803-276-5010, Ext 300

Summerlin, Lena, *Librn,* Sumiton Public Library, Sumiton AL. 205-648-3261

Summers, Brian, *Librn,* Foundation for Economic Education Library, Irvington NY. 914-591-7230

Summers, Eunice, *Ad,* Peters Township Library, McMurray PA. 412-941-9430

Summers, Eva, *Dir & Ad,* Iroquois Public Library, Brinston Public Library, Iroquois ON. 613-652-2045

Summers, F William, *Dean,* University of South Carolina, College of Librarianship, SC. 803-777-3858

Summers, George V, *Dir,* Loma Linda University Library, Riverside CA. 714-785-2022

Summers, Jean, *Ad,* Hutchinson Public Library, Hutchinson KS. 316-663-5441

Summers, Marilyn, *Ref,* Wake Forest University (Bowman Gray School of Medicine Library), Winston-Salem NC. 919-727-4691

Summers, Nancy, *Spec Coll,* Virginia Commonwealth University (Tompkins-McCaw Library), Richmond VA. 804-786-0629

Summers, Ruth O, *Dir,* Pittsford Community Library, Pittsford NY. 716-586-1251

Summers, Sheryl, *Pub Servs,* Detroit College of Law Library, Detroit MI. 313-965-0150

Summers, Jr, Robert L, *Asst Librn,* Loyola University Library (School of Law), New Orleans LA. 504-865-3426, 865-3427, 865-3136

Summit, Roger K, *Prog Dir,* Lockheed Dialog Information Retrieval Service, CA. 415-858-3810

Sumner, Bettie, *Asst Dir & Media,* Shorter College, Livingston Library, Rome GA. 404-291-2121, Ext 43

Sumner, Cynthia, *Asst Librn,* Putney Public Library, Putney VT. 802-387-4407

Sumner, Ellen, *Hist,* University of Georgia Libraries, Athens GA. 404-542-2716

Sumner, Katie, *Librn,* Marquette Heights Public Library, Marquette Heights IL. 309-382-3778

Sumner, Linda, *Readers' Advisors,* Louisville Free Public Library (Talking Book Library), Louisville KY. 502-587-1069, 587-1085

Sumner, Mary Ann, *Assoc Librn & On-Line Servs,* Educational Testing Service, Carl Campbell Brigham Library, Princeton NJ. 609-921-9000, Ext 2667

Sumner, Wanda, *Librn,* Coastal Plain Regional Library (Irwin County), Ocilla GA. 912-468-5456

Sump, Gretchem, *Dir,* Concordia Lutheran College, Hirschi Library, Austin TX. 512-452-7661

Sumpf, Seely, *Dir,* Watsonville Public Library, Watsonville CA. 408-722-2408

Sumrell, Marjorie W, *Asst Librn,* United States Marine Corps (Air Station Library), Cherry Point NC. 919-466-3571, 466-3552

Sumter, Beatrice, *Cat,* Benedict College, Benjamin F Payton Learning Resources Ctr, Columbia SC. 803-256-4220

Sun, Aurora, *Librn,* Saint John's Hospital School of Nursing, Jean Dickson Devlin Memorial Library, Springfield MO. 417-885-2104

Sun, Chester Y, *Asst Librn,* Blue Ridge Community College Library, Weyers Cave VA. 703-234-9261, Ext 247

Sun, Cossette T, *Librn,* Alameda County Law Library, Oakland CA. 415-874-5823

Sun, Cossette T, *Dir,* Alameda County Law Library, South County Branch, Hayward CA. 415-881-6380, 783-5044

Sun, Lan C, *Librn, On-Line Servs & Bibliog Instr,* Shell Canada Ltd, Research Centre Library, Oakville ON. 416-827-1141, Ext 339

Sun, Shirley, *Dir,* Chinese Culture Foundation of San Francisco, Chinese Culture Center Library, San Francisco CA. 415-986-1822

Sunaitis, Irma, *Librn,* Lambton County Library (Corunna Branch), Corunna ON. 519-862-1132

Sund, Mary, *Actg Librn,* Virginia Public Library, Virginia MN. 218-741-2260

Sunday, Donald R, *Dir & Acq,* Centre County Library & Historical Museum, Bellefonte PA. 814-355-3131

Sundberg, Burton, *Dir,* Crow River Regional Library, Willmar MN. 612-235-3162

Sundberg, Eloise, *Librn,* Galen State Hospital, Deer Lodge MT. 406-693-2281

Sundberg, Mrs O E, *Librn,* Polk Public Library, Polk NE. 402-765-3381

Sundberg, Phyllis, *Librn,* Bridger Public Library, Bridger MT. 406-662-3598

Sundbye, Delores, *AV,* Saint Paul Public Library, Saint Paul MN. 612-292-6311

Sundeen, Patricia, *Librn,* Black River Falls Public Library (Childrens Room), Black River Falls WI. 715-284-4112

Sunder, Mary Jane, *Dir & Bibliog Instr,* Point Park College Library, Helen-Jean Moore Library, Pittsburgh PA. 412-391-4100, Ext 361

Sunder-Raj, P E, *Librn,* Canada Employment & Immigration Commission Library, Hull PQ. 819-994-2603

Sunderland, Barbara, *Librn,* Watseka Public Library, Watseka IL. 815-432-4544

Sunderland, Isabel K, *Dir,* Porterville College Library, Porterville CA. 209-781-0177, Ext 57

Sunderman, JoAnne, *Asst Dir,* Pioneer Memorial Library, Colby KS. 913-462-3881

Sundermeyer, Ann, *Dir,* Hannibal-LaGrange College, Hannibal MO. 314-221-3675, Ext 24

Sundfort, Linda, *Information Specialist,* Minot Public Library, Minot ND. 701-852-1045

Sundquist, Kenneth E, *Librn,* Ontario Ministry of Agriculture & Food Library, Toronto ON. 416-965-1816

Sundstrand, Jacque, *Ref Coordr,* Metropolitan Cooperative Library System, Pasadena CA. 213-577-4081

Sundstrom, Donna G, *Chief Librn,* Harvey Public Library, Harvey IL. 312-331-0757

Sundstrom, Grace, *Librn,* Operation's Research, Inc Library, Silver Spring MD. 301-588-6180, Ext 270

Sundvold, Glenn, *Dir & Media,* Mount Marty College Library, Yankton SD. 605-668-1555

Sung, Carin, *Chief Librn,* Orange County Public Library (University Park), Irvine CA. 714-552-1602

Suokaite, Christine, *Asst Librn,* Brescia College Library, London ON. 519-432-8353

Suos, Barbara, *Ch,* Burbank Public Library, Burbank CA. 213-847-9744

Supinski, Ellen J, *Acq,* Forbes Library, Northampton MA. 413-584-8399

Supple, Sister Michael Patrick, *Media,* Mount Saint Mary's College, Charles Willard Coe Memorial Library, Los Angeles CA. 213-476-2237, Ext 233

Suput, Ray R, *Dir,* Ball State University, Alexander M Bracken Library, Muncie IN. 317-285-6261

Surace, Cecily J, *Librn,* Los Angeles Times Editorial Library, Los Angeles CA. 213-972-7184

Surber, Gale, *ILL & Pub Serv,* Bethany College, T L Phillips Memorial Library, Bethany WV. 304-829-7000

Surber, Melissa, *Asst Librn,* Midlands Technical College (Airport Campus), Columbia SC. 803-782-5471, Ext 265

Surenkamp, M, *Tech Asst,* Blue Cross of Southern California Library, Woodland Hills CA. 213-703-3160

Surette, JoAnn, *Librn,* Macro Systems, Inc Library, Silver Spring MD. 301-588-5484

Surface, Laura, *Librn,* Tazewell County Public Library, Tazewell VA. 703-988-2541

Suri, Raj, *Br Coordr,* Palliser Regional Library, Moose Jaw SK. 306-693-3669

Surles, Jr, Richard H, *Librn,* University of Oregon Library (Law), Eugene OR. 503-686-3088

Surprenant, Neil, *Cat,* Paul Smiths College of Arts & Sciences, Frank L Cubley Library, Paul Smiths NY. 518-327-6313

Surprenant, Thomas, *Asst Prof,* University of Rhode Island, Graduate Library School, RI. 401-792-2878 or 792-2947

Surrey, Joan, *ILL, Archivist & Pub Servs,* Rockford College, Howard Colman Library, Rockford IL. 815-226-4035, 226-4036, 266-4037

Sus, Maryann, *Ref,* Lake County Public Library, Merrillville IN. 219-769-3541

Suseland, Mary, *Librn,* Cass County Library (Newberg-Porter), Jones MI. 616-445-8651

Susman, Beatrice, *Librn,* First Manhattan Co Research Library, New York NY. 212-949-8130

Susman, Renee, *Cat,* Saint Francis College, McGarry Library, Brooklyn NY. 212-522-2300, Ext 205, 207

Susser, Judy, *Librn,* Brooklyn Public Library (Highlawn), Brooklyn NY. 212-837-1700

Sussman, Jody, *Librn,* Illinois Bureau of Employment Security, Research & Analysis Library, Chicago IL. 312-793-2316

Sussman, Norma, *Cat,* United States Army Medical Center (Post-Patients' Library), Washington DC. 202-576-1314

Sustar, Ethel, *Librn,* Union County Public Library (Indian Trail Branch), Indian Trail NC. 704-821-7475

Sustek, Charlotte, *Librn,* Central Florida Regional Library (Floral City), Ocala FL. 904-726-3671

Sutch, Sonia, *Librn,* Jackson District Library (Hanover Branch), Hanover MI. 517-788-4087

Sutcliffe, Priscilla H, *Spec Coll,* Clemson University, Robert Muldrow Cooper Library, Clemson SC. 803-656-3026

Sutcliffe, Virginia W, *Dir,* First Baptist Church, I C Anderson Library, Waco TX. 817-754-0328

Suter, Cindy, *Asst Librn,* Saint Jude Children's Research Hospital, Medical Library, Memphis TN. 901-522-0388

Suter, Joanna, *Ch,* Rock Island Public Library, Rock Island IL. 309-788-7627

Suter, Jon M, *Tech Serv,* East Central State University, Linscheid Library, Ada OK. 405-332-8000

Suter, Marcia, *Dir,* Northwest Technical College Library, Archbold OH. 419-267-5511, Ext 243

Sutherland, Alison, *Br Coordr,* Pictou Antigonish Regional Library, New Glasgow NS. 902-752-6217

Sutherland, Carol, *Ch,* Vigo County Public Library, Terre Haute IN. 812-232-1113

Sutherland, Dick, *Per,* Foothill College, Hubert H Semans Library, Los Altos Hills CA. 415-948-8590, Ext 390, 391

Sutherland, J Elizabeth, *Acting Head Libr Servs,* Canada Department Fisheries & Oceans, Bedford Institute of Oceanography Library, Dartmouth NS. 902-426-3675

Sutherland, Joan, *Chief Librn,* Alberta Department of Energy & Natural Resources Library, Edmonton AB. 403-427-7425

Sutherland, John, *Maps,* University of Georgia Libraries, Athens GA. 404-542-2716

Sutherland, Karen, *Ch,* La Grange Park Public Library District, La Grange Park IL. 312-352-0100

Sutherland, Margaret, *Librn,* Umatilla County Library (Weston Branch), Weston OR. 503-566-2378

Sutherland, Michael, *Spec Coll,* Occidental College, Mary Norton Clapp Library, Los Angeles CA. 213-259-2640

Sutherland, Mrs K, *Supvr,* Elgin County Public Library (Port Burwell Branch), Port Burwell ON. 519-633-0815

Sutherland, Sandra, *Asst Librn,* Wythe-Grayson Regional Library, Independence VA. 703-773-2761

Sutherland, Terry, *Librn,* Northeastern Regional Library System (Calstock Lake Bend Branch), Calstock ON. 705-567-7043

Sutherland, Thomas A, *Dir,* Paducah Public Library, Paducah KY. 502-442-2510, 443-2664

Sutherland, Tim, *Ref,* Goshen Public Library, Goshen IN. 219-533-9531

Sutherland, Zena, *Assoc Prof,* University of Chicago, Graduate Library School, IL. 312-753-3482

Sutherlin, Susie, *Commun Servs,* Montgomery County Department of Public Libraries, Rockville MD. 301-279-1401

Sutliff, M E, *Librn,* Kimberly-Clark Corp, Research & Engineering Library, Neenah WI. 414-729-5261

Sutor, Gertrude, *Tech Serv,* Thornton Community College, Learning Resources Center, South Holland IL. 312-596-2000, Ext 240

Sutphin, Sue, *Librn,* Mason & Hanger-Silas Mason Co, Inc, Pantex Plant Technical Library, Amarillo TX. 806-335-1581, Ext 2643

Sutrick, Anita, *Asst Librn,* Oklahoma College of Osteopathic Medicine & Surgery, College Library, Tulsa OK. 918-582-1972, Ext 351

Sutter, Carolyn, *Dir,* Long Beach Public Library System, Long Beach CA. 213-436-9225

Sutter, Daniel, *Asst Prof,* Southern Illinois University at Carbondale, Educational Media Program, IL. 618-453-5764

Sutter, Deborah, *Coordr,* Providence Hospital, School of Nursing Media Center, Sandusky OH. 419-625-8450, Ext 291

Sutter, Dorothy, *Ad,* Bryan Public Library, Bryan OH. 419-636-2937

Sutter, Mary, *Librn,* Martin Township Public Library, Colfax IL. 309-723-2541

Sutterfield, Barbara, *Ch,* Marion County Public Library, Fairmont WV. 304-366-4831

Suttle, Juanita, *Librn,* Atlanta Public Library (Collier Heights), Atlanta GA. 404-691-1988

Sutton, Betty, *Asst Dir,* Roxana Public Library, Roxana IL. 618-254-6713

Sutton, Carolyn A, *Librn,* Pitt Community College, Learning Resources Center, Greenville NC. 919-756-3130, Ext 213, 229, 259 & 273

Sutton, Diane, *Librn,* Eddyville Public Library, Eddyville IA. 515-969-4815

Sutton, Doris, *Dir,* Barrett Memorial Library, Williams Bay WI. 414-245-6161

Sutton, Edie, *Learning Resource Ctr,* Maysville Community College Library, Maysville KY. 606-759-7141, Ext 28

Sutton, Evelyn, *Librn,* United Methodist Church, Commission on Archives & History Library, Lake Junaluska NC. 704-456-9433

Sutton, Gary C, *Librn,* United States Air Force (Medical Library), Reese AFB TX. 806-885-4511

Sutton, Gloria W, *Bibliog Instr,* Sampson Technical College Library, Clinton NC. 919-592-8081, Ext 250

Sutton, James E, *Dir,* Morse Institute Library, Natick MA. 617-653-4252

Sutton, Josephine, *Doc,* Fresno County Free Library, Fresno CA. 209-488-3191

Sutton, Judith K, *Assoc Dir,* Public Library of Charlotte & Mecklenburg County, Inc, Charlotte NC. 704-374-2725

Sutton, Mary Lou, *Tech Serv,* Barberton Public Library, Barberton OH. 216-745-1194

Sutton, Nona, *Circ,* Western Texas College, Learning Resource Center, Snyder TX. 915-573-8511, Ext 265

Sutton, Phyllis, *Dir,* Dodge Memorial Library, Rouses Point NY. 518-297-5503

Sutton, Robert, *Dir,* University of Illinois Library at Urbana-Champaign (Illinois State Historical Survey), Urbana IL. 217-333-1777

Sutton, Robert F, *Asst Dir,* Monmouth College, Guggenheim Library, West Long Branch NJ. 201-222-6600, Ext 264

Sutton, Ruth E, *Librn,* Alexander Memorial Library, Cotulla TX. 512-879-2601

Sutton, Suzanne, *Dep Dir & Ad,* Bloomfield Township Public Library, Bloomfield Hills MI. 313-642-5800

Sutton, William, *Br Head,* Lancaster Public Library, Lancaster NY. 716-683-1120

Suttorp, MaryLou, *Fiction,* Grand Rapids Public Library, Grand Rapids MI. 616-456-4400

Suvak, Daniel S, *Dir,* Mideastern Ohio Library Organization, (MOLO), OH. 216-875-4269

Suvak, Nancy Jean, *Librn,* United States Steel Corporation (Commercial Information Center), Pittsburgh PA. 412-433-1121

Suvak, Jr, William A, *Librn,* Mayview State Hospital (Professional Library), Bridgeville PA. 412-221-7500, Ext 496

Suvak, Jr, William A, *Librn,* Pennsylvania Department of Public Welfare, Mayview State Hospital Professional Library, Bridgeville PA. 412-221-7500, Ext 496

Suvarnamani, Nuj, *Tech Asst,* Beatrice Foods Co, Research Center Library, Chicago IL. 312-791-8292

Suwinski, Marie, *Asst Librn,* Elma Public Library, Elma NY. 716-652-2719

Suyematsu, Kiyo, *Music,* Mankato State University, Memorial Library, Mankato MN. 507-389-6201

Suzuki, Dawn, *Librn,* Hawaii State Library System (Lanai Community-School), Lanai HI. 808-565-6996

Suzuki, May, *Coop Servs,* University of Hawaii (University of Hawaii Library), Honolulu HI. 808-948-7205

Suzuki, Yukihisa, *Prof,* University of Hawaii, Graduate School of Library Studies, HI. 808-948-7321

Sved, Alexander, *Cat,* Loyola University of Chicago Libraries (Law School Library), Chicago IL. 312-670-2952

Sved, Dana, *Librn,* Chicago Public Library (Mount Greenwood), Chicago IL. 312-239-2805

Sveda, Clara, *ILL & Acq,* Northland College, Dexter Library, Ashland WI. 715-682-4531, Ext 297

Svee, Elizabeth C, *Dir,* San Bruno Public Library, San Bruno CA. 415-877-8878

Svenningsen, Robert, *Dir,* National Archives & Records Service, Denver Federal Archives & Records Center Library, Lakewood CO. 303-234-3187

Svenonius, Elaine, *Instr,* University of Denver, Graduate School of Librarianship and Information Management, CO. 303-753-2557

Svenson, Alf, *Admin & Planning,* Catholic University of America, John K Mullen of Denver Memorial Library, Washington DC. 202-635-5055

Svenson, Leigh, *Operations Mgr,* Hampshire College, Harold F Johnson Library Center, Amherst MA. 413-549-4600

Svetich, Tony, *Ref,* Blue Mountain Community College Library, Pendleton OR. 503-276-1260, Ext 234

Svinth, Mila, *Br Asst,* Timberland Regional Library (Taholah Branch), Taholah WA. 206-276-8211

Svoboda, Joseph G, *Archives & Spec Coll,* University of Nebraska-Lincoln, University Libraries, Lincoln NE. 402-472-2526

Swackhammer, Margaret, *Commun Servs,* Stratford Library Association, Stratford CT. 203-378-7345

Swadener, Marc, *Instr,* University of Colorado, Educational Technology Program, CO. 303-492-5141 & 492-6715

Swafford, Ethel, *Dir,* McAllen Memorial Library, McAllen TX. 512-682-4531

Swaim, Elizabeth, *Rare Bks & Spec Coll,* Wesleyan University, Olin Memorial Library, Middletown CT. 203-347-9411, Ext 296

Swaim, Mrs Mike, *ILL,* White River Regional Library, Batesville AR. 501-793-7347

Swain, Ann, *ILL, Spec Coll & On-Line Servs,* Radford University, John Preston McConnell Library, Radford VA. 703-731-5471, 5472

Swain, Barbara C, *Librn,* University of Illinois Library at Urbana-Champaign (Home Economics), Urbana IL. 217-333-0748

Swain, Christine, *Chief Librn,* Orange County Public Library (Cypress Branch), Cypress CA. 714-826-0350

Swain, Constance, *Acq,* McDonnell Douglas Corp (Corporate Library), Saint Louis MO. 314-232-8515

Swain, Dorothy, *Librn,* Gary Public Library (Brunswick), Gary IN. 219-949-9109

Swain, Marvel J, *Librn,* Chicago Public Library (Lorraine Hansberry), Chicago IL. 312-373-2221
Swain, R H, *Humanities,* Cleveland State University Libraries, Cleveland OH. 216-687-2486
Swain, Richard H, *Bibliog Instr,* Cleveland State University Libraries, Cleveland OH. 216-687-2486
Swainbank, Mary, *Actg Dir,* University of Wisconsin Center, Washington County Library, West Bend WI. 414-338-8753, Ext 60
Swaine, Cynthia, *Bibliog Instr,* Old Dominion University Library, Norfolk VA. 804-440-4141
Swaine, Lynne, *Librn,* Rockingham County Public Library (Eden Branch), Eden NC. 919-623-3168
Swalboski, Marlys, *Librn,* Mountain Lake Public Library, Mountain Lake MN. 507-427-2506
Swalboski, Martin L, *Head Librn,* Litchfield Public Library, Litchfield MN. 612-693-2483, 693-2484
Swan, Carla, *Ch,* Athol Public Library, Athol MA. 617-249-9515
Swan, Deloris J, *Supvr,* United States Navy (Naval Air Engineering Center, Technical Library), Lakehurst NJ. 201-323-2893
Swan, Frank F, *Asst Dir & Br Coordr,* Jackson County Library System, Medford OR. 503-776-7281
Swan, James, *Dir,* Central Kansas Library System, Great Bend KS. 316-792-4865
Swan, James A, *Dir,* Great Bend Public Library, Great Bend KS. 316-792-2409
Swan, John, *Ref,* Wabash College, Lilly Library, Crawfordsville IN. 317-362-1400, Ext 215, 216
Swan, Louise G, *Ref,* Marlboro County Library, Bennettsville SC. 803-479-6201
Swan, Martha, *Per,* University of Mississippi Library, University MS. 601-232-7091
Swan, Ruth, *Media,* Oakwood College, Eva B Dykes Library, Huntsville AL. 205-837-1630, Ext 275
Swan, Zona, *Cat,* Los Angeles City College Library, Los Angeles CA. 213-663-9141, Ext 412
Swanbeck, Janet, *Doc,* Boston College Libraries (Bapst (Central Library)), Chestnut Hill MA. 617-969-0100, Ext 3205
Swanigan, Meryl H, *Librn,* Atlantic Richfield Co (Headquarters Library), Los Angeles CA. 213-486-2400
Swanigan, Reita, *ILL,* Cass County Public Library, Harrisonville MO. 816-884-3483
Swank, Chet, *Chief, Mgt Info Systs,* National Agricultural Library, Beltsville MD. 301-344-4248
Swank, Mildred, *Commun Servs,* Jackson District Library, Jackson MI. 517-788-4087
Swank, Ruth, *Circ,* Midlands Technical College, Beltline Campus Library, Columbia SC. 803-782-5471, Ext 265
Swank, Theron, *Prof,* Central Missouri State University, Dept of Library Science and Instructional Technology, MO. 816-429-4835
Swann, Arthur, *Librn,* University of the Pacific (Methodist Archives), Stockton CA. 209-946-2269
Swann, Arthur, *Librn,* University of the Pacific (Science Library), Stockton CA. 209-946-2568
Swann, Arthur, *Librn,* United Methodist Church, J A B Fry Research Library, Stockton CA. 209-946-2269
Swann, Mrs Ben, *Spec Coll,* Chattanooga-Hamilton County Bicentennial Library, Chattanooga TN. 615-757-5320
Swanner, Ronnie C, *Media,* Trinity University Library, San Antonio TX. 512-736-8121
Swanner, Sallieann, *Acq,* University of Texas Health Science Center at San Antonio Library, San Antonio TX. 512-691-6271
Swanson, Ann, *Circ,* Minnesota Valley Regional Library, Mankato MN. 507-387-1856
Swanson, Ann, *Dir,* North Central Regional Library System, Mason City IA. 515-423-6917
Swanson, Barbara, *Librn,* Kern County Library (Baker Street), Bakersfield CA. 805-861-2130
Swanson, Barbara, *Dir,* Southeast Community College-Lincoln Campus, Learning Resource Center, Lincoln NE. 402-471-3333, Ext 249
Swanson, Byron, *Ref,* Butler University, Irwin Library, Indianapolis IN. 317-283-9225
Swanson, Carol J, *Librn,* United States Navy (Engineering Library), Bremerton WA. 206-478-2767

Swanson, Carribelle, *Librn,* Sugar Grove Free Library, Sugar Grove PA. 814-489-7872
Swanson, Clara, *Tech Serv,* Oakland Public Library, Oakland CA. 415-273-3281
Swanson, Constance L, *Ch,* Atlantic City Free Public Library, Atlantic City NJ. 609-345-2269
Swanson, Cordelia, *Health Sci,* Indiana Vocational Technical College, Learning Resource Center, Gary IN. 219-981-1111, Ext 28
Swanson, Cynthia, *Librn,* Contra Costa County Library (Orinda Branch), Orinda CA. 415-254-2184
Swanson, Don R, *Prof,* University of Chicago, Graduate Library School, IL. 312-753-3482
Swanson, Donna, *On-Line Servs,* Kentucky Department of Education Materials Center Library, Frankfort KY. 502-564-5513
Swanson, Dorothy, *Spec Coll,* New York University, Elmer Holmes Bobst Library, New York NY. 212-598-2484
Swanson, Dorothy, *Archivist,* New York University (Tamiment Library & Robert F Wagner Labor Archive), New York NY. 212-598-2484
Swanson, Dorothy A, *Librn,* Town Center Library at Tanasbourne, Portland OR. 503-645-3597
Swanson, Eileen, *Cat,* La Crosse County Library, La Crosse WI. 608-785-9638
Swanson, Ellen W, *In Charge,* Augustana Lutheran Church Library, Denver CO. 303-388-4678
Swanson, Elliott, *AV,* Kitsap Regional Library, Bremerton WA. 206-377-7601
Swanson, Jane, *Young Ad,* Richardson Public Library, Richardson TX. 214-238-8251
Swanson, Jane Cary, *Ref,* Public Library of Pine Bluff & Jefferson County, Pine Bluff AR. 501-534-4802, 534-4818
Swanson, Kenneth G, *Dir,* Indian Trails Public Library District, Wheeling IL. 312-537-4011
Swanson, Madeline, *Asst Dir,* Prairie Trails Public Library District, Burbank IL. 312-430-3688
Swanson, Patricia K, *ILL & Ref,* University of Chicago, Joseph Regenstein Library, Chicago IL. 312-753-2977
Swanson, Paul, *Tech Serv & Cat,* Brockton Public Library System, Brockton MA. 617-587-2515
Swanson, Phoebe A, *Librn,* Quidnick Baptist Church Library, Coventry RI. 401-821-2465
Swanson, Ronald J, *Asst Dean Tech Servs,* University of Nebraska-Lincoln, University Libraries, Lincoln NE. 402-472-2526
Swanson, Rowena, *Instr,* University of Denver, Graduate School of Librarianship and Information Management, CO. 303-753-2557
Swanson, Scott, *Spec Coll,* Northeast Louisiana University, Sandel Library, Monroe LA. 318-342-2195
Swanson, Sheila, *Librn,* Academy of Medicine, William Boyd Library, Toronto ON. 416-964-7088
Swanson, Stanley S, *Bibliog Selection,* Oregon State University, William Jasper Kerr Library, Corvallis OR. 503-754-3411
Swanson, Winifred L, *Ad,* Sonoma County Library, Santa Rosa CA. 707-545-0831
Swanton, James, *Cat,* Albert Einstein College of Medicine, D Samuel Gottesman Library, Bronx NY. 212-430-3108
Swanton, Susan, *Dir,* Gates Public Library, Gates Robert Abbott Memorial Library, Rochester NY. 716-247-6446
Swanton, W, *Librn,* Saskatchewan Department of Tourism & Renewable Resources, Forestry Branch Library, Prince Albert SK. 306-764-6848
Swarm, Mrs C L, *Librn,* Third Baptist Church Library, Saint Louis MO. 314-533-7340, Ext 25
Swarr, Anne, *Ch,* Rockville Public Library, George Maxwell Memorial Library, Vernon CT. 203-875-5892
Swart, Joanna, *Genealogy,* Killeen Public Library, Killeen TX. 817-526-6527
Swartley, Eunice, *YA,* Downey City Library, Downey CA. 213-923-3256
Swartout, Douglas H, *Acq,* Mohawk Valley Community College Library, Utica NY. 315-792-5337
Swartz, Gloria, *YA,* Prince William Public Library, Manassas VA. 703-361-8211
Swartz, Jeanne, *ILL,* North Dakota State School of Science, Mildred Johnson Library, Wahpeton ND. 701-671-2298
Swartz, Lois, *Asst Librn,* Montgomery House Library, McEwensville PA. 717-538-1381

Swartz, Mary Ann, *Dir Libr Serv,* Sheppard & Enoch Pratt Hospital (Lawrence S Kubie Medical Library), Towson MD. 301-823-8200
Swartz, Roderick G, *State Librn,* Washington State Library, Olympia WA. 206-753-5592
Swartz, Sylvia, *Librn,* Malden Public Library (Maplewood), Malden MA. 617-322-0373
Swartzlander, June, *Ch,* Kendallville Public Library, Kendallville IN. 219-347-3554
Swaskiw, Christine, *Librn,* University of Alberta (Weir Memorial Law Library), Edmonton AB. 403-432-5560
Swauncy, Emmer, *Bkkeeper,* State Technical Institute at Memphis, George E Freeman Library, Memphis TN. 901-377-4106
Swe, Kendra K, *Cat,* Louisiana State University (Law Center Library), Baton Rouge LA. 504-388-8802
Swe, Thein, *Bibliographer,* Louisiana Mississippi Microform Network, LA. 504-388-2217
Swe, Thein, *Chief Biblog,* Louisiana State University (Troy II Middleton Library), Baton Rouge LA. 504-388-2217
Sweaney, W, *Librn,* University of Saskatchewan Library (Health Sciences), Saskatoon SK. 306-343-3168
Swearingen, Peggy, *Humanities,* Forsyth County Public Library, Winston-Salem NC. 919-727-2556
Swearingen, Richard, *Cat,* Milwaukee County Federated Library System, Milwaukee WI. 414-278-3210
Swearingen, Wilba, *Ser,* Marquette University Memorial Library, Milwaukee WI. 414-224-7214
Sweat, Anne, *Dir,* Washington Bible College-Capital Bible Seminary, Oyer Memorial Library, Lanham MD. 301-552-1400, Ext 232
Sweat, Edith, *Librn,* Oconee Regional Library (Sparks Memorial), Soperton GA. 912-529-6683
Sweat, Grace, *Bkmobile Coordr,* Southwest Georgia Regional Library, Gilbert H Gragg Library, Bainbridge GA. 912-246-3887, 3894, 3895
Sweat, Mary Lee, *Pub Servs & On-Line Servs,* Loyola University Library, Main Library, New Orleans LA. 504-865-3346
Swedburg, Loren T, *Dir,* Nebraska Christian College Library, Norfolk NE. 402-371-5960
Swedenberg, Anne, *Coll Develop,* Georgetown University (John Vinton Dahlgren Memorial Library), Washington DC. 202-625-7577
Swedish, Alexandra, *Cat,* Loyola University of Chicago Libraries (Medical Center), Maywood IL. 312-531-3192
Swedlund, Iris, *Librn,* Velva School & Public Library, Velva ND. 701-338-2022
Sweely, Edna, *Curator,* Delaware County Historical Society Library, Chester PA. 215-874-6444
Sween, Roger, *Instr,* Saint Cloud State University, Center for Library & Audiovisual Education, MN. 612-255-2022
Sweeney, Carolyn, *Info Mgr,* Digital Equipment Corp, Corporate Library, Maynard MA. 617-493-6231, 493-5821
Sweeney, Grace, *Librn,* Blackhawk Vocational Technical Institute, Tech-Beloit Campus Library, Beloit WI. 608-365-6663
Sweeney, Grace, *Librn,* Blackhawk Vocational Technical Institute, Learning Materials Center, Janesville WI. 608-756-4121
Sweeney, Hester, *Librn,* Burnham Memorial Library, Colchester VT. 802-879-7576
Sweeney, Julia, *Asst Librn,* Pillsbury Free Library, Warner NH. 603-456-2289
Sweeney, Mary, *Librn,* Tampa-Hillsborough County Public Library System (Brandon Public), Brandon FL. 813-689-7074
Sweeney, Richard T, *Dir,* Public Library of Columbus & Franklin County, Columbus OH. 614-864-8050
Sweeney, Suzanne, *Cat,* Beaumont Public Library, Beaumont TX. 713-838-0812
Sweeney, Urban J, *Librn,* General Dynamics Corp, Convair Div, Research Library, San Diego CA. 714-277-8900, Ext 1073
Sweeny, June D, *Librn,* Public Library of the District of Columbia (Georgetown (Regional)), Washington DC. 202-727-1353
Sweeny, Mary K, *Ref,* John Carroll University, Grasselli Library, University Heights OH. 491-4233 & 491-4231
Sweet, Ann, *Asst Librn,* Milan Public Library, Milan MI. 313-439-1240

Sweet, Charlene B, *Librn,* Watertown Township Library, Fostoria MI. 517-795-2127

Sweet, Delilah, *Librn,* Grenola Public Library, Grenola KS. 316-358-3100

Sweet, Donald G, *Tech Serv & Cat,* Colgate Rochester-Bexley Hall-Crozer Theological Seminaries, Ambrose Swasey Library, Rochester NY. 716-271-1320, Ext 24

Sweet, Edith, *Librn,* New York State Department of Law Library, Albany NY. 518-474-3840

Sweet, Herman R, *In Charge,* Harvard University Library (Oakes Ames Orchid Library), Cambridge MA. 617-495-2360

Sweet, Reen, *Asst Dir & ILL,* Bennington Free Library, Bennington VT. 802-442-9051

Sweet, Sister Mary, *Lectr,* Marywood College, Dept of Librarianship, PA. 717-342-6521

Sweetland, James, *Ref,* Tulane University of Louisiana, Howard-Tilton Memorial Library, New Orleans LA. 504-865-5131

Sweigart, Susan, *ILL,* Amos Memorial Public Library, Sidney Public Library, Sidney OH. 513-492-8354

Sweitzer, Helen I, *Asst Librn,* Warren State Hospital (Patients' Library), Warren PA. 814-723-5500, Ext 356

Sweitzer, James, *Astronomer,* Adler Planetarium Library, Chicago IL. 312-322-0304

Sweitzer, Muriel, *Tech Serv,* River Forest Public Library, River Forest IL. 312-366-5205

Sweitzer, Peggy, *Dir,* Foundation Center Library, New York NY. 212-975-1120

Swenson, Alan, *Media,* Lee College, Learning Resources Center, Baytown TX. 713-427-5611, Ext 279, 277

Swenson, Betty, *ILL & Cat,* Franklin Library, Ray Memorial Library, Franklin MA. 617-528-0371

Swenson, Bruce P, *Dir,* Wenatchee Valley College, John A Brown Library Media Center, Wenatchee WA. 509-662-1651

Swenson, Evelyn J, *Chairperson,* Moorhead State University, Media Education Dept, MN. 218-236-2922

Swentosky, Josie, *Librn,* Pittsburgh Regional Planning Association Library, Pittsburgh PA. 412-263-3594

Sweny, Edward J, *Dir,* New England Deposit Library, MA. 617-782-8441

Swerbrick, Betty F, *Librn,* Du Pont Canada Inc, Research Center Library, Kingston ON. 613-544-6400, Ext 504, 578

Swetek, Alice, *Librn,* Ventura County Library Services Agency (Port Hueneme Branch), Port Hueneme CA. 805-486-5460

Swetell, Marilyn, *Librn,* Diamond Shamrock, Process Chemicals Div Library, Morristown NJ. 201-267-1000, Ext 220

Swett, Gladys, *Cat,* New Britain Public Library, New Britain CT. 203-224-3155

Swiddle, Mrs L, *Asst Dir,* Pinawa Public Library, Pinawa MB. 204-753-2496

Swift, Allison, *Dir,* Cerro Coso Community College, Learning Resources Center, Ridgecrest CA. 714-375-5001, Ext 47

Swift, Ardyce, *Librn,* Deschutes County Library (Redmond Public), Redmond OR. 503-548-3141

Swift, Janet M, *Asst Dir,* University of Connecticut, Waterbury Branch, Edward H Kirschbaum Library, Waterbury CT. 203-757-6795, Ext 50

Swift, Jill, *Community Relations,* East Saint Louis Public Library, East Saint Louis IL. 618-874-7280

Swift, Lee, *Asst Librn,* Oliver Wolcott Library, Litchfield Public Library, Litchfield CT. 203-567-8030

Swift, Leonard W, *Dir,* Charles M White Memorial Public Library, Stevens Point WI. 715-346-2841

Swift, Marion T, *Librn,* West Dennis Free Public Library, West Dennis MA. 617-398-2050

Swift, Virginia, *Librn,* New York Public Library (Chatham Square), New York NY. 212-964-6598

Swiger, LeMoyne, *Per,* Lee College Library, Cleveland TN. 615-472-2111, Ext 329

Swilley, Alice, *Librn,* Orlando Public Library (Washington Shores Station), Orlando FL. 305-293-8562

Swilley, Diane, *Librn,* South Georgia Regional Library (Statenville Branch), Statenville GA. 912-559-5734

Swinarski, Mary L, *Librn,* Greeley Public Library, Greeley NE. 308-428-2545

Swinchoski, Elisabeth, *Librn,* Stowe Free Library, Stowe VT. 802-253-4808

Swinehart, David, *Tech Serv,* Gary Public Library, Gary IN. 219-886-2484

Swinehart, Katharine Jean, *Ref,* Barberton Public Library, Barberton OH. 216-745-1194

Swiney, Ethel, *Librn,* Farmer City Public Library, Farmer City IL. 309-928-9532

Swingle, Ruth, *In Charge,* Hastings Regional Center (Patients), Hastings NE. 402-463-2471

Swinney, Sara Carter, *Dir,* South Mississippi Regional Library, Columbia MS. 601-736-5516

Swinson, Ruth, *Ser,* Armstrong State College, Lane Memorial Library, Savannah GA. 912-927-5332

Swinson, Ruth, *Instr,* Armstrong State College, Library Media, GA. 912-927-5332

Swinson, William R, *Dir,* Walter Cecil Rawls Regional Library System, Courtland VA. 804-653-2821

Swint, Gary, *Media,* Augusta Regional Library, Augusta-Richmond County Public Library, Augusta GA. 404-724-1871

Swint, Gary, *Librn,* Augusta Regional Library (Talking Book Center), Augusta GA. 404-724-1871

Swint, Katherine, *Tech Serv,* Georgia Department of Education (Div of Public Library Services), Atlanta GA. 404-656-2461

Swinton, Cordelia, *Lending Servs,* Pennsylvania State University, Fred Lewis Pattee Library, University Park PA. 814-865-0401

Swinton, Jeanne, *Librn,* Planned Parenthood of New York City, Abraham Stone Memorial Library, Margaret Sanger, New York NY. 212-677-6474, Ext 3158, 3159

Swinton, Sylvia, *Media,* Morris College, Pinson Memorial Library, Sumter SC. 803-775-9371, Ext 216

Swisher, Christopher, *Media,* Lutheran Theological Seminary, Krauth Memorial Library, Philadelphia PA. 215-248-4616

Swisher, Violet D, *Dir,* United States Office of Personnel Management Library, Washington DC. 202-632-4432

Swist, Ann C, *On-Line Servs,* Bristol-Myers Products, Technical Information Center, Hillside NJ. 201-926-6691

Switser, Edith, *Librn,* Dalton Public Library, Dalton NH. 603-837-9821

Switzer, Wilma M, *Librn,* Brenizer Public Library, Merna NE. 308-643-2268

Swofford, Gloria, *Reader Serv & Ref,* Saint Louis County Library, Saint Louis MO. 314-994-3300

Swope, C Hermas, *Libr Adminr,* American Optical Corp, Warner-Lambert Company Research Center Library, Southbridge MA. 617-765-9711, Ext 2669

Swope, Cynthia, *Cat,* Harford Community College Learning Resources Center, Bel Air MD. 301-838-1000, Ext 268

Swope, Donald, *Archivist,* Eastern Illinois University, Booth Library, Charleston IL. 217-581-2210

Sydnor, Mary Anne, *Librn, ILL & Bibliog Instr,* Tidewater Community College, Frederick Campus Library, Portsmouth VA. 804-484-2121, Ext 226

Sydnor, William, *Learning Ctr,* Marymount Palos Verdes College Library, Rancho Palos Verdes CA. 213-377-5501, Ext 29

Sydro, Laura, *Librn,* Mooney Chemicals Inc Library, Cleveland OH. 216-781-8383

Syke, Mae, *Nursing Coll Librn,* Durham College of Applied Arts & Technology Library, Oshawa ON. 416-576-0210, Ext 214

Sykes, Barbara, *Bus,* Fordham University Library at Lincoln Center, New York NY. 212-841-5130, 841-5133

Sykes, Carol S, *Dir,* Laconia Public Library, Laconia NH. 603-524-4775

Sykes, Jean, *Librn,* Thelma Dingus Bryant Library, Wallace NC. 919-285-3796

Sykes, Laurence, *Tech Serv,* University of Arkansas, Pine Bluff, Watson Memorial Library, Pine Bluff AR. 501-541-6825

Sykes, Maggie Faye, *Librn,* Bladen County Public Library (Bridger Memorial), Bladenboro NC. 919-863-4586

Sykes, Margaret, *Dir,* Paris-Henry County Library, Paris TN. 901-642-1702

Sykes, Sue, *Librn,* Gila Bend Public Library, Gila Bend AZ. 602-683-2061

Sylvester, Joan, *Librn,* Parsons Memorial Library, Alfred ME. 207-324-2001

Sylvestre, J G, *Nat Librn,* National Library of Canada, Ottawa ON. 613-995-9481

Sylvestre, W Roger, *Dir,* Chateauguay Municipal Library, Chateauguay PQ. 514-691-1934

Symeonoglou, Rheba, *Librn,* Saint Louis Psychoanalytic Institute, Betty Golde Smith Memorial Library, Saint Louis MO. 314-361-7075

Symington, Margo, *Dir,* Devine Public Library, Devine TX. 512-663-2993

Symon, Beverly, *Librn,* Rockport-Ohio Township Public Library, Rockport IN. 812-649-4866

Symon, Carol, *Librn,* General Foods Ltd, Information Center, Toronto ON. 416-484-5492

Symonds, Leola, *Dir,* Metuchen Public Library, Metuchen NJ. 201-548-1526

Symonds, Mrs John, *Pres,* Historic Annapolis, Inc Library, Annapolis MD. 267-7619 & 269-0432

Synan, Ruth, *Dir,* Taunton Public Library, Subregional Headquarters for Eastern Massachusetts Regional Library System, Taunton MA. 617-823-3570

Synerholm, Chris, *On-Line Servs,* Syntex USA, Inc, Corporate Library-Information Services, Palo Alto CA. 415-855-5814

Sypolt, Terri, *Pub Servs,* Defiance College, Anthony Wayne Library & Instructional Resource Ctr, Defiance OH. 419-784-4010, Ext 132-135

Syracruse, Richard, *Cat,* College of Charleston, Robert Scott Small Library, Charleston SC. 803-792-5530

Syrette, Darlene, *Librn,* Batchewana Band Library, Sault Sainte Marie ON. 705-949-5322

Sysak, Maria, *Adult Independent Learner, Info & Referral,* Elmont Public Library, Elmont NY. 516-354-5280, 354-4091

Sytsma, Helen H, *Dir,* Washburn Public Library, Washburn WI. 715-373-2185

Syverson, Pansy, *Actg Librn,* Benson Public Library, Benson MN. 612-842-7981

Syverson, Ruby M, *Librn,* Christian Board of Publication, Marion Stevenson Library, Saint Louis MO. 314-371-6900, Ext 254

Sywak, Myron, *Assoc Prof,* Long Island University, Palmer Graduate Library School, NY. 516-299-2855 & 299-2856

Szabo, Ann, *Cat,* Sinte Gleska College Library, Mission SD. 605-856-4550

Szabo, Charles, *Western European Langs & Lit,* University of Wisconsin-Madison, Memorial Library, Madison WI. 608-262-3521

Szabo, Charlotte H, *Asst Dir,* White Plains Public Library, White Plains NY. 914-682-4400

Szach, Eugene, *On-Line Servs & Bibliog Instr,* University of Manitoba Libraries (Law), Winnipeg MB. 204-474-9773

Szachlenicz, Alina, *Librn,* COMINCO Ltd, Product Research Centre Library, Mississauga ON. 416-822-2022, Ext 32

Szasz, Debby, *Acq,* Columbia Union College, Theofield G Weis Library, Takoma Park MD. 301-270-4999

Szczepaniak, Adam, *On-Line Servs,* Medical & Chirurgical Faculty of the State of Maryland Library, Baltimore MD. 301-539-0872

Szczesiul, Mary, *Tech Serv,* Kirkwood Public Library, Kirkwood MO. 314-821-5770

Sze, Melanie C, *Librn, On-Line Servs & Bibliog Instr,* Standard Brands Inc Library, Wilton CT. 203-762-2500, Ext 414, 416

Szegedi, Laszlo, *Cat,* Loyola Marymount University (Loyola Law School Library), Los Angeles CA. 213-642-2934

Szeghy, Dean, *Ref,* Olive-Harvey College, City Colleges of Chicago, Olive-Harvey College Library, Chicago IL. 312-568-3700

Szekely, Yoram, *Librn,* Cornell University Libraries (Uris Undergraduate Library), Ithaca NY. 607-256-3414

Szeliga, Gail, *Dir,* Fenton Free Library, Moody Memorial Library Building, Binghamton NY. 607-724-8649

Szeman, Frances E, *Librn,* Presbyterian Hospital, Medical Library, Albuquerque NM. 505-243-9411

Szemes, Patricia, *Media,* Georgetown University (John Vinton Dahlgren Memorial Library), Washington DC. 202-625-7577

Szentendrey, Julius, *Foreign Law,* University of Houston (Law Library), Houston TX. 713-749-3119

Szeplaki, Joseph, *Tech Serv,* Brookdale Community College, Learning Resources Center, Lincroft NJ. 201-842-1900, Ext 392

Szerenyi, B Joseph, *Dir,* Eastern Illinois University, Booth Library, Charleston IL. 217-581-2210

Szesko, Gerald, *Tech,* Chicago Public Library (Business, Science & Technology Div), Chicago IL. 312-269-2814, 269-2865

Szilard, Paula, *Science Bibliogr,* University of Hawaii (University of Hawaii Library), Honolulu HI. 808-948-7205

Szilassy, Sandor, *Dir,* Glassboro State College, Savitz Learning Resource Center, Glassboro NJ. 609-445-6101

Szivos, M, *Asst Librn,* Brandon University, John E Robbins Library, Brandon MB. 204-728-9520

Szkudlarek, Thomas, *Librn,* Dana Corp, Technical Information Center, Ottawa Lake MI. 313-856-5111

Szladits, Lola L, *Curator,* New York Public Library (Berg Collection), New York NY. 212-790-6281

Szmuk, Szilvia, *Rare Bks, Spec Coll & Bibliog Instr,* Saint John's University Library, Jamaica NY. 212-969-8000, Ext 201

Szollosy, Les, *Ref,* Smiths Falls Public Library, Smiths Falls ON. 613-283-2911

Szopinski, Jim, *Media,* Joliet Junior College, Learning Resource Center, Joliet IL. 815-729-9020, Ext 282

Szostak, Mary I, *Dir,* Cheektowaga Public Library, Cheektowaga NY. 716-892-8089

Szot, Irene, *Asst Librn,* Saint Anthony Hospital, Sprafka Memorial Health Science Library, Chicago IL. 312-521-1710, Ext 331

Szpakowska, Janina-Klara, *Assoc Prof,* University of Montreal, Ecole de Bibliotheconomie, PQ. 514-343-6044

Sztorc, Sister Mary Virginia, *Lectr,* Felician College, Dept of Library Science, IL. 312-539-2328

Szymarski, Lucyna, *Ser,* Rush-Presbyterian-Saint Luke's Medical Center (Library of Rush University), Chicago IL. 312-942-2271, 942-5950

Szymczak, Doreen B, *Dir,* Albert Wisner Public Library, Warwick NY. 914-986-1047

Szynaka, Edward M, *Dir,* Grace A Dow Memorial Library, Midland Public Library, Midland MI. 517-835-7151

T

Tabachnik, Miriam, *Librn,* Alfred Adler Institute Library, Chicago IL. 312-346-3458

Tabaka, Sharon, *Librn,* Saint Clair County Library System (Marine City Public), Marine City MI. 313-765-5233

Tabakin, Rhea, *Librn,* Deloitte, Haskins & Sells, Executive Office Library, New York NY. 212-790-0639

Taber, John, *Ser,* Texas College of Osteopathic Medicine Library, Fort Worth TX. 817-735-2465

Taber, Sharon, *Circ,* University of Maryland at College Park (Theodore R McKeldin Library), College Park MD. 301-454-2853, 454-5977

Tabit, Edith, *Ref,* West Virginia Institute of Technology, Vining Library, Montgomery WV. 304-442-3141

Tabler, Grayson B, *Librn,* United States Food & Drug Administration, Bureau of Foods Library, Washington DC. 202-245-1235

Tabor, Dotty, *Dir,* Chatfield Public Library, Chatfield MN. 507-867-3480

Tabor, Karel, *ILL & Ad,* Farmers Branch Public Library, Farmers Branch TX. 214-247-3131, Ext 60, 61

Tabor, Loren, *Librn,* Denver Public Library (Hampden), Denver CO. 303-573-5152, Ext 271

Tabor, Susan, *ILL,* Hebrew Union College-Jewish Institute of Religion, The Klau Library, New York NY. 212-674-5300

Taborsky, Theresa, *Asst Dir,* University of Utah (Spencer S Eccles Health Sciences Library), Salt Lake City UT. 801-581-8771

Taboy, Enriqueta, *Dir,* Tri-State University, Perry T Ford Library, Angola IN. 219-665-3141, Ext 225

Tabron, Lynda, *Per,* Community College of Baltimore, Bard Library, Baltimore MD. 301-396-0432, 0433

Tacha, Michael L, *Librn,* Neosho County Community Junior College, Chapman Library, Chanute KS. 316-431-2820, Ext 9

Tache, Louis, *Dir,* Commission Des Accidents Du Travail Du Quebec Bibliotheque, Quebec PQ. 418-643-5850

Tachihata, Chieko, *Librn,* University of Hawaii (Gregg M Sinclair Library), Honolulu HI. 808-948-8422

Tacia, David G, *Dir,* Big Rapids Community Library, Big Rapids MI. 616-796-5234

Tackaberry, Sister Mary Liguori, *Tech Serv, Cat & On-Line Servs,* Fontbonne College Library, Saint Louis MO. 314-862-3456, Ext 352

Tackett, Evelyn, *Assoc Librn,* Belhaven College, Warren Hood Library, Jackson MS. 601-353-0012

Tackett, Evelyn, *Librn,* Central Presbyterian Church Library, Jackson MS. 601-353-2757

Tackett, Mrs P, *Librn,* Greenwood-Leflore Public Library System (City Library), Minter City MS. 601-658-4430

Tacy, Gillian, *Librn,* San Patricio County Library System, Sinton TX. 512-364-4863

Taddeo, Linda, *Ch,* Carnegie Free Library, Beaver Falls PA. 412-846-4340

Tadlock, Phyllis, *Librn,* Sperry Rand Corporation, Sperry Univac Division Library, Salt Lake City UT. 801-328-8066

Taff, Billie L, *Librn,* Dallas County Public Library (Veterans Memorial), Lancaster TX. 214-227-1080

Taff, Edith, *Dir,* Southeastern Bible College, Rowe Memorial Library, Birmingham AL. 205-251-2311, Ext 51

Taff, Irma, *Librn,* Scott Sebastian Regional Library (Scott County), Waldron AR. 501-637-3516

Taffe, Maureen, *Asst Dir & Ad,* Johnson Free Public Library, Hackensack NJ. 201-343-4169

Tafoya, Herlinda, *Librn,* Cochise County Law Library, Bisbee AZ. 602-432-5703, Ext 448

Taft, Gwen M, *On-Line Servs,* Samuel Roberts Noble Foundation, Inc, Biomedical Library, Ardmore OK. 405-223-5810, Ext 230

Taft, Lynne A, *Librn,* Ernst & Ernst Library, Detroit MI. 313-354-4600, Ext 325

Taggart, Thoburn, *ILL,* Wichita State University, Library & Media Resources Center, Wichita KS. 316-689-3586

Taggart, W R, *Spec Coll,* University of Victoria, McPherson Library, Victoria BC. 604-477-6911, Ext 4466

Tahiliani, Moti, *Chief Librn,* Lindsay Public Library, Lindsay ON. 705-324-5632

Taillon, Micheline, *Librn,* Canadian National Institute for the Blind, Quebec Division Library, Montreal PQ. 514-931-7221

Taillon, Yolande, *Agr & Nutrition,* Universite Laval Bibliotheque, Quebec PQ. 418-656-3344

Taipole, Joyce, *Asst Dir,* Fairport Public Library, Fairport Harbor OH. 216-354-8191

Tait, George, *Chief Librn,* Orange County Public Library (Leisure World), Seal Beach CA. 213-598-2431

Tait, Mary M, *Dir,* Upper Darby Township & Sellers Free Public Library, Upper Darby PA. 215-789-4400

Tait, Nancy, *Librn,* Fairview Municipal Library, Fairview AB. 403-835-2613

Tait, Susan, *YA,* Seattle Public Library, Seattle WA. 206-625-2665

Taitano, Magdalena S, *Dir,* Guam Public Library, Nieves M Flores Memorial Library, Agana, Guam PI. 472-6417

Tajima, Marie, *Acq,* Altadena Library District, Altadena CA. 213-798-0833

Takaci, Elda, *Doc,* Bowdoin College Library, Brunswick ME. 207-725-8731, Ext 281

Takeda, Nobuko, *Acq,* Boise Public Library & Information Center, Boise ID. 208-384-4466

Takemoto, Hazel, *In Charge,* Hilo Hospital (Fred Irwin Medical Library), Hilo HI. 808-961-4331

Takemoto, Hazel, *In Charge,* Hilo Hospital (Patients' Library Media Center), Hilo HI. 808-961-4331

Takita, Jim, *Soc Sci & Sci,* Library Association of Portland, Multnomah County Library, Portland OR. 503-223-7201, Ext 40

Talar, Sister Anita, *Dir & Bibliog Instr,* Georgian Court College, Farley Memorial Library, Lakewood NJ. 201-364-2200, Ext 19

Talat-Kielpsz, Janina, *Librn,* Ohio State University Libraries (Mathematics Library), Columbus OH. 614-422-2009

Talbert, Dorothy, *Librn,* Salt Lake County Library System (East Mill Creek), Salt Lake City UT. 801-278-4625

Talbert, Edward, *Librn,* Prince George's County Memorial Library System (New Carrollton Branch), New Carrollton MD. 301-459-6900

Talbert, Lena, *In Charge,* Milwaukee Public Library (Center Branch), Milwaukee WI. 414-278-3090

Talbert, Margaret, *Librn,* Milaca Community College, Milaca MN. 612-983-3677

Talbot, Carl A, *Dir,* Monroe Community College, LeRoy V Good Library, Rochester NY. 716-442-9950, Ext 2310

Talbot, Franklin, *ILL, Ref & Bibliog Instr,* University of Southern Maine, Gorham ME. 207-780-3340, 780-4273

Talbot, Jarold D, *Curator,* Hill-Stead Museum Library, Farmington CT. 203-677-9064

Talbot, Mary J, *Librn,* Hennepin County Library (Brooklyn Center Branch), Brooklyn Center MN. 612-537-6716

Talbot, Mrs M, *Librn,* Ajax Public Library (Village), Pickering ON. 416-683-1140

Talbot, Richard J, *President,* Boston Library Consortium, MA. 617-262-0380

Talbot, Richard J, *Dir,* University of Massachusetts at Amherst Library, Amherst MA. 413-545-0284

Talbot, William, *Ref & Bibliog Instr,* Boston State College Library, Boston MA. 617-731-3300

Talcott, A W, *Libr Supvr,* Bell Telephone Laboratories (Bell Telephone Laboratories Technical Library), Murray Hill NJ. 582-4612 (Supvr); 582-3740 (Circ); 582-3604 (Info Alerting Servs); 582-3901 (Systs Design Program); 582-3453 (Computing Info Serv); 582-7330 (Computing)

Talcott, Ann, *Cat,* Williamsburg Regional Library, Williamsburg VA. 804-229-7326

Talentine, Bill, *ILL & Ref,* Swampscott Public Library, Swampscott MA. 617-593-8380

Taler, Izabella, *ILL,* Queens College Library, Flushing NY. 212-520-7616

Taliaferro, Helen, *Librn,* United States Air Force (Military Airlift Command Library), Scott AFB IL. 618-256-3228

Talis, Ross M, *Asst Dir,* Oak Creek Public Library, Oak Creek WI. 414-764-4400

Talkington, Donald, *Ad & YA,* Kalamazoo Public Library, Kalamazoo MI. 616-342-9837

Tallar, Georgia, *Spec Coll,* Palmer College of Chiropractic, Davenport IA. 319-324-1611, Ext 242

Tallard, Inez, *Asst Librn,* Sandy Public Library, Sandy OR. 503-668-5537

Tallent, Elizabeth, *Librn,* Clinton County Public Library, Albany KY. 606-387-5989

Tallentire, Thomas L, *Cat,* University of Cincinnati Libraries (Robert S Marx Law Library), Cincinnati OH. 513-475-3016

Tallerico, Phyllis, *Cat,* Kean College of New Jersey, Nancy Thompson Library, Union NJ. 201-527-2017

Talley, Marcia, *Cat,* Saint John's College, Woodward Hall Library, Annapolis MD. 301-263-2371, Ext 71, 72

Tallichet, Marjorie, *Deputy Dir,* Alexandria Library, Alexandria VA. 703-750-6351

Tallman, Carol W, *Librn,* Pennsylvania Historical & Museum Commission, Reference Library, Harrisburg PA. 717-787-2701

Tallman, Johanna E, *Dir,* California Institute of Technology, Robert A Millikan Memorial Library, Pasadena CA. 213-795-6811

Tallman, Marna C, *Librn,* University of Washington Libraries (Business Administration), Seattle WA. 206-543-4360

Tallman, Nancy, *Librn,* Trinity United Presbyterian Church Library, Santa Ana CA. 714-544-7850

Talmadge, Paula, *Ch,* Worcester Public Library, Worcester MA. 617-752-3751

Talmage, J Philip, *Ref,* Marquette University Memorial Library, Milwaukee WI. 414-224-7214

Talrico, Sister Joanne, *Librn,* Ottumwa Heights College, Learning Resource Center, Ottumwa IA. 515-682-4551

Tam, Billy K, *In Charge,* United States Army (Corps of Engineers, North Atlantic Div Library), New York NY. 212-264-7698

Tam, Delia, *ILL,* Florida State University, Robert Manning Strozier Library, Tallahassee FL. 904-644-5211

Tam, Miriam, *Asst Librn & Tech Serv,* American Museum of Natural History Library, New York NY. 212-873-1300, Ext 494

Tama, Inge, *Librn,* Ajax Magnethermic Corp, Research & Development Library, Warren OH. 216-372-8511

Tamaus, Marcia, *Dir,* United Nations Information Center, Washington DC. 202-296-5370

Tamblyn, Eldon, *Cat,* Portland State University, Branford Price Millar Library, Portland OR. 503-229-4424

Tamblyn, Sylvia, *Asst Librn,* Churchill County Library, Fallon NV. 702-423-4623

Tambo, David C, *Delaware County Archives,* Ball State University, Alexander M Bracken Library, Muncie IN. 317-285-6261

Tamir, Emanuel, *Cat,* New York Public Library (The Branch Libraries), New York NY. 212-790-6262

Tamkevicz, Julia, *Chief Librn,* University of Pittsburgh at Greensburg, Powers Hall Library, Greensburg PA. 412-837-7040, Ext 133

Tamminen, Paul, *Commun Servs,* Pocatello Public Library, Information and Video Center, Pocatello ID. 208-232-1263

Tamura, Marilyn, *Dir of Branches,* Los Angeles Public Library System, Los Angeles CA. 213-626-7555

Tan, Victoria, *Circ,* Marianopolis College Library, Montreal PQ. 514-931-8792

Tanaka, Momoe, *Librn,* Hawaii Supreme Court Law Library, Honolulu HI. 808-548-7434

Tanaka, Momoe, *Librn,* State of Hawaii, Supreme Court, Fifth Circuit Court, Law Library, Lihue HI. 808-548-7432

Tandowsky, Eleanor, *Librn,* Alameda County Library (Pleasanton Branch), Pleasanton CA. 415-462-3535

Tanen, Lee, *On-Line Servs,* USV Pharmaceutical Corp, Information Services Department, Tuckahoe NY. 914-779-6300, Ext 2592

Tanfani, Tillie, *Acq,* Edgecliff College, Brennan Memorial Library, Cincinnati OH. 513-961-3770

Tang, Debbie, *Asst Librn,* Itawamba Junior College Vocational-Technical Center, Itawamba Junior College-Tupelo Branch, Learning Resources Ctr, Tupelo MS. 601-842-5621, Ext 25

Tang, Donna Taxco, *Coordr,* Pima Community College (Downtown Campus Learning Resource Center), Tucson AZ. 602-884-6649

Tanguay, Guy, *Dir,* Universite De Sherbrooke Bibliotheque (Bibliotheque de Droit), Sherbrooke PQ. 819-565-2905

Tanis, James, *Dir,* Bryn Mawr College, Canaday Library, Bryn Mawr PA. 215-645-5279

Tanis, Norman E, *Dir,* California State University, Northridge, Delmar T Oviatt & South Libraries, Northridge CA. 213-885-2271

Tank, Robert G, *In Charge,* Kaiser Steel Corp, Steel Manufacturing Division, Management Library, Fontana CA. 714-829-3359

Tankersley, Carolyn, *Acq,* El Paso Public Library, El Paso TX. 915-543-3804

Tannberg, Kersti, *Fine Arts,* Wheaton College Library, Norton MA. 617-285-7722, Ext 518

Tannberg, Kersti H, *Librn,* Wheaton College Library (Fine Arts), Norton MA. 617-285-7722

Tannehill, Courtney, *Dir,* Neshoba County Public Library, Philadelphia MS. 601-656-4911

Tannehill, Jr, Robert S, *Libr Mgr,* Chemical Abstracts Service Library, Columbus OH. 614-421-6940, Ext 2028

Tannenbaum, Authur, *Building Servs,* New York University, Elmer Holmes Bobst Library, New York NY. 212-598-2484

Tannenbaum, Earl, *Pub Serv,* Indiana State University, Cunningham Memorial Library, Terre Haute IN. 812-232-6311, Ext 2451

Tannenbaum, Maria A Gargotta, *Dir,* Istituto Italiano Di Cultura Biblioteca, New York NY. 212-879-4242

Tanner, Gary, *Homebound Serv,* Nevada County Library, Nevada City CA. 916-265-2461, Ext 244

Tanner, George, *Chmn,* Utah College Library Council, UT. 801-533-5875

Tanner, George, *Dir,* Utah Technical College at Provo Library, Provo UT. 801-224-6161

Tanner, George W, *Librn,* Utah Technical College at Provo, Orem Campus Library, Orem UT. 801-224-6161, Ext 265

Tanner, Jean, *Chief Librn,* Claremore Junior College, Thunderbird Library, Claremore OK. 918-341-7510, Ext 278

Tanner, Mary C, *Dir,* Mondovi Public Library, Mondovi WI. 715-926-4403

Tanner, Nancy, *Librn,* Dayton & Montgomery County Public Library (Westwood), Dayton OH. 513-224-1651, Ext 230

Tanner, Nancy, *Librn,* Dayton & Montgomery County Public Library (Madden Hills), Dayton OH. 513-224-1651, Ext 231

Tanner, Sandra H, *Dir,* Arlington Baptist College, Earl K Oldham Library, Arlington TX. 817-265-6331

Tanner, Thomas M, *Assoc Librn,* Lincoln Christian College & Seminary Library, Lincoln IL. 217-732-3168, Ext 234

Tannich, Jean B, *Librn,* Southern Maine Vocational Technical Institute Library, South Portland ME. 207-799-7303, Ext 230

Tanno, John, *Librn,* University of California, Riverside (Music), Riverside CA. 714-787-3137

Tanno, John, *Asst Librn,* University of California, Riverside, University Library, Riverside CA. 714-787-3221

Tanofsky, Mildred, *Dir,* Quinnipiac College Library, Hamden CT. 203-288-5251, Ext 271

Tanski, Jr, Henry M, *Interpretive Spec,* Crater Lake National Park, Research Library, Crater Lake OR. 503-594-2211

Tao, Clinton, *Tech Serv,* Robbins Library, Arlington MA. 617-643-0026

Taormina, Anthony P, *Asst Dir,* Lodi Memorial Library, Lodi NJ. 201-777-9195

Taperzer, Thomas R, *Dir,* Rochester Art Center Library, Rochester MN. 507-282-8629

Tapley, Frances W, *Actg Dir,* Alexander City State Junior College, Thomas D Russell Library, Alexander City AL. 205-234-6346, Ext 290

Taplin, Franklin P, *Dir,* Westfield Athenaeum, Westfield MA. 413-568-7833

Taplinger, Beverly R, *Libr Technician,* United States Department of Housing & Urban Development, Region III Library, Philadelphia PA. 215-597-2685

Tapp, Joan E, *Librn,* Argos Public Library, Argos IN. 219-892-5818

Tappenden, Shirley, *Asst Librn,* Pigeon District Library, Pigeon MI. 517-453-2341

Tarala, Marina, *ILL,* University of the Pacific, Irving Martin Library, Stockton CA. 209-946-2431

Taran, Nadia, *Regional Librn,* Southern Maryland Regional Library Association, La Plata MD. 301-934-9442

Tararin, Peter A, *Librn,* Los Angeles Psychoanalytic Society & Institute, Simmel-Fenichel Library, Los Angeles CA. 213-478-6851

Tarbell, Ellen S, *Librn,* United States Air Force (Francis E Warren Air Force Base Library), F E Warren AFB WY. 307-775-1110

Tarbell, Susan A, *Tech Serv,* Bellevue College, F Hoyte Freeman Library, Bellevue NE. 291-8100 Ext 64

Tarbert, Anita W, *Libr Tech,* United States Department of the Interior (US Geological Survey, Mineral Resources Library), Spokane WA. 509-456-4677

Tarbox, Barbara, *Dir,* Bill Memorial Library, Groton CT. 203-445-0392

Tarbox, Jr, G L, *Dir,* Brookgreen Gardens Library, Murrells Inlet SC. 803-237-4218

Tarbutton, Betty, *Asst Librn,* West Point Public Library, West Point NE. 402-372-3831

Tarczy, Stephen I, *Cat,* University of California Library, San Francisco CA. 415-666-2334

Tardif, L Gagne, *Ch,* LaSalle Municipal Library, Bibliotheque Municipale La Salle, La Salle PQ. 514-366-2582

Targo, Alice D, *Dir & Acq,* North Suburban District Library, Loves Park IL. 815-633-4247, 633-4248

Tarjan, Agnes, *Librn,* Cleveland Public Library (Nottingham), Cleveland OH. 216-481-5588

Tarlin, Harry, *Dir & Media,* Utica College of Syracuse University, Frank E Gannett Memorial Library, Utica NY. 315-792-3041

Tarlton, Shirley M, *Dir,* Winthrop College, Ida Jane Dacus Library, Rock Hill SC. 803-323-2131

Tarman, Mary Sandra, *Librn,* Ramsey County Medical Society, Boeckmann Library, Saint Paul MN. 612-224-3346

Tarnawsky, Ostap, *Cat,* Community College of Philadelphia, Division of Educational Resources, Philadelphia PA. 215-972-7250

Tarr, Andrea, *Ch,* Fiske Free Library, Claremont NH. 603-542-4393

Tarr, E Whitney, *Librn,* Richard Salter Storrs Library, Longmeadow MA. 413-567-5500

Tarrant, Doris M, *Asst Dir,* Mahopac Library, Mahopac NY. 914-628-2009

Tart, Barbara, *Librn,* Wake County Department of the Public Library (Halifax Court Neighborhood), Raleigh NC. 919-755-6121

Tarter, Theodore, *Curator,* Conde Nast Publications Library, New York NY. 212-880-8245

Tarwater, Katherine, *Acq & Per,* Brevard Community College, Learning Resources Center, Cocoa FL. 305-632-1111, Ext 295, 298

Tarwater, Leah, *Librn,* Montgomery County Department of Public Libraries (Gaithersburg Branch), Gaithersburg MD. 301-840-2381

Tash, Steve, *ILL & On-Line Servs,* Saddleback Community College Library, Mission Viejo CA. 714-831-4515

Tashima, Marie, *Supervisor,* Nalco Chemical Company, Information Services, Naperville IL. 312-961-9500

Tashjian, Sharon, *Dir,* University of Oregon Health Sciences Center (Dental Library), Portland OR. 503-225-8822

Tashjian, Virginia, *Lectr,* Simmons College, Graduate School of Library & Information Science, MA. 617-738-2225

Tashjian, Virginia A, *Dir,* Newton Free Library, Newton MA. 617-527-7700, Ext 24

Tasker, Ida, *Dir,* Roche Memorial Library, Wyoming IA. 319-488-3975

Tasker, Margaret, *Cat,* Hobbs Public Library, Hobbs NM. 505-397-2451

Tassia, Margaret R, *Asst Prof,* Millersville State College, Dept of Library Science, PA. 717-872-5411, Ext 416

Tassin, Anthony G, *Circ,* University of New Orleans, Earl K Long Library, New Orleans LA. 504-283-0353

Tassin, Anthony G, *Automation,* University of New Orleans, Earl K Long Library, New Orleans LA. 504-283-0353

Tate, Billie, *Libr Technician,* San Diego County Library (Crest), El Cajon CA. 714-565-5100

Tate, David, *Librn,* Van Buren County Library, Webster Memorial Library, Decatur MI. 616-423-4771

Tate, Joanne, *Chief Librn,* Ajax Public Library, Ajax ON. 416-683-6911

Tate, Lucy, *Librn,* Moore Memorial Library, Hillsdale IL. 309-658-2666

Tate, Nancy, *Ch,* Erie County Library System, Erie PA. 814-452-2333

Tatman, Mary Ann, *On-Line Servs,* Veterans Administration (Hospital Library), Salem VA. 703-982-2463, Ext 358

Tatman, Sandra, *Archit Librn,* Athenaeum of Philadelphia, Philadelphia PA. 215-925-2688

Tatro, Hildred, *Librn,* Enosburg Public Library, Enosburg Falls VT. 802-933-2328

Tatsch, Helen, *On-Line Servs,* Raytheon Company, Missle Systems Div, Bedford Laboratories Technical Information Center Library, Bedford MA. 617-274-7100, Ext 2231

Tattershall, S, *Librn,* Shell Canada Limited, Technical Library, Toronto ON. 416-597-7985

Tatum, Barbara, *Tech Serv & Cat,* Brunswick Junior College, Clara Wood Gould Memorial Library, Brunswick GA. 912-264-7270

Tatum, Constance M, *Cat,* Duke University (Medical Center Library), Durham NC. 919-684-2092

Tatum, Jennie S, *Ch,* Abilene Public Library, Abilene TX. 915-677-2474

Taub, Diane I, *Librn,* Industrial Nucleonics Corp, Technical Library, Columbus OH. 614-261-3442

Taub, Edith A, *Dir,* Methodist Hospital, Medical Library, Brooklyn NY. 212-780-3000

Taub, Sonia, *Cat & Ref,* Saratoga Springs Public Library, Saratoga Springs NY. 518-584-7860

Taube, Frances, *Dir,* Sturgis Public Library, Sturgis MI. 616-651-7907, 651-2321

Taubel, Sandra, *Lectr,* University of Wisconsin-Oshkosh, Dept of Library Science, WI. 414-424-2313

Tauber, Anna R, *Librn,* Carnegie Museum of Natural History Library, Pittsburgh PA. 412-622-3264

Tauber, Margery A, *Dir,* Watertown Regional Library, Watertown SD. 605-886-8521, 886-8282

Taubman, Susan, *Librn,* Creedmoor Psychiatric Center (Health Sciences Library), Queens Village NY. 212-464-7500, Ext 1322

Taubman, Susan, *Librn,* Creedmoor Psychiatric Center (Patients Library), Queens Village NY. 212-464-7500, Ext 1303

Taugher, Carol A, *Librn,* Volusia County Public Libraries (Holly Hill Branch), Holly Hill FL. 904-252-8374

Taulman, Marian, *Ch,* Carnegie Public Library District, Fortville IN. 317-485-5432

Taus, Nina G, *Librn,* Beth El Ner Tamid Synagogue, Sampson Library, Milwaukee WI. 414-442-4520

Tavai, Lauolive, *Bkmobile Coordr,* American Samoa-Office of Library Services, Pago Pago, Samoa PI. 633-5869

Tavai, Lauolive, *Librn,* American Samoa-Office of Library Services (Main), Utulei Village PI. 633-5423

Tavares, Onalee, *Cat,* Grove City College, Henry Buhl Library, Grove City PA. 412-458-6600, Ext 270

Tavino, Mrs Ralph, *Librn,* Circleville Presbyterian Church Library, Circleville NY. 914-361-9552

Tawil, Adrienne, *ILL,* Joint Free Public Library of the Chathams, Chatham NJ. 201-635-0603

Taybert, Joyce M, *Librn,* R T French Co, Technical Department Library, Rochester NY. 716-482-8000, Ext 106

Tayler, Susan, *Tech Serv,* United States Equal Employment Opportunity Commission Library, Washington DC. 202-634-6990

Taylor, A R, *Librn,* National Research Council of Canada, Atlantic Regional Laboratory Library, Halifax NS. 902-429-6450, Ext 138

Taylor, Adele, *Librn,* Moultonboro Public Library, Moultonboro NH. 603-476-8895

Taylor, Alice J, *Librn,* Price Waterhouse & Co Library, Detroit MI. 313-259-0500

Taylor, Aline H, *Librn,* General Telephone Co of the Southwest, E H Danner Library of Telephony, San Angelo TX. 915-944-5149

Taylor, Amanda, *Librn,* Concordia Parish Library, Ferriday LA. 318-757-3550

Taylor, Ann, *Asst Librn & Br Coordr,* Washington County Library System, William Alexander Percy Memorial Library, Greenville MS. 601-335-2331

Taylor, Anne, *Ch,* Farmers Branch Public Library, Farmers Branch TX. 214-247-3131, Ext 60, 61

Taylor, Anne, *Librn,* Lennox & Addington County Public Library (Amherstview Branch), Amherstview ON. 613-389-6006

Taylor, Anne M, *Chief Librn,* Veterans Administration, Hospital Library, Madison WI. 608-256-1901

Taylor, Arthur R, *Dir,* Thomas More College, Learning Resources Center, Fort Mitchell KY. 606-341-5800, Ext 61

Taylor, Barbara, *Librn,* Baker Free Public Library, Inc, Macclenny FL. 904-259-6464

Taylor, Barbara, *YA,* Carnegie Free Library, Beaver Falls PA. 412-846-4340

Taylor, Barbara, *Ad,* Cedar Falls Public Library, Cedar Falls IA. 319-266-2629

Taylor, Barbara, *Cat,* University of Tennessee at Martin, Paul Meek Library, Martin TN. 901-587-7060

Taylor, Barbara P, *Bus & Tech,* Stark County District Library, Canton OH. 216-452-0665, Ext 31

Taylor, Betsy, *Chief Librn,* Veterans Administration, Hospital Library Service, Danville IL. 217-442-8000, Ext 523

Taylor, Betty, *Librn,* Vassalboro Public Library, East Vassalboro ME. 207 923 3533

Taylor, Betty W, *Dir,* University of Florida Libraries (Legal Information Center), Gainesville FL. 904-392-0417

Taylor, Bonnie M, *Tech Serv,* Portland Public Library, Baxter Library, Portland ME. 207-773-4761

Taylor, Brenda, *Ch & YA,* Temple Public Library, Temple TX. 817-778-5555

Taylor, Byron C, *Librn,* United States Air Force (Whiteman Air Force Base Library), Whiteman AFB MO. 816-687-1110, Ext 3089

Taylor, Caro, *Librn,* Montgomery County Department of Public Libraries (Sherwood), Sandy Spring MD. 301-774-4245

Taylor, Carol, *Acq, Tech Serv & Cat,* Concord Free Public Library, Concord MA. 617-369-5324

Taylor, Carol F, *Librn,* Smith-Corona Laboratory Library, Cortland NY. 607-753-6011, Ext 278

Taylor, Carole, *Dir,* Dillard University, Will W Alexander Library, New Orleans LA. 504-949-2123, Ext 256, 257

Taylor, Carolyn C, *Acq,* Florida State University, Robert Manning Strozier Library, Tallahassee FL. 904-644-5211

Taylor, Carolyn L, *Asst Dir,* Saint Louis University (Medical Center Library), Saint Louis MO. 314-664-9800

Taylor, Cecilia S, *Librn,* Westminster West Public Library, Westminster West VT. 802-387-5710

Taylor, Charles, *Educ,* California State University, Long Beach, University Library, Long Beach CA. 213-498-4047

Taylor, Charlotte, *Acq & Per,* Cheyney State College, Leslie Pinckney Hill Library, Cheyney PA. 215-758-2000, Ext 2203, 2208, 2245

Taylor, Christine, *Asst Librn,* Snohomish County Law Library, Everett WA. 206-259-5326

Taylor, Clellie M, *Dir,* Halifax Community College, Learning Resources Center, Weldon NC. 919-536-2551

Taylor, Dan, *Ref,* University of Texas Health Science Center at San Antonio Library, San Antonio TX. 512-691-6271

Taylor, Dan, *Ref,* University of Texas Health Science Center at San Antonio Library, San Antonio TX. 512-691-6271

Taylor, David, *Librn,* University of North Carolina at Chapel Hill (Robert B House Undergraduate Library), Chapel Hill NC. 919-933-1355

Taylor, Deborah D, *Librn,* Enoch Pratt Free Library (Broadway), Baltimore MD. 301-396-5430, 396-5395

Taylor, Desmond, *Dir,* University of Puget Sound, Collins Memorial Library, Tacoma WA. 206-756-3257

Taylor, Diana, *Ch,* Portsmouth Public Library, Portsmouth NH. 603-431-2000, Ext 252

Taylor, Dianne, *ILL & Circ,* North Carolina Wesleyan College Library, Rocky Mount NC. 919-442-7121, Ext 280, 283

Taylor, Dolores, *Dir,* Pennsylvania College of Optometry, Albert Fitch Memorial Library, Philadelphia PA. 215-424-5900, Ext 231

Taylor, Don, *Asst Dir,* Church of Jesus Christ of Latter Day Saints, Arizona Branch Genealogical Library, Mesa AZ. 602-964-1200

Taylor, Dora Jean, *Tech Serv,* Westfield Memorial Library, Westfield NJ. 201-233-1515

Taylor, Eleanor, *Processing,* Chicago Public Library, Chicago IL. 312-269-2900

Taylor, Elizabeth, *Youth Specialist,* Chicago Public Library, Chicago IL. 312-269-2900

Taylor, Elizabeth, *Reader Serv,* Elyria Public Library, Elyria OH. 216-323-5747

Taylor, Elizabeth, *ILL,* Gaston-Lincoln Regional Library, Gastonia NC. 704-866-3756

Taylor, Elizabeth, *Cat,* New England College, H Raymond Danforth Library, Henniker NH. 603-428-2344

Taylor, Ellyn, *ILL,* Kansas State University, Farrell Library, Manhattan KS. 913-532-6516

Taylor, Ethel S, *Dir,* Brielle Public Library, Brielle NJ. 201-528-9381

Taylor, France B, *Librn,* Uinta County Library (Mountain View Branch), Mountain View WY. 307-782-3161

Taylor, Frances, *Librn,* Federal Aviation Administration, Western Region Library, Hawthorne CA. 213-536-6427

Taylor, Gladys, *Archivist,* Rochester Institute of Technology, Wallace Memorial Library, Rochester NY. 716-475-2566

Taylor, Helen, *Acq,* Chesterfield County Central Library, Chesterfield VA. 804-748-1601

Taylor, Helen, *Ad & YA,* Saint Louis Public Library, Saint Louis MO. 314-241-2288

Taylor, Holly H, *Ref,* West Deptford Public Library, Thorofare NJ. 609-845-5593

Taylor, Hugh A, *Prov Archivist,* Public Archives of Nova Scotia, Halifax NS. 902-423-9915

Taylor, Jack, *AV,* Bucks County Community College Library, Newtown PA. 215-968-5861, Ext 306, 307

Taylor, James, *Bus & Sci,* Seattle Public Library, Seattle WA. 206-625-2665

Taylor, Jan, *Librn,* Uinta County Library (Lyman Branch), Lyman WY. 307-787-3814

Taylor, Jean, *Media,* East Tennessee State University, Sherrod Library, Johnson City TN. 615-929-4338

Taylor, Jeanette, *Asst Librn,* New York Psychoanalytic Institute, Abraham A Brill Library, New York NY. 212-879-6900

Taylor, Jeanie, *Librn,* Doddridge County Public Library (Center Point Branch), Center Point WV. 304-873-1941

Taylor, Jeri, *Librn,* Bureau of Land Management Library, Vernal UT. 801-789-1362

Taylor, Jerry, *Librn,* Northland Pioneer College, Show Low Center Library, Show Low AZ. 602-537-2976

Taylor, Jo, *Circ,* Pickens County Library, Easley SC. 803-859-9679

Taylor, Joann, *Dir,* Joseph and Elizabeth Shaw Public Library, Clearfield PA. 814-765-3271

Taylor, Jose, *Librn,* Los Angeles Public Library System (Lincoln Heights), Los Angeles CA. 213-225-3977

Taylor, Joy, *Librn,* Caudill Rowlett Scott Library, Houston TX. 713-621-9600

Taylor, Joyce, *Librn,* University of Mississippi Library (Education), University MS. 601-232-7040

Taylor, Juanita W, *Chief Librn,* United States Army (Presidio of San Francisco Post Library System), Presidio of San Francisco CA. 415-561-3448, 561-5037

Taylor, Julia, *Librn,* Wetumpka Public Library, Wetumpka AL. 205-567-8966

Taylor, Julie A, *Tech Serv,* Edgecliff College, Brennan Memorial Library, Cincinnati OH. 513-961-3770

Taylor, Karen, *Asst Coordr,* South County Interrelated Library System, Westerly RI. 401-596-2877

Taylor, Karren, *Asst Dir,* East Greenwich Free Library, East Greenwich RI. 401-884-9511

Taylor, Kathy, *Asst Librn,* Bloomsburg Public Library, Bloomsburg PA. 717-784-0883

Taylor, Kay, *Ch,* Durham County Library, Durham NC. 919-683-2626

Taylor, Kay, *Asst Dir,* Jackson Metropolitan Library, Jackson MS. 601-352-3677

Taylor, Kenneth I, *Assoc Prof,* Villanova University, Graduate Dept of Library Science, PA. 215-527-2100, Ext 354, 355

Taylor, Larry, *Cat,* Drexel University Library, Philadelphia PA. 215-895-2750

Taylor, Leah, *Librn,* Pamunkey Regional Library (Mechanicsville Branch), Mechanicsville VA. 804-746-9615

Taylor, Lillian M, *Librn,* Columbia Theological Seminary, John Bulow Campbell Library, Decatur GA. 404-378-8821, Ext 67

Taylor, Linda, *Librn,* Louisville Free Public Library (Bon Air), Louisville KY. 502-459-5242

Taylor, Linda, *ILL & Circ,* Newmarket Public Library, Newmarket ON. 416-895-5196

Taylor, Loretta, *Librn,* Ozark Regional Library (Recklein Memorial), Cuba MO. 314-885-3431

Taylor, M, *Tech Serv,* Lancaster Town Library, Lancaster MA. 617-365-2008

Taylor, M D, *Chief Librn,* Ontario Hydro Library, Toronto ON. 416-529-5111

Taylor, M Robin, *Librn,* Preston Hills Presbyterian Church Library, Dallas TX. 214-233-2622

Taylor, Madeline, *Ser,* College of Medicine & Dentistry of New Jersey, George F Smith Library of the Health Sciences, Newark NJ. 201-456-4580

Taylor, Margaret Jean, *Librn,* United States Forest Service, Southeastern Forest Experiment Station Library, Asheville NC. 704-258-2850, Ext 632

Taylor, Margaret T, *Lectr,* University of Michigan, School of Library Science, MI. 313-764-9376

Taylor, Marguerite S, *Librn,* Missouri Division of Corrections Libraries (Renz Correctional Center Library), Jefferson City MO. 314-751-3050

Taylor, Marion, *Assoc Prof,* Emory University, Div of Librarianship, GA. 404-329-6840

Taylor, Marion, *Soc Sci, Music,* University of California, University Library, Santa Cruz CA. 408-429-2076

Taylor, Marion W, *Chmn,* Chicago State University, Dept of Library Science & Communications Media, IL. 312-995-2278

Taylor, Mark-Allen, *Tech Serv,* Massachusetts General Hospital (Treadwell Library), Boston MA. 617-726-8600

Taylor, Martha, *ILL,* New York Medical College, Westchester Medical Center Library, Valhalla NY. 914-347-5237

Taylor, Martha H, *Ad & Ref,* Dalton Public Library, Inc, Dalton Regional Library, Dalton GA. 404-278-4507, 278-9247, 226-2039

Taylor, Mary, *ILL,* ITT Research Institute, Technical Information Services Library, Annapolis MD. 301-267-2251

Taylor, Mary, *Circ,* Western Michigan University, Dwight B Waldo Library, Kalamazoo MI. 616-383-4961

Taylor, Mary Ann, *ILL,* Southeast Kansas Library System, Iola KS. 316-365-3833

Taylor, Mary Virginia, *On-Line Servs,* Veterans Administration, Health Sciences Library, Little Rock AR. 501-372-8361, Ext 1294

Taylor, Mary-Stuart, *Cat,* National Defense University Library, Washington DC. 202-693-8437

Taylor, Maurice, *Ref,* New Hanover County Public Library, Wilmington NC. 919-763-3303

Taylor, Mercedes, *Ref,* Antelope Valley College, Roy A Knapp Library, Lancaster CA. 805-943-3241, Ext 234

Taylor, Merrily, *Servs Group Dir,* Columbia University (University Libraries), New York NY. 212-280-2241

Taylor, Mimi, *Librn,* First Regional Library (Emily Jones Pointer Library), Como MS. 601-526-5673

Taylor, Molly, *Libr Tech,* Alberta Alcoholism & Drug Abuse Commission Library, Calgary AB. 403-269-6101, Ext 42

Taylor, Mrs C, *Librn,* Windsor Public Library (Nikola Budimir Memorial), Windsor ON. 519-969-5880

Taylor, Mrs Charles, *Librn,* Bolivar-Hardeman County Public Library, Bolivar TN. 901-658-3436

Taylor, Mrs Everett, *Tech Serv,* Abilene Christian University, Margarett & Herman Brown Library, Abilene TX. 915-677-1911, Ext 2344

Taylor, Mrs K F, *Librn,* Curve Lake Indian Reserve Public Library, Curve Lake ON. 705-657-3217

Taylor, Mrs M, *Br Supvr,* Scarborough Public Library (Port Union), Scarborough ON. 416-282-7428

Taylor, Mrs V, *Dir,* Cobalt Public Library, Cobalt ON. 705-679-8120

Taylor, Nancy, *Actg Dir,* University of Wisconsin-Madison (Instructional Materials Center), Madison WI. 608-262-3521

Taylor, Naomi L, *Librn,* Enterprise Public Library, Enterprise KS. 913-934-2351

Taylor, Nettie B, *Asst State Supt for Libr & Dir Div Libr Develop & Servs,* Maryland State Department of Education, Division of Library Development & Services, Baltimore MD. 301-796-8300, Ext 284

Taylor, Norma, *Ch,* Benedum Civic Center Library, Bridgeport WV. 304-842-6201, Ext 33

Taylor, Prudence, *Ch,* Athens Regional Library, Athens GA. 404-543-0134

Taylor, Rebbecca, *Ref,* Howard County Library, Big Spring TX. 915-267-5295

Taylor, Rebecca, *Librn,* Boulder Public Library (George R Reynolds), Boulder CO. 303-441-3120

Taylor, Rebecca, *Ch & Bkmobile Coordr,* Saint Charles Parish Library, Luling LA. 504-785-8471

Taylor, Rebecca S, *Librn,* New Hanover County Public Library (Red Cross Street), Wilmington NC. 919-763-5215

Taylor, Renee, *Per,* Cumberland County Public Library, Anderson Street Library, Frances Brooks Stein Memorial Library, Fayetteville NC. 919-483-1580

Taylor, Richard L, *Dir,* Wilbur Wright College of the City Colleges of Chicago Library, Chicago IL. 312-777-7900, Ext 83

Taylor, Robert, *Music,* Greensboro Public Library, Greensboro NC. 373-2474; 373-2471

Taylor, Robert, *Commun Arts Coordr,* Olean Public Library, Olean NY. 716-372-0200

Taylor, Robert S, *Dean,* Syracuse University, School of Information Studies, NY. 315-423-2911

Taylor, Rose, *Librn,* Manatee County Public Library System (Palmetto Branch), Palmetto FL. 813-722-3333

Taylor, Rosemarie Kazda, *Dir,* Wilkes-Barre General Hospital Library, Wilkes-Barre PA. 717-829-8111, Ext 2180

Taylor, Rosemary, *Ref,* El Segundo Public Library, El Segundo CA. 213-322-4121

Taylor, Ruth, *Asst Head,* Wayne State University Libraries (Vera P Shiffman Medical Library), Detroit MI. 313-577-1088

Taylor, Sandra, *Consultant,* Prince Edward Island Provincial Library, Charlottetown PE. 902-892-3504, Ext 54

Taylor, Sarah, *Ser,* Kentucky Department of Library & Archives, Frankfort KY. 502-564-7910

Taylor, Sarah, *Ref & Per,* Lakewood Community College Library, White Bear Lake MN. 612-770-1331, Ext 129

Taylor, Sharon, *Dir,* Reformed Theological Seminary Library, Jackson MS. 601-922-4988, Ext 52

Taylor, Simeon P, *Mgr Info Serv,* National Education Association, Information Center Library, Washington DC. 202-833-5462

Taylor, Stillman K, *Dir,* Great River Library System, Quincy IL. 217-223-2560

Taylor, Sue, *Circ,* West Chester State College, Francis Harvey Green Library, West Chester PA. 215-436-2643

Taylor, Susan, *ILL, Ref & Bibliog Instr,* Salem College, Dale H Gramley Library, Winston-Salem NC. 919-721-2649

Taylor, Susan D, *Law Librn,* Indiana Supreme Court Law Library, Indianapolis IN. 317-633-4640

Taylor, Ted, *Cat & On-Line Servs,* Azusa Pacific College, Marshburn Memorial Library, Azusa CA. 213-969-3434, Ext 198

Taylor, Tom, *Ref,* Fort Vancouver Regional Library, Vancouver WA. 206-695-1561

Taylor, Tucker Neel, *Ref,* Newberry College, Wessels Library, Newberry SC. 803-276-5010, Ext 300

Taylor, Vickie, *Asst Librn,* Peat, Marwick, Mitchell & Co Library, Los Angeles CA. 213-972-4000, Ext 405

Taylor, Warren, *Spec Coll,* Topeka Public Library, Topeka KS. 913-233-2040

Taylor, Warren, *Topeka Hist,* Topeka Public Library, Topeka KS. 913-233-2040

Taylor, Warren G, *Asst Dir Admin Serv,* Auraria Libraries, Denver CO. 303-629-2805

Taylor, Yvonne, *Asst Librn, ILL & Circ,* Norristown State Hospital, Professional & Staff Library System, Norristown PA. 215-631-2879, 631-2948

Taylor-Vaisey, A, *ILL, Circ & Ref,* Trent University, Thomas J Bata Library, Peterborough ON. 705-748-1550

Taynton, Virginia, *Acq,* Thomas Jefferson University (Scott Memorial Library), Philadelphia PA. 215-928-8848

Tchen, Agnete, *Health Sci,* Long Island University, Brooklyn Center Libraries, Brooklyn NY. 212-834-6060, 834-6064

Tchiyuka, Evelyn, *Librn,* Prince George's County Memorial Library System (Accokeek Branch), Accokeek MD. 301-283-2521

Tchiyuka, Evelyn, *Librn,* Prince George's County Memorial Library System (Baden Branch), Brandywine MD. 301-888-1152

Tchobanoff, James B, *In Charge, On-Line Servs & Bibliog Instr,* Pillsbury Company (Technical Information Center), Minneapolis MN. 612-330-4750

Teachout, Margaret H, *Dir,* Standing Rock Community College Library, Fort Yates ND. 701-854-2901, Ext 2

Teagarden, Milton A, *Instr,* Alabama State University, Library Educational Media Program, AL. 205-832-6072, Ext 502

Teague, Grace, *Ad,* Crandall Library, Glens Falls NY. 518-792-6508

Teague, Janet E, *Circ,* Pearl River County Library System, Margaret Reed Crosby Memorial Library, Picayune MS. 601-798-5081

Teague, Phil, *County Dept,* Birmingham Public & Jefferson County Free Library, Birmingham AL. 205-254-2551

Teague, Phil, *Librn,* Birmingham Public & Jefferson County Free Library (Bookmobile Center), Birmingham AL. 205-254-2551

Teague, Jr, Sidney P, *Dir,* Shelby County Regional Library, Columbiana AL. 205-669-7851

Teahan, John, *Asst Librn,* Wadsworth Atheneum, Auerbach Art Library, Hartford CT. 203-278-2670, Ext 257

Teahan, Shirley, *In Charge,* Albert-Westmorland-Kent Regional Library (Hopewell Cape Public), Hopewell Cape NB. 506-389-2631

Teall, Bette Jeanne, *Librn,* Lawton Public Library, Lawton MI. 616-624-5481

Teall, Eileen, *Ch,* Way Public Library, Perrysburg OH. 419-874-3135

Teare, Robert F, *Asst Dir,* Claremont Colleges Libraries, Claremont CA. 714-621-8000, Ext 3721

Tease, Mrs B, *Librn,* Canada Department of National Defense, Canadian Forces Base Bushell Park School Resource Center Library, Bushell Park SK. 306-693-5311

Teather, Linda, *Ser,* University of Manitoba Libraries, Winnipeg MB. 204-474-9881

TeBay, Marilou, *Librn,* First Federal Savings & Loan Association, Research & Management Division Library, Miami FL. 305-577-6120

Tebbetts, Diane, *On-Line Servs,* University of New Hampshire, Ezekiel W Dimond Library, Durham NH. 603-862-1540

Tebbetts, Don S, *Tech Serv,* Idaho State University Library, Pocatello ID. 208-236-3202

Tebbutt, Jean, *Chief Librn,* Spectator Library, Hamilton ON. 416-526-3315

Tebo, Marlene, *Librn,* State University of New York at Binghamton Library (Science), Binghamton NY. 607-798-2528

Teckenbrock, Vicki, *Ch,* Little Rock Township Public Library, Plano IL. 312-552-3310

Teclaff, Ludwik A, *Dir,* Fordham University, School of Law Library, New York NY. 212-841-5223

Tedards, Helen, *Librn,* Greenville News-Piedmont Library, Multimedia Newspaper, Greenville SC. 803-298-4323

Tedeschi, John A, *Curator Rare Bks & Mss,* Newberry Library, Chicago IL. 312-943-9090

Tedeschi, John A, *Dir, Ctr for Renaissance Studies,* Newberry Library, Chicago IL. 312-943-9090

Tedesco, Claire R, *Asst for Libr Operations,* Veterans Administration (Library Division), Washington DC. 202-389-2781

Tedesco, Eileen, *On-Line Servs,* Stone & Webster Engineering Corporation, Technical Information Center Library, Boston MA. 617-973-2103

Tedesco, Eleanor, *Ser,* University of New Mexico General Library (Medical Center Library), Albuquerque NM. 505-277-2311

Tedman, Vernelia, *Librn,* Micro Switch, Engineering Library, Freeport IL. 815-235-5500

Teel, Roger, *Tech Serv,* Albany Public Library, Albany OR. 503-967-4304

Teeple, Marcella, *Librn,* Akron-Summit County Public Library (Manchester), Akron OH. 216-882-3840

Teeselink, Evangeline, *Dir,* Kewaskum Public Library, Kewaskum WI. 414-626-4312

Teeter, Enola Jane N, *Librn,* Longwood Gardens Inc Library, Kennett Square PA. 215-388-6741, Ext 510

Teffeau, Harriet L, *ILL,* National Defense University Library, Washington DC. 202-693-8437

Tefft, Carol, *Librn,* Santa Clara County Free Library (Las Altas Public), Los Altos CA. 415-948-7683

Tefft, Carol, *Librn,* Santa Clara County Free Library (Woodland), Los Altos CA. 415-969-6030

Tefs, Debbie, *Librn,* Ohio Brass Co, Frank B Black Research Center Library, Wadsworth OH. 216-336-3541

Tega, Vasile, *Ref,* Ecole Des Hautes Etudes Commerciales De Montreal Bibliotheque, Montreal PQ. 514-343-4481

Tegler, P, *Libr Sci, Comm & Communicative Disorders,* State University of New York at Buffalo, University Libraries, Buffalo NY. 716-636-2965

Tegler, Patricia, *Instr,* State University of New York at Buffalo, School of Information & Library Studies, NY. 716-636-2412

Tegler, Patricia, *Librn,* State University of New York at Buffalo (Library Studies), Buffalo NY. 716-636-2386

Teichman, Norma, *Acq,* Stamford's Public Library, Ferguson Library, Stamford CT. 203-325-4354

Teichman, Raymond, *AV,* General Services Administration - National Archives & Records Service, Franklin D Roosevelt Library, Hyde Park NY. 914-229-8114

Teigen, Philip, *Librn,* McGill University Libraries (Osler Library), Montreal PQ. 514-392-4331

Teigland, Laurel, *Ch,* Glendale Public Library, Glendale CA. 213-956-2030

Teigler, Elaine, *Asst Dir & Ref,* Northwestern University, Chicago (School of Law Library), Chicago IL. 312-649-8450

Teisberg, Daniel, *Bk Selection Librn,* Minneapolis Public Library & Information Center, Minneapolis MN. 612-372-6500

Teitelbaum, Gene, *Dir,* University of Louisville Library (Law), Louisville KY. 502-588-6392

Teitelbaum, Priscilla, *Info Servs,* New York University, Elmer Holmes Bobst Library, New York NY. 212-598-2484

Teko, Jay, *ILL & Ref,* Automation Industries, Inc, Vitro Laboratories Division Library, Silver Spring MD. 301-871-7200

Telatnik, George M, *Dir,* Niagara University Library, Niagara University NY. 716-285-1212, Ext 376

Tellor, Mrs Raymond J, *Dir,* Catholic Information Center, Philadelphia PA. 215-587-3520

Teloh, Mary H, *Rare Bks & Spec Coll,* Vanderbilt University Medical Center Library, Nashville TN. 615-322-2292

Tema, William, *Dir,* Altadena Library District, Altadena CA. 213-798-0833

Temkin, Edward A, *Asst Prof,* Kean College of New Jersey, Library-Media Program, NJ. 201-527-2626, 527-2071

Temkin, Sara, *Asst Dir & Acq,* Cranford Public Library, Cranford NJ. 201-276-1826

Tempkin, Lillian, *Librn,* Temple Beth Israel Library, Phoenix AZ. 602-264-4428, Ext 9

Temple, Byron, *Librn,* Tensas Parish Library, Saint Joseph LA. 318-766-3781

Temple, Harold, *On-Line Servs,* College of DuPage, Learning Resources Center, Glen Ellyn IL. 312-858-2800, Ext 2351

Temple, Janet A, *Librn & On-Line Servs,* GPU Service Corporation (Technical Library), Parsippany NJ. 201-263-6500, Ext 459

Temple, Julie, *Librn,* Brazoria County Library (Brazoria Branch), Brazoria TX. 713-798-2372

Temple, Nancy, *Spec Coll,* Altoona Area Public Library, Altoona PA. 814-946-0417

Temple, Patricia, *Librn,* County of Henrico Public Library (Dumbarton), Richmond VA. 804-262-6506

Temple, William A, *Librn,* Mitchell College Library, New London CT. 203-443-2811

Templeton, Carol, *ILL,* Santa Barbara Public Library, Santa Barbara CA. 805-962-7653

Templeton, Dan, *Media,* Aims Community College Library, Greeley CO. 303-330-8008, Ext 326

Templeton, Etheldra, *Asst Dir & On-Line Servs,* Medical College of Pennsylvania, Florence A Moore Library of Medicine, Philadelphia PA. 215-842-6910

Templeton, S J, *Librn,* Ridgetown College of Agriculture Technology Library, Ridgetown ON. 519-674-5456, Ext 61

Templin, Dorothy, *Dir,* Central Ontario Regional Library, Richmond Hill ON. 416-884-4395

Templin, Frances, *Librn,* Atlanta Public Library (Highland), Atlanta GA. 404-872-4291

Templin, Mrs Forest, *Librn,* Shelby County Regional Library (Alabaster), Alabaster AL. 205-669-7851

Temsky, Marlene, *Librn,* Worcester Public Library (Talking Book Library), Worcester MA. 617-752-3751, Ext 33

Tench, Terry, *Tech Serv,* Brunswick-Glynn County Regional Library, Brunswick GA. 912-264-7360

Tendallen, Eugene J, *Dir,* Standard Insurance Co, Home Office Library, Portland OR. 503-248-2885

Tener, Jean, *Archivist,* University of Calgary Library, Calgary AB. 403-284-5954

Tenhoff, Melody, *Asst Librn,* Dodge Center Public Library, Dodge Center MN. 507-374-2275

Tenhoff, Virginia, *Librn,* Dodge Center Public Library, Dodge Center MN. 507-374-2275

Tennant, Roy, *Media,* Columbia College Library, Columbia CA. 209-532-3141, Ext 228

Tennes, Debbie, *Media,* Evansville Public Library & Vanderburgh County Public Library, Evansville IN. 812-425-2621

Tenney, Kim, *Asst Librn,* Boston Architectural Center Library, Boston MA. 617-536-9018

Tenning, L, *Librn,* Okanagan Regional Library District (Osoyoos Branch), Osoyoos BC. 604-495-7637

Tensaw, Anna May, *On-Line Servs,* Smithsonian Science Information Exchange, DC. 202-745-4600

Teo, Elizabeth, *Ref,* Moraine Valley Community College, Learning Resources Center, Palos Hills IL. 312-974-4300, Ext 222

Tepedino, Ruth, *Circ,* Miami-Dade Public Library System, Miami FL. 305-579-5001

Tepper, Herbert J, *Cat,* State Historical Society of Wisconsin Library, Madison WI. 608-262-3421

Tepper, Krysta, *ILL,* Corn Belt Library System, Normal IL. 309-452-4485

Terauds, Susan, *Librn,* Houston Department of Aviation Technical Library, Houston TX. 713-443-4361

Terbille, Charles, *Librn,* Ohio University-Zanesville Campus, Herrold Hall Learning Resource Center Library, Zanesville OH. 614-453-0762

Terhaar, Florene, *Ch,* Westwood Free Public Library, Westwood NJ. 201-664-0583

Terhune, Dorothy, *Cat,* Grand Rapids Junior College, Arthur Andrews Memorial Library, Grand Rapids MI. 616-456-4841

Terhune, Joy, *Assoc Prof,* University of Kentucky, College of Library Science, KY. 606-258-8876

Terhune, Stanford, *Chmn,* Essex County Cooperating Libraries, MA. 617-774-5000, Ext 146

Terhune, Stanford, *Tech Serv & Bibliog Instr,* Gordon College, Winn Library, Wenham MA. 617-927-2300, Ext 233

Terkos, Beatrice, *Librn,* Dowagiac Public Library (Chestnut Towers), Dowagiac MI. 616-782-2195, Ext 49

Terlecky, John, *Librn,* Saint Basil's College Library, Stamford CT. 203-327-7899

Termine, Jack E, *Librn,* New York Orthopaedic Hospital, Russell A Hibbs Memorial Library, New York NY. 212-694-3294

Ternberg, Milt, *Govt Publications, Maps & Municipal Ref,* Dallas Public Library, Dallas TX. 214-748-9071

Terni, Anna, *Librn,* Harvard University Library (Biblioteca Berenson), Florence, Italy MA. 617-495-3650

Terpo, Mary A, *Librn,* Worcester County Law Library, Worcester MA. 617-756-2441, Ext 227, 254

Terrell, Alice, *YA,* Ralph Chandler Harrison Memorial Library, Carmel CA. 408-624-4629

Terrell, Darrell, *Librn,* Kent State University, Ashtabula Campus Library, Ashtabula OH. 216-964-3322, Ext 137

Terrell, Jane, *Librn,* Jacksonville Public Library System (Jacksonville Beach), Jacksonville FL. 904-246-7376

Terrell, Mary Sue, *Actg Dir,* Western Nevada Community College, Learning Resources Library, Carson City NV. 702-885-5070

Terrell, Myra, *Ref,* Grayson County Junior College Library, Denison TX. 214-465-6030, Ext 237

Terrill, Henry, *ILL, Reader Serv & Doc,* Harding University, Beaumont Memorial Library, Searcy AR. 501-268-6161, Ext 354

Terrill, Marjorie L, *Librn,* Menorah Medical Center, Robert Uhlmann Medical Library, Kansas City MO. 816-276-8171, 8172

Terry, Anita, *Reader Serv,* Mayo Foundation (Medical Library), Rochester MN. 507-284-2061

Terry, Ann Scott, *Commun Servs,* York County Library, Headquarters Rock Hill Public Library, Rock Hill SC. 803-328-8402

Terry, Constance, *In Charge,* Oysterponds Historical Society Library, Orient NY. 516-323-2480

Terry, Donna I, *ILL, Tech Serv & Cat,* West Shore Public Library, Camp Hill PA. 717-761-3900, 761-3901

Terry, Edice, *Librn,* Shoals Public Library, Shoals IN. 812-247-3591

Terry, Joan N, *Librn,* Northeast Utilities Service Co Library, Berlin CT. 203-666-6911, Ext 5141

Terry, Josephine R, *Dir,* Butte County Library, Oroville CA. 916-534-4525

Terry, Juan, *Media,* University of Florida Libraries (J Hillis Miller Health Center), Gainesville FL. 904-392-4011

Terry, M Nancy, *Per,* Grand Valley State Colleges, Zumberge Library, Allendale MI. 313-895-6611, Ext 252

Terry, Mary Jo, *Librn,* Walt Disney Productions Library, Burbank CA. 213-845-3141, Ext 2326

Terry, Mary-Isabel, *Instr,* Dalhousie University, School of Library Service, NS. 902-424-3656

Terry, Mildred, *Librn,* Chattahoochee Valley Regional Library (Fourth Avenue), Columbus GA. 404-322-1423

Terry, Spurgeon D, *Librn,* National Agricultural Library (Law), Washington DC. 202-447-7751

Terry, Steve, *Radio Readers Serv,* Memphis-Shelby County Public Library & Information Center (Science, Business, Social Sciences), Memphis TN. 901-528-2950

Terstegge, Mary Anne, *Spec Coll,* Tulare County Library System, Visalia CA. 209-733-8440

Terstegge, Mary Anne, *Librn,* Tulare County Library System (Ivanhoe Branch), Ivanhoe CA. 209-798-1264

Terukina, Charlene, *In Charge,* Hawaii State Library System (Waialua Branch), Waialua HI. 808-637-4876

Terwillegar, Jane, *Instr,* University of Georgia, Dept of Educational Media & Librarianship, GA. 404-542-3810

Terwilliger, Gail, *Ch,* Cumberland County Public Library, Anderson Street Library, Frances Brooks Stein Memorial Library, Fayetteville NC. 919-483-1580

Terzian, Sherry, *Librn,* Neuropsychiatric Institute, Professional Staff Library, Los Angeles CA. 213-825-0597, 825-0374

Terzis, Anthony, *Librn,* O M Scott & Son, Information Services, Marysville OH. 513-644-0011

Tesar, Elizabeth, *Tech Serv,* Saint Leo College Library, Saint Leo FL. 904-588-8258

Tesar, Wanita D, *Librn,* Johns Hopkins University Libraries (School of Hygiene & Public Health Interdepartmental Library), Baltimore MD. 301-955-3028

Teske, Sharon, *Asst Librn,* Grundy Center Public Library, Grundy Center IA. 319-824-3607

Teslow, Gladys, *Syst Secy,* Serra Cooperative Library System, San Diego CA. 714-278-8090

Tesoriere, Connie, *ILL,* Guernsey Memorial Library, Norwich NY. 607-334-4034

Tesseo, Edith D, *Librn,* Hampden Regional Library, Hampden ME. 207-862-3550

Tessier, Diane, *ILL,* Laurentian University Library, Bibliotheque de l'Universite Laurentienne, Sudbury ON. 705-675-1151, Ext 251 & 252

Tessier, Dorothy, *Librn,* Elk Lake Public Library, Elk Lake ON. 705-678-2340

Tessier, Judy, *Asst Prof,* Syracuse University, School of Information Studies, NY. 315-423-2911

Tessier, Yves, *Reader Serv,* Universite Laval Bibliotheque, Quebec PQ. 418-656-3344

Tessmer, Loralee, *Bkmobile Coordr,* Menominee County Library, Stephenson MI. 906-753-6923

Tessmer, Martin, *Ref,* Richland Community College, Learning Resources Center, Decatur IL. 217-875-7200

Test, Lyn, *ILL,* Steele Memorial Library, Chemung-Southern Tier Library System, Elmira NY. 607-733-9173, 733-9174, 733-9175

Testa, Dana D, *AV,* University of Oklahoma Health Sciences Center Library, Oklahoma City OK. 405-271-2285

Testa, E, *Librn,* California Postsecondary Education Commission Library, Sacramento CA. 916-445-7933

Tester, Evelyn, *Librn,* Black River Falls Public Library, Black River Falls WI. 715-284-4112

Tester, Ronald L, *Librn,* Howard County Library, Big Spring TX. 915-267-5295

Teter, Mrs Roy, *Librn,* Asbury United Methodist Church Library, Tacoma WA. 206-472-4239

Tetove, Judith, *Librn,* Los Angeles Public Library System (Vermont Square), Los Angeles CA. 213-293-7138

Tetrault, Ruth, *Acq,* Bibliotheque Nationale Du Quebec, Montreal PQ. 514-873-4553

Tetrault, Yvette, *Ch,* Glenview Public Library, Glenview IL. 312-724-5200

Tetreau, Richard D, *Dir,* Saint Peter's College, Theresa & Edward O'Tool Library, Jersey City NJ. 201-333-4400, Ext 228

Tetrick, Arthur F, *Asst Dir & ILL,* Warner Southern College, Learning Resource Center, Lake Wales FL. 813-638-1426, Ext 28

Tetrick, Jean, *Bkmobile Coordr,* Paris-Bourbon County Library, Paris KY. 606-987-4419

Tetzlaff, Charles, *Dir,* Gogebic Community College, Alex D Chisholm Learning Resource Center, Ironwood MI. 906-932-4231, Ext 211

Teverbaugh, Mac, *Chief Librn,* Orange County Public Library (West Garden Grove Branch), Garden Grove CA. 714-897-2594

Tevis, Raymond H, *Assoc Prof,* Ball State University, Dept of Library Science, IN. 317-285-7180, 285-7189

Tew, Robin, *Cat,* Kansas City Kansas Public Library, Kansas City KS. 913-621-3073

Tewksbury, Geneva, *Cat,* Saugus Public Library, Saugus MA. 617-233-0530

Texter, Dorothy, *Librn,* Delton District Library, Delton MI. 616-623-8040

Thacker, Mrs Carl, *Librn,* Hart County Public Library, Munfordville KY. 502-524-9953

Thaden, Irma, *Librn,* Angie Williams Cox Library, Pardeeville WI. 608-429-2354

Thaden, June, *Tech Serv,* Central Methodist College, George M Smiley Memorial Library, Fayette MO. 816-248-3391, Ext 261

Thakore, Manhar, *Acq,* Illinois State University, Milner Library, Normal IL. 309-438-3675

Thal, Esther, *Dir,* Bank of America (Law Library), San Francisco CA. 415-622-6040

Thal, Esther G, *Librn,* Thelen, Marrin, Johnson & Bridges, Law Library, San Francisco CA. 415-392-6320, Ext 306

Thalken, Thomas T, *Dir,* General Services Administration - National Archives & Records Service, Herbert Hoover Presidential Library, West Branch IA. 319-643-5301

Thapar, Shashi P, *Librn,* Maryland State Department of Natural Resources Library, Annapolis MD. 301-269-3015

Tharand, Cynthia M, *Librn,* Mesa County Medical Society, Medical Library, Grand Junction CO. 303-242-1550, Ext 721

Tharp, Mrs Ralph, *Dir,* Alamosa Southern Peaks Public Library, Alamosa CO. 303-589-6592

Thatcher, Edward P, *Librn,* University of Oregon Library (Map), Eugene OR. 503-686-3051

Thatcher, Linda, *Librn,* Utah State Historical Society Library, Salt Lake City UT. 801-533-5808, 533-5809

Thaxter, Pamela, *Pre-Cat,* Temple University of the Commonwealth System of Higher Education, Samuel Paley Library, Philadelphia PA. 215-787-8231

Thaxton, Carlton J, *Asst Dir,* Lake Blackshear Regional Library, Americus GA. 912-924-8091

Thaxton, Carol J, *Librn,* Federal Reserve Bank of Saint Louis, Saint Louis MO. 314-444-8552

Thayer, Richard, *Ref,* Janesville Public Library, Janesville WI. 608-752-8934, Ext B

Thayer, Shirley, *Spec Coll,* Maine State Library, Augusta ME. 207-289-3561

Thayer, W Gaye, *Librn,* Paw Paw Public Library, Paw Paw WV. 304-947-7013

The-Mulliner, Lian, *Southeast Asia,* Ohio University, Vernon R Alden Library, Athens OH. 614-594-5228

Theall, John N, *Pub Servs,* University of Illinois at the Medical Center, Library of the Health Sciences, Chicago IL. 312-996-8974

Theberge, Elaine, *On-Line Servs & Bibliog Instr,* Seminaire Saint-Augustin Bibliotheque, Cap-Rouge PQ. 418-872-0954

TheBerge, Marjorie, *Dir,* Ranger Junior College, Learning Resource Center Library, Ranger TX. 817-647-3234

Thede, Barbara, *Circ,* Tarrant County Junior College System (Northeast Campus Learning Resource Center), Hurst TX. 817-281-7860, Ext 477

Theilman, Jim, *Dir,* Mesa Community College, Library Technician Program, AZ. 602-833-1261

Theilmann, James W, *Dir,* Mesa Community College Library, Mesa AZ. 602-833-1261, Ext 291, 201

Theisen, Jeannette, *Adm Asst,* Great River Regional Library, Saint Cloud MN. 612-251-7282

Thelin, Sonya R, *ILL, Ref & Bibliog Instr,* Robert Morris College Library, Coraopolis PA. 412-264-9300

Theobald, H Rupert, *Bureau Chief,* Wisconsin Legislative Reference Bureau Library, Madison WI. 608-266-0341

Theobold, Sister Joanice, *Librn,* Briar Cliff College Library, Sioux City IA. 712-279-5450

Theodorakopoulos, Danae, *Librn,* Centre Hospitalier Maisonneuve-Rosemont, Bibliotheque Medicale, Montreal PQ. 514-254-8341

Theodos, Cytheria, *Dir,* Dreyfus Corp Library, New York NY. 212-935-8405

Theologides, Maro, *Librn,* Honeywell, Inc (Systems & Research Center Library), Minneapolis MN. 612-378-4238

Theriault, Anita, *Libr Asst I,* Chaleur Regional Library (Msgr Paquet), Caraquet NB. 506-727-2070

Theriault, Betty, *In Charge,* Eastern Counties Regional Library (Sherbrooke Branch), Sherbrooke NS. 902-747-2597

Theriault, Emile, *Tech Serv,* Dartmouth Regional Library, Dartmouth NS. 902-466-7623

Theriault, Susan, *Ch,* Leominster Public Library, Leominster MA. 617-537-0941

Therien, Madeleine, *Librn,* Bibliotheque Municipale, Lachute PQ. 514-562-4092

Therriault, Linda L, *Librn,* Griffin Free Public Library, Auburn NH. 603-483-2400

Therriault, Susan A, *Librn,* Millbury Public Library, Millbury MA. 617-865-2291

Therrien, Elyse, *Librn,* Domtar Ltd Library, Montreal PQ. 514-282-5039

Therrien, Frances, *Librn,* Sundridge-Strong Union Public Library, Sundridge ON. 705-384-5222

Thery, Kenneth, *Ch,* Okmulgee Public Library, Okmulgee OK. 918-756-1448

Thews, Dorothy, *Lit,* Minneapolis Public Library & Information Center, Minneapolis MN. 612-372-6500

Thibeault, Margaret, *Bkmobile Coordr,* Maine State Library, Augusta ME. 207-289-3561

Thibodaux, Goldie, *ILL,* Saint Mary Parish Library, Franklin LA. 318-828-5364

Thibodeau, Patricia L, *Librn,* Women & Infants Hospital of Rhode Island, Medical Library, Providence RI. 401-274-1100, Ext 578

Thibodeau, Ralph A, *Librn,* Del Mar College Library (Music), Corpus Christi TX. 512-881-6308

Thibodeaux, Diane, *ILL, Ref & Commun Servs,* Jefferson County Library, Nederland TX. 713-727-2735, 727-2736

Thiedeman, Mary P, *Instr,* West Virginia Wesleyan College, Dept of Library Science, WV. 304-473-8059

Thiedeman, Mary P, *Ref,* West Virginia Wesleyan College, Annie Merner Pfeiffer Library, Buckhannon WV. 304-473-8059

Thiel, Clara, *Secy,* Salmo Public Library, Salmo BC. 604-357-2312

Thiel, Elinor, *Tech Serv & Ref,* Dallas Public Library, Dallas OR. 503-623-2633

Thiel, Lucie A, *Librn,* Weyauwega Public Library, Weyauwega WI. 414-867-3742

Thiele, Joel K, *Ref,* Malden Public Library, Malden MA. 617-324-0218

Thiele, Judith C, *Ref & Spec Coll,* University of British Columbia Library (Charles Crane Memorial Library), Vancouver BC. 604-228-6111

Thiele, Paul E, *Chief Librn,* University of British Columbia Library (Charles Crane Memorial Library), Vancouver BC. 604-228-6111

Thielke, Eva, *Librn,* Ackley Public Library, Ackley IA. 515-847-2503

Thielman, Paul, *YA,* Musser Public Library, Muscatine IA. 319-263-3065

Thiesen, Clara, *ILL,* Vancouver Community College Libraries, Vancouver BC. 604-688-1111

Thigpen, Ann, *Asst Dir,* Sampson-Clinton Public Library, Clinton NC. 919-592-4153

Thigpen, M, *Circ,* Georgia Institute of Technology, Price Gilbert Memorial Library, Atlanta GA. 404-894-4510

Thigpen, Nettie H, *Ref,* Fayetteville State University, Charles W Chesnutt Library, Fayetteville NC. 919-486-1232

Thigpen, Ruth, *Librn,* Louisiana College, Norton Memorial Library, Pineville LA. 318-487-7201

Thodeson, Kathryn, *Ref,* Case Western Reserve University & Cleveland Medical Library Association, Cleveland Health Sciences Library, Cleveland OH. 216-368-3426

Thogersen, Elmer H, *Librn,* United States Department of Housing & Urban Development, Region V Library, Chicago IL. 312-353-0623

Tholfsen, Jean, *Ref,* Whatcom County Public Library, Bellingham WA. 206-384-3150

Thollon, Therese, *Librn,* Bibliotheque Municipale, Repenetigny PQ. 514-581-3320

Thom, Rupert C, *Librn,* United States Air Force (England Air Force Base Library), England AFB LA. 318-448-2100

Thomann, Dorothy, *Librn,* Huffman Memorial United Methodist Church Library, Saint Joseph MO. 816-233-0239

Thomas, Alan W, *Ext,* Free Library of Philadelphia, Philadelphia PA. 215-686-5322

Thomas, Alice, *Circ,* Lake City Community College, G T Melton Learning Resources Center, Lake City FL. 904-752-1822, Ext 260

Thomas, Ann, *Asst Librn,* George P & Susan Platt Cady Library, Nichols NY. 607-699-3835

Thomas, Anne White, *Huntsville Heritage,* Huntsville-Madison County Public Library, Huntsville AL. 205-536-0021

Thomas, Arthur, *Ref,* Southern University Library (Law Library), Baton Rouge LA. 504-771-3776

Thomas, Barbara, *Med Res,* Texas A&m University Libraries (Medical Sciences), College Station TX. 713-845-7427, 845-7428

Thomas, Bernadine C, *Dir,* Northern Virginia Community College Libraries (Loudoun Campus), Sterling VA. 703-323-4657

Thomas, Bess, *Librn,* Tellico Plains Public Library, Tellico Plains TN. 615-253-7388

Thomas, Bonnie, *Librn,* New Virginia Public Library, New Virginia IA. 515-449-3614

Thomas, Bruce, *Dir & ILL,* Antioch College, Olive Kettering Memorial Library, Yellow Springs OH. 513-767-7331, Ext 229

Thomas, Bruce E, *Head Reader Serv,* Lock Haven State College, George B Stevenson Library, Lock Haven PA. 717-893-2309

Thomas, C Diane, *Cat,* Ohio County Public Library, Wheeling WV. 304-232-0244

Thomas, Carol Jean, *Librn,* Hale & Dorr Library, Boston MA. 617-742-9100

Thomas, Caroline D, *Dir,* New Martinsville Public Library, New Martinsville WV. 304-455-4545

Thomas, Carrie, *ILL,* Monmouth County Library, Freehold NJ. 201-431-7220

Thomas, Cathlyn, *Librn,* Fort Sanders Presbyterian Hospital, Nursing-Medical Library, Knoxville TN. 615-546-2811, Ext 1293

Thomas, D A, *Tech Serv,* University of Kansas Medical Center, College of Health Sciences & Hospital, Clendening Library, Kansas City KS. 913-588-7166

Thomas, Dathine, *Librn,* Paragould Public Library (Randolph County), Pocahontas AR. 501-892-5617

Thomas, David, *Librn,* Cornell University Libraries (Entomology), Ithaca NY. 607-256-3265

Thomas, David A, *Dir,* Brigham Young University (Law Library), Provo UT. 801-378-3593

Thomas, David H, *Cat,* Michigan Technological University Library, Houghton MI. 906-487-2500

Thomas, Dorothy L, *Librn,* Community Library, Ketchum ID. 208-726-3493

Thomas, Ellen, *Librn,* Cornell University Libraries (Physical Sciences), Ithaca NY. 607-256-5288

Thomas, Eugenie St, *Reader Serv,* County College of Morris, Sherman H Masten Learning Resource Center, Randolph Township NJ. 201-361-5000, Ext 470

Thomas, Evelyne B, *Acq,* Davidson College, E H Little Library, Davidson NC. 704-892-2000, Ext 331

Thomas, Florence, *Tech Serv,* Idaho Falls Public Library, Idaho Falls ID. 208-529-1450

Thomas, Georgette, *Ch,* Bolivar County Library, Robinson-Carpenter Memorial Library, Cleveland MS. 601-843-2774

Thomas, Gillian M V, *Lectr,* Dalhousie University, School of Library Service, NS. 902-424-3656

Thomas, Greg, *Librn,* Amarillo Public Library (North), Amarillo TX. 806-378-3048, 378-3049

Thomas, Helen Lind, *Ch,* Kanawha County Public Library, Kanawha County Service Center, Charleston WV. 304-343-4646

Thomas, Helena, *Librn,* Newark Public Library (Weequahic), Newark NJ. 201-733-7751

Thomas, Henry, *Dir,* Maurice M Pine Free Public Library, Fair Lawn NJ. 201-796-3400

Thomas, Howard, *Librn,* Saint Louis Public Library (Divoll), Saint Louis MO. 314-534-0313

Thomas, J Donald, *Head,* University of Maryland at College Park (Undergraduate), College Park MD. 301-454-4743

Thomas, James L, *Instr,* North Texas State University, School of Library & Information Sciences, TX. 817-788-2445

Thomas, Janet, *Commun Servs,* Salt Lake City Public Library, Salt Lake City UT. 801-363-5733

Thomas, Janice, *Asst Dir,* Pacific Northwest Bibliographic Center, (PNBC), WA. 206-543-1878

Thomas, Jean, *Librn,* Iowa Veteran's Home Library, Marshalltown IA. 515-752-1510

Thomas, Jean L, *Ref,* Santa Fe Community College Library, Gainesville FL. 904-377-5161, Ext 315

Thomas, Jeanete, *AV,* Hanover College, Duggan Library, Hanover IN. 812-866-2151, Ext 333

Thomas, Jeanne F, *Librn,* Merrill-Palmer Institute (Kresge Historical Library in Child Development & Family Life), Detroit MI. 313-875-7450

Thomas, Jeanne F, *Librn,* Merrill-Palmer Institute (Edna Noble White Library), Detroit MI. 313-875-7450

Thomas, Jennifer E, *Librn,* Holy Cross Hospital Library, Calgary AB. 403-266-7231

Thomas, Joann, *Ch,* Satilla Regional Library, Douglas GA. 912-384-4667, 384-1172

Thomas, John B, *Dean,* Davidson County Community College, Grady E Love Learning Resources Center, Lexington NC. 704-249-8186, Ext 270

Thomas, Karen, *Ref,* Woolworth Community Library, Jal NM. 505-395-3268

Thomas, Lawrence, *Dir,* Seattle University, A A Lemieux Library, Seattle WA. 206-626-6859

Thomas, Leah D, *Librn,* H B Maynard & Company, Inc Library, Pittsburgh PA. 412-351-4100

Thomas, Lois, *Librn,* Santa Clara County Free Library (Saratoga Community), Saratoga CA. 408-293-2326

Thomas, Lois, *Librn,* Santa Clara County Free Library (Saratoga Village Branch), Saratoga CA. 408-867-3893

Thomas, Lorna L, *Librn,* Knoxville Public Library, Knoxville IA. 515-842-5512

Thomas, Lou, *Librn,* Capital City Press, State-Times & Morning Advocate Newspapers Library, Baton Rouge LA. 504-383-1111

Thomas, Lynda, *Asst Dir, Ad & On-Line Servs,* Cheshire Public Library, Cheshire CT. 203-272-2245

Thomas, M Rosemary, *Dir,* Schreiner College, W M Logan Library, Kerrville TX. 512-896-5411, Ext 64

Thomas, Mabel, *Reader Serv,* National Defense University Library, Washington DC. 202-693-8437

Thomas, Mae, *Acq,* Kanawha County Public Library, Kanawha County Service Center, Charleston WV. 304-343-4646

Thomas, Marcia, *Tech Serv,* Bloomington Public Library, Bloomington IL. 309-828-6091

Thomas, Marcine, *Librn,* Patrick Henry School District Public Library (Hamler), Hamler OH. 419-274-3821

Thomas, Mark, *Central Libr Supvr,* Aurora Public Library, Aurora CO. 303-750-5000, Ext 410

Thomas, Martha, *Dir,* Buena Vista Public Library, Northern Chaffee County Regional Library, Buena Vista CO. 303-395-8700

Thomas, Marvin, *Dir,* Howard County Library, Columbia MD. 301-997-8000

Thomas, Mary, *Circ,* Belmont Abbey College, Abbot Vincent Taylor Library, Belmont NC. 704-825-3711, Ext 342

Thomas, Mary, *Ref,* Burlington County Library, Mount Holly NJ. 609-267-9660

Thomas, Mary, *Cat,* Talbot County Free Library, Easton MD. 301-822-1626

Thomas, Mary, *Coll Development,* University of North Carolina at Chapel Hill (Health Sciences Library), Chapel Hill NC. 919-966-2111

Thomas, Mary A, *Librn,* First United Methodist Church, Jennie E Weaver Memorial Library, Gloversville NY. 518-725-9313

Thomas, Mary Ann, *Acq,* Lakewood Public Library, Lakewood OH. 216-226-8275

Thomas, Mary Elizabeth, *Librn,* Missouri Division of Corrections Libraries (State Correctional Pre-Release Center), Jefferson City MO. 314-751-3050

Thomas, Mary F, *Librn,* Yorkville Public Library, Yorkville IL. 312-553-5513

Thomas, Mary Lou, *Librn,* New York Genealogical & Biographical Society Library, New York NY. 212-755-8532

Thomas, Milton U, *Media,* Palm Beach Junior College, Library Learning Resources Center, Lake Worth FL. 305-965-8000, Ext 213

Thomas, Mrs Frankie T, *Ref,* University of Alabama, Amelia Gayle Gorgas Library, University AL. 205-348-5298

Thomas, Mrs Gordon, *Librn,* Laurel-Jones County Library (Victoria Park Library), Laurel MS. 601-428-4313

Thomas, Mrs Kodell M, *Librn,* Veterans Administration, Hospital Library, Dublin GA. 912-272-1210, Ext 229

Thomas, Mrs M H, *Tech Serv,* Savannah State College Library, Savannah GA. 912-356-2183, 356-2184

Thomas, Mrs Martin, *Librn,* First Christian Church Library, Saint Joseph MO. 816-233-2556

Thomas, Naomi T, *Inner City Servs,* Carnegie Library of Pittsburgh, Pittsburgh PA. 412-622-3100

Thomas, Oretha, *Books-By-Mail Coordr,* Eastern Oklahoma District Library System, Muskogee OK. 918-683-2846

Thomas, Page, *ILL,* Southern Methodist University Libraries (Bridwell Theology), Dallas TX. 692-3258 (Off), 692-3230 (Ref)

Thomas, Patricia, *Tech Serv & Cat,* Burlingame Public Library, Burlingame CA. 415-344-7107

Thomas, Patricia U, *Dir,* Tidewater Community College, Chesapeake Campus Library, Chesapeake VA. 804-547-9271, Ext 261-269

Thomas, Patsy, *Research Spec,* Sterling Drug, Inc, Sterling-Winthrop Research Institute Library, Rensselaer NY. 518-445-8260

Thomas, Paul W, *Dir,* Wesleyan Church, Archives & Historical Library, Marion IN. 317-674-3301, Ext 189

Thomas, Pearl M, *Librn,* Philosophical Research Society Library, Los Angeles CA. 213-663-2167

Thomas, Rhonda, *Dir,* California Christian College Library, Fresno CA. 209-251-4215

Thomas, Ritchie, *Dir,* Wright State University Library, Dayton OH. 513-873-2380

Thomas, Ritchie D, *Chmn Libr Div,* Dayton-Miami Valley Consortium, OH. 513-278-9105

Thomas, Ruth, *Librn,* Shreve Memorial Library (Means), Ida LA. 318-221-2614

Thomas, Sam, *ILL,* Fort Worth Public Library, Fort Worth TX. 817-870-7700

Thomas, Satoko, *Per,* Merrimack College, McQuade Library, North Andover MA. 617-683-7111, Ext 210

Thomas, Sidney S, *Acq,* Georgia State University, William Russell Pullen Library, Atlanta GA. 404-658-2185, 658-2172

Thomas, Susan, *Librn,* Alexander Grant & Co Library (Chicago Office Library), Chicago IL. 312-856-0001

Thomas, Susan, *Librn,* Holmes Library, Boonton NJ. 201-334-2980

Thomas, Sylvia F, *Dir, Ad & Acq,* Vestavia Hills Library, Vestavia Hills AL. 205-823-0520, 823-0521

Thomas, Victoria M, *Ser,* University of North Florida Library, Jacksonville FL. 904-646-2553

Thomas, Virginia, *Cat,* Pensacola Junior College, Learning Resource Center, Pensacola FL. 904-476-5410

Thomas, Sr, Robert D, *Librn,* Sauk Valley College, Learning Resources Center, Dixon IL. 815-288-5511, Ext 247

Thomas-Jackson, Penny, *Asst Dir,* Illinois College of Podiatric Medicine Library, Chicago IL. 312-280-2891

Thomason, Nevada, *Asst Prof,* University of New Mexico, Library Media Education, NM. 505-277-5141

Thomassen, Cora, *Assoc Prof,* University of Illinois, Graduate School of Library Science, IL. 217-333-3280

Thomasson, Carmen S, *Spec Coll,* South Carolina State College, Miller F Whittaker Library, Orangeburg SC. 803-536-7045, 536-7046

Thomasson, Zelma M, *On-Line Servs,* Sampson Technical College Library, Clinton NC. 919-592-8081, Ext 250

Thomen, Harold, *Rare Bks,* Centre County Library & Historical Museum, Bellefonte PA. 814-355-3131

Thommes, Bonnie Kay, *Librn,* Danvers Township Library, Danvers IL. 309-963-4269

Thommes, Dorothy, *ILL,* Morton Grove Public Library, Morton Grove IL. 312-965-4220

Thompson, Alleen, *Librn,* General Electric Co, Nuclear Energy Group Library, San Jose CA. 408-925-3522

Thompson, Allie, *Teacher Educ Mat Ctr,* North Carolina Agricultural & Technical State University, F D Bluford Library, Greensboro NC. 919-379-7782, 379-7783

Thompson, Alma, *Librn,* Sterling Public Library, Sterling NE. 402-866-2421

Thompson, Amelia, *Asst Dir,* Bartlesville Wesleyan College Library, Bartlesville OK. 918-333-6151, Ext 225

Thompson, Ann, *Ext Adminr,* Clark County Library District, Las Vegas NV. 702-733-7810

Thompson, Ann, *Coll Develop,* University of Texas at San Antonio Library, San Antonio TX. 512-691-4570

Thompson, Anne, *Dir,* Butler Public Library, Butler WI. 414-781-3180

Thompson, Annie, *Music,* University of Puerto Rico Library, Jose M Lazaro Memorial Library, Rio Piedras PR. 809-764-0000, Ext 3296

Thompson, Arlene, *Librn,* Kitsap Regional Library (Kingston Station), Kingston WA. 206-297-3330

Thompson, B, *Librn,* Cambridge Municipal Public Library (Preston), Cambridge ON. 519-653-3632

Thompson, B Dolores, *Dir,* Fenton Historical Society, Historical Center Library, Jamestown NY. 716-661-2296

Thompson, Barbara, *Librn,* Economics Research Associates Library, Los Angeles CA. 213-477-9585

Thompson, Barbara, *Cat,* Olivet College Burrage Library, Olivet MI. 616-749-7608

Thompson, Barbara E, *ILL & Circ,* Hood College of Frederick, Joseph Henry Apple Library, Frederick MD. 301-663-3131, Ext 364, 365

Thompson, Becky, *MLS & Records Asst,* Southern Natural Gas Co, Corporate Library, Birmingham AL. 205-325-7409

Thompson, Berneice, *Dir,* Husson College Library, Bangor ME. 207-945-5641, Ext 322

Thompson, Bert A, *Dir,* Illinois Benedictine College, Theodore Lownik Library, Lisle IL. 312-968-7270, Ext 286

Thompson, Betty L, *Asst Dir,* North Baltimore Public Library, North Baltimore OH. 419-257-2196

Thompson, Bill, *Dir,* Performing Arts Foundation, Arts-In-Education Resource Center, Huntington Station NY. 516-261-0050

Thompson, Bryan, *Chief Librn,* American Samoa Community College, Learning Resources Center, Pago Pago, Samoa PI. 688-9155, Ext 24

Thompson, C, *In Charge,* British Columbia Ministry of Forests, Branch Library, Nelson BC. 604-354-4181, Ext 278

Thompson, Celestine, *Librn,* Perry Memorial Library, Perryton TX. 806-435-5801

THOMPSON

Thompson, Charles, *Dir,* Patterson Library, Westfield NY. 716-326-2154

Thompson, Charlotte, *Librn,* Tombigbee Regional Library (Nettleton Public), Nettleton MS. 601-963-2014

Thompson, Christine E, *Tech Serv & Cat,* Tarleton State University Library, Stephenville TX. 817-968-9246

Thompson, Clare T, *Librn,* Sperry Corp, Business Planning Library, New York NY. 212-956-3476

Thompson, Cleo B, *Ref,* Washington County Public Library, Abingdon VA. 703-628-2971

Thompson, Corinne, *Librn,* Nortonville Public Library, Nortonville KS. 913-886-2060

Thompson, D, *Ch,* Chatham Public Library, Chatham ON. 519-354-2940

Thompson, Deborah, *Med Ref & Search Analyst,* Indiana University (School of Medicine Library), Indianapolis IN. 317-264-7182

Thompson, Devona, *Cat,* Greenville Area Public Library, Greenville PA. 412-588-5490

Thompson, Diane, *Ch,* Pierce County Rural Library District, Tacoma WA. 206-572-6760

Thompson, Dianne, *Dir,* United States Navy (Navy Environmental Support Office, Information Retrieval Branch), Port Hueneme CA. 805-982-5952, Ext 4822

Thompson, Don, *Dir,* Merced College, Lesher Library, Merced CA. 209-723-4321, Ext 274

Thompson, Don, *Ref,* University of Southern California, Edward L Doheny Memorial Library, Los Angeles CA. 213-743-6050

Thompson, Donald, *Business,* Southern Illinois University at Edwardsville, Elijah P Lovejoy Library, Edwardsville IL. 618-692-2711

Thompson, Donna, *Librn,* Chestatee Regional Library (Lula Branch), Lula GA. 404-869-7172

Thompson, Doris L, *Dir,* Velma Teague Library, Glendale Public Library, Glendale AZ. 602-931-5576

Thompson, Dorothea, *ILL,* Carnegie-Mellon University, Hunt Library, Pittsburgh PA. 412-578-2446, 578-2447

Thompson, Dorothea, *Asst Librn,* Creighton Public Library, Creighton NE. 402-358-5115

Thompson, Earle C, *Dir Libr Serv,* University of Montana, Maureen & Mike Mansfield Library, Missoula MT. 406-243-6800

Thompson, Eleanor E, *Dir,* Wenham Historical Association & Museum Inc, Col Timothy Pickering Library, Wenham MA. 617-468-2377

Thompson, Elizabeth J, *Circ,* Alabama State University, Library & Learning Resources, Montgomery AL. 205-832-6072

Thompson, Elizabeth M, *Dir,* Ilion Free Public Library, Ilion NY. 315-894-2151

Thompson, Ellen, *Outreach & AV Coordr,* Riverside City & County Public Library, Riverside CA. 714-787-7211

Thompson, Elliott, *Dir,* Dixie Regional Library, Pontotoc MS. 601-489-3522

Thompson, Elsie, *Librn,* Abbott Memorial Library, South Pomfret VT. 802-457-2046

Thompson, Emma W, *Librn,* Enterprise Public Library, Enterprise AL. 205-347-2636

Thompson, Evan, *Br Coordr,* Detroit Public Library, Detroit Associated Libraries, Detroit MI. 313-833-1000

Thompson, F H, *Dir,* South Texas College of Law Library, Houston TX. 713-659-8040, Ext 35

Thompson, Florence, *Librn,* Montgomery Memorial Library, Jewell IA. 515-827-5112

Thompson, Frances, *ILL,* Medford Public Library, Medford MA. 617-395-7950

Thompson, Gary B, *Pub Servs, On-Line Servs & Bibliog Instr,* Hobart & William Smith Colleges, Warren Hunting Smith Library, Geneva NY. 315-789-5500, Ext 224

Thompson, Geneva, *Librn,* Effingham Free Public Library, Effingham NH. 603-539-6370

Thompson, Georgia, *Librn,* Cass County Library (Mason-Union), Edwardsburg MI. 616-445-8651

Thompson, Glayce, *ILL,* Whitman County Library, Colfax WA. 509-397-4366

Thompson, Glee, *Librn,* Blakesburg Public Library, Blakesburg IA. 515-938-2845

Thompson, Glenn, *Chmn,* University of Wisconsin-Eau Claire, Dept of Library Science & Media Education, WI. 715-836-2635

Thompson, Helen, *Librn,* Commonwealth Edison Co Library, Chicago IL. 312-294-4321

Thompson, Helen, *Librn,* Robbins Library (Victoria Dallin), Arlington MA. 617-643-3005

Thompson, Irene, *Librn,* Tufts Library (Franklin N Pratt Library), East Weymouth MA. 617-337-1677

Thompson, J, *Media,* Halton Hills Public Libraries, Georgetown ON. 416-877-2631

Thompson, J A, *Circ,* University of Alabama in Birmingham (Lister Hill Library of the Health Sciences), Birmingham AL. 205-934-5460

Thompson, James C, *Tech Serv,* Johns Hopkins University Libraries (Milton S Eisenhower Library), Baltimore MD. 301-338-8325

Thompson, James H, *Dir,* University of North Carolina at Greensboro, Walter Clinton Jackson Library, Greensboro NC. 919-379-5880

Thompson, James J, *Chmn,* University of South Alabama, Dept of Educational Media, AL. 205-460-6201

Thompson, Jane, *Ser Libr,* University of Oregon Health Sciences Center (Health Sciences Library), Portland OR. 503-225-8026

Thompson, Jane E, *Librn,* Colorado State District Court Law Library, Denver CO. 303-575-2233

Thompson, Janice, *Librn,* Buffalo General Hospital (A H Aaron Medical Library), Buffalo NY. 716-845-2888

Thompson, Jean, *ILL & Ref,* Columbia Basin College, Library Media Center, Pasco WA. 509-547-0511, Ext 287

Thompson, Jean, *Info Specialists,* Digital Equipment Corp, Corporate Library, Maynard MA. 617-493-6231, 493-5821

Thompson, Jean, *Librn,* Fort Vancouver Regional Library (Goldendale Community), Goldendale WA. 509-773-4487

Thompson, Jean, *ILL, Circ & Ref,* Middlesex Community College Library, Middletown CT. 203-344-3062, 344-3063, 344-3064

Thompson, Jean, *Chief Librn,* Orange County Public Library (Villa Park Branch), Villa Park CA. 714-998-0861

Thompson, Jean, *Librn,* Public Service Company of Oklahoma, Reference Center, Tulsa OK. 918-583-3611, Ext 2367

Thompson, Jean, *Asst Librn,* Rock Springs Public Library, Rock Springs WY. 307-362-6212

Thompson, Jean T, *Soc Sci,* Virginia Polytechnic Institute & State University Library, Blacksburg VA. 703-961-5593

Thompson, Jennifer, *Ad,* Chillicothe & Ross County Public Library, Chillicothe OH. 614-773-4145

Thompson, Jennifer, *Asst Dir,* Chillicothe & Ross County Public Library, Chillicothe OH. 614-773-4145

Thompson, Jesse R, *Chief Librn,* Orange County Public Library (Brea Branch), Brea CA. 714-529-3277

Thompson, Jo-Anne, *In Charge,* Parks Canada, Prairie Region Library, Winnipeg MB. 204-949-5941

Thompson, Johanna, *Ref & Doc,* Delaware Law School Library of Widener University, Wilmington DE. 302-478-5280

Thompson, John, *Tech Serv,* Citrus College, Hayden Memorial Library, Azusa CA. 213-335-0521, Ext 290, 291

Thompson, John, *Librn,* United States Navy (Naval Ship Engineering Center Library), Norfolk VA. 804-444-1521

Thompson, John M, *Dir,* Spokane Falls Community College, Library Media Services, Spokane WA. 509-456-2860

Thompson, Judith A, *Ref,* California State College, Stanislaus Library, Turlock CA. 209-633-2232

Thompson, Judy, *Asst Librn,* Federal Reserve Bank of Saint Louis, Saint Louis MO. 314-444-8552

Thompson, K, *Cat,* Atlantic Christian College, Hackney Library, Wilson NC. 919-237-3161, Ext 330

Thompson, Karen, *Dir,* Piedmont Technical College, Learning Resources Center, Roxboro NC. 919-599-1181, Ext 266

Thompson, Karolyn, *ILL,* University of Southern Mississippi, Cook Memorial Library, Hattiesburg MS. 601-266-7301

Thompson, Katherine, *Ref,* Niagara County Community College, Library Learning Center, Sanborn NY. 716-731-3271, Ext 145

Thompson, Kathleen, *Dir,* Cass County Library, Cassopolis MI. 616-445-8651

Thompson, Kathy, *Ref,* Carrollton Public Library, Carrollton TX. 214-323-5014

Thompson, Kathy, *Librn,* Honeywell, Inc, Solid State Electronics Library, Plymouth MN. 612-541-2075

Thompson, LaDonna, *Librn,* MTS Systems Corp, Information Services, Minneapolis MN. 612-944-4000

Thompson, Linda, *Cat,* University of Texas at San Antonio Library, San Antonio TX. 512-691-4570

Thompson, Linda L, *Librn,* World Bank Law Library, Washington DC. 202-676-1288

Thompson, Lois, *Librn,* Stey-Nevant Public Library, Farrell PA. 412-347-7295

Thompson, Lola, *Dir,* Saint Mary Parish Library, Franklin LA. 318-828-5364

Thompson, Loren, *Sch Librn,* Community Library, Roundup MT. 406-323-1802

Thompson, Lucille, *Ref,* Montana State University, Roland R Renne Library, Bozeman MT. 406-994-3119

Thompson, M A, *Info Chemist,* El Paso Products Co Library, Odessa TX. 915-337-2811

Thompson, Margaret, *Librn,* Eckels Memorial Library, Oakland Public Library, Oakland IA. 712-482-6668

Thompson, Marie, *Actg Dir,* Banning Public Library, Banning CA. 714-849-3192

Thompson, Marilyn, *Dir,* Ledding Library of Milwaukie, Milwaukie Public Library, Milwaukie OR. 503-659-3911

Thompson, Marilyn L, *Librn,* United States Air Force (Fairchild Air Force Base Library), Fairchild AFB WA. 509-247-5556, 247-5228

Thompson, Marilyn T, *Dir Libr Serv & Acq,* George Williams College Library, Downers Grove IL. 312-964-3100, Ext 242

Thompson, Martha, *Spec Coll,* Brookdale Community College, Learning Resources Center, Lincroft NJ. 201-842-1900, Ext 392

Thompson, Martin L, *Chmn,* Slippery Rock State College, Dept of Library Science, PA. 412-794-7321

Thompson, Mary, *Librn,* Woodville State Hospital, Professional Library, Carnegie PA. 412-279-2000, Ext 487

Thompson, Mary E, *Pub Servs,* Tidewater Community College, Frederick Campus Library, Portsmouth VA. 804-484-2121, Ext 226

Thompson, Mary Sue, *Librn,* Oregon State Water Resources Department Library, Salem OR. 503-378-3671

Thompson, Mrs D E, *Librn,* Anthon Public Library, Anthon IA. 712-373-5275

Thompson, Mrs Don, *Cat,* Crawfordsville District Public Library, Crawfordsville IN. 317-362-2242

Thompson, Mrs Hugh, *Librn,* Columbia-Lafayette-Ouachita-Calhoun Regional Library (Bearden Branch), Bearden AR. 501-234-1991

Thompson, Mrs M M, *Librn,* Bloomfield Hallowell Public Library, Bloomfield ON. 613-393-3400

Thompson, Nadine, *Trade Ref Ass't,* United States Department of Commerce, Saint Louis District Office Library, Saint Louis MO. 314-425-3302

Thompson, Orin, *Microforms,* University of Wisconsin-La Crosse, Murphy Library, La Crosse WI. 608-785-8505

Thompson, Pat, *Media,* Brookhaven College, Learning Resources Center, Farmers Branch TX. 214-746-5250

Thompson, Patricia, *Circ,* Citizens Library, Washington PA. 412-222-2400

Thompson, Patricia A, *Librn,* Bryant & Stratton Business Institute Library, Buffalo NY. 716-884-9120

Thompson, Paul F, *Dir,* Lompoc Public Library, Lompoc CA. 805-736-3477

Thompson, Phillis D, *Librn,* Daniels County Free Library, Scobey MT. 406-487-5502

Thompson, Phyllis, *Ch,* Public Library of Columbus & Franklin County, Columbus OH. 614-864-8050

Thompson, R, *Librn,* Hamilton Public Library (Westdale), Hamilton ON. 416-528-1668

Thompson, Richard E, *Dir,* Wilmette Public Library District, Wilmette IL. 312-256-5025

Thompson, Richard M, *Librn,* Georgia-Pacific Historical Museum Library, Portland OR. 503-222-5561, Ext 7981

Thompson, Robert, *Librn,* Oregon State Penitentiary Library, Salem OR. 503-378-2454, Ext 276

Thompson, Robert D, *Librn,* Florida Beacon College & Seminary, Joel O Stephens Library, Largo FL. 813-531-4498

Thompson, Robert D, *Librn,* Tampa College, Clearwater Campus Library, Clearwater FL. 813-443-6491

Thompson, Roger, *Mgr,* Fermi National Accelerator Laboratory Library, Batavia IL. 312-840-3401

Thompson, Rosanne, *Ch,* Roxanne Whipple Memorial-Navajo County Library, Winslow City-Navajo County Library, Winslow AZ. 602-289-4982

Thompson, Rose, *Librn,* Barlow Hospital, Elks Tuberculosis Library, Los Angeles CA. 213-628-4165, Ext 58

Thompson, Rosemary, *Librn,* Perry County District Library (Somerset Branch), Somerset OH. 614-743-1161

Thompson, Ruth, *Librn,* Simmonds Precision Products, Inc, Instrument Systems Div, Engineering Dept Library, Vergennes VT. 802-877-2911

Thompson, Ruth M, *Dir,* Canadian Department of External Affairs Library, Ottawa ON. 613-996-9134

Thompson, Sally, *Librn,* New York Public Library (Mott Haven), New York NY. 212-665-4878

Thompson, Sandra, *Librn,* Carnegie Library of Pittsburgh (Downtown), Pittsburgh PA. 412-622-3100

Thompson, Sandra R, *Librn,* Indiana State Planning Services Agency Library, Indianapolis IN. 317-633-4346

Thompson, Sara, *Ref, Rare Bks & Spec Coll,* Stanislaus County Free Library, Modesto CA. 209-526-6821

Thompson, Sharon D, *ILL,* Louisville Presbyterian Theological Seminary Library, Louisville KY. 502-895-3413, Ext 52

Thompson, Shirley, *Librn,* Midland College, Learning Resources Center, Midland TX. 915-684-7851, Ext 214

Thompson, Shirley, *Supvr,* Shell Oil Co, Shell Development Co, Westhollow Research Center Library, Houston TX. 713-493-7530

Thompson, Sidney, *Librn,* Cerritos College Library, Learning Materials Center, Norwalk CA. 213-860-2451, Ext 286

Thompson, Sister M Eva, *Media,* Brescia College Library, Owensboro KY. 502-685-3131, Ext 213

Thompson, Susan, *Prof,* Columbia University in the City of New York, School of Library Service, NY. 212-280-2292

Thompson, Susan, *Librn,* Los Angeles Public Library System (El Sereno), Los Angeles CA. 213-225-9201

Thompson, Susan, *Dir,* Valley City Public Library, Valley City ND. 701-845-3821

Thompson, T, *Dir,* Northern Montana College Library, Havre MT. 406-265-7821, Ext 3306, 3307

Thompson, Vivian, *ILL,* University of Alaska, Fairbanks (Biomedical Library), Fairbanks AK. 907-479-7442

Thompson, Wendell, *Dir,* Bartlesville Wesleyan College Library, Bartlesville OK. 918-333-6151, Ext 225

Thompson, William, *Doc,* University of Massachusetts at Amherst Library, Amherst MA. 413-545-0284

Thompson, William P, *Librn,* Piedmont Bible College, George M Manuel Memorial Library, Winston-Salem NC. 919-725-8345, Ext 311

Thompson, Wilma, *Asst Librn,* Washoe County Law Library, Reno NV. 702-785-4188

Thompson, Jr, Harold W, *Dir,* Free Public Library of the City of Trenton, Trenton NJ. 609-392-7188

Thomsen, Helen F, *Dir,* Mendocino Community Library, Mendocino CA. 937-5773

Thomsen, Linda, *Libr Technicians,* Veterans Administration, Hospital Library, Miles City MT. 406-232-3060, Ext 305

Thomsen, Mary H, *Librn,* Marsh & McLennan Management Co, Inc, Putnam Management Co Investment Library, Boston MA. 617-423-4960, Ext 210

Thomsen, Odelta, *Librn,* Billings Gazette Library, Billings MT. 406-245-3071, Ext 271

Thomson, Ashley, *Orientation,* Laurentian University Library, Bibliotheque de l'Universite Laurentienne, Sudbury ON. 705-675-1151, Ext 251 & 252

Thomson, Ashley, *Orientation,* Laurentian University Library, Bibliotheque de l'Universite Laurentienne, Sudbury ON. 705-675-1151, Ext 251 & 252

Thomson, Betty, *Cat,* East Texas State University, James Gilliam Gee Library, Commerce TX. 214-886-5717

Thomson, Carol, *ILL,* Union Carbide Corp, Haynes-Becket Memorial Library, Niagara Falls NY. 716-278-3474, 278-3475

Thomson, Charlotte, *Librn,* Red Hook Public Library, Red Hook NY. 914-758-3241

Thomson, Dale, *Regional Director,* Library Services Branch, East Kookenay Regional Office, Cranbrook BC. 604-489-3521, Ext 285

Thomson, Dorothy, *Cat & On-Line Servs,* Point Loma College, Ryan Library, San Diego CA. 714-222-6474, Ext 355, 338

Thomson, Isabel, *Ref,* Dekalb Library System, Maud M Burrus Library, Decatur GA. 404-378-7569

Thomson, J G, *Cat,* University of Victoria, McPherson Library, Victoria BC. 604-477-6911, Ext 4466

Thomson, Katherine, *Per & Doc,* Saint Clair County Library System, Port Huron MI. 313-987-7323

Thomson, Marian, *Exec Secy,* Mariposa County Historical Society Research Library, Mariposa CA. 209-966-2924

Thomson, Marion, *Librn,* Canada Department of National Defence (Medical Library), Borden ON. 705-424-1200, Ext 2624

Thomson, Mrs G, *Ad,* Ottawa Public Library, Ottawa ON. 613-236-0301

Thomson, Sheila, *Librn,* Orford Social Library, Orford NH. 603-353-4488

Thonis, Anne H, *Dir,* Leominster Public Library, Leominster MA. 617-537-0941

Thorburn, Marian, *Asst Librn,* Spruce Grove Public Library, Spruce Grove AB. 403-962-4423

Thorkildson, Terry A, *Dir,* University of Virginia (Claude Moore Health Sciences Library), Charlottesville VA. 804-924-5444

Thorland, Charlotte, *Librn,* Thompson Public Library, Thompson IA. 515-584-2829

Thorleifson, Mary C, *Asst Librn,* North Dakota State University-Bottineau Branch, Institute of Forestry Library, Bottineau ND. 701-228-2277, Ext 54

Thorn, Janet, *Cat,* Lyndon State College, Samuel Read Hall Library, Lyndonville VT. 802-626-3555

Thorn, Lynne, *ILL, On-Line Servs & Bibliog Instr,* Friends University, Edmund Stanley Library, Wichita KS. 316-263-9131, Ext 220

Thorn, Lynne, *Per,* Kansas Newman College, Ryan Library, Wichita KS. 316-942-4291, Ext 40

Thorn, Muriel J, *Librn,* Dickinson Library, Deerfield MA. 413-774-4541

Thornberry, Nancye H, *Dir,* Polk Public Museum Library, Lakeland FL. 813-688-7744

Thornblom, Jeanie, *Coordr,* New Mexico Military Institute, Learning Resource Center, Roswell NM. 505-622-6250, Ext 227, 213

Thornbrough, Gayle, *Dir,* Indiana Historical Society Library, Indianapolis IN. 317-232-1879

Thornburg, Phyllis, *Librn,* Umatilla County Library (Umatilla Branch), Umatilla OR. 503-276-1881

Thornbury, Victoria, *Librn,* Akron-Summit County Public Library (East), Akron OH. 216-784-7522

Thorne, Bonnie B, *Assoc Prof,* Sam Houston State University, Library Science Department, TX. 713-295-6211, Ext 1151

Thorne, Hazel M, *Ad,* Wayne Township Library, Morrison-Reeves Library, Richmond IN. 317-966-8291

Thorne, Herbert, *Librn,* New York Public Library (Columbia), New York NY. 212-864-2530

Thorne, Larry, *Librn,* Alva Public Library, Alva OK. 405-327-1833

Thorne, M Margaret, *Librn,* Northwest Regional Education Laboratory, Information Center Library, Portland OR. 503-248-6922

Thorne, Nancy H, *Librn,* Middlesex Memorial Hospital, Health Sciences Library, Middletown CT. 203-347-9471, Ext 387

Thorne, Shirley, *Circ,* Northwestern Oklahoma State University Library, Alva OK. 405-327-1700, Ext 219

Thornhill, Annette, *Librn,* Fairfield Hills State Hospital, Medical Library, Newtown CT. 203-426-2531, Ext 488

Thornley, Anita, *Librn,* John Cheetham Memorial Library, Ashland IL. 217-476-3417

Thornlow, Bruce S, *Chmn,* Southeastern Massachusetts Health Sciences Libraries Consortium, (SEMCO), MA. 617-583-4500, Ext 321

Thornton, Anne, *Librn,* Veterans Administration, Hospital Library, Saint Louis MO. 314-652-4100

Thornton, Elizabeth, *Acting Ch Librn,* Guernsey Memorial Library, Norwich NY. 607-334-4034

Thornton, Ellen, *Librn,* Nottawa Township Library, Centreville MI. 616-467-6289

Thornton, Gayle, *ILL,* The 49-99 Cooperative Library System, Stockton CA. 209-944-8649

Thornton, Gladys, *Tech Serv,* Olean Public Library, Olean NY. 716-372-0200

Thornton, Glenda, *Tech Serv & Acq,* Adams State College Library, Alamosa CO. 303-589-7781

Thornton, Glenda A, *Instr,* Adams State College, Masters in Educational Media with the University of Northern Colorado, CO. 303-589-7781

Thornton, Judy, *Ad,* Grove City Public Library, Grove City OH. 614-875-6716

Thornton, Kanella, *Bkmobile,* Chesterfield County Library, Chesterfield SC. 803-623-7489

Thornton, Karen, *Bkmobile Coordr,* Saint Joseph Public Library, Saint Joseph MO. 816-232-7729, 232-7720

Thornton, Michael V, *Librn,* Mary Immaculate Seminary Library, Northampton PA. 215-262-7866, Ext 19

Thornton, Phyllis, *Librn,* Norcen Energy Resources Ltd Library, Calgary AB. 403-231-0151, 0152

Thornton, Ruth, *Cat,* Bridgeton Free Public Library, Bridgeton NJ. 609-451-2620

Thornton, Sheila F, *Libr Servs Chief,* California State Library, Sacramento CA. 916-445-2585

Thornycroft, Alice, *Ch,* Maud Preston Palenske Memorial Library, Saint Joseph Public Library, Saint Joseph MI. 616-983-7106

Thoroughman, Doris, *Asst Librn,* Lewis County Public Library, Vanceburg KY. 606-796-2532

Thorpe, Cathy, *Schools,* Louisville Public Library, Louisville OH. 216-875-1696

Thorpe, M, *Tech Serv,* University of Missouri-Rolla Library, Rolla MO. 314-341-4227

Thorpe, Marjorie, *Librn,* Community Hospital of the Monterey Peninsula, Medical Staff Library, Carmel CA. 408-624-5311

Thorpe, Suzanne, *Cat,* Hamline University (School of Law Library), Saint Paul MN. 612-641-2344

Thorsen, Nancy, *ILL,* University of Wisconsin-Green Bay, Library Learning Center, Green Bay WI. 414-465-2382

Thorsen, Patricia, *YA,* White Plains Public Library, White Plains NY. 914-682-4400

Thorson, Beverly, *Librn,* Klemme Public Library, Klemme IA. 515-587-2369

Thorson, Connie, *Acq & Spec Coll,* University of New Mexico General Library, Albuquerque NM. 505-277-4241

Thorson, Robert, *Microforms,* Ohio State University Libraries (William Oxley Thompson Memorial Library), Columbus OH. 614-422-6151

Thorson, Robert, *Circ & ILL,* Ohio State University Libraries (William Oxley Thompson Memorial Library), Columbus OH. 614-422-6151

Thrall, Sharilyn, *Ch,* Riverhead Free Library, Riverhead NY. 516-727-3228

Thrash, James R, *Dir,* Salisbury State College, Blackwell Library, Salisbury MD. 301-546-3261, Ext 351

Thrash, Mrs Woodson, *Librn,* Southwest Arkansas Regional Library (Ashdown Branch), Ashdown AR. 501-777-4564

Thrasher, Deborah, *Librn,* Edison State Community College Library, Piqua OH. 513-778-8600

Thrasher, Jerry A, *Librn,* Cumberland County Public Library, Anderson Street Library, Frances Brooks Stein Memorial Library, Fayetteville NC. 919-483-1580

Thrasher, Joyce, *Dir,* W A Rankin Memorial Library, Neodesha KS. 316-325-3275

Thrasher, Margaret, *Ad,* Prince George's County Memorial Library System, Hyattsville MD. 301-699-3500

Thrasher, Ray, *Tech Serv & On-Line Servs,* Trevecca Nazarene College, Mackey Library, Nashville TN. 615-244-6000, Ext 214

Threadgill, Mary C, *Europe & Soviet Union,* National Defense University Library, Washington DC. 202-693-8437

Threlfall, Joan, *Ch,* Midland County Public Library, Midland TX. 915-683-2708

Threlkeld, Leone, *Cat,* Mount Vernon Public Library, Mount Vernon IL. 618-242-6322

Threndyle, Sherleyan, *Librn,* Saint Josephs Seminary, Newman Theological College Library, Edmonton AB. 459-6656 & 458-6555

Thresher, Jacquelyn, *Ad,* Westchester Library System, Hartsdale NY. 914-761-7620

Throckmorton, Georgie, *Ref,* Public Library of Enid & Garfield County, Enid Public Library, Enid OK. 405-234-6313

Throgmorton, Dorothy, *Cat,* Southwest Baptist College, Estep Library, Bolivar MO. 417-326-5281, Ext 228

Thronberg, Tom, *Dir,* Veterans Administration, Hospital Library, Indianapolis IN. 317-635-7401

Thrower, Anne, *County Librn,* Richmond County Library, Rockingham NC. 919-895-4343

Thrower, Anne E, *Asst Dir,* Sandhill Regional Library System, Rockingham NC. 919-997-3388

Thrower, Jane B, *Librn,* McMillian Memorial Hospital, Red Springs NC. 919-843-4205

Thubauville, Jeanine, *On-Line Servs,* University of Wisconsin-Madison, Memorial Library, Madison WI. 608-262-3521

Thuesen, Mary, *Circ,* Lenoir-Rhyne College, Carl A Rudisill Library, Hickory NC. 704-328-1741, Ext 221

Thull, Frances K, *Dir,* Hesperian Library, Cawker City Public Library, Cawker City KS. 913-781-4925

Thuma, Marion G, *Dir,* Lower Columbia College, Learning Resource Center, Longview WA. 206-577-2310

Thums, Lillian, *Dir, Acq & Cat,* Rib Lake Public Library, Rib Lake WI. 715-427-5769

Thurber, Mary C, *Ref,* Bergenfield Free Public Library, Bergenfield NJ. 201-384-2765

Thurber, Patricia, *Librn,* Magnetic Metals United States of America, Business Library, Camden NJ. 609-964-7842

Thurheimer, David C, *Dir,* Brick Store Museum, Edith Cleaves Barry Library, Kennebunk ME. 207-985-4802

Thuringer, Florence G, *Librn,* United States Navy (Fletcher Library), Seattle WA. 907-579-8215

Thurklesen, Mildred, *Librn,* Ho-Ho-Kus Public Library, Ho-Ho-Kus NJ. 201-445-8078

Thurman, Elizabeth, *Asst Librn,* Duerson-Oldham County Public Library, La Grange KY. 502-222-1133

Thurman, Estelle, *Asst Librn,* United Technologies Corp, Norden Systems Inc Technical Library, Norwalk CT. 203-838-4471

Thurman, Odell, *Dir,* Church Hill Public Library, Church Hill TN. 615-357-4591

Thurman, Sheryl, *ILL & Tech Serv,* Oklahoma Christian College Library, Oklahoma City OK. 405-478-1661, Ext 337

Thurmond, Anne, *Dir,* Shiloh Regional Library, Jackson TN. 901-668-0710

Thurmond, Emma Sue, *Librn,* Piedmont Regional Library (Jefferson Branch), Jefferson GA. 404-867-2762

Thurston, Eleanor, *Librn,* Freedom Public Library, Freedom NH. 603-539-4880

Thurston, Hilda, *Ch,* Pitkin County Library, Aspen CO. 303-925-7124

Thurston, Minnie G, *Supvr Libr Servs,* Westinghouse Electric Corporation, Offshore Power Systems Library, Jacksonville FL. 904-724-3441

Thurston, Mrs R J, *Dir,* Indianfields Public Library, Caro MI. 517-673-4329

Thurston, Nancy, *Librn,* Ontario Ministry of Natural Resources, Mines Library, Toronto ON. 416-965-1352

Thurston, Virginia, *Ad,* Mount Vernon Public Library, Mount Vernon WA. 206-336-2418

Thweatt, Elizabeth, *Acq & Doc,* Gonzaga University (Law Library), Spokane WA. 509-328-4220, Ext 3781

Thwing, Valerie, *ILL,* Central Arkansas Library System, Little Rock AR. 501-374-7546

Thyer, Judith, *Librn,* Linn County District Library Three, Blue Mound KS. 913-756-2614

Thysell, Gloria, *Ref,* John Tyler Community College Library, Chester VA. 804-748-6481, Ext 251

Tibayan, Arlene S, *Librn,* United States Army (Army Support Command Headquarters), Ft Shafter HI. 438-1935 or 438-2906

Tibayan, Arlene S, *Librn,* United States Army (Sergeant Rodney J Yano Post Library), Schofield Barracks HI. 655-9143 or 655-0145

Tibbals, John M, *Head, External Libr Operations,* California State College, San Bernardino Library, San Bernardino CA. 714-887-7321

Tibbetts, James C, *Bkmobile Coordr,* Leavenworth Public Library, Leavenworth KS. 913-682-5666

Tibbetts, Robert A, *Rare Bks & Spec Coll,* Ohio State University Libraries (William Oxley Thompson Memorial Library), Columbus OH. 614-422-6151

Tibbits, Edith, *Tech Serv,* Gustavus Adolphus College, Folke Bernadotte Memorial Library, Saint Peter MN. 507-931-4300, Ext 2301

Tiberg, Ethel, *Mgt Libr Serv,* Edison Electric Institute Library, Washington DC. 202-828-7520, 828-7521

Tibesar, Leo J, *Dir,* Saint Paul Seminary, John Ireland Memorial Library, Saint Paul MN. 612-690-4355

Tibesar, Leo J, *Bibliog Instr,* Saint Paul Seminary, John Ireland Memorial Library, Saint Paul MN. 612-690-4355

Tice, Kathy, *Mat Mgt,* Public Library of Annapolis & Anne Arundel County Inc, Annapolis MD. 301-224-7371

Tice, Margaret, *Ch,* Leonia Public Library, Leonia NJ. 201-944-1444

Tice, Mary, *Circ,* University of Tennessee at Martin, Paul Meek Library, Martin TN. 901-587-7060

Tice, Mary T, *In Charge,* Raytheon Company, Business Information Center, Lexington MA. 617-862-6600, Ext 579

Tice, Ruth B, *Dir,* Winter Public Library, Winter WI. 715-266-4721

Tichbourne, Mrs V, *Librn,* Queensway General Hospital, Medical Library, Etobicoke ON. 416-259-6671, Ext 211

Tichelaar, George R, *Chief,* California State Department of Food & Agriculture, Chemistry Laboratory Services Library, Sacramento CA. 916-445-3196

Tickner, Bernita, *Librn,* Siskiyou County Public Library (Etna Branch), Etna CA. 916-467-3661

Tidball, Ellen, *Commun Servs,* Morley Library, Painesville OH. 216-352-3383

Tidd, Mrs George, *Librn,* Slate Memorial Library, Gill MA. 413-863-2591

Tidd, Peggy, *Librn,* Greene County District Library (Jamestown Branch), Jamestown OH. 513-675-4411

Tidemann, Viola, *Coll Develop,* Wichita Public Library, Wichita KS. 316-262-0611

Tidlow, Marylin, *Librn,* Spalding Memorial Library, Athens PA. 717-888-7117

Tidona, Kathleen, *Acq,* Longwood Gardens Inc Library, Kennett Square PA. 215-388-6741, Ext 510

Tidwell, Hugh H, *Librn,* American Irish Historical Society Library, New York NY. 212-288-2263

Tidwell, Janet P, *Librn,* Curtis, Mallet-Prevost, Colt & Mosle Library, New York NY. 212-248-8111, Ext 368, 365

Tidwell, Mrs D H, *Librn,* Statesboro Regional Library (Richmond Hill Branch), Richmond Hill GA. 912-756-3580

Tidwell, R L, *Librn,* Portland Community College, Media Center, Portland OR. 503-244-6111, Ext 367

Tidwell, Rose, *Librn,* California & Hawaiian Sugar Co Library, Crockett CA. 415-787-2121

Tidwell, Ruth, *Cat,* Carl Elliott Regional Library, Jasper AL. 205-221-2567

Tieben, Sharon, *Tech Serv,* Saint Francis College Library, Fort Wayne IN. 219-432-3551, Ext 263

Tiedemann, David, *Media,* University of San Diego, James S Copley Library, San Diego CA. 714-291-6480, Ext 4312, 4313, 4314

Tiedemann, Mary, *Cat,* University of San Diego, James S Copley Library, San Diego CA. 714-291-6480, Ext 4312, 4313, 4314

Tiedrich, Ellen, *Ad,* Camden County Free Library, Voorhees NJ. 609-772-1636

Tiedrich, Ellen, *On-Line Servs,* Camden County Free Library, Voorhees NJ. 609-772-1636

Tiefel, Virginia, *Undergrad Librn,* Ohio State University Libraries (William Oxley Thompson Memorial Library), Columbus OH. 614-422-6151

Tiemann, Loreta, *Film Servs,* Lincoln City Libraries, Lincoln NE. 402-435-2146

Tien, Mary Anna, *Head,* Connecticut State Library (Middletown Library Service Center), Middletown CT. 203-346-7779

Tiensvold, Darleen, *Librn,* Montana State Library, Division for the Blind & Physically Handicapped, Helena MT. 406-339-3004

Tierney, Catherine, *Tech Serv,* Boston University Libraries (School of Law), Boston MA. 617-353-3151

Tierney, Catherine M, *Librn,* Akron Beacon Journal Reference Library, Akron OH. 216-375-8515, 375-8514

Tierney, Clifford L, *Mgr Info Ctr,* Whirlpool Corporation Technical Information Center Library, Benton Harbor MI. 616-926-5323

Tierney, Diane, *Librn,* Community Legal Services Library, Philadelphia PA. 215-893-5368

Tierney, Gerry, *Ref,* Lake Michigan College Library, Benton Harbor MI. 616-927-3571, Ext 261

Tierney, Joseph, *Ref,* Newark Free Library, Newark DE. 302-731-7550

Tierney, Judith, *Librn Blind,* Bur Oak Library System, Shorewood IL. 815-729-3345, 729-3346

Tierney, Judith, *ILL, Ref & Spec Coll,* King's College, D Leonard Corgan Library, Wilkes-Barre PA. 717-824-9931, Ext 245

Tierney, Sister Jeanne, *Librn,* Saint Peter's College Library, Englewood Cliffs NJ. 201-568-7730

Tietgen, Marlene, *Ch,* Larchwood Public Library, Larchwood IA. 712-477-2583

Tietjen, Anna N, *In Charge,* Bureau of Land Management, Arizona Strip, District Office Library, Saint George UT. 801-673-3545, Ext 40

Tietjen, Mildred, *Dir,* Georgia Southwestern College, James Earl Carter Library, Americus GA. 912-928-1352

Tieuli, Anthony F, *Asst Dir, Personnel & Br Coordr,* Malden Public Library, Malden MA. 617-324-0218

Tieuli, Athony, *On-Line Servs,* Malden Public Library, Malden MA. 617-324-0218

Tiff, Arthur, *Asst Dir,* Presentation College Library, Aberdeen SD. 605-225-0420, Ext 368

Tiff, Georgiana, *In Charge,* Denver Public Library (Arts & Recreation), Denver CO. 303-573-5152, Ext 271

Tiff, John T, *Historian,* National Park Service, Lyndon B Johnson National Historical Site Library, Johnson City TX. 512-868-7128

Tighe, Pauline J, *Librn,* California State Automobile Association Library, San Francisco CA. 415-565-2012

Tijunelis, Gus, *Librn,* Chicago Public Library (East Side), Chicago IL. 312-721-5500

Tildesley, Rebecca E, *Dir,* Roger Williams College Library, Bristol RI. 401-255-2361

Tilford, Diana, *Extension,* Pamunkey Regional Library, Hanover VA. 804-798-6081, Ext 285, 287

Tilghman, Ann, *Librn,* Peoria Public Library, Peoria AZ. 602-979-3282

Till, Mildred, *Librn,* Copiah-Jefferson Regional Library (Wesson Branch), Wesson MS. 601-643-5221

Tiller, Colen, *In Charge,* Central Arizona College, Instructional Materials Center, Coolidge AZ. 602-723-4141

Tiller, Francine, *Ref,* Central Michigan University, Charles V Park Library, Mount Pleasant MI. 517-774-3500

Tilles, E Doris, *ILL,* Oregon State University, William Jasper Kerr Library, Corvallis OR. 503-754-3411

Tillett, Donald, *Dir,* Miami Memorial-Gila County Library, Miami AZ. 602-473-2621

Tilley, Lou W, *Librn,* Environmental Protection Agency, Region V Library, Chicago IL. 312-353-2022

Tillinger, Frances, *Librn,* Morristown Jewish Center Library, Morristown NJ. 201-538-9292

Tillis, Jennifer, *Coll Develop,* University of Wisconsin-Green Bay, Library Learning Center, Green Bay WI. 414-465-2382

Tillman, Ann, *Librn,* Crockett Memorial Library, Alamo TN. 901-696-4220

Tillman, James S, *Cat,* University of South Florida (Medical Center Library), Tampa FL. 813-974-2399

Tillman, Jeanne, *Librn,* Webber College, Grace & Roger Babson Learning Center, Babson Park FL. 813-638-1431

Tillman, Laura, *Ch,* Monrovia Public Library, Monrovia CA. 213-358-0174

Tillotson, Patricia, *Librn,* Groveton Public Library, Northumberland NH. 603-636-2066

Tillson, Marion, *Librn,* Jackson Metropolitan Library (Raleigh Library), Raleigh MS. 601-352-3677

Tilson, Marie, *Librn,* Manalytics, Inc Library, San Francisco CA. 415-788-4143

Tilson, Phyllis, *Asst Librn,* Arkansas City Public Library, Arkansas City KS. 316-442-1280

Tilson, Sarah, *Reader Serv & Spec Coll,* Transylvania County Library, Inc, Brevard NC. 704-883-9880

Tilton, James J, *Dir Computerized Servs Div,* Bibliographical Center for Research, Rocky Mountain Region, Inc, Denver CO. 303-388-9261

Tilton, James J, *Asst Exec Dir,* Bibliographical Center for Research, Rocky Mountain Region, Inc (Computerized Services Division), CO. 303-388-9261

Tilton, Loretta J, *Dir & Acq,* Norwalk Public Library, Norwalk IA. 515-981-0217

Timberlake, Cynthia, *Librn,* Bernice P Bishop Museum Library, Honolulu HI. 808-847-3511

Timberlake, Patricia, *Ref Asst,* Missouri State Library, Jefferson City MO. 314-751-4214

Timbers, Elaine B, *Dir,* Emmaus Public Library, Emmaus PA. 215-965-9284

Timian, Sylvia, *Librn,* North Memorial Medical Center, Medical Library, Minneapolis MN. 612-588-0616, Ext 431

Timian, Talley, *Librn,* North Memorial Medical Center, Medical Library, Minneapolis MN. 612-588-0616, Ext 431

Timken, William, *Ch,* Gogebic Community College, Alex D Chisholm Learning Resource Center, Ironwood MI. 906-932-4231, Ext 211

Timko, Georgene A, *Tech Serv, Acq & Cat,* Marietta College, Dawes Memorial Library, Marietta OH. 614-373-4643, Ext 215, 216, 285

Timko, Patricia, *Asst Librn,* Windber Public Library, Inc, Windber PA. 814-467-4950

Timm, D Ivan, *Media,* Asbury Theological Seminary, B L Fisher Library, Wilmore KY. 606-858-3581, Ext 246

Timmer, Joan, *Asst Librn,* Papillion Public Library, Papillion NE. 402-339-3177

Timmer, Julia, *Librn,* East Chicago Public Library (Baring Avenue), East Chicago IN. 219-397-2453

Timmerman, Dolores, *Dir,* Bell Public Library, Portland TX. 512-643-6527

Timmerman, Mildred D, *Librn,* Central New York Academy of Medicine Inc Library, New Hartford NY. 315-735-2204

Timmerman, Wayne, *Lit & Lang,* Phoenix Public Library, Phoenix AZ. 602-262-6451

Timmesch, Joann, *Librn,* Colwich City-Union Township Library, Colwich KS. 316-796-1521

Timmons, Dorothy, *Librn,* Omaha Public Library (Millard), Omaha NE. 402-444-4848

Timmons, Martha J, *Librn,* Sheridan Public Library, Sheridan IN. 317-758-5201

Timmons, Sadie, *Rare Bks & Spec Coll,* Public Library of Anniston & Calhoun County, Liles Memorial Library, Anniston AL. 205-237-8501, Ext 8503

Timmons, Sarah, *Librn,* McDowell Public Library (Northfork Branch), Northfork WV. 304-862-2343

Timms, Carolyn, *Librn,* Wentworth Library (Binbrook Branch), Binbrook ON. 416-526-4126

Timour, John A, *Dir,* Thomas Jefferson University (Scott Memorial Library), Philadelphia PA. 215-928-8848

Timperley, Doris, *Cat,* Kearney State College, Calvin T Ryan Library, Kearney NE. 308-236-4218

Timperley, Jane M, *Circ,* Trinity University Library, San Antonio TX. 512-736-8121

Tims, Glenn, *Cat,* Tyler Public Library, Tyler TX. 214-595-4267

Tincovich, Mary E, *Librn,* Connecticut State Library, Library for the Blind & Physically Handicapped, Hartford CT. 203-566-3028

Tindall, Mildred D, *Librn,* Roseville Community Hospital, Medical Library, Roseville CA. 916-783-9111, Ext 580

Tiner, Helen, *Per,* Merced College, Lesher Library, Merced CA. 209-723-4321, Ext 274

Ting, Florence, *Cat,* Princeton Public Library, Princeton NJ. 609-924-9529

Ting, Robert N, *Coordr & Bibliog Instr,* National Oceanic & Atmospheric Administration, Miami-Coral Gables Library Center, Miami FL. 305-361-3361, Ext 330 & 331

Tingen, James D, *Reader Serv,* Tennessee Wesleyan College, Merner-Pfeiffer Library, Athens TN. 615-745-2363

Tingle, Mavis, *Circ,* Neshoba County Public Library, Philadelphia MS. 601-656-4911

Tinio, Cecilia, *Researcher,* William Douglas McAdams Medical Library Medical Library, New York NY. 212-759-6300, Ext 276

Tinkham, Edith, *Librn,* Sargent Township Library, Sargent NE. 308-527-4241

Tinkham, Natalie, *Lit & Soc Sci,* Madison Public Library, Madison WI. 608-266-6300

Tinkler, Ellen, *Exten Servs,* Medical University of South Carolina Library, Charleston SC. 803-792-2374

Tino, Carmela, *Pers,* University of Bridgeport, Magnus Wahlstrom Library, Bridgeport CT. 203-576-4740

Tinsley, Margie B, *Dir,* Bacon Memorial Public Library, Wyandotte MI. 313-282-7660

Tinsley, Marilyn S, *ILL,* University of Tennessee at Chattanooga Library, Chattanooga TN. 615-755-4701

Tinsman, Emma, *Dir,* Westville Public Library, Westville NJ. 609-456-0357

Tipka, Donald, *In Charge,* Cleveland Public Library (History & Geography), Cleveland OH. 216-623-2864

Tippet, Harriet, *Ref,* Lawrence University, Seeley G Mudd Library, Appleton WI. 414-739-3681, Ext 264

Tippet, Harriet, *ILL,* Lawrence University, Seeley G Mudd Library, Appleton WI. 414-739-3681, Ext 264

Tippets, Ruth, *Librn,* Calaveras County Law Library, San Andreas CA. 209-754-4252

Tippett, Edythe, *Librn,* Wake County Department of the Public Library (Zebulon Public), Zebulon NC. 919-269-9301

Tippit, Myrna, *DP Lab Tech,* State Technical Institute at Memphis, George E Freeman Library, Memphis TN. 901-377-4106

Tipple, Cynda, *Asst Dir,* Onondaga Free Library, Syracuse NY. 315-492-1727

Tipple, David C, *Actg Dir,* Bard College, Kellogg-Hoffman Memorial Library, Annandale-on-Hudson NY. 914-758-6822, Ext 231

Tipps, Wilma, *Ch,* Pioneer Multi-County Library, Norman OK. 405-321-1481

Tippy, Thelma, *Media Production,* Tri-County Technical College, Learning Resource Center, Pendleton SC. 803-646-3227

Tipsword, Wilma, *Dir,* Lake Land College, Virgil H Judge Learning Resource Center, Mattoon IL. 217-235-3131, Ext 267

Tipton, Lois M, *Dir,* Girard Township Library, Girard IL. 217-627-2414

Tipton, Mary, *Asst Coordr,* Wisconsin Library Consortium, (WLC), WI. 608-263-5051

Tipton, Roberta, *Librn,* John F Kennedy Medical Center, Medical Library, Edison NJ. 201-321-7000

Tirada, Nellie, *Librn,* Lebanon County Library System (Spanish Reading Ctr), Lebanon PA. 717-273-4755

Tirmenstein, Adrienne, *Tech Serv, Acq & Cat,* Evansville Public Library & Vanderburgh County Public Library, Evansville IN. 812-425-2621

Tirpak, Mary Ellen, *Librn,* Lackawanna Junior College - Wilkes Barre Center Library, Wilkes-Barre PA. 717-823-3123

Tirpok, Mary Ellen, *Br Coordr,* Lackawanna Junior College, Seeley Memorial Library, Scranton PA. 717-961-7831

Tirrell, Brenda Peabody, *Librn,* Houston Public Library (Business, Science & Technology), Houston TX. 713-224-5441

Tirrell-McLaughlin, Anne, *Librn,* Frederick E Parlin Memorial Library (East Everett), Everett MA. 617-389-9282

Tisby, Pamela, *Cat,* Southern University, Shreveport-Bossier City Campus Library, Shreveport LA. 318-424-6552, Ext 238

Tischelman, Beulah, *Actg Librn,* Yeshiva University Libraries (Belfer Graduate School of Science Library), New York NY. 212-960-5451

Tisdale, Barbara, *Librn,* Great Neck Library (Lakeville), Great Neck NY. 516-466-8055, Ext 231

Tisdale, Carol, *Circ,* Saugus Public Library, Saugus MA. 617-233-0530

Tisdale, Janice, *Librn,* Edward C Jordan Co, Inc Library, Portland ME. 207-775-5401, Ext 295

Tisdale, Jeanne, *AV,* Coe College, Stewart Memorial Library, Cedar Rapids IA. 319-399-8585, 399-8586

Tise, Barbara, *Bkmobile Coordr,* California Lutheran College Library, Thousand Oaks CA. 805-492-2411, Ext 205

Tishkoff, Helen, *Ref,* San Bernardino County Library, San Bernardino CA. 714-383-1734

Tishler, Myrr, *Librn,* Congregation Beth Jacob, Goodwin Family Library, Merchantville NJ. 609-662-4509

Tisthammer, Dana, *Asst Dir & Tech Serv,* Saint Louis University, Pius XII Memorial Library, Saint Louis MO. 314-658-3100

Titchenal, Marcia, *ILL,* Spokane Falls Community College, Library Media Services, Spokane WA. 509-456-2860

Titman, Gisela M, *Librn,* Perkins School for the Blind, Regional Library for the Blind & Physically Handicapped, Watertown MA. 617-924-3434, Ext 240

Tittelman, Lynn R, *Libr Technician,* Regional Counsel of United States Customs Service, Law Library, New York NY. 212-466-4579

Titterington, James, *Media,* University of Nebraska-Lincoln (Instructional Media Center), Lincoln NE. 402-472-1910

Titterson, Beth, *Research Tech,* Peel Board of Education, J A Turner Professional Library, Mississauga ON. 416-279-6010

Tittley, Remi J, *Dir,* College Bourget Bibliotheque, Rigaud PQ. 514-451-5311

Titus, Betty, *Librn,* Galesburg Memorial Library, Galesburg MI. 616-665-7839

Titus, Charlcie, *Librn,* Euclid Public Library (Euclid Central), Euclid OH. 216-531-0812

Titus, David, *Ch & YA,* Portage County District Library, Hiram OH. 216-569-7666

Titus, Elizabeth, *Computer Search,* Oakland University, Kresge Library, Rochester MI. 313-377-2486, 377-2474

Titus, Isabel, *Librn,* Fairlee Public Library, Fairlee VT. 802-333-4343

Titus, Jane, *Personnel,* Temple University of the Commonwealth System of Higher Education, Samuel Paley Library, Philadelphia PA. 215-787-8231

Titus, Pearl, *Librn,* Tangipahoa Parish Library (Kentwood Branch), Kentwood LA. 504-229-3596

Titus, Penny, *Librn,* Tampa-Hillsborough County Public Library System (Citrus Park), Odessa FL. 813-920-3155

Titus, Robert, *Prof,* East Texas State University, Educational Media & Technology (Library & Information Science), TX. 214-886-5496

Tiwana, Jagpal S, *Acq,* Nova Scotia Teachers College Library, Truro NS. 902-895-5347, Ext 30

Tizol, Elba, *Spec Coll,* University of Puerto Rico, Humacao University College Library, Humacao PR. 809-852-2525, Ext 200

Tjaden, Kathy, *Outreach Servs Coordr,* Mid-Wisconsin Federated Library System, Fond du Lac WI. 414-921-3670

Tjaden, Margaret B, *Coordr Bibliog Control,* University of Washington Libraries, Seattle WA. 206-543-1760

Tjarks, Connor, *Cent Proc Div,* Virginia Commonwealth University (James Branch Cabell Library), Richmond VA. 804-257-1105

Tkaczuk, Lydia, *Chief,* Veterans Administration (Lakeside Medical Center Medical Library), Chicago IL. 312-943-6600, Ext 259

Tobey, Ilene, *Consult,* Uncas-On-Thames Hospital, Mary Lerou Memorial Medical Library, Norwich CT. 203-889-1321, Ext 296

Tobey, Marieta, *Pub Servs,* Mercy College Libraries, Dobbs Ferry NY. 914-693-4500, Ext 260

Tobin, Jayne Culver, *Librn,* Towanda Public Library, Towanda PA. 717-265-2470

Tobin, Jean E, *Librn,* New York Stock Exchange, Research Library, New York NY. 212-623-5049

Tobin, Margaret M, *Dir,* Saint Francis College, Library Science Program, PA. 814-472-7000, Ext 265

Tobin, Margaret M, *Dir,* Saint Francis College, Pius XII Memorial Library, Loretto PA. 814-472-7000, Ext 264, 265 & 266

Tobin, Roberta, *Librn,* McDonald Free Library, McDonald PA. 412-926-8400

Tobin, Shirley, *Librn,* Onslow County Public Library (Sneads Ferry Branch), Sneads Ferry NC. 919-347-2592, 347-5495

Tobler, Helen, *ILL,* Wesley College, Parker Library, Dover DE. 302-736-2413

Tobler, June, *Librn,* Spiro Public Library, Spiro OK. 918-962-3461

Tod, Mary, *Librn,* Dallas Public Library (Polk-Wisdom), Dallas TX. 214-224-5586

Toda, Seichi, *Dir,* Hawaii State Library System (Administrative Services), Honolulu HI. 808-548-6280

Todd, Alma P, *Acq,* Mississippi Valley State University, James Herbert White Library, Itta Bena MS. 601-254-9041, Ext 6340

Todd, Cynthia, *Librn,* International Brotherhood of Teamsters Library, Washington DC. 202-624-6978

Todd, Ellen V, *Head Reference Servs,* University of Texas Health Science Center at San Antonio Library, San Antonio TX. 512-691-6271

Todd, Fred W, *Chief Librn,* United States Air Force (Strughold Aeromedical Library), Brooks AFB TX. 512-536-3321

Todd, Georgette, *Librn,* Los Angeles Public Library System (Hollywood), Los Angeles CA. 213-464-3101

Todd, Hal W, *Dir,* Albany Dougherty Public Library, Albany GA. 912-435-2104

Todd, J M, *Librn,* Okanagan Regional Library District (Peachland Branch), Peachland BC. 604-767-9111

Todd, Jack M, *Dir & Media,* Sul Ross State University, Bryan Wildenthal Memorial Library, Alpine TX. 915-837-3461

Todd, Janice, *Librn,* West Georgia Regional Library (Heard County Public), Franklin GA. 404-832-1381

Todd, Joanna, *Reader Serv,* Stephens College, Hugh Stephens Library, Columbia MO. 314-442-2211, Ext 428

Todd, Kay Moller, *Librn,* Kilpatrick & Cody, Law Library, Atlanta GA. 404-572-6397

Todd, Marie, *Librn,* Ira C Reed Public Library, Lafayette IL. 309-995-3927

Todd, Mary, *Ch,* Joplin Public Library, Joplin MO. 417-623-7953

Todd, Mary, *Bkmobile Coordr,* Lagrange County Library, Lagrange IN. 219-463-2841

Todd, Mary, *Ch & YA,* Mercer County Library, Trenton NJ. 609-989-6917

Todd, Millie, *Cat,* Lincoln Library, Springfield Public Library, Springfield IL. 217-753-4900

Todd, Mrs J, *Librn,* Russel Public Library, Russel ON. 613-445-5331

Todd, Priscilla, *Librn,* Kinchafoonee Regional Library (Clay County), Ft Gaines GA. 912-995-2902

Todd, R A, *Assoc Librn & On-Line Searcher,* National Film Board of Canada, Reference Library, Montreal PQ. 514-333-3141, 333-3142

Todd, Jr, A W, *Dir,* Fountaindale Public Library District, Bolingbrook IL. 312-759-2102

Todor, Jacqueline, *YA,* Spartanburg County Public Library, Spartanburg SC. 582-4123 & 585-2441

Todoroki, Earline, *Librn,* Hawaii State Library System (Waipahu Branch), Waipahu HI. 808-677-3742

Todt, Martha, *Media,* Burbank Public Library, Burbank CA. 213-847-9744

Toeppe, Joan M, *Dir,* Diamond Shamrock Corp Research Library, Painesville OH. 216-352-9311, Ext 293

Tofalo, Anne, *Coordr,* National Micrographics Association, Resource Center, Silver Spring MD. 301-587-8202

Toft, A M, *Librn,* Red Lake Public Library, Red Lake ON. 807-727-2230

Tognarelli, Marilou, *ILL,* Colorado Mountain College, Learning Resources Center, Leadville CO. 303-486-2015, Ext 36

Toifel, Peggy W, *Ref & Bibliog Instr,* University of West Florida, John C Pace Library, Pensacola FL. 904-476-9500, Ext 261

Tokarczyk, Wm, *Circ,* Oshkosh Public Library, Oshkosh WI. 414-424-0473

Tolefree, Shirley, *Librn,* Philander Smith College, M L Harris Library, Little Rock AR. 501-375-7859

Toler, Donna J, *Asst Prof,* University of Central Florida, Educational Media Programs, FL. 305-275-2426

Toler, Elizabeth, *Per,* Maywood Public Library, Maywood NJ. 201-845-7755

Tolford, Janice J, *Cat,* Heidelberg College, Beeghly Library, Tiffin OH. 419-448-2104

Toliver, Virginia, *On-Line Servs,* University of Southern Mississippi, Cook Memorial Library, Hattiesburg MS. 601-266-7301

Toll, Anne, *Librn,* Newport Hospital, Ina Mosher Memorial Library, Newport RI. 401-846-6400, Ext 249

Toll, Mary E, *Doc,* South Carolina State Library, Columbia SC. 803-758-3181

Tollafield, Ronald, *Dir,* Franklin Sylvester Library, Medina OH. 216-725-0588

Tollefson, Alan, *Dir,* Beloit Public Library, Beloit WI. 608-364-6715

Tollefson, Dean E, *Exec Dir,* Union of Independent Colleges of Art, MO. 816-753-6654

Tolles, Jr, Bryant F, *Dir,* Essex Institute, James Duncan Phillips Library, Salem MA. 617-744-3390

Tolleson, Sue, *Circ,* Ector County Library, Odessa TX. 915-332-0633

Tolliver, Barbara, *Transcription & Broadcast,* Washington Regional Library for the Blind & Physically Handicapped, Seattle WA. 464-6930. SCAN 576-6930

Tolliver, Don L, *Dean Libr & Learning Resources,* University of Wisconsin-Whitewater, Library & Learning Resources, Whitewater WI. 414-472-1000

Tollman, Gerry, *Dir,* Niobrara County Library, Lusk WY. 307-334-3490

Tollman, Thomas, *Ref,* University of Nebraska at Omaha, University Library, Omaha NE. 402-554-2361

Tolmachev, Mirjana, *Gen Libr Bur, Actg Dir & User Servs,* State Library of Pennsylvania, Harrisburg PA. 717-787-2646

Tolman, Lorraine E, *Assoc Prof,* Boston University, Dept of Instructional Development-Educational Media, MA. 617-353-3176

Tolotti, F C, *Librn,* Shell Oil Co (Legal Library), Houston TX. 713-241-3514

Tolzmann, Don, *Germanic Lang & Lit,* University of Cincinnati Libraries, Central Library, Cincinnati OH. 513-475-2218

Tolzmann, Lynne, *Media & Bkmobile Coordr,* Le Sueur-Waseca Regional Library, Waseca MN. 507-835-2910

Tom, Abraham, *Librn,* San Jose Public Library (East San Jose Carnegie), San Jose CA. 408-998-2069

Tom, Chow Loy, *Instr,* University of Denver, Graduate School of Librarianship and Information Management, CO. 303-753-2557

Toma, Rita, *Per,* University of North Dakota, Chester Fritz Library, Grand Forks ND. 701-777-2617

Toman, Vera, *Rare Bks & Spec Coll,* Smithtown Library, Smithtown NY. 516-265-2072

Tomann, Stephen G, *In Charge,* Putnam County Historical Society Library, Cold Spring NY. 914-265-2781

Tomas, Ann, *Librn,* Jefferson County Public Library (Lakewood Regional), Lakewood CO. 303-238-8411

Tomas, Elizabeth, *Librn,* Northern Telecom Ltd, Library & Information Center, Montreal PQ. 514-931-5711

Tomazic, Marion, *Supvr Cent Tiles,* Diamond Shamrock Corp, Corporate Library, Cleveland OH. 216-694-6253

Tomczak, Thomas, *Gen Mat & Servs,* Milwaukee Public Library, Milwaukee WI. 414-278-3000

Tomczyk, Charmaine, *Tech Serv,* University of South Carolina, Coastal Carolina College Kimbel Library, Conway SC. 803-347-3161, Ext 242

Tomeo, Susan, *Media,* Medford Public Library, Medford MA. 617-395-7950

Tomer, Christinger, *Asst Prof,* Case Western Reserve University, School of Library Science, OH. 216-368-3500

Tomer, Edel, *Librn,* York Regional Library (Plaster Rock Public), Plaster Rock NB. 506-356-8642

Tomes, Julia, *Librn,* New York Public Library (South Beach), New York NY. 212-442-7420

Tomforde, Joan, *Librn,* Edgewater Free Public Library, Edgewater NJ. 201-943-1778

Tomich, Nicholas, *Librn,* Union County Law Library, Elizabeth NJ. 201-527-4194

Tomie, J, *Asst Dir,* Calgary Public Library, Calgary AB. 403-268-2880

Tomikawa, Kathryn, *Librn,* Sanderson & Porter, Inc, Library, New York NY. 212-344-5550, Ext 336, 337

Tomillo, Patricia, *Dir,* Reuben McMillan Free Library Free Library Association (Special Outgoing Services), Youngstown OH. 216-792-3869

Tomillo, Patricia, *Special Outgoing Serv,* Reuben McMillan Free Library Free Library Association, Public Library of Youngstown & Mahoning County, Youngstown OH. 216-744-8636

Tominc, Kathleen, *Learning Lab Instr,* Western Wyoming Community College, Library Learning Resources Center, Rock Springs WY. 307-382-2121, Ext 154

Tomlin, Celia K, *Librn,* American Fork City Library, American Fork UT. 801-756-4681

Tomlin, Harold, *Media Production,* Wright State University Library (Fordham Library, Cox Heart Institute Library & Fels Research Institute Library), Dayton OH. 513-873-2266

Tomlin, Mary Evelyn, *Asst Mgr & On Line Search Coord,* Mississippi Research & Development Center, Information Services Divison, Jackson MS. 601-982-6324

Tomlinson, Betty, *Science Libr,* Carleton College Library, Northfield MN. 507-645-4431

Tomlinson, C Edmund, *Tech Serv & Acq,* High Point Public Library, High Point NC. 919-885-8411

Tomlinson, Calvin, *Librn,* California State Department of Corrections, Deuel Vocational Institution Library, Tracy CA. 209-466-5114

Tomlinson, Edwin, *Librn,* Sherman Research Library, Corona del Mar CA. 714-673-1880

Tomlinson, Elizabeth, *Librn,* Saint Olaf College (Science), Northfield MN. 507-663-3099

Tomlinson, Frances, *Ad,* Midland County Public Library, Midland TX. 915-683-2708

Tomlinson, Gail, *Pub Relations,* Dallas Public Library, Dallas TX. 214-748-9071

Tomlinson, Janie, *Librn,* Satilla Regional Library (Pearson Public), Pearson GA. 912-422-3500

Tomlinson, Josie, *Dir,* Wilson County Public Library, Wilson NC. 919-237-3818

Tomlinson, Mrs J, *Media,* Ajax Public Library, Ajax ON. 416-683-6911

Tommela, Joann M, *Mgr,* Computer Sciences Corp, Technical Library, El Segundo CA. 213-678-0311, Ext 1078

Tommell, Anthony Wayne, *Actg Chief Historian,* National Park Service, Saratoga National Historical Park Library, Stillwater NY. 518-664-9821

Tommey, Richard J, *Librn,* General Atomic Company Library, La Jolla CA. 714-455-3322

Tompkins, Dorothy C, *Chief Librn,* United States Army (Post Library System), Fort Huachuca AZ. 602-538-3041

Tompkins, Edgar, *Dir,* Albany Public Library, Albany NY. 518-449-3380

Tompkins, Edgar, *Librn,* Upper Hudson Library Federation, Albany NY. 518-449-3387, 449-3380

Tompkins, Eleanor E, *Dir & Acq,* Middleboro Public Library, Middleboro MA. 617-947-0613

Tompkins, Louise, *Librn,* Princeton University Library (Pliney Fisk Library of Economics & Finance), Princeton NJ. 609-452-3180

Tompkins, Margaret, *Ref,* Russell Sage College, James Wheelock Clark Library, Troy NY. 518-270-2249

Tompkins, Marjorie M, *Asst, Budget Planning & Admin,* University of Michigan Libraries (University Library), Ann Arbor MI. 313-764-9356

Tompkins, T Philip, *Assoc Dir,* University of Missouri-Kansas City Libraries, Kansas City MO. 816-276-1531

Tomposki, Philip, *Librn,* United States Navy, Newport RI. 401-841-4338

Toms, Alicia, *Librn,* San Mateo Public Library (Hillsdale), San Mateo CA. 415-574-6955

Toms, Alicia, *Librn,* San Mateo Public Library (Marina), San Mateo CA. 415-574-6955

Toms, Merrill, *Supvr Br,* Kansas City Public Library, Kansas City MO. 816-221-2685

Toms, Merrill, *Librn,* Kansas City Public Library (Plaza), Kansas City MO. 816-753-6114

Tondee, Sara W, *Librn,* Lake Blackshear Regional Library (Schley County Public), Ellaville GA. 912-937-2004

Tondi, Lorraine, *Dir,* Kingsborough Historical Society Library, Brooklyn NY. 212-934-5122

Tondo, Peter, *Librn,* Miami Beach Public Library (South Shore), Miami Beach FL. 305-673-7541

Toner, Mary Anne, *Librn,* Worcester City Hospital (Medical Library), Worcester MA. 617-756-1551, Ext 248

Toner, Michael P, *Dir,* Presbyterian University of Pennsylvania Medical Center, Scheie Eye Institute Library, Philadelphia PA. 215-662-8100, Ext 8148

Toney, Bernard J, *Assoc Prof,* Shippensburg State College, Dept of Library Science, PA. 717-532-1472

Toney, Sherrill F, *Librn,* Universities Center Library, Jackson MS. 601-982-6226

Tongate, John, *Assoc Libr & Pub Servs,* Southeastern Massachusetts University, Library Communications Center, North Dartmouth MA. 617-999-8662

Tongue, Marie, *Dir Libr Serv,* First United Methodist Church Library, Tulsa OK. 918-587-9481

Tonian, Helen, *Readers' Advisors,* Louisville Free Public Library (Talking Book Library), Louisville KY. 502-587-1069, 587-1085

Tonji, Virginia, *On-Line Servs,* Hawaii Medical Library, Inc, Honolulu HI. 808-536-9302

Tonkery, Dan, *Assoc Univ Librn for Tech & Bibliog Product Servs,* University of California Los Angeles Library, Los Angeles CA. 213-825-1201

Tonkin, Helen R, *Dir, On-Line Servs & Bibliog Instr,* Bakerville Library, New Hartford CT. 203-482-8806

Tonkyn, Virginia, *Librn,* Whatcom County Public Library (Diablo Dam Libr), Rockport WA. 206-397-5569

Tonne, Margaret I, *Librn,* Anamosa Public Library, Anamosa IA. 319-462-2183

Tonnes, Evelyn L, *Ad,* Middletown Free Library, Middletown RI. 846-1573 & 846-1584

Tonseth, Phebe, *Media,* Portland Public Library, Baxter Library, Portland ME. 207-773-4761

Tontar, Silvia, *YA,* Winchester Public Library, Winchester MA. 617-729-3770

Toohey, Douglas, *Tech Serv & Ref,* Santa Ana College, Nealley Library, Santa Ana CA. 714-835-3000, Ext 357

Toohey, Elizabeth L, *Dir,* Adams Free Library, Adams MA. 413-743-0540

Tooker, Anna Lisa, *Chief Librn,* Red Wing Public Library, Red Wing MN. 612-388-2884

Tooker, Barbara D, *Program Info Librn,* High Plains Regional Library System, Greeley CO. 303-330-7691

Tooker, G Calvin, *Librn,* Metropolitan State Hospital (Patients Library), Norwalk CA. 213-863-7011, Ext 3274

Tooker, G Calvin, *Librn,* Metropolitan State Hospital (Staff Library), Norwalk CA. 213-863-7011, Ext 295, 4334

Tooker, Kathleen, *Dir,* Wayne Public Library, Wayne NE. 402-375-3135

Tooley, Bonita, *Librn,* Seton Memorial Library & Museum, Cimarron NM. 505-376-2281, Ext 46

Tooley, Robert E, *Asst Dir,* New Castle-Henry County Public Library, New Castle IN. 317-529-0362

Tooly, Irene L, *Librn,* Dolgeville Public Library, Dolgeville NY. 315-429-3421

Toomajian, Janice, *YA,* Downers Grove Public Library, Downers Grove IL. 312-960-1200

Toombs, Kenneth E, *Dir,* University of South Carolina, Thomas Cooper Library, Columbia SC. 803-777-3142

Toombs, Sylvia, *ILL,* Washington University Libraries, Saint Louis MO. 314-889-5400

Toombs, William, *Acq,* Saint Louis University (Omer Poos Law Library), Saint Louis MO. 314-658-2755

Toomey, Gail M, *Dir,* Corunna Public Library, Corunna MI. 517-743-4800

Toomey, Kathleen, *Librn,* McGill University Libraries (Marvin Duchow Music Library), Montreal PQ. 514-392-4281

Toomey, Sister Mary, *Librn,* Saint Francis General Hospital, Medical Library, Pittsburgh PA. 412-622-4343

Toon, Jo, *Librn,* Alberta Department of Culture (Historical Resources Library), Edmonton AB. 403-427-1750

Tooth, John, *Librn,* Manitoba Department of Education Library, Winnipeg MB. 204-786-0218

Topa, Mrs M, *Librn,* Borough of Etobicoke Public Library (Richview Library), Etobicoke ON. 416-248-5681

Topcik, Evelyn, *Librn,* Bureau of Jewish Education, Israel T Naamani Library, Louisville KY. 502-454-5416

Tope, Diana Ray, *Dir,* Robeson County Public Library, Lumberton NC. 919-738-4859

Topel, A Robert, *Dir,* Grayslake Area Public Library District, Grayslake IL. 312-223-5313

Topfer, Sue A, *Ser & Micro,* Wilkes College, Eugene Shedden Farley Library, Wilkes-Barre PA. 717-824-4651, Ext 331 & 332

Topham, Elsie, *Librn,* San Diego Public Library (Pacific Beach), San Diego CA. 714-273-9581

Topham, Patricia, *Librn,* Plymouth Public Library, Plymouth NH. 603-536-2616

Toplin, Barbara, *Ch,* Teaneck Public Library, Teaneck NJ. 201-837-4171

Topper, Judith M, *Librn,* Lawrence Hospital, Ashley Baker Morrill Library, Bronxville NY. 914-337-7300, Ext 306

Topping, Solonge, *Tech Serv & Acq,* Long Branch Public Library, Long Branch NJ. 201-222-3900

Torbett, Mina, *Librn,* Flint River Regional Library (Hawkes), Jackson GA. 404-775-7524

Torgersen, Christine, *Librn,* Highland Falls Library (Frances Tracey Morgan Memorial), Fort Montgomery NY. 914-446-5220

Torgerson, Yvonne, *Librn,* Elkford Public Library, Elkford BC. 604-865-2912

Torgeson, Mary Jo, *YA,* Sheridan County Fulmer Public Library, Sheridan WY. 307-674-8585, 674-9898

Torkelsen, Ivy Jo, *AV,* Union College Library, Lincoln NE. 402-488-2331, Ext 316

Tormay, Katherine A, *Commun Servs,* Florence County Library, Florence SC. 803-662-8424

Tornabene, Jr, Charles, *Librn,* Southwest Florida Water Management District Library, Brooksville FL. 904-796-7211, Ext 1279

Tornell, Helen, *Librn,* Textile Research Institute Library, Princeton NJ. 609-924-3150, Ext 21

Torney, Mildred, *Librn,* Alleghany County Public Library, Sparta NC. 919-372-5573

Torok, Andrew, *Asst Prof,* Northern Illinois University, Dept of Library Science, IL. 815-753-1735

Torr, Lydia M, *Dir & Acq,* Meredith Public Library, Benjamin M Smith Memorial Library, Meredith NH. 603-279-4303

Torrance, Lois, *Circ,* Southwestern College, Memorial Library, Winfield KS. 316-221-4150, Ext 25

Torrence, Carolyn Armold, *ILL, Ref & Doc,* Southwestern Oklahoma State University, Al Harris Library, Weatherford OK. 405-772-6611, Ext 5311

Torrente, Michael J, *Asst Dir Southeastern Regional Med Libr Program,* Emory University Libraries (A W Calhoun Medical Library), Atlanta GA. 404-329-5810

Torrente, Michael J, *Assoc Dir,* Southeastern Regional Medical Library Program, (SERMLP), GA. 404-329-5818

Torres, Cecilia C, *Librn,* Pima County Law Library, Tucson AZ. 602-792-8456

Torres, Elsie, *Cat,* Wells College, Louis Jefferson Long Library, Aurora NY. 315-364-3351

Torres, Irva, *Librn,* New Bedford Free Public Library (Wilks), New Bedford MA. 617-995-5288

Torres, Julia Sanchez, *Librn,* Catholic University of Puerto Rico, Guayama Branch Library, Guayama PR. 809-864-0550, Ext 18 & 23

Torres, Marta, *Librn,* University of Puerto Rico Library (Graduate School of Planning), Rio Piedras PR. 809-764-0000, Ext 3186

Torres, Myrtis, *Librn,* Pointe Coupee Parish Library (Livonia Branch), Maringouin LA. 504-638-7593

Torres, Olga R, *Asst Dir & Tech Serv,* University of Puerto Rico Library, Jose M Lazaro Memorial Library, Rio Piedras PR. 809-764-0000, Ext 3296

Torres, Rita, *Librn,* San Jose Public Library (Biblioteca Latina Americana), San Jose CA. 408-294-1237

Torrey, Charlotte, *Ref,* Bangor Public Library, Bangor ME. 207-947-8336

Torréy, Mary, *Dir,* Park Ridge Public Library, Park Ridge NJ. 201-391-5151

Torstenbo, Laurence H, *Librn,* Miles Community College Library, Miles City MT. 406-232-3031

Tortora, Eileen, *Ser,* Hoechst-Roussel Pharmaceuticals, Inc Library, Div of American Hoechst Corp Library, Somerville NJ. 201-685-2394

Tortorelli, Ann E, *Dir,* Community College of Allegheny County Library, South Campus Library, West Mifflin PA. 412-469-1100, Ext 290

Tosi, Laura, *Assoc Librn,* Museum of Bronx History, The Bronx County Historical Society Library, Bronx NY. 212-881-8900

Tostevin, Patricia A, *Librn,* ITT Rayonier Inc, Olympic Research Div Library, Shelton WA. 206-426-4461, Ext 224

Toth, Alex, *Ref,* Pacific University, Harvey W Scott Memorial Library, Forest Grove OR. 503-357-6151, Ext 301

Toth, Ben, *Design, Mech Eng & Mgt Sci,* University of Waterloo Library, Waterloo ON. 519-885-1211

Toth, Betty, *ILL,* Shaker Heights Public Library, Shaker Heights OH. 216-991-2030

Toth, Carol G, *ILL, Acq & Per,* Cuyahoga Community College (Western Campus Library), Parma OH. 216-845-4000, Ext 278

Toth, Gregory, *Humanities & Bibliographic Instr,* Rochester Institute of Technology, Wallace Memorial Library, Rochester NY. 716-475-2566

Toth, Luann, *Ch,* Free Public Library of Summit, Summit NJ. 201-273-0350

Toth, Robert W, *Dir,* Wellsville-Carnegie Public Library, Wellsville OH. 532-1526 & 532-1264

Totten, Doris, *Asst Librn,* Rathbun Free Memorial Library, East Haddam CT. 203-873-8210

Totten, Herman L, *Instr,* North Texas State University, School of Library & Information Sciences, TX. 817-788-2445

Totten, Shirley, *Librn,* Mingo County Library, Delbarton WV. 304-475-2749

Totura, June, *Ad & YA,* Boca Raton Public Library, Boca Raton FL. 395-2980 & 395-1110, Ext 285, 286, 336

Touhey, John F, *Dir,* Fashion Institute of Technology, Library-Media Services Dept, New York NY. 212-760-7695

Toupin, C, *Librn,* Bibliotheque Pinocchio, Montreal PQ. 514-254-6891

Toupin, Juanita, *Librn,* Montreal Museum of Fine Arts, Art Reference Library, Montreal PQ. 514-285-1600

Toups, Patricia, *Librn,* Life Office Management Association, Information Center, Atlanta GA. 404-892-7272

Tousley, Edna, *Librn,* Elbert County Library (Elizabeth Library), Elizabeth CO. 303-621-2041

Tousley, Rebecca P, *Doc,* Mississippi University for Women, John Clayton Fant Memorial Library, Columbus MS. 601-328-4808

Toussaint, George, *Institutional Servs Librn,* Corn Belt Library System, Normal IL. 309-452-4485

Toussaint, Mecheline, *Ref,* Bibliotheque De Quebec, Quebec PQ. 418-694-6356

Toutsis, Ellen, *Bibliog Instr,* United States Army (Materials & Mechanics Research Center Library), Watertown MA. 617-923-3460

Tower, Kathie, *Cat & On-Line Servs,* Mesa College, Learning Resource Services, Lowell Heiny Library, Grand Junction CO. 303-248-1436

Tower, Mary L, *Ad & Ref,* Lower Merion Library Association, Bryn Mawr PA. 215-527-3889

Tower, Mary L, *Ad & Acq,* Ludington Public Library, Bryn Mawr PA. 215-527-1550, 525-1776

Tower, Terri, *Acq,* Willard Library, Battle Creek MI. 616-968-8166

Tower, Thelma, *Asst Dir,* York Public Library, York ME. 207-363-2818

Towers, A Carol, *Librn,* Binghamton Public Library (East), Binghamton NY. 607-722-4342

Towery, Mrs Dick, *Librn,* First Methodist Church, Bliss Memorial Library, Shreveport LA. 318-425-4586

Towery, Raunda, *Librn,* John Portman & Associates Library, Atlanta GA. 404-522-8811, Ext 394

Towery, Stephen, *Tech Serv,* Walla Walla Public Library, Walla Walla WA. 509-525-5353

Towery, Suzanne M, *Librn,* Surrey Township Public Library, Farwell MI. 517-588-9782

Towle, Elnora, *Cat,* Lenawee County Library, Adrian MI. 517-263-1011

Towle, Jean Ann, *Librn,* Tamaqua Public Library, Tamaqua PA. 717-668-4660

Towle, Judith, *Librn,* Island Resources Foundation, Saint Thomas VI. 809-775-3225

Towles, Lorraine, *Automated Systems Librn,* Richland College, Learning Resource Center, Dallas TX. 214-746-4460

Town, T, *Asst Librn User Servs,* Toronto Public Library, Toronto ON. 416-484-8015

Towner, Lawrence W, *Librn,* Newberry Library, Chicago IL. 312-943-9090

Towner, Lorena, *Librn,* Chouteau County Free Library, Fort Benton MT. 406-622-5222

Townley, Charles, *Dir,* Pennsylvania State University, Capitol Campus Heindel Library, Middletown PA. 717-787-7771

Towns, Bobby, *Asst Librn,* Mayer, Brown & Platt Law Library, Chicago IL. 312-782-0600

Towns, Rose Mary, *Ref Coordr,* North Bay Cooperative Library System, Santa Rosa CA. 707-545-0831

Townsend, Alice, *Librn,* Brooklyn Public Library (Leonard), Brooklyn NY. 212-387-3800

Townsend, Catherine, *Dir,* Watervliet Public Library, Watervliet NY. 518-274-4471

Townsend, Constance, *Asst Dir,* Teton County Library, Huff Memorial Library, Jackson WY. 307-733-2164

Townsend, Dorothy, *Librn,* Skaneateles Library Association, Skaneateles NY. 315-685-5135

Townsend, Lorraine, *Asst Librn,* Northern Telecom Ltd, Library & Information Center, Montreal PQ. 514-931-5711

Townsend, Martha, *Ad & Ref,* Santa Monica Public Library, Santa Monica CA. 213-451-5751

Townsend, Mary, *Asst Librn & Ref,* University of Michigan Libraries (Public Health), Ann Arbor MI. 313-764-5473

Townsend, Robert, *On-Line Servs,* Illinois State University, Milner Library, Normal IL. 309-438-3675

Townsend, Ruth, *Librn,* Powell County Public Library, Stanton KY. 606-663-4511

Townsley, Patricia, *Instr,* Southeast Missouri State University, Library Science Program, MO. 314-651-2235

Towriss, Sharon, *Ad,* Meridian Public Library, Meridian MS. 601-693-6771, 693-4913

Towry, Lucy, *Librn,* Tulsa World-Tulsa Tribune, Library Department, Tulsa OK. 918-583-2161

Towse, Karyl, *Librn,* Kern County Library (Wasco Branch), Wasco CA. 805-861-2130

Towsley, Ruth, *Librn,* Rockingham Memorial Hospital Library, Bellows Falls VT. 802-463-3903

Toy, Beverly, *Assoc Dir,* University of California Library, Irvine CA. 714-833-5212

Toy, Jacqueline B, *Librn,* Providence Public Library (Rochambeau), Providence RI. 401-421-1499

Toy, Jr, Ernest W, *Librn,* California State University Fullerton Library, Fullerton CA. 714-773-2714

Toyama, Sally, *Librn,* Hawaii State Library System (Aina Haina), Honolulu HI. 808-373-3888

Tozer, Peggy M, *Dir,* Eastern New Mexico University Library, Portales NM. 505-562-2624

Tozier, Coralie, *Dir,* Lawrence Public Library, Fairfield ME. 207-453-6867

Tra, John, *Librn,* Divine Word College, Mat Jacoby Library, Epworth IA. 319-876-3354

Trabert, W Douglas, *Media,* Lake-Sumter Community College, Learning Resources Center, Leesburg FL. 904-787-3747, Ext 33

Trace, Sally A, *Adv,* State Library of Pennsylvania, Harrisburg PA. 717-787-2646

Trachinger, Helga, *In Charge,* University of California, Los Angeles (Office of Instructional Development, Instructional Media Library), Los Angeles CA. 213-825-0755

Tracy, Constance J M, *Librn,* Virginia State Penitentiary Library, Richmond VA. 804-786-2101

Tracy, Helen, *Librn,* Billings & East Allan Public Library, Kagawong ON. 705-282-2611

Tracy, Hugh, *On-Line Servs,* Creighton University, Alumni Memorial Library, Omaha NE. 402-449-2705

Tracy, Joan, *Asst Dir & Tech Serv,* Eastern Washington University, John F Kennedy Memorial Library, Cheney WA. 509-359-2261

Tracy, Karen B, *Ref Dept Head,* Harvard University Library (Baker Library), Boston MA. 617-495-3650

Tracy, Kenneth L, *Librn,* Southern California College, O Cope Budge Library, Costa Mesa CA. 714-556-3610, Ext 264

Tracy, Norman E, *Dir,* Harford Community College Learning Resources Center, Bel Air MD. 301-838-1000, Ext 268

Tracy, Phyllis, *Librn,* Lexington Public Library, Lexington IL. 309-365-7801

Tracy, Sherri, *Librn,* Las Vegas Mental Health Center, NV. 702-870-7211

Traeger, Bill, *Pub Servs,* Tempe Public Library, Tempe AZ. 602-968-8231

Trafford, Mabel A, *Librn,* National Marine Fisheries Service, Lionel A Walford Library, Sandy Hook Laboratory, Highlands NJ. 201-872-0200

Trafton, William, *Ref,* Stanly County Public Library, Albemarle NC. 704-982-0115

Tragesser, Susan, *Acq,* Indiana University at Kokomo, Learning Resource Center, Kokomo IN. 317-453-2000, Ext 237

Tragitt, Pete, *Consortium Dir,* Coastal Bend Health Sciences Library Consortium, TX. 512-881-4198

Trahan, Kathryn P, *Librn,* Holiday House Corp, Media Center, De Land FL. 904-734-8800, Ext 171

Traina, Helen J, *Chief Librn,* Chemical Bank Research Library, New York NY. 212-770-3127

Trainer, C W, *Librn,* Irion County Public Library, Mertzon TX. 915-835-3671

Trainer, Karin, *Tech Serv,* New York University, Elmer Holmes Bobst Library, New York NY. 212-598-2484

Traister, Alice, *Media,* Wayne County Library System, Newark NY. 315-331-2176

Traister, Alice S, *Media,* Ontario Cooperative Library System, Newark NY. 315-331-2176

Traks, Carole, *Librn,* Poudre Valley Memorial Hospital, Media Resources, Fort Collins CO. 303-482-4111, Ext 1559

Tramdack, Philip J, *Cat,* Trinity University Library, San Antonio TX. 512-736-8121

Trammell, Anne, *Dir,* North Harris County College, Learning Resource Center, Houston TX. 713-443-6640, Ext 270, 271

Trammer, Onetha, *Librn,* Eaton Corp Library, Cleveland OH. 216-523-5269

Tran, Thuan, *Librn,* Western Wisconsin Technical Institute Library, La Crosse WI. 608-785-9412

Trant, Dorothy, *Asst Dir,* Woonsocket Harris Public Library, Woonsocket RI. 401-769-9044

Trapani, Jean, *Librn,* Libby, McNeill & Libby, Research & Product Development Center Library, Chicago IL. 312-568-3300, Ext 259

Trapnell, Lucile, *Librn,* Brunswick-Glynn County Regional Library (Wayne County), Saint Mary's GA. 912-885-4450

Trappoli, Dianne, *Doc,* East Brunswick Public Library, East Brunswick NJ. 201-254-1220

Trash, Julia, *Librn,* Smith Center Public Library, Smith Center KS. 913-282-3361

Trask, Carole A, *Librn,* Teledyne Water Pik, Information Center Library, Fort Collins CO. 303-493-8600

Trask, Richard, *Rare Bks & Spec Coll,* Peabody Institute Library, Danvers Public Library, Danvers MA. 617-774-0554

Trask, Richard B, *Archivist,* Peabody Institute Library (Danvers Archival Center), Danvers MA. 617-777-2821

Tratt, Grace, *Humanities, Soc Sci,* Dalhousie University, Izaak Walton Killam Memorial Library (Humanities & Social Sciences), Macdonald Memorial Library (Science), Halifax NS. 902-424-3601

Trauner, Meg, *Librn,* Ohio State University Libraries (Vocational Education Research Library), Columbus OH. 614-486-3655, Ext 221

Trauner, Meg, *Librn,* Ohio State University, National Center for Research in Vocational Education, Research Library, Columbus OH. 614-486-3655, Ext 221, 329

Traute, Barbara, *Ad & Cat,* Fairfield Public Library, Fairfield NJ. 201-227-3575

Trautman, Dorothy, *Commun Servs,* Augusta Regional Library, Augusta-Richmond County Public Library, Augusta GA. 404-724-1871

Trautman, Wilbur, *Post-Cat,* Temple University of the Commonwealth System of Higher Education, Samuel Paley Library, Philadelphia PA. 215-787-8231

Trautwein, R C, *Dir,* Columbus Public Library, Pawnee Regional Library, Columbus NE. 402-564-7116

Travaline, Marjorie, *Librn,* Glassboro State College (Wilson Music), Glassboro NJ. 609-445-7306

Traven, Lee W, *Dir Libr Serv,* Exxon Co USA (Information Center), New York NY. 212-398-3000

Traver, Paula, *Tech Serv,* Concordia Theological Seminary Library, Fort Wayne IN. 219-482-9611, Ext 226

Travillian, J Maurice, *Network Coordr,* Maryland State Department of Education, Division of Library Development & Services, Baltimore MD. 301-796-8300, Ext 284

Travis, Eileen, *Regional Librn,* Saint John Regional Library, Saint John NB. 506-693-1191

Travis, Irene L, *Asst Prof,* University of Maryland, College of Library & Information Services, MD. 301-454-5441

Travis, Jessica, *Librn,* Rockingham County Public Library (Reidsville Branch), Reidsville NC. 919-349-8476

Travis, Jo Ann, *Librn,* King's College Library, Charlotte NC. 704-372-0266

Travis, Kay, *Tech Serv,* Purchase Regional Library, Murray KY. 502-753-6461

Travis, Lucille, *Instr,* Blue Mountain College, Dept of Library Science, MS. 601-685-5711, Ext 47

Travis, Lucille W, *Acq,* Blue Mountain College, Guyton Library, Blue Mountain MS. 601-685-5711, Ext 47

Travis, Marguerite W, *Librn,* Saint Thomas Seminary Library, Denver CO. 303-722-4687, Ext 50

Travis, Marjorie, *Librn,* Loup City Township Library, Loup City NE. 308-745-1630

Travis, Terry, *Dir,* Indiana Vocational Technical College, Region 4, Lafayette, Learning Resources Center, Lafayette IN. 317-477-7401

Trawick, Clara, *Librn,* Conecuh County Public Library, Evergreen AL. 205-578-2670

Traxel, Ellen, *District Libr,* United States Army (Corps of Engineers, Seattle District Library), Seattle WA. 206-764-3728

Trayling, Karen, *Ch,* Acorn Public Library District, Oak Forest IL. 312-687-3700

Trayling, Karen, *Ch,* Dolton Public Library District, Dolton IL. 312-849-2385

Traylor, Margaret, *Ref,* College of Alameda Library & Resources Center, Alameda CA. 415-522-7221, Ext 365

Treadway, Cleo, *Dir,* Tusculum College Library, Greeneville TN. 615-639-1481

Treat, William, *Dir Tech Servs/Systs,* Bowling Green State University Library, Bowling Green OH. 419-372-2856

Trebbi, Jean, *Pub Servs Syst Librn,* Broward County Division of Libraries, Broward County Library, Pompano Beach FL. 305-972-1100

Treble, Joan, *Borough Coordr Staten Island,* New York Public Library (The Branch Libraries), New York NY. 212-790-6262

Treciokas, Anne C, *Librn,* Norwood Hospital, Youngdahl Library, Norwood MA. 617-769-4000, Ext 235

Treece, Regina, *Asst Dir,* Sugar Grove Public Library, Sugar Grove IL. 312-466-4686

Treffner, Walter S, *Mgr,* General Refractories Co, Research Center Library, Baltimore MD. 301-355-3400

Trefry, Timothy, *Circ,* University of Nebraska at Omaha, University Library, Omaha NE. 402-554-2361

Tregilgas, Kathleen, *In Charge,* Saint Paul Public Library (Saint Anthony Park), Saint Paul MN. 612-292-6635

Trehub, Elaine, *College Hist,* Mount Holyoke College, Williston Memorial Library, South Hadley MA. 413-538-2226

Trejo, Arnulfo D, *Prof,* University of Arizona, Graduate Library School, AZ. 602-626-3565

Trejo, Tamiye, *Chief Northeast District Br,* Chicago Public Library, Chicago IL. 312-269-2900

Tremaine, Laurine, *Dir,* Parry Sound Public Library, Parry Sound ON. 705-746-9601

Tremblay, Caryl A, *Dir,* Berlin Township Library, West Berlin NJ. 609-767-6727

Tremblay, Francine, *Ad & Tech Serv,* Bibliotheque Municipale De Lachine, Lachine PQ. 514-637-2568

Tremblay, Levis, *Tech Serv & Cat,* College Du Nord-Quest La Bibliotheque, Rouyn PQ. 819-762-0931, Ext 134

Tremblay, Levis, *Tech Serv & Cat,* Universite Du Quebec: Centre d'etudes Universitaires Dans L'ouest Quebecois Bibliotheque, Rouyn PQ. 819-762-0971, Ext 350

Tremblay, Louise, *Ch,* Confederation Des Caisses Populaires Et D'economie Des Jardins Du Quebec, Centre De Documentation, Levis PQ. 418-835-2468

Tremblay, Maud Pomerleau, *ILL,* CEGEP de Chicoutimi, Centre De Documentation, Chicoutimi PQ. 418-549-9520, Ext 212, 312

Tremblay, Maude L, *Per,* CEGEP de Chicoutimi, Centre De Documentation, Chicoutimi PQ. 418-549-9520, Ext 212, 312

Tremblay, Mrs Bernie, *Librn,* Kent County Municipal Public Library (Merlin Public), Merlin ON. 519-689-4944

Tremblay, R-Marcuerite, *AV,* CEGEP de Chicoutimi, Centre De Documentation, Chicoutimi PQ. 418-549-9520, Ext 212, 312

Trench, Mrs Ray, *Librn,* Northeast Georgia Regional Library System (Cornelia), Clarkesville GA. 404-754-4413

Trenery, Frank E, *Dir,* Pompano Beach City Library, Pompano Beach FL. 305-942-7220

Trenholme, Margery W, *Dir,* Fraser-Hickson Institute, Montreal, Free Library, Montreal PQ. 514-489-5301

Trenner, Claudine, *Librn,* Livonia Public Library (Carl Sandburg Branch), Livonia MI. 313-476-0700

Trent, Helen, *Librn,* Methodist Hospital, School of Nursing Library, Mitchell SD. 605-996-5716

Trepanier, Luc, *Ref,* Ecole Polytechnique De Montreal Bibliotheque, Montreal PQ. 514-344-4847

Trepanier, Rose, *Librn,* Rehabilitation Institute of Montreal Library, Montreal PQ. 514-735-3741, Ext 212

Trepman, Paul, *Dir,* Bibliotheque Publique Juive, Jewish Public Library, Montreal PQ. 514-735-6535

Trepp, George, *Acting Dir,* Long Beach Public Library, Long Beach NY. 516-432-7201

Tressler, Laura, *Tech Serv,* Glen Ellyn Public Library, Glen Ellyn IL. 312-469-0879

Trethewey, Willeen, *Media,* Wisconsin Department of Public Instruction (Reference & Loan Library), Madison WI. 608-266-7270266-1053

Treude, Mai, *Librn,* University of Minnesota Libraries-Twin Cities (Maps), Minneapolis MN. 612-373-2825

Trevanion, Margaret, *Librn,* North Hills Passavant Hospital, Medical Library, Pittsburgh PA. 412-366-1000, Ext 340

Trevaskis, Lee, *Librn,* Celanese Canada Ltd Library, Montreal PQ. 514-878-1581, Ext 264

Trevathan, Margaret, *Dir,* Calloway County Public Library, Murray KY. 502-753-2288

Trevino, Raquel, *Librn,* Houston Public Library (Carnegie), Houston TX. 713-227-9177

Trevorrow, Todd, *Ref & Bibliog Instr,* Westbrook College Library, Portland ME. 207-797-7261, Ext 280

Trew, James R, *Dir, Libr Environ Resources Off,* Library of Congress, Washington DC. 202-287-5000

Trew, Joan, *Ch,* Thomas Hackney Braswell Memorial Library, Rocky Mount NC. 442-1937 & 442-1951

Trexell, Arlene, *Dir,* First Southern Baptist Church Library, Tucson AZ. 602-623-5858

Trexler, Mrs Hollis B, *Librn,* North Davidson Public Library, Welcome NC. 704-249-1586

Treyz, Joseph H, *Dir,* University of Wisconsin-Madison, Memorial Library, Madison WI. 608-262-3521

Trezevant, Caroline, *On-Line Servs & Bibliog Instr,* East Texas State University, James Gilliam Gee Library, Commerce TX. 214-886-5717

Trezza, Alphonse F, *Exec Dir,* National Commission on Libraries & Information Science, (NCLIS), DC. 202-653-6252

Triay, Paulette, *Ref & Spec Coll,* Fullerton City Library, Fullerton CA. 714-738-6333, Ext 301

Trible, Bruce, *Cat,* University of Southwestern Louisiana, Dupre Library, Lafayette LA. 318-264-6396

Tribley, Edna, *Tech Serv & Cat,* Northport Public Library, Northport NY. 516-261-6930

Tricarico, Maryann, *Asst Dir,* Lynn Public Library, Lynn MA. 617-595-0567

Tridao, Nellie, *Librn,* Lebanon Community Library (Spanish Reading Center), Lebanon PA. 717-273-7624

Trieber, B, *Asst Librn,* Redcliff Centennial Library, Redcliff AB. 403-548-3335

Triemstra, Brenda, *Asst Librn,* First Christian Reformed Church Library, Kalamazoo MI. 616-345-4280

Triffin, Nicholas, *Asst Librn & Ref,* University of Connecticut at Hartford (Law Library), West Hartford CT. 203-523-4841, Ext 347, 370

Triggs, Jo, *Intertype Coordr,* Mid-Wisconsin Federated Library System, Fond du Lac WI. 414-921-3670

Trimarche, Joan, *Pub Relations,* Herrick Public Library, Holland MI. 616-392-3114

Trimble, Eleanor, *Librn,* Sunflower County Library System (Horace Stansel Memorial), Ruleville MS. 601-756-2226

Trimble, Kathleen, *Librn,* Toledo Blade Co Library, Toledo OH. 419-259-6000

Trimble, Robert, *Librn,* Southwestern Baptist Theological Seminary (AV Learning Center), Fort Worth TX. 817-923-1921, Ext 277

Trimboli, Sister Teresa, *Assoc Dir, On-Line Servs & Bibliog Instr,* Saint Mary's University (School of Law Library), San Antonio TX. 512-436-3435

Trimboli, Teresa, *Ref,* University of Dayton Libraries (Law School Library), Dayton OH. 513-229-2314

Trimingham, Robert, *Acq,* California State University, Sacramento Library, Sacramento CA. 916-454-6466

Trimm, Maureen D, *Dir,* South Bay Cooperative Library System, Santa Clara CA. 408-984-3278

Trimmell, Theresa, *Librn,* Wichita Public Library (Westlink), Wichita KS. 316-262-0611

Trinca, Margaret, *Ad & Tech Serv,* Liverpool Public Library, Liverpool NY. 315-457-0310

Trinkle, Robert, *Dir,* Monroe County Public Library, Bloomington IN. 812-339-2271

Trinklein, Lois, *Librn,* Shippensburg Public Library, Shippensburg PA. 717-532-4508

Triolo, Victor, *Assoc Prof,* Southern Connecticut State College, Div of Library Science & Instructional Technology, CT. 203-397-4532

Triplehorn, Judie, *On-Line Servs,* University of Alaska, Fairbanks, Elmer E Rasmuson Library, Fairbanks AK. 907-479-7224

Triplett, Margaret S, *Librn,* Bucks County Free Library, Doylestown PA. 215-348-9081

Triplett, Margaret S, *Librn,* Bucks County Free Library (Center County), Doylestown PA. 215-348-9081

Triplett, Nan, *Librn,* Judith Basin County Free Library (Geyser Library Station), Geyser MT. 406-566-2389

Tripp, Donna L, *Dir,* Emerson College, Abbot Memorial Library, Boston MA. 617-262-2010, Ext 281

Tripp, Donna L, *Coordr,* Fenway Library Consortium, MA. 617-262-2010, Ext 281

Tripp, Margaret S, *Ref,* Florida International University, Tamiami Campus, Athenaeum, Miami FL. 305-552-2461

Tripp, Wendell, *Librn,* New York State Historical Association Library, Cooperstown NY. 607-547-2509

Trippett, Sandra K, *Dir,* First Baptist Church, John L Whorton Media Center Library, Longview TX. 214-758-0681, Ext 31

Tripplett, M Glenn, *Dir,* Miami Dade Community College (New World Center Campus), Miami FL. 305-577-6890

Trisdale, Raymon, *Chief Librn,* United States Army (The Army Logistics Library), Fort Lee VA. 804-734-1797, 734-4286

Trisdale, Raymon, *Chief Librn,* United States Department of the Army Logistics Management Center, Defense Logistics Studies Information Exchange (DLSIE), Fort Lee VA. 804-734-1797

Trishman, Judith, *Ext Dir,* Public Library of Columbus & Franklin County, Columbus OH. 614-864-8050

Trisler, Donna, *Librn,* Brook Lane Psychiatric Center Library, Hagerstown MD. 301-733-0330

Tritch, Colleen, *Librn,* Southeast Butler County Library Association, Saxonburg PA. 412-352-4810

Trithart, David, *Bibliog Instr,* State University of New York College at Potsdam, Frederick W Crumb Memorial Library, Potsdam NY. 315-268-2940

Trivedi, Harish, *Librn,* Journal Herald, Reference Library, Dayton OH. 513-225-2430

Trivision, Margaret, *Regional Coordr,* San Diego County Library (Region B), San Diego CA. 714-565-5100

Trivison, Donna, *ILL & Tech Serv,* Lake Erie College, James F Lincoln Learning Resource Center, Painesville OH. 216-352-3361, Ext 280

Trobaugh, Nellie, *Librn,* Edward Chipman Public Library, Momence IL. 815-472-2581

Troester, Zala, *Asst Librn,* Garnavillo Public Library, Garnavillo IA. 319-964-2119

Troiano, Wendy E, *Librn,* Bangor Mental Health Institute, Health Science Library, Bangor ME. 207-947-6981, Ext 349

Troisi, Barbara, *Ref,* South San Francisco Public Library, South San Francisco CA. 415-877-8521

Trolander, Judith, *Dir,* Northeast Minnesota Historical Center, Duluth MN. 218-726-8526

Trolinger, Sara, *Librn,* Brooklyn Public Library (East Flatbush), Brooklyn NY. 212-498-0033

Trollinger, Deborah, *Ser,* Rockingham Community College Library, Learning Resources Center, Wentworth NC. 919-342-4261, Ext 245

Tromater, Ray, *Dir,* Green Gold Library System, Shreveport LA. 318-221-0101

Trombatore, Dennis, *Common Curric,* Loyola University Library, Main Library, New Orleans LA. 504-865-3346

Trombitas, Ildiko, *Librn,* Burroughs Wellcome Co Library, Research Triangle Park NC. 919-549-8371, Ext 305

Trombley, Ivan C, *Librn,* PPG Industries Inc, Chemical Div, Research Library, Corpus Christi TX. 512-883-4301, Ext 556

Trombly, Pat, *ILL,* Upland Public Library, Upland CA. 714-982-1561

Trombly, Robert, *Dept Head,* New York State Library (Educational Programs & Studies Information Service), Albany NY. 518-474-3759

Troop, Anne, *Mgr Info Servs,* CPC International, Inc, Best Food Information Center, Union NJ. 201-688-9000

Troost, F William, *Media,* Los Angeles Trade Technical College Library, Los Angeles CA. 213-746-0800, Ext 217

Troph, Lucille, *In Charge,* Cleveland Public Library (Literature), Cleveland OH. 216-623-2881

Trost, Keith R, *Dir,* Barton County Community College Library, Great Bend KS. 316-792-2701

Trott, Margaret, *Librn,* Humber College of Applied Arts & Technology (Lakeshore Campus II Resource Center), Toronto ON. 416-252-5571

Trott, Margaret, *Librn,* Humber College of Applied Arts & Technology (Keelesdale Campus Resource Center), Toronto ON. 416-763-4571, Ext 42

Trott, Margaret, *Coordr Lakeshore Libr,* Humber College, Learning Resource Centre, Rexdale ON. 416-675-3111, Ext 331

Trotta, Victoria, *Head of Tech Servs,* University of Southern California (Asa V Call Law Library), Los Angeles CA. 213-743-6487
Trotter, Debbie, *Spec Coll,* Morris Public Library, Morris IL. 815-942-6880
Trotter, Mrs J, *Librn,* Stayner Public Library, Stayner ON. 705-428-3595
Trotti, John B, *Dir,* Union Theological Seminary in Virginia Library, Richmond VA. 804-355-0671, Ext 311
Trotti, Louise, *Dir,* Dekalb Library System, Maud M Burrus Library, Decatur GA. 404-378-7569
Trouba, Marianne, *Asst Librn,* Dwight Community Library, Dwight NE. 402-566-2755
Troust, Warren, *Reader Serv,* Bucks County Community College Library, Newtown PA. 215-968-5861, Ext 306, 307
Trout, Anne, *Media,* Midland County Public Library, Midland TX. 915-683-2708
Trout, Frank E, *Curator, Winsor Memorial Map Room,* Harvard University Library (Harvard College Library (Headquarters in Harry Elkins Widener Memorial Library)), Cambridge MA. 617-495-2401
Trout, Ina S, *Asst Dir,* Ina Pullen Smallwood Memorial Library, Chickasaw AL. 205-452-3912
Troutman, Naomi E, *Librn,* Trevorton Public Library, Trevorton PA. 717-797-8011
Troutman, Vivian S, *Dir,* Annville Free Library, Annville PA. 717-867-1802
Troutt, Harriett, *Dir,* Tallahatchie County Library, Charleston MS. 601-647-2638
Trowbridge, Ann, *Librn,* Fairfax County Public Library (Woodrow Wilson), Falls Church VA. 703-820-8774
Trowbridge, Leslie, *Librn,* Weber County Library (Emerson Stone), Ogden UT. 801-399-8397
Troy, Jane, *Librn,* Sandy Lake Community Library, Sandy Lake PA. 412-376-3766
Troy, Juel, *Ref,* La Porte Public Library, La Porte IN. 219-362-6156
Troy, Margaret H, *Librn,* Bolt Beranek & Newman Inc Library, Cambridge MA. 617-491-1850, Ext 3277
Troyer, F L, *Librn,* Royal Astronomical Society of Canada Library, Toronto ON. 416-484-4960
Truck, L Lorna, *Extension Serv,* Public Library of Des Moines, Des Moines IA. 515-283-4152
Trucksess, Joseph, *Librn,* Salem County Historical Society Library, Salem NJ. 609-935-5004
Trucksis, Theresa, *Dir,* Northeastern Ohio Library Association, (NOLA), OH. 216-746-7042
Trudeau, Janice, *Tech Serv & Cat,* Monroe Community College, LeRoy V Good Library, Rochester NY. 716-442-9950, Ext 2310
Trudell, Robert J, *Dir,* Greenburgh Public Library, Elmsford NY. 914-682-5265
Trudell, Sister Margaret, *Bibliog Instr,* Rivier College, Regina Library, Nashua NH. 603-888-1311, Ext 42
True, Beverly, *Chief Librn,* Cumberland Regional Library, Amherst NS. 902-667-2135
Truec, Nymah L, *Chief Librn,* Veterans Administration, Hospital Library, Vancouver WA. 206-696-4061, Ext 254
Truelson, J, *Librn,* University of Southern California (Crocker Business), Los Angeles CA. 213-743-7348
Truelson, Stanley, *Dir,* Alaska Health Sciences Library, Anchorage AK. 907-263-1870
Truelson, Stanley, *Alaska Health Sciences,* Alaska State Library, Juneau AK. 907-465-2910
Truesdell, Eugenia, *Cat,* West Chester State College, Francis Harvey Green Library, West Chester PA. 215-436-2643
Truesdell, Walter G, *Librn,* Theological Seminary of the Reformed Episcopal Church, Kuehner Memorial Library, Philadelphia PA. 215-222-5158
Truitt, Lucille, *Librn,* Shelby County, Fannie Brown Booth Memorial Library, Center TX. 713-598-5522
Truitt, Margaret H, *ILL,* Medical College of Georgia Library, Augusta GA. 404-828-3441
Trull, Jo Ann, *Librn,* Lithium Corp of America, Inc, Ellestad Research Library, Bessemer City NC. 704-629-2282
Trulock, Joy B, *ILL,* Valdosta State College Library, Valdosta GA. 912-247-3228
Truman, Gloria F, *Librn,* Howard Public Library, Howard SD. 605-772-4761

Truman, Susan, *Habilitation Tech II,* Arizona Training Program at Coolidge Library (Client Library), Coolidge AZ. 602-723-4151
Trumbly, Lindeke Schurmeier, *Librn,* Stone & Webster Engineering Corp, Technical Information Center Library, Denver CO. 303-770-7700, Ext 494
Trumbore, Jean, *Doc,* University of Delaware, Hugh M Morris Library, Newark DE. 302-738-2231
Trump, Anne, *Ref,* Brookings Public Library, Brookings SD. 605-692-9407, 692-9408
Trumpeter, Margo, *Mgt,* University of New Mexico General Library, Albuquerque NM. 505-277-4241
Truro, James C, *Librn,* Immaculate Conception Seminary Library, Mahwah NJ. 201-327-0300
Truschel, Patricia A, *Librn,* Federal Reserve Bank of Cleveland, Pittsburgh Branch Library, Pittsburgh PA. 412-281-5981
Truscott, Dee Ann, *Dir,* Republic-Michigamme Public Library, Republic MI. 906-376-8401
Truscott, Jean, *Librn,* Saint Mary's Hospital, Memorial Library, Milwaukee WI. 414-289-7000, Ext 2223
Truscott, Kamala, *Tech Serv,* Rutgers University (Kilmer Area Library), New Brunswick NJ. 201-932-3610
Truscott, Myfanwy, *Librn,* Saskatchewan Alcoholism Commission Library, Regina SK. 306-565-4656
Tryon, Elena, *Dir,* Cheektowaga Public Library, Cheektowaga NY. 716-892-8089
Tryon, Jonathan, *Assoc Prof,* University of Rhode Island, Graduate Library School, RI. 401-792-2878 or 792-2947
Tryon, Roy H, *Dir,* Balch Institute for Ethnic Studies Library, Philadelphia PA. 215-925-8090
Trzyna, Thaddens C, *Dir,* California Institute of Public Affairs Library, Claremont CA. 714-624-5212
Tsai, Betty, *Tech Serv,* Bucks County Community College Library, Newtown PA. 215-968-5861, Ext 306, 307
Tsai, Elizabeth, *Ser,* Our Lady of the Lake University Libraries, San Antonio TX. 512-434-6711, Ext 272
Tsai, Ernest J, *Librn,* Washington University Libraries (East Asian Library), Saint Louis MO. 314-889-5155
Tsai, Sheng-Luen, *Tech Serv & Acq,* Brigham Young University-Hawaii Campus, Joseph F Smith Library, Laie HI. 808-293-9211, Ext 260, 264
Tsang, Walter M, *Librn,* Canada Department of Energy, Mines & Resources (Earth Physics Branch Library), Ottawa ON. 613-995-5558
Tsao, Jennifer, *Asst Librn,* New York Institute of Technology, Metropolitan Center Library, New York NY. 212-399-8340, 399-8341
Tschudi, Carol, *On-Line Servs,* Engineering Societies Library, New York NY. 212-644-7611
Tschudi, Phyllis, *Tech Serv,* Schools of Theology in Dubuque Library, Dubuque IA. 319-589-3100, 556-8151
Tschudy, Karen D, *Chief Librn,* Cleveland Institute of Art, Jessica Gund Memorial Library, Cleveland OH. 216-421-4322, Ext 30
Tse, Joyce, *Cat,* West Liberty State College, Paul N Elbin Library, West Liberty WV. 304-336-8035
Tseng, Evelina, *Tech Serv,* Catawba College, Corriher-Linn-Black Library, Salisbury NC. 704-637-4448, 637-4449
Tseng, Henry P, *Dir,* Capital University Library (Law School Library), Columbus OH. 614-445-8634
Tseou, Carolyn, *Librn,* Xerox Corp (Xerox Square Library), Rochester NY. 716-423-5223
Tsikata, Marcella, *Librn,* Houston Public Library (Fifth Ward Branch), Houston TX. 713-236-0759
Tsuchida, Himeko, *Cat,* Laney College Library-Learning Resources Center, Oakland CA. 415-763-4791
Tsui, Theresa, *Per & Doc,* Jersey City State College, Forrest A Irwin Library, Jersey City NJ. 201-547-3026
Tsukamoto, Jack, *Tech Serv,* Ball State University, Alexander M Bracken Library, Muncie IN. 317-285-6261

Tsuneishi, David, *Acq,* United States Commission on Civil Rights, National Clearinghouse Library, Washington DC. 202-254-6636
Tsuneishi, Warren, *Dir for Area Studies,* Library of Congress, Washington DC. 202-287-5000
Tsusaki, Edna, *Adminr,* Hawaii State Library System (East Oahu Library District), Honolulu HI. 808-988-2194
Tu, Carol, *Per,* West Virginia Institute of Technology, Vining Library, Montgomery WV. 304-442-3141
Tu, Susan, *Dir,* Saints College, Alumni Library, Lexington MS. 601-834-3416
Tubandt, Dianne, *ILL,* John Packard Library of Yuba County, Marysville CA. 916-674-6241
Tubb, Sara, *Acq,* Mississippi Library Commission, Jackson MS. 601-354-6369
Tubbs, Barbara C, *ILL,* Warren Library Association, Warren Library, Warren PA. 814-723-4650
Tubbs, William, *Tech Serv,* Wesleyan University, Olin Memorial Library, Middletown CT. 203-347-9411, Ext 296
Tubesing, Richard, *Dir,* Lewis University Library, Romeoville IL. 815-838-0500, Ext 302
Tubio, Manuel, *Asst Dir,* Bucks County Community College Library, Newtown PA. 215-968-5861, Ext 306, 307
Tucci, Valerie, *Mgr Info Servs,* Air Products & Chemicals, Inc (Corporate Library), Allentown PA. 215-398-7288
Tucciarone, Marlene, *Libr Technician,* San Diego County Library (Pine Valley Branch), Pine Valley CA. 714-473-8022
Tucey, Richard K, *Tech Serv,* Pueblo Library District, Pueblo CO. 303-544-1940
Tuchalski, Yvonne, *Dir,* Glendale Adventist Medical Center Library, Glendale CA. 213-240-8000, Ext 531, 532
Tuchman, Maurice, *Dir,* Hebrew College, Jacob & Rose Grossman Library, Brookline MA. 617-232-8710, 232-8711
Tucht, Alice, *Ch,* Old Bridge Public Library, Old Bridge NJ. 201-679-5622
Tuck, Weldon W, *Librn,* United States Department of Commerce - Industry and Trade Administration, Richmond District Office Library, Richmond VA. 804-782-2246
Tucker, Benjamin R, *Chief, Office of Descriptive Cat Policy,* Library of Congress, Washington DC. 202-287-5000
Tucker, Bonita J, *Chief Librn,* United States Army (Madigan Army Medical Center, Recreation Services Library), Tacoma WA. 206-967-6198
Tucker, Carol M, *ILL,* Orange Public Library, Orange CT. 203-795-0288
Tucker, Cathy, *Instr,* East Tennessee State University, Library Service Division, TN. 615-929-4244
Tucker, Eddie, *Instr,* Alabama State University, Library Educational Media Program, AL. 205-832-6072, Ext 502
Tucker, Eddie T, *Media,* Alabama State University, Library & Learning Resources, Montgomery AL. 205-832-6072
Tucker, Ellis E, *Dir,* University of Mississippi, Graduate School of Library & Information Science, MS. 601-232-7440
Tucker, Florence R, *Assoc Dir Support Serv,* Detroit Public Library, Detroit Associated Libraries, Detroit MI. 313-833-1000
Tucker, Frances, *Asst Librn,* Carnegie Public Library, Perry OK. 405-336-4721
Tucker, Frances, *Librn,* Darlington County Library (Society Hill Branch), Society Hill SC. 803-393-5864
Tucker, Gladys, *Librn,* Southeast Arkansas Regional Library (Star City Public), Star City AR. 501-628-4711
Tucker, James, *Librn,* Montgomery-Floyd Regional Library (Blacksburg Branch), Blacksburg VA. 703-552-8246
Tucker, Joan, *Cat,* Iowa City Public Library, Iowa City IA. 319-354-1265
Tucker, Kittrell L, *Tech Serv,* Newberry College, Wessels Library, Newberry SC. 803-276-5010, Ext 300
Tucker, Linda, *Librn,* Oakboro Library, Oakboro NC. 704-485-4310
Tucker, Linda, *Librn,* Stanly County Public Library (Oakboro), Oakboro NC. 704-485-4310
Tucker, Lorene, *Administrator,* Dallas County Library, Buffalo MO. 417-345-2647

Tucker, Lori D, *Doc,* United States Army (Gaffey Hall Library), Fort Knox KY. 502-624-5449
Tucker, Mae S, *Asst Dir (Main),* Public Library of Charlotte & Mecklenburg County, Inc, Charlotte NC. 704-374-2725
Tucker, Margaret, *Ref,* Catawba County Library, Newton NC. 704-464-2421
Tucker, Margaret B, *Tech Serv,* Northwestern Regional Library, Elkin NC. 919-835-4894
Tucker, Martha, *Asst Dir,* Kansas State Library, Topeka KS. 913-296-3296
Tucker, Mary Ellen, *Acq,* Columbia University (Barnard College), New York NY. 212-280-3846
Tucker, Mary Steele, *Dir,* East Hartford Public Library, Raymond Memorial Library, East Hartford CT. 203-289-6429
Tucker, Mrs C, *ILL,* Institute for Advanced Study Libraries, Princeton NJ. 609-924-4400
Tucker, Pat, *Librn,* Oklahoma Gas & Electric Co Library, Oklahoma City OK. 405-272-3191
Tucker, Patricia, *ILL,* Berkshire Community College, Jonathan Edwards Library, Pittsfield MA. 413-499-4660, Ext 201, 202, 203
Tucker, Penny, *Ser,* University of South Dakota, Christian P Lommen Health Sciences Library, Vermillion SD. 605-677-5347
Tucker, Rose Ann, *ILL,* Jackson Metropolitan Library, Jackson MS. 601-352-3677
Tucker, Ruth, *In Charge, Tech Serv & Circ,* Beth Israel Synagogue, Beth Israel Congregation Library, Vineland NJ. 609-691-0852
Tucker, Sandra, *Librn,* Wyoming County Library System (Pineville), Pineville WV. 304-732-6228
Tucker, Shirley C, *Dir,* Mid-Columbia Regional Library, Kennewick WA. 509-586-3156
Tucker, Susan, *Librn,* Middlebury College (Science Center Library), Middlebury VT. 802-388-4122
Tucker, Susan, *Ref,* Middlebury College, Egbert Starr Library, Middlebury VT. 802-388-7621
Tucker, Yema, *Librn,* Public Library of the District of Columbia (Cleveland Park), Washington DC. 202-727-1345
Tuculet, Ronald, *Librn,* California Correctional Institution Library, Tehachapi CA. 805-822-4402, Ext 508
Tudiver, Lillian, *Soc Sci & Philos,* Brooklyn Public Library (Central Library), Brooklyn NY. 212-780-7712
Tudor, Dean, *Chmn,* Ryerson Polytechnical Institute, Library Arts Dept, ON. 416-595-5285
Tudor, Nancy, *Cat,* Toronto Public Library, Toronto ON. 416-484-8015
Tudryn, Dora, *Admin Asst,* HILC, Inc, MA. 413-549-0135
Tufano, Sister Anne Louise, *Dir,* Molloy College, James Edward Tobin Library, Rockville Centre NY. 678-5000 Ext 234
Tuffli, Richard, *Dir,* Clackamas County Library, Oregon City OR. 503-655-8543
Tufts, Aileen, *Ref,* Vancouver Public Library, Vancouver BC. 604-682-5911
Tuggle, Herbert, *Ref,* Middle Georgia Regional Library, Macon GA. 912-745-5813
Tuke, Donna M, *Librn,* Friedman & Koven Library, Chicago IL. 312-346-8500, Ext 260, 261
Tule, Howard S, *Librn,* Nicholson Memorial Library (Walnut Creek Branch), Garland TX. 214-494-7168
Tuley, Carolyn, *Librn,* Sulphur Springs Public Library, Sulphur Springs TX. 214-885-4926
Tull, Elva, *Librn,* Lower Arkansas Valley Regional Library, Las Animas CO. 303-456-1770
Tullis, Louise H, *Librn,* Rangeley Public Library, Rangeley ME. 207-864-5529
Tully, James, *Dean,* Western Texas College, Learning Resource Center, Snyder TX. 915-573-8511, Ext 265
Tumbler, Laurel J, *Mgr,* Girard Bank, Girard Information Center, Philadelphia PA. 215-585-3313
Tumey, Ronald C, *Dir,* Rapides Parish Library, Alexandria LA. 318-445-2411
Tumilty, Mary D, *Librn,* Sierra Madre Public Library, Sierra Madre CA. 213-355-7186
Tumiski, Walter, *ILL, Ref & Spec Coll,* Ocean County College, Learning Resources Center, Toms River NJ. 201-255-4298
Tumulty, Patricia, *ILL & Ref,* Cumberland County Library, Bridgeton NJ. 609-455-0080
Tung, Sandra, *Librn,* Center for Early Education, Laura M Ellis Memorial Library, Los Angeles CA. 213-655-4878

Tung, Shirley, *Cat,* State University of New York, College at New Paltz, Sojourner Truth Library, New Paltz NY. 914-257-2204
Tunious, Goldie D, *Head Info Resources,* 3D-International, Library, Houston TX. 713-871-7141
Tunnell, Juanita, *Librn,* Saint Louis County Library (Eliza Heidbrink), St Louis MO. 314-428-5424
Tunstell, Irene, *Proc,* New York Public Library (The Branch Libraries), New York NY. 212-790-6262
Tunze, Jean, *Asst Librn,* Columbia Public Library, Columbia IL. 618-281-4237
Tuohy, Nancy L, *Ref,* Loyola University of Chicago Libraries (Law School Library), Chicago IL. 312-670-2952
Tuominen, Julie, *Librn,* Carver County Library System (Watertown Branch), Watertown MN. 612-955-2939
Tupper, Ardenia, *Tech Serv,* North Platte Public Library, Lincoln Keith Perkins Regional Library, North Platte NE. 308-532-6560
Tupper, Pat, *Dir,* Minnesota Department of Education Professional Library, Saint Paul MN. 612-296-6104
Tupper, Pat, *Librn,* Minnesota State Planning Agency Library, Saint Paul MN. 612-296-2007
Tupps, Charlotte, *Librn,* Adams County Public Library (Bennett), North Glenn CO. 303-644-3303
Turak, Steve, *Bus Servs,* Wayne Oakland Library Federation, Wayne MI. 313-326-8910
Turbeville, Marjorie H, *Bkmobile Coordr,* Horry County Memorial Library, Conway SC. 803-248-4898
Turbide, Raymonde, *Dir,* Bibliotheque Municipale, Montreal-Nord PQ. 514-325-4655
Turcott, Irene, *Acq,* Kalamazoo Valley Community College, Learning Resources Center, Kalamazoo MI. 616-372-5000, Ext 328
Turcotte, Mildred, *Head,* University of Cincinnati Medical Center Libraries (Solomon W Levi Memorial Library), Cincinnati OH. 513-872-5543
Turek, Mary Monica, *Librn,* Le Sueur-Waseca Regional Library (Montgomery Public), Montgomery MN. 612-364-7615
Turek, Mrs M, *Librn,* Pierce Public Library, Pierce NE. 402-329-6324
Turk, Beatrice U, *Adjunct Prof,* Case Western Reserve University, School of Library Science, OH. 216-368-3500
Turk, Wilbur, *Cat & Data Proc Dept Head,* Harvard University Library (Baker Library), Boston MA. 617-495-3650
Turkal, Margie, *Librn,* Solon Public Library, Solon IA. 319-644-2678
Turkington, Mrs N, *Sci & Eng,* Royal Military College of Canada, Massey Arts & Science-Engineering Library, Kingston ON. 613-545-7305
Turkman, Aydin Y, *Ref,* Grand Lodge Free & Accepted Masons of the State of New York Library & Museum, New York NY. 212-741-4500
Turkos, Joseph, *ILL,* Loyola-Notre Dame Library, Inc, Baltimore MD. 301-532-8787
Turley, Frances, *Librn,* Texas State Department of Human Resources Library, Austin TX. 512-475-3753
Turman, Barbara, *Doc,* University of Texas Libraries (Perry-Castaneda Library (Main Library)), Austin TX. 512-471-3811
Turnbull, Robert, *Reader Serv,* Concord College, J Frank Marsh Library, Athens WV. 304-384-3115, Ext 247
Turner, A M, *Department Head,* Mansfield State College Library (Acquisitions), Mansfield PA. 717-662-4257
Turner, Albert M, *Acq,* Mansfield State College Library, Mansfield PA. 717-662-4071
Turner, Alice, *Asst Dir,* Saskatoon Public Library, Saskatoon SK. 306-664-9555
Turner, Ann, *Dir,* Norwich University, Henry Prescott Chaplin Memorial Library, Northfield VT. 802-485-5011, Ext 48
Turner, Ann, *Cat Records,* University of British Columbia Library, Vancouver BC. 604-228-3871
Turner, Ann, *Dir,* Vermont College Division of Norwich University, Gary Memorial Library, Montpelier VT. 802-229-0522, Ext 53

Turner, Annetta, *Librn,* Centennial College of Applied Arts & Technology (Warden Woods Resource Centre), Scarborough ON. 416-694-3241
Turner, Arthur F, *Librn,* Yolo County Library (West Sacramento Branch), West Sacramento CA. 916-371-5612
Turner, Audrey, *Tech Serv,* Spokane Falls Community College, Library Media Services, Spokane WA. 509-456-2860
Turner, Avis, *Librn,* Lutheran Brotherhood Insurance Society, Martin Luther Library, Minneapolis MN. 612-340-7269
Turner, Betty A, *Librn,* Arkansas Gazette News Library, Little Rock AR. 501-371-3740
Turner, Beulah R, *Librn,* Adair County Public Library, Columbia KY. 502-384-2472
Turner, Brenda, *Bkmobile Coordr,* Cynthiana Public Library, Harrison County Library District, Cynthiana KY. 606-234-4881
Turner, Bruce, *Spec Coll,* State University of New York, College of Arts & Science at Oswego, Penfield Library, Oswego NY. 315-341-4232
Turner, Carann, *Search Anaylist,* Carolina Population Center Library, Chapel Hill NC. 919-933-3081
Turner, Carol, *Govt Docs,* Stanford University Libraries, Stanford CA. 415-497-2016
Turner, Carol C, *Dir,* Mildred G Fields Library, Milan Public Library, Milan TN. 901-686-8268
Turner, Celestine, *Librn,* Public Library of Nashville & Davidson County (Bordeaux), Nashville TN. 615-255-1648
Turner, Charles T, *Ref,* Pueblo Library District, Pueblo CO. 303-544-1940
Turner, David, *Media,* Amarillo Art Center Library, Amarillo TX. 806-372-8356
Turner, Decherd, *Dir,* University of Texas Libraries (Humanities Research Center), Austin TX. 512-471-1833
Turner, Donald A, *ILL,* Florence-Lauderdale Public Library, Florence AL. 205-764-6563
Turner, Donald A, *ILL,* Muscle Shoals Regional Library System, Florence AL. 205-764-6563
Turner, Elizabeth W, *Ref,* Dekalb Community College, North Campus, Learning Resources Center, Dunwoody GA. 404-393-3300, Ext 233
Turner, Elnora H, *Pub Health Librn,* Department of Human Resources, Health Services Division, Public Health Library, Raleigh NC. 919-733-7389
Turner, Emily, *Librn,* Brooklyn Public Library (Brownsville), Brooklyn NY. 212-345-1212
Turner, Evelyne, *Librn,* Wellington County Public Library (Palmerston Branch), Palmerston ON. 519-343-2573
Turner, Frank L, *Prof,* Texas Woman's University, School of Library Science, TX. 817-387-2418 & 566-1455
Turner, Gene, *Media,* Oklahoma Christian College Library, Oklahoma City OK. 405-478-1661, Ext 337
Turner, George G, *Asst Dir,* University of Alberta (University Libraries), Edmonton AB. 403-432-3790
Turner, Gladys, *Acq,* Cooke County Library, Gainesville TX. 817-665-2401
Turner, Gladys W, *ILL & Ref,* Roosevelt University, Murray-Green Library, Chicago IL. 312-341-3639
Turner, Gurley, *Dir Libr Serv,* Catalyst Library, New York NY. 212-759-9700
Turner, Hilda A, *Librn,* East Bethel Octagon Library, East Bethel VT. 802-763-7659
Turner, J E, *Librn,* Frankford Public Library, Frankford ON. 613-398-7572
Turner, Joan B, *Dir,* Westport Library Association, Westport Public Library, Westport CT. 203-227-8411
Turner, John, *Instr,* Jacksonville State University, College of Library Science, Communications & Instructional Media, AL. 205-435-6390
Turner, Judith, *Ad,* Marlborough Public Library, Marlborough MA. 617-485-0494
Turner, Judith Campbell, *Museum Librn,* Milwaukee Public Museum Reference Library, Milwaukee WI. 414-278-2736
Turner, Karen, *Librn,* Dallas Museum of Natural History Library, Dallas TX. 214-421-2169
Turner, Kathleen, *Librn,* Sno-Isle Regional Library (Edmonds Branch), Edmonds WA. 206-778-1221

Turner, Kay, *Ch,* Ecorse Public Library, Ecorse MI. 313-381-6630
Turner, Linda, *Librn,* Marfa Public Library, Marfa TX. 915-729-4631
Turner, Linda A, *Librn,* Esterline Angus Instrument Corp Library, Indianapolis IN. 317-244-7611
Turner, Louise, *Ch,* Fort Smith Public Library, Fort Smith AR. 501-783-0229
Turner, Lucille, *Librn,* Thomas Jefferson Library (Osage County Library Service Center), Linn MO. 314-897-2951
Turner, M L, *Media,* Medical College of Georgia Library, Augusta GA. 404-828-3441
Turner, Margaret, *Supvr,* Elgin County Public Library (Shedden Branch), Shedden ON. 519-633-0815
Turner, Margaret, *On-Line Servs & Bibliog Instr,* Gellman Research Associates Library, Jenkintown PA. 215-884-7500
Turner, Margaret A, *Librn,* Lambton College of Applied Arts & Technology Library, Resource Center, Sarnia ON. 519-542-7751
Turner, Mary E, *Librn,* Veterans Administration, Medical Center Library, Montrose NY. 914-737-4400, Ext 578
Turner, Mimi W, *Dir,* Petersburg Public Library, Petersburg VA. 804-732-3851
Turner, Mrs Scott, *Librn,* Brownsville-Haywood County Public Library, Brownsville TN. 901-772-9534
Turner, Mrs Winifred, *Librn,* Tonganoxie Public Library, Tonganoxie KS. 913-845-3281
Turner, Nancy, *Librn,* Caryville Public Library, Caryville TN. 615-562-1108
Turner, Patricia, *Librn,* United States Air Force (Shaw Air Force Base Library), Shaw AFB SC. 803-668-8110
Turner, Philip, *Asst Prof,* University of Alabama, Graduate School of Library Service, AL. 205-348-4610
Turner, Rebecca, *Ref, On-Line Servs & Bibliog Instr,* Eastern Kentucky University, John Grant Crabbe Library, Richmond KY. 606-622-3606
Turner, Richard, *Instr,* University of Colorado, Educational Technology Program, CO. 303-492-5141 & 492-6715
Turner, Rose, *Dir,* Carnegie Library, Fitzgerald-Ben Hill County Library, Fitzgerald GA. 912-423-3642
Turner, Ruth, *Asst Librn,* International Minerals & Chemical Corp, R & D Library, Terre Haute IN. 812-232-0121, Ext 349 & 405
Turner, Ruth E, *On-Line Servs,* Weber State College Library, Stewart Library, Ogden UT. 801-626-6403
Turner, Stephen W, *Ad,* Lake Oswego Public Library, Lake Oswego OR. 503-636-7628
Turner, Tamara A, *Dir,* Children's Orthopedic Hospital & Medical Center, Hospital Library, Seattle WA. 206-634-5081, 634-5497
Turner, Jr, James M, *Exec Dir,* Central New York Library Resources Council, NY. 315-478-6080, 724-4044
Turner, Jr, Robert L, *Ref & On-Line Servs,* University of Texas of the Permian Basin, Learning Resources Center, Odessa TX. 915-367-2114
Turner, Jr, Roger F, *AV,* Dean Junior College, E Ross Anderson Library, Franklin MA. 617-528-9100, Ext 261
Turney, Ruth A, *Librn,* Trinity Episcopal Church Library, Newtown CT. 203-426-9070
Turnipseed, Geraldine, *Asst Librn,* Brenizer Public Library, Merna NE. 308-643-2268
Turnquist, Reba, *Asst Dir & Acq,* University of Washington Libraries (Law Library), Seattle WA. 206-543-4089
Turock, Betty, *Asst Dir,* Monroe County Library System, Rochester NY. 716-428-7345
Turpin, Sue, *Circ,* Southwestern at Memphis, Burrow Library, Memphis TN. 901-274-1800, Ext 365, 366
Tursi, Carol A, *Asst Librn,* Eastern State School & Hospital Professional Library, Trevose PA. 215-671-3129, 671-3389
Tursi, Laraine, *Librn,* Saint John's Episcopal Hospital, Medical Library, Brooklyn NY. 212-467-7000
Tusler, Doris, *Librn,* Mount Ascutney Hospital, Agatha Young Medical Library, Windsor VT. 802-674-6711

Tussey, Helen, *Librn,* Coraopolis Memorial Library, Coraopolis PA. 412-264-3502
Tussin, Sandra H, *Acq & Bibliog Instr,* Louisiana State University at Alexandria Library, Alexandria LA. 318-445-3672, Ext 46
Tustison, Beulah, *Librn,* Public Library of Fort Wayne & Allen County (Harlan Branch), Harlan IN. 219-657-5719
Tuthill, Barbara, *Art, Hist & Music,* San Diego Public Library, San Diego CA. 714-236-5800
Tuthill, Mary, *Dir,* Abington Community Library, Clarks Summit PA. 717-587-3411
Tutt, Celestine, *Librn,* Columbia University (Social Work), New York NY. 212-280-2241
Tuttle, Dorothy, *Librn,* Chamberlin Free Public Library, Greenville NH. 603-878-1105
Tuttle, Florance, *Librn,* Defiance Public Library (Johnson Memorial), Hicksville OH. 419-782-1456
Tuttle, Irene, *Librn,* Andover College Library, Portland ME. 207-774-6126
Tuttle, Irma S, *Administrator,* Masonic Medical Research Laboratory Library, Utica NY. 315-735-2217
Tuttle, Judy, *Circ,* University of Wisconsin-Madison, Memorial Library, Madison WI. 608-262-3521
Tuttle, Leah, *Ref,* Baldwin Public Library, Birmingham MI. 313-647-1700
Tuttle, Rodmilla, *Head of Central,* Onondaga County Public Library System, Syracuse NY. 315-473-2702
Tuttle, Sister Mary Jean, *Librn,* College of Saint Scholastica Library (Music), Duluth MN. 218-723-6077
Tuttle, Walter Alan, *Dir,* National Humanities Center Library, Research Triangle Park NC. 919-549-0661, Ext 219
Tutton, Mary, *Bkmobile Coordr,* Warren-Newport Public Library District, Gurnee IL. 312-244-5150
Tutwiler, Margaret, *Librn,* Birmingham Public & Jefferson County Free Library (Huffman), Birmingham AL. 205-254-2551
Tuveson, Mimi, *Acq,* Mobile Public Library, Mobile AL. 205-438-7073
Tveit, Carol, *Librn,* Whatcom County Public Library (Sudden Valley Library), Bellingham WA. 206-734-6434
Twaddle, Dan, *Asst Prof,* Western Kentucky University, Dept of Library Science & Instructional Media, KY. 502-745-3446
Tweed, Venetia, *Librn,* Hagaman Memorial Library, East Haven CT. 203-467-0810
Tweedy, Albert Vincent, *Dir,* Alpha Regional Library, Spencer WV. 304-927-1770
Tweedy, Sue, *Ch,* Norton Public Library, Norton MA. 617-285-4761
Twelves, Diana, *Bibliog Instr,* University of Texas at El Paso Library, El Paso TX. 747-5683; 747-5684
Twelves, June, *Librn,* Salt Lake County Library System (Ruth V Tyler Branch), Midvale UT. 801-255-7168
Twerdochlib, Suzanne, *Bkmobile Librn,* Manatee County Public Library System, Bradenton FL. 813-748-5555
Twiest, David A, *Dir,* Trinity Western College, Vernon Strombeck Library, Langley BC. 604-888-7511, Ext 267
Twiggs, Brenda, *Tech Serv & On-Line Servs,* Hudson Valley Community College Learning Resources Center, Dwight Marvin Library, Troy NY. 518-283-1100, Ext 629
Twing, Ella, *Librn,* Port Byron Township Library, Port Byron IL. 309-523-3440
Twitchel, Joanne, *Tech Serv,* John F Kennedy University Library, Orinda CA. 415-254-0200, Ext 36
Twitchell, Anne, *ILL,* Selby Public Library, Sarasota County Federated Library System, Sarasota FL. 814-366-7303
Twitchell, Phyllis B, *Ch,* Winchester Public Library, Winchester MA. 617-729-3770
Tyau, Sonja O, *Librn,* Hawaii Employers Council Library, Honolulu HI. 808-836-1511
Tyce, Richard, *Ref,* Wright State University Library, Dayton OH. 513-873-2380
Tycer, Maxie, *Librn,* Iberia Parish Public Library (Loreauville Branch), Loreauville LA. 318-229-6348
Tyer, Lois, *Acq,* Lincoln Library, Springfield Public Library, Springfield IL. 217-753-4900

Tyger, B, *On-Line Servs,* San Francisco Academy of Comic Art Library, San Francisco CA. 415-681-1737
Tylecki, Mary F, *Librn,* Sussex County Superior Court Law Library, Georgetown DE. 302-734-5473
Tyler, Audrey, *Branches,* Atlanta Public Library, Atlanta GA. 404-688-4636
Tyler, Carolyn, *Educ,* University of South Carolina, Thomas Cooper Library, Columbia SC. 803-777-3142
Tyler, Christine, *Librn,* Howard Whittemore Memorial Library (Children's Department), Naugatuck CT. 203-729-0313
Tyler, Jean, *Dir,* Milwaukee Legislative Reference Bureau Library, Milwaukee WI. 414-278-2295
Tyler, Mildred, *Librn,* Monroeville Public Library, Monroeville OH. 419-465-2035
Tym, Deborah, *Librn,* Shenandoah Area Free Public Library, Shenandoah PA. 717-462-9829
Tynan, Elizabeth R, *Ref,* Denison University, William Howard Doane Library, Granville OH. 614-587-0810, Ext 225
Tynan, Laurie, *Asst Dir & Ref,* Meadville Library Art & Historical Association, Meadville PA. 814-336-1773
Tyndall, Randolph R, *Media,* Dekalb Community College, North Campus, Learning Resources Center, Dunwoody GA. 404-393-3300, Ext 233
Tyner, Mary, *Info Spec,* Kraft, Inc (Corporate Library), Glenview IL. 312-998-2465
Tynes, Jacqueline, *Ad,* Greenburgh Public Library, Elmsford NY. 914-682-5265
Tyra, Rose, *Librn,* Fresno County Department of Health, Public Health Service Library, Fresno CA. 209-488-3781
Tyre, Virginia, *Tech Serv & Acq,* Northeast Georgia Regional Library System, Clarkesville GA. 404-754-4413
Tyrrell, Maryann, *Instr,* Lansing Community College, Library Media Technology Program, MI. 517-373-9978
Tyson, Christy, *YA,* Spokane Public Library, Comstock Building Library, Spokane WA. 509-838-3361, Ext 65
Tyson, Edwin L, *Librn,* Nevada County Historical Society, Searls Historical Library, Nevada City CA. 916-265-9901
Tyson, Elizabeth, *Asst Librn,* Delray Beach Public Library Association, Inc, Delray Beach FL. 305-276-6482
Tyson, Elizabeth M, *Asst Dir,* Augusta Regional Library, Augusta-Richmond County Public Library, Augusta GA. 404-724-1871
Tyson, Jean, *Librn,* Birchard Public Library of Sandusky County (Green Springs Memorial), Green Springs OH. 419-332-1121
Tyson, Roberta S, *Asst Prof,* Southern University, Dept of Library Science, LA. 504-771-3282, Ext 2970
Tywoniak, Edward, *Media,* Saint Mary's College of California, Saint Albert Hall Library, Moraga CA. 415-376-4411, Ext 229, 230
Tzeng, John, *Instr,* University of the District of Columbia-Mount Vernon Square Campus, Dept of Library Science & Instructional Systems Technology, DC. 202-727-2756, 727-2757 & 727-2758

U

U, Anna, *Librn,* University of Toronto Libraries (East Asian Library), Toronto ON. 416-978-3300
Ubaldini, Michael W, *Res Librn,* Tennessee Eastman Co (Research Library), Kingsport TN. 615-246-2111, Ext 2541, 3870
Ubel, James A, *Dir,* Shawnee Library System, Carterville IL. 618-985-3711
Ubois, Josephine, *Tech Serv & Cat,* San Mateo Public Library, San Mateo CA. 415-574-6955
Uden, Janet, *Acq,* University of Massachusetts at Amherst Library, Amherst MA. 413-545-0284
Uebelacker, Susan, *Librn,* Prince George's County Memorial Library System (Hillcrest Heights Branch), Temple Heights MD. 301-630-4900
Ueligitone, Alofa, *Librn,* American Samoa-Office of Library Services (Manu'a), Tau Village PI. 633-4660

Uglow, Sadie, *Ref,* Tacoma Art Museum Reference Library, Tacoma WA. 206-272-4258

Uehane, Sister Suzanne, *Dir,* Ohio Dominican College Library, Columbus OH. 614-253-2741, Ext 258, 210&219

Uhler, Edward H, *Librn,* Western Electric Library, Greensboro NC. 919-697-5012

Uhlmann, Marie L, *Librn,* Westvaco Corp, Research Library, Laurel MD. 301-776-5400

Uhreen, Rosellen, *Librn,* Washington County Cooperative Library Services (West Slope Community), Portland OR. 503-292-6416

Uhrich, Lois, *In Charge,* Cessna Aircraft Co (Marketing Div Library), Wichita KS. 316-685-9111, Ext 4241

Uhrig, Judith, *YA,* Cary Memorial Library, Lexington MA. 617-862-6288

Uick, Helen, *Librn,* S C Johnson & Son Inc, Technical & Business Information Center, Racine WI. 414-554-2372

Ujhelyi, Michael, *Cat,* Fordham University, Duane Library, Bronx NY. 212-933-2233, Ext 230, 259

Ulinski, Audrey A, *Librn,* Monroe Developmental Center (Staff-Parent Library), Rochester NY. 716-461-2800, Ext 362

Ulitz, Jean, *Librn,* Cook Memorial Library, Tamworth NH. 603-323-8510

Ullrick, Doris B, *Librn,* Hall Memorial Library, Tilton NH. 603-286-8971

Ulm, Marquita, *Ch,* Central Kansas Library System, Great Bend KS. 316-792-4865

Ulmer, Beverly R, *Dir,* Orangeburg County Library, Orangeburg SC. 803-534-1429

Ulmer, Mary C, *Librn,* South Carolina Department of Health Library, Columbia SC. 803-758-5448

Ulmer, Mary C, *Librn,* State Park Health Center, Patients' & Professional Library, State Park SC. 803-758-4694

Ulmer, Mary Lewis, *Librn,* Houston Public Library (Clayton Library), Houston TX. 713-224-5441

Ulrich, B Elizabeth, *Gen Ref & ILL,* State Library of Pennsylvania, Harrisburg PA. 717-787-2646

Ulrich, Jane, *Coordr,* Texas Panhandle Library System, Amarillo TX. 806-378-3043

Ulrich, Josephine, *Librn,* Morton Township Public Library, Mecosta MI. 616-972-8315

Ultang, Joanne, *Librn,* Brown Brothers Harriman & Co Library, New York NY. 212-483-5517

Umbach, Stephanie, *Tech Serv,* Valparaiso University, Henry F Moellering Memorial Library, Valparaiso IN. 219-464-5364

Umbarger, Judy, *Asst Dir,* Albany County Public Library, Laramie WY. 307-745-3365

Umberger, Sheila, *Asst Librn,* Lutheran Theological Southern Seminary, Lineberger Memorial Library, Columbia SC. 803-786-5750

Umenhofer, Kenneth, *Tech Serv,* Gordon-Conwell Theological Seminary, Burton L Goddard Library, South Hamilton MA. 617-468-7111, Ext 255, 256

Umhoefer, Aural, *Dir,* University of Wisconsin Center, Baraboo-Sauk County Library, Baraboo WI. 608-356-8351, Ext 49

Umi, Paese, *Librn,* American Samoa-Office of Library Services (Leone), Vailoa Village PI. 688-7119

Unciano, Elena, *Librn,* Hawaii Department of Education, Technical Assistance Center Library, Honolulu HI. 808-548-6250

Uncrau, Sharon, *Librn,* Nampa Community Library, Nampa AB. 403-322-3805

Underbrink, Robert, *Dir,* Blackburn College, Lumpkin Library, Carlinville IL. 217-854-3231

Underhill, Carolyn, *Librn,* Lincoln County Library-Caliente, Caliente NV. 702-726-3104

Underhill, Jeanne, *Pub serv,* Nova University Libraries (Law Center Library), Fort Lauderdale FL. 522-2300 Ext 113

Underhill, Nancy, *Asst Librn,* Piermont Public Library, Piermont NH. 603-272-4964

Underwood, Barbara, *Circ,* University of Wyoming, William Robertson Coe Library, Laramie WY. 307-766-3279

Underwood, Ed M, *Supvr,* University of the District of Columbia (Van Ness Campus), Washington DC. 202-282-7501

Underwood, Mrs K G, *Supvr,* Huron County Public Library (Gorrie Branch), Gorrie ON. 519-335-3987

Underwood, Rosalind, *Ref,* Gordon Junior College Library, Barnesville GA. 404-385-1700, Ext 271, 272, 276

Underwood, Teresa A, *Librn,* Newman Township Library, Newman IL. 217-837-2412

Ungar, Carmen, *Art,* Thomas Crane Public Library, Subregional Headquarters for Eastern Massachusetts Regional Library System, Quincy MA. 617-471-2400

Ungarelli, Donald L, *Dir,* C W Post Center of Long Island University, B Davis Schwartz Memorial Library, Greenvale NY. 516-299-0200

Ungarelli, Louis, *Asst Dir,* Concord Public Library, Concord NH. 603-225-2743

Unger, Agnes, *Librn,* Richardson Securities of Canada, Research Library, Winnipeg MB. 204-988-5940

Unger, Amy, *Librn,* Leander Public Library, Chris Marshall Library, Leander TX. 512-259-1178

Unger, Bigelane A, *Ch & YA,* North Olympic Library System, Port Angeles WA. 206-457-4464

Unger, Donald, *Math-Physics,* Oregon State University, William Jasper Kerr Library, Corvallis OR. 503-754-3411

Ungurait, Karen, *Resource Ctr Coordr,* Florida Department of Health & Rehabilitative Services, Resource Center, Tallahassee FL. 904-488-0500

Unrau, Ruth, *Librn,* Bethel College Library (Mennonite Library & Archives), North Newton KS. 316-283-2500, Ext 310

Unrue, Michelle, *Ref,* Franklin-Johnson County Public Library, Franklin IN. 317-738-2833

Unruh, Carolyn V, *Librn,* Reading Hospital & Medical Center (School of Nursing Library), Reading PA. 215-378-6359

Unterborn, Lee R, *Tech Serv, Acq & Ref,* Saint Mary's University (School of Law Library), San Antonio TX. 512-436-3435

Unterburger, George, *Gen Ref,* Detroit Public Library, Detroit Associated Libraries, Detroit MI. 313-833-1000

Unterburger, Mrs George, *Librn,* Bushnell Congregational Church Library, Detroit MI. 313-272-3550

Unterholzner, Dennis L, *ILL & Ser,* Carthage College, John Mosheim Ruthrauff Library, Kenosha WI. 414-551-8500, Ext 530

Unthank, Frances L, *Dir,* United States Air Force (Strategic Air Command, McConnell Air Force Base Library), McConnell AFB KS. 316-681-5414

Upadhyaya, Prakash D, *Librn,* Central State Hospital (Medical Library), Petersburg VA. 804-861-7000

Upchurch, Sharon, *Instr,* Culver-Stockton College, Dept of Library Science, MO. 314-288-5221

Upchurch, Sharon, *Librn,* Culver-Stockton College, Carl Johann Memorial Library, Canton MO. 314-288-5221, Ext 21

Uppgard, Jeanine, *Educ Res,* Westfield State College Library, Westfield MA. 413-568-3311

Upson, Ruth S, *Asst Dir,* Middlebury Public Library, Middlebury CT. 203-758-2634

Uptigrove, Kenneth R, *Dir,* Owosso Public Library, Owosso MI. 517-725-5134

Upton, Elinor I, *Bus & Tech,* Yonkers Public Library, Yonkers NY. 914-337-1500

Upton, Elinor L, *Spec Coll,* Yonkers Public Library, Yonkers NY. 914-337-1500

Upton, Mrs Merle B, *In Charge,* Mississippi State Law Library, Jackson MS. 601-354-7113

Upton, Samuel M, *Actg Dir, On-Line Servs & Bibliog Instr,* Cass County Historical Society Museum Library, Logansport IN. 219-753-3866

Urban, Gloria, *Spec Coll,* Washington County Free Library, Hagerstown MD. 301-739-3250

Urbanowicz, Jadwiga, *Ref,* Radio Free Europe-Radio Liberty Reference Library, New York NY. 212-867-5200, Ext 210

Urbassik, M J, *Acq,* University of Pittsburgh, Johnstown Campus Library, Johnstown PA. 814-266-9661, Ext 314

Urbina, Eileen, *Asst Librn,* Charles Camsell Hospital, Peter Wilcock Library, Edmonton AB. 403-452-8770, Ext 271

Uricchio, William J, *Tech Serv,* West Hartford Public Library, Noah Webster Memorial Library, West Hartford CT. 203-236-6286

Urie, Kathryn, *Ch,* Islip Public Library, Islip NY. 516-581-5933

Urling, Anna, *Librn,* Barry Research Corp Library, Sunnyvale CA. 408-734-1600

Urquhart, Kenneth, *Archivist,* Historic New Orleans Collection Library, New Orleans LA. 504-523-7146

Urquiza, Rosina, *Cat,* Florida Southern College, Roux Library, Lakeland FL. 813-683-5521, Ext 211

UrregodeAshton, Ruth M, *Tech Serv,* Inter-American University of Puerto Rico, Metropolitan Campus Library, Hato Rey PR. 809-754-7215, Ext 246, 245, 256

Urry, Norma, *Librn,* Malheur County Library (Nyssa Public), Nyssa OR. 503-372-2978

Urschel, Joan, *Ref,* County of Strathcona Municipal Library, Sherwood Park AB. 403-467-3513

Urtz, Nancy S, *Tech Serv,* Nashua Public Library, Nashua NH. 603-883-4141, 883-4142

Uselton, Marilyn, *Actg Librn,* Sugar Hill-Lauderdale County Library, Ripley TN. 901-635-1872

Usher, Elizabeth R, *Chief Librn,* Metropolitan Museum of Art (Thomas J Watson Memorial Library), New York NY. 212-879-5500, Ext 221, 224

Usher, Esther, *Librn,* United Engineers & Constructors Inc, Boston Office Library, Boston MA. 617-338-6000, Ext 2362

Utley, Mrs Edie, *On-Line Servs,* Chattanooga-Hamilton County Bicentennial Library, Chattanooga TN. 615-757-5320

Utpatel, Mrs Frank, *Dir,* Mazomanie Free Library, Mazomanie WI. 608-795-2544

Utsunomiya, Leslie, *ILL & Ad,* Coquitlam Public Library, Coquitlam BC. 604-931-2416

Utt, Joann, *Librn,* Troup Harris Coweta Regional Library (East Coweta Public), Senoia GA. 404-599-3256

Utterback, Myrl, *Librn,* Tabor Public Library, Tabor IA. 712-629-2735

Utterback, Nancy, *On-Line Servs & Pub Servs,* University of Louisville Library (Kornhauser Health Sciences), Louisville KY. 502-588-5771

Utterback, Robert T, *Cat,* Southwestern College Library, Chula Vista CA. 714-421-6700, Ext 237

Utz, Mary Lee, *Librn,* Hillsborough Community College Library, Tampa FL. 813-247-6641, Ext 261

Utz, Peter, *Media,* County College of Morris, Sherman H Masten Learning Resource Center, Randolph Township NJ. 201-361-5000, Ext 470

Utzinger, Nancy, *Media & Ser,* Weld County Library, Greeley CO. 303-330-7691

Utzinger, Pauline, *Commun Servs,* Rochester Public Library, Olmsted County Library System, Rochester MN. 507-285-8000

Uunila, Edith H, *In Charge,* Editorial Projects for Education, Chronicle of Higher Education, Washington DC. 202-223-3225

Uyehara, Harry, *Asst Prof,* University of Hawaii, Graduate School of Library Studies, HI. 808-948-7321

Uyehara, Loretta, *Librn,* Brooklyn Public Library (Windsor Terrace), Brooklyn NY. 212-853-7265

Uyematsu, Kaley, *Ch,* Caldwell Public Library, Caldwell ID. 208-459-3242

Uzee, Phillip D, *Spec Coll,* Nicholls State University, Allen J Ellender Memorial Library, Thibodaux LA. 504-446-8111, Ext 401, 402

Uzes, F D, *In Charge,* California State Lands Commission Library, Sacramento CA. 916-322-5137

Uzzo, Beatrice, *Librn,* Holzmacher, McLendon & Murrell, Farmingdale NY. 516-694-3410, Ext 6

Uzzo, Beatrice, *Librn,* Holzmacher, McLendon & Murrell Library, Melville NY. 516-694-3040

V

Vaag, Henry O, *In Charge,* Denver Public Library (Literature & History), Denver CO. 303-573-5152, Ext 271

Vaaler, Nan S, *Dir,* Napa Community College Library, Napa CA. 707-255-2100, Ext 311

Vaaler, Nan Stormont, *Dir,* Napa City - County Library, Napa CA. 707-253-4241

Vaca, Wilson A, *Librn,* Hartford Public Library (Ropkins), Hartford CT. 203-246-9780

Vacca, Pasquale, *Exten Servs,* Boston Public Library, Eastern Massachusetts Library System, Boston MA. 617-536-5400

Vaccaro, MaryAnn, *Asst Libm,* New England Institute Library, Ridgefield CT. 203-438-6591

Vachereau, Georgette, *Libm,* Vermont State Hospital (Community Library), Waterbury VT. 802-241-3246

Vadnais, Ginette, *Tech Serv, Acq & Cat,* Saint-Laurent Municipal Library, Saint Laurent PQ. 514-744-6411, Ext 220

Vadnais, Sandy, *Libm,* Carver County Library System (Chanhassen Branch), Chanhassen MN. 612-934-8689

Vaeth, Helen, *Acq,* Milwaukee Public Library, Milwaukee WI. 414-278-3000

Vagianos, Louis G, *Prof,* Dalhousie University, School of Library Service, NS. 902-424-3656

Vago, M, *Libm, On-Line Servs & Bibliog Instr,* National Starch & Chemical Corp Library, Bridgewater NJ. 201-658-5082

Vagt, J Paul, *District Dir,* Tarrant County Junior College System, Fort Worth TX. 817-281-7860, Ext 485

Vaida, Marie E, *Dir,* Gilbert Public Library, Gilbert MN. 218-741-6023

Vail, Irma, *Libm,* Oregon Metallurgical Corp Library, Albany OR. 503-926-4281

Vail, Keith R, *Assoc Dir,* Salisbury State College, Blackwell Library, Salisbury MD. 301-546-3261, Ext 351

Vail, Rebecca, *Acq,* Guilford College Library, Greensboro NC. 919-292-5511, Ext 250

Vaillancourt, Joan, *Ref,* Ridgefield Library & Historical Association, Ridgefield CT. 203-438-2282

Vaillancourt, Pauline M, *Assoc Prof,* State University of New York at Albany, School of Library & Information Science, NY. 518-455-6288

Vainstein, Rose, *Prof,* University of Michigan, School of Library Science, MI. 313-764-9376

Vaisey, Doug, *Bibliog Instr,* Saint Mary's University, Patrick Power Library, Halifax NS. 902-422-7361

Vaisey, G Douglas, *Convenor,* Nova Scotia On-Line Consortium, NS. 902-422-7361, Ext 219

Vaive, Sharon, *Asst Libm,* McGregor Public Library, Highland Park Library, Highland Park MI. 313-252-0288

Vajda, Carolyn, *Cat,* Greenwich Library, Greenwich CT. 203-622-7900

Vajda, Elizabeth A, *Chief Libm,* Cooper Union for Advancement of Science & Art Library, New York NY. 212-254-6300, Ext 323

Vajda, John, *Asst Libm,* United States Department of the Navy (Navy Dept Library), Washington DC. 202-433-4131

Valance, Marsha, *Libm,* Dubuque County Library, Dubuque IA. 319-583-3511, Ext 20

Valasek, Lillian, *Libm,* Shiawassee County Library (Lennon Village), Lennon MI. 313-621-4285

Valbert, Louis H, *Dir,* Richland Community College, Learning Resources Center, Decatur IL. 217-875-7200

Valder, Al, *Libm,* Commonwealth Microfilm Library, Calgary AB. 403-263-2555, 245-2555

Valdez, Brother Patrick, *Libm,* Saint Andrew Seminary Library, Denver CO. 303-756-5522

Valdez, Mina, *Media,* Weslaco Public Library, Porter Doss Memorial Library, Weslaco TX. 512-968-4533

Valdez, Tony, *Acq,* University of Houston (Clear Lake City), Houston TX. 713-488-9280

Valdez, Veronica, *Tech Serv,* Durango Public Library, Durango CO. 303-247-2492

Valee, Emilien, *Libm,* Bibliotheque De La Ville De Montreal (Lorimier Adult), Montreal PQ. 514-872-4885

Valen, Robert, *Park Interpreter,* National Park Service, Cabrillo National Monument Library, San Diego CA. 714-293-5450

Valence, Joselyne, *Ref,* Bibliotheque Municipale De Sherbrooke, Sherbrooke Municipal Library, Sherbrooke PQ. 819-565-5860, 565-5861 & 565-5862

Valencia, Maria L, *Libm,* Luis Munoz rivera Library & Museum, Barranquitas PR. 809-857-0205

Valente, John Bosco, *Libm,* Saint Francis Chapel Library, Providence RI. 401-331-6510

Valenti, Nancy, *Circ,* Manatee County Public Library System, Bradenton FL. 813-748-5555

Valentin, Gloria Luna, *Per,* University of Puerto Rico - Bayamon Regional College, Learning Resources Center, Bayamon PR. 809-786-5225

Valentine, Alexander, *Ref,* City College of San Francisco Library, San Francisco CA. 415-239-3404

Valentine, Gaynell, *Media,* Southern University Library, Baton Rouge LA. 504-771-4990, 771-4991, 771-4992

Valentine, Mary, *Libm,* Kansas City Public Library (Southeast), Kansas City MO. 816-363-3088

Valeri, John R, *Dir,* Catholic University of America (Robert J White Law), Washington DC. 202-635-5155

Valerie, Sister M, *AV,* Maria Regina College Library-Media Center, Syracuse NY. 315-474-4891, Ext 28

Valerie, Sister M, *Asst Prof,* Mary Regina College, Library Service Program, NY. 315-474-4891

Valgemae, Mare, *On-Line Servs,* Manufacturers Hanover Trust Co, Corporate Library: Financial Library Division, New York NY. 212-350-4733

Valigura, Frances, *Cat,* Brazoria County Library, Angleton TX. 713-849-0591

Valint, Nancy, *Libm,* Foster Associates Inc Library, Washington DC. 202-296-2380

Vallely, John, *Tech Serv,* Siena College, Jerome Dawson Memorial Library, Loudonville NY. 518-783-2522

Vallely, Mary, *YA & Ref,* Wyckoff Public Library, Wyckoff NJ. 201-891-4866

Valois, Richard, *Media,* Bibliotheque Municipale Des Trois-Rivieres, Trois-Rivieres PQ. 819-374-3521, Ext 71

Valone, Gloria, *Asst Dir & ILL,* Kean College of New Jersey, Nancy Thompson Library, Union NJ. 201-527-2017

Valtier, Delma, *Libm,* El Paso Public Library (Armijo), El Paso TX. 915-543-3867

Valunas, Madelyn, *Ser,* Shippensburg State College, Ezra Lehman Memorial Library, Shippensburg PA. 717-532-1463

Valutas, Naomi, *Libm,* Darby Free Library, Darby PA. 215-586-7310

Valvo, Francine, *Libm,* Buffalo & Erie County Public Library System (Fairfield), Buffalo NY. 716-834-7500

Vambery, Joseph T, *Libm,* Pace University, School of Law Library, White Plains NY. 914-682-7272

VanAartsen, Marlys, *Tech Serv,* Northwestern College, Ramaker Library, Orange City IA. 712-737-4821, Ext 57, 58

Vanags, E N, *In Charge,* Aluminum Co of Canada, Ltd, Technical Information Centre, Arvida PQ. 418-548-1121, Ext 2817

vanAllen, Neil, *Gen Supvr,* General Motors Corp (System on Automotive Safety Information Research Laboratories Library), Warren MI. 313-575-3125

VanAllen, Russell E, *Asst Libm,* Utah State Law Library, Salt Lake City UT. 801-533-5280

VanAlstyne, Joan, *Libm,* Chaumont Free Library, Chaumont NY. 315-649-5454

VanAmringe, Patricia, *Admin Asst,* Trumbull Library, Trumbull CT. 203-261-6421

VanAntwerp, Adeline, *Tech Serv & Acq,* Olivet Nazarene College, Benner Library & Resource Center, Bourbonnais IL. 815-939-5354

VanAradale, Dennis, *Asst Libm,* North Arkansas Regional Library, Harrison AR. 501-741-3665

VanArsdale, William, *Pub Servs,* Austin Peay State University, Felix G Woodward Library, Clarksville TN. 615-648-7346

VanAtta, Cathaleen, *Libm,* Kitt Peak National Observatory Library, Tucson AZ. 602-327-5511, Ext 381

VanAuken, Mary, *Dir,* Johnson County Library, Buffalo WY. 307-684-7888

VanBaalen, C J, *Ch,* Fountaindale Public Library District, Bolingbrook IL. 312-759-2102

vanBenten, Sister Lucia, *Dir,* Donnelly Community College, Saint Jerome Library, Kansas City KS. 913-621-6070, Ext 35

VanBenthuysen, Robert, *Dir,* Monmouth Consortium, NJ. 201-222-6600

VanBenthuysen, Robert F, *Dir,* Monmouth College, Guggenheim Library, West Long Branch NJ. 201-222-6600, Ext 264

VanBergen, Robert, *Film Dept,* Linden Free Public Library, Linden NJ. 201-486-3888

VanBraam, William, *Tech Serv,* Finkelstein Memorial Library, Spring Valley NY. 914-352-5700, Ext 230

VanBrocklin, Jackie, *Commun Servs,* Fort Worth Public Library, Fort Worth TX. 817-870-7700

vanBronkhorst, Margaret, *Asst Dir,* New Rochelle Public Library, New Rochelle NY. 914-632-7878

VanBuren, John, *Libm,* Monroe County Department of Health, Health Education Library, Rochester NY. 716-442-4000

VanBurgh, Nora, *Acq & Ref,* Casper College, Goodstein Foundation Library, Casper WY. 307-268-2269

VanCamp, Ann, *Search Analyst & Coordr,* Indiana University (School of Medicine Library), Indianapolis IN. 317-264-7182

VanCamp, Beverly G, *Syst Coordr,* South Texas Library System, Corpus Christi TX. 512-882-6502

VanCamp, George, *Dir,* Mesa County Public Library, Grand Junction CO. 303-243-4442

Vance, Ann, *Dir,* Thomas Ford Memorial Library, Western Springs Library, Western Springs IL. 312-246-0520

Vance, Carole, *Dir,* Paoli Public Library, Paoli IN. 812-723-3841

Vance, Janet, *Ch,* Richardson Public Library, Richardson TX. 214-238-8251

Vance, Kenneth E, *Prof,* University of Michigan, School of Library Science, MI. 313-764-9376

Vance, Richard L, *Chief Park Naturalist,* National Park Service, Lassen Volcanic National Park Library, Mineral CA. 916-595-4444

Vance, Sandra L, *Libm,* Illinois State Journal & Register Editorial Library, Springfield IL. 217-788-8769

Vance, Sharon, *Tech Serv,* Wheaton College Library, Wheaton IL. 312-682-5101

Vance, Sharon, *On-Line Servs,* Wheaton College Library, Wheaton IL. 312-682-5101

Vance, Susan, *Ref,* Atlantic County Library, Pleasantville NJ. 609-646-8699, 645-7121, 625-2776

Vancini, Linda, *Commun Servs,* North Kingstown Free Library, North Kingstown RI. 401-294-2521

Vanco, John, *Exec Dir,* Erie Art Center Library, Erie PA. 814-459-5477

Vandale, Elsie H, *Asst Libm & Media,* Azusa City Library, Azusa CA. 213-334-0338

Vandall, Marion, *Asst Dir & Cat,* Oil City Library, Oil City PA. 814-646-8771

VanDam, Thomas, *Libm,* Pine Rest Christian Hospital, Professional Library, Grand Rapids MI. 616-455-5000, Ext 202

VanDamme, Joan, *Libm,* Kent County Municipal Public Library (Wallaceburg Public), Wallaceburg ON. 519-627-5292

VandeBrink, Jake, *Libm,* Edmonton General Hospital Health Sciences Library, Edmonton AB. 403-482-4421

VanDeCarr, Janet, *Ch,* Park Ridge Public Library, Park Ridge IL. 312-825-3123

Vandegrift, J R, *Dir,* Pontifical Faculty of the Immaculate Conception, Dominican House of Studies, Washington DC. 202-529-5300, Ext 11

Vandehaar, Helen, *Libm,* Mitchellville Public Library, Mitchellville IA. 515-967-3339

VandenBerg, Emma, *ILL, Ref & Per,* Dordt College Library, Sioux Center IA. 712-722-3771, Ext 139

VandenBerge, Peter N, *Dir,* Colgate Rochester-Bexley Hall-Crozer Theological Seminaries, Ambrose Swasey Library, Rochester NY. 716-271-1320, Ext 24

VanDenBorre, Beverly, *Ref,* Cass County Library, Cassopolis MI. 616-445-8651

VandenTop, Jeraldine, *ILL,* Alaska Health Sciences Library, Anchorage AK. 907-263-1870

VanderBellen, L, *Chief Rare Bks & Mss Div,* National Library of Canada, Ottawa ON. 613-995-9481

Vanderberg, Thelma, *Libm,* Regional Plan Association, Inc Library, New York NY. 212-682-7750, Ext 34

Vanderbloemen, Ruth, *Tech Serv & Cat,* Joseph Mann Library, Two Rivers WI. 414-794-7121

Vanderburg, Mary Alice, *Libm,* United States Navy (Mayport Naval Station Library), Jacksonville FL. 904-246-5393

Vandercook, Sharon, *Dir Info Serv,* Area Wide Library Network, (AWLNET), CA. 209-488-3230

Vandercook, Sharon, *Ref,* San Joaquin Valley Library System, Fresno CA. 201-488-3185

Vanderford, Mary E, *In Charge*, Lowry Nature Center Library, Carver Park Reserve, Hennepin County Park Reserve District, Excelsior MN. 612-472-4911

Vandergrift, Kay, *Asst Prof*, Columbia University in the City of New York, School of Library Service, NY. 212-280-2292

Vanderheyden, Sally, *Acq*, Saint Norbert College, Todd Wehr Library, De Pere WI. 414-337-3280

Vanderhoff, Barbara, *Per*, Arizona State University Library, Tempe AZ. 602-965-3417

Vanderhoff, Doris, *Librn*, Horry County Memorial Library (Aynor Branch), Aynor SC. 803-358-3324

VanderKaay, Mme F J, *Librn*, Bibliotheque Municipale, Rosemere PQ. 514-622-7035

VanderKooy, Dianne, *Asst Dir*, Georgetown Township Public Library, Jenison MI. 616-457-9620, 457-9140

VanderLaan, Bernice, *Librn*, Missaukee County Library, Lake City MI. 616-839-2166

Vanderlaan, Robert, *Cat*, Muskegon Community College, Allen G Umbreit Library, Muskegon MI. 616-773-9131, Ext 260

Vanderlee, Kris, *Ref*, Moraine Valley Community College, Learning Resources Center, Palos Hills IL. 312-974-4300, Ext 222

VanderLyke, Barbara, *Dir*, Connecticut State Library, Library Development Division, Willimantic Library Service Center, Willimantic CT. 203-456-1717

VanderLyke, Barbara, *Dir*, Connecticut State Library (Willimantic Library Service Center), Willimantic CT. 203-456-1717

Vandermade, Claudia, *Dir*, Analytic Sciences Corporation, Reading MA. 617-944-6850

Vandermark, Sondra H, *Asst Librn*, Morse Institute Library, Natick MA. 617-653-4252

Vandermeulen, Christie, *ILL, AV & Ref*, Branch County Library, Coldwater MI. 517-278-2341

Vandermolen, John, *Sci-Tech*, Auburn University, Ralph Brown Draughton Library, Auburn AL. 205-826-4500

VanderPol, Diane, *Librn*, Somerset County Library (Hillsborough Public), Belle Mead NJ. 201-359-3916

Vanderpool, Janet, *Librn*, Hamilton County Library, Syracuse KS. 316-384-5622

Vanderpoorten, Mary Beth, *Acq*, Texas Woman's University, Bralley Memorial Library, Denton TX. 817-566-6415

VanderPyle, Jeanne, *Media & Acq*, Sandwich Public Library, Sandwich MA. 617-888-0625

vanderSchalk, H, *In Charge*, Netherlands Embassy Library, Washington DC. 202-244-5300

Vanderspool, Constance, *Circ*, Warren-Newport Public Library District, Gurnee IL. 312-244-5150

Vandersteen, Elizabeth, *Soc Sci*, Louisiana Tech University, Prescott Memorial Library, Ruston LA. 318-257-2577

VanderVeen, Eunice, *Ad & Br Coordr*, Kent County Library System, Grand Rapids MI. 616-774-3250

VanderVelde, John J, *Spec Proj & Editorial Consult*, Kansas State University, Farrell Library, Manhattan KS. 913-532-6516

VanDerVoorn, Neal, *Librn*, Washington State Library (Eastern State Hospital Library), Medical Lake WA. 509-299-4276, Ext 276

VanDerVoorn, Neal, *Librn*, Washington State Library (Lakeland Village Library), Medical Lake WA. 509-299-5089

VanderVoort, A, *Acq*, University of Victoria, McPherson Library, Victoria BC. 604-477-6911, Ext 4466

Vanderwerff, Dennis I, *Librn & Bibliog Instr*, Taft College Library, Taft CA. 805-765-4191

VanderZyl, Madeline, *Acq*, Central College, Geisler Learning Resource Center, Pella IA. 515-628-4151, Ext 233

VandeStreek, David, *Librn*, University of Southern California, Information Sciences Institute Library, Marina del Rey CA. 213-822-1511, Ext 117

VanDeusen, Eric, *Acq*, Columbia-Greene Community College Library, Hudson NY. 518-828-4181

vandeVelde, Catherine, *Reader Serv*, Bentley College, Solomon R Baker Library, Waltham MA. 617-891-2231

VanDeVoorde, Philip, *Doc*, Iowa State University Library, Ames IA. 515-294-1442

VanDeVoorde, Ronald A, *Assoc Prof*, University of Arizona, Graduate Library School, AZ. 602-626-3565

VanDiest, Doris, *Librn*, Sunshine City Library, Prairie View City Library, Prairie View KS. 913-973-2706

VanDine, Ann, *Asst Mgr, Libr Servs*, Hoechst-Roussel Pharmaceuticals, Inc Library, Div of American Hoechst Corp Library, Somerville NJ. 201-685-2394

VanDinter, Nancy, *Librn*, Idaho Statesman Library, Boise ID. 208-377-6435

VanDolah, Imogene, *Librn*, Harper Public Library, Harper KS. 316-896-2959

Vandon, Gwendolyn R, *Circ*, Bethany & Northern Baptist Theological Seminaries Library, Oak Brook IL. 312-620-2214

VanDreser, R J, *Coordr*, University of Wisconsin-Stevens Point, Instructional Resources Curriculum, WI. 715-346-2540

VanDrisse, Sherm, *Librn*, Wisconsin State Prison Library, Waupun WI. 414-324-5571

VanDyck, Carolyn, *Librn*, Montgomery County Department of Public Libraries (Aspen Hill), Rockville MD. 301-942-2421

VanDyk, Stephon, *Archit*, New Jersey Institute of Technology, Robert W Van Houten Library, Newark NJ. 201-645-5306

VanDyke, Marilyn, *Tech Serv*, Geneva College, McCartney Library, Beaver Falls PA. 412-846-5100, Ext 297

VanDyke, Ruth L, *Librn*, Dames & Moore Library, Seattle WA. 206-523-0560

Vaneck, Louisa, *Circ*, Saint Mary's University (School of Law Library), San Antonio TX. 512-436-3435

VanEgdom, Deborah, *Librn*, Iowa Hospital Association Library, Des Moines IA. 515-288-1955

VanEpps, Myrna, *Media*, Grand Ledge Public Library, Grand Ledge MI. 517-627-7014

VanEtten, Margaret K, *Curator*, Mary Ball Washington Museum & Library Inc, Lancaster VA. 804-462-7280

VanFossen, Evelyn, *Librn*, Benton Township-Potterville District Library, Potterville MI. 517-645-2989

VanGeel, Nancy, *In Charge*, Oxford County Library (Thamesford Branch), Thamesford ON. 519-285-3482

VanGieson, Marilyn, *Librn*, Hawaii State Library System (Pearl City Regional), Pearl City HI. 808-455-4134

VanGinkel, C, *Librn*, United Way of the Lower Mainland, Social Planning & Res Dept Library, Vancouver BC. 604-731-7781

VanGoldwick, Marie, *Librn*, Northeastern Regional Library System (Albany Bend Branch), Fort Albany ON. 705-567-7043

VanGrasstek, Jean, *Librn*, University of Minnesota, Freshwater Biological Library, Navarre MN. 612-471-8407

VanGrasstek, Jean, *Librn*, University of Minnesota (Tennant Memorial Library), Navarre MN. 612-471-7715

Vanhaften-Mackler, Susan, *On-Line Servs*, Smithsonian Institution Libraries, Washington DC. 202-381-5496, 381-5421

VanHandel, Ralph A, *Dir*, Albert A Wells Memorial Library, Tippecanoe County Contractual Library, Lafayette IN. 317-423-2602

VanHassel, Ann, *ILL & Circ*, University of Washington Libraries (Law Library), Seattle WA. 206-543-4089

VanHess, Regina, *Asst Dir*, Anacortes Public Library, Anacortes WA. 206-293-2700

VanHeurn, Helen, *Cat*, University of Miami (Louis Calder Memorial Library), Miami FL. 305-547-6441

VanHoesen, Lois, *Ref*, Public Library of Brookline, Brookline MA. 617-734-0100

VanHook, Nell, *Ch*, Florence County Library, Florence SC. 803-662-8424

VanHoorn, Audra, *Dir*, Mount Hope Township Library, McLean IL. 309-874-2291

VanHorn, Elizabeth K, *Librn*, Bar Association of the District of Columbia Library, Washington DC. 202-426-7087, 426-7088

VanHorn, Grace, *Librn*, Castle Rock Public Library, Castle Rock WA. 206-274-6961

VanHorn, Mabel, *Librn*, Jackson County Library System (Central Point Branch), Central Point OR. 503-664-3228

VanHorn, Martha, *Rare Bks, Tech Serv & Cat*, Kern County Library, Bakersfield CA. 805-861-2130

VanHorn, Maureen, *Dir*, Carpenter Memorial Library, Pittsfield NH. 603-435-8406

VanHorn, Peggy, *Librn*, North Loup Public Library, North Loup NE. 308-496-3151

VanHorne, Geneva, *Assoc Prof*, University of Montana, School of Education, MT. 406-243-4911

VanHouten, Michael, *ILL, Ref & Bibliog Instr*, Adrian College, Shipman Library, Adrian MI. 517-265-5161, Ext 220

VanHoven, William D, *Dir*, North Carolina School of the Arts, Semans Library, Winston-Salem NC. 919-784-7170, Ext 2566

VanHuss, Mary, *Acq*, Taylor County Public Library, Campbellsville KY. 502-465-2562

VanInman, Dorothy, *Bkmobile Coordr*, Transylvania County Library, Inc, Brevard NC. 704-883-9880

VanKersen, Lionel, *Librn*, Masonic Temple, Masonic Library of Southern California, Los Angeles CA. 213-747-0819

VanKirk, Bernyce T, *Librn*, Monmouth County Library (Allentown Branch), Allentown NJ. 201-259-7565

VanKleek, Laurie M, *Librn*, Western Pentecostal Bible College Library, Clayburn BC. 604-853-7491, Ext 20

VanKlompenberg, Ruth, *Exten*, Herrick Public Library, Holland MI. 616-392-3114

VanLehn, Elsie, *Acq & Per*, Salem College, Dale H Gramley Library, Winston-Salem NC. 919-721-2649

VanLierde, Mrs I, *Ser*, National Gallery of Canada Library, Ottawa ON. 613-995-6245

VanLihn, Tran, *Foreign, Comparative & International Law*, Louisiana State University (Law Center Library), Baton Rouge LA. 504-388-8802

VanLoo, Dana, *Acq & Ref*, Depauw University, Roy O West Library, Greencastle IN. 317-653-9721, Ext 250

VanLoo, Viola A, *Librn*, Brookville Public Library, Brookville IN. 317-647-4031

VanMaanen, Lorna, *Asst Librn*, Rock Valley Community Library, Rock Valley IA. 712-476-5651

VanMason, Pat, *Cat*, University of Washington Libraries (Law Library), Seattle WA. 206-543-4089

VanMason, Pat, *Ref*, University of Washington Libraries (Law Library), Seattle WA. 206-543-4089

VanMater, John, *Dir*, Theosophical University Library, Altadena CA. 213-798-8020, Ext 5

VanMater, R K, *Hist*, Theosophical University Library, Altadena CA. 213-798-8020, Ext 5

VanMater, Sarah B, *Asst Dir*, Theosophical University Library, Altadena CA. 213-798-8020, Ext 5

VanMeeveren, Dawn, *Asst Dir*, Toccoa Falls College, Seby Jones Library, Toccoa Falls GA. 404-886-6831, Ext 229

VanMeeveren, Rebecca, *Dir*, Bryan College, H A Ironside Memorial Library, Dayton TN. 615-775-2041, Ext 228

vanMelle, Patricia, *Tech Serv & Cat*, Homewood Public Library, Homewood IL. 312-798-0121

VanMeter, Johanna, *Librn*, WED Enterprises, Inc (Walt E Disney), Research Library, Glendale CA. 213-956-7263

Vann, Edna L, *Per*, Chipola Junior College Library, Marianna FL. 904-526-2761, Ext 122

Vann, J Daniel, *Librn*, State University of New York at Buffalo (Lockwood Library), Buffalo NY. 716-636-2816

Vann, Sarah K, *Prof*, University of Hawaii, Graduate School of Library Studies, HI. 808-948-7321

VanNatta, Margaret W, *Librn*, First Presbyterian Church, D R A Carson Memorial Library, Lansdowne PA. 215-622-0800

VanNatten, Janet, *Librn*, Monmouth County Library (Wall Public), Sea Girt NJ. 201-431-7220

Vanndy, Jackie, *Asst Dir*, Sherman Public Library, Sherman TX. 214-892-4545, Ext 242

VanNess, Susan, *Ch*, Elwood Public Library, Elwood IN. 317-552-5001

VanNest, Dee, *Law,* Maryland State Law Library, Annapolis MD. 301-269-3395

VanNiekerken, William, *ILL,* Burlingame Public Library, Burlingame CA. 415-344-7107

VanNord, Joan, *Librn,* University of Illinois Library at Urbana-Champaign (University High School), Urbana IL. 217-333-1589

Vannorsdall, Mildred, *Head, Prof Libr,* Chicago Public Library (Central Library), Chicago IL. 312-269-2900

VanNort, Mary C, *Dir,* Keystone Junior College, Miller Library, La Plume PA. 717-945-5141, Ext 275

VanNortwick, Barbara, *Dir,* New York State Nurses Association Library, Guilderland NY. 518-456-9352, 456-9354

VanNote, Roy Nelson, *ILL,* University of Wisconsin-La Crosse, Murphy Library, La Crosse WI. 608-785-8505

VanOgtrop, Stefanie, *Librn,* Contra Costa County Library (San Ramon Valley), Danville CA. 415-837-4889

VanOosbree, Charlyne, *Librn,* Mid-Continent Public Library (Platte Woods), Kansas City MO. 816-741-4721

VanOrden, Phyllis, *Prof,* Florida State University, School of Library Science, FL. 904-644-5775

VanOss, Elsie, *Librn,* Auglaize County District Library (Francis J Stallo Memorial), Minster OH. 419-628-2925

VanOss, Jane, *ILL,* Central College, Geisler Learning Resource Center, Pella IA. 515-628-4151, Ext 233

VanOsten, Linda, *Asst Librn,* Meservey Public Library, Meservey IA. 515-358-6408

VanPelt, Jane, *Librn,* Highland County District (Leesburg Branch), Leesburg OH. 513-780-7295

VanPelt, Rita, *Tech Serv,* Muscle Shoals Regional Library System, Florence AL. 205-764-6563

vanPeski, Evelyn, *Librn,* Flushing Hospital & Medical Center, Medical & School of Nursing Library, Flushing NY. 212-670-5653

VanPickett, Richard, *Librn,* Brooklyn Public Library (Gravesend), Brooklyn NY. 212-376-9311

VanPolen, Susan, *Ch,* Mount Vernon Public Library, Mount Vernon WA. 206-336-2418

VanPuffelen, John, *Dir,* Appalachian Bible College Library, Bradley WV. 304-877-6428, Ext 11

VanRavensway, Leila, *Librn,* Albany Public Library (Pine Hills), Albany NY. 518-482-7911

VanReed, Suzanne, *Librn,* Vigo County Public Library (Southland Libr), Terre Haute IN. 812-232-8460

VanReken, Don, *Local Hist,* Herrick Public Library, Holland MI. 616-392-3114

vanRossem, Karen, *Ref,* North Babylon Public Library, North Babylon NY. 516-669-4020

VanRyzin, Elizabeth, *Mgr,* Institute of Gas Technology Library, Technical Information Center, Chicago IL. 312-567-3650

VanSant, Kay, *Dir,* American Cancer Society Library, Honolulu HI. 808-531-1662

VanSciver, Ruth, *Acq,* Asbury College, Morrison-Kenyon Library, Wilmore KY. 606-858-3511

VanScoy, Dorothy, *Spec Coll,* Frostburg State College Library, Frostburg MD. 301-689-4396

VanScoyoc, Lilas, *Librn,* Evart Public Library, Evart MI. 616-734-5542

VanSell, Janice, *Librn,* Montrose County Regional District Library (Uravan Branch), Uravan CO. 303-862-7301, Ext 233

VanSickle, Elsie, *Librn,* Shelby Public Library, Shelby MI. 616-861-4565

VanSickle, Jean L, *Librn,* Sac City Public Library, Sac City IA. 712-662-7276

VanSlooten, Arthur, *Media,* Ridgewood Public Library, Ridgewood NJ. 201-652-5200

VanSluys, Loralie, *Librn,* Hewitt Associates Library, Lincolnshire IL. 312-295-5000

VanSlyke, D, *Librn,* Niagara Falls Public Library, Niagara Falls ON. 416-356-8080

VanSonnenberg, Catherine, *Asst Dir,* Peabody Institute Library, Danvers Public Library, Danvers MA. 617-774-0554, Ext 0557, 0555

Vanstaareren, Elizabeth, *Bibliog Instr,* United States Department of Labor Library, Washington DC. 202-523-6988

Vanstone, H Charlotte, *Libr Tech,* Agriculture Canada (Research Station Regina Saskatchewan Library), Regina SK. 306-585-0255

Vansweden, Jesse, *Librn,* Tremonton City Library, Tremonton UT. 801-257-3213

VanTassell, Fred, *Business Mgr,* Mid-Hudson Library System, Poughkeepsie NY. 914-471-6060

VanTilburg, Constance, *Librn,* New York Public Library (Washington Heights), New York NY. 212-923-6054

VanToll, Faith, *Assoc Regional Librn,* Wayne State University Libraries (Vera P Shiffman Medical Library), Detroit MI. 313-577-1088

VanValen, Julie, *Serials, Docs & Libr Sci,* Beloit College, Col Robert H Morse Library, Beloit WI. 608-365-3391, Ext 230

VanValkenburg, Wanda, *Serials,* West Texas State University, Cornette Library, Canyon TX. 806-656-2761

VanVelzer, Verna, *Librn,* ESL Inc, Research Library, Sunnyvale CA. 408-734-2244, Ext 6796

vanVugt, Andre, *Dir,* Whitchurch-Stouffville Public Library, Stouffville ON. 416-640-2395

VanVuren, Darcy D, *AV Program Specialist,* Veterans Administration (Library Division), Washington DC. 202-389-2781

VanWart, Thomas, *Librn, On-Line Servs & Bibliog Instr,* United States Army (Corps of Engineers, Buffalo District Library), Buffalo NY. 716-876-5454

VanWeringh, Janet, *On-Line Servs,* Clarkson College of Technology, Harriet Call Burnap Memorial Library, Potsdam NY. 315-268-6645

VanWhy, Joseph S, *Dir,* Stowe-Day Library, Hartford CT. 203-522-9258

vanWinkle, Mary, *Ref,* Bentley College, Solomon R Baker Library, Waltham MA. 617-891-2231

VanZanten, Frank, *Dir,* Mid-Hudson Library System, Poughkeepsie NY. 914-471-6060

VanZee, Trudy, *Librn,* Central College (Music), Pella IA. 515-628-4151, Ext 233

vanZelm, Susan, *Ch,* Elizabeth Sanford Botsford Memorial Library, Williamstown Public Library, Williamstown MA. 413-458-5369

VanZetta, Carmella, *ILL & Acq,* Ladycliff College, Msgr C Hugo Doyle Library, Highland Falls NY. 914-446-4747, Ext 21

VanZilen, Eunice, *Librn,* East Norwalk Improvement Association Library, Norwalk CT. 203-857-8619

VanZuilen, Darlene, *Dir,* Mendon Township Library, Mendon MI. 616-496-4865

VanZwalenburg, Joyce, *Adminr,* Hawaii State Library System (Maui Library District), Wailuku HI. 808-244-3945

Vaprin, David, *Librn,* National Association of Insurance Commissioners, Central Office Library, Milwaukee WI. 414-271-4464

Vara, Wilson A, *Librn,* Hartford Public Library (Barbour), Hartford CT. 203-527-2257

Varani, Barbara, *Acq,* University of Connecticut at Hartford (Law Library), West Hartford CT. 203-523-4841, Ext 347, 370

Varga, Carol C, *Librn,* Burton Public Library, Burton OH. 216-834-4258

Vargas, Gwen S, *Librn,* Kirkpatrick, Lockhart, Johnson & Hutchison, Law Library, Pittsburgh PA. 412-355-6517

Vargas, Patricia, *Asst Dir,* Groton Public Library, Groton CT. 203-448-1552, 445-8551

Vargas, Sonia, *Study Center Librn,* Puerto Rico Junior College (Cupey Campus Learning Resources Center), Rio Piedras PR. 809-765-1716

Varghese, Grace, *Librn,* Rhode Island Medical Center (General Hospital Core Medical Library), Cranston RI. 401-464-3439

Vargo, Jeri, *Acq,* University of Massachusetts at Boston Library, Boston MA. 617-287-1900, Ext 2224

Varieur, Normand L, *Librn,* United States Army (Armament R & D Command, Scientific & Technical Information Div), Dover NJ. 201-328-2914

Varin, Kim, *Librn,* Washington County Library, Plymouth NC. 919-793-2113

Varin, Ruth, *Librn,* Shiawassee County Library (Shiawassee Township), Bancroft MI. 517-743-3421, Ext 278

Varineau, Teddi, *Cat,* Albany County Public Library, Laramie WY. 307-745-3365

Varland, Janet, *Librn,* Augusta Community Library, Augusta MT. 406-362-3348

Varland, Janet, *Librn,* Lewis & Clark Library (Augusta Community), Augusta MT. 406-562-3348

Varlejs, Jana, *Lectr,* Rutgers-The State University of New Jersey, Graduate School of Library & Information Studies, NJ. 201-932-7500

Varley, Eileen, *Librn,* Yachats Public Library, Yachats OR. 503-547-3741

Varner, Carroll, *Cat,* University of Nebraska at Omaha, University Library, Omaha NE. 402-554-2361

Varner, J H, *Libr Supvr,* Bell Telephone Laboratories (Western Electric Technical Library), Denver CO. 303-451-4275

Varner, Roberta, *Dir & Media,* Worch Memorial Public Library, Versailles OH. 513-526-3416

Varnes, O Charles, *Acq,* Mount San Antonio College, Learning Resources Center, Walnut CA. 714-594-5611, Ext 260

Varnes, Richard, *Media,* Boulder Public Library, Boulder CO. 303-441-3100

Varrelman, Sallie, *Librn,* Gulf South Research Institute Library, New Iberia LA. 318-356-2411

Varty, Beverly, *Librn,* Kimberley Public Library, Kimberley BC. 604-427-3112

Vary, Sue, *Supvr,* Elgin County Public Library (Port Stanley Branch), Port Stanley ON. 519-633-0815

Vasco, Gerhard, *Coordr Coll Develop,* State University of New York, Frank Melville Jr Memorial Library, Stony Brook NY. 516-246-5650

Vasenius, Linda, *Librn,* Aims Community College Library, Greeley CO. 303-330-8008, Ext 326

Vasey, Maureen, *Dir Info Servs,* Canadian Rehabilitation Council for the Disabled Library, Toronto ON. 416-862-0340

Vasey, Regina, *Librn,* Mott Public Library, Mott ND. 701-824-2163

Vasi, John, *Research & Planning,* University of Colorado at Boulder (University Libraries), Boulder CO. 303-492-7511

Vasilakis, Mary, *Libr Mgr,* Westinghouse Electric Corp (Nuclear Energy Systems, Information Resources), Pittsburgh PA. 412-373-4200

Vaslef, Irene, *Librn Ctr for Byzantine Studies,* Harvard University Library (Dumbarton Oaks Research Library, Bliss Pre-Columbian Collection & Garden Library), Washington DC. 202-232-3101

Vasquez, Christine, *Chief Librn,* Orange County Public Library (Fountain Valley Branch), Fountain Valley CA. 714-962-1324

Vassallo, Paul, *Chmn,* Council of New Mexico Academic Libraries, NM. 505-277-4241

Vassallo, Paul, *Dean,* University of New Mexico General Library, Albuquerque NM. 505-277-4241

Vassilakos, Marion, *Ref,* San Bernardino Public Library, San Bernardino CA. 714-889-0264

Vassios, Dora Mae, *Dir,* Hugo Public Library, Hugo CO. 303-743-2485

Vastine, James, *Bibliog Instr,* University of South Florida (University Library), Tampa FL. 813-974-2721

Vath, Hope, *ILL,* Corning Community College, Arthur A Houghton, Jr Library, Corning NY. 607-962-9251

Vaughan, Anne, *Librn,* Litton Industries, Electron Tube Div of San Carlos Library, San Carlos CA. 415-591-8411, Ext 231

Vaughan, Carolyn, *Asst Librn & YA,* Henderson County Public Library, Hendersonville NC. 704-693-8427

Vaughan, Frances, *Bkmobile Coordr,* Thomas Hackney Braswell Memorial Library, Rocky Mount NC. 442-1937 & 442-1951

Vaughan, James, *ILL, On-Line Servs & Bibliog Instr,* Elmhurst College, A C Buehler Library, Elmhurst IL. 312-279-4100, Ext 255

Vaughan, Ted, *Media,* University of Wyoming (Jayne Media Center), Laramie WY. 307-766-6391

Vaughan, Ted, *Asst Prof,* University of Wyoming, Library Media Program, WY. 307-766-2349

Vaughn, Elvina, *Librn,* Plaquemines Parish Library (Happy Jack), Port Sulphur LA. 504-657-7121

Vaughn, Florence, *Cat,* Texas College, D R Glass Library, Tyler TX. 214-593-8311, Ext 37

Vaughn, Grady, *Librn,* Adamsville Public Library, Adamsville TN. 901-632-3572

Vaughn, Maude L, *Bkmobile Coordr,* Henry County Library, Eminence KY. 502-845-5682

Vaughn, Mrs Orville, *Librn,* Dulany Memorial Library, Salisbury MO. 816-388-5712

Vaughn, Nancy, *Librn,* Veterans Administration, Medical Center Library, Topeka KS. 913-272-3111, Ext 271

Vaughn, Robert V, *Chief Librn & On-Line Servs,* Good Hope School Library, Saint Croix VI. 809-772-0022

Vaughn, Victor R, *Librn,* Wesley College Library, Florence MS. 601-845-6019

Vaughn, W A, *Dir,* Arkansas Tech University, Tomlinson Library, Russellville AR. 501-968-0304

Vaught, Anne M, *Reader Serv,* Horry County Memorial Library, Conway SC. 803-248-4898

Vaught, Edwin F, *Librn,* Southwest Research Institute, Thomas Baker Slick Memorial Library, San Antonio TX. 512-684-5111, Ext 2125

Vavra, Agnes, *Librn, AV & Commun Servs,* Ely Public Library, Ely IA. 319-848-9197

Vavrek, Bernard, *Prof,* Clarion State College, School of Library Science, PA. 814-226-2271

Vavricka, Karen, *ILL, Ad & Ref,* Tom Green County Library System, San Angelo TX. 915-655-7321

Vayssie, Wilifred Louise, *Librn,* Reedley College Library, Reedley CA. 209-638-3641, Ext 239

Vazquez, Martha W, *Dir,* Williamsburg Regional Library, Williamsburg VA. 804-229-7326

Vazquez, Noris, *Commun Servs,* University of Puerto Rico Library, Jose M Lazaro Memorial Library, Rio Piedras PR. 809-764-0000, Ext 3296

Vdovin, George, *Librn,* University of California, Berkeley (Chemistry), Berkeley CA. 415-642-3753

Vealey, George, *Bkmobile Coordr,* Albany Public Library, Albany NY. 518-449-3380

Vealey, George, *Librn,* Albany Public Library (Howe), Albany NY. 518-472-9485

Veaner, Allen B, *Dir,* University of California, Santa Barbara Library, Santa Barbara CA. 805-961-2741

Veatch, Lamar, *Dir,* High Plains Regional Library System, Greeley CO. 303-330-7691

Veatch, Van, *Dir,* Jackson Area Colleges, TN. 901-424-3520

Veatch, Van H, *Dir,* Jackson State Community College Library, Jackson TN. 901-424-3520, Ext 248

Veath, Marian, *Librn,* National Society, Sons of the American Revolution Library, Louisville KY. 502-589-1776

Veath, Marian S, *Librn,* General Electric Co, Major Appliance Laboratory Library, Louisville KY. 502-452-4613

Vebra, Dr Genevieve, *Assoc Prof,* Southern Connecticut State College, Div of Library Science & Instructional Technology, CT. 203-397-4532

Veenstra, John G, *Dir,* George Mason University Libraries, Fairfax VA. 703-323-2616

Veenstra, Joyce, *Ser Cat,* Columbia University (University Libraries), New York NY. 212-280-2241

Vega, Cyndi, *Librn,* John F Kennedy Center, National Park Service Library, Washington DC. 202-254-3850

Vegeler, Robert H, *Dir,* Public Library of Fort Wayne & Allen County, Fort Wayne IN. 219-424-7241

Veiham, Robert, *Tech Serv,* College of DuPage, Learning Resources Center, Glen Ellyn IL. 312-858-2800, Ext 2351

Veit, Henri, *Hist, Biol & Relig,* Brooklyn Public Library (Central Library), Brooklyn NY. 212-780-7712

Veitch, Carol J, *Asst Prof,* East Carolina University, Dept of Library Science, NC. 919-757-6621, 757-6627

Veitch, Karen, *Librn,* Frederick E Parlin Memorial Library (Woodlawn), Everett MA. 617-387-1228

Veith, Victoria, *Librn,* Hortonville Public Library, Hortonville WI. 414-779-4279

Velantzas, Tina, *Info Scientist,* Colgate-Palmolive Co, Technical Information Center Library, Piscataway NJ. 201-463-1212, Ext 277

Velez, A, *Librn,* La Crete Community Library, La Crete AB. 403-928-3913

Velez, Roberto, *Asst Librn,* Inter-American University of Puerto Rico, Aguadilla Regional College Branch Library, Ramey AFB PR. 809-890-5118

Velics, Laszlo, *Acq,* Michigan Technological University Library, Houghton MI. 906-487-2500

Velie, Jan, *Asst Librn,* Meadowlane Community Library, Melbourne FL. 305-727-7181

Vella, Frances G, *Dir & Acq,* West Los Angeles College Library, Culver City CA. 213-836-7110, Ext 301

Venable, Andrew, *Commun Servs,* Cleveland Public Library, Cleveland OH. 216-623-2800

Venable, Harriet C, *Dir,* Troy State University, Fort Rucker-Dothan Branch Library, Fort Rucker AL. 205-598-6110

Venable, Mrs Dell, *Librn,* Acadia Parish Library (Church Point Branch), Church Point LA. 318-788-1880

Venator, Mary Jane, *Ch,* Ringwood Public Library, Ringwood NJ. 201-962-6256

Veneziano, Patricia, *Fine Arts,* Silas Bronson Library, Waterbury CT. 203-574-8200

Veneziano, Velma, *Syst Analyst,* Northwestern University Library, Evanston IL. 312-492-7658

Veno, Mrs A, *Librn,* Nickel Centre Public Library, Garson ON. 705-693-2727

Veno, Phil, *Spec Servs,* Kentucky Department of Library & Archives, Frankfort KY. 502-564-7910

Venter, Lori, *Librn,* Corning Laboratories, Inc, Library, Cedar Falls IA. 319-277-2401

Ventgen, Carol, *Librn,* Coos Bay Public Library, Coos Bay OR. 503-269-1101

Ventres, Mary, *Ch,* Conant Free Public Library, Sterling MA. 617-422-6409

Ventresca, Donna, *ILL,* Turner Free Library, Randolph MA. 617-963-3000

Venturini, Corinne, *Assoc Dir Cent Servs,* Fort Vancouver Regional Library, Vancouver WA. 206-695-1561

Venzke, Jane, *Ch,* Williamsburg Regional Library, Williamsburg VA. 804-229-7326

Venzke, Patricia, *ILL,* New Brunswick Theological Seminary, Gardner A Sage Library, New Brunswick NJ. 201-247-5241, Ext 6

Vequist, Jim, *Media,* Fort Hays State University, Forsyth Library, Hays KS. 913-628-4431

Vera, Mercedes, *Cat,* Puerto Rico Junior College (Cupey Campus Learning Resources Center), Rio Piedras PR. 809-765-1716

Veracka, Peter G, *Dir,* Pontifical College Josephinum, Wehrle Memorial Library, Worthington OH. 614-885-2376

Verberne, Linda, *Supvr,* Middlesex County Library (Delaware Branch), Delaware ON. 519-438-8368

Verbesey, J Robert, *Dir,* Mastics-Moriches-Shirley Community Library, Shirley NY. 516-339-1511

Verble, Frances, *Cat,* University of Tennessee Center for the Health Sciences Library, Memphis TN. 901-528-5638

Vercellino, Ray, *Dir,* Cameron County Public Library, Emporium PA. 814-486-8011

Verch, Peggy, *Spec Coll,* Garfield Memorial Library, Clare Public Library, Clare MI. 517-386-7576

Verd, E Thomas, *Ref,* Spokane Public Library, Comstock Building Library, Spokane WA. 509-838-3361, Ext 65

Verdesi, Lida, *Coordr Adult Programs,* Finkelstein Memorial Library, Spring Valley NY. 914-352-5700, Ext 230

Verdi, Ann, *Librn,* Lewis & Clark Library (Lincoln Community), Lincoln MT. 406-362-4300

Verdi, Ann, *Librn,* Lincoln Community Library, Lincoln MT. 406-362-4300

Verdugo, Karen, *Pub Serv,* Loyola Marymount University (Loyola Law School Library), Los Angeles CA. 213-642-2934

Verdugo, Kathy, *Librn,* Presbyterian Intercommunity Hospital, Anna Siegrist Medical Library, Whittier CA. 213-298-0811

Vereecke, Melanie, *Librn,* Chicago Public Library (Roosevelt), Chicago IL. 312-666-5656

Verge, Colleen Richards, *Ref,* Petoskey Public Library, Petoskey MI. 616-347-4211

Vergonet, Diane, *AV,* Roseville Public Library, Roseville CA. 916-783-7158

Vergzmini, Tom, *Librn,* Northern Kentucky University, S P Chase College of Law Library, Covington KY. 606-292-5394

Verian, Joan, *Librn,* Mason County Public Library (Mason City Public), Mason WV. 304-773-5580

Verich, Thomas, *Spec Coll,* University of Mississippi Library, University MS. 601-232-7091

Verity, John B, *Libr Mgr,* University of California Lawrence Livermore Laboratory, Technical Information Department Library, Livermore CA. 415-422-5277

Verkade, Katherine, *Asst Dir,* Marstons Mills Public Library, Marstons Mills MA. 617-428-5175

Vermeulen, Eloise, *In Charge,* First Presbyterian Church Library, Kalamazoo MI. 616-344-0119

Vermillion, Jane E, *Librn,* Engineers Club of Dayton Library, Dayton OH. 513-228-2148

Vermillion, Judy, *Librn,* Children's Mercy Hospital, Medical Library, Kansas City MO. 816-234-3001

Vermillion, Judy, *Librn,* Rusk State Hospital Library (Texas Department of Mental Health & Mental Retardation Patient Library), Rusk TX. 214-683-3120

Vermillion, Judy, *Librn,* Rusk State Hospital Library (Texas Department of Mental Health & Mental Retardation Medical Library), Rusk TX. 214-683-3120

Vermillion, William, *Dir,* Western Evangelical Seminary, G Hallauer Memorial Library, Portland OR. 503-654-5182

Vernei, Barbara, *Ref,* Seattle Public Library, Seattle WA. 206-625-2665

Vernerder, Gloria, *Ch,* Hinsdale Public Library, Hinsdale IL. 312-986-1976

Verniero, Joan E, *In Charge,* Arthur Brisbane Child Treatment Center Library, Farmingdale NJ. 201-938-5061

Vernon, Christie D, *Dir,* Thomas Nelson Community College Library, Hampton VA. 804-825-2868, 825-2876

Vernon, Merry Ann, *Librn,* Denver Public Library (Ross-Cherry Creek), Denver CO. 303-573-5152, Ext 271

Verny, Roger, *Head,* University of Cincinnati Medical Center Libraries (Media Resources Center), Cincinnati OH. 513-872-4173

Veronica, Sister Mary, *Curric Libr,* Notre Dame College, Clara Fritzsche Library, Cleveland OH. 216-381-1680, Ext 59

Verrill, Mrs James, *Ch,* Baxter Memorial Library, Gorham ME. 207-839-4653

Versailles, Joseph, *Librn,* Societe D'archeologie Et De Numismatique De Montreal, Chateau Ramezay Bibliotheque, Montreal PQ. 514-861-7182

Verspoor, F, *On-Line Servs,* British Columbia Government, Legislative Library, Victoria BC. 604-387-6500

Versteeg, Jean, *Ad,* Township of Shaler North Hills Library, Glenshaw PA. 412-486-0211, 486-0212

Vertun, Lenore, *Ch,* Beverly Hills Public Library, Beverly Hills CA. 213-550-4711

Verzaro, Mary Ellen, *Pub Servs & Bibliog Instr,* Lycoming College Library, Williamsport PA. 717-326-8153

Vesely, Marilyn, *Pub Info Officer,* Oklahoma Department of Libraries, Oklahoma City OK. 405-521-2502

Vesper, Carolyn, *Tech Serv,* Colby Community College, H F Davis Memorial Library, Colby KS. 913-462-3984, Ext 265

Vest, Cathye, *Librn,* Meade County Public Library, Meade KS. 316-873-2522

Vest, Stephen C, *Assoc Librn,* Shenandoah College & Conservatory of Music, Howe Library, Winchester VA. 703-667-8714, Ext 453

Vestal, Alice M, *Rare Bks & Spec Coll,* University of Cincinnati Libraries, Central Library, Cincinnati OH. 513-475-2218

Veth, Terry R, *Acq,* Minneapolis Public Library & Information Center, Minneapolis MN. 612-372-6500

Vettese, Jan, *Tech Serv,* Yorba Linda Library District, Yorba Linda CA. 714-528-7039

Vettese, Richard, *Librn,* Muskegon County Library (Norton Shores), Muskegon MI. 616-780-2322

Vey, Jeffrey A, *Info Specialist,* Bucks County Planning Commission, Staff Library, Doylestown PA. 215-348-2911

Vezina, Allene, *Circ,* Allerton Public Library, Monticello IL. 217-762-4676

Via, John, *Acq,* Wake Forest University, Z Smith Reynolds Library, Winston-Salem NC. 919-761-5480

Via, Nancy, *Info,* Southern Connecticut State College, Hilton C Buley Library, New Haven CT. 203-397-4505

Viabec, Donald, *In Charge,* Geisinger Medical Center (Davison Library), Danville PA. 717-275-6211

Viacava, Doris, *On-Line Servs & Bibliog Instr,* Iona College, Ryan Library, New Rochelle NY. 914-636-2100

Viana, Jaqueline, *Librn,* Midlothian Public Library, Midlothian IL. 312-388-4119

Viar, Bridget, *ILL,* Canon City Public Library, Canon City CO. 303-275-3669

Viarengo, Theresa, *Dir & Bibliog Instr,* Waynesburg College Library, Waynesburg PA. 412-627-8191, Ext 278

Vicars, Phyllis, *Acq,* University of Texas at Arlington Library, Arlington TX. 817-273-3391

Viccars, Marion, *Spec Coll,* University of West Florida, John C Pace Library, Pensacola FL. 904-476-9500, Ext 261

Vick, Kathleen, *Project Coordr,* Consortium for Health Information & Library Services, PA. 215-872-6575

Vick, Mary B, *Cat,* United States Naval War College Library, Newport RI. 401-841-2641

Vick, Mary Ellen, *Tech Serv, Cat & On-Line Servs,* Whittier College (Bonnie Bell Wardman Library), Whittier CA. 213-693-0771, Ext 223

Vick, Mrs James, *Librn,* White Pine Public Library, White Pine TN. 615-674-2557

Vick, Peggy, *Asst Librn,* Logan County Public Library, Russellville KY. 502-726-6129

Vick, Robert, *Librn,* UNCAP International, Inc, Project Collector's Research Library, Los Angeles CA. 213-222-2012

Vickers, Ann, *Cat,* Elon College, Iris Holt McEwen Library, Elon College NC. 919-584-9711, Ext 230 or 242

Vickers, Rebecca, *Tech Serv & Cat,* Lubbock Christian College, Moody Library, Lubbock TX. 806-792-3221, Ext, 241, 242

Vickery, Byrdean, *Dir & Acq,* Columbia Basin College, Library Media Center, Pasco WA. 509-547-0511, Ext 287

Vickery, George, *AV,* George S Houston Memorial Library, Dothan AL. 205-793-9767

Vickrey, Caroline, *Librn,* Nazareth Memorial Library, Nazareth PA. 215-759-4932

Vickrey, J William, *AV,* Flint Public Library, Flint MI. 313-232-7111

Vickrey, Marie, *Librn,* Graves Public Library, Mendota Library, Mendota IL. 815-538-5142

Victor, Doris H, *Acq,* Nassau Community College Library, Garden City NY. 516-222-7400

Victor, Mary O'Neill, *Dir,* Fine Arts Museum of the South Library, Mobile AL. 205-342-4642

Victor, Renea, *Asst Dir,* Teaneck Public Library, Teaneck NJ. 201-837-4171

Victor, Stephen, *Deputy Dir,* Old Slater Mill Association, Slater Mill Historic Site Library, Pawtucket RI. 401-725-8638

Victoria, Judy, *Librn,* Kings County Library (Stratford), Hanford CA. 209-947-3003

Victors, Betty, *Librn,* Wasilla Public Library, Wasilla AK. 907-376-5913

Vidalin, Mrs C, *Supvr,* Edmonton Public Library (Calder), Edmonton AB. 403-454-9321

Vidalin, Mrs C, *Librn,* Edmonton Public Library (Dickinsfield), Edmonton AB. 403-478-2811

Vidmanis, Val, *Dir,* Becker Junior College at Leicester, Paul Swan Library, Leicester MA. 617-892-3784

Vidmanis, Val, *Dir,* Becker Junior College at Worcester, Alumni Library, Worcester MA. 617-791-9241, Ext 26

Vidor, David, *Cat,* Federal Reserve Bank of Atlanta, Research Library, Atlanta GA. 404-586-8829

Vidovich, Susan Reilly, *Dir,* Raleigh County Public Library, Beckley WV. 304-255-0511

Vidrine, Jacqueline, *Dir & Acq,* Lincoln Parish Library, Ruston LA. 318-255-1920

Viegut, Marlyn, *Librn,* Marathon County Public Library (Athens Branch), Athens WI. 715-845-7214, Ext 21

Viehdorfer, Alreeta, *Librn,* United States Air Force (Accounting & Finance Center), Denver CO. 303-320-7566

Viele, George B, *Dir,* Greensboro Public Library, Greensboro NC. 373-2474; 373-2471

Vierich, Richard, *Librn,* University of California, Riverside (Physical Sciences), Riverside CA. 714-787-3511

Vierich, Richard, *Physical Sci,* University of California, Riverside, University Library, Riverside CA. 714-787-3221

Vierich, Richard W, *Chmn,* Inland Empire Academic Libraries Cooperative, CA. 714-787-3511

Vierra, B, *Br Coordr,* Napa City - County Library, Napa CA. 707-253-4241

Vierria, Ruth, *Ch,* Sutter County Free Library, Yuba City CA. 916-673-5773

Vieser, Kathleen, *ILL,* Des Plaines Public Library, Des Plaines IL. 312-827-5551

Vieten, Martha, *ILL,* Hemet Public Library, Hemet CA. 714-658-7293

Viewig, Nancy, *Librn,* Ohio County Public Library (Warwood Community), Wheeling WV. 304-277-1800

Vigars, Linda, *Ref,* General Electric Co (Main Library), Schenectady NY. 518-385-2117

Vigeant, Robert J, *Dir,* Saint Joseph's College Library, Rensselaer IN. 219-866-7111, Ext 187

Viger, Veronica, *Ref,* Equitable Life Assurance Society of the United States (General Library), New York NY. 212-554-2491

Viggiano, Leonard, *Librn,* New York Public Library (Throg's Neck), New York NY. 212-792-2612

Vigil, Peter, *On-Line Servs,* University of California at Davis (Health Sciences Library), Davis CA. 916-752-1214

Vigil, Peter J, *Health Sci,* University of California at Davis, General Library, Davis CA. 916-752-2110

Vigil, Susie, *Cat,* New Mexico State Library, Santa Fe NM. 505-827-2033

Viher, Mrs Joseph, *Cat,* Carnegie Public Library, Ironwood MI. 906-932-0203

Vijay, Girija, *Dir,* Crawford W Long Memorial Hospital, Medical Library, Atlanta GA. 404-892-4411, Ext 678

Vikre, David, *Librn,* Smith College Library (Science), Northampton MA. 413-584-2700, Ext 638

Vilcins, M, *Ref,* National Gallery of Canada Library, Ottawa ON. 613-995-6245

Viles, Ann, *Dir,* Curtis Institute of Music Library, Philadelphia PA. 215-893-5265

Vileta, James, *Archivist,* University of Minnesota, Duluth, Duluth MN. 218-726-8100

Viljoen, John, *ILL,* Los Angeles County Public Library System, South State Cooperative Library System, Los Angeles CA. 213-974-6501

Villabona, Dulce, *Pub Servs,* Yale University Library (Ira V Hiscock Library), New Haven CT. 203-436-3148

Villamora, G A, *Librn,* Ogilvy & Mather Inc, Chicago Library, Chicago IL. 312-861-1166

Villanueva, Dorothy, *ILL,* Roxanne Whipple Memorial-Navajo County Library, Winslow City-Navajo County Library, Winslow AZ. 602-289-4982

Villanueva, Alicia, *Asst Librn,* San Benito Public Library, San Benito TX. 512-399-2311

Villarreal, L Guen, *Asst Dir,* Washburn University of Topeka (School of Law Library), Topeka KS. 913-295-6688

Villavecchia, Maria, *Cat & Spec Coll,* Union City Free Public Library, Union City NJ. 201-866-7500

Villegas, Alberto, *AV,* El Paso Public Library, El Paso TX. 915-543-3804

Villegas, Gertrude, *Librn,* Santa Maria Public Library (Guadalupe Station), Guadalupe CA. 805-343-1405

Villemarette, Francis, *Librn,* Avoyelles Parish Library (Hessmer Branch), Hessmer LA. 318-253-7559

Villemarie, Gabrielle, *Librn,* Canadian Centre for Ecumenism, Montreal PQ. 514-937-9176

Villeneuve, Charles, *Ref,* CEGEP de Chicoutimi, Centre De Documentation, Chicoutimi PQ. 418-549-9520, Ext 212, 312

Villeneuve, Madeleine, *Librn,* Bibliotheque Municipale, Rimouski PQ. 418-724-3164

Villere, Dawn N, *Tech Librn,* ITT Corp, Gilfillan Div, Technical Library, Van Nuys CA. 213-988-2600

Villers, Alta, *ILL,* Parkersburg & Wood County Public Library, Wood County Service Center, Parkersburg WV. 304-485-6564

Villines, Dorothy, *Bkmobile Coordr,* North Arkansas Regional Library, Harrison AR. 501-741-3665

Vilnins, Raita, *Asst Librn,* Elmhurst Public Library, Elmhurst IL. 312-279-8696

Vinakmans, Cathy, *ILL,* Midwestern Regional Library System, Kitchener ON. 519-576-5061

Vince, Thomas L, *Dir,* Hudson Library & Historical Society, Hudson OH. 216-653-6658

Vincelli, Sue, *Librn,* General Electric Co (Lighting Research & Technical Services Operation Library), Cleveland OH. 216-266-2121

Vincent, Alice C, *Asst Dir,* Park Falls Public Library, Park Falls WI. 715-762-3121

Vincent, Donald E, *Dir,* University of New Hampshire, Ezekiel W Dimond Library, Durham NH. 603-862-1540

Vincent, John, *Librn Blind,* South Dakota State Library, Pierre SD. 605-773-3131

Vincent, John J, *Librn,* South Dakota State Library for the Handicapped, Pierre SD. 605-773-3514

Vincent, Joseph G, *Exec Dir,* Rome Historical Society, William E & Elaine Scripture Memorial Library, Rome NY. 315-336-5870

Vincent, Kathy, *Acq,* Wake Forest University (Bowman Gray School of Medicine Library), Winston-Salem NC. 919-727-4691

Vincent, Louise, *Librn,* Muhlenberg County Libraries (Central City Branch), Central City KY. 502-754-4630

Vincent, Margaret, *Asst Dir,* North Syracuse Free Library, North Syracuse NY. 315-458-6184

Vincent, Mary, *Tech Serv,* Lucius Beebe Memorial Library, Wakefield MA. 617-245-0790

Vincent, Mary T, *Ad,* Floral Park Public Library, Floral Park NY. 516-354-0666

Vincent, Thelma, *Librn,* Lockyear College Library, Evansville IN. 812-425-8157

Vinci, Lorraine, *In Charge,* Old Bridge Public Library (Laurence Harbor Branch), Laurence Harbor NJ. 201-566-2227

Vines, Robert, *Sr Libr,* New York State Library, Albany NY. 518-474-5930

Viney, Devra, *Ch,* Great Bend Public Library, Great Bend KS. 316-792-2409

Vingren, Margaret, *Circ,* Roselle Public Library District, Roselle IL. 312-529-1641

Vinicombe, Marie, *Spec Coll,* Baldwin Public Library, Baldwin NY. 516-223-6228

Vinkemulder, Don, *Cat,* Kellogg Community College, Emory W Morris Learning Resource Center, Battle Creek MI. 616-965-3931, Ext 333

Vinkemulder, John, *Distribution Dept,* Ferris State College Library, Big Rapids MI. 616-796-9494, 796-9971, Ext 323

Vinnes, Norman, *Dir,* Ramsey County Public Library, Roseville MN. 612-631-0494

Vinokur, Caroline, *Dir,* New Hyde Park Public Library, New Hyde Park NY. 516-354-1413

Vinsant, Gwendolyn, *Librn,* Summerfield Public Library, Summerfield KS. 913-244-6543

Vinson, Charlotte W, *Chief Librn,* Lone Star Gas Co, Reference Library, Dallas TX. 214-741-3711

Vinson, Dyan, *Acq,* Thomas Nelson Community College Library, Hampton VA. 804-825-2868, 825-2876

Vinson, Kate, *Tech Serv,* Thomas Public Library, Peach Public Libraries, Fort Valley GA. 912-825-8540

Vinson, Lisa, *Circ,* Bentley College, Solomon R Baker Library, Waltham MA. 617-891-2231

Vinson, Margaret, *Librn,* Macon County Library (Red Boiling Springs Branch Library), Red Boiling Springs TN. 615-699-3701

Vinson, Ruby H, *Acq,* Alabama State University, Library & Learning Resources, Montgomery AL. 205-832-6072

Vint, Lucile, *Librn,* Glen Elder Library, Glen Elder KS. 913-545-3632

Violet, Jane, *Dir,* Community Hospital of Springfield & Clark County, Health Science Library, Springfield OH. 513-325-0531, Ext 321, 383

Violette, Judith, *Ref & Bibliog Instr,* Indiana University-Purdue University at Fort Wayne Library, Walter E Helmke Library, Fort Wayne IN. 219-482-5456

Vipond, Alva, *Asst Librn & Cat,* Atwater Library of Mechanics Institute of Montreal, Montreal PQ. 514-935-7344, 935-1960

Vipond, S, *In Charge,* Bell Canada (Information Resource Centre), Montreal PQ. 514-870-8922

Vires, Geneva K, *Asst Librn,* Lincoln Memorial University Library, Harrogate TN. 615-869-3611, Ext 57
Virostek, Frank, *Dir,* Washoe County Library, Reno NV. 702-785-4039
Virostek, Frank E, *Dir,* B F Jones Memorial Library, Aliquippa District Center, Aliquippa PA. 412-375-7174
Virta, Marilyn, *Librn,* Sno-Isle Regional Library (Monroe Branch), Monroe WA. 206-794-7851
Virtue, Mary, *ILL & Ref,* Ryerson Polytechnical Institute, Donald Mordell Learning Resources Centre, Toronto ON. 416-595-5331
Vis, Marcia, *ILL,* Northwestern College, Ramaker Library, Orange City IA. 712-737-4821, Ext 57, 58
Viscarra, Joseph R, *Cat,* New York City Community College, Namm Hall Library, Brooklyn NY. 212-643-5240
Viscuso, Viola, *Asst Dir,* Coloma Public Library, Coloma MI. 616-468-3431
Vishnefske, Vic, *AV,* Kansas Wesleyan, Memorial Library, Salina KS. 913-827-5541, Ext 233
Vita, Susan H, *Chief,* Library of Congress (Cataloging in Publications Division), Washington DC. 202-287-5000
Vitek, Clement G, *Chief Librn,* Baltimore Sun Papers Library, Baltimore MD. 301-332-6250
Viti, Thomas, *Librn,* Norton Public Library, Norton MA. 617-285-4761
Vitriol, Malvin, *Librn,* Veterans Administration, Hospital Library, New York NY. 212-686-7500, Ext 445, 279
Vittands, Gunta, *ILL & Ref,* Wheaton College Library, Norton MA. 617-285-7722, Ext 518
Vittek, Mary, *Tech Serv,* Public Library of Annapolis & Anne Arundel County Inc, Annapolis MD. 301-224-7371
Vitters, Lynn, *Ch,* South Huntington Public Library, Huntington Station NY. 516-549-4411
Vitters, Roy, *Media & YA,* Harborfields Public Library, Greenlawn NY. 516-757-4200
Vittitow, Maudie, *Librn,* Texas Gas Transmission Corp, Technical & Law Libraries, Owensboro KY. 502-926-8686
Vixie, Anne, *Librn,* Lamb-Weston Inc, Business Research Center, Portland OR. 503-639-8612
Vizoyan, Barbara B, *Info Mgr,* Georgeson & Co Library, New York NY. 212-440-9949, 440-9950
Vlach, Milada, *Rare Bks,* Bibliotheque Nationale Du Quebec, Montreal PQ. 514-873-4553
Vladick, Mark, *Media,* University of Wisconsin Center, Baraboo-Sauk County Library, Baraboo WI. 608-356-8351, Ext 49
Vladimir, V Abbot, *Librn,* Holy Trinity Orthodox Seminary Library, Jordanville NY. 315-858-1332
Vlahon, Linda, *Ch,* Selby Public Library, Sarasota County Federated Library System, Sarasota FL. 814-366-7303
Vlantikas, Mary, *Librn,* Federal Reserve Bank of Boston, Research Library, Boston MA. 617-973-3393
Vlasic, Ivan, *Librn Tech,* Tulane University of Louisiana, Howard-Tilton Memorial Library, New Orleans LA. 504-865-5131
Vlcansky, Dorcas, *Personnel,* Milwaukee Public Library, Milwaukee WI. 414-278-3000
Vlcek, Charles, *IMC,* Central Washington University Library, Ellensburg WA. 509-963-1901
Vlcek, Randall, *Librn,* Chicago Public Library (Albany Park), Chicago IL. 312-588-3901
Vlechek, Cecelia, *Asst Librn,* Kirtland Public Library, Kirtland OH. 216-256-3747
Vlielstra, Lois B, *Librn,* Kalamazoo County Law Library, Kalamazoo MI. 616-383-8839
Vocelka, Mary, *In Charge,* National Park Service, Yosemite National Park, Research Library, Yosemite National Park CA. 209-372-4461, Ext 61
Vocelli, Virginia, *Ref,* Meriden Public Library, Meriden CT. 203-238-2344
Vodde, Nan, *Asst Dir,* Madison County-Canton Public Library, Canton MS. 601-859-3202
Voegel, George H, *Dean,* William Rainey Harper College, Harper Learning Resource Ctr, Palatine IL. 312-397-3000
Voegele, Marlyn, *ILL,* University of Missouri-Columbia, Elmer Ellis Library, Columbia MO. 314-882-4701

Voegtle, Mary Guittard, *Librn,* Meyers, Miller, Middleton, Weiner, & Warren, Law Library, Dallas TX. 214-651-1700
Voelker, Linda, *Ref & On-Line Servs,* University of Western Ontario (Health Sciences Library), London ON. 519-679-6175
Voelker, Marie, *Librn,* University of Minnesota Libraries-Twin Cities (Mathematics), Minneapolis MN. 612-376-7207
Vogal, Vernon W, *Reader Serv,* Edinboro State College, Baron-Forness Library, Edinboro PA. 814-732-2780
Vogan, Elizabeth F, *Dir,* Mooers Free Library, Mooers NY. 518-236-7744
Voge, Susan, *Librn,* Equitable Life Assurance Society of the United States (Medical Library), New York NY. 212-554-2935
Vogel, Albert W, *Chairperson,* University of New Mexico, Library Media Education, NM. 505-277-5141
Vogel, Becky, *ILL,* Seguin-Guadalupe County Public Library, Seguin TX. 312-379-1331
Vogel, Bruce, *Ch,* Alameda County Library, Hayward CA. 415-881-6337
Vogel, Helen M, *Librn,* Rochester Psychiatric Center, Rehabilitation Center Library, Rochester NY. 716-473-3230, Ext 640
Vogel, Joanne, *Doc,* Saint Louis University (Omer Poos Law Library), Saint Louis MO. 314-658-2755
Vogel, K Chris, *Librn,* San Jose Public Library (Calabazas), San Jose CA. 408-996-1535
Vogel, Loualta, *Dir,* Centralia College Library, Centralia WA. 206-736-9391, Ext 241
Vogel, Marion L, *Learning Resources Dean,* Trident Technical College (North Campus Learning Resources Center), Charleston SC. 803-572-6094
Vogel, Marion L, *Dean of Learning Resources,* Trident Technical College (Palmer Campus Learning Resource Center), Charleston SC. 803-792-7135
Vogel, Mrs Robert, *Ch,* Schmaling Memorial Public Library District, Fulton IL. 815-589-2045
Vogel, Phyllis, *Tech Serv,* Allentown College of Saint Francis De Sales Library, Center Valley PA. 215-282-1100, Ext 266
Vogelback, Judith, *Cat,* Lynchburg Public Library, Lynchburg VA. 804-847-1565
Vogelhuber, Heather, *Circ,* San Jose Public Library, San Jose CA. 408-277-4822
Vogelstein, Susan, *Dir,* Buttenwieser Library, 92nd St YM & YWHA, New York NY. 212-427-6000
Vogrin, Jean, *Librn,* Ocean County Library (Barnegat Branch), Barnegat NJ. 609-698-3331
Vogt, Donna, *Librn,* Town of Hamburg Public Library (Lake Shore), Hamburg NY. 716-627-3017
Vogt, Howard S, *Dir,* Bloomfield Public Library, Northwest Essex Area Library, Bloomfield NJ. 201-429-9292
Vogt, Richard, *Servs Coordr,* Viking Library System, Fergus Falls MN. 218-739-2896
Vogt, Sheryl, *Acting Head,* Richard B Russell Library, University of Georgia Libraries, Athens GA. 404-542-2716
Vohra, Pran, *Supvr & Chief Librn,* Wascana Institute of Applied Arts & Sciences, Resource & Information Center, Regina SK. 306-565-4321
Voight, Randall L, *Librn,* International Research & Evaluation, Information & Research Resources Library-Data Base, Eagan MN. 612-869-2675
Voigt, Ann, *Chief Librn,* Lockheed Corporation (Lockheed-California Company Central Library), Burbank CA. 213-847-5646
Voigt, Audry, *AV,* Alpena Community College Library, Alpena MI. 517-356-9021, Ext 249
Voigt, John, *Dir,* Berklee College of Music Library, Boston MA. 617-266-1400, Ext 158
Voigt, Kathleen, *Ref & On-Line Servs,* University of Toledo, William S Carlson Library, Toledo OH. 419-537-2324
Voigt, Louise, *Librn,* Oklahoma Well Log Library, Inc, Tulsa OK. 918-582-6188
Voisin, Patricia, *Librn,* Colorado State Department of Natural Resources (Div of Water Resources Library), Denver CO. 303-839-3581
Voit, Betty, *ILL & Ref,* Jefferson Community College, Learning Resources Center, Louisville KY. 502-584-0181, Ext 305
Vojtech, Kathryn, *Ad,* Villa Park Public Library, Villa Park IL. 312-834-1164

Volc, Judith, *Ch,* Boulder Public Library, Boulder CO. 303-441-3100
Volk, Mary Jane, *Librn,* Carnegie-Mellon University (Mellon Institute Library), Pittsburgh PA. 412-578-3172
Volk, Susan, *Ch,* Riviera Beach Public Library, Riviera Beach FL. 305-845-4194, 845-4195, 845-4196
Volk, Ulla, *ILL & Ref,* Fairleigh Dickinson University, Friendship Library, Madison NJ. 201-377-4700, Ext 234
Volk, Ulla, *Bus & Legal,* Fairleigh Dickinson University, Friendship Library, Madison NJ. 201-377-4700, Ext 234
Volkenburgh, Jean Van, *Acq,* Public Library of Nashville & Davidson County, Nashville TN. 615-244-4700
Volkening, Jane, *Circ,* Cadillac-Wexford Public Library, Cadillac MI. 616-775-6541
Volkering, Virginia, *Librn,* Decorah Public Library, Decorah IA. 319-382-3717
Volkersz, Evert, *Spec Coll,* State University of New York, Frank Melville Jr Memorial Library, Stony Brook NY. 516-246-5650
Volkman, Carl W, *Assoc Dir,* Lincoln Library, Springfield Public Library, Springfield IL. 217-753-4900
Volkman, Virginia, *Librn,* Sedona Public Library, Sedona AZ. 602-282-7714
Vollmayer, Karl, *Dir,* Redwood City Public Library, Redwood City CA. 415-369-6251, Ext 288
Vollmer, Darlene, *ILL,* Benedictine College (North Campus Library), Atchison KS. 913-367-5340, Ext 290
Vollmer, Eileen, *Librn,* Allen Science Research, Inc Library, Charlotte NC. 704-376-1015
Vollmer, Helen, *Librn,* Francesville-Salem Township Public Library, Francesville IN. 219-567-9433
Volny, James G, *Dir,* Centenary College of Louisiana, Magale Library, Shreveport LA. 318-869-5170
Volpe, Ann, *Sci,* New York University, Elmer Holmes Bobst Library, New York NY. 212-598-2484
Volpe, Florence, *Acq & Circ,* Cumberland County College Library, Vineland NJ. 609-691-8600, Ext 44, 45
Volpi, Louis J, *Bus Mgr,* Yale University Library (University Library), New Haven CT. 203-436-8335
Volstad, Evelyn, *Librn,* Claresholm Municipal Library, Claresholm AB. 403-625-4168
Volz, Robert L, *In Charge,* Williams College (Chapin Library), Williamstown MA. 413-597-2462
VonArb, Glenda, *Asst Librn,* Alton Public Library, Alton IA. 712-756-4516
VonBalen, John, *Circ,* University of South Dakota, I D Weeks Library, Vermillion SD. 605-677-5371
vonBrauchitsch, Ilse, *Ref,* University of Oklahoma Health Sciences Center Library, Oklahoma City OK. 405-271-2285
vonBriesen, Susan, *Ref,* Portsmouth Public Library, Portsmouth NH. 603-431-2000, Ext 252
vonBrockdorff, Eric, *Dir,* Hartwick College Library, Oneonta NY. 607-432-4200, Ext 324
vonBrockdorff, Hans, *Dir,* State University of New York Agricultural & Technical College at Canton, Southworth Library, Canton NY. 315-386-7229
VonBruck, Marion, *Coordr,* Pierce County Medical Library Consortium, WA. 206-597-7664
VonderLindt, Alice M, *Chief Librn,* Veterans Administration, Medical Center Library, Coatesville PA. 215-384-7711, Ext 333
Vondra, Anne, *Ref,* Wilson College, John Stewart Memorial Library, Chambersburg PA. 717-264-4141, Ext 344
Vondrasek, Bets, *Curator,* Walt Whitman House State Historic Site, Research Library & Museum, Huntington Station NY. 516-427-5240
Vondruska, Eloise, *Tech Serv,* Parkland College, Learning Resource Center, Champaign IL. 217-351-2241
VonGlahn, A Stephen, *Evening Librn,* Chesapeake College Library, Learning Resources Center, Wye Mills MD. 301-758-1537, 822-5400, Ext 56, 57
vonGodany, Ursula, *Humanities,* Iowa State University Library, Ames IA. 515-294-1442

Vongpaisal, S, *Acq,* Laurentian University Library, Bibliotheque de l'Universite Laurentienne, Sudbury ON. 705-675-1151, Ext 251 & 252

vonGunten, Louis E, *Asst Librn,* Alameda County Law Library, Oakland CA. 415-874-5823

vonHake, Margaret J, *Dir & Acq,* Columbia Union College, Theofield G Weis Library, Takoma Park MD. 301-270-4999

vonHassell, Rose, *Cat,* Howard County Library, Big Spring TX. 915-267-5295

VonLang, Frederick, *Dir,* Hibbing Public Library, Hibbing MN. 218-262-1038

VonLaue, Hildegarde, *ILL,* University of Massachusetts at Boston Library, Boston MA. 617-287-1900, Ext 2224

Vonnes, John, *Asst Dir,* Central Technical Community College, Nuckolls Study Lounge, Hastings NE. 402-463-9811, Ext 363

vonNussbaumer, Aliyah, *Librn,* Dresser Industries, Inc, Magcobar Research Library, Houston TX. 713-972-6011

VonPfeil, Helene, *Librn,* District of Columbia Office of the Corporation Counsel, Law Library, Washington DC. 202-727-6274

vonRosen, Margaret, *Librn,* Chrysler Corp Defense Engineering Library, Center Line MI. 313-497-0495

vonRosenberg, Jo, *In Charge,* Texas Education Agency (Region XII), Waco TX. 817-756-7494

vonSchrader, Julie L, *Librn,* Pitney, Hardin & Kipp, Law Library, Morristown NJ. 201-267-3333, Ext 311

vonSlagle, Allison, *Media,* University of Tennessee at Chattanooga Library, Chattanooga TN. 615-755-4701

VonStralendorff, Vicco, *ILL, Ref & Bibliog Instr,* Franklin College Library, Franklin IN. 317-736-8441, Ext 257

VonVogt, Steve, *Dir,* Parmly Billings Library, South Central Federation of Libraries, Billings MT. 406-248-7393

VonWald, Katherine, *Asst Librn,* North Central Regional Library System, Mason City IA. 515-423-6917

VonWeise, Jutta, *Librn,* J Walter Thompson Co, Research Library, Los Angeles CA. 213-553-8383

Voor, Patricia A, *Librn,* Meadowlane Community Library, Melbourne FL. 305-727-7181

Voorhees, Donald, *Acq,* Corning Community College, Arthur A Houghton, Jr Library, Corning NY. 607-962-9251

Voorhees, Edward H, *Librn for Staff Develop & Training,* Dallas Public Library, Dallas TX. 214-748-9071

Voos, Henry, *Prof,* Rutgers-The State University of New Jersey, Graduate School of Library & Information Studies, NJ. 201-932-7500

Vorderstrasse, Donald C, *Ref,* Clackamas Community College, Marshall N Dana Memorial Library, Oregon City OR. 503-656-2631, Ext 288

Vorhees, Joan, *Tech Serv,* Mary H Weir Public Library, Weirton WV. 304-748-7070

Vork, D, *In Charge,* Uniroyal, Inc, Oxford Managment & Research Center, Technical Library, Middlebury CT. 203-573-4509

Vorndran, Catherine M, *Librn,* Bucks County Free Library (James A Michener), Quakertown PA. 215-536-8574

Vorp, Donald, *Theol Librn,* Drew University, Rose Memorial Library, Madison NJ. 201-377-3000, Ext 469

Vorse, Elinore, *ILL,* State University of New York College at Potsdam, Frederick W Crumb Memorial Library, Potsdam NY. 315-268-2940

Vorss, Esther, *Librn,* Kice Metal Products Co, Inc, Library, Wichita KS. 316-267-4281

Vorwald, Doris, *Educ,* Queens College Library, Flushing NY. 212-520-7616

Voskuil, Marion, *Dir,* Hammond Community Library, Hammond WI. 715-796-2281

Vosper, Dena, *Librn,* Yale University Library (Ira V Hiscock Library), New Haven CT. 203-436-3148

Vosper, Robert, *Dir,* University of California Los Angeles Library (William Andrews Clark Memorial Library), Los Angeles CA. 213-731-8529

Voss, Allie Flo, *Circ Mgr,* Dallas Public Library, Dallas TX. 214-748-9071

Voss, Anne E, *Coordr Sch & Col Media Servs,* New Jersey State Library, Trenton NJ. 609-292-6200

Voss, Joyce, *Ref,* Franklin Park Public Library District, Franklin Park IL. 312-455-6016

Voss, Kathryn, *Librn,* Trails Regional Library (Lexington Branch), Lexington MO. 816-259-3071

Voss, Nancy, *Librn,* Southern Tier Library System (Middlesex Reading Center), Middlesex NY. 607-962-3141

Voss, Ruth, *Dir,* Faulkner-Van Buren Regional Library, Conway AR. 501-327-7482

Vossenberg, Andrea A, *Librr,* Scranton Public Library (Providence), Scranton PA. 717-347-5414

Votaw, Floyd, *ILL & Tech Serv,* Grace College & Grace Theological Seminary, Betty Zimmer Morgan Library, Winona Lake IN. 219-267-8191, Ext 182

Voth, Sally, *Assoc Dir for Tech Servs, Budget & Automation,* Kansas State University, Farrell Library, Manhattan KS. 913-532-6516

Vowles, Carole, *Ch & YA,* Kings County Library, Hanford CA. 209-582-0261

Voyer, Mrs R F, *Dir,* Honey Grove Memorial Library, Honey Grove TX. 214-378-2206

Vrabel, Donald A, *ILL,* Allegheny College, Lawrence Lee Pelletier Library, Meadville PA. 814-724-3363

Vrabel, Patricia, *Asst Librn,* Teinert Memorial Public Library, Bartlett TX. 817-527-3208

Vratil, Evelyn W, *Librn,* Limon Memorial Public Library, Limon CO. 303-775-2163

Vrecenak, Robert, *ILL,* University of Connecticut Library, Storrs CT. 203-486-2219

Vreeland, Mrs E, *ILL,* Freehold Public Library, Freehold NJ. 201-462-5135

Vreeze, Assia B De, *Dir,* National Theatre School of Canada Library, Montreal PQ. 514-842-7954, Ext 38

Vriesacker, Jane, *Ad,* Reedsburg Public Library, Reedsburg WI. 608-524-3316

Vroom, Olga, *Librn,* Paterson Free Public Library (People's Park-Lakeview), Paterson NJ. 201-881-3786

Vrooman, George K, *Chief Librn,* United States Army Armament Research & Development Command, Benet Weapons Laboratory Technical Library, Watervliet NY. 518-266-5613

Vrugtman, Ina, *Bot-Hort Librn,* Royal Botanical Gardens Library, Hamilton ON. 416-527-1158

Vuckovich, C Y, *Dir,* Community College of Beaver County Library, Monaca PA. 412-775-8561, Ext 249

Vugrinecz, Anna-Elizabeth, *Librn,* Western Electric Co Inc, Technical Library, Kearny NJ. 201-344-7700, Ext 4875

Vukazich, Anna, *Librn,* Osborne Laboratories, Inc, Library, Santa Fe Springs CA. 213-944-6435

Vuturo, Robert, *Dir,* Kansas City Kansas Community College Library, Kansas City KS. 913-334-1100, Ext 38

Vyas, Shanker H, *Dir,* Philadelphia College of Osteopathic Medicine, O J Snyder Memorial Library, Philadelphia PA. 215-581-6526

Vyas, Veena, *Dir,* Orthopaedic Hospital, Lt Robert J Rubel Memorial Library, Los Angeles CA. 213-742-1530, 742-1531

W

Wachel, Kathleen B, *Acq,* University of Iowa Libraries, Iowa City IA. 319-353-4450

Wachna, Jane, *Librn,* Financial Times of Canada Library, Toronto ON. 416-922-1133

Wachter, Carrie, *Librn,* Glasgow Public Library, Glasgow MO. 816-338-2395

Wachter, John, *Asst Dir,* Catonsville Community College, Learning Resources Div, Baltimore MD. 301-455-4586

Wack, Helen M, *Librn,* Colorado State Hospital (Professional Library), Pueblo CO. 303-543-1170, Ext 2677

Wacker, Mrs Alfred J, *Librn,* Teinert Memorial Public Library, Bartlett TX. 817-527-3208

Wacker, Thelma, *ILL,* Phoenix Public Library, Phoenix AZ. 602-262-6451

Waddel, Dean A, *Asst Dean, Pub Servs,* University of Nebraska-Lincoln, University Libraries, Lincoln NE. 402-472-2526

Waddell, Bonnie, *Ad,* Colchester-East Hants Regional Library, Truro NS. 902-895-4183

Waddell, Carol, *Asst Dir,* Tippecanoe County Historical Association, Alameda McCollough Library, Lafayette IN. 317-742-8411

Waddell, Carolyn, *Librn,* Columbus County Public Library (Fair Bluff Community), Fair Bluff NC. 919-649-7098

Waddell, Gene, *Dir,* South Carolina Historical Society Library, Charleston SC. 803-723-3225

Waddell, Jay, *Eng,* California Polytechnic State University Library, San Luis Obispo CA. 805-546-2345

Waddell, Mina Jean, *Educ,* Wichita State University, Library & Media Resources Center, Wichita KS. 316-689-3586

Waddell, Richard E, *Dir, ILL, Acq & Cat,* Virginia Intermont College, J F Hicks Memorial Library, Bristol VA. 703-669-6101, Ext 26

Waddell, Rose, *Ch & Cat,* Clinton-Essex-Franklin Library System, Plattsburgh NY. 518-563-5190

Waddell, Samuel J, *Dir,* Hunter College of the City University of New York Library (Health Professions), New York NY. 212-481-4326

Wadden, Emily, *Librn,* Spokane County Law Library, Spokane WA. 509-456-3680

Waddington, Elaine, *Librn,* Royal Victoria Hospital (Women's Pavilion Library), Montreal PQ. 514-842-1251, Ext 1971

Waddington, R C, *Dir,* Fargo Public Library, Fargo ND. 701-241-1490

Waddington, Susan R, *Art & Music,* Providence Public Library, Providence RI. 401-521-7722

Waddle, Richard, *Tech Serv & Acq,* Central Washington University Library, Ellensburg WA. 509-963-1901

Waddle, Richard L, *Dean,* Central Washington State College, Dept of Education, WA. 509-963-1111

Wade, Anne, *Cat,* East Baton Rouge Parish Library, Baton Rouge LA. 504-389-3360

Wade, Carol, *Librn,* Florida Board of Regents Library, Tallahassee FL. 904-488-6826

Wade, Catherine, *Librn,* Sno-Isle Regional Library (Oak Harbor Branch), Oak Harbor WA. 206-675-5115

Wade, Diana M, *Head Ref,* National Archives & Records Service (National Audiovisual Center), Washington DC. 301-763-1896

Wade, Dianna, *Cat,* University of Tampa, Merl Kelce Library, Tampa FL. 813-253-8861, Ext 385

Wade, Elaine, *Ch,* Edison Free Public Library, Edison NJ. 201-287-2298

Wade, Gordon S, *Dir, On-Line Servs & Bibliog Instr,* Carroll Public Library, Carroll IA. 712-792-3432

Wade, Idella B, *Tech Serv,* Palm Beach Junior College, Library Learning Resources Center, Lake Worth FL. 305-965-8000, Ext 213

Wade, Judy, *Asst Librn,* Lamont Memorial Free Library, McGraw NY. 607-836-6767

Wade, MariAlice, *ILL & Ref,* Pequannock Township Public Library, Pompton Plains NJ. 201-835-7460

Wade, Marjorie, *Dir,* Riga Free Library, Churchville NY. 716-293-2009

Wade, Pam, *Asst Librn,* Haskell County Public Library, Stigler OK. 918-967-4801

Wade, Tina, *Librn,* Cass County Public Library (Creighton Branch), Creighton MO. 816-499-2340

Wade, Virginia, *Librn,* Brunswick-Glynn County Regional Library (Charlton County), Folkston GA. 912-296-2041

Wade, Willie, *Ref,* Tuskegee Institute, Hollis Burke Frissell Library, Tuskegee Institute AL. 205-727-8894

Wadhwa, Om P, *Dir,* Wethersfield Public Library, Wethersfield CT. 203-563-5348

Wadian, Becky, *Actg Dir & Acq,* Upper Iowa University, Henderson-Wilder Library, Fayette IA. 319-425-3311, Ext 270

Wadley, Carol, *Librn,* Stormont-Vail Hospital, School of Nursing Library, Topeka KS. 913-354-6930

Wadnizak, Lillian M, *Librn,* North Dakota State Film Library, Div of Independent Study, Fargo ND. 701-237-8907

Wadsworth, Anne, *Librn,* William A Farnsworth Library & Art Museum, Rockland ME. 207-596-6457

Wadsworth, Carol, *Librn,* Brooklyn Public Library (Bay Ridge), Brooklyn NY. 212-748-3042

Wadsworth, Lynn, *AV,* Northwestern College of Chiropractic Library, Saint Paul MN. 612-690-1735, Ext 22

Wadsworth, Pauline, *Talking Bks Coordr,* Greater Vancouver Library Federation, Vancouver BC. 604-251-1147

Waesche, Betty, *Ref,* Spokane Community College, East Mission Campus Library, Spokane WA. 509-455-7699

Waffle, Jan, *Pub Servs,* Harris County Public Library, Houston TX. 713-221-5350

Waffle, Lois, *Librn,* Toledo-Lucas County Public Library (Waterville Branch), Waterville OH. 419-878-2091, 878-4961

Wageman, Lynette, *SE Asia Area Specialist,* University of Hawaii (University of Hawaii Library), Honolulu HI. 808-948-7205

Wagener, Elsie, *ILL & Circ,* United States Air Force (Strughold Aeromedical Library), Brooks AFB TX. 512-536-3321

Wagener, Henry, *AV Coordr,* Minnesota Department of Public Welfare Library, Saint Paul MN. 612-296-6117

Wagener, Mary, *Tech Serv,* Brookfield Public Library, Brookfield WI. 414-782-4140

Wagenknecht, Robert E, *Dir,* City Library, Springfield MA. 413-739-3871

Wagenveld, Linda, *Librn,* Herman Miller Inc, Resource Center, Zeeland MI. 616-772-3629

Wager, Judith, *Media,* Saint Clair County Library System, Port Huron MI. 313-987-7323

Wager, Judy, *AV,* Blue Water Library Federation, Port Huron MI. 313-987-7323

Wagers, Laurel, *Cat,* Sandpoint-East Bonner County Free Public Library District, Sandpoint ID. 208-263-6930

Wagers, Robert, *Asst Prof,* San Jose State University, Division of Library Science, CA. 408-277-2292

Wages, Orland, *Dir,* Bridgewater College, Alexander Mack Memorial Library, Bridgewater VA. 703-828-2501, Ext 510

Wages, Virginia M, *Librn,* Barber-Nichols Engineering Co Library, Arvada CO. 303-421-8111

Waggener, Jean B, *Dir Archives & Mss,* Tennessee State Library & Archives, Nashville TN. 615-741-2764

Waggoner, Mrs Spencer, *Asst Dir,* Lowndes County Library System, Columbus Public Library, Columbus MS. 601-328-1056

Waggoner, Phyllis A, *Librn,* Federal Reserve Bank of San Francisco, Research Library, San Francisco CA. 415-544-2358

Waggoner, Ruth, *Asst Dir,* Willard Memorial Library, Willard OH. 419-933-8564

Wagman, Frederick H, *Prof,* University of Michigan, School of Library Science, MI. 313-764-9376

Wagner, Ann, *Librn,* Espanola Public Library, Espanola ON. 705-869-2940

Wagner, Betty L, *Librn,* University of Washington Libraries (Architecture & Urban Planning), Seattle WA. 206-543-4067

Wagner, Beulah, *Librn,* Illinois Prairie District Public Library (Benson Branch), Benson IL. 309-394-2542

Wagner, Bonnie, *Librn,* Port Orford Public Library, Port Orford OR. 503-332-5622

Wagner, Byron M, *Assoc Prof,* Millersville State College, Dept of Library Science, PA. 717-872-5411, Ext 416

Wagner, Carolyn, *Dir,* Glenwood-Lynwood Public Library District, Glenwood IL. 312-758-0090

Wagner, Charlene M, *Ch,* Gardiner Public Library, Gardiner ME. 207-582-3312

Wagner, Charles A, *Dir,* Peru Public Library, Peru IN. 317-473-3069

Wagner, Dietmar, *ILL,* Ann Arbor Public Library, Ann Arbor MI. 313-994-2333

Wagner, Edward, *ILL,* University of Northern Iowa Library, Cedar Falls IA. 319-273-2737

Wagner, Edward C, *Librn,* Supreme Court Library, Staten Island NY. 212-447-4748

Wagner, Elaine, *Pub Info Office,* Saint Paul Public Library, Saint Paul MN. 612-292-6311

Wagner, Ernest C, *Dir,* College of the Virgin Islands, Ralph M Paiewonsky Library, Saint Thomas VI. 809-774-1252, Ext 483

Wagner, Felicia, *ILL,* Thomas Jefferson University (Scott Memorial Library), Philadelphia PA. 215-928-8848

Wagner, Frank, *Info Specialist,* Celanese Corp, Celanese Chemical Company, Inc-Technical Center-Library, Corpus Christi TX. 512-241-2343

Wagner, George L, *Ad,* Port Jefferson Free Library Association, Port Jefferson NY. 516-473-0022

Wagner, Gertrude, *Librn,* Jackson District Library (Eastern), Jackson MI. 517-788-4074

Wagner, Grace, *Librn,* Rockbridge Regional Library (Buena Vista Branch), Buena Vista VA. 703-261-2715

Wagner, Heather, *Dir,* Middleton Public Library, Middleton WI. 608-831-5564

Wagner, Helen, *ILL,* Elmwood Park Public Library, Elmwood Park NJ. 201-796-8888

Wagner, Ilene M, *Librn,* United States Navy (Norfolk Naval Shipyard, Technical Library), Portsmouth VA. 804-393-5580, 393-3480

Wagner, Jan, *In Charge,* Milwaukee Public Library (Oklahoma Branch), Milwaukee WI. 414-278-3055

Wagner, Jane, *Educ & Relig,* Public Library of Cincinnati & Hamilton County, Cincinnati Public Library, Cincinnati OH. 513-369-6000

Wagner, Janet, *ILL,* Hofstra University Library, Hempstead NY. 516-560-3475

Wagner, Johnice, *Librn,* Public Library of the District of Columbia (R L Christian), Washington DC. 202-727-1347

Wagner, Judy, *On-Line Servs,* Ohio State University Libraries (Vocational Education Research Library), Columbus OH. 614-486-3655, Ext 221

Wagner, Lloyd Felix, *Dir,* Hood College of Frederick, Joseph Henry Apple Library, Frederick MD. 301-663-3131, Ext 364, 365

Wagner, Louise, *Acq,* Pace University, Pleasantville-Briarcliff Library, Pleasantville NY. 914-769-3200, Ext 382

Wagner, Mary, *Chairperson,* College of Saint Catherine, Dept of Library Science, MN. 612-690-6651

Wagner, Murray L, *Librn,* Bethany & Northern Baptist Theological Seminaries Library, Oak Brook IL. 312-620-2214

Wagner, Nancy, *Asst Librn,* Murphy Memorial Library, Monona IA. 319-539-2356

Wagner, Patricia, *Homebound Serv,* Quincy Public Library, Quincy IL. 217-223-1309

Wagner, Patricia M, *In Charge,* Canada Employment & Immigration Commission, Saskatchewan Regional Library, Regina SK. 306-569-6532

Wagner, Richard L, *Librn,* The Dalles City-Wasco County Library, The Dalles OR. 503-296-2815

Wagner, Rita, *Ch,* Elk Grove Village Public Library, Elk Grove Village IL. 312-439-0447

Wagner, Robert, *Ref,* Skyline College Library, San Bruno CA. 415-355-7000, Ext 311

Wagner, Rod, *Deputy Dir,* Nebraska Library Commission, Lincoln NE. 402-471-2045

Wagner, Rod, *NEBASE,* NE. 402-471-2045

Wagner, Sister Mary Patricia, *Ser,* College of Mount Saint Joseph on the Ohio, Archbishop Alter Library, Mount Saint Joseph OH. 513-244-4216

Wagoner, Ora M, *Librn,* Bureau of Land Management (Denver Service Center Library), Denver CO. 303-234-4578

Wahl, K Jane, *Bus Admin & Hist,* University of Portland, Wilson W Clark Memorial Library, Portland OR. 503-283-7111

Wahl, K Jane, *ILL, Ref & Bibliog Instr,* University of Portland, Wilson W Clark Memorial Library, Portland OR. 503-283-7111

Wahl, Karl H, *In Charge,* Thunder Bay Public Library (Waverley Resource Library), Thunder Bay ON. 807-344-3585

Wahlborg, Ruth, *Acq,* Santa Barbara City College Library, Santa Barbara CA. 805-965-0581, Ext 242

Wahls, Elsie, *Dir,* Gridley Township Public Library, Gridley IL. 309-747-2284

Wahrow, Lillian A, *Librn,* New York Hospital-Cornell Medical Center, Westchester Div Medical Library, White Plains NY. 914-682-9100, Ext 2396

Waibel, Grace, *On-Line Servs,* Bureau of the Census Library, Suitland MD. 301-763-5040, 763-5042

Waickman, Sister Anna M, *Librn,* Marygrove College Library, Detroit MI. 313-862-8000

Waidelich, A, *Librn,* Madison Public Library (Municipal Reference Service), Madison WI. 608-266-6316

Wailes, Lucile H, *Dir,* Adams County Public Library, North Glenn CO. 303-452-7532

Wainer, Margaret, *Dir,* Carl Sandburg College, Learning Resources Center, Galesburg IL. 309-344-2518, Ext 247 & 257

Wainio, Betty Dent, *Dir,* Somerville Free Public Library, Somerville NJ. 201-725-1336

Wainwright, Alexander, *Asst Librn for Coll Develop,* Princeton University Library, Princeton NJ. 609-452-3180

Wainwright, Judith, *Ref & Bibliog Instr,* University of San Francisco, Richard A Gleeson Library, San Francisco CA. 415-666-6167

Wainwright, Nicholas B, *Dir Emeritus & Ed,* Historical Society of Pennsylvania Library, Philadelphia PA. 215-732-6200

Wainwright, Tom A, *Librn,* American Cyanamid Co, Lederle Laboratories Division, Y SubbaRow Memorial Library, Pearl River NY. 914-735-5000, Ext 3401

Waisanen, Ofelia Q, *Acq,* Imperial Valley College, Spencer Library Media Center, Imperial CA. 714-352-8320, Ext 270

Wait, Carol D, *Ser,* Capital District Library Council Bibliographic Center-Library, Troy NY. 518-272-8834

Waite, Amy, *Dir,* Alfred Dickey Public Library, Jamestown ND. 701-252-2990

Waite, Crimora Y, *Dir,* Culpeper Town & County Library, Culpeper VA. 703-825-8691

Waite, Joan, *Lectr,* Concordia University, Library Studies Program, PQ. 514-482-0320, Ext 324

Waite, M, *Librn,* Hazeltine Corp Library, Greenlawn NY. 516-261-7000

Waite, Patricia, *Librn,* Coca-Cola Company Foods Division, Citrus Research & Development Technical Library, Plymouth FL. 305-886-1568

Wajima, Masakatsio, *Librn,* Consulate General of Japan in New York, Japan Information Center Library, New York NY. 212-986-1600, Ext 56

Wakasugi, Amy, *Circ,* Miami Beach Public Library, Miami Beach FL. 305-673-7535

Wakefield, Anna Mae, *Librn,* Public Library of Fort Wayne & Allen County (Little Turtle), Fort Wayne IN. 219-426-6214

Wakefield, Carol, *Ch,* Hillsboro Public Library, Hillsboro OR. 503-648-6669

Wakefield, D'Anna, *In Charge,* Clay County Public Library (Orange Park), Green Cove Springs FL. 904-284-3822

Wakefield, David M, *Systems Analyst,* Fairfax County Public Library, Administrative Offices, Springfield VA. 703-321-9810

Wakefield, Diane, *Librn,* Beaver Area Memorial Library, Beaver PA. 412-775-1132

Wakefield, Elizabeth, *Dir,* Saint Joseph Hospital, Medical Staff Library, Lorain OH. 216-245-6851, Ext 160

Wakefield, Jacqueline M, *Ch & East Br Coordr,* Ventura County Library Services Agency, Ventura County Library, Ventura CA. 805-654-2627

Wakefield, June, *Librn,* Kerbs Memorial Hospital, Information Center, Saint Albans VT. 802-524-2161

Wakefield, Lynn, *Librn,* Thompson Falls Public Library, Thompson Falls MT. 406-827-3557

Wakefield, Marie, *Librn,* Harris-Stowe State College Library, Saint Louis MO. 314-533-3366, Ext 36

Wakeford, C, *Librn,* Canada Department of National Defense (Chief Construction & Properties Technical Library), Ottawa ON. 613-996-0930

Wakeley, Deborah, *Dir,* Fort Wright College of the Holy Names Library, Spokane WA. 509-328-2970, Ext 20, 456-5087

Wakeman, Joan, *Librn,* Lehigh Public Library, Lehigh IA. 515-359-2967

Wakeman, Marjory, *ILL,* Bennington College, Crossett Library, Bennington VT. 802-442-5401, Ext 278, 279, 290

Wakevainen, Alden, *Librn,* Houston Public Library (Social Sciences), Houston TX. 713-224-5441

WALCH

Walch, David B, *Dir,* State University College at Buffalo, Edward H Butler Library, Buffalo NY. 716-878-6302

Walch, Irene, *Ref,* Clark University, Robert Hutchings Goddard Library, Worcester MA. 617-793-7573

Walck, Marion, *Librn,* Linn Grove Public Library, Linn Grove IA. 712-296-3919

Walcott, Dee, *Librn,* Mancelona Township Library, Mancelona MI. 616-587-9451

Walcott, Roger, *Dir,* Herrick Public Library, Holland MI. 616-392-3114

Walcott, Rosalind, *Librn,* State University of New York (Earth & Space Sciences), Stony Brook NY. 516-246-3616

Wald, Edyth F, *Librn,* Mount Dora Public Library, Mount Dora FL. 904-383-3326

Wald, G, *Librn,* Pharmaco-Medical Documentation, Inc, Research Library, Chatham NJ. 201-635-9500

Waldbillig, Martha, *Tech Serv,* Hemet Public Library, Hemet CA. 714-658-7293

Waldecker, Alice V, *Curator,* Norfolk Historical Society Library, Norfolk CT. 203-542-5761

Waldemar, David, *Commun Servs, North Area,* Hennepin County Library, Edina MN. 612-830-4944

Waldemer, Susan, *Librn,* Wilder District Library, Wilder ID. 208-482-7880

Walden, Barbara, *Chairperson,* University of Minnesota Libraries-Twin Cities (Reference-Resources), Minneapolis MN. 612-373-3082

Walden, Bette K, *Dir,* Indiana State University, Evansville Library, Evansville IN. 812-464-1824

Walden, Bonnie, *Librn,* Choctawhatchee Regional Library (Louisville Public), Louisville AL. 205-266-5210

Walden, Elaine B, *Librn,* Dallas Times Herald Library, Dallas TX. 214-744-6240

Walden, Harriet, *Circ,* Royal Oak Public Library, Royal Oak MI. 313-541-1470

Walden, R M, *Librn,* Canada Department of Agriculture, Experiment Farm Library, Indian Head SK. 306-695-2274

Walden, Ralph H, *Librn,* Avon Park Correctional Institution Library, Avon Park FL. 813-453-3174, Ext 368

Walden, Winston, *Coordr Tech Servs,* Southeast Missouri State University, Kent Library, Cape Girardeau MO. 314-651-2235

Waldenberg, Gloria, *Librn,* Beth David Congregation, Harry Simons Library, Miami FL. 305-854-3911

Walder, Antoinette, *Acq,* Xavier University, McDonald Memorial Library, Cincinnati OH. 513-745-3881

Waldern, D E, *Dir,* Agriculture Canada, Research Station Library, Lacombe AB. 403-782-3316

Waldhart, Thomas, *Assoc Prof,* University of Kentucky, College of Library Science, KY. 606-258-8876

Waldhorn, Katharine Wohl, *Dir,* Ypsilanti Area Public Library, Ypsilanti MI. 313-482-4110

Waldhour, Grace, *Acq,* Newberry College, Wessels Library, Newberry SC. 803-276-5010, Ext 300

Waldman, Betty, *Librn,* Akron-Summit County Public Library (Ayres), Akron OH. 216-762-7621

Waldman, Ruth, *Ch,* City of Inglewood Public Library, Inglewood CA. 213-649-7380

Waldner, J Dudley, *Exec Secy,* Comics Magazine Association of America, Inc Library, New York NY. 212-682-8144

Waldner, Janet, *Librn,* Boyne City Public Library, Boyne City MI. 616-582-7861

Waldo, Alma, *Asst Dir,* E C Scranton Memorial Library, Madison CT. 203-245-7365

Waldo, Michael, *Instr,* Illinois State University, Department of Information Sciences, IL. 309-438-3671

Waldoch, Mary Beth, *Dir,* Rawlins Municipal Library, Pierre SD. 605-224-7421

Waldow, Betty, *Librn,* Arlington County Bar Association, Walter T McCarthy Law Library, Arlington VA. 703-558-2243

Waldrep, Pamela, *Ad,* Washington Carnegie Library, Washington Court House OH. 614-335-2540

Waldrip, Maryalice, *ILL & Ref,* Kingsport Public Library, J Fred Johnson Memorial Library, Kingsport TN. 615-245-3141

Waldron, Donna, *Circ & Ref,* George W Norris Regional Library, McCook Public Library, McCook NE. 308-345-1906

Waldron, Elizabeth, *Librn,* Life Sciences, Inc Library, Saint Petersburg FL. 813-345-9371

Waldron, Esther, *Head Cat,* University of Pittsburgh (Maurice & Laura Falk Library of the Health Sciences), Pittsburgh PA. 412-624-2521

Waldron, Richard, *Assoc Exec Dir,* New Jersey State Library (New Jersey Historical Commission), Trenton NJ. 609-292-6062

Waldron, Rodney K, *Dir,* Oregon State University, William Jasper Kerr Library, Corvallis OR. 503-754-3411

Waldron, Shirley, *Librn,* Cultural Arts Center, Arts Library, Ocean City NJ. 609-399-7628

Waldschmidt, Marilyn, *Asst Librn,* Sage Public Library, Osage IA. 515-732-3323

Waldsmith, Ruth, *Ch,* Marshall Community Library, Marshall WI. 414-655-3123

Waldvogel, Ruth, *Dir,* Lockport Township Public Library, Lockport IL. 815-838-0755

Walensky, Lucile, *Libr Adminr,* Southwest Iowa Regional Library System, Missouri Valley IA. 712-642-4131

Wales, Mary Lynne, *Librn,* Blue Ridge Regional Library (Collinsville Branch), Collinsville VA. 703-647-1112

Walf, Bette, *ILL,* State University of New York at Buffalo (Charles B Sears Law Library), Buffalo NY. 716-636-2043

Walia, Rajinder S, *Librn,* Northeastern University Libraries (School of Law), Boston MA. 617-437-3338

Walk, Mary, *Ch,* Spencer Public Library, Spencer IA. 712-262-2960

Walker, A Lorraine, *ILL,* Birmingham Public & Jefferson County Free Library, Birmingham AL. 205-254-2551

Walker, Alan, *Librn,* Saskatchewan Department of Continuing Education, Research & Planning Branch Library, Regina SK. 306-565-5614

Walker, Alberta, *Cat,* Claremont Colleges Libraries, Claremont CA. 714-621-8000, Ext 3721

Walker, Alice, *Ext Servs,* Dearborn Department of Libraries, Henry Ford Centennial Library, Dearborn MI. 313-271-1000

Walker, Alice L, *Librn,* Fremont County Library (Pavillion Branch), Pavillion WY. 307-332-5194

Walker, Almena, *Librn,* Durham County Library (Salvation Army Boys Club), Durham NC. 919-682-7842

Walker, Ann, *Librn,* Lake Lanier Regional Library (Lilburn Public), Lilburn GA. 404-921-7346

Walker, Annalise, *Archit Archives,* University of Calgary Library, Calgary AB. 403-284-5954

Walker, B A, *Librn,* Southwestern Manitoba Regional Library, Melita MB. 204-522-3923

Walker, Barbara, *Dir,* Beaufort, Hyde, Martin Regional Library, Washington NC. 919-946-6401

Walker, Barbara, *Librn,* Farmington Community Library (Farmington), Farmington Hills MI. 313-477-4770

Walker, Barbara E, *Dir,* Fort Walton Beach Public Library, Fort Walton Beach FL. 904-244-5361

Walker, Betty, *Lectr,* Lambuth College, Library Science Program, TN. 901-427-6743

Walker, Blanche, *Librn,* Tangipahoa Parish Library (Clark), Kentwood LA. 318-229-8204

Walker, Bonieta, *ILL,* Alamogordo Public Library, Alamogordo NM. 505-437-9058

Walker, Bonnie, *Cat,* Abilene Christian University, Margaret & Herman Brown Library, Abilene TX. 915-677-1911, Ext 2344

Walker, Bonnie L, *Dir,* Valdez Public Library, Valdez AK. 907-835-4632

Walker, Brooks, *Dir,* Walker Museum Library, Fairlee VT. 802-333-9572

Walker, Carma, *Acq,* Murray Public Library, Murray UT. 801-266-1137

Walker, Celine, *Sci,* Stanford University Libraries, Stanford CA. 415-497-2016

Walker, Celine, *Librn,* Stanford University Libraries (Engineering), Stanford CA. 415-497-1513

Walker, Clara M, *Dir,* Selma University, Stone-Robinson Library, Selma AL. 205-894-8673

Walker, Clare M, *Dir,* Mechanicsburg Area Public Library, Mechanicsburg PA. 717-766-0171

Walker, Constance, *Dir,* University of Saint Thomas, Robert Pace & Ada Mary Doherty Library, Houston TX. 713-522-7911, Ext 325

Walker, Danny, *Librn,* Jackson Sun Library, Jackson TN. 901-427-3333, Ext 157

Walker, Donald, *Coordr Ad Servs,* New York Public Library (The Branch Libraries), New York NY. 212-790-6262

Walker, Donna, *Ref,* Grandview Heights School District Public Library, Columbus OH. 614-486-2951

Walker, Doris L, *Dir,* Manasquan Public Library, Manasquan NJ. 201-223-1503

Walker, Dorothy, *Ad, On-Line Servs & Bibliog Instr,* Northport Public Library, Northport NY. 516-261-6930

Walker, Edna, *Librn,* Prince Edward Island Provincial Library (Tyne Valley Branch), Tyne Valley PE. 902-892-3504, Ext 54

Walker, Elaine, *Ser,* Cornell University Libraries (University Libraries), Ithaca NY. 607-256-4144

Walker, Elizabeth, *Asst Dir,* Curtis Institute of Music Library, Philadelphia PA. 215-893-5265

Walker, Eunice, *Tech Serv & Cat,* Fashion Institute of Technology, Library-Media Services Dept, New York NY. 212-760-7695

Walker, Flora, *Asst Dir,* Sioux City Public Library, Sioux City IA. 712-279-6179

Walker, Frances, *Art,* Jericho Public Library, Jericho NY. 516-935-6790

Walker, Frank, *Head, Adult Servs,* George S Houston Memorial Library, Dothan AL. 205-793-9767

Walker, Frank, *Coordr,* Southeast Alabama Cooperative Library System, Dothan AL. 205-793-9767

Walker, Frank X, *Coll Develop Officer,* New York University, Elmer Holmes Bobst Library, New York NY. 212-598-2484

Walker, George, *Dir,* SCM Corp, Glidden Pigments Group Library, Baltimore MD. 301-633-6400

Walker, H T, *Pub Servs,* Public Library of Annapolis & Anne Arundel County Inc, Annapolis MD. 301-224-7371

Walker, Jane, *Acq,* Jenkintown Library, Abington Library Society, Jenkintown PA. 215-884-0593

Walker, Jean, *ILL,* Kern County Library, Bakersfield CA. 805-861-2130

Walker, Jean, *Librn,* Public Library of Columbus & Franklin County (Dublin Branch), Dublin OH. 614-889-2366

Walker, John, *Librn,* National Park Service, Southeast Archaeological Center Library, Tallahassee FL. 904-222-1167

Walker, John A, *Librn,* East Central State University, Linscheid Library, Ada OK. 405-332-8000

Walker, John T, *Ref,* Sinclair Community College, Learning Resources Center, Dayton OH. 513-226-2855

Walker, John T, *On-Line Servs & Bibliog Instr,* Sinclair Community College, Learning Resources Center, Dayton OH. 513-226-2855

Walker, Joseph L, *Cat,* Saint Clair Shores Public Library, Saint Clair Shores MI. 313-771-9020

Walker, Joyce, *Librn,* San Diego Public Library (Otay Mesa), San Diego CA. 714-424-5841

Walker, Judith, *Ser,* University of South Carolina (School of Medicine Library), Columbia SC. 803-777-4858

Walker, Judy, *Media,* Burlington Public Library, Burlington ON. 416-639-3611

Walker, June, *Librn,* Court of Civil Appeals Law Library, El Paso TX. 915-543-2917

Walker, Kaye Coke, *Librn,* New York Public Library (Castle Hill), New York NY. 212-824-3838

Walker, L B, *Librn,* Bellaire Public Library, Bellaire OH. 614-676-9421

Walker, Laura, *Ref,* Brookings Institution Library, Washington DC. 202-797-6240

Walker, Lewis J, *Dir,* College of the Sequoias Library, Visalia CA. 209-733-2050, Ext 314

Walker, Lillie, *Librn,* Dearborn Department of Libraries (Bryant), Dearborn MI. 313-278-8288

Walker, Lillie S, *On-Line Servs & Bibliog Instr,* South Carolina State College, Miller F Whittaker Library, Orangeburg SC. 803-536-7045, 536-7046

Walker, Loretta, *Info Servs,* Union College, Schaffer Library, Schenectady NY. 518-370-6278

Walker, Louise, *Librn,* Suwannee River Regional Library, Seven-County Region (Branford (Suwannee County)), Live Oak FL. 904-935-1556

Walker, Luise E, *Librn,* University of Oregon Library (Science), Eugene OR. 503-686-3075

Walker, Lynn W, *Dir,* University of Central Florida Library, Orlando FL. 305-275-2564

Walker, Marella, *Acq,* Emory University Libraries (General Libraries), Atlanta GA. 404-329-6861

Walker, Marguerite W, *Librn,* Akron Public Library, Akron AL. 205-372-9215

Walker, Marie D, *Librn,* Reynolds Metals Co (Flexible Packaging Division, Technology Center Library), Richmond VA. 804-743-6649

Walker, Marie D, *Librn,* Reynolds Metals Co, Materials & Product Development Library, Grottoes VA. 703-249-5711

Walker, Martha, *Mgr Human Servs & Relations,* Blue Water Library Federation, Port Huron MI. 313-987-7323

Walker, Martha, *Human Serv & Relations Mgr,* Saint Clair County Library System, Port Huron MI. 313-987-7323

Walker, Mary, *Librn,* British Consulate-General, Information Section, San Francisco CA. 415-981-3030

Walker, Mary Ann, *On-Line Servs,* University of Dayton Libraries, Roesch Library, Dayton OH. 513-229-4221

Walker, Mary Faith, *Dir,* Belfast Free Library, Belfast ME. 207-338-3884

Walker, Mary Jo, *Spec Coll,* Eastern New Mexico University Library, Portales NM. 505-562-2624

Walker, Michael, *Sci & Ref,* Alabama Agricultural & Mechanical University, Joseph F Drake Memorial Learning Resources Center, Normal AL. 205-859-7309

Walker, Mrs E R, *Librn,* Stokely Memorial Library, Newport TN. 615-623-3832

Walker, Mrs M, *Supvr,* Edmonton Public Library (Highlands), Edmonton AB. 403-478-1303

Walker, Mrs Norman, *Librn,* Judith Basin County Free Library (Benchland Library Station), Benchland MT. 406-566-2389

Walker, Nadine, *Librn,* Hickman County Memorial Library, Clinton KY. 502-653-4684

Walker, Nadine, *Dir,* Litchfield Carnegie Public Library, Litchfield IL. 217-324-3866

Walker, Nancy, *Asst Librn,* Winnetka Public Library District, Winnetka IL. 312-446-5085

Walker, Noel, *Asst Dir,* Walker Museum Library, Fairlee VT. 802-333-9572

Walker, Orrin M, *Librn,* University of South Dakota (McKusick Law Library), Vermillion SD. 605-677-5259

Walker, Patricia, *Librn,* Los Angeles Public Library System (Benjamin Franklin), Los Angeles CA. 213-263-6901

Walker, Paula M, *Bibliog Instr,* University of Washington Libraries, Seattle WA. 206-543-1760

Walker, Phoebe, *Acq,* Evergreen State College, Daniel J Evans Library, Olympia WA. 206-866-6262

Walker, R Gay, *Curator Arts of the Book Coll,* Yale University Library (Sterling Memorial Library), New Haven CT. 203-436-8335

Walker, R Gay, *Head Librn Preservations & Preparations Dept,* Yale University Library (Sterling Memorial Library), New Haven CT. 203-436-8335

Walker, Richard, *Ad,* Davidson County Public Library System, Lexington NC. 704-246-2520

Walker, Russell, *Dir,* Upper Arlington Public Library, Upper Arlington OH. 614-486-9621

Walker, Ruth, *Librn,* Central Florida Regional Library (Dunnellon), Ocala FL. 904-489-4196

Walker, Ruth, *Librn,* Cleveland Public Library (Superior), Cleveland OH. 216-795-4249

Walker, Shirley, *Br Coordr,* Champaign Public Library & Information Center, Champaign IL. 217-356-7243

Walker, Shirley, *Librn,* Champaign Public Library & Information Center (Douglass), Champaign IL. 217-356-4455

Walker, Sonia, *Librn,* Callahan County Public Library, Baird TX. 915-854-1718

Walker, Stephen, *Cat,* Central Missouri State University, Ward Edwards Library, Warrensburg MO. 816-429-4141

Walker, Sue E, *Dir,* Rocky Mountain College, Paul M Adams Memorial Library, Billings MT. 406-245-6151, Ext 260

Walker, Sue R, *Librn,* First United Methodist Church, Epworth Library, Gainesville FL. 904-372-8523

Walker, Susan P, *In Charge,* United States Army (Keller Army Hospital Library), West Point NY. 914-938-2722

Walker, T, *Tech Serv,* London Public Libraries & Museums, London ON. 519-432-7166

Walker, Terry, *Tech Serv,* Sampson-Clinton Public Library, Clinton NC. 919-592-4153

Walker, Theresa, *Ref, On-Line Servs & Bibliog Instr,* Grinnell College, Burling Library, Grinnell IA. 515-236-6181, Ext 598

Walker, Verdelle, *Ch,* Broward County Division of Libraries, Broward County Library, Pompano Beach FL. 305-972-1100

Walker, Virginia, *Librn,* Cairo Public Library, Cairo IL. 618-734-1840

Walker, Vivian, *Librn,* Annapolis Valley Regional Library Headquarters (Annapolis Royal Branch), Annapolis Royal NS. 902-532-2260

Walker, William B, *Dir,* Metropolitan Museum of Art (Thomas J Watson Memorial Library), New York NY. 212-879-5500, Ext 221, 224

Walker, William B, *Librn,* Smithsonian Institution Libraries (Library of the National Collection of Fine Arts & the National Portrait Gallery), Washington DC. 202-357-1886

Walker, William D, *Dir,* Medical Library Center of New York, New York NY. 212-427-1630

Walker, Zetta, *Ad,* Marion Public Library, Marion OH. 614-387-0992

Walker, II, Robert E, *TV servs,* Portland State University, Branford Price Millar Library, Portland OR. 503-229-4424

Walker, Jr, Mrs John B, *Dir,* First Baptist Church, Witherspoon Memorial Library, Marion NC. 704-652-6030

Walker-Atchison, Susan, *Asst Curator,* Art Museum of South Texas Library, Corpus Christi TX. 512-884-3844

Walker-Hitt, Sarah, *Librn,* Lyndon Carnegie Library, Lyndon KS. 913-828-4520

Walkonen, Helvi E, *Libr Dir,* Northern Michigan University, Dept of Library Science, MI. 906-227-2250

Walkonen, Helvi E, *Dir,* Northern Michigan University, Lydia M Olson Library, Marquette MI. 906-227-2250

Wall, Brenda, *Librn,* De Soto Trail Regional Library (Early County), Blakely GA. 912-723-6561

Wall, C Edward, *Dir,* University of Michigan-Dearborn Library, Dearborn MI. 313-593-5400

Wall, Carol, *Asst Librn,* Youngstown State University Library, William F Maag Library, Youngstown OH. 216-742-3676

Wall, Celia, *Librn,* News & Observer Library, Raleigh NC. 919-821-1234

Wall, Constance, *Librn,* Detroit Institute of Arts Research Library, Detroit MI. 313-833-7900

Wall, Elaine, *Per,* Christian Brothers College Library, Memphis TN. 901-278-0100, Ext 220

Wall, Estelle, *Actg Dir, On-Line Servs & Bibliog Instr,* United States Navy (Technical Library), Indian Head MD. 301-743-4742, 743-4743

Wall, H Duncan, *Dir,* Cleveland State University Libraries, Cleveland OH. 216-687-2486

Wall, James, *Per,* Thomas More College, Learning Resources Center, Fort Mitchell KY. 606-341-5800, Ext 61

Wall, Janice, *Librn,* Moscow-Latah County Library System (Potlatch Branch), Potlatch ID. 208-875-1036

Wall, Norma, *Librn,* Hinds Junior College, Jackson Branch Library, Jackson MS. 601-366-1405

Wall, Norma, *Admin Libr,* Hinds Junior College, George M McLendon Library, Raymond MS. 601-857-5261, Ext 253

Wall, Robert B, *Asst Dir,* Sacramento Public Library, Sacramento CA. 916-440-5926

Wall, Roger, *Librn,* National Science Teachers Association, Glenn O Blough Library, Washington DC. 202-265-4150, Ext 60

Wall, Virginia, *Librn,* Chicago Horticultural Society Botanic Garden Library, Glencoe IL. 312-835-5440, Ext 27

Wallace, Angelo, *Humanities,* University of Toledo, William S Carlson Library, Toledo OH. 419-537-2324

Wallace, Atarrha, *Tech Serv,* Manitoba Department of Education Library, Winnipeg MB. 204-786-0218

Wallace, Bernice Z, *Librn,* Michigan State University Library (Chemistry), East Lansing MI. 517-355-2344

Wallace, Burma, *Dir Libr Serv,* Jefferson Davis State Junior College, Leigh Library, Brewton AL. 205-867-4832, Ext 32

Wallace, Burma, *Dir,* Jefferson State Junior College, James B Allen Library, Birmingham AL. 205-853-1200, Ext 280

Wallace, Carolyn, *Southern Hist,* University of North Carolina at Chapel Hill, Louis Round Wilson Academic Affairs Library, Chapel Hill NC. 919-933-1301

Wallace, Christine, *Ch,* Franklin Township Free Public Library, Somerset NJ. 201-545-8032

Wallace, Delores, *Librn,* University of Illinois Library at Urbana-Champaign (Architecture), Urbana IL. 217-333-0224

Wallace, Diane, *Asst Librn,* Brockton Hospital Library, Brockton MA. 617-586-2600, Ext 375

Wallace, Elizabeth, *Reader Serv & On-Line Servs,* Stephen F Austin State University, Ralph W Steen Library, Nacogdoches TX. 713-569-4109

Wallace, Gladys, *Librn,* Brewster Public Library, Brewster WA. 509-689-3521

Wallace, Glenn, *Chief Librn,* Veterans Administration, Hospital Library, Columbia MO. 314-443-2511, Ext 330

Wallace, Harriet, *Librn,* University of Illinois Library at Urbana-Champaign (Geology), Urbana IL. 217-333-1266

Wallace, I W, *Librn,* Moncton Hospital, Medical Library, Moncton NB. 506-858-3232

Wallace, Isabel, *Librn,* Cranston Public Library (Auburn), Cranston RI. 401-781-6116

Wallace, Jacquelyn, *Ch,* Peter White Public Library, Marquette MI. 906-228-9510

Wallace, James O, *Dir,* San Antonio College Library, San Antonio TX. 512-734-7311, Ext 2480

Wallace, James O, *Dept Head,* San Antonio College, Library Technology Program, TX. 512-734-7311, Ext 2482

Wallace, Janie M, *Librn,* Choctawhatchee Regional Library (Brundidge Public), Brundidge AL. 205-735-2145

Wallace, Jennifer, *Ad,* Los Angeles Public Library System, Los Angeles CA. 213-626-7555

Wallace, Katharine R, *Chief Librn,* NASA, NSTL Research Library, Bay Saint Louis MS. 601-688-3244

Wallace, Kathleen, *Librn,* Carbon County Public Library (Sinclair Branch), Sinclair WY. 307-324-4756

Wallace, Linda, *Community Relations,* Mideastern Michigan Library Cooperative, Flint MI. 313-232-7119

Wallace, Linda, *Librn,* Strawberry Point Public Library, Strawberry Point IA. 319-933-4340

Wallace, Lorraine J, *Librn,* AVCO Corp, Lycoming Division Library & Information Center, Stratford CT. 203-378-8211

Wallace, Madeleine, *Librn,* Lambton County Library (Forest Branch), Forest ON. 519-873-5152

Wallace, Margaret B, *Dir,* Brookhaven Free Library, Brookhaven NY. 516-286-1923

Wallace, Marie G, *Librn,* Kindel & Anderson, Law Library, Los Angeles CA. 213-680-2222, Ext 295

Wallace, Martha, *Librn,* Craighead County & Jonesboro Public Library (Kohn Memorial), Monette AR. 501-486-5736

Wallace, Martha, *Librn,* Crowley Ridge Regional Library (Kohn Memorial), Monette AR. 501-486-5736

Wallace, Mary Troy, *Librn,* Cambridge Public Library (North Cambridge), Cambridge MA. 617-498-9086

Wallace, Mary-Ann, *Librn,* Santa Clara County Free Library (Cupertino Public), Cupertino CA. 408-253-6212

Wallace, Mildred, *Asst Prof,* George Peabody College for Teachers, Department of Library Science, TN. 615-327-8037

Wallace, Mildred, *Bkmobile Coordr,* Scott County Library, Eldridge IA. 319-285-4794

Wallace, Patricia, *Ser,* Slippery Rock State College Library, Slippery Rock PA. 412-794-2510

Wallace, Patte, *AV & Ref,* Pioneer Multi-County Library, Norman OK. 405-321-1481
Wallace, Pearl, *Circ,* Scarborough Public Library, Scarborough ME. 207-883-4723
Wallace, Phyllis, *Ch,* Bloomington Public Library, Bloomington IL. 309-828-6091
Wallace, Rebecca, *Tech Serv,* Bay County Public Library Association, Northwest Regional Library System, Panama City FL. 904-785-3457
Wallace, Richard E, *Mgr Info Serv,* Archer Daniels Midland Co, Research Library, Decatur IL. 217-424-5397
Wallace, Robert B, *Librn,* Dade County Law Library, Miami FL. 305-579-5422
Wallace, Ruth, *Librn,* Phoenix Public Library (Palo Verde), Phoenix AZ. 602-262-6805
Wallace, Salvador B, *Deputy Chief,* National Institutes of Health (NIH Library), Bethesda MD. 301-496-4000
Wallace, Sandy, *ILL,* Carl Sandburg College, Learning Resources Center, Galesburg IL. 309-344-2518, Ext 247 & 257
Wallace, Stella, *Librn,* Lambton County Library (Brights Grove), Camlachie ON. 519-869-2351
Wallace, Susan, *Media,* Eastern Washington University, John F Kennedy Memorial Library, Cheney WA. 509-359-2261
Wallace, Tish, *Librn,* Farmers Insurance Group Library, Los Angeles CA. 213-932-3200
Wallace, Victoria, *Dir,* Northport Public Library, Northport NY. 516-261-6930
Wallach, John S, *Dir,* Dayton & Montgomery County Public Library, Dayton OH. 513-224-1651
Walle, Dennis, *Archives & Ms,* University of Alaska, Anchorage Library, Anchorage AK. 907-263-1825
Wallen, Joyce M, *Dir,* Miami Public Library, Miami OK. 918-542-3064
Wallen, Judith, *Commun Servs,* Fayette County Public Library, Oakhill WV. 304-465-0121, 465-0311
Wallen, Mary Ann, *Librn,* Sacramento Public Library (North Highlands Branch), North Highlands CA. 916-331-0675
Wallen, Regina, *Tech Serv, On-Line Servs & Bibliog Instr,* University of Santa Clara (Heafey Law Library), Santa Clara CA. 408-984-4451
Wallen, Wayne, *Per,* Sacramento Public Library, Sacramento CA. 916-440-5926
Wallenberg, Barbara, *Librn,* Austin Public Library (Brownsdale Public), Brownsdale MN. 507-567-2177
Wallens, Nancy G, *Ref,* Lake Forest Library, Lake Forest IL. 312-234-0636
Waller, Aline, *Ad,* Haltom City Public Library, Haltom City TX. 817-834-7341
Waller, Annelle, *Librn,* Oconee Regional Library (Harlie Fulford Memorial), Wrightsville GA. 912-864-2263
Waller, Carolyn A, *Librn,* Emma Pendleton Bradley Hospital, Austin T & June Rockwell Levy Library, Riverside RI. 401-434-3400, Ext 165 & 152
Waller, Elaine, *Librn,* Andrews University (Music Library), Berrien Springs MI. 616-471-3114
Waller, Gerry E, *Librn Blind,* Cabell County Public Library, Western Counties Regional Library System, Huntington WV. 304-523-9451
Waller, Hope, *Dir,* Sherman Public Library, Sherman TX. 214-892-4545, Ext 242
Waller, Jeanne P, *Dir & Ref,* Westhampton Free Library, Westhampton Beach NY. 516-288-3335
Waller, Judith, *Ref,* Boulder Public Library, Boulder CO. 303-441-3100
Waller, Pauline, *Asst Librn,* Nathaniel Hawthorne College, Silver Library, Antrim NH. 603-588-6341, Ext 235
Waller, S Lee, *Librn,* Chesapeake Public Library (Indian River), Chesapeake VA. 804-420-5804
Waller, Wayne, *Librn,* Sacramento Public Library (McKinley), Sacramento CA. 916-442-0598
Walley, Georgia, *Circ,* University of Arkansas, Pine Bluff, Watson Memorial Library, Pine Bluff AR. 501-541-6825
Walley, Ruth, *Librn,* Jackson Metropolitan Library (Taylorsville Library), Taylorsville MS. 601-352-3677
Wallhead, Margaret E, *Librn,* Lorain County Law Library, Elyria OH. 216-322-5024
Wallick, Mary E, *Dir,* Charlevoix Public Library, Charlevoix MI. 616-547-2651

Wallin, Janet L, *Librn,* University of Toledo (Law), Toledo OH. 419-537-2733
Wallin, Karen, *Volunteer Servs & Commun Relations,* Washington Regional Library for the Blind & Physically Handicapped, Seattle WA. 464-6930. SCAN 576-6930
Wallin, Ragnhild, *Librn,* Swedish Information Service, New York NY. 212-751-5900, Ext 205
Wallin, Richard L, *Asst Dir,* University of Missouri-Kansas City Libraries, Kansas City MO. 816-276-1531
Walling, Mrs H C, *Librn,* First United Methodist Church, Gertrude Callihan Memorial Library, San Marcos TX. 512-392-3848
Wallis, C Lamar, *Dir,* Memphis-Shelby County Public Library & Information Center, Memphis TN. 901-528-2950
Wallis, Lillian G, *Chief Tech Servs,* Minneapolis Public Library & Information Center, Minneapolis MN. 612-372-6500
Walls, Edwina, *Hist of Med,* University of Arkansas for Medical Sciences Library, Little Rock AR. 501-661-5980
Walls, Esther J, *Assoc Dir,* State University of New York, Frank Melville Jr Memorial Library, Stony Brook NY. 516-246-5650
Walls, Francine E, *Librn,* Seattle Pacific University, Weter Memorial Library, Seattle WA. 206-284-2000
Walls, Jackie, *Librn,* Floyd County Library, Floydada TX. 806-983-3578
Walls, Madelyn, *Asst Dir & Circ,* Mason City Public Library, Mason City IA. 515-423-7552
Walls, Nina, *Bibliog Instr,* Balch Institute for Ethnic Studies Library, Philadelphia PA. 215-925-8090
Walls, Susan, *Librn,* Vermilion Community College Library, Ely MN. 218-365-3256
Walls, T, *Libr Tech,* Queen's University at Kingston (Documents Library & Local Government), Kingston ON. 613-547-2620
Walluk, Ann, *Librn,* Burlington Public Library, Burlington CT. 203-673-3331
Wally, Margarette, *Librn,* Saint Luke's Hospital Association, Medical & Nursing Library, Jacksonville FL. 904-356-1992, Ext 285
Walmsley, S A, *Chaplain,* Manitoba School for Retardates, Memorial Library, Portage La Prairie MB. 204-857-3403, Ext 363
Walrod, Ronald C, *Dir,* Baker County Public Library, Baker OR. 503-523-6414, 523-6419
Walsh, Barbara, *Librn,* Carleton Place Public Library, Carleton Place ON. 613-257-2702
Walsh, Bertrand M, *Librn,* E I Du Pont De Nemours & Co, Inc (Jackson Laboratory Library), Wilmington DE. 609-299-5000, Ext 486
Walsh, Carmela, *Dir,* Goshen Public Library, Goshen MA. 413-268-7856
Walsh, Carol Jean, *Ref,* New Milford Public Library, New Milford NJ. 201-262-1221
Walsh, Carol S, *Librn & Ad,* Kellogg Free Library, Cincinnatus NY. 607-863-4300
Walsh, Carolyn C, *Dir,* Villanova University (Library Science), Villanova PA. 215-527-2100, Ext 355
Walsh, Catherine, *Librn,* General Electric Co, Aircraft Equipment Div, Engineering Library, Utica NY. 315-797-1000, Ext 5170
Walsh, Deborah, *ILL, On-Line Servs & Bibliog Instr,* Rosary College, Rebecca Crown Library, River Forest IL. 312-366-2490, Ext 305
Walsh, Dennis, *Asst Dir & Tech Serv,* Saint Thomas Aquinas College Library, Sparkill NY. 359-9500 Ext 246, 245
Walsh, Donald, *Librn,* Grand Rapids Public Library (Ottawa Hills), Grand Rapids MI. 616-456-4434
Walsh, E Elizabeth, *Actg Chmn,* Villanova University, Graduate Dept of Library Science, PA. 215-527-2100, Ext 354, 355
Walsh, Edward, *Cat,* Central Michigan University, Charles V Park Library, Mount Pleasant MI. 517-774-3500
Walsh, Florence C, *Actg Dir,* Union Township Public Library, Union NJ. 201-686-0420
Walsh, Frances H, *Asst Prof,* Slippery Rock State College, Dept of Library Science, PA. 412-794-7321
Walsh, Francis, *Dir,* Tucker Memorial Library, Alexandria NE. 402-749-3550
Walsh, Gretchen, *Librn,* Boston University Libraries (African Studies Library), Boston MA. 617-353-3726

Walsh, Irene, *Media,* D'Youville College, Library Resources Center, Buffalo NY. 716-886-8100, Ext 304
Walsh, James, *Instr,* Northern Michigan University, Dept of Library Science, MI. 906-227-2250
Walsh, James, *Doc,* Northern Michigan University, Lydia M Olson Library, Marquette MI. 906-227-2250
Walsh, James F, *Cat Dept: Keeper of Printed Books,* Harvard University Library (Houghton Library-Rare Books & Manuscripts), Cambridge MA. 617-495-2441
Walsh, Jan, *Librn,* Washington State Library (Cascadia JRDC Library), Tacoma WA. 206-383-4771
Walsh, Jan, *Librn,* Washington State Library (Western State Hospital Resident Library), Fort Steilacoom WA. 206-756-9668
Walsh, Jeanne, *Ref,* River Forest Public Library, River Forest IL. 312-366-5205
Walsh, Joanna M, *Coordr,* Boston Library Consortium, MA. 617-262-0380
Walsh, Joseph E, *Bus Branch Librn,* Boston Public Library, Eastern Massachusetts Library System, Boston MA. 617-536-5400
Walsh, Joseph E, *Librn,* Boston Public Library (Kirstein Business), Boston MA. 617-523-0860
Walsh, K, *Librn,* Grace General Hospital, School of Nursing Library, Saint John's NF. 709-778-6643
Walsh, Lea, *ILL,* South Carolina State Library, Columbia SC. 803-758-3181
Walsh, Marcia, *Librn,* Wittenberg University (Science), Springfield OH. 513-327-7408
Walsh, Margaret, *In Charge,* Butte County Law Library, Oroville CA. 916-534-4611
Walsh, Mary, *ILL,* New City Free Library, New City NY. 914-634-4997
Walsh, Mary, *Chief Librn,* Sun Life Assurance Co of Canada, Reference Library, Toronto ON. 416-364-1541
Walsh, Michael, *AV,* Massachusetts Bay Community College Library, Wellesley MA. 617-237-1100, Ext 193
Walsh, Mrs Frederick R, *In Charge,* Rensselaer County Historical Society Library, Troy NY. 518-272-7232
Walsh, Phyllis, *Dir,* University of Wisconsin Center-Richland, Miller Memorial Library, Richland Center WI. 608-647-6186, Ext 20
Walsh, Sister Emily, *Dir,* Saint Mary-Of-The-Woods College Library, Saint Mary-of-the-Woods IN. 812-535-4141, Ext 223
Walsh, Sister Leona, *Cat,* Saint Mary-Of-The-Woods College Library, Saint Mary-of-the-Woods IN. 812-535-4141, Ext 223
Walsh, Sylvia, *Librn,* Rutgers University (Mathematics Library), New Brunswick NJ. 201-932-3735
Walsh, Wanda T, *Librn,* County of Carleton Law Library, Ottawa ON. 613-722-2163
Walsh, William R, *Librn,* Saint Ignatius Loyola Church, S J Memorial Library, New York NY. 212-288-3588
Walsh, Jr, Maurice D, *Dir,* Jefferson Parish Library Division, Metairie LA. 504-834-5850
Walshak, M Lynn, *Doc,* Georgia Southern College Library, Statesboro GA. 912-681-5115
Walstad, Kay, *Librn,* Eureka-Humboldt County Library (Klamath-Trinity), Willow Creek CA. 707-629-2146
Walt, Mary Ann, *Assoc Dir,* University of Southern Mississippi (Teaching-Learning Resources Center), Hattiesburg MS. 601-266-7307
Waltemade, Anna, *Librn,* Contra Costa County Library (Walnut Creek Branch), Walnut Creek CA. 415-934-5373
Walter, David, *Ref,* Montana Historical Society Library & Archives, Helena MT. 406-449-2681
Walter, Gary D, *Dir,* Defense Language Institute, Learning Resources Center, Presidio of Monterey CA. 408-242-8206
Walter, Gaye, *Media,* Idaho State Library, Boise ID. 208-334-2150
Walter, Gaye, *Volunteer Coordr,* Idaho State Library - Blind & Physically Handicapped Services, Boise ID. 208-334-2150
Walter, Georgia, *Dir,* Kirksville College of Osteopathic Medicine, A T Still Memorial Library, Kirksville MO. 816-626-2345
Walter, Imogene, *Dir,* Swanton Public Library, Swanton OH. 419-826-2760

Walter, James, *Spec Coll,* Columbia College, Kirtley Library, Columbia MO. 314-449-0531, Ext 221

Walter, JoAnn M, *Dir,* McKune Memorial Library, Chelsea MI. 313-475-8732

Walter, Kenneth G, *Chmn,* East Georgia Library Triangle, GA. 912-681-5115

Walter, Kenneth G, *Dir,* Georgia Southern College Library, Statesboro GA. 912-681-5115

Walter, Mary, *Librn,* Madison Police Department Library, Madison WI. 608-266-4275

Walter, Otto W, *Supvr of Libr Servs,* Missouri Division of Corrections Libraries, Jefferson City MO. 314-751-3050

Walter, Otto W, *Librn,* Missouri Division of Corrections Libraries (Missouri State Penitentiary Library), Jefferson City MO. 314-751-3050

Walter, Ruth, *Librn,* Meadowlark Public Library, Lewis KS. 316-324-5678

Walter, Stephen B, *Dir,* Tri-County Technical College, Learning Resource Center, Pendleton SC. 803-646-3227

Walters, Clarence R, *County Librn,* Contra Costa County Library, Pleasant Hill CA. 415-944-3423

Walters, Corky, *Coll Develop & Continuing Educ,* Wyoming State Library, Cheyenne WY. 307-777-7281

Walters, Dan, *Exten Servs,* North Central Regional Library, Wenatchee WA. 509-663-1117

Walters, E H, *Librn,* Nelson Municipal Library, Nelson BC. 604-352-6333

Walters, E M, *Dir,* East Tennessee State University, Kingsport University Center Library, Kingsport TN. 615-247-6181

Walters, Edward, *Dir,* East Tennessee State University, Sherrod Library, Johnson City TN. 615-929-4338

Walters, Elizabeth, *Librn,* Santa Clara County Health Department Library, San Jose CA. 408-279-6021

Walters, Frances, *Ch,* Niles Community Library, Niles MI. 616-683-8545, 683-8546

Walters, Gladys, *Librn,* Roanoke County Public Library (Bent Mountain Branch), Bent Mountain VA. 703-929-4700

Walters, Helen, *Bkmobile Coordr,* Burlington County Library, Mount Holly NJ. 609-267-9660

Walters, Irene, *Ch,* Carnegie Bookmobile Library, Grafton ND. 701-352-2754

Walters, Kenneth, *Media,* Henry Ford Community College, Eshleman Library, Dearborn MI. 313-271-2750, Ext 378

Walters, LeRoy, *Dir,* Kennedy Institute (Center for Bioethics Library), Washington DC. 202-625-0100

Walters, Mary, *Coll Develop,* California State University, John F Kennedy Memorial Library, Los Angeles CA. 213-224-2201

Walters, Patricia, *Librn,* Newark Public Library (Hebron Branch), Hebron OH. 345-1750 & 345-8972

Walters, Raquel A, *Chief Librn,* Veterans Administration, Hospital Library, San Juan PR. 809-764-4545

Walters, Roberta A, *Tech Serv,* Alameda County Law Library, Oakland CA. 415-874-5823

Walters, Sandra, *Ch,* Sedalia Public Library, Sedalia MO. 816-826-1314

Walters, Sharon, *Cat,* West Hills Community College Library, Coalinga CA. 209-935-0801, Ext 47

Walth, Allison, *ILL, On-Line Servs & Bibliog Instr,* Three Rivers Regional Library Service System, New Castle CO. 303-984-2887

Walthall, Harry, *In Charge,* College of the Desert Library, Palm Desert CA. 714-346-8041, Ext 258

Walther, Jane, *Librn,* Moraine Park Technical Institute Library, West Bend WI. 414-334-3413

Walther, Mary, *Ref & Doc,* Benton Harbor Public Library, Benton Harbor MI. 616-926-6139

Walther, Mary, *Ch,* Canal Fulton Public Library, Canal Fulton OH. 216-854-4148

Walther, Richard E, *Dir & AV,* Ambassador College Library, Pasadena CA. 213-577-5540

Walther, Yvonne, *Librn,* Free Public Library of the City of Trenton (Skelton), Trenton NJ. 609-392-7188

Waltman, Elizabeth, *Dir,* Perry Public Library, Perry OH. 216-259-3300

Waltman, Rosemary, *Librn,* Brown Memorial Library, Lewisburg OH. 513-962-2377

Waltner, Lenore, *ILL,* Bloomington Public Library, Bloomington IL. 309-828-6091

Waltner, Nellie L, *Acq,* North Carolina State University, D H Hill Library, Raleigh NC. 919-737-2843, 2595

Walton, Clyde C, *Dir,* University of Colorado at Boulder (University Libraries), Boulder CO. 303-492-7511

Walton, Delores, *Librn Supvr,* La Porte County Library, La Porte IN. 219-362-6156

Walton, Frances L, *Libr Asst,* Upper Dublin Public Library (North Hills Community), North Hills PA. 215-884-4760

Walton, Gloria, *Asst Dir,* Fern Ridge Community Library, Veneta OR. 503-935-7512

Walton, Gloria, *Librn,* San Diego Public Library (Oak Park), San Diego CA. 714-262-8249

Walton, Homer, *Cat,* University of South Carolina, Thomas Cooper Library, Columbia SC. 803-777-3142

Walton, Jan, *Librn,* Saint John's Hospital (Frederick J Plondke Medical Library), Saint Paul MN. 612-228-3255

Walton, Jewell, *Dir,* Half Hollow Hills Community Public Library, Dix Hills NY. 516-421-4530

Walton, Joan, *Ad & Commun Servs,* Champaign Public Library & Information Center, Champaign IL. 217-356-7243

Walton, Josie, *Acq,* Emory University, Oxford College Library, Oxford GA. 404-786-7051, Ext 281

Walton, Judy, *Ch,* Mobile Public Library, Mobile AL. 205-438-7073

Walton, L R, *Librn,* Pet Inc, Corporate Library, Saint Louis MO. 314-621-5400

Walton, Lee H, *Dir,* William H Clark Associates Inc, Library, New York NY. 212-661-8760

Walton, Lonita, *Educ,* Seattle Public Library, Seattle WA. 206-625-2665

Walton, Mrs Artence, *Librn,* Pitney Bowes, Monarch Marketing System Library, Miamisburg OH. 513-865-2082

Walton, Nancy Kay, *Librn,* General Telephone & Electronics, GTE Lenkurt Inc, Technical Library, San Carlos CA. 415-595-3000, Ext 2293

Walton, Richard A, *Dir,* Goddard College, William Shipman Library, Plainfield VT. 802-454-8311, Ext 232

Walton, Terence, *Tech Serv,* Old Dominion University Library, Norfolk VA. 804-440-4141

Waltos, Rosemary, *Circ,* Digital Equipment Corp, Corporate Library, Maynard MA. 617-493-6231, 493-5821

Walz, Carolyn L, *Dir,* Estherville Public Library, Estherville IA. 712-362-3869

Walz, Josephine, *In Charge,* Royalton Library, Royalton MN. 612-584-8151

Walzer, H, *Cat,* Georgia Institute of Technology, Price Gilbert Memorial Library, Atlanta GA. 404-894-4510

Wamble, Mrs H E, *Librn,* Tombigbee Regional Library (Amory Municipal), Amory MS. 601-256-5261

Wan, Wei-Ying, *Librn,* University of Michigan Libraries (Asia), Ann Arbor MI. 313-764-0406

Wan, William W, *ILL,* Texas Woman's University, Bralley Memorial Library, Denton TX. 817-566-6415

Wanat, Camille, *Librn,* University of California, Berkeley (Physics), Berkeley CA. 415-642-3122

Wand, Annette, *Librn,* Elbert County Library (Bowman Branch), Bowman GA. 404-283-5375

Wandersee, Mary, *Librn,* Maine State Department of Human Services Library, Augusta ME. 207-289-3055

Wang, A, *Libr Supvr,* Bell Telephone Laboratories (Western Electric Technical Library), Indianapolis IN. 317-352-3347

Wang, Albert, *Per,* Montclair State College, Harry A Sprague Library, Upper Montclair NJ. 201-893-4291

Wang, Amy, *Librn,* John Hancock Mutual Life Insurance Co Library, Boston MA. 617-421-4524

Wang, Anna, *Cat,* Margaret Woodbury Strong Museum Library, Rochester NY. 716-381-1818, Ext 23

Wang, Chester C I, *Far East,* University of Wisconsin-Madison, Memorial Library, Madison WI. 608-262-3521

Wang, Chih, *Asst Prof,* Atlanta University, School of Library & Information Studies, GA. 404-681-0251, Ext 312

Wang, Chin Ling, *Acq,* Saint John's University Library, Jamaica NY. 212-969-8000, Ext 201

Wang, Eunice, *Cat,* Saint Anselm's College, Geisel Library, Manchester NH. 603-669-1030, Ext 240, 249

Wang, George, *Doc & Rare Bks,* New Mexico Highlands University, Donnelly Library, Las Vegas NM. 505-425-7511, Ext 331

Wang, Hazel, *Librn,* Orange Public Library (Charles P Taft), Orange CA. 714-532-0421

Wang, Jo Sung-chun, *Chief Cat,* Harvard University Library (Francis A Countway Library of Medicine), Boston MA. 617-732-2142

Wang, Josephine, *Ch,* Kingsport Public Library, J Fred Johnson Memorial Library, Kingsport TN. 615-245-3141

Wang, Leo, *Librn,* Sault College of Applied Arts & Technology Library, Sault Sainte Marie ON. 705-949-2050, Ext 240

Wang, Mrs A B, *Librn,* Canada Department of National Defence, Defence Research Establishment Atlantic Library, Dartmouth NS. 902-426-3100, Ext 135 or 161

Wang, Peter, *Cat,* Morton Arboretum, Sterling Morton Library, Lisle IL. 312-968-0074

Wang, Richard, *Librn,* University of Minnesota Libraries-Twin Cities (East Asian Library), Minneapolis MN. 612-373-3737

Wang, Rosalind C, *Librn,* Fort Vancouver Regional Library (Vancouver Community (Headquarters)), Vancouver WA. 206-695-1566

Wang, Ruth, *Cat,* Montclair State College, Harry A Sprague Library, Upper Montclair NJ. 201-893-4291

Wang, Sidney, *Asst Dir,* Rapid City Public Library, Rapid City SD. 605-394-4171

Wang, Yi-lien, *Cat,* Binghamton Public Library, Binghamton NY. 607-723-6457

Wang, Yi-lien, *Tech Serv,* Binghamton Public Library, Binghamton NY. 607-723-6457

Wangerin, Mark, *Pub Servs,* Concordia Seminary Library, Ludwig E Fuerbringer Hall Library, Saint Louis MO. 314-721-5934, Ext 293

Wangsgard, Lynnda, *Asst Dir, Ref & Commun Servs,* Weber County Library, Ogden UT. 801-399-8516

Wannarka, Marjorie, *Dir,* Creighton University (Health Sciences), Omaha NE. 402-449-2908

Wannemacher, Jacqueline M, *Mgr,* General Electric Co, Aircraft Engine Group, Technical Information Center, Lynn MA. 617-594-5363

Wannemacher, Maxyne M, *Librn,* Riverside County Law Library, Riverside CA. 714-787-2460

Wanner, Alice, *Dir,* Sublette County Library, Pinedale WY. 307-367-2240

Wantman, Linda, *Asst Dir & Cat,* Delaware Valley College of Science and Agriculture, Krauskopf Memorial Library, Doylestown PA. 215-345-1500, Ext 255

Wantz, Michael, *Br Coordr,* Franklin Sylvester Library, Medina OH. 216-725-0588

Wantz, Michael, *Librn,* Franklin Sylvester Library (Brunswick Branch), Brunswick OH. 216-225-2770

Wany, Doris, *Searches-Publications,* Airco Inc, Information Center, Murray Hill NJ. 201-464-2400

Wanza, Maggie P, *Cat & On-Line Servs,* Morgan State University, Morris A Soper Library, Baltimore MD. 301-444-3488, 444-3489

Wanzer, Janet, *Acq,* Phillips University, Zollars Memorial Library, Enid OK. 405-237-4433, Ext 251

Waranius, Francis B, *Libr-Info Ctr Mgr,* Lunar and Planetary Institute (Library-Information Center), Houston TX. 713-486-2134, 486-2135

Warburton, Roberta, *Cat,* Harris-Stowe State College Library, Saint Louis MO. 314-533-3366, Ext 36

Ward, A E, *Dir,* Center for Anthropological Studies Library, Albuquerque NM. 505-296-4836

Ward, Annette, *Br Coordr,* Elbert County Library, Elberton GA. 404-283-5375

Ward, B M, *Librn,* Powell River District Libraries, Powell River BC. 604-485-4796

Ward, Barbara, *Coordr,* California State University at Long Beach, Library Education Program, CA. 213-498-4966

Ward, Betty, *ILL & Acq,* Garfield County Public Library, New Castle CO. 303-984-2346
Ward, Charlotte, *Librn,* Canadian Government Office of Tourism, Tourism Reference and Data Center, Ottawa ON. 613-995-2754
Ward, Cheryl, *Syst Coordr,* Carolina Population Center Library, Chapel Hill NC. 919-933-3081
Ward, Colleen, *Librn,* Western Electric Co, Technical Library, Oklahoma City OK. 405-781-3415
Ward, Conaire, *Tech Serv,* Waterford Public Library, Waterford CT. 203-442-8551
Ward, Dennis F, *Librn,* Sierra Conservation Center, Inmate Library, Jamestown CA. 209-984-5291
Ward, Dianne, *Librn,* Public Library of Nashville & Davidson County (Madison Branch), Madison TN. 615-868-7302
Ward, Eileen, *Branch Librn,* Honeywell Information Systems Inc, System Technical Library, Waltham MA. 617-890-8400
Ward, Elizabeth P, *Dir,* Indiana Free Library Inc, Indiana PA. 412-465-8841
Ward, Estelle, *Dir,* Plattsburgh Public Library, Plattsburgh NY. 518-563-0921
Ward, Frank J, *Asst Dir,* University of Toledo, William S Carlson Library, Toledo OH. 419-537-2324
Ward, Gladys, *Circ,* Athens State College Library, Athens AL. 205-232-1802, Ext 291
Ward, Helen, *Circ,* Burlingame Public Library, Burlingame CA. 415-344-7107
Ward, Heloise, *Librn,* Coolidge Library, Solon ME. 207-643-2388
Ward, Irene, *Ch,* Pasquotank-Camden Library, Elizabeth City NC. 919-335-2473
Ward, James E, *Dir & Bibliog Instr,* David Lipscomb College, Crisman Memorial Library, Nashville TN. 615-385-3855, Ext 282, 283
Ward, James G, *Co Librn,* Union Gas Ltd Library, Chatham ON. 519-352-3100, Ext 2594
Ward, Jane, *Librn,* Thompson & Knight Law Firm Library, Dallas TX. 214-655-7568
Ward, Joyce, *Librn,* Martin Memorial Library, Williamston NC. 919-792-5966
Ward, Joyce, *Librn,* Trudeau Institute Library, Saranac Lake NY. 518-891-3080
Ward, Judi, *Ch & YA,* Roswell Public Library, Roswell NM. 505-622-7101
Ward, Judy, *Librn,* Developmental Sciences, Inc Library, City of Industry CA. 213-330-6865
Ward, Leslie, *Libr Technician,* San Diego County Library (Fletcher Hills), El Cajon CA. 714-466-1132
Ward, Loraine, *Librn,* United States Air Force (US Air Force Regional Hospital Carswell (SAC)), Carswell AFB TX. 817-735-7579
Ward, Louise, *Commun Servs,* Lane Public Library, Hamilton OH. 513-894-7156
Ward, Lucinda, *Tech Serv,* Fond Du Lac City-County Library Service, Fond du Lac WI. 414-921-3670
Ward, Lucinda, *Tech Serv & On-Line Servs,* Mid-Wisconsin Federated Library System, Fond du Lac WI. 414-921-3670
Ward, Marietta M, *Librn,* University of Washington Libraries (Art), Seattle WA. 206-543-0648
Ward, Martha E, *Ch,* Quincy Public Library, Quincy IL. 217-223-1309
Ward, Mary Margaret, *Librn,* Ruth Enlow Library of Garrett County (Finzel Community Ctr), Frostburg MD. 301-689-8388
Ward, Mildred, *Librn,* Dalton Public Library, Inc (Catoosa County Library-Ringgold), Ringold GA. 404-935-3800
Ward, Mildred, *Librn,* Fletcher Town Library, Cavendish VT. 802-226-7369
Ward, Mrs Clarence, *Librn,* S M Dunlap Memorial Library, Italy TX. 214-483-6481
Ward, Myrtle, *Librn,* Clarendon Hills Public Library, Clarendon Hills IL. 312-323-8188
Ward, N, *Librn,* London Public Libraries & Museums (Central Children's Branch), London ON. 519-432-7166
Ward, Nancy E, *Librn,* Lafayette Clinic Library, Detroit MI. 313-256-9596
Ward, O C, *Asst Dir,* Beaumont Public Library, Beaumont TX. 713-838-0812
Ward, Patricia, *ILL,* Frostburg State College Library, Frostburg MD. 301-689-4396
Ward, Peggy, *Asst Librn,* Tucker Free Library, Henniker NH. 603-428-3471
Ward, Richard, *ILL & Ref,* Clinton-Essex-Franklin Library System, Plattsburgh NY. 518-563-5190
Ward, Robert, *Asst Adminr,* Central Iowa Regional Library, Des Moines IA. 515-280-9092
Ward, Rose O, *Librn,* New York Public Library (One Hundred & Twenty-Fifth Street), New York NY. 212-534-5050
Ward, Rosemary, *Commun Servs,* Lakewood Public Library, Lakewood OH. 216-226-8275
Ward, S M, *Cat,* British Columbia Government, Legislative Library, Victoria BC. 604-387-6500
Ward, SallyAnn, *Ad,* Collier County Free Public Library, Naples FL. 813-262-4130, 261-8208
Ward, Susan, *Regional Coordr,* San Diego County Library (Region E), San Diego CA. 714-565-5100
Ward, Thelma, *In Charge,* Students Museum Library, Knoxville TN. 615-637-1121
Ward, Ursula, *Tech Serv, Acq & Cat,* Dodge City Public Library, Dodge City KS. 316-225-0248
Ward, Velma, *Librn,* Tulsa City-County Library (Owasso Branch), Owasso OK. 918-272-5022
Ward, Victoria, *Librn,* Morgan, Lewis & Bockius Law Library, Washington DC. 202-872-7691
Ward, III, Dederick, *Librn,* University of Colorado at Boulder (Earth Science Library), Boulder CO. 303-492-6133
Ward, III, Dederick, *Acting Librn,* University of Colorado at Boulder (Science Library), Boulder CO. 303-492-5136
Warde, William D, *Dir,* Fall River Public Library, Fall River MA. 617-676-8541
Warden, Jeannie, *Librn,* Waco-McLennan County Library (R B Hoover), Waco TX. 817-776-1581
Warden, Marjorie, *Librn,* Wittman Public Library, Wittman AZ. 602-388-2321
Wardian, Vivienne, *Circ,* Marion County Public Library, Fairmont WV. 304-366-4831
Wardlaw, Janet A, *ILL & Ser,* University of Cincinnati Libraries (Robert S Marx Law Library), Cincinnati OH. 513-475-3016
Wardlaw, Ruth, *Cat,* Grady C Hogue Library, Learning Resource Center, Beeville TX. 512-358-7032
Wardrop, Elaine L, *Librn,* 3M (The 236 Technical Library), Saint Paul MN. 612-733-5751
Ware, Aletha, *Librn,* Kings County Library (Kettleman City Branch), Kettleman City CA. 209-386-9804
Ware, Elva M, *Staff Asst-Admin Servs,* United States Steel Corporation (Law Library), Pittsburgh PA. 412-433-1121
Ware, Ethel, *Librn,* Texas College, D R Glass Library, Tyler TX. 214-593-8311, Ext 37
Ware, Jimmy Nell, *Librn,* Cordova Public Library, Cordova AL. 205-483-7637
Ware, Malcolm S, *Librn,* Gulf Coast Research Laboratory, Gunter Library, Ocean Springs MS. 601-875-2244, Ext 253, 264
Ware, Mrs L R, *Librn,* Marshall County Memorial Library, Lewisburg TN. 615-359-3335
Ware, Nellie, *Ch,* Scotch Plains Public Library, Scotch Plains NJ. 201-322-5007
Ware, Rebecca, *Ser,* Elizabeth City State University, G R Little Library, Elizabeth City NC. 919-335-0551, Ext 332
Ware, Susan, *Ref,* Pennsylvania State University, Delaware County Campus Library, Media PA. 215-565-3300, Ext 24
Wareham, Nancy, *Exec Dir,* Cleveland Area Metropolitan Library System, (CAMLS), OH. 216-368-2642
Warehime, Helen, *Librn,* Wedsworth Memorial Library, Cascade MT. 406-468-2848
Waren, Doris J, *Librn,* Keeneland Association, Keeneland Library, Lexington KY. 606-254-3412, Ext 223
Warfield, Ken, *Bkmobile Coordr,* Santa Barbara Public Library, Santa Barbara CA. 805-962-7653
Warfield, Marsha, *Ch,* North Palm Beach Public Library, North Palm Beach FL. 305-848-0445
Warg, Eleanor, *Circ,* Cedar Crest College, Cressman Library, Allentown PA. 215-437-4471, Ext 264
Wargo, Cynthia, *Ref,* Evanston Public Library, Evanston IL. 312-866-0300
Wargo, Lucy, *Librn,* Children's Hospital of Buffalo, Emily Foster Memorial Library, Buffalo NY. 716-878-7000
Waring, Judy, *Ser,* Saint John Fisher College, Lavery Library, Pittsford NY. 716-586-4140, Ext 222
Waring, Margaret, *Librn,* Comanche Public Library, Comanche TX. 915-356-2122
Warkentin, Kathryn, *Doc,* Shippensburg State College, Ezra Lehman Memorial Library, Shippensburg PA. 717-532-1463
Warkoczewski, Edith, *Librn,* Lutheran Social Services of Wisconsin & Upper Michigan Library, Milwaukee WI. 414-342-7175
Warmack, Geraldine, *Librn,* Will Rogers Library, Claremore OK. 918-341-1564
Warne, Keith, *Instr,* Northern State College, Library Science Program, SD. 605-622-2645
Warne, Keith, *Pub Servs,* Northern State College, Williams Library & Learning Resource Center, Aberdeen SD. 605-622-2645
Warnement, Judy, *Media,* Northeastern Ohio Universities College of Medicine, Basic Medical Sciences Library, Rootstown OH. 216-325-2511
Warner, Annie K, *Tech Serv,* Lexington County Circulating Library, Batesburg SC. 803-532-9223
Warner, Betty, *Acq,* University of Puget Sound (Law Library), Tacoma WA. 206-756-3322
Warner, Bro Thomas, *Dir,* La Salle College, David Leo Lawrence Library, Philadelphia PA. 215-951-1292
Warner, Bruno, *Librn,* Sacred Heart Hospital, Medical Library, Eau Claire WI. 715-839-4330
Warner, Claudette, *Librn,* Bank Administration Institute, Information Center, Park Ridge IL. 312-693-7300
Warner, Edward S, *Dir,* University of North Dakota, Chester Fritz Library, Grand Forks ND. 701-777-2617
Warner, Elizabeth R, *Ext Librn for Doc Delivery & On-Line Servs,* Mid-Eastern Regional Medical Library Service, PA. 215-561-6050
Warner, F Eleanor, *Librn,* New England College of Optometry Library, Boston MA. 617-261-3430, Ext 42, 43
Warner, Frank L, *Actg Dir,* New Orleans Consortium, LA. 504-866-4826
Warner, Gail P, *Asst Dir,* H Grady Bradshaw Chambers County Library and Cobb Memorial Archives, Shawmut AL. 205-768-3150
Warner, Geneva, *Bkmobile Coordr,* Pickens County Library, Easley SC. 803-859-9679
Warner, Grant, *Dir,* Ciba - Geigy Corp, Cranston Library, Cranston RI. 401-941-3000
Warner, Helen J, *Librn,* Bethesda Memorial Hospital, Medical Library, Boynton Beach FL. 305-737-7733, Ext 4439
Warner, Jeannie, *Acting Br Coordr,* Umatilla County Library, Pendleton OR. 503-276-1881
Warner, Judith A, *Librn, On-Line Servs & Bibliog Instr,* Ontario Ministry of Agriculture & Food, Horticultural Research Institute of Ontario Library, Vineland Station ON. 416-562-4141, Ext 61
Warner, Karen, *Dir,* Northeast Technical Community College, Library Resource Center, Norfolk NE. 402-371-2020
Warner, Kathleen, *On-Line Servs,* MTS Systems Corp, Information Services, Minneapolis MN. 612-944-4000
Warner, Marie, *Servs to the Disadvantaged Consult,* Massachusetts Board of Library Commissioners, Office for the Development of Library Services, Boston MA. 617-267-9400
Warner, Michelle, *Asst Dir,* Appalachian Bible College Library, Bradley WV. 304-877-6428, Ext 11
Warner, Mrs C R, *Librn,* Solomon Public Library, Solomon KS. 913-655-3831
Warner, Pat, *Pub Info Specialist,* Alabama Public Library Service, Montgomery AL. 205-832-5743
Warner, Rebecca L, *Dir,* Thompson Home Public Library, Ithaca MI. 517-875-4184
Warner, Richard, *Asst Prof,* Shippensburg State College, Dept of Library Science, PA. 717-532-1472
Warner, Richard, *Dept Chmn,* Trenton State College, Media Communication Science, NJ. 609-771-1855
Warner, Robert, *In Charge,* Cobb County Public Library System (Acworth Branch), Acworth GA. 404-974-3341
Warner, Robert D, *Dir,* Ketchikan Community College Library, Ketchikan AK. 907-225-4722
Warner, Robert M, *Dir,* University of Michigan (Michigan Historical Collections), Ann Arbor MI. 313-764-3482

Warner, Robert M, *Prof,* University of Michigan, School of Library Science, MI. 313-764-9376
Warner, Ruth, *Ch,* Itasca Community Library, Itasca IL. 312-773-1699
Warner, Sandra, *Circ,* Waterloo Public Library, Waterloo IA. 319-291-4521
Warner, Sister M Reginald, *Assoc Librn,* Saint Mary's Dominican College, John XXIII Library, New Orleans LA. 504-865-7761, Ext 225
Warner, Truman A, *Archivist,* Danbury Scott-Fanton Museum & Historical Society Research Library, Danbury CT. 203-743-5200
Warner, Velda, *Librn,* Bonaparte Public Library, Bonaparte IA. 319-592-3677
Warner, Lorena, *Librn,* Burley Public Library, Burley ID. 208-678-7708
Warnke, Nancy, *Librn,* United States District Court Law Library, San Francisco CA. 415-556-7979
Warnken, Kimberley, *ILL & Acq,* Tennessee Wesleyan College, Merner-Pfeiffer Library, Athens TN. 615-745-2363
Warnock, Carol, *Bibliog Instr,* Memphis State University Libraries, Memphis TN. 901-454-2201
Warnock, Doreen, *Librn,* Picture Butte Municipal Library, Picture Butte AB. 403-732-9710
Warnock, Phyllis, *Librn,* Somersworth Public Library, Somersworth NH. 603-692-4587
Warpeha, Rita C, *Chief Librn, On-Line Servs & Bibliog Instr,* Action Library, Washington DC. 202-254-3307
Warran, Leslie, *Bkmobile Coordr & Br Coordr,* Warren Public Library, Warren OH. 216-399-8807
Warren, B, *Librn,* DeCordova & Dana Museum Library, Lincoln MA. 617-259-8355
Warren, Betty H, *Dir,* Muscle Shoals Regional Library System, Florence AL. 205-764-6563
Warren, Bobbye, *Dir,* Waller County Library, Hempstead TX. 713-826-2521
Warren, C David, *Dir,* Richland County Public Library, Columbia SC. 803-799-9084
Warren, Catherine, *Librn,* First Regional Library (Senatobia Public), Senatobia MS. 601-562-6791
Warren, Dianne, *Instr,* Alderson-Broaddus College, Media Education Program, WV. 304-457-1700, Ext 258
Warren, Dianne, *Tech Serv & Cat,* Alderson-Broaddus College, Pickett Library Media Center, Philippi WV. 304-457-1700, Ext 229, 258
Warren, Donna, *Librn,* Harris Trust & Savings, Bank Research Library, Chicago IL. 312-461-7625
Warren, Dorothea, *Ref,* Washburn University of Topeka (School of Law Library), Topeka KS. 913-295-6688
Warren, E Louise, *Asst Librn Tech Servs,* Emory University Libraries (A W Calhoun Medical Library), Atlanta GA. 404-329-5810
Warren, Emma A, *Dir,* Rutgers University (Kilmer Area Library), New Brunswick NJ. 201-932-3610
Warren, Erma Lou, *Librn,* Fairfield Public Library, Fairfield IL. 618-842-4516
Warren, Frank, *Ext Coordr,* Davenport Public Library, Davenport IA. 319-326-7832
Warren, G Garry, *Dir,* Henderson State University, Huie Library, Arkadelphia AR. 501-246-5511, Ext 200
Warren, George E, *Dir,* Colorado State Department of Administration, Colorado State Archives, Denver CO. 303-839-2055
Warren, Janet, *Librn,* Goodland Public Library, Goodland KS. 913-899-5461
Warren, Joanne, *Ch,* New City Free Library, New City NY. 914-634-4997
Warren, John, *In Charge,* North Alabama Biomedical Information Network, (NABIN), AL. 205-895-6540
Warren, John, *Dir,* North Alabama Library Alliance, AL. 205-895-6540
Warren, John, *Dir,* University of Alabama in Huntsville Library, Huntsville AL. 205-895-6540
Warren, Julia, *Cat,* Tyler Junior College, Edgar H Vaughn Memorial Library, Tyler TX. 214-592-5993, 593-3342
Warren, Kenneth, *Asst Dir,* Leonia Public Library, Leonia NJ. 201-944-1444
Warren, Laura B, *Dir,* Erwin Library & Institute, Boonville NY. 315-942-4834

Warren, Lois, *Acq,* Indiana University at South Bend Library, South Bend IN. 219-237-4440
Warren, Lorraine, *On-Line Servs,* Southern Utah State College Library, Cedar City UT. 801-586-4411, Ext 351
Warren, Majel, *Ref,* Portland State University, Branford Price Millar Library, Portland OR. 503-229-4424
Warren, Margaret, *Librn for Serv Evaluation & Grants,* Dallas Public Library, Dallas TX. 214-748-9071
Warren, Marlea, *Art-Music-Films,* Minneapolis Public Library & Information Center, Minneapolis MN. 612-372-6500
Warren, Mary F, *Librn,* Randall Memorial Library, Stow MA. 617-897-8572
Warren, Mrs W E, *Librn,* Hickman County Public Library, Centerville TN. 615-729-5130
Warren, Mrs W K, *Bkmobile Coordr,* Ocmulgee Regional Library, Eastman GA. 912-374-4711
Warren, Nanella, *Librn,* Brooklyn Public Library (Bedford), Brooklyn NY. 212-638-9544
Warren, Phillis, *Acq,* Arlington Public Library, Arlington TX. 817-275-2763, 265-3311, Ext 347
Warren, Ruth, *Rare Bks & Spec Coll,* Mobile Public Library, Mobile AL. 205-438-7073
Warren, Jr, Richard, *Curator Hist Sound Rec Coll,* Yale University Library (Sterling Memorial Library), New Haven CT. 203-436-8335
Warrick, Francis R, *Dir & ILL,* Adirondack Community College Library, Glens Falls NY. 518-793-4491, Ext 60
Warrington, Carol, *Dir,* Saint Louis Community College (Forest Park Campus), Saint Louis MO. 314-644-9209
Warro, Edward A, *Acq,* Southwest Texas State University, Learning Resources Center, San Marcos TX. 512-245-2132
Warron, Hugh P, *Personnel,* South Bend Public Library, South Bend IN. 219-288-4413
Warshasky, Stanford, *Dir,* Silas Bronson Library, Waterbury CT. 203-574-8200
Warshaw, P, *Bibliog Instr,* Cabrillo College, Robert E Swenson Library, Aptos CA. 408-425-6473, 688-6458
Warshaw, Peter, *Asst Librn,* Cabrillo College, Robert E Swenson Library, Aptos CA. 408-425-6473, 688-6458
Warso, Ruby L, *Librn,* Hebrew Theological College (Liberal Arts), Skokie IL. 312-267-9800
Warthen, Lee, *ILL & Ref,* Brigham Young University (Law Library), Provo UT. 801-378-3593
Wartluft, David J, *Dir,* Lutheran Theological Seminary, Krauth Memorial Library, Philadelphia PA. 215-248-4616
Wartman, William, *Instr,* Glenville State College, Library Science Program, WV. 304-462-7361, Ext 291, 292
Wartman, III, William, *Tech Serv,* Glenville State College, Robert F Kidd Library, Glenville WV. 304-462-7361, Ext 291
Wartzok, Susan G, *Cat,* Community College of Baltimore, Bard Library, Baltimore MD. 301-396-0432, 0433
Warwick, James, *Ad,* Mid-Wisconsin Federated Library System, Fond du Lac WI. 414-921-3670
Warwick, James F, *Coord Libr Servs,* Fond Du Lac City-County Library Service, Fond du Lac WI. 414-921-3670
Wasden, Mrs Charles, *Librn,* Monroe County Public Library, Monroeville AL. 205-743-3818
Waser, Grace, *Librn,* La Vina Hospital for Respiratory Diseases, Medical Library, Altadena CA. 213-791-1241
Waserman, Barbara, *Librn,* Fairfax County Public Library (George Mason Regional), Annandale VA. 703-256-3800
Wash, Eleanor, *Librn,* F D Lanterman State Hospital (Staff Library), Pomona CA. 714-595-1221, Ext 2264
Wash, Melba, *Regional Dir,* Reelfoot Regional Library Center, Martin TN. 901-587-2347
Washburn, Anne, *Asst Dir, ILL & Ref,* Greensboro College, James Addison Jones Library, Greensboro NC. 919-272-7102, Ext 234
Washburn, Barbara P, *Dir,* Austin Community College Library, Austin TX. 512-476-6381
Washburn, David B, *Librn,* New Hampshire Hospital, Professional Library, Concord NH. 603-224-6531, Ext 2042

Washburn, Keith E, *Dir Pub Servs,* Hamilton College, Burke Library, Clinton NY. 315-859-4478
Washburn, Lucille, *Librn,* West Lafayette Public Library, West Lafayette IN. 317-743-2261
Washburn, Lynda, *Librn,* Pamunkey Regional Library (Rockville Branch), Rockville VA. 804-749-3146
Washburn, Mildred L, *Librn,* California State Board of Equalization, Law Library, Sacramento CA. 916-445-7356
Washington, Ada, *Librn,* Norfolk Botanical Gardens Library, Norfolk VA. 804-855-0194
Washington, Alice, *Media,* Mesa County Public Library, Grand Junction CO. 303-243-4442
Washington, Clannie H, *Librn,* Midlands Center Library, Columbia SC. 803-758-4434
Washington, Dollie E, *Librn,* Wichita Public Library (Seneca), Wichita KS. 316-262-0611
Washington, Freedia, *Bkmobile Coordr,* Indianapolis Marion County Public Library, Indianapolis IN. 317-635-5662
Washington, Harold, *Asst Librn,* Albuquerque Technical-Vocational Institute, Instructional Materials Center, Albuquerque NM. 505-843-7250, Ext 243
Washington, Isaac, *Librn,* Atlanta Public Library (Fulton County Jail), Atlanta GA. 404-572-2425
Washington, Mary, *Tech Serv & Acq,* Albany Junior College, Library-Learning Resources Ctr, Albany GA. 912-439-4332
Washington, Penny C, *Asst Chief, Central Libr,* Dallas Public Library, Dallas TX. 214-748-9071
Washington, Sigrid M, *Regional Librn,* Public Library of the District of Columbia (Woodridge (Regional)), Washington DC. 202-727-1401
Washington, Wendy, *Librn,* Lambton County Library (Camlachie Branch), Camlachie ON. 519-899-2202
Washuleski, Bennie, *Tech Serv,* Hurst Public Library, Hurst TX. 817-485-5320
Wasick, Lucille J, *Dir,* Wolcott Public Library, Wolcott CT. 203-879-3663
Wasielewski, Eleanor B, *Asst Dir,* Harford County Library, Bel Air MD. 301-838-7484
Wasmer, Carmenia Ann, *Cat,* Glen Rock Public Library, Glen Rock NJ. 201-445-4222, 445-4223
Wasnidge, Theresa, *Librn,* Prince Edward Island Provincial Library (Tignish Branch), Tignish PE. 902-892-3504, Ext 54
Wass, Janice Tauer, *Librn,* Rochester Museum & Science Center, Museum Library, Rochester NY. 716-271-4320, Ext 30
Wassam, Ann, *Ref,* Santa Maria Public Library, Santa Maria CA. 805-925-0994, Ext 261
Wasserman, Alice, *Dir,* Calhoun County Library, Port Lavaca TX. 512-552-2661
Wasserman, Morton N, *Asst Dir,* Paterson Free Public Library, Danforth Memorial Library, Paterson NJ. 201-881-3770
Wasserman, Paul, *Prof,* University of Maryland, College of Library & Information Services, MD. 301-454-5441
Wassom, Earl, *Dir,* Kentucky Cooperative Library Information Project, KY. 502-745-4875
Wassom, Earl, *Dir,* State Assisted Academic Library Council of Kentucky, KY. 502-745-4875
Wassom, Earl, *Dir,* Western Kentucky University, Helm-Cravens Library, Bowling Green KY. 502-745-4875
Wasson, Betty, *Dir,* Washington College, Clifton M Miller Library, Chestertown MD. 301-778-2800, Ext 242
Wasson, Eunice S, *ILL, On-Line Servs & Bibliog Instr,* Ohio University, Chillicothe Library, Chillicothe OH. 775-9500 Ext 215, 260
Wasson, Joan, *Dir,* Somonauk Public Library, Somonauk IL. 815-498-2440
Wasson, Marjorie, *Librn,* Linden Public Library, Linden IA. 515-744-2387
Wasylyk, Marcia, *Librn,* Winnipeg Public Library (Cornish), Winnipeg MB. 204-783-5223
Wasylyk, Marcia, *Librn,* Winnipeg Public Library (Osborne), Winnipeg MB. 204-475-5832
Watanabe, Fumiko, *Librn,* Kula Hospital, Occupational Therapy Dept Library, Kula HI. 808-878-1221
Watanabe, Ruth, *Librn,* University of Rochester (Sibley Music Library), Rochester NY. 716-275-3018

Watanabe, Ruth T, *Adjunct Prof,* State University of New York, College of Arts & Science, School of Library & Information Science, NY. 716-245-5322

Watanabe, Stella K, *Librn,* United States Air Force (Hickam Base Library), Hickam AFB HI. 808-449-2831

Watchurst, Rita, *Asst Librn,* Town of Caledon Public Libraries (Alton Branch), Alton ON. 416-857-1400

Waterbury, Eleanor, *Librn,* J J Hands Library, Lohrville IA. 712-465-4115

Waterhouse, Jo, *Asst Dir,* Palatka Public Library, Palatka FL. 904-328-2385

Waterloo, Jean E, *Librn,* Lenox Township Library, New Haven MI. 313-749-3430

Waterman, Agness, *Librn;* North Thetford Public Library, North Thetford VT. 802-333-9184

Waterman, Ann M, *Dir,* Adams County Library, Adams WI. 608-339-3211

Waterman, Enid, *Acq,* University of Waterloo Library, Waterloo ON. 519-885-1211

Waterman, Fred, *Bus,* Western Washington University, Mabel Zoe Wilson Library, Bellingham WA. 206-676-3050

Waterman, Gertrude E, *Assoc Dir,* Chester County Library & District Center, Exton PA. 215-363-0884

Waterman, Sophia, *Asst Librn,* Bay Path Junior College, Frank & Marian Hatch Library, Longmeadow MA. 413-567-0621, Ext 444

Watermulder, Dale, *Librn,* Knoxville-Knox County Public Library (Fountain City), Knoxville TN. 615-689-2681

Waters, Betsy M, *Librn,* Moore Business Forms, Inc, Research Center Library, Grand Island NY. 716-773-0557

Waters, Francis B, *Librn,* New York State Court of Appeals Library, Albany NY. 518-474-3624

Waters, Helen, *Librn,* Scott Sebastian Regional Library (Hartford Library), Hartford AR. 501-996-2856

Waters, Joyce, *Circ,* Boynton Beach City Library, Boynton Beach FL. 732-2624 or 732-8111, Ext 223, 224 & 225

Waters, Martin F, *Geog & Maps Cur,* Boston Public Library, Eastern Massachusetts Library System, Boston MA. 617-536-5400

Waters, Patricia A, *Librn,* Hamburg Township Library, Hamburg MI. 313-231-1771

Waters, Richard L, *Assoc Dir, Pub Servs,* Dallas Public Library, Dallas TX. 214-748-9071

Waters, Samuel T, *Assoc Dep Dir,* National Agricultural Library, Beltsville MD. 301-344-4248

Waters, Shirley V, *Asst Librn,* Newport Public Library, Newport RI. 401-847-8720

Waters, Will, *Dir,* University of Florida, Agricultural Research & Education Center Library, Bradenton FL. 813-755-1568

Waters, Wilma, *Asst Librn,* Mccreary County Public Library District, Whitley City KY. 606-376-8738

Waterstreet, Nan, *Librn,* Winkler County Library, Kermit TX. 915-586-3841

Wathen, Donald L, *Dir,* Henderson County Public Library, Henderson KY. 502-826-3712

Watkins, Barbara, *Librn & Ad,* Williams Lake Library, Williams Lake BC. 604-392-3630

Watkins, Betty, *Librn,* Wisconsin School for the Deaf, John R Gant Library, Delavan WI. 414-728-6477

Watkins, Carolyn K, *Librn,* Walker Memorial Library, Westbrook ME. 207-854-2391

Watkins, Cheryl, *Br Coordr,* Flathead County Free Library, Kalispell MT. 406-755-5300, Ext 357

Watkins, Dorothy, *Asst Librn,* Southwestern Christian College Library, Hogan-Steward Learning Center, Terrell TX. 214-563-3341

Watkins, Geraldine, *Archivist,* University of Baltimore, Langsdale Library, Baltimore MD. 301-727-6350, Ext 444

Watkins, Janeen Nelson, *Librn,* Lehi City Library, Lehi UT. 801-768-3961

Watkins, Karen, *Librn,* Santa Fe Public Library (Agua Fria), Santa Fe NM. 505-982-4471

Watkins, Karen, *Librn,* Santa Fe Public Library (Alto Street), Santa Fe NM. 505-982-4471

Watkins, Lou P, *Circ,* Richard H Thornton Library, Oxford NC. 919-693-1121

Watkins, Lucretia, *Ref,* Davis County Library, Farmington UT. 801-867-2322

Watkins, Melvin, *Librn,* Town of Hamburg Public Library, Hamburg NY. 716-649-4415

Watkins, Susan, *Staff Libr,* University of Notre Dame Library (Law School Library), Notre Dame IN. 219-283-7024

Watkins, Susan J, *Librn,* Eastern Nazarene College, Nease Library, Wollaston MA. 617-773-6350, Ext 251

Watkins, Thomas, *Librn,* Columbia University (Music Library), New York NY. 212-280-2241

Watkins, William, *Dir,* Green Free Library, Wellsboro PA. 717-724-4876

Watley, Ann, *Cat,* University of Texas Health Science Center at Dallas Library, Dallas TX. 214-688-3368

Watrous, Mary Ann, *ILL,* Miami-Dade Public Library System, Miami FL. 305-579-5001

Watson, Adele L, *Librn,* Coalinga District Library, Coalinga CA. 209-935-1676

Watson, Allen, *Coordr,* Grant MacEwan Community College, Learning Resource Centres, Edmonton AB. 403-484-7791

Watson, Ann, *Media,* East Carolina University, J Y Joyner Library, Greenville NC. 919-757-6514

Watson, Barbara, *Asst Dir,* Howard County Library, Columbia MD. 301-997-8000

Watson, Betty, *Librn,* Firestone Tire & Rubber Co (Corp Business Library), Akron OH. 216-379-6650

Watson, Betty S, *Librn,* Amherst Town Library, Amherst NH. 603-673-2288

Watson, Carol, *Cat,* Washington Bible College-Capital Bible Seminary, Oyer Memorial Library, Lanham MD. 301-552-1400, Ext 232

Watson, Cheryl L, *Librn,* Transco Inc, Transcontinental Gas Pipe Line Corp Library, Houston TX. 713-871-2321

Watson, Cynthia Cummings, *Dir,* Ericson Public Library, Boone IA. 515-432-3727, 432-7010, 432-3738

Watson, Delores, *In Charge,* Outwood State Hospital Library, Dawson Springs KY. 502-797-3771

Watson, Douglas, *Tech Serv & Cat,* Macomb County Library, Mount Clemens MI. 313-469-5300

Watson, Elizabeth J, *Librn,* Agriculture Canada, Research Station Library, Saskatoon SK. 306-343-8214, Ext 51

Watson, Elizabeth S, *Ch,* Fitchburg Public Library, Fitchburg MA. 617-343-3096

Watson, Ellen, *ILL & Ref,* Community College of Baltimore, Bard Library, Baltimore MD. 301-396-0432, 0433

Watson, Elma, *ILL,* Johnson Free Public Library, Hackensack NJ. 201-343-4169

Watson, George F, *Dir,* Columbia State Community College, John W Finney Memorial Library, Columbia TN. 615-388-0120, Ext 234

Watson, Guy, *Assoc Prof,* University of New Mexico, Library Media Education, NM. 505-277-5141

Watson, Halbert, *Dir,* Pomona Public Library, Pomona CA. 714-620-2033

Watson, Jan, *Librn,* Kingsley Public Library, Kingsley IA. 712-378-6521

Watson, Jean, *Librn,* Beaver County Bar Association, Law Library, Beaver PA. 412-728-5700

Watson, Jean, *Asst Librn,* Harcum Junior College Library, Bryn Mawr PA. 215-525-4100, Ext 221

Watson, Jeanette, *Ch & Tech Serv,* Cherokee Regional Library, LaFayette-Walker County Library, LaFayette GA. 404-638-2992

Watson, Joyce M, *Dir,* Norwin Public Library Association Inc, Irwin PA. 412-863-4700

Watson, Judith, *Dir,* Phelps Community Memorial Library, Phelps NY. 315-548-3120

Watson, Justine, *Asst Dir & Tech Serv,* Sioux Falls Public Library, Sioux Falls SD. 605-339-7081

Watson, Letha, *Dir,* De Kalb County Library, Fort Payne AL. 205-845-2671

Watson, Linda, *Dir,* National College Library, Rapid City SD. 605-394-4943

Watson, Linda, *Librn,* York Regional Library (Nackawic Public & School), Nackawic NB. 506-575-2136

Watson, Lorraine B, *Adminr,* Lucile L Morgan Public Library of Cleburne County, Heflin AL. 205-463-2259

Watson, Louise M, *Librn,* Concord Hospital, School of Nursing Library, Concord NH. 603-225-2711

Watson, Margaret, *Librn,* First Baptist Church Library of West Terre Haute, Terre Haute IN. 812-232-2772

Watson, Margaret C, *Ch,* Richmond Memorial Library, Batavia NY. 716-343-9550

Watson, Melissa, *Ch & YA,* Barry-Lawrence Regional Library, Monett MO. 417-235-6646

Watson, Mildred, *ILL,* Marple Public Library, Broomall PA. 215-356-1510, 356-0550

Watson, Nancy, *Genealogy,* Middle Georgia Regional Library, Macon GA. 912-745-5813

Watson, Norma, *Librn,* Cary Library (Sub-Regional Library for the Blind & Physically Handicapped), Houlton ME. 207-532-3967

Watson, Norman, *Librn,* Tuba City Public Library, Tuba City AZ. 602-283-6280

Watson, Odber, *ILL, Rare Bks & Bibliog Instr,* Evergreen Valley College Library, San Jose CA. 408-274-7900, Ext 310

Watson, Patricia, *Asst Librn,* Grandfield Public Library, Grandfield OK. 405-479-5533

Watson, Patricia, *Librn,* Knoxville-Knox County Public Library (West Knoxville), Knoxville TN. 615-588-8813

Watson, Paula, *Librn,* University of Illinois Library at Urbana-Champaign (City Planning & Landscape Architecture), Urbana IL. 217-333-7181

Watson, Paulette Skirbunt, *Dir,* James Monroe Law Office Museum & Memorial Library, Fredericksburg VA. 703-373-8426

Watson, Peggy, *Librn,* Agriculture Canada, Research Station Library, Sidney BC. 604-656-1173

Watson, Peggy D, *Dir,* Columbia Junior College Library, Columbia SC. 803-799-9082

Watson, Peter G, *On-Line Servs,* California State University, Chico Library, Chico CA. 916-895-6212

Watson, Priscilla M, *Dir,* Lawrence Hall of Science, Science & Mathematics Education Library, Berkeley CA. 415-642-1334

Watson, Richard, *Chmn,* Wichita State University, College of Education-School Library Program, KS. 316 689 3324

Watson, Robert J, *Asst Dir,* Denison University, William Howard Doane Library, Granville OH. 614-587-0810, Ext 225

Watson, Rosalie, *Librn,* Piedmont Regional Library (Monroe-Walton County Branch), Monroe GA. 404-867-2762

Watson, Ruth H, *Dir,* Fort Vancouver Regional Library, Vancouver WA. 206-695-1561

Watson, Sandra, *Asst Dir,* Guilford Free Library, Guilford CT. 203-453-6561

Watson, Thomas, *Ref,* East Saint Louis Public Library, East Saint Louis IL. 618-874-7280

Watson, Tom G, *Dir,* University of the South, Jessie Ball duPont Library, Sewanee TN. 615-598-5931, Ext 265, 267

Watson, Vera J, *Librn,* Michael Reese Medical Center (Psychosomatic-Psychiatric Institute), Chicago IL. 312-791-3800

Watson, Warren E, *Dir,* Thomas Crane Public Library, Subregional Headquarters for Eastern Massachusetts Regional Library System, Quincy MA. 617-471-2400

Watson, William, *Asst Librn,* University of British Columbia Library, Vancouver BC. 604-228-3871

Watstein, Sarah, *Bibliog Instr,* Teachers College - Columbia University Library, New York NY. 212-678-3022, 678-3020

Watt, C R, *Asst Librn & Spec Coll,* Royal Military College of Canada, Massey Arts & Science-Engineering Library, Kingston ON. 613-545-7305

Watt, John, *Librn,* Stockton-San Joaquin County Public Library (Manteca Branch), Manteca CA. 209-944-8415

Watt, Mary Morris, *Librn,* Richmond Newspapers, Inc Library, Richmond VA. 804-649-6283

Watt, Nancy, *Media,* Palm Springs Public Library, Palm Springs CA. 714-323-8291

Watters, Phyllis, *Libr Technician,* San Diego County Library (Alpine Branch), Alpine CA. 714-445-4221

Watters, Sister Dolores, *Ref,* Incarnate Word College, Saint Pius X Library, San Antonio TX. 512-828-1261, Ext 215

Watters, Stephen P, *Librn,* United States Court of Appeals, Eighth Circuit Library, Saint Paul MN. 612-725-7177

Watters, Vona, *Librn,* United States Department of Labor, Atterbury Job Corps Center Library, Edinburg IN. 812-526-5581

Watterson, R M, *Librn,* Medical College of Ohio at Toledo, Raymon H Mulford Library, Toledo OH. 419-381-4223

Watts, Anne, *Reader Serv & Doc,* Saint Louis Public Library, Saint Louis MO. 314-241-2288

Watts, Doris E, *Supvry Librn,* Interstate Commerce Commission Library, Washington DC. 275-7327; 275-7328

Watts, Grace, *Librn,* Bethesda United Methodist Church Library, Bethesda MD. 301-652-2990

Watts, Henrietta, *Cat,* Moody Bible Institute Library, Chicago IL. 312-329-4138

Watts, Judith G, *Mgr Info & Libr Servs,* Martin Marietta Corp, Laboratories Library, Baltimore MD. 301-247-0700

Watts, June, *Acq,* Foothill College, Hubert H Semans Library, Los Altos Hills CA. 415-948-8590, Ext 390, 391

Watts, Marjory R, *Dir,* Kingston Public Library, Kingston TN. 615-376-9905

Watts, Mary, *AV,* Valparaiso-Porter County Public Library System & Administrative Headquarters, Valparaiso IN. 219-462-0524

Watts, Mary E, *Librn,* Alabama Department of Mental Health, Thomasville Adult Adjustment Center Library, Thomasville AL. 205-636-5421, Ext 265

Watts, Mrs James D, *Librn,* Pleasanton Public Library, Pleasanton TX. 512-569-3622

Watts, Peggy, *Librn,* Primghar Public Library, Primghar IA. 712-757-8981

Watts, Richard, *Librn,* San Bernardino County Library (East Base Line), Highland CA. 714-862-8549

Watts, Sharon, *Librn,* Kentucky State Department for Human Resources Library (Educational Materials Library), Frankfort KY. 606-564-2366, 987-4984

Watts, Shirley, *Librn,* Vanderbilt University Library (Music), Nashville TN. 615-327-8081

Waudby-Smith, Mrs J, *Librn,* Canada Institute for Scientific & Technical Information (Physics), Ottawa ON. 613-993-1600

Waugaman, Marcia, *Asst Dir & Acq,* Avon Lake Public Library, Avon Lake OH. 216-933-8128

Waugh, A, *Bus & Sci,* Calgary Public Library, Calgary AB. 403-268-2880

Waugh, Arthur, *Librn,* University of California, Berkeley (Environmental Design), Berkeley CA. 415-642-4818

Waugh, Lucky, *Dir,* Norfolk Public Library, Lewis & Clark Regional Library, Norfolk NE. 402-371-4590

Waugh, Richard P, *Ref,* Albany Public Library, Albany NY. 518-449-3380

Waugh, Shirley, *Asst Librn,* Centralia College Library, Centralia WA. 206-736-9391, Ext 241

Wavada, Margaret, *Ad,* Grundy County-Jewett Norris Library, Trenton MO. 816-359-3577

Waverchak, Gail, *Librn,* Saint Joseph's Hospital of Atlanta, Russell Bellman Library, Atlanta GA. 404-256-7040

Wavering, Marie, *Ch & YA,* Addison Public Library, Addison IL. 312-543-3617

Wawack, Judith, *Info Specialist,* American Can Co, Business Information Center, Greenwich CT. 203-552-2160, 552-2161 & 552-3685

Way, Catherine, *Asst to Dir,* James Prendergast Library Association, Jamestown NY. 716-484-7135

Way, Nick, *Media,* Pamlico Technical College Library, Grantsboro NC. 919-249-1851, Ext 22

Way, Susan, *Asst Librn,* Providence Hospital, Medical Library & Learning Resource Center, Seattle WA. 206-326-5621

Way, William, *Head, Tech Servs,* Riverside City & County Public Library, Riverside CA. 714-787-7211

Waybright, Joyce, *Tech Serv & Cat,* United States Army (Abrams Library), Fort McClellan AL. 205-238-3715

Wayland, Shirley, *Ch & YA,* Phoenix Public Library, Phoenix AZ. 602-262-6451

Wayne, Patricia, *Asst Dir,* Roxbury Public Library, Succasunna NJ. 201-584-2400, 584-2401

Wckman, Lloyd D, *Exec Dir,* San Francisco Consortium, CA. 415-543-9580

Weadick, M, *Librn,* Hamilton Public Library (Red Hill), Hamilton ON. 416-561-2835

Weant, Rebecca E, *ILL & Ref,* Rowan Public Library, Salisbury NC. 704-633-5578

Weant, Robert A, *Librn,* Eno Foundation for Transportation Library, Westport CT. 203-227-4852

Wear, Betty, *Cat,* Jacksonville State University Library, Jacksonville AL. 205-435-9820, Ext 213, 214

Wearmouth, Judith, *Librn,* Castlegar & District Public Library, Castlegar BC. 604-365-6611

Wearstler, Emogene, *Bkmobile Coordr,* Albert A Wells Memorial Library, Tippecanoe County Contractual Library, Lafayette IN. 317-423-2602

Weary, Richard L, *Media,* United States Army War College Library, Carlisle Barracks PA. 717-245-4319

Weast, Janice, *Librn,* Morrill Free Public Library, Hiawatha KS. 913-742-3831

Weatherbe, Mrs K, *Tech Serv & Acq,* Saint Catharines Public Library, Saint Catharines ON. 416-688-6103

Weatherell, Betty, *In Charge,* Carnegie Library of Pittsburgh (Hazelwood), Pittsburgh PA. 412-622-3100

Weatherford, John W, *Dir,* Central Michigan University, Charles V Park Library, Mount Pleasant MI. 517-774-3500

Weatherhead, B A B, *Dir,* Ontario Ministry of Treasury, Economics & Intergovernmental Affairs, Library Service Branch, Toronto ON. 416-965-2314, 965-2315 & 965-6296

Weatherill, Helene A, *Librn,* Sullivan & Cromwell Law Library, New York NY. 212-558-3778

Weatherley, Anne, *Acq,* Goucher College, Julia Rogers Library, Towson MD. 301-825-3300, Ext 360

Weatherly, Carolyn, *Librn,* Brazoria County Library (Freeport Branch), Freeport TX. 713-233-3622

Weatherly, Margaret B, *Dir,* Camden County Historical Society, Charles S Boyer Memorial Library, Camden NJ. 609-964-3333

Weathers, Azilee, *Reader Serv,* Samford University (Cordell Hull Law), Birmingham AL. 205-870-2714

Weathers, Edra M, *Dir,* John Tomay Memorial Library, Georgetown Library, Georgetown CO. 303-569-2620

Weatherwax, John R, *Lab Dir,* United States Food & Drug Administration Library, Los Angeles CA. 213-688-3771

Weatherwax, Philip E, *Head Tech Librn,* NASA, Langley Research Center Technical Library MS 185, Hampton VA. 804-827-2786

Weaver, Anna, *Librn,* University of Florida Libraries (Architecture & Fine Arts), Gainesville FL. 904-392-0222

Weaver, Barbara F, *Asst Commissioner of Educ & State Librn,* New Jersey State Library, Trenton NJ. 609-292-6200

Weaver, Betty, *Librn,* Paw Paw Public Library, Paw Paw WV. 304-947-7013

Weaver, Bobbett A, *Asst Librn,* National Park Service, Midwest Archeological Center Library, Lincoln NE. 402-471-5392

Weaver, Brenda, *Librn,* Gaston County Public Library (Stanley Branch), Stanley NC. 704-263-4166

Weaver, Carolyn G, *Ref & On-Line Servs,* University of Nebraska Medical Center, Library of Medicine, Omaha NE. 402-541-4006

Weaver, Christine, *Genealogist,* Lebanon County Historical Society Library, Lebanon PA. 717-272-1473

Weaver, Clarice, *Ch,* Ashe County Public Library, West Jefferson NC. 919-246-2041

Weaver, David, *Rare Bk Room,* Saint Louis Public Library, Saint Louis MO. 314-241-2288

Weaver, Debbie J, *In Charge,* Governor's Office of Budget & Administration, Bureau of Personnel Library, Harrisburg PA. 717-787-7869

Weaver, Enid Jean, *Cat,* Victoria College - University of Houston Victoria Campus Library, Victoria TX. 512-575-7436

Weaver, Esther, *Cat,* Pioneer Memorial City-County Library, Fredericksburg TX. 512-997-4604

Weaver, Gerry, *Tech Serv,* Clermont County Public Library, Batavia OH. 513-732-2128

Weaver, Gloria, *ILL,* North Baltimore Public Library, North Baltimore OH. 419-257-2196

Weaver, Jerry W, *Dir,* Surry Community College, Learning Resources Center, Dobson NC. 919-386-8121, Ext 52

Weaver, Josephine E, *Librn,* Ayer Public Library, Ayer MA. 617-772-2257

Weaver, Josephine E, *Chief Librn,* United States Army (Davis Library), Fort Devens MA. 617-796-2431

Weaver, Joyce, *Librn,* Robersonville Public Library, Robersonville NC. 919-795-3591

Weaver, Linza, *Tech Serv & Cat,* Morris College, Pinson Memorial Library, Sumter SC. 803-775-9371, Ext 216

Weaver, Lola, *Librn,* Allen County Public Library, Scottsville KY. 502-237-3861

Weaver, Lyn, *Flms,* Chester County Library & District Center, Exton PA. 215-363-0884

Weaver, Margaret, *ILL,* University of Tennessee at Martin, Paul Meek Library, Martin TN. 901-587-7060

Weaver, Mary Ann, *Librn,* Champion International (Business Library), Hamilton OH. 513-868-4552

Weaver, Marycatharine, *Dir,* Martin Memorial Library, York PA. 717-843-3978

Weaver, Marycatharine, *Dir,* York County Library System, York PA. 717-846-0677

Weaver, Mrs Thomas, *Asst Librn,* Alabama Christian College, Gus Nichols Library, Montgomery AL. 205-272-5820, Ext 47

Weaver, Priscilla, *Libr Assts,* Cumberland Valley Regional Library, Subheadquarters, London KY. 606-864-9346

Weaver, Richard, *Sr Librns,* New York State Library (Serials Processing), Albany NY. 518-474-6280, 474-7868

Weaver, Ron, *Tech Serv,* Los Angeles Times Editorial Library, Los Angeles CA. 213-972-7184

Weaver, Ruby, *Chief, Cent Libr,* Houston Public Library, Houston TX. 713-224-5441

Weaver, Serena, *Acq,* Hampshire College, Harold F Johnson Library Center, Amherst MA. 413-549-4600

Weaver, Thelma, *Librn,* Franklin Sylvester Library (Lodi Branch), Lodi OH. 216-948-1885

Weaver, Thomas W, *Chief Librn,* Alabama Christian College, Gus Nichols Library, Montgomery AL. 205-272-5820, Ext 47

Weaver, Virginia, *Coordr Res Training,* Atlanta Public Library, Atlanta GA. 404-688-4636

Weaver, William B, *Asst Librn,* University of Florida Libraries (Agriculture), Gainesville FL. 904-392-1934

Weaver, Zella, *ILL,* Plano Public Library System, Plano TX. 214-423-6502, 867-1002

Web, Marek, *Archivist,* Yivo Institute for Jewish Research Library & Archives, New York NY. 212-535-6700

Webb, Andy, *AV,* Surry Community College, Learning Resources Center, Dobson NC. 919-386-8121, Ext 52

Webb, Ann B, *Librn,* Coastal Carolina Community College Library, Jacksonville NC. 919-455-1221

Webb, Anna Blanche, *Librn,* Madisonville Public Library, Madisonville TN. 615-442-4500

Webb, Beth, *Music & Art,* Brigham Young University, Harold B Lee Library, Provo UT. 801-378-2905

Webb, Bettye W, *Bkmobile Coordr,* City Library, Springfield MA. 413-739-3871

Webb, Bettye W, *Librn,* City Library (Winchester Square), Springfield MA. 413-732-6294

Webb, C Ty, *Data Base Searcher,* Mobay Chemical Corp, Agricultural Chemicals Division Library, Kansas City MO. 816-242-2236

Webb, David A, *Instr,* North Texas State University, School of Library & Information Sciences, TX. 817-788-2445

Webb, Dorothy, *Editorial Res Supvr,* Canadian National Railways (Public Affairs Library), Montreal PQ. 514-877-5584

Webb, Dorothy, *Cat,* Hughes Aircraft Co (Company Technical Document Center Library), Culver City CA. 213-391-0711, Ext 6187

Webb, Frances, *Ad,* Miami Public Library, Miami OK. 918-542-3064

Webb, Hildegard, *Ref & Bibliog Instr,* Monmouth College, Guggenheim Library, West Long Branch NJ. 201-222-6600, Ext 264

Webb, Jack, *Reader Serv & Bibliog Instr,* Kansas City Kansas Community College Library, Kansas City KS. 913-334-1100, Ext 38

Webb, Jane, *Asst Librn,* Detroit College of Business Library, Dearborn MI. 313-582-6983, Ext 24

Webb, Jane, *Dir,* Oxford County Library, Woodstock ON. 519-537-3322

Webb, Jane, *Supervisor,* University of Texas Libraries (Film Library), Austin TX. 512-471-3573

Webb, Jane W, *Acq,* David Lipscomb College, Crisman Memorial Library, Nashville TN. 615-385-3855, Ext 282, 283

Webb, Janice, *ILL,* Missouri Western State College, Hearnes Learning Resources Center, Saint Joseph MO. 816-271-4368

Webb, John, *Tech Serv,* Oregon State Library, Salem OR. 503-378-4243

Webb, Linda, *Fine Arts,* Adams Library, Chelmsford MA. 617-256-5521

Webb, Linda H, *Librn,* ABT Associates Inc Library, Cambridge MA. 617-492-7100, Ext 535, 612

Webb, Lois, *Admin Asst,* Bacone College Library, Muskogee OK. 918-683-4581, Exts 214,227,246

Webb, Lorrayne B, *Librn,* University of Texas (Dental Branch Library), Houston TX. 713-792-4094

Webb, M Jane, *Librn,* Calgary Board of Education, Professional Library, Calgary AB. 403-287-1880, Ext 381

Webb, Margaret L, *Librn,* New Jersey Department of Transportation Library, Trenton NJ. 609-292-3082

Webb, Marlene, *Librn,* Aerospace Research Corp Library, Roanoke VA. 703-342-2961

Webb, Mary E, *On-Line Servs,* University of Kansas Regents Center Library, Overland Park KS. 913-341-4554

Webb, Nancy, *Doc,* University of Arkansas Libraries, Fayetteville AR. 501-575-4101

Webb, Pat, *Learning Resource Ctr,* Maysville Community College Library, Maysville KY. 606-759-7141, Ext 28

Webb, Phyllis, *Asst Librn,* Robert R Jones Public Library, Coal Valley IL. 309-799-3047

Webb, Priscilla, *Ch,* Elkhart Public Library, Elkhart IN. 219-294-5463

Webb, Rodney, *ILL,* Laredo Junior College, Harold R Yeary Library, Laredo TX. 512-724-7544, 722-0521

Webb, Rodney, *ILL,* Laredo State University, Harold R Yeary Library, Laredo TX. 512-722-8001, Ext 42

Webb, Rozelle B, *Med Librn,* Veterans Administration, Library Service, Chillicothe OH. 614-773-1141, Ext 281

Webb, Sara S, *Librn,* Demopolis Public Library, Demopolis AL. 205-289-1595

Webb, Sharon, *ILL,* Fond Du Lac City-County Library Service, Fond du Lac WI. 414-921-3670

Webb, Sharon, *ILL,* Mid-Wisconsin Federated Library System, Fond du Lac WI. 414-921-3670

Webb, Sherrill, *Librn,* Edgecombe Technical Institute, R M Fountain Learning Resources Center, Tarboro NC. 919-823-5166

Webb, Susan M, *Librn,* Ingersoll-Rand Co, Engineering Library, Nashua NH. 603-882-2711

Webb, William H, *Coll Div,* University of California, San Diego, University Libraries, La Jolla CA. 714-452-3336

Webber, Charles A, *Spec Coll & Archivist,* University of Idaho Library, Moscow ID. 208-885-6534

Webber, E, *Cat,* Ipswich Public Library, Ipswich MA. 617-356-4646

Webber, Lorraine, *Librn,* Union Mutual Life Insurance Co, Information Center, Portland ME. 207-780-2347

Webber, Lorraine E, *Librn,* Union Mutual Life Insurance Co (Law Library), Portland ME. 207-780-2211

Webber, Margaret, *Tech Serv,* Saint Louis County Library, Saint Louis MO. 314-994-3300

Webber, Marjorie, *Instr,* Phillips University, Education & Library Science Study Area, OK. 405-237-4433, Ext 417

Webber, Marjorie, *ILL & On-Line Servs,* Phillips University, Zollars Memorial Library, Enid OK. 405-237-4433, Ext 251

Webber, Nancy R, *Acq,* Oregon State University, William Jasper Kerr Library, Corvallis OR. 503-754-3411

Webber, Ruth, *Cat,* Worcester State College, Learning Resources Center, Worcester MA. 617-752-7700, Ext 132, 135

Webber, Sylvia J, *Chief Librn,* United States Army (Army Intelligence Center & School Library), Fort Huachuca AZ. 602-538-5930

Webby, Jr, Ernest J, *Dir,* Brockton Public Library System, Brockton MA. 617-587-2515

Weber, Ami, *YA & Commun Servs,* Prosser Public Library, Bloomfield CT. 203-243-9721

Weber, Barbara, *Bkmobile Coordr,* Fullerton City Library, Fullerton CA. 714-738-6333, Ext 301

Weber, Benita, *Ser,* University of New Mexico General Library, Albuquerque NM. 505-277-4241

Weber, Carol, *Librn,* Dresser Industries, Inc, Dresser Clark Division Engineering Library, Olean NY. 716-375-3000

Weber, Clara, *Librn,* Cascade Public Library, Cascade IA. 319-852-3011, 852-3222

Weber, Cynthia, *Librn,* American Paper Institute Library, New York NY. 212-340-0612

Weber, David C, *Dir,* Stanford University Libraries, Stanford CA. 415-497-2016

Weber, Donald John, *Dir,* Florida Regional Library for the Blind & Physically Handicapped, Daytona Beach FL. 904-252-4722

Weber, Dorothy, *In Charge,* Melrose Library, Melrose MN. 612-256-3885

Weber, Dorothy, *Ch,* Redwood City Public Library, Redwood City CA. 415-369-6251, Ext 288

Weber, E Sue, *Tech Serv,* University of Texas Health Science Center at San Antonio Library, San Antonio TX. 512-691-6271

Weber, Elizabeth, *AV,* Framingham Public Library, Framingham MA. 617-879-3570

Weber, Elizabeth, *Librn,* Seneca Free Library, Seneca KS. 913-336-2377

Weber, Ellen, *Circ,* Geneva College, McCartney Library, Beaver Falls PA. 412-846-5100, Ext 297

Weber, Ellen C, *Librn,* Mildred Johnston Memorial Library, Jacksonville AL. 205-435-6332

Weber, Ellenjoy, *Ch,* Elko County Library, Elko NV. 702-738-3066

Weber, Harry, *Ref & Ad,* Massapequa Public Library, Massapequa NY. 516-798-4607

Weber, Helen, *Librn,* Abbotsford Public Library, Abbotsford WI. 715-223-3444

Weber, Joan L, *Dir & Bibliog Instr,* Northeastern Junior College, Learning Resource Center, Sterling CO. 303-522-6600, Ext 613

Weber, L, *Media,* Eastern Michigan University, Center of Educational Resources, Ypsilanti MI. 313-487-0020

Weber, L L, *Dir,* Fort Collins Public Library, Fort Collins CO. 303-493-4422

Weber, Louise, *Libr Tech,* Milwaukee Technical College, South Region Campus Library, Oak Creek WI. 414-762-2500, Ext 720

Weber, Lynne, *Librn,* Le Sueur-Waseca Regional Library (Le Sueur Public), Le Sueur MN. 612-665-2662

Weber, Marian, *Ref,* Kitchener Public Library, Kitchener ON. 519-743-0271

Weber, Milada, *Tech Serv,* Northwestern University, Chicago (School of Law Library), Chicago IL. 312-649-8450

Weber, Paul, *Librn,* State Library of Ohio (Adams-Brown Counties Bookmobile Center), Winchester OH. 513-695-0990

Weber, Paul M, *Librn,* Adams-Brown Counties Bookmobile, Winchester OH. 513-695-0990

Weber, Ron, *Photo-Carto Data Mgr,* Lunar and Planetary Institute (Photo Map Library), Houston TX. 713-486-2172, 486-2136

Weber, Ruth A, *Dir,* Westchester Library System, Hartsdale NY. 914-761-7620

Weber, Victoria, *Ser,* Vermont Law School Library, South Royalton VT. 802-763-8307

Webreck, Susan J, *Commun Servs,* Salem College, Benedum Learning Resources Center, Salem WV. 304-782-5238

Webster, Agnes, *Park Tech,* National Park Service, Ocmulgee National Monument Resource Center, Macon GA. 912-742-0447

Webster, Ann B, *Ch,* Rockingham Public Library, Harrisonburg VA. 703-434-4475

Webster, Dennis B, *Instrnl TV Mgr,* University of Southern Mississippi (Teaching-Learning Resources Center), Hattiesburg MS. 601-266-7307

Webster, Diana R, *Librn,* Richland Public Library, Gibsonia PA. 412-443-1930

Webster, Donald F, *Dir,* State University of New York, College of Environmental Science & Forestry, F Franklin Moon Library, Syracuse NY. 315-473-8696

Webster, Ellen, *ILL & Ref,* Halifax City Regional Library, Halifax NS. 902-426-6980

Webster, Evon, *Librn,* Wasatch County Library, Heber UT. 801-654-1511

Webster, Harriet A, *On-Line Servs,* Duke Power Co, David Nabow Library, Charlotte NC. 704-373-4095

Webster, Howard B, *Prof,* Eastern New Mexico University, Library Science, Dept of Instructional Resources, NM. 505-562-3111

Webster, James, *Dir,* State University of New York at Buffalo (Science & Engineering), Buffalo NY. 716-636-2946

Webster, Janne, *Tech Serv,* Davis County Library, Farmington UT. 801-867-2322

Webster, Joan, *Supvr,* Sir Sandford Fleming College of Applied Arts & Technology Library (Peterborough), Peterborough ON. 705-799-6617

Webster, Joan, *Supvr,* Sir Sandford Fleming College, Frost Campus Library, Lindsay ON. 705-799-6617

Webster, Joseph S, *Dir,* Seminary of Saint Pius X, Ackerman Library, Erlanger KY. 606-371-4448

Webster, Judy, *Monographs,* University of Tennessee, Knoxville, James D Hoskins Library, Knoxville TN. 615-974-0111

Webster, Judy, *Head,* University of Tennessee, Knoxville (Monographs Order), Knoxville TN. 615-974-4431

Webster, Linda, *Learning Lab Instr,* Western Wyoming Community College, Library Learning Resources Center, Rock Springs WY. 307-382-2121, Ext 154

Webster, Lois, *Librn,* American Nuclear Society Library, La Grange Park IL. 312-352-6611, Ext 26

Webster, Mrs B, *Librn,* Wellington Public Library, Wellington ON. 613-399-2023

Webster, Norman D, *Tech Serv,* Smith College Library, Northampton MA. 413-584-2700, Ext 501

Webster, Patricia, *ILL,* Lyndon State College, Samuel Read Hall Library, Lyndonville VT. 802-626-3555

Webster, Sarah, *Tech Serv,* Bartholomew County Library, Cleo Rogers Memorial Library, Columbus IN. 812-379-1255

Webster, Valerie, *Dir,* Arizona Public Service Company, Central Files Library, Phoenix AZ. 602-271-7900

Webster, Wenda, *Health Sci,* Northeast Louisiana University, Sandel Library, Monroe LA. 318-342-2195

Webster, William G, *Dir,* Hayward Public Library, Hayward CA. 415-581-2545

Wechtler, Stephen, *Asst Dir,* Free Public Library of the Borough of Fort Lee, Fort Lee NJ. 201-461-8020

Wecker, Steven, *Mgr,* National Bank of Detroit Library, Detroit MI. 313-225-2840

Weckerle, Kilda M, *Librn,* Royalton Memorial Library, South Royalton VT. 802-763-7165

Wecks, M, *Librn,* Marshalltown Community College, Learning Resource Center, Marshalltown IA. 515-752-7106

Weddell, Doris, *Librn,* Kern County Library (Lamont Branch), Lamont CA. 805-861-2130

Weddle, Georgia Moc, *Chief Librn,* Orange County Public Library (Dana Niguel), Laguna Niguel CA. 714-496-5517

Weddle, Margaret, *Cat,* Carl Elliott Regional Library, Jasper AL. 205-221-2567

Wedel, Linda, *Asst Librn & Tech Serv,* Texas Medical Association, Memorial Library, Austin TX. 512-477-6704, Ext 191

Wedel, Ruth A, *Librn,* Carver Bible Institute & College Library, Atlanta GA. 404-524-0291

Wedig, Bro Vincent, *Librn,* Saint Benedict's Abbey, Benet Library, Benet Lake WI. 414-396-4311

Wedin, Darlene, *Programs Coordr,* Superiorland Library Cooperative, Marquette MI. 906-228-7697

Weech, Jane, *Media,* Marycrest College, Cone Library, Davenport IA. 319-326-9254

Weech, Terry, *Asst Prof,* University of Iowa, School of Library Science, IA. 319-353-3644

Weed, Kathleen C, *Librn,* Sutton Free Public Library, Sutton VT. 802-467-3746

Weed, Lois, *Asst Dir,* Taylor University, Ayres Alumni Memorial Library, Upland IN. 317-998-2751, Ext 241

Weedenhorn, Marj, *Tech Serv,* Westchester Community College Library, Valhalla NY. 914-347-6939

Weedman, Dorothy, *Asst Librn,* Oak Park Public Library, Scoville Institute, Oak Park IL. 312-383-8200

Weekes, David, *Dir,* Midwestern Baptist Theological Seminary Library, Kansas City MO. 816-453-4600, Ext 248

Weekes, Mrs N H, *Librn,* Saint Luke United Methodist Church Library, Enterprise AL. 205-347-9023

Weekly, Jon, *On-Line Servs,* State University of New York College, Daniel A Reed Library, Fredonia NY. 716-673-3183

Weekly, Suzann, *Ref,* Nyack Library, Nyack NY 914-358-3370

Weeks, Art, *AV,* Forsyth County Public Library, Winston-Salem NC. 919-727-2556

Weeks, Barbara K, *Dir,* Kirkwood Highway Library, Wilmington DE. 302-999-0161

Weeks, Ethel, *Asst Dir & ILL,* Holbrook Public Library, Holbrook MA. 617-767-3644

Weeks, G, *Ref,* British Columbia Institute of Technology Library, Burnaby BC. 604-434-5734, Ext 360

Weeks, Harry S, *Dir,* Bucks County Free Library, Doylestown PA. 215-348-9081

Weeks, Jane, *Asst Librn,* Edward C Jordan Co, Inc Library, Portland ME. 207-775-5401, Ext 295

Weeks, Mary C, *Librn,* Ellsworth Community College Library, Learning Resource Center, Iowa Falls IA. 515-648-4611, Ext 33

Weeks, Olivia, *Librn,* Edgecombe Technical Institute, R M Fountain Learning Resources Center, Tarboro NC. 919-823-5166

Weeks, Jr, Arnold D, *Librn,* Union Correctional Institution Library, Raiford FL. 904-431-1212, Ext 141

Weens, Charles, *Librn,* Seattle Medical Surgical Clinic Library, Seattle WA. 206-392-0200

Weer, Mildred B, *Libr Specialist,* University of Delaware, Marine Studies Library, Lewes DE. 302-645-4290

Weersing, Hermine, *Ref,* Grand Rapids Junior College, Arthur Andrews Memorial Library, Grand Rapids MI. 616-456-4841

Weerts, Mary Jane, *Librn,* Kern County Library (Oildale Branch), Oildale CA. 805-861-2130

Weese, Florence, *Librn,* Triton College Library, River Grove IL. 312-456-0300

Wegener, Judith, *Exec Dir,* Central Indiana Area Library Services Authority, IN. 317-926-6561

Wegman, Marie A, *Librn,* United States Public Health Service, Hospital Medical Library, San Francisco CA. 415-752-1400, Ext 308

Wegman, Robert L, *Dir,* Normal Public Library, Normal IL. 309-452-1757

Wegner, Mary, *Librn,* Iowa Methodist Medical Center (Oliver J Fay Medical Library), Des Moines IA. 515-283-6490, 283-6173

Wegner, Mary, *Coordr,* Polk County Biomedical Consortium, IA. 515-283-6173

Wegner, Sandra, *ILL,* Midland County Public Library, Midland TX. 915-683-2708

Wehlacz, Cherilyn A, *Librn,* Greenfield Public Library, Greenfield IN. 317-462-5141

Wehmer, Marie, *Librn,* Harris County Public Library (West University), Houston TX. 713-668-7180

Wehr, Sally, *Ch,* Westfield Memorial Library, Westfield NJ. 201-233-1515

Wehrlen, Dorothy G, *ILL,* Middletown Township Public Library, Middletown NJ. 201-671-3700

Wehrley, Kathy, *Exten Coordr,* Troy-Miami County Public Library, Troy OH. 513-339-0502

Wehrly, Bernadette, *Instr,* California State University-Los Angeles, Library Services Credential Program, CA. 213-224-3765

Wehrung, Janet J, *Dir,* Three Rivers Public Library, Three Rivers MI. 616-279-2245

Wehtje, Renate, *Per,* Atlantic Union College, G Eric Jones Library, South Lancaster MA. 617-365-4561

Wei, Anna, *Tech Serv,* Santa Monica Public Library, Santa Monica CA. 213-451-5751

Wei, Carl K, *Librn,* Ontario Research Foundation Library, Mississauga ON. 416-822-4111, Ext 268

Wei, Esther, *Ser,* Ohio State University Libraries (Health Sciences Library), Columbus OH. 614-422-9810

Wei, Philip, *Acq,* Mankato State University, Memorial Library, Mankato MN. 507-389-6201

Weibel, Carol, *Librn,* University of Washington Libraries (Philosophy), Seattle WA. 206-543-5856

Weibel, Kathleen, *Consult,* New York State Library, Albany NY. 518-474-5930

Weible, Dorothy, *Librn,* Knox Public Library, Knox PA. 814-797-1054

Weichert, Lorna, *Tech Serv,* Midland County Public Library, Midland TX. 915-683-2708

Weichlein, William J, *Prof,* University of Michigan, School of Library Science, MI. 313-764-9376

Weida, William A, *Dir,* American Society for Metals Library, Metals Park OH. 216-338-5151, Ext 557

Weide, Brenda, *Librn,* Winnipeg Public Library (Windsor Park), Winnipeg MB. 204-253-1168

Weidenburner, Kathleen, *Asst Dir,* Westville Public Library, Westville IL. 217-267-3170

Weidenhamer, Bradley, *Seminary,* Ashland College Library, Ashland OH. 419-289-4067

Weidenhamer, Bradley E, *Dir,* Ashland Theological Seminary, Roger E Darling Memorial Library, Ashland OH. 419-289-4126

Weiding, Kay, *Librn,* West Point Public Library, West Point IA. 319-837-6315

Weidl, Beverly, *Curator,* Hopewell Museum Library, Hopewell NJ. 609-466-0103

Weidle, Catherine, *Rare Bks,* Saint Louis University, Pius XII Memorial Library, Saint Louis MO. 314-658-3100

Weidlein, Kay, *Librn,* Seattle Public Library (South Region), Seattle WA. 206-625-2665

Weidner, Ruth, *Media,* Ormond Beach Public Library, Ormond Beach FL. 904-677-0328, Ext 270-243

Weidner, Ruth, *Librn,* West Chester State College (Music), West Chester PA. 215-436-2430

Weidt, Mary Ann Nieberle, *Ch,* Duluth Public Library, Duluth MN. 218-723-3800

Weigel, Jack W, *Librn,* University of Michigan, McMath-Hulbert Observatory Library, Pontiac MI. 313-335-6434

Weigel, Patricia A, *Cat & On-Line Servs,* Bloomsburg State College, Harvey A Andruss Library, Bloomsburg PA. 717-389-2716

Weigel, II, John W, *Librn,* University of Michigan Libraries (Mathematics), Ann Arbor MI. 313-764-7266

Weigel, II, John W, *Librn,* University of Michigan Libraries (Physics-Astronomy), Ann Arbor MI. 313-764-3442

Weigh, Samuel, *Ref,* Rider College, Franklin F Moore Library, Lawrenceville NJ. 609-896-5111

Weigley, Louise, *Librn,* Richland Community Library, Richland PA. 717-866-4939

Weiherer, Patricia, *Ref,* Reading Public Library, Reading Public Library District, Reading PA. 215-374-4548

Weihs, Jean, *Dir,* Seneca College of Applied Arts & Technology, Library Techniques, ON. 416-491-5050

Weihs, Mary, *Dir & Media,* Saint Joseph Hospital (Sister Mary Alvina Nursing Library), Baltimore MD. 301-828-5800, Ext 2409

Weikert, Barbara, *Exten Servs (incl Br & Bkmobile),* Pierce County Rural Library District, Tacoma WA. 206-572-6760

Weil, Kathy G, *Asst Dir,* Medford Public Library, Medford MA. 617-395-7950

Weil, Kenneth S, *Dir,* Oyster Bay-East Norwich Public Library, Oyster Bay NY. 516-922-1212

Weil, Mrs Francis, *Librn,* Waukee Public Library, Waukee IA. 515-987-4522

Weil, Peter E, *Dir, ILL & Acq,* Illinois College of Optometry, Carl F Shepard Memorial Library, Chicago IL. 312-225-1700, Ext 566

Weiland, Sue, *Ref,* Great Neck Library, Great Neck NY. 516-466-8055

Weilerstein, Deborah, *Ch,* Arlington County Department of Libraries, Arlington Public Library, Arlington VA. 703-527-4777

Weill, Ann, *Circ,* Mississippi College, Leland Speed Library, Clinton MS. 601-924-5131, Ext 232, 307

Weill, David, *Dir,* East Brunswick Public Library, East Brunswick NJ. 201-254-1220

Weill, Marianne, *Acq,* Greenwich Library, Greenwich CT. 203-622-7900

Weimann, Jr, William H, *Coordr,* Planned Parenthood of Cambria-Somerset, Resource Library, Johnstown PA. 814-535-5545

Weimer, Jane, *Acq,* Ohio Northern University, Heterick Memorial Library, Ada OH. 419-634-9921, Ext 370, 490

Weimer, Judith, *Librn,* United States Army (Logistics Center Library), Fort Lee VA. 804-734-4749

Weimerskirch, Philip J, *Historian Archivist,* University of Rochester (Edward G Miner Library, School of Medicine & Dentistry), Rochester NY. 716-275-3364

Wein, Sheldon, *Asst Librn & On-Line Search Coordr,* Peat, Marwick, Mitchell & Co (Accounting & Auditing Library), New York NY. 212-758-9700

Weinbaum, Alex, *Head,* Free Library of Philadelphia (Business, Science & Industry), Philadelphia PA. 215-686-5322

Weinberg, Alan, *City Archivist,* Philadelphia City Archives, Philadelphia PA. 215-686-2276, 686-2249

Weinberg, Cheryl, *Ref,* Chapman College, Thurmond Clarke Memorial Library, Orange CA. 714-997-6806

Weinberg, Fleur, *Librn,* Wills Eye Hospital Library, Philadelphia PA. 215-928-3000

Weinberger, Maria, *Media,* Hamilton Public Library, Hamilton ON. 416-529-8111

Weinberger, Wendy, *Ch & YA,* West Nyack Free Library, West Nyack NY. 914-358-6081

Weinbrecht, Ruby Y, *Dir,* Mary Washington College, E Lee Trinkle Library, Fredericksburg VA. 703-899-4666

Weindel, Kenneth, *Librn Deaf & Librn Blind,* South Georgia Regional Library, Valdosta-Lowndes County Public Library, Valdosta GA. 912-247-3405

Weindel, Kenneth J, *Librn,* South Georgia Regional Library (Talking Book Center), Valdosta GA. 912-247-3405

Weine, Mae, *Librn,* Congregation Beth Abraham-Hillel-Moses, Judge Nathan J Kaufman Library, West Bloomfield MI. 313-851-6880, Ext 27

Weiner, Herbert, *Dir,* Franklin Square Public Library, Franklin Square NY. 516-488-3444

Weiner, Victoria Y, *Librn,* Lilian S Besore Memorial Library, Greencastle PA. 717-597-7920

Weinerth, David, *Ser,* California State University, Sacramento Library, Sacramento CA. 916-454-6466

Weingartz, Emily M, *Information Specialist,* Kellogg Co, Technical Information Center, Battle Creek MI. 616-966-2000

Weingold, Frieda, *Bkmobile Coordr,* Peninsula Public Library, Lawrence NY. 516-239-3262

Weinheimer, Fredricka, *Pres,* Our Lady of Light Catholic Center & Library, Santa Barbara CA. 805-962-9708

Weinhold, David, *Dir,* Sheboygan Falls Memorial Library, Sheboygan Falls WI. 414-467-6771

Weinles, Carol, *Librn,* United States Army (Fort Myer Post Library), Fort Myer VA. 703-692-9574, 692-9650

Weinrebe, Laura, *Librn,* Massachusetts Department of Public Health, Div of Health Education Library, Boston MA. 617-727-7170

Weinrich, Gloria, *Librn,* New York State Department of Labor (Research Library New York City), New York NY. 212-488-6295, 6296

Weinstein, Daniel, *On-Line Servs,* West Hartford Public Library, Noah Webster Memorial Library, West Hartford CT. 203-236-6286

Weinstein, Dora, *On-Line Servs,* United States Patent and Trademark Office, Science Library, Arlington VA. 703-557-2957

Weinstein, Jill, *Librn,* Salomon Brothers Library (International Division), New York NY. 212-747-7932, 747-6146

Weinstein, Lois, *Librn,* General Foods Corp, Technical Center, Research Information Center, Tarrytown NY. 914-683-2500

Weinstein, Neha, *Ser,* Rutgers University (Archibald Stevens Alexander Library), New Brunswick NJ. 201-932-7129

503

Weinstein, Robert J, *Tech Serv, Acq & Cat,* Yonkers Public Library, Yonkers NY. 914-337-1500

Weinstein, Saul, *Dir,* Edinboro State College, Baron-Forness Library, Edinboro PA. 814-732-2780

Weinstein, Sue, *Asst Librn & Pub Servs,* University of Denver (Westminster Law Library), Denver CO. 303-753-3405

Weinstock, Carolynn, *Ref & Ad,* Massapequa Public Library, Massapequa NY. 516-798-4607

Weinstock, Joanna, *Dir,* Highland Falls Library, Highland Falls NY. 914-446-3113

Weinstock, Nancy L, *Rare Bks,* Philadelphia College of Pharmacy & Science, Joseph W England Library, Philadelphia PA. 215-386-5800, Ext 296

Weintraub, Benjamin, *Assoc Prof,* Rutgers-The State University of New Jersey, Graduate School of Library & Information Studies, NJ. 201-932-7500

Weintraub, D Kathryn, *Assoc Prof,* University of Chicago, Graduate Library School, IL. 312-753-3482

Weir, Arvella, *Librn,* Environmental Protection Agency, Region X Library, Seattle WA. 206-442-1289

Weir, Birdie O, *Dir,* Alabama Agricultural & Mechanical University, Joseph F Drake Memorial Learning Resources Center, Normal AL. 205-859-7309

Weir, Brenda, *Librn,* Houston Public Library (Children's Carousel), Houston TX. 713-869-1307

Weir, Gay, *Asst Dir,* Oakland City College, Founders Memorial Library, Oakland City IN. 812-749-4781, Ext 21

Weir, Gertrude B, *Librn,* University of New England (Saint Francis College Library), Biddeford ME. 207-282-1515, Ext 35

Weir, K, *Archit & Environ Design,* State University of New York at Buffalo, University Libraries, Buffalo NY. 716-636-2965

Weir, Kathy, *Librn,* State University of New York at Buffalo (Architecture & Environmental Design), Buffalo NY. 716-831-4609

Weir, Mary Jean, *Asst Prof,* San Diego State University, Dept of Educational Technology & Librarianship, CA. 714-265-6718

Weir, Morton, *Dir,* Father Flanagan's Boys' Home, Center for the Study of Youth Development, Boys Town NE. 402-498-1420

Weirbach, James L, *Librn,* Lehigh County Law Library, Allentown PA. 215-820-3308

Weirich, Helen, *Commun Servs,* Pioneer Memorial City-County Library, Fredericksburg TX. 512-997-4604

Weirman, Leslie S, *Dir,* Cornwall Public Library, Cornwall-on-Hudson NY. 914-534-8282

Weis, Aimee, *ILL & Ref,* Community College of Philadelphia, Division of Educational Resources, Philadelphia PA. 215-972-7510

Weis, Ann Marie, *Supvr,* Sterling Drug, Inc, Sterling-Winthrop Research Institute Library, Rensselaer NY. 518-445-8260

Weis, Helene H, *Librn,* Willet Stained Glass Studios Library, Philadelphia PA. 215-247-5721

Weis, Ina, *Adminr Info Servs,* University of Toledo, William S Carlson Library, Toledo OH. 419-537-2324

Weis, Mabel, *Librn,* Bird Island Public Library, Bird Island MN. 612-365-4640

Weisberg, Elizabeth, *Dir,* Middletown Free Library, Middletown RI. 846-1573 & 846-1584

Weisblatt, Maureen, *Librn,* Cleveland Heights-University Heights Public Library (University Heights), University Heights OH. 216-932-3600

Weisbrod, David L, *Head Systs Office,* Yale University Library (Sterling Memorial Library), New Haven CT. 203-436-8335

Weisbrod, Mrs Dale, *Librn,* Fenton Public Library, Fenton IA. 515-889-2333

Weischedel, Elaine, *Ch,* Kirkwood Highway Library, Wilmington DE. 302-999-0161

Weisel, Juanita, *Dir,* Ursuline College Library, Cleveland OH. 216-449-4200, Ext 276

Weisenberg, Renee, *Librn,* Los Angeles Public Library System (Palisades), Pacific Palisades CA. 213-459-2754

Weisenborne, James, *Librn,* Oakland Community College, Martin Luther King Jr Learning Resources Center, Farmington Hills MI. 476-9400. Ext 401, 402

Weiser, Douglas E, *Head, Info Servs,* Wayne Oakland Library Federation, Wayne MI. 313-326-8910

Weisgerber, William, *Dir,* Saddleback Community College Library, Mission Viejo CA. 714-831-4515

Weisgram, Sister Stefanie, *Commun Servs,* College of Saint Benedict Library, Saint Joseph MN. 612-363-5011

Weisling, Alice, *Librn,* Mead Johnson Research Library, Evansville IN. 812-426-6546

Weismiller, David, *Librn,* Belleville Public Library, Belleville ON. 613-968-7536

Weisrock, Tom, *Circ,* Saddleback Community College Library, Mission Viejo CA. 714-831-4515

Weiss, A Dorothy, *Dir,* Orange City Public Library, Orange City IA. 712-737-4302

Weiss, Barb, *Librn,* Calamus Public Library, Calamus IA. 319-246-2265

Weiss, Bernadette, *Librn,* Fort Lauderdale College, Virginia Judson Memorial Library, Fort Lauderdale FL. 305-462-3761, Ext 51

Weiss, Betty, *Librn,* Washington University Libraries (Earth & Planetary Science), Saint Louis MO. 314-889-5406

Weiss, Betty Page, *Media,* Rappahannock Community College, North Campus Learning Resource Center, Warsaw VA. 804-333-4024, Ext 208, 209

Weiss, Bruce, *Librn,* Beth David Reform Congregation, Jewel K Markowitz Library, Philadelphia PA. 215-913-3438

Weiss, Carole, *Ref,* University of Toronto Libraries (University Library), Toronto ON. 416-978-2294

Weiss, Cynthia, *Consulting Servs Dir,* Rolling Prairie Library System, Decatur IL. 217-429-2586

Weiss, David, *Law,* University of Florida Libraries (Legal Information Center), Gainesville FL. 904-392-0417

Weiss, Dianne, *Librn,* Saint Clare's Hospital & Health Center, Medical Library, New York NY. 212-586-1500, Ext 294

Weiss, Egon A, *Dir,* United States Military Academy Library, West Point NY. 914-938-2230

Weiss, Glenda, *Ch,* Bettendorf Public Library & Information Center, Bettendorf IA. 319-359-4427

Weiss, Henry A, *Dir,* Palm Springs Public Library, Palm Springs CA. 714-323-8291

Weiss, Jack, *Dir,* Elgin Community College, Renner Learning Resources Center, Elgin IL. 312-697-1000, Ext 258

Weiss, Lynn, *Asst Supvr,* Waterloo Regional Library (New Dundee), New Dundee ON. 519-696-3041

Weiss, Marcia, *Librn,* American Cyanamid Co, Sholton Incorporated Research & Development Library, Clifton NJ. 201-365-6000

Weiss, Marianne, *Ad,* Louis Bay Library, Hawthorne NJ. 201-427-5745

Weiss, Melanie, *Program,* North Babylon Public Library, North Babylon NY. 516-669-4020

Weiss, Paula, *Ad,* Pekin Public Library, Pekin IL. 309-347-7111

Weiss, Richard A, *Spec Coll,* Kentucky Wesleyan College, Library Learning Center, Owensboro KY. 502-926-3111, Ext 113, 117

Weiss, Roberta, *Ad,* W E Walter Memorial Library, Bremen Public Library, Bremen IN. 219-546-2849

Weiss, Sarah, *Acq,* Yeshiva University Libraries (Hedi Steinberg Library), New York NY. 212-481-0570

Weiss, Stanley, *In Charge,* Interboro General Hospital, Alyn M Steinhardt Memorial Library, Brooklyn NY. 212-277-5100

Weiss, Susan, *Supvr,* E-Systems, Inc-ECI Division, Technical Information Center, Saint Petersburg FL. 813-381-2000, Ext 2182

Weiss, Susan, *Bibliog Instr,* Florida International University, North Miami Campus Library, North Miami FL. 305-940-5730

Weiss, Susan, *Ref,* Hofstra University Library, Hempstead NY. 516-560-3475

Weiss, Virginia, *Librn,* Licking County Law Library Association, Newark OH. 614-345-6400

Weiss, Virginia, *Acq,* Monroe County Library System, Monroe MI. 313-241-5277

Weiss, William, *Cat,* Russell Sage College, James Wheelock Clark Library, Troy NY. 518-270-2249

Weiss, Wynne, *Bkmobile Coordr,* Des Plaines Public Library, Des Plaines IL. 312-827-5551

Weissbord, E Ramona, *Senior Librn,* New York State Department of Labor Research Library, Albany NY. 518-451-2741

Weisser, Margaret S, *Librn,* Geneseo Township Public Library, Geneseo IL. 309-944-2643

Weissman, Aaron, *Asst Dir,* Bowdoin College Library, Brunswick ME. 207-725-8731, Ext 281

Weissman, Dorothea Y, *Librn,* Rockefeller Family & Associates Inc, Office Library, New York NY. 212-247-3700, Ext 606, 607

Weissman, Elaine, *Tech Serv,* Free Public Library of Roselle Park, Veterans Memorial Library, Roselle Park NJ. 201-245-2456, 245-7171

Weissman, Sue, *Dir,* Captain John Curtis Memorial Library, Brunswick Public Library, Brunswick ME. 207-725-5242

Weissmann, Steven L, *Asst Librn & Ref,* Port Authority of New York & New Jersey Library, New York NY. 212-466-4067, 4068

Weitkemper, Harry, *Chief Librn,* Veterans Administration Medical Center, Library Service, Dallas TX. 214-376-5451, Ext 214

Weitkemper, Larry, *President,* Central Indiana Health Science Libraries Consortium, IN. 317-365-7401

Weitting, June, *Ref,* Wheaton College Library, Wheaton IL. 312-682-5101

Weitz, Jay, *Rare Bks,* Capital University Library, Columbus OH. 614-236-6718

Weitzel, Thomas R, *Librn,* Dayton & Montgomery County Public Library (East), Dayton OH. 513-224-1651, Ext 260

Weitzel, Thomas R, *Librn,* Dayton & Montgomery County Public Library (Electra C Doren), Dayton OH. 513-224-1651, Ext 270

Weixel, Kathleen, *Librn,* Rose, Schmidt, Dixon, Hasley, Whyte & Hardesty, Law Library, Pittsburgh PA. 412-434-8649

Welburn, William, *Actg Librn,* Indiana University at Bloomington (Journalism), Bloomington IN. 812-337-3517

Welch, Anne, *Librn,* Savannah News-Press Library, Savannah GA. 912-236-9511

Welch, Carolyn J, *Librn,* Knoll Pharmaceutical Co, Research Library, Whippany NJ. 201-887-8300, Ext 168

Welch, Cynthia, *ILL,* University of Wisconsin-Stout, Pierce Library, Menomonie WI. 715-232-1184

Welch, Dale, *Librn,* Patrick Henry State Junior College, John Dennis Forte Library, Monroeville AL. 205-575-3156, Ext 27

Welch, Doreen, *Govt Doc,* Angelo State University, Porter Henderson Library, San Angelo TX. 915-942-2222

Welch, Eleonore, *Cat,* Ringling School of Art Library, Sarasota FL. 813-355-1232

Welch, Elizabeth, *Ch,* Spokane County Library, Spokane WA. 509-924-4122

Welch, Eric C, *Ref, On-Line Servs & Bibliog Instr,* University of Illinois, Woodruff L Crawford Branch Library of Health Sciences, Rockford IL. 815-987-7382

Welch, Gary, *Ad & Media,* Jennings County Public Library, North Vernon IN. 812-346-2091

Welch, Grace M, *Dir,* Poynette Public Library, Poynette WI. 608-635-2269

Welch, Ingrid, *Tech Serv,* San Antonio College Library, San Antonio TX. 512-734-7311, Ext 2480

Welch, Janet L, *Dir,* Clinton Township Public Library, Clinton MI. 517-456-4192

Welch, Janet M, *Dir,* Rochester Regional Research Library Council, (RRRLC), NY. 716-232-7930

Welch, Jeanie M, *Asst Dir & ILL,* American Graduate School of International Management, Barton Kyle Yount Memorial Library, Glendale AZ. 602-978-7232

Welch, Jeanne, *ILL,* Saint Anselm's College, Geisel Library, Manchester NH. 603-669-1030, Ext 240, 249

Welch, Jim, *Syst Programmer,* Metropolitan Library System, Oklahoma City OK. 405-235-0571

Welch, Jimmie L, *Librn,* Chickasha Public Library, Chickasha OK. 405-224-5424

Welch, John, *Asst Dir,* Chatham-Effingham-Liberty Regional Library, Savannah Public Library, Savannah GA. 912-234-5127

Welch, John D, *ILL & Ref,* Virginia Western Community College, Brown Library, Roanoke VA. 703-982-7303

Welch, Liz, *Librn,* Van Horn City-County Library, Van Horn TX. 915-283-2855

Welch, M, *Ref,* University of Western Ontario (Law Library), London ON. 519-679-2857

Welch, Marian, *Librn,* Lower Gilmanton Library, Gilmanton NH. 603-435-8882

Welch, Marty, *Media,* Pocatello Public Library, Information and Video Center, Pocatello ID. 208-232-1263

Welch, Mrs Louis, *Librn,* Bales Memorial Library, Jefferson City TN. 615-475-9094

Welch, Sharon, *In Charge,* Texas Education Agency (Region XVIII), Midland TX. 915-563-2380

Welch, Steven, *Inst Serv Coordr,* Bur Oak Library System, Shorewood IL. 815-729-3345, 729-3346

Welch, Sue, *Cat,* College of William & Mary in Virginia (Marshall-Wythe Law Library), Williamsburg VA. 804-253-4680

Welch, Sue C, *Librn,* Schenectady Museum Library, Schenectady NY. 518-382-7890

Welch, Theodore F, *Develop,* Northwestern University Library, Evanston IL. 312-492-7658

Welch, Thomas Larry, *Chief Librn,* Organization of American States, Columbus Memorial Library, Washington DC. 789-6040; 789-6041

Welch, Walter L, *Dir-Thomas Alva Edison Re-recording Laboratory,* Syracuse University Libraries, Ernest S Bird Library, Syracuse NY. 315-423-2575

Welchance, Joyce, *Per & Bibliog Instr,* Northeast Missouri State University, Pickler Memorial Library, Kirksville MO. 816-665-5121, Ext 7186

Welchert, Mary, *Acq,* Yankton College, James M Lloyd Library, Yankton SD. 605-665-4662

Welchman, J Nicholas, *Ref,* Eastern Connecticut State College, J Eugene Smith Library, Willimantic CT. 203-456-2231, Ext 374, 422

Weldon, Janice A, *Ch,* Allegany County Library, Cumberland MD. 301-777-1200

Weldon, Stephanie, *Actg Librn,* New York State Library (Law-Social Sciences Reference Service), Albany NY. 518-474-5957

Weliever, Emma Lou, *Librn,* Darlington Public Library, Darlington IN. 312-794-4813

Welk, Judy, *Librn,* McLean-Mercer Regional Library, Riverdale ND. 701-654-7652

Welk, Leann, *Librn,* Sayre Junior College Library, Sayre OK. 405-928-5533

Welker, Betty E, *Ref,* Port Authority of New York & New Jersey Library, New York NY. 212-466-4067, 4068

Welker, Kathy J, *Asst Dir,* Indiana University (School of Law Library), Indianapolis IN. 317-264-4028

Welker, Mary, *Media,* Greensboro Public Library, Greensboro NC. 373-2474; 373-2471

Well, Maureen D, *In Charge,* Connecticut State Library (Law Library), Hartford CT. 203-566-4301

Welland, Marilyn, *Br Coordr,* Dartmouth Regional Library, Dartmouth NS. 902-466-7623

Welland, Marilyn, *In Charge,* Dartmouth Regional Library (Woodlawn Branch), Dartmouth NS. 902-434-6196

Wellborn, Cecil, *Libr Sci,* University of Arizona Library, Tucson AZ. 602-626-2101

Wellborn, Cecil, *Librn,* University of Arizona Library (Library Science Collection), Tucson AZ. 602-626-3383

Welle, Jacob, *Asst Librn,* Allentown College of Saint Francis De Sales Library, Center Valley PA. 215-282-1100, Ext 266

Weller, Bev, *Librn,* Dinsmore, Shohl, Coates & Deupree Library, Cincinnati OH. 513-621-6747

Weller, Elizabeth, *Prof,* Indiana State University, Dept of Library Science, IN. 812-232-6311, Ext 2834

Weller, Marian L, *Asst Librn,* Granby Free Public Library, Granby MA. 413-467-3320

Weller, Verna A, *Librn,* Mount Carmel Lutheran Church Library, Milwaukee WI. 414-771-1270

Weller, Jr, Russell E, *In Charge,* Office of the Attorney General, Law Library, Agana PI. 472-6841

Welles, A L, *Curator,* Learning Inc Library, Manset-Seawall ME. 207-244-5015

Wellings, Virginia M, *Circ,* Darien Library, Inc, Darien CT. 203-655-2568

Wellington, Flora H, *Tech Serv,* University of Miami (Louis Calder Memorial Library), Miami FL. 305-547-6441

Wellington, Jean, *Head,* University of Cincinnati Libraries (Classics), Cincinnati OH. 513-475-6724

Wellins, Cindi, *Admin Asst,* North Bergen Federation, Ridgewood NJ. 201-445-0848

Wellisch, Hans, *Assoc Prof,* University of Maryland, College of Library & Information Services, MD. 301-454-5441

Wellnitz, Bertha, *Librn,* McLaughlin Gormley King Co Library, Minneapolis MN. 612-544-0341

Wells, A, *On-Line Servs,* Lee Pharmaceuticals Library, South El Monte CA. 213-442-3141

Wells, Anne R, *Circ & Spec Coll,* Brevard Community College, Learning Resources Center, Cocoa FL. 305-632-1111, Ext 295, 298

Wells, Benita, *Librn,* Mallard Public Library, Mallard IA. 712-425-3527

Wells, Betty M, *Ch,* Marlboro County Library, Bennettsville SC. 803-479-6201

Wells, Carolyn, *Librn,* Environmental Systems Corp Library, Knoxville TN. 615-637-4741

Wells, Cathey, *Br Coordr,* Craighead County & Jonesboro Public Library, Jonesboro AR. 501-935-5133

Wells, Cathey, *Br Coordr,* Crowley Ridge Regional Library, Jonesboro AR. 501-935-5133

Wells, Christine, *In Charge,* State Journal Library, Lansing MI. 517-487-4608

Wells, Clare, *Librn,* First Church of Christian Scientist, Reading Room Library, Honolulu HI. 808-949-1421

Wells, Doris, *Commun Servs,* Dekalb Library System, Maud M Burrus Library, Decatur GA. 404-378-7569

Wells, Eileen, *Librn,* Fresno County Free Library (Sunnyside), Fresno CA. 209-255-6594

Wells, Elgin A, *Librn,* Elgin County Public Library, Saint Thomas ON. 519-633-0815

Wells, H Lea, *Personnel,* University of Tennessee, Knoxville, James D Hoskins Library, Knoxville TN. 615-974-0111

Wells, Harold F, *Dir,* California State Polytechnic University Library, Pomona CA. 714-598-4671

Wells, Jack C, *Indian,* University of Wisconsin-Madison, Memorial Library, Madison WI. 608-262-3521

Wells, James L, *Dir,* Washington County Library, Lake Elmo MN. 612-777-8143

Wells, James M, *Vice President,* Newberry Library, Chicago IL. 312-943-9090

Wells, Jane B, *Dir,* University Hospital, Medical Library, Augusta GA. 404-722-9011, Ext 2329, 2335

Wells, Joy, *Librn,* Oconee Regional Library (Wheeler County), Alamo GA. 912-568-3231

Wells, Joyce A, *Dir,* Nekoosa Public Library, Nekoosa WI. 715-886-3109

Wells, Judy, *Head,* University of Minnesota Libraries-Twin Cities (INFORM), Minneapolis MN. 612-373-5938

Wells, Judy, *Librn,* University of Minnesota Libraries-Twin Cities (Business Reference Service), Minneapolis MN. 612-373-4109

Wells, L Ada, *Dir,* Napoleon Public Library, Napoleon OH. 419-592-2531

Wells, L Ada, *Librn,* Napoleon Public Library (McClure Community), McClure OH. 419-592-2531

Wells, Leah, *Librn,* West Burke Library, West Burke VT. 802-467-3022

Wells, Lois E, *Librn,* Jacksonville Mental Health & Development Center, Resident Library, Jacksonville IL. 217-245-2111, Ext 373

Wells, Lou, *Cat,* Greenwood-Leflore Public Library System, Greenwood MS. 601-453-3634

Wells, M Paula Armstrong, *Dir,* Lamar Community College, Learning Resources Center, Lamar CO. 303-336-2733

Wells, Marianna, *Head,* University of Cincinnati Libraries (Physics), Cincinnati OH. 513-475-2331

Wells, Marihelen, *Librn,* Lordsburg-Hidalgo Library, Lordsburg NM. 505-542-9646

Wells, Mary Lou, *Mgr,* Richardson-Merrell Inc, Vick Chemical Co Div Library, Wilton CT. 203-762-2222

Wells, Merle, *Librn,* Idaho State Historical Society Libraries (Historical Library), Boise ID. 208-334-3356

Wells, Mrs Hans, *In Charge,* First Baptist Church Library, McAllen TX. 512-686-7418

Wells, Mrs V G, *Librn,* Thomas Wilhite Memorial Library, Perkins OK. 405-547-2509

Wells, Nancy, *Ch,* Alexander Mitchell Library, Aberdeen Public Library, Aberdeen SD. 605-225-4186

Wells, R, *Dir,* Davenport Library, Bath NY. 607-776-4613

Wells, Rhuenella, *ILL, Ad & Ref,* Paterson Free Public Library, Danforth Memorial Library, Paterson NJ. 201-881-3770

Wells, Richard, *Librn,* Randolph Technical Institute, Learning Resources Center, Asheboro NC. 919-629-1471, Ext 27

Wells, Ruth E, *Librn,* Toledo Public Library, Toledo IA. 515-484-4362

Wells, Shirley, *Librn,* Armour Pharmaceutical Co, Technical Division Library, Kankakee IL. 815-932-6771

Wells, Stewart, *Asst Dir,* East Chicago Public Library, East Chicago IN. 219-397-2453

Wells, Susan Conrad, *Tech Serv & Cat,* Western New England College (Law Library), Springfield MA. 413-782-3111, Ext 454, 455

Wells, Suzanne M, *Librn,* Devry Institute of Technology Library, Chicago IL. 312-929-8500, Ext 272

Wells, Vicki, *Librn,* Tangipahoa Parish Library (Ponchatoula Branch), Ponchatoula LA. 504-386-6554

Wells, William, *CEF,* University of Virginia (Law Library), Charlottesville VA. 804-924-3384

Wells, Wilma, *Acq,* Grand Canyon College, Fleming Library, Phoenix AZ. 602-249-3300, Ext 207

Welmaker, Roland B, *Branches,* Atlanta Public Library, Atlanta GA. 404-688-4636

Welsch, Erwin, *Soc Studies,* University of Wisconsin-Madison, Memorial Library, Madison WI. 608-262-3521

Welsch, Lynn, *Asst Dir,* Fennville District Library, Fennville Area Public Library, Fennville MI. 616-561-5050

Welsch, Mrs Clyde, *Librn,* Williams Public Library, Williams IA. 515-854-2488

Welsh, Donna, *Librn,* Interstudy Library, Excelsior MN. 612-474-1176

Welsh, Ellen F, *Librn,* Skidompha Library, Damariscotta ME. 207-563-5513

Welsh, Eric, *Ref,* Dade County Law Library, Miami FL. 305-579-5422

Welsh, Harry E, *Dir,* South Dakota School of Mines & Technology, Devereaux Library, Rapid City SD. 605-394-2418

Welsh, Jim, *Librn,* Seattle Public Library (Northwest Region), Seattle WA. 206-625-2665

Welsh, William J, *Deputy Librn of Congress,* Library of Congress, Washington DC. 202-287-5000

Welshhans, Janice B, *Librn,* King & Spalding, Law Library, Washington DC. 202-466-7640

Welshhans, Janice B, *Librn,* King & Spalding Law Library, Atlanta GA. 404-572-4808

Welt, Mary, *Asst Dir,* Lena Community District Library, Lena IL. 815-369-4211

Weltsch, Patricia, *Doc,* Smithtown Library, Smithtown NY. 516-265-2072

Welty, D, *Librn,* Prescott Public-Yavapai County Library System (Mayer Public), Mayer AZ. 602-445-8110

Welwood, Frances J, *Librn,* British Columbia Law Library Foundation, Nelson Branch Library, Nelson BC. 604-352-2211, Ext 200

Welwood, Ronald J, *Dir,* David Thompson University Centre, Nelson BC. 604-352-2241, Ext 29

Welykochy, Donna, *Librn,* Saskatoon Mental Health Centre Library, Saskatoon SK. 306-664-6500

Wember, Bertha, *Librn,* Temple Israel Library, Detroit MI. 313-863-7769

Wember, Lawrence, *Dir,* Oak Park Public Library, Oak Park MI. 313-548-7230

Wemett, Lisa, *Librn,* Fairport Public Library, Fairport NY. 716-223-9091

Wende, Frances, *Circ,* Lewisville Public Library, Lewisville TX. 214-436-1812

Wender, Ruth W, *Extension Serv,* University of Oklahoma Health Sciences Center Library, Oklahoma City OK. 405-271-2285

Wenderoth, Leota E, *Librn,* H A Peine Memorial Library, Minier IL. 309-392-3220

Wendling, Corlice, *ILL,* Santa Barbara Public Library, Santa Barbara CA. 805-962-7653

Wendling, Phyllis J, *Actg Librn,* Walton-Tipton Township Public Library, Walton IN. 219-626-2234

Wendt, Kris Adams, *Ch,* Rhinelander Public Library, Rhinelander WI. 715-369-1070

Wendt, Lillian, *Librn,* Modesto Bee Library, Editorial Library, Modesto CA. 209-524-4041, Ext 565

Wendtland, Frances, *Coordr & Bkmobile Coordr,* Sheboygan County Federated Library System, Sheboygan WI. 414-459-3412

Wengel, Linda, *Librn,* Emergency Care Research Institute Library, Plymouth Meeting PA. 215-825-6000, Ext 192

Wenger, Anne J, *Asst Dir,* Bexley Public Library, Columbus OH. 614-231-2784

Wenger, Charles B, *Chief Librn,* National Center for Atmospheric Research (Mesa Library), Boulder CO. 303-494-5151, Ext 428

Wenger, Larry B, *Dir,* University of Virginia (Law Library), Charlottesville VA. 804-924-3384

Wenger, M B, *Dir,* Chem Systems, Inc, Information Center, New York NY. 212-421-9460

Wenger, Margaret H, *Librn,* Second English Lutheran Church Library, Baltimore MD. 301-945-2350

Wenger, Martin, *Circ,* Mesa College, Learning Resource Services, Lowell Heiny Library, Grand Junction CO. 303-248-1436

Weniger, Reva, *Librn,* Kingman Carnegie Public Library, Kingman KS. 316-532-3061

Wenneis, Jane, *Acq,* Fairleigh Dickinson University, Friendship Library, Madison NJ. 201-377-4700, Ext 234

Wennrich, Susan, *Commun Servs,* Bangor Public Library, Bangor ME. 207-947-8336

Wente, Joyce, *Librn,* Broward County Division of Libraries (Fort Lauderdale), Coral Springs FL. 305-752-4080

Wente, Norman, *Dir,* Consortium of Minnesota Seminary Libraries, MN. 612-641-3224

Wente, Norman G, *Dir,* Luther-Northwestern Seminary Library, Saint Paul MN. 612-641-3225

Wentworth, Ann Marie, *Librn,* San Bernardino County Library (Hesperia Branch), Hesperia CA. 714-244-4898

Wentworth, Jennifer, *Librn,* Polar Gas Project Library, Toronto ON. 416-869-2675

Wentworth, Margaret, *Asst Librn & Ch,* Auburn Public Library, Auburn ME. 207-782-3191

Wentworth, Jr, Don, *Bkmobile Coordr,* South Brunswick Public Library, Monmouth Junction NJ. 201-821-8224, 821-8225

Wentz, Charlotte, *Dir,* Southwestern Michigan College, Fred L Mathews Library, Dowagiac MI. 616-782-5113, Ext 27

Wentz, Frances, *Doc,* Catawba College, Corriher-Linn-Black Library, Salisbury NC. 704-637-4448, 637-4449

Wentzel, Barbara, *Dir,* Kimberly Public Library, Kimberly WI. 414-788-2906

Wentzell, Catherine, *Ch,* Bedford Public Library, Bedford IN. 812-275-4471

Wentzell, Judy, *Fine Arts,* Portland Public Library, Baxter Library, Portland ME. 207-773-4761

Wenz, Robert E, *Tech Serv,* Floyd Junior College Library, Rome GA. 404-295-6318

Wenzel, Betty, *Dir,* Hartford Public Library, Hartford WI. 414-673-3750

Wenzel, Glee, *Dir,* Santa Fe Public Library, Santa Fe NM. 505-982-4471

Wenzl, Sister Mary Louise, *Clerk,* Saint Francis Hospital, Medical Library, Colorado Springs CO. 303-473-6830, Ext 508

Werbel, Cherie Sherman, *In Charge,* Letchworth Village Developmental Center, Isaac N Wolfson Library, Thiells NY. 914-947-1000, Ext 517

Werich, Georgia, *Librn,* Mount Sinai Hospital Medical Center (I J Goldberg School of Nursing), Chicago IL. 312-542-2561

Werk, William R, *Chief Librn,* United States Army (ERADCOM Technical Library), Fort Monmouth NJ. 201-544-4231

Werking, Melvin W, *AV,* Colorado Mountain College-West Campus, Learning Center, Glenwood Springs CO. 303-945-7481, Ext 66

Werking, Richard, *Asst Dir,* University of Mississippi Library, University MS. 601-232-7091

Werle, Carolyn, *Librn,* Papeterie Reed Ltd, Technical Library, Quebec PQ. 418-694-7802

Wermcrantz, Sally, *ILL,* Lincoln Trail Libraries System, Champaign IL. 217-352-0047

Wermuth, Barbara, *AV,* Swampscott Public Library, Swampscott MA. 617-593-8380

Werner, Betty, *Librn,* Cozad Public Library, Cozad NE. 308-784-2019

Werner, Doris, *Asst Administrator,* Standard Oil Co (Indiana), Amoco Production Co, Exploration Library, Houston TX. 713-652-5222

Werner, Dorothy, *Librn,* Anderson County Library (Jennie Erwin), Honea Path SC. 803-369-7751

Werner, Elizabeth, *Librn,* Clearwater Christian College Library, Clearwater FL. 813-726-1153, Ext 20

Werner, Gloria, *Dir,* Pacific Southwest Regional Medical Library Service, CA. 213-825-1200

Werner, Gloria, *Librn,* University of California Los Angeles Library (Biomedical), Los Angeles CA. 213-825-5781

Werner, Hedy L, *Librn,* Cuyahoga County Public Library (Parma Heights Branch), Parma Heights OH. 216-884-2313

Werner, JoAnne, *Cat,* Mohawk Valley Community College Library, Utica NY. 315-792-5337

Werner, Joyce C, *Ref & Bibliog Instr,* University of South Carolina, Thomas Cooper Library, Columbia SC. 803-777-3142

Werner, Judy, *Cat,* Mason City Public Library, Mason City IA. 515-423-7552

Werner, Lawrence, *Librn,* Honeywell Inc, Defense Systems Div Engineering Library, Hopkins MN. 612-931-6603

Werner, O James, *Librn,* San Diego County Law Library, San Diego CA. 714-236-2231

Werner, O James, *President of Board of Directors,* San Diego Greater Metropolitan Area Library & Information Agency Council, (SD METRO), CA. 714-236-2234

Werner, Rosemary, *Acq,* New College of the University of South Florida, Sarasota Campus Library, Sarasota FL. 813-355-7671, Ext 214

Werner, Sally, *Librn,* Ecology Information Center, Sacramento CA. 916-444-3174

Werner, Sister Mary Dionette, *Lectr,* Felician College, Dept of Library Science, IL. 312-539-2328

Werner, Stuart, *Tech Info Specialist,* United States Department of Commerce, New York District Office Library, New York NY. 212-264-0630

Werner, W, *Asst Librn,* Carpenter Technology Corp Research & Development Center Library, Reading PA. 215-372-4511, Ext 695, 583

Wersching, Yolande, *Soc Work & Educ,* Loyola University of Chicago Libraries (Julia Deal Lewis Library), Chicago IL. 312-670-2875

Wert, Alice, *Tech Serv,* Vigo County Public Library, Terre Haute IN. 812-232-1113

Wert, Lucille, *Librn,* University of Illinois Library at Urbana-Champaign (Chemistry), Urbana IL. 217-333-3737

Wertenbaker, Adelle, *Actg Librn,* Warren County Library (Catherine Dickson Hofman), Blairstown NJ. 201-362-8376

Wertenbaker, Jr, Mrs Thomas J, *Actg Librn,* Catherine Dickson Hofman Library, Blairstown NJ. 201-362-8376

Wery, Madeline, *Ref,* Sacred Heart College, McCarthy Library, Belmont NC. 704-825-5146

Wescoat, Bonna B, *In Charge,* Beaumont Art Museum Library, Beaumont TX. 713-832-3432

Wescott, Eloise, *Librn,* Norway Memorial Library, Norway ME. 207-743-5145

Wescott, Eula, *Librn,* Arlington Public Library, Arlington IA. 319-633-3475

Wescott, Karen, *Librn,* Equitable Life Assurance Society of the United States (Investments Library), New York NY. 212-554-1234

Weseloh, Todd S, *Librn,* Canal Museum Research Library, Syracuse NY. 315-471-0593

Weselteer, Ruth, *Librn,* Lebhar-Friedman Inc Library, New York NY. 212-371-9400

Wesley, Dianna L, *Librn,* Northville Regional Psychiatric Hospital, Professional Library, Northville MI. 313-349-1800, Ext 209

Wesley, Emmalyn F, *Acq,* Fayetteville State University, Charles W Chesnutt Library, Fayetteville NC. 919-486-1232

Wesley, Kathryn Rice, *Librn,* Wadsworth Library, Geneseo NY. 716-243-0440

Wesley, Nancy M, *Librn,* Children's Hospital, Pediatric Library, Saint Paul MN. 612-298-8831

Wesley, Phillip, *Dean,* California State University Dominguez Hills, Educational Resources Center, Carson CA. 213-515-3700

Wesley, Scott, *Tech Serv,* Mesa College, Learning Resource Services, Lowell Heiny Library, Grand Junction CO. 303-248-1436

Wesling, Angela, *Librn,* San Francisco Psychoanalytic Institute Library, San Francisco CA. 415-563-5815

Wessel, Janet, *Tech Serv,* Contra Costa County Library, Pleasant Hill CA. 415-944-3423

Wessel, Joyce, *Librn & Cat,* Watertown Free Public Library, Watertown WI. 414-261-5757

Wessell, Carolyn Moyer, *Ad,* Randolph Township Free Public Library, Randolph NJ. 201-366-0518

Wessell, Laura, *Ad & Ref,* Sandusky Library Association, Sandusky OH. 419-625-3834

Wessells, Robert S, *Asst Librn,* United States Navy (Naval Education & Training Center), Newport RI. 401-841-3044, 841-4352

Wessels, Margaret, *Librn,* Somonauk Public Library, Somonauk IL. 815-498-2440

Wessels, Margie, *Asst Librn,* Northwest General Hospital, Health Science Library, Milwaukee WI. 414-447-8599, 447-8600

Wessels, Nina, *Librn,* Mulvane Public Library, Mulvane KS. 316-777-1211

Wessler, Carol, *Ref, ILL & On-Line Servs,* Wisconsin Valley Library Service, System Headquarters, Wausau WI. 715-845-7214, Ext 35

Wessling, Catholeen, *Librn,* Wall Lake Public Library, Wall Lake IA. 712-664-2983

Wessling, Julie, *ILL,* Colorado State University, William E Morgan Library, Fort Collins CO. 303-491-5911

Wessling, Mary, *Asst Dir,* Falmouth Public Library, Subregional Headquarters for Eastern Massachusetts Regional System, Falmouth MA. 617-548-0280

Wesson, Ruby, *Librn,* Assemblies of God Graduate School Library, Cordas C Burnett Library, Springfield MO. 417-862-2781, Ext 5505

West, Barbara, *Dir,* Anchor Foundation, Library of Social History, New York NY. 212-255-1767

West, Barbara, *Librn,* Harden Memorial Library, Hamlin TX. 915-576-3763

West, Barbara, *Info Serv,* Prairie Trails Public Library District, Burbank IL. 312-430-3688

West, Barbara, *Librn,* Stanly County Public Library (Badin), Badin NC. 704-422-3218

West, Barbara A, *Cat,* Northern Illinois University, College Law Library, Glen Ellyn IL. 312-858-7200

West, Betty, *Librn,* Birmingham Public & Jefferson County Free Library (Wylam Branch), Birmingham AL. 205-254-2551

West, Carol, *Dir,* Mississippi College (Law Library), Clinton MS. 601-924-5131, Ext 280

West, Carol, *ILL,* New Hampshire College, Shapiro Library, Manchester NH. 603-668-2211, Ext 211

West, Colleen, *Librn,* Bettsville Public Library, Bettsville OH. 419-986-5198

West, David J, *Dir,* Cumberland County Library, Bridgeton NJ. 609-455-0080

West, Dona, *Librn,* U-Haul International Library and Research Services, Phoenix AZ. 602-263-6606

West, Eleanora F, *Curator,* Library of the Fitchburg Historical Society, Fitchburg MA. 617-345-1157

West, Esther, *Dir,* Marion Public Library, Marion WI. 715-754-5368

West, Frances, *Librn,* East Mississippi Regional Library (Quitman Public), Quitman MS. 601-776-2492

West, Gwen, *Librn,* Iberia Parish Public Library (Morton), New Iberia LA. 318-364-7355

West, James, *Librn,* Mid-Continent Public Library (South Independence Branch), Independence MO. 816-461-2050

West, Janice, *Librn,* Minburn Public Library, Minburn IA. 515-677-2340

West, Jo Anne, *Librn,* Jackson-George Regional Library System (Kathleen McIlwain Public), Goutier MS. 601-497-4531

West, Joyce M, *Outreach,* Richard H Thornton Library, Oxford NC. 919-693-1121

West, Judith, *Pub Servs,* Stanislaus County Free Library, Modesto CA. 209-526-6821

West, L Clinton, *Dir,* United States International University, Walter Library, San Diego CA. 714-271-4300

West, Leah, *Ad,* Grand Prairie Memorial Library, Grand Prairie TX. 214-264-1571

West, Louise, *Bus,* Texas Southern University Library, Houston TX. 713-527-7121

West, Lynne, *Br Coordr,* Western Counties Regional Library, Yarmouth NS. 902-742-2486

West, Lynne, *Librn,* Western Counties Regional Library (Yarmouth Branch), Yarmouth NS. 902-742-5040

West, Mabel, *On-Line Servs & Bibliog Instr,* Fermi National Accelerator Laboratory Library, Batavia IL. 312-840-3401

West, Margaret, *Dir,* Andalusia Public Library, Andalusia AL. 205-222-6612

West, Marion, *ILL,* Milton Public Library, Milton MA. 617-698-5707

West, Mary Ellen, *In Charge,* Ohio Historical Society Library, Columbus OH. 614-466-1500, Ext 326

West, Sharon M, *Cat,* University of Alaska, Fairbanks, Elmer E Rasmuson Library, Fairbanks AK. 907-479-7224

West, Shirley, *Coordr Libr Servs,* Camden Free Public Library, Camden NJ. 609-963-4807

West, Suzanne, *Extention Serv,* New Rochelle Public Library, New Rochelle NY. 914-632-7878

West, Suzanne, *Librn,* New Rochelle Public Library (Columbus), New Rochelle NY. 914-632-5136

West, Wanda, *Librn,* New Mexico School for the Visually Handicapped, Alamogordo NM. 505-437-3505, Ext 50

West, Wilfred L, *Tech Serv,* Jefferson County Public Library, Lakewood CO. 303-238-8411

West, Jr, Rayford L, *Librn,* Palmyra Public Library, Palmyra MO. 314-769-2830

Westall, John, *Tech Serv,* Illinois Wesleyan University Library, Bloomington IL. 309-556-3172

Westbrook, Betty Sue, *Cat,* University of North Carolina at Wilmington, William Madison Randall Library, Wilmington NC. 919-791-4330, Ext 2270

Westbrook, Donna, *Tech Serv,* Weatherford Public Library, Weatherford TX. 817-594-2767

Westbrook, Mrs Warren G, *Librn,* Menard Public Library, Menard TX. 915-396-2473

Westbrook, Patricia C, *Librn,* Meriden-Wallingford Hospital, Health Sciences Library, Meriden CT. 203-238-0771, Ext 342

Westbrooks, Allegra M, *Asst Dir (Branch),* Public Library of Charlotte & Mecklenburg County, Inc, Charlotte NC. 704-374-2725

Westburg, Alma, *Media,* Santa Cruz Public Library, Santa Cruz CA. 408-429-3533

Westby, Barbara M, *Chief, Cat Mgt Div,* Library of Congress, Washington DC. 202-287-5000

Westby, Gerald, *Assoc Prof,* Saint Cloud State University, Center for Library & Audiovisual Education, MN. 612-255-2022

Westcott, Mary, *Instr,* Southern Alberta Institute of Technology, Library Arts Program, AB. 403-284-8328

Westendorf, Vicki, *Librn,* Cass County Public Library (Harrisonville Branch), Harrisonville MO. 816-884-3483

Wester, Karen, *Librn,* Distilled Spirits Council of the United States Library, Washington DC. 202-628-3544

Wester, Martha, *Asst Librn,* North Haledon Free Public Library, North Haledon NJ. 201-427-6213

Wester, Wilma, *Dir,* Hutchinson County Library, Borger TX. 806-274-6221

Wester-House, Mary, *Librn,* Tennessee Department of Public Health, MCH-HWP Resource Center, Nashville TN. 615-741-7276

Westergard, Jackie, *YA,* Weber County Library, Ogden UT. 801-399-8516

Westergard, Marjorie, *Librn,* Wisconsin Department of Public Instruction (Dept of Public Instruction Library), Madison WI. 608-266-2529

Westerhaus, Martin O, *Dir,* Wisconsin Lutheran Seminary Library, Mequon WI. 414-242-2331

Westerman, Melvin E, *Bus & Econ,* Pennsylvania State University, Fred Lewis Pattee Library, University Park PA. 814-865-0401

Westerman, Susan, *Asst Dir & Ref,* Concordia College, Scheele Memorial Library, Bronxville NY. 914-337-9300, Ext 138

Westermann, Mary L, *Librn,* Nassau Academy of Medicine, John N Shell Library, Garden City NY. 516-832-2320, 832-2321

Westermeyer, Carroll L, *Cat,* Loma Linda University, Vernier Radcliffe Memorial Library, Loma Linda CA. 714-796-7311, Ext 2916

Western, Gladys M, *Chief Librn & Ch,* Grimsby Public Library, Grimsby ON. 416-945-5142

Westervelt, Ann, *Librn,* B H Bartol Library, Freeport ME. 207-865-3307

Westervelt, Barbara, *Admin,* Rose Memorial Library Association, Stony Point NY. 914-786-2100

Westfall, Beverly, *Br Asst,* Timberland Regional Library (Westport Branch), Westport WA. 206-268-0521

Westfall, Edna Lucille, *Librn,* Hertzler Research Foundation Library, Halstead KS. 316-835-2662

Westfall, Elizabeth, *Librn,* Federal Home Loan Bank of San Francisco Library, San Francisco CA. 415-393-1000

Westfall, Susanne, *Dir,* University of Wisconsin Center-Sheboygan, Battig Memorial Library, Sheboygan WI. 414-459-3725

Westfall, Wendell, *Acq,* Orange Coast College Library, Costa Mesa CA. 714-556-5885

Westgate, Hazel, *Ch,* Iowa City Public Library, Iowa City IA. 319-354-1265

Westhuis, Judy, *Tech Serv,* Albany Law School Library, Albany NY. 518-445-2311, 445-2340

Westhuis, Mary, *Ch,* Schlow Memorial Library, State College PA. 814-237-6236

Westlake, Margaret W, *Monographs,* Vanderbilt University Medical Center Library, Nashville TN. 615-322-2292

Westley, Donna, *ILL,* Marquette University Memorial Library, Milwaukee WI. 414-224-7214

Westley, Donna, *Ref,* Marygrove College Library, Detroit MI. 313-862-8000

Westling, Ellen, *Info-Circ Servs,* Massachusetts General Hospital (Treadwell Library), Boston MA. 617-726-8600

Westmoreland, Sybil, *Librn,* Village Library, Wimberley TX. 512-847-2188

Westnedge, Jean, *Librn,* Atlanta Public Library (Ida Williams), Atlanta GA. 404-233-2108

Weston, Beverlee, *Librn,* Anchorage Municipal Libraries (Mountain View), Anchorage AK. 907-276-0543

Weston, Helen, *Librn,* Bureau of Land Management, Ely District Office Library, Ely NV. 702-289-4865

Weston, Janice C, *Chief Librn,* United States Army (Ordnance Center & School Library), Aberdeen Proving Ground MD. 301-278-4991, 5615

Weston, Katherine, *Librn,* Roddenbery Memorial Library (Oak Reading Center), Cairo GA. 912-377-4944

Weston, Maude, *Supvr,* Huron County Public Library (Bayfield Branch), Bayfield ON. 519-565-2886

Weston, Muriel, *Librn,* Canadian Nazarene College, Winnipeg MB. 204-269-2120

Weston, Priscilla, *Dir,* Mansfield Public Library, Temple NH. 603-878-3100

Weston, Ruby D, *Supvr,* Maryland State Department of Transportation, State Highway Administration Library, Baltimore MD. 301-383-4200

Westover, Jane, *Librn,* Bridgewater Public Library, Bridgewater VT. 802-672-5168

Westover, Pauline, *Clerk,* Mid-Columbia Regional Library (Benton City Branch), Benton City WA. 509-588-3916

Westover, Robert C, *Acq,* Portland State University, Branford Price Millar Library, Portland OR. 503-229-4424

Westra, Jane, *Circ,* Sussex County Library System, Sussex County Area Reference Library, Newton NJ. 201-948-3660

Westsbal, Gene, *Librn,* Triton College Library, River Grove IL. 312-456-0300

Westwood, Anita, *Librn,* Denver Public Library (Health & Hospitals, Denver General Hospital), Denver CO. 303-573-5152, Ext 271

Westwood, Anita F, *Librn,* Denver General Hospital Library, Denver CO. 303-893-6000

Wetherall, Robert S, *Asst Dir,* Cumberland County Library, Bridgeton NJ. 609-455-0080

Wetherby, Ivor, *Librn,* Miami Dade Community College (Medical Center Campus Library), Miami FL. 305-547-1256

Wetherell, Erla, *Chief Librn,* Orange County Public Library (San Juan Capistrano Branch), San Juan Capistrano CA. 714-493-1752

Wethey, Connee Chandler, *Librn,* Piedmont Hospital, Sauls Memorial Library, Atlanta GA. 404-355-7611, Ext 3305

Wetmore, Madelyn E, *Ch,* Weston Public Library, Weston MA. 617-893-3312

Wetmore, Maggie, *Ch,* Albany Public Library, Albany OR. 503-967-4304

Wetmore, Rosamond B, *Prof,* Ball State University, Dept of Library Science, IN. 317-285-7180, 285-7189

Wetterau, Charlotte, *Librn,* Fort Plain Free Library, Fort Plain NY. 518-993-4646

Wettig, Joan, *Asst Librn & Media,* Bellarmine College Library, Louisville KY. 502-452-8137

Wetton, Ellen E, *Librn,* Lantana Community Library, Lantana FL. 305-586-4320

Wetz, Marion, *Librn,* Syracuse Public Library, Syracuse NE. 402-269-2336

Wetzbarger, Cissy, *Bibliog Instr,* Central State University Library, Edmond OK. 405-341-2980, Ext 494, 495 & 496

Wetzel, Frank, *Dir,* Lincoln Educational Foundation Inc, Business History Library, New York NY. 212-697-2236

Wetzel, Mary, *Librn,* Tuscola Public Library, Tuscola IL. 217-253-3812

Wetzel, Mrs O, *Dir,* Rock Hill Public Library, Rock Hill MO. 314-962-4723

Wetzel, Norman P, *Dir,* Dover Public Library, Dover OH. 216-343-6123

Weum, Colleen M, *Coll Develop,* University of Washington Libraries (Health Sciences), Seattle WA. 206-543-5530

Wever, Susan M, *ILL & Ref,* Deer Park Public Library, Deer Park TX. 713-479-5276

Wewler, Johanna, *On-Line Servs,* Mount Royal College Library, Calgary AB. 403-246-6111

Wexler, Jack, *Law Librarian,* New York City Law Department, Corp Counsels Library, New York NY. 212-566-4418, 566-5772

Weyant, Nancy S, *ILL,* Bucknell University, Ellen Clarke Bertrand Library, Lewisburg PA. 717-524-3056

Weyh, Sue, *Tech Serv,* Sperry Corp, Sperry UNIVAC Div, Information Service Center, Roseville MN. 612-631-5386

Weyhrauch, Ernest E, *Dir,* Eastern Kentucky University, John Grant Crabbe Library, Richmond KY. 606-622-3606

Weymouth, Laura, *Libr Resources,* Lincoln City Libraries, Lincoln NE. 402-435-2146

Weyrick, Margaret A, *Bkmobile Coordr,* Ashland Public School District Library, Ashland OH. 419-289-8188

Wezeman, Claire, *Dir,* Warner Baird Spring Lake Township Library, Spring Lake MI. 616-846-5770

Wezeman, Frederick, *Dir,* University of Iowa, School of Library Science, IA. 319-353-3644

Whalen, Alice, *ILL,* Carnegie Free Library, McKeesport PA. 412-672-0625

Whalen, Cathy, *Tech Serv,* State University of New York Agricultural & Technical College at Canton, Southworth Library, Canton NY. 315-386-7229

Whalen, Jane, *Librn,* Deaconess Hospital, Drusch Professional Library, Saint Louis MO. 645-8510, Ext 2194

Whalen, Jean R, *Dir,* Ansonia Library, Ansonia CT. 203-734-6275

Whalen, Lucille, *Prof,* State University of New York at Albany, School of Library & Information Science, NY. 518-455-6288

Whalen, Mary Kenneth, *Per,* Cardinal Ritter Library, Saint Louis MO. 314-544-0455, Ext 56

Whalen, Pauline K, *Librn,* Salk Institute for Biological Studies Library, La Jolla CA. 453-4100 Ext 235

Whalen, Wm F, *Dir,* United States Air Force (6585th Test Group Technical Information Center), Holloman AFB NM. 505-679-2463

Whaley, Harold, *Dir,* Unity School of Christianity Library, Unity Village MO. 816-524-3550, Ext 333

Whaley, Jay, *Bibliog Instr,* University of North Carolina at Charlotte, J Murrey Atkins Library, Charlotte NC. 704-597-2221

Whaley, Martha, *Librn,* First National Bank of Chicago Library, Chicago IL. 312-732-3590

Whaley, Mike, *Ser,* Pensacola Junior College, Learning Resource Center, Pensacola FL. 904-476-5410

Whalin, Kathleen, *Librn,* Kanawha County Public Library (Elk Valley), Charleston WV. 304-965-3636

Whalon, Marion K, *Fine Arts & Humanities,* University of California at Davis, General Library, Davis CA. 916-752-2110

Whartenby, Allen, *Govt Doc, Petroleum & Geol,* Shreve Memorial Library, Shreveport LA. 318-221-2614

Whartenby, Wrenette, *Genealogy,* Shreve Memorial Library, Shreveport LA. 318-221-2614

Whartnaby, Eva, *Ch,* Marple Public Library, Broomall PA. 215-356-1510, 356-0550

Wharton, Donald, *Acting Head Librn,* Pennsylvania State University Altoona Campus, Robert E Eiche Library, Altoona PA. 814-946-4321

Wharton, Martha, *ILL & Ref,* Wofford College, Sandor Teszler Library, Spartanburg SC. 803-585-4821, Ext 396

Wharton, Nancy E K, *Acq,* Warwick Public Library and Regional Center, Warwick RI. 401-739-5440

Whatley, Della, *In Charge,* Texas Education Agency (Region XII), Waco TX. 817-756-7494

Whealler, Cynthia J, *Ref & Bibliog Instr,* Emmanuel College, Cardinal Cushing Library, Boston MA. 617-277-9340, Ext 126

Wheat, Frances, *Librn,* United States Army (Ireland Army Hospital Library), Fort Knox KY. 502-624-2752

Wheat, Helen, *Pub Servs,* Northeastern Oklahoma State University, John Vaughan Library-Learning Resource Center, Tahlequah OK. 918-456-5511, Ext 385

Wheat, Joyce, *Outreach & Home Servs,* Mideastern Michigan Library Cooperative, Flint MI. 313-232-7119

Wheat, Joyce, *Librn,* Mideastern Michigan Library Cooperative (Home Services Library for the Blind & Physically Handicapped), Flint MI. 313-732-1120

Wheat, Nan, *Pres,* Middletown Fine Arts Center Library, Middletown OH. 513-424-2416

Wheaton, Leslie Anne, *Head Librn,* Donaldson, Lufkin & Jenrette Securities Corp, Corporate Library, New York NY. 212-943-0300, Ext 1356-9

Wheelbarger, J J, *Dir,* Trevecca Nazarene College, Mackey Library, Nashville TN. 615-244-6000, Ext 214

Wheeler, Allison, *Ch,* Russell Public Library, Russell NY. 315-347-3210

Wheeler, Anne, *Librn,* Brooklyn Public Library (Macon), Brooklyn NY. 212-453-3333

Wheeler, Arlene, *Librn,* Sutter County Free Library (Barber), Live Oak CA. 916-659-2021

Wheeler, Bea, *Librn,* Lucius Beebe Memorial Library (Montrose), Wakefield MA. 617-245-0193

Wheeler, Betty A, *Bkmobile Librns,* Mercer County Public Library, Harrodsburg KY. 606-734-3680

Wheeler, Beverly, *Dir,* Arizona Department of Education, Educational Information Center, Phoenix AZ. 602-255-5391

Wheeler, Charys, *Ad & Ref,* Saint Charles Public Library District, Saint Charles IL. 312-584-0076

Wheeler, Connie, *Cat,* Illinois Wesleyan University Library, Bloomington IL. 309-556-3172

Wheeler, Diane L, *Librn,* Grand Rapids Press Library, Grand Rapids MI. 616-459-1474

Wheeler, Evelyn H, *Librn,* Isaac Umberhine Library, Richmond ME. 207-737-2770

Wheeler, Florence E, *Librn,* Egremont Free Library, South Egremont MA. 413-528-0182

Wheeler, George, *Librn,* Muskogee Law Library Association, Muskogee OK. 918-682-0248

Wheeler, Gerald, *Librn,* Southern Publishing Association of Seventh-Day Adventists, Editorial Library, Nashville TN. 615-889-8000

Wheeler, James, *Ad,* Volusia County Public Libraries, Daytona Beach FL. 904-252-8374

Wheeler, Jean, *Instr,* San Jose State University, Division of Library Science, CA. 408-277-2292

Wheeler, Jean-Philippe, *Acq Proc,* Harvard University Library (Harvard College Library (Headquarters in Harry Elkins Widener Memorial Library)), Cambridge MA. 617-495-2401

Wheeler, Joan, *Librn,* Newfoundland Public Library Services (Community Library Services Dept), Saint John's NF. 709-737-3964

Wheeler, Joan E, *Librn,* Dr Charles A Janeway Child Health Centre, Medical Library, Saint John's NF. 709-722-5100, Ext 310

Wheeler, Joan M, *Ch,* Ansonia Library, Ansonia CT. 203-734-6275

Wheeler, Julia, *Librn,* Sequoyah Regional Library (Pickens County Public), Jasper GA. 404-692-5411

Wheeler, Leonard, *Local Hist,* Ontario Public Library, Ontario CA. 984-2758 Ext 38

Wheeler, Lora Jeanne, *Dir,* American Graduate School of International Management, Barton Kyle Yount Memorial Library, Glendale AZ. 602-978-7232

Wheeler, Mrs Charlie, *Dir,* Crosby County Pioneer Memorial Museum Library, Crosbyton TX. 806-675-2331

Wheeler, Mrs D, *Br Supvr,* Scarborough Public Library (Taylor), Scarborough ON. 416-698-3481

Wheeler, Robin, *Ch,* Poplar Creek Public Library District, Streamwood IL. 312-837-6800

Wheeler, Velma, *Cat,* Garrett-Evangelical Theological Seminary Library, Evanston IL. 312-866-3911

Wheeley, Nancy J, *Cat,* Mississippi University for Women, John Clayton Fant Memorial Library, Columbus MS. 601-328-4808

Whelan, Alice H, *Dir,* Saint John's College in Santa Fe Library, Santa Fe NM. 505-982-3691, Ext 21

Whelan, Elizabeth M, *Circ,* Stoneham Public Library, Stoneham MA. 617-438-1324

Whelan, John F, *Librn,* Williams & Connolly Library, Washington DC. 202-331-5519

Whelan, Mary, *Tech Serv & On-Line Servs,* Wheaton College Library, Norton MA. 617-285-7722, Ext 518

Whelan, Sister M Emily, *Asst Librn,* Brescia College Library, Owensboro KY. 502-685-3131, Ext 213

Whelchel, Mrs Earl, *ILL,* Chestatee Regional Library, Gainesville GA. 404-532-3311

Whelden, Suzanne, *Librn,* Chicago Public Library (Southeast), Chicago IL. 312-221-7177

Wherry, Mrs Del, *Librn,* Exxon Co USA (Headquarters Law Dept Library), Houston TX. 713-221-2019

Whetstone, Ethel, *Departmental Coll,* Bryn Mawr College, Canaday Library, Bryn Mawr PA. 215-645-5279

Whetstone, Suzanne, *Librn,* Deerfield Public Library, Deerfield IL. 312-945-3311

Whetzel, Jane L, *Dir,* Uncle Remus Regional Library, Madison GA. 404-342-1206, 342-2955

Whiddon, Carrie C, *Dir,* Pine Forest Regional Library, Richton MS. 601-788-6539

Whiddon, Douglas, *Bkmobile Coordr,* South Georgia Regional Library, Valdosta-Lowndes County Public Library, Valdosta GA. 912-247-3405

Whiffin, J, *Ser,* University of Victoria, McPherson Library, Victoria BC. 604-477-6911, Ext 4466

Whigham, Mrs Entice, *Librn,* Samson Public Library, Samson AL. 205-898-7806

Whildin, Sara Lou, *Head Librn,* Pennsylvania State University, Delaware County Campus Library, Media PA. 215-565-3300, Ext 24

Whipple, Caroline B, *Tech Serv,* Juniata College, L A Beeghly & O R Myers Science Library, Huntingdon PA. 814-643-4310, Ext 57

Whipple, Marcia J, *Chief Librn,* United States Army (Morale Support Activities Library), Fort Leonard Wood MO. 314-368-5431

Whipple, Michael, *Ref,* University of Denver (Westminster Law Library), Denver CO. 303-753-3405

Whipple, Wendy, *Br Coordr & Bkmobile Coordr,* Sussex County Library System, Sussex County Area Reference Library, Newton NJ. 201-948-3660

Whisenhunt, Helen, *Cat,* Bay County Public Library Association, Northwest Regional Library System, Panama City FL. 904-785-3457

Whisenton, Andre C, *Dir,* United States Department of Labor Library, Washington DC. 202-523-6988

Whisenton, Kenneth, *Ref,* University of Arkansas, Pine Bluff, Watson Memorial Library, Pine Bluff AR. 501-541-6825

Whisler, Barbara, *Librn,* Mount Washington Baptist Church Library, Independence MO. 816-254-5688

Whisler, Lois, *Librn,* Dudley Township Public Library, Satanta KS. 316-649-2213

Whistance-Smith, Ronald, *Curator,* University of Alberta (University Map Collection), Edmonton AB. 403-432-4760

Whistler, Alice, *ILL & Ref,* University of Santa Clara, Michel Orradre Library, Santa Clara CA. 408-984-4415

Whistler, Brandon, *Asst Prof,* University of Nebraska-Lincoln, School Media Specialist Program, NE. 402-472-3726

Whistler, Donn, *Ref,* Gavilan College Library, Gilroy CA. 408-847-1400, Ext 312

Whit, Chester, *Asst Librn,* Broome Community College, Cecil C Tyrrell Learning Resources Center, Binghamton NY. 607-772-5020

Whitacre, Margaret, *Librn,* Port of Houston World Trade Center Library, Houston TX. 713-225-0671

Whitacre, Teddie C, *Librn,* Jonesboro Public Library, Jonesboro IL. 618-833-8121

Whitaker, Carl, *Librn,* Morrison & Foerster Law Library, San Francisco CA. 415-777-6000

Whitaker, Carolyn, *Patients' Librs,* Veterans Administration, Hospital Library, Perry Point MD. 301-642-2411

Whitaker, Douglas A, *Dep Dir,* Wayne Oakland Library Federation, Wayne MI. 313-326-8910

Whitaker, Geraldine, *Doc,* Lincoln Library, Springfield Public Library, Springfield IL. 217-753-4900

Whitaker, Lesley, *On-Line Servs,* NASA (Technical Library), Moffett Field CA. 415-965-5157

Whitaker, Linda, *Librn,* Reading Area Community College, Learning Resources Center, Reading PA. 215-372-4721

Whitaker, R Reed, *Chief, Archives,* National Archives & Records Service, Federal Archives & Records Center, Kansas City MO. 816-926-7271

Whitaker, Susanne, *Librn,* Cornell University Libraries (Flower Veterinary Library), Ithaca NY. 607-256-2083

Whitbeck, Margaret, *Librn,* Mount Washington Public Library, Mount Washington MA. 413-528-0406

Whitbeck, Vicki, *ILL,* University of Southern Colorado Library, Pueblo CO. 303-549-2361

Whitby, Thomas, *Instr,* University of Denver, Graduate School of Librarianship and Information Management, CO. 303-753-2557

Whitchurch, Elizabeth, *Dir,* Clarence Public Library, Clarence NY. 716-759-6651

Whitcomb, Dorothy, *Asst Librn,* Hobart Public Library, Hobart OK. 405-726-2535

Whitcomb, Nancy, *Librn,* Lake County Public Library (Dyer Public), Dyer IN. 219-865-1337

Whitcomb, Peggy, *Asst Librn,* La Roche College, John J Wright Library, Pittsburgh PA. 412-931-9333, Ext 175

Whitcomb, Virginia, *Asst Dir,* Emporia Public Library, Emporia KS. 316-342-6524

White, Allison, *Syst Coordr,* Dekalb Library System, Maud M Burrus Library, Decatur GA. 404-378-7569

White, Anita, *Ref,* Community College of Allegheny County, Allegheny Campus Library, Pittsburgh PA. 412-237-2585

White, Ann, *Media,* Wright State University Library, Dayton OH. 513-873-2380

White, Ann, *ILL,* Centenary College of Louisiana, Magale Library, Shreveport LA. 318-869-5170

White, Anne, *Media,* North Country Community College, Learning Resource Center, Saranac Lake NY. 518-891-2915, Ext 222

White, Barbara A, *Librn,* Nevada State Supreme Court Library, Carson City NV. 702-885-5140

White, Barbara C, *Librn,* Blyth Eastman Dillon & Co Inc, Research Library, New York NY. 212-785-9086

White, Barbara E, *Supvr,* Rockwell International Corp, Seal Beach Information Systems Center, Seal Beach CA. 213-594-3311

White, Barbara E, *Mgr,* Rockwell International Corp, Space Systems Group, Technical Information Center, Downey CA. 213-922-3807

White, Beryl, *Librn,* International Telephone & Telegraph Corp (Legal Dept Library), New York NY. 212-940-1766

White, Betty J, *Librn,* University of Texas Libraries (Science (Biology, Pharmacy)), Austin TX. 512-471-1475

White, Bonda L, *Asst Librn & On-Line Servs,* Hunton & Williams Law Library, Richmond VA. 804-788-8245

White, Carol J, *Original Cat,* University of Wyoming, William Robertson Coe Library, Laramie WY. 307-766-3279

White, Carolyn M, *Librn,* Fairfax County Public Library (Tysons Pimmit Branch), Falls Church VA. 703-790-8088

White, Catherine, *Librn,* Irell & Manella Library, Los Angeles CA. 213-277-1010

White, Cecil R, *Dir,* Golden Gate Baptist Theological Seminary Library, Mill Valley CA. 415-388-8080, Ext 37

White, Cecil R, *Theol & Biblical Studies,* Southwestern Baptist Theological Seminary, Fleming Library, Fort Worth TX. 817-923-1921, Ext 277

White, Cecil R, *Asst Dir & Bibliog Instr,* Southwestern Baptist Theological Seminary, Fleming Library, Fort Worth TX. 817-923-1921, Ext 277

White, Christine, *Librn,* Lennox & Addington County Public Library (Tamworth Branch), Tamworth ON. 613-379-2511

White, Cynthia A, *Dir,* East Point Public Library, East Point GA. 404-761-1222

White, D, *Bibliog Instr,* University of Victoria, McPherson Library, Victoria BC. 604-477-6911, Ext 4466

White, D A, *Librn,* Canadian Rehabilitation Council for the Disabled Library, Toronto ON. 416-862-0340

White, David, *Mus,* Connecticut State Library, Hartford CT. 203-566-4301

White, Deborah, *ILL,* Albany Junior College, Library-Learning Resources Ctr, Albany GA. 912-439-4332

White, Delores, *Librn,* Ulysses Township Library, Ulysses NE. 402-549-2451

White, Donald B, *AV,* Public Library of Charlotte & Mecklenburg County, Inc, Charlotte NC. 704-374-2725

White, Donna Jean, *Librn,* Willard Memorial Library (Greenwich Branch), Greenwich OH. 419-752-2441

White, Edna R, *Librn,* Fairfield Public Library, Fairfield AL. 205-787-0425

White, Ernest M, *Librn,* Louisville Presbyterian Theological Seminary Library, Louisville KY. 502-895-3413, Ext 52

White, F, *Cat,* Bristol Myers Co, Bristol Laboratories Library & Information Service, Syracuse NY. 315-432-2232

White, Florence, *Librn,* Carter Lake Public Library, Carter Lake IA. 712-347-5492

White, Frances, *ILL & Ref,* Randolph-Macon Woman's College, Lipscomb Library, Lynchburg VA. 804-846-7392, Ext 242

White, Frances J, *Librn,* East Millinocket Public Library, East Millinocket ME. 207-746-3392

White, Fred T, *Dir,* Vancouver Island Regional Library, Nanaimo BC. 604-754-6327

White, G Travis, *Instr,* University of Denver, Graduate School of Librarianship and Information Management, CO. 303-753-2557

White, George R, *Instr Serv,* Lynchburg College, Knight Memorial & Capron Libraries, Lynchburg VA. 804-845-9071, Ext 271

White, Harriet, *Librn,* Fort Vancouver Regional Library (Ridgefield Community), Ridgefield WA. 206-887-8281

White, Hazel, *Librn,* Northern Nevada Community College, Learning Resources Center, Elko NV. 702-738-8493, Ext 225

White, Henry O, *Cat,* Mississippi Valley State University, James Herbert White Library, Itta Bena MS. 601-254-9041, Ext 6340

White, Howard, *Assoc Prof,* Drexel University, School of Library & Information Science, PA. 215-895-2474

White, Inez, *Librn,* Jackson Metropolitan Library (Utica Library), Utica MS. 601-352-3677

White, J Kenneth, *Coord Inst Tech Serv,* Allegany Community College, Library (Division of Learning Resources), Cumberland MD. 301-724-7700, Ext 35, 36

White, James, *Dir,* La Crosse Public Library, La Crosse WI. 608-784-8623

White, James William, *Dir,* Winding Rivers Library System, La Crosse WI. 608-784-3151

White, Jane, *Bibliog Instr,* District One Technical Institute Library, Eau Claire WI. 715-836-3971

White, Jane, *Librn,* University of Kentucky (Education), Lexington KY. 606-258-4939

White, Jane M, *Librn,* Mead Corp, Central Research Library, Chillicothe OH. 614-772-3588

White, Janet F, *Ref,* University of Michigan Libraries (University Library), Ann Arbor MI. 313-764-9356

White, Jean, *Ch,* Kellogg Free Library, Cincinnatus NY. 607-863-4300

White, Jeronell, *Librn,* Florence-Darlington Technical College Library, Florence SC. 803-662-8151, Ext 224

White, John, *Pub Serv,* Hudson Valley Community College Learning Resources Center, Dwight Marvin Library, Troy NY. 518-283-1100, Ext 629

White, John G, *Circ,* Fordham University, School of Law Library, New York NY. 212-841-5223

White, Josephine, *Bkmobile Coordr,* Fort Smith Public Library, Fort Smith AR. 501-783-0229

White, Joyce G, *In Charge,* Hunterdon Medical Center, Medical Library, Flemington NJ. 201-782-2121, Ext 257,657

White, Judy, *Acq,* Bryan Public Library, Bryan TX. 713-823-8021

White, Julia, *Librn,* New Mexico State University at Carlsbad Library, Carlsbad NM. 505-885-8831, Ext 27

White, Julia F, *Librn,* Beals Memorial Library, Winchendon MA. 617-297-0300

White, June, *Librn,* Westminster Presbyterian Church Library, Oklahoma City OK. 405-524-2204

White, Katherine, *Librn,* Montgomery County Department of Public Libraries (Western County), Poolesville MD. 301-349-2118

White, Kathy, *Librn,* Dearborn Department of Libraries (Snow), Dearborn MI. 313-565-4323

White, Kay, *Librn,* Alexander County Public Library, Taylorsville NC. 704-632-4058

White, Larry, *Ref,* University of North Carolina at Chapel Hill (Chemistry), Chapel Hill NC. 919-933-1188

White, Lelia, *Dir,* Oakland Public Library, Oakland CA. 415-273-3281

White, Libby K, *YA,* Schenectady County Public Library, Schenectady NY. 518-382-3500

White, Lillian, *Extention Serv,* Durham County Library, Durham NC. 919-683-2626

White, Linda, *ILL & Ref,* Carnegie Public Library, Clarksdale MS. 601-624-4461

White, Linda, *On-Line Servs & Bibliog Instr,* Perrot Memorial Library, Old Greenwich CT. 203-637-1066

White, Lionel, *Media,* Fashion Institute of Technology, Library-Media Services Dept, New York NY. 212-760-7695

White, Margaret, *Librn,* Malvern Public Library, Malvern IA. 712-624-8554

White, Marilyn D, *Asst Prof,* University of Maryland, College of Library & Information Services, MD. 301-454-5441

White, Marion, *Asst Librn,* Starr Library, Rhinebeck NY. 914-876-4030

White, Martha U, *Dir,* Yarmouth Library Association, Yarmouth Port MA. 617-362-3717

White, Mary, *Ch,* Marion County Library, Marion SC. 803-423-2244

White, Mary C, *Dir,* Delaware Free Library, Callicoon NY. 914-887-4040

White, Mary Ellen, *Asst Librn,* Dennison Manufacturing Co Research Library, Framingham MA. 617-879-0511, Ext 509

White, Mary Jane, *Info Spec,* Michigan Education Association Library, East Lansing MI. 517-332-6551

White, Melvin, *Circ,* College of Medicine & Dentistry of New Jersey, George F Smith Library of the Health Sciences, Newark NJ. 201-456-4580

White, Mildred F, *Afro Am Studies,* Nassau Community College Library, Garden City NY. 516-222-7400

White, Mona, *Librn,* Sutter County Free Library (Browns), Rio Oso CA. 916-633-2170

White, Mrs William E, *Librn,* Davie County Public Library (Cooleemee Branch), Cooleemee NC. 704-284-2102

White, Nancy, *Ch,* Morgan Memorial Library, Suffolk VA. 804-539-3175

White, Nancy P, *Asst Dir,* Spokane Public Library, Comstock Building Library, Spokane WA. 509-838-3361, Ext 65

White, Nellie, *Asst Dir & Media,* Texarkana Community College, Palmer Memorial Library, Texarkana TX. 214-838-4541, Ext 215, 231

White, Neva, *Cat,* Kansas State University, Farrell Library, Manhattan KS. 913-532-6516

White, Ouida, *Librn,* Crittendale County Library, Marion AR. 501-739-3238

White, Pamela K, *Dir,* Oakland City-Columbia Township Public Library, Oakland City IN. 812-749-3559

White, Patsy, *Tech Serv & Cat,* Grayson County Junior College Library, Denison TX. 214-465-6030, Ext 237

White, Paul A, *Librn,* Kinderhook Regional Library, Lebanon MO. 417-532-2148

White, Paula, *Dir,* Eastern Plains Regional Library, Tucumcari NM. 505-461-1206

White, Pauline, *Librn,* Lincoln County Free Library (Troy Branch), Troy MT. 406-295-4040

White, Peggy, *Coordr,* Algonquin College of Applied Arts & Technology, Library Technician's Program, ON. 613-725-7413

White, Phillip M, *On-Line Servs,* Southwest Texas State University, Learning Resources Center, San Marcos TX. 512-245-2132

White, Phyllis, *Librn,* Louisville Free Public Library (Fairdale), Louisville KY. 502-361-7843

White, Rex A, *Assoc Librn,* Idaho State University Library, Pocatello ID. 208-236-3202

White, Robert L, *Planning,* Virginia Commonwealth University (James Branch Cabell Library), Richmond VA. 804-257-1105

White, Robert W, *Head Serials Librn,* Brown University (University Library), Providence RI. 401-863-2167

White, Roberta S, *Librn & Bibliog Instr,* New River Community College, Learning Resource Center, Dublin VA. 703-674-4121, Ext 303

White, Ross, *Ref,* Shreve Memorial Library, Shreveport LA. 318-221-2614

White, Ruth, *Librn,* Southwest Arkansas Regional Library (Dierks Branch), Dierks AR. 501-777-4564

White, Ruth I, *Dir,* Linden Public Library, Linden IN. 317-339-4239

White, Sally, *Librn,* Manatee County Public Library System (Island), Holmes Beach FL. 813-778-6341

White, Sandra, *ILL,* Andrews University, James White Library, Berrien Springs MI. 616-471-3264, 471-3275

White, Sandy, *Librn,* Portales Public Library, Portales NM. 505-356-3940

White, Sumner, *City Librn,* New Haven Free Public Library, New Haven CT. 203-787-8130

White, Susan E, *Tech Serv,* Sequoyah Regional Library, R T Jones Memorial Library, Canton GA. 404-479-3090

White, Tera B, *Mgr,* Blue Cross & Blue Shield of North Carolina, Information Center, Durham NC. 919-489-7431, Ext 2460

White, Theresa, *ILL & Acq,* Becker Junior College at Worcester, Alumni Library, Worcester MA. 617-791-9241, Ext 26

White, Theresa, *Commun Servs,* Saint Louis Public Library, Saint Louis MO. 314-241-2288

White, Theresa J, *Dir,* North Olympic Library System, Port Angeles WA. 206-457-4464

WHITE

White, Virgine, *Librn,* Marathon County Public Library (Schofield Branch), Schofield WI. 715-359-5230

White, Virginia, *Cat,* Digital Equipment Corp, Corporate Library, Maynard MA. 617-493-6231, 493-5821

White, Virginia M, *Librn,* Lynchburg Training School & Hospital (Professional Library), Lynchburg VA. 804-528-6171

White, Virginia W, *Librn,* New London Public Library, New London OH. 419-929-3981

White, W L, *Librn,* Arizona State Prison, Central Unit Library, Florence AZ. 602-868-4011, Ext 301

White, Wallace, *Dir,* Flesh Public Library, Piqua OH. 513-773-6753

White, Wini W, *Acq,* Cornwall Public Library, Cornwall-on-Hudson NY. 914-534-8282

Whitehead, Alice, *Librn,* Dunklin County Library (Campbell Branch), Campbell MO. 314-246-2112

Whitehead, Catherine, *Librn,* Gloucester Public Library (Blackburn Hamlet), Ottawa ON. 613-824-6926

Whitehead, Emma, *Tech Serv,* Tuxedo Park Library, Tuxedo Park NY. 914-351-2207

Whitehead, Gladys, *Tech Serv,* Northeast Regional Library, Corinth MS. 601-287-2441

Whitehead, James, *Dir,* Bloomington Public Library, Bloomington IL. 309-828-6091

Whitehead, James, *Cat,* Malone College, Everett L Cattell Library, Canton OH. 216-454-3011, Ext 311

Whitehead, James M, *Asst Prof,* State University of New York, College of Arts & Science, School of Library & Information Science, NY. 716-245-5322

Whitehead, Jane R, *In Charge,* B F Goodrich Co, Charles Cross Goodrich Library, Brecksville OH. 216-526-4311

Whitehead, Jill, *Librn,* Erie Community College-South Campus, Library Learning Resources Center, Orchard Park NY. 716-648-5400, Ext 270, 274

Whitehead, Nell, *Librn,* Ridgely Public Library, Ridgely TN. 901-264-5809

Whitehead, Olive F, *Librn,* RCA Corp, Government Communications Systems Library, Camden NJ. 609-338-3488

Whitehead, Susan, *Info Servs,* University of Colorado Health Sciences Center (Denison Memorial Library), Denver CO. 303-394-5125

Whitehead, Thomas, *Spec Coll,* Temple University of the Commonwealth System of Higher Education, Samuel Paley Library, Philadelphia PA. 215-787-8231

Whitehead, Wm A, *Librn,* Tennessee Valley Authority (Knoxville Technical Library), Knoxville TN. 615-632-3464

Whitehill, Mary Evelyn, *Circ,* Newburgh Free Library, Newburgh NY. 914-561-1836

Whitehorne, Lorna Z, *Librn,* Brandon Training School Library, Brandon VT. 802-247-5711, Ext 273

Whitehouse, Anna B, *Librn,* Winter Harbor Public Library, Winter Harbor ME. 207-963-2235

Whitehouse, Christine, *Librn,* San Antonio Public Library (Pan American), San Antonio TX. 512-924-8164

Whitehouse, Helen, *Librn,* Washington State Library (Rainier School Staff Library), Buckley WA. 206-829-1111

Whitelaw, Marjorie, *Librn,* El Dorado County Library (Georgetown Branch), Georgetown CA. 916-333-4724

Whitelock, Alfred T, *Dir,* Roanoke City Public Library System, Roanoke VA. 703-981-2475, Ext 2476

Whiteman, M B, *Asst Librn,* Borough of Etobicoke Public Library, Weston ON. 416-248-5681

Whiteman, Merlin, *Reader Serv,* Indiana University (School of Law Library), Indianapolis IN. 317-264-4028

Whitesel, George, *Art, Music & Lang,* Jacksonville State University Library, Jacksonville AL. 205-435-9820, Ext 213, 214

Whitesell, Edith, *ILL,* University of the South, Jessie Ball duPont Library, Sewanee TN. 615-598-5931, Ext 265, 267

Whiteside, Betty, *Librn,* Potwin Public Library, Potwin KS. 316-752-3253

Whiteside, S, *Librn,* Nova Scotia Museum Library, Halifax NS. 902-429-4610, Ext 44

Whitesides, Daisy, *Ch,* Hyconeechee Regional Library, Yanceyville NC. 919-694-6241

Whitesides, William L, *Dir Libr Serv,* Fairfax County Public Library, Administrative Offices, Springfield VA. 703-321-9810

Whitfield, Frances S, *Librn,* Speed Art Museum Library, Louisville KY. 502-637-6363

Whitfill, Margaret, *Chief Librn,* Arthur Young & Co Library (Tax Library), New York NY. 212-922-3131

Whiting, John, *Media,* Sinte Gleska College Library, Mission SD. 605-856-4550

Whiting, Marvin, *Archivist,* Birmingham Public & Jefferson County Free Library, Birmingham AL. 205-254-2551

Whiting, Nancy W, *Librn,* West Tisbury Free Public Library, West Tisbury MA. 617-693-3366

Whiting, Ralph, *Supvr Instrnl Media & Tech,* Wisconsin Department of Public Instruction (Bureau of Instructional Media Program), Madison WI. 608-266-1965

Whitinger, Elaine H, *Nursing & Allied Health,* Indiana University (School of Medicine Library), Indianapolis IN. 317-264-7182

Whitlatch, Jo, *ILL,* San Jose State University Library, San Jose CA. 408-277-3377

Whitley, Bernice, *Media,* Grand Rapids Junior College, Arthur Andrews Memorial Library, Grand Rapids MI. 616-456-4841

Whitley, Nettie, *Admin,* Cheaha Regional Library, Anniston AL. 205-238-1581

Whitley, Sr, E J, *AV,* First Baptist Church Library, Gainesville FL. 904-376-2131

Whitlock, C C, *Dir,* Royal Roads Military College, Coronel Memorial Library, Victoria BC. 604-388-1483

Whitlow, Gayna, *Media,* Midland College, Learning Resources Center, Midland TX. 915-684-7851, Ext 214

Whitlow, Hubert H, *Librn,* Floyd Junior College Library, Rome GA. 404-295-6318

Whitman, Beverly, *Assoc Librn,* Yellowstone Library & Museum Association, Yellowstone National Park WY. 307-344-7381

Whitman, Dorothy, *Librn,* Louisville Free Public Library (Portland), Louisville KY. 502-778-6531

Whitman, Elsie, *Librn,* Annapolis Valley Regional Library Headquarters (Lawrencetown Branch), Lawrencetown NS. 902-532-2260

Whitman, Eunice, *Ref,* Franklin Library, Ray Memorial Library, Franklin MA. 617-528-0371

Whitman, Evelyn A, *Dir,* Manatee Junior College Library, Sara Scott Harller Library, Bradenton FL. 813-755-1511, Ext 304

Whitman, Jean, *Exten,* Robeson County Public Library, Lumberton NC. 919-738-4859

Whitman, Jean, *Adult Literacy,* Robeson County Public Library, Lumberton NC. 919-738-4859

Whitman, Joan T, *Librn,* Jameson Memorial Hospital, School of Nursing Library, New Castle PA. 412-658-9001, Ext 312

Whitman, Kathi, *Archivist,* Kansas City Museum of History and Science, Library and Archives, Kansas City MO. 816-241-3660, Ext 21

Whitman, Phyllis G, *Ch,* Woburn Public Library, Woburn MA. 617-933-0148

Whitmarsh, Doris, *Br Asst,* Timberland Regional Library (South Mason Branch), Shelton WA. 206-426-1362

Whitmer, Nick, *Ad,* Rockingham Public Library, Harrisonburg VA. 703-434-4475

Whitmore, Ellie, *ILL,* North Texas State University Library, Denton TX. 817-788-2411

Whitmore, Harry E, *Libr Develop Coordr,* Northwest Wisconsin Library System, Ashland WI. 715-682-8027

Whitmore, Jane, *Evening Librn,* Eager Free Public Library, Evansville WI. 608-882-4230

Whitmore, Laurence, *Librn,* Indianapolis-Marion County Public Library (Prospect), Indianapolis IN. 317-635-5662

Whitmore, Maxine, *Librn,* Center Point Public Library, Center Point IA. 319-849-1508

Whitmore, Richard, *Librn,* Saint Peter State Hospital, Elizabeth Seaquist Library, Saint Peter MN. 507-931-3000, Ext 349

Whitmore, Victor, *Cat,* University of New Mexico General Library (Law Library), Albuquerque NM. 505-277-6236

Whitney, Byron V, *Tech Serv,* Clarkson College of Technology, Harriet Call Burnap Memorial Library, Potsdam NY. 315-268-6645

Whitney, Ellen, *Head,* Free Library of Philadelphia (Central Children's), Philadelphia PA. 215-686-5322

Whitney, Genevieve, *Dir,* Henderson Free Library, Henderson NY. 315-938-5032

Whitney, Janet, *Supv Librn,* California Department of Justice Library, Los Angeles CA. 213-736-2196

Whitney, Josephine J, *Librn,* United Air Lines, Engineering Dept Library, San Francisco CA. 415-876-3730

Whitney, Kenneth, *Curator,* Aurora Historical Society, Elbert Hubbard Library Museum, East Aurora NY. 716-652-6000

Whitney, Mrs Kenneth, *Curator,* Aurora Historical Society, Elbert Hubbard Library Museum, East Aurora NY. 716-652-6000

Whitney, Ruth, *Ad,* Lincolnwood Public Library, Lincolnwood IL. 312-677-5277

Whitney, Shirley, *Librn,* Kent County Memorial Hospital, Medical Library, Warwick RI. 401-737-7000

Whitney, Stephen L, *Librn,* San Bernardino Public Library, San Bernardino CA. 714-889-0264

Whitney, Virginia B, *Librn,* Wake County Medical Center Library, Raleigh NC. 919-755-8528

Whitney, William, *Ref & Bibliog Instr,* Fullerton College, William T Boyce Library, Fullerton CA. 714-871-8000

Whiton, Paul, *Per,* Darien Library, Inc, Darien CT. 203-655-2568

Whitson, Alice, *Librn,* Jackson District Library (Summit), Jackson MI. 517-783-4030

Whitson, Carolyn, *Media,* Tennessee Technological University, Jere Whitson Memorial Library, Cookeville TN. 615-528-3408

Whitson, Randolph L, *Asst Dir,* University of Tennessee at Chattanooga Library, Chattanooga TN. 615-755-4701

Whitson, Vivienne, *Chief Librn,* Metropolitan Hospital Center (Frederick M Dearborn Medical Library), New York NY. 212-360-6262

Whitt, Cynthia, *Librn,* Public Library of Cincinnati & Hamilton County (Sharonville), Cincinnati OH. 513-369-6049

Whitt, Elizabeth, *Cat,* John Tyler Community College Library, Chester VA. 804-748-6481, Ext 251

Whitt, Esther, *Asst Dir,* Jetmore Municipal Library, Jetmore KS. 316-357-8336

Whittaker, Barbara, *Librn,* Louis B Goodall Memorial Library (Carpentier), Sanford ME. 207-324-6338

Whittaker, Brenda, *Ch,* Rochester Public Library, Olmsted County Library System, Rochester MN. 507-285-8000

Whittaker, Claire B, *Librn,* Institute of Textile Technology, Roger Milliken Textile Library, Charlottesville VA. 804-296-5511, Ext 54

Whittaker, Edward L, *Dir,* Genesee District Library, Flint MI. 313-732-0110

Whittaker, Kathleen, *Librn,* Dartmouth Public Libraries (Dartmouth Free Public), Dartmouth MA. 617-636-2661

Whittaker, Kathleen, *ILL,* Dartmouth Public Libraries, Southworth Library, South Dartmouth MA. 617-997-1252

Whittaker, Mary Jean, *Ref,* University of Maryland Baltimore County Library, Baltimore MD. 301-455-2457

Whittemore, C, *Inst Media,* Northern Montana College Library, Havre MT. 406-265-7821, Ext 3306, 3307

Whittemore, Dorothy, *Pub Serv,* Tulane University of Louisiana, Howard-Tilton Memorial Library, New Orleans LA. 504-865-5131

Whittemore, Lios, *Co-Dir,* Grout Museum of History & Science Library, Waterloo IA. 319-234-6357

Whitten, Denis, *ILL & Ref,* Madison County-Canton Public Library, Canton MS. 601-859-3202

Whitten, Jennie, *Librn,* Central Florida Regional Library (Herman B Oberman), Ocala FL. 904-489-4716

Whitten, Joseph N, *Prof,* Long Island University, Palmer Graduate Library School, NY. 516-299-2855 & 299-2856

Whitten, Mrs Winston, *Ad,* Bixby Memorial Free Library, Vergennes VT. 802-877-2211

Whitten, Ruth Lutz, *Asst Librn & Ref,* Athens State College Library, Athens AL. 205-232-1802, Ext 291

Whittenberg, Barbara, *Librn,* Hutchinson Public Library, Hutchinson MN. 612-587-2368
Whittfield, Equella, *Librn,* Cass County Public Library (Pleasant Hill Branch), Pleasant Hill MO. 816-987-2231
Whittington, Aletha, *Dir,* Gentry County Library, Stanberry MO. 816-782-2335
Whittington, Mae, *Librn,* Breckenridge Public Library, Breckenridge TX. 817-559-5505
Whittle, Karin, *Archivist,* Calaveras County Museum & Archives Library, San Andreas CA. 209-754-4203
Whittle, Lona T, *Librn,* Aiken-Bamberg-Barnwell-Edgefield Regional Library (Johnston Branch), Johnston SC. 803-648-8961
Whittle, Susan, *Manpower Cont Educ & Trustees,* State Library of Florida, Div of Library Services, Dept of State, Tallahassee FL. 904-487-2651
Whittman, Sandra, *Acq,* Oakton Community College, Learning Resources Center, Morton Grove IL. 312-967-5120, Ext 331
Whittock, Jr, John M, *Librn,* University of Pennsylvania Libraries (Dental), Philadelphia PA. 215-243-8969
Whittom, Gilles, *Dir,* Francois-Xavier Garneau College Library, Quebec PQ. 418-688-8310, Ext 256
Whitton, Harriet, *Librn,* Sheffield Township Library, Sheffield PA. 814-968-3439
Whitworth, Virginia, *Librn,* Benton County Library, Camden TN. 901-584-4772
Wiacek, Elma, *Acq,* Southern Connecticut State College, Hilton C Buley Library, New Haven CT. 203-397-4505
Wiant, Sarah K, *Librn,* Washington & Lee University (Wilbur C Hall Library), Lexington VA. 703-463-3157
Wiberley, Stephen E, *Social Sci,* University of Illinois at Chicago Circle Library, Chicago IL. 312-996-2716
Wible, Marion, *Acq,* Conococheague District Library System, Chambersburg PA. 717-263-1054
Wichard, Loma D, *ILL & Ad,* Saint Louis County Library, Saint Louis MO. 314-994-3300
Wicher, Aleene, *Supvr,* Department of Public Libraries & Information (Subregional Library for the Blind, Special Services Division), Virginia Beach VA. 804-464-9175
Wichers, Jean E, *Assoc Prof,* San Jose State University, Division of Library Science, CA. 408-277-2292
Wichmann, Dorothy, *Ch & Media,* Lodi Public Library, Lodi CA. 209-334-3973
Wichmann, Jane, *YA & Media,* North Bellmore Public Library, North Bellmore NY. 516-785-6260
Wick, Bonnie, *Librn,* Clearfield County Public Library Federation (Osceola Mills Branch), Osceola Mills PA. 814-339-7229
Wick, Donald E, *Actg Librn,* University of Lethbridge Library, Lethbridge AB. 403-329-2261
Wick, Dwan, *Prof,* University of Wisconsin-LaCrosse, Educational Media Dept, WI. 608-784-8134
Wick, Hilda, *Ref,* Ohio Wesleyan University, L A Beeghly Library, Delaware OH. 614-369-4431, Ext 509
Wick, Kris, *Asst Librn & Ref,* Contra Costa County Library (Central Library), Pleasant Hill CA. 415-935-6420
Wick, Mary, *Librn,* Marin County Free Library (Woodacre Branch), Woodacre CA. 415-479-1100, Ext 2577
Wicker, Barbara, *Librn,* Boston Public Library (Hyde Park Branch), Hyde Park MA. 617-361-2524
Wicker, Eddith, *Librn,* Lyon County Public Library, Eddyville KY. 502-388-7720
Wicker, W Walter, *Dir,* University of Houston (Clear Lake City), Houston TX. 713-488-9280
Wicker, Walter, *Instr,* University of Houston at Clear Lake City, Learning Resources Specialist Program, TX. 713-488-9405
Wickham, Rose Marie, *Tech Serv,* State University of New York College at Purchase Library, Purchase NY. 914-253-5085
Wickins, Mary Clare, *Ref,* Regis College, Dayton Memorial Library, Denver CO. 303-458-4030

Wickizer, Alice, *Govt Pubs,* Indiana University at Bloomington, University Libraries, Bloomington IN. 812-337-3403
Wicklund, Nancy, *Asst Librn & Ref,* Westminster Choir College, Talbott Library, Princeton NJ. 921-3658 (Dir), 921-7826 (Publ Servs), 921-3659 (Choral Libr), 921-7148 (Media Servs)
Wicklund, Shirley, *Ad,* Crow River Regional Library, Willmar MN. 612-235-3162
Wicklund, Shirley, *Instr,* Pima Community College, Library Technology Program, AZ. 602-884-6821
Wicklund, Shirley, *Tech Serv,* Pima Community College, West Campus Learning Resource Center, Tucson AZ. 602-884-6821
Wickman, Doreen, *Librn,* Environmental Protection Agency, Technical Library, Las Vegas NV. 702-736-2969
Wickman, John E, *Dir,* General Services Administration - National Archives & Records Service, Dwight D Eisenhower Library, Abilene KS. 913-263-4751
Widdicomb, Ruth, *Librn,* Rock County Historical Society, Research Library, Janesville WI. 608-752-4519
Widdicombe, Richard P, *Dir,* Stevens Institute of Technology, Samuel C Williams Library, Hoboken NJ. 201-420-5198
Widmaier, Jean, *Cat,* Mercer County Community College Library, Trenton NJ. 609-586-4800, Ext 358
Widman, Rudolph P, *Dir,* Indian River Community College, Charles S Miley Learning Resources Center, Fort Pierce FL. 305-464-2000, Ext 347
Wiebe, Margaret, *Asst Librn,* Tabor College Library, Hillsboro KS. 316-947-3121
Wiebe, V, *Ref,* University of Saskatchewan Library, Saskatoon SK. 306-343-4216
Wiebel, Machele, *Librn,* Lowden Public Library, Lowden IA. 319-944-7705
Wieben, Helen M, *Librn,* Dysart Public Library, Dysart IA. 319-476-5210
Wieben, Susan, *Dir,* Carnegie Public Library, Perry Public Library, Perry IA. 515-465-2805
Wiedenhoefer, Joyce, *Librn,* Cleveland Public Library (Eastman), Cleveland OH. 216-251-9433
Wieder, Amelia, *In Charge,* Jewish Community Center of Staten Island, William Rosenthal Judaica Library, Staten Island NY. 212-981-1500
Wiederholt, Kathleen, *Ref,* Lane Community College Library, Eugene OR. 503-747-4501, Ext 2354
Wiegand, Doris, *Librn,* Franklin Public Library, Franklin MI. 313-851-2254
Wiegand, Wayne, *Asst Prof,* University of Kentucky, College of Library Science, KY. 606-258-8876
Wiegenstein, Faye, *Librn,* Ozark Regional Library (Annapolis Branch), Annapolis MO. 314-546-2615
Wiegert, Roy H, *Librn,* Iowa Lakes Community Colleges Library, Estherville IA. 712-362-2554
Wiehe, Janet, *Fiction,* Public Library of Cincinnati & Hamilton County, Cincinnati Public Library, Cincinnati OH. 513-369-6000
Wielage, Beth P, *Ref,* Dekalb Community College, South Campus, Learning Resources Center, Decatur GA. 404-243-3860, Ext 12
Wieland, Larry, *Librn,* United States Department of Labor, Employment & Training Administration Technical Resource Library, Denver CO. 303-837-4571
Wiemann, Barbara, *Tech Serv & Cat,* Easton Area Public Library, Easton PA. 215-258-2917
Wiencko, Bonnie L, *Librn,* Smith, Cohen, Ringel, Kohler & Martin, Law Library, Atlanta GA. 404-656-1800, Ext 1876
Wieneke, Dorothy, *Librn,* Middletown Hospital Association, Ada Leonard Memorial Library, Middletown OH. 513-422-5411
Wiener, Dr Israel, *Librn,* Congregation Beth Achim, Joseph Katkowsky Library, Southfield MI. 313-352-8670
Wiener, Harry, *Dir,* Pfizer Inc, Pharmaceuticals Library, New York NY. 212-573-2323
Wieners, Sharon, *On-Line Servs,* Rochester Community College, Goddard Library, Rochester MN. 507-285-7233
Wienmeyer, Ellen, *Circ,* County of Strathcona Municipal Library, Sherwood Park AB. 403-467-3513

Wiens, Allan L, *Dir,* Olivet Nazarene College, Benner Library & Resource Center, Bourbonnais IL. 815-939-5354
Wiens, Elizabeth, *Cat,* Southern Connecticut State College, Hilton C Buley Library, New Haven CT. 203-397-4505
Wiens, P, *Asst Dir, Admin,* University of Manitoba Libraries, Winnipeg MB. 204-474-9881
Wieranga, W, *Librn,* Neerlandia Library, Neerlandia AB. 403-674-2160
Wierenga, Janice, *Ch,* Herrick Public Library, Holland MI. 616-392-3114
Wierzba, Christine M, *Dir,* Franklin Lakes Free Public Library, Franklin Lakes NJ. 201-891-2224
Wiese, Sister Berdelle, *Prof,* Silver Lake College, School Librarianship Program, WI. 414-684-6691, Ext 34
Wieseman, Glenna, *Asst Librn,* Osceola Public Library, Osceola NE. 402-747-4301
Wiesen, Yvonne, *Librn,* Whatcom County Public Library (Mountain View), Ferndale WA. 206-384-1472
Wiesenthal, Diane, *Librn,* Veterans Administration Medical Center, Medical Center Library, Phoenix AZ. 602-277-5551, Ext 248
Wiesman, Dorothy, *Librn,* Marathon County Public Library (Stratford Branch), Stratford WI. 715-687-4166
Wiesner, Peter, *Coordr,* Essex County College, Learning Resources Center, Newark NJ. 201-877-3233
Wigent, Evelyn, *Librn,* Saint Elizabeth Hospital Medical Center (School of Nursing), Lafayette IN. 317-423-6408
Wigersma, Helen, *Dir,* Missouri Western State College, Hearnes Learning Resources Center, Saint Joseph MO. 816-271-4368
Wigg, Ristiina, *Ch,* Mid-Hudson Library System, Poughkeepsie NY. 914-471-6060
Wiggans, Cynthia, *Ad,* Elkhart Public Library, Elkhart IN. 219-294-5463
Wiggin, Frances M, *Librn,* Bedford Public Library, Bedford NH. 603-472-3023
Wiggin, Kendall, *Chief Librn,* Merrimack Public Library, Merrimack NH. 603-424-5021
Wiggins, Amy, *Supvr,* Huron County Public Library (Dungannon Branch), Dungannon ON. 519-529-7901
Wiggins, Barbara B, *Librn,* Cove City Public Library, Cove City NC. 919-638-6363
Wiggins, Carolyn, *Librn,* Dauphin County Library System (Kline Village), Harrisburg PA. 717-234-3934
Wiggins, Gary, *Librn,* Indiana University at Bloomington (Chemistry), Bloomington IN. 812-337-9452
Wiggins, Jean, *Humanities,* Morehead State University, Johnson Camden-Julian Carroll Library, Morehead KY. 606-783-2250
Wiggins, Joanne, *Ref & Commun Servs,* Hudson Public Library, Hudson MA. 617-562-7521, 7522
Wiggins, Marvin, *ILL & Ref,* Brigham Young University, Harold B Lee Library, Provo UT. 801-378-2905
Wiggins, Pat, *Ch & Tech Serv,* Jefferson County Library, Nederland TX. 713-727-2735, 727-2736
Wiggins, Theresa, *Librn,* Princeton University Library (Psychology), Princeton NJ. 609-452-3180
Wiggs, William H, *Dir,* James Sprunt Institute Library, Kenansville NC. 919-296-1341, Ext 27
Wight, Susan B, *Ad & On-Line Servs,* Bangor Public Library, Bangor ME. 207-947-8336
Wight, Wanda, *Librn,* Tucson Public Library (Green Valley), Green Valley AZ. 602-622-8660
Wightman, Brad, *Acq,* Provo City Public Library, Provo UT. 801-373-1494
Wightman, Doris S, *Librn,* Norborne Public Library, Norborne MO. 816-594-3514
Wightman, Dorris O, *Dir,* Kinchafoonee Regional Library, Dawson GA. 912-995-2902
Wightman, Kingsley W, *In Charge,* Chabot Observatory Library, Oakland CA. 415-531-4560, Ext 4
Wigley, Lisa, *Librn,* Hopkins County-Madisonville Public Library (Dawson Springs Branch), Dawson Springs KY. 502-797-8990
Wigley, Mary, *Librn,* Wilson County Public Library (Elm City Branch), Elm City NC. 919-236-4269

Wigley, Mary Lou, *Supvry Librn,* Ventura County Library Services Agency (Conejo), Thousand Oaks CA. 805-495-1039

Wigmore, S, *Librn,* University of Toronto Libraries (Ontario Institute for Studies in Education), Toronto ON. 416-923-6641

Wignall, Marcella, *Librn,* Traer Public Library, Traer IA. 319-478-2180

Wikander, Lawrence E, *Dir,* Williams College, Sawyer Library, Williamstown MA. 413-597-2501

Wiker, Carolyn M, *Dir,* Adams County Public Library, East Berlin Community, Gettysburg PA. 717-334-5716

Wiktor, Christian L, *Librn,* Dalhousie University (Sir James Dunn Law Library), Halifax NS. 902-424-2124

Wilander, Ardis, *Cat,* Bemidji State University, A C Clark Library, Bemidji MN. 218-755-2955

Wilbanks, Faye, *Librn,* Piedmont Regional Library (Nicholson Branch), Nicholson GA. 404-867-2762

Wilbee, Roy, *Media,* Bethel College, Learning Resource Center, Saint Paul MN. 612-641-6222

Wilber, Isabel, *Ch,* Lucius Beebe Memorial Library, Wakefield MA. 617-245-0790

Wilber, Kaylene, *Chief Librn,* Tri-County Technical College, Learning Resource Center, Pendleton SC. 803-646-3227

Wilber, Mary D, *Librn,* Addressograph-Multigraph Corp, Multigraphics Division, Information Document Control Center, Mount Prospect IL. 312-398-1900

Wilbert, Jo, *Rare Bks,* Natrona County Public Library, Casper WY. 307-235-9272

Wilbert, Jo, *Gov Pubs,* Natrona County Public Library, Casper WY. 307-235-9272

Wilbert, Shirley, *Asst Prof,* University of Wisconsin-Oshkosh, Dept of Library Science, WI. 414-424-2313

Wilbracht, Marilyn, *Librn,* Milwaukee Food Laboratories Inc Library, Germantown WI. 414-251-6146

Wilbur, Helen L, *Librn & Mgr Info Servs,* Zinc Institute, Lead Industries Association Libr, New York NY. 212-578-4750

Wilbur, Lowell R, *Librn,* Iowa State Historical Department, Division of Museum & Archives, Des Moines IA. 515-281-5472

Wilbur, Ruth, *Librn,* Society of Mayflower Descendants in the State of California Library, San Francisco CA. 415-781-8324

Wilburn, Gene, *Chief Librn,* Royal Ontario Museum Library, Toronto ON. 416-978-3671

Wilckens, Marla, *Acq,* Great Falls Public Library, Pathfinder Federation of Libraries Headquarters, Great Falls MT. 406-453-0349

Wilcox, Alice E, *Dir,* Minnesota Interlibrary Telecommunications Exchange, (MINITEX), MN. 612-376-3925, 376-3926

Wilcox, Barbara, *Dir,* Lima Public Library, Lima NY. 716-582-1311

Wilcox, David, *Bkmobile Coordr,* Atlantic County Library, Pleasantville NJ. 609-646-8699, 645-7121, 625-2776

Wilcox, Doris, *Media,* Cedar Rapids Public Library, Cedar Rapids IA. 319-398-5123

Wilcox, Harold E, *Supvr,* United Technologies Corp, Chemical Systems Div Library, Sunnyvale CA. 408-739-4880, Ext 2563

Wilcox, Marilyn, *Ref,* Tulsa Junior College, Learning Resource Center, Tulsa OK. 918-587-6561, Ext 363

Wilcox, Marjorie C, *Dir,* Grand Rapids Bar Association Law Library, Grand Rapids MI. 616-454-9493

Wilcox, Mildred, *Dir,* Ashville Free Library, Ashville NY. 716-763-9906

Wilcox, Opal, *ILL,* Sheridan College, Kooi Library, Instructional Resource Center, Sheridan WY. 307-674-6446, Ext 170

Wilcox, Virginia, *Cat,* Oakland Community College, Highland Lakes Campus Library, Union Lake MI. 313-363-7191, Ext 335

Wilcoxen, Patricia, *Circ,* University of Chicago, Joseph Regenstein Library, Chicago IL. 312-753-2977

Wild, Lynn Charles, *Librn Deaf,* Villa Park Public Library, Villa Park IL. 312-834-1164

Wilde, John H, *Librn,* Erskine College, McCain Library, Due West SC. 803-379-8898

Wilde, Lucy, *Ref,* Kansas State University, Farrell Library, Manhattan KS. 913-532-6516

Wilde, Nila, *Librn,* Sweetwater County Library (McKinnon Branch), McKinnon WY. 307-875-3615

Wilder, Alice, *Instr,* Foothill College, Library-Media Technical Assistant Program, CA. 415-948-8590, Ext 390

Wilder, Bernice, *Dir,* Gary Public Library, Gary IN. 219-886-2484

Wilder, Charlotte, *Librn,* Worcester District Medical Society, Worcester Medical Library, Worcester MA. 617-753-1579

Wilder, David, *Regional Libr Dir,* Cumberland Valley Regional Library, Harlan KY. 606-573-5124

Wilder, David, *Dir,* Long Island Library Resources Council, NY. 516-286-0400

Wilder, Ellen, *Librn,* Dartmouth Public Libraries (North Dartmouth Branch), North Dartmouth MA. 617-996-6471

Wilder, Mrs S, *Librn,* Middle Georgia Regional Library (Crawford County Public), Musella GA. 912-836-3315

Wilder, Ulah, *Dir,* Oakland City College, Founders Memorial Library, Oakland City IN. 812-749-4781, Ext 21

Wilder, Virginia C, *Circ,* Winthrop Public Library, Frost Public Library, Winthrop MA. 617-846-1703

Wilder-Jones, Joyce, *On-Line Servs,* California State University Fullerton Library, Fullerton CA. 714-773-2714

Wildes, Elizabeth S, *Librn,* Saint Luke's Hospital, Health Sciences Library, New Bedford MA. 617-997-1515, Ext 267

Wildin, Nancy, *Lang, Philos & Relig,* Seattle Public Library, Seattle WA. 206-625-2665

Wilding-White, Frederic H, *Librn,* New Mexico State University, Grants Branch Library, Grants NM. 505-287-7981, Ext 14

Wildman, Doreen A, *Librn,* Lighthouse Point Library, Lighthouse Point FL. 305-946-6398

Wilensky, Elsie, *Librn,* North Shore University Hospital, Daniel Carroll Payson Medical Library, Manhasset NY. 516-562-4324

Wilensky, Yvonne, *Tech Serv & Acq,* State University of New York College, Daniel A Reed Library, Fredonia NY. 716-673-3183

Wiler, Linda, *Ref,* Florida Atlantic University, S E Wimberly Library, Boca Raton FL. 305-395-5100, Ext 2448

Wiler, Linda, *Soc Sci,* Florida Atlantic University, S E Wimberly Library, Boca Raton FL. 305-395-5100, Ext 2448

Wiler, Louise, *Librn,* Wenonah Free Public Library, Wenonah NJ. 609-468-6323

Wiles, Pauline, *Librn,* Greenwood Public Library, Greenwood NE. 402-789-2300

Wiles, Susan B, *Ad,* Bartow Public Library, Bartow FL. 813-533-4985

Wiley, Bettie, *ILL,* Vicksburg-Warren County Public Library, Vicksburg MS. 601-636-6411

Wiley, Carol, *Actg Librn,* Watchung Public Library, Watchung NJ. 201-561-0117

Wiley, Carolyn, *Librn,* Warren Free Public Library, Warren ME. 207-273-2900

Wiley, Don D, *Advisor,* Eastern Washington University, Library Science-Media, WA. 509-359-7023

Wiley, Opal L, *Dir,* Camanche Public Library, Camanche IA. 319-259-1106

Wiley, Phyllis B, *Librn,* Grace Presbyterian Church Library, Jenkintown PA. 215-887-6117

Wiley, Terese, *ILL & Acq,* Kenrick Seminary, Charles L Souvay Memorial Library, Saint Louis MO. 314-961-4320, Ext 28,29

Wilford, Enid L, *Librn,* United States Air Force (Baker Library), Castle AFB CA. 209-726-2011

Wilford, Jane, *ILL,* Columbia University (University Libraries), New York NY. 212-280-2241

Wilford, Valerie J, *Instr,* Illinois State University, Department of Information Sciences, IL. 309-438-3671

Wilgus, Anne, *Tech Serv,* North Carolina Wesleyan College Library, Rocky Mount NC. 919-442-7121, Ext 280, 283

Wilhelm, Diane, *Ref,* Illinois State Historical Library, Springfield IL. 217-782-4836

Wilhelm, Laurn, *Instr,* University of Wyoming, Library Media Program, WY. 307-766-2349

Wilhelm, M, *Research Dir,* Ciba-Geigy Corp, Pharmaceuticals Div, Scientific Information Center, Summit NJ. 201-277-5544

Wilhelm, Mary, *Librn,* Amherst County Public Library (Seminole), Madison Heights VA. 804-846-8171

Wilhelm, Mary Lou, *Dir,* Cuesta College, Library Learning Center, San Luis Obispo CA. 805-544-2943, Ext 280

Wilhelm, Mrs Herbert, *Librn,* Plainville Public Library, Plainville KS. 913-434-2786

Wilhelm, Paula, *Assoc Librn,* Cleveland Electric Illuminating Co Library, Cleveland OH. 216-622-9800, Ext 2046

Wilhelm, Ruth I, *Assoc Prof,* Slippery Rock State College, Dept of Library Science, PA. 412-794-7321

Wilhelmi, Charlotte, *Adminr,* Consortium for Continuing Higher Education in Northern Virginia, VA. 703-323-2155

Wilhide, Betsy B, *On-Line Servs,* Pennwalt Corp, Technical Div Library, King of Prussia PA. 215-265-3200

Wilhite, Carolyn, *Librn,* W R Grace & Co Agricultural Chemicals Group, Planning Services Library, Memphis TN. 901-522-2385

Wilhite, Flora Richardson, *Dir,* Sterling Municipal Library, Baytown TX. 713-427-7331

Wilhite, Linda, *Media,* Union County Public Library, Liberty IN. 317-458-5355

Wilimovsky, Diana, *Librn,* MacMillan Bloedel Research Ltd Library, Vancouver BC. 604-254-5151, Ext 213

Wilk, Edward, *Loan Servs,* California Polytechnic State University Library, San Luis Obispo CA. 805-546-2345

Wilk, Susan, *Dir,* Florida Public Library, Florida NY. 914-651-7659

Wilkas, Lenore, *Acq,* University of South Carolina, Thomas Cooper Library, Columbia SC. 803-777-3142

Wilke, Bonnie, *Dir,* Forest Park Public Library, Forest Park IL. 312-366-2530

Wilke, Janet Stoeger, *Circ & Doc,* Doane College, Perkins Library, Crete NE. 402-826-2161, Ext 224, 287

Wilken, Madeleine, *Assoc Librn,* Western New England College (Law Library), Springfield MA. 413-782-3111, Ext 454, 455

Wilkenfeld, Polly, *Librn,* Mayfield Hillcrest Synagogue, Rabbi Enoch H Kronheim Memorial Library, Mayfield Heights OH. 216-449-6200

Wilkens, Betsy, *Ch & YA,* Windsor Public Library, Windsor CT. 203-688-6433

Wilkens, Betty, *Ch,* Martin County Public Library, Stuart FL. 305-287-2257

Wilkens, E C, *Librn,* Collectors Club Library, New York NY. 212-683-0559

Wilkens, Lea-Ruth C, *Assoc Prof,* University of Houston at Clear Lake City, Learning Resources Specialist Program, TX. 713-488-9405

Wilkerson, Carolyn, *Librn,* Cambridge Community Library, Cambridge ID. 208-257-3434

Wilkerson, James R, *Dir,* Arkansas Valley Regional Library Service System, Pueblo CO. 303-542-2156

Wilkerson, Robert C, *Mgr, Admin Systs,* Celanese Corp, Celanese Chemical Company, Inc-Technical Center-Library, Corpus Christi TX. 512-241-2343

Wilkes, Adeline W, *Librn,* Florida State University (Library Science), Tallahassee FL. 904-644-1803

Wilkes, Mrs H B, *Librn,* Clinton Junior College Library, Rock Hill SC. 803-327-7402

Wilkes, Mrs Lamar, *Librn,* Brooks County Library, Quitman GA. 912-263-4412

Wilkey, Roberta, *Librn,* Moore Memorial Library, Christiana PA. 215-593-6683

Wilkie, Elizabeth, *Chief Librn,* United States Navy (Naval Weapons Center Library), China Lake CA. 714-939-3278, 939-2595

Wilkie, Lorna C, *Librn,* Dames & Moore Cincinnati Library, Cincinnati OH. 513-651-3440, Ext 64

Wilkin, Darlene K, *Librn,* Stark County District Library (Sandy Valley), Magnolia OH. 216-866-3633

Wilkin, Marta, *Bkmobile Coordr,* Franklin-Johnson County Public Library, Franklin IN. 317-738-2833

Wilkin, Martha, *Librn,* Highland County District (Lynchburg Branch), Lynchburg OH. 513-364-2511

Wilkins, Alice, *Dir,* Robeson Technical Institute Library, Lumberton NC. 919-738-7101, Ext 66

Wilkins, Barratt, *State Librn,* Florida Computer Catalog of Monographic Holdings, (FLORIDA COMCAT), FL. 904-487-2651
Wilkins, Barratt, *State Librn,* Florida Library Information Network, FL. 904-487-2651
Wilkins, Barratt, *Dir,* State Library of Florida, Div of Library Services, Dept of State, Tallahassee FL. 904-487-2651
Wilkins, Diane, *On-Line Servs,* Wilfrid Laurier University Library, Waterloo ON. 519-884-1970
Wilkins, Donna J, *ILL,* Hazel Park Memorial Library, Hazel Park MI. 313-542-0940
Wilkins, Eleanore E, *Librn,* United States Geological Survey Library, Menlo Park CA. 415-323-8111, Ext 2207
Wilkins, Elizabeth R, *Assoc Librn,* University of Washington Libraries (Law Library), Seattle WA. 206-543-4089
Wilkins, Joyce, *Librn,* Whitehall City Library, Whitehall MI. 616-894-4048
Wilkins, June, *ILL & Acq,* Woodstock Public Library & Art Gallery, Woodstock ON. 519-537-4801
Wilkins, Karen, *Asst Librn,* Aliceville Public Library, Aliceville AL. 205-373-6691
Wilkins, Madeleine, *Librn,* National Recreation & Park Association, Joseph Lee Memorial Library & Information Center, Arlington VA. 703-525-0606
Wilkins, Madge L, *Librn,* Hughes Tool Co, Business & Technical Library, Houston TX. 713-924-2583
Wilkins, Marilyn, *Media,* New Orleans Public Library, Simon Heinsheim & Fisk Libraries, New Orleans LA. 504-586-4905
Wilkins, Mary Ann, *Librn,* Duke University (Math-Physics), Durham NC. 919-684-8118
Wilkins, Mary I, *Asst Dir,* Linden Public Library, Linden IN. 317-339-4239
Wilkins, Mrs DeWight, *Librn,* Dallas County Library (Sparkman Branch), Sparkman AR. 501-352-3592
Wilkins, Ruth W, *Librn,* University of Utah (Law Library), Salt Lake City UT. 801-581-6438
Wilkins, Shirley, *Dir,* Johnson C Smith University, James B Duke Memorial Library, Charlotte NC. 704-372-2370, Ext 211, 212
Wilkinson, Betty A, *Dir,* Providence Saint Margaret Health Center, Health Center Library, Kansas City KS. 913-596-4795
Wilkinson, Billy R, *Dir,* University of Maryland Baltimore County Library, Baltimore MD. 301-455-2457
Wilkinson, Bro Brendan, *Dir,* College of Santa Fe, Fogelson Library Center, Santa Fe NM. 505-473-6011
Wilkinson, E E, *AV,* Abraham Baldwin Agricultural College, Baldwin Library, Tifton GA. 912-386-3223
Wilkinson, Elizabeth L, *Librn,* San Miguel County Public Library, Telluride CO. 303-728-4519
Wilkinson, Evon, *Ref,* Tangipahoa Parish Library, Amite LA. 504-748-9387
Wilkinson, Gene L, *Assoc Prof,* University of Georgia, Dept of Educational Media & Librarianship, GA. 404-542-3810
Wilkinson, Irene A, *Tech Serv,* Public Library of Brookline, Brookline MA. 617-734-0100
Wilkinson, Jane, *Cat,* Gloucester County College, Library-Media Center, Sewell NJ. 609-468-5000, Ext 294
Wilkinson, Marjorie, *Librn,* Fairbury Public Library, Fairbury NE. 402-729-2843
Wilkinson, Marjorie, *Librn,* Knightstown Public Library, Knightstown IN. 317-345-5095
Wilkinson, Mrs Gary W, *Librn,* North Dakota Memorial Mental Health & Retardation Center Library, Mandan ND. 701-663-6575
Wilkinson, Nancy, *In Charge,* Alexander Grant & Co Library, Chicago IL. 312-856-0001
Wilkinson, Natasha, *Librn,* Pacific-Union Club Library, San Francisco CA. 415-775-1233
Wilkinson, Patrick, *Doc,* University of Northern Iowa Library, Cedar Falls IA. 319-273-2737
Wilkinson, Patrick, *Maps,* University of Northern Iowa Library, Cedar Falls IA. 319-273-2737
Wilkinson, Tom, *Media,* New River Community College, Learning Resource Center, Dublin VA. 703-674-4121, Ext 303
Wilkinson, Tom, *Circ,* Richland College, Learning Resources Center, Dallas TX. 214-746-4460

Wilkinson, Virginia, *Assoc Prof,* Middle Tennessee State University, Department of Library Service, TN. 615-898-2740 & 898-5555
Wilkinson, Virginia, *Acq,* Middle Tennessee State University, Andrew L Todd Library, Murfreesboro TN. 615-898-2622
Wilkinson, William A, *Mgr,* Monsanto Co, Information Center Library, Saint Louis MO. 694-4736
Wilkinson, Zera, *Librn,* Frio Public Library, Pearsall TX. 512-334-2496
Wilkish, Susan, *ILL & Ad,* Ipswich Public Library, Ipswich MA. 617-356-4646
Wilks, Brian B, *Librn,* York University (Steacie Science Library), Downsview ON. 416-667-3927
Will, Barbara, *Ch & YA,* Mid-York Library System, Utica NY. 315-735-8328
Will, Elizabeth J, *Librn,* First Lutheran Church, Parish Library, Johnstown PA. 814-539-1179
Will, LaVerne, *Dir,* Sherwood Public Library, Sherwood OR. 503-625-5322
Will, Lavina K, *Librn,* Mount Jewett Memorial Library, Mount Jewett PA. 814-778-5588
Will, Mary, *Librn,* Priest River Library, Priest River ID. 208-418-5501
Will, Mary Kay, *Ch,* Union City Free Public Library, Union City NJ. 201-866-7500
Willan, Donna, *Asst Librn & Ch,* Williams Lake Library, Williams Lake BC. 604-392-3630
Willar, Arline, *Reader Serv & Bibliog Instr,* Northeastern University Libraries, Boston MA. 617-437-2350
Willard, Barbara B, *Spec Coll,* Hays Public Library, Hays KS. 913-625-9014
Willard, Barbara J, *Librn,* IBM Corp, Burlington Technical Information Center, Essex Junction VT. 802-769-3931
Willard, Charles, *Dir,* Princeton Theological Seminary, Speer Library, Princeton NJ. 609-921-8300
Willard, D Dean, *Dept Head,* Fort Hays State University, Dept of Library Science, KS. 913-628-4431
Willard, D Dean, *Dir,* Fort Hays State University, Forsyth Library, Hays KS. 913-628-4431
Willard, Linda R, *ILL & Tech Serv,* Trinity College Library, Burlington VT. 802-658-0337, Ext 343
Willbanks, Nella, *Circ,* Tyler Junior College, Edgar H Vaughn Memorial Library, Tyler TX. 214-592-5993, 593-3342
Willberg, Carolyn S, *Dir,* Ellensburg Public Library, Ellensburg WA. 509-962-9863, Ext 250
Willbern, Jo, *Ref,* Coffeyville Public Library, Coffeyville KS. 316-251-1370
Willbur, Norma, *Librn,* Marcellus Township Library, Marcellus MI. 616-646-9654
Wille, Clara Ann, *Asst Dir,* Garfield County Free Library, Jordan MT. 406-557-2297
Wille, Kathy, *Tech Serv,* Inver Hills Community College, Learning Resource Center, Inver Grove Heights MN. 612-455-9621, Ext 58
Willes, Glenda, *Dir,* Eagle Public Library, Eagle ID. 208-939-6813
Willet, Ruth, *Hist,* Buffalo & Erie County Public Library System, Buffalo NY. 716-856-7525
Willett, Charles, *Acq,* University of Florida Libraries, Gainesville FL. 904-392-0341
Willett, Edward J, *Exec Officer,* United States Office of Personnel Management, Federal Executive Institute Library, Charlottesville VA. 804-296-0181
Willett, Holly G, *Ch,* New Bedford Free Public Library, Subregional Headquarters for Eastern Massachusetts Regional Library System, New Bedford MA. 617-999-6291
Willett, Martha, *Tech Serv & Bibliog Instr,* Indiana State University, Evansville Library, Evansville IN. 812-464-1824
Willett, Mary, *Asst Dir,* Harbor Beach Public Library, Harbor Beach MI. 517-479-5284
Willey, Darro C, *Dir,* Great River Regional Library, Saint Cloud MN. 612-251-7282
Willey, Darro C, *In Charge,* Saint Cloud Library, Saint Cloud MN. 612-251-7282
Willey, Mary E, *Librn,* Knox College (Science), Galesburg IL. 309-343-0112, Ext 246
Willey, Mary E, *Spec Coll,* Knox College, Henry W Seymour Library, Galesburg IL. 309-343-0112, Ext 246
Willford, Joanne, *On-Line Servs,* General Dynamics, Pomona Division Library, Pomona CA. 714-629-5111, Ext 4151, 4161

Willhite, Dorothy, *Dir,* Pearl City Memorial Library, Pearl City IL. 815-443-2832
Williammee, Lenora, *Librn,* Union Public Library, Union OR. 503-562-5811
Williams, Ada, *Circ,* Paine College, Warren A Candler Memorial Library, Augusta GA. 404-722-4471, Ext 253
Williams, Adele P, *Dir,* Allegany Public Library, Allegany NY. 716-373-1056
Williams, Agnes, *Librn,* Chatham-Effingham-Liberty Regional Library (W W Law Neighborhood Facility), Savannah GA. 912-236-8040
Williams, Alice, *Librn,* Lynn Public Library (Wyoma Branch), Lynn MA. 617-595-3735
Williams, Anita, *ILL,* Washington & Lee University, The University Library, Lexington VA. 703-463-9111, Ext 403
Williams, Ann T, *Asst Librn,* University of Texas (Dental Branch Library), Houston TX. 713-792-4094
Williams, Anne, *Bibliog Instr,* University of Texas at Tyler, Tyler TX. 214-566-1471
Williams, Anne E, *Librn,* Hopkins, Sutter, Mulroy, Davis & Cromartie, Law Library, Chicago IL. 312-558-6732
Williams, Autha S, *Chief Librn,* United States Army (Transportation School Technical Information & Research Center), Fort Eustis VA. 804-878-5563
Williams, B M, *Acq,* University of Missouri-Rolla Library, Rolla MO. 314-341-4227
Williams, Barbara, *Cat,* Canal Fulton Public Library, Canal Fulton OH. 216-854-4148
Williams, Barbara, *Asst Dir & ILL,* Roddenbery Memorial Library, Cairo GA. 912-377-3632
Williams, Barbara K, *Librn,* Prudential Insurance Co of America, Prudential Recreation & Business Library, Jacksonville FL. 904-399-2711
Williams, Barbara M, *State Librn, Dir Dept Libr & Arch,* Kentucky Department of Library & Archives, Frankfort KY. 502-564-7910
Williams, Bernice, *Librn,* Kinchafoonee Regional Library (Lee County), Leesburg GA. 912-995-2902
Williams, Betsy, *Asst Librn,* East Tennessee State University (Medical Library), Johnson City TN. 615-928-6426, Ext 252
Williams, Betty, *Dir,* Webster County Public Library, Dixon KY. 502-639-9171
Williams, Betty H, *Cat,* Lander College Library, Larry A Jackson Library, Greenwood SC. 803-229-8366
Williams, Betty Lu, *Librn,* Antioch Township Library, Antioch IL. 312-395-0874
Williams, Bonnie, *Librn,* New York Public Library (Grand Concourse), New York NY. 212-583-6611
Williams, Brenda M, *Tech Serv & Ref,* Lewiston City Library, Lewiston ID. 208-743-6519
Williams, Brian, *Bibliog Instr,* University of California, University Library, Santa Cruz CA. 408-429-2076
Williams, Calvin, *Ref & Bibliog Instr,* Saginaw Valley State College Library & Learning Resources Center, University Center MI. 517-790-4237
Williams, Carol, *Outreach,* Chesterfield County Library, Chesterfield SC. 803-623-7489
Williams, Catherine, *Asst Librn,* Argos Public Library, Argos IN. 219-892-5818
Williams, Charles, *Librn,* Public Library of Charlotte & Mecklenburg County, Inc (South), Charlotte NC. 704-374-2011
Williams, Clara B, *Librn,* Public Library of the District of Columbia (Garnet C Wilkinson), Washington DC. 202-767-7338
Williams, Constance D, *Tech Librn,* Gilbert-Commonwealth Associates, Inc, Corp Library, Reading PA. 215-775-2600, Ext 3130
Williams, Cynthia, *Chmn,* Health Science Library & Information Cooperative, ME. 207-622-4794
Williams, Cynthia, *Librn,* Regional Memorial Hospital, Health Sciences Library, Brunswick ME. 207-729-0181, Ext 365
Williams, Danby O, *Librn,* Winchester-Clark County Public Library, Winchester KY. 606-744-5661
Williams, Daniel T, *Spec Coll,* Tuskegee Institute, Hollis Burke Frissell Library, Tuskegee Institute AL. 205-727-8894

WILLIAMS

Williams, David R, *Dir,* Douglas College Tech & Vocational Institute Library, New Westminster BC. 604-521-4851

Williams, David S, *Librn,* Marion Correctional Institution, Adrean Memorial Library, Marion OH. 614-382-5781, Ext 345

Williams, Davide B, *Librn,* United States Department of Housing & Urban Development, Region IV Library, Atlanta GA. 404-221-4576

Williams, Dean, *ILL, Commun Servs & On-Line Servs,* Pembroke State University, Mary Livermore Library, Pembroke NC. 919-521-4214, Ext 238

Williams, Debbie, *Tech Serv,* Lee College, Learning Resources Center, Baytown TX. 713-427-5611, Ext 279, 277

Williams, Deborah, *Ch,* Binghamton Public Library, Binghamton NY. 607-723-6457

Williams, Delmus, *Asst Dir,* Western Illinois University Libraries, Macomb IL. 309-298-2411

Williams, DeWitt, *ILL,* Jackson County Public Library, Ripley WV. 304-372-2831

Williams, Dianne McAfee, *Dir,* Wisconsin Department of Public Instruction (Bureau of Instructional Media Program), Madison WI. 608-266-1965

Williams, Dinah, *Educ,* Northeast Louisiana University, Sandel Library, Monroe LA. 318-342-2195

Williams, Dinah, *On-Line Servs,* Northeast Louisiana University, Sandel Library, Monroe LA. 318-342-2195

Williams, Donna, *ILL & Circ,* Le Sueur-Waseca Regional Library, Waseca MN. 507-835-2910

Williams, Donna E, *Cat,* Purdue University, North Central Campus Library, Westville IN. 219-785-2541

Williams, Doris, *Librn,* State University of New York (Biological Sciences), Stony Brook NY. 516-246-5662

Williams, Dorothy, *Asst Librn,* Northland Pioneer College, Snowflake Center Library, Snowflake AZ. 602-536-7871

Williams, Dorothy, *Dir,* Presbyterian Hospital, Medical Library, Oklahoma City OK. 405-271-4266

Williams, Dorothy J, *Acq,* Bennett College, Thomas F Holgate Library, Greensboro NC. 919-273-4431, Ext 139

Williams, Dorothy P, *Asst Dir,* University of North Florida Library, Jacksonville FL. 904-646-2553

Williams, Dorothy P, *Assoc Prof,* University of North Florida, Library Science Program, FL. 904-646-2553

Williams, Earlon, *Librn,* Angelina College Library, Lufkin TX. 713-639-1301

Williams, Edna, *In Charge,* East Chicago Public Library (Calumet), East Chicago IN. 219-397-2453

Williams, Edna, *Acq,* Tuskegee Institute, Hollis Burke Frissell Library, Tuskegee Institute AL. 205-727-8894

Williams, Edna J, *Chief Librn,* Florida Memorial College Library, Miami FL. 305-625-4141, Ext 148

Williams, Elizabeth, *Librn,* Brazoria County Library (Pearland Branch), Pearland TX. 713-485-4876

Williams, Elizabeth, *ILL,* Medical University of South Carolina Library, Charleston SC. 803-792-2374

Williams, Elizabeth D, *Librn,* Safeway Stores Library, Oakland CA. 415-891-3000

Williams, Elsie M, *Librn,* Veterans Memorial Library, Garwood TX. 713-758-3251

Williams, Emily, *Librn,* Forsyth County Public Library (Southside), Winston-Salem NC. 919-727-2577

Williams, Emma Inman, *Spec Coll,* Jackson-Madison County Library, Jackson TN. 901-423-0225

Williams, Ethelynn, *Ad,* New Rochelle Public Library, New Rochelle NY. 914-632-7878

Williams, Etta, *Librn,* Ethyl Corp, Research Laboratories Library, Ferndale MI. 313-399-9600

Williams, Evan, *Spec Coll,* Kansas State University, Farrell Library, Manhattan KS. 913-532-6516

Williams, Faye, *Librn,* Kemper-Newton Regional Library (Scooba Branch), Scooba MS. 601-476-3611

Williams, Faye, *Coll Develop,* Virginia Commonwealth University (Tompkins-McCaw Library), Richmond VA. 804-786-0629

Williams, Florence, *Asst Librn,* Chicago Board of Education Library, Chicago IL. 312-641-4105

Williams, Frances, *Asst Librn,* Gardendale Public Library, Gardendale AL. 205-631-6639

Williams, Frances G, *Reader Serv,* Wheaton College Library, Norton MA. 617-285-7722, Ext 518

Williams, Francine, *Tech Serv,* Kearney Public Library, Kearney NE. 308-237-5133

Williams, Fred E, *Prof,* Bowling Green State University, Dept of Library & Educational Media, OH. 419-372-2461

Williams, Gary, *ILL,* Warder Public Library, Springfield OH. 323-8616 & 323-9751

Williams, Geneva, *ILL & Ref,* Western State College of Colorado, Leslie J Savage Library, Gunnison CO. 303-943-2053

Williams, Geneva, *Bibliog Instr,* Western State College of Colorado, Leslie J Savage Library, Gunnison CO. 303-943-2053

Williams, Genevieve, *Acq,* Lee County Library System Administrative Office, Fort Myers FL. 813-334-3221

Williams, George L, *Dir,* Nova Scotia Institute of Technology Library, Halifax NS. 902-424-4333

Williams, George W, *Dir,* University of Michigan Libraries (Ford L Lemler Educational Film Library), Ann Arbor MI. 313-764-5360

Williams, Gloria, *Acq,* Scarborough Public Library, Scarborough ON. 416-291-1991

Williams, Gloria B, *Tech Serv,* Mercer University in Atlanta Library, Atlanta GA. 404-451-0331, Ext 47, 66

Williams, Gordon, *Librn,* Center for Health Administration Studies, Chicago IL. 312-753-4191

Williams, Gudrun, *ILL & Ref,* Loma Linda University, Vernier Radcliffe Memorial Library, Loma Linda CA. 714-796-7311, Ext 2916

Williams, Gussie, *Librn,* Salt River Tribal Library, Scottsdale AZ. 602-949-7234

Williams, Gwendolyn, *Dir,* Prichard Public Library, Prichard AL. 205-452-4395

Williams, Helen F, *Pub Serv,* Morgan State University, Morris A Soper Library, Baltimore MD. 301-444-3488, 444-3489

Williams, Helen M, *Librn,* United States Air Force (Wheeler Air Force Base Library), Wheeler AFB HI. 808-471-7411

Williams, Helen W, *Librn,* York General Hospital Library, Rock Hill SC. 803-324-4200, Ext 387

Williams, Henry L, *Dir,* Moravian College, Reeves Library, Bethlehem PA. 215-865-0741, Ext 200

Williams, Herbert, *Tech Serv,* Meredith College, Carlyle Campbell Library, Raleigh NC. 919-833-6461, Ext 231

Williams, James, *Media,* Elmhurst College, A C Buehler Library, Elmhurst IL. 312-279-4100, Ext 255

Williams, James, *Prof,* University of Pittsburgh, School of Library & Information Science, PA. 412-624-5230

Williams, James F, *Librn,* Federal Aviation Administration, National Aviation Facilities Experimental Center Library, Atlantic City NJ. 609-641-8200, Ext 2124

Williams, James F, *Head,* Wayne State University Libraries (Vera P Shiffman Medical Library), Detroit MI. 313-577-1088

Williams, James M, *Dir Libr Serv,* Philips Roxane, Inc Library, Saint Joseph MO. 816-233-2571

Williams, Jan E, *Supvr Tech Libr,* Monsanto Co, Information Center Library, Saint Louis MO. 694-4736

Williams, Jane, *Asst Librn,* Eastern New Mexico University Library (Instructional Resources Center), Portales NM. 505-562-2258

Williams, Jane, *Dir,* Jordaan Memorial Library, Larned KS. 316-285-2876

Williams, Jane, *Librn,* Wallowa County Library, Enterprise OR. 503-426-3969

Williams, Janet, *Librn,* Educational Testing Service, Carl Campbell Brigham Library, Princeton NJ. 609-921-9000, Ext 2667

Williams, Janet, *Ad,* A Holmes Johnson Memorial Library, Kodiak Public Library, Kodiak AK. 907-486-3312

Williams, Janet, *Ch,* Moore Memorial Public Library, Texas City TX. 713-948-3111, Ext 160

Williams, Janet, *Dir,* Scott County Library System, Shakopee MN. 612-445-7750

Williams, Janice, *Librn,* Charles F Kettering Foundation, Research Laboratory Library, Yellow Springs OH. 513-767-7271

Williams, Janis, *Librn,* Blue Cross Association-Blue Shield Association, Corporate Library Blue Cross NE Ohio, Cleveland OH. 216-687-7527

Williams, Jean, *In Charge,* American Medical Systems Inc, Information Center, Minneapolis MN. 612-927-4211

Williams, Jean, *Asst Chief Librn & Ch,* Belleville Public Library, Belleville ON. 613-968-7536

Williams, Jean, *Ad,* Kelley Library, Salem Public Library, Salem NH. 603-898-7064

Williams, Jean, *Asst Librn,* Stockton Township Public Library, Stockton IL. 815-947-2030

Williams, Jean, *Acq,* Virginia State College, Johnston Memorial Library, Petersburg VA. 804-520-6171

Williams, Jerre Roe, *Librn,* Corsicana Public Library, Corsicana TX. 214-872-3071, Ext 3072

Williams, Jimmie Nell, *Doc,* Jacksonville State University Library, Jacksonville AL. 205-435-9820, Ext 213, 214

Williams, Joan, *Ch,* El Centro Public Library, El Centro CA. 714-352-0751

Williams, Joan, *Librn,* Mercer County Library (Lawrence Branch), Lawrence NJ. 609-882-9246

Williams, Joan N, *Dir,* Elmwood Public Library, Elmwood NE. 402-994-4125

Williams, John, *Acq & Cat,* Mesquite Public Library, Mesquite TX. 214-285-6369

Williams, John, *Pub Servs,* Wright State University Library, Dayton OH. 513-873-2380

Williams, John Clemens, *Dir,* Shawnee State College Library, Portsmouth OH. 614-354-3205, Ext 29

Williams, Johnette, *Educ Servs,* Glendale Community College, John F Prince Library, Glendale AZ. 602-934-2211, Ext 239, 242

Williams, Judith, *Librn,* Southborough Public Library, Southborough MA. 617-485-5031

Williams, Judy, *Asst Dir,* Jacksonville Public Library System, Haydon Burns Library, Jacksonville FL. 904-633-6870

Williams, Julia, *Librn,* Jackson-George Regional Library System (Vancleave Public), Ocean Springs MS. 601-826-5857

Williams, Julie, *Ch, YA & Bkmobile Coordr,* LaSalle Parish Library, Jena LA. 318-992-5675

Williams, K Jill, *Dir,* American Humane Association, Roberta Wright Reeves Memorial Library, Englewood CO. 303-779-1400

Williams, Karin, *Librn,* Weyerhaeuser Corporate Library, Federal Way WA. 206-924-2345

Williams, Karin H, *Librn,* Weyerhaeuser Co, Corporate Library, Tacoma WA. 206-924-2345

Williams, Kay, *Librn,* Berkeley County Library (Goose Creek Branch), Goose Creek SC. 803-899-2218

Williams, Kenneth, *Per,* Hudson Valley Community College Learning Resources Center, Dwight Marvin Library, Troy NY. 518-283-1100, Ext 629

Williams, Kenneth, *Librn,* Institute for Behavioral Research, Inc Library, Silver Spring MD. 301-585-3915

Williams, Lauren, *Doc,* Florida State University, Robert Manning Strozier Library, Tallahassee FL. 904-644-5211

Williams, Lawrence, *Media,* West Liberty State College, Paul N Elbin Library, West Liberty WV. 304-336-8035

Williams, Leonette, *Acq,* University of Southern California (Asa V Call Law Library), Los Angeles CA. 213-743-6487

Williams, Lillian, *Coordr Libr Serv,* J Sargeant Reynolds Community College (Downtown Campus-Learning Resources Center), Richmond VA. 804-786-6249

Williams, Linda, *Librn,* Manhattan Christian College, B D Phillips Memorial Library, Manhattan KS. 913-539-7582, Ext 27

Williams, Linda, *Acq,* Northern Arizona University Libraries, Flagstaff AZ. 602-523-9011

Williams, Linda L, *Ref,* West Lafayette Public Library, West Lafayette IN. 317-743-2261

Williams, Luester, *In Charge,* Tuskegee Institute (Architecture), Tuskegee Institute AL. 205-727-8330

Williams, Lula M, *Acq,* Tougaloo College, L Zenobia Coleman Library, Tougaloo MS. 601-956-4941, Ext 271

Williams, Lydia S, *Librn,* Public Library of Charlotte & Mecklenburg County, Inc (Independence), Charlotte NC. 704-568-3151

Williams, Lynda, *Spec Coll,* Marion Public Library, Marion OH. 614-387-0992

Williams, M Alexia, *Ch,* Jefferson-Madison Regional Library, McIntire Public Library, Charlottesville VA. 804-296-6157

Williams, Madeline, *Circ,* Cherry Hill Free Public Library, Cherry Hill NJ. 609-667-0300

Williams, Mae E, *Librn,* Mercer Medical Center, David B Ackley Medical Library, Trenton NJ. 609-396-4070, Ext 206, 207

Williams, Marcia, *Data Process,* EG&G Idaho, Inc, INEL Technical Library, Idaho Falls ID. 208-526-1185

Williams, Marcia, *Info Assts,* Marsteller Inc Library, New York NY. 212-752-6500, Ext 829

Williams, Marcia J, *Per,* Hughes Aircraft Co (Technical Library), Culver City CA. 213-391-0711, Ext 2615

Williams, Margaret, *Librn,* Flint Public Library (Downtown), Flint MI. 313-235-4619

Williams, Margaret, *Assoc Librn,* Memorial University of Newfoundland Library, Saint John's NF. 709-753-1200

Williams, Margot, *Govt Doc,* Long Island University, Brooklyn Center Libraries, Brooklyn NY. 212-834-6060, 834-6064

Williams, Margot, *On-Line Servs & Bibliog Instr,* Long Island University, Brooklyn Center Libraries, Brooklyn NY. 212-834-6060, 834-6064

Williams, Margot G, *AV,* Gloucester Lyceum & Sawyer Free Library, Gloucester MA. 617-283-0376

Williams, Marguerite, *Librn,* Vanceboro Public Library, Vanceboro NC. 919-244-0571

Williams, Marjorie, *Librn,* Flint River Regional Library (Margaret Mitchell Branch), Fayetteville GA. 404-461-8841

Williams, Marjorie, *ILL,* Stoughton Public Library, Stoughton MA. 617-344-2711

Williams, Marvin, *Cat,* Tennessee State Library & Archives, Nashville TN. 615-741-2764

Williams, Mary, *Librn,* Ontario Civil Service Commission Library, Toronto ON. 416-965-7096

Williams, Mary, *Librn,* Trenton Public Library, Trenton IL. 618-224-7662

Williams, Mary Ann, *Regional Librn,* Tulsa City-County Library, Tulsa OK. 918-581-5221

Williams, Mary C, *Librn,* Clayton Environmental Consultants, Inc, Library, Southfield MI. 313-424-8860, Ext 35

Williams, Mary E, *Dir,* Clarion State College, Venango Campus Library, Oil City PA. 814-676-6591, Ext 42

Williams, Mary E, *Librn,* Poteet Public Library, Poteet TX. 512-742-8917

Williams, Mary Ellen, *Bkmobile Coordr,* Autauga-Prattville Public Library System, Prattville AL. 205-365-3396

Williams, Mary G, *Librn,* Church of the Incarnation, Marmion Library, Dallas TX. 214-521-5101

Williams, Mary-Lois, *Cat,* Canadian Imperial Bank of Commerce, Information Centre Library, Toronto ON. 416-862-3053

Williams, Maudine, *Art,* Indiana University-Purdue University at Indianapolis (Herron School of Art), Indianapolis IN. 317-923-3651

Williams, Maureen, *Spec Coll,* Saint Francis Xavier University, Angus L Macdonald Library, Antigonish NS. 902-867-2267

Williams, Melissa, *Librn,* Miller, Anderson, Nash, Yerke & Wiener Library, Portland OR. 503-224-5858

Williams, Michael, *Cat,* United States Commission on Civil Rights, National Clearinghouse Library, Washington DC. 202-254-6636

Williams, Michelle, *Ref,* Chickasaw Library System, Ardmore OK. 405-223-3164

Williams, Mildred M, *Personnel,* Dallas Public Library, Dallas TX. 214-748-9071

Williams, Mrs Avery, *Ref,* Roosevelt University, Murray-Green Library, Chicago IL. 312-341-3639

Williams, Mrs Lynwood, *Circ,* Kurth Memorial Library, Lufkin TX. 713-634-7923

Williams, Mrs R L, *Asst Dir,* Vaughan Memorial Library, Galax Public Library, Galax VA. 703-236-2351

Williams, N, *Per,* Atlantic Christian College, Hackney Library, Wilson NC. 919-237-3161, Ext 330

Williams, Nadine, *Librn,* Contra Costa County Library (Brentwood Branch), Brentwood CA. 415-634-4101

Williams, Nancy, *Acq,* Decatur Public Library, Decatur IL. 217-428-6617, Ext 33

Williams, Nancy, *Ref & Bibliog Instr,* Mercer University in Atlanta Library, Atlanta GA. 404-451-0331, Ext 47, 66

Williams, Nancy, *Tech Serv,* Oak Brook Free Public Library, Oak Brook IL. 312-654-2222

Williams, Nancy, *Cat,* University of Florida Libraries, Gainesville FL. 904-392-0341

Williams, Nell, *Circ,* Dallas Public Library, Dallas OR. 503-623-2633

Williams, Nell K, *Librn,* Refugio County Public Library, Refugio TX. 512-526-2608

Williams, Norma, *Doc,* Columbus College, Simon Schwob Memorial Library, Columbus GA. 404-560-2042

Williams, Nyal Z, *Librn,* Ball State University (Music), Muncie IN. 317-285-7356

Williams, Odessa, *Acq,* Elizabeth City State University, G R Little Library, Elizabeth City NC. 919-335-0551, Ext 332

Williams, P, *Libr Asst,* Oakland Public Library (Brookfield Village), Oakland CA. 415-562-8282

Williams, Pam, *Librn,* Shelby County Regional Library (Pelham), Pelham AL. 205-669-7851

Williams, Pamela, *Asst Librn,* Brunswick-Glynn County Regional Library (Talking Book Center), Brunswick GA. 912-264-7360

Williams, Patricia, *Dir,* Georgetown Public Library, Georgetown DE. 302-856-7958

Williams, Patricia, *Chmn,* Twin Cities Biomedical Consortium, MN. 612-920-4400, Ext 333

Williams, Patricia A, *Chief Librn,* Hennepin County Medical Center, Thomas Lowry Library, Minneapolis MN. 612-347-2710

Williams, Patricia A, *Librn,* Thomas Lowry Health Sciences Library, Hennepin County Medical Center, Minneapolis MN. 612-347-2710

Williams, Peggy Sue, *Dir,* Upton County Public Library, McCamey TX. 915-652-8718

Williams, Phillip, *Ad,* Jefferson-Madison Regional Library, McIntire Public Library, Charlottesville VA. 804-296-6157

Williams, Richard C, *Cat,* New York Public Library (Preparation Services), New York NY. 212-790-6262

Williams, Richmond D, *Dir,* Eleutherian Mills-Hagley Foundation, Eleutherian Mills Historical Library, Greenville DE. 302-658-2400

Williams, Robert, *Ref,* Ohio State University Libraries (Health Sciences Library), Columbus OH. 614-422-9810

Williams, Robert Bruce, *Dir,* Cumberland College, Norma Perkins Hagan Memorial Library, Williamsburg KY. 606-549-0558

Williams, Robert C, *Librn,* University of Alaska, Fairbanks (Institute of Marine Science), Fairbanks AK. 907-479-7740

Williams, Roberta S, *Dir,* Duplin County Library, Dorothy Wightman Library, Kenansville NC. 919-296-1333

Williams, Roger M, *Dir,* Nazarene Bible College Library, Colorado Springs CO. 303-596-5110, Ext 29, 46

Williams, Ronald David, *Asst Prof,* Emory University, Div of Librarianship, GA. 404-329-6840

Williams, Ruby, *In Charge,* Washington County Historical Society Library, Salem IN. 812-883-6495

Williams, Ruth, *ILL,* Washington County Library System, William Alexander Percy Memorial Library, Greenville MS. 601-335-2331

Williams, Ruth J, *Librn,* Michael Baker Jr, Inc Library, Beaver PA. 412-495-7711, Ext 357

Williams, Sally F, *Budget & Planning Officer,* Harvard University Library (Harvard College Library (Headquarters in Harry Elkins Widener Memorial Library)), Cambridge MA. 617-495-2401

Williams, Sandra, *Cat,* Saint John's University, Alcuin Library, Collegeville MN. 612-363-2119

Williams, Sandra C, *ILL,* Central Virginia Community College Library, Lynchburg VA. 804-239-0321, Ext 231

Williams, Sheila, *AV,* Grand Prairie Memorial Library, Grand Prairie TX. 214-264-1571

Williams, Sheryl, *Librn,* University of Kansas Libraries (Kansas Collection), Lawrence KS. 913-864-4274

Williams, Sieglinde, *Doc,* Geauga County Public Library, Chardon OH. 216-285-7601

Williams, Stephanie V, *On-Line Servs,* United States Department of the Navy (Naval Sea Systems Command, Library Documentation Branch), Washington DC. 202-692-3305

Williams, Sue, *Librn,* American Automobile Association Library, Falls Church VA. 703-222-6466

Williams, Sue, *Eng Secy,* Kollmorgen Corp, Photo Research Division Library, Burbank CA. 213-843-6100

Williams, Sue, *Asst Librn,* Malakoff Public Library, Malakoff TX. 214-489-1818

Williams, Susan S, *Asst Dir,* Northland Library Cooperative, Alpena MI. 517-356-4444

Williams, Suzanne, *Ch,* Asheville-Buncombe Library System, Asheville NC. 704-252-8701

Williams, Suzanne, *Librn,* Spring Grove Free Public Library, Spring Grove PA. 717-225-3220

Williams, Sylvia, *Librn,* Phoenix Public Library (Harmon), Phoenix AZ. 602-262-6362

Williams, Telva, *Librn,* Arcola Public Library, Arcola IL. 217-268-4477

Williams, Tim, *Ref,* J Sargeant Reynolds Community College (Parham Campus Learning Resources Center), Richmond VA. 804-264-3220

Williams, Timothy, *Dir,* Garland County Community College, Learning Resource Center, Hot Springs AR. 501-767-9371, 767-4553

Williams, Todd, *Ref & Doc & Bibliog Instr,* San Jose City College Library, San Jose CA. 408-298-2181, Ext 410

Williams, Vaneesa, *Pub Servs,* Flint River Regional Library, Griffin GA. 404-227-2756

Williams, Velma S, *Asst Dir & Ch,* Nevada Public Library, Nevada MO. 417-667-2831

Williams, Verna, *Dir,* Normal Memorial Library, Fayette OH. 419-237-2115

Williams, Vicki, *Librn,* Dekalb Library System (Scott Candler Branch), Decatur GA. 404-284-7848

Williams, Vina, *Librn,* Dunklin County Library (Cardwell Branch), Cardwell MO. 314-654-3366

Williams, Vina, *Librn,* Dunklin County Library (Honersville Branch), Hornersville MO. 314-737-2728

Williams, Virginia T, *Librn,* First United Methodist Church Library, Palo Alto CA. 415-323-6167

Williams, Vivian J, *Librn,* Pearl River County Library System, Margaret Reed Crosby Memorial Library, Picayune MS. 601-798-5081

Williams, Wallace, *Librn,* Florence A Williams Public Library, Saint Croix VI. 809-773-5715

Williams, Wiley J, *Prof,* Kent State University, School of Library Science, OH. 216-672-2782, 672-7988

Williams, Wilma A, *Librn,* United States Army (Oakland Army Base Post Library), Oakland CA. 415-466-2906

Williams, Wynelle H, *Librn,* Phillips-Lee-Monroe Regional Library, Helena AR. 501-338-3537

Williams, II, James F, *Dir,* Kentucky-Ohio-Michigan-Regional Medical Library, (KOMRML), MI. 313-577-1101

Williams, Jr, Hugh E, *Dir,* Stoneham Public Library, Stoneham MA. 617-438-1324

Williams, Jr, Lee M, *Curator Latin Am Coll,* Yale University Library (Sterling Memorial Library), New Haven CT. 203-436-8345

Williamsen, Nancy, *YA,* Pocatello Public Library, Information and Video Center, Pocatello ID. 208-232-1263

Williamson, Ann, *Ch,* Central State University Library, Edmond OK. 405-341-2980, Ext 494, 495 & 496

Williamson, Anne K, *Rare Bks & Spec Coll,* Jones Library, Inc, Amherst MA. 413-256-0246

Williamson, Betty, *Dir,* Fayetteville Technical Institute, Paul H Thompson Library, Fayetteville NC. 919-323-1961

Williamson, Blanche, *Circ,* Carterville Public Library, Carterville IL. 618-985-3298

Williamson, Duane E, *Chief Librn,* United States Army (Technical Library), Dugway UT. 801-522-3565

WILLIAMSON

Williamson, Estelle B, *Sch Libr Media Specialists,* Maryland State Department of Education, Division of Library Development & Services, Baltimore MD. 301-796-8300, Ext 284

Williamson, Harriet, *Coordr,* Champaign-Urbana Consortium, IL. 217-337-2283 & 337-2299

Williamson, Harriet, *Dir,* Mercy Hospital, Library, Urbana IL. 217-337-2283, Ext. 199

Williamson, Jane, *Ser,* Memphis Theological Seminary Library, Memphis TN. 901-458-8232

Williamson, Jane, *Librn,* Womens Action Alliance Library, New York NY. 212-532-8330

Williamson, Jo Ann, *Chief Archivist,* National Archives & Records Service, Archives Branch, San Bruno CA. 415-876-9003

Williamson, John G, *Dir,* Saint Mary's College of Maryland Library, Saint Mary's City MD. 301-994-1600, Ext 216

Williamson, Josephine, *Cat,* Wofford College, Sandor Teszler Library, Spartanburg SC. 803-585-4821, Ext 396

Williamson, Larry, *Acq,* Seattle Public Library, Seattle WA. 206-625-2665

Williamson, Lil, *Admn Servs Officer,* University of Texas at Arlington Library, Arlington TX. 817-273-3391

Williamson, Linda, *Doc,* Vanderbilt University Library (Central-Science), Nashville TN. 615-322-6603

Williamson, Lydia, *Librn,* Phoenix Public Library (Saguaro), Phoenix AZ. 602-262-6801

Williamson, Mary, *WILS,* University of Wisconsin-Madison, Memorial Library, Madison WI. 608-262-3521

Williamson, Mary, *Coordr,* Wisconsin Interlibrary Loan Service, (WILS), WI. 608-263-4962

Williamson, Mildred E, *In Charge,* Pennsylvania State Supreme & Superior Courts Library, Harrisburg PA. 717-787-6199

Williamson, Miriam B, *Librn,* Blount Memorial Hospital, L R Lingeman Memorial Medical Library, Maryville TN. 615-983-7211, Ext 529

Williamson, Naja, *ILL & On-Line Servs,* Western Carolina University, Hunter Memorial Library, Cullowhee NC. 704-293-7306

Williamson, Naja, *ILL,* Western Carolina University (Interlibrary Loan), Cullowhee NC. 704-293-7306

Williamson, Peggy, *Librn,* Meriden Town Library, Meriden NH. 603-469-3252

Williamson, Rick, *Media,* Bethany College, T L Phillips Memorial Library, Bethany WV. 304-829-7000

Williamson, Ron, *Bkmobile Coordr,* Greenwood-Leflore Public Library System, Greenwood MS. 601-453-3634

Williard, Raelen, *Librn,* National Center for Appropriate Technology, Research Library, Butte MT. 406-494-4572, Ext 251

Williford, Doxie, *Acq,* University of Mississippi Library, University MS. 601-232-7091

Williford, John, *Pub Rel,* Elbert County Library, Elberton GA. 404-283-5375

Williford;, Evelyn I, *Asst Dir,* Bladen County Public Library, Elizabethtown NC. 919-862-8171

Willig, Maureen T, *Librn,* Taft, Stettinius & Hollister Library, Cincinnati OH. 513-381-2838

Willingham, Elizabeth, *Spec Educ Teacher-Librn,* South Carolina Department of Mental Retardation, Whitten Center Library & Media Resource Services, Clinton SC. 803-833-2736

Willingham, Louise, *Cat,* Atlanta Public Library, Atlanta GA. 404-688-4636

Willis, A G, *Commun Servs,* Fountaindale Public Library District, Bolingbrook IL. 312-759-2102

Willis, Anne, *Asst Librns,* Stamford Village Library, Stamford NY. 607-652-5001

Willis, Cheryl J, *Acq,* Allegany County Library, Cumberland MD. 301-777-1200

Willis, Constance, *Dir,* Saugus Public Library, Saugus MA. 617-233-0530

Willis, Dorothy B, *Librn,* Palmer Public Library, Palmer ME. 308-894-5305

Willis, Eileen, *Genealogy,* Orlando Public Library, Orlando FL. 305-425-4694

Willis, Elizabeth, *Librn,* Tucson Public Library (Marana), Tucson AZ. 602-682-4216

Willis, Esme, *Dir,* Sturgis Library, Barnstable MA. 617-362-6636

Willis, Gussie B, *Librn,* Webster Parish Library (Doyline Branch), Doyline LA. 318-377-1411

Willis, Hazel, *Librn,* J V Willis Special Library, Hammond IN. 219-931-2672

Willis, Irma, *Ch,* Okefenokee Regional Library, Waycross GA. 912-283-3126

Willis, Jeffrey A, *Librn,* Talladega County Law Library, Talladega AL. 205-362-2050

Willis, Joan, *Dir,* Gill Memorial Library, Paulsboro NJ. 609-423-5155

Willis, John, *Media,* Hartwick College Library, Oneonta NY. 607-432-4200, Ext 324

Willis, Joyce, *Librn,* Somerset County Library (Mary Jacobs Memorial Library), Rocky Hill NJ. 609-924-7073

Willis, Madelyn B, *Librn,* Doddridge County Public Library, West Union WV. 304-873-1941

Willis, Mary, *Cat,* Kirkwood Public Library, Kirkwood MO. 314-821-5770

Willis, Mary Fay, *Asst Dir,* Carnegie Public Library, Washington IN. 812-254-4586

Willis, Nell P, *Circ,* Richard H Thornton Library, Oxford NC. 919-693-1121

Willis, Patricia C, *Curator, Marianne Moore Coll,* Rosenbach Museum & Library, Philadelphia PA. 215-732-1600

Willis, Paul A, *Dir,* University of Kentucky, Margaret I King Library, Lexington KY. 606-257-3801

Willis, Sara, *Librn,* De Soto Trail Regional Library (Worth County), Sylvester GA. 912-776-2096

Willison, Maureen, *Asst,* Greater Vancouver Library Federation, Vancouver BC. 604-251-1147

Willits, Jane, *Tech Serv, Cat & On-Line Servs,* Trinity College Library, Hartford CT. 203-527-3151, Ext 396

Willits, Robert, *Regional Librn,* Eastern Shore Regional Library, Salisbury MD. 301-742-1537

Willmering, William, *Ser,* Northwestern University Library, Evanston IL. 312-492-7658

Willmert, J Allen, *Instr,* Manchester College, Educational Media Specialist Program, IN. 219-982-2141, Ext 231

Willmert, J Allen, *Dir,* Manchester College, Funderburg Library, North Manchester IN. 219-982-2141, Ext 231

Willocks, R Max, *Assoc Dir Pub Serv,* University of Florida Libraries, Gainesville FL. 904-392-0341

Willoughby, Mrs B, *Librn,* Borough of Etobicoke Public Library (Mimico Centennial), Toronto ON. 416-248-5681

Willoughby, Nona C, *Librn,* Northern Westchester Hospital Center Health Sciences Library, Mount Kisco NY. 914-666-1259

Willower, Paul, *Ch,* Corning Public Library, Corning NY. 607-936-3713

Wills, A, *Librn,* Quebec Ministere Des Affaires Sociales, Informatheque-Montreal, Montreal PQ. 514-873-3695

Wills, Alice, *Asst Dir,* Marion College Library, Marion IN. 317-674-6901, Ext 228

Wills, Ethel, *Bkmobile Coordr,* Bath County Memorial Library, Owingsville KY. 606-674-2531

Wills, Jo, *Librn,* Kent County Library System (Wyoming Branch), Wyoming MI. 616-538-4380

Wills, Keith C, *Dir,* Southwestern Baptist Theological Seminary, Fleming Library, Fort Worth TX. 817-923-1921, Ext 277

Wills, Lila, *Librn,* Mesa County Public Library (Fruita Public), Fruita CO. 303-858-7703

Wills, Margaret, *Cat,* Richard Bland College Library, Petersburg VA. 804-732-0111, Ext 226

Wills, Morris, *Tech Serv,* Utica College of Syracuse University, Frank E Gannett Memorial Library, Utica NY. 315-792-3041

Wills, Paul, *Chief Librn,* Florida Department of Agriculture & Consumer Services (Division of Forestry Library), Tallahassee FL. 904-488-8220

Wills, Richard D, *Librn,* Western State Hospital (Professional/Medical Library), Staunton VA. 703-886-2343

Wills, Richard D, *Librn,* Western State Hospital (Stribling Library), Staunton VA. 703-885-9340

Willsey, Katherine, *Librn,* Schenectady County Public Library (Woodlawn), Schenectady NY. 518-382-3508

Willson, Georgia L, *Dir,* Manchester Township Library, Manchester MI. 313-428-8045

Willson, Katherine H, *Librn,* Futures Group, Inc Library, Glastonbury CT. 203-633-3501

Willson, Paula, *Libr Asst,* Kalamazoo Institute of Arts Library, Kalamazoo MI. 616-349-7775, Ext 5

Willson, Raymond L, *Dir,* Southeast Kansas Library System, Iola KS. 316-365-3833

Wilma, Sheila, *Dir,* North Bend Public Library, North Bend OR. 503-756-6712

Wilmer, Kathryn G, *Librn,* Cuyahoga County Public Library (Brecksville Branch), Brecksville OH. 216-526-1102

Wilmeth, V, *Admin Servs,* Carleton University, Murdoch Maxwell MacOdrum Library, Ottawa ON. 613-231-4357

Wilowaty, Joyce, *Doc,* Montclair State College, Harry A Sprague Library, Upper Montclair NJ. 201-893-4291

Wilroy, Jo Ann, *Asst Dir,* First Regional Library, DeSoto County Library, Hernando MS. 601-368-4439

Wilshusen, John, *AV,* Purdue University Libraries & Audio-Visual Center, West Lafayette IN. 317-749-2571

Wilson, A, *Educ & Curric,* California State College, San Bernardino Library, San Bernardino CA. 714-887-7321

Wilson, Alice S, *Librn,* Steamship Historical Society of America, Inc, Baltimore MD. 301-727-6350

Wilson, Ann L, *Librn,* Jersey Shore Library, Jersey Shore PA. 717-398-1560

Wilson, Ann M, *Librn,* Astra Pharmaceutical Products, Inc, Technical Information Center Library, Framingham MA. 617-620-0600

Wilson, Annette, *Librn,* Hanson-McCook County Regional Library, Spencer SD. 605-246-2740

Wilson, Anthony, *Tech Serv,* Highline Community College Library, Midway WA. 206-878-3710, Ext 230

Wilson, Anthony, *Coordr,* Highline Community College Library, Library Technician Program, WA. 206-878-3710, Ext 233

Wilson, Ashby, *Ad,* Greensboro Public Library, Greensboro NC. 373-2474; 373-2471

Wilson, Audrey, *Spec Coll,* Monmouth College, Guggenhcim Library, West Long Branch NJ. 201-222-6600, Ext 264

Wilson, Barbara, *Ref,* Beaverton City Library, Beaverton OR. 503-644-2197

Wilson, Barbara, *ILL,* Bur Oak Library System, Shorewood IL. 815-729-3345, 729-3346

Wilson, Barbara, *Librn,* Plain City Public Library, Plain City OH. 614-873-4912

Wilson, Barbara A, *Chmn,* Medical Library Consortium of Santa Clara County, CA. 408-279-5650

Wilson, Barbara A, *Librn,* Santa Clara Valley Medical Center, Medical Library, San Jose CA. 408-279-5650, 279-5651

Wilson, Barbara J, *Lectr,* University of Michigan, School of Library Science, MI. 313-764-9376

Wilson, Barbara L, *Dir,* Hackley Public Library, Muskegon MI. 616-722-7276

Wilson, Barbara L, *Chief, Div of Special Libr Servs,* Rhode Island Department of State Library Services, Providence RI. 401-277-2726

Wilson, Beth, *Cat,* Missouri Historical Society Library, Saint Louis MO. 314-361-1424

Wilson, Betty J, *Acq,* Southeast Kansas Library System, Iola KS. 316-365-3833

Wilson, Betty S, *Librn,* Saint Francis Hospital, Medical Library, Poughkeepsie NY. 914-471-2000, Ext 1132

Wilson, Beverly, *Tech Serv & Acq,* Columbus Technical Institute, Educational Resources Center, Columbus OH. 614-227-2463

Wilson, Bob, *Commun Servs,* Southern Alberta Institute of Technology, Learning Resources Centre, Calgary AB. 284-8647; 284-8648

Wilson, Bobbi, *Librn,* Ottawa Institute, Irene Holm Memorial Library, Columbus OH. 614-486-5028

Wilson, Bonnie, *Head Librn,* Minnesota Historical Society (Special Libraries), Saint Paul MN. 612-296-2489

Wilson, Bonnie, *AV,* Rock Island Public Library, Rock Island IL. 309-788-7627

Wilson, Bonnie L, *Librn,* Franklin Institute of Boston Library, Boston MA. 617-423-4630, Ext 28

Wilson, Brady, *Ga Hist & Genealogy,* Chattahoochee Valley Regional Library, W C Bradley Memorial Library, Headquarters, Columbus GA. 404-327-0211

Wilson, C Daniel, *Assoc Dir, Central Libr,* Birmingham Public & Jefferson County Free Library, Birmingham AL. 205-254-2551

Wilson, Carol, *Librn,* Dorchester Community Library, Dorchester NH. 603-523-7088

Wilson, Carol, *Librn,* University of Michigan (Center for Research on Economic Development Library), Ann Arbor MI. 313-763-6609

Wilson, Carolyn, *Asst Librn,* United Methodist Publishing House Library, Nashville TN. 615-749-6437

Wilson, Catherine E, *Librn,* Charles W Gibson Public Library, Buckhannon WV. 304-472-2339

Wilson, Christine, *Dir,* Living Learning Library Center, Frostproof FL. 813-635-3264

Wilson, Clement, *Pres,* Pejepscot Historical Society, Curtis Memorial Library, Brunswick ME. 207-729-4622

Wilson, Clyde W, *Chief Librn,* United States Army (William Beaumont Army Medical Center Library), El Paso TX. 915-569-2537, 569-2580

Wilson, Cora R, *Librn,* Spokane County Medical Society Library, Spokane WA. 509-747-5777

Wilson, Cynthia, *Ext Servs Div Coordr,* Bethlehem Public Library, Bethlehem PA. 215-867-3761

Wilson, David, *ILL,* Salt Lake County Library System, Whitmore Library, Salt Lake City UT. 801-943-7614

Wilson, David, *Tech Serv & Coordr,* Salt Lake County Library System, Whitmore Library, Salt Lake City UT. 801-943-7614

Wilson, David C, *Tech Serv,* Ocmulgee Regional Library, Eastman GA. 912-374-4711

Wilson, David K, *Librn,* Custer County Historical Society Inc, Broken Bow Historical Library, Broken Bow NE. 308-872-2203

Wilson, Dean, *Librn,* Missouri Institute of Technology Library, Kansas City MO. 816-363-7030

Wilson, DeEtta C, *Dir,* Windward Community College Library, Kaneohe HI. 808-235-0077, Ext 136

Wilson, Diana, *Tech Serv,* Barrington Public Library District, Barrington IL. 312-382-1300

Wilson, Diane, *Ch,* McGregor Public Library, Highland Park Library, Highland Park MI. 313-252-0288

Wilson, Don, *YA,* Lindenhurst Memorial Library, Lindenhurst NY. 516-888-7575

Wilson, Don, *Virginiana,* Prince William Public Library, Manassas VA. 703-361-8211

Wilson, Donald H, *Bkmobile Coordr,* North Olympic Library System, Port Angeles WA. 206-457-4464

Wilson, Doris Jean, *Librn,* Washington County Library System (Avon Library), Avon MS. 601-335-1419

Wilson, Dorothy, *Asst Librn,* Colby Memorial Library, Danville NH. 603-382-6733

Wilson, Dorothy, *Librn,* Kent County Municipal Public Library (Thamesville Public), Town Hall ON. 519-692-4251

Wilson, Dorothy, *Librn,* Western Electric Co, Inc, Technical Library, Shreveport LA. 318-683-2543

Wilson, Dorothy T, *Librn,* United States Pipe & Foundry Co, Research Department Library, Burlington NJ. 609-386-1850

Wilson, Douglas L, *Dir,* Knox College, Henry W Seymour Library, Galesburg IL. 309-343-0112, Ext 246

Wilson, Dunning S, *Near Eastern,* University of California Los Angeles Library, Los Angeles CA. 213-825-1201

Wilson, E, *Actg Librn,* Texas Memorial Museum Library, Austin TX. 512-471-1604

Wilson, Eatha, *Librn,* Houston Public Library (Martin Luther King), Houston TX. 713-659-4672

Wilson, Eileen, *ILL,* EG&G Idaho, Inc, INEL Technical Library, Idaho Falls ID. 208-526-1185

Wilson, Elaine F, *Dir,* Siloam Springs Public Library, Siloam Springs AR. 501-524-4236

Wilson, Eleanor, *Dir & ILL,* Barrington College Library, Barrington RI. 401-246-1200, Ext 291

Wilson, Eleanor A, *Librn,* Alpine Public Library, Alpine TX. 915-837-2621

Wilson, Eleanor E, *Dir,* Orrville Public Library, Orrville OH. 216-683-1065

Wilson, Elizabeth, *Librn,* Pasadena Public Library (Santa Catalina), Pasadena CA. 213-794-1219

Wilson, Elizabeth, *Ref,* Surry Community College, Learning Resources Center, Dobson NC. 919-386-8121, Ext 52

Wilson, Emily, *Librn,* Silvis Public Library, Silvis IL. 309-755-3393

Wilson, Emmy-Lou, *Librn,* Detroit Public Library (Franklin), Detroit MI. 313-833-9162

Wilson, Erma, *Commun Servs,* Franklin-Johnson County Public Library, Franklin IN. 317-738-2833

Wilson, Esther, *Librn,* Moline Public Library, Moline KS. 316-647-9989

Wilson, Eunice, *Librn,* Maynard Community Library, Maynard IA. 319-637-2269

Wilson, Evelyn, *Tech Serv & Cat,* Valparaiso-Porter County Public Library System & Administrative Headquarters, Valparaiso IN. 219-462-0524

Wilson, Evie, *YA,* Tampa-Hillsborough County Public Library System, Tampa FL. 813-223-8947

Wilson, Faye, *ILL,* Saginaw Public Libraries, Hoyt Public Library, Saginaw MI. 517-755-0904

Wilson, Florabelle, *Dir,* Indiana Central University Library, Krannert Memorial Library, Indianapolis IN. 317-788-3268

Wilson, Florence, *Circ,* George Mason University Libraries, Fairfax VA. 703-323-2616

Wilson, Gene B, *Dir,* Ann Arbor Public Library, Ann Arbor MI. 313-994-2333

Wilson, George, *Media Cntr Tech,* Tyler Junior College, Edgar H Vaughn Memorial Library, Tyler TX. 214-592-5993, 593-3342

Wilson, Gordon G, *Librn,* Harper Woods Public Library, John F Kennedy Memorial Library, Harper Woods MI. 313-886-4080

Wilson, Hattie, *In Charge,* Cobb County Public Library System (Fort Hill), Marietta GA. 404-428-2665

Wilson, Hazel, *Librn,* Tampa College Library, Saint Petersburg FL. 813-527-8464, Ext 6

Wilson, Helen, *Ch,* Salem Public Library, Salem OR. 503-588-6071

Wilson, Helen, *Librn,* Shreve Memorial Library (Oil City Branch), Oil City LA. 318-221-2614

Wilson, Helen M, *Librn,* Historical Society of Western Pennsylvania Library, Pittsburgh PA. 412-681-5533

Wilson, Helen N, *Dir,* Northwestern Medical Center Library, Information Center, Saint Albans VT. 802-524-2161, 524-5238

Wilson, Hilda, *Spec Coll,* Ottumwa Public Library, Ottumwa IA. 515-682-7563

Wilson, Ian A, *City Librn,* Saint John Regional Library, Saint John NB. 506-693-1191

Wilson, J A, *Librn,* Canada Defence Research Establishment, Pacific Library, Victoria BC. 604-388-1665

Wilson, Jack T, *Librn,* Harnischfeger Corp, Engineer's Club Library, Milwaukee WI. 414-671-4400, Ext 2057

Wilson, Jane, *Librn,* Farnhamville Public Library, Farnhamville IA. 712-462-3660

Wilson, Jane P, *Librn,* Grafton Public Library, Grafton MA. 617-839-4649

Wilson, Janice E, *Librn,* Truett-McConnell College, Cofer Library, Cleveland GA. 404-865-5633

Wilson, Jeffrey L, *Dir,* Pacific Christian College, Hurst Memorial Library, Fullerton CA. 714-879-3901, Ext 34

Wilson, Jerry R, *Ref, On-Line Servs & Bibliog Instr,* Fort Hays State University, Forsyth Library, Hays KS. 913-628-4431

Wilson, Jo, *Cat,* Delta State University, W B Roberts Library, Cleveland MS. 601-843-2483

Wilson, Joan, *Librn & On-Line Servs,* Fred Hutchinson Cancer Research Center Library, Seattle WA. 206-292-2168

Wilson, Joyce, *Dir,* Indiana Vocational Technical College, Learning Resource Center, Sellersburg IN. 812-246-3301

Wilson, Joyce, *Librn,* Montrose County Regional District Library (Redvale Branch), Redvale CO. 303-327-4694

Wilson, Judith, *Dir,* Sandy Corporation, Research & Retrieval Center, Southfield MI. 313-569-4000, Ext 391

Wilson, Judith L, *Dir,* Mary Lou Johnson-Hardin County District Library, Kenton OH. 419-673-2278

Wilson, Karen, *Librn,* Bob Jones University (Music), Greenville SC. 803-242-5100, Ext 277

Wilson, Kay, *Librn,* Graysville Public Library, Graysville TN. 615-775-9242

Wilson, Kenneth S, *Assoc Dir for Colls,* Howard University Libraries, Founders Library, Washington DC. 202-636-7253

Wilson, Larry, *Dean,* Brookhaven College, Learning Resources Center, Farmers Branch TX. 214-746-5250

Wilson, Linda, *Dist Dir,* Lake Agassiz Regional Library, Moorhead MN. 218-233-7594

Wilson, Linda, *Librn,* Polk County Library, Crookston MN. 218-281-4522

Wilson, Linda L, *Librn,* Methodist Hospitals of Dallas, Medical Library, Dallas TX. 214-946-8181, Ext 321

Wilson, Lise, *Ref,* College De Maisonneuve Bibliotheque, Montreal PQ. 514-254-7131, 254-4035

Wilson, Lois, *Librn,* Delaware Township Library, Valley Falls KS. 913-945-3990

Wilson, Lorraine, *Commun Servs,* Ryerson Polytechnical Institute, Donald Mordell Learning Resources Centre, Toronto ON. 416-595-5331

Wilson, Louis C, *Dir,* Community College of Baltimore (Harbor Campus), Baltimore MD. 301-396-1860

Wilson, Lucy, *Commun Servs,* Laney College Library-Learning Resources Center, Oakland CA. 415-763-4791

Wilson, Lucy, *Dir & On-Line Servs,* University of Cincinnati Libraries (Raymond Walters General & Technical College Library), Blue Ash OH. 513-745-4313

Wilson, Madelyn M, *Librn,* Irondale Public Library, Irondale AL. 205-956-4250

Wilson, Margaret, *ILL,* Covina Public Library, Covina CA. 213-967-3935

Wilson, Margaret, *In Charge,* Florida Agricultural & Mechanical University (School of Technology Library), Tallahassee FL. 904-599-3022

Wilson, Marian, *Librn,* Essential Club Free Library, Canaseraga NY. 607-545-6443

Wilson, Marietta, *Librn,* Mercy Medical Center, Medical Library, Springfield OH. 513-390-5000, Ext 2293

Wilson, Marilyn, *Acq,* University of California, San Diego, University Libraries, La Jolla CA. 714-452-3336

Wilson, Martha, *Dir,* Franklin Furnace Archive, Inc, New York NY. 212-925-4671

Wilson, Martha B, *In Charge,* Enoch Pratt Free Library (Clifton), Baltimore MD. 301-396-5430, 396-5395

Wilson, Martin, *Asst Prof,* University of Guam, Library Science Program, GU. 734-2921

Wilson, Martin P, *Actg Dean,* University of Guam, Robert F Kennedy Memorial Library, Agana, Guam PI. 734-2461

Wilson, Marty, *Media,* Gaston County Public Library, Gastonia NC. 704-866-3756

Wilson, Mary, *Librn,* Mercer County Library (East Windsor), Hightstown NJ. 609-448-1330

Wilson, Mary, *Cat,* Novi Public Library, Novi MI. 313-349-0720

Wilson, Mary W, *Dir,* Public Relations Society of America, Research Information Center, New York NY. 212-826-1776

Wilson, Maureen, *Maps,* University of British Columbia Library, Vancouver BC. 604-228-3871

Wilson, Melanie, *Ref,* Fondulac Public Library District, East Peoria IL. 309-699-3917

Wilson, Mrs Howard, *Librn,* Vassar Brothers Hospital, Medical Library, Poughkeepsie NY. 914-454-7900

Wilson, Mrs R, *ILL & Ref,* Baptist Bible College Library, G B Vick Memorial Library, Springfield MO. 417-869-9811, Ext 375, 376

Wilson, Mrs Robert, *ILL & Ref,* East Lyme Public Library, Inc, Niantic CT. 203-739-6926

Wilson, Mrs S, *Rare Bks & Spec Coll,* Saint Catharines Public Library, Saint Catharines ON. 416-688-6103

Wilson, Muriel, *Librn,* Victoria County Public Library (Manilla Branch), Manilla ON. 705-324-3104

Wilson, Nancy I, *Mgr,* Boeing Co (Renton Technical Library), Seattle WA. 206-237-8311

Wilson, Norma, *Librn,* Elgin Public Library, Elgin IA. 319-426-5313

Wilson, Norman B, *Dir,* Pfeiffer College, Gustavus Adolphus Pfeiffer Library, Misenheimer NC. 704-463-7343, Ext 278

Wilson, Pamela J, *Dir,* Morris Public Library, Morris IL. 815-942-6880

Wilson, Patricia, *Ref & On-Line Servs,* Alaska State Library, Juneau AK. 907-465-2910

Wilson, Patricia, *Trustee,* Andover Public Library, , Andover VT. 802-875-2765

Wilson, Patricia, *Librn,* Los Angeles Public Library System (Arroyo Seco), Los Angeles CA. 213-256-3178

Wilson, Patricia, *Librn,* Newfoundland Public Library Services (Gander Region), Saint John's NF. 709-651-2781

Wilson, Patsy L, *Dir,* Cooke County College, Mary Josephine Cox Memorial Library, Gainesville TX. 817-668-7731, Ext 237

Wilson, Pauline C, *Assoc Prof,* University of Tennessee, Knoxville, Graduate School of Library & Information Science, TN. 615-974-2148

Wilson, Peggy, *Chief Librn,* United California Bank (Library & Research Dept), Los Angeles CA. 213-614-4097

Wilson, Phillis M, *Dir,* Rochester Public Library, Olmsted County Library System, Rochester MN. 507-285-8000

Wilson, Ralph, *Dean,* Southern Arkansas University, School of Education Library Science Program, AR. 501-234-5120, Ext 260

Wilson, Reina M, *Librn,* Brown City Public Library, Brown City MI. 313-346-2511

Wilson, Richard, *Librn,* Eureka-Humboldt County Library (Garberville), Garberville CA. 707-923-2230

Wilson, Richard, *Continuing Educ & Spec Programs,* Idaho State Library, Boise ID. 208-334-2150

Wilson, Richard E, *Dir,* Starved Rock Library System, Ottawa IL. 815-434-7537

Wilson, Robert, *Reader Serv,* Winona State University, Maxwell Library, Winona MN. 507-457-2040

Wilson, Robert M, *Librn,* Laurentian University Library (Science), Sudbury ON. 705-675-1151, Ext 456

Wilson, Robert R, *Librn,* Jackson County Library System (Ashland Branch), Ashland OR. 503-482-1151

Wilson, Ruth W, *Librn,* Shelton College Library, Cape May NJ. 305-783-4280

Wilson, Sandra, *Tech Serv,* Ramsey County Public Library, Roseville MN. 612-631-0494

Wilson, Sharonn, *YA,* Plattsburgh Public Library, Plattsburgh NY. 518-563-0921

Wilson, Shirley, *Librn,* Notus Public Library, Notus ID. 208-459-7889

Wilson, Sue Ellen, *Librn,* Spokane County Library (North Argonne), Spokane WA. 509-924-4122

Wilson, Susan, *Librn,* Honey Brook Community Library, Honey Brook PA. 215-273-3303

Wilson, Susan W, *Dir & On-Line Servs,* Daniel Freeman Hospital, Victor J Wacha Medical Library, Inglewood CA. 213-674-7050, Ext 3230, 3235

Wilson, Theresa, *Ch,* Huron County Public Library, Goderich ON. 519-524-7751

Wilson, Thomas, *Assoc Prof,* University of South Florida, Graduate Department of Library, Media & Information Studies, FL. 813-974-2557

Wilson, Thomas B, *Dir,* Lambertville Free Public Library, Lambertville NJ. 609-397-0275

Wilson, Virginia, *Acq,* Kitsap Regional Library, Bremerton WA. 206-377-7601

Wilson, Virginia, *Librn,* Kitsap Regional Library (Poulsbo), Bremerton WA. 206-779-2951

Wilson, Vivian L, *Librn,* Wake Forest University (Law Library), Winston-Salem NC. 919-761-5438

Wilson, Wesley, *Southwest & Art,* El Paso Public Library, El Paso TX. 915-543-3804

Wilson, William, *Assoc Dir,* Winding Rivers Library System, La Crosse WI. 608-784-3151

Wilson, William G, *Librn,* University of Maryland at College Park (College of Library & Information Services Library), College Park MD. 301-454-6003

Wilson, William G, *Lectr,* University of Maryland, College of Library & Information Services, MD. 301-454-5441

Wilson, Yvonne, *ILL,* University of California Library, Irvine CA. 714-833-5212

Wilson, Jr, Fred L, *Librn,* Conemaugh Valley Memorial Hospital, Medical Staff Library, Johnstown PA. 814-536-6671

Wilsted, Thomas, *In Charge,* Salvation Army Education Department, Archives Library, New York NY. 212-620-4392

Wilt, Geraldine, *Librn,* Bagley Public Library, Bagley IA. 515-427-5214

Wilt, Jean-Marie, *Librn,* Eva K Bowlby Public Library, Waynesburg PA. 412-627-9776

Wilt, Jean-Marie, *Dir,* Greene County Library System, Waynesburg PA. 412-627-9776

Wilt, Larry, *Ref & Bibliog Instr,* Dickinson College, Boyd Lee Spahr Library, Carlisle PA. 717-245-1396

Wilthew, Velma, *Librn,* Arenberg Ultrasonic, Inc Library, Jamaica Plain MA. 617-522-7800

Wilton, Elaine B, *Librn,* Temple Israel Library, Boston MA. 617-566-3960, Ext 26

Wilton, K E, *Librn,* Canada Department of Agriculture, Research Station Library, Swift Current SK. 306-773-4621

Wilts, Joan, *Ad,* Waukegan Public Library, Waukegan IL. 312-623-2041

Wiltzen, Sheril, *Librn,* De Soto Public Library, De Soto IA. 515-834-2233

Wiman, Raymond V, *Instr,* Illinois State University, Department of Information Sciences, IL. 309-438-3671

Wiman, W, *Ad,* Carnegie-Stout Public Library, Dubuque Public Library, Dubuque IA. 319-583-9197

Wimber, Patricia A, *Dir,* Connors State College, Jacob Johnson Library, Warner OK. 918-463-2931

Wimberly, Claude A, *Librn,* Florida State University (Education), Tallahassee FL. 904-644-1583

Wimbish, Jr, Emery, *Dir,* Lincoln University, Langston Hughes Memorial Library, Lincoln University PA. 215-932-8300, Ext 261

Wimer, Barney, *Librn,* Puget Sound College of the Bible Library, Edmonds WA. 206-775-8686, Ext 29

Wimmer, Katherine, *Dir & On-Line Servs,* Saint Joseph Hospital, Medical Library, Chicago IL. 312-975-3038

Winans, Diane, *Cat, On-Line Servs & Bibliog Instr,*Shaker Heights Public Library, Shaker Heights OH. 216-991-2030

Winar, Martin P, *Dir & Br Coordr,* Mercer County Library, Trenton NJ. 609-989-6917

Winard, Judith, *Ch,* Huntington Public Library, Huntington NY. 516-427-5165

Winberry, Carolyn, *Sci,* University of South Carolina, Thomas Cooper Library, Columbia SC. 803-777-3142

Wince, Barbara, *Ref & Bibliog Instr,* University of Cincinnati Libraries (Raymond Walters General & Technical College Library), Blue Ash OH. 513-745-4313

Winch, Susan L, *Ch,* Scarborough Public Library, Scarborough ME. 207-883-4723

Winchell, Dave *Love & Wilcey, Learning Skills,* Clark College Library, Vancouver WA. 206-699-0251

Winchell, Peggy, *Librn,* Glendive Public Library, Dawson County Library, Glendive MT. 406-365-3633

Winckler, Paul A, *Prof,* Long Island University, Palmer Graduate Library School, NY. 516-299-2855 & 299-2856

Windels, Gene, *Librn,* Information Access Corp Library, Menlo Park CA. 415-941-1100

Winder, Jimmet, *Acq,* Dillard University, Will W Alexander Library, New Orleans LA. 504-949-2123, Ext 256, 257

Windes, Billy, *Media,* Mid-Continent Public Library, Independence MO. 816-836-5200

Windfelder, Claire, *Librn,* Public Library of Annapolis & Anne Arundel County Inc (Linthicum), Linthicum Heights MD. 301-789-6250

Windham, Carol, *Librn,* Baptist Hospital Fund, Midway School of Nursing Library, Saint Paul MN. 612-641-5500

Windham, Eula, *Librn,* Middle Georgia College, Library Technical Assistant Program, GA. 912-934-6221, Ext 271

Windham, Eula, *Dir,* Middle Georgia College, Roberts Memorial Library, Cochran GA. 912-934-6221, Ext 274

Windham, Mary, *Librn,* Cheaha Regional Library, Anniston AL. 205-238-1581

Windham, Shirley, *Ref,* Greensboro Public Library, Greensboro NC. 373-2474; 373-2471

Windisch, Rita, *ILL,* South County Interrelated Library System, Westerly RI. 401-596-2877

Windle, Shirley, *Asst Librn,* Claremore Junior College, Thunderbird Library, Claremore OK. 918-341-7510, Ext 278

Windler, Jacqueline M, *Dir,* Catholic Health Association of the U S, Information Resource Center, Saint Louis MO. 314-773-0646

Windmeyer, Nora, *Librn,* Trails Regional Library (Waverly Branch), Waverly MO. 816-493-2987

Windrem, Laurel, *Instr,* Grossmont College, Library Technology Program, CA. 714-465-1700, Ext 319

Windsor, Donald A, *Dir & Spec Coll,* Norwich-Eaton Pharmaceuticals, Research Library, Norwich NY. 607-335-2539

Wine, Evelyn, *Librn,* Panora Public Library, Panora IA. 515-755-2529

Wineman, Walter R, *Rare Bks,* Lynchburg College, Knight Memorial & Capron Libraries, Lynchburg VA. 804-845-9071, Ext 271

Winemiller, Lynnette, *Tech Serv,* Akron-Summit County Public Library, Akron OH. 216-762-7621

Winer, Mark J, *Librn,* Stewartstown Public Library, Stewartstown NH. 603-237-8874

Wines, Mrs E, *Librn,* Creemore Public Library, Creemore ON. 705-466-3011

Wines, R L, *Librn,* White Consolidated Industries Inc, Sarco Corp, Harrisonburg Works Library, Harrisonburg VA. 703-434-3591

Winfrey, Dorman H, *Dir,* Texas State Library, Austin TX. 512-475-2166

Wing, Mary C, *Dir,* Lincoln Library, Medicine Lodge KS. 316-886-5746

Wingate, Dawn A, *Librn,* Max Factor & Co, Research & Development Laboratory Library, Los Angeles CA. 213-462-6131, Ext 527

Wingate, Margaret, *Pub Servs & Archivist,* Broome Community College, Cecil C Tyrrell Learning Resources Center, Binghamton NY. 607-772-5020

Wingate, Margaret, *Cat,* Your Home Public Library, Johnson City NY. 607-797-4816

Wingenroth, Janet, *Circ & Ref,* Carroll College Library, Helena MT. 406-442-3450, Ext 245, 247 & 442-1295

Winger, Anna K, *Librn,* Defense Logistics Agency, Defense Logistics Services Center Library, Battle Creek MI. 616-962-6511, Ext 6787

Winger, Howard W, *Prof,* University of Chicago, Graduate Library School, IL. 312-753-3482

Wingert, Carole A, *Librn,* Missouri Court of Appeals, Southern District Library, Springfield MO. 417-862-6314

Wingertsahn, Gerard, *Dir,* Cheaha Regional Library, Anniston AL. 205-238-1581

Wingertsahn, Gerard, *Dir,* Public Library of Anniston & Calhoun County, Liles Memorial Library, Anniston AL. 205-237-8501, Ext 8503

Wingfield, Ms Tommie, *On-Line Servs,* University of Texas at Dallas, University Library, Richardson TX. 214-690-2950

Wingfield-Digby, Valerie, *Br Coordr,* Parkland Regional Library, Yorkton SK. 306-783-2876

Wingo, Betty, *Librn,* Lake Lanier Regional Library (Norcross Public), Norcross GA. 404-448-4938

Winiarski, Joanne, *In Charge,* Ogilvy & Mather, Inc Library, New York NY. 212-688-6100, Ext 542

Winiecki, Mary Alice, *Ref,* Canisius College, Andrew L Bouwhuis Library, Buffalo NY. 716-883-7000, Ext 253, 254, 290

Winkel, Kathy, *Librn,* Flagstaff City-Coconino County Public Library System (Subregional Library for the Blind & Physically Handicapped), Flagstaff AZ. 602-774-0270

Winkelman, John H, *Assoc Prof,* State University of New York, College of Arts & Science, School of Library & Information Science, NY. 716-245-5322

Winkels, Mary, *Mgr,* Brookhaven National Laboratory, Research Library, Upton NY. 516-345-3489

Winkle, Sharon L, *Dir,* Englewood Public Library, Englewood CO. 303-761-4376

Winkler, Faye, *Asst Librn,* Estill County Public Library, Irvine KY. 606-723-3030

Winkler, Margaret, *Coordr,* Florida Educators' Information Service, Tallahassee FL. 904-644-6454

Winkler, Marianne, *Librn,* Temple Emanu-El, Ivan M Stettenheim Library, New York NY. 212-744-1400
Winkler, Walter J, *Acq,* Canisius College, Andrew L Bouwhuis Library, Buffalo NY. 716-883-7000, Ext 253, 254, 290
Winks, Isla Dale, *Librn,* Gaines County Library, Seminole TX. 915-758-5668
Winn, Carolyn P, *Librn,* Woods Hole Oceanographic Institution (General Library), Woods Hole MA. 617-548-1400, Ext 2512, 2708
Winn, Cynthia, *Media & YA,* Sioux Falls Public Library, Sioux Falls SD. 605-339-7081
Winn, F, *Libr Asst,* Oakland Public Library (Golden Gate), Oakland CA. 415-652-3584
Winn, Frank, *Librn,* Mankind Research Foundation, Inc, Silver Spring MD. 202-882-4000
Winn, Herbert E, *Librn,* Bartlesville Public Library, Bartlesville OK. 918-336-2133
Winn, Karyl, *Mss,* University of Washington Libraries, Seattle WA. 206-543-1760
Winn, Kimberly Anne, *Librn,* Louis T Graves Memorial Public Library, Kennebunkport ME. 207-967-2778
Winn, LaVerne, *Sci,* Bates College, George and Helen Ladd Library, Lewiston ME. 207-784-2949
Winn, Louise, *Librn,* Frederick Eugene Lykes Jr Memorial County Library (Ridge Manor Branch), Ridge Manor FL. 904-796-3480
Winn, Marilyn, *ILL,* Yeshiva University Libraries (Pollack Branch), New York NY. 212-960-5380
Winn, Ruth E, *Tech Serv,* Suffolk University College Library, Boston MA. 617-723-4700, Ext 241
Winner, Ann, *Ad & Commun Servs,* Willingboro Public Library, Willingboro NJ. 609-877-6668
Winner, Marian, *Librn,* Miami University (Science Library), Oxford OH. 513-529-7526
Winner, Neale, *Coordr Media Prod-Instrnl Tech,* Williamsport Area Community College Library, Williamsport PA. 717-326-3761, Ext 211
Winning, Amy, *Asst Librn,* Griggs County Library, Cooperstown ND. 701-797-2214
Winowich, Nicholas, *Dir,* Kanawha County Public Library, Kanawha County Service Center, Charleston WV. 304-343-4646
Winsche, Richard A, *Historian,* Nassau County Museum Reference Library, East Meadow NY. 516-292-4292
Winscott, Marcia, *Dir,* Rockford Carnegie Library, Rockford OH. 419-363-2630
Winship, Connie, *Librn,* Kent County Municipal Public Library (Dresden Public), Dresden ON. 519-683-4922
Winship, Robert, *Acting Cat,* Temple University of the Commonwealth System of Higher Education, Samuel Paley Library, Philadelphia PA. 215-787-8231
Winship, Sheila G, *ILL & Ref,* Del Mar College Library, Corpus Christi TX. 512-881-6308
Winslow, Katharine H, *Dir, Acq & Commun Servs,* Narragansett Pier Free Library, Narragansett RI. 401-789-9507
Winslow, Lisa, *Librn,* Greenberg & Glusker, Law Library, Los Angeles CA. 213-553-3610
Winslow, Olive B, *Librn,* Joseph H Plumb Memorial Library, Rochester MA. 617-763-8600
Winslow, Patricia, *Asst Librn,* Lisbon Public Library, Lisbon NH. 603-838-6615
Winslow, Vaughn, *Media,* Indiana University at Kokomo, Learning Resource Center, Kokomo IN. 317-453-2000, Ext 237
Winslow, Vaughn, *Media,* Indiana University Southeast Library, New Albany IN. 812-945-2731
Winsome, Geneva, *Librn,* Poplar Bluff Public Library (Twin Towers), Poplar Bluff MO. 314-785-8593
Winsor, Donald L, *Media,* Southern Illinois University at Carbondale, Delyte W Morris Library, Carbondale IL. 618-453-2522
Winstead, G Alvis, *Dir,* Tennessee State Law Library, Nashville TN. 615-741-2016
Winstead, Mamie H, *Dir,* Supreme Court Law Library, Knoxville TN. 615-524-4537
Winstead, Mrs H G, *Librn,* Jackson Metropolitan Library (Burns Library), Raleigh MS. 601-352-3677

Winston, Carol, *Librn,* Lincoln Library (East), Springfield IL. 217-753-4975
Winston, Christina, *Librn,* Rushville Public Library, Rushville NE. 308-327-2740
Winter, Amy, *Asst Librn,* West Branch Public Library, West Branch MI. 517-345-2235
Winter, Carol, *Librn,* Gee & Jensen Inc Library, West Palm Beach FL. 305-683-3301, Ext 205
Winter, Darlene, *Ref,* Herrick Public Library, Holland MI. 616-392-3114
Winter, Darlene, *Genealogy,* Herrick Public Library, Holland MI. 616-392-3114
Winter, Eugenia, *ILL & Ad,* Stockton-San Joaquin County Public Library, Stockton Public Libr, Stockton CA. 209-944-8415
Winter, Kay, *Dir,* Hendrick Hudson Free Library, Montrose NY. 914-739-5654
Winter, Madeline F, *Librn,* Eagle Publishing Co, Berkshire Eagle Library, Pittsfield MA. 413-447-7311, Ext 141
Winter, Michael B, *Chief Librn,* Western Conservative Baptist Seminary, Cline-Tunnell Library, Portland OR. 503-233-8561, Ext 23
Winter, Patricia, *Asst Dir & Media,* Westfield Memorial Library, Westfield NJ. 201-233-1515
Winter, Priscilla, *ILL,* Martin County Library, Fairmont MN. 507-238-4207
Winter, Roland A, *Librn,* Middlesex County Law Library, New Brunswick NJ. 201-745-3357
Winter, Trudy, *On-Line Servs,* Glencoe Public Library, Glencoe IL. 312-835-5056
Winter, William O, *Dir Govt Res,* University of Colorado at Boulder (Bureau of Government Research & Service Library), Boulder CO. 303-492-8586
Winterfeldt, Henry, *Asst Prof,* University of Wisconsin-Oshkosh, Dept of Library Science, WI. 414-424-2313
Wintermeyer, Mary, *Dir,* Winfield Public Library, Winfield IA. 319-257-3247
Winternitz, Emanuel, *Co-Directors,* Research Center for Musical Iconography, New York NY. 212-790-4282
Winterroth, T, *Tech Serv,* West Valley College, Learning Resource Center, Saratoga CA. 408-867-2200, Ext 284
Winters, Frances, *Tech Serv,* Louisiana Tech University, Prescott Memorial Library, Ruston LA. 318-257-2577
Winters, Gladys A, *Librn,* United States Army (Medical Library), Fort Hood TX. 817-685-4237
Winters, Jacqueline, *Librn,* Gary Public Library (Ora L Wildermuth), Gary IN. 219-938-3941
Winters, Jeannette E, *Librn,* Red Oak Public Library, Red Oak IA. 712-623-3570
Winters, Murl M, *Dir,* Southwestern Assemblies of God College, P C Nelson Memorial Library, Waxahachie TX. 214-937-4010, Ext 59
Winters, Robert, *Asst Dir,* Charles City Public Library, Charles City IA. 515-228-5532
Winters, Wilma, *Librn,* Harvard University Library (Center for Population Studies), Boston MA. 617-495-3650
Winters, Zdenka, *Asst Dir Tech Serv,* Montclair State College, Harry A Sprague Library, Upper Montclair NJ. 201-893-4291
Wintersteen, Teddy, *Dir,* Kuskokwim Consortium Library, Bethel Public Library, Bethel AK. 907-543-2118
Winton, Barbara, *Dir,* Gafney Library, Inc, Wakefield NH. 603-522-3401
Wintrode, Ann, *Coordr,* Area 3 Library Service Authority, (TRI-ALSA), IN. 219-424-6664
Wintter, J E, *Dir,* Samford University (Drug Information Center), Birmingham AL. 205-870-2721
Winzenburg, Kathryn, *Tech Serv,* Martin County Library, Fairmont MN. 507-238-4207
Winzenried, Juanita, *Acq,* Kansas City Kansas Community College Library, Kansas City KS. 913-334-1100, Ext 38
Wiren, Harold N, *Librn,* University of Washington Libraries (Engineering), Seattle WA. 206-543-0740
Wirkus, Barbara, *Librn,* Flathead County Free Library (Columbia Falls Branch), Columbia Falls MT. 406-892-5919
Wirt, Michael J, *Dir,* Spokane County Library, Spokane WA. 509-924-4122
Wirth, Linda, *Cat,* Georgetown University (Fred O Dennis Law Library), Washington DC. 202-624-8260

Wirth, Mary K, *Dir,* New England College, H Raymond Danforth Library, Henniker NH. 603-428-2344
Wirtz, Donna, *Librn,* Ward County Public Library (Kenmare Branch), Kenmare ND. 701-385-4232
Wisbeski, Dorothy, *Ch,* Bound Brook Memorial Library, Bound Brook NJ. 201-356-0043
Wischmann, Bonnie J, *Librn,* George McCone Memorial County Library Memorial County Library, Circle MT. 406-485-2350
Wischmeyer, Laurie, *Librn,* Florida Department of Commerce, Research Library, Tallahassee FL. 904-487-2971
Wisdom, Donald, *Chief, Serial Div & Govt Publ,* Library of Congress, Washington DC. 202-287-5000
Wisdom, Wanda, *Librn,* Douglas County Library System (Oakland Public), Oakland OR. 503-459-9784
Wise, Anne S, *Coordr,* El Paso Natural Gas Co, Technical Information Center, El Paso TX. 915-543-3067, 3085
Wise, Carroll, *Librn,* Grove Public Library, Grove OK. 918-786-2945
Wise, Edith C, *Bibliog,* Port Authority of New York & New Jersey Library, New York NY. 212-466-4067, 4068
Wise, Jo, *Asst Dir,* Panhandle State University, Marvin E McKee Library, Goodwell OK. 405-349-2611
Wise, Julia B, *Head Librn,* Trident Technical College (Palmer Campus Learning Resource Center), Charleston SC. 803-792-7135
Wise, Mary P, *Per,* University of Miami, Otto G Richter Library, Coral Gables FL. 305-284-3551
Wise, Merl L, *Librn,* Indiana Reformatory Library, Pendleton IN. 317-778-2107
Wise, Ronnie, *Bkmobile Coordr,* Bolivar County Library, Robinson-Carpenter Memorial Library, Cleveland MS. 601-843-2774
Wise, Ruth H, *Librn,* Far East Merchants Association Library, Berkeley CA. 415-527-3455
Wise, Sally, *Asst Librn,* University of Puget Sound (Law Library), Tacoma WA. 206-756-3322
Wise, Sunny, *Librn,* Southam Business Publications Ltd Library, Don Mills ON. 416-445-6641
Wise, Suzanne, *On-Line Servs & Bibliog Instr,* Appalachian State University, Carol Grotnes Belk Library, Boone NC. 704-262-2186
Wise, Jr, Mrs L H, *Librn,* Webster Parish Library (Shongaloo Branch), Shongaloo LA. 318-377-1411
Wiseblood, Edward, *Dir,* Allan Hancock Joint Community College Library, Santa Maria CA. 805-922-6966, Ext 215, 242
Wisel, Lee Marie, *Cat,* Columbia Union College, Theofield G Weis Library, Takoma Park MD. 301-270-4999
Wisely, Forrest G, *Instr,* Illinois State University, Department of Information Sciences, IL. 309-438-3671
Wiseman, Frances M, *Dir,* Beech Grove Public Library, Beech Grove IN. 317-788-4203
Wiseman, J A, *Assoc Librn,* Trent University, Thomas J Bata Library, Peterborough ON. 705-748-1550
Wiseman, Lynda M, *Info Specialist,* Celanese Corp (Environmental & Health Affairs Information Center), New York NY. 212-764-8829
Wiseman, Margaret, *YA,* Fullerton City Library, Fullerton CA. 714-738-6333, Ext 301
Wiseman, Mary Jane, *Ch,* Neenah Public Library, Neenah WI. 414-729-4728
Wiseman, Robert, *Dept Chmn,* Eastern Illinois University, Dept of School Service Personnel, IL. 217-581-5112
Wiseman, Teko, *Commun Servs,* Mobile Public Library, Mobile AL. 205-438-7073
Wishart, Lynn, *Assoc Librn,* Washington & Lee University (Wilbur C Hall Library), Lexington VA. 703-463-3157
Wishinsky, Janet, *Ref,* De Paul University Libraries (Law Library), Chicago IL. 312-321-7710
Wisler, Martha, *Media,* New England Baptist Hospital (Helene Fuld Library), Boston MA. 617-738-5800, Ext 349
Wisler, Vesta, *Librn,* New Carlisle Public Library, New Carlisle OH. 513-845-3601
Wismer, Don, *Circ, State Agency Coordr & On-Line Servs,* Maine State Library, Augusta ME. 207-289-3561

Wisner, L Harriet, *Librn,* Kuhn, Loeb & Co Library, New York NY. 212-797-2100
Wisniewski, Eleanor, *Asst Dir,* Burlington County Library, Mount Holly NJ. 609-267-9660
Wisniewski, Eleanor, *Br Coordr,* Burlington County Library, Mount Holly NJ. 609-267-9660
Wisniewski, Helen H, *ILL,* California Western School of Law, San Diego CA. 714-239-0391, Ext 36
Wisniewski, Joseph, *Bkmobile Coordr,* Fall River Public Library, Fall River MA. 617-676-8541
Wissel, Melanie, *Ch,* Shelbyville-Shelby County Public Library, Shelbyville IN. 317-398-7121
Wissel, Ruth, *Dir,* Kiowa County Public Library, Eads CO. 303-438-5581
Wissler, Doris, *Librn,* Fremont County Library (Jeffrey City Branch), Jeffrey City WY. 307-544-2690
Wissman, Rita A, *Librn,* Public Library of Fort Wayne & Allen County (New Haven Branch), New Haven IN. 219-493-1616
Wiswall, Marcia, *Dir,* Lynnfield Public Library, Lynnfield MA. 617-334-5411
Wiswall, Marcia, *Genealogical Res,* Lynnfield Public Library, Lynnfield MA. 617-334-5411
Witcher, Kerry, *Librn,* Saint Joseph's Hospital, Medical Library, San Francisco CA. 415-431-3900, Ext 205
Witczak, Matthew W, *Libr Administrator,* Cicero Public Library, Cicero IL. 312-652-8084
Witham, Carol, *Ref,* Framingham Public Library, Framingham MA. 617-879-3570
Witham, Margaret, *Libr Asst,* Lemuel Shattuck Hospital (Medical Library), Jamaica Plain MA. 617-522-8110, Ext 307
Witherell, Julian, *Chief, African & Middle Eastern Div,* Library of Congress, Washington DC. 202-287-5000
Witherill, Melody, *In Charge,* Enoch Pratt Free Library (Morrell Park), Baltimore MD. 301-396-5430, 396-5395
Witherly, David, *Librn,* Annapolis Valley Regional Library Headquarters, Annapolis Royal NS. 902-532-2260
Withers, Jean, *Acq,* Attleboro Public Library, Joseph L Sweet Memorial, Attleboro MA. 617-222-0157
Witherspoon, Ronald E, *Media,* Atlanta Junior College Library, Atlanta GA. 404-656-6649
Withgott, Irene, *Librn,* Woodward City Library, Woodward OK. 405-254-3401
Withington, Marian, *ILL,* Clemson University, Robert Muldrow Cooper Library, Clemson SC. 803-656-3026
Withington, Marion H, *Ref,* Clemson University, Robert Muldrow Cooper Library, Clemson SC. 803-656-3026
Withrow, Faye, *Librn,* Dallas County Public Library (De Soto Branch), De Soto TX. 214-223-8406
Witiak, Joanne L, *On-Line Servs,* Rohm & Haas Co, Research Div, Information Services Dept, Spring House PA. 215-643-0200
Witker, Catherine, *Librn,* Toledo Edison Co Library, Toledo OH. 419-259-5000, Ext 5279
Witkowski, Dianne, *Librn,* Schiff, Hardin & Waite Library, Chicago IL. 312-876-1000
Witmer, Elaine, *ILL,* Geauga County Public Library, Chardon OH. 216-285-7601
Witmer, John A, *Dir,* Dallas Theological Seminary, Mosher Library, Dallas TX. 214-824-3094, Ext 285
Witt, Dora, *Librn,* Churchill County Library, Fallon NV. 702-423-4623
Witt, Jane, *Asst Librn,* La Crosse County Library, La Crosse WI. 608-785-9638
Witt, Muriel M, *Dir,* Theda Clark Regional Medical Center, Health Sciences Library, Neenah WI. 414-729-2190
Witte, Anne, *Acq & Cat,* Boca Raton Public Library, Boca Raton FL. 395-2980 & 395-1110, Ext 285, 286, 336
Witte, Irene, *Admin Asst,* La Porte Public Library, La Porte IN. 219-362-6156
Witte, Karen, *Asst Librn,* Nicholas P Sims Library, Waxahachie TX. 214-937-2671
Witten, Carol Ann, *Chief Librn,* Orange County Public Library (Tustin Branch), Tustin CA. 714-544-7725
Wittenberg, Eleanor, *Librn,* Lowell Public Library, Lowell IN. 219-696-7704
Wittenberg, Ronda, *Circ,* Eureka-Humboldt County Library, Eureka CA. 707-445-7284, 445-7513

Wittenmyer, Oleta, *Ser,* Texas Christian University, Mary Couts Burnett Library, Fort Worth TX. 817-921-7106
Wittenmyer, Oleta, *Librn,* Texas Christian University (Serials Department), Fort Worth TX. 817-921-7106, Ext 6114
Witters, Maryanne, *Dir,* Danbury Hospital, Health Sciences Library, Danbury CT. 203-744-2300, Ext 279
Wittgow, Barbara J, *Dir,* Stanton Public Library, Stanton NE. 402-439-2230
Wittgren, Maurine, *Librn,* Valparaiso-Porter County Public Library System & Administrative Headquarters (South Haven Public Library), Valparaiso IN. 219-759-4474
Wittig, June E, *Librn,* Shell Rock Public Library, Shell Rock IA. 319-885-4453
Wittke, Carol, *Librn,* Douglas County Law Library, Superior WI. 715-394-0237
Wittkopf, Frances, *Librn,* Bay County Public Library Association (North Bay), Lynn Haven FL. 904-265-2781
Wittlin, Denise M, *Dir,* Lake Worth Public Library, Lake Worth FL. 305-585-9882
Wittman, Elizabeth, *Spec Coll & Archivist,* University of Illinois at the Medical Center, Library of the Health Sciences, Chicago IL. 312-996-8974
Wittman, Paul, *Media,* Montgomery County Community College, Learning Resources Center, Blue Bell PA. 215-643-6000, Ext 340
Wittman, Sister Patricia, *Librn,* Holy Family College Library, Fremont CA. 415-651-1764
Witucke, Virginia, *Assoc Prof,* University of Arizona, Graduate Library School, AZ. 602-626-3565
Witzke, Carmela, *Librn,* Central Rappahannock Regional Library (North Stafford Branch), Stafford VA. 703-371-3311
Wiwel, Pam, *Librn,* United States Army (Army Corps of Engineers, Philadelphia District Library), Philadelphia PA. 215-597-3610
Wocelka, Corinne, *Acq,* Lawrence University, Seeley G Mudd Library, Appleton WI. 414-739-3681, Ext 264
Woeckel, Allan J, *Dir,* Reddick Library, Ottawa IL. 815-434-0509
Woehl, Yvehe, *ILL,* North Dakota State University Library, Fargo ND. 701-237-8876
Woehrmann, Paul, *Local Hist,* Milwaukee Public Library, Milwaukee WI. 414-278-3000
Woelflein, Ann, *Librn,* Greenwich Public Schools, Educational Reference Library, Greenwich CT. 203-869-9400
Woelflin, Leslie E, *Dir,* United States Department of Labor, National Mine Health & Safety Academy Learning Resource Center, Beckley WV. 304-255-0451, Ext 266
Woeller, Richard, *Ser,* Wilfrid Laurier University Library, Waterloo ON. 519-884-1970
Woerner, W Robert, *Dir,* Ithaca College Library, Ithaca NY. 607-274-3182
Woffenden, Mary, *Librn,* Victoria County Public Library (Dunsford Branch), Kirkfield ON. 705-324-3104
Wogoman, Lillian, *Librn,* Dayton & Montgomery County Public Library (Brookville Branch), Brookville OH. 513-833-2553
Wohlers, Karon, *Ch,* Missouri Valley Public Library, Missouri Valley IA. 712-642-4111
Wohlers, Mrs Ted, *Librn,* Logan Public Library, Logan IA. 712-644-2551
Wohlschlag, Sarah, *On-Line Servs,* Houston Public Library, Houston TX. 713-224-5441
Wohlsen, Theodore, *Doc,* Connecticut State Library, Hartford CT. 203-566-4301
Woike, Glenn V, *Acq,* Niagara University Library, Niagara University NY. 716-285-1212, Ext 376
Woinowsk, Orrine L, *Admin Librn,* United States Air Force (Human Resources Laboratory Library), Brooks AFB TX. 512-536-1110
Wojahn, Marvin, Colorado State Department of Labor & Employment, Division of Employment & Training, Research & Analysis Section Library, Denver CO. 303-839-5833, Ext 441
Wolak, Theresa, *Librn,* Institute of Chartered Accountants of Ontario, Merrilees Library, Toronto ON. 416-962-1841, Ext 43
Wolaruk, Dianne, *Librn,* Elk Point Municipal Public Library, Elk Point AB. 403-724-3737
Wolcott, Jane, *AV,* Washington State Library, Olympia WA. 206-753-5592

Wolcott, Jane, *Librn,* Washington State Library (Audio-Visual Film Library), Olympia WA. 206-866-6472
Wolcott, Merlin D, *Dir,* Stark County District Library, Canton OH. 216-452-0665, Ext 31
Wold, Michael, *Librn,* Carthage Public Library, Carthage IL. 217-357-3232
Wold, Shelley, *Doc,* University of Arkansas at Little Rock Library, Little Rock AR. 501-569-3120
Wolek, Joan T, *ILL,* Hamilton College, Burke Library, Clinton NY. 315-859-4478
Wolf, Alicia, *Spec Coll,* Thomas Branigan Memorial Library, Las Cruces Public Library, Las Cruces NM. 505-526-0347
Wolf, Amy, *Librn,* Caterpillar Tractor Co (Business Library), Peoria IL. 309-675-4622
Wolf, Carolyn E, *Circ,* Hartwick College Library, Oneonta NY. 607-432-4200, Ext 324
Wolf, Carolyn E, *ILL, Ref, On-Line Servs & Bibliog Instr,* Hartwick College Library, Oneonta NY. 607-432-4200, Ext 324
Wolf, Connie, *Librn, On-Line Servs & Bibliog Instr,* Missouri Institute of Psychiatry Library, Saint Louis MO. 314-644-8838
Wolf, Coralie, *Librn,* Tucson Public Library (Wilmot), Tucson AZ. 602-296-7158
Wolf, Edward, *Media,* Indiana University of Pennsylvania, Rhodes R Stabley Library, Indiana PA. 412-357-2340
Wolf, Edythe, *Dir,* Jewish Federation of Omaha Library, Omaha NE. 402-334-8200, Ext 30
Wolf, Frances, *Librn,* Beth Shalom Congregation, Blanche & Ira Rosenblum Memorial Library, Kansas City MO. 816-363-3331
Wolf, Frances, *Asst Librn,* Richland Community Library, Richland PA. 717-866-4939
Wolf, Gretchen, *Cat,* Duke University (Law School Library), Durham NC. 919-684-2847
Wolf, Harriet, *Librn,* American Power Jet Co Library, Ridgefield NJ. 201-945-8204
Wolf, Janice L, *Librn,* Minatare Public Library, Minatare NE. 308-783-2514
Wolf, Kathleen, *Librn,* Bleyhl Community Library, Grandview Public Library, Grandview WA. 509-882-2807
Wolf, Milton, *Coll Develop,* University of Nevada-Reno, Noble H Getchell Library, Reno NV. 702-784-6533
Wolf, Patricia M, *Librn,* General Research Corp Library, McLean VA. 703-893-5900, Ext 574
Wolf, Sally, *Librn,* Los Angeles Public Library System (City Planning), Los Angeles CA. 213-485-5077, 485-5038
Wolf, Sara H, *Librn,* Mint Museum of Art Library, Charlotte NC. 704-334-9723
Wolf, Timothy, *Librn,* Mortgage Bankers Association Library, Washington DC. 202-785-8333, Ext 260
Wolf, William, *Librn,* Hebrew Educational Alliance Library, Denver CO. 303-629-0410
Wolf, II, Edwin, *Librn,* Library Co of Philadelphia, Philadelphia PA. 215-546-3181
Wolfe, Bardie, *Librn,* University of Tennessee, Law Library, Knoxville TN. 615-974-4381
Wolfe, C F, *Research Librn,* Dow Chemical USA, Texas Div Library, Freeport TX. 713-238-3513
Wolfe, Catherine, *Supvr,* Elgin County Public Library (Straffordville Branch), Straffordville ON. 519-633-0815
Wolfe, D Jane, *Ch,* Anaheim Public Library, Anaheim CA. 714-533-5221
Wolfe, Gary D, *District Adminr,* Centre County Library & Historical Museum, Bellefonte PA. 814-355-3131
Wolfe, Ginger, *Chief Librn,* Scott County Bar Association, Grant Law Library, Davenport IA. 319-326-8677
Wolfe, Glenna, *Librn,* Herbert J Thomas Memorial Hospital Library, South Charleston WV. 304-768-3961, Ext 212
Wolfe, Helen E, *Dir,* John R Kauffman Jr Public Library, Sunbury PA. 717-286-2461
Wolfe, Ithmer, *Librn,* Presbyterian Church Library, Tenafly NJ. 201-567-0111
Wolfe, Jean, *Librn,* Jefferson-Madison Regional Library (Crozet Branch), Crozet VA. 804-823-4050
Wolfe, Jean, *Librn,* Lawrenceville Township Public Library, Lawrenceville IL. 618-943-3016
Wolfe, Jo Anne, *Librn,* John Wesley College, Learning Resources Center, Owosso MI. 517-723-8141

Wolfe, Judith, *Coordr Resources,* Missouri State Library, Jefferson City MO. 314-751-4214

Wolfe, Lou, *Asst Dir,* San Francisco Conservatory of Music Library, San Francisco CA. 415-564-8086

Wolfe, M, *ILL,* University of Windsor, Leddy Library, Windsor ON. 519-253-4232, Ext 198

Wolfe, M, *Ref,* University of Windsor, Leddy Library, Windsor ON. 519-253-4232, Ext 198

Wolfe, Marice A, *Librn,* Vanderbilt University Library (Special Collections), Nashville TN. 615-322-2807

Wolfe, Mary, *Tech Serv,* University of Southern Mississippi, Cook Memorial Library, Hattiesburg MS. 601-266-7301

Wolfe, Mary Lou, *Librn,* Pennsylvania Horticultural Society Library, Philadelphia PA. 215-625-8268

Wolfe, Phyllis, *Librn,* Des Moines Register & Tribune Newsroom Library, Des Moines IA. 515-284-8000

Wolfe, Richard J, *Rare Bks,* Harvard University Library (Francis A Countway Library of Medicine), Boston MA. 617-732-2142

Wolfe, Shirley, *Dir,* Central Agency for Jewish Education, Educational Resource Center, Miami FL. 305-573-5720

Wolfe, Virginia, *Librn,* Arlington County Department of Libraries (Cherrydale), Arlington VA. 703-527-2358

Wolfender, D, *Librn,* Canadian Pacific Limited, Corporate Library Information Centre, Montreal PQ. 514-395-6762

Wolfermann, Nancy, *Cat,* Mount Sinai School of Medicine of City University of New York, Gustave L & Janet W Levy Library, New York NY. 212-650-6671

Wolfert, Richard J, *State Librn,* North Dakota Network for Knowledge, ND. 701-224-2490

Wolfert, Richard J, *Librn,* North Dakota State Library, Bismarck ND. 701-224-2490

Wolff, Emily, *Cat,* Borough of Manhattan Community College Library, Martin B Dworkis Library, New York NY. 212-262-3530

Wolff, Lynell, *Librn,* New Carlisle & Olive Township Public Library, New Carlisle IN. 219-654-3046

Wolff, Walter, *Sci & Indust,* Brooklyn Public Library (Central Library), Brooklyn NY. 212-780-7712

Wolffe, Harriette, *ILL,* University of Cincinnati Libraries (Raymond Walters General & Technical College Library), Blue Ash OH. 513-745-4313

Wolford, Joanne, *Dir,* Ohio University-Lancaster, Library Media Technology, OH. 614-654-6711

Wolford, Linda, *ILL,* Central Florida Regional Library, Ocala Public Library, Ocala FL. 904-629-8551

Wolfsehr, Cliff, *Acq,* Southern Oregon State College Library, Ashland OR. 503-482-6445

Wolfson, Catherine, *Acq,* University of Arizona Library (Arizona Health Sciences Center Library), Tucson AZ. 602-626-6121

Wolfteich, Alice, *Ad, YA & Ref,* Franklin Square Public Library, Franklin Square NY. 516-488-3444

Wolgemuth, Henry, *Acq,* Southwestern University, Cody Memorial Library, Georgetown TX. 512-863-6511, Ext 338

Wolk, Josephine, *Librn,* Ingham County Library (Haslett Branch), Haslett MI. 517-339-2324

Wolk, Robert G, *Dir,* Nature Science Center Library, Winston-Salem NC. 919-767-6730

Wolk, Robert S, *Librn,* Seamen's Church Institute of New York, Joseph Conrad Library, New York NY. 212-269-2710, Ext 215

Wolkenstein, Zigmund, *Dir,* Toronto Jewish Congress, Jewish Public Library of Toronto, Toronto ON. 416-781-6282, 781-8065

Wolkoff, Regina, *ILL,* Boca Raton Public Library, Boca Raton FL. 395-2980 & 395-1110, Ext 285, 286, 336

Wollen, Sid, *Librn,* Saskatchewan Power Corp, Library-Archives, Regina SK. 306-525-7650, 527-7611

Wollenburg, Ruth, *Dir,* L D Fargo Public Library, Lake Mills WI. 414-648-2166

Woller, Charles P, *In Charge,* Cleveland Public Library, Braille & Talking Book Department, Cleveland OH. 216-623-2911

Wollerman, June, *Librn,* Lorain Public Library (Avon Branch), Avon OH. 216-934-4743

Wolleson, Ethel, *Librn,* San Clemente Presbyterian Church, Sutherland Memorial Library, San Clemente CA. 714-492-6158

Wollet, Bonnie, *Media,* University of Arizona Library, Tucson AZ. 602-626-2101

Wolpe, Katharine B, *Librn,* New York Psychoanalytic Institute, Abraham A Brill Library, New York NY. 212-879-6900

Wolper, Frieda, *Librn,* Congregation Tifereth Israel Library, Everett MA. 617-387-0200

Wolpert, Alice H, *Librn,* Massachusetts Mental Health Center, Charles MacFie Campbell Memorial Library, Boston MA. 617-734-1300, Ext 260

Wolpert, Ann J, *Librn,* Arthur D Little Inc, Research Library, Cambridge MA. 617-864-5770, Ext 3019

Wolski, Jean, Wisconsin School for the Visually Handicapped Library, Janesville WI. 608-755-2950

Wolter, Audrey, *YA,* Saint Clair County Library System, Port Huron MI. 313-987-7323

Wolter, John A, *Chief, Geog & Map Div,* Library of Congress, Washington DC. 202-287-5000

Wolter, Susan, *Librn,* Walker Library, Walker MN. 218-547-1019

Wolters, Virginia, *Librn,* University of Wisconsin-Madison (Social Science Graduate Reference Room), Madison WI. 608-262-3521

Woltz, Martha, *ILL & Ref,* University of Science & Arts of Oklahoma, Nash Library, Chickasha OK. 405-224-3140, Ext 260

Wolverton, Dorothy, *Dir,* Peshtigo Public Library, Peshtigo WI. 715-582-4905

Womack, Beverly, *Librn,* Dekalb Library System (Newton County), Covington GA. 404-786-3936

Womack, Sharon G, *Actg Dir,* Arizona State Library, Dept of Library, Archives & Public Records, Phoenix AZ. 602-255-4035

Womboldt, Mary Ellen, *Bkmobile Coordr,* Morse Institute Library, Natick MA. 617-653-4252

Womeldorf, Ann C, *Asst Librn,* United States Senate Library, Washington DC. 202-224-7106

Wonderly, Judson, *Dir,* United States Department of Commerce - Industry and Trade Administration, Seattle District Office Library, Seattle WA. 206-442-5615

Wondriska, Rebecca, *ILL,* Trinity College Library, Hartford CT. 203-527-3151, Ext 396

Wong, Anita, *Dir,* Saint Michael's Hospital, Health Science Library, Toronto ON. 416-360-4941

Wong, Carol, *Librn,* United States Army (Hospital Library), Honolulu HI. 433-6968 or 433-6745

Wong, Chuck C, *Cat,* Laurentian University Library, Bibliotheque de l'Universite Laurentienne, Sudbury ON. 705-675-1151, Ext 251 & 252

Wong, Clark, *Dir,* Community College of Denver, North Campus Learning Materials Center, Westminster CO. 303-466-8811, Ext 500

Wong, Ed, *Media,* Okanagan College, Muriel Ffoulkes Learning Resource Center, Kelowna BC. 604-762-5445, Ext 293

Wong, Eugenia, *Tech Serv,* Champaign Public Library & Information Center, Champaign IL. 217-356-7243

Wong, Lana, *Ad & Ref,* Anaheim Public Library, Anaheim CA. 714-533-5221

Wong, Madeline, *Librn,* Signatron Library, Lexington MA. 617-861-1500

Wong, Marlene M, *Music,* University of California at Davis, General Library, Davis CA. 916-752-2110

Wong, Maureen, *On-Line Servs,* University of Ottawa Libraries (Vanier Library (Medicine, Science & Engineering)), Ottawa ON. 613-231-2324

Wong, Monica, *Librn,* Southern West Virginia Community College, Williamson Campus Library, Williamson WV. 304-235-2800

Wong, Roberta S, *Librn,* Saint Paul's Hospital, Health Sciences Library, Vancouver BC. 604-682-2344, Ext 405, 406

Wong, Tony, *Dir,* Grace College of the Bible, Omaha NE. 402-342-3377, Ext 225

Wong, Virginia, *ILL,* Houston Area Library System, Houston TX. 713-222-4704

Wong, Virginia, *ILL,* Houston Public Library, Houston TX. 713-224-5441

Wong, Wesley, *Librn,* Harvard University Library (Economic Botany Library), Cambridge MA. 617-495-2326

Wong, William, *Asia,* University of Illinois Library at Urbana-Champaign, Urbana IL. 217-333-0790

Wong-Cross, Philip, *Tel-Ref,* Public Library of the District of Columbia, Martin Luther King Memorial Library, Washington DC. 202-727-1101

Wonsek, Pamela, *Cat,* Mercy College Libraries, Dobbs Ferry NY. 914-693-4500, Ext 260

Wonsmos, Dorothy, *ILL,* University of New Mexico General Library, Albuquerque NM. 505-277-4241

Wonson, Theresa O, *Asst Dir & YA,* Gloucester Lyceum & Sawyer Free Library, Gloucester MA. 617-283-0376

Woo, Helen, *Exten, Tech Servs,* Manitoba Department of Cultural Affairs & Historical Resources, Public Library Services Branch, Winnipeg MB. 204-453-7549

Woo, Janet, *Librn,* Pasadena Public Library (Allendale), Pasadena CA. 213-799-2519

Wood, Alberta Auringer, *Ref,* Memorial University of Newfoundland Library, Saint John's NF. 709-753-1200

Wood, Alice, *Dir,* Nineveh Public Library of Colesville Township, Nineveh NY. 607-693-1858

Wood, Ann, *Asst Dir,* Hamilton Public Library, Hamilton MT. 406-363-1670

Wood, Annabelle, *Servs to Blind & Physically Handicapped Dir,* Broward County Division of Libraries, Broward County Library, Pompano Beach FL. 305-972-1100

Wood, Annabelle, *Librn,* Broward County Division of Libraries (Library for the Blind & Physically Handicapped), Hollywood FL. 305-765-5999, 987-0042

Wood, Betty, *Librn,* Saint Francis Hospital, Medical Library, Wichita KS. 316-262-6211

Wood, Beulah C, *Assoc Librn,* Union Carbide Corp (Library & Technical Information Serv), Tarrytown NY. 914-789-3700

Wood, Caroline, *Librn,* Craighead County & Jonesboro Public Library (Caraway Branch), Caraway AR. 501-482-3394

Wood, Caroline, *Librn,* Crowley Ridge Regional Library (Caraway Public), Caraway AR. 501-482-3394

Wood, Carolyn C, *Cat,* Palomar Community College, Phil H Putnam Memorial Library, San Marcos CA. 714-744-1150, Ext 275, 276 & 473

Wood, Cathy, *Ch,* Kellogg-Hubbard Library, Montpelier VT. 802-223-3338

Wood, Christal, *Ref,* Largo Library, Largo FL. 813-584-8671, Ext 281, 282

Wood, Connie, *Librn,* Warren Schloat Productions, Prentice-Hall, Inc Reference Library, Tarrytown NY. 914-631-8300

Wood, Cynthia, *Cat & Film Coordr,* Waycross Junior College Library, Waycross GA. 912-285-6136

Wood, Dan, *Librn,* Manhattan State Hospital, Medical Library, New York NY. 212-369-0500

Wood, Darrow C, *Acq,* New York City Community College, Namm Hall Library, Brooklyn NY. 212-643-5240

Wood, David A, *Humanities & Soc Sci,* University of Washington Libraries, Seattle WA. 206-543-1760

Wood, David A, *Librn,* University of Washington Libraries (Music), Seattle WA. 206-543-1168

Wood, Dee, *Librn,* Wyoming School for the Deaf Library, Casper WY. 307-237-3634

Wood, Diane, *Librn,* Barryton Public Library, Barryton MI. 517-382-5288

Wood, Dorothy, *Ch,* Bryant Library, Roslyn NY. 516-621-2240

Wood, Dorothy, *Libr Asst,* Emergency Care Research Institute Library, Plymouth Meeting PA. 215-825-6000, Ext 192

Wood, Dorothy, *Chief Librn,* Orange County Public Library (Chapman), Garden Grove CA. 714-539-2115, 539-2116

Wood, Edythe Edwards, *Dir,* Grace Balloch Memorial Library, Spearfish Public, Spearfish SD. 605-642-4645

Wood, Elizabeth, *Tech Serv,* Asheville-Buncombe Library System, Asheville NC. 704-252-8701

Wood, Florence, *Librn,* Public Library of Cincinnati & Hamilton County (Norwood), Cincinnati OH. 513-369-6037

Wood, Floris, *Ser,* Bowling Green State University Library, Bowling Green OH. 419-372-2856

Wood, Gail, *Asst Librs,* East Central Junior College, Burton Library, Decatur MS. 601-635-2111, Ext 219

Wood, Harold B, *Librn,* T O H P Burnham Public Library, Essex MA. 617-768-7410

Wood, Helen, *Spec Coll,* Friends University, Edmund Stanley Library, Wichita KS. 316-263-9131, Ext 220

Wood, Idelle S, *Librn,* Temple University of the Commonwealth System of Higher Education (Woodhaven Staff Library), Philadelphia PA. 215-671-5106

Wood, Jeanne, *Librn,* Employers Reinsurance Corp Library, Kansas City MO. 816-283-5000, Ext 5176

Wood, John, *Per,* California State University, John F Kennedy Memorial Library, Los Angeles CA. 213-224-2201

Wood, John R, *Acq,* Essex County College, Learning Resources Center, Newark NJ. 201-877-3233

Wood, Judy, *Acq,* Fashion Institute of Technology, Library-Media Services Dept, New York NY. 212-760-7695

Wood, Katharine M, *Ref,* University of Delaware, Hugh M Morris Library, Newark DE. 302-738-2231

Wood, Katherine, *ILL, Circ & Ref,* Chowan College, Whitaker Library, Murfreesboro NC. 919-398-4101, Ext 241

Wood, Kathleen A, *Libr Servs & Programs,* Public Library of the District of Columbia, Martin Luther King Memorial Library, Washington DC. 202-727-1101

Wood, Kathy, *Librn,* Pocatello Public Library (Raymond), Pocatello ID. 208-232-9463

Wood, Lawrence R, *Acq & Ser,* Clemson University, Robert Muldrow Cooper Library, Clemson SC. 803-656-3026

Wood, Linda, *Asst Dir,* Los Angeles Public Library System, Los Angeles CA. 213-626-7555

Wood, Linda, *Ref,* Public Library of Columbus & Franklin County, Columbus OH. 614-864-8050

Wood, M J, *Dir,* Katherine Hamilton Mental Health Care Center Library, Terre Haute IN. 812-232-5681

Wood, M Sandra, *Ref,* Pennsylvania State University, Milton S Hershey Medical Center, George T Harrell Library, Hershey PA. 717-534-8626

Wood, Margaret D, *In Charge,* Perkin-Elmer Corp, Corporate Library, Norwalk CT. 203-762-6022

Wood, Marie P, *Librn,* East Greenbush Community Library, East Greenbush NY. 518-477-7476

Wood, Marlene, *Cat,* Findlay College, Shafer Library, Findlay OH. 419-422-8313, Ext 327

Wood, Mary, *County Librn,* Saint Mary's County Memorial Library, Leonardtown MD. 301-475-2846

Wood, Mary Lou, *Ch,* Homewood Public Library, Homewood IL. 312-798-0121

Wood, Mary Ruth, *Librn,* Little Dixie Regional Libraries (Madison Branch), Madison MO. 816-291-3695

Wood, Mrs V, *Librn,* Capreol Public Library, Capreol ON. 705-858-1622

Wood, Muriel B, *Asst Dir,* University of Washington Libraries (Health Sciences), Seattle WA. 206-543-5530

Wood, Norma, *Tech Serv,* East Chicago Public Library, East Chicago IN. 219-397-2453

Wood, Pamela, *Asst Dir,* Mount Olive College, Moye Library, Mount Olive NC. 919-658-2502, 658-2503, Ext 25, 26

Wood, Phyllis, *Asst Librn,* Englehart Public Library, Englehart ON. 705-544-2100

Wood, Phyllis P, *Dir,* Sun City Library, Sun City AZ. 602-974-2569

Wood, Richard, *Ref,* Texas College of Osteopathic Medicine Library, Fort Worth TX. 817-735-2465

Wood, Richard, *Librn,* Wesleyan University (Art), Middletown CT. 347-9411; Ext 697

Wood, Robert, *Div Chmn,* Chabot College, Library Media Technology Program, CA. 415-786-6600

Wood, Robert D, *Dir,* East Chicago Public Library, East Chicago IN. 219-397-2453

Wood, Robert S, *On-Line Servs,* United States Army War College Library, Carlisle Barracks PA. 717-245-4319

Wood, Ron, *Librn,* Centennial College of Applied Arts & Technology (East York Resource Centre), Scarborough ON. 416-469-5981

Wood, Shirley, *Libr Asst,* Kentucky Department for Finance Library, Frankfort KY. 502-564-7300

Wood, Sister Mary John, *Librn,* Silver Lake College Library, Manitowoc WI. 414-684-6691, Ext 34

Wood, Sister Mary John, *Dept Head,* Silver Lake College, School Librarianship Program, WI. 414-684-6691, Ext 34

Wood, Stephen, *Librn & ILL,* Cleveland Heights-University Heights Public Library, Cleveland Heights OH. 216-932-3600

Wood, Suzanne, *Tech Serv,* State University of New York, Agricultural & Technical College at Alfred, Walter C Hinkle Memorial Library, Alfred NY. 607-871-6313

Wood, Teresa, *ILL,* Sandhills Community College Library, Carthage NC. 919-692-6185, Ext 221, 223

Wood, Thomas, *Humanities,* Tulane University of Louisiana, Howard-Tilton Memorial Library, New Orleans LA. 504-865-5131

Wood, Thor E, *Chief,* New York Public Library (Performing Arts Research Center (Lincoln Center)), New York NY. 212-799-2200

Wood, Virginia, *Librn,* Willoughby-Eastlake Public Library (Eastlake Branch), Eastlake OH. 216-942-7880

Wood, Vivian, *Ref & Bibliog Instr,* Rutgers University (Kilmer Area Library), New Brunswick NJ. 201-932-3610

Woodall, Frances, *Asst Dir,* Hollifield Memorial Library, Auburn Public Library, Auburn AL. 205-887-8497

Woodall, Nancy C, *Ad,* Fairfax County Public Library, Administrative Offices, Springfield VA. 703-321-9810

Woodams, L, *Supervisor,* State University of New York at Buffalo (New Ridge Lea), Buffalo NY. 716-831-1120

Woodard, Alberta, *Librn,* Elkland Public Library, Elkland PA. 814-258-7576

Woodard, Anne, *Acq,* Tidewater Community College, Virginia Beach Campus Library, Virginia Beach VA. 804-427-3070, Ext 123, 126

Woodard, Frances, *Librn,* Aurora Community Library, Aurora NC. 919-322-5046

Woodard, Helen, *Librn,* Newark Public Library (Roseville), Newark NJ. 201-733-7770

Woodard, J Lamar, *Librn,* Stetson University College of Law, Charles A Dana Law Library, Saint Petersburg FL. 813-345-1335

Woodard, J Russell, *Ref,* Mercer University, Stetson Memorial Library, Macon GA. 912-745-6811, Ext 284

Woodard, John, *Baptist Coll,* Wake Forest University, Z Smith Reynolds Library, Winston-Salem NC. 919-761-5480

Woodard, Marion L, *Librn,* Glover Public Library, Glover VT. 802-525-3054

Woodard, Mrs George, *ILL,* Beaufort, Hyde, Martin Regional Library, Washington NC. 919-946-6401

Woodard, Paul E, *Dir,* New England Baptist Hospital (Patients' Library), Boston MA. 617-738-5800, Ext 108

Woodard, Paul Esty, *Dir,* New England Baptist Hospital (Medical Staff Library), Boston MA. 617-738-5800, Ext 107

Woodard, Ruth, *Dir,* Saint Clair County Library (Pell City), Pell City AL. 205-884-1685

Woodard, Ruth, *Librn,* Umatilla County Library (Hermiston Branch), Hermiston OR. 503-567-6493

Woodard, Suzanne, *Librn,* Saint John's Episcopal Cathedral, Kadey Memorial Library, Albuquerque NM. 505-247-1581

Woodbridge, Kristin, *Acq,* Connecticut State Library, Hartford CT. 203-566-4301

Woodburn, David, *Asst Dir,* Mississippi Library Commission, Jackson MS. 601-354-6369

Woodburn, Deborah L, *Librn,* Cabell-Huntington Hospital, Health Science Library, Huntington WV. 304-696-2605

Woodburn, Judy, *Coll Develop,* Duke University (Medical Center Library), Durham NC. 919-684-2092

Woodbury, Ella, *Ref,* State Library of Florida, Div of Library Services, Dept of State, Tallahassee FL. 904-487-2651

Woodbury, Juliet, *Librn,* New York Public Library (Hudson Park), New York NY. 212-243-6876

Woodbury, Linda, *Ch,* Beatrice Public Library, Beatrice NE. 402-223-3584

Woodbury, Ruth B, *Asst Librn, Tech Serv & Cat,* Milton Public Library, Milton MA. 617-698-5707

Woodbury, Virginia, *Ch,* Kelley Library, Salem Public Library, Salem NH. 603-898-7064

Woodcock, Mildred, *Ch,* Fenton Historical Society, Historical Center Library, Jamestown NY. 716-661-2296

Wooden, Howard E, *Dir,* Wichita Art Museum Library, Wichita KS. 316-268-4621

Wooden, Martha H, *Librn,* Vernon Parish Library, Leesville LA. 318-239-2027

Woodfill, Jean, *Doc,* University of Washington Libraries (Law Library), Seattle WA. 206-543-4089

Woodford, Arthur M, *Dir,* Saint Clair Shores Public Library, Saint Clair Shores MI. 313-771-9020

Woodford, Vanessa, *Librn,* Summit County Library (Dillon Branch), Dillon CO. 303-468-2403

Woodger, Carol, *Ad & Ref,* Port Chester Public Library, Port Chester NY. 914-939-6710, 939-6711

Woodke, Bonnie, *Admin Asst,* LeMars Public Library, Le Mars IA. 712-546-5004

Woodland, Alan, *Dir,* New Westminster Public Library, New Westminster BC. 604-521-8874

Woodle, Virginia, *Librn,* City Library, Winnsboro TX. 214-342-6866

Woodley, John, *Cat,* Queen's University at Kingston (Education), Kingston ON. 613-547-6286

Woodman, Doris E, *Librn,* Lebanon Area Library, Lebanon ME. 207-457-1184

Woodman, Grace D, *Librn,* Hartland Free Library, Hartland ME. 207-938-4702

Woodman, Mary, *Adminr & Adult Librn,* Elk City Carnegie Library, Elk City OK. 405-225-0136

Woodman, Sandra C, *Librn,* Texas State Technical Institute, Rolling Plains Campus Learning Resource Center, Sweetwater TX. 915-235-8441, Ext 66, 67

Woodrell, Kathy, *Ch,* Rowan Public Library, Salisbury NC. 704-633-5578

Woodruff, Bill, *Tech Communications Specialist,* Hershey Foods Corp, Communications Center, Hershey PA. 717-534-5106

Woodruff, Brenda, *Librn,* Wood County Law Library, Bowling Green OH. 419-353-3921

Woodruff, Cynthia, *Ch,* Meadville Library Art & Historical Association, Meadville PA. 814-336-1773

Woodrum, Frances L, *Dir,* Jacksonville Public Library, Jacksonville IL. 217-243-5435

Woodrum, Pat, *Dir,* Tulsa City-County Library, Tulsa OK. 918-581-5221

Woods, Anita, *Libr Tech,* Interstate Commerce Commission Library, Washington DC. 275-7327; 275-7328

Woods, Ann, *Dir,* Cooke County Library, Gainesville TX. 817-665-2401

Woods, Barry F, *General Ref & Spec Servs,* Connecticut State Library, Hartford CT. 203-566-4301

Woods, Dale, *Asst to Dir & Serials,* Johnson State College, John Dewey Library, Johnson VT. 802-635-2356, Ext 248

Woods, Diane, *Librn,* Maryville Public Library, Maryville MO. 816-582-5281

Woods, Don E, *Ser,* Southern Illinois University at Carbondale, Delyte W Morris Library, Carbondale IL. 618-453-2522

Woods, Eini, *Circ,* Fitchburg State College Library, Fitchburg MA. 617-345-2151, Ext 137

Woods, Elizabeth M, *Librn,* Chicago Public Library (Chicago Lawn), Chicago IL. 312-476-0639

Woods, Elmer, *ILL & Ref,* Atlantic Community College, Daniel Leeds Learning Resources Center, Mays Landing NJ. 625-1111 & 646-4950

Woods, Emma, *Librn,* Southwest Arkansas Regional Library (Murfreesboro Branch), Murfreesboro AR. 501-777-4564

Woods, Frances A, *Librn,* Nez Perce County Free Library District (Kamiah Community), Kamiah ID. 208-935-2672

Woods, Francis, *AV,* State of Vermont Department of Libraries, Montpelier VT. 802-828-3261

Woods, Hortense, *Librn,* Los Angeles Public Library System (Vernon Branch), Los Angeles CA. 213-234-9106

Woods, Jackie, *Acq,* Paducah Public Library, Paducah KY. 502-442-2510, 443-2664

Woods, Jan, *AV,* National College Library, Rapid City SD. 605-394-4943

Woods, Janice T, *Interim Dir,* Half Hollow Hills Community Public Library, Dix Hills NY. 516-421-4530

Woods, Joyce, *Dir,* Saline Public Library, Saline MI. 313-429-5450

Woods, Julia A, *Tech Serv,* Florida International University, Tamiami Campus, Athenaeum, Miami FL. 305-552-2461

Woods, Karen, *Librn,* Lutheran Hospital of Milwaukee, Inc, Evans Memorial Library, Milwaukee WI. 414-344-8800, Ext 251

Woods, L B, *Asst Prof,* University of Rhode Island, Graduate Library School, RI. 401-792-2878 or 792-2947

Woods, Laurie, *Asst Librn,* Taylor County Public Library, Perry FL. 904-584-4807

Woods, Linda, *ILL & Ref,* Kutztown State College, Rohrbach Library, Kutztown PA. 215-683-4480

Woods, Margaret S, *Librn,* Jackson County Library System (Prospect Branch), Prospect OR. 503-560-3668

Woods, Marjorie, *Asst Librn, ILL & Bkmobile Coordr,* Jennings County Public Library, North Vernon IN. 812-346-2091

Woods, Mary G, *Head, Doc Branch,* International Communication Agency (Agency Library), Washington DC. 202-724-9214

Woods, Mary S, *Chairperson,* Council of Research & Academic Libraries (San Antonio Area Online Users Group (SOLUG)), San Antonio TX. 512-690-2698

Woods, Mary S, *President,* Council of Research & Academic Libraries (Coral Periodicals-Serials Librarians Group (CORPSE)), San Antonio TX. 512-690-2698

Woods, Mary S, *Mgr, Libr Servs,* United Services Automobile Association Library, San Antonio TX. 512-690-2698, 690-2982

Woods, Mattie, *Circ,* Harrisburg Area Community College, McCormick Library, Harrisburg PA. 717-236-9533, Ext 257

Woods, Maureen, *Librn, On-Line Servs & Bibliog Instr,* National Marine Fisheries Service, Southwest Fisheries Center Library, Tiburon CA. 415-435-3149

Woods, Maureen, *Librn,* Regina Public Library (Connaught), Regina SK. 306-569-7615

Woods, Mayris, *Circ,* McDonnell Douglas Corp (Corporate Library), Saint Louis MO. 314-232-8515

Woods, Muriel E, *Dir,* Community College of Denver, Learning Materials Center, Red Rocks Campus, Golden CO. 303-988-6160, Ext 281

Woods, Nora, *Asst Librn,* Southern University, Shreveport-Bossier City Campus Library, Shreveport LA. 318-424-6552, Ext 238

Woods, Sister Angela, *Assoc Librn,* Saint John's Seminary, Edward Laurence Doheny Memorial Library, Camarillo CA. 805-482-4697

Woods, Sister Regina Clare, *Coordr,* Catholic Medical Center of Brooklyn & Queens Inc, Central Medical Library, Jamaica NY. 212-291-3300

Woods, William E, *Coordr,* Richard J Daley College, Library Technologies Program, IL. 312-735-3000

Woods, William R, *Ref,* College of the Sequoias Library, Visalia CA. 209-733-2050, Ext 314

Woodson, Almeta, *Media,* Atlanta University, Trevor Arnett Library, Atlanta GA. 404-681-0251, Ext 225

Woodson, E, *Geol & Maps,* State University of New York at Buffalo, University Libraries, Buffalo NY. 716-636-2965

Woodson, Nancy, *Ref,* Georgia Department of Education (Div of Public Library Services), Atlanta GA. 404-656-2461

Woodson, Wiletta, *Reader Serv,* Northwest Christian College, Learning Resource Center, Eugene OR. 503-343-1641, Ext 35

Woodstrom, Linda, *Librn,* Minnesota Office of Economic Opportunity Library, Saint Paul MN. 612-296-5740

Woodsworth, Anne, *Dir,* York University, Scott Library, Downsview ON. 416-667-2235

Woodward, Cathy, *AV,* Lima Public Library, Lima OH. 419-228-5113

Woodward, Cathy, *Coordr,* Western Ohio Film Circuit, OH. 419-228-5113

Woodward, Daniel H, *Librn,* Huntington Library, Art Gallery & Botanical Gardens, San Marino CA. 213-792-6141

Woodward, David A, *Dir, Hermon Dunlap Smith Ctr for Hist of Cartography,* Newberry Library, Chicago IL. 312-943-9090

Woodward, Edith S, *Librn,* Ohio Legislative Service Commission Library, Columbus OH. 614-466-5312

Woodward, Jeannette, *Dir,* Gardner-Webb College, Dover Memorial Library, Boiling Springs NC. 704-434-2361

Woodward, Julia, *Librn,* Deaconess Hospital, Health Science Library, Milwaukee WI. 414-933-9600, Ext 3314

Woodward, Julie, *Ref,* Marion County Public Library, Fairmont WV. 304-366-4831

Woodward, Mary Ellen, *Libr Program Officer (North Africa & Near East),* International Communication Agency (Education & Cultural Affairs), Washington DC. 202-632-5346, 632-6752

Woodward, Nanette, *Commun Servs,* Ocmulgee Regional Library, Eastman GA. 912-374-4711

Woodward, Phyllis, *Librn,* Lake County Public Library (Highland Public), Highland IN. 219-838-2394

Woodward, Robert C, *Dir,* Bangor Public Library, Bangor ME. 207-947-8336

Woodward, Sallie, *Librn,* Crockett Public Library, Crockett TX. 713-544-3089

Woodward, Wayne, *Dir,* Wesley Biblical Seminary Library, Jackson MS. 601-957-1276

Woodworth, Bonnie Jean, *Librn,* Hartford Insurance Group (Corporate Library), Hartford CT. 203-547-5516

Woodworth, Edith, *Librn,* Annapolis Valley Regional Library Headquarters (Port Williams Branch), Port Williams NS. 902-542-3005

Woodworth, Eileen B, *Ad,* Enoch Pratt Free Library, Baltimore MD. 301-396-5430, 396-5395

Woodworth, Elizabeth, *Librn,* British Columbia Ministry of Health Library, Victoria BC. 604-387-6627, 387-6777

Woody, Jacqueline, *Librn,* Prince George's County Memorial Library System (Glenarden Branch), Glenarden MD. 301-772-5477

Woody, Kennerly, *Hist & Rel,* Princeton University Library, Princeton NJ. 609-452-3180

Woody, Nadine, *Librn,* Douglass Public Library, Douglass KS. 316-746-2200

Woodyard, Nancy, *Librn,* El Paso Public Library (Richard Burges Branch), El Paso TX. 915-543-3846

Wool, Susan E, *Per,* Hispanic Society of America Library, New York NY. 212-926-2234

Woolard, Kathryn A, *Librn,* Republic Steel Corporation, Research Center Library, Independence OH. 216-524-5100, Ext 261, 262

Wooldridge, Steven, *Media,* Loyola-Notre Dame Library, Inc, Baltimore MD. 301-532-8787

Wooley, Kathy, *Ad,* Public Library of Columbus & Franklin County, Columbus OH. 614-864-8050

Woolf, Nadene M, *Dir,* Spencer Public-Owen County Contractual Library, Spencer IN. 812-829-3392

Woolfe, Marianne, *Dir,* Danbury Public Library, Danbury CT. 203-797-4505

Woolfenden, William E, *Dir,* Archives of American Art, National Headquarters, New York NY. 212-826-5722

Woollard, Isabel, *Librn,* North American Life Assurance Co Library, Toronto ON. 416-362-6011

Woollet, Bonnie, *Librn,* University of Arizona Library (Media Center), Tucson AZ. 602-626-3441

Woollett, Raymond J, *Librn,* Bentley Memorial Library, Bolton CT. 203-646-7349

Woolley, Robert, *Curriculum Ctr,* Utah State University, Merrill Library & Learning Resources Program, Logan UT. 801-750-2637

Woolley, Robert D, *Librn,* Utah State University (Curriculum Center), Logan UT. 801-750-2749

Woolls, Blanche, *Assoc Prof,* University of Pittsburgh, School of Library & Information Science, PA. 412-624-5230

Woolsey, John L, *Librn,* International Fabricare Institute Research Center Library, Silver Spring MD. 301-622-1900

Woolsey, Mable L, *Dir,* Knoxville Public Library, Knoxville IL. 309-289-2113

Woolson, Barbara, *Dir,* Oceanic Free Public Library, Rumson NJ. 201-842-2692

Woolworth, Alan R, *Head Archaeol Dept,* Minnesota Historical Society, Fort Snelling Branch Library, Fort Snelling MN. 612-726-1630

Wooten, Jacqueline, *Librn,* Flathead County Free Library (Whitefish Branch), Whitefish MT. 406-862-3273

Wooten, Jeannine, *Librn,* Humboldt Public Library, Humboldt TN. 901-784-2383

Wooters, Shirley, *Dir,* Gowrie Public Library, Gowrie IA. 515-352-3315

Wootton, Norris, *Dir,* Chesterfield County Library, Chesterfield SC. 803-623-7489

Worcester, Bonnie, *Librn,* Lulejian & Associates Inc Library, Falls Church VA. 703-820-6100

Worcester, Bonnie, *On-Line Servs,* Urban Institute Library, Washington DC. 202-223-1950, Ext 362

Worcester, Dorothy, *Librn,* Dublin Public Library, Dublin NH. 603-563-8137

Word, Alberta, *Commun Servs,* Nutley Public Library, Nutley NJ. 201-667-0405

Wordell, Edith G, *Librn,* Brownell Library, Home of Little Compton Free Public Library, Little Compton RI. 401-635-8562

Wordell, Madeline H, *Librn,* Newport Historical Society Library, Newport RI. 401-846-0813

Worden, Diane D, *Dir,* Kalamazoo Nature Center, Environmental Information Center Library, Kalamazoo MI. 616-381-1575, Ext 28

Work, Helen, *Asst Librn,* American Baptist Theological Seminary, College of the Bible, T L Holcomb Library, Nashville TN. 615-228-7877

Workman, Garnet, *Librn,* Lewistown Carnegie Public Library, Lewistown IL. 309-547-2860

Workman, Laraine, *Circ,* Lake County Public Library, Leadville CO. 303-486-0569

Workman, Stan, *Pub Servs & On-Line Servs,* Salt Lake County Library System, Whitmore Library, Salt Lake City UT. 801-943-7614

Workman, Virginia, *In Charge,* University of Missouri Saint Louis (Education Library), Saint Louis MO. 314-553-5571

Worley, Betty, *Librn,* Delta County Public Library (Cedaredge Public), Cedaredge CO. 303-874-9630

Worley, Betty, *Dir,* Sequatchie County Public Library, Dunlap TN. 615-949-2357

Worley, L W, *Asst to Vice Pres-Law,* Seaboard Coast Line Railroad Co, Law Library, Jacksonville FL. 904-353-2011

Worley, Mrs Larry Jo, *Ref,* University of Dallas, William A Blakley Library, Irving TX. 214-438-1123, Ext 328

Worley, Parker, *Dir,* Rutgers University (Camden Arts & Science Library), Camden NJ. 609-757-6036

Worley, Penny, *On-Line Servs,* Houston Academy of Medicine, Texas Medical Center Library, Houston TX. 713-797-1230

Worley, Ross, *Media,* Fort Lewis College Library, Durango CO. 303-247-7738

Worley, S Nelson, *Dir,* Appomattox Regional Library, Maud Langhorne Nelson Library, Hopewell VA. 804-458-6329

Worman, Lillian, *Librn,* Paterson Free Public Library (Grand Street), Paterson NJ. 201-881-3780

Worrell, Jr, Donald E, *Asst Dir,* Mount Clemens Public Library, Mount Clemens MI. 313-465-1906

Worsham, Beverly B, *Asst Dir,* Walter Cecil Rawls Regional Library System, Courtland VA. 804-653-2821

Worsham, Helen, *Ch,* Washington County Library System, William Alexander Percy Memorial Library, Greenville MS. 601-335-2331

Worsham, Patricia, *Librn,* Volusia County Public Libraries (Campbell Community Center), Daytona Beach FL. 904-252-8374

Worsley, Dorcas, *Librn,* Tucson Museum of Art Library, Tucson AZ. 602-623-4881

Worsley, Florence, *Librn,* Victoria County Public Library (Cambray Branch), Cambray ON. 705-324-3104

Worstell, Carl E, *Dir Libr Serv,* Veterans Administration, Medical Center Library Service, North Chicago IL. 312-689-1900, Ext 2547 (General), 2737 (Medical)

Wortelboer, Loraine, *Libm,* Onondaga County Public Library System (Hazard), Syracuse NY. 315-473-2638

Worth, Gertrude, *Libm,* Cardston Municipal Library, Cardston AB. 403-653-3366

Worthen, Isabella P, *Libm,* Old Forge Library, Old Forge NY. 315-369-6008

Worthen, Kate, *Libm,* Frederick County Public Library (Emmitsburg), Frederick MD. 301-694-1613

Worthen, Marion A, *Libm,* Gates Memorial Library, White River Junction VT. 802-295-7402

Worthington, Peri, *Ref,* United States Navy (Thompson Medical Library), San Diego CA. 714-233-2367

Worthington, Sandra, *Cat,* Florida Memorial College Library, Miami FL. 305-625-4141, Ext 148

Worthley, Dr Harold F, *Libm,* American Congregational Association, Congregational Library, Boston MA. 617-523-0470

Wortley, Aileen, *Libm,* Mississauga Public Library (Port Credit), Mississauga ON. 416-278-3437

Wortman, Lois, *Circ,* Cumberland College, Norma Perkins Hagan Memorial Library, Williamsburg KY. 606-549-0558

Wortzel, Murray, *Per,* Herbert H Lehman College Library, Bronx NY. 212-960-8577, 960-8582

Wos, Midge, *Libm,* Saint Luke's Hospital, Medical Library, Milwaukee WI. 414-647-6608

Wosh, Peter J, *Archivist,* Seton Hall University, McLaughlin Library, South Orange NJ. 201-762-9000, Ext 282, 276

Wotherspoon, Shelash, *Reader Serv,* Memorial University of Newfoundland Library (Health Sciences Library), Saint John's NF. 709-737-6670

Wotipka, Pam, *Outreach Servs,* Lewis & Clark Library, Helena MT. 406-442-2380

Woudenberg, Emily, *Ref,* Ralph Chandler Harrison Memorial Library, Carmel CA. 408-624-4629

Wournell, Doug, *Bkmobile Coordr,* Dartmouth Regional Library, Dartmouth NS. 902-466-7623

Woy, James B, *Libm,* Free Library of Philadelphia (Mercantile), Philadelphia PA. 215-686-5449

Woy, Sara G, *Dir,* Friends Free Library of Germantown, Philadelphia PA. 215-438-6023

Wozniak, Grace I, *Prof Coll,* State Library of Pennsylvania, Harrisburg PA. 717-787-2646

Wozny, Jay, *Dir,* Pettigrew Regional Library, Plymouth NC. 919-793-2113

Wrage, Joyce, *Ch,* Brookings Public Library, Brookings SD. 605-692-9407, 692-9408

Wray, Dorothy, *ILL,* Volusia County Public Libraries, Daytona Beach FL. 904-252-8374

Wray, H Donley, *Dir & Bkmobile Coordr,* Goffstown Public Library, Goffstown NH. 603-497-2102

Wray, Thelma J, *Dir,* Fort Smith Public Library, Fort Smith AR. 501-783-0229

Wray, Wendell, *Prof,* University of Pittsburgh, School of Library & Information Science, PA. 412-624-5230

Wreath, April, *Cat,* University of North Carolina at Chapel Hill (Health Sciences Library), Chapel Hill NC. 919-966-2111

Wrede, Richard, *Asst Dir & Ref,* Lyndhurst Free Public Library, Lyndhurst NJ. 201-939-6548

Wreford, S, *In Charge,* University of Toronto Libraries (Dept of Chemistry), Toronto ON. 416-978-3587

Wren, Daniel, *Bus Hist,* University of Oklahoma MUniversity Libraries, Norman OK. 405-325-2611

Wren, James, *Mgr,* Motor Vehicle Manufacturers Association of the United States, Inc (Patent & Trademark), Detroit MI. 313-872-4311, Ext 238

Wrenn, Christy J, *Libm,* Times Library, Shreveport LA. 318-424-0373, Ext 310

Wrenn, John P, *Libr Facilities & Equipment,* Chicago Public Library, Chicago IL. 312-269-2900

Wrenn, Teresa, *Editorial Asst,* National Municipal League, Murray Seasongood Library, New York NY. 212-535-5700

Wrenn, Thomas, *Ad,* Kanawha County Public Library, Kanawha County Service Center, Charleston WV. 304-343-4646

Wrigglesworth, Doreen, *Ref,* Collingswood Free Public Library, Collingswood NJ. 609-858-0649

Wright, Amy, *Libm,* Phoenicia Library, Phoenicia NY. 914-688-7811

Wright, Ann, *ILL,* San Diego State University Library, San Diego CA. 714-286-6014

Wright, Ann Finley, *Libm,* United States Geological Survey, Water Resources Division Library, Albuquerque NM. 505-766-2841

Wright, Barbara, *Admin Asst,* Los Angeles County Public Library System, South State Cooperative Library System, Los Angeles CA. 213-974-6501

Wright, Bernice, *Acq,* Stephen F Austin State University, Ralph W Steen Library, Nacogdoches TX. 713-569-4109

Wright, Bernice, *Libm,* Town of Berne Free Library, Berne NY. 518-872-1246

Wright, C Dan, *Actg Head,* Auburn University, Dept of Educational Media, AL. 205-826-4529

Wright, Carol, *Regional Libm,* Ozarks Regional Library, Fayetteville AR. 501-442-6253

Wright, Carol K, *Libm,* Heermance Memorial Library, Coxsackie NY. 518-731-8084

Wright, Catherine, *Dir,* Leisure World-Laguna Hills Library, Laguna Hills CA. 714-951-2274, Ext 274

Wright, Catherine, *Libm,* West Greenwich Public Library, West Greenwich RI. 401-397-3434

Wright, Charlotte, *Libm,* Monroe County Library System (Erie Branch), Erie MI. 313-848-4420

Wright, Corawayne, *Assoc Libm & Bibliog Instr,* Wesleyan College, Willet Memorial Library, Macon GA. 912-477-1110, Ext 200

Wright, Daisy O, *In Charge,* Stone & Webster Management Consultants, Inc, Information Center, New York NY. 212-269-4224, Ext 298

Wright, David, *Asst Dir,* Bryan College, H A Ironside Memorial Library, Dayton TN. 615-775-2041, Ext 228

Wright, David T, *Dir,* Idaho Museum of Natural History, Pocatello ID. 208-236-3168

Wright, Dolores, *ILL,* Berkeley Public Library, Berkeley CA. 415-644-6095

Wright, Dolores, *Circ,* Free Public Library of Oakland, Oakland NJ. 201-337-3742

Wright, Dolores, *Libm,* Rock Island Public Library (Thirtieth St & Thirty First Ave Branch), Rock Island IL. 309-788-2469

Wright, Donald E, *Dir,* Evanston Public Library, Evanston IL. 312-866-0300

Wright, Doris, *Ad, Acq & Ref,* Spartanburg County Public Library, Spartanburg SC. 582-4123 & 585-2441

Wright, Dr Gwendolyn, *Asst Prof,* Southern Connecticut State College, Div of Library Science & Instructional Technology, CT. 203-397-4532

Wright, Frances, *Libm,* Valley Publishing Co Library, Kent WA. 206-872-6600

Wright, Gerry, *Ser,* University of Texas Libraries (General), Austin TX. 512-471-3811

Wright, Gladys H, *Libm,* Casco Public Library, Casco ME. 207-627-4541

Wright, Gwen, *Libm,* Queen's University at Kingston (Education), Kingston ON. 613-547-6286

Wright, H Curtis, *Prof,* Brigham Young University, School of Library & Information Sciences, UT. 801-378-2976

Wright, Heather, *Libm,* Welland Public Library (Northwest), Welland ON. 416-735-4231

Wright, Helen, *ILL,* Boynton Beach City Library, Boynton Beach FL. 732-2624 or 732-8111, Ext 223, 224 & 225

Wright, Helen H, *Dir,* Pittsfield Public Library, Pittsfield IL. 217-285-2200

Wright, Helena, *Libm & Curator,* Merrimack Valley Textile Museum Library, North Andover MA. 617-686-0191

Wright, Hope, *Dir,* Sussex County Department of Libraries (Bethany Beach Public), Bethany Beach DE. 302-539-5231

Wright, I Marlene, *Libm,* Loudoun County Public Library (Sterling Public), Sterling VA. 703-430-9500

Wright, J, *Prof,* University of Alberta, Faculty of Library Science, AB. 403-432-4578

Wright, Jacqueline S, *Dir,* Arkansas Supreme Court Library, Little Rock AR. 501-374-2512

Wright, James B, *Libm,* University of New Mexico General Library (Fine Arts), Albuquerque NM. 505-277-2357

Wright, Janet, *Cat,* College of the Virgin Islands, Ralph M Paiewonsky Library, Saint Thomas VI. 809-774-1252, Ext 483

Wright, Janet, *Dir,* Menlo Public Library, Menlo IA. 515-524-4201

Wright, Janetta, *Libr Tech Asst,* Randolph Technical Institute, Learning Resources Center, Asheboro NC. 919-629-1471, Ext 27

Wright, Jean, *Ser,* Vanderbilt University Library, Nashville TN. 615-322-2834

Wright, Jeanne, *ILL,* A K Smiley Public Library, Redlands CA. 714-793-2201

Wright, Jill, *Tech Serv,* Franklin-Johnson County Public Library, Franklin IN. 317-738-2833

Wright, Joan, *Ch,* Orchard Park Public Library, Orchard Park NY. 716-662-9851

Wright, Joan M, *Libm,* C F Lawrence Memorial Library, Pepperell MA. 617-433-6933

Wright, Joe, *Libm,* Miami News Library, Miami FL. 305-350-2189

Wright, Joe, *Libm,* Trenton Times Library, Trenton NJ. 609-396-3232

Wright, John L, *Libm,* Cuyahoga County Public Library (North Royalton Branch), North Royalton OH. 216-237-3800

Wright, Joyce, *Per,* Memphis-Shelby County Public Library & Information Center (Science, Business, Social Sciences), Memphis TN. 901-528-2950

Wright, Joyce, *Head, Asia Coll,* University of Hawaii (University of Hawaii Library), Honolulu HI. 808-948-7205

Wright, Judith M, *Dir,* University of Chicago (Law Library), Chicago IL. 312-753-3425

Wright, Judy, *Libm,* Texas Research League Library, Austin TX. 512-472-3127

Wright, Karen, *Ch & AV,* Mount Laurel Free Public Library, Mount Laurel NJ. 609-234-7319

Wright, Kathryn, *Libm,* Dallas County Library, Fordyce AR. 501-352-3592

Wright, Kieth, *Dean,* University of Maryland, College of Library & Information Services, MD. 301-454-5441

Wright, Leona, *Ch,* Washoe County Library, Reno NV. 702-785-4039

Wright, Lillian, *Tech Serv,* Kentucky State University, Blazer Library, Frankfort KY. 502-564-5852

Wright, Linda, *Ref,* Brewer State Junior College, Main Campus Library, Fayette AL. 205-922-3221, Ext 244

Wright, Linda, *Libm,* Central Arkansas Library System (Fletcher), Little Rock AR. 501-663-5457

Wright, Linda, *Asst Dir,* Gaston County Public Library, Gastonia NC. 704-866-3756

Wright, Linda, *Ch,* Watertown Free Public Library, Watertown MA. 617-924-5390

Wright, Lynda, *Exten Serv,* Borough of Etobicoke Public Library, Weston ON. 416-248-5681

Wright, M Eugene, *Dir,* Southeast Louisiana Library Network Cooperative, (SEALLINC), LA. 504-586-4896

Wright, Mareda, *Tech Serv,* Twin Falls Public Library, Twin Falls ID. 208-733-2965

Wright, Margaret, *Bkmobile Coordr,* Everett Public Library, Everett WA. 206-259-8858

Wright, Margaret, *Libm,* LeRoy Public Library, LeRoy KS. 316-964-2245

Wright, Margery, *Libm,* Shreve Memorial Library (South Caddo), Shreveport LA. 318-687-6824

Wright, Marie, *Libm,* Harris County Public Library (Galena Park Branch), Galena Park TX. 713-674-2245

Wright, Marie, *Asst Libm,* Oakland Park City Library, Oakland Park FL. 305-561-6287

Wright, Marjorie, *Libm,* Crawford Public Library, Crawford NE. 308-665-1780

Wright, Marjorie, *Tech Serv,* Rock Springs Public Library, Rock Springs WY. 307-362-6212

Wright, Mary, *Tech Serv,* Field Library, Peekskill Library, Peekskill NY. 914-737-0010

Wright, Mary F, *Asst Dir,* Itawamba Junior College, Learning Resource Center, Fulton MS. 601-862-3101, Ext 237

Wright, Meredith S, *Mgr,* Union Carbide Corp-Parma Technical Center, Technical Information Service, Parma OH. 216-676-2263

Wright, Michael D, *Dir,* Dakota Wesleyan University, Layne Library, Mitchell SD. 605-996-6511, Ext 203

Wright, Mildred, *Librn,* Akron-Summit County Public Library (Wooster), Akron OH. 216-434-8726

Wright, Morton S, *Dir,* Shawnee College Library, Ullin IL. 618-634-2242, Ext 36

Wright, Myrna, *Librn,* Minnesota Library for the Blind & Physically Handicapped, Faribault MN. 507-332-3279

Wright, Myrna, *Librn Blind,* Minnesota State Library Agency, Office of Public Libraries & Interlibrary Cooperation, Saint Paul MN. 612-296-2821

Wright, Nan, *Ref,* Free Public Library of the City of Trenton, Trenton NJ. 609-392-7188

Wright, Nancy D, *Mgr,* Herner & Co Library, Arlington VA. 703-558-8238

Wright, Nancy M, *Librn,* H J Heinz Co, Research & Development Laboratory Library, Pittsburgh PA. 412-237-5948, 237-5949

Wright, Nanette, *Pub Servs,* Detroit College of Law Library, Detroit MI. 313-965-0150

Wright, Pat, *Librn,* Burlington Public Library (New Appleby), Burlington ON. 416-639-3611, Ext 56

Wright, Patricia, *ILL,* Arlington Public Library, Arlington TX. 817-275-2763, 265-3311, Ext 347

Wright, Patricia, *Cat,* Sweet Briar College Library, Sweet Briar VA. 804-381-5541

Wright, Patricia C, *Dir,* University of Saint Thomas (Cardinal Beran Library at Saint Mary's Seminary), Houston TX. 713-681-5544

Wright, Pauline M, *Dir,* Pulteney Free Library, Pulteney NY. 607-868-3652

Wright, Ray, *In Charge,* National Chamber of Commerce for Women, Inc Library, New York NY. 212-685-3454

Wright, Raymond, *ILL,* Albert Einstein College of Medicine, D Samuel Gottesman Library, Bronx NY. 212-430-3108

Wright, Raymond, *Pub Servs,* Church of Jesus Christ of Latter-Day Saints (Genealogical Society of Utah), Salt Lake City UT. 801-531-2323

Wright, Raymond C, *Chief Librn,* University of Winnipeg Library, Winnipeg MB. 204-786-7811, Ext 520

Wright, Rhona A, *Librn,* Saskatchewan Department of Agriculture Library, Regina SK. 306-565-5151

Wright, Richard J, *Dir,* Bowling Green State University Library (Center for Archival Collections), Bowling Green OH. 419-372-2411

Wright, Robert, *Lectr,* University of Pittsburgh, School of Library & Information Science, PA. 412-624-5230

Wright, Roberta M, *Ch,* Laramie County Library System, Cheyenne WY. 307-634-3561

Wright, Rosa G, *Librn,* Law Library Association of Saint Louis, Saint Louis MO. 314-622-4386

Wright, Roseann Anderson, *Librn,* Akron-Summit County Public Library (Tallmadge Branch), Tallmadge OH. 216-633-4345

Wright, Ruth E, *Ch,* Gloucester Lyceum & Sawyer Free Library, Gloucester MA. 617-283-0376

Wright, S, *Prof,* University of Alberta, Faculty of Library Science, AB. 403-432-4578

Wright, Scott, *Dir,* College of Saint Thomas, O'Shaughnessy Library, Saint Paul MN. 612-647-5720

Wright, Sharon Kay, *Librn,* Chillicothe & Ross County Public Library (South Salem Branch), South Salem OH. 614-981-2400

Wright, Shirley, *Librn,* Woodbury County Rural Library (Danbury Branch), Danbury IA. 712-873-3322

Wright, Sue, *Tech Serv & Cat,* Bowling Green Public Library, Bowling Green KY. 502-781-4882

Wright, Susan, *Ch,* Cherokee County Public Library, Gaffney SC. 803-489-4381

Wright, Susan, *Dir,* Freehold Public Library, Freehold NJ. 201-462-5135

Wright, Sylvia H, *Librn,* City College of the City University of New York (Architecture), New York NY. 212-690-5329

Wright, Thomas, *Dir,* Northern College of Applied Art & Technology Library, Kirkland Lake ON. 705-567-9291

Wright, Thomas, *Librn,* University of California Los Angeles Library (William Andrews Clark Memorial Library), Los Angeles CA. 213-731-8529

Wright, Viola, *Librn,* Richland County Public Library (Latimer Manor), Columbia SC. 803-799-9084

Wright, Virginia A, *Librn,* Humphreys College Library, Stockton CA. 209-478-0800

Wright, Walter W, *Rare Bks & Spec Coll,* Dartmouth College, Baker Memorial Library, Hanover NH. 603-646-2235

Wright, Wanda, *Ch,* Weatherford Public Library, Weatherford TX. 817-594-2767

Wright, William C, *Archivist & Hist Bureau Head,* New Jersey State Library, Trenton NJ. 609-292-6200

Wright, Jr, M Eugene, *Dir,* New Orleans Public Library, Simon Heinsheim & Fisk Libraries, New Orleans LA. 504-586-4905

Wrigley, Elizabeth S, *Dir,* Francis Bacon Library, Francis Bacon Foundation Inc, Claremont CA. 714-624-6305

Wrinkle, Barbara D, *Librn,* United States Air Force (Luke Air Force Base Library), Luke AFB AZ. 602-935-6301, 935-7191

Wrobel, Hilda, *In Charge,* Milwaukee Public Library (Atkinson Branch), Milwaukee WI. 414-278-3068

Wrobleski, Iretha, *Librn,* McDowell Public Library (Bradshaw Branch), Bradshaw WV. 304-967-5140

Wroblewski, Christine, *Dir,* Fairfield Public Library, Fairfield NJ. 201-227-3575

Wroblewski, Maureen, *Ad,* Newark Public Library, Newark NY. 315-331-4370

Wrocklage, Pauline, *Asst Dir,* Delphos Public Library, Delphos OH. 419-692-1339

Wrotenbery, Carl R, *Dir,* Houston Baptist University, Moody Memorial Library, Houston TX. 713-774-7661, Ext 303

Wryn, Ruth, *Librn,* Hawaii State Library System (Maui Regional), Wailuku HI. 808-244-3945

Wszolek, Sister Mary Maurita, *Librn,* Saint Anthony Medical Center, Medical Library, Crown Point IN. 219-663-8120

Wu, Celia, *Dir & Ref,* Academy of Aeronautics Library, East Elmhurst NY. 212-429-6600

Wu, Elsa, *Ref & Ser,* Alabama Agricultural & Mechanical University, Joseph F Drake Memorial Learning Resources Center, Normal AL. 205-859-7309

Wu, Ethel, *Librn,* New York Public Library (City Island), New York NY. 212-885-1703

Wu, Eugene W, *Librn,* Harvard University Library (Harvard-Yenching Library), Cambridge MA. 617-495-3327

Wu, Frances, *Cat,* University of Dayton Libraries (Law School Library), Dayton OH. 513-229-2314

Wu, Grace, *Tech Serv & Cat,* Cumberland County College Library, Vineland NJ. 609-691-8600, Ext 44, 45

Wu, Grace, *Cat,* Wartburg College, Engelbrecht Library, Waverly IA. 319-352-1200, Ext 244

Wu, Harry P, *Dir,* Blue Water Library Federation, Port Huron MI. 313-987-7323

Wu, Harry P, *Dir,* Saint Clair County Library System, Port Huron MI. 313-987-7323

Wu, Jeanette, *Cat,* Bentley College, Solomon R Baker Library, Waltham MA. 617-891-2231

Wu, Pei-ling, *Tech Serv,* Macomb County Community College-South Campus, Max Thompson Learning Media Center, Warren MI. 313-445-7401

Wu, Phillip, *Bernard Fall Coll,* Howard University Libraries, Founders Library, Washington DC. 202-636-7253

Wu, Tinna, *Soc Sci,* Hamline University, Bush Memorial Library, Saint Paul MN. 612-641-2373

Wu, William S, *Chief Research,* Ontario Legislative Library, Research & Information Services, Toronto ON. 416-965-4545

Wudyaka, Mark, *Librn,* Gowanda Psychiatric Center, Health Sciences Library, Helmuth NY. 716-532-3311

Wudzki, James, *AV,* Ocean County Library, Toms River NJ. 201-349-6200

Wulff, Jacqueline, *On-Line Servs,* North Memorial Medical Center, Medical Library, Minneapolis MN. 612-588-0616, Ext 431

Wulff, L Yvonne, *Head,* University of Michigan Libraries (Medical Center), Ann Arbor MI. 313-764-1210

Wulffenstein, Pauline C, *Dir, Acq & Spec Coll,* Washington County Library, Saint George UT. 801-673-2562

Wunder, Juanita, *Librn,* Fonda Public Library, Fonda IA. 712-288-6618

Wunder, Richard, *Dir,* Westminster College, William T Nightingale Memorial Library, Salt Lake City UT. 801-484-7651, Ext 305

Wunderlich, Gretchen, *Commun Servs, South Area,* Hennepin County Library, Edina MN. 612-830-4944

Wunderlich, Gretchen, *Librn,* Hennepin County Library (Southdale-Hennepin), Edina MN. 612-830-4900

Wunn, Dolores, *Coordr,* Estherville Public Library, Estherville IA. 712-362-3869

Wunsh, Stephanie Q, *Tech Serv,* Horry County Memorial Library, Conway SC. 803-248-4898

Wuori, Ruth, *Librn,* Clovis-Carver Public Library, Clovis NM. 505-769-1973

Wurfel, Clifford, *Spec Coll,* University of California, Riverside, University Library, Riverside CA. 714-787-3221

Wurster, Ann Marie, *Ad,* Fremont Public Library District, Mundelein IL. 312-566-8702

Wurzburger, Marilyn, *Rare Bks,* Arizona State University Library, Tempe AZ. 602-965-3417

Wurzel, Denise, *Cat,* Girard Free Public Library, Girard OH. 216-545-2508

Wusnack, Prima, *Dir,* City-County Public Library, Bay Saint Louis MS. 601-467-5282, 467-6836

Wuthrick, Virginia, *Ref,* Fort Bend County Library, Richmond TX. 713-342-4455

Wyatt, Diane, *Librn,* Flesherton Public Library, Flesherton ON. 519-924-2241

Wyatt, James F, *Dean,* University of Alabama, Amelia Gayle Gorgas Library, University AL. 205-348-5298

Wyatt, JoAnn, *Librn,* Clanton Public Library, Clanton AL. 205-755-1768

Wyatt, Marie, *Librn,* United States Navy (Naval Air Station & Missile Center Library), Point Mugu CA. 805-982-1110

Wyatt, Marjorie, *Supvr,* Middlesex County Library (Arva Branch), Arva ON. 519-438-8368

Wyatt, Sue, *Librn,* Marshall County Public Library (Hardin Branch), Hardin KY. 502-437-4275

Wyche, Floyd E, *Librn,* Hartford Public Library (Albany), Hartford CT. 203-527-2076

Wyche, Floyd E, *Librn,* Hartford Public Library (Blue Hills), Hartford CT. 203-242-4634

Wyche, Margery, *Librn,* Shreve Memorial Library (Belcher Branch), Belcher LA. 318-221-2614

Wyckert, Paul V, *Superintendent,* National Park Service, Travertine Nature Center Library, Sulphur OK. 405-622-3165

Wycoff, Carolyn, *Librn,* Caldwell Public Library, Caldwell OH. 614-732-4506

Wyeth, John, *Bibliog Instr,* Framingham State College, Henry Whittemore Library, Framingham MA. 617-620-1220, Ext 273

Wygant, Larry J, *Hist of Med & Archives,* University of Texas Medical Branch, Moody Medical Library, Galveston TX. 713-765-1971

Wygant, Virginia, *Librn, Servs to Homebound,* Montgomery County Department of Public Libraries, Rockville MD. 301-279-1401

Wygergangs, J, *Librn,* Protestant School Board of Greater Montreal, Professional Library, Montreal PQ. 514-482-6000, Ext 223

Wygnanski, Jadwiga, *Librn,* McGill University Libraries (Engineering), Montreal PQ. 514-392-5913

Wyker, Shirley, *Librn,* Onondaga County Public Library System (Children's), Syracuse NY. 315-473-2702

Wykert, Todd, *Media,* University of Wyoming (Jayne Media Center), Laramie WY. 307-766-6391

Wykoff, Leslie, *Librn,* Kaiser Foundation Hospital (Health Services Research Center), Portland OR. 503-233-5631

Wykoff, Paula, *Ref & On-Line Servs,* University of Texas (M D Anderson Hospital & Tumor Institute), Houston TX. 713-792-2282

Wyks, Margaret, *Librn,* Sterck School for the Hearing Impaired, Newark DE. 302-454-2301

Wylie, Dorothy, *Librn,* Decatur County Library, Decaturville TN. 901-852-2863

Wylie, Kathy, *On-Line Servs & Bibliog Instr,* Delta State University, W B Roberts Library, Cleveland MS. 601-843-2483

Wyllie, Elizabeth T, *Dir,* Cobleigh Public Library, Lyndonville VT. 802-626-5475

Wylot, Connie, *ILL,* Grand Forks Public City-County Library, Grand Forks ND. 701-772-8116

Wyly, Mary P, *Dep Dir Libr Servs,* Newberry Library, Chicago IL. 312-943-9090

Wymore, Jan, *Librn,* Washington State Library (Western State Hospital Staff Library), Fort Steilacoom WA. 206-756-9715

Wynar, Lubomyr R, *Prof,* Kent State University, School of Library Science, OH. 216-672-2782, 672-7988

Wynder, Leslie, *Secy,* Invermere Public Library, Invermere BC. 604-342-6416

Wynecoop, Joseph, *Dir,* Jet Propulsion Laboratory Library, California Institute of Technology, Pasadena CA. 213-354-4200

Wynen, Nancy H, *Dir,* Hillsdale Free Public Library, Hillsdale NJ. 201-664-0020

Wyngaard, Susan, *Dir,* International Museum of Photography at George Eastman House Archives, Rochester NY. 716-271-3361, Ext 24, 28

Wyngaarden, Joyce, *Tech Serv & Cat,* Chattahoochee Valley Regional Library, W C Bradley Memorial Library, Headquarters, Columbus GA. 404-327-0211

Wynkoop, Lois, *Librn,* Newton Falls Public Library, Newton Falls OH. 216-872-1282

Wynn, Barbara J, *Ch,* Temple Terrace Public Library, Temple Terrace FL. 813-988-4731

Wynn, Barbara L, *Librn,* Monterey County Library, Salinas CA. 408-424-8611, Ext 395-396

Wynn, Elizabeth, *Librn,* United States Railroad Retirement Board Library, Chicago IL. 312-751-4500

Wynn, Linda, *Librn,* Camp Hill Public Library, Camp Hill AL. 205-896-2291

Wynn, Margaret, *Librn,* Orange County Transit District, Resource Center, Garden Grove CA. 714-971-6200

Wynn, Nancy, *Librn,* De Soto Trail Regional Library (Pelham Branch), Pelham GA. 912-294-4811

Wynne, Allen, *Librn,* University of Colorado at Boulder (Math/Physics Library), Boulder CO. 303-492-8231

Wynne, Joseph, *Cat,* University of Virginia (Law Library), Charlottesville VA. 804-924-3384

Wynne, Judith A, *Librn,* International Paper Co, Science & Technology-Information Services, Mobile AL. 205-457-8911, Ext 375

Wynne, Marjorie G, *Res Librn,* Yale University Library (Beinecke Rare Book & Manuscript), New Haven CT. 203-436-0234

Wynne, Nancy G, *Librn,* Amon Carter Museum of Western Art Library, Fort Worth TX. 817-738-1933, Ext 45

Wyppich, Margaret H, *Ch,* Springfield Township Library, Springfield PA. 215-543-2113

Wypyski, Eugene, *Librn,* Hofstra University Library (Law School Library), Hempstead NY. 516-560-3638

Wyrick, Jeannette, *Ad,* Fresno County Free Library, Fresno CA. 209-488-3191

Wyrwicz, Julia, *ILL,* Nashua Public Library, Nashua NH. 603-883-4141, 883-4142

Wyscarver, Deborah A, *Ref,* Pacific Christian College, Hurst Memorial Library, Fullerton CA. 714-879-3901, Ext 34

Wyser, Theresa A, *Librn,* Connecticut Police Academy, Resource Center, Meriden CT. 203-238-6531

Wysocki, Mary, *ILL,* Saint Joseph College, Pope Pius XII Library, West Hartford CT. 203-232-4571, Ext 208

Wysong, Rebecca, *Manager,* Preble County District Library, Eaton OH. 513-456-4331

Wysor, Blanche, *Librn,* County of Henrico Public Library (Sandston Branch), Sandston VA. 804-737-6670

Wyttenhove, Phyllis, *Librn,* Carver County Library System (Waconia Branch), Waconia MN. 612-442-4714

X

Xydias, Ellen, *Ch,* Webster Public Library, Webster NY. 872-3251 & 872-0240

Y

Yacko, Beverly C, *Dir,* Brookfield Free Public Library, Brookfield IL. 312-485-6917

Yadlosky, Elizabeth, *Assoc Dir Research Anal & Rev,* Library of Congress, Washington DC. 202-287-5000

Yaffee, Rachel, *Librn,* Kesher Zion Synagogue Sisterhood-Library, Reading PA. 215-372-3818

Yagello, Virginia E, *Librn,* Ohio State University Libraries (Chemistry Library), Columbus OH. 614-422-1118

Yagello, Virginia E, *Librn,* Ohio State University Libraries (Physics Library), Columbus OH. 614-422-7894

Yagendorf, Sanford S, *Librn,* Veterans Administration (Medical Library), Bedford MA. 617-275-7500

Yahn, Ellen, *Ch, Tech Serv & Cat,* Springfield Town Library, Springfield VT. 802-885-3108

Yakel, Grace, *Sr Libm,* New York State Library (Documents Processing), Albany NY. 518-474-5563

Yakerson, Amy, *AV,* Hamden Library, Miller Memorial, Hamden CT. 203-248-7747

Yakey, Marion, *Acq,* Lincoln Christian College & Seminary Library, Lincoln IL. 217-732-3168, Ext 234

Yakura, Thelma, *Dir,* Wright Memorial, Oakwood Library, Oakwood OH. 513-294-7171

Yakura, Thelma P, *Dir,* Wright Memorial Library, Dayton OH. 513-294-7171

Yamada, Shirley, *Naval Regional Libm,* United States Navy (Office of Naval Regional Librarian), Pearl Harbor HI. 808-471-8391

Yamada, Shirley H, *Libm,* United States Navy (Marine Corps Air Station Library), Kaneohe MCAS HI. 808-257-3583

Yamamoto, Andrea, *Asst Dir,* Owatonna Free Public Library, Owatonna MN. 507-451-4660

Yamamoto, Carol, *Comm Info,* Peninsula Library Systems, Daly City CA. 415-878-5577

Yamamoto, Catherine, *Ch,* Lake County Public Library, Merrillville IN. 219-769-3541

Yamane, Takeko Y, *Libr Tech,* Hawaii State Library System (Kapaa Branch), Kapaa HI. 808-822-5041

Yamashita, Hisako, *Libm,* New York Public Library (Ninety-Sixth Street), New York NY. 212-289-0908

Yamashita, Sumika, *Admin Libm,* Oakland Public Library, Oakland CA. 415-273-3281

Yampokky, Robert, *Bibliographer,* Carl and Lily Pforzheimer Foundation, Inc, Carl H Pforzheimer Library, New York NY. 212-697-7217

Yan, Mrs R, *Libm,* IBM Canada-Ltd, Laboratory Library, Don Mills ON. 416-443-3136

Yanarella, Marie, *Prof,* Northwestern Connecticut Community College, Library Technology Program, CT. 203-379-8543

Yancey, Beatrice, *Libm,* Waterford Township Free Public Library, Atco NJ. 609-767-7727

Yanchison, Daniel, *Spec Coll,* Virginia Commonwealth University (James Branch Cabell Library), Richmond VA. 804-257-1105

Yancich, David, *Controller,* Gary Public Library, Gary IN. 219-886-2484

Yancy, Kevin, *Supvr,* Chicago Public Library (Stateway Gardens Reading & Study Center), Chicago IL. 312-538-7218

Yandle, Anne, *Spec Coll,* University of British Columbia Library, Vancouver BC. 604-228-3871

Yang, Jackson, *Libm,* Michigan State University Library (Engineering), East Lansing MI. 517-355-2344

Yang, Lily, *Libm,* Queen of Angels Hospital, Medical Library, Los Angeles CA. 213-413-3000

Yang, Louise, *Actg Dir & Tech Serv,* Berea College, Hutchins Library, Berea KY. 606-986-9341, Ext 289

Yang, Monica, *Libm,* Maryland General Hospital (School of Nursing Library), Baltimore MD. 301-728-7900, Ext 2403

Yang, Myrtle, *Libm,* Carnegie Library of Pittsburgh (Lawrenceville), Pittsburgh PA. 412-622-3100

Yang, Ruth, *AV,* Pace University, Pleasantville-Briarcliff Library, Pleasantville NY. 914-769-3200, Ext 382

Yanicke, Joanne, *Libm,* Saint Michael Hospital, Regner Health Science Library, Milwaukee WI. 414-263-8477

Yankielun, Judith, *ILL, Ad & Ref,* Scotch Plains Public Library, Scotch Plains NJ. 201-322-5007

Yannotta, Peter J, *Dir,* Joint Free Public Library of the Chathams, Chatham NJ. 201-635-0603

Yannuci, D A, *Mgr,* Westinghouse Electric Corp, Transformer Division Engineering Library, Sharon PA. 412-981-1611, Ext 3306

Yanover, Abraham F, *Exec Dir,* Bureau of Jewish Education Library, Williamsville NY. 716-689-8844

Yao, Linda, *Dir,* Upland Public Library, Upland CA. 714-982-1561

Yao-Tang, Ta-liang (Daisey), *Libm,* Dixmont State Hospital, Personnel Library, Sewickley PA. 412-761-1780, Ext 228

Yaple, Henry, *Acq,* University of Wyoming, William Robertson Coe Library, Laramie WY. 307-766-3279

Yaple, Marilyn V, *Dir,* Bellaire City Library, Bellaire TX. 713-664-4098

Yarborough, Maxine, *Ad, Br Coordr & Bkmobile Coordr,* Jacksonville Public Library System, Haydon Burns Library, Jacksonville FL. 904-633-6870

Yarbrough, H V, *Mgr,* G D Searle & Co, Research Library, Skokie IL. 312-982-7884

Yarbrough, Linda, *Libm,* Mississippi County Library System, Blytheville AR. 501-762-2431

Yarbrough, Mayme, *Libm,* Shelby County Regional Library (Montevallo), Montevallo AL. 205-669-7851

Yarbrough, Valerie, *Ref,* Kennesaw College Library, Marietta GA. 404-422-8770, Ext 250

Yardley, Mrs Tommy M, *Libm,* Texas Woman's University, F W & Bessie Dye Memorial Library, Dallas TX. 214-631-3836

Yardum, Barbara, *Ch,* Monroeville Public Library, Monroeville PA. 412-372-0500

Yardumian, Alice J, *Dir,* Delanco Free Library Association, Delanco NJ. 609-461-6850

Yare, Yvonne, *Cat,* New City Free Library, New City NY. 914-634-4997

Yarnall, Jean, *Circ,* Warwick Public Library and Regional Center, Warwick RI. 401-739-5440

Yasson, Barbara, *Tech Serv,* Chesapeake Public Library, Chesapeake VA. 804-547-6579, 547-6592

Yasukawa, Leilani, *Asst Libm,* Hawaiian Telephone Co Library, Honolulu HI. 808-546-2600

Yasunari, Wakako, *Research Libm,* WED Enterprises, Inc (Walt E Disney), Research Library, Glendale CA. 213-956-7263

Yates, Charlene, *Libm,* Stamping Ground Public Library, Stamping Ground KY. 502-863-3566

Yates, Diane G, *YA & Ref,* Township of Shaler North Hills Library, Glenshaw PA. 412-486-0211, 486-0212

Yates, Dudley, *Dir,* Tennessee Technological University, Jere Whitson Memorial Library, Cookeville TN. 615-528-3408

Yates, Dudley V, *Dir & Prof,* Tennessee Technological University, Library Science Program, TN. 615-528-3124

Yates, Ella Gaines, *Dir,* Atlanta Public Library, Atlanta GA. 404-688-4636

Yates, Eva, *YA,* Birmingham Public & Jefferson County Free Library, Birmingham AL. 205-254-2551

Yates, Margaret, *Acq,* Mid-Mississippi Regional Library System, Kosciusko MS. 601-289-5141, 289-5146

Yates, Millicent E, *Libm,* E-Systems Inc, Melpar Division Technical Library, Falls Church VA. 703-560-5000

Yates, Sophia, *Libm,* Sheridan County Fulmer Public Library (Clearmont Community), Clearmont WY. 307-758-2282

Yates, Stanley, *Spec Coll,* Iowa State University Library, Ames IA. 515-294-1442

Yates, Sue, *Libm,* Dallas County Public Library (Seagoville Branch), Seagoville TX. 214-287-1022

Yates, Sue, *Libm,* Seagoville Public Library, Seagoville TX. 214-287-2911

Yates, T B, *Dir,* Rockwell International Corp, North American Aircraft Division Technical Information Center, El Segundo CA. 213-647-2961

Yates, W C, *Mgr,* Cities Service Co (Chemicals & Minerals Group Market Research Library), Tulsa OK. 918-586-4889

Yatrofsky, Katherine, *ILL,* Eastern Virginia Medical School, Moorman Memorial Library, Norfolk VA. 804-446-5840

Yaun, Gloria A, *Chief Librn,* Orfordville Public Library, Orfordville WI. 608-879-9229

Yavarkovsky, Jerome, *Asst Univ Librn, Planning,* Columbia University (University Libraries), New York NY. 212-280-2241

Yax, Lawrence D, *Dir,* Pensacola Junior College, Learning Resource Center, Pensacola FL. 904-476-5410

Yazgoor, Donald, *Dir,* Norwalk Public Library, Norwalk CT. 203-866-5559

Yeager, Cynthia Miller, *Librn,* Military Order of the Loyal Legion of the United States, War Library & Museum, Philadelphia PA. 215-735-8196

Yeager, Jacqueline, *Ch,* Tiffin-Seneca Public Library, Tiffin OH. 419-447-3751

Yeager, Marie, *Ch,* Haddon Heights Public Library, Haddon Heights NJ. 609-547-7132

Yeager, William, *Curator,* Norfolk Historical Society, Eva Brook Donly Museum Library, Simcoe ON. 519-426-1583

Yeamans, George T, *Prof,* Ball State University, Dept of Library Science, IN. 317-285-7180, 285-7189

Yeates, Elizabeth J, *Chief Librn,* National Oceanic & Atmospheric Administration, Library & Information Services Division, Rockville MD. 301-655-4000

Yeaton, Lorraine, *Librn,* Acton Public Library, Acton ME. 207-636-3839

Yeats, Naomi, *Spec Coll,* Arlington Public Library, Arlington TX. 817-275-2763, 265-3311, Ext 347

Yedlin, Deborah, *Tech Serv & Cat,* Washington University Libraries (School of Medicine Library), Saint Louis MO. 314-454-3711

Yee, Cynthia, *In Charge,* Valley National Bank, Financial Research Library, Phoenix AZ. 602-261-2456

Yee, Dale, *Resource Specialist,* Sierra Club, William E Colby Memorial Library, San Francisco CA. 415-981-8634, Ext 505

Yee, Hazel, *In Charge,* California Air Resources Board Library, El Monte CA. 213-575-6721

Yee, Janet I, *Ser,* University of Washington Libraries (Health Sciences), Seattle WA. 206-543-5530

Yee, Janice, *Ch & Bkmobile Coordr,* Santa Clara County Free Library, San Jose CA. 408-293-2326

Yee, Joyce V, *Cat,* University of Calgary Library (Faculty of Medicine Medical Library), Calgary AB. 403-284-6858

Yee, Kenneth, *Tech Serv & Cat,* Long Island University, Brooklyn Center Libraries, Brooklyn NY. 212-834-6060, 834-6064

Yee, Kenneth, *Automation Activities,* Long Island University, Brooklyn Center Libraries, Brooklyn NY. 212-834-6060, 834-6064

Yee, Kenneth, *Bus, Chinese Computer Tech & Spanish,* Long Island University, Brooklyn Center Libraries, Brooklyn NY. 212-834-6060, 834-6064

Yee, Margaret, *Ad,* Brookfield Free Public Library, Brookfield IL. 312-485-6917

Yee, Sandra, *Coordr & Bibliog Instr,* Muskegon Community College, Allen G Umbreit Library, Muskegon MI. 616-773-9131, Ext 260

Yegerlehner, Shirley, *Bus,* Indiana University-Purdue University at Indianapolis, University Library, Indianapolis IN. 317-264-4101

Yeh, Daniel, *Bus,* West Chester State College, Francis Harvey Green Library, West Chester PA. 215-436-2643

Yeh, Emily, *Coll Develop & Volunteer Coordr,* Georgia Regional Library for the Blind & Physically Handicapped, Atlanta GA. 404-656-2465

Yeh, Jessie, *Librn,* Brooklyn Public Library (Flatbush), Brooklyn NY. 212-282-2017

Yeh, Nah Lin, *Tech Serv & Cat,* Letourneau College, Margaret Estes Library, Longview TX. 214-753-0231, Ext 230

Yeh, Nah Lin, *On-Line Servs & Bibliog Instr,* Letourneau College, Margaret Estes Library, Longview TX. 214-753-0231, Ext 230

Yeh, Pauline, *Acq,* Montclair State College, Harry A Sprague Library, Upper Montclair NJ. 201-893-4291

Yeh, Rita, *Librn,* United Technologies Corp Library, East Hartford CT. 203-727-7120

Yeh, Thomas, *Cat,* Central Washington University Library, Ellensburg WA. 509-963-1901

Yeley, Donna K, *Librn,* Larue D Carter Memorial Hospital (Patients' Library), Indianapolis IN. 317-634-8401, Ext 314

Yelverton, John R, *Chief Bibliographer,* Georgia State University, William Russell Pullen Library, Atlanta GA. 404-658-2185, 658-2172

Yelverton, Mildred G, *Dir,* Judson College, Bowling Library, Marion AL. 205-683-2011, Ext 22

Yen, David S, *Dir,* Southwestern University, School of Law Library, Los Angeles CA. 213-738-0723

Yen, Marylynn Woo, *Librn,* Inner-City Business Improvement Forum, Consult & Systems Library, Detroit MI. 313-875-4700

Yenney, Patricia, *Ref & On-Line Servs,* Alaska Health Sciences Library, Anchorage AK. 907-263-1870

Yeno, Anne, *ILL,* Silas Bronson Library, Waterbury CT. 203-574-8200

Yeno, Anne, *Librn,* Silas Bronson Library (Bunker Hill), Waterbury CT. 203-574-8240

Yensen, Sandra C, *Ad,* Weston Public Library, Weston MA. 617-893-3312

Yeoh, Jo, *Dir & On-Line Servs,* Riverside Methodist Hospital, Medical Library, Columbus OH. 614-261-5230

Yeoman, Eunice, *Asst Librn,* Jasper County Public Library, Rensselaer Public Library (Hq), Rensselaer IN. 219-866-5881

Yeoman, Mrs John, *In Charge,* Oxford County Library (East Oxford), Woodstock ON. 519-537-5127

Yeoman, Mrs Robert, *In Charge,* Oxford County Library (Burgessville Branch), Burgessville ON. 519-424-9360

Yeomans, A, *Librn,* Okanagan Regional Library District (Summerland Branch), Summerland BC. 604-494-5591

Yeomans, Eleanor, *Ad,* Danville Public Library, Danville IL. 217-446-7420

Yerke, Theodor B, *Coordr,* Western Forestry Information Network, (WESTFORNET), CA. 415-584-3173

Yerkey, A Neil, *Asst Prof,* State University of New York at Buffalo, School of Information & Library Studies, NY. 716-636-2412

Yers, James N, *Asst Dir,* Stanford University Libraries, Stanford CA. 415-497-2016

Yeske, Loraine A, *Librn,* United States Army (Fort McCoy Post Library), Sparta WI. 608-388-2410

Yetman, Jeannette, *Librn,* Saugus Public Library (East Saugus), Saugus MA. 617-233-1710

Yetman, Nancy, *Tech Librn,* Donnelly Mirrors, Inc Library, Holland MI. 616-394-2268

Yetter, Cathleen L, *Syst Coordr,* Texas Trans Pecos Library System, El Paso Public Library, El Paso TX. 915-544-6772

Yetter, Cathy, *Tex Trans-Pecos Syst Coordr,* El Paso Public Library, El Paso TX. 915-543-3804

Yew, June, *Cat,* Rush-Presbyterian-Saint Luke's Medical Center (Library of Rush University), Chicago IL. 312-942-2271, 942-5950

Yewell, Eugenia, *Tech Serv,* Jacksonville State University Library, Jacksonville AL. 205-435-9820, Ext 213, 214

Yi, Soong, *Tech Serv,* Skokie Public Library, Skokie IL. 312-673-7774

Yien, Helen, *Acq,* University of Nebraska-Lincoln, University Libraries, Lincoln NE. 402-472-2526

Yingling, Ann, *Adminr Libr, Support Serv,* Sunnyvale Public Library, Sunnyvale CA. 408-738-5585

Yirka, Carl A, *Acq,* Northwestern University, Chicago (School of Law Library), Chicago IL. 312-649-8450

Ykelenstam, Priscilla, *Tech Serv,* Prince Edward Island Provincial Library, Charlottetown PE. 902-892-3504, Ext 54

Ylinen, Julie, *Ch,* Ela Area Public Library District, Lake Zurich IL. 312-438-3433

Yngve, Victor H, *Prof,* University of Chicago, Graduate Library School, IL. 312-753-3482

Yoakam, Eva, *Asst Dir,* Homer Public Library, Homer OH. 614-892-2020, Ext 1

Yockman, Helen K, *Librn,* Greensburg Library, Greensburg PA. 412-837-5620

Yoder, Cynthia A, *Librn,* United States Army (Corps of Engineers, Jacksonville District Library), Jacksonville FL. 904-791-3643

Yoder, Devon J, *Asst Dir,* Goshen College (Harold & Wilma Good Library), Goshen IN. 219-533-3161, Ext 257

Yoder, Elizabeth, *Librn,* Mifflin County Library (Allensville Branch), Allensville PA. 717-483-6968

Yoder, Eunice, *Ref,* Azusa Pacific College, Marshburn Memorial Library, Azusa CA. 213-969-3434, Ext 198

Yoder, Keith E, *Chmn,* Millersville State College, Dept of Library Science, PA. 717-872-5411, Ext 416

Yoder, Myra S, *Asst Dir,* Florida, State University System, Extension Library, Saint Petersburg FL. 813-893-9120

Yoder, Paula, *Asst, Children's Libr,* Eckhart Public Library, Auburn IN. 219-925-2414

Yoder, Robert A, *Asst Dir,* Kent State University Libraries (Audio-Visual Services), Kent OH. 216-672-3456

Yoder, Roman, *Asst Librn,* Stetson University College of Law, Charles A Dana Law Library, Saint Petersburg FL. 813-345-1335

Yoder, Saida, *Librn,* Weatherford Public Library, Weatherford TX. 817-594-2767

Yoelson, Martin I, *Chief Park Historian,* National Park Service, Independence National Historical Park Library, Philadelphia PA. 215-597-8047

Yoemans, Ruby, *Librn,* Oconee County Library (Westminster Branch), Westminster SC. 803-638-5837

Yogmour, Olga, *Head Main Libr,* Akron-Summit County Public Library, Akron OH. 216-762-7621

Yoke, Shirley, *Cat,* University of Charleston, Andrew S Thomas Memorial Library, Charleston WV. 304-346-1400

Yomada, Ken, *Dir,* Hiwassee College, Hardwick Johnston Memorial Library, Madisonville TN. 615-442-3343

Yonce, Barbara, *Librn,* Greenville Technical College, Learning Resources Center, Greenville SC. 803-242-3170, Ext 321

Yoo, Tae Jung, *Librn,* Windels, Marx, Davies & Ives Library, New York NY. 212-977-9600, Ext 333

Yoo, Yushin, *Assoc Prof,* Murray State University, Dept of Library Science, KY. 502-762-2291

Yoo, Yuskin, *ILL & Media,* Murray State University, Harry Lee Waterfield Library, Murray KY. 502-762-2291

Yoon, Choong Nam, *Tech Serv,* Central Young Men's Christian Association Community College, Stanley G Harris Library, Chicago IL. 312-222-8212

Yorgey, Jessica, *Librn,* Corvallis Public Library (Adair), Corvallis OR. 503-757-6928

York, D A, *Librn,* Georgia Supreme Court Library, Atlanta GA. 404-656-3470

York, Donald A, *Rare Bks,* Cambridge Public Library, Cambridge MA. 617-498-9080

York, H E, *Soc Sci,* Cleveland State University Libraries, Cleveland OH. 216-687-2486

York, Michael, *Asst Dir & Ref,* Castleton State College, Calvin Coolidge Library, Castleton VT. 802-468-5611, Ext 255

York, Myra, *Media,* Tyler Junior College, Edgar H Vaughn Memorial Library, Tyler TX. 214-592-5993, 593-3342

York, Nevada, *Rec Mgr,* Bureau of Land Management Library, Winnemucca NV. 702-623-3676

York, Peggy Ann, *Librn,* Forsyth Township Public Library, Gwinn MI. 906-346-3433

York, Sue, *Librn,* Boeing Co, Technical Library, Houston TX. 713-488-0910

Yorkdale, A H, *Dir,* Brick Institute of America Library, McLean VA. 703-893-4010

Yorks, Ruth E, *Librn,* Harmony Foundation, Old Songs Library, Kenosha WI. 414-654-9111, Ext 30

Yorston, Melissa, *Librn,* Prince Edward Island Provincial Library (Montague Branch), Montague PE. 902-892-3504, Ext 54

Yorty, Faith Ann, *Librn,* Springfield Art Museum Library, Springfield MO. 417-866-2716

Yosowitz, Ruth, *Ch,* Fairmount Temple, Sam & Emma Miller Library, Cleveland OH. 216-464-1330, Ext 37

Yost, Charles E, *Dir,* Sacred Heart School of Theology, Leo Dehon Library, Hales Corners WI. 425-8300 & 425-8301, Ext 27

Yost, Charles E, *Theology,* Sacred Heart School of Theology, Leo Dehon Library, Hales Corners WI. 425-8300 & 425-8301, Ext 27

Yother, Larry W, *Librn,* Hartford State Technical College Library, Hartford CT. 203-527-4111

Youmans, Alice, *Ref,* University of California, Berkeley (Law Library), Berkeley CA. 415-642-4044

Youmans, Diana, *Librn,* Ausley Memorial Library, Wauchula FL. 813-773-6438

Youmans, Mary, *Ser,* Western Carolina University (Serials), Cullowhee NC. 704-293-7306

Youmans, Mary M, *Ser,* Western Carolina University, Hunter Memorial Library, Cullowhee NC. 704-293-7306

Young, Alberta, *Admin Sec,* Sedalia Public Library, Sedalia MO. 816-826-1314

Young, Alene, *Head, Div of Pub Servs,* North Carolina Agricultural & Technical State University, F D Bluford Library, Greensboro NC. 919-379-7782, 379-7783

Young, Annie, *Asst Librn,* De Kalb County Library, Fort Payne AL. 205-845-2671

Young, Arthur, *Asst Dean,* University of Alabama, Amelia Gayle Gorgas Library, University AL. 205-348-5298

Young, B, *Core & Admin,* British Columbia Institute of Technology Library, Burnaby BC. 604-434-5734, Ext 360

Young, Barbara, *Dir,* Presentation College Library (Nursing Learning Laboratory), Aberdeen SD. 605-225-0420, Ext 382

Young, Barbara, *Librn,* Riley E Wright Library, Coventry VT. 802-754-6690

Young, Bessie H, *Librn,* Mary Holmes College, Barr Library, West Point MS. 601-494-6820, Ext 59

Young, Betty, *Actg Librn,* Duke University (East Campus), Durham NC. 919-684-3144

Young, Bill, *Librn,* Arkansas Division of Rehabilitation Services, Little Rock AR. 501-371-2411

Young, Catharine K, *Librn,* Catharine Young Library, Margate FL. 972-1188 & 972-1196

Young, Catherine, *Librn,* Palmer Public Library, Palmer MA. 413-283-3330

Young, Charles F J, *Head, Cent Libr,* Queens Borough Public Library, Jamaica NY. 212-990-0700

Young, Christopher, *Curator,* Library of the Flint Institute of Arts, Flint MI. 313-234-1695

Young, Dorothy, *Librn,* Ethel Briggs Memorial Library, Barnsdall OK. 918-847-2980, Ext 2980

Young, Dottie, *Librn,* Arcair Co Library, Lancaster OH. 614-653-5618, Ext 288

Young, Eddie Mae, *Dir,* Southern University in New Orleans Library, New Orleans LA. 504-282-4401, Ext 224

Young, Elma, *Librn,* Crane Public Library, Crane MO. 417-723-8261

Young, Faith, *Cat,* Westchester Community College Library, Valhalla NY. 914-347-6939

Young, Florence H, *Br Coordr & Bkmobile Coordr,* Abbeville-Greenwood Regional Library, Greenwood SC. 803-223-4515

Young, Francis, *Librn,* Wheatland Regional Library, Saskatoon SK. 306-652-5077

Young, Gail, *Per,* Schenectady County Community College Library, Library Resources Center, Schenectady NY. 518-346-6211, Ext 240, 241

Young, Gail B, *Librn,* Tift College, Hardin Memorial Library, Forsyth GA. 912-994-6587

Young, Gordon, *Supvr Info Serv,* Hercules Inc, Systems Division, Bacchus Plant Lab Library, Magna UT. 801-250-5911

Young, Harold C, *Dir,* University of Minnesota Libraries-Twin Cities (Wilson Library), Minneapolis MN. 612-373-5370

Young, Harvey E, *Asst Librn,* Marion Correctional Institution, Adrean Memorial Library, Marion OH. 614-382-5781, Ext 345

Young, Helen, *Coordr,* Barberton Citizens Hospital, Medical Library, Barberton OH. 216-745-1611, Ext 369

Young, Helen W, *Librn,* Nelsonville Public Library, Nelsonville OH. 614-753-2118

Young, Jack, *Bkmobile Coordr,* Ashe County Public Library, West Jefferson NC. 919-246-2041

Young, Jackie, *Librn,* Shreve Memorial Library (Broadmoor), Shreveport LA. 318-861-1370

Young, Jean, *Asst Dir,* Bristol-Washington Township Public Library, Bristol Public Library, Bristol IN. 219-848-7214

Young, Jerry F, *Dir,* Anoka County Library, Blaine MN. 612-784-1100

Young, JoAnne, *Dir,* Pennsylvania Department of Commerce, Economic Development Research Library, Harrisburg PA. 717-787-9610

Young, John, *Archivist,* Saint John's University Library, Jamaica NY. 212-969-8000, Ext 201

Young, John P, *Dir,* William Jewell College, Curry Library, Liberty MO. 816-781-3806

Young, Joyce, *Librn,* Onondaga County Public Library System (Paine), Syracuse NY. 315-473-4390

Young, Juana, *Ad & Circ,* University of Arkansas Libraries, Fayetteville AR. 501-575-4101

Young, Juanita, *Tech Serv,* Palos Verdes Library District, Palos Verdes Peninsula CA. 213-541-2559, 2550

Young, Judy, *Librn,* Iberville Parish Library (Bayou Sorrel), Plaquemine LA. 504-687-2520

Young, Katharine, *Librn,* Broward County Division of Libraries (Riverland), Margate FL. 305-972-1188

Young, Kathryn A, *Dir,* Gavilan College Library, Gilroy CA. 408-847-1400, Ext 132

Young, Kathy, *Librn,* Keystone Custodian Funds Library, Boston MA. 617-338-3435

Young, Lafayette, *Media,* Maui Community College, Learning Resource Center, Kahului HI. 808-242-5433, 242-5498

Young, Laura, *ILL & Ref,* Bob Jones University, J S Mack Library, Greenville SC. 803-242-5100, Ext 296

Young, Linda, *Ch,* Monessen Public Library, Monessen PA. 412-684-4750

Young, Louise, *Branch Asst,* Abbeville-Greenwood Regional Library (Ware Shoals Branch), Ware Shoals SC. 803-456-2813

Young, Louise, *Personnel Supvr,* West Virginia Library Commission, Science & Cultural Center, Charleston WV. 304-348-2041

Young, Lyn, *ILL,* California State College, San Bernardino Library, San Bernardino CA. 714-887-7321

Young, Lynette C, *Librn,* Granby Free Public Library, Granby MA. 413-467-3320

Young, Margarat, *Librn,* TRW Inc, Research & Development Library, Philadelphia PA. 215-922-8900

Young, Margaret H, *Librn,* Lahontan Basin Medical Library, Carson-Tahoe Hospital, Carson City NV. 702-882-1361, Ext 268

Young, Maria, *Ch,* Terrace Public Library, Terrace BC. 604-638-8177

Young, Marna, *Circ,* Wichita State University, Library & Media Resources Center, Wichita KS. 316-689-3586

Young, Martha L, *Dir,* Mediapolis Public Library, Mediapolis IA. 319-394-3895

Young, Mary, *Librn,* Yancey County Library, Burnsville NC. 704-682-2600

Young, Mary Ellen, *Librn,* Western Geophysical Company of America Library, Houston TX. 713-789-9600, Ext 2312

Young, Melissa L, *Librn,* Defense Technical Information Center, Alexandria VA. 202-274-6833, 6834

Young, Mildred, *Films,* Seneca College of Applied Arts & Technology, Finch Campus Learning Resource Centre, Willowdale ON. 416-491-5050, Ext 381

Young, Morris N, *Dir,* M N & C V Young Library of Mnemonics, New York NY. 212-227-4714

Young, Mrs Vaughty, *Librn,* Mitchell County Library, Bakersville NC. 704-688-2511

Young, Nancy, *Asst Dir, Main Libr,* Dekalb Library System, Maud M Burrus Library, Decatur GA. 404-378-7569

Young, Nancy T, *Ad & Ref,* White Plains Public Library, White Plains NY. 914-682-4400

Young, Nelle, *Librn,* Chestatee Regional Library (Lumpkin County), Dahlonega GA. 404-864-3668

Young, Olivia, *Dir Libr Develop & Extension Serv,* Tennessee State Library & Archives, Nashville TN. 615-741-2764

Young, Patricia, *Asst Librn,* Butler Memorial Library, Cambridge NE. 308-697-3836

Young, Patricia A, *Instr,* State University of New York, College of Arts & Science, School of Library & Information Science, NY. 716-245-5322

Young, Paul M, *Ref,* Texas Tech University Library, Lubbock TX. 806-742-2261

Young, Pearl, *Librn,* First Baptist Church Library, Kennett MO. 314-888-4689

Young, Phyllis, *Commun Servs, Br Coordr & Bkmobile Coordr,* Greensboro Public Library, Greensboro NC. 373-2474; 373-2471

Young, Randy, *Media,* Public Library of Anniston & Calhoun County, Liles Memorial Library, Anniston AL. 205-237-8501, Ext 8503

Young, Rich, *ILL,* West Virginia Library Commission, Science & Cultural Center, Charleston WV. 304-348-2041

Young, Richard, *Ref,* Seminole Community College Library, Sanford FL. 305-323-1450, Ext 450

Young, Rita K, *Tech Serv,* West Virginia Institute of Technology, Vining Library, Montgomery WV. 304-442-3141

Young, Robert, *Librn,* Burnaby Municipal Library (Kingsway), Burnaby BC. 604-522-3971

Young, Rosemary, *YA & Ch,* Denver Public Library, Denver CO. 303-573-5152, Ext 271

Young, Ruth A, *Librn,* Edgerton Public Library, Edgerton WI. 608-884-4511

Young, S L, *Librn,* Huntsville Museum of Art Library, Huntsville AL. 205-534-4566

Young, Sandra, *Librn,* Allen County Law Library, Fort Wayne IN. 219-423-7638

Young, Susan, *Librn,* Arkansas Geology Commission Library, Little Rock AR. 501-371-1309

Young, Sybil, *Asst Librn,* High River Centennial Library, High River AB. 403-652-2917

Young, Thomas Elton, *Librn,* Philbrook Art Center Library, Tulsa OK. 918-749-7941

Young, Valerie M, *Coordr,* Saint Mary's University (Community Tape Resource Library), Halifax NS. 902-422-7361, Ext 183

Young, Victor, *Cat,* University of Toledo, William S Carlson Library, Toledo OH. 419-537-2324

Young, Victor C, *Dir,* West Virginia Institute of Technology, Vining Library, Montgomery WV. 304-442-3141

Young, William H, *Librn,* Cedar Springs Library, Auberry CA. 209-855-2438

Young, Wilma, *Dir,* Brimfield Public Library, Brimfield IL. 309-446-9575

Young, Winifred C, *Librn,* Altoona Public Library, Altoona KS. 316-568-3706

Youngblood, Jacqueline, *Ch,* Fort Vancouver Regional Library, Vancouver WA. 206-695-1561

Youngblut, Cindy, *Librn,* Sage Public Library, Osage IA. 515-732-3323

Youngck, Marlys, *Curric Lab,* Winona State University, Maxwell Library, Winona MN. 507-457-2040

Younger, Barbra K, *Ch,* Dedham Public Library, Dedham MA. 617-326-0583

Younger, Freda, *Commun Servs,* Caldwell Public Library, Caldwell ID. 208-459-3242

Younger, William C, *Dir,* Alabama Supreme Court, Supreme Court & State Law Library, Montgomery AL. 205-832-6410

Youngholm, Philip, *Librn,* Connecticut College Library (Greer Music), New London CT. 203-447-1911, Ext 525

Youngman, Charles, *Asst Dir,* Yuma City-County Library, Yuma AZ. 602-782-1871

Youngman, Clifton, *Acq,* Jefferson Community College, Learning Resources Center, Louisville KY. 502-584-0181, Ext 305

Youngman, M Patricia, *Asst Dir & Ch,* Ellensburg Public Library, Ellensburg WA. 509-962-9863, Ext 250

Youngquist, Jo, *Media,* Troy-Miami County Public Library, Troy OH. 513-339-0502

Yount, Diana, *Spec Coll,* Andover Newton Theological School, Franklin Trask Library, Newton Centre MA. 617-964-1100, Ext 140

Yount, Leon, *Program Mgr,* DOE-RECON, TN. 615-574-5391

Youree, Beverly W, *Asst Prof,* Middle Tennessee State University, Department of Library Service, TN. 615-898-2740 & 898-5555

Yourman, Madeline C, *Pub Servs,* Brooklyn College Library, Brooklyn NY. 212-780-5342

Youssef, C, *District Librn,* Scarborough Public Library, Scarborough ON. 416-291-1991
Youssef, Mrs C, *Libr n,* Scarborough Public Library (Albert Campbell District), Scarborough ON. 416-698-1194
Youssif, Nassif, *Head,* University of Minnesota Libraries-Twin Cities (Middle East Library), Minneapolis MN. 612-373-7804
Yovanovitch, Nadia, *Librn,* Sherman Library, Sherman CT. 203-354-2455
Yowell, Jerry, *Mgr Industrial Div,* NASA, Technology Application Center, Albuquerque NM. 505-277-3622
Yowell, Pat, *Br Coordr,* Palo Alto City Library, Palo Alto CA. 415-329-2436
Yu, Amanda, *Libr n,* York Technical College Library, Rock Hill SC. 803-324-3130
Yu, Chilin, *Librn,* Columbus College of Art & Design, Packard Library, Columbus OH. 614-224-9101
Yu, Francis, *Instructional Mat,* Wright State University Library, Dayton OH. 513-873-2380
Yu, H C, *Acq,* Texas A&m University Libraries (Medical Sciences), College Station TX. 713-845-7427, 845-7428
Yu, Lorraine, *Media,* Reading Public Library, Reading Public Library District, Reading PA. 215-374-4548
Yu, Lucy C, *Libr n,* University of Michigan Libraries (Public Health), Ann Arbor MI. 313-764-5473
Yu, Robert, *Bibliog Centre & ILL,* Metropolitan Toronto Library Board, Metropolitan Toronto Library, Toronto ON. 416-928-5150
Yu, Winnie, *Asst Libr n,* Kaiser Permanente Medical Care Program, Medical Library, Los Angeles CA. 213-667-4011
Yuan, Christina, *Bibliographer,* Worcester Polytechnic Institute, George C Gordon Library, Worcester MA. 617-753-1411, Ext 410
Yucht, Donald, *Instr Media Ctr,* New York University, Elmer Holmes Bobst Library, New York NY. 212-598-2484
Yucht, Harriet, *Libr n,* New Castle County Law Library, Wilmington DE. 302-571-2437
Yucupicio, Phyllis, *Asst Libr n,* Coolidge Public Library, Coolidge AZ. 602-723-4538
Yueh, Norma, *Dir,* Ramapo College of New Jersey Library, Mahwah NJ. 201-825-2800, Ext 260
Yun, Mrs Kyung, *Ref,* Emma S Clark Memorial Library, Setauket NY. 516-941-4080
Yunag, Monica, *ILL & Ref,* Wright State University Library (Fordham Library, Cox Heart Institute Library & Fels Research Institute Library), Dayton OH. 513-873-2266
Yundt, Cecilia L, *Dir,* Plaquemines Parish Library, Buras LA. 504-657-7121
Yung, J, *Libr n,* Oakland Public Library (Asian Community), Oakland CA. 415-273-3400

Z

Zabel, Nancy, *Asst Dir,* Rice Lake Public Library, Rice Lake WI. 715-234-4861
Zablocki, Audrey B, *Dir,* Forsyth Technical Institute Library, Winston-Salem NC. 919-723-0371, Ext 216
Zaborowski, Julia, *On-Line Servs & Bibliog Instr,* Fermi National Accelerator Laboratory Library, Batavia IL. 312-840-3401
Zaborski, Jacqueline M, *Dir,* North Palm Beach Public Library, North Palm Beach FL. 305-848-0445
Zacher, Elaine, *Asst Libr n,* Kaiser Engineers Library, Oakland CA. 415-271-4357
Zacherl, Alice, *Libr n,* Palm Beach Junior College, Glades Center Campus Library, Belle Glade FL. 305-996-3055
Zachery, Imogene, *Libr n,* Bowie State College, Thomas G Pullen Jr Library, Bowie MD. 301-464-3237
Zachowski, Julie, *Dir,* Beaufort County Library, Beaufort SC. 803-524-0762
Zachry, Virginia, *Per,* Union University, Emma Waters Summar Library, Jackson TN. 901-668-1818, Ext 269
Zack, Daniel, *Dir,* Burlington Public Library, Burlington IA. 319-753-1649
Zack, Phyllis G, *ILL & Ref,* Berkshire Athenaeum, Pittsfield Public Library, Pittsfield MA. 413-442-1559

Zack, Sylvia, *Chmn of Learning Resources,* Horry-Georgetown Technical College Library, Conway SC. 803-347-3186, Ext 35
Zacker, Gail, *Tech Serv,* Kalamazoo Valley Community College, Learning Resources Center, Kalamazoo MI. 616-372-5000, Ext 328
Zackheim, Michael, *Circ,* State University of New York, College at New Paltz, Sojourner Truth Library, New Paltz NY. 914-257-2204
Zacks, Goldie, *Libr n,* Torrance Public Library (Walteria), Torrance CA. 213-375-8418
Zadner, Paul, *Circ & Per,* State University College at Buffalo, Edward H Butler Library, Buffalo NY. 716-878-6302
Zadnikar, Vili, *Tech Serv,* Case Western Reserve University Libraries (School of Law Library), Cleveland OH. 216-368-2792
Zadrozny, Yvette, *Tech Servs Asst,* Honeywell Information Systems Inc, System Technical Library, Waltham MA. 617-890-8400
Zaehringer, David, *Libr n,* University of California, Berkeley (Institute of Industrial Relations Library), Berkeley CA. 415-642-4441
Zaenger, Kathleen, *Libr n,* Howell Carnegie Library, Howell MI. 517-546-0720
Zafren, Herbert C, *Dir,* Hebrew Union College-Jewish Institute of Religion Library, Cincinnati OH. 513-221-1875
Zaganczyk, Joseph, *ETV Production,* Edison Community College, Learning Resources Center, Fort Myers FL. 813-481-2121, Ext 219, 220, 360
Zagorski, Sara, *Libr n,* Day, Berry & Howard Library, Hartford CT. 203-278-1330
Zaichick, Norman, *Libr n,* Argonne National Laboratory (General Reference & ILL), Argonne IL. 312-972-4228
Zaidel, John, *Libr n,* Baltimore County Public Library (Catonsville Area Branch), Catonsville MD. 301-747-3551
Zairay, Paula, *Tech Serv,* Logan Library, Logan UT. 801-752-2365
Zajac, Irene, *Acq,* Nichols College, Conant Library, Dudley MA. 617-943-1560
Zajackowski, Janet, *Libr n,* Baden Memorial Library, Baden PA. 412-869-3960
Zak, Debby, *Interlibr Loan & Ref,* Cleveland Public Library, Braille & Talking Book Department, Cleveland OH. 216-623-2911
Zak, Debby, *Acting Asst Dept Head,* Cleveland Public Library, Braille & Talking Book Department, Cleveland OH. 216-623-2911
Zale, Phyllis, *Ch,* Marin County Free Library, San Rafael CA. 415-479-1100, Ext 2577
Zalenski, Barbara V, *Libr n,* Belding Memorial Library, Ashfield MA. 413-628-4414
Zalenski, Kathleen, *Ref,* Garfield Free Public Library, Garfield NJ. 201-478-3800
Zaleski, Joan, *Dir,* Connetquot Public Library, Bohemia NY. 516-567-5115
Zaleskie, Joan, *Ad,* North Merrick Public Library, North Merrick NY. 516-378-7474
Zaletel, Hank, *Ref,* Iowa Department of Transportation Library, Ames IA. 515-296-1200
Zaletel, Hank, *Libr n,* Northwest Hospital, Medical Library, Chicago IL. 312-282-7000
Zalewski, Cecilia, *Libr n,* Redford Township Public Library, Detroit MI. 313-531-5960
Zalewski, Wojciech, *Eastern European & Russian,* Stanford University Libraries, Stanford CA. 415-497-2016
Zalin, Fern, *Dir,* Philadelphia Psychiatric Center, Professional Library, Philadelphia PA. 215-877-2000
Zalme, Gabriel, *Libr n,* Rutgers University (Chemistry), New Brunswick NJ. 201-932-2625
Zalubas, Karen I, *Ch,* Reading Public Library, Reading MA. 617-944-0840
Zamarelli, Calvin A, *Chief Libr n,* Veterans Administration, Hospital Library, East Orange NJ. 201-676-1000, Ext 388
Zamboky, Agnes E, *Cat,* Towson State University, Albert S Cook Library, Towson MD. 301-321-2450
Zambotti, Marguerite, *Libr n,* CIT Financial Corp, Reference Library, New York NY. 212-572-6412
Zambusi, W, *Asst Dir,* Midwestern Regional Library System, Kitchener ON. 519-576-5061
Zamora, Gloria, *Asst Ref,* United States Air Force (Air Force Weapons Laboratory Technical Library), Kirtland AFB NM. 505-844-7449

Zamora, Olga, *Asst Libr n,* El Progreso Memorial Library, Uvalde TX. 512-278-2017
Zampier, Kathy, *Ref,* Talbot County Free Library, Easton MD. 301-822-1626
Zanan, Arthur S, *Libr n,* Law Library of Montgomery County, Norristown PA. 215-278-3805, 278-3806
Zane, Sena, *AV,* Volusia County Public Libraries, Daytona Beach FL. 904-252-8374
Zangerle, Mary G, *Dir,* Lee-Whedon Memorial Library, Medina NY. 716-798-3430
Zannetti, Phyllis, *Dir,* Orwell Public Library, Orwell OH. 216-437-6545
Zapf, Cynthia A, *Libr n,* Polychrome Corp, Research & Development Library, Yonkers NY. 914-965-8800, Ext 135
Zaphiris, Nancy P, *End Proc & Bd Preparation Div Head,* Harvard University Library (Harvard College Library (Headquarters in Harry Elkins Widener Memorial Library)), Cambridge MA. 617-495-2401
Zapszalka, Barbara, *Dir,* Saint Francis Hospital (School of Nursing Library), Evanston IL. 312-492-6268
Zar, Kathleen, *Geophysics, Anthrop & Maps,* University of Chicago, Joseph Regenstein Library, Chicago IL. 312-753-2977
Zarabi, Ali, *Gen Asst,* University Club Library, New York NY. 212-572-3418
Zaragoza, Lois, *Reader Serv,* Pensacola Junior College, Learning Resource Center, Pensacola FL. 904-476-5410
Zarate, Geraldine, *Libr n,* Clark County Library District (Virgin Valley), Mesquite NV. 702-346-5348
Zarella, Ruth, *Tech Serv & Cat,* Melrose Public Library, Melrose MA. 617-665-2313
Zaremba, Andrew, *Libr n,* Century Association Library, New York NY. 212-944-0090
Zaremski, Andrea, *ILL & YA,* Fairfield Public Library, Fairfield CT. 203-259-8303
Zarins, Pavils, *On-Line Servs,* University of California, San Diego, University Libraries, La Jolla CA. 714-452-3336
Zartman, Ann, *Libr n,* Fulton County Public Library (Phyllis Meyer), Fulton IN. 219-857-3895
Zartman, Kelly D, *Ad,* Nevada Public Library, Nevada MO. 417-667-2831
Zartner, Rebecca L, *Asst Libr n,* Miami University-Hamilton Campus, Rentschler Learning Resources Center, Hamilton OH. 513-863-8833, Ext 232
Zaslow, Barry, *Tech Serv,* Staley Library, Millikin University, Decatur IL. 217-424-6214
Zastera, Alice, *Acq & Cat,* Free Public Library of Stratford, Stratford NJ. 609-783-0602
Zastera, Barbara B, *Dir,* Onawa Public Library, Onawa IA. 712-423-1733
Zaunbrecher, Helen, *Libr n,* Acadia Parish Library (Crowley Branch), Crowley LA. 318-788-1880
Zavala, Antonio, *In Charge,* Chicago Public Library (El Centro de la Causa Reading & Study Center), Chicago IL. 312-243-7638
Zavish, Gloria, *Libr n,* North Miami Public Library, North Miami FL. 305-891-5535
Zavodny, Joseph, *Asst Dir,* Atlanta Public Library, Atlanta GA. 404-688-4636
Zavortink, David, *Media, Tech Serv & Cat,* Valley City State College, Allen Memorial Library, Valley City ND. 701-845-7276
Zawacki, Lee, *Libr n,* Orlando Public Library (North Orange), Apopka FL. 305-889-3335
Zawadzki, Danuta M, *Acq, Circ & Ref,* Hughes Aircraft Co (Company Technical Document Center Library), Culver City CA. 213-391-0711, Ext 6187
Zbrozek, Stephanie, *YA,* Edwin A Bemis Public Library, Littleton Public Library, Littleton CO. 303-795-3826
Zdon, Elizabeth, *ILL & Ref,* Dakota County Library System, Burnsville MN. 612-435-8111
Zeagler, Ethel Mae, *Libr n,* East Mississippi Regional Library (Heidelberg Municipal), Heidelberg MS. 601-787-3857
Zeak, Mary Ann, *Libr n,* Penn Hills Library, Pittsburgh PA. 412-793-8049
Zealand, Josephine P, *Asst Libr n,* Louisburg College, C W Robbins Library, Louisburg NC. 496-2521 Ext 279, 280, 281
Zealberg, Catherine L, *Dir,* United States Army War College Library, Carlisle Barracks PA. 717-245-4319

ZECK

Zeck, Nancy, *Librn,* Del Norte County Law Library, Crescent City CA. 707-464-4139

Zeenkov, Joan, *Asst Librn,* San Diego Historical Society, Library & Manuscripts Collection, San Diego CA. 714-297-3258

Zegel, Kay, *YA & Ref,* Islip Public Library, Islip NY. 516-581-5933

Zehner, Claire, *Dir,* Fulton County Public Library, Rochester IN. 219-223-2713

Zehner, Ethel, *Asst Librn,* White Haven Center (Resident Library), White Haven PA. 717-443-9564, Ext 251

Zeidberg, David, *Spec Coll,* George Washington University Library, Washington DC. 202-676-6455

Zeigfinger, Susan, *Tech Serv,* Goddard College, William Shipman Library, Plainfield VT. 802-454-8311, Ext 232

Zeimet, E J, *Prof,* University of Wisconsin-LaCrosse, Educational Media Dept, WI. 608-784-8134

Zeind, Samir, *Asst Librn,* Huntington Memorial Hospital, Health Sciences Information Center, Pasadena CA. 213-440-5161

Zeirke, Norma G, *Librn,* Hartland Public Library, Hartland WI. 414-367-3350

Zeiss, Beth, *Librn,* American Technological University Library, Killeen TX. 817-526-1244

Zeitlhofer, Friederike, *Librn,* Austrian Institute Library, New York NY. 212-759-5165

Zeitlin, Stanley, *President,* Zeitlin Periodicals Co, Inc Library, Los Angeles CA. 213-933-7175

Zeleny, Julia, *Librn,* Sigourney Public Library, Sigourney IA. 515-622-2890

Zelfde, Anthonia Van't, *ILL & Ref,* Van Buren County Library, Webster Memorial Library, Decatur MI. 616-423-4771

Zelinsky, Sherman, *Dean,* Danville Junior College Library, Danville IL. 217-443-1811, Ext 245

Zell, Diana, *Librn,* Five Towns College Library, Merrick NY. 516-379-1400

Zell, Stanley D, *Librn,* Dayton & Montgomery County Public Library (Belmont), Dayton OH. 513-224-1651, Ext 220

Zellar, Carol, *Dir,* Roy Pickard Cicero Free Library, Cicero NY. 315-699-2032

Zeller, Fae, *Librn,* Louis Latzer Memorial Public Library, Highland IL. 618-654-5066

Zeller, Hortense, *Librn,* Haight, Gardner, Poor & Havens Law Library, New York NY. 212-344-6800, Ext 193

Zellers, Ledell, *Librn,* Mendota Mental Health Institute, Library-Media Center, Madison WI. 608-244-2411, Ext 466

Zellmer, Katherine, *ILL & Ref,* Iosco-Arenac Regional Library, Tawas City MI. 517-362-2651

Zelman, Jacqueline, *Cat,* Florida International University, Tamiami Campus, Athenaeum, Miami FL. 305-552-2461

Zeman, Dorothy F, *Librn,* Marine Midland Bank, Technical Information Center, Buffalo NY. 716-843-5011

Zembicki, Christine R, *ILL,* New Jersey Institute of Technology, Robert W Van Houten Library, Newark NJ. 201-645-5306

Zemmin, Sister William Anne, *Tech Serv & Acq,* Barry College, Monsignor William Barry Memorial Library, Miami Shores FL. 305-758-3392, Ext 263

Zenan, Joan, *Librn,* University of Nevada-Reno (Medical Library), Reno NV. 702-784-4625

Zenchoff, Adele, *Planning & Develop Coordr,* Bureau of Libraries, Museums & Archaeological Services, Saint Thomas VI. 809-774-3407

Zenke, Mary H, *Dir,* Dolton Public Library District, Dolton IL. 312-849-2385

Zenner, Hans, *Tech Serv,* North Dakota State University Library, Fargo ND. 701-237-8876

Zenor, Stanley, *Media,* Saint Louis Community College (Forest Park Campus), Saint Louis MO. 314-644-9209

Zentner, Elire, *Librn,* Congregation Beth Am Library, Los Altos Hills CA. 415-493-4661

Zenzen, Jeanne, *Librn,* Tillamook County Public Library (Garibaldi Branch), Garibaldi OR. 503-322-3327

Zera, Hortense, *Librn,* American Academy & Institute of Arts & Letters Library, New York NY. 212-368-1900

Zerkel, Elizabeth J, *Librn,* Decatur Public Library, Decatur IN. 219-724-2605

Zerkow, Syma, *Film,* Houston Area Library System, Houston TX. 713-222-4704

Zerkow, Syma, *Librn,* Houston Public Library (Film Library), Houston TX. 713-224-5441

Zermuehlen, D, *Librn,* Madison Public Library (South Madison), Madison WI. 608-266-6395

Zeroles, Linda, *Bkmobile Coordr,* Sussex County Department of Libraries, Georgetown DE. 302-856-7701, Ext 292

Zerwekh, Charles E, *Dept Mgr,* Polaroid Corporation, Research Library, Cambridge MA. 617-864-6000

Zeta, Elinore, *Actg Dir & Cat,* University of Evansville, Clifford Memorial Library & Learning Resources, Evansville IN. 812-479-2462

Zettel, Jenelle, *Asst Librn,* Bellville Public Library, Bellville TX. 713-865-3731

Zetterberg, Judy, *Tech Serv,* Saint Louis Community College (Administrative Center), Saint Louis MO. 314-644-9589

Zeugner, Lorenzo A, *Acq,* University of Notre Dame Library, Notre Dame IN. 219-283-7317

Zeydel, Jeanne R, *Agency Librn,* International Communication Agency (Agency Library), Washington DC. 202-724-9214

Zgainer, Margaret, *Acq,* Chatham College, Jennie King Mellon Library, Pittsburgh PA. 412-441-8200, Ext 220 & 221

Zia, Dora, *Librn,* Becton, Dickinson & Co, Research Center Library, Research Triangle Park NC. 919-549-8641, Ext 113

Ziaya, Alana, *Asst Librn,* Marshfield Clinic, Medical Center Library, Marshfield WI. 715-387-5183

Zibell, Joel, *Asst Librn,* Waterloo Public Memorial Library, Waterloo WI. 414-478-3344

Zibilich, Bernice, *Ch,* New Orleans Public Library, Simon Heinsheim & Fisk Libraries, New Orleans LA. 504-586-4905

Zibrat, Jan, *Librn, On-Line Servs & Bibliog Instr,* Swedish Covenant Hospital, Joseph G Stromberg Library of the Health Sciences, Chicago IL. 312-878-8200, Ext 5312

Ziccardi, Gerald J, *Librn,* Defense Personnel Support Center, Directorate of Medical Material Library, Philadelphia PA. 215-952-2110

Zich, Bonnie, *Librn,* Indiana County Law Library, Indiana PA. 412-465-2661, Ext 317

Zick, II, Kenneth A, *Dir,* Wake Forest University (Law Library), Winston-Salem NC. 919-761-5438

Zickgraf, Sister Therese M, *Dir,* Loyola Marymount University, Orange Campus, Loyola Marymount Library, Orange CA. 714-633-8495, Ext 7765

Ziebarth, Alan, *Librn,* Chicago Public Library (West Lawn), Chicago IL. 312-284-7381

Ziegenfuss, Donald G, *Librn,* Carlton, Fields, Ward, Emmanuel, Smith & Cutler, Law Library, Tampa FL. 813-223-5366, Ext 228

Ziegler, Elaine, *Genealogy,* Alamosa Southern Peaks Public Library, Alamosa CO. 303-589-6592

Ziegler, Elizabeth, *Librn,* Teletype Corp, Research & Development Library, Skokie IL. 312-982-3000

Ziegler, Roma, *Spec Coll,* Muhlenberg College, John A W Haas Library, Allentown PA. 215-433-3191, Ext 214

Ziegler, Jr, Arthur P, *Pres,* Pittsburgh History & Landmarks Foundation, James D Van Trump Library, Pittsburgh PA. 412-322-1204

Ziehli, Rosemary, *Dir,* Belleville Public Library, Belleville WI. 608-424-3545

Zielinska, M F, *Chief, Multilingual Biblioserv,* National Library of Canada, Ottawa ON. 613-995-9481

Zielinski, Helene, *Dir,* Terra Technical College, Learning Resource Center, Fremont OH. 419-334-3886

Ziemer, Opal, *Ch,* Dearborn Department of Libraries, Henry Ford Centennial Library, Dearborn MI. 313-271-1000

Zientek, Jane, *Ref,* Cadillac-Wexford Public Library, Cadillac MI. 616-775-6541

Zierold, Karolyn, *Tech Serv,* Idaho State Library, Boise ID. 208-334-2150

Zieselman, Paula, *ILL,* New Rochelle Public Library, New Rochelle NY. 914-632-7878

Zieske, Kathleen, *Librn,* Fulda Public Library, Fulda MN. 507-425-3277

Zietlow, Myrtle, *Acq,* Kalamazoo College, Upjohn Library, Kalamazoo MI. 616-383-8481

Zietz, Stephen, *Cat,* Pratt Institute Library, Brooklyn NY. 212-636-3684

Zilles, Anna, *On-Line Servs,* State University of New York Agricultural & Technical College at Delhi, Delhi College Library, Delhi NY. 607-746-4107

Zilliox, Robert E, *Asst Dir,* Hanover College, Duggan Library, Hanover IN. 812-866-2151, Ext 333

Zimmer, Gail, *Ref,* Maurice M Pine Free Public Library, Fair Lawn NJ. 201-796-3400

Zimmer, Iris M, *Librn,* Carlinville Public Library, Carlinville IL. 217-854-3505

Zimmer, Judith L, *Librn,* Rhode Island Medical Society Library, Providence RI. 401-331-3208

Zimmer, Naomi, *Gen Serv Consult,* Mohawk Valley Library Association, Schenectady NY. 518-355-2010

Zimmer, R, *Asst Librn,* Saint Charles Scholasticate Library, Battleford SK. 306-937-2355

Zimmer, Stephen, *Curator,* Seton Memorial Library & Museum, Cimarron NM. 505-376-2281, Ext 46

Zimmerburg, Helen, *Librn,* Princeton University Library (Biology), Princeton NJ. 609-452-3180

Zimmerer, Katherine, *Commun Servs,* Long Branch Public Library, Long Branch NJ. 201-222-3900

Zimmerly, Joyce C, *Librn,* Lima Public Library (Lafayette Branch), Lafayette OH. 419-228-5113

Zimmerman, Alan, *Res Analyst & Aids Coordr,* Wisconsin Department of Public Instruction, Division of Library Services, Madison WI. 608-266-2205

Zimmerman, Albert, *Librn,* Marshfield Clinic, Medical Center Library, Marshfield WI. 715-387-5183

Zimmerman, Bernardine M, *In Charge,* ERT-Ecology Consultants Life Sciences Information Center, Fort Collins CO. 303-493-8878

Zimmerman, Betty, *Librn,* Public Library of Charlotte & Mecklenburg County, Inc (Northwest), Charlotte NC. 704-394-7820

Zimmerman, Carolee, *Librn & Secy,* University of Florida, Florida Institute of Food & Agriculture Sciences, Medical Entomology Laboratory, Vero Beach FL. 305-562-5435, Ext 55

Zimmerman, Carolyn, *Librn,* Hatboro Baptist Church Library, Hatboro PA. 215-675-8400

Zimmerman, Cheryl, *Chief Librn,* Ontario Educational Communications Authority, Media Resource Centre, Toronto ON. 416-484-2651

Zimmerman, David, *Media,* James Madison University, Madison Memorial Library, Harrisonburg VA. 703-433-6150

Zimmerman, E, *W Long Branch Info Librn,* Bell Telephone Laboratories (Bell Telephone Laboratories Technical Library), Holmdel NJ. 949-3912 (Supvr); 949-5966 (Libr Network Support); 949-7986 (Cat); 229-7810 (W Long Branch Info)

Zimmerman, Gaynelle, *Cat,* Plymouth State College, Herbert H Lamson Library, Plymouth NH. 603-536-1550, Ext 257

Zimmerman, Gerald, *Asst Chief,* Chicago Public Library (Literature & Philosophy Div), Chicago IL. 312-269-2880

Zimmerman, Glen A, *Dir, Personnel & Labor Relations Off,* Library of Congress, Washington DC. 202-287-5000

Zimmerman, H Neil, *Librn,* Population Council Library, New York NY. 212-644-1620

Zimmerman, John, *Dir,* Frostburg State College Library, Frostburg MD. 301-689-4396

Zimmerman, Mary, *Tech Processes,* Frostburg State College Library, Frostburg MD. 301-689-4396

Zimmerman, Mary, *Librn,* Sioux Falls Newspapers, Inc, Sioux Falls Argus-Leader Library, Sioux Falls SD. 605-331-2200

Zimmerman, Roxy, *Tech Serv & On-Line Servs,* Beloit College, Col Robert H Morse Library, Beloit WI. 608-365-3391, Ext 230

Zimmerman, Velma, *Librn,* Martin County Library, Stanton TX. 915-756-2472

Zimmerman, Walter, *On-Line Servs,* University of Western Ontario, A B Weldon Library, London ON. 519-679-6191

Zimmermann, Jane M, *Librn,* Granby Public Library, Granby CT. 203-653-2800

Zimmermann, Lawrence, *Dir,* Black Hawk College-East Campus, Learning Resource Center, Kewanee IL. 309-852-5671, Ext 215

Zimmers, Linda, *In Charge,* Pennsylvania State University (Architecture Reading Room), University Park PA. 814-863-0511
Zimon, Kathy, *Fine Arts,* University of Calgary Library, Calgary AB. 403-284-5954
Zimpfer, William E, *Dir,* Boston University Libraries (School of Theology Library), Boston MA. 617-353-3034
Zimring, Vicki, *Ref,* United Bank of Denver, Information Center-Library, Denver CO. 303-861-8811, Ext 2703
Zindel, David L, *Dir,* Labette Community Junior College Library, Parsons KS. 316-421-1250, 421-6700
Zingales, Philip, *Cat,* Adelphi University Library, Garden City NY. 516-294-8700
Zini, Maria, *Pennsylvania,* Carnegie Library of Pittsburgh, Pittsburgh PA. 412-622-3100
Zink, Esther, *Dir,* Trinity Bible Institute, Fred J Graham Library, Ellendale ND. 701-349-3408
Zink, James, *Dir,* Southeast Missouri State University, Kent Library, Cape Girardeau MO. 314-651-2235
Zink, Teddy, *Librn,* Trails Regional Library (Knob Noster Branch), Knob Noster MO. 816-563-2997
Zinkl, Andy, *On-Line Servs,* University of Wisconsin-Green Bay, Library Learning Center, Green Bay WI. 414-465-2382
Zinn, Mary, *Br Coordr,* Salem College, Benedum Learning Resources Center, Salem WV. 304-782-5238
Zinn, Nancy, *Spec Coll,* University of California Library, San Francisco CA. 415-666-2334
Zinser, Terry, *Dir,* College of the Siskiyous Library, Weed CA. 916-938-4463
Zinsser, Katherine, *Librn,* Montgomery County Department of Public Libraries (Little Falls), Washington DC. 301-320-4880
Ziolko, Joseph F, *Dir,* Mississippi County Library System, Blytheville AR. 501-762-2431
Ziolkowski, Darlene, *Librn,* Chicago Public Library (Damen Avenue), Chicago IL. 312-486-6022
Ziolkowski, Ruth, *In Charge,* Indian Museum of North America Library, Black Hills SD. 605-673-4681
Zipkowitz, Fay, *Coordr,* Worcester Area Cooperating Libraries, MA. 617-754-3964, 752-7700, Ext 159
Zipp, Louise S, *Librn,* University of Iowa Libraries (Chemistry-Botany), Iowa City IA. 319-353-3707
Zipp, Louise S, *Librn,* University of Iowa Libraries (Geology), Iowa City IA. 319-353-4225
Zipper, Masha, *On-Line Servs,* Price Waterhouse & Company, National Office Library, New York NY. 212-489-8900
Zipsie, Josephine, *Dir,* Baraboo Public Library, Baraboo WI. 608-356-6166
Zirbes, Sister Colette, *Dir, Acq & Bibliog Instr,* Cardinal Stritch College Library, Milwaukee WI. 414-352-5400, Ext 356
Zirk, Marjorie, *Librn,* Hardy County Public Library, Moorefield WV. 304-538-6560
Zirkle, Ailene A, *Pub Servs,* College of William & Mary in Virginia, Earl Gregg Swem Library, Williamsburg VA. 804-253-4404
Zislin, Phyllis, *Cat,* Beth Israel Synagogue, Beth Israel Congregation Library, Vineland NJ. 609-691-0852
Zitko, Howard John, *Librn,* World University Library, Tucson AZ. 602-622-2170
Zito, Anthony, *Univ Archivist,* Catholic University of America (Archives & Manuscripts Division), Washington DC. 202-635-5065
Zito, Valerie, *Ref,* Lodi Public Library, Lodi CA. 209-334-3973
Zittrauer, Gloria, *Librn,* Jacksonville Public Library System (Westbrook), Jacksonville FL. 904-633-6135
Zittrich, Harriett, *Asst Librn,* Terril Community Library, Terril IA. 712-853-6224
Ziyad, Dawud, *Instr,* University of the District of Columbia-Mount Vernon Square Campus, Dept of Library Science & Instructional Systems Technology, DC. 202-727-2756, 727-2757 & 727-2758
Zizka, George E A, *Librn,* Victoria General Hospital, Health Sciences Library, Victoria BC. 604-388-9121, Ext 330
Zlatos, Christy, *Ref,* Indiana State University, Evansville Library, Evansville IN. 812-464-1824
Zobrist, Benedict K, *Dir,* Harry S Truman Library, General Services Admin, Independence MO. 816-833-1400
Zoccola, Donna M, *Librn, On-Line Servs & Bibliog Instr,* Friends Hospital, Norman D Weiner Professional Library, Philadelphia PA. 215-831-4763
Zoch, Ruth, *Librn,* Saline County Public Library (Bryant Branch), Bryant AR. 501-847-2166
Zoch, Virginia, *Librn,* Middleburgh Library Association, Middleburg NY. 518-827-5142
Zoelle, Virginia M, *Dir,* Waterford Public Library, Waterford WI. 414-534-3988
Zoellick, Ruthann, *Environ Info Ctr,* East Central State University, Linscheid Library, Ada OK. 405-332-8000
Zoellner, Alan F, *ILL & Ref,* Hampden Sydney College, Eggleston Library, Hampden Sydney VA. 804-223-4381, Ext 190
Zoellner, Donna, *Librn,* Santa Maria Public Library (Los Alamos Station), Los Alamos CA. 805-925-0994, Ext 261
Zolich, Joseph, *Librn,* Arter & Hadden Law Library, Cleveland OH. 216-696-1144
Zolin, Ronnie, *Dir,* Nyack Library, Nyack NY. 914-358-3370
Zolkowski, Sue, *Bks By Mail Coord,* Outagamie Waupaca Counties Federated Library System, Appleton WI. 414-734-8873
Zoller, C E, *In Charge,* McDonnell Douglas Corp (McDonnell Aircraft Library), Saint Louis MO. 314-232-6134
Zonlight, Martin, *Exten Servs,* Stanislaus County Free Library, Modesto CA. 209-526-6821
Zonnelfeld, Lena, *Librn,* Sanborn Public Library, Sanborn IA. 712-729-3215
Zook, Leona, *Librn,* Fairfield Public Library, Fairfield NE. 402-726-2220
Zook, Lois Ann, *Librn,* Lancaster Mennonite Historical Society Library, Lancaster PA. 717-393-9745
Zorach, Margaret B, *Chief Librn,* Brooklyn Museum (Art Reference Library), Brooklyn NY. 212-638-5000, Ext 307 & 308
Zorbas, Elaine, *Librn,* Pasadena Public Library (Hastings), Pasadena CA. 213-792-0945
Zortman, Denise, *ILL & Ref,* Iowa Western Community College, Hoover Media Library, Council Bluffs IA. 712-325-3247
Zschock, Suzanne, *Dir,* Stafford Public Library, Stafford Springs CT. 203-684-2852
Zschunke, William J, *Librn,* United States Department of the Air Force (Office of the Judge Advocate General Library), Washington DC. 202-693-5638
Zubrow, Marcia, *Ref,* State University of New York at Buffalo (Charles B Sears Law Library), Buffalo NY. 716-636-2043
Zuchak, Marguerite, *ILL,* Wayne County Public Library, Wooster OH. 216-262-0916
Zuck, Rosemary, *Tech Serv,* Kansas City College of Osteopathic Medicine, Mazzacano Hall Library, Kansas City MO. 816-283-2451, 2454
Zucker, Donna, *Asst Librn,* Temple Emanu-El, William P Engel Library, Birmingham AL. 205-933-8037
Zuckerman, Janet, *AV,* City College of the City University of New York, Morris Raphael Cohen Library, New York NY. 212-690-6612
Zuckerman, Sandra, *Librn,* Washington Hebrew Congregation, Hurston Adult Library, Washington DC. 202-362-7100
Zuckerman, Sara, *Librn,* New York City Commission on Human Rights Library, New York NY. 212-566-5050
Zuehlke, Lois, *Librn,* Mercy Hospital, Medical Library, Janesville WI. 608-756-6749
Zufan, Donna, *On-Line Servs,* California State University, Fresno Library, Fresno CA. 209-487-2403
Zugby, Lillian C, *ILL, Reader Serv & Ref,* Montgomery College-Takoma Park Campus Library, Takoma Park MD. 301-587-4090, Ext 242
Zuger, Joy E, *Librn,* Veterans Administration, Hospital Library, Marion IN. 317-674-3321
Zuiderveld, Sharon, *Dir,* Southwest Area Multi-County Multi-Type Interlibrary Exchange, (SAMMIE), MN. 507-537-6108
Zuk, S, *Bibliog Instr,* University of Winnipeg Library, Winnipeg MB. 204-786-7811, Ext 520
Zukowski, Frances, *Librn,* Lake County Superior Court Library, Gary IN. 219-886-3621, Ext 204
Zukowski, Stanley, *Sci & Bus,* Buffalo & Erie County Public Library System, Buffalo NY. 716-856-7525
Zukowsky, John, *Archit Archivist,* Art Institute of Chicago (Ryerson & Burnham Libraries), Chicago IL. 312-443-6666
Zukroff, Carl, *Media,* Beverly Public Library, Beverly MA. 617-922-0310
Zula, Floyd M, *Acq,* Christopher Newport College, Captain John Smith Library, Newport News VA. 804-599-7130
Zulinski, Jean D, *Librn,* Osceola Township Public & School Library, Dollar Bay MI. 906-482-5800
Zumbrunnen, Donna, *Librn,* Mount Zion Township Public Library, Mount Zion IL. 217-864-3622
Zumpfe, Rose, *Dir,* Crete Public Library, Crete NE. 402-826-3809
Zumstein, Marjorie, *Librn,* Purdue University Libraries & Audio-Visual Center (Psychological Sciences), West Lafayette IN. 317-749-2131
Zumstein, Marjorie, *Librn,* Purdue University Libraries & Audio-Visual Center (Educational Learning Resources Center), West Lafayette IN. 317-494-8620
Zumwalt, George M, *Chief Librn,* Veterans Administration, Health Sciences Library, Little Rock AR. 501-372-8361, Ext 1294
Zunder, Marjorie, *Tech Serv,* State of Vermont Department of Libraries, Montpelier VT. 802-828-3261
Zunker, Alice L, *Asst Librn,* Dittlinger Memorial Library, New Braunfels TX. 512-625-8919
Zupanick, Adina, *Info Specialist,* Leeds & Northrup Co, Technical Center Library, North Wales PA. 215-643-2000, Ext 2035
Zupfer, Betty, *Ref Mat,* Southwest State University Library, Marshall MN. 507-537-7021
Zuppa, Theodore C, *Cat & On-Line Servs,* Francis Marion College, James A Rogers Library, Florence SC. 803-669-4121, Ext 321
Zuraw, Cathy, *Chief Librn,* Sheridan College of Applied Arts & Technology Library, Library Learning Centre, Oakville ON. 416-845-9430, Ext 166
Zussman, M, *AV,* Lansing Community College Library, Lansing MI. 517-373-9978
Zussy, Nancy, *Dir,* Clearwater Public Library, Clearwater FL. 813-462-6800
Zuvers, Cynthia, *Dir,* McLaughlin Memorial Public Library, Archbold OH. 419-445-4781
Zuzack, Zenon, *Tech Serv,* Saskatoon Public Library, Saskatoon SK. 306-664-9555
Zuzick, Kathryn T, *Chief Librn,* United States Department of Defense, Defense Communications Agency, Command & Control Technical Center Library, Washington DC. 202-697-6469
Zweibach, Allan, *Tech Serv,* Grand Lodge Free & Accepted Masons of the State of New York Library & Museum, New York NY. 212-741-4500
Zweifel, LeRoy G, *Librn,* University of Wisconsin-Madison (Kurt Wendt Engineering Library), Madison WI. 608-262-3521
Zweizig, Douglas, *Asst Prof,* University of Washington, School of Librarianship, WA. 206-543-1794
Zwetell, Marina, *Librn,* Moritz Community Hospital, Dean Pierose Memorial Health Sciences Library, Sun Valley ID. 208-622-3323
Zwick, John W, *Dir,* Tidewater Community College, Virginia Beach Campus Library, Virginia Beach VA. 804-427-3070, Ext 123, 126
Zwick, Susan, *Librn,* Norfolk Public Library (Janaf), Norfolk VA. 804-461-0734
Zych, Carol, *Senior Info Scientists,* Schering-Plough Pharmaceutical Research Div, Library Information Center, Bloomfield NJ. 201-743-6000, Ext 781
Zylstra, Sigrid, *Ref,* Whatcom County Public Library, Bellingham WA. 206-384-3150
Zylstra, Sigrid, *Librn,* Whatcom County Public Library (Lynden Branch), Lynden WA. 206-354-4883
Zysk, Larry W, *Dir,* Aquinas College, Learning Resource Center, Grand Rapids MI. 616-459-8281, Ext 234

Ref
Z
720
A4
L5
1981